PASSENGER AND IMMIGRATION LISTS INDEX

1999 Supplement
Part 2

Passenger and Immigration Lists Series

Passenger and Immigration Lists Index, First Edition

Passenger and Immigration Lists Index: 1982 Supplement

Passenger and Immigration Lists Index: 1983 Supplement

Passenger and Immigration Lists Index: 1984 Supplement

Passenger and Immigration Lists Index: 1985 Supplement

Passenger and Immigration Lists Index: 1982-85 Cumulated Supplements

Passenger and Immigration Lists Index: 1986 Supplement

Passenger and Immigration Lists Index: 1987 Supplement

Passenger and Immigration Lists Index: 1988 Supplement

Passenger and Immigration Lists Index: 1989 Supplement

Passenger and Immigration Lists Index: 1990 Supplement

Passenger and Immigration Lists Index: 1986-90 Cumulated Supplements

Passenger and Immigration Lists Index: 1991 Supplement

Passenger and Immigration Lists Index: 1992 Supplement

Passenger and Immigration Lists Index: 1993 Supplement

Passenger and Immigration Lists Index: 1994 Supplement

Passenger and Immigration Lists Index: 1995 Supplement

Passenger and Immigration Lists Index: 1991-95 Cumulated Supplements

Passenger and Immigration Lists Index: 1996 Supplement

Passenger and Immigration Lists Index: 1997 Supplement

Passenger and Immigration Lists Index: 1998 Supplement Part 1

Passenger and Immigration Lists Index: 1998 Supplement Part 2

Passenger and Immigration Lists Index: 1999 Supplement Part 1

Passenger and Immigration Lists Index: 1999 Supplement Part 2

Passenger and Immigration Lists Bibliography, 1538-1900, Second Edition

Philadelphia Naturalization Records

ISSN 0736-8267

PASSENGER AND IMMIGRATION LISTS INDEX

A Guide to Published Records
of More Than 3,176,000 Immigrants Who Came
to the New World between the Sixteenth
and the Mid-Twentieth Centuries

1999 Supplement
Part 2

Edited by P. William Filby
and Frank V. Castronova

GALE

DETROIT · LONDON

Staff

Editors: P. William Filby, Frank V. Castronova
Managing Editor: Neil E. Walker
Senior Editor: Paula K. Byers
Contributing Editors: Jennifer Mossman, Katherine H. Nemeh
Associate Editors: Luann Brennan, Catt Slovey
Proofreaders: Sheri L. Chewning, Karen Kaus Nicolli, Amy L. Unterburger
Marker: Heidi Denler
Researcher: Lois Haile Petras

Production Director: Mary Beth Trimper
Production Assistants: Carolyn A. Fischer, Deborah Milliken

Data Entry Manager: Eleanor Allison
Data Entry Coordinator: Janine Whitney

Manager, Technical Support Services: Theresa Rocklin
Oracle Applications Specialist: Carolin V. Jones

Copyright ©1999
Gale Research
27500 Drake Rd.
Farmington Hills, MI 48331-3535

Library of Congress Catalog Card Number 84-15404
ISBN 0-7876-1937-X
ISSN 0736-8267
Printed in the United States of America

235⁰⁰ NC

Contents

Highlights ix

Introduction xi

User's Guide: How to Read a Citation xiii

How to Locate Sources Indexed xvii

Bibliography of Sources Indexed xix

Passenger and Immigration Lists Index: 1999 Supplement Part 2 1

Highlights

Passenger and Immigration Lists Index: 1999 Supplement Part 2 brings together in one alphabet more than 126,000 immigrants who arrived in the New World between the sixteenth and the mid-twentieth centuries. This book is the twentieth supplement to the base set of *Passenger and Immigration Lists Index (PILI)* published in 1981. These names appear in a broad collection of more than 160 published passenger lists, naturalization records, church records, family and local histories, voter and land registrations, etc.

For the user's convenience, the following features appear in this supplement:

- The **User's Guide: How to Read a Citation** section, which begins on page xiii, gives examples which show the user how index and bibliographic citations should be interpreted.

- Information as to where to find the sources indexed in *PILI* may be found in the **How to Locate Sources Indexed** section beginning on page xvii.

- Complete bibliographic citations to the sources indexed in *PILI 1999 Supplement Part 2*, and the codes used to refer to them, may be found in the **Bibliography of Sources Indexed** section, beginning on page xix.

Introduction

Passenger and Immigration Lists Index (PILI) was first published in 1981 in three volumes which indexed more than 300 published lists covering about 500,000 persons. *PILI* and its twenty supplements now cover more than 3,176,000 persons—still only a fraction of the over 35,000,000 immigrants who came to the New World. For the user's convenience, all material in the first four annual supplements to the *PILI* base set is also available in one alphabet in *PILI 1982-85 Cumulated Supplements.* The material indexed in the *PILI 1986* through *1990* and *1991* through *1995 Supplements* is also available in one alphabet in *PILI 1986-90 Cumulated Supplements* and *PILI 1991-95 Cumulated Supplements*, respectively. Beginning with the 1998 supplements, two volumes are published annually. At this time publication plans include a cumulation of supplements every five years.

Concept and Scope

Passenger lists, naturalization records, church records, etc. are primary sources for genealogists, since, in the case of passenger lists, almost all passengers arriving in the New World during the period covered were not casual travelers but immigrants intending to remain in America as permanent residents. Information which documents a specific time and location of an immigrant in the New World is an invaluable aid to research on the history of a family in America. In addition, any of the lists that furnish this information may also furnish clues to the country of origin and other crucial bits of genealogical information. This is true of all the lists indexed in *PILI,* and researchers will want to make certain to consult the sources themselves for additional information.

It should be noted that in some cases variant versions of lists have been indexed in *PILI,* since copying is notoriously inaccurate and it is not unusual to note variations from list to list. Likewise, different information is frequently given about the circumstances of the immigration. Since no library holds all of the lists, the researcher will have a better opportunity to locate one of the versions.

Most of the sources indexed in the three-volume base set of *PILI* were identified by Harold Lancour's *Bibliography of Ship Passenger Lists, 1538-1825: Being a Guide to Published Lists of Early Immigrants to North America* (third edition revised by Richard J. Wolfe, New York: New York Public Library, 1963). In 1981, P. William Filby edited a revised and updated edition of the Lancour bibliography, *Passenger and Immigration Lists Bibliography, 1538-1900: Being a Guide to Published Lists of Arrivals in the United States and Canada* (Detroit: Gale Research, 1981). Now in its second edition (published 1988), this bibliography identifies more than 2,550 published passenger and immigration lists, completely superseding Lancour's work. Many of the sources indexed in the earlier volumes of *PILI* are listed in *Passenger and Immigration Lists Bibliography,* Second Edition.

Editorial Practices

All names listed in *PILI* have been compiled directly from published sources; unpublished sources are never indexed. The information given in a source about each immigrant and those accompanying him or her was edited to a standard format. Cross-references were made for each of those individuals who accompanied the primary listee since, without those cross-references, much valuable information would be lost.

PILI does not index passenger lists only. Naturalization lists and other publications where immigration to the New World can be determined to have occurred are indexed as well. Early in the project, the editors decided that all names, including alternate forms of the surname, in a given source would be indexed unless there was a definite reason for omission. Examples of names that would not be indexed are those whose data reflects birth in America or those with no listed surname.

The date and place appearing in *PILI* do *not* necessarily equate to the date and port of *arrival.* Locations referred to in some sources are in fact sometimes destinations, the area where naturalization was filed, or the particular location of the immigrant on the date cited. Dates may reflect the date of death, the date the listee

requested permission to emigrate, or the point in time when documents place that person in the New World at the location specified. Although they are not ports and dates of arrival, these references are retained because the editors feel that when someone is searching for an elusive ancestor, all information is helpful. It is felt that no researcher will object to the inclusion of her or his ancestor even if the person did not arrive precisely on the date listed in *PILI*. By consulting the complete bibliographic citation for the source cited in a *PILI* entry in the section "Bibliography of Sources Indexed" which begins on page xix, researchers can determine exactly what information the listed date and place represent.

While every attempt has been made to ensure accuracy, it has been impossible to search for corrections or errata in articles published after the ones indexed. Similarly, all names have been copied exactly as printed, even in cases where they might appear to be erroneous. Abbreviations, such as "Jno.," have been retained. Van, Van der, De, De La, von, van, etc. have been left as given in the source. Letters sometimes umlauted (¨) in German names (ü, ä, ö) have been spelled out (ue, ae, oe) in the bibliography but have *not* been spelled out in the index unless they are spelled out in the source document. The ess-tset symbol (ß) has been anglicized as "ss".

It should be remembered that names of emigrants were often recorded as they were heard, that many emigrants could not spell their own names, and that authorities were not as literate as one would wish. Thus, variations in spelling of names occur and members of the same family arriving at different times or places may be found under more than one spelling. In using *PILI*, the researcher should search for every conceivable spelling of the name sought as well as adaptations of the surname based on the customs of the ancestor's country of origin. (For example, if the ancestor is a female of German extraction, the surname may be listed with an "in" appended at the end. Thus, "Mayer" is listed as "Mayerin.")

When ages given in the source books contain fractions of years, these fractions have been dropped. (For example, 14 ½ will appear in *PILI* as 14.) Ages of children of less than a year have been shown in months, weeks, or days.

Suggestions Are Welcome

PILI, which indexes only published material, has had an effect on genealogical publishing. Researchers have responded to *PILI* by increasing their efforts to have new lists published. Librarians and researchers are encouraged to inform the editors of further lists that could be indexed in the future. Questions, comments, and suggestions may be sent to Gale Research, *Passenger and Immigration Lists Index,* 27500 Drake Rd., Farmington Hills, MI 48331-3535 [phone: (248) 699-4253, toll-free (800) 347-4253, fax: (248) 699-8062].

User's Guide:
How to Read a Citation

There are two main types of citations in *Passenger and Immigration Lists Index (PILI)*: Citations listing names of immigrants which appear in the main body or index portion of the book (beginning on page 1) and bibliographic citations which appear in the section "Bibliography of Sources Indexed" (beginning on page xix).

Index Citations

Citations in the main body of *PILI* can be of two types. The first type, the main entry, may read as follows:

```
    (1)        (2)      (3)        (4)  (5)  (6)
Bender, George 20; New York, NY, 1852 8506 p224
            Wife: Catharine 27
(7)         Son: Jacob 4
            Daughter: Catharine 2
```

The numbers in parentheses appearing in the above entry refer to the following explanations:

(1)   Name of the immigrant, as spelled in the original published source
(2)   Immigrant's age, when given
(3)   Place of arrival, naturalization, or other record of immigration
(4)   Year of arrival, naturalization, or other record of immigration
(5)   Code that refers to the source in which the particular list can be found. **Complete bibliographic citations to the sources indexed which include an explanation as to what information is provided by the place and year cited, and the codes used to refer to them, may be found in the "Bibliography of Sources Indexed" section, beginning on page xix.**
(6)   Page number on which that particular name is listed in the source cited
(7)   Accompanying family members, if there are any, together with each person's relationship to the primary listee, and his or her age.

Occasionally a published list will not indicate a year of arrival or other reference year. In those instances the abbreviation *n.d.* (no date) is inserted:

Altomore, Mauro; Galveston, TX, n.d. **1004.5** *p17*

Some immigration lists note that the main listee was accompanied by other persons, with only the relationships indicated, and possibly the ages. Such information is included in the *PILI* listing:

Jacobs, Jan; New Netherland(s), 1659 **9143** *p174*
        With wife & mother
        With child 2
        With child 4

The second type of citation found in *PILI* is the cross-reference. Cross-references have been generated by the computer for every accompanying relative whose name is provided in the source indexed in *PILI*. The only exception would be those lists where a relationship seemed obvious, but was not specified. Cross-references may read as follows:

```
    (1)        (2)     (3)
Bauer, Katharina 6 SEE Bauer, Peter
```

The numbers in parentheses appearing in the preceding entry refer to the following explanations:

(1) Name of accompanying family member
(2) Family member's age, when given
(3) Name of the primary listee

Since cross-references are generated each time an accompanying individual is listed, duplicate cross-references will appear in *PILI* for names listed in more than one source or page:

Robertson, Jane *SEE* Robertson, James
Robertson, Jane *SEE* Robertson, James
Robertson, Jane *SEE* Robertson, James
Robertson, Jane *SEE* Robertson, James

This indicates to the researcher that there are four separate listings for Isaack Allerton in *PILI* in which Mary is given as someone who accompanied him.

A wife whose maiden name is supplied in a source document may appear in three places in *PILI:* a) in the husband's main listing, b) under the maiden name, and c) as a cross-reference under the married name:

a) **Gardner,** Simeon; Nova Scotia, 1762 **8750.40** *p90*
      Wife: Sarah Long

b) **Long,** Sarah; Nova Scotia, 1762 **8750.40** *p90*

c) **Gardner,** Sarah Long *SEE* Gardner, Simeon

For information concerning how names are selected and indexed in *PILI,* see the "Editorial Practices" section of the Introduction beginning on page xi.

Bibliographic Citations

Citations in the bibliography of *PILI* can also be of two types. The first type, indicating that the source indexed was a book, may read as follows:

(1)
*778.5
(2)   (3)
BRASSEAUX, CARL A. *The "Foreign French:" Nineteenth-Century French Immigra-*
            (4)   (5)   (6)
tion into Louisiana. Vol. 1: 1820-1839. Lafayette, LA: The Center for Louisiana Studies,
                              (7)   (8)
University of Southwestern Louisiana, 1990. 569p.

The numbers in parentheses appearing in the above entry refer to the following explanations:

(1)   Code cited in index citation referencing this source
(2)   Author, editor, or compiler
(3)   Title of book, pamphlet, or monograph
(4)   Subtitle, volume, or edition information
(5)   Place where source was published
(6)   Name of publisher
(7)   Year when published
(8)   Number of pages in the source

The second type of bibliographic citation, indicating that the source indexed was a magazine or newspaper article or a chapter of a book may read as follows:

(1)
*7129

(2)   (3)   (4)   (5)

RACINE, JUANITA. "Caddo Parish Courthouse, Shreveport, LA. In *The Genie* (Ark-La-Tex

                               (6)   (7)   (8)

Genealogical Association, Shreveport), vol. 15:1 (Jan. 1981), pp. 44-46.

The numbers in parentheses appearing in the above entry refer to the following explanations:

- (1)   Code cited in index citation referencing this source
- (2)   Author or compiler of article
- (3)   Name of magazine article, book chapter, or newspaper article
- (4)   Name of the magazine, book, or newspaper in which the article or text appears
- (5)   Publisher of magazine or book and city (and, sometimes, state) where source was published
- (6)   Volume and issue number of magazine or newspaper
- (7)   Date when magazine, book, or newspaper was published
- (8)   Pages of article or chapter which were indexed

Both types of bibliographic citations will also have an annotation immediately following the citation:

(1)   (2)

Date and place of first mention of residence in the New World. Extracted from records found

                                               (3)

among the Bradford papers in the archives of the Pennsylvania Historical Society. Regiment,

company, place of birth, and other information provided.

The numbers in parentheses appearing in the above entry refer to the following explanations:

- (1)   Denotes what the date and place cited in the index citation represent
- (2)   Where the compiler or author of this source found his or her information
- (3)   What other information (not indexed in *PILI*) is provided by the compiler or author

Annotations may also contain other information:

English translation of the title if source is in a foreign language
The location of the original records
Address of author or compiler if source was self-published
Additional information that the staff of *PILI* feels will be of aid to the researcher

How to Locate Sources Indexed

Large public libraries, state libraries, libraries with genealogical or history collections, and libraries of family associations and genealogical or historical societies are excellent places to check for the sources listed in the "Bibliography of Sources Indexed" section of *PILI*. It should be noted that while many libraries do not have the staff to research sources, librarians can provide guidance to assist researchers in their own investigations. Some libraries may provide lists of researchers for hire. The publisher of the magazine or book indexed can also be contacted; magazine publishers often offer reprints of articles they publish. Also, the bibliographic citation in *PILI* (*see* "Bibliography of Sources Indexed," which begins on page xix) may provide information as to where the source may be found.

Many of the books and periodicals containing articles indexed in *PILI* are among the holdings of some of the institutions listed below. The *Bibliography of Genealogy and Local History Periodicals with Union List of Major U.S. Collections* edited by Michael Barren Clegg and published by the Allen County Public Library Foundation in Fort Wayne, Indiana, is helpful in determining which of the major genealogical libraries hold a specific periodical (those libraries surveyed by Clegg are indicated below by an asterisk).

A sampling of institutions and organizations with major holdings of genealogical publications follows:

*Allen County Public Library**
  Genealogy Department
  900 Webster Street
  P.O. Box 2270
  Fort Wayne, IN 46801-2270

*Atlanta-Fulton Public Library**
  Special Collections Department
  1 Margaret Mitchell Square NW
  Atlanta, GA 30303-1089

Berkshire Athenaeum
  Local History and Literature Services
  1 Wendell Avenue
  Pittsfield, MA 01201-6385

California State Library
  Sutro Library Branch
  480 Winston Drive
  San Francisco, CA 94132-1777

The Church of Jesus Christ of Latter-day Saints
  *Family History Library**
  35 North West Temple Street
  Salt Lake City, UT 84150-1003

The Connecticut Historical Society
  1 Elizabeth Street
  Hartford, CT 06105-2292

*Dallas Public Library**
  Genealogy Collection
  1515 Young Street
  Dallas, TX 75201-5499

Denver Public Library
  Western History/Genealogy Department
  10 West 14th Avenue Parkway
  Denver, CO 80204-2731

Detroit Public Library
  Burton Historical Collection
  5201 Woodward Avenue
  Detroit, MI 48202-4093

The Filson Club Historical Society
  1310 South Third Street
  Louisville, KY 40208-5506

Houston Public Library
  Clayton Library
  Center for Genealogical Research
  5300 Caroline Street
  Houston, TX 77004-6896

*Library of Congress**
  Local History and Genealogy Reading Room
  Humanities and Social Sciences Division
  Thomas Jefferson Building, Room LJ G42
  Washington, DC 20540-5554

Library of Michigan
  Michigan Library and Historical Center
  717 W. Allegan Street
  P.O. Box 30007
  Lansing, MI 48909-7507

Los Angeles Public Library*
History and Genealogy Department
630 West Fifth Street
Los Angeles, CA 90071-2097

National Society, Daughters of the
American Revolution Library
1776 D Street, N.W.
Washington, DC 20006-5392

New England Historic Genealogical Society*
101 Newbury Street
Boston, MA 02116-3007

The New York Public Library*
Center for the Humanities
U.S. History, Local History
 and Genealogy Division
Fifth Avenue and 42nd Street, Room 315S
New York, NY 10018-2788

Newberry Library*
Local & Family History Room
60 West Walton Street
Chicago, IL 60610-3380

Onondaga County Public Library
Local History and Special Collections
447 South Salina Street
Syracuse, NY 13202-2494

Orange County Library System
Genealogy Department
101 East Central Boulevard
Orlando, FL 32801-2471

Public Library of Cincinnati and Hamilton County*
History Department
800 Vine Street
Library Square
Cincinnati, OH 45202-2071

The State Historical Society of Wisconsin*
816 State Street
Madison, WI 53706-1482

Western Reserve Historical Society
Ohio Network of American History
 Research Centers
10825 East Boulevard
Cleveland, OH 44106-1777

Bibliography of Sources Indexed

★*Source Number*

★**90.20**

ALBERTS, JAN, and LYNDEN E. REYNOLDS. "Voyage of the *April* — Amsterdam to New Castle . . . ." In *The Palatine Immigrant,* vol. 19:3 (June, 1994), pp. 144-155.

Date and port of arrival. Village, canton, and state of origin, and family data may also be provided.

★**117.5**

ANDERSON, ROBERT CHARLES. "The *Mary & John*: Developing Objective Criteria for a Synthetic Passenger List." In *The New England Historical and Genealogical Register,* vol. CXLVII (April 1993), pp. 148-161.

Date and port of arrival or date and place of first mention of residence in the New World. Extracted from several sources, mainly passenger lists, and records of the Massachusetts Bay General Court, and Dorchester Town Records. Name of ship, place of origin, and other genealogical and historical information may also be provided.

★**121.35**

"ANNOUNCEMENT OF NATURALIZATION." In *Lake County (IL) Genealogical Society Quarterly,* vol. 15:3 (Spring 1995), pp. 100-101.

Date and place of naturalization. Extracted from the newspaper *Independent-Register,* September 16, 1930. Place of residence at the time of naturalization is also provided.

★**152.20**

ARRAS, THERON H.L. "Shipwreck." In *The Palatine Immigrant,* vol. 13:2 (July 1988), pp. 54-71.

Date and port of arrival. The microfilm of the ship list is on file at the U.S. National Archives. Date and place of birth, family information, and other genealogical information may also be provided. Historical data on the shipwreck is also provided.

★**170.15**

AUERBACH, INGE. *Hessische Auswanderer (Hesaus): Index nach Familiennamen. Bd. I: Auswanderer aus Hanau im 18. Jahrhundert.* Marburg: Archivschule Marburg, 1987. 48p. (Veroeffentlichungen der Archivschule Marburg. . ., Nr. 12)

Hessian Immigrants: Index to Family Names. Book I: Immigrants from Hanau in the 18th Century. Date and port of arrival. Hometown, assets, occupation, and code of dossier may also be provided.

★**179.55**

"AUSWANDERER AUS DEM OBERAMT GAILDORF." In *Rundschau fuer den Schwaebischen Wald,* no. 40 (02-18-93), p. 19.

"Immigrants from the Gaildorf District." Date and port of arrival. Place of origin and other historical data are also provided.

★**358.56**

BARNETT, LE ROY. "The Immigration Records of Rudolph Diepenbeck." In *The Detroit Society for Genealogical Research Magazine,* Part I, vol. 60:2 (Winter 1997), pp. 51-55; Part II, vol. 60:3 (Spring 1997), pp. 99-102; Part III, vol. 60:4 (Summer 1997), pp. 147-150. Part IV, vol. 61:1 (Fall 1997), pp. 3-8.

Date and port arrival. Country of origin and value of personal property are also provided; occupation and other historical and genealogical data may also be provided.

★**471.10**

BEEKMAN, JANE KYHL, and JOYCE COLLEEN LIBES. "Delaware County, Indiana, Declaration of Intention & Application for Citizenship Records." In *Delaware County Genealogist and Historian,* vol. 4:3 (September 1995), pp. 61-62; vol. 4:4 (December 1995), pp. 86-88.

Date and port of arrival, date and place of declaration of intention, or date and place of first mention of residence in the New World. Extracted from records at the Civil Court Order Books available in Archives and Special Collections, Bracken Library, Ball State University, Indiana. Place of origin, physical description, port of embarkation, and other genealogical information may also be provided.

★**554.30**

"BIRTH REGISTER OF THE GERMAN BAPTIST CONGREGATION, Carrington, Dakota." In *Heritage Review* (Germans from Russia Heritage Society), vol. 23:1 (March 1993), pp. 25-26.

Date of birth and place of church record. Extracted from church records. Place of origin may also be provided.

★**571.7**

BLAHA, ALBERT. "Vessels of 1855." In *PGST News* (Polish Genealogical Society of Texas), vol. 11:3 (Fall 1994), pp. 16-18.

Date and port of arrival of the *Miles* from Hamburg, the *Mississippi* from Bremen, and the *Gessner* from Bremen. Place of last residence in the Old World is also provided.

★**609.10**

BOARDMAN, EDNA. "What He Starts, He Finishes: Jacob and Johanna Wirtz: From Russia to North Dakota via Argentina." In *Heritage Review* (Germans from Russia Heritage Society), vol. 27:1 (March 1997), pp. 13-16.

Date and port of arrival. Extensive biographical and historical information is also provided.

★**777.40**

BRANIGAR, THOMAS. "Swedes in the 1880 Census of Dickinson County, Kansas." In *Swedish American Genealogist,* vol. 14:1 (March 1994), pp. 1-33.

Date and place of census or dates of arrival in the New World and census and place of census. Refer-

ence to original record, family number, sex of the immigrant, occupation, family data, and other genealogical information are also provided.

★778.6

BRASSEAUX, CARL A. *The "Foreign French:" Nineteenth-Century French Immigration into Louisiana.* Volume 2: 1840-1848. Lafayette, LA: The Center for Louisiana Studies, University of Southwestern Louisiana, 1992. 363p.

Date and port of arrival. Sex of the immigrant, occupation, country of nativity, name of ship, and port of embarkation are also provided; other historical data may also be provided. Volume 1 was indexed as source number 778.5 in *PILI 1996.*

★927.31

BREITBARD, GAIL. "Some Names from Revolutionary Census of New Jersey." In *The Lost Palatine,* no. 39 (December 1987), pp. 2-3.

Date of arrival and place of census. Name of ship and other historical information may also be provided.

★930.50

BRESCOLL, STANLEY, JR. "Polish Troops Arriving at New York Aboard the SS Rochambeau on 14 March 1920." In *Polish Eaglet* (Polish Genealogical Society of Michigan), vol. 16:2 (May 1996), pp. 48-49.

Date and port of arrival. Copied from the ship's manifest. Intended destination, marital status, and place of birth are also provided.

★970.38

BROSZ, ALLYN. "Passenger Ship Lists." In *Clues* (American Historical Society of Germans from Russia), 1995, pp. 75-82.

Date and port of arrival. Extracted from records at the U.S. National Archives. Name of ship, place of origin, and intended destination are also provided.

★1002.51

BUECHER, ROBERT. "Passenger List: Ship *Ruthelin,* 17 Nov. 1834." In *St. Clair County Genealogical Society Quarterly,* vol. 11:2 (1988), pp. 110-114.

Date and port of arrival. Extracted from "Quarterly Abstracts of Passenger Lists of Vessels Arriving at New Orleans, 1820-1875." Sex of the immigrant, occupation, and place of origin may also be provided.

★1029.59

BURDICK, LIZ, JULIE McKEOWN, MABELLE NEWMAN, and NITA PUGH. *Jefferson County, Colorado Natrualization Records—1862-1920.* Lakewood, CO: Foothills Genealogical Society of Colorado, Inc., 1989. 97p.

Date and port of arrival, date and place of declaration of intention, or date and place of oath. Extracted from original records located at the Colorado State Archives in Denver. Place of birth is also provided.

★1053.15

BYRNE, CYRIL. "The Brig *Thomas Farrell.*" In *An Nasc: The Newsletter of the D'Arcy McGee Chair of Irish Studies,* vol. 4:1 (Winter 1991), pp. 6-7.

Date and port of arrival. Original records are located at the Colonial Office, London, item CO194/71 f. 322-323, and is available on microfilm at Canada's National Archives at Ottawa, Ontario.

★1053.20

BYRNE, CYRIL J. "The Case of the Schooner *Fanny* from Waterford to St. John's, 1811." In *An Nasc: The Newsletter of the D'Arcy McGee Chair of Irish Studies,* vol. 3:1 (Spring/Summer 1990), pp. 19-22.

Date and port of arrival. Extracted from records located in the Colonial Office Materials for Newfoundland, Canada, and cited as CO 194/51 f.17ff. Original list is located at the British Library, Kew, England. Physical description and other genealogical information are also provided.

★1088.45

CAMIN, BETTY J. *North Carolina Naturalization Index 1792-1862.* Mt. Airy, NC: the author, 1989. 38p.

Date and place of naturalization. Extracted from North Carolina County and State court minutes and county miscellaneous records. Place of residence at naturalization is also provided; country of origin may also be provided.

★1131.61

CARR, PETER E. "Passenger Arrivals in San Luis Obispo in 1868." In *San Luis Obispo County Genealogical Society Bulletin,* vol. 28:3 (Fall 1995), pp. 89-90.

Date and port of arrival. Extracted from various issues of the newspaper *San Luis Obispo Pioneer.* Newspaper date and name of ship are also provided.

★1132.30

CARVELL, KENNETH L. "Early German Settlements in Present-Day West Virginia." In *The Palatine Immigrant,* vol. 13:3 (September 1988), pp. 146-152.

Date and place of first mention of residence in the New World or date and port of arrival. Much genealogical and historical information is also provided.

★1142.10

CHARBONNEAU, HUBERT. "Femmes de moeurs legeres au XVIIe siecle." In *Memoires* (Societe Genealogique Canadienne-Francaise, Montreal, Quebec), vol. 47:2 (Summer 1996), pp. 127-134.

"Women of light morals in the 17th century." Date and port of arrival; a few are date and place of banishment. Additional information may be found in *La vie libertine en Nouvelle-France au dix-septieme siecle* by R.-L. Seguin (Montreal: Lemeac, 1972).

★1173.1

"CITIZENSHIP DAY SEPT. 17, 1926." In *Nyando Roots* (Nyando Roots Genealogical Club, Massena, NY), vol. 11:2 (April 1994), p. 2.

Date and place of naturalization.

★1183.3

CLARK, ROLAND. "Early Boats: Passengers to Virginia on the *Speedwell.*" In *Prospector* (Antelope Valley Genealogical Society [CA]), vol. 16:2 (Spring 1994), pp. 30-31.

Date and port of arrival. Excerpted from *A Consolidation of Ship Passenger Lists from The New England Historical and Genealogical Record,* by Michael Tepper (1980).

★1192.4

CLASEN, ARMIN. "Deutsche Auswanderung nach Chile, 1853-1856." In *Zeitschrift fuer Niedersaechsische Familienkunde,* 33. Jahrgang, Heft 4 (Juli 1958), pp. 86-101.

"German Immigrants to Chile, 1853-1856." Date and port of arrival.

★1211.15

"CLAY CO. NATURALIZATIONS 1866-1932." In *ILGS Teaser* (Iowa Lakes Genealogical Society, Spencer, IA), vol. 10:2 (September 1994), pp. 8-11 (A-I); vol. 10:3 (December 1994), pp. 15-20 (J-Z).

Date and place of naturalization.

★1211.45

CLEGG, HELEN T. "The Mormon Battalion Company C." In *Genealogical Journal* (Utah Genealogical Association), vol. 25:3 (1997), pp. 129-136.

Date and place of death. Date of birth, places of birth and death, and other genealogical information may also be provided.

★1220.12

COLDHAM, PETER WILSON. *The Complete Book of Emigrants in Bondage, 1614-1775.* Baltimore: Genealogical Publishing Co., Inc., 1988. pp. 462-920.

Date and port of arrival, or date of sentencing or reprieve for transport and port of arrival. Name of ship, crime convicted of, and other information may also be provided. The first part of this book was indexed as source number 1220.11 in *PILI 1999 Part 1.*

★1236.25

COLDHAM, PETER WILSON. "Maryland Land-Patent Records, 1671-80: Correlated Evidence Identifying Transported Convicts." In *National Genealogical Quarterly,* vol. 83:1 (March 1995), pp. 44-53.

Date and place where patent was granted. Extracted from information on the Patent Rolls at the British Public Record Office. Place of origin and date of order of transportation may also be provided; reference to location in Patent Books is also provided.

★1276.15

COMFORT, MAURICE E. "Disbanded Troops, Settled Loyalists and Emigrants in the Niagara District in 1787." In *Families* (Ontario Genealogical Society, Toronto), vol. 27:4 (November 1988), pp. 227-232.

Date and place of settlement. Extracted from film C3002 of R.G.4 A I vol. 34 in the National Archives of Canada. Other genealogical and historical information may also be provided.

★1416.15

CROWDER, NORMAN K. "Ship *MacDonald* 1786." In *Clan Donald Canada,* vol. 2:1 (January/February 1994), pp. 8-9.

Date and port of arrival. Some historical information is also provided.

★1422.10

CURRY, LOUISE. "Some Records of Emigrants to North Carolina." In *Argyll Colony Plus* (Journal of the North Carolina Scottish Heritage Society), vol. 9:1 (March 1995), pp. 54-63.

Date and port of arrival. Port of embarkation, name of ship, occupation, country of origin, and other genealogical information are also provided.

★1447.20

DANIEL, WILLIAM D., MRS. "Naturalization Records, District Court, Gray County, Kansas, 1887-1906." In *The Treesearcher* (Kansas Genealogical Society), vol. 34:2 (Summer 1992), pp. 62-65.

Date and place of naturalization or date and place of declaration of intention. Country of birth and other genealogical information are also provided.

★1451.56

DAVIS, ROBERT S., JR. "Some Frenchmen Become United States Citizens, Wilkes County, 1795." In *Contents* (Georgia Genealogical Society), vol. 30:2 (Summer 1994), p. 118.

Date and place of petition for citizenship. The original record is located in the Joseph M. Toomey Collection, Acquisition 78-528, Box 4, Georgia Department of

Archives and History. Names of witnesses are also provided.

★1494.20

DEFNET, MARY ANN. "Declarations of Intention—Door County." In *Belgian Laces,* vol. 17:62 (1995-1), pp. 11-12.

Date and port of arrival; one is date and place of declaration of intention. Original declarations are on file at the Area Research Center, University of Wisconsin/Green Bay. Year of birth and date of declaration of intention are also provided.

★1494.21

DEFNET, MARY ANN. "Declaration of Intention—Kewaunee County." In *Belgian Laces,* vol. 17:63 (1995-2), p. 31.

Date and port of arrival. Original declarations are on file at the Area Research Center, University of Wisconsin/Green Bay. Year of birth and date of declaration of intention are also provided.

★1495.20

DEFNET, MARY ANN., and OTHERS "Belgian Emigrants." In *Belgian Laces,* vol. 11:3 (1989), pp. 49-50; vol. 11:4 (1989), pp. 66-67; vol. 12:1 (1990), p. 12; vol. 12:2 (1990), p. 29; vol. 12:3 (1990), p. 40-41; vol. 12:4 (1990) pp. 55-56; vol. 13:1 (1991), pp. 7-8; vol. 13:2 (1991), p. 28; vol. 13:3/4 (1991), pp. 45-46.

Date of emigration and port of arrival. Place of origin, date of birth, and family data may also be provided.

★1640.8

DOBSON, DAVID. "Scotland: British-Army Deserters in America, circa 1750." In *National Genealogical Society Quarterly,* vol. 76:3 (September 1988), pp. 233-34.

Date and place of desertion or of discharge. Extracted from file GD45.2.35 at the Scottish Record Office (SRO) in Edinburgh. Name of company served in is also provided.

★1640.55

DOLEGA, FLORENCE, JAMES DUNBECK, THERESA KALINSKI, and JAN ZALESKI. "Poles Filing Naturalization Petitions (Federal) in Detroit, MI, in October, 1929." In *Polish Eaglet* (Polish Genealogical Society of Michigan), vol. 15:3 (September 1995), pp. 112-117.

Date and place of naturalization. Extracted from LDS microfilm numbers 1509870 (petitions 44827 to 45094), 1509871 (petitions 45102 to 45677), and 1509872 (petitions 45680 to 45868). Petition number, race, date of birth, and place of birth are also provided.

★1640.60

DOLEGA, FLORENCE, and JAN ZALESKI. "Poles Filing Naturalization Petitions (Federal) in Detroit, MI, in March & April, 1930." In *Polish Eaglet* (Polish Genealogical Society of Michigan), vol. 17:2 (May 1997), pp. 76-83.

Date and place of naturalization. Extracted from LDS microfilm numbers 1510080 (petitions 48429 to 48648), 1510081 (petitions 48666 to 49238), and 1510082 (petitions 49241 to 49635). Petition number, race, place of birth, and date pf birth are also provided; indication of military service may also be provided.

★1642

DONOVAN, GEORGE FRANCIS. *The Pre-Revolutionary Irish in Massachusetts, 1620-1775.* Menasha, WI: George Banta Publishing Co., 1932. 158p.

Date and port of arrival, date and place of marriage, or date and place of first mention of residence in the New World. All names indexed unless birth in U.S. was specifically mentioned. Author extracted only names of Irish origin almost entirely from Whitmore's *Port Arrivals. . .Boston, 1715-1716 and 1762-1769* (indexed as source no. 9750 in *PILI,* 1st edition). Donovan's work was originally a doctoral dissertation, St. Louis University, 1931.

★1658.20

DOYLE, JAMES W., JR. "The *Mayflower* Comes to Virginia, 1633." In *Tidewater Virginia Families,* vol. 3:4 (February/March 1995), pp. 208-216.

Date and port of arrival. Extracted from the Burwell-Vause Head Right List. Much historical information is also provided.

★1766.1

EDDINS, BETTY. ["Addition to Passenger List of SS *David Hoadley* from Antwerp to N.Y., 17 April 1856."] In *Belgian Laces,* vol. 12:3/44 (1990), p. 45.

Date and port of arrival. Country of origin and sex of the immigrant are also provided; occupation may also be provided.

★1766.20

EDER, LINDA. "Notice of Application for Admission to Citizenship." In *The Kane County [IL] Chronicles,* vol. 15:4 (September-December 1994), pp. 34-37; vol. 16:1 (January-March 1995), pp. 3-4; vol. 16:2 (April-June 1995), pp. 14-19; vol. 16:3 (July-September 1995), pp. 23-28.

Date and port of arrival. Extracted from records at the Kane County Circuit Court. Place of birth; residence at the time of application; filing, posting, and hearing dates; and names of witnesses are also provided.

★1822.55

ELLINGSON, IRMGARD HEIN. "Declarations of Intext, Marathon County, Wisconsin." In *Wandering Volhynians,* vol. 8:1 (March 1995), p. 10.

Date and place of declaration of intention. Date and place of birth and residence at the time of declaration may also be provided.

★1823.17

ELLIOTT, BRUCE S. *Index to the 1871 Census of Ontario: Lambton.* Toronto: Ontario Genealogical Society, 1986. 181p. There are two pages on each leaf.

Date and place of census. Census records are on microfilm at the Public Archives of Canada. Sex of the immigrant, country of birth, religion, ethnicity, occupation, district, subdistrict, division, and page number of record in census are also provided.

★1823.21

ELLIOTT, BRUCE S. *Index to the 1871 Census of Ontario: London, Middlesex.* Toronto: Ontario Genealogical Society, 1990. 405p.

Date and place of census. Census films are available from the National Archives of Canada. Place of birth, religion, ethnicity, occupation, district, subdistrict, division, and page of original record are also provided.

★1826.15

"ELLIS COUNTY ALIEN REGISTRATION, 1917-1918." In *The Kansas Review* (The Kansas Council of Genealogical Societies), vol. 17:4 (April 1992), p 81.

Date and place of registration. These affidavits were submitted by local registrars of the Chief Registrar for the District of Kansas under provisions of proclamations of the President of the United States dated No-

vember 16, 1917-April 19, 1918. Date of birth and country of origin are also provided.

★1833.5

"EMIGRANTS TO CAPE BRETON, 1906." In *The Cape Breton Genealogical Society Newsletter* (Sydney, Nova Scotia), vol. 4:23 (January 1995), p. 7.

Date and port of arrival. Ticket number, marital status, place of birth, occupation, and port of embarkation may also be provided.

★1860.4

ENGLAND, LOUISE C. "Canadian Passenger Lists." In *Clues* (American Historical Society of Germans from Russia), 1987, part 2, pp. 39-44.

Date and port of arrival. Microfilms of these passenger lists are available at the Public Archives of Canada. Occupation, intended destination, and name of ship may also be provided.

★1865.50

ERICKSON, JAMES E. "First Covenant Church, St. Paul, MN, Members, 1874-1905." In *Swedish American Genealogist,* vol. 13:1 (March 1993), pp. 23-52; vol. 13:2 (June 1993), pp. 91-115; vol. 13:3 (Sept 1993), pp. 156-179; vol. 13:4 (December 1993), pp. 201-215.

Date of emigration and place of first mention of residence in the New World or date and place when joined church. Occupation, date and place of birth, and other genealogical and historical information may also be provided.

★1883.7

ESSIG, ALICE. "Passenger Lists." In *Heritage Review* (Germans from Russia Heritage Society), vol. 18:2 (May 1988), pp. 37-48.

Date and port of arrival. Occupation, sex of the immigrant, place of origin, intended destination, and name of ship may also be provided.

★1920.45

"FAMILY & CREW OF THE ORIGINAL *MAYFLOWER*." In *Shiawassee Steppin' Stones* (Shiawassee County Genealogical Society), vol. 24:2 (January 1995), p. 5.

Date and port of arrival. Occupation may also be provided; number of persons on board and other information are also provided. Also appears in *Michigan Genealogical Council Newsletter,* vol. 23:3 (Summer 1995), pp. 48-49.

★1937.10

FARR, ROBIN MARLATT. "List of Saloon Passengers on the *S.S. Circassian* (Allan Line), Bound for Quebec, 18 June 1885." In *Families* (Ontario Genealogical Society, Toronto), vol. 36:1 (February 1997), p. 52.

Date and port of arrival. Extracted from a brochure printed for the voyage.

★2054.10

"FINNEY COUNTY ALIEN REGISTRATION RECORDS." In *The Kansas Review* (The Kansas Council of Genealogical Societies), vol. 18:2 (October 1992), p. 48.

Date and place of registration of affidavit of alien enemy or alien female.

★2094.25

"FORD COUNTY ALIEN REGISTRATION." In *The Kansas Review* (The Kansas Council of Genealogical Societies), vol. 18:2 (October 1992), p. 50.

Date and place of registration. These affidavits were submitted by local registrars of the Chief Registrar for the District of Kansas under provisions of proclamations of the President of the United States dated No-

vember 16, 1917-April 19, 1918. Place registered from, date of birth, and country of origin are also provided.

★2314.30

GADOURY, LORRAINE. *La Noblesse de Nouvelle-France: Familles et Alliances.* Ville La Salle, Quebec: Editions Hurtubise, 1991. 212p. Annexes 2 through 5, pp. 166-197.

> *The Nobles of New France.* Date and port of arrival (pp. 166-170), date and place of marriage (p. 171), date and port of arrival or place of marriage (p. 172), or date and port of arrival or place of ennoblement (pp. 173-197). This book is among the holdings of the Family History Library in Salt Lake City.

★2526.42

GIEG, ELLA. *Auswanderungen aus dem Odenwaldkreis.* Band 1. Luetzelbach: Ella Gieg, 1988. 204p.

> *Immigrants from the Odenwald District of Hesse. Book 1.* Date and port of arrival. Other genealogical and historical information are also provided.

★2526.43

GIEG, ELLA. *Auswanderungen aus dem Odenwaldkreis.* Band 2. Luetzelbach: Ella Gieg, 1989. 240p.

> *Immigrants from the Odenwald District of Hesse. Book 2.* Date and port of arrival. Occupation and family data may also be provided.

★2763.1

GRAY, MARY PARKER. ''Naturalizations from Lorain County Common Pleas Court Journals.'' Two parts. In *Lorain County Researcher* (Lorain County Chapter, Ohio Genealogical Society), vol. 8:1 (Winter 1991), pp. 7-9; vol. 8:2 (Spring 1992), pp. 20-22.

> Date and place of naturalization. Book and page number of original record and country of former allegiance are also provided.

★2769.54

GREEN, STINA B. ''Citizenship Class Attendance Records, St. Louis County Board of Education.'' In *Minnesota Genealogical Journal,* no. 14 (September 1995), pp. 1377-1386.

> Date and place of class. Extracted from records at the State Archives at the Minnesota Historical Society. Number of classes attended, course(s) of study, grades, and name of teacher may also be provided.

★2770.40

GREENING, DELL, and VELMA H. RICE. ''Superior Court of King Co., Seattle, Wa., Naturalization Papers.'' In *Seattle Genealogical Society Bulletin,* vol. 37:3 (Spring 1988), pp. 134-137; vol. 37:4 (Summer 1988), pp. 192-195); vol. 38:1 (Autumn 1988), pp. 24-27; vol. 38:2 (Winter 1988/89), pp. 79-81.

> Date and place of declaration of intention or of naturalization. Original volumes are housed at the Seattle Branch of the Federal Archives at Sandpoint Way. Country of origin is also provided.

★2853.20

HABENICHT, JAN. *History of Czechs in America.* St. Paul, MN: Czechoslovak Genealogical Society International, 1996. 581p.

> Date and port of arrival or date and place of first mention of residence in the New World. Much genealogical and historical information are also provided. The editors only indexed names of persons who the source stated were immigrants. Originally published as *Dejiny Cechuv Americkych* by the Hlas (Voice) Publishing Co., St. Louis, Missouri, in 1910.

★2897.7

HARDING, MARY-LYNNE. ''Destination Kamloops & Other Points in the B.C. Interior.'' In *Family Footsteps* (Kamloops Family History Society), vol. 7:1 (April 1991), pp. 7-10.

> Date and port of arrival. Extracted from National Archives of Canada Ship Manifests, Reel T-4767: Quebec/Montreal 17 May 1910-17 June 1910. Name of ship, intended destination, and place of birth are also provided; occupation may also be provided.

★2910.35

HARRISON, MICHAEL. ''Nominal List of Repealers From the *Toronto Mirror* 2 Feburary 1844.'' In *Families* (Ontario Genealogical Society), vol. 36:2 (June 1997), pp. 111-116.

> Date and place when list was published. Irish county of origin is also provided.

★2978.15

HAYWARD, GEORGE H. ''Provincial Secretary Immigration Records.'' In *Generations* (New Brunswick Genealogical Society), issue 66 (Winter 1995), pp. 35-41.

> Date and port of arrival. Extracted from Provincial Archives of New Brunswick, RS555, Provincial Secretary: Immigration Administration Records, Blc, Sick Immigrants, microfilm reel F16226. Place of nativity, place of origin, name of ship, and other genealogical data are also provided.

★2978.20

HAYWARD, GEORGE H. ''St. Andrews Immigration Records.'' In *Generations* (New Brunswick Genealogical Society), vol. 18:1 (Spring 1996), pp. 6-10.

> Date and port of arrival. Place of origin is provided; other genealogical and historical information is also provided.

★3004.30

HEINSOHN, MARLENE. ''Full Fledged Citizens.'' In *Roots and Leaves* (Eastern Nebraska Genealogical Society, Fremont), vol. 15:3 (Fall 1992), p. 46.

> Date and place of naturalization. Extracted from the *West Point [NE] Republican,* 22 Dec. 1905.

★3036.5

HENNESSEY, G. P. ''The Yorkshire Migration.'' In *The Flowing Stream* (Sheffield and District Family History Society), vol. 9:2 (Winter 1988), pp. 40-42; vol. 9:3 (Spring 1989), pp. 67-78.

> Date and port of arrival of the ships *Albion* and *Jenny* from Hull, England. Occupations and other historical and genealogical data are also provided.

★3051

HERPIN, JULIEN. ''Les Malouins colonisateurs au Canada: les Acadiens deportes dans la region Malouine.'' (Les Provinces de France et la Nouvelle France.) In *Nova Francia,* Vol. 3:2 (December 1927), pp. 111-118; vol. 3:5 (June 1928), pp. 309-314.

> ''Colonizers from St. Malo [France] in Canada: deported Canadians in the St. Malo region.'' Date and place where the Reverend Father Isidore created a register listing some of the original settlers of Louisbourg who eventually retired to Saint-Servan. Earlier parts of this article were indexed in *PILI 1993.*

★3160.1

HINDS, A. LEONE. ''Destitute and Sick Emigrants at Prescott, 1835.'' In *Families* (Ontario Genealogical Society, Toronto), vol. 33:3 (August 1994), p.150.

> Date and place of medical treatment. Extracted from National Archives microfilm C-9824, pp. 85852-85857, finding aid 881, page 157.

★3208.30

THE HISTORICAL CENTER OF YORK COUNTY. "New Citizens in York District." In *The Quarterly* (The York County Genealogical and Historical Society, Rock Hill, SC), vol. 3:3 (December 1991), pp. 31-32; vol. 4:3 (December 1992), pp. 18-19.

Date and place of naturalization. Some historical information is also provided. Both articles cited here appear to be the same.

★3274.55—3274.56

HOLMES, JAMES M. "Worcester County Superior Court Naturalizations, Vol. 1: 1837-1848." In *Massog* (Massachusetts Society of Genealogists).

★3274.55

vol. 14:3 (September 1990), pp. 65-75 (1-121); vol. 15:1 (March 1991), pp. 22-27 (122-198); vol. 15:2 (June 1991), pp. 42-44 (199-231).

★3274.56

vol. 15:3 (September 1991), pp. 69-72 (232-274); vol. 15:4 (December 1991)), pp. 96-101 (275-340).

Date and port of arrival. Extracted from court records located at the Worcester Court Building at Lincoln Square. Place of residence at naturalization, date of naturalization, date and place of birth, age upon naturalization, date of declaration of intention, names of witnesses, and other genealogical information may also be provided.

★3276.1

HOLT COUNTY, MISSOURI NATURALIZATIONS, 1850-1900. St. Joseph, MO: Northwest Missouri Genealogical Society, [1991]. 4p.

Date and place of declaration of intention or of naturalization. Page number of record in original source and country of origin are also provided. Indexers paginated this source.

★3276.8

HOLTZMAN, MIMI LOZANO. "The Basque: From the Pyrenees of France and Spain to Orange County, CA 1860-1890." In *Orange County California Genealogical Society Journal,* vol. 33:1 (April 1996), pp. 17-21.

Date and port of arrival or date and place of first mention of residence in the New World. Much genealogical information is also provided.

★3289.1

HOUSTON, CECIL J. and WILLIAM J. SMYTH. "Immigrants Assisted at Prescott, Upper Canada, 1835." In *Irish Emigration and Canadian Settlement: Patterns, Links, and Letters,* University of Toronto Press, Toronto, 1990, pp. 60-62, 347.

Date and place of assistance. Extracted from record C-6887, Upper Canada Sundries, at the National Archives of Canada. Country of origin, intended destination, and other genealogical information are also provided.

★3331.4

HURLBERT, GEORGIANA. "Bryan County, Oklahoma, Naturalization Papers." In *Bryan County Heritage Quarterly* (Bryan County Heritage Association, Calera, OK), May 1992, pp. 11-12.

Date and port of arrival. Age at naturalization, place of birth, and port of embarkation are also provided; date of birth may also be provided.

★3366.30

"HUTCHINSON COUNTY NATURALIZATION: Volume V00347, Declaration of Intent." In *South Dakota Genealogical Society Quarterly,* vol. 14:2 (October 1995), p. 70.

Most are date and port of arrival; a few are place of naturalization, in which case indexers assumed a range of dates as a date was not given. Original records are at the South Dakota State Archives. Country of birth, date of birth, and page number of record in original source are also provided.

★3435.45

"INDEX TO NATURALIZATION RECORDS, NACOGDOCHES COUNTY, TEXAS, District Court." In *Yesterdays* (Nacogdoches Genealogical Society), vol. 14:2 (September 1994), pp. 35-37.

Date and place of naturalization. Country of birth may also be provided.

★3476.10

JACKMAN, DIANNE C. "Notices Appearing in *The Royal Gazette*-1814." In *The Newfoundland Ancestor* (Newfoundland and Labrador Genealogical Society), vol. 9:1 (May 1993), p. 54.

Date and port of arrival. Name of ship is also provided; port of embarkation and other information may also be provided.

★3476.25

JACKSON, GEORGE C. "Some Louisiana Immigrants to Puerto Rico." In *New Orleans Genesis,* (Genealogical Research Society of New Orleans), vol. 36:142 (April 1997), pp. 111-114.

Date and place of receipt of letter of citizenship or date and place of first mention of residence in the New World. Place of origin and other genealogical information are also provided.

★3476.30

JACKSON, LOUISE. "British Aliens Seek Naturalization in War of 1812." In *The Quarterly* (The York County Genealogical and Historical Society, Rock Hill, SC), vol. 4:4 (March 1993), pp. 11-13.

Date and place of petition for naturalization. Extracted from Kenneth Scott, *British Aliens in the United States During the War of 1812,* indexed in *PILI 1982* as source number 8195. Number of years resident of the U.S., nationality, family data, and residence may also be provided.

★3580.20

JOHNSON, WM. C. "Naturalizations from Jefferson County, Ohio, 1818-1879." In *Jefferson County Lines* (Jefferson County Chapter, Ohio Genealogical Society), vol. 9:3 (Fall 1995), pp. 31-34.

Date and place of naturalization; a few are date and place of declaration of intention. Extracted from Superior Court Journal, 1818-1831, Supreme Court Journal, 1832-1850, and District Court Journal, 1852-1879. Place of origin and reference to original source are also provided.

★3629.40

JONES, VICTOR T., JR. "Swiss-Palatines to New Bern: A List of Known Persons Who Left Switzerland and Germany to Settle New Bern, N. C., in 1710." In *North Carolina Genealogical Society Journal,* vol. 23:1 (February 1997), pp. 3-10.

Date and place of first mention of residence in the New World. Historical and family information may also be provided.

★3665.20

JORDAN, RENE. "Some Knox County, Tennessee, Naturalizations, 1876-1906." In *Tennessee Ancestors* (East Tennessee Historical Society, Knoxville), vol. 8:2 (August 1992), pp. 111-112.

Date and place where petition for naturalization was filed or date and port of arrival. Country of origin and other genealogical information are also provided.

★3675.1
JOYNER, U.P., JR. "Orange County Notes." In *Orange County [Orange, VA] Historical Society Newsletter,* vol. 20:3 (March 1989), unpaginated.

Date and place of assignment of land. Extracted from Orange County Order Book 5, page 234, March 22, 1749. This article appears on the back cover of the newsletter.

★3687.1
JUSTESEN, ELAINE. "The Mormon Batallion." In *Genealogical Journal* (Utah Genealogical Association), vol. 25:1 (1997), pp. 33-40.

Date and place of death. Date and place of birth and family information is also provided.

★3799.30
KENNEDY, MICHAEL. "Emigrants on the *Edinburgh,* 1771: A New Passenger List for Prince Edward Island." In *The Island Magazine,* no. 39 (Spring/Summer 1996), pp. 39-42.

Date and port of arrival. Other genealogical and historical information are also provided.

★3845.2
KLETT, JOSEPH R. "Middlesex County Records, Naturalization Petitions and Declarations of Intention, 1794-1812." In *Genealogical Magazine of New Jersey,* vol. 69:3 (September 1994), pp. 128-130.

Date and place of declaration of intention. Extracted from papers of the Middlesex County Court of Common Pleas at the New Jersey State Archives. Place of origin, name of monarch renouncing allegiance to, names of court officials, and other genealogical information are also provided.

★3899.5
KLUEBER, KARL WERNER. "Badische Auswanderer nach Venezuela." In *Genealogie,* Band 7, 13/14 Jahrgang (1964/65), pp. 538-547.

"Immigrants from Baden to Venezuela." Date and port of arrival. Family information is also provided.

★3967.10
KLUEBER, KARL WERNER. "Westeuropaeische Castro-Kolonisten fuer Texas, 1843-1847." In *Genealogie,* Band 12, 23. Jahrgang, Heft 12 (December 1974), pp. 369-379.

"Western European Colonists to Texas, 1843-1847." Date and port of arrival. Date and place of transport, name of ship, and other genealogical and historical information are also provided.

★4022.20
KNOWLES, ANNE KELLY. *Calvinists Incorporated: Welsh Immigrants on Ohio's Industrial Frontier.* Chicago: University of Chicago Press, 1997. pp. 271-294.

Date and place of first mention of residence in the New World. Place of origin in Wales and other genealogical information are also provided. This section of the book is called Appendix D, which is not paginated. The editors assigned page numbers beginning with 271 and ending with 294 for this portion.

★4487.25
KVIST, ROGER. "The Galesburg Light Guards During the Civil War." In *Swedish American Genealogist,* vol. 17:2 (July 1997), pp. 49-77.

Date and place where joined service. Marital status, occupation, physical description, place of birth, and military data are also provided.

★4491.30
LADD, DALE A., and ELEANOR CROSS KOEPKE. *1880 Federal Census . . . Genesse County, Michigan.* Flint, MI: The Flint Genealogical Society (PO Box 1217, 48501-1217). *Genesee Township* (1996), 34p.

Date and place of census. Place of birth and page number of census record are also provided.

★4491.33
LADDD, DALE A., and ELEANOR CROSS KOEPKE. *1880 Federal Census . . . Genesse County, Michigan.* Flint, MI: The Flint Genealogical Society (PO Box 1217, 48501-1217). *Grand Blanc Township* (1996), 25p.

Date and place of census. Place of birth and page number of census record are also provided.

★4491.36
LADD, DALE A., and ELEANOR CROSS KOEPKE. *1880 Federal Census . . . Genesse County, Michigan.* Flint, MI: The Flint Genealogical Society (PO Box 1217, 48501-1217). *Montrose Township* (1996), 25p.

Date and place of census. Place of birth and page number of census record are also provided.

★4491.39
LADD, DALE A., and ELEANOR CROSS KOEPKE. *1880 Federal Census . . . Genesse County, Michigan.* Flint, MI: The Flint Genealogical Society (PO Box 1217, 48501-1217). *Mt. Morris Township* (1996), 33p.

Date and place of census. Place of birth and page number of census record are also provided.

★4491.42
LADD, DALE A., and ELEANOR CROSS KOEPKE. *1880 Federal Census . . . Genessee County, Michigan.* Flint, MI: The Flint Genealogical Society (PO Box 1217, 48501-1217). *Mundy Township* (1997), 30p.

Date and place of census. Place of birth and page number of census record are also provided.

★4511.35
LANDIS, LAUREN K. *Index to the Naturalization Records of Stark County, Ohio (1809-1852).* Canton, OH: The Stark County District Library, 1994. 62p.

Date and place of declaration of intention or of naturalization. Extracted from Stark County Common Pleas Journals, on microfilm at the Stark County District Library. Page reference to original record is also provided.

★4514.3
LANDRY, YVES. *Orphelines en France, pionnieres au Canada: Les Filles du roi au XVIIe siecle.* Montreal: Lemeac Editeur, 1992. 438p. Part 2: *Repertoire Biographique Des Filles Du Roi,* pp. 265-379.

Orphans in France, Pioneers in Canada: The King's Daughters in the 17th Century. Part 2: Biographical List of the King's Daughters. Most are date and port of arrival; a few are date and place of first mention of residence in the New World. This book is among the holdings of the Family History Library in Salt Lake City.

★4514.4
LANE, JOY. "Lost Relatives?" In *Hamilton Branch* (Ontario Genealogical Society), vol. 25:2 (May 1994), p. 32.

Date and port of arrival.

★4812.1
LOFGREEN, JUNE. ["Copied from *The Clayton Citizen . . . .*"] In *New Mexico Genealogist* (New Mexico Gene-

alogical Society, Albuquerque, NM), vol. 34:3 (September 1995), p. 87.

Date and place of naturalization. Country of origin is also provided.

★**4879.40**

LUCAS, ELAINE M. "Canadians in Paulding County, Ohio, 1880, Census of the United States." In *Families* (Ontario Genealogical Society), vol. 35:4 (November 1996), pp. 257-260.

Date and place of census. Name of township of residence and page number of record in original census are also provided; occupation may also be provided.

★**4981.45**

McELROY, VIRGINIA VANDERHEYDEN. "Second District Court Register of Naturalizations, Oaths of Applicants and Witnesses, October 15, 1874-December 21, 1875." In *L'Heritage* (St. Bernard Genealogical Society, Chalmette, LA), vol. 13:51 (July 1990), pp. 208-213 (Vols. 1-4: A-Z) (NO VOL. 5); vol. 13:52 (October 1990), pp. 295-298 (Vol. 6: A-Z, Vol. 7: A-G); vol. 14:53 (January 1991), pp. 29-31 (Vol. 7: G-S); vol. 14:54 (April 1991), pp. 130-134 (Vol. 7: S-Z; Vol. 8: A-Z).

Date and place of naturalization. Extracted from microfilm at the New Orleans Public Library. Volume and page number references to original records are also provided.

★**4984.12**

McFADDEN, ANN JOSBERG. "U.S. Citizenship Granted to 72." In *Heritage* (The Genealogical Society of Greater Miami, FL), vol. 20:2 (April 1994), p. 39.

Date and place of naturalization. Extracted from *Miami News,* November 8, 1935, page 12.

★**4984.15**

McFADDEN, ANN JOSBERGER. ["Wednesday, April 28, 1920, *Miami Metropolis.*"] In *Heritage* (Miami, FL), vol. 21:2 (April 1995), p. 38.

Date and place of naturalization. City of residence at the time of naturalization is also provided; race or nationality may also be provided.

★**5024.1**

McWILLIAMS, PAUL F. "*Lady of the Lake* Passenger List." In *The Report* (Ohio Genealogical Society), vol. 29:3 (Fall 1989), pp. 136-139.

Date and port of arrival. Copied from Genealogical Society of Utah film number 2271, *New York Customs Passenger Lists, 1820-1835.* Port of embarkation, sex of the immigrant, and other genealogical information are also provided.

★**5475.1**

MERGEN, JOSEF. *Die Auswanderungen aus den ehemals preussischen Teilen des Saarlandes im 19. Jahrhundert* (II): Die Auswanderer. Saarbruecken: Institut fuer Landeskunde im Saarland, 1987. 646p. (Veroeffentlichungen des Instituts fuer Landeskunde im Saarland, Band 28)

Emigrations from the former Prussian part of Saarland in the 19th cnetury. Date and port of arrival. Extracted from archives in Saarland, county archives in Saarbrucken, and the main archives in Koblenz. Date and place of birth, port of emigration, information on family members, and other genealogical information may also be provided.

★**5720.10**

MOAK, JEFFERSON M. "The WPA Index of Naturalizations." In *The Pennsylvania Genealogical Magazine,* "An Explanation," vol. 36:2 (1989), pp. 109-116; "Ad-

ditions and Corrections," vol. 38:4 (Fall/Winter 1994), pp. 375-382.

Date and place where declaration of intention to become a citizen was filed or where citizenship was granted. Author seeks to clarify and correct information published in *Philadelphia Naturalization Records* (P.W. Filby) and indexed as source numbers 9290-9314 (see *PILI,* first edition).

★**6007.60**

"NATURALIZATION DAY — February 06, 1918." In *Macoupin County Searcher* (Macoupin County [Staunton, IL] Genealogical Society), vol. 12:4 (April 1992), p. 9.

Date and place of naturalization. Extracted from the *Gillespie News,* February 6, 1918, page 8. Nationality is also provided.

★**6015.10**

"NATURALIZATION RECORDS." In *Kittitas Kinfolk* (Kittitas County [WA] Genealogical Society), vol. 8:2, p. 16.

Date and place of naturalization. Country of former allegiance and page number of record in original source are also provided.

★**6015.15**

"NATURALIZAION RECORDS." In *Polish Footprints* (Polish Genealogical Society of Texas), vol. 12:2 (Summer 1995), pp. 9-13 (Caldwell County, Washington County); vol. 12:3 (Fall 1995), pp. 23-30 (Brazos County).

Most are date and port of arrival; some are date and place of declaration of intention or date and place of naturalization. Date of birth, place of birth, name of ship, name of court, and reference to original record may also be provided.

★**6020.5**

"NATURALIZATIONS FOUND IN THE *INDEX TO THE McLEAN COUNTY PROBATE RECORDS, 1834-1900.*" In *Gleanings from the Heart of the Cornbelt* (McLean County Genealogical Society, Normal, IL), vol. 29:4 (Winter 1995), pp. 131-133.

Date and place of naturalization. Extracted from probate holdings for McLean County located at the Illinois Regional Archives Depository at Illinois State University. Volume and page number reference to original records are also provided.

★**6020.12**

"NATURALIZATIONS FROM JEFFERSON CO., OHIO, COURT RECORDS, 1818-79, Including Declaration of Intention to be a Citizen & Bar Admission." In *Jefferson County Lines* (Jefferson County Chapter of the Ohio Genealogical Society), vol. 6:1 (Spring 1992), pp. 6-7 (A-G); vol. 6:2 (Summer 1992), pp. 12-13 (H-M); vol. 6:3 (Fall 1992), pp. 21-23 (M-Z). Title varies.

Date and place of naturalization or of declaration of intent. Place of origin may also be provided.

★**6079.1**

NEILL, MICHAEL JOHN. *Index to Declarations of Intention to Hancock County, Illinois, 1851-1866.* Carthage, IL: Neill, 1987. 15p.

Date and place of declaration of intention. Extracted from information on file at the Circuit Clerk of Hancock County, second floor, Courthouse. Book and page number of original record are also provided.

★**6155.4**

"NEWBERRY [SC] NATURALIZATION PAPERS." In *Upper South Carolina Genealogy and History Quar-*

terly (Piedmont Historical Society), vol. 9:1 (January 1995), pp. 18-19.

Date and place of naturalization. Extracted from Newberry County Clerk of Court records in the South Carolina Department of Archives and History, Columbia, SC.

★6178.50

NICHOLS, JOAN M. "Oaths of Intention to Become Citizens, Kings County Court of Common Pleas, September 18, 1821 to May 8, 1849." In *New York Genealogical and Biographical Record,* vol. 123:2 (April 1992), pp. 75-78; vol. 123:3 (July 1992), pp. 148-152.

Date and place of oath. Extracted from volume labelled "Circuit Court, Kings County No. 1" at the New York City Municipal Archives. Sex of the immigrant, country of origin, occupation, residence at time of oath, and other genealogical information may also be provided.

★6212.1

"NOTICE OF APPLICATION FOR ADMISSION TO CITIZENSHIP." In *Ozar'kin* (Ozarks Genealogical Society), vol. 14:1 (Spring 1992), 13-16.

Most are date and port of arrival; some are date and place of naturalization. Place of birth, residence at naturalization, and names and residences of witnesses are also provided.

★6214.5

NOVAK, CLARENCE, ET AL. "Poles Filing Naturalization Petitions (Federal) in Detroit, MI, in December, 1929 & January, 1930." In *Polish Eaglet* (Polish Genealogical Society of Michigan), vol. 16:2 (May 1996), pp. 60-71.

Date and place of naturalization; one is date and port of arrival. Extracted from LDS microfilm number 1509873 (petitions 46639 to 46809), 1509874 (petitions 46810 to 47250), 1509875 (petitions 47251 to 47498), and 1510079 (petitions 47504 to 47778). Petition number, race, date of birth, place of birth, and other genealogical information are also provided.

★6254.4

"OATHS OF ALLEGIANCE, NORTHUMBERLAND COUNTY, 1652." In *Tidewater Virginia Families: A Magazine of History and Genealogy,* vol. 3:4 (February/March 1995), pp. 243-244.

Date and place of oath of allegiance. Extracted from records at the Northumberland County Circuit Court.

★6406.6

OLSON, LOLA. "Passenger Lists." In *Heritage Review* (Germans from Russia Heritage Society), vol. 13:3 (September 1983), p. 47.

Date and port of arrival; one is date and place of first mention of residence in the New World. Name of ship, date and port of embarkation, and intended destination are also provided.

★6410.15

OLSSON, NILS WILLIAM. "Emigrants from Gotland [Sweden] to America, 1819-1890." In *Swedish American Genealogist,* vol. 2:3 (September 1982), pp. 102-109.

Date and port of arrival. Extracted from the *Gotlands Landskansli,* signum C III:1-3, held at the Provincial Archives of Visby, Sweden. Occupation and other genealogical information may also be provided.

★6412.40

OLSSON, NILS WILLIAM. "Swedish Seamen Who Deserted in U.S. Ports, 1841-1858." In *Swedish American Genealogist,* vol. 3:4 (Dec. 1983), pp. 141-157.

Date and port of sailor's abandoning ship. Extracted from records loacted in the Stockholm, Sweden, City Archives, signum D1h:1 (1841-1859). Date of registration, rank, place of birth, residence, and other genealogical information may also be provided.

★6424.55

OVERTON, JULIE M. "German Immigrant Arrivals in Boston — 1835." In *The Palatine Immigrant,* vol. 21:1 (December 1995), p. 30-31.

Date and port of arrival. Extracted from NARA microfilm series M277, roll 9, list nos. 38-285. Sex of the immigrant is also provided; occupation and country of origin may also be provided.

★6442.17

PALMER, MICHAEL. "19th-Century Emigrants from Schwarzenbach/Saarland to America." In *German Genealogical Society of America Bulletin,* vol. 3:6 (June 1989), pp. 65, 69.

Date and port of arrival or span of years immigrant was alive during the nineteenth century. Extracted from Petto, *Ortsgeschichte von Schwarzenbach,* Nonnweiler: Verein fur Heimatkunde Nonnweiler, 1987, pp. 136-138. Date of birth, marital status, and name of spouse may also be provided.

★6469.7

"PASSENGER LIST FOT THE BRIG *AMBASSADOR,* Londonderry, Ireland, to Saint John, N.B., 1834." In *Generations* (New Brunswick Genealogical Society), vol. 19:1 (Spring 1997), pp. 4-6.

Date and port of arrival. Names of crew members, occupations, place of origin, and other genealogical information are provided.

★6512.1

"PASSENGER LISTS." In *The Melting Pot* (Melting Pot Genealogical Society, Hot Springs, AR), vol. 3:3 (July 1987), pp. 181-186; vol. 3:4 (October 1987), pp. 228-232.

Date and port of arrival. Name of ship and port of embarkation are also provided; sex of the immigrant, place of origin, intended destination, and occupation may also be provided.

★6529.11

"PASSENGER MANIFEST OF THE BARK *CAROLINA* Which Arrived in New York 27 Oct. 1856, Saefstroem, Master." In *Swedish American Genealogist,* vol. 7:1 (March 1987), pp. 19-26.

Date and port of arrival. Place of origin, occupation, and other genealogical information are also provided.

★6533.11

"PASSENGER SHIP ARRIVALS." In *Pathways and Passages* (Polish Genealogical Society of Conencticut), vol. 13:1 (Fall 1996), pp. 9-10.

Date and port of arrival. Extracted from information at the U.S. National Archives. Birthplace and intended destination are also provided. The information contained in this source was submitted by several persons.

★6795.8

PODOLL, BRIAN A. *Prussian Netzelanders and Other German Immigrants in Green Lake, Marquette & Waushara Counties, Wisconsin.* Bowie, MD: Heritage Books, Inc., 1994. 241p.

Date and place of marriage, death, declaration of intent, or naturalization. Volume, page, and/or record number of original source, place of birth, and other genealogical and historical data may also be provided.

★6954.7

PRITZKAU, GWEN. "Passenger Lists." In *Heritage Review* (Germans from Russia Heritage Society), vol. 17:3 (September 1987), pp. 37-41.

Date and port of arrival. Name of ship and port of embarkation are also provided; name of colony of origin may also be provided.

★7009.9

PUNCH, TERRENCE M. "Finding Our Irish." In *Nova Scotia Historical Review*, vol. 6:1 (1986), pp. 57-62.

Date and port of arrival. Occupation, date of burial, and place of birth are also provided.

★7074.20

PUNCH, TERRENCE M. "Nova Scotians Naturalized at Philadelphia, 1807-1880." In *The Nova Scotia Genealogist*, vol. 10:3 (Fall 1992), pp. 132-133.

Date and place of naturalization. Extracted from Filby, *Philadelphia Naturalization Records*, which was indexed in *PILI* first edition as United States Works Projects Administration, *Index to Records of Aliens' Declarations of Intention and/or Oaths of Allegiance, 1789-1880, in United States Circuit Court, United States District Court, Supreme Court of Pennsylvania, Quarter Sessions Court, Court of Common Pleas, Philadelphia*, source nos. 9290-9314.

★7078

PUNCH, TERRENCE M. "Passengers on the *Aide-de-Camp*." In *Genealogical Research in Nova Scotia*, Halifax, NS: Petheric Press, 1978, p. 80.

Date and port of arrival. Extracted from *The Novascotian*, 29 June 1839, p. 306.

★7085.8

PUNCH, TERRENCE M. "Scots Settlers to Long Point [Cape Breton Island], 1816: the Ship *Tartar*." In *The Nova Scotia Genealogist*, vol. 2:2 (1984), pp. 88-89.

Date and port of arrival. Extracted from PANS, RG 20, Series "A," post-1800.

★7100

PUNCH, TERRENCE M. "Sutherlandshire Settlers on the Brigantine *Prince William*." In *The Nova Scotia Genealogist*, vol. 3:1 (1985), p. 20.

Date and port of arrival. Extracted from PANS, RG 20, Series "A," post-1800.

★7105

PUNCH, TERRENCE M. "Wann Sie in Harrietsfeld Deutsch Sprachen." In *The Nova Scotia Genealogist*, vol. 1:1 (1983), pp. 22-27.

"When in Harrietsfield Speak German." Date and place of land grant. Military data and other genealogical information are also provided.

★7242.30

REES, JIM. *A Farewell to Famine*. Arklow, Ireland: Arklow Enterprise Centre, 1994.

Date and port of arrival. Name of ship and other genealogical informaion are also provided. Also included in "The Luck of the Irish Researcher" by Patrick Coleman in *The Septs* (Irish Genealogical Society, International), vol. 18:2 (April 1997), pp. 8-15.

★7420.1

RIECKENBERG, HEINRICH, editor. *Schaumburger Auswanderer, 1820-1914*. Rinteln: Verlag C. Boesendahl, 1988 (Schaumburger Studien, 48). 535p.

Schaumburg Immigrants, 1820-1914. Date and port of arrival. Place of origin, date of birth, and other genealogical information may also be provided.

★7710.1

ROSS, EVELYN MATHEWS. "Naturalization Record Book A, Carroll Parish, Records of East Carroll Parish, Louisiana." In *Louisiana Genealogical Register*, vol. 44:2 (June 1997), pp. 149-162.

Date and port of arrival and/or date and place of naturalization. Country of origin and other genealogical information are also provided.

★7919.3

SCHAIDL, NORBERT. "Auswanderer aus dem Herzogtum Sachsen-Meiningen 1867/68." In *Mitteldeutsche Familienkunde*, Band 7, 23-25 Jahrgang (1982-1984), pp. 524-535.

"Immigrants from the Duchy of Saxe-Meiningen 1867/68." Date and port of arrival. Place of origin is also provided.

★7951.13

SCHALL, NED. "Passenger Lists." In *Heritage Review*, vol. 17:3 (September 1987), pp. 41-44.

Date and port of arrival. Name of ship, port of embarkation, place of origin, intended destination, and sex of the immigrant are also provided; occupation may also be provided.

★8023.44

SCHEELE, NORBERT. "Zum drittenmal: Der Kreis Olpe und Amerika." In *Heimatstimmen aus dem Kreise Olpe* (*Voice from Home from the Olpe Community*, 6 Folge (1950), pp. 370-381.

"For the Third Time: The Olpe Community and America." Date and port of arrival or date and place of first mention of residence in the New World. Place of origin, intended destination, and other genealogical information may also be provided.

★8115.12

SCHMIDT-BIEBERTAL, ERNST. "Die Auswanderer aus dem Kirchspiel Rodheim an der Bieber nach Nordamerika." In *Hessische Familienkunde*, Band 19, Heft 7 (September 1989), col. 317-328.

"Immigrants from Rodheim Parish on the River to North America." Date and port of arrival. Other genealogical and historical information may also be provided.

★8277.31

"SCOTTISH SETTLERS FROM ISLAY AND JURA (in the Western Isles of Scotland) Who Were Awarded Lots in the Argyle Patent in Washington County, New York." In *New York Lost & Found* (J.W. Enterprises, Highlands Ranch, CO), vol. 2:4 (July 1996), pp. 113-120.

Date and port of arrival. Extracted from *History of Washington County, New York*, Washington Historical Society, 1956. Number of acres in lot and family data are also provided.

★8355.1

SEMANSKE, DIANE and ODETTE, BARBARA. "Passenger Ship Arrivals." In *Pathways and Passages: Official Publication of the Polish of the Polish Genealogical Society of Connecticut/Polish Genealogical Society of the Northeast*, vol. 12:1 (Fall 1995), pp. 15-16.

Date and port of arrival. Place of birth and intended destination are also provided.

★8364.32

SHEARON, JIM. "'Home Children' Passenger List for the Year 1870." In *Anglo Celtic Roots* (British Family History Society of Greater Ottawa), vol. 3:3 (Summer 1997), pp. 11, 21-26.

A

Aai, James 50; Ontario, 1871 *1823.17 p1*
Aaker, A.F.; Iowa, 1877 *1211.15 p8*
Aaron, Chas.; Louisiana, 1874-1875 *4981.45 p297*
Abadie, Mr. 20; America, 1846 *778.6 p1*
Abadie, Mr. 24; America, 1848 *778.6 p1*
Abadie, Mr. 25; Port uncertain, 1844 *778.6 p1*
Abadie, Mr. 36; Port uncertain, 1845 *778.6 p1*
Abadie, C. 30; New Orleans, 1840 *778.6 p1*
Abadie, C. 34; New Orleans, 1840 *778.6 p1*
Abadie, Dominique; Louisiana, 1874 *4981.45 p130*
Abadie, Ferdinand 22; New Orleans, 1848 *778.6 p1*
Abadie, Francois 19; America, 1845 *778.6 p1*
Abadie, J. 40; America, 1848 *778.6 p1*
Abadie, J. B. 18; New Orleans, 1848 *778.6 p1*
Abadie, Jean; New Orleans, 1848 *778.6 p1*
Abadie, Jean 21; New Orleans, 1845 *778.6 p1*
Abadie, Joseph; Louisiana, 1874-1875 *4981.45 p297*
Abadie, Joseph 30; New Orleans, 1843 *778.6 p1*
Abadie, Louis 24; New Orleans, 1848 *778.6 p1*
Abadie, Philippe 18; New Orleans, 1845 *778.6 p1*
Abadie, Raymond Bigobert 21; New Orleans, 1845 *778.6 p1*
Abals, Henry; New York, NY, 1881 *7710.1 p159*
Abarbanell, Eliza 40; Ontario, 1871 *1823.21 p1*
Abat, Octave 19; America, 1846 *778.6 p1*
Abat, Paul 17; America, 1846 *778.6 p1*
Abbey, Thomas Francis 43; Indiana, 1873-1874 *9076.20 p68*
Abbis, Ferdinand 29; America, 1855 *2526.43 p163*
Abbis, Wilhelm; America, 1856 *2526.43 p163*
Abbot, Alexander S. 58; Ontario, 1871 *1823.21 p1*
Abbot, Benjamin 60; Ontario, 1871 *1823.21 p1*
Abbot, Thomas 55; Ontario, 1871 *1823.21 p1*
Abbott, Charles 23; Ontario, 1871 *1823.17 p1*
Abbott, Hodson G. 30; Ontario, 1871 *1823.21 p1*
Abbott, Lawrence; Long Island, 1778 *8529.30 p9A*
Abbott, Richard 62; Ontario, 1871 *1823.21 p1*
Abbott, Robert 32; Michigan, 1880 *4491.39 p1*
Abbott, Samuel 31; Ontario, 1871 *1823.21 p1*
Abbott, Thomas 39; Ontario, 1871 *1823.21 p1*
Abboutt, Francis 73; Ontario, 1871 *1823.17 p1*
Abdt, G. K.; New York, 1859 *358.56 p101*
Abe, Caspar Michael; America, 1868 *7919.3 p526*
Abe, Friedrich; America, 1867 *7919.3 p526*
  With wife & 3 children
Abegg, H. 6; New Orleans, 1834 *1002.51 p112*
Abegg, J. 15; New Orleans, 1834 *1002.51 p112*
Abegg, J. 42; New Orleans, 1834 *1002.51 p112*
Abegg, Miss S. 41; New Orleans, 1834 *1002.51 p112*
Abel, Albert Herm. Edward; Wisconsin, 1895 *6795.8 p148*
Abel, Anna Frantz *SEE* Abel, Michel
Abel, Anna Maria 18; New York, NY, 1898 *7951.13 p42*
Abel, Carl Hermann Leopold; Wisconsin, 1899 *6795.8 p83*
Abel, Catharine; Philadelphia, 1874 *7420.1 p303*
Abel, Conrad; Ohio, 1809-1852 *4511.35 p1*
Abel, Elisabeth *SEE* Abel, Michel
Abel, Friedrich *SEE* Abel, Michel
Abel, Friedrich Gottlieb; America, 1847 *7420.1 p51*
Abel, Heinrich Gottlieb; America, 1855 *7420.1 p134*
Abel, Heinrich Hans Hermann; America, 1851 *7420.1 p78*
  *Wife:*Ida Auguste Eleonore Oppermann
Abel, Ida Auguste Eleonore Oppermann *SEE* Abel, Heinrich Hans Hermann
Abel, Johann; America, 1872 *5475.1 p231*
Abel, Johann *SEE* Abel, Michel

Abel, John 24; New York, NY, 1835 *5024.1 p137*
Abel, Josef; New York, 1880 *5475.1 p420*
Abel, Maria; America, 1880 *5475.1 p172*
Abel, Michel *SEE* Abel, Michel
Abel, Michel; America, 1882 *5475.1 p214*
  *Wife:*Anna Frantz
  *Son:*Michel
  *Son:*Peter
  *Son:*Johann
  *Daughter:*Elisabeth
  *Son:*Friedrich
Abel, Nicholas 25; New York, NY, 1898 *7951.13 p42*
Abel, Peter *SEE* Abel, Michel
Abele, Anna Maria; America, 1858 *179.55 p19*
Abele, Christina; America, 1872 *179.55 p19*
Abele, Johannes; America, 1857 *179.55 p19*
Abele, John; Missouri, 1890 *3276.1 p1*
Abele, Rosina; America, 1700-1899 *179.55 p19*
Abele, Sophia; America, 1857 *179.55 p19*
Abell, Robt.; Maryland, 1673 *1236.25 p49*
Abelmann, Heinrich Wilhelm; America, 1892 *7420.1 p364*
Abendroth, Mary Louisa; Wisconsin, 1888 *6795.8 p66*
Abercrombie, William; Ohio, 1836 *3580.20 p31*
Abercrombie, William; Ohio, 1836 *6020.12 p6*
Abernethy, James 48; Ontario, 1871 *1823.21 p1*
Abernethy, William 39; Ontario, 1871 *1823.17 p1*
Abernruel, Mr. 18; New Orleans, 1848 *778.6 p1*
Abil, Albert Herm. Edward; Wisconsin, 1895 *6795.8 p148*
Able, George 48; Ontario, 1871 *1823.21 p1*
Able, Richard 51; Ontario, 1871 *1823.17 p1*
Ableson, Mary 59; Ontario, 1871 *1823.21 p1*
Abraham, Antonias; Texas, 1906 *3435.45 p35*
Abraham, Antonin; Nebraska, 1876 *2853.20 p172*
Abraham, Benoit; Quebec, 1642 *9221.17 p111*
Abraham, Durgen 45; Ontario, 1871 *1823.21 p1*
Abraham, Gustav Friedrich Albert; Wisconsin, 1903 *6795.8 p130*
Abraham, Jeanne 31; Quebec, 1636 *9221.17 p54*
Abraham, John 35; Ontario, 1871 *1823.21 p1*
Abraham, Julius Wilhelm; Wisconsin, 1893 *6795.8 p133*
Abraham, Leib 65; America, 1866 *5475.1 p160*
  *Son:*Moses
Abraham, Marguerite; Quebec, 1665 *4514.3 p269*
Abraham, Moses *SEE* Abraham, Leib
Abraham, Pauline O.; Wisconsin, 1888 *6795.8 p133*
Abraham, Richard 45; Ontario, 1871 *1823.17 p1*
Abraham, Samuel; Wisconsin, 1878 *6795.8 p200*
Abraham, William 37; Ontario, 1871 *1823.21 p1*
Abraham, Wm 45; Ontario, 1871 *1823.21 p1*
Abrahmson, Gustaf Alexcius; Boston, 1901 *1766.20 p18*
Abram, Jacob 50; Ontario, 1871 *1823.21 p1*
Abram, Jane 42; Ontario, 1871 *1823.21 p1*
Abram, John 30; Ontario, 1871 *1823.21 p1*
Abram, Rebecca 40; Ontario, 1871 *1823.21 p1*
Abramowitz, Henoch 36; New York, NY, 1878 *9253.2 p45*
Abramowitz, Julius 26; New York, NY, 1878 *9253.2 p45*
Abray, Thomas 59; Ontario, 1871 *1823.21 p1*
Abri, Mary; New York, 1860 *358.56 p149*
Abromowski, Joseph; Galveston, TX, 1911 *6015.15 p9*
Abrozaitis, Peter 28; New York, NY, 1890 *1883.7 p48*
Abselius, Antoinette *SEE* Abselius, George
Abselius, Desiree *SEE* Abselius, George
Abselius, Francois *SEE* Abselius, George

Abselius, George; Wisconsin, 1855 *1495.20 p8*
  *Wife:*Marie Joseph Robat
  *Child:*Josephine
  *Child:*Virginie
  *Child:*Justine
  *Child:*Marie Barbe
  *Child:*Francois
  *Child:*Desiree
  *Child:*Antoinette
Abselius, Josephine *SEE* Abselius, George
Abselius, Justine *SEE* Abselius, George
Abselius, Marie Barbe *SEE* Abselius, George
Abselius, Marie Joseph Robat *SEE* Abselius, George
Abselius, Virginie *SEE* Abselius, George
Acard, Charles 20; Louisiana, 1848 *778.6 p1*
Acard, Constant 48; Louisiana, 1848 *778.6 p1*
Acard, Eugene 16; Louisiana, 1848 *778.6 p1*
Acard, Fois. 10; Louisiana, 1848 *778.6 p1*
Acard, Fois. 18; Louisiana, 1848 *778.6 p1*
Acard, Leon 9; Louisiana, 1848 *778.6 p1*
Acard, Marie Jos. 50; Louisiana, 1848 *778.6 p1*
Acarie, Jean; Quebec, 1643 *9221.17 p128*
Acarie, Louise; Quebec, 1643 *9221.17 p128*
Accarias, Henry; America, 1842 *778.6 p1*
Accola, Valentin 33; Port uncertain, 1840 *778.6 p1*
Acess, Ann 80; Ontario, 1871 *1823.21 p1*
Ach, Lyon; Louisiana, 1836-1841 *4981.45 p208*
Achander, Bror Albert; North America, 1890 *6410.15 p106*
Achapt, Charles 23; Quebec, 1656 *9221.17 p330*
Achard, Samuel; Salem, MA, 1577-1652 *9228.50 p75*
Acheson, George; Ohio, 1831 *3580.20 p31*
Acheson, George W.; Ohio, 1831 *6020.12 p6*
Acheson, Thomas; Boston, 1774 *8529.30 p6*
Achilles, . . .; America, 1846 *7420.1 p42*
Achilles, Ms.; America, 1853 *7420.1 p102*
  With son
Achilles, Carl Heinrich August; America, 1872 *7420.1 p293*
Achon, Ozanne-Jeanne 27; Quebec, 1657 *9221.17 p350*
Achsell, C.W.; Boston, 1847 *6412.40 p150*
Achtenberg, Friedr. 24; New York, NY, 1883 *8427.14 p44*
Achterberg, Emilie Maasz *SEE* Achterberg, Wilhelm
Achterberg, Emma Martha *SEE* Achterberg, Wilhelm
Achterberg, Gustav August *SEE* Achterberg, Wilhelm
Achterberg, Minna Auguste *SEE* Achterberg, Wilhelm
Achterberg, Wilhelm; Dakota, 1887 *554.30 p25*
  *Wife:*Emilie Maasz
  *Child:*Emma Martha
  *Child:*Minna Auguste
  *Child:*Gustav August
Acidis, Margaret; New Orleans, 1851 *7242.30 p134*
Acidis, Robert; New Orleans, 1851 *7242.30 p134*
Ackemann, Caroline Friederike *SEE* Ackemann, Heinrich Wilhelm August
Ackemann, Engel Sophie Wilhelmine; America, 1893 *7420.1 p369*
Ackemann, Friederike Wilhelmine Justine *SEE* Ackemann, Heinrich Wilhelm August
Ackemann, Heinrich Wilhelm *SEE* Ackemann, Heinrich Wilhelm August
Ackemann, Heinrich Wilhelm August; America, 1871 *7420.1 p288*
  *Daughter:*Friederike Wilhelmine Justine
  *Daughter:*Caroline Friederike
  *Daughter:*Heinrich Wilhelm
  With wife

Acker, Margaritha 60; Port uncertain, 1848 ***778.6*** *p1*
Acker, Mary Ann 58; Ontario, 1871 ***1823.21*** *p1*
Ackerly, Norbert; Ohio, 1840-1897 ***8365.35*** *p15*
Ackerman, John; Ohio, 1809-1852 ***4511.35*** *p1*
Ackerman, John D.; Ohio, 1809-1852 ***4511.35*** *p1*
Ackerman, Mathias; Ohio, 1809-1852 ***4511.35*** *p1*
Ackermann, Anna 42 *SEE* Ackermann, Peter
Ackermann, Anna Maria *SEE* Ackermann, Josef
Ackermann, Auguste 33; New York, NY, 1894 ***6512.1*** *p182*
Ackermann, Barbara Rausch *SEE* Ackermann, Josef
Ackermann, Johann *SEE* Ackermann, Peter
Ackermann, Johann Georg; America, 1866 ***179.55*** *p19*
Ackermann, Josef; America, 1868 ***5475.1*** *p262*
*Wife:*Barbara Rausch
*Son:*Peter
*Daughter:*Anna Maria
Ackermann, Joseph; New York, NY, 1893 ***1883.7*** *p39*
Ackermann, Katharina *SEE* Ackermann, Peter
Ackermann, Louis; Illinois, 1855 ***6079.1*** *p1*
Ackermann, Maria *SEE* Ackermann, Peter
Ackermann, Maria; New York, NY, 1893 ***1883.7*** *p39*
Ackermann, Mathias *SEE* Ackermann, Peter
Ackermann, Peter *SEE* Ackermann, Peter
Ackermann, Peter *SEE* Ackermann, Josef
Ackermann, Peter 46; America, 1868 ***5475.1*** *p253*
*Wife:*Anna 42
*Son:*Peter
*Daughter:*Maria
*Daughter:*Katharina
*Son:*Mathias
*Son:*Johann
Ackermann, Peter; New York, 1884 ***5475.1*** *p263*
Ackersmann, Friedrich Humbracht; America, 1852 ***7420.1*** *p91*
Ackland, Henry 55; Ontario, 1871 ***1823.17*** *p1*
Ackland, Louisa 10; Quebec, 1870 ***8364.32*** *p22*
Ackley, Harvey 50; Ontario, 1871 ***1823.21*** *p1*
Ackley, S. E. 30; Ontario, 1871 ***1823.17*** *p1*
Ackmann, . . .; America, 1846 ***7420.1*** *p42*
*Son:*Friedrich
Ackmann, Widow; America, 1882 ***7420.1*** *p327*
With family
Ackmann, Carl; America, 1854 ***7420.1*** *p114*
Ackmann, Carl Ludwig Wilhelm *SEE* Ackmann, Hanna Justine Wilhelmine Booge
Ackmann, Caroline; America, 1854 ***7420.1*** *p114*
Ackmann, Christ. Ludwig; America, 1885 ***7420.1*** *p346*
Ackmann, Christoph; America, 1848 ***7420.1*** *p58*
*Wife:*Engel Sophie Caroline Scheibe
*Daughter:*Engel Sophie Dorothee
*Son:*Hans Heinr. Christ
*Son:*Heinr. Christ. Konr.
*Son:*Johann Heinr.
*Son:*Friedr. Aug.
*Daughter:*Engel Marie Sophie
Ackmann, Engel Marie Sophie *SEE* Ackmann, Christoph
Ackmann, Engel Sophie Caroline Scheibe *SEE* Ackmann, Christoph
Ackmann, Engel Sophie Dorothee *SEE* Ackmann, Christoph
Ackmann, Friedr. Aug. *SEE* Ackmann, Christoph
Ackmann, Friedrich *SEE* Ackmann, . . .
Ackmann, Friedrich; America, 1857 ***7420.1*** *p156*
Ackmann, Friedrich Christian Wilhelm; America, 1886 ***7420.1*** *p350*
Ackmann, Friedrich Wilhelm *SEE* Ackmann, Hanna Justine Wilhelmine Booge
Ackmann, Hanna Justine Wilhelmine; America, 1882 ***7420.1*** *p328*
*Son:*Heinrich Friedrich Wilhelm
With mother-in-law
*Son:*Friedrich Wilhelm
*Son:*Carl Ludwig Wilhelm
*Son:*Heinrich Friedrich Wilhelm
Ackmann, Hans Heinr. Christ *SEE* Ackmann, Christoph
Ackmann, Heinr. Christ. Konr. *SEE* Ackmann, Christoph
Ackmann, Heinrich Friedrich Wilhelm *SEE* Ackmann, Hanna Justine Wilhelmine Booge
Ackmann, Johann Heinr. *SEE* Ackmann, Christoph
Ackmann, Karl Heinrich Christian; America, 1890 ***7420.1*** *p360*
Ackmann, Louise; America, 1857 ***7420.1*** *p156*
Ackmann, Sophie; America, 1854 ***7420.1*** *p114*
Ackmann, Sophie; America, 1857 ***7420.1*** *p156*
With daughter
Ackmann, Wilhelm; America, 1854 ***7420.1*** *p114*
With wife & daughter
Ackmann, Wilhelmine Justine; America, 1868 ***7420.1*** *p267*
Ackne, Nicholas; Ohio, 1809-1852 ***4511.35*** *p1*
Ackroid, John 44; Ontario, 1871 ***1823.17*** *p1*
A'Court, . . .; Ontario, n.d. ***9228.50*** *p75*
Acourt, . . .; Ontario, n.d. ***9228.50*** *p75*
Acre, George 29; Michigan, 1880 ***4491.39*** *p1*
Acres, Esther 65; Ontario, 1871 ***1823.21*** *p1*
Acres, Henry W. 41; Ontario, 1871 ***1823.21*** *p1*
Acton, James 34; Ontario, 1871 ***1823.17*** *p1*
Acton, William 35; Ontario, 1871 ***1823.17*** *p1*
Acton, William 40; Ontario, 1871 ***1823.17*** *p1*
Acuri, Mr. 38; America, 1845 ***778.6*** *p1*
Adair, Alexander; Washington, 1889 ***2770.40*** *p26*
Adair, Ann 28; Ontario, 1871 ***1823.21*** *p1*
Adair, Benjamin 33; Ontario, 1871 ***1823.21*** *p1*
Adair, Carson 5; Ontario, 1871 ***1823.21*** *p1*
Adair, Elisha 30; Ontario, 1871 ***1823.21*** *p1*
Adair, Ellen 50; Ontario, 1871 ***1823.21*** *p1*
Adair, James 60; Ontario, 1871 ***1823.21*** *p1*
Adair, Jeanette 40; Ontario, 1871 ***1823.21*** *p1*
Adair, Mary 26; Ontario, 1871 ***1823.21*** *p2*
Adair, Robert 48; Ontario, 1871 ***1823.21*** *p2*
Adam, Mr. 38; Louisiana, 1840 ***778.6*** *p1*
Adam, Andreas; America, 1845 ***7420.1*** *p34*
Adam, Anna 1 *SEE* Adam, Philipp
Adam, Anna Maria; Venezuela, 1843 ***3899.5*** *p541*
Adam, Anne; Quebec, 1671 ***4514.3*** *p269*
Adam, Barbara; America, 1872 ***5475.1*** *p304*
Adam, Camg. 57; Jacksonville, FL, 1840 ***778.6*** *p1*
Adam, Catha. 22; Jacksonville, FL, 1840 ***778.6*** *p2*
Adam, Charles 12; Jacksonville, FL, 1840 ***778.6*** *p2*
Adam, Christine Wilhelm; America, 1842 ***7420.1*** *p24*
*Daughter:*Sophie Caroline
Adam, Chubert 32; Jacksonville, FL, 1840 ***778.6*** *p2*
Adam, Claude 67; Jacksonville, FL, 1840 ***778.6*** *p2*
Adam, Gustav; Cleveland, OH, 1848 ***2853.20*** *p475*
Adam, Helene; Dakota, 1884-1918 ***554.30*** *p25*
Adam, Hubert 19; Jacksonville, FL, 1840 ***778.6*** *p2*
Adam, Jacques; Quebec, 1639 ***9221.17*** *p84*
Adam, Jakob; America, 1882 ***5475.1*** *p228*
*Wife:*Maria Gadomsky
Adam, James 24; Ontario, 1871 ***1823.21*** *p2*
Adam, Jean 18; Quebec, 1662 ***9221.17*** *p478*
Adam, Johann; America, 1872 ***5475.1*** *p216*
Adam, Johann *SEE* Adam, Magdalene Ludwig
Adam, Johannes 44; Portland, ME, 1911 ***970.38*** *p76*
Adam, Johannes; Venezuela, 1843 ***3899.5*** *p542*
Adam, John 25; America, 1841 ***778.6*** *p2*
Adam, John; Marston's Wharf, 1781 ***8529.30*** *p9*
Adam, Katharina 62; America, 1878 ***5475.1*** *p147*
Adam, Louise 23; Jacksonville, FL, 1840 ***778.6*** *p2*
Adam, Magdalene; America, 1883 ***5475.1*** *p303*
*Son:*Michel
*Son:*Johann
*Son:*Nikolaus
*Son:*Peter
Adam, Magnus Wilhelm; America, 1867 ***7919.3*** *p526*
Adam, Maria Gadomsky *SEE* Adam, Jakob
Adam, Maria K. 34; Portland, ME, 1911 ***970.38*** *p76*
Adam, Marianna 23; Portland, ME, 1910 ***970.38*** *p76*
Adam, Marie 29 *SEE* Adam, Philipp
Adam, Marie Josephe; Wisconsin, 1887 ***1495.20*** *p12*
Adam, Michel *SEE* Adam, Magdalene Ludwig
Adam, Nicolas 47; Quebec, 1636 ***9221.17*** *p50*
Adam, Nikolaus *SEE* Adam, Magdalene Ludwig
Adam, Peter *SEE* Adam, Magdalene Ludwig
Adam, Philipp 29; America, 1882 ***2526.43*** *p159*
*Wife:*Marie 29
*Daughter:*Anna 1
Adam, Sebastian 37; Missouri, 1847 ***778.6*** *p2*
Adam, Sophie Caroline *SEE* Adam, Christine Wilhelm
Adam, Valentine; Washington, 1882 ***2770.40*** *p135*
Adaman, Mrs. 26; New Orleans, 1843 ***778.6*** *p2*
Adaman, Mrs. 33; New Orleans, 1843 ***778.6*** *p2*
Adamczak, John; Wisconsin, 1900 ***6795.8*** *p36*
Adams, Alexander 30; Ontario, 1871 ***1823.21*** *p2*
Adams, Anna Maria; Arkansas, 1880 ***5475.1*** *p299*
Adams, Benjiman 60; Ontario, 1871 ***1823.21*** *p2*
Adams, Charles E.; Tennessee, 1897 ***3665.20*** *p111*
Adams, Christian Henry; Louisiana, 1874 ***4981.45*** *p295*
Adams, Daniel 35; Ontario, 1871 ***1823.21*** *p2*
Adams, Edward 27; Ontario, 1871 ***1823.17*** *p1*
Adams, Elizabeth 55; Ontario, 1871 ***1823.17*** *p1*
Adams, Elizabeth 72; Ontario, 1871 ***1823.21*** *p2*
Adams, Francis 36; Ontario, 1871 ***1823.21*** *p2*
Adams, Francis 42; Ontario, 1871 ***1823.21*** *p2*
Adams, Henry 36; Michigan, 1880 ***4491.42*** *p1*
Adams, Henry 40; Ontario, 1871 ***1823.21*** *p2*
Adams, Henry 54; Ontario, 1871 ***1823.21*** *p2*
Adams, Henry 75; Ontario, 1871 ***1823.21*** *p2*
Adams, Issa 42; Ontario, 1871 ***1823.21*** *p2*
Adams, James; North Carolina, 1837 ***1088.45*** *p1*
Adams, James; Philadelphia, 1850 ***8513.31*** *p293*
Adams, Jane 72; Ontario, 1871 ***1823.21*** *p2*
Adams, Johann; America, 1881 ***5475.1*** *p315*
*Wife:*Katharina Thiel
*Daughter:*Katharina
Adams, John; Marston's Wharf, 1781 ***8529.30*** *p9*
Adams, John 40; Ontario, 1871 ***1823.21*** *p2*
Adams, John 43; Ontario, 1871 ***1823.21*** *p2*
Adams, John 59; Ontario, 1871 ***1823.17*** *p1*
Adams, John H.; Ohio, 1840-1897 ***8365.35*** *p15*
Adams, Karl; America, 1870 ***5475.1*** *p43*
Adams, Katharina *SEE* Adams, Johann
Adams, Katharina Thiel *SEE* Adams, Johann
Adams, Laura Georgina 66; Ontario, 1871 ***1823.17*** *p1*
Adams, Lewis 49; Ontario, 1871 ***1823.21*** *p2*
Adams, Mary Ann 48; Ontario, 1871 ***1823.17*** *p1*
Adams, Mary Ann 50; Ontario, 1871 ***1823.17*** *p1*
Adams, Meridith 46; Ontario, 1871 ***1823.21*** *p2*
Adams, Robert 55; Ontario, 1871 ***1823.17*** *p1*
Adams, Tho.; Jamestown, VA, 1633 ***1658.20*** *p211*
Adams, Thomas 42; Ontario, 1871 ***1823.17*** *p1*
Adams, Thomas 64; Ontario, 1871 ***1823.21*** *p2*
Adams, Thomas 70; Ontario, 1871 ***1823.21*** *p2*
Adams, William 32; Ontario, 1871 ***1823.17*** *p1*
Adams, William 52; Ontario, 1871 ***1823.21*** *p2*
Adamska, Mary; Detroit, 1929 ***1640.55*** *p117*
Adamski, Walter; Detroit, 1929 ***1640.55*** *p117*
Adamson, Adam 18; New York, NY, 1835 ***5024.1*** *p136*
Adamson, Adam; Washington, 1887 ***6015.10*** *p16*
Adamson, Dora 34; Ontario, 1871 ***1823.17*** *p1*
Adamson, George; North Carolina, 1846 ***1088.45*** *p1*
Adamson, George 62; Ontario, 1871 ***1823.17*** *p1*
Adamson, James 45; Ontario, 1871 ***1823.21*** *p2*
Adamson, Janet 28; New York, NY, 1835 ***5024.1*** *p137*
Adamson, John 23; New York, NY, 1835 ***5024.1*** *p136*
Adamson, Mabel 38; Quebec, 1910 ***2897.7*** *p8*
Adamson, Mary 64; Ontario, 1871 ***1823.21*** *p2*
Adamson, Thomas 6; New York, NY, 1835 ***5024.1*** *p137*
Adamson, Thomas 20; New York, NY, 1835 ***5024.1*** *p136*
Adamson, William 22; New York, NY, 1835 ***5024.1*** *p136*
Adamsson, Johannes; North America, 1859 ***6410.15*** *p105*
Adamy, Anne Marie 1; Missouri, 1845 ***778.6*** *p2*
Adamy, Anne Marie 23; Missouri, 1845 ***778.6*** *p2*
Adamy, Barbara 5; Missouri, 1845 ***778.6*** *p2*
Adamy, Catherine 2; Missouri, 1845 ***778.6*** *p2*
Adamy, Marie 30; Missouri, 1845 ***778.6*** *p2*
Adamy, Mathis 33; Missouri, 1845 ***778.6*** *p2*
Adan, Juan Bautista; Puerto Rico, 1816 ***3476.25*** *p111*
Adare, William 50; Ontario, 1871 ***1823.21*** *p2*
Adcock, William 25; Ontario, 1871 ***1823.21*** *p2*
Addair, John; Marston's Wharf, 1779 ***8529.30*** *p9*
Addenbrook, Richard; Colorado, 1888 ***1029.59*** *p1*
Addenbrook, Richard; Colorado, 1902 ***1029.59*** *p1*
Addenbrooke, Bernard; Colorado, 1898 ***1029.59*** *p1*
Addenbrooke, Bernard; Colorado, 1898 ***1029.59*** *p1*
Addick, Herbert 28; Ontario, 1871 ***1823.21*** *p2*
Addison, George 50; Ontario, 1871 ***1823.17*** *p1*
Addisson, Honorato 32; New Orleans, 1843 ***778.6*** *p2*
Addix, John H. D.; North Carolina, 1858 ***1088.45*** *p1*
Addotta, Santo; Louisiana, 1874 ***4981.45*** *p130*
Adelberger, Adam; America, 1866 ***2526.42*** *p138*
Adelberger, Elise Margaretha 20 *SEE* Adelberger, Georg, III
Adelberger, Eva Maria; America, 1869 ***2526.42*** *p138*
Adelberger, Genovefa 5 *SEE* Adelberger, Johannes
Adelberger, Georg 13 *SEE* Adelberger, Jakob
Adelberger, Georg, III 49; America, 1844 ***2526.42*** *p138*
With wife 46
*Child:*Johannes 7
*Child:*Katharina 14
*Child:*Elise Margaretha 20
*Child:*Johannes 17
Adelberger, Jakob 39; America, 1882 ***2526.42*** *p187*
*Son:*Georg 13
Adelberger, Johannes; America, 1836 ***2526.42*** *p187*
With wife & 2 children
Adelberger, Johannes 7 *SEE* Adelberger, Georg, III
Adelberger, Johannes 17 *SEE* Adelberger, Georg, III
Adelberger, Johannes 42; America, 1846 ***2526.42*** *p187*
With wife
*Son:*Nikolaus 9
*Daughter:*Genovefa 5
*Daughter:*Rosina 7
*Daughter:*Marie 11
Adelberger, Katharina 14 *SEE* Adelberger, Georg, III
Adelberger, Marie 11 *SEE* Adelberger, Johannes
Adelberger, Nikolaus 9 *SEE* Adelberger, Johannes
Adelberger, Philipp; America, 1868 ***2526.42*** *p187*
Adelberger, Rosina 7 *SEE* Adelberger, Johannes
Adelberger, Wilhelm; America, 1866 ***2526.42*** *p138*
Adelhied, Jules 20; Mississippi, 1847 ***778.6*** *p2*
Ademar, Count 28; Port uncertain, 1843 ***778.6*** *p2*
Aden, John; Iowa, 1898 ***1211.15*** *p8*
Ader, Francis 24; New Orleans, 1848 ***778.6*** *p2*
Aderholz, Elise; New York, 1860 ***358.56*** *p3*
Adermann, William; New York, 1860 ***358.56*** *p5*

2 *FOR A COMPLETE EXPLANATION OF ENTRY, SEE "HOW TO READ A CITATION" SECTION*

Ades, Meyer 22; Indiana, 1885-1896 ***9076.20*** *p74*
Adhemar deLantagnac, Gaspard; Quebec, 1712 ***2314.30*** *p169*
Adhemar deLantagnac, Gaspard; Quebec, 1712 ***2314.30*** *p173*
Aditajs, Michael; Detroit, 1929-1930 ***6214.5*** *p70*
Adkins, David 22; North Carolina, 1774 ***1422.10*** *p55*
Adkins, John 54; Ontario, 1871 ***1823.21*** *p2*
Adkins, Richard 24; Ontario, 1871 ***1823.21*** *p2*
Adlemann, Forencz 24; America, 1847 ***778.6*** *p2*
Adler, Anna 41; Iowa, 1882 ***5475.1*** *p350*
Adler, Anton 4; New York, NY, 1893 ***1883.7*** *p41*
Adler, Caspar; America, 1867 ***7919.3*** *p531*
Adler, Friedrich Wilhelm; Wisconsin, 1892 ***6795.8*** *p96*
Adler, Henry; North Carolina, 1852 ***1088.45*** *p1*
Adler, Jacob 30; New York, NY, 1893 ***1883.7*** *p41*
Adler, Jacob; Ohio, 1809-1852 ***4511.35*** *p1*
Adler, Johann; America, 1843 ***5475.1*** *p263*
Adler, Johann 2; New York, NY, 1893 ***1883.7*** *p41*
Adler, Leo 11 months; New York, NY, 1893 ***1883.7*** *p41*
Adler, Ludwig; America, 1849 ***5475.1*** *p402*
Adler, Magdalena 6; New York, NY, 1893 ***1883.7*** *p41*
Adler, Magdalena 28; New York, NY, 1893 ***1883.7*** *p41*
Adler, Peter; America, 1869 ***5475.1*** *p417*
Adler, Samuel 36; Port uncertain, 1841 ***778.6*** *p2*
Adler, Wallburga 2; New York, NY, 1893 ***1883.7*** *p41*
Adler, William 56; Ontario, 1871 ***1823.17*** *p1*
Adolph, August; America, 1867 ***7919.3*** *p530*
With wife & child
Adolph, George; Ohio, 1809-1852 ***4511.35*** *p1*
Adolph, Peter; Ohio, 1809-1852 ***4511.35*** *p1*
Adolphe, Charles 17; America, 1843 ***778.6*** *p2*
Adouc, P...re 27; New Orleans, 1840 ***778.6*** *p2*
Adrian, Albridge; North Carolina, 1857 ***1088.45*** *p1*
Adrian, Emil August Julius; America, 1882 ***2526.43*** *p137*
Adrian, Jacob; Iowa, 1895 ***1211.15*** *p8*
Adrian, Lorenz; Port uncertain, 1800-1900 ***5475.1*** *p340*
Adrian, Max Richard; Iowa, 1913 ***1211.15*** *p9*
Adrien, Hareq; Louisiana, 1874 ***4981.45*** *p130*
Adruz, Jean 55; Mississippi, 1846 ***778.6*** *p2*
Adshead, George 33; Ontario, 1871 ***1823.21*** *p2*
Adson, Francis 48; Ontario, 1871 ***1823.21*** *p2*
Aebly, Henry; Iowa, 1878 ***1211.15*** *p8*
Affleck, Jane Ann; Vancouver, B.C., 1906-1926 ***9228.50*** *p321*
af Klint, E.J.; North America, 1837 ***6410.15*** *p103*
Agacinski, John; Detroit, 1930 ***1640.60*** *p81*
Agamaite, Felicien; Boston, 1871 ***1494.21*** *p31*
Agan, Hugh; Ipswich, MA, 1737 ***1642*** *p70*
Agan, Hugh; Ipswich, MA, 1737 ***1642*** *p71*
Agate, Michael; Ohio, 1840 ***2763.1*** *p7*
Agathe, Marie-Anne; Quebec, 1663 ***4514.3*** *p269*
Ageraige, Antoine 35; America, 1841 ***778.6*** *p2*
Agne, Christian; Ohio, 1809-1852 ***4511.35*** *p1*
Agnee, David; Ohio, 1809-1852 ***4511.35*** *p1*
Agner, Georg 34; America, 1832 ***2526.43*** *p163*
With wife & child
Agnew, . . .; America, n.d. ***9228.50*** *p75*
Agnew, . . .; Canada, n.d. ***9228.50*** *p75*
Agnew, John E.; Ohio, 1809-1852 ***4511.35*** *p1*
Agnew, John W. 70; Ontario, 1871 ***1823.21*** *p2*
Agnew, Margaret; Ohio, 1797-1805 ***9228.50*** *p121*
Agoste, Ch. 20; America, 1840 ***778.6*** *p2*
Agostin, Francis M.; North Carolina, 1848 ***1088.45*** *p1*
Agostin, Francisco; North Carolina, 1846 ***1088.45*** *p1*
Agostin, Joseph M.; North Carolina, 1855 ***1088.45*** *p1*
Agranove, Nathan; Detroit, 1929 ***1640.55*** *p117*
Agrell, Carl Christian; Charleston, SC, 1834 ***6410.15*** *p103*
Agren, Anna Ch. Peterson *SEE* Agren, Petrus
Agren, Petrus; New York, 1881-1888 ***1865.50*** *p101*
*Wife:*Anna Ch. Peterson
Ahern, J.; Quebec, 1870 ***8364.32*** *p22*
Ahern, James J.; North Carolina, 1857 ***1088.45*** *p1*
Ahern, Patrick 39; Ontario, 1871 ***1823.21*** *p2*
A'Herne, Thomas; Toronto, 1844 ***2910.35*** *p113*
Aherns, Frederic William; North Carolina, 1853 ***1088.45*** *p1*
Ahier, . . .; Canada, n.d. ***9228.50*** *p75*
Ahier, John; America, n.d. ***9228.50*** *p75*
Ahier, John; Portsmouth, NH, 1688 ***9228.50*** *p75*
Ahier Family ; California, 1900-1983 ***9228.50*** *p75*
Ahier Family ; Toronto, 1900-1983 ***9228.50*** *p75*
Ahiers, . . .; New England, n.d. ***9228.50*** *p75*
Ahires, John; Portsmouth, NH, 1688 ***9228.50*** *p75*
Ahl, Charlotta O.; St. Paul, MN, 1879 ***1865.50*** *p115*
Ahl, Christina; St. Paul, MN, 1874 ***1865.50*** *p35*
Ahl, Emil C.; St. Paul, MN, 1879 ***1865.50*** *p35*
Ahlen, C. Edward F.; Cleveland, OH, 1892-1894 ***9722.10*** *p115*
Ahlert, Fred Wilhelm; Louisiana, 1841-1844 ***4981.45*** *p210*
Ahlqvist, David; Savannah, GA, 1851 ***6412.40*** *p153*
Ahlstrom, John; Colorado, 1889 ***1029.59*** *p1*
Ahnefeld, Mr.; America, 1851 ***7420.1*** *p78*
Aho, Lusiana 33; Minnesota, 1925 ***2769.54*** *p1382*
Aho, Lydia 23; Minnesota, 1926 ***2769.54*** *p1381*
Aho, Mrs. Sam 48; Minnesota, 1925 ***2769.54*** *p1380*
Aho, William 42; Minnesota, 1925 ***2769.54*** *p1382*
Ahorn, John; New York, 1860 ***358.56*** *p148*
Ahr, Christine Schneider *SEE* Ahr, Peter
Ahr, Peter; America, 1841 ***5475.1*** *p56*
*Wife:*Christine Schneider
With 4 children
Ahrend, Heinrich; Nebraska, 1883 ***7420.1*** *p334*
*Wife:*Minna Steinwentel
Ahrend, Karl; Nebraska, 1884 ***7420.1*** *p341*
Ahrend, Karl Friedrich; America, 1884 ***7420.1*** *p341*
Ahrend, Leopold Wilhelm; Nebraska, 1878 ***7420.1*** *p310*
Ahrend, Ludwig; Nebraska, 1887 ***7420.1*** *p352*
Ahrend, Minna Steinwentel *SEE* Ahrend, Heinrich
Ahrens, Christ.; Valdivia, Chile, 1851 ***1192.4*** *p50*
Ahrens, Sophie Louise; America, 1881 ***7420.1*** *p319*
Aichenbener, Camilins 6; Halifax, N.S., 1902 ***1860.4*** *p44*
Aichenbener, Catha 3; Halifax, N.S., 1902 ***1860.4*** *p44*
Aichenbener, Eliz. 31; Halifax, N.S., 1902 ***1860.4*** *p44*
Aichenbener, Leopold 33; Halifax, N.S., 1902 ***1860.4*** *p44*
Aichenbener, Magdalene 11; Halifax, N.S., 1902 ***1860.4*** *p44*
Aichorn, Charles 52; Ontario, 1871 ***1823.17*** *p1*
Aid, Edwd 19; St. Johns, N.F., 1811 ***1053.20*** *p21*
Aide, James 28; Ontario, 1871 ***1823.17*** *p1*
Aigron, Pierre 43; Quebec, 1658 ***9221.17*** *p383*
Aikens, John 32; Ontario, 1871 ***1823.21*** *p3*
Aikin, David 27; Ontario, 1871 ***1823.21*** *p3*
Aikin, James 40; Ontario, 1871 ***1823.17*** *p2*
Aikin, John 65; Ontario, 1871 ***1823.21*** *p3*
Aikins, Sarah 45; Ontario, 1871 ***1823.21*** *p3*
Aikins, William 57; Ontario, 1871 ***1823.21*** *p3*
Ailleboust DeCoulonge, Barbe de Boullonge 25 *SEE* Ailleboust DeCoulonge, Louis
Ailleboust DeCoulonge, Louis 31; Montreal, 1643 ***9221.17*** *p136*
*Wife:*Barbe de Boullonge 25
Ailleboust deCoulonges, Louis d'; Quebec, 1643 ***2314.30*** *p166*
Ailleboust deCoulonges, Louis d'; Quebec, 1643 ***2314.30*** *p173*
Ailleboust DeManthet, Roger; Quebec, 1657 ***9221.17*** *p350*
Ailleboust desMuceaux, Charles d'; Quebec, 1648 ***2314.30*** *p166*
Ailleboust desMuceaux, Charles d'; Quebec, 1648 ***2314.30*** *p173*
Ailleboust DesMuceaux, Charles-Joseph 21; Montreal, 1648 ***9221.17*** *p205*
Ainscough, Rich 54; Ontario, 1871 ***1823.17*** *p2*
Ainson, Mary *SEE* Ainson, Miles
Ainson, Mary *SEE* Ainson, Miles
Ainson, Miles *SEE* Ainson, Miles
Ainson, Miles; Canada, 1774 ***3036.5*** *p41*
*Wife:*Mary
*Child:*Mary
*Child:*Thomas
*Child:*Miles
Ainson, Thomas *SEE* Ainson, Miles
Ainsthrope, Henry 29; Ontario, 1871 ***1823.17*** *p2*
Aires, . . .; New England, n.d. ***9228.50*** *p75*
Aires, Edward; Boston, 1716 ***9228.50*** *p75*
Aires, John; Boston, 1794 ***9228.50*** *p75*
Airs, John; Virginia, 1652 ***6254.4*** *p243*
Aisenbrey, Jakob; New York, NY, 1889 ***3366.30*** *p70*
Aisthorp, Reuben 31; Ontario, 1871 ***1823.17*** *p2*
Ait, Catharina 26; America, 1747 ***778.6*** *p2*
Ait, Johann 18; America, 1747 ***778.6*** *p2*
Aitchison, George 50; Ontario, 1871 ***1823.21*** *p3*
Aitken, David 43; Ontario, 1871 ***1823.17*** *p2*
Aitken, John; New Jersey, 1807 ***3845.2*** *p128*
Aitken, John 57; Ontario, 1871 ***1823.21*** *p3*
Aitken, John 70; Ontario, 1871 ***1823.17*** *p2*
Aitkens, William 43; Ontario, 1871 ***1823.17*** *p2*
Akarmaprn, Isidore; Louisiana, 1841-1844 ***4981.45*** *p210*
Ake, Elias F. 24; Kansas, 1893 ***1447.20*** *p62*
Ake, Richard E. 21; Kansas, 1893 ***1447.20*** *p62*
Akens, James 62; Ontario, 1871 ***1823.21*** *p3*
Akens, Jane; New York, 1858 ***8513.31*** *p418*
Akerbach, Mr. 20; America, 1841 ***778.6*** *p2*
Akerhielm, Johan Fredrik Georg Rickard; North America, 1860 ***6410.15*** *p105*
Akerlund, Brita 26; New York, 1856 ***6529.11*** *p21*
Akeson, Betty; Iowa, 1898-1900 ***1865.50*** *p35*
Akeson, Gothe; New York, NY, 1849 ***6412.40*** *p152*
Akeson, John Charles; Kansas, 1870 ***777.40*** *p21*
Akesson, Betty; Iowa, 1898-1900 ***1865.50*** *p35*
Akesson, Charles; Kansas, 1870 ***777.40*** *p21*
Akings, John 35; Ontario, 1871 ***1823.21*** *p3*
Akmann, Carl Ernst Wilhelm; Indianapolis, 1877 ***7420.1*** *p308*
Akmann, Ernst Heinrich; Indianapolis, 1874 ***7420.1*** *p302*
Akroyd, Margaret 50; Ontario, 1871 ***1823.21*** *p3*
Aksamit, Antonin; Nebraska, 1836-1910 ***2853.20*** *p157*
Aksmann, Johannes 25; New York, NY, 1905 ***8425.16*** *p34*
Alaimo, Antonio; Louisiana, 1874-1875 ***4981.45*** *p297*
Alaire, Pierre; Quebec, 1659 ***9221.17*** *p412*
Alanson, John 41; Ontario, 1871 ***1823.21*** *p3*
Albach, Peter; Ohio, 1809-1852 ***4511.35*** *p1*
Alban, Alban; Ohio, 1834 ***4022.20*** *p272*
*Wife:*Mary Ann Davies
*Child:*Thomas
With 3 children
Alban, Ann Morgan *SEE* Alban, Thomas
Alban, Catherine; Ohio, 1834-1835 ***4022.20*** *p272*
With siblings
Alban, Isaac *SEE* Alban, Thomas A.
Alban, John; Ohio, 1834 ***4022.20*** *p272*
*Wife:*Mary Morgan
With siblings
Alban, Mary Morgan *SEE* Alban, John
Alban, Mary Ann Davies *SEE* Alban, Alban
Alban, Thomas *SEE* Alban, Alban
Alban, Thomas; Ohio, 1835 ***4022.20*** *p272*
*Wife:*Ann Morgan
With 5 children & brother-in-law
Alban, Thomas A.; Ohio, 1858 ***4022.20*** *p272*
*Son:*Isaac
Albanel, Charles 33; Quebec, 1649 ***9221.17*** *p207*
Albans, Mary; Ohio, 1836 ***4022.20*** *p275*
Albas, Henry; Ohio, 1840-1897 ***8365.35*** *p15*
Alberpson, Paul; Washington, 1880 ***2770.40*** *p134*
Alberry, Donato 30; New Orleans, 1843 ***778.6*** *p2*
Albers, John D.; Illinois, 1854 ***6079.1*** *p1*
Albert, Andre 22; Quebec, 1659 ***9221.17*** *p393*
Albert, Anna 9 *SEE* Albert, Nikolaus
Albert, Antoine Joseph *SEE* Albert, Charles Joseph
Albert, Charles Joseph; Wisconsin, 1855-1858 ***1495.20*** *p67*
*Wife:*Marie Francoise Ramoisy
*Child:*Victor Joseph
*Child:*Jacques Joseph
*Child:*Isidore Joseph
*Child:*Antoine Joseph
Albert, E. 20; Port uncertain, 1843 ***778.6*** *p3*
Albert, Elisabeth *SEE* Albert, Johann
Albert, Guillaume 21; Quebec, 1656 ***9221.17*** *p331*
Albert, Gustav 26; New York, NY, 1893 ***1883.7*** *p38*
Albert, H.; Illinois, 1852 ***6079.1*** *p1*
Albert, Isidore Joseph *SEE* Albert, Charles Joseph
Albert, J. J.; New York, NY, 1871 ***1494.20*** *p12*
Albert, Jacob; Louisiana, 1841-1844 ***4981.45*** *p210*
Albert, Jacques Joseph *SEE* Albert, Charles Joseph
Albert, Jean; New Castle, DE, 1817-1818 ***90.20*** *p150*
Albert, Jean 18; Quebec, 1657 ***9221.17*** *p350*
Albert, Johann; Brazil, 1861 ***5475.1*** *p489*
*Wife:*Karoline Moosmann
*Daughter:*Philippine
*Daughter:*Luise
*Daughter:*Elisabeth
Albert, Josephine; Wisconsin, 1854-1858 ***1495.20*** *p66*
Albert, Karoline Moosmann *SEE* Albert, Johann
Albert, Katharina; America, 1883 ***5475.1*** *p176*
Albert, Katharina Meyer 27 *SEE* Albert, Nikolaus
Albert, Louis 29; Louisiana, 1848 ***778.6*** *p3*
Albert, Luise *SEE* Albert, Johann
Albert, Magdalena 3 *SEE* Albert, Nikolaus
Albert, Margarethe 5 *SEE* Albert, Nikolaus
Albert, Maria 3 *SEE* Albert, Nikolaus
Albert, Maria Ursula; Venezuela, 1843 ***3899.5*** *p541*
Albert, Marie; Quebec, 1663 ***4514.3*** *p269*
Albert, Marie 14; Quebec, 1657 ***9221.17*** *p351*
Albert, Marie Francoise Ramoisy *SEE* Albert, Charles Joseph
Albert, Martin; Venezuela, 1843 ***3899.5*** *p541*
Albert, Nikolaus 29; America, 1851 ***5475.1*** *p68*
*Wife:*Katharina Meyer 27
*Daughter:*Magdalena 3 months
*Daughter:*Anna 9
*Daughter:*Margarethe 5
*Daughter:*Maria 3
Albert, P. J.; Detroit, 1872 ***1494.20*** *p12*
Albert, Paul; Washington, 1880 ***2770.40*** *p134*
Albert, Philippine *SEE* Albert, Johann
Albert, Pierre 20; Quebec, 1647 ***9221.17*** *p172*
Albert, Victor Joseph *SEE* Albert, Charles Joseph
Alberti, L. 21; Port uncertain, 1848 ***778.6*** *p3*
Albertsen, John Oskar; Oregon, 1941 ***9157.47*** *p2*
Albes, A. 33; New Orleans, 1848 ***778.6*** *p2*

Albes, Carl; America, 1857 7420.1 p157
Albesser, Andrew; Illinois, 1860 6079.1 p1
Albieri, Pavel; Chicago, 1889 2853.20 p507
Albison, John; Marston's Wharf, 1782 8529.30 p9
Albitz, Jaques; New Castle, DE, 1817-1818 90.20 p150
Albo, Joseph; New York, 1860 358.56 p149
Albo De Bernales, Lucy Maria; New York, 1845-1870 9228.50 p76
Albrecht, Anna 53; America, 1847 778.6 p3
Albrecht, Anna Catharine 40; America, 1847 778.6 p3
Albrecht, August 3; America, 1840 778.6 p3
Albrecht, Barb 20; America, 1840 778.6 p3
Albrecht, Barbara; Philadelphia, 1856 8513.31 p421
Albrecht, Bonrad; Galveston, TX, 1855 571.7 p16
Albrecht, Catharine 2 months; America, 1847 778.6 p3
Albrecht, Catharine 16; America, 1847 778.6 p3
Albrecht, Eva 24; America, 1840 778.6 p3
Albrecht, Eva 52; America, 1840 778.6 p3
Albrecht, F.; Galveston, TX, 1855 571.7 p17
Albrecht, Hermann Martin; Wisconsin, 1888 6795.8 p92
Albrecht, Jan 16; America, 1847 778.6 p3
Albrecht, Jan 53; America, 1847 778.6 p3
Albrecht, Jean 2; America, 1840 778.6 p3
Albrecht, Julius Friedrich; Port uncertain, 1888 7420.1 p355
Albrecht, Louise 16; America, 1840 778.6 p3
Albrecht, Magd. 18; America, 1840 778.6 p3
Albrecht, Magdaline 14; America, 1847 778.6 p3
Albrecht, Margaretha 14; America, 1847 778.6 p3
Albrecht, Marian 19; America, 1847 778.6 p3
Albrecht, Martin 35; America, 1840 778.6 p3
Albrecht, Mathias 9; America, 1847 778.6 p3
Albrecht, Nathanael Samuel; Wisconsin, 1874 6795.8 p33
Albrecht, Peter 28; America, 1840 778.6 p3
Albrecht, Peter 46; America, 1847 778.6 p3
Albrecht, Peter 58; America, 1840 778.6 p3
Albrecht, Plazenz 45; Galveston, TX, 1844 3967.10 p370
Albrecht, Samuel Nathanael; Wisconsin, 1888 6795.8 p33
Albrecht, Wilh.; Galveston, TX, 1855 571.7 p16
Albrecht, Wladyslaw; Detroit, 1930 1640.60 p81
Albregt, Paul; Washington, 1880 2770.40 p134
Albright, Charles; Ohio, 1809-1852 4511.35 p1
Albright, Frederick; Ohio, 1809-1852 4511.35 p1
Albright, Hermann Martin; Wisconsin, 1888 6795.8 p92
Albright, John; Ohio, 1809-1852 4511.35 p1
Albright, Michael; Ohio, 1809-1852 4511.35 p1
Albro, Mary J. 36; Michigan, 1880 4491.39 p1
Albroy, Carl 29; New York, NY, 1894 6512.1 p182
Albucht, John; Ohio, 1809-1852 4511.35 p1
Albury, Charles Eugene Lloyd; Miami, 1935 4984.12 p39
Albus, Christian *SEE* Albus, Christian, Jr.
Albus, Christian, Jr.; Dakota, 1883 554.30 p25
*Wife:*Katharina Edinger
*Child:*Friedrich
*Child:*Christian
Albus, Christine Lutz *SEE* Albus, Franz
Albus, Dorothea; Dakota, 1883 554.30 p25
Albus, Franz *SEE* Albus, Franz
Albus, Franz; Dakota, 1885 554.30 p25
*Wife:*Christine Lutz
*Child:*Franz
Albus, Friedrich *SEE* Albus, Christian, Jr.
Albus, Karolina; Dakota, 1884 554.30 p25
Albus, Katharina Edinger *SEE* Albus, Christian, Jr.
Alby de Bress de Croses, C. A.; Louisiana, 1874-1875 4981.45 p297
Alcazar, Gonzales; Louisiana, 1874 4981.45 p295
Alcock, John; Maryland, 1672 1236.25 p47
Alconchel, Antonio; Louisiana, 1836-1840 4981.45 p212
Aldag, Carl; America, 1854 7420.1 p114
With wife son & daughter
Aldag, Carl; America, 1870 7420.1 p395
Aldag, Caroline; America, 1852 7420.1 p84
Aldag, Friedrich; America, 1854 7420.1 p114
With son
Aldag, Georg Jeremias; New York, NY, 1891 7420.1 p362
Aldag, Louis; America, 1852 7420.1 p84
Aldag, Wilhelm Conrad; America, 1860 7420.1 p190
Aldak, Paul; Washington, 1884 2770.40 p192
Aldarton, Henry 56; Ontario, 1871 1823.21 p3
Alden, John; Plymouth, MA, 1620 1920.45 p5
Aldenberger, Peter; Ohio, 1809-1852 4511.35 p1
Aldenhoven, Katharina; America, 1867 5475.1 p321
Alder, Henry 23; Ontario, 1871 1823.21 p3
Alder, Henry 43; Ontario, 1871 1823.21 p3
Alder, Thomas 42; Ontario, 1871 1823.21 p3
Alder, Ulrich 22; Missouri, 1845 778.6 p3
Alderchurch, Edward; Boston, 1737 1642 p26
Alderman, Carline 60; Ontario, 1871 1823.21 p3
Alderson, John 61; Ontario, 1871 1823.17 p2
Aldfield, Elizabeth; Canada, 1775 3036.5 p67
Aldmeyer, John 20; America, 1841 778.6 p3
Aldmeyer, Mary 21; America, 1841 778.6 p3
Aldorf, Christina 26; America, 1848 778.6 p3
Aldred, Thomas 15; Quebec, 1870 8364.32 p22
Aldridge, Fanny 11; Quebec, 1870 8364.32 p22
Aleaume, Jean; Quebec, 1635 9221.17 p43
Alegri, Pierre 24; America, 1846 778.6 p3
Alegris, Francois 38; Tennessee, 1845 778.6 p3
Alemand, Miss 12; America, 1844 778.6 p3
Alenson, Jean; Quebec, 1659 9221.17 p412
Alester, William 36; Ontario, 1871 1823.21 p3
Alet, Michael; New York, 1859 358.56 p53
Alexande, John 32; Ontario, 1871 1823.21 p3
Alexande, Thomas 48; Ontario, 1871 1823.21 p3
Alexande, Wm 56; Ontario, 1871 1823.21 p3
Alexander, . . .; Massachusetts, 1663 1642 p90
Alexander, . . .; Topsham, MA, 1719 9228.50 p76
Alexander, Miss; St. Louis, 1870 2853.20 p23
Alexander, Adolf; New York, 1855 5475.1 p403
Alexander, Adolph; New York, 1885 5475.1 p383
Alexander, Alexander 71; Ontario, 1871 1823.17 p2
Alexander, Andrew 49; Ontario, 1871 1823.17 p2
Alexander, Benj 20; Ontario, 1871 1823.21 p3
Alexander, Catherine; Boston, 1769 1642 p40
Alexander, Charles 45; Ontario, 1871 1823.21 p3
Alexander, Charles; St. Louis, n.d. 9228.50 p17A
Alexander, David 50; Ontario, 1871 1823.17 p2
Alexander, David 65; Ontario, 1871 1823.17 p2
Alexander, Donald 25; Ontario, 1871 1823.17 p2
Alexander, Eliza 45; Ontario, 1871 1823.21 p3
Alexander, Francis 69; Ontario, 1871 1823.21 p3
Alexander, George 27; Mississippi, 1847 778.6 p3
Alexander, George 43; Ontario, 1871 1823.21 p3
Alexander, Gin *SEE* Alexander, William
Alexander, Hugo; Rio Grande do Sul, Brazil, 1892 5475.1 p424
Alexander, J. 15; Quebec, 1870 8364.32 p22
Alexander, James; Maine, 1600-1699 9228.50 p76
Alexander, James 38; Ontario, 1871 1823.21 p3
Alexander, James 51; Ontario, 1871 1823.17 p2
Alexander, James 13; Quebec, 1870 8364.32 p22
Alexander, John *SEE* Alexander, William
Alexander, John 60; Ontario, 1871 1823.21 p3
Alexander, John; Philadelphia, 1778 8529.30 p2
Alexander, Joseph 45; Ontario, 1871 1823.21 p3
Alexander, Lawrence; Ohio, 1838 3580.20 p31
Alexander, Lawrence; Ohio, 1838 6020.12 p6
Alexander, Lawrence; Ohio, 1840 3580.20 p31
Alexander, Lawrence; Ohio, 1840 6020.12 p6
Alexander, Lazarus 16; America, 1862 5475.1 p30
Alexander, Leopold; New York, 1885 5475.1 p383
With family
Alexander, Lydia *SEE* Alexander, William
Alexander, Marcus; America, 1883 5475.1 p407
Alexander, Mary 58; Ontario, 1871 1823.21 p3
Alexander, Michael; America, 1854 5475.1 p403
Alexander, Moritz; America, 1883 5475.1 p383
Alexander, Richard; New Hampshire, 1674 9228.50 p76
Alexander, Ronald 7; Quebec, 1870 8364.32 p22
Alexander, Samuel; Ohio, 1844 2763.1 p7
Alexander, Seligman; Illinois, 1856 6079.1 p1
Alexander, Thomas; New York, 1776 8529.30 p6
Alexander, Thomas 40; Ontario, 1871 1823.21 p3
Alexander, William; Massachusetts, 1765 1642 p117
*Son:*John
*Daughter:*Gin
*Daughter:*Lydia
Alexander, William 19; Ontario, 1871 1823.21 p4
Alexander, William 52; Ontario, 1871 1823.21 p3
Alexander, William 71; Ontario, 1871 1823.21 p3
Alexandre, Mr. 26; America, 1842 778.6 p4
Alexandre, Mr. 35; America, 1847 778.6 p4
Alexandre, Miss A.; New York, NY, 1932 9228.50 p76
Alexandre, Alice; Maine, n.d. 9228.50 p76
Alexandre, Arthur Herbert; British Columbia, 1882-1982 9228.50 p76
Alexandre, Arthur Herbert; San Francisco, 1882-1982 9228.50 p76
Alexandre, Emily; Maine, n.d. 9228.50 p76
Alexandre, Estelle; Massachusetts, n.d. 9228.50 p76
Alexandre, Francis; Maine, n.d. 9228.50 p76
Alexandre, George; Maine, n.d. 9228.50 p76
Alexandre, Jacques; Quebec, 1654 9221.17 p304
Alexandre, James; Maine, 1600-1699 9228.50 p76
Alexandre, Jane; Maine, n.d. 9228.50 p76
Alexandre, Josephine; Massachusetts, n.d. 9228.50 p76
Alexandre, Michel 20; Port uncertain, 1842 778.6 p4
Alexandre, Raymonde; Massachusetts, n.d. 9228.50 p76
Alexandre, William; Maine, n.d. 9228.50 p76
Alexandre Family ; Canada, n.d. 9228.50 p76
Alexandre Family ; New England, n.d. 9228.50 p76
Alexy, Gustav; New York, NY, 1868 2853.20 p113
Alfele, William; Ohio, 1840-1897 8365.35 p15
Alff, Edgar Max Ferd. Franz; America, 1882 5475.1 p406
Alff, Gottfried August; Wisconsin, 1896 6795.8 p160
Alfonso, August 18; Ontario, 1871 1823.21 p4
Algar, Frank C.; Washington, 1884 2770.40 p192
Algate, William 68; Michigan, 1880 4491.30 p1
Alger Family ; New England, n.d. 9228.50 p86
Algover, Ulrich 28; America, 1840 778.6 p4
Algrove, Nicholas; North Carolina, 1702 9228.50 p76
Algrove, Nicholas 49; North Carolina, 1702 9228.50 p257
Alguley, J. B. 23; America, 1746 778.6 p4
Alimo, Peter; Washington, 1886 2770.40 p195
Alin, Jean 51; America, 1843 778.6 p4
Aliomet, Isabelle; Montreal, 1650 9221.17 p232
Alis, Josef *SEE* Alis, Karel
Alis, Karel; St. Louis, 1852 2853.20 p21
*Father:*Josef
Alison, Hugh 59; Ontario, 1871 1823.21 p4
Alison, Peter John 40; Ontario, 1871 1823.21 p4
Alison, Rustan 58; Ontario, 1871 1823.17 p2
Allaire, Charles 18; Quebec, 1658 9221.17 p375
*Brother:*Jean 23
Allaire, Jean 23 *SEE* Allaire, Charles
Allan, Alexr 22; North Carolina, 1774 1422.10 p62
Allan, Alexr. 22; North Carolina, 1774 1422.10 p58
Allan, Bradrick 66; Ontario, 1871 1823.21 p4
Allan, David 30; Ontario, 1871 1823.17 p2
Allan, David 62; Ontario, 1871 1823.21 p4
Allan, Edward 50; Ontario, 1871 1823.17 p2
Allan, George; Louisiana, 1836-1841 4981.45 p208
Allan, Henry 33; Ontario, 1871 1823.21 p4
Allan, James 30; Ontario, 1871 1823.17 p2
Allan, James 59; Ontario, 1871 1823.21 p4
Allan, James 69; Ontario, 1871 1823.21 p4
Allan, James G.; Washington, 1889 2770.40 p26
Allan, Martha 38; Ontario, 1871 1823.21 p4
Allan, Mary; Toronto, 1860 9228.50 p76
Allan, Robert 30; Ontario, 1871 1823.21 p4
Allan, Robert 60; Ontario, 1871 1823.17 p2
Allan, Robert; Washington, 1886 2770.40 p195
Allan, William 40; Ontario, 1871 1823.17 p2
Allan, Willis 21; Michigan, 1880 4491.39 p1
Allbricht, Geo. F.; Ohio, 1840-1897 8365.35 p15
Allcock, James 26; Ontario, 1871 1823.17 p2
Allday, Jonathan 66; Ontario, 1871 1823.21 p4
Allebrodt, Jos.; America, 1923 8023.44 p371
Alleher, Richard 40; Ontario, 1871 1823.17 p2
Alleman, Mr. 16; New Orleans, 1845 778.6 p4
Allemand, Marie Marg. 20; New Orleans, 1847 778.6 p4
Allemann, J. G. A.; Ohio, 1809-1852 4511.35 p1
Allen, Alex 60; Ontario, 1871 1823.17 p2
Allen, Alexander; North Carolina, 1805 1088.45 p1
Allen, Archibald 42; Ontario, 1871 1823.17 p2
Allen, Austin; Ohio, 1809-1852 4511.35 p1
Allen, Catherine 31; Ontario, 1871 1823.21 p4
Allen, Charles 36; Ontario, 1871 1823.21 p4
Allen, Daniel 34; Ontario, 1871 1823.21 p4
Allen, Edmund 10; Ontario, 1871 1823.21 p4
Allen, Edward 18; Ontario, 1871 1823.17 p2
Allen, Edward P. 31; Ontario, 1871 1823.21 p4
Allen, George 64; Ontario, 1871 1823.21 p4
Allen, George Worsley; Colorado, 1887 1029.59 p1
Allen, George Worsley; Colorado, 1895 1029.59 p1
Allen, Hannah; New England, 1666-1750 9228.50 p317
Allen, Hannah 23; Ontario, 1871 1823.21 p4
Allen, Henry 28; Ontario, 1871 1823.21 p4
Allen, Henry 52; Ontario, 1871 1823.21 p4
Allen, Henry Samuel; Washington, 1879 2770.40 p134
Allen, James 45; Ontario, 1871 1823.21 p4
Allen, James 63; Ontario, 1871 1823.17 p2
Allen, Jno A. 61; Ontario, 1871 1823.17 p2
Allen, John; North America, 1750 1640.8 p234
Allen, John 51; Ontario, 1871 1823.17 p2
Allen, John 67; Ontario, 1871 1823.21 p4
Allen, Jonathan; New York, 1776 8529.30 p2A
Allen, Lewis 25; Ontario, 1871 1823.21 p4
Allen, Lousia 21; Ontario, 1871 1823.21 p4
Allen, Mary 7; Quebec, 1870 8364.32 p22
Allen, Mary Ann 40; Ontario, 1871 1823.17 p2
Allen, Neil 20; Minnesota, 1925 2769.54 p1378
Allen, Richard 57; Ontario, 1871 1823.21 p4
Allen, Richard; Philadelphia, 1777 8529.30 p2A
Allen, Samuel; Boston, 1766 1642 p36
Allen, Samuel 32; Ontario, 1871 1823.17 p2
Allen, Sarah 11; Quebec, 1870 8364.32 p22
Allen, Sylvester 25; Michigan, 1880 4491.36 p1
Allen, Theophilus 40; Ontario, 1871 1823.21 p4
Allen, Thomas; Boston, 1774 8529.30 p6
Allen, Thomas; Marston's Wharf, 1782 8529.30 p9
Allen, Thomas; Ontario, 1871 1823.17 p2
Allen, Vaino 18; Minnesota, 1925 2769.54 p1378

Allen, W.H.; Oregon, 1862 *9228.50 p76*
  With wife
Allen, Wheaton; North America, 1842 *6410.15 p103*
Allen, William 21; Ontario, 1871 *1823.21 p4*
Allen, William 51; Ontario, 1871 *1823.17 p2*
Allen, William A. 11; Ontario, 1871 *1823.21 p4*
Allen, William M.; Colorado, 1879 *1029.59 p1*
Allenbacher, Joh. Nikolaus; America, 1865 *5475.1 p541*
Allence, Marie; Quebec, 1669 *4514.3 p269*
Allenet, Philippe 50; New Orleans, 1848 *778.6 p4*
Allen Family ; Utah, 1863 *9228.50 p76*
Allenson, William; Virginia, 1652 *6254.4 p243*
Allerton, Barheolomew SEE Allerton, Isaak
Allerton, Isaak; Plymouth, MA, 1620 *1920.45 p5*
  *Wife:*Mary
  *Child:*Remember
  *Child:*Mary
  *Child:*Barheolomew
Allerton, John; Plymouth, MA, 1620 *1920.45 p5*
Allerton, Mary SEE Allerton, Isaak
Allerton, Mary SEE Allerton, Isaak
Allerton, Remember SEE Allerton, Isaak
Alles, . . .; New England, n.d. *9228.50 p77*
Alles, . . .; New York, NY, 1834 *9228.50 p449*
Alles, . . .; Salem, MA, n.d. *9228.50 p77*
Alles, Elizabeth; Michigan, 1833-1856 *9228.50 p77*
Alles, Frederick Mansell; New York, NY, 1834 *9228.50 p77*
Alles, H.; New York, 1860 *358.56 p149*
Alles, Jacob; Ohio, 1809-1852 *4511.35 p1*
Alles, Jakob 29; Brazil, 1864 *5475.1 p501*
  *Wife:*Maria Koch 24
Alles, Johann 6 SEE Alles, Michel
Alles, Margarethe Schmitt 22 SEE Alles, Michel
Alles, Maria Koch 24 SEE Alles, Jakob
Alles, Michel 26; Brazil, 1864 *5475.1 p501*
  *Wife:*Margarethe Schmitt 22
  *Son:*Johann 6 months
Alles, Peter 46; Brazil, 1864 *5475.1 p500*
Allet, Eugene; New Orleans, 1871 *1494.21 p31*
Allet, Victor; New Orleans, 1871 *1494.21 p31*
Allett, Peter; Iowa, 1887 *1211.15 p8*
Alley, . . .; New England, n.d. *9228.50 p77*
Alley, Benjamin; Salem, MA, 1619-1719 *9228.50 p79*
Alley, H. Bb 46; Ontario, 1871 *1823.21 p4*
Alley, June; New Orleans, 1851 *7242.30 p134*
Alley, Thomas; Marblehead, MA, 1675 *9228.50 p5*
Alley, Thomas; Marblehead, MA, 1675 *9228.50 p77*
Alley, William; New Orleans, 1851 *7242.30 p134*
Allez, . . .; New England, n.d. *9228.50 p77*
Allez, Eliz.; Wisconsin, 1846 *9228.50 p19A*
Allez, Emilie; Ontario, 1856-1898 *9228.50 p79*
Allez, Emilie; Ontario, 1880-1894 *9228.50 p477*
Allgaeber, John; Philadelphia, 1858 *8513.31 p293*
  *Wife:*Louise Herner
Allgaeber, Louise Herner SEE Allgaeber, John
Allgate, Daniel 29; Ontario, 1871 *1823.21 p4*
Allgrow, Nicholas 49; North Carolina, 1702 *9228.50 p257*
Allin, James 45; Ontario, 1871 *1823.17 p2*
Allin, Thomas 32; Ontario, 1871 *1823.21 p5*
Allingham, Agnes 36; Ontario, 1871 *1823.17 p2*
Allingham, Andrew 55; Ontario, 1871 *1823.17 p2*
Allingham, John 49; Ontario, 1871 *1823.17 p2*
Allingham, Thomas 40; Ontario, 1871 *1823.21 p5*
Allingham, William 35; Ontario, 1871 *1823.21 p5*
Allinia, Abraham; Louisiana, 1874 *4981.45 p130*
Allison, Alfred; Cleveland, OH, 1888-1894 *9722.10 p118*
Allison, Anthony 56; Ontario, 1871 *1823.21 p5*
Allison, Charles 55; Ontario, 1871 *1823.21 p5*
Allison, George 36; Ontario, 1871 *1823.21 p5*
Allison, James 64; Ontario, 1871 *1823.21 p5*
Allison, Mary 11; Quebec, 1870 *8364.32 p22*
Allison, Willm.; Maryland, 1674-1675 *1236.25 p51*
Allister, John 35; Ontario, 1871 *1823.21 p5*
Allister, John 48; Ontario, 1871 *1823.21 p5*
Allister, John 64; Ontario, 1871 *1823.21 p5*
Allister, Peter 34; Ontario, 1871 *1823.21 p5*
Allivant, J. D. 43; America, 1846 *778.6 p4*
Allivellatorf; Texas, 1885 *3435.45 p35*
Allmann, Andreas 42; America, 1836 *2526.43 p159*
  With wife 40
Allmanritter, Eva Maria 37; America, 1854 *2526.43 p149*
Allmanritter, Wilhelm 27; America, 1883 *2526.43 p145*
Allnutt, Henry F. 29; Ontario, 1871 *1823.21 p5*
Allonas, Joseph; Ohio, 1809-1852 *4511.35 p1*
Allord, Mr. 35; Louisiana, 1848 *778.6 p4*
Allord, Jules 4; Louisiana, 1848 *778.6 p4*
Allouez, Claude 36; Quebec, 1658 *9221.17 p375*
Allovon, . . .; Port uncertain, 1843 *778.6 p4*
Allovon, . . .; Port uncertain, 1843 *778.6 p4*
Allovon, Alfred 16; Port uncertain, 1843 *778.6 p4*

Allovon, Francoise 34; Port uncertain, 1843 *778.6 p4*
Alloway, Thomas 60; Ontario, 1871 *1823.21 p5*
Allsop, George 40; Ontario, 1871 *1823.17 p3*
Allspach, Aug. Karl; America, 1881 *5475.1 p14*
Allsup, George 40; Ontario, 1871 *1823.17 p3*
Allum, Ann 70; Ontario, 1871 *1823.21 p5*
Allum, Samuel 46; Ontario, 1871 *1823.17 p3*
Allwood, Sarah; Maryland, 1672 *1236.25 p48*
Allworth, J. 35; Ontario, 1871 *1823.21 p5*
Alm, Andrew H.; St. Paul, MN, 1874-1905 *1865.50 p35*
  *Wife:*Augusta
Alm, Augusta SEE Alm, Andrew H.
Alman, John; Ohio, 1809-1852 *4511.35 p1*
Almayer, Pierre 19; America, 1847 *778.6 p4*
Almen, Gustaf; Minneapolis, 1888-1891 *1865.50 p35*
Almen, Hulda; St. Paul, MN, 1900 *1865.50 p35*
Almen, Maria C.; Minneapolis, 1891 *1865.50 p35*
Almer, Anna Maria; St. Paul, MN, 1890-1892 *1865.50 p35*
Almer, F.O.; St. Paul, MN, 1874-1905 *1865.50 p35*
Almquist, Herman; St. Paul, MN, 1902 *1865.50 p35*
Almqvist, Herman; St. Paul, MN, 1902 *1865.50 p35*
Almstedt, John N.; Illinois, 1861 *4487.25 p50*
Aloigny deLa Groye, Charles-Henri d'; Quebec, 1683-1688 *2314.30 p168*
Aloigny deLa Groye, Charles-Henri d'; Quebec, 1683 *2314.30 p174*
Alpach, William; New Jersey, 1734-1774 *927.31 p3*
Alpack, William; New Jersey, 1734-1774 *927.31 p3*
Alquier, Ulrich 29; Missouri, 1845 *778.6 p4*
Alray, John 47; Ontario, 1871 *1823.21 p5*
Alsdorf, Heinrich; Valdivia, Chile, 1850 *1192.4 p48*
Alsdorf, Johanna; Valdivia, Chile, 1850 *1192.4 p48*
Alsen, David Einar; Boston, 1902 *1766.20 p34*
Alsfasser, Johann; America, 1847 *5475.1 p475*
Alsford, James; Quebec, 1870 *8364.32 p22*
Alson, Charles; Cleveland, OH, 1888-1891 *9722.10 p115*
Alsop, Thomas 48; Indiana, 1848-1880 *9076.20 p69*
Alstin, Jac'b V.; Ontario, 1787 *1276.15 p230*
Alston, Alice 10; Quebec, 1870 *8364.32 p22*
Alstrom, Gus; Kansas, 1868-1871 *777.40 p4*
Alt, Christian 16 SEE Alt, Johann
Alt, Friedrich 6 SEE Alt, Johann
Alt, Johann; America, 1882 *5475.1 p184*
Alt, Johann 26; America, 1843 *5475.1 p430*
  With wife
Alt, Johann 43; America, 1849 *5475.1 p415*
  *Wife:*Maria Wilhelm 45
  *Daughter:*Katharina 11
  *Son:*Friedrich 6
  *Son:*Wilhelm 18
  *Son:*Christian 16
Alt, Katharina 11 SEE Alt, Johann
Alt, Maria Wilhelm 45 SEE Alt, Johann
Alt, Maria 56; America, 1863 *5475.1 p49*
  *Son:*Karl
Alt, Peter; Brazil, 1881 *5475.1 p184*
Alt, Regina; America, 1867 *7919.3 p525*
Alt, Wilhelm; America, 1849 *5475.1 p464*
Alt, Wilhelm; America, 1852-1862 *5475.1 p411*
Alt, Wilhelm 18 SEE Alt, Johann
Alten, Johann 31; America, 1875 *5475.1 p362*
Altenburg, Mr.; America, 1864 *7420.1 p222*
Altenburg, Friederike; America, 1859 *7420.1 p183*
Altenburg, Friedrich Wilhelm; America, 1859 *7420.1 p183*
Altenburg, Michael; Wisconsin, 1869 *6795.8 p125*
Altenburg, Wilhelm; America, 1857 *7420.1 p157*
Althafer, Andreas 25; Port uncertain, 1847 *778.6 p4*
Althans, August; America, 1853 *7420.1 p102*
  *Brother:*Wilhelm
Althans, Carl Heinrich Adolph Dietrich; America, 1856 *7420.1 p144*
Althans, Friederike; America, 1854 *7420.1 p114*
Althans, Friedrich Wilhelm Hermann; America, 1858 *7420.1 p176*
Althans, Johann Heinrich; America, 1864 *7420.1 p222*
Althans, Leopold; America, 1854 *7420.1 p114*
Althans, Louise SEE Althans, Wilhelmine
Althans, Maria; America, 1884 *7420.1 p341*
Althans, Rudolf Georg Wilhelm; New York, NY, 1880 *7420.1 p314*
Althans, Wilhelm SEE Althans, August
Althans, Wilhelm Gottfried; America, 1851 *7420.1 p78*
  With wife & 4 children
Althans, Wilhelmine; America, 1888 *7420.1 p399*
  *Daughter:*Louise
Altheimer, Anna Maria 21; New Orleans, 1848 *778.6 p4*
Altheimer, Clementine 7; New Orleans, 1848 *778.6 p4*
Altheimer, Emile 6; New Orleans, 1848 *778.6 p4*
Altheimer, Joseph 33; New Orleans, 1848 *778.6 p4*
Altheimer, Jules 4; New Orleans, 1848 *778.6 p4*
Altheimer, Lorence 2; New Orleans, 1848 *778.6 p4*

Altheimer, Virginie 9; New Orleans, 1848 *778.6 p4*
Altheimer, Wolf 8; New Orleans, 1848 *778.6 p4*
Alther, Nikolaus; America, 1847 *5475.1 p234*
Altikrose, Everhard; Ohio, 1809-1852 *4511.35 p1*
Altikrose, Rudolph; Ohio, 1809-1852 *4511.35 p1*
Altikrose, William; Ohio, 1809-1852 *4511.35 p1*
Altman, Anna 6; Michigan, 1880 *4491.30 p1*
Altman, Caroline 32; Michigan, 1880 *4491.30 p1*
Altman, George 2; Michigan, 1880 *4491.30 p1*
Altman, Lavina F. 4; Michigan, 1880 *4491.30 p1*
Altman, Mary 9; Michigan, 1880 *4491.30 p1*
Altman, Nicholas 32; Michigan, 1880 *4491.30 p1*
Altmann, Anton; Galveston, TX, 1855 *571.7 p16*
Altmann, Barb; Galveston, TX, 1855 *571.7 p16*
Altmayer, Georg; America, 1881 *5475.1 p193*
Altmeyer, Barbara; America, 1836 *5475.1 p65*
Altmeyer, Jakob; America, 1836 *5475.1 p64*
  With wife & 5 children
Altmeyer, Jakob; America, 1848 *5475.1 p486*
Altmeyer, Jakob 36; America, 1857 *5475.1 p68*
  *Wife:*Maria Speicher 26
  *Daughter:*Maria 6 months
  *Daughter:*Margarethe 4
Altmeyer, Johann; Missouri, 1884 *5475.1 p194*
Altmeyer, Katharina 49; America, 1851 *5475.1 p106*
Altmeyer, Margarethe 4 SEE Altmeyer, Jakob
Altmeyer, Maria 6 SEE Altmeyer, Jakob
Altmeyer, Maria Speicher 26 SEE Altmeyer, Jakob
Altmeyer, Peter; America, 1836 *5475.1 p66*
Alton, Etiennette 21; Montreal, 1659 *9221.17 p415*
Alton, Joseph D.; Florida, 1844 *8481.1 p18*
Alton, Ralph; Philadelphia, 1865 *8513.31 p293*
Altpeter, Sophia; America, 1882 *5475.1 p51*
Altringer, Chretien 31; Louisiana, 1848 *778.6 p4*
Altringer, Marie 30; Louisiana, 1848 *778.6 p4*
Altschaffl, Dorinda; Kansas, 1917-1918 *1826.15 p81*
Altstatter, Augusta SEE Altstatter, Georg Friedrich
Altstatter, Christina SEE Altstatter, Georg Friedrich
Altstatter, Emma SEE Altstatter, Georg Friedrich
Altstatter, Georg Friedrich; America, 1851 *2526.43 p145*
  *Wife:*Susanna Ganzert
  *Son:*Heinrich
  *Daughter:*Emma
  *Daughter:*Augusta
  *Daughter:*Maria
  *Son:*Hermann
  *Daughter:*Christina
Altstatter, Heinrich SEE Altstatter, Georg Friedrich
Altstatter, Hermann SEE Altstatter, Georg Friedrich
Altstatter, Ludwig; Ohio, 1850 *2526.43 p145*
  *Brother:*Wilhelm
Altstatter, Maria SEE Altstatter, Georg Friedrich
Altstatter, Susanna Ganzert SEE Altstatter, Georg Friedrich
Altstatter, Wilhelm 14 SEE Altstatter, Ludwig
Alves, Ludwig; America, 1861 *7420.1 p202*
Alves, Wilhelm; America, 1864 *7420.1 p222*
  With family
Alward, Samuel 53; Ontario, 1871 *1823.21 p5*
Alway, Elizabeth 63; Ontario, 1871 *1823.21 p5*
Alway, George 71; Ontario, 1871 *1823.21 p5*
Alway, Mary Ann 35; Ontario, 1871 *1823.21 p5*
Alway, William 72; Ontario, 1871 *1823.21 p5*
Alzina, Pablo; Louisiana, 1836-1840 *4981.45 p212*
Alzino, Jose; Louisiana, 1836-1840 *4981.45 p212*
Amable, Mr. 26; Texas, 1840 *778.6 p4*
Amais, Katharina; Venezuela, 1843 *3899.5 p542*
Aman, Joh.; Baltimore, 1846 *6412.40 p149*
Amann, Bernard 28; America, 1840 *778.6 p4*
Amann, Joseph 24; Louisiana, 1848 *778.6 p4*
Amark, Anna Christina SEE Amark, Kerstin Jonsdotter
Amark, J.C.; New York, NY, 1843 *6412.40 p147*
Amark, Kerstin; New York, 1857 *6529.11 p25*
  *Daughter:*Anna Christina
Amark, Pehr 32; New York, 1856 *6529.11 p21*
Amaus, Jacques; Louisiana, 1836-1841 *4981.45 p208*
Amberg, Ludwig; America, 1850 *5475.1 p29*
Ambert, Mr. 36; America, 1840 *778.6 p5*
Ambler, Ignatz 19; America, 1847 *778.6 p5*
Ambler, Richard; Ohio, 1855 *3580.20 p31*
Ambler, Richard; Ohio, 1855 *6020.12 p6*
Ambos, Jacob; Ohio, 1840-1897 *8365.35 p15*
Amboy, Alfred 40; Ohio, 1880 *4879.40 p257*
Ambrehl, Joseph 40; Indiana, 1870-1883 *9076.20 p70*
Ambros, Mary; Boston, 1767 *1642 p39*
Ambrose, P. 13; Quebec, 1870 *8364.32 p22*
Ambrosewicz, Josef 25; New York, NY, 1878 *9253.2 p45*
Ambrunn, Friedrich Melchior; America, 1869 *7919.3 p526*
Ambs, Philip; Ohio, 1809-1852 *4511.35 p1*
Ameat, Vinct.; North Carolina, 1710 *3629.40 p3*
Ameau, Severin 28; Quebec, 1648 *9221.17 p194*

Ameen, George; Louisiana, 1874 ***4981.45*** *p295*
Ameis, Katharina; Venezuela, 1843 ***3899.5*** *p542*
Amelin, Nicolas; Quebec, 1639 ***9221.17*** *p84*
Ameline, Jean; Quebec, 1639 ***9221.17*** *p84*
Amelung, Engel; America, 1883 ***7420.1*** *p334*
Amelung, Johann Heinrich Christian; America, 1910 ***7420.1*** *p387*
Amend, Heinrich; America, 1844 ***2526.42*** *p187*
With wife
With child 12
With child 9
With child 5
With child 14
Amend, Konrad 42; America, 1837 ***2526.42*** *p113*
Amend, Mrs. Michael; America, 1844 ***2526.42*** *p187*
Ames, Ann 35; Ontario, 1871 ***1823.21*** *p5*
Ames, Nikolaus; Brazil, 1879 ***5475.1*** *p431*
Amherse, Danl. 35; New York, NY, 1884 ***8427.14*** *p45*
Amieu, Pierre 42; Port uncertain, 1842 ***778.6*** *p5*
Amiot, Anne Convent 33 *SEE* Amiot, Philippe
Amiot, Jean 10 *SEE* Amiot, Philippe
Amiot, Jeanne; Quebec, 1673 ***4514.3*** *p270*
Amiot, Mathieu 6 *SEE* Amiot, Philippe
Amiot, Philippe; Quebec, 1636 ***9221.17*** *p51*
*Wife:*Anne Convent
*Son:*Jean
*Son:*Mathieu
Amiraux, Delicia; Boston, 1787 ***9228.50*** *p80*
Amiraux, Emma; Virginia, 1873-1962 ***9228.50*** *p80*
Amiraux, Jane; Massachusetts, 1767-1837 ***9228.50*** *p80*
Amiraux, Pierre; New Brunswick, 1772-1804 ***9228.50*** *p80*
Amiraux, Timothy 65; Ontario, 1871 ***1823.21*** *p5*
Amlor, Oskar; London, Eng., 1886 ***5475.1*** *p86*
Ammel, Charles; Louisiana, 1841-1844 ***4981.45*** *p210*
Ammon, Johann; America, 1867 ***7919.3*** *p527*
Amon, John; North Carolina, 1710 ***3629.40*** *p3*
Amon, Philip; North Carolina, 1710 ***3629.40*** *p6*
Amor, James 48; Ontario, 1871 ***1823.21*** *p5*
Amor, William 50; Ontario, 1871 ***1823.21*** *p5*
Amory, Thomas; South Carolina, 1719 ***1642*** *p22*
Amos, Thomas 71; Ontario, 1871 ***1823.21*** *p5*
Amos, William 50; Ontario, 1871 ***1823.21*** *p5*
Amour, Richard 22; Indiana, 1881-1890 ***9076.20*** *p72*
Amsden, Edwin 32; Ontario, 1871 ***1823.17*** *p3*
Amthauser, Conrad; Chile, 1852 ***1192.4*** *p51*
Amthor, Bernhardina; America, 1868 ***7919.3*** *p525*
Amundson, J.P.; New York, NY, 1851 ***6412.40*** *p153*
Amy, . . .; New England, n.d. ***9228.50*** *p81*
Amy, Henry; Uruguay, 1800-1899 ***9228.50*** *p81*
Amy, Thomas; Carolina, 1650-1699 ***9228.50*** *p55*
Amy, Walter; Uruguay, 1800-1899 ***9228.50*** *p81*
Amyault, Raymond; Quebec, 1698 ***2314.30*** *p171*
Amyett, Vinct.; North Carolina, 1710 ***3629.40*** *p3*
Anacker, Catharina Elisabeth; America, 1867 ***7919.3*** *p530*
Anceaume, Pierre; Quebec, 1639 ***9221.17*** *p85*
Ancelin, Francoise; Quebec, 1669 ***4514.3*** *p270*
Ancerne, Aglae 50; New Orleans, 1848 ***778.6*** *p5*
Ancerne, Pierre Noel 47; New Orleans, 1848 ***778.6*** *p5*
Anchell, Lewin; Valdivia, Chile, 1850 ***1192.4*** *p49*
Anciaux, Anne Joseph; Wisconsin, 1856 ***1495.20*** *p46*
*Child:*Eugenie
*Child:*Lambert Emmanuel
Anciaux, Eugenie *SEE* Anciaux, Anne Joseph Barras
Anciaux, Lambert Emmanuel *SEE* Anciaux, Anne Joseph Barras
Ancinelle, B. A. 18; New Orleans, 1848 ***778.6*** *p5*
Ancinelle, P. J. 26; New Orleans, 1848 ***778.6*** *p5*
Ancliff, John 40; Ontario, 1871 ***1823.21*** *p5*
Ancquetin, Elie; Quebec, 1656 ***9221.17*** *p331*
Andberg, John P.; America, 1854 ***4487.25*** *p50*
With family
Andel, Jiri; Nebraska, 1874 ***2853.20*** *p172*
Andel, Josef; Chicago, 1897 ***2853.20*** *p419*
Anderegg, . . .; West Virginia, n.d. ***1132.30*** *p151*
Anderle, Josef Frantisek; Milwaukee, 1853 ***2853.20*** *p308*
Anders, Bertha 30; Galveston, TX, 1855 ***571.7*** *p16*
Anders, Gottlieb 32; Galveston, TX, 1855 ***571.7*** *p16*
Andersdotter, Anna 21; New York, 1856 ***6529.11*** *p20*
Andersdotter, Anna 24; New York, 1856 ***6529.11*** *p22*
Andersdotter, Anna S.; Kansas, 1870 ***777.40*** *p13*
Andersdotter, Brita; Iowa, 1866-1869 ***777.40*** *p8*
Andersdotter, Brita 22; New York, 1856 ***6529.11*** *p21*
Andersdotter, Brita 25; New York, 1856 ***6529.11*** *p22*
Andersdotter, Brita 27; New York, 1856 ***6529.11*** *p21*
Andersdotter, Christina Charlotte; Kansas, 1868 ***777.40*** *p14*
Andersdotter, Christine C.; Kansas, 1868 ***777.40*** *p14*
Andersdotter, Hannah; Kansas, 1844-1871 ***777.40*** *p4*
Andersdotter, Kerstin; New York, 1857 ***6529.11*** *p25*
Andersdotter, Lisa; New York, 1856 ***6529.11*** *p19*
Andersdotter, Lisa 30; New York, 1856 ***6529.11*** *p19*
Andersdotter, Maria Lisa; America, 1869 ***777.40*** *p27*
Andersen, Andrew 23; New York, NY, 1844 ***6178.50*** *p151*
Andersen, Edward Michael; Iowa, 1926 ***1211.15*** *p9*
Andersen, Gustaf; Cleveland, OH, 1869 ***9722.10*** *p115*
Anderson, Mr.; Canada, 1775 ***3036.5*** *p68*
Anderson, A.B. 45; Kansas, 1880 ***777.40*** *p6*
*Wife:*C.M. 30
Anderson, A.G.; Iowa, 1886 ***1211.15*** *p9*
Anderson, Aaron; Cleveland, OH, 1901-1902 ***9722.10*** *p115*
Anderson, Adolf Hugo; Cleveland, OH, 1903-1904 ***9722.10*** *p115*
Anderson, Adolph; St. Paul, MN, 1883 ***1865.50*** *p35*
Anderson, Albert; Colorado, 1888 ***1029.59*** *p1*
Anderson, Albert; Colorado, 1897 ***1029.59*** *p1*
Anderson, Albert; Colorado, 1903 ***1029.59*** *p1*
Anderson, Albert; Iowa, 1897 ***1211.15*** *p8*
Anderson, Albert; New York, NY, 1886 ***1029.59*** *p1*
Anderson, Albert Christian George Hartleman; Iowa, 1927 ***1211.15*** *p9*
Anderson, Albert Gottfried; Cleveland, OH, 1903-1904 ***9722.10*** *p115*
Anderson, Alex 32; Ontario, 1871 ***1823.21*** *p5*
Anderson, Alex 59; Ontario, 1871 ***1823.21*** *p5*
Anderson, Alexander; America, 1849 ***4487.25*** *p50*
With parents
Anderson, Alexander; Colorado, 1886 ***1029.59*** *p1*
Anderson, Alexander 35; Ontario, 1871 ***1823.21*** *p5*
Anderson, Alexander 53; Ontario, 1871 ***1823.21*** *p5*
Anderson, Alexander 67; Ontario, 1871 ***1823.21*** *p5*
Anderson, Alexd 60; Ontario, 1871 ***1823.17*** *p3*
Anderson, Alfred; Cleveland, OH, 1891-1896 ***9722.10*** *p116*
Anderson, Alfred; Iowa, 1905 ***1211.15*** *p9*
Anderson, Alfred J. 30; Kansas, 1880 ***777.40*** *p20*
Anderson, Amalia; St. Paul, MN, 1898-1899 ***1865.50*** *p35*
Anderson, Amanda; Illinois, 1887-1888 ***1865.50*** *p42*
Anderson, Andars G.; Colorado, 1888 ***1029.59*** *p1*
Anderson, Andeas; Washington, 1882 ***2770.40*** *p135*
Anderson, Anders; Iowa, 1865-1878 ***777.40*** *p4*
*Wife:*Martha Jansdotter
*Daughter:*Margaret
Anderson, Andreas 46; Kansas, 1880 ***777.40*** *p12*
Anderson, Andrew; America, 1869 ***777.40*** *p12*
Anderson, Andrew; Colorado, 1873 ***1029.59*** *p2*
Anderson, Andrew; Colorado, 1888 ***1029.59*** *p2*
Anderson, Andrew; Colorado, 1892 ***1029.59*** *p2*
Anderson, Andrew; Colorado, 1898 ***1029.59*** *p2*
Anderson, Andrew; Colorado, 1898 ***1029.59*** *p2*
Anderson, Andrew; Iowa, 1896 ***1211.15*** *p8*
Anderson, Andrew 23; New York, NY, 1844 ***6178.50*** *p151*
Anderson, Andrew; St. Paul, MN, 1900 ***1865.50*** *p35*
Anderson, Andrew; Washington, 1885 ***2770.40*** *p193*
Anderson, Andrew; Washington, 1887 ***2770.40*** *p24*
Anderson, Andrew Bernahrd; Boston, 1900 ***1766.20*** *p16*
Anderson, Andrew G.J.; St. Paul, MN, 1882 ***1865.50*** *p35*
Anderson, Andrew J.; Illinois, 1861 ***4487.25*** *p51*
Anderson, Andrew Ludvig; St. Paul, MN, 1888 ***1865.50*** *p36*
Anderson, Andrew M.; St. Paul, MN, 1874-1905 ***1865.50*** *p36*
*Wife:*Christina
Anderson, Andrew M.; St. Paul, MN, 1902 ***1865.50*** *p36*
Anderson, Andrew P.; Colorado, 1892 ***1029.59*** *p2*
Anderson, Andrew P.; St. Paul, MN, 1887 ***1865.50*** *p36*
Anderson, Andrew R.R. 3 *SEE* Anderson, John
Anderson, Andrew W. 29; Indiana, 1884-1888 ***9076.20*** *p71*
Anderson, Andrew W.; St. Paul, MN, 1873 ***1865.50*** *p36*
Anderson, Ann 23; Ontario, 1871 ***1823.21*** *p5*
Anderson, Ann 40; Ontario, 1871 ***1823.17*** *p3*
Anderson, Anna; St. Paul, MN, 1884 ***1865.50*** *p109*
Anderson, Anna Augusta; St. Paul, MN, 1896-1897 ***1865.50*** *p36*
Anderson, Anna G. *SEE* Anderson, John
Anderson, Anna Sophia *SEE* Anderson, Lars E.
Anderson, Annie Maria *SEE* Anderson, Ulrika S.
Anderson, Antone; Iowa, 1900 ***1211.15*** *p9*
Anderson, Arthur Beander; Cleveland, OH, 1904 ***9722.10*** *p116*
Anderson, August; Cleveland, OH, 1887-1890 ***9722.10*** *p116*
Anderson, August; Colorado, 1893 ***1029.59*** *p2*
Anderson, August; St. Paul, MN, 1888 ***1865.50*** *p36*
Anderson, August; Washington, 1884 ***2770.40*** *p192*
Anderson, Augusta; St. Paul, MN, 1874-1905 ***1865.50*** *p36*
Anderson, Axel; Boston, 1903 ***1766.20*** *p34*
Anderson, Axel L.; Cleveland, OH, 1896-1904 ***9722.10*** *p116*
Anderson, Axel Luther; New York, 1902 ***1766.20*** *p14*
Anderson, Axel Wilhelm; Cleveland, OH, 1889-1892 ***9722.10*** *p116*
Anderson, Baltzar Isidor; Boston, 1901 ***1766.20*** *p3*
Anderson, Baron; Washington, 1889 ***2770.40*** *p26*
Anderson, Benjamin; Michigan, 1881-1882 ***1865.50*** *p36*
Anderson, Bernhard; Cleveland, OH, 1898-1901 ***9722.10*** *p116*
Anderson, Betty; St. Paul, MN, 1890 ***1865.50*** *p36*
Anderson, C.G.; Iowa, 1896 ***1211.15*** *p8*
Anderson, C.M. 30 *SEE* Anderson, A.B.
Anderson, Carl; Cleveland, OH, 1906 ***9722.10*** *p116*
Anderson, Carl; Colorado, 1892 ***1029.59*** *p2*
Anderson, Carl; Colorado, 1892 ***1029.59*** *p2*
Anderson, Carl A.H.; Cleveland, OH, 1878-1890 ***9722.10*** *p116*
Anderson, Carl Johan 17; New York, NY, 1894 ***6512.1*** *p184*
Anderson, Carl John; Cleveland, OH, 1894-1897 ***9722.10*** *p116*
Anderson, Carl L.; Iowa, 1903 ***1211.15*** *p9*
Anderson, Carl Otto 27; Indiana, 1887-1888 ***9076.20*** *p71*
Anderson, Carolina; Buffalo, NY, 1893-1901 ***1865.50*** *p101*
Anderson, Caroline Jonsdotter 40 *SEE* Anderson, John
Anderson, Catarina; St. Paul, MN, 1886 ***1865.50*** *p99*
Anderson, Charles; Cleveland, OH, 1889-1901 ***9722.10*** *p116*
Anderson, Charles; Cleveland, OH, 1891-1894 ***9722.10*** *p116*
Anderson, Charles; Colorado, 1890 ***1029.59*** *p2*
Anderson, Charles; Colorado, 1897 ***1029.59*** *p2*
Anderson, Charles 43; Ontario, 1871 ***1823.21*** *p5*
Anderson, Charles 68; Ontario, 1871 ***1823.17*** *p3*
Anderson, Charles; St. Paul, MN, 1881 ***1865.50*** *p36*
*Wife:*Maria M. Larson
With 4 children
Anderson, Charles E. 9; Kansas, 1845-1870 ***777.40*** *p21*
Anderson, Charles Emil; St. Paul, MN, 1880 ***1865.50*** *p36*
Anderson, Charles F.; St. Paul, MN, 1883 ***1865.50*** *p36*
*Wife:*Rebecka
Anderson, Charles John 14 *SEE* Anderson, John
Anderson, Charles U.; St. Paul, MN, 1887 ***1865.50*** *p37*
Anderson, Charley; Colorado, 1890 ***1029.59*** *p2*
Anderson, Charlotta; Minnesota, 1893-1895 ***1865.50*** *p37*
Anderson, Chris; Iowa, 1894 ***1211.15*** *p8*
Anderson, Christian; Chile, 1852 ***1192.4*** *p51*
Anderson, Christian; Iowa, 1890 ***1211.15*** *p8*
Anderson, Christian Scott; Iowa, 1914 ***1211.15*** *p9*
Anderson, Christina *SEE* Anderson, Andrew M.
Anderson, Christina; St. Paul, MN, 1874-1905 ***1865.50*** *p37*
Anderson, Christina; St. Paul, MN, 1880 ***1865.50*** *p113*
Anderson, Christina *SEE* Anderson, Lars E.
Anderson, Christina; St. Paul, MN, 1888 ***1865.50*** *p104*
Anderson, Christina; St. Paul, MN, 1894 ***1865.50*** *p37*
Anderson, Christina C.; St. Paul, MN, 1882 ***1865.50*** *p36*
Anderson, Christopher 35; Toronto, 1862 ***9228.50*** *p156*
Anderson, David; Cleveland, OH, 1889-1893 ***9722.10*** *p116*
Anderson, David; Cleveland, OH, 1889-1901 ***9722.10*** *p116*
Anderson, David; Ohio, 1809-1852 ***4511.35*** *p1*
Anderson, David 50; Ontario, 1871 ***1823.21*** *p5*
Anderson, David 62; Ontario, 1871 ***1823.21*** *p5*
Anderson, Denis 18; St. John, N.B., 1834 ***6469.7*** *p4*
Anderson, Donald 35; Ontario, 1871 ***1823.21*** *p5*
Anderson, Donald 60; Ontario, 1871 ***1823.21*** *p5*
Anderson, Duncan 85; Ontario, 1871 ***1823.17*** *p3*
Anderson, Edw 23; Ontario, 1871 ***1823.21*** *p6*
Anderson, Edward 25; Ontario, 1871 ***1823.21*** *p6*
Anderson, Edward 30; Ontario, 1871 ***1823.21*** *p6*
Anderson, Elias; Cleveland, OH, 1872-1897 ***9722.10*** *p116*
Anderson, Elizabeth; Canada, 1775 ***3036.5*** *p68*
*Child:*Mary
*Child:*Janes
*Child:*William
*Child:*John
*Child:*Moses
Anderson, Ellen; St. Paul, MN, 1880 ***1865.50*** *p37*
Anderson, Ellen; St. Paul, MN, 1898 ***1865.50*** *p35*
Anderson, Ellen M. 12 *SEE* Anderson, John
Anderson, Emil; St. Paul, MN, 1880 ***1865.50*** *p37*
Anderson, Emil; Washington, 1882 ***2770.40*** *p135*
Anderson, Emma; Colorado, 1896 ***1029.59*** *p2*
Anderson, Emma *SEE* Anderson, John A.
Anderson, Emma; St. Paul, MN, 1874-1905 ***1865.50*** *p37*
Anderson, Emma; St. Paul, MN, 1890 ***1865.50*** *p97*
Anderson, Emma Lovisa; St. Paul, MN, 1902 ***1865.50*** *p37*
Anderson, Erick August 8 *SEE* Anderson, John

Anderson, Erick G.; St. Paul, MN, 1881 *1865.50 p37*
Anderson, Erick J.; Dakota, 1881-1883 *1865.50 p37*
Anderson, Erl; Washington, 1888 *2770.40 p25*
Anderson, Ezekiel; North Carolina, 1823 *1088.45 p1*
Anderson, Fannie; St. Paul, MN, 1889-1890 *1865.50 p37*
Anderson, Frank; Cleveland, OH, 1894-1897 *9722.10 p116*
Anderson, Frank; New York, 1862-1920 *1029.59 p2*
Anderson, Frank; New York, 1899 *1766.20 p25*
Anderson, Frans Oscar; Cleveland, OH, 1899-1900 *9722.10 p116*
Anderson, Fred; Cleveland, OH, 1887-1891 *9722.10 p116*
Anderson, Fredrick 52; Ontario, 1871 *1823.21 p6*
Anderson, George; North Carolina, 1832-1837 *1088.45 p1*
Anderson, George 30; Ontario, 1871 *1823.17 p3*
Anderson, Gerda Maria; St. Paul, MN, 1883 *1865.50 p105*
Anderson, Gottfried; Cleveland, OH, 1901-1906 *9722.10 p116*
Anderson, Gus; Iowa, 1875 *1211.15 p8*
Anderson, Gust; Iowa, 1896 *1211.15 p9*
Anderson, Gustaf; Cleveland, OH, 1891-1892 *9722.10 p116*
Anderson, Gustaf; Colorado, 1903 *1029.59 p2*
Anderson, Gustaf 30; Colorado, 1903 *1029.59 p3*
Anderson, Gustaf Adolf; Cleveland, OH, 1900-1905 *9722.10 p116*
Anderson, Gustaf Adolph; Illinois, 1861 *4487.25 p51*
Anderson, Gustav; Cleveland, OH, 1891 *9722.10 p116*
Anderson, Gustav; Cleveland, OH, 1896-1898 *9722.10 p116*
Anderson, Gustav O. 10 *SEE* Anderson, John
Anderson, Gustavus 56; Ontario, 1871 *1823.21 p6*
Anderson, Gustof; Washington, 1889 *2770.40 p26*
Anderson, Hannah; St. Paul, MN, 1894-1897 *1865.50 p37*
Anderson, Hannah M.; Minnesota, 1901 *1865.50 p109*
Anderson, Hans; Iowa, 1897 *1211.15 p8*
Anderson, Hans; New York, 1902 *1766.20 p16*
Anderson, Hans; Washington, 1887 *2770.40 p24*
Anderson, Harry; Cleveland, OH, 1898-1901 *9722.10 p116*
Anderson, Henry 52; Ontario, 1871 *1823.21 p6*
Anderson, Hilma M.; St. Paul, MN, 1881 *1865.50 p50*
Anderson, Hjalmar Erik *SEE* Anderson, Lars E.
Anderson, Hugh 77; Ontario, 1871 *1823.21 p6*
Anderson, Hulda; St. Paul, MN, 1885-1899 *1865.50 p40*
Anderson, Hulda M.; Illinois, 1881-1885 *1865.50 p38*
Anderson, Miss I.; Montreal, 1922 *4514.4 p32*
Anderson, Ida 25; New York, NY, 1883 *8427.14 p44*
Anderson, J.A.; Cleveland, OH, 1901 *9722.10 p116*
Anderson, J.P.; Iowa, 1890 *1211.15 p8*
Anderson, James; Illinois, 1864 *4487.25 p51*
Anderson, James; Iowa, 1890 *1211.15 p8*
Anderson, James; Iowa, 1896 *1211.15 p8*
Anderson, James; Missouri, 1885 *3276.1 p1*
Anderson, James; Ohio, 1809-1852 *4511.35 p1*
Anderson, James 39; Ontario, 1871 *1823.21 p6*
Anderson, James 40; Ontario, 1871 *1823.21 p6*
Anderson, James 49; Ontario, 1871 *1823.21 p6*
Anderson, James 55; Ontario, 1871 *1823.21 p6*
Anderson, James 59; Ontario, 1871 *1823.21 p6*
Anderson, James 76; Ontario, 1871 *1823.17 p3*
Anderson, Jane 40; Ontario, 1871 *1823.21 p6*
Anderson, Janes *SEE* Anderson, Elizabeth
Anderson, Jennie *SEE* Anderson, Peter
Anderson, Jessey; New Orleans, 1851 *7242.30 p134*
Anderson, Johan; Cleveland, OH, 1886-1888 *9722.10 p116*
Anderson, Johan; Cleveland, OH, 1902-1903 *9722.10 p116*
Anderson, Johan; Washington, 1882 *2770.40 p135*
Anderson, Johan Edward; Cleveland, OH, 1892 *9722.10 p116*
Anderson, Johan Martin; New York, 1901 *1766.20 p27*
Anderson, Johanna; St. Paul, MN, 1874-1905 *1865.50 p37*
Anderson, John *SEE* Anderson, Elizabeth
Anderson, John; Cleveland, OH, 1892-1895 *9722.10 p116*
Anderson, John; Cleveland, OH, 1895-1902 *9722.10 p116*
Anderson, John; Cleveland, OH, 1901-1904 *9722.10 p116*
Anderson, John; Colorado, 1888 *1029.59 p3*
Anderson, John; Colorado, 1895 *1029.59 p3*
Anderson, John; Iowa, 1891 *1211.15 p9*
Anderson, John; Iowa, 1898 *1211.15 p8*
Anderson, John 23; Kansas, 1880 *777.40 p19*
Anderson, John 30; Kansas, 1880 *777.40 p6*

Anderson, John 40; Kansas, 1880 *777.40 p13*
  *Wife:*Caroline Jonsdotter 40
  *Son:*Andrew R.R. 3
  *Daughter:*Wandle C. 5
  *Daughter:*Ellen M. 12
  *Son:*Gustav O. 10
  *Son:*Charles John 14
  *Son:*Erick August 8
Anderson, John; Louisiana, 1874 *4981.45 p295*
Anderson, John; Minneapolis, 1888-1892 *1865.50 p38*
Anderson, John; New York, 1904 *1766.20 p34*
Anderson, John 28; New York, NY, 1894 *6512.1 p185*
Anderson, John; Ohio, 1809-1852 *4511.35 p1*
Anderson, John 20; Ontario, 1871 *1823.21 p6*
Anderson, John 30; Ontario, 1871 *1823.17 p3*
Anderson, John 32; Ontario, 1871 *1823.21 p6*
Anderson, John 44; Ontario, 1871 *1823.17 p3*
Anderson, John 59; Ontario, 1871 *1823.21 p6*
Anderson, John 70; Ontario, 1871 *1823.17 p3*
Anderson, John 75; Ontario, 1871 *1823.21 p6*
Anderson, John; St. Paul, MN, 1894 *1865.50 p38*
  *Wife:*Anna G.
Anderson, John; Washington, 1884 *2770.40 p192*
Anderson, John; Washington, 1889 *2770.40 p26*
Anderson, John A.; Illinois, 1864 *4487.25 p51*
Anderson, John A.; St. Paul, MN, 1869 *1865.50 p38*
  *Wife:*Emma
Anderson, John Adolph; St. Paul, MN, 1883 *1865.50 p38*
Anderson, John Albert; Boston, 1883 *1766.20 p34*
Anderson, John Alfred; Washington, 1888 *2770.40 p25*
Anderson, John E.; Colorado, 1891 *1029.59 p3*
Anderson, John E. 25; Indiana, 1885-1888 *9076.20 p72*
Anderson, John L. 44; Ontario, 1871 *1823.21 p6*
Anderson, John Peter *SEE* Anderson, Ulrika S.
Anderson, Jonas 18; New York, 1856 *6529.11 p21*
Anderson, Jonas; Washington, 1884 *2770.40 p192*
Anderson, Jos.; Colorado, 1899 *1029.59 p3*
Anderson, Joseph 50; Ontario, 1871 *1823.21 p6*
Anderson, Joseph 65; Ontario, 1871 *1823.17 p3*
Anderson, K.E.; Iowa, 1897 *1211.15 p8*
Anderson, Karl; Cleveland, OH, 1892-1903 *9722.10 p116*
Anderson, Karl Enoch; Boston, 1903 *1766.20 p25*
Anderson, Karl Peter; Cleveland, OH, 1891-1899 *9722.10 p116*
Anderson, Karl Simon; Illinois, 1930 *121.35 p100*
Anderson, Karolina M.; St. Paul, MN, 1874-1905 *1865.50 p38*
Anderson, Larry 30; Kansas, 1880 *777.40 p5*
Anderson, Lars; Iowa, 1911 *1211.15 p9*
Anderson, Lars E.; St. Paul, MN, 1882 *1865.50 p38*
  *Wife:*Christina
  *Daughter:*Anna Sophia
  *Son:*Hjalmar Erik
Anderson, Lars G.; St. Paul, MN, 1882 *1865.50 p38*
Anderson, Lars Jorgen; Iowa, 1896 *1211.15 p8*
Anderson, Levin; St. Paul, MN, 1890 *1865.50 p38*
Anderson, Linda 37; Minnesota, 1925 *2769.54 p1379*
Anderson, Louis 25; Ontario, 1871 *1823.17 p3*
Anderson, Louis C.; Washington, 1882 *2770.40 p135*
Anderson, Louis J.; Illinois, 1861 *4487.25 p52*
Anderson, Lovisa J.; St. Paul, MN, 1874-1905 *1865.50 p38*
Anderson, Maja K.; St. Paul, MN, 1894 *1865.50 p38*
Anderson, Margaret *SEE* Anderson, Anders
Anderson, Margaret 54; Ontario, 1871 *1823.17 p3*
Anderson, Maria; Minnesota, 1881-1883 *1865.50 p50*
Anderson, Maria; St. Paul, MN, 1872 *1865.50 p36*
Anderson, Maria; St. Paul, MN, 1883 *1865.50 p38*
Anderson, Maria; St. Paul, MN, 1890 *1865.50 p36*
Anderson, Maria M. Larson *SEE* Anderson, Charles
Anderson, Martha Jansdotter *SEE* Anderson, Anders
Anderson, Martha 63; Ontario, 1871 *1823.17 p3*
Anderson, Martin; Cleveland, OH, 1891-1897 *9722.10 p116*
Anderson, Mary *SEE* Anderson, Elizabeth
Anderson, Mary; New York, 1740 *8277.31 p113*
  With 2 daughters
Anderson, Mary 52; Ontario, 1871 *1823.21 p6*
Anderson, Mary 69; Ontario, 1871 *1823.21 p6*
Anderson, Mary; St. Paul, MN, 1894 *1865.50 p38*
Anderson, Mary; Wisconsin, 1840-1900 *9228.50 p81*
Anderson, Mary C.; St. Paul, MN, 1894 *1865.50 p38*
Anderson, Mathew; Washington, 1883 *2770.40 p136*
Anderson, Mathilda; St. Paul, MN, 1874-1905 *1865.50 p39*
Anderson, Mathilda; St. Paul, MN, 1881 *1865.50 p99*
Anderson, Mathilda; St. Paul, MN, 1882 *1865.50 p107*
Anderson, Mathilda; St. Paul, MN, 1888 *1865.50 p92*
Anderson, Mathilda; St. Paul, MN, 1901 *1865.50 p39*
Anderson, Mathilda Josephina; Cleveland, OH, 1887-1904 *9722.10 p130*

Anderson, Moses *SEE* Anderson, Elizabeth
Anderson, N.M.; Iowa, 1888 *1211.15 p8*
Anderson, Neils; Cleveland, OH, 1895-1905 *9722.10 p116*
Anderson, Nels; Illinois, 1861 *4487.25 p52*
Anderson, Nels; Iowa, 1885 *1211.15 p8*
Anderson, Nils Alfred; New York, 1901 *1766.20 p36*
Anderson, Nils Aug.; Cleveland, OH, 1897-1898 *9722.10 p116*
Anderson, Nils L.; Colorado, 1887 *1029.59 p3*
Anderson, Nils Steffen; Washington, 1884 *2770.40 p192*
Anderson, O.M.; Cleveland, OH, 1881-1904 *9722.10 p116*
Anderson, Olaus; Cleveland, OH, 1889-1893 *9722.10 p116*
Anderson, Ole; Iowa, 1868 *1211.15 p8*
Anderson, Olga Victoria *SEE* Anderson, Ulrika S.
Anderson, Oliver; Colorado, 1886 *1029.59 p3*
Anderson, Olof 25; Kansas, 1880 *777.40 p7*
Anderson, Olof; St. Paul, MN, 1874-1905 *1865.50 p39*
Anderson, Olson; Colorado, 1862-1920 *1029.59 p3*
Anderson, Oly; Colorado, 1888 *1029.59 p3*
Anderson, Oscar; New York, 1884 *1766.20 p34*
Anderson, Osmund; Iowa, 1924 *1211.15 p9*
Anderson, Otto; Cleveland, OH, 1889-1892 *9722.10 p116*
Anderson, Otto S.; St. Paul, MN, 1887-1888 *1865.50 p39*
Anderson, Pete; Cleveland, OH, 1903-1905 *9722.10 p116*
Anderson, Peter; Colorado, 1873 *1029.59 p3*
Anderson, Peter; Illinois, 1861 *4487.25 p52*
Anderson, Peter; Iowa, 1876 *1211.15 p8*
Anderson, Peter 21; Ontario, 1871 *1823.17 p3*
Anderson, Peter 59; Ontario, 1871 *1823.17 p3*
Anderson, Peter; St. Paul, MN, 1894 *1865.50 p39*
  *Wife:*Jennie
Anderson, Peter; St. Paul, MN, 1897 *1865.50 p39*
Anderson, Peter D.; America, 1849 *4487.25 p52*
  With family
Anderson, Petter Anton; Washington, 1888 *2770.40 p25*
Anderson, Ralph 40; Ontario, 1871 *1823.17 p3*
Anderson, Rebecka *SEE* Anderson, Charles F.
Anderson, Richard 39; Ontario, 1871 *1823.21 p6*
Anderson, Robert; Cleveland, OH, 1884-1892 *9722.10 p117*
Anderson, Robert 20; Ontario, 1871 *1823.21 p6*
Anderson, Robert 20; Ontario, 1871 *1823.21 p6*
Anderson, Robert 24; Ontario, 1871 *1823.21 p6*
Anderson, Robert 41; Ontario, 1871 *1823.21 p6*
Anderson, Robert 46; Ontario, 1871 *1823.21 p6*
Anderson, Robert 60; Ontario, 1871 *1823.17 p3*
Anderson, Robert; Toronto, 1844 *2910.35 p115*
Anderson, Robt. 50; Ontario, 1871 *1823.17 p3*
Anderson, Samuel 38; Ontario, 1871 *1823.17 p3*
Anderson, Sophia; St. Paul, MN, 1881 *1865.50 p35*
Anderson, Sophia; St. Paul, MN, 1889 *1865.50 p37*
Anderson, Sven Elof; Colorado, 1893 *1029.59 p3*
Anderson, Sven Elof; Colorado, 1893 *1029.59 p4*
Anderson, Thomas 72; Ontario, 1871 *1823.21 p6*
Anderson, Tobias 58; Ohio, 1859 *9722.10 p115*
Anderson, Tollef; Iowa, 1903 *1211.15 p9*
Anderson, Ulrika S.; St. Paul, MN, 1886 *1865.50 p39*
  *Child:*Annie Maria
  *Child:*John Peter
  *Child:*Olga Victoria
Anderson, Victor; Cleveland, OH, 1867-1882 *9722.10 p117*
Anderson, Victor; Colorado, 1887 *1029.59 p4*
Anderson, Walter 63; Ontario, 1871 *1823.17 p3*
Anderson, Wandle C. 5 *SEE* Anderson, John
Anderson, William *SEE* Anderson, Elizabeth
Anderson, William; Cleveland, OH, 1860-1869 *9722.10 p117*
Anderson, William; Illinois, 1861 *4487.25 p52*
Anderson, William; New York, 1776 *8529.30 p2*
Anderson, William; North Carolina, 1841 *1088.45 p1*
Anderson, William; North Carolina, 1843 *1088.45 p1*
Anderson, William; Ohio, 1809-1852 *4511.35 p1*
Anderson, William 19; Ontario, 1871 *1823.21 p7*
Anderson, William 28; Ontario, 1871 *1823.21 p7*
Anderson, William 31; Ontario, 1871 *1823.21 p7*
Anderson, William 36; Ontario, 1871 *1823.17 p3*
Anderson, William 38; Ontario, 1871 *1823.17 p3*
Anderson, William 40; Ontario, 1871 *1823.17 p3*
Anderson, William 43; Ontario, 1871 *1823.17 p3*
Anderson, William 53; Ontario, 1871 *1823.17 p3*
Anderson, William 60; Ontario, 1871 *1823.21 p7*
Anderson, William 77; Ontario, 1871 *1823.21 p7*
Anderson, William; Wisconsin, 1840 *9228.50 p81*
Anderson, William G.; Washington, 1889 *2770.40 p26*
Anderson, Wm 55; Ontario, 1871 *1823.21 p7*
Anderssen, Andreas; Valdivia, Chile, 1850 *1192.4 p49*

Anderssen, J.; Valparaiso, Chile, 1850 ***1192.4*** *p50*
Anderssen, L.; Valparaiso, Chile, 1850 ***1192.4*** *p50*
Andersson, A.; Cleveland, OH, 1897 ***9722.10*** *p117*
Andersson, A. F.; Valparaiso, Chile, 1850 ***1192.4*** *p50*
Andersson, A. Fr.; Savannah, GA, 1851 ***6412.40*** *p153*
Andersson, A.J.; New York, NY, 1844 ***6412.40*** *p147*
Andersson, And.; New York, NY, 1844 ***6412.40*** *p147*
Andersson, Anders; New Orleans, 1851 ***6412.40*** *p153*
Andersson, Anders 25; New York, 1856 ***6529.11*** *p21*
Andersson, Anders 46; New York, 1856 ***6529.11*** *p21*
*Wife:*Ingrid Hansdotter 43
*Daughter:*Carin 19
*Daughter:*Margaretha 10
*Son:*Pehr 16
Andersson, Anders Fredrik 10 *SEE* Andersson, Hans
Andersson, Andrew *SEE* Andersson, Hans
Andersson, Andrew R.R. 3 *SEE* Andersson, Johannes
Andersson, Anna Christina *SEE* Andersson, Kerstin Jonsdotter
Andersson, Birger; Colorado, 1887 ***1029.59*** *p4*
Andersson, Brita Erickson *SEE* Andersson, Hans
Andersson, C. Aug.; San Francisco, 1855 ***6412.40*** *p153*
Andersson, C.E.; New York, NY, 1843 ***6412.40*** *p148*
Andersson, C.G.; New York, NY, 1846 ***6412.40*** *p149*
Andersson, Carin 19 *SEE* Andersson, Anders
Andersson, Carl 15 *SEE* Andersson, Hans
Andersson, Carolina Jonsdotter 40 *SEE* Andersson, Johannes
Andersson, Charles John 14 *SEE* Andersson, Johannes
Andersson, Daniel; America, 1855 ***6529.11*** *p25*
Andersson, E.M.; New York, NY, 1845 ***6412.40*** *p148*
Andersson, Ellen M. 12 *SEE* Andersson, Johannes
Andersson, Emanuel; Boston, 1847 ***6412.40*** *p150*
Andersson, Emanuel; San Francisco, 1855 ***6412.40*** *p153*
Andersson, Erick August 8 *SEE* Andersson, Johannes
Andersson, F.; Valparaiso, Chile, 1850 ***1192.4*** *p50*
Andersson, Gustaf; Charleston, SC, 1850 ***6412.40*** *p152*
Andersson, Gustav O. 10 *SEE* Andersson, Johannes
Andersson, Hans; Kansas, 1876 ***777.40*** *p14*
*Wife:*Brita Erickson
With father-in-law & mother-in-law
*Son:*Andrew
Andersson, Hans 43; New York, 1856 ***6529.11*** *p21*
*Son:*Anders Fredrik 10
*Son:*Carl 15
Andersson, Ingrid Hansdotter 43 *SEE* Andersson, Anders
Andersson, J.; New Orleans, 1851 ***6412.40*** *p152*
Andersson, J.; New York, NY, 1843 ***6412.40*** *p147*
Andersson, J.; New York, NY, 1845 ***6412.40*** *p148*
Andersson, J.; New York, NY, 1847 ***6412.40*** *p150*
Andersson, J.P.; New York, NY, 1849 ***6412.40*** *p151*
Andersson, Joh. Ludv.; New York, NY, 1851 ***6412.40*** *p151*
Andersson, Johannes 40; Kansas, 1880 ***777.40*** *p13*
*Wife:*Carolina Jonsdotter 40
*Son:*Charles John 14
*Son:*Gustav O. 10
*Son:*Andrew R.R. 3
*Daughter:*Wandle C. 5
*Son:*Erick August 8
*Daughter:*Ellen M. 12
Andersson, Jon 19; New York, 1856 ***6529.11*** *p20*
Andersson, Jon 37; New York, 1856 ***6529.11*** *p21*
Andersson, Kerstin; New York, 1857 ***6529.11*** *p25*
*Daughter:*Anna Christina
Andersson, L.; New York, NY, 1847 ***6412.40*** *p150*
Andersson, L.G.; New Orleans, 1843 ***6412.40*** *p147*
Andersson, Margaretha 10 *SEE* Andersson, Anders
Andersson, Martin; Colorado, 1887 ***1029.59*** *p4*
Andersson, N.P.; Charleston, SC, 1850 ***6412.40*** *p152*
Andersson, Nils; New York, NY, 1849 ***6412.40*** *p151*
Andersson, P.; New York, NY, 1845 ***6412.40*** *p149*
Andersson, Pehr 16 *SEE* Andersson, Anders
Andersson, Pehr 32; New York, 1856 ***6529.11*** *p21*
Andersson, Soen P.; Colorado, 1884 ***1029.59*** *p4*
Andersson, Sv.; New York, NY, 1843 ***6412.40*** *p147*
Andersson, W.; Valparaiso, Chile, 1850 ***1192.4*** *p50*
Andersson, Wandle C. 5 *SEE* Andersson, Johannes
Anderten, Friedrich Christian Albrecht; America, 1857 ***7420.1*** *p157*
Anderten, Johann Friedrich Wilhelm; America, 1868 ***7420.1*** *p267*
Anderton, William 71; Ontario, 1871 ***1823.17*** *p4*
Anding, Jean; Chile, 1852 ***1192.4*** *p51*
With wife
Anding, Sebastian; Ohio, 1809-1852 ***4511.35*** *p1*
Andler, Carl Fr.; Valdivia, Chile, 1852 ***1192.4*** *p55*
With wife 5 children & baby
With child 12
Andler, Jacob; Ohio, 1809-1852 ***4511.35*** *p1*
Andler, Margarethe; America, 1843 ***5475.1*** *p453*
Andrap, Casper Heinrich 23; New York, NY, 1864 ***8425.62*** *p195*
Andras, Peter; North Carolina, 1710 ***3629.40*** *p3*
Andraszewitz, Joseph 27; New York, NY, 1893 ***1883.7*** *p37*
Andre, Mrs. 38; New Orleans, 1846 ***778.6*** *p5*
Andre, Catherina 13; America, 1840 ***778.6*** *p5*
Andre, Catherina 38; America, 1840 ***778.6*** *p5*
Andre, Catherine 8; Missouri, 1845 ***778.6*** *p5*
Andre, Chna. 4; America, 1840 ***778.6*** *p5*
Andre, Christine 16; Missouri, 1845 ***778.6*** *p5*
Andre, Cora 8; New Orleans, 1846 ***778.6*** *p5*
Andre, Gariel 17; Port uncertain, 1843 ***778.6*** *p5*
Andre, Georg; America, 1847 ***7420.1*** *p51*
With wife & 2 sons
Andre, Henry; Illinois, 1860 ***6079.1*** *p1*
Andre, Jacques; Montreal, 1653 ***9221.17*** *p280*
Andre, Jean 6; Missouri, 1845 ***778.6*** *p5*
Andre, Joseph 3; Missouri, 1845 ***778.6*** *p5*
Andre, L...s F. 30; America, 1842 ***778.6*** *p5*
Andre, Louise; Quebec, 1667 ***4514.3*** *p270*
Andre, Madelaine 42; Missouri, 1845 ***778.6*** *p5*
Andre, Marie 11; Missouri, 1845 ***778.6*** *p5*
Andre, Mathias; America, 1853 ***5475.1*** *p235*
Andre, Michel 23; Montreal, 1662 ***9221.17*** *p495*
Andre, Nicolas 10; Missouri, 1845 ***778.6*** *p5*
Andre, Pierre 40; Missouri, 1845 ***778.6*** *p5*
Andre, Regnault 30; Quebec, 1651 ***9221.17*** *p236*
Andre, Salome 22; America, 1840 ***778.6*** *p5*
Andrea, Caroline; America, 1867 ***7919.3*** *p527*
With child
Andrea, Johanne Friederike; America, 1867 ***7919.3*** *p530*
With granddaughter & 4 children
Andreas, Auguste 3; New Orleans, 1848 ***778.6*** *p5*
Andreas, Barbe 21; New Orleans, 1848 ***778.6*** *p5*
Andreas, Hermann; Valdivia, Chile, 1850 ***1192.4*** *p50*
Andreas, Joseph 42; New Orleans, 1848 ***778.6*** *p5*
Andreas, Josephine 4; New Orleans, 1848 ***778.6*** *p5*
Andreas, Sophie 1; New Orleans, 1848 ***778.6*** *p5*
Andreau, Julian 50; New Orleans, 1847 ***778.6*** *p5*
Andrecht, Johann Heinrich; America, 1867 ***7420.1*** *p252*
With family
Andre deLeigne, Pierre; Quebec, 1718 ***2314.30*** *p169*
Andre deLeigne, Pierre; Quebec, 1718 ***2314.30*** *p174*
Andreen, John A.; Washington, 1886 ***2770.40*** *p195*
Andreen, Kirsten; America, 1918-1966 ***9228.50*** *p122*
Andres, Benedikt 31; Galveston, TX, 1846 ***3967.10*** *p378*
Andres, Daniel; America, 1895 ***170.15*** *p18*
Andres, Elisabeth 6 months; Galveston, TX, 1846 ***3967.10*** *p378*
Andres, Elisabeth 41; Galveston, TX, 1846 ***3967.10*** *p378*
Andres, Jean 37; New Orleans, 1848 ***778.6*** *p5*
Andres, Nikolaus 19; Galveston, TX, 1846 ***3967.10*** *p378*
Andres, Nikolaus 37; Galveston, TX, 1846 ***3967.10*** *p378*
Andres, Nikolaus 63; Galveston, TX, 1846 ***3967.10*** *p378*
Andres, Wilhelm; Colorado, 1881 ***5475.1*** *p33*
Andresson, Anders; Washington, 1885 ***2770.40*** *p193*
Andrew, Mr. 45; America, 1845 ***778.6*** *p5*
Andrew, Alexander; Philadelphia, 1778 ***8529.30*** *p2*
Andrew, Giles; New York, NY, 1830 ***3274.55*** *p74*
Andrew, Jacob 30; Ontario, 1871 ***1823.17*** *p4*
Andrew, John 42; Ontario, 1871 ***1823.21*** *p7*
Andrew, M.; Louisiana, 1874 ***4981.45*** *p295*
Andrew, Matthew 50; Ontario, 1871 ***1823.17*** *p4*
Andrews, Adolphus 49; Ontario, 1871 ***1823.21*** *p7*
Andrews, Alexander; Philadelphia, 1778 ***8529.30*** *p2*
Andrews, Annie 16; Ontario, 1871 ***1823.17*** *p4*
Andrews, Charles H.; North Carolina, 1858 ***1088.45*** *p1*
Andrews, Charles H. 28; Ontario, 1871 ***1823.21*** *p7*
Andrews, David 25; Ontario, 1871 ***1823.21*** *p7*
Andrews, Edwin; Ohio, 1876 ***3580.20*** *p31*
Andrews, Edwin S.; Ohio, 1876 ***6020.12*** *p6*
Andrews, Elizabeth 60; Ontario, 1871 ***1823.21*** *p7*
Andrews, Ella M. 20; Michigan, 1880 ***4491.30*** *p1*
Andrews, Garvis 46; Ontario, 1871 ***1823.21*** *p7*
Andrews, George 35; Ontario, 1871 ***1823.17*** *p4*
Andrews, George 52; Ontario, 1871 ***1823.17*** *p4*
Andrews, Henry 15; Quebec, 1870 ***8364.32*** *p22*
Andrews, Isaac 63; Ontario, 1871 ***1823.17*** *p4*
Andrews, Israel 59; Ohio, 1880 ***4879.40*** *p258*
Andrews, John; Colorado, 1880 ***1029.59*** *p4*
Andrews, John; Colorado, 1903 ***1029.59*** *p4*
Andrews, John; Illinois, 1864 ***6079.1*** *p1*
Andrews, John; New York, 1775 ***8529.30*** *p9*
Andrews, John 20; Ontario, 1871 ***1823.17*** *p4*
Andrews, John 40; Ontario, 1871 ***1823.21*** *p7*
Andrews, John 45; Ontario, 1871 ***1823.21*** *p7*
Andrews, Joseph; Ohio, 1809-1852 ***4511.35*** *p1*
Andrews, Joseph 40; Ontario, 1871 ***1823.21*** *p7*
Andrews, Kenedy 13; Ontario, 1871 ***1823.17*** *p4*
Andrews, Ms. M. A. 14; Quebec, 1870 ***8364.32*** *p22*
Andrews, Margret 35; Ontario, 1871 ***1823.21*** *p7*
Andrews, Nils P.; Washington, 1885 ***2770.40*** *p193*
Andrews, Peter; New York, 1776 ***8529.30*** *p2*
Andrews, Peter; North Carolina, 1710 ***3629.40*** *p3*
Andrews, Rebina 18; Ontario, 1871 ***1823.17*** *p4*
Andrews, Richard; Colorado, 1882 ***1029.59*** *p4*
Andrews, Richard; Colorado, 1893 ***1029.59*** *p4*
Andrews, Richard 49; Ontario, 1871 ***1823.21*** *p7*
Andrews, Thomas 35; North Carolina, 1774 ***1422.10*** *p55*
Andrews, Thomas 34; Ontario, 1871 ***1823.21*** *p7*
Andrews, Thomas 52; Ontario, 1871 ***1823.21*** *p7*
Andrews, William 31; North Carolina, 1774 ***1422.10*** *p55*
Andrews, William T.; Colorado, 1903 ***1029.59*** *p4*
Andrews, William T.; South Dakota, 1892 ***1029.59*** *p4*
Andrews, Wm 28; Ontario, 1871 ***1823.21*** *p7*
Andrieu, Antoine 18; Quebec, 1660 ***9221.17*** *p430*
Andrieu, F. Elise 24; New Orleans, 1840 ***778.6*** *p6*
Andrieu, Marguerite; Quebec, 1673 ***4514.3*** *p270*
Andrin, Pierre Jos.; Louisiana, 1874-1875 ***4981.45*** *p297*
Andrle, Frantisek; Wisconsin, 1850 ***2853.20*** *p303*
Andros, . . .; Massachusetts, 1774-1780 ***9228.50*** *p81*
Andros, . . .; New Brunswick, n.d. ***9228.50*** *p81*
Andros, Edmond; New York, 1678 ***9228.50*** *p656*
Andros, Edmund; Carolina, 1650-1699 ***9228.50*** *p55*
Andros, Edmund; New York, 1674 ***9228.50*** *p18*
Andros, Edmund; West Indies, 1637-1672 ***9228.50*** *p18*
Androzjewska, Marianna 14; New York, NY, 1894 ***6512.1*** *p231*
Androzjewska, Stanislawa 17; New York, NY, 1894 ***6512.1*** *p231*
Andrus, Charles W. 37; Ontario, 1871 ***1823.21*** *p7*
Andrus, W. P. 44; Ontario, 1871 ***1823.21*** *p7*
Andry, Mrs. 25; New Orleans, 1844 ***778.6*** *p6*
Andry, Ms. 50; New Orleans, 1848 ***778.6*** *p6*
Andry, A. 29; New Orleans, 1844 ***778.6*** *p6*
Andy, William 27; Ontario, 1871 ***1823.21*** *p7*
Andziewitz, Bachmiel 6 *SEE* Andziewitz, Malke
Andziewitz, Malke 23; New York, NY, 1878 ***9253.2*** *p45*
*Child:*Bachmiel 6 months
Anes, Thomas; Montreal, 1662 ***9221.17*** *p495*
Anest, Elisabeth Lerat 50 *SEE* Anest, Robert
Anest, Jacques 8 *SEE* Anest, Robert
Anest, Marie 4 *SEE* Anest, Robert
Anest, Robert 38; Quebec, 1654 ***9221.17*** *p304*
*Wife:*Elisabeth Lerat 50
*Son:*Jacques 8
*Daughter:*Marie 4
Anestas, George; Louisiana, 1874 ***4981.45*** *p295*
Angel, Mrs. Johann; Pennsylvania, 1880 ***5475.1*** *p23*
*Son:*Peter
Angel, Karl; Philadelphia, 1840 ***5475.1*** *p470*
Angel, Peter *SEE* Angel, Mrs. Johann
Angelier, Marie; Quebec, 1669 ***4514.3*** *p270*
Angeliere, Elazabet; Virginia, 1700 ***9230.15*** *p80*
Angelo, Geo.; Louisiana, 1874-1875 ***4981.45*** *p297*
Angelot, Jn. Bte. 25; Louisiana, 1848 ***778.6*** *p6*
Angerman, John 30; Ontario, 1871 ***1823.21*** *p7*
Angeto, Nicola; Illinois, 1918 ***6007.60*** *p9*
Anglade, Paul 23; New Orleans, 1845 ***778.6*** *p6*
Anglairo, Joseph; Louisiana, 1836-1840 ***4981.45*** *p212*
Angles, Samuel 50; Ontario, 1871 ***1823.21*** *p7*
Anglim, Timothy; Ohio, 1856 ***3580.20*** *p31*
Anglim, Timothy; Ohio, 1856 ***6020.12*** *p6*
Anglom, Daniel; Boston, 1834 ***3274.56*** *p98*
Angne, John; Ohio, 1809-1852 ***4511.35*** *p1*
Angus, James 50; Ontario, 1871 ***1823.21*** *p7*
Angus, Mary 60; Ontario, 1871 ***1823.21*** *p7*
Angus, W.G.; Quebec, 1885 ***1937.10*** *p52*
Anhauser, Wilhelm; Brazil, 1899 ***5475.1*** *p26*
Aniballi, Franch; New York, 1894 ***1766.20*** *p36*
Anicich, Antone; Washington, 1889 ***2770.40*** *p26*
Anjou, Pierre; Montreal, 1653 ***9221.17*** *p280*
Ankel, Robert 24; Ontario, 1871 ***1823.21*** *p7*
Ankele, Joseph 35; New York, NY, 1920 ***930.50*** *p49*
Anklam, Adolph; Wisconsin, 1883 ***6795.8*** *p200*
Anklam, Michael; Wisconsin, 1842 ***6795.8*** *p200*
Anley, . . .; America, n.d. ***9228.50*** *p81*
Anley, . . .; New York, 1850-1859 ***9228.50*** *p81*
Anley, . . .; Virginia, 1635 ***9228.50*** *p17A*
Annaly, Luke; Boston, 1775 ***8529.30*** *p2A*
Annand, George 22; Colorado, 1902 ***1029.59*** *p4*
Annand, George 22; Colorado, 1902 ***1029.59*** *p4*
Annen, Adam 44; America, 1843 ***5475.1*** *p252*
Annest, Jeanne 54; Quebec, 1659 ***9221.17*** *p393*
Annet, Philip; Quebec, 1859 ***9228.50*** *p82*
Annet Family ; Ohio, 1824 ***9228.50*** *p82*
Annett, Dorothy; America, 1964-1983 ***9228.50*** *p365*
Annett, George 50; Ontario, 1871 ***1823.17*** *p4*
Annett, James 45; Ontario, 1871 ***1823.21*** *p7*
Annett, Joseph 46; Ontario, 1871 ***1823.17*** *p4*
Annett, Margaret 78; Ontario, 1871 ***1823.21*** *p7*
Annett, Phillip 60; Ontario, 1871 ***1823.17*** *p4*
Annett, Stephen 49; Ontario, 1871 ***1823.17*** *p4*
Annette, Noah 55; Ontario, 1871 ***1823.21*** *p7*
Annundson, Chris 48; Ontario, 1871 ***1823.21*** *p7*
Anoil, Jacob; Texas, 1855-1884 ***9980.22*** *p16*
Anrud, Ole E.; Washington, 1883 ***2770.40*** *p136*

8 *FOR A COMPLETE EXPLANATION OF ENTRY, SEE "HOW TO READ A CITATION" SECTION*

Anseau, Benjamin 12; Quebec, 1647 ***9221.17*** *p173*
Anselin, Pierre; Montreal, 1653 ***9221.17*** *p280*
Anselm, Ablima 1; America, 1846 ***778.6*** *p6*
Anselm, Adelaide 8; America, 1846 ***778.6*** *p6*
Anselm, Herbert 3; America, 1846 ***778.6*** *p6*
Anselm, Joseph 42; America, 1846 ***778.6*** *p6*
Anselm, Martin 68; America, 1846 ***778.6*** *p6*
Anselm, Pauline 6; America, 1846 ***778.6*** *p6*
Anselm, Rosine 5; America, 1846 ***778.6*** *p6*
Anselm, Therese 40; America, 1846 ***778.6*** *p6*
Anslinger, Anton 26; Port uncertain, 1846 ***778.6*** *p6*
Anson, John; Philadelphia, 1778 ***8529.30*** *p2A*
Ansorge, Carl Heinrich; Valdivia, Chile, 1850 ***1192.4*** *p49*
Anstaett, Joseph 21; America, 1846 ***778.6*** *p6*
Ansteth, Wilhelmine 35; America, 1846 ***5475.1*** *p401*
Anstey, John S. 36; Ontario, 1871 ***1823.21*** *p7*
Anstey, Philip; Washington, 1881 ***2770.40*** *p134*
Anstie, Mary Ann 42; Ontario, 1871 ***1823.21*** *p7*
Antes, Johann Jakob 21; America, 1849 ***5475.1*** *p538*
Anthes, Marton 35; Ontario, 1871 ***1823.21*** *p7*
Anthoine, Denise; Quebec, 1670 ***4514.3*** *p270*
Anthoine, John; Marblehead, MA, 1768 ***9228.50*** *p82*
Anthoine, John; Marblehead, MA, n.d. ***9228.50*** *p82*
Anthoine, John 23; Virginia, 1624 ***9228.50*** *p82*
Anthoine, Nicholas; Maine, 1787 ***9228.50*** *p82*
Anthoine, Nicholas; Marblehead, MA, 1750 ***9228.50*** *p82*
Anthoine, Richard; Philadelphia, 1700 ***9228.50*** *p82*
  *Wife:*Sarah
Anthoine, Richard; Philadelphia, 1708 ***9228.50*** *p17A*
  *Relative:*Sarah
Anthoine, Sarah *SEE* Anthoine, Richard
Anthoine, Sarah *SEE* Anthoine, Richard
Anthoney, Charles 54; Ontario, 1871 ***1823.21*** *p7*
Anthonies, Jacob 43; Ontario, 1871 ***1823.21*** *p7*
Anthony, . . .; Massachusetts, 1790 ***9228.50*** *p83*
Anthony, . . .; Rhode Island, n.d. ***9228.50*** *p82*
Anthony, Frederick; Philadelphia, 1790 ***9228.50*** *p82*
Anthony, Jacob; Philadelphia, 1790 ***9228.50*** *p82*
Anthony, John 21; North Carolina, 1774 ***1422.10*** *p55*
Anthony, John; Portsmouth, 1607-1675 ***9228.50*** *p82*
Anthony, Joseph; Philadelphia, 1790 ***9228.50*** *p82*
Anthony, Michael; Philadelphia, 1790 ***9228.50*** *p82*
Anthony, Nicholas; Boston, 1722 ***9228.50*** *p82*
Anthony, Nicholas; Philadelphia, 1790 ***9228.50*** *p82*
Anthony, Richard; Portsmouth, NH, 1690-1699 ***9228.50*** *p82*
Anthony, Richard; Portsmouth, NH, 1697 ***9228.50*** *p82*
Anthony, William C.; Marblehead, MA, n.d. ***9228.50*** *p82*
Antich, Stephen; Washington, 1884 ***2770.40*** *p192*
Antick, Neck; Washington, 1885 ***2770.40*** *p193*
Antien, John 54; America, 1845 ***778.6*** *p6*
Antl, Frantisek J.; America, 1869 ***2853.20*** *p68*
Antl, Frantisek J.; Illinois, 1910 ***2853.20*** *p471*
Antoine, . . .; Quebec, 1534 ***9228.50*** *p3*
Antoine, . . .; Quebec, 1635 ***9221.17*** *p43*
Antoine, . . .; Quebec, 1636 ***9221.17*** *p51*
Antoine, Charles 24; America, 1846 ***778.6*** *p6*
Antoine, Eve 25; Port uncertain, 1846 ***778.6*** *p6*
Antoine, Francois; Prince Edward Island, 1771-1871 ***9228.50*** *p287*
Antoine, G. 37; Port uncertain, 1846 ***778.6*** *p6*
Antoine, Jean 24; America, 1843 ***778.6*** *p6*
Antoine, Jean 29; America, 1840 ***778.6*** *p6*
Antoine, John 21; New Orleans, 1840 ***778.6*** *p6*
Antoine, Marc 21; Quebec, 1661 ***9221.17*** *p446*
Antoine, Sebastien 35; Cuba, 1841 ***778.6*** *p6*
Antoine, Vietn; Louisiana, 1874 ***4981.45*** *p130*
Anton, Angela *SEE* Anton, Michel
Anton, Katharina *SEE* Anton, Michel
Anton, Margarethe Friedrich *SEE* Anton, Michel
Anton, Michel 47; America, 1873 ***5475.1*** *p269*
  *Wife:*Margarethe Friedrich
  *Daughter:*Katharina
  *Daughter:*Angela
  *Daughter:*Peter
Anton, Peter *SEE* Anton, Michel
Antone, Aaron 25; Ontario, 1871 ***1823.21*** *p7*
Antone, Henry 44; Ontario, 1871 ***1823.21*** *p8*
Antone, Henry 59; Ontario, 1871 ***1823.21*** *p8*
Antone, Henry 60; Ontario, 1871 ***1823.21*** *p8*
Antone, Isaac 29; Ontario, 1871 ***1823.21*** *p8*
Antone, Jacob 37; Ontario, 1871 ***1823.21*** *p8*
Antone, Jacob 99; Ontario, 1871 ***1823.21*** *p8*
Antoni, Frank; Washington, 1885 ***2770.40*** *p193*
Antoni, Franziska; America, 1862 ***5475.1*** *p495*
Antonia, Joseph D.; Louisiana, 1874-1875 ***4981.45*** *p297*
Antonia, Peter 39; New Orleans, 1843 ***778.6*** *p6*
Antonio, Bernard 28; New Orleans, 1847 ***778.6*** *p6*
Antosik, Teofila; Detroit, 1930 ***1640.60*** *p77*
Antwistle, Arthur; Philadelphia, 1777 ***8529.30*** *p2A*
Anwaerter, Henry; Ohio, 1809-1852 ***4511.35*** *p1*
Anwandter, Carl; Valdivia, Chile, 1850 ***1192.4*** *p48*
  With child 12
  With child 17
Anwandter, Hermann; Valdivia, Chile, 1850 ***1192.4*** *p48*
Anwandter, Otto 14; Valdivia, Chile, 1850 ***1192.4*** *p48*
Anwandter, Wilhelm; Valdivia, Chile, 1850 ***1192.4*** *p48*
Anweiler, Anna; Pennsylvania, 1851 ***170.15*** *p18*
  With family
Anweiler, Michael; Pennsylvania, 1851 ***170.15*** *p18*
  With family
Anwetler, Jacob; Ohio, 1809-1852 ***4511.35*** *p1*
Anye, Jose; Louisiana, 1836-1840 ***4981.45*** *p212*
Aoenicka, Adam; Washington, 1888 ***2770.40*** *p25*
Aoldan, James 49; Ontario, 1871 ***1823.21*** *p8*
Apel, David; Chile, 1852 ***1192.4*** *p51*
Apel, Georg; America, 1867 ***7919.3*** *p527*
Apel, Lorenze; North Carolina, 1855 ***1088.45*** *p1*
Apell, John; Ohio, 1844 ***2763.1*** *p7*
Apfel, William; Illinois, 1865 ***6079.1*** *p1*
Apking, Caroline; Port uncertain, 1884 ***7420.1*** *p345*
Apking, Engel Sophie Wilhelmine Nolting *SEE* Apking, Friedrich Wilhelm
Apking, Ernst Heinrich; America, 1848 ***7420.1*** *p58*
Apking, Friedrich Wilhelm; America, 1886 ***7420.1*** *p350*
  *Wife:*Engel Sophie Wilhelmine Nolting
  *Son:*Heinrich Friedrich
Apking, Heinrich Friedrich *SEE* Apking, Friedrich Wilhelm
Apking, Karl; Port uncertain, 1895 ***7420.1*** *p371*
Apleman, Catharine 65; Michigan, 1880 ***4491.36*** *p1*
Apley, Charles; Massachusetts, 1830-1870 ***9228.50*** *p17A*
Aponde, Auguste 18; Mississippi, 1845 ***778.6*** *p6*
App, Daniel; Ohio, 1809-1852 ***4511.35*** *p1*
Appe, Fred; Louisiana, 1874-1875 ***4981.45*** *p297*
Appel, Boas; Philadelphia, 1856 ***8513.31*** *p293*
  *Wife:*Clara Leipheimer
Appel, Clara Leipheimer *SEE* Appel, Boas
Appelmann, Benjamin; Ohio, 1840-1897 ***8365.35*** *p15*
Appenzeller, Jacob; New York, 1860 ***358.56*** *p148*
Appleby, Wm. 32; Virginia, 1635 ***1183.3*** *p31*
Applegate, William 39; Ontario, 1871 ***1823.21*** *p8*
Appleman, John; Ohio, 1844 ***2763.1*** *p7*
Appleton, Frederick 36; Ontario, 1871 ***1823.21*** *p8*
Appleton, Luke 83; Ontario, 1871 ***1823.21*** *p8*
Appleton, Robert; Canada, 1774 ***3036.5*** *p41*
Appleton, Thomas 45; Ontario, 1871 ***1823.21*** *p8*
Appo, Lee 22; New Orleans, 1870 ***7710.1*** *p162*
Appolt, Georg 35; America, 1873 ***5475.1*** *p72*
Apprederis, Carolina; America, 1874 ***5475.1*** *p372*
Apsey, James E. 12; Quebec, 1910 ***2897.7*** *p9*
Apsey, Lizzie 30; Quebec, 1910 ***2897.7*** *p9*
Apsey, Thomas 26; Quebec, 1910 ***2897.7*** *p9*
Aquila, Miss 22; Texas, 1848 ***778.6*** *p6*
Aquila, Antoine 56; Texas, 1848 ***778.6*** *p6*
Aquila, Jan 6 months; Texas, 1848 ***778.6*** *p6*
Aquilmo, Baja 14; New York, NY, 1894 ***6512.1*** *p230*
Arambell, Ysabel; California, 1860-1890 ***3276.8*** *p20*
Arand, Jakob; America, 1881 ***5475.1*** *p273*
  *Wife:*Johannetta Wolff
  *Daughter:*Katharina
Arand, Johannetta Wolff *SEE* Arand, Jakob
Arand, Katharina *SEE* Arand, Jakob
Arbenz, Anna; Philadelphia, 1861 ***8513.31*** *p313*
Arbige, John; Marston's Wharf, 1782 ***8529.30*** *p12*
Arbinson, James; Jamaica, 1778 ***8529.30*** *p13A*
Arbogaste, Auguste; Louisiana, 1841-1844 ***4981.45*** *p210*
Arbruster, Eve 24; America, 1845 ***778.6*** *p6*
Arbuckle, Donald 62; Ontario, 1871 ***1823.21*** *p8*
Arbuckle, John; Ohio, 1809-1852 ***4511.35*** *p1*
Archambault, Anne 16 *SEE* Archambault, Jacques
Archambault, Denis 17 *SEE* Archambault, Jacques
Archambault, Francoise Tourault 47 *SEE* Archambault, Jacques
Archambault, Jacques 43; Quebec, 1647 ***9221.17*** *p173*
  *Wife:*Francoise Tourault 47
  *Daughter:*Jacquette 15
  *Daughter:*Louise
  *Daughter:*Marie 3
  *Son:*Laurent 5
  *Daughter:*Marie 11
  *Son:*Denis 17
  *Daughter:*Anne 16
Archambault, Jacquette 15 *SEE* Archambault, Jacques
Archambault, Laurent 5 *SEE* Archambault, Jacques
Archambault, Louise *SEE* Archambault, Jacques
Archambault, Marie 3 *SEE* Archambault, Jacques
Archambault, Marie 11 *SEE* Archambault, Jacques
Archer, . . .; Massachusetts, 1774-1780 ***9228.50*** *p83*
Archer, Ann 48; Ontario, 1871 ***1823.21*** *p8*
Archer, Edward 48; Ontario, 1871 ***1823.17*** *p4*
Archer, Edward A. 23; Ontario, 1871 ***1823.17*** *p4*
Archer, Henry 60; Ontario, 1871 ***1823.21*** *p8*
Archer, Henry R. 45; Ontario, 1871 ***1823.21*** *p8*
Archer, James 31; Ontario, 1871 ***1823.21*** *p8*
Archer, James; Texas, 1878 ***3435.45*** *p35*
Archer, John 36; Ontario, 1871 ***1823.17*** *p4*
Archer, John J. 39; Ontario, 1871 ***1823.21*** *p8*
Archer, Joseph 42; Ontario, 1871 ***1823.17*** *p4*
Archer, Joseph 50; Ontario, 1871 ***1823.21*** *p8*
Archer, Mary 45; Ontario, 1871 ***1823.21*** *p8*
Archer, Robert 50; Ontario, 1871 ***1823.21*** *p8*
Archer, Samuel; North Carolina, 1854 ***1088.45*** *p1*
Archer, Thomas 38; Ontario, 1871 ***1823.21*** *p8*
Archer, Thomas 56; Ontario, 1871 ***1823.21*** *p8*
Archer, William 38; Ontario, 1871 ***1823.21*** *p8*
Archer, William 48; Ontario, 1871 ***1823.21*** *p8*
Archibald, Edward 28; Louisiana, 1831-1850 ***7710.1*** *p152*
Archibald, Smyth Allen; North Carolina, 1815 ***1088.45*** *p1*
Arckepele, John 26; New Orleans, 1840 ***778.6*** *p6*
Arcoat, George 52; Ontario, 1871 ***1823.21*** *p8*
Arcular, Marie; Quebec, 1669 ***4514.3*** *p270*
Ardell, Isabella 36; Ontario, 1871 ***1823.21*** *p8*
Ardell, James 55; Ontario, 1871 ***1823.21*** *p8*
Ardell, Sarah 40; Ontario, 1871 ***1823.21*** *p8*
Ardell, Susan 60; Ontario, 1871 ***1823.21*** *p8*
Ardell, William 60; Ontario, 1871 ***1823.21*** *p8*
Ardery, William; South Carolina, 1813 ***3208.30*** *p19*
Ardery, William; South Carolina, 1813 ***3208.30*** *p31*
Ardiel, Jane 49; Ontario, 1871 ***1823.21*** *p8*
Ardiel, Laucelot 60; Ontario, 1871 ***1823.21*** *p8*
Ardile, Henery 48; Ontario, 1871 ***1823.21*** *p8*
Ardill, James 41; Ontario, 1871 ***1823.21*** *p8*
Ardion, Marguerite; Quebec, 1663 ***4514.3*** *p271*
  *Son:*Laurent
Ardle, Catherine 25; Ontario, 1871 ***1823.21*** *p8*
Arend, Charlotte Schuch *SEE* Arend, Friedrich
Arend, Friedrich; America, 1862 ***5475.1*** *p524*
  *Wife:*Charlotte Schuch
  *Daughter:*Karoline
Arend, Karoline *SEE* Arend, Friedrich
Arends, Henrich August Wilhelm; America, 1857 ***7420.1*** *p157*
Arendsee, Paul F.W.; Wisconsin, 1876 ***6795.8*** *p229*
Arendt, David 11; Portland, ME, 1911 ***970.38*** *p76*
Arendt, Edward 16; Portland, ME, 1911 ***970.38*** *p76*
Arendt, Louisa 37; Portland, ME, 1911 ***970.38*** *p76*
Arendt, Nathaniel 13; Portland, ME, 1911 ***970.38*** *p76*
Arendt, Reinhold 9; Portland, ME, 1911 ***970.38*** *p76*
Arens, August; New York, 1860 ***358.56*** *p5*
Arens, Frank; Colorado, 1897 ***1029.59*** *p4*
Aretaine, Jacques; Quebec, 1646 ***9221.17*** *p160*
Arfvidson, N.; New York, NY, 1843 ***6412.40*** *p148*
Argencourt, Denis; Quebec, 1646 ***9221.17*** *p162*
Argencourt, Simon; Quebec, 1646 ***9221.17*** *p163*
Argonis, F.; California, 1868 ***1131.61*** *p90*
Argulus, P. 30; America, 1848 ***778.6*** *p7*
Argus, Adam 2 *SEE* Argus, Georg Adam
Argus, Bernard; Louisiana, 1841-1844 ***4981.45*** *p210*
Argus, Christine 28 *SEE* Argus, Georg Adam
Argus, Georg Adam 38; America, 1882 ***2526.43*** *p217*
  *Daughter:*Christine 28
  *Son:*Heinrich 1
  *Son:*Adam 2
Argus, Heinrich 1 *SEE* Argus, Georg Adam
Argust, John 51; Ontario, 1871 ***1823.21*** *p8*
Argyle, Edward 49; Ontario, 1871 ***1823.21*** *p8*
Arias, Sergio; Miami, 1935 ***4984.12*** *p39*
Arias y Garcia, Ramon Sergio; Miami, 1935 ***4984.12*** *p39*
Arila, Joseph R. 40; Mexico, 1843 ***778.6*** *p9*
Arinart, Anne; Quebec, 1671 ***4514.3*** *p271*
Ariot, Marie; Quebec, 1670 ***4514.3*** *p271*
Aristack, Marie 26; Port uncertain, 1840 ***778.6*** *p7*
Ark, Mary; Chicago, 1930 ***121.35*** *p100*
Arkell, Robert 42; Ontario, 1871 ***1823.21*** *p8*
Arkteffa, Andrew 20; Port uncertain, 1840 ***778.6*** *p7*
Arkteffa, Elizabeth 19; Port uncertain, 1840 ***778.6*** *p7*
Armance, Samuel; North Carolina, 1831 ***1088.45*** *p1*
Armand, . . .; Quebec, 1646 ***9221.17*** *p161*
Armand, Marie 19; Quebec, 1657 ***9221.17*** *p355*
Armbotin, Wilhe.m 23; America, 1840 ***778.6*** *p7*
Armbruster, J. M. 27; America, 1847 ***778.6*** *p7*
Armendariz, Carlos; El Paso, TX, 1909 ***3331.4*** *p11*
Armer, James 59; Ontario, 1871 ***1823.21*** *p8*
Armes, Malvina 44; Ontario, 1871 ***1823.21*** *p9*
Armes, Nicolas 50; Ontario, 1871 ***1823.21*** *p9*
Armington, Joseph; Roxbury, MA, 1680-1715 ***9228.50*** *p83*
  *Wife:*Rachel
Armington, Rachel *SEE* Armington, Joseph
Armitage, Edward 20; Ontario, 1871 ***1823.21*** *p9*
Armitage, George 40; Ontario, 1871 ***1823.21*** *p9*
Armitage, John 72; Ontario, 1871 ***1823.21*** *p9*
Armitage, Joseph 65; Ontario, 1871 ***1823.21*** *p9*

Armitage, Rody 58; Ontario, 1871 ***1823.21*** *p9*
Armitage, Thomas 52; Ontario, 1871 ***1823.21*** *p9*
Armitage, Thomas R.; Ontario, 1871 ***1823.21*** *p9*
Armitage, William 20; Ontario, 1871 ***1823.17*** *p4*
Armitage, William 64; Ontario, 1871 ***1823.21*** *p9*
Armour, Isabella 24; Ontario, 1871 ***1823.21*** *p9*
Armour, Robert 31; Ontario, 1871 ***1823.17*** *p4*
Arms, William; America, 1600-1699 ***9228.50*** *p83*
Arms, William; Massachusetts, 1654-1684 ***9228.50*** *p84*
Armsbruster, Fred. 30; America, 1841 ***778.6*** *p7*
Armstrong, Adam 42; Ontario, 1871 ***1823.17*** *p4*
Armstrong, Adam 50; Ontario, 1871 ***1823.21*** *p9*
Armstrong, Alex 80; Ontario, 1871 ***1823.21*** *p9*
Armstrong, Alfred J.; Colorado, 1880 ***1029.59*** *p4*
Armstrong, Alice 70; Ontario, 1871 ***1823.21*** *p9*
Armstrong, Allen 28; Ontario, 1871 ***1823.21*** *p9*
Armstrong, Barbara 11; Quebec, 1870 ***8364.32*** *p22*
Armstrong, Catharine 22; Michigan, 1880 ***4491.33*** *p1*
Armstrong, Charles 47; Ontario, 1871 ***1823.17*** *p4*
Armstrong, Cilia 38; Ontario, 1871 ***1823.21*** *p9*
Armstrong, David 28; Ontario, 1871 ***1823.17*** *p4*
Armstrong, David 36; Ontario, 1871 ***1823.17*** *p4*
Armstrong, Edward 65; Ontario, 1871 ***1823.17*** *p4*
Armstrong, Ellenor; Philadelphia, 1852 ***8513.31*** *p430*
Armstrong, Emily 8; Quebec, 1870 ***8364.32*** *p22*
Armstrong, Florence; Ottawa, 1800-1899 ***9228.50*** *p306*
Armstrong, G. W.; Louisiana, 1874 ***4981.45*** *p295*
Armstrong, George 43; Ontario, 1871 ***1823.17*** *p4*
Armstrong, George 59; Ontario, 1871 ***1823.21*** *p9*
Armstrong, Hanah 52; Ontario, 1871 ***1823.21*** *p9*
Armstrong, Henry 39; Ontario, 1871 ***1823.17*** *p4*
Armstrong, James 32; Ontario, 1871 ***1823.21*** *p9*
Armstrong, James 46; Ontario, 1871 ***1823.17*** *p4*
Armstrong, James 50; Ontario, 1871 ***1823.17*** *p4*
Armstrong, James 22; St. John, N.B., 1834 ***6469.7*** *p6*
Armstrong, Jane 52; Ontario, 1871 ***1823.21*** *p9*
Armstrong, Jane 80; Ontario, 1871 ***1823.21*** *p9*
Armstrong, Jeriad 68; Ontario, 1871 ***1823.21*** *p9*
Armstrong, John; Ohio, 1809-1852 ***4511.35*** *p1*
Armstrong, John; Ontario, 1835 ***3160.1*** *p150*
Armstrong, John; Ontario, 1835 ***3160.1*** *p150*
Armstrong, John 13; Ontario, 1871 ***1823.21*** *p9*
Armstrong, John 32; Ontario, 1871 ***1823.21*** *p9*
Armstrong, John 35; Ontario, 1871 ***1823.21*** *p9*
Armstrong, John 41; Ontario, 1871 ***1823.21*** *p9*
Armstrong, John 45; Ontario, 1871 ***1823.21*** *p9*
Armstrong, John 49; Ontario, 1871 ***1823.17*** *p4*
Armstrong, John 54; Ontario, 1871 ***1823.17*** *p4*
Armstrong, John 64; Ontario, 1871 ***1823.21*** *p9*
Armstrong, John 70; Ontario, 1871 ***1823.21*** *p9*
Armstrong, John; Prescott, Ont., 1835 ***3289.1*** *p62*
Armstrong, Joseph 23; Ontario, 1871 ***1823.17*** *p4*
Armstrong, Joseph 38; Ontario, 1871 ***1823.21*** *p9*
Armstrong, Moses 70; Ontario, 1871 ***1823.17*** *p4*
Armstrong, Rebeca 85; Ontario, 1871 ***1823.21*** *p10*
Armstrong, Rebecca 85; Ontario, 1871 ***1823.21*** *p10*
Armstrong, Robert 39; Ontario, 1871 ***1823.21*** *p10*
Armstrong, Robert 39; Ontario, 1871 ***1823.21*** *p10*
Armstrong, Robert 40; Ontario, 1871 ***1823.21*** *p10*
Armstrong, Robert 5; Quebec, 1870 ***8364.32*** *p22*
Armstrong, Sylvester 21; Ontario, 1871 ***1823.21*** *p10*
Armstrong, Thomas 34; Ontario, 1871 ***1823.21*** *p10*
Armstrong, Thomas 48; Ontario, 1871 ***1823.21*** *p10*
Armstrong, Thomas 54; Ontario, 1871 ***1823.21*** *p10*
Armstrong, Thomas 55; Ontario, 1871 ***1823.21*** *p10*
Armstrong, Thomas 65; Ontario, 1871 ***1823.17*** *p5*
Armstrong, Thomas 65; Ontario, 1871 ***1823.21*** *p10*
Armstrong, Thomas 74; Ontario, 1871 ***1823.21*** *p10*
Armstrong, Thomas K.; Illinois, 1834-1900 ***6020.5*** *p131*
Armstrong, Thomas L. 53; Ontario, 1871 ***1823.21*** *p10*
Armstrong, Violet 22; St. John, N.B., 1834 ***6469.7*** *p6*
Armstrong, Walter 49; Ontario, 1871 ***1823.21*** *p10*
Armstrong, William 26; Ontario, 1871 ***1823.17*** *p5*
Armstrong, William 31; Ontario, 1871 ***1823.17*** *p5*
Armstrong, William 32; Ontario, 1871 ***1823.21*** *p10*
Armstrong, William 37; Ontario, 1871 ***1823.17*** *p5*
Armstrong, William 43; Ontario, 1871 ***1823.21*** *p10*
Armstrong, William 48; Ontario, 1871 ***1823.17*** *p5*
Armstrong, William 59; Ontario, 1871 ***1823.17*** *p5*
Armstrong, William 62; Ontario, 1871 ***1823.21*** *p10*
Armstrong, William 80; Ontario, 1871 ***1823.21*** *p10*
Armstrong, William H. 39; Ontario, 1871 ***1823.21*** *p10*
Armstrong, William J. 30; Ontario, 1871 ***1823.21*** *p10*
Arnandin, H. 14; Quebec, 1870 ***8364.32*** *p22*
Arnard Sen, Simon; Virginia, 1652 ***6254.4*** *p243*
Arnaud, Mr. 22; New Orleans, 1845 ***778.6*** *p7*
Arnaud, Mr. 43; New Orleans, 1840 ***778.6*** *p7*
Arnaud, Chas. 51; America, 1842 ***778.6*** *p7*
Arnaud, Delphine Adele 19; New Orleans, 1848 ***778.6*** *p7*
Arnaud, G. 30; New Orleans, 1844 ***778.6*** *p7*
Arnaud, Isaac; Virginia, 1700 ***9230.15*** *p81*
With wife
Arnaud, Jacques 63; Port uncertain, 1841 ***778.6*** *p7*
Arnaud, Jean 47; New Orleans, 1848 ***778.6*** *p7*
Arnaud, Julie Cecile 15; New Orleans, 1848 ***778.6*** *p7*
Arnaud, Louis 25; America, 1848 ***778.6*** *p7*
Arnaud, Marie 45; Port uncertain, 1840 ***778.6*** *p7*
Arnaux, Antoine; Quebec, 1636 ***9221.17*** *p51*
*Wife:*Madeleine
Arnaux, Madeleine *SEE* Arnaux, Antoine
Arnaux, O. M. 21; America, 1843 ***778.6*** *p7*
Arnberg, Carolina; Minneapolis, 1896-1898 ***1865.50*** *p39*
Arnbler, Ignatz 19; America, 1847 ***778.6*** *p5*
Arndt, August 37; New York, NY, 1893 ***1883.7*** *p40*
Arndt, August 37; New York, NY, 1893 ***1883.7*** *p47*
Arndt, August Friedrich; New York, 1859 ***358.56*** *p99*
Arndt, August William; Wisconsin, 1899 ***6795.8*** *p71*
Arndt, Gustav; Wisconsin, 1890 ***6795.8*** *p170*
Arndt, Hugo 25; New York, NY, 1893 ***1883.7*** *p39*
Arndt, Hugo 25; New York, NY, 1893 ***1883.7*** *p47*
Arneheartte, Ba. 22; Port uncertain, 1846 ***778.6*** *p7*
Arnes, John 36; America, 1842 ***778.6*** *p7*
Arnes, Marie 35; America, 1842 ***778.6*** *p7*
Arnes, Marthe 2; America, 1842 ***778.6*** *p7*
Arnet, James 55; South Carolina, 1812 ***3476.30*** *p11*
Arnet, John; Ohio, 1809-1852 ***4511.35*** *p1*
Arnew, John 48; Ontario, 1871 ***1823.17*** *p5*
Arnichel, Antoine 24; Quebec, 1641 ***9221.17*** *p107*
Arnie, John 19; America, 1848 ***778.6*** *p7*
Arning, C.; America, 1852 ***7420.1*** *p84*
With family
Arnkvarn, Carolina; Chicago, 1891 ***1865.50*** *p110*
Arnold, . . .; Pennsylvania, 1854 ***170.15*** *p18*
Arnold, . . .; Pennsylvania, 1854 ***170.15*** *p18*
Arnold, . . .; Pennsylvania, 1854 ***170.15*** *p18*
Arnold, Mrs. 29; New Orleans, 1843 ***778.6*** *p8*
Arnold, Mrs. 53; New Orleans, 1843 ***778.6*** *p8*
Arnold, Adam; America, 1867 ***2526.43*** *p125*
Arnold, Adam 25; America, 1845 ***2526.43*** *p125*
With wife
*Son:*Johann Nikolaus 3
*Daughter:*Elisabetha Katharina 6 months
Arnold, Agathe 25; Galveston, TX, 1844 ***3967.10*** *p372*
Arnold, Ana 26; America, 1747 ***778.6*** *p7*
Arnold, Andre 20; New Orleans, 1843 ***778.6*** *p7*
Arnold, Andre Lyon; New Orleans, 1843 ***778.6*** *p7*
Arnold, Anna Margaretha; America, 1867 ***2526.43*** *p125*
Arnold, August; America, 1867 ***2526.43*** *p125*
Arnold, August; America, 1883 ***2526.43*** *p125*
Arnold, Charles 13; New Orleans, 1843 ***778.6*** *p7*
Arnold, Christine 38; America, 1745 ***778.6*** *p7*
Arnold, Didier 33; New Orleans, 1848 ***778.6*** *p7*
Arnold, Elisabetha; America, 1871 ***2526.43*** *p125*
Arnold, Elisabetha Katharina 6 *SEE* Arnold, Adam
Arnold, Eva; America, 1854 ***2526.42*** *p110*
Arnold, Florgnie 9; St. Louis, 1844 ***778.6*** *p7*
Arnold, Frederic 17; New Orleans, 1843 ***778.6*** *p7*
Arnold, Frederick 17; Quebec, 1870 ***8364.32*** *p22*
Arnold, Friedrike; Brazil, 1862 ***5475.1*** *p561*
Arnold, Gabriel 27; America, 1841 ***778.6*** *p8*
Arnold, Gabriel 45; America, 1745 ***778.6*** *p7*
Arnold, Georg 40; Galveston, TX, 1844 ***3967.10*** *p370*
Arnold, George; New York, 1783 ***8529.30*** *p9*
Arnold, George; Ohio, 1809-1852 ***4511.35*** *p1*
Arnold, George 40; Ontario, 1871 ***1823.21*** *p10*
Arnold, George 43; St. Louis, 1844 ***778.6*** *p8*
Arnold, Georges 58; New Orleans, 1843 ***778.6*** *p8*
Arnold, Henri 22; New Orleans, 1843 ***778.6*** *p8*
Arnold, Isaac 70; Ontario, 1871 ***1823.21*** *p10*
Arnold, Jakob 6 *SEE* Arnold, Nikolaus
Arnold, James 44; Ontario, 1871 ***1823.21*** *p10*
Arnold, James; South Carolina, 1813 ***3208.30*** *p18*
Arnold, James; South Carolina, 1813 ***3208.30*** *p31*
Arnold, James 55; South Carolina, 1812 ***3476.30*** *p11*
Arnold, Johann; America, 1884 ***2526.43*** *p127*
Arnold, Johann Nikolaus; America, 1867 ***2526.43*** *p125*
With father & siblings
Arnold, Johann Nikolaus 3 *SEE* Arnold, Adam
Arnold, Johanna 33; New York, NY, 1893 ***1883.7*** *p42*
Arnold, Johannes; America, 1867 ***2526.43*** *p125*
Arnold, Johannes 9 *SEE* Arnold, Nikolaus
Arnold, Johannes 12; New York, NY, 1893 ***1883.7*** *p42*
Arnold, John 42; Ontario, 1871 ***1823.21*** *p10*
Arnold, John 43; Ontario, 1871 ***1823.21*** *p10*
Arnold, Joseph 25; Ontario, 1871 ***1823.21*** *p10*
Arnold, Joseph G. 28; Ontario, 1871 ***1823.17*** *p5*
Arnold, Josephe 8; St. Louis, 1844 ***778.6*** *p8*
Arnold, Lorenz 8; Galveston, TX, 1844 ***3967.10*** *p370*
Arnold, Lorenz; Pennsylvania, 1854 ***170.15*** *p18*
With wife & 2 children
Arnold, Ludwig; Brazil, 1862 ***5475.1*** *p540*
Arnold, Madeline 30; St. Louis, 1844 ***778.6*** *p8*
Arnold, Magdalena 33; Galveston, TX, 1844 ***3967.10*** *p370*
Arnold, Magdeline 8; St. Louis, 1844 ***778.6*** *p8*
Arnold, Maria Margaretha 37 *SEE* Arnold, Nikolaus
Arnold, Marianne 5; America, 1745 ***778.6*** *p8*
Arnold, Michael 2; Galveston, TX, 1844 ***3967.10*** *p370*
Arnold, Michel 18; America, 1846 ***778.6*** *p8*
Arnold, Natalia 7; New York, NY, 1893 ***1883.7*** *p42*
Arnold, Nikolaus 48; America, 1867 ***2526.43*** *p125*
*Wife:*Maria Margaretha 37
*Son:*Johannes 9
*Son:*Jakob 6
Arnold, Olivia 13; New York, NY, 1893 ***1883.7*** *p42*
Arnold, Peter; America, 1833 ***5475.1*** *p64*
Arnold, Philip 40; New York, NY, 1893 ***1883.7*** *p42*
Arnold, Robert 28; Ontario, 1871 ***1823.21*** *p10*
Arnold, Rose 9; America, 1745 ***778.6*** *p8*
Arnold, Salomea 20; America, 1846 ***778.6*** *p8*
Arnold, Theobald 10; New York, NY, 1893 ***1883.7*** *p42*
Arnold, Thomas 80; Ontario, 1871 ***1823.21*** *p10*
Arnold, William; Ohio, 1840 ***2763.1*** *p7*
Arnold, Xaver 6; Galveston, TX, 1844 ***3967.10*** *p370*
Arnold, Zelstinne 15; New York, NY, 1893 ***1883.7*** *p42*
Arnoul, Jean 20; Montreal, 1659 ***9221.17*** *p427*
Arnould, Elisabeth 12; America, 1846 ***778.6*** *p8*
Arnould, Elisabeth 42; America, 1846 ***778.6*** *p8*
Arnould, Jean 8; America, 1846 ***778.6*** *p8*
Arnould, Jean 51; America, 1846 ***778.6*** *p8*
Arnould, Marianne 4; America, 1846 ***778.6*** *p8*
Arnould, Marie 15; America, 1846 ***778.6*** *p8*
Arnould, Michel 17; America, 1846 ***778.6*** *p8*
Arns, Norbert Alois; South America, 1923 ***8023.44*** *p371*
Arnsdorf, August Julius Eduard; Wisconsin, 1882 ***6795.8*** *p89*
Arnsdorf, Auguste Minna; Wisconsin, 1884 ***6795.8*** *p89*
Arnsdorf, Nicolas 23; America, 1846 ***778.6*** *p8*
Arnsdorff, Anna Maria; Wisconsin, 1892 ***6795.8*** *p83*
Arnsinger, George 18; America, 1840 ***778.6*** *p8*
Arnsler, Samuel 26; Louisiana, 1848 ***778.6*** *p8*
Arnt, Georg 18; America, 1847 ***778.6*** *p8*
Arnt, Jacque 35; America, 1847 ***778.6*** *p8*
Arnt, Margaretha 4; America, 1847 ***778.6*** *p8*
Arnt, Margaretha 31; America, 1847 ***778.6*** *p8*
Arnt, Michel 18; America, 1847 ***778.6*** *p8*
Arnue, Louise Brodeur 48; Montreal, 1658 ***9221.17*** *p391*
*Daughter:*Marthe 26
Arnue, Marthe 26 *SEE* Arnue, Louise Brodeur
Arnum, Benjam 34; Ontario, 1871 ***1823.21*** *p10*
Arold, August Jakob; America, 1881 ***2526.43*** *p163*
Arold, Mrs. Jakob; America, 1848 ***2526.43*** *p163*
Arold, Johann 28; America, 1853 ***2526.43*** *p163*
Arolere, Leroy 19; America, 1847 ***778.6*** *p8*
Aron, Judith; Ohio, 1894 ***5475.1*** *p162*
*Child:*Helena
*Child:*Leopold
*Child:*Simon
Aron, Tomas; New York, NY, 1867 ***2853.20*** *p156*
Aronsson, Olof; New York, NY, 1843 ***6412.40*** *p147*
Arosenius, Carl; Illinois, 1862 ***4487.25*** *p53*
Arpeling, John; Ohio, 1840-1897 ***8365.35*** *p15*
Arrand, George 65; Ontario, 1871 ***1823.21*** *p10*
Arrand, Thomas 36; Ontario, 1871 ***1823.21*** *p10*
Arras, Anna Eva *SEE* Arras, Johann Georg
Arras, Anna Eva *SEE* Arras, Johann Peter
Arras, Anna Eva *SEE* Arras, Johann Adam
Arras, Anna Eva *SEE* Arras, Johannes
Arras, Anna Eva; Virginia, 1831 ***152.20*** *p61*
Arras, Anna Katharina Hofmann *SEE* Arras, Johann Georg
Arras, Anna Margarethe *SEE* Arras, Johann Peter
Arras, Anna Margarethe *SEE* Arras, Johann Adam
Arras, Anna Margarethe Hofmann *SEE* Arras, Johann Peter
Arras, Anna Margarethe *SEE* Arras, Johannes
Arras, Anna Margarethe; Virginia, 1831 ***152.20*** *p64*
Arras, Conrad; Ohio, 1809-1852 ***4511.35*** *p1*
Arras, Elisabeth Weber *SEE* Arras, Johs.
Arras, Eva Elisabeth Lauer *SEE* Arras, Johannes
Arras, Eva Maria Dascher *SEE* Arras, Johannes
Arras, Francois; Montreal, 1650 ***9221.17*** *p231*
Arras, Joh. Peter *SEE* Arras, Johann Georg
Arras, Joh. Peter; Virginia, 1831 ***152.20*** *p61*
Arras, Johann Adam *SEE* Arras, Johann Georg
Arras, Johann Adam; Virginia, 1831 ***152.20*** *p60*
*Wife:*Margarethe Elisabeth Hochgenug
*Child:*Anna Eva
*Child:*Anna Margarethe
Arras, Johann Georg; Virginia, 1831 ***152.20*** *p60*
*Wife:*Anna Katharina Hofmann
*Child:*Johann Peter
*Child:*Johann Adam
*Child:*Johannes
*Child:*Joh. Peter
*Child:*Anna Eva
With child
Arras, Johann Peter *SEE* Arras, Johann Georg

Arras, Johann Peter *SEE* Arras, Johann Peter
Arras, Johann Peter; Virginia, 1831 ***152.20*** *p60*
*Wife:*Anna Margarethe Hofmann
*Child:*Anna Eva
*Child:*Johann Peter
*Child:*Anna Margarethe
*Child:*Johannes
Arras, Johannes *SEE* Arras, Johann Georg
Arras, Johannes *SEE* Arras, Johann Peter
Arras, Johannes; Virginia, 1831 ***152.20*** *p61*
*Wife:*Eva Elisabeth Lauer
*Child:*Anna Margarethe
Arras, Johannes; Virginia, 1831 ***152.20*** *p61*
*Wife:*Eva Maria Dascher
*Child:*Anna Eva
Arras, Johs. 6 months; Virginia, 1831 ***152.20*** *p61*
*Wife:*Elisabeth Weber
*Child:*Margareth
Arras, Margareth *SEE* Arras, Johs.
Arras, Margarethe Elisabeth Hochgenug *SEE* Arras, Johann Adam
Arrese, Pascuala; America, 1889 ***3276.8*** *p20*
Arrive, Jean 30; Quebec, 1660 ***9221.17*** *p430*
Arrive, Maurice 49; Quebec, 1650 ***9221.17*** *p222*
Arrive, Pierre 15; Quebec, 1661 ***9221.17*** *p446*
Arroues, Bernard 18; America, 1892 ***3276.8*** *p21*
Arscott, Ann 26; Ontario, 1871 ***1823.21*** *p10*
Arscott, George 23; Ontario, 1871 ***1823.21*** *p10*
Arscott, George 31; Ontario, 1871 ***1823.21*** *p10*
Arscott, Richard 47; Ontario, 1871 ***1823.21*** *p10*
Arscott, Samuel 22; Ontario, 1871 ***1823.21*** *p10*
Arscott, Samuel 45; Ontario, 1871 ***1823.21*** *p10*
Arsenault, Mr.; New England, 1675-1676 ***9228.50*** *p268*
Arsian, Barbara 8; Missouri, 1847 ***778.6*** *p8*
Arsian, Catherine 6; Missouri, 1847 ***778.6*** *p8*
Arsian, Christine 17; Missouri, 1847 ***778.6*** *p8*
Arsian, Johann 9; Missouri, 1847 ***778.6*** *p9*
Arsian, Margareth 13; Missouri, 1847 ***778.6*** *p9*
Arslinger, Joseph 26; Port uncertain, 1846 ***778.6*** *p9*
Arst, Christian; Ohio, 1809-1852 ***4511.35*** *p1*
Arta, Michael; Ohio, 1809-1852 ***4511.35*** *p1*
Arter, Michael; Ohio, 1809-1852 ***4511.35*** *p1*
Arter, Michael; Ohio, 1809-1852 ***4511.35*** *p2*
Artes, Jean Loussales 20; America, 1845 ***778.6*** *p9*
Artha, James 35; Ontario, 1871 ***1823.21*** *p10*
Arthur, Alfred *SEE* Arthur, Charles
Arthur, Charles 43; Quebec, 1881 ***9228.50*** *p85*
*Wife:*Jane 37
*Child:*Laura
*Child:*George
*Child:*Alfred
*Child:*Charles, Jr.
*Child:*John
Arthur, Charles, Jr. *SEE* Arthur, Charles
Arthur, George *SEE* Arthur, Charles
Arthur, Jane 37 *SEE* Arthur, Charles
Arthur, John; Maine, 1653 ***9228.50*** *p85*
Arthur, John; Massachusetts, 1713 ***9228.50*** *p84*
Arthur, John *SEE* Arthur, Charles
Arthur, Joseph; Colorado, 1870 ***1029.59*** *p5*
Arthur, Joseph; Colorado, 1894 ***1029.59*** *p5*
Arthur, Joseph 38; Ontario, 1871 ***1823.17*** *p5*
Arthur, Laura *SEE* Arthur, Charles
Arthur, William; Boston, 1831 ***3274.55*** *p44*
Arthurs, Mrs.; Toronto, 1844 ***2910.35*** *p114*
Arthurs, John 75; Ontario, 1871 ***1823.21*** *p10*
Artigue, Joseph 25; New Orleans, 1845 ***778.6*** *p9*
Artiguenave, Amedee 20; Port uncertain, 1846 ***778.6*** *p9*
Artigues, Jean; Louisiana, 1874 ***4981.45*** *p295*
Artois, E. Ernst; New York, 1884 ***5475.1*** *p381*
Artois, Edmund August; Philadelphia, 1874 ***5475.1*** *p32*
Arton, P.; New Orleans, 1850 ***7242.30*** *p134*
Artus, M. E. 33; New York, NY, 1894 ***6512.1*** *p181*
Artus, Mrs. M. E. 26; New York, NY, 1894 ***6512.1*** *p181*
Artus, Michelle 26; Quebec, 1654 ***9221.17*** *p304*
Artus DeSailly, Anne-Francoise Bourduceau 20 *SEE* Artus DeSailly, Louis
Artus DeSailly, Louis 33; Montreal, 1658 ***9221.17*** *p387*
*Wife:*Anne-Francoise Bourduceau 20
Arua, Joseph R. 40; Mexico, 1843 ***778.6*** *p9*
Arunel, Auguste 19; Louisiana, 1847 ***778.6*** *p9*
Arvidson, Christina *SEE* Arvidson, Peter
Arvidson, Lars P.; Colorado, 1883 ***1029.59*** *p5*
Arvidson, Peter; St. Paul, MN, 1888-1890 ***1865.50*** *p39*
*Wife:*Christina
Arvist, Francis; North Carolina, 1852 ***1088.45*** *p1*
Arweiler, Susanna 24; Philadelphia, 1866 ***5475.1*** *p178*
Arzt, Christian Karl 25 *SEE* Arzt, Friedrich Karl
Arzt, Ferdinand Friedrich 23 *SEE* Arzt, Friedrich Karl
Arzt, Frantisek J.; Iowa, 1866 ***2853.20*** *p51*
Arzt, Friedrich Karl 59; America, 1845 ***2526.43*** *p163*
With wife
*Son:*Johann Michael 34
*Son:*Johann Peter 28
*Son:*Ferdinand Friedrich 23
*Son:*Johann Jakob 13
*Son:*Georg Ludwig 18
*Son:*Christian Karl 25
Arzt, Friedrich Ludwig; America, 1888 ***2526.43*** *p163*
Arzt, Georg Ludwig 18 *SEE* Arzt, Friedrich Karl
Arzt, Johann Jakob 13 *SEE* Arzt, Friedrich Karl
Arzt, Johann Michael 34 *SEE* Arzt, Friedrich Karl
Arzt, Johann Peter 28 *SEE* Arzt, Friedrich Karl
Arzt, Ludwig; America, 1832 ***2526.43*** *p163*
Aschaffenburg, Leopold; Louisiana, 1883 ***7710.1*** *p158*
Aschen, Carl Julius Theodor; Port uncertain, 1884 ***7420.1*** *p341*
Aschenbach, Jacob; America, 1868 ***7919.3*** *p533*
*Daughter:*Maria
Aschenbach, Maria *SEE* Aschenbach, Jacob
Ascher, Isaac; North Carolina, 1859 ***1088.45*** *p1*
Aschermann, Siegmund; America, 1891 ***7420.1*** *p362*
With family
Aseke, Joest; Iowa, 1890 ***1211.15*** *p8*
Aselage, Bernard; Ohio, 1840-1897 ***8365.35*** *p15*
Ash, Aaron 40; Ontario, 1871 ***1823.21*** *p10*
Ash, Christian; Ohio, 1809-1852 ***4511.35*** *p2*
Ash, Elizabeth; St. John, N.B., 1842 ***2978.20*** *p7*
Ash, Elizabeth; St. John, N.B., 1842 ***2978.20*** *p9*
Ash, James; St. John, N.B., 1842 ***2978.20*** *p9*
Ash, Mary; St. John, N.B., 1842 ***2978.20*** *p7*
Ash, Mary; St. John, N.B., 1842 ***2978.20*** *p9*
Ash, Winifred; St. John, N.B., 1842 ***2978.20*** *p9*
Ashbury, William 56; Ontario, 1871 ***1823.21*** *p10*
Ashby, Annie 38; Ontario, 1871 ***1823.17*** *p5*
Ashby, William; Marston's Wharf, 1782 ***8529.30*** *p9*
Ashcroft, James; Indiana, 1802-1849 ***471.10*** *p88*
Ashe, Richard; Ohio, 1809-1852 ***4511.35*** *p2*
Ashelford, William 50; Ontario, 1871 ***1823.21*** *p10*
Ashly, John W. 60; Ontario, 1871 ***1823.21*** *p10*
Ashman, Mark 43; Ontario, 1871 ***1823.21*** *p10*
Ashmuty, Robert; Boston, 1740 ***1642*** *p26*
Ashton, Charles; Virginia, 1652 ***6254.4*** *p243*
Ashton, Charles J. 43; Ontario, 1871 ***1823.21*** *p11*
Ashton, John 12; Ontario, 1871 ***1823.21*** *p11*
Ashton, John 50; Ontario, 1871 ***1823.17*** *p5*
Ashton, John 68; Ontario, 1871 ***1823.21*** *p11*
Ashton, John 73; Ontario, 1871 ***1823.21*** *p11*
Ashton, Thomas 41; Ontario, 1871 ***1823.21*** *p11*
Ashwell, John 52; Ontario, 1871 ***1823.17*** *p5*
Ashworth, John 37; Ontario, 1871 ***1823.21*** *p11*
Ashworth, Jonathan 57; Ontario, 1871 ***1823.21*** *p11*
Ashworth, Samuel; Philadelphia, 1778 ***8529.30*** *p2A*
Askenberg, Conrad F.; Cleveland, OH, 1880-1894 ***9722.10*** *p117*
Askengren, Hugo; Philadelphia, 1848 ***6412.40*** *p151*
Asker, Catherine 35; America, 1845 ***778.6*** *p9*
Asker, Franz 42; America, 1845 ***778.6*** *p9*
Asker, Salome 4; America, 1845 ***778.6*** *p9*
Askerberg, Conrad F.; Cleveland, OH, 1880-1894 ***9722.10*** *p117*
Askie, John 45; Ontario, 1871 ***1823.21*** *p11*
Askin, Eliza 77; Ontario, 1871 ***1823.21*** *p11*
Askin, James; Toronto, 1844 ***2910.35*** *p112*
Askins, . . .; Ontario, 1871 ***1823.21*** *p11*
Askins, George 55; Ontario, 1871 ***1823.17*** *p5*
Askworth, Samuel; Philadelphia, 1778 ***8529.30*** *p2A*
Aspenleiter, Marie; Wisconsin, 1897 ***6795.8*** *p234*
Asper, Henry; West Virginia, 1869 ***1132.30*** *p151*
Aspgren, Bron Oscar; Philadelphia, 1902 ***1766.20*** *p23*
Asplet, Charles; Massachusetts, 1830-1870 ***9228.50*** *p17A*
Asplund, Olof; New York, NY, 1851 ***6412.40*** *p152*
Ass, John 43; New Orleans, 1843 ***778.6*** *p9*
Assant, Elise 2; New Orleans, 1846 ***778.6*** *p9*
Assant, George 36; New Orleans, 1846 ***778.6*** *p9*
Assant, Marie 32; New Orleans, 1846 ***778.6*** *p9*
Asselin, David; Quebec, 1600-1670 ***4514.3*** *p310*
With brother
Asselin, Jacques; Quebec, 1600-1670 ***4514.3*** *p310*
With brother
Asseline, David 34; Quebec, 1661 ***9221.17*** *p446*
Asseline, Jacques 29; Quebec, 1659 ***9221.17*** *p394*
Assenmacher, Heinrich 20; Galveston, TX, 1846 ***3967.10*** *p378*
Asserin, Fleurance; Quebec, 1667 ***4514.3*** *p271*
Assinuor, Johann Baptist 36; Galveston, TX, 1844 ***3967.10*** *p375*
Assiunes, Johannes 9; America, 1747 ***778.6*** *p9*
Assiunes, Joseph 20; America, 1747 ***778.6*** *p9*
Assiunes, Louis 60; America, 1747 ***778.6*** *p9*
Assiunes, Magdalena 55; America, 1747 ***778.6*** *p9*
Assiunes, Magdelena 18; America, 1747 ***778.6*** *p9*
Assiunes, Margarette 14; America, 1747 ***778.6*** *p9*
Assmann, August 19; Detroit, 1912 ***8023.44*** *p371*
Assmus, Adolph; America, 1867 ***7919.3*** *p528*
With wife & child
Assmus, Barbara Rosina; America, 1868 ***7919.3*** *p529*
With daughter
Assmuss, Christian; America, 1867 ***7919.3*** *p526*
With wife & 8 children
Asswald, . . .; New Orleans, 1840 ***778.6*** *p9*
Asswald, Mr.; New Orleans, 1840 ***778.6*** *p9*
Ast, Christian; Ohio, 1809-1852 ***4511.35*** *p2*
Astain, Felix 35; America, 1843 ***778.6*** *p9*
Astfulck, Lothar; Valdivia, Chile, 1850 ***1192.4*** *p49*
Aston, Jemima 17; Ontario, 1871 ***1823.17*** *p5*
Astrom, A.F.; New York, NY, 1850 ***6412.40*** *p152*
Astrom, Anders Fredrik 10 *SEE* Astrom, Hans
Astrom, C. Jac.; New York, NY, 1849 ***6412.40*** *p152*
Astrom, C.J.; New York, NY, 1850 ***6412.40*** *p152*
Astrom, Carl 15 *SEE* Astrom, Hans
Astrom, Hans 43; New York, 1856 ***6529.11*** *p21*
*Son:*Anders Fredrik 10
*Son:*Carl 15
Astrom, Hans; New York, NY, 1847 ***6412.40*** *p150*
Astrom, Margareta; New York, 1857 ***6529.11*** *p24*
Astrup, Christine; Minnesota, 1891-1895 ***1865.50*** *p112*
Asume, John; Colorado, 1873 ***1029.59*** *p5*
Asworth, Samuel; Philadelphia, 1778 ***8529.30*** *p2A*
Atcheson, Ann 79; Ontario, 1871 ***1823.21*** *p11*
Atchison, Ebenezer 30; Ontario, 1871 ***1823.21*** *p11*
Athastla, John 63; Ontario, 1871 ***1823.21*** *p11*
Athenasia, Nicholas; New York, NY, 1913 ***3331.4*** *p12*
Atherton, James 42; Ontario, 1871 ***1823.21*** *p11*
Athis, Nicholas; New York, NY, 1913 ***3331.4*** *p12*
Athonaud, Jean 22; America, 1846 ***778.6*** *p10*
Atkins, Edward; Marston's Wharf, 1782 ***8529.30*** *p9*
Atkins, George 60; Ontario, 1871 ***1823.21*** *p11*
Atkins, John 39; Ontario, 1871 ***1823.21*** *p11*
Atkins, John; Washington, 1882 ***2770.40*** *p135*
Atkins, Joseph 34; Ontario, 1871 ***1823.21*** *p11*
Atkins, Moses 62; Ontario, 1871 ***1823.21*** *p11*
Atkins, Ritchon 34; Ontario, 1871 ***1823.21*** *p11*
Atkins, Samuel 30; Ontario, 1871 ***1823.21*** *p11*
Atkins, William; New York, 1776 ***8529.30*** *p2A*
Atkins, William 27; Ontario, 1871 ***1823.21*** *p11*
Atkinson, Ann; Canada, 1774 ***3036.5*** *p40*
Atkinson, Ann *SEE* Atkinson, Robert
Atkinson, Catharine 74; Ontario, 1871 ***1823.21*** *p11*
Atkinson, Charles *SEE* Atkinson, John
Atkinson, Edward S.; Illinois, 1834-1900 ***6020.5*** *p131*
Atkinson, Elizabeth 53; Ontario, 1871 ***1823.21*** *p11*
Atkinson, Ella 23; Ontario, 1871 ***1823.21*** *p11*
Atkinson, Ellen 83; Ontario, 1871 ***1823.21*** *p11*
Atkinson, Enoch 21; Indiana, 1870 ***9076.20*** *p66*
Atkinson, Frances *SEE* Atkinson, John
Atkinson, George 48; Ontario, 1871 ***1823.17*** *p5*
Atkinson, Henry M. 35; Ontario, 1871 ***1823.17*** *p5*
Atkinson, Ida Estell 5; Ontario, 1871 ***1823.17*** *p5*
Atkinson, James 42; Indiana, 1863-1880 ***9076.20*** *p70*
Atkinson, James 50; Ontario, 1871 ***1823.21*** *p11*
Atkinson, John 50; America, 1841 ***778.6*** *p10*
Atkinson, John *SEE* Atkinson, John
Atkinson, John; Canada, 1774 ***3036.5*** *p40*
*Wife:*Frances
*Child:*Martha
*Child:*John
*Child:*Michael
*Child:*Charles
Atkinson, John 33; Ontario, 1871 ***1823.21*** *p11*
Atkinson, John 38; Ontario, 1871 ***1823.21*** *p11*
Atkinson, John 60; Ontario, 1871 ***1823.21*** *p11*
Atkinson, Joseph 41; Ontario, 1871 ***1823.21*** *p11*
Atkinson, Joseph 52; Ontario, 1871 ***1823.21*** *p11*
Atkinson, Martha *SEE* Atkinson, John
Atkinson, Michael *SEE* Atkinson, John
Atkinson, Mosas 45; Ontario, 1871 ***1823.17*** *p5*
Atkinson, Richard 34; Ontario, 1871 ***1823.21*** *p12*
Atkinson, Richard 64; Ontario, 1871 ***1823.21*** *p12*
Atkinson, Robert; Canada, 1774 ***3036.5*** *p41*
*Wife:*Ann
Atkinson, Robert; Havana, 1782 ***8529.30*** *p9A*
Atkinson, Sarah Jane 17; Ontario, 1871 ***1823.21*** *p12*
Atkinson, Thomas 20; Ontario, 1871 ***1823.21*** *p12*
Atkinson, Thomas 67; Ontario, 1871 ***1823.21*** *p12*
Atkinson, Thomas 67; Ontario, 1871 ***1823.21*** *p12*
Atkinson, Thomas 74; Ontario, 1871 ***1823.17*** *p5*
Atkinson, William; Canada, 1774 ***3036.5*** *p41*
Atkinson, William; Illinois, 1834-1900 ***6020.5*** *p131*
Atkinson, William 30; Ontario, 1871 ***1823.17*** *p5*
Atkinson, William 40; Ontario, 1871 ***1823.21*** *p12*
Atkinson, William 52; Ontario, 1871 ***1823.21*** *p12*
Atkinson, William 54; Ontario, 1871 ***1823.21*** *p12*
Atkinson, William H.; Illinois, 1834-1900 ***6020.5*** *p131*
Atkinson, William Kirby 32; Ontario, 1871 ***1823.21*** *p12*
Atlante, V. E.; Montreal, 1922 ***4514.4*** *p32*
Atrill, Edward 48; Ontario, 1871 ***1823.21*** *p12*
Atrill, William 25; Ontario, 1871 ***1823.21*** *p12*
Atschit, Karl Josef; Chicago, 1894 ***5475.1*** *p39*

Attane, Jose 15; America, 1843 ***778.6*** *p10*
Attane, Louis 32; America, 1843 ***778.6*** *p10*
Attaway, Thomas; Marston's Wharf, 1782 ***8529.30*** *p9*
Atter, John 28; Ontario, 1871 ***1823.21*** *p12*
Atthel, Ms. 32; America, 1847 ***778.6*** *p10*
Attwood, Adolphus 36; Ontario, 1871 ***1823.21*** *p12*
Attwood, John 32; Ontario, 1871 ***1823.17*** *p5*
Attwood, Peter H. 43; Ontario, 1871 ***1823.21*** *p12*
Atweel, John 51; Ontario, 1871 ***1823.21*** *p12*
Atwell, John F. 50; Ontario, 1871 ***1823.21*** *p12*
Atwell, Thomas 29; Ontario, 1871 ***1823.21*** *p12*
Atwell, William 28; Ontario, 1871 ***1823.21*** *p12*
Atwood, Robert 65; Ontario, 1871 ***1823.17*** *p5*
Atz, Elisabeth; Brazil, 1846 ***5475.1*** *p438*
Atz, Jakob; America, 1856 ***5475.1*** *p440*
Atz, Michael; America, 1852 ***5475.1*** *p439*
Atz, Nikolaus; America, 1856 ***5475.1*** *p440*
Atz-Rausch, Maria Dewes *SEE* Atz-Rausch, Michel
Atz-Rausch, Michel; America, 1833 ***5475.1*** *p436*
*Wife:*Maria Dewes
With 5 children
Aube, Francoise; Quebec, 1668 ***4514.3*** *p271*
Aube, Thomas; Quebec, 1659 ***9221.17*** *p412*
Aubel, Conrad; Valdivia, Chile, 1852 ***1192.4*** *p55*
Aubele, Pier.e 22; New Orleans, 1846 ***778.6*** *p10*
Auber, Claude 32; Quebec, 1647 ***9221.17*** *p174*
*Wife:*Jacqueline Lucas 30
*Son:*Felix 3
Auber, Felix 3 *SEE* Auber, Claude
Auber, Jacqueline Lucas 30 *SEE* Auber, Claude
Auber, Marguerite 15; Quebec, 1635 ***9221.17*** *p43*
Auber, Richard; Massachusetts, 1664 ***9228.50*** *p479*
Aubert, . . .; New England, n.d. ***9228.50*** *p85*
Aubert, B. 80; Port uncertain, 1845 ***778.6*** *p10*
Aubert, Clatharina 27; America, 1842 ***778.6*** *p10*
Aubert, Elisabeth; Quebec, 1670 ***4514.3*** *p271*
Aubert, Francois; Quebec, 1635 ***9221.17*** *p43*
Aubert, Jacob 26; America, 1842 ***778.6*** *p10*
Aubert, Jeanne; Quebec, 1669 ***4514.3*** *p271*
Aubert, Richard; Massachusetts, 1664 ***9228.50*** *p479*
Aubert deLa Chesnaye, Charles; Quebec, 1655 ***2314.30*** *p167*
Aubert deLa Chesnaye, Charles; Quebec, 1693 ***2314.30*** *p174*
Aubert DeLaChesnaye, Charles 29; Quebec, 1659 ***9221.17*** *p394*
Aubertin, Francois 30; America, 1841 ***778.6*** *p10*
Aubertin, Jan 18; America, 1847 ***778.6*** *p10*
Aubertin, Julien; Louisiana, 1874-1875 ***4981.45*** *p297*
Aubet, Jn. Bte. 24; Louisiana, 1848 ***778.6*** *p10*
Aubin, . . .; Philadelphia, 1874 ***9228.50*** *p17A*
Aubin, Catherine Jane; Nebraska, 1858-1885 ***9228.50*** *p659*
Aubin, Catherine Jane *SEE* Aubin, Philip
Aubin, Eliz. de Sainte Croix *SEE* Aubin, Philip
Aubin, Francis; Georgia, 1795 ***1451.56*** *p118*
Aubin, Jacques; Quebec, 1651 ***9221.17*** *p236*
Aubin, Jean; Quebec, 1658 ***9221.17*** *p375*
Aubin, John; California, 1850-1950 ***9228.50*** *p659*
Aubin, Philip; Newburyport, MA, 1767 ***9228.50*** *p85*
Aubin, Philip *SEE* Aubin, Philip
Aubin, Philip; Toronto, 1860-1869 ***9228.50*** *p659*
*Child:*Catherine Jane
*Wife:*Eliz. de Sainte Croix
*Child:*Philip
Aubineau, Suzanne; Quebec, 1666 ***4514.3*** *p272*
*Son:*Pierre
*Son:*Andre
Aubrecht, J.; Cleveland, OH, 1873 ***2853.20*** *p498*
Aubrecht, Jan; Cleveland, OH, 1810-1910 ***2853.20*** *p476*
Aubrecht, Jan; Cleveland, OH, 1868-1910 ***2853.20*** *p498*
Aubrenan, Thecle-Cornelius 22; Montreal, 1660 ***9221.17*** *p440*
Aubry, Adelaide 8; New Orleans, 1848 ***778.6*** *p10*
Aubry, Anne; Quebec, 1671 ***4514.3*** *p272*
Aubry, Auguste 6; America, 1840 ***778.6*** *p10*
Aubry, Etienne 10; America, 1840 ***778.6*** *p10*
Aubry, Felicia 2; Galveston, TX, 1845 ***3967.10*** *p377*
Aubry, Francois Lucien 3; New Orleans, 1848 ***778.6*** *p10*
Aubry, Francoise; Quebec, 1673 ***4514.3*** *p272*
Aubry, Henriette 50; Galveston, TX, 1845 ***3967.10*** *p377*
Aubry, J. B. 30; Port uncertain, 1846 ***778.6*** *p10*
Aubry, Jacqueline; Quebec, 1670 ***4514.3*** *p272*
Aubry, Jacques 47; Quebec, 1659 ***9221.17*** *p394*
Aubry, Jean 38; America, 1840 ***778.6*** *p10*
Aubry, Jean Pierre; Illinois, 1852 ***6079.1*** *p1*
Aubry, Marie 4; America, 1840 ***778.6*** *p10*
Aubry, Marie 9; New Orleans, 1848 ***778.6*** *p10*
Aubry, Martine 40; America, 1840 ***778.6*** *p10*
Aubry, Pauline 41; New Orleans, 1848 ***778.6*** *p10*
Aubry, Sophia 25; Galveston, TX, 1845 ***3967.10*** *p377*
Aubuchon, Jacques 25; Quebec, 1642 ***9221.17*** *p111*
Aubuchon, Jean 14; Montreal, 1648 ***9221.17*** *p205*
Auch, Jean 20; America, 1840 ***778.6*** *p10*
Auch, Joseph 27; America, 1840 ***778.6*** *p10*
Aucher, Aaron 23; America, 1846 ***778.6*** *p10*
Auckland, George 47; Ontario, 1871 ***1823.21*** *p12*
Auckland, Sarah 19; Ontario, 1871 ***1823.21*** *p12*
Auclair, Andre *SEE* Auclair, Suzanne Aubineau
Auclair, Pierre *SEE* Auclair, Suzanne Aubineau
Auclair, Suzanne; Quebec, 1666 ***4514.3*** *p272*
*Son:*Pierre
*Son:*Andre
Auden, Pierre; Quebec, 1662 ***9221.17*** *p479*
Audes, John 25; America, 1843 ***778.6*** *p10*
Audesirk, Barbara; America, 1880 ***5475.1*** *p70*
*Son:*Joh. Nikolaus
*Daughter:*Emilie
*Son:*Ph. Konrad
*Daughter:*Katharina
Audesirk, Emilie *SEE* Audesirk, Barbara Werner
Audesirk, Joh. Nikolaus *SEE* Audesirk, Barbara Werner
Audesirk, Katharina *SEE* Audesirk, Barbara Werner
Audesirk, Ph. Konrad *SEE* Audesirk, Barbara Werner
Audiffert, Dominique 23; Port uncertain, 1842 ***778.6*** *p10*
Auding, Sebastian; Ohio, 1809-1852 ***4511.35*** *p2*
Audler, Jacob; Ohio, 1809-1852 ***4511.35*** *p2*
Audoin Family ; Massachusetts, 1870-1879 ***9228.50*** *p86*
Audol, George 18; America, 1844 ***778.6*** *p10*
Audon, Esprit 26; America, 1841 ***778.6*** *p10*
Audouart, Guillaume; Quebec, 1647 ***9221.17*** *p174*
Audouin, Louis; Quebec, 1642 ***9221.17*** *p111*
Audouy, Charles 22; America, 1843 ***778.6*** *p10*
Audru, Jacques; Montreal, 1653 ***9221.17*** *p280*
Aue, Caroline; America, 1854 ***7420.1*** *p114*
Auer, Anton 21; America, 1849 ***5475.1*** *p477*
Auer, August; America, 1846 ***5475.1*** *p472*
Auer, Conrad; Ohio, 1809-1852 ***4511.35*** *p2*
Auer, Frederick; Ohio, 1809-1852 ***4511.35*** *p2*
Auer, Friedrich; America, 1846 ***5475.1*** *p472*
Auer, Johann Adolf; America, 1844 ***5475.1*** *p471*
Auer, Michael; Ohio, 1809-1852 ***4511.35*** *p2*
Auer, Peter Joseph; New York, 1859 ***358.56*** *p54*
Aufroix, Cesaire 20; America, 1843 ***778.6*** *p10*
Aufroix, Charles 21; America, 1843 ***778.6*** *p10*
Augan, Joseph 35; New Orleans, 1848 ***778.6*** *p11*
Auger, Catherine; Quebec, 1671 ***4514.3*** *p272*
Auger, Denis; Quebec, 1652 ***9221.17*** *p253*
Auger, Jean 33; Montreal, 1653 ***9221.17*** *p281*
Auger, Jeanne; Quebec, 1671 ***4514.3*** *p272*
Auger, Louis 9 *SEE* Auger, Louise Grisard
Auger, Louis; Quebec, 1659 ***9221.17*** *p412*
Auger, Louise 27; Montreal, 1660 ***9221.17*** *p440*
*Son:*Louis 9
Augereau, Pierre 20; Quebec, 1657 ***9221.17*** *p351*
Auger Family ; New England, n.d. ***9228.50*** *p86*
Aughey, David; Ohio, 1838 ***3580.20*** *p31*
Aughey, David; Ohio, 1838 ***6020.12*** *p6*
Augier, Christophe 25; Montreal, 1659 ***9221.17*** *p416*
Augier, Jn. Romain 33; Louisiana, 1848 ***778.6*** *p11*
Augnel, Mr. 23; America, 1841 ***778.6*** *p11*
Augostine, Joseph M.; North Carolina, 1853 ***1088.45*** *p1*
Augrin, Jean; Montreal, 1659 ***9221.17*** *p416*
August, Aaron; America, 1882 ***5475.1*** *p421*
August, Alexand.e 8; New Orleans, 1845 ***778.6*** *p11*
August, Edward 3; New Orleans, 1845 ***778.6*** *p11*
August, Emma; Chicago, 1885 ***5475.1*** *p423*
August, Frances 34; New Orleans, 1845 ***778.6*** *p11*
August, George; Washington, 1889 ***2770.40*** *p26*
August, Hermann; Madison, WI, 1877 ***5475.1*** *p433*
August, Justien 6; New Orleans, 1845 ***778.6*** *p11*
August, Leopold; America, 1889 ***5475.1*** *p424*
August, Lucien 40; New Orleans, 1845 ***778.6*** *p11*
August, M.; Valdivia, Chile, 1850 ***1192.4*** *p48*
*Child:*Paul
*Child:*Maria
With baby
August, Maria 3 *SEE* August, M.
August, Mary 9 months; New Orleans, 1845 ***778.6*** *p11*
August, Paul 6 *SEE* August, M.
August, R. 41; America, 1848 ***778.6*** *p11*
August, Simon; America, 1884 ***5475.1*** *p422*
August, Simon 17; New Orleans, 1848 ***778.6*** *p11*
Auguste, Mr. 23; America, 1841 ***778.6*** *p11*
Auguste, M. 17; New Orleans, 1840 ***778.6*** *p11*
Auguste, Math.e 25; Mississippi, 1846 ***778.6*** *p11*
Augustin, Andreas; Rochester, NY, 1870 ***5475.1*** *p143*
Augustin, Barbara 43; America, 1859 ***5475.1*** *p251*
Augustin, Hermann; Illinois, 1851 ***6079.1*** *p1*
Augustin, J. 19; America, 1846 ***778.6*** *p11*
Augustine, Joseph; Ohio, 1809-1852 ***4511.35*** *p2*
Augustinsky, Father; New York, NY, 1875 ***2853.20*** *p254*
Augustos, Mr. 26; New Orleans, 1843 ***778.6*** *p11*
Auhn, Gaspard 21; America, 1846 ***778.6*** *p11*
Aukerman, John; Ohio, 1809-1852 ***4511.35*** *p2*
Aukland, Mary 48; Ontario, 1871 ***1823.21*** *p12*
Aukland, Peter 40; Ontario, 1871 ***1823.21*** *p12*
Aul, Ad.; New York, 1859 ***358.56*** *p55*
Aulart, Nicolas; Quebec, 1641 ***9221.17*** *p100*
Auld, Adam 40; Ontario, 1871 ***1823.21*** *p12*
Auld, Adam C.; Colorado, 1904 ***1029.59*** *p5*
Auld, Adum 65; Ontario, 1871 ***1823.21*** *p12*
Auld, Ann; Philadelphia, 1860 ***8513.31*** *p293*
Auld, Euphamia 40; Ontario, 1871 ***1823.21*** *p12*
Auld, James; Colorado, 1904 ***1029.59*** *p5*
Auld, John 37; Ontario, 1871 ***1823.21*** *p12*
Auld, Margaret 59; Ontario, 1871 ***1823.21*** *p12*
Auld, Mary 40; Ontario, 1871 ***1823.21*** *p12*
Auld, Robert 35; Ontario, 1871 ***1823.17*** *p5*
Auld, William 45; Ontario, 1871 ***1823.17*** *p5*
Auld, William C.; Colorado, 1904 ***1029.59*** *p5*
Auldjo, Alexr. 16; North Carolina, 1774 ***1422.10*** *p56*
Auldjo, John 15; North Carolina, 1774 ***1422.10*** *p56*
Aullm, Joshua 27; Ontario, 1871 ***1823.21*** *p12*
Ault, John B.; Washington, 1883 ***2770.40*** *p136*
Aumann, Christian; America, 1842 ***7420.1*** *p24*
Aumann, Christian; America, 1853 ***7420.1*** *p102*
Aumann, Christine Louise; America, 1853 ***7420.1*** *p105*
Aumann, Ernst Heinrich Friedrich; America, 1878 ***7420.1*** *p310*
Aumann, Heinrich; America, 1846 ***7420.1*** *p42*
Aumann, Heinrich Ernst; America, 1871 ***7420.1*** *p288*
Aumeau, Louis 35; Montreal, 1661 ***9221.17*** *p470*
Aumueller, Konrad; Pennsylvania, 1854 ***170.15*** *p18*
With 2 children & wife
Aunas, Wilhelm; Valdivia, Chile, 1850 ***1192.4*** *p48*
Auneau, Jeanne 22; Quebec, 1645 ***9221.17*** *p150*
Aunois, Jeanne 22; Quebec, 1645 ***9221.17*** *p150*
Aupe, Isabelle; Quebec, 1670 ***4514.3*** *p272*
Aurard, Catherine 31; Montreal, 1659 ***9221.17*** *p428*
Aurey, Pierre; Quebec, 1635 ***9221.17*** *p43*
Aurianne, P...re 21; New Orleans, 1840 ***778.6*** *p11*
Auroire, Mr. 42; America, 1747 ***778.6*** *p11*
Ausbury, Patrick; Louisiana, 1874 ***4981.45*** *p295*
Austin, C. 18; America, 1848 ***778.6*** *p11*
Austin, Edward; Louisiana, 1874-1875 ***4981.45*** *p297*
Austin, Edward 26; Virginia, 1635 ***1183.3*** *p31*
Austin, George; Ohio, 1840 ***2763.1*** *p7*
Austin, Granis W.; Washington, 1885 ***2770.40*** *p193*
Austin, Henry; Pennsylvania, 1860 ***8513.31*** *p293*
*Wife:*Margaret Williams
Austin, James 42; Ontario, 1871 ***1823.17*** *p5*
Austin, Jane 47; Ontario, 1871 ***1823.17*** *p5*
Austin, John; Ohio, 1840 ***2763.1*** *p7*
Austin, John 36; Ontario, 1871 ***1823.21*** *p12*
Austin, John 37; Ontario, 1871 ***1823.17*** *p5*
Austin, John 44; Ontario, 1871 ***1823.21*** *p12*
Austin, Joseph 42; Ontario, 1871 ***1823.21*** *p12*
Austin, Margaret Williams *SEE* Austin, Henry
Austin, Robert 49; Ontario, 1871 ***1823.17*** *p5*
Austin, William 37; Ontario, 1871 ***1823.21*** *p12*
Auterson, James 50; Ontario, 1871 ***1823.21*** *p12*
Authaway, Thomas; Marston's Wharf, 1782 ***8529.30*** *p9*
Autio, Amalja 37; Minnesota, 1926 ***2769.54*** *p1383*
Autio, John 38; Minnesota, 1926 ***2769.54*** *p1383*
Autour, Clemence 24; America, 1847 ***778.6*** *p11*
Autreiller, Marie; Missouri, 1845 ***778.6*** *p11*
Autreuil, Marthe 15; Montreal, 1658 ***9221.17*** *p387*
Autzen, Peter; Washington, 1889 ***2770.40*** *p26*
Auvray, Madeleine; Quebec, 1671 ***4514.3*** *p273*
Auvray, Marie; Quebec, 1660 ***9221.17*** *p436*
Auvrey, Adelaise 34; Port uncertain, 1841 ***778.6*** *p11*
Auvrey, Charles 45; Port uncertain, 1841 ***778.6*** *p11*
Auzies, Jacques 29; Port uncertain, 1846 ***778.6*** *p11*
Avegnen, J. B. 40; America, 1843 ***778.6*** *p11*
Aveline, Mr. 27; America, 1841 ***778.6*** *p11*
Aveline, Ms. 19; America, 1841 ***778.6*** *p11*
Avenel, Robert; Quebec, 1637 ***9221.17*** *p67*
Averill, Theodore 60; Ontario, 1871 ***1823.21*** *p12*
Averill, Theodore 70; Ontario, 1871 ***1823.21*** *p12*
Averta, Susanna; Portsmouth, NH, 1672 ***9228.50*** *p86*
Averty, . . .; New England, n.d. ***9228.50*** *p86*
Averty, John; Massachusetts, 1751-1790 ***9228.50*** *p654*
Averty, Julien 26; Montreal, 1659 ***9221.17*** *p416*
Averty, Maurice 21; Montreal, 1653 ***9221.17*** *p281*
Averty, Susanna; Portsmouth, NH, 1672 ***9228.50*** *p86*
Avery, James 34; Ontario, 1871 ***1823.21*** *p12*
Avery, Thomas; Marston's Wharf, 1782 ***8529.30*** *p9*
Avery, Tindell 39; Ontario, 1871 ***1823.17*** *p5*
Avery, William 36; Ontario, 1871 ***1823.21*** *p12*
Avery, William 46; Ontario, 1871 ***1823.21*** *p12*
Avet, Celina 2; America, 1841 ***778.6*** *p11*
Avet, F. 40; America, 1841 ***778.6*** *p11*
Avet, Jean 24; America, 1746 ***778.6*** *p11*
Avet, M. 20; America, 1841 ***778.6*** *p11*
Aveyron, Paul; Illinois, 1852 ***6079.1*** *p1*
Avilla, Mrs.; California, 1868 ***1131.61*** *p89*
Avorta, Susanna; Portsmouth, NH, 1672 ***9228.50*** *p86*
Avott, John; Marston's Wharf, 1782 ***8529.30*** *p9*

Axelson, Nels F.; Illinois, 1861 *4487.25 p52*
Axford, George 57; Ontario, 1871 *1823.21 p12*
Axford, John 32; Ontario, 1871 *1823.17 p6*
Axford, Marion 57; Ontario, 1871 *1823.17 p6*
Axin, Thomas 22; Ontario, 1871 *1823.21 p12*
Axtel, John 46; Ontario, 1871 *1823.17 p6*
Axtell, Sarah M. 44; Michigan, 1880 *4491.42 p2*
Axtman, Elisabeth 32; New York, NY, 1898 *7951.13 p43*
Axtman, Franz 7; New York, NY, 1898 *7951.13 p43*
Axtman, Franz 27; New York, NY, 1898 *7951.13 p43*
Axtman, Ignatz 11 months; New York, NY, 1898 *7951.13 p43*
Axtman, Joseph 32; New York, NY, 1898 *7951.13 p43*
Axtman, Kunigunda 27; New York, NY, 1898 *7951.13 p43*
Axtman, Marianna 19; New York, NY, 1898 *7951.13 p43*
Axtman, Martin 19; New York, NY, 1898 *7951.13 p43*
Axtman, Otillia 3; New York, NY, 1898 *7951.13 p43*
Axtman, Peter 6; New York, NY, 1898 *7951.13 p43*

Axtman, Rochus 11 months; New York, NY, 1898 *7951.13 p43*
Aye, Elizabeth 14; Quebec, 1870 *8364.32 p22*
Ayer, Robert 37; Ontario, 1871 *1823.21 p12*
Ayers, . . .; Canada, n.d. *9228.50 p75*
Ayers, . . .; New England, n.d. *9228.50 p75*
Ayers, Charles F. 27; Ontario, 1871 *1823.21 p12*
Ayers, John; Portsmouth, NH, 1688 *9228.50 p75*
Ayers, Trfima 77; Ontario, 1871 *1823.21 p13*
Ayers, William 34; Ontario, 1871 *1823.21 p13*
Ayet, Christoph 10; America, 1840 *778.6 p12*
Ayet, Joseph 35; America, 1840 *778.6 p12*
Ayet, Lucie 34; America, 1840 *778.6 p12*
Ayet, Marie 1; America, 1840 *778.6 p12*
Ayet, Nicolas 6; America, 1840 *778.6 p12*
Ayet, Rose 4; America, 1840 *778.6 p12*
Ayet, Sebastian 12; America, 1840 *778.6 p12*
Aykroid, James; North Carolina, 1823 *1088.45 p1*
Ayling, William 20; Ontario, 1871 *1823.21 p13*
Aynaud, Anna 57; Mississippi, 1847 *778.6 p12*
Aynaud, Etienne 29; Mississippi, 1847 *778.6 p12*

Aynaud, Josephine 21; Mississippi, 1847 *778.6 p12*
Aynsworth, Joshua 57; Ontario, 1871 *1823.21 p13*
Ayoob, M. R. 19; New York, NY, 1894 *6512.1 p181*
Ayoob, M. R. 23; New York, NY, 1894 *6512.1 p181*
Ayre, Fred M. 25; New York, NY, 1894 *6512.1 p183*
Ayre, Joshua 25; Ontario, 1871 *1823.21 p13*
Ayres, John; America, n.d. *9228.50 p75*
Ayres, Philip; Boston, 1708 *9228.50 p75*
Ayry, Athia; Maryland, 1672 *1236.25 p47*
Azarie, Jean; Quebec, 1643 *9221.17 p128*
Azarie, Louise; Quebec, 1643 *9221.17 p128*
Azicq, Alce 8; Port uncertain, 1845 *778.6 p12*
Azicq, Evelina 14; Port uncertain, 1845 *778.6 p12*
Azicq, Ferdinand 12; Port uncertain, 1845 *778.6 p12*
Azicq, Ferdinand 12; Port uncertain, 1845 *778.6 p12*
Azicq, Lisca 4; Port uncertain, 1845 *778.6 p12*
Azicq, Lisca 4; Port uncertain, 1845 *778.6 p12*
Azicq, Rachel 33; Port uncertain, 1845 *778.6 p12*
Azicq, Rachel 33; Port uncertain, 1845 *778.6 p12*

B

Baader, Rasso; Miami, 1935 *4984.12 p39*
Baake, Carl; America, 1868 *7420.1 p267*
  With wife
Baake, Ernst; America, 1882 *7420.1 p327*
Baal, . . .; New England, n.d. *9228.50 p86*
Baal, Edward Manwaring; Maine, n.d. *9228.50 p87*
Baal, Nicholas; Maine, n.d. *9228.50 p87*
Baal, Peter; Philadelphia, 1741 *9228.50 p86*
Baal, Wm.; Maine, n.d. *9228.50 p87*
Baal, Wm., Jr.; Maine, n.d. *9228.50 p87*
Baal Family ; Ontario, 1930-1939 *9228.50 p17A*
Baas, Joachim; New York, 1859 *358.56 p54*
Babage, Edwin 23; Ontario, 1871 *1823.21 p13*
Babaghette, Joseph Antoine 70; New Orleans, 1848
  778.6 p12
Babb, Mark W.; Ohio, 1809-1852 *4511.35 p2*
Babb, Mark Wescombe; Ohio, 1809-1852 *4511.35 p2*
Babbage, Gilbert 28; Ontario, 1871 *1823.21 p13*
Babbington, John 62; Ontario, 1871 *1823.17 p6*
Babcock, David 60; Ontario, 1871 *1823.21 p13*
Babcock, H. W. 34; Ontario, 1871 *1823.21 p13*
Babel, Joseph Denis; Colorado, 1876 *1029.59 p5*
Babey, Sophia 42; Ontario, 1871 *1823.17 p6*
Babiarz, Joseph; Detroit, 1929-1930 *6214.5 p65*
Babin, Michel 29; New Orleans, 1848 *778.6 p12*
Babington, John 63; Ontario, 1871 *1823.17 p6*
Babington, Thomas 57; Ontario, 1871 *1823.21 p13*
Babinsay, Henry 33; Ontario, 1871 *1823.21 p13*
Babois, Pierre; Quebec, 1649 *9221.17 p208*
Babst, Daniel; Ohio, 1809-1852 *4511.35 p2*
Babst, Jacob; Ohio, 1809-1852 *4511.35 p2*
Babst, Joseph; Ohio, 1809-1852 *4511.35 p2*
Babst, Lawrence; Ohio, 1809-1852 *4511.35 p2*
Baby, Peter 23; Ontario, 1871 *1823.21 p13*
Bacarisse, Mr. 24; New Orleans, 1841 *778.6 p12*
Baccus-Charlier, Adrienne *SEE* Baccus-Charlier,
  Henriette
Baccus-Charlier, Augustine *SEE* Baccus-Charlier,
  Henriette
Baccus-Charlier, Henriette *SEE* Baccus-Charlier,
  Henriette
Baccus-Charlier, Henriette; Wisconsin, 1857 *1495.20*
  p41
  Child: Rosalie
  Child: Augustine
  Child: Marie Louise
  Child: Adrienne
  Child: Josephine
  Child: Henriette
  Child: Marie Joseph
Baccus-Charlier, Honore; Wisconsin, 1856 *1495.20 p41*
Baccus-Charlier, Josephine *SEE* Baccus-Charlier,
  Henriette
Baccus-Charlier, Marie Joseph *SEE* Baccus-Charlier,
  Henriette
Baccus-Charlier, Marie Louise *SEE* Baccus-Charlier,
  Henriette
Baccus-Charlier, Rosalie *SEE* Baccus-Charlier, Henriette
Bach, Adam *SEE* Bach, Jakob
Bach, Agatha 35; Port uncertain, 1843 *778.6 p12*
Bach, Anna *SEE* Bach, Jakob
Bach, Anna Jost *SEE* Bach, Jakob
Bach, Anna Maria; America, 1846 *5475.1 p61*
Bach, Barbara *SEE* Bach, Jakob
Bach, Carl 11; Port uncertain, 1843 *778.6 p12*
Bach, David 5; Port uncertain, 1843 *778.6 p12*
Bach, Elisabeth *SEE* Bach, Johann Wilhelm

Bach, Elisabeth; England, 1867 *170.15 p18*
  With family
Bach, Elisabeth *SEE* Bach, Jakob
Bach, Henry 2; Port uncertain, 1843 *778.6 p12*
Bach, Jacob; Louisiana, 1874-1875 *4981.45 p297*
Bach, Jacob 46; Mississippi, 1847 *778.6 p12*
Bach, Jakob *SEE* Bach, Jakob
Bach, Jakob; Minnesota, 1884 *5475.1 p142*
  Wife: Anna Jost
  Daughter: Elisabeth
  Daughter: Anna
  Son: Adam
  Daughter: Barbara
  Daughter: Maria
  Son: Nikolaus
  Son: Jakob
Bach, Jean 8; Port uncertain, 1843 *778.6 p12*
Bach, Joh. Eduard *SEE* Bach, Margarethe Jochum
Bach, Joh.Pet.; England, 1867 *170.15 p18*
  With 3 siblings
Bach, Johan 37; Port uncertain, 1843 *778.6 p12*
Bach, Johann Wilhelm; America, 1832 *5475.1 p457*
  Wife: Elisabeth
  With family
Bach, Katharina; America, 1884 *2526.43 p159*
  With son
Bach, Katharina; America, 1884 *2526.43 p162*
Bach, Margareta 25; Mississippi, 1847 *778.6 p12*
Bach, Margarethe; America, 1854 *5475.1 p57*
  Son: Nikolaus
  Daughter: Sus. Veronika
  Son: Joh. Eduard
Bach, Margarethe 28; America, 1864 *5475.1 p282*
Bach, Maria; America, 1879 *5475.1 p186*
Bach, Maria *SEE* Bach, Jakob
Bach, Nikolaus *SEE* Bach, Margarethe Jochum
Bach, Nikolaus *SEE* Bach, Jakob
Bach, Paulus; America, 1883 *5475.1 p142*
Bach, Peter; Chicago, 1852 *5475.1 p235*
  With wife & 5 children
Bach, Sus. Veronika *SEE* Bach, Margarethe Jochum
Bachand, William 29; Ontario, 1871 *1823.21 p13*
Bacharisse, Charles 24; New Orleans, 1842 *778.6 p12*
Bache, Benjamin 59; Ontario, 1871 *1823.21 p13*
Bachelier, Karl Peter; America, 1871 *5475.1 p62*
Bachelier, Peter; America, 1836 *5475.1 p70*
  With family
Bachelin, Adrien; Quebec, 1659 *9221.17 p412*
Bacher, Jacob; Ohio, 1809-1852 *4511.35 p2*
Bacher, Nikolaus 38; Brazil, 1828 *5475.1 p233*
Bacherer, Jacob; Ohio, 1809-1852 *4511.35 p2*
Bachler, Anna *SEE* Bachler, Auguste
Bachler, Auguste *SEE* Bachler, Auguste
Bachler, Auguste; America, 1889 *7420.1 p400*
  Daughter: Anna
  Son: Hermann
  Daughter: Therese
  Daughter: Caroline
  Daughter: Auguste
  Son: Wilhelm
Bachler, Bernhard; America, 1889 *7420.1 p400*
Bachler, Caroline *SEE* Bachler, Auguste
Bachler, Friedrich; America, 1889 *7420.1 p358*
Bachler, Hermann *SEE* Bachler, Auguste
Bachler, Therese *SEE* Bachler, Auguste
Bachler, Wilhelm *SEE* Bachler, Auguste
Bachli, Gabriel 27; New Castle, DE, 1817-1818 *90.20*
  p150

Bachman, Christian; Ohio, 1809-1852 *4511.35 p2*
Bachman, Emil; Chicago, 1888 *2853.20 p419*
Bachman, Johannes 27; New York, NY, 1893 *1883.7*
  p43
Bachman, Josef 25; New York, NY, 1893 *1883.7 p43*
Bachman, Katharina 22; New York, NY, 1893 *1883.7*
  p43
Bachman, Margaretha 22; New York, NY, 1893 *1883.7*
  p43
Bachman, R.; Louisiana, 1874-1875 *4981.45 p297*
Bachmann, August Herman; Wisconsin, 1884 *6795.8*
  p128
Bachmann, Carl Christian; America, 1868 *7919.3 p524*
Bachmann, Emil; New York, 1860 *358.56 p150*
Bachmann, Johann *SEE* Bachmann, Karl
Bachmann, Johann Christian; America, 1868 *7919.3*
  p524
Bachmann, Karl *SEE* Bachmann, Karl
Bachmann, Karl; Pittsburgh, 1882 *5475.1 p35*
  Wife: Maria Heinen
  Son: Johann
  Son: Nikolaus
  Daughter: Maria
  Son: Karl
  Son: Wilhelm
Bachmann, Maria *SEE* Bachmann, Karl
Bachmann, Maria Heinen *SEE* Bachmann, Karl
Bachmann, Nikolaus *SEE* Bachmann, Karl
Bachmann, Wilhelm *SEE* Bachmann, Karl
Bachmeier, Augustine 21; New York, NY, 1898 *7951.13*
  p43
Bachmeier, Helena 7 months; New York, NY, 1898
  7951.13 p43
Bachmeier, Margaret 21; New York, NY, 1898 *7951.13*
  p43
Bachmeyer, Anna Maria *SEE* Bachmeyer, Maria Gerard
Bachmeyer, Elisabeth *SEE* Bachmeyer, Maria Gerard
Bachmeyer, J. Kaspar *SEE* Bachmeyer, Maria Gerard
Bachmeyer, Johann; England, 1867 *5475.1 p146* .
Bachmeyer, Jos. Mathias *SEE* Bachmeyer, Maria Gerard
Bachmeyer, Maria *SEE* Bachmeyer, Maria Gerard
Bachmeyer, Maria 47; America, 1868 *5475.1 p146*
  Daughter: Elisabeth
  Daughter: Maria
  Daughter: Anna Maria
  Son: J. Kaspar
  Son: Jos. Mathias
Bach-Nielson, Adolf K.; Colorado, 1921 *1029.59 p5*
Bachnman, Gottfried; Wisconsin, 1877 *6795.8 p225*
Bachoie deBarraute, Jean-Pierre; Quebec, 1755-1757
  2314.30 p170
Bachoie deBarraute, Jean-Pierre; Quebec, 1755 *2314.30*
  p174
Bachus, John; Ontario, 1787 *1276.15 p231*
Back, John Henry; Louisiana, 1836-1841 *4981.45 p208*
Backe, Dorothea Charlotte; America, 1867 *7420.1 p252*
Backer, Elisabeth *SEE* Backer, Jakob
Backer, Elisabeth *SEE* Backer, Jakob
Backer, Franciska 62; Ontario, 1871 *1823.17 p6*
Backer, Jakob; America, 1895 *5475.1 p425*
  Wife: Elisabeth
  Son: Karl
  Daughter: Elisabeth
Backer, Karl *SEE* Backer, Jakob
Backer, M. Elisabeth; America, 1836 *5475.1 p457*
Backer, Nels; St. Paul, MN, 1887 *1865.50 p39*
Backert, Margaretha; America, 1856 *2526.43 p145*
Backert, Rozalia; Detroit, 1929 *1640.55 p116*

Backes, Angela 41; America, 1872 *5475.1 p446*
Backes, Anna *SEE* Backes, Johann
Backes, Anna Muller *SEE* Backes, Johann
Backes, Anna Weber 27 *SEE* Backes, Peter
Backes, Anna 27; Brazil, 1872 *5475.1 p442*
Backes, Anna Maria *SEE* Backes, Johann
Backes, Anna Maria 31; America, 1864 *5475.1 p544*
Backes, Anton *SEE* Backes, Johann
Backes, Barbara Lauer *SEE* Backes, Michel
Backes, Barbara Lauer 36 *SEE* Backes, Michael
Backes, Barbara Bommer 24 *SEE* Backes, Peter
Backes, Elisabeth *SEE* Backes, Mathias
Backes, Gertrud Reiber *SEE* Backes, Johann
Backes, Gertrud Schuetz *SEE* Backes, Johann
Backes, Ida 2 *SEE* Backes, Michael
Backes, Jakob *SEE* Backes, Johann
Backes, Johann *SEE* Backes, Johann
Backes, Johann *SEE* Backes, Johann
Backes, Johann; America, 1873 *5475.1 p22*
  *Wife:*Anna Muller
  *Granddaughter:*Anna
  *Daughter-In-Law:*Maria Leinen
  *Son:*Mathias
  *Son:*Johann
  *Son:*Anton
  *Daughter:*Susanna
  *Son:*Karl
Backes, Johann; America, 1887 *5475.1 p333*
  *Wife:*Gertrud Reiber
Backes, Johann 44; America, 1857 *5475.1 p492*
  *Wife:*Katharina Henkes 34
  *Son:*Johann
  *Son:*Jakob
  *Daughter:*Katharina
  *Daughter:*Anna Maria
Backes, Johann; Brazil, 1846 *5475.1 p439*
  *Wife:*Gertrud Schuetz
  With 6 children
Backes, Josef 15 *SEE* Backes, Peter
Backes, Karl *SEE* Backes, Johann
Backes, Katharina *SEE* Backes, Johann
Backes, Katharina Henkes 34 *SEE* Backes, Johann
Backes, Katharina; Brazil, 1846 *5475.1 p438*
Backes, Katharina *SEE* Backes, Mathias
Backes, Katharina 43; Brazil, 1879 *5475.1 p444*
Backes, Margarethe 31 *SEE* Backes, Theodor
Backes, Margarethe; Brazil, 1863 *5475.1 p502*
Backes, Margarethe; Brazil, 1873 *5475.1 p371*
Backes, Maria Leinen *SEE* Backes, Johann
Backes, Maria 28; America, 1873 *5475.1 p389*
Backes, Maria; Brazil, 1857 *5475.1 p441*
Backes, Maria *SEE* Backes, Mathias
Backes, Maria Kuhn 54 *SEE* Backes, Peter
Backes, Mathias *SEE* Backes, Johann
Backes, Mathias; Brazil, 1879 *5475.1 p390*
Backes, Mathias; Brazil, 1879 *5475.1 p390*
  *Daughter:*Maria
  *Daughter:*Elisabeth
  *Daughter:*Katharina
Backes, Mathias 23; Brazil, 1872 *5475.1 p389*
Backes, Michael 39; America, 1860 *5475.1 p482*
  *Wife:*Barbara Lauer 36
  *Daughter:*Ida 2
Backes, Michel; America, 1853 *5475.1 p481*
  *Wife:*Barbara Lauer
Backes, Michel; America, 1857 *5475.1 p388*
Backes, Michel 1 *SEE* Backes, Peter
Backes, Michel 25; Brazil, 1872 *5475.1 p389*
Backes, Nikolaus; America, 1847 *5475.1 p439*
Backes, Nikolaus; America, 1867 *5475.1 p279*
Backes, Nikolaus 27 *SEE* Backes, Theodor
Backes, Nikolaus; Brazil, 1879 *5475.1 p390*
  With parents
Backes, Nikolaus; England, 1887 *5475.1 p356*
Backes, Peter 28; America, 1867 *5475.1 p357*
Backes, Peter 31; America, 1851 *5475.1 p317*
  *Wife:*Anna Weber 27
Backes, Peter; Brazil, 1857 *5475.1 p441*
Backes, Peter; Brazil, 1872 *5475.1 p443*
Backes, Peter 32; Brazil, 1873 *5475.1 p389*
  *Wife:*Barbara Bommer 24
  *Brother:*Josef 15
  *Son:*Michel 1
  *Mother:*Maria Kuhn 54
Backes, Susanna *SEE* Backes, Johann
Backes, Theodor 36; America, 1871 *5475.1 p353*
  *Sister:*Margarethe 31
  *Brother:*Nikolaus 27
Backhaus, Franz; Chile, 1852 *1192.4 p54*
Backle, Georg 9 months; New York, NY, 1893 *1883.7 p40*
Backle, Georg 26; New York, NY, 1893 *1883.7 p40*
Backle, Hendr. 4; New York, NY, 1893 *1883.7 p40*

Backle, Louise 2; New York, NY, 1893 *1883.7 p40*
Backle, Louise 23; New York, NY, 1893 *1883.7 p40*
Backlund, And 30; New York, 1856 *6529.11 p22*
  *Wife:*Great Lisa Jonsdotter 27
  *Daughter:*Chatar Elisabeth 1
Backlund, And.; Boston, 1847 *6412.40 p150*
Backlund, Anders 5 *SEE* Backlund, Jon
Backlund, Cajsa Stina 1 *SEE* Backlund, Jon
Backlund, Chatar Elisabeth 1 *SEE* Backlund, And
Backlund, Great Lisa Jonsdotter 27 *SEE* Backlund, And
Backlund, Jon 43; New York, 1856 *6529.11 p19*
  *Wife:*Martha Jonsdotter 34
  *Son:*Jonas 7
  *Son:*Anders 5
  *Daughter:*Cajsa Stina 1
  *Son:*Lars 3
  *Son:*Pehr 9
Backlund, Jonas 7 *SEE* Backlund, Jon
Backlund, Lars 3 *SEE* Backlund, Jon
Backlund, Martha Jonsdotter 34 *SEE* Backlund, Jon
Backlund, Pehr 9 *SEE* Backlund, Jon
Backman, Alma Lovisa; St. Paul, MN, 1900 *1865.50 p91*
Backman, And.; Philadelphia, 1847 *6412.40 p150*
Backman, Andrew; Washington, 1889 *2770.40 p26*
Backman, Frank Gustaf; St. Paul, MN, 1887 *1865.50 p39*
Backman, John Alfred; Chicago, 1889-1890 *1865.50 p40*
Backowski, Josef 25; New York, NY, 1920 *930.50 p48*
Backrod, William 40; Ontario, 1871 *1823.21 p13*
Backstrom, Andrew; St. Paul, MN, 1894 *1865.50 p39*
  *Wife:*Augusta
Backstrom, Augusta *SEE* Backstrom, Andrew
Backstrom, Charles Fr.; Kansas, 1879 *777.40 p11*
  *Wife:*Christine B. Pehrsdotter
  *Son:*John Peter
  *Daughter:*Jennie Cath.
Backstrom, Christine B. Pehrsdotter *SEE* Backstrom, Charles Fr.
Backstrom, J.; New York, NY, 1845 *6412.40 p148*
Backstrom, Jennie Cath. *SEE* Backstrom, Charles Fr.
Backstrom, John Peter *SEE* Backstrom, Charles Fr.
Backstrom, Peter; Kansas, 1865-1868 *777.40 p16*
Backwitz, Helena 18; New York, NY, 1885 *1883.7 p45*
Backwitz, Magda. 18; New York, NY, 1885 *1883.7 p45*
Bacle, Pierre 23; Port uncertain, 1840 *778.6 p12*
Bacleine, Desire Eugene *SEE* Bacleine, Eugene
Bacleine, Eloise Josephe *SEE* Bacleine, Eugene
Bacleine, Eugene; Wisconsin, 1854-1858 *1495.20 p66*
  *Wife:*Hortense Meuron
  *Child:*Marie Therese
  *Child:*Zenon Joseph
  *Child:*Nestor
  *Child:*Desire Eugene
  *Child:*Eloise Josephe
Bacleine, Henri; Wisconsin, 1854-1858 *1495.20 p66*
Bacleine, Hortense Meuron *SEE* Bacleine, Eugene
Bacleine, Marie Josephe; Wisconsin, 1854-1858 *1495.20 p66*
Bacleine, Marie Therese *SEE* Bacleine, Eugene
Bacleine, Nestor *SEE* Bacleine, Eugene
Bacleine, Zenon Joseph *SEE* Bacleine, Eugene
Bacon, Mr.; Dedham, MA, 1640 *1642 p101*
Bacon, Charles 36; Ontario, 1871 *1823.21 p13*
Bacon, Daniel *SEE* Bacon, Michael
Bacon, Daniel 64; Ontario, 1871 *1823.21 p13*
Bacon, John *SEE* Bacon, Michael
Bacon, Michael *SEE* Bacon, Michael
Bacon, Michael; Dedham, MA, 1640 *1642 p101*
  With wife
  *Child:*Sarah
  *Child:*Michael
  *Child:*Daniel
  *Child:*John
Bacon, Pierre Thomas; Illinois, 1852 *6079.1 p1*
Bacon, Sarah *SEE* Bacon, Michael
Bacon, William; Salem, MA, 1640 *1642 p78*
Baconier, Jean-Baptiste 44; New Orleans, 1848 *778.6 p12*
Bacot, Benoist 42; America, 1846 *778.6 p13*
Bacot, Prudent 22; America, 1846 *778.6 p13*
Bacque, Peter 30; New Orleans, 1847 *778.6 p13*
Baczko, Morris; Detroit, 1929 *1640.55 p115*
Badcock, Maria 25; Ontario, 1871 *1823.21 p13*
Badcock, Samuel 31; Ontario, 1871 *1823.21 p13*
Bade, . . .; New York, NY, 1856 *7420.1 p144*
  With family
Bade, Engel Marie; America, 1856 *7420.1 p154*
Bade, Engel Marie Sophie *SEE* Bade, Heinrich Christoph
Bade, Engel Marie Sophie Toineboin *SEE* Bade, Heinrich Christoph
Bade, Hans Heinrich; America, 1860 *7420.1 p190*

Bade, Heinrich Christoph; America, 1856 *7420.1 p144*
  *Wife:*Engel Marie Sophie Toineboin
  *Daughter:*Engel Marie Sophie
  With children
Bade, Heinrich Friedrich Wilhelm; Chicago, 1886 *7420.1 p350*
Bade, Johann Tonnies; America, 1854 *7420.1 p114*
Badeau, Anne Hardouin 32 *SEE* Badeau, Jacques
Badeau, Francois 15 *SEE* Badeau, Jacques
Badeau, Jacques; Quebec, 1647 *9221.17 p175*
  *Wife:*Anne Hardouin
  *Son:*Jean
  *Son:*Francois
  *Daughter:*Jeanne
  *Daughter:*Madeleine
Badeau, Jean 6 *SEE* Badeau, Jacques
Badeau, Jeanne 8 *SEE* Badeau, Jacques
Badeau, Madeleine 13 *SEE* Badeau, Jacques
Bader, Andre 17; America, 1846 *778.6 p13*
Bader, Anton 18; New York, NY, 1885 *1883.7 p46*
Bader, August; America, 1867 *7919.3 p528*
Bader, Christina; Philadelphia, 1852 *8513.31 p417*
Bader, Christn. 48; New York, NY, 1885 *1883.7 p46*
Bader, Constantin; America, 1868 *7919.3 p528*
  With family
Bader, Fidel; New Castle, DE, 1817-1818 *90.20 p150*
Bader, Georg; America, 1867 *7919.3 p528*
  With 2 daughters
Bader, Heinrich 7; New York, NY, 1885 *1883.7 p46*
Bader, Johanne 48; New York, NY, 1885 *1883.7 p46*
Bader, John; Ohio, 1852 *3580.20 p31*
Bader, John; Ohio, 1852 *6020.12 p6*
Bader, Joseph 10; Galveston, TX, 1844 *3967.10 p373*
Bader, Joseph 43; Galveston, TX, 1844 *3967.10 p373*
Bader, Katherine 16; New York, NY, 1885 *1883.7 p46*
Bader, Maria Anna 18; Galveston, TX, 1844 *3967.10 p373*
Bader, Wilhelm 10; New York, NY, 1885 *1883.7 p46*
Bader, William C.; New York, 1883 *1029.59 p5*
Badger, Arnold; Illinois, 1852 *6079.1 p1*
Badger, George; West Indies, 1740 *9228.50 p88*
Badger, Giles; New England, n.d. *9228.50 p88*
Badger, Mary; Portsmouth, NH, n.d. *9228.50 p88*
Badger, William; Illinois, 1852 *6079.1 p1*
Badier, George; West Indies, 1740 *9228.50 p88*
Badier, Mary; Portsmouth, NH, n.d. *9228.50 p88*
Badkie, Frank; Detroit, 1890 *9980.23 p97*
Badouet, Estienne; Virginia, 1700 *9230.15 p80*
Badshook, Philip; Ohio, 1809-1852 *4511.35 p2*
Badshuck, Philip; Ohio, 1809-1852 *4511.35 p2*
Badtke, H.; Valdivia, Chile, 1850 *1192.4 p48*
Bae, Emile 30; New Orleans, 1848 *778.6 p13*
Baebler, Oswald; Wisconsin, 1875 *6795.8 p101*
Baechel, Michael; Ohio, 1809-1852 *4511.35 p2*
Baechel, Philip; Ohio, 1809-1852 *4511.35 p2*
Baegelen, Joseph; Ohio, 1809-1852 *4511.35 p2*
Baehrens, Engel Maria *SEE* Baehrens, Hans Heinrich
Baehrens, Engel Maria Sophia Reese *SEE* Baehrens, Hans Heinrich
Baehrens, Hans Heinrich; America, 1848 *7420.1 p58*
  *Wife:*Engel Maria Sophia Reese
  *Daughter:*Engel Maria
Baehy, Clarence; Louisiana, 1874 *4981.45 p131*
Baensch, Berthold; Wisconsin, 1903 *6795.8 p212*
Baer, Andre 22; America, 1847 *778.6 p13*
Baer, Antoine 1; America, 1846 *778.6 p13*
Baer, Catherine 24; America, 1846 *778.6 p13*
Baer, Delphine 5; New Orleans, 1848 *778.6 p13*
Baer, Jeanette 22; New Orleans, 1848 *778.6 p13*
Baer, Marie; America, 1870 *7420.1 p395*
Baer, Mathilde 17; New Orleans, 1848 *778.6 p13*
Baer, Michel 3; New Orleans, 1848 *778.6 p13*
Baer, Nicolas 26; America, 1846 *778.6 p13*
Baer, Peter; America, 1846 *5475.1 p67*
Baer, Rachel 29; New Orleans, 1848 *778.6 p13*
Baer, Roselle 34; America, 1846 *778.6 p13*
Baer, Solomon; North Carolina, 1856 *1088.45 p1*
Baermann, Abraham *SEE* Baermann, Ernst
Baermann, Cacilia *SEE* Baermann, Ernst
Baermann, Elisabeth; America, 1842 *5475.1 p397*
Baermann, Ernst 38; America, 1860 *5475.1 p561*
  *Wife:*Ester Haimann 37
  *Son:*Abraham
  *Daughter:*Cacilia
Baermann, Ester Haimann 37 *SEE* Baermann, Ernst
Baermann, Friedrich 32; America, 1847 *5475.1 p396*
  *Wife:*Maria Schwartz 26
  *Son:*Leonhard 2
Baermann, Jakob; Port uncertain, 1845 *5475.1 p397*
Baermann, Leonhard 2 *SEE* Baermann, Friedrich
Baermann, Maria Schwartz 26 *SEE* Baermann, Friedrich
Baersch, Albert; Washington, 1886 *2770.40 p195*
Baetke, John; New York, 1859 *358.56 p101*

           FOR A COMPLETE EXPLANATION OF ENTRY, SEE "HOW TO READ A CITATION" SECTION

Bagau, Antoinette; Quebec, 1671 ***4514.3*** *p273*
Bager, Fred W. 25; New York, NY, 1894 ***6512.1*** *p185*
Bagley, Robert 35; Ontario, 1871 ***1823.17*** *p6*
Bagnell, Susan Alma; Cambridge, MA, 1880-1894 ***9228.50*** *p314*
Bagstrom, Mary; Illinois, 1869-1872 ***777.40*** *p5*
Bahan, M.; New Orleans, 1850 ***7242.30*** *p134*
Bahan, Simon 60; Ontario, 1871 ***1823.17*** *p6*
Bahe, Mr.; America, 1854 ***7420.1*** *p114*
Bahe, Carl Heinrich Conrad *SEE* Bahe, Johann Heinrich Christian
Bahe, Caroline Wilhelmine Sophie *SEE* Bahe, Johann Friedrich Ludwig
Bahe, Christian Conrad; America, 1855 ***7420.1*** *p134*
Bahe, Christian Wilhelm Conrad *SEE* Bahe, Johann Heinrich Christian
Bahe, Engel Marie; America, 1857 ***7420.1*** *p157*
Bahe, Engel Marie Dorothea; America, 1864 ***7420.1*** *p222*
*Sister:*Engel Sophie
*Sister:*Sophie Dorothea
*Brother:*Johann Heinrich
Bahe, Engel Marie Dorothea; America, 1867 ***7420.1*** *p252*
Bahe, Engel Marie Sophie *SEE* Bahe, Heinrich Christoph
Bahe, Engel Marie Sophie Toineboin *SEE* Bahe, Heinrich Christoph
Bahe, Engel Marie Sophie *SEE* Bahe, Johann Friedrich Ludwig
Bahe, Engel Sophie *SEE* Bahe, Engel Marie Dorothea
Bahe, Ernst; America, 1856 ***7420.1*** *p144*
*Brother:*Friedrich
Bahe, Friedrich *SEE* Bahe, Ernst
Bahe, Heinrich; America, 1855 ***7420.1*** *p134*
Bahe, Heinrich Chr; America, 1875 ***7420.1*** *p304*
Bahe, Heinrich Chr.; America, 1855 ***7420.1*** *p134*
Bahe, Heinrich Christoph; America, 1856 ***7420.1*** *p144*
*Wife:*Engel Marie Sophie Toineboin
*Daughter:*Engel Marie Sophie
With children
Bahe, Heinrich Christoph; America, 1868 ***7420.1*** *p267*
Bahe, Heinrich Ludwig Wilhelm *SEE* Bahe, Johann Friedrich Ludwig
Bahe, Johann Conrad Wilhelm; America, 1882 ***7420.1*** *p327*
Bahe, Johann Friedrich; America, 1870 ***7420.1*** *p282*
Bahe, Johann Friedrich Christian Ludwig *SEE* Bahe, Johann Friedrich Ludwig
Bahe, Johann Friedrich Ludwig; America, 1882 ***7420.1*** *p327*
*Wife:*Engel Marie Sophie
*Daughter:*Caroline Wilhelmine Sophie
*Son:*Johann Friedrich Christian Ludwig
*Son:*Heinrich Ludwig Wilhelm
Bahe, Johann Heinrich *SEE* Bahe, Engel Marie Dorothea
Bahe, Johann Heinrich Christian; America, 1875 ***7420.1*** *p304*
With wife
*Son:*Christian Wilhelm Conrad
*Son:*Carl Heinrich Conrad
*Son:*Johann Heinrich Wilhelm
Bahe, Johann Heinrich Friedrich; America, 1854 ***7420.1*** *p114*
Bahe, Johann Heinrich Wilhelm *SEE* Bahe, Johann Heinrich Christian
Bahe, Sophie Dorothea *SEE* Bahe, Engel Marie Dorothea
Bahe, Sophie Dorothea; America, 1886 ***7420.1*** *p350*
Bahe Family ; America, 1855 ***7420.1*** *p144*
Bahl, Babette 37; New Orleans, 1843 ***778.6*** *p13*
Bahlmann, Caroline Marie Sophie *SEE* Bahlmann, Hans Heinrich Christoph
Bahlmann, Engel Marie Meyer *SEE* Bahlmann, Hans Heinrich Christoph
Bahlmann, Engel Marie Sophie Meyer *SEE* Bahlmann, Johann Heinrich
Bahlmann, Engel Marie Sophie; America, 1852 ***7420.1*** *p84*
*Son:*Heinr. Konrad
Bahlmann, Hans Heinrich *SEE* Bahlmann, Johann Heinrich
Bahlmann, Hans Heinrich Christoph *SEE* Bahlmann, Hans Heinrich Christoph
Bahlmann, Hans Heinrich Christoph; America, 1845 ***7420.1*** *p34*
*Wife:*Engel Marie Meyer
*Daughter:*Caroline Marie Sophie
*Son:*Hans Heinrich Christoph
Bahlmann, Heinr. Konrad *SEE* Bahlmann, Engel Marie Sophie
Bahlmann, Johann Heinrich; America, 1846 ***7420.1*** *p42*
*Wife:*Engel Marie Sophie Meyer
*Son:*Hans Heinrich
Bahmit, Mr. 24; America, 1843 ***778.6*** *p13*
Bahn, John; Wisconsin, 1892 ***6795.8*** *p125*
Bahn, Luise; Wisconsin, 1883 ***6795.8*** *p29*
Bahnle, Emilie Clara; America, 1867 ***7919.3*** *p530*
Bahr, Heinrich Ludwig; America, 1871 ***7420.1*** *p288*
Bahr, Hermann; Wisconsin, 1877 ***6795.8*** *p43*
Bahr, Jean 22; America, 1843 ***778.6*** *p13*
Bahr, Josephine; America, 1874 ***7420.1*** *p302*
Bahr, Pierre 18; America, 1843 ***778.6*** *p13*
Bahre, Johann Heinrich Christian; America, 1866 ***7420.1*** *p239*
With family
Bahrilien, Peter 41; Port uncertain, 1844 ***778.6*** *p13*
Bahring, Emil *SEE* Bahring, Henriette
Bahring, Henriette; America, 1867 ***7919.3*** *p534*
*Son:*Emil
Baier, Anna 23; Portland, ME, 1910 ***970.38*** *p76*
Baier, Dorothea; America, 1869 ***179.55*** *p19*
With child
Baier, Josef F.; Missouri, 1852 ***2853.20*** *p49*
With parents
Baierle, Charles; Louisiana, 1874 ***4981.45*** *p130*
Baies, Joseph; Colorado, 1880 ***1029.59*** *p5*
Bailes, John; Virginia, 1652 ***6254.4*** *p243*
Bailes, Tho; Virginia, 1652 ***6254.4*** *p243*
Bailess, William; Boston, 1774 ***8529.30*** *p2*
Bailey, Adam 50; Ontario, 1871 ***1823.21*** *p13*
Bailey, Addison; America, 1908 ***1211.45*** *p131*
Bailey, Arthur H.; Washington, 1886 ***2770.40*** *p195*
Bailey, Augustine 3; New Orleans, 1848 ***778.6*** *p13*
Bailey, Charles; Maryland, 1673 ***1236.25*** *p48*
Bailey, Claude 35; New Orleans, 1848 ***778.6*** *p13*
Bailey, Francis; Washington, 1883 ***2770.40*** *p136*
Bailey, Henry 34; Indiana, 1894-1896 ***9076.20*** *p74*
Bailey, Hugh 40; Ontario, 1871 ***1823.21*** *p13*
Bailey, James 62; Ontario, 1871 ***1823.21*** *p13*
Bailey, James 70; Ontario, 1871 ***1823.21*** *p13*
Bailey, John 35; Ontario, 1871 ***1823.21*** *p13*
Bailey, John 43; Ontario, 1871 ***1823.21*** *p13*
Bailey, John C.; North Carolina, 1814-1818 ***1088.45*** *p1*
Bailey, Joseph R. 30; Ontario, 1871 ***1823.17*** *p6*
Bailey, Louisa 9; New Orleans, 1848 ***778.6*** *p13*
Bailey, Marie Esther 30; New Orleans, 1848 ***778.6*** *p13*
Bailey, Mary 9; Quebec, 1870 ***8364.32*** *p22*
Bailey, Mary Ann 31; Ontario, 1871 ***1823.21*** *p13*
Bailey, Mathew; New York, NY, 1829 ***3274.56*** *p70*
Bailey, Pauline 6; New Orleans, 1848 ***778.6*** *p13*
Bailey, Richard 22; Quebec, 1870 ***8364.32*** *p22*
Bailey, Thomas; New York, 1750 ***1640.8*** *p234*
Bailey, Thomas 40; Ontario, 1871 ***1823.21*** *p13*
Bailey, Thomas 77; Ontario, 1871 ***1823.21*** *p13*
Bailey, Walter 17; Quebec, 1870 ***8364.32*** *p22*
Bailey, William 14; Ontario, 1871 ***1823.17*** *p6*
Bailey, William 35; Ontario, 1864 ***9228.50*** *p88*
Bailhache, John; Massachusetts, 1774-1780 ***9228.50*** *p88*
Bailhache, Mary; Massachusetts, 1755 ***9228.50*** *p579*
Bailhache, Mary; Massachusetts, 1755 ***9228.50*** *p593*
Bailhache, Nicholas; Ohio, 1825 ***9228.50*** *p88*
Bailhache, Philip; Marblehead, MA, 1790 ***9228.50*** *p88*
Bailie, Elijah 47; Ontario, 1871 ***1823.17*** *p6*
Baillargeon, Jean 39; Quebec, 1650 ***9221.17*** *p223*
Baillargeon, Mathurin 25; Quebec, 1648 ***9221.17*** *p194*
Baille, Alex. 35; New Orleans, 1846 ***778.6*** *p13*
Baille, Bernard 34; Port uncertain, 1840 ***778.6*** *p13*
Baille, Joseph 37; New York, NY, 1894 ***6512.1*** *p182*
Baillet, Adolph 43; America, 1843 ***778.6*** *p13*
Bailleur, Christophe; Quebec, 1659 ***9221.17*** *p412*
Bailleur, Nicolas; Quebec, 1659 ***9221.17*** *p412*
Bailley, Isabella 38; Ontario, 1871 ***1823.21*** *p13*
Baillie, Edward; Marston's Wharf, 1782 ***8529.30*** *p9*
Bailloquet, Pierre 34; Quebec, 1647 ***9221.17*** *p171*
Baillot, Charles 2; America, 1843 ***778.6*** *p13*
Baillot, Constance 3 months; America, 1843 ***778.6*** *p13*
Baillot, Justin 4; America, 1843 ***778.6*** *p13*
Baillot, Louis 28; America, 1843 ***778.6*** *p14*
Baillot, Marie 30; America, 1843 ***778.6*** *p14*
Bailly, Francois 32; Montreal, 1659 ***9221.17*** *p416*
*Wife:*Marie Fonteneau 28
Bailly, Madeleine; Quebec, 1671 ***4514.3*** *p273*
Bailly, Marie Fonteneau 28 *SEE* Bailly, Francois
Bailly deMessein, Nicolas; Quebec, 1700 ***2314.30*** *p172*
Baily, Anne; New Orleans, 1850 ***7242.30*** *p134*
Baily, Benjamin 63; Ontario, 1871 ***1823.21*** *p13*
Baily, Catherine; New Orleans, 1850 ***7242.30*** *p134*
Baily, Dorothea 63; Ontario, 1871 ***1823.17*** *p6*
Baily, Elizabeth 65; Ontario, 1871 ***1823.17*** *p6*
Baily, Ellen; New Orleans, 1850 ***7242.30*** *p134*
Baily, John 50; Ontario, 1871 ***1823.21*** *p13*
Baily, Margaret 48; Ontario, 1871 ***1823.21*** *p13*
Baily, Michael; New Orleans, 1850 ***7242.30*** *p134*
Baily, Wm 65; Ontario, 1871 ***1823.21*** *p13*
Bain, Bruce; Miami, 1920 ***4984.15*** *p38*
Bain, John 34; Ontario, 1871 ***1823.21*** *p13*
Bain, Robert 24; Ontario, 1871 ***1823.17*** *p6*
Bain, Robert 28; Ontario, 1871 ***1823.21*** *p13*
Bain, William 37; North Carolina, 1774 ***1422.10*** *p59*
Bain, William 31; Ontario, 1871 ***1823.17*** *p6*
Bain, William 50; Ontario, 1871 ***1823.17*** *p6*
Baina, Jan 22; New York, NY, 1911 ***6533.11*** *p10*
Bainard, David 29; Ontario, 1871 ***1823.21*** *p13*
Bainard, Luther 50; Ontario, 1871 ***1823.21*** *p13*
Bainberry, Nicholes 30; Ontario, 1871 ***1823.17*** *p6*
Bainberry, Nicholes 80; Ontario, 1871 ***1823.17*** *p6*
Baines, George 36; Ontario, 1871 ***1823.17*** *p6*
Baines, William 41; Ontario, 1871 ***1823.17*** *p6*
Bainsberry, Samuel 25; Ontario, 1871 ***1823.17*** *p6*
Bair, Andrew A.; Ohio, 1842 ***3580.20*** *p31*
Bair, Andrew A.; Ohio, 1842 ***6020.12*** *p6*
Baird, George; Colorado, 1893 ***1029.59*** *p5*
Baird, Hugh C. 36; Ontario, 1871 ***1823.21*** *p14*
Baird, James; Illinois, 1861 ***6079.1*** *p1*
Baird, John; Nova Scotia, 1839 ***7078*** *p80*
Baird, John 33; Ontario, 1871 ***1823.21*** *p14*
Baird, William 26; Ontario, 1871 ***1823.21*** *p14*
Bairns, John 55; Ontario, 1871 ***1823.21*** *p14*
Baiselat, Francoise; Quebec, 1668 ***4514.3*** *p273*
Baish, Ernest Henry; Iowa, 1909 ***1211.15*** *p9*
Baitlet, Fanny 29; Ontario, 1871 ***1823.21*** *p14*
Bajard, Albert; New York, NY, 1844 ***6412.40*** *p148*
Bajda, Antonina; Detroit, 1930 ***1640.60*** *p77*
Bajenski, John; Texas, 1871-1892 ***6015.15*** *p23*
Bajenski, Thomas; Texas, 1894 ***6015.15*** *p23*
Bajenski, Thomas; Texas, 1895 ***6015.15*** *p23*
Bajko, Leon; Detroit, 1929 ***1640.55*** *p115*
Bajon, Mr. 20; Port uncertain, 1844 ***778.6*** *p14*
Bak, Jean 22; New Orleans, 1846 ***778.6*** *p24*
Bake, James 38; Ontario, 1871 ***1823.21*** *p14*
Bake, Johann Heinrich Christoph; New York, NY, 1879 ***7420.1*** *p312*
Bake, Sophie Dorothea; New York, NY, 1879 ***7420.1*** *p313*
Bake, Sophie Wilhelmine Louise; America, 1860 ***7420.1*** *p190*
Bakelew, Dewalt; Ohio, 1809-1852 ***4511.35*** *p2*
Bakelin, Dewalt; Ohio, 1809-1852 ***4511.35*** *p2*
Baker, Andrew 27; Ontario, 1871 ***1823.21*** *p14*
Baker, August; Wisconsin, 1886 ***6795.8*** *p172*
Baker, Barnhart; Ohio, 1809-1852 ***4511.35*** *p2*
Baker, Charles 32; Michigan, 1880 ***4491.33*** *p1*
Baker, Charles 34; Ontario, 1871 ***1823.21*** *p14*
Baker, Charles 60; Ontario, 1871 ***1823.21*** *p14*
Baker, Charles 16; Quebec, 1870 ***8364.32*** *p22*
Baker, Christian; Wisconsin, 1890 ***6795.8*** *p173*
Baker, Conrad; Ohio, 1809-1852 ***4511.35*** *p2*
Baker, Daniel 27; Michigan, 1880 ***4491.36*** *p1*
Baker, Diana; California, 1867-1937 ***9228.50*** *p320*
Baker, Dominick; Ohio, 1809-1852 ***4511.35*** *p2*
Baker, Dominick M.; Ohio, 1809-1852 ***4511.35*** *p2*
Baker, Edward; Maryland, 1673 ***1236.25*** *p48*
Baker, Edward 59; Ontario, 1871 ***1823.21*** *p14*
Baker, Elijah 55; Ontario, 1871 ***1823.21*** *p14*
Baker, Elisa 52; Ontario, 1871 ***1823.21*** *p14*
Baker, Elisabeth 27; Ontario, 1871 ***1823.21*** *p14*
Baker, Frederick 38; Ontario, 1871 ***1823.17*** *p6*
Baker, George 36; Michigan, 1880 ***4491.42*** *p2*
Baker, George; Ohio, 1844 ***2763.1*** *p7*
Baker, George 30; Ontario, 1871 ***1823.21*** *p14*
Baker, George Lloyd; North Carolina, 1832 ***1088.45*** *p1*
Baker, George M.; North Carolina, 1858-1859 ***1088.45*** *p1*
Baker, Grace 31; Michigan, 1880 ***4491.33*** *p1*
Baker, Hannah; Miami, 1935 ***4984.12*** *p39*
Baker, Henry 24; Ontario, 1871 ***1823.21*** *p14*
Baker, Henry 35; Ontario, 1871 ***1823.21*** *p14*
Baker, Henry 55; Ontario, 1871 ***1823.21*** *p14*
Baker, Isaac Nc 27; Ontario, 1871 ***1823.21*** *p14*
Baker, J. W.C. 27; Ontario, 1871 ***1823.21*** *p14*
Baker, James Lewis 50; Ontario, 1871 ***1823.21*** *p14*
Baker, Jeremiah 48; Ontario, 1871 ***1823.21*** *p14*
Baker, Jesse 52; Ontario, 1871 ***1823.21*** *p14*
Baker, John; Boston, 1767 ***1642*** *p38*
Baker, John; Charlestown, MA, 1636 ***9228.50*** *p89*
Baker, John 44; Ontario, 1871 ***1823.17*** *p6*
Baker, John 48; Ontario, 1871 ***1823.21*** *p14*
Baker, John 55; Ontario, 1871 ***1823.21*** *p14*
Baker, John 64; Ontario, 1871 ***1823.21*** *p14*
Baker, John P. 24; Indiana, 1880 ***9076.20*** *p69*
Baker, Keith Philip; Ontario, 1945-1983 ***9228.50*** *p89*
Baker, Lewis; Virginia, 1718 ***1220.12*** *p793*
Baker, Majni Elvor; Oregon, 1941 ***9157.47*** *p2*
Baker, Mary E. 59; Michigan, 1880 ***4491.39*** *p2*
Baker, Nicholas; Marblehead, MA, 1696 ***9228.50*** *p88*
Baker, Philip; Died enroute, 1851 ***9228.50*** *p192*
Baker, Philip; Died enroute, 1851 ***9228.50*** *p359*
Baker, Richard 42; Ontario, 1871 ***1823.21*** *p14*
Baker, Richard; South Carolina, 1740-1760 ***9228.50*** *p89*
Baker, Robert 45; Ontario, 1871 ***1823.21*** *p14*
Baker, Robert 63; Ontario, 1871 ***1823.21*** *p14*
Baker, Samuel 37; Ontario, 1871 ***1823.21*** *p14*

Baker, Samuel 43; Ontario, 1871 ***1823.21*** *p14*
Baker, Sarah 63; Ontario, 1871 ***1823.21*** *p14*
Baker, Sophia; America, 1800-1859 ***9228.50*** *p89*
Baker, Stephen 22; Michigan, 1880 ***4491.36*** *p1*
Baker, Susan; North Carolina, 1839 ***1088.45*** *p1*
Baker, Thomas; Massachusetts, 1679 ***9228.50*** *p88*
Baker, William; Marston's Wharf, 1780 ***8529.30*** *p9*
Baker, William; Ontario, 1871 ***1823.21*** *p14*
Baker, William 30; Ontario, 1871 ***1823.21*** *p14*
Baker, William 45; Ontario, 1871 ***1823.21*** *p14*
Baker, William; Wisconsin, 1864 ***6795.8*** *p173*
Baklarz, Eva Chudy *SEE* Baklarz, Frank
Baklarz, Frank; Detroit, 1929-1930 ***6214.5*** *p70*
*Wife:*Eva Chudy
Bakman, Louis 25; Port uncertain, 1841 ***778.6*** *p14*
Bakor, John 33; Indiana, 1902-1906 ***9076.20*** *p74*
Bal, Constant 20; Missouri, 1848 ***778.6*** *p14*
Balaine, John; Salem, MA, 1650-1699 ***9228.50*** *p87*
Balaine, John; Salem, MA, 1650-1699 ***9228.50*** *p93*
Balanrch, Christopher; Louisiana, 1874 ***4981.45*** *p130*
Balbe, Adam 28; America, 1841 ***778.6*** *p14*
Balbier, Karl Friedrich; America, 1848 ***5475.1*** *p476*
Balcam, . . .; Connecticut, 1790 ***9228.50*** *p89*
Balcam, . . .; Massachusetts, 1790 ***9228.50*** *p89*
Balcar, Josef; Wisconsin, 1890 ***2853.20*** *p229*
Balcom, . . .; Connecticut, 1697-1804 ***9228.50*** *p268*
Balcom, . . .; Connecticut, 1790 ***9228.50*** *p89*
Balcom, . . .; Massachusetts, 1790 ***9228.50*** *p89*
Balcomb, . . .; Connecticut, 1790 ***9228.50*** *p89*
Balcomb, . . .; Massachusetts, 1790 ***9228.50*** *p89*
Baldauf, Barbara Karrenbauer *SEE* Baldauf, Johann
Baldauf, Georg; America, 1838 ***5475.1*** *p67*
With wife & 2 children
Baldauf, Heinrich; America, 1846 ***5475.1*** *p68*
Baldauf, Johann 50; America, 1836 ***5475.1*** *p64*
*Wife:*Barbara Karrenbauer
With child 15
With child 13
With child 10
Baldauf, Peter; Pennsylvania, 1846 ***5475.1*** *p68*
Balde, Hans Heinrich; America, 1855 ***7420.1*** *p144*
Balder, Max Philip; Colorado, 1905 ***1029.59*** *p6*
Baldescheims, Helena 18; New York, NY, 1847 ***9176.15*** *p49*
Baldeschweiler, Blasius 34; Galveston, TX, 1844 ***3967.10*** *p373*
Baldeschweiler, Maria Anna 30; Galveston, TX, 1844 ***3967.10*** *p373*
Baldewein, Erich; Port uncertain, 1889 ***7420.1*** *p400*
Baldewein, Wilhelm; America, 1886 ***7420.1*** *p350*
Baldewein, Wilhelm Emil; America, 1852 ***7420.1*** *p84*
Baldie, John 55; Ontario, 1871 ***1823.21*** *p14*
Baldinger, Jacob 70; Ontario, 1871 ***1823.21*** *p14*
Baldinger, John; Ohio, 1809-1852 ***4511.35*** *p2*
Baldinger, Susana 63; Ontario, 1871 ***1823.21*** *p15*
Baldinger, Xaveri 40; New Castle, DE, 1817-1818 ***90.20*** *p150*
Baldwin, Cecilia *SEE* Baldwin, T.
Baldwin, Celenie *SEE* Baldwin, T.
Baldwin, Fanny *SEE* Baldwin, T.
Baldwin, Henry 37; Ontario, 1871 ***1823.21*** *p15*
Baldwin, Louisa *SEE* Baldwin, T.
Baldwin, Maurice 30; Ontario, 1871 ***1823.21*** *p15*
Baldwin, Peter; Salem, MA, 1672 ***9228.50*** *p159*
Baldwin, Roxina *SEE* Baldwin, T.
Baldwin, T.; Toronto, 1844 ***2910.35*** *p115*
*Relative:*Celenie
*Relative:*Cecilia
*Relative:*Roxina
*Relative:*Louisa
*Relative:*Fanny
Baldwin Family ; Massachusetts, n.d. ***9228.50*** *p126*
Bale, Edward Manwaring; Maine, n.d. ***9228.50*** *p87*
Bale, James 35; Ontario, 1871 ***1823.21*** *p15*
Bale, Nicholas; Maine, n.d. ***9228.50*** *p87*
Bale, William 28; Ontario, 1871 ***1823.21*** *p15*
Bale, Wm.; Maine, n.d. ***9228.50*** *p87*
Bale, Wm., Jr.; Maine, n.d. ***9228.50*** *p87*
Balenski, Catharine 9; New York, NY, 1874 ***6954.7*** *p37*
Balenski, Catherine 35; New York, NY, 1874 ***6954.7*** *p37*
Balenski, Conrad 20; New York, NY, 1874 ***6954.7*** *p37*
Balenski, Georg 8; New York, NY, 1874 ***6954.7*** *p37*
Balenski, Georg 41; New York, NY, 1874 ***6954.7*** *p37*
Balenski, Michel 20; New York, NY, 1874 ***6954.7*** *p37*
Balentyne, James 46; Ontario, 1871 ***1823.17*** *p6*
Baler, Conrad; New Jersey, 1749-1774 ***927.31*** *p3*
Bales, Elizabeth; Philadelphia, 1842 ***8513.31*** *p294*
Bales, Jean Bernard 22; New Orleans, 1848 ***778.6*** *p14*
Bales, Victoire 21; New Orleans, 1847 ***778.6*** *p14*
Balestier, Joseph; Massachusetts, 1788-1816 ***9228.50*** *p328*
Baletka, Jan; Texas, 1855 ***2853.20*** *p78*
Baleuski, Balthasar 20; New York, NY, 1874 ***6954.7*** *p37*

Balfe, M. A. 45; Ontario, 1871 ***1823.21*** *p15*
Balfour, Rutherford 32; Ontario, 1871 ***1823.17*** *p6*
Balge, Nikolaus; America, 1881 ***5475.1*** *p210*
Balhachet, Thomas; Boston, 1707 ***9228.50*** *p88*
Balie, Christopher 45; Michigan, 1880 ***4491.30*** *p2*
Balik, . . .; Pennsylvania, 1750-1799 ***2853.20*** *p17*
Balin, Josef; St. Louis, 1887 ***2853.20*** *p28*
Balin, Xavier; Ohio, 1809-1852 ***4511.35*** *p2*
Balis, Caroline 5; Missouri, 1846 ***778.6*** *p14*
Balis, Catherine 1; Missouri, 1846 ***778.6*** *p14*
Balis, Catherine 9; Missouri, 1846 ***778.6*** *p14*
Balis, Eve 7; Missouri, 1846 ***778.6*** *p14*
Balis, George 9; Missouri, 1846 ***778.6*** *p14*
Balis, George 42; Missouri, 1846 ***778.6*** *p14*
Balis, Louis 10; Missouri, 1846 ***778.6*** *p14*
Balis, Louis 14; Missouri, 1846 ***778.6*** *p14*
Balis, Louis 45; Missouri, 1846 ***778.6*** *p14*
Balis, Louise 3; Missouri, 1846 ***778.6*** *p14*
Balis, Madeleine 8; Missouri, 1846 ***778.6*** *p14*
Balis, Madeleine 17; Missouri, 1846 ***778.6*** *p14*
Balis, Madeleine 36; Missouri, 1846 ***778.6*** *p14*
Balis, Sophie 7; Missouri, 1846 ***778.6*** *p14*
Balis, Sophie 37; Missouri, 1846 ***778.6*** *p14*
Baliset, John 40; Texas, 1843 ***778.6*** *p14*
Balk, Barbara; New York, 1860 ***358.56*** *p148*
Balkhaus, Helene; Philadelphia, 1868 ***8513.31*** *p421*
Balkwell, Isaac 27; Ontario, 1871 ***1823.21*** *p15*
Balkwell, William 40; Ontario, 1871 ***1823.21*** *p15*
Balkwell, William 60; Ontario, 1871 ***1823.21*** *p15*
Ball, . . .; Massachusetts, n.d. ***9228.50*** *p86*
Ball, . . .; New England, n.d. ***9228.50*** *p86*
Ball, . . .; New Hampshire, n.d. ***9228.50*** *p86*
Ball, Charles; Philadelphia, 1778 ***8529.30*** *p2A*
Ball, David W. 38; Ontario, 1871 ***1823.21*** *p15*
Ball, Eliz.; Maryland, 1674-1675 ***1236.25*** *p52*
Ball, Emma W. 21; Ontario, 1871 ***1823.21*** *p15*
Ball, George; Colorado, 1876 ***1029.59*** *p6*
Ball, Henry 34; Ontario, 1871 ***1823.21*** *p15*
Ball, Henry 19; Quebec, 1870 ***8364.32*** *p22*
Ball, Jacob; Ontario, 1787 ***1276.15*** *p230*
With 2 children & 3 relatives
Ball, John 48; Ontario, 1871 ***1823.21*** *p15*
Ball, John 49; Ontario, 1871 ***1823.21*** *p15*
Ball, John 53; Ontario, 1871 ***1823.17*** *p6*
Ball, John; Watertown, MA, n.d. ***9228.50*** *p86*
Ball, Mary 30; Ontario, 1871 ***1823.21*** *p15*
Ball, Melvell 29; Ontario, 1871 ***1823.17*** *p6*
Ball, Michael; Washington, 1888 ***2770.40*** *p25*
Ball, Peter; Ontario, 1787 ***1276.15*** *p230*
With 3 relatives
Ball, Richard 45; Ontario, 1871 ***1823.17*** *p6*
Ball, Stearns 50; Ontario, 1871 ***1823.21*** *p15*
Ball, Thomas 40; Ontario, 1871 ***1823.21*** *p15*
Ball, Thomas 49; Ontario, 1871 ***1823.17*** *p6*
Ball, William H. 33; Ontario, 1871 ***1823.21*** *p15*
Ballah, Moses 40; Ontario, 1871 ***1823.21*** *p15*
Ballaine, . . .; America, n.d. ***9228.50*** *p143*
Ballam, Miss; Nova Scotia, n.d. ***9228.50*** *p92*
With 2 sisters
Ballam, Thomas; Nova Scotia, 1877 ***9228.50*** *p92*
Ballantine, George 64; Ontario, 1871 ***1823.21*** *p15*
Ballast, John; Massachusetts, 1774-1780 ***9228.50*** *p88*
Ballat, Maria Katharina Christine; America, 1857 ***5475.1*** *p518*
Ballay, Francis; Ohio, 1840-1897 ***8365.35*** *p15*
Balle, Soren P.; Iowa, 1903 ***1211.15*** *p9*
Ballein, John; Illinois, 1860 ***6079.1*** *p1*
Balleine, . . .; America, n.d. ***9228.50*** *p143*
Balleine, . . .; Canada, n.d. ***9228.50*** *p93*
Balleine, Anne Vauquellin *SEE* Balleine, James
Balleine, Edward; Iowa, 1854 ***9228.50*** *p331*
Balleine, Edward; San Francisco, 1829-1853 ***9228.50*** *p92*
Balleine, Frank; America, 1840-1849 ***9228.50*** *p92*
Balleine, James; New Jersey, 1655 ***9228.50*** *p647*
*Wife:*Anne Vauquellin
*Daughter:*Mary
Balleine, John; Salem, MA, 1650-1699 ***9228.50*** *p93*
Balleine, Mary *SEE* Balleine, James
Balleine, Peter; Pennsylvania, 1745-1800 ***9228.50*** *p127*
Ballem, Priscilla Jane; Maine, 1906 ***9228.50*** *p304*
Baller, Barbara 43; America, 1863 ***5475.1*** *p283*
Baller, Elisabeth; America, 1864 ***5475.1*** *p264*
Baller, Mathias; America, 1879 ***5475.1*** *p265*
Ballesen, Peter; Valdivia, Chile, 1851 ***1192.4*** *p51*
With wife & child
Balley, Eleaner; Ohio, 1809-1852 ***4511.35*** *p2*
Balley, Francis; Ohio, 1809-1852 ***4511.35*** *p2*
Balli, . . .; West Virginia, 1865-1879 ***1132.30*** *p150*
Ballie, Catherine; Quebec, 1667 ***4514.3*** *p273*
Ballie, Samuel 46; Ontario, 1871 ***1823.17*** *p6*
Balliet, Johanna 20; Portland, ME, 1910 ***970.38*** *p76*
Ballimann, Charles F.; Louisiana, 1841-1844 ***4981.45*** *p210*

Ballin, James; New Jersey, 1666 ***9228.50*** *p124*
Ballintine, Sam L. 40; Ontario, 1871 ***1823.17*** *p7*
Ballmert, Adam 19 *SEE* Ballmert, Jakob
Ballmert, Adam; Argentina, 1855 ***2526.43*** *p207*
With family of 9
Ballmert, Jakob 59; America, 1881 ***2526.43*** *p207*
*Wife:*Karoline 42
*Son:*Adam 19
Ballmert, Jakob; Argentina, 1855 ***2526.43*** *p207*
With family of 2
Ballmert, Johannes 25; America, 1854 ***2526.43*** *p133*
Ballmert, Karoline 42 *SEE* Ballmert, Jakob
Balloffet, Jean Marie; Illinois, 1852 ***6079.1*** *p1*
Ballon, Francois; Quebec, 1657 ***9221.17*** *p351*
Ballon, T. B. 19; New Orleans, 1843 ***778.6*** *p14*
Ballon, Tomas; Iowa, 1910 ***2853.20*** *p240*
Balls, Edmund 17; Quebec, 1870 ***8364.32*** *p22*
Balls, Gater 37; Ontario, 1871 ***1823.17*** *p7*
Balls, William 29; Ontario, 1871 ***1823.17*** *p7*
Ballum, . . .; Prince Edward Island, n.d. ***9228.50*** *p92*
Balme, Marc Jean 22; America, 1848 ***778.6*** *p14*
Balmer, George; Toronto, 1844 ***2910.35*** *p113*
Balmer, Henry 71; Ontario, 1871 ***1823.21*** *p15*
Balmer, Richard; Texas, 1851 ***3435.45*** *p35*
Balmer, Robert 33; Ontario, 1871 ***1823.21*** *p15*
Balmer, Thomas 60; Ontario, 1871 ***1823.21*** *p15*
Balmer, Ulrich; Ohio, 1809-1852 ***4511.35*** *p2*
Balmer, Ulrick; Ohio, 1809-1852 ***4511.35*** *p2*
Balmert, Katharina 29; Pennsylvania, 1867 ***2526.43*** *p137*
Balmot, Alexander; Ohio, 1809-1852 ***4511.35*** *p2*
Balon, John; Detroit, 1923 ***6214.5*** *p67*
Balon, Victoria; Detroit, 1929-1930 ***6214.5*** *p67*
Balonier, Anna Marie; America, 1853 ***2526.42*** *p141*
Balonier, Nanna; America, 1853 ***2526.42*** *p138*
Balonier, Peter Bonifatius; Dayton, OH, 1882 ***2526.42*** *p139*
Balot, Samuel; Ohio, 1809-1852 ***4511.35*** *p2*
Balster, John C. 38; Ontario, 1871 ***1823.17*** *p7*
Balt, Staneli William; Baltimore, 1903 ***1766.20*** *p36*
Baltasard, Mr. 29; America, 1843 ***778.6*** *p14*
Baltasard, Charles 4; America, 1843 ***778.6*** *p14*
Baltasard, Marie 29; America, 1843 ***778.6*** *p14*
Baltes, Anna 11 *SEE* Baltes, Johann
Baltes, Elisabeth 3 *SEE* Baltes, Johann
Baltes, Elisabeth 57; America, 1857 ***5475.1*** *p548*
Baltes, Georg; America, 1837 ***5475.1*** *p67*
Baltes, Johann; America, 1836 ***5475.1*** *p545*
With wife
*Son:*Nikolaus
*Son:*Valentin
*Daughter:*Elisabeth
*Daughter:*Margarethe
*Son:*Johann
*Daughter:*Anna
Baltes, Johann 7 *SEE* Baltes, Johann
Baltes, Johann 26; America, 1868 ***5475.1*** *p247*
Baltes, Margarethe 6 *SEE* Baltes, Johann
Baltes, Nikolaus 9 *SEE* Baltes, Johann
Baltes, Rudolf; New York, 1898 ***5475.1*** *p40*
Baltes, Valentin 5 *SEE* Baltes, Johann
Balthasar, Caspar Melchior; America, 1889 ***5475.1*** *p424*
Baltimore, Lord; Maryland, 1662 ***9228.50*** *p283*
Baltimore, Cecilius Calvert; Maryland, 1632 ***2853.20*** *p124*
*Brother:*Philip
Baltimore, Philip *SEE* Baltimore, Cecilius Calvert
Baltiner, Andre 40; Louisiana, 1848 ***778.6*** *p14*
Baltiner, Anne Marie 36; Louisiana, 1848 ***778.6*** *p14*
Baltiner, Elias 5; Louisiana, 1848 ***778.6*** *p14*
Baltiner, Jacob 40; Louisiana, 1848 ***778.6*** *p15*
Baltrias, Kanners 22; New York, NY, 1878 ***9253.2*** *p44*
Baltruhonis, Magdalena 28; New York, NY, 1894 ***6512.1*** *p183*
Baltruhonis, Petronela 3; New York, NY, 1894 ***6512.1*** *p183*
Baltruhonis, Wencas 1; New York, NY, 1894 ***6512.1*** *p183*
Baltsly, Nicholas; Ohio, 1809-1852 ***4511.35*** *p2*
Baltus, Anna Meilchen *SEE* Baltus, Michel
Baltus, Barbara *SEE* Baltus, Michel
Baltus, Maria *SEE* Baltus, Michel
Baltus, Michel; America, 1883 ***5475.1*** *p164*
*Wife:*Anna Meilchen
*Daughter:*Barbara
*Daughter:*Maria
Baltz, Pierre 18; America, 1842 ***778.6*** *p15*
Baltzby, Nicholas; Ohio, 1809-1852 ***4511.35*** *p2*
Baltzer, Andreas; America, 1881 ***5475.1*** *p227*
*Wife:*Elisabeth Schulz
*Daughter:*Bertha
*Daughter:*Susanna
*Daughter:*Barbara
*Son:*Peter

Baltzer, Barbara *SEE* Baltzer, Andreas
Baltzer, Bertha *SEE* Baltzer, Andreas
Baltzer, Elisabeth Schulz *SEE* Baltzer, Andreas
Baltzer, Julius; Canada, 1887 ***5475.1*** *p131*
Baltzer, Peter *SEE* Baltzer, Andreas
Baltzer, Susanna *SEE* Baltzer, Andreas
Balza, A.; New York, NY, 1880 ***1494.20*** *p13*
Balza, Auguste; Chicago, 1857 ***1494.20*** *p11*
Balza, Eugene; Detroit, 1869 ***1494.20*** *p13*
Balzat, Alexandre; Wisconsin, 1857 ***1495.20*** *p46*
*Wife:*Catherine Joseph Prevot
*Child:*Marie Therese
*Child:*Eugene
*Child:*Auguste
*Child:*Aurelie
*Child:*Leopold
Balzat, Antoine; Wisconsin, 1880 ***1495.20*** *p46*
*Wife:*Pauline Louis
*Child:*Marie
*Child:*Francoise
*Child:*Ernest Joseph
*Child:*Henriette
Balzat, Auguste *SEE* Balzat, Alexandre
Balzat, Aurelie *SEE* Balzat, Alexandre
Balzat, Catherine Joseph Prevot *SEE* Balzat, Alexandre
Balzat, Ernest Joseph *SEE* Balzat, Antoine
Balzat, Eugene *SEE* Balzat, Alexandre
Balzat, Francoise *SEE* Balzat, Antoine
Balzat, Henriette *SEE* Balzat, Antoine
Balzat, Leopold *SEE* Balzat, Alexandre
Balzat, Marie *SEE* Balzat, Antoine
Balzat, Marie Therese *SEE* Balzat, Alexandre
Balzat, Pauline Louis *SEE* Balzat, Antoine
Balzer, Adam; America, 1843 ***5475.1*** *p428*
With wife
With daughter
With 2 sons
Balzer, Magdalena 25; America, 1867 ***5475.1*** *p160*
Balzer, Nik.; America, 1840 ***5475.1*** *p169*
Balzle, Christian; Ohio, 1809-1852 ***4511.35*** *p2*
Balzly, Christian; Ohio, 1809-1852 ***4511.35*** *p2*
Bamberg, Barbara; America, 1867 ***7919.3*** *p533*
*Grandchild:*Gottlieb
*Grandchild:*Emilie
Bamberg, Emilie *SEE* Bamberg, Barbara
Bamberg, Gottlieb *SEE* Bamberg, Barbara
Bamberger, Mr. 33; America, 1843 ***778.6*** *p15*
Bamberger, Xavier; Ohio, 1809-1852 ***4511.35*** *p2*
Bambreck, Thom; New Orleans, 1851 ***7242.30*** *p134*
Bambridge, Joseph 40; Ontario, 1871 ***1823.21*** *p15*
Bambridge, M. T. 36; Ontario, 1871 ***1823.17*** *p7*
Bambridge, Robert 37; Ontario, 1871 ***1823.17*** *p7*
Bamerlin, Ernst F.; Ohio, 1809-1852 ***4511.35*** *p2*
Bamfield, James; Philadelphia, 1778 ***8529.30*** *p2A*
Bamont, Marie-Anne; Quebec, 1673 ***4514.3*** *p273*
Bampon, C. 40; Port uncertain, 1843 ***778.6*** *p15*
Bamrick, Fanny 2; Ontario, 1871 ***1823.21*** *p15*
Bamrick, William 3; Ontario, 1871 ***1823.21*** *p15*
Bamstier, J. 29; America, 1846 ***778.6*** *p15*
Bamstier, M. Frederic 22; America, 1846 ***778.6*** *p15*
Bamstier, Rosin 29; America, 1846 ***778.6*** *p15*
Ban, Jean-Baptiste 29; New Orleans, 1848 ***778.6*** *p15*
Banaghan, Teddy 70; Ontario, 1871 ***1823.17*** *p7*
Banasiak, John; Detroit, 1929-1930 ***6214.5*** *p70*
Bancherons, Henry; Quebec, 1646 ***9221.17*** *p161*
Bancroft, C. A.; California, 1868 ***1131.61*** *p89*
Bandeen, Jean Yule *SEE* Bandeen, John
Bandeen, John; Ohio, 1843-1876 ***5024.1*** *p139*
*Wife:*Jean Yule
Bandeen, Rachel; Ohio, 1843 ***5024.1*** *p139*
Bandel, George; Louisiana, 1836-1840 ***4981.45*** *p212*
Bandel, George; Louisiana, 1836-1841 ***4981.45*** *p208*
Bandel, Jacob; Louisiana, 1836-1841 ***4981.45*** *p208*
Bander, Alexander 48; New York, NY, 1885 ***1883.7*** *p46*
Bander, Alisie 5; New York, NY, 1885 ***1883.7*** *p46*
Bander, Auguste 14; New York, NY, 1885 ***1883.7*** *p46*
Bander, Julius 19; New York, NY, 1885 ***1883.7*** *p46*
Bander, Justine 48; New York, NY, 1885 ***1883.7*** *p46*
Bander, Mechthild; Venezuela, 1843 ***3899.5*** *p543*
Bander, Pauline 7; New York, NY, 1885 ***1883.7*** *p46*
Bandhauer, Vaclav; St. Louis, 1852 ***2853.20*** *p21*
Bands, Mary 35; North Carolina, 1774 ***1422.10*** *p55*
Bang, Niels C.; Iowa, 1896 ***1211.15*** *p9*
Bang, Walter; Iowa, 1916 ***1211.15*** *p9*
Bangert, Francis; North Carolina, 1840 ***1088.45*** *p1*
Banghart, Sarah 79; Ontario, 1871 ***1823.21*** *p15*
Bangle, Mary 86; Ontario, 1871 ***1823.21*** *p15*
Bangmier, J. 19; New Orleans, 1834 ***1002.51*** *p112*
Banham, John 40; Ontario, 1871 ***1823.21*** *p15*
Banik, Christian; Dakota, 1886 ***554.30*** *p25*
*Wife:*Mariane Leitner
*Child:*Lisbeth
*Child:*Maria
Banik, Lisbeth *SEE* Banik, Christian
Banik, Maria *SEE* Banik, Christian
Banik, Mariane Leitner *SEE* Banik, Christian
Banik, Wilhelmine; Dakota, 1888 ***554.30*** *p26*
Banin, John; Toronto, 1844 ***2910.35*** *p115*
Banister, James 54; Ontario, 1871 ***1823.17*** *p7*
Banister, John 59; Ontario, 1871 ***1823.17*** *p7*
Bankerel, Emelie 37; New Orleans, 1848 ***778.6*** *p15*
Banko, Michael; Chicago, 1930 ***121.35*** *p100*
Banks, David; North Carolina, 1844 ***1088.45*** *p1*
Banks, David; Ohio, 1809-1852 ***4511.35*** *p2*
Banks, George 50; Ontario, 1871 ***1823.21*** *p15*
Banks, Hannah; America, 1722 ***1220.12*** *p635*
Banks, Henry 36; Ontario, 1871 ***1823.21*** *p15*
Banks, James; North Carolina, 1836 ***1088.45*** *p1*
Banks, John; North Carolina, 1834 ***1088.45*** *p1*
Banks, John 24; Ontario, 1871 ***1823.21*** *p15*
Banks, John 19; Quebec, 1870 ***8364.32*** *p22*
Banks, Thomas; Ohio, 1809-1852 ***4511.35*** *p2*
Banks, Thomas 42; Ontario, 1871 ***1823.21*** *p15*
Banks, Thomas; Philadelphia, 1777 ***8529.30*** *p7A*
Banks, William 26; Ontario, 1871 ***1823.21*** *p15*
Bannard, Jean 31; Port uncertain, 1843 ***778.6*** *p15*
Bannasek, Tomas; Detroit, 1930 ***1640.60*** *p81*
Bannatine, Hector 38; Ontario, 1871 ***1823.21*** *p15*
Banner, John; Marston's Wharf, 1782 ***8529.30*** *p9*
Bannholzer, Matthias; Valdivia, Chile, 1850 ***1192.4*** *p50*
Bannister, Benjamin; Washington, 1883 ***2770.40*** *p136*
Bannister, Joseph; Massachusetts, 1788-1816 ***9228.50*** *p328*
Bannon, John 45; Ontario, 1871 ***1823.17*** *p7*
Bannon, William 55; Ontario, 1871 ***1823.21*** *p16*
Banse, Francoise; Quebec, 1667 ***4514.3*** *p274*
Banser, Heinrich Daniel; America, 1856 ***7420.1*** *p144*
Banser, J. G.; Louisiana, 1836-1840 ***4981.45*** *p212*
Banson, Peter; Jamestown, VA, 1633 ***1658.20*** *p211*
Bansser, Carl 19; America, 1847 ***778.6*** *p15*
Bansser, Elizabeth 22; America, 1847 ***778.6*** *p15*
Bansser, Georg 12; America, 1847 ***778.6*** *p15*
Bansser, Georg 52; America, 1847 ***778.6*** *p15*
Bansser, Joseph 5; America, 1847 ***778.6*** *p15*
Bansser, Madaline 10; America, 1847 ***778.6*** *p15*
Bansser, Maria 8; America, 1847 ***778.6*** *p15*
Bansser, Rosina 48; America, 1847 ***778.6*** *p15*
Bante, Dietrich Heinrich Wilhelm; America, 1865 ***7420.1*** *p228*
With family
Bantte, Catharine F.; Philadelphia, 1855 ***8513.31*** *p305*
Banwarth, Fidelis; Wisconsin, 1872-1877 ***2853.20*** *p346*
Banweg, Nikolaus; America, 1846 ***5475.1*** *p234*
Bany, Georg Adolf; America, 1884 ***2526.42*** *p168*
Banzhof, Michael; Valdivia, Chile, 1852 ***1192.4*** *p52*
Baptist, John 75; New Orleans, 1842 ***778.6*** *p15*
Baptiste, Jean 16; New Orleans, 1848 ***778.6*** *p15*
Baptiste, P. T.; Louisiana, 1874-1875 ***4981.45*** *p297*
Baptiste, Pierre 20; Port uncertain, 1846 ***778.6*** *p15*
Baque, Dominique 20; New Orleans, 1845 ***778.6*** *p15*
Baquis, J. A. 34; New Orleans, 1845 ***778.6*** *p15*
Bar, Anna 11; New York, NY, 1885 ***1883.7*** *p46*
Bar, Christn. 7; New York, NY, 1885 ***1883.7*** *p46*
Bar, John 28; South Carolina, 1812 ***3476.30*** *p11*
Bar, Johs. 23; New York, NY, 1885 ***1883.7*** *p46*
Bar, Reinhold 5; New York, NY, 1885 ***1883.7*** *p46*
Bar, Susanne 14; New York, NY, 1885 ***1883.7*** *p46*
Barachon, Francis 25; America, 1848 ***778.6*** *p15*
Baranger, Urbain; Quebec, 1661 ***9221.17*** *p446*
Baranowska, Anne; Wisconsin, 1890 ***6795.8*** *p54*
Baranowski, Anne; Wisconsin, 1890 ***6795.8*** *p54*
Baranowski, Anthony; Detroit, 1930 ***1640.60*** *p81*
Baranowski, Bronislawa; Wisconsin, 1890 ***6795.8*** *p54*
Baranowski, Cornel; Detroit, 1929-1930 ***6214.5*** *p71*
Baranowski, Joseph; Wisconsin, 1881 ***6795.8*** *p54*
Barasse, Daunay 30; America, 1843 ***778.6*** *p15*
Barate, Joseph; Illinois, 1856 ***6079.1*** *p1*
Baratgin, Dominique 22; Port uncertain, 1846 ***778.6*** *p15*
Baratgin, Louis 25; Port uncertain, 1843 ***778.6*** *p15*
Baratgin, Pierre 24; Port uncertain, 1843 ***778.6*** *p15*
Baraton, Michel 26; America, 1848 ***778.6*** *p15*
Baraty, Francois 20; New Orleans, 1845 ***778.6*** *p15*
Barba, Jno.; Louisiana, 1874 ***4981.45*** *p295*
Barbant, Marie; Quebec, 1666 ***4514.3*** *p274*
Barbaret, Adelheit 33; New Orleans, 1847 ***778.6*** *p15*
Barbaret, Francois 3; New Orleans, 1847 ***778.6*** *p15*
Barbaret, Jean Philippe 32; New Orleans, 1847 ***778.6*** *p16*
Barbaret, Jules 1; New Orleans, 1847 ***778.6*** *p16*
Barbat, Mr. 25; New Orleans, 1840 ***778.6*** *p16*
Barbat, J. 16; America, 1841 ***778.6*** *p16*
Barbe, J. Pierre 22; Mississippi, 1845 ***778.6*** *p16*
Barbe, Jean Francois; Louisiana, 1841-1844 ***4981.45*** *p210*
Barbe, Victor 22; America, 1748 ***778.6*** *p16*
Barbea, Louis 32; New Orleans, 1843 ***778.6*** *p16*
Barbeau, Andre 20; Quebec, 1661 ***9221.17*** *p446*
Barbeau, Elie; Quebec, 1651 ***9221.17*** *p237*
Barbeau, Suzanne; Quebec, 1649 ***9221.17*** *p208*
Barbencq, Jacq. 41; America, 1841 ***778.6*** *p16*
Barbenoire, August 39; America, 1843 ***778.6*** *p16*
Barber, Agnes 34; Ontario, 1871 ***1823.21*** *p16*
Barber, Alex 66; Ontario, 1871 ***1823.21*** *p16*
Barber, Andrew H. 31; Ontario, 1871 ***1823.21*** *p16*
Barber, Anna 40; Michigan, 1880 ***4491.30*** *p2*
Barber, Claud; Virginia, 1665 ***9228.50*** *p53*
Barber, Claude; New Jersey, 1665 ***9228.50*** *p93*
Barber, Edwin M. 14; Ontario, 1871 ***1823.21*** *p16*
Barber, George; Maryland, 1671-1672 ***1236.25*** *p45*
Barber, Henry 71; Michigan, 1880 ***4491.39*** *p2*
Barber, James 43; Ontario, 1871 ***1823.21*** *p16*
Barber, Jane 50; Ontario, 1871 ***1823.17*** *p7*
Barber, Margaret 56; Ontario, 1871 ***1823.21*** *p16*
Barber, Matthew 60; Ontario, 1871 ***1823.21*** *p16*
Barber, Mitchel 48; Ontario, 1871 ***1823.17*** *p7*
Barber, Robert 15; Quebec, 1870 ***8364.32*** *p22*
Barber, Robert B. 37; Ontario, 1871 ***1823.21*** *p16*
Barber, William 36; Ontario, 1871 ***1823.17*** *p7*
Barber, William 36; Ontario, 1871 ***1823.21*** *p16*
Barberack, Francois 30; Louisiana, 1848 ***778.6*** *p16*
Barberack, Marie 28; Louisiana, 1848 ***778.6*** *p16*
Barbereau, Jeanne; Quebec, 1666 ***4514.3*** *p274*
Barberie, Pietro; Colorado, 1889 ***1029.59*** *p6*
Barberot, Alexandrine 15; America, 1843 ***778.6*** *p16*
Barberot, Francois 32; America, 1843 ***778.6*** *p16*
Barberot, Francois 39; America, 1843 ***778.6*** *p16*
Barberot, Stephani 2; America, 1843 ***778.6*** *p16*
Barberot, Victor 22; America, 1847 ***778.6*** *p16*
Barberot, Virginie 18; America, 1843 ***778.6*** *p16*
Barbery, Francoise; Quebec, 1668 ***4514.3*** *p274*
Barbet, Mr. 32; America, 1846 ***778.6*** *p16*
Barbet, Francois; Quebec, 1659 ***9221.17*** *p394*
Barbet, John; Marblehead, MA, 1751 ***9228.50*** *p93*
Barbey, Emanuel; New York, 1855 ***5475.1*** *p283*
Barbian, Angela 47; Brazil, 1857 ***5475.1*** *p368*
Barbian, Anton; America, 1843 ***5475.1*** *p365*
With wife
With daughter
Barbian, Anton 24; America, 1843 ***5475.1*** *p363*
Barbian, Barbara Reuter *SEE* Barbian, Johann
Barbian, Elisabeth *SEE* Barbian, Johann
Barbian, Jakob; America, 1843 ***5475.1*** *p333*
Barbian, Jakob 30; America, 1843 ***5475.1*** *p365*
Barbian, Johann; America, 1872 ***5475.1*** *p331*
Barbian, Johann 57; America, 1843 ***5475.1*** *p363*
Barbian, Johann *SEE* Barbian, Johann
Barbian, Johann; Brazil, 1880 ***5475.1*** *p373*
*Son:*Mathias
*Daughter:*Nikolaus
*Daughter:*Elisabeth
*Wife:*Barbara Reuter
*Son:*Johann
*Son:*Peter
*Daughter:*Magdalena
Barbian, Magdalena *SEE* Barbian, Johann
Barbian, Margarethe; Brazil, 1881 ***5475.1*** *p373*
Barbian, Margarethe 19; Brazil, 1857 ***5475.1*** *p368*
Barbian, Mathias 59; America, 1843 ***5475.1*** *p366*
Barbian, Mathias *SEE* Barbian, Johann
Barbian, Nikolaus *SEE* Barbian, Johann
Barbian, Peter *SEE* Barbian, Johann
Barbian, Stephan; Brazil, 1880 ***5475.1*** *p373*
Barbiaux, August Joseph *SEE* Barbiaux, Jean Francois
Barbiaux, Charles Antoine *SEE* Barbiaux, Jean Francois
Barbiaux, Jean Francois; Wisconsin, 1856 ***1495.20*** *p46*
*Wife:*Marie Therese Vandermeuse
*Son:*August Joseph
*Son:*Charles Antoine
Barbiaux, Marie Therese Vandermeuse *SEE* Barbiaux, Jean Francois
Barbier, Alphonse 36; New Orleans, 1848 ***778.6*** *p16*
Barbier, Amice; America, 1800-1901 ***9228.50*** *p94*
*Wife:*Mary Anne Collas
Barbier, Amice; America, 1814-1900 ***9228.50*** *p394*
*Wife:*Mary Anne Le Rossignol
Barbier, Amice; America, n.d. ***9228.50*** *p94*
*Wife:*Mary Ann Le Rossignol
Barbier, Claud; Virginia, 1665 ***9228.50*** *p53*
Barbier, Ferdinand Gaspard; Illinois, 1852 ***6079.1*** *p1*
Barbier, Gilbert 20; Montreal, 1642 ***9221.17*** *p122*
Barbier, Jean Francois; Illinois, 1852 ***6079.1*** *p1*
Barbier, Jeanne 35; Missouri, 1845 ***778.6*** *p16*
Barbier, Jeanne; Quebec, 1670 ***4514.3*** *p274*
Barbier, Julienne; Wisconsin, 1855 ***1495.20*** *p8*
Barbier, Mary 25; Ohio, 1880 ***4879.40*** *p260*
Barbier, Mary Ann Le Rossignol *SEE* Barbier, Amice
Barbier, Mary Anne Collas *SEE* Barbier, Amice
Barbier, Mary Anne Le Rossignol *SEE* Barbier, Amice
Barbot, Leonard; Montreal, 1642 ***9221.17*** *p124*

Barbour, Claud; Virginia, 1665 ***9228.50*** *p53*
Barbour, Claude; New Jersey, 1665 ***9228.50*** *p93*
Barbousson, Valeric de; Montreal, 1653 ***9221.17*** *p281*
Barbridge, R. 16; Quebec, 1870 ***8364.32*** *p22*
Barc, Peter; Detroit, 1930 ***1640.60*** *p81*
Barcal, Frantisek *SEE* Barcal, Matej
Barcal, Matej; Chicago, 1854 ***2853.20*** *p388*
*Son:*Frantisek
Barchard, Judas 31; America, 1847 ***778.6*** *p16*
Barclay, . . .; Ontario, 1871 ***1823.21*** *p16*
Barclay, Alexander 48; Ontario, 1871 ***1823.21*** *p16*
Barclay, George 70; Ontario, 1871 ***1823.21*** *p16*
Barclay, John; Illinois, 1860 ***6079.1*** *p1*
Barclay, John 59; Ontario, 1871 ***1823.21*** *p16*
Barclay, Patrick; Ontario, 1871 ***1823.17*** *p7*
Barclay, Terry 13; Quebec, 1870 ***8364.32*** *p22*
Barclay, William 45; Ontario, 1871 ***1823.17*** *p7*
Barcley, Isabella 60; Ontario, 1871 ***1823.17*** *p7*
Bard, Barbara *SEE* Bard, Jakob
Bard, Barbara 27; Brazil, 1872 ***5475.1*** *p443*
Bard, Daniel 59; Ontario, 1871 ***1823.21*** *p16*
Bard, Jakob; Brazil, 1846 ***5475.1*** *p437*
*Brother:*Johann
*Sister:*Barbara
Bard, Johann *SEE* Bard, Jakob
Bard, Katharina; Brazil, 1846 ***5475.1*** *p438*
Bardel, Catherina 19; New Orleans, 1848 ***778.6*** *p16*
Bardel, Dominique 18; New Orleans, 1848 ***778.6*** *p16*
Bardel, Jacob 18; America, 1846 ***778.6*** *p16*
Bardet, Anne; Quebec, 1665 ***4514.3*** *p274*
Bardon, Claud; Virginia, 1700 ***9230.15*** *p81*
With wife
Bardon, Louis; Quebec, 1642 ***9221.17*** *p111*
Bardonner, Adam; America, 1836 ***2526.43*** *p159*
*Brother:*Jakob
Bardonner, Adam 25; America, 1836 ***2526.43*** *p137*
With wife 19
Bardonner, Heinrich; America, 1831 ***2526.43*** *p120*
With wife & child
Bardonner, Jakob *SEE* Bardonner, Adam
Bardonner, Jakob 36; America, 1836 ***2526.43*** *p159*
With wife 30
With child 11
With child 7
With child 3
With child 9
Bardonner, Nikolaus; America, 1831 ***2526.43*** *p120*
Bardorf, Gottlieb Eduard; America, 1867 ***7919.3*** *p529*
With wife & child
Bardou, Marie; Quebec, 1669 ***4514.3*** *p274*
Bardout, Edmond 31; America, 1847 ***778.6*** *p16*
Bardout, Jules 23; America, 1847 ***778.6*** *p16*
Bardoux, Julien 22; America, 1846 ***778.6*** *p16*
Bardsley, Henry 35; Indiana, 1879-1888 ***9076.20*** *p72*
Bardsley, Levi 32; Indiana, 1862-1870 ***9076.20*** *p67*
Bardwell, Daniel 37; Ontario, 1871 ***1823.17*** *p7*
Bardwell, Harriet 68; Michigan, 1880 ***4491.30*** *p2*
Bare, Jean 39; New Orleans, 1846 ***778.6*** *p16*
Barefoot, Walter F.; New York, 1921-1974 ***9228.50*** *p120*
Bareiss, Gottlieb; America, 1885 ***179.55*** *p19*
Bareiss, Johannes; America, 1885 ***179.55*** *p19*
Barencon, Mr. 38; America, 1841 ***778.6*** *p16*
Bares, Ambroisine 28; America, 1842 ***778.6*** *p16*
Barese, Dominio; Louisiana, 1874 ***4981.45*** *p131*
Bareth, Catharina 8; New York, NY, 1874 ***6954.7*** *p38*
Bareth, Christina 6 months; New York, NY, 1874 ***6954.7*** *p38*
Bareth, Conrad 34; New York, NY, 1874 ***6954.7*** *p38*
Bareth, Margaretha 32; New York, NY, 1874 ***6954.7*** *p38*
Bareth, Sophia 10; New York, NY, 1874 ***6954.7*** *p38*
Barette, Antoinette; Wisconsin, 1854-1858 ***1495.20*** *p66*
Barette, Barbe; Wisconsin, 1854-1858 ***1495.20*** *p66*
With son
Barette, Guillaume 27; Quebec, 1660 ***9221.17*** *p431*
Barette, Jean 16; Quebec, 1646 ***9221.17*** *p161*
Barette, Josephine; Wisconsin, 1854-1858 ***1495.20*** *p66*
Barette, Marie Barbe; Wisconsin, 1854-1858 ***1495.20*** *p66*
Barford, George 61; Ontario, 1871 ***1823.21*** *p16*
Barford, Rebecca 61; Ontario, 1871 ***1823.21*** *p16*
Barg, Ethel; Miami, 1935 ***4984.12*** *p39*
Barg, Etta; Miami, 1935 ***4984.12*** *p39*
Bargen, J. H. von; Valdivia, Chile, 1852 ***1192.4*** *p52*
Barger, Claes; Colorado, 1882 ***1029.59*** *p6*
Barger, Claus; Colorado, 1887 ***1029.59*** *p6*
Barger, Per Otto; Colorado, 1882 ***1029.59*** *p6*
Barger, Per Otto; Colorado, 1887 ***1029.59*** *p6*
Barglof, Gustaf; Iowa, 1876 ***1211.15*** *p9*
Bargmann, J. G. W.; Chile, 1852 ***1192.4*** *p51*
Bargot, Barbe 41; America, 1847 ***778.6*** *p16*
Bargot, Francois 16; America, 1847 ***778.6*** *p16*
Bargot, Jeanne 10; America, 1847 ***778.6*** *p17*
Bargot, Nicolas 50; America, 1847 ***778.6*** *p17*
Bargsted, Christiana; Wisconsin, 1889 ***6795.8*** *p105*
Barham, Thomas 34; Ontario, 1871 ***1823.21*** *p16*
Barholzer, Magnus; New Castle, DE, 1817-1818 ***90.20*** *p150*
Barhr, Florent 70; America, 1840 ***778.6*** *p17*
Baril, Marie; Quebec, 1670 ***4514.3*** *p275*
Barillet, Anne; Quebec, 1671 ***4514.3*** *p275*
Barillet, Jean; Quebec, 1644 ***9221.17*** *p139*
Barincon, Mr. 26; New Orleans, 1840 ***778.6*** *p17*
Barincou, Mr. 34; Port uncertain, 1844 ***778.6*** *p17*
Barincou, B. 30; New Orleans, 1843 ***778.6*** *p17*
Barincou, B. 35; New Orleans, 1847 ***778.6*** *p17*
Barington, Fra; Jamestown, VA, 1633 ***1658.20*** *p211*
Baris, Mrs. Alc. 35; America, 1840 ***778.6*** *p17*
Bark, John; Ohio, 1844 ***2763.1*** *p7*
Bark, Peter 48; Ontario, 1871 ***1823.21*** *p16*
Barker, Charles 25; Ontario, 1871 ***1823.21*** *p16*
Barker, Henry 60; Michigan, 1880 ***4491.39*** *p2*
Barker, Henry; Washington, 1883 ***2770.40*** *p136*
Barker, John 65; Michigan, 1880 ***4491.39*** *p2*
Barker, Jonathan; New York, 1782 ***8529.30*** *p9*
Barker, Joseph 16; America, 1847 ***778.6*** *p17*
Barker, Marie 40; America, 1847 ***778.6*** *p17*
Barker, Marvyn Albert; Montana, 1915 ***1029.59*** *p6*
Barker, Matthew 58; Ontario, 1871 ***1823.17*** *p7*
Barker, Nicolas 46; America, 1847 ***778.6*** *p17*
Barker, Samuel 34; Ontario, 1871 ***1823.17*** *p7*
Barker, William; Havana, 1782 ***8529.30*** *p9A*
Barker, William; New York, 1778 ***8529.30*** *p6*
Barker, William 28; Ontario, 1871 ***1823.17*** *p7*
Barker, William 40; Ontario, 1871 ***1823.21*** *p16*
Barker, William 60; Ontario, 1871 ***1823.21*** *p16*
Barker, William 74; Ontario, 1871 ***1823.21*** *p16*
Barkhaus, Diedr.; Valdivia, Chile, 1852 ***1192.4*** *p52*
With wife
Barkhaus, Friedrich 16; Valdivia, Chile, 1852 ***1192.4*** *p52*
Barkhausen, Heinrich; America, 1863 ***7420.1*** *p217*
With family
Barkhold, Falden; Ohio, 1809-1852 ***4511.35*** *p2*
Barkley, H. G.; Louisiana, 1836-1840 ***4981.45*** *p212*
Barkow, Hermann Carl Julius; Wisconsin, 1884 ***6795.8*** *p89*
Barkowski, Johann Julius; Wisconsin, 1892 ***6795.8*** *p67*
Barks, James 39; Ontario, 1871 ***1823.17*** *p7*
Barlee, Frederick; Ohio, 1809-1852 ***4511.35*** *p2*
Barley, John 52; Ontario, 1871 ***1823.21*** *p16*
Barlow, Henry 18; Quebec, 1870 ***8364.32*** *p22*
Barlow, Robert 51; Michigan, 1880 ***4491.33*** *p2*
Barmann, Alois 24; New Orleans, 1848 ***778.6*** *p17*
Barmann, Anna Keller *SEE* Barmann, Martin
Barmann, Martin 29; America, 1897 ***5475.1*** *p25*
*Wife:*Anna Keller
Barmite, George 60; Ontario, 1871 ***1823.21*** *p16*
Barn, William; North Carolina, 1710 ***3629.40*** *p3*
Barna, Misko 40; New York, NY, 1894 ***6512.1*** *p232*
Barnabee, Charles; Washington, 1879 ***2770.40*** *p134*
Barnard, Edith Anne 29; Quebec, 1910 ***2897.7*** *p8*
Barnard, Henry 28; Quebec, 1910 ***2897.7*** *p8*
Barnard, John B. 48; Ontario, 1871 ***1823.21*** *p16*
Barnard, Norman 70; Ontario, 1871 ***1823.21*** *p16*
Barnard, Peter C. 50; Ontario, 1871 ***1823.21*** *p16*
Barnard, Solomon 22; America, 1842 ***778.6*** *p17*
Barnard, William 33; New York, NY, 1825 ***6178.50*** *p77*
Barnawell, Keeran 21; Indiana, 1856-1860 ***9076.20*** *p66*
Barnbeck, Carl August Albrecht; America, 1890 ***7420.1*** *p360*
Barnes, Charles M. 57; Ontario, 1871 ***1823.17*** *p7*
Barnes, Danll.; Maryland, 1672 ***1236.25*** *p47*
Barnes, Edward 34; Ontario, 1871 ***1823.21*** *p16*
Barnes, Edward 35; Ontario, 1871 ***1823.17*** *p7*
Barnes, Emma 54; Michigan, 1880 ***4491.33*** *p2*
Barnes, George 27; Ontario, 1871 ***1823.17*** *p7*
Barnes, George 14; Quebec, 1870 ***8364.32*** *p22*
Barnes, Hen; Virginia, 1652 ***6254.4*** *p243*
Barnes, Henry 35; Ontario, 1871 ***1823.21*** *p16*
Barnes, J.; Louisiana, 1874 ***4981.45*** *p295*
Barnes, John 28; Ontario, 1871 ***1823.21*** *p16*
Barnes, Lily 8; Michigan, 1880 ***4491.33*** *p2*
Barnes, Mary 50; Ontario, 1871 ***1823.21*** *p16*
Barnes, Oliver 63; Ontario, 1871 ***1823.21*** *p17*
Barnes, Robert; Illinois, 1834-1900 ***6020.5*** *p131*
Barnes, Robert 55; Michigan, 1880 ***4491.33*** *p2*
Barnes, Samuel 61; Ontario, 1871 ***1823.17*** *p7*
Barnes, Thomas; Maryland, 1674-1675 ***1236.25*** *p52*
Barnes, Thomas 69; Ontario, 1871 ***1823.21*** *p17*
Barnes, William 63; Ontario, 1871 ***1823.21*** *p17*
Barnet, Anastasia; St. Johns, N.F., 1825 ***1053.15*** *p6*
Barnet, Thomas; St. Johns, N.F., 1825 ***1053.15*** *p6*
Barnett, Anne 72; America, 1843 ***778.6*** *p17*
Barnett, Edwin 36; Michigan, 1880 ***4491.30*** *p2*
Barnett, Ferdinand; Wisconsin, 1873 ***6795.8*** *p89*
Barnett, Henry 32; Ontario, 1871 ***1823.17*** *p7*
Barnett, Jacob; New York, NY, 1847 ***7710.1*** *p152*
Barnett, James; Ohio, 1809-1852 ***4511.35*** *p2*
Barnett, James; Ohio, 1809-1852 ***4511.35*** *p3*
Barnett, Johann Carl.; Wisconsin, 1886 ***6795.8*** *p92*
Barnett, Louis V. 68; America, 1843 ***778.6*** *p17*
Barnett, William; Philadelphia, 1778 ***8529.30*** *p2A*
Barnfather, William 43; Ontario, 1871 ***1823.21*** *p17*
Barnfield, James; Philadelphia, 1778 ***8529.30*** *p2A*
Barnhart, Michael; Ohio, 1809-1852 ***4511.35*** *p3*
Barnhart, Peter; Ohio, 1809-1852 ***4511.35*** *p3*
Barnmann, Paul; North Carolina, 1835 ***1088.45*** *p1*
Barns, Elias 44; Ontario, 1871 ***1823.17*** *p7*
Barns, John 60; Ontario, 1871 ***1823.21*** *p17*
Barns, John 71; Ontario, 1871 ***1823.21*** *p17*
Barns, Walter 45; Ontario, 1871 ***1823.17*** *p7*
Barnslan, Bernard 32; America, 1840 ***778.6*** *p17*
Barnstead, Robert P.; Philadelphia, 1842 ***7074.20*** *p132*
Barnstead, Thomas S.; Philadelphia, 1844-1849 ***7074.20*** *p132*
Barnstin, Simon 22; America, 1846 ***778.6*** *p17*
Barnum, Martha M. 20; Michigan, 1880 ***4491.30*** *p2*
Barnwell, Gilbert 36; Ontario, 1871 ***1823.21*** *p17*
Barnyard, F. 22; New Orleans, 1840 ***778.6*** *p17*
Baro, Antoinette; Quebec, 1665 ***4514.3*** *p347*
Baroldi, Isidore 48; New York, NY, 1894 ***6512.1*** *p230*
Baron, Alexander; Detroit, 1930 ***1640.60*** *p83*
Baron, Barbe; Quebec, 1667 ***4514.3*** *p275*
Baron, Emil; Washington, 1888 ***2770.40*** *p25*
Baron, Francoise; Quebec, 1664 ***4514.3*** *p289*
Baron, J. 45; Port uncertain, 1842 ***778.6*** *p17*
Baron, J. B. 22; America, 1841 ***778.6*** *p17*
Baron, Jean 25; New Orleans, 1848 ***778.6*** *p17*
Baron, John 42; Cuba, 1841 ***778.6*** *p17*
Baron, Joseph 28; America, 1841 ***778.6*** *p17*
Baron, Louis; Quebec, 1642 ***9221.17*** *p111*
Baron, Simon; Acadia, 1632 ***9221.17*** *p28*
Baronowski, Alexander; Detroit, 1930 ***1640.60*** *p83*
Barousse, B.; Louisiana, 1874-1875 ***4981.45*** *p297*
Barr, Alexander 26; Ontario, 1871 ***1823.21*** *p17*
Barr, Alexander 60; Ontario, 1871 ***1823.21*** *p17*
Barr, Allan 40; Ontario, 1871 ***1823.21*** *p17*
Barr, Andrew 14; Quebec, 1870 ***8364.32*** *p22*
Barr, David; South Carolina, 1813 ***3208.30*** *p19*
Barr, David; South Carolina, 1813 ***3208.30*** *p32*
Barr, David 52; South Carolina, 1812 ***3476.30*** *p11*
Barr, James; Washington, 1887 ***2770.40*** *p24*
Barr, Janet 71; Ontario, 1871 ***1823.21*** *p17*
Barr, John P.; Illinois, 1834-1900 ***6020.5*** *p131*
Barr, Sarah; Canada, 1774 ***3036.5*** *p41*
Barr, William 72; Ontario, 1871 ***1823.21*** *p17*
Barraco, Feidele; Louisiana, 1874-1875 ***4981.45*** *p297*
Barraguet, Jean 42; New Orleans, 1848 ***778.6*** *p17*
Barraguet, Rose 30; New Orleans, 1848 ***778.6*** *p17*
Barralier, F. 35; America, 1842 ***778.6*** *p17*
Barras, Anne Joseph; Wisconsin, 1856 ***1495.20*** *p46*
*Child:*Eugenie
*Child:*Lambert Emmanuel
Barras, Jeanne Joseph; Wisconsin, 1856 ***1495.20*** *p46*
Barras, Marie Therese; Wisconsin, 1856 ***1495.20*** *p46*
Barrasin Family ; America, n.d. ***9228.50*** *p94*
Barratt, William 15; Quebec, 1870 ***8364.32*** *p22*
Barratta, A.; Louisiana, 1874 ***4981.45*** *p295*
Barrau, Ph. 17; New Orleans, 1842 ***778.6*** *p17*
Barraud, Aug. 36; Louisiana, 1848 ***778.6*** *p17*
Barrault, Simon; Montreal, 1644 ***9221.17*** *p146*
Barre, Andre 33; New Orleans, 1848 ***778.6*** *p17*
Barre, Catherine; Quebec, 1663 ***4514.3*** *p275*
Barre, Catherine; Quebec, 1664 ***4514.3*** *p275*
Barre, Charlotte 19; Quebec, 1639 ***9221.17*** *p85*
Barre, Denis; Quebec, 1649 ***9221.17*** *p208*
Barre, Gabrielle 18; Quebec, 1658 ***9221.17*** *p376*
Barre, Henriette 36; New Orleans, 1848 ***778.6*** *p17*
Barreau, Auguste 35; America, 1843 ***778.6*** *p17*
Barreau, Marc 30; Quebec, 1651 ***9221.17*** *p237*
Barreau, Pierre 14; Montreal, 1653 ***9221.17*** *p281*
Barrel, Jean-Baptiste 30; New Orleans, 1848 ***778.6*** *p17*
Barrell, Elizabeth 43; Ontario, 1871 ***1823.21*** *p17*
Barrera, J. 25; America, 1847 ***778.6*** *p18*
Barrere, J. B. 19; Port uncertain, 1843 ***778.6*** *p18*
Barrere, J. Marie 22; New Orleans, 1848 ***778.6*** *p18*
Barret, Ellen; New Orleans, 1851 ***7242.30*** *p134*
Barret, John; Louisiana, 1841-1844 ***4981.45*** *p210*
Barret, Ralph; Maryland, 1671 ***1236.25*** *p46*
Barrett, Andrew; Boston, 1764 ***1642*** *p34*
Barrett, Ellen; Ontario, 1835 ***3160.1*** *p150*
Barrett, Ellen; Prescott, Ont., 1835 ***3289.1*** *p61*
Barrett, Jeremiah; New Orleans, 1851 ***7242.30*** *p134*
Barrett, Johanna Henrietta; Chicago, 1854-1868 ***9228.50*** *p197*
Barrett, John; Boston, 1736 ***9228.50*** *p94*
Barrett, John 13; Quebec, 1870 ***8364.32*** *p22*
Barrett, Joseph; America, 1754 ***1220.12*** *p675*
Barrett, Joseph 37; Ontario, 1871 ***1823.17*** *p7*

Barrett, Mary Anne; Toronto, 1844 *2910.35 p112*
Barrett, Patrick 40; Ontario, 1871 *1823.21 p17*
Barrett, Phillip; North Carolina, 1811-1812 *1088.45 p2*
Barrett, Samuel 42; Ontario, 1871 *1823.21 p17*
Barrett, William 18; Quebec, 1870 *8364.32 p22*
Barrett, Wm.; Toronto, 1844 *2910.35 p112*
Barrey, James; Boston, 1739 *1642 p44*
Barrey, John 46; Ontario, 1871 *1823.21 p17*
Barrey, Joseph; Massachusetts, 1748 *1642 p84*
Barrey, Joseph M.; Worcester, MA, 1835 *3274.55 p74*
Barrey, Patrick 31; Ontario, 1871 *1823.21 p17*
Barrey, Thomas; Boston, 1744 *1642 p45*
Barrey, Thomas; Boston, 1766 *1642 p37*
Barriball, John 24; Ontario, 1871 *1823.21 p17*
Barrick, William; Colorado, 1873 *1029.59 p6*
Barrick, William Henry; Colorado, 1891 *1029.59 p6*
Barrie, Miss 18; Texas, 1848 *778.6 p18*
Barrie, James 42; Ontario, 1871 *1823.17 p7*
Barrie, Jean Numa 42; Texas, 1848 *778.6 p18*
Barriere, J..ques 28; America, 1841 *778.6 p18*
Barrigan, John; Boston, 1837 *3274.56 p96*
Barrile, Luis. 53; New Orleans, 1847 *778.6 p18*
Barrington, Fra; Jamestown, VA, 1633 *1658.20 p211*
Barrington, John 36; Ontario, 1871 *1823.21 p17*
Barrington, Thomas 45; Ontario, 1871 *1823.17 p7*
Barris, Charles 12; Ontario, 1871 *1823.21 p17*
Barris, James; Nova Scotia, 1839 *7078 p80*
Barritt, Patrick; Boston, 1763 *1642 p48*
Barrois, Anna Maria 48; America, 1837 *5475.1 p450*
Barrois, Anna Maria 48; America, 1837 *5475.1 p450*
Barroise, Thomas 47; Ontario, 1871 *1823.17 p7*
Barron, David 12; Ontario, 1871 *1823.17 p7*
Barron, Henry 30; Ontario, 1871 *1823.17 p8*
Barron, Isaac 49; Ontario, 1871 *1823.21 p17*
Barron, Jacob; Wisconsin, 1902 *6795.8 p232*
Barron, Jean Pierre 29; New Orleans, 1847 *778.6 p18*
Barron, John 29; Ontario, 1871 *1823.17 p8*
Barron, John F. 44; Ontario, 1871 *1823.21 p17*
Barron, Thomas 42; Ontario, 1871 *1823.17 p8*
Barroux, Francois 35; Texas, 1848 *778.6 p18*
Barrow, Joseph 25; Ontario, 1871 *1823.21 p17*
Barrow, Josiah; New York, 1779 *8529.30 p9*
Barrow, Josiah; New York, 1779 *8529.30 p10*
Barrows, Frances 37; Ontario, 1871 *1823.21 p17*
Barrows, Irie 49; Ontario, 1871 *1823.21 p17*
Barrows, Owen; Colorado, 1873 *1029.59 p6*
Barrufre, Francis 28; New Orleans, 1848 *778.6 p18*
Barry, Mr.; Boston, 1766 *1642 p36*
Barry, Burdie 22; Ontario, 1871 *1823.21 p17*
Barry, Charles; Boston, 1728 *1642 p25*
Barry, Cicely; Boston, 1739 *1642 p44*
Barry, Cicely; Boston, 1745 *1642 p45*
Barry, David 50; St. Johns, N.F., 1811 *1053.20 p20*
Barry, Edward; North Carolina, 1858 *1088.45 p2*
Barry, Elizabeth 70; Massachusetts, 1765 *1642 p99*
Barry, Gabriel Daniel; Iowa, 1925 *1211.15 p9*
Barry, George 24; Ontario, 1871 *1823.21 p17*
Barry, George 16; Quebec, 1870 *8364.32 p22*
Barry, Hannah; Boston, 1725 *1642 p25*
Barry, Hannah; Ipswich, MA, 1676 *1642 p71*
  *Husband:*John
Barry, James; Boston, 1707 *1642 p24*
Barry, James; Boston, 1721 *1642 p25*
Barry, James; Boston, 1736 *1642 p44*
Barry, James; Boston, 1752-1759 *1642 p31*
Barry, James; Massachusetts, 1735-1741 *1642 p116*
Barry, James 24; Ontario, 1871 *1823.21 p17*
Barry, James 27; Ontario, 1871 *1823.21 p17*
Barry, James 54; Ontario, 1871 *1823.17 p8*
Barry, Jean 32; New Orleans, 1840 *778.6 p18*
Barry, Jean; Quebec, 1658 *9221.17 p376*
Barry, John; Boston, 1713 *1642 p24*
Barry, John; Boston, 1726 *1642 p25*
Barry, John; Boston, 1757 *1642 p47*
Barry, John; Boston, 1766 *1642 p37*
Barry, John; Dorchester, MA, 1770 *1642 p102*
Barry, John *SEE* Barry, Hannah
Barry, John; Ipswich, MA, 1676 *1642 p71*
Barry, John; Ipswich, MA, 1678 *1642 p70*
Barry, John; Lynn, MA, 1767 *1642 p71*
  *Wife:*Rachael
Barry, John 60; Ontario, 1871 *1823.21 p17*
Barry, John 63; Ontario, 1871 *1823.21 p18*
Barry, John 68; Ontario, 1871 *1823.21 p17*
Barry, John 23; St. Johns, N.F., 1811 *1053.20 p20*
Barry, Julia 33; Ontario, 1871 *1823.21 p18*
Barry, Larence 60; Ontario, 1871 *1823.21 p18*
Barry, Mary; New Orleans, 1851 *7242.30 p134*
Barry, Michael 54; Ontario, 1871 *1823.21 p18*
Barry, Patrick 31; Ontario, 1871 *1823.21 p18*
Barry, Patrick 78; Ontario, 1871 *1823.21 p18*
Barry, Peter; New Orleans, 1850 *7242.30 p134*
Barry, Peter 45; Ontario, 1871 *1823.21 p18*

Barry, Pierre 48; New Orleans, 1848 *778.6 p18*
Barry, Rachael; Boston, 1719 *1642 p25*
Barry, Rachael *SEE* Barry, John
Barry, Richard; Boston, 1740 *1642 p45*
Barry, Richard 42; Ontario, 1871 *1823.21 p18*
Barry, Richard 60; Ontario, 1871 *1823.21 p18*
Barry, Richard; Toronto, 1844 *2910.35 p116*
Barry, Susanna; Boston, 1719 *1642 p25*
Barry, Thomas; Boston, 1724 *1642 p25*
Barry, Thomas 45; Ontario, 1871 *1823.17 p8*
Barry, Thomas 60; Ontario, 1871 *1823.21 p18*
Barry, Thomas; Toronto, 1844 *2910.35 p113*
Barrydel, Ann; Roxbury, MA, 1645 *1642 p107*
Barrye, John; Ipswich, MA, 1719 *1642 p71*
Barsaloux, Joseph; Colorado, 1884 *1029.59 p6*
Barsch, Ludwick; Ohio, 1809-1852 *4511.35 p3*
Barsch, Madelaine 27; America, 1844 *778.6 p18*
Barsfield, Titus; Ontario, 1871 *1823.21 p18*
Barszczewski, Carolina; Detroit, 1929 *1640.55 p116*
Bart, Anna 22; Ohio, 1847 *778.6 p18*
Bart, Frank; Washington, 1866 *2770.40 p134*
Bart, Frank G.; Washington, 1881 *2770.40 p134*
Bart, Pierre; Louisiana, 1874-1875 *4981.45 p297*
Barta, Alois; New York, NY, 1895 *2853.20 p236*
Bartel, Anthony; Ohio, 1809-1852 *4511.35 p3*
Bartel, August; New York, 1859 *358.56 p101*
Bartel, Emil P.; Wisconsin, 1903 *6795.8 p217*
Bartel, Ewald; Wisconsin, 1881 *6795.8 p200*
Bartel, George; New York, 1860 *358.56 p149*
Bartel, Gustav; Wisconsin, 1876 *6795.8 p225*
Bartel, Nicholas; Ohio, 1809-1852 *4511.35 p3*
Bartel, Peter 24; America, 1843 *5475.1 p261*
Bartel, Peter 16; New York, 1854 *5475.1 p236*
Bartelot, Richard; Newbury, MA, 1635 *9228.50 p94*
Bartels, Mr.; America, 1856 *7420.1 p144*
  With wife & 2 children
Bartels, Mr.; America, 1862 *7420.1 p210*
Bartels, Mr.; America, 1869 *7420.1 p279*
  With wife & 5 sons
Bartels, Anne Marie Cathar. Sophie Stiefelmeier *SEE* Bartels, Ernst Heinrich Wilhelm
Bartels, Carl Conrad Leopold; America, 1890 *7420.1 p400*
Bartels, Catharine Marie Dorothee; America, 1851 *7420.1 p83*
Bartels, Christoph Aug. Conrad Gottl. *SEE* Bartels, Hans Heinrich Christoph
Bartels, Dorette; America, 1861 *7420.1 p202*
Bartels, Engel Marie Caroline *SEE* Bartels, Ernst Heinrich Gottlieb
Bartels, Engel Marie Ernestine Kromer *SEE* Bartels, Ernst Heinrich Gottlieb
Bartels, Engel Marie Sophie Reese *SEE* Bartels, Johann Friedrich
Bartels, Engel Sophie Charlotte; America, 1867 *7420.1 p252*
Bartels, Engel Sophie Doroth. *SEE* Bartels, Johann Friedrich
Bartels, Ernst Heinrich Gottlieb; America, 1870 *7420.1 p282*
  *Wife:*Engel Marie Ernestine Kromer
  *Son:*Friedrich Wilhelm
  *Daughter:*Engel Marie Caroline
Bartels, Ernst Heinrich Wilhelm; America, 1867 *7420.1 p252*
  *Wife:*Anne Marie Cathar. Sophie Stiefelmeier
  With 6 children
Bartels, Friedrich Christian Wilhelm; America, 1874 *7420.1 p302*
Bartels, Friedrich Wilhelm *SEE* Bartels, Ernst Heinrich Gottlieb
Bartels, Hans Heinr. Conr. *SEE* Bartels, Johann Friedrich
Bartels, Hans Heinrich Christoph; America, 1865 *7420.1 p228*
Bartels, Hans Heinrich Christoph *SEE* Bartels, Hans Heinrich Christoph
Bartels, Hans Heinrich Christoph; America, 1871 *7420.1 p288*
  With family
  *Son:*Hans Heinrich Christoph
  *Son:*Christoph Aug. Conrad Gottl.
Bartels, Heinr. Christoph *SEE* Bartels, Johann Friedrich
Bartels, Heinrich; Illinois, 1864 *6079.1 p1*
Bartels, Heinrich Christoph; America, 1868 *7420.1 p267*
Bartels, Heinrich Conrad; America, 1868 *7420.1 p267*
Bartels, Joh. Friedr. *SEE* Bartels, Johann Friedrich
Bartels, Johann Friedrich; America, 1846 *7420.1 p42*
Bartels, Johann Friedrich; America, 1847 *7420.1 p51*
  *Wife:*Engel Marie Sophie Reese
  *Son:*Joh. Friedr.
  *Son:*Hans Heinr. Conr.
  *Son:*Heinr. Christoph

  *Daughter:*Engel Sophie Doroth.
  With stepchild
Bartels, Thrine Marie Sophie; America, 1856 *7420.1 p144*
Bartely, John 40; Ontario, 1871 *1823.17 p8*
Barter, Elie 44; Ontario, 1871 *1823.21 p18*
Barter, John; Baltimore, 1828 *9228.50 p94*
Barth, Abraham; America, 1859 *5475.1 p403*
Barth, Adam 30; Galveston, TX, 1844 *3967.10 p373*
Barth, Alexander; America, 1848 *5475.1 p402*
Barth, Angela *SEE* Barth, Johann
Barth, Anna *SEE* Barth, Nikolaus
Barth, Anna Maria 3 *SEE* Barth, Michel
Barth, August; Iowa, 1909 *1211.15 p9*
Barth, Barbara Dittgen *SEE* Barth, Mathias
Barth, Barbara Gastauer *SEE* Barth, Michel
Barth, Barbara 15 *SEE* Barth, Mathias
Barth, Barbara 31; America, 1854 *2526.42 p116*
Barth, Berthold 25; Galveston, TX, 1844 *3967.10 p370*
Barth, Christian; Illinois, 1859 *6079.1 p1*
Barth, Christiane 36; New York, NY, 1874 *6954.7 p37*
Barth, Christine 17; New York, NY, 1874 *6954.7 p37*
Barth, Elisabeth 58; Indiana, 1885 *5475.1 p555*
Barth, Elisabeth 3 months; New York, NY, 1874 *6954.7 p37*
Barth, Eva 14; New York, NY, 1874 *6954.7 p37*
Barth, Felix; Missouri, 1889 *5475.1 p381*
Barth, Ferd.; Valdivia, Chile, 1852 *1192.4 p52*
Barth, Friedrich; America, 1881 *2526.43 p137*
Barth, Georg; America, 1831 *2526.43 p137*
Barth, Georg 8; New York, NY, 1874 *6954.7 p37*
Barth, Mrs. Georg; America, 1854 *2526.42 p118*
Barth, Gottlieb 29; Missouri, 1852 *5475.1 p403*
Barth, Gustav; Missouri, 1872 *5475.1 p405*
Barth, Heinrich; America, 1854 *2526.42 p118*
Barth, Heinrich *SEE* Barth, Heinrich
Barth, Heinrich; Brazil, 1862 *5475.1 p540*
  *Wife:*Margarethe Schmoll
  *Daughter:*Margarethe
  *Son:*Heinrich
  *Son:*Jakob
Barth, Henry; Iowa, 1913 *1211.15 p9*
Barth, Jacob 18; New York, NY, 1874 *6954.7 p37*
Barth, Jakob *SEE* Barth, Heinrich
Barth, Johann; America, 1874 *5475.1 p348*
  *Mother:*Angela
Barth, Johann; America, 1881 *5475.1 p55*
  *Wife:*Katharina Becker
  *Daughter:*Karoline
  *Son:*Ludwig
  *Daughter:*Maria
Barth, Johann 4 *SEE* Barth, Michel
Barth, Johann Michael 29; Galveston, TX, 1844 *3967.10 p374*
Barth, Johanna; America, 1891 *5475.1 p407*
Barth, Josef; New York, 1881 *5475.1 p434*
Barth, Joseph; America, 1865-1870 *5475.1 p405*
Barth, Karl *SEE* Barth, Nikolaus
Barth, Karl Ludwig 23; Ohio, 1884 *5475.1 p55*
Barth, Karoline *SEE* Barth, Nikolaus
Barth, Karoline *SEE* Barth, Johann
Barth, Katharina Becker *SEE* Barth, Johann
Barth, Leonhard; America, 1871 *2526.42 p149*
Barth, Louise 36; New York, NY, 1893 *1883.7 p40*
Barth, Ludwig *SEE* Barth, Johann
Barth, Ludwig; Pittsburgh, 1880 *5475.1 p54*
Barth, Margar. Schwambach *SEE* Barth, Nikolaus
Barth, Margaretha 10; New York, NY, 1874 *6954.7 p37*
Barth, Margarethe *SEE* Barth, Heinrich
Barth, Margarethe Schmoll *SEE* Barth, Heinrich
Barth, Maria *SEE* Barth, Johann
Barth, Maria 52; America, 1882 *5475.1 p555*
Barth, Maria Meyer *SEE* Barth, Peter
Barth, Maria; New York, 1881 *5475.1 p434*
  With son
Barth, Maria Magdalena; Venezuela, 1843 *3899.5 p542*
Barth, Mathias; America, 1864 *5475.1 p264*
  *Wife:*Barbara Dittgen
  *Daughter:*Barbara
Barth, Mathias; America, 1874 *5475.1 p347*
Barth, Mathias 27; America, 1843 *5475.1 p366*
Barth, Max Frederick; Iowa, 1891 *1211.15 p9*
Barth, Michel; America, 1864 *5475.1 p264*
  *Wife:*Barbara Gastauer
  *Daughter:*Anna Maria
  *Son:*Johann
Barth, Michel; Brazil, 1881 *5475.1 p306*
Barth, Michel; New York, 1887 *5475.1 p246*
Barth, Moses; Missouri, 1880 *5475.1 p406*
Barth, Nikolaus; America, 1865 *5475.1 p498*
  With mother-in-law 53
  *Wife:*Margar. Schwambach
  *Daughter:*Karoline

*Son:*Karl
*Son:*Peter
Barth, Nikolaus; Chicago, 1876 5475.1 p363
*Sister:*Anna
Barth, Peter *SEE* Barth, Nikolaus
Barth, Peter 36; America, 1843 5475.1 p347
Barth, Peter; Chicago, 1880 5475.1 p347
*Wife:*Maria Meyer
With sister-in-law
Barth, Philip 43; New York, NY, 1893 1883.7 p40
Barth, Salome 30; Galveston, TX, 1844 3967.10 p373
Barth, Salomon; Missouri, 1880 5475.1 p406
Barth, Sebastian; America, 1831 2526.43 p137
With wife & 7 children
Barth, Simon; America, 1866 5475.1 p404
Barth, Simon; Philadelphia, 1866 5475.1 p404
Barth, Thomas; Louisiana, 1841-1844 4981.45 p210
Barth, Yast; Illinois, 1866 6079.1 p1
Barthat, M. 35; America, 1843 778.6 p18
Barthe, Mr. 18; America, 1840 778.6 p18
Barthe, Mr. 30; America, 1846 778.6 p18
Barthe, Bernard 18; America, 1847 778.6 p18
Barthe, Bondidier 29; Texas, 1848 778.6 p18
Barthe, Emile; Louisiana, 1836-1841 4981.45 p208
Barthel, George 44; St. Louis, 1847 778.6 p18
Barthel, J. J.; Louisiana, 1874-1875 4981.45 p297
Barthel, Johann; America, 1881 5475.1 p336
*Wife:*Katharina Jager
*Son:*Nikolaus
*Daughter:*Margarethe
*Son:*Peter
*Daughter:*Katharina
*Daughter:*Maria
Barthel, Jos. 36; America, 1842 778.6 p18
Barthel, Katharina *SEE* Barthel, Johann
Barthel, Katharina Jager *SEE* Barthel, Johann
Barthel, Margarethe *SEE* Barthel, Johann
Barthel, Maria *SEE* Barthel, Johann
Barthel, Nikolaus *SEE* Barthel, Johann
Barthel, Peter; America, 1833 5475.1 p27
With family
Barthel, Peter *SEE* Barthel, Johann
Barthel, Phil. Joh.; America, 1897 5475.1 p48
Barthelemi, Mr. 18; New Orleans, 1840 778.6 p18
Barthelemy, Catherine 38; America, 1846 778.6 p18
Barthelemy, J. L. 25; New Orleans, 1840 778.6 p18
Barthelemy, Jean Baptiste 5; America, 1846 778.6 p18
Barthelemy, Joseph 42; America, 1846 778.6 p18
Barthelemy, Joseph 25; New Orleans, 1845 778.6 p18
Barthelme, Wilhelm; America, 1869 5475.1 p138
Barthels, Catharina Engel Dorothea; America, 1867 7420.1 p253
Barthet, Jean; Louisiana, 1874-1875 4981.45 p298
Bartholemy, Jean Marie 22; New Orleans, 1848 778.6 p18
Bartholet, . . .; Massachusetts, n.d. 9228.50 p99
Bartholomew, Nicholas; Ohio, 1809-1852 4511.35 p3
Bartholomew, Robert; Marston's Wharf, 1782 8529.30 p9
Bartholomew, Thomas; Marston's Wharf, 1782 8529.30 p9
Bartik, Josef; Nebraska, 1857-1910 2853.20 p188
Bartik, Josef; Wisconsin, 1889 2853.20 p332
Bartlay, George 49; Ontario, 1871 1823.21 p18
Bartle, Anthony; Ohio, 1809-1852 4511.35 p3
Bartle, James 45; Ontario, 1871 1823.21 p18
Bartless, Matthew; Toronto, 1844 2910.35 p115
Bartlet, Eliz.; Maryland, 1674-1675 1236.25 p51
Bartlet, Eliza 44; Ontario, 1871 1823.21 p18
Bartlet, Frank 46; Ontario, 1871 1823.17 p8
Bartlet, Franklin 49; Ontario, 1871 1823.21 p18
Bartlett, Experience 72; Ontario, 1871 1823.21 p18
Bartlett, Florence 3; Ontario, 1871 1823.21 p18
Bartlett, Francis 54; Ontario, 1871 1823.17 p8
Bartlett, John 29; Ontario, 1871 1823.21 p18
Bartlett, John H. 44; Ontario, 1871 1823.21 p18
Bartlett, Jonathan; Toronto, 1844 2910.35 p116
Bartlett, Mary 28; Ontario, 1871 1823.21 p18
Bartlett, Richard; Newbury, MA, 1635 9228.50 p94
Bartlett, Thomas 65; Ontario, 1871 1823.21 p18
Bartlett, William 17; Ontario, 1871 1823.17 p8
Bartlett, William 28; Ontario, 1871 1823.21 p18
Bartley, John 46; Ontario, 1871 1823.17 p8
Bartley, John 66; Ontario, 1871 1823.21 p18
Bartling, Carl August Ludwig; America, 1859 7420.1 p183
Bartling, Carl Friedrich Daniel; Port uncertain, 1852 7420.1 p84
Bartling, Carl Gerhard; America, 1868 7420.1 p268
Bartling, Conrad; America, 1852 7420.1 p84
With wife 3 sons & daughter
Bartling, Friedrich Wilhelm; America, 1859 7420.1 p183
Bartling, Friedrich Wilhelm; America, 1868 7420.1 p268
With family
Bartling, Hanna Christine Caroline; America, 1867 7420.1 p253
Bartling, Heinrich; Port uncertain, 1854 7420.1 p115
Bartling, Ludwig; America, 1868 7420.1 p268
With family
Barto, Bruce; Anchorage, AK, 1979 9228.50 p592
Bartocha, Anna 28; New York, NY, 1911 6533.11 p10
Bartol, . . .; Massachusetts, n.d. 9228.50 p99
Barton, . . .; Boston, 1769 9228.50 p5
Barton, . . .; New England, n.d. 9228.50 p94
Barton, Angelina 14; Quebec, 1870 8364.32 p22
Barton, Annie 12; Quebec, 1870 8364.32 p22
Barton, Daniel 50; Ontario, 1871 1823.21 p18
Barton, F. J.; Nebraska, 1905 3004.30 p46
Barton, Francoise-Marthe; Quebec, 1670 4514.3 p275
Barton, Henry 44; Ontario, 1871 1823.21 p18
Barton, John; Boston, 1769 9228.50 p48
Barton, John; Boston, 1769 9228.50 p95
Barton, John 19; Ontario, 1871 1823.21 p18
Barton, John 53; Ontario, 1871 1823.17 p8
Barton, John S.; Louisiana, 1874 4981.45 p130
Barton, Matthew; Salem, MA, 1671 9228.50 p95
Barton, Richard; New York, 1810 9228.50 p95
Barton, Sarah 14; Quebec, 1870 8364.32 p22
Barton, Thomas 25; Ontario, 1871 1823.21 p18
Barton, Thomas 27; Ontario, 1871 1823.21 p18
Barton, Thomas 75; Ontario, 1871 1823.21 p18
Barton, William G.; North Carolina, 1842 1088.45 p2
Bartonoux, Mr. 30; Port uncertain, 1840 778.6 p18
Bartosek, Dr.; America, 1810-1910 2853.20 p513
Bartosek, Frantisek; New York, NY, 1883 2853.20 p115
Bartosiewicz, Walter; Detroit, 1929-1930 6214.5 p67
Bartosz, Joseph 37; New York, NY, 1920 930.50 p48
Bartoszkiewitz, Johann; Galveston, TX, 1855 571.7 p16
Bartram, . . .; New England, n.d. 9228.50 p95
Bartram, . . .; New England, n.d. 9228.50 p95
Bartram, . . .; Ohio, n.d. 9228.50 p95
Bartram, Ebenezer 52; Fairfield, CT, 1783 9228.50 p95
Bartram, Robert J. 21; Ontario, 1871 1823.21 p18
Bartram, Thomas 48; Ontario, 1871 1823.17 p8
Bartram, William 50; Ontario, 1871 1823.21 p18
Bartram, William H. 22; Ontario, 1871 1823.21 p18
Bartram Family ; Newfoundland, n.d. 9228.50 p95
Bartsch, Johann August; New York, NY, 1905 6212.1 p14
Bartsop, Ernst. August; Wisconsin, 1865 6795.8 p62
Bartwhistler, Richard 71; Ontario, 1871 1823.21 p18
Bartz, Barbara 1 *SEE* Bartz, Philipp
Bartz, Friederike Regine; America, 1836 7420.1 p11
Bartz, Georg 13 *SEE* Bartz, Philipp
Bartz, George; Illinois, 1852 6079.1 p1
Bartz, Maria 10 *SEE* Bartz, Philipp
Bartz, Nikolaus 4 *SEE* Bartz, Philipp
Bartz, Peter 6 *SEE* Bartz, Philipp
Bartz, Philipp; America, 1836 5475.1 p549
With wife
*Daughter:*Maria
*Son:*Nikolaus
*Daughter:*Barbara
*Son:*Peter
*Son:*Philipp
*Son:*Georg
Bartz, Philipp 15 *SEE* Bartz, Philipp
Baruzzine, Guiseppi; Illinois, 1918 6007.60 p9
Barwyse, Margret 52; Ontario, 1871 1823.21 p18
Bary, Mr.; Massachusetts, 1764 1642 p99
Bary, Francois; Quebec, 1644 9221.17 p139
Bary, Jeanne 45; New Orleans, 1848 778.6 p18
Bary, Joseph; Ohio, 1809-1852 4511.35 p3
Barycki, Adam; Detroit, 1929 1640.55 p116
Baschat, John; Ohio, 1809-1852 4511.35 p3
Bascon, Gilles; Quebec, 1645 9221.17 p150
Basenach, Franz; New York, 1880 5475.1 p325
Baset, Mrs. 37; America, 1844 778.6 p18
Basford, Willm 19; Virginia, 1635 1183.3 p30
Bash, Ferdinand D.; Louisiana, 1841-1844 4981.45 p210
Basin, A.; America, 1846 778.6 p18
Basin, A. 4; America, 1846 778.6 p19
Basin, A. 35; America, 1846 778.6 p19
Basin, F. 57; America, 1846 778.6 p19
Basin, Matthias; Ohio, 1809-1852 4511.35 p3
Baskerville, Christopher 40; Ontario, 1871 1823.21 p18
Baskerville, James 32; Ontario, 1871 1823.21 p18
Baskerville, John W. 29; Ontario, 1871 1823.21 p18
Baskerville, William 47; Ontario, 1871 1823.21 p18
Baskerville, William 80; Ontario, 1871 1823.21 p18
Basle, Frantz 37; America, 1845 778.6 p19
Basler, Antoine 13; New Orleans, 1848 778.6 p19
Basler, Barbara 15; New Orleans, 1848 778.6 p19
Basler, Franz 9; New Orleans, 1848 778.6 p19
Basler, Franz 47; New Orleans, 1848 778.6 p19
Basler, Peter 11; New Orleans, 1848 778.6 p19
Basman, John 44; Ontario, 1871 1823.21 p18
Basque, Jean; Quebec, 1646 9221.17 p161
Basquien, Jeannin; Quebec, 1646 9221.17 p161
Basquier, Francois 25; Missouri, 1845 778.6 p19
Bass, Elizabeth 53; Ontario, 1871 1823.17 p8
Bass, James 29; Ontario, 1871 1823.21 p19
Bass, John; Ohio, 1809-1852 4511.35 p3
Bass, Robert W. 29; Ontario, 1871 1823.17 p8
Bassany, Joseph; Quebec, 1654 9221.17 p304
*Wife:*Marie-Madeleine Breman
Bassany, Marie-Madeleine Breman *SEE* Bassany, Joseph
Bassaux, Julian 3; New Orleans, 1842 778.6 p19
Bassaux, Poline 39; New Orleans, 1842 778.6 p19
Bassaux, Zacharie 34; New Orleans, 1842 778.6 p19
Bassclerin, Barbara; New Castle, DE, 1817-1818 90.20 p150
Bassedeau, Jean 40; New Orleans, 1844 778.6 p19
Bassen, Paul; Washington, 1887 2770.40 p24
Basser, Hy. 24; America, 1843 778.6 p19
Basset, Benigne 23; Montreal, 1657 9221.17 p372
Basset, Catherine; Quebec, 1667-1675 1142.10 p128
Basset, Catherine; Quebec, 1667 4514.3 p275
Basset, Jean 17; Quebec, 1657 9221.17 p351
Basset, Matthew; Marblehead, MA, 1763 9228.50 p95
Basset, Pierre; Quebec, 1657 9221.17 p351
Bassett, John 16; Quebec, 1870 8364.32 p22
Bassett, Ralph 53; Ontario, 1871 1823.17 p8
Bassfrelo, Titus 70; Ontario, 1871 1823.21 p19
Bassich, John; Louisiana, 1874 4981.45 p295
Bassina, E.; Louisiana, 1874 4981.45 p295
Bassompierre, Antoine; Quebec, 1649 9221.17 p216
Basson, Jean 25; Port uncertain, 1841 778.6 p19
Bassot, Francois 42; Quebec, 1643 9221.17 p128
Bast, Barbara; America, 1830 5475.1 p410
Bast, Josef; St. Paul, MN, 1872 2853.20 p278
Bast, Mina Avline Helema; Wisconsin, 1890 6795.8 p236
Bastam, Marianne 18; America, 1845 778.6 p19
Bastanchury, Domingo; California, 1860 3276.8 p18
Bastard, Harry; Ohio, 1840 2763.1 p7
Bastard, Joseph; Fairfield, CT, 1685 9228.50 p95
Bastard, Michel; Quebec, 1659 9221.17 p394
Bastard, Thomas 36; Ontario, 1871 1823.21 p19
Bastard, Thomas C.; Ohio, 1841 2763.1 p7
Bastard, William 51; Ontario, 1871 1823.21 p19
Bastard, Yves; Montreal, 1653 9221.17 p281
Bastel, Bedrich Bohdan; Wisconsin, 1870 2853.20 p323
Bastien, Mrs.; Port uncertain, 1844 778.6 p19
Bastien, V.; Port uncertain, 1844 778.6 p19
Baston, . . .; Montreal, 1652 9221.17 p267
Baston, Simon; Quebec, 1657 9221.17 p351
Bastune, Robert J.; Ohio, 1844 2763.1 p7
Basueldo, J. M.; Louisiana, 1836-1840 4981.45 p212
Bataglia, Geuiseppe; Louisiana, 1874-1875 4981.45 p298
Bataillard, Christophe 34; America, 1845 778.6 p19
Bataille, Miss 20; New Orleans, 1848 778.6 p19
Bataille, Ms. 23; New Orleans, 1845 778.6 p19
Bataille, Anatole 2; New Orleans, 1845 778.6 p19
Bataille, Anne 26; Quebec, 1642 9221.17 p111
Bataille, Antoine 57; Havana, 1848 778.6 p19
Bataille, Georg 35; New Orleans, 1848 778.6 p19
Bataille, Guillaume 71; Quebec, 1656 9221.17 p331
Bataille, Jules 1; New Orleans, 1845 778.6 p19
Batais, Lamange 25; Mississippi, 1847 778.6 p19
Batanville, Angelique *SEE* Batanville, Louis
Batanville, Louis; Quebec, 1665 4514.3 p298
*Wife:*Suzanne Debure
*Daughter:*Angelique
With sister-in-law
Batanville, Suzanne Debure *SEE* Batanville, Louis
Batchelor, Benjamin 55; Ontario, 1871 1823.17 p8
Batchko, Morris; Detroit, 1929 1640.55 p115
Bate, George 14; Quebec, 1870 8364.32 p22
Bate, Humphrey 30; Ontario, 1871 1823.21 p19
Bate, Royle; North Carolina, 1855 1088.45 p2
Bate, Thomas 15; Quebec, 1870 8364.32 p22
Batelsdotter, Catherine; Kansas, 1868 777.40 p11
Batelsson, Bertha L. Ohman *SEE* Batelsson, Goran Johannes
Batelsson, Goran Johannes; Kansas, 1869 777.40 p15
*Wife:*Bertha L. Ohman
*Son:*John
Batelsson, John *SEE* Batelsson, Goran Johannes
Bateman, Charles 60; Ontario, 1871 1823.21 p19
Bateman, Edward 67; Ontario, 1871 1823.21 p19
Bateman, Edward C. 32; Ontario, 1871 1823.21 p19
Bateman, John 56; Ontario, 1871 1823.21 p19
Bateman, John 61; Ontario, 1871 1823.21 p19
Bateman, John 68; Ontario, 1871 1823.21 p19
Bateman, Robert 59; Ontario, 1871 1823.21 p19
Bateman, Sarah 19; Quebec, 1870 8364.32 p22
Bateman, William 45; Ontario, 1871 1823.21 p19
Batenhorst, Anton; Nebraska, 1905 3004.30 p46

Batenhorst, Frank; Nebraska, 1905 *3004.30 p46*
Batenhorst, Joe; Nebraska, 1905 *3004.30 p46*
Bates, Elizabeth; St. Johns, N.F., 1825 *1053.15 p6*
Bates, George 60; Ontario, 1871 *1823.21 p19*
Bates, Henry; Ohio, 1844 *2763.1 p7*
Bates, Henry 51; Ontario, 1871 *1823.21 p19*
Bates, Mary 67; Ontario, 1871 *1823.21 p19*
Bates, Nicholas; Nova Scotia, 1784 *7105 p22*
Bates, Robert 32; Ontario, 1871 *1823.21 p19*
Bates, Thomas 37; Ontario, 1871 *1823.21 p19*
Bates, William H. 38; Ontario, 1871 *1823.21 p19*
Bath, John; Canada, 1775 *3036.5 p68*
Bath, Philippe 28; Louisiana, 1848 *778.6 p19*
Bathe, Georg Heinrich; Pennsylvania, 1840 *7420.1 p17*
Bathel, Mr. 25; Louisiana, 1848 *778.6 p19*
Bathel, Mrs. 20; Louisiana, 1848 *778.6 p19*
Batinger, F. A. 28; New Orleans, 1843 *778.6 p19*
Batinger, Julia 17; New Orleans, 1843 *778.6 p20*
Batinger, Urania 13; New Orleans, 1843 *778.6 p20*
Batista, J. 25; America, 1844 *778.6 p20*
Batiste, . . .; New England, n.d. *9228.50 p96*
Batko, John; Detroit, 1930 *1640.60 p83*
Batla, Tomas; Texas, 1881 *2853.20 p63*
Batman, Thomas 53; Ontario, 1871 *1823.21 p19*
Baton, Louis Charles 34; New Orleans, 1848 *778.6 p20*
Batot, Constant 22; America, 1847 *778.6 p20*
Batovec, Frantisek; Cleveland, OH, 1880-1889 *2853.20 p509*
Batovec, Frantisek; Michigan, 1810-1910 *2853.20 p370*
Batram, Joshua 48; Ontario, 1871 *1823.21 p19*
Batt, Abraham 19; New York, NY, 1878 *9253.2 p45*
Batt, Joseph; Louisiana, 1874 *4981.45 p295*
Batt, Joseph; Wisconsin, 1884 *6795.8 p134*
Battaglia, S.; Louisiana, 1874 *4981.45 p295*
Batten, . . .; New England, n.d. *9228.50 p96*
Batten Family ; Newfoundland, 1500-1599 *9228.50 p96*
Battermann, Albert; England, 1881 *7420.1 p320*
Battermann, August; America, 1882 *7420.1 p398*
Battermann, Charlotte; America, 1865 *7420.1 p228*
Battermann, Engel Sophie Dorothea; Illinois, 1880 *7420.1 p315*
Battermann, Friedrich Christ. August; America, 1883 *7420.1 p334*
Battermann, Friedrich Wilhelm; America, 1887 *7420.1 p352*
Battermann, Georg Heinrich Christoph; America, 1848 *7420.1 p58*
Battermann, Hans Heinrich Christ.; America, 1862 *7420.1 p210*
Battermann, Heinrich Ludwig; America, 1884 *7420.1 p341*
Battermann, Hermann; America, 1907 *7420.1 p402*
Battermann, Johann Friederich; America, 1839 *7420.1 p15*
Battermann, Johann Heinrich; America, 1854 *7420.1 p115*
Battermann, Sophia Dorothea; America, 1850 *7420.1 p69*
Battin, George; Ohio, 1845 *2763.1 p7*
Battin, William; Ohio, 1845 *2763.1 p7*
Battis, . . .; New England, n.d. *9228.50 p96*
Battisti, Pietro 26; New York, NY, 1894 *6512.1 p182*
Battle, James; New York, 1783 *8529.30 p9*
Battle, John; Marston's Wharf, 1782 *8529.30 p9*
Battle, Levi 18; Ontario, 1871 *1823.17 p8*
Battle, Mary Ann 40; Ontario, 1871 *1823.17 p8*
Battle, R. R. 30; Ontario, 1871 *1823.21 p19*
Battle, William 7; Ontario, 1871 *1823.17 p8*
Batty, Eliza. 16; North Carolina, 1774 *1422.10 p56*
Batty, Thomas 19; Quebec, 1870 *8364.32 p22*
Batty, William 29; Ontario, 1871 *1823.21 p19*
Batys, Frank; Detroit, 1929 *1640.55 p117*
Batz, Nicolas; Nova Scotia, 1784 *7105 p22*
Batzenhofer, Antoine 8; America, 1746 *778.6 p20*
Batzenhofer, Antoine 38; America, 1746 *778.6 p20*
Batzenhofer, Barb. 22; America, 1746 *778.6 p20*
Batzenhofer, Elisabeth 30; America, 1746 *778.6 p20*
Batzenhofer, Georg 6; America, 1746 *778.6 p20*
Batzenhofer, Joseph 7; America, 1746 *778.6 p20*
Batzenhofer, Joseph 42; America, 1746 *778.6 p20*
Batzenhofer, Louise 3; America, 1746 *778.6 p20*
Batzenhofer, Louise 8; America, 1746 *778.6 p20*
Batzenhofer, Mag. 36; America, 1746 *778.6 p20*
Batzer, John; Ohio, 1809-1852 *4511.35 p3*
Bauban, Lucas; Louisiana, 1874-1875 *4981.45 p298*
Bauben, George 27; Port uncertain, 1846 *778.6 p20*
Bauchaft, Henri 17; Louisiana, 1848 *778.6 p20*
Bauchaft, Margt. 25; Louisiana, 1848 *778.6 p20*
Baucher, . . . 27; Quebec, 1655 *9221.17 p320*
Bauchery, J. 33; America, 1845 *778.6 p20*
Baucholet, Marie 26; Missouri, 1848 *778.6 p20*
Baucker, Ernst; America, 1867 *7919.3 p531*

Baud, Adam 59; Missouri, 1840 *778.6 p20*
Baud, Michael 19; Missouri, 1840 *778.6 p20*
Baud, Richard 17; Missouri, 1840 *778.6 p20*
Baud, Richard 57; Missouri, 1840 *778.6 p20*
Baudain, . . .; New England, n.d. *9228.50 p127*
Baudain, Francis; Marblehead, MA, 1650-1750 *9228.50 p126*
Baudains, Capt.; America, 1645-1745 *9228.50 p96*
Baudains Family ; Massachusetts, n.d. *9228.50 p126*
Baudemont, Henry 5; Mississippi, 1847 *778.6 p20*
Baudemont, Marie 38; Mississippi, 1847 *778.6 p20*
Baudenon, Leonard 33; New Orleans, 1848 *778.6 p20*
Bauder, Alexander 48; New York, NY, 1885 *1883.7 p46*
Bauder, Alisie 5; New York, NY, 1885 *1883.7 p46*
Bauder, Auguste 14; New York, NY, 1885 *1883.7 p46*
Bauder, Julius 19; New York, NY, 1885 *1883.7 p46*
Bauder, Justine 48; New York, NY, 1885 *1883.7 p46*
Bauder, Pauline 7; New York, NY, 1885 *1883.7 p46*
Baudereau, Urbain 20; Montreal, 1653 *9221.17 p281*
Baudet, . . .; Quebec, 1652 *9221.17 p253*
Baudet, Antoine 16; Quebec, 1654 *9221.17 p304*
Baudhuin, D. J.; Boston, 1870 *1494.20 p11*
Baudhuin, Joseph; Boston, 1870 *1494.20 p11*
Baudhuin, Marcellin; Detroit, 1870 *1494.20 p12*
Baudhuin, Martin; Detroit, 1870 *1494.20 p12*
Baudhuin, Pierre; Detroit, 1870 *1494.20 p12*
Baudhuin, Prosper; Boston, 1870 *1494.20 p11*
Baudin, C. 38; America, 1843 *778.6 p20*
Baudin, Clemence 35; America, 1843 *778.6 p20*
Baudin Family ; Massachusetts, n.d. *9228.50 p126*
Baudin Family ; Newfoundland, 1500-1599 *9228.50 p96*
Baudoin, Ant. 28; America, 1841 *778.6 p20*
Baudoin, Pierre; Salem, MA, 1600-1687 *9228.50 p181*
Baudon, Charles; Quebec, 1661 *9221.17 p447*
Baudon, Jacques 26; Quebec, 1661 *9221.17 p447*
Baudouin, Mr. 11; New Orleans, 1842 *778.6 p20*
Baudouin, Antoine; Quebec, 1649 *9221.17 p209*
Baudouin, Francois; Quebec, 1659 *9221.17 p412*
Baudouin, Jean 20; Montreal, 1658 *9221.17 p387*
Baudouin, Jean; Quebec, 1658 *9221.17 p376*
Baudouin, Madeleine 21; Quebec, 1660 *9221.17 p431*
Baudouin, Olivier; Montreal, 1653 *9221.17 p282*
Baudouin, Rene 16; Quebec, 1662 *9221.17 p479*
Baudran, Jean; Quebec, 1642 *9221.17 p111*
Baudrie, Jacques; Quebec, 1659 *9221.17 p394*
Baudry, Antoine 15; Montreal, 1653 *9221.17 p282*
Baudry, Jean 58; America, 1840 *778.6 p20*
Baudry, Louis; Quebec, 1661 *9221.17 p447*
Baudry, Louis Francher; North Carolina, 1858 *1088.45 p2*
Baudry, Perrine; Quebec, 1649 *9221.17 p209*
  Son:Pierre
Baudry, Urbain 30; Quebec, 1645 *9221.17 p151*
Baudry, William F.; North Carolina, 1852 *1088.45 p2*
Bauer, Adam 45; America, 1846 *778.6 p21*
Bauer, Adam 63; America, 1846 *778.6 p21*
Bauer, Alfred 38; Galveston, TX, 1845 *3967.10 p376*
Bauer, Alois; America, 1867 *7919.3 p524*
  With 2 children
Bauer, Anna 11; New York, NY, 1894 *6512.1 p183*
Bauer, Anna Barbara Rauch SEE Bauer, Michael
Bauer, Anna Katharina SEE Bauer, Georg Heinrich
Bauer, Anna Margaretha; America, 1852 *2526.42 p188*
Bauer, Anna Maria 46; New Orleans, 1848 *778.6 p21*
Bauer, Anna Regina Schmidt SEE Bauer, Georg Heinrich
Bauer, Anton; Wisconsin, 1888 *6795.8 p234*
Bauer, August 17; New Orleans, 1848 *778.6 p21*
Bauer, Balthasar; America, 1831 *2526.43 p133*
Bauer, Beata 3; New York, NY, 1893 *1883.7 p41*
Bauer, Carl 12; New Orleans, 1848 *778.6 p21*
Bauer, Carl 18; New York, NY, 1894 *6512.1 p183*
Bauer, Carl 49; New York, NY, 1894 *6512.1 p183*
Bauer, Caroline 3; Galveston, TX, 1845 *3967.10 p376*
Bauer, Caspar; Washington, 1887 *6015.10 p16*
Bauer, Catherine 7; America, 1846 *778.6 p21*
Bauer, Christ. 19; Port uncertain, 1840 *778.6 p21*
Bauer, Christine 3; America, 1846 *778.6 p21*
Bauer, Egidius 28; Mississippi, 1847 *778.6 p21*
Bauer, Elisabeth 4; America, 1846 *778.6 p21*
Bauer, Elisabeth; Pittsburgh, 1863 *5475.1 p541*
Bauer, Emil 7; New Orleans, 1848 *778.6 p21*
Bauer, Ernst 5; New York, NY, 1894 *6512.1 p183*
Bauer, Eva Elisabeth SEE Bauer, Georg Heinrich
Bauer, Felix; Detroit, 1873 *1494.20 p13*
Bauer, Ferdinand 4; New Orleans, 1848 *778.6 p21*
Bauer, Franz 10; Mississippi, 1847 *778.6 p21*
Bauer, Friedrich 26; Halifax, N.S., 1902 *1860.4 p42*
Bauer, Georg; America, 1848 *2526.43 p145*
  With wife
  Son:Philipp
Bauer, Georg 6 SEE Bauer, Oswald
Bauer, Georg Friedrich; America, 1867 *7919.3 p527*

Bauer, Georg Heinrich; Virginia, 1831 *152.20 p62*
  Wife:Anna Regina Schmidt
  Child:Anna Katharina
  Child:Eva Elisabeth
Bauer, Georg Nikolaus; America, 1880 *2526.43 p137*
Bauer, Georg Paul; America, 1862-1882 *179.55 p19*
Bauer, George; Illinois, 1852 *6079.1 p1*
Bauer, George; Louisiana, 1836-1841 *4981.45 p208*
Bauer, George; Ohio, 1809-1852 *4511.35 p3*
Bauer, Gertrud Sachs 39 SEE Bauer, Oswald
Bauer, Gttfr.; New York, 1860 *358.56 p150*
Bauer, Heinrich; America, 1891 *179.55 p19*
Bauer, Heinrike; America, 1845-1882 *179.55 p19*
Bauer, Henriette 1 months; America, 1846 *778.6 p21*
Bauer, Hermann 17; New York, NY, 1894 *6512.1 p183*
Bauer, Hubert 5; America, 1847 *778.6 p21*
Bauer, Ida C. 22; Kansas, 1880 *777.40 p20*
Bauer, J. D. H.; Louisiana, 1874 *4981.45 p295*
Bauer, Jacques 10; New Orleans, 1848 *778.6 p21*
Bauer, Jakob SEE Bauer, Jakob
Bauer, Jakob; America, 1865 *5475.1 p510*
  Wife:Magdalena Hornung
  Son:Jakob
  Daughter:Mathilde
  Daughter:Magdalena
Bauer, Jakob 38; Galveston, TX, 1845 *3967.10 p376*
Bauer, Jakob 68; Galveston, TX, 1845 *3967.10 p376*
Bauer, Jean 10; Mississippi, 1847 *778.6 p21*
Bauer, Jean J.; Illinois, 1852 *6079.1 p1*
Bauer, Johann; America, 1836 *5475.1 p527*
  With wife
Bauer, Johann; America, 1846-1847 *5475.1 p67*
Bauer, Johann; America, 1846 *5475.1 p233*
Bauer, Johann 15 SEE Bauer, Oswald
Bauer, Johann; Cincinnati, 1852 *5475.1 p235*
Bauer, Johann Abraham; America, 1834 *5475.1 p503*
Bauer, Johann Friedrich Wilhelm Heinrich; America, 1884 *2526.43 p137*
  With grandmother
Bauer, Johann Georg; America, 1885 *179.55 p19*
Bauer, Johann Gottlieb; America, 1882 *179.55 p19*
Bauer, Johann Nikolaus SEE Bauer, Michael
Bauer, Johannes; Pennsylvania, 1866 *170.15 p18*
  With 3 daughters
Bauer, Johannes 41; Pennsylvania, 1866 *170.15 p18*
  With wife & 4 sons
Bauer, Josef; America, 1864 *5475.1 p237*
Bauer, Joseph 20; America, 1847 *778.6 p21*
Bauer, Joseph 24; Louisiana, 1848 *778.6 p21*
Bauer, Karl; America, 1877-1882 *179.55 p19*
Bauer, Karl 4; New York, NY, 1893 *1883.7 p41*
Bauer, Karl 38; New York, NY, 1893 *1883.7 p41*
Bauer, Katharina; America, 1854 *179.55 p19*
Bauer, Katharina 9 SEE Bauer, Oswald
Bauer, Katharina 22; America, 1854 *5475.1 p264*
Bauer, Katharina; Rio Grande do Sul, Brazil, 1881 *5475.1 p533*
Bauer, Lisette 47; New York, NY, 1894 *6512.1 p183*
Bauer, Ludwig; America, 1855 *5475.1 p360*
Bauer, M. Josephine; America, 1881 *5475.1 p152*
Bauer, Madalain 70; Missouri, 1845 *778.6 p21*
Bauer, Madeleine 3; America, 1846 *778.6 p21*
Bauer, Magdalena SEE Bauer, Jakob
Bauer, Magdalena Hornung 26 SEE Bauer, Jakob
Bauer, Magdalena 36; Galveston, TX, 1845 *3967.10 p376*
Bauer, Maria 36; America, 1846 *778.6 p21*
Bauer, Maria Louise; America, 1869-1882 *179.55 p19*
Bauer, Marie 9; America, 1846 *778.6 p21*
Bauer, Mathilde SEE Bauer, Jakob
Bauer, Michael; Virginia, 1831 *152.20 p62*
  Wife:Anna Barbara Rauch
  Child:Johann Nikolaus
Bauer, Michel 52; New Orleans, 1848 *778.6 p21*
Bauer, Nicolas 26; New Orleans, 1848 *778.6 p21*
Bauer, Oswald 36; America, 1863 *5475.1 p45*
  Wife:Gertrud Sachs 39
  Daughter:Katharina 9
  Son:Johann 15 months
  Son:Georg 6
Bauer, Philipp 16 SEE Bauer, Georg
Bauer, Pierre 23; New Orleans, 1846 *778.6 p21*
Bauer, Regina 23; Halifax, N.S., 1902 *1860.4 p42*
Bauer, Regine 30; Mississippi, 1847 *778.6 p21*
Bauer, Rosina 27; New York, NY, 1893 *1883.7 p41*
Bauer, Salomea 34; Galveston, TX, 1845 *3967.10 p376*
Bauer, Sophie; America, 1867 *7919.3 p527*
  With child
Bauer, Sophie 6; America, 1846 *778.6 p21*
Bauer, Sophie Caroline Charlotte; America, 1867 *7420.1 p253*
Bauer, Stephan; America, 1868 *7919.3 p527*
Bauer, Tobias F.; America, 1844-1882 *179.55 p19*

Bauer, Valentin; America, 1837 *5475.1 p549*
  With wife
  With child
Bauer, Wilhelm; America, 1892 *5475.1 p407*
Bauer, Wilhelm Heinrich; America, 1868 *7919.3 p525*
Bauerfeind, William Henry; North Carolina, 1855 *1088.45 p2*
Bauerfeldt, Adolph; Wisconsin, 1869 *7420.1 p279*
Bauerle, Johann Georg; America, 1854 *179.55 p19*
Bauerle, John; Ohio, 1809-1852 *4511.35 p3*
Bauerle, Katharina; America, 1854 *179.55 p19*
Bauerlein, Heinrich; America, 1884 *2526.43 p207*
Bauermann, Georg 47; New Orleans, 1848 *778.6 p21*
Bauermann, Henry 21; Missouri, 1846 *778.6 p21*
Bauermeister, Mr.; America, 1871 *7420.1 p289*
  *Wife:*B. Schmidt
Bauermeister, B. Schmidt *SEE* Bauermeister, Mr.
Bauermeister, C.; America, 1863 *7420.1 p217*
Bauermeister, Franz Carl Adolph; America, 1868 *7420.1 p268*
Bauernfeind, Vincent de; New York, 1859 *358.56 p99*
Bauers, Peter 50; Ontario, 1871 *1823.17 p8*
Bauge, Anne; Canada, 1673 *1142.10 p128*
Bauge, Anne; Quebec, 1673 *4514.3 p276*
Baugeois, . . .; Louisiana, 1874-1875 *4981.45 p297*
Baugh, Jacob; Ohio, 1809-1852 *4511.35 p3*
Baughman, Mathias; Ohio, 1809-1852 *4511.35 p3*
Baugis, Denise Mercier *SEE* Baugis, Francois
Baugis, Francois 55; Quebec, 1641 *9221.17 p101*
  *Wife:*Denise Mercier
  *Son:*Michel 3
Baugis, Michel 3 *SEE* Baugis, Francois
Baugniet, Augustine Paquet *SEE* Baugniet, Clement
Baugniet, Clement; Wisconsin, 1856 *1495.20 p28*
  *Wife:*Augustine Paquet
  *Child:*Francois
  *Child:*Florent
  *Child:*Frederic
Baugniet, Florent *SEE* Baugniet, Clement
Baugniet, Francois *SEE* Baugniet, Clement
Baugniet, Frederic *SEE* Baugniet, Clement
Baulard, Daniel 21; America, 1845 *778.6 p21*
Baulde, Anne; Quebec, 1662 *9221.17 p479*
Bauldin, Peter; Salem, MA, 1672 *9228.50 p159*
Baule, Wilhelmine Sophia; America, 1852 *7420.1 p93*
Baulig, Donolus; Kansas, 1917-1918 *1826.15 p81*
Baulle, Ebenezar 40; Ontario, 1871 *1823.17 p8*
Baum, Apoline 24; America, 1846 *778.6 p21*
Baum, Bernhard 52; America, 1833 *5475.1 p27*
  With wife sons & 3 daughters
Baum, Daniel 24; America, 1847 *778.6 p22*
Baum, Franklin; North Carolina, 1856 *1088.45 p2*
Baum, Maria Friedrichs *SEE* Baum, Mathias
Baum, Mathias; America, 1881 *5475.1 p276*
  *Wife:*Maria Friedrichs
Baum, Philip; Illinois, 1851 *6079.1 p1*
Bauman, Emilie; Wisconsin, 1898 *6795.8 p85*
Bauman, Johannes; Venezuela, 1843 *3899.5 p542*
Bauman, Karl Fredrich Ernst; Wisconsin, 1895 *6795.8 p92*
Baumann, Adam; America, 1854 *2526.43 p133*
Baumann, Carl; America, 1840 *7420.1 p17*
  With son 6
  With daughter 6 months
  With son 2
Baumann, Emilie; Wisconsin, 1898 *6795.8 p85*
Baumann, Gregori; Ohio, 1840-1897 *8365.35 p15*
Baumann, H. L.; Valdivia, Chile, 1852 *1192.4 p55*
Baumann, Herman; Wisconsin, 1892 *6795.8 p173*
Baumann, Herman Jul.; Wisconsin, 1899 *6795.8 p105*
Baumann, Ignatz 23; America, 1847 *778.6 p22*
Baumann, Karl Fredrich Ernst; Wisconsin, 1895 *6795.8 p92*
Baumann, Lina *SEE* Baumann, Maria Sorge
Baumann, Magdalena 21; America, 1847 *778.6 p22*
Baumann, Maria *SEE* Baumann, Maria Sorge
Baumann, Maria; America, 1868 *7919.3 p531*
  *Daughter:*Lina
  *Granddaughter:*Maria
Baumann, Maria Josepha; Venezuela, 1843 *3899.5 p542*
Baumann, Martin 9; America, 1847 *778.6 p22*
Baumann, Regina 8; America, 1847 *778.6 p22*
Baumann, Regina 48; America, 1847 *778.6 p22*
Baumbach, Jacob; America, 1867 *7919.3 p525*
Baumbach, Samuel; America, 1867 *7919.3 p525*
Baumbach, Wilhelm; America, 1868 *7919.3 p532*
  With 3 children
Baumer, Blen. 30; Missouri, 1845 *778.6 p22*
Baumer, John; Boston, 1774 *8529.30 p6*
Baumert, Michael; Illinois, 1854 *6079.1 p1*
Baumfoht, Max M.; New York, NY, 1906 *3331.4 p11*
Baumgarten, Christine; Galveston, TX, 1855 *571.7 p16*

Baumgarten, Friedrich August; Port uncertain, 1839 *7420.1 p15*
Baumgarter, Michel 28; America, 1841 *778.6 p22*
Baumgartner, A. 64; New Orleans, 1834 *1002.51 p112*
Baumgartner, Miss E. 60; New Orleans, 1834 *1002.51 p112*
Baumgartner, Miss M. 34; New Orleans, 1834 *1002.51 p112*
Baumgartner, Mathias 23; New Castle, DE, 1817-1818 *90.20 p150*
Baumhard, Johann Peter; Brazil, 1862 *5475.1 p551*
Baumhardt, Abraham; America, 1863 *5475.1 p557*
  *Wife:*Marg. Elisabeth Neu
  *Daughter:*M. Elisabeth
  *Daughter:*Karoline
Baumhardt, Heinrich; America, 1865 *5475.1 p557*
Baumhardt, Karoline *SEE* Baumhardt, Abraham
Baumhardt, M. Elisabeth *SEE* Baumhardt, Abraham
Baumhardt, Marg. Elisabeth Neu *SEE* Baumhardt, Abraham
Baumhofener, August Heinrich Leopold; America, 1850 *7420.1 p69*
  *Wife:*Sophie Leonore Rosener
Baumhofener, Sophie Leonore Rosener *SEE* Baumhofener, August Heinrich Leopold
Baumont, Augustine 16; Louisiana, 1848 *778.6 p22*
Baumont, Eugenie 50; Louisiana, 1848 *778.6 p22*
Baumont, Fois. 11; Louisiana, 1848 *778.6 p22*
Baumont, Fois. 54; Louisiana, 1848 *778.6 p22*
Baumont, Genevieve 18; Louisiana, 1848 *778.6 p22*
Baumont, Joseph 20; Louisiana, 1848 *778.6 p22*
Baumont, Marie 24; Louisiana, 1848 *778.6 p22*
Baumont, Marie Therese; Wisconsin, 1855 *1495.20 p41*
Baumstark, Valentin 21; America, 1846 *778.6 p22*
Baunach, Jacob; New York, 1872 *1132.30 p150*
Baune, Gillette 18; Quebec, 1649 *9221.17 p209*
Baune, Robert; Quebec, 1659 *9221.17 p412*
Baunum, Bernard 28; Ohio, 1880 *4879.40 p257*
  *Daughter:*Mary E. 1
Baunum, Mary E. 1 *SEE* Baunum, Bernard
Bauques, Sophie 21; America, 1845 *778.6 p22*
Bausbach, Carolina 20; America, 1840 *778.6 p22*
Bausbach, Sebast. 27; America, 1840 *778.6 p22*
Bausch, Anna Margaretha 18 *SEE* Bausch, Johannes
Bausch, Anna Maria 11 *SEE* Bausch, Johannes
Bausch, Elisabetha 15 *SEE* Bausch, Johannes
Bausch, Georg; America, 1883 *2526.42 p180*
Bausch, Johannes; America, 1854 *2526.42 p199*
  With wife
  *Daughter:*Anna Maria
  With stepchild 27
  *Daughter:*Elisabetha
  *Daughter:*Anna Margaretha
Bausch, Wilhelmine Auguste Louise; Wisconsin, 1891 *6795.8 p71*
Bausemier, Ludwig 31; Portland, ME, 1911 *970.38 p76*
Bausher, Jacob; Ohio, 1809-1852 *4511.35 p3*
Bauss, Pierre 25; New Orleans, 1848 *778.6 p22*
Bausse, Aime 27; Port uncertain, 1843 *778.6 p22*
Bausum, Johannes 47; Pennsylvania, 1850 *170.15 p19*
  With son 20
  With son 17
Bautel, Therese 35; New Orleans, 1748 *778.6 p22*
Bautien, Christian; New York, 1859 *358.56 p101*
Bautz, Johann Philipp; Carolina, 1841 *170.15 p19*
  With wife & 4 children
Bauwin, Anne Joseph; Wisconsin, 1856 *1495.20 p45*
Baver, Abraham; North Carolina, 1710 *3629.40 p3*
Baver, Christian; North Carolina, 1710 *3629.40 p3*
Bavereit, Casp 36; Port uncertain, 1840 *778.6 p22*
Bavlur, Sloan 31; Ontario, 1871 *1823.21 p19*
Bawden, George 24; Ontario, 1871 *1823.21 p19*
Bawden, William 37; Ontario, 1871 *1823.21 p19*
Bax, Mr.; America, 1865 *7420.1 p228*
Bax, Widow; America, 1866 *7420.1 p239*
  With child 17
  With child 10
  With child 7
Bax, Friedrich; America, 1854 *7420.1 p115*
Baxler, Cecile 2; America, 1840 *778.6 p22*
Baxler, Etienne 37; America, 1840 *778.6 p22*
Baxler, Julie 6; America, 1840 *778.6 p22*
Baxler, Nicolas 7; America, 1840 *778.6 p22*
Baxler, Therese 40; America, 1840 *778.6 p22*
Baxter, Bernard; North Carolina, 1827-1832 *1088.45 p2*
Baxter, Edward; New Jersey, 1777 *8529.30 p6*
Baxter, Francis 32; Ontario, 1871 *1823.17 p8*
Baxter, George; Philadelphia, 1777 *8529.30 p6*
Baxter, H. A. 46; Ontario, 1871 *1823.21 p19*
Baxter, Isaac 32; Ontario, 1871 *1823.17 p8*
Baxter, James 47; Ontario, 1871 *1823.21 p19*
Baxter, John; North Carolina, 1847 *1088.45 p2*
Baxter, John 36; Ontario, 1871 *1823.17 p8*

Baxter, John 37; Ontario, 1871 *1823.17 p8*
Baxter, John 55; Ontario, 1871 *1823.21 p19*
Baxter, Michael 22; New York, NY, 1849 *6178.50 p152*
Baxter, Owen 17; Quebec, 1870 *8364.32 p22*
Baxter, Robert 35; Ontario, 1871 *1823.17 p8*
Baxter, Robert 43; Ontario, 1871 *1823.17 p8*
Baxter, Sarah; Maryland, 1674-1675 *1236.25 p51*
Baxter, William 40; Ontario, 1871 *1823.17 p8*
Baxter, William 55; Ontario, 1871 *1823.21 p19*
Baxtrom, Charles Fr.; Kansas, 1879 *777.40 p11*
  *Wife:*Christine B. Pehrsdotter
  *Daughter:*Jennie Cath.
  *Son:*John Peter
Baxtrom, Christine B. Pehrsdotter *SEE* Baxtrom, Charles Fr.
Baxtrom, Jennie Cath. *SEE* Baxtrom, Charles Fr.
Baxtrom, John Peter *SEE* Baxtrom, Charles Fr.
Bay, Gotthilf; America, 1882 *179.55 p19*
Bayard, Jean-Baptiste 37; New Orleans, 1748 *778.6 p22*
Baye, Marie Therese; Wisconsin, 1856 *1495.20 p41*
Bayer, Mr.; New England, 1675-1676 *9228.50 p268*
Bayer, Bernhard; America, 1923 *8023.44 p371*
Bayer, John; Louisiana, 1836-1841 *4981.45 p208*
Bayerle, Caroline; New York, 1859 *358.56 p54*
Bayh, Gottliebin; America, 1891 *179.55 p19*
Bayiche, Pierre; Louisiana, 1841-1844 *4981.45 p210*
Baylar, F. 36; New Orleans, 1840 *778.6 p22*
Bayle, Samuel W.; Philadelphia, 1858 *8513.31 p294*
Bayles, Thomas 68; Ontario, 1871 *1823.21 p19*
Bayley, Thomas 17; Ontario, 1871 *1823.21 p20*
Bayley, William 44; Ontario, 1871 *1823.21 p20*
Baylie, Richard 22; Virginia, 1635 *1183.3 p30*
Bayliffe, George W. 64; Ontario, 1871 *1823.21 p20*
Baylis, John 46; Ontario, 1871 *1823.17 p8*
Baylis, Thomas 27; Ontario, 1871 *1823.17 p8*
Baylor, Peter; Iowa, 1891 *1211.15 p9*
Bayls, Robert 29; Ontario, 1871 *1823.17 p8*
Bayly, George; Maryland, 1672 *1236.25 p47*
Bayly, James; Maryland, 1674-1675 *1236.25 p51*
Bayly, Richard 36; Ontario, 1871 *1823.21 p20*
Bayly, Sarah; Maryland, 1674-1675 *1236.25 p52*
Bayly, Thomas; North Carolina, 1812 *1088.45 p2*
Bayly, William 35; Ontario, 1871 *1823.21 p20*
Baynes, Oswald 46; Ontario, 1871 *1823.21 p20*
Baynham, Agnes 9; Ontario, 1871 *1823.21 p20*
Baynham, Eleanor Catherine 11; Ontario, 1871 *1823.21 p20*
Baynton, Christiana 56; Ontario, 1871 *1823.21 p20*
Baynton, Foster 38; Ontario, 1871 *1823.17 p8*
Baynton, William 63; Ontario, 1871 *1823.21 p20*
Bayon, R. 27; America, 1845 *778.6 p22*
Bayot, Cecile; Wisconsin, 1880 *1495.20 p56*
Bays, Joseph 52; Ontario, 1871 *1823.17 p8*
Bazin, Andre; Quebec, 1653 *9221.17 p269*
Bazire, Charles 20; Quebec, 1661 *9221.17 p447*
Bazonlet, Marie 21; Port uncertain, 1843 *778.6 p23*
Bazze, Marie 25; New Orleans, 1845 *778.6 p23*
Bazzi, Marie 25; New Orleans, 1845 *778.6 p23*
Beach, Jane 17; Ontario, 1871 *1823.21 p20*
Beach, Joseph 60; Ontario, 1871 *1823.21 p20*
Beach, Sarah 50; Michigan, 1880 *4491.33 p2*
Beach, Truman 36; Michigan, 1880 *4491.39 p2*
Beach, William 36; Ontario, 1871 *1823.21 p20*
Beach, William S. 31; Michigan, 1880 *4491.39 p2*
Beacroft, John 28; Ontario, 1871 *1823.21 p20*
Beacroft, John 58; Ontario, 1871 *1823.21 p20*
Beadle, George 45; Ontario, 1871 *1823.21 p20*
Beadle, John; Boston, 1745 *9228.50 p652*
Beadle, Samuel; Charlestown, MA, 1623-1664 *9228.50 p96*
Beahl, Dewalt; Ohio, 1809-1852 *4511.35 p3*
Beahneen, John William; Texas, 1900 *3435.45 p35*
Beal, George 14; Quebec, 1870 *8364.32 p22*
Beal, Samuel 14; Quebec, 1870 *8364.32 p22*
Beale, Charlotte 13; Quebec, 1870 *8364.32 p22*
Beale, Jacob; Ohio, 1809-1852 *4511.35 p3*
Bealen, Caroline 18; New Orleans, 1847 *778.6 p23*
Bealen, Johann 50; New Orleans, 1847 *778.6 p23*
Bealey, Thomas; Maryland, 1680 *1236.25 p53*
Beall, John 50; Ontario, 1871 *1823.17 p8*
Beals, Philip; Ohio, 1844 *2763.1 p7*
Beamer, Franklin 19; Ontario, 1871 *1823.21 p20*
Beamish, E. 25; Ontario, 1871 *1823.21 p20*
Beamish, John 45; Ontario, 1871 *1823.21 p20*
Beamish, John 49; Ontario, 1871 *1823.21 p20*
Beamish, Robert 30; Ontario, 1871 *1823.21 p20*
Beamish, Samuel 71; Ontario, 1871 *1823.17 p8*
Bean, Betsy 17; Ontario, 1871 *1823.21 p20*
Bean, Charles 32; Ontario, 1871 *1823.21 p20*
Bean, George 28; Ontario, 1871 *1823.21 p20*
Bean, James 36; Port uncertain, 1846 *778.6 p23*
Bean, Robert 45; Ontario, 1871 *1823.17 p8*
Bean, William 56; Ontario, 1871 *1823.21 p20*

Beanclerk, Mrs.; America, 1840 ***778.6*** *p23*
Beanclerk, V. 40; America, 1840 ***778.6*** *p23*
Beanish, Frank 24; Ontario, 1871 ***1823.21*** *p20*
Beant, Marie Eleon. 31; America, 1847 ***778.6*** *p23*
Beaquet, B. 17; America, 1841 ***778.6*** *p23*
Bear, Andrew; Illinois, 1858 ***6079.1*** *p1*
Bear, Samuel; North Carolina, 1859-1860 ***1088.45*** *p2*
Bear, Thomas; Ohio, 1838 ***3580.20*** *p31*
Bear, Thomas; Ohio, 1838 ***6020.12*** *p6*
Bear, Thomas 73; Ontario, 1871 ***1823.21*** *p20*
Bearcley, George 56; Ontario, 1871 ***1823.21*** *p20*
Beard, Andred; Boston, 1766 ***1642*** *p36*
With 4 children
Beard, Charles 25; Ontario, 1871 ***1823.17*** *p8*
Beard, Cornelius Collins *SEE* Beard, Joseph Antony
Beard, Ellie 25; St. John, N.B., 1834 ***6469.7*** *p6*
Beard, G. R.; Louisiana, 1836-1840 ***4981.45*** *p212*
Beard, Hugh 20; Ontario, 1871 ***1823.21*** *p20*
Beard, J. A.; Louisiana, 1836-1840 ***4981.45*** *p212*
Beard, Joseph Antony; Atlanta, GA, 1830 ***9228.50*** *p256*
*Wife:*May Grover
*Child:*Cornelius Collins
*Child:*Joseph Robert
Beard, Joseph Robert *SEE* Beard, Joseph Antony
Beard, Mary; Maryland, 1672 ***1236.25*** *p47*
Beard, May Grover *SEE* Beard, Joseph Antony
Beard, Oliver J.; Ohio, 1877 ***3580.20*** *p31*
Beard, Oliver J.; Ohio, 1877 ***6020.12*** *p6*
Beare, Elizab.; Maryland, 1673 ***1236.25*** *p48*
Bearman, Abraham; North Carolina, 1853 ***1088.45*** *p2*
Bearman, Isaac; North Carolina, 1850 ***1088.45*** *p2*
Bearman, Samuel; North Carolina, 1855 ***1088.45*** *p2*
Bears, Cassie May Hume *SEE* Bears, Ralph Rosco
Bears, Cyrus Wilfred; Boston, 1875-1925 ***9228.50*** *p277*
Bears, Della Beatrice; Florida, 1918-1974 ***9228.50*** *p277*
Bears, Elizabeth Ann; Boston, 1869-1919 ***9228.50*** *p277*
Bears, Henry Alline; Massachusetts, 1890-1914 ***9228.50*** *p277*
Bears, Inez *SEE* Bears, Ralph Rosco
Bears, Ralph Rosco; Massachusetts, 1910-1912 ***9228.50*** *p277*
*Wife:*Cassie May Hume
*Child:*Inez
*Child:*William Russell
Bears, William Russell *SEE* Bears, Ralph Rosco
Beasford, Joshua F. 24; Ontario, n.d. ***9228.50*** *p97*
Beasler, Joseph; Ohio, 1809-1852 ***4511.35*** *p3*
Beason Family ; America, n.d. ***9228.50*** *p113*
Beasor, Richard 22; Ontario, 1871 ***1823.21*** *p20*
Beasyere, Martin; Ohio, 1809-1852 ***4511.35*** *p3*
Beath, Chas. 46; Ontario, 1871 ***1823.17*** *p9*
Beath, Donald 42; Ontario, 1871 ***1823.17*** *p9*
Beath, John 45; Ontario, 1871 ***1823.17*** *p9*
Beath, Peter 44; Ontario, 1871 ***1823.17*** *p9*
Beatie, Benjamin 42; Ontario, 1871 ***1823.17*** *p9*
Beaton, Annie 20; Ontario, 1871 ***1823.21*** *p20*
Beaton, Archy 36; Ontario, 1871 ***1823.21*** *p21*
Beaton, David 28; North Carolina, 1774 ***1422.10*** *p58*
Beaton, David 28; North Carolina, 1774 ***1422.10*** *p62*
Beaton, David 23; Ontario, 1871 ***1823.17*** *p9*
Beaton, Flora 29; North Carolina, 1774 ***1422.10*** *p58*
Beaton, Flora 29; North Carolina, 1774 ***1422.10*** *p62*
Beaton, James 54; Ontario, 1871 ***1823.17*** *p9*
Beaton, John 29; Ontario, 1871 ***1823.21*** *p21*
Beaton, Mary; New York, 1738 ***8277.31*** *p113*
With son
Beaton, Peter 60; Ontario, 1871 ***1823.17*** *p9*
Beattie, Andrew 60; Ontario, 1871 ***1823.21*** *p21*
Beattie, Benjamin 26; Ontario, 1871 ***1823.21*** *p21*
Beattie, Benjamin 52; Ontario, 1871 ***1823.21*** *p21*
Beattie, Charles 35; Ontario, 1871 ***1823.21*** *p21*
Beattie, Christina Davie *SEE* Beattie, George
Beattie, David 76; Ontario, 1871 ***1823.21*** *p21*
Beattie, Elizabeth 68; Ontario, 1871 ***1823.21*** *p21*
Beattie, George; New York, NY, 1836 ***5024.1*** *p138*
*Wife:*Christina Davie
Beattie, James 25; Ontario, 1871 ***1823.17*** *p9*
Beattie, James 59; Ontario, 1871 ***1823.21*** *p21*
Beattie, James; Washington, 1889 ***2770.40*** *p26*
Beattie, John 36; Ontario, 1871 ***1823.21*** *p21*
Beattie, John 50; Ontario, 1871 ***1823.21*** *p21*
Beattie, John 50; Ontario, 1871 ***1823.21*** *p21*
Beattie, Joseph 28; Ontario, 1871 ***1823.17*** *p9*
Beattie, Margaret 60; Ontario, 1871 ***1823.21*** *p21*
Beattie, Margaret Boyle; Virginia, 1911-1920 ***9228.50*** *p330*
Beattie, Margaret Boyle; Virginia, 1911-1920 ***9228.50*** *p330*
Beattie, Marthia 64; Ontario, 1871 ***1823.21*** *p21*
Beattie, Mary 44; Ontario, 1871 ***1823.17*** *p9*
Beattie, Robert 52; Ontario, 1871 ***1823.21*** *p21*
Beattie, Robert 57; Ontario, 1871 ***1823.17*** *p9*
Beattie, Sarah; New York, NY, 1836 ***5024.1*** *p138*
Beattie, Wm 76; Ontario, 1871 ***1823.21*** *p21*
Beatty, John; Ohio, 1838 ***3580.20*** *p31*
Beatty, John; Ohio, 1838 ***6020.12*** *p6*
Beatty, John 38; Ontario, 1871 ***1823.21*** *p21*
Beatty, Thomas 50; Ontario, 1871 ***1823.17*** *p9*
Beaty, James 34; Ontario, 1871 ***1823.17*** *p9*
Beaty, James 40; Ontario, 1871 ***1823.21*** *p21*
Beau, . . .; America, 1841 ***778.6*** *p23*
Beau, Mr. 26; America, 1841 ***778.6*** *p23*
Beau, Mrs.; America, 1841 ***778.6*** *p23*
Beau, C. 20; New Orleans, 1848 ***778.6*** *p23*
Beauchamp, Edmund; Maryland, 1666 ***9228.50*** *p97*
Beauchamp, Edward; Ipswich, MA, 1642 ***9228.50*** *p97*
Beauchamp, Jacques 1 *SEE* Beauchamp, Jacques
Beauchamp, Jacques 24; Montreal, 1659 ***9221.17*** *p416*
*Wife:*Marie Dardenne 22
*Son:*Jacques 1
Beauchamp, Jean; Ontario, n.d. ***9228.50*** *p17A*
Beauchamp, Marie Dardenne 22 *SEE* Beauchamp, Jacques
Beauchamp, Mary; Ipswich, MA, 1642 ***9228.50*** *p97*
Beauchange, A.; Louisiana, 1874 ***4981.45*** *p295*
Beauchemin, . . .; Canada, n.d. ***9228.50*** *p97*
Beauchemin Family ; Utah, 1800-1899 ***9228.50*** *p17A*
Beaucise, Stanislas 30; America, 1844 ***778.6*** *p23*
Beaucourt, Joseph 40; America, 1846 ***778.6*** *p23*
Beaucourt, Marie 36; America, 1846 ***778.6*** *p23*
Beaude, Jean 33; America, 1847 ***778.6*** *p23*
Beaudet, Laurent *SEE* Beaudet, Marguerite Ardion
Beaudet, Marguerite; Quebec, 1663 ***4514.3*** *p271*
*Son:*Laurent
Beaudin, Ambrose; Massachusetts, 1700-1750 ***9228.50*** *p122*
Beaudin, Catherine; Quebec, 1671 ***4514.3*** *p276*
Beaudin Family ; Massachusetts, n.d. ***9228.50*** *p126*
Beaudin Family ; Newfoundland, 1500-1599 ***9228.50*** *p96*
Beaudon, Etiennette; Quebec, 1671 ***4514.3*** *p276*
Beaufaux, Charlotte Josepine *SEE* Beaufaux, Pierre Joseph
Beaufaux, Jean Joseph *SEE* Beaufaux, Pierre Joseph
Beaufaux, Marie Francoise Socquet *SEE* Beaufaux, Pierre Joseph
Beaufaux, Marie Sylvie *SEE* Beaufaux, Pierre Joseph
Beaufaux, Pierre Joseph; Wisconsin, 1855-1857 ***1495.20*** *p41*
*Wife:*Marie Francoise Socquet
*Child:*Marie Sylvie
*Child:*Jean Joseph
*Child:*Charlotte Josepine
*Child:*Pierre Joseph Desire
Beaufaux, Pierre Joseph Desire *SEE* Beaufaux, Pierre Joseph
Beaufour, Antoine; Quebec, 1649 ***9221.17*** *p209*
Beauger, . . .; New England, n.d. ***9228.50*** *p97*
Beaugie, . . .; New England, n.d. ***9228.50*** *p97*
Beaugrand, Marie; Quebec, 1673 ***4514.3*** *p276*
Beaugy, . . .; New England, n.d. ***9228.50*** *p97*
Beaujean, Elie-Joseph 34; Montreal, 1659 ***9221.17*** *p417*
*Wife:*Suzanne Couignon 33
*Daughter:*Suzanne 3
Beaujean, Francois 35; Louisiana, 1848 ***778.6*** *p23*
Beaujean, Francoise 39; Louisiana, 1848 ***778.6*** *p23*
Beaujean, Marie-Jeanne; Quebec, 1666 ***4514.3*** *p276*
Beaujean, Pierre 6; Louisiana, 1848 ***778.6*** *p23*
Beaujean, Pierre 10; Louisiana, 1848 ***778.6*** *p23*
Beaujean, Suzanne 3 *SEE* Beaujean, Elie-Joseph
Beaujean, Suzanne Couignon 33 *SEE* Beaujean, Elie-Joseph
Beaujean, Thomas 9; Louisiana, 1848 ***778.6*** *p23*
Beaulieu, . . .; Quebec, 1636 ***9221.17*** *p52*
Beaumont, . . .; Ontario, n.d. ***9228.50*** *p97*
Beaumont, Eduard; Valparaiso, Chile, 1850 ***1192.4*** *p50*
Beaumont, Eugen Jakob; America, 1880 ***5475.1*** *p129*
Beaumont, Franc. 38; America, 1840 ***778.6*** *p23*
Beaumont, George 13; Quebec, 1870 ***8364.32*** *p22*
Beaumont, Jean de; Quebec, 1651 ***9221.17*** *p237*
Beaumont, Sebastian Julius; Pittsburgh, 1885 ***5475.1*** *p131*
Beaupre, Nicolas 33; Quebec, 1640 ***9221.17*** *p95*
Beauregard, Claude; Quebec, 1657 ***9221.17*** *p353*
Beauregard, Marguerite; Quebec, 1671 ***4514.3*** *p358*
Beauregard, Marin; Quebec, 1653 ***9221.17*** *p270*
Beauregard, Marthe; Quebec, 1671 ***4514.3*** *p276*
Beausang, Richard 47; Ontario, 1871 ***1823.17*** *p9*
Beausaque deBrillemont, Michel-Honore; Quebec, 1729 ***2314.30*** *p171*
Beausier, Jeanne 29; Quebec, 1658 ***9221.17*** *p376*
Beausieur, Joseph; Montreal, 1651 ***9221.17*** *p251*
Beaussaut, Alexandre 39; Port uncertain, 1847 ***778.6*** *p23*
Beauvais, Jacques 29; Montreal, 1653 ***9221.17*** *p282*
Beauvais, Pierre; Montreal, 1653 ***9221.17*** *p282*
Beauvalais, Mr. 32; Louisiana, 1848 ***778.6*** *p23*
Beauveau, Jeanne; Quebec, 1672 ***4514.3*** *p276*
Beaux, Mr. 20; Port uncertain, 1844 ***778.6*** *p23*
Beavington, William 19; Ontario, 1871 ***1823.21*** *p21*
Beaynam, John 47; Ontario, 1871 ***1823.21*** *p21*
Bebbings, James 22; Ontario, 1871 ***1823.17*** *p9*
Bebendee, J. P. 18; New Orleans, 1848 ***778.6*** *p23*
Bebenet, Mr. 45; America, 1841 ***778.6*** *p23*
Beber, Nicolas 22; New Orleans, 1846 ***778.6*** *p23*
Bebeza, Henry; Louisiana, 1874-1875 ***4981.45*** *p298*
Bebo, Joseph; Washington, 1884 ***2770.40*** *p192*
Bec, Jn. Pre. 21; Havana, 1848 ***778.6*** *p23*
Becak, Jan; Texas, 1856 ***2853.20*** *p64*
Becard deGrandville, Pierre; Quebec, 1665 ***2314.30*** *p167*
Becard deGrandville, Pierre; Quebec, 1665 ***2314.30*** *p174*
Becart, Mr. 21; Louisiana, 1848 ***778.6*** *p23*
Beccard, Louis Amedee 23; America, 1846 ***778.6*** *p23*
Bechan, Robert 30; Ontario, 1871 ***1823.17*** *p9*
Bechel, Fred. 17; America, 1846 ***778.6*** *p24*
Bechel, George; Ohio, 1809-1852 ***4511.35*** *p3*
Bechel, Mathias; Ohio, 1809-1852 ***4511.35*** *p3*
Bechel, Matthais; Ohio, 1809-1852 ***4511.35*** *p3*
Bechel, Michael; Ohio, 1809-1852 ***4511.35*** *p3*
Bechel, Nicholas; Ohio, 1809-1852 ***4511.35*** *p3*
Bechele, Theobald; Ohio, 1809-1852 ***4511.35*** *p3*
Bechen, John H. P.; Illinois, 1852 ***6079.1*** *p1*
Becher, Andrew; Ohio, 1809-1852 ***4511.35*** *p3*
Becher, Constantine; Ohio, 1809-1852 ***4511.35*** *p3*
Becher, Henry Cr 53; Ontario, 1871 ***1823.21*** *p21*
Becher, Philip; Ohio, 1809-1852 ***4511.35*** *p3*
Becher, Sophie Wilhelmine Friederike; America, 1881 ***7420.1*** *p322*
Becherel, Mr.; Port uncertain, 1844 ***778.6*** *p24*
Becherel, Emile 36; Port uncertain, 1846 ***778.6*** *p24*
Bechler, Florian; Ohio, 1809-1852 ***4511.35*** *p3*
Bechlinger, Andreas; America, n.d. ***8115.12*** *p317*
Bechlinger, Anna Margarethe; America, 1848 ***8115.12*** *p317*
Bechlinger, Anna Marie; America, 1847 ***8115.12*** *p319*
*Child:*Johann Georg
Bechlinger, Elisabeth; America, 1870 ***8115.12*** *p317*
Bechlinger, Elisabeth; America, 1870 ***8115.12*** *p320*
*Child:*Louise
Bechlinger, Johann Georg *SEE* Bechlinger, Anna Marie
Bechlinger, Louise *SEE* Bechlinger, Elisabeth
Bechlinger, Marie Katharine; America, 1848 ***8115.12*** *p317*
Bechman, John; Ohio, 1809-1852 ***4511.35*** *p3*
Bechon, J. 30; America, 1848 ***778.6*** *p24*
Becht, Marg. A. 27; New York, NY, 1847 ***9176.15*** *p50*
Becht, Nicolaus 22; New York, NY, 1847 ***9176.15*** *p50*
Bechtel, Carl; America, 1852 ***7420.1*** *p84*
Bechtel, Herman; Illinois, 1851 ***6079.1*** *p1*
Bechtel, Isaac K.; Washington, 1889 ***2770.40*** *p26*
Bechtel, Maria 24; America, 1881 ***5475.1*** *p429*
Bechthold, Andreas *SEE* Bechthold, Elisabeth Margarethe
Bechthold, Anna Margarethe *SEE* Bechthold, Elisabeth Margarethe
Bechthold, Anna Marie *SEE* Bechthold, Elisabeth Margarethe
Bechthold, Anna Marie; America, n.d. ***8115.12*** *p323*
Bechthold, Elisabeth *SEE* Bechthold, Elisabeth Margarethe
Bechthold, Elisabeth Margarethe; America, 1842 ***8115.12*** *p326*
*Child:*Johannes
*Child:*Anna Margarethe
*Child:*Elisabeth
*Child:*Anna Marie
*Child:*Andreas
*Child:*Georg Philipp
Bechthold, Georg Philipp *SEE* Bechthold, Elisabeth Margarethe
Bechthold, Johannes *SEE* Bechthold, Elisabeth Margarethe
Bechtler, August; North Carolina, 1832 ***1088.45*** *p2*
Bechtler, Christ. 39; America, 1840 ***778.6*** *p24*
Bechtler, Christopher; North Carolina, 1832 ***1088.45*** *p2*
Bechtler, Eliza 35; America, 1840 ***778.6*** *p24*
Bechtler, Joseph 13; America, 1840 ***778.6*** *p24*
Bechtler, Karl 7; America, 1840 ***778.6*** *p24*
Bechtler, Marie 9; America, 1840 ***778.6*** *p24*
Bechtler, Nicolas 5; America, 1840 ***778.6*** *p24*
Bechtmeyer, Joseph 22; New York, NY, 1847 ***9176.15*** *p50*
Bechtold, Christian *SEE* Bechtold, Christian
Bechtold, Christian; America, 1882 ***5475.1*** *p16*
*Wife:*Sophie Gleichmann
*Son:*Christian
Bechtold, Dorothea 1 *SEE* Bechtold, Jakob
Bechtold, Elisabetha 14 *SEE* Bechtold, Jakob

Bechtold, Eva Elisabetha 10 *SEE* Bechtold, Jakob
Bechtold, Friedrich; Pennsylvania, 1848 *170.15 p19*
  With wife & 5 children
Bechtold, Jakob; America, 1853 *2526.43 p145*
  Wife: Maria Katharina Stein
  Stepchild: Eva Elisabetha
  Stepchild: Johannes
  Daughter: Dorothea
  Stepchild: Leonhard
  Stepchild: Katharina
  Stepchild: Elisabetha
Bechtold, Johann Adam; America, 1883 *2526.43 p203*
Bechtold, Johannes 6 *SEE* Bechtold, Jakob
Bechtold, John; Illinois, 1856 *6079.1 p1*
Bechtold, Katharina 12 *SEE* Bechtold, Jakob
Bechtold, Leonhard 8 *SEE* Bechtold, Jakob
Bechtold, Maria Katharina Stein *SEE* Bechtold, Jakob
Bechtold, Martin; Illinois, 1856 *6079.1 p1*
Bechtold, Samuel; Illinois, 1856 *6079.1 p1*
Bechtold, Sophie Gleichmann 22 *SEE* Bechtold, Christian
Bechtold, Wilhelm 26; New York, NY, 1893 *1883.7 p42*
Beck, Mr.; Wisconsin, 1882 *5475.1 p277*
Beck, Adam; America, 1886 *2526.43 p137*
Beck, Adam 17; America, 1881 *2526.42 p135*
Beck, Andreas; New York, NY, 1893 *3366.30 p70*
Beck, Anna Remark *SEE* Beck, Nikolaus
Beck, Anna Elisabetha; America, 1872 *2526.43 p137*
Beck, Anna Maria Backes 31 *SEE* Beck, Jakob
Beck, Antoine 2; New Orleans, 1848 *778.6 p24*
Beck, Antoinette 6; New Orleans, 1848 *778.6 p24*
Beck, Aurelia 5; New Orleans, 1848 *778.6 p24*
Beck, Catharine 35; New Orleans, 1848 *778.6 p24*
Beck, Christian 15 *SEE* Beck, Christina
Beck, Christina; America, 1844 *2526.42 p187*
  Son: Friedrich
  Son: Christian
Beck, Christina 3; New York, NY, 1898 *7951.13 p42*
Beck, Conrad 28; New York, NY, 1885 *1883.7 p45*
Beck, Elisabeth *SEE* Beck, Elisabetha
Beck, Elisabeth 27 *SEE* Beck, Johannes
Beck, Elisabetha; America, 1855 *2526.42 p113*
  Child: Elisabeth
Beck, Francois 49; New Orleans, 1848 *778.6 p24*
Beck, Frederick; Ohio, 1809-1852 *4511.35 p3*
Beck, Friedrich; America, 1836 *2526.42 p104*
Beck, Friedrich; America, 1853 *2526.42 p187*
Beck, Friedrich; America, 1871 *5475.1 p219*
Beck, Friedrich 25 *SEE* Beck, Christina
Beck, Friedrich 27; Cadiz,, 1888 *5475.1 p215*
Beck, Fritz; America, 1854 *2526.43 p163*
Beck, Georg; Colorado, 1888 *5475.1 p214*
Beck, Georg; New York, NY, 1894 *3366.30 p70*
Beck, George; Illinois, 1865 *6079.1 p1*
Beck, George 37; New York, NY, 1898 *7951.13 p42*
Beck, Gottlieb; New York, NY, 1888 *3366.30 p70*
Beck, Heinrich; America, 1882 *2526.43 p137*
Beck, Henry; Wisconsin, 1906 *6795.8 p234*
Beck, Hugh 60; Ontario, 1871 *1823.21 p21*
Beck, J. David; Wisconsin, 1872 *6795.8 p100*
Beck, Jacob; New York, NY, 1888 *3366.30 p70*
Beck, Jacques 6 months; New Orleans, 1848 *778.6 p24*
Beck, Jakob 30; America, 1864 *5475.1 p544*
  Wife: Anna Maria Backes 31
  Niece: Katharina 8
Beck, James; Miami, 1920 *4984.15 p38*
Beck, Jean 22; New Orleans, 1846 *778.6 p24*
Beck, Johann; America, 1872 *5475.1 p171*
Beck, Johann; America, 1882 *5475.1 p221*
Beck, Johann Henrich; America, 1854 *170.15 p19*
Beck, Johann Peter 29; Pennsylvania, 1850 *170.15 p19*
  With wife
Beck, Johannes 29; America, 1871 *2526.42 p135*
  Wife: Elisabeth 27
  With child 1
Beck, John; Ohio, 1840-1897 *8365.35 p15*
Beck, John 38; Ontario, 1871 *1823.21 p21*
Beck, John 40; Ontario, 1871 *1823.21 p21*
Beck, John Christopher; Illinois, 1854 *6079.1 p1*
Beck, Julia A. 49; Ontario, 1871 *1823.21 p21*
Beck, Julius; Washington, 1882 *2770.40 p135*
Beck, Karl; New York, NY, 1894 *3366.30 p70*
Beck, Karolina 7; New York, NY, 1898 *7951.13 p42*
Beck, Katharina 8 *SEE* Beck, Jakob
Beck, Konrad; America, 1836 *2526.42 p187*
  With wife
  With child 9
Beck, Konrad; America, 1882 *5475.1 p174*
Beck, Magdalena; America, 1838 *2526.42 p178*
Beck, Magdalena; America, 1841 *2526.42 p172*
Beck, Magdalena 38; America, 1837 *2526.43 p137*
  Daughter: Margaretha 4
Beck, Margaretha 4 *SEE* Beck, Magdalena
Beck, Maria *SEE* Beck, Nikolaus

Beck, Maria 36; New York, NY, 1898 *7951.13 p42*
Beck, Mary A. 21; Ontario, 1871 *1823.21 p21*
Beck, Mary Ann Darby; Providence, RI, 1875-1911 *9228.50 p413*
Beck, Mathias 22; America, 1846 *778.6 p24*
Beck, Nikolaus; America, 1872 *5475.1 p172*
  Wife: Anna Remark
  Daughter: Maria
Beck, Nikolaus; America, 1888 *2526.43 p137*
Beck, Nikolaus 27; Galveston, TX, 1844 *3967.10 p374*
Beck, Paul; Iowa, 1892 *1211.15 p9*
Beck, Pauline 7; New Orleans, 1848 *778.6 p24*
Beck, Peter 30; America, 1890 *5475.1 p221*
Beck, Rasmus M.; Iowa, 1894 *1211.15 p9*
Beck, Sebastian Andrew; Illinois, 1854 *6079.1 p1*
Beck, Sophie 28; New York, NY, 1885 *1883.7 p45*
Beck, Thomas; North Carolina, 1853 *1088.45 p2*
Beck, Vaclav; Iowa, 1855 *2853.20 p156*
Beck, Wilhelm; Illinois, 1854 *6079.1 p1*
Beck, Wilhelm; New York, NY, 1888 *3366.30 p70*
Beck, William 25; Ontario, 1871 *1823.21 p21*
Beck, Wolfgang; Ohio, 1809-1852 *4511.35 p3*
Becka, Jan; Texas, 1856 *2853.20 p64*
Beckard, Adam; America, 1870 *5475.1 p405*
Beckel, Caroline Wilhelmine Charlotte *SEE* Beckel, Friedrich Wilhelm
Beckel, Friederike Charlotte *SEE* Beckel, Friedrich Wilhelm
Beckel, Friedrich Wilhelm *SEE* Beckel, Friedrich Wilhelm
Beckel, Friedrich Wilhelm; America, 1867 *7420.1 p253*
  Wife: Wilhelmine Justine Charlotte Pock
  Daughter: Friederike Charlotte
  Son: Heinrich Friedrich Wilhelm
  Son: Friedrich Wilhelm
  Daughter: Caroline Wilhelmine Charlotte
Beckel, Heinrich Friedrich Wilhelm *SEE* Beckel, Friedrich Wilhelm
Beckel, Wilhelmine Justine Charlotte Pock *SEE* Beckel, Friedrich Wilhelm
Beckenbach, August; America, 1881 *5475.1 p34*
Beckend, Ellen 19; Ontario, 1871 *1823.21 p22*
Beckendorf, Georg *SEE* Beckendorf, Jakob
Beckendorf, Jakob 34; New Orleans, 1860 *5475.1 p328*
  Wife: Katharina Uhrmacher 27
  Son: Georg
Beckendorf, Katharina; America, 1891 *5475.1 p79*
Beckendorf, Katharina Uhrmacher 27 *SEE* Beckendorf, Jakob
Beckenhoupt, George; Ohio, 1809-1852 *4511.35 p3*
Becker, Miss; Chicago, 1865 *7420.1 p228*
Becker, Mr.; Chicago, 1865 *7420.1 p228*
Becker, Adrian; America, 1861 *5475.1 p482*
  Daughter: Anna
  Son: Johanna
  Daughter: Helena
  Son: Nikolaus
  Son: Heinrich
Becker, Albert *SEE* Becker, Wilhelm
Becker, Albert; Valdivia, Chile, 1850 *1192.4 p48*
Becker, Amalie Wunn 27 *SEE* Becker, Karl
Becker, Angela; America, 1875 *5475.1 p213*
Becker, Angela Kettenhofen 28 *SEE* Becker, Anton
Becker, Angela *SEE* Becker, Michel
Becker, Anna *SEE* Becker, Adrian
Becker, Anna 6 *SEE* Becker, Mathias
Becker, Anna Kolling 28 *SEE* Becker, Mathias
Becker, Anna; Texas, 1881 *5475.1 p202*
Becker, Anna 7; Texas, 1913 *8425.16 p31*
Becker, Anna 34; Texas, 1913 *8425.16 p31*
Becker, Anna Maria *SEE* Becker, Bernhard
Becker, Anna Maria 16 *SEE* Becker, Johann
Becker, Anna Maria 50; America, 1872 *5475.1 p354*
  Daughter: Karoline
  Son: Karl Alexander
  Son: Friedrich
Becker, Anne Sophie Wilhelmine Caroline *SEE* Becker, Johann Conrad
Becker, Anton 26; America, 1855 *5475.1 p317*
  Wife: Angela Kettenhofen 28
  Son: Peter 1
Becker, August *SEE* Becker, Nikolaus
Becker, Barbara *SEE* Becker, Nikolaus
Becker, Barbara *SEE* Becker, Nikolaus
Becker, Barbara *SEE* Becker, Nikolaus
Becker, Barbara *SEE* Becker, Bernhard
Becker, Barbara *SEE* Becker, Margarethe Steffensky
Becker, Barbara 30; America, 1800-1899 *5475.1 p314*
Becker, Barbara Minas 40 *SEE* Becker, Johann
Becker, Barbara 50; America, 1857 *5475.1 p500*
Becker, Barbara 41; Brazil, 1857 *5475.1 p368*
Becker, Barbara 55; Brazil, 1862 *5475.1 p289*
Becker, Barbara 17 *SEE* Becker, Elisabeth Zeiger
Becker, Barbara *SEE* Becker, Nikolaus

Becker, Bernhard; America, 1872 *5475.1 p134*
  Wife: Maria Hermann
  Daughter: Anna Maria
  Daughter: Barbara
Becker, Carl; America, 1857 *7420.1 p157*
Becker, Carl; Chile, 1852 *1192.4 p51*
Becker, Carl; Ohio, 1893 *7420.1 p367*
Becker, Catarine Engel; America, 1867 *7420.1 p264*
  Son: Johann Heinrich
  Daughter: Engel Marie Sophie
  Daughter: Engel Marie Dorothea
  Son: Hans Heinrich Otto
  Daughter: Engel Marie Dorothea
Becker, Catharine Marie; America, 1868 *7420.1 p278*
Becker, Catharine Marie *SEE* Becker, Sophie Louise Charlotte Schaefer
Becker, Charles; Washington, 1885 *2770.40 p193*
Becker, Charlotte Escher; America, 1868 *7420.1 p268*
  With children
Becker, Christian; America, 1855 *7420.1 p134*
Becker, Christine; America, 1874 *5475.1 p361*
Becker, Christine Sarter *SEE* Becker, Friedrich
Becker, Christine 4 *SEE* Becker, Mathias
Becker, Claudius; America, 1883 *5475.1 p70*
Becker, Constantine; Ohio, 1809-1852 *4511.35 p3*
Becker, David 2; Texas, 1913 *8425.16 p31*
Becker, Dorothea 32; America, 1837 *5475.1 p120*
Becker, Eleonore; America, 1856 *7420.1 p144*
  With 3 sons
Becker, Elisabeth *SEE* Becker, Philipp
Becker, Elisabeth; America, 1873 *5475.1 p140*
  Son: Johann
  Daughter: Eva
  Son: Peter
  Mother-In-Law: Kath. Engstler
Becker, Elisabeth; America, 1881 *5475.1 p307*
Becker, Elisabeth; America, 1881 *5475.1 p336*
Becker, Elisabeth 14 *SEE* Becker, Johann
Becker, Elisabeth 22; America, 1837 *5475.1 p63*
Becker, Elisabeth 29; America, 1837 *5475.1 p63*
Becker, Elisabeth Beiling 29 *SEE* Becker, Josef
Becker, Elisabeth Heiser 40 *SEE* Becker, Johann
Becker, Elisabeth *SEE* Becker, Heinrich
Becker, Elisabeth Kollet *SEE* Becker, Mathias
Becker, Elisabeth; Chicago, 1875 *5475.1 p384*
  Son: Johann
  Daughter: Barbara
  Daughter: Elisabeth
Becker, Elisabeth 10 *SEE* Becker, Elisabeth Zeiger
Becker, Elisabeth; Ohio, 1880 *5475.1 p373*
Becker, Engel Dorothea; America, 1867 *7420.1 p255*
Becker, Engel Marie Dorothee *SEE* Becker, Sophie Louise Charlotte Schaefer
Becker, Engel Marie Sophie; America, 1866 *7420.1 p239*
Becker, Engel Marie Sophie; America, 1868 *7420.1 p268*
Becker, Engel Marie Sophie Caroline *SEE* Becker, Johann Conrad
Becker, Engel Marie Sophie Charlotte Spindler *SEE* Becker, Johann Conrad
Becker, Engel Marie Sophie Dorothee *SEE* Becker, Johann Conrad
Becker, Ernest; New York, 1859 *358.56 p101*
Becker, Eva *SEE* Becker, Elisabeth Jung
Becker, Eva Streit *SEE* Becker, Michel
Becker, Frank; Louisiana, 1874 *4981.45 p131*
Becker, Franz 23; America, 1863 *5475.1 p269*
Becker, Franz 64; America, 1860 *5475.1 p269*
  Wife: Katharina Muller 54
  Son: Mathias 19
  Daughter: Maria 14
Becker, Franz; New York, 1849 *5475.1 p477*
Becker, Franz Josef; America, 1839 *5475.1 p470*
Becker, Friedrich; America, 1854 *7420.1 p115*
Becker, Friedrich 21; America, 1856 *5475.1 p503*
Becker, Friedrich *SEE* Becker, Friedrich
Becker, Friedrich; Brazil, 1859 *5475.1 p523*
  Wife: Christine Sarter
  Son: Friedrich
Becker, Friedrich 11; Texas, 1913 *8425.16 p31*
Becker, Friedrich 48; Texas, 1913 *8425.16 p31*
Becker, Friedrich Christian; America, 1854 *7420.1 p115*
Becker, Friedrich Wilhelm; America, 1854 *7420.1 p115*
Becker, Friedrich Wilhelm; Port uncertain, 1853 *7420.1 p102*
Becker, Fritz; Chicago, 1865 *7420.1 p228*
Becker, Georg 3; Texas, 1913 *8425.16 p31*
Becker, Georg Konrad; America, n.d. *8115.12 p325*
Becker, George; Nova Scotia, 1784 *7105 p22*
Becker, Gertrud 27; America, 1860 *5475.1 p314*
Becker, H. P.; Valdivia, Chile, 1852 *1192.4 p55*
  With wife & baby
Becker, H. W.; Valdivia, Chile, 1852 *1192.4 p55*

Becker, Hans H. Conrad Otto *SEE* Becker, Johann
Conrad
Becker, Hans Heinrich; America, 1855 *7420.1 p134*
  *Wife:*Sophie Eleonore Dopking
  *Son:*Heinrich Friedr. Christian
  *Son:*Heinrich Conrad Wilh.
Becker, Heinrich *SEE* Becker, Philipp
Becker, Heinrich *SEE* Becker, Adrian
Becker, Heinrich; America, 1867 *7420.1 p253*
  With family
Becker, Heinrich; America, 1876 *5475.1 p350*
Becker, Heinrich; Brazil, 1859 *5475.1 p523*
  *Wife:*Philippine Reis
  *Daughter:*Elisabeth
  *Daughter:*Luise
  *Daughter:*Katharina
  *Daughter:*Philippine
  *Son:*Karl
Becker, Heinrich Conrad Wilh. *SEE* Becker, Hans
Heinrich
Becker, Heinrich Fr. Conrad *SEE* Becker, Johann Conrad
Becker, Heinrich Friedr. Christian *SEE* Becker, Hans
Heinrich
Becker, Helena *SEE* Becker, Adrian
Becker, Helena *SEE* Becker, Michel
Becker, Helene; America, 1846 *5475.1 p472*
Becker, J. Baptist *SEE* Becker, Michel
Becker, Jacob; Illinois, 1834-1900 *6020.5 p131*
Becker, Jakob; America, 1844 *5475.1 p472*
Becker, Jakob; America, 1852 *5475.1 p538*
Becker, Jakob *SEE* Becker, Nikolaus
Becker, Jakob *SEE* Becker, Nikolaus
Becker, Jakob; America, 1879 *5475.1 p44*
Becker, Jakob 11 *SEE* Becker, Johann
Becker, Jakob *SEE* Becker, Michel
Becker, Johann; America, 1854 *7420.1 p115*
Becker, Johann *SEE* Becker, Nikolaus
Becker, Johann *SEE* Becker, Nikolaus
Becker, Johann *SEE* Becker, Josef
Becker, Johann *SEE* Becker, Elisabeth Jung
Becker, Johann; America, 1873 *5475.1 p172*
  *Wife:*Magdalena Burgard
  *Daughter:*Katharina
  *Daughter:*Magdalena
Becker, Johann; America, 1881 *5475.1 p202*
Becker, Johann; America, 1881 *5475.1 p276*
Becker, Johann 6 *SEE* Becker, Johann
Becker, Johann 29; America, 1877 *5475.1 p517*
Becker, Johann 41; America, 1855 *5475.1 p244*
  *Wife:*Barbara Minas 40
  *Daughter:*Margarethe 2
  *Son:*Jakob 11
  *Son:*Johann 6
Becker, Johann 42; America, 1855 *5475.1 p317*
  *Wife:*Elisabeth Heiser 40
  *Daughter:*Elisabeth 14
  With mother-in-law 75
  *Daughter:*Anna Maria 16
Becker, Johann 20 *SEE* Becker, Elisabeth Zeiger
Becker, Johann *SEE* Becker, Michel
Becker, Johann *SEE* Becker, Michel
Becker, Johann Conrad; America, 1855 *7420.1 p134*
  *Wife:*Engel Marie Sophie Charlotte Spindler
  *Daughter:*Anne Sophie Wilhelmine Caroline
  *Son:*Hans H. Conrad Otto
  *Son:*Johann Friedrich Christoph
  *Daughter:*Sophie Philippine
  *Daughter:*Engel Marie Sophie Caroline
  *Son:*Heinrich Fr. Conrad
  *Daughter:*Engel Marie Sophie Dorothee
Becker, Johann Conrad Ludwig; America, 1860 *7420.1
p191*
Becker, Johann Friedrich Christoph *SEE* Becker, Johann
Conrad
Becker, Johann Heinr. Conrad *SEE* Becker, Sophie
Louise Charlotte Schaefer
Becker, Johann Heinrich Conrad; America, 1857 *7420.1
p157*
Becker, Johann Heinrich Wilhelm; America, 1846 *7420.1
p42*
Becker, Johann Karl *SEE* Becker, Philipp
Becker, Johann Nikolaus 30; America, 1886 *5475.1 p485*
  *Wife:*Maria Lambert
  *Daughter:*M. Katharina
  *Son:*Josef Wilhelm
Becker, Johann Philipp; America, 1834 *8115.12 p325*
Becker, Johanna *SEE* Becker, Adrian
Becker, Johannes; America, 1799-1834 *8115.12 p317*
Becker, Josef; America, 1840 *5475.1 p471*
Becker, Josef 31; America, 1869 *5475.1 p315*
Becker, Josef 31; America, 1872 *5475.1 p336*
  *Wife:*Elisabeth Beiling 29
  *Son:*Lambert

  *Daughter:*Katharina
  *Son:*Nikolaus
  *Son:*Johann
Becker, Josef Wilhelm *SEE* Becker, Johann Nikolaus
Becker, Karl; America, 1864 *5475.1 p45*
  *Wife:*Amalie Wunn
  *Son:*Peter
  *Son:*Karl
  *Son:*Ludwig
Becker, Karl 7 *SEE* Becker, Karl
Becker, Karl *SEE* Becker, Heinrich
Becker, Karl Wilhelm *SEE* Becker, Philipp
Becker, Kath. Engstler *SEE* Becker, Elisabeth Jung
Becker, Katharina; America, 1837 *5475.1 p66*
Becker, Katharina *SEE* Becker, Josef
Becker, Katharina *SEE* Becker, Johann
Becker, Katharina; America, 1881 *5475.1 p55*
Becker, Katharina Muller 54 *SEE* Becker, Franz
Becker, Katharina; Arkansas, 1880 *5475.1 p299*
Becker, Katharina *SEE* Becker, Heinrich
Becker, Katharina 3 *SEE* Becker, Mathias
Becker, Katharina 4 *SEE* Becker, Mathias
Becker, Katharina *SEE* Becker, Nikolaus
Becker, Katharina 4; Texas, 1913 *8425.16 p31*
Becker, Katharina *SEE* Becker, Michel
Becker, Konrad; America, 1843 *5475.1 p270*
Becker, Lambert *SEE* Becker, Josef
Becker, Lewis; Ohio, 1809-1852 *4511.35 p3*
Becker, Ludwig 5 *SEE* Becker, Karl
Becker, Ludwig Adolph August; America, 1859 *7420.1
p183*
Becker, Luise *SEE* Becker, Philipp
Becker, Luise 70; America, 1843 *5475.1 p529*
Becker, Luise *SEE* Becker, Heinrich
Becker, Luise Juliana; Rio Grande do Sul, Brazil, 1861
5475.1 p505
Becker, M. Josef *SEE* Becker, Nikolaus
Becker, M. Katharina *SEE* Becker, Johann Nikolaus
Becker, Magdalena *SEE* Becker, Johann
Becker, Magdalena Burgard 29 *SEE* Becker, Johann
Becker, Magdalena 30; America, 1837 *5475.1 p70*
Becker, Magrethe 14; America, 1880 *5475.1 p420*
Becker, Margarethe *SEE* Becker, Philipp
Becker, Margarethe *SEE* Becker, Nikolaus
Becker, Margarethe Bitzer *SEE* Becker, Nikolaus
Becker, Margarethe; America, 1880 *5475.1 p220*
Becker, Margarethe; America, 1881 *5475.1 p203*
  *Daughter:*Barbara
  *Son:*Peter
  *Daughter:*Maria
Becker, Margarethe 2 *SEE* Becker, Johann
Becker, Marguerite 28; Louisiana, 1848 *778.6 p24*
Becker, Maria; America, 1861 *5475.1 p482*
  *Daughter:*Katharina
  *Daughter:*Anna Maria
  *Daughter:*Elisabeth
  *Daughter:*Helena
  *Son:*Christoph
Becker, Maria; America, 1871 *5475.1 p212*
Becker, Maria Hermann *SEE* Becker, Bernhard
Becker, Maria; America, 1873 *5475.1 p167*
Becker, Maria *SEE* Becker, Margarethe Steffensky
Becker, Maria Lambert *SEE* Becker, Johann Nikolaus
Becker, Maria 14 *SEE* Becker, Franz
Becker, Maria *SEE* Becker, Wilhelm
Becker, Maria *SEE* Becker, Nikolaus
Becker, Maria Klein *SEE* Becker, Nikolaus
Becker, Maria Kiefer *SEE* Becker, Michel
Becker, Maria 6 months; Texas, 1913 *8425.16 p31*
Becker, Marie Sophie Dorothea; America, 1868 *7420.1
p268*
Becker, Mathias; America, 1863 *5475.1 p302*
Becker, Mathias; America, 1872 *6442.17 p65*
Becker, Mathias; America, 1879 *5475.1 p44*
Becker, Mathias 19 *SEE* Becker, Franz
Becker, Mathias 2 *SEE* Becker, Mathias
Becker, Mathias 28; Brazil, 1873 *5475.1 p517*
  *Wife:*Elisabeth Kollet
  *Daughter:*Katharina 3 months
Becker, Mathias 39; Brazil, 1864 *5475.1 p370*
  *Wife:*Anna Kolling 28
  *Son:*Mathias 2
  *Daughter:*Christine 4 months
  *Daughter:*Anna 6
  *Daughter:*Katharina 4
Becker, Mathias *SEE* Becker, Michel
Becker, Michel; America, 1856 *5475.1 p365*
Becker, Michel; America, 1866 *5475.1 p185*
Becker, Michel; America, 1882 *5475.1 p293*
Becker, Michel; New York, 1899 *5475.1 p426*
Becker, Michel; Pennsylvania, 1886 *5475.1 p265*
  *Wife:*Maria Kiefer
  *Daughter:*Angela

  *Son:*Johann
  *Daughter:*Helena
  *Son:*Jakob
Becker, Michel *SEE* Becker, Michel
Becker, Michel; Wisconsin, 1887 *5475.1 p268*
  *Wife:*Eva Streit
  *Son:*Michel
  *Son:*Mathias
  *Daughter:*Katharina
  *Son:*Nikolaus
  *Son:*J. Baptist
  *Son:*Peter
  *Son:*Johann
Becker, Moritz *SEE* Becker, Nikolaus
Becker, Nathalia 9; Texas, 1913 *8425.16 p31*
Becker, Nels; St. Paul, MN, 1887 *1865.50 p39*
Becker, Nik.; Pennsylvania, 1883 *5475.1 p293*
Becker, Nikolaus; America, 1838 *5475.1 p469*
Becker, Nikolaus; America, 1857 *5475.1 p321*
Becker, Nikolaus *SEE* Becker, Nikolaus
Becker, Nikolaus; America, 1860 *5475.1 p314*
  *Wife:*Barbara
  *Son:*Jakob
  *Son:*Johann
  *Son:*Nikolaus
  *Daughter:*Barbara
  *Son:*Peter
Becker, Nikolaus *SEE* Becker, Adrian
Becker, Nikolaus *SEE* Becker, Nikolaus
Becker, Nikolaus; America, 1872 *5475.1 p212*
  *Wife:*Margarethe Bitzer
  *Daughter:*Margarethe
  *Son:*Jakob
  *Son:*Nikolaus
  *Son:*Johann
  *Son:*Peter
  *Son:*Moritz
Becker, Nikolaus *SEE* Becker, Josef
Becker, Nikolaus 20; America, 1855 *5475.1 p317*
Becker, Nikolaus 36; America, 1855 *5475.1 p244*
Becker, Nikolaus *SEE* Becker, Nikolaus
Becker, Nikolaus; Ohio, 1884 *5475.1 p316*
  *Wife:*Maria Klein
  *Son:*M. Josef
  *Son:*August
  *Daughter:*Barbara
  *Son:*Nikolaus
  *Daughter:*Maria
  *Daughter:*Katharina
Becker, Nikolaus *SEE* Becker, Michel
Becker, Peter *SEE* Becker, Philipp
Becker, Peter *SEE* Becker, Nikolaus
Becker, Peter; America, 1868 *5475.1 p350*
Becker, Peter *SEE* Becker, Nikolaus
Becker, Peter *SEE* Becker, Elisabeth Jung
Becker, Peter; America, 1876 *5475.1 p151*
Becker, Peter *SEE* Becker, Margarethe Steffensky
Becker, Peter 1 *SEE* Becker, Anton
Becker, Peter 9 *SEE* Becker, Karl
Becker, Peter 33; America, 1843 *5475.1 p257*
Becker, Peter 29; Brazil, 1857 *5475.1 p516*
Becker, Peter; Iowa, 1880 *5475.1 p275*
Becker, Peter *SEE* Becker, Michel
Becker, Phil. Wilhelm *SEE* Becker, Philipp
Becker, Philip; Ohio, 1809-1852 *4511.35 p3*
Becker, Philipp; America, 1833 *5475.1 p11*
  *Son:*Simon Philipp
  *Son:*Karl Wilhelm
  *Daughter:*Luise
  *Son:*Johann Karl
  *Son:*Phil. Wilhelm
  *Daughter:*Elisabeth
  *Son:*Peter
  *Son:*Heinrich
  *Daughter:*Margarethe
Becker, Philippine *SEE* Becker, Heinrich
Becker, Philippine Reis *SEE* Becker, Heinrich
Becker, Pierre 20; America, 1842 *778.6 p24*
Becker, Rachel 18; New York, NY, 1893 *1883.7 p42*
Becker, Reisel 6; New York, NY, 1893 *1883.7 p42*
Becker, Sara 44; New York, NY, 1893 *1883.7 p42*
Becker, Schael 10; New York, NY, 1893 *1883.7 p42*
Becker, Simon Philipp *SEE* Becker, Philipp
Becker, Sophie; America, 1854 *7420.1 p115*
Becker, Sophie; America, 1856 *7420.1 p144*
  With 2 sons & daughter
Becker, Sophie Charlotte *SEE* Becker, Sophie Louise
Charlotte Schaefer
Becker, Sophie Charlotte *SEE* Becker, Sophie Louise
Charlotte Schaefer
Becker, Sophie Eleonore Dopking *SEE* Becker, Hans
Heinrich

Becker, Sophie Louise Charlotte; America, 1870 ***7420.1*** *p282*
*Daughter:*Sophie Charlotte
*Granddaughter:*Engel Marie Dorothee
*Granddaughter:*Catharine Marie
*Son:*Johann Heinr. Conrad
*Granddaughter:*Sophie Charlotte
Becker, Sophie Philippine *SEE* Becker, Johann Conrad
Becker, Susanna; Arkansas, 1880 ***5475.1*** *p299*
Becker, Wilhelm; Brazil, 1904-1950 ***8023.44*** *p371*
With wife
*Daughter:*Maria
*Son:*Albert
Becker, Wilhelm Friedrich; Chicago, 1870 ***7420.1*** *p282*
Beckeran, Fredrick; New York, 1860 ***358.56*** *p4*
Beckerhof, Johann 29; New York, 1855 ***5475.1*** *p481*
Beckerll, William; North Carolina, 1811-1812 ***1088.45*** *p2*
Beckers, Josep; Valdivia, Chile, 1851 ***1192.4*** *p51*
Becker-Schmitz, Anna *SEE* Becker-Schmitz, Peter
Becker-Schmitz, Peter *SEE* Becker-Schmitz, Peter
Becker-Schmitz, Peter 45; America, 1857 ***5475.1*** *p517*
*Daughter:*Anna
*Son:*Peter
Beckert, Joseph; Illinois, 1857 ***6079.1*** *p1*
Becket, . . .; Salem, MA, n.d. ***9228.50*** *p97*
Becket, Francis; New York, 1834 ***9228.50*** *p97*
Becket, Hilda; Seattle, 1910-1950 ***9228.50*** *p653*
Becket, Michael 40; Ontario, 1871 ***1823.21*** *p22*
Beckett, Lucy; Colorado, 1897 ***1029.59*** *p7*
Beckett, Lucy; Colorado, 1902 ***1029.59*** *p6*
Beckett, Robert Henry; Colorado, 1900 ***1029.59*** *p7*
Beckett, William; Colorado, 1897 ***1029.59*** *p7*
Beckett, William; Colorado, 1902 ***1029.59*** *p7*
Beckhardt, Fr. Wilhelm; America, 1867 ***5475.1*** *p417*
Becking, Franz; America, 1866 ***5475.1*** *p123*
Becking, Franz; America, 1867 ***5475.1*** *p124*
Beckinger, Elisabeth Zugage 20 *SEE* Beckinger, Peter
Beckinger, Peter; America, 1868 ***5475.1*** *p282*
*Wife:*Elisabeth Zugage
Beckley, John 44; Ontario, 1871 ***1823.21*** *p22*
Beckman, A.F.; Cleveland, OH, 1887-1901 ***9722.10*** *p117*
Beckman, Carl L.; Washington, 1887 ***2770.40*** *p24*
Beckman, Frank Gustaf; St. Paul, MN, 1887 ***1865.50*** *p39*
Beckman, Henry; Ohio, 1840-1897 ***8365.35*** *p15*
Beckman, Hilda; Minnesota, 1925 ***2769.54*** *p1381*
Beckman, Hilda 35; Minnesota, 1923 ***2769.54*** *p1381*
Beckman, Hulda; St. Paul, MN, 1885-1899 ***1865.50*** *p40*
Beckman, John; Cleveland, OH, 1884-1894 ***9722.10*** *p117*
Beckman, John Alfred; Chicago, 1889-1890 ***1865.50*** *p40*
Beckman, Mary; North Carolina, 1792-1862 ***1088.45*** *p6*
Beckman, Mary; North Carolina, 1856 ***1088.45*** *p2*
Beckman, Theodore; Minnesota, 1925 ***2769.54*** *p1381*
Beckman, Theodore 43; Minnesota, 1923 ***2769.54*** *p1381*
Beckmann, Allien 23; New Orleans, 1841 ***778.6*** *p24*
Beckmann, Friederich August; Wisconsin, 1871 ***6795.8*** *p92*
Beckmann, Friedrich Wilhelm; America, 1867 ***7420.1*** *p253*
Beckmann, Henry; Illinois, 1860 ***6079.1*** *p1*
Beckmann, Julian 25; New Orleans, 1841 ***778.6*** *p24*
Beckmann, Peter; America, 1873 ***8023.44*** *p371*
Becknell, Charles; Ohio, 1809-1852 ***4511.35*** *p3*
Beckrich, Antona 36; America, 1847 ***778.6*** *p24*
Beckrich, Jacob 2; America, 1847 ***778.6*** *p24*
Beckrich, Lorenz 35; America, 1847 ***778.6*** *p24*
Beckrich, Louisa 35; America, 1847 ***778.6*** *p24*
Beckrich, Magdalena 6 months; America, 1847 ***778.6*** *p24*
Beckstead, Gordon S.; Idaho, 1891 ***3687.1*** *p35*
Beckstead, Orin M.; Nevada, 1912 ***3687.1*** *p35*
Beckstead, William E.; California, 1909 ***1211.45*** *p131*
Beckstran, A. O.; Washington, 1889 ***2770.40*** *p26*
Beckstrom, J.P.; New York, NY, 1848 ***6412.40*** *p151*
Becktert, Peter; Illinois, 1854-1855 ***6079.1*** *p1*
Beckton, George 45; Ontario, 1871 ***1823.21*** *p22*
Beckton, George 70; Ontario, 1871 ***1823.21*** *p22*
Beckton, George 71; Ontario, 1871 ***1823.21*** *p22*
Beckwith, William 54; Ontario, 1871 ***1823.21*** *p22*
Becomcey, Nicolas 36; America, 1841 ***778.6*** *p24*
Becourt, Auguste 30; Texas, 1843 ***778.6*** *p24*
Becquet, Francois 33; Quebec, 1659 ***9221.17*** *p395*
Bectman, John; Philadelphia, 1778 ***8529.30*** *p2*
Becton, John 80; Ontario, 1871 ***1823.21*** *p22*
Beczkala, Mary; Wisconsin, 1891 ***6795.8*** *p54*
Bedard, Isaac 44; Quebec, 1660 ***9221.17*** *p431*
*Son:*Jacques 15
Bedard, Jacques 15 *SEE* Bedard, Isaac
Bedard, Marie 23; Montreal, 1658 ***9221.17*** *p388*
Beddome, Fostick B. 50; Ontario, 1871 ***1823.21*** *p22*
Bedeaux, Silvester; Ohio, 1809-1852 ***4511.35*** *p3*
Bederage, Wm 26; Ontario, 1871 ***1823.21*** *p22*
Bedford, Gordon 21; Ontario, 1871 ***1823.17*** *p9*
Bedford, James 38; Ontario, 1871 ***1823.21*** *p22*
Bedford, John 36; Ontario, 1871 ***1823.21*** *p22*
Bedford, Suzanne 19; Quebec, 1649 ***9221.17*** *p210*
Bedgegood, Jerry 20; Ontario, 1871 ***1823.21*** *p22*
Bedier, Hercule J. B. A.; Illinois, 1852 ***6079.1*** *p1*
Bedier, Jean Francis; Illinois, 1853 ***6079.1*** *p1*
Bedke, John August; Wisconsin, 1892 ***6795.8*** *p29*
Bedle, Daniel; Louisiana, 1797 ***9228.50*** *p96*
Bednar, Antonin; Omaha, NE, 1900 ***2853.20*** *p153*
Bednar, Martin Fr.; Nebraska, 1847-1910 ***2853.20*** *p182*
Bednarova, Marie; Iowa, 1850-1910 ***2853.20*** *p218*
Bednarski, Stephen; Detroit, 1930 ***1640.60*** *p78*
Bedoni, Joseph 12; New Orleans, 1848 ***778.6*** *p24*
Bedot, Mary 20; New Orleans, 1846 ***778.6*** *p24*
Bedwell, Charles 16; Quebec, 1870 ***8364.32*** *p22*
Bee, Detlef; Washington, 1873 ***2770.40*** *p134*
Beeby, Jo. 17; Virginia, 1635 ***1183.3*** *p31*
Beech, Henry 30; Ontario, 1871 ***1823.21*** *p22*
Beech, Rosa 34; Ontario, 1871 ***1823.21*** *p22*
Beecom, Irving; Ohio, 1844 ***3580.20*** *p31*
Beecom, Irving; Ohio, 1844 ***6020.12*** *p6*
Beede, Eli 14; New England, 1713-1715 ***9228.50*** *p98*
Beedle, Lawrence; Maryland, 1673 ***1236.25*** *p49*
Beehan, . . .; Newfoundland, n.d. ***9228.50*** *p98*
Been, Walfrid; Philadelphia, 1847 ***6412.40*** *p150*
Beer, Amalia Schneider *SEE* Beer, Henry
Beer, Anna 44; America, 1858 ***5475.1*** *p310*
Beer, Barbara 58; America, 1881 ***5475.1*** *p420*
Beer, Carl Ludwig; America, 1868 ***7919.3*** *p531*
Beer, Christopher 80; Ontario, 1871 ***1823.21*** *p22*
Beer, Friedrich; America, 1868 ***7919.3*** *p526*
Beer, Henry; Baltimore, 1853 ***8513.31*** *p294*
*Wife:*Amalia Schneider
Beer, Henry 40; Ontario, 1871 ***1823.21*** *p22*
Beer, Henry 50; Ontario, 1871 ***1823.21*** *p22*
Beer, Jacob C. 41; Ontario, 1871 ***1823.21*** *p22*
Beer, John Phillip; North Carolina, 1855 ***1088.45*** *p2*
Beer, Thomas 35; Ontario, 1871 ***1823.17*** *p9*
Beerberg, Caroline Louise Wilhelmine; America, 1867 ***7420.1*** *p253*
Beere, Henry 24; Virginia, 1635 ***1183.3*** *p30*
Beers, Charles 71; Ontario, 1871 ***1823.21*** *p22*
Beers, Daniel; Massachusetts, 1675-1676 ***1642*** *p130*
Beers, Robert; Massachusetts, 1675-1676 ***1642*** *p130*
Bees, Eliza 24; Ontario, 1871 ***1823.21*** *p22*
Beffield, Sarah 85; Ontario, 1871 ***1823.21*** *p22*
Begair, William 17; Michigan, 1880 ***4491.39*** *p3*
Begarrie, Becie; Washington, 1886 ***2770.40*** *p195*
Begemann, Heinrich; America, 1858 ***7420.1*** *p176*
Beger, Edward 29; Ontario, 1871 ***1823.21*** *p22*
Begg, Alexander 36; Ontario, 1871 ***1823.21*** *p22*
Begg, James G. 33; Ontario, 1871 ***1823.21*** *p22*
Begg, John 30; Ontario, 1871 ***1823.21*** *p22*
Begg, William 69; Ontario, 1871 ***1823.21*** *p22*
Begg, William 72; Ontario, 1871 ***1823.21*** *p22*
Beggendorff, Fr.; Venezuela, 1843 ***3899.5*** *p546*
Beggs, John C.; Boston, 1829 ***3274.55*** *p27*
Beggs, John N. 24; Michigan, 1880 ***4491.33*** *p2*
Begin, Diane Meloque *SEE* Begin, Jacques
Begin, Jacques; Quebec, 1656 ***9221.17*** *p331*
*Wife:*Diane Meloque
*Son:*Louis
Begin, Louis 25 *SEE* Begin, Jacques
Beglau, Friedr. 6 months; New York, NY, 1886 ***8425.16*** *p33*
Beglau, Friedr. 35; New York, NY, 1886 ***8425.16*** *p33*
Beglau, Gottl. 5; New York, NY, 1886 ***8425.16*** *p33*
Beglau, Johannes 7; New York, NY, 1886 ***8425.16*** *p33*
Beglau, Katha 2; New York, NY, 1886 ***8425.16*** *p33*
Beglau, Katha 33; New York, NY, 1886 ***8425.16*** *p33*
Beglen, J. 22; America, 1845 ***778.6*** *p25*
Begly, Ann Marie 24; New Orleans, 1845 ***778.6*** *p25*
Begly, John 31; New Orleans, 1845 ***778.6*** *p25*
Begnier, Joseph-Masse 35; Quebec, 1660 ***9221.17*** *p431*
Begon, Claude-Michel; Quebec, 1712 ***2314.30*** *p169*
Begon, Claude-Michel; Quebec, 1712 ***2314.30*** *p174*
Begourdan, Osmyn 34; America, 1843 ***778.6*** *p25*
Beguein, Robert; Quebec, 1659 ***9221.17*** *p412*
Beguin, D. H.; Louisiana, 1836-1841 ***4981.45*** *p208*
Beh, Josifeh 22; New York, NY, 1847 ***9176.15*** *p49*
Beh, Peter 29; New York, NY, 1847 ***9176.15*** *p49*
Beh, Rosina 25; New York, NY, 1847 ***9176.15*** *p49*
Behan, Bridget; St. Johns, N.F., 1825 ***1053.15*** *p6*
Behan, Cornelius; Boston, 1832 ***3274.55*** *p66*
Behan, Eliza; St. Johns, N.F., 1825 ***1053.15*** *p7*
Behan, Johanne; St. Johns, N.F., 1825 ***1053.15*** *p7*
Behan, John; New Orleans, 1850 ***7242.30*** *p134*
Behan, Patrick; New Orleans, 1850 ***7242.30*** *p134*
Behan, Thomas; St. Johns, N.F., 1825 ***1053.15*** *p6*
Behan, William; St. Johns, N.F., 1825 ***1053.15*** *p7*
Behler, Conrad; New Jersey, 1749-1774 ***927.31*** *p3*
Behler, Valentine; New Jersey, 1749-1774 ***927.31*** *p3*
Behles, Angela *SEE* Behles, Christoph
Behles, Anna 51; America, 1856 ***5475.1*** *p352*
Behles, Anna *SEE* Behles, Christoph
Behles, Barbara Schommer *SEE* Behles, Peter
Behles, Christoph; Ohio, 1880 ***5475.1*** *p373*
*Wife:*Elisabeth Becker
*Daughter:*Anna
*Daughter:*Irmina
*Son:*Josef
*Son:*Mathias
*Son:*Johann
*Daughter:*Angela
Behles, Elisabeth Becker *SEE* Behles, Christoph
Behles, Franz; America, 1892 ***5475.1*** *p76*
Behles, Irmina *SEE* Behles, Christoph
Behles, Jakob 38; America, 1843 ***5475.1*** *p366*
Behles, Johann; America, 1868 ***5475.1*** *p363*
Behles, Johann *SEE* Behles, Christoph
Behles, Johann; Ohio, 1880 ***5475.1*** *p373*
Behles, Josef *SEE* Behles, Christoph
Behles, Margarethe; Brazil, 1874 ***5475.1*** *p371*
Behles, Margarethe 22; Brazil, 1862 ***5475.1*** *p370*
Behles, Maria; Brazil, 1880 ***5475.1*** *p372*
Behles, Mathias *SEE* Behles, Christoph
Behles, Peter; Chicago, 1880 ***5475.1*** *p373*
*Wife:*Barbara Schommer
Behling, H.; New York, 1859 ***358.56*** *p55*
Behling, Heinrich Conrad Wilhelm; America, 1872 ***7420.1*** *p293*
Behling, Heinrich Friedrich Conrad; Iowa, 1878 ***7420.1*** *p310*
Behling, Marie Dorothee Louise; America, 1893 ***7420.1*** *p369*
Behling, Wilhelm; America, 1868 ***7420.1*** *p268*
Behm, Albert R.; Wisconsin, 1904 ***6795.8*** *p178*
Behm, August; Wisconsin, 1897 ***6795.8*** *p178*
Behm, Carl Ernst August; Wisconsin, 1891 ***6795.8*** *p221*
Behm, Dorothea; Miami, 1935 ***4984.12*** *p39*
Behm, Wilhelm Friedrich; Wisconsin, 1889 ***6795.8*** *p221*
Behme, Friedrich Ferdinand August; America, 1872 ***7420.1*** *p293*
Behme, Wilhelm Ludwig; America, 1856 ***7420.1*** *p145*
Behner, Cathe. 30; America, 1841 ***778.6*** *p25*
Behner, Jean 10; America, 1841 ***778.6*** *p25*
Behner, Joseph 39; America, 1841 ***778.6*** *p25*
Behner, Marie 18; America, 1841 ***778.6*** *p25*
Behnke, Carl 32; Galveston, TX, 1855 ***571.7*** *p16*
Behnke, Gottfried; Galveston, TX, 1855 ***571.7*** *p16*
Behnke, Johann; Wisconsin, 1873 ***6795.8*** *p63*
Behnke, John; Illinois, 1864 ***6079.1*** *p1*
Behnos, Bernard 24; America, 1847 ***778.6*** *p25*
Behr, Charles; Ohio, 1840-1897 ***8365.35*** *p15*
Behrend, Mr.; America, 1854 ***7420.1*** *p115*
Behrend, Adolph; America, 1864 ***7420.1*** *p222*
Behrend, Jakob; America, 1853 ***7420.1*** *p102*
Behrend, Michael; America, 1854 ***7420.1*** *p115*
Behrend, Peter; Iowa, 1885 ***5475.1*** *p319*
Behrend, Wilhelm; America, 1854 ***7420.1*** *p115*
Behrend, Wolf; America, 1858 ***7420.1*** *p176*
Behrendt, Christina 64; New York, NY, 1887 ***6954.7*** *p41*
Behrendt, Heinrich 22; New York, NY, 1887 ***6954.7*** *p41*
Behrendt, Heinrich 68; New York, NY, 1887 ***6954.7*** *p41*
Behrendt, Maria 3 months; New York, NY, 1887 ***6954.7*** *p41*
Behrendt, Maria 23; New York, NY, 1887 ***6954.7*** *p41*
Behrens, Henry; Nebraska, 1905 ***3004.30*** *p46*
Behrens, Henry; Washington, 1889 ***2770.40*** *p26*
Behrens, Konrad; Wisconsin, 1895 ***6795.8*** *p155*
Behrens, W.; America, 1857 ***7420.1*** *p157*
With wife
Behring, William; Washington, 1889 ***2770.40*** *p26*
Behringer, David; New York, 1860 ***358.56*** *p149*
Behrling, J.H.; Philadelphia, 1848 ***6412.40*** *p150*
Behu, August; Louisiana, 1874 ***4981.45*** *p131*
Beickmann, Mr.; America, 1855 ***7420.1*** *p134*
With wife stepchild & 2 daughters
Beickmann, Carl Friedrich Wilhelm; America, 1854 ***7420.1*** *p115*
Beidler, Samuel; Ohio, 1809-1852 ***4511.35*** *p3*
Beidler, Ulrich; Ohio, 1809-1852 ***4511.35*** *p3*
Beidner, Mollie; Detroit, 1929-1930 ***6214.5*** *p67*
Beier, Eduard Julius; America, 1868 ***7919.3*** *p530*
With wife & son
Beier, Erik; New York, 1923 ***8023.44*** *p371*
*Wife:*Hedwig Viegener
Beier, Hedwig Viegener *SEE* Beier, Erik
Beier, Helene; America, 1923 ***8023.44*** *p371*
Beierlein, Erich; New York, 1923 ***8023.44*** *p371*
*Wife:*Hedwig Viegener
Beierlein, Hedwig Viegener *SEE* Beierlein, Erich
Beiersdorfer, Georg; America, 1868 ***7919.3*** *p532*
With wife & 3 children

Beig, Theodore 20; America, 1747 ***778.6*** *p25*
Beiher, Lewis 39; America, 1843 ***778.6*** *p25*
Beihmann, A.; Galveston, TX, 1855 ***571.7*** *p17*
Beik, Carolin 6; New Orleans, 1843 ***778.6*** *p25*
Beik, Catharine 10; New Orleans, 1843 ***778.6*** *p25*
Beik, Margrate 4; New Orleans, 1843 ***778.6*** *p25*
Beik, Maria 20; New Orleans, 1843 ***778.6*** *p25*
Beik, Una 16; New Orleans, 1843 ***778.6*** *p25*
Beik, Una Maria 18; New Orleans, 1843 ***778.6*** *p25*
Beil, Frederick; Ohio, 1809-1852 ***4511.35*** *p4*
Beil, Frederick; Ohio, 1809-1852 ***4511.35*** *p6*
Beil, Jacob; Valdivia, Chile, 1852 ***1192.4*** *p52*
Beiling, Elisabeth 29; America, 1872 ***5475.1*** *p336*
Bein, Thomas; Louisiana, 1836-1840 ***4981.45*** *p212*
Beinhardt, Maria Wilhelmine Amanda; America, 1868 ***7919.3*** *p525*
Beinix, John; New York, 1895 ***1766.20*** *p3*
Beire, Jean 39; New Orleans, 1846 ***778.6*** *p16*
Beirich, Nikolaus; America, 1881 ***5475.1*** *p136*
Beirich, Peter 28; America, 1894 ***5475.1*** *p39*
Beisheim, Gustav Adolf Hermann; America, 1881 ***7420.1*** *p319*
Beisner, Ernst; America, 1883 ***7420.1*** *p334*
Beisner, Friedrich Christian; America, 1866 ***7420.1*** *p239*
Beisner, Heinrich Wilhelm; Port uncertain, 1858 ***7420.1*** *p176*
Beisner, Johanne; America, 1861 ***7420.1*** *p202*
Beisner, Ludwig Welsede; America, 1848 ***7420.1*** *p58*
With son 18
With son 11
With son 5
With daughter 3
With son 8
With son 13
Beisner, Sophie Louise; America, 1855 ***7420.1*** *p143*
Beisner, Wilhelmine; America, 1860 ***7420.1*** *p191*
Beissner, Widow; America, 1859 ***7420.1*** *p183*
*Son:*Carl Wilhelm
Beissner, August; America, 1867 ***7420.1*** *p253*
*Brother:*Heinrich
Beissner, C. Hr.; America, 1860 ***7420.1*** *p191*
Beissner, Carl; America, 1869 ***7420.1*** *p279*
Beissner, Carl Heinrich Ludwig; America, 1854 ***7420.1*** *p115*
Beissner, Carl Wilhelm *SEE* Beissner, Widow
Beissner, Christian Friedrich August; America, 1883 ***7420.1*** *p334*
Beissner, Ernst Friedrich Wilhelm *SEE* Beissner, Johann Friedrich Christian
Beissner, Fr.; America, 1861 ***7420.1*** *p202*
With parents & wife & children
Beissner, Franz Friedrich Ludwig; America, 1902 ***7420.1*** *p378*
Beissner, Friedrich; America, 1884 ***7420.1*** *p398*
Beissner, Friedrich Conrad; America, 1868 ***7420.1*** *p268*
Beissner, Georg Philipp; America, 1867 ***7420.1*** *p253*
Beissner, Heinrich; America, 1857 ***7420.1*** *p157*
With son daughter & wife
Beissner, Heinrich; America, 1858 ***7420.1*** *p176*
With family
Beissner, Heinrich *SEE* Beissner, August
Beissner, Johann Friedrich Christian; America, 1881 ***7420.1*** *p319*
*Son:*Ernst Friedrich Wilhelm
Beissner, Johanne Karoline Wilhelmine *SEE* Beissner, Karl Friedrich August
Beissner, Karl Friedrich August; America, 1865 ***7420.1*** *p229*
*Sister:*Johanne Karoline Wilhelmine
Beissner, Ludwig Hermann Wilhelm; America, 1902 ***7420.1*** *p378*
Beissner, Wilhelmine; America, 1854 ***7420.1*** *p115*
With sister
Beisswenger, Gottlieb; America, 1880 ***179.55*** *p19*
Beisswenger, Jakob; America, 1866 ***179.55*** *p19*
Beisswenger, Jakob; America, 1883 ***179.55*** *p19*
Beisswenger, Johann; America, 1881 ***179.55*** *p19*
Beisswenger, Johann Georg; America, 1881 ***179.55*** *p19*
Beisswenger, Johann Georg; America, 1894 ***179.55*** *p19*
Beisswenger, Karl Heinrich; America, 1889 ***179.55*** *p19*
Beisswenger, Rebekka; America, 1853 ***179.55*** *p19*
Beitner, Rose; Detroit, 1929 ***1640.55*** *p115*
Beitz, David 33; Portland, ME, 1911 ***970.38*** *p76*
Bejcek, Jan; Cleveland, OH, 1838-1910 ***2853.20*** *p476*
Bejick, Carl Eduard; Wisconsin, 1873 ***6795.8*** *p89*
Bejoutet, Leon 25; Port uncertain, 1846 ***778.6*** *p25*
Bejtz, David 33; Portland, ME, 1911 ***970.38*** *p76*
Bekedorf, Franz August Georg Simon; Port uncertain, 1898 ***7420.1*** *p374*
Beker, Rudolph; Colorado, 1898 ***1029.59*** *p7*
Bekmann, Friederich August; Wisconsin, 1871 ***6795.8*** *p92*
Belair, Mathurin; Quebec, 1658 ***9221.17*** *p381*
Belame, Jean 33; Port uncertain, 1843 ***778.6*** *p25*
Beland, Miss 6; New Orleans, 1845 ***778.6*** *p25*
Beland, Bapt...e Marie 27; New Orleans, 1845 ***778.6*** *p25*
Belanger, Francois 24; Quebec, 1636 ***9221.17*** *p52*
Belanger, Michel 30; Quebec, 1658 ***9221.17*** *p376*
Belanger, Nicolas 19; Quebec, 1655 ***9221.17*** *p320*
Belanger, Noel; Quebec, 1643 ***9221.17*** *p128*
Belanger, Rene; Montreal, 1653 ***9221.17*** *p282*
Belanger, Suzanne; Quebec, 1662 ***9221.17*** *p483*
Belard, Martin 22; America, 1843 ***778.6*** *p32*
Belard, Michel 18; America, 1843 ***778.6*** *p32*
Belash, Betsey; Marblehead, MA, 1804 ***9228.50*** *p88*
Belash, Philip; Marblehead, MA, 1790 ***9228.50*** *p88*
Belchamber, James 57; Ontario, 1871 ***1823.17*** *p9*
Beldt, C.; Venezuela, 1843 ***3899.5*** *p546*
Belestat, Jean; Quebec, 1638 ***9221.17*** *p76*
Belet, Philippe; Quebec, 1659 ***9221.17*** *p412*
Belford, Ailce; Maryland, 1672 ***1236.25*** *p47*
Belford, Charlotte; Ontario, 1835 ***9228.50*** *p98*
Belford, John 60; Ontario, 1871 ***1823.17*** *p9*
Belg, Carl 29; America, 1847 ***778.6*** *p25*
Belg, Michel 18; America, 1847 ***778.6*** *p25*
Belgen, Solomen; Colorado, 1871 ***1029.59*** *p7*
Belhomme, Marie 34; Quebec, 1644 ***9221.17*** *p140*
Belhomme, Mathurin; Quebec, 1647 ***9221.17*** *p175*
Belin, Joe; Texas, 1884 ***3435.45*** *p35*
Beliot, Charles-Jean; Montreal, 1653 ***9221.17*** *p282*
Beliveau, Joseph 40; Ohio, 1880 ***4879.40*** *p257*
With son
Belk, Jonathan; Philadelphia, 1778 ***8529.30*** *p2A*
Belkiu, Peter; Louisiana, 1874 ***4981.45*** *p130*
Belknap, Jane Dickie; Boston, 1740 ***1642*** *p26*
Bell, A. Maria Schwindling *SEE* Bell, Johann Peter
Bell, Adam 47; Ontario, 1871 ***1823.17*** *p9*
Bell, Agnes 20; New York, NY, 1835 ***5024.1*** *p136*
Bell, Alexander 49; Ontario, 1871 ***1823.21*** *p22*
Bell, Andrew 38; Ontario, 1871 ***1823.17*** *p10*
Bell, Andrew 69; Ontario, 1871 ***1823.17*** *p9*
Bell, Anna *SEE* Bell, Johann Peter
Bell, Archibald 62; Ontario, 1871 ***1823.21*** *p22*
Bell, Catharine 50; Ontario, 1871 ***1823.17*** *p10*
Bell, Christena 56; Ontario, 1871 ***1823.17*** *p10*
Bell, Christopher 44; Ontario, 1871 ***1823.17*** *p10*
Bell, David 89; Ontario, 1871 ***1823.21*** *p22*
Bell, Francis 54; Ontario, 1871 ***1823.21*** *p22*
Bell, George 23; New York, NY, 1835 ***5024.1*** *p136*
Bell, H. 40; Ontario, 1871 ***1823.21*** *p22*
Bell, Hannah 59; Ontario, 1871 ***1823.17*** *p10*
Bell, Harray 32; Ontario, 1871 ***1823.21*** *p22*
Bell, Henry 43; Ontario, 1871 ***1823.21*** *p22*
Bell, J.H. Forrest; Washington, 1886 ***2770.40*** *p195*
Bell, James 30; New York, NY, 1825 ***6178.50*** *p148*
Bell, James; North America, 1750 ***1640.8*** *p234*
Bell, James 34; Ontario, 1871 ***1823.21*** *p22*
Bell, James 42; Ontario, 1871 ***1823.17*** *p10*
Bell, James 43; Ontario, 1871 ***1823.21*** *p22*
Bell, James 58; Ontario, 1871 ***1823.21*** *p22*
Bell, James 60; Ontario, 1871 ***1823.21*** *p22*
Bell, James 63; Ontario, 1871 ***1823.17*** *p10*
Bell, James 82; Ontario, 1871 ***1823.21*** *p22*
Bell, Johann Peter; Chicago, 1887 ***5475.1*** *p244*
*Wife:*A. Maria Schwindling
*Son:*Peter
*Daughter:*Anna
*Daughter:*Maria
Bell, John; Jamestown, VA, 1633 ***1658.20*** *p211*
Bell, John 30; Ontario, 1871 ***1823.17*** *p10*
Bell, John 31; Ontario, 1871 ***1823.17*** *p10*
Bell, John 37; Ontario, 1871 ***1823.21*** *p23*
Bell, John 50; Ontario, 1871 ***1823.17*** *p10*
Bell, John 52; Ontario, 1871 ***1823.21*** *p23*
Bell, John 60; Ontario, 1871 ***1823.21*** *p23*
Bell, John Thomas; Washington, 1882 ***2770.40*** *p135*
Bell, Joseph 19; Ontario, 1871 ***1823.21*** *p23*
Bell, Joseph 32; Ontario, 1871 ***1823.17*** *p10*
Bell, Joshua 40; Ontario, 1871 ***1823.21*** *p23*
Bell, Louis; Florida, 1829-1839 ***8481.1*** *p18*
Bell, Maria *SEE* Bell, Johann Peter
Bell, Matilda 26; Michigan, 1880 ***4491.42*** *p3*
Bell, Mina 7; Quebec, 1870 ***8364.32*** *p22*
Bell, Niel 55; Ontario, 1871 ***1823.21*** *p23*
Bell, Peter *SEE* Bell, Johann Peter
Bell, Peter 31; Michigan, 1880 ***4491.36*** *p2*
Bell, Richard; Marston's Wharf, 1782 ***8529.30*** *p9*
Bell, Richard 40; Ontario, 1871 ***1823.21*** *p23*
Bell, Robert; Marston's Wharf, 1782 ***8529.30*** *p9*
Bell, Sarah 32; Ontario, 1871 ***1823.21*** *p23*
Bell, Seymour; Colorado, 1900 ***1029.59*** *p7*
Bell, Seymour 27; Colorado, 1900 ***1029.59*** *p7*
Bell, Thomas; Ontario, 1871 ***1823.17*** *p10*
Bell, Thomas 28; Ontario, 1871 ***1823.21*** *p23*
Bell, William; North Carolina, 1839 ***1088.45*** *p2*
Bell, William 22; Ontario, 1871 ***1823.21*** *p23*
Bell, William 43; Ontario, 1871 ***1823.21*** *p23*
Bell, William 43; Ontario, 1871 ***1823.21*** *p23*
Bell, William 50; Ontario, 1871 ***1823.21*** *p23*
Bell, William 54; Ontario, 1871 ***1823.21*** *p23*
Bell, William 56; Ontario, 1871 ***1823.17*** *p10*
Bell, William 70; Ontario, 1871 ***1823.21*** *p23*
Bell, William C. 40; Ontario, 1871 ***1823.21*** *p23*
Bell, Wm 68; Ontario, 1871 ***1823.21*** *p23*
Bellars, Oswald 54; Ontario, 1871 ***1823.21*** *p23*
Bellavance, Louis 32; Quebec, 1644 ***9221.17*** *p142*
*Wife:*Marie Michel 22
*Daughter:*Louise 2
Bellavance, Louise 2 *SEE* Bellavance, Louis
Bellavance, Marie Michel 22 *SEE* Bellavance, Louis
Bellefeuille, Anthony 12 *SEE* Bellefeuille, Frank
Bellefeuille, Frank 36; Ohio, 1880 ***4879.40*** *p258*
*Wife:*Philomen 31
*Son:*Anthony 12
*Son:*Tennis 8
*Son:*Joseph 15
Bellefeuille, Joseph 15 *SEE* Bellefeuille, Frank
Bellefeuille, Philomen 31 *SEE* Bellefeuille, Frank
Bellefeuille, Tennis 8 *SEE* Bellefeuille, Frank
Bellefleur, . . .; Quebec, 1657 ***9221.17*** *p351*
Bellefleur, Jean; Quebec, 1660 ***9221.17*** *p432*
Bellefond, Charles-Guillaume de; Quebec, 1733 ***2314.30*** *p171*
Bellefontaine, Julien 29; Quebec, 1650 ***9221.17*** *p225*
Bellehache, Marie; Quebec, 1673 ***4514.3*** *p276*
Bellehumeur, Antoine 19; Montreal, 1662 ***9221.17*** *p496*
Bellemant, Francois; Quebec, 1654 ***9221.17*** *p304*
Bellenot, Francis 27; America, 1846 ***778.6*** *p25*
Bellepoire, Vincent 25; Quebec, 1652 ***9221.17*** *p264*
Beller, Elisabetha 22; Brazil, 1858 ***2526.43*** *p193*
Beller, Johann Jakob; America, 1862 ***2526.43*** *p194*
Beller, Katharina; America, 1883 ***5475.1*** *p35*
Beller, Leonhard; America, 1872 ***2526.43*** *p193*
*Mother:*Margaretha
Beller, Margaretha 63 *SEE* Beller, Leonhard
Bellerive, Pierre; Quebec, 1650 ***9221.17*** *p223*
Bellersen, Wilhelmine Christine; America, 1868 ***7420.1*** *p270*
Belles, Katharina; America, 1881-1900 ***5475.1*** *p228*
Bellesoeur, Anne; Quebec, 1665 ***4514.3*** *p277*
Bellet, Jean 23; Quebec, 1657 ***9221.17*** *p351*
Bellet, Jean 48; Texas, 1848 ***778.6*** *p25*
Belleville, Francois 17; Montreal, 1653 ***9221.17*** *p283*
Bellevue, Mr. 36; New Orleans, 1848 ***778.6*** *p25*
Bellew, Edward; Washington, 1887 ***2770.40*** *p24*
Bellew, Peter; Louisiana, 1874-1875 ***4981.45*** *p297*
Belli, Frank; Louisiana, 1874 ***4981.45*** *p131*
Bellieud, J. 35; New Orleans, 1840 ***778.6*** *p25*
Bellingham, Thomas; Philadelphia, 1777 ***8529.30*** *p7A*
Bellington, Nathan 47; Ontario, 1871 ***1823.21*** *p23*
Bellion, Alexius; America, 1881 ***5475.1*** *p133*
Belliot, J. Martin 32; Louisiana, 1848 ***778.6*** *p25*
Belliquet, Armand 30; Louisiana, 1848 ***778.6*** *p25*
Bellman, Eleanor 6; Quebec, 1870 ***8364.32*** *p22*
Belloc, Mr.; America, 1842 ***778.6*** *p25*
Belloc, A. 20; America, 1842 ***778.6*** *p25*
Belloc, J. T. 29; New Orleans, 1848 ***778.6*** *p26*
Bellocq, Mr. 19; Port uncertain, 1845 ***778.6*** *p26*
Bellocq, John; Louisiana, 1874-1875 ***4981.45*** *p297*
Belloir, Louis 30; Missouri, 1845 ***778.6*** *p26*
Bellon, Jacques; Quebec, 1661 ***9221.17*** *p447*
Bellon, Joseph; New Orleans, 1840 ***778.6*** *p26*
Belloquest, August; Louisiana, 1874 ***4981.45*** *p131*
Bellot, Anna 6 months; New Orleans, 1847 ***778.6*** *p26*
Bellot, Anne 41; New Orleans, 1846 ***778.6*** *p26*
Bellot, Antoine-Joseph de; Quebec, 1755-1757 ***2314.30*** *p170*
Bellot, Antoine-Joseph de; Quebec, 1755 ***2314.30*** *p175*
Bellot, Christine 30; New Orleans, 1847 ***778.6*** *p26*
Bellot, Ferdinand; Ohio, 1809-1852 ***4511.35*** *p4*
Bellot, Francois; Quebec, 1653 ***9221.17*** *p269*
Bellot, Joseph 8; New Orleans, 1846 ***778.6*** *p26*
Bellot, Joseph 41; New Orleans, 1846 ***778.6*** *p26*
Bellot, Marie 6; New Orleans, 1846 ***778.6*** *p26*
Bellot, Pierre 2; New Orleans, 1847 ***778.6*** *p26*
Bellot, Pierre 28; New Orleans, 1847 ***778.6*** *p26*
Bellott, Otto; Ohio, 1840-1897 ***8365.35*** *p15*
Bellouard, Mathurin 16; Quebec, 1658 ***9221.17*** *p376*
Bellwood, Monah 21; Ontario, 1871 ***1823.21*** *p23*
Belmont, Adolphe 31; America, 1846 ***778.6*** *p26*
Beloo, John F.; North Carolina, 1816 ***1088.45*** *p2*
Belot, Charles-Jean; Montreal, 1653 ***9221.17*** *p282*
Below, August; Wisconsin, 1886 ***6795.8*** *p29*
Below, Joe; Wisconsin, 1904 ***6795.8*** *p155*
Belrose, Jean 25; Port uncertain, 1842 ***778.6*** *p26*
Belsher, Richard 60; Ontario, 1871 ***1823.21*** *p23*
Belshi, Betsey; Marblehead, MA, 1804 ***9228.50*** *p88*
Belshi, Mary; Massachusetts, 1755 ***9228.50*** *p579*
Belshi, Mary; Massachusetts, 1755 ***9228.50*** *p593*

Belstiler, Jacob; North Carolina, 1710 ***3629.40*** *p3*
Belt, George 42; Ontario, 1871 ***1823.21*** *p23*
Belton, George 60; Ontario, 1871 ***1823.21*** *p23*
Belton, George 72; Ontario, 1871 ***1823.21*** *p23*
Belton, James; Marston's Wharf, 1782 ***8529.30*** *p9*
Belton, Janet 20; North Carolina, 1774 ***1422.10*** *p55*
Belton, John 45; Ontario, 1871 ***1823.21*** *p23*
Beltz, George; Ohio, 1809-1852 ***4511.35*** *p4*
Beltz, Henry 63; Ontario, 1871 ***1823.21*** *p23*
Belville, William 18; Quebec, 1870 ***8364.32*** *p22*
Belz, Michel 18; Mississippi, 1847 ***778.6*** *p26*
Belzle, Pierre 25; America, 1844 ***778.6*** *p26*
Belzner, John; Ohio, 1809-1852 ***4511.35*** *p4*
Bem, Frantisek; Chicago, 1857 ***2853.20*** *p389*
Bem, Frantisek; South Dakota, 1850-1910 ***2853.20*** *p246*
Bemeike, Nikols 21; New York, NY, 1893 ***1883.7*** *p41*
Bemmington, William 21; Ontario, 1871 ***1823.21*** *p23*
Benacis, Anne Dupuy 46; Quebec, 1642 ***9221.17*** *p121*
Benacis, Catherine 5 *SEE* Benacis, Guillaume
Benacis, Francoise 1 *SEE* Benacis, Guillaume
Benacis, Guillaume; Quebec, 1642 ***9221.17*** *p112*
  *Wife:*Jeanne Sauvaget
  *Daughter:*Madeleine
  *Daughter:*Catherine
  *Daughter:*Francoise
Benacis, Jeanne Sauvaget 31 *SEE* Benacis, Guillaume
Benacis, Madeleine 7 *SEE* Benacis, Guillaume
Benai, James 25; New York, NY, 1835 ***5024.1*** *p137*
Benalle, Francoise 17; America, 1840 ***778.6*** *p26*
Benard, Henry Joseph; Illinois, 1856 ***6079.1*** *p1*
Benard, Jeanne; Quebec, 1664 ***4514.3*** *p277*
Benard, Marin; Quebec, 1653 ***9221.17*** *p270*
Benatiare, Mr. 17; New Orleans, 1848 ***778.6*** *p26*
Bench, Jemimah; Ontario, 1871 ***1823.21*** *p23*
Bencini, Anthony; North Carolina, 1838 ***1088.45*** *p2*
Benckeser, John; Illinois, 1834-1900 ***6020.5*** *p131*
Benda, Vaclav; St. Louis, 1896 ***2853.20*** *p54*
Bendall, Nicholas; Marston's Wharf, 1782 ***8529.30*** *p9*
Bendel, August; New York, 1860 ***358.56*** *p150*
Bendel, Louis 35; Missouri, 1848 ***778.6*** *p26*
Bendele, Jakob 17; Galveston, TX, 1846 ***3967.10*** *p377*
Bendelin, Jaques; New Castle, DE, 1817-1818 ***90.20*** *p150*
Benden, Joseph; New York, 1860 ***358.56*** *p5*
Bender, Adolph; Ohio, 1809-1852 ***4511.35*** *p4*
Bender, Alfred 1; Portland, ME, 1911 ***970.38*** *p76*
Bender, Andreas *SEE* Bender, Anna Margarethe
Bender, Andrew; New York, 1859 ***358.56*** *p54*
Bender, Anna 32; America, 1862 ***5475.1*** *p495*
Bender, Anna Elisabeth *SEE* Bender, Anna Magdalene
Bender, Anna Elisabeth *SEE* Bender, Anna Elisabeth
Bender, Anna Elisabeth; America, 1836 ***8115.12*** *p327*
  *Child:*Katharine Margarethe
  *Child:*Anna Elisabeth
  *Child:*Johann Georg
  *Child:*Wilhelm Andreas
Bender, Anna Magdalene *SEE* Bender, Anna Magdalene
Bender, Anna Magdalene; America, 1835 ***8115.12*** *p325*
  *Child:*Anna Magdalene
  *Child:*Anna Elisabeth
  *Child:*Johann Jakob
Bender, Anna Magdalene; America, 1855 ***8115.12*** *p318*
Bender, Anna Margaretha; America, 1854 ***8115.12*** *p318*
Bender, Anna Margarethe; America, 1840 ***8115.12*** *p325*
  *Child:*Katharine
  *Child:*Andreas
Bender, August *SEE* Bender, Jakob
Bender, August *SEE* Bender, Christine
Bender, Christian; Ohio, 1809-1852 ***4511.35*** *p4*
Bender, Christine *SEE* Bender, Christine
Bender, Christine; America, 1880 ***8115.12*** *p320*
  *Child:*August
  *Child:*Christine
  *Child:*Louise
  *Child:*Friedrich
  *Child:*Karl
Bender, Elisabeth 12; Portland, ME, 1911 ***970.38*** *p76*
Bender, Elisabeth 32; Portland, ME, 1911 ***970.38*** *p76*
Bender, Elisabeth Margar.; America, 1835 ***8115.12*** *p318*
Bender, Eva 63; New York, NY, 1874 ***6954.7*** *p37*
Bender, Friedr. Hartmann; America, 1835 ***8115.12*** *p318*
Bender, Friedrich *SEE* Bender, Jakob
Bender, Friedrich *SEE* Bender, Christine
Bender, Georg 43; America, 1860 ***5475.1*** *p519*
  *Wife:*Margrethe Henn
  *Son:*Peter 17
Bender, Georg Christian; America, 1854 ***8115.12*** *p317*
Bender, Helene; America, n.d. ***8115.12*** *p318*
Bender, Hieronymus 45; Ontario, 1871 ***1823.21*** *p23*
Bender, Jakob; America, 1865 ***5475.1*** *p562*
  *Wife:*Katharina Stenzhorn
  *Son:*August
  *Son:*Friedrich
Bender, Jakob; America, n.d. ***8115.12*** *p318*
Bender, Johann 19; New York, NY, 1874 ***6954.7*** *p37*
Bender, Johann Friedrich; America, 1854 ***8115.12*** *p317*
Bender, Johann Friedrich; America, n.d. ***8115.12*** *p326*
Bender, Johann Georg *SEE* Bender, Anna Elisabeth
Bender, Johann Georg; America, 1852 ***8115.12*** *p326*
  With brother
Bender, Johann Jakob *SEE* Bender, Anna Magdalene
Bender, Johann Jakob; America, 1854 ***8115.12*** *p318*
Bender, Johannes; America, 1834 ***8115.12*** *p318*
Bender, Johannes; America, n.d. ***8115.12*** *p326*
Bender, John; Ohio, 1809-1852 ***4511.35*** *p4*
Bender, John Frederick; Ohio, 1809-1852 ***4511.35*** *p4*
Bender, Karl *SEE* Bender, Christine
Bender, Karl 32; Portland, ME, 1911 ***970.38*** *p76*
Bender, Karl Emil 17; America, 1853 ***2526.43*** *p145*
Bender, Katharina Stenzhorn 27 *SEE* Bender, Jakob
Bender, Katharine *SEE* Bender, Anna Margarethe
Bender, Katharine *SEE* Bender, Katharine
Bender, Katharine; America, 1870 ***8115.12*** *p328*
  *Child:*Katharine
Bender, Katharine Margarethe *SEE* Bender, Anna Elisabeth
Bender, Konrad; America, 1851 ***8115.12*** *p318*
Bender, Louise *SEE* Bender, Christine
Bender, Ludwig; America, 1852 ***8115.12*** *p326*
Bender, Ludwig; America, 1886 ***8115.12*** *p318*
Bender, Ludwig Wilhelm Eduard 15; America, 1853 ***2526.43*** *p145*
Bender, Magdalene; America, 1860 ***8115.12*** *p318*
Bender, Margaretha; Baltimore, 1855 ***2526.43*** *p163*
Bender, Margarethe; America, 1884 ***8115.12*** *p326*
  With siblings
Bender, Margrethe Henn *SEE* Bender, Georg
Bender, Marie Katharine; America, 1859 ***8115.12*** *p318*
Bender, Patrick 50; Ontario, 1871 ***1823.17*** *p10*
Bender, Peter 17 *SEE* Bender, Georg
Bender, Philipp; America, 1883 ***8115.12*** *p326*
Bender, Philipp; America, n.d. ***8115.12*** *p318*
Bender, Philipp 60; New York, NY, 1874 ***6954.7*** *p37*
Bender, Sophie Dorothea; Ohio, 1865 ***5475.1*** *p21*
Bender, Wilhelm Andreas *SEE* Bender, Anna Elisabeth
Bendewald, Charles; Illinois, 1859 ***6079.1*** *p1*
Bendite, Conrad; America, 1857 ***7420.1*** *p157*
Bendix, Mrs. B.; America, 1861 ***7420.1*** *p202*
  *Daughter:*Sophie
  *Daughter:*Line
Bendix, Hermann; America, 1860 ***7420.1*** *p191*
Bendix, Line *SEE* Bendix, Mrs. B.
Bendix, Sophie *SEE* Bendix, Mrs. B.
Bendle, Elizabeth 66; Michigan, 1880 ***4491.30*** *p2*
Bendle, Thomas 65; Michigan, 1880 ***4491.30*** *p2*
Bendrath, Mr.; America, 1854 ***7420.1*** *p115*
Benedict, Adolf 18; New Orleans, 1847 ***778.6*** *p26*
Benedict, Charles; Louisiana, 1841-1844 ***4981.45*** *p210*
Benedict, Laure 3; America, 1844 ***778.6*** *p26*
Benedict, Leone 7; America, 1844 ***778.6*** *p26*
Benedict, Mathilde 34; America, 1844 ***778.6*** *p26*
Benedict, Petry 5; America, 1844 ***778.6*** *p26*
Benedixon, Andreas; Valparaiso, Chile, 1850 ***1192.4*** *p50*
Benedixon, Mag.; Valparaiso, Chile, 1850 ***1192.4*** *p50*
Benee, Andrew; St. Paul, MN, 1894 ***1865.50*** *p40*
Benes, . . .; Iowa, 1870 ***2853.20*** *p202*
Benes, C.J.; Texas, 1889 ***2853.20*** *p70*
Benes, Frantisek; Arkansas, 1892 ***2853.20*** *p376*
Benes, Jan; Nebraska, 1876 ***2853.20*** *p172*
Benes, Jan Josef; Cleveland, OH, 1870 ***2853.20*** *p405*
  With parents
Benest, Amice; Marblehead, MA, 1780-1787 ***9228.50*** *p99*
Benest, Clarence; Massachusetts, 1884-1899 ***9228.50*** *p99*
Benest, Francis G.; Massachusetts, 1850-1899 ***9228.50*** *p99*
Benest, Philip; Boston, 1776 ***9228.50*** *p99*
Benest, Philip; Nova Scotia, 1776 ***9228.50*** *p99*
Benest, Sarah; Boston, 1776 ***9228.50*** *p99*
Benetaud, Oscar 28; Louisiana, 1848 ***778.6*** *p26*
Benett, William 14; Quebec, 1870 ***8364.32*** *p22*
Beneys, Louise Rose Magdel. 23; New Orleans, 1840 ***778.6*** *p26*
Benford, Ailce; Maryland, 1672 ***1236.25*** *p47*
Bengert, Jean 21; America, 1846 ***778.6*** *p26*
Bengin, James; St. Johns, N.F., 1825 ***1053.15*** *p6*
Bengson, Andrew; Colorado, 1880 ***1029.59*** *p7*
Bengson, August; Colorado, 1880 ***1029.59*** *p7*
Bengson, Nels A.; Colorado, 1902 ***1029.59*** *p7*
Bengson, Nil A.; Colorado, 1880 ***1029.59*** *p7*
Bengson, Nils; Colorado, 1879 ***1029.59*** *p7*
Bengson, Nils A.; Colorado, 1880 ***1029.59*** *p7*
Bengson, Oliver A.; Colorado, 1889 ***1029.59*** *p8*
Bengstron, Emil; New York, 1901 ***1766.20*** *p14*
Bengtsen, Andrew; Colorado, 1879 ***1029.59*** *p8*
Bengtson, Anders; Colorado, 1879 ***1029.59*** *p8*
Bengtson, Carl; Cleveland, OH, 1896-1903 ***9722.10*** *p117*
Bengtson, John; Cleveland, OH, 1901-1903 ***9722.10*** *p117*
Bengtson, Olof; Illinois, 1861 ***4487.25*** *p53*
Bengtson, Peter; Illinois, 1861 ***4487.25*** *p53*
Bengtson, Sara; St. Paul, MN, 1894 ***1865.50*** *p40*
Bengtson, Tilda; St. Paul, MN, 1874-1905 ***1865.50*** *p40*
Bengtsson, And.; New York, NY, 1850 ***6412.40*** *p152*
Bengtsson, Anders; New York, NY, 1849 ***6412.40*** *p152*
Bengtsson, Carl A.; Colorado, 1871 ***1029.59*** *p8*
Benhall, Ed.; Maryland, 1672 ***1236.25*** *p47*
Benham, John; Massachusetts, 1630 ***117.5*** *p156*
Benhard, George; Philadelphia, 1777 ***8529.30*** *p6*
Benhlam, John 29; Ontario, 1871 ***1823.17*** *p10*
Beni, Godfred 14; New Orleans, 1846 ***778.6*** *p26*
Beni, Ludwic 19; New Orleans, 1846 ***778.6*** *p26*
Beni, Mag.alena 47; New Orleans, 1846 ***778.6*** *p26*
Beni, Michel 7; New Orleans, 1846 ***778.6*** *p26*
Beni, Stephen 47; New Orleans, 1846 ***778.6*** *p26*
Benington, William 18; Quebec, 1870 ***8364.32*** *p22*
Benington, Wm 44; Ontario, 1871 ***1823.21*** *p23*
Benjamin, Jacob 23; America, 1848 ***778.6*** *p27*
Benjamin, William 67; Ontario, 1871 ***1823.21*** *p23*
Benjamins, Matie; New Castle, DE, 1817-1818 ***90.20*** *p150*
Benke, Franz; New York, 1859 ***358.56*** *p99*
Benn, Angela 47; America, 1846 ***5475.1*** *p463*
Benn, George 38; Ontario, 1871 ***1823.21*** *p23*
Benn, Hugh 66; Ontario, 1871 ***1823.21*** *p23*
Benn, Katharina 45; America, 1846 ***5475.1*** *p401*
Benn, Thomas 30; Ontario, 1871 ***1823.21*** *p23*
Bennar, Robert 37; Ontario, 1871 ***1823.17*** *p10*
Benner, Jacob; Ohio, 1809-1852 ***4511.35*** *p4*
Bennest, Francis 30; Ontario, 1871 ***1823.17*** *p10*
Bennest, Francis 54; Ontario, 1871 ***1823.17*** *p10*
Bennet, Amos; Marblehead, MA, 1780-1787 ***9228.50*** *p99*
Bennet, John; Maryland, 1674-1675 ***1236.25*** *p51*
Bennet, Joseph; Ohio, 1809-1852 ***4511.35*** *p4*
Bennet, Philip; Boston, 1730 ***9228.50*** *p421*
Bennet, Philip; Boston, 1745 ***9228.50*** *p99*
Bennet, Rachel; Massachusetts, 1772 ***9228.50*** *p99*
Bennet, Robert; New York, 1778 ***8529.30*** *p2A*
Bennet, Thomas; Boston, 1745 ***9228.50*** *p99*
Bennet, Thomas 40; Ontario, 1871 ***1823.21*** *p23*
Bennet, William; Connecticut, 1676 ***9228.50*** *p99*
Bennett, Ann; Philadelphia, 1856 ***8513.31*** *p412*
Bennett, Charles 58; Ontario, 1871 ***1823.21*** *p23*
Bennett, Clara 5; Quebec, 1870 ***8364.32*** *p22*
Bennett, David; Canada, 1774 ***3036.5*** *p41*
  *Wife:*Mary
Bennett, Edward 57; Ontario, 1871 ***1823.21*** *p23*
Bennett, Elizabeth 56; Ontario, 1871 ***1823.21*** *p24*
Bennett, Emma 11; Quebec, 1870 ***8364.32*** *p22*
Bennett, George 50; Ontario, 1871 ***1823.21*** *p24*
Bennett, Henry 42; Ontario, 1871 ***1823.21*** *p24*
Bennett, James 52; Ontario, 1871 ***1823.21*** *p24*
Bennett, John; Maryland, 1673 ***1236.25*** *p49*
Bennett, John 20; Ontario, 1871 ***1823.21*** *p24*
Bennett, John 25; Ontario, 1871 ***1823.21*** *p24*
Bennett, John 69; Ontario, 1871 ***1823.17*** *p10*
Bennett, John; Virginia, 1652 ***6254.4*** *p243*
Bennett, John N.; Colorado, 1880 ***1029.59*** *p8*
Bennett, Mary *SEE* Bennett, David
Bennett, Mary 43; Ontario, 1871 ***1823.21*** *p24*
Bennett, Mary 75; Ontario, 1871 ***1823.21*** *p24*
Bennett, Mary 9; Quebec, 1870 ***8364.32*** *p22*
Bennett, Philip; Louisiana, 1874-1875 ***4981.45*** *p297*
Bennett, Rachel; Marblehead, MA, 1772 ***9228.50*** *p539*
Bennett, Richard 53; Ontario, 1871 ***1823.21*** *p24*
Bennett, Thomas; Boston, 1737 ***1642*** *p26*
Bennett, Thomas 26; Ontario, 1871 ***1823.21*** *p24*
Bennett, Thomas 39; Ontario, 1871 ***1823.21*** *p24*
Bennett, Thomas 39; Ontario, 1871 ***1823.21*** *p24*
Bennett, William 25; Ontario, 1871 ***1823.21*** *p24*
Bennick, Christopher; Philadelphia, 1778 ***8529.30*** *p2*
Benningham, William; Boston, 1833 ***3274.56*** *p71*
Bennington, John 63; Ontario, 1871 ***1823.21*** *p24*
Bennington, Thomas; Ohio, 1843 ***2763.1*** *p7*
Bennions, Thomas 15; Quebec, 1870 ***8364.32*** *p22*
Bennis, John 24; Ontario, 1871 ***1823.21*** *p24*
Bennison, Eliza.; Jamestown, VA, 1633 ***1658.20*** *p211*
Bennoi, Charle 18; America, 1848 ***778.6*** *p27*
Benois, Mr. 45; New Orleans, 1841 ***778.6*** *p27*
Benoist, Abel 23; Quebec, 1650 ***9221.17*** *p223*
Benoist, Antoine-Gabriel-Francois; Quebec, 1735 ***2314.30*** *p170*
Benoist, Antoine-Gabriel-Francois; Quebec, 1735 ***2314.30*** *p175*
Benoist, Bernard; Quebec, 1656 ***9221.17*** *p331*
Benoist, Gabriel 26; Quebec, 1662 ***9221.17*** *p479*
Benoist, Jean 18; Quebec, 1657 ***9221.17*** *p352*
Benoist, Jean 24; Quebec, 1655 ***9221.17*** *p320*
Benoist, Laurent 18; Quebec, 1657 ***9221.17*** *p352*
Benoist, Paul 27; Montreal, 1653 ***9221.17*** *p282*

Benoit, Mr. 25; America, 1843 ***778.6*** *p27*
Benoit, Mrs. 24; America, 1843 ***778.6*** *p27*
Benoit, Mrs. 31; Port uncertain, 1843 ***778.6*** *p27*
Benoit, David 35; America, 1840 ***778.6*** *p27*
Benoit, Emelie 3 months; Port uncertain, 1843 ***778.6*** *p27*
Benoit, Ernestine 16; Port uncertain, 1843 ***778.6*** *p27*
Benoit, J. C.; Port uncertain, 1843 ***778.6*** *p27*
Benoit, Joseph 26; America, 1840 ***778.6*** *p27*
Benoit, Jules 3; Port uncertain, 1843 ***778.6*** *p27*
Benoit, Julie Joseph; Wisconsin, 1856 ***1495.20*** *p41*
Benoit, Marie; Quebec, 1667 ***4514.3*** *p277*
Benoit, Servente 18; Port uncertain, 1843 ***778.6*** *p27*
Benoit, T. 36; America, 1846 ***778.6*** *p27*
Benrit, Francisco; Puerto Rico, 1816 ***3476.25*** *p111*
Bense, Guillaume; Quebec, 1639 ***9221.17*** *p85*
*Wife:*Jeanne Jerome
*Son:*Philippe
*Daughter:*Marguerite
Bense, Jeanne Jerome *SEE* Bense, Guillaume
Bense, Marguerite *SEE* Bense, Guillaume
Bense, Philippe *SEE* Bense, Guillaume
Bense, Wilhelmine Charlotte; America, 1847 ***7420.1*** *p53*
Bensen, Joseph C.; Colorado, 1876 ***1029.59*** *p8*
Benskin, John M.; Ohio, 1809-1852 ***4511.35*** *p4*
Benson, Adolph; Cleveland, OH, 1895-1900 ***9722.10*** *p117*
Benson, Alfred W.; Cleveland, OH, 1881-1893 ***9722.10*** *p117*
Benson, Andrew; Cleveland, OH, 1888-1893 ***9722.10*** *p117*
Benson, Brita Stina Svenson *SEE* Benson, John
Benson, Carl; Cleveland, OH, 1896-1903 ***9722.10*** *p117*
Benson, Charles 22; Ontario, 1871 ***1823.21*** *p24*
Benson, Charles A.; Iowa, 1900 ***1211.15*** *p9*
Benson, Edward 50; Ontario, 1871 ***1823.21*** *p24*
Benson, Eleanor; Boston, 1764 ***1642*** *p33*
Benson, Hannah; Minnesota, 1889-1902 ***1865.50*** *p40*
Benson, John; Minnesota, 1867-1891 ***1865.50*** *p40*
*Wife:*Brita Stina Svenson
Benson, Joseph 27; Port uncertain, 1845 ***778.6*** *p27*
Benson, Joseph C.; Colorado, 1876 ***1029.59*** *p8*
Benson, Karl J.; Colorado, 1900 ***1029.59*** *p8*
Benson, Lovisa; St. Paul, MN, 1892 ***1865.50*** *p40*
Benson, Malkom Hjalmer; Cleveland, OH, 1903-1906 ***9722.10*** *p117*
Benson, Maria 9; Quebec, 1870 ***8364.32*** *p22*
Benson, Mathilda; Wisconsin, 1883 ***1865.50*** *p40*
Benson, Nels; St. Paul, MN, 1887 ***1865.50*** *p40*
Benson, Samuel 36; Michigan, 1880 ***4491.30*** *p2*
Benson, William 31; Ontario, 1871 ***1823.21*** *p24*
Benssen, Karl J.; Nebraska, 1888 ***1029.59*** *p8*
Benstein, William; Illinois, 1860 ***6079.1*** *p1*
Benston, Augustus; Colorado, 1882 ***1029.59*** *p8*
Bentayon, L.; Louisiana, 1874 ***4981.45*** *p295*
Benter, Colobanne 54; Missouri, 1845 ***778.6*** *p27*
Benter, Julius 6; Missouri, 1845 ***778.6*** *p27*
Benter, Willina 32; Missouri, 1845 ***778.6*** *p27*
Bentjerodt, Heinr.; Chile, 1852 ***1192.4*** *p54*
With wife & 2 children
With child 8
With child 25
Bentley, Allen 18; Ontario, 1871 ***1823.21*** *p24*
Bentley, Bengiman 62; Ontario, 1871 ***1823.17*** *p10*
Bentley, Henry 60; Ontario, 1871 ***1823.21*** *p24*
Bentley, John; Boston, 1826 ***3274.55*** *p74*
Bentley, John 32; Ontario, 1871 ***1823.17*** *p10*
Bentley, Mark H.; Colorado, 1891 ***1029.59*** *p8*
Bentley, Pat; St. John, N.B., 1848 ***2978.15*** *p40*
Bentley, Peter; Boston, 1775 ***8529.30*** *p2*
Bentley, Robert 51; Ontario, 1871 ***1823.21*** *p24*
Bentley, Robt; St. John, N.B., 1848 ***2978.15*** *p40*
Bentley, Samuel; New Mexico, 1914 ***4812.1*** *p87*
Bentley, Thomas 16; Quebec, 1870 ***8364.32*** *p22*
Bentley, William 23; Ontario, 1871 ***1823.21*** *p24*
Benton, Austin 42; Ontario, 1871 ***1823.21*** *p24*
Benton, Barbara 9; New York, NY, 1835 ***5024.1*** *p137*
Benton, George Henry; Kansas, 1917-1918 ***1826.15*** *p81*
Benton, Henry Herman; Kansas, 1917-1918 ***1826.15*** *p81*
Benton, Herman; Kansas, 1917-1918 ***1826.15*** *p81*
Benton, Herman George; Kansas, 1917-1918 ***1826.15*** *p81*
Benton, Isabella 4; New York, NY, 1835 ***5024.1*** *p137*
Benton, Isabella Davidson 33 *SEE* Benton, William
Benton, James 8; New York, NY, 1835 ***5024.1*** *p137*
Benton, James 29; New York, NY, 1835 ***5024.1*** *p137*
Benton, Joseph 14 *SEE* Benton, William
Benton, William 16 *SEE* Benton, William
Benton, William 44; New York, NY, 1835 ***5024.1*** *p137*
*Wife:*Isabella Davidson 33
*Son:*William 16
*Son:*Joseph 14
Bentz, Flerion 24; New York, NY, 1847 ***9176.15*** *p50*
Bentz, J. C.; Valdivia, Chile, 1852 ***1192.4*** *p52*
Bentz, John; Illinois, 1855 ***6079.1*** *p1*
Benz, Bertha; Wisconsin, 1892 ***6795.8*** *p71*
Benz, Therese; America, 1867 ***7919.3*** *p533*
Benz, Wilhelm; Wisconsin, 1895 ***6795.8*** *p148*
Benzel, Jog. Georg; Rio Grande do Sul, Brazil, 1861 ***5475.1*** *p505*
*Wife:*Luise Juliana Becker
*Daughter:*Klara
Benzel, Klara *SEE* Benzel, Jog. Georg
Benzel, Luise Juliana Becker *SEE* Benzel, Jog. Georg
Benzel, Rud. Philipp; New York, 1890 ***5475.1*** *p381*
Benziger, Thomas 20; New York, NY, 1894 ***6512.1*** *p182*
Beoffre, Auguste 3; New Orleans, 1848 ***778.6*** *p27*
Beoffre, Cambry 19; New Orleans, 1848 ***778.6*** *p27*
Beover, Elizabeth; Canada, 1775 ***3036.5*** *p67*
Bepler, Anna Elisabeth; America, 1840 ***8115.12*** *p318*
Bepler, Anna Elisabeth; America, 1870 ***8115.12*** *p318*
Bepler, Johann Jakob; America, n.d. ***8115.12*** *p318*
Bepler, Johann Philipp; America, 1847 ***8115.12*** *p318*
Bepler, Konrad; America, 1870 ***8115.12*** *p318*
Beque, J. M. 50; New Orleans, 1841 ***778.6*** *p27*
Ber, Leon 27; New Orleans, 1847 ***778.6*** *p27*
Beran, Jan; Nebraska, 1870 ***2853.20*** *p193*
Beran, Jan; Nebraska, 1879 ***2853.20*** *p190*
Beran, Jan W.; Pennsylvania, 1900 ***2853.20*** *p122*
Beranek, Frantisek; Iowa, 1855 ***2853.20*** *p239*
Beranek, Karel; Chicago, 1905 ***2853.20*** *p421*
Beranger, Alexis 40; Montreal, 1662 ***9221.17*** *p495*
Berard, Marie; Quebec, 1637 ***9221.17*** *p67*
Beraud, Agatha 16; New Orleans, 1848 ***778.6*** *p27*
Beraud, Anna 20; New Orleans, 1848 ***778.6*** *p27*
Beraud, Anne 52; New Orleans, 1848 ***778.6*** *p27*
Beraud, Anne; Quebec, 1673 ***4514.3*** *p277*
Beraud, Dominique 8; New Orleans, 1848 ***778.6*** *p27*
Beraud, Etienne 17; New Orleans, 1848 ***778.6*** *p27*
Beraud, Etienne 46; New Orleans, 1848 ***778.6*** *p27*
Beraud, Joseph 14; New Orleans, 1848 ***778.6*** *p27*
Berberich, Therese 24; America, 1871 ***5475.1*** *p153*
Berbero, Antonio; Louisiana, 1874-1875 ***4981.45*** *p298*
Berbes, Mr. 46; America, 1841 ***778.6*** *p27*
Berbier, Adele 9; Mississippi, 1847 ***778.6*** *p27*
Berbier, Francois 8; Mississippi, 1847 ***778.6*** *p27*
Berbier, Henry 5; Mississippi, 1847 ***778.6*** *p28*
Berbier, Joseph 48; Mississippi, 1847 ***778.6*** *p28*
Berbier, Louise 6; Mississippi, 1847 ***778.6*** *p28*
Berbier, Marianne 2; Mississippi, 1847 ***778.6*** *p28*
Berbier, Marie 39; Mississippi, 1847 ***778.6*** *p28*
Berbier, Victoire 11; Mississippi, 1847 ***778.6*** *p28*
Berbiquier, Mr. 40; America, 1843 ***778.6*** *p28*
Berblinger, Andreas; Venezuela, 1843 ***3899.5*** *p540*
Berblinger, Joseph; Venezuela, 1843 ***3899.5*** *p540*
Berblinger, Kaspar; Venezuela, 1843 ***3899.5*** *p540*
Berblinger Children, . . .; Venezuela, 1843 ***3899.5*** *p540*
Berch, C.; Cleveland, OH, 1891-1895 ***9722.10*** *p117*
Berchtold, Henry; Ohio, 1809-1852 ***4511.35*** *p4*
Bercier, Louis *SEE* Bercier, Louise
Bercier, Louise; Quebec, 1668 ***4514.3*** *p277*
*Uncle:*Louis
Berckmans, Jean; Wisconsin, 1855-1858 ***1495.20*** *p67*
*Wife:*Therese Mercenier
*Daughter:*Marie Philippine
Berckmans, Marie Philippine *SEE* Berckmans, Jean
Berckmans, Therese Mercenier *SEE* Berckmans, Jean
Berdelle, Catharina 2; America, 1848 ***778.6*** *p28*
Berdelle, Joseph 33; America, 1848 ***778.6*** *p28*
Berdelle, Louis 1; America, 1848 ***778.6*** *p28*
Berdelle, Mariana 24; America, 1848 ***778.6*** *p28*
Berdelle, Marie 4; America, 1848 ***778.6*** *p28*
Berden, Jacob; New York, NY, 1905 ***3331.4*** *p11*
Berdien, Auguste 18; Chile, 1852 ***1192.4*** *p51*
Berdow, J. L.; Louisiana, 1874 ***4981.45*** *p295*
Berdun, Lester 17; Ontario, 1871 ***1823.17*** *p10*
Bere, Benjamin 26; Ontario, 1871 ***1823.21*** *p24*
Bere, George 68; Ontario, 1871 ***1823.21*** *p24*
Bere, William 34; Ontario, 1871 ***1823.21*** *p24*
Bereau, Jean; Quebec, 1653 ***9221.17*** *p270*
Berend, Maria 30; America, 1868 ***5475.1*** *p274*
Berendt, Jacob; Dakota, 1876-1918 ***554.30*** *p26*
*Wife:*Rosina
Berendt, Rosina *SEE* Berendt, Jacob
Berendts, Friedrich August; Wisconsin, 1879 ***6795.8*** *p33*
Berenger, John; Iowa, 1889 ***1211.15*** *p9*
Berens, John; Colorado, 1896 ***1029.59*** *p8*
Berer, Jh. 21; America, 1847 ***778.6*** *p28*
Berey desEssarts, Francois de; Quebec, 1703 ***2314.30*** *p169*
Berey desEssarts, Francois de; Quebec, 1703 ***2314.30*** *p175*
Berg, Alb. Robt. Edward; Wisconsin, 1899 ***6795.8*** *p233*
Berg, And.; New York, NY, 1847 ***6412.40*** *p150*
Berg, Andreas von; Wisconsin, 1872 ***6795.8*** *p97*
Berg, Barbe 27; America, 1840 ***778.6*** *p28*
Berg, Charles 35; America, 1840 ***778.6*** *p28*
Berg, Clara 2; America, 1840 ***778.6*** *p28*
Berg, Elisabeth; Iowa, 1905 ***8023.44*** *p372*
*Relative:*Martin
Berg, Emily 2 weeks; Halifax, N.S., 1902 ***1860.4*** *p43*
Berg, Eva 59; America, 1856 ***5475.1*** *p348*
Berg, Frederick; Ohio, 1844 ***2763.1*** *p7*
Berg, George; Ohio, 1844 ***2763.1*** *p7*
Berg, Gert. 29; Halifax, N.S., 1902 ***1860.4*** *p43*
Berg, Gustaf Ragner; Illinois, 1930 ***121.35*** *p100*
Berg, Gustav; Wisconsin, 1905 ***6795.8*** *p209*
Berg, Jacob; Ohio, 1844 ***2763.1*** *p7*
Berg, Julius 33; Indiana, 1868-1880 ***9076.20*** *p69*
Berg, Kate 4; Halifax, N.S., 1902 ***1860.4*** *p43*
Berg, Katharina; America, 1881 ***5475.1*** *p227*
Berg, Louisa 26; America, 1840 ***778.6*** *p28*
Berg, Louise 6; America, 1840 ***778.6*** *p28*
Berg, M.; New Orleans, 1844 ***6412.40*** *p147*
Berg, Magdalena; Brazil, 1882 ***5475.1*** *p391*
Berg, Marguerite 8; America, 1840 ***778.6*** *p28*
Berg, Maria; America, 1873 ***5475.1*** *p346*
Berg, Maria Louisa; Wisconsin, 1892 ***6795.8*** *p216*
Berg, Marie; Wisconsin, 1905 ***6795.8*** *p196*
Berg, Martin *SEE* Berg, Elisabeth
Berg, Ole Andras; Iowa, 1877 ***1211.15*** *p9*
Berg, Pauline 9 months; Halifax, N.S., 1902 ***1860.4*** *p43*
Berg, Peter 32; Halifax, N.S., 1902 ***1860.4*** *p43*
Berg, Peter; Illinois, 1856 ***6079.1*** *p1*
Berg, Pierre 10; America, 1840 ***778.6*** *p28*
Berg, Pierre 29; America, 1840 ***778.6*** *p28*
Berg, Sven Alfred; St. Paul, MN, 1903 ***1865.50*** *p40*
Berg, Terese 3; Halifax, N.S., 1902 ***1860.4*** *p43*
Bergan, John; Louisiana, 1874 ***4981.45*** *p131*
Bergananini, A.; Louisiana, 1836-1840 ***4981.45*** *p212*
Bergans, Patrick 65; Ontario, 1871 ***1823.21*** *p24*
Bergeman, Jacob; Ohio, 1809-1852 ***4511.35*** *p4*
Bergen, Ellen; Colorado, 1894 ***1029.59*** *p8*
Bergen, John J.; Ohio, 1809-1852 ***4511.35*** *p4*
Bergen, Lawrence 35; Ontario, 1871 ***1823.21*** *p24*
Bergen, Patrick 50; Ontario, 1871 ***1823.21*** *p24*
Berger, Adolphine Josephine Prevot *SEE* Berger, Ferdinand Joseph
Berger, Adrien Joseph; Wisconsin, 1880 ***1495.20*** *p55*
*Wife:*Rosalie Lombeau
Berger, Barthelemy; Wisconsin, 1880 ***1495.20*** *p28*
Berger, Bernard; Ohio, 1809-1852 ***4511.35*** *p4*
Berger, Ch.; New York, 1860 ***358.56*** *p4*
Berger, Claus; Colorado, 1887 ***1029.59*** *p8*
Berger, Desire; Wisconsin, 1854-1858 ***1495.20*** *p66*
With wife
Berger, Ernst; Illinois, 1851 ***6079.1*** *p1*
Berger, Ferdinand Joseph; Wisconsin, 1880 ***1495.20*** *p55*
*Wife:*Adolphine Josephine Prevot
*Daughter:*Marie Florentine
Berger, Frances *SEE* Berger, Jacob
Berger, Frances *SEE* Berger, Jacob
Berger, Frank *SEE* Berger, Jacob
Berger, Frank *SEE* Berger, Jacob
Berger, Franz Christian Gerhard; Port uncertain, 1859 ***7420.1*** *p183*
Berger, Friedr. 21; New York, NY, 1893 ***1883.7*** *p43*
Berger, Friedrich Eduard; America, 1859 ***7420.1*** *p183*
Berger, Georg Carl Heinrich Otto; America, 1866 ***7420.1*** *p239*
Berger, George *SEE* Berger, Jacob
Berger, George *SEE* Berger, Jacob
Berger, Heine; North Carolina, 1710 ***3629.40*** *p3*
Berger, J. F.; Chile, 1852 ***1192.4*** *p51*
With wife
Berger, Jacob; New York, NY, 1904 ***609.10*** *p14*
*Wife:*Frances
With daughter son-in-law & 3 grandchildren
*Child:*Frank
*Daughter-In-Law:*Magdalina
*Child:*Philip
*Child:*George
Berger, Jacob; Uruguay, 1895 ***609.10*** *p13*
*Wife:*Frances
*Daughter-In-Law:*Magdalina
*Child:*George
With daughter son-in-law & granddaughter
*Child:*Frank
Berger, Jean-Baptiste; Quebec, 1661 ***9221.17*** *p447*
Berger, Johanna; Uruguay, 1895 ***609.10*** *p13*
Berger, John; Ohio, 1840-1897 ***8365.35*** *p15*
Berger, John; Ohio, 1852 ***3580.20*** *p31*
Berger, John; Ohio, 1852 ***6020.12*** *p6*
Berger, John; Philadelphia, 1778 ***8529.30*** *p2A*
Berger, Jules 25; Port uncertain, 1841 ***778.6*** *p28*
Berger, Magdalina *SEE* Berger, Jacob
Berger, Magdalina *SEE* Berger, Jacob
Berger, Marguerite; Quebec, 1670 ***4514.3*** *p277*
Berger, Marie Florentine *SEE* Berger, Ferdinand Joseph
Berger, Marie Louise; Wisconsin, 1869 ***1495.20*** *p55*

Berger, Modeste 28; New Orleans, 1848 ***778.6*** *p28*
Berger, Pauline; North Dakota, 1904 ***609.10*** *p14*
Berger, Philip *SEE* Berger, Jacob
Berger, Philip; Uruguay, 1895 ***609.10*** *p13*
Berger, Rosalie Lombeau *SEE* Berger, Adrien Joseph
Berger, Rudolph Carl Heinrich Ludwig; Chicago, 1882 ***7420.1*** *p327*
Berger, Stanislaus; Port uncertain, 1905 ***7420.1*** *p380*
Berger, Victoire; Wisconsin, 1854-1858 ***1495.20*** *p50*
Bergerac, Jacques 18; Quebec, 1656 ***9221.17*** *p339*
Bergeron, J. P. Paul 18; New Orleans, 1848 ***778.6*** *p28*
Bergeron, Pierre; Illinois, 1852 ***6079.1*** *p1*
Bergeronne, Marie-Madeleine 31; Quebec, 1647 ***9221.17*** *p186*
*Son:*Robert 5
*Son:*Etienne 2
Bergerot, Jean; Louisiana, 1874 ***4981.45*** *p130*
Bergerot, John; Louisiana, 1874-1875 ***4981.45*** *p297*
Berges, E.; Louisiana, 1874 ***4981.45*** *p130*
Berges, Jean 47; New Orleans, 1844 ***778.6*** *p28*
Bergfeld, Carolina; America, 1856 ***2526.43*** *p145*
Berggren, Anna Nilsdotter 26 *SEE* Berggren, Jan E.
Berggren, Anna Christina Neilsen *SEE* Berggren, Olof Pehrsson
Berggren, Anna Stina 30; New York, 1856 ***6529.11*** *p20*
Berggren, August Verner 17 *SEE* Berggren, Joh.
Berggren, Bror 13 *SEE* Berggren, Joh.
Berggren, C. Axel L.; New York, NY, 1851 ***6412.40*** *p151*
Berggren, Carin 2 *SEE* Berggren, Jan E.
Berggren, Carl; America, 1857 ***6529.11*** *p23*
Berggren, Herman; Cleveland, OH, 1893-1898 ***9722.10*** *p117*
Berggren, J. A.; Valparaiso, Chile, 1850 ***1192.4*** *p50*
Berggren, Jan E. 26; New York, 1856 ***6529.11*** *p20*
*Wife:*Anna Nilsdotter 26
*Daughter:*Carin 2
Berggren, Joh. 59; New York, 1856 ***6529.11*** *p20*
*Son:*August Verner 17
*Son:*Bror 13
Berggren, John; Colorado, 1899 ***1029.59*** *p8*
Berggren, John; Colorado, 1899 ***1029.59*** *p9*
Berggren, John A.; Colorado, 1899 ***1029.59*** *p9*
Berggren, Lars 25; New York, 1856 ***6529.11*** *p20*
Berggren, Olof Pehrsson; St. Paul, MN, 1867 ***1865.50*** *p40*
*Wife:*Anna Christina Neilsen
Berggren, Per Anton 23; New York, 1856 ***6529.11*** *p20*
Berghof, Mr.; America, 1870 ***7420.1*** *p283*
Berghold, A. 24; America, 1846 ***778.6*** *p28*
Bergilez, Marie Julie; Wisconsin, 1880 ***1495.20*** *p56*
Bergin, Patrick; Toronto, 1844 ***2910.35*** *p113*
Bergin, Stephen; New York, NY, 1841 ***3274.56*** *p71*
Bergland, John; Colorado, 1882 ***1029.59*** *p9*
Bergling, Bror Josef; Illinois, 1930 ***121.35*** *p100*
Berglof, Lars O.; Illinois, 1861 ***4487.25*** *p53*
Berglund, Adolf; Colorado, 1893 ***1029.59*** *p9*
Berglund, Adolph; Colorado, 1893 ***1029.59*** *p9*
Berglund, Brita; America, 1855 ***6529.11*** *p25*
Berglund, Jacob Petter; North America, 1888 ***6410.15*** *p106*
Berglund, John; Colorado, 1882 ***1029.59*** *p9*
Berglund, Pehr 25; New York, 1856 ***6529.11*** *p22*
Bergman, Anna 12 *SEE* Bergman, Anna
Bergman, Anna 55; New York, 1856 ***6529.11*** *p22*
*Daughter:*Anna 12
Bergman, Karl; Cleveland, OH, 1892-1894 ***9722.10*** *p117*
Bergman, Olof; Colorado, 1886 ***1029.59*** *p9*
Bergmann, Anthony; Long Island, 1781 ***8529.30*** *p9A*
Bergmann, Arnost; Texas, 1849 ***2853.20*** *p58*
With family
Bergmann, Charlotte 18; New York, NY, 1864 ***8425.62*** *p198*
Bergmann, E.; Venezuela, 1843 ***3899.5*** *p546*
Bergmann, Franz; Galveston, TX, 1855 ***571.7*** *p16*
Bergmann, Friedrich August; America, 1868 ***7420.1*** *p268*
Bergmann, Friedrich August; Port uncertain, 1853 ***7420.1*** *p102*
Bergmann, Georg Ludwig; America, 1866 ***7420.1*** *p239*
Bergmann, Gerh. H. 51; New York, NY, 1864 ***8425.62*** *p198*
Bergmann, H. E.; Ohio, 1809-1852 ***4511.35*** *p4*
Bergmann, Heinrich August; America, 1867 ***7420.1*** *p253*
Bergmann, Johann Heinrich Friedrich; America, 1867 ***7420.1*** *p253*
Bergmann, Louise 9; New York, NY, 1864 ***8425.62*** *p198*
Bergmann, Ludwig; America, 1853 ***7420.1*** *p102*
Bergmann, P.; New York, 1860 ***358.56*** *p149*
Bergmann, Sophie Dorothea; America, 1886 ***7420.1*** *p350*
Bergmann, Wilhelmine; America, 1852 ***7420.1*** *p85*
Bergmann, Wilhelmine 15; New York, NY, 1864 ***8425.62*** *p198*
Bergmeier, Carl Heinrich Gottlieb; Port uncertain, 1840 ***7420.1*** *p17*
*Wife:*Engel Marie Wilhelm Eleonore Moller
With 2 sons & 2 daughters
Bergmeier, Daniel; New York, 1778 ***8529.30*** *p6*
Bergmeier, Engel Marie Wilhelm Eleonore Moller *SEE* Bergmeier, Carl Heinrich Gottlieb
Bergmeier, Wilhelm Friedrich; St. Paul, MN, 1888 ***7420.1*** *p355*
Bergmeyer, Gottlieb; America, 1860 ***7420.1*** *p191*
With wife son & 4 daughters
Bergmuller, Gregor; America, 1846 ***5475.1*** *p472*
Bergmuller, Johann; America, 1843 ***5475.1*** *p471*
Bergmyer, Daniel; New York, 1778 ***8529.30*** *p6*
Bergot, Eug. D.; Louisiana, 1874 ***4981.45*** *p295*
Bergquist, A. G.; Washington, 1885 ***2770.40*** *p193*
Bergquist, Andrew Peter; Minneapolis, 1882-1891 ***1865.50*** *p40*
*Wife:*Katarina Sophia
Bergquist, Henry; St. Paul, MN, 1894 ***1865.50*** *p41*
Bergquist, Henry H.; Chicago, 1881-1887 ***1865.50*** *p41*
Bergquist, Katarina Sophia *SEE* Bergquist, Andrew Peter
Bergquist, Samuel A.; America, 1849 ***4487.25*** *p53*
With parents
Bergqvist, Anders Gustaf *SEE* Bergqvist, Jan
Bergqvist, Anders P.; Minneapolis, 1882-1891 ***1865.50*** *p40*
*Wife:*Katarina Sophia
Bergqvist, Anna Margareta *SEE* Bergqvist, Jan
Bergqvist, Henry; St. Paul, MN, 1894 ***1865.50*** *p41*
Bergqvist, Henry H.; Chicago, 1881-1887 ***1865.50*** *p41*
Bergqvist, Jan *SEE* Bergqvist, Jan
Bergqvist, Jan; New York, 1857 ***6529.11*** *p25*
*Wife:*Margta Pehrsdotter
*Child:*Jan
*Child:*Anna Margareta
*Child:*Lars Erik
*Child:*Anders Gustaf
*Child:*Peter Olof
*Child:*Maja Helena
Bergqvist, Jon 19; New York, 1856 ***6529.11*** *p21*
Bergqvist, Katarina Sophia *SEE* Bergqvist, Anders P.
Bergqvist, Lars Erik *SEE* Bergqvist, Jan
Bergqvist, Maja Helena *SEE* Bergqvist, Jan
Bergqvist, Margta Pehrsdotter *SEE* Bergqvist, Jan
Bergqvist, Peter Olof *SEE* Bergqvist, Jan
Bergriah, Linas; Louisiana, 1874-1875 ***4981.45*** *p297*
Bergstedt, C.G.; New York, NY, 1844 ***6412.40*** *p147*
Bergstrom, Aug. Th.; Baltimore, 1851 ***6412.40*** *p152*
Bergstrom, C.F.; New York, NY, 1843 ***6412.40*** *p146*
Bergstrom, Charlotta; St. Paul, MN, 1881 ***1865.50*** *p39*
Bergstrom, Edward Leander; Boston, 1902 ***1766.20*** *p16*
Bergstrom, J.P.; New York, NY, 1846 ***6412.40*** *p149*
Bergstrom, John 53; Minnesota, 1925 ***2769.54*** *p1378*
Bergstrom, Mary C.; St. Paul, MN, 1889-1890 ***1865.50*** *p41*
Bergstrom, Olof 21; Kansas, 1880 ***777.40*** *p9*
Bergstrom, Samuel M.; Colorado, 1888 ***1029.59*** *p9*
Bergtold, Catherine 19; Port uncertain, 1843 ***778.6*** *p28*
Bergunder, Emilian 35; Halifax, N.S., 1902 ***1860.4*** *p42*
Bergunder, Josef 24; Halifax, N.S., 1902 ***1860.4*** *p42*
Bergunder, Paul; Louisiana, 1836-1841 ***4981.45*** *p208*
Berham, William; Iowa, 1888 ***1211.15*** *p9*
Berhardt, Mary; Wisconsin, 1900 ***6795.8*** *p67*
Beriau, Jacques; Montreal, 1659 ***9221.17*** *p417*
Beriau, Jean; Quebec, 1653 ***9221.17*** *p270*
Berich, Adam 23; Baltimore, 1889 ***8425.16*** *p36*
Berich, Jacob 4; Baltimore, 1889 ***8425.16*** *p36*
Berich, Josef 6 months; Baltimore, 1889 ***8425.16*** *p36*
Berich, Marie 2; Baltimore, 1889 ***8425.16*** *p36*
Berich, Veronika 25; Baltimore, 1889 ***8425.16*** *p36*
Berillon, Marcel Aug. F. A. 50; America, 1841 ***778.6*** *p28*
Berisford, William 27; Ontario, 1871 ***1823.21*** *p24*
Berisset, Jean 25; Quebec, 1657 ***9221.17*** *p352*
Berk, John; Illinois, 1851 ***6079.1*** *p1*
Berka, Josef; Illinois, 1853-1910 ***2853.20*** *p471*
Berka, Ludvik; America, 1862 ***2853.20*** *p155*
With parents & 4 siblings
Berke, Albert; Miami, 1920 ***4984.15*** *p38*
Berkel, Adam 25; Halifax, N.S., 1902 ***1860.4*** *p44*
Berkel, Anast... 16; Halifax, N.S., 1902 ***1860.4*** *p44*
Berkel, Constantin; Halifax, N.S., 1902 ***1860.4*** *p44*
Berkel, Frederick 11; Halifax, N.S., 1902 ***1860.4*** *p44*
Berkel, Helena 18; Halifax, N.S., 1902 ***1860.4*** *p44*
Berkel, Johrist 3; Halifax, N.S., 1902 ***1860.4*** *p44*
Berkel, Margn 23; Halifax, N.S., 1902 ***1860.4*** *p44*
Berkel, Valentine 18; Halifax, N.S., 1902 ***1860.4*** *p44*
Berkenbusch, Th.; Galveston, TX, 1855 ***571.7*** *p16*
Berkenhaur, Josephine; Valdivia, Chile, 1852 ***1192.4*** *p55*
Berkner, Eduard 24; America, 1872 ***5475.1*** *p14*
Berle, Adam 27 *SEE* Berle, Leonhard
Berle, Dieter 17 *SEE* Berle, Leonhard
Berle, Elisabetha 31 *SEE* Berle, Leonhard
Berle, Leonhard 59; America, 1854 ***2526.42*** *p118*
*Child:*Elisabetha 31
With wife 51
*Child:*Adam 27
*Child:*Peter 19
*Child:*Ludwig 9
*Child:*Dieter 17
*Child:*Maria Magdalena 23
Berle, Ludwig 9 *SEE* Berle, Leonhard
Berle, Maria Magdalena 23 *SEE* Berle, Leonhard
Berle, Peter 19 *SEE* Berle, Leonhard
Berlier, Jacob 23; America, 1847 ***778.6*** *p53*
Berlier, Michel 28; New Orleans, 1848 ***778.6*** *p28*
Berlier, Regina 20; America, 1847 ***778.6*** *p53*
Berling, Frederich; Ohio, 1840-1897 ***8365.35*** *p15*
Berlinger, Barron; North Carolina, 1850 ***1088.45*** *p2*
Berlinger, Jacob; North Carolina, 1849 ***1088.45*** *p2*
Berlingere, P.; Louisiana, 1874-1875 ***4981.45*** *p298*
Bermacher, Miss 6; America, 1843 ***778.6*** *p29*
Bermacher, Miss 8; America, 1843 ***778.6*** *p29*
Bermacher, Miss 10; America, 1843 ***778.6*** *p29*
Bermacher, Mr. 20; America, 1843 ***778.6*** *p28*
Bermacher, Mr. 49; America, 1843 ***778.6*** *p28*
Bermacher, Mrs. 40; America, 1843 ***778.6*** *p29*
Bermacher, Ms. 20; America, 1843 ***778.6*** *p28*
Bermann, Friedrich; America, 1854 ***5475.1*** *p398*
Bermann, Katharina; America, 1843 ***5475.1*** *p463*
With 4 children
Bermatin, Mr. 36; New Orleans, 1841 ***778.6*** *p29*
Bermen, Laurent; Quebec, 1645 ***9221.17*** *p151*
Bermen DeLaMartiniere, Claude 26; Quebec, 1662 ***9221.17*** *p479*
Bermen deLa Martiniere, Claude de; Quebec, 1662 ***2314.30*** *p166*
Bermen deLa Martiniere, Claude de; Quebec, 1662 ***2314.30*** *p175*
Bermenstein, Leonhart 28; America, 1843 ***778.6*** *p29*
Bernard, . . .; New England, n.d. ***9228.50*** *p99*
Bernard, . . .; New Orleans, 1840 ***778.6*** *p29*
Bernard, . . .; New Orleans, 1840 ***778.6*** *p29*
Bernard, Mr. 31; America, 1845 ***778.6*** *p29*
Bernard, Mr. 75; America, 1846 ***778.6*** *p29*
Bernard, Mrs. 57; America, 1843 ***778.6*** *p30*
Bernard, Adolf 32; New Orleans, 1848 ***778.6*** *p29*
Bernard, Aglaie 3; New Orleans, 1848 ***778.6*** *p29*
Bernard, Alexis 1; America, 1843 ***778.6*** *p29*
Bernard, Alphonsin 8; America, 1843 ***778.6*** *p29*
Bernard, Amand 24; New Orleans, 1840 ***778.6*** *p29*
Bernard, Amelie 2; New Orleans, 1848 ***778.6*** *p29*
Bernard, Ann Mary; North Carolina, 1849 ***1088.45*** *p2*
Bernard, Anna; San Antonio, TX, 1886 ***5475.1*** *p161*
Bernard, C. 23; America, 1842 ***778.6*** *p29*
Bernard, Catherine 9; Missouri, 1846 ***778.6*** *p29*
Bernard, Celestin 24; America, 1847 ***778.6*** *p29*
Bernard, Celestin 30; America, 1843 ***778.6*** *p29*
Bernard, Celina 26; America, 1843 ***778.6*** *p29*
Bernard, Charles 28; America, 1841 ***778.6*** *p29*
Bernard, D. 25; America, 1843 ***778.6*** *p29*
Bernard, David; Virginia, 1700 ***9230.15*** *p80*
Bernard, Dupeche 23; New Orleans, 1840 ***778.6*** *p29*
Bernard, Elemore 28; New Orleans, 1848 ***778.6*** *p29*
Bernard, Francois 43; America, 1844 ***778.6*** *p29*
Bernard, Georg 26; New Orleans, 1848 ***778.6*** *p29*
Bernard, Henri; Louisiana, 1836-1841 ***4981.45*** *p208*
Bernard, Henri 29; New Orleans, 1848 ***778.6*** *p29*
Bernard, J. 57; America, 1843 ***778.6*** *p29*
Bernard, Jean 47; America, 1842 ***778.6*** *p29*
Bernard, Jean Francois; New Orleans, 1840 ***778.6*** *p29*
Bernard, Jeanne 29; New Orleans, 1840 ***778.6*** *p29*
Bernard, Jeanne; Quebec, 1668 ***4514.3*** *p277*
Bernard, John Baptist; Ohio, 1809-1852 ***4511.35*** *p4*
Bernard, Joseph 40; America, 1840 ***778.6*** *p30*
Bernard, Joseph 47; America, 1841 ***778.6*** *p30*
Bernard, Julie Catherine 25; New Orleans, 1848 ***778.6*** *p30*
Bernard, Leonie 4; New Orleans, 1848 ***778.6*** *p30*
Bernard, Marie 7; America, 1843 ***778.6*** *p30*
Bernard, Marie Henriette 62; New Orleans, 1848 ***778.6*** *p30*
Bernard, Mary 40; America, 1841 ***778.6*** *p30*
Bernard, Michael 10; New York, NY, 1821-1849 ***6178.50*** *p77*
Bernard, Peter; Ohio, 1809-1852 ***4511.35*** *p4*
Bernard, Philipp 30; New Orleans, 1848 ***778.6*** *p30*
Bernard, William 8; New York, NY, 1821-1849 ***6178.50*** *p77*
Bernard, William 33; New York, NY, 1825 ***6178.50*** *p77*
Bernard, William 50; Ontario, 1871 ***1823.21*** *p24*
Bernarding, Ferdinand *SEE* Bernarding, Peter

32 *FOR A COMPLETE EXPLANATION OF ENTRY, SEE "HOW TO READ A CITATION" SECTION*

Bernarding, Katharina *SEE* Bernarding, Peter
Bernarding, Katharina Truar *SEE* Bernarding, Peter
Bernarding, Katharina Zimmer *SEE* Bernarding, Mathias
Bernarding, Mathias; America, 1882 ***5475.1*** *p168*
  *Wife:*Katharina Zimmer
Bernarding, Peter; America, 1871 ***5475.1*** *p168*
  *Wife:*Katharina Truar
  *Son:*Ferdinand
  *Sister:*Katharina
Bernardy, A. Maria 27; America, 1863 ***5475.1*** *p347*
Bernardy, Helena Meiers *SEE* Bernardy, Johann
Bernardy, Jakob *SEE* Bernardy, Johann
Bernardy, Johann *SEE* Bernardy, Johann
Bernardy, Johann; Brazil, 1880 ***5475.1*** *p373*
  *Wife:*Helena Meiers
  With child
  *Daughter:*Maria
  *Son:*Jakob
  *Son:*Johann
  *Son:*Peter
  *Son:*P. Mathias
  *Daughter:*Rosina
  *Son:*Mathias
Bernardy, Maria *SEE* Bernardy, Johann
Bernardy, Mathias; America, 1879 ***5475.1*** *p315*
Bernardy, Mathias *SEE* Bernardy, Johann
Bernardy, P. Mathias *SEE* Bernardy, Johann
Bernardy, Peter *SEE* Bernardy, Johann
Bernardy, Rosina *SEE* Bernardy, Johann
Bernas, Jan; Minnesota, 1857 ***2853.20*** *p259*
Bernasco, Eduard; America, 1846 ***5475.1*** *p234*
Bernasco, Emil Josef 35; America, 1847 ***5475.1*** *p234*
Bernatz, Jacob 24; Ontario, 1871 ***1823.17*** *p10*
Bernauer, Ott. 27; America, 1840 ***778.6*** *p30*
Bernbeck, Berna.d 40; New Orleans, 1843 ***778.6*** *p30*
Berndt, Anna 21; New York, NY, 1876 ***6954.7*** *p39*
Berndt, Dorothea 48; New York, NY, 1886 ***6954.7*** *p40*
Berndt, Emmanuel 8; New York, NY, 1876 ***6954.7*** *p39*
Berndt, Ephriam 9; New York, NY, 1876 ***6954.7*** *p39*
Berndt, Friedrich 16; New York, NY, 1876 ***6954.7*** *p39*
Berndt, Heinrich 22; New York, NY, 1876 ***6954.7*** *p39*
Berndt, Johann 19; New York, NY, 1876 ***6954.7*** *p39*
Berndt, Johann 55; New York, NY, 1876 ***6954.7*** *p39*
Berndt, Karl 9; New York, NY, 1886 ***6954.7*** *p40*
Berndt, Katherina 20; New York, NY, 1886 ***6954.7*** *p40*
Berndt, Maria 53; New York, NY, 1876 ***6954.7*** *p39*
Berndt, Michael 27; New York, NY, 1876 ***6954.7*** *p39*
Berndt, Michael 56; New York, NY, 1886 ***6954.7*** *p40*
Berndt, Rudolph Heinrich; Wisconsin, 1893 ***6795.8*** *p115*
Berndt, Theador 4 months; New York, NY, 1876 ***6954.7*** *p39*
Berndt, Theador 17; New York, NY, 1876 ***6954.7*** *p39*
Berndt, Wilhelm 25; New York, NY, 1876 ***6954.7*** *p39*
Berndt, William; Colorado, 1889 ***1029.59*** *p9*
Berndtsson, A.; New York, NY, 1847 ***6412.40*** *p150*
Berne, Christian; Philadelphia, 1854 ***8513.31*** *p294*
  *Wife:*Maria Ana Capuret
Berne, Felix; Louisiana, 1874-1875 ***4981.45*** *p297*
Berne, Maria Ana Capuret *SEE* Berne, Christian
Bernede, Ernest 25; Port uncertain, 1841 ***778.6*** *p30*
Berner, Carl Joseph; Louisiana, 1841-1844 ***4981.45*** *p210*
Berner, Frans Jacob; Louisiana, 1841-1844 ***4981.45*** *p210*
Berner, Leopold; Louisiana, 1874-1875 ***4981.45*** *p298*
Berner, P. F.; Valdivia, Chile, 1852 ***1192.4*** *p52*
  With wife
Bernet, John; Illinois, 1861 ***6079.1*** *p1*
Berney, John 35; Ontario, 1871 ***1823.21*** *p24*
Bernhagen, Michael; Iowa, 1878 ***1211.15*** *p9*
Bernhalzer, Franz; Colorado, 1879 ***1029.59*** *p9*
Bernhard, Mr.; America, 1887 ***7420.1*** *p352*
  With brother & 2 sisters
Bernhard, Mr.; Port uncertain, 1866 ***7420.1*** *p239*
Bernhard, Anne 42; Missouri, 1846 ***778.6*** *p30*
Bernhard, Anne Marie 7; Missouri, 1846 ***778.6*** *p30*
Bernhard, Antoine 8; Missouri, 1846 ***778.6*** *p30*
Bernhard, Catharine 6; America, 1847 ***778.6*** *p30*
Bernhard, Catharine 43; America, 1847 ***778.6*** *p30*
Bernhard, Charles 24; Mississippi, 1847 ***778.6*** *p30*
Bernhard, Christian; America, 1853 ***179.55*** *p19*
Bernhard, Elisabeth 5; Missouri, 1846 ***778.6*** *p30*
Bernhard, Friedrich Gottlieb; America, 1867 ***7420.1*** *p253*
Bernhard, Georg 15; America, 1847 ***778.6*** *p30*
Bernhard, George 40; Missouri, 1846 ***778.6*** *p30*
Bernhard, Jacob 18; America, 1847 ***778.6*** *p30*
Bernhard, Jacob 45; America, 1847 ***778.6*** *p30*
Bernhard, Jan; Chicago, 1875-1879 ***2853.20*** *p458*
Bernhard, Johann 2 *SEE* Bernhard, Johann
Bernhard, Johann 28; America, 1864 ***5475.1*** *p45*
  *Wife:*Lucia Wall 27
  *Son:*Johann 2
Bernhard, Katharine; America, 1886 ***8115.12*** *p328*
Bernhard, Lucia Wall 27 *SEE* Bernhard, Johann
Bernhard, Margaretha 3; America, 1847 ***778.6*** *p30*
Bernhard, Maria 3 months; America, 1847 ***778.6*** *p30*
Bernhard, Marie 14; Missouri, 1846 ***778.6*** *p30*
Bernhard, Michel 13; America, 1847 ***778.6*** *p30*
Bernhard, Therese 2; Missouri, 1846 ***778.6*** *p30*
Bernheim, Moses; America, 1867 ***5475.1*** *p417*
Bernier, Alfred; Washington, 1889 ***2770.40*** *p26*
Bernier, Jacques 16; Quebec, 1652 ***9221.17*** *p254*
Bernieres, Henri de 24; Quebec, 1659 ***9221.17*** *p393*
Bernir, Mrs. 19; Port uncertain, 1845 ***778.6*** *p30*
Bernir, Marin 25; Port uncertain, 1845 ***778.6*** *p30*
Bernlohr, Johannes; America, 1854 ***179.55*** *p19*
Bernot, Jques. 30; New Orleans, 1840 ***778.6*** *p30*
Bernour, Conrad; Ohio, 1809-1852 ***4511.35*** *p4*
Bernowitz, Hermann; America, 1867 ***7919.3*** *p527*
  With 4 children
Bernsee, Ernest; Colorado, 1901 ***1029.59*** *p9*
Bernt, Jean Pierre 15; New Orleans, 1848 ***778.6*** *p30*
Bernt, Joseph 38; New Orleans, 1848 ***778.6*** *p31*
Bernusse, Bernard; Louisiana, 1836-1840 ***4981.45*** *p212*
Bernzeau, Antoine 37; Port uncertain, 1843 ***778.6*** *p31*
Bero, Frank; New York, NY, 1855 ***1494.20*** *p13*
Bero, Louis; New York, NY, 1856 ***1494.20*** *p12*
Bero, Theophile; New York, NY, 1857 ***1494.20*** *p13*
Beroffre, Adele 40; New Orleans, 1848 ***778.6*** *p31*
Beroffre, Anton 35; New Orleans, 1848 ***778.6*** *p31*
Beroz, Mr. 27; America, 1847 ***778.6*** *p31*
Berranger, Jean Baptista Louis Reni du Bois; Georgia, 1795 ***1451.56*** *p118*
Berranger, Jean Baptista du Bois; Georgia, 1795 ***1451.56*** *p118*
Berranger, Pierre Rene du Bois; Georgia, 1795 ***1451.56*** *p118*
Berrenger, Jean Baptista du Bois; Georgia, 1795 ***1451.56*** *p118*
Berrenger, Jean-Baptiste; Quebec, 1741 ***2314.30*** *p170*
Berrenger, Jean-Baptiste; Quebec, 1741 ***2314.30*** *p175*
Berres, Adam 2 *SEE* Berres, Mrs. Peter
Berres, Elisabetha 5 *SEE* Berres, Leonhard
Berres, Eva Schuler 27 *SEE* Berres, Leonhard
Berres, Eva Elisabetha 20; America, 1844 ***2526.43*** *p207*
Berres, Georg Peter 16; America, 1880 ***2526.42*** *p135*
Berres, Katharina 4 *SEE* Berres, Mrs. Peter
Berres, Leonhard 26; America, 1740-1899 ***2526.42*** *p135*
  *Wife:*Eva Schuler 27
  *Child:*Margaretha 1
  *Child:*Philipp 4
  *Child:*Elisabetha 5
Berres, Leonhard; Argentina, 1855 ***2526.43*** *p207*
  With family of 5
Berres, Margaretha 1 *SEE* Berres, Leonhard
Berres, Marie Elisabetha 49; America, 1872 ***2526.43*** *p217*
Berres, Peter; America, 1852 ***2526.43*** *p217*
Berres, Peter; America, 1880 ***2526.42*** *p135*
Berres, Mrs. Peter; America, 1853 ***2526.43*** *p217*
  *Daughter:*Katharina
  *Son:*Adam
Berres, Philipp 4 *SEE* Berres, Leonhard
Berres, Philipp 17; America, 1881 ***2526.42*** *p135*
Berres, Wilhelm; America, 1906 ***2526.43*** *p207*
Berridge, Thomas 21; Indiana, 1895-1896 ***9076.20*** *p74*
Berridge, Thomas 21; Indiana, 1895-1896 ***9076.20*** *p74*
Berrigan, Patrick 43; Ontario, 1871 ***1823.21*** *p24*
Berrill, John 70; Ontario, 1871 ***1823.21*** *p24*
Berrin, Marguerite; Quebec, 1672 ***4514.3*** *p278*
Berroth, Jacob; America, 1853 ***179.55*** *p19*
Berroth, Jakob; America, 1882 ***179.55*** *p19*
Berry, . . .; Ohio, 1800-1850 ***9228.50*** *p99*
Berry, Benjamin 12; Quebec, 1647 ***9221.17*** *p173*
Berry, Charlotte 48; New York, NY, 1894 ***6512.1*** *p228*
Berry, Duncan 26; Michigan, 1880 ***4491.36*** *p2*
Berry, Eliz.; New Jersey, 1922-1951 ***9228.50*** *p527*
Berry, Gerit 29; Ontario, 1871 ***1823.21*** *p24*
Berry, James 50; New York, NY, 1894 ***6512.1*** *p228*
Berry, James 38; Ontario, 1871 ***1823.17*** *p10*
Berry, James 44; Ontario, 1871 ***1823.21*** *p24*
Berry, John; Ipswich, MA, 1754-1763 ***1642*** *p70*
Berry, John 52; Michigan, 1880 ***4491.36*** *p2*
Berry, Joseph 28; Michigan, 1880 ***4491.36*** *p2*
Berry, Margaret 52; Michigan, 1880 ***4491.36*** *p2*
Berry, Patrick; North Carolina, 1829 ***1088.45*** *p2*
Berry, Richard 58; Ontario, 1871 ***1823.21*** *p24*
Berry, Simon; Montreal, 1653 ***9221.17*** *p288*
Berry, William 56; Michigan, 1880 ***4491.39*** *p3*
Berryhill, Ann 74; Ontario, 1871 ***1823.21*** *p24*
Berryhill, Samuel 44; Ontario, 1871 ***1823.21*** *p24*
Berryman, James 32; Ontario, 1871 ***1823.21*** *p25*
Bersch, George; Ohio, 1809-1852 ***4511.35*** *p4*
Bersch, Jacob; Washington, 1885 ***2770.40*** *p193*
Berse, Pierre 46; America, 1846 ***778.6*** *p31*
Berseigle, Elisabet 22; America, 1847 ***778.6*** *p31*
Bersh, John; Illinois, 1851 ***6079.1*** *p2*
Berson, Antoine; Quebec, 1657 ***9221.17*** *p352*
Berson, Jacques 50; Texas, 1848 ***778.6*** *p31*
Bertalino, Serafino; Illinois, 1918 ***6007.60*** *p9*
Bertault, Anne; Quebec, 1669 ***4514.3*** *p278*
Bertaut, Barthelemy 30; Quebec, 1653 ***9221.17*** *p270*
Bertaut, Jacques 24; Quebec, 1650 ***9221.17*** *p223*
Berte, Bernard; Montreal, 1642 ***9221.17*** *p123*
Berteaux, . . .; Canada, n.d. ***9228.50*** *p99*
Bertel, Elisabeth 6 months; America, 1846 ***778.6*** *p31*
Bertel, Elisabeth 30; America, 1846 ***778.6*** *p31*
Bertel, Ignatz 7; America, 1846 ***778.6*** *p31*
Bertel, Jean 36; America, 1846 ***778.6*** *p31*
Bertel, John; Ohio, 1809-1852 ***4511.35*** *p4*
Bertel, Julie 5; America, 1846 ***778.6*** *p31*
Berth, Elisabeth; America, 1867 ***7919.3*** *p531*
Berthand, Francis; Ohio, 1809-1852 ***4511.35*** *p4*
Berthe, Alex.; Philadelphia, 1881 ***8513.31*** *p294*
  *Wife:*Eugenia Patin
Berthe, Eugenia Patin *SEE* Berthe, Alex.
Berthelon, Claude 28; Missouri, 1845 ***778.6*** *p31*
Berthelot, Andre 16; Quebec, 1656 ***9221.17*** *p331*
Berthelot, Guillaume; Quebec, 1659 ***9221.17*** *p412*
Berthelot, Jean; Quebec, 1659 ***9221.17*** *p412*
Berthelot, Marie; Quebec, 1669 ***4514.3*** *p359*
  *Daughter:*Marie-Madeleine
Berthelot, Marie-Madeleine *SEE* Berthelot, Marie Prevost
Berthelot, Pierre; Quebec, 1636-1669 ***4514.3*** *p360*
Berthier, Alexandre; Quebec, 1665 ***2314.30*** *p167*
Berthier, Alexandre; Quebec, 1665 ***2314.30*** *p175*
Berthier, Jules 29; America, 1848 ***778.6*** *p31*
Berthilemy, Jacob; Ohio, 1809-1852 ***4511.35*** *p4*
Berthoud, Mr. 25; America, 1846 ***778.6*** *p31*
Berthoumier, Francs. 26; America, 1840 ***778.6*** *p31*
Bertin, Benoit 21; Mississippi, 1847 ***778.6*** *p31*
Bertin, Eugene 5; Mississippi, 1847 ***778.6*** *p31*
Bertin, Francois 25; America, 1843 ***778.6*** *p31*
Bertin, Francois 31; Mississippi, 1847 ***778.6*** *p31*
Bertin, Marie 31; Mississippi, 1847 ***778.6*** *p31*
Bertin, Marie; Quebec, 1669 ***4514.3*** *p278*
Bertin, Virginie 32; America, 1843 ***778.6*** *p31*
Bertler, Johann 49; Galveston, TX, 1846 ***3967.10*** *p378*
Bertoch, Andrew 32; Halifax, N.S., 1902 ***1860.4*** *p44*
Bertoch, Catherine 21; Halifax, N.S., 1902 ***1860.4*** *p44*
Bertoch, Elias 58; Halifax, N.S., 1902 ***1860.4*** *p44*
Bertolet, . . .; Massachusetts, n.d. ***9228.50*** *p99*
Berton, Anselme 22; America, 1846 ***778.6*** *p31*
Bertot, J. 25; America, 1844 ***778.6*** *p31*
Bertram, . . .; Ohio, n.d. ***9228.50*** *p95*
Bertram, Amice; Canada, 1849 ***9228.50*** *p100*
  *Wife:*Elizabeth Le Neveu
  *Daughter:*Louisa
Bertram, Elizabeth *SEE* Bertram, John
Bertram, Elizabeth Le Neveu *SEE* Bertram, Amice
Bertram, Friedrich Hermann; America, 1882 ***7420.1*** *p327*
Bertram, George *SEE* Bertram, John
Bertram, George; Massachusetts, 1843 ***9228.50*** *p100*
Bertram, Jane *SEE* Bertram, John
Bertram, John *SEE* Bertram, John
Bertram, John; Baltimore, 1807 ***9228.50*** *p19*
  *Son:*John
  With 5 children
  *Wife:*Mary Perchard
Bertram, John *SEE* Bertram, John
Bertram, John; Baltimore, 1807 ***9228.50*** *p99*
  *Wife:*Mary Perchard
  *Child:*John
  *Child:*Philip
  *Child:*Jane
  *Child:*Elizabeth
  *Child:*George
  *Child:*Mary Ann
Bertram, John; Boston, 1807 ***9228.50*** *p122*
  With family of 8
Bertram, John; Massachusetts, 1775-1820 ***9228.50*** *p122*
Bertram, Joseph; Brazil, 1910 ***8023.44*** *p372*
Bertram, Louisa; British Columbia, 1890 ***9228.50*** *p592*
Bertram, Louisa; California, 1890 ***9228.50*** *p592*
Bertram, Louisa *SEE* Bertram, Amice
Bertram, Mary Perchard *SEE* Bertram, John
Bertram, Mary Perchard *SEE* Bertram, John
Bertram, Mary Ann *SEE* Bertram, John
Bertram, Philip *SEE* Bertram, John
Bertrand, Mr. 59; New Orleans, 1840 ***778.6*** *p31*
Bertrand, Bertrand 3; Mississippi, 1847 ***778.6*** *p31*
Bertrand, Catherine 27; Mississippi, 1847 ***778.6*** *p31*
Bertrand, Charles 18; Mississippi, 1847 ***778.6*** *p31*
Bertrand, Conler 25; Port uncertain, 1843 ***778.6*** *p31*
Bertrand, J. B. 42; Port uncertain, 1846 ***778.6*** *p31*
Bertrand, Jacob 1; Mississippi, 1847 ***778.6*** *p31*
Bertrand, Jean Georges 4; Mississippi, 1847 ***778.6*** *p32*
Bertrand, John 28; New Orleans, 1840 ***778.6*** *p32*
Bertrand, Louis 35; Louisiana, 1848 ***778.6*** *p32*

Bertrand, Marie-Antoine 47; New Orleans, 1848 *778.6 p32*
Bertrand, Michel 27; Port uncertain, 1845 *778.6 p32*
Bertrand, Nicolas 33; Mississippi, 1847 *778.6 p32*
Bertrand, Nicolas 64; Mississippi, 1847 *778.6 p32*
Bertrand, Nicolas 39; Port uncertain, 1846 *778.6 p32*
Bertrand, Peroline 44; New Orleans, 1848 *778.6 p32*
Bertrand, Pierre Francis; Illinois, 1852 *6079.1 p2*
Bertrand, Porte 20; New Orleans, 1848 *778.6 p32*
Bertrand, Victorine Helene 13; New Orleans, 1848 *778.6 p32*
Bertrand DeLafreminiere, Francois 23; Montreal, 1661 *9221.17 p471*
Bertrande, Alcide 22; America, 1842 *778.6 p32*
Bertsch, Anna 11 months; New York, NY, 1886 *8425.16 p33*
Bertsch, Anna 23; New York, NY, 1886 *8425.16 p33*
Bertsch, Elisabeth 3; New York, NY, 1874 *6954.7 p39*
Bertsch, Friedriecke 23; New York, NY, 1874 *6954.7 p39*
Bertsch, Gottlieb 6 months; New York, NY, 1874 *6954.7 p39*
Bertsch, Johannes 28; New York, NY, 1874 *6954.7 p39*
Bertsch, John; Washington, 1888 *2770.40 p25*
Bertsch, Mag. 1 months; New York, NY, 1886 *8425.16 p33*
Bertsch, Stanisl. 28; New York, NY, 1886 *8425.16 p33*
Bertschi, Soloman; Illinois, 1861 *6079.1 p2*
Bertschi, William; Illinois, 1852 *6079.1 p2*
Bertucci, Guacio; Louisiana, 1874-1875 *4981.45 p298*
Bertuch, Joseph; Louisiana, 1874 *4981.45 p131*
Bertz, George; New York, 1859 *358.56 p101*
Berwald, Oswald Eugene; Oregon, 1941 *9157.47 p2*
Berwanger, Barbara Adam *SEE* Berwanger, Johann
Berwanger, Johann *SEE* Berwanger, Johann
Berwanger, Johann; America, 1872 *5475.1 p304*
    *Wife:*Barbara Adam
    *Son:*Peter
    *Son:*Johann
Berwanger, Josef 34; Brazil, 1872 *5475.1 p442*
Berwanger, Nikolaus; America, 1865 *5475.1 p518*
Berwanger, Peter *SEE* Berwanger, Johann
Berwanger, Peter 29; America, 1800-1899 *5475.1 p518*
Berwart, Antoine; New York, NY, 1869 *1494.20 p11*
Berwian, Nikolaus; America, 1878 *5475.1 p435*
Berwick, Nathaniel 68; Ontario, 1871 *1823.21 p25*
Besancon, Jean 18; America, 1842 *778.6 p32*
Besancon, N. 25; America, 1842 *778.6 p32*
Besch, Mr.; America, 1846 *5475.1 p455*
Besch, Anton; Venezuela, 1843 *3899.5 p540*
Besch, Peter Karl; America, 1847 *5475.1 p473*
Besche, Marie; Quebec, 1670 *4514.3 p278*
Besilide, Clement 58; New Orleans, 1848 *778.6 p32*
Besilide, Elise 32; New Orleans, 1848 *778.6 p32*
Besnard, Catherine 31; Quebec, 1661 *9221.17 p447*
Besnard, Denis *SEE* Besnard, Denis
Besnard, Denis; Quebec, 1647 *9221.17 p176*
    *Wife:*Marie Michelet
    *Daughter:*Marie
    *Son:*Pierre
    *Son:*Denis
    *Daughter:*Marguerite
Besnard, Francoise 27; Montreal, 1654 *9221.17 p316*
Besnard, Jacques; Quebec, 1655 *9221.17 p321*
Besnard, Marguerite 15 *SEE* Besnard, Denis
Besnard, Marie Michelet *SEE* Besnard, Denis
Besnard, Marie 16 *SEE* Besnard, Denis
Besnard, Nicolas; Quebec, 1649 *9221.17 p209*
Besnard, Nicolas; Quebec, 1659 *9221.17 p412*
Besnard, Pierre *SEE* Besnard, Denis
Besnard, Rene 26; Montreal, 1653 *9221.17 p282*
Besold, Fred 49; Ontario, 1871 *1823.21 p25*
Besome, Joseph; North America, 1766 *9228.50 p112*
    *Nephew:*Nicholas
Besome, Nicholas *SEE* Besome, Joseph
Besse, Mr. 30; New Orleans, 1840 *778.6 p32*
Besse, Paul 40; Port uncertain, 1845 *778.6 p32*
Besselun, William; Philadelphia, 1891 *1766.20 p36*
Besser, Elisabeth 38; America, 1847 *5475.1 p327*
Besser, Friedrich August; America, 1845 *7420.1 p34*
Besship, Francis 25; Ontario, 1871 *1823.17 p10*
Bessi, Charles 28; Louisiana, 1848 *778.6 p32*
Bessin, . . .; Boston, 1769 *9228.50 p5*
Bessin, . . .; Maryland, 1600-1699 *9228.50 p113*
Bessin, Alphonse 39; Louisiana, 1848 *778.6 p32*
Bessin, Daniel; Boston, 1769 *9228.50 p48*
Bessin, Jacques 28; New Orleans, 1748 *778.6 p32*
Bessom, . . .; Marblehead, MA, 1749 *9228.50 p109*
Bessom, Mr.; New London, CT, 1669 *9228.50 p112*
Bessom, John; Marblehead, MA, 1793 *9228.50 p112*
Bessom, Joseph *SEE* Bessom, Nicholas
Bessom, Nicholas 11; Massachusetts, 1766 *9228.50 p112*
    *Uncle:*Joseph

Bessom, Richard; Marblehead, MA, 1753 *9228.50 p112*
Besson, Andre 25; New Orleans, 1848 *778.6 p32*
Besson, Epolet 33; America, 1848 *778.6 p32*
Besson, Joseph; Quebec, 1654 *9221.17 p305*
Besson, Thomas; Virginia, 1640 *9228.50 p113*
Bessonnet, Marie; Quebec, 1658 *9221.17 p376*
Bessonnet, Pierre 32; Montreal, 1658 *9221.17 p388*
Best, Mr.; America, n.d. *9228.50 p532*
    *Wife:*Elizabeth Rabey
Best, Mr.; New York, NY, 1904 *9228.50 p100*
Best, Alfred 18; Michigan, 1880 *4491.39 p3*
Best, Alice 16; Michigan, 1880 *4491.39 p3*
Best, Elizabeth Rabey *SEE* Best, Mr.
Best, Emeline 46; Michigan, 1880 *4491.39 p3*
Best, Harvey 12; Michigan, 1880 *4491.39 p3*
Best, John; Salem, MA, 1670 *9228.50 p201*
Best, Katharina 30; America, 1872 *5475.1 p41*
Best, Susan Elizabeth; Canada, n.d. *9228.50 p100*
Best, Thomas 30; Ontario, 1871 *1823.17 p10*
Best, Walter E. 22; Michigan, 1880 *4491.39 p3*
Bestecker, Ose; New York, 1859 *358.56 p101*
Betard, Martin 22; America, 1843 *778.6 p32*
Betard, Michel 18; America, 1843 *778.6 p32*
Betaz, Ida Wilhelmine Marie von; America, 1851 *7420.1 p78*
Beteetee, Maria 9; Santa Clara Co., CA, 1852 *8704.1 p22*
Bethame, Donald 35; Ontario, 1871 *1823.21 p25*
Bethel, Charles Theodore; Miami, 1935 *4984.12 p39*
Bethele, Jeanne 19; New Orleans, 1848 *778.6 p32*
Bethell, Elizabeth 17; Quebec, 1870 *8364.32 p22*
Bethell, Emily 16; Quebec, 1870 *8364.32 p22*
Bethke, Emma; Wisconsin, 1971 *6795.8 p130*
Bethune, Niel; Quebec, 1786 *1416.15 p8*
Betini, Celeste; Illinois, 1930 *121.35 p101*
Betison, John 30; Ontario, 1871 *1823.17 p10*
Betler, Frederick; Ohio, 1809-1852 *4511.35 p4*
Beton, Mary; New York, 1738 *8277.31 p113*
    With son
Bettcher, August 31; New York, NY, 1893 *1883.7 p42*
Bettcher, Elisabeth 3; New York, NY, 1893 *1883.7 p42*
Bettcher, Louise 24; New York, NY, 1893 *1883.7 p42*
Bettcher, Mathilde 4; New York, NY, 1893 *1883.7 p42*
Bettcher, Sofia 9 months; New York, NY, 1893 *1883.7 p42*
Bette, . . .; New England, n.d. *9228.50 p96*
Bettee, . . .; New England, n.d. *9228.50 p96*
Bettenburger, Elisabeth Moos 19 *SEE* Bettenburger, Franz
Bettenburger, Franz 18; America, 1858 *5475.1 p310*
    *Wife:*Elisabeth Moos 19
Bettencourt, Emanuel; North Carolina, 1852 *1088.45 p2*
Bettencourt, William C.; North Carolina, 1817 *1088.45 p2*
Bettes, . . .; New England, n.d. *9228.50 p96*
Bettien, Catharine Sophie Dorothee; America, 1860 *7420.1 p191*
Bettin, Gustav; Wisconsin, 1886 *6795.8 p69*
Bettinger, Andreas 12 *SEE* Bettinger, Andreas
Bettinger, Andreas 43; America, 1847 *5475.1 p531*
    *Wife:*Katharina Scherer 35
    *Daughter:*Elisabeth 14
    *Son:*Andreas 12
Bettinger, Anna Maria Stahl 36 *SEE* Bettinger, Jakob
Bettinger, Elisabeth 1 *SEE* Bettinger, Jakob
Bettinger, Elisabeth 14 *SEE* Bettinger, Andreas
Bettinger, J. Georg 4 *SEE* Bettinger, Jakob
Bettinger, Jakob 10 *SEE* Bettinger, Karoline Leweck
Bettinger, Jakob 36; America, 1847 *5475.1 p531*
    *Wife:*Anna Maria Stahl 36
    *Son:*J. Georg 4
    *Daughter:*Elisabeth 1
    *Daughter:*Katharina 7
Bettinger, Karoline 20 *SEE* Bettinger, Karoline Leweck
Bettinger, Karoline 42; America, 1852 *5475.1 p495*
    *Daughter:*Karoline 20
    *Son:*Theobald 14
    *Son:*Jakob 10
    *Son:*Konrad 7
    *Son:*Nikolaus 11
    *Daughter:*Katharina 16
Bettinger, Katharina 7 *SEE* Bettinger, Jakob
Bettinger, Katharina 16 *SEE* Bettinger, Karoline Leweck
Bettinger, Katharina Scherer 35 *SEE* Bettinger, Andreas
Bettinger, Konrad 7 *SEE* Bettinger, Karoline Leweck
Bettinger, Nikolaus 11 *SEE* Bettinger, Karoline Leweck
Bettinger, Peter; America, 1852 *5475.1 p495*
Bettinger, Theobald 14 *SEE* Bettinger, Karoline Leweck
Bettis, . . .; New England, n.d. *9228.50 p96*
Bettke, Louis Wilhelm August Moritz; America, 1871 *7420.1 p396*
Bettner, William; Ohio, 1809-1852 *4511.35 p4*
Betts, Thomas 49; Ontario, 1871 *1823.21 p25*
Betz, Anna Katharina; Venezuela, 1843 *3899.5 p543*

Betz, Catherine 24; Missouri, 1848 *778.6 p32*
Betz, Daniel; Louisiana, 1836-1841 *4981.45 p208*
Betz, Elisabetha 52 *SEE* Betz, Otto
Betz, Heinrich 22; Texas, 1913 *8425.16 p31*
Betz, Katharina; Venezuela, 1843 *3899.5 p544*
Betz, Ludwig; Valdivia, Chile, 1851 *1192.4 p50*
Betz, Marie 32; Chile, 1852 *1192.4 p54*
Betz, Otto 42; America, 1864 *2526.43 p145*
    *Wife:*Elisabetha 52
Betzner, John; Ohio, 1809-1852 *4511.35 p4*
Beuerlein, E.; Valdivia, Chile, 1850 *1192.4 p49*
Beuerlein, Elisabeth 12 *SEE* Beuerlein, Friedrich
Beuerlein, Friedrich 21 *SEE* Beuerlein, Friedrich
Beuerlein, Friedrich 48; America, 1872 *5475.1 p446*
    *Wife:*Katharina Schafer 48
    *Daughter:*Elisabeth 12
    *Son:*Michael 7
    *Son:*Friedrich 21
    *Son:*Urban 17
Beuerlein, Katharina Schafer 48 *SEE* Beuerlein, Friedrich
Beuerlein, Michael 7 *SEE* Beuerlein, Friedrich
Beuerlein, Urban 17 *SEE* Beuerlein, Friedrich
Beugnot, Peter F.; Ohio, 1809-1852 *4511.35 p4*
Beuriger, Margaretha; America, 1886 *5475.1 p243*
    *Son:*Karl
    *Son:*Peter
Beutel, Anna Elisabeth Preiss *SEE* Beutel, Johann Blasius
Beutel, Anna Katharina *SEE* Beutel, Johann Blasius
Beutel, Anna Margarethe *SEE* Beutel, Johann Blasius
Beutel, Johann Blasius; Virginia, 1831 *152.20 p62*
    *Wife:*Anna Elisabeth Preiss
    *Child:*Anna Margarethe
    *Child:*Susanne
    *Child:*Anna Katharina
Beutel, Susanne *SEE* Beutel, Johann Blasius
Beuthe, Johann Wilhelm Leonhard; America, 1867 *7919.3 p533*
Beuthler, Julius; Wisconsin, 1877 *6795.8 p200*
Beuzelin, Catherine; Quebec, 1671 *4514.3 p278*
Bevan, James; Utah, 1894 *3687.1 p35*
Bevan, John; Colorado, 1894 *1029.59 p9*
Bevans, Robert 40; Ontario, 1871 *1823.17 p11*
Bevens, Peter 64; Ontario, 1871 *1823.21 p25*
Bever, Jo. 24; Virginia, 1635 *1183.3 p31*
Beverage, Jacob 70; Ontario, 1871 *1823.21 p25*
Beveridge, Mrs.; Montreal, 1922 *4514.4 p32*
Beveridge, Bridget 65; Ontario, 1871 *1823.21 p25*
Beveridge, G.; Montreal, 1922 *4514.4 p32*
Beveridge, Miss M.; Montreal, 1922 *4514.4 p32*
Beveridge, Thomas 45; Ontario, 1871 *1823.21 p25*
Beveridge, William; Washington, 1879 *2770.40 p134*
Beverly, George 72; Ontario, 1871 *1823.21 p25*
Beverreau, Mr. 52; New Orleans, 1848 *778.6 p32*
Bevintasson, Robert; Louisiana, 1836-1840 *4981.45 p212*
Bevrungen, Charles; Illinois, 1851 *6079.1 p2*
Bewley, P.; Quebec, 1885 *1937.10 p52*
Beyer, Adam Ernst; America, 1868 *7919.3 p528*
    With wife
Beyer, Anna Christiane Henriette; America, 1868 *7919.3 p530*
Beyer, August 50; Ontario, 1871 *1823.17 p11*
Beyer, Bruno Alvin; Kansas, 1917-1918 *2054.10 p48*
Beyer, Carl 27; New York, NY, 1893 *1883.7 p40*
Beyer, Carl 27; New York, NY, 1893 *1883.7 p47*
Beyer, Charles 28; Ontario, 1871 *1823.17 p11*
Beyer, Clara; Kansas, 1917 *2054.10 p48*
Beyer, Johanna 23; New York, NY, 1893 *1883.7 p40*
Beyer, Johanna 23; New York, NY, 1893 *1883.7 p47*
Beyer, John; Philadelphia, 1777 *8529.30 p2A*
Beyer, Lizzie; Wisconsin, 1906 *6795.8 p221*
Beyer, Maria Barbara; America, 1868 *7919.3 p526*
Beyer, William Fred; Wisconsin, 1889 *6795.8 p29*
Beyersdorf, Sophia; America, 1867 *7919.3 p535*
    With 2 children
Beyhan, Andrew 60; Ontario, 1871 *1823.21 p25*
Beyl, Paul J.; Wisconsin, 1900 *6795.8 p101*
Beyrau, Laurau; Illinois, 1859 *6079.1 p2*
Beys, John; Canada, 1774 *3036.5 p41*
Bez, Anna Katharina; Venezuela, 1843 *3899.5 p543*
Bez, Katharina; Venezuela, 1843 *3899.5 p544*
Biamont, Auguste *SEE* Biamont, Joachim
Biamont, Joachim; Illinois, 1880 *1495.20 p28*
    *Brother:*Auguste
Biansky, John; Texas, 1871-1892 *6015.15 p23*
Biards, Gilles; Montreal, 1653 *9221.17 p283*
Biarnes, Adolphe 36; America, 1848 *778.6 p32*
Biarues, Jean Adam 35; Port uncertain, 1840 *778.6 p32*
Bibault, Francois 24; Quebec, 1656 *9221.17 p332*
Bibb, William; New York, 1783 *8529.30 p9*
Bibbeau, Jaques; Virginia, 1700 *9230.15 p81*
Bibber, James; New Hampshire, 1724-1725 *9228.50 p100*
Bice, Joseph; America, 1859 *9076.20 p68*

Bich, Wendel; America, 1847 *5475.1 p485*
Bichard, Mr.; North America, n.d. *9228.50 p103*
Bichard, Anne; Ohio, 1789-1849 *9228.50 p103*
Bichard, Anne; Ohio, 1807 *9228.50 p567*
Bichard, Daniel *SEE* Bichard, James
Bichard, James; Norfolk, VA, 1806 *9228.50 p56*
  With wife & children
Bichard, James *SEE* Bichard, James
Bichard, James; Ohio, 1807 *9228.50 p101*
  Wife: Rachel Sarchet
  Child: Rachel
  Child: Martha
  Child: Nicholas
  Child: Daniel
  Child: James
Bichard, James; Ohio, 1807 *9228.50 p103*
  Wife: Rachel De La Rue
Bichard, James; Ohio, 1807 *9228.50 p516*
Bichard, James, Family; Ohio, 1807 *9228.50 p57*
Bichard, John 14; Wisconsin, 1830-1860 *9228.50 p103*
Bichard, Martha *SEE* Bichard, James
Bichard, Nicholas; Ohio, 1807 *9228.50 p57*
Bichard, Nicholas *SEE* Bichard, James
Bichard, Nicholas; Ohio, 1825 *9228.50 p147*
Bichard, Peter; Ohio, 1807 *9228.50 p57*
Bichard, Rachel *SEE* Bichard, James
Bichard, Rachel Sarchet *SEE* Bichard, James
Bichard, Rachel De La Rue *SEE* Bichard, James
Bichart, Achille 25; America, 1847 *778.6 p33*
Bicher, Willy 26; Milwaukee, 1926 *8023.44 p372*
Bichler, Andrew; Ohio, 1809-1852 *4511.35 p4*
Bick, Elisabeth 20 *SEE* Bick, Wendel
Bick, Georg 21 *SEE* Bick, Georg
Bick, Georg 49; America, 1880 *5475.1 p456*
  Wife: Katharina Mohr 49
  Son: Josef 17
  Daughter: Magdalena 14
  Son: Stephan 8
  Son: Georg 21
Bick, Jakob; America, 1863 *5475.1 p508*
Bick, Jakob 22; America, 1864 *5475.1 p550*
Bick, Jakob 19 *SEE* Bick, Wendel
Bick, Josef 17 *SEE* Bick, Georg
Bick, Katharina Mohr 49 *SEE* Bick, Georg
Bick, Katharina 9 *SEE* Bick, Wendel
Bick, Magdalena 14 *SEE* Bick, Georg
Bick, Margarethe 13 *SEE* Bick, Wendel
Bick, Margarethe 56 *SEE* Bick, Wendel
Bick, Mathias 27 *SEE* Bick, Wendel
Bick, Nikolaus 24 *SEE* Bick, Wendel
Bick, Stephan 8 *SEE* Bick, Georg
Bick, Wendel; America, 1855 *5475.1 p487*
Bick, Wendel 55; New York, 1855 *5475.1 p487*
  Wife: Margarethe 56
  Son: Jakob 19
  Daughter: Katharina 9
  Daughter: Margarethe 13
  Daughter: Elisabeth 20
  Son: Mathias 27
  Son: Nikolaus 24
Bickel, Christopher; Baltimore, 1841 *471.10 p62*
Bickele, William; New Orleans, 1851 *7242.30 p134*
Bickelhaupt, Adam 5 *SEE* Bickelhaupt, Hieronymus
Bickelhaupt, Anna Elisabetha; America, 1788 *2526.43 p137*
Bickelhaupt, Georg 13 *SEE* Bickelhaupt, Hieronymus
Bickelhaupt, Hieronymus; New York, 1853 *2526.43 p125*
  Wife: Margaretha Hartmann
  Son: Leonhard
  Son: Georg
  Son: Adam
Bickelhaupt, Leonhard 15 *SEE* Bickelhaupt, Hieronymus
Bickelhaupt, Margaretha Hartmann *SEE* Bickelhaupt, Hieronymus
Bickelhaupt, Peter; New York, 1853 *2526.43 p125*
Bickelhaupt, Mrs. Peter; America, 1842 *2526.43 p125*
  With daughter 19
Bickelmann, Franz Carl Conrad; America, 1874 *7420.1 p302*
Bickelmann, Georg Conrad; America, 1871 *7420.1 p289*
Bickelmann, Otto Conrad; America, 1872 *7420.1 p293*
Bickle, John 29; Ontario, 1871 *1823.21 p25*
Bickler, Christine *SEE* Bickler, Johann Jakob
Bickler, Joh. Philipp *SEE* Bickler, Johann Jakob
Bickler, Johann Jakob 54; America, 1865 *5475.1 p518*
  Wife: Maria Katharina Klein 57
  Son: Joh. Philipp
  Daughter: Christine
Bickler, Maria Katharina; America, 1865 *5475.1 p517*
  Son: Philipp
  With parents

Bickler, Maria Katharina Klein 57 *SEE* Bickler, Johann Jakob
Bickler, Philipp *SEE* Bickler, Maria Katharina
Bickley, Francis 35; Ontario, 1871 *1823.21 p25*
Bicknase, Wilhelmine Justine; America, 1854 *7420.1 p116*
Bicknell, Benjamin 56; Ontario, 1871 *1823.21 p25*
Bicknell, Lucy 14; Ontario, 1871 *1823.21 p25*
Bicknell, Timothy 18; Ontario, 1871 *1823.21 p25*
Bicknell, Walt; Colorado, 1891 *1029.59 p10*
Bicknell, Walter H.; Colorado, 1899 *1029.59 p10*
Bicksay, Elizabeth 14; Quebec, 1870 *8364.32 p22*
Bicksay, Jane 16; Quebec, 1870 *8364.32 p22*
Bidault, Antoine 40; Port uncertain, 1840 *778.6 p33*
Bidault, J. F. 44; America, 1845 *778.6 p33*
Biddle, John 31; New York, 1821 *9228.50 p103*
  Wife: Mary 27
  Daughter: Mary Ann 5
Biddle, Mary 27 *SEE* Biddle, John
Biddle, Mary Ann 5 *SEE* Biddle, John
Biddle, Philip; California, 1868 *1131.61 p89*
Biddulph, Thomas; Ohio, 1844 *2763.1 p7*
Biddulph, Walter 59; Ontario, 1871 *1823.21 p25*
Bidegood, Robert 65; Ontario, 1871 *1823.21 p25*
Bidekofer, John; Ohio, 1809-1852 *4511.35 p4*
Biden, Etienne 15; Mississippi, 1846 *778.6 p33*
Biden, Francois 48; Mississippi, 1846 *778.6 p33*
Biden, Hiasinth 20; Mississippi, 1846 *778.6 p33*
Biden, Madalaine 48; Mississippi, 1846 *778.6 p33*
Bidet, Jean; Quebec, 1642 *9221.17 p112*
Bidnall, John 36; Ontario, 1871 *1823.21 p25*
Bidon, Louis 24; Quebec, 1655 *9221.17 p325*
Bidulph, Richard 60; Ontario, 1871 *1823.21 p25*
Biebe, Kilian; America, 1867 *7919.3 p535*
Bieberbach, Mathilde; America, 1867 *7919.3 p529*
Bieberbach, Wilhelm; America, 1867 *7919.3 p529*
Biechele, Carl 22; Port uncertain, 1848 *778.6 p33*
Biechele, Charles; Ohio, 1809-1852 *4511.35 p4*
Biede, Charles; Ohio, 1809-1852 *4511.35 p4*
Biedebach, Franz Anton; America, 1860 *7420.1 p191*
Biedermann, Famille; New Castle, DE, 1817-1818 *90.20 p150*
Biedermann, Justine 72; New York, NY, 1878 *9253.2 p45*
Bieganek, Valentine; Wisconsin, 1891 *6795.8 p54*
Biegel, Andreas; America, 1836 *5475.1 p527*
  With wife
Biegel, Peter; America, 1853 *5475.1 p481*
Bieger, Charles; Colorado, 1873 *1029.59 p10*
Biegler, Barbara 28; New York, NY, 1898 *7951.13 p43*
Biegler, Bartholomaus 6 months; New York, NY, 1898 *7951.13 p43*
Biegler, Elisabeth 7; New York, NY, 1898 *7951.13 p43*
Biegler, Johann 33; New York, NY, 1898 *7951.13 p43*
Biegler, Katherine 31; New York, NY, 1898 *7951.13 p43*
Biegler, Magdalena 9; New York, NY, 1898 *7951.13 p43*
Biegler, Margaret 4; New York, NY, 1898 *7951.13 p43*
Biegler, Michael 33; New York, NY, 1898 *7951.13 p43*
Biegler, Susanna; America, 1872 *5475.1 p153*
  Son: Johann
  Daughter: Ottilie
Biegler, Theresia 9; New York, NY, 1898 *7951.13 p43*
Biehl, Andreas 9 *SEE* Biehl, Andreas
Biehl, Andreas 34; America, 1833 *5475.1 p393*
  Wife: Sophia Gross 29
  Daughter: Maria 5
  Son: Wilhelm 1
  Son: Valentin 7
  Son: Andreas 9
Biehl, Anna *SEE* Biehl, Peter
Biehl, Anna Thiel *SEE* Biehl, Peter
Biehl, Anna; America, 1881 *5475.1 p287*
Biehl, Barbara *SEE* Biehl, Peter
Biehl, Jakob; America, 1883 *5475.1 p377*
  Brother: Joh. Jakob
Biehl, Joh. Jakob *SEE* Biehl, Jakob
Biehl, Magdalena; America, 1869 *5475.1 p307*
Biehl, Maria 5 *SEE* Biehl, Andreas
Biehl, Michael; Philadelphia, 1851 *5720.10 p377*
Biehl, Nikolaus 25; America, 1880 *5475.1 p339*
Biehl, Peter; America, 1879 *5475.1 p187*
  Daughter: Anna
  Daughter: Barbara
  Mother: Anna Thiel
Biehl, Sophia Gross 29 *SEE* Biehl, Andreas
Biehl, Valentin 7 *SEE* Biehl, Andreas
Biehl, Wilhelm 1 *SEE* Biehl, Andreas
Biehler, Maria Anna; Venezuela, 1843 *3899.5 p542*
Biehlmann, Eva Magdalena; Venezuela, 1843 *3899.5 p543*
Biel, Georg 20; New York, NY, 1893 *1883.7 p44*
Biel, Johann; America, 1847 *5475.1 p537*
Biel, Margarethe 47; Cincinnati, 1863 *5475.1 p281*

Bielas, Wladyslaw; Detroit, 1929 *1640.55 p115*
Bielaszka, Jan 25; New York, NY, 1911 *6533.11 p10*
Bielecki, Agnes; Detroit, 1929 *1640.55 p116*
Bielenberg, P. D.; Valdivia, Chile, 1852 *1192.4 p52*
Bieler, Maria Anna; Venezuela, 1843 *3899.5 p542*
Bielhuber, Otto; Valparaiso, Chile, 1850 *1192.4 p50*
Bielicki, Stanislaw; Detroit, 1929-1930 *6214.5 p63*
Bieling, Carl Friedrich Josef; America, 1868 *7420.1 p268*
Bielinski, Veronica; Wisconsin, 1893 *6795.8 p54*
Bielitz, Johann Friedrich Wilhelm; Port uncertain, 1839 *7420.1 p15*
Bielmaier, John; Wisconsin, 1896 *6795.8 p234*
Bielmann, Anna Maria; Venezuela, 1843 *3899.5 p541*
Bielstein, Frederick; Illinois, 1859 *6079.1 p2*
Biemkowski, Adalbertus; Wisconsin, 1894 *6795.8 p54*
Bienek, Michael; Baltimore, 1881 *6015.15 p9*
Bienski, John; Texas, 1871-1892 *6015.15 p23*
Bienski, Thomas; Texas, 1894 *6015.15 p23*
Bienski, Thomas; Texas, 1895 *6015.15 p23*
Bienvenue, Hermann; Louisiana, 1874 *4981.45 p130*
Bienvenue, Ruest; Louisiana, 1874 *4981.45 p130*
Bier, A. Maria 8 *SEE* Bier, Jakob
Bier, A. Maria Gregorius 40 *SEE* Bier, Jakob
Bier, Carla; America, 1870 *179.55 p19*
Bier, Elisabeth Haupenthal *SEE* Bier, Jakob
Bier, Jakob; Brazil, 1867 *5475.1 p505*
  Wife: Elisabeth Haupenthal
Bier, Jakob 18 *SEE* Bier, Jakob
Bier, Jakob 44; Brazil, 1864 *5475.1 p501*
  Wife: A. Maria Gregorius 40
  Son: Karl 2
  Daughter: Phillippine 4
  Son: Peter 2 months
  Son: Jakob 18
  Son: Nikolaus 10
  Son: Josef 9
  Daughter: A. Maria 8
  Son: Johann 13
  Daughter: Maria 19
Bier, Johann 13 *SEE* Bier, Jakob
Bier, Josef 9 *SEE* Bier, Jakob
Bier, Karl; America, 1846 *5475.1 p537*
Bier, Karl 2 *SEE* Bier, Jakob
Bier, Karoline *SEE* Bier, Nikolaus
Bier, Katharina 38 *SEE* Bier, Nikolaus
Bier, M. Katharina 10 *SEE* Bier, Nikolaus
Bier, Maria 19 *SEE* Bier, Jakob
Bier, Maria 7 *SEE* Bier, Nikolaus
Bier, Nikolaus; America, 1872 *5475.1 p205*
Bier, Nikolaus 10 *SEE* Bier, Jakob
Bier, Nikolaus 3 *SEE* Bier, Nikolaus
Bier, Nikolaus 39; Rio Grande do Sul, Brazil, 1854 *5475.1 p539*
  Wife: Katharina 38
  Son: Nikolaus 3
  Daughter: Karoline
  Daughter: M. Katharina 10
  Daughter: Maria 7
Bier, Peter; America, 1852 *5475.1 p538*
Bier, Peter 2 *SEE* Bier, Jakob
Bier, Phillippine 4 *SEE* Bier, Jakob
Bier, Salome 24; Louisiana, 1848 *778.6 p33*
Bier, Simon 28; Louisiana, 1848 *778.6 p33*
Bierbrauer, Barbara; Brazil, 1880 *5475.1 p373*
Bierdeman, Augustus B.; Ohio, 1809-1852 *4511.35 p4*
Biermacher, Karl; America, 1896 *5475.1 p18*
Bierman, August; Missouri, 1891 *3276.1 p3*
Bierman, Otto; Missouri, 1882 *3276.1 p3*
Biermann, August; America, 1861 *7420.1 p203*
Biermann, Joseph; Galveston, TX, 1855 *571.7 p16*
Biermann, Louise; Port uncertain, 1882 *7420.1 p102*
Biermann, Peter; America, 1867 *5475.1 p238*
Biermann, Wilhelm Gerhard; America, 1861 *7420.1 p203*
Bierwart, Guillaume; Baltimore, 1873 *1494.20 p12*
Bierwirth, Hanna Sophie; New York, NY, 1858 *7420.1 p176*
  With husband
Biery, Joseph; Ohio, 1809-1852 *4511.35 p4*
Bies, Anna *SEE* Bies, Johann
Bies, Anna Massone *SEE* Bies, Jakob
Bies, Elisabeth *SEE* Bies, Johann
Bies, Jakob *SEE* Bies, Jakob
Bies, Jakob; America, 1872 *5475.1 p205*
  Wife: Anna Massone
  Son: Jakob
  Son: Johann
Bies, Johann *SEE* Bies, Jakob
Bies, Johann; America, 1872 *5475.1 p205*
  Wife: Maria Anna Knauf
  Son: Johannes
  Daughter: Anna

*Daughter:*Elisabeth
With 2 children
Bies, Johannes *SEE* Bies, Johann
Bies, Katharina 25; America, 1860 ***5475.1*** *p266*
Bies, Maria Anna Knauf *SEE* Bies, Johann
Bies, Peter; England, 1864 ***5475.1*** *p266*
Biesantz, August; Port uncertain, 1903 ***7420.1*** *p378*
Biesantz, Louise; London, Eng., 1850 ***7420.1*** *p69*
Biesdorf, Anna *SEE* Biesdorf, Christine Reith
Biesdorf, Christine; Philadelphia, 1883 ***5475.1*** *p36*
*Child:*Rosa
*Child:*Anna
*Child:*Theodor
Biesdorf, Rosa *SEE* Biesdorf, Christine Reith
Biesdorf, Theodor *SEE* Biesdorf, Christine Reith
Biesel, Carl Wilhelm Alexander; America, 1845 ***7420.1*** *p34*
Biesel, Caroline; America, 1852 ***7420.1*** *p85*
Biesel, Dorothea; Philadelphia, 1904 ***7420.1*** *p401*
Biesel, Friederike; Philadelphia, 1904 ***7420.1*** *p401*
Biesen, Josef; America, 1847 ***5475.1*** *p439*
Bieslada, Carolina; Detroit, 1929 ***1640.55*** *p116*
Biessmann, Margarethe; America, 1868 ***7919.3*** *p524*
Biesterfeld, Caroline Sophie; America, 1867 ***7420.1*** *p253*
Biesterfeld, Conrad; America, 1856 ***7420.1*** *p145*
Biesterfeld, Engel Marie *SEE* Biesterfeld, Johann Christoph
Biesterfeld, Engel Marie Hecht *SEE* Biesterfeld, Johann Christoph
Biesterfeld, Engel Marie; America, 1865 ***7420.1*** *p229*
Biesterfeld, Engel Marie Sophie; America, 1847 ***7420.1*** *p51*
Biesterfeld, Engel Sophie; America, 1863 ***7420.1*** *p217*
Biesterfeld, Hans Heinrich; America, 1867 ***7420.1*** *p254*
Biesterfeld, Hans Heinrich Christoph; America, 1845 ***7420.1*** *p34*
Biesterfeld, Heinrich; America, 1858 ***7420.1*** *p176*
With wife & 2 sons
Biesterfeld, Heinrich Conrad; America, 1857 ***7420.1*** *p157*
Biesterfeld, Johann Christoph; America, 1850 ***7420.1*** *p69*
*Wife:*Engel Marie Hecht
*Daughter:*Marie Sophie Dorothee
*Daughter:*Engel Marie
Biesterfeld, Johann Friedrich; America, 1865 ***7420.1*** *p229*
Biesterfeld, Johann Friedrich; America, 1866 ***7420.1*** *p239*
Biesterfeld, Johann Friedrich Wilhelm; America, 1866 ***7420.1*** *p239*
Biesterfeld, Johann Heinrich; America, 1866 ***7420.1*** *p239*
Biesterfeld, Johann Heinrich Conrad; New York, NY, 1856 ***7420.1*** *p145*
Biesterfeld, Johann Heinrich Friedrich Gottlieb; America, 1860 ***7420.1*** *p191*
Biesterfeld, Johann W.; America, 1866 ***7420.1*** *p239*
Biesterfeld, Marie Sophie Dorothee *SEE* Biesterfeld, Johann Christoph
Biethel, James 35; Ontario, 1871 ***1823.21*** *p25*
Biewer, Johann; America, 1873 ***5475.1*** *p324*
*Wife:*Margarethe Fox
*Son:*Johann
*Son:*Nikolaus
*Son:*Mathias
*Daughter:*Maria
Biewer, Johann 14 *SEE* Biewer, Johann
Biewer, Josef; America, 1871 ***5475.1*** *p304*
Biewer, Josef *SEE* Biewer, Peter
Biewer, Margarethe Fox *SEE* Biewer, Johann
Biewer, Maria 16 *SEE* Biewer, Johann
Biewer, Mathias 8 *SEE* Biewer, Johann
Biewer, Nikolaus; America, 1882 ***5475.1*** *p277*
Biewer, Nikolaus 10 *SEE* Biewer, Johann
Biewer, Peter; America, 1867 ***5475.1*** *p311*
Biewer, Peter; America, 1871 ***5475.1*** *p311*
*Son:*Josef
Biewer, Peter; America, 1881 ***5475.1*** *p241*
Biey, Bartholemy; Illinois, 1852 ***6079.1*** *p2*
Bigelow, Isaac N.; Washington, 1885 ***2770.40*** *p193*
Bigelow, Margaret 60; Michigan, 1880 ***4491.42*** *p4*
Biggar, Annabel; Washington, 1885 ***2770.40*** *p193*
Biggio, G.; Louisiana, 1874 ***4981.45*** *p295*
Biggs, Elizabeth 10; Virginia, 1635 ***1183.3*** *p31*
Biggs, James 50; Ontario, 1871 ***1823.21*** *p25*
Biggs, Joseph; New York, 1776 ***8529.30*** *p9*
Biggs, Phillipp 6 months; Virginia, 1635 ***1183.3*** *p31*
Bigler, Ambrocius 8; New York, NY, 1893 ***1883.7*** *p41*
Bigler, Anna 6; New York, NY, 1893 ***1883.7*** *p41*
Bigler, Anton 31; New York, NY, 1893 ***1883.7*** *p41*
Bigler, Balthasar 36; New York, NY, 1893 ***1883.7*** *p41*
Bigler, Catharina 11; New York, NY, 1893 ***1883.7*** *p41*
Bigler, Jacob 9; New York, NY, 1893 ***1883.7*** *p41*
Bigler, Josef 2; New York, NY, 1893 ***1883.7*** *p41*
Bigler, Julia 2; New York, NY, 1893 ***1883.7*** *p41*
Bigler, Katharina 4; New York, NY, 1893 ***1883.7*** *p41*
Bigler, Louisa 29; New York, NY, 1893 ***1883.7*** *p41*
Bigler, Magdalena 4 months; New York, NY, 1893 ***1883.7*** *p41*
Bigler, Magdalena 11 months; New York, NY, 1893 ***1883.7*** *p41*
Bigler, Maria 3; New York, NY, 1893 ***1883.7*** *p41*
Bigler, Regina 8; New York, NY, 1893 ***1883.7*** *p41*
Bigler, Regina 35; New York, NY, 1893 ***1883.7*** *p41*
Bignall, Thomas 57; Ontario, 1871 ***1823.21*** *p26*
Bignell, Jane 47; North Carolina, 1774 ***1422.10*** *p56*
Bigot, Francois 39; Quebec, 1660 ***9221.17*** *p431*
Bigot, Francoise 16 *SEE* Bigot, Thomine Chastel
Bigot, Guillaume 25; Quebec, 1638 ***9221.17*** *p75*
Bigot, Jacques; Quebec, 1659 ***9221.17*** *p395*
Bigot, Jean 13 *SEE* Bigot, Thomine Chastel
Bigot, Jeanne *SEE* Bigot, Thomine Chastel
Bigot, Marguerite; Quebec, 1648 ***9221.17*** *p195*
Bigot, Perrine 20; Quebec, 1637 ***9221.17*** *p70*
Bigot, Pierre; Montreal, 1643 ***9221.17*** *p136*
Bigot, Thomine; Quebec, 1647 ***9221.17*** *p176*
*Daughter:*Francoise
*Daughter:*Jeanne
*Son:*Jean
Bigras, Francois; Quebec, 1671 ***4514.3*** *p353*
Biguinot, Francois 27; America, 1847 ***778.6*** *p33*
Bihan, . . .; Newfoundland, n.d. ***9228.50*** *p98*
Bihl, Joseph 31; Galveston, TX, 1846 ***3967.10*** *p377*
Bihl, Katharina 28; Galveston, TX, 1846 ***3967.10*** *p377*
Bihl, Marie 20; Galveston, TX, 1846 ***3967.10*** *p377*
Bihl, Michael 50; Galveston, TX, 1846 ***3967.10*** *p377*
Bihl, Rosa 10 months; Galveston, TX, 1846 ***3967.10*** *p377*
Bihler, Katharina; Venezuela, 1843 ***3899.5*** *p544*
Bik, Anna 34; New York, NY, 1911 ***6533.11*** *p10*
Biksen, S.S.; Iowa, 1880 ***1211.15*** *p9*
Bilair, Eli 19; Ohio, 1880 ***4879.40*** *p257*
Bilais, J. B. 42; America, 1843 ***778.6*** *p33*
Bilar, F.; Galveston, TX, 1855 ***571.7*** *p17*
Bilbrough, Thomas 24; Ontario, 1871 ***1823.17*** *p11*
Bilder, Christian 5 months; New York, NY, 1886 ***8425.16*** *p33*
Bilder, Johs 33; New York, NY, 1886 ***8425.16*** *p33*
Bilder, Katha 28; New York, NY, 1886 ***8425.16*** *p33*
Bilder, Maria 4; New York, NY, 1886 ***8425.16*** *p33*
Bilder, Martin 3; New York, NY, 1886 ***8425.16*** *p33*
Bildhauer, Felix; America, 1891 ***5475.1*** *p204*
Bildstern, Jacques 31; New Orleans, 1848 ***778.6*** *p33*
Bileck, Nicholas; Detroit, 1929 ***1640.55*** *p117*
Biler, George; Ohio, 1809-1852 ***4511.35*** *p4*
Biler, Katharina; Venezuela, 1843 ***3899.5*** *p544*
Bilger, Micah 28; New Orleans, 1840 ***778.6*** *p33*
Bilges, Johann Heinrich Conrad; America, 1867 ***7420.1*** *p254*
With family
Bilicka, Valeria; Detroit, 1890 ***9980.23*** *p96*
Bilik, Antonin; Wisconsin, 1903 ***2853.20*** *p342*
Bilk, Jonathan; Philadelphia, 1778 ***8529.30*** *p2A*
Bill, Barbara 1 *SEE* Bill, Heinrich
Bill, Georg 23 *SEE* Bill, Heinrich
Bill, Georg Christian; America, 1846 ***5475.1*** *p530*
Bill, Gertrud 30; America, 1843 ***5475.1*** *p529*
Bill, Heinrich; America, 1836 ***5475.1*** *p527*
With wife
*Daughter:*Katharina
*Daughter:*Maria
*Daughter:*Barbara
*Son:*Konrad
*Son:*Georg
Bill, Katharina 17 *SEE* Bill, Heinrich
Bill, Konrad 5 *SEE* Bill, Heinrich
Bill, Konrad 27; America, 1884 ***5475.1*** *p534*
Bill, Maria 14 *SEE* Bill, Heinrich
Billaud, A. 28; Port uncertain, 1845 ***778.6*** *p33*
Billaud, Marie; Quebec, 1649 ***9221.17*** *p215*
Billaud, Marie; Quebec, 1649 ***9221.17*** *p215*
Biller, Catharina 31; New Orleans, 1847 ***778.6*** *p33*
Biller, John; Ohio, 1809-1852 ***4511.35*** *p4*
Biller, Julie 22; New Orleans, 1847 ***778.6*** *p33*
Billet, Francois 34; America, 1843 ***778.6*** *p33*
Billet, Francois 35; Quebec, 1661 ***9221.17*** *p448*
Billet, Lily 37; Louisiana, 1848 ***778.6*** *p33*
Billet, Wm 22; Ontario, 1871 ***1823.21*** *p26*
Billiar, Baptiste 30; America, 1842 ***778.6*** *p33*
Billiau, Mr. 10; New Orleans, 1840 ***778.6*** *p33*
Billing, Ellick; Wisconsin, 1903 ***6795.8*** *p149*
Billinger, George Jacob; Ohio, 1809-1852 ***4511.35*** *p4*
Billinghurst, Alfred 33; Ontario, 1871 ***1823.17*** *p11*
Billings, John 38; Ontario, 1871 ***1823.21*** *p26*
Billington, Elen *SEE* Billington, John
Billington, Francis *SEE* Billington, John
Billington, George 54; Ontario, 1871 ***1823.21*** *p26*
Billington, John *SEE* Billington, John
Billington, John; Plymouth, MA, 1620 ***1920.45*** *p5*
*Wife:*Elen
*Son:*John
*Son:*Francis
Billins, George 26; Ontario, 1871 ***1823.21*** *p26*
Billius, Christian; America, 1853 ***7420.1*** *p102*
Billmann, Friedr.; Chile, 1852 ***1192.4*** *p51*
Billmann, Philipp 17; Port uncertain, 1847 ***778.6*** *p33*
Billo, Anna Maria; America, 1894 ***5475.1*** *p551*
*Son:*Johann
*Son:*Friedrich
Billo, John 19; New Orleans, 1842 ***778.6*** *p33*
Billon, James; Marston's Wharf, 1782 ***8529.30*** *p9*
Billot, Catharine; Virginia, 1700 ***9230.15*** *p81*
Billot, Catherine; Quebec, 1670 ***4514.3*** *p278*
Billot, Francois; Virginia, 1700 ***9230.15*** *p81*
Billot, Genevieve; Quebec, 1670 ***4514.3*** *p278*
Billot, Lucrece; Quebec, 1667 ***4514.3*** *p279*
Billot, Marie Ann; Salt Lake City, 1855 ***9228.50*** *p552*
*Child:*Jane Nancy
*Child:*Sophia Jane
*Child:*Charles Abraham
*Child:*Fanny Mary Ann
Bilodeau, Jacques 20; Quebec, 1654 ***9221.17*** *p305*
Bilodeau, Jeanne; Quebec, 1665 ***4514.3*** *p279*
Bilodeau, Jerome 19; Quebec, 1657 ***9221.17*** *p352*
Bilton, Edward S. 30; Ontario, 1871 ***1823.21*** *p26*
Bilton, James; Marston's Wharf, 1782 ***8529.30*** *p9*
Bilton, Oliver 61; Ontario, 1871 ***1823.17*** *p11*
Bily, Tomas; South Dakota, 1886 ***2853.20*** *p247*
Bilz, Cerf 31; Texas, 1848 ***778.6*** *p33*
Bilz, Johannes; Port uncertain, 1887 ***170.15*** *p20*
Bilz, Moise 25; Texas, 1848 ***778.6*** *p33*
Bilzinger, Anna Maria 10 *SEE* Bilzinger, Mathias
Bilzinger, Katharina 1 *SEE* Bilzinger, Mathias
Bilzinger, Maria 7 *SEE* Bilzinger, Mathias
Bilzinger, Maria Braun 31 *SEE* Bilzinger, Mathias
Bilzinger, Mathias 36; America, 1846 ***5475.1*** *p301*
*Wife:*Maria Braun 31
*Daughter:*Katharina 1
*Daughter:*Anna Maria 10
*Daughter:*Maria 7
Bimer, Bernhard; Ohio, 1840-1897 ***8365.35*** *p15*
Binaudiere, Marguerite; Quebec, 1670 ***4514.3*** *p279*
Bindbeutel, Miss; America, 1872 ***7420.1*** *p297*
Bindel, Sabine; Philadelphia, 1865 ***8513.31*** *p309*
Binder, Anna; Kansas, 1917-1918 ***1826.15*** *p81*
Binder, Ellen 21; Ontario, 1871 ***1823.21*** *p26*
Binder, Joakim; Colorado, 1868 ***1029.59*** *p10*
Binder, Joe; Kansas, 1917-1918 ***1826.15*** *p81*
Binder, Sebastian; Kansas, 1917-1918 ***1826.15*** *p81*
Binder, Theresia; Venezuela, 1843 ***3899.5*** *p544*
Bindewald, Johannes 3; New York, NY, 1886 ***8425.16*** *p33*
Bindewald, Johannes 28; New York, NY, 1886 ***8425.16*** *p33*
Bindewald, Katha 4; New York, NY, 1886 ***8425.16*** *p33*
Bindewald, Marg. 25; New York, NY, 1886 ***8425.16*** *p33*
Bindewald, Michael 3 months; New York, NY, 1886 ***8425.16*** *p33*
Bindler, Antony; Philadelphia, 1778 ***8529.30*** *p2*
Bindre, Mr.; Louisiana, 1847 ***778.6*** *p33*
Binet, Frederic 30; Port uncertain, 1843 ***778.6*** *p33*
Binet, Jean; Salem, MA, 1675 ***9228.50*** *p104*
Binet, Marie; Quebec, 1670 ***4514.3*** *p332*
Binet, Marie-Suzanne 18; Quebec, 1661 ***9221.17*** *p448*
Binferd, . . . 29; Baltimore, 1889 ***8425.16*** *p35*
Binferd, Katherina 28; Baltimore, 1889 ***8425.16*** *p35*
Binferd, Stephan 3; Baltimore, 1889 ***8425.16*** *p35*
Binferd, Theresa 2; Baltimore, 1889 ***8425.16*** *p35*
Bing, Friedrich Wilhelm; America, 1867 ***7919.3*** *p531*
With wife & 5 children
Bing, Henriette; America, 1849 ***7420.1*** *p64*
Bing, Maria 37; St. Louis, 1847 ***778.6*** *p33*
Bing, Stephen; Ohio, 1809-1852 ***4511.35*** *p4*
Bingel, Jakob; America, 1887 ***2526.42*** *p118*
Bingel, Johannes; America, 1884 ***170.15*** *p20*
Bingen, Anna; America, 1867 ***5475.1*** *p327*
Bingen, Johann 22; America, 1882 ***5475.1*** *p376*
Bingen, Michel; America, 1883 ***5475.1*** *p377*
Bingham, Hyram C. 40; Ontario, 1871 ***1823.21*** *p26*
Bingham, Tho.; Maryland, 1674 ***1236.25*** *p50*
Bingham, Thomas; Boston, 1769 ***9228.50*** *p48*
Bingham, Thomas; Boston, 1769 ***9228.50*** *p104*
Bingham, Thomas; Maryland, 1680 ***1236.25*** *p53*
Bingley, Ann Breeden *SEE* Bingley, Richard
Bingley, Richard; Germantown, PA, 1856 ***8513.31*** *p294*
*Wife:*Ann Breeden
Bingmer, Anton; America, 1839 ***5475.1*** *p470*
Binkeley, Nicholas; Ohio, 1809-1852 ***4511.35*** *p4*
Binkhi, John 36; Ontario, 1871 ***1823.21*** *p26*
Binoche, L. 41; New Orleans, 1844 ***778.6*** *p33*

Binoche, Louis 40; America, 1843 *778.6 p33*
Binotto, Francesco; Illinois, 1930 *121.35 p101*
Binski, Thomas; Texas, 1894 *6015.15 p23*
Binski, Thomas; Texas, 1895 *6015.15 p23*
Biquetie, J. 3; America, 1846 *778.6 p33*
Bira, Guillaume; Illinois, 1852 *6079.1 p2*
Birard, Marie; Quebec, 1669 *4514.3 p279*
Biras, Guillaume 28; Texas, 1848 *778.6 p34*
Birch, John 52; Michigan, 1880 *4491.30 p3*
Birch, Mary 43; Michigan, 1880 *4491.30 p3*
Birch, Willm.; Maryland, 1674-1675 *1236.25 p52*
Birchall, Elizabeth 45; Ontario, 1871 *1823.21 p26*
Birchard, Nicholas; Ohio, 1825 *9228.50 p147*
Birck, Florentina 2; New York, NY, 1847 *9176.15 p49*
Birck, Florentina 25; New York, NY, 1847 *9176.15 p49*
Birck, Martin 27; New York, NY, 1847 *9176.15 p49*
Bird, Ann E. 57; Ontario, 1871 *1823.21 p26*
Bird, Brenda Christine; New York, NY, 1935 *9228.50 p104*
Bird, Donald SEE Bird, Walter G.
Bird, Frank Cyril; Detroit, 1914 *9228.50 p104*
Bird, Jane 75; Ontario, 1871 *1823.17 p11*
Bird, John 70; Ontario, 1871 *1823.17 p11*
Bird, John, Jr. 47; Ontario, 1871 *1823.17 p11*
Bird, Margaret; Boston, 1656 *1642 p9*
Bird, Michael 42; Ontario, 1871 *1823.21 p26*
Bird, Michaell; Maryland, 1674-1675 *1236.25 p52*
Bird, Nicholas; Ohio, 1856 *9228.50 p104*
Bird, Samuel; Virginia, 1749 *3675.1 p*
Bird, Stanley William; Detroit, 1903-1950 *9228.50 p104*
Bird, Walter; Canada, 1900 *9228.50 p653*
Bird, Walter G.; Los Angeles, 1900-1983 *9228.50 p104*
*Son:*Donald
Bire, Marguerite 40; Quebec, 1657 *9221.17 p368*
*Son:*Etienne 15
Bires, Pierre 21; Quebec, 1657 *9221.17 p352*
Biret, Renee; Quebec, 1671 *4514.3 p279*
Birk, Barbara 41; America, 1855 *5475.1 p309*
*Daughter:*Magdalena 18
*Daughter:*Elisabeth 13
*Son:*Jakob 12
*Son:*Peter
Birk, Elisabeth 13 SEE Birk, Barbara Schmitt
Birk, Jakob 12 SEE Birk, Barbara Schmitt
Birk, Katharina 15 SEE Birk, Katharina Gier
Birk, Katharina 47; America, 1858 *5475.1 p251*
*Son:*Peter 20
*Son:*Philipp 17
*Daughter:*Katharina 15
Birk, Magdalena 18 SEE Birk, Barbara Schmitt
Birk, Peter SEE Birk, Barbara Schmitt
Birk, Peter 20 SEE Birk, Katharina Gier
Birk, Philipp 17 SEE Birk, Katharina Gier
Birkel, Jacob 46; New Orleans, 1848 *778.6 p34*
Birkelbach, Valeska; Chile, 1885 *5475.1 p37*
Birkenbach, Juliana 10 SEE Birkenbach, Peter
Birkenbach, Karl 8 SEE Birkenbach, Peter
Birkenbach, Peter; America, 1860 *5475.1 p548*
*Daughter:*Juliana
*Son:*Karl
Birkholz, Ernestine; Wisconsin, 1887 *6795.8 p71*
Birmann, Modeste 36; New Orleans, 1848 *778.6 p34*
Birmingham, West Thomas 44; Ontario, 1871 *1823.21 p26*
Birminghauss, Fr. William; New York, 1860 *358.56 p3*
Birnbach, Otto; America, 1853 *2526.43 p164*
Birnbach, Mrs. Otto; America, 1855 *2526.43 p164*
With 4 children
Birnstill, Joseph; Ohio, 1809-1852 *4511.35 p4*
Biron, Pierre 23; Quebec, 1648 *9221.17 p195*
Birr, Bertha Auguste Alwine; Wisconsin, 1892 *6795.8 p217*
Birrell, Henry 36; Ontario, 1871 *1823.21 p26*
Birrer, John; New York, 1944 *1766.20 p34*
Birt, Mary 63; Ontario, 1871 *1823.21 p26*
Birtel, Anna; America, 1871 *5475.1 p291*
*Sister:*Elisabeth
*Brother:*Peter
Birtel, Elisabeth SEE Birtel, Anna
Birtel, Elisabeth 23; America, 1856 *5475.1 p290*
*Sister:*Gertrud 19
*Sister:*Susanna 10
*Sister:*Maria 10
Birtel, Gertrud 19 SEE Birtel, Elisabeth
Birtel, Johann; America, 1857 *5475.1 p290*
Birtel, Maria; America, 1872 *5475.1 p292*
Birtel, Maria 10 SEE Birtel, Elisabeth
Birtel, Michel; America, 1867 *5475.1 p291*
Birtel, Nikolaus; America, 1867 *5475.1 p291*
Birtel, Peter SEE Birtel, Anna
Birtel, Peter; America, 1871 *5475.1 p292*
Birtel, Susanna 10 SEE Birtel, Elisabeth
Birten, Thomas 40; Ontario, 1871 *1823.17 p11*

Birth, Mary; New York, 1859 *358.56 p100*
Bisbee, James B. 42; Ontario, 1871 *1823.21 p26*
Bisbee, Reuben 66; Ontario, 1871 *1823.21 p26*
Bisch, Johann; America, 1879 *5475.1 p156*
Bisch, Nikolaus; America, 1881 *5475.1 p156*
Bisch, Peter Josef; America, 1880 *5475.1 p156*
Bischof, Adolf 24; New York, NY, 1893 *1883.7 p42*
Bischof, Christina 26; New York, NY, 1893 *1883.7 p42*
Bischoff, Anton 30; Galveston, TX, 1844 *3967.10 p370*
Bischoff, Catharina; America, 1867 *7919.3 p526*
Bischoff, E. G.; Valdivia, Chile, 1852 *1192.4 p54*
Bischoff, Edmund; America, 1867 *7919.3 p531*
Bischoff 32; America, 1844 *2526.42 p136*
Bischoff, Louis 28; Galveston, TX, 1844 *3967.10 p370*
Bischoff, Oskar Julius; America, 1868 *7919.3 p531*
Bischoff 13; America, 1883 *2526.42 p136*
Bischofshausen, Gustav von; Valdivia, Chile, 1852 *1192.4 p52*
With wife & 3 children
With child 8
With child 18
Bischoppe, Eleazar; New London, CT, 1676 *9228.50 p105*
Bischoppe, Frederick Primrose; Massachusetts, 1883-1983 *9228.50 p106*
Bischoppe, George Dolbeare SEE Bischoppe, John
Bischoppe, James; America, 1740-1800 *9228.50 p108*
Bischoppe, John; Nova Scotia, 1760 *9228.50 p108*
With family
*Nephew:*George Dolbeare
Bischoppe, John, Jr.; Nova Scotia, 1729-1815 *9228.50 p105*
Bischoppe, Mary; Nova Scotia, 1741-1800 *9228.50 p108*
Bischoppe, Peter; Nova Scotia, 1735-1826 *9228.50 p106*
Bischoppe, Timothy; Nova Scotia, 1740-1827 *9228.50 p107*
Bischoppe, William; Nova Scotia, 1732-1761 *9228.50 p105*
Bisdon, James 45; Ontario, 1871 *1823.21 p26*
Biseuil, Josephine; Canada, 1871-1971 *9228.50 p287*
Bisher, John 14; Wisconsin, 1830-1860 *9228.50 p103*
Bisher, Nicholas; Ohio, 1825 *9228.50 p147*
Bishoop, James; North Carolina, 1837 *1088.45 p2*
Bishop, Agnes 31; New York, NY, 1885 *1883.7 p46*
Bishop, Agnes 54; Ontario, 1871 *1823.21 p26*
Bishop, Anna 2; New York, NY, 1885 *1883.7 p46*
Bishop, Daniel SEE Bishop, John
Bishop, Ebenezer SEE Bishop, John
Bishop, Edward Greentree 2 SEE Bishop, Thomas
Bishop, Eleazar; New London, CT, 1676 *9228.50 p105*
Bishop, Elizabeth 36 SEE Bishop, Thomas
Bishop, Fr. 10; New York, NY, 1885 *1883.7 p46*
Bishop, Frederick Primrose; Massachusetts, 1883-1983 *9228.50 p106*
Bishop, George 57; Ontario, 1871 *1823.21 p26*
Bishop, George Dolbeare SEE Bishop, John
Bishop, Henry 64; Ontario, 1871 *1823.17 p11*
Bishop, Henry 65; Ontario, 1871 *1823.17 p11*
Bishop, Jacob H.; Colorado, 1868 *1029.59 p10*
Bishop, James; America, 1740-1800 *9228.50 p108*
Bishop, John; Connecticut, n.d. *9228.50 p104*
*Brother:*Ebenezer
*Brother:*Nathaniel
*Brother:*Daniel
Bishop, John; Nova Scotia, 1760 *9228.50 p108*
With family
*Nephew:*George Dolbeare
Bishop, John 20; Ontario, 1871 *1823.17 p11*
Bishop, John 50; Ontario, 1871 *1823.17 p11*
Bishop, John, Jr.; Nova Scotia, 1729-1815 *9228.50 p105*
Bishop, Mar. 4; New York, NY, 1885 *1883.7 p46*
Bishop, Mariah 40; Michigan, 1880 *4491.30 p3*
Bishop, Mary; Nova Scotia, 1741-1800 *9228.50 p108*
Bishop, Nathaniel SEE Bishop, John
Bishop, Peter; Nova Scotia, 1735-1826 *9228.50 p106*
Bishop, Samuel 28; Ontario, 1871 *1823.17 p11*
Bishop, Thomas; New York, NY, 1821 *9228.50 p108*
*Wife:*Elizabeth
*Son:*Edward Greentree
Bishop, Thomas 57; Ontario, 1871 *1823.17 p11*
Bishop, Timothy; Nova Scotia, 1740-1827 *9228.50 p107*
Bishop, Victor 23; New York, 1842 *778.6 p34*
Bishop, Webone; Virginia, 1652 *6254.4 p243*
Bishop, William; Nova Scotia, 1732-1761 *9228.50 p105*
Bishop, William 28; Ontario, 1871 *1823.21 p26*
Bishop, William 37; Ontario, 1871 *1823.17 p11*
Bishop, William 50; Ontario, 1871 *1823.17 p11*
Bishop, William 53; Ontario, 1871 *1823.21 p26*
Bishop, William W.; Burlington, VT, 1836 *3274.55 p75*
Bishopric, George 15; Ontario, 1871 *1823.21 p26*
Bishuti, Antonio; Louisiana, 1874 *4981.45 p130*
Bisker, Henry; Ohio, 1809-1852 *4511.35 p4*
Bissel, Wm 63; Ontario, 1871 *1823.21 p26*

Bissell, Charles 32; Ontario, 1871 *1823.17 p11*
Bissell, Hermione 46; Ontario, 1871 *1823.21 p26*
Bissell, James 40; Ontario, 1871 *1823.17 p11*
Bissell, Susanna 30; Ontario, 1871 *1823.17 p11*
Bissett, Donald 55; Ontario, 1871 *1823.21 p26*
Bissett, George; North Carolina, 1860 *1088.45 p2*
Bissett, Horatio N.; Ohio, 1842 *2763.1 p7*
Bissett, Maria 22; New York, 1895 *5475.1 p485*
*Child:*Willy 2
*Child:*Nik. Franz 4 months
Bissett, Nik. Franz 4 SEE Bissett, Maria
Bissett, Willy 2 SEE Bissett, Maria
Bissien, Miss 45; New Orleans, 1848 *778.6 p34*
Bissiere, Joseph 43; New Orleans, 1848 *778.6 p34*
Bisson, . . .; America, n.d. *9228.50 p109*
Bisson, . . .; Maryland, 1600-1699 *9228.50 p113*
Bisson, . . .; New London, CT, 1676 *9228.50 p105*
Bisson, Mr.; New London, CT, 1669 *9228.50 p112*
Bisson, Mrs.; America, 1896-1952 *9228.50 p182*
With 2 sons & daughter
Bisson, Austin; Miami, 1920 *4984.15 p38*
Bisson, Daniel; Quebec, 1822-1842 *9228.50 p113*
Bisson, Edward; Michigan, 1862-1962 *9228.50 p115*
Bisson, Elizabeth Jenry SEE Bisson, Nicolas
Bisson, James Almond; Michigan, 1863-1911 *9228.50 p115*
Bisson, Jane; Ohio, 1806-1843 *9228.50 p113*
Bisson, John; Marblehead, MA, 1793 *9228.50 p112*
Bisson, Joseph SEE Bisson, Nicholas
Bisson, Joshua; America, 1652-1675 *9228.50 p112*
Bisson, Luena Shirley; New York, 1926-1949 *9228.50 p115*
Bisson, Nicholas 11; Massachusetts, 1766 *9228.50 p112*
*Uncle:*Joseph
Bisson, Nicolas; Massachusetts, 1716-1750 *9228.50 p113*
*Wife:*Elizabeth Jenry
Bisson, Philip; Marblehead, MA, 1749 *9228.50 p109*
With brothers
Bisson, Philippe John; Quebec, 1866 *9228.50 p116*
Bisson, Richard; Marblehead, MA, 1753 *9228.50 p112*
Bisson Des Landes, Elizabeth Jenry SEE Bisson Des Landes, Nicolas
Bisson Des Landes, Nicolas; Massachusetts, 1716-1750 *9228.50 p113*
*Wife:*Elizabeth Jenry
Bissoon, . . .; Maryland, 1600-1699 *9228.50 p113*
Bissot, Francois 27; Quebec, 1639 *9221.17 p85*
Bissot deVincennes, Jean-Baptiste; Quebec, 1696 *2314.30 p172*
Bisterfeld, Christian; Kansas, 1896 *1447.20 p65*
Bisterfeld, Heinrich Conrad; America, 1860 *7420.1 p201*
Biston, Ms.; Wisconsin, 1872 *1495.20 p12*
Biszewski, Stanley; Detroit, 1929 *1640.55 p116*
Biteau, Louis 23; Montreal, 1653 *9221.17 p283*
Bitman, William; Ohio, 1809-1852 *4511.35 p4*
Bitner, Eliz.; Minnesota, 1813-1900 *9228.50 p336*
Biton, Jean B.; Illinois, 1852 *6079.1 p2*
Bitouset, Jeanne 18; Quebec, 1652 *9221.17 p254*
Bittalava, Vincent; Louisiana, 1874-1875 *4981.45 p297*
Bittelmann, Gottfried; Wisconsin, 1858 *6795.8 p41*
Bitter, Wilhelm; America, 1868 *7420.1 p276*
Bitterlich, J. G.; Valdivia, Chile, 1852 *1192.4 p54*
With wife baby & child
With child 3
Bittermann, Caroline 21; New York, NY, 1885 *1883.7 p46*
Bittermann, Lisbeth; New York, NY, 1885 *1883.7 p46*
Bittermann, Peter 25; New York, NY, 1885 *1883.7 p46*
Bitterstadt, Carl 58; New York, NY, 1890 *1883.7 p47*
Bitterstadt, Carole 6; New York, NY, 1890 *1883.7 p47*
Bitterstadt, Johann G. 7; New York, NY, 1890 *1883.7 p47*
Bitterstadt, Johanne 56; New York, NY, 1890 *1883.7 p47*
Bittmann, Christian; New York, 1860 *358.56 p4*
Bittner, Bartos; New York, NY, 1885 *2853.20 p400*
Bittner, Carl; Valdivia, Chile, 1852 *1192.4 p55*
With wife & 4 children
With child 2
With child 20
Bittner, Peter; Port uncertain, 1866 *170.15 p20*
Bittorf, Catharine Elisabeth; America, 1868 *7919.3 p532*
Bittorf, M.; Venezuela, 1843 *3899.5 p546*
Bitzer, John; New York, 1859 *358.56 p55*
Bitzer, Margarethe; America, 1872 *5475.1 p212*
Biwer, Anna; Philadelphia, 1880 *1088.45 p2*
Biwer, Jakob; America, 1869 *5475.1 p169*
Biwer, Margarethe 36; America, 1836 *5475.1 p259*
Biwer, Peter 33; America, 1836 *5475.1 p259*
Biz, Giacoma; Louisiana, 1874 *4981.45 p131*
Bizard, Jacques; Quebec, 1672 *2314.30 p166*
Bizard, Jacques; Quebec, 1672 *2314.30 p175*
Bizette, Jeanne 37; Montreal, 1658 *9221.17 p390*

Bjalek, Frantisek; Texas, 1860 ***2853.20*** *p74*
Bjcblin, John; Washington, 1889 ***2770.40*** *p79*
Bjocklin, John; Washington, 1889 ***2770.40*** *p27*
Bjoerkander, Nicholas 28; Kansas, 1879-1880 ***777.40*** *p15*
Bjorck, Arvid Herman; New York, NY, 1856 ***6412.40*** *p154*
Bjork, Agnes; St. Paul, MN, 1901 ***1865.50*** *p41*
Bjork, Chas.; Cleveland, OH, 1899 ***9722.10*** *p117*
Bjork, Gustaf; Illinois, 1861 ***4487.25*** *p54*
Bjorkander, Andreas Nickolas 28; Kansas, 1879-1880 ***777.40*** *p15*
Bjorkander, O.; New York, NY, 1851 ***6412.40*** *p152*
Bjorkander, Salomon Carl Johan; North America, 1856 ***6410.15*** *p105*
Bjorkgren, A.; New York, NY, 1851 ***6412.40*** *p152*
Bjorkgren, C.G.; New York, NY, 1843 ***6412.40*** *p147*
Bjorklund, Alexander A.; St. Paul, MN, 1889-1890 ***1865.50*** *p41*
*Wife:*Anna
Bjorklund, Anna *SEE* Bjorklund, Alexander A.
Bjorklund, Arvid; Cleveland, OH, 1906 ***9722.10*** *p117*
Bjorklund, John; St. Paul, MN, 1882-1885 ***1865.50*** *p41*
Bjorklund, Jonas; New York, NY, 1844 ***6412.40*** *p147*
Bjorklund, Martha; St. Paul, MN, 1883-1885 ***1865.50*** *p41*
Bjorkman, Sophia; St. Paul, MN, 1902 ***1865.50*** *p41*
Bjorling, Gustaf L.; Cleveland, OH, 1902-1904 ***9722.10*** *p117*
Bjorling, Lisa Samuelsson 25 *SEE* Bjorling, Matts
Bjorling, Matts 25; New York, 1856 ***6529.11*** *p20*
*Sister:*Lisa Samuelsson 25
Bjornberg, Erland; Cleveland, OH, 1900-1906 ***9722.10*** *p117*
Bjornsen, Friedrich August; Valdivia, Chile, 1850 ***1192.4*** *p50*
Bjornstad, Bjorn O.; Iowa, 1884 ***1211.15*** *p9*
Bjurquist, Sofia; St. Paul, MN, 1894 ***1865.50*** *p41*
Bjurqvist, Emma; St. Paul, MN, 1886 ***1865.50*** *p52*
Bjurqvist, Maria Ch.; Minnesota, 1880-1881 ***1865.50*** *p102*
Bjurqvist, Sofia; St. Paul, MN, 1894 ***1865.50*** *p41*
Blaach, Julius; North Carolina, 1850 ***1088.45*** *p2*
Blaasch, Rudolph; Illinois, 1834-1900 ***6020.5*** *p131*
Blabe, Johanna; Maryland, 1672 ***1236.25*** *p47*
Blach, Daniel 24; Missouri, 1845 ***778.6*** *p34*
Blachier, Mr. 49; Louisiana, 1848 ***778.6*** *p34*
Blachier, Camille 8; Louisiana, 1848 ***778.6*** *p34*
Blachier, Louise 2; Louisiana, 1848 ***778.6*** *p34*
Blachier, Louise 35; Louisiana, 1848 ***778.6*** *p34*
Blachuta, Franciszek 40; New York, NY, 1920 ***930.50*** *p48*
Blacich, John; Louisiana, 1874-1875 ***4981.45*** *p297*
Black, Alexander 45; Ontario, 1871 ***1823.21*** *p27*
Black, Alexander 54; Ontario, 1871 ***1823.21*** *p27*
Black, Alexander 60; Ontario, 1871 ***1823.21*** *p27*
Black, Angus 24; Ontario, 1871 ***1823.21*** *p27*
Black, Ann 4; North Carolina, 1775 ***1422.10*** *p60*
Black, Arch Ray; Cape Fear, NC,, 1754 ***1422.10*** *p62*
Black, Archibald 38; Ontario, 1871 ***1823.21*** *p27*
Black, Archibald 40; Ontario, 1871 ***1823.21*** *p27*
Black, Archibald 44; Ontario, 1871 ***1823.21*** *p27*
Black, Archibald; Washington, 1884 ***2770.40*** *p192*
Black, Christian 8; North Carolina, 1775 ***1422.10*** *p60*
Black, Donald 45; North Carolina, 1775 ***1422.10*** *p60*
Black, Donald 51; Ontario, 1871 ***1823.21*** *p27*
Black, Donald 67; Ontario, 1871 ***1823.17*** *p11*
Black, Dond; Cape Fear, NC,, 1754 ***1422.10*** *p61*
Black, Duncan; Cape Fear, NC,, 1754 ***1422.10*** *p62*
Black, Duncan 1; North Carolina, 1775 ***1422.10*** *p60*
Black, Duncan 29; Ontario, 1871 ***1823.21*** *p27*
Black, Duncan 48; Ontario, 1871 ***1823.21*** *p27*
Black, Eliza 26; New York, NY, 1884 ***8427.14*** *p45*
Black, Elizabeth *SEE* Black, William
Black, Ewen 4; North Carolina, 1775 ***1422.10*** *p60*
Black, George 35; Ontario, 1871 ***1823.21*** *p27*
Black, George 36; Ontario, 1871 ***1823.21*** *p27*
Black, Henry 32; Ontario, 1871 ***1823.17*** *p11*
Black, James; Illinois, 1851 ***6079.1*** *p2*
Black, James 28; Ontario, 1871 ***1823.21*** *p27*
Black, James 45; Ontario, 1871 ***1823.21*** *p27*
Black, James 50; Ontario, 1871 ***1823.21*** *p27*
Black, Jane 30; Santa Clara Co., CA, 1860 ***8704.1*** *p22*
Black, Jannet 34; North Carolina, 1775 ***1422.10*** *p60*
Black, John *SEE* Black, William
Black, John; Iowa, 1893 ***1211.15*** *p9*
Black, John 14; North Carolina, 1775 ***1422.10*** *p60*
Black, John 40; Ontario, 1871 ***1823.17*** *p11*
Black, John 49; Ontario, 1871 ***1823.21*** *p27*
Black, Joseph; Colorado, 1862-1894 ***1029.59*** *p10*
Black, Joseph; North Carolina, 1806 ***1088.45*** *p2*
Black, Malcum; North Carolina, 1844 ***1088.45*** *p2*
Black, Mary 16; North Carolina, 1775 ***1422.10*** *p60*
Black, Mary 35; Ontario, 1871 ***1823.21*** *p27*
Black, Richard *SEE* Black, William
Black, Samuel; Boston, 1752 ***1642*** *p30*
Black, Sarah *SEE* Black, William
Black, Sarah 30; Ontario, 1871 ***1823.21*** *p27*
Black, Thomas *SEE* Black, William
Black, Thomas 54; Ontario, 1871 ***1823.21*** *p27*
Black, Walter 36; New York, NY, 1884 ***8427.14*** *p45*
Black, William *SEE* Black, William
Black, William; Canada, 1775 ***3036.5*** *p67*
*Wife:*Elizabeth
*Child:*William
*Child:*Richard
*Child:*John
*Child:*Thomas
*Child:*Sarah
Black, William 32; Ontario, 1871 ***1823.21*** *p27*
Black, William 34; Ontario, 1871 ***1823.21*** *p27*
Black, William 63; Ontario, 1871 ***1823.21*** *p27*
Black, Wm J. 50; Ontario, 1871 ***1823.21*** *p27*
Blackall, John; Ontario, 1871 ***1823.21*** *p27*
Blackbird, Joseph 50; Ontario, 1871 ***1823.17*** *p11*
Blackburn, Benjamin 28; North Carolina, 1774 ***1422.10*** *p54*
Blackburn, Eliza 55; Ontario, 1871 ***1823.17*** *p11*
Blackburn, Jacob; Canada, 1774 ***3036.5*** *p42*
Blackburn, Jacob O.; Ohio, 1867 ***3580.20*** *p31*
Blackburn, Jacob O.; Ohio, 1867 ***6020.12*** *p6*
Blackburn, Josiah 48; Ontario, 1871 ***1823.21*** *p27*
Blackburn, Stephen 44; Ontario, 1871 ***1823.21*** *p27*
Blackburn, Thomas; Ohio, 1809-1852 ***4511.35*** *p4*
Blackburn, Thomas 30; Ontario, 1871 ***1823.17*** *p11*
Blackburn, Thomas 46; Ontario, 1871 ***1823.21*** *p27*
Blackburn, William 30; Ontario, 1871 ***1823.21*** *p27*
Blacke, Moses; Boston, 1784 ***1642*** *p26*
Blacker, Edward; New Jersey, 1810 ***3845.2*** *p128*
Blackett, Tobiah 25; North Carolina, 1774 ***1422.10*** *p55*
Blackhall, Alexander 45; Ontario, 1871 ***1823.17*** *p11*
Blackhall, Joshua 44; Ontario, 1871 ***1823.21*** *p27*
Blackler, . . .; Montreal, 1830-1899 ***9228.50*** *p116*
Blackler, . . .; Ontario, 1830-1899 ***9228.50*** *p116*
Blackley, Andrew 44; Indiana, 1852-1860 ***9076.20*** *p66*
Blackley, John 23; Ontario, 1871 ***1823.21*** *p27*
Blacklock, John; Marston's Wharf, 1782 ***8529.30*** *p9*
Blacklock, John 41; Ontario, 1871 ***1823.17*** *p11*
Blackman, Lewis 28; Ontario, 1871 ***1823.17*** *p12*
Blackman, Tracey 16; Michigan, 1880 ***4491.30*** *p3*
Blackmore, Elisa 54; Ontario, 1871 ***1823.21*** *p27*
Blackmore, Philip; Boston, 1715 ***9228.50*** *p116*
Blackmore, Richard 32; Ontario, 1871 ***1823.21*** *p27*
Blackmore, Robert 28; Ontario, 1871 ***1823.21*** *p27*
Blackstock, George 40; Ontario, 1871 ***1823.21*** *p27*
Blackstock, James 56; Ontario, 1871 ***1823.21*** *p27*
Blackstock, Moses 50; Ontario, 1871 ***1823.17*** *p12*
Blackstock, Moses 50; Ontario, 1871 ***1823.21*** *p27*
Blackstock, Sarah J. 19; Ontario, 1871 ***1823.17*** *p12*
Blackwell, Benjamin 59; Ontario, 1871 ***1823.21*** *p27*
Blackwell, Crick; Ohio, 1844 ***2763.1*** *p7*
Blackwell, Jane 50; Ontario, 1871 ***1823.21*** *p28*
Blackwell, John 23; Ontario, 1871 ***1823.21*** *p28*
Blackwell, John 47; Ontario, 1871 ***1823.21*** *p28*
Blackwell, Ritchard 40; Ontario, 1871 ***1823.21*** *p28*
Blackwell, Robert 36; Ontario, 1871 ***1823.21*** *p28*
Blackwell, Smith; Ohio, 1840 ***2763.1*** *p7*
Blackwell, Thomas 38; Ontario, 1871 ***1823.21*** *p28*
Blackwell, William 27; Ontario, 1871 ***1823.21*** *p28*
Blackwill, Benjamin 35; Ontario, 1871 ***1823.21*** *p28*
Blackwill, George 60; Ontario, 1871 ***1823.21*** *p28*
Blackwill, George 87; Ontario, 1871 ***1823.21*** *p28*
Blackwill, Robert 50; Ontario, 1871 ***1823.21*** *p28*
Blackwill, Samuel 52; Ontario, 1871 ***1823.21*** *p28*
Blackwood, William 50; Ontario, 1871 ***1823.21*** *p28*
Blaczynska, Anna 18; New York, NY, 1912 ***8355.1*** *p15*
Blades, Thomas 45; Ontario, 1871 ***1823.21*** *p28*
Bladow, Richard; Wisconsin, 1880 ***6795.8*** *p225*
Blaes, Andreas; America, 1846 ***5475.1*** *p546*
Blaes, Jakob; America, 1848 ***5475.1*** *p532*
Blaesius, Ernst Leopold; America, 1867 ***5475.1*** *p505*
Blaesius, Leopoldine; America, 1867 ***5475.1*** *p504*
Blagelon, Charles 19; Michigan, 1880 ***4491.42*** *p4*
Blahe, Friedrich Christoph; Port uncertain, 1855 ***7420.1*** *p134*
Blahnik, Vavrinec; Chicago, 1866 ***2853.20*** *p391*
Blahs, Peter; America, 1881 ***5475.1*** *p148*
Blaikie, Francis; Ontario, 1871 ***1823.17*** *p12*
Blaileu, Francis 48; Ontario, 1871 ***1823.17*** *p12*
Blain, James 55; Ontario, 1871 ***1823.21*** *p28*
Blain, Marie-Anne; Quebec, 1665 ***4514.3*** *p279*
Blain, Thomas 57; Ontario, 1871 ***1823.17*** *p12*
Blainvillain, Anne; Quebec, 1671 ***4514.3*** *p279*
Blair, Andrew 61; Ontario, 1871 ***1823.21*** *p28*
Blair, James 40; Ontario, 1871 ***1823.17*** *p12*
Blair, James 45; Ontario, 1871 ***1823.21*** *p28*
Blair, James 56; Ontario, 1871 ***1823.21*** *p28*
Blair, James 75; Ontario, 1871 ***1823.21*** *p28*
Blair, John 48; Ontario, 1871 ***1823.21*** *p28*
Blair, John 55; Ontario, 1871 ***1823.21*** *p28*
Blair, Jos. 35; South Carolina, 1812 ***3476.30*** *p11*
Blair, Lewis; St. John, N.B., 1848 ***2978.15*** *p38*
Blair, Maria 19; Ontario, 1871 ***1823.21*** *p28*
Blair, Ogle B. 45; Ontario, 1871 ***1823.21*** *p28*
Blair, Ople 21; Ontario, 1871 ***1823.21*** *p28*
Blair, Robert 30; Ontario, 1871 ***1823.21*** *p28*
Blair, Saml. 45; South Carolina, 1812 ***3476.30*** *p11*
Blair, William 34; Ontario, 1871 ***1823.21*** *p28*
Blais, Elisabeth; Quebec, 1669 ***4514.3*** *p279*
Blais, Louis T. J.; Colorado, 1880 ***1029.59*** *p10*
Blaise, A.; Louisiana, 1874-1875 ***4981.45*** *p297*
Blaise, Anne Josephine 40; New Orleans, 1848 ***778.6*** *p34*
Blaise, Belgrese 57; New Orleans, 1848 ***778.6*** *p34*
Blaise, Gaspar 43; New Orleans, 1848 ***778.6*** *p34*
Blaise, Gaspard; Illinois, 1852 ***6079.1*** *p2*
Blaise, Marguerite; Quebec, 1669 ***4514.3*** *p280*
Blaise desBergeres, Raymond; Quebec, 1683-1688 ***2314.30*** *p168*
Blaise desBergeres, Raymond; Quebec, 1685 ***2314.30*** *p175*
Blaize, Mr. 19; America, 1841 ***778.6*** *p34*
Blaize, Mr. 32; America, 1841 ***778.6*** *p34*
Blake, Bridget 51; Ontario, 1871 ***1823.17*** *p12*
Blake, Charles; Colorado, 1873 ***1029.59*** *p10*
Blake, Frances 65; Ontario, 1871 ***1823.17*** *p12*
Blake, James 60; Ontario, 1871 ***1823.21*** *p28*
Blake, James 60; Ontario, 1871 ***1823.21*** *p28*
Blake, James; Toronto, 1844 ***2910.35*** *p115*
Blake, Johanna; Maryland, 1672 ***1236.25*** *p47*
Blake, John 68; Ontario, 1871 ***1823.21*** *p28*
Blake, Richard 37; Ontario, 1871 ***1823.17*** *p12*
Blake, Robert 31; Michigan, 1880 ***4491.42*** *p4*
Blake, Thomas 21; Ontario, 1871 ***1823.21*** *p28*
Blake, Tompins; Illinois, 1866 ***6079.1*** *p2*
Blake, William 31; Ontario, 1871 ***1823.21*** *p28*
Blake, William 43; Ontario, 1871 ***1823.21*** *p28*
Blake, William 52; Ontario, 1871 ***1823.17*** *p12*
Blake, William 62; Ontario, 1871 ***1823.21*** *p28*
Blakeley, Joseph 46; Ontario, 1871 ***1823.17*** *p12*
Blakely, John 36; Ontario, 1871 ***1823.21*** *p28*
Blakely, Robert; Ohio, 1809-1852 ***4511.35*** *p4*
Blakely, William; New Jersey, 1776 ***8529.30*** *p6*
Blaker, John; New York, 1775 ***8529.30*** *p9*
Blakie, Catherine 2; Ontario, 1871 ***1823.21*** *p28*
Blakie, James 42; Ontario, 1871 ***1823.21*** *p28*
Blakie, James 66; Ontario, 1871 ***1823.21*** *p28*
Blakie, William 37; Ontario, 1871 ***1823.21*** *p28*
Blakley, William; Ontario, 1871 ***1823.17*** *p12*
Blakre, Antone; Iowa, 1896 ***1211.15*** *p9*
Blakswik, James 21; North Carolina, 1774 ***1422.10*** *p54*
Blakwell, John 65; Ontario, 1871 ***1823.21*** *p28*
Blam, F. 26; America, 1846 ***778.6*** *p34*
Blampey, Walter F.; New York, 1921-1974 ***9228.50*** *p120*
Blampied, . . .; Nova Scotia, 1800-1899 ***9228.50*** *p120*
Blampied, Abraham 65; Ontario, 1871 ***1823.17*** *p12*
Blampied, Annie *SEE* Blampied, Judith
Blampied, Charles 35; Boston, 1870-1970 ***9228.50*** *p120*
*Wife:*Mary Ann
*Son:*Joshua
Blampied, Elisha; Ohio, 1813-1820 ***9228.50*** *p116*
Blampied, Elisha; Ohio, 1813 ***9228.50*** *p43*
Blampied, Eliza Jane *SEE* Blampied, Judith
Blampied, Elizabeth; Ohio, 1805-1836 ***9228.50*** *p119*
Blampied, John; Boston, 1816 ***9228.50*** *p119*
Blampied, John; Salem, MA, 1678 ***9228.50*** *p653*
Blampied, Joshua *SEE* Blampied, Charles
Blampied, Judith; America, 1830-1900 ***9228.50*** *p119*
*Sister:*Virginia
*Sister:*Eliza Jane
*Sister:*Annie
Blampied, Judith; Ohio, 1823 ***9228.50*** *p434*
Blampied, Margaret; Ohio, 1834 ***9228.50*** *p119*
Blampied, Mary A. 60; Ontario, 1871 ***1823.17*** *p12*
Blampied, Mary Ann *SEE* Blampied, Charles
Blampied, Nicholas; Ohio, 1800-1899 ***9228.50*** *p119*
Blampied, Virginia *SEE* Blampied, Judith
Blampied, Walter F.; New York, 1921-1974 ***9228.50*** *p120*
Blan, John 17; New York, NY, 1835 ***5024.1*** *p137*
Blanc, Mr. 40; Louisiana, 1848 ***778.6*** *p34*
Blanc, Elisabeth 30; America, 1843 ***778.6*** *p34*
Blanc, Francois 31; Mississippi, 1845 ***778.6*** *p34*
Blanc, Henri 18; New Orleans, 1840 ***778.6*** *p34*
Blanc, Henry 9; Louisiana, 1848 ***778.6*** *p34*
Blanc, Jean 34; America, 1840 ***778.6*** *p34*
Blanc, Joseph 30; America, 1843 ***778.6*** *p34*
Blanc, Julie 26; New Orleans, 1847 ***778.6*** *p34*
Blancat, Martin 19; New Orleans, 1845 ***778.6*** *p34*
Blanchard, Mr. 8; New Orleans, 1843 ***778.6*** *p34*

Blanchard, Mr. 29; New Orleans, 1840 *778.6 p34*
Blanchard, Mrs. 37; America, 1844 *778.6 p35*
Blanchard, Mrs. 42; America, 1844 *778.6 p35*
Blanchard, Mrs. 43; America, 1844 *778.6 p34*
Blanchard, Ms. 40; New Orleans, 1843 *778.6 p34*
Blanchard, Abraham; Ohio, 1809-1852 *4511.35 p4*
Blanchard, Francois 17; Montreal, 1653 *9221.17 p283*
Blanchard, Hypolite; North Carolina, 1834 *1088.45 p2*
Blanchard, Jean 33; America, 1842 *778.6 p34*
Blanchard, John L.; North Carolina, 1853 *1088.45 p3*
Blanchard, Joseph I.; North Carolina, 1853 *1088.45 p3*
Blanchard, Julia 26; America, 1848 *778.6 p34*
Blanchard, Louis; Quebec, 1755-1757 *2314.30 p170*
Blanchard, Louis; Quebec, 1755-1757 *2314.30 p176*
Blanchard, Louis 15; Quebec, 1656 *9221.17 p332*
Blanchard, Marie; Quebec, 1667 *4514.3 p280*
Blanchard, Philias 32; Ohio, 1880 *4879.40 p259*
Blanchard, Victor 31; Port uncertain, 1841 *778.6 p35*
Blanchard, William; Washington, 1888 *2770.40 p25*
Blanchard, William A. 18; Ontario, 1871 *1823.21 p29*
Blanche, C.; Louisiana, 1874-1875 *4981.45 p298*
Blanche, Cornelia B.; Costa Rica, 1910-1972 *9228.50
p662*
Blanche, Francois; Quebec, 1640 *9221.17 p94*
Blanche, James *SEE* Blanche, John
Blanche, John; America, 1859 *9228.50 p662*
  *Uncle:*James
Blanche, Marguerite; America, 1848-1911 *9228.50 p659*
Blanche, Marguerite; America, 1848-1911 *9228.50 p661*
Blanche, Robert; Quebec, 1648 *9221.17 p195*
Blanchet, Franz August; Port uncertain, 1894 *7420.1
p370*
Blanchet, Jean 30; America, 1840 *778.6 p35*
Blanchet, Rene 23; Quebec, 1662 *9221.17 p480*
Blanchett, Henry; Ohio, 1840 *2763.1 p7*
Blanchett, John; Ohio, 1840 *2763.1 p7*
Blanchon, Nicolas; Quebec, 1643 *9221.17 p129*
Blancpied, Walter F.; New York, 1921-1974 *9228.50
p120*
Bland, Ann 40; Ontario, 1871 *1823.21 p29*
Bland, Mrs. J.; Montreal, 1922 *4514.4 p2*
Blande, Adam 18; Halifax, N.S., 1902 *1860.4 p43*
Blande, Adam 24; Halifax, N.S., 1902 *1860.4 p43*
Blande, Christine 17; Halifax, N.S., 1902 *1860.4 p43*
Blande, Clemens 19; Halifax, N.S., 1902 *1860.4 p43*
Blande, Franz 24; Halifax, N.S., 1902 *1860.4 p43*
Blaney, John; St. John, N.B., 1847 *2978.15 p36*
Blaney, Patrick; Philadelphia, 1859 *8513.31 p295*
Blang, Adam; Ohio, 1809-1852 *4511.35 p4*
Blank, Dorothea 10 *SEE* Blank, Josef
Blank, Dorothea 36 *SEE* Blank, Josef
Blank, Henry 30; Boston, 1835 *6424.55 p30*
Blank, Jakob; America, 1882 *179.55 p19*
Blank, Johann 9 *SEE* Blank, Josef
Blank, Jos.; Louisiana, 1874-1875 *4981.45 p297*
Blank, Josef 35; America, 1853 *5475.1 p53*
  *Wife:*Dorothea 36
  *Daughter:*Dorothea 10
  *Son:*Valentin 8
  *Son:*Johann 9 months
  *Son:*Peter 5
Blank, Peter 5 *SEE* Blank, Josef
Blank, Ursula; America, 1848-1892 *179.55 p19*
Blank, Valentin 8 *SEE* Blank, Josef
Blank, William; Ohio, 1809-1852 *4511.35 p4*
Blanke, Miss; America, 1852 *7420.1 p85*
Blanke, Mr.; America, 1852 *7420.1 p85*
Blankemeyer, Hermann D.; Colorado, 1879 *1029.59 p10*
Blankenburg, Alexander D. 24; Portland, ME, 1911
970.38 p76
Blanket, Jane 90; Ontario, 1871 *1823.21 p29*
Blanknagel, Ferd; Nebraska, 1905 *3004.30 p46*
Blanot, Elisabeth; Quebec, 1647 *9221.17 p177*
Blanot, Michel; Quebec, 1645 *9221.17 p151*
Blanpied, Elisha; Ohio, 1813-1820 *9228.50 p116*
Blanquet, Adrien 54; Quebec, 1658 *9221.17 p376*
Blanquet, Marie 29; Quebec, 1660 *9221.17 p437*
Blanquet, Marie 29; Quebec, 1660 *9221.17 p437*
Blanqueteau, Nicolas; Quebec, 1662 *9221.17 p480*
Blanvit, Walter F.; New York, 1921-1974 *9228.50 p120*
Blaquiere, Mary Ann 51; Ontario, 1871 *1823.21 p29*
Blaschke, Jan; Wisconsin, 1886 *2853.20 p331*
Blaschke, Jan Alois; Chicago, 1877 *2853.20 p347*
Blasdell, Thomas; New York, 1776 *8529.30 p9*
Blase, Catherine 46; Port uncertain, 1841 *778.6 p35*
Blaser, Christoph; America, 1883 *5475.1 p462*
Blaser, Christoph 54; America, 1833 *5475.1 p454*
  *Wife:*Maria 40
  With daughter 9 months
  With daughter 8
  With son 10
  With son 6
Blaser, Maria 40 *SEE* Blaser, Christoph

Blaser, Nicolas 18; America, 1846 *778.6 p35*
Blashale, Henry 69; Ontario, 1871 *1823.17 p12*
Blashill, James 28; Ontario, 1871 *1823.21 p29*
Blashill, Tindale 36; Ontario, 1871 *1823.17 p12*
Blashill, William 34; Ontario, 1871 *1823.21 p29*
Blasinson, Gustof; Colorado, 1891 *1029.59 p10*
Blasius, Friedrich; America, 1834 *5475.1 p503*
  With wife
  With 2 children
Blasius, Gertrud 65; America, 1860 *5475.1 p314*
Blasius, Maria; America, 1837 *5475.1 p395*
Blassill, William 58; Ontario, 1871 *1823.21 p29*
Blaston, Wm 25; Ontario, 1871 *1823.21 p29*
Blatchford, James 41; Ontario, 1871 *1823.21 p29*
Blatiner, Johannes 43; New Castle, DE, 1817-1818 *90.20
p150*
Blatow, Michael; Ohio, 1809-1852 *4511.35 p5*
Blatt, . . .; West Virginia, 1850-1860 *1132.30 p149*
Blatt, Elisabeth; America, 1880 *5475.1 p398*
Blatt, Johann 43; America, 1846 *5475.1 p401*
  *Wife:*Katharina Benn 45
  With stepchild 18
  With stepchild 20
Blatt, Katharina Benn 45 *SEE* Blatt, Johann
Blatt, Wilhelm; Pittsburgh, 1896 *5475.1 p426*
Blatz, Lawrence; South Carolina, 1852 *6155.4 p18*
Blatz, Wilhelm; New York, 1882 *2526.43 p125*
Blau, Catharina 11; New York, NY, 1856 *1766.1 p45*
Blau, Gustav; Venezuela, 1843 *3899.5 p546*
Blau, Maria 35; New York, NY, 1856 *1766.1 p45*
Blau, Nikolaus 42; America, 1843 *5475.1 p305*
Blau, Pierre 35; New York, NY, 1856 *1766.1 p45*
Blau, Wilhelm 25; New York, NY, 1894 *6512.1 p182*
Blaue, Carl Heinrich; America, 1893 *7420.1 p367*
Blaue, Wilhelm; America, 1893 *7420.1 p367*
  With family
Blaume, W.; America, 1866 *7420.1 p239*
Blaume, Wilhelm; America, 1854 *7420.1 p115*
  With wife
Blazejewska, Elizabeth; Wisconsin, 1890 *6795.8 p54*
Blazejewski, Elizabeth; Wisconsin, 1890 *6795.8 p54*
Blazejowski, Jozef 17; New York, NY, 1903 *8355.1 p15*
Blazucki, Michael 30; New York, NY, 1920 *930.50 p49*
Blean, Alexander 40; Ontario, 1871 *1823.21 p29*
Blean, Isaac 50; Ontario, 1871 *1823.21 p29*
Blean, James 52; Ontario, 1871 *1823.21 p29*
Blean, John 49; Ontario, 1871 *1823.21 p29*
Blearean, Paul; Louisiana, 1874 *4981.45 p131*
Blecha, Matej; Iowa, 1855-1856 *2853.20 p237*
Bledow, August Ferdinand Franz; Wisconsin, 1869
6795.8 p152
Blee, William; Washington, 1875 *2770.40 p134*
Bleeney, Dan; St. John, N.B., 1847 *2978.15 p37*
Blees, Nikolaus; America, 1862 *5475.1 p353*
Bleha, Karel A.; New Orleans, 1891 *2853.20 p32*
Bleidistel, Engel Charlotte; America, 1846 *7420.1 p47*
Bleimehl, Johann Peter; America, 1847 *5475.1 p538*
Bleimehl, Peter; America, 1852 *5475.1 p556*
Bleiweiss, George; Detroit, 1929 *1640.55 p117*
Blench, John 37; Ontario, 1871 *1823.21 p29*
Blennerhassett, Herman; Ohio, 1797-1805 *9228.50 p121*
  *Wife:*Margaret Agnew
Blennerhassett, Margaret Agnew *SEE* Blennerhassett,
  Herman
Blenz, Ignace 39; America, 1840 *778.6 p35*
Blenz, Maria 17; America, 1840 *778.6 p35*
Blenz, Maria 39; America, 1840 *778.6 p35*
Blery, Francois; Quebec, 1670 *4514.3 p332*
  *Wife:*Marie Binet Langlois
Blery, Marie Binet Langlois *SEE* Blery, Francois
Blesene, G. D.; Illinois, 1861 *6079.1 p2*
Bleses, Christine; America, 1882 *5475.1 p206*
Blesine, A.J.D.B.; Louisiana, 1836-1840 *4981.45 p212*
Bless, Adam; America, 1847 *2526.43 p164*
Blessing, Catherina 5; New York, NY, 1874 *6954.7 p39*
Blessing, Christiane 45; New York, NY, 1874 *6954.7
p39*
Blessing, Johann 17; New York, NY, 1874 *6954.7 p39*
Blessing, Maria 15; New York, NY, 1874 *6954.7 p39*
Blessing, Wilhelm 51; New York, NY, 1874 *6954.7 p39*
Blesson, Ellen; Philadelphia, 1851 *8513.31 p423*
Blethen, John; Salem, MA, 1659-1674 *9228.50 p425*
Blewer, James 36; Ontario, 1871 *1823.21 p29*
Blickas, Marie 21; New Orleans, 1845 *778.6 p35*
Blickle, Josef; America, 1850 *5475.1 p479*
Blidham, George 60; Ontario, 1871 *1823.17 p12*
Blieder, Johann; Galveston, TX, 1855 *571.7 p16*
Blieske, Robert 25; New York, NY, 1893 *1883.7 p38*
Bligh, Joanna 48; Ontario, 1871 *1823.21 p29*
Blight, George 32; Ontario, 1871 *1823.21 p29*
Blight, Harriett 46; Michigan, 1880 *4491.39 p3*
Blight, William 48; Michigan, 1880 *4491.39 p3*
Bligne, Mrs.; America, 1844 *778.6 p35*

Blikre, Nels T.; Iowa, 1901 *1211.15 p9*
Blilelor, Jacob; North Carolina, 1710 *3629.40 p3*
Blin, August 22; New York, NY, 1890 *1883.7 p47*
Blina, Chaney 29; Ontario, 1871 *1823.21 p29*
Blind, Christian; America, 1870 *179.55 p19*
Blind, Christian; America, 1870 *179.55 p19*
  With wife
Blind, Dorothea; America, 1854 *179.55 p19*
Blind, Jakob *SEE* Blind, Peter
Blind, Johann *SEE* Blind, Peter
Blind, Johann; America, 1870 *179.55 p19*
Blind, Katharina *SEE* Blind, Peter
Blind, Margarethe Morgenstern 49 *SEE* Blind, Peter
Blind, Marin; America, 1854 *179.55 p19*
Blind, Peter 48; America, 1856 *5475.1 p496*
  *Wife:*Margarethe Morgenstern 49
  *Daughter:*Katharina
  *Son:*Johann
  *Son:*Jakob
Blind, Philippine; America, 1866 *5475.1 p556*
Blind, Sophie; America, 1700-1899 *179.55 p19*
Blindauer, Adam 47; America, 1855 *5475.1 p359*
  *Wife:*Helena Boos 46
  *Son:*Mathias
  *Daughter:*Helena 8
  *Daughter:*Margarethe 13
  *Daughter:*Eva 20
Blindauer, Eva 20 *SEE* Blindauer, Adam
Blindauer, Helena 8 *SEE* Blindauer, Adam
Blindauer, Helena Boos 46 *SEE* Blindauer, Adam
Blindauer, Johann; New York, 1888 *5475.1 p301*
Blindauer, Margarethe 13 *SEE* Blindauer, Adam
Blindauer, Mathias *SEE* Blindauer, Adam
Blindauer, Mathias; America, 1878 *5475.1 p298*
Blindeau, Rene; Louisiana, 1874 *4981.45 p130*
Blineau, Isaac; Quebec, 1647 *9221.17 p177*
Blinham, Hannah 33; Ontario, 1871 *1823.21 p29*
Blinkey, Charles; Canada, 1774 *3036.5 p41*
  *Wife:*Sarah
  *Child:*Mary
  *Child:*Jane
Blinkey, Jane *SEE* Blinkey, Charles
Blinkey, Mary *SEE* Blinkey, Charles
Blinkey, Sarah *SEE* Blinkey, Charles
Blinkhorn, Walter 26; Ontario, 1871 *1823.21 p29*
Blinn, Christian; Ohio, 1809-1852 *4511.35 p5*
Blinn, Warren 72; Ontario, 1871 *1823.21 p29*
Blinzer, Mrs. 37; America, 1844 *778.6 p35*
Bliske, Friedrich; Wisconsin, 1867 *6795.8 p17*
  *Wife:*Julianna Henriette Borkenhagen
  With 5 sons & 4 daughters
Bliske, Julianna Henriette Borkenhagen *SEE* Bliske,
  Friedrich
Bliss, Charles; Ohio, 1809-1852 *4511.35 p5*
Bliss, E. C. 35; Ontario, 1871 *1823.21 p29*
Bliss, Emma Elizabeth; Wisconsin, 1897 *6795.8 p193*
Blitray, A. 46; New Orleans, 1844 *778.6 p35*
Blitz, Anna Elisabeth Hotz *SEE* Blitz, Paulus
Blitz, Elisabeth; America, 1853 *2526.42 p139*
Blitz, Georg; America, 1854 *2526.42 p113*
Blitz, Heinrich 18; America, 1850 *2526.42 p113*
Blitz, Johann Leonhard; America, 1766 *2526.42 p139*
Blitz, Katharina; America, 1868 *2526.42 p139*
Blitz, Paulus; America, 1753 *2526.42 p139*
  *Wife:*Anna Elisabeth Hotz
Blix, Nels 25; Minnesota, 1923 *2769.54 p1378*
Blizky, . . .; Pennsylvania, 1750-1799 *2853.20 p17*
Bloch, Mr. 18; America, 1847 *778.6 p35*
Bloch, Adolph; New York, NY, 1853 *5475.1 p31*
Bloch, Arthur; America, 1872 *5475.1 p419*
Bloch, David 23; Port uncertain, 1847 *778.6 p35*
Bloch, Emilie; Wisconsin, 1892 *6795.8 p24*
Bloch, Emmanuel 23; Port uncertain, 1847 *778.6 p35*
Bloch, Eva 48; America, 1865 *5475.1 p417*
Bloch, Eva 24; Port uncertain, 1847 *778.6 p35*
Bloch, Fredrick; America, 1898 *6795.8 p200*
Bloch, Isidor; New York, 1879 *5475.1 p420*
Bloch, Johann; Wisconsin, 1895 *6795.8 p176*
Bloch, Josef; New York, 1878 *5475.1 p420*
Bloch, Leon 24; New Orleans, 1848 *778.6 p35*
Bloch, Maria 23; New Orleans, 1848 *778.6 p35*
Bloch, Monz 18; New Orleans, 1848 *778.6 p35*
Bloch, Samuel; New York, 1877 *5475.1 p420*
Blochinger, Auguste 5; America, 1747 *778.6 p35*
Blochinger, Francisca 30; America, 1747 *778.6 p35*
Blochinger, Francisca 7; America, 1747 *778.6 p35*
Blochinger, Francisca 58; America, 1747 *778.6 p35*
Blochinger, Franzisca 60; New Orleans, 1847 *778.6 p35*
Blochinger, Joseph 8; America, 1747 *778.6 p35*
Blochinger, Louis 13; America, 1747 *778.6 p35*
Blochinger, Louis 37; America, 1747 *778.6 p35*
Blochinger, Louisa 9; America, 1747 *778.6 p35*
Blochinger, Lucas 22; America, 1747 *778.6 p35*

Blochinger, Pierre 64; America, 1747 ***778.6*** *p35*
Blochinger, Pierre 64; New Orleans, 1847 ***778.6*** *p35*
Blochinger, Zizilia 19; America, 1747 ***778.6*** *p36*
Blochman, A.; California, 1868 ***1131.61*** *p89*
With wife & child
Blochman, Lisette 21; Port uncertain, 1843 ***778.6*** *p36*
Block, Abraham 20; Mississippi, 1848 ***778.6*** *p36*
Block, Abraham 28; New Orleans, 1846 ***778.6*** *p36*
Block, Adele 11; Port uncertain, 1841 ***778.6*** *p36*
Block, Albert 9 months; New York, NY, 1893 ***1883.7*** *p38*
Block, Baratte 18; Port uncertain, 1841 ***778.6*** *p36*
Block, Caroline 30; New York, NY, 1893 ***1883.7*** *p38*
Block, Emil 11; New York, NY, 1893 ***1883.7*** *p38*
Block, Esther 49; Port uncertain, 1841 ***778.6*** *p36*
Block, Frederich; Louisiana, 1841-1844 ***4981.45*** *p210*
Block, Friedrich 9; New York, NY, 1893 ***1883.7*** *p38*
Block, Godlief; Wisconsin, 1901 ***6795.8*** *p213*
Block, Henriette 23; Port uncertain, 1841 ***778.6*** *p36*
Block, Henry; North Carolina, 1852 ***1088.45*** *p3*
Block, Henry; Washington, 1881 ***2770.40*** *p134*
Block, Jonas 20; New Orleans, 1879 ***7710.1*** *p158*
Block, Joseph; Louisiana, 1883 ***7710.1*** *p158*
Block, Julius 21; New York, NY, 1882 ***7710.1*** *p160*
Block, M.; Louisiana, 1874-1875 ***4981.45*** *p298*
Block, Martin; Illinois, 1855 ***6079.1*** *p2*
Block, Michel 20; New York, NY, 1881 ***7710.1*** *p159*
Block, Pauline 7; New York, NY, 1893 ***1883.7*** *p38*
Blockly, John; North Carolina, 1844 ***1088.45*** *p3*
Blockwitz, Peter; Wisconsin, 1855 ***6795.8*** *p99*
Bloean, Remy 18; America, 1840 ***778.6*** *p36*
Bloedel, Anton; Wisconsin, 1899 ***6795.8*** *p158*
Bloeden, Julius Rudolph Edward; Wisconsin, 1878 ***6795.8*** *p217*
Blohm, Peter; Missouri, 1895 ***3276.1*** *p3*
Blohm, Wilhelm; Missouri, 1898 ***3276.1*** *p3*
Blohorn, George; New York, 1860 ***358.56*** *p148*
Blois, Julien 20; Montreal, 1659 ***9221.17*** *p417*
Bloising, Jean 16; America, 1840 ***778.6*** *p36*
Blom, Anna 36; Minnesota, 1925 ***2769.54*** *p1379*
Blom, Betse Jacobsdotter *SEE* Blom, Henry
Blom, Casp. Leon.; Philadelphia, 1847 ***6412.40*** *p150*
Blom, Elise; Chicago, 1881-1882 ***1865.50*** *p41*
Blom, Erick Olof *SEE* Blom, Henry
Blom, Henry; Iowa, 1866-1870 ***777.40*** *p9*
*Wife:*Betse Jacobsdotter
*Son:*Erick Olof
*Son:*Jacob J.
Blom, Jacob J. *SEE* Blom, Henry
Blom, Olof; Illinois, 1881-1883 ***1865.50*** *p41*
Blomberg, Anton Friedrich; America, 1880 ***7420.1*** *p314*
Blomberg, Eleonore *SEE* Blomberg, Ernst Friedrich Wilhelm
Blomberg, Eleonore Robke *SEE* Blomberg, Ernst Friedrich Wilhelm
Blomberg, Engel Marie Sophie; Chicago, 1875 ***7420.1*** *p304*
Blomberg, Ernst; America, 1867 ***7420.1*** *p254*
Blomberg, Ernst Friedrich Wilhelm; America, 1882 ***7420.1*** *p327*
*Wife:*Eleonore Robke
*Son:*Wilhelm Carl Heinrich
*Daughter:*Eleonore
Blomberg, Wilhelm Carl Heinrich *SEE* Blomberg, Ernst Friedrich Wilhelm
Blome, Dorothea Sophie Louise Kersten *SEE* Blome, Heinrich Wilhelm August
Blome, Heinrich Wilhelm August; America, 1893 ***7420.1*** *p368*
*Wife:*Dorothea Sophie Louise Kersten
*Daughter:*Marie Louise Wilhelmine
*Son:*Konrad Heinrich August
*Daughter:*Marie Louise Auguste
Blome, Konrad Heinrich August *SEE* Blome, Heinrich Wilhelm August
Blome, Marie Louise Auguste *SEE* Blome, Heinrich Wilhelm August
Blome, Marie Louise Wilhelmine *SEE* Blome, Heinrich Wilhelm August
Blomeke, Christian *SEE* Blomeke, Elisabeth
Blomeke, Elisabeth; America, 1880 ***8115.12*** *p321*
*Child:*Heinrich Christian Gustav
*Child:*Marie
*Child:*Karoline
*Child:*Christian
*Child:*Luise
Blomeke, Heinrich Christian Gustav *SEE* Blomeke, Elisabeth
Blomeke, Karoline *SEE* Blomeke, Elisabeth
Blomeke, Luise *SEE* Blomeke, Elisabeth
Blomeke, Marie *SEE* Blomeke, Elisabeth
Blomphe, Walter F.; New York, 1921-1974 ***9228.50*** *p120*
Blomphee, Walter F.; New York, 1921-1974 ***9228.50*** *p120*
Blomquist, Petter; Cleveland, OH, 1886-1893 ***9722.10*** *p117*
Blomster, A.W.; New York, NY, 1844 ***6412.40*** *p148*
Blondat, C. 24; New Orleans, 1848 ***778.6*** *p36*
Blondeau, Bernard S.; Illinois, 1852 ***6079.1*** *p2*
Blondeau, Francois 10; Quebec, 1641 ***9221.17*** *p101*
Blondeau, Jeanne; Quebec, 1671 ***4514.3*** *p280*
Blondel, Alizon Gourdin *SEE* Blondel, Pierre
Blondel, Claude 40; Quebec, 1642 ***9221.17*** *p112*
Blondel, John; New York, 1885 ***9228.50*** *p121*
Blondel, Marie 45; Quebec, 1657 ***9221.17*** *p370*
Blondel, Marie 45; Quebec, 1657 ***9221.17*** *p370*
Blondel, Nicolas 30; Quebec, 1637 ***9221.17*** *p67*
Blondel, Peter; New York, 1821 ***9228.50*** *p121*
Blondel, Pierre; Quebec, 1636 ***9221.17*** *p52*
*Wife:*Alizon Gourdin
Blondel, Pierre; Quebec, 1643 ***9221.17*** *p129*
Blondel, Thomas; Boston, 1760-1769 ***9228.50*** *p122*
Blondell, C.E.; Iowa, 1884 ***1211.15*** *p9*
Blondelu, Louis 51; Port uncertain, 1842 ***778.6*** *p36*
Blondin, M. 39; England, 1841 ***778.6*** *p36*
Blondlet, Joseph 23; Kansas, 1888 ***1447.20*** *p62*
Blong, John Baptiste; Ohio, 1809-1852 ***4511.35*** *p5*
Blonzer, Genovefa 15; Galveston, TX, 1844 ***3967.10*** *p372*
Blonzer, Leo 17; Galveston, TX, 1844 ***3967.10*** *p372*
Blonzer, Magdalena 6 months; Galveston, TX, 1844 ***3967.10*** *p372*
Blonzer, Nikolaus 9; Galveston, TX, 1844 ***3967.10*** *p372*
Blonzer, Peter 37; Galveston, TX, 1844 ***3967.10*** *p372*
Blonzer, Siplus 2; Galveston, TX, 1844 ***3967.10*** *p372*
Blonzer, Therese 7; Galveston, TX, 1844 ***3967.10*** *p372*
Blonzer, Therese 39; Galveston, TX, 1844 ***3967.10*** *p372*
Blonzer, Urban 12; Galveston, TX, 1844 ***3967.10*** *p372*
Blonzer, Veronika 5; Galveston, TX, 1844 ***3967.10*** *p372*
Bloom, Boruch; Detroit, 1929 ***1640.55*** *p115*
Bloom, Charles; Illinois, 1859 ***6079.1*** *p2*
Bloom, Joseph; Ohio, 1871 ***1029.59*** *p10*
Bloom, Manuel Paul; Detroit, 1929-1930 ***6214.5*** *p63*
Bloom, Margaret S. 44; Michigan, 1880 ***4491.33*** *p2*
Bloomberg, Eric 21; Minnesota, 1923 ***2769.54*** *p1378*
Bloome, John; Maryland, 1671-1672 ***1236.25*** *p45*
Bloomer, Charles; Iowa, 1888 ***1211.15*** *p9*
Bloomfield, Daniel 67; Ontario, 1871 ***1823.21*** *p29*
Bloomfield, Eleanor 35; Ontario, 1871 ***1823.21*** *p29*
Bloomfield, Henry 25; Ontario, 1871 ***1823.21*** *p29*
Bloum, Joseph; Ohio, 1871 ***1029.59*** *p10*
Blova, James; Louisiana, 1874 ***4981.45*** *p131*
Blovel, John; Boston, 1769 ***9228.50*** *p48*
Blow, Henry 35; Ontario, 1871 ***1823.21*** *p29*
Blow, John 70; Ontario, 1871 ***1823.21*** *p29*
Blow, Wm 60; Ontario, 1871 ***1823.21*** *p29*
Blows, John 55; Ontario, 1871 ***1823.21*** *p29*
Bloy, Louis 30; New Orleans, 1848 ***778.6*** *p36*
Blu, William; Washington, 1875 ***2770.40*** *p134*
Bluch, Barbara; Brazil, 1855 ***5475.1*** *p440*
Bluch, Katharina; America, 1840 ***5475.1*** *p437*
Bluch-Kosters, Anna 30; America, 1856 ***5475.1*** *p440*
Blue, Sarah 49; Ontario, 1871 ***1823.21*** *p29*
Bluemke, Gottlied; Wisconsin, 1877 ***6795.8*** *p216*
Bluesz, John; Ohio, 1809-1852 ***4511.35*** *p5*
Blufert, Carl 8; Valdivia, Chile, 1850 ***1192.4*** *p48*
Blufert, Louise E.; Valdivia, Chile, 1850 ***1192.4*** *p48*
Bluhm, L.; Louisiana, 1874 ***4981.45*** *p130*
Blule, Mr. 36; Halifax, N.S., 1902 ***1860.4*** *p44*
Blule, Bernhart 2; Halifax, N.S., 1902 ***1860.4*** *p44*
Blule, Elizabeth 35; Halifax, N.S., 1902 ***1860.4*** *p44*
Blule, Joseph 16; Halifax, N.S., 1902 ***1860.4*** *p44*
Blule, Juliana; Halifax, N.S., 1902 ***1860.4*** *p44*
Blule, Rosine 4; Halifax, N.S., 1902 ***1860.4*** *p44*
Blum, Mr. 28; America, 1846 ***778.6*** *p36*
Blum, Aron 28; Port uncertain, 1847 ***778.6*** *p36*
Blum, G. 4; America, 1846 ***778.6*** *p36*
Blum, Herman; Philadelphia, 1846 ***5720.10*** *p377*
Blum, Jacob 25; America, 1845 ***778.6*** *p36*
Blum, Jacob; Colorado, 1880 ***1029.59*** *p10*
Blum, Jacob; Colorado, 1880 ***1029.59*** *p10*
Blum, Jacob; Colorado, 1892 ***1029.59*** *p10*
Blum, Jacob; Ohio, 1809-1852 ***4511.35*** *p5*
Blum, Johann Heinrich Christoph; America, 1876 ***7420.1*** *p306*
Blum, John; Ohio, 1809-1852 ***4511.35*** *p5*
Blum, John; Philadelphia, 1853 ***5720.10*** *p377*
Blum, Joseph 20; America, 1847 ***778.6*** *p36*
Blum, Justin 12; America, 1845 ***778.6*** *p36*
Blum, Minette 24; Port uncertain, 1847 ***778.6*** *p36*
Blumanhost, Herman; Ohio, 1840-1897 ***8365.35*** *p15*
Blumberg, Clara 19; New York, NY, 1878 ***9253.2*** *p45*
Blumberg, Salomon 21; New York, NY, 1878 ***9253.2*** *p45*
Blume, Catharina Engel; America, 1867 ***7420.1*** *p254*
*Son:*Hans Heinrich Conrad
Blume, Catharine Maria Dorothea; America, 1859 ***7420.1*** *p184*
Blume, Conrad; America, 1856 ***7420.1*** *p145*
With wife & daughter
Blume, Cyril; Ohio, 1809-1852 ***4511.35*** *p5*
Blume, Dorothee Charlotte Steege *SEE* Blume, Johann Conrad
Blume, Engel Maria Sophia *SEE* Blume, Johann Heinrich
Blume, Engel Marie Charlotte; America, 1865 ***7420.1*** *p229*
Blume, Engel Marie Dorothee; America, 1848 ***7420.1*** *p58*
Blume, Engel Marie Sophie *SEE* Blume, Hans Heinrich Christoph
Blume, Hans Heinrich Christoph; America, 1855 ***7420.1*** *p134*
*Sister:*Engel Marie Sophie
Blume, Hans Henrich *SEE* Blume, Johann Heinrich
Blume, Heinrich; America, 1868 ***7420.1*** *p268*
Blume, Johann Conrad; America, 1856 ***7420.1*** *p145*
*Wife:*Dorothee Charlotte Steege
*Son:*Johann Heinrich
*Daughter:*Sophie Charlotte
*Son:*Johann Friedrich
Blume, Johann Friedrich *SEE* Blume, Johann Conrad
Blume, Johann Heinrich; America, 1848 ***7420.1*** *p59*
*Daughter:*Engel Maria Sophia
*Son:*Hans Henrich
*Son:*Johann Heinrich Conrad
*Wife:*Thrine Engel Wilkening
*Son:*Johann Wilhelm
Blume, Johann Heinrich; America, 1854 ***7420.1*** *p115*
Blume, Johann Heinrich *SEE* Blume, Johann Conrad
Blume, Johann Heinrich Conrad *SEE* Blume, Johann Heinrich
Blume, Johann Wilhelm *SEE* Blume, Johann Heinrich
Blume, Marie 22; New Orleans, 1848 ***778.6*** *p36*
Blume, Marie Sophie; America, 1865 ***7420.1*** *p229*
Blume, Melchior 26; New Orleans, 1848 ***778.6*** *p36*
Blume, Sophie; America, 1854 ***7420.1*** *p116*
Blume, Sophie; America, 1856 ***7420.1*** *p145*
Blume, Sophie; America, 1856 ***7420.1*** *p145*
With 2 sons
Blume, Sophie Charlotte *SEE* Blume, Johann Conrad
Blume, Sophie Friederike Dorothea; America, 1860 ***7420.1*** *p191*
Blume, Thrine Engel Wilkening *SEE* Blume, Johann Heinrich
Blume, Trine Marie Dorothee; America, 1851 ***7420.1*** *p78*
Blume, Victor; Ohio, 1809-1852 ***4511.35*** *p5*
Blume, W.; America, 1853 ***7420.1*** *p102*
Blumel, Gustav; Valdivia, Chile, 1851 ***1192.4*** *p50*
Blumemthan, Jacob; North Carolina, 1845-1851 ***1088.45*** *p3*
Blumenschein, Adam 27; America, 1846 ***2526.43*** *p122*
With wife
*Son:*Peter 3
Blumenschein, Anna Barbara Goetz *SEE* Blumenschein, Johann Adam
Blumenschein, Johann Adam; Virginia, 1831 ***152.20*** *p62*
*Wife:*Anna Barbara Goetz
Blumenschein, Peter 3 *SEE* Blumenschein, Adam
Blumhagen, Christina 66; New York, NY, 1899 ***6406.6*** *p47*
Blumhagen, Christoph; North Dakota, 1899 ***6406.6*** *p47*
Blumhard, Jean 30; Mississippi, 1847 ***778.6*** *p36*
Blumhardt, Elizabeth Wacker *SEE* Blumhardt, G. Frederick
Blumhardt, G. Frederick; Philadelphia, 1853 ***8513.31*** *p295*
*Wife:*Elizabeth Wacker
Blumquet, Louis 24; Mississippi, 1846 ***778.6*** *p36*
Blundel, Henry; North Carolina, 1841 ***1088.45*** *p3*
Blundell, Henry S.; North Carolina, 1842 ***1088.45*** *p3*
Blunden, Catherine 61; Ontario, 1871 ***1823.17*** *p12*
Blunden, Christopher 64; Ontario, 1871 ***1823.17*** *p12*
Blunden, Thomas; New York, 1775 ***8529.30*** *p10*
Blunden, Trevor 35; Ontario, 1871 ***1823.17*** *p12*
Blunie, Joseph; Louisiana, 1874 ***4981.45*** *p130*
Blunket, Richard; North Carolina, 1835 ***1088.45*** *p3*
Blunket, William; North Carolina, 1835 ***1088.45*** *p3*
Blunt, David 18; Quebec, 1870 ***8364.32*** *p22*
Blunt, Ruth; Massachusetts, 1766 ***1642*** *p109*
Blush, Frederick; Ohio, 1809-1852 ***4511.35*** *p5*
Blust, Nicholas; Ohio, 1809-1852 ***4511.35*** *p5*
Bluteau, Antoinette; Quebec, 1671 ***4514.3*** *p280*
Bluthard, Gottl.; Chile, 1852 ***1192.4*** *p51*
Blyth, Robert 27; Ontario, 1871 ***1823.17*** *p12*
Blythe, Charles 22; Ontario, 1871 ***1823.17*** *p12*
Blythe, John 32; North Carolina, 1774 ***1422.10*** *p56*
Blythen, John; Salem, MA, 1659-1674 ***9228.50*** *p425*

40 *FOR A COMPLETE EXPLANATION OF ENTRY, SEE "HOW TO READ A CITATION" SECTION*

Boachaud, Mrs. 43; Port uncertain, 1845 ***778.6*** *p36*
Boachaud, A. 29; Port uncertain, 1845 ***778.6*** *p36*
Boachaud, J. 30; Port uncertain, 1845 ***778.6*** *p36*
Boahret, John Christopher; Ohio, 1809-1852 ***4511.35*** *p5*
Boakin, Alfred 6; Quebec, 1870 ***8364.32*** *p22*
Boakin, Harriet 13; Quebec, 1870 ***8364.32*** *p22*
Boakin, Thomas 7; Quebec, 1870 ***8364.32*** *p22*
Boanne, Yves; Quebec, 1660 ***9221.17*** *p432*
With son
Boar, Mary J. 60; Ontario, 1871 ***1823.21*** *p29*
Board, Gregory; Colorado, 1882 ***1029.59*** *p10*
Board, Gregory; St. Clair Co., IL, 1874 ***1029.59*** *p10*
Boardman, Thomas 35; Ontario, 1871 ***1823.21*** *p29*
Boas, Marie 34; America, 1846 ***778.6*** *p36*
Boass, James; Ontario, 1871 ***1823.17*** *p12*
Boasso, Joachim; Louisiana, 1836-1840 ***4981.45*** *p212*
Bobal, Frantisek; Chicago, 1877 ***2853.20*** *p427*
Bobal, Frantisek; Omaha, NE, 1872 ***2853.20*** *p148*
Bobal, Tomas J.; Wisconsin, 1883 ***2853.20*** *p445*
Bobb, Conrad; Ohio, 1809-1852 ***4511.35*** *p5*
Bobenrieth, Jakob 32; Galveston, TX, 1844 ***3967.10*** *p375*
Bober, Magdalena; Detroit, 1929 ***1640.55*** *p114*
Boberg, Lena; St. Paul, MN, 1893 ***1865.50*** *p41*
Bobicar, John; St. Johns, N.F., 1825 ***1053.15*** *p6*
Bobicar, Joshua; St. Johns, N.F., 1825 ***1053.15*** *p6*
Bobicar, Margaret; St. Johns, N.F., 1825 ***1053.15*** *p6*
Bobicar, Margaret; St. Johns, N.F., 1825 ***1053.15*** *p7*
Bobicar, Thomas; St. Johns, N.F., 1825 ***1053.15*** *p6*
Bobier, John 66; Ontario, 1871 ***1823.17*** *p12*
Bobier, Joshua; St. Johns, N.F., 1825 ***1053.15*** *p6*
Boblier, Stanisl. 21; New York, NY, 1893 ***1883.7*** *p43*
Boboeuf, Medard 27; Port uncertain, 1840 ***778.6*** *p36*
Bobowski, Albert; Detroit, 1929 ***1640.55*** *p116*
Bobst, Joseph; Ohio, 1809-1852 ***4511.35*** *p5*
Boch, Andre 8; America, 1840 ***778.6*** *p36*
Boch, Franz 6; America, 1840 ***778.6*** *p36*
Boch, Jacob; Ohio, 1809-1852 ***4511.35*** *p5*
Boch, Jean 9; America, 1840 ***778.6*** *p37*
Boch, Jean 47; America, 1840 ***778.6*** *p37*
Boch, Johann 4; America, 1840 ***778.6*** *p37*
Boch, Maria 2; America, 1840 ***778.6*** *p37*
Boch, Mary 36; America, 1840 ***778.6*** *p37*
Bochart, Denis; Quebec, 1647 ***9221.17*** *p177*
Bochatey, Frederic Cam; New York, NY, 1905 ***1029.59*** *p11*
Bochholz, Lorenz Hubert 28; Galveston, TX, 1844 ***3967.10*** *p375*
Bochholz, Maria Margarethe 22; Galveston, TX, 1844 ***3967.10*** *p375*
Bochholz, Martin 1; Galveston, TX, 1844 ***3967.10*** *p375*
Bocinski, George; Detroit, 1929 ***1640.55*** *p114*
Bocinski, Wojciech; Detroit, 1929 ***1640.55*** *p114*
Bock, . . .; Port uncertain, 1866 ***170.15*** *p20*
Bock, Mr.; America, 1854 ***7420.1*** *p116*
Bock, Mr.; America, 1867 ***7420.1*** *p254*
Bock, Adam 18; America, 1851 ***2526.43*** *p190*
Bock, Adam; Illinois, 1855 ***6079.1*** *p2*
Bock, Agnes *SEE* Bock, Mina Kleine
Bock, Anna Kathar. Marie Homeier *SEE* Bock, Johann Heinrich Conrad
Bock, Anna Maria; America, 1880 ***5475.1*** *p241*
Bock, Bernhard; America, 1923 ***8023.44*** *p372*
With wife
Bock, Christoph; America, 1862 ***7420.1*** *p210*
With family
Bock, Elisabeth; Iowa, 1924 ***8023.44*** *p372*
Bock, Engel Marie; America, 1854 ***7420.1*** *p116*
Bock, Engel Marie; Illinois, 1880 ***7420.1*** *p315*
Bock, Engel Marie Dorothea; America, 1874 ***7420.1*** *p302*
Bock, Engel Marie Sophie Koeneke *SEE* Bock, Hans Heinrich Conrad
Bock, Engel Rosine Wilhelmine; America, 1850 ***7420.1*** *p69*
Bock, Eugen *SEE* Bock, Mina Kleine
Bock, Eugen von; Chile, 1852 ***1192.4*** *p54*
Bock, Friedrich Ludwig; America, 1878 ***7420.1*** *p310*
Bock, Friedrich Wilhelm; Illinois, 1880 ***7420.1*** *p314*
Bock, Georg; America, 1857 ***2526.43*** *p190*
Bock, Georg 23; America, 1884 ***2526.43*** *p190*
Bock, Georg Heinrich; America, 1868 ***7919.3*** *p525*
Bock, Georg Wilhelm; Port uncertain, 1854 ***7420.1*** *p116*
Bock, Hans Heinrich; Illinois, 1880 ***7420.1*** *p315*
Bock, Hans Heinrich Conrad *SEE* Bock, Hans Heinrich Conrad
Bock, Hans Heinrich Conrad; America, 1866 ***7420.1*** *p239*
*Wife:*Engel Marie Sophie Koeneke
*Son:*Hans Heinrich Conrad
Bock, Heinrich; America, 1867 ***7420.1*** *p254*
Bock, Heinrich Conrad; America, 1857 ***7420.1*** *p157*
Bock, Heinrich Conrad; America, 1865 ***7420.1*** *p229*
Bock, Heinrich Friedr. Conr. *SEE* Bock, Johann Heinrich Conrad
Bock, Heinrich Friedrich Wilhelm; America, 1882 ***7420.1*** *p327*
Bock, Heinrich Ludwig Eduard; America, 1887 ***7420.1*** *p352*
Bock, Heinrich Wilh. Konrad *SEE* Bock, Johann Heinrich Conrad
Bock, Herman 25; Ontario, 1871 ***1823.21*** *p29*
Bock, Ilse Marie Sophie Charlotte; America, 1857 ***7420.1*** *p157*
Bock, Jack; Detroit, 1929 ***1640.55*** *p115*
Bock, Jakob, II; America, 1842 ***2526.43*** *p137*
With wife
With child 10
With child 5
With child 3
With child 8
Bock, Johann Christian; America, 1857 ***7420.1*** *p157*
Bock, Johann Christoph; America, 1862 ***7420.1*** *p210*
Bock, Johann Friedrich; America, 1857 ***7420.1*** *p157*
With family
Bock, Johann Friedrich Conrad; America, 1866 ***7420.1*** *p239*
With family
Bock, Johann Heinrich; America, 1868 ***7420.1*** *p268*
Bock, Johann Heinrich Conrad; America, 1845 ***7420.1*** *p34*
*Wife:*Anna Kathar. Marie Homeier
*Son:*Heinrich Friedr. Conr.
*Daughter:*Sophie Dorothee Just. Frieder.
*Son:*Heinrich Wilh. Konrad
Bock, Johann Heinrich Friedr. Christoph; America, 1850 ***7420.1*** *p69*
Bock, Johann Otto; America, 1866 ***7420.1*** *p240*
Bock, Johann Philipp; America, 1864 ***7420.1*** *p222*
Bock, Johannes; Pennsylvania, 1899 ***170.15*** *p20*
With wife & 2 children
Bock, Leonhard 17; America, 1852 ***2526.43*** *p190*
Bock, Marie; Illinois, 1880 ***7420.1*** *p315*
Bock, Marie Sophie; America, 1850 ***7420.1*** *p73*
Bock, Mina; Chicago, 1926 ***8023.44*** *p372*
*Daughter:*Agnes
*Son:*Otto
*Son:*Eugen
Bock, Otto *SEE* Bock, Mina Kleine
Bock, Sophie; America, 1857 ***7420.1*** *p158*
Bock, Sophie Dorothee Just. Frieder. *SEE* Bock, Johann Heinrich Conrad
Bock, Wilhelm Carl Johan Friedrich; Wisconsin, 1875 ***6795.8*** *p225*
Bock, Wilhelm Christoph; Illinois, 1880 ***7420.1*** *p315*
Bockel, Amalia 4; New York, NY, 1898 ***7951.13*** *p41*
Bockel, Elisabeth 6; New York, NY, 1898 ***7951.13*** *p41*
Bockel, Elisabeth 59; New York, NY, 1898 ***7951.13*** *p41*
Bockel, Emilia 1 months; New York, NY, 1898 ***7951.13*** *p41*
Bockel, Johann 35; New York, NY, 1898 ***7951.13*** *p41*
Bockel, Joseph 29; New York, NY, 1898 ***7951.13*** *p41*
Bockel, Karolina 31; New York, NY, 1898 ***7951.13*** *p41*
Bockel, Ludwig 18; New York, NY, 1898 ***7951.13*** *p41*
Bockel, Peter 15; New York, NY, 1898 ***7951.13*** *p41*
Bockeloh, Heinrich Wilhelm; Port uncertain, 1886 ***7420.1*** *p350*
Bocquet, Charles 27; Quebec, 1656 ***9221.17*** *p332*
Bocquet, Pierre; Quebec, 1640 ***9221.17*** *p94*
Bocquet, Vincent; Quebec, 1659 ***9221.17*** *p395*
Bocquil, Joseph 27; New Orleans, 1848 ***778.6*** *p37*
Boczak, Gustave 27; New York, NY, 1920 ***930.50*** *p49*
Bodaly, John 45; Ontario, 1871 ***1823.17*** *p12*
Bodden, George 26; Ontario, 1871 ***1823.21*** *p29*
Boddie, Mr.; Boston, n.d. ***9228.50*** *p124*
Boddy, Guy D. 29; Quebec, 1910 ***2897.7*** *p9*
Boddy, William 48; Ontario, 1871 ***1823.21*** *p29*
Bode, Auguste; New York, NY, 1874 ***7420.1*** *p302*
Bode, Friedrich; America, 1858 ***7420.1*** *p176*
Bode, Heinrich August; England, 1880 ***7420.1*** *p315*
Bode, Henry W.; Washington, 1888 ***2770.40*** *p25*
Bode, Johannes; Louisiana, 1841-1844 ***4981.45*** *p210*
Bodean, Louis; Louisiana, 1874-1875 ***4981.45*** *p297*
Bodechtel, Frederick E.; Louisiana, 1841-1844 ***4981.45*** *p210*
Bodecker, Caroline Louise *SEE* Bodecker, Christian Friedrich Conrad
Bodecker, Catharine Wilhelmine Elisabeth Spangenberg *SEE* Bodecker, Christian Friedrich Conrad
Bodecker, Christian Friedrich Conrad; America, 1853 ***7420.1*** *p102*
*Wife:*Catharine Wilhelmine Elisabeth Spangenberg
*Son:*Christian Ludwig
*Daughter:*Dorothee Lou. Wilh.
*Daughter:*Caroline Louise
*Son:*Friedrich August
Bodecker, Christian Ludwig *SEE* Bodecker, Christian Friedrich Conrad
Bodecker, Dorothee Lou. Wilh. *SEE* Bodecker, Christian Friedrich Conrad
Bodecker, Friedrich; America, 1852 ***7420.1*** *p85*
Bodecker, Friedrich August *SEE* Bodecker, Christian Friedrich Conrad
Bodecker, Georg Moritz Victor; America, 1880 ***7420.1*** *p315*
Bodecker, Moritz; America, 1852 ***7420.1*** *p85*
Bodecker, Wilhelm; America, 1868 ***7420.1*** *p268*
Bodee, Mr.; Boston, n.d. ***9228.50*** *p124*
Bodeker, Engel Dorothea Eleonore; America, 1873 ***7420.1*** *p397*
Bodeker, Mrs. Franz; America, 1873 ***7420.1*** *p397*
Bodeker, Friedrich; America, 1857 ***7420.1*** *p158*
Bodeker, Fritz 16; New York, NY, 1864 ***8425.62*** *p195*
Bodeker, Gard; Iowa, 1890 ***1211.15*** *p9*
Bodeker, Johann Daniel; America, 1857 ***7420.1*** *p158*
Bodeker, Sophie; America, 1854 ***7420.1*** *p116*
Bodemer, Elisabeth 19; New York, NY, 1886 ***8425.16*** *p33*
Bodemer, Gottl. 55; New York, NY, 1886 ***8425.16*** *p33*
Bodemer, Justine 57; New York, NY, 1886 ***8425.16*** *p33*
Boden, . . .; America, n.d. ***9228.50*** *p126*
Boden, Ambrose; Massachusetts, 1700-1750 ***9228.50*** *p122*
Boden, Charles; Boston, 1769 ***9228.50*** *p48*
Boden, Edward; Nantucket, MA, 1782-1807 ***9228.50*** *p123*
Boden, Johann 40; America, 1843 ***5475.1*** *p252*
Boden, Johann 60; America, 1843 ***5475.1*** *p293*
Boden, William; Boston, 1769 ***9228.50*** *p48*
Boden, William; Salem, MA, 1783 ***9228.50*** *p122*
Boden, Wm.; New England, 1775-1807 ***9228.50*** *p122*
Bodenbery, John; Louisiana, 1874-1875 ***4981.45*** *p297*
Boden Family ; Massachusetts, n.d. ***9228.50*** *p126*
Bodenstein, Andrew F.; Philadelphia, 1867 ***8513.31*** *p296*
*Wife:*Charlote Truemper
*Son:*George
Bodenstein, Charlote Truemper *SEE* Bodenstein, Andrew F.
Bodenstein, George *SEE* Bodenstein, Andrew F.
Bodes, Heinrich Ludwig; America, 1870 ***7420.1*** *p283*
Bodes, Hermann; America, 1874 ***7420.1*** *p302*
Bodge, . . .; New England, n.d. ***9228.50*** *p97*
Bodger, John 26; Indiana, 1858-1859 ***9076.20*** *p65*
Bodie, Catherine; Ohio, 1850 ***9228.50*** *p490*
Bodier, Adam 25; Louisiana, 1848 ***778.6*** *p37*
Bodin, Jacques; Quebec, 1642 ***9221.17*** *p112*
Bodine, Nicholas 82; Ontario, 1871 ***1823.21*** *p29*
Bodinet, Ambrosius; America, 1881 ***5475.1*** *p154*
Bodinet, Ambrosius; Chicago, 1890 ***5475.1*** *p155*
Bodinet, P. Eduard; Chicago, 1891 ***5475.1*** *p156*
Boding, Nils; Colorado, 1880 ***1029.59*** *p11*
Boding, Nils; Colorado, 1887 ***1029.59*** *p11*
Boding, Nils; Colorado, 1894 ***1029.59*** *p11*
Boding, Nils, Sr.; Colorado, 1887 ***1029.59*** *p11*
Boding, Nils, Sr.; Colorado, 1894 ***1029.59*** *p11*
Bodinson, Fredrik John; Boston, 1902 ***1766.20*** *p34*
Bodken, Jane 24; Ontario, 1871 ***1823.21*** *p29*
Bodkin, Alexander 31; Ontario, 1871 ***1823.21*** *p29*
Bodkin, John 29; Ontario, 1871 ***1823.21*** *p30*
Bodkin, Minnie 3; Ontario, 1871 ***1823.21*** *p30*
Bodkin, William 58; Ontario, 1871 ***1823.21*** *p30*
Bodley, Anna; St. Paul, MN, 1880 ***1865.50*** *p41*
Bodley, Edward 26; Ontario, 1871 ***1823.21*** *p30*
Bodmer, Charles; Ohio, 1840-1897 ***8365.35*** *p15*
Bodot, Antoinette *SEE* Bodot, Lambert
Bodot, Josephine *SEE* Bodot, Lambert
Bodot, Lambert; Wisconsin, 1855 ***1495.20*** *p8*
*Wife:*Marie Therese Lejeune
*Daughter:*Antoinette
*Daughter:*Josephine
Bodot, Marie Therese Lejeune *SEE* Bodot, Lambert
Bodret, Michael; Maine, n.d. ***9228.50*** *p17A*
Bodris, Louis 22; New Orleans, 1848 ***778.6*** *p37*
Body, Catherine; Ohio, 1850 ***9228.50*** *p490*
Boe, Detlef; Washington, 1873 ***2770.40*** *p134*
Boe, Detlef; Washington, 1884 ***2770.40*** *p192*
Boedefeld, M.; New York, 1859 ***358.56*** *p54*
Boegel, Augustus; Ohio, 1809-1852 ***4511.35*** *p5*
Boeglin, John; Ohio, 1809-1852 ***4511.35*** *p5*
Boehl, John; Ohio, 1809-1852 ***4511.35*** *p5*
Boehle, William; New York, 1860 ***358.56*** *p3*
Boehler, Barbara 19; New Orleans, 1848 ***778.6*** *p37*
Boehler, F.; Galveston, TX, 1855 ***571.7*** *p18*
Boehler, Xavier 25; New Orleans, 1848 ***778.6*** *p37*
Boehm, Elisabeth Margareth; Virginia, 1831 ***152.20*** *p63*
Boehm, Gottlieb; New York, 1859 ***358.56*** *p100*
Boehm, Johann; Wisconsin, 1885 ***6795.8*** *p69*
Boehm, Johann Blasius *SEE* Boehm, Johann Georg

Boehm, Johann Georg; Virginia, 1831 *152.20 p63*
*Wife:*Marie Freudenberger
*Child:*Johann Blasius
*Child:*Johannes
Boehm, Johannes *SEE* Boehm, Johann Georg
Boehm, Katherine; North Dakota, 1905 *609.10 p15*
Boehm, Marie Freudenberger *SEE* Boehm, Johann Georg
Boehmer, Jacob; Ohio, 1809-1852 *4511.35 p5*
Boehning, Ferdinand; Wisconsin, 1881 *6795.8 p71*
Boekel, Anne 37; America, 1847 *778.6 p37*
Boekel, Celina 2; America, 1847 *778.6 p37*
Boekel, Clemence 6; America, 1847 *778.6 p37*
Boekel, Elisa 13; America, 1847 *778.6 p37*
Boekel, Francois 9; America, 1847 *778.6 p37*
Boekel, George 45; America, 1847 *778.6 p37*
Boekel, Louis 10 months; America, 1847 *778.6 p37*
Boekel, Marie 14; America, 1847 *778.6 p37*
Boeker, Christoph 25; New Orleans, 1846 *778.6 p37*
Boeker, Herman F.; Wisconsin, 1892 *6795.8 p120*
Boelke, Frederick; Wisconsin, 1881 *6795.8 p14*
Boelter, Adeline Ernestine; Wisconsin, 1895 *6795.8 p137*
Boelter, August Carl; Wisconsin, 1868 *6795.8 p137*
Boelter, August Hermann; Wisconsin, 1870 *6795.8 p44*
Boelter, David Hermann; Wisconsin, 1875 *6795.8 p36*
Boelter, Franz Edward; Wisconsin, 1900 *6795.8 p137*
Boelter, Friedrich Wilhelm; Wisconsin, 1889 *6795.8 p71*
Boelter, Herman August; Wisconsin, 1898 *6795.8 p36*
Boelter, Johannes; Wisconsin, 1881 *6795.8 p200*
Boelter, Wilhelm; Wisconsin, 1902 *6795.8 p200*
Boerner, Huelda; Philadelphia, 1856 *8513.31 p422*
Boerner, Johannes; Nova Scotia, 1852 *170.15 p21*
With wife & child
Boerner, John; Ohio, 1809-1852 *4511.35 p5*
Boescher, A. W.; Texas, 1884 *3435.45 p35*
Boeschler, Ba.bara 62; Mississippi, 1846 *778.6 p37*
Boese, Wilhelm; Wisconsin, 1869 *6795.8 p85*
Boesen, Anna *SEE* Boesen, Johann
Boesen, Anna Maria *SEE* Boesen, Johann
Boesen, Johann *SEE* Boesen, Johann
Boesen, Johann; America, 1883 *5475.1 p275*
*Wife:*Margarethe Fisch
*Son:*Peter
*Daughter:*Anna Maria
*Daughter:*Anna
*Daughter:*Magdalena
*Daughter:*Maria
*Son:*Sebastian
*Son:*Johann
Boesen, Magdalena *SEE* Boesen, Johann
Boesen, Margarethe Fisch *SEE* Boesen, Johann
Boesen, Maria *SEE* Boesen, Johann
Boesen, Nikoaus; America, 1881 *5475.1 p275*
Boesen, Nikolaus; America, 1872 *5475.1 p275*
Boesen, Peter *SEE* Boesen, Johann
Boesen, Peter; Dakota, 1888 *5475.1 p275*
Boesen, Sebastian *SEE* Boesen, Johann
Boessel, Jacob; Louisiana, 1874-1875 *4981.45 p298*
Boessel, Jacques 31; Quebec, 1639 *9221.17 p86*
*Wife:*Marie Heripel 17
Boessel, Marie Heripel 17 *SEE* Boessel, Jacques
Boessel, Marie 2; Quebec, 1654 *9221.17 p305*
Boesser, Frederick; North Carolina, 1859 *1088.45 p3*
Boesser, George; North Carolina, 1851 *1088.45 p3*
Boesser, William; North Carolina, 1852 *1088.45 p3*
Boetcher, August; Iowa, 1905 *1211.15 p9*
Boettcher, Agathe Anna; Wisconsin, 1899 *6795.8 p137*
Boettcher, Robert Otto; Wisconsin, 1896 *6795.8 p167*
Boettcher, Wilhelm; Wisconsin, 1874 *6795.8 p29*
Boeuf, Appalline 30; America, 1841 *778.6 p37*
Boeuf, Clarisse 3; America, 1841 *778.6 p37*
Boeuf, Francois 27; America, 1841 *778.6 p37*
Boeuf, Leontine 6 months; America, 1841 *778.6 p37*
Boeuf, Melanie 24; America, 1841 *778.6 p37*
Boeuf, Pierre 34; America, 1841 *778.6 p37*
Bogacz, Jozef 18; New York, NY, 1912 *8355.1 p16*
Bogdan, Martin; Washington, 1882 *2770.40 p135*
Boge, Jurgen; Valdivia, Chile, 1852 *1192.4 p55*
Bogee, . . .; New England, n.d. *9228.50 p97*
Bogen, Frederick; Ohio, 1809-1852 *4511.35 p5*
Bogen, Ludwig; America, 1853 *2526.43 p164*
Bogenschurtz, Michel 19; America, 1847 *778.6 p37*
Bogenschutz, Felix; Colorado, 1893 *1029.59 p11*
Bogenschutz, Felix; Colorado, 1893 *1029.59 p11*
Boger, Carl Heinrich; America, 1855 *7420.1 p134*
Boger, Carl Otto Heinrich; America, 1857 *7420.1 p158*
Boger, Catharine Sophie Redecker *SEE* Boger, Johann Heinrich
Boger, Catharine Sophie; America, 1847 *7420.1 p52*
With sister
Boger, Christine Wilhelmine Charlotte; America, 1860 *7420.1 p191*
Boger, Christoph; America, 1857 *7420.1 p158*
With wife & 2 sons

Boger, Friedrich Adolph; America, 1850 *7420.1 p69*
Boger, Friedrich Wilhelm; America, 1857 *7420.1 p158*
With wife 2 sons & 2 daughters
Boger, Friedrich Wilhelm; Port uncertain, 1840 *7420.1 p17*
Boger, Hanna Sophie Caroline *SEE* Boger, Johann Heinrich
Boger, Heinrich; Port uncertain, 1860 *7420.1 p191*
Boger, Johann Heinrich; America, 1845 *7420.1 p35*
*Wife:*Catharine Sophie Redecker
*Daughter:*Hanna Sophie Caroline
Boger, Wilhelm; America, 1852 *7420.1 p85*
Bogershausen, Heinrich Conrad; America, 1867 *7420.1 p254*
With family
Bogershausen, Johann Friedrich; America, 1865 *7420.1 p229*
Bogershausen, Johann Heinrich Conrad; America, 1866 *7420.1 p240*
Bogershausen, Wilhelm; America, 1866 *7420.1 p240*
Boggan, John; New Orleans, 1850 *7242.30 p134*
Boggan, Patrick; New Orleans, 1850 *7242.30 p134*
Boggs, Johan McCole *SEE* Boggs, Joseph
Boggs, Joseph; Philadelphia, 1861 *8513.31 p296*
*Wife:*Johan McCole
Bogle, Jacob; Washington, 1889 *2770.40 p26*
Bogle, Mary; Ohio, 1824 *9228.50 p592*
Bogr, Frantisek; Nebraska, 1873 *2853.20 p171*
Bogucki, Karol; Detroit, 1929 *1640.55 p114*
Bogue, John 43; Ontario, 1871 *1823.21 p30*
Bogue, John 70; Ontario, 1871 *1823.21 p30*
Boguet, Pierre; Quebec, 1640 *9221.17 p94*
Bogus, William; Ohio, 1809-1852 *4511.35 p5*
Boguslaw, Peter; Detroit, 1930 *1640.60 p81*
Boh, Bte. 17; America, 1745 *778.6 p37*
Bohacek, Josef, Sr.; Nebraska, 1910 *2853.20 p157*
Bohannan, Patrick 49; Ontario, 1871 *1823.21 p12*
Bohl, Gertrude 24; America, 1844 *778.6 p37*
Bohl, Peter; Louisiana, 1841-1844 *4981.45 p210*
Bohl, Theobald 14; America, 1844 *778.6 p37*
Bohle, Mr.; America, 1889 *7420.1 p400*
Bohle, Henry; Washington, 1889 *2770.40 p26*
Bohlender, William; Louisiana, 1874 *4981.45 p295*
Bohler, Andreas 44; New York, NY, 1893 *1883.7 p37*
Bohler, Bartholomaus 9; New York, NY, 1893 *1883.7 p37*
Bohler, Elisabeth 21; New York, NY, 1893 *1883.7 p37*
Bohler, Grigori 10; New York, NY, 1893 *1883.7 p37*
Bohler, Hermann Karl; America, 1866 *2526.43 p145*
Bohler, Karl; America, 1867 *2526.43 p145*
Bohler, Marianna 34; New York, NY, 1893 *1883.7 p37*
Bohler, Wincent 13; New York, NY, 1893 *1883.7 p37*
Bohlert, Friedrich; Pennsylvania, 1887 *5475.1 p17*
Bohling, Martin; North Carolina, 1859-1860 *1088.45 p3*
Bohm, Adam; America, 1881 *2526.43 p137*
Bohm, Balthasar 7 *SEE* Bohm, Nikolaus, II
Bohm, Elisabetha 12 *SEE* Bohm, Nikolaus, II
Bohm, Emanuel; America, 1867 *7919.3 p529*
Bohm, Gretchen 19 *SEE* Bohm, Nikolaus, II
Bohm, Johannes; America, 1891 *2526.43 p137*
Bohm, John George; New York, 1860 *358.56 p148*
Bohm, Katharina 15 *SEE* Bohm, Nikolaus, II
Bohm, Katharina Balmert 29 *SEE* Bohm, Nikolaus, III
Bohm, Katharina Kaufmann 44 *SEE* Bohm, Nikolaus, II
Bohm, Maria 9 *SEE* Bohm, Nikolaus, II
Bohm, Nikolaus, II 41; Pennsylvania, 1867 *2526.43 p137*
*Wife:*Katharina Kaufmann 44
*Son:*Peter 4
*Son:*Balthasar 7
*Daughter:*Gretchen 19
*Daughter:*Katharina 15
*Daughter:*Elisabetha 12
*Daughter:*Maria 9
Bohm, Nikolaus, III 28; Pennsylvania, 1867 *2526.43 p137*
*Wife:*Katharina Balmert 29
Bohm, Peter 4 *SEE* Bohm, Nikolaus, II
Bohm, Wilhelm Ferdinand; Wisconsin, 1893 *6795.8 p105*
Bohmann, Anna Maria; America, 1856 *2526.43 p194*
Bohme, Aug.; Chile, 1852 *1192.4 p51*
Bohme, Heinrich; America, 1874 *8023.44 p372*
Bohme, Wilhelm Ludwig; America, 1856 *7420.1 p145*
Bohmers, Marie; America, 1856 *7420.1 p145*
Bohmke, Carl; Washington, 1887 *2770.40 p24*
Bohmwald, C. G.; Valdivia, Chile, 1850 *1192.4 p49*
With wife & child
With child 3
With child 8
Bohn, A. 22; America, 1846 *778.6 p37*
Bohn, Andreas *SEE* Bohn, Johann Adam
Bohn, Christian; America, 1865-1885 *179.55 p19*
Bohn, Jakob; America, 1853 *179.55 p19*
Bohn, Jakob; America, 1883 *179.55 p19*

Bohn, Jakob *SEE* Bohn, Johann Adam
Bohn, Johann; New York, 1853 *5475.1 p481*
Bohn, Johann *SEE* Bohn, Johann Adam
Bohn, Johann Adam; St. Louis, 1893 *5475.1 p409*
*Wife:*Margarethe Holzer
*Son:*Johann
*Son:*Andreas
*Daughter:*Margarethe
*Son:*Jakob
*Daughter:*Maria
*Son:*Wilhelm
Bohn, Josef 22; America, 1882 *5475.1 p485*
Bohn, Margarethe *SEE* Bohn, Johann Adam
Bohn, Margarethe Holzer *SEE* Bohn, Johann Adam
Bohn, Maria *SEE* Bohn, Johann Adam
Bohn, Michel 34; Port uncertain, 1843 *778.6 p37*
Bohn, N. 18; America, 1846 *778.6 p38*
Bohn, N., Jr. 16; America, 1846 *778.6 p38*
Bohn, Nicolas 21; Mississippi, 1847 *778.6 p38*
Bohn, Peter; Ohio, 1809-1852 *4511.35 p5*
Bohn, Wilhelm *SEE* Bohn, Johann Adam
Bohn, Wilhelm; Wisconsin, 1873 *6795.8 p41*
Bohn, Wilhelm Friedrich; America, 1881 *179.55 p19*
Bohne, . . .; America, 1870 *7420.1 p395*
With family
Bohne, Carl; America, 1892 *7420.1 p365*
Bohne, Carl Ludwig *SEE* Bohne, Heinrich
Bohne, Charles; Illinois, 1851 *6079.1 p2*
Bohne, Ernst Heinrich; Port uncertain, 1888 *7420.1 p355*
Bohne, Gerhard; America, 1883 *7420.1 p335*
Bohne, Heinrich; America, 1866 *7420.1 p240*
With wife
With child
*Son:*Carl Ludwig
Bohne, Heinrich Friedrich Wilhelm; America, 1866 *7420.1 p240*
Bohnenberger, Barbara Gregorius *SEE* Bohnenberger, Philipp
Bohnenberger, Friedrich *SEE* Bohnenberger, Philipp
Bohnenberger, Georg; America, 1865 *5475.1 p521*
Bohnenberger, Jakob; America, 1861 *5475.1 p520*
Bohnenberger, Johann *SEE* Bohnenberger, Philipp
Bohnenberger, Karoline *SEE* Bohnenberger, Philipp
Bohnenberger, Katharina 30; America, 1865 *5475.1 p521*
Bohnenberger, Katharina *SEE* Bohnenberger, Philipp
Bohnenberger, Ludwig; America, 1865 *5475.1 p521*
Bohnenberger, Nikolaus *SEE* Bohnenberger, Philipp
Bohnenberger, Philipp; Pittsburgh, 1893 *5475.1 p409*
*Wife:*Barbara Gregorius
*Son:*Johann
*Son:*Nikolaus
*Daughter:*Karoline
*Son:*Friedrich
*Daughter:*Katharina
Bohnenberger, Wilhelm 54; Brazil, 1865 *5475.1 p521*
Bohnenkamp, Arnold 45; Galveston, TX, 1845 *3967.10 p376*
Bohnenkamp, Maria Katharina 50; Galveston, TX, 1845 *3967.10 p376*
Bohnert, August; America, 1867 *7919.3 p525*
Bohnet, Anna *SEE* Bohnet, Christian
Bohnet, Christian; Colorado, 1906 *1029.59 p11*
*Wife:*Katharina
*Child:*Hedvig
*Child:*Frieda
*Child:*Anna
Bohnet, Christian; New Jersey, 1906 *1029.59 p1A*
Bohnet, Elisabeth *SEE* Bohnet, Martin
Bohnet, Frieda *SEE* Bohnet, Christian
Bohnet, Friedrich *SEE* Bohnet, Martin
Bohnet, Hedvig *SEE* Bohnet, Christian
Bohnet, Jakob *SEE* Bohnet, Martin
Bohnet, Katharina 34 *SEE* Bohnet, Christian
Bohnet, Katharina Leitner *SEE* Bohnet, Martin
Bohnet, Maria *SEE* Bohnet, Martin
Bohnet, Martin; Dakota, 1888 *554.30 p25*
*Wife:*Katharina Leitner
*Child:*Friedrich
*Child:*Rosina
*Child:*Jakob
*Child:*Elisabeth
*Child:*Maria
Bohnet, Rosina *SEE* Bohnet, Martin
Bohnholzer, M.; Valparaiso, Chile, 1850 *1192.4 p50*
Bohning, Mrs. B., Sr.; America, 1868 *7420.1 p268*
Bohning, Carl; America, 1853 *7420.1 p103*
Bohning, Carl Heinrich Daniel; America, 1868 *7420.1 p269*
Bohning, Caroline; America, 1868 *7420.1 p269*
Bohning, Ferdinand; Mexico, 1902 *7420.1 p378*
Bohnsack, D.; Venezuela, 1843 *3899.5 p546*
Bohr, Miss; Chicago, 1882 *5475.1 p350*
Bohr, Anna *SEE* Bohr, Nikolaus

Bohr, Elisabeth *SEE* Bohr, Nikolaus
Bohr, Jakob *SEE* Bohr, Nikolaus
Bohr, Katharina Weber 43 *SEE* Bohr, Nikolaus
Bohr, Louis 20; America, 1747 ***778.6*** *p38*
Bohr, Michel *SEE* Bohr, Nikolaus
Bohr, Nikolaus *SEE* Bohr, Nikolaus
Bohr, Nikolaus; America, 1883 ***5475.1*** *p270*
*Wife:*Katharina Weber
*Daughter:*Anna
*Daughter:*Elisabeth
*Son:*Michel
*Son:*Nikolaus
*Son:*Jakob
Bohr, Peter; Wisconsin, 1882 ***5475.1*** *p350*
Bohrey, Ignatz; Ohio, 1809-1852 ***4511.35*** *p5*
Bohringer, G. 30; New York, NY, 1847 ***9176.15*** *p50*
Bohrmann, Margarethe 35; America, 1849 ***5475.1*** *p415*
Bohrmann, Peter 33; America, 1843 ***5475.1*** *p294*
Bohstedt, Theodore E.; North Carolina, 1858-1859 ***1088.45*** *p3*
Boht, August 22; Halifax, N.S., 1902 ***1860.4*** *p41*
Bohun, Richard; South Carolina, 1740-1760 ***9228.50*** *p89*
Boid, John 48; Ontario, 1871 ***1823.21*** *p30*
Boil, Edward 27; New York, NY, 1825 ***6178.50*** *p76*
Boileau, Marguerite; Canada, 1662 ***1142.10*** *p128*
Boileau, Marguerite; Quebec, 1662 ***9221.17*** *p480*
Boileau, Marie; Quebec, 1666 ***4514.3*** *p280*
Boillargeon, Joseph Arthur; Washington, 1884 ***2770.40*** *p192*
Boillin, Joseph 28; New Orleans, 1843 ***778.6*** *p38*
Boillot, Charles 21; Port uncertain, 1842 ***778.6*** *p38*
Boillot, Elisabeth 30; Port uncertain, 1842 ***778.6*** *p38*
Boillot, Eugene 21; Port uncertain, 1842 ***778.6*** *p38*
Boillot, Juenne 59; Port uncertain, 1842 ***778.6*** *p38*
Boillot, Justine 24; Port uncertain, 1842 ***778.6*** *p38*
Bois, Mathurin; Quebec, 1648 ***9221.17*** *p195*
Boisbuisson, Louis-Marin 5; Quebec, 1635 ***9221.17*** *p45*
Boisdon, Jacques; Quebec, 1648 ***9221.17*** *p195*
Boiseux, Nicolas; Quebec, 1659 ***9221.17*** *p413*
Boiseux, Pierre; Quebec, 1659 ***9221.17*** *p413*
Boishebert, Pierre; Quebec, 1645 ***9221.17*** *p153*
Boisseau, Elisabeth 43; America, 1840 ***778.6*** *p38*
Boisseau, Hubert 17; America, 1840 ***778.6*** *p38*
Boisseau, Jacques 22; Montreal, 1659 ***9221.17*** *p417*
Boisseau, Jacques 15; Quebec, 1645 ***9221.17*** *p151*
Boisseau, Jean 40; America, 1840 ***778.6*** *p38*
Boisseau, Joseph 23; America, 1840 ***778.6*** *p38*
Boisseau, Marie 10; America, 1840 ***778.6*** *p38*
Boisseau, Nicolas 13; America, 1840 ***778.6*** *p38*
Boisseau, Rosalie 8; America, 1840 ***778.6*** *p38*
Boissel, Anne 7; Missouri, 1845 ***778.6*** *p38*
Boissel, Anne 44; Missouri, 1845 ***778.6*** *p38*
Boissel, Catherine 5; Missouri, 1845 ***778.6*** *p38*
Boissel, Dominique 15; Missouri, 1845 ***778.6*** *p38*
Boissel, Francois; Quebec, 1652 ***9221.17*** *p254*
Boissel, Hypolite 10; Missouri, 1845 ***778.6*** *p38*
Boissel, Marie 10; Missouri, 1845 ***778.6*** *p38*
Boissel, Nicolas 57; Missouri, 1845 ***778.6*** *p38*
Boissenin, Esther 8; Port uncertain, 1842 ***778.6*** *p38*
Boissenin, Feline 9; Port uncertain, 1842 ***778.6*** *p38*
Boissenin, Glondrine 12; Port uncertain, 1842 ***778.6*** *p38*
Boissenin, Isidore 7; Port uncertain, 1842 ***778.6*** *p38*
Boissenin, Josette 44; Port uncertain, 1842 ***778.6*** *p38*
Boissenin, Nicolas 45; Port uncertain, 1842 ***778.6*** *p38*
Boissenin, Silvin 14; Port uncertain, 1842 ***778.6*** *p38*
Boissey, Eugenie 16; New Orleans, 1848 ***778.6*** *p38*
Boissey, Josephine 41; New Orleans, 1848 ***778.6*** *p39*
Boissier, Francois 46; Texas, 1848 ***778.6*** *p39*
Boissier, Guillaume; Montreal, 1642 ***9221.17*** *p123*
Boisson, Jean; Virginia, 1700 ***9230.15*** *p80*
Boissonet, Claudine 7; New Orleans, 1848 ***778.6*** *p39*
Boissonet, Marie 8; New Orleans, 1848 ***778.6*** *p39*
Boissonnet, Ja.ques 36; Texas, 1848 ***778.6*** *p39*
Boisverdun, Charles 11; Quebec, 1636 ***9221.17*** *p64*
Boisvert, Joseph de; Quebec, 1647 ***9221.17*** *p177*
Boit, John; America, 1774-1874 ***9228.50*** *p123*
With family
Boit, John; Marblehead, MA, 1743 ***9228.50*** *p123*
Boivin, Charles 39; Quebec, 1640 ***9221.17*** *p94*
Boivin, Francois 32; Quebec, 1646 ***9221.17*** *p161*
Boivin, Francoise; Quebec, 1668 ***4514.3*** *p281*
Boivin, Guillaume 29; Quebec, 1639 ***9221.17*** *p86*
Boivin, Jacques 29; Montreal, 1653 ***9221.17*** *p283*
Boivin, Pierre 18; Quebec, 1661 ***9221.17*** *p448*
Bojaris, Alexander 25; New York, NY, 1894 ***6512.1*** *p184*
Bojet, Mr. 17; America, 1846 ***778.6*** *p39*
Boker, Heinrich Wilhelm Friedrich Christoph; America, 1858 ***7420.1*** *p176*
Bokies, Biad; New York, NY, 1906 ***3331.4*** *p12*
Bokies, Sam; New York, NY, 1922 ***3331.4*** *p12*
Bokowsky, John; Texas, 1896-1904 ***6015.15*** *p9*
Bolaender, Jakob; Pennsylvania, 1854 ***170.15*** *p21*
With wife & 2 children
Boland, Beatrice 30; Minnesota, 1923 ***2769.54*** *p1378*
Boland, Cornelius; Colorado, 1869 ***1029.59*** *p11*
Boland, Johanna 46; Ontario, 1871 ***1823.21*** *p30*
Boland, John; New Orleans, 1851 ***7242.30*** *p134*
Boland, Patrick 30; Ontario, 1871 ***1823.21*** *p30*
Boland, Peter; North Carolina, 1855 ***1088.45*** *p3*
Boland, Richard 21; Ontario, 1871 ***1823.21*** *p30*
Boland, Tobias; New York, NY, 1825 ***3274.55*** *p66*
Bolarorn, Constant 18; America, 1846 ***778.6*** *p39*
Bolay, Friedrich; America, 1865 ***5475.1*** *p30*
Bolch, Anna Maria Barrois 48 *SEE* Bolch, Johann
Bolch, Jakob 24 *SEE* Bolch, Johann
Bolch, Johann 17 *SEE* Bolch, Johann
Bolch, Johann 53; America, 1837 ***5475.1*** *p450*
With sister-in-law 25
With daughter 21
*Son:*Johann 17
*Wife:*Anna Maria Barrois 48
*Son:*Jakob 24
*Son:*Mathias 16
Bolch, Mathias 16 *SEE* Bolch, Johann
Boldt, Gottfried; Galveston, TX, 1855 ***571.7*** *p16*
Bole, William 46; Ontario, 1871 ***1823.21*** *p30*
Bolei, Frederick; Ohio, 1809-1852 ***4511.35*** *p5*
Bolen, John 32; Ontario, 1871 ***1823.21*** *p30*
Bolene, Emma 22; Kansas, 1879-1880 ***777.40*** *p15*
Boles, James 42; Ontario, 1871 ***1823.17*** *p12*
Boley, Adele 7; Missouri, 1848 ***778.6*** *p39*
Boley, Emilie 38; Missouri, 1848 ***778.6*** *p39*
Boley, Francois 10; Missouri, 1848 ***778.6*** *p39*
Boley, Gustave 5; Missouri, 1848 ***778.6*** *p39*
Boley, Lucie 6; Missouri, 1848 ***778.6*** *p39*
Boley, Nicolas 41; Missouri, 1848 ***778.6*** *p39*
Bolg, Anna Maria Barrois 48 *SEE* Bolg, Johann
Bolg, Jakob 24 *SEE* Bolg, Johann
Bolg, Johann; America, 1837 ***5475.1*** *p449*
Bolg, Johann; America, 1837 ***5475.1*** *p450*
Bolg, Johann 17 *SEE* Bolg, Johann
Bolg, Johann 53; America, 1837 ***5475.1*** *p450*
*Wife:*Anna Maria Barrois 48
*Son:*Mathias 16
With sister-in-law 25
With daughter 21
*Son:*Jakob 24
*Son:*Johann 17
Bolg, Mathias 16 *SEE* Bolg, Johann
Bolger, Edward; New Orleans, 1850 ***7242.30*** *p134*
Bolger, John; St. Johns, N.F., 1825 ***1053.15*** *p6*
Bolger, Michael 42; Indiana, 1880-1882 ***9076.20*** *p70*
Bolger, Michael; New Orleans, 1850 ***7242.30*** *p134*
Bolibrzuch, Frank; Detroit, 1930 ***1640.60*** *p83*
Bolin, Daniel; Philadelphia, 1863 ***8513.31*** *p296*
*Wife:*Margaret Morse
Bolin, Emma 22; Kansas, 1879-1880 ***777.40*** *p15*
Bolin, F.W.; New Orleans, 1845 ***6412.40*** *p148*
Bolin, James; Nova Scotia, 1785 ***9228.50*** *p145*
Bolin, John; Nova Scotia, 1784 ***9228.50*** *p145*
Bolin, Margaret Morse *SEE* Bolin, Daniel
Bolin, Maria; Kansas, 1871 ***777.40*** *p15*
*Daughter:*Dina
*Son:*Charles
Bolinger, Ignatius; Ohio, 1809-1852 ***4511.35*** *p5*
Bolis, Joseph; New Orleans, 1840 ***778.6*** *p39*
Bolitho, William; Colorado, 1862-1894 ***1029.59*** *p11*
Boliver, Frank; Detroit, 1930 ***1640.60*** *p83*
Boll, Adam; America, 1883 ***2526.42*** *p168*
*Wife:*Anna Margaretha Geist
*Stepchild:*Anna Margaretha
Boll, Anna Margaretha Geist *SEE* Boll, Adam
Boll, Anna Margaretha 5 *SEE* Boll, Adam
Boll, Elisabetha 9 *SEE* Boll, Mrs. Michael
Boll, Johannes 23 *SEE* Boll, Mrs. Michael
Boll, Marie 26 *SEE* Boll, Mrs. Michael
Boll, Marie Elisabeth 29 *SEE* Boll, Mrs. Michael
Boll, Mrs. Michael 48; America, 1860 ***2526.42*** *p139*
*Child:*Marie Elisabeth 29
*Child:*Valentin 17
*Child:*Elisabetha 9
*Child:*Johannes 23
*Child:*Marie 26
Boll, Valentin 17 *SEE* Boll, Mrs. Michael
Boll, Wilhelm; America, 1854 ***2526.42*** *p107*
Bollandret, Aimable 10; America, 1843 ***778.6*** *p39*
Bollandret, Alexis 59; America, 1843 ***778.6*** *p39*
Bollandret, Charles 14; America, 1843 ***778.6*** *p39*
Bollandret, Christina 48; America, 1843 ***778.6*** *p39*
Bollandret, Hilare 12; America, 1843 ***778.6*** *p39*
Bollbach, Baptist; America, 1881 ***5475.1*** *p210*
Bollen, . . .; America, n.d. ***9228.50*** *p143*
Bollen, Anne Vauquellin *SEE* Bollen, James
Bollen, James; New Jersey, 1655 ***9228.50*** *p647*
*Wife:*Anne Vauquellin
*Daughter:*Mary
Bollen, James; New Jersey, 1666 ***9228.50*** *p124*
Bollen, John; Salem, MA, 1650-1699 ***9228.50*** *p93*
Bollen, Mary *SEE* Bollen, James
Bollenbacher, Carolina Elisabeth 29; America, 1843 ***5475.1*** *p516*
Bollheimer, Joseph; Ohio, 1840-1897 ***8365.35*** *p15*
Bollin, John; Illinois, 1858 ***6079.1*** *p2*
Bollinder, Jacob 15; New York, NY, 1874 ***6954.7*** *p37*
Bollinger, Miss A. 22; New Orleans, 1834 ***1002.51*** *p114*
Bollinger, Miss B. 2; Died enroute, 1834 ***1002.51*** *p114*
Bollinger, Miss J. 6 months; Died enroute, 1834 ***1002.51*** *p114*
Bolper, Marie-Louise; Quebec, 1671 ***4514.3*** *p281*
Bolsewig, Johann Friedrich Wilhelm; America, 1856 ***7420.1*** *p145*
Bolstef, Catharine 60; Ontario, 1871 ***1823.21*** *p30*
Bolt, George 33; Ontario, 1871 ***1823.21*** *p30*
Bolt, James 32; Ontario, 1871 ***1823.21*** *p30*
Bolt, John G. 33; Ontario, 1871 ***1823.17*** *p12*
Bolte, Mr.; America, 1871 ***7420.1*** *p289*
*Daughter:*Sophie Wilhelmine Christine
With wife & mother-in-law
Bolte, Carl Heinrich Wilhelm; America, 1876 ***7420.1*** *p306*
Bolte, Heinrich; London, Eng., 1898 ***7420.1*** *p374*
Bolte, Heinrich Christoph; America, 1888 ***7420.1*** *p355*
Bolte, Heinrich Wilhelm; America, 1870 ***7420.1*** *p283*
Bolte, Johann Heinrich Philipp; America, 1854 ***7420.1*** *p116*
*Wife:*Wilhelmine Justine Bicknase
With 4 sons & 3 daughters
Bolte, Johann Konrad; America, 1881 ***7420.1*** *p319*
Bolte, Lorenz; Port uncertain, 1836 ***7420.1*** *p10*
Bolte, Otto Eduard Heinrich; London, Eng., 1897 ***7420.1*** *p373*
Bolte, Richard 64; Ontario, 1871 ***1823.17*** *p13*
Bolte, Sophie Wilhelmine Christine *SEE* Bolte, Mr.
Bolte, Wilhelm; America, 1855 ***7420.1*** *p135*
With family & sister
Bolte, Wilhelmine Justine Bicknase *SEE* Bolte, Johann Heinrich Philipp
Bolten, Thomas 39; Ontario, 1871 ***1823.17*** *p13*
Bolter, Richard 64; Ontario, 1871 ***1823.17*** *p13*
Bolting, C.H.T.; Cleveland, OH, 1892-1893 ***9722.10*** *p117*
Bolton, Alexander; Illinois, 1860 ***6079.1*** *p2*
Bolton, Charles; Illinois, 1851 ***6079.1*** *p2*
Bolton, Charles 25; Ontario, 1871 ***1823.17*** *p13*
Bolton, Charles 37; Ontario, 1871 ***1823.21*** *p30*
Bolton, Eleanor 4; Quebec, 1870 ***8364.32*** *p22*
Bolton, George; Illinois, 1855 ***6079.1*** *p2*
Bolton, James; Illinois, 1851 ***6079.1*** *p2*
Bolton, James 36; Ontario, 1871 ***1823.21*** *p30*
Bolton, James 37; Ontario, 1871 ***1823.21*** *p30*
Bolton, James 46; Ontario, 1871 ***1823.17*** *p13*
Bolton, John 49; Ontario, 1871 ***1823.17*** *p13*
Bolton, John 69; Ontario, 1871 ***1823.21*** *p30*
Bolton, John Orange 33; Ontario, 1871 ***1823.17*** *p13*
Bolton, Richard 73; Ontario, 1871 ***1823.21*** *p30*
Bolund, F.A.W.; New York, NY, 1843 ***6412.40*** *p147*
Boly, James 43; Ontario, 1871 ***1823.21*** *p30*
Boman, J. O.; North America, 1886 ***6410.15*** *p106*
Boman, Johan Jonasson; North America, 1859 ***6410.15*** *p105*
Boman, Mathias; Cleveland, OH, 1886-1895 ***9722.10*** *p117*
Boman, P.; New York, NY, 1845 ***6412.40*** *p149*
Boman, P. Edv.; New York, NY, 1851 ***6412.40*** *p152*
Bomard, Catharine; Virginia, 1700 ***9230.15*** *p80*
Bombeck, Friedrich Daniel; America, 1857 ***7420.1*** *p158*
With 4 sons & 2 daughters
Bomberger, Andrew; Ohio, 1809-1852 ***4511.35*** *p5*
Bomberger, Nicholas; Ohio, 1809-1852 ***4511.35*** *p5*
Bomberry, John; Toronto, 1844 ***2910.35*** *p113*
Bombrehler, E.; Louisiana, 1874 ***4981.45*** *p295*
Bomerlin, Ernest F.; Ohio, 1809-1852 ***4511.35*** *p5*
Bomers, . . .; Port uncertain, 1835 ***7420.1*** *p8*
Bomers, Hermann Heinrich; England, 1867 ***7420.1*** *p254*
Bomm, Conrad; Ohio, 1809-1852 ***4511.35*** *p5*
Bommer, Barbara 24; Brazil, 1873 ***5475.1*** *p389*
Bommerly, John; Ohio, 1809-1852 ***4511.35*** *p5*
Bomont, William 35; Ontario, 1871 ***1823.21*** *p30*
Bon, C. 30; America, 1840 ***778.6*** *p39*
Bon, Louiss; Virginia, 1700 ***9230.15*** *p81*
Bon, Philipp 27; New Orleans, 1848 ***778.6*** *p39*
Bonacoursy, Jean; Quebec, 1645 ***9221.17*** *p155*
Bonamy, Jean; Quebec, 1654 ***9221.17*** *p305*
Bonander, Alice *SEE* Bonander, John
Bonander, John; St. Paul, MN, 1894 ***1865.50*** *p41*
*Wife:*Alice

Bonar, Nicolas 43; America, 1844 ***778.6*** *p39*
Bonas, Michael; Wisconsin, 1901 ***6795.8*** *p176*
Bond, Abraham 32; Ontario, 1871 ***1823.21*** *p30*
Bond, Benjamin; Jamaica, 1778 ***8529.30*** *p12A*
Bond, Bridget 32; Ontario, 1871 ***1823.21*** *p30*
Bond, Henry; New York, NY, 1840 ***3274.56*** *p100*
Bond, J.; Quebec, 1870 ***8364.32*** *p22*
Bond, James 54; Ontario, 1871 ***1823.21*** *p30*
Bond, John 40; Ontario, 1871 ***1823.21*** *p30*
Bond, John 60; Ontario, 1871 ***1823.21*** *p30*
Bond, Robert 38; Ontario, 1871 ***1823.21*** *p30*
Bond, Stephen 62; Ontario, 1871 ***1823.21*** *p30*
Bond, Thomas 50; Ontario, 1871 ***1823.21*** *p30*
Bond, Walter 18; Quebec, 1870 ***8364.32*** *p22*
Bond, William J. 24; Indiana, 1889-1895 ***9076.20*** *p74*
Bonde, Jean N.; Louisiana, 1874-1875 ***4981.45*** *p298*
Bondel, Hermann Friedrich; America, 1861 ***7420.1*** *p203*
Bondel, Karl; America, 1897 ***7420.1*** *p373*
Bondenet, Claude 46; America, 1842 ***778.6*** *p39*
Bondes, Elisabetha; America, 1865 ***2526.43*** *p164*
Bondes, Margaretha; America, 1855 ***2526.43*** *p164*
Bondies, A.; Texas, 1852 ***3435.45*** *p35*
Bonditz, Carl 26; Mississippi, 1847 ***778.6*** *p39*
Bonditz, Georg 18; Mississippi, 1847 ***778.6*** *p39*
Bondu, Rene; Montreal, 1653 ***9221.17*** *p283*
Bondy, Jacques; Montreal, 1658 ***9221.17*** *p388*
Bondy, Rene; Montreal, 1653 ***9221.17*** *p283*
Bone, James 62; Ontario, 1871 ***1823.21*** *p30*
Bone, Philippe; Quebec, 1659 ***9221.17*** *p413*
Bone, William; Ohio, 1809-1852 ***4511.35*** *p5*
Bone, William 33; Ontario, 1871 ***1823.21*** *p31*
Bonel, Nicolas 41; America, 1847 ***778.6*** *p39*
Bonemer, L. 40; New Orleans, 1840 ***778.6*** *p39*
Bonenfant, Mathurin 25; Montreal, 1648 ***9221.17*** *p205*
Boner, Hugh; Philadelphia, 1778 ***8529.30*** *p2A*
Boner, James; Illinois, 1852 ***6079.1*** *p2*
Boner, John D.; Ohio, 1809-1852 ***4511.35*** *p5*
Boner, Peter; Ohio, 1809-1852 ***4511.35*** *p5*
Boners, Arthur G.; North Carolina, 1850 ***1088.45*** *p3*
Bones, Friedrich; Wisconsin, 1882 ***6795.8*** *p225*
Bonet, Mr. 19; America, 1846 ***778.6*** *p39*
Boney, Thomas; Boston, 1775 ***8529.30*** *p2*
Bongoust, Etienne; Quebec, 1645 ***9221.17*** *p151*
Bonheim, David; America, 1865 ***7420.1*** *p229*
Bonheim, Lina; America, 1865 ***7420.1*** *p229*
Bonheur, Marie; Quebec, 1669 ***4514.3*** *p281*
Bonhey, Armand 8; Missouri, 1845 ***778.6*** *p39*
Bonhey, Caroline 5; Missouri, 1845 ***778.6*** *p39*
Bonhey, Charles 43; Missouri, 1845 ***778.6*** *p39*
Bonhey, Emelie 10; Missouri, 1845 ***778.6*** *p40*
Bonhey, Marie 20; Missouri, 1845 ***778.6*** *p40*
Bonhire, Elizabeth 58; Ontario, 1871 ***1823.21*** *p31*
Bonhomme, Guillaume; Quebec, 1645 ***9221.17*** *p151*
*Brother:*Ignace
Bonhomme, Ignace *SEE* Bonhomme, Guillaume
Bonhomme, Nicolas 33; Quebec, 1640 ***9221.17*** *p95*
Boni, Fr. Joseph 64; New Castle, DE, 1817-1818 ***90.20*** *p150*
Boni, Jacques; Montreal, 1642 ***9221.17*** *p123*
Boni, Wendel 63; New Castle, DE, 1817-1818 ***90.20*** *p150*
Bonidon, G. T. 45; New Orleans, 1847 ***778.6*** *p40*
Bonin, Charles 24; Quebec, 1659 ***9221.17*** *p395*
Bonin, Francois; Quebec, 1651 ***9221.17*** *p237*
Bonin, Jacques 30; Quebec, 1647 ***9221.17*** *p172*
Bonin, Marie 20; Quebec, 1657 ***9221.17*** *p354*
Boning, Mr.; America, 1860 ***7420.1*** *p192*
With family
Boning, Carl Wilhelm August; America, 1869 ***7420.1*** *p279*
Boning, Georg Friedrich Wilhelm; America, 1873 ***7420.1*** *p299*
Boning, Heinrich Ernst; America, 1858 ***7420.1*** *p176*
Boning, Sophie Justine Charlotte; America, 1862 ***7420.1*** *p210*
Boniotte, Mr. 45; New Orleans, 1848 ***778.6*** *p40*
Bonis, Theodore 18; New Orleans, 1840 ***778.6*** *p40*
Bonjeu, Hilaire; Quebec, 1642 ***9221.17*** *p113*
Bonker, John 16; Quebec, 1870 ***8364.32*** *p22*
Bonkowski, Jan; Texas, 1896-1904 ***6015.15*** *p9*
Bonkowski, Wladyslaw; Galveston, TX, 1906 ***6015.15*** *p9*
Bonnafourche, Mr. 35; New Orleans, 1840 ***778.6*** *p40*
Bonnard, Nikolaus; America, 1881 ***5475.1*** *p133*
Bonnart, Jean; Quebec, 1646 ***9221.17*** *p161*
*Wife:*Jeanne Richer
Bonnart, Jeanne Richer 45 *SEE* Bonnart, Jean
Bonnat, Barbe 36; America, 1840 ***778.6*** *p40*
Bonnault, Isaac; Quebec, 1643 ***9221.17*** *p129*
Bonnaveau, Jean-Bte. 21; New Orleans, 1840 ***778.6*** *p40*
Bonnaveau, Jeanne Boileau 20; New Orleans, 1840 ***778.6*** *p40*
Bonnaveau, Pierre 45; New Orleans, 1840 ***778.6*** *p40*
Bonneau, Andre; Quebec, 1658 ***9221.17*** *p376*
Bonneau, Helene; Quebec, 1667 ***4514.3*** *p281*
Bonneau, Jean 34; America, 1845 ***778.6*** *p40*
Bonneau, Jean Dominique 34; New Orleans, 1845 ***778.6*** *p40*
Bonneau, Pierre; Quebec, 1654 ***9221.17*** *p305*
Bonnecaze, Eloina 21; New Orleans, 1848 ***778.6*** *p40*
Bonne deMissegle, Louis de; Quebec, 1749 ***2314.30*** *p170*
Bonne deMissegle, Louis de; Quebec, 1749 ***2314.30*** *p176*
Bonnefons, Pierre; Montreal, 1661 ***9221.17*** *p471*
Bonnefoy, Marguerite; Quebec, 1667 ***4514.3*** *p281*
Bonnell, George 33; Ontario, 1871 ***1823.21*** *p31*
Bonnem, Bernhard; America, 1882 ***5475.1*** *p447*
Bonnem, Gustav; America, 1882 ***5475.1*** *p206*
Bonnem, Henriette; Cleveland, OH, 1885 ***5475.1*** *p209*
Bonnem, Julius; America, 1890 ***5475.1*** *p448*
Bonnem, Moses; America, 1880 ***5475.1*** *p209*
Bonnemer, Florent 47; Quebec, 1647 ***9221.17*** *p172*
Bonner, Charles; Ohio, 1843 ***2763.1*** *p7*
Bonner, Emme Pfeifer *SEE* Bonner, Jakob
Bonner, Hugh; Philadelphia, 1778 ***8529.30*** *p2A*
Bonner, Jakob; New York, 1898 ***5475.1*** *p426*
*Wife:*Emme Pfeifer
Bonner, John; Marston's Wharf, 1782 ***8529.30*** *p10*
Bonner, Michel; America, 1800-1899 ***5475.1*** *p50*
Bonner, Peter Michel; America, 1895 ***5475.1*** *p425*
Bonner, Peter Michel; New York, 1885 ***5475.1*** *p423*
Bonner, Thomas; Toronto, 1844 ***2910.35*** *p113*
Bonnet, Mr. 23; America, 1843 ***778.6*** *p40*
Bonnet, Alexandre 34; New Orleans, 1848 ***778.6*** *p40*
Bonnet, Augustus; Ohio, 1809-1852 ***4511.35*** *p5*
Bonnet, Eliza 50; America, 1844 ***778.6*** *p40*
Bonnet, Etienne 35; America, 1843 ***778.6*** *p40*
Bonnet, Francoise 8; America, 1843 ***778.6*** *p40*
Bonnet, Guillaume; Quebec, 1658 ***9221.17*** *p377*
Bonnet, J. P. 45; America, 1842 ***778.6*** *p40*
Bonnet, Jacques; Quebec, 1649 ***9221.17*** *p209*
Bonnet, Jeanne 3; America, 1843 ***778.6*** *p40*
Bonnet, Jeanne 39; America, 1843 ***778.6*** *p40*
Bonnet, Joseph 53; America, 1844 ***778.6*** *p40*
Bonnet, Louis 3 months; America, 1843 ***778.6*** *p40*
Bonnet, Marie 4; America, 1843 ***778.6*** *p40*
Bonney, John F.; Illinois, 1918 ***6007.60*** *p9*
Bonnoront, George; Ohio, 1840-1897 ***8365.35*** *p15*
Bonnot, Adele 13; America, 1843 ***778.6*** *p40*
Bonnot, Appoline 15; America, 1843 ***778.6*** *p40*
Bonnot, Charles 6 months; America, 1843 ***778.6*** *p40*
Bonnot, Emil 3; America, 1843 ***778.6*** *p40*
Bonnot, Francois 7; America, 1843 ***778.6*** *p40*
Bonnot, Francoise 34; America, 1843 ***778.6*** *p40*
Bonnot, Jean 42; America, 1843 ***778.6*** *p40*
Bonnot, Joseph 5; America, 1843 ***778.6*** *p40*
Bonnot, Jules 9; America, 1843 ***778.6*** *p41*
Bononio, Autmino; Louisiana, 1874 ***4981.45*** *p131*
Bonorden, C.; America, 1852 ***7420.1*** *p85*
Bonorden, Fr. W.; America, 1855 ***7420.1*** *p135*
Bonorden, Fr.W.; America, 1854 ***7420.1*** *p116*
Bonorden, Friedrich Christian; America, 1840 ***7420.1*** *p17*
Bonsevard, Adelle 15; America, 1848 ***778.6*** *p41*
Bonsevard, Adelle 38; America, 1848 ***778.6*** *p41*
Bonsevard, Joseph 17; America, 1848 ***778.6*** *p41*
Bonsignes, Mr. 33; America, 1745 ***778.6*** *p41*
Bonsold, James; North Carolina, 1852 ***1088.45*** *p3*
Bonsor, John 58; Ontario, 1871 ***1823.21*** *p31*
Bonsor, Matilda 37; Ontario, 1871 ***1823.21*** *p31*
Bonstead, Charles H.; North Carolina, 1853 ***1088.45*** *p3*
Bont, Leonard; Illinois, 1834-1900 ***6020.5*** *p131*
Bontaup, J.; Louisiana, 1836-1840 ***4981.45*** *p212*
Bontemps, Francois 32; Quebec, 1646 ***9221.17*** *p161*
Bontemps, Joseph 28; America, 1846 ***778.6*** *p41*
Bonvalet, Mr. 40; America, 1846 ***778.6*** *p41*
Bonvie, H. 21; America, 1848 ***778.6*** *p41*
Bonville, Pierre 30; New Orleans, 1848 ***778.6*** *p41*
Bonwitt, Therese; America, 1863 ***7420.1*** *p217*
Bony, Fr. Joseph 64; New Castle, DE, 1817-1818 ***90.20*** *p150*
Bony, Jos. 26; Port uncertain, 1846 ***778.6*** *p41*
Bony, Wendel 63; New Castle, DE, 1817-1818 ***90.20*** *p150*
Bonyfee, M. 37; Port uncertain, 1745 ***778.6*** *p41*
Bonyfer, M. 37; Port uncertain, 1745 ***778.6*** *p41*
Bonzon, Ferdinand; Louisiana, 1836-1841 ***4981.45*** *p208*
Boodey, Zechariah; New Hampshire, 1703-1803 ***9228.50*** *p124*
Boodman, Bessie; Detroit, 1929-1930 ***6214.5*** *p69*
Boody, Mr.; Boston, n.d. ***9228.50*** *p124*
Boody, John; Salem, MA, 1674 ***9228.50*** *p646*
Boody, Moses; Massachusetts, 1616-1716 ***9228.50*** *p646*
Boody, Nicholas; Massachusetts, 1730 ***9228.50*** *p139*
Booge, Hanna Justine Wilhelmine; America, 1882 ***7420.1*** *p328*
*Son:*Heinrich Friedrich Wilhelm
With mother-in-law
*Son:*Friedrich Wilhelm
*Son:*Carl Ludwig Wilhelm
*Son:*Heinrich Friedrich Wilhelm
Bookham, Mary A. 39; Michigan, 1880 ***4491.42*** *p5*
Bookman, Henry 27; Ontario, 1871 ***1823.21*** *p31*
Booland, Michael; Ohio, 1856 ***3580.20*** *p31*
Booland, Michael; Ohio, 1856 ***6020.12*** *p6*
Booland, William 19; Halifax, N.S., n.d. ***1833.5*** *p7*
Booland, William 19; Halifax, N.S., n.d. ***8445.10*** *p7*
Boom, Elias; Colorado, 1896 ***1029.59*** *p11*
Boom, Oeda Vos; Colorado, 1896 ***1029.59*** *p11*
Boone, Joshua C.; Ohio, 1878 ***3580.20*** *p31*
Boone, Joshua C.; Ohio, 1878 ***6020.12*** *p6*
Booren, August P.; Minnesota, 1882-1885 ***1865.50*** *p41*
Boory, Daniel; Ohio, 1809-1852 ***4511.35*** *p5*
Boos, Etienne 60; America, 1844 ***778.6*** *p41*
Boos, Helena 46; America, 1855 ***5475.1*** *p359*
Boos, Jacob; Illinois, 1860 ***6079.1*** *p2*
Boos, Johann; America, 1881 ***5475.1*** *p332*
Boos, Katharina *SEE* Boos, Nikolaus
Boos, Katharina Huwer *SEE* Boos, Nikolaus
Boos, Mathias; America, 1855 ***5475.1*** *p331*
Boos, Nik. Wilhelm; America, 1867 ***5475.1*** *p225*
Boos, Nikolaus *SEE* Boos, Nikolaus
Boos, Nikolaus; America, 1867 ***5475.1*** *p225*
*Wife:*Katharina Huwer
*Daughter:*Katharina
*Son:*Nikolaus
Boos, Susanna; Iowa, 1880 ***5475.1*** *p272*
Boost, Charles 47; Ontario, 1871 ***1823.21*** *p31*
Boote, William Rowland; New Jersey, 1795 ***3845.2*** *p128*
Booth, Charles 17; Quebec, 1870 ***8364.32*** *p22*
Booth, Edward 30; Ontario, 1871 ***1823.21*** *p31*
Booth, Edward 44; Ontario, 1871 ***1823.17*** *p13*
Booth, Eliza; Jamestown, VA, 1633 ***1658.20*** *p211*
Booth, George 40; Ontario, 1871 ***1823.21*** *p31*
Booth, George 45; Ontario, 1871 ***1823.17*** *p13*
Booth, James 32; Ontario, 1871 ***1823.17*** *p13*
Booth, James 56; Ontario, 1871 ***1823.17*** *p13*
Booth, James 19; Quebec, 1870 ***8364.32*** *p22*
Booth, Joseph 37; Ontario, 1871 ***1823.21*** *p31*
Booth, Joseph, Jr. 67; Ontario, 1871 ***1823.17*** *p13*
Booth, Ralph 49; Ontario, 1871 ***1823.17*** *p13*
Booth, Richard 40; Ontario, 1871 ***1823.21*** *p31*
Booth, Robert 50; Ontario, 1871 ***1823.21*** *p31*
Booth, Sarah Jane 36; Ontario, 1871 ***1823.21*** *p31*
Booth, Thomas 69; Ontario, 1871 ***1823.17*** *p13*
Booth, W. 14; Quebec, 1870 ***8364.32*** *p22*
Booth, William 35; Ontario, 1871 ***1823.21*** *p31*
Booth, Wineford 70; Ontario, 1871 ***1823.21*** *p31*
Boothby, Joseph 37; Ontario, 1871 ***1823.21*** *p31*
Boothe, William 60; Ontario, 1871 ***1823.17*** *p13*
Booty, John; Detroit, 1929-1930 ***6214.5*** *p61*
Booz, Leonhard M. Lorenz; America, 1883 ***179.55*** *p19*
Bopp, Johann Georg; Port uncertain, 1887 ***170.15*** *p21*
Bopp, Nikolaus 19; Pennsylvania, 1863 ***170.15*** *p21*
Bopp, Valentin 23; Pennsylvania, 1899 ***170.15*** *p21*
Bor, Matej; Milwaukee, 1888 ***2853.20*** *p163*
Boran, Mr. 18; New Orleans, 1848 ***778.6*** *p41*
Boran, Peter; Ohio, 1809-1852 ***4511.35*** *p5*
Borawski, Israel 27; New York, NY, 1878 ***9253.2*** *p45*
Borchard, F.A.; Iowa, 1896 ***1211.15*** *p9*
Borchard, J. 25; Montreal, 1844 ***778.6*** *p41*
Borcherding, Mr.; America, 1854 ***7420.1*** *p116*
Borcherding, Carl; America, 1850 ***7420.1*** *p69*
Borcherding, Christine *SEE* Borcherding, Eleonore
Borcherding, Eleonore; America, 1851 ***7420.1*** *p78*
*Daughter:*Louise
*Daughter:*Christine
Borcherding, Louise *SEE* Borcherding, Eleonore
Borchers, Miss; America, 1867 ***7420.1*** *p254*
Borchers, Mr.; America, 1853 ***7420.1*** *p103*
Borchers, Catharina Engel; America, 1867 ***7420.1*** *p254*
*Son:*Hans Heinrich Conrad
Borchers, Christian; Ohio, 1809-1852 ***4511.35*** *p5*
Borchers, Gottlieb; America, 1868 ***7420.1*** *p269*
Borchers, Hans Heinrich Conrad *SEE* Borchers, Catharina Engel Blume
Borchers, Johann Philipp; America, 1850 ***7420.1*** *p69*
Borchert, Anna 22; New York, NY, 1894 ***6512.1*** *p231*
Borchert, August 50; New York, NY, 1894 ***6512.1*** *p231*
Borchert, Emilie 40; New York, NY, 1894 ***6512.1*** *p231*
Borchert, Emma 4; New York, NY, 1894 ***6512.1*** *p231*
Borchert, Gustav 8; New York, NY, 1894 ***6512.1*** *p231*
Borchert, Helene 6; New York, NY, 1894 ***6512.1*** *p231*
Borchert, Julius 12; New York, NY, 1894 ***6512.1*** *p231*
Borchert, Marie 18; New York, NY, 1894 ***6512.1*** *p231*
Bordages, Francois 20; Montreal, 1845 ***778.6*** *p41*
Bordas, E. 60; New Orleans, 1840 ***778.6*** *p41*

Bordat, Denis; Quebec, 1642 ***9221.17*** *p113*
Bordat, Jean; Quebec, 1660 ***9221.17*** *p432*
Borde, Jacqueline; Quebec, 1651 ***9221.17*** *p237*
Bordel, Jean; Quebec, 1659 ***9221.17*** *p413*
Bordenave, J. J. 29; New Orleans, 1843 ***778.6*** *p41*
Bordenave, Paul; Louisiana, 1874-1875 ***4981.45*** *p298*
Borders, Charles; Louisiana, 1874 ***4981.45*** *p131*
Bordes, Bertrand 23; New Orleans, 1845 ***778.6*** *p41*
Bordes, Francois 20; New Orleans, 1845 ***778.6*** *p41*
Bordiat, M. 18; America, 1848 ***778.6*** *p41*
Bordier, Francois; Montreal, 1661 ***9221.17*** *p471*
Bordis, C. J. 30; America, 1843 ***778.6*** *p41*
Borecky, Jan; Chicago, 1828-1910 ***2853.20*** *p405*
Borecky, Jan; Milwaukee, 1854 ***2853.20*** *p292*
Borecky, Joe; Texas, 1896-1904 ***6015.15*** *p23*
Borel, Eugenie 5; New Orleans, 1848 ***778.6*** *p41*
Borel, Expert 38; New Orleans, 1848 ***778.6*** *p41*
Borel, J. 50; Port uncertain, 1844 ***778.6*** *p41*
Borel, Rosalie 50; New Orleans, 1848 ***778.6*** *p41*
Borella, Albert 22; America, 1846 ***778.6*** *p41*
Borello, Savano; Louisiana, 1874-1875 ***4981.45*** *p298*
Borelly, Jean 45; Port uncertain, 1842 ***778.6*** *p41*
Boren, August P.; Minnesota, 1882-1885 ***1865.50*** *p41*
Borens, Johannetta *SEE* Borens, Peter
Borens, M. Susanna *SEE* Borens, Peter
Borens, Maria Jager *SEE* Borens, Peter
Borens, Michel *SEE* Borens, Peter
Borens, Peter; America, 1879 ***5475.1*** *p267*
*Wife:*Maria Jager
*Son:*Michel
*Daughter:*Johannetta
*Daughter:*M. Susanna
Borg, Mr. 19; America, 1841 ***778.6*** *p41*
Borg, Agathe 5; New York, NY, 1893 ***1883.7*** *p40*
Borg, Anna 8; New York, NY, 1893 ***1883.7*** *p40*
Borg, Barbara 20; New York, NY, 1893 ***1883.7*** *p40*
Borg, Barbara 40; New York, NY, 1893 ***1883.7*** *p40*
Borg, David 4; New York, NY, 1893 ***1883.7*** *p40*
Borg, Gerhard 18; New York, NY, 1893 ***1883.7*** *p40*
Borg, Isaak; America, 1866 ***5475.1*** *p507*
Borg, Jacob 16; New York, NY, 1893 ***1883.7*** *p40*
Borg, Jacob 47; New York, NY, 1893 ***1883.7*** *p40*
Borg, Johann 10; New York, NY, 1893 ***1883.7*** *p40*
Borg, Johannetta *SEE* Borg, Moses Simon
Borg, Katharina 11; New York, NY, 1893 ***1883.7*** *p40*
Borg, Marie 14; New York, NY, 1893 ***1883.7*** *p40*
Borg, Moses Simon; America, 1856 ***5475.1*** *p508*
*Sister:*Johannetta
Borgens, Constins 23; Halifax, N.S., 1902 ***1860.4*** *p39*
Borgens, Jacob; Halifax, N.S., 1902 ***1860.4*** *p39*
Borgens, Johannes 24; Halifax, N.S., 1902 ***1860.4*** *p39*
Borger, Anna Maria; America, 1894 ***5475.1*** *p551*
*Son:*Johann
*Son:*Friedrich
Borger, Franz; South America, 1923 ***8023.44*** *p372*
Borger, Friedrich *SEE* Borger, Anna Maria Billo
Borger, Johann; America, 1879 ***5475.1*** *p447*
Borger, Johann *SEE* Borger, Anna Maria Billo
Borger, Johannes; America, 1842 ***2526.42*** *p199*
With wife
With daughter 19
With daughter 17
With daughter 14
With son 24
With son 12
Borgesson, Carl M.; Cleveland, OH, 1871-1889 ***9722.10*** *p117*
Borghard, Wilhelm; America, 1855 ***7420.1*** *p135*
With wife & daughter
Borghardt, Caroline; America, 1867 ***7420.1*** *p254*
Borglund, John C.; Colorado, 1884 ***1029.59*** *p11*
Borgstrom, P.; New York, NY, 1846 ***6412.40*** *p149*
Borgstrom, Sigfrid; New York, NY, 1849 ***6412.40*** *p151*
Borgward, Leo; America, 1892 ***7420.1*** *p365*
With mother
Borhofen, Maria; Iowa, 1880 ***5475.1*** *p350*
Borhofen, Mathias; America, 1868 ***5475.1*** *p349*
Borhofen, Peter; America, 1867 ***5475.1*** *p349*
Boria, Pierre 19; America, 1847 ***778.6*** *p41*
Boriskie, Joe; Texas, 1896-1904 ***6015.15*** *p23*
Borjerson, John A.; Colorado, 1887 ***1029.59*** *p11*
Borjeson, Carl; New Orleans, 1847 ***6412.40*** *p149*
Borjesson, Joseph Alban; Miami, 1935 ***4984.12*** *p39*
Borjesson, Petter; New York, NY, 1844 ***6412.40*** *p148*
Bork, Bertha Mathilde; Wisconsin, 1900 ***6795.8*** *p221*
Bork, Felix 25; Louisiana, 1840 ***778.6*** *p41*
Bork, Johann Friederick; Wisconsin, 1894 ***6795.8*** *p221*
Borkenhagen, Julianna Henriette; Wisconsin, 1867 ***6795.8*** *p17*
Borking, Ernst; America, 1868 ***7420.1*** *p277*
With wife & family
Borkorky, Cancilie 2; New York, NY, 1894 ***6512.1*** *p183*
Borkorky, Michaline 20; New York, NY, 1894 ***6512.1*** *p182*
Borkoski, Gabrala; Wisconsin, 1886 ***6795.8*** *p137*
Borkowska, Kazimiera 23; New York, NY, 1911 ***6533.11*** *p9*
Borland, James 37; Ontario, 1871 ***1823.21*** *p31*
Born, August Herman; Wisconsin, 1896 ***6795.8*** *p85*
Born, August Julius; Wisconsin, 1886 ***6795.8*** *p168*
Born, Johann; America, 1847 ***5475.1*** *p485*
Born, Otto Julius; Wisconsin, 1914 ***6795.8*** *p165*
Borne, Carolina 16; America, 1844 ***778.6*** *p41*
Borne, Georges 24; America, 1844 ***778.6*** *p42*
Borne, Julius; New York, 1860 ***358.56*** *p3*
Borne, Jullie 1; New Orleans, 1848 ***778.6*** *p42*
Borne, Louis 22; America, 1844 ***778.6*** *p42*
Borne, Louise 23; New Orleans, 1848 ***778.6*** *p42*
Bornemann, . . .; America, 1851 ***7420.1*** *p78*
With family
Bornemann, . . .; America, 1852 ***7420.1*** *p86*
Bornemann, Widow; America, 1852 ***7420.1*** *p86*
Bornemann, Anton Heinrich; America, 1883 ***7420.1*** *p335*
Bornemann, Carl Friedrich *SEE* Bornemann, Carl Heinrich
Bornemann, Carl Friedrich Wilhelm; America, 1871 ***7420.1*** *p289*
Bornemann, Carl Heinrich; America, 1882 ***7420.1*** *p327*
*Brother:*Carl Friedrich
Bornemann, Caroline Sophie; America, 1883 ***7420.1*** *p335*
Bornemann, Franz; America, 1870 ***7420.1*** *p286*
Bornemann, Franz; Port uncertain, 1858 ***7420.1*** *p176*
Bornemann, Heinrich; America, 1851 ***7420.1*** *p78*
With wife
Bornemann, Sophie; America, 1857 ***7420.1*** *p158*
Bornemann, Mrs. Wilhelm; America, 1868 ***7420.1*** *p269*
Borner, Georg; America, 1867 ***7919.3*** *p531*
With family
Bornhagen, John Herman; Wisconsin, 1891 ***6795.8*** *p71*
Bornick, August; Wisconsin, 1890 ***6795.8*** *p41*
Bornick, Wilhelmine; Wisconsin, 1866 ***6795.8*** *p46*
Bornicke, August; Wisconsin, 1876 ***6795.8*** *p115*
Bornie, Martin; North Carolina, 1843 ***1088.45*** *p3*
Bornson, Peter; Illinois, 1855 ***6079.1*** *p2*
Bornstein, Leon; Miami, 1935 ***4984.12*** *p39*
Bornstock, James 50; Ontario, 1871 ***1823.17*** *p13*
Borova, Marie; Wisconsin, 1876 ***2853.20*** *p336*
Borowski, Walter; Detroit, 1929-1930 ***6214.5*** *p65*
Borowy, Jozef 20; New York, NY, 1911 ***6533.11*** *p10*
Borq, Mr. 18; America, 1841 ***778.6*** *p42*
Borq, Mr. 18; America, 1841 ***778.6*** *p42*
Borreau, Mr. 18; America, 1842 ***778.6*** *p42*
Borrel, Antoine 40; America, 1842 ***778.6*** *p42*
Borremans, Laurent; Illinois, 1856 ***6079.1*** *p2*
Borriden, Mr. 50; America, 1846 ***778.6*** *p42*
Borrilum, Ange 45; America, 1847 ***778.6*** *p42*
Borroughs, George 31; Ontario, 1871 ***1823.21*** *p31*
Borrowdale, Ann; Roxbury, MA, 1645 ***1642*** *p107*
Borschneck, Marie 27; America, 1846 ***778.6*** *p42*
Borsing, Carl Ernst; America, 1885 ***7420.1*** *p347*
Bortel, Anthony; Ohio, 1809-1852 ***4511.35*** *p5*
Bortel, Nicholas; Ohio, 1809-1852 ***4511.35*** *p5*
Borthwick, Alexander 59; Ontario, 1871 ***1823.17*** *p13*
Borthwick, Christopher 34; Ontario, 1871 ***1823.21*** *p31*
Bortle, Anthony; Ohio, 1809-1852 ***4511.35*** *p3*
Bortle, Anthony; Ohio, 1809-1852 ***4511.35*** *p3*
Bortmann, Jean P. 32; New Orleans, 1848 ***778.6*** *p42*
Bory, Dr.; America, 1847 ***778.6*** *p42*
Bory, Laurent 24; Montreal, 1662 ***9221.17*** *p496*
Bosack, Bridget; Detroit, 1929 ***1640.55*** *p117*
Bosak, Frantisek; Texas, 1860 ***2853.20*** *p74*
Bosan, Theodore; Colorado, 1879 ***1029.59*** *p12*
Bosau, Theodore; Colorado, 1893 ***1029.59*** *p12*
Bosc, Victor 30; America, 1848 ***778.6*** *p42*
Bosch, Adam 45; New York, NY, 1893 ***1883.7*** *p38*
Bosch, Anna 17; New York, NY, 1893 ***1883.7*** *p38*
Bosch, Antoine 30; New Orleans, 1848 ***778.6*** *p42*
Bosch, Anton; Venezuela, 1843 ***3899.5*** *p540*
Bosch, Barbara 33; New Orleans, 1848 ***778.6*** *p42*
Bosch, Catharina 44; New York, NY, 1893 ***1883.7*** *p38*
Bosch, Georg 12; New York, NY, 1893 ***1883.7*** *p38*
Bosch, Georg Heinrich 26; America, 1897 ***5475.1*** *p40*
Bosch, Ignac 16; New York, NY, 1893 ***1883.7*** *p38*
Bosch, Joseph 19; New York, NY, 1893 ***1883.7*** *p38*
Bosch, Joseph; Venezuela, 1843 ***3899.5*** *p540*
Bosch, Nicolaus 1 months; New York, NY, 1893 ***1883.7*** *p38*
Bosch, Peter 3; New York, NY, 1893 ***1883.7*** *p38*
Bosch, Wilhelm; Venezuela, 1843 ***3899.5*** *p540*
Bosch, Xavier 6 months; New Orleans, 1848 ***778.6*** *p42*
Bosch Children, . . .; Venezuela, 1843 ***3899.5*** *p540*
Boschen, Amrhen; Wisconsin, 1892 ***6795.8*** *p233*
Boschliss, Louis 25; Louisiana, 1847 ***778.6*** *p42*
Boscker, Elias; Ohio, 1809-1852 ***4511.35*** *p5*
Bosdet, Barnard; Portsmouth, NH, 1719 ***9228.50*** *p125*
Bosdet, Nicholas; Massachusetts, 1730 ***9228.50*** *p139*
Bose, Mr.; America, 1856 ***7420.1*** *p145*
*Son:*Carl Friedrich
*Son:*Christian Heinrich
*Son:*Carl Friedrich Wilhelm
With wife & daughter
*Son:*Anton Heinrich
*Son:*Ernst Wilhelm Ferdinand
Bose, Anton Heinrich *SEE* Bose, Mr.
Bose, Carl Friedrich *SEE* Bose, Mr.
Bose, Carl Friedrich Wilhelm *SEE* Bose, Mr.
Bose, Christian; America, 1865 ***7420.1*** *p229*
With wife & 3 daughters
With son 18
With son 5
Bose, Christian Heinrich *SEE* Bose, Mr.
Bose, Ernst Wilhelm Ferdinand *SEE* Bose, Mr.
Bose, Friedrich Gottlieb; America, 1853 ***7420.1*** *p103*
Bose, Gottlieb Heinrich; America, 1870 ***7420.1*** *p283*
Bosecker, Elias; Ohio, 1809-1852 ***4511.35*** *p5*
Bose Family ; America, 1854 ***7420.1*** *p117*
Bosen, Elisabeth 7 *SEE* Bosen, Mathias
Bosen, Magdalena Breiter 31 *SEE* Bosen, Mathias
Bosen, Margarethe 5 *SEE* Bosen, Mathias
Bosen, Maria 1 *SEE* Bosen, Mathias
Bosen, Mathias 33; America, 1846 ***5475.1*** *p345*
*Wife:*Magdalena Breiter 31
*Daughter:*Margarethe 5
*Daughter:*Maria 1
*Daughter:*Elisabeth 7
Bosendahl, Rudolph Eduard Viktor; Port uncertain, 1835 ***7420.1*** *p8*
Boset, Annie 22; Halifax, N.S., 1902 ***1860.4*** *p43*
Boset, Christine 8 months; Halifax, N.S., 1902 ***1860.4*** *p44*
Boset, Johan 30; Halifax, N.S., 1902 ***1860.4*** *p43*
Boset, Joseph 59; Halifax, N.S., 1902 ***1860.4*** *p43*
Boset, Katrina 53; Halifax, N.S., 1902 ***1860.4*** *p43*
Boset, Marie 24; Halifax, N.S., 1902 ***1860.4*** *p43*
Boset, Mary 28; Halifax, N.S., 1902 ***1860.4*** *p44*
Boset, Paoli 3; Halifax, N.S., 1902 ***1860.4*** *p44*
Boset, Walter 19; Halifax, N.S., 1902 ***1860.4*** *p43*
Boset, Wawara 20; Halifax, N.S., 1902 ***1860.4*** *p44*
Boskett, John; New York, 1776 ***8529.30*** *p10*
Bosman, Adolphe; Philadelphia, 1880 ***1494.20*** *p13*
Bosman, Adolphe *SEE* Bosman, Louis Joseph
Bosman, Auguste *SEE* Bosman, Louis Joseph
Bosman, Dieudonne Joseph *SEE* Bosman, Louis Joseph
Bosman, Gustave *SEE* Bosman, Louis Joseph
Bosman, Jeanne *SEE* Bosman, Louis Joseph
Bosman, Louis Joseph; Wisconsin, 1854-1858 ***1495.20*** *p50*
*Wife:*Marie Catherine Liesse
*Child:*Dieudonne Joseph
*Child:*Veronique
*Child:*Marie Antoinette
*Child:*Marie Catherine
*Child:*Auguste
*Child:*Gustave
*Child:*Adolphe
*Child:*Jeanne
Bosman, Marie Antoinette *SEE* Bosman, Louis Joseph
Bosman, Marie Catherine *SEE* Bosman, Louis Joseph
Bosman, Marie Catherine Liesse *SEE* Bosman, Louis Joseph
Bosman, Veronique *SEE* Bosman, Louis Joseph
Bosovski, Mathilda 28; Portland, ME, 1910 ***970.38*** *p76*
Bosovski, Peter 6; Portland, ME, 1910 ***970.38*** *p76*
Bosovski, Samuel 2; Portland, ME, 1910 ***970.38*** *p76*
Boss, Jacob; Ohio, 1809-1852 ***4511.35*** *p5*
Boss, John; Ohio, 1840-1897 ***8365.35*** *p15*
Boss, Joseph; South Carolina, 1860 ***6155.4*** *p18*
Boss, Katharina; America, 1881 ***5475.1*** *p273*
Bossamannick, Jacob 19; New York, NY, 1878 ***9253.2*** *p44*
Bossay, Charles; Illinois, 1852 ***6079.1*** *p2*
Bosse, Francois; Virginia, 1700 ***9230.15*** *p80*
Bosse, Henry; North Carolina, 1854 ***1088.45*** *p3*
Bossen, Hans; Iowa, 1892 ***1211.15*** *p9*
Bossen, Peter; Iowa, 1896 ***1211.15*** *p9*
Bosset, Pierre; Quebec, 1662 ***9221.17*** *p480*
Bossey, Sarah 27; Ontario, 1871 ***1823.17*** *p13*
Bossong, Jakob 52; America, 1881 ***5475.1*** *p420*
Bossuat, Louis; Quebec, 1641 ***9221.17*** *p101*
Bosswald, Mrs. Johann Anton; America, 1856 ***2526.42*** *p139*
With 7 children
Bosswald, Johannes; America, 1847 ***2526.42*** *p139*
With wife & 4 children
Bost, Dorothea; America, 1881 ***5475.1*** *p429*
Bost, Elisabeth 15 *SEE* Bost, Valentin

Bost, Johann 11 *SEE* Bost, Valentin
Bost, Johann, III; America, 1860 ***5475.1*** *p412*
Bost, John; Colorado, 1889 ***1029.59*** *p12*
Bost, John; Colorado, 1895 ***1029.59*** *p12*
Bost, Katharina 18 *SEE* Bost, Valentin
Bost, Louis 10 *SEE* Bost, Valentin
Bost, Ludwig; America, 1850 ***5475.1*** *p403*
Bost, Ludwig; America, 1865-1870 ***5475.1*** *p412*
Bost, Luise 22 *SEE* Bost, Valentin
Bost, Maria 13 *SEE* Bost, Valentin
Bost, Maria 20 *SEE* Bost, Valentin
Bost, Valentin; America, 1852 ***5475.1*** *p387*
*Sister:*Luise
*Sister:*Elisabeth
*Brother:*Johann
*Brother:*Louis
*Sister:*Maria
*Sister:*Maria
*Sister:*Katharina
Bostian, George; Ohio, 1809-1852 ***4511.35*** *p5*
Bostick, Thomas 18; Ontario, 1871 ***1823.17*** *p13*
Bostick, Thomas 49; Ontario, 1871 ***1823.17*** *p13*
Bostrom, C.; New York, NY, 1845 ***6412.40*** *p149*
Boswell, Eliza 50; Ontario, 1871 ***1823.21*** *p31*
Boswell, George 57; Ontario, 1871 ***1823.21*** *p31*
Boswell, Mary; America, 1750 ***1220.12*** *p874*
Boswell, Nathaniel 37; Ontario, 1871 ***1823.17*** *p13*
Boszen, George; Washington, 1882 ***2770.40*** *p135*
Botell, Alfred 13; Quebec, 1870 ***8364.32*** *p22*
Botelson, Nels; Illinois, 1861 ***4487.25*** *p54*
Botfaite, Suzanne 19; Quebec, 1649 ***9221.17*** *p210*
Both, Johann; Brazil, 1846 ***5475.1*** *p438*
*Sister:*Margarethe
*Sister:*Magdalena
Both, Magdalena *SEE* Both, Johann
Both, Margarethe *SEE* Both, Johann
Both, Maria; America, 1856 ***5475.1*** *p440*
With 3 children
Both, Maria; Brazil, 1846 ***5475.1*** *p438*
Bothey, Lulien 34; New Orleans, 1848 ***778.6*** *p42*
Bothey, Margaretha 44; New Orleans, 1848 ***778.6*** *p42*
Bothey, Victor 10; New Orleans, 1848 ***778.6*** *p42*
Both-Neubauers, Anna Moersdorf *SEE* Both-Neubauers, Michel
Both-Neubauers, Michel; Brazil, 1846 ***5475.1*** *p438*
*Wife:*Anna Moersdorf
With 2 children
Botschi, Johan Jacob; North Carolina, 1710 ***3629.40*** *p3*
Bott, . . .; America, n.d. ***9228.50*** *p125*
Bott, Mr.; Detroit, 1890-1990 ***9228.50*** *p125*
With brother & 2 sisters
Bott, Eliz.; Canada, 1800-1857 ***9228.50*** *p184*
Bott, Johannes; Illinois, 1854 ***6079.1*** *p2*
Bott, John; Ontario, 1880 ***9228.50*** *p125*
Bott, L.; New York, 1859 ***358.56*** *p54*
Bott, Nicholas; Ontario, 1890 ***9228.50*** *p125*
Botta, John; Washington, 1888 ***2770.40*** *p25*
Bottcher, August; America, 1881 ***7420.1*** *p319*
Bottcher, Barbara 24; Halifax, N.S., 1902 ***1860.4*** *p41*
Bottcher, Christian 43; Halifax, N.S., 1902 ***1860.4*** *p41*
Bottcher, Dorathea 33; Halifax, N.S., 1902 ***1860.4*** *p41*
Bottcher, Eva 3; Halifax, N.S., 1902 ***1860.4*** *p41*
Bottcher, Friedr. 42; Halifax, N.S., 1902 ***1860.4*** *p41*
Bottcher, Friedr.; Valdivia, Chile, 1851 ***1192.4*** *p50*
Bottcher, Jacob; Halifax, N.S., 1902 ***1860.4*** *p41*
Bottcher, Louise 2; Halifax, N.S., 1902 ***1860.4*** *p41*
Bottcher, Magdalena 23; Halifax, N.S., 1902 ***1860.4*** *p41*
Bottcher, Magdlene; Halifax, N.S., 1902 ***1860.4*** *p41*
Bottcher, Maria; Valdivia, Chile, 1851 ***1192.4*** *p50*
Bottcher, Pauline 8; Halifax, N.S., 1902 ***1860.4*** *p41*
Bottcher, Wilhelm 32; Halifax, N.S., 1902 ***1860.4*** *p41*
Botte, Jean 21; Quebec, 1661 ***9221.17*** *p448*
Botte, Michel 24; Quebec, 1659 ***9221.17*** *p400*
Bottens, Jakobus T.; Illinois, 1861 ***6079.1*** *p2*
Bottes, Joseph 48; America, 1848 ***778.6*** *p42*
Bottier, Blaise 9; Ohio, 1747 ***778.6*** *p42*
Bottier, Isidore 18; Ohio, 1747 ***778.6*** *p42*
Bottier, Joseph 23; Ohio, 1747 ***778.6*** *p42*
Bottier, Joseph 48; Ohio, 1747 ***778.6*** *p42*
Bottier, Louis 24; New Orleans, 1847 ***778.6*** *p42*
Bottier, Rose 7; Ohio, 1747 ***778.6*** *p42*
Bottier, Victoire 48; Ohio, 1747 ***778.6*** *p42*
Bottiley, John; South Carolina, 1678 ***9228.50*** *p125*
Botting, Lizzie 24; Ontario, 1871 ***1823.17*** *p13*
Botton, Jean 32; Quebec, 1661 ***9221.17*** *p448*
Bottow, Friderich; Wisconsin, 1883 ***6795.8*** *p225*
Botz, Anasta.ie 24; Louisiana, 1848 ***778.6*** *p42*
Bouart, Marie; Quebec, 1668 ***4514.3*** *p281*
Boubion, S. P.; Louisiana, 1874-1875 ***4981.45*** *p297*
Boucard, Benj. 11; New Orleans, 1843 ***778.6*** *p42*
Boucard, Elie 2; Port uncertain, 1843 ***778.6*** *p43*
Boucard, Francis 43; New Orleans, 1843 ***778.6*** *p43*
Boucard, Hyppolite 4; Port uncertain, 1843 ***778.6*** *p43*
Boucard, Jean 36; Port uncertain, 1843 ***778.6*** *p43*
Boucard, Jeanne 63; Port uncertain, 1843 ***778.6*** *p43*
Boucard, Marie 34; Port uncertain, 1843 ***778.6*** *p43*
Boucard, Pauline 11; New Orleans, 1843 ***778.6*** *p43*
Boucard, Pauline 31; New Orleans, 1843 ***778.6*** *p43*
Boucard, Stephanie 10; Port uncertain, 1843 ***778.6*** *p43*
Boucault, Jeanne; Quebec, 1668 ***4514.3*** *p282*
Boucaut, Nicolas; Quebec, 1659 ***9221.17*** *p413*
Bouch, James; Marston's Wharf, 1782 ***8529.30*** *p10*
Bouchard, Claude 26; Quebec, 1650 ***9221.17*** *p223*
Bouchard, Etienne 31; Montreal, 1653 ***9221.17*** *p283*
Bouchard, Gabriel; Quebec, 1642 ***9221.17*** *p113*
Bouchard, Jeanne; Quebec, 1665 ***4514.3*** *p282*
Bouchard, Louise; Quebec, 1667 ***4514.3*** *p282*
Bouchard, Michel 21; Quebec, 1657 ***9221.17*** *p352*
*Brother:*Nicolas 22
Bouchard, Nicolas 22 *SEE* Bouchard, Michel
Bouchart, Claude 31; Quebec, 1643 ***9221.17*** *p129*
Bouche, . . . 20; Galveston, TX, 1845 ***3967.10*** *p377*
Bouche, Mr. 27; America, 1841 ***778.6*** *p43*
Bouche, Joseph 28; New Orleans, 1848 ***778.6*** *p43*
Bouchel Dorceval, Jacques-Francois de; Quebec, 1732 ***2314.30*** *p170*
Bouchel Dorceval, Jacques-Francois de; Quebec, 1732 ***2314.30*** *p176*
Boucher, . . .; Boston, 1769 ***9228.50*** *p5*
Boucher, Mr. 3; America, 1846 ***778.6*** *p43*
Boucher, Mr.; New Orleans, 1840 ***778.6*** *p43*
Boucher, Arthur; Washington, 1889 ***2770.40*** *p26*
Boucher, Augustine *SEE* Boucher, Francois Joseph
Boucher, Christine 29; St. Louis, 1847 ***778.6*** *p43*
Boucher, Claude; Quebec, 1640 ***9221.17*** *p95*
Boucher, Constantin *SEE* Boucher, Francois Joseph
Boucher, Daniel 62; Ontario, 1871 ***1823.21*** *p31*
Boucher, Eleonore *SEE* Boucher, Francois Joseph
Boucher, Elisabeth 27; America, 1843 ***778.6*** *p43*
Boucher, Francis 14; Quebec, 1870 ***8364.32*** *p22*
Boucher, Francois 21; Port uncertain, 1842 ***778.6*** *p43*
Boucher, Francois 17 *SEE* Boucher, Marin
Boucher, Francois 19; Quebec, 1651 ***9221.17*** *p237*
Boucher, Francois 33; St. Louis, 1847 ***778.6*** *p43*
Boucher, Francois *SEE* Boucher, Francois Joseph
Boucher, Francois Joseph; Wisconsin, 1855-1858 ***1495.20*** *p67*
*Wife:*Julie Laduron
*Child:*Eleonore
*Child:*Leon Joseph
*Child:*Francois
*Child:*Augustine
*Child:*Constantin
*Child:*Louis Joseph
*Child:*Jean Baptiste
Boucher, Gaspard 36; Quebec, 1635 ***9221.17*** *p43*
*Wife:*Nicole Lemer
*Son:*Pierre 13
*Daughter:*Marie 6
*Son:*Nicolas 10
*Daughter:*Madeleine 1
*Daughter:*Marguerite 4
Boucher, Gaspard; Wisconsin, 1854 ***1495.20*** *p29*
*Wife:*Marie
Boucher, Geo.; Boston, 1727 ***9228.50*** *p421*
Boucher, Georg Heinrich; Chicago, 1884 ***5475.1*** *p17*
Boucher, George; Boston, 1727 ***9228.50*** *p125*
Boucher, Jean Baptiste *SEE* Boucher, Francois Joseph
Boucher, Jean-Galleran 1 *SEE* Boucher, Perrine Mallet
Boucher, Jeanne 31; Quebec, 1638 ***9221.17*** *p77*
Boucher, John 50; America, 1841 ***778.6*** *p43*
Boucher, Joseph; Boston, 1769 ***9228.50*** *p48*
Boucher, Joseph; Boston, 1769 ***9228.50*** *p125*
Boucher, Josephine; Wisconsin, 1856 ***1495.20*** *p41*
Boucher, Julie Laduron *SEE* Boucher, Francois Joseph
Boucher, Leon Joseph *SEE* Boucher, Francois Joseph
Boucher, Louis Joseph *SEE* Boucher, Francois Joseph
Boucher, Louis-Marin 5 *SEE* Boucher, Perrine Mallet
Boucher, Madeleine; Quebec, 1665 ***4514.3*** *p282*
Boucher, Madeleine 1 *SEE* Boucher, Gaspard
Boucher, Marguerite 4 *SEE* Boucher, Gaspard
Boucher, Maria 6 months; St. Louis, 1847 ***778.6*** *p43*
Boucher, Marie 6 *SEE* Boucher, Gaspard
Boucher, Marie *SEE* Boucher, Gaspard
Boucher, Marin; Quebec, 1639 ***9221.17*** *p44*
Boucher, Marin 46; Quebec, 1634 ***9221.17*** *p33*
*Relative:*Francois 17
Boucher, Melanie; Wisconsin, 1846-1856 ***1495.20*** *p29*
Boucher, Nicolas 10 *SEE* Boucher, Gaspard
Boucher, Nicolas; Wisconsin, 1856 ***1495.20*** *p46*
Boucher, Nicole Lemer *SEE* Boucher, Gaspard
Boucher, Perrine; Quebec, 1635 ***9221.17*** *p33*
Boucher, Perrine 30; Quebec, 1635 ***9221.17*** *p44*
*Son:*Louis-Marin 5
*Son:*Jean-Galleran 1
Boucher, Pierre 13 *SEE* Boucher, Gaspard
Boucher, Victoire; Wisconsin, 1857 ***1495.20*** *p45*
Boucher deBoucherville, Pierre; Quebec, 1634-1635 ***2314.30*** *p167*
Boucher deBoucherville, Pierre; Quebec, 1661 ***2314.30*** *p176*
Boucherie, Edouard 44; America, 1843 ***778.6*** *p43*
Bouches, Mr. 23; America, 1841 ***778.6*** *p43*
Bouchet, Jean; Virginia, 1700 ***9230.15*** *p80*
Bouchet, Jules 30; New Orleans, 1848 ***778.6*** *p43*
Bouchet, Mathurin; Quebec, 1655 ***9221.17*** *p321*
Bouchonville, Isidore; Wisconsin, 1880 ***1494.20*** *p13*
Bouchot, Pre. 27; Louisiana, 1848 ***778.6*** *p43*
Boucquet, Guillaume 30; Quebec, 1657 ***9221.17*** *p353*
Boudart, Catherine Mercier *SEE* Boudart, Jean
Boudart, Jean; Montreal, 1649 ***9221.17*** *p221*
*Wife:*Catherine Mercier
Boudeau, Francoise 14; Quebec, 1647 ***9221.17*** *p177*
Bouden, Francis; Marblehead, MA, 1650-1750 ***9228.50*** *p126*
Boudet, Mr. 25; New Orleans, 1848 ***778.6*** *p43*
Boudet, Romaine; Quebec, 1661 ***9221.17*** *p448*
Boudier, Mr.; Boston, n.d. ***9228.50*** *p124*
Boudier, Eleonore de Grandmaison 22; Quebec, 1641 ***9221.17*** *p102*
Boudin, Ambrose; Massachusetts, 1700-1750 ***9228.50*** *p122*
Boudon, Henry 24; New Orleans, 1845 ***778.6*** *p43*
Boudroit, Frederick; Ohio, 1809-1852 ***4511.35*** *p6*
Boudrot, Anselme; Nova Scotia, 1753 ***3051*** *p112*
*Wife:*Ursule Daigre
Boudrot, Ursule Daigre *SEE* Boudrot, Anselme
Boue, Mr. 38; America, 1846 ***778.6*** *p43*
Boue, Phiippe 37; Texas, 1848 ***778.6*** *p43*
Bouencha, Pierre 17; Quebec, 1646 ***9221.17*** *p162*
Bouencheau, Pierre 17; Quebec, 1646 ***9221.17*** *p162*
Bouer, Katharina 20; Galveston, TX, 1844 ***3967.10*** *p375*
Bouer, Magdalena 33; Galveston, TX, 1844 ***3967.10*** *p375*
Bouet, Francoise 19; Montreal, 1659 ***9221.17*** *p427*
Bouet, Marie; Quebec, 1667 ***4514.3*** *p282*
Boufilhon, Hipolit 24; New Orleans, 1845 ***778.6*** *p43*
Bouge, David 75; Ontario, 1871 ***1823.21*** *p31*
Bouge, James 45; Ontario, 1871 ***1823.21*** *p31*
Boughton, Henry 40; Ontario, 1871 ***1823.17*** *p13*
Bougon, Baptist 70; New Orleans, 1846 ***778.6*** *p43*
Bougourd, Charles; Quebec, 1659 ***9221.17*** *p413*
Bougourd, John; Massachusetts, 1890-1920 ***9228.50*** *p125*
Bouhallier, Victor 33; New Orleans, 1843 ***778.6*** *p43*
Bouiard, Auguste 35; Louisiana, 1848 ***778.6*** *p43*
Bouiard, Felicie 5; Louisiana, 1848 ***778.6*** *p43*
Bouiard, Francoise 27; Louisiana, 1848 ***778.6*** *p44*
Bouiard, Josephine 1; Louisiana, 1848 ***778.6*** *p44*
Bouillard, Pierre 19; Louisiana, 1847 ***778.6*** *p44*
Bouillet deChevalet, Claude; Quebec, 1739 ***2314.30*** *p170*
Bouillet deChevalet, Claude; Quebec, 1739 ***2314.30*** *p176*
Bouillet deLa Chassaigne, Jean; Quebec, 1683-1688 ***2314.30*** *p168*
Bouillet deLa Chassaigne, Jean; Quebec, 1687 ***2314.30*** *p177*
Bouillon, Helena *SEE* Bouillon, Reinhard
Bouillon, Katharina 29 *SEE* Bouillon, Reinhard
Bouillon, Maria Harig 50 *SEE* Bouillon, Reinhard
Bouillon, Marie; Quebec, 1668 ***4514.3*** *p282*
Bouillon, Nikolaus *SEE* Bouillon, Reinhard
Bouillon, Reinhard 59; America, 1867 ***5475.1*** *p344*
*Wife:*Maria Harig 50
*Son:*Nikolaus
*Daughter:*Katharina 29
*Daughter:*Helena
Bouillon, Virginia; Philadelphia, 1858 ***8513.31*** *p305*
Bouin, Jacques 37; Montreal, 1659 ***9221.17*** *p417*
Boujonnier, Flour; Quebec, 1648 ***9221.17*** *p195*
Boul, Caspar 2; New Orleans, 1847 ***778.6*** *p44*
Boul, Catharina 17; New Orleans, 1847 ***778.6*** *p44*
Boul, Elisabeth 45; New Orleans, 1847 ***778.6*** *p44*
Boul, Magdalena 15; New Orleans, 1847 ***778.6*** *p44*
Boul, Marianna 7; New Orleans, 1847 ***778.6*** *p44*
Boul, Nicolas 54; New Orleans, 1847 ***778.6*** *p44*
Boul, Peter 8; New Orleans, 1847 ***778.6*** *p44*
Boulan, . . .; Quebec, 1649 ***9221.17*** *p210*
Boulanger, Desire; New York, NY, 1858 ***1494.21*** *p31*
Boulanger, Francois 24; Montreal, 1661 ***9221.17*** *p471*
Boulanger, Sophia; America, 1800-1859 ***9228.50*** *p89*
Boulard, Francois 37; New Orleans, 1840 ***778.6*** *p44*
Boulard, Martin 22; Quebec, 1661 ***9221.17*** *p449*
Boules, John 66; Ontario, 1871 ***1823.17*** *p13*
Boulet, Mr. 25; New Orleans, 1841 ***778.6*** *p44*
Boulet, Alexandre 39; New Orleans, 1848 ***778.6*** *p44*
Boulet, Emile 18; America, 1842 ***778.6*** *p44*
Boulet, Homroset 29; New Orleans, 1848 ***778.6*** *p44*

Boulet, Marie 24; New Orleans, 1848 778.6 p44
Boulet, Olympe 28; New Orleans, 1848 778.6 p44
Boulgar, Richard; Ohio, 1809-1852 4511.35 p6
Boulic, Marie-Renee 25; Quebec, 1654 9221.17 p303
Boulle, Francois; Quebec, 1637 9221.17 p68
With wife
Boulle, Francoise Garnier 25 SEE Boulle, Robert
Boulle, Helene; Quebec, 1608 9221.17 p26
Boulle, Jacqueline 3 SEE Boulle, Robert
Boulle, Robert 32; Quebec, 1662 9221.17 p480
Wife:Francoise Garnier 25
Daughter:Jacqueline 3
Boullonge, Barbe de 25; Montreal, 1643 9221.17 p136
Boullongne, Barbe de SEE Boullongne, Philippine-Gertrude
Boullongne, Philippine-Gertrude; Montreal, 1643 9221.17 p136
Sister:Barbe de
Boullosa, Simon; Louisiana, 1836-1840 4981.45 p212
Boulogne, Mrs. 26; America, 1843 778.6 p44
Boulogne, Barbe de; Quebec, 1600-1671 4514.3 p345
Boulogne, Juan 28; America, 1843 778.6 p44
Boulogne, Philippe-Gertrude de; Quebec, 1600-1671 4514.3 p345
Boulton, Alfred 64; Ontario, 1871 1823.21 p31
Boulton, George 50; Ontario, 1871 1823.17 p13
Boumerster, Joseph; Washington, 1889 2770.40 p26
Boumin, Jacques 37; Montreal, 1659 9221.17 p417
Bouquet, Estevan 26; America, 1843 778.6 p44
Bouquet, John; Missouri, 1890 1029.59 p12
Bour, F. 50; America, 1748 778.6 p44
Bour, Nicholas; Ohio, 1809-1852 4511.35 p6
Bour, Philip 45; Cuba, 1842 778.6 p44
Bourasseau, Jean 23; Quebec, 1657 9221.17 p353
Bourbault, Elie 24; Quebec, 1650 9221.17 p223
Bourbault, Paul; Montreal, 1652 9221.17 p267
Bourbault, Simon 36; Quebec, 1662 9221.17 p481
Bourbonell, John; Boston, 1769 9228.50 p48
Bourbonell, John; Boston, 1769 9228.50 p125
Bourbonniere, Charlotte 46; Quebec, 1647 9221.17 p181
Son:Nicolas 27
Son:Jacques 10
Bourbonniere, Jacques 10 SEE Bourbonniere, Charlotte Chevalier
Bourbonniere, Nicolas 27 SEE Bourbonniere, Charlotte Chevalier
Bourcier, Etienne; Quebec, 1642 9221.17 p113
Bourda, Louis 22; New Orleans, 1846 778.6 p44
Bourdeau, Jean; Quebec, 1657 9221.17 p353
Bourdel, Edward O.; Illinois, 1852 6079.1 p2
Bourdelais, Jean 23; Quebec, 1657 9221.17 p353
Bourdet, J. 27; New Orleans, 1842 778.6 p44
Bourdet, Michel; Quebec, 1653 9221.17 p270
Bourdet, Pierre 17; America, 1848 778.6 p44
Bourdie, G. 50; America, 1846 778.6 p44
Bourdier, Elie 28; America, 1840 778.6 p44
Bourdier, Marie Therese 22; America, 1840 778.6 p44
Bourdoin, Francois 47; Port uncertain, 1847 778.6 p44
Bourdoin, Franz 3 months; Port uncertain, 1847 778.6 p44
Bourdoin, Georg 4; Port uncertain, 1847 778.6 p45
Bourdoin, Jean 29; Port uncertain, 1847 778.6 p45
Bourdon, Edward; Nantucket, MA, 1782-1807 9228.50 p123
Bourdon, Jean 30; Quebec, 1661 9221.17 p449
Bourdon, Jean 32; Quebec, 1634 9221.17 p33
Bourdon, Marie 14; Quebec, 1648 9221.17 p196
Bourdon, William; Salem, MA, 1783 9228.50 p122
Bourdon, Wm.; New England, 1775-1807 9228.50 p122
Bourduceau, Anne-Francoise 20; Montreal, 1658 9221.17 p387
Bourduceau DeLaBouchardiere, Genevieve Butin SEE Bourduceau DeLaBouchardiere, Mederic
Bourduceau DeLaBouchardiere, Mederic; Montreal, 1658 9221.17 p388
Wife:Genevieve Butin
Bourens, Mathias; America, 1877 5475.1 p257
Bourg, Cecile 36; New Orleans, 1848 778.6 p45
Bourg, Chas. 17; Port uncertain, 1840 778.6 p45
Bourg, Jean 50; New Orleans, 1848 778.6 p45
Bourg, Jean-Marie 34; New Orleans, 1848 778.6 p45
Bourg, Josephine 38; New Orleans, 1848 778.6 p45
Bourg, Salome 20; Port uncertain, 1840 778.6 p45
Bourgaize, Mr.; Quebec, n.d. 9228.50 p593
Bourgaize, Nicholas; Salem, MA, 1600-1699 9228.50 p125
Bourgaize Children, . . .; Quebec, 1880-1950 9228.50 p125
Bourgaize Children, . . .; Washington, 1880-1950 9228.50 p125
Bourgard, Bon. 24; Missouri, 1846 778.6 p45
Bourgard, Claude; Quebec, 1657 9221.17 p353
Bourgard, Georg; America, 1865 5475.1 p122
Bourgeois, Miss 21; Louisiana, 1848 778.6 p45
Bourgeois, Catherine; Quebec, 1667 4514.3 p282
Bourgeois, Francoise; Quebec, 1669 4514.3 p283
Bourgeois, Hubert; New York, NY, 1871 1494.20 p13
Bourgeois, Jeanne; Quebec, 1665 4514.3 p283
Bourgeois, Joseph Simon 50; Galveston, TX, 1844 3967.10 p371
Bourgeois, Louis; Illinois, 1861 6079.1 p2
Bourgeois, Luc 31; Texas, 1848 778.6 p45
Bourgeois, Marie; Quebec, 1667 4514.3 p283
Bourgeois, Nikolaus 30; America, 1843 5475.1 p357
Bourgeot, Joachim; Quebec, 1659 9221.17 p413
Bourgeoys, Claude 19; Montreal, 1662 9221.17 p496
Bourgeoys, Marguerite 33; Montreal, 1653 9221.17 p284
Bourgery, Jean-Baptiste; Quebec, 1652 9221.17 p254
Son:Pierre
Wife:Marie Gendre
Bourgery, Marie Gendre 45 SEE Bourgery, Jean-Baptiste
Bourgery, Pierre 8 SEE Bourgery, Jean-Baptiste
Bourget, Andre 30; Quebec, 1655 9221.17 p321
Bourgjoly, Rene 26; Montreal, 1653 9221.17 p282
Bourgoian, Joseph; Virginia, 1700 9230.15 p80
Bourgoin, Mrs. 30; New Orleans, 1848 778.6 p45
Bourgoin, Olivier; Quebec, 1653 9221.17 p270
Bourgois, Mr. 38; Missouri, 1846 778.6 p45
Bourgois, Bon. 41; Missouri, 1846 778.6 p45
Bourgois, G. G.; North Carolina, 1827 1088.45 p3
Bourgon, Nicolas 26; New Orleans, 1748 778.6 p45
Bourgouin, Marie-Marthe 24; Quebec, 1661 9221.17 p449
Bourgouin, Pierre 20; Quebec, 1661 9221.17 p449
Bourguignolle, Pierre; Quebec, 1661 9221.17 p449
Bourguignon, Barthelemy 31; Montreal, 1662 9221.17 p500
Bourguignon, Edward; Wisconsin, 1854-1858 1495.20 p49
Wife:Melanie Pos
Child:Seraphine
Child:Xavier
Bourguignon, Jamen; Quebec, 1636 9221.17 p52
Bourguignon, Karl Ludwig; America, 1858 5475.1 p552
Bourguignon, Margarethe Hess 40 SEE Bourguignon, Nikolaus
Bourguignon, Melanie Pos SEE Bourguignon, Edward
Bourguignon, Nikolaus SEE Bourguignon, Nikolaus
Bourguignon, Nikolaus; America, 1867 5475.1 p224
Wife:Margarethe Hess
Son:Nikolaus
Bourguignon, Pierre 20; Quebec, 1661 9221.17 p449
Bourguignon, Rosalie; Wisconsin, 1855 1495.20 p56
Bourguignon, Seraphine SEE Bourguignon, Edward
Bourguignon, Seraphine; Wisconsin, 1855 1495.20 p56
Bourguignon, Xavier SEE Bourguignon, Edward
Bouring, Jeremie 28; America, 1840 778.6 p45
Bourk, Elizabeth 75; Ontario, 1871 1823.21 p31
Bourk, Michael; Boston, 1745 1642 p45
Bourke, John; Boston, 1766 1642 p37
Bourke, Richard; Boston, 1764 1642 p33
Bourlard, Josephine 35; Galveston, TX, 1844 3967.10 p374
Bourlie, Thomas 56; Ontario, 1871 1823.21 p31
Bourlier, Leonard 21; Quebec, 1655 9221.17 p321
Bourman, Mr. 37; America, 1846 778.6 p45
Bourmault, Benjamin; Quebec, 1652 9221.17 p254
Bourne, Caroline 43; Ontario, 1871 1823.21 p31
Bourne, Charles 67; Ontario, 1871 1823.17 p13
Bourne, Hannam 41; Ontario, 1871 1823.17 p13
Bourne, Harvey 36; Ontario, 1871 1823.17 p13
Bourne, Joseph F. 42; Ontario, 1871 1823.21 p31
Bourne, William 43; Ontario, 1871 1823.17 p14
Bourner, William Bako 24; Ontario, 1871 1823.17 p14
Bournonville, Hubert; America, 1869 1494.20 p12
Bournonville, Joseph; Milwaukee, 1871 1494.20 p11
Bournonville, Pierre; Milwaukee, 1871 1494.20 p11
Bourret, Francois; Quebec, 1661 9221.17 p449
Bourrot, Emmanuel; Quebec, 1661 9221.17 p449
Bourru, Jean; Virginia, 1700 9230.15 p80
Boursier, Joseph 19; Quebec, 1646 9221.17 p162
Bouschere, Nikolaus; Chicago, 1887 5475.1 p243
Bousfield, William Henry 52; Ontario, 1871 1823.21 p31
Bousier, John 50; America, 1843 778.6 p45
Bouska, Emanuel; Nebraska, 1889 2853.20 p160
Bouska, Frantisek; Iowa, 1854 2853.20 p230
Bouska, Martin; Iowa, 1854 2853.20 p230
Bousonville, Christina 34; America, 1854 5475.1 p64
Bousquet, A. 33; America, 1846 778.6 p45
Bousquet, Francois 30; New Orleans, 1848 778.6 p45
Bousquet, Jean; Quebec, 1642 9221.17 p113
Bousse, Mrs. 25; America, 1844 778.6 p45
Boussiques, Mr. 20; Port uncertain, 1844 778.6 p45
Boussot, Louis; Montreal, 1652 9221.17 p267
Boutard, Marie; Quebec, 1669 4514.3 p283
Boute-En-Train, Francoise Delamare SEE Boute-En-Train, Michel
Boute-En-Train, Michel 2 SEE Boute-En-Train, Michel
Boute-En-Train, Michel 31; Quebec, 1657 9221.17 p356
Wife:Francoise Delamare
Son:Michel 2
Boutefeu, Mathurin; Montreal, 1644 9221.17 p146
Boutelaud, Antoine 20; Quebec, 1656 9221.17 p332
Bouteloupe, Vincent; Massachusetts, 1900-1940 9228.50 p126
Boutereau, Vincent 33; Montreal, 1660 9221.17 p440
Boutet, Catherine SEE Boutet, Martin
Boutet, Catherine Soulage SEE Boutet, Martin
Boutet, Catherine; Quebec, 1650 9221.17 p223
Daughter:Catherine
Daughter:Marie
Boutet, Catherine 8 SEE Boutet, Catherine Soulage
Boutet, Eugene 14; America, 1840 778.6 p45
Boutet, Josephine 18; America, 1840 778.6 p45
Boutet, Marie SEE Boutet, Martin
Boutet, Marie 7 SEE Boutet, Catherine Soulage
Boutet, Marie-Madeleine; Quebec, 1664 4514.3 p283
Boutet, Martin; Quebec, 1600-1664 4514.3 p283
Child:Catherine
Child:Marie
Wife:Catherine Soulage
Boutet, Martin 31; Quebec, 1643 9221.17 p129
Boutet, Paul 22; America, 1840 778.6 p45
Boutin, Antoine 20; Quebec, 1662 9221.17 p481
Boutin, Jean; Quebec, 1652 9221.17 p254
Boutin, Jean 19; Quebec, 1656 9221.17 p332
Boutleu, Francoise 17; America, 1841 778.6 p45
Boutloup, Rosine 43; Kentucky, 1846 778.6 p45
Bouton, John; Massachusetts, 1635 9228.50 p126
Bouton, William; New Hampshire, 1693 9228.50 p126
Boutonville, Henry; Quebec, 1646 9221.17 p161
Boutz, Francois 47; New York, NY, 1894 6512.1 p181
Bouvard, A. 20; America, 1848 778.6 p45
Bouvier, Hippolyte; Illinois, 1852 6079.1 p2
Bouvier, Jacques; Quebec, 1653 9221.17 p270
Bouvier, Mathias 33; New Orleans, 1848 778.6 p45
Bouvier, Michel 20; Montreal, 1653 9221.17 p284
Bouvot, Emmanuel; Quebec, 1661 9221.17 p449
Bouvret, Auguste; New Orleans, 1848 778.6 p45
Bouvvret, Clemence; New Orleans, 1848 778.6 p45
Bouvy, Jakob; America, 1868 5475.1 p169
Bouy, Julie 25; America, 1846 778.6 p45
Bouy, Marie 2; America, 1846 778.6 p46
Bouyer, Jean 16; Tennessee, 1848 778.6 p46
Bouza, Jan; South Dakota, 1871 2853.20 p247
Bouze, Pierre; Montreal, 1653 9221.17 p284
Bovers, Carl Louis August; America, 1891 7420.1 p362
Bovers, Christoph Wilhelm; America, 1866 7420.1 p240
With stepchild
Bovers, Engel Marie Dorothee; America, 1846 7420.1 p51
Bovers, Ernst Friedrich Wilhelm; America, 1880 7420.1 p315
Bovers, Friedrich; America, 1855 7420.1 p134
With wife
With 2 children mother-in-law & sister
Bovers, Johann Heinrich; America, 1868 7420.1 p269
With family
Boversen, Mr.; America, 1852 7420.1 p85
With wife 3 daughters & son
Boversen, Ernst; America, 1854 7420.1 p116
With family
Boverssen, Mr.; America, 1852 7420.1 p85
With wife 3 daughters & son
Bovets, Robert 58; Michigan, 1880 4491.30 p3
Bovets, Sally 58; Michigan, 1880 4491.30 p3
Bovin, Louis; Colorado, 1884 1029.59 p12
Bow, Johannah 48; Ontario, 1871 1823.21 p31
Bowdedge, John Smith; Salt Lake City, 1939 9228.50 p127
Bowdedge Family ; Utah, 1863 9228.50 p127
Bowden, . . .; America, n.d. 9228.50 p126
Bowden, Capt.; America, 1645-1745 9228.50 p96
Bowden, Ambrose; Massachusetts, 1700-1750 9228.50 p122
Bowden, Charles 40; Ontario, 1871 1823.21 p31
Bowden, Elizabeth; Maryland, 1671-1672 1236.25 p45
Bowden, Francis; Marblehead, MA, 1650-1750 9228.50 p126
Bowden, John; Boston, 1764 1642 p33
Bowden, John 27; Ontario, 1871 1823.21 p31
Bowden, Joseph; Colorado, 1891 1029.59 p12
Bowden, Joseph; Colorado, 1896 1029.59 p12
Bowden, William Goldsworthy; North Carolina, 1845 1088.45 p3
Bowden Family ; Massachusetts, n.d. 9228.50 p126
Bowdidge, Alice; Utah, 1862 9228.50 p127
Bowdidge, Elizabeth; Utah, 1865 9228.50 p127

Bowdle, Elizabeth; Maryland, 1673 *1236.25 p49*
Bowdley, Elizabeth; Maryland, 1673 *1236.25 p49*
Bowdoin, . . .; New England, n.d. *9228.50 p127*
Bowdoin, Peter; FalmoutH ME, 1700-1740 *9228.50 p335*
Bowel, Thomas; New York, 1778 *8529.30 p10*
Bowen, Harriet 29; Ontario, 1871 *1823.21 p32*
Bowen, Henry; Washington, 1884 *2770.40 p192*
Bowen, Honor; Barbados, 1671 *1220.12 p593*
Bowen, James 23; Ontario, 1871 *1823.21 p32*
Bowen, Margaret; Maryland, 1674-1675 *1236.25 p51*
Bowen, Nelson 36; Ontario, 1871 *1823.17 p14*
Bowen, William; Ohio, 1838 *4022.20 p272*
Bower, Alexander 54; Ontario, 1871 *1823.21 p32*
Bower, Anna Maria; America, 1854 *179.55 p19*
Bower, Christopher; Ohio, 1809-1852 *4511.35 p6*
Bower, Geo.; Ohio, 1840-1897 *8365.35 p15*
Bower, Georg Matthaus; America, 1854 *179.55 p19*
Bower, Henry; Ohio, 1809-1852 *4511.35 p6*
Bower, Jacob; America, 1854 *179.55 p19*
With wife
Bower, Johann Georg; America, 1854 *179.55 p19*
Bower, Johann Georg A. Julius; America, 1854 *179.55 p19*
Bower, John; Ohio, 1809-1852 *4511.35 p6*
Bower, John 38; Ontario, 1871 *1823.21 p32*
Bower, Maria Catharine; America, 1854 *179.55 p19*
Bowerice, Ludwick; Ohio, 1809-1852 *4511.35 p6*
Bowering, Thomas 61; Ontario, 1871 *1823.21 p32*
Bowers, Andrew; North Carolina, 1855 *1088.45 p3*
Bowers, Arthur G.; North Carolina, 1850 *1088.45 p3*
Bowers, Charles E.; North Carolina, 1830 *1088.45 p3*
Bowers, Francis 57; Ontario, 1871 *1823.21 p32*
Bowers, George A.; North Carolina, 1857 *1088.45 p3*
Bowers, Johann Friedrich; America, 1868 *7420.1 p269*
With family
Bowers, John; Ohio, 1809-1852 *4511.35 p6*
Bowers, Louise Albertine Christine; America, 1859 *7420.1 p184*
Bowers, Mary 77; Ontario, 1871 *1823.21 p32*
Bowers, William; America, 1782 *8529.30 p10*
Bowes, Jane D. 64; Ontario, 1871 *1823.17 p14*
Bowes, Johannah 16; Ontario, 1871 *1823.21 p32*
Bowes, John 54; Ontario, 1871 *1823.21 p32*
Bowey, James 48; Ontario, 1871 *1823.21 p32*
Bowey, John 40; Ontario, 1871 *1823.21 p32*
Bowey, William 40; Ontario, 1871 *1823.21 p32*
Bowgren, Otto Servatius; New York, 1892 *1766.20 p34*
Bowie, Ann 36; North Carolina, 1774 *1422.10 p56*
Bowie, John 39; Ontario, 1871 *1823.21 p32*
Bowie, John 40; Ontario, 1871 *1823.17 p14*
Bowie, Margaret; Cape Fear, NC,, 1754 *1422.10 p62*
Bowie, William 43; Ontario, 1871 *1823.17 p14*
Bowin, Elisabeth; New Orleans, 1851 *7242.30 p134*
Bowing, Elijah 23; Ontario, 1871 *1823.21 p32*
Bowler, Charlotte 70; Ontario, 1871 *1823.21 p32*
Bowler, John; Boston, 1766 *1642 p37*
Bowler, Walter 28; Ontario, 1871 *1823.21 p32*
Bowles, James 62; Ontario, 1871 *1823.17 p14*
Bowles, Thomas; Boston, 1823 *3274.56 p99*
Bowley, George 32; Ontario, 1871 *1823.21 p32*
Bowley, Henry 37; Ontario, 1871 *1823.21 p32*
Bowlin, James 40; Ontario, 1871 *1823.21 p32*
Bowlin, Paterick 76; Ontario, 1871 *1823.21 p32*
Bowlin, Peter; Pennsylvania, 1745-1800 *9228.50 p127*
Bowls, Lanchelet 30; Ontario, 1871 *1823.21 p32*
Bowly, Jacob; Ohio, 1809-1852 *4511.35 p6*
Bowman, Andrew; North Carolina, 1809 *1088.45 p3*
Bowman, Anthony; Ohio, 1809-1852 *4511.35 p6*
Bowman, Antney 50; Ontario, 1871 *1823.21 p32*
Bowman, Christian; Ohio, 1840-1897 *8365.35 p15*
Bowman, Gustav; Ohio, 1809-1852 *4511.35 p6*
Bowman, Henry 54; Ontario, 1871 *1823.21 p32*
Bowman, James 41; Ontario, 1871 *1823.21 p32*
Bowman, James 70; Ontario, 1871 *1823.21 p32*
Bowman, John; North Carolina, 1850 *1088.45 p3*
Bowman, John 54; Ontario, 1871 *1823.21 p32*
Bowman, Joseph 44; Ontario, 1871 *1823.21 p32*
Bowman, William 51; Ontario, 1871 *1823.21 p32*
Bowness, Henry; Missouri, 1894 *3276.1 p1*
Bowrice, Ludwik; Ohio, 1809-1852 *4511.35 p6*
Bowring, Charles; North Carolina, 1818 *1088.45 p3*
Bows, John 68; Ontario, 1871 *1823.21 p32*
Bowser, John 46; Ontario, 1871 *1823.21 p32*
Bowyers, Matthew; Jamaica, 1779 *8529.30 p12A*
Box, Daniel Thomas 25; Ontario, 1871 *1823.21 p32*
Boy, Emil Carl Leopold; Wisconsin, 1869 *6795.8 p147*
Boy, James O.; Ohio, 1809-1852 *4511.35 p6*
Boy, Joseph; New York, 1778 *8529.30 p10*
Boyce, Henry 40; Ontario, 1871 *1823.21 p32*
Boyce, Henry 42; Ontario, 1871 *1823.21 p32*
Boyce, James 21; Ontario, 1871 *1823.21 p32*
Boyce, James 64; Ontario, 1871 *1823.21 p32*
Boyce, John 40; Ontario, 1871 *1823.21 p32*
Boyce, Peter; Washington, 1886 *2770.40 p195*
Boyce, William 40; Ontario, 1871 *1823.21 p32*
Boyce, William 44; Ontario, 1871 *1823.17 p14*
Boyd, Adam; Boston, 1737 *1642 p26*
Boyd, Alex 29; Ontario, 1871 *1823.21 p32*
Boyd, Andrew 33; Ontario, 1871 *1823.21 p33*
Boyd, Francis S. 47; Ontario, 1871 *1823.21 p33*
Boyd, Hamelton; Missouri, 1889 *3276.1 p1*
Boyd, Henry 50; Ontario, 1871 *1823.21 p33*
Boyd, Hugh; Philadelphia, 1777 *8529.30 p2A*
Boyd, James T. 37; Ontario, 1871 *1823.21 p33*
Boyd, Jane 11; Ontario, 1871 *1823.21 p33*
Boyd, John 29; New York, NY, 1835 *5024.1 p136*
Boyd, John; Ohio, 1846 *3580.20 p31*
Boyd, John; Ohio, 1846 *6020.12 p6*
Boyd, John 38; Ontario, 1871 *1823.21 p33*
Boyd, Joseph 13; Ontario, 1871 *1823.21 p33*
Boyd, Joseph 42; Ontario, 1871 *1823.17 p14*
Boyd, Mary 45; Ontario, 1871 *1823.21 p33*
Boyd, Mary Ann 16; Ontario, 1871 *1823.21 p33*
Boyd, Matthew; North Carolina, 1838 *1088.45 p3*
Boyd, Rachael 29; Ontario, 1871 *1823.21 p33*
Boyd, Robert 47; Ontario, 1871 *1823.21 p33*
Boyd, Robert 50; Ontario, 1871 *1823.21 p33*
Boyd, Robert 57; Ontario, 1871 *1823.17 p14*
Boyd, Robt. 50; Ontario, 1871 *1823.17 p14*
Boyd, Thomas 21; Ontario, 1871 *1823.21 p33*
Boyd, Thomas 23; Ontario, 1871 *1823.21 p33*
Boyd, Thomas 53; Ontario, 1871 *1823.21 p33*
Boyd, William; Boston, 1766 *1642 p35*
Boyd, William; Boston, 1775 *8529.30 p2A*
Boyd, William 18; Ontario, 1871 *1823.21 p33*
Boyd, William 23; Ontario, 1871 *1823.21 p33*
Boyd, William 42; Ontario, 1871 *1823.21 p33*
Boyde, Violet; Massachusetts, 1947 *9228.50 p528*
Boyer, Achile 16; New Orleans, 1840 *778.6 p46*
Boyer, Anne 25; Quebec, 1657 *9221.17 p353*
Boyer, Barbe; Quebec, 1673 *4514.3 p283*
Boyer, Catherine; Quebec, 1662 *9221.17 p481*
*Daughter:*Marie
Boyer, Charles 12; New Orleans, 1840 *778.6 p46*
Boyer, Eva 24; America, 1747 *778.6 p46*
Boyer, Florence 1; Ohio, 1880 *4879.40 p257*
Boyer, J. D. J. 38; New Orleans, 1841 *778.6 p46*
Boyer, Jean; Quebec, 1649 *9221.17 p210*
Boyer, Joseph; Louisiana, 1836-1840 *4981.45 p212*
Boyer, Julie 19; America, 1840 *778.6 p46*
Boyer, Lucas; Quebec, 1648 *9221.17 p196*
Boyer, Mad. 38; New Orleans, 1840 *778.6 p46*
Boyer, Magdalena 28; New Orleans, 1848 *778.6 p46*
Boyer, Marie 28 *SEE* Boyer, Catherine Vinet
Boyer, Noelie 9; New Orleans, 1840 *778.6 p46*
Boyer, Pierre; Montreal, 1649 *9221.17 p221*
Boyer, Pierre 24; New Orleans, 1842 *778.6 p46*
Boyer, Thos 25; Ontario, 1871 *1823.21 p33*
Boyer, Zelima 18; New Orleans, 1840 *778.6 p46*
Boyers, Matthew; Jamaica, 1779 *8529.30 p12A*
Boyk, Anna; Wisconsin, 1898 *6795.8 p67*
Boyl, Micheal 40; Ontario, 1871 *1823.21 p33*
Boyl, Susanna; Boston, 1756 *1642 p47*
Boyle, Adam 40; Ontario, 1871 *1823.17 p14*
Boyle, Andrew 35; Ontario, 1871 *1823.21 p33*
Boyle, Barnabas; Nantucket, MA, 1764 *1642 p89*
Boyle, Daniel; St. Johns, N.F., 1825 *1053.15 p6*
Boyle, David; Washington, 1887 *2770.40 p24*
Boyle, George 79; Ontario, 1871 *1823.21 p33*
Boyle, Henry; Philadelphia, 1778 *8529.30 p6*
Boyle, J. B. 56; Ontario, 1871 *1823.21 p33*
Boyle, James; Louisiana, 1836-1841 *4981.45 p208*
Boyle, James 45; Ontario, 1871 *1823.17 p14*
Boyle, Jane; Boston, 1769 *1642 p49*
Boyle, John 24; Ontario, 1871 *1823.21 p33*
Boyle, John 52; Ontario, 1871 *1823.21 p33*
Boyle, John; St. Johns, N.F., 1825 *1053.15 p7*
Boyle, John L.; Washington, 1883 *2770.40 p136*
Boyle, Judith; St. Johns, N.F., 1825 *1053.15 p6*
Boyle, Judy; St. Johns, N.F., 1825 *1053.15 p6*
Boyle, Margaret 12; Quebec, 1870 *8364.32 p22*
Boyle, Mary; Nantucket, MA, 1764 *1642 p89*
Boyle, Matthew 42; Ontario, 1871 *1823.17 p14*
Boyle, Matthew 64; Ontario, 1871 *1823.21 p33*
Boyle, Michael 55; Ontario, 1871 *1823.17 p14*
Boyle, Patrick 30; Ontario, 1871 *1823.21 p33*
Boyle, Rose 60; St. John, N.B., 1834 *6469.7 p5*
Boyle, Samuel 25; Ontario, 1871 *1823.17 p14*
Boyle, Samuel; St. Johns, N.F., 1825 *1053.15 p6*
Boyle, Walter 43; Ontario, 1871 *1823.17 p14*
Boyle, William 31; Ontario, 1871 *1823.21 p33*
Boyle, William 36; Ontario, 1871 *1823.17 p14*
Boyles, Dan; Boston, 1766 *1642 p36*
With wife
Boyles, John; Boston, 1772 *1642 p49*
Boylevre DeFaVerole, Gilles; Quebec, 1645 *9221.17 p152*
Boyner, M. 28; New Orleans, 1847 *778.6 p46*
Boys, Willm.; Maryland, 1674 *1236.25 p49*
Boysse, Guillaume; Quebec, 1652 *9221.17 p255*
Bozenhardt, John; Ohio, 1840-1897 *8365.35 p15*
Brabant, Antoine Joseph; Wisconsin, 1854-1858 *1495.20 p50*
*Wife:*Marie Antoinette Rosy
*Child:*Beatrice
*Child:*Therese
*Child:*Josephine
*Child:*Antoine Joseph, Jr.
*Child:*Marie
*Child:*Emerence
Brabant, Antoine Joseph, Jr. *SEE* Brabant, Antoine Joseph
Brabant, Beatrice *SEE* Brabant, Antoine Joseph
Brabant, Emerence *SEE* Brabant, Antoine Joseph
Brabant, Josephine *SEE* Brabant, Antoine Joseph
Brabant, Marie *SEE* Brabant, Antoine Joseph
Brabant, Marie Antoinette Rosy *SEE* Brabant, Antoine Joseph
Brabant, Therese *SEE* Brabant, Antoine Joseph
Brabason, Robert 41; Ontario, 1871 *1823.21 p33*
Brabazon, John M.; Louisiana, 1874 *4981.45 p131*
Brabek, . . .; Pennsylvania, 1750-1799 *2853.20 p17*
Brabenec, Antonin; New York, NY, 1866 *2853.20 p101*
Brabphy, Thomas 58; Ontario, 1871 *1823.21 p33*
Bracconier, Mr. 35; Port uncertain, 1848 *778.6 p46*
Brace, Wm 73; Ontario, 1871 *1823.21 p33*
Bracey, Elizabeth 11; Quebec, 1870 *8364.32 p22*
Brach, Gustav; America, 1867 *5475.1 p124*
Brach, Julius; America, 1867 *5475.1 p124*
Brach, Victor; Mexico, 1869 *5475.1 p126*
Brachet, M. 41; Ohio, 1847 *778.6 p46*
Brachetty, Christine Lutz *SEE* Brachetty, Jakob
Brachetty, Jakob; America, 1859 *5475.1 p522*
*Wife:*Christine Lutz
Brachmann, Anton; America, 1843 *5475.1 p366*
With 3 sons
With 5 daughters
Braciszewska, Catharine; Detroit, 1890 *9980.23 p97*
Brack, Janet 43; Ontario, 1871 *1823.17 p14*
Brack, John; Ohio, 1809-1852 *4511.35 p6*
Bracken, John 41; Ontario, 1871 *1823.21 p33*
Brackenbush, Charles; Ohio, 1809-1852 *4511.35 p6*
Bracker, Francois; Louisiana, 1836-1841 *4981.45 p208*
Brackhagen, Friedrich; America, 1882 *7420.1 p398*
Brackhagen, Heinrich; America, 1882 *7420.1 p327*
With family
Braconnier, Jeanne; Quebec, 1673 *4514.3 p284*
Bracouar, Robert; Quebec, 1659 *9221.17 p413*
Bracrzk, Stanislas; New York, NY, 1891 *6015.15 p23*
Bradburry, George; Jamaica, 1783 *8529.30 p12A*
Bradbury, David; New York, NY, 1836 *3274.56 p70*
Bradbury, Isaac; Portsmouth, NH, 1827 *3274.55 p69*
Bradbury, James; Boston, 1827 *3274.55 p68*
Bradbury, John 30; Indiana, 1853-1865 *9076.20 p66*
Bradbury, John; New York, NY, 1829 *3274.55 p68*
Bradbury, John; North Carolina, 1824 *1088.45 p3*
Braddon, J. G. 38; Ontario, 1871 *1823.21 p33*
Bradford, Amos 31; Ontario, 1871 *1823.21 p33*
Bradford, Dorothy *SEE* Bradford, Wm.
Bradford, Wm.; Plymouth, MA, 1620 *1920.45 p5*
*Wife:*Dorothy
Bradley, Alexander 39; Ontario, 1871 *1823.21 p33*
Bradley, Alexander 42; Ontario, 1871 *1823.21 p33*
Bradley, Anne 50; Ontario, 1871 *1823.21 p33*
Bradley, Anne; St. Johns, N.F., 1825 *1053.15 p6*
Bradley, Charles 13; Quebec, 1870 *8364.32 p22*
Bradley, Charles; South Carolina, 1813 *3208.30 p19*
Bradley, Charles; South Carolina, 1813 *3208.30 p31*
Bradley, Dennis 38; Ontario, 1871 *1823.21 p33*
Bradley, James 37; Michigan, 1880 *4491.42 p5*
Bradley, James 53; Ontario, 1871 *1823.21 p34*
Bradley, Jane McDade *SEE* Bradley, William
Bradley, John 42; Ontario, 1871 *1823.21 p34*
Bradley, John 73; Ontario, 1871 *1823.21 p34*
Bradley, Mary 33; Ontario, 1871 *1823.21 p34*
Bradley, Mary J. 28; Michigan, 1880 *4491.42 p5*
Bradley, Michael; South Carolina, 1813 *3208.30 p19*
Bradley, Michael; South Carolina, 1813 *3208.30 p31*
Bradley, Samuel 40; Ontario, 1871 *1823.21 p34*
Bradley, Samuel 40; Ontario, 1871 *1823.21 p34*
Bradley, Tamar; Boston, 1832 *3274.55 p70*
Bradley, William; Philadelphia, 1852 *8513.31 p296*
*Wife:*Jane McDade
Bradshaw, Charles 14; Quebec, 1870 *8364.32 p22*
Bradshaw, James 49; Ontario, 1871 *1823.21 p34*
Bradshaw, John; Maryland, 1674-1675 *1236.25 p51*
Bradshaw, John 56; Ontario, 1871 *1823.21 p34*
Bradshaw, John 60; Ontario, 1871 *1823.21 p34*

Bradshaw, John; Philadelphia, 1778 *8529.30 p2A*
Bradshaw, Richard 47; Ontario, 1871 *1823.21 p34*
Bradshaw, Samuel 35; Ontario, 1871 *1823.21 p34*
Bradshaw, Tho.; Maryland, 1672 *1236.25 p47*
Bradshaw, Wm; Jamestown, VA, 1633 *1658.20 p211*
Bradshawe, John; Virginia, 1652 *6254.4 p243*
Bradshawe, Robart; Virginia, 1652 *6254.4 p243*
Bradt, Carl Friedrich; America, 1861 *7420.1 p203*
Bradt, Carl Ludwig Friedrich; America, 1861 *7420.1 p203*
Bradt, John; Ontario, 1787 *1276.15 p230*
Bradt, Louis; America, 1860 *7420.1 p192*
Bradt, Peter; Ontario, 1787 *1276.15 p230*
Bradt, Rejer; Ontario, 1787 *1276.15 p230*
Brady, Bernard 45; Ontario, 1871 *1823.21 p34*
Brady, Edward; Philadelphia, 1847 *8513.31 p296*
  Wife:Mary Ann Sharp
Brady, Henry; Maryland, 1671 *1236.25 p46*
Brady, Hugh; Louisiana, 1852-1854 *7710.1 p154*
Brady, Hugh; New Orleans, 1849 *7710.1 p152*
Brady, James; Illinois, 1834-1900 *6020.5 p131*
Brady, James; Marblehead, MA, 1731 *1642 p73*
Brady, James 41; Ontario, 1871 *1823.21 p34*
Brady, Jane 21; Ontario, 1871 *1823.17 p14*
Brady, John; Louisiana, 1874 *4981.45 p130*
Brady, John; Ohio, 1842 *2763.1 p7*
Brady, John 54; Ontario, 1871 *1823.21 p34*
Brady, Joseph; Ohio, 1809-1852 *4511.35 p6*
Brady, Joseph 71; Ontario, 1871 *1823.21 p34*
Brady, Margaret Ellen; Miami, 1935 *4984.12 p39*
Brady, Mary Ann Sharp *SEE* Brady, Edward
Brady, Michael; Louisiana, 1874-1875 *4981.45 p298*
Brady, Owen 56; Ontario, 1871 *1823.17 p14*
Brady, Peter; New Orleans, 1851 *7242.30 p134*
Brady, Peter 30; Ontario, 1871 *1823.21 p34*
Brady, Thomas; New York, NY, 1888 *6212.1 p14*
Brady, Thomas 42; Ontario, 1871 *1823.21 p34*
Brady, Thomas 45; Ontario, 1871 *1823.21 p34*
Brady, William; Plymouth, MA, 1755 *1642 p90*
Bragg, Charles 22; Ontario, 1871 *1823.21 p34*
Bragg, Frederick 25; Ontario, 1871 *1823.21 p34*
Bragg, George 1; Ontario, 1871 *1823.17 p14*
Bragg, Hannah 11; Ontario, 1871 *1823.17 p14*
Bragg, James 36; Ontario, 1871 *1823.21 p34*
Bragg, Jane 18; Ontario, 1871 *1823.21 p34*
Bragg, John 26; Ontario, 1871 *1823.21 p34*
Braham, Guss; Washington, 1886 *2770.40 p195*
Braidle, Leonard; Ohio, 1809-1852 *4511.35 p6*
Braidy, Chazkel C.; Missouri, 1894 *3276.1 p1*
Brainard, Celia 12; Michigan, 1880 *4491.33 p3*
Brainard, Mary A. 20; Michigan, 1880 *4491.33 p3*
Braisville, Mr. 25; America, 1840 *778.6 p46*
Braithwaite, Elijah 41; Ontario, 1871 *1823.21 p34*
Braithwaite, John; Ohio, 1845 *2763.1 p7*
Braithwaite, Mary 50; Ontario, 1871 *1823.21 p34*
Brajelongne, Etienne de; Quebec, 1702 *2314.30 p169*
Brajelongne, Etienne de; Quebec, 1702 *2314.30 p177*
Brake, Alfred *SEE* Brake, Elisha, Jr.
Brake, Alice; Massachusetts, 1907 *9228.50 p127*
Brake, Elisha, Jr.; Massachusetts, 1907-1910 *9228.50 p127*
  Brother:Alfred
  Sister:Mary Ann
Brake, Elisha, Sr.; Massachusetts, 1907 *9228.50 p127*
Brake, J. 15; Quebec, 1870 *8364.32 p22*
Brake, John 40; Ontario, 1871 *1823.17 p14*
Brake, Mary Ann *SEE* Brake, Elisha, Jr.
Brake, Mary Ann; Massachusetts, 1910 *9228.50 p127*
Brake, Philip; Massachusetts, 1910 *9228.50 p127*
Brakebusch, Gustav; Wisconsin, 1910 *6795.8 p174*
Brakebush, Heinrich; Wisconsin, 1903 *6795.8 p158*
Brakel, Ferdinand; Iowa, 1875 *1211.15 p9*
Brakhagen, Friedrich Wilhelm; America, 1870 *7420.1 p283*
Braley, David; Massachusetts, 1768 *1642 p90*
Braley, Lydia; Massachusetts, 1767 *1642 p90*
Bralski, Maryanna; Detroit, 1929-1930 *6214.5 p61*
Bram, John; Iowa, 1868-1875 *777.40 p6*
Bram, John 30; Kansas, 1880 *777.40 p7*
  Wife:Mary 28
Bram, Mary 28 *SEE* Bram, John
Braman, Thomas; New England, 1745 *1642 p28*
Bramer, Reca 45; Michigan, 1880 *4491.36 p2*
Bramhall, Elizabeth 10; Quebec, 1870 *8364.32 p22*
Bramhall, Sarah 12; Quebec, 1870 *8364.32 p22*
Bramley, Amelia 18; Ontario, 1871 *1823.17 p14*
Bramley, Mary; Maryland, 1674 *1236.25 p50*
Brammer, Edward 50; Ontario, 1871 *1823.21 p34*
Brammer, Heinrich; Wisconsin, 1881 *6795.8 p233*
Brampton, Peter 17; Quebec, 1870 *8364.32 p22*
Bramspach, Friederike; New York, NY, 1855 *7420.1 p135*
Bran, Sarah; Lynn, MA, 1694 *1642 p71*

Branagan, Ellen; St. John, N.B., 1842 *2978.20 p6*
Branagan, Terence; St. John, N.B., 1842 *2978.20 p7*
Branan, John W. 44; Ontario, 1871 *1823.17 p14*
Branan, Moses 54; Ontario, 1871 *1823.21 p34*
Branche, Rene 20; Quebec, 1661 *9221.17 p449*
Brancheu, Rene 20; Quebec, 1661 *9221.17 p449*
Branchflower, George 30; Ontario, 1871 *1823.17 p15*
Brancias, Joseph; Illinois, 1852 *6079.1 p2*
Brand, . . .; Port uncertain, 1883 *7420.1 p335*
Brand, Mr.; America, 1857 *7420.1 p158*
Brand, Adolf; Brazil, 1869 *5475.1 p13*
Brand, Alexander 11 months; Portland, ME, 1906 *970.38 p76*
Brand, Alexander 26; Portland, ME, 1906 *970.38 p76*
Brand, Anton Christian Ludwig; America, 1888 *7420.1 p355*
Brand, Carl; America, 1865 *7420.1 p229*
  With wife & 3 children
Brand, Charles; North Carolina, 1854 *1088.45 p3*
Brand, Christian; America, 1856 *7420.1 p145*
Brand, David 64; Ontario, 1871 *1823.17 p15*
Brand, Dietrich Heinrich Wilhelm; America, 1846 *7420.1 p42*
Brand, Ernst; America, 1868 *7420.1 p269*
  With wife & daughter
Brand, Frederick 56; Ontario, 1871 *1823.21 p34*
Brand, Friedrich Wilhelm; Chicago, 1887 *7420.1 p352*
  Uncle:Koritz
  With aunt
Brand, Heinrich Wilhelm; America, 1846 *7420.1 p42*
Brand, Johann Friedrich; Port uncertain, 1836 *7420.1 p10*
Brand, Kata 34; Portland, ME, 1906 *970.38 p76*
Brand, Koritz *SEE* Brand, Friedrich Wilhelm
Brand, Peter; Ohio, 1809-1852 *4511.35 p6*
Brand, Vincent; Kansas, 1917-1918 *1826.15 p81*
Brandbourg, Franc. 36; Port uncertain, 1840 *778.6 p46*
Brandeau, Francis 36; Port uncertain, 1840 *778.6 p46*
Brandebourg, Francs. 29; Port uncertain, 1846 *778.6 p46*
Brandenburger, Elisabeth 35; Brazil, 1862 *5475.1 p551*
Brander, Henry; Illinois, 1857 *6079.1 p2*
Brandes, Anna Sophie Marie; America, 1868 *7420.1 p269*
Brandes, Engel Marie Sophie; America, 1856 *7420.1 p147*
Brandes, Hans Heinrich; America, 1856 *7420.1 p145*
Brandes, Hans Heinrich; America, 1856 *7420.1 p145*
Brandes, Heinrich Anton; Port uncertain, 1824 *7420.1 p1*
Brandes, Johann Conrad; America, 1852 *7420.1 p86*
Brandes, Johann Conrad; America, 1857 *7420.1 p158*
Brandes, Johann Friedrich; America, 1868 *7420.1 p269*
  With family
Brandey, Mr. 30; New Orleans, 1848 *778.6 p46*
Brandey, Jean 22; New Orleans, 1848 *778.6 p46*
Brandey, Jean 38; New Orleans, 1845 *778.6 p46*
Brandie, Adam; New York, 1900 *1766.20 p23*
Brandly, Abs 20; Mississippi, 1847 *778.6 p46*
Brandly, Ann 24; Mississippi, 1847 *778.6 p46*
Brandly, Johann 21; Mississippi, 1847 *778.6 p46*
Brando, William; Ohio, 1844 *2763.1 p7*
Brandon, Anne; Quebec, 1665 *4514.3 p284*
Brandon, James 59; Ontario, 1871 *1823.17 p15*
Brandon, Michel 60; Ontario, 1871 *1823.21 p34*
Brandon, Thomas 34; Ontario, 1871 *1823.17 p15*
Brandorff, Alexander Philipp; New Jersey, 1879 *7420.1 p312*
Brandorff, Arnold *SEE* Brandorff, Carl
Brandorff, Carl; America, 1872 *7420.1 p293*
  Brother:Arnold
Brands, Engel Marie; America, 1868 *7420.1 p271*
  Daughter:Ernestine
  Son:Heinrich Conrad Wilhelm
Brands, Heinrich Christoph; America, 1868 *7420.1 p269*
  With wife & daughter
  With son 10
  With son 6
  With son 16
  With son 22
Brandt, Miss; America, 1871 *7420.1 p292*
Brandt, Adolf 22; New York, NY, 1893 *1883.7 p43*
Brandt, Adolph Georg; America, 1888 *7420.1 p355*
Brandt, Anna; Indianapolis, 1886 *7420.1 p350*
Brandt, Anna; St. Paul, MN, 1884 *1865.50 p42*
  Child:Carolina
  Child:Hilma Augusta
  Child:Otto Conrad
Brandt, Anna Caroline *SEE* Brandt, August Friedrich
Brandt, Anton Friedrich Wilhelm; America, 1893 *7420.1 p368*
  Wife:Christine Sophie Schmidt
Brandt, August Friedrich; America, 1881 *7420.1 p319*
  Sister:Anna Caroline

Brandt, Bertha; America, 1853 *7420.1 p103*
Brandt, Carl August Walerius; Cleveland, OH, 1902-1905 *9722.10 p317*
Brandt, Carl Heinrich; America, 1858 *7420.1 p176*
Brandt, Carolina; Colorado, 1892 *1029.59 p12*
Brandt, Carolina *SEE* Brandt, Anna
Brandt, Caroline; Colorado, 1885 *1029.59 p12*
Brandt, Christian Friedrich; America, 1872 *7420.1 p294*
Brandt, Christine Sophie Schmidt *SEE* Brandt, Anton Friedrich Wilhelm
Brandt, Conrad; Port uncertain, 1859 *7420.1 p184*
Brandt, D.; America, 1845 *7420.1 p35*
  With wife & 4 children
Brandt, Daniel; America, 1894 *7420.1 p370*
Brandt, Daniel Friedrich Alexander; America, 1889 *7420.1 p358*
Brandt, Daniel Wilhelm; America, 1897 *7420.1 p373*
Brandt, Edward G.; Colorado, 1904 *1029.59 p12*
Brandt, Edward G.; Colorado, 1904 *1029.59 p12*
Brandt, Engel Marie; America, 1867 *7420.1 p254*
Brandt, Ernst; America, 1868 *7420.1 p269*
  With wife & daughter
Brandt, Friedrich; America, 1853 *7420.1 p103*
Brandt, Friedrich; America, 1857 *7420.1 p158*
Brandt, Friedrich; Indiana, 1908 *7420.1 p383*
Brandt, Friedrich; Kansas, 1880 *7420.1 p315*
Brandt, Friedrich; Pennsylvania, 1908 *7420.1 p383*
Brandt, Friedrich Wilhelm; America, 1871 *7420.1 p289*
Brandt, Friedrich Wilhelm Christoph; America, 1897 *7420.1 p373*
Brandt, George; Louisiana, 1841-1844 *4981.45 p210*
Brandt, George; North Carolina, 1848 *1088.45 p3*
Brandt, Heinrich; Port uncertain, 1865 *7420.1 p229*
Brandt, Heinrich Anton; America, 1880 *7420.1 p315*
Brandt, Hilma Augusta *SEE* Brandt, Anna
Brandt, Jacob; Halifax, N.S., 1902 *1860.4 p44*
Brandt, Jacob; North Carolina, 1859 *1088.45 p3*
Brandt, John; North Carolina, 1835 *1088.45 p3*
Brandt, Jon; Colorado, 1885 *1029.59 p12*
Brandt, Karl Daniel; America, 1890 *7420.1 p360*
Brandt, Karl Reinhard; New York, NY, 1885 *5475.1 p17*
Brandt, Leon; North Carolina, 1836 *1088.45 p3*
Brandt, Louise Marie Christine; America, 1883 *7420.1 p335*
Brandt, Nels O.; New York, NY, 1881-1883 *1865.50 p42*
Brandt, Otto Conrad *SEE* Brandt, Anna
Brandt, Wilhelm; Ohio, 1840-1897 *8365.35 p15*
Brandy, Daniel 30; Ontario, 1871 *1823.17 p15*
Brandy, Duncan 37; Ontario, 1871 *1823.17 p15*
Brandy, John 40; Ontario, 1871 *1823.17 p15*
Branecky, Frantisek; Texas, 1860-1865 *2853.20 p67*
Branem, John; Ohio, 1809-1852 *4511.35 p6*
Branen, Mr.; North Carolina, 1710 *3629.40 p3*
  With 4 children & relative
Braner, Johann Friedrich; America, 1882 *2526.43 p164*
Branfield, John; Boston, 1764 *1642 p33*
Branley, William; St. John, N.B., 1847 *2978.15 p35*
Brannagh, Samuel; New York, 1836 *3274.55 p75*
Brannah, John; Boston, 1826 *3274.55 p72*
Brannan, John; Ohio, 1844 *2763.1 p7*
Brannen, John; St. John, N.B., 1848 *2978.15 p38*
Brannigan, William 30; Toronto, 1867 *9228.50 p255*
Brannstrom, Erik Johan; New York, NY, 1848 *6412.40 p155*
Brans, George; Toronto, 1844 *2910.35 p114*
Branston, I. S. 20; Ontario, 1871 *1823.17 p15*
Branston, Mary Ann 50; Ontario, 1871 *1823.21 p34*
Branston, William 27; Ontario, 1871 *1823.21 p34*
Branstrom, E.J.; New York, NY, 1845 *6412.40 p149*
Brant, Henry Grover 33; Ontario, 1871 *1823.17 p15*
Brantin, John 45; Ontario, 1871 *1823.21 p35*
Brantingham, Martin; Ohio, 1809-1852 *4511.35 p6*
Branton, George E. 39; Ontario, 1871 *1823.21 p35*
Branton, Henry 53; Ontario, 1871 *1823.17 p15*
Branton, John 30; Ontario, 1871 *1823.17 p15*
Branton, Rich 35; Ontario, 1871 *1823.21 p35*
Branton, Thomas 25; Ontario, 1871 *1823.21 p35*
Branton, William 30; Ontario, 1871 *1823.21 p35*
Branton, William 56; Ontario, 1871 *1823.21 p35*
Brapf, Valentine; Ohio, 1809-1852 *4511.35 p6*
Braquet, Hilla.re 22; New Orleans, 1845 *778.6 p46*
Braraton, John 60; Ontario, 1871 *1823.21 p35*
Brarly, James; Massachusetts, 1675-1676 *1642 p128*
Brasche, Henry; Illinois, 1853 *6079.1 p2*
Bras-De-Fer DeChateaufort, Marc-Antoine; Quebec, 1634 *9221.17 p31*
Braselmann, Peter; South Carolina, 1808 *6155.4 p18*
Brass, Anton; New York, 1859 *358.56 p54*
Brass, P.; New Orleans, 1850 *7242.30 p134*
Brassard, Antoine 1; Quebec, 1641 *9221.17 p101*
  With parents
  Sister:Jeanne 3 months

Brassard, Antoine 27; Quebec, 1636 *9221.17 p52*
Brassard, Jeanne 3 *SEE* Brassard, Antoine
Brassard, Louis 28; Quebec, 1658 *9221.17 p377*
Brassard, Paul; Quebec, 1642 *9221.17 p113*
Brassen, N. H.; Washington, 1880 *2770.40 p134*
Brassi, Miss 3; America, 1842 *778.6 p46*
Brassi, Miss 6; America, 1842 *778.6 p46*
Brassi, Mrs. 30; America, 1842 *778.6 p46*
Brassi, F. 35; America, 1842 *778.6 p46*
Brassier, Jacques 22; Montreal, 1653 *9221.17 p284*
Brat, Aaron; Ontario, 1787 *1276.15 p230*
   With relative
Bratczyk, Stanislaus; New York, NY, 1891 *6015.15 p23*
Brats, A. 34; Port uncertain, 1843 *778.6 p46*
Bratt, G.W.; San Francisco, 1855 *6412.40 p153*
Bratt, Jonas 40; Ontario, 1871 *1823.21 p35*
Bratt, Samuel 54; Ontario, 1871 *1823.21 p35*
Bratts, Enoch 56; Ontario, 1871 *1823.21 p35*
Bratty, John 38; New York, NY, 1825 *6178.50 p148*
Bratz, . . .; Port uncertain, 1843 *778.6 p46*
Bratz, . . .; Port uncertain, 1843 *778.6 p47*
Brau, Henri 24; Quebec, 1659 *9221.17 p395*
Braubach, Miss; Port uncertain, 1828 *170.15 p21*
Braubach, Gertraud; Port uncertain, 1828 *170.15 p21*
Brauder, J. F.; Louisiana, 1874 *4981.45 p295*
Braudreth, Wm. 39; Ontario, 1871 *1823.21 p35*
Brauer, Carl 31; New York, NY, 1893 *1883.7 p39*
Brauer, Philipp; Chile, 1852 *1192.4 p51*
Braumuller, Johan 29; America, 1840 *778.6 p47*
Braun, Adam; America, 1869 *5475.1 p297*
Braun, Adam 34; Port uncertain, 1846 *778.6 p47*
Braun, Alexander 18 months; New York, NY, 1898
   7951.13 p41
Braun, Andreas *SEE* Braun, Johann
Braun, Anna Gertrud; America, 1800-1899 *5475.1 p140*
   Daughter: Katharina
   Daughter: Barbara
   Grandchild: Johann
Braun, Apolonia 15; New York, NY, 1893 *1883.7 p42*
Braun, Aug.; Louisiana, 1874-1875 *4981.45 p297*
Braun, August; Wisconsin, 1873 *6795.8 p63*
Braun, August; Wisconsin, 1880 *6795.8 p63*
Braun, Barbara *SEE* Braun, Anna Gertrud Schmitt
Braun, Barbara 64; America, 1869 *5475.1 p170*
Braun, Bertha; Wisconsin, 1883 *6795.8 p89*
Braun, Cecile 24; Louisiana, 1848 *778.6 p47*
Braun, Charlotte; America, 1833 *2526.43 p164*
Braun, Elisabeth *SEE* Braun, Johann
Braun, Elisabeth *SEE* Braun, Johann
Braun, Elisabeth 9; New York, NY, 1898 *7951.13 p41*
Braun, Elisabeth 38; New York, NY, 1898 *7951.13 p41*
Braun, Emanuel 3; New York, NY, 1893 *1883.7 p42*
Braun, Emanuel/Rob 16; New York, NY, 1898 *7951.13
   p41*
Braun, Fransica 1; New York, NY, 1893 *1883.7 p42*
Braun, Friedrich Ludwig; America, 1857 *2526.43 p164*
Braun, Geo 18; New York, NY, 1898 *7951.13 p41*
Braun, Georg *SEE* Braun, Johann
Braun, Georg Friedrich; America, 1850 *2526.43 p164*
Braun, Georg Wilhelm; America, 1883 *2526.43 p164*
Braun, George 26; Texas, 1913 *8425.16 p31*
Braun, Gertrud 4 *SEE* Braun, Peter
Braun, Gertrud Jung 27 *SEE* Braun, Peter
Braun, Gustav; Wisconsin, 1888 *6795.8 p24*
Braun, Helena 48; America, 1843 *5475.1 p294*
Braun, Helena 22; Texas, 1913 *8425.16 p31*
Braun, J. Peter *SEE* Braun, Johann
Braun, Jacob 8 months; Texas, 1913 *8425.16 p31*
Braun, Jakob *SEE* Braun, Johann
Braun, Jakob; New York, 1873 *5475.1 p127*
Braun, Jakob; New York, NY, 1893 *3366.30 p70*
Braun, Jean 30; Louisiana, 1848 *778.6 p47*
Braun, Joh. Jakob *SEE* Braun, Johann
Braun, Johan 19; New York, NY, 1893 *1883.7 p42*
Braun, Johann *SEE* Braun, Anna Gertrud Schmitt
Braun, Johann; America, 1872 *5475.1 p171*
Braun, Johann *SEE* Braun, Johann
Braun, Johann; America, 1872 *5475.1 p212*
   Wife: Margarethe Mang
   Son: J. Peter
   Daughter: Margarethe
   Son: Johann
   Son: Georg
   Son: Peter
   Daughter: Maria
Braun, Johann *SEE* Braun, Johann
Braun, Johann; America, 1874 *5475.1 p451*
   Wife: Katharina Schramm
   Daughter: Elisabeth
   Daughter: Katharina
   Son: Andreas
   Son: Jakob
   Daughter: Maria

   Daughter: Margarethe
   Son: Peter
   Son: Johann
   Son: Mathias
Braun, Johann *SEE* Braun, Johann
Braun, Johann; America, 1877 *5475.1 p452*
   Wife: Margarethe Neu
   Child: Maria
   Child: Johann
   Child: Elisabeth
   Child: Joh. Jakob
   Child: Jos. Peter
Braun, Johann 4; New York, NY, 1898 *7951.13 p41*
Braun, Johann 4; Texas, 1913 *8425.16 p31*
Braun, Johann Friedrich; America, 1867 *2526.43 p164*
Braun, Johannes 43; New York, NY, 1893 *1883.7 p42*
Braun, Jos. Peter *SEE* Braun, Johann
Braun, Josef 9; New York, NY, 1893 *1883.7 p42*
Braun, Ju.ia 31; Port uncertain, 1846 *778.6 p47*
Braun, Karl; Colorado, 1890 *1029.59 p13*
Braun, Karl; Colorado, 1894 *1029.59 p13*
Braun, Karoline; America, 1866 *5475.1 p557*
Braun, Katharina *SEE* Braun, Anna Gertrud Schmitt
Braun, Katharina; America, 1858 *5475.1 p556*
Braun, Katharina *SEE* Braun, Johann
Braun, Katharina Schramm *SEE* Braun, Johann
Braun, Katharina 12; New York, NY, 1893 *1883.7 p42*
Braun, Katharina 39; New York, NY, 1893 *1883.7 p42*
Braun, Louis 17; New Orleans, 1848 *778.6 p47*
Braun, Ludwig Albrecht; America, 1859 *2526.43 p164*
Braun, Madelaine 28; Mississippi, 1848 *778.6 p47*
Braun, Margarethe *SEE* Braun, Johann
Braun, Margarethe Mang *SEE* Braun, Johann
Braun, Margarethe *SEE* Braun, Johann
Braun, Margarethe Neu *SEE* Braun, Johann
Braun, Margarethe; America, 1883 *5475.1 p174*
Braun, Margueritte 24; America, 1842 *778.6 p47*
Braun, Maria *SEE* Braun, Johann
Braun, Maria *SEE* Braun, Johann
Braun, Maria *SEE* Braun, Johann
Braun, Maria Klahm *SEE* Braun, Mathias
Braun, Maria 1 *SEE* Braun, Peter
Braun, Maria 31; America, 1846 *5475.1 p301*
Braun, Maria 58; America, 1847 *778.6 p47*
Braun, Marie 4; Mississippi, 1848 *778.6 p47*
Braun, Martin 27; Philadelphia, 1912 *8425.16 p34*
Braun, Mathias *SEE* Braun, Johann
Braun, Mathias 41; America, 1890 *5475.1 p76*
   Wife: Maria Klahm
Braun, Michael 19; New York, NY, 1901 *8425.16 p34*
Braun, Michel; America, 1883 *5475.1 p174*
Braun, Monica 25; Philadelphia, 1912 *8425.16 p34*
Braun, Nikolaus; America, 1846 *5475.1 p301*
Braun, Nikolaus; America, 1866 *5475.1 p190*
Braun, Paul 10; New York, NY, 1893 *1883.7 p42*
Braun, Peter; America, 1857 *5475.1 p507*
Braun, Peter *SEE* Braun, Johann
Braun, Peter *SEE* Braun, Johann
Braun, Peter 29; America, 1856 *5475.1 p295*
   Wife: Gertrud Jung 27
   Daughter: Maria 1
   Daughter: Gertrud 4
Braun, Peter 25; Pennsylvania, 1888 *5475.1 p286*
Braun, Philipp; Galveston, TX, 1855 *571.7 p16*
Braun, Rob 39; New York, NY, 1898 *7951.13 p41*
Braun, Sebastian 22; America, 1846 *778.6 p47*
Braun, Thiebaut 1; Mississippi, 1848 *778.6 p47*
Braun, Valentin 17; New York, NY, 1893 *1883.7 p42*
Braun, Wilhelm C.; Wisconsin, 1889 *6795.8 p221*
Braun, Wilhelm Carl F.; Wisconsin, 1889 *6795.8 p152*
Braun, Wm.; Nebraska, 1905 *3004.30 p46*
Braun, Xavier 34; Mississippi, 1848 *778.6 p47*
Braund, George 38; Ontario, 1871 *1823.21 p35*
Braund, John Q. 46; Ontario, 1871 *1823.17 p15*
Braunelle, Yves; Quebec, 1660 *9221.17 p432*
   With son
Brauner, L.; Louisiana, 1874 *4981.45 p295*
Braunheim, Walter; Miami, 1935 *4984.12 p39*
Braunig, Jakob; America, 1887 *2526.43 p164*
Braunle, Jean 19; America, 1847 *778.6 p47*
Braunmiller, Ludwick; Philadelphia, 1778 *8529.30 p2*
Braunmueller, Ludwick; Philadelphia, 1778 *8529.30 p2*
Braunner, A. 19; Port uncertain, 1845 *778.6 p47*
Braunung, G.; Chile, 1852 *1192.4 p51*
   With wife
   With child 16
   With child 11
Braunwerth, Babette; Valdivia, Chile, 1852 *1192.4 p55*
   With daughter 15
Brausch, Elisabeth Besser 38 *SEE* Brausch, Franz

Brausch, Franz 40; America, 1847 *5475.1 p327*
   Wife: Elisabeth Besser 38
   Son: Heinrich 1
   Daughter: Maria 4
Brausch, Heinrich 1 *SEE* Brausch, Franz
Brausch, Johann; America, 1868 *5475.1 p262*
Brausch, Maria 4 *SEE* Brausch, Franz
Brausch, Nikolaus; America, 1867 *5475.1 p284*
Braut, Stephan 25; Galveston, TX, 1844 *3967.10 p372*
Bravinder, Robert 51; Ontario, 1871 *1823.21 p35*
Brawday, Jacob 65; Ontario, 1871 *1823.17 p15*
Brawley, Michael; Toronto, 1844 *2910.35 p112*
Brawn, Aron; Ohio, 1840-1897 *8365.35 p15*
Bray, Frederick; Ontario, 1831-1912 *9228.50 p128*
   Wife: Margaret D. Scott
Bray, Margaret D. Scott *SEE* Bray, Frederick
Bray, Patrick 36; Ontario, 1871 *1823.21 p35*
Bray, Thomas; Newfoundland, 1814 *3476.10 p54*
Bray, Thomas 40; Ontario, 1871 *1823.21 p35*
Braybeal, Ruth; Toronto, 1921-1962 *9228.50 p467*
Brazeau, Andre; Montreal, 1662 *9221.17 p496*
Brazeau, Marie; Canada, 1681 *1142.10 p128*
   With family
Brazier, Robert; North Carolina, 1824 *1088.45 p4*
Brazil, Oliver 40; Ontario, 1871 *1823.21 p35*
Brazill, Patrick 42; Ontario, 1871 *1823.21 p35*
Breacher, John 63; Ontario, 1871 *1823.21 p35*
Bready, James; Boston, 1752 *1642 p46*
Breakey, John 50; Ontario, 1871 *1823.17 p15*
Breathwale, Thomas 50; Ontario, 1871 *1823.21 p35*
Breau, Vincent; Quebec, 1647 *9221.17 p177*
Breber, Cath. 22; America, 1841 *778.6 p47*
Brebeuf, Jean de; Quebec, 1625 *9221.17 p27*
Brebner, Charles 66; Ontario, 1871 *1823.17 p15*
Brechlin, Herman Franz; Wisconsin, 1897 *6795.8 p71*
Brechmann, Franz; Colorado, 1881 *1029.59 p13*
Brechmann, Franz; Colorado, 1884 *1029.59 p13*
Brechtelsbauer, Elise; New York, 1860 *358.56 p5*
Breckenridge, Caroline 1; Santa Clara Co., CA, 1860
   8704.1 p22
Breckle, Gottlieb; Chile, 1852 *1192.4 p54*
Bred, Adolph; South Carolina, 1800-1899 *6155.4 p18*
Bredael, Jean; Wisconsin, 1857 *1495.20 p41*
Bredemeier, Carl Friedrich Wilhelm; America, 1867
   7420.1 p254
Bredemeier, Carl Heinrich Friedrich; America, 1889
   7420.1 p358
Bredemeier, Carl Wilhelm Christian; America, 1882
   7420.1 p327
Bredemeier, Caroline Rosine Charlotte; America, 1867
   7420.1 p254
Bredemeier, Ernestine; America, 1846 *7420.1 p42*
Bredemeier, Ferdinand; America, 1896 *7420.1 p372*
Bredemeier, Friedrich Christian Wilhelm; America, 1867
   7420.1 p254
Bredemeier, Friedrich Christian Wilhelm; America, 1882
   7420.1 p328
Bredemeier, Friedrich Wilhelm; America, 1887 *7420.1
   p353*
Bredemeier, Hans Heinrich Conrad *SEE* Bredemeier,
   Johann Conrad
Bredemeier, Heinrich; America, 1858 *7420.1 p176*
Bredemeier, Heinrich Ludwig; America, 1853 *7420.1
   p103*
Bredemeier, Heinrich Wilhelm *SEE* Bredemeier, Johann
   Conrad
Bredemeier, Johann Conrad; Illinois, 1873 *7420.1 p299*
   With wife
   Son: Johann Friedrich
   Son: Heinrich Wilhelm
   Son: Hans Heinrich Conrad
Bredemeier, Johann Friedrich *SEE* Bredemeier, Johann
   Conrad
Bredemeier, Ludwig; America, 1854 *7420.1 p116*
Bredemeier, Sophie; America, 1854 *7420.1 p116*
Bredemeier, Wilhelm; America, 1854 *7420.1 p116*
Bredemeyer, Christine Luise Leonore; America, 1837
   7420.1 p14
Bredemeyer, Ludwig; America, 1868 *7420.1 p269*
   With family
Bredenberg, Oscar; Cleveland, OH, 1890-1893 *9722.10
   p117*
Bredler, John 41; Ontario, 1871 *1823.21 p35*
Bredthauer, August; Port uncertain, 1904 *7420.1 p379*
Bredthauer, H.W.; America, 1857 *7420.1 p158*
   With wife & 3 children
Breeden, Ann; Germantown, PA, 1856 *8513.31 p294*
Breeland, Charles D.; North Carolina, 1821 *1088.45 p4*
Breen, Anne; New Orleans, 1850 *7242.30 p135*
Breen, Bridget 40; Ontario, 1871 *1823.21 p35*
Breen, Fanny; New Orleans, 1850 *7242.30 p135*
Breen, Hanna; St. Johns, N.F., 1825 *1053.15 p6*
Breen, James; New Orleans, 1850 *7242.30 p135*

Breen, John; New Orleans, 1850 **7242.30** *p135*
Breen, John 51; Ontario, 1871 *1823.21* *p35*
Breen, John; Toronto, 1844 *2910.35* *p116*
Breen, John P.; Toronto, 1844 *2910.35* *p116*
Breen, Joseph 46; Ontario, 1871 *1823.21* *p35*
Breen, Lizzie; Portsmouth, NH, 1899-1926 **9228.50** *p243*
Breen, Margaret; New Orleans, 1850 **7242.30** *p135*
Breen, Mary; New Orleans, 1850 **7242.30** *p135*
Breen, Mary; St. Johns, N.F., 1825 *1053.15* *p6*
Breen, Michael 40; Ontario, 1871 *1823.21* *p35*
Breen, Patrick; New Orleans, 1850 **7242.30** *p135*
Breen, Patrick; Toronto, 1844 *2910.35* *p113*
Breen, Patrick; Toronto, 1844 *2910.35* *p114*
Breen, Peter; New Orleans, 1850 **7242.30** *p135*
Breen, Philip 65; Ontario, 1871 *1823.21* *p35*
Breen, William; New Orleans, 1850 **7242.30** *p135*
Breenan, Edward 80; Ontario, 1871 *1823.21* *p35*
Breese, Thomas 24; Ontario, 1871 *1823.21* *p35*
Breet, Mathias; Boston, 1766 *1642* *p37*
Breffulh, Mr. 23; America, 1841 *778.6* *p47*
Breffulh, Mr. 33; America, 1841 *778.6* *p47*
Bregenzer, Conrad 6; America, 1845 *778.6* *p47*
Bregenzer, Elize 8; America, 1845 *778.6* *p47*
Bregenzer, Frederica 40; America, 1845 *778.6* *p47*
Breggs, William 34; Ontario, 1871 *1823.21* *p35*
Breglel, Joseph; Ohio, 1809-1852 *4511.35* *p6*
Breham, Margaret 44 *SEE* Breham, Oliver
Breham, Oliver 45; Ohio, 1880 *4879.40* *p259*
　*Wife:*Margaret 44
Brehant DeL'Isle, Achille; Quebec, 1636 *9221.17* *p49*
Brehaut, Benjamin; Massachusetts, 1796-1896 **9228.50** *p128*
Brehaut, Benjamin Noble; America, 1855-1888 **9228.50** *p130*
Brehaut, Daniel; America, 1850-1900 **9228.50** *p130*
Brehaut, Daniel *SEE* Brehaut, Henry
Brehaut, Daniel *SEE* Brehaut, Henry
Brehaut, Eliz. Pulham *SEE* Brehaut, Henry
Brehaut, Elizabeth; Massachusetts, 1796-1896 **9228.50** *p128*
Brehaut, Elizabeth Pullam *SEE* Brehaut, Henry
Brehaut, Elizabeth Pulham *SEE* Brehaut, Henry
Brehaut, Elizabeth *SEE* Brehaut, Henry
Brehaut, Elizabeth Pulham *SEE* Brehaut, Henry
Brehaut, Elizabeth Hannah Brooks *SEE* Brehaut, William John
Brehaut, G. Herbert *SEE* Brehaut, William John
Brehaut, Henry; Dorchester, MA, 1796-1896 **9228.50** *p128*
Brehaut, Henry *SEE* Brehaut, Henry
Brehaut, Henry; Prince Edward Island, 1792-1823 **9228.50** *p128*
　*Wife:*Elizabeth Pullam
　*Son:*Henry
Brehaut, Henry *SEE* Brehaut, Henry
Brehaut, Henry; Prince Edward Island, 1806 **9228.50** *p128*
　*Wife:*Elizabeth Pulham
　*Child:*Henry
　*Child:*Thomas Smith
Brehaut, Henry; Prince Edward Island, 1806 **9228.50** *p129*
　*Wife:*Elizabeth Pulham
　*Child:*Daniel
　*Child:*Elizabeth
Brehaut, Henry; Prince Edward Island, 1806 **9228.50** *p659*
　*Wife:*Eliz. Pulham
　*Child:*Daniel
　*Child:*Henry, II
Brehaut, Henry, II *SEE* Brehaut, Henry
Brehaut, Joseph Watson; America, 1853-1900 **9228.50** *p130*
Brehaut, Peter; Quebec, 1788-1792 **9228.50** *p128*
Brehaut, Thomas Smith *SEE* Brehaut, Henry
Brehaut, William John; Nebraska, 1873-1878 **9228.50** *p128*
　*Wife:*Elizabeth Hannah Brooks
　*Child:*G. Herbert
Brehen, Adam; Ohio, 1809-1852 *4511.35* *p6*
Brehen, Jacob; Ohio, 1809-1852 *4511.35* *p6*
Brehier, Jean; Quebec, 1643 *9221.17* *p130*
Brehm, Johann Nicolaus; America, 1868 *7919.3* *p530*
Brehm, Philip; Illinois, 1856 *6079.1* *p2*
Brehmeier, Friedrich August; America, 1840 *7420.1* *p18*
Brehmer, Wilhelmine; Wisconsin, 1893 *6795.8* *p160*
Brehmeyer, Johann Heinrich August; Port uncertain, 1858 *7420.1* *p177*
Breid, Johann; America, 1879 *5475.1* *p306*
Breidling, Joh. 16; New York, NY, 1886 *8425.16* *p33*
Breidt, Anna Katharina; Brazil, 1848 *5475.1* *p439*
Breier, Johann Jakob *SEE* Breier, Nikolaus
Breier, Margarethe Jochum *SEE* Breier, Nikolaus

Breier, Maria *SEE* Breier, Nikolaus
Breier, Nikolaus; Pittsburgh, 1891 *5475.1* *p393*
　*Wife:*Margarethe Jochum
　*Daughter:*Maria
　*Son:*Johann Jakob
Breimeier, Ernestine Wilhelmine; America, 1862 *7420.1* *p214*
　With son & 3 daughters
Breimer, Georg; America, 1889 *2526.43* *p164*
Breimer, Jakob 16; America, 1879 *2526.43* *p164*
Breiner, Christine 21; America, 1847 *778.6* *p47*
Breiner, Franz Jos. 18; America, 1847 *778.6* *p47*
Breit, Anna 50; America, 1855 *5475.1* *p318*
Breit, Elisabeth *SEE* Breit, Johann Georg
Breit, Elisabeth Hoffmann *SEE* Breit, Johann Georg
Breit, Helma 36; Brazil, 1837 *5475.1* *p367*
Breit, Jakob; America, 1883 *5475.1* *p396*
Breit, Johann Georg 32; New York, NY, 1868 *5475.1* *p26*
　*Wife:*Elisabeth Hoffmann
　*Daughter:*Elisabeth
　*Daughter:*Louise
　*Daughter:*Sophie
Breit, Louise *SEE* Breit, Johann Georg
Breit, Peter; America, 1880 *5475.1* *p396*
Breit, Sophie *SEE* Breit, Johann Georg
Breit, Valentin 20; America, 1880 *5475.1* *p456*
Breitbarth, John Adam; Illinois, 1852 *6079.1* *p2*
Breiter, Magdalena 31; America, 1846 *5475.1* *p345*
Breitung, Caroline; America, 1867 *7919.3* *p535*
Brelau, Henriette; Wisconsin, 1890 *6795.8* *p71*
Brele, Charles 23; Missouri, 1846 *778.6* *p47*
Brellat, Louisa 11; Quebec, 1870 *8364.32* *p22*
Bremaille, Marie; Quebec, 1666 *4514.3* *p284*
Breman, Cdne; Colorado, 1872 *1029.59* *p13*
Breman, Marie-Madeleine; Quebec, 1654 *9221.17* *p304*
Breman, Marie-Madeleine; Quebec, 1654 *9221.17* *p304*
Bremer, Anna Maria 68; Pennsylvania, 1848 *170.15* *p21*
　With family
Bremer, Anne Sophie Dorothee *SEE* Bremer, Johann Heinrich Christoph
Bremer, Catharina Sophia *SEE* Bremer, Johann Heinrich
Bremer, Catharine; America, 1866 *7420.1* *p240*
Bremer, Christian; New York, 1777 *8529.30* *p6*
Bremer, Engel Maria Dorothea *SEE* Bremer, Johann Heinrich
Bremer, Engel Maria Hinze *SEE* Bremer, Johann Heinrich
Bremer, Engel Marie Sophie; America, 1866 *7420.1* *p240*
Bremer, Gustav; America, 1856 *7420.1* *p145*
Bremer, Heinrich Christoph; America, 1856 *7420.1* *p146*
Bremer, Heinrich Dietrich Wilhelm; America, 1884 *7420.1* *p342*
Bremer, Heinrich Friedrich; America, 1882 *7420.1* *p328*
Bremer, Heinrich Wilhelm; America, 1865 *7420.1* *p229*
Bremer, Herm.; Valdivia, Chile, 1852 *1192.4* *p55*
　With wife
Bremer, Johann Christian; America, 1856 *7420.1* *p146*
Bremer, Johann Friedrich; America, 1858 *7420.1* *p177*
Bremer, Johann Georg; America, n.d. *8115.12* *p319*
Bremer, Johann Georg; America, n.d. *8115.12* *p326*
Bremer, Johann Heinr. Christoph *SEE* Bremer, Johann Heinrich Christoph
Bremer, Johann Heinr. Conrad *SEE* Bremer, Johann Heinrich Christoph
Bremer, Johann Heinrich *SEE* Bremer, Johann Heinrich
Bremer, Johann Heinrich; America, 1848 *7420.1* *p59*
　*Wife:*Engel Maria Hinze
　*Son:*Johann Heinrich
　*Daughter:*Engel Maria Dorothea
　*Daughter:*Catharina Sophia
Bremer, Johann Heinrich *SEE* Bremer, Johann Heinrich Christoph
Bremer, Johann Heinrich; America, 1866 *7420.1* *p240*
Bremer, Johann Heinrich Christoph; America, 1850 *7420.1* *p69*
Bremer, Johann Heinrich Christoph; America, 1850 *7420.1* *p69*
　*Brother:*Johann Heinr. Conrad
　*Brother:*Johann Heinr. Christoph
　*Sister:*Anne Sophie Dorothee
Bremer, Johann Heinrich Christoph; America, 1860 *7420.1* *p192*
　*Brother:*Johann Heinrich
Bremer, Johann Heinrich Gustav; America, 1856 *7420.1* *p146*
Bremer, John Mathias; North Carolina, 1855 *1088.45* *p4*
Bremer, Nicholas; North Carolina, 1858 *1088.45* *p4*
Bremer, Peter; Pennsylvania, 1848 *170.15* *p21*
　With 5 siblings
Bremer, Trine Maria; America, 1867 *7420.1* *p254*
Bremner, Alexander 40; Ontario, 1871 *1823.17* *p15*

Bremner, Alexander 46; Ontario, 1871 *1823.21* *p35*
Bremner, Catherine 32; Ontario, 1871 *1823.21* *p35*
Bremner, James 68; Ontario, 1871 *1823.21* *p35*
Bremner, John 40; Ontario, 1871 *1823.17* *p15*
Bremner, John 57; Ontario, 1871 *1823.21* *p35*
Bremner, Peter 30; Ontario, 1871 *1823.21* *p35*
Bremner, Robert 31; Ontario, 1871 *1823.21* *p35*
Bremner, Robert 66; Ontario, 1871 *1823.21* *p35*
Bremner, Wilhelmine; Wisconsin, 1893 *6795.8* *p160*
Bremner, William 38; Ontario, 1871 *1823.21* *p35*
Bren, Josef; Wisconsin, 1891 *2853.20* *p303*
Brenan, Patrick 31; Ontario, 1871 *1823.21* *p35*
Brender, G.; Valdivia, Chile, 1852 *1192.4* *p55*
　With wife & 3 children
　With child 8
　With child 1
Brendle, Joseph; Louisiana, 1874 *4981.45* *p131*
Brenen, L. Jean Batiste 21; New Orleans, 1845 *778.6* *p47*
Brenens, Paul 25; Port uncertain, 1846 *778.6* *p47*
Brenez, Joseph; Colorado, 1895 *1029.59* *p13*
Brenez, Joseph; Colorado, 1899 *1029.59* *p13*
Brengle, Anna Maria; Venezuela, 1843 *3899.5* *p541*
Brengle, Johannes; Venezuela, 1843 *3899.5* *p541*
Brengle, Philipp 26; America, 1848 *778.6* *p47*
Brenglerin, Anna Maria; Venezuela, 1843 *3899.5* *p541*
Brenglin, Anna Maria; Venezuela, 1843 *3899.5* *p541*
Brenil, Noel de 24; Quebec, 1661 *9221.17* *p449*
Brenk, Mike; Louisiana, 1874 *4981.45* *p131*
Brenna, James 23; Michigan, 1880 *4491.30* *p4*
Brennan, Mrs.; Toronto, 1844 *2910.35* *p112*
Brennan, Alley; St. Johns, N.F., 1825 *1053.15* *p7*
Brennan, Anne; St. Johns, N.F., 1825 *1053.15* *p6*
Brennan, Catherine; Halifax, N.S., 1827 *7009.9* *p62*
　*Husband:*Nicholas
Brennan, Catherine; New Orleans, 1850 *7242.30* *p135*
Brennan, Catherine; St. Johns, N.F., 1825 *1053.15* *p7*
Brennan, Daniel; St. Johns, N.F., 1825 *1053.15* *p7*
Brennan, Dennis 60; Ontario, 1871 *1823.21* *p35*
Brennan, Edward 28; Ontario, 1871 *1823.21* *p36*
Brennan, Edward 63; Ontario, 1871 *1823.21* *p35*
Brennan, Ellen; St. Johns, N.F., 1825 *1053.15* *p7*
Brennan, James; New Orleans, 1850 *7242.30* *p135*
Brennan, James; St. Johns, N.F., 1825 *1053.15* *p7*
Brennan, John; New Orleans, 1850 *7242.30* *p135*
Brennan, John 30; Ontario, 1871 *1823.21* *p36*
Brennan, John; St. Johns, N.F., 1825 *1053.15* *p6*
Brennan, Jon; New Orleans, 1851 *7242.30* *p135*
Brennan, Kearn; St. Johns, N.F., 1825 *1053.15* *p6*
Brennan, Mary; Miami, 1935 *4984.12* *p39*
Brennan, Mary; St. Johns, N.F., 1825 *1053.15* *p7*
Brennan, Michael; New Orleans, 1851 *7242.30* *p135*
Brennan, Michael 32; Ontario, 1871 *1823.21* *p36*
Brennan, Michael 44; Ontario, 1871 *1823.17* *p15*
Brennan, Michael; Toronto, 1844 *2910.35* *p114*
Brennan, Michael Mary; Miami, 1935 *4984.12* *p39*
Brennan, Mogue; New Orleans, 1850 *7242.30* *p135*
Brennan, Murtagh; St. Johns, N.F., 1825 *1053.15* *p7*
Brennan, Pat; St. Johns, N.F., 1825 *1053.15* *p7*
Brennan, Patrick; New Orleans, 1850 *7242.30* *p135*
Brennan, Patrick 76; Ontario, 1871 *1823.21* *p36*
Brennan, Thomas; New Orleans, 1850 *7242.30* *p135*
Brenner, Albert 24; New York, NY, 1894 *6512.1* *p183*
Brenner, Anna 3; America, 1847 *778.6* *p47*
Brenner, Chas 25; Ontario, 1871 *1823.21* *p36*
Brenner, Christian Heinrich 16; America, 1833 *5475.1* *p27*
Brenner, Georg Philipp; America, 1833 *5475.1* *p11*
　*Son:*Ludwig Karl
　*Son:*Wilh. Friedrich
Brenner, Henry 17; America, 1847 *778.6* *p47*
Brenner, Henry 48; America, 1847 *778.6* *p47*
Brenner, Jacques 9; America, 1847 *778.6* *p47*
Brenner, Jean 18; America, 1847 *778.6* *p48*
Brenner, Ludwig Karl *SEE* Brenner, Georg Philipp
Brenner, Maria 11; America, 1847 *778.6* *p48*
Brenner, Salome 40; America, 1847 *778.6* *p48*
Brenner, Wilh. Friedrich *SEE* Brenner, Georg Philipp
Brennin, George; North Carolina, 1844 *1088.45* *p4*
Brenning, Bridget; Boston, 1746 *1642* *p46*
Brensecke, Adam 29; America, 1865 *5475.1* *p504*
Brensecke, Karoline 35; America, 1865 *5475.1* *p504*
Brent, George 36; Ontario, 1871 *1823.17* *p15*
Brent, William 35; Ontario, 1871 *1823.17* *p15*
Brent, William 71; Ontario, 1871 *1823.21* *p36*
Brentigny, Etienne 22; Quebec, 1649 *9221.17* *p212*
Brenton, Sarah A. 46; Ontario, 1871 *1823.21* *p36*
Brenton, Thomas 40; Ontario, 1871 *1823.21* *p36*
Brereton, William 39; Ontario, 1871 *1823.17* *p15*
Breschon DeBellefond, Jacques; Quebec, 1662 *9221.17* *p481*
Brescote, Judith 1 *SEE* Brescote, Pierre
Brescote, Marguerite Maillet *SEE* Brescote, Pierre

Brescote, Marie 4 *SEE* Brescote, Pierre
Brescote, Pierre 44; Quebec, 1659 ***9221.17*** *p395*
*Wife:*Marguerite Maillet
*Daughter:*Marie 4
*Daughter:*Judith 1
Breslan, Michael 30; Ontario, 1871 ***1823.17*** *p15*
Bresler, David Leib; Detroit, 1929-1930 ***6214.5*** *p67*
Bresler, Heinrich 9; Portland, ME, 1911 ***970.38*** *p76*
Bresler, Heinrich 42; Portland, ME, 1911 ***970.38*** *p76*
Bresler, Katerina M. 40; Portland, ME, 1911 ***970.38*** *p76*
Bresler, Konrad 47; Portland, ME, 1911 ***970.38*** *p76*
Bresler, Martin 2; Portland, ME, 1911 ***970.38*** *p76*
Bresler, Wilhelm 4; Portland, ME, 1911 ***970.38*** *p76*
Breslin, James 35; Ontario, 1871 ***1823.17*** *p15*
Bress, Mr. 33; America, 1846 ***778.6*** *p48*
Bress, Auguste 18 months; America, 1846 ***778.6*** *p48*
Bress, Etienne 8; America, 1846 ***778.6*** *p48*
Bressani, Francois-Joseph 30; Quebec, 1642 ***9221.17*** *p110*
Bressel, Mr.; America, 1843 ***778.6*** *p48*
Bresser, Sophie; America, 1869 ***5475.1*** *p13*
*Son:*Johann
Bressett, Jefry 35; Ontario, 1871 ***1823.17*** *p15*
Bressey, James 66; Ontario, 1871 ***1823.17*** *p15*
Bressy, Adolph 13; America, 1843 ***778.6*** *p48*
Bressy, Theodule 10; America, 1843 ***778.6*** *p48*
Brest, . . .; Quebec, 1638 ***9221.17*** *p75*
Breton, Mr. 24; America, 1843 ***778.6*** *p13*
Breton, Francois 22; Quebec, 1661 ***9221.17*** *p450*
Breton, Henriette 16; Port uncertain, 1841 ***778.6*** *p48*
Breton, Louis 43; Port uncertain, 1841 ***778.6*** *p48*
Breton, Marguerite; Quebec, 1649-1664 ***4514.3*** *p377*
Breton, Marguerite 15; Quebec, 1651 ***9221.17*** *p237*
Breton, Peter; Salem, MA, 1677 ***9228.50*** *p135*
Breton Family ; Massachusetts, 1790 ***9228.50*** *p334*
Breton Family ; Ontario, n.d. ***9228.50*** *p131*
Bretoon, John; Maine, 1668 ***9228.50*** *p135*
With wife
Bretoon Family ; Massachusetts, 1790 ***9228.50*** *p334*
Brett, George 50; Ontario, 1871 ***1823.21*** *p36*
Brett, James 50; Ontario, 1871 ***1823.21*** *p36*
Brett, Walton 33; Ontario, 1871 ***1823.21*** *p36*
Bretthauer, D.; America, 1867 ***7420.1*** *p254*
With wife
With son 22
With daughter 14
With son 16
With daughter 12
With daughter 6
With daughter 23
With daughter 9
Bretthauer, Heinrich; America, 1867 ***7420.1*** *p255*
*Wife:*Maria Schwabe
*Son:*Heinrich Conrad Georg
With daughter & son
Bretthauer, Heinrich Conrad Georg *SEE* Bretthauer, Heinrich
Bretthauer, Maria Schwabe *SEE* Bretthauer, Heinrich
Brettnacher, Margarethe Moll 21 *SEE* Brettnacher, Philipp
Brettnacher, Philipp 21; America, 1866 ***5475.1*** *p143*
*Wife:*Margarethe Moll 21
Bretton, Benjamin; Salem, MA, 1685 ***9228.50*** *p135*
Bretton Family ; Ontario, n.d. ***9228.50*** *p131*
Bretueil, Lienard; Quebec, 1640 ***9221.17*** *p95*
Breuer, Carl; Galveston, TX, 1855 ***571.7*** *p16*
Breuer, Karel H.; Minnesota, 1876 ***2853.20*** *p510*
With parents
Breugde, Jean Francois Corneille; Wisconsin, 1857 ***1495.20*** *p41*
Breugne, H. 44; America, 1845 ***778.6*** *p48*
Breunig, Anna *SEE* Breunig, Peter
Breunig, Anna Philippi *SEE* Breunig, Peter
Breunig, Eva Katharina; America, 1855 ***2526.43*** *p194*
Breunig, Heinrich *SEE* Breunig, Peter
Breunig, Katharina 43; America, 1856 ***2526.43*** *p132*
Breunig, Margarete; America, 1871 ***2526.42*** *p94*
Breunig, Mathias *SEE* Breunig, Peter
Breunig, Peter *SEE* Breunig, Peter
Breunig, Peter; Pittsburgh, 1881 ***5475.1*** *p69*
*Wife:*Anna Philippi
*Son:*Peter
*Son:*Heinrich
*Son:*Mathias
*Daughter:*Anna
Breunig, Philipp; America, 1853 ***2526.42*** *p94*
Breuning, Jacob; Chile, 1852 ***1192.4*** *p51*
Breuning, Nikolaus; America, 1872 ***5475.1*** *p205*
Breval, Marie; Quebec, 1669 ***4514.3*** *p278*
Brewer, Mr.; New York, NY, 1830 ***9228.50*** *p131*
Brewer, Mrs.; Toronto, 1844 ***2910.35*** *p114*
Brewer, Agnes 29; Michigan, 1880 ***4491.42*** *p5*
Brewer, Charles W.; Wisconsin, 1853 ***9228.50*** *p131*
*Wife:*Jane Matthews
Brewer, Elisabeth 25; Michigan, 1880 ***4491.36*** *p2*
Brewer, Henry 32; Ontario, 1871 ***1823.21*** *p36*
Brewer, J. Isaac; South Carolina, 1832 ***6155.4*** *p18*
Brewer, Jane Matthews *SEE* Brewer, Charles W.
Brewer, John; Washington, 1881 ***2770.40*** *p134*
Brewer, Oscar 55; Ontario, 1871 ***1823.21*** *p36*
Brewer, Tho; Virginia, 1652 ***6254.4*** *p243*
Brewer, Willm.; Maryland, 1674 ***1236.25*** *p50*
Brewett, Willm.; Maryland, 1674 ***1236.25*** *p50*
Brewster, Love *SEE* Brewster, Wm.
Brewster, Mary *SEE* Brewster, Wm.
Brewster, Wm.; Plymouth, MA, 1620 ***1920.45*** *p5*
*Wife:*Mary
*Son:*Wrasling
*Son:*Love
Brewster, Wrasling *SEE* Brewster, Wm.
Breyer, Adam; Brazil, 1863 ***5475.1*** *p497*
*Wife:*Elisabeth Simon
*Son:*Paul
Breyer, Carl Ludwig; America, 1836 ***7420.1*** *p10*
Breyer, Elisabeth Simon *SEE* Breyer, Adam
Breyer, Elisabeth; Brazil, 1863 ***5475.1*** *p497*
Breyer, Jakob 60; Brazil, 1863 ***5475.1*** *p497*
*Wife:*Karoline
Breyer, Karoline *SEE* Breyer, Jakob
Breyer, Paul *SEE* Breyer, Adam
Breyer, Theodore 22; America, 1847 ***778.6*** *p48*
Breymeier, Engel Marie Philippine Schonbeck *SEE* Breymeier, Heinrich Christian Gottlieb
Breymeier, Heinrich Christian Gottlieb; America, 1862 ***7420.1*** *p211*
*Wife:*Engel Marie Philippine Schonbeck
With 3 daughters & 3 sons
Brezieux, Michel; Quebec, 1647 ***9221.17*** *p177*
Briam, Magdalena; America, 1881 ***5475.1*** *p44*
Brian, Anne Byrne *SEE* Brian, Charles
Brian, C.; New Orleans, 1850 ***7242.30*** *p135*
Brian, Charles; Halifax, N.S., 1827 ***7009.9*** *p61*
*Father:*John
*Mother:*Anne Byrne
Brian, Elizabeth 58; Michigan, 1880 ***4491.30*** *p4*
Brian, J.; New Orleans, 1850 ***7242.30*** *p135*
Brian, James; New Orleans, 1850 ***7242.30*** *p135*
Brian, Jean; New Orleans, 1840 ***778.6*** *p48*
Brian, John; Boston, 1754 ***1642*** *p47*
Brian, John *SEE* Brian, Charles
Brian, John; Massachusetts, 1739 ***1642*** *p109*
*Wife:*Ruth
Brian, John O.; Ohio, 1840-1897 ***8365.35*** *p15*
Brian, Lawarnes 56; Michigan, 1880 ***4491.30*** *p4*
Brian, Mary; Boston, 1756 ***1642*** *p47*
Brian, Micah; Lancaster, MA, 1770 ***1642*** *p105*
Brian, Peter; Marblehead, MA, 1776 ***1642*** *p73*
Brian, Richard; Massachusetts, 1675-1676 ***1642*** *p127*
Brian, Ruth *SEE* Brian, John
Brian, Thadeus; Lynn, MA, 1670 ***1642*** *p71*
Brian, Thomas; Massachusetts, 1675-1676 ***1642*** *p128*
Brian, Thomas; New Orleans, 1850 ***7242.30*** *p135*
Brian, Timothy; Boston, 1760 ***1642*** *p48*
Briand, . . .; Edmonton, Alberta, n.d. ***9228.50*** *p131*
Briand Family ; Nova Scotia, 1700-1799 ***9228.50*** *p132*
Briant, . . .; Edmonton, Alberta, n.d. ***9228.50*** *p131*
Briant, Elizabeth; Boston, 1724 ***1642*** *p25*
Briant, M.L.; Philadelphia, 1847 ***6412.40*** *p150*
Briant, Patrick; Boston, 1769 ***1642*** *p40*
Briant, Robert; Massachusetts, 1675-1676 ***1642*** *p128*
Briant, Thomas; Boston, 1642 ***1642*** *p7*
Briant, Thomas; Massachusetts, 1675-1676 ***1642*** *p128*
Briant, William 18; Quebec, 1870 ***8364.32*** *p22*
Briar, Alexandre 47; America, 1840 ***778.6*** *p48*
Briar, Francoise 48; America, 1840 ***778.6*** *p48*
Briard, . . .; New England, n.d. ***9228.50*** *p132*
Briard, Charles 18; Louisiana, 1848 ***778.6*** *p48*
Briard, Elias; Marblehead, MA, 1700-1799 ***9228.50*** *p132*
Briard, Elias, Sr. 16; Quebec, 1854 ***9228.50*** *p133*
Briard, Ella; Florida, 1974 ***9228.50*** *p133*
Briard, John; Portsmouth, NH, 1726 ***9228.50*** *p132*
Briard, Odile 27; Louisiana, 1848 ***778.6*** *p48*
Briard, Philip 37; Louisiana, 1848 ***778.6*** *p48*
Briard, Stanley; Quebec, 1860-1960 ***9228.50*** *p134*
Briard Family ; Quebec, 1800-1899 ***9228.50*** *p133*
Briarly, James; Massachusetts, 1675-1676 ***1642*** *p128*
Brice, Andrew; Ohio, 1840-1897 ***8365.35*** *p15*
Brice, Harry; Kansas, 1885 ***1447.20*** *p63*
Brice, Harry 27; Kansas, 1887 ***1447.20*** *p62*
Brice, John 60; Ontario, 1871 ***1823.17*** *p15*
Brice, Patrick; Ohio, 1840-1897 ***8365.35*** *p15*
Brice, Ted; Chicago, 1900-1950 ***9228.50*** *p134*
Brick, William J. 22; Ontario, 1871 ***1823.21*** *p36*
Bricken, Methias; Ohio, 1840-1897 ***8365.35*** *p15*
Brickenhanz, Chat. Carlot. 17; New York, NY, 1864 ***8425.62*** *p197*
Bricker, George; Illinois, 1852 ***6079.1*** *p2*
Brickinridge, Rachel 64; Ontario, 1871 ***1823.21*** *p36*
Brickler, Carolina 19; Port uncertain, 1843 ***778.6*** *p48*
Brickler, Catharina 27; Port uncertain, 1843 ***778.6*** *p48*
Brickler, Catharina 53; Port uncertain, 1843 ***778.6*** *p48*
Brickler, Charles 16; Port uncertain, 1843 ***778.6*** *p48*
Brickler, Isidor 13; Port uncertain, 1843 ***778.6*** *p48*
Brickler, Margaretha 23; Port uncertain, 1843 ***778.6*** *p48*
Brickler, Nicolas 53; Port uncertain, 1843 ***778.6*** *p48*
Brickler, Therese 7; Port uncertain, 1843 ***778.6*** *p48*
Brickley, Bess; New Orleans, 1850 ***7242.30*** *p135*
Brickley, Daniel; New Orleans, 1850 ***7242.30*** *p135*
Brickley, James; New Orleans, 1850 ***7242.30*** *p135*
Brickley, John; New Orleans, 1850 ***7242.30*** *p135*
Brickley, Mary; New Orleans, 1850 ***7242.30*** *p135*
Brickley, Paul; New Orleans, 1850 ***7242.30*** *p135*
Brickley, Richard; New Orleans, 1850 ***7242.30*** *p135*
Brickley, William; New Orleans, 1850 ***7242.30*** *p135*
Brickmann, W.; New York, 1860 ***358.56*** *p3*
Bridant, Edward Louis; Miami, 1920 ***4984.15*** *p38*
Bride, Chirst 52; North Carolina, 1774 ***1422.10*** *p62*
Bride, Chirst. 52; North Carolina, 1774 ***1422.10*** *p57*
Bride, Flora 29; North Carolina, 1774 ***1422.10*** *p58*
Bride, Flora 29; North Carolina, 1774 ***1422.10*** *p62*
Bride, Jollin; Quebec, 1637 ***9221.17*** *p68*
With wife
Brideaux, . . .; Marblehead, MA, 1700-1799 ***9228.50*** *p134*
Brideaux, Edwin Charles; Quebec, 1887-1910 ***9228.50*** *p134*
Brideaux, Walter Pirouet; America, n.d. ***9228.50*** *p134*
Brideaux Family ; Utah, 1852 ***9228.50*** *p135*
Bridge, Hanna 76; Ontario, 1871 ***1823.21*** *p36*
Bridge, Ralph; Ohio, 1834 ***3580.20*** *p31*
Bridge, Ralph; Ohio, 1834 ***6020.12*** *p6*
Bridgehood Family ; Utah, 1852 ***9228.50*** *p135*
Bridgeman, Robert 53; Ontario, 1871 ***1823.21*** *p36*
Bridges, George; Ontario, 1835 ***3160.1*** *p150*
Bridges, George; Prescott, Ont., 1835 ***3289.1*** *p61*
Bridges, Thomas 25; Ontario, 1871 ***1823.17*** *p15*
Bridgewater, T. O. 41; Ontario, 1871 ***1823.21*** *p36*
Bridgo, . . .; Marblehead, MA, 1700-1799 ***9228.50*** *p134*
Bridgwater, Thomas; Boston, 1696 ***1642*** *p17*
Bridle, John 31; New York, 1821 ***9228.50*** *p103*
*Wife:*Mary 27
*Daughter:*Mary Ann 5
Bridle, John 31; New York, 1821 ***9228.50*** *p104*
*Wife:*Mary 27
*Daughter:*Mary Ann 5
Bridle, Mary 27 *SEE* Bridle, John
Bridle, Mary 27 *SEE* Bridle, John
Bridle, Mary Ann 5 *SEE* Bridle, John
Bridle, Mary Ann 5 *SEE* Bridle, John
Brie, Maurice; Quebec, 1662 ***9221.17*** *p481*
Briede, F. W.; Chile, 1852 ***1192.4*** *p51*
Briee, Mary 11; Quebec, 1870 ***8364.32*** *p22*
Brieheler, Barbe 20; America, 1847 ***778.6*** *p48*
Brieheler, Barbe 30; America, 1847 ***778.6*** *p48*
Brieheler, Joseph 33; America, 1847 ***778.6*** *p48*
Brieheler, Madeleine 19; America, 1847 ***778.6*** *p48*
Brieheler, Nicolas 9; America, 1847 ***778.6*** *p48*
Brieka, Catharine 22; Kentucky, 1846 ***778.6*** *p49*
Brieka, Jacob 25; Kentucky, 1846 ***778.6*** *p49*
Brien, Catherine; New Orleans, 1850 ***7242.30*** *p135*
Brien, Dennis; New Orleans, 1850 ***7242.30*** *p135*
Brien, Elizabeth; Boston, 1767 ***1642*** *p38*
Brien, Honora; New Orleans, 1851 ***7242.30*** *p135*
Brien, James; Boston, 1764 ***1642*** *p33*
Brien, James O.; Colorado, 1878 ***1029.59*** *p13*
Brien, John 50; Ontario, 1871 ***1823.21*** *p36*
Brien, Martin; New Orleans, 1851 ***7242.30*** *p135*
Brien, Matthew; New Orleans, 1851 ***7242.30*** *p135*
Brien, Michael; New Orleans, 1850 ***7242.30*** *p135*
Brien, Stephen; Boston, 1776 ***8529.30*** *p2A*
Briere, Denis 25; Quebec, 1657 ***9221.17*** *p353*
Briere, Jeanne-Angelique 21; Quebec, 1661 ***9221.17*** *p450*
Briere, Marie; Quebec, 1670 ***4514.3*** *p284*
Brierley, James Bell 55; Ontario, 1871 ***1823.21*** *p36*
Brierley, John; New York, NY, 1827 ***3274.55*** *p73*
Brierly, Benjamin; Boston, 1828 ***3274.55*** *p73*
Brierly, John; Philadelphia, 1821 ***3274.55*** *p70*
Brierly, John, Jr.; Boston, 1828 ***3274.55*** *p73*
Brierre, Jean Louis; Illinois, 1852 ***6079.1*** *p2*
Briese, August; Wisconsin, 1914 ***6795.8*** *p170*
Briese, August Julius; Wisconsin, 1885 ***6795.8*** *p66*
Briese, Caroline H.; Wisconsin, 1888 ***6795.8*** *p144*
Briese, Wilhelmine; Wisconsin, 1882 ***6795.8*** *p46*
Brietzke, Ottelie; Wisconsin, 1894 ***6795.8*** *p236*
Brieugne, Francois 28; Port uncertain, 1846 ***778.6*** *p49*
Briez, Christian; North Carolina, 1812 ***1088.45*** *p4*

Brigacum, Jesse 26; Ohio, 1880 ***4879.40*** *p257*
Brigeac, Claude de 30; Montreal, 1659 ***9221.17*** *p418*
Briger, Francois 21; America, 1847 ***778.6*** *p49*
Brigg, Mrs. F.; Montreal, 1922 ***4514.4*** *p32*
Briggs, Benjamin 11; Michigan, 1880 ***4491.36*** *p2*
Briggs, Caleb 18; Michigan, 1880 ***4491.36*** *p2*
Briggs, Eugene 10; Michigan, 1880 ***4491.36*** *p2*
Briggs, George; New York, 1777 ***8529.30*** *p6*
Briggs, Hannah 40; Michigan, 1880 ***4491.36*** *p2*
Briggs, Jay 44; Michigan, 1880 ***4491.36*** *p2*
Briggs, John 13; Michigan, 1880 ***4491.36*** *p2*
Briggs, John 13; Michigan, 1880 ***4491.36*** *p3*
Briggs, John 63; Ontario, 1871 ***1823.21*** *p36*
Briggs, Larone 3; Michigan, 1880 ***4491.36*** *p2*
Briggs, William; Ohio, 1857 ***3580.20*** *p31*
Briggs, William; Ohio, 1857 ***6020.12*** *p6*
Briggs, Willm.; Maryland, 1674 ***1236.25*** *p49*
Brigham, Levi; Vermont, 1837 ***3274.56*** *p96*
Brigham, Samuel C.; Vermont, 1837 ***3274.56*** *p96*
Bright, George G.; Ohio, 1878 ***3580.20*** *p31*
Bright, George G.; Ohio, 1878 ***6020.12*** *p6*
Bright, Henry 34; Ontario, 1871 ***1823.21*** *p36*
Bright, James G. 40; Ontario, 1871 ***1823.17*** *p15*
Bright, John 48; Ontario, 1871 ***1823.17*** *p15*
Bright, John 65; Ontario, 1871 ***1823.17*** *p15*
Brighton, John 52; Ontario, 1871 ***1823.21*** *p36*
Brijat, Claude de 30; Montreal, 1659 ***9221.17*** *p418*
Brika, Jacques 7; America, 1847 ***778.6*** *p49*
Brika, Josia 56; America, 1847 ***778.6*** *p49*
Bril, Frederick; Ohio, 1809-1852 ***4511.35*** *p6*
Bril, Timothy O.; Ohio, 1809-1852 ***4511.35*** *p6*
Briliau, Michel 23; Mississippi, 1847 ***778.6*** *p49*
Brill, A. Maria *SEE* Brill, Johann
Brill, Angela Klesen *SEE* Brill, Johann
Brill, August; Wisconsin, 1879 ***6795.8*** *p200*
Brill, Jacob; North Carolina, 1845 ***1088.45*** *p4*
Brill, Joh. Friedr.; Pittsburgh, 1861 ***5475.1*** *p488*
Brill, Johann *SEE* Brill, Johann
Brill, Johann; Brazil, 1883 ***5475.1*** *p416*
*Wife:*Angela Klesen
*Daughter:*A. Maria
*Daughter:*Maria
*Daughter:*Katharina
*Son:*Michel
*Son:*Johann
Brill, Johann 21; Port uncertain, 1840 ***778.6*** *p49*
Brill, Katharina *SEE* Brill, Johann
Brill, Maria; Arkansas, 1880 ***5475.1*** *p245*
Brill, Maria *SEE* Brill, Johann
Brill, Michel *SEE* Brill, Johann
Brill, Peter; Illinois, 1851 ***6079.1*** *p2*
Brilley, Thomas; Illinois, 1858 ***6079.1*** *p2*
Brilliant, . . .; Edmonton, Alberta, n.d. ***9228.50*** *p131*
Brilliard, Sophia 22; Ontario, 1871 ***1823.21*** *p36*
Brillord, Henry 23; New Orleans, 1845 ***778.6*** *p49*
Brilowski, Peter; Wisconsin, 1885 ***6795.8*** *p54*
Brimer, Harm Matthias; North Carolina, 1853 ***1088.45*** *p4*
Brimican, William 30; Ontario, 1871 ***1823.21*** *p36*
Brinckhoff, Anna 68; Galveston, TX, 1845 ***3967.10*** *p376*
Brinckhoff, Bernhard 8; Galveston, TX, 1845 ***3967.10*** *p376*
Brinckhoff, Gerhard 6; Galveston, TX, 1845 ***3967.10*** *p376*
Brinckhoff, Gertrud 29; Galveston, TX, 1845 ***3967.10*** *p376*
Brinckhoff, Heinrich 39; Galveston, TX, 1845 ***3967.10*** *p376*
Brinckhoff, Heinrich 69; Galveston, TX, 1845 ***3967.10*** *p376*
Brinckhoff, Theodor 3 months; Galveston, TX, 1845 ***3967.10*** *p376*
Brindelierre, Masse 26; Quebec, 1641 ***9221.17*** *p104*
Brindley, James; Boston, 1774 ***8529.30*** *p2*
Brine, James 53; Ontario, 1871 ***1823.21*** *p36*
Bringart, Anne Marie 27; Lexington, TN, 1848 ***778.6*** *p49*
Bringeer, Joseph; Ohio, 1839 ***3580.20*** *p31*
Bringeer, Joseph; Ohio, 1839 ***6020.12*** *p6*
Bringel, Geo.; Louisiana, 1874-1875 ***4981.45*** *p298*
Bringel, Henry; Louisiana, 1874-1875 ***4981.45*** *p298*
Bringele, Valentin 17; Missouri, 1848 ***778.6*** *p49*
Bringer, Joseph; Ohio, 1839 ***3580.20*** *p31*
Bringmann, Georg Wilhelm; America, 1871 ***7420.1*** *p289*
Bringmann, Johann Heinrich; America, 1857 ***7420.1*** *p159*
Bringodin, Judith 1 *SEE* Bringodin, Pierre
Bringodin, Marguerite Maillet *SEE* Bringodin, Pierre
Bringodin, Marie 4 *SEE* Bringodin, Pierre
Bringodin, Pierre 44; Quebec, 1659 ***9221.17*** *p395*
*Wife:*Marguerite Maillet
*Daughter:*Marie 4
*Daughter:*Judith 1
Bringold, Adele 3; America, 1846 ***778.6*** *p49*
Bringold, Baptiste 6; America, 1846 ***778.6*** *p49*
Bringold, Constant 18; America, 1846 ***778.6*** *p49*
Bringold, Elisabeth 45; America, 1846 ***778.6*** *p49*
Bringold, Emile 9; America, 1846 ***778.6*** *p49*
Bringold, Florine 8; America, 1846 ***778.6*** *p49*
Bringold, Gertrude 4; America, 1846 ***778.6*** *p49*
Bringold, Marguerite 5; America, 1846 ***778.6*** *p49*
Bringold, Marie 17; America, 1846 ***778.6*** *p49*
Bringold, Nicolas 42; America, 1846 ***778.6*** *p49*
Brink, Anna; St. Paul, MN, 1888 ***1865.50*** *p46*
Brink, Hermann Otto; America, 1890 ***7420.1*** *p360*
Brink, Vera Kathleen; Oregon, 1941 ***9157.47*** *p2*
Brink, Wilhelm Heinrich; America, 1892 ***7420.1*** *p365*
Brinkman, Carl Edward; Illinois, 1851 ***6079.1*** *p2*
Brinkmann, Adolf; America, 1906 ***7420.1*** *p401*
Brinkmann, Alexander; Galveston, TX, 1855 ***571.7*** *p16*
Brinkmann, Auguste; America, 1866 ***7420.1*** *p240*
Brinkmann, Caroline; America, 1853 ***7420.1*** *p103*
Brinkmann, Christian Friedrich Anton; America, 1881 ***7420.1*** *p320*
Brinkmann, Christine Dorothee Amalie Fuhring *SEE* Brinkmann, Ernst Heinrich
Brinkmann, Christine Wilhelmine Charl. Teigeler *SEE* Brinkmann, Heinrich Gottlieb
Brinkmann, Ernst Heinrich; America, 1851 ***7420.1*** *p78*
*Wife:*Christine Dorothee Amalie Fuhring
*Sister:*Sophie
*Sister:*Philippine
Brinkmann, Friedrich Wilhelm; America, 1859 ***7420.1*** *p184*
Brinkmann, Heinrich Gottlieb; America, 1850 ***7420.1*** *p69*
*Wife:*Christine Wilhelmine Charl. Teigeler
*Daughter:*Sophie Wilhelm Charlotte
Brinkmann, Justine; America, 1870 ***7420.1*** *p395*
Brinkmann, L.; New York, 1860 ***358.56*** *p3*
Brinkmann, Philippine *SEE* Brinkmann, Ernst Heinrich
Brinkmann, Sophie *SEE* Brinkmann, Ernst Heinrich
Brinkmann, Sophie Wilhelm Charlotte *SEE* Brinkmann, Heinrich Gottlieb
Brinnen, Patt; Boston, 1766 ***1642*** *p38*
Brinton, Philip; FalmoutH ME, 1700-1740 ***9228.50*** *p335*
Brinton Family ; Massachusetts, 1790 ***9228.50*** *p334*
Brintz, Henry; Ohio, 1809-1852 ***4511.35*** *p6*
Briody, James 62; Ontario, 1871 ***1823.21*** *p36*
Briohet, Francois 28; New Orleans, 1848 ***778.6*** *p49*
Briol, Jn. 20; America, 1847 ***778.6*** *p49*
Briot, Claude 41; America, 1840 ***778.6*** *p49*
Briot, Jean 19; Port uncertain, 1846 ***778.6*** *p49*
Brisacher, John George; Ohio, 1809-1852 ***4511.35*** *p6*
Brisacker, John George; Ohio, 1809-1852 ***4511.35*** *p6*
Brisebois, Rene 29; Quebec, 1658 ***9221.17*** *p378*
Briset, Marie; Quebec, 1670 ***4514.3*** *p284*
Brishan, Wellington 58; Ontario, 1871 ***1823.17*** *p15*
Brisiau, Michel; Quebec, 1647 ***9221.17*** *p177*
Brisiere, Michel; Quebec, 1647 ***9221.17*** *p177*
Brisley, Charles 48; Ontario, 1871 ***1823.17*** *p15*
Brismonker, Jacques 25; Missouri, 1845 ***778.6*** *p49*
Brison, William 50; Ontario, 1871 ***1823.17*** *p15*
Brisquignau, Mr. 56; Port uncertain, 1844 ***778.6*** *p49*
Brisse, Antoine 22; New Orleans, 1840 ***778.6*** *p49*
Brisset, . . . 38; Quebec, 1662 ***9221.17*** *p481*
*Wife:*Jeanne Fetine
*Son:*Jacques 14
*Son:*Jean
Brisset, Jacques 14 *SEE* Brisset, . . .
Brisset, Jacques 28; Quebec, 1651 ***9221.17*** *p237*
Brisset, Jean *SEE* Brisset, . . .
Brisset, Jeanne Fetine *SEE* Brisset, . . .
Brissin, Francois; Quebec, 1660 ***9221.17*** *p432*
Brisson, Rene 24; Quebec, 1659 ***9221.17*** *p396*
Brit, Jacob 26; America, 1846 ***778.6*** *p49*
Britain, John; Marblehead, MA, 1762 ***9228.50*** *p135*
Brites, A. 48; New Orleans, 1844 ***778.6*** *p49*
Britley, John; Louisiana, 1841-1844 ***4981.45*** *p210*
Briton Family ; Massachusetts, 1790 ***9228.50*** *p334*
Britt, Catharine 38; Ontario, 1871 ***1823.21*** *p36*
Britt, David; North Carolina, 1844 ***1088.45*** *p4*
Britt, David 48; Ontario, 1871 ***1823.21*** *p36*
Britt, James 40; Ontario, 1871 ***1823.17*** *p15*
Britt, Kate 18; Ontario, 1871 ***1823.21*** *p36*
Britt, Letitia 70; Ontario, 1871 ***1823.21*** *p36*
Brittain, Jane; Massachusetts, 1730 ***1642*** *p82*
Brittain, William; New York, 1782 ***8529.30*** *p10*
Brittaine Family ; Massachusetts, 1790 ***9228.50*** *p334*
Britten, Franz; America, 1871 ***5475.1*** *p274*
Britten, Mathias; America, 1872 ***5475.1*** *p274*
Britten, Nikolaus; America, 1869 ***5475.1*** *p273*
Britteridge, Richard; Plymouth, MA, 1620 ***1920.45*** *p5*
Brittian, Mary 40; Ontario, 1871 ***1823.21*** *p36*
Brittle, Thomas 32; Ontario, 1871 ***1823.21*** *p36*
Britton, Mr.; California, 1868 ***1131.61*** *p89*
Britton, J.; California, 1868 ***1131.61*** *p89*
Britton, James 62; Ontario, 1871 ***1823.21*** *p36*
Britton, Joseph 38; Ontario, 1871 ***1823.17*** *p15*
Britton, Liman 69; Ontario, 1871 ***1823.17*** *p15*
Britton, Peter; Salem, MA, 1677 ***9228.50*** *p135*
Britton, Philip; FalmoutH ME, 1700-1740 ***9228.50*** *p335*
Britton Family ; Massachusetts, 1790 ***9228.50*** *p334*
Britz, Anna 3 *SEE* Britz, Michel
Britz, Barbara Dewes 27 *SEE* Britz, Michel
Britz, Elisabeth 1 *SEE* Britz, Michel
Britz, Michel 27; Brazil, 1872 ***5475.1*** *p442*
*Wife:*Barbara Dewes 27
*Daughter:*Anna 3
*Daughter:*Elisabeth 1
*Son:*Nikolaus 6
Britz, Nikolaus 6 *SEE* Britz, Michel
Britzke, Ida Alvina; Wisconsin, 1903 ***6795.8*** *p216*
Broach, Peter; Quebec, 1815-1834 ***9228.50*** *p660*
Broad, James 40; Ontario, 1871 ***1823.21*** *p36*
Broad, Richard; Colorado, 1877 ***1029.59*** *p13*
Broad, Richard; Colorado, 1894 ***1029.59*** *p13*
Broad, Robert B.; Colorado, 1894 ***1029.59*** *p13*
Broadbent, Ammon; New York, NY, 1832 ***3274.55*** *p23*
Broadbent, John 31; Indiana, 1870-1872 ***9076.20*** *p67*
Broadbent, John 30; Ontario, 1871 ***1823.17*** *p16*
Broadbent, Joseph 31; Ontario, 1871 ***1823.21*** *p36*
Broadbent, Joseph; Philadelphia, 1816 ***3274.55*** *p72*
Broadbent, Nathan 48; Ontario, 1871 ***1823.21*** *p36*
Broaderick, Daniel; New York, NY, 1778 ***8529.30*** *p2*
Broadhead, Samuel; New York, 1776 ***8529.30*** *p2*
Broadhurst, Wat; Virginia, 1652 ***6254.4*** *p243*
Broadley, John 38; Ontario, 1871 ***1823.21*** *p37*
Broadway, Edwin; Washington, 1886 ***2770.40*** *p195*
Broadwood, Jane 60; Ontario, 1871 ***1823.21*** *p37*
Broadwood, Kate 19; Ontario, 1871 ***1823.21*** *p37*
Brobstfield, Francis; Ohio, 1809-1852 ***4511.35*** *p6*
Brocamp Family ; West Virginia, 1850 ***1132.30*** *p147*
Brocard DeBelle-Isle, Guillaume; Quebec, 1652 ***9221.17*** *p255*
Brocette, Emile 19; New Orleans, 1846 ***778.6*** *p49*
Brochan, John; St. John, N.B., 1848 ***2978.15*** *p39*
Brochat, Louis 24; Texas, 1843 ***778.6*** *p49*
Broche, Peter; Quebec, 1815-1834 ***9228.50*** *p660*
Broche, Rachel; Ohio, 1840-1847 ***9228.50*** *p135*
Brochet, . . .; Canada, n.d. ***9228.50*** *p135*
Brochet, Peter; Quebec, 1815-1834 ***9228.50*** *p660*
Brochet, Rachel; Ohio, 1840-1847 ***9228.50*** *p135*
Brock, . . .; Venezuela, 1843 ***3899.5*** *p546*
Brock, Alexander 35; Ontario, 1871 ***1823.21*** *p37*
Brock, Archibald 30; Ontario, 1871 ***1823.21*** *p37*
Brock, David 59; Ontario, 1871 ***1823.21*** *p37*
Brock, Elizabeth; Maryland, 1673 ***1236.25*** *p48*
Brock, Ferdinand; Nova Scotia, 1816 ***9228.50*** *p636*
Brock, George 65; Ontario, 1871 ***1823.21*** *p37*
Brock, Isaac; Ontario, 1810 ***9228.50*** *p20*
Brock, Isaac 42; Ontario, 1871 ***1823.21*** *p37*
Brock, Isaac; Quebec, 1750-1850 ***9228.50*** *p553*
Brock, Jacob; Ohio, 1809-1852 ***4511.35*** *p6*
Brock, John; Marblehead, MA, 1600-1699 ***9228.50*** *p137*
Brock, John; Marblehead, MA, 1758 ***9228.50*** *p137*
Brock, John; New York, 1783-1805 ***9228.50*** *p137*
Brock, John 33; Ontario, 1871 ***1823.17*** *p16*
Brock, John 55; Ontario, 1871 ***1823.21*** *p37*
Brock, Martha; Beverly, MA, 1698 ***9228.50*** *p335*
Brock, Nickodan; Wisconsin, 1898 ***6795.8*** *p46*
Brock, Robert 30; Ontario, 1871 ***1823.21*** *p37*
Brock, Robert 34; Ontario, 1871 ***1823.17*** *p16*
Brock, Thomas 23; Ontario, 1871 ***1823.21*** *p37*
Brock, Thomas 47; Ontario, 1871 ***1823.21*** *p37*
Brock, Thomas 72; Ontario, 1871 ***1823.17*** *p16*
Brock, William 63; Ontario, 1871 ***1823.17*** *p16*
Brockdorff, Count 57; Ontario, 1871 ***1823.17*** *p16*
Brocker, Elisabeth; America, 1893 ***5475.1*** *p425*
Brocker, Karl 23; America, 1886 ***5475.1*** *p423*
Brockhuisen, Gerret 19; Galveston, TX, 1844 ***3967.10*** *p375*
Brockington, H. 18; Quebec, 1870 ***8364.32*** *p22*
Brockman, Emma; Missouri, 1904 ***3276.1*** *p3*
Brockman, Frederick; Missouri, 1906 ***3276.1*** *p3*
Brockmann, Carl Heinrich Julius; America, 1850 ***7420.1*** *p70*
Brockmann, Carl Victor Ferdinand; America, 1850 ***7420.1*** *p70*
Brockmann, Clamor Adolph Theodor; America, 1851 ***7420.1*** *p79*
Brockmann, Hermann Lucien Ferdinand; America, 1892 ***7420.1*** *p365*
Brockmann, Wilhelm Dietrich Friedrich; Port uncertain, 1885 ***7420.1*** *p347*
Brockmeier, Wilhelm; America, 1854 ***7420.1*** *p116*
Brockriede, Henry; Ohio, 1840-1897 ***8365.35*** *p15*
Brockriede, Wm.; Ohio, 1840-1897 ***8365.35*** *p15*

Brod, Anna Maria 17; Galveston, TX, 1844 ***3967.10*** *p371*
Brod, Anton 19; Galveston, TX, 1844 ***3967.10*** *p371*
Brod, Jakob 15; Galveston, TX, 1844 ***3967.10*** *p371*
Brod, Johann 21; Galveston, TX, 1844 ***3967.10*** *p371*
Brod, Johann 50; Galveston, TX, 1844 ***3967.10*** *p371*
Brod, Katharina 43; Galveston, TX, 1844 ***3967.10*** *p371*
Brod, Nikolaus 9; Galveston, TX, 1844 ***3967.10*** *p371*
Brod, Peter 1; Galveston, TX, 1844 ***3967.10*** *p371*
Brod, Philipp 12; Galveston, TX, 1844 ***3967.10*** *p371*
Broddie, John 55; Ontario, 1871 ***1823.21*** *p37*
Broderdorf, Ernst Wilhelm; Wisconsin, 1896 ***6795.8*** *p160*
Broderick, Ansty; St. Johns, N.F., 1825 ***1053.15*** *p6*
Broderick, Daniel 35; Ontario, 1871 ***1823.17*** *p16*
Broderick, John; Colorado, 1873 ***1029.59*** *p13*
Broderick, John; St. Johns, N.F., 1825 ***1053.15*** *p7*
Broderick, Judy; St. Johns, N.F., 1825 ***1053.15*** *p7*
Broderick, Mary; St. Johns, N.F., 1825 ***1053.15*** *p7*
Broderick, Pat; St. Johns, N.F., 1825 ***1053.15*** *p6*
Brodersen, Carl Chr.; Iowa, 1899 ***1211.15*** *p9*
Brodeur, Louise 48; Montreal, 1658 ***9221.17*** *p391*
Brodhon, Marie 37; America, 1840 ***778.6*** *p50*
Brodie, Alexander 42; Ontario, 1871 ***1823.21*** *p37*
Brodie, Flora 55; Ontario, 1871 ***1823.21*** *p37*
Brodie, Hugh 40; Ontario, 1871 ***1823.21*** *p37*
Brodie, Hugh 65; Ontario, 1871 ***1823.21*** *p37*
Brodie, James 53; Ontario, 1871 ***1823.21*** *p37*
Brodie, John 30; Ontario, 1871 ***1823.17*** *p16*
Brodie, Malcolm 40; Ontario, 1871 ***1823.17*** *p16*
Brodin, Lovisa B.; St. Paul, MN, 1889 ***1865.50*** *p42*
Brodin, Oscar F.A.; St. Paul, MN, 1887 ***1865.50*** *p42*
Brodsky, Frantisek; New York, NY, 1836-1910 ***2853.20*** *p103*
Brodsky, Frantisek; New York, NY, 1850 ***2853.20*** *p100*
Broermann, Francis; Ohio, 1840-1897 ***8365.35*** *p15*
Broess, Anne 52; America, 1841 ***778.6*** *p50*
Broesse, Ja.ques 27; America, 1841 ***778.6*** *p50*
Brogan, Michael 45; Ontario, 1871 ***1823.21*** *p37*
Brogan, W. Fred.; Louisiana, 1874-1875 ***4981.45*** *p298*
Brogelmann, Karl Rudolf; Chicago, 1883 ***2526.42*** *p172*
Brogen, John 44; Ontario, 1871 ***1823.21*** *p37*
Broh, John; New York, 1859 ***358.56*** *p54*
Brohl, M.; New York, 1859 ***358.56*** *p54*
Brohm, Johann Georg; America, 1836 ***2526.43*** *p207*
Brohm, Johannes; America, n.d. ***2526.43*** *p221*
Brohm, Konrad Georg 18; America, 1853 ***2526.43*** *p207*
Brohm, Wilhelm; America, 1887 ***2526.43*** *p221*
Broker, Joseph; New Castle, DE, 1817-1818 ***90.20*** *p150*
Broklady, John 36; New Orleans, 1843 ***778.6*** *p50*
Broks, Edwin John 24; Ontario, 1871 ***1823.21*** *p37*
Brolin, Johan August; Colorado, 1891 ***1029.59*** *p14*
Brolley, A. P.; South Carolina, 1848 ***6155.4*** *p18*
Brom, Frantisek; St. Paul, MN, 1863 ***2853.20*** *p277*
Broman, Alfriede *SEE* Broman, Frank M.
Broman, Charlotte Sandstedt *SEE* Broman, Frank M.
Broman, Emma Ottilia; Kansas, 1867-1868 ***777.40*** *p16*
Broman, Frank M.; Kansas, 1867-1870 ***777.40*** *p8*
*Wife:*Charlotte Sandstedt
*Daughter:*Winried M.
*Daughter:*Alfriede
Broman, Gust; Iowa, 1891 ***1211.15*** *p9*
Broman, Isaac *SEE* Broman, Johanna
Broman, Johanna; Kansas, 1865-1870 ***777.40*** *p16*
*Husband:*Isaac
Broman, Winried M. *SEE* Broman, Frank M.
Brombacher, William; Ohio, 1809-1852 ***4511.35*** *p6*
Bromberek, Michael; Wisconsin, 1893 ***6795.8*** *p54*
Bromell, Joseph G.; North Carolina, 1858 ***1088.45*** *p4*
Bromer, Barbara 5; America, 1846 ***778.6*** *p50*
Bromer, Chatherine 9; America, 1846 ***778.6*** *p50*
Bromer, Hen.y 3; America, 1846 ***778.6*** *p50*
Bromer, Ma.garette 34; America, 1846 ***778.6*** *p50*
Bromer, Pierre 4; America, 1846 ***778.6*** *p50*
Bromer, Pierre 45; America, 1846 ***778.6*** *p50*
Bromfere, J.; Quebec, 1870 ***8364.32*** *p22*
Bromley, James; Boston, 1720 ***1642*** *p25*
Bromley, Mary; Maryland, 1674 ***1236.25*** *p50*
Brommer, Caroline; New York, 1859 ***358.56*** *p99*
Brommes, Henry; New York, 1860 ***358.56*** *p149*
Brona, Joseph; New York, 1885 ***1766.20*** *p36*
Bronan, Henry L.; Louisiana, 1836-1841 ***4981.45*** *p208*
Bronaugh, Mr.; Jamestown, VA, 1600-1699 ***9228.50*** *p137*
Bronaugh Family ; Virginia, n.d. ***9228.50*** *p137*
Brondza, Joseph 28; New York, NY, 1894 ***6512.1*** *p232*
Brone, A. 21; America, 1848 ***778.6*** *p50*
Bronn, Rosina 33; New York, NY, 1847 ***9176.15*** *p49*
Bronson, Robinson 55; Ontario, 1871 ***1823.21*** *p37*
Brook, Charlott 45; Ontario, 1871 ***1823.21*** *p37*
Brook, Samuel 28; Ontario, 1871 ***1823.21*** *p37*
Brook, William 47; Ontario, 1871 ***1823.21*** *p37*
Brooke, Jane 11; Quebec, 1870 ***8364.32*** *p22*
Brooke, Mary 20; Quebec, 1870 ***8364.32*** *p22*
Brooker, Robert; Ohio, 1834 ***3580.20*** *p31*
Brooker, Robert; Ohio, 1834 ***6020.12*** *p6*
Brooks, Andrew 19; Ontario, 1871 ***1823.17*** *p16*
Brooks, Anne 48; Ontario, 1871 ***1823.21*** *p37*
Brooks, Baptiste; Louisiana, 1874 ***4981.45*** *p130*
Brooks, Charles 35; Ontario, 1871 ***1823.17*** *p16*
Brooks, Edward; Philadelphia, 1777 ***8529.30*** *p7A*
Brooks, Edwin 50; Ontario, 1871 ***1823.21*** *p37*
Brooks, Elisabeth 73; Ontario, 1871 ***1823.21*** *p37*
Brooks, Eliza; Ontario, 1890-1930 ***9228.50*** *p125*
Brooks, Elizabeth Hannah; Nebraska, 1873-1878 ***9228.50*** *p128*
Brooks, George; Boston, 1774 ***8529.30*** *p6*
Brooks, James 37; Ontario, 1871 ***1823.21*** *p37*
Brooks, James 51; Ontario, 1871 ***1823.21*** *p37*
Brooks, James 63; Ontario, 1871 ***1823.17*** *p16*
Brooks, John 26; Ontario, 1871 ***1823.21*** *p37*
Brooks, John 67; Ontario, 1871 ***1823.17*** *p16*
Brooks, Joseph; New York, 1778 ***8529.30*** *p10*
Brooks, Julia 56; Ontario, 1871 ***1823.17*** *p16*
Brooks, Leonard 32; Ontario, 1871 ***1823.21*** *p37*
Brooks, Robert 26; Ontario, 1871 ***1823.21*** *p37*
Brooks, Robert 55; Ontario, 1871 ***1823.17*** *p16*
Brooks, Thomas; Louisiana, 1874 ***4981.45*** *p130*
Brooks, William 63; Ontario, 1871 ***1823.21*** *p37*
Broom, Elizabeth 62; Ontario, 1871 ***1823.21*** *p38*
Broom, Thomas 50; Ontario, 1871 ***1823.21*** *p38*
Brophey, Mary A. 33; Ontario, 1871 ***1823.21*** *p38*
Brophy, James; Newfoundland, 1814 ***3476.10*** *p54*
Brophy, James 45; Ontario, 1871 ***1823.21*** *p38*
Brophy, Mary 72; Ontario, 1871 ***1823.21*** *p38*
Brophy, Patrick 67; Ontario, 1871 ***1823.21*** *p38*
Brophy, Thomas 80; Ontario, 1871 ***1823.21*** *p38*
Brophy, Thos 40; Ontario, 1871 ***1823.21*** *p38*
Broquiere, Pierre 39; New Orleans, 1848 ***778.6*** *p50*
Broret, Jaques; Virginia, 1700 ***9230.15*** *p81*
With wife & 2 children
Broschat, Adolf Gustav *SEE* Broschat, Friedrich
Broschat, Auguste *SEE* Broschat, Friedrich
Broschat, C. L.; North Dakota, 1908 ***554.30*** *p26*
*Wife:*Minna
Broschat, Ernst *SEE* Broschat, Friedrich
Broschat, Fred. Wilm *SEE* Broschat, Friedrich
Broschat, Friederike *SEE* Broschat, Karl
Broschat, Friedrich; North Dakota, 1892 ***554.30*** *p26*
*Wife:*Marie
*Child:*Ernst
*Child:*Fred. Wilm
*Child:*Maria
*Child:*Adolf Gustav
*Child:*Johannes
*Child:*Auguste
Broschat, Johannes *SEE* Broschat, Friedrich
Broschat, Karl; Dakota, 1859-1918 ***554.30*** *p26*
*Wife:*Friederike
Broschat, Maria *SEE* Broschat, Friedrich
Broschat, Marie *SEE* Broschat, Friedrich
Broschat, Minna *SEE* Broschat, C. L.
Brose, Caroline Wilhelmine; Wisconsin, 1898 ***6795.8*** *p120*
Brose, Fr. Ferdinand; America, 1876 ***5475.1*** *p251*
Brose, Pauline Bertha; Wisconsin, 1885 ***6795.8*** *p123*
Brose, Wm.; Wisconsin, 1891 ***6795.8*** *p105*
Brosnihan, John; Boston, 1840 ***3274.56*** *p69*
Broson, William 38; Ontario, 1871 ***1823.17*** *p16*
Brossard, Julien 4; New Orleans, 1848 ***778.6*** *p50*
Brossard, Julien 24; Quebec, 1661 ***9221.17*** *p450*
Brossard, Marie Anne 34; New Orleans, 1848 ***778.6*** *p50*
Brossard, Pierre 8; New Orleans, 1848 ***778.6*** *p50*
Brossard, Pierre 40; New Orleans, 1848 ***778.6*** *p50*
Brossard, Urbain 19; Montreal, 1653 ***9221.17*** *p284*
Brossart, Denis; Quebec, 1646 ***9221.17*** *p161*
Brossier, Jean; Quebec, 1638 ***9221.17*** *p75*
Brostrom, Andrew; Colorado, 1884 ***1029.59*** *p14*
Brostrom, Gust A.; Cleveland, OH, 1891-1893 ***9722.10*** *p117*
Brosvat, Anna 16; New York, NY, 1894 ***6512.1*** *p182*
Brot, Josephine 21; America, 1846 ***778.6*** *p50*
Brot, Louis 24; America, 1846 ***778.6*** *p50*
Brotechi, Jean-Baptiste 18; New Orleans, 1848 ***778.6*** *p50*
Brothers, George 67; Ontario, 1871 ***1823.21*** *p38*
Brotherstone, Thomas 64; Ontario, 1871 ***1823.17*** *p16*
Brothier, Jean 18; Quebec, 1659 ***9221.17*** *p396*
Brouard, . . .; Massachusetts, n.d. ***9228.50*** *p138*
Brouard, Henry; New Jersey, 1852 ***9228.50*** *p138*
Brouard, John Guy Lowe; America, 1800-1900 ***9228.50*** *p138*
Broue, A. 21; America, 1848 ***778.6*** *p50*
Broueil, Joseph 29; New Orleans, 1840 ***778.6*** *p50*
Brouer, Ephram 58; Ontario, 1871 ***1823.17*** *p16*
Brouet, Ambroise 42; Quebec, 1641 ***9221.17*** *p100*
Brough, C. C. 76; Ontario, 1871 ***1823.21*** *p38*
Brough, Elizabeth 55; Ontario, 1871 ***1823.21*** *p38*
Brough, Robert 57; Ontario, 1871 ***1823.21*** *p38*
Brough, William 40; Ontario, 1871 ***1823.17*** *p16*
Broughton, James 31; Ontario, 1871 ***1823.17*** *p16*
Broughton, John; America, 1615-1662 ***9228.50*** *p138*
Broughton, John; Marblehead, MA, 1718 ***9228.50*** *p138*
Broughton, John; Philadelphia, 1778 ***8529.30*** *p10*
Broughton, Tho; Virginia, 1652 ***6254.4*** *p243*
Broughton, Thomas; Charleston, SC, 1699 ***9228.50*** *p138*
Broulain, Joseph 21; New Orleans, 1848 ***778.6*** *p50*
Brous, Henry 20; Ohio, 1847 ***778.6*** *p50*
Broussard, Jean; Nova Scotia, 1753 ***3051*** *p112*
*Wife:*Ozite Landrin
Broussard, Louis 28; Quebec, 1658 ***9221.17*** *p377*
Broussard, Ozite Landrin *SEE* Broussard, Jean
Broussaud, Louis; Quebec, 1658 ***9221.17*** *p7*
Brousse, . . .; New Orleans, 1848 ***778.6*** *p50*
Brousse, . . .; New Orleans, 1848 ***778.6*** *p50*
Brousse, Mr. 38; New Orleans, 1848 ***778.6*** *p50*
Brousse, Mrs.; New Orleans, 1848 ***778.6*** *p50*
Brousse, Jaques; Virginia, 1700 ***9230.15*** *p81*
With child
Brousseau, Julien 24; Quebec, 1661 ***9221.17*** *p450*
Brovings, Carl Johan Carlsson; North America, 1858 ***6410.15*** *p105*
*Wife:*Christina Larsdotter
*Daughter:*Johanna Christina Carolina
Brovings, Christina Larsdotter *SEE* Brovings, Carl Johan Carlsson
Brovings, Johanna Christina Carolina *SEE* Brovings, Carl Johan Carlsson
Brown, Agnes 34; Ontario, 1871 ***1823.21*** *p38*
Brown, Albert; Texas, 1907 ***3435.45*** *p35*
Brown, Alexander 34; Ontario, 1871 ***1823.21*** *p38*
Brown, Alfred 22; Ontario, 1871 ***1823.21*** *p38*
Brown, Andrew 26; Ontario, 1871 ***1823.17*** *p16*
Brown, Andrew 27; Ontario, 1871 ***1823.17*** *p16*
Brown, Andrew 63; Ontario, 1871 ***1823.21*** *p38*
Brown, Andrew; Washington, 1889 ***2770.40*** *p26*
Brown, Ann 2; New York, NY, 1835 ***5024.1*** *p136*
Brown, Ann 20; Ontario, 1871 ***1823.21*** *p38*
Brown, Ann 37; Ontario, 1871 ***1823.17*** *p16*
Brown, Ann 67; Ontario, 1871 ***1823.21*** *p38*
Brown, Annie 23; Ontario, 1871 ***1823.17*** *p16*
Brown, Annie 9; Quebec, 1870 ***8364.32*** *p22*
Brown, Archibald 45; Ontario, 1871 ***1823.17*** *p16*
Brown, Arthur 42; Ontario, 1871 ***1823.21*** *p38*
Brown, Arthur 71; Ontario, 1871 ***1823.17*** *p16*
Brown, Ash; North Carolina, 1859 ***1088.45*** *p4*
Brown, Augustus 44; Ontario, 1871 ***1823.21*** *p38*
Brown, Bridget 55; Ontario, 1871 ***1823.21*** *p38*
Brown, Catherine 75; Michigan, 1880 ***4491.39*** *p3*
Brown, Catherine 50; Ontario, 1871 ***1823.21*** *p38*
Brown, Cathn 24; St. John, N.B., 1834 ***6469.7*** *p5*
Brown, Charles; Maryland, 1673 ***1236.25*** *p49*
Brown, Charles 1; Ontario, 1871 ***1823.21*** *p38*
Brown, Charles; Washington, 1883 ***2770.40*** *p136*
Brown, Charles A. 33; Ontario, 1871 ***1823.17*** *p16*
Brown, Christian *SEE* Brown, Duncan
Brown, Cornelius 34; Ontario, 1871 ***1823.21*** *p38*
Brown, Dan 30; Ontario, 1871 ***1823.17*** *p16*
Brown, Daniel 66; Ontario, 1871 ***1823.17*** *p16*
Brown, Daniel *SEE* Brown, John
Brown, David 25; Ontario, 1871 ***1823.17*** *p16*
Brown, David 36; Ontario, 1871 ***1823.17*** *p16*
Brown, David 51; Ontario, 1871 ***1823.21*** *p38*
Brown, David 64; Ontario, 1871 ***1823.21*** *p38*
Brown, David 71; Ontario, 1871 ***1823.17*** *p16*
Brown, Donald *SEE* Brown, Duncan
Brown, Dugal 57; Ontario, 1871 ***1823.21*** *p38*
Brown, Duncan; New York, 1739 ***8277.31*** *p119*
*Wife:*Mary McIlepheder
*Child:*Gilbert
*Child:*Christian
*Child:*Donald
*Child:*John
Brown, Duncan 51; Ontario, 1871 ***1823.21*** *p38*
Brown, E. R. 35; Ontario, 1871 ***1823.17*** *p16*
Brown, Edward; Ohio, 1836 ***2763.1*** *p7*
Brown, Edward 51; Ontario, 1871 ***1823.21*** *p38*
Brown, Elias; New York, NY, 1840 ***3274.56*** *p71*
Brown, Elisabeth; New Orleans, 1851 ***7242.30*** *p136*
Brown, Eliza 53; Ontario, 1871 ***1823.21*** *p38*
Brown, Eliza 60; Ontario, 1871 ***1823.21*** *p38*
Brown, Eliza 64; Ontario, 1871 ***1823.21*** *p38*
Brown, Elizabeth; Minnesota, 1880 ***9228.50*** *p139*
Brown, Elizabeth; Ohio, 1813-1892 ***9228.50*** *p43*
Brown, Elizabeth 70; Ontario, 1871 ***1823.21*** *p38*
Brown, Elizabeth, Family; Marlborough, MA, 1657-1757 ***9228.50*** *p138*
Brown, Ella 24; Michigan, 1880 ***4491.33*** *p3*
Brown, Ellen 12; Quebec, 1870 ***8364.32*** *p22*
Brown, Emily 74; Ontario, 1871 ***1823.17*** *p17*

Brown, Francis 36; Ontario, 1871 ***1823.17*** *p17*
Brown, Francis 52; Ontario, 1871 ***1823.21*** *p38*
Brown, Frederick; Toronto, 1844 ***2910.35*** *p114*
Brown, G. N.; California, 1868 ***1131.61*** *p89*
Brown, Geo 45; Ontario, 1871 ***1823.21*** *p38*
Brown, George; New York, NY, 1826 ***3274.55*** *p26*
Brown, George; North Carolina, 1795 ***1088.45*** *p4*
Brown, George; Ohio, 1809-1852 ***4511.35*** *p6*
Brown, George; Ohio, 1840 ***3580.20*** *p31*
Brown, George; Ohio, 1840 ***6020.12*** *p6*
Brown, George 29; Ontario, 1871 ***1823.21*** *p39*
Brown, George 33; Ontario, 1871 ***1823.21*** *p39*
Brown, George 39; Ontario, 1871 ***1823.21*** *p39*
Brown, George 48; Ontario, 1871 ***1823.17*** *p17*
Brown, George 60; Ontario, 1871 ***1823.21*** *p39*
Brown, George 81; Ontario, 1871 ***1823.21*** *p39*
Brown, Gilbert *SEE* Brown, Duncan
Brown, H'y.; Ontario, 1787 ***1276.15*** *p230*
With 2 relatives
Brown, Hannah; New Haven, CT, 1703-1704 ***9228.50*** *p523*
Brown, Harry Raymond; Massachusetts, 1915 ***9228.50*** *p408*
Brown, Helen 11; New York, NY, 1835 ***5024.1*** *p136*
Brown, Henry 28; Ontario, 1871 ***1823.21*** *p39*
Brown, Henry 43; Ontario, 1871 ***1823.17*** *p17*
Brown, Henry 43; Ontario, 1871 ***1823.21*** *p39*
Brown, Henry 50; Ontario, 1871 ***1823.17*** *p17*
Brown, Henry 14; Quebec, 1870 ***8364.32*** *p22*
Brown, Hugh 23; Ontario, 1871 ***1823.21*** *p39*
Brown, Hugh 42; Ontario, 1871 ***1823.21*** *p39*
Brown, Ida Elizabeth; Hartford, CT, 1952 ***9228.50*** *p408*
Brown, Isaac 45; Ontario, 1871 ***1823.21*** *p39*
Brown, James; Boston, 1764 ***1642*** *p34*
Brown, James; Halifax, N.S., 1781 ***9228.50*** *p444*
Brown, James 7; New York, NY, 1835 ***5024.1*** *p136*
Brown, James 25; New York, NY, 1884 ***8427.14*** *p45*
Brown, James 20; Ontario, 1871 ***1823.21*** *p39*
Brown, James 30; Ontario, 1871 ***1823.17*** *p17*
Brown, James 34; Ontario, 1871 ***1823.21*** *p39*
Brown, James 35; Ontario, 1871 ***1823.21*** *p39*
Brown, James 36; Ontario, 1871 ***1823.21*** *p39*
Brown, James 40; Ontario, 1871 ***1823.21*** *p39*
Brown, James 43; Ontario, 1871 ***1823.21*** *p39*
Brown, James 45; Ontario, 1871 ***1823.17*** *p17*
Brown, James 51; Ontario, 1871 ***1823.21*** *p39*
Brown, James 55; Ontario, 1871 ***1823.21*** *p39*
Brown, James 62; Ontario, 1871 ***1823.21*** *p39*
Brown, James 65; Ontario, 1871 ***1823.21*** *p39*
Brown, James 66; Ontario, 1871 ***1823.21*** *p39*
Brown, James 1; St. John, N.B., 1834 ***6469.7*** *p5*
Brown, James H. 28; Ontario, 1871 ***1823.21*** *p39*
Brown, Jane 27; Ontario, 1871 ***1823.17*** *p17*
Brown, Jane 47; Ontario, 1871 ***1823.21*** *p39*
Brown, Janet 14; New York, NY, 1835 ***5024.1*** *p136*
Brown, Janet 56; Ontario, 1871 ***1823.21*** *p39*
Brown, Jean 37; New York, NY, 1835 ***5024.1*** *p136*
Brown, John; Illinois, 1859 ***6079.1*** *p2*
Brown, John; Minnesota, 1862 ***9228.50*** *p336*
*Brother:*Peter
Brown, John *SEE* Brown, Duncan
Brown, John; New York, 1778 ***8529.30*** *p10*
Brown, John 10; New York, NY, 1835 ***5024.1*** *p136*
Brown, John 45; New York, NY, 1835 ***5024.1*** *p136*
Brown, John; North Carolina, 1828 ***1088.45*** *p4*
Brown, John; North Carolina, 1856 ***1088.45*** *p4*
Brown, John 21; North Carolina, 1774 ***1422.10*** *p55*
Brown, John; Ohio, 1809-1852 ***4511.35*** *p6*
Brown, John 21; Ontario, 1871 ***1823.17*** *p17*
Brown, John 21; Ontario, 1871 ***1823.21*** *p39*
Brown, John 23; Ontario, 1871 ***1823.21*** *p39*
Brown, John 31; Ontario, 1871 ***1823.21*** *p40*
Brown, John 32; Ontario, 1871 ***1823.21*** *p39*
Brown, John 33; Ontario, 1871 ***1823.17*** *p17*
Brown, John 34; Ontario, 1871 ***1823.17*** *p17*
Brown, John 35; Ontario, 1871 ***1823.17*** *p17*
Brown, John 35; Ontario, 1871 ***1823.21*** *p39*
Brown, John 36; Ontario, 1871 ***1823.17*** *p17*
Brown, John 40; Ontario, 1871 ***1823.17*** *p17*
Brown, John 50; Ontario, 1871 ***1823.21*** *p39*
Brown, John 53; Ontario, 1871 ***1823.21*** *p39*
Brown, John 53; Ontario, 1871 ***1823.21*** *p40*
Brown, John 56; Ontario, 1871 ***1823.17*** *p17*
Brown, John 59; Ontario, 1871 ***1823.21*** *p39*
Brown, John 62; Ontario, 1871 ***1823.17*** *p17*
Brown, John 63; Ontario, 1871 ***1823.21*** *p40*
Brown, John; Portsmouth, NH, 1698 ***9228.50*** *p17A*
*Brother:*Daniel
Brown, John; Salem, MA, 1660 ***9228.50*** *p138*
Brown, John; St. John, N.B., 1847 ***2978.15*** *p36*
Brown, John 4; St. John, N.B., 1834 ***6469.7*** *p5*
Brown, John 20; St. John, N.B., 1834 ***6469.7*** *p5*
Brown, John 56; St. John, N.B., 1834 ***6469.7*** *p5*
Brown, John 60; St. John, N.B., 1834 ***6469.7*** *p5*
Brown, John; Utah, 1888 ***3687.1*** *p36*
Brown, John J. 40; Ontario, 1871 ***1823.17*** *p17*
Brown, John S.; Washington, 1889 ***2770.40*** *p26*
Brown, Jonathon 27; Ontario, 1871 ***1823.21*** *p40*
Brown, Joseph 52; Ontario, 1871 ***1823.21*** *p40*
Brown, Joseph 54; Ontario, 1871 ***1823.17*** *p17*
Brown, Joseph; Toronto, 1844 ***2910.35*** *p115*
Brown, Joseph F.; Washington, 1882 ***2770.40*** *p135*
Brown, Karl; Colorado, 1890 ***1029.59*** *p14*
Brown, Katrine 26; North Carolina, 1774 ***1422.10*** *p57*
Brown, Lewis 53; Ontario, 1871 ***1823.21*** *p40*
Brown, Lilian Elsie; America, 1868-1947 ***9228.50*** *p352*
Brown, Lizzie 21; Ontario, 1871 ***1823.21*** *p40*
Brown, Louis; Ohio, 1841 ***2763.1*** *p7*
Brown, Luther 47; Michigan, 1880 ***4491.30*** *p4*
Brown, Margaret 4; New York, NY, 1835 ***5024.1*** *p136*
Brown, Margaret 17; Quebec, 1870 ***8364.32*** *p22*
Brown, Margarett 40; Michigan, 1880 ***4491.39*** *p3*
Brown, Martha 26; Ontario, 1871 ***1823.21*** *p40*
Brown, Martin 62; Ontario, 1871 ***1823.21*** *p40*
Brown, Mary 10; Michigan, 1880 ***4491.39*** *p3*
Brown, Mary McIlepheder *SEE* Brown, Duncan
Brown, Mary 30; Ontario, 1871 ***1823.21*** *p40*
Brown, Mary 32; Ontario, 1871 ***1823.21*** *p40*
Brown, Mary 59; Ontario, 1871 ***1823.21*** *p40*
Brown, Mary 67; Ontario, 1871 ***1823.21*** *p40*
Brown, Mary 77; Ontario, 1871 ***1823.21*** *p40*
Brown, Mary 13; Quebec, 1870 ***8364.32*** *p22*
Brown, Mathew 31; Ontario, 1871 ***1823.21*** *p40*
Brown, Matthew 39; Ontario, 1871 ***1823.17*** *p17*
Brown, Matthew 28; St. John, N.B., 1834 ***6469.7*** *p5*
Brown, Merran; New York, 1740 ***8277.31*** *p119*
Brown, Mic; St. John, N.B., 1848 ***2978.15*** *p39*
Brown, Michael; Toronto, 1844 ***2910.35*** *p116*
Brown, Minnie M.; Quebec, 1915-1916 ***9228.50*** *p408*
Brown, Moses 53; Ontario, 1871 ***1823.21*** *p40*
Brown, Nancy 58; Ontario, 1871 ***1823.21*** *p40*
Brown, Neil 50; Ontario, 1871 ***1823.21*** *p40*
Brown, Neil 63; Ontario, 1871 ***1823.21*** *p40*
Brown, Olaf J.; Washington, 1887 ***2770.40*** *p24*
Brown, Olive A. 34; Michigan, 1880 ***4491.36*** *p3*
Brown, Patrick 70; Ontario, 1871 ***1823.21*** *p40*
Brown, Peter 70; Michigan, 1880 ***4491.39*** *p3*
Brown, Peter; Minnesota, 1830-1862 ***9228.50*** *p139*
Brown, Peter *SEE* Brown, John
Brown, Peter 46; Ontario, 1871 ***1823.17*** *p17*
Brown, Peter 54; Ontario, 1871 ***1823.21*** *p40*
Brown, Peter; Plymouth, MA, 1620 ***1920.45*** *p5*
Brown, Prescott Libbey; New Jersey, 1938 ***9228.50*** *p408*
Brown, R. M.; California, 1868 ***1131.61*** *p89*
Brown, Rebc Jane 2; St. John, N.B., 1834 ***6469.7*** *p5*
Brown, Rebecca 56; St. John, N.B., 1834 ***6469.7*** *p5*
Brown, Richard; New York, 1776 ***8529.30*** *p10*
Brown, Robert 30; Ontario, 1871 ***1823.21*** *p40*
Brown, Robert 38; Ontario, 1871 ***1823.21*** *p40*
Brown, Robert 39; Ontario, 1871 ***1823.17*** *p17*
Brown, Robert 40; Ontario, 1871 ***1823.21*** *p40*
Brown, Robert 53; Ontario, 1871 ***1823.21*** *p40*
Brown, Robert 75; Ontario, 1871 ***1823.17*** *p17*
Brown, Sam 24; Ontario, 1871 ***1823.21*** *p40*
Brown, Samson 47; Ontario, 1871 ***1823.17*** *p17*
Brown, Samuel 41; Michigan, 1880 ***4491.39*** *p3*
Brown, Samuel 28; Ontario, 1871 ***1823.21*** *p40*
Brown, Samuel 43; Ontario, 1871 ***1823.21*** *p40*
Brown, Samuel 71; Ontario, 1871 ***1823.21*** *p40*
Brown, T. S.; California, 1868 ***1131.61*** *p89*
Brown, Tho.; Maryland, 1674-1675 ***1236.25*** *p51*
Brown, Thomas; Illinois, 1854 ***6079.1*** *p2*
Brown, Thomas; New York, 1777 ***8529.30*** *p10*
Brown, Thomas; North Carolina, 1842 ***1088.45*** *p4*
Brown, Thomas 20; Ontario, 1871 ***1823.21*** *p40*
Brown, Thomas 31; Ontario, 1871 ***1823.17*** *p17*
Brown, Thomas 34; Ontario, 1871 ***1823.17*** *p17*
Brown, Thomas 35; Ontario, 1871 ***1823.17*** *p17*
Brown, Thomas 40; Ontario, 1871 ***1823.21*** *p40*
Brown, Thomas 41; Ontario, 1871 ***1823.21*** *p40*
Brown, Thomas 43; Ontario, 1871 ***1823.17*** *p17*
Brown, Thomas 44; Ontario, 1871 ***1823.17*** *p17*
Brown, Thomas 45; Ontario, 1871 ***1823.21*** *p40*
Brown, Thomas 52; Ontario, 1871 ***1823.17*** *p17*
Brown, Thomas 62; Ontario, 1871 ***1823.17*** *p17*
Brown, Thomas Joseph; Colorado, 1873 ***1029.59*** *p14*
Brown, Vesey A. 45; Ontario, 1871 ***1823.21*** *p40*
Brown, Walter 36; Ontario, 1871 ***1823.21*** *p40*
Brown, Walter 6; Quebec, 1870 ***8364.32*** *p22*
Brown, Wendel 56; Ontario, 1871 ***1823.17*** *p17*
Brown, William; Boston, 1827 ***3274.55*** *p43*
Brown, William; Marston's Wharf, 1782 ***8529.30*** *p10*
Brown, William 25; Ontario, 1871 ***1823.21*** *p41*
Brown, William 27; Ontario, 1871 ***1823.21*** *p40*
Brown, William 33; Ontario, 1871 ***1823.21*** *p40*
Brown, William 33; Ontario, 1871 ***1823.21*** *p41*
Brown, William 35; Ontario, 1871 ***1823.21*** *p41*
Brown, William 36; Ontario, 1871 ***1823.21*** *p41*
Brown, William 37; Ontario, 1871 ***1823.21*** *p41*
Brown, William 38; Ontario, 1871 ***1823.17*** *p17*
Brown, William 39; Ontario, 1871 ***1823.17*** *p17*
Brown, William 41; Ontario, 1871 ***1823.21*** *p41*
Brown, William 44; Ontario, 1871 ***1823.17*** *p18*
Brown, William 45; Ontario, 1871 ***1823.21*** *p41*
Brown, William 46; Ontario, 1871 ***1823.21*** *p40*
Brown, William 47; Ontario, 1871 ***1823.21*** *p41*
Brown, William 50; Ontario, 1871 ***1823.21*** *p40*
Brown, William 51; Ontario, 1871 ***1823.17*** *p18*
Brown, William 51; Ontario, 1871 ***1823.21*** *p41*
Brown, William 59; Ontario, 1871 ***1823.17*** *p17*
Brown, William 61; Ontario, 1871 ***1823.17*** *p18*
Brown, William 13; St. John, N.B., 1834 ***6469.7*** *p5*
Brown, William 25; St. John, N.B., 1834 ***6469.7*** *p5*
Brown, William H.; Tennessee, 1854 ***3665.20*** *p111*
Brown, William John; Washington, 1881 ***2770.40*** *p134*
Brown, William L. 28; Ontario, 1871 ***1823.21*** *p41*
Brown, William T.; Massachusetts, 1825 ***3274.55*** *p66*
Brown, Wm.; Maryland, 1674-1675 ***1236.25*** *p52*
Brown, Zachariah; Philadelphia, 1778 ***8529.30*** *p6*
Brown, Ziriak; New York, NY, 1847 ***7710.1*** *p152*
Browne, George 17; Ontario, 1871 ***1823.21*** *p41*
Browne, Honor; St. Johns, N.F., 1825 ***1053.15*** *p6*
Browne, John; Massachusetts, 1686 ***9228.50*** *p350*
Browne, John; Salem, MA, 1660 ***9228.50*** *p138*
Browne, Moses; New England, 1686 ***9228.50*** *p336*
Browne, Richard 56; Ontario, 1871 ***1823.21*** *p41*
Browne, Richard 19; Virginia, 1635 ***1183.3*** *p31*
Browne, Rose; New Orleans, 1850 ***7242.30*** *p136*
Browne, William; New York, 1778 ***8529.30*** *p6*
Brown Family ; West Virginia, 1850 ***1132.30*** *p147*
Browngate, Mathew; Long Island, 1781 ***8529.30*** *p9A*
Browning, George; New York, NY, 1830 ***3274.55*** *p71*
Brownlee, Agnes 67; Ontario, 1871 ***1823.21*** *p41*
Brownlee, Andrew 52; Ontario, 1871 ***1823.21*** *p41*
Brownlee, Christopher 62; Ontario, 1871 ***1823.17*** *p18*
Brownlee, Henry 44; Ontario, 1871 ***1823.17*** *p18*
Brownlee, John 37; Ontario, 1871 ***1823.17*** *p18*
Brownlee, Mary 38; Ontario, 1871 ***1823.21*** *p41*
Brownlee, Robert; North Carolina, 1837 ***1088.45*** *p4*
Brownlee, Robert 50; Ontario, 1871 ***1823.17*** *p18*
Brownlee, William 38; Ontario, 1871 ***1823.17*** *p18*
Brownlee, William 60; Ontario, 1871 ***1823.17*** *p18*
Brownllee, John 54; Ontario, 1871 ***1823.17*** *p18*
Brownmiller, Ludwick; Philadelphia, 1778 ***8529.30*** *p2*
Brownmullier, Ludwick; Philadelphia, 1778 ***8529.30*** *p2*
Broz, . . .; Pennsylvania, 1750-1799 ***2853.20*** *p17*
Broz, Anton 43; Minnesota, 1925 ***2769.54*** *p1384*
Broz, Frantisek; Iowa, 1870 ***2853.20*** *p202*
Broz, Jan; Iowa, 1855 ***2853.20*** *p217*
Broz, Jan Petr; Iowa, 1900 ***2853.20*** *p224*
Broz, Jan Stepan; Nebraska, 1890 ***2853.20*** *p187*
Broz, Josef; St. Louis, 1854 ***2853.20*** *p21*
Brozdeniez, Josefa 23; New York, NY, 1894 ***6512.1*** *p231*
Brozdeniez, Stanislawa 1 months; New York, NY, 1894 ***6512.1*** *p231*
Brozek, Frantisek; New York, NY, 1852 ***2853.20*** *p386*
Bruce, Mr. 26; America, 1848 ***778.6*** *p50*
Bruce, Mrs. 28; America, 1848 ***778.6*** *p50*
Bruce, A. 3; America, 1848 ***778.6*** *p50*
Bruce, Adam 34; Ontario, 1871 ***1823.17*** *p18*
Bruce, Adam 43; Ontario, 1871 ***1823.17*** *p18*
Bruce, Alexander 65; Ontario, 1871 ***1823.21*** *p41*
Bruce, Allan 50; Ontario, 1871 ***1823.17*** *p18*
Bruce, David 32; Ontario, 1871 ***1823.21*** *p41*
Bruce, David Dickey; Boston, 1882 ***1029.59*** *p1A*
Bruce, Henry 30; Ontario, 1871 ***1823.21*** *p41*
Bruce, Henry 60; Ontario, 1871 ***1823.21*** *p41*
Bruce, James 11; Michigan, 1880 ***4491.36*** *p3*
Bruce, James 64; Ontario, 1871 ***1823.21*** *p41*
Bruce, James E.; Ohio, 1809-1852 ***4511.35*** *p6*
Bruce, John 14; Michigan, 1880 ***4491.36*** *p3*
Bruce, John 50; Ontario, 1871 ***1823.21*** *p41*
Bruce, Julia 42; Michigan, 1880 ***4491.36*** *p3*
Bruce, Thomas 8; Michigan, 1880 ***4491.36*** *p3*
Bruce, Thomas 49; Michigan, 1880 ***4491.36*** *p3*
Bruch, August; Wisconsin, 1873 ***6795.8*** *p16*
*Wife:*Wilhelmine Knaack
Bruch, Elisabeth *SEE* Bruch, Johann
Bruch, Johann; Rio Grande do Sul, Brazil, 1861 ***5475.1*** *p489*
*Wife:*Maria El. Schussler
*Daughter:*Elisabeth
Bruch, Maria El. Schussler *SEE* Bruch, Johann
Bruch, Peter; America, 1846 ***5475.1*** *p234*
Bruch, Wilhelmine Knaack *SEE* Bruch, August
Bruchel, Joseph 46; Galveston, TX, 1844 ***3967.10*** *p375*
Bruchel, Margarethe 36; Galveston, TX, 1844 ***3967.10*** *p375*

Brucher, Johann Nikolaus; America, 1877 ***5475.1*** *p309*
*Wife:*Josephine Hirzig
*Daughter:*Margarethe
Brucher, Josephine Hirzig 25 *SEE* Brucher, Johann Nikolaus
Brucher, Margarethe *SEE* Brucher, Johann Nikolaus
Bruck, A. Maria 20; America, 1847 ***5475.1*** *p393*
Bruck, Barbara 11; America, 1847 ***5475.1*** *p393*
Bruck, Hermann Michael; Wisconsin, 1894 ***6795.8*** *p189*
Bruck, Isadore; Detroit, 1929 ***1640.55*** *p117*
Bruck, Johann; America, 1879 ***5475.1*** *p187*
*Wife:*Margarethe Buchheit
*Son:*Mathias
*Son:*Josef
*Daughter:*Maria
*Son:*Peter
Bruck, Josef *SEE* Bruck, Johann
Bruck, Karl; America, 1839 ***5475.1*** *p27*
Bruck, Katharina; Brazil, 1881 ***5475.1*** *p42*
Bruck, Margarethe Buchheit *SEE* Bruck, Johann
Bruck, Maria *SEE* Bruck, Johann
Bruck, Mathias *SEE* Bruck, Johann
Bruck, Peter *SEE* Bruck, Johann
Bruck, Peter 25; America, 1865 ***5475.1*** *p516*
Bruckel, George; New York, 1860 ***358.56*** *p149*
Brucken, Conrad; Ohio, 1840-1897 ***8365.35*** *p15*
Brucken, Michael Peter; America, 1847 ***5475.1*** *p439*
With 4 children
Bruckener, Heinrich 21; America, 1858 ***5475.1*** *p482*
Brucker, Anton 39; Galveston, TX, 1844 ***3967.10*** *p371*
Brucker, Carl; Valdivia, Chile, 1852 ***1192.4*** *p52*
Brucker, Jacob; Ohio, 1809-1852 ***4511.35*** *p6*
Brucker, Jacob 22; Port uncertain, 1843 ***778.6*** *p50*
Brucker, Louis Philippe 6 months; Galveston, TX, 1844 ***3967.10*** *p371*
Brucker, Theresa 36; Galveston, TX, 1844 ***3967.10*** *p371*
Bruckman, Matias; Puerto Rico, 1839 ***3476.25*** *p111*
Bruckman Duliebre, Matias; Puerto Rico, 1853 ***3476.25*** *p112*
Bruckner, August 2 *SEE* Bruckner, Friedrich Michael
Bruckner, C. F.; Valdivia, Chile, 1852 ***1192.4*** *p54*
Bruckner, Elisabeth 2 *SEE* Bruckner, Friedrich Michael
Bruckner, Friedrich Michael 26; America, 1846 ***2526.42*** *p159*
With wife
*Child:*August 2 months
*Child:*Elisabeth 2
Bruckner, Hermann; America, 1867 ***7919.3*** *p529*
Brucks, Elisabeth 7; Galveston, TX, 1845 ***3967.10*** *p376*
Brucks, Gertrud 11; Galveston, TX, 1845 ***3967.10*** *p376*
Brucks, Gertrud 45; Galveston, TX, 1845 ***3967.10*** *p376*
Brucks, Heinrich 7; Galveston, TX, 1845 ***3967.10*** *p376*
Brucks, Johann Bernhard 8; Galveston, TX, 1845 ***3967.10*** *p376*
Brucks, Johann Bernhard 49; Galveston, TX, 1845 ***3967.10*** *p376*
Brudeau, J. Marie 20; New Orleans, 1848 ***778.6*** *p50*
Bruder, Barbara Mohr *SEE* Bruder, Heinrich
Bruder, Georg, III; Illinois, 1872 ***2526.42*** *p149*
Bruder, Heinrich; Illinois, 1865 ***2526.42*** *p149*
*Wife:*Barbara Mohr
Bruder, Hieronymus; Illinois, 1867 ***2526.42*** *p149*
Bruder, Jacob; New York, NY, 1855 ***8513.31*** *p297*
*Wife:*Louise Kuenzel
Bruder, Louise Kuenzel *SEE* Bruder, Jacob
Bruderly, Joseph; New Castle, DE, 1817-1818 ***90.20*** *p150*
Brudi, Joh.; Valdivia, Chile, 1851 ***1192.4*** *p51*
Brudnacher, Jean 31; New Orleans, 1848 ***778.6*** *p50*
Brue, Andrew A.; Washington, 1883 ***2770.40*** *p136*
Brue, Andrew J.; Washington, 1883 ***2770.40*** *p136*
Bruel, Pierre; Quebec, 1648 ***9221.17*** *p196*
Bruen, Leopold; Louisiana, 1874 ***4981.45*** *p295*
Bruer, . . .; Massachusetts, n.d. ***9228.50*** *p138*
Brug, Peter; Ohio, 1809-1852 ***4511.35*** *p6*
Brugera, Felix; Louisiana, 1874-1875 ***4981.45*** *p297*
Brugge, A. W.; Louisiana, 1836-1841 ***4981.45*** *p208*
Bruggemann, Anna 3; Galveston, TX, 1845 ***3967.10*** *p376*
Bruggemann, Bernhard 8; Galveston, TX, 1845 ***3967.10*** *p376*
Bruggemann, Bernhard 38; Galveston, TX, 1845 ***3967.10*** *p376*
Bruggemann, Eva; New York, 1859-1860 ***358.56*** *p102*
Bruggemann, Gottfried; America, 1854 ***7420.1*** *p117*
Bruggemann, Heinrich Ludwig; Port uncertain, 1837 ***7420.1*** *p12*
Bruggemann, Hermann 7; Galveston, TX, 1845 ***3967.10*** *p376*
Bruggemann, Johann Theodor 5; Galveston, TX, 1845 ***3967.10*** *p376*
Bruggemann, Ludovica 34; Galveston, TX, 1845 ***3967.10*** *p376*
Bruggemann, Walburga 1; Galveston, TX, 1845 ***3967.10*** *p376*
Brugger, Benedict; Illinois, 1861 ***6079.1*** *p2*
Brugger, Christian; Illinois, 1851 ***6079.1*** *p2*
Brugger, John Ulrich; Illinois, 1859 ***6079.1*** *p2*
Brugherm, Mary 20; Ontario, 1871 ***1823.17*** *p18*
Brugier, Mr. 40; America, 1844 ***778.6*** *p51*
Brugler, Magdalena 19; Akron, OH, 1880 ***5475.1*** *p240*
Brugman, Joseph; North Carolina, 1839 ***1088.45*** *p4*
Brugne, Pierre 24; America, 1847 ***778.6*** *p51*
Bruhen, Francois 23; America, 1847 ***778.6*** *p51*
Bruhling, Mrs. Severin; America, 1838 ***2526.42*** *p118*
With daughter 22
With son 16
Bruhn, F.L.D.; Venezuela, 1843 ***3899.5*** *p546*
Bruin, John 66; Ontario, 1871 ***1823.21*** *p41*
Bruin, Pierre 44; America, 1843 ***778.6*** *p51*
Bruire, Mr. 45; New Orleans, 1848 ***778.6*** *p51*
Bruitiere, Jean; Nova Scotia, 1753 ***3051*** *p112*
Brulard, Etinne; Louisiana, 1836-1840 ***4981.45*** *p212*
Brulche, Xavier; Ohio, 1809-1852 ***4511.35*** *p6*
Brule, Etienne; Quebec, 1608 ***9221.17*** *p17*
Brumby, James; Philadelphia, 1777 ***8529.30*** *p2*
Brumby, Thomas; Philadelphia, 1777 ***8529.30*** *p2*
Brumell, Robt. 37; Ontario, 1871 ***1823.17*** *p18*
Brumen, George; North Carolina, 1844 ***1088.45*** *p4*
Bruming, John 40; Ontario, 1871 ***1823.17*** *p18*
Brummit, Reuban 41; Ontario, 1871 ***1823.21*** *p41*
Brun, Bernard 7; America, 1840 ***778.6*** *p51*
Brun, Bernard 41; America, 1840 ***778.6*** *p51*
Brun, Brigitte 31; America, 1840 ***778.6*** *p51*
Brun, Jean 24; America, 1847 ***778.6*** *p51*
Brun, Johannes 1; America, 1840 ***778.6*** *p51*
Brun, Joseph; Ohio, 1840-1897 ***8365.35*** *p15*
Brun, Josephine 6; America, 1840 ***778.6*** *p51*
Brun, Marcelin 44; America, 1848 ***778.6*** *p51*
Brun, Pierre 23; New Orleans, 1840 ***778.6*** *p51*
Brun, R. 35; America, 1841 ***778.6*** *p51*
Brun, Veronika 8; America, 1840 ***778.6*** *p51*
Brune, Boris 18; New Orleans, 1848 ***778.6*** *p51*
Brune, Wilh. 17; New York, NY, 1864 ***8425.62*** *p197*
Bruneau, Mr.; Jamestown, VA, 1600-1699 ***9228.50*** *p137*
Bruneau, Catherine; Quebec, 1670 ***4514.3*** *p284*
Bruneau Family ; Virginia, n.d. ***9228.50*** *p137*
Brunel, Denaise 3; New Orleans, 1848 ***778.6*** *p51*
Brunel, Elisa 31; New Orleans, 1848 ***778.6*** *p51*
Brunel, Louis; Colorado, 1895 ***1029.59*** *p14*
Brunel, Louis; Illinois, 1890 ***1029.59*** *p14*
Bruner, Christian; Missouri, 1898 ***3276.1*** *p1*
Bruner, Maria 32; America, 1845 ***778.6*** *p51*
Brunet, Anne; Quebec, 1665 ***4514.3*** *p284*
Brunet, Antoine 19; Montreal, 1662 ***9221.17*** *p496*
Brunet, Francois 17; Quebec, 1661 ***9221.17*** *p450*
Brunet, Francoise; Quebec, 1663 ***4514.3*** *p284*
*Child:*Jeanne
*Child:*Francoise
Brunet, Isaac 32; Quebec, 1662 ***9221.17*** *p482*
Brunet, Jacques 16; Quebec, 1661 ***9221.17*** *p450*
Brunet, Marie-Jeanne; Quebec, 1667 ***4514.3*** *p322*
Brunet, Michel-Mathieu 20; Quebec, 1657 ***9221.17*** *p353*
Brunet, Pierre 19; Quebec, 1661 ***9221.17*** *p450*
Brunette, Jean 18; Missouri, 1847 ***778.6*** *p51*
Brunette, Marie 21; Missouri, 1847 ***778.6*** *p51*
Brunger, Henry; Illinois, 1861 ***6079.1*** *p2*
Brungne, Fc. 26; America, 1847 ***778.6*** *p51*
Brunier, . . .; Montreal, 1662 ***9221.17*** *p496*
Brunier, Christian 24; America, 1848 ***778.6*** *p51*
Brunket, Richard; North Carolina, 1837 ***1088.45*** *p4*
Brunket, William; North Carolina, 1837 ***1088.45*** *p4*
Brunkhorst, Engel Marie Charlotte Meierhoff Wille *SEE* Brunkhorst, Friedrich Christian
Brunkhorst, Friedrich Christian; America, 1864 ***7420.1*** *p222*
*Wife:*Engel Marie Charlotte Meierhoff Wille
Brunkhorst, Heinrich Christian Wilhelm; America, 1864 ***7420.1*** *p222*
Brunnemeyer, Catha. 5; New York, NY, 1885 ***1883.7*** *p46*
Brunnemeyer, Conrad 11 months; New York, NY, 1885 ***1883.7*** *p46*
Brunnemeyer, Georg 8; New York, NY, 1885 ***1883.7*** *p46*
Brunnemeyer, Georg 33; New York, NY, 1885 ***1883.7*** *p46*
Brunnemeyer, Jacob 2; New York, NY, 1885 ***1883.7*** *p46*
Brunnemeyer, Liesbeth 11 months; New York, NY, 1885 ***1883.7*** *p46*
Brunnemeyer, Marga. 31; New York, NY, 1885 ***1883.7*** *p46*
Brunnemeyer, Sofia 4; New York, NY, 1885 ***1883.7*** *p46*
Brunner, Adam 1 *SEE* Brunner, Jakob
Brunner, Anna Maria 30; America, 1854 ***2526.43*** *p217*
Brunner, Antonin; Nebraska, 1874 ***2853.20*** *p172*
Brunner, Christian; Missouri, 1893 ***3276.1*** *p1*
Brunner, Elisabetha 3 *SEE* Brunner, Jakob
Brunner, Elisabetha 35; America, 1857 ***2526.43*** *p154*
*Daughter:*Elise 13
*Son:*Theodor 11
*Daughter:*Jeanette 9
*Daughter:*Maria 4
*Daughter:*Anna 7
Brunner, Ernst Heinrich Daniel; Pittsburgh, 1882 ***2526.43*** *p164*
Brunner, Eva Maria 25; America, 1853 ***2526.43*** *p165*
Brunner, Ferdinand; Valdivia, Chile, 1851 ***1192.4*** *p50*
Brunner, Georg; America, 1885 ***2526.43*** *p165*
Brunner, Georg; Wisconsin, 1870 ***2853.20*** *p326*
Brunner, Heinrich; America, 1842 ***2526.43*** *p165*
With wife
With daughter 4
Brunner, Heinrich; Pennsylvania, 1877 ***2526.43*** *p165*
Brunner, Jakob 27; America, 1846 ***2526.43*** *p138*
With wife
*Daughter:*Elisabetha 3
*Son:*Adam 1
Brunner, Jakob; Pittsburgh, 1879 ***2526.43*** *p165*
Brunner, Jakob, II; America, 1846 ***2526.43*** *p159*
With family & mother-in-law
Brunner, Jakob, II; America, 1846 ***2526.43*** *p162*
Brunner, Katharina; America, 1871 ***2526.43*** *p146*
Brunner, Ludwig, II; Pennsylvania, 1853 ***2526.43*** *p165*
Brunner, Margaret 56; Michigan, 1880 ***4491.36*** *p3*
Brunnett, Lisette; Philadelphia, 1859 ***8513.31*** *p324*
Bruno, Andrew; Philadelphia, 1867 ***8513.31*** *p297*
Bruns, Mr.; America, 1852 ***7420.1*** *p86*
Bruns, Mr.; America, 1860 ***7420.1*** *p192*
With family
Bruns, Mr.; America, 1864 ***7420.1*** *p222*
Bruns, Auguste Marie Dorothee *SEE* Bruns, Johann Heinrich Conrad
Bruns, Carl Friedrich; America, 1850 ***7420.1*** *p70*
*Wife:*Engel Marie Sophie Eleon. Wustenfeld
*Son:*Heinrich Friedrich Carl
*Son:*Johann Heinrich Carl
Bruns, Christian Ludwig; America, 1835 ***7420.1*** *p8*
Bruns, Dorothea; America, 1893 ***7420.1*** *p368*
Bruns, Engel Marie Dorothea; America, 1868 ***7420.1*** *p269*
Bruns, Engel Marie Sophie Eleon. Wustenfeld *SEE* Bruns, Carl Friedrich
Bruns, Ernst Friedrich Wilhelm; New York, NY, 1878 ***7420.1*** *p310*
Bruns, Ernst Heinrich Conrad; Port uncertain, 1835 ***7420.1*** *p8*
Bruns, Friedrich Heinrich Philipp; America, 1867 ***7420.1*** *p255*
Bruns, Gerke 20; New York, NY, 1885 ***1883.7*** *p45*
Bruns, Hans Heinrich; America, 1850 ***7420.1*** *p70*
*Sister:*Thrine Sophie
Bruns, Hans Heinrich; New York, NY, 1856 ***7420.1*** *p146*
Bruns, Heinrich; America, 1854 ***7420.1*** *p117*
Bruns, Heinrich; New York, NY, 1856 ***7420.1*** *p146*
Bruns, Heinrich Christoph; Port uncertain, 1838 ***7420.1*** *p14*
Bruns, Heinrich Friedrich Carl *SEE* Bruns, Carl Friedrich
Bruns, Heinrich Wilhelm Ludwig; America, 1850 ***7420.1*** *p70*
Bruns, Herm. Philipp 18; New York, NY, 1864 ***8425.62*** *p197*
Bruns, Johann Heinrich Carl *SEE* Bruns, Carl Friedrich
Bruns, Johann Heinrich Christoph; America, 1850 ***7420.1*** *p70*
Bruns, Johann Heinrich Conrad; America, 1882 ***7420.1*** *p328*
*Sister:*Auguste Marie Dorothee
Bruns, Philippine; America, 1857 ***7420.1*** *p159*
Bruns, Thrine Sophie *SEE* Bruns, Hans Heinrich
Bruns, Wilhelm; America, 1854 ***7420.1*** *p117*
Brunskill, Thomas 45; Ontario, 1871 ***1823.21*** *p41*
Brunssen, Friedrich; Iowa, 1914 ***1211.15*** *p9*
Brunstead, Dora 25; Ontario, 1871 ***1823.21*** *p41*
Brunstead, Henry 51; Ontario, 1871 ***1823.21*** *p41*
Brunsteller, Jean 26; America, 1844 ***778.6*** *p51*
Brunswick, Mrs. C. 23; America, 1844 ***778.6*** *p51*
Brunt, James 44; Ontario, 1871 ***1823.21*** *p41*
Brunton, William 45; Ontario, 1871 ***1823.21*** *p41*
Brus, Peter; America, 1882 ***5475.1*** *p203*
*Wife:*Susanna Fell
Brus, Susanna Fell *SEE* Brus, Peter
Brusa, Ange 27; America, 1842 ***778.6*** *p51*
Brusanhan, Edward; Ohio, 1840-1897 ***8365.35*** *p15*
Brush, James 26; Ontario, 1871 ***1823.17*** *p18*
Brush, James 30; Ontario, 1871 ***1823.17*** *p18*
Brush, James 55; Ontario, 1871 ***1823.17*** *p18*

56 *FOR A COMPLETE EXPLANATION OF ENTRY, SEE "HOW TO READ A CITATION" SECTION*

Brush, Thomas 42; Ontario, 1871 ***1823.17*** *p18*
Brushal, Frank S.; Louisiana, 1874 ***4981.45*** *p131*
Bruson, Peter 43; America, 1843 ***778.6*** *p51*
Bruster, Antone 7; America, 1847 ***778.6*** *p51*
Bruster, Catharina 41; America, 1847 ***778.6*** *p51*
Bruster, Johanis 8; America, 1847 ***778.6*** *p51*
Bruster, Joseph 9; America, 1847 ***778.6*** *p51*
Bruster, Nicolas 43; America, 1847 ***778.6*** *p51*
Bruster, Nicolaus 3; America, 1847 ***778.6*** *p52*
Brustmann, Adolf; Wisconsin, 1902 ***6795.8*** *p134*
Brustmann, Gustav; Wisconsin, 1898 ***6795.8*** *p160*
Brustmann, Theodor; Wisconsin, 1904 ***6795.8*** *p137*
Brutche, Xavier; Ohio, 1809-1852 ***4511.35*** *p6*
Bruterel, Lienard; Quebec, 1640 ***9221.17*** *p95*
Brutscher, Angela *SEE* Brutscher, Jakob
Brutscher, Anna Maria Sinnwell *SEE* Brutscher, Jakob
Brutscher, Jakob; Rio Grande do Sul, Brazil, 1860 ***5475.1*** *p368*
*Wife:*Anna Maria Sinnwell
*Daughter:*Angela
Brutschi, Johann 56; New Castle, DE, 1817-1818 ***90.20*** *p150*
Brutto, Catharina 52; Port uncertain, 1843 ***778.6*** *p52*
Brutto, Jean 83; Port uncertain, 1843 ***778.6*** *p52*
Bruun, T. O.; Valparaiso, Chile, 1850 ***1192.4*** *p50*
Bruxmeier, Johann; America, 1881 ***5475.1*** *p145*
Bruyer, Ant. 23; Port uncertain, 1840 ***778.6*** *p52*
Bruyer, Isdore 36; Michigan, 1880 ***4491.36*** *p3*
Bruyer, Mary 65; Michigan, 1880 ***4491.36*** *p3*
Bruyer, Ophenia 24; Michigan, 1880 ***4491.36*** *p3*
Bruyere, James 63; Ontario, 1871 ***1823.21*** *p41*
Bruza, . . .; New Orleans, 1848 ***778.6*** *p52*
Bruza, Mrs.; New Orleans, 1848 ***778.6*** *p52*
Bruza, Jean 26; New Orleans, 1848 ***778.6*** *p52*
Bruze, Pierre; Montreal, 1653 ***9221.17*** *p284*
Bruzek, Frantisek; Minnesota, 1857 ***2853.20*** *p259*
Bruzgd, Ynozas 20; New York, NY, 1894 ***6512.1*** *p231*
Bruzon, Jean Jacques; Louisiana, 1841-1844 ***4981.45*** *p210*
Bry, Antoine; Quebec, 1654 ***9221.17*** *p305*
Bryan, Ann; Boston, 1744 ***1642*** *p45*
Bryan, Biddy; New Orleans, 1850 ***7242.30*** *p136*
Bryan, Henry 45; Ontario, 1871 ***1823.21*** *p41*
Bryan, Jane; Boston, 1745 ***1642*** *p45*
Bryan, Jeremiah 40; Ontario, 1871 ***1823.21*** *p41*
Bryan, John; Boston, 1741 ***1642*** *p45*
Bryan, John; Boston, 1765 ***1642*** *p35*
Bryan, John 32; Ontario, 1871 ***1823.21*** *p41*
Bryan, John 40; Ontario, 1871 ***1823.21*** *p41*
Bryan, John; St. Johns, N.F., 1825 ***1053.15*** *p7*
Bryan, Kittie 22; Michigan, 1880 ***4491.39*** *p3*
Bryan, Lucy; New Orleans, 1850 ***7242.30*** *p136*
Bryan, N. Joseph; Colorado, 1867 ***1029.59*** *p14*
Bryan, Richard; Massachusetts, 1675-1676 ***1642*** *p128*
Bryan, Robert; Massachusetts, 1675-1676 ***1642*** *p128*
Bryan, Robert 69; Ontario, 1871 ***1823.21*** *p41*
Bryan, Sarah 65; Ontario, 1871 ***1823.21*** *p41*
Bryan, Thomas 30; Ontario, 1871 ***1823.21*** *p41*
Bryan, Thomas 64; Ontario, 1871 ***1823.21*** *p41*
Bryan, Timothy 17; Quebec, 1870 ***8364.32*** *p22*
Bryann, George 76; Michigan, 1880 ***4491.39*** *p3*
Bryann, Henry 36; Michigan, 1880 ***4491.39*** *p3*
Bryans, William 67; Ontario, 1871 ***1823.21*** *p41*
Bryans, Wm 56; Ontario, 1871 ***1823.21*** *p41*
Bryant, Charles 39; Santa Clara Co., CA, 1870 ***8704.1*** *p24*
Bryant, Charles; Washington, 1884 ***2770.40*** *p192*
Bryant, Clara 6; Ontario, 1871 ***1823.21*** *p42*
Bryant, Elizabeth 72; Ontario, 1871 ***1823.21*** *p42*
Bryant, Geo 60; Ontario, 1871 ***1823.21*** *p42*
Bryant, George 35; Ontario, 1871 ***1823.17*** *p18*
Bryant, Henry 30; Ontario, 1871 ***1823.21*** *p42*
Bryant, Jane 31; Ontario, 1871 ***1823.21*** *p42*
Bryant, John 31; Ontario, 1871 ***1823.21*** *p42*
Bryant, John 16; Quebec, 1870 ***8364.32*** *p22*
Bryant, Lydia 42; Ontario, 1871 ***1823.21*** *p42*
Bryant, Michael; Boston, 1766 ***1642*** *p36*
With wife
Bryant, Nathaniel; Ohio, 1845 ***2763.1*** *p7*
Bryant, Richard 44; Ontario, 1871 ***1823.21*** *p42*
Bryant, Spineer 50; Ontario, 1871 ***1823.21*** *p42*
Bryant, Thomas; Massachusetts, 1675-1676 ***1642*** *p129*
Bryant, Thomas 90; Ontario, 1871 ***1823.21*** *p42*
Bryant, Timothy; Boston, 1766 ***1642*** *p37*
Bryant, William; Boston, 1761 ***1642*** *p48*
Bryant, William 14; Quebec, 1870 ***8364.32*** *p22*
Bryanton, Robert 58; Ontario, 1871 ***1823.21*** *p42*
Bryants, Dehilia 22; Ontario, 1871 ***1823.21*** *p42*
Bryants, Jane 20; Ontario, 1871 ***1823.21*** *p42*
Bryar, Elias; Marblehead, MA, 1700-1799 ***9228.50*** *p132*
Bryar, Richard; Massachusetts, 1675-1676 ***1642*** *p128*
Bryce, Ellen 8; Quebec, 1870 ***8364.32*** *p22*
Bryce, Hugh 62; Ontario, 1871 ***1823.17*** *p18*
Bryce, John M. 31; Ontario, 1871 ***1823.21*** *p42*
Bryce, Robert 54; Ontario, 1871 ***1823.17*** *p18*
Bryce, Thomas 35; Ontario, 1871 ***1823.21*** *p42*
Bryce, William 28; Ontario, 1871 ***1823.17*** *p18*
Bryce, William 40; Ontario, 1871 ***1823.17*** *p18*
Bryce, William 54; Ontario, 1871 ***1823.21*** *p42*
Brydges, Thomas 32; Ontario, 1871 ***1823.17*** *p18*
Brydges, William 40; Ontario, 1871 ***1823.17*** *p18*
Bryen, John; Boston, 1764 ***1642*** *p33*
Brygger, John; Washington, 1881 ***2770.40*** *p134*
Bryla, Marcin 17; New York, NY, 1911 ***6533.11*** *p9*
Brylowski, Anne; Wisconsin, 1891 ***6795.8*** *p54*
Brylowski, Michael; Wisconsin, 1891 ***6795.8*** *p54*
Brylowski, Veronica; Wisconsin, 1881 ***6795.8*** *p54*
Bryn, Mr.; Boston, 1767 ***1642*** *p38*
Bryon, Mary; Boston, 1734 ***1642*** *p44*
Bryson, James; North Carolina, 1855 ***1088.45*** *p4*
Bryson, James 41; Ontario, 1871 ***1823.17*** *p18*
Brzeski, Francis; Wisconsin, 1884 ***6795.8*** *p54*
Brzeski, Franciszek; Wisconsin, 1885 ***6795.8*** *p55*
Brzoska, Frank; Detroit, 1929 ***1640.55*** *p112*
Brzozowski, Jan 23; New York, NY, 1911 ***6533.11*** *p10*
Brzozowski, John; Detroit, 1890 ***9980.23*** *p96*
Brzuszek, Ferdinand; Detroit, 1929 ***1640.55*** *p115*
Buallet, J. 25; Port uncertain, 1843 ***778.6*** *p52*
Bubb, William; Colorado, 1871 ***1029.59*** *p14*
Bubb, William; Colorado, 1880 ***1029.59*** *p14*
Bubeck, J. F.; Valdivia, Chile, 1852 ***1192.4*** *p52*
Bubel, Francis 25; America, 1847 ***778.6*** *p52*
Bubien, Bronislaw; Detroit, 1929-1930 ***6214.5*** *p60*
Bubier, Joseph; Marblehead, MA, 1668 ***9228.50*** *p139*
Bublitz, August F.; Wisconsin, 1885 ***6795.8*** *p85*
Bubolz, Emilie Auguste; Wisconsin, 1897 ***6795.8*** *p46*
Buce, David 33; Ontario, 1871 ***1823.17*** *p18*
Buch, Andreas 35; America, 1747 ***778.6*** *p52*
Buch, Francisca 3; America, 1747 ***778.6*** *p52*
Buch, Georg; America, 1872 ***2526.43*** *p146*
Buch, Jacobinia 25; America, 1747 ***778.6*** *p52*
Buch, Madeleine 1; America, 1747 ***778.6*** *p52*
Buch, Margaretha 4; America, 1747 ***778.6*** *p52*
Buch, Richard 5; America, 1747 ***778.6*** *p52*
Buchanan, Alex 32; Ontario, 1871 ***1823.21*** *p42*
Buchanan, Alexander 29; Ontario, 1871 ***1823.17*** *p18*
Buchanan, Angus 26; Ontario, 1871 ***1823.17*** *p19*
Buchanan, Archibald; Illinois, 1834-1900 ***6020.5*** *p131*
Buchanan, Daniel 47; Ontario, 1871 ***1823.21*** *p42*
Buchanan, Donald 45; Ontario, 1871 ***1823.17*** *p19*
Buchanan, Duncan 40; Ontario, 1871 ***1823.17*** *p19*
Buchanan, George 34; Ontario, 1871 ***1823.21*** *p42*
Buchanan, Hugh 39; Ontario, 1871 ***1823.17*** *p19*
Buchanan, Hugh 57; Ontario, 1871 ***1823.17*** *p19*
Buchanan, Hugh 80; Ontario, 1871 ***1823.17*** *p19*
Buchanan, James 40; Ontario, 1871 ***1823.21*** *p42*
Buchanan, James 74; Ontario, 1871 ***1823.17*** *p19*
Buchanan, John 32; Ontario, 1871 ***1823.17*** *p19*
Buchanan, John 41; Ontario, 1871 ***1823.17*** *p19*
Buchanan, Mary Ann; Philadelphia, 1867 ***8513.31*** *p422*
Buchanan, Thomas 31; St. John, N.B., 1834 ***6469.7*** *p6*
Buchanan, William 58; Ontario, 1871 ***1823.21*** *p42*
Buchanan, William 60; Ontario, 1871 ***1823.21*** *p42*
Buchanan, William S.; Ohio, 1843 ***3580.20*** *p31*
Buchanan, William S.; Ohio, 1843 ***6020.12*** *p6*
Buchannan, James 30; Ontario, 1871 ***1823.21*** *p42*
Buchannon, Archibald 32; Ontario, 1871 ***1823.21*** *p42*
Buchannon, Duncan 33; Ontario, 1871 ***1823.21*** *p42*
Buchanon, Duncan; Washington, 1889 ***2770.40*** *p26*
Buche, Elisabeth Peifer *SEE* Buche, Peter
Buche, Franz *SEE* Buche, Peter
Buche, Johann 70 *SEE* Buche, Peter
Buche, Joseph; Ohio, 1809-1852 ***4511.35*** *p6*
Buche, Katharina 45 *SEE* Buche, Peter
Buche, Nikolaus *SEE* Buche, Peter
Buche, Peter *SEE* Buche, Peter
Buche, Peter; Brazil, 1873 ***5475.1*** *p371*
*Wife:*Elisabeth Peifer
*Daughter:*Susanna
*Son:*Franz
*Sister:*Katharina
*Father:*Johann
*Son:*Peter
*Son:*Nikolaus
Buche, Susanna *SEE* Buche, Peter
Buchel, Conrad; Louisiana, 1841-1844 ***4981.45*** *p210*
Buchels, James; New York, 1860 ***358.56*** *p150*
Bucher, . . .; Died enroute, 1847 ***778.6*** *p52*
Bucher, Alexandre 7; Louisiana, 1848 ***778.6*** *p52*
Bucher, Catherine 45; Louisiana, 1848 ***778.6*** *p52*
Bucher, Jean 44; Louisiana, 1848 ***778.6*** *p52*
Bucher, Jn. Bte. 9; Louisiana, 1848 ***778.6*** *p52*
Bucher, Joseph 17; America, 1844 ***778.6*** *p52*
Bucher, Lorenz 40; New Orleans, 1847 ***778.6*** *p52*
Bucher, Ludwig; America, 1855 ***7420.1*** *p135*
Bucher, Pauline 6; Louisiana, 1848 ***778.6*** *p52*
Bucher, Philip 4; Louisiana, 1848 ***778.6*** *p52*
Bucher, Regina 3; New Orleans, 1847 ***778.6*** *p52*
Bucher, Regina 40; New Orleans, 1847 ***778.6*** *p52*
Bucher, Theresa 15; New Orleans, 1847 ***778.6*** *p52*
Bucher, Wilhelm 31; America, 1844 ***778.6*** *p52*
Buchheit, Anna *SEE* Buchheit, Peter Josef
Buchheit, Anna Biehl *SEE* Buchheit, Peter
Buchheit, Anna Maria Endres *SEE* Buchheit, Peter Josef
Buchheit, Josef *SEE* Buchheit, Peter Josef
Buchheit, Katharina *SEE* Buchheit, Peter
Buchheit, Margarethe *SEE* Buchheit, Peter Josef
Buchheit, Margarethe; America, 1879 ***5475.1*** *p187*
Buchheit, Maria *SEE* Buchheit, Peter Josef
Buchheit, Mathias *SEE* Buchheit, Peter Josef
Buchheit, Peter *SEE* Buchheit, Peter Josef
Buchheit, Peter *SEE* Buchheit, Peter
Buchheit, Peter; America, 1881 ***5475.1*** *p287*
*Wife:*Anna Biehl
*Daughter:*Katharina
*Son:*Peter
Buchheit, Peter Josef; America, 1879 ***5475.1*** *p186*
*Wife:*Anna Maria Endres
*Son:*Mathias
*Son:*Peter
*Daughter:*Anna
*Daughter:*Maria
*Daughter:*Margarethe
*Son:*Josef
Buchholtz, Charles Robert; Wisconsin, 1913 ***6795.8*** *p165*
Buchholtz, Hermann Rudolf; Wisconsin, 1905 ***6795.8*** *p115*
Buchholz, Anna 4; New York, NY, 1879 ***6954.7*** *p40*
Buchholz, Anna 12; New York, NY, 1876 ***6954.7*** *p39*
Buchholz, Anna 17; New York, NY, 1876 ***6954.7*** *p39*
Buchholz, Anna 28; New York, NY, 1886 ***6954.7*** *p40*
Buchholz, Anna 48; New York, NY, 1879 ***6954.7*** *p40*
Buchholz, Anna Maria 24; New York, NY, 1886 ***6954.7*** *p40*
Buchholz, August; Wisconsin, 1880 ***6795.8*** *p92*
Buchholz, August; Wisconsin, 1885 ***6795.8*** *p46*
Buchholz, Carl 9 months; New York, NY, 1885 ***6954.7*** *p40*
Buchholz, Carl; Wisconsin, 1881 ***6795.8*** *p225*
Buchholz, Carl; Wisconsin, 1882 ***6795.8*** *p167*
Buchholz, Carl Robert; Wisconsin, 1907 ***6795.8*** *p115*
Buchholz, Carolina 7; New York, NY, 1879 ***6954.7*** *p40*
Buchholz, Catharina 17; New York, NY, 1879 ***6954.7*** *p40*
Buchholz, Charlotte; Port uncertain, 1881 ***7420.1*** *p320*
*Daughter:*Engel
Buchholz, Christina 2 months; New York, NY, 1886 ***6954.7*** *p40*
Buchholz, Dorothea 4 months; New York, NY, 1876 ***6954.7*** *p39*
Buchholz, Dorothea 6; New York, NY, 1879 ***6954.7*** *p40*
Buchholz, Dorothea 9; New York, NY, 1885 ***6954.7*** *p40*
Buchholz, Dorothea 19; New York, NY, 1877 ***6954.7*** *p39*
Buchholz, Dorothea 37; New York, NY, 1876 ***6954.7*** *p39*
Buchholz, Edward; Wisconsin, 1882 ***6795.8*** *p200*
Buchholz, Elisabeth 33; New York, NY, 1876 ***6954.7*** *p39*
Buchholz, Emmanuel 2; New York, NY, 1885 ***6954.7*** *p40*
Buchholz, Emmanuel 8; New York, NY, 1879 ***6954.7*** *p40*
Buchholz, Engel *SEE* Buchholz, Charlotte
Buchholz, Ephriam 42; New York, NY, 1885 ***6954.7*** *p40*
Buchholz, Fredrick; Wisconsin, 1859 ***6795.8*** *p149*
Buchholz, Friedrich; Rio Grande do Sul, Brazil, 1883 ***5475.1*** *p36*
Buchholz, Heinrich 12; New York, NY, 1876 ***6954.7*** *p39*
Buchholz, Heinrich 14; New York, NY, 1876 ***6954.7*** *p39*
Buchholz, Heinrich 18; New York, NY, 1886 ***6954.7*** *p41*
Buchholz, Heinrich 35; New York, NY, 1876 ***6954.7*** *p39*
Buchholz, Heinrich Friedrich Conrad; America, 1865 ***7420.1*** *p230*
Buchholz, Johann 5; New York, NY, 1876 ***6954.7*** *p39*
Buchholz, Johann 9; New York, NY, 1876 ***6954.7*** *p39*
Buchholz, Johann 28; New York, NY, 1886 ***6954.7*** *p40*
Buchholz, Johann 39; New York, NY, 1876 ***6954.7*** *p39*
Buchholz, Johann 50; New York, NY, 1879 ***6954.7*** *p40*
Buchholz, Johannes 9; New York, NY, 1879 ***6954.7*** *p40*
Buchholz, Josephine Hulda; Wisconsin, 1907 ***6795.8*** *p115*
Buchholz, Katherina 5; New York, NY, 1876 ***6954.7*** *p39*
Buchholz, Katherina 13; New York, NY, 1885 ***6954.7*** *p40*
Buchholz, Leonore 29; New York, NY, 1879 ***6954.7*** *p40*
Buchholz, Margaretha 36; New York, NY, 1885 ***6954.7*** *p40*
Buchholz, Maria 7; New York, NY, 1876 ***6954.7*** *p39*

Buchholz, Maria 20; New York, NY, 1879 ***6954.7*** *p40*
Buchholz, Michael 26; New York, NY, 1877 ***6954.7*** *p39*
Buchholz, Michael 32; New York, NY, 1886 ***6954.7*** *p40*
Buchholz, Paul 3; New York, NY, 1876 ***6954.7*** *p39*
Buchholz, Paulina 2; New York, NY, 1876 ***6954.7*** *p39*
Buchholz, Paulina 2; New York, NY, 1886 ***6954.7*** *p40*
Buchholz, Paulina 7; New York, NY, 1879 ***6954.7*** *p40*
Buchholz, Theador 4; New York, NY, 1879 ***6954.7*** *p40*
Buchholz, Theador 11 months; New York, NY, 1876 ***6954.7*** *p39*
Buchholz, Theador 19; New York, NY, 1876 ***6954.7*** *p39*
Buchholz, Wilhelm 7; New York, NY, 1876 ***6954.7*** *p39*
Buchholz, Wilhelm 33; New York, NY, 1879 ***6954.7*** *p40*
Buchhorn, Mr.; America, 1846 ***7420.1*** *p43*
*Sister:*Eleonore B.
*Nephew:*Wilhelm
*Sister:*Louise B.
Buchhorn, Eleonore B. *SEE* Buchhorn, Mr.
Buchhorn, Friedrich 20; Portland, ME, 1912 ***970.38*** *p76*
Buchhorn, Louise; America, 1846 ***7420.1*** *p46*
With family
Buchhorn, Louise B. *SEE* Buchhorn, Mr.
Buchhorn, Wilhelm *SEE* Buchhorn, Mr.
Buchleitner, Anna Maria; America, 1854 ***5475.1*** *p57*
Buchleitner, Georg 22; America, 1854 ***5475.1*** *p57*
Buchleitner, Gertrud; America, 1854 ***5475.1*** *p57*
Buchleitner, Katharina; America, 1840 ***5475.1*** *p56*
Buchleitner, Katharina Mayer *SEE* Buchleitner, Nikolaus
Buchleitner, Nikolaus; America, 1852 ***5475.1*** *p56*
*Wife:*Katharina Mayer
Buchler, Miss; America, 1868 ***2526.43*** *p212*
Buchler, Anna 49; New York, NY, 1893 ***1883.7*** *p45*
Buchler, Elisabeth; America, 1854 ***2526.43*** *p138*
Buchler, Friedrich Karl; Baltimore, 1884 ***2526.43*** *p165*
Buchler, Georg August; Brazil, 1904 ***2526.43*** *p194*
Buchler, Jacob 49; New York, NY, 1893 ***1883.7*** *p45*
Buchler, Jacob 51; New York, NY, 1893 ***1883.7*** *p45*
Buchler, Johann Jakob 19; America, 1852 ***2526.43*** *p165*
Buchler, Katha. 6; New York, NY, 1893 ***1883.7*** *p45*
Buchler, Marga. 10; New York, NY, 1893 ***1883.7*** *p45*
Buchler, Maria 17; New York, NY, 1893 ***1883.7*** *p45*
Buchler, Peter 13; New York, NY, 1893 ***1883.7*** *p45*
Buchler, Wilhelm; America, 1854 ***2526.43*** *p138*
Buchmann, A. Maria 9 *SEE* Buchmann, Johann
Buchmann, Helena Schneider *SEE* Buchmann, Johann
Buchmann, Helene 10 *SEE* Buchmann, Mathias
Buchmann, Johann; America, 1864 ***5475.1*** *p264*
*Wife:*Helena Schneider
*Son:*Mathias
*Daughter:*Margarethe
*Daughter:*A. Maria
Buchmann, Johann 27; America, 1854 ***5475.1*** *p264*
*Wife:*Katharina Bauer 22
Buchmann, Johann; Cincinnati, 1884 ***5475.1*** *p246*
Buchmann, Katharina Bauer 22 *SEE* Buchmann, Johann
Buchmann, Katharina Leuck 33 *SEE* Buchmann, Mathias
Buchmann, Magdalene 1 *SEE* Buchmann, Mathias
Buchmann, Margarethe 2 *SEE* Buchmann, Johann
Buchmann, Mathias; America, 1881 ***5475.1*** *p245*
Buchmann, Mathias 4 *SEE* Buchmann, Johann
Buchmann, Mathias 7 *SEE* Buchmann, Mathias
Buchmann, Mathias 35; America, 1857 ***5475.1*** *p244*
*Wife:*Katharina Leuck 33
*Son:*Mathias 7
*Daughter:*Magdalene 1
*Daughter:*Helene 10
Buchmeier, Barbara 11 months; New York, NY, 1893 ***1883.7*** *p43*
Buchmeier, Barbara 25; New York, NY, 1893 ***1883.7*** *p43*
Buchmeier, Carl Friedrich; America, 1846 ***7420.1*** *p43*
Buchmeier, Carl Friedrich August; America, 1881 ***7420.1*** *p320*
Buchmeier, Christian; America, 1866 ***7420.1*** *p240*
With family
Buchmeier, Friedrich Ferdinand; America, 1856 ***7420.1*** *p146*
Buchmeier, Georg; America, 1868 ***7420.1*** *p269*
Buchmeier, Philipp August; America, 1860 ***7420.1*** *p192*
Buchmeier, Sophie Wilhelmine Charlotte; America, 1865 ***7420.1*** *p230*
Buchmeier, Ursula 13; New York, NY, 1893 ***1883.7*** *p43*
Buchmeier, Valentin 30; New York, NY, 1893 ***1883.7*** *p43*
Buchmeier, Wilhelm; America, 1861 ***7420.1*** *p203*
Buchmeier, Wilhelm; America, 1870 ***7420.1*** *p395*
With family
Buchmeyer, Carl Wilhelm Heinrich August; America, 1866 ***7420.1*** *p240*
Buchmeyer, Wilhelmine Charlotte; America, 1864 ***7420.1*** *p222*
Buchner, Adam; America, 1854 ***2526.42*** *p107*
Buchner, Johannes 4 *SEE* Buchner, Michael, II
Buchner, Mrs. Johannes; America, 1884 ***2526.43*** *p137*
Buchner, Katharina Wiesmann 47 *SEE* Buchner, Michael, II
Buchner, Magdalena 16 *SEE* Buchner, Michael, II
Buchner, Michael; America, 1873 ***2526.43*** *p138*
Buchner, Michael; America, 1883 ***2526.42*** *p168*
Buchner, Michael 9 *SEE* Buchner, Michael, II
Buchner, Michael, II 43; America, 1874 ***2526.42*** *p168*
*Wife:*Katharina Wiesmann 47
*Son:*Johannes 4
*Son:*Michael 9
*Daughter:*Magdalena 16
Buchner, Peter 24; America, 1836 ***2526.42*** *p159*
Buchnvitz, Christine 17; Halifax, N.S., 1902 ***1860.4*** *p41*
Buchnvitz, Christof 45; Halifax, N.S., 1902 ***1860.4*** *p41*
Buchnvitz, Elisabeth 4; Halifax, N.S., 1902 ***1860.4*** *p41*
Buchnvitz, Elisabeth 39; Halifax, N.S., 1902 ***1860.4*** *p41*
Buchnvitz, Jakob 11; Halifax, N.S., 1902 ***1860.4*** *p41*
Buchnvitz, Johann 2; Halifax, N.S., 1902 ***1860.4*** *p41*
Buchnvitz, Natalia 5; Halifax, N.S., 1902 ***1860.4*** *p41*
Buchnvitz, Samuel 15; Halifax, N.S., 1902 ***1860.4*** *p41*
Buchnvitz, Sara 13; Halifax, N.S., 1902 ***1860.4*** *p41*
Buchnvitz, Sophia; Halifax, N.S., 1902 ***1860.4*** *p41*
Buchold, Konrad; Port uncertain, 1866 ***170.15*** *p21*
With wife 2 daughters & father
Buchrvitz, Christine 17; Halifax, N.S., 1902 ***1860.4*** *p41*
Buchrvitz, Christof 45; Halifax, N.S., 1902 ***1860.4*** *p41*
Buchrvitz, Elisabeth 4; Halifax, N.S., 1902 ***1860.4*** *p41*
Buchrvitz, Elisabeth 39; Halifax, N.S., 1902 ***1860.4*** *p41*
Buchrvitz, Jakob 11; Halifax, N.S., 1902 ***1860.4*** *p41*
Buchrvitz, Johann 2; Halifax, N.S., 1902 ***1860.4*** *p41*
Buchrvitz, Natalia 5; Halifax, N.S., 1902 ***1860.4*** *p41*
Buchrvitz, Samuel 15; Halifax, N.S., 1902 ***1860.4*** *p41*
Buchrvitz, Sara 13; Halifax, N.S., 1902 ***1860.4*** *p41*
Buchrvitz, Sophia; Halifax, N.S., 1902 ***1860.4*** *p41*
Buchsott, Herrmann 26; New York, NY, 1864 ***8425.62*** *p198*
Buck, Eidel; Valdivia, Chile, 1850 ***1192.4*** *p49*
With wife
Buck, George; Massachusetts, 1775 ***1642*** *p116*
Buck, George 42; Ontario, 1871 ***1823.17*** *p19*
Buck, Heinrich; America, 1846 ***7420.1*** *p43*
With wife & 2 children
Buck, Jacob; Iowa, 1888 ***1211.15*** *p9*
Buck, John; Ohio, 1809-1852 ***4511.35*** *p6*
Buck, Mary 14; Quebec, 1870 ***8364.32*** *p22*
Buck, William 50; Michigan, 1880 ***4491.33*** *p3*
Buck, William 54; Ontario, 1871 ***1823.17*** *p19*
Buckel, Joseph; Ohio, 1840-1897 ***8365.35*** *p15*
Buckeley, Michael; Marblehead, MA, 1764 ***1642*** *p33*
Bucker, Jean 38; America, 1747 ***778.6*** *p52*
Bucker, Joseph 2; America, 1747 ***778.6*** *p52*
Bucker, Louis 6; America, 1747 ***778.6*** *p52*
Bucker, Madelaine 9; America, 1747 ***778.6*** *p53*
Bucker, Madelaine 40; America, 1747 ***778.6*** *p52*
Bucker, Margaretha 7; America, 1747 ***778.6*** *p53*
Bucker, Susana 8; America, 1747 ***778.6*** *p53*
Buckert, Frederick; Illinois, 1851 ***6079.1*** *p2*
Buckert, John; Illinois, 1865 ***6079.1*** *p2*
Buckhole, Fredrick; Wisconsin, 1859 ***6795.8*** *p149*
Buckholz, Albert L.; Wisconsin, 1895 ***6795.8*** *p125*
Buckholz, Wilhem; Wisconsin, 1858 ***6795.8*** *p137*
Buckingham, Clara 6; Quebec, 1870 ***8364.32*** *p22*
Buckingham, Ellen 21; Ontario, 1871 ***1823.17*** *p19*
Buckingham, George 65; Ontario, 1871 ***1823.17*** *p19*
Buckingham, John 25; Ontario, 1871 ***1823.21*** *p42*
Buckingham, Miss S. J. 9; Quebec, 1870 ***8364.32*** *p22*
Buckius, John Jacob Charles; Ohio, 1809-1852 ***4511.35*** *p6*
Buckle, Georg; Valdivia, Chile, 1852 ***1192.4*** *p52*
With wife
With child 6
With child 4
Buckle, Hannah 60; Ontario, 1871 ***1823.21*** *p42*
Buckler, David 30; Ontario, 1871 ***1823.21*** *p42*
Buckleter, Henry 27; America, 1847 ***778.6*** *p53*
Buckley, Anders 5 *SEE* Buckley, Jon
Buckley, C. 13; Quebec, 1870 ***8364.32*** *p22*
Buckley, Cajsa Stina 1 *SEE* Buckley, Jon
Buckley, Christina; Cleveland, OH, 1883-1895 ***9722.10*** *p117*
Buckley, James 43; New York, NY, 1825 ***6178.50*** *p78*
Buckley, John; North America, 1750 ***1640.8*** *p234*
Buckley, John; St. John, N.B., 1848 ***2978.15*** *p37*
Buckley, John; St. John, N.B., 1848 ***2978.15*** *p37*
Buckley, Jon 43; New York, 1856 ***6529.11*** *p19*
*Wife:*Martha Jonsdotter 34
*Daughter:*Cajsa Stina 1
*Son:*Lars 3
*Son:*Pehr 9
*Son:*Anders 5
*Son:*Jonas 7
Buckley, Jonas 7 *SEE* Buckley, Jon
Buckley, Lars 3 *SEE* Buckley, Jon
Buckley, Martha Jonsdotter 34 *SEE* Buckley, Jon
Buckley, Michael; Toronto, 1844 ***2910.35*** *p113*
Buckley, Paul 42; Indiana, 1856-1880 ***9076.20*** *p70*
Buckley, Pehr 9 *SEE* Buckley, Jon
Buckley, T. M.; Louisiana, 1836-1840 ***4981.45*** *p212*
Buckley, Thomas; New York, NY, 1830 ***3274.56*** *p100*
Buckley, Thomas; North America, 1750 ***1640.8*** *p234*
Buckley, William; Boston, 1768 ***1642*** *p39*
Buckley, William; Ipswich, MA, 1669 ***1642*** *p70*
Buckly, William 50; Ontario, 1871 ***1823.17*** *p19*
Bucknell, Bell 27; Michigan, 1880 ***4491.30*** *p4*
Bucknell, John 28; Michigan, 1880 ***4491.30*** *p4*
Buckner, Henry 42; Ontario, 1871 ***1823.21*** *p42*
Buckpitt, Thomas 47; Ontario, 1871 ***1823.17*** *p19*
Bucks, Michael; North Carolina, 1822-1828 ***1088.45*** *p4*
Buctzer, Christopher; Missouri, 1885 ***3276.1*** *p1*
Budar, Antonia; California, 1868 ***1131.61*** *p89*
Budd, Joseph; Ohio, 1809-1852 ***4511.35*** *p6*
Budd, Rich; Virginia, 1652 ***6254.4*** *p243*
Budde, Louise; America, 1853 ***7420.1*** *p103*
Budde, Otto; Kansas, 1917-1918 ***2094.25*** *p50*
Budde, William; New York, 1859 ***358.56*** *p54*
Buddensiek, . . .; America, 1868 ***7420.1*** *p269*
Buddensiek, Miss; America, 1873 ***7420.1*** *p299*
Buddensiek, Friedrich Wilhelm; America, 1846 ***7420.1*** *p43*
With wife & 5 children
Buddensiek, Heinrich Christian August; America, 1892 ***7420.1*** *p365*
Buddensiek, Heinrich Christian August; Port uncertain, 1893 ***7420.1*** *p368*
Buddy, Nicholas; Massachusetts, 1730 ***9228.50*** *p139*
Budenbach, Amalia *SEE* Budenbach, Elisabeth Weber
Budenbach, Charlotte *SEE* Budenbach, Elisabeth Weber
Budenbach, Elisabeth; America, 1867 ***5475.1*** *p491*
*Daughter:*Karoline
*Daughter:*Amalia
*Daughter:*Florina
*Son:*Wilhelm
*Daughter:*Charlotte
Budenbach, Florina *SEE* Budenbach, Elisabeth Weber
Budenbach, Karoline *SEE* Budenbach, Elisabeth Weber
Budenbach, Wilhelm *SEE* Budenbach, Elisabeth Weber
Budendick, Bernard; Ohio, 1840-1897 ***8365.35*** *p15*
Budia, Annia; Oklahoma, 1893 ***3331.4*** *p12*
Budkova, Anna; Iowa, 1857 ***2853.20*** *p228*
Budner, Joseph 49; Ontario, 1871 ***1823.21*** *p42*
Budz, John; Detroit, 1929-1930 ***6214.5*** *p67*
Budziewicz, Franciszek 24; New York, NY, 1911 ***6533.11*** *p10*
Buea, Archibald; Brunswick, NC, 1767 ***1422.10*** *p61*
Buea, Duncan; Brunswick, NC, 1767 ***1422.10*** *p61*
Buea, Duncan; Brunswick, NC, 1767 ***1422.10*** *p61*
Buea, Malcolm; Brunswick, NC, 1767 ***1422.10*** *p61*
Buea, Mary; Brunswick, NC, 1767 ***1422.10*** *p61*
Buea, Neill; Brunswick, NC, 1767 ***1422.10*** *p61*
Bueb, George; Colorado, 1896 ***1029.59*** *p14*
Bueb, Joseph; Ohio, 1809-1852 ***4511.35*** *p6*
Buechel, George; Illinois, 1852 ***6079.1*** *p2*
Buechler, Christine *SEE* Buechler, George
Buechler, George *SEE* Buechler, George
Buechler, George; South Dakota, 1885 ***554.30*** *p26*
*Wife:*Christine
*Child:*George
*Child:*Gottlieb
*Child:*Heinrich
Buechler, Gottlieb *SEE* Buechler, George
Buechler, Heinrich *SEE* Buechler, George
Buechler, Margarethe; Dakota, 1918 ***554.30*** *p26*
Buechner, Pauline; Philadelphia, 1855 ***8513.31*** *p418*
Buel, Jared R.; Ohio, 1852 ***3580.20*** *p31*
Buel, Jared R.; Ohio, 1852 ***6020.12*** *p6*
Buel, Lewis; New York, 1860 ***358.56*** *p4*
Buelock, John; Illinois, 1860 ***6079.1*** *p2*
Buelow, Ernst Adolph; Wisconsin, 1884 ***6795.8*** *p160*
Buene, Wm.; Nebraska, 1905 ***3004.30*** *p46*
Buerhagen, Marie Caroline Juliane; America, 1870 ***7420.1*** *p395*
With daughter
Buesnel, Ann Jane Louise; Canada, n.d. ***9228.50*** *p19A*
Buesnel, R.G.; Louisiana, 1900-1990 ***9228.50*** *p139*
Buesnel, Winifred Norah; Port uncertain, 1926 ***9228.50*** *p311*
Buesnel, Winnifred Norah; Edmonton, Alberta, 1906-1990 ***9228.50*** *p139*
Buetighaver, Jacob, Jr.; Ohio, 1809-1852 ***4511.35*** *p7*
Buettner, Henry; Wisconsin, 1908 ***1822.55*** *p10*
Buettner, Justine; Wisconsin, 1901 ***6795.8*** *p176*
Buetzer, Jacob; Missouri, 1895 ***3276.1*** *p1*
Buffet, Mr.; Wisconsin, 1875-1925 ***9228.50*** *p139*
Buffet, Antoine 18; America, 1840 ***778.6*** *p53*
Buffet, Francois 39; America, 1843 ***778.6*** *p53*

Buffey, George 42; Ontario, 1871 *1823.17 p19*
Buffington, Resind 32; Ontario, 1871 *1823.17 p19*
Bufli, Joseph 21; Missouri, 1848 *778.6 p53*
Bugajski, John; Detroit, 1929-1930 *6214.5 p65*
Bugalatri, Stanislaw 23; New York, NY, 1894 *6512.1 p183*
Bugeaux, Suzanne; Quebec, 1648 *9221.17 p196*
Bugg, George 15; Quebec, 1870 *8364.32 p22*
Bugg, John; New York, 1783 *8529.30 p10*
Bugges, Bernardine; San Francisco, 1880-1899 *8023.44 p372*
Bugges, Therese; San Francisco, 1880-1899 *8023.44 p372*
Buggy, John; Died enroute, 1827 *7009.9 p61*
Buggy, John; Halifax, N.S., 1827 *7009.9 p62*
  *Wife:*Mary Canfill
Buggy, John; St. Johns, N.F., 1825 *1053.15 p6*
Buggy, Mary Crawley SEE Buggy, Mary
Buggy, Mary; Halifax, N.S., 1827 *7009.9 p61*
  *Mother:*Mary Crawley
Buggy, Mary Canfill SEE Buggy, John
Buggy, Patrick 60; Ontario, 1871 *1823.17 p19*
Bugler, Richard 45; Ontario, 1871 *1823.21 p42*
Bugler, Richard 76; Ontario, 1871 *1823.21 p42*
Bugniard, Virginie 38; New Orleans, 1848 *778.6 p53*
Bugon, Francoise 14; Montreal, 1644 *9221.17 p149*
Bugsad, A.; New York, 1860 *358.56 p3*
Buguiard, Victor 46; New Orleans, 1848 *778.6 p53*
Buhat, Joseph 34; America, 1847 *778.6 p53*
Buhel, Michael; Ohio, 1809-1852 *4511.35 p7*
Buher, Philip; Ohio, 1809-1852 *4511.35 p7*
Buhert, Joseph 34; America, 1847 *778.6 p53*
Buhl, Maria; America, 1871 *5475.1 p139*
  *Daughter:*Barbara
Buhler, Catherine; New York, 1860 *358.56 p5*
Buhler, Charles 16; Missouri, 1845 *778.6 p53*
Buhler, Fritz; Valparaiso, Chile, 1850 *1192.4 p50*
Buhler, Katharina Sturm 30 SEE Buhler, Michael
Buhler, Maximilian Oswald Rich.; Cincinnati, 1890 *5475.1 p18*
Buhler, Michael 33; Galveston, TX, 1844 *3967.10 p372*
  *Wife:*Katharina Sturm 30
Buhler, Otto; America, 1923 *8023.44 p372*
Buhlmann, Peter; North Carolina, 1710 *3629.40 p6*
Buhner, Christian; America, 1867 *7919.3 p534*
Buhr, Carl; America, 1854 *7420.1 p117*
  With wife & 3 sons
Buhr, Christian; America, 1852 *7420.1 p86*
  With wife 2 sons & 2 daughters
Buhr, Engel Christine Dorothea; America, 1868 *7420.1 p270*
Buhr, Engel Maria Catharina Sophia; Port uncertain, 1850 *7420.1 p76*
Buhr, Johann; America, 1884 *5475.1 p346*
Buhr, Johann Peter; America, 1884 *5475.1 p346*
Buhr, Ludwig Friedrich Arnold; America, 1885 *7420.1 p347*
Buhr, Peter 19; Louisiana, 1848 *778.6 p53*
Buhre, Engel Marie Charlotte Geistfeld SEE Buhre, Heinrich Christian
Buhre, Hans Heinr. Konrad; America, 1850 *7420.1 p70*
Buhre, Heinrich Christian; America, 1851 *7420.1 p79*
  *Wife:*Engel Marie Charlotte Geistfeld
Buhre, Heinrich Christoph; America, 1850 *7420.1 p70*
  *Wife:*Thrine Engel Buhre
  *Son:*Hans Heinr. Konrad
Buhre, Johann Otto; America, 1846 *7420.1 p43*
Buhre, Thrine Engel; America, 1850 *7420.1 p70*
Buhrisy, Caroline 2; Mississippi, 1847 *778.6 p53*
Buhrisy, Cathrine 5; Mississippi, 1847 *778.6 p53*
Buhrisy, Cathrine 32; Mississippi, 1847 *778.6 p53*
Buhrisy, Christine 4; Mississippi, 1847 *778.6 p53*
Buhrisy, Pierre 27; Mississippi, 1847 *778.6 p53*
Buhrmann, Heinrich Wilhelm; America, 1854 *7420.1 p117*
Buhrow, Ferdinand; Wisconsin, 1882 *6795.8 p212*
Buhs, Mr.; America, 1869 *7420.1 p279*
  With family
Buhse, Fritz; Valdivia, Chile, 1852 *1192.4 p55*
Buhsi, Carl; Louisiana, 1874-1875 *4981.45 p297*
Buie, Dond; Cape Fear, NC,, 1754 *1422.10 p61*
Buie, George S.; North Carolina, 1854 *1088.45 p4*
Buigler, Barbe 2; America, 1847 *778.6 p53*
Buigler, Josepha 5 months; America, 1847 *778.6 p53*
Buileont, E. 22; Port uncertain, 1845 *778.6 p53*
Buirer, Francis; Ohio, 1809-1852 *4511.35 p7*
Buison, B. 28; New Orleans, 1841 *778.6 p53*
Buisson, Antoine 6 SEE Buisson, Marie Lereau
Buisson, Elizabeth Jenry SEE Buisson, Nicolas
Buisson, Florent; Quebec, 1652 *9221.17 p255*
  *Wife:*Jeanne
  *Daughter:*Mathurine
  *Son:*Michel

Buisson, Gervais 10 SEE Buisson, Marie Lereau
Buisson, Gervais 48; Quebec, 1650 *9221.17 p224*
Buisson, Jean Jacques 31; Texas, 1848 *778.6 p53*
Buisson, Jeanne 32 SEE Buisson, Florent
Buisson, Marie 47; New Orleans, 1848 *778.6 p53*
Buisson, Marie; Quebec, 1652 *9221.17 p255*
  *Son:*Gervais
  *Son:*Antoine
Buisson, Mathurine 15 SEE Buisson, Florent
Buisson, Michel 13 SEE Buisson, Florent
Buisson, Nicolas; Massachusetts, 1716-1750 *9228.50 p113*
  *Wife:*Elizabeth Jenry
Buisson, Onesime; America, 1840 *778.6 p53*
Buissonneau, Jean; Quebec, 1661 *9221.17 p450*
Buker, Georges 29; Louisiana, 1848 *778.6 p53*
Bukowski, Andreas; Wisconsin, 1882 *6795.8 p55*
Bukowski, Frank; Texas, 1884 *6015.15 p23*
Buksiel, Caroline 3; New York, NY, 1885 *1883.7 p45*
Buksiel, Jacob 36; New York, NY, 1885 *1883.7 p45*
Buksiel, Rosine 31; New York, NY, 1885 *1883.7 p45*
Buksiel, Theodor 7; New York, NY, 1885 *1883.7 p45*
Bulacher, Franziska 18; Galveston, TX, 1844 *3967.10 p370*
Bulacher, Franziska 45; Galveston, TX, 1844 *3967.10 p370*
Bulacher, Johann 21; Galveston, TX, 1844 *3967.10 p370*
Bulacher, Justin 50; Galveston, TX, 1844 *3967.10 p370*
Bulard, Ephrim 71; Ontario, 1871 *1823.21 p43*
Bulauer, John G.; New York, 1860 *358.56 p6*
Bulawa, Aniela 18; New York, NY, 1911 *6533.11 p10*
Bulb, George; Colorado, 1896 *1029.59 p14*
Bulford, Clara Martha SEE Bulford, George
Bulford, Edward Charles SEE Bulford, George
Bulford, Emily Ada SEE Bulford, George
Bulford, George; Ontario, 1866-1869 *9228.50 p139*
  *Wife:*Jane Hallett
  *Child:*Clara Martha
  *Child:*Edward Charles
  *Child:*Melinda Elizabeth
  *Child:*Emily Ada
  *Child:*John T.
  *Child:*George Aquilla
Bulford, George Aquilla SEE Bulford, George
Bulford, Jane Hallett SEE Bulford, George
Bulford, John T. SEE Bulford, George
Bulford, Melinda Elizabeth SEE Bulford, George
Bulger, Ellen; New Orleans, 1850 *7242.30 p136*
Bulger, Fanny; New Orleans, 1850 *7242.30 p136*
Bulger, James 29; Indiana, 1856-1866 *9076.20 p66*
Bulger, James; New Orleans, 1851 *7242.30 p136*
Bulger, James; Ohio, 1809-1852 *4511.35 p7*
Bulger, James; Toronto, 1844 *2910.35 p115*
Bulger, John; New Orleans, 1850 *7242.30 p136*
Bulger, Kate; New Orleans, 1850 *7242.30 p136*
Bulger, Mary; New Orleans, 1850 *7242.30 p136*
Bulger, Mary 75; Ontario, 1871 *1823.21 p43*
Bulger, Michael; New Orleans, 1850 *7242.30 p136*
Bulger, Patt; New Orleans, 1850 *7242.30 p136*
Bulicek, . . .; Pennsylvania, 1750-1799 *2853.20 p17*
Bulier, Jacob 23; America, 1847 *778.6 p53*
Bulier, Regina 20; America, 1847 *778.6 p53*
Bulkeley, Daniel; Boston, 1766 *1642 p37*
Bulkley, Patrick; Massachusetts, 1773 *1642 p116*
Bull, George; Boston, 1774 *8529.30 p6*
Bull, John 22; Ontario, 1871 *1823.17 p19*
Bull, John 34; Ontario, 1871 *1823.17 p19*
Bull, John 50; Ontario, 1871 *1823.17 p19*
Bull, Thomas; Maryland, 1673 *1236.25 p48*
Bull, William 28; Ontario, 1871 *1823.17 p19*
Bull, William; Washington, 1885 *2770.40 p193*
Bull, Zebedee 46; Ontario, 1871 *1823.17 p19*
Bullaigne, James; New Jersey, 1666 *9228.50 p124*
Bullein, James; Nova Scotia, 1785 *9228.50 p145*
Bullein, John; Nova Scotia, 1784 *9228.50 p145*
Bullein, Nathaniel; Nova Scotia, 1783 *9228.50 p145*
Bullen, . . .; America, n.d. *9228.50 p143*
Bullen, Anne Vauquellin SEE Bullen, James
Bullen, F. W. 34; Ontario, 1871 *1823.21 p43*
Bullen, James; New Jersey, 1655 *9228.50 p647*
  *Wife:*Anne Vauquellin
  *Daughter:*Mary
Bullen, James; New Jersey, 1665 *9228.50 p143*
Bullen, John 51; Ontario, 1871 *1823.21 p43*
Bullen, Mary SEE Bullen, James
Bullen, Philip; Charlestown, MA, 1710-1747 *9228.50 p144*
Bullen, William 62; Ontario, 1871 *1823.21 p43*
Buller, Andres; Colorado, 1862-1894 *1029.59 p14*
Buller, William 31; Ontario, 1871 *1823.21 p43*
Bulling, Christian; America, 1882 *179.55 p19*
Bullinger, Georg Karl; America, 1848-1895 *179.55 p19*
Bullinger, Martin; Ohio, 1809-1852 *4511.35 p7*

Bullinger, Pauline; North Dakota, 1904 *609.10 p14*
Bullmann, Caroline; America, 1868 *7420.1 p270*
Bullock, Clyde SEE Bullock, Herbert
Bullock, Herb SEE Bullock, Herbert
Bullock, Herbert; Colorado, 1920 *1029.59 p14*
Bullock, Herbert; Colorado, 1920 *1029.59 p14*
  *Wife:*Lillian
  *Child:*Olive
  *Child:*Clyde
  *Child:*Herb
  *Child:*Lillian
Bullock, John 37; Ontario, 1871 *1823.21 p43*
Bullock, John 60; Ontario, 1871 *1823.21 p43*
Bullock, Lillian SEE Bullock, Herbert
Bullock, Lillian SEE Bullock, Herbert
Bullock, Olive SEE Bullock, Herbert
Bullock, Robert 45; Ontario, 1871 *1823.17 p19*
Bullot, Benjamin 25; Port uncertain, 1842 *778.6 p53*
Bullot, Francois 50; Port uncertain, 1842 *778.6 p53*
Bullot, Joseph 29; Port uncertain, 1842 *778.6 p53*
Bulman, Alexander; Watertown, MA, 1690 *1642 p112*
Bulman, Thomas 50; Ontario, 1871 *1823.17 p19*
Bulmann, Mr.; America, 1868 *7420.1 p270*
  With brother & sister
Bulmanski, Frank; Texas, 1878 *6015.15 p23*
Bulmuski, Frank; Texas, 1878 *6015.15 p23*
Bulot, Adeline 32; New Orleans, 1847 *778.6 p53*
Bulow, Louis Frhr. von; Argentina, 1895 *7420.1 p371*
Bulsh, Alle; Wisconsin, 1842 *9228.50 p145*
  With wife & 4 children
Bulte, Anne SEE Bulte, Marguerite
Bulte, Jeanne Charron SEE Bulte, Marguerite
Bulte, Marguerite; Quebec, 1670 *4514.3 p285*
  *Father:*Pierre
  *Stepmother:*Jeanne Charron
  *Sister:*Anne
  *Sister:*Peyronne
Bulte, Peyronne SEE Bulte, Marguerite
Bulte, Pierre SEE Bulte, Marguerite
Bultin, T.; California, 1868 *1131.61 p89*
Bultman, A. J.; Louisiana, 1874 *4981.45 p131*
Buluske, Thomas; Texas, 1892 *6015.15 p23*
Buma, John; Louisiana, 1874 *4981.45 p131*
Bumberger, Anthony; Ohio, 1809-1852 *4511.35 p7*
Bumberger, Joseph; Ohio, 1809-1852 *4511.35 p7*
Bunata, Josef; New York, NY, 1870 *2853.20 p115*
Bunata, Josef; New York, NY, 1870 *2853.20 p223*
Bunce, George 36; Ontario, 1871 *1823.21 p43*
Bund, Martin 20; Port uncertain, 1843 *778.6 p53*
Bunde, Carl; Wisconsin, 1883 *6795.8 p160*
Bundiker, Joseph; Illinois, 1863 *6079.1 p2*
Bunding, Wilhelm; Wisconsin, 1874 *6795.8 p71*
Bundt, Herman Friedrich; Wisconsin, 1896 *6795.8 p115*
Bunelic, Henry 29; Ontario, 1871 *1823.21 p43*
Bunelle, Vivienne 38; Quebec, 1660 *9221.17 p468*
  *Son:*Pierre 16
  *Daughter:*Marie-Anne 14
  *Daughter:*Anne 11
Bungy, Joshua; Marston's Wharf, 1782 *8529.30 p10*
Bunn, George 35; Ontario, 1871 *1823.21 p43*
Bunn, Jeremiah 56; Ontario, 1871 *1823.21 p43*
Bunn, John; Illinois, 1860 *6079.1 p3*
Bunn, Joseph 28; Ontario, 1871 *1823.21 p43*
Bunney, Robert; Colorado, 1886 *1029.59 p14*
Bunningham, James 50; Ontario, 1871 *1823.17 p19*
Bunnsiek, Friedrich; America, 1866 *7420.1 p241*
Bunny, Rob; Colorado, 1869 *1029.59 p14*
Bunschler, Ernestine; Valdivia, Chile, 1850 *1192.4 p48*
Bunsil, Henry 22; Ontario, 1871 *1823.17 p19*
Bunson, Geroge; New York, 1901 *1766.20 p36*
Bunte, August SEE Bunte, Carl Friedrich Conrad
Bunte, Carl Friedrich Conrad; America, 1866 *7420.1 p241*
  *Wife:*Wilhelmine
  *Son:*Conrad Hermann
  *Son:*August
Bunte, Caroline; America, 1852 *7420.1 p86*
Bunte, Conrad Hermann SEE Bunte, Carl Friedrich Conrad
Bunte, Heinrich; America, 1856 *7420.1 p146*
Bunte, Heinrich Ludwig; Port uncertain, 1840 *7420.1 p18*
Bunte, Johann Dietrich; America, 1866 *7420.1 p241*
  With family
Bunte, John de; New York, 1860 *358.56 p148*
Bunte, Ludwig 20; New York, NY, 1864 *8425.62 p198*
Bunte, Sophie Amalie; Iowa, 1880 *7420.1 p315*
Bunte, Wilhelmine SEE Bunte, Carl Friedrich Conrad
Bunting, Thomas; New York, 1775 *8529.30 p10*
Bunting, Wesley 45; Ontario, 1871 *1823.21 p43*
Buon, Amalie 9; Mississippi, 1848 *778.6 p54*
Buon, Edouard 8; Mississippi, 1848 *778.6 p54*
Buon, Marie 5; Mississippi, 1848 *778.6 p54*
Buon, Marie Anne 15; Mississippi, 1848 *778.6 p54*

Buon, Marie Anne 38; Mississippi, 1848 ***778.6*** *p54*
Buot, Marie; Quebec, 1670 ***4514.3*** *p285*
Bupe, John; Ohio, 1809-1852 ***4511.35*** *p7*
Bur, Jakob; America, 1865 ***5475.1*** *p553*
Bur, Josef; America, 1864 ***5475.1*** *p61*
Bur, Lorenz; Philadelphia, 1860 ***5475.1*** *p552*
Burat, Joseph P.; Louisiana, 1874 ***4981.45*** *p131*
Burban, Tessie; Detroit, 1930 ***1640.60*** *p78*
Burbeck, Carl 18; New York, NY, 1876 ***6954.7*** *p39*
Burbeck, Johann 18; New York, NY, 1876 ***6954.7*** *p39*
Burbes, Heinrich Wilhelm *SEE* Burbes, Joh. Ferd.
Burbes, Joh. Ferd.; America, 1892 ***5475.1*** *p79*
*Wife:*Maria Schneider
*Son:*Heinrich Wilhelm
*Son:*Philipp Ferdinand
Burbes, Maria Schneider *SEE* Burbes, Joh. Ferd.
Burbes, Philipp Ferdinand *SEE* Burbes, Joh. Ferd.
Burbidge, Ann; Maryland, 1672 ***1236.25*** *p47*
Burch, . . .; Massachusetts, 1719 ***1642*** *p99*
Burch, Abigail; Massachusetts, 1751 ***1642*** *p106*
Burch, Alexander; Wisconsin, 1842 ***9228.50*** *p145*
*Wife:*Jane Cargan
Burch, Elizabeth; Massachusetts, 1708 ***1642*** *p106*
Burch, James; Boston, 1752-1760 ***1642*** *p30*
Burch, James; Ipswich, MA, 1754-1763 ***1642*** *p70*
Burch, James; Ipswich, MA, 1754 ***1642*** *p71*
Burch, James; Massachusetts, 1727 ***1642*** *p72*
*Wife:*Sarah
Burch, James; Massachusetts, 1754 ***1642*** *p63*
Burch, James; Massachusetts, 1757 ***1642*** *p82*
Burch, James; Massachusetts, 1760 ***1642*** *p82*
Burch, Jane Cargan *SEE* Burch, Alexander
Burch, Jedidiah; Massachusetts, 1759 ***1642*** *p82*
Burch, Margaret; Boston, 1760 ***1642*** *p48*
Burch, Mary; Boston, 1765 ***1642*** *p48*
Burch, Mary; Massachusetts, 1744 ***1642*** *p106*
Burch, Mary 4; Ontario, 1871 ***1823.21*** *p43*
Burch, Michael; Boston, 1765 ***1642*** *p48*
Burch, Peggy; Boston, 1752-1760 ***1642*** *p30*
Burch, Sarah *SEE* Burch, James
Burch, Sarah; Massachusetts, 1748 ***1642*** *p82*
Burch, Sarah Lewis; Chicago, 1830-1900 ***9228.50*** *p145*
Burch, Thomas; Massachusetts, 1717 ***1642*** *p106*
Burch, William 19; Ontario, 1871 ***1823.21*** *p43*
Burch, Willm.; Maryland, 1674-1675 ***1236.25*** *p52*
Burchardt, Otto Curt Carl von; America, 1883 ***7420.1*** *p335*
Burchel, Abraham 60; Ontario, 1871 ***1823.21*** *p43*
Burchell, Sarah E.; New Hampshire, 1900 ***9228.50*** *p294*
Burchell, Thomas 12; New York, NY, 1894 ***6512.1*** *p228*
Burchell, William 44; New York, NY, 1894 ***6512.1*** *p228*
Burchert, Emma 1; Portland, ME, 1912 ***970.38*** *p76*
Burchert, Matilde 8; Portland, ME, 1912 ***970.38*** *p76*
Burchert, Pauline 30; Portland, ME, 1912 ***970.38*** *p76*
Burchert, Wilhelm 4; Portland, ME, 1912 ***970.38*** *p76*
Burchfield, John A.; Ohio, 1879 ***3580.20*** *p31*
Burchfield, John A.; Ohio, 1879 ***6020.12*** *p6*
Burchill, George; Washington, 1884 ***2770.40*** *p192*
Burck, Elizabeth; Boston, 1750 ***1642*** *p46*
Burck, Mary; Massachusetts, 1744 ***1642*** *p100*
Burckard, Maria Barbara; America, 1753 ***2526.42*** *p139*
With 3 children
Burckensteck, Jean 20; America, 1847 ***778.6*** *p54*
Burckhard, Barbara 2; New York, NY, 1893 ***1883.7*** *p41*
Burckhard, Catharina 38; New York, NY, 1893 ***1883.7*** *p41*
Burckhard, Ignaz 13; New York, NY, 1893 ***1883.7*** *p41*
Burckhard, Paul 38; New York, NY, 1893 ***1883.7*** *p41*
Burckhard, Peter 4; New York, NY, 1893 ***1883.7*** *p41*
Burckhard, Philippine 10; New York, NY, 1893 ***1883.7*** *p41*
Burckhard, Sylvester; Pennsylvania, 1849 ***170.15*** *p21*
With wife & 5 children
Burckhardt, Christian; America, 1867 ***7919.3*** *p534*
With wife mother & 2 children
Burda, Frantisek; Ohio, 1881-1889 ***2853.20*** *p505*
Burda, Vojtech; Ohio, 1881-1889 ***2853.20*** *p505*
Burdan, Benjamin 52; Ontario, 1871 ***1823.21*** *p43*
Burdan, James 69; Ontario, 1871 ***1823.21*** *p43*
Burden, Richard 48; Ontario, 1871 ***1823.17*** *p19*
Burdett, George 46; Ontario, 1871 ***1823.21*** *p43*
Burdett, William 19; Quebec, 1870 ***8364.32*** *p22*
Burdette, Chastene; Jamestown, VA, 1633 ***1658.20*** *p211*
Burdic, Louisa 23; Ontario, 1871 ***1823.21*** *p43*
Burdick, Charles 21; Ontario, 1871 ***1823.21*** *p43*
Burdick, George 48; Ontario, 1871 ***1823.21*** *p43*
Burdick, Ira 25; Ontario, 1871 ***1823.21*** *p43*
Burdick, Sarah 45; Ontario, 1871 ***1823.21*** *p43*
Bureau, Mr. 23; New Orleans, 1842 ***778.6*** *p54*
Bureau, Catherine; Quebec, 1669 ***4514.3*** *p285*
Bureau, Louise 36; New Orleans, 1848 ***778.6*** *p54*
Burel, Gilbert; Quebec, 1625 ***9221.17*** *p23*
Burel, Jeanne; Quebec, 1667 ***4514.3*** *p285*
Burens, Peter; America, 1863 ***5475.1*** *p349*
Burenz, Johann 18; America, 1859 ***5475.1*** *p348*
Bures, Jan; Wisconsin, 1853 ***2853.20*** *p303*
Bures, Vaclav; Nebraska, 1860-1910 ***2853.20*** *p168*
Buresquet, Reaux 45; America, 1842 ***778.6*** *p54*
Burford, Ann 48; Ontario, 1871 ***1823.21*** *p43*
Burford, George; Boston, 1835 ***3274.55*** *p23*
Burford, John 45; Ontario, 1871 ***1823.21*** *p43*
Burfurd, John 19; Ontario, 1871 ***1823.21*** *p43*
Burg, Andre 25; Missouri, 1846 ***778.6*** *p54*
Burg, Felix 30; New Orleans, 1845 ***778.6*** *p54*
Burg, Georg; Valdivia, Chile, 1851 ***1192.4*** *p51*
With wife
Burg, Johann; America, 1867 ***5475.1*** *p144*
Burg, Joseph 33; New Orleans, 1845 ***778.6*** *p54*
Burg, Karl; America, 1880 ***5475.1*** *p220*
Burg, Katharina Schemel *SEE* Burg, Nikolaus
Burg, Michel 28; America, 1866 ***5475.1*** *p150*
Burg, Nikolaus; America, 1858-1900 ***5475.1*** *p164*
*Wife:*Katharina Schemel
Burg, Nikolaus; America, 1881 ***5475.1*** *p164*
Burg, Philipp 33; America, 1843 ***778.6*** *p54*
Burg, Stephen; Ohio, 1809-1852 ***4511.35*** *p7*
Burgard, Christian *SEE* Burgard, Heinrich
Burgard, Elisabeth 20; New York, NY, 1893 ***1883.7*** *p41*
Burgard, Gertrud; America, 1881 ***5475.1*** *p50*
Burgard, Heinrich; America, 1836 ***5475.1*** *p44*
*Brother:*Christian
Burgard, Magdalena 29; America, 1873 ***5475.1*** *p172*
Burgard, Marguerite 25; Missouri, 1846 ***778.6*** *p54*
Burgard, Nikolaus; America, 1880 ***5475.1*** *p173*
Burgard, Peter; America, 1833 ***5475.1*** *p43*
Burgart, Dominick; Ohio, 1809-1852 ***4511.35*** *p7*
Burgel, Antoin 3; America, 1847 ***778.6*** *p54*
Burgel, August 5; America, 1847 ***778.6*** *p54*
Burgel, Carolina 27; America, 1847 ***778.6*** *p54*
Burgel, Christian 29; America, 1847 ***778.6*** *p54*
Burgel, Christina 7; America, 1847 ***778.6*** *p54*
Burgel, Dominique 37; America, 1847 ***778.6*** *p54*
Burgel, Jean 27; America, 1847 ***778.6*** *p54*
Burgel, Nicolas 1; America, 1847 ***778.6*** *p54*
Burgeois, Armand; Illinois, 1852 ***6079.1*** *p3*
Burger, A. Maria *SEE* Burger, Jakob
Burger, Adam; Ohio, 1809-1852 ***4511.35*** *p7*
Burger, Adolphe 25; Ontario, 1871 ***1823.21*** *p43*
Burger, Anna *SEE* Burger, Mathias
Burger, Anna *SEE* Burger, Jakob
Burger, Barbara *SEE* Burger, Mathias
Burger, Franz *SEE* Burger, Jakob
Burger, Godfrey; Missouri, 1888 ***3276.1*** *p1*
Burger, Henry 38; Ontario, 1871 ***1823.21*** *p43*
Burger, Henry M.; Ohio, 1809-1852 ***4511.35*** *p7*
Burger, Henry Michael; Ohio, 1809-1852 ***4511.35*** *p7*
Burger, Jakob *SEE* Burger, Mathias
Burger, Jakob 36; America, 1872 ***5475.1*** *p153*
*Wife:*Margarethe Flesch
*Son:*Franz
*Daughter:*Anna
*Daughter:*A. Maria
*Daughter:*Margaretha
*Son:*Johann
*Son:*Joh. Jakob
*Son:*Peter
Burger, Joh. Jakob *SEE* Burger, Jakob
Burger, Johann; America, 1847 ***5475.1*** *p475*
Burger, Johann *SEE* Burger, Mathias
Burger, Johann *SEE* Burger, Jakob
Burger, Johann *SEE* Burger, Susanna Biegler
Burger, Johann; Wisconsin, 1873 ***6795.8*** *p200*
Burger, Katharina *SEE* Burger, Mathias
Burger, Margaretha *SEE* Burger, Jakob
Burger, Margarethe Flesch *SEE* Burger, Jakob
Burger, Maria *SEE* Burger, Mathias
Burger, Maria Kiefer *SEE* Burger, Mathias
Burger, Marie; Wisconsin, 1897 ***6795.8*** *p234*
Burger, Mathias 41; America, 1872 ***5475.1*** *p153*
*Wife:*Maria Kiefer
*Daughter:*Maria
*Daughter:*Barbara
*Son:*Johann
*Son:*Jakob
*Daughter:*Anna
*Daughter:*Katharina
Burger, Ottilie *SEE* Burger, Susanna Biegler
Burger, Peter *SEE* Burger, Jakob
Burger, Susanna; America, 1872 ***5475.1*** *p153*
Burger, Susanna; America, 1872 ***5475.1*** *p153*
*Son:*Johann
*Daughter:*Ottilie
Burgert, Adam; Ohio, 1809-1852 ***4511.35*** *p7*
Burges, Alex 18; Ontario, 1871 ***1823.17*** *p19*
Burges, Alex 34; Ontario, 1871 ***1823.21*** *p43*
Burges, Anny 70; Ontario, 1871 ***1823.21*** *p43*
Burges, Richard; Maryland, 1672 ***1236.25*** *p47*
Burgeson, Carl Alfred; Cleveland, OH, 1889-1892 ***9722.10*** *p117*
Burgess, Albert 18; Ontario, 1871 ***1823.21*** *p44*
Burgess, Alexander 18; Ontario, 1871 ***1823.17*** *p19*
Burgess, Allman 4; Michigan, 1880 ***4491.39*** *p3*
Burgess, Anna 17; Michigan, 1880 ***4491.39*** *p3*
Burgess, Edward 67; Ontario, 1871 ***1823.17*** *p19*
Burgess, Elsia 19; Ontario, 1871 ***1823.17*** *p19*
Burgess, Fanny 30; Michigan, 1880 ***4491.39*** *p4*
Burgess, James 50; Ontario, 1871 ***1823.21*** *p44*
Burgess, Jessie 3 months; Michigan, 1880 ***4491.39*** *p4*
Burgess, John 33; Michigan, 1880 ***4491.39*** *p4*
Burgess, John 36; Ontario, 1871 ***1823.17*** *p20*
Burgess, John 40; Ontario, 1871 ***1823.17*** *p20*
Burgess, John 46; Ontario, 1871 ***1823.21*** *p44*
Burgess, John 65; Ontario, 1871 ***1823.21*** *p44*
Burgess, John Gibson, Daughter; Canada, 1793-1893 ***9228.50*** *p146*
Burgess, Julia; Wisconsin, 1850-1859 ***9228.50*** *p146*
Burgess, Julia; Wisconsin, 1860 ***9228.50*** *p631*
Burgess, Ruth H. 3; Michigan, 1880 ***4491.39*** *p4*
Burgess, Thomas 60; Ontario, 1871 ***1823.21*** *p44*
Burgess, Wilfred De Lisle; Wisconsin, 1919 ***9228.50*** *p146*
Burgess, William 35; Ontario, 1871 ***1823.21*** *p44*
Burggraff, William; Illinois, 1853 ***6079.1*** *p3*
Burghardt, Kasper 6; New York, NY, 1898 ***7951.13*** *p43*
Burghardt, Kasper 62; New York, NY, 1898 ***7951.13*** *p43*
Burghardt, Katherina 19; New York, NY, 1898 ***7951.13*** *p44*
Burghardt, Lawrence; Ohio, 1809-1852 ***4511.35*** *p7*
Burghardt, Margarethe 46; New York, NY, 1898 ***7951.13*** *p43*
Burghardt, Michael 18; New York, NY, 1898 ***7951.13*** *p43*
Burgi, Friederich 22; New Castle, DE, 1817-1818 ***90.20*** *p150*
Burgi, Joseph 28; America, 1844 ***778.6*** *p54*
Burgin, Augustin 33; New Castle, DE, 1817-1818 ***90.20*** *p150*
Burgin, Friederich 22; New Castle, DE, 1817-1818 ***90.20*** *p150*
Burgin, Johann 20; New Castle, DE, 1817-1818 ***90.20*** *p150*
Burgner, Fredric Christopher; North Carolina, 1813 ***1088.45*** *p4*
Burgner, John; Ohio, 1809-1852 ***4511.35*** *p7*
Burgold, Ernst; Ohio, 1840-1897 ***8365.35*** *p15*
Burgren, Charles; Cleveland, OH, 1891-1895 ***9722.10*** *p117*
Burgstahler, Susanna; Dakota, 1859-1918 ***554.30*** *p26*
Burgtorff, Aug.; Valdivia, Chile, 1852 ***1192.4*** *p53*
Burgun, Elisabeth; America, 1880 ***5475.1*** *p220*
Burgunder, Marie 28; America, 1842 ***778.6*** *p54*
Burgunter, Franziska 28; Texas, 1848 ***778.6*** *p54*
Burgunter, Jean-Baptiste 17; Texas, 1848 ***778.6*** *p54*
Burgunter, Seraphin 32; Texas, 1848 ***778.6*** *p54*
Burgurt, Laurenz 18; America, 1847 ***778.6*** *p54*
Burhardt, Anthony; Wisconsin, 1903 ***6795.8*** *p137*
Burhmann, Henry; New Orleans, 1869 ***6212.1*** *p16*
Burian, Gottlieb; Washington, 1884 ***2770.40*** *p192*
Buric, Severin; Iowa, 1856-1858 ***2853.20*** *p211*
Burk, Family; Massachusetts, 1727 ***1642*** *p99*
Burk, Abigail; Massachusetts, 1709 ***1642*** *p110*
Burk, Abigail; Massachusetts, 1744 ***1642*** *p101*
Burk, Anthony; Boston, 1768 ***1642*** *p39*
Burk, David; Ohio, 1840 ***2763.1*** *p7*
Burk, Deliverance; Ipswich, MA, 1740 ***1642*** *p71*
Burk, Dorothea; America, 1871 ***179.55*** *p19*
Burk, Edward; Boston, 1656 ***1642*** *p9*
Burk, Elizabeth; Boston, 1760 ***1642*** *p48*
Burk, Elizabeth; Massachusetts, 1749 ***1642*** *p110*
Burk, George; Illinois, 1855 ***6079.1*** *p3*
Burk, James; Boston, 1752-1760 ***1642*** *p30*
Burk, James; Massachusetts, 1773 ***1642*** *p106*
Burk, John; Boston, 1736 ***1642*** *p26*
Burk, John; Boston, 1764 ***1642*** *p33*
Burk, John; Boston, 1765 ***1642*** *p35*
Burk, John; Boston, 1768 ***1642*** *p39*
Burk, John; Illinois, 1853 ***6079.1*** *p3*
Burk, John; Illinois, 1860-1872 ***777.40*** *p5*
Burk, John; Long Island, 1781 ***8529.30*** *p9A*
Burk, John; Massachusetts, 1752 ***1642*** *p117*
*Wife:*Sary
Burk, John; Massachusetts, 1775 ***1642*** *p100*
Burk, John; St. John, N.B., 1848 ***2978.15*** *p38*
Burk, Jonathan *SEE* Burk, Richard
Burk, Jonathan; Massachusetts, 1732 ***1642*** *p106*
With 7 children
Burk, Mary *SEE* Burk, Richard
Burk, Mathew; Marblehead, MA, 1737 ***1642*** *p73*

Burk, Mehitable; Massachusetts, 1742 ***1642*** *p117*
Burk, Michael; Boston, 1772 ***1642*** *p49*
Burk, Patrick; Boston, 1740 ***1642*** *p45*
Burk, Peter; Illinois, 1860 ***6079.1*** *p3*
Burk, Richard; Boston, 1727 ***1642*** *p25*
Burk, Richard; Boston, 1745 ***1642*** *p28*
Burk, Richard; Massachusetts, 1675-1676 ***1642*** *p128*
Burk, Richard; Massachusetts, 1676 ***1642*** *p110*
*Wife:*Mary
Burk, Richard *SEE* Burk, Richard
Burk, Richard; Massachusetts, 1727 ***1642*** *p106*
*Son:*Richard
*Son:*Jonathan
With child
Burk, Richard; Newbury, MA, 1728 ***1642*** *p75*
Burk, Samuel; Ohio, 1840 ***2763.1*** *p7*
Burk, Sarah; Boston, 1771 ***1642*** *p49*
Burk, Sarah; Massachusetts, 1739 ***1642*** *p106*
Burk, Sary *SEE* Burk, John
Burk, Thomas; Massachusetts, 1753 ***1642*** *p109*
Burk, Thos.; Louisiana, 1874-1875 ***4981.45*** *p298*
Burk, Ulick; New York, 1782 ***8529.30*** *p10*
Burk, William; Boston, 1738 ***1642*** *p44*
Burk, William; Lynn, MA, 1772 ***1642*** *p71*
Burk, William; Salem, MA, 1738 ***1642*** *p78*
Burkard, Amalia; Kansas, 1917-1918 ***1826.15*** *p81*
Burkard, Michel 46; America, 1880 ***5475.1*** *p420*
Burke, Abigail; Massachusetts, 1744 ***1642*** *p111*
Burke, Angus 49; Ontario, 1871 ***1823.21*** *p44*
Burke, Ann; Pennsylvania, 1864 ***8513.31*** *p415*
Burke, Conrad 37; Ontario, 1871 ***1823.17*** *p20*
Burke, David 28; St. Johns, N.F., 1811 ***1053.20*** *p20*
Burke, Edward; Salem, MA, 1687 ***1642*** *p79*
Burke, Harvey 66; Ontario, 1871 ***1823.17*** *p20*
Burke, Henry; Louisiana, 1874 ***4981.45*** *p130*
Burke, James; Boston, 1836 ***3274.56*** *p70*
Burke, James; Colorado, 1862-1894 ***1029.59*** *p15*
Burke, Jas.; California, 1868 ***1131.61*** *p89*
Burke, John; Boston, 1763 ***1642*** *p32*
Burke, John; Boston, 1764 ***1642*** *p33*
Burke, John; Illinois, 1860-1872 ***777.40*** *p5*
Burke, John; North Carolina, 1853 ***1088.45*** *p4*
Burke, Katharina; America, 1872 ***5475.1*** *p370*
Burke, Mary; New Orleans, 1850 ***7242.30*** *p136*
Burke, Mary 9; Quebec, 1870 ***8364.32*** *p22*
Burke, Maurice R. 33; Ontario, 1871 ***1823.17*** *p20*
Burke, Patrick; Louisiana, 1874 ***4981.45*** *p131*
Burke, Patrick; Toronto, 1844 ***2910.35*** *p114*
Burke, Patt; New Orleans, 1850 ***7242.30*** *p136*
Burke, Peter C. 22; New York, NY, 1869 ***7710.1*** *p157*
Burke, Richard 53; Ontario, 1871 ***1823.21*** *p44*
Burke, Thomas 45; Ontario, 1871 ***1823.17*** *p20*
Burke, Walter; Boston, 1667 ***1642*** *p10*
Burke, Walter; Toronto, 1844 ***2910.35*** *p116*
Burke, William; Boston, 1767 ***1642*** *p38*
Burke, William; Marblehead, MA, 1772 ***1642*** *p73*
Burke, William 21; Ontario, 1871 ***1823.21*** *p44*
Burke, William 16; Quebec, 1870 ***8364.32*** *p22*
Burke, William; Salem, MA, 1766 ***1642*** *p78*
Burke, Wm 56; Ontario, 1871 ***1823.21*** *p44*
Burkel, Georg 27; Mississippi, 1847 ***778.6*** *p54*
Burker, Alexandria; America, 1854 ***2526.43*** *p217*
Burker, Ignaz 20; New Orleans, 1848 ***778.6*** *p54*
Burker, Johannes; America, 1854 ***2526.43*** *p217*
Burket, C.; Louisiana, 1874 ***4981.45*** *p295*
Burkett, James 71; Ontario, 1871 ***1823.17*** *p20*
Burkett, Jesse 45; Ontario, 1871 ***1823.17*** *p20*
Burkett, William 18; Ontario, 1871 ***1823.21*** *p44*
Burkhard, Alexander 39; Mississippi, 1847 ***778.6*** *p54*
Burkhard, Anastasias 36; Mississippi, 1847 ***778.6*** *p54*
Burkhard, Franziska 6; Mississippi, 1847 ***778.6*** *p55*
Burkhard, Henry 3; Mississippi, 1847 ***778.6*** *p55*
Burkhard, Mathias 28; America, 1846 ***778.6*** *p55*
Burkhard, Regine 6; Mississippi, 1847 ***778.6*** *p55*
Burkhard, Sophie 2; Mississippi, 1847 ***778.6*** *p55*
Burkhardsmaier, Friedrich; Chile, 1852 ***1192.4*** *p51*
Burkhardt, Eleonore; America, 1857 ***179.55*** *p19*
Burkhardt, Ida; Illinois, 1930 ***121.35*** *p101*
Burkhardt, Joh. 9; America, 1846 ***778.6*** *p55*
Burks, John; New England, 1745 ***1642*** *p27*
Burky, . . .; West Virginia, 1865-1879 ***1132.30*** *p150*
Burl, Herman Rudolf; Iowa, 1915 ***1211.15*** *p9*
Burley, Francis 40; Ontario, 1871 ***1823.21*** *p44*
Burley, Jerimiah 50; Ontario, 1871 ***1823.21*** *p44*
Burley, Joseph; New York, NY, 1839 ***3274.55*** *p43*
Burley, Nelson 59; Ontario, 1871 ***1823.17*** *p20*
Burley, William 36; Ontario, 1871 ***1823.21*** *p44*
Burman, Arthur *SEE* Burman, Charles
Burman, Charles *SEE* Burman, Charles
Burman, Charles 39; Quebec, 1881 ***9228.50*** *p146*
*Wife:*Ellen 39
*Child:*George
*Child:*Charles
*Child:*Arthur
*Child:*Clara
*Child:*Mary
Burman, Charles G.; St. Paul, MN, 1880 ***1865.50*** *p42*
Burman, Clara *SEE* Burman, Charles
Burman, Ellen 39 *SEE* Burman, Charles
Burman, Fredrick W.; North Carolina, 1843 ***1088.45*** *p4*
Burman, George *SEE* Burman, Charles
Burman, Mary *SEE* Burman, Charles
Burmann, Karl; Wisconsin, 1878 ***6795.8*** *p62*
Burn, Elinor; Boston, 1743 ***1642*** *p45*
Burn, John; Ohio, 1809-1852 ***4511.35*** *p7*
Burn, Lizzie 7; Quebec, 1870 ***8364.32*** *p22*
Burn, Patrick; New England, 1745 ***1642*** *p28*
Burn, Richard; Philadelphia, 1778 ***8529.30*** *p2*
Burn, Robert 14; Quebec, 1870 ***8364.32*** *p22*
Burn, Silence; Massachusetts, 1773 ***1642*** *p91*
Burnard, Richard 79; Ontario, 1871 ***1823.21*** *p44*
Burnas, Louis; Louisiana, 1874 ***4981.45*** *p131*
Burne, Jas 28; St. Johns, N.F., 1811 ***1053.20*** *p21*
Burne, Patrick; Massachusetts, 1730 ***1642*** *p82*
Burnel, Charles 2; New Orleans, 1848 ***778.6*** *p55*
Burnel, Dessire 29; New Orleans, 1848 ***778.6*** *p55*
Burnes, Patrick; Washington, 1887 ***2770.40*** *p24*
Burnett, George 34; Ontario, 1871 ***1823.21*** *p44*
Burnett, John 40; Ontario, 1871 ***1823.21*** *p44*
Burnett, John 50; Ontario, 1871 ***1823.21*** *p44*
Burnett, Nathan; Tennessee, 1906 ***3665.20*** *p111*
Burnett, Thomas 28; Indiana, 1865-1870 ***9076.20*** *p67*
Burnette, Christena 55; Ontario, 1871 ***1823.21*** *p44*
Burney, Thomas; New York, NY, 1819 ***3274.55*** *p72*
Burnham, Elishi 31; Ontario, 1871 ***1823.17*** *p20*
Burnham, Jemima 74; Ontario, 1871 ***1823.17*** *p20*
Burnham, M. L. 58; Ontario, 1871 ***1823.17*** *p20*
Burnham, Roll 24; Michigan, 1880 ***4491.30*** *p4*
Burnham, Samu'l 31; Ontario, 1871 ***1823.17*** *p20*
Burnie, Alfred R. 34; Ontario, 1871 ***1823.21*** *p44*
Burnie, William 29; Ontario, 1871 ***1823.17*** *p20*
Burning, Jean 28; America, 1847 ***778.6*** *p55*
Burnison, James; Ohio, 1809-1852 ***4511.35*** *p7*
Burnit, William 30; Ontario, 1871 ***1823.17*** *p20*
Burnley, John 33; Ontario, 1871 ***1823.17*** *p20*
Burnona, Claude 25; New Orleans, 1848 ***778.6*** *p55*
Burns, Allis 18; Ontario, 1871 ***1823.21*** *p44*
Burns, Andrew 30; Ontario, 1871 ***1823.21*** *p44*
Burns, Ann; Boston, 1753 ***1642*** *p47*
Burns, Ann Jane 44; Ontario, 1871 ***1823.21*** *p44*
Burns, Charles 34; Ontario, 1871 ***1823.17*** *p20*
Burns, Daniel; Toronto, 1844 ***2910.35*** *p115*
Burns, David; Dorchester, MA, 1770 ***1642*** *p102*
Burns, Edward; Louisiana, 1874 ***4981.45*** *p130*
Burns, Eliza 56; Ontario, 1871 ***1823.21*** *p44*
Burns, Eliza Jane 16; Ontario, 1871 ***1823.21*** *p44*
Burns, George; North Carolina, 1825 ***1088.45*** *p4*
Burns, George 33; Ontario, 1871 ***1823.21*** *p44*
Burns, George 36; Ontario, 1871 ***1823.21*** *p44*
Burns, George 50; Ontario, 1871 ***1823.21*** *p44*
Burns, Hariett 82; Ontario, 1871 ***1823.21*** *p44*
Burns, Henry 51; Ontario, 1871 ***1823.21*** *p44*
Burns, James; Colorado, 1884 ***1029.59*** *p15*
Burns, James 16; Ontario, 1871 ***1823.21*** *p44*
Burns, James 18; Ontario, 1871 ***1823.21*** *p44*
Burns, James 50; Ontario, 1871 ***1823.21*** *p44*
Burns, James 57; Ontario, 1871 ***1823.21*** *p45*
Burns, James 58; Ontario, 1871 ***1823.17*** *p20*
Burns, Jeremiah 34; Ontario, 1871 ***1823.17*** *p20*
Burns, John; Massachusetts, 1769 ***1642*** *p66*
Burns, John; Ohio, 1840-1897 ***8365.35*** *p15*
Burns, John 34; Ontario, 1871 ***1823.21*** *p45*
Burns, John 37; Ontario, 1871 ***1823.17*** *p20*
Burns, John 40; Ontario, 1871 ***1823.17*** *p20*
Burns, John 40; Ontario, 1871 ***1823.21*** *p45*
Burns, John 50; Ontario, 1871 ***1823.21*** *p45*
Burns, John 73; Ontario, 1871 ***1823.21*** *p45*
Burns, John 74; Ontario, 1871 ***1823.21*** *p45*
Burns, John; Washington, 1887 ***2770.40*** *p24*
Burns, John K.; Iowa, 1895 ***1211.15*** *p9*
Burns, Joseph 80; Ontario, 1871 ***1823.21*** *p45*
Burns, Margaret *SEE* Burns, Olive
Burns, Margarett 43; Michigan, 1880 ***4491.39*** *p4*
Burns, Mary 17; Ontario, 1871 ***1823.17*** *p20*
Burns, Mary 35; Ontario, 1871 ***1823.21*** *p45*
Burns, Mary 59; Ontario, 1871 ***1823.21*** *p45*
Burns, Mary 10; Quebec, 1870 ***8364.32*** *p22*
Burns, Mary A. 35; Ontario, 1871 ***1823.21*** *p45*
Burns, Michael; Illinois, 1858 ***6079.1*** *p3*
Burns, Olive; Shrewsbury, MA, 1708 ***1642*** *p108*
*Wife:*Margaret
Burns, Owen; Illinois, 1918 ***6007.60*** *p9*
Burns, P. M. 52; Ontario, 1871 ***1823.21*** *p45*
Burns, Patrick; Illinois, 1860 ***6079.1*** *p3*
Burns, Patrick 31; Ontario, 1871 ***1823.17*** *p20*
Burns, Patrick 52; Ontario, 1871 ***1823.21*** *p45*
Burns, Pearce 80; Ontario, 1871 ***1823.21*** *p45*
Burns, Peter 42; Ontario, 1871 ***1823.17*** *p20*
Burns, Peter 58; Ontario, 1871 ***1823.21*** *p45*
Burns, Robert 57; Ontario, 1871 ***1823.21*** *p45*
Burns, Rodger; Toronto, 1844 ***2910.35*** *p112*
Burns, Samuel; Massachusetts, 1765 ***1642*** *p91*
Burns, Sarah 8; Quebec, 1870 ***8364.32*** *p22*
Burns, Simon 36; Ontario, 1871 ***1823.17*** *p20*
Burns, T. P.; Louisiana, 1874-1875 ***4981.45*** *p297*
Burns, Thomas 28; Ontario, 1871 ***1823.17*** *p20*
Burns, Thomas 48; Ontario, 1871 ***1823.21*** *p45*
Burns, Thomas 63; Ontario, 1871 ***1823.17*** *p20*
Burns, William; Louisiana, 1874 ***4981.45*** *p295*
Buron, A. 20; New Orleans, 1847 ***778.6*** *p55*
Burphoff, Nicholas 47; Ontario, 1871 ***1823.21*** *p45*
Burque, Jean 40; New Orleans, 1848 ***778.6*** *p55*
Burr, James 48; Ontario, 1871 ***1823.21*** *p45*
Burr, Jeremy 20; Virginia, 1635 ***1183.3*** *p30*
Burr, John; New York, 1783 ***8529.30*** *p10*
Burr, John 35; Ontario, 1871 ***1823.21*** *p45*
Burr, John 60; Ontario, 1871 ***1823.21*** *p45*
Burr, Michael 80; Ontario, 1871 ***1823.17*** *p20*
Burr, Richard; New York, 1800-1850 ***9228.50*** *p246*
Burr, Richard; New York, 1822 ***9228.50*** *p146*
Burr, Saml. 62; Ontario, 1871 ***1823.17*** *p20*
Burr, William 58; Ontario, 1871 ***1823.17*** *p20*
Burren, George; Maine, 1665 ***9228.50*** *p146*
Burren, George; Massachusetts, 1640 ***9228.50*** *p149*
Burren, Hannah 46; Michigan, 1880 ***4491.42*** *p6*
Burren, James 57; Michigan, 1880 ***4491.42*** *p6*
Burrett, Peter; Ontario, 1871 ***1823.21*** *p45*
Burrichter, Wilhelm; Miami, 1935 ***4984.12*** *p39*
Burridge, Evans A. 15; Ontario, 1871 ***1823.21*** *p45*
Burridge, John 48; Ontario, 1871 ***1823.21*** *p45*
Burrill, George; Ohio, 1809-1852 ***4511.35*** *p7*
Burris, William 38; Ontario, 1871 ***1823.21*** *p45*
Burriss, James W. 21; Ontario, 1871 ***1823.21*** *p45*
Burriss, Jane 18; Ontario, 1871 ***1823.21*** *p45*
Burriss, Margeret 16; Ontario, 1871 ***1823.21*** *p45*
Burro, Theophile; New York, NY, 1857 ***1494.20*** *p13*
Burroney, Joseph; St. Johns, N.F., 1825 ***1053.15*** *p7*
Burrow, John; New York, 1776 ***8529.30*** *p2*
Burrow, Josiah; New York, 1779 ***8529.30*** *p9*
Burrow, Josiah; New York, 1779 ***8529.30*** *p10*
Burrows, Charles 21; Ontario, 1871 ***1823.21*** *p45*
Burrows, Frank 23; Indiana, 1887-1890 ***9076.20*** *p72*
Burrows, George 43; Ontario, 1871 ***1823.21*** *p45*
Burrows, Henry 37; Ontario, 1871 ***1823.17*** *p20*
Burrows, James 35; Ontario, 1871 ***1823.21*** *p45*
Burrows, John; New York, 1776 ***8529.30*** *p2*
Burrows, Margt; St. Johns, N.F., 1825 ***1053.15*** *p6*
Burrows, Phillip 33; Ontario, 1871 ***1823.21*** *p45*
Burrows, Thomas 35; Ontario, 1871 ***1823.17*** *p20*
Burrows, William 70; Ontario, 1871 ***1823.21*** *p45*
Burschel, Mrs. 44; Valdivia, Chile, 1852 ***1192.4*** *p53*
With child 14
With child 8
With child 7
Burschel, J. J.; Valdivia, Chile, 1852 ***1192.4*** *p53*
Bursgstahler, Albert *SEE* Bursgstahler, Friedrich
Bursgstahler, Christian Gustav *SEE* Bursgstahler, Friedrich
Bursgstahler, Eva Maron *SEE* Bursgstahler, Friedrich
Bursgstahler, Friedrich; Dakota, 1866-1918 ***554.30*** *p26*
*Wife:*Eva Maron
*Child:*Albert
*Child:*Christian Gustav
Burshell, Maria 71; Ontario, 1871 ***1823.21*** *p45*
Burshell, William J. 20; New York, NY, 1894 ***6512.1*** *p186*
Bursson, O. 26; America, 1840 ***778.6*** *p55*
Burstein, Louis; Detroit, 1929-1930 ***6214.5*** *p69*
Burt, Charles 42; Ontario, 1871 ***1823.21*** *p45*
Burt, David; Ohio, 1810 ***9228.50*** *p17A*
Burt, H. Joseph; Philadelphia, 1865 ***5720.10*** *p377*
Burt, J. L. 37; Ontario, 1871 ***1823.21*** *p45*
Burt, James; Ohio, 1846 ***3580.20*** *p31*
Burt, James; Ohio, 1846 ***6020.12*** *p6*
Burt, Marg.; Ohio, 1854 ***9228.50*** *p17A*
Burt, Nicholas; Boston, 1830 ***3274.55*** *p26*
Burt, Nicholas; Marston's Wharf, 1782 ***8529.30*** *p10*
Burt, Samuel 23; Ontario, 1871 ***1823.21*** *p45*
Burtenwood, Wm.; Jamestown, VA, 1633 ***1658.20*** *p211*
Burth, John Peter; Illinois, 1856 ***6079.1*** *p3*
Burthra, Janet 17; Ontario, 1871 ***1823.17*** *p21*
Burtin, Clemintis 21; Ontario, 1871 ***1823.17*** *p21*
Burtin, F. 36; Louisiana, 1847 ***778.6*** *p55*
Burton, Miss 20; America, 1847 ***778.6*** *p55*
Burton, Mr. 50; America, 1847 ***778.6*** *p55*
Burton, Allan 46; Ontario, 1871 ***1823.17*** *p21*
Burton, Duke; New York, 1776 ***8529.30*** *p2*
Burton, George 29; Ontario, 1871 ***1823.21*** *p45*
Burton, George 47; Ontario, 1871 ***1823.17*** *p21*

Burton, Isaac; Marston's Wharf, 1782 *8529.30 p10*
Burton, James; New York, 1783 *8529.30 p10*
Burton, James 57; Ontario, 1871 *1823.21 p45*
Burton, James 18; Quebec, 1870 *8364.32 p22*
Burton, John 28; Ontario, 1871 *1823.21 p45*
Burton, Th. 25; America, 1847 *778.6 p55*
Burton, Thomas; Colorado, 1889 *1029.59 p15*
Burton, Thomas; Pennsylvania, 1876 *1029.59 p15*
Burtz, Magdalena 46; Galveston, TX, 1844 *3967.10 p372*
Burtz, Moritz 36; Galveston, TX, 1844 *3967.10 p372*
Burwell, Dorothy; Jamestown, VA, 1633 *1658.20 p211*
Burwell, Dorothy; Jamestown, VA, 1633 *1658.20 p211*
Burwell, Lewis; Virginia, 1648 *1658.20 p208*
Burwell, Wm; Jamestown, VA, 1633 *1658.20 p211*
Bury, Joseph; Ohio, 1809-1852 *4511.35 p7*
Bury, Nicholas; Ohio, 1809-1852 *4511.35 p7*
Bury, William 82; Ontario, 1871 *1823.17 p21*
Burzynska, Maryanna; Wisconsin, 1882 *6795.8 p55*
Busbee, Elen 17; Ontario, 1871 *1823.21 p45*
Busby, Eliza 60; Ontario, 1871 *1823.21 p45*
Busby, Henry; Maryland, 1674-1675 *1236.25 p52*
Busby, Mary 52; Ontario, 1871 *1823.21 p45*
Busby, Samuel 68; Ontario, 1871 *1823.21 p46*
Busby, Tho. 19; Virginia, 1635 *1183.3 p31*
Buscano, S.; Louisiana, 1874-1875 *4981.45 p298*
Busch, Anthony; Ohio, 1809-1852 *4511.35 p7*
Busch, Charles; Louisiana, 1841-1844 *4981.45 p210*
Busch, Danl. 21; New Orleans, 1847 *778.6 p55*
Busch, Ferdinand; Wisconsin, 1877 *6795.8 p89*
Busch, Friedrich Wilhelm Carl Victor; America, 1889 *7420.1 p358*
Busch, George; Ohio, 1809-1852 *4511.35 p7*
Busch, Heinrich Ludwig; Ohio, 1887 *7420.1 p353*
Busch, Katharina 37; Pittsburgh, 1880 *5475.1 p434*
Busch, Maria; America, 1897 *5475.1 p426*
Busch, Nikolaus 46; America, 1846 *5475.1 p397*
  With family
Busch, Peter 30; Port uncertain, 1840 *778.6 p55*
Busch, Wilhelm; Port uncertain, 1883 *7420.1 p335*
Buschbaum, Adam, III; Argentina, 1855 *2526.43 p207*
  With family of 4
Buschbaum, Georg Adam; America, 1883 *2526.43 p207*
Busche, . . .; America, 1837 *7420.1 p12*
Busche, . . .; Port uncertain, 1845 *7420.1 p35*
Busche, Carl; America, 1857 *7420.1 p159*
Busche, Carl Friedrich; America, 1846 *7420.1 p43*
  With son 25
  With son 13
Busche, Carl Wilhelm; America, 1836 *7420.1 p10*
Busche, Carl Wilhelm; America, 1857 *7420.1 p159*
  With wife 3 sons & 4 daughters
Busche, Engel Marie Sophie SEE Busche, Johann Heinrich Christoph
Busche, Engel Sophie Dorothee SEE Busche, Johann Heinrich Christoph
Busche, Ernst Heinrich Wilhelm; Indiana, 1888 *7420.1 p356*
Busche, Friedrich; America, 1853 *7420.1 p103*
Busche, Friedrich; America, 1900 *7420.1 p376*
Busche, Friedrich Wilhelm; America, 1857 *7420.1 p159*
Busche, Friedrich Wilhelm Gottlieb; America, 1868 *7420.1 p270*
Busche, Heinrich; America, 1867 *7420.1 p255*
Busche, Johann Conrad Heinrich; America, 1846 *7420.1 p43*
Busche, Johann Heinrich Christoph SEE Busche, Johann Heinrich Christoph
Busche, Johann Heinrich Christoph; America, 1872 *7420.1 p294*
  Son:Johann Heinrich Christoph
  Daughter:Engel Marie Sophie
  Daughter:Engel Sophie Dorothee
Busche, Johann Heinrich Otto; America, 1864 *7420.1 p223*
Busche, Katharina 21; America, 1870 *5475.1 p185*
Busche, Thrine Marie Charl; America, 1848 *7420.1 p59*
Buschel, Anna Maria SEE Buschel, Mathias
Buschel, C.; Venezuela, 1843 *3899.5 p546*
Buschel, Elisabeth SEE Buschel, Mathias
Buschel, Maria Barbara Strass SEE Buschel, Mathias
Buschel, Mathias; America, 1872 *5475.1 p186*
  Wife:Maria Barbara Strass
  Daughter:Elisabeth
  Daughter:Anna Maria
Buscher, Albert; Washington, 1889 *2770.40 p26*
Buschke, Friedrich; Wisconsin, 1898 *6795.8 p115*
Buschke, Hulda; Wisconsin, 1893 *6795.8 p115*
Buschmann, Franz Heinrich Ferdinand Wilhelm; America, 1852 *7420.1 p86*
Buschmann, Friederike SEE Buschmann, Ludwig
Buschmann, Heinrich Christian; Port uncertain, 1837 *7420.1 p12*

Buschmann, Heinrich Wilhelm; America, 1854 *7420.1 p117*
Buschmann, Henry; Ohio, 1840-1897 *8365.35 p15*
Buschmann, Johann Heinrich Christoph; Port uncertain, 1840 *7420.1 p18*
Buschmann, Ludwig; America, 1868 *7420.1 p270*
  Daughter:Friederike
Buschow, Martin Jacob; Wisconsin, 1855 *6795.8 p24*
Buse, Samuel 37; Ontario, 1871 *1823.17 p21*
Bush, Anthony; Ohio, 1809-1852 *4511.35 p7*
Bush, Chisstian; Louisiana, 1874 *4981.45 p131*
Bush, George; Ohio, 1809-1852 *4511.35 p7*
Bush, George; Ohio, 1809-1852 *4511.35 p7*
Bush, Henry 42; Ontario, 1871 *1823.21 p46*
Bush, Wilko; Louisiana, 1874 *4981.45 p131*
Bush, William; Miami, 1920 *4984.15 p38*
Bush, Wm.; Maryland, 1672 *1236.25 p46*
Bushbaum, John G.; North Carolina, 1857 *1088.45 p4*
Bushbie Family ; Bermuda, 1703-1803 *9228.50 p124*
Bushbie Family ; Boston, 1703-1803 *9228.50 p124*
Bushel, Caspar 28; America, 1844 *778.6 p55*
Bushert, Pierre 26; America, 1847 *778.6 p55*
Bushmann, George; Ohio, 1840-1897 *8365.35 p15*
Busho, Martin Jacob; Wisconsin, 1855 *6795.8 p24*
Bushong, John Alan; New York, 1969 *9228.50 p408*
Bushong, Lawrence Fansler; Panama, 1938 *9228.50 p408*
Bushong, Philip Lewis; Virginia, 1965 *9228.50 p408*
Busing, Friedrich Wilhelm; America, 1868 *7420.1 p269*
Busing, Gustava 19; Valdivia, Chile, 1852 *1192.4 p55*
Businger, Martin; Died enroute, 1817-1818 *90.20 p150*
Businger, Martin; New Castle, DE, 1817-1818 *90.20 p150*
Busit, Abraham; North Carolina, 1710 *3629.40 p3*
Busoch, Christian; Valdivia, Chile, 1850 *1192.4 p48*
Busque, Jean; Illinois, 1852 *6079.1 p3*
Buss, Eva; America, 1873 *5475.1 p361*
Buss, Frederick; Wisconsin, 1889 *6795.8 p193*
Bussac, Marie 38; New Orleans, 1848 *778.6 p55*
Bussac, Michael F.; Illinois, 1852 *6079.1 p3*
Bussac, Michel Francois 49; New Orleans, 1848 *778.6 p55*
Bussall, Elizabeth 80; Ontario, 1871 *1823.17 p21*
Bussar, Antoine; New York, NY, 1869 *1494.20 p11*
Busse, Mr.; America, 1854 *7420.1 p117*
  With wife & son
Busse, August Johann Ludwig SEE Busse, Carl Friedrich August
Busse, Bertram Heinrich; America, 1847 *7420.1 p52*
Busse, Carl Friedrich August; America, 1874 *7420.1 p302*
  Daughter:Friederike Christiane
  Son:August Johann Ludwig
  Son:Karl Friedrich
  Son:Hermann Gustav
Busse, Carl Gustav SEE Busse, Christian
Busse, Christian; America, 1870 *7420.1 p286*
  Son:Carl Gustav
  With family
Busse, Emma Alvine Martha; Wisconsin, 1888 *6795.8 p105*
Busse, Friederike Christiane SEE Busse, Carl Friedrich August
Busse, Friedrich; America, 1861 *7420.1 p203*
Busse, George; Maine, 1665 *9228.50 p146*
Busse, Hanna; Massachusetts, 1630-1683 *9228.50 p18A*
Busse, Hermann; America, 1890 *7420.1 p400*
Busse, Hermann Gustav SEE Busse, Carl Friedrich August
Busse, Karl Friedrich SEE Busse, Carl Friedrich August
Busse, Louisa; Wisconsin, 1891 *6795.8 p33*
Busse, Louise; America, 1861 *7420.1 p203*
Busse, Richard Robert; Wisconsin, 1896 *6795.8 p41*
Busse, Samuel; New York, 1860 *358.56 p5*
Busselberg, Friedrich; America, 1868 *7420.1 p269*
Busselberg, Heinrich; America, 1868 *7420.1 p270*
  With wife
  With daughter 9
  With daughter 3
  With son 1
  With son 6
Bussell, John; New Hampshire, 1650 *9228.50 p147*
Bussell, Simon; Maine, 1668 *9228.50 p147*
Bussett, Abraham; North Carolina, 1710 *3629.40 p3*
Bussey, . . .; Maryland, 1669 *9228.50 p149*
Bussian, Albert; Wisconsin, 1874 *6795.8 p83*
Bussier, Modeste 22; America, 1843 *778.6 p55*
Bussieres, Jacques 15; Quebec, 1643 *9221.17 p130*
Bussing, Engel Marie Sophie Schelhorn SEE Bussing, Johann Wilhelm
Bussing, Engel Marie Sophie; New York, NY, 1856 *7420.1 p146*
Bussing, Johann Wilhelm; America, 1857 *7420.1 p159*
  Wife:Engel Marie Sophie Schelhorn

Bussner, Carl; Illinois, 1860 *6079.1 p3*
Busson, Francois 34; Port uncertain, 1846 *778.6 p55*
Bussy, . . .; Maine, 1665 *9228.50 p146*
Bussy, Charlemagne 42; New Orleans, 1848 *778.6 p55*
Bussy, George; Massachusetts, 1640 *9228.50 p149*
Bussy, John; New Hampshire, 1650 *9228.50 p147*
Bussy, Justine 35; New Orleans, 1848 *778.6 p55*
Bussy, Simon; Maine, 1668 *9228.50 p147*
Bustien, Ja.ques 30; Mississippi, 1846 *778.6 p55*
Buston, Fidele 35; America, 1842 *778.6 p55*
Butcher, Benjamin 53; Ontario, 1871 *1823.21 p46*
Butcher, Charles 38; Port uncertain, 1840 *778.6 p55*
Butcher, William F. 37; Ontario, 1871 *1823.21 p46*
Bute, Miss; America, 1852 *7420.1 p86*
Bute, Mrs.; America, 1847 *7420.1 p52*
  With 2 children
Bute, Engel Marie Dorothea; Iowa, 1876 *7420.1 p308*
Butel, Mary; Salem, MA, 1675 *9228.50 p149*
Buteux, Jacques 35; Quebec, 1634 *9221.17 p32*
Butha, Henry 32; Missouri, 1845 *778.6 p55*
Butha, Philippe 18; Missouri, 1845 *778.6 p55*
Buthe, August; America, 1854 *7420.1 p117*
Buthe, Carl; America, 1858 *7420.1 p177*
  With wife 3 sons & 4 daughters
Buthe, Christian; Port uncertain, 1837 *7420.1 p12*
Buthe, Christian Ludwig; America, 1853 *7420.1 p103*
Buthe, Conrad; America, 1865 *7420.1 p230*
  With wife
Buthe, Conrad Ludwig; America, 1862 *7420.1 p211*
  Daughter:Louise Caroline Sophie
  With wife
Buthe, Engel Sophie Friederike; America, 1891 *7420.1 p364*
Buthe, Hans Heinrich; America, 1852 *7420.1 p86*
  With family
Buthe, Hans Heinrich; America, 1858 *7420.1 p177*
Buthe, Hans Heinrich; Port uncertain, 1858 *7420.1 p177*
Buthe, Heinrich; America, 1854 *7420.1 p117*
Buthe, Heinrich Wilhelm; America, 1861 *7420.1 p203*
  With family
Buthe, Louise Caroline Sophie SEE Buthe, Conrad Ludwig
Buthe, Philipp; Port uncertain, 1854 *7420.1 p117*
Buthe, Reinhold Heinrich; America, 1857 *7420.1 p159*
  With wife
Buthe, Sophie; America, 1857 *7420.1 p159*
Buthe, Sophie; America, 1884 *7420.1 p344*
  Daughter:Engel
Buthe, Wilhelm Christian; America, 1892 *7420.1 p365*
Buthe, Wilhelmine; America, 1857 *7420.1 p159*
Buthmann, Charles; Missouri, 1886 *3276.1 p1*
Buthmen, Charles; Missouri, 1896 *3276.1 p1*
Buti, Mr. 27; America, 1846 *778.6 p56*
Butikofer, Jacob; Ohio, 1809-1852 *4511.35 p7*
Butin, Genevieve; Montreal, 1658 *9221.17 p388*
Butkiewicz, Constantin 44; New York, NY, 1920 *930.50 p49*
Butler, Abraham 77; Ontario, 1871 *1823.17 p21*
Butler, Alfred 50; Ontario, 1871 *1823.21 p46*
Butler, Alfred SEE Butler, Hugh
Butler, Andrew 34; Ontario, 1871 *1823.21 p46*
Butler, Ann 25; North Carolina, 1774 *1422.10 p55*
Butler, Ann 42; Ontario, 1871 *1823.21 p46*
Butler, Ann Jane SEE Butler, Hugh
Butler, Anne Le Sueur SEE Butler, Charles
Butler, Caleb; Massachusetts, 1700-1799 *1642 p138*
Butler, Charles SEE Butler, Charles
Butler, Charles; Iowa, 1851 *9228.50 p330*
  Wife:Anne Le Sueur
  Child:Charles
  Child:Mary
  Child:Elizabeth
  Child:Philip
  Child:Rachel
  Child:John
  Child:Esther
Butler, Colonel; Ontario, 1787 *1276.15 p230*
  With child & 4 relatives
Butler, Cornelius 40; Ontario, 1871 *1823.21 p46*
Butler, David; Boston, 1839 *3274.55 p26*
Butler, Edmund; Boston, 1763 *1642 p32*
Butler, Edward; Roxbury, MA, 1743 *1642 p108*
Butler, Eliza.; Maryland, 1674 *1236.25 p50*
Butler, Elizabeth SEE Butler, Charles
Butler, Esther SEE Butler, Charles
Butler, Francis; Boston, 1763 *1642 p48*
Butler, Frederick 21; Ontario, 1871 *1823.17 p21*
Butler, Georgina SEE Butler, Hugh
Butler, Hugh; Virginia, 1911-1920 *9228.50 p330*
  Child:Georgina
  Wife:Margaret Boyle Beattie
  Child:Ann Jane
  Child:Alfred

Butler, Ira 63; Ontario, 1871 *1823.21 p46*
Butler, James; Boston, 1771 *1642 p49*
Butler, James; Colorado, 1862-1894 *1029.59 p15*
Butler, James; Massachusetts, 1675-1676 *1642 p128*
Butler, James 51; Ontario, 1871 *1823.17 p21*
Butler, James 55; Ontario, 1871 *1823.21 p46*
Butler, James 83; Ontario, 1871 *1823.17 p21*
Butler, James; Woburn, MA, 1676 *1642 p113*
Butler, James, Sr.; Massachusetts, 1681 *1642 p64*
Butler, Jane Elizabeth Le Boutillier Le Sueur *SEE* Butler, Jean
Butler, Jaques 52; New Castle, DE, 1817-1818 *90.20 p150*
Butler, Jean; Iowa, 1870 *9228.50 p330*
　*Wife:*Jane Elizabeth Le Boutillier Le Sueur
　With stepchild
Butler, Jean; New Castle, DE, 1817-1818 *90.20 p150*
Butler, John *SEE* Butler, Charles
Butler, John; New England, 1745 *1642 p28*
Butler, John; New England, 1745 *1642 p28*
Butler, John; New England, 1745 *1642 p28*
Butler, John 25; North Carolina, 1774 *1422.10 p55*
Butler, John 47; Ontario, 1871 *1823.17 p21*
Butler, Margaret Boyle Beattie *SEE* Butler, Hugh
Butler, Mary; Boston, 1766 *1642 p36*
　With daughter
Butler, Mary *SEE* Butler, Charles
Butler, Mary; Salem, MA, 1675 *9228.50 p149*
Butler, Mary; Salem, MA, 1675 *9228.50 p469*
Butler, Michael; Boston, 1752 *1642 p46*
Butler, Moses; New England, 1745 *1642 p28*
Butler, Patrick 36; Ontario, 1871 *1823.21 p46*
Butler, Peter 42; Ontario, 1871 *1823.21 p46*
Butler, Peter 71; Ontario, 1871 *1823.17 p21*
Butler, Philip *SEE* Butler, Charles
Butler, Philip; Massachusetts, 1675-1676 *1642 p128*
Butler, Philip; Massachusetts, 1675-1676 *1642 p128*
Butler, Rachel 7 *SEE* Butler, Charles
Butler, Richard; New England, 1745 *1642 p27*
Butler, Richard; New England, 1745 *1642 p28*
Butler, Richard; New England, 1745 *1642 p28*
Butler, Richard; New England, 1745 *1642 p28*
Butler, Richard; Newfoundland, 1814 *3476.10 p54*
Butler, Richard 65; Ontario, 1871 *1823.21 p46*
Butler, Robert 63; Ontario, 1871 *1823.21 p46*
Butler, Sarah; New Orleans, 1850 *7242.30 p136*
Butler, Stephen; Massachusetts, 1675-1676 *1642 p128*
Butler, Steven; Massachusetts, 1675-1676 *1642 p127*
Butler, Susan; Jamaica, 1665 *1220.12 p767*
Butler, Thomas 27; Ontario, 1871 *1823.21 p46*
Butler, Thomas 41; Ontario, 1871 *1823.17 p21*
Butler, William; Massachusetts, 1675-1676 *1642 p129*
Butler, William 30; Ontario, 1871 *1823.21 p46*
Butler, William 35; Ontario, 1871 *1823.17 p21*
Butlin, George; Oswego, NY, 1859-1959 *9228.50 p149*
Butlin, Thomas; Quebec, 1830-1859 *9228.50 p149*
Butner, Ernestine 15; Portland, ME, 1910 *970.38 p76*
Buton, Mr. 29; New Orleans, 1848 *778.6 p56*
Buton, Ms. 22; New Orleans, 1848 *778.6 p56*
Butow, Elnoald; Wisconsin, 1896 *6795.8 p89*
Butsch, George; Ohio, 1809-1852 *4511.35 p7*

Butsch, John; Ohio, 1809-1852 *4511.35 p7*
Butsch, Joseph; Ohio, 1809-1852 *4511.35 p7*
Butt, Edward; Massachusetts, n.d. *9228.50 p150*
Butt, Emma Blanche; Massachusetts, 1900-1990 *9228.50 p150*
Butt, Hermann Ferdinand Erdmann; Wisconsin, 1892 *6795.8 p231*
Butt, John; Massachusetts, n.d. *9228.50 p150*
Butt, John; Newfoundland, 1706 *9228.50 p149*
Butt, Joseph; Newfoundland, 1837 *9228.50 p150*
Butt, Michael; America, 1885-1956 *9228.50 p150*
Butt, Roger; Newfoundland, 1675 *9228.50 p149*
Butt, William Henry; Massachusetts, 1872-1938 *9228.50 p150*
Butten, William; Plymouth, MA, 1620 *1920.45 p5*
Butter, Andrew; Louisiana, 1836-1841 *4981.45 p208*
Butter, Friedrich; Wisconsin, 1875 *6795.8 p29*
Butter, Jaques 52; New Castle, DE, 1817-1818 *90.20 p150*
Butterfield, Abram 33; Michigan, 1880 *4491.30 p4*
Butterfield, Margret 53; Michigan, 1880 *4491.30 p4*
Butters, John; Illinois, 1860 *6079.1 p3*
Butterworth, William 50; Ontario, 1871 *1823.17 p21*
Buttery, W. H. 61; Ontario, 1871 *1823.21 p46*
Buttin, William 22; Ontario, 1871 *1823.17 p21*
Buttler, George 33; Ontario, 1871 *1823.21 p46*
Buttman, Christ; Missouri, 1886 *3276.1 p1*
Buttner, Bertha E.; Pennsylvania, 1855 *8513.31 p416*
Buttner, Dorothea; America, 1867 *7919.3 p526*
　With child
Buttner, Friedrich; America, 1867 *7919.3 p527*
Buttner, Michel; America, 1884 *5475.1 p413*
Buttner, Peter; America, 1887 *5475.1 p413*
Button, Claude; Maine, n.d. *9228.50 p18A*
Button, William; New Hampshire, 1693 *9228.50 p126*
Buttry, Georg 50; Ontario, 1871 *1823.21 p46*
Butz, Georg; America, 1889 *179.55 p19*
Butz, Marianna; Venezuela, 1843 *3899.5 p542*
Butz, Michael; Venezuela, 1843 *3899.5 p542*
Buxbaum, Joseph; North Carolina, 1859-1860 *1088.45 p4*
Buxbaum, Sebastian; America, 1852 *2526.43 p221*
Buxbeaum, Henry; North Carolina, 1814-1820 *1088.45 p4*
Buxer, Samuel; Ohio, 1809-1852 *4511.35 p7*
Buxtell, Philip; Ohio, 1809-1852 *4511.35 p7*
Buz, Marianna; Venezuela, 1843 *3899.5 p542*
Buzby, John; Ohio, 1809-1852 *4511.35 p7*
Buzie, Simon; Maine, 1667 *9228.50 p147*
Byam, Amelia Beatrice; Honduras, 1982 *9228.50 p360*
Byant, James; New Orleans, 1850 *7242.30 p136*
Byerly, Casper; Ohio, 1809-1852 *4511.35 p7*
Byers, Andrew 31; Ontario, 1871 *1823.21 p46*
Byers, James 42; Ontario, 1871 *1823.17 p21*
Byggere, Frederick; Iowa, 1890 *1211.15 p9*
Byhain, F. W.; Chile, 1852 *1192.4 p51*
Byhain, Johanna 34; Valdivia, Chile, 1852 *1192.4 p54*
　With 3 children
　With child 8
　With child 3 months
Byhan, Gottlieb; North Carolina, 1819 *1088.45 p4*

Bymion, Patrick; Hingham, MA, 1685 *1642 p15*
Bynes, James 60; Ontario, 1871 *1823.21 p46*
Byram, Abraha; Virginia, 1652 *6254.4 p243*
Byrar, James; Ohio, 1809-1852 *4511.35 p7*
Byrdziak, Jennie; Detroit, 1929 *1640.55 p117*
Byrdziak, Josephine; Detroit, 1929 *1640.55 p116*
Byrne, A.; New Orleans, 1850 *7242.30 p137*
Byrne, Anne; Halifax, N.S., 1827 *7009.9 p61*
Byrne, Anne; New Orleans, 1850 *7242.30 p136*
Byrne, Betsy; New Orleans, 1850 *7242.30 p136*
Byrne, Betty; New Orleans, 1850 *7242.30 p136*
Byrne, Biddy; New Orleans, 1850 *7242.30 p136*
Byrne, Bridget; New Orleans, 1850 *7242.30 p136*
Byrne, Charles; New Orleans, 1850 *7242.30 p136*
Byrne, Eliza; New Orleans, 1850 *7242.30 p136*
Byrne, Ellen; New Orleans, 1850 *7242.30 p136*
Byrne, George; New Orleans, 1850 *7242.30 p136*
Byrne, H.; New Orleans, 1850 *7242.30 p136*
Byrne, James; New Orleans, 1850 *7242.30 p136*
Byrne, James; New Orleans, 1850 *7242.30 p137*
Byrne, John; New Orleans, 1850 *7242.30 p137*
Byrne, John; New Orleans, 1851 *7242.30 p137*
Byrne, Laurence; New Orleans, 1850 *7242.30 p137*
Byrne, Laurence; New Orleans, 1851 *7242.30 p137*
Byrne, Loughlin; New Orleans, 1850 *7242.30 p137*
Byrne, Martin; Washington, 1886 *6015.10 p16*
Byrne, Mary; New Orleans, 1850 *7242.30 p137*
Byrne, Michael; New Orleans, 1850 *7242.30 p137*
Byrne, Miles; New Orleans, 1850 *7242.30 p137*
Byrne, Murtogh; New Orleans, 1850 *7242.30 p137*
Byrne, P. O.; California, 1868 *1131.61 p89*
Byrne, Patrick 35; Michigan, 1880 *4491.30 p4*
Byrne, Patrick; New Orleans, 1850 *7242.30 p137*
Byrne, Patt; New Orleans, 1850 *7242.30 p137*
Byrne, Patt; New Orleans, 1851 *7242.30 p137*
Byrne, Peggy; New Orleans, 1850 *7242.30 p137*
Byrne, Richard; New Orleans, 1850 *7242.30 p137*
Byrne, Rose; New Orleans, 1850 *7242.30 p137*
Byrne, S.; New Orleans, 1850 *7242.30 p137*
Byrne, Sally; New Orleans, 1850 *7242.30 p137*
Byrne, William; Louisiana, 1841-1844 *4981.45 p210*
Byrne, William; New Orleans, 1850 *7242.30 p137*
Byrne, William; New York, NY, 1841 *3274.56 p100*
Byrnes, Catharine Welsh *SEE* Byrnes, Peter
Byrnes, Peter; Philadelphia, 1857 *8513.31 p297*
　*Wife:*Catharine Welsh
Byrnes, Thomas 27; Louisiana, 1838-1847 *7710.1 p150*
Byrney, G.; New Orleans, 1850 *7242.30 p137*
Byrns, Lawrance J.; Kansas, 1887 *1447.20 p63*
Byron, Valentine 70; Ontario, 1871 *1823.21 p46*
Byshop, Mary; Maryland, 1674-1675 *1236.25 p51*
Bysse, . . .; Maryland, 1669 *9228.50 p149*
Bysse, George; Massachusetts, 1640 *9228.50 p149*
Byssy, . . .; Maryland, 1669 *9228.50 p149*
Bystrek, Jan 41; New York, NY, 1904 *8355.1 p15*
Byvon, Daniel; New York, NY, 1832 *3274.55 p70*
Bzdzinek, Aniela 20; New York, NY, 1911 *6533.11 p10*
Bzymek, Anna; Detroit, 1929 *1640.55 p115*

C

Cabanes, Joseph 19; America, 1845 *778.6 p56*
Cabanis, Henry; Virginia, 1700 *9230.15 p80*
  With wife & child
Cabanne, Louis 25; Port uncertain, 1840 *778.6 p56*
Cabannes, J. 19; New Orleans, 1848 *778.6 p56*
Cabannet, Jean 19; New Orleans, 1843 *778.6 p56*
Cabaret, Pierre 26; New Orleans, 1845 *778.6 p56*
Cabaski, Martin; Washington, 1886 *2770.40 p195*
Cabbell, S.A. 19; New York, NY, 1835 *5024.1 p136*
Cabet, Etienne; Illinois, 1852 *6079.1 p3*
Cabiro, Louis A.; Louisiana, 1836-1841 *4981.45 p208*
Cable, David F.; Ohio, 1861 *3580.20 p31*
Cable, David F.; Ohio, 1861 *6020.12 p6*
Cabol, J. B. 28; New Orleans, 1841 *778.6 p56*
Cabot, Elias; Massachusetts, 1775-1820 *9228.50 p122*
Cabot, Francis; Massachusetts, 1700 *9228.50 p150*
  *Brother:*George
  *Brother:*John
Cabot, George *SEE* Cabot, Francis
Cabot, John *SEE* Cabot, Francis
Cabot, John; Salem, MA, 1700 *9228.50 p21*
Cabot, Robert; Louisiana, 1836-1840 *4981.45 p212*
Cabreillac, Denis 31; New Orleans, 1848 *778.6 p56*
Cabryar, Francois 27; America, 1846 *778.6 p56*
Caburet, Jean 28; America, 1840 *778.6 p56*
Caces, Mr. 30; Port uncertain, 1846 *778.6 p56*
Cacey, Henry 60; Ontario, 1871 *1823.21 p46*
Cacey, John 49; Ontario, 1871 *1823.21 p46*
Cachot, Claude 48; America, 1847 *778.6 p56*
Cacker, Abraham; New York, NY, 1823 *3274.55 p69*
Cada, Josef; New York, NY, 1884 *2853.20 p421*
Cade, Robert 49; Ontario, 1871 *1823.21 p46*
Cadell, Zacharias; Maryland, 1680 *1236.25 p53*
Cadenhead, Alex 11; Quebec, 1910 *2897.7 p7*
Cadenhead, George 16; Quebec, 1910 *2897.7 p7*
Cadenhead, Isabella 43; Quebec, 1910 *2897.7 p7*
Cadenhead, James 2; Quebec, 1910 *2897.7 p7*
Cadenhead, John 10; Quebec, 1910 *2897.7 p7*
Cadenhead, Symian 43; Quebec, 1910 *2897.7 p7*
Cadenhead, W. 7; Quebec, 1910 *2897.7 p7*
Cadet, Rene; Montreal, 1653 *9221.17 p285*
Cadham, Charles 58; Ontario, 1871 *1823.21 p46*
Cadieu, Charles 13; Quebec, 1641 *9221.17 p101*
Cadieu, Jean 19; Montreal, 1653 *9221.17 p285*
Cadieu, Michelle-Madeleine 17; Quebec, 1654 *9221.17 p305*
Cadillon, G. 41; America, 1843 *778.6 p56*
Cadman, James 60; Ontario, 1871 *1823.21 p46*
Cadmore, Elizabeth 70; Ontario, 1871 *1823.21 p46*
Cadoret, Daniel; Utah, 1855 *9228.50 p151*
  *Relative:*Mary
Cadoret, Georges 20; Quebec, 1651 *9221.17 p238*
Cadoret, Mary *SEE* Cadoret, Daniel
Cadray, Mr. 17; America, 1747 *778.6 p56*
Cael, Francois 20; Montreal, 1662 *9221.17 p496*
Caen, Emery de; Quebec, 1624 *9221.17 p22*
Caffary, John 70; Ontario, 1871 *1823.21 p47*
Caffiero, Joseph; Louisiana, 1841-1844 *4981.45 p210*
Caffrey, Catherine; New Orleans, 1850 *7242.30 p137*
Caffrey, Edward; New Orleans, 1850 *7242.30 p137*
Cagnet, Mr. 24; New Orleans, 1840 *778.6 p56*
Cagny, Michael 40; Ontario, 1871 *1823.21 p47*
Caha, Ant.; Oklahoma, 1889 *2853.20 p372*
Caha, Josef; Oklahoma, 1889 *2853.20 p372*
Cahil, Thomas; Boston, 1746 *1642 p44*
Cahill, Anastasia 43; Ontario, 1871 *1823.21 p47*
Cahill, Bridget; New Orleans, 1851 *7242.30 p137*
Cahill, Daniel; Marblehead, MA, 1768 *1642 p73*

Cahill, Daniel; Marblehead, MA, 1768 *1642 p73*
Cahill, John; Marblehead, MA, 1732 *1642 p73*
Cahill, John; New Orleans, 1851 *7242.30 p137*
Cahill, John; Salem, MA, 1752 *1642 p78*
Cahill, John A. 41; Ontario, 1871 *1823.17 p21*
Cahill, Joseph 40; Ontario, 1871 *1823.17 p21*
Cahill, Joseph Zouch; Illinois, 1930 *121.35 p101*
Cahill, Margret 40; Ontario, 1871 *1823.21 p47*
Cahill, Martin; St. John, N.B., 1834 *2978.15 p38*
Cahill, Mary; Canada, 1856-1859 *8513.31 p417*
Cahill, Mary; Trenton, NJ, 1856 *8513.31 p417*
Cahill, Thomas; St. Johns, N.F., 1825 *1053.15 p6*
Cahn, Bonoum; Louisiana, 1856 *7710.1 p156*
Cahn, Bonoum; New Orleans, 1849 *7710.1 p154*
Cahn, Lambert 23; America, 1847 *778.6 p56*
Cahn, Michael; Louisiana, 1855 *7710.1 p155*
Cahn, Michael; New Orleans, 1850 *7710.1 p154*
Cahn, Simon 18; New Orleans, 1848 *778.6 p56*
Cahuzac, J. B. R. 27; New Orleans, 1844 *778.6 p56*
Cailhaut DeLaTesserie, Jacques 32; Quebec, 1661 *9221.17 p445*
Cailhaut deLa Tesserie, Jacques de; Quebec, 1662 *2314.30 p166*
Cailhaut deLa Tesserie, Jacques de; Quebec, 1662 *2314.30 p177*
Cailhe, Antoine 29; New Orleans, 1846 *778.6 p56*
Caillard, Francois 27; New Orleans, 1848 *778.6 p56*
Caillard, Louis 30; America, 1846 *778.6 p56*
Caillard, Louise Felicitre 21; New Orleans, 1848 *778.6 p56*
Caillard, Theodie 15; New Orleans, 1848 *778.6 p56*
Caillau, Pierre 17; Quebec, 1649 *9221.17 p210*
Caillaud, Andree; Quebec, 1665 *4514.3 p285*
Caille, Jacques; Quebec, 1665 *4514.3 p292*
  *Wife:*Marie-Andre Gervais
  *Child:*Jean
Caille, Jean *SEE* Caille, Jacques
Caille, Jeanne; Quebec, 1670 *4514.3 p285*
Caille, Marie; Quebec, 1668 *4514.3 p285*
Caille, Marie-Andre Gervais *SEE* Caille, Jacques
Caille, Marie-Jeanne; Quebec, 1671 *4514.3 p286*
Caille, Pierre; Montreal, 1661 *9221.17 p471*
Caille, Pierre Ehe; Illinois, 1852 *6079.1 p3*
Cailleret, Augustine 40; Port uncertain, 1840 *778.6 p56*
Cailleret, Florentin 36; Port uncertain, 1840 *778.6 p56*
Caillet, . . .; New England, 1788-1888 *9228.50 p151*
Cailleteau, Emery; Quebec, 1642 *9221.17 p113*
Cailliot, Jean 23; Montreal, 1641 *9221.17 p107*
Cailloteau, Emery; Quebec, 1642 *9221.17 p113*
Caillouet, Simon 25; Quebec, 1656 *9221.17 p332*
Cain, . . .; New England, n.d. *9228.50 p151*
Cain, Albert; Missouri, 1891 *3276.1 p1*
Cain, Arthur; Massachusetts, 1675 *9228.50 p151*
Cain, Bridget 60; Ontario, 1871 *1823.21 p47*
Cain, Catherine 78; Ontario, 1871 *1823.17 p21*
Cain, Charles 67; Ontario, 1871 *1823.21 p47*
Cain, James 28; Ontario, 1871 *1823.17 p21*
Cain, James 50; Ontario, 1871 *1823.21 p47*
Cain, James 65; Ontario, 1871 *1823.17 p21*
Cain, Jane 48; Ontario, 1871 *1823.21 p47*
Cain, Jeremiah; Boston, 1833 *3274.55 p43*
Cain, John 26; Ontario, 1871 *1823.21 p47*
Cain, John 26; Ontario, 1871 *1823.21 p47*
Cain, John 52; Ontario, 1871 *1823.21 p47*
Cain, Margrett 30; Ontario, 1871 *1823.21 p47*
Cain, Mary; New Orleans, 1851 *7242.30 p137*
Cain, Michael 33; Ontario, 1871 *1823.21 p47*
Cain, Michael 33; Ontario, 1871 *1823.21 p47*

Cain, Michael 39; Ontario, 1871 *1823.17 p21*
Cain, Owen 35; Ontario, 1871 *1823.21 p47*
Cain, Patrick 30; Ontario, 1871 *1823.17 p21*
Cain, Richard 65; Ontario, 1871 *1823.17 p21*
Cain, William 20; Ontario, 1871 *1823.21 p47*
Caines, Tom; St. John, N.B., n.d. *3331.4 p11*
Cains, Thomas; Burlington, VT, 1836 *3274.56 p96*
Caire, Ed.; Mississippi, 1848 *778.6 p56*
Caire, Francois de; Quebec, 1759 *2314.30 p170*
Caire, Francois de; Quebec, 1759 *2314.30 p177*
Caire, L. G.; Mississippi, 1848 *778.6 p56*
Cairncross, Walters 45; Ontario, 1871 *1823.21 p47*
Cairney, Michael 28; Ontario, 1871 *1823.17 p21*
Cairns, David A.; Colorado, 1897 *1029.59 p15*
Cairns, Elizabeth 84; Ontario, 1871 *1823.17 p22*
Cairns, George 28; Ontario, 1871 *1823.17 p22*
Cairns, James 56; Ontario, 1871 *1823.17 p22*
Cairns, James J.; Iowa, 1904 *1211.15 p10*
Cairns, John; Ohio, 1809-1852 *4511.35 p7*
Cairns, John 45; Ontario, 1871 *1823.17 p22*
Cairns, John 62; Ontario, 1871 *1823.21 p47*
Cairns, Peter 53; Ontario, 1871 *1823.17 p22*
Cairns, Robert; Washington, 1886 *2770.40 p195*
Cairns, Thomas 60; Ontario, 1871 *1823.17 p22*
Caittat, H. S. M.; Louisiana, 1836-1840 *4981.45 p212*
Cake, Elias 24; Ontario, 1871 *1823.21 p47*
Calahan, Dennis; Newfoundland, 1814 *3476.10 p54*
Calahan, Timothy; Massachusetts, 1756 *1642 p111*
Calais, Helene; Quebec, 1673 *4514.3 p286*
Calback, Marie 60; New Orleans, 1846 *778.6 p56*
Calbat, Gustave; New York, NY, 1868 *1494.20 p11*
Calbeck, John; Ohio, 1809-1852 *4511.35 p7*
Calbeck, Joseph; Ohio, 1809-1852 *4511.35 p7*
Calbert, Charles; Illinois, 1858 *6079.1 p3*
Calcott, George W. 34; Ontario, 1871 *1823.21 p47*
Calder, Agnes 27; Ontario, 1871 *1823.21 p47*
Calder, Alexander 28; Ontario, 1871 *1823.21 p47*
Calder, Duncan 73; Ontario, 1871 *1823.21 p47*
Calder, Hugh 80; Ontario, 1871 *1823.21 p47*
Calder, Janet; New York, 1739 *8277.31 p117*
Calder, John 32; Ontario, 1871 *1823.21 p47*
Calder, John 88; Ontario, 1871 *1823.21 p47*
Calder, William 31; Ontario, 1871 *1823.21 p47*
Calderwood, Robert 45; Ontario, 1871 *1823.21 p47*
Caldwell, Alexander *SEE* Caldwell, John
Caldwell, Elizabeth 25; Ontario, 1871 *1823.21 p47*
Caldwell, Henry; Marston's Wharf, 1782 *8529.30 p10*
Caldwell, James *SEE* Caldwell, John
Caldwell, John; New York, 1739 *8277.31 p113*
  *Wife:*Mary Nutt
  *Son:*Alexander
  *Son:*James
Caldwell, Mary Nutt *SEE* Caldwell, John
Caldwell, Robert 25; Ontario, 1871 *1823.17 p22*
Caldwell, Thomas 50; Ontario, 1871 *1823.21 p47*
Caldwell, William 20; South Carolina, 1812 *3476.30 p11*
Calene, Anna *SEE* Calene, Louis E.
Calene, Christine Pehrsdotter *SEE* Calene, Louis E.
Calene, Erick; Kansas, 1868 *777.40 p9*
Calene, Johanna; Kansas, 1873 *777.40 p16*
Calene, John 22; Kansas, 1870-1880 *777.40 p17*
Calene, Louis E.; Kansas, 1870 *777.40 p14*
  *Wife:*Christine Pehrsdotter
  *Daughter:*Anna
  *Son:*Peter L.
Calene, Louis L.; Kansas, 1870 *777.40 p14*
Calene, Martha Ersdotter *SEE* Calene, Olof

Calene, Olof; Kansas, 1869-1871 777.40 p9
*Wife:*Martha Ersdotter
Calene, Peter Erick; America, 1854 777.40 p15
Calene, Peter L. *SEE* Calene, Louis E.
Calet, Chas. 20; New Orleans, 1846 778.6 p56
Calevill, Moses 36; Ontario, 1871 1823.21 p47
Calewell, Danl. 18; North Carolina, 1774 1422.10 p58
Caley, Robert; Ohio, 1840 2763.1 p7
Caley, Thomas; Ohio, 1844 2763.1 p7
Calhone, Alexander; Massachusetts, 1755-1761 1642 p110
Calhoun, Mary 23; Ontario, 1871 1823.21 p47
Calhoven, Gilbert 59; Ontario, 1871 1823.21 p47
Calihan, Ann 35; Michigan, 1880 4491.39 p4
Calina, John Leon; North Carolina, 1827-1832 1088.45 p4
Calkeen, Mary; Ontario, 1835 3160.1 p150
Calkeen, Nancy; Ontario, 1835 3160.1 p150
Call, N.; California, 1868 1131.61 p89
Callaghan, James; Worcester, MA, 1822-1840 3274.55 p74
Callaghan, Jas 19; Ontario, 1871 1823.21 p47
Callaghan, John 35; Ontario, 1871 1823.17 p22
Callaghan, Owen; Iowa, 1876 1211.15 p9
Callaghan, Terence 36; Ontario, 1871 1823.21 p47
Callaghan, William 56; Ontario, 1871 1823.21 p47
Callahan, Catherine 41; Michigan, 1880 4491.39 p4
Callahan, Catherine 28; Ontario, 1871 1823.21 p47
Callahan, Charles; Boston, 1762 1642 p48
Callahan, Dan 47; Michigan, 1880 4491.39 p4
Callahan, Danl 20; St. Johns, N.F., 1811 1053.20 p21
Callahan, James 69; Michigan, 1880 4491.39 p4
Callahan, James; Quebec, 1834 471.10 p87
Callahan, James; Vermont, 1834 471.10 p87
Callahan, John; Boston, 1764 1642 p33
Callahan, John; Boston, 1764 1642 p33
Callahan, John; Boston, 1765 1642 p35
Callahan, John; Boston, 1773 1642 p49
Callahan, John; Boston, 1774 1642 p50
Callahan, Newport; Boston, 1752-1760 1642 p30
Callahan, Patrick 10; Ontario, 1871 1823.21 p47
Callahan, Rebecca; Boston, 1752-1760 1642 p30
Callahan, Rose T. 60; Michigan, 1880 4491.39 p4
Callahane, Mary; Boston, 1767 1642 p38
Callanan, Mary; Boston, 1758 1642 p47
Callanan, Thomas 28; Ontario, 1871 1823.17 p22
Callault, Abraham; Quebec, 1661 9221.17 p451
Callault, Mrs. Abraham; Quebec, 1662 9221.17 p482
With 2 children
Callehan, Ann; Boston, 1766 1642 p37
With 2 children
Callehan, Daniel; Marblehead, MA, 1768 1642 p73
Callehand, Mary; Roxbury, MA, 1734 1642 p108
Callemont, Jean; Quebec, 1642 9221.17 p113
Callen, James; Massachusetts, 1675-1676 1642 p128
Callen, James; New Orleans, 1850 7242.30 p137
Callen, John; New Orleans, 1850 7242.30 p137
Callen, M.; New Orleans, 1850 7242.30 p137
Callen, Wm.; Ohio, 1840-1897 8365.35 p15
Callender, Thomas 38; Ontario, 1871 1823.17 p22
Callerand, Franz 47; Port uncertain, 1843 778.6 p57
Calley, . . .; New England, 1788-1888 9228.50 p151
Callihan, Margaret; Boston, 1744 1642 p45
Calliman, Thomas 27; Ontario, 1871 1823.17 p22
Callinan, Thomas; Louisiana, 1841-1844 4981.45 p210
Callio, Jos.; North Carolina, 1710 3629.40 p8
Callisen, Ernst; Chile, 1852 1192.4 p54
Callison, Wm.; Illinois, 1834-1900 6020.5 p131
Callohue, Hugh; Massachusetts, 1675-1676 1642 p127
Callow, James; Missouri, 1890 3276.1 p1
Callow, John; Missouri, 1887 3276.1 p1
Callow, Thomas; Marston's Wharf, 1782 8529.30 p10
Callowan, W. 32; Ontario, 1871 1823.21 p47
Callum, Donald 55; Ontario, 1871 1823.17 p22
Callum, Duncan 64; Ontario, 1871 1823.17 p22
Callum, Francis 32; Ontario, 1871 1823.17 p22
Callum, William 50; Ontario, 1871 1823.17 p22
Calmel, Francois 27; Port uncertain, 1848 778.6 p57
Calmelat, Jacob 43; Port uncertain, 1845 778.6 p57
Calmelat, Margarite 26; Port uncertain, 1845 778.6 p57
Calmelat, Maria 18; Port uncertain, 1845 778.6 p57
Calmillon, John Baptist; Ohio, 1809-1852 4511.35 p7
Calonne, Desiree; Wisconsin, 1878 1495.20 p12
Calonne, Desiree; Wisconsin, 1878 1495.20 p12
Calonne, Isidore; Wisconsin, 1871 1495.20 p12
Calonne, Marie Agnes Josephe; Wisconsin, 1871 1495.20 p12
Caltaut, Emery; Quebec, 1642 9221.17 p113
Caltenbaugh, Martin; Washington, 1884 2770.40 p192
Calvert, David 49; Ontario, 1871 1823.17 p22
Calvert, John 47; Ontario, 1871 1823.21 p47
Calvert, John 66; Ontario, 1871 1823.17 p22
Calvert, Peter; North Carolina, 1710 3629.40 p8
*Wife:*Saloma
Calvert, Saloma *SEE* Calvert, Peter
Calvi, Mr. 28; New Orleans, 1848 778.6 p57
Calvignac, Mr. 24; America, 1846 778.6 p57
Cam, Michael; Nova Scotia, 1839 7078 p80
Cam, William 18; Ontario, 1871 1823.17 p22
Cambarre, . . .; Quebec, 1660 9221.17 p432
Cambas, Francois 4; America, 1846 778.6 p57
Cambeilh, Mr. 39; America, 1747 778.6 p57
Cambell, Charles 36; Ontario, 1871 1823.17 p22
Cambell, J.R.; New York, NY, 1843 6412.40 p147
Camber, Veuve Antoinette 52; New Orleans, 1843 778.6 p57
Cambert, Augt. 26; America, 1848 778.6 p57
Camblat, Charol 38; America, 1841 778.6 p57
Camble, Donald 50; Ontario, 1871 1823.21 p48
Camble, Duncan 26; Ontario, 1871 1823.21 p48
Camble, Duncan 57; Ontario, 1871 1823.21 p48
Cambot, Louis 23; Port uncertain, 1848 778.6 p57
Cambre, Eugene; Illinois, 1856 6079.1 p3
Camelon, David 40; Ontario, 1871 1823.21 p48
Camerallo, Petune; Louisiana, 1874 4981.45 p131
Cameran, Hugh 40; Ontario, 1871 1823.17 p22
Cameron, . . . 35; Ontario, 1871 1823.21 p48
Cameron, . . . 40; Ontario, 1871 1823.17 p22
Cameron, Alexander 40; Ontario, 1871 1823.21 p48
Cameron, Allan 28; North Carolina, 1774 1422.10 p58
Cameron, Allan 28; North Carolina, 1774 1422.10 p62
Cameron, Allan 70; Ontario, 1871 1823.21 p48
Cameron, Angus 18; North Carolina, 1774 1422.10 p58
Cameron, Angus 18; North Carolina, 1774 1422.10 p62
Cameron, Angus 40; Ontario, 1871 1823.21 p48
Cameron, Angus 59; Ontario, 1871 1823.17 p22
Cameron, Archibald 58; Ontario, 1871 1823.21 p48
Cameron, Archibald A. 30; Ontario, 1871 1823.21 p48
Cameron, Archy 47; Ontario, 1871 1823.21 p48
Cameron, Catherine 50; Ontario, 1871 1823.21 p48
Cameron, Charles 40; Michigan, 1880 4491.33 p4
Cameron, Christina 62; Ontario, 1871 1823.17 p22
Cameron, Colin 73; Ontario, 1871 1823.17 p22
Cameron, Donald 41; New York, NY, 1835 5024.1 p136
Cameron, Donald 34; Ontario, 1871 1823.21 p48
Cameron, Donald 36; Ontario, 1871 1823.21 p48
Cameron, Donald 45; Ontario, 1871 1823.17 p22
Cameron, Donald 73; Ontario, 1871 1823.21 p48
Cameron, Donald 74; Ontario, 1871 1823.21 p48
Cameron, Donald; Toronto, 1844 2910.35 p113
Cameron, Duff 52; Ontario, 1871 1823.21 p48
Cameron, Duncan 52; Ontario, 1871 1823.17 p22
Cameron, Ewin; North Carolina, 1835 1088.45 p4
Cameron, George 3; New York, NY, 1835 5024.1 p136
Cameron, George 30; Ontario, 1871 1823.17 p22
Cameron, H. D. 37; Ontario, 1871 1823.21 p48
Cameron, Hector 51; Ontario, 1871 1823.21 p48
Cameron, Hugh 44; Ontario, 1871 1823.21 p48
Cameron, Isabella 34; Ontario, 1871 1823.17 p22
Cameron, James 10; New York, NY, 1835 5024.1 p136
Cameron, James 51; Ontario, 1871 1823.21 p48
Cameron, James 57; Ontario, 1871 1823.17 p22
Cameron, Jannet 52; Ontario, 1871 1823.17 p22
Cameron, Jean 12; New York, NY, 1835 5024.1 p136
Cameron, Jean 32; New York, NY, 1835 5024.1 p136
Cameron, Jeannette 44; Ontario, 1871 1823.17 p22
Cameron, John 7; New York, NY, 1835 5024.1 p136
Cameron, John; North Carolina, 1830 1088.45 p4
Cameron, John; Ohio, 1809-1852 4511.35 p9
Cameron, John 37; Ontario, 1871 1823.17 p23
Cameron, John 37; Ontario, 1871 1823.21 p48
Cameron, John 40; Ontario, 1871 1823.21 p48
Cameron, John 40; Ontario, 1871 1823.21 p48
Cameron, John 41; Ontario, 1871 1823.21 p48
Cameron, John 46; Ontario, 1871 1823.17 p23
Cameron, John 47; Ontario, 1871 1823.17 p22
Cameron, John 56; Ontario, 1871 1823.17 p22
Cameron, John 64; Ontario, 1871 1823.21 p48
Cameron, John 66; Ontario, 1871 1823.21 p48
Cameron, John 76; Ontario, 1871 1823.21 p48
Cameron, John B. 25; Michigan, 1880 4491.36 p3
Cameron, John Wilson; North Carolina, 1840 1088.45 p4
Cameron, Katrine 21; North Carolina, 1774 1422.10 p58
Cameron, Katrine 21; North Carolina, 1774 1422.10 p62
Cameron, Malcolm 48; Ontario, 1871 1823.21 p48
Cameron, Malcolm 50; Ontario, 1871 1823.17 p23
Cameron, Malcolm 80; Ontario, 1871 1823.21 p48
Cameron, Margaret 47; Ontario, 1871 1823.17 p23
Cameron, Mary 2; New York, NY, 1835 5024.1 p136
Cameron, Mary 80; Ontario, 1871 1823.21 p48
Cameron, Mary Ann 34; Ontario, 1871 1823.21 p48
Cameron, William 34; Ontario, 1871 1823.21 p48
Cameron, William 55; Ontario, 1871 1823.21 p48
Camille, Niclaus 35; New Orleans, 1848 778.6 p57
Camis, James 32; Ontario, 1871 1823.21 p48
Cammeron, Alexander 40; Ontario, 1871 1823.17 p23
Cammeron, Ann 36; Ontario, 1871 1823.21 p49
Cammeron, Donald 60; Ontario, 1871 1823.17 p23
Cammeron, Donald 80; Ontario, 1871 1823.21 p49
Cammeron, Duncan 55; Ontario, 1871 1823.17 p23
Cammeron, John 47; Ontario, 1871 1823.21 p49
Cammeron, Margaret 30; Ontario, 1871 1823.21 p49
Cammeron, Margaret 70; Ontario, 1871 1823.21 p49
Camobat, Juan; Louisiana, 1874-1875 4981.45 p298
Camois, P. 14; America, 1846 778.6 p57
Camors, P. 14; America, 1846 778.6 p57
Camort, Bertrand 18; Port uncertain, 1846 778.6 p57
Campagne, Celestin 16; America, 1845 778.6 p57
Campagne, P. 17; New Orleans, 1848 778.6 p57
Campball, Robert 67; Ontario, 1871 1823.21 p49
Campbell, Albert 25; Ontario, 1871 1823.17 p23
Campbell, Alex 25; Ontario, 1871 1823.21 p49
Campbell, Alex 62; Ontario, 1871 1823.21 p49
Campbell, Alexander; New York, 1738 8277.31 p114
Campbell, Alexander 3; Ontario, 1871 1823.17 p23
Campbell, Alexander 29; Ontario, 1871 1823.21 p49
Campbell, Alexander 40; Ontario, 1871 1823.21 p49
Campbell, Alexander 40; Ontario, 1871 1823.21 p49
Campbell, Alexander 46; Ontario, 1871 1823.17 p23
Campbell, Alexander 60; Ontario, 1871 1823.21 p49
Campbell, Alexr. 12; North Carolina, 1774 1422.10 p58
Campbell, Almeda 13; Michigan, 1880 4491.39 p4
Campbell, Amos 14; Michigan, 1880 4491.39 p4
Campbell, Ann 19; North Carolina, 1774 1422.10 p58
Campbell, Ann 19; North Carolina, 1774 1422.10 p62
Campbell, Ann 19; Ontario, 1871 1823.21 p49
Campbell, Anna McDougall *SEE* Campbell, James
Campbell, Anna; New York, 1739 8277.31 p117
*Child:*Mary
*Child:*James
*Child:*Duncan
*Child:*Archibald
*Child:*Isabel
Campbell, Anna *SEE* Campbell, Duncan
Campbell, Anna; New York, 1740 8277.31 p114
Campbell, Archabald 41; Ontario, 1871 1823.21 p49
Campbell, Archabald 55; Ontario, 1871 1823.21 p49
Campbell, Archd 6; Ontario, 1871 1823.21 p49
Campbell, Archibald 58; Michigan, 1880 4491.39 p4
Campbell, Archibald *SEE* Campbell, James
Campbell, Archibald *SEE* Campbell, Anna
Campbell, Archibald; New York, 1740 8277.31 p114
Campbell, Archibald 38; North Carolina, 1774 1422.10 p60
Campbell, Archibald 38; North Carolina, 1774 1422.10 p62
Campbell, Archibald 37; Ontario, 1871 1823.21 p49
Campbell, Archibald 50; Ontario, 1871 1823.21 p49
Campbell, Archibald 50; Ontario, 1871 1823.21 p49
Campbell, Archibald 53; Ontario, 1871 1823.21 p49
Campbell, C. 20; Ontario, 1871 1823.21 p49
Campbell, Catarine *SEE* Campbell, Duncan
Campbell, Catharine; New York, 1739 8277.31 p117
Campbell, Catherine; New York, 1739 8277.31 p114
Campbell, Catherine 62; Ontario, 1871 1823.17 p23
Campbell, Cathn 46; North Carolina, 1774 1422.10 p62
Campbell, Cathn. 46; North Carolina, 1774 1422.10 p58
Campbell, Charles 28; Ontario, 1871 1823.21 p49
Campbell, Charles 45; Ontario, 1871 1823.17 p23
Campbell, Charles C. 22; Michigan, 1880 4491.39 p4
Campbell, Colin; North Carolina, 1774 1422.10 p54
Campbell, Colin 38; Ontario, 1871 1823.21 p49
Campbell, Colin 41; Ontario, 1871 1823.21 p49
Campbell, Colin 45; Ontario, 1871 1823.21 p49
Campbell, Colin 54; Ontario, 1871 1823.21 p49
Campbell, D. B. 56; Ontario, 1871 1823.21 p49
Campbell, D. W. 65; Ontario, 1871 1823.21 p49
Campbell, Daniel 25; North Carolina, 1774 1422.10 p62
Campbell, Daniel 41; Ontario, 1871 1823.17 p23
Campbell, Daniel 55; Ontario, 1871 1823.21 p49
Campbell, Daniel; Philadelphia, 1778 8529.30 p2A
Campbell, Danl. 25; North Carolina, 1774 1422.10 p58
Campbell, David 47; Ontario, 1871 1823.21 p49
Campbell, David 57; Ontario, 1871 1823.21 p49
Campbell, Donald; New York, 1738 8277.31 p114
*Wife:*Mary McKay
*Child:*Robert
*Child:*James
*Child:*Isabel
*Child:*Margaret
Campbell, Donald 50; North Carolina, 1774 1422.10 p59
Campbell, Donald 40; Ontario, 1871 1823.17 p23
Campbell, Donald 40; Ontario, 1871 1823.21 p50
Campbell, Donald 41; Ontario, 1871 1823.21 p50
Campbell, Donald 44; Ontario, 1871 1823.21 p50
Campbell, Donald 44; Ontario, 1871 1823.21 p50
Campbell, Donald 53; Ontario, 1871 1823.21 p50

66 *FOR A COMPLETE EXPLANATION OF ENTRY, SEE "HOW TO READ A CITATION" SECTION*

Campbell, Donald 58; Ontario, 1871 ***1823.21*** *p50*
Campbell, Donald 60; Ontario, 1871 ***1823.17*** *p23*
Campbell, Donald 60; Ontario, 1871 ***1823.21*** *p50*
Campbell, Donald 66; Ontario, 1871 ***1823.21*** *p49*
Campbell, Dugal 49; Ontario, 1871 ***1823.17*** *p23*
Campbell, Dugd.; Prince Edward Island, 1771 ***3799.30*** *p41*
Campbell, Duncan; New York, 1739 ***8277.31*** *p114*
*Wife:*Sara Fraser
Campbell, Duncan *SEE* Campbell, Anna
Campbell, Duncan; New York, 1740 ***8277.31*** *p114*
*Wife:*Anna
*Daughter:*Catarine
Campbell, Duncan; New York, 1740 ***8277.31*** *p114*
Campbell, Duncan; North Carolina, 1775 ***1422.10*** *p59*
Campbell, Duncan; North Carolina, 1811-1812 ***1088.45*** *p4*
Campbell, Duncan 31; Ontario, 1871 ***1823.21*** *p50*
Campbell, Duncan 40; Ontario, 1871 ***1823.17*** *p23*
Campbell, Duncan 41; Ontario, 1871 ***1823.17*** *p23*
Campbell, Duncan 42; Ontario, 1871 ***1823.17*** *p23*
Campbell, Duncan 49; Ontario, 1871 ***1823.21*** *p50*
Campbell, Duncan 50; Ontario, 1871 ***1823.17*** *p23*
Campbell, Duncan 58; Ontario, 1871 ***1823.21*** *p50*
Campbell, Duncan 60; Ontario, 1871 ***1823.21*** *p50*
Campbell, Duncan 64; Ontario, 1871 ***1823.21*** *p50*
Campbell, Duncan 69; Ontario, 1871 ***1823.21*** *p50*
Campbell, Duncan 78; Ontario, 1871 ***1823.17*** *p23*
Campbell, Duncan; Toronto, 1844 ***2910.35*** *p113*
Campbell, Edward 34; Ontario, 1871 ***1823.17*** *p23*
Campbell, Edward M. 26; Michigan, 1880 ***4491.39*** *p4*
Campbell, Edwd. 57; Ontario, 1871 ***1823.17*** *p23*
Campbell, Elen 47; Ontario, 1871 ***1823.21*** *p50*
Campbell, Elizabeth *SEE* Campbell, James
Campbell, Elizabeth; New York, 1738 ***8277.31*** *p118*
Campbell, Elizabeth 84; Ontario, 1871 ***1823.21*** *p50*
Campbell, Emily R. 37; Ontario, 1871 ***1823.21*** *p50*
Campbell, Euphemia 55; Ontario, 1871 ***1823.21*** *p50*
Campbell, Flory 54; Ontario, 1871 ***1823.21*** *p50*
Campbell, Gavin 23; Ontario, 1871 ***1823.17*** *p23*
Campbell, George 50; Ontario, 1871 ***1823.17*** *p23*
Campbell, George 60; Ontario, 1871 ***1823.21*** *p50*
Campbell, Girzie 6; North Carolina, 1774 ***1422.10*** *p60*
Campbell, Grizel 6; North Carolina, 1774 ***1422.10*** *p62*
Campbell, Hector 16; North Carolina, 1774 ***1422.10*** *p58*
Campbell, Hugh; North Carolina, 1821 ***1088.45*** *p5*
Campbell, Humphrey 35; Ontario, 1871 ***1823.17*** *p23*
Campbell, Humphrey 61; Ontario, 1871 ***1823.21*** *p50*
Campbell, Isabel *SEE* Campbell, Donald
Campbell, Isabel *SEE* Campbell, Anna
Campbell, Issabella 67; Ontario, 1871 ***1823.17*** *p23*
Campbell, J. C. 44; Ontario, 1871 ***1823.21*** *p50*
Campbell, J.R.; New York, NY, 1843 ***6412.40*** *p147*
Campbell, James *SEE* Campbell, Donald
Campbell, James; New York, 1738 ***8277.31*** *p114*
*Wife:*Anna McDougall
*Child:*Laughlin
*Child:*Elizabeth
*Child:*Janet
*Child:*Archibald
Campbell, James *SEE* Campbell, Anna
Campbell, James; North Carolina, 1808-1813 ***1088.45*** *p5*
Campbell, James; North Carolina, 1830 ***1088.45*** *p5*
Campbell, James; Ohio, 1809-1852 ***4511.35*** *p7*
Campbell, James 24; Ontario, 1871 ***1823.17*** *p23*
Campbell, James 38; Ontario, 1871 ***1823.17*** *p23*
Campbell, James 38; Ontario, 1871 ***1823.21*** *p50*
Campbell, James 41; Ontario, 1871 ***1823.21*** *p50*
Campbell, James 60; Ontario, 1871 ***1823.21*** *p50*
Campbell, James 68; Ontario, 1871 ***1823.21*** *p50*
Campbell, James; Washington, 1883 ***2770.40*** *p136*
Campbell, James; Washington, 1889 ***2770.40*** *p26*
Campbell, James A.; North Carolina, 1838 ***1088.45*** *p5*
Campbell, Jane 55; Ontario, 1871 ***1823.21*** *p50*
Campbell, Janet *SEE* Campbell, James
Campbell, Janette 40; Ontario, 1871 ***1823.21*** *p51*
Campbell, Jannette 19; Ontario, 1871 ***1823.21*** *p51*
Campbell, Jean 24; North Carolina, 1774 ***1422.10*** *p57*
Campbell, Jean 32; North Carolina, 1774 ***1422.10*** *p60*
Campbell, Jean 32; North Carolina, 1774 ***1422.10*** *p62*
Campbell, Jesse 36; Ontario, 1871 ***1823.21*** *p51*
Campbell, John; Brunswick, NC, 1767 ***1422.10*** *p61*
Campbell, John; New York, 1740 ***8277.31*** *p114*
Campbell, John; North Carolina, 1835 ***1088.45*** *p5*
Campbell, John; Ohio, 1809-1852 ***4511.35*** *p7*
Campbell, John 23; Ontario, 1871 ***1823.21*** *p51*
Campbell, John 38; Ontario, 1871 ***1823.21*** *p51*
Campbell, John 40; Ontario, 1871 ***1823.17*** *p23*
Campbell, John 40; Ontario, 1871 ***1823.21*** *p51*
Campbell, John 43; Ontario, 1871 ***1823.17*** *p23*
Campbell, John 44; Ontario, 1871 ***1823.21*** *p51*
Campbell, John 47; Ontario, 1871 ***1823.21*** *p51*
Campbell, John 48; Ontario, 1871 ***1823.21*** *p51*
Campbell, John 50; Ontario, 1871 ***1823.21*** *p51*
Campbell, John 50; Ontario, 1871 ***1823.21*** *p51*
Campbell, John 53; Ontario, 1871 ***1823.21*** *p51*
Campbell, John 55; Ontario, 1871 ***1823.21*** *p51*
Campbell, John 57; Ontario, 1871 ***1823.17*** *p23*
Campbell, John 57; Ontario, 1871 ***1823.21*** *p51*
Campbell, John 58; Ontario, 1871 ***1823.21*** *p51*
Campbell, John 59; Ontario, 1871 ***1823.21*** *p51*
Campbell, John 60; Ontario, 1871 ***1823.17*** *p23*
Campbell, John 60; Ontario, 1871 ***1823.21*** *p51*
Campbell, John 61; Ontario, 1871 ***1823.21*** *p51*
Campbell, John 63; Ontario, 1871 ***1823.21*** *p51*
Campbell, John 70; Ontario, 1871 ***1823.17*** *p23*
Campbell, John 74; Ontario, 1871 ***1823.17*** *p23*
Campbell, John 75; Ontario, 1871 ***1823.21*** *p51*
Campbell, John 79; Ontario, 1871 ***1823.21*** *p51*
Campbell, John; Philadelphia, 1862 ***8513.31*** *p298*
Campbell, John P. 52; Ontario, 1871 ***1823.21*** *p51*
Campbell, John R. 62; Ontario, 1871 ***1823.21*** *p51*
Campbell, John S. 55; Ontario, 1871 ***1823.21*** *p51*
Campbell, Joseph 30; Ontario, 1871 ***1823.17*** *p24*
Campbell, Katherine 32; North Carolina, 1775 ***1422.10*** *p59*
Campbell, Lachlan 2; North Carolina, 1774 ***1422.10*** *p60*
Campbell, Lachlan 2; North Carolina, 1774 ***1422.10*** *p62*
Campbell, Laughlin *SEE* Campbell, James
Campbell, Laura 10; Ontario, 1871 ***1823.21*** *p51*
Campbell, Laura 9; Quebec, 1870 ***8364.32*** *p22*
Campbell, Lewis K.; Ohio, 1868 ***3580.20*** *p31*
Campbell, Lewis K.; Ohio, 1868 ***6020.12*** *p6*
Campbell, Lily 34; Ontario, 1871 ***1823.21*** *p51*
Campbell, Malcolm; New York, 1740 ***8277.31*** *p114*
Campbell, Malcolm 37; Ontario, 1871 ***1823.17*** *p24*
Campbell, Malcolm 52; Ontario, 1871 ***1823.21*** *p51*
Campbell, Malcolm 56; Ontario, 1871 ***1823.21*** *p51*
Campbell, Malcolm 58; Ontario, 1871 ***1823.21*** *p51*
Campbell, Malcom 52; Ontario, 1871 ***1823.17*** *p24*
Campbell, Margaret *SEE* Campbell, Donald
Campbell, Margret 20; Ontario, 1871 ***1823.21*** *p51*
Campbell, Mary 47; Michigan, 1880 ***4491.39*** *p4*
Campbell, Mary McKay *SEE* Campbell, Donald
Campbell, Mary; New York, 1738 ***8277.31*** *p114*
Campbell, Mary; New York, 1738 ***8277.31*** *p116*
Campbell, Mary *SEE* Campbell, Anna
Campbell, Mary 7; North Carolina, 1774 ***1422.10*** *p60*
Campbell, Mary 7; North Carolina, 1774 ***1422.10*** *p62*
Campbell, Mary 45; Ontario, 1871 ***1823.21*** *p51*
Campbell, Mary 50; Ontario, 1871 ***1823.21*** *p51*
Campbell, Mary 83; Ontario, 1871 ***1823.21*** *p51*
Campbell, Mary 11; Quebec, 1870 ***8364.32*** *p22*
Campbell, Neil 32; Ontario, 1871 ***1823.21*** *p51*
Campbell, Neil 38; Ontario, 1871 ***1823.17*** *p24*
Campbell, Neil 45; Ontario, 1871 ***1823.17*** *p24*
Campbell, Niel; Quebec, 1786 ***1416.15*** *p8*
Campbell, Norman 35; Ontario, 1871 ***1823.21*** *p52*
Campbell, Peter 41; Ontario, 1871 ***1823.21*** *p52*
Campbell, Peter 53; Ontario, 1871 ***1823.17*** *p24*
Campbell, Peter 56; Ontario, 1871 ***1823.21*** *p52*
Campbell, Peter 70; Ontario, 1871 ***1823.21*** *p52*
Campbell, Richard 51; Ontario, 1871 ***1823.21*** *p52*
Campbell, Robert *SEE* Campbell, Donald
Campbell, Robert; North Carolina, 1835 ***1088.45*** *p5*
Campbell, Robert 2; North Carolina, 1775 ***1422.10*** *p59*
Campbell, Robert 38; Ontario, 1871 ***1823.17*** *p24*
Campbell, Robert 40; Ontario, 1871 ***1823.21*** *p52*
Campbell, Robert 46; Ontario, 1871 ***1823.17*** *p24*
Campbell, Robert 48; Ontario, 1871 ***1823.17*** *p24*
Campbell, Robert 50; Ontario, 1871 ***1823.21*** *p52*
Campbell, Robert 52; Ontario, 1871 ***1823.17*** *p24*
Campbell, Robert 71; Ontario, 1871 ***1823.21*** *p52*
Campbell, Robert 75; Ontario, 1871 ***1823.17*** *p24*
Campbell, Robert; Washington, 1879 ***2770.40*** *p134*
Campbell, Robt. 39; Ontario, 1871 ***1823.17*** *p24*
Campbell, Ronald; New York, 1738 ***8277.31*** *p114*
Campbell, Samuel 24; Indiana, 1881-1884 ***9076.20*** *p71*
Campbell, Samuel 26; Ontario, 1871 ***1823.17*** *p24*
Campbell, Sara Fraser *SEE* Campbell, Duncan
Campbell, Sarah 16; Michigan, 1880 ***4491.39*** *p4*
Campbell, Sarah A.; Long Island, 1853 ***8513.31*** *p306*
Campbell, Sylvester 72; Ontario, 1871 ***1823.21*** *p52*
Campbell, Thomas; Ohio, 1841 ***3580.20*** *p31*
Campbell, Thomas; Ohio, 1841 ***6020.12*** *p6*
Campbell, Thomas 54; Ontario, 1871 ***1823.21*** *p52*
Campbell, Thomas 54; Ontario, 1871 ***1823.21*** *p52*
Campbell, Thomas; Philadelphia, 1777 ***8529.30*** *p7A*
Campbell, W. H. 21; Ontario, 1871 ***1823.17*** *p24*
Campbell, William 18; Michigan, 1880 ***4491.39*** *p5*
Campbell, William 28; North Carolina, 1775 ***1422.10*** *p59*
Campbell, William; Ohio, 1870 ***3580.20*** *p31*
Campbell, William 31; Ontario, 1871 ***1823.21*** *p52*
Campbell, William 33; Ontario, 1871 ***1823.21*** *p52*
Campbell, William 35; Ontario, 1871 ***1823.21*** *p52*
Campbell, William 37; Ontario, 1871 ***1823.17*** *p24*
Campbell, William 43; Ontario, 1871 ***1823.21*** *p52*
Campbell, William 50; Ontario, 1871 ***1823.21*** *p52*
Campbell, William 51; Ontario, 1871 ***1823.21*** *p52*
Campbell, William 53; Ontario, 1871 ***1823.17*** *p24*
Campbell, William 57; Ontario, 1871 ***1823.21*** *p52*
Campbell, William; Washington, 1884 ***2770.40*** *p192*
Campbell, William T.; Ohio, 1870 ***6020.12*** *p6*
Campbell, Wm 52; Ontario, 1871 ***1823.21*** *p52*
Campeau, Etienne 25; Montreal, 1662 ***9221.17*** *p496*
Camphil, John; North Carolina, 1860 ***1088.45*** *p5*
Campion, Jean; Quebec, 1659 ***9221.17*** *p413*
Campion, John; Marston's Wharf, 1782 ***8529.30*** *p10*
Campion, Marie; Quebec, 1670 ***4514.3*** *p286*
Campion, Rene; Quebec, 1659 ***9221.17*** *p413*
Campistrons, Dominique 25; New Orleans, 1845 ***778.6*** *p57*
Campistrons, Jn. Marie 23; New Orleans, 1845 ***778.6*** *p57*
Cample, Daniel; Philadelphia, 1778 ***8529.30*** *p2A*
Campo, Thomas; Louisiana, 1874 ***4981.45*** *p131*
Campo, Vincent 30; America, 1842 ***778.6*** *p57*
Camus, Catherine 20; Quebec, 1656 ***9221.17*** *p333*
Camus, Claude 23; Quebec, 1652 ***9221.17*** *p256*
Camus, Claude 23; Quebec, 1652 ***9221.17*** *p256*
Camus, Eugene T.; Illinois, 1852 ***6079.1*** *p3*
Camus, Henri M.; Illinois, 1852 ***6079.1*** *p3*
Camus, Jean-Baptiste 19; Texas, 1843 ***778.6*** *p57*
Camus, Pierre 35; Texas, 1843 ***778.6*** *p57*
Can, Andrew 60; Ontario, 1871 ***1823.17*** *p24*
Canabe, Dame 32; New Orleans, 1843 ***778.6*** *p57*
Canada, Daniel; Massachusetts, 1675-1676 ***1642*** *p127*
Canada, Daniel 58; Ontario, 1871 ***1823.21*** *p52*
Canada, George 79; Ontario, 1871 ***1823.21*** *p52*
Canada, Moses 45; Ontario, 1871 ***1823.21*** *p52*
Canada, Sally 38; Ontario, 1871 ***1823.21*** *p52*
Canada, Sarah 19; Ontario, 1871 ***1823.21*** *p52*
Canadou, Pierre 30; Quebec, 1661 ***9221.17*** *p451*
Canard, Marie-Madeleine; Quebec, 1671 ***4514.3*** *p286*
Canaway, John; New England, 1745 ***1642*** *p27*
Candelaria, Mr. 6 months; Texas, 1848 ***778.6*** *p57*
Candelaria, Rovira 22; Texas, 1848 ***778.6*** *p57*
Candelea, Patrick; Massachusetts, 1771 ***1642*** *p66*
Candide, Mr. 45; New Orleans, 1848 ***778.6*** *p57*
Candidus, Lisette Reiniger *SEE* Candidus, William
Candidus, William; Philadelphia, 1843 ***8513.31*** *p298*
*Wife:*Lisette Reiniger
Candler, Charles 14; Quebec, 1870 ***8364.32*** *p22*
Candon, Saml M. 47; Ontario, 1871 ***1823.21*** *p52*
Candwell, Edmund J. 27; Ontario, 1871 ***1823.21*** *p52*
Candy, William 36; Ontario, 1871 ***1823.17*** *p24*
Caneat, Jean 19; New Orleans, 1848 ***778.6*** *p57*
Canelon, J. B. 17; America, 1846 ***778.6*** *p57*
Caney, James; Philadelphia, 1849-1851 ***5720.10*** *p377*
Caney, James; Philadelphia, 1849 ***5720.10*** *p377*
Canfill, Mary; Halifax, N.S., 1827 ***7009.9*** *p62*
Canitz, Sebastian; Philadelphia, 1778 ***8529.30*** *p2A*
Canivet, Elisabeth Esther; Idaho, 1822-1912 ***9228.50*** *p151*
Canivet, Elizabeth Esther; Utah, 1855 ***9228.50*** *p656*
Canmun, Nathan 22; Ontario, 1871 ***1823.21*** *p52*
Cann, Jane Langlois *SEE* Cann, John
Cann, John; Nova Scotia, 1731-1800 ***9228.50*** *p321*
*Wife:*Jane Langlois
Cann, Samuel 47; Ontario, 1871 ***1823.17*** *p24*
Cann, William 30; Ontario, 1871 ***1823.21*** *p52*
Cann, William 50; Ontario, 1871 ***1823.21*** *p52*
Cannaly, John; Boston, 1714 ***1642*** *p24*
Canne, Franz Thomas; America, 1882 ***5475.1*** *p229*
Cannell, Philip 60; Ontario, 1871 ***1823.21*** *p52*
Cannell, Roger 25; St. Johns, N.F., 1811 ***1053.20*** *p20*
Cannell-Cross Family ; Massachusetts, n.d. ***9228.50*** *p170*
Canning, Thomas 52; Ontario, 1871 ***1823.21*** *p52*
Cannino, Salvatore; Louisiana, 1874-1875 ***4981.45*** *p298*
Cannivet, Margarethe; America, 1874 ***5475.1*** *p140*
Cannom, John 55; Ontario, 1871 ***1823.21*** *p52*
Cannon, George; Boston, 1775 ***8529.30*** *p2A*
Cannon, John; Louisiana, 1841-1844 ***4981.45*** *p210*
Cannon, John; Plymouth, MA, 1621 ***1642*** *p1*
Cannon, Michael; America, 1779 ***8529.30*** *p10*
Cannon, Obadia 23; Ontario, 1871 ***1823.21*** *p52*
Cano, Ludwig; Philadelphia, 1876 ***8513.31*** *p298*
*Wife:*Wilhelmina Walzinger
Cano, Wilhelmina Walzinger *SEE* Cano, Ludwig
Canon, Thomas; Boston, 1832 ***3274.55*** *p72*
Canon, Thomas 27; Ontario, 1871 ***1823.21*** *p52*
Canonge, Placide 26; New Orleans, 1848 ***778.6*** *p57*
Canot, Guillom 28; New Orleans, 1840 ***778.6*** *p58*
Canot, Joseph 27; New Orleans, 1840 ***778.6*** *p58*
Cansoan, Bernard 36; Ontario, 1871 ***1823.17*** *p24*
Canterre, Mr. 28; New Orleans, 1840 ***778.6*** *p58*
Canto, Francois; Quebec, 1660 ***9221.17*** *p432*

Canton, Elloner 58; Ontario, 1871 ***1823.17*** *p24*
Canton, F. 24; America, 1840 ***778.6*** *p58*
Canton, John; Maryland, 1673 ***1236.25*** *p49*
Canton, Peter 42; Ontario, 1871 ***1823.17*** *p24*
Canton, William 33; Ontario, 1871 ***1823.17*** *p24*
Cantwell, Pat; St. Johns, N.F., 1825 ***1053.15*** *p6*
Canty, Francois 34; America, 1843 ***778.6*** *p58*
Canty, John; Louisiana, 1874-1875 ***4981.45*** *p298*
Cap, Daniel; South Dakota, 1850-1910 ***2853.20*** *p246*
Cap, Jan; Iowa, 1870 ***2853.20*** *p202*
Capaeirelle, Philipe; Louisiana, 1874 ***4981.45*** *p131*
Capanady, F. 22; New Orleans, 1843 ***778.6*** *p58*
Capdevelle, P. 22; America, 1846 ***778.6*** *p58*
Capdeville, Mr. 20; Port uncertain, 1844 ***778.6*** *p58*
Capdeville, Augustin; Louisiana, 1836-1840 ***4981.45*** *p212*
Capdeville, John; Louisiana, 1874 ***4981.45*** *p131*
Capek, Alois; Wisconsin, 1858 ***2853.20*** *p327*
Capek, Jan V.; Cleveland, OH, 1871 ***2853.20*** *p503*
Capek, Jan V.; New York, NY, 1880 ***2853.20*** *p101*
Capek, Josef Horymir *SEE* Capek, Petr
Capek, Petr; Milwaukee, 1867 ***2853.20*** *p309*
*Son:*Josef Horymir
Capek, Tomas; New York, NY, 1880 ***2853.20*** *p101*
Capelle, Francoise 24; Quebec, 1650 ***9221.17*** *p224*
Capelle, Marie M. 23; America, 1846 ***778.6*** *p58*
Capen, Bernard; Dorchester, MA, 1633 ***117.5*** *p158*
Capereau, J. P. 26; New Orleans, 1843 ***778.6*** *p58*
Capes, James 54; Ontario, 1871 ***1823.17*** *p24*
Capesuis, J. P. 22; New York, NY, 1894 ***6512.1*** *p182*
Capey, James; Louisiana, 1874 ***4981.45*** *p131*
Capigns, S.; Louisiana, 1874-1875 ***4981.45*** *p298*
Capon, Mrs. 30; America, 1843 ***778.6*** *p58*
Capon, Ernest 26; America, 1843 ***778.6*** *p58*
Cappel, Dorothea; America, 1867 ***5475.1*** *p522*
Cappel, Karl; America, 1924 ***8023.44*** *p372*
Cappel, Luise; America, 1856 ***5475.1*** *p520*
Capprone, Louis 22; New Orleans, 1848 ***778.6*** *p58*
Caps, Anna Maria 5 *SEE* Caps, Martin
Caps, Barbara 11 *SEE* Caps, Martin
Caps, Katharina 14 *SEE* Caps, Martin
Caps, Margaretha 9 *SEE* Caps, Martin
Caps, Margaretha Saal 45 *SEE* Caps, Martin
Caps, Martin 42; America, 1858 ***2526.42*** *p199*
*Wife:*Margaretha Saal 45
*Daughter:*Barbara 11
*Daughter:*Margaretha 9
*Daughter:*Anna Maria 5
*Son:*Wilhelm 9
*Daughter:*Katharina 14
Caps, Wilhelm 9 *SEE* Caps, Martin
Capstick, Christopher 64; Ontario, 1871 ***1823.21*** *p52*
Capstick, Edward; Iowa, 1876 ***1211.15*** *p9*
Capstick, Johnathan 39; Ontario, 1871 ***1823.21*** *p52*
Capuret, Maria Ana; Philadelphia, 1854 ***8513.31*** *p294*
Car, Louis Joseph; Illinois, 1852 ***6079.1*** *p3*
Carace, Vincent; Quebec, 1655 ***9221.17*** *p321*
Carbery, Robert; Nova Scotia, 1839 ***7078*** *p80*
Carbery, Thomas; Nova Scotia, 1839 ***7078*** *p80*
Carbonai, Dn. 50; New Orleans, 1845 ***778.6*** *p58*
Carbonner, Jean-Baptiste 34; New Orleans, 1848 ***778.6*** *p58*
Carbonnet, Madeleine; Quebec, 1664 ***4514.3*** *p286*
Carcagno, Joachno; Louisiana, 1874-1875 ***4981.45*** *p298*
Carcelen, B.; Louisiana, 1836-1840 ***4981.45*** *p212*
Carcireux, Sylvine; Quebec, 1667 ***4514.3*** *p286*
Carcy, John; St. John, N.B., 1847 ***2978.15*** *p40*
Cardaillac, Mr. 42; Port uncertain, 1844 ***778.6*** *p58*
Cardeillai, Mr. 27; New Orleans, 1840 ***778.6*** *p58*
Cardell, Henry; Iowa, 1887 ***1211.15*** *p9*
Carden, Joseph; North Carolina, 1840 ***1088.45*** *p5*
Cardenas, Salvadore; Louisiana, 1874 ***4981.45*** *p131*
Carder, Isaac; Marston's Wharf, 1780 ***8529.30*** *p10*
Cardier, Celestin 10; America, 1840 ***778.6*** *p58*
Cardier, Constantin 12; America, 1840 ***778.6*** *p58*
Cardier, Eugene 14; America, 1840 ***778.6*** *p58*
Cardier, Hypolite 17; America, 1840 ***778.6*** *p58*
Cardier, Paul 45; America, 1840 ***778.6*** *p58*
Cardier, Pauline 6; America, 1840 ***778.6*** *p58*
Cardier, Sophie 43; America, 1840 ***778.6*** *p58*
Cardier, Virginie 2; America, 1840 ***778.6*** *p58*
Cardillon, Marguerite; Quebec, 1665 ***4514.3*** *p286*
Cardina, Claude 32; America, 1841 ***778.6*** *p58*
Cardina, Laura 23; America, 1841 ***778.6*** *p58*
Cardinal, Mr.; America, 1854 ***7420.1*** *p117*
With family
Cardinal, Adolphe 32; America, 1843 ***778.6*** *p58*
Cardinal, Anne-Michelle Garnier 26 *SEE* Cardinal, Simon
Cardinal, Jacques 5 *SEE* Cardinal, Simon
Cardinal, Jean 1 *SEE* Cardinal, Simon
Cardinal, Simon 35; Montreal, 1659 ***9221.17*** *p418*
*Wife:*Anne-Michelle Garnier 26
*Son:*Jacques 5
*Son:*Jean 1
Cardine, Adele 22; Louisiana, 1840 ***778.6*** *p58*
Cardry, Daniel; Utah, 1855 ***9228.50*** *p151*
*Relative:*Mary
Cardry, Mary *SEE* Cardry, Daniel
Careille, Marie 26; America, 1844 ***778.6*** *p58*
Carelius, William F.; Washington, 1880 ***2770.40*** *p134*
Carell, . . .; Boston, 1769 ***9228.50*** *p5*
Carell, Joseph; Boston, 1769 ***9228.50*** *p48*
Caresse, Vincent; Quebec, 1655 ***9221.17*** *p321*
Carey, . . .; Massachusetts, n.d. ***9228.50*** *p151*
Carey, Amelius 21; Ontario, 1871 ***1823.21*** *p53*
Carey, Anne; New Orleans, 1850 ***7242.30*** *p138*
Carey, Bernard; Ohio, 1809-1852 ***4511.35*** *p7*
Carey, Edward; Boston, 1766 ***1642*** *p37*
Carey, Elizabeth 54; Ontario, 1871 ***1823.21*** *p53*
Carey, James; New Orleans, 1850 ***7242.30*** *p138*
Carey, James; Ohio, 1809-1852 ***4511.35*** *p7*
Carey, John; Iowa, 1860 ***9228.50*** *p151*
Carey, John; New Orleans, 1850 ***7242.30*** *p138*
Carey, John 68; Ontario, 1871 ***1823.21*** *p53*
Carey, John E. 59; Ontario, 1871 ***1823.21*** *p53*
Carey, Mary; New Orleans, 1850 ***7242.30*** *p138*
Carey, Mary; Ontario, 1835 ***3160.1*** *p150*
Carey, Mary 12; Quebec, 1870 ***8364.32*** *p22*
Carey, Michael; New Orleans, 1850 ***7242.30*** *p138*
Carey, Mike; Louisiana, 1874-1875 ***4981.45*** *p298*
Carey, Patrick 34; Ontario, 1871 ***1823.17*** *p24*
Carey, Peggy; New Orleans, 1850 ***7242.30*** *p138*
Carey, Robert; New Orleans, 1850 ***7242.30*** *p138*
Carey, Sally; Massachusetts, 1797 ***9228.50*** *p489*
Carey, Thomas; New Orleans, 1850 ***7242.30*** *p138*
Carey, Timothy 39; Ontario, 1871 ***1823.21*** *p53*
Carfrae, Robert 67; Ontario, 1871 ***1823.21*** *p53*
Carfriee, Jane 77; Ontario, 1871 ***1823.17*** *p24*
Cargan, Jane; Wisconsin, 1842 ***9228.50*** *p145*
Carger, B.M.; Iowa, 1884 ***1211.15*** *p9*
Cargill, Elizabeth; New York, 1740 ***8277.31*** *p114*
Cargill, Hugh; Massachusetts, 1774-1799 ***1642*** *p101*
Cargill, James; New York, 1740 ***8277.31*** *p114*
Cargill, Jean; New York, 1739 ***8277.31*** *p114*
Cargill, John; New England, 1745 ***1642*** *p28*
Cargill, John; New York, 1740 ***8277.31*** *p114*
Cargonja, A.; Montreal, 1922 ***4514.4*** *p32*
Cargyle, Don.; Cape Fear, NC,, 1754 ***1422.10*** *p61*
Cargyle, John; Cape Fear, NC,, 1754 ***1422.10*** *p61*
Carian, Joseph 23; America, 1842 ***778.6*** *p58*
Carigan, Patrick 64; Ontario, 1871 ***1823.17*** *p24*
Carigan, Timothy 57; Ontario, 1871 ***1823.17*** *p24*
Carion duFresnoy, Philippe; Quebec, 1665 ***2314.30*** *p167*
Carion duFresnoy, Philippe; Quebec, 1665 ***2314.30*** *p177*
Carl, Alexander 17; Mississippi, 1847 ***778.6*** *p59*
Carl, August; Louisiana, 1836-1841 ***4981.45*** *p208*
Carl, Dennis 45; Ontario, 1871 ***1823.17*** *p24*
Carl, George 64; Mississippi, 1847 ***778.6*** *p59*
Carl, James 65; Ontario, 1871 ***1823.21*** *p53*
Carl, John; Illinois, 1856 ***6079.1*** *p3*
Carl, Maria; America, 1857 ***5475.1*** *p375*
Carl, Maria 18; Ontario, 1871 ***1823.17*** *p24*
Carl, Peter; America, 1889 ***5475.1*** *p343*
Carl, Theodore; Iowa, 1888 ***1211.15*** *p10*
Carl, Thomas 32; Michigan, 1880 ***4491.30*** *p5*
Carl, Wilhelmine 66; America, 1864 ***5475.1*** *p45*
Carla, John; Washington, 1884 ***2770.40*** *p192*
Carlaion, John; Boston, 1754 ***1642*** *p47*
Carland, William; Philadelphia, 1858 ***5720.10*** *p378*
Carlbeck, C.W.; New Orleans, 1847 ***6412.40*** *p149*
Carleton, Mary; Maryland, 1672 ***1236.25*** *p47*
Carlier, Francoise; Montreal, 1679 ***4514.3*** *p286*
Carlier, Marie; Quebec, 1670 ***4514.3*** *p286*
Carling, Bernard 30; Ontario, 1871 ***1823.21*** *p53*
Carling, Edward 48; Ontario, 1871 ***1823.21*** *p53*
Carling, Margaret 84; Ontario, 1871 ***1823.21*** *p53*
Carling, Peter 31; Ontario, 1871 ***1823.21*** *p53*
Carling, Thomas 44; Ontario, 1871 ***1823.21*** *p53*
Carling, Thomas 73; Ontario, 1871 ***1823.21*** *p53*
Carlinofski, Gottfried; America, 1834 ***5475.1*** *p467*
*Son:*Nikolaus
*Niece:*Maria Wilhelma
Carlinofski, Maria Wilhelma *SEE* Carlinofski, Gottfried
Carlinofski, Nikolaus; America, 1833 ***5475.1*** *p467*
Carlinofski, Nikolaus *SEE* Carlinofski, Gottfried
Carlinoski, Gottfried; America, 1834 ***5475.1*** *p467*
*Son:*Nikolaus
*Niece:*Maria Wilhelma
Carlinoski, Maria Wilhelma *SEE* Carlinoski, Gottfried
Carlinoski, Nikolaus *SEE* Carlinoski, Gottfried
Carlisle, Mary A.; New York, 1856 ***8513.31*** *p426*
Carll, Hugh 22; Ontario, 1871 ***1823.17*** *p24*
Carlo, Jno.; Louisiana, 1874-1875 ***4981.45*** *p298*
Carlo, John; Ohio, 1807 ***9228.50*** *p152*
Carlogh, Adolof; New Jersey, 1773-1774 ***927.31*** *p2*
Carlogh, John; New Jersey, 1773-1774 ***927.31*** *p2*
Carlon, Henry; Louisiana, 1874 ***4981.45*** *p131*
Carlough, Henry; New Jersey, 1773-1774 ***927.31*** *p3*
Carlow, John; Ohio, 1807 ***9228.50*** *p57*
Carlow, John; Ohio, 1807 ***9228.50*** *p152*
Carlson, A.; Cleveland, OH, 1891-1896 ***9722.10*** *p117*
Carlson, Albert; Cleveland, OH, 1888-1895 ***9722.10*** *p117*
Carlson, Alfred; Cleveland, OH, 1892-1902 ***9722.10*** *p117*
Carlson, Alfred; Cleveland, OH, 1893-1903 ***9722.10*** *p118*
Carlson, Anna Augusta; St. Paul, MN, 1888 ***1865.50*** *p42*
Carlson, Anna Ulrika; Minnesota, 1887-1888 ***1865.50*** *p42*
Carlson, August 24; Kansas, 1880 ***777.40*** *p6*
Carlson, Augusta J.; Colorado, 1895 ***1029.59*** *p15*
Carlson, Axel S.; Colorado, 1882 ***1029.59*** *p15*
Carlson, C. O.; Washington, 1889 ***2770.40*** *p26*
Carlson, Carl; Boston, 1903 ***1766.20*** *p25*
Carlson, Carl; Cleveland, OH, 1892-1896 ***9722.10*** *p118*
Carlson, Carl A.; Cleveland, OH, 1894-1900 ***9722.10*** *p118*
Carlson, Carl A.; Minnesota, 1880-1881 ***1865.50*** *p42*
Carlson, Carl Emil; New York, 1902 ***1766.20*** *p18*
Carlson, Carl F.; St. Paul, MN, 1880 ***1865.50*** *p42*
Carlson, Carl Gustaf; Minnesota, 1886-1889 ***1865.50*** *p42*
Carlson, Carl J.; Colorado, 1882 ***1029.59*** *p15*
Carlson, Carl Johan; Omaha, NE, 1903-1905 ***1865.50*** *p42*
Carlson, Carl Severin; St. Paul, MN, 1888 ***1865.50*** *p42*
Carlson, Carolina; St. Paul, MN, 1874-1905 ***1865.50*** *p42*
Carlson, Carolina; St. Paul, MN, 1886 ***1865.50*** *p97*
Carlson, Carolina; St. Paul, MN, 1888 ***1865.50*** *p115*
Carlson, Charles; Louisiana, 1895 ***7710.1*** *p161*
Carlson, Charles G.; Washington, 1889 ***2770.40*** *p26*
Carlson, Charlotta; St. Paul, MN, 1874-1905 ***1865.50*** *p42*
Carlson, Charlotta; St. Paul, MN, 1882 ***1865.50*** *p115*
Carlson, Clas; Colorado, 1891 ***1029.59*** *p15*
Carlson, Claus; Colorado, 1891 ***1029.59*** *p15*
Carlson, Claus; Colorado, 1894 ***1029.59*** *p15*
Carlson, Edwin; St. Paul, MN, 1894 ***1865.50*** *p43*
Carlson, Emma; St. Paul, MN, 1894 ***1865.50*** *p43*
Carlson, Emma C.; St. Paul, MN, 1894 ***1865.50*** *p43*
Carlson, Eva Christina; Minnesota, 1887-1888 ***1865.50*** *p43*
Carlson, Frank G.; Iowa, 1894 ***1211.15*** *p9*
Carlson, Frank M.; Cleveland, OH, 1902-1905 ***9722.10*** *p118*
Carlson, Fred N.; Cleveland, OH, 1894-1897 ***9722.10*** *p118*
Carlson, Fredrick; Washington, 1889 ***2770.40*** *p26*
Carlson, Gus; Cleveland, OH, 1887-1893 ***9722.10*** *p118*
Carlson, Gust; Cleveland, OH, 1897-1899 ***9722.10*** *p118*
Carlson, Gust; Colorado, 1891 ***1029.59*** *p15*
Carlson, Gust; Iowa, 1900 ***1211.15*** *p9*
Carlson, Herman; Colorado, 1873 ***1029.59*** *p15*
Carlson, Johan Alfred; Cleveland, OH, 1903-1906 ***9722.10*** *p118*
Carlson, Johan August; New York, 1898 ***1766.20*** *p27*
Carlson, Johanna *SEE* Carlson, John
Carlson, John; Colorado, 1901 ***1029.59*** *p15*
Carlson, John 42; Minnesota, 1925 ***2769.54*** *p1380*
Carlson, John; South Dakota, 1876-1901 ***1865.50*** *p43*
*Wife:*Johanna
Carlson, John; Washington, 1886 ***2770.40*** *p195*
Carlson, John Alfred; Iowa, 1900 ***1211.15*** *p9*
Carlson, John E.; Washington, 1889 ***2770.40*** *p26*
Carlson, John P.; Colorado, 1882 ***1029.59*** *p16*
Carlson, Jon Lottie; Michigan, 1897-1898 ***1865.50*** *p43*
Carlson, Justina Wilhelmina; Minnesota, 1887-1889 ***1865.50*** *p42*
Carlson, Knute Arthur; Boston, 1902 ***1766.20*** *p3*
Carlson, Lars 29; Minnesota, 1925 ***2769.54*** *p1383*
Carlson, Lavina; Minnesota, 1887-1890 ***1865.50*** *p43*
Carlson, Louise 31; Minnesota, 1925 ***2769.54*** *p1379*
Carlson, Lovisa E.; Seattle, 1890-1892 ***1865.50*** *p43*
Carlson, Nellie; Minnesota, 1868-1882 ***1865.50*** *p43*
Carlson, O. F.; Washington, 1888 ***2770.40*** *p25*
Carlson, Per; Cleveland, OH, 1893 ***9722.10*** *p118*
Carlson, Robert 33; Minnesota, 1925 ***2769.54*** *p1383*
Carlson, S.; Cleveland, OH, 1893-1896 ***9722.10*** *p118*
Carlson, Sophia; St. Paul, MN, 1888 ***1865.50*** *p50*
Carlson, Sven A.; Wisconsin, 1880-1881 ***1865.50*** *p43*
Carlson, Victor; Colorado, 1891 ***1029.59*** *p16*
Carlson, Victor 34; Minnesota, 1925 ***2769.54*** *p1379*
Carlson, Victor; New York, 1899 ***1766.20*** *p14*

Carlson, Wilhelmina; St. Paul, MN, 1874-1905 ***1865.50*** *p43*
Carlsson, A.; New York, NY, 1847 ***6412.40*** *p149*
Carlsson, Anders; North America, 1854 ***6410.15*** *p104*
*Wife:*Fredrika Pehrsdotter
*Son:*Carl Alfred
Carlsson, C.G.; New York, NY, 1847 ***6412.40*** *p150*
Carlsson, Carl Alfred *SEE* Carlsson, Anders
Carlsson, Carl Emil; Colorado, 1892 ***1029.59*** *p16*
Carlsson, Frank; Cleveland, OH, 1878-1892 ***9722.10*** *p118*
Carlsson, Fredrika Pehrsdotter *SEE* Carlsson, Anders
Carlsson, Gustaf; New York, NY, 1844 ***6412.40*** *p147*
Carlsson, Henrik; New York, NY, 1851 ***6412.40*** *p152*
Carlsson, J.E.; San Francisco, 1849 ***6412.40*** *p151*
Carlsson, J.O.; New York, NY, 1846 ***6412.40*** *p149*
Carlsson, Olof; Philadelphia, 1847 ***6412.40*** *p150*
Carlsson, Petter; New York, NY, 1844 ***6412.40*** *p148*
Carlstell, Frederick; Ohio, 1809-1852 ***4511.35*** *p8*
Carlston, Fred N.; Cleveland, OH, 1894-1897 ***9722.10*** *p118*
Carlstrom, Andrew August; St. Paul, MN, 1880 ***1865.50*** *p43*
Carlstrom, Mina; St. Paul, MN, 1881 ***1865.50*** *p37*
Carlstrom, Otto; St. Paul, MN, 1882 ***1865.50*** *p43*
Carlstrom, Sophia; St. Paul, MN, 1881 ***1865.50*** *p35*
Carlwagen, A.F.; New York, NY, 1846 ***6412.40*** *p149*
Carly, William; Louisiana, 1836-1840 ***4981.45*** *p212*
Carmack, Peter; New York, 1782 ***8529.30*** *p10*
Carman, Edward 53; Ontario, 1871 ***1823.21*** *p53*
Carmichael, Allan 12; North Carolina, 1775 ***1422.10*** *p60*
Carmichael, Angus 40; Ontario, 1871 ***1823.17*** *p24*
Carmichael, Ann J. King *SEE* Carmichael, Joseph
Carmichael, Archibald 14; North Carolina, 1775 ***1422.10*** *p60*
Carmichael, Archibald 26; North Carolina, 1775 ***1422.10*** *p60*
Carmichael, Archibald 24; Ontario, 1871 ***1823.17*** *p24*
Carmichael, Archibald 66; Ontario, 1871 ***1823.17*** *p24*
Carmichael, Catharine *SEE* Carmichael, Dugald
Carmichael, Catherine McEuen *SEE* Carmichael, Dugald
Carmichael, Catherine 7; North Carolina, 1775 ***1422.10*** *p60*
Carmichael, Christian 14; North Carolina, 1775 ***1422.10*** *p60*
Carmichael, Dugald; New York, 1739 ***8277.31*** *p115*
*Wife:*Catherine McEuen
*Child:*Neil
*Child:*Catharine
*Child:*Janet
*Child:*Mary
Carmichael, Dugald 55; North Carolina, 1775 ***1422.10*** *p60*
Carmichael, Dugald 70; Ontario, 1871 ***1823.17*** *p24*
Carmichael, Evan 40; North Carolina, 1775 ***1422.10*** *p60*
Carmichael, Hugh 75; Ontario, 1871 ***1823.21*** *p53*
Carmichael, Janet *SEE* Carmichael, Dugald
Carmichael, John 51; Ontario, 1871 ***1823.21*** *p53*
Carmichael, Joseph; Philadelphia, 1857 ***8513.31*** *p298*
*Wife:*Ann J. King
Carmichael, Katherine 3; North Carolina, 1775 ***1422.10*** *p60*
Carmichael, Margaret 38; North Carolina, 1775 ***1422.10*** *p60*
Carmichael, Mary *SEE* Carmichael, Dugald
Carmichael, Mary 26; North Carolina, 1775 ***1422.10*** *p60*
Carmichael, Mary 55; North Carolina, 1775 ***1422.10*** *p60*
Carmichael, Neil *SEE* Carmichael, Dugald
Carmichael, Peter 59; Ontario, 1871 ***1823.21*** *p53*
Carmichael, Thomas 43; Ontario, 1871 ***1823.17*** *p25*
Carmichael, William 38; Ontario, 1871 ***1823.17*** *p25*
Carmichail, Donald 22; North Carolina, 1775 ***1422.10*** *p60*
Carmichel, M. 27; New York, NY, 1894 ***6512.1*** *p181*
Carmichel, Mrs. M. 21; New York, NY, 1894 ***6512.1*** *p181*
Carmoody, Thomas; Ohio, 1853 ***3580.20*** *p31*
Carmoody, Thomas; Ohio, 1853 ***6020.12*** *p6*
Carmoody, Thomas 33; Ontario, 1871 ***1823.21*** *p53*
Carnagan, Daniel 47; Ontario, 1871 ***1823.17*** *p25*
Carnahan, Margaret 75; Ontario, 1871 ***1823.17*** *p25*
Carnahan, Samuel H. 56; Ontario, 1871 ***1823.17*** *p25*
Carnahan, William 21; Louisiana, 1831-1846 ***7710.1*** *p149*
Carnecki, John; Galveston, TX, 1890 ***6015.15*** *p9*
Carnegie, Miss; Quebec, 1885 ***1937.10*** *p52*
Carnegie, J.H.; Quebec, 1885 ***1937.10*** *p52*
Carnel, Henry 55; Ontario, 1871 ***1823.21*** *p53*
Carnell, Henry; Missouri, 1889 ***3276.1*** *p1*
Carnepy, George; North Carolina, 1710 ***3629.40*** *p5*
Carnes, William; Washington, 1882 ***2770.40*** *p135*
Carnet, Fois. 19; Missouri, 1848 ***778.6*** *p59*
Carney, Eliza 60; Ontario, 1871 ***1823.21*** *p53*
Carney, John 34; Ontario, 1871 ***1823.21*** *p53*
Carney, John; Vermont, 1836 ***3274.55*** *p26*
Carney, Mary; New Orleans, 1851 ***7242.30*** *p138*
Carney, Mathew; New Orleans, 1851 ***7242.30*** *p138*
Carney, Michael; Illinois, 1863 ***6079.1*** *p3*
Carney, Patrick 29; Ontario, 1871 ***1823.21*** *p53*
Carney, Reuben 35; Ontario, 1871 ***1823.21*** *p53*
Carney, Robert; New Orleans, 1851 ***7242.30*** *p138*
Carny, Thomas; Newfoundland, 1814 ***3476.10*** *p54*
Caro, Mr. 33; America, 1846 ***778.6*** *p59*
Caro, Emilie 20; New Orleans, 1848 ***778.6*** *p59*
Caro, Pierre 30; New Orleans, 1848 ***778.6*** *p59*
Caroff, Louis 35; New Orleans, 1848 ***778.6*** *p59*
Carognas, D.; Louisiana, 1874 ***4981.45*** *p295*
Carol, J.; Toronto, 1844 ***2910.35*** *p111*
Carolane, Dan; St. John, N.B., 1847 ***2978.15*** *p36*
Carolane, Roger; St. John, N.B., 1847 ***2978.15*** *p37*
Carolane, Thos; St. John, N.B., 1847 ***2978.15*** *p36*
Caroll, James 25; Ontario, 1871 ***1823.21*** *p53*
Caroll, John 60; Ontario, 1871 ***1823.21*** *p53*
Caroll, Michael 60; Ontario, 1871 ***1823.21*** *p53*
Caroll, Robert 63; Ontario, 1871 ***1823.21*** *p53*
Carolus, Heinrich; America, 1854 ***7420.1*** *p117*
Caron, Alex. Louis 30; Missouri, 1846 ***778.6*** *p59*
Caron, Francois; Montreal, 1659 ***9221.17*** *p418*
Caron, Jean 45; Quebec, 1659 ***9221.17*** *p396*
Caron, Jean-Baptiste 24; Quebec, 1638 ***9221.17*** *p75*
Caron, Robert; Quebec, 1636 ***9221.17*** *p53*
Caroussel, Jerome 23; America, 1846 ***778.6*** *p59*
Carpenter, . . .; Rhode Island, 1670-1699 ***9228.50*** *p632*
Carpenter, Anthony; Boston, 1832 ***3274.56*** *p70*
Carpenter, Anthony E.; Boston, 1832 ***3274.55*** *p43*
Carpenter, Charles 21; Ontario, 1871 ***1823.17*** *p25*
Carpenter, Elijah 71; Ontario, 1871 ***1823.17*** *p25*
Carpenter, Mary; Boston, 1832 ***3274.56*** *p96*
Carpenter, Patrick; Louisiana, 1874 ***4981.45*** *p131*
Carpenter, Philip; Maine, 1688 ***9228.50*** *p152*
Carpenter, Philip; Virginia, 1652 ***6254.4*** *p243*
Carpenter, William 42; Ontario, 1871 ***1823.17*** *p25*
Carpentier, Jean 20; Quebec, 1652 ***9221.17*** *p256*
Carper, Henry; Ohio, 1809-1852 ***4511.35*** *p8*
Carpiaux, Eloi *SEE* Carpiaux, Pierre Joseph
Carpiaux, Josephine *SEE* Carpiaux, Pierre Joseph
Carpiaux, Julie Joseph Benoit *SEE* Carpiaux, Pierre Joseph
Carpiaux, Pierre Joseph; Wisconsin, 1856 ***1495.20*** *p41*
*Wife:*Julie Joseph Benoit
*Child:*Josephine
*Child:*Eloi
Carpon, Elisabeth 4 *SEE* Carpon, Elise
Carpon, Elise; America, 1836 ***5475.1*** *p536*
*Daughter:*Elisabeth
*Son:*Johann Georg
Carpon, Johann Georg 2 *SEE* Carpon, Elise
Carr, Andrew; Ontario, 1871 ***1823.17*** *p25*
Carr, Angus 50; Ontario, 1871 ***1823.21*** *p54*
Carr, Bertie Leonard Chas. 25; Quebec, 1910 ***2897.7*** *p8*
Carr, Duncan 42; Ontario, 1871 ***1823.21*** *p54*
Carr, Emely 41; Ohio, 1880 ***4879.40*** *p260*
Carr, Esther 50; Ontario, 1871 ***1823.17*** *p25*
Carr, George 32; Michigan, 1880 ***4491.30*** *p5*
Carr, Isebela 61; Ontario, 1871 ***1823.21*** *p54*
Carr, James 24; Ontario, 1871 ***1823.21*** *p54*
Carr, James 30; Ontario, 1871 ***1823.21*** *p54*
Carr, James 52; Ontario, 1871 ***1823.17*** *p25*
Carr, Jerry; Philadelphia Co., PA, 1860 ***5720.10*** *p377*
Carr, John; Marston's Wharf, 1782 ***8529.30*** *p10*
Carr, John 28; Ontario, 1871 ***1823.21*** *p54*
Carr, Joseph 46; Ontario, 1871 ***1823.17*** *p25*
Carr, Patrick 30; Boston, 1770 ***1642*** *p42*
Carr, William; Marston's Wharf, 1782 ***8529.30*** *p10*
Carr, William 36; Ontario, 1871 ***1823.21*** *p54*
Carr, William 49; Ontario, 1871 ***1823.17*** *p25*
Carr, William 51; Ontario, 1871 ***1823.21*** *p54*
Carr, Winifred 19; Quebec, 1870 ***8364.32*** *p22*
Carragan, Patrick; North Carolina, 1858 ***1088.45*** *p5*
Carran, John; Newfoundland, 1814 ***3476.10*** *p54*
Carrathons, Peter 43; Ontario, 1871 ***1823.17*** *p25*
Carrau, Joseph 24; New Orleans, 1746 ***778.6*** *p59*
Carre, Mr. 3; Texas, 1848 ***778.6*** *p59*
Carre, Mr. 37; Texas, 1848 ***778.6*** *p59*
Carre, Anne; Illinois, 1799-1872 ***9228.50*** *p152*
Carre, Claire 64; Port uncertain, 1846 ***778.6*** *p59*
Carre, Ella; Massachusetts, 1928 ***9228.50*** *p383*
Carre, Ellen J.; Massachusetts, 1870-1899 ***9228.50*** *p153*
Carre, Ezekiel; Rhode Island, 1686 ***9228.50*** *p152*
Carre, Henry; Alabama, 1818 ***9228.50*** *p152*
Carre, John; New York, 1825 ***9228.50*** *p153*
Carre, Joseph 19; Port uncertain, 1846 ***778.6*** *p59*
Carre, Louise; Wisconsin, 1842 ***9228.50*** *p153*
Carre, Susan; America, 1818 ***9228.50*** *p152*
Carre, Walter William; New Orleans, 1829-1900 ***9228.50*** *p152*
Carreau, Mr. 19; Port uncertain, 1844 ***778.6*** *p59*
Carreau, J. 19; New Orleans, 1846 ***778.6*** *p59*
Carreau, Louis 27; Quebec, 1645 ***9221.17*** *p152*
Carrel, Samuel 34; Ontario, 1871 ***1823.21*** *p54*
Carrell, . . .; Maryland, 1600-1699 ***9228.50*** *p153*
Carrell, . . .; Prince Edward Island, 1800-1840 ***9228.50*** *p153*
Carrell, Hannah; Massachusetts, 1720-1729 ***9228.50*** *p153*
Carrell, Joseph; America, 1769 ***9228.50*** *p153*
Carrell, Michael; Boston, 1766 ***1642*** *p38*
Carrell, Patrick; Massachusetts, 1754-1763 ***1642*** *p74*
Carrell, Patrick; Massachusetts, 1756-1763 ***1642*** *p64*
Carrelon, J. B. 17; America, 1846 ***778.6*** *p57*
Carrere, Mrs.; New Orleans, 1845 ***778.6*** *p59*
Carrere, Ms.; New Orleans, 1845 ***778.6*** *p59*
Carrere, D...que 24; New Orleans, 1840 ***778.6*** *p59*
Carrere, J. B. 22; America, 1840 ***778.6*** *p59*
Carrere, Pierre 25; New Orleans, 1845 ***778.6*** *p59*
Carrere, Pierre 33; New Orleans, 1845 ***778.6*** *p59*
Carrey, Thomas; New England, 1745 ***1642*** *p28*
Carrick, William 56; Ontario, 1871 ***1823.17*** *p25*
Carrico, Peter; West Virginia, 1787 ***1132.30*** *p146*
Carrie, Richard 32; Ontario, 1871 ***1823.21*** *p54*
Carrie, Richard 33; Ontario, 1871 ***1823.21*** *p54*
Carrier, Jean 24; Montreal, 1660 ***9221.17*** *p441*
Carrigan, James 34; Ontario, 1871 ***1823.21*** *p54*
Carrigan, John 39; Ontario, 1871 ***1823.17*** *p25*
Carrigan, Phillip; Boston, 1741 ***1642*** *p45*
Carrigue, Richard; Long Island, 1781 ***8529.30*** *p9A*
Carrill, Cather; Boston, 1766 ***1642*** *p37*
Carrington, Jack; Indiana, 1900-1990 ***9228.50*** *p153*
Carrington, Stanley; Florida, 1900 ***9228.50*** *p153*
Carrique, Richard; Long Island, 1781 ***8529.30*** *p9A*
Carrison, Arthur 26; Ontario, 1871 ***1823.21*** *p54*
Carrmann, Nicolas 33; St. Louis, 1847 ***778.6*** *p59*
Carrol, Christian; Ohio, 1809-1852 ***4511.35*** *p8*
Carrol, Edward; Ohio, 1809-1852 ***4511.35*** *p8*
Carrol, James; Boston, 1763 ***1642*** *p32*
Carrol, James 23; Ontario, 1871 ***1823.21*** *p54*
Carrol, James 30; Ontario, 1871 ***1823.21*** *p54*
Carrol, John; Boston, 1770 ***1642*** *p43*
Carrol, John 38; Ontario, 1871 ***1823.21*** *p54*
Carrol, Pat; St. John, N.B., 1847 ***2978.15*** *p39*
Carrol, Phelix; St. John, N.B., 1847 ***2978.15*** *p39*
Carrol, Thomas 45; Ontario, 1871 ***1823.21*** *p54*
Carroll, A.; Louisiana, 1874-1875 ***4981.45*** *p298*
Carroll, Alexander J.; Ohio, 1846 ***3580.20*** *p31*
Carroll, Alexander J.; Ohio, 1846 ***6020.12*** *p6*
Carroll, Catherine; St. Johns, N.F., 1825 ***1053.15*** *p6*
Carroll, David; Boston, 1840 ***3274.56*** *p70*
Carroll, Eliza 46; Ontario, 1871 ***1823.17*** *p25*
Carroll, Henry; Washington, 1887 ***2770.40*** *p24*
Carroll, James 70; Ontario, 1871 ***1823.21*** *p54*
Carroll, John; Halifax, N.S., 1827 ***7009.9*** *p62*
Carroll, John; Louisiana, 1874 ***4981.45*** *p131*
Carroll, John; Louisiana, 1874 ***4981.45*** *p131*
Carroll, John; Louisiana, 1874 ***4981.45*** *p295*
Carroll, John 60; Ontario, 1871 ***1823.17*** *p25*
Carroll, Karns 54; Ontario, 1871 ***1823.17*** *p25*
Carroll, Liddy 57; Ontario, 1871 ***1823.17*** *p25*
Carroll, Luke; Iowa, 1892 ***1211.15*** *p9*
Carroll, Margaret; Ontario, 1835 ***3160.1*** *p150*
Carroll, Martin; Illinois, 1860 ***6079.1*** *p3*
Carroll, Mary 19; Ontario, 1871 ***1823.21*** *p54*
Carroll, Patrick; St. Johns, N.F., 1825 ***1053.15*** *p6*
Carroll, Patrick; Washington, 1882 ***2770.40*** *p135*
Carroll, Robert 18; Ontario, 1871 ***1823.21*** *p54*
Carroll, William 78; Ontario, 1871 ***1823.21*** *p54*
Carron, J. 32; America, 1843 ***778.6*** *p59*
Carrothers, David 60; Ontario, 1871 ***1823.21*** *p54*
Carrothers, Eliza 40; Ontario, 1871 ***1823.21*** *p54*
Carrothers, James 30; Ontario, 1871 ***1823.17*** *p25*
Carrothers, Jas. 78; Ontario, 1871 ***1823.17*** *p25*
Carrothers, John 34; Ontario, 1871 ***1823.21*** *p54*
Carrothers, Michael 53; Ontario, 1871 ***1823.21*** *p54*
Carrothers, Nathaniel 66; Ontario, 1871 ***1823.21*** *p54*
Carrothers, Patrick 52; Ontario, 1871 ***1823.21*** *p54*
Carrothers, Robert 62; Ontario, 1871 ***1823.21*** *p54*
Carrothers, Samuel 71; Ontario, 1871 ***1823.21*** *p54*
Carrothers, Thomas 60; Ontario, 1871 ***1823.21*** *p54*
Carrothers, Wm. 38; Ontario, 1871 ***1823.17*** *p25*
Carrothors, Jane; Ontario, 1871 ***1823.17*** *p25*
Carruthers, Chris 34; Ontario, 1871 ***1823.21*** *p54*
Carruthers, Delilah 60; Ontario, 1871 ***1823.21*** *p54*
Carruthers, Eliza; Ontario, 1871 ***1823.21*** *p54*
Carruthers, Francis 65; Ontario, 1871 ***1823.17*** *p25*
Carry, James 70; Ontario, 1871 ***1823.21*** *p55*
Carry, James; Philadelphia, 1849 ***5720.10*** *p377*
Carry, John; St. John, N.B., 1847 ***2978.15*** *p38*
Carry, W. S. 32; Ontario, 1871 ***1823.21*** *p55*
Carry, William 66; Ontario, 1871 ***1823.21*** *p55*
Carryl, Hannah; Massachusetts, 1720-1729 ***9228.50*** *p153*

Carson, Andrew 44; Ontario, 1871 ***1823.17*** *p25*
Carson, Elizabeth; North Carolina, 1792-1862 ***1088.45*** *p5*
Carson, Frank; Louisiana, 1874-1875 ***4981.45*** *p298*
Carson, John; North Carolina, 1840 ***1088.45*** *p5*
Carson, John 41; Ontario, 1871 ***1823.21*** *p55*
Carson, John 64; Ontario, 1871 ***1823.21*** *p55*
Carson, John Alexander; North Carolina, 1792-1862 ***1088.45*** *p5*
Carson, John Kit; Colorado, 1873 ***1029.59*** *p16*
Carson, Margaret; North Carolina, 1824 ***1088.45*** *p5*
Carson, Samuel; Philadelphia, 1777 ***8529.30*** *p2A*
Carson, Smith; North Carolina, 1824 ***1088.45*** *p5*
Carson, Thomas 31; Ontario, 1871 ***1823.21*** *p55*
Carson, William; Ohio, 1856 ***3580.20*** *p31*
Carson, William; Ohio, 1856 ***6020.12*** *p6*
Carson, William 38; Ontario, 1871 ***1823.17*** *p25*
Carstensen, Joachim Friedrich; Iowa, 1916 ***1211.15*** *p9*
Carstensen, Paul; Iowa, 1921 ***1211.15*** *p9*
Carswell, George 50; Ontario, 1871 ***1823.21*** *p55*
Carswell, Giles 49; Ontario, 1871 ***1823.21*** *p55*
Carswell, John 77; Ontario, 1871 ***1823.21*** *p55*
Carswell, Neil 25; Ontario, 1871 ***1823.21*** *p55*
Cartee, Philip; Maine, 1668 ***9228.50*** *p153*
Carter, Ann 62; Ontario, 1871 ***1823.21*** *p55*
Carter, Catherine 69; Ontario, 1871 ***1823.21*** *p55*
Carter, Charles 30; Ontario, 1871 ***1823.17*** *p25*
Carter, Charles 34; Ontario, 1871 ***1823.21*** *p55*
Carter, Christine 15; Quebec, 1870 ***8364.32*** *p22*
Carter, Daniel 58; Ontario, 1871 ***1823.17*** *p26*
Carter, David 45; Ontario, 1871 ***1823.21*** *p55*
Carter, George; Marston's Wharf, 1780 ***8529.30*** *p10*
Carter, George; Ontario, 1871 ***1823.17*** *p26*
Carter, George 35; Ontario, 1871 ***1823.21*** *p55*
Carter, George H. 31; Ontario, 1871 ***1823.21*** *p55*
Carter, George William 39; Ontario, 1871 ***1823.17*** *p26*
Carter, Gilbert 58; Ontario, 1871 ***1823.21*** *p55*
Carter, Henry; Washington, 1885 ***2770.40*** *p194*
Carter, James; Albany, NY, 1832 ***3274.55*** *p75*
Carter, James; Long Island, 1780 ***8529.30*** *p9A*
Carter, James 50; Ontario, 1871 ***1823.21*** *p55*
Carter, James 50; Ontario, 1871 ***1823.21*** *p55*
Carter, Jeremiah 48; Ontario, 1871 ***1823.21*** *p55*
Carter, John 40; Ontario, 1871 ***1823.17*** *p26*
Carter, Margaret; British Columbia, 1810-1886 ***9228.50*** *p153*
Carter, Margaret; Quebec, 1862 ***9228.50*** *p466*
Carter, Maria 22; Ontario, 1871 ***1823.21*** *p55*
Carter, Mary; Montreal, 1869-1951 ***9228.50*** *p153*
Carter, Philip; Maine, 1668 ***9228.50*** *p153*
Carter, Richard; Canada, 1774 ***3036.5*** *p41*
Carter, Richard 60; Ontario, 1871 ***1823.21*** *p55*
Carter, Robert 23; Ontario, 1871 ***1823.21*** *p55*
Carter, Robert 38; Ontario, 1871 ***1823.21*** *p55*
Carter, Robert 49; Ontario, 1871 ***1823.21*** *p55*
Carter, Sarah 20; Ontario, 1871 ***1823.17*** *p26*
Carter, William 53; Ontario, 1871 ***1823.17*** *p26*
Carteret, . . .; New Jersey, 1665 ***9228.50*** *p159*
Carteret, . . .; New Jersey, 1665 ***9228.50*** *p180*
Carteret, Lord; New Jersey, 1665 ***9228.50*** *p218*
Carteret, Ann *SEE* Carteret, Hugh
Carteret, Edward; Maine, 1763 ***9228.50*** *p155*
*Son:*Nicholas
Carteret, George; Carolina, 1650-1699 ***9228.50*** *p55*
Carteret, Hugh; South Carolina, 1671 ***9228.50*** *p155*
*Wife:*Ann
Carteret, James; Carolina, 1622 ***9228.50*** *p55*
Carteret, James; Carolina, 1650-1699 ***9228.50*** *p55*
Carteret, James; Carolina, 1671 ***9228.50*** *p154*
Carteret, James; Georgia, 1622 ***9228.50*** *p4*
With wife
Carteret, John; Carolina, 1650-1699 ***9228.50*** *p55*
Carteret, John De; Massachusetts, 1870 ***9228.50*** *p50*
Carteret, Nicholas *SEE* Carteret, Edward
Carteret, Nicholas; North Carolina, 1670 ***9228.50*** *p55*
Carteret, Nicholas; South Carolina, 1672 ***9228.50*** *p156*
With family
Carteret, Peter; Carolina, 1650-1699 ***9228.50*** *p55*
Carteret, Peter; Carolina, 1664 ***9228.50*** *p55*
Carteret, Peter; Virginia, 1664 ***9228.50*** *p156*
Carteret, Peter; Virginia, 1664 ***9228.50*** *p156*
Carteret, Philip; Boston, 1703-1767 ***9228.50*** *p153*
Carteret, Philip; New York, 1665 ***9228.50*** *p156*
Carteret Brothers, . . .; Connecticut, 1690 ***9228.50*** *p265*
Carteron, Daniel; Quebec, 1644 ***9221.17*** *p139*
Carteron, Peter; Missouri, 1898 ***3276.1*** *p3*
Cartes, Jakob; America, 1883 ***5475.1*** *p452*
Cartes, Johann; America, 1830 ***5475.1*** *p449*
Cartes, Johann; America, 1877 ***5475.1*** *p452*
Cartes, Katharina Doerr *SEE* Cartes, Mathias
Cartes, Mathias; America, 1830 ***5475.1*** *p449*
*Father:*Nikolaus
*Mother:*Katharina Doerr
Cartes, Nikolaus *SEE* Cartes, Mathias
Carthy, Ellen Gallagher *SEE* Carthy, John
Carthy, John; Philadelphia, 1854 ***8513.31*** *p298*
*Wife:*Ellen Gallagher
Carthy, Maria 17; Quebec, 1870 ***8364.32*** *p22*
Cartier, A. 35; New Orleans, 1846 ***778.6*** *p60*
Cartier, Adolphe 25; America, 1840 ***778.6*** *p60*
Cartier, Apoline 37; New Orleans, 1847 ***778.6*** *p59*
Cartier, August 13; New Orleans, 1847 ***778.6*** *p59*
Cartier, Augustine 19; Port uncertain, 1843 ***778.6*** *p60*
Cartier, Francois 24; New Orleans, 1848 ***778.6*** *p60*
Cartier, Francois 28; New Orleans, 1847 ***778.6*** *p59*
Cartier, Jacques; Quebec, 1534 ***9228.50*** *p3*
Cartier, Joseph 10; New Orleans, 1847 ***778.6*** *p59*
Cartier, Laurent 28; Port uncertain, 1843 ***778.6*** *p60*
Cartier, Louis 3; New Orleans, 1847 ***778.6*** *p59*
Cartier, Marie 9; New Orleans, 1847 ***778.6*** *p59*
Cartier, Philip; Maine, 1668 ***9228.50*** *p153*
Cartier, Philipp 5; New Orleans, 1847 ***778.6*** *p59*
Cartier, Robert; Plymouth, MA, 1620 ***1920.45*** *p5*
Cartier, Serinne 1; New Orleans, 1847 ***778.6*** *p59*
Cartignier, Marie; Quebec, 1669 ***4514.3*** *p287*
Cartjohn, Carson; North Carolina, 1858 ***1088.45*** *p5*
Cartlidge, Elizabeth 65; Ontario, 1871 ***1823.21*** *p55*
Cartner, Johann; Brazil, 1825 ***5475.1*** *p461*
With daughter 19
With son 8
Cartois, Henriette; Quebec, 1671 ***4514.3*** *p287*
Carton, John; Boston, 1764 ***1642*** *p33*
Cartwright, Hinery; Virginia, 1652 ***6254.4*** *p243*
Cartwright, William 65; Ontario, 1871 ***1823.21*** *p55*
Cartwright, William 14; Quebec, 1870 ***8364.32*** *p22*
Cartwrights, Edward; Maine, 1763 ***9228.50*** *p155*
*Son:*Nicholas
Cartwrights, Nicholas *SEE* Cartwrights, Edward
Carty, Mr.; Boston, 1768 ***1642*** *p40*
Carty, Andrew 43; Ontario, 1871 ***1823.21*** *p55*
Carty, Denis 61; Ontario, 1871 ***1823.21*** *p55*
Carty, Dennis 49; Ontario, 1871 ***1823.21*** *p55*
Carty, Elizabeth; Boston, 1753 ***1642*** *p47*
Carty, Florence; Boston, 1738 ***1642*** *p44*
Carty, John; Newfoundland, 1814 ***3476.10*** *p54*
Carty, Mary; Boston, 1738 ***1642*** *p44*
Carty, Michael; New Orleans, 1851 ***7242.30*** *p138*
Carty, Robert 60; Ontario, 1871 ***1823.21*** *p56*
Cartzy, Honer; Boston, 1743 ***1642*** *p45*
Carus, Nicholas 23; America, 1845 ***778.6*** *p60*
Caruthers, Andrew 31; Ontario, 1871 ***1823.21*** *p56*
Carvanel, . . .; Plymouth, MA, 1621 ***9228.50*** *p4*
Carvanell, . . .; Plymouth, MA, 1621 ***9228.50*** *p156*
Carvanyell, . . .; Plymouth, MA, 1621 ***9228.50*** *p4*
Carvanyell, . . .; Plymouth, MA, 1621 ***9228.50*** *p156*
Carvarte, John; Washington, 1882 ***2770.40*** *p135*
Carver, John; North Carolina, 1826 ***1088.45*** *p5*
Carver, John; Plymouth, MA, 1620 ***1920.45*** *p5*
*Wife:*Katherine
Carver, Katherine *SEE* Carver, John
Carver, Thomas 55; Ontario, 1871 ***1823.21*** *p56*
Carvill, Patrick; Boston, 1831 ***3274.55*** *p70*
Cary, Charles 22; Michigan, 1880 ***4491.30*** *p5*
Cary, George; New England, 1745 ***1642*** *p28*
Cary, Henry 47; Ontario, 1871 ***1823.21*** *p56*
Cary, James 36; Ontario, 1871 ***1823.17*** *p26*
Cary, John 50; Ontario, 1871 ***1823.21*** *p56*
Cary, Patrick; Ontario, 1871 ***1823.21*** *p56*
Cary, R. T. 52; Ontario, 1871 ***1823.17*** *p26*
Cary, Thomas 84; Ontario, 1871 ***1823.21*** *p56*
Casaly, Mr. 20; Port uncertain, 1844 ***778.6*** *p60*
Casanaze, B.; Louisiana, 1874-1875 ***4981.45*** *p298*
Cascaden, David 43; Ontario, 1871 ***1823.17*** *p26*
Cascur, Patrick; Newfoundland, 1814 ***3476.10*** *p54*
Case, Albert; Washington, 1887 ***2770.40*** *p24*
Case, Charles L.; North Carolina, 1868 ***1088.45*** *p5*
Case, Cicero 57; Ontario, 1871 ***1823.17*** *p26*
Case, Edward 20; Quebec, 1910 ***2897.7*** *p7*
Case, Ira 45; Ontario, 1871 ***1823.21*** *p56*
Case, John 59; Ontario, 1871 ***1823.21*** *p56*
Case, Margaret 43; Ontario, 1871 ***1823.21*** *p56*
Case, William H. 31; Ontario, 1871 ***1823.17*** *p26*
Caseaux, Louis 27; Port uncertain, 1840 ***778.6*** *p60*
Casee, John; Massachusetts, 1744 ***1642*** *p82*
Casem, Marie C. 22; New Orleans, 1844 ***778.6*** *p60*
Casenave, L. 24; America, 1848 ***778.6*** *p60*
Casey, Charles 51; Ontario, 1871 ***1823.21*** *p56*
Casey, Con; Boston, 1765 ***1642*** *p34*
Casey, Edward; Boston, 1766 ***1642*** *p36*
Casey, Johanna; New Orleans, 1851 ***7242.30*** *p138*
Casey, John; Boston, 1675-1676 ***1642*** *p130*
Casey, John; Boston, 1762 ***1642*** *p31*
Casey, John; Massachusetts, 1675-1676 ***1642*** *p127*
Casey, John; Massachusetts, 1675-1676 ***1642*** *p128*
Casey, John S. 83; Ontario, 1871 ***1823.17*** *p26*
Casey, Mary; Boston, 1761 ***1642*** *p48*
Casey, Mary; New Orleans, 1851 ***7242.30*** *p138*
Casey, Mary 15; Ontario, 1871 ***1823.17*** *p26*
Casey, Michael; Toronto, 1844 ***2910.35*** *p116*
Casey, Patt; New Orleans, 1851 ***7242.30*** *p138*
Casey, Robert; Philadelphia, 1777 ***8529.30*** *p3A*
Casey, Samuel 17; Quebec, 1870 ***8364.32*** *p22*
Casey, Sarah 20; Ontario, 1871 ***1823.21*** *p56*
Casey, Susan 18; Quebec, 1870 ***8364.32*** *p22*
Casey, Thomas; Boston, 1758 ***1642*** *p47*
Casey, Thomas; Boston, 1759 ***1642*** *p47*
Casey, Thomas 50; Ontario, 1871 ***1823.21*** *p56*
Casey, Timothy; Ohio, 1856 ***3580.20*** *p31*
Casey, Timothy; Ohio, 1856 ***6020.12*** *p6*
Casey, William; Ohio, 1856 ***3580.20*** *p31*
Casey, William; Ohio, 1856 ***6020.12*** *p6*
Casey, William 41; Ontario, 1871 ***1823.21*** *p56*
Casgrain-Gagnon, Luce; New York, 1858 ***9228.50*** *p515*
Casgrain-Gagnon, Luce; New York, 1858 ***9228.50*** *p515*
Casgrove, Francis; Vermont, 1832 ***3274.55*** *p43*
Cashen, Francis 65; Ontario, 1871 ***1823.21*** *p56*
Casher, James 42; Ontario, 1871 ***1823.17*** *p26*
Cashin, Nichols 40; Michigan, 1880 ***4491.30*** *p5*
Cashion, John; Ohio, 1840-1897 ***8365.35*** *p15*
Casidy, Edward 53; Ontario, 1871 ***1823.17*** *p26*
Casidy, Johnson 54; Ontario, 1871 ***1823.21*** *p56*
Casimere, Mr. 29; America, 1746 ***778.6*** *p60*
Casin, Etienne; Louisiana, 1836-1840 ***4981.45*** *p212*
Casis, Darmien; Louisiana, 1836-1840 ***4981.45*** *p212*
Casitan, Ann Marie 23; Mississippi, 1846 ***778.6*** *p60*
Casitan, Cristian 21; Mississippi, 1846 ***778.6*** *p60*
Casitan, Georg 10; Mississippi, 1846 ***778.6*** *p60*
Casitan, Joseph 54; Mississippi, 1846 ***778.6*** *p60*
Casitan, Marie 24; Mississippi, 1846 ***778.6*** *p60*
Casky, Samuel; Ohio, 1809-1852 ***4511.35*** *p8*
Caslake, Thomas 40; Ontario, 1871 ***1823.21*** *p56*
Casmann, Carl; Valdivia, Chile, 1852 ***1192.4*** *p55*
Caspar, Anna 30; America, 1840 ***778.6*** *p60*
Caspar, Appolonia 24; America, 1844 ***2526.43*** *p207*
*Son:*Johann Philipp 3 months
Caspar, Bernhard; Ohio, 1809-1852 ***4511.35*** *p8*
Caspar, Carl Gottlob 29; America, 1846 ***778.6*** *p60*
Caspar, Jacob 40; America, 1840 ***778.6*** *p60*
Caspar, Johann; Galveston, TX, 1855 ***571.7*** *p16*
Caspar, Johann Philipp 3 *SEE* Caspar, Appolonia
Caspar, Peter; America, 1882 ***5475.1*** *p148*
Caspar, Philipp 27; America, 1844 ***2526.43*** *p207*
Caspel, Edouard 3; Missouri, 1845 ***778.6*** *p60*
Caspel, Felix 12; Missouri, 1845 ***778.6*** *p60*
Caspel, Jean 33; Missouri, 1845 ***778.6*** *p60*
Caspel, Joseph 9; Missouri, 1845 ***778.6*** *p60*
Caspel, Joseph 60; Missouri, 1845 ***778.6*** *p60*
Caspel, Louis 23; Missouri, 1845 ***778.6*** *p60*
Caspel, Marie 60; Missouri, 1845 ***778.6*** *p60*
Casper, George; Ohio, 1809-1852 ***4511.35*** *p8*
Casper, John; Colorado, 1867 ***1029.59*** *p16*
Casper, John; Colorado, 1891 ***1029.59*** *p16*
Casper, Joseph; Colorado, 1885 ***1029.59*** *p16*
Casper, Philip; Ohio, 1809-1852 ***4511.35*** *p8*
Cass, Mrs. M.; Montreal, 1922 ***4514.4*** *p32*
Cassa, Jacques; Quebec, 1642 ***9221.17*** *p114*
Cassada, Charles 67; Newbury, MA, 1764 ***1642*** *p76*
Cassaday, Elizabeth; Newburyport, MA, 1772 ***1642*** *p76*
Cassaday, Philemon; Salem, MA, 1766 ***1642*** *p78*
Cassaday, Robert; Colorado, 1871 ***1029.59*** *p16*
Cassady, James 36; Ontario, 1871 ***1823.21*** *p56*
Cassady, Robert; Colorado, 1888 ***1029.59*** *p16*
Cassady, Robert; Colorado, 1894 ***1029.59*** *p16*
Cassagne, Mr. 34; America, 1841 ***778.6*** *p60*
Cassagne, Frank; Louisiana, 1874-1875 ***4981.45*** *p298*
Cassagne, Marie Denis 19; New Orleans, 1848 ***778.6*** *p60*
Cassaigne, Mr. 38; America, 1846 ***778.6*** *p60*
Cassair, L.; Louisiana, 1874-1875 ***4981.45*** *p298*
Cassalar, Dque. 32; New Orleans, 1840 ***778.6*** *p60*
Cassalar, Fr. 25; New Orleans, 1840 ***778.6*** *p60*
Cassard, Mr. 19; America, 1846 ***778.6*** *p60*
Cassel, Caroline 28; Missouri, 1845 ***778.6*** *p61*
Cassel, Christian 4; Missouri, 1845 ***778.6*** *p61*
Cassel, George 9; Missouri, 1845 ***778.6*** *p61*
Cassel, Louise 1; Missouri, 1845 ***778.6*** *p61*
Cassel, Philippe 11; Missouri, 1845 ***778.6*** *p61*
Cassel, Philippe 32; Missouri, 1845 ***778.6*** *p61*
Casselle, Pietro; Louisiana, 1874-1875 ***4981.45*** *p298*
Cassenave, Pierre 32; Port uncertain, 1842 ***778.6*** *p61*
Casses, Mr. 24; New Orleans, 1840 ***778.6*** *p61*
Casset, Jean Joseph 60; New Orleans, 1848 ***778.6*** *p61*
Casset, Pauline 22; New Orleans, 1848 ***778.6*** *p61*
Casset, Therese 60; New Orleans, 1848 ***778.6*** *p61*
Cassey, Johanna; New Orleans, 1851 ***7242.30*** *p138*
Cassidy, Andrew 73; Ontario, 1871 ***1823.21*** *p56*
Cassidy, Catherine 20; Ontario, 1871 ***1823.21*** *p56*
Cassidy, Charles 67; Newbury, MA, 1764 ***1642*** *p76*
Cassidy, Elizabeth 48; Ontario, 1871 ***1823.21*** *p56*

Cassidy, Jane 34; Ontario, 1871 ***1823.21*** *p56*
Cassidy, John 40; Ontario, 1871 ***1823.21*** *p56*
Cassidy, Kate 28; New York, NY, 1894 ***6512.1*** *p229*
Cassidy, Margaret; Philadelphia, 1867 ***8513.31*** *p300*
Cassidy, Margaret 32; Toronto, 1862 ***9228.50*** *p156*
Cassidy, Michael 23; Ontario, 1871 ***1823.21*** *p56*
Cassidy, Patrick; New York, NY, 1820 ***3274.55*** *p24*
Cassidy, Patrick 27; Ontario, 1871 ***1823.21*** *p56*
Cassidy, Patrick 60; Ontario, 1871 ***1823.17*** *p26*
Cassidy, Thos 25; Ontario, 1871 ***1823.21*** *p56*
Cassie, James G. 35; Ontario, 1871 ***1823.21*** *p56*
Cassin, Michael 54; Ontario, 1871 ***1823.17*** *p26*
Cassle, James 50; Ontario, 1871 ***1823.21*** *p56*
Cassody, Mary; Newburyport, MA, 1766 ***1642*** *p76*
Casson, John 6; Ontario, 1871 ***1823.21*** *p56*
Casson, M. A. 42; New York, NY, 1894 ***6512.1*** *p181*
Castaille, Franc. 24; America, 1840 ***778.6*** *p61*
Castaing, Mr. 18; America, 1848 ***778.6*** *p61*
Castaing, Jean 36; America, 1845 ***778.6*** *p61*
Castairest, Baptiste 30; New Orleans, 1845 ***778.6*** *p61*
Castalon, Lewis 35; America, 1843 ***778.6*** *p61*
Castany, Louis Godfrey 30; Indiana, 1854-1876 ***9076.20*** *p68*
Castar, J. 33; America, 1848 ***778.6*** *p61*
Castel, Antoine; New Orleans, 1840 ***778.6*** *p61*
Castelas, Thomas 32; New Orleans, 1848 ***778.6*** *p61*
Castel Bon, Mr. 33; America, 1843 ***778.6*** *p61*
Castelbon, Lewis 33; America, 1841 ***778.6*** *p61*
Castelhau, Mr.; Port uncertain, 1844 ***778.6*** *p61*
Castell, Edward 35; New York, NY, 1844 ***6178.50*** *p151*
Castelle, Don 31; Port uncertain, 1841 ***778.6*** *p61*
Castello, Mary 18; Ontario, 1871 ***1823.21*** *p56*
Caster, Mr. 33; New Orleans, 1847 ***778.6*** *p61*
Castey, Bernard 23; America, 1845 ***778.6*** *p61*
Castillo, Louis 28; America, 1848 ***778.6*** *p61*
Castillon, Casimir 23; America, 1844 ***778.6*** *p61*
Castillon, L. 34; America, 1843 ***778.6*** *p61*
Castine, John 30; America, 1848 ***778.6*** *p61*
Casting, Charles; North Carolina, 1856 ***1088.45*** *p5*
Castle, Jane 33; Ontario, 1871 ***1823.17*** *p26*
Castle, Joseph 35; Ontario, 1871 ***1823.21*** *p56*
Castle, William 40; Ontario, 1871 ***1823.17*** *p26*
Castleton, Robt.; Maryland, 1673 ***1236.25*** *p49*
Castlo, Michael; Ohio, 1840-1897 ***8365.35*** *p15*
Castre, Jsoeph 21; America, 1847 ***778.6*** *p61*
Casurave, Jean 37; Louisiana, 1848 ***778.6*** *p61*
Casurave, Marie 20; Louisiana, 1848 ***778.6*** *p61*
Caswell, Andrew 70; Ontario, 1871 ***1823.21*** *p56*
Caswell, John 26; Ontario, 1871 ***1823.21*** *p56*
Caswell, Joseph 35; Ontario, 1871 ***1823.21*** *p56*
Caswell, Simon; Marblehead, MA, 1700-1799 ***9228.50*** *p156*
Caswell Family ; New England, 1704-1714 ***9228.50*** *p156*
Casy, Mary 41; Ontario, 1871 ***1823.17*** *p26*
Casy, Mary; Salem, MA, 1714 ***1642*** *p78*
Casy, Sarah 30; Ontario, 1871 ***1823.17*** *p26*
Casy, Thomas 65; Ontario, 1871 ***1823.17*** *p26*
Catalagne, Mr. 26; America, 1841 ***778.6*** *p62*
Catalogne, Gedeon de; Quebec, 1683-1688 ***2314.30*** *p168*
Catalogne, Gedeon de; Quebec, 1683 ***2314.30*** *p177*
Catalon, Mr. 33; Port uncertain, 1845 ***778.6*** *p62*
Catanoch, John 50; North Carolina, 1774 ***1422.10*** *p58*
Catanzarite, Dominick; New York, 1926 ***1173.1*** *p2*
Catanzarite, Frank; New York, 1926 ***1173.1*** *p2*
Catchpole, Henry 18; Quebec, 1870 ***8364.32*** *p22*
Catderan, Louis de; Quebec, 1687 ***2314.30*** *p171*
Caterer, Char; Jamestown, VA, 1633 ***1658.20*** *p211*
Cates, Charles; Ontario, 1871 ***1823.17*** *p26*
Cates, Elizabeth 12; Quebec, 1870 ***8364.32*** *p22*
Cates, William 29; Ontario, 1871 ***1823.17*** *p26*
Cathburt, Alexander 22; Ontario, 1871 ***1823.21*** *p56*
Cathburt, Anne 22; Ontario, 1871 ***1823.21*** *p57*
Cathcart, George 33; Ontario, 1871 ***1823.21*** *p57*
Cathcart, Issac; Washington, 1883 ***2770.40*** *p136*
Cathcart, John 23; Ontario, 1871 ***1823.21*** *p57*
Cathcart, Robert 40; Ontario, 1871 ***1823.17*** *p26*
Catherine, Nicolas 19; Quebec, 1655 ***9221.17*** *p320*
Cathers, Alexander 24; Ontario, 1871 ***1823.21*** *p57*
Cathing, Louisa 9; Quebec, 1870 ***8364.32*** *p22*
Cathing, Norah 11; Quebec, 1870 ***8364.32*** *p22*
Cathro, Peter 76; Ontario, 1871 ***1823.21*** *p57*
Cathro, Thomas R. 44; Ontario, 1871 ***1823.21*** *p57*
Cathyet, August 1; Missouri, 1845 ***778.6*** *p62*
Cathyet, Joseph 6; Missouri, 1845 ***778.6*** *p62*
Cathyet, Joseph 30; Missouri, 1845 ***778.6*** *p62*
Cathyet, Marie Els. 29; Missouri, 1845 ***778.6*** *p62*
Cathyet, Marie F. 4; Missouri, 1845 ***778.6*** *p62*
Cato, Dominiuque 45; America, 1848 ***778.6*** *p62*
Caton, Daniel; Salem, MA, 1716 ***1642*** *p79*
Catre, Antoine; Quebec, 1644 ***9221.17*** *p139*
Catrein, Elisabeth *SEE* Catrein, Jakob
Catrein, Elisabeth Muller *SEE* Catrein, Jakob
Catrein, Jakob; Brazil, 1862 ***5475.1*** *p561*
*Wife:*Elisabeth Muller
*Daughter:*Katharina
*Daughter:*Elisabeth
Catrein, Katharina *SEE* Catrein, Jakob
Catt, Mr. 29; New Orleans, 1840 ***778.6*** *p62*
Catt, Henry 35; Ontario, 1871 ***1823.17*** *p26*
Catt, Henry 52; Ontario, 1871 ***1823.17*** *p26*
Catt, Stephen 30; Ontario, 1871 ***1823.17*** *p26*
Cattanach, Peter 65; Ontario, 1871 ***1823.17*** *p26*
Cattermole, James 62; Ontario, 1871 ***1823.21*** *p57*
Cattley, Harriet 46; Ontario, 1871 ***1823.21*** *p57*
Catton, John; Maryland, 1673 ***1236.25*** *p49*
Cattrell, Bessie 11; Quebec, 1870 ***8364.32*** *p22*
Cattula, C.; Galveston, TX, 1855 ***571.7*** *p18*
Caubere, Catherine 30; Port uncertain, 1846 ***778.6*** *p62*
Caubere, Jean 26; New Orleans, 1845 ***778.6*** *p62*
Caubert, Mr. 23; Port uncertain, 1845 ***778.6*** *p62*
Caubin, Miss; New Orleans, 1845 ***778.6*** *p62*
Caubin, Mrs.; New Orleans, 1845 ***778.6*** *p62*
Caubin, D...que 45; New Orleans, 1845 ***778.6*** *p62*
Caubine, Jane 9; Quebec, 1870 ***8364.32*** *p22*
Cauchois, Michel; Quebec, 1642 ***9221.17*** *p114*
Caudellou, . . .; America, 1840 ***778.6*** *p62*
Caudellou, Mrs. 30; America, 1840 ***778.6*** *p62*
Caudellou, Bernard 38; America, 1840 ***778.6*** *p62*
Caudron, J. B. Casimir; Illinois, 1852 ***6079.1*** *p3*
Caughey, Alex; Louisiana, 1874-1875 ***4981.45*** *p298*
Caughlin, Daniel; Toronto, 1844 ***2910.35*** *p115*
Caughlin, Elizabeth 66; Ontario, 1871 ***1823.21*** *p57*
Caughlin, Hariet 27; Ontario, 1871 ***1823.21*** *p57*
Caughlin, Lucenda 60; Ontario, 1871 ***1823.21*** *p57*
Caughlin, Michael 60; Ontario, 1871 ***1823.17*** *p26*
Caul, . . .; Boston, 1769 ***9228.50*** *p5*
Caul, Geo.; Boston, 1769 ***9228.50*** *p48*
Caul, Geo.; Boston, 1769 ***9228.50*** *p111*
Caul, George; Boston, 1769 ***9228.50*** *p157*
Caul, John; Wisconsin, 1800-1899 ***9228.50*** *p164*
Cauldre, Elizabeth 54; Ontario, 1871 ***1823.21*** *p57*
Caulfield, Francis; Toronto, 1844 ***2910.35*** *p116*
Caulfield, James 36; Ontario, 1871 ***1823.21*** *p57*
Caulfield, John; New Orleans, 1851 ***7242.30*** *p138*
Caulfield, Mary; New Orleans, 1851 ***7242.30*** *p138*
Caulfield, William; Toronto, 1844 ***2910.35*** *p116*
Caumartin, Nic. 29; America, 1841 ***778.6*** *p62*
Caumont, Jacques; Quebec, 1636 ***9221.17*** *p53*
*Brother:*Robert
Caumont, Pierre; Quebec, 1642 ***9221.17*** *p114*
Caumont, Robert *SEE* Caumont, Jacques
Caurot, Mrs. 25; New Orleans, 1844 ***778.6*** *p62*
Caurot, P. 27; New Orleans, 1844 ***778.6*** *p62*
Caurse, Charles, Sr. 72; Ontario, 1871 ***1823.21*** *p57*
Causinier, Perrine; Quebec, 1649 ***9221.17*** *p209*
*Son:*Pierre
Causinier, Pierre 11 *SEE* Causinier, Perrine Baudry
Causley, Malisa 62; Ontario, 1871 ***1823.17*** *p26*
Caust, William 53; Ontario, 1871 ***1823.21*** *p57*
Cautane, Mr. 25; New Orleans, 1840 ***778.6*** *p62*
Cautau, Anne 22; America, 1848 ***778.6*** *p62*
Cautegrille, Pierre 19; New Orleans, 1843 ***778.6*** *p62*
Cautepie, Jean; Virginia, 1700 ***9230.15*** *p81*
Cautepie, Michell; Virginia, 1700 ***9230.15*** *p81*
With wife & 2 children
Cauvet, Ambroise; Quebec, 1633 ***9221.17*** *p28*
Cauvin, Pierre; Montreal, 1660 ***9221.17*** *p440*
Caux, Eliz; Boston, 1716 ***9228.50*** *p273*
Cavalgieri, Domino; Washington, 1883 ***2770.40*** *p136*
Cavalier, Charles 9; Port uncertain, 1846 ***778.6*** *p62*
Cavalier, Pablo 27; New Orleans, 1841 ***778.6*** *p62*
Cavalier, Pr. Charles 45; Port uncertain, 1846 ***778.6*** *p62*
Cavallier, Francois 40; America, 1845 ***778.6*** *p62*
Cavallier, Jean 48; America, 1845 ***778.6*** *p62*
Cavallier, Jean Baptiste 17; America, 1845 ***778.6*** *p62*
Cavallier, Victoria 10; America, 1845 ***778.6*** *p62*
Cavan, Hugh 51; Ontario, 1871 ***1823.21*** *p57*
Cavana, John; North Carolina, 1859 ***1088.45*** *p5*
Cavanagh, Edward; Ohio, 1809-1852 ***4511.35*** *p8*
Cavanagh, Edward 45; Ontario, 1871 ***1823.21*** *p57*
Cavanagh, Fobe 102; Ontario, 1871 ***1823.21*** *p57*
Cavanagh, James; Louisiana, 1841-1844 ***4981.45*** *p210*
Cavanagh, Miles; Toronto, 1844 ***2910.35*** *p115*
Cavanagh, Priscila 61; Ontario, 1871 ***1823.21*** *p57*
Cavanagh, William 27; Ontario, 1871 ***1823.21*** *p57*
Cavanah, F. D.; North Carolina, 1861 ***1088.45*** *p5*
Cavanah, John 60; Ontario, 1871 ***1823.21*** *p57*
Cavanaugh, Chs. 42; Ontario, 1871 ***1823.17*** *p26*
Cavanaugh, John 41; Ontario, 1871 ***1823.17*** *p26*
Cavanaugh, Margaret 31; Ontario, 1871 ***1823.17*** *p26*
Cavanaugh, Thomas; Ohio, 1840-1897 ***8365.35*** *p15*
Cavaner, Peter 42; Ontario, 1871 ***1823.21*** *p57*
Cavannah, P.; New Orleans, 1850 ***7242.30*** *p138*
Cave, Alfred 33; Ontario, 1871 ***1823.21*** *p57*
Cave, Joesph 61; Ontario, 1871 ***1823.21*** *p57*
Cave, John; New York, 1783 ***8529.30*** *p10*
Cave, Thomas; Salem, MA, 1700 ***9228.50*** *p157*
Cave, William 42; Ontario, 1871 ***1823.21*** *p57*
Cavelier, Robert 24; Montreal, 1650 ***9221.17*** *p230*
Cavelier deLa Salle, Rene-Robert; Quebec, 1667 ***2314.30*** *p167*
Cavelier deLa Salle, Rene-Robert; Quebec, 1675 ***2314.30*** *p177*
Cavelius, Adam; America, 1882 ***5475.1*** *p229*
*Wife:*Susanna Eglin
*Daughter:*Anna
Cavelius, Anna *SEE* Cavelius, Adam
Cavelius, Nikolaus; America, 1882 ***5475.1*** *p228*
Cavelius, Susanna Eglin *SEE* Cavelius, Adam
Caven, William; Philadelphia, 1853 ***5720.10*** *p377*
Cavenah, Adam; Boston, 1756 ***1642*** *p47*
Cavenaugh, Adam; Boston, 1747 ***1642*** *p46*
Cavenaugh, Charles; Massachusetts, 1745 ***1642*** *p28*
Cavenaugh, Charles; New England, 1745 ***1642*** *p28*
Cavenaugh, Daniel; Boston, 1736 ***1642*** *p44*
Cavenaugh, Daniel; Boston, 1745 ***1642*** *p28*
Cavenaugh, Maurice; Boston, 1766 ***1642*** *p38*
Cavenaugh, Maurice; Boston, 1767 ***1642*** *p39*
Cavener, Danby; Boston, 1744 ***1642*** *p45*
Cavener, John; Massachusetts, 1718 ***1642*** *p85*
Cavennaigh, Lucy; Beverly, MA, 1765 ***1642*** *p64*
Cavennigh, James; Beverly, MA, 1760 ***1642*** *p64*
Cavenno, Arthur; Boston, 1736 ***1642*** *p44*
Cavenough, Captain; Boston, 1764 ***1642*** *p33*
Caverhill, Archibald 54; Ontario, 1871 ***1823.21*** *p57*
Caverhill, Thomas 59; Ontario, 1871 ***1823.21*** *p57*
Caverner, Catherine *SEE* Caverner, James
Caverner, James; Newburyport, MA, 1765 ***1642*** *p76*
*Wife:*Catherine
Caves, James 43; Ontario, 1871 ***1823.21*** *p57*
Caves, John 56; Ontario, 1871 ***1823.21*** *p57*
Cavet, Thomas; Salem, MA, 1700 ***9228.50*** *p157*
Cavey, Thomas; Salem, MA, 1700 ***9228.50*** *p157*
Caville, D. B. 38; Ontario, 1871 ***1823.21*** *p57*
Cavin, Peter 34; Ontario, 1871 ***1823.21*** *p57*
Cavinah, Tim 31; Ontario, 1871 ***1823.17*** *p26*
Caviot, Joseph 27; New Orleans, 1840 ***778.6*** *p58*
Cavit, Patrick; Ohio, 1841 ***2763.1*** *p7*
Cavner, William; Philadelphia, 1856 ***5720.10*** *p379*
Caw, William 28; Ontario, 1871 ***1823.21*** *p57*
Cawruthers, George 36; Ontario, 1871 ***1823.21*** *p57*
Cawthorpe, William 41; Ontario, 1871 ***1823.21*** *p57*
Cawthrope, Thomas 49; Ontario, 1871 ***1823.21*** *p57*
Cayer, Jean; Quebec, 1653 ***9221.17*** *p270*
Caylus, E. 27; New York, 1840 ***778.6*** *p62*
Cayol, Andre 30; Port uncertain, 1843 ***778.6*** *p63*
Cayot, Francis; Ohio, 1809-1852 ***4511.35*** *p8*
Caza, Marguerite; Nova Scotia, 1753 ***3051*** *p112*
Cazale, Mr. 20; New Orleans, 1840 ***778.6*** *p63*
Cazanova, A.; Louisiana, 1874-1875 ***4981.45*** *p298*
Cazaux, . . .; New Orleans, 1845 ***778.6*** *p63*
Cazaux, John Marie; North Carolina, 1824 ***1088.45*** *p5*
Cazaux, Paule 30; New Orleans, 1845 ***778.6*** *p210*
Cazaux, Pierre 23; New Orleans, 1845 ***778.6*** *p63*
Caze, Mr. 30; New Orleans, 1840 ***778.6*** *p63*
Cazeau, Dominique 20; New Orleans, 1848 ***778.6*** *p63*
Cazeau, Dominique 38; New Orleans, 1844 ***778.6*** *p63*
Cazeaux, Charles 37; Texas, 1845 ***778.6*** *p63*
Cazeaux, J. J. 20; America, 1848 ***778.6*** *p63*
Cazelle, Francois 28; Port uncertain, 1845 ***778.6*** *p63*
Cazelle, Rosa 31; Port uncertain, 1845 ***778.6*** *p63*
Cazenave, J. P. 16; Port uncertain, 1843 ***778.6*** *p63*
Cazenave, Jean 26; New Orleans, 1840 ***778.6*** *p63*
Cazentre, J.Marie 29; New Orleans, 1848 ***778.6*** *p63*
Cazeres, E. 39; Port uncertain, 1748 ***778.6*** *p63*
Cazeres, Francois 18; New Orleans, 1848 ***778.6*** *p63*
Cazes, Hypolite 29; Port uncertain, 1846 ***778.6*** *p63*
Cearney, William; Toronto, 1844 ***2910.35*** *p115*
Ceasedorf, Charles; Ohio, 1809-1852 ***4511.35*** *p8*
Ceaton, John; America, 1767 ***1220.12*** *p709*
Cebula, Mary; Detroit, 1929-1930 ***6214.5*** *p61*
Cech, Martin; Chicago, 1857 ***2853.20*** *p389*
Cechlinska, Zofia 26; New York, NY, 1911 ***6533.11*** *p10*
Cechova, A.; America, 1899 ***2853.20*** *p512*
Cecks, Jeab 29; Ontario, 1871 ***1823.21*** *p57*
Cedarholm, Peter; Iowa, 1877 ***1211.15*** *p9*
Cederberg, Erik; Colorado, 1891 ***1029.59*** *p16*
Cederblom, J. Isaac; Minnesota, 1866-1867 ***1865.50*** *p44*
Cedik, Josef; Chicago, 1870 ***2853.20*** *p405*
Cellane, Jean Pierre; Illinois, 1852 ***6079.1*** *p3*
Cellard, Jean 23; America, 1841 ***778.6*** *p63*
Cellberg, Erick 25; Kansas, 1880 ***777.40*** *p9*
Celle DuClos, Gabriel 19; Quebec, 1645 ***9221.17*** *p152*
Celles Duclos, Gabriel; Quebec, 1643 ***2314.30*** *p172*
Cellier, Jean; Montreal, 1659 ***9221.17*** *p418*
Celoron deBlainville, Jean-Baptiste; Quebec, 1683-1688 ***2314.30*** *p168*

Celoron deBlainville, Jean-Baptiste; Quebec, 1684 ***2314.30*** *p177*
Cemmer, George; Ohio, 1809-1852 ***4511.35*** *p8*
Cemus, Frantisek; New York, NY, 1881 ***2853.20*** *p301*
Cenac, Raymond 30; New Orleans, 1843 ***778.6*** *p63*
Censedorf, Charles; Ohio, 1809-1852 ***4511.35*** *p8*
Cerdaiman, Thievaut 36; New Orleans, 1848 ***778.6*** *p63*
Cere, Michel; Quebec, 1640 ***9221.17*** *p95*
Ceretto, Jim; Illinois, 1918 ***6007.60*** *p9*
Cerf, Mr. 22; Louisiana, 1848 ***778.6*** *p63*
Cermak, Jaroslav; St. Paul, MN, 1891 ***2853.20*** *p264*
Cermak, Josef; Chicago, 1858-1910 ***2853.20*** *p405*
Cermak, Josef; Chicago, 1910 ***2853.20*** *p415*
Cermak, Karel; Cleveland, OH, 1867 ***2853.20*** *p498*
Cermak, Tomas; Baltimore, 1847 ***2853.20*** *p125*
Cernin, Jan; Idaho, 1853 ***2853.20*** *p211*
Cerny, Frantisek V.; New York, NY, 1848 ***2853.20*** *p308*
Cerny, Jan; Iowa, 1853 ***2853.20*** *p211*
Cerny, Jan; Oklahoma, 1889 ***2853.20*** *p372*
Cerny, Josef; Oklahoma, 1889 ***2853.20*** *p372*
Cerny, Matej; Illinois, 1853-1910 ***2853.20*** *p471*
Cerny, Vojtech; Chicago, 1871-1910 ***2853.20*** *p465*
Cerre, Jacques; Montreal, 1661 ***9221.17*** *p471*
Certain, Manuel; North Carolina, 1826 ***1088.45*** *p5*
Certive, L. 33; America, 1848 ***778.6*** *p63*
Cerveny, Frantisek; New York, NY, 1848 ***2853.20*** *p100*
Cerveny, Frantisek; New York, NY, 1858 ***2853.20*** *p103*
Cerveny, Petr M.; Cleveland, OH, 1892 ***2853.20*** *p487*
Cerves, Johan 28; America, 1840 ***778.6*** *p63*
Ceryon, Casimir; Wisconsin, 1878 ***1495.20*** *p12*
*Wife:*Desiree Calonne
*Child:*Florimond
*Child:*Nicolas Joseph
*Child:*Henri
*Child:*Desire George
*Child:*Oscar
*Child:*Gustave Ferdinand
Ceryon, Desire George *SEE* Ceryon, Casimir
Ceryon, Desiree Calonne *SEE* Ceryon, Casimir
Ceryon, Florimond *SEE* Ceryon, Casimir
Ceryon, Gustave Ferdinand *SEE* Ceryon, Casimir
Ceryon, Henri *SEE* Ceryon, Casimir
Ceryon, Nicolas Joseph *SEE* Ceryon, Casimir
Ceryon, Oscar *SEE* Ceryon, Casimir
Cesak, Blazij; Texas, 1896 ***6015.15*** *p23*
Ceserac, Franc.s 35; America, 1841 ***778.6*** *p63*
Cesey, Catherine; Boston, 1763 ***1642*** *p32*
Cespa, Antonio; Illinois, 1918 ***6007.60*** *p9*
Cessac, Mr. 19; America, 1747 ***778.6*** *p63*
Cestia, A. 14; New Orleans, 1848 ***778.6*** *p63*
Cetto, Max; America, 1847 ***5475.1*** *p474*
Ceutre, Frederich; Louisiana, 1874 ***4981.45*** *p131*
Ceverne, Janette; America, 1673 ***9228.50*** *p157*
Chabanas, Isaac; Virginia, 1700 ***9230.15*** *p80*
With sons
Chabanel, Noel 30; Quebec, 1643 ***9221.17*** *p127*
Chabaud, A. 29; America, 1841 ***778.6*** *p63*
Chabaud, Anais 30; Louisiana, 1848 ***778.6*** *p63*
Chabaud, Pierre August 20; New Orleans, 1845 ***778.6*** *p63*
Chabert De La Chariere, Marguerite; Quebec, 1668 ***4514.3*** *p287*
Chabol, J. 30; America, 1840 ***778.6*** *p63*
Chabot, Hy. 20; America, 1845 ***778.6*** *p63*
Chabot, Mathurin 20; Quebec, 1657 ***9221.17*** *p354*
Chabrito, Andrew; Boston, 1766 ***1642*** *p36*
Chace, James; Marston's Wharf, 1781 ***8529.30*** *p10*
Chackley, Francis L. 40; Ontario, 1871 ***1823.17*** *p26*
Chadeffaud, Camille 21; New Orleans, 1848 ***778.6*** *p64*
Chadina, Frantisek; Michigan, 1858 ***2853.20*** *p370*
Chadville, Nicholas 42; America, 1841 ***778.6*** *p64*
Chadwick, Catharin 55; Ontario, 1871 ***1823.21*** *p57*
Chadwick, John U.; New York, NY, 1832 ***3274.55*** *p71*
Chadwick, Samuel 31; Ontario, 1871 ***1823.21*** *p57*
Chaevelot, John Francis; Illinois, 1860 ***6079.1*** *p3*
Chagneau, Jean; Quebec, 1650 ***9221.17*** *p224*
Chagniau, Louise *SEE* Chagniau, Nicolas
Chagniau, Nicolas; Quebec, 1642 ***9221.17*** *p114*
*Wife:*Louise
Chagnolet, Gilles 24; Quebec, 1643 ***9221.17*** *p131*
Chaigne, Mr. 36; America, 1746 ***778.6*** *p64*
Chaigneau, Louise *SEE* Chaigneau, Nicolas
Chaigneau, Nicolas; Quebec, 1642 ***9221.17*** *p114*
*Wife:*Louise
Chaigneau, Nicolas; Quebec, 1651 ***9221.17*** *p238*
Chaillet, Louis 20; America, 1841 ***778.6*** *p64*
Chaillet, Mathurin 18; Quebec, 1657 ***9221.17*** *p354*
Chaillet, Menart 30; America, 1841 ***778.6*** *p64*
Chaillon, . . .; Quebec, 1652 ***9221.17*** *p256*
Chaineau, Rene; Quebec, 1649 ***9221.17*** *p210*
Chaineux, Francois 28; New Orleans, 1848 ***778.6*** *p64*
Chaineux, Louise 21; New Orleans, 1848 ***778.6*** *p64*
Chaineywoolfe, John Bernard; North Carolina, 1710 ***3629.40*** *p6*
Chairriere, Eugene; Louisiana, 1836-1841 ***4981.45*** *p208*
Chaise, Etienne 29; New Orleans, 1848 ***778.6*** *p64*
Chaise, Marie 25; New Orleans, 1848 ***778.6*** *p64*
Chaix, Henry 30; America, 1841 ***778.6*** *p64*
Chaix, Sebastian 20; Port uncertain, 1842 ***778.6*** *p64*
Chakiris, Anastasios Aristotadis; Miami, 1935 ***4984.12*** *p39*
Chakiris, Andy; Miami, 1935 ***4984.12*** *p39*
Chalan, Mrs. 41; New Orleans, 1843 ***778.6*** *p64*
Chalan, Adelia 12; New Orleans, 1843 ***778.6*** *p64*
Chalan, Louisa 2; New Orleans, 1843 ***778.6*** *p64*
Chalard, J. 27; New Orleans, 1843 ***778.6*** *p64*
Chalard, N. 25; Port uncertain, 1841 ***778.6*** *p64*
Chalatinon, F. 55; America, 1848 ***778.6*** *p64*
Chalberg, Carl Gustaf; Boston, 1899 ***1766.20*** *p16*
Chalet, Felix 22; New Orleans, 1848 ***778.6*** *p64*
Chalette, F. C.; Louisiana, 1836-1840 ***4981.45*** *p212*
Chaleut, Marie 20; Quebec, 1657 ***9221.17*** *p354*
Chaleut, Pierre 24; Quebec, 1654 ***9221.17*** *p305*
Chalfont, Roy; Chicago, 1947-1970 ***9228.50*** *p174*
Chalifour, Paul 34; Quebec, 1647 ***9221.17*** *p177*
Chalk, Henry 45; Ontario, 1871 ***1823.17*** *p26*
Challavant, Auguste 29; New Orleans, 1848 ***778.6*** *p64*
Challenger, Thomas 25; Ontario, 1871 ***1823.21*** *p58*
Challiner, George; Marston's Wharf, 1782 ***8529.30*** *p10*
Challinor, George; Marston's Wharf, 1782 ***8529.30*** *p10*
Challoner, Thomas S. 40; Ontario, 1871 ***1823.17*** *p26*
Chalmer, Alexander 68; Ontario, 1871 ***1823.17*** *p26*
Chalmer, John 24; Indiana, 1869-1870 ***9076.20*** *p67*
Chalmers, Alexander 41; Ontario, 1871 ***1823.17*** *p27*
Chalmers, Alexander; South Carolina, 1808 ***6155.4*** *p18*
Chalmers, David; South Carolina, 1808 ***6155.4*** *p18*
Chalmers, James; Jamaica, 1783 ***8529.30*** *p12A*
Chalmers, James; Ontario, 1871 ***1823.21*** *p58*
Chalmers, James 70; Ontario, 1871 ***1823.17*** *p27*
Chalmers, James; South Carolina, 1808 ***6155.4*** *p18*
Chalmers, Margaret 16; Ontario, 1871 ***1823.17*** *p27*
Chalmers, Margaret 18; Ontario, 1871 ***1823.17*** *p27*
Chalmers, Robert 60; Ontario, 1871 ***1823.17*** *p27*
Chalmers, Robert S. 43; Ontario, 1871 ***1823.17*** *p27*
Chalmers, William 61; Ontario, 1871 ***1823.21*** *p58*
Chalmers, William; South Carolina, 1808 ***6155.4*** *p18*
Chaloner, George O. 50; Ontario, 1871 ***1823.21*** *p58*
Chaloner, N. K. 54; Ontario, 1871 ***1823.21*** *p58*
Chaloupka, Antonin; Nebraska, 1868 ***2853.20*** *p156*
Chaloupka, Frantisek; Nebraska, 1871 ***2853.20*** *p157*
Chaloupka, Martin; Texas, 1860 ***2853.20*** *p74*
Chalupsky, Josef; Minnesota, 1870 ***2853.20*** *p265*
Chamare, Pierre 24; Quebec, 1662 ***9221.17*** *p482*
Chambaudt, Claud 23; America, 1846 ***778.6*** *p64*
Chambelle, C. 18; America, 1846 ***778.6*** *p64*
Chamberlain, . . .; Ontario, 1871 ***1823.17*** *p27*
Chamberlain, Capt.; America, 1600-1699 ***9228.50*** *p157*
Chamberlain, Albert 6; Michigan, 1880 ***4491.30*** *p5*
Chamberlain, Daniel; Massachusetts, 1776-1785 ***9228.50*** *p157*
*Relative:*Eli
Chamberlain, Ebenezer; North Carolina, 1715 ***9228.50*** *p157*
Chamberlain, Eli *SEE* Chamberlain, Daniel
Chamberlain, Mary 70; Ontario, 1871 ***1823.17*** *p27*
Chamberlain, Richard; Salem, MA, 1699 ***9228.50*** *p19A*
Chamberlain, Richard; Salem, MA, 1700 ***9228.50*** *p18A*
Chamberlayne, Abram; New Jersey, n.d. ***9228.50*** *p157*
Chamberlin, Sam.; Maryland, 1672 ***1236.25*** *p46*
Chamberlyne, Hannah; Boston, n.d. ***9228.50*** *p392*
Chambers, Ann 36; Ontario, 1871 ***1823.21*** *p58*
Chambers, Charles 30; Ontario, 1871 ***1823.17*** *p27*
Chambers, Charles 32; Ontario, 1871 ***1823.21*** *p58*
Chambers, Charles 73; Ontario, 1871 ***1823.17*** *p27*
Chambers, David 51; Ontario, 1871 ***1823.21*** *p58*
Chambers, David 60; Ontario, 1871 ***1823.21*** *p58*
Chambers, Edgar 26; Ontario, 1871 ***1823.17*** *p27*
Chambers, James; New York, 1859 ***358.56*** *p100*
Chambers, James 33; Ontario, 1871 ***1823.21*** *p58*
Chambers, James 38; Ontario, 1871 ***1823.17*** *p27*
Chambers, Richard; Philadelphia, 1778 ***8529.30*** *p2A*
Chambers, Robert 58; Ontario, 1871 ***1823.21*** *p58*
Chambers, William; New York, NY, 1840 ***3274.56*** *p100*
Chambers, William 40; Ontario, 1871 ***1823.21*** *p58*
Chambers, William 42; Ontario, 1871 ***1823.21*** *p58*
Chambers, William 60; Ontario, 1871 ***1823.17*** *p27*
Chambers, William G. 54; Ontario, 1871 ***1823.21*** *p58*
Chambert, Elie; Quebec, 1659 ***9221.17*** *p396*
Chamblain, J. L.; California, 1868 ***1131.61*** *p89*
Chambord, Paul; Montreal, 1644 ***9221.17*** *p146*
Chambot, Mathurin 20; Quebec, 1657 ***9221.17*** *p354*
Chamboux, Jedron; Virginia, 1700 ***9230.15*** *p80*
With wife
Chamboy, Jacqueline 26; Quebec, 1648 ***9221.17*** *p202*
*Daughter:*Louise 2
*Daughter:*Jeanne-Francoise 6 months
Chambry, Amelie 49; New Orleans, 1848 ***778.6*** *p64*
Chambry, Charles 27; New Orleans, 1848 ***778.6*** *p64*
Chambry, Eugene Jean 32; New Orleans, 1848 ***778.6*** *p64*
Chambry, Felicite 27; New Orleans, 1848 ***778.6*** *p64*
Chambry, Joseph 52; New Orleans, 1848 ***778.6*** *p64*
Chambry, Marguerite 26; New Orleans, 1848 ***778.6*** *p64*
Chambry, Maria 3; New Orleans, 1848 ***778.6*** *p64*
Chambry, Paul 5; New Orleans, 1848 ***778.6*** *p64*
Chambry, Pierre 28; Missouri, 1848 ***778.6*** *p64*
Chamebers, Thomas 63; Ontario, 1871 ***1823.21*** *p58*
Chamet, Mrs. 36; America, 1844 ***778.6*** *p64*
Chamfrau, B. 20; America, 1848 ***778.6*** *p65*
Chamois, Marie-Claude; Quebec, 1670 ***4514.3*** *p287*
Chamont, Prospere 22; America, 1846 ***778.6*** *p65*
Champagne, . . . 24; Quebec, 1661 ***9221.17*** *p451*
Champagne, Francois; Quebec, 1641 ***9221.17*** *p102*
Champagne, Gilles; Quebec, 1654 ***9221.17*** *p313*
Champagne, Michel; Quebec, 1658 ***9221.17*** *p383*
Champagne, Nicolas; Quebec, 1638 ***9221.17*** *p79*
Champagne, Noel; Quebec, 1657 ***9221.17*** *p369*
Champagne, Peter; Ontario, 1871 ***1823.17*** *p27*
Champagne, Potor; Ontario, 1871 ***1823.17*** *p27*
Champale, Etienne 40; America, 1842 ***778.6*** *p65*
Champale, Pierre 17; America, 1842 ***778.6*** *p65*
Champeau, Francois; Illinois, 1856 ***6079.1*** *p3*
Champeau, Francois 41; Texas, 1848 ***778.6*** *p65*
Champeau, Pierre Marie Prudent; Illinois, 1855 ***6079.1*** *p3*
Champeau, Pre. Francois 17; Texas, 1848 ***778.6*** *p65*
Champeaux, Marie Louise 37; New Orleans, 1848 ***778.6*** *p65*
Champeaux, Pierre Francois 10; New Orleans, 1848 ***778.6*** *p65*
Champeaux, Pierre Marie 15; New Orleans, 1848 ***778.6*** *p65*
Champflour, Amable de *SEE* Champflour, Francois de
Champflour, Francois de; Quebec, 1639 ***9221.17*** *p82*
*Son:*Amable de
*Son:*Marcel de
Champflour, Marcel de *SEE* Champflour, Francois de
Champfort, . . .; Quebec, 1636 ***9221.17*** *p53*
Champigny, . . .; Quebec, 1646 ***9221.17*** *p162*
Champion, Alex 34; Ontario, 1871 ***1823.17*** *p27*
Champion, Charles 29; New Orleans, 1847 ***778.6*** *p65*
Champion, Francis 44; Ontario, 1871 ***1823.21*** *p58*
Champion, Francis 69; Ontario, 1871 ***1823.21*** *p58*
Champion, Frederick; Ontario, 1871 ***1823.17*** *p27*
Champion, Mary Ann; New York, 1843-1871 ***9228.50*** *p213*
Champion, Mary Ann; New York, 1853-1910 ***9228.50*** *p157*
Champlain, Helene Boulle *SEE* Champlain, Samuel de
Champlain, Samuel de; Quebec, 1608 ***9221.17*** *p26*
*Wife:*Helene Boulle
Champoux, Cphriam; Washington, 1884 ***2770.40*** *p192*
Chancel, Antoine 29; America, 1841 ***778.6*** *p65*
Chancelier, Francois; Quebec, 1653 ***9221.17*** *p270*
Chancy, Marie; Quebec, 1673 ***4514.3*** *p287*
Chandel, Andreas 6; America, 1846 ***778.6*** *p65*
Chandel, Georges 4; America, 1846 ***778.6*** *p65*
Chandel, Laurent 40; America, 1846 ***778.6*** *p65*
Chandel, Magdalena 38; America, 1846 ***778.6*** *p65*
Chandel, Miston 8; America, 1846 ***778.6*** *p65*
Chandel, Wilhelm 1; America, 1846 ***778.6*** *p65*
Chandet, Joseph 18; Kentucky, 1846 ***778.6*** *p65*
Chandler, Burdett 34; Ontario, 1871 ***1823.17*** *p27*
Chandler, George; New York, 1783 ***8529.30*** *p10*
Chandler, Melville D. 24; Kansas, 1892 ***1447.20*** *p62*
Chandoiseau, Nicole; Quebec, 1670 ***4514.3*** *p287*
Chandriau, Jean 23; Quebec, 1659 ***9221.17*** *p396*
Chaney, M.; New Orleans, 1850 ***7242.30*** *p138*
Chaney Wolfe, John Bernard; North Carolina, 1710 ***3629.40*** *p6*
Chaneywoolfe, John Bernard; North Carolina, 1710 ***3629.40*** *p6*
Chanfrain, Renee; Quebec, 1669 ***4514.3*** *p288*
Changelon, Angeline Joseph *SEE* Changelon, Jean Joseph
Changelon, Florent *SEE* Changelon, Jean Joseph
Changelon, Gaspar Joseph *SEE* Changelon, Jean Joseph
Changelon, Henri *SEE* Changelon, Jean Joseph
Changelon, Jean Joseph *SEE* Changelon, Jean Joseph
Changelon, Jean Joseph; Wisconsin, 1856 ***1495.20*** *p41*
*Wife:*Rose Melon
*Child:*Marie Therese
*Child:*Gaspar Joseph
*Child:*Angeline Joseph
*Child:*Victor Joseph
*Child:*Florent

*Child:*Jean Joseph
*Child:*Henri
*Child:*Victoire
Changelon, Marie Therese *SEE* Changelon, Jean Joseph
Changelon, Rose Melon *SEE* Changelon, Jean Joseph
Changelon, Victoire *SEE* Changelon, Jean Joseph
Changelon, Victor Joseph *SEE* Changelon, Jean Joseph
Chang-Eng, . . .; North Carolina, 1839 ***1088.45*** *p5*
Chanleon, Adolphe 23; America, 1841 ***778.6*** *p65*
Channiler, George; Marston's Wharf, 1782 ***8529.30*** *p10*
Channitz, Johann Aug.; Wisconsin, 1868 ***6795.8*** *p137*
Channot Pourret, Victor 32; America, 1842 ***778.6*** *p65*
Chanrion, Antony 23; America, 1846 ***778.6*** *p65*
Chanson, Louis 25; Missouri, 1848 ***778.6*** *p65*
Chant, Benjamin; Colorado, 1874 ***1029.59*** *p16*
Chantini, J. 22; New Orleans, 1840 ***778.6*** *p65*
Chantinne, Marie Barbe; Wisconsin, 1887 ***1495.20*** *p12*
Chantracq, Mr. 34; Port uncertain, 1840 ***778.6*** *p65*
Chanut, Mr. 8; America, 1844 ***778.6*** *p65*
Chanverlange, Jeanne-Madeleine 18; Quebec, 1655 ***9221.17*** *p321*
Chanvreux, Renee; Quebec, 1669 ***4514.3*** *p288*
Chaon, Auguste 6; Louisiana, 1848 ***778.6*** *p65*
Chaon, Fcois. Xavier 27; Louisiana, 1848 ***778.6*** *p65*
Chaon, Josephine 33; Louisiana, 1848 ***778.6*** *p65*
Chaon, Pre. Amedee 5; Louisiana, 1848 ***778.6*** *p65*
Chapacou, Marie; Canada, 1664 ***1142.10*** *p128*
With family
Chapeau, Pierre 25; Quebec, 1648 ***9221.17*** *p196*
Chapel, A. 38; America, 1843 ***778.6*** *p65*
Chapel, Mrs. 24; America, 1843 ***778.6*** *p65*
Chapelain, Bernard 13 *SEE* Chapelain, Louis
Chapelain, Francoise 14 *SEE* Chapelain, Louis
Chapelain, Francoise Dechaux 39 *SEE* Chapelain, Louis
Chapelain, Jacques; Quebec, 1658 ***9221.17*** *p377*
*Son:*Jacques
Chapelain, Jacques 27 *SEE* Chapelain, Jacques
Chapelain, Louis 42; Quebec, 1660 ***9221.17*** *p432*
*Wife:*Francoise Dechaux 39
*Daughter:*Francoise 14
*Son:*Bernard 13
Chapeleau, Jean 26; Quebec, 1653 ***9221.17*** *p270*
Chapelier, Louis 31; New Orleans, 1843 ***778.6*** *p65*
Chapelier, Marie 25; Quebec, 1649 ***9221.17*** *p210*
Chapelle, Jeanne Joseph Barras *SEE* Chapelle, Pierre
Chapelle, Pierre; Wisconsin, 1856 ***1495.20*** *p46*
*Wife:*Jeanne Joseph Barras
Chapelle, S. 32; America, 1848 ***778.6*** *p66*
Chaperon, Jean 19; Quebec, 1656 ***9221.17*** *p333*
Chapiteau, Pierre 49; Quebec, 1654 ***9221.17*** *p306*
Chaplain, Charles T.; Louisiana, 1841-1844 ***4981.45*** *p210*
Chaplain, Louis Pierre; Louisiana, 1841-1844 ***4981.45*** *p210*
Chaplin, Ephrim 44; Ontario, 1871 ***1823.21*** *p58*
Chaplin, Richard 42; Ontario, 1871 ***1823.21*** *p58*
Chapman, Alfred 41; Ontario, 1871 ***1823.21*** *p58*
Chapman, Andrew 65; Ontario, 1871 ***1823.21*** *p58*
Chapman, Ann *SEE* Chapman, Lancelot
Chapman, Ann *SEE* Chapman, William
Chapman, Charles 29; Ontario, 1871 ***1823.21*** *p58*
Chapman, Charles 44; Ontario, 1871 ***1823.21*** *p58*
Chapman, Elizabeth 21; Ontario, 1871 ***1823.21*** *p58*
Chapman, Frances *SEE* Chapman, Lancelot
Chapman, Frances *SEE* Chapman, Lancelot
Chapman, George 22; Ontario, 1871 ***1823.21*** *p58*
Chapman, Hannah *SEE* Chapman, Lancelot
Chapman, Henry *SEE* Chapman, William
Chapman, Henry 30; North Carolina, 1774 ***1422.10*** *p54*
Chapman, Henry 30; Ontario, 1871 ***1823.21*** *p58*
Chapman, Jane *SEE* Chapman, William
Chapman, John *SEE* Chapman, William
Chapman, John 35; Ontario, 1871 ***1823.21*** *p58*
Chapman, John 53; Ontario, 1871 ***1823.21*** *p58*
Chapman, Jonathan *SEE* Chapman, William
Chapman, Joseph 63; Michigan, 1880 ***4491.30*** *p5*
Chapman, Joseph 29; Ontario, 1871 ***1823.21*** *p58*
Chapman, Lancelot *SEE* Chapman, Lancelot
Chapman, Lancelot; Canada, 1774 ***3036.5*** *p40*
*Wife:*Frances
*Child:*Martin
*Child:*Lancelot
*Child:*Hannah
*Child:*Ann
*Child:*Frances
*Child:*Thomas
*Child:*Rachael
Chapman, Leicester; North Carolina, 1852 ***1088.45*** *p5*
Chapman, Martin *SEE* Chapman, Lancelot
Chapman, Martin; Ohio, 1840 ***2763.1*** *p7*
Chapman, Mary *SEE* Chapman, William
Chapman, Mary *SEE* Chapman, William
Chapman, Mary; Ipswich, MA, 1676 ***1642*** *p71*
Chapman, Rachael *SEE* Chapman, Lancelot
Chapman, Robert 47; Ontario, 1871 ***1823.21*** *p58*
Chapman, Rosenna 60; Ontario, 1871 ***1823.17*** *p27*
Chapman, Sarah *SEE* Chapman, William
Chapman, Sarah 59; Ontario, 1871 ***1823.21*** *p58*
Chapman, Simpson; Colorado, 1882 ***1029.59*** *p16*
Chapman, Thomas *SEE* Chapman, Lancelot
Chapman, Thomas *SEE* Chapman, William
Chapman, Thomas 44; Ontario, 1871 ***1823.17*** *p27*
Chapman, William *SEE* Chapman, William
Chapman, William; Canada, 1774 ***3036.5*** *p41*
*Wife:*Mary
*Child:*Mary
*Child:*Jonathan
*Child:*Ann
*Child:*Sarah
*Child:*Henry
*Child:*John
*Child:*William
*Child:*Thomas
*Child:*Jane
Chapman, William 34; Ontario, 1871 ***1823.17*** *p27*
Chapman, William 35; Ontario, 1871 ***1823.21*** *p58*
Chapman, Wm 65; Ontario, 1871 ***1823.21*** *p58*
Chapnis, Pierre 24; Ohio, 1847 ***778.6*** *p66*
Chapois, Auguste 42; Texas, 1843 ***778.6*** *p66*
Chapois, Felix Lyon; Texas, 1843 ***778.6*** *p66*
Chapon, Guillaume; Quebec, 1660 ***9221.17*** *p433*
Chapontot, Auguste 30; America, 1846 ***778.6*** *p66*
Chappais, D. 20; New Orleans, 1848 ***778.6*** *p66*
Chappius, Daniel; Ohio, 1809-1852 ***4511.35*** *p8*
Chappreis, Daniel; Ohio, 1809-1852 ***4511.35*** *p8*
Chappuis, Alfonce 18; Missouri, 1846 ***778.6*** *p66*
Chappuis, Genevieve 28; Missouri, 1846 ***778.6*** *p66*
Chapront, Louis 32; Missouri, 1848 ***778.6*** *p66*
Chapud, John 23; America, 1848 ***778.6*** *p66*
Chapuis, Catherine 36; Mississippi, 1847 ***778.6*** *p66*
Chapuis, Jean 56; Mississippi, 1847 ***778.6*** *p66*
Chapuis, Marie 11; Mississippi, 1847 ***778.6*** *p66*
Chapuis, Theodor 9; Mississippi, 1847 ***778.6*** *p66*
Chapus, Mrs.; New Orleans, 1840 ***778.6*** *p66*
Chapus, Ms.; New Orleans, 1840 ***778.6*** *p66*
Chapus, J. Fs. 45; New Orleans, 1840 ***778.6*** *p66*
Chapus, Jean; Louisiana, 1874 ***4981.45*** *p295*
Chapuy, Mary 27; America, 1848 ***778.6*** *p66*
Chapuy, Urbin 29; America, 1848 ***778.6*** *p66*
Charbonneau, Anne 2 *SEE* Charbonneau, Olivier
Charbonneau, Marie Garnier 34 *SEE* Charbonneau, Olivier
Charbonneau, Olivier 36; Montreal, 1659 ***9221.17*** *p419*
*Wife:*Marie Garnier 34
*Daughter:*Anne 2
Charbonnett, Mr. 19; America, 1846 ***778.6*** *p66*
Charbonnier, Johann; America, 1883 ***5475.1*** *p63*
Charbonnier, Marie-Madeleine; Quebec, 1672 ***4514.3*** *p288*
Chard, Sarah 24; Ontario, 1871 ***1823.17*** *p27*
Charde, Elizabeth; Massachusetts, 1630 ***117.5*** *p153*
Chardier, A.; Wisconsin, 1858 ***1494.20*** *p11*
Chardon, Eugenio; Puerto Rico, 1872 ***3476.25*** *p112*
Chardonneau, Hilaire 36; Quebec, 1657 ***9221.17*** *p354*
Chardy, E.; Louisiana, 1874-1875 ***4981.45*** *p298*
Charebert, Marie; Quebec, 1672 ***4514.3*** *p288*
Chareio, Barney; Ohio, 1809-1852 ***4511.35*** *p8*
Charelton, Thomas; Philadelphia, 1778 ***8529.30*** *p2A*
Charf, A.; Cleveland, OH, 1893-1900 ***9722.10*** *p118*
Chargneau, Daniel; Quebec, 1661 ***9221.17*** *p451*
Charias, Caliste 18; New Orleans, 1840 ***778.6*** *p66*
Charieo, Barney; Ohio, 1809-1852 ***4511.35*** *p8*
Charier, R. 31; New Orleans, 1842 ***778.6*** *p66*
Charland, Claude 20; Quebec, 1646 ***9221.17*** *p162*
Charles, . . . 25; Ontario, 1871 ***1823.21*** *p1*
Charles, Mrs. 39; America, 1844 ***778.6*** *p66*
Charles, Ms. 16; America, 1844 ***778.6*** *p66*
Charles, Catherine 22; Montreal, 1659 ***9221.17*** *p419*
Charles, Geo.; Louisiana, 1874-1875 ***4981.45*** *p298*
Charles, Guillaume; Quebec, 1662 ***9221.17*** *p482*
*Wife:*Marie Guillot
Charles, Henri; Quebec, 1659 ***9221.17*** *p396*
Charles, Jno. 23; New Orleans, 1845 ***778.6*** *p66*
Charles, John 64; Ontario, 1871 ***1823.21*** *p58*
Charles, Joseph; America, 1779 ***8529.30*** *p10*
Charles, Marie Guillot *SEE* Charles, Guillaume
Charles, Thomas 48; Ontario, 1871 ***1823.21*** *p58*
Charles, William 20; Ontario, 1871 ***1823.21*** *p59*
Charles, William 70; Ontario, 1871 ***1823.21*** *p59*
Charlet, Jean; Quebec, 1660 ***9221.17*** *p433*
With wife
Charleton, John 52; Ontario, 1871 ***1823.21*** *p59*
Charleton, Thomas; Philadelphia, 1778 ***8529.30*** *p2A*
Charlier, A.; Wisconsin, 1858 ***1494.20*** *p11*
Charlier, Charles Alfred *SEE* Charlier, Louis
Charlier, Jean Baptiste *SEE* Charlier, Louis
Charlier, Louis; New York, NY, 1869 ***1494.21*** *p31*
Charlier, Louis; Wisconsin, 1869 ***1495.20*** *p55*
*Wife:*Marie Louise Berger
*Child:*Victor
*Child:*Pierre Joseph
*Child:*Charles Alfred
*Child:*Louis Joseph
*Child:*Jean Baptiste
Charlier, Louis Joseph *SEE* Charlier, Louis
Charlier, Marie Louise Berger *SEE* Charlier, Louis
Charlier, Michelle; Quebec, 1668 ***4514.3*** *p288*
Charlier, Pierre Joseph *SEE* Charlier, Louis
Charlier, Victor *SEE* Charlier, Louis
Charlier, Virginie; Wisconsin, 1872 ***1495.20*** *p12*
Charlot, Madeleine; Quebec, 1639 ***9221.17*** *p88*
Charlot, Madeleine; Quebec, 1639 ***9221.17*** *p88*
Charlot, Marguerite 16; Montreal, 1647 ***9221.17*** *p191*
Charlsen, Gustaf E.; Colorado, 1903 ***1029.59*** *p16*
Charlsen, Gustaf E.; New York, NY, 1889 ***1029.59*** *p16*
Charlton, Charles F.; Iowa, 1885 ***1211.15*** *p9*
Charlton, John 52; Ontario, 1871 ***1823.21*** *p59*
Charlton, Joseph 56; Ontario, 1871 ***1823.21*** *p59*
Charlton, Robert; Canada, 1774 ***3036.5*** *p41*
Charlton, Robert 69; Ontario, 1871 ***1823.21*** *p59*
Charlton, Thomas; Philadelphia, 1778 ***8529.30*** *p2A*
Charlton, William 56; Ontario, 1871 ***1823.21*** *p59*
Charly, Andre 19; Quebec, 1651 ***9221.17*** *p238*
Charmick, Henry; Canada, 1774 ***3036.5*** *p41*
Charmy, . . . 50; Ontario, 1871 ***1823.17*** *p27*
Charnier, A.; Wisconsin, 1858 ***1494.20*** *p11*
Charnier, Victor; New York, NY, 1870 ***1494.20*** *p13*
Charnock, Robert 40; Ontario, 1871 ***1823.21*** *p59*
Charonnet, Hilaire 36; Quebec, 1657 ***9221.17*** *p354*
Charoset, Chyprien 19; Missouri, 1845 ***778.6*** *p66*
Charouleau, August 18; New Orleans, 1845 ***778.6*** *p66*
Charpentier, Bernard 33; America, 1843 ***778.6*** *p66*
Charpentier, Francois 28; America, 1843 ***778.6*** *p66*
Charpentier, Jacques 15; Quebec, 1660 ***9221.17*** *p433*
Charpentier, Jean 20; Quebec, 1652 ***9221.17*** *p256*
Charpentier, Marguerite; Quebec, 1668 ***4514.3*** *p288*
Charpentier, Marguerite; Quebec, 1668 ***4514.3*** *p288*
Charpentier, Marie; Quebec, 1671 ***4514.3*** *p289*
Charpentier, Marie-Reine; Quebec, 1671 ***4514.3*** *p289*
Charpentier, Nicolas; Quebec, 1662 ***9221.17*** *p482*
Charpentier, Octavie 4; America, 1843 ***778.6*** *p66*
Charpentier, Victor 5; America, 1843 ***778.6*** *p66*
Charpin, Baptiste 38; Mississippi, 1846 ***778.6*** *p66*
Charrie, Mr. 32; America, 1843 ***778.6*** *p67*
Charrier, Elie 37; Quebec, 1659 ***9221.17*** *p396*
Charrier, Louise; Quebec, 1663 ***4514.3*** *p289*
Charrier, Marie; Quebec, 1665 ***4514.3*** *p289*
Charron, Claude Camus 23 *SEE* Charron, Claude
Charron, Claude 26; Quebec, 1652 ***9221.17*** *p256*
*Wife:*Claude Camus 23
Charron, Francoise; Quebec, 1664 ***4514.3*** *p289*
Charron, Jean 16; Quebec, 1657 ***9221.17*** *p354*
Charron, Jeanne; Quebec, 1670 ***4514.3*** *p285*
Charron, Marie; Quebec, 1667 ***4514.3*** *p289*
Charron, Pierre 21; Montreal, 1661 ***9221.17*** *p471*
Charroux, Thomas; Quebec, 1648 ***9221.17*** *p196*
Charte, Pierre; Illinois, 1852 ***6079.1*** *p3*
Chartener, Karl; Pittsburgh, 1883 ***5475.1*** *p130*
Chartener, Peter Nik.; America, 1872 ***5475.1*** *p126*
Chartener, Vict. Math.; America, 1880 ***5475.1*** *p227*
Charter, Elizabeth C. 18; Ontario, 1871 ***1823.21*** *p59*
Charter, Mary Ann 13; Ontario, 1871 ***1823.21*** *p59*
Charters, Miss C. M.; Montreal, 1922 ***4514.4*** *p32*
Chartier, Mr. 29; America, 1841 ***778.6*** *p67*
Chartier, Alphe 30; America, 1845 ***778.6*** *p67*
Chartier, Guillaume 15; Montreal, 1653 ***9221.17*** *p285*
Chartier, Jeanne; Quebec, 1669 ***4514.3*** *p290*
Chartier, Jeanne; Quebec, 1670 ***4514.3*** *p289*
Chartier, Julien 32; America, 1843 ***778.6*** *p67*
Chartier, Julien 33; America, 1844 ***778.6*** *p67*
Chartier, Julien 25; Louisiana, 1848 ***778.6*** *p67*
Chartier, Louis 20; Montreal, 1653 ***9221.17*** *p285*
Chartier, Noel; Quebec, 1647 ***9221.17*** *p178*
Chartier, Rene; Quebec, 1642-1643 ***9221.17*** *p128*
Chartier, Rosa 24; America, 1845 ***778.6*** *p67*
Chartier DeLaBrocquerye, Louis; Quebec, 1652 ***9221.17*** *p257*
Chartier DeLotbiniere, Elisabeth Damours DesChaufours 39 *SEE* Chartier DeLotbiniere, Louis-Theandre
Chartier deLotbiniere, Louis-Theandre; Quebec, 1651 ***2314.30*** *p166*
Chartier deLotbiniere, Louis-Theandre; Quebec, 1651 ***2314.30*** *p177*
Chartier DeLotbiniere, Louis-Theandre 39; Quebec, 1651 ***9221.17*** *p238*
*Wife:*Elisabeth Damours DesChaufours 39
*Son:*Rene-Louis 10
*Daughter:*Marie-Francoise 4

Chartier DeLotbiniere, Marie-Francoise 4 *SEE* Chartier DeLotbiniere, Louis-Theandre
Chartier DeLotbiniere, Rene-Louis 10 *SEE* Chartier DeLotbiniere, Louis-Theandre
Charton, Genevieve 30; Port uncertain, 1846 ***778.6*** *p67*
Charton, Jeanne; Quebec, 1667 ***4514.3*** *p290*
Charton, Nicolas; Quebec, 1657 ***9221.17*** *p354*
Charton, Pierre 45; Port uncertain, 1846 ***778.6*** *p67*
Charvat, Josef; Iowa, 1854 ***2853.20*** *p211*
Charvat, Otakar; America, 1810-1910 ***2853.20*** *p513*
Charvat, Otakar; Omaha, NE, 1910 ***2853.20*** *p517*
Charvin, Amedee 23; New Orleans, 1848 ***778.6*** *p67*
Charvin, Celina 8; Louisiana, 1848 ***778.6*** *p67*
Charvin, Henry 7; Louisiana, 1848 ***778.6*** *p67*
Charvin, Julie 40; Louisiana, 1848 ***778.6*** *p67*
Charworth, Elizabeth 9; Quebec, 1870 ***8364.32*** *p22*
Chase, Aggie 25; Michigan, 1880 ***4491.36*** *p4*
Chase, Dolly 15; Ontario, 1871 ***1823.21*** *p59*
Chase, James; New York, 1779 ***8529.30*** *p10*
Chase, Thomas 16; Quebec, 1870 ***8364.32*** *p22*
Chasenan, Maria L. 23; Port uncertain, 1841 ***778.6*** *p67*
Chasholm, George 45; Ontario, 1871 ***1823.21*** *p59*
Chassainy, Frs. 40; New Orleans, 1840 ***778.6*** *p67*
Chassard, Pierre Francois 31; Texas, 1843 ***778.6*** *p67*
Chassees, Antoin 30; America, 1848 ***778.6*** *p67*
Chassees, Julie 35; America, 1848 ***778.6*** *p67*
Chassidoux, Jean-Louis 27; Texas, 1848 ***778.6*** *p67*
Chastain, Estienne; Virginia, 1700 ***9230.15*** *p80*
Chastain, Pierre; Virginia, 1700 ***9230.15*** *p80*
With wife & 5 children
Chastatain, Quintin; Virginia, 1700 ***9230.15*** *p80*
Chasteau, Jean; Quebec, 1653 ***9221.17*** *p271*
Chasteauneuf, Jean; Quebec, 1662 ***9221.17*** *p488*
Chasteigny, Marie 34; Quebec, 1656 ***9221.17*** *p333*
Chastel, Antoine; Quebec, 1661 ***9221.17*** *p451*
Chastel, Edmee 39; Montreal, 1659 ***9221.17*** *p419*
Chastel, Helene; Quebec, 1641 ***9221.17*** *p102*
Chastel, Michel; Quebec, 1661 ***9221.17*** *p451*
Chastel, Thomine; Quebec, 1647 ***9221.17*** *p176*
*Daughter:*Francoise
*Daughter:*Jeanne
*Son:*Jean
Chastelain, Francois; Quebec, 1719 ***2314.30*** *p169*
Chastelain, Francois; Quebec, 1719 ***2314.30*** *p178*
Chastellain, Pierre 30; Quebec, 1636 ***9221.17*** *p50*
Chastereau, . . .; Quebec, 1660 ***9221.17*** *p433*
Chastillon, Antoine; Quebec, 1657 ***9221.17*** *p352*
Chastillon, Jean 16; Quebec, 1643 ***9221.17*** *p133*
Chastillon, Pierre 23; Montreal, 1653 ***9221.17*** *p290*
Chatanier, Pierre; Virginia, 1700 ***9230.15*** *p81*
With wife & father
Chateauneuf, Jacques 23; Quebec, 1662 ***9221.17*** *p490*
Chatelet, Nicolas 29; America, 1843 ***778.6*** *p67*
Chaton, Marie; Quebec, 1666 ***4514.3*** *p290*
Chattlewe, Francis 38; Ohio, 1880 ***4879.40*** *p258*
Chaubet, Jean 19; New Orleans, 1848 ***778.6*** *p67*
Chaudet, Jean 28; Kentucky, 1846 ***778.6*** *p67*
Chaudoir, Gregoire Alexa; Detroit, 1871 ***1494.20*** *p12*
Chaudoir, Justin Pierre; Detroit, 1873 ***1494.20*** *p12*
Chaudon, Philibert 47; Quebec, 1647 ***9221.17*** *p178*
Chaudron, Pierre 29; America, 1844 ***778.6*** *p67*
Chaudronnier, Jean; Montreal, 1653 ***9221.17*** *p285*
Chaulet, Marie 21; Montreal, 1659 ***9221.17*** *p419*
Chaumartin, Paul; Quebec, 1660 ***9221.17*** *p433*
Chaumonot, Joseph-Marie 28; Quebec, 1639 ***9221.17*** *p83*
Chaupat, Celestine 2; Missouri, 1845 ***778.6*** *p67*
Chauret, Mathieu; Quebec, 1645 ***9221.17*** *p152*
Chauret, Sebastienne 16; Quebec, 1647 ***9221.17*** *p178*
Chaussee, Francois 30; Quebec, 1662 ***9221.17*** *p482*
Chaussegros de Lery, Gaspard; Quebec, 1716 ***2314.30*** *p169*
Chaussegros deLery, Gaspard; Quebec, 1716 ***2314.30*** *p178*
Chausseur, Fredrik Herman; America, 1839 ***6410.15*** *p103*
Chaussiau, Mr. 24; Port uncertain, 1840 ***778.6*** *p67*
Chauveau, Jean 21; Quebec, 1656 ***9221.17*** *p333*
Chauveng, Jules 19; Port uncertain, 1843 ***778.6*** *p67*
Chauvet, Jean 22; Quebec, 1656 ***9221.17*** *p333*
Chauvet, Marie; Quebec, 1668 ***4514.3*** *p290*
Chauvigny DeLaPeltrie, Marie-Madeleine 36; Quebec, 1639 ***9221.17*** *p86*
Chauvin, Francois; Louisiana, 1841-1844 ***4981.45*** *p210*
Chauvin, Marin; Quebec, 1648 ***9221.17*** *p196*
Chauvin, Michel; Montreal, 1644 ***9221.17*** *p146*
Chauvin, Pierre 18; Montreal, 1653 ***9221.17*** *p285*
Chavalia, Alexander; Ohio, 1842 ***2763.1*** *p7*
Chavanne, Aimy John Baptist; Illinois, 1860 ***6079.1*** *p3*
Chavant, Marin; Illinois, 1852 ***6079.1*** *p3*
Chavaribeyre, Mr. 26; America, 1841 ***778.6*** *p67*
Chavaux, Claudine 8; New Orleans, 1848 ***778.6*** *p67*
Chavaux, Marie 52; New Orleans, 1848 ***778.6*** *p67*
Chaveau, T. H. 21; New Orleans, 1845 ***778.6*** *p67*
Chavelle, Catherine 29; Louisiana, 1848 ***778.6*** *p67*
Chavelle, Francois 6; Louisiana, 1848 ***778.6*** *p68*
Chavelle, Joseph 8; Louisiana, 1848 ***778.6*** *p68*
Chavelle, N...as 33; Louisiana, 1848 ***778.6*** *p68*
Chavery, Frederic 37; Port uncertain, 1843 ***778.6*** *p68*
Chavey, Edouard 17; Missouri, 1846 ***778.6*** *p68*
Chavey, Louise 27; Missouri, 1846 ***778.6*** *p68*
Chavigneaux, Nicolas 19; Quebec, 1658 ***9221.17*** *p377*
Chavigny, Francois de; Quebec, 1641 ***2314.30*** *p166*
Chavigny, Francois de; Quebec, 1641 ***2314.30*** *p178*
Chavigny DeBerchereau, Eleonore de Grandmaison Boudier 22 *SEE* Chavigny DeBerchereau, Francois
Chavigny DeBerchereau, Francois; Quebec, 1641 ***9221.17*** *p102*
*Wife:*Eleonore de Grandmaison Boudier
Chavin, Rene; Quebec, 1658 ***9221.17*** *p377*
Chavois, Joseph 29; Texas, 1848 ***778.6*** *p68*
Chazelle, Mathey 26; America, 1846 ***778.6*** *p68*
Chazot, E. B.; Louisiana, 1874-1875 ***4981.45*** *p298*
Cheaty, Joseph 14; Quebec, 1870 ***8364.32*** *p22*
Chebandier, Mr. 29; America, 1842 ***778.6*** *p68*
Chebret, Eliza 9; Mississippi, 1846 ***778.6*** *p68*
Chebret, Jean 40; Mississippi, 1846 ***778.6*** *p68*
Chebret, Sosten 6; Mississippi, 1846 ***778.6*** *p68*
Checkley, Thomas; Ohio, 1809-1852 ***4511.35*** *p8*
Chedon, Ms. 29; Port uncertain, 1845 ***778.6*** *p68*
Chedville, V. P.; Louisiana, 1836-1841 ***4981.45*** *p208*
Cheek Family ; Utah, 1852 ***9228.50*** *p158*
Cheever, H. A.; North America, 1843 ***6410.15*** *p103*
Cheevers, Thos.; Louisiana, 1874 ***4981.45*** *p295*
Chefdeville, Marie 17; Montreal, 1650 ***9221.17*** *p231*
Chegremond, Olive; Quebec, 1637 ***9221.17*** *p73*
Cheile, Miss; Quebec, 1885 ***1937.10*** *p52*
Cheiney, George 35; Ontario, 1871 ***1823.17*** *p27*
Chela, Anna; Wisconsin, 1886 ***6795.8*** *p38*
Chelchowska, Klementyna; Detroit, 1929 ***1640.55*** *p117*
Chelcott, Frederick 33; Ontario, 1871 ***1823.21*** *p59*
Chellgren, Anna Elisabeth *SEE* Chellgren, Hedvig Lovisa
Chellgren, Anna Elisabeth; St. Paul, MN, 1889 ***1865.50*** *p52*
*Mother:*Hedvig L.
Chellgren, Gustaf F.; St. Paul, MN, 1887 ***1865.50*** *p44*
Chellgren, Hedvig L. *SEE* Chellgren, Anna Elisabeth
Chellgren, Hedvig Lovisa; St. Paul, MN, 1889 ***1865.50*** *p44*
*Daughter:*Anna Elisabeth
Chemalvide, Catherine 26; New Orleans, 1846 ***778.6*** *p68*
Chemenes, Joseph 27; New Orleans, 1848 ***778.6*** *p68*
Chemereau, Marguerite; Quebec, 1669 ***4514.3*** *p290*
Chemin, . . . 40; New Orleans, 1843 ***778.6*** *p68*
Chemin, Jean; Quebec, 1648 ***9221.17*** *p197*
Chemin, Rene; Quebec, 1658 ***9221.17*** *p377*
Chemine, J. 23; Port uncertain, 1843 ***778.6*** *p68*
Chemouker, Mrs. 48; Cincinnati, 1843 ***778.6*** *p68*
Chemouker, Catherine 17; Cincinnati, 1843 ***778.6*** *p68*
Chemouker, Joseph 48; Cincinnati, 1843 ***778.6*** *p68*
Chemouker, Madeleine 20; Cincinnati, 1843 ***778.6*** *p68*
Chemouker, Marie 10; Cincinnati, 1843 ***778.6*** *p68*
Chemouker, Marie Barbe 12; Cincinnati, 1843 ***778.6*** *p68*
Chenard, Jean 18; New York, NY, 1894 ***6512.1*** *p181*
Chenau, William 35; Ontario, 1871 ***1823.21*** *p59*
Cheneman, G. S.; Iowa, 1894 ***1211.15*** *p10*
Cheney, Fleurant; Quebec, 1661 ***9221.17*** *p451*
Cheney, John 46; Ontario, 1871 ***1823.21*** *p59*
Chenierce, Pierre 28; America, 1847 ***778.6*** *p68*
Chenillart, Denis; Quebec, 1646 ***9221.17*** *p162*
Chenry, Mary; Watertown, MA, 1745 ***1642*** *p112*
Cheray, Franc. 42; America, 1840 ***778.6*** *p68*
Cheray, Rose 37; America, 1840 ***778.6*** *p68*
Cheray, Victor 17; America, 1840 ***778.6*** *p68*
Chereau, Jacques; Quebec, 1651 ***9221.17*** *p239*
Cherfault, Denise; Quebec, 1665 ***4514.3*** *p290*
Cherier, Alex. 42; Port uncertain, 1846 ***778.6*** *p68*
Cherit, Mr. 49; America, 1846 ***778.6*** *p68*
Cherit, Josephine 20; America, 1846 ***778.6*** *p68*
Cherit, Justin 19; America, 1846 ***778.6*** *p69*
Cherit, Rose 20; America, 1846 ***778.6*** *p69*
Cherny, Joseph 42; Ontario, 1871 ***1823.17*** *p27*
Cherof, Amelie 5; America, 1840 ***778.6*** *p69*
Cheron, Marie Josephine; Wisconsin, 1856 ***1495.20*** *p28*
Cherq, Amelie 5; America, 1840 ***778.6*** *p69*
Cherry, Francis; North Carolina, 1848 ***1088.45*** *p5*
Cherry, James; Ohio, 1819 ***9228.50*** *p157*
Cherry, Michael; Ohio, 1864 ***3580.20*** *p31*
Cherry, Michael; Ohio, 1864 ***6020.12*** *p6*
Cherry, Thomas; Ohio, 1809-1852 ***4511.35*** *p8*
Chervay, Jean 26; New Orleans, 1847 ***778.6*** *p69*
Chesher, Edmund 61; Ontario, 1871 ***1823.17*** *p27*
Cheske, Fr. A.; Galveston, TX, 1855 ***571.7*** *p16*
Cheskey, Addie Bertha; Wisconsin, 1881 ***6795.8*** *p105*
Cheslir, John; North Carolina, 1792-1862 ***1088.45*** *p5*
Chesnaye, Bertrand 31; Quebec, 1656 ***9221.17*** *p333*
Chesneau, Jean; Quebec, 1650 ***9221.17*** *p224*
Chesneau, Louise *SEE* Chesneau, Nicolas
Chesneau, Nicolas; Quebec, 1642 ***9221.17*** *p114*
*Wife:*Louise
Chesney, John 45; Ontario, 1871 ***1823.17*** *p27*
Chesnier, Jean 27; Quebec, 1651 ***9221.17*** *p239*
Chessell, Susannah; Prince Edward Island, 1799-1839 ***9228.50*** *p275*
Chessler, Benjamin; Detroit, 1929-1930 ***6214.5*** *p71*
Chester, William; Ohio, 1840 ***2763.1*** *p7*
Chesterfield, William; Boston, 1775 ***8529.30*** *p2*
Cheton, Achille 34; America, 1844 ***778.6*** *p69*
Cheunier, Pierre; Quebec, 1641 ***9221.17*** *p102*
Chevalier, Adolf 23; New Orleans, 1848 ***778.6*** *p69*
Chevalier, Charles; Quebec, 1644 ***9221.17*** *p139*
Chevalier, Charlotte 46; Quebec, 1647 ***9221.17*** *p181*
*Son:*Nicolas 27
*Son:*Jacques 10
Chevalier, Charlotte 46; Quebec, 1647 ***9221.17*** *p181*
*Son:*Nicolas 27
*Son:*Jacques 10
Chevalier, David 16; Montreal, 1661 ***9221.17*** *p471*
Chevalier, Edward 55; Salem, MA, 1700-1799 ***9228.50*** *p157*
Chevalier, Etienne; Quebec, 1644 ***9221.17*** *p139*
Chevalier, Francoise; Quebec, 1667 ***4514.3*** *p290*
Chevalier, Guillaume; Quebec, 1648 ***9221.17*** *p197*
Chevalier, J. Bap. 28; Mississippi, 1847 ***778.6*** *p69*
Chevalier, Jacques; New England, 1676 ***9228.50*** *p157*
Chevalier, Jean 26; Montreal, 1661 ***9221.17*** *p472*
Chevalier, Jean 66; Port uncertain, 1848 ***778.6*** *p69*
Chevalier, Jean; Quebec, 1648 ***9221.17*** *p197*
Chevalier, Jeanne; Quebec, 1671 ***4514.3*** *p290*
Chevalier, John *SEE* Chevalier, Thomas
Chevalier, John; Martinique, 1659-1759 ***9228.50*** *p313*
Chevalier, John; New Hampshire, 1770 ***9228.50*** *p348*
Chevalier, John *SEE* Chevalier, Thomas
Chevalier, Joseph 18; Montreal, 1662 ***9221.17*** *p496*
Chevalier, Julien 23; New Orleans, 1840 ***778.6*** *p69*
Chevalier, Louis 24; Montreal, 1653 ***9221.17*** *p286*
Chevalier, Marie; Utah, 1823-1884 ***9228.50*** *p183*
Chevalier, Marie; Utah, 1852 ***9228.50*** *p157*
Chevalier, Marie Josephine 29; New Orleans, 1848 ***778.6*** *p69*
Chevalier, Nicholas; Massachusetts, 1600-1699 ***9228.50*** *p158*
Chevalier, Rene 26; Quebec, 1653 ***9221.17*** *p271*
Chevalier, Richard; New England, 1650-1706 ***9228.50*** *p300*
Chevalier, Suzanne; Quebec, 1669 ***4514.3*** *p291*
Chevalier, Thomas; Boston, 1760-1769 ***9228.50*** *p158*
*Relative:*John
Chevalier, Thomas; Newfoundland, 1760-1769 ***9228.50*** *p158*
*Relative:*John
Chevalier, Wm.; New England, 1635 ***9228.50*** *p313*
Chevallie, Mar. Cath. 33; Missouri, 1848 ***778.6*** *p69*
Chevallier, Eugene Victor 56; New Orleans, 1848 ***778.6*** *p69*
Chevas, Jean; Virginia, 1700 ***9230.15*** *p80*
With wife
Chevasset, Antoine 17; Montreal, 1653 ***9221.17*** *p286*
Chevens, John 64; Ontario, 1871 ***1823.21*** *p59*
Chevet, Miss; Louisiana, 1845 ***778.6*** *p69*
Chevet, Mr.; Louisiana, 1845 ***778.6*** *p69*
Chevillard, Guillaume 53; New Orleans, 1848 ***778.6*** *p69*
Chevillart, Denis; Quebec, 1646 ***9221.17*** *p162*
Chevillon, Eugene; Illinois, 1856 ***6079.1*** *p3*
Chevillon, Laurent 25; New Orleans, 1848 ***778.6*** *p69*
Cheviotti, Danuto 31; New York, NY, 1894 ***6512.1*** *p230*
Chevons, John 22; Ontario, 1871 ***1823.21*** *p59*
Chevreau, Marie; Quebec, 1665 ***4514.3*** *p291*
Chew, Sarah 11; Quebec, 1870 ***8364.32*** *p22*
Chewt, George 35; Ontario, 1871 ***1823.21*** *p59*
Chiard, P. 24; America, 1846 ***778.6*** *p69*
Chiasson, Francoise *SEE* Chiasson, Guyon
Chiasson, Guyon; Quebec, 1666 ***4514.3*** *p291*
*Child:*Michel
*Child:*Jean
*Child:*Francoise
Chiasson, Jean *SEE* Chiasson, Guyon
Chiasson, Louise; Quebec, 1666 ***4514.3*** *p291*
Chiasson, Michel *SEE* Chiasson, Guyon
Chicaut, Guillaume 25; Missouri, 1847 ***778.6*** *p69*
Chichozewski, Ignacy 42; New York, NY, 1920 ***930.50*** *p49*
Chick, Anna 63; Ontario, 1871 ***1823.21*** *p59*
Chick, Elizabeth 26; Ontario, 1871 ***1823.21*** *p59*
Chick Family ; Utah, 1852 ***9228.50*** *p158*
Chicoisne, Pierre 27; Montreal, 1662 ***9221.17*** *p497*
Chidraoni, Daniel 41; New York, NY, 1894 ***6512.1*** *p232*

Chidraoni, Fanoud 13; New York, NY, 1894 ***6512.1*** *p232*
Chidraoni, Lubathi 30; New York, NY, 1894 ***6512.1*** *p232*
Chiedziewica, Keawery; Chicago, 1930 ***121.35*** *p100*
Chigal, Pierre 19; America, 1841 ***778.6*** *p69*
Chigish, Kisnigua 43; Ontario, 1871 ***1823.17*** *p27*
Chigon, Mr. 25; New Orleans, 1840 ***778.6*** *p69*
Chilberg, Jacob; America, 1849 ***4487.25*** *p54*
With family
Childs, George 39; Ontario, 1871 ***1823.21*** *p59*
Childs, George 45; Ontario, 1871 ***1823.17*** *p27*
Childs, Tho. 30; Virginia, 1635 ***1183.3*** *p30*
Chillard, Jean 29; America, 1840 ***778.6*** *p69*
Chillingworth, William 4; Quebec, 1870 ***8364.32*** *p22*
Chillot, Francois 30; Louisiana, 1840 ***778.6*** *p69*
Chilos, Joseph 39; Ontario, 1871 ***1823.17*** *p27*
Chilos, William 71; Ontario, 1871 ***1823.17*** *p27*
Chilton, James; Plymouth, MA, 1620 ***1920.45*** *p5*
With wife
*Daughter:*Mary
Chilton, Mary *SEE* Chilton, James
Chimenes, Charles 19; New Orleans, 1848 ***778.6*** *p69*
Chimento, Philipo; Louisiana, 1874 ***4981.45*** *p131*
Chimlewski, Sam; New Orleans, 1875 ***6015.15*** *p23*
Chimrery, Nellie 17; Ontario, 1871 ***1823.21*** *p59*
China, Percival John; Miami, 1935 ***4984.12*** *p39*
Chinard, Francois A.; Illinois, 1852 ***6079.1*** *p3*
Chinaue, Isadore 28; New Orleans, 1842 ***778.6*** *p69*
Chinmark, Nicholas; Cleveland, OH, 1842 ***9722.10*** *p118*
Chinn, John; Marblehead, MA, 1700-1799 ***9228.50*** *p158*
Chinnery, Richard 43; Ontario, 1871 ***1823.21*** *p59*
Chinnick, John 52; Ontario, 1871 ***1823.21*** *p59*
Chintel, Francois 25; New Orleans, 1840 ***778.6*** *p69*
Chipchase, William 20; Quebec, 1870 ***8364.32*** *p22*
Chiperowski, Francois 57; New Orleans, 1848 ***778.6*** *p69*
Chipret, Marie 45; New Orleans, 1843 ***778.6*** *p69*
Chipron, . . .; New Orleans, 1848 ***778.6*** *p69*
Chipron, . . .; New Orleans, 1848 ***778.6*** *p70*
Chipron, Mr. 26; New Orleans, 1848 ***778.6*** *p69*
Chipron, Mrs. 46; New Orleans, 1848 ***778.6*** *p70*
Chiquet, . . .; Quebec, 1652 ***9221.17*** *p257*
Chirey, Robert 65; Ontario, 1871 ***1823.21*** *p59*
Chirsuge, Constante 31; Port uncertain, 1842 ***778.6*** *p70*
Chisholm, Andrew 38; Ontario, 1871 ***1823.21*** *p59*
Chisholm, Colin; Quebec, 1786 ***1416.15*** *p8*
Chisholm, John; Ontario, 1787 ***1276.15*** *p230*
With child & relative
Chisholm, John 56; Ontario, 1871 ***1823.21*** *p59*
Chisholm, Mary 36; Ontario, 1871 ***1823.21*** *p59*
Chisholm, Willm; Quebec, 1786 ***1416.15*** *p8*
Chislett, John 55; Ontario, 1871 ***1823.17*** *p27*
Chism, William 50; Ontario, 1871 ***1823.21*** *p60*
Chisolm, Allan 40; Ontario, 1871 ***1823.21*** *p60*
Chisom, Finley 42; Ontario, 1871 ***1823.17*** *p27*
Chison, John 23; New Orleans, 1848 ***778.6*** *p70*
Chisorenes, Mathilde 19; New Orleans, 1848 ***778.6*** *p70*
Chissens, C. 15; Quebec, 1870 ***8364.32*** *p22*
Chissol, Joseph Honore 28; New Orleans, 1848 ***778.6*** *p70*
Chittenden, Sarah 65; Michigan, 1880 ***4491.30*** *p5*
Chitter, Claude 27; America, 1842 ***778.6*** *p70*
Chittick, Francis 42; Ontario, 1871 ***1823.21*** *p60*
Chittick, George 40; Ontario, 1871 ***1823.21*** *p60*
Chittick, John 32; Ontario, 1871 ***1823.17*** *p27*
Chittick, William H. 24; Ontario, 1871 ***1823.17*** *p28*
Chittrik, George 70; Ontario, 1871 ***1823.21*** *p60*
Chladek, Dr.; Chicago, 1859 ***2853.20*** *p390*
Chladek, Alois; South Dakota, 1850-1910 ***2853.20*** *p246*
Chlapik, Vaclav; Texas, 1881-1887 ***2853.20*** *p66*
Chloupek, Antonin; Wisconsin, 1851 ***2853.20*** *p312*
Chloupek, Emanuel; Wisconsin, 1851 ***2853.20*** *p312*
Chloupek, Jan; Wisconsin, 1851 ***2853.20*** *p312*
Chloupek, Josef; Wisconsin, 1851 ***2853.20*** *p312*
Chloupek, Martin; Nebraska, 1876 ***2853.20*** *p172*
Chloupek, Vaclav; Wisconsin, 1851 ***2853.20*** *p312*
Chlumsky, Adolf; Texas, 1889 ***2853.20*** *p80*
Chlumsky, Jaroslav Ludvik; Texas, 1874 ***2853.20*** *p65*
Chlumsky, Ludvik Jaroslav; Texas, 1874 ***2853.20*** *p79*
Chmelar, Frantisek; Iowa, 1864-1869 ***2853.20*** *p224*
Chmelesky, Peter; New Orleans, 1872 ***6015.15*** *p24*
Chmelka, Matej; Nebraska, 1866-1900 ***2853.20*** *p161*
Chmielewski, Sam; New Orleans, 1875 ***6015.15*** *p23*
Chmielewsky, Peter; New Orleans, 1872 ***6015.15*** *p24*
Chmielowska, Stefania 19; New York, NY, 1904 ***8355.1*** *p15*
Chodaki, Szczepan; Detroit, 1929 ***1640.55*** *p115*
Choden, Caesar; Detroit, 1930 ***1640.60*** *p82*
Chodorowski, Caesar; Detroit, 1930 ***1640.60*** *p82*
Choffert, Cath. 37; America, 1844 ***778.6*** *p70*
Choffert, Celini 3; America, 1844 ***778.6*** *p70*
Choffert, Eugene 14; America, 1844 ***778.6*** *p70*
Choffert, Melanie 7; America, 1844 ***778.6*** *p70*
Chojnacki, Michal 31; New York, NY, 1912 ***8355.1*** *p16*
Chomedey DeMaisonneuve, Paul 29; Montreal, 1641 ***9221.17*** *p107*
Chon, M. 30; America, 1842 ***778.6*** *p70*
Chonik, Letzko 25; New York, NY, 1894 ***6512.1*** *p232*
Chopard, Louis A.; Louisiana, 1836-1841 ***4981.45*** *p208*
Choppart, Celestine 40; Missouri, 1845 ***778.6*** *p70*
Choppart, Philippe 41; Missouri, 1845 ***778.6*** *p70*
Chotard, Jeanne 26; Quebec, 1662 ***9221.17*** *p483*
Chotart, Olivier; Quebec, 1646 ***9221.17*** *p162*
Choteau, Francis 40; Ontario, 1871 ***1823.21*** *p60*
Chotek, Hugo; New York, NY, 1875 ***2853.20*** *p181*
Chotel, Frederic 22; Missouri, 1847 ***778.6*** *p70*
Chott, Frantisek; St. Louis, 1896 ***2853.20*** *p54*
Chott, Jan; St. Louis, 1896 ***2853.20*** *p54*
Chou, M. 30; America, 1842 ***778.6*** *p70*
Chouart, Medard 23; Quebec, 1641 ***9221.17*** *p103*
Chouleur, Nicolas 40; America, 1848 ***778.6*** *p70*
Chouquet, Simon; Quebec, 1654 ***9221.17*** *p306*
Chouremoun, Pierre 24; New Orleans, 1844 ***778.6*** *p70*
Chovanec, Konstantin; Texas, 1856 ***2853.20*** *p64*
Chrastil, Frantisek; Nebraska, 1857-1904 ***2853.20*** *p182*
Chrestiennot, Mongin; Quebec, 1645 ***9221.17*** *p152*
Chretian, Peter; Ohio, 1809-1852 ***4511.35*** *p8*
Chretien, Eugene 22; America, 1846 ***778.6*** *p70*
Chretien, Josephine 28; America, 1846 ***778.6*** *p70*
Chretien, Madeleine; Quebec, 1670 ***4514.3*** *p291*
Chretien, Marie; Quebec, 1670 ***4514.3*** *p291*
Chretien, Napoleon 36; Louisiana, 1848 ***778.6*** *p70*
Chrichton, David; Prince Edward Island, 1839 ***9228.50*** *p130*
Chrichton, James; San Francisco, 1848-1900 ***9228.50*** *p131*
Chrichton, John Robert; California, 1873 ***9228.50*** *p130*
Chris, Marie 23; Mississippi, 1845 ***778.6*** *p70*
Chrisgan, John George; North Carolina, 1853 ***1088.45*** *p5*
Chrisjahnsen, H.; Venezuela, 1843 ***3899.5*** *p546*
Chrislor, Constant 41; America, 1840 ***778.6*** *p70*
Chrislor, Henry 11; America, 1840 ***778.6*** *p70*
Chrislor, Phillippe 17; America, 1840 ***778.6*** *p70*
Chrisostom, Elisabeth 15; America, 1846 ***778.6*** *p70*
Chrisostom, Justin 17; America, 1846 ***778.6*** *p70*
Chrisostom, Lucie 9; America, 1846 ***778.6*** *p70*
Chrisostom, Marie 6; America, 1846 ***778.6*** *p70*
Chrisostom, Marie 47; America, 1846 ***778.6*** *p70*
Chrisostom, Nicolas 7; America, 1846 ***778.6*** *p70*
Chrisostom, Nicolas 39; America, 1846 ***778.6*** *p70*
Christ, Christian Heinrich; America, 1867 ***7919.3*** *p530*
With wife & 6 children
Christ, Maria 64; America, 1872 ***5475.1*** *p354*
Christ, Nikolaus 58; Port uncertain, 1848 ***170.15*** *p22*
With 4 children
Christeen, Marian; North Carolina, 1812 ***1088.45*** *p5*
Christen, Ignaz 30; Port uncertain, 1843 ***778.6*** *p71*
Christensen, Agnes *SEE* Christensen, Hans
Christensen, Chris Peter; Iowa, 1911 ***1211.15*** *p9*
Christensen, Christen Lauritsen; Iowa, 1896 ***1211.15*** *p9*
Christensen, Christen Skadhede; Iowa, 1900 ***1211.15*** *p9*
Christensen, Christian; Colorado, 1877 ***1029.59*** *p16*
Christensen, Eli Karl; Missouri, 1903 ***3276.1*** *p4*
Christensen, Frncis *SEE* Christensen, Hans
Christensen, Hans; Colorado, 1920 ***1029.59*** *p17*
*Wife:*Marie
*Child:*Justna
*Child:*John
*Child:*Frncis
*Child:*Agnes
*Child:*Louis
Christensen, Hans; Iowa, 1875 ***1211.15*** *p9*
Christensen, Herman Christian; Iowa, 1920 ***1211.15*** *p9*
Christensen, John *SEE* Christensen, Hans
Christensen, Justna *SEE* Christensen, Hans
Christensen, Louis *SEE* Christensen, Hans
Christensen, Marie *SEE* Christensen, Hans
Christensen, Nels Peter; Iowa, 1920 ***1211.15*** *p9*
Christensen, Peter; Colorado, 1877 ***1029.59*** *p17*
Christensen, Peter; Colorado, 1885 ***1029.59*** *p17*
Christensen, Peter; Iowa, 1871 ***1029.59*** *p17*
Christensen, Peter; Iowa, 1890 ***1211.15*** *p10*
Christenson, Andrew; Iowa, 1888 ***1211.15*** *p9*
Christenson, Christian; Colorado, 1887 ***1029.59*** *p17*
Christenson, Godfrey C.; Iowa, 1891 ***1211.15*** *p9*
Christenson, John; Iowa, 1897 ***1211.15*** *p9*
Christenson, Julius W.; Iowa, 1884 ***1211.15*** *p9*
Christenson, Loren; Iowa, 1893 ***1211.15*** *p9*
Christenson, Martin; Iowa, 1897 ***1211.15*** *p9*
Christenson, Ole; Iowa, 1887 ***1211.15*** *p9*
Christenson, Peter; Iowa, 1875 ***1211.15*** *p9*
Christian, C. 25; America, 1846 ***778.6*** *p71*
Christian, Cole 54; Ontario, 1871 ***1823.21*** *p60*
Christian, Fred; Wisconsin, 1885 ***6795.8*** *p101*
Christian, Helen; New Brunswick, 1830-1852 ***9228.50*** *p403*
Christian, Jacob 17; Missouri, 1845 ***778.6*** *p71*
Christian, Jean 32; Louisiana, 1848 ***778.6*** *p71*
Christian, Michael; New Jersey, 1773-1774 ***927.31*** *p3*
Christian, Nels; Colorado, 1892 ***1029.59*** *p17*
Christian, Peter; Ohio, 1809-1852 ***4511.35*** *p8*
Christiansen, H.; Venezuela, 1843 ***3899.5*** *p546*
Christiansen, Holger Bernhardt; Iowa, 1930 ***1211.15*** *p10*
Christiansen, Soren C.; Iowa, 1897 ***1211.15*** *p9*
Christianson, Andrew M.; Iowa, 1904 ***1211.15*** *p9*
Christianson, Knuelt; Iowa, 1881 ***1211.15*** *p9*
Christianson, Lars; Washington, 1881 ***2770.40*** *p134*
Christianson, T.; New York, NY, 1846 ***6412.40*** *p149*
Christie, Mr.; Massachusetts, 1741 ***1642*** *p67*
Christie, Daniel 25; Indiana, 1855-1861 ***9076.20*** *p66*
Christie, G. R. 24; Ontario, 1871 ***1823.21*** *p60*
Christie, George 39; Ontario, 1871 ***1823.17*** *p28*
Christie, Helen; New Brunswick, 1830-1852 ***9228.50*** *p403*
Christie, James; New Orleans, 1851 ***7242.30*** *p138*
Christie, John 49; Ontario, 1871 ***1823.21*** *p60*
Christie, Nora Marjorie; Vancouver, B.C., 1910-1912 ***9228.50*** *p175*
Christie, Nora Marjorie; Vancouver, B.C., 1910-1912 ***9228.50*** *p175*
Christie, William; New Orleans, 1851 ***7242.30*** *p138*
Christler, Christian; Ohio, 1809-1852 ***4511.35*** *p8*
Christler Jantz, Christina; North Carolina, 1710 ***3629.40*** *p5*
Christman, Daniel; Ohio, 1809-1852 ***4511.35*** *p8*
Christman, He.nrich 21; America, 1845 ***778.6*** *p71*
Christman, Jean 18; America, 1845 ***778.6*** *p71*
Christman, Peter; Ohio, 1809-1852 ***4511.35*** *p8*
Christman, Reid 19; America, 1845 ***778.6*** *p71*
Christmar, Etienne 36; New Orleans, 1848 ***778.6*** *p71*
Christofel, George; Ohio, 1809-1852 ***4511.35*** *p8*
Christoph, Barbara 41; New Orleans, 1847 ***778.6*** *p71*
Christoph, Carl Friedrich August; London, Eng., 1877 ***7420.1*** *p308*
Christoph, Charles 42; America, 1848 ***778.6*** *p71*
Christoph, Claude 3; New Orleans, 1847 ***778.6*** *p71*
Christoph, Jean Cl. 42; New Orleans, 1847 ***778.6*** *p71*
Christoph, John; Louisiana, 1874 ***4981.45*** *p131*
Christoph, Pierre 11; New Orleans, 1847 ***778.6*** *p71*
Christoph, Wilhelmine Charlotte; America, 1883 ***7420.1*** *p338*
Christophe, Henri; Louisiana, 1874 ***4981.45*** *p131*
Christophel, Adam; Ohio, 1809-1852 ***4511.35*** *p8*
Christopher, Jacob; Ohio, 1809-1852 ***4511.35*** *p8*
Christopher, John; Illinois, 1834-1900 ***6020.5*** *p131*
Christopherson, Hans; Colorado, 1887 ***1029.59*** *p17*
Christy, Hannah *SEE* Christy, John
Christy, Isabel McArthur *SEE* Christy, John
Christy, John; New York, 1740 ***8277.31*** *p115*
*Wife:*Isabel McArthur
*Daughter:*Mary
*Daughter:*Hannah
Christy, Mary *SEE* Christy, John
Christy, Peter; Massachusetts, 1741 ***1642*** *p67*
Chromcik, Josef; Texas, 1870-1875 ***2853.20*** *p64*
Chronaberry, Philip; Ohio, 1840-1897 ***8365.35*** *p15*
Chrostek, Ozok Zofia; Detroit, 1929-1930 ***6214.5*** *p69*
Chubb, Alan T. 19; Quebec, 1910 ***2897.7*** *p9*
Chubb, Charles 30; Ontario, 1871 ***1823.17*** *p28*
Chubb, Thomas 52; Ontario, 1871 ***1823.17*** *p28*
Chuchro, Stanislaw; Detroit, 1929-1930 ***6214.5*** *p65*
Chudy, Eva; Detroit, 1929-1930 ***6214.5*** *p70*
Chuig, William 25; Ontario, 1871 ***1823.21*** *p60*
Chulley, Vincent; Louisiana, 1874 ***4981.45*** *p131*
Chumley, Claude 36; Missouri, 1845 ***778.6*** *p71*
Chummer, Eugen; Wisconsin, 1869 ***6795.8*** *p99*
Chundelak, Josef; Omaha, NE, 1893 ***2853.20*** *p153*
Chupik, Jiri; Texas, 1856 ***2853.20*** *p78*
Church, Elizabeth Jervois *SEE* Church, George Dalimore
Church, Frank 40; Ontario, 1871 ***1823.21*** *p60*
Church, George Dalimore; Columbus, OH, 1852 ***9228.50*** *p158*
*Wife:*Elizabeth Jervois
*Child:*Richard Howard
With 3 siblings
Church, Henry L. 49; Ontario, 1871 ***1823.21*** *p60*
Church, Richard Howard *SEE* Church, George Dalimore
Church, Robert 27; Ontario, 1871 ***1823.21*** *p60*
Church, Stephen 17; Quebec, 1870 ***8364.32*** *p22*
Church, William 35; Ontario, 1871 ***1823.21*** *p60*
Churcher, Thomas 59; Ontario, 1871 ***1823.21*** *p60*
Churchill, Fannie; Portland, OR, 1835-1890 ***9228.50*** *p642*
Churchill, P. J.; Louisiana, 1874 ***4981.45*** *p295*
Chuto, Domingo Jean 38; New Orleans, 1841 ***778.6*** *p71*
Chvatal, Josef; Chicago, 1897 ***2853.20*** *p433*
Chyna, Percival John; Miami, 1935 ***4984.12*** *p39*

Ciasnocha, Wojciech 19; New York, NY, 1912 ***8355.1*** *p16*
Cibery, J. 31; America, 1840 ***778.6*** *p71*
Cibulka, Vaclav; St. Louis, 1848 ***2853.20*** *p21*
Cichon, Maryanna 20; New York, NY, 1911 ***6533.11*** *p9*
Cicot, Jean 19; Montreal, 1650 ***9221.17*** *p231*
Cientar, Louis 20; New Orleans, 1845 ***778.6*** *p71*
Ciervinski, Jan 27; New York, NY, 1920 ***930.50*** *p49*
Cierzmowski, August; Wisconsin, 1897 ***6795.8*** *p55*
Ciesak, Blazey; Texas, 1896-1904 ***6015.15*** *p24*
Ciesak, Blazij; Texas, 1896 ***6015.15*** *p23*
Cieslack, Juzef 40; New York, NY, 1920 ***930.50*** *p48*
Cieszynski, Frank; Wisconsin, 1898 ***6795.8*** *p67*
Cigrend, Bernard; Ohio, 1840-1897 ***8365.35*** *p15*
Cihak, Josef V. 16; Baltimore, 1872-1873 ***2853.20*** *p131*
Cilinsky, Josef; New York, NY, 1848 ***2853.20*** *p100*
Cilley, Robert; New Jersey, 1665 ***9228.50*** *p578*
Cimenge, Pepper; Louisiana, 1874 ***4981.45*** *p131*
Cimer, J.; North Dakota, 1909 ***2853.20*** *p252*
Cince, Benjamin 24; Ontario, 1871 ***1823.17*** *p28*
Ciompertik, Anton 28; Texas, 1887 ***9980.22*** *p17*
Ciondafiglis, Elias 35; New York, NY, 1894 ***6512.1*** *p186*
Cipin, Vojtech; Wisconsin, 1873 ***2853.20*** *p318*
Cisar, Jiri; Wisconsin, 1855 ***2853.20*** *p333*
Cisik, Katrin; Detroit, 1929 ***1640.55*** *p117*
Ciszek, Piotre 37; New York, NY, 1894 ***6512.1*** *p231*
Ciszke, Anton S.; Wisconsin, 1876 ***6795.8*** *p46*
Ciuchna, Jozef; Detroit, 1929 ***1640.55*** *p113*
Civa, Joseph; Texas, 1876-1915 ***6015.15*** *p24*
Cizek, Jan; Wisconsin, 1852 ***2853.20*** *p312*
Cizek, Matej; Nebraska, 1868 ***2853.20*** *p161*
Cizek, Vojtech; Wisconsin, 1866 ***2853.20*** *p251*
Cizek Brothers, . . .; New York, NY, 1848 ***2853.20*** *p100*
Claar, Frederick; Quebec, 1925-1953 ***9228.50*** *p343*
Claassen, Gerhard; Louisiana, 1874-1875 ***4981.45*** *p298*
Clabes, Adolph Johannes Ludolph; America, 1887 ***7420.1*** *p353*
Clabes, Albert Christian; America, 1868 ***7420.1*** *p270*
Clabes, Charlotte Louise; St. Louis, 1886 ***7420.1*** *p350*
Clabes, Friedrich Wilhelm; Buenos Aires, 1884 ***7420.1*** *p342*
Clach, Sarah 20; Ontario, 1871 ***1823.21*** *p60*
Clack, Robert; North Carolina, 1856 ***1088.45*** *p5*
Claesing, Christine; America, 1851 ***7420.1*** *p79*
*Sister:*Leonore C.
Claesing, Leonore C. *SEE* Claesing, Christine
Clague, Thomas Henry; Iowa, 1917 ***1211.15*** *p9*
Clain, George; Philadelphia, 1777 ***8529.30*** *p4A*
Clainpell, George 50; Ontario, 1871 ***1823.21*** *p60*
Clair, Eugene 28; New Orleans, 1845 ***778.6*** *p71*
Clair, James; Louisiana, 1874-1875 ***4981.45*** *p298*
Clair, Louis 20; Ontario, 1871 ***1823.21*** *p60*
Clairambault d'Aigremont, Francois; Quebec, 1701 ***2314.30*** *p169*
Clairambault d'Aigremont, Francois; Quebec, 1701 ***2314.30*** *p178*
Claire, Francois 32; New Orleans, 1848 ***778.6*** *p71*
Claire, Michael; Boston, 1764 ***1642*** *p33*
Clampet, James 47; Ontario, 1871 ***1823.21*** *p60*
Clampit, B. G. 45; Ontario, 1871 ***1823.21*** *p60*
Clanahan, James 67; Ontario, 1871 ***1823.21*** *p60*
Clancey, Annie 18; Ontario, 1871 ***1823.17*** *p28*
Clancey, Catherine 78; Ontario, 1871 ***1823.17*** *p28*
Clancey, Ellen 30; Ontario, 1871 ***1823.21*** *p60*
Clancey, James 25; Ontario, 1871 ***1823.17*** *p28*
Clancey, James 40; Ontario, 1871 ***1823.21*** *p60*
Clancey, John 60; Ontario, 1871 ***1823.21*** *p60*
Clancy, Daniel; St. Johns, N.F., 1825 ***1053.15*** *p6*
Clancy, John 33; Ontario, 1871 ***1823.17*** *p28*
Clancy, John 42; Ontario, 1871 ***1823.17*** *p28*
Clancy, John 66; Ontario, 1871 ***1823.21*** *p60*
Clancy, John; St. Johns, N.F., 1825 ***1053.15*** *p6*
Clancy, Kearn; St. Johns, N.F., 1825 ***1053.15*** *p6*
Clancy, Sarah 34; Ontario, 1871 ***1823.21*** *p60*
Clap, Roger; Dorchester, MA, 1635-1636 ***117.5*** *p152*
Clar, James; Boston, 1737 ***1642*** *p26*
Clare, John H. 40; Ontario, 1871 ***1823.21*** *p60*
Clare, Mary Jane 30; Ontario, 1871 ***1823.21*** *p60*
Clare, Rich; Virginia, 1652 ***6254.4*** *p243*
Clare, Robert 40; Ontario, 1871 ***1823.21*** *p60*
Clare, Thomas 27; Ontario, 1871 ***1823.21*** *p60*
Claree, L. 45; America, 1845 ***778.6*** *p71*
Clares, Thomas B.; North Carolina, 1830 ***1088.45*** *p5*
Claret, V. 23; America, 1745 ***778.6*** *p71*
Clarey, James; South Carolina, 1808 ***6155.4*** *p18*
Clarey, John; South Carolina, 1808 ***6155.4*** *p18*
Clarez, Alfred 23; America, 1846 ***778.6*** *p71*
Clarins, Francis 55; Ontario, 1871 ***1823.21*** *p60*
Clark, . . .; Nebraska, n.d. ***9228.50*** *p18A*
Clark, A. Q.; South Carolina, 1855 ***6155.4*** *p18*
Clark, Abraham 74; Ontario, 1871 ***1823.21*** *p60*
Clark, Alex 27; Ontario, 1871 ***1823.21*** *p60*
Clark, Alex 59; Ontario, 1871 ***1823.21*** *p60*
Clark, Andrew; North Carolina, 1813 ***1088.45*** *p5*
Clark, Andrew 41; Ontario, 1871 ***1823.17*** *p28*
Clark, Angus; New York, 1740 ***8277.31*** *p115*
*Wife:*Mary McCollum
*Daughter:*Catherine
*Daughter:*Mary
Clark, Ann; Philadelphia, 1855 ***8513.31*** *p299*
Clark, Ann McGinty *SEE* Clark, John
Clark, Archd; Cape Fear, NC,, 1754 ***1422.10*** *p61*
Clark, Asahel 61; Ontario, 1871 ***1823.17*** *p28*
Clark, Brant 27; Ontario, 1871 ***1823.17*** *p28*
Clark, C.; Montreal, 1922 ***4514.4*** *p32*
Clark, Caroline 49; Ontario, 1871 ***1823.21*** *p60*
Clark, Cath. 32; New York, NY, 1884 ***8427.14*** *p45*
Clark, Catherine *SEE* Clark, Angus
Clark, Charles 52; Ontario, 1871 ***1823.17*** *p28*
Clark, Christopher 35; Ontario, 1871 ***1823.21*** *p61*
Clark, Christy; New York, 1739 ***8277.31*** *p119*
Clark, Christy; New York, 1739 ***8277.31*** *p119*
Clark, Curtis; Ontario, 1871 ***1823.17*** *p28*
Clark, David 24; Ontario, 1871 ***1823.17*** *p28*
Clark, Donald 34; Ontario, 1871 ***1823.21*** *p61*
Clark, Dond; Cape Fear, NC,, 1754 ***1422.10*** *p61*
Clark, Edmond 16; Virginia, 1635 ***1183.3*** *p30*
Clark, Edward; Illinois, 1863 ***6079.1*** *p3*
Clark, Edwin; North Carolina, 1872 ***1088.45*** *p5*
Clark, Ellenor 66; Ontario, 1871 ***1823.17*** *p28*
Clark, Esther Ann 28; Michigan, 1880 ***4491.30*** *p6*
Clark, Francis; Illinois, 1852 ***6079.1*** *p3*
Clark, Genoha 7; Michigan, 1880 ***4491.30*** *p6*
Clark, Geo.; St. John, N.B., 1848 ***2978.15*** *p39*
Clark, George; Illinois, 1851 ***6079.1*** *p3*
Clark, George 31; Michigan, 1880 ***4491.30*** *p6*
Clark, George 29; Ontario, 1871 ***1823.17*** *p28*
Clark, George 39; Ontario, 1871 ***1823.21*** *p61*
Clark, Gilbert; Cape Fear, NC,, 1754 ***1422.10*** *p61*
Clark, Hannah 56; Ontario, 1871 ***1823.17*** *p28*
Clark, Hanora 57; Ontario, 1871 ***1823.21*** *p61*
Clark, Henry 39; Quebec, 1910 ***2897.7*** *p9*
Clark, Hugh; Massachusetts, 1675-1676 ***1642*** *p129*
Clark, Hugh 30; Ontario, 1871 ***1823.21*** *p61*
Clark, Hugh 40; Ontario, 1871 ***1823.21*** *p61*
Clark, Hugh 46; Ontario, 1871 ***1823.17*** *p28*
Clark, Hugh 74; Ontario, 1871 ***1823.21*** *p61*
Clark, James; Colorado, 1862-1894 ***1029.59*** *p17*
Clark, James; Colorado, 1870 ***1029.59*** *p17*
Clark, James 42; North Carolina, 1774 ***1422.10*** *p55*
Clark, James 36; Ontario, 1871 ***1823.21*** *p61*
Clark, James 39; Ontario, 1871 ***1823.21*** *p61*
Clark, James; Salem, MA, 1757 ***1642*** *p80*
Clark, James 14; Salem, MA, 1756 ***1642*** *p80*
Clark, James W.; Ohio, 1879 ***3580.20*** *p31*
Clark, James W.; Ohio, 1879 ***6020.12*** *p6*
Clark, Jewet; Ohio, 1843 ***2763.1*** *p9*
Clark, John; Boston, 1737 ***1642*** *p26*
Clark, John; Colorado, 1862-1894 ***1029.59*** *p17*
Clark, John 15; Michigan, 1880 ***4491.30*** *p6*
Clark, John 54; Michigan, 1880 ***4491.30*** *p6*
Clark, John; New Jersey, 1665 ***9228.50*** *p159*
Clark, John *SEE* Clark, William
Clark, John; North Carolina, 1860 ***1088.45*** *p5*
Clark, John 27; Ontario, 1871 ***1823.21*** *p61*
Clark, John 33; Ontario, 1871 ***1823.21*** *p61*
Clark, John 44; Ontario, 1871 ***1823.17*** *p28*
Clark, John 45; Ontario, 1871 ***1823.17*** *p28*
Clark, John 68; Ontario, 1871 ***1823.17*** *p28*
Clark, John; Philadelphia, 1857 ***8513.31*** *p299*
*Wife:*Ann McGinty
Clark, John; Virginia, 1665 ***9228.50*** *p53*
Clark, John, Jr.; Massachusetts, 1757-1763 ***1642*** *p117*
Clark, John, Sr.; Massachusetts, 1757-1763 ***1642*** *p117*
Clark, John Allen; Ohio, 1835 ***471.10*** *p86*
Clark, John S. 23; Ontario, 1871 ***1823.17*** *p28*
Clark, John W. 35; Ontario, 1871 ***1823.17*** *p28*
Clark, Joseph 49; Ontario, 1871 ***1823.17*** *p28*
Clark, Joseph 56; Ontario, 1871 ***1823.21*** *p61*
Clark, Lizzie 18; Ontario, 1871 ***1823.21*** *p61*
Clark, Marg 37; Ontario, 1871 ***1823.21*** *p61*
Clark, Margaret; Boston, 1742 ***1642*** *p45*
Clark, Margret 39; Michigan, 1880 ***4491.30*** *p6*
Clark, Mary; Boston, 1758 ***1642*** *p47*
Clark, Mary *SEE* Clark, William
Clark, Mary *SEE* Clark, Angus
Clark, Mary McCollum *SEE* Clark, Angus
Clark, Mary 82; Ontario, 1871 ***1823.21*** *p61*
Clark, Matilda 11; Quebec, 1870 ***8364.32*** *p22*
Clark, Michael; Baltimore, 1841 ***3274.56*** *p100*
Clark, Michal 39; Ontario, 1871 ***1823.17*** *p28*
Clark, Nancy 46; Ontario, 1871 ***1823.17*** *p28*
Clark, Nathanil 53; Ontario, 1871 ***1823.21*** *p61*
Clark, Neill; Brunswick, NC, 1767 ***1422.10*** *p61*
Clark, Newtown 56; Ontario, 1871 ***1823.21*** *p61*
Clark, P. W.; Louisiana, 1874 ***4981.45*** *p295*
Clark, Pat 22; St. Johns, N.F., 1811 ***1053.20*** *p21*
Clark, Rachael *SEE* Clark, William
Clark, Richard *SEE* Clark, William
Clark, Robert 26; Ontario, 1871 ***1823.21*** *p61*
Clark, Robert 37; Ontario, 1871 ***1823.17*** *p28*
Clark, Robert 37; Ontario, 1871 ***1823.21*** *p61*
Clark, Robert 52; Ontario, 1871 ***1823.21*** *p61*
Clark, Samuel; Ohio, 1840-1897 ***8365.35*** *p15*
Clark, Samuel 22; Ontario, 1871 ***1823.21*** *p61*
Clark, Samuel 29; Ontario, 1871 ***1823.21*** *p61*
Clark, Samuel 30; Ontario, 1871 ***1823.17*** *p28*
Clark, Samuel 66; Ontario, 1871 ***1823.17*** *p28*
Clark, Sarah; Boston, 1718 ***1642*** *p25*
Clark, Sarah; Maine, n.d. ***9228.50*** *p467*
Clark, Stephan 60; Ontario, 1871 ***1823.17*** *p28*
Clark, Susanna; Boston, 1763 ***1642*** *p48*
Clark, Thomas; Boston, 1774 ***8529.30*** *p2A*
Clark, Thomas 38; Ontario, 1871 ***1823.17*** *p29*
Clark, Thomas 41; Ontario, 1871 ***1823.17*** *p29*
Clark, Thomas; St. John, N.B., 1848 ***2978.15*** *p39*
Clark, Thomas W. 25; Ontario, 1871 ***1823.17*** *p29*
Clark, W. A.; California, 1868 ***1131.61*** *p89*
Clark, William *SEE* Clark, William
Clark, William; Canada, 1775 ***3036.5*** *p67*
*Child:*Mary
*Child:*Richard
*Child:*Rachael
*Child:*William
Clark, William; Massachusetts, 1757-1763 ***1642*** *p117*
Clark, William; New York, 1739 ***8277.31*** *p115*
With wife
*Son:*John
Clark, William; North Carolina, 1837 ***1088.45*** *p5*
Clark, William 30; Ontario, 1871 ***1823.17*** *p29*
Clark, William 35; Ontario, 1871 ***1823.21*** *p61*
Clark, William 42; Ontario, 1871 ***1823.17*** *p29*
Clark, William 61; Ontario, 1871 ***1823.17*** *p29*
Clark, William 62; Ontario, 1871 ***1823.21*** *p61*
Clark, William A. 29; Michigan, 1880 ***4491.36*** *p4*
Clark, William George 37; Ontario, 1871 ***1823.21*** *p61*
Clark, Wm 59; Ontario, 1871 ***1823.17*** *p29*
Clarke, Adam 36; Ontario, 1871 ***1823.21*** *p61*
Clarke, Albert 30; Ontario, 1871 ***1823.21*** *p61*
Clarke, Alexander 62; Ontario, 1871 ***1823.21*** *p61*
Clarke, Andrew 19; New York, NY, 1894 ***6512.1*** *p186*
Clarke, Ann 40; Ontario, 1871 ***1823.21*** *p61*
Clarke, Archibald; Illinois, 1851 ***6079.1*** *p3*
Clarke, B. R.; Marston's Wharf, 1782 ***8529.30*** *p10*
Clarke, Bridget 28; New York, NY, 1894 ***6512.1*** *p186*
Clarke, Charles 40; Ontario, 1871 ***1823.21*** *p61*
Clarke, Daniel 47; Ontario, 1871 ***1823.17*** *p29*
Clarke, David 50; Ontario, 1871 ***1823.21*** *p61*
Clarke, David 64; Ontario, 1871 ***1823.21*** *p61*
Clarke, Edward; Colorado, 1893 ***1029.59*** *p17*
Clarke, Elizabeth; Ipswich, MA, 1629-1651 ***9228.50*** *p324*
Clarke, George 30; Ontario, 1871 ***1823.21*** *p62*
Clarke, George 45; Ontario, 1871 ***1823.21*** *p62*
Clarke, George 57; Ontario, 1871 ***1823.17*** *p29*
Clarke, George 57; Ontario, 1871 ***1823.21*** *p61*
Clarke, Henry 63; Ontario, 1871 ***1823.17*** *p29*
Clarke, James 25; Ontario, 1871 ***1823.21*** *p62*
Clarke, James 30; Ontario, 1871 ***1823.21*** *p62*
Clarke, James 40; Ontario, 1871 ***1823.17*** *p29*
Clarke, James 42; Ontario, 1871 ***1823.21*** *p62*
Clarke, Jennet 69; Ontario, 1871 ***1823.21*** *p62*
Clarke, Jno.; Louisiana, 1874-1875 ***4981.45*** *p298*
Clarke, Johana 50; Ontario, 1871 ***1823.21*** *p62*
Clarke, John; North Carolina, 1844 ***1088.45*** *p5*
Clarke, John 34; Ontario, 1871 ***1823.17*** *p29*
Clarke, John 36; Ontario, 1871 ***1823.21*** *p62*
Clarke, John 93; Ontario, 1871 ***1823.21*** *p62*
Clarke, John; Toronto, 1844 ***2910.35*** *p113*
Clarke, Mary 45; Ontario, 1871 ***1823.21*** *p62*
Clarke, Rachel 70; Ontario, 1871 ***1823.21*** *p62*
Clarke, Richard; Plymouth, MA, 1620 ***1920.45*** *p5*
Clarke, Robert 28; Ontario, 1871 ***1823.21*** *p62*
Clarke, Robert 32; Ontario, 1871 ***1823.21*** *p62*
Clarke, Robert 72; Ontario, 1871 ***1823.21*** *p62*
Clarke, Saml Jn 22; Ontario, 1871 ***1823.21*** *p62*
Clarke, Thomas; Philadelphia, 1778 ***8529.30*** *p10*
Clarke, W. G.; Florida, 1842 ***8481.1*** *p18*
Clarke, William; Boston, 1831 ***3274.56*** *p97*
Clarke, William; New York, 1860 ***358.56*** *p148*
Clarke, William 26; Ontario, 1871 ***1823.21*** *p62*
Clarke, William 31; Ontario, 1871 ***1823.21*** *p62*
Clarke, William 43; Ontario, 1871 ***1823.21*** *p62*
Clarke, William 81; Ontario, 1871 ***1823.21*** *p62*
Clarke, William L. 58; Ontario, 1871 ***1823.21*** *p62*
Clarkson, Charles; Canada, 1774 ***3036.5*** *p41*
Clarkson, George 26; Ontario, 1871 ***1823.21*** *p62*

Clary, Bridget; New Brunswick, 1842 ***2978.20*** *p9*
Clary, Catherine; New Brunswick, 1842 ***2978.20*** *p9*
Clary, Margaret; New Brunswick, 1842 ***2978.20*** *p9*
Clary, Michael; Boston, 1764 ***1642*** *p33*
Clary, Michael; New Brunswick, 1842 ***2978.20*** *p9*
Clasing, Christoph; America, 1857 ***7420.1*** *p159*
With wife son & 3 daughters
Clason, N.; Philadelphia, 1847 ***6412.40*** *p150*
Classon, Jacob; Kansas, 1869-1871 ***777.40*** *p7*
Clasz, Jacob; Ohio, 1809-1852 ***4511.35*** *p8*
Clattersy, Michael; Ohio, 1840-1897 ***8365.35*** *p15*
Clattery, Mary; Marblehead, MA, 1700 ***1642*** *p72*
Claud, Victor 18; America, 1847 ***778.6*** *p71*
Claude, Le Petit 26; Quebec, 1642 ***9221.17*** *p118*
Claude, Claude; Quebec, 1647 ***9221.17*** *p178*
Claude, Elisabeth 44; America, 1846 ***778.6*** *p71*
Claude, Emile 14; America, 1846 ***778.6*** *p71*
Claude, H. A.; Louisiana, 1874-1875 ***4981.45*** *p298*
Claude, Joseph 16; America, 1846 ***778.6*** *p71*
Claude, Joseph 54; America, 1846 ***778.6*** *p71*
Claude, Josephine 8; America, 1846 ***778.6*** *p71*
Claude, Jsoeph 25; America, 1846 ***778.6*** *p71*
Claude, Julien 5; America, 1846 ***778.6*** *p71*
Claude, Marianne 38; America, 1846 ***778.6*** *p71*
Claude, Marie 18; America, 1846 ***778.6*** *p72*
Claudel, Charles; New York, 1902 ***1766.20*** *p18*
Claudin, Adele 12; Missouri, 1846 ***778.6*** *p72*
Claudin, August 8; Missouri, 1846 ***778.6*** *p72*
Claudin, Charles 17; Missouri, 1846 ***778.6*** *p72*
Claudin, Eugen 18; Missouri, 1846 ***778.6*** *p72*
Claudin, J. Louis 47; Missouri, 1846 ***778.6*** *p72*
Claudin, Jacques 15; Missouri, 1846 ***778.6*** *p72*
Claudin, Jean 15; Missouri, 1846 ***778.6*** *p72*
Claudin, Justine 13; Missouri, 1846 ***778.6*** *p72*
Claudin, Justine 20; Missouri, 1846 ***778.6*** *p72*
Claudin, Marie 9; Missouri, 1846 ***778.6*** *p72*
Claudin, Marie 49; Missouri, 1846 ***778.6*** *p72*
Claudy, Albert; Colorado, 1899 ***1029.59*** *p17*
Claudy, Albert; Colorado, 1901 ***1029.59*** *p17*
Claudy, Hypolitte; Illinois, 1858 ***6079.1*** *p3*
Claughlin, Patrick 60; Ontario, 1871 ***1823.21*** *p62*
Claughton, Mrs.; California, 1868 ***1131.61*** *p89*
With daughter
Claughton, David; Virginia, 1652 ***6254.4*** *p243*
Claus, Caroline; America, 1866 ***7420.1*** *p241*
Claus, Dorothee; America, 1854 ***7420.1*** *p117*
With son
Claus, Fred; Colorado, 1890 ***1029.59*** *p17*
Claus, Fred; Colorado, 1890 ***1029.59*** *p18*
Claus, Friedrich; Illinois, 1856 ***2526.43*** *p165*
Claus, Georg; America, 1866 ***5475.1*** *p490*
*Wife:*Juliane Linder
Claus, Georg Conrad; America, 1865 ***5475.1*** *p490*
Claus, Hans Heinrich; America, 1866 ***7420.1*** *p241*
*Brother:*Heinrich Conrad
Claus, Heinrich Conrad *SEE* Claus, Hans Heinrich
Claus, Henry; Ohio, 1841 ***2763.1*** *p9*
Claus, Jacob; Ohio, 1844 ***2763.1*** *p9*
Claus, Johann Heinrich Conrad; America, 1867 ***7420.1*** *p255*
With family
Claus, Juliane Linder 52 *SEE* Claus, Georg
Claus, Louise Wilhelmine; America, 1850 ***7420.1*** *p70*
Claus, Phillip 28; Ontario, 1871 ***1823.21*** *p62*
Clausen, Carl; Washington, 1882 ***2770.40*** *p135*
Clausen, Lars 26; New York, NY, 1894 ***6512.1*** *p185*
Clausen, Leo; New York, 1898 ***1766.20*** *p27*
Claushen, Emil; Iowa, 1925 ***1211.15*** *p9*
Clausing, Caroline; America, 1854 ***7420.1*** *p117*
With daughter
Clausing, Caroline Sophie Louise; America, 1857 ***7420.1*** *p159*
Clausing, Charlotte Dorothee Oltrogge *SEE* Clausing, Johann Christoph Ludwig
Clausing, Friederike Amalie Elisabeth *SEE* Clausing, Heinrich Conrad Ludwig
Clausing, Friedrich; America, 1852 ***7420.1*** *p86*
Clausing, Friedrich Christian Wilhelm; America, 1861 ***7420.1*** *p203*
With wife & son & 2 daughters
Clausing, Heinrich Conrad Ludwig; America, 1851 ***7420.1*** *p79*
*Sister:*Friederike Amalie Elisabeth
Clausing, Johann Christoph Ludwig; America, 1856 ***7420.1*** *p146*
*Wife:*Charlotte Dorothee Oltrogge
With family
Clausing, Johann Friedrich; America, 1857 ***7420.1*** *p159*
Clausing, Sophie Wilhelmine Caroline; America, 1857 ***7420.1*** *p159*
Clauson, Anna; Kansas, 1870-1875 ***777.40*** *p9*
Clauson, Jacob Nicklas; Kansas, 1869-1871 ***777.40*** *p7*
Clausse, B.; Valdivia, Chile, 1851 ***1192.4*** *p51*
With wife & child
Clausson, Elisabeth; New York, NY, 1845-1870 ***777.40*** *p7*
Claut, Louise 29; America, 1841 ***778.6*** *p72*
Clavei, Wilhelm; America, 1852 ***7420.1*** *p87*
With wife son & daughter
Clavel, Pierre 15; New Orleans, 1846 ***778.6*** *p72*
Claverie, Chs. Octave 18; New Orleans, 1846 ***778.6*** *p72*
Claverie, Jean 19; America, 1845 ***778.6*** *p72*
Claverie, Joseph 22; New Orleans, 1843 ***778.6*** *p72*
Claverie, P. 19; New Orleans, 1848 ***778.6*** *p72*
Clavey, August; America, 1856 ***7420.1*** *p146*
Clavey, Justine; America, 1891 ***7420.1*** *p364*
Clavey, Ludwig; America, 1867 ***7420.1*** *p255*
With family
Clavey, Wilhelmine Auguste; America, 1886 ***7420.1*** *p350*
Claxton, Sarah 43; Ontario, 1871 ***1823.17*** *p29*
Clay, Daniel 55; Ontario, 1871 ***1823.21*** *p62*
Clay, Elvas; Jamestown, VA, 1633 ***1658.20*** *p211*
Clay, James; Philadelphia, 1850 ***8513.31*** *p299*
*Wife:*Jane Eakin
Clay, Jane Eakin *SEE* Clay, James
Clay, Peter; Washington, 1881 ***2770.40*** *p135*
Claydon, John 30; Ontario, 1871 ***1823.17*** *p29*
Claydon, Joseph 43; Ontario, 1871 ***1823.21*** *p62*
Claypole, Mary A. 47; Ontario, 1871 ***1823.21*** *p62*
Clayson, William 44; Ontario, 1871 ***1823.21*** *p62*
Clayton, Ellen 12; Quebec, 1870 ***8364.32*** *p22*
Clayton, Mark 28; Indiana, 1868-1870 ***9076.20*** *p66*
Clayton, Robert; Marston's Wharf, 1782 ***8529.30*** *p10*
Clayton, Robert 74; Ontario, 1871 ***1823.21*** *p62*
Clayton, Sarah 18; Ontario, 1871 ***1823.21*** *p62*
Clear, Annie 26; Ontario, 1871 ***1823.21*** *p62*
Clear, Margaret Delaney *SEE* Clear, Pierce
Clear, Pierce; Halifax, N.S., 1827 ***7009.9*** *p62*
*Father:*William
*Mother:*Margaret Delaney
Clear, Thomas 30; Ontario, 1871 ***1823.21*** *p62*
Clear, William *SEE* Clear, Pierce
Cleary, John; Boston, 1764 ***1642*** *p34*
Cleary, Pat; St. Johns, N.F., 1825 ***1053.15*** *p6*
Cleary, Patrick 59; Ontario, 1871 ***1823.21*** *p62*
Cleary, Timothy; Vermont, 1835 ***3274.55*** *p75*
Cleary, Walter; Toronto, 1844 ***2910.35*** *p112*
Cleaveland, W. P. 50; Ontario, 1871 ***1823.21*** *p62*
Cleckner, Peter; New Jersey, 1773-1774 ***927.31*** *p2*
Clede, Jacob; Ohio, 1809-1852 ***4511.35*** *p8*
Clegg, Letitia 40; Ontario, 1871 ***1823.21*** *p62*
Cleghorn, George 29; Ontario, 1871 ***1823.17*** *p29*
Clein, William; Nova Scotia, 1784 ***7105*** *p24*
Cleland, John W. 56; Ontario, 1871 ***1823.17*** *p29*
Clelland, Robert 62; Ontario, 1871 ***1823.21*** *p62*
Clelland, Wiley 40; Ontario, 1871 ***1823.21*** *p63*
Clemens, Angela *SEE* Clemens, Mathias
Clemens, Barbara; America, 1880 ***5475.1*** *p358*
Clemens, Elisabeth Gimler *SEE* Clemens, Mathias
Clemens, Francis 44; Ontario, 1871 ***1823.17*** *p29*
Clemens, Jakob *SEE* Clemens, Mathias
Clemens, John; Ohio, 1809-1852 ***4511.35*** *p8*
Clemens, Margaret 40; Ontario, 1871 ***1823.21*** *p63*
Clemens, Margret; America, 1927 ***8023.44*** *p372*
Clemens, Maria *SEE* Clemens, Mathias
Clemens, Mathias; New York, 1880 ***5475.1*** *p378*
*Wife:*Elisabeth Gimler
*Son:*Jakob
*Daughter:*Angela
*Daughter:*Maria
Clemens, Peter; America, 1868 ***5475.1*** *p378*
Clemens, Richard; Marston's Wharf, 1782 ***8529.30*** *p10*
Clemensson, G.; Philadelphia, 1848 ***6412.40*** *p151*
Clement, Charles 59; Ontario, 1871 ***1823.21*** *p63*
Clement, Claude; Louisiana, 1841-1844 ***4981.45*** *p210*
Clement, Edward 14; Quebec, 1870 ***8364.32*** *p22*
Clement, Eisner 30; America, 1842 ***778.6*** *p72*
Clement, Frederick 33; America, 1842 ***778.6*** *p72*
Clement, Georgette; Quebec, 1661 ***9221.17*** *p452*
Clement, Henry; South Carolina, 1675 ***9228.50*** *p158*
Clement, Isaac; Salem, MA, 1700-1730 ***9228.50*** *p158*
Clement, Jacob; Salem, MA, 1700-1730 ***9228.50*** *p158*
Clement, Jean 22; America, 1846 ***778.6*** *p72*
Clement, Jean 33; Quebec, 1659 ***9221.17*** *p396*
Clement, Jim; Newfoundland, n.d. ***9228.50*** *p273*
Clement, John 45; America, 1841 ***778.6*** *p72*
Clement, John; Newfoundland, 1865 ***9228.50*** *p158*
Clement, Louis 27; America, 1846 ***778.6*** *p72*
Clement, Maria Sophia 19; America, 1841 ***778.6*** *p72*
Clement, Marie 34; New Orleans, 1848 ***778.6*** *p72*
Clement, Pierre 28; Quebec, 1656 ***9221.17*** *p333*
Clement, Seivery; Marblehead, MA, 1758 ***9228.50*** *p158*
Clement, Sidonie 24; New Orleans, 1848 ***778.6*** *p72*
Clement, Voutier 23; New Orleans, 1848 ***778.6*** *p72*
Clement DuVault, Claire-Francoise; Quebec, 1649 ***9221.17*** *p220*
Clement duVuault deValrennes, Philippe; Quebec, 1687 ***2314.30*** *p171*
Clements, Albert 29; Michigan, 1880 ***4491.36*** *p4*
Clements, Anne 54; Michigan, 1880 ***4491.36*** *p4*
Clements, Benje 27; Ontario, 1871 ***1823.17*** *p29*
Clements, Cecelia; America, 1831-1931 ***9228.50*** *p414*
Clements, Elisabeth 19; Michigan, 1880 ***4491.36*** *p4*
Clements, Ellen 27; Ontario, 1871 ***1823.17*** *p29*
Clements, Francis; North Carolina, 1806 ***1088.45*** *p5*
Clements, George 25; Michigan, 1880 ***4491.36*** *p4*
Clements, James; Boston, 1774 ***8529.30*** *p6*
Clements, James 52; Ontario, 1871 ***1823.21*** *p63*
Clements, John; Marblehead, MA, 1715-1776 ***9228.50*** *p158*
Clements, John 29; Michigan, 1880 ***4491.36*** *p4*
Clements, John; Nova Scotia, 1776-1805 ***9228.50*** *p158*
Clements, Mrs. John; Massachusetts, n.d. ***1642*** *p66*
With children
*Brother-In-Law:*Robert
Clements, Louisa 19; Michigan, 1880 ***4491.36*** *p4*
Clements, Rachel H. 16; Michigan, 1880 ***4491.36*** *p4*
Clements, Richard; Marston's Wharf, 1782 ***8529.30*** *p10*
Clements, Richard; New England, n.d. ***9228.50*** *p158*
Clements, Robert *SEE* Clements, Mrs. John
Clements, William 56; Michigan, 1880 ***4491.36*** *p4*
Clements, William 25; Ontario, 1871 ***1823.21*** *p63*
Clements, William 56; Ontario, 1871 ***1823.21*** *p63*
Clements, William 68; Ontario, 1871 ***1823.21*** *p63*
Clements, William R. 28; Michigan, 1880 ***4491.36*** *p4*
Clementz, Carolus 6; America, 1846 ***778.6*** *p72*
Clementz, Georges 32; America, 1846 ***778.6*** *p72*
Clementz, Marie 1; America, 1846 ***778.6*** *p72*
Clementz, Marie 31; America, 1846 ***778.6*** *p72*
Clementz, Ruppert 7; America, 1846 ***778.6*** *p73*
Clemenz, David 30; Port uncertain, 1846 ***778.6*** *p73*
Clemenz, David 62; Port uncertain, 1846 ***778.6*** *p73*
Clemmens, John; Ohio, 1809-1852 ***4511.35*** *p8*
Clemmens, Richard; Marston's Wharf, 1782 ***8529.30*** *p10*
Clemonn, Henry; Ohio, 1809-1852 ***4511.35*** *p8*
Clemons, Isaac; Salem, MA, 1700-1730 ***9228.50*** *p158*
Clemons, Jacob; Salem, MA, 1700-1730 ***9228.50*** *p158*
Clench, Serena 71; Ontario, 1871 ***1823.21*** *p63*
Clendenning, Georgina 25; Ontario, 1871 ***1823.17*** *p29*
Clenhenine, Margaret 27; Ontario, 1871 ***1823.17*** *p29*
Clerc, Caro; America, 1868 ***7919.3*** *p527*
Clerc, Jean 30; New Orleans, 1845 ***778.6*** *p73*
Clerc, P. Daniel; New Castle, DE, 1817-1818 ***90.20*** *p150*
Clere, Francois; Virginia, 1700 ***9230.15*** *p80*
Clere, Jeremy 29; Missouri, 1845 ***778.6*** *p73*
Clerice, Catherine; Quebec, 1671 ***4514.3*** *p292*
Clerit, Amelie 9; America, 1846 ***778.6*** *p73*
Clerk, George; Utah, 1863 ***9228.50*** *p338*
Clerk, John 40; Ontario, 1871 ***1823.17*** *p29*
Cless, Henry; Ohio, 1809-1852 ***4511.35*** *p8*
Clesson, Matthew; Massachusetts, 1678 ***1642*** *p116*
Cleve, Edward; North Carolina, 1850 ***1088.45*** *p6*
Cleve, William; North Carolina, 1860 ***1088.45*** *p6*
Cleveland, John D. 47; Ontario, 1871 ***1823.21*** *p63*
Cleverton, Lawrence 32; Ontario, 1871 ***1823.21*** *p63*
Click, Ludwick; Ohio, 1809-1852 ***4511.35*** *p8*
Clifford, Charles 40; Ontario, 1871 ***1823.21*** *p63*
Clifford, Cornelius 30; Ontario, 1871 ***1823.21*** *p63*
Clifford, James; Illinois, 1855 ***6079.1*** *p3*
Clifford, James 38; Ontario, 1871 ***1823.17*** *p29*
Clifford, Jeramiah 39; Ontario, 1871 ***1823.21*** *p63*
Clifford, John 34; Ontario, 1871 ***1823.17*** *p29*
Clifford, Tom; St. John, N.B., 1848 ***2978.15*** *p38*
Clifford, William 50; Ontario, 1871 ***1823.21*** *p63*
Clifford, William 61; Ontario, 1871 ***1823.21*** *p63*
Clifford, William 70; Ontario, 1871 ***1823.21*** *p63*
Clifsold, Thomas S.; New York, NY, 1827 ***3274.55*** *p70*
Clifton, Jane; Jamestown, VA, 1633 ***1658.20*** *p211*
Climie, Thomas 63; Ontario, 1871 ***1823.17*** *p29*
Climie, William 53; Ontario, 1871 ***1823.17*** *p29*
Clinard, William; Philadelphia, 1777 ***8529.30*** *p2A*
Clinch, Biddy; New Orleans, 1850 ***7242.30*** *p138*
Clinch, Eliza; New Orleans, 1850 ***7242.30*** *p138*
Clinch, Ellen; New Orleans, 1850 ***7242.30*** *p138*
Clinch, Mary; New Orleans, 1850 ***7242.30*** *p138*
Clinch, Michael; New Orleans, 1850 ***7242.30*** *p138*
Cline, George 55; Ontario, 1871 ***1823.21*** *p63*
Cline, Jacob; North Carolina, 1839 ***1088.45*** *p6*
Cline, Peter 81; Ontario, 1871 ***1823.17*** *p29*
Cline, Robert H. 29; Ontario, 1871 ***1823.21*** *p63*
Cline, Wm 30; Ontario, 1871 ***1823.21*** *p63*
Cling, Charles; Illinois, 1861 ***4487.25*** *p54*
Clingan, James 50; Ontario, 1871 ***1823.17*** *p29*
Clink, John 61; Ontario, 1871 ***1823.17*** *p29*
Clinkman, James 37; Ontario, 1871 ***1823.17*** *p30*
Clinton, Lucy Hannah 24; Ontario, 1871 ***1823.21*** *p63*
Cliper, Henry; New Jersey, 1767-1774 ***927.31*** *p2*

Clipperton, James 33; Ontario, 1871 1823.21 p63
Clipton, Chas 21; Ontario, 1871 1823.21 p63
Clique, Jacques; Quebec, 1646 9221.17 p163
Clissold, Catherine 39; Ontario, 1871 1823.21 p63
Cllenill, Edwin 33; Ontario, 1871 1823.17 p30
Cloche, John; New Jersey, 1665 9228.50 p159
Cloche, John; Virginia, 1665 9228.50 p53
Cloche, Rachel; Salem, MA, 1672 9228.50 p159
Clochecy, Joseph P. 26; New York, NY, 1825 6178.50 p149
Clochey, Joseph P. 26; New York, NY, 1825 6178.50 p149
Clochnessy, Patrick 42; Ontario, 1871 1823.21 p63
Clock, J.M.; San Francisco, 1851 9228.50 p159
Clock, John; New Jersey, 1665 9228.50 p159
Clock, John; Virginia, 1665 9228.50 p53
Clockecy, Joseph P. 26; New York, NY, 1825 6178.50 p149
Clocksey, Joseph P. 26; New York, NY, 1825 6178.50 p149
Clogg, Bessy 17; Ontario, 1871 1823.21 p63
Clohesey, Patrick; Vermont, 1830 3274.55 p75
Clomann, Anna Maria *SEE* Clomann, Nikolaus
Clomann, Nikolaus; Louisville, KY, 1859 5475.1 p534
*Sister:*Anna Maria
Clonid, A. A. 22; New Orleans, 1843 778.6 p73
Cloos, Jacob; Missouri, 1898 3276.1 p1
Cloos, Jacob; Missouri, 1900 3276.1 p1
Clopet, Antoine 27; Missouri, 1848 778.6 p73
Clopin, Jules Francis 24; America, 1846 778.6 p73
Clos, Barthelemy 18; New Orleans, 1848 778.6 p73
Clos, F.; Louisiana, 1874 4981.45 p295
Close, Elizabeth 56; Michigan, 1880 4491.39 p5
Close, John 60; Ontario, 1871 1823.21 p63
Close, Robert 22; Ontario, 1871 1823.17 p30
Closen, Johann *SEE* Closen, Mathias
Closen, Maria Bach *SEE* Closen, Mathias
Closen, Mathias *SEE* Closen, Mathias
Closen, Mathias; America, 1879 5475.1 p186
*Wife:*Maria Bach
*Son:*Peter
*Son:*Johann
*Son:*Mathias
Closen, Peter *SEE* Closen, Mathias
Closse, Lambert 29; Montreal, 1647 9221.17 p191
Clossner, Clara; Baltimore, 1853 8513.31 p305
Closz, Jacob; Ohio, 1809-1852 4511.35 p8
Closz, Jacob; Ohio, 1809-1852 4511.35 p8
Cloth, Boye; North Carolina, 1826 1088.45 p6
Clouard, Aman 17; America, 1843 778.6 p73
Cloude, John; Ohio, 1809-1852 4511.35 p8
Clouse, Michael; Ohio, 1809-1852 4511.35 p8
Clout, Henry; Ontario, 1787 1276.15 p230
Cloutier, Anne 11 *SEE* Cloutier, Xaintes Dupont
Cloutier, Charles 7 *SEE* Cloutier, Xaintes Dupont
Cloutier, Jean 16 *SEE* Cloutier, Xaintes Dupont
Cloutier, Louise 4 *SEE* Cloutier, Xaintes Dupont
Cloutier, Madeleine 22; Quebec, 1648 9221.17 p197
Cloutier, Xaintes 40; Quebec, 1636 9221.17 p53
*Son:*Jean 16
*Daughter:*Louise 4
*Son:*Charles 7
*Daughter:*Anne 11
Cloutier, Zacharie 17 *SEE* Cloutier, Zacharie
Cloutier, Zacharie 44; Quebec, 1634 9221.17 p34
*Son:*Zacharie 17
Clouton, Robert 53; New York, NY, 1835 5024.1 p137
Clow, Alfred 24; Ontario, 1871 1823.21 p63
Clow, Janet; Prince Edward Island, 1826-1874 9228.50 p128
Clow, Janet; Prince Edward Island, 1849 9228.50 p660
Clow, William 20; Ontario, 1871 1823.21 p63
Clowe, Peter; Ontario, 1787 1276.15 p230
With 3 children & 3 relatives
Clowsman, H. H.; California, 1868 1131.61 p89
Cloyse, Nicho.; Maryland, 1674-1675 1236.25 p51
Clubb, Alexander 52; Ontario, 1871 1823.21 p63
Clubb, John 46; Ontario, 1871 1823.21 p63
Cluch, William Robert 30; Ontario, 1871 1823.21 p63
Cluckman, John 30; Ontario, 1871 1823.17 p30
Cluff, John; Marston's Wharf, 1782 8529.30 p10
Clune, Joseph 34; Michigan, 1880 4491.33 p5
Clune, Martin 18; Michigan, 1880 4491.33 p5
Clune, Mary; Ontario, 1835 3160.1 p150
Clunes, John 66; Ontario, 1871 1823.21 p63
Cluness, David 69; Ontario, 1871 1823.21 p63
Cluness, John 38; Ontario, 1871 1823.21 p63
Cluney, John 50; Ontario, 1871 1823.21 p63
Clunn, Edward 30; Ontario, 1871 1823.21 p63
Clust, Pierre; Quebec, 1634 9221.17 p35
Clusz, Jacob; Ohio, 1809-1852 4511.35 p8
Cluth, C.; Galveston, TX, 1855 571.7 p18
Clutier, Pierre; Louisiana, 1874 4981.45 p131
Clutterham, Samuel 60; Ontario, 1871 1823.21 p63
Cluzeaux, Francois 21; New Orleans, 1840 778.6 p73
Clyne, Jos.; Ontario, 1787 1276.15 p230
Clys, Alphonse 31; America, 1746 778.6 p73
Coad, Richard 53; Ontario, 1871 1823.21 p63
Coady, Anne; Halifax, N.S., 1827 7009.9 p60
*Father:*William
*Mother:*Mary McDonald
Coady, Martha Le Brocq *SEE* Coady, Philip
Coady, Mary McDonald *SEE* Coady, Anne
Coady, Philip; Beverly, MA, 1698 9228.50 p159
*Wife:*Martha Le Brocq
Coady, Philip, Family; America, 1600-1699 9228.50 p337
Coady, William *SEE* Coady, Anne
Coagy, Patrick 89; Ontario, 1871 1823.17 p30
Coakley, Henry; North Carolina, 1804 1088.45 p6
Coakley, Mary 12; Quebec, 1870 8364.32 p23
Coakley, Sarah 6; Quebec, 1870 8364.32 p23
Coalman, Cathrine 9; Ontario, 1871 1823.21 p63
Coan, Mrs.; Toronto, 1844 2910.35 p114
Coasten, Eliza 48; Ontario, 1871 1823.21 p64
Coate, Leonard; Maryland, 1673 1236.25 p48
Coates, Mark 56; Ontario, 1871 1823.21 p64
Coates, Mary 51; Ontario, 1871 1823.17 p30
Coats, James; Toronto, 1844 2910.35 p112
Coats, Moses 70; Ontario, 1871 1823.21 p64
Coats, William 45; Ontario, 1871 1823.21 p64
Cobb, Susan 30; Ontario, 1871 1823.21 p64
Cobb, William 16; Quebec, 1870 8364.32 p23
Cobban, Helen Webster 30 *SEE* Cobban, James
Cobban, James 24; New York, NY, 1835 5024.1 p137
*Wife:*Helen Webster 30
Cobban, James 28; Ontario, 1871 1823.21 p64
Cobban, John 1; New York, NY, 1835 5024.1 p137
Cobban, William 37; Ontario, 1871 1823.21 p64
Cobbin, Daniel 18; Ontario, 1871 1823.21 p64
Cobbin, William 36; Ontario, 1871 1823.21 p64
Cobble, James 60; Ontario, 1871 1823.21 p64
Cobbledick, Samuel 48; Ontario, 1871 1823.21 p64
Cobbledick, Thomas 35; Ontario, 1871 1823.21 p64
Cobbledick, William 34; Ontario, 1871 1823.21 p64
Cobbushack, Francis; Long Island, 1780 8529.30 p9A
Coben, John 41; Ontario, 1871 1823.21 p64
Cobleigh, Ratio 60; Ontario, 1871 1823.21 p64
Coblenz, Daniel; America, 1865-1870 5475.1 p404
Coburn, Hazlit 32; Ohio, 1880 4879.40 p259
*Wife:*Isabella McOnaughy 33
Coburn, Isabella McOnaughy 33 *SEE* Coburn, Hazlit
Cobwill, John 36; Ontario, 1871 1823.21 p64
Cochard, Charles 44; Texas, 1848 778.6 p73
Cochare, John *SEE* Cochare, Samuel
Cochare, Samuel; Dorchester, MA, 1770 1642 p102
*Relative:*John
Cochelier, Respin 29; Quebec, 1659 9221.17 p397
Cocher, John; Ohio, 1809-1852 4511.35 p8
Cochereau, Pierre 27; Quebec, 1662 9221.17 p483
Cochet, Andre; Virginia, 1700 9230.15 p80
Cochlin, James; Illinois, 1834-1900 6020.5 p131
Cochlin, Marey 60; Ontario, 1871 1823.17 p30
Cochlin, Margaret 65; Ontario, 1871 1823.17 p30
Cochman, John 45; Ontario, 1871 1823.21 p64
Cochon, Guillaume; Quebec, 1644 9221.17 p139
Cochon, Jacques *SEE* Cochon, Jean
Cochon, Jean 10 *SEE* Cochon, Jean
Cochon, Jean 45; Quebec, 1636 9221.17 p54
*Daughter:*Marguerite 16
*Wife:*Jeanne Abraham 31
*Son:*Pierre 5
*Son:*Jean 10
*Son:*Jacques
Cochon, Jeanne Abraham 31 *SEE* Cochon, Jean
Cochon, Laurent 30; New Orleans, 1848 778.6 p73
Cochon, Marguerite 16 *SEE* Cochon, Jean
Cochon, Pierre 5 *SEE* Cochon, Jean
Cochon, Prosper 4; New Orleans, 1848 778.6 p73
Cochon, Rose 24; New Orleans, 1848 778.6 p73
Cochore, Teague; Boston, 1640 1642 p6
Cochran, Mr. 18; Massachusetts, 1725 1642 p23
Cochran, Agnes; Massachusetts, 1766 1642 p120
Cochran, Agnes 30; New York, NY, 1835 5024.1 p137
Cochran, Andrew; Salem, MA, 1739 1642 p78
Cochran, Elenor 17; St. John, N.B., 1834 6469.7 p5
Cochran, Hamilton 5; St. John, N.B., 1834 6469.7 p5
Cochran, James; Ohio, 1854 3580.20 p31
Cochran, James; Ohio, 1854 6020.12 p6
Cochran, James 16; St. John, N.B., 1834 6469.7 p5
Cochran, Jane 14; St. John, N.B., 1834 6469.7 p5
Cochran, John; Massachusetts, 1733 1642 p85
Cochran, John; Massachusetts, 1765 1642 p100
Cochran, John 40; Ontario, 1871 1823.21 p64
Cochran, John; Salem, MA, 1756 1642 p78
Cochran, John 9; St. John, N.B., 1834 6469.7 p5
Cochran, Margaret *SEE* Cochran, Thomas
Cochran, Michael; Massachusetts, 1757 1642 p66
Cochran, Nathaniel; Salem, MA, 1753 1642 p78
Cochran, Rebecca 2; St. John, N.B., 1834 6469.7 p5
Cochran, Robert; Massachusetts, 1767 1642 p120
Cochran, Robert 12; St. John, N.B., 1834 6469.7 p5
Cochran, Sarah 40; St. John, N.B., 1834 6469.7 p5
Cochran, Sarah Ann 6; St. John, N.B., 1834 6469.7 p5
Cochran, Thomas; Massachusetts, 1741 1642 p119
*Wife:*Margaret
Cochran, William; Massachusetts, 1758 1642 p85
Cochran, William 20; St. John, N.B., 1834 6469.7 p5
Cochrane, Bridget 70; Ontario, 1871 1823.17 p30
Cochrane, James 23; Ontario, 1871 1823.21 p64
Cochrane, James 39; Ontario, 1871 1823.21 p64
Cochrane, Thomas 43; Ontario, 1871 1823.17 p30
Cochrane, William; Massachusetts, 1772 1642 p68
Cochrane, William; Ontario, 1871 1823.21 p64
Cochrane, William 18; Quebec, 1870 8364.32 p23
Cochren, James; Massachusetts, 1735 1642 p63
*Wife:*Sarah
Cochren, Sarah *SEE* Cochren, James
Cock, Anth.; Maryland, 1672 1236.25 p47
Cock, Mary; Boston, 1745 1642 p45
Cock, Thomas; Boston, 1740 9228.50 p159
Cock, Thomas 33; Ontario, 1871 1823.17 p30
Cock, Wm.; New England, 1688 9228.50 p338
Cockans, Edward; Ontario, 1835 3160.1 p150
Cockburn, John 50; Ontario, 1871 1823.21 p64
Cocke, Willm; Virginia, 1652 6254.4 p243
Cocker, William 55; Ontario, 1871 1823.21 p64
Cockery, Mary; Boston, 1766 1642 p37
Cocking, Francis; Barbados or St. Christopher, 1780 8529.30 p7A
Cockle, Horace 39; Ontario, 1871 1823.21 p64
Cockle, John 54; Ontario, 1871 1823.21 p64
Cockram, Mr. 18; Massachusetts, 1725 1642 p23
Cockran, Mary *SEE* Cockran, William
Cockran, William; Watertown, MA, 1773 1642 p112
*Wife:*Mary
Cockrane, David 26; New York, NY, 1835 5024.1 p137
Cockrane, Margaret 22; Ontario, 1871 1823.17 p30
Cockrill, George; Quebec, 1870 8364.32 p23
Cockrill, William 39; Ontario, 1871 1823.21 p64
Cocks, Mary; Boston, 1756 1642 p47
Cocquelin, Nicolas; Quebec, 1649 9221.17 p210
Cocu, Louise 24; Quebec, 1659 9221.17 p397
Codd, Matthew; Toronto, 1844 2910.35 p112
Codd, Nicholas; New Orleans, 1850 7242.30 p138
Coddington, Phoebe F.; Ontario, 1871 1823.21 p64
Coddou, Victor 21; America, 1845 778.6 p73
Code, Deborah 48; Ontario, 1871 1823.21 p64
Code, Nicholas; North Carolina, 1838 1088.45 p6
Code, William 33; Ontario, 1871 1823.21 p64
Code, William G. 62; Ontario, 1871 1823.21 p64
Codie, Martha Le Brocq *SEE* Codie, Philip
Codie, Philip; Beverly, MA, 1698 9228.50 p159
*Wife:*Martha Le Brocq
Codie, Philip, Family; America, 1600-1699 9228.50 p337
Codlin, Mathew; Ontario, 1871 1823.17 p30
Codlin, Matthew; Ontario, 1871 1823.17 p30
Codman, James; Louisiana, 1874 4981.45 p131
Codrjrs, Thomas; Louisiana, 1836-1841 4981.45 p208
Cody, Mrs.; Toronto, 1844 2910.35 p114
Cody, Eugene; Colorado, 1918 1029.59 p18
Cody, Eugene; Vermont, 1870 1029.59 p18
Cody, Martha Le Brocq *SEE* Cody, Philip
Cody, Martha LeBrocq *SEE* Cody, Philippe
Cody, Martha LeBrocq *SEE* Cody, Philip
Cody, Patrick 71; Ontario, 1871 1823.17 p30
Cody, Philip; Beverly, MA, 1698 9228.50 p159
*Wife:*Martha Le Brocq
Cody, Philip; Beverly, MA, 1698 9228.50 p335
*Wife:*Martha LeBrocq
Cody, Philip, Family; America, 1600-1699 9228.50 p337
Cody, Philippe; Massachusetts, 1743 9228.50 p23
*Wife:*Martha LeBrocq
Cody, William 17; Michigan, 1880 4491.39 p6
Cody, Wm 21; St. Johns, N.F., 1811 1053.20 p22
Coe, Robert; Massachusetts, 1634 9228.50 p228
Coeffe, Vincent; Illinois, 1852 6079.1 p3
Coellard, Jn. Pre. 36; Louisiana, 1848 778.6 p73
Coellard, Madelaine 24; Louisiana, 1848 778.6 p73
Coesfeld, Ernst; America, 1874 7420.1 p302
Coffe, James; Boston, 1764 1642 p33
Coffee, Thomas 25; Ontario, 1871 1823.21 p64
Coffee, Thomas 75; Ontario, 1871 1823.21 p64
Coffey, James; Colorado, 1895 1029.59 p18
Coffey, Patrick; North Carolina, 1824 1088.45 p6
Coffey, Patrick Joseph; North Carolina, 1845 1088.45 p6
Coffey, Stephen 60; Ontario, 1871 1823.17 p30
Coffie, Mrs.; Port uncertain, 1844 778.6 p73
Coffie, G.; Port uncertain, 1844 778.6 p73

Coffino, Blanche 44; America, 1844 ***778.6*** *p73*
Coflin, Edmund; Boston, 1765 ***1642*** *p35*
Cogan, Henry; Boston, 1638 ***1642*** *p6*
Cogan, James; Louisiana, 1874-1875 ***4981.45*** *p298*
Cogan, John; Boston, 1620-1775 ***1642*** *p138*
Cogan, John; Boston, 1620-1775 ***1642*** *p138*
Cogan, John; Boston, 1633 ***1642*** *p3*
Cogan, John 55; Ontario, 1871 ***1823.21*** *p64*
Cogan, Ruth; Springfield, MA, 1675 ***1642*** *p120*
Cogan, Samuel; Marblehead, MA, 1714 ***1642*** *p73*
Cogeault, August; Louisiana, 1836-1840 ***4981.45*** *p212*
Coggan, . . .; Boston, 1630-1644 ***1642*** *p3*
Coggan, Henry; Beverly, MA, 1764 ***1642*** *p64*
Coggan, Henry; Boston, 1638 ***1642*** *p6*
Coggan, John; Boston, 1633 ***1642*** *p4*
Coggan, John; Dorchester, MA, 1633 ***117.5*** *p158*
Coggan, John W.; Colorado, 1887 ***1029.59*** *p18*
Cogger, Elizabeth *SEE* Cogger, John
Cogger, John; Woburn, MA, 1693 ***1642*** *p113*
*Wife:*Elizabeth
Coggin, Henry; Massachusetts, 1756 ***1642*** *p110*
Coggin, Henry; Massachusetts, 1756 ***1642*** *p113*
Coggin, John; Charlestown, MA, 1664 ***1642*** *p100*
Coggin, Mary; Massachusetts, 1732 ***1642*** *p102*
Coggin, Mary; Worcester, MA, 1732 ***1642*** *p114*
Coggin, Silence; Massachusetts, 1750 ***1642*** *p111*
Coggin, Tho; Virginia, 1652 ***6254.4*** *p243*
Coghlan, John 30; New York, NY, 1825 ***6178.50*** *p77*
Coghlan, Michael 60; Ontario, 1871 ***1823.21*** *p64*
Coghlin, Felix; North Carolina, 1838 ***1088.45*** *p6*
Coghlin, James; Boston, 1766 ***1642*** *p37*
Coghlin, John 30; New York, NY, 1825 ***6178.50*** *p77*
Cogin, Henry; Massachusetts, 1725 ***1642*** *p113*
Cogin, Henry; Massachusetts, 1730 ***1642*** *p102*
Cogin, Heny; Massachusetts, 1730 ***1642*** *p110*
Cogin, John; Massachusetts, 1725 ***1642*** *p113*
Cogin, Josiah; Massachusetts, 1752 ***1642*** *p63*
Cogin, Thomas; Boston, 1751 ***1642*** *p46*
Coglan, Lillian De Broder *SEE* Coglan, Wm.
Coglan, Lillian De Broder *SEE* Coglan, Wm.
Coglan, Wm.; Canada, 1964 ***9228.50*** *p160*
*Wife:*Lillian De Broder
Coglan, Wm.; Wisconsin, 1964 ***9228.50*** *p160*
*Wife:*Lillian De Broder
Cogswell, Mason; North Carolina, 1820-1825 ***1088.45*** *p6*
Cogut, Mary; Detroit, 1929 ***1640.55*** *p112*
Cohan, Charles; Massachusetts, 1675-1676 ***1642*** *p129*
Cohane, Walter; Massachusetts, 1675-1676 ***1642*** *p127*
Cohas, Charles 37; America, 1846 ***778.6*** *p73*
Cohen, Mr. 50; New Orleans, 1840 ***778.6*** *p73*
Cohen, Mrs. 28; New York, NY, 1894 ***6512.1*** *p228*
Cohen, Auguste 20; Kentucky, 1846 ***778.6*** *p73*
Cohen, C. 31; America, 1848 ***778.6*** *p73*
Cohen, Hodah 11 months; New York, NY, 1894 ***6512.1*** *p228*
Cohen, Hyman 16; New York, NY, 1894 ***6512.1*** *p228*
Cohen, Jonas; North Carolina, 1820 ***1088.45*** *p6*
Cohen, Joseph 3; New York, NY, 1894 ***6512.1*** *p228*
Cohen, Morris 30; New York, NY, 1894 ***6512.1*** *p228*
Cohen, Samuel; South Carolina, 1861 ***6155.4*** *p18*
Cohetine, Daniel 66; Port uncertain, 1840 ***778.6*** *p73*
Cohilas, Barnis; Louisiana, 1874 ***4981.45*** *p295*
Cohn, Isaak; America, 1848 ***7420.1*** *p59*
Cohn, Julius; America, 1855 ***7420.1*** *p135*
Cohn, Mary; North Carolina, 1792-1862 ***1088.45*** *p6*
Cohn, Solomon; Louisiana, 1836-1841 ***4981.45*** *p208*
Cohu, Paul; Salem, MA, 1762 ***9228.50*** *p164*
Cohu, Peter; New York, 1765-1815 ***9228.50*** *p162*
Cohu, Susan; New York, 1815 ***9228.50*** *p405*
Cohu, Thomas Ashburn; Philadelphia, 1869 ***9228.50*** *p160*
Cohu, William; New York, 1831 ***9228.50*** *p164*
Coignac, Marthe 42; Quebec, 1648 ***9221.17*** *p198*
Coignard, Marie; Quebec, 1669 ***4514.3*** *p292*
Coignat, Marthe 42; Quebec, 1648 ***9221.17*** *p198*
Coignon, Etienne 31; America, 1847 ***778.6*** *p73*
Coignon, Jean 3; America, 1847 ***778.6*** *p73*
Coignon, Marie 4; America, 1847 ***778.6*** *p73*
Coignon, Rosalie 31; America, 1847 ***778.6*** *p74*
Coil, Edward 32; St. John, N.B., 1834 ***6469.7*** *p5*
Coil, Nancy 30; St. John, N.B., 1834 ***6469.7*** *p5*
Coil, Patrick 9 months; St. John, N.B., 1834 ***6469.7*** *p5*
Coin, Thomas; Ohio, 1809-1852 ***4511.35*** *p9*
Coinarblo, Pierre S. 33; New Orleans, 1842 ***778.6*** *p74*
Coindet, Gedeon; Quebec, 1644 ***9221.17*** *p140*
Coipel, Marie; Quebec, 1669 ***4514.3*** *p292*
Coirier, Perrine; Quebec, 1665 ***4514.3*** *p292*
*Brother:*Pierre
Coirier, Pierre *SEE* Coirier, Perrine
Coisman, Celestine Taillet *SEE* Coisman, Louis
Coisman, Constant; Wisconsin, 1854-1858 ***1495.20*** *p66*
Coisman, Emile Joseph *SEE* Coisman, Louis
Coisman, Louis; Wisconsin, 1854-1858 ***1495.20*** *p66*
*Wife:*Celestine Taillet
*Child:*Emile Joseph
*Child:*Marie Antoinette
Coisman, Marie Antoinette *SEE* Coisman, Louis
Coka, Vilem; Chicago, 1871 ***2853.20*** *p426*
Coka, Vilem; Omaha, NE, 1889 ***2853.20*** *p150*
Cokelin, John 30; Ontario, 1871 ***1823.17*** *p30*
Colard, Francois; Quebec, 1661 ***9221.17*** *p452*
Colart, Louis; New York, NY, 1870 ***1494.20*** *p11*
Colas, . . .; Quebec, 1534 ***9228.50*** *p3*
Colas, Charles 36; America, 1843 ***778.6*** *p74*
Colas, Charles; Louisiana, 1836-1840 ***4981.45*** *p212*
Colbaker, Florioen; Ohio, 1809-1852 ***4511.35*** *p8*
Colbeck, William 35; Ontario, 1871 ***1823.17*** *p30*
Colbert, J. J. 34; Port uncertain, 1843 ***778.6*** *p74*
Colbert, Robert 40; Ontario, 1871 ***1823.21*** *p64*
Colbert, Thomas; Louisiana, 1874 ***4981.45*** *p131*
Colbourne, Margaret 45; Ontario, 1871 ***1823.21*** *p64*
Colburn, John 52; Ontario, 1871 ***1823.21*** *p65*
Colby, Henry 37; Ontario, 1871 ***1823.17*** *p30*
Colclough, George; Virginia, 1652 ***6254.4*** *p243*
Colclough, John 58; Ontario, 1871 ***1823.17*** *p30*
Colcombe, . . .; Boston, 1769 ***9228.50*** *p5*
Colcombe, Charles; Boston, 1769 ***9228.50*** *p168*
Colden, Elizabeth; Philadelphia, 1849 ***8513.31*** *p420*
Coldrick Family ; Canada, n.d. ***9228.50*** *p164*
Coldsnow, Frederick; Ohio, 1809-1852 ***4511.35*** *p8*
Coldwater, Charles; Illinois, 1857 ***6079.1*** *p3*
Cole, Abraham 67; Ontario, 1871 ***1823.21*** *p65*
Cole, Agnes 48; Ontario, 1871 ***1823.21*** *p65*
Cole, Alwynd; Ohio, 1809-1852 ***4511.35*** *p8*
Cole, Arthur 17; Quebec, 1870 ***8364.32*** *p23*
Cole, Benjamin 45; Ontario, 1871 ***1823.17*** *p30*
Cole, David 18; Michigan, 1880 ***4491.30*** *p6*
Cole, Edwin 44; Ontario, 1871 ***1823.21*** *p65*
Cole, Eliza Jane; Saskatchewan, 1921 ***9228.50*** *p565*
Cole, Harvey 26; Ontario, 1871 ***1823.17*** *p30*
Cole, James 14; Michigan, 1880 ***4491.30*** *p6*
Cole, John; Ohio, 1809-1852 ***4511.35*** *p8*
Cole, John 32; Ontario, 1871 ***1823.21*** *p65*
Cole, John 78; Ontario, 1871 ***1823.17*** *p30*
Cole, John; Wisconsin, 1800-1899 ***9228.50*** *p164*
Cole, Mary Ann; Havana, 1817-1900 ***9228.50*** *p581*
Cole, Mary J. 12; Ontario, 1871 ***1823.17*** *p30*
Cole, Moray 30; Ontario, 1871 ***1823.21*** *p65*
Cole, Robert 26; Ontario, 1871 ***1823.21*** *p65*
Cole, Samuel 71; Ontario, 1871 ***1823.17*** *p30*
Cole, Sarah 18; Michigan, 1880 ***4491.30*** *p6*
Cole, Sarah; Philadelphia, 1857 ***8513.31*** *p314*
Cole, Thomas 35; Ontario, 1871 ***1823.21*** *p65*
Cole, William 36; Ontario, 1871 ***1823.21*** *p65*
Cole, William 16; Quebec, 1870 ***8364.32*** *p23*
Coleen, John 42; Ontario, 1871 ***1823.21*** *p65*
Coleman, Edward 60; Ontario, 1871 ***1823.21*** *p65*
Coleman, George 76; Ontario, 1871 ***1823.21*** *p65*
Coleman, Henry 22; Ontario, 1871 ***1823.17*** *p30*
Coleman, James 28; Ontario, 1871 ***1823.21*** *p65*
Coleman, Jas 28; Ontario, 1871 ***1823.21*** *p65*
Coleman, Jeremiah; Boston, 1833 ***3274.56*** *p69*
Coleman, John; Ohio, 1809-1852 ***4511.35*** *p8*
Coleman, John; Ohio, 1835 ***2763.1*** *p9*
Coleman, John 25; Ontario, 1871 ***1823.17*** *p30*
Coleman, John 43; Ontario, 1871 ***1823.17*** *p30*
Coleman, John 60; Ontario, 1871 ***1823.21*** *p65*
Coleman, John; Philadelphia, 1777 ***8529.30*** *p2*
Coleman, Joshua; Ohio, 1842 ***2763.1*** *p9*
Coleman, Lewis 24; Ontario, 1871 ***1823.17*** *p30*
Coleman, Michael; Boston, 1763 ***1642*** *p32*
Coleman, Michael; Boston, 1763 ***1642*** *p32*
Coleman, Michael; Boston, 1768 ***1642*** *p39*
Coleman, Michael 42; Ontario, 1871 ***1823.17*** *p30*
Coleman, Michl 23; St. Johns, N.F., 1811 ***1053.20*** *p21*
Coleman, Miles 30; Ontario, 1871 ***1823.17*** *p30*
Coleman, Pat 34; St. Johns, N.F., 1811 ***1053.20*** *p20*
Coleman, Thomas 35; Ontario, 1871 ***1823.17*** *p30*
Coleman, William 31; Michigan, 1880 ***4491.42*** *p8*
Coleman, William 58; Ontario, 1871 ***1823.21*** *p65*
Coleman, William 60; Ontario, 1871 ***1823.21*** *p65*
Coleman, William, Jr.; Ohio, 1809-1852 ***4511.35*** *p8*
Coleman, William B.; Ohio, 1809-1852 ***4511.35*** *p8*
Colen, Patrick; Massachusetts, 1768 ***1642*** *p90*
Coleraine, Daniel 13; Quebec, 1870 ***8364.32*** *p23*
Colerick, Mary 58; Ontario, 1871 ***1823.21*** *p65*
Coles, Edward 21; Ontario, 1871 ***1823.21*** *p65*
Coles, Elizabeth 19; Ontario, 1871 ***1823.21*** *p65*
Coles, Frank 30; Ontario, 1871 ***1823.21*** *p65*
Coles, John I. 22; Ontario, 1871 ***1823.21*** *p65*
Coles, Robert 32; Ontario, 1871 ***1823.21*** *p65*
Coley, Hugh; Worcester, MA, 1733 ***1642*** *p114*
*Wife:*Sarah
Coley, Sarah *SEE* Coley, Hugh
Colgan, James Patrick; Louisiana, 1841-1844 ***4981.45*** *p210*
Colgan, Michael; Toronto, 1844 ***2910.35*** *p112*
Colgrove, Robert 34; Ontario, 1871 ***1823.21*** *p65*
Coli, A.; New York, 1860 ***358.56*** *p5*
Colier, Henry 27; Boston, 1835 ***6424.55*** *p30*
Colier, Samuel 49; Ontario, 1871 ***1823.17*** *p30*
Colignon, Sophie 45; New Orleans, 1848 ***778.6*** *p74*
Colin, Anne; Quebec, 1669 ***4514.3*** *p292*
Colin, Denise; Quebec, 1673 ***4514.3*** *p292*
Colin, Marie-Rose; Quebec, 1670 ***4514.3*** *p292*
Colin, Marisse 40; Mississippi, 1845 ***778.6*** *p74*
Colin, Victor 21; Mississippi, 1845 ***778.6*** *p74*
Colkeen, Mary; Ontario, 1835 ***3160.1*** *p150*
Coll, John; Long Island, 1778 ***8529.30*** *p9A*
Collaert, Jean F. 10; New York, NY, 1856 ***1766.1*** *p45*
Collahan, Ann; Boston, 1770 ***1642*** *p49*
Collais, Claude 19; New Orleans, 1848 ***778.6*** *p74*
Collard, Norman Ernest Charles; Miami, 1935 ***4984.12*** *p39*
Collard, William 21; Ontario, 1871 ***1823.21*** *p65*
Collart, Albertine Fronville *SEE* Collart, Eugene
Collart, Eugene; Illinois, 1856 ***1495.20*** *p8*
*Wife:*Albertine Fronville
*Daughter:*Eugenie
Collart, Eugenie *SEE* Collart, Eugene
Collas, Harry; Montreal, 1900-1930 ***9228.50*** *p164*
Collas, Mary Anne; America, 1800-1901 ***9228.50*** *p94*
Collas, T.; New York, NY, 1897 ***9228.50*** *p37*
Collas, T.; New York, NY, 1897 ***9228.50*** *p446*
Colle, Peter; Ohio, 1809-1852 ***4511.35*** *p8*
Colleau, Lewis 25; New Orleans, 1842 ***778.6*** *p74*
Colledge, W. Wilson 44; Ontario, 1871 ***1823.21*** *p65*
Collehan, Dennis; Boston, 1733 ***1642*** *p44*
Collemy, Jeremiah; Massachusetts, 1772 ***1642*** *p87*
Collen, William 19; Ontario, 1871 ***1823.21*** *p65*
Collenbaugh, Peter; Ohio, 1809-1852 ***4511.35*** *p8*
Collens, D.; Boston, 1728 ***1642*** *p23*
Collens, Timothy; Boston, 1764 ***1642*** *p33*
Collet, Augusta Leonie *SEE* Collet, Jean Baptiste
Collet, Edmond Jules *SEE* Collet, Jean Baptiste
Collet, Jean; Quebec, 1659 ***9221.17*** *p397*
Collet, Jean Baptiste; Wisconsin, 1887 ***1495.20*** *p12*
*Wife:*Marie Josephe Adam
*Child:*Augusta Leonie
*Child:*Edmond Jules
Collet, Jean Joseph; Wisconsin, 1887 ***1495.20*** *p12*
*Wife:*Marie Barbe Chantinne
Collet, Jeanne; Quebec, 1668 ***4514.3*** *p293*
Collet, John; Philadelphia, 1777 ***8529.30*** *p7A*
Collet, Julien; Wisconsin, 1869 ***1495.20*** *p12*
With wife
Collet, Lorenz 23; America, 1864 ***5475.1*** *p553*
Collet, Louis 36; Texas, 1848 ***778.6*** *p74*
Collet, Marguerite; Quebec, 1670 ***4514.3*** *p293*
Collet, Marie Barbe Chantinne *SEE* Collet, Jean Joseph
Collet, Marie Josephe Adam *SEE* Collet, Jean Baptiste
Collet, Mathieu-Benoit; Quebec, 1712 ***2314.30*** *p169*
Collet, Mathieu-Benoit; Quebec, 1712 ***2314.30*** *p178*
Collett, . . .; Maryland, 1600-1699 ***9228.50*** *p164*
Collett, Charles 30; Ontario, 1871 ***1823.21*** *p65*
Collett, Edward S. 44; Ontario, 1871 ***1823.21*** *p65*
Collett, Harold; Illinois, 1930 ***121.35*** *p101*
Collette, Thomas; Quebec, 1871 ***9228.50*** *p349*
Colley, Arabella; Ohio, 1800-1858 ***9228.50*** *p245*
Colley, Benj.; Marblehead, MA, 1756 ***9228.50*** *p164*
Collhon, Henry 20; Boston, 1835 ***6424.55*** *p30*
Collicott, Richard; Dorchester, MA, 1632 ***117.5*** *p158*
Collier, Charles B.; Ohio, 1855 ***3580.20*** *p31*
Collier, Charles Beatty; Ohio, 1855 ***6020.12*** *p6*
Collier, Daniel Lewis; Ohio, 1818 ***3580.20*** *p31*
Collier, Daniel Lewis; Ohio, 1818 ***6020.12*** *p6*
Collier, David L.; Ohio, 1852 ***3580.20*** *p31*
Collier, David L.; Ohio, 1852 ***6020.12*** *p7*
Collier, Frederick; Long Island, 1778 ***8529.30*** *p9A*
Collier, Henry 17; Ontario, 1871 ***1823.17*** *p30*
Collier, Jane 24; Ontario, 1871 ***1823.21*** *p65*
Collier, John; America, 1709 ***9228.50*** *p165*
Collier, John; Boston, 1705 ***9228.50*** *p164*
Collier, John Charles 37; Ontario, 1871 ***1823.17*** *p30*
Collier, Robert 40; Ontario, 1871 ***1823.21*** *p65*
Collieshaw, William 23; Ontario, 1871 ***1823.21*** *p65*
Colligan, James; New Hampshire, 1819 ***3274.55*** *p22*
Collignon, Miss 2; New Orleans, 1848 ***778.6*** *p74*
Collignon, Mr. 30; New Orleans, 1848 ***778.6*** *p74*
Collignon, Mrs. 24; New Orleans, 1848 ***778.6*** *p74*
Collin, Catherine 16; Quebec, 1654 ***9221.17*** *p306*
Collin, Charles; Detroit, 1856 ***1494.21*** *p31*
Collin, Emma; Kansas, 1870-1871 ***777.40*** *p16*
Collin, Eugene; Louisiana, 1874-1875 ***4981.45*** *p298*
Collin, Jean 31; America, 1846 ***778.6*** *p74*
Collin, Jean; Quebec, 1661 ***9221.17*** *p452*
Collin, Jean B. 33; Port uncertain, 1842 ***778.6*** *p74*

Collin, Johanna; Kansas, 1873 ***777.40*** *p16*
Collin, Karl; America, 1867 ***5475.1*** *p125*
Collin, Perpetue 22; America, 1845 ***778.6*** *p74*
Collin, Pierre; Louisiana, 1874 ***4981.45*** *p131*
Collin, Wendel; America, 1867 ***5475.1*** *p125*
Collin, William; Colorado, 1886 ***1029.59*** *p18*
Colline, Mr. 16; Port uncertain, 1841 ***778.6*** *p74*
Colline, Mrs. 40; Port uncertain, 1841 ***778.6*** *p74*
Colline, Emilie 14; Port uncertain, 1841 ***778.6*** *p74*
Collinet, Claudine Elisabeth 17; New Orleans, 1848 ***778.6*** *p74*
Collinet, Emile Louis 7; New Orleans, 1848 ***778.6*** *p74*
Collinet, Marie Desiree 47; New Orleans, 1848 ***778.6*** *p74*
Collinet, Pierre; Quebec, 1648 ***9221.17*** *p197*
Colling, Dorothea; America, 1847-1899 ***6442.17*** *p69*
Colling, Johann; America, 1844-1899 ***6442.17*** *p65*
*Wife:*Margaretha Maier
Colling, Margaretha Maier *SEE* Colling, Johann
Collinge, Mary; Ontario, 1871 ***1823.17*** *p31*
Collings, Daniel; Boston, 1693 ***9228.50*** *p165*
Collings, Francis D'Auvergne; Ontario, 1953 ***9228.50*** *p166*
Collings, Francis D'Auvergne; Washington, D.C., 1953-1990 ***9228.50*** *p166*
Collings, H.; Boston, 1728 ***1642*** *p23*
Collings, Philip D'Auvergne; Vancouver, B.C., 1955 ***9228.50*** *p166*
Collings Family ; Kentucky, 1808 ***9228.50*** *p165*
Collingwood, L. 15; Quebec, 1870 ***8364.32*** *p23*
Collins, Alexander; Boston, 1678-1679 ***1642*** *p11*
Collins, Allen; Maine, 1835 ***3274.55*** *p23*
Collins, Andrew 60; Ontario, 1871 ***1823.21*** *p65*
Collins, Andrew 60; Ontario, 1871 ***1823.21*** *p65*
Collins, Ann; Boston, 1767 ***1642*** *p38*
Collins, Ann 20; Ontario, 1871 ***1823.21*** *p65*
Collins, Anna 32; Michigan, 1880 ***4491.39*** *p6*
Collins, Benjamin; Massachusetts, 1675-1676 ***1642*** *p128*
Collins, Briget 51; Ontario, 1871 ***1823.21*** *p66*
Collins, C. 33; America, 1843 ***778.6*** *p74*
Collins, Catharine 51; Ontario, 1871 ***1823.21*** *p66*
Collins, Daniel; Boston, 1693 ***9228.50*** *p165*
Collins, Daniel; Ohio, 1809-1852 ***4511.35*** *p8*
Collins, Daniel 40; Ontario, 1871 ***1823.21*** *p66*
Collins, Daniel 49; Ontario, 1871 ***1823.17*** *p31*
Collins, David 30; Ontario, 1871 ***1823.21*** *p66*
Collins, Dennis; Toronto, 1844 ***2910.35*** *p115*
Collins, Elizabeth 10; Ontario, 1871 ***1823.21*** *p66*
Collins, Elmira 24; Ontario, 1871 ***1823.17*** *p31*
Collins, George 23; Ontario, 1871 ***1823.21*** *p66*
Collins, H.; Boston, 1728 ***1642*** *p23*
Collins, Hanorah 22; Ontario, 1871 ***1823.21*** *p66*
Collins, Henry 72; Ontario, 1871 ***1823.21*** *p66*
Collins, James 24; Ontario, 1871 ***1823.21*** *p66*
Collins, James 30; Ontario, 1871 ***1823.21*** *p66*
Collins, James 39; Ontario, 1871 ***1823.21*** *p66*
Collins, James; Virginia, 1749 ***3675.1*** *p*
Collins, Jared 52; Ontario, 1871 ***1823.17*** *p31*
Collins, Jeremiah; Ohio, 1857 ***3580.20*** *p31*
Collins, Jeremiah; Ohio, 1857 ***6020.12*** *p7*
Collins, Jeremiah 40; Ontario, 1871 ***1823.21*** *p66*
Collins, Jeremiah 60; Ontario, 1871 ***1823.21*** *p66*
Collins, Jeremiah 75; Ontario, 1871 ***1823.21*** *p66*
Collins, John; New York, NY, 1830 ***3274.55*** *p70*
Collins, John 26; Ontario, 1871 ***1823.21*** *p66*
Collins, John 27; Ontario, 1871 ***1823.21*** *p66*
Collins, John 30; Ontario, 1871 ***1823.21*** *p66*
Collins, John 44; Ontario, 1871 ***1823.21*** *p66*
Collins, John 45; Ontario, 1871 ***1823.21*** *p66*
Collins, John 61; Ontario, 1871 ***1823.21*** *p66*
Collins, John 64; Ontario, 1871 ***1823.21*** *p66*
Collins, Joseph; Massachusetts, 1675-1676 ***1642*** *p128*
Collins, Joseph 35; Ontario, 1871 ***1823.21*** *p66*
Collins, Judith; Boston, 1744 ***1642*** *p45*
Collins, Manus 78; Ontario, 1871 ***1823.21*** *p66*
Collins, Mary 26; Ontario, 1871 ***1823.21*** *p66*
Collins, Mary 28; Ontario, 1871 ***1823.21*** *p66*
Collins, Mary 60; Ontario, 1871 ***1823.21*** *p66*
Collins, Mary A. 45; Michigan, 1880 ***4491.42*** *p8*
Collins, Mary Ann 56; Ontario, 1871 ***1823.17*** *p31*
Collins, Maryann 13; Ontario, 1871 ***1823.21*** *p66*
Collins, Mathew 59; Ontario, 1871 ***1823.17*** *p31*
Collins, Michael 26; Indiana, 1886-1890 ***9076.20*** *p72*
Collins, Michael; Ohio, 1809-1852 ***4511.35*** *p8*
Collins, Michael 48; Ontario, 1871 ***1823.17*** *p31*
Collins, Michl 22; St. Johns, N.F., 1811 ***1053.20*** *p21*
Collins, Nathaniel; New England, 1745 ***1642*** *p28*
Collins, Neil 60; Ontario, 1871 ***1823.21*** *p66*
Collins, Patrick; Louisiana, 1874 ***4981.45*** *p131*
Collins, Peter; Louisiana, 1874 ***4981.45*** *p131*
Collins, Richard 50; Ontario, 1871 ***1823.21*** *p66*
Collins, Robert; North Carolina, 1832 ***1088.45*** *p6*
Collins, Stephen; New York, NY, 1830 ***3274.55*** *p70*
Collins, T. 40; Ontario, 1871 ***1823.21*** *p66*
Collins, Thom; New Orleans, 1851 ***7242.30*** *p138*
Collins, Thomas; Boston, 1745 ***1642*** *p28*
Collins, Thomas 19; Ontario, 1871 ***1823.21*** *p66*
Collins, Thomas 24; Ontario, 1871 ***1823.17*** *p31*
Collins, Thomas 55; Ontario, 1871 ***1823.21*** *p66*
Collins, Thomas 65; Ontario, 1871 ***1823.21*** *p66*
Collins, Thomas M.; New York, NY, 1832 ***3274.55*** *p73*
Collins, Timothy 17; Ontario, 1871 ***1823.21*** *p67*
Collins, William; Boston, 1776 ***8529.30*** *p2A*
Collins, William 46; Michigan, 1880 ***4491.42*** *p8*
Collins, William 27; Ontario, 1871 ***1823.17*** *p31*
Collins, William 50; Ontario, 1871 ***1823.21*** *p67*
Collins, William 52; Ontario, 1871 ***1823.21*** *p67*
Collins, William B. 27; Ontario, 1871 ***1823.17*** *p31*
Collinson, Mary J. 32; Ontario, 1871 ***1823.21*** *p67*
Collinwalk, . . . 41; Ontario, 1871 ***1823.17*** *p31*
Collis, Sidney John; Illinois, 1930 ***121.35*** *p101*
Collison, Dan'l 39; Ontario, 1871 ***1823.21*** *p67*
Collison, James 48; Ontario, 1871 ***1823.21*** *p67*
Collison, Jane 41; Ontario, 1871 ***1823.21*** *p67*
Collison, Martin 41; Ontario, 1871 ***1823.21*** *p67*
Collison, Mary 80; Ontario, 1871 ***1823.21*** *p67*
Collison, Mary Ann 32; Ontario, 1871 ***1823.21*** *p67*
Collison, Michael 47; Ontario, 1871 ***1823.21*** *p67*
Collison, Robert 97; Ontario, 1871 ***1823.21*** *p67*
Collison, Timothy 35; Ontario, 1871 ***1823.21*** *p67*
Collmann, Barbara Augustin 43 *SEE* Collmann, Johann
Collmann, Johann *SEE* Collmann, Johann
Collmann, Johann 40; America, 1859 ***5475.1*** *p251*
*Wife:*Barbara Augustin 43
*Son:*Peter
*Son:*Johann
*Son:*Mathias
*Daughter:*Margarethe
Collmann, Margarethe *SEE* Collmann, Johann
Collmann, Mathias *SEE* Collmann, Johann
Collmann, Peter *SEE* Collmann, Johann
Collmon, G. 10; America, 1848 ***778.6*** *p74*
Collmon, H. 47; America, 1848 ***778.6*** *p74*
Collogan, Bartholomew; Boston, 1746 ***1642*** *p46*
Collom, Edward; Colorado, 1880 ***1029.59*** *p18*
Collonghues, Pierre 21; New Orleans, 1848 ***778.6*** *p74*
Collons, Charley 26; Ontario, 1871 ***1823.17*** *p31*
Collot, Charles 30; Ontario, 1871 ***1823.17*** *p31*
Collum, John; Toronto, 1844 ***2910.35*** *p112*
Colly, John; Barbados, 1679 ***1220.12*** *p815*
Collyer, John; Boston, 1705 ***9228.50*** *p164*
Collyes, Nicholas 35; Ontario, 1871 ***1823.17*** *p31*
Colman, John 43; Ontario, 1871 ***1823.17*** *p31*
Colmorgan, Fred K. 43; Ontario, 1871 ***1823.21*** *p67*
Colnex, George 32; Ontario, 1871 ***1823.21*** *p67*
Colodone, James 29; New Orleans, 1843 ***778.6*** *p74*
Colombe, . . .; Boston, 1769 ***9228.50*** *p5*
Colombe, Charles; Boston, 1769 ***9228.50*** *p168*
Colombe, Claire; Quebec, 1670 ***4514.3*** *p342*
Colombel, Paul; Louisiana, 1836-1840 ***4981.45*** *p212*
Colony, Elizabeth; Massachusetts, 1773 ***1642*** *p86*
Coloven, Charles 61; Ontario, 1871 ***1823.21*** *p67*
Colovin, Mary 45; Ontario, 1871 ***1823.21*** *p67*
Colpits, Robert; Canada, 1775 ***3036.5*** *p67*
Colquhoun, Ann 20; North Carolina, 1775 ***1422.10*** *p60*
Colquhoun, Archibald 22; North Carolina, 1775 ***1422.10*** *p60*
Colquhoun, Catherine 59; Ontario, 1871 ***1823.21*** *p67*
Colquitt, Henry *SEE* Colquitt, John
Colquitt, Henry *SEE* Colquitt, John
Colquitt, James *SEE* Colquitt, John
Colquitt, James *SEE* Colquitt, John
Colquitt, John *SEE* Colquitt, John
Colquitt, John; Virginia, 1638-1668 ***9228.50*** *p166*
*Brother:*Henry
*Son:*Henry
*Son:*John
With son
*Son:*James
*Brother:*Samuel
*Brother:*James
*Brother:*Robert
Colquitt, Robert *SEE* Colquitt, John
Colquitt, Samuel *SEE* Colquitt, John
Colson, Carl; Port uncertain, 1822 ***7420.1*** *p1*
Colson, Henry 25; Ontario, 1871 ***1823.17*** *p31*
Colson, Nicolas; Quebec, 1635 ***9221.17*** *p45*
Colstead, Major; New York, 1750 ***1640.8*** *p234*
Colston, George; Cleveland, OH, 1881-1897 ***9722.10*** *p118*
Colter, John 60; Ontario, 1871 ***1823.21*** *p67*
Colter, William 40; Ontario, 1871 ***1823.21*** *p67*
Coltman, Samuel; North Carolina, 1836 ***1088.45*** *p6*
Colton, Annie 22; Ontario, 1871 ***1823.21*** *p67*
Colton, Henry; Philadelphia, 1777 ***8529.30*** *p2*
Colton, John; Ohio, 1809-1852 ***4511.35*** *p9*
Colton, John 20; Ontario, 1871 ***1823.21*** *p67*
Columbus, Anton; Washington, 1889 ***2770.40*** *p26*
Colvil, Jno.; Prince Edward Island, 1771 ***3799.30*** *p41*
Colville, Charles 44; Ontario, 1871 ***1823.21*** *p67*
Colville, James 57; Ontario, 1871 ***1823.21*** *p67*
Colville, John; North Carolina, 1859-1860 ***1088.45*** *p6*
Colville, Thomas L.; North Carolina, 1856 ***1088.45*** *p6*
Colwell, Stephen; Ohio, 1821 ***3580.20*** *p31*
Colwell, Stephen; Ohio, 1821 ***6020.12*** *p7*
Coman, James; North Carolina, 1821 ***1088.45*** *p6*
Combas, Constant 18; America, 1846 ***778.6*** *p74*
Combers, William 38; Ontario, 1871 ***1823.21*** *p67*
Combes, Magdalena 30; New Orleans, 1848 ***778.6*** *p74*
Combez, Joseph 32; Texas, 1848 ***778.6*** *p74*
Combier, J. Philippe 24; America, 1843 ***778.6*** *p74*
Combs, Bengiman 24; Ontario, 1871 ***1823.17*** *p31*
Combs, Joseph 53; Ontario, 1871 ***1823.17*** *p31*
Comden, George W. 5 *SEE* Comden, Mary Ann
Comden, Mary Ann 28; Ohio, 1880 ***4879.40*** *p258*
*Son:*George W. 5
Come, Henry 60; Ontario, 1871 ***1823.17*** *p31*
Comeford, Edwa 50; St. Johns, N.F., 1811 ***1053.20*** *p20*
Comeford, James 19; St. Johns, N.F., 1811 ***1053.20*** *p20*
Comeford, Thos. 17; St. Johns, N.F., 1811 ***1053.20*** *p20*
Comeinge, Ferdinand 20; New Orleans, 1746 ***778.6*** *p74*
Comens, August; America, 1849 ***7420.1*** *p63*
Comens, Eduard; America, 1851 ***7420.1*** *p79*
Comens, Heinrich August; America, 1845 ***7420.1*** *p35*
Comens, Hermann; Port uncertain, 1853 ***7420.1*** *p103*
Comer, Morris 63; Ontario, 1871 ***1823.17*** *p31*
Comerford, Peter; Maine, 1833 ***3274.55*** *p26*
Comet, H.P.; New York, NY, 1844 ***6412.40*** *p148*
Comfort, Andrew I. 72; Ontario, 1871 ***1823.21*** *p67*
Comfort, Jesse 51; Ontario, 1871 ***1823.21*** *p67*
Comfort, John; Ontario, 1787 ***1276.15*** *p231*
With 2 children & 5 relatives
Comike, Joseph; Louisiana, 1874 ***4981.45*** *p131*
Comings, William; Boston, 1766 ***1642*** *p37*
Comins, Martin T. J.; Colorado, 1881 ***1029.59*** *p18*
Comins, Martin T. J.; Colorado, 1883 ***1029.59*** *p18*
Comisky, Michael; Louisiana, 1874-1875 ***4981.45*** *p298*
Comite, Isabelle 19; America, 1843 ***778.6*** *p75*
Commenge, Jean Louis 24; New Orleans, 1845 ***778.6*** *p75*
Commer, Alwine 10; New York, NY, 1893 ***1883.7*** *p39*
Commer, Augusta 30; New York, NY, 1893 ***1883.7*** *p39*
Commeran, John; Ohio, 1809-1852 ***4511.35*** *p9*
Comming, Ann 75; Ontario, 1871 ***1823.17*** *p31*
Commons, James 29; Ontario, 1871 ***1823.21*** *p67*
Communay, Mr. 27; America, 1843 ***778.6*** *p75*
Compagno, A.; Louisiana, 1874-1875 ***4981.45*** *p298*
Compagnon, Antoinette; Quebec, 1668 ***4514.3*** *p293*
Compain, Anne; Quebec, 1644 ***9221.17*** *p138*
Complin, Charles F. 31; Ontario, 1871 ***1823.21*** *p67*
Compo, Susan 21; Ohio, 1880 ***4879.40*** *p260*
Compton, Henry 20; Ontario, 1871 ***1823.21*** *p67*
Comstock, Harvey 50; Ontario, 1871 ***1823.21*** *p67*
Comte, Jacques 34; Mississippi, 1847 ***778.6*** *p75*
Comte, Pierre; Virginia, 1700 ***9230.15*** *p81*
Comtesse, Franz; America, 1867 ***5475.1*** *p189*
Comuelli, Jacques Victor 30; New Orleans, 1848 ***778.6*** *p75*
Comyn, Lewis 66; Ontario, 1871 ***1823.17*** *p31*
Comyn, Maurice; New Jersey, 1795-1802 ***3845.2*** *p129*
Conah, Jeremiah; Massachusetts, 1675-1676 ***1642*** *p128*
Conally, Eleanor; Boston, 1746 ***1642*** *p46*
Conaly, Arthur; Jamaica, 1778 ***8529.30*** *p12A*
Conaway, Elizabeth; Massachusetts, 1744 ***1642*** *p87*
Conbetta, Vincenzo; Washington, 1888 ***2770.40*** *p25*
Conboy, James 40; Ontario, 1871 ***1823.17*** *p31*
Conboy, John; Illinois, 1860 ***6079.1*** *p3*
Conboy, Thomas; Illinois, 1860 ***6079.1*** *p3*
Conception, Mere de la 31; Quebec, 1657 ***9221.17*** *p350*
Conche, Dame 45; Mobile, AL, 1840 ***778.6*** *p75*
Conche, Miss 14; Mobile, AL, 1840 ***778.6*** *p75*
Conche, Miss 17; Mobile, AL, 1840 ***778.6*** *p75*
Condave, Peter 50; America, 1848 ***778.6*** *p75*
Conday, Charles; Ontario, 1871 ***1823.17*** *p31*
Conden, David; Massachusetts, 1771 ***1642*** *p106*
Condick, Charles 23; Ontario, 1871 ***1823.17*** *p31*
Condon, Cath; New Orleans, 1851 ***7242.30*** *p138*
Condon, Constantia; Boston, 1768 ***1642*** *p49*
Condon, Daniel John 28; Ontario, 1871 ***1823.21*** *p68*
Condon, John; Boston, 1770 ***1642*** *p49*
Condon, Mary; Boston, 1763 ***1642*** *p48*
Condon, Michael; Boston, 1762 ***1642*** *p48*
Condon, Richard; Boston, 1774 ***1642*** *p50*
Condon, Samuel; Boston, 1770 ***1642*** *p49*
Condon, Thomas 55; Ontario, 1871 ***1823.21*** *p68*
Condon, Thos; New Orleans, 1850 ***7242.30*** *p138*
Condon, Wallace 24; Ontario, 1871 ***1823.17*** *p32*
Condran, Alexander; New Orleans, 1850 ***7242.30*** *p138*
Condran, Edward; New Orleans, 1850 ***7242.30*** *p138*

Condran, Mary; New Orleans, 1850 ***7242.30*** *p138*
Condrick, Thomas 35; Ontario, 1871 ***1823.21*** *p68*
Condroy, Adolphe; Louisiana, 1836-1840 ***4981.45*** *p212*
Condroy, Caroline 16; Quebec, 1870 ***8364.32*** *p23*
Condun, Honour; Boston, 1755 ***1642*** *p47*
Cone, Patrick; Louisiana, 1874-1875 ***4981.45*** *p298*
Coneau, A. 18; New Orleans, 1844 ***778.6*** *p75*
Conefray, Jean 41; Texas, 1848 ***778.6*** *p75*
Conefray, Jean L. D.; Illinois, 1852 ***6079.1*** *p3*
Conefray, Pierre James; Illinois, 1852 ***6079.1*** *p3*
Conelin, John; Boston, 1752-1760 ***1642*** *p30*
Conell, Eliza 9; Quebec, 1870 ***8364.32*** *p23*
Conell, John; Newfoundland, 1814 ***3476.10*** *p54*
Conell, Mary; Boston, 1664 ***1642*** *p10*
Conely, Anthony 40; Ontario, 1871 ***1823.17*** *p32*
Conely, Daniel; Boston, 1758 ***1642*** *p47*
Coner, Francis; Boston, 1754 ***1642*** *p47*
Coner, William; Plymouth, MA, 1621 ***1642*** *p1*
Coners, Antony 50; Ontario, 1871 ***1823.17*** *p32*
Coners, Mical 60; Ontario, 1871 ***1823.17*** *p32*
Conery, James; New York, NY, 1832 ***3274.56*** *p71*
Coney, Peter 31; New Orleans, 1843 ***778.6*** *p75*
Coney, William; New England, 1745 ***1642*** *p28*
Conflans, Francoise; Quebec, 1667 ***4514.3*** *p293*
Congdon, John 29; Ontario, 1871 ***1823.21*** *p68*
Congdon, Richard 30; Ontario, 1871 ***1823.21*** *p68*
Congdon, William 40; Ontario, 1871 ***1823.21*** *p68*
Conget, Mr. 25; New Orleans, 1840 ***778.6*** *p78*
Conigland, Andrew; North Carolina, 1840 ***1088.45*** *p6*
Coning, Thomas 12; Ontario, 1871 ***1823.21*** *p68*
Conitz, Sebastian; Philadelphia, 1778 ***8529.30*** *p2A*
Conkey, Margrett 80; Ontario, 1871 ***1823.21*** *p68*
Conkey, Robert 47; Ontario, 1871 ***1823.21*** *p68*
Conkey, Thomas; Iowa, 1886 ***1211.15*** *p9*
Conkey, William 55; Ontario, 1871 ***1823.21*** *p68*
Conley, Alexander 52; Ontario, 1871 ***1823.21*** *p68*
Conley, John 30; Ontario, 1871 ***1823.17*** *p32*
Conley, Jolitha; Palmer, MA, 1771 ***1642*** *p119*
Conlin, Bernard; Toronto, 1844 ***2910.35*** *p113*
Conlon, Andrew; Burlington, VT, 1834 ***3274.55*** *p27*
Conlon, Bridgit 43; Ontario, 1871 ***1823.17*** *p32*
Conlon, Michael; New York, NY, 1836 ***3274.56*** *p71*
Conlon, Michael 45; Ontario, 1871 ***1823.17*** *p32*
Conlon, Michel 60; Ontario, 1871 ***1823.17*** *p32*
Conloy, John; Worcester, MA, 1745 ***1642*** *p114*
Conly, Miles; Boston, 1766 ***1642*** *p36*
Conn, Fletcher W.; Washington, 1885 ***2770.40*** *p194*
Conn, George *SEE* Conn, John
Conn, Hugh 45; Ontario, 1871 ***1823.21*** *p68*
Conn, James 32; Ontario, 1871 ***1823.21*** *p68*
Conn, James 64; Ontario, 1871 ***1823.21*** *p68*
Conn, Jane 23; Ontario, 1871 ***1823.21*** *p68*
Conn, John; Massachusetts, 1620-1775 ***1642*** *p138*
Conn, John *SEE* Conn, John
Conn, John; Massachusetts, 1747 ***1642*** *p102*
*Wife:*Rosanna
*Son:*Thomas
*Son:*George
*Daughter:*Margaret
*Son:*John
Conn, Margaret *SEE* Conn, John
Conn, Margaret 46; Ontario, 1871 ***1823.21*** *p68*
Conn, Robert 60; Ontario, 1871 ***1823.21*** *p68*
Conn, Rosanna *SEE* Conn, John
Conn, Thomas *SEE* Conn, John
Conn, William 46; Ontario, 1871 ***1823.17*** *p32*
Connally, Arthur; Jamaica, 1778 ***8529.30*** *p12A*
Connaly, Thomas; Jamaica, 1783 ***8529.30*** *p12A*
Connard, Antoine; Detroit, 1856 ***1494.20*** *p12*
Connaway, Mary; Ipswich, MA, 1729 ***1642*** *p71*
Connaway, Mary; Newbury, MA, 1729 ***1642*** *p75*
Connegue, George; North Carolina, 1710 ***3629.40*** *p5*
Connel, Bella 22; Ontario, 1871 ***1823.21*** *p68*
Connel, Bridget 60; Ontario, 1871 ***1823.21*** *p68*
Connel, Dan; Boston, 1768 ***1642*** *p39*
Connel, John; Marblehead, MA, 1749 ***1642*** *p73*
Connel, Philip; Massachusetts, 1688 ***1642*** *p105*
Connel, Valentine; Boston, 1763 ***1642*** *p32*
Connell, David; Ontario, 1871 ***1823.17*** *p32*
Connell, Duncan 30; Ontario, 1871 ***1823.21*** *p68*
Connell, Duncan 50; Ontario, 1871 ***1823.21*** *p68*
Connell, Flora 13; Ontario, 1871 ***1823.21*** *p68*
Connell, James; Boston, 1766 ***1642*** *p35*
Connell, James 44; Ontario, 1871 ***1823.21*** *p68*
Connell, John; Boston, 1768 ***1642*** *p49*
Connell, John 24; Ontario, 1871 ***1823.21*** *p68*
Connell, John 45; Ontario, 1871 ***1823.21*** *p68*
Connell, John 50; Ontario, 1871 ***1823.21*** *p68*
Connell, John 50; Ontario, 1871 ***1823.21*** *p68*
Connell, Joseph 26; Ontario, 1871 ***1823.21*** *p68*
Connell, Joseph 50; Ontario, 1871 ***1823.17*** *p32*
Connell, Margaret; Boston, 1774 ***1642*** *p50*
Connell, Margaret; New Brunswick, 1842 ***2978.20*** *p8*
Connell, Mary; Boston, 1763 ***1642*** *p48*
Connell, Mary; Boston, 1764 ***1642*** *p33*
Connell, Mathew C.; New York, NY, 1829 ***3274.55*** *p69*
Connell, Patrick; New Brunswick, 1842 ***2978.20*** *p8*
Connell, Peter; Vermont, 1829 ***3274.55*** *p26*
Connell, Robert 48; Ontario, 1871 ***1823.17*** *p32*
Connell, William; St. John, N.B., 1847 ***2978.15*** *p36*
Connelley, Henry 64; Ontario, 1871 ***1823.21*** *p68*
Connellson, Christian; North Carolina, 1846 ***1088.45*** *p6*
Connelly, Catherine; Massachusetts, 1744 ***1642*** *p66*
Connelly, Catherine; Newbury, MA, 1744 ***1642*** *p75*
Connelly, Edward; Washington, 1887 ***2770.40*** *p24*
Connelly, Elizabeth; Philadelphia, 1854 ***8513.31*** *p413*
Connelly, James; Boston, 1743 ***1642*** *p45*
Connelly, Jesse; Boston, 1766 ***1642*** *p38*
Connelly, John; Salem, MA, 1773 ***1642*** *p78*
Connelly, Mary; Philadelphia, 1861 ***8513.31*** *p315*
Connelly, Patrick; Boston, 1756 ***1642*** *p47*
Connelly, Patrick 60; Michigan, 1880 ***4491.39*** *p6*
Connelly, Rebecca; Dedham, MA, 1769 ***1642*** *p102*
Connelly, Thomas 36; Ontario, 1871 ***1823.21*** *p68*
Connelly, Thomas 40; Ontario, 1871 ***1823.17*** *p32*
Connelly, William; Ohio, 1840 ***3580.20*** *p31*
Connelly, William; Ohio, 1840 ***6020.12*** *p7*
Connelly, William; Toronto, 1844 ***2910.35*** *p114*
Connely, Henry; Jamaica, 1779 ***8529.30*** *p12A*
Connely, Philip 62; Ontario, 1871 ***1823.17*** *p32*
Connely, Sarah; Boston, 1731 ***1642*** *p44*
Conner, Ann; Boston, 1751 ***1642*** *p46*
Conner, Ann; Massachusetts, 1743 ***1642*** *p63*
Conner, Anna; Boston, 1769 ***1642*** *p49*
Conner, Catharine; Boston, 1766 ***1642*** *p37*
Conner, Charles; Boston, 1758 ***1642*** *p47*
Conner, Charles; Toronto, 1844 ***2910.35*** *p114*
Conner, Cornelius; Massachusetts, 1666 ***1642*** *p64*
Conner, Cornelius; Salisbury, MA, 1675 ***1642*** *p81*
*Wife:*Sarah
Conner, Daniel; Boston, 1714 ***1642*** *p24*
Conner, Darby; Boston, 1767 ***1642*** *p38*
Conner, Dennis; Toronto, 1844 ***2910.35*** *p116*
Conner, Dorothy; Massachusetts, 1721 ***1642*** *p63*
Conner, Eleanor; Boston, 1749 ***1642*** *p46*
Conner, Elisebeth; Massachusetts, 1758 ***1642*** *p63*
Conner, Elizabeth *SEE* Conner, John
Conner, Enoch 24; Ontario, 1871 ***1823.21*** *p68*
Conner, Henry; Massachusetts, 1669 ***1642*** *p64*
Conner, James; Boston, 1767 ***1642*** *p38*
Conner, John; Boston, 1746 ***1642*** *p46*
Conner, John; Nantucket, MA, 1772 ***1642*** *p89*
Conner, John; New England, 1745 ***1642*** *p27*
Conner, John 41; Ontario, 1871 ***1823.21*** *p68*
Conner, John 52; Ontario, 1871 ***1823.17*** *p32*
Conner, John; Salisbury, MA, 1659 ***1642*** *p81*
*Wife:*Elizabeth
Conner, Katharine; Boston, 1742 ***1642*** *p45*
Conner, Mary; Boston, 1727 ***1642*** *p25*
Conner, Mary; Massachusetts, 1727 ***1642*** *p63*
Conner, Mary; Newbury, MA, 1743 ***1642*** *p75*
Conner, Michael; Boston, 1768 ***1642*** *p39*
Conner, Michael; Boston, 1768 ***1642*** *p39*
Conner, Mitchel; Boston, 1773 ***1642*** *p49*
Conner, Moses; Newbury, MA, 1721 ***1642*** *p75*
Conner, Nathanial; Ipswich, MA, 1754-1763 ***1642*** *p70*
Conner, Patrick; Boston, 1765 ***1642*** *p35*
Conner, Patrick; Boston, 1768 ***1642*** *p39*
Conner, Patrick; Newbury, MA, 1743 ***1642*** *p75*
Conner, Patrick; North Carolina, 1843 ***1088.45*** *p6*
Conner, Sarah *SEE* Conner, Cornelius
Conner, Thomas; Salem, MA, 1774 ***1642*** *p78*
Conner, Timothy; Boston, 1766 ***1642*** *p36*
Conner, Timothy; Ohio, 1840-1897 ***8365.35*** *p15*
Conner, Volt; Boston, 1765 ***1642*** *p35*
Conner, William; Massachusetts, 1669 ***1642*** *p64*
Conner, William 34; New York, NY, 1821 ***6178.50*** *p75*
Connerey, Content; Massachusetts, 1761 ***1642*** *p87*
Conners, Barney 60; Ontario, 1871 ***1823.21*** *p68*
Conners, Edward; Louisiana, 1874 ***4981.45*** *p131*
Conners, John 22; Ontario, 1871 ***1823.17*** *p32*
Conners, Michael 53; Ontario, 1871 ***1823.21*** *p68*
Conners, Moses; Philadelphia, 1777 ***8529.30*** *p2A*
Conners, Thomas; Colorado, 1871 ***1029.59*** *p18*
Connery, Mr.; Massachusetts, 1754 ***1642*** *p108*
Connery, John *SEE* Connery, John
Connery, John; Massachusetts, 1761 ***1642*** *p64*
*Relative:*Lydia
*Relative:*Sarah
*Relative:*John
*Relative:*Lydia
Connery, Lawrence; Louisiana, 1836-1840 ***4981.45*** *p212*
Connery, Lydia *SEE* Connery, John
Connery, Sarah *SEE* Connery, John
Connery, William; Ipswich, MA, 1754-1763 ***1642*** *p70*
Conniars, James; Boston, 1696 ***1642*** *p17*
Connil, Eleanor; Boston, 1753 ***1642*** *p47*
Connin, John; Ohio, 1840-1897 ***8365.35*** *p15*
Connis, Naomi; Boston, 1702 ***1642*** *p24*
Connley, Cornelius 37; Ontario, 1871 ***1823.21*** *p68*
Connole, Elizabeth *SEE* Connole, John
Connole, John; Massachusetts, 1745 ***1642*** *p105*
*Wife:*Elizabeth
Connolly, Widow; Newburyport, MA, 1771 ***1642*** *p76*
Connolly, Anna; Boston, 1740 ***1642*** *p45*
Connolly, Elizabeth *SEE* Connolly, John
Connolly, John; Massachusetts, 1745 ***1642*** *p105*
*Wife:*Elizabeth
Connolly, John; St. John, N.B., 1847 ***2978.15*** *p35*
Connolly, Margaret 64; Ontario, 1871 ***1823.21*** *p68*
Connolly, Mary *SEE* Connolly, William
Connolly, William; Ipswich, MA, 1754-1763 ***1642*** *p70*
Connolly, William; Massachusetts, 1772 ***1642*** *p105*
*Wife:*Mary
Connolly, William; Salem, MA, 1774 ***1642*** *p78*
Connoly, Elizabeth *SEE* Connoly, John
Connoly, John; Massachusetts, 1751 ***1642*** *p111*
*Wife:*Elizabeth
Connon, John 62; Ontario, 1871 ***1823.21*** *p68*
Connont, Pierre 36; New Orleans, 1848 ***778.6*** *p75*
Connor, Benjamin; Massachusetts, 1733 ***1642*** *p66*
Connor, Bernard 19; New York, NY, 1894 ***6512.1*** *p229*
Connor, Charles 28; Ontario, 1871 ***1823.21*** *p68*
Connor, Daniel 12; Quebec, 1870 ***8364.32*** *p23*
Connor, Edward 74; Ontario, 1871 ***1823.17*** *p32*
Connor, Hannah; Massachusetts, 1695 ***1642*** *p85*
Connor, Issaic 44; Ontario, 1871 ***1823.17*** *p32*
Connor, James; Newburyport, MA, 1772 ***1642*** *p76*
Connor, James 60; Ontario, 1871 ***1823.21*** *p68*
Connor, Jane 12; Quebec, 1870 ***8364.32*** *p23*
Connor, John 60; Ontario, 1871 ***1823.17*** *p32*
Connor, John 66; Ontario, 1871 ***1823.21*** *p68*
Connor, Julia 15; Quebec, 1870 ***8364.32*** *p23*
Connor, Mary; Boston, 1757 ***1642*** *p47*
Connor, Michael 40; Ontario, 1871 ***1823.21*** *p69*
Connor, Miles; Massachusetts, 1756 ***1642*** *p66*
Connor, Mossis; Rowley, MA, 1721 ***1642*** *p77*
Connor, Patrick; Lynn, MA, 1732 ***1642*** *p71*
Connor, Patrick; New Orleans, 1851 ***7242.30*** *p138*
Connor, Patrick 36; Ontario, 1871 ***1823.21*** *p69*
Connor, Patrick 51; Ontario, 1871 ***1823.17*** *p32*
Connor, Patrick 60; Ontario, 1871 ***1823.21*** *p69*
Connor, Patt; New Orleans, 1850 ***7242.30*** *p139*
Connor, Peg; Massachusetts, 1766 ***1642*** *p102*
Connor, Robert 34; Ontario, 1871 ***1823.17*** *p32*
Connor, Samuel; New England, 1745 ***1642*** *p28*
Connor, Simon 16; Quebec, 1870 ***8364.32*** *p23*
Connor, Thomas; New York, 1832 ***3274.56*** *p72*
Connor, William; Newbury, MA, 1755 ***1642*** *p75*
Connord, Pierre 62; America, 1840 ***778.6*** *p75*
Connors, Catherine; St. Johns, N.F., 1825 ***1053.15*** *p6*
Connors, John 50; Ontario, 1871 ***1823.21*** *p69*
Connors, Mical 40; Ontario, 1871 ***1823.17*** *p32*
Connors, Michael; Newfoundland, 1814 ***3476.10*** *p54*
Connors, Pat; St. John, N.B., 1848 ***2978.15*** *p40*
Connors, Thomas; St. Johns, N.F., 1825 ***1053.15*** *p6*
Connors, William; Boston, 1736 ***1642*** *p44*
Connory, Daniel; Lynn, MA, 1763 ***1642*** *p71*
Connory, Pat; St. John, N.B., 1847 ***2978.15*** *p38*
Connsel, Joseph; Louisiana, 1874 ***4981.45*** *p131*
Conole, Elizabeth *SEE* Conole, John
Conole, John; Massachusetts, 1745 ***1642*** *p105*
*Wife:*Elizabeth
Conolly, John 66; Ontario, 1871 ***1823.21*** *p69*
Conolly, Katharine; Boston, 1744 ***1642*** *p45*
Conolly, Pat; St. John, N.B., 1847 ***2978.15*** *p39*
Conover, Elizabeth C.; Philadelphia, 1858 ***8513.31*** *p300*
Conoway, Mary *SEE* Conoway, Robert
Conoway, Robert; Ipswich, MA, 1687 ***1642*** *p71*
*Wife:*Mary
Conrad, Miss 1; New Orleans, 1748 ***778.6*** *p75*
Conrad, Ms. 28; New Orleans, 1748 ***778.6*** *p75*
Conrad, Adam; America, 1850-1899 ***6442.17*** *p65*
*Wife:*Anna Gard
With 8 children
Conrad, Andreas; America, 1845-1899 ***6442.17*** *p65*
Conrad, Anna Gard *SEE* Conrad, Adam
Conrad, Anna Maria; Pittsburgh, 1866 ***5475.1*** *p433*
Conrad, Anton 33; Portland, ME, 1906 ***970.38*** *p76*
Conrad, Casper; Ohio, 1809-1852 ***4511.35*** *p9*
Conrad, Charles Fabian; Washington, 1883 ***2770.40*** *p136*
Conrad, Christian 26; Missouri, 1846 ***778.6*** *p75*
Conrad, Clark Willem; Wisconsin, 1896 ***6795.8*** *p105*
Conrad, Elisabeth Rausch *SEE* Conrad, Peter
Conrad, F. I. 24; New York, NY, 1847 ***9176.15*** *p50*
Conrad, F. R.; Valdivia, Chile, 1852 ***1192.4*** *p53*
Conrad, Franz; Cincinnati, 1878 ***5475.1*** *p22*
Conrad, Frederic 28; Missouri, 1846 ***778.6*** *p75*

Conrad, Jacob; Ohio, 1809-1852 ***4511.35*** *p9*
Conrad, Jakob; America, 1898-1899 ***6442.17*** *p65*
Conrad, Johann; America, 1845-1899 ***6442.17*** *p65*
*Wife:*Maria Elisabeth Kuhr
*Son:*Peter
Conrad, Johann; Brazil, 1857 ***5475.1*** *p441*
*Wife:*Maria Backes
With 5 children
Conrad, Johann August; Wisconsin, 1870 ***6795.8*** *p123*
Conrad, John George; Texas, 1892 ***3435.45*** *p35*
Conrad, Katharina; America, 1852-1899 ***6442.17*** *p69*
Conrad, Maria Backes *SEE* Conrad, Johann
Conrad, Maria Elisabeth Kuhr *SEE* Conrad, Johann
Conrad, Maria Elisabeth Sophie Saar *SEE* Conrad, Mathias
Conrad, Mathias; America, 1850-1899 ***6442.17*** *p65*
*Wife:*Maria Elisabeth Sophie Saar
With 5 children
Conrad, Matthais; Ohio, 1809-1852 ***4511.35*** *p9*
Conrad, Matthias; Ohio, 1809-1852 ***4511.35*** *p9*
Conrad, Michael; America, 1890-1899 ***6442.17*** *p65*
Conrad, Nicholas; Illinois, 1856 ***6079.1*** *p3*
Conrad, Peter *SEE* Conrad, Johann
Conrad, Peter; America, 1850-1899 ***6442.17*** *p65*
*Wife:*Elisabeth Rausch
With 4 children
Conradi, Miss 3; New Orleans, 1848 ***778.6*** *p75*
Conradi, Miss 5; New Orleans, 1848 ***778.6*** *p75*
Conradi, Mr. 40; New Orleans, 1848 ***778.6*** *p75*
Conradi, Ms. 35; New Orleans, 1848 ***778.6*** *p75*
Conradini, Francesco 38; New York, NY, 1894 ***6512.1*** *p182*
Conrads, Maria 58; New York, NY, 1893 ***1883.7*** *p39*
Conradt, Frederico; Miami, 1935 ***4984.12*** *p39*
Conradt y Bernal, Frederico; Miami, 1935 ***4984.12*** *p39*
Conran, Stephen; Louisiana, 1874-1875 ***4981.45*** *p298*
Conrath, Barbara; Brazil, 1846 ***5475.1*** *p438*
Conray, James; St. John, N.B., 1847 ***2978.15*** *p37*
Conreny, James; St. John, N.B., 1847 ***2978.15*** *p35*
Conrod, Peter; Ohio, 1809-1852 ***4511.35*** *p9*
Conron, Daniel 62; Ontario, 1871 ***1823.21*** *p69*
Conroy, Aggie 21; Michigan, 1880 ***4491.42*** *p8*
Conroy, Bridget 17; Michigan, 1880 ***4491.42*** *p8*
Conroy, Denis; Washington, 1884 ***2770.40*** *p192*
Conroy, John; Ohio, 1840-1897 ***8365.35*** *p15*
Conroy, Patrick 30; New York, NY, 1849 ***6178.50*** *p152*
Conroy, Philip 60; Ontario, 1871 ***1823.21*** *p69*
Conroy, Susan; America, 1832-1932 ***9228.50*** *p168*
Conroy, Thomas; New Orleans, 1851 ***7242.30*** *p139*
Consell, John 35; Ontario, 1871 ***1823.17*** *p32*
Constable, William 29; Ontario, 1871 ***1823.21*** *p69*
Constansohn, Jean 28; Missouri, 1848 ***778.6*** *p75*
Constant, Ms. 32; America, 1843 ***778.6*** *p75*
Constant, Alix 34; America, 1843 ***778.6*** *p75*
Constant, Louis 2; New Orleans, 1848 ***778.6*** *p75*
Constantin, Claude 29; America, 1845 ***778.6*** *p75*
Constantin, Eliakakos 26; New York, NY, 1894 ***6512.1*** *p186*
Constantin, Guilaume 10; Montreal, 1648 ***9221.17*** *p206*
Constantin, Jean; Quebec, 1644 ***9221.17*** *p140*
Constantin, Jean; Virginia, 1700 ***9230.15*** *p81*
Constantin, Joseph 35; Ontario, 1871 ***1823.21*** *p69*
Constantine, Nick; Colorado, 1899 ***1029.59*** *p18*
Constantion, Nick; Colorado, 1901 ***1029.59*** *p18*
Constanz, Carolina 9; Louisiana, 1842 ***778.6*** *p75*
Constanz, Carolina 33; Louisiana, 1842 ***778.6*** *p75*
Constanz, Charles 2; Louisiana, 1842 ***778.6*** *p75*
Constanz, Charlotte 7; Louisiana, 1842 ***778.6*** *p75*
Constanz, Christine 5; Louisiana, 1842 ***778.6*** *p75*
Constanz, Louise 11; Louisiana, 1842 ***778.6*** *p76*
Constanzer, John; Philadelphia, 1857 ***8513.31*** *p300*
*Wife:*Margaret Lampater
Constanzer, Margaret Lampater *SEE* Constanzer, John
Conte, Alexandrine 7; Port uncertain, 1843 ***778.6*** *p76*
Conte, Arcene 5; Port uncertain, 1843 ***778.6*** *p76*
Conte, Elie 23; Missouri, 1846 ***778.6*** *p76*
Conte, Emanuel 29; Missouri, 1846 ***778.6*** *p76*
Conte, Jean 34; Missouri, 1846 ***778.6*** *p76*
Conte, Louis 29; Port uncertain, 1843 ***778.6*** *p76*
Conte, Marie 29; Missouri, 1846 ***778.6*** *p76*
Conte, Victoire 34; Port uncertain, 1843 ***778.6*** *p76*
Conter, Katharina Zehren *SEE* Conter, Nikolaus
Conter, Margarethe *SEE* Conter, Nikolaus
Conter, Nikolaus; San Francisco, 1857 ***5475.1*** *p255*
*Wife:*Katharina Zehren
*Daughter:*Margarethe
Contesse, Gertrud Kronenberger *SEE* Contesse, Peter
Contesse, Peter; America, 1873 ***5475.1*** *p158*
*Wife:*Gertrud Kronenberger
Contier, August 22; New Orleans, 1848 ***778.6*** *p76*
Conum, Mary; Boston, 1767 ***1642*** *p38*
Convent, Anne 33; Quebec, 1636 ***9221.17*** *p51*
Convery, John; Washington, 1885 ***2770.40*** *p194*
Conway, Mrs.; Toronto, 1844 ***2910.35*** *p114*
Conway, Francis V.; North Carolina, 1841 ***1088.45*** *p6*
Conway, Henry 16; Quebec, 1870 ***8364.32*** *p23*
Conway, Jno.; Louisiana, 1874-1875 ***4981.45*** *p298*
Conway, John 17; Quebec, 1870 ***8364.32*** *p23*
Conway, P.; Louisiana, 1874 ***4981.45*** *p295*
Conway, Patrick; Boston, 1833 ***3274.55*** *p24*
Conway, Peterat; North Carolina, 1844 ***1088.45*** *p6*
Conway, Thomas 67; Ontario, 1871 ***1823.21*** *p69*
Conway, Thos; New Orleans, 1851 ***7242.30*** *p139*
Conwell, Daniel 60; Ontario, 1871 ***1823.17*** *p32*
Conwell, John; Washington, 1888 ***2770.40*** *p25*
Cooeny, John 60; Ontario, 1871 ***1823.21*** *p69*
Coogan, Michael; Boston, 1835 ***3274.55*** *p43*
Cook, Miss; California, 1868 ***1131.61*** *p90*
Cook, Abraham B. 59; Ontario, 1871 ***1823.21*** *p69*
Cook, Alexander; Iowa, 1888 ***1211.15*** *p9*
Cook, Andrew; Iowa, 1895 ***1211.15*** *p9*
Cook, Ann; Utah, 1863 ***9228.50*** *p168*
Cook, Benjamin 60; Ontario, 1871 ***1823.21*** *p69*
Cook, Edward; Marston's Wharf, 1781 ***8529.30*** *p10*
Cook, Edward 43; Ontario, 1871 ***1823.17*** *p32*
Cook, Eliza 12; Quebec, 1870 ***8364.32*** *p23*
Cook, Elizabeth 22; Ontario, 1871 ***1823.21*** *p69*
Cook, Elizabeth 67; Ontario, 1871 ***1823.17*** *p32*
Cook, Frederick Wm.; Illinois, 1857 ***6079.1*** *p3*
Cook, George 59; Ontario, 1871 ***1823.21*** *p69*
Cook, Harrett 55; Ontario, 1871 ***1823.21*** *p69*
Cook, Henry 30; Ontario, 1871 ***1823.17*** *p32*
Cook, Jabez 43; Ontario, 1871 ***1823.21*** *p69*
Cook, Jacob; Illinois, 1856 ***6079.1*** *p3*
Cook, James; Iowa, 1891 ***1211.15*** *p9*
Cook, James 17; Ontario, 1871 ***1823.21*** *p69*
Cook, James 32; Ontario, 1871 ***1823.21*** *p69*
Cook, James; Quebec, 1870 ***8364.32*** *p23*
Cook, John 34; Ontario, 1871 ***1823.21*** *p69*
Cook, John 35; Ontario, 1871 ***1823.21*** *p69*
Cook, John 48; Ontario, 1871 ***1823.17*** *p32*
Cook, John 55; Ontario, 1871 ***1823.21*** *p69*
Cook, Jonathan 70; Ontario, 1871 ***1823.17*** *p32*
Cook, Lawrence 44; Ontario, 1871 ***1823.17*** *p32*
Cook, Mary; Marblehead, MA, 1743 ***9228.50*** *p345*
Cook, Mary Ann 36; Ontario, 1871 ***1823.21*** *p69*
Cook, Mary Riley 64; Ontario, 1871 ***1823.21*** *p69*
Cook, Matthew; North Carolina, 1841 ***1088.45*** *p6*
Cook, Morton 30; Boston, 1835 ***6424.55*** *p30*
Cook, Owen 60; Ontario, 1871 ***1823.21*** *p69*
Cook, Peter; New York, 1775 ***8529.30*** *p2*
Cook, Phillip 38; Ontario, 1871 ***1823.21*** *p69*
Cook, Robert 45; Ontario, 1871 ***1823.17*** *p32*
Cook, S. F. 58; Ontario, 1871 ***1823.17*** *p32*
Cook, Sarah 68; Ontario, 1871 ***1823.21*** *p69*
Cook, Thomas; Boston, 1764 ***1642*** *p33*
Cook, Thomas 29; Ontario, 1871 ***1823.21*** *p69*
Cook, Valentine; Ohio, 1809-1852 ***4511.35*** *p9*
Cook, William; Marston's Wharf, 1782 ***8529.30*** *p10*
Cook, William 28; Ontario, 1871 ***1823.21*** *p69*
Cook, William 36; Ontario, 1871 ***1823.17*** *p33*
Cook, William 37; Ontario, 1871 ***1823.21*** *p69*
Cook, William 44; Ontario, 1871 ***1823.21*** *p69*
Cook, William 44; Ontario, 1871 ***1823.21*** *p70*
Cook, William 50; Ontario, 1871 ***1823.21*** *p70*
Cook, William 54; Ontario, 1871 ***1823.21*** *p70*
Cook, William 55; Ontario, 1871 ***1823.21*** *p70*
Cook, William 59; Ontario, 1871 ***1823.21*** *p70*
Cook, William 60; Ontario, 1871 ***1823.21*** *p69*
Cook, William; Philadelphia, 1778 ***8529.30*** *p2A*
Cooke, Miss A.; Montreal, 1922 ***4514.4*** *p32*
Cooke, Aaron; Massachusetts, 1630 ***117.5*** *p153*
*Mother:*Elizabeth Charde
With stepfather
Cooke, Alfred J. 43; Louisiana, 1816-1848 ***7710.1*** *p150*
Cooke, Elizabeth Charde *SEE* Cooke, Aaron
Cooke, Francis; Plymouth, MA, 1620 ***1920.45*** *p5*
*Son:*John
Cooke, George 34; Ontario, 1871 ***1823.21*** *p70*
Cooke, James; Jamestown, VA, 1633 ***1658.20*** *p211*
Cooke, Jeffery 25; Ontario, 1871 ***1823.21*** *p70*
Cooke, John *SEE* Cooke, Francis
Cooke, Samuel; Dedham, MA, 1640 ***1642*** *p101*
Cookman, William; North Carolina, 1857 ***1088.45*** *p6*
Cooledge, Elizabeth; Watertown, MA, 1715 ***1642*** *p112*
Cooley, Hellen A. 36; Michigan, 1880 ***4491.30*** *p6*
Cooley, Hiram 37; Ontario, 1871 ***1823.17*** *p33*
Cooley, John 62; Ontario, 1871 ***1823.17*** *p33*
Cooly, Richd.; Maryland, 1674 ***1236.25*** *p50*
Coombe, John; Washington, 1889 ***2770.40*** *p26*
Coombs, Ann 71; Ontario, 1871 ***1823.21*** *p70*
Coombs, Charles C. 55; Ontario, 1871 ***1823.21*** *p70*
Coombs, Charlott 55; Ontario, 1871 ***1823.17*** *p33*
Coombs, Christopher C. 59; Ontario, 1871 ***1823.21*** *p70*
Coombs, Elizabeth C. 97; Ontario, 1871 ***1823.17*** *p33*
Coombs, George 32; Ontario, 1871 ***1823.21*** *p70*
Coombs, Henry 51; Ontario, 1871 ***1823.21*** *p70*
Coombs, Henry 57; Ontario, 1871 ***1823.21*** *p70*
Coombs, Jane 40; Ontario, 1871 ***1823.21*** *p70*
Coombs, John 39; Ontario, 1871 ***1823.21*** *p70*
Coombs, John 40; Ontario, 1871 ***1823.21*** *p70*
Coombs, Samuel 25; Ontario, 1871 ***1823.21*** *p70*
Coombs, William 42; Ontario, 1871 ***1823.21*** *p70*
Coon, Thomas 38; Ontario, 1871 ***1823.17*** *p33*
Cooney, Mr.; St. John, N.B., 1848 ***2978.15*** *p39*
Cooney, John; Colorado, 1880 ***1029.59*** *p18*
Cooney, Margret 50; Ontario, 1871 ***1823.21*** *p70*
Cooney, Mary 23; Ontario, 1871 ***1823.21*** *p70*
Cooney, Patrick; Boston, 1744 ***1642*** *p45*
Cooney, Patrick 61; Ontario, 1871 ***1823.21*** *p70*
Cooney, Robert; Louisiana, 1836-1841 ***4981.45*** *p208*
Coons, George; North Carolina, 1710 ***3629.40*** *p3*
Coop, Hen'y; Ontario, 1787 ***1276.15*** *p230*
With 2 relatives
Cooper, Mrs.; Toronto, 1844 ***2910.35*** *p114*
Cooper, Abraham; North Carolina, 1851 ***1088.45*** *p6*
Cooper, Benjamin 43; Ontario, 1871 ***1823.21*** *p70*
Cooper, Catharine Malone *SEE* Cooper, Joseph
Cooper, David T. 42; New York, NY, 1822 ***6178.50*** *p76*
Cooper, David W.; Ohio, 1875 ***3580.20*** *p31*
Cooper, David W.; Ohio, 1875 ***6020.12*** *p7*
Cooper, Edmond H. 30; Ontario, 1871 ***1823.21*** *p70*
Cooper, Edward; Marston's Wharf, 1780 ***8529.30*** *p10*
Cooper, Emilea 61; Ontario, 1871 ***1823.21*** *p70*
Cooper, Francis; Philadelphia, 1777 ***8529.30*** *p2A*
Cooper, George; Colorado, 1882 ***1029.59*** *p18*
Cooper, George; New York, NY, 1897 ***9228.50*** *p446*
Cooper, George 22; Ontario, 1871 ***1823.17*** *p33*
Cooper, George 40; Ontario, 1871 ***1823.17*** *p33*
Cooper, George C.; Colorado, 1880 ***1029.59*** *p19*
Cooper, George C.; Colorado, 1886 ***1029.59*** *p19*
Cooper, Grant; Philadelphia, 1777 ***8529.30*** *p2A*
Cooper, Harry J.; Colorado, 1887 ***1029.59*** *p19*
Cooper, Harry J.; Colorado, 1891 ***1029.59*** *p19*
Cooper, Henry 43; Ontario, 1871 ***1823.21*** *p70*
Cooper, Humillity; Plymouth, MA, 1620 ***1920.45*** *p5*
Cooper, James; Illinois, 1834-1900 ***6020.5*** *p131*
Cooper, James; North Carolina, 1850 ***1088.45*** *p6*
Cooper, James 35; Ontario, 1871 ***1823.21*** *p70*
Cooper, James 58; Ontario, 1871 ***1823.21*** *p70*
Cooper, James 78; Ontario, 1871 ***1823.21*** *p70*
Cooper, Jbr; California, 1798-1898 ***9228.50*** *p168*
Cooper, John; North Carolina, 1837 ***1088.45*** *p6*
Cooper, John 67; Ontario, 1871 ***1823.21*** *p70*
Cooper, John 69; Ontario, 1871 ***1823.21*** *p70*
Cooper, John; Washington, 1889 ***2770.40*** *p27*
Cooper, John H.; Colorado, 1894 ***1029.59*** *p19*
Cooper, Joseph; Baltimore, 1860 ***8513.31*** *p300*
*Wife:*Catharine Malone
Cooper, Joseph 72; Ontario, 1871 ***1823.21*** *p71*
Cooper, Mary 57; Ontario, 1871 ***1823.21*** *p71*
Cooper, Mary A. 45; Ontario, 1871 ***1823.21*** *p71*
Cooper, Maryann 40; Ontario, 1871 ***1823.21*** *p71*
Cooper, Matthias; Ohio, 1809-1852 ***4511.35*** *p9*
Cooper, Pheobe 59; Ontario, 1871 ***1823.21*** *p71*
Cooper, Samuel 32; Ontario, 1871 ***1823.21*** *p71*
Cooper, Samuel 50; Ontario, 1871 ***1823.17*** *p33*
Cooper, Sarah 51; Ontario, 1871 ***1823.21*** *p71*
Cooper, Sarah 60; Ontario, 1871 ***1823.21*** *p71*
Cooper, Stephen 57; Ontario, 1871 ***1823.21*** *p71*
Cooper, Theop; Havana, 1782 ***8529.30*** *p9A*
Cooper, Thomas 14; New York, NY, 1822 ***6178.50*** *p76*
Cooper, W. D. 36; Ontario, 1871 ***1823.21*** *p71*
Cooper, William 36; Ontario, 1871 ***1823.21*** *p71*
Cooper, William 37; Ontario, 1871 ***1823.21*** *p71*
Cooper, William 44; Ontario, 1871 ***1823.21*** *p71*
Cooper, William 46; Ontario, 1871 ***1823.21*** *p71*
Cooper, William 47; Ontario, 1871 ***1823.17*** *p33*
Cooper, William 14; Quebec, 1870 ***8364.32*** *p23*
Cooper, Wm.; Ohio, 1799-1812 ***9228.50*** *p621*
Coopland, John; Marston's Wharf, 1782 ***8529.30*** *p10*
Coors, Adolph; Colorado, 1889 ***1029.59*** *p19*
Coors, Adolph; Illinois, 1870 ***1029.59*** *p19*
Coote, Elizabeth 53; Ontario, 1871 ***1823.21*** *p71*
Coote, John 42; Ontario, 1871 ***1823.21*** *p71*
Coote, Robert 54; Ontario, 1871 ***1823.21*** *p71*
Cootes, David 35; Ontario, 1871 ***1823.21*** *p71*
Coots, David 30; Ontario, 1871 ***1823.21*** *p71*
Cope, Francis; Illinois, 1858 ***6079.1*** *p3*
Cope, John 40; Ontario, 1871 ***1823.17*** *p33*
Cope, Kennedy 38; Ontario, 1871 ***1823.21*** *p71*
Cope, Richard 50; Ontario, 1871 ***1823.17*** *p33*
Cope, Samuel 60; Ontario, 1871 ***1823.17*** *p33*
Cope, Stephen 33; Ontario, 1871 ***1823.21*** *p71*
Cope, Thomas 30; Ontario, 1871 ***1823.21*** *p71*
Copeland, James 56; Ontario, 1871 ***1823.21*** *p71*
Copeland, James; South Carolina, 1810 ***6155.4*** *p18*
Copeland, John; Marston's Wharf, 1782 ***8529.30*** *p10*
Copeland, Joseph 28; Ontario, 1871 ***1823.21*** *p71*

Copland, James 51; Ontario, 1871 ***1823.17*** *p33*
Copland, Jane 77; Ontario, 1871 ***1823.17*** *p33*
Copland, Robert 40; Ontario, 1871 ***1823.17*** *p33*
Copland, William; Washington, 1882 ***2770.40*** *p135*
Copler, David; Ohio, 1809-1852 ***4511.35*** *p9*
Copp, . . .; Boston, 1635 ***1642*** *p27*
Copp, Thomas 53; Ontario, 1871 ***1823.21*** *p71*
Coppenger, Mary 20; Ontario, 1871 ***1823.21*** *p71*
Coppens, John; New York, NY, 1854 ***1494.21*** *p31*
Coppersmith, Alexis; Wisconsin, 1854-1858 ***1495.20*** *p66*
*Wife:*Desiree Meuron
*Child:*Ferdinand
*Child:*Flora
*Child:*Stephanie
*Child:*Victorine Desiree
*Child:*Isidore
*Child:*Elvire
*Child:*Clotilde
*Child:*Marcel Henri
Coppersmith, Clotilde *SEE* Coppersmith, Alexis
Coppersmith, Desiree Meuron *SEE* Coppersmith, Alexis
Coppersmith, Elvire *SEE* Coppersmith, Alexis
Coppersmith, Ferdinand *SEE* Coppersmith, Alexis
Coppersmith, Flora *SEE* Coppersmith, Alexis
Coppersmith, Isidore *SEE* Coppersmith, Alexis
Coppersmith, Marcel Henri *SEE* Coppersmith, Alexis
Coppersmith, Stephanie *SEE* Coppersmith, Alexis
Coppersmith, Victorine Desiree *SEE* Coppersmith, Alexis
Coppesmette, Alexis; Wisconsin, 1854-1858 ***1495.20*** *p66*
*Wife:*Desiree Meuron
*Child:*Stephanie
*Child:*Flora
*Child:*Ferdinand
*Child:*Elvire
*Child:*Victorine Desiree
*Child:*Isidore
*Child:*Clotilde
*Child:*Marcel Henri
Coppesmette, Clotilde *SEE* Coppesmette, Alexis
Coppesmette, Desiree Meuron *SEE* Coppesmette, Alexis
Coppesmette, Elvire *SEE* Coppesmette, Alexis
Coppesmette, Ferdinand *SEE* Coppesmette, Alexis
Coppesmette, Flora *SEE* Coppesmette, Alexis
Coppesmette, Isidore *SEE* Coppesmette, Alexis
Coppesmette, Marcel Henri *SEE* Coppesmette, Alexis
Coppesmette, Stephanie *SEE* Coppesmette, Alexis
Coppesmette, Victorine Desiree *SEE* Coppesmette, Alexis
Coppinger, Walter 60; Ontario, 1871 ***1823.21*** *p71*
Copporsea, Louis 22; New Orleans, 1848 ***778.6*** *p76*
Copron, Michelis 25; Louisiana, 1846 ***778.6*** *p76*
Coquel, Nicolas; Quebec, 1649 ***9221.17*** *p210*
Coquelet, Mr. 25; Louisiana, 1848 ***778.6*** *p76*
Coquelin, Julie 28; America, 1848 ***778.6*** *p76*
Coquelin, L. Nicolas 58; America, 1848 ***778.6*** *p76*
Coquelin, Mrs. L. Nicolas 47; America, 1848 ***778.6*** *p76*
Coquelin, Melanie 25; America, 1848 ***778.6*** *p76*
Coqueret, Jacques; Quebec, 1636 ***9221.17*** *p64*
Coquigene, John 53; Michigan, 1880 ***4491.42*** *p8*
Coquigene, Peter B. 60; Michigan, 1880 ***4491.42*** *p8*
Coram, William 51; Ontario, 1871 ***1823.17*** *p33*
Corbach, Friedrich Wilhelm; America, 1865 ***7420.1*** *p230*
With wife
Corbe, Madalaine 22; Louisiana, 1848 ***778.6*** *p76*
Corbe, Pierre; Louisiana, 1848 ***778.6*** *p76*
Corbet, Abraham; New England, 1674 ***9228.50*** *p168*
Corbet, Celestin *SEE* Corbet, Desire
Corbet, Desire; Wisconsin, 1856 ***1495.20*** *p41*
*Wife:*Therese Malaise
*Child:*Francois Joseph
*Child:*Marie Therese
*Child:*Eugene
*Child:*Victorine
*Child:*Celestin
*Child:*Julie
*Child:*Florence
Corbet, Eliza; Ohio, 1838-1874 ***9228.50*** *p168*
Corbet, Eugene *SEE* Corbet, Desire
Corbet, Florence *SEE* Corbet, Desire
Corbet, Francois Joseph *SEE* Corbet, Desire
Corbet, John 54; Ontario, 1871 ***1823.21*** *p71*
Corbet, Julie *SEE* Corbet, Desire
Corbet, Marie Therese *SEE* Corbet, Desire
Corbet, Peter; Ohio, 1807 ***9228.50*** *p57*
Corbet, Peter; Ohio, 1820 ***9228.50*** *p168*
Corbet, Therese Malaise *SEE* Corbet, Desire
Corbet, Victorine *SEE* Corbet, Desire
Corbett, Mrs. 38; Ontario, 1871 ***1823.21*** *p71*
Corbett, Eliza; Ohio, 1838-1874 ***9228.50*** *p168*
Corbett, John; Philadelphia, 1844 ***7074.20*** *p132*
Corbett, Laur 13; Ontario, 1871 ***1823.21*** *p71*
Corbett, Minnie 11; Ontario, 1871 ***1823.21*** *p71*
Corbett, Wm. Ed. Percival 16; Quebec, 1910 ***2897.7*** *p8*
Corbier, Charles 23; New Orleans, 1847 ***778.6*** *p76*
Corbin, Clement; New England, 1637-1696 ***9228.50*** *p169*
Corbin, David 17; Quebec, 1661 ***9221.17*** *p452*
Corbitt, John; California, 1868 ***1131.61*** *p89*
Corbitt, John; Philadelphia, 1844 ***7074.20*** *p132*
Corbusier, Oliver; New York, NY, 1856 ***1494.20*** *p12*
Corby, Francis; Ohio, 1809-1852 ***4511.35*** *p9*
Corby, James 29; Ontario, 1871 ***1823.21*** *p71*
Corchoran, William 49; Ontario, 1871 ***1823.21*** *p71*
Corcoran, Bartholomew 45; Ontario, 1871 ***1823.17*** *p33*
Corcoran, Bryan; Louisiana, 1841-1844 ***4981.45*** *p210*
Corcoran, Dennis 70; Ontario, 1871 ***1823.21*** *p71*
Corcoran, James 45; Ontario, 1871 ***1823.21*** *p71*
Corcoran, Robert 33; Ontario, 1871 ***1823.21*** *p71*
Corcoran, Thomas; Toronto, 1844 ***2910.35*** *p113*
Corde, Catherine; Quebec, 1636 ***9221.17*** *p58*
*Son:*Pierre
*Grandson:*Jean-Baptiste
*Granddaughter:*Catherine
*Granddaughter:*Marie-Madeleine
*Daughter-In-Law:*Marie Favery
*Son:*Charles
Corde, Catherine; Quebec, 1636 ***9221.17*** *p58*
Cordeau, Jean 24; Quebec, 1659 ***9221.17*** *p397*
Corder, Joseph 38; America, 1843 ***778.6*** *p76*
Cordes, Joseph 38; America, 1843 ***778.6*** *p76*
Cordier, . . .; America, 1843 ***778.6*** *p76*
Cordier, Mrs. 30; America, 1843 ***778.6*** *p76*
Cordier, Christian; Ohio, 1809-1852 ***4511.35*** *p9*
Cordier, Christian, Jr.; Ohio, 1809-1852 ***4511.35*** *p9*
Cordier, Claire 17; America, 1847 ***778.6*** *p76*
Cordier, Clautilde 40; America, 1847 ***778.6*** *p76*
Cordier, E. 32; New Orleans, 1844 ***778.6*** *p76*
Cordier, John Adam; Ohio, 1809-1852 ***4511.35*** *p9*
Cordier, Laurent; Louisiana, 1836-1840 ***4981.45*** *p212*
Cordier, Remis 33; Galveston, TX, 1844 ***3967.10*** *p371*
Cording, Mr.; America, 1884 ***7420.1*** *p342*
Cording, Carl Friedrich Christian; America, 1853 ***7420.1*** *p103*
Cording, Ernst Fr. Ch.; America, 1853 ***7420.1*** *p104*
Cording, Friedrich August Ferdinand; America, 1885 ***7420.1*** *p347*
Cordonnier, Nicholas 40; Port uncertain, 1845 ***778.6*** *p76*
Cordor, Clara 11; Port uncertain, 1847 ***778.6*** *p76*
Cordor, Desir 24; Port uncertain, 1847 ***778.6*** *p76*
Cordor, Ida 24; Port uncertain, 1847 ***778.6*** *p76*
Core, Edward 32; Ontario, 1871 ***1823.17*** *p33*
Core, Grace; Boston, 1766 ***1642*** *p36*
With 4 children
Core, Thomas 59; Ontario, 1871 ***1823.17*** *p33*
Core, Walter 43; Ontario, 1871 ***1823.17*** *p33*
Corey, Hiram Chancey 27; Ontario, 1871 ***1823.17*** *p33*
Corino, Jos.; Louisiana, 1874 ***4981.45*** *p295*
Corkery, Eliza; Boston, 1743 ***1642*** *p45*
Corkery, Patrick; Boston, 1741 ***1642*** *p45*
Corkhill, Thomas Alfred; Missouri, 1867 ***3276.1*** *p3*
Corleit, Robert; North Carolina, 1811-1812 ***1088.45*** *p6*
Corljahan, Richard; North Carolina, 1852 ***1088.45*** *p6*
Corly, Francis; Ohio, 1809-1852 ***4511.35*** *p9*
Corman, Peter; Ohio, 1809-1852 ***4511.35*** *p9*
Cormel, Sebastian 33; Port uncertain, 1844 ***778.6*** *p76*
Corn, Theadore; Ohio, 1840-1897 ***8365.35*** *p15*
Cornberg, Ernst Christian Ludwig; America, 1889 ***7420.1*** *p400*
Cornbert, Mrs. 22; Port uncertain, 1843 ***778.6*** *p77*
Corne, John; Portsmouth, NH, 1700-1730 ***9228.50*** *p169*
*Relative:*Susannah
*Relative:*Thomas
Corne, Pierre 24; America, 1840 ***778.6*** *p77*
Corne, Susannah *SEE* Corne, John
Corne, Thomas *SEE* Corne, John
Cornecki, John; Galveston, TX, 1890 ***6015.15*** *p9*
Corneicki, John; Galveston, TX, 1890 ***6015.15*** *p9*
Corneil, Adam 49; Ontario, 1871 ***1823.21*** *p72*
Corneil, Christopher 67; Ontario, 1871 ***1823.21*** *p72*
Corneil, Daniel 44; Ontario, 1871 ***1823.21*** *p72*
Corneil, George 58; Ontario, 1871 ***1823.21*** *p72*
Corneil, Gideon 54; Ontario, 1871 ***1823.21*** *p72*
Corneil, Julius D. 53; Ontario, 1871 ***1823.21*** *p72*
Corneil, Philip 63; Ontario, 1871 ***1823.21*** *p72*
Cornelius, A. Maria 7 *SEE* Cornelius, Johann
Cornelius, Anna Maria Meiser 25 *SEE* Cornelius, Johann
Cornelius, Augustus 64; Ontario, 1871 ***1823.21*** *p72*
Cornelius, Barbara 26 *SEE* Cornelius, Johann
Cornelius, Catherine 53; Ontario, 1871 ***1823.21*** *p72*
Cornelius, Cornelius 32; Ontario, 1871 ***1823.21*** *p72*
Cornelius, Dennis 37; Ontario, 1871 ***1823.21*** *p72*
Cornelius, Dorothea 22 *SEE* Cornelius, Johann
Cornelius, Eleazer 31; Ontario, 1871 ***1823.21*** *p72*
Cornelius, Gertrud 4 *SEE* Cornelius, Johann
Cornelius, Johann 1 *SEE* Cornelius, Johann
Cornelius, Johann 20 *SEE* Cornelius, Johann
Cornelius, Johann 34; America, 1846 ***5475.1*** *p402*
*Wife:*Anna Maria Meiser 25
*Son:*Johann 1
*Daughter:*A. Maria 7
*Daughter:*Gertrud 4
Cornelius, Johann 48; America, 1833 ***5475.1*** *p398*
With wife 52
*Daughter:*Katharina 12
*Daughter:*Dorothea 22
*Son:*Johann 20
*Son:*Peter 18
*Daughter:*Barbara 26
Cornelius, Katharina; America, 1883 ***5475.1*** *p20*
Cornelius, Katharina 12 *SEE* Cornelius, Johann
Cornelius, Mary 29; Ontario, 1871 ***1823.21*** *p72*
Cornelius, Nicholas 35; Ontario, 1871 ***1823.21*** *p72*
Cornelius, Peter 18 *SEE* Cornelius, Johann
Cornelius, William 36; Ontario, 1871 ***1823.21*** *p72*
Cornelius, William 57; Ontario, 1871 ***1823.21*** *p72*
Corneliuson, Paul Oscar; Cleveland, OH, 1886-1890 ***9722.10*** *p118*
Cornell, Aaron 75; Ontario, 1871 ***1823.21*** *p72*
Cornell, Eliza 48; Ontario, 1871 ***1823.17*** *p33*
Cornell, Elizabeth 71; Ontario, 1871 ***1823.21*** *p72*
Cornelson, Christian; North Carolina, 1852 ***1088.45*** *p6*
Corner, Jacob 42; Ontario, 1871 ***1823.17*** *p33*
Corner, Thomas 10; Ontario, 1871 ***1823.21*** *p72*
Corners, John; Weymouth, MA, 1772 ***1642*** *p92*
*Wife:*Sarah
Corners, Sarah *SEE* Corners, John
Cornet, J. 37; New Orleans, 1846 ***778.6*** *p77*
Cornew, Catherine; Maine, 1680 ***9228.50*** *p339*
Cornforth, Elizabeth *SEE* Cornforth, William
Cornforth, Mary *SEE* Cornforth, William
Cornforth, Mary *SEE* Cornforth, William
Cornforth, Paul; Canada, 1774 ***3036.5*** *p40*
*Wife:*Phillis
Cornforth, Phillis *SEE* Cornforth, Paul
Cornforth, William; Canada, 1774 ***3036.5*** *p40*
*Wife:*Mary
*Child:*Elizabeth
*Child:*Mary
Cornibert, Mrs. 20; Port uncertain, 1843 ***778.6*** *p77*
Cornibert, Christophe 27; Port uncertain, 1843 ***778.6*** *p77*
Cornibert, Jean Florin 63; New Orleans, 1843 ***778.6*** *p77*
Cornibert, Jean Florin 26; Port uncertain, 1843 ***778.6*** *p77*
Cornick, Charles; Detroit, 1929 ***1640.55*** *p113*
Cornier, Nicolas; Montreal, 1653 ***9221.17*** *p286*
Cornish, Elizabeth K. 67; Ontario, 1871 ***1823.21*** *p72*
Cornish, Frederick 33; Ontario, 1871 ***1823.21*** *p72*
Cornish, Frederick 14; Quebec, 1870 ***8364.32*** *p23*
Cornish, John 65; Ontario, 1871 ***1823.21*** *p72*
Cornish, Mary 21; Ontario, 1871 ***1823.21*** *p72*
Cornish, Thomas 45; Ontario, 1871 ***1823.21*** *p72*
Cornish, Wm; Virginia, 1652 ***6254.4*** *p243*
Cornman, Henry; Ohio, 1809-1852 ***4511.35*** *p9*
Cornnel, Louis 24; Port uncertain, 1846 ***778.6*** *p77*
Cornu, Peter; New York, 1730-1739 ***9228.50*** *p338*
Cornu, Pierre; Virginia, 1700 ***9230.15*** *p81*
Cornuel, Louis 24; Port uncertain, 1846 ***778.6*** *p77*
Cornwall, Ann; Maryland, 1673 ***1236.25*** *p49*
Cornwall, Dan'l; Ontario, 1787 ***1276.15*** *p231*
With 3 children & 3 relatives
Cornwall, John 33; Ontario, 1871 ***1823.17*** *p33*
Cornwall, Nelson 31; Ontario, 1871 ***1823.17*** *p33*
Cornwall, Robert 76; Ontario, 1871 ***1823.21*** *p72*
Coro, Juan; Louisiana, 1874-1875 ***4981.45*** *p298*
Coronne, Jean; Quebec, 1654 ***9221.17*** *p306*
Corpe, John 75; Ontario, 1871 ***1823.21*** *p73*
Corran, D.; New Orleans, 1850 ***7242.30*** *p139*
Corran, Margaret; Boston, 1733 ***1642*** *p44*
Corre, Frank; Washington, 1884 ***2770.40*** *p192*
Corre, Pierre; Quebec, 1638 ***9221.17*** *p76*
Corrigan, Agnes *SEE* Corrigan, Hugh
Corrigan, Ann 64; Ontario, 1871 ***1823.21*** *p73*
Corrigan, Ellen *SEE* Corrigan, Hugh
Corrigan, Hugh; Philadelphia, 1867 ***8513.31*** *p300*
*Wife:*Margaret Cassidy
*Daughter:*Ellen
*Daughter:*Jane
*Son:*Thomas
*Daughter:*Agnes
Corrigan, Jane *SEE* Corrigan, Hugh
Corrigan, Margaret Cassidy *SEE* Corrigan, Hugh
Corrigan, Richard 22; Ontario, 1871 ***1823.21*** *p73*
Corrigan, Thomas *SEE* Corrigan, Hugh
Corris, Thomas 77; Ontario, 1871 ***1823.21*** *p73*
Corristine, John 29; Ontario, 1871 ***1823.17*** *p33*
Corristine, R. D. 55; Ontario, 1871 ***1823.17*** *p33*

Corrivault, Marguerite 22; Quebec, 1648 ***9221.17*** *p201*
Corrivault Lefranc, Marguerite 22; Quebec, 1648 ***9221.17*** *p201*
*Son:*Jean-Paul Corrivault 1
Corroy, A. 40; New Orleans, 1844 ***778.6*** *p77*
Corroy, Celine Marie *SEE* Corroy, Marie Catherine
Corroy, Donat D. *SEE* Corroy, Jean Baptiste
Corroy, Jean Baptiste; Wisconsin, 1880 ***1495.20*** *p55*
*Wife:*Marie Victorine Matagne
*Son:*Donat D.
Corroy, Marie Catherine; Wisconsin, 1882 ***1495.20*** *p55*
*Daughter:*Celine Marie
Corroy, Marie Victorine Matagne *SEE* Corroy, Jean Baptiste
Corroy, Virginie; Wisconsin, 1800-1857 ***1495.20*** *p56*
Corry, Honor 70; Ontario, 1871 ***1823.21*** *p73*
Corsant, Christopher F. 72; Ontario, 1871 ***1823.21*** *p73*
Corse, James; Massachusetts, n.d. ***9228.50*** *p169*
Corson, William 32; Ontario, 1871 ***1823.21*** *p73*
Corssen, Arndt; New Netherland, 1633 ***2853.20*** *p11*
Corston, Malcolm 30; Ontario, 1871 ***1823.17*** *p34*
Cort, Matilda Ann; Ontario, 1880-1894 ***9228.50*** *p477*
Cortetz, Frederick William; Ohio, 1809-1852 ***4511.35*** *p9*
Cortschot, Margaretha 40; America, 1747 ***778.6*** *p77*
Cortschot, Pierre 38; America, 1747 ***778.6*** *p77*
Corught, Adam 44; Ontario, 1871 ***1823.17*** *p34*
Coruman, Henry; Ohio, 1809-1852 ***4511.35*** *p9*
Corus, Jasper; Ontario, 1787 ***1276.15*** *p230*
Cory, Thomas 36; Ontario, 1871 ***1823.21*** *p73*
Coscomb, Thomas; Marston's Wharf, 1782 ***8529.30*** *p10*
Coscomb, Thomas; Marston's Wharf, 1782 ***8529.30*** *p12*
Coscon, James; New York, NY, 1819 ***3274.55*** *p69*
Coscon, Richard; New York, NY, 1819 ***3274.55*** *p69*
Coscon, William; New York, NY, 1819 ***3274.55*** *p69*
Cosfevar, Ramia 50; Ontario, 1871 ***1823.17*** *p34*
Cosgrove, William 29; Ontario, 1871 ***1823.21*** *p73*
Cosimier, Francois 43; America, 1842 ***778.6*** *p77*
Cosmorgen, Caspar Luntly von; North Carolina, 1710 ***3629.40*** *p5*
Cosnard, Martin; Quebec, 1648 ***9221.17*** *p197*
Cosquer, James; Boston, 1753 ***1642*** *p31*
Cosse, Pierre; Quebec, 1638 ***9221.17*** *p76*
Cosset, Daniel; Quebec, 1655 ***9221.17*** *p321*
Cosset, Rene 25; Quebec, 1656 ***9221.17*** *p334*
Cosson, Pierre; Quebec, 1656 ***9221.17*** *p334*
*Brother:*Thomas
Cosson, Thomas *SEE* Cosson, Pierre
Costello, Andrew 48; Michigan, 1880 ***4491.30*** *p7*
Costello, Elen 21; Ontario, 1871 ***1823.21*** *p73*
Costello, Elizabeth 49; Michigan, 1880 ***4491.30*** *p7*
Costello, John; San Francisco, 1902 ***3665.20*** *p111*
Costello, John; St. John, N.B., 1847 ***2978.15*** *p37*
Costello, Martin 45; Ontario, 1871 ***1823.17*** *p34*
Costello, Michael; Toronto, 1844 ***2910.35*** *p114*
Costello, Patrick 40; Ontario, 1871 ***1823.21*** *p73*
Costelloe, Thomas 72; Ontario, 1871 ***1823.17*** *p34*
Costelo, M.; Toronto, 1844 ***2910.35*** *p113*
Costels, William; Louisiana, 1874 ***4981.45*** *p131*
Coster, Else 53; America, 1847 ***778.6*** *p77*
Coster, Heinrich; America, 1864 ***5475.1*** *p508*
*Wife:*Katharina Klein
*Son:*Julius
*Daughter:*Katharina
Coster, Julius *SEE* Coster, Heinrich
Coster, Katharina *SEE* Coster, Heinrich
Coster, Katharina Klein *SEE* Coster, Heinrich
Costigan, Bridget; St. Johns, N.F., 1825 ***1053.15*** *p6*
Costigan, James; St. Johns, N.F., 1825 ***1053.15*** *p6*
Costolo, John; Boston, 1764 ***1642*** *p33*
Costoloe, Thomas; Ohio, 1840-1897 ***8365.35*** *p15*
Costot, Emile 17; Mississippi, 1845-1846 ***778.6*** *p77*
Costreau, Pierre 23; America, 1841 ***778.6*** *p77*
Costrick, Mr.; America, 1852 ***7420.1*** *p86*
Costy, Wm.; Ohio, 1840-1897 ***8365.35*** *p15*
Cota, Eugene; Washington, 1885 ***2770.40*** *p194*
Cote, Mr. 56; America, 1841 ***778.6*** *p77*
Cote, Jean; Quebec, 1634 ***9221.17*** *p35*
Coti, Pierre 30; New Orleans, 1846 ***778.6*** *p77*
Coto, Alfred; New York, 1926 ***1173.1*** *p2*
Cotrell, William 22; Ontario, 1871 ***1823.21*** *p73*
Cottan, Rene; Quebec, 1643 ***9221.17*** *p130*
Cotteney, Julie 33; New Orleans, 1848 ***778.6*** *p77*
Cotteney, Pierre 35; New Orleans, 1848 ***778.6*** *p77*
Cotter, John; Boston, 1764 ***1642*** *p33*
Cotter, Patrick; Illinois, 1857 ***6079.1*** *p3*
Cotter, Richard 65; Ontario, 1871 ***1823.21*** *p73*
Cotter, Timothy 55; Ontario, 1871 ***1823.21*** *p73*
Cotter, William; Jamaica, 1783 ***8529.30*** *p12A*
Cottereau, Jean 24; Quebec, 1657 ***9221.17*** *p354*
Cotterell, Samuel 5; Quebec, 1870 ***8364.32*** *p23*
Cotteril, Patrick 48; Ontario, 1871 ***1823.21*** *p73*
Cotteron, Jacques; Illinois, 1852 ***6079.1*** *p3*
Cottet, George; Ohio, 1840-1897 ***8365.35*** *p15*
Cottet, Jules L.; Illinois, 1856 ***6079.1*** *p3*
Cottier, James; Colorado, 1879 ***1029.59*** *p19*
Cottier, James; Colorado, 1894 ***1029.59*** *p19*
Cottilla, Brigid Dorian *SEE* Cottilla, Edward F.
Cottilla, Edward F.; Philadelphia, 1855 ***8513.31*** *p301*
*Wife:*Brigid Dorian
Cottin, Marie-Catherine; Quebec, 1664 ***4514.3*** *p293*
Cotton, Charles 70; Ontario, 1871 ***1823.17*** *p34*
Cotton, Elizabeth 79; Ontario, 1871 ***1823.17*** *p34*
Cotton, Henry; Philadelphia, 1777 ***8529.30*** *p2*
Cottrell, Ellen Welsh *SEE* Cottrell, Joseph
Cottrell, George 23; Ontario, 1871 ***1823.21*** *p73*
Cottrell, Henry 14; Quebec, 1870 ***8364.32*** *p23*
Cottrell, John 21; Quebec, 1870 ***8364.32*** *p23*
Cottrell, Joseph; Philadelphia, 1857 ***8513.31*** *p301*
*Wife:*Ellen Welsh
Cottrell, Susan 16; Quebec, 1870 ***8364.32*** *p23*
Cottret, Jacques; Quebec, 1653 ***9221.17*** *p271*
Cottrill, John 22; Ontario, 1871 ***1823.21*** *p73*
Cottrill, Valentine 31; Ontario, 1871 ***1823.21*** *p73*
Cottron, Eleonore Angelique 26; New Orleans, 1848 ***778.6*** *p77*
Cottron, Jacques 39; New Orleans, 1848 ***778.6*** *p77*
Cotwell, Richard 62; Michigan, 1880 ***4491.42*** *p8*
Cou, Louis 46; Port uncertain, 1845 ***778.6*** *p77*
Couanee, Pierre; Montreal, 1660 ***9221.17*** *p441*
Couba, Laurent 47; America, 1842 ***778.6*** *p77*
Coubret, Guillaume 23; Quebec, 1656 ***9221.17*** *p334*
Coubrough, James 40; Ontario, 1871 ***1823.17*** *p34*
Couc, Pierre 24; Quebec, 1651 ***9221.17*** *p239*
Couch, Julia 17; Quebec, 1870 ***8364.32*** *p23*
Couch, Richard 40; Ontario, 1871 ***1823.21*** *p73*
Couchot, Francois 13; America, 1840 ***778.6*** *p77*
Couchot, Jean 45; America, 1840 ***778.6*** *p77*
Couchot, Joseph 9; America, 1840 ***778.6*** *p77*
Couchot, Marie 4; America, 1840 ***778.6*** *p77*
Couchot, Marie 42; America, 1840 ***778.6*** *p77*
Couchot, Nicolas 7; America, 1840 ***778.6*** *p77*
Couder, . . . 31; Port uncertain, 1843 ***778.6*** *p77*
Couder, Clementine 8; Port uncertain, 1843 ***778.6*** *p77*
Coudon, Patrick; Ohio, 1809-1852 ***4511.35*** *p9*
Coudret, Andre 16; Quebec, 1658 ***9221.17*** *p377*
Coudrin, Elie 24; New Orleans, 1848 ***778.6*** *p77*
Couet, Marie; Quebec, 1669 ***4514.3*** *p293*
Couget, Mr. 25; New Orleans, 1840 ***778.6*** *p78*
Cougetau, Catherine 27; New Orleans, 1848 ***778.6*** *p78*
Coughlin, John 74; Ontario, 1871 ***1823.21*** *p73*
Coughlin, Joseph 37; Ontario, 1871 ***1823.21*** *p73*
Coughlin, Margaret 55; Ontario, 1871 ***1823.21*** *p73*
Coughlin, Matthew 65; Ontario, 1871 ***1823.21*** *p73*
Couglan, Euriah; Newfoundland, 1814 ***3476.10*** *p54*
Couglin, James 50; Ontario, 1871 ***1823.17*** *p34*
Couglin, Richard 50; Ontario, 1871 ***1823.17*** *p34*
Cougot, Louis 20; New Orleans, 1848 ***778.6*** *p78*
Couignon, Antoine-Jacques 15; Montreal, 1659 ***9221.17*** *p419*
Couignon, Suzanne 33; Montreal, 1659 ***9221.17*** *p417*
Couillard, Louis; Quebec, 1721 ***2314.30*** *p172*
Couillard deBeaumont, Charles; Quebec, 1668 ***2314.30*** *p172*
Couillard deSecors, Joseph; Quebec, 1725 ***2314.30*** *p172*
Couillart, Guillaume; Quebec, 1613 ***9221.17*** *p17*
Couillart, Michel; Quebec, 1659 ***9221.17*** *p413*
Couillart, Pierre 21; Quebec, 1658 ***9221.17*** *p378*
Couise, Henry 20; Ontario, 1871 ***1823.21*** *p73*
Coulange, Etienne 16; America, 1847 ***778.6*** *p78*
Coule, Jean 20; New Orleans, 1848 ***778.6*** *p78*
Couliccich, Alex; Louisiana, 1874-1875 ***4981.45*** *p298*
Coullard, Louis; New York, NY, 1870 ***1494.20*** *p11*
Coullard, Robert; Quebec, 1652 ***9221.17*** *p257*
Coullaud, Jean 18; Quebec, 1657 ***9221.17*** *p355*
Coulombe, Charles; Boston, 1769 ***9228.50*** *p48*
Coulombier, A. 27; America, 1843 ***778.6*** *p78*
Coulon, Claude 25; America, 1842 ***778.6*** *p78*
Coulon, Francoise 60; America, 1842 ***778.6*** *p78*
Coulon, Joseph 21; America, 1842 ***778.6*** *p78*
Coulon, Marie Victoire; Wisconsin, 1846-1856 ***1495.20*** *p29*
Coulon, Pierre; Louisiana, 1874 ***4981.45*** *p295*
Coulon deVilliers, Nicolas-Antoine; Quebec, 1700 ***2314.30*** *p169*
Coulon deVilliers, Nicolas-Antoine; Quebec, 1700 ***2314.30*** *p178*
Couloy, Francois; Illinois, 1852 ***6079.1*** *p3*
Couloy, Germain Francois; Illinois, 1852 ***6079.1*** *p3*
Couloy, Isadore; Illinois, 1852 ***6079.1*** *p4*
Coulson, John; Canada, 1774 ***3036.5*** *p40*
*Wife:*Mary
Coulson, Joseph 74; Ontario, 1871 ***1823.21*** *p73*
Coulson, Mary *SEE* Coulson, John
Coulson, Oscar T.; Cleveland, OH, 1880-1888 ***9722.10*** *p118*
Coulson, Walter D. 32; Indiana, 1879-1896 ***9076.20*** *p74*
Coulter, Andrew 58; Ontario, 1871 ***1823.21*** *p73*
Coulter, George 16; Quebec, 1870 ***8364.32*** *p23*
Coulter, James 66; Ontario, 1871 ***1823.21*** *p73*
Coulter, John; North Carolina, 1853 ***1088.45*** *p6*
Coulter, John 49; Ontario, 1871 ***1823.17*** *p34*
Coulter, Mary 49; Ontario, 1871 ***1823.21*** *p73*
Coulter, Rose 82; Ontario, 1871 ***1823.17*** *p34*
Coulter, Thomas 58; Ontario, 1871 ***1823.21*** *p73*
Coultered, John; Barbados or St. Christopher, 1780 ***8529.30*** *p7A*
Coulthard, Andrew 66; Ontario, 1871 ***1823.21*** *p73*
Coulthard, Robert 57; Ontario, 1871 ***1823.21*** *p73*
Coultis, William 59; Ontario, 1871 ***1823.21*** *p73*
Coultor, Robert Isiah 43; Ontario, 1871 ***1823.21*** *p73*
Counart, Emile; Wisconsin, 1856 ***1494.20*** *p11*
Counart, Joseph; Wisconsin, 1856 ***1494.20*** *p11*
Counart, Maximilian; New York, NY, 1856 ***1494.20*** *p11*
Counter, Edward; Salem, MA, 1668 ***9228.50*** *p169*
Counter, Edward; Salem, MA, 1668 ***9228.50*** *p340*
Coupet, Francoise; Virginia, 1700 ***9230.15*** *p80*
Courade, Mr. 18; America, 1841 ***778.6*** *p78*
Courage, D. 28; America, 1847 ***778.6*** *p78*
Courage, Hilaire 32; America, 1847 ***778.6*** *p78*
Courault, Pierre; Quebec, 1662 ***9221.17*** *p483*
*Wife:*Suzanne Belanger
Courault, Suzanne Belanger *SEE* Courault, Pierre
Courbelaise, . . . 18; New Orleans, 1840 ***778.6*** *p78*
Courbelaise, Joachim 29; New Orleans, 1840 ***778.6*** *p78*
Courbelaise, Rosalie D. 20; New Orleans, 1840 ***778.6*** *p78*
Courbet, Guillaume 23; Quebec, 1656 ***9221.17*** *p334*
Courcoul, Madeleine; Quebec, 1668 ***4514.3*** *p363*
Courege, Jean 21; America, 1845 ***778.6*** *p78*
Coureges, E. 21; New Orleans, 1847 ***778.6*** *p78*
Courenburg, Constance 36; America, 1847 ***778.6*** *p78*
Courenburg, Marie 1; America, 1847 ***778.6*** *p78*
Courenburg, Marie Eliza 35; America, 1847 ***778.6*** *p78*
Courney, Daniel; Boston, 1835 ***3274.55*** *p25*
Couron, Annie 14; Quebec, 1870 ***8364.32*** *p23*
Courrege, Bernard 24; New Orleans, 1840 ***778.6*** *p78*
Courrege, Paul 40; New Orleans, 1848 ***778.6*** *p78*
Courreges, Fer. 16; New Orleans, 1846 ***778.6*** *p78*
Course, Charles 36; Ontario, 1871 ***1823.21*** *p73*
Coursey, Jane 54; Ontario, 1871 ***1823.21*** *p73*
Coursey, John 60; Ontario, 1871 ***1823.21*** *p73*
Court, A. 40; Mexico, 1845 ***778.6*** *p78*
Court, John 65; Ontario, 1871 ***1823.21*** *p73*
Court, Louis Alexandre 43; America, 1847 ***778.6*** *p78*
Court, William 68; Ontario, 1871 ***1823.21*** *p74*
Courtade, Mr. 22; America, 1841 ***778.6*** *p78*
Courtade, Francois 21; New Orleans, 1845 ***778.6*** *p78*
Courtade, J. 25; America, 1846 ***778.6*** *p78*
Courtade, J. B. 17; New Orleans, 1848 ***778.6*** *p78*
Courtade, P. 29; America, 1846 ***778.6*** *p78*
Courtelmont, Victorine 30; Missouri, 1845 ***778.6*** *p78*
Courtemanche, Antoine 18; Montreal, 1659 ***9221.17*** *p419*
Courtice, John 38; Ontario, 1871 ***1823.21*** *p74*
Courtier, Francis 50; Ontario, 1871 ***1823.21*** *p74*
Courtier, Matilda 19; Ontario, 1871 ***1823.21*** *p74*
Courtigne, Pierre 33; America, 1846 ***778.6*** *p78*
Courtil, William 32; Ontario, 1871 ***1823.21*** *p74*
Courtneidge, William G. 26; Ontario, 1871 ***1823.17*** *p34*
Courtney, Dennis; Illinois, 1860 ***6079.1*** *p4*
Courtney, Humphrey 41; Ontario, 1871 ***1823.21*** *p74*
Courtney, Joseph; Toronto, 1844 ***2910.35*** *p112*
Courtney, Margaret; New Orleans, 1851 ***7242.30*** *p139*
Courtney, Mary; New Orleans, 1851 ***7242.30*** *p139*
Courtney, Thomas; Louisiana, 1874 ***4981.45*** *p131*
Courtois, Ms. 27; Port uncertain, 1845 ***778.6*** *p79*
Courtois, Charles 10; Quebec, 1657 ***9221.17*** *p355*
Courtois, Joseph 23; New Orleans, 1847 ***778.6*** *p79*
Courtois, Michel; Quebec, 1657 ***9221.17*** *p355*
Courtonne, Pierre 31; Louisiana, 1848 ***778.6*** *p79*
Courts, Ann 62; Michigan, 1880 ***4491.30*** *p7*
Courts, Loise 23; Michigan, 1880 ***4491.30*** *p7*
Courts, Philipp B. 59; Michigan, 1880 ***4491.30*** *p7*
Courts, William 30; Michigan, 1880 ***4491.30*** *p7*
Courville, Charles; Quebec, 1646 ***9221.17*** *p164*
Courville, Charles 13; Quebec, 1641 ***9221.17*** *p101*
Courvoisier, Gaspar 21; Texas, 1843 ***778.6*** *p79*
Coury, A. 40; New Orleans, 1844 ***778.6*** *p79*
Couse, George; Ohio, 1809-1852 ***4511.35*** *p9*
Cousens, Anne; New Orleans, 1850 ***7242.30*** *p139*
Cousin, Francoise; Quebec, 1665 ***4514.3*** *p293*
Cousinet, Amandus; Chile, 1852 ***1192.4*** *p51*
Cousin Family ; America, n.d. ***9228.50*** *p169*
Cousins, Eliza 54; Ontario, 1871 ***1823.21*** *p74*
Cousins, Job 43; Ontario, 1871 ***1823.21*** *p74*
Cousins, John 42; Ontario, 1871 ***1823.21*** *p74*
Cousins, John 16; Quebec, 1870 ***8364.32*** *p23*
Cousins, Thomas 57; Ontario, 1871 ***1823.21*** *p74*
Cousins, William 45; Ontario, 1871 ***1823.21*** *p74*

Cousins, William; Washington, 1889 2770.40 p27
Coussant, Jean; Quebec, 1644 9221.17 p140
Cousseau, Pierre; Quebec, 1600-1663 4514.3 p375
Cousseau, Pierre; Quebec, 1655 9221.17 p321
Cousteau, Marie-Madeleine 41; Quebec, 1647 9221.17 p178
Cousture, Guillaume 21; Quebec, 1637 9221.17 p68
Cousturier, Francois; Quebec, 1659 9221.17 p397
Coutanceau, Jacob; Virginia, 1652 6254.4 p243
Coutanch, Jane; Utah, 1855 9228.50 p169
Coutanche, John *SEE* Coutanche, John
Coutanche, John; Utah, 1839-1911 9228.50 p169
*Wife:*Mary Eliz.
*Child:*Mary Ann
*Child:*Philip
*Child:*John
Coutanche, Mary Ann *SEE* Coutanche, John
Coutanche, Mary Eliz. *SEE* Coutanche, John
Coutanche, Michael; North Carolina, 1762 9228.50 p170
Coutanche, Philip *SEE* Coutanche, John
Coutellier, Prosper 36; Louisiana, 1840 778.6 p79
Couter, George 50; Ontario, 1871 1823.17 p34
Couterot, Hubert; Quebec, 1750 2314.30 p170
Couterot, Hubert; Quebec, 1750 2314.30 p178
Couteur, Clement; Nova Scotia, 1753 3051 p112
Coutis, William; Boston, 1764 1642 p33
Coutts, Charles 50; Ontario, 1871 1823.17 p34
Coutts, William 23; New York, NY, 1835 5024.1 p137
Couture, Anne; Quebec, 1665 4514.3 p294
Couturey, Eugene 27; New Orleans, 1840 778.6 p79
Couturier, Isabelle; Quebec, 1670 4514.3 p294
Couturier de Versan, Ed. 24; America, 1842 778.6 p79
Coveney, Honer; Boston, 1767 1642 p39
Coveney, John; Philadelphia, 1778 8529.30 p2A
Coventry, John 35; Ontario, 1871 1823.21 p74
Coveny, John; Philadelphia, 1778 8529.30 p2A
Coveny, Michael 45; Ontario, 1871 1823.21 p74
Covert, Sarah 65; Ontario, 1871 1823.17 p34
Covert, William 28; Ontario, 1871 1823.17 p34
Covroie, Ms. 50; New Orleans, 1847 778.6 p79
Cow, Peter; Portsmouth, NH, 1735 9228.50 p170
Cowan, Alexander 40; Ontario, 1871 1823.21 p74
Cowan, Alexander 42; Ontario, 1871 1823.17 p34
Cowan, David 40; Ontario, 1871 1823.21 p74
Cowan, Dougald 45; Ontario, 1871 1823.21 p74
Cowan, Edward 40; Ontario, 1871 1823.17 p34
Cowan, Edward 53; Ontario, 1871 1823.21 p74
Cowan, Ellen 36; Ontario, 1871 1823.17 p34
Cowan, Hugh 49; Ontario, 1871 1823.21 p74
Cowan, James 39; Ontario, 1871 1823.21 p74
Cowan, James 58; Ontario, 1871 1823.17 p34
Cowan, James 64; Ontario, 1871 1823.17 p34
Cowan, Jane 12; Ontario, 1871 1823.21 p74
Cowan, John 32; Ontario, 1871 1823.17 p34
Cowan, John 78; Ontario, 1871 1823.17 p34
Cowan, John Alexander *SEE* Cowan, William
Cowan, Joseph 23; Michigan, 1880 4491.33 p6
Cowan, Joseph 23; Ontario, 1871 1823.17 p34
Cowan, Mary 21; Ontario, 1871 1823.21 p74
Cowan, Mary 35; Ontario, 1871 1823.21 p74
Cowan, Rebecca Fowler *SEE* Cowan, William
Cowan, Richard 60; Ontario, 1871 1823.21 p74
Cowan, Robert 67; Ontario, 1871 1823.21 p74
Cowan, Ronald 40; Ontario, 1871 1823.21 p74
Cowan, Thomas 37; Ontario, 1871 1823.17 p34
Cowan, William 38; Ontario, 1871 1823.21 p74
Cowan, William 52; Ontario, 1871 1823.17 p34
Cowan, William 64; Ontario, 1871 1823.17 p34
Cowan, William; Philadelphia, 1874 8513.31 p301
*Wife:*Rebecca Fowler
*Son:*John Alexander
Cowe, Peter; Portsmouth, NH, 1735 9228.50 p170
Cowell, Thomas; Barbados or Jamaica, 1696 1220.12 p527
Cowen, James; Boston, 1763 1642 p32
Cowen, John 72; Ontario, 1871 1823.17 p34
Cowen, Peter 50; America, 1841 778.6 p79
Cowen, Robert 32; Ontario, 1871 1823.17 p34
Cowen, Sarah 25; Ontario, 1871 1823.21 p74
Cowie, George; Quebec, 1885 1937.10 p52
Cowie, John 36; Ontario, 1871 1823.21 p74
Cowie, John 75; Ontario, 1871 1823.21 p74
Cowie, Robert 35; Ontario, 1871 1823.21 p74
Cowie, William 45; Ontario, 1871 1823.17 p34
Cowin, Duncan 50; Ontario, 1871 1823.17 p35
Cowin, Elizabeth 7; Ontario, 1871 1823.17 p35
Cowin, James 35; Ontario, 1871 1823.17 p35
Cowin, John 35; Ontario, 1871 1823.17 p35
Cowin, Malcolm 32; Ontario, 1871 1823.17 p35
Cowin, William 40; Ontario, 1871 1823.17 p35
Cowing, John 15; Ontario, 1871 1823.21 p74
Cowing, Prince; Massachusetts, 1775 1642 p116
Cowing, Thomas 42; Ontario, 1871 1823.21 p74
Cowits, William 17; Ontario, 1871 1823.21 p74
Cowley, Edward 47; Ontario, 1871 1823.21 p74
Cowley, John; New York, NY, 1842 3274.56 p100
Cowley, Mary 75; Ontario, 1871 1823.21 p74
Cowley, Michael; Colorado, 1903 1029.59 p19
Cowley, Richard B.; New York, 1819 9228.50 p170
Cowley, Richd.; Maryland, 1674 1236.25 p50
Cowley, Robert W. 46; Ontario, 1871 1823.21 p74
Cowling, John 29; Ontario, 1871 1823.21 p74
Cowling, John 46; Ontario, 1871 1823.21 p74
Cowling, William 19; Ontario, 1871 1823.21 p74
Cowly, Sera 60; Ontario, 1871 1823.21 p75
Cowper, Arthur 18; Ontario, 1871 1823.21 p75
Cox, Esq; Virginia, 1652 6254.4 p243
Cox, Andrew 63; Ontario, 1871 1823.17 p35
Cox, Anne 50; Ontario, 1871 1823.17 p35
Cox, Catharine G. 25; Ontario, 1871 1823.21 p75
Cox, Charles 17; Quebec, 1870 8364.32 p23
Cox, Eliz; Boston, 1716 9228.50 p273
Cox, Eliza 48; Ontario, 1871 1823.21 p75
Cox, George 21; Ontario, 1871 1823.21 p75
Cox, George 52; Ontario, 1871 1823.21 p75
Cox, Harriett 35; Quebec, 1870 8364.32 p23
Cox, James 49; Ontario, 1871 1823.21 p75
Cox, James J. 50; Ontario, 1871 1823.17 p35
Cox, John 40; Michigan, 1880 4491.42 p9
Cox, John 19; Ontario, 1871 1823.21 p75
Cox, John 28; Ontario, 1871 1823.21 p75
Cox, Martha 36; Michigan, 1880 4491.42 p9
Cox, Mary 50; Ontario, 1871 1823.21 p75
Cox, Mary Ann 47; Ontario, 1871 1823.17 p35
Cox, Michael; North Carolina, 1834 1088.45 p6
Cox, Peter 43; Ontario, 1871 1823.21 p75
Cox, Peter; Portsmouth, NH, 1735 9228.50 p170
Cox, Richard 70; Ontario, 1871 1823.21 p75
Cox, Ruth 60; Ontario, 1871 1823.21 p75
Cox, Sam'l; Ontario, 1787 1276.15 p230
With 2 children & 2 relatives
Cox, Thomas 45; Ontario, 1871 1823.21 p75
Cox, Thomas W. 21; Ontario, 1871 1823.21 p75
Cox, W. M. 40; Ontario, 1871 1823.17 p35
Cox, William 35; Ontario, 1871 1823.21 p75
Cox, William 60; Ontario, 1871 1823.17 p35
Cox, William C. 17; Ontario, 1871 1823.21 p75
Coxe, Jno.; Maryland, 1674 1236.25 p50
Coy, Charlotte; Quebec, 1669 4514.3 p294
Coy, John 40; Ontario, 1871 1823.21 p75
Coy, Richard 67; Ontario, 1871 1823.21 p75
Coyer, John W. 44; Ontario, 1871 1823.21 p75
Coyle, Charles 27; Ontario, 1871 1823.17 p35
Coyle, James; New York, NY, 1827 3274.55 p68
Coyle, Jane 21; St. John, N.B., 1834 6469.7 p4
Coyle, John 46; Ontario, 1871 1823.17 p35
Coyle, Mary; Philadelphia, 1855 8513.31 p304
Coyle, Patrick 45; Ontario, 1871 1823.17 p35
Coyle, Thomas; Marston's Wharf, 1782 8529.30 p10
Coyles, Thomas; Marston's Wharf, 1782 8529.30 p10
Coyne, John 65; Ontario, 1871 1823.21 p75
Coyne, John; St. John, N.B., 1848 2978.15 p40
Coyne, Peter 45; Ontario, 1871 1823.17 p35
Coyne, Thimias; Louisiana, 1874 4981.45 p131
Coyne, Thomas; Ohio, 1809-1852 4511.35 p9
Coyne, William 29; Ontario, 1871 1823.21 p75
Coysy, Michel; Quebec, 1634 9221.17 p35
Coz, Sarah Dera.; Jamestown, VA, 1633 1658.20 p211
Cozens, Ferrand 65; Ontario, 1871 1823.21 p75
Crabb, Fredd 21; Ontario, 1871 1823.21 p75
Crabb, Lewis Ellis; Canada, 1882-1982 9228.50 p380
Crack, Frank 28; Ontario, 1871 1823.21 p75
Crackle, John 38; Ontario, 1871 1823.21 p75
Crackston, John *SEE* Crackston, John
Crackston, John; Plymouth, MA, 1620 1920.45 p5
*Son:*John
Craddock, Albert 18; Quebec, 1870 8364.32 p23
Craddock, George 41; Ontario, 1871 1823.21 p75
Craditon, Martha 22; Ontario, 1871 1823.21 p75
Crafford, Sarah; Virginia, 1752 9228.50 p170
Crafford, Stephen; Maine, 1642 9228.50 p170
Craffy, Mark; North Carolina, 1844 1088.45 p6
Craft, Benjamin 64; Michigan, 1880 4491.36 p5
Craft, Herman Friedrich; Wisconsin, 1903 6795.8 p236
Craft, Jane 70; Michigan, 1880 4491.36 p5
Craft, Joseph; South Carolina, 1837 6155.4 p18
Craft, Thomas; Marston's Wharf, 1782 8529.30 p10
Crafts, Eliz.; Maryland, 1674 1236.25 p50
Cragg, John; Louisiana, 1836-1840 4981.45 p212
Cragie, James 36; Ontario, 1871 1823.21 p75
Cragorski, Stanislaw 28; New York, NY, 1894 6512.1 p183
Craib, Alexander 30; Ontario, 1871 1823.21 p75
Craig, Mr.; Prince Edward Island, 1771 3799.30 p41
Craig, Andrew W. 34; Ontario, 1871 1823.17 p35
Craig, Charles; North Carolina, 1854-1856 1088.45 p6
Craig, David 58; Ontario, 1871 1823.21 p75
Craig, Elizabeth 34; Ontario, 1871 1823.17 p35
Craig, James 38; Ontario, 1871 1823.17 p35
Craig, James 42; Ontario, 1871 1823.21 p75
Craig, James 81; Ontario, 1871 1823.21 p75
Craig, Jane 22; Ontario, 1871 1823.21 p76
Craig, Janet 52; Ontario, 1871 1823.21 p76
Craig, John; Charleston, SC, 1820 3274.55 p68
Craig, John; North Carolina, 1825 1088.45 p6
Craig, John 27; Ontario, 1871 1823.21 p76
Craig, John 40; Ontario, 1871 1823.21 p76
Craig, John 45; Ontario, 1871 1823.21 p76
Craig, John 54; Ontario, 1871 1823.17 p35
Craig, John J. 36; Ontario, 1871 1823.21 p76
Craig, Samuel 45; Ontario, 1871 1823.17 p35
Craig, Thomas 30; Michigan, 1880 4491.39 p6
Craig, Thomas 45; Ontario, 1871 1823.21 p76
Craig, William; North Carolina, 1817 1088.45 p6
Craig, William 32; Ontario, 1871 1823.21 p76
Craig, William 64; Ontario, 1871 1823.17 p35
Craik, James 35; Ontario, 1871 1823.21 p76
Craine, Dr. 30; Ontario, 1871 1823.21 p76
Craine, Thomas 37; Ontario, 1871 1823.17 p35
Craine, William 32; Ontario, 1871 1823.21 p76
Cram, Simeon 46; Ohio, 1880 4879.40 p258
Cramer, Albert 32; Indiana, 1866-1870 9076.20 p67
Cramer, Christian; Ohio, 1809-1852 4511.35 p9
Cramer, Cornelius; Ohio, 1809-1852 4511.35 p9
Cramer, Eduard Johann; America, 1867 7919.3 p535
Cramer, Elisabeth; America, 1864 8115.12 p326
Cramer, Marie; America, 1864 8115.12 p326
With sisters
Cramer, Ullrich; Brazil, 1902 7420.1 p378
Cramer, Ullrich; Brazil, 1904 7420.1 p379
Crampon, Catherine 20; Quebec, 1662 9221.17 p483
Cran, Robert 40; Ontario, 1871 1823.17 p35
Crandall, Auguste; Louisiana, 1874 4981.45 p131
Crane, Benjamin 67; Michigan, 1880 4491.36 p5
Crane, Jean; Quebec, 1659 9221.17 p413
Crane, William 60; Ontario, 1871 1823.21 p76
Craney, Michael; Toronto, 1844 2910.35 p113
Crannell, Anna 30; Michigan, 1880 4491.36 p5
Cranney, George James; Washington, 1882 2770.40 p135
Cranston, Hamilton 41; Ontario, 1871 1823.17 p35
Cranston, James 60; Ontario, 1871 1823.21 p76
Cranston, Sam'l 33; Ontario, 1871 1823.17 p35
Cranston, Thomas 74; Ontario, 1871 1823.17 p35
Crapa, Francis; Wisconsin, 1878 6795.8 p46
Crapaud, Pierre; New England, n.d. 9228.50 p170
Crapo, Pierre; New England, n.d. 9228.50 p170
Crapper, Thomas 51; Ontario, 1871 1823.17 p35
Crautmann, Guillaume 21; New York, NY, 1894 6512.1 p182
Crauz, Charles F.; Ohio, 1809-1852 4511.35 p9
Craven, Miss; California, 1924 9228.50 p576
Craven, James 47; Michigan, 1880 4491.39 p6
Craven, Linwood 52; Ontario, 1871 1823.21 p76
Cravin, Bridget; New Orleans, 1851 7242.30 p139
Cravin, Honora; New Orleans, 1851 7242.30 p139
Cravin, Martin; New Orleans, 1851 7242.30 p139
Cravin, Mary; New Orleans, 1851 7242.30 p139
Cravin, Michael; New Orleans, 1851 7242.30 p139
Crawford, Alexander 52; Ontario, 1871 1823.21 p76
Crawford, Allen 60; Ontario, 1871 1823.17 p35
Crawford, Andrew 24; Ontario, 1871 1823.21 p76
Crawford, Andrew 37; Ontario, 1871 1823.21 p76
Crawford, Andrew 38; Ontario, 1871 1823.21 p76
Crawford, Annie 9; Quebec, 1870 8364.32 p23
Crawford, Archibald 50; Ontario, 1871 1823.21 p76
Crawford, Charles 28; Ontario, 1871 1823.21 p76
Crawford, Christena 66; Ontario, 1871 1823.21 p76
Crawford, David 45; Ontario, 1871 1823.17 p35
Crawford, Dennis 46; Ontario, 1871 1823.21 p76
Crawford, Donald 42; Ontario, 1871 1823.17 p35
Crawford, Donald 46; Ontario, 1871 1823.21 p76
Crawford, Dugald 53; Ontario, 1871 1823.21 p76
Crawford, Duncan 42; Ontario, 1871 1823.21 p76
Crawford, Georgiana 9; New York, NY, 1835 5024.1 p137
Crawford, Grace 55; Ontario, 1871 1823.21 p76
Crawford, Helen 18; New York, NY, 1835 5024.1 p137
Crawford, Isabella 24; New York, NY, 1835 5024.1 p137
Crawford, Isabella 29; Ontario, 1871 1823.21 p76
Crawford, James; North America, 1750 1640.8 p234
Crawford, James 36; Ontario, 1871 1823.21 p76
Crawford, James 52; Ontario, 1871 1823.21 p76
Crawford, James 56; Ontario, 1871 1823.21 p76
Crawford, James; South Carolina, 1861 6155.4 p18
Crawford, John 45; Ontario, 1871 1823.17 p35
Crawford, John 50; Ontario, 1871 1823.21 p76
Crawford, John 51; Ontario, 1871 1823.17 p35

Crawford, John 68; Ontario, 1871 ***1823.21*** *p76*
Crawford, Mary 54; Ontario, 1871 ***1823.21*** *p76*
Crawford, Niel 26; Ontario, 1871 ***1823.17*** *p35*
Crawford, Robert; New York, NY, 1778 ***8529.30*** *p2*
Crawford, Robert 35; Ontario, 1871 ***1823.17*** *p35*
Crawford, Samuel 34; Ontario, 1871 ***1823.21*** *p76*
Crawford, Samuel 53; Ontario, 1871 ***1823.17*** *p36*
Crawford, Sarah; Virginia, 1752 ***9228.50*** *p170*
Crawford, Stephen; Maine, 1642 ***9228.50*** *p170*
Crawford, Thomas 46; Ontario, 1871 ***1823.17*** *p36*
Crawford, Thomas 50; Ontario, 1871 ***1823.17*** *p36*
Crawford, William 21; New York, NY, 1835 ***5024.1*** *p137*
Crawford, William 32; Ontario, 1871 ***1823.17*** *p36*
Crawford, William 35; Ontario, 1871 ***1823.17*** *p36*
Crawley, Dennis 23; Ontario, 1871 ***1823.17*** *p36*
Crawley, Mary; Halifax, N.S., 1827 ***7009.9*** *p61*
Crawley, Phillip 50; Ontario, 1871 ***1823.21*** *p76*
Crawley, Timothy 63; Ontario, 1871 ***1823.21*** *p76*
Crawthers, Ellen 40; Ontario, 1871 ***1823.17*** *p36*
Crayton, Abraham 43; Ontario, 1871 ***1823.21*** *p76*
Craze, Dorothy 7; Quebec, 1910 ***2897.7*** *p8*
Craze, Ethel 1; Quebec, 1910 ***2897.7*** *p8*
Craze, Julia 37; Quebec, 1910 ***2897.7*** *p8*
Craze, Wm. 3; Quebec, 1910 ***2897.7*** *p8*
Craze, Wm. 43; Quebec, 1910 ***2897.7*** *p8*
Creagh, Ann; Boston, 1739 ***1642*** *p44*
Creane, Sarah 62; Ontario, 1871 ***1823.17*** *p36*
Creasey, Moses 50; Ontario, 1871 ***1823.17*** *p36*
Creaton, James; Jamaica, 1780 ***8529.30*** *p12A*
Crebbs, John; Ohio, 1809-1852 ***4511.35*** *p9*
Crebo, Grace; Colorado, 1902 ***1029.59*** *p19*
Crebo, Grace 39; Colorado, 1902 ***1029.59*** *p19*
Credeford, John; Nova Scotia, 1709-1745 ***9228.50*** *p148*
Creech, Annie 15; Quebec, 1870 ***8364.32*** *p23*
Creech, Susan 14; Quebec, 1870 ***8364.32*** *p23*
Creed, George; Illinois, 1858 ***6079.1*** *p4*
Creef, Corat; North Carolina, 1806 ***1088.45*** *p7*
Creegan, Miles; Washington, 1889 ***2770.40*** *p27*
Creeke, Edwd.; Maryland, 1672 ***1236.25*** *p47*
Crehan, William; Newfoundland, 1814 ***3476.10*** *p54*
Crehore, Timothy; Massachusetts, 1688 ***1642*** *p106*
Creig, William 36; Ontario, 1871 ***1823.21*** *p77*
Creighton, David; Prince Edward Island, 1839 ***9228.50*** *p130*
Creighton, Francis 54; Ontario, 1871 ***1823.17*** *p36*
Creighton, Hugh; Ohio, 1809-1852 ***4511.35*** *p9*
Creighton, James; San Francisco, 1848-1900 ***9228.50*** *p131*
Creighton, John; Philadelphia, 1856 ***8513.31*** *p301*
*Wife:*Margaret Kenney
Creighton, John Robert; California, 1873 ***9228.50*** *p130*
Creighton, Margaret Kenney *SEE* Creighton, John
Creighton, Rebecca; New York, 1739 ***8277.31*** *p119*
Cremer, Anton 23; Galveston, TX, 1844 ***3967.10*** *p375*
Crenel, Jean; Quebec, 1651 ***9221.17*** *p244*
Crepel, Francoise 17; Quebec, 1662 ***9221.17*** *p483*
Crepin, Marie; Quebec, 1667 ***4514.3*** *p294*
Creps, John; Ohio, 1809-1852 ***4511.35*** *p9*
Crescen, Abel 23; Port uncertain, 1844 ***778.6*** *p79*
Cresob, John; Maryland, 1672 ***1236.25*** *p47*
Crespeau, Jean 19; Quebec, 1656 ***9221.17*** *p334*
Crespeau, Jeanne 43; Montreal, 1659 ***9221.17*** *p424*
Crespeau, Maurice 21; Quebec, 1661 ***9221.17*** *p452*
Cress, Johann Peter 28; Nova Scotia, 1852 ***170.15*** *p22*
With wife & 2 children
Cress, William B. 38; Ontario, 1871 ***1823.21*** *p77*
Creste, Jean 23; Quebec, 1649 ***9221.17*** *p211*
Cretel, Elisabeth; Quebec, 1671 ***4514.3*** *p294*
Cretien, Donna 19; New Orleans, 1848 ***778.6*** *p79*
Cretien, Johann Michel; America, 1837 ***5475.1*** *p73*
Cretien, Veuve 55; New Orleans, 1848 ***778.6*** *p79*
Cretien, Victorine 17; New Orleans, 1848 ***778.6*** *p79*
Cretin, Constant 35; America, 1843 ***778.6*** *p79*
Cretin, Mary 23; America, 1843 ***778.6*** *p79*
Cretitlo, L.; Louisiana, 1874-1875 ***4981.45*** *p298*
Creton, Henri 28; New Orleans, 1848 ***778.6*** *p79*
Creuset, Mr. 25; America, 1846 ***778.6*** *p79*
Creutz, Sophie Elisabeth 51; America, 1857 ***2526.43*** *p176*
Creux, Charles 2; Louisiana, 1848 ***778.6*** *p79*
Creux, Francois 32; Louisiana, 1848 ***778.6*** *p79*
Creux, Francoise 9; Louisiana, 1848 ***778.6*** *p79*
Creux, Francoise 33; Louisiana, 1848 ***778.6*** *p79*
Creux, Justine 4; Louisiana, 1848 ***778.6*** *p79*
Creux, Theodore 6; Louisiana, 1848 ***778.6*** *p79*
Creven, Patrick; New York, NY, 1828 ***3274.55*** *p71*
Crevet, Marie 16; Quebec, 1637 ***9221.17*** *p68*
Crevier, Andre; Quebec, 1642 ***9221.17*** *p114*
Crevier, Antoine; Quebec, 1649 ***9221.17*** *p211*
*Sister:*Marguerite
*Brother:*Jean-Baptiste
*Sister:*Marie
*Brother:*Jerome
Crevier, Christophe 27; Quebec, 1639 ***9221.17*** *p86*
*Wife:*Jeanne Enart 16
*Daughter:*Jeanne 2
Crevier, Jean-Baptiste *SEE* Crevier, Antoine
Crevier, Jeanne 2 *SEE* Crevier, Christophe
Crevier, Jeanne Enart 16 *SEE* Crevier, Christophe
Crevier, Jerome *SEE* Crevier, Antoine
Crevier, Marguerite 4 *SEE* Crevier, Antoine
Crevier, Marie *SEE* Crevier, Antoine
Crews, Thomas 49; Ontario, 1871 ***1823.21*** *p77*
Creyton, James 49; Ontario, 1871 ***1823.21*** *p77*
Crichton, David; Prince Edward Island, 1839 ***9228.50*** *p130*
Crichton, James; San Francisco, 1848-1900 ***9228.50*** *p131*
Crichton, John Robert; California, 1873 ***9228.50*** *p130*
Crick, Sarah 22; Quebec, 1870 ***8364.32*** *p23*
Cricket, George 59; Ontario, 1871 ***1823.21*** *p77*
Crimiti, Jadwiga; Detroit, 1929 ***1640.55*** *p115*
Crimma, Joseph 27; Louisiana, 1848 ***778.6*** *p79*
Crinklaw, John 61; Ontario, 1871 ***1823.21*** *p77*
Crinshaw, Thos 34; Ontario, 1871 ***1823.21*** *p77*
Cripps, Eliza 29; Quebec, 1870 ***8364.32*** *p23*
Crisafy, Antoine de; Quebec, 1683-1688 ***2314.30*** *p168*
Crisafy, Antoine de; Quebec, 1684 ***2314.30*** *p178*
Crisafy, Thomas de; Quebec, 1683-1688 ***2314.30*** *p168*
Crisafy, Thomas de; Quebec, 1684 ***2314.30*** *p179*
Crisman, Jean; New Orleans, 1840 ***778.6*** *p79*
Crisman, M. 20; Halifax, N.S., 1902 ***1860.4*** *p44*
Crisp, S. A.; Washington, 1887 ***2770.40*** *p24*
Crispin, George 66; Ontario, 1871 ***1823.21*** *p77*
Crispin, Maria 24; New York, NY, 1885 ***1883.7*** *p45*
Crispin, Thomas 44; Ontario, 1871 ***1823.21*** *p77*
Crissey, Christian; Ohio, 1809-1852 ***4511.35*** *p9*
Crisswell, James; New York, 1778 ***8529.30*** *p2A*
Crissy, Christian, Jr.; Ohio, 1809-1852 ***4511.35*** *p9*
Cristy, Elizabeth; Philadelphia, 1868 ***8513.31*** *p416*
Critchton, Robert; North Carolina, 1835 ***1088.45*** *p7*
Criton, John; North America, 1750 ***1640.8*** *p234*
Crivel, Angelite 20; New Orleans, 1848 ***778.6*** *p79*
Croake, Johanna 58; Ontario, 1871 ***1823.21*** *p77*
Crockard, Alexander 38; Ontario, 1871 ***1823.17*** *p36*
Crocker, Edmund; New York, NY, 1834 ***3274.55*** *p26*
Crocker, James 58; Ontario, 1871 ***1823.21*** *p77*
Crocker, John 33; Ontario, 1871 ***1823.21*** *p77*
Crocker, Jonathan; New York, NY, 1834 ***3274.55*** *p75*
Crocker, Sarah; Nova Scotia, 1795 ***9228.50*** *p640*
Crocker, William 29; Ontario, 1871 ***1823.21*** *p77*
Crocker, William 50; Ontario, 1871 ***1823.17*** *p36*
Crocket, Joseph 32; America, 1846 ***778.6*** *p79*
Crocket, William; North Carolina, 1842 ***1088.45*** *p7*
Crockett, Elena 20; Ontario, 1871 ***1823.21*** *p77*
Crockett, John 60; Ontario, 1871 ***1823.21*** *p77*
Croft, Eliz.; Maryland, 1674 ***1236.25*** *p50*
Croft, Elizabeth 17; Ontario, 1871 ***1823.21*** *p77*
Croft, John 34; Ontario, 1871 ***1823.17*** *p36*
Croft, Robert 37; Ontario, 1871 ***1823.21*** *p77*
Croft, Thomas; Marston's Wharf, 1782 ***8529.30*** *p10*
Crofts, Daniel W.; Ohio, 1850 ***3580.20*** *p31*
Crofts, Daniel W.; Ohio, 1850 ***6020.12*** *p7*
Crogan, Thomas; Toronto, 1844 ***2910.35*** *p114*
Croggin, Cornelius; Barnstable, MA, 1664 ***1642*** *p84*
Croggin, Thomas; Barnstable, MA, 1650 ***1642*** *p84*
Croghn, Davis 40; Ontario, 1871 ***1823.17*** *p36*
Crohave, Jn. Pierre 18; New Orleans, 1846 ***778.6*** *p79*
Crohoar, Teag; Boston, 1620-1775 ***1642*** *p138*
Croin, James F. 10; Ontario, 1871 ***1823.17*** *p36*
Croiset, Marie; Quebec, 1671 ***4514.3*** *p294*
Croix, . . .; Massachusetts, n.d. ***9228.50*** *p170*
Croley, Jeremiah; Toronto, 1844 ***2910.35*** *p113*
Crolley, Sarah; Lexington, MA, 1738 ***1642*** *p105*
Crolo, Catherine 41; Montreal, 1659 ***9221.17*** *p415*
Cromby, John 51; Ontario, 1871 ***1823.21*** *p77*
Cromer, Carl Heinrich; America, 1868 ***7420.1*** *p270*
*Wife:*Wilhelmine Christine Bellersen
With children
*Son:*Heinrich Ferdinand
Cromer, Heinrich Ferdinand *SEE* Cromer, Carl Heinrich
Cromer, Heinrich Wilhelm; America, 1872 ***7420.1*** *p294*
Cromer, Wilhelmine Christine Bellersen *SEE* Cromer, Carl Heinrich
Cromgouan, A. 21; America, 1846 ***778.6*** *p79*
Crompton, George 43; Michigan, 1880 ***4491.30*** *p7*
Cromwell, Gershon; Virginia, 1652 ***6254.4*** *p244*
Cron, Anna *SEE* Cron, Josef
Cron, August; New York, 1886 ***5475.1*** *p48*
Cron, Francis; Ohio, 1809-1852 ***4511.35*** *p9*
Cron, Johann *SEE* Cron, Josef
Cron, John; Ohio, 1809-1852 ***4511.35*** *p9*
Cron, Josef; America, 1874 ***5475.1*** *p175*
*Wife:*Kath. Kramer
*Son:*Johann
*Son:*Peter
*Daughter:*Anna
*Daughter:*Maria
Cron, Kath. Kramer *SEE* Cron, Josef
Cron, Louise *SEE* Cron, Peter Christian
Cron, Maria *SEE* Cron, Josef
Cron, Peter *SEE* Cron, Josef
Cron, Peter Christian; America, 1870 ***5475.1*** *p43*
*Wife:*Sophie Rink
*Daughter:*Louise
*Son:*Peter Ludwig
Cron, Peter Ludwig *SEE* Cron, Peter Christian
Cron, Sophie Rink 32 *SEE* Cron, Peter Christian
Cronan, J.; California, 1868 ***1131.61*** *p89*
Crone, Francis 51; Ontario, 1871 ***1823.17*** *p36*
Crone, John 46; Ontario, 1871 ***1823.21*** *p77*
Crone, Samuel 51; Ontario, 1871 ***1823.21*** *p77*
Croney, Thomas Martin; Washington, 1887 ***2770.40*** *p24*
Cronholm, C.; New York, NY, 1847 ***6412.40*** *p149*
Cronin, Francis; St. John, N.B., 1847 ***2978.15*** *p36*
Cronin, James 76; Ontario, 1871 ***1823.17*** *p36*
Cronin, John; New York, NY, 1907 ***6212.1*** *p14*
Cronland, Charles R. F.; North Carolina, 1856 ***1088.45*** *p7*
Cronney, Mack; Springfield, MA, 1725 ***1642*** *p120*
Cronney, William Mack; Springfield, MA, 1685 ***1642*** *p120*
Cronnon, Susanna; Massachusetts, 1745 ***1642*** *p85*
Cronyn, Anne 16; Ontario, 1871 ***1823.17*** *p36*
Cronyn, John 60; Ontario, 1871 ***1823.17*** *p36*
Cronyn, John; Toronto, 1844 ***2910.35*** *p115*
Cronyn, Martha 44; Ontario, 1871 ***1823.21*** *p77*
Crook, John 39; Ontario, 1871 ***1823.17*** *p36*
Crook, John 61; Ontario, 1871 ***1823.21*** *p77*
Crooks, John 32; Ontario, 1871 ***1823.21*** *p77*
Crooks, Robert 15; Quebec, 1870 ***8364.32*** *p23*
Crooks, William 43; Ontario, 1871 ***1823.21*** *p77*
Crookshank, George 55; Ontario, 1871 ***1823.21*** *p77*
Croper, Thomas; New York, 1776 ***8529.30*** *p10*
Cropp, Adam; Illinois, 1856 ***6079.1*** *p4*
Croquart, Jules 28; America, 1843 ***778.6*** *p79*
Crosbey, Margaret 60; Ontario, 1871 ***1823.17*** *p36*
Crosby, Christopher 28; Ontario, 1871 ***1823.21*** *p77*
Crosby, Ewen K.; Washington, 1884 ***2770.40*** *p192*
Crosby, George; Ontario, 1787 ***1276.15*** *p230*
With child & relative
Crosby, John 30; Indiana, 1878-1880 ***9076.20*** *p69*
Crosby, Robert 26; Ontario, 1871 ***1823.21*** *p77*
Crosby, William 52; Ontario, 1871 ***1823.21*** *p77*
Croskell, Mary Hargreaves; Texas, 1885 ***9228.50*** *p476*
Crosnier, Andre; Quebec, 1642 ***9221.17*** *p114*
Crosnier, Jeanne; Quebec, 1669 ***4514.3*** *p294*
Crosnier, Martine; Quebec, 1669 ***4514.3*** *p295*
Cross, . . .; Massachusetts, n.d. ***9228.50*** *p170*
Cross, Abraham; Marblehead, MA, 1700 ***9228.50*** *p170*
Cross, Benjamin *SEE* Cross, William
Cross, Cabot *SEE* Cross, William
Cross, Charles 40; Michigan, 1880 ***4491.30*** *p7*
Cross, Christian; Ohio, 1809-1852 ***4511.35*** *p9*
Cross, Eveline E. 14; Michigan, 1880 ***4491.30*** *p7*
Cross, Henry; Ohio, 1809-1852 ***4511.35*** *p9*
Cross, Jacob; Ohio, 1809-1852 ***4511.35*** *p9*
Cross, James *SEE* Cross, William
Cross, John; Virginia, 1652 ***6254.4*** *p243*
Cross, Joseph 53; Ontario, 1871 ***1823.17*** *p36*
Cross, Ludwig; Ohio, 1809-1852 ***4511.35*** *p9*
Cross, Mary E. 17; Michigan, 1880 ***4491.30*** *p7*
Cross, Moses, Jr. *SEE* Cross, William
Cross, Noah; New York, 1776 ***8529.30*** *p10*
Cross, Rowland 27; Ontario, 1871 ***1823.17*** *p36*
Cross, Sarah J. 16; Michigan, 1880 ***4491.30*** *p7*
Cross, William; Maine, 1715-1716 ***9228.50*** *p132*
Cross, William; Maine, 1778 ***9228.50*** *p170*
*Relative:*James
*Relative:*Benjamin
*Relative:*Moses, Jr.
*Relative:*Cabot
Crosse, William 23; Ontario, 1871 ***1823.21*** *p77*
Crossen, Richard 19; Ontario, 1871 ***1823.21*** *p77*
Crossly, Mary Ann 75; Ontario, 1871 ***1823.21*** *p77*
Crothers, Joseph 47; Ontario, 1871 ***1823.21*** *p77*
Crothers, Wm 36; Ontario, 1871 ***1823.21*** *p78*
Crotty, Con 23; St. Johns, N.F., 1811 ***1053.20*** *p19*
Crouch, James; Washington, 1889 ***2770.40*** *p27*
Crouch, William 36; Ontario, 1871 ***1823.17*** *p36*
Croucher, George 26; Ontario, 1871 ***1823.21*** *p78*
Crouchman, Edward 47; Ontario, 1871 ***1823.21*** *p78*
Croudy, Charles 50; Ontario, 1871 ***1823.21*** *p78*
Crouigneau, J. A. 23; New Orleans, 1848 ***778.6*** *p79*
Crouse, George; Ohio, 1809-1852 ***4511.35*** *p9*

Crout, N. C.; Ohio, 1809-1852 ***4511.35*** *p9*
Crouzeilles, Louis 24; New Orleans, 1746 ***778.6*** *p80*
Crovetto, C. J.; Louisiana, 1874 ***4981.45*** *p295*
Crow, Andrew; St. John, N.B., 1847 ***2978.15*** *p38*
Crow, Braithwait 55; Ontario, 1871 ***1823.21*** *p78*
Crow, Charles; Marston's Wharf, 1782 ***8529.30*** *p10*
Crow, Elizabeth 66; Ontario, 1871 ***1823.21*** *p78*
Crow, James J. 37; Ontario, 1871 ***1823.21*** *p78*
Crow, John; New Orleans, 1851 ***7242.30*** *p139*
Crow, John; North Carolina, 1818 ***1088.45*** *p7*
Crow, John 55; Ontario, 1871 ***1823.21*** *p78*
Crow, Mary 50; Ontario, 1871 ***1823.21*** *p78*
Crow, Moses 20; Ontario, 1871 ***1823.21*** *p78*
Crow, Solomon 60; Ontario, 1871 ***1823.17*** *p36*
Crowden, Thomas 6; Ontario, 1871 ***1823.21*** *p78*
Crowe, Charlotte 41; New York, NY, 1884 ***8427.14*** *p45*
Crowe, Wm. 10; New York, NY, 1884 ***8427.14*** *p45*
Crowe, Wm. 13; New York, NY, 1884 ***8427.14*** *p45*
Crowill, Samuel; Ontario, 1787 ***1276.15*** *p230*
With child & 2 relatives
Crowl, John G.; Colorado, 1882 ***1029.59*** *p20*
Crowley, Bartholomew; New England, 1745 ***1642*** *p28*
Crowley, Cornelius; Marston's Wharf, 1782 ***8529.30*** *p10*
Crowley, Darby; New England, 1745 ***1642*** *p28*
Crowley, James; Marston's Wharf, 1782 ***8529.30*** *p10*
Crowley, Jeremiah 49; Ontario, 1871 ***1823.21*** *p78*
Crowley, Jeremiah; Trenton, NJ, 1829 ***3274.56*** *p97*
Crowley, John; Roxbury, MA, 1756 ***1642*** *p107*
Crowley, Katharine; Boston, 1740 ***1642*** *p45*
Crowley, Mary; Salem, MA, 1708 ***1642*** *p78*
Crowley, Patrick 40; Ontario, 1871 ***1823.21*** *p78*
Crowley, Timothy; Massachusetts, 1766 ***1642*** *p66*
Crown, George 39; Ontario, 1871 ***1823.17*** *p36*
Crowther, Richard 17; Quebec, 1870 ***8364.32*** *p23*
Crowthers, Joseph 48; Ontario, 1871 ***1823.21*** *p78*
Crozat, Pierre; Illinois, 1852 ***6079.1*** *p4*
Crozier, Fanny; Pennsylvania, 1858 ***8513.31*** *p312*
Crozier, John B. 36; Ontario, 1871 ***1823.21*** *p78*
Crozier, Robert 60; Ontario, 1871 ***1823.21*** *p78*
Cruan, Pierre 40; America, 1841 ***778.6*** *p80*
Crues, Joseph 47; Ontario, 1871 ***1823.21*** *p78*
Cruickshank, Alexander D. 30; Ontario, 1871 ***1823.21*** *p78*
Cruickshank, Geo 48; Ontario, 1871 ***1823.17*** *p37*
Cruickshank, John 60; Ontario, 1871 ***1823.21*** *p78*
Cruickshank, Lewis 50; Ontario, 1871 ***1823.21*** *p78*
Cruikshank, Catherine 59; Ontario, 1871 ***1823.21*** *p78*
Cruikshank, James 60; Ontario, 1871 ***1823.17*** *p37*
Cruikshank, John 35; Ontario, 1871 ***1823.21*** *p78*
Cruikshank, Peter 31; Ontario, 1871 ***1823.21*** *p78*
Cruikshank, Robert 65; Ontario, 1871 ***1823.21*** *p78*
Cruise, Joseph 55; Ontario, 1871 ***1823.17*** *p37*
Crummer, John 46; Ontario, 1871 ***1823.21*** *p78*
Crumsee, George; New Orleans, 1851 ***7242.30*** *p139*
Crundewell, Thomas 40; Ontario, 1871 ***1823.17*** *p37*
Crunicon, Michael 48; Ontario, 1871 ***1823.21*** *p78*
Cruse, John; New York, 1776 ***8529.30*** *p2A*
Crusson, Francois 17; Montreal, 1653 ***9221.17*** *p286*
Crust, Joseph 42; New York, NY, 1894 ***6512.1*** *p182*
Crutchell, William; Jamaica, 1783 ***8529.30*** *p12A*
Crutin, P. M.; Louisiana, 1874 ***4981.45*** *p131*
Cruttenden, Benjamin 18; Quebec, 1870 ***8364.32*** *p23*
Cryens, John 59; Indiana, 1893 ***9076.20*** *p73*
Crynes, James 31; Indiana, 1892-1893 ***9076.20*** *p73*
Crynes, Patrick; Louisiana, 1847-1855 ***7710.1*** *p155*
Crysler, Lucry 66; Ontario, 1871 ***1823.17*** *p37*
Cryton, Emily 74; Ontario, 1871 ***1823.21*** *p78*
Cuadiado, Vincent; Louisiana, 1874 ***4981.45*** *p131*
Cubeck, Mrs. 40; New Orleans, 1843 ***778.6*** *p80*
Cubeck, Emily 5; New Orleans, 1843 ***778.6*** *p80*
Cubeck, Sophia 7; New Orleans, 1843 ***778.6*** *p80*
Cubelar, John; New York, 1778 ***8529.30*** *p6*
Cuccia, Antonio; Louisiana, 1874 ***4981.45*** *p131*
Cuche, Emelie 29; America, 1843 ***778.6*** *p80*
Cuche, Pierre 38; America, 1843 ***778.6*** *p80*
Cucinelli, John; Minnesota, 1925 ***2769.54*** *p1384*
Cucinelli, Robert 20; Minnesota, 1925 ***2769.54*** *p1384*
Cucinneu, Antoin 46; America, 1847 ***778.6*** *p80*
Cucinneu, Cath. 9; America, 1847 ***778.6*** *p80*
Cucinneu, Guntor 8; America, 1847 ***778.6*** *p80*
Cucinneu, Marie 46; America, 1847 ***778.6*** *p80*
Cucinneu, Ross 16; America, 1847 ***778.6*** *p80*
Cucumber, Thomas 35; Ontario, 1871 ***1823.17*** *p37*
Cuddy, James 63; Ontario, 1871 ***1823.21*** *p78*
Cuddy, Thomas 57; Ontario, 1871 ***1823.21*** *p78*
Cudlin, Matthew 46; Ontario, 1871 ***1823.17*** *p37*
Cudney, Pharas 70; Ontario, 1871 ***1823.21*** *p78*
Cuevas, Pedro; Florida, 1843 ***8481.1*** *p18*
Cuff, John; Boston, 1753 ***1642*** *p31*
Cuilhe, Francois 23; New Orleans, 1844 ***778.6*** *p80*
Cuilhe, J. Pierre 19; New Orleans, 1848 ***778.6*** *p80*
Cuillerier, Rene 20; Montreal, 1659 ***9221.17*** *p420*
Culbert, James 53; Ontario, 1871 ***1823.21*** *p78*
Culbert, Richard 50; Ontario, 1871 ***1823.17*** *p37*
Culbert, Thomas 27; Ontario, 1871 ***1823.21*** *p78*
Culbort, William 46; Ontario, 1871 ***1823.21*** *p79*
Culburt, John 64; Ontario, 1871 ***1823.21*** *p79*
Culburt, Thomas 38; Ontario, 1871 ***1823.21*** *p79*
Culer, Christoph 9; America, 1846 ***778.6*** *p80*
Culer, Jean 2; America, 1846 ***778.6*** *p80*
Culer, Marguerite 4; America, 1846 ***778.6*** *p80*
Culer, Marie 35; America, 1846 ***778.6*** *p80*
Culer, Nanette 3; America, 1846 ***778.6*** *p80*
Culer, Nicolas 36; America, 1846 ***778.6*** *p80*
Culkeen, Mary; Ontario, 1835 ***3160.1*** *p150*
Culkeen, Mary; Prescott, Ont., 1835 ***3289.1*** *p61*
Culkeen, Michael; Ontario, 1835 ***3160.1*** *p150*
Culkeen, Michael; Prescott, Ont., 1835 ***3289.1*** *p61*
Culken, William; South Carolina, 1846 ***6155.4*** *p18*
Cull, Martin; Illinois, 1855 ***6079.1*** *p4*
Cull, P. J.; Washington, 1883 ***2770.40*** *p136*
Cullane, Martin; Illinois, 1855 ***6079.1*** *p4*
Cullen, Ambrose; New Orleans, 1850 ***7242.30*** *p139*
Cullen, Ann 33; Ontario, 1871 ***1823.21*** *p79*
Cullen, Anne; New Orleans, 1850 ***7242.30*** *p139*
Cullen, Anne; New Orleans, 1851 ***7242.30*** *p139*
Cullen, Bridget; New Orleans, 1851 ***7242.30*** *p139*
Cullen, Honora; New Orleans, 1851 ***7242.30*** *p139*
Cullen, James; New Orleans, 1851 ***7242.30*** *p139*
Cullen, James 28; Ontario, 1871 ***1823.17*** *p37*
Cullen, James 18; Quebec, 1870 ***8364.32*** *p23*
Cullen, Jane; New Orleans, 1851 ***7242.30*** *p139*
Cullen, John 50; Ontario, 1871 ***1823.21*** *p79*
Cullen, Peter 34; Ontario, 1871 ***1823.17*** *p37*
Cullen, Thomas; New Orleans, 1851 ***7242.30*** *p139*
Cullen, Thomas 46; Ontario, 1871 ***1823.17*** *p37*
Culley, Patrick 61; Ontario, 1871 ***1823.17*** *p37*
Cullidon, David; Philadelphia, 1857 ***8513.31*** *p302*
*Wife:*Mary McLaughlin
*Son:*Thomas
Cullidon, Mary McLaughlin *SEE* Cullidon, David
Cullidon, Thomas *SEE* Cullidon, David
Cullier, John; Maryland, 1672 ***1236.25*** *p47*
Culligan, Michael 49; Ontario, 1871 ***1823.21*** *p79*
Cullin, John; New York, 1836 ***471.10*** *p61*
Cullinan, James 27; Ontario, 1871 ***1823.17*** *p37*
Cullivan, William; Ohio, 1840-1897 ***8365.35*** *p15*
Cully, Barney; Illinois, 1834-1900 ***6020.5*** *p131*
Cully, John 85; Ontario, 1871 ***1823.21*** *p79*
Cully, Robert 38; Ontario, 1871 ***1823.17*** *p37*
Culmann, Ludwig; America, 1847 ***5475.1*** *p473*
Culmer, James Whitford; Miami, 1920 ***4984.15*** *p38*
Culnane, Patt; New Orleans, 1851 ***7242.30*** *p139*
Culp, Benjamin H.; Ohio, 1861 ***3580.20*** *p31*
Culp, Benjamin H.; Ohio, 1861 ***6020.12*** *p7*
Culp, John; New Jersey, 1773-1774 ***927.31*** *p3*
Culver, Elias 29; Ontario, 1871 ***1823.21*** *p79*
Culvert, Thos 35; Ontario, 1871 ***1823.21*** *p79*
Culy, Ann 60; Ontario, 1871 ***1823.21*** *p79*
Cumb, William 53; Ontario, 1871 ***1823.21*** *p79*
Cumberland, . . . 50; Ontario, 1871 ***1823.21*** *p79*
Cumberlidge, George 62; Ontario, 1871 ***1823.21*** *p79*
Cume, Henry 25; Boston, 1835 ***6424.55*** *p30*
Cumming, Farquarson 11; New York, NY, 1835 ***5024.1*** *p137*
Cumming, Jean 7; New York, NY, 1835 ***5024.1*** *p137*
Cumming, Jean 37; New York, NY, 1835 ***5024.1*** *p137*
Cumming, Johnathan 33; New York, NY, 1835 ***5024.1*** *p137*
Cumming, Margaret 13; New York, NY, 1835 ***5024.1*** *p137*
Cummings, Charles; North Carolina, 1845 ***1088.45*** *p7*
Cummings, David 38; Ontario, 1871 ***1823.17*** *p37*
Cummings, H.; California, 1868 ***1131.61*** *p89*
Cummings, J. H.; California, 1868 ***1131.61*** *p90*
Cummings, James; New York, NY, 1839 ***3274.56*** *p97*
Cummings, John 27; Ontario, 1871 ***1823.17*** *p37*
Cummings, John 41; Ontario, 1871 ***1823.21*** *p79*
Cummings, Mary 33; Michigan, 1880 ***4491.36*** *p5*
Cummings, Mary 20; Ontario, 1871 ***1823.21*** *p79*
Cummings, Mary 45; Ontario, 1871 ***1823.21*** *p79*
Cummings, Sarah C. 22; Michigan, 1880 ***4491.30*** *p7*
Cummings, Thomas; New York, NY, 1839 ***3274.56*** *p97*
Cummins, Alfred 41; Ontario, 1871 ***1823.21*** *p79*
Cummins, Anthony 35; New York, NY, 1825 ***6178.50*** *p148*
Cummins, John 35; Ontario, 1871 ***1823.21*** *p79*
Cummins, John 54; Ontario, 1871 ***1823.21*** *p79*
Cummins, Joseph 34; Ontario, 1871 ***1823.21*** *p79*
Cummins, Margaret 7 months; New York, NY, 1821-1849 ***6178.50*** *p148*
Cummins, Mary; Boston, 1741 ***1642*** *p45*
Cummins, Michael 67; Ontario, 1871 ***1823.17*** *p37*
Cummins, Thomas; Ohio, 1809-1852 ***4511.35*** *p9*
Cummins, William; Boston, 1747 ***1642*** *p29*
Cummins, William; Boston, 1765 ***1642*** *p35*
Cummuskey, John 26; Michigan, 1880 ***4491.39*** *p7*
Cummuskey, Mary 18; Michigan, 1880 ***4491.39*** *p7*
Cummuskey, Michael 53; Michigan, 1880 ***4491.39*** *p7*
Cummuskey, Sarah 58; Michigan, 1880 ***4491.39*** *p7*
Cuniff, Thomas; Ohio, 1856 ***3580.20*** *p31*
Cuniff, Thomas; Ohio, 1856 ***6020.12*** *p7*
Cuningham, . . .; Massachusetts, 1740-1800 ***1642*** *p108*
Cuningham, Peleg; Tyringham, MA, 1772 ***1642*** *p120*
Cuningham, Thomas; Edgartown, MA, 1739 ***1642*** *p86*
*Wife:*Zilpah
Cuningham, Zilpah *SEE* Cuningham, Thomas
Cuningim, Catherine *SEE* Cuningim, John
Cuningim, John; Massachusetts, 1721 ***1642*** *p85*
*Wife:*Catherine
Cunliffe, James; Florida, 1843 ***8481.1*** *p18*
Cunmont, Maria 45; America, 1842 ***778.6*** *p80*
Cunnigan, Robert 55; Ontario, 1871 ***1823.21*** *p79*
Cunning, William 37; Ontario, 1871 ***1823.21*** *p79*
Cunningham, . . .; Canada, n.d. ***9228.50*** *p171*
Cunningham, Colonel; Boston, 1766 ***1642*** *p35*
Cunningham, Alexander; Nantucket, MA, 1733 ***1642*** *p89*
Cunningham, Anna; Massachusetts, 1742 ***1642*** *p66*
Cunningham, Charles; Washington, 1883 ***2770.40*** *p136*
Cunningham, David; Massachusetts, 1755-1761 ***1642*** *p110*
Cunningham, David; Massachusetts, 1766 ***1642*** *p66*
Cunningham, David 26; Ontario, 1871 ***1823.17*** *p37*
Cunningham, David; Worcester, MA, 1760 ***1642*** *p114*
*Wife:*Eleanor
Cunningham, Duncan 27; Ontario, 1871 ***1823.17*** *p37*
Cunningham, Edward; Marblehead, MA, 1769 ***1642*** *p73*
Cunningham, Mrs. Edward; Marblehead, MA, 1770 ***1642*** *p73*
Cunningham, Eleanor *SEE* Cunningham, David
Cunningham, Henry 50; Ontario, 1871 ***1823.21*** *p79*
Cunningham, James; Massachusetts, 1768 ***1642*** *p100*
Cunningham, James; North Carolina, 1852 ***1088.45*** *p7*
Cunningham, James; Ohio, 1827 ***3580.20*** *p31*
Cunningham, James; Ohio, 1827 ***6020.12*** *p7*
Cunningham, James 30; Ontario, 1871 ***1823.21*** *p79*
Cunningham, James 70; Ontario, 1871 ***1823.21*** *p79*
Cunningham, James; Rutland, MA, 1736 ***1642*** *p108*
Cunningham, James H. 28; Ontario, 1871 ***1823.21*** *p79*
Cunningham, James Scott; Missouri, 1888 ***3276.1*** *p3*
Cunningham, John; Boston, 1765 ***1642*** *p35*
Cunningham, John; Edgartown, MA, 1748 ***1642*** *p86*
Cunningham, John; Ipswich, MA, 1757 ***1642*** *p71*
Cunningham, John; Massachusetts, 1757 ***1642*** *p66*
Cunningham, John; Massachusetts, 1765 ***1642*** *p66*
Cunningham, John 40; Ontario, 1871 ***1823.17*** *p37*
Cunningham, John 73; Ontario, 1871 ***1823.21*** *p79*
Cunningham, John; Washington, 1884 ***2770.40*** *p192*
Cunningham, John; Watertown, MA, 1715 ***1642*** *p112*
Cunningham, John, Jr.; Massachusetts, 1770 ***1642*** *p106*
Cunningham, Jonathan; Massachusetts, 1771 ***1642*** *p106*
Cunningham, Judah; Boston, 1766 ***1642*** *p48*
Cunningham, Kate 20; New York, NY, 1894 ***6512.1*** *p186*
Cunningham, Katharine; Boston, 1732 ***1642*** *p44*
Cunningham, Mart 50; Ontario, 1871 ***1823.21*** *p79*
Cunningham, Mary; Massachusetts, 1741 ***1642*** *p66*
Cunningham, Mary; Massachusetts, 1759 ***1642*** *p100*
Cunningham, Mary; Massachusetts, 1759 ***1642*** *p120*
Cunningham, Mary 70; Ontario, 1871 ***1823.21*** *p79*
Cunningham, Mary 12; Quebec, 1870 ***8364.32*** *p23*
Cunningham, Mary; Roxbury, MA, 1772 ***1642*** *p108*
Cunningham, N.; Boston, 1728 ***1642*** *p23*
Cunningham, Owen 43; Florida, 1830-1846 ***8481.1*** *p18*
Cunningham, Owin; New England, 1745 ***1642*** *p28*
Cunningham, Robert; Massachusetts, 1740-1800 ***1642*** *p109*
Cunningham, Robert; Massachusetts, 1763 ***1642*** *p112*
Cunningham, Robert; New England, 1745 ***1642*** *p28*
Cunningham, Robert 25; Ontario, 1871 ***1823.17*** *p37*
Cunningham, Stephen; Massachusetts, 1773 ***1642*** *p91*
Cunningham, Thomas 32; Ontario, 1871 ***1823.17*** *p37*
Cunningham, Thos 30; Ontario, 1871 ***1823.21*** *p79*
Cunningham, William; Massachusetts, 1774 ***1642*** *p100*
Cunningham, Wm 60; Ontario, 1871 ***1823.21*** *p80*
Cunningham, Wm 65; Ontario, 1871 ***1823.21*** *p80*
Cunningham, Wm. 21; Virginia, 1635 ***1183.3*** *p31*
Cunninghan, Robert; Woburn, MA, 1745 ***1642*** *p114*
Cunot, Stephen; Ohio, 1809-1852 ***4511.35*** *p9*
Cunse, N. 20; Port uncertain, 1842 ***778.6*** *p80*
Cuntzenhizer, Jacob; Ohio, 1809-1852 ***4511.35*** *p9*
Cuny Dauterive, Philippe-Antoine de; Quebec, 1749 ***2314.30*** *p171*
Cunze, C.; Galveston, TX, 1855 ***571.7*** *p18*
Cupette, F. 20; America, 1847 ***778.6*** *p80*
Cupit, James 61; Michigan, 1880 ***4491.42*** *p9*
Cupit, John G. 25; Michigan, 1880 ***4491.42*** *p9*
Cupit, Joseph 22; Michigan, 1880 ***4491.42*** *p9*

Cupper, Pierre; Virginia, 1700 *9230.15 p81*
Cupples, Camille 52; Galveston, TX, 1845 *3967.10 p376*
Cupples, Charles 20; Galveston, TX, 1845 *3967.10 p376*
Cupples, Christine 27; Galveston, TX, 1844 *3967.10 p374*
Cupples, George 28; Galveston, TX, 1844 *3967.10 p374*
Cupples, Jane 23; Galveston, TX, 1845 *3967.10 p376*
Cupples, Robert 5; Galveston, TX, 1844 *3967.10 p374*
Cupron, Elnaria Wellinger 49 *SEE* Cupron, Samuel
Cupron, Samuel 31; Ohio, 1880 *4879.40 p259*
    *Wife:*Elnaria Wellinger 49
Cur, Mary Ann 33; Ontario, 1871 *1823.21 p80*
Curaillon, Francois 24; Quebec, 1659 *9221.17 p397*
Curby, Paul; America, 1767 *1220.12 p473*
Curden, Jo. 22; Virginia, 1635 *1183.3 p30*
Cure, Francoise; Quebec, 1669 *4514.3 p295*
Curee, Adelaide 7; New Orleans, 1844 *778.6 p80*
Curee, Francis 8; New Orleans, 1844 *778.6 p80*
Curee, Francis 49; New Orleans, 1844 *778.6 p80*
Curee, Justin 9; New Orleans, 1844 *778.6 p80*
Curee, Melanie 2; New Orleans, 1844 *778.6 p80*
Curee, Nicholas 19; New Orleans, 1844 *778.6 p80*
Curette, Johann Friedrich; New York, NY, 1882 *5475.1 p15*
Curey, Adolphe 9; America, 1747 *778.6 p80*
Curey, Celestine 5; America, 1747 *778.6 p80*
Curey, Christine 17; America, 1747 *778.6 p81*
Curey, Christine 42; America, 1747 *778.6 p81*
Curey, Francois 1; America, 1747 *778.6 p81*
Curey, Justine 4; America, 1747 *778.6 p81*
Curey, Nicolas 42; America, 1747 *778.6 p81*
Curjes, Mr. 47; America, 1846 *778.6 p81*
Curling, William 66; Ontario, 1871 *1823.21 p80*
Curn, Hugh 30; Michigan, 1880 *4491.30 p7*
Curn, Margrett 27; Michigan, 1880 *4491.30 p7*
Curnan, Charles; Ohio, 1853 *3580.20 p31*
Curnan, Charles; Ohio, 1853 *6020.12 p7*
Curne, . . .; Massachusetts, 1790 *9228.50 p339*
Curney, . . .; Massachusetts, 1790 *9228.50 p339*
Curnillon, Mr. 46; Port uncertain, 1844 *778.6 p81*
Curnow, Catherine; Maine, 1680 *9228.50 p339*
Currah, Joseph 37; Ontario, 1871 *1823.17 p37*
Curran, George 9; Ontario, 1871 *1823.17 p37*
Curran, Henry 48; Ontario, 1871 *1823.17 p37*
Curran, Mary Anne 36; Ontario, 1871 *1823.17 p37*
Curren, Charles 55; Ontario, 1871 *1823.17 p37*
Curren, Edward; Philadelphia, 1778 *8529.30 p2A*
Curren, John 45; Ontario, 1871 *1823.21 p80*
Currey, James; Ohio, 1834 *3580.20 p31*
Currey, James; Ohio, 1834 *6020.12 p7*
Currie, Agnes 66; Ontario, 1871 *1823.17 p37*
Currie, Alex 40; Ontario, 1871 *1823.21 p80*
Currie, Archibald 24; Ontario, 1871 *1823.17 p37*
Currie, Archibald 30; Ontario, 1871 *1823.17 p37*
Currie, Archibald 44; Ontario, 1871 *1823.21 p80*
Currie, Catharine 62; North Carolina, 1774 *1422.10 p60*

Currie, Catherine 62; North Carolina, 1774 *1422.10 p63*
Currie, Catherine 74; Ontario, 1871 *1823.21 p80*
Currie, Daniel; Washington, 1884 *2770.40 p192*
Currie, Donald 42; Ontario, 1871 *1823.21 p80*
Currie, Duncan 35; Ontario, 1871 *1823.21 p80*
Currie, Edward 56; Ontario, 1871 *1823.21 p80*
Currie, George 59; Ontario, 1871 *1823.21 p80*
Currie, Jannet 82; Ontario, 1871 *1823.21 p80*
Currie, John 50; Ontario, 1871 *1823.21 p80*
Currie, Lachlan 35; Ontario, 1871 *1823.17 p37*
Currie, Lachlin 61; Ontario, 1871 *1823.17 p37*
Currie, Neil 50; Ontario, 1871 *1823.21 p80*
Currie, Peter 75; Ontario, 1871 *1823.21 p80*
Currie, Robert 45; Ontario, 1871 *1823.21 p80*
Currie, Robert 60; Ontario, 1871 *1823.21 p80*
Currie, Roger 48; Ontario, 1871 *1823.17 p37*
Currie, William 42; Ontario, 1871 *1823.21 p80*
Currin, Edward; Philadelphia, 1778 *8529.30 p2A*
Curry, Archibald 50; Ontario, 1871 *1823.21 p80*
Curry, Frederick G. 33; Ontario, 1871 *1823.21 p80*
Curry, Gardner J. 25; Ontario, 1871 *1823.21 p80*
Curry, James; Philadelphia, 1849-1851 *5720.10 p377*
Curry, John 40; Ontario, 1871 *1823.17 p37*
Curry, John 65; Ontario, 1871 *1823.21 p80*
Curry, Mary 63; Ontario, 1871 *1823.21 p80*
Curry, Michael 45; Ontario, 1871 *1823.21 p80*
Curry, Miles 48; Ontario, 1871 *1823.21 p80*
Curtain, Bartholomew; Boston, 1763 *1642 p48*
Curtain, Michael; Toronto, 1844 *2910.35 p116*
Curtain, Micheal 55; Ontario, 1871 *1823.21 p80*
Curtain, Richard 51; Ontario, 1871 *1823.21 p80*
Curtice, Edward; Marston's Wharf, 1782 *8529.30 p10*
Curtice, Richard; Marston's Wharf, 1782 *8529.30 p10*
Curtin, Anna 61; Ontario, 1871 *1823.21 p80*
Curtin, John; Toronto, 1844 *2910.35 p112*
Curtin, Thomas; Toronto, 1844 *2910.35 p113*
Curtin, William; Ohio, 1809-1852 *4511.35 p9*
Curtis, Alfred 50; Ontario, 1871 *1823.21 p80*
Curtis, Charles 25; Ontario, 1871 *1823.21 p80*
Curtis, Chas.; California, 1868 *1131.61 p89*
Curtis, David D.; Ohio, 1840-1897 *8365.35 p15*
Curtis, Edward; Marston's Wharf, 1782 *8529.30 p10*
Curtis, George 26; Ontario, 1871 *1823.21 p80*
Curtis, Henry 33; Ontario, 1871 *1823.21 p80*
Curtis, John 60; Ontario, 1871 *1823.21 p80*
Curtis, John 14; Quebec, 1870 *8364.32 p23*
Curtis, Patrick; Illinois, 1834-1900 *6020.5 p131*
Curtis, Richard 20; Ontario, 1871 *1823.21 p81*
Curtis, Richard 40; Ontario, 1871 *1823.21 p80*
Curtis, Rowland P.; Toronto, 1844 *2910.35 p113*
Curts, John 50; Ontario, 1871 *1823.21 p81*
Cusack, Ellen 58; Ontario, 1871 *1823.21 p81*
Cusack, James 33; Ontario, 1871 *1823.21 p81*
Cushing, William 45; Ontario, 1871 *1823.21 p81*
Cushion, John; Toronto, 1844 *2910.35 p113*
Cushion, Patt; New Orleans, 1851 *7242.30 p139*

Cushner, Alexander; New York, 1783 *8529.30 p10*
Cusick, Christpher 35; Ontario, 1871 *1823.21 p81*
Cusick, John; Colorado, 1891 *1029.59 p20*
Cuson, Christopher; North America, 1750 *1640.8 p234*
Cussick, John 40; Ontario, 1871 *1823.17 p38*
Cusson, Jean 21; Quebec, 1655 *9221.17 p322*
Custin, Jeremiah 27; Ontario, 1871 *1823.21 p81*
Custy, Mike; Colorado, 1886 *1029.59 p20*
Cutcut, Moses 55; Ontario, 1871 *1823.21 p81*
Cutguhan, Richard; North Carolina, 1852 *1088.45 p7*
Cuthbert, Andrew 43; Ontario, 1871 *1823.21 p81*
Cuthbert, James G.; North Carolina, 1814 *1088.45 p7*
Cuthbert, William; North Carolina, 1823 *1088.45 p7*
Cuthbertson, Peter 44; Ontario, 1871 *1823.17 p38*
Cuthburt, Alex 18; Ontario, 1871 *1823.21 p81*
Cutherbertson, John 34; Ontario, 1871 *1823.17 p38*
Cutherbertson, William 42; Ontario, 1871 *1823.17 p38*
Cutler, Augustus W. 41; Ontario, 1871 *1823.17 p38*
Cutler, Benjamin 91; Ontario, 1871 *1823.21 p81*
Cutraio, Giacomo; Louisiana, 1874 *4981.45 p131*
Cutt, John 18; Quebec, 1870 *8364.32 p23*
Cutter, . . .; Massachusetts, 1790 *9228.50 p171*
Cutter, George 52; Ontario, 1871 *1823.21 p81*
Cutter, J. H.; California, 1868 *1131.61 p89*
Cuttle, William 47; Ontario, 1871 *1823.21 p81*
Cutts, William 13; Quebec, 1870 *8364.32 p23*
Cuxey, William 58; Ontario, 1871 *1823.21 p81*
Cuzes, Jean; Quebec, 1661 *9221.17 p452*
Cwicklinsky, N.; New York, 1859 *358.56 p101*
Cwikla, Michael; Detroit, 1929-1930 *6214.5 p70*
Cyman, Anna; Wisconsin, 1890 *6795.8 p55*
Cyman, Mary; Wisconsin, 1891 *6795.8 p55*
Cymann, Martin; Wisconsin, 1881 *6795.8 p55*
Cyr, Jean; Nova Scotia, 1753 *3051 p112*
    *Wife:*Marie Hebert
    *Relative:*Joseph
Cyr, Joseph *SEE* Cyr, Jean
Cyr, Marie Hebert *SEE* Cyr, Jean
Cyrene, M. 46; Ontario, 1871 *1823.17 p38*
Czajkowski, John; Detroit, 1929 *1640.55 p117*
Czajkowski, Thomas; Wisconsin, 1884 *6795.8 p33*
Czajkowski, Valentin; Wisconsin, 1886 *6795.8 p46*
Czapka, Marcin 25; New York, NY, 1912 *8355.1 p16*
Czapla, Maria 23; New York, NY, 1911 *6533.11 p10*
Czarnuta, Frank; Detroit, 1930 *1640.60 p82*
Czech, Stanislaw 23; New York, NY, 1912 *8355.1 p16*
Czeiholinski, Valeria; Wisconsin, 1893 *6795.8 p55*
Czerniecki, Joseph; Detroit, 1929 *1640.55 p113*
Czerniewska, Adela 19; New York, NY, 1911 *6533.11 p10*
Czich, Hermann; Wisconsin, 1895 *6795.8 p229*
Czolnecki, Valentin; Wisconsin, 1886 *6795.8 p46*
Czop, Franciszek 24; New York, NY, 1912 *8355.1 p16*
Czoska, Frank; Wisconsin, 1882 *6795.8 p55*
Czuchna, Stanley; Detroit, 1930 *1640.60 p78*
Czyzak, Sophia; Wisconsin, 1899 *6795.8 p55*

FOR A COMPLETE EXPLANATION OF ENTRY, SEE "HOW TO READ A CITATION" SECTION

D

Dabancourt, Adrien; Quebec, 1635 *9221.17 p45*
  *Wife:*Simone Orville
  *Daughter:*Marie
Dabancourt, Marie 17 *SEE* Dabancourt, Adrien
Dabancourt, Simone Orville *SEE* Dabancourt, Adrien
Dabien, John 19; America, 1845 *778.6 p81*
Dablon, Claude 36; Quebec, 1655 *9221.17 p320*
Dabney, William; Marston's Wharf, 1782 *8529.30 p11*
Dabora, B. 32; Port uncertain, 1843 *778.6 p81*
Daboval, Mr. 42; America, 1846 *778.6 p81*
Daboval, Mr. 23; Louisiana, 1840 *778.6 p81*
Dabrowski, Jan 25; New York, NY, 1920 *930.50 p48*
Dabuis, Claude 29; America, 1846 *778.6 p81*
Dabzall, Willson 25; North Carolina, 1774 *1422.10 p56*
Dach, Peter 23; Port uncertain, 1840 *778.6 p81*
Dachelet, Catherine; Wisconsin, 1870 *1495.20 p12*
Dachelet-Gheyne, Julien *SEE* Dachelet-Gheyne, Marie Anne
Dachelet-Gheyne, Marcellin *SEE* Dachelet-Gheyne, Marie Anne
Dachelet-Gheyne, Marie Anne; Wisconsin, 1856 *1495.20 p41*
  *Child:*Julien
  *Child:*Marcellin
  *Child:*Rosalie Joseph
Dachelet-Gheyne, Rosalie Joseph *SEE* Dachelet-Gheyne, Marie Anne
Dacis, Francois; New York, NY, 1868 *1494.21 p31*
Da Costa, . . .; Boston, 1758 *9228.50 p175*
Dadd, William 23; Ontario, 1871 *1823.21 p81*
Dadd, William 50; Ontario, 1871 *1823.21 p81*
Dadenkoeff, Cath. 26; America, 1840 *778.6 p81*
Dadenkoeff, Lorentz 28; America, 1840 *778.6 p81*
Dadenkoeff, Maria 3 months; America, 1840 *778.6 p81*
Daeges, Fr. Josef *SEE* Daeges, Michel
Daeges, Jakob *SEE* Daeges, Michel
Daeges, Johann *SEE* Daeges, Michel
Daeges, Johannetta Schmitt *SEE* Daeges, Michel
Daeges, Michel; America, 1881 *5475.1 p364*
  *Wife:*Johannetta Schmitt
  *Son:*Jakob
  *Son:*Peter
  *Son:*Nikolaus
  *Son:*Johann
  *Son:*Fr. Josef
Daeges, Nikolaus *SEE* Daeges, Michel
Daeges, Peter *SEE* Daeges, Michel
Daffy, James 14; Ontario, 1871 *1823.17 p38*
Dafo, James H. 23; Michigan, 1880 *4491.30 p8*
Dafroso, Henry 54; Ontario, 1871 *1823.21 p81*
Daferment, John; Colorado, 1868 *1029.59 p20*
Dagathaud, Dani.l 28; America, 1841 *778.6 p81*
Dageney, Marie *SEE* Dageney, Pierre
Dageney, Pierre 15; Montreal, 1650 *9221.17 p231*
  *Wife:*Marie
Dages, Francis; Ohio, 1809-1852 *4511.35 p9*
Dagg, James 46; Ontario, 1871 *1823.21 p81*
Dagg, John 27; Ontario, 1871 *1823.21 p81*
Dagg, John 36; Ontario, 1871 *1823.21 p81*
Dagg, Mary; New Orleans, 1850 *7242.30 p139*
Dagg, Richard 45; Ontario, 1871 *1823.21 p81*
Dagg, Richard 46; Ontario, 1871 *1823.21 p81*
Dagg, Richard 62; Ontario, 1871 *1823.21 p81*
Dagg, Thomas; Boston, 1774 *8529.30 p2A*
Dagg, William; New Orleans, 1850 *7242.30 p139*
Daggett, Henry A.; Washington, 1886 *2770.40 p195*
Dagis, Jacob; Ohio, 1809-1852 *4511.35 p9*
Dagneau, Joseph; New York, NY, 1856 *1494.20 p12*

Dagneau Douville, Michel; Quebec, 1683-1688 *2314.30 p168*
Dagneau Douville, Michel; Quebec, 1687 *2314.30 p179*
Dagoreau, Urbain; Quebec, 1637 *9221.17 p68*
Daguerre, Helene; California, 1906 *3276.8 p20*
Daguerre, Jean Pierre 18; California, 1874 *3276.8 p19*
Daher, Gustav L.; Wisconsin, 1891 *6795.8 p137*
Dahint, Margarethe; America, 1868 *7919.3 p528*
Dahl, Julia; St. Paul, MN, 1881 *1865.50 p42*
Dahlberg, Botvid 56; Kansas, 1870-1880 *777.40 p21*
  *Wife:*Caroline 48
Dahlberg, C. G. 40; New York, NY, 1844 *6410.15 p103*
  With wife 38
  With son 13
  With 4 sons
  With son 1
Dahlberg, Caroline 48 *SEE* Dahlberg, Botvid
Dahlberg, Charles 22; Kansas, 1879-1880 *777.40 p21*
Dahlberg, Mary; St. Paul, MN, 1893 *1865.50 p44*
Dahlberg, Nels; Colorado, 1887 *1029.59 p20*
Dahlberg, Nels; Colorado, 1901 *1029.59 p20*
Dahlberg, Olof; New York, NY, 1847 *6412.40 p150*
Dahlberg, Swan P.; Colorado, 1891 *1029.59 p20*
Dahlbom, Oscar Walfrid; North America, 1887 *6410.15 p106*
Dahlburg, August; New York, 1901 *1766.20 p14*
Dahler, Math.; America, 1840 *5475.1 p169*
Dahlgren, Adolph Jacob; North America, 1857 *6410.15 p105*
Dahlin, Alma Elisabeth; St. Paul, MN, 1900 *1865.50 p44*
Dahlin, Andrew; St. Paul, MN, 1882 *1865.50 p44*
Dahlin, August; Minnesota, 1892-1897 *1865.50 p44*
Dahlin, J.A.; San Francisco, 1849 *6412.40 p151*
Dahlin, John; St. Paul, MN, 1903 *1865.50 p44*
Dahlin, John Adolph; St. Paul, MN, 1886 *1865.50 p44*
Dahlin, Karin Eliasson *SEE* Dahlin, Magnus
Dahlin, Magnus *SEE* Dahlin, Magnus
Dahlin, Magnus; St. Paul, MN, 1888 *1865.50 p44*
  *Wife:*Karin Eliasson
  *Son:*Magnus
Dahlin, Peter; Cleveland, OH, 1887-1893 *9722.10 p118*
Dahlke, August William; Wisconsin, 1880 *6795.8 p168*
Dahlke, Herman; Wisconsin, 1892 *6795.8 p168*
Dahlke, Herman Reinhold; Wisconsin, 1894 *6795.8 p134*
Dahlke, Julius; Wisconsin, 1911 *6795.8 p167*
Dahlke, Julius Herman; Wisconsin, 1879 *6795.8 p200*
Dahlmann, Charles William; Wisconsin, 1873 *6795.8 p85*
Dahlmann, Peter; New Jersey, 1752-1774 *927.31 p3*
Dahlquist, Betty; St. Paul, MN, 1891 *1865.50 p44*
Dahlquist, Olaf Peter; Washington, 1889 *2770.40 p27*
Dahlqvist, A.G.; New York, NY, 1856 *6412.40 p154*
Dahlqvist, Betty; St. Paul, MN, 1891 *1865.50 p44*
Dahlqvist, C.G.; Philadelphia, 1848 *6412.40 p150*
Dahlstrand, Hanna Theresia; Cleveland, OH, 1903 *9722.10 p129*
Dahlstrand, Oscar L.O.; America, 1891 *9722.10 p118*
Dahlstrom, A.G.; Charleston, SC, 1850 *6412.40 p152*
Dahlstrom, Charlotte 32; Kansas, 1880 *777.40 p18*
Dahlstrom, Erick S.; St. Paul, MN, 1891 *1865.50 p44*
Dahlstrom, Johan; Philadelphia, 1848 *6412.40 p150*
Dahlstrom, Matilda 40; Kansas, 1880 *777.40 p18*
Dahlstrom, Oscar; New York, 1902 *1766.20 p18*
Dahlstrom, Philip F. 37; Kansas, 1865-1880 *777.40 p18*
Dahlstrom, Sigrid 37; Kansas, 1871-1880 *777.40 p18*
Dahlstrom, Stafva 72; Kansas, 1880 *777.40 p18*
Dahm, Andrew Sorenson; Iowa, 1917 *1211.15 p10*
Dahm, Johan Sorensen; Iowa, 1929 *1211.15 p10*

Dahmen, Clara 44; Galveston, TX, 1844 *3967.10 p375*
Dahms, Alvina E.; Wisconsin, 1905 *6795.8 p177*
Dahms, Auguste; Wisconsin, 1893 *6795.8 p160*
Dahms, Bertha; Wisconsin, 1899 *6795.8 p128*
Dahms, Gustav Ferdinand; Wisconsin, 1913 *6795.8 p167*
Dahus, Jacob Augustinus Olofsson; New York, NY, 1856 *6410.15 p105*
Daic, Josef; Nebraska, 1866 *2853.20 p156*
Daiges, Jacob; Ohio, 1809-1852 *4511.35 p9*
Daignous, Mr. 35; New Orleans, 1845 *778.6 p81*
Daigre, Ursule; Nova Scotia, 1753 *3051 p112*
Dailey, Mary 50; Ontario, 1871 *1823.17 p38*
Dailey, Thomas; North Carolina, 1855 *1088.45 p7*
D'Aille-Boust, Charles *SEE* D'Aille-Boust, Louis
D'Aille-Boust, Louis; Quebec, 1600-1671 *4514.3 p345*
  *Son:*Charles
D'Aille-Boust, Philippe-Gertrude de; Quebec, 1600-1671 *4514.3 p345*
Dailly, Anne; Quebec, 1671 *4514.3 p295*
Daily, Danl 48; St. Johns, N.F., 1811 *1053.20 p22*
Dain, Marie; Quebec, 1669 *4514.3 p295*
Daire, Marie; Quebec, 1669 *4514.3 p315*
Daisoreather, Abraham 34; New Orleans, 1848 *778.6 p81*
Daisoreather, Edouard 38; New Orleans, 1848 *778.6 p81*
Daisoreather, Sophia 38; New Orleans, 1848 *778.6 p81*
Dake, Carl Heinrich Wilhelm; America, 1877 *7420.1 p308*
Dake, Heinrich Christian; America, 1880 *7420.1 p315*
  *Wife:*Sophie Louise Charlotte Schutte
  *Daughter:*Johanna Luise Wilhelmine
  *Son:*Heinrich Friedrich
  *Son:*Heinrich Friedrich Wilhelm
  *Daughter:*Wilhelmine Friederike Charlotte
Dake, Heinrich Friedrich *SEE* Dake, Heinrich Christian
Dake, Heinrich Friedrich Wilhelm *SEE* Dake, Heinrich Christian
Dake, Johanna Luise Wilhelmine *SEE* Dake, Heinrich Christian
Dake, Sophie Louise Charlotte Schutte *SEE* Dake, Heinrich Christian
Dake, Wilhelmine Friederike Charlotte *SEE* Dake, Heinrich Christian
Dakers, Miss; Quebec, 1885 *1937.10 p52*
Dakin, David 37; Ontario, 1871 *1823.21 p81*
Dakupio, John; Galveston, TX, 1912 *3331.4 p12*
Dalacker, Michael; America, 1700-1899 *179.55 p19*
Daland, . . .; Portsmouth, NH, 1636 *9228.50 p184*
Dalbeck, John; Iowa, 1895 *1211.15 p10*
Dalberg, Mary; St. Paul, MN, 1894 *1865.50 p44*
Dalbergati Vezza, Francois-Marie-Luc; Quebec, 1755-1757 *2314.30 p170*
Dalbergati Vezza, Francois-Marie-Luc; Quebec, 1755 *2314.30 p170*
Dalbert, Martin; Quebec, 1657 *9221.17 p355*
Dalbsmeier, Caroline Wilhelmine; America, 1882 *7420.1 p334*
Dale, Henry Frank; Colorado, 1891 *1029.59 p20*
Dale, Jacob 65; Ontario, 1871 *1823.21 p82*
Dale, James 33; Ontario, 1871 *1823.21 p82*
Dale, Jane 30; Ontario, 1871 *1823.17 p38*
Dale, John 68; Ontario, 1871 *1823.21 p82*
Dale, John B. 26; Ontario, 1871 *1823.17 p38*
Dale, Joseph 61; Ontario, 1871 *1823.17 p38*
Dale, Lawrence 49; Ontario, 1871 *1823.17 p38*
Dale, R. 15; Quebec, 1870 *8364.32 p23*
Dale, Robert 49; Ontario, 1871 *1823.17 p38*
Dale, Soloman 33; Ontario, 1871 *1823.21 p82*

Dale, William H. 25; Ontario, 1871 ***1823.17*** *p38*
Daleae, Joseph; Louisiana, 1874 ***4981.45*** *p131*
Dalemont, Joseph; New York, NY, 1856 ***1494.20*** *p12*
Dalesto, Michael 41; America, 1842 ***778.6*** *p81*
Daleth, Philippe 24; Mississippi, 1845-1846 ***778.6*** *p81*
Daley, Catherine 8; Quebec, 1870 ***8364.32*** *p23*
Daley, James; Ohio, 1836 ***2763.1*** *p9*
Daley, James 40; Ontario, 1871 ***1823.21*** *p82*
Daley, John; Ohio, 1835 ***2763.1*** *p9*
Daley, Stephen 67; Ontario, 1871 ***1823.21*** *p82*
Dalhausen, William; Illinois, 1851 ***6079.1*** *p4*
Dalhgreen, Axel; Louisiana, 1874-1875 ***4981.45*** *p298*
Dalie, Ann 45; Michigan, 1880 ***4491.30*** *p8*
Dalie, Patrick 63; Michigan, 1880 ***4491.30*** *p8*
Dallany, Patrick; Boston, 1765 ***1642*** *p35*
Dallarosa, Eliz *SEE* Dallarosa, Leo
Dallarosa, Joseph *SEE* Dallarosa, Leo
Dallarosa, Karl *SEE* Dallarosa, Leo
Dallarosa, Leo; Denver, CO, 1917 ***1029.59*** *p20*
*Wife:*Mary
*Child:*Eliz
*Child:*Leona
*Child:*Joseph
*Child:*Karl
*Child:*Mary
Dallarosa, Leona *SEE* Dallarosa, Leo
Dallarosa, Mary *SEE* Dallarosa, Leo
Dallarosa, Mary *SEE* Dallarosa, Leo
Dalled, Dennis; Toronto, 1844 ***2910.35*** *p116*
Dalleret, Marin 25; Quebec, 1661 ***9221.17*** *p452*
D'Allet, Antoine 23; Montreal, 1657 ***9221.17*** *p372*
Dalley, John 39; America, 1848 ***778.6*** *p81*
Dallinger, Charles; Illinois, 1852 ***6079.1*** *p4*
Dallis, John 39; Ontario, 1871 ***1823.17*** *p38*
Dallman, Andrew; North Carolina, 1855 ***1088.45*** *p7*
Dallman, Heinrich C.F.; Wisconsin, 1877 ***6795.8*** *p225*
Dallmeier, Arnold; Galveston, TX, 1855 ***571.7*** *p16*
Dallon, Marie; Quebec, 1668 ***4514.3*** *p295*
Dalloue, Charles; Montreal, 1659 ***9221.17*** *p420*
Dalmage, Adam 40; Ontario, 1871 ***1823.21*** *p82*
Dalman, Peter; New Jersey, 1752-1774 ***927.31*** *p3*
Daloux, Pierre; Quebec, 1643 ***9221.17*** *p130*
Daloux, Rene; Quebec, 1643 ***9221.17*** *p130*
Dalrymple, Ann 9; North Carolina, 1775 ***1422.10*** *p57*
Dalrymple, Archd. 15; North Carolina, 1775 ***1422.10*** *p57*
Dalrymple, Janet 7; North Carolina, 1775 ***1422.10*** *p57*
Dalrymple, Jas. 11; North Carolina, 1775 ***1422.10*** *p57*
Dalrymple, Jean 5; North Carolina, 1775 ***1422.10*** *p57*
Dalrymple, Jn. 17; North Carolina, 1775 ***1422.10*** *p57*
Dalrymple, Jno. 40; North Carolina, 1775 ***1422.10*** *p57*
Dalrymple, Marg. 39; North Carolina, 1775 ***1422.10*** *p57*
Dalrymple, Mary 19; North Carolina, 1775 ***1422.10*** *p57*
Dalrymple, Roy 40; Ontario, 1871 ***1823.17*** *p38*
Dalrymple, Wm. 2; North Carolina, 1775 ***1422.10*** *p57*
Dalsheines, Caroline 28; America, 1842 ***778.6*** *p81*
Dalsheines, David 30; America, 1842 ***778.6*** *p81*
Dalstrom, Betse Hansdotter *SEE* Dalstrom, Olof E.
Dalstrom, Olof E.; Kansas, 1868-1869 ***777.40*** *p8*
*Wife:*Betse Hansdotter
Dalton, Anne; New Orleans, 1850 ***7242.30*** *p139*
Dalton, Betty; New Orleans, 1850 ***7242.30*** *p139*
Dalton, Bridget 39; Ontario, 1871 ***1823.21*** *p82*
Dalton, Dukes 38; Ontario, 1871 ***1823.21*** *p82*
Dalton, Edmund; Newfoundland, 1814 ***3476.10*** *p54*
Dalton, James; Boston, 1766 ***1642*** *p37*
Dalton, James 30; New York, NY, 1849 ***6178.50*** *p152*
Dalton, James; Washington, 1885 ***2770.40*** *p194*
Dalton, John 51; Ontario, 1871 ***1823.21*** *p82*
Dalton, Joseph 60; Ontario, 1871 ***1823.21*** *p82*
Dalton, Marg; Jamestown, VA, 1633 ***1658.20*** *p211*
Dalton, Margaret; New Orleans, 1850 ***7242.30*** *p139*
Dalton, Mary 63; Ontario, 1871 ***1823.21*** *p82*
Dalton, Michael; New Orleans, 1851 ***7242.30*** *p139*
Dalton, Michael; Newfoundland, 1814 ***3476.10*** *p54*
Dalton, Michael 32; Ontario, 1871 ***1823.17*** *p38*
Dalton, Patrick 60; Ontario, 1871 ***1823.17*** *p38*
Dalton, Philip; Ipswich, MA, 1661 ***1642*** *p69*
Dalton, Thomas; New Orleans, 1850 ***7242.30*** *p139*
Dalton, William 40; Ontario, 1871 ***1823.21*** *p82*
Dalton, William 69; Ontario, 1871 ***1823.21*** *p82*
Dalton, William; Salem, MA, 1654 ***1642*** *p78*
Daltroff, Solomon; New Orleans, 1846 ***7710.1*** *p154*
Dalumaire, Brunette 35; Louisiana, 1847 ***778.6*** *p81*
Daluzeau, Jean 24; Montreal, 1662 ***9221.17*** *p497*
Dalvine, James; Massachusetts, 1675-1676 ***1642*** *p128*
Dalwig, Albert; Chicago, 1888 ***7420.1*** *p399*
Daly, Ann 39; Ontario, 1871 ***1823.21*** *p82*
Daly, Ann 10; Quebec, 1870 ***8364.32*** *p23*
Daly, Celia 38; Michigan, 1880 ***4491.39*** *p7*
Daly, Christopher 54; Michigan, 1880 ***4491.39*** *p7*
Daly, Dennis 48; Ontario, 1871 ***1823.21*** *p82*
Daly, Henry; Toronto, 1844 ***2910.35*** *p115*
Daly, James 45; Michigan, 1880 ***4491.39*** *p7*
Daly, James 30; Ontario, 1871 ***1823.17*** *p38*
Daly, James 34; Ontario, 1871 ***1823.17*** *p38*
Daly, James; Toronto, 1844 ***2910.35*** *p115*
Daly, John 50; Ontario, 1871 ***1823.21*** *p82*
Daly, John; Washington, 1884 ***2770.40*** *p192*
Daly, Julia 45; Michigan, 1880 ***4491.39*** *p7*
Daly, Lydia A. 58; Michigan, 1880 ***4491.39*** *p7*
Daly, Marie 68; New Orleans, 1848 ***778.6*** *p81*
Daly, Mary 48; Ontario, 1871 ***1823.21*** *p82*
Daly, Michael; Illinois, 1834-1900 ***6020.5*** *p131*
Daly, Mickal 35; Ontario, 1871 ***1823.21*** *p82*
Daly, Patrick 30; Ontario, 1871 ***1823.21*** *p82*
Daly, Patrick J.; Colorado, 1889 ***1029.59*** *p20*
Daly, Terence; Toronto, 1844 ***2910.35*** *p116*
Daly, William 17; Quebec, 1870 ***8364.32*** *p23*
Dalziel, James 29; Ontario, 1871 ***1823.17*** *p38*
Dalziel, John 38; Ontario, 1871 ***1823.17*** *p38*
Dam, Martin Anderson; Iowa, 1911 ***1211.15*** *p10*
Damane, Denise; Quebec, 1665 ***4514.3*** *p295*
Damange, Louis 23; Port uncertain, 1846 ***778.6*** *p81*
Damann, K. Ch.; New York, 1859 ***358.56*** *p99*
Damarre, Mrs. 22; New Orleans, 1843 ***778.6*** *p82*
Damarre, Chs. 5; New Orleans, 1843 ***778.6*** *p81*
Damarre, J. L. 36; New Orleans, 1843 ***778.6*** *p81*
Damarre, Jean 6; New Orleans, 1843 ***778.6*** *p82*
Damarre, Julia 2; New Orleans, 1843 ***778.6*** *p82*
Dambach, Henriette 17; Port uncertain, 1843 ***778.6*** *p82*
Dambach, Louis 14; Port uncertain, 1843 ***778.6*** *p82*
Dambach, Louis 44; Port uncertain, 1843 ***778.6*** *p82*
Dambremont, Ferdinand; Wisconsin, 1872 ***1495.20*** *p12*
*Wife:*Virginie Charlier
*Child:*Josephine
*Child:*Ferdinande Desiree
*Child:*Marie Therese
*Child:*Francois
Dambremont, Ferdinande Desiree *SEE* Dambremont, Ferdinand
Dambremont, Francois *SEE* Dambremont, Ferdinand
Dambremont, Josephine *SEE* Dambremont, Ferdinand
Dambremont, Marie Therese *SEE* Dambremont, Ferdinand
Dambremont, Virginie Charlier *SEE* Dambremont, Ferdinand
Dambrun, Ls. 21; America, 1848 ***778.6*** *p82*
Damer, Magdalena; New England, 1867 ***170.15*** *p22*
Damerell, Emmanuel; Illinois, 1856 ***6079.1*** *p4*
Damerell, John C.; Illinois, 1856 ***6079.1*** *p4*
Dames, Frank; New York, NY, 1870 ***1494.20*** *p13*
Damiens, Antoine; Quebec, 1640 ***9221.17*** *p95*
Damise, Claude; Quebec, 1668 ***4514.3*** *p295*
Dammarell, Edward; Boston, 1767 ***1642*** *p38*
Dammeier, Widow; America, 1853 ***7420.1*** *p104*
With son
Dammeier, Caroline; America, 1852 ***7420.1*** *p87*
Dammeier, Gottlieb; America, 1867 ***7420.1*** *p255*
With family
Dammeier, Louis; America, 1853 ***7420.1*** *p104*
Dammon, Conrade; Philadelphia, 1778 ***8529.30*** *p2A*
Damois, Marie; Quebec, 1669 ***4514.3*** *p296*
Damon, Conrade; Philadelphia, 1778 ***8529.30*** *p2A*
Damouche, Antonio 28; America, 1848 ***778.6*** *p82*
Damours, Helene; Quebec, 1668 ***4514.3*** *p296*
Damours, Leon Andre 23; Texas, 1848 ***778.6*** *p82*
Damours deChauffours, Mathieu; Quebec, 1651 ***2314.30*** *p166*
Damours deChauffours, Mathieu; Quebec, 1651 ***2314.30*** *p179*
Damours DesChaufours, Elisabeth 39; Quebec, 1651 ***9221.17*** *p238*
Damours DesChaufours, Mathieu 33; Quebec, 1651 ***9221.17*** *p239*
Damoux, Baptiste 19; America, 1845 ***778.6*** *p82*
Damozet, Mr. 28; America, 1841 ***778.6*** *p82*
Damrohse, Martha Ann; Wisconsin, 1899 ***6795.8*** *p189*
Dams, Anna 17; Portland, ME, 1906 ***970.38*** *p76*
Dams, Karl 15 *SEE* Dams, Luise Schug
Dams, Luise 19 *SEE* Dams, Luise Schug
Dams, Luise 41; America, 1866 ***5475.1*** *p490*
*Daughter:*Luise 19
*Son:*Karl 15
Damson, William 45; Ontario, 1871 ***1823.21*** *p82*
Dan, Huin 30; Ontario, 1871 ***1823.21*** *p82*
Dancey, John 50; Ontario, 1871 ***1823.21*** *p82*
Danckert, Joh. A.; Valdivia, Chile, 1852 ***1192.4*** *p55*
Danckert, Joh. Leonhard; Valdivia, Chile, 1852 ***1192.4*** *p55*
Dancosse, Pierre 18; Quebec, 1662 ***9221.17*** *p483*
Dandanne Dansville deLetandart, Nicolas-Antoine; Quebec, 1758 ***2314.30*** *p170*
Dandanne Dansville deLetandart, Nicolas-Antoine; Quebec, 1758 ***2314.30*** *p179*
Dandonneau, Pierre 23; Quebec, 1647 ***9221.17*** *p178*
Dandonneau duSable, Louis-Adrien; Quebec, 1718 ***2314.30*** *p172*
Dands, Evan; Maryland, 1674 ***1236.25*** *p49*
Dandue, Guillaume 29; America, 1848 ***778.6*** *p82*
Danduque, Mrs. 40; New Orleans, 1848 ***778.6*** *p82*
Dandy, Geo 30; Ontario, 1871 ***1823.21*** *p82*
Dandy, John; Marston's Wharf, 1782 ***8529.30*** *p11*
Dandy, John 39; Ontario, 1871 ***1823.17*** *p38*
Dane, Thomas; North Carolina, 1858 ***1088.45*** *p7*
Daneau, Antoine 23; Quebec, 1649 ***9221.17*** *p211*
Daneau deMuy, Nicolas; Quebec, 1683-1688 ***2314.30*** *p168*
Daneau deMuy, Nicolas; Quebec, 1685 ***2314.30*** *p179*
Danek, Frantisek; America, 1852 ***2853.20*** *p272*
Danek, Frantisek; Wisconsin, 1852 ***2853.20*** *p303*
Danek, Jan; Wisconsin, 1852 ***2853.20*** *p303*
Danet, Charles; Quebec, 1664 ***4514.3*** *p326*
Danford, John 37; Ontario, 1871 ***1823.21*** *p82*
Danford, William; Ipswich, MA, 1678 ***1642*** *p70*
Dange, Francois; Quebec, 1662 ***9221.17*** *p483*
D'Angelo, Francisco; Louisiana, 1874-1875 ***4981.45*** *p298*
D'Angelo, Guiseppe; Louisiana, 1874-1875 ***4981.45*** *p298*
Dangla, Guillaume; Louisiana, 1874 ***4981.45*** *p131*
Daniau, Francois 20; Quebec, 1661 ***9221.17*** *p452*
Daniel, Ann *SEE* Daniel, David
Daniel, Anne; Ohio, 1832 ***4022.20*** *p280*
Daniel, Antoine; Quebec, 1632 ***9221.17*** *p27*
Daniel, David; Ohio, 1847 ***4022.20*** *p272*
*Wife:*Elizabeth
*Child:*Ann
Daniel, Elizabeth *SEE* Daniel, David
Daniel, John; Ohio, 1809-1852 ***4511.35*** *p9*
Daniel, McLaren 35; Ontario, 1871 ***1823.17*** *p38*
Daniel, Thomas 62; Ontario, 1871 ***1823.21*** *p82*
Danielak, Jan; Detroit, 1930 ***1640.60*** *p82*
Danielek, Bernard; New York, 1893 ***1766.20*** *p23*
Daniell, G. J. 15; New York, NY, 1894 ***6512.1*** *p228*
Daniell, John 18; New York, NY, 1894 ***6512.1*** *p228*
Daniell, Rachel 16; New York, NY, 1894 ***6512.1*** *p228*
Daniels, Edward 22; Ontario, 1871 ***1823.21*** *p82*
Daniels, Henry 17; Quebec, 1870 ***8364.32*** *p23*
Daniels, John; Ohio, 1809-1852 ***4511.35*** *p9*
Daniels, John 75; Ontario, 1871 ***1823.21*** *p82*
Daniels, Mark 41; Ontario, 1871 ***1823.17*** *p38*
Daniels, Rachael 18; Quebec, 1870 ***8364.32*** *p23*
Daniels, William 40; Ontario, 1871 ***1823.17*** *p38*
Daniels, William 15; Quebec, 1870 ***8364.32*** *p23*
Danielsdotter, Brita; America, 1855 ***6529.11*** *p25*
Danielsdotter, Maria 32; New York, 1856 ***6529.11*** *p22*
Danielson, Carl; Iowa, 1900 ***1211.15*** *p10*
Danielson, Claes; Illinois, 1861 ***4487.25*** *p55*
Danielson, Gustaf; Kansas, 1845-1878 ***777.40*** *p12*
Danielson, Gustavus; Iowa, 1887 ***1211.15*** *p10*
Danielsson, Anders Johan 6 *SEE* Danielsson, Marten
Danielsson, Brita Strom 27 *SEE* Danielsson, Marten
Danielsson, Brita Cajsa 4 *SEE* Danielsson, Marten
Danielsson, Johan Petter; North America, 1887 ***6410.15*** *p106*
Danielsson, Marten 30; New York, 1856 ***6529.11*** *p21*
*Wife:*Brita Strom 27
*Son:*Marten August 1
*Son:*Anders Johan 6
*Daughter:*Brita Cajsa 4
Danielsson, Marten August 1 *SEE* Danielsson, Marten
Danielsson, Pehr 25; New York, 1856 ***6529.11*** *p22*
Danill, William 68; Ontario, 1871 ***1823.21*** *p83*
Danimiller, Bennedict; Ohio, 1809-1852 ***4511.35*** *p9*
Danin, August; Utah, 1855 ***9228.50*** *p171*
*Relative:*Nancy
Danin, Nancy *SEE* Danin, August
Danis, Honore 26; Montreal, 1653 ***9221.17*** *p286*
Danisewicz, Joseph; Detroit, 1930 ***1640.60*** *p82*
Danjan, B. 19; New Orleans, 1848 ***778.6*** *p82*
Danjou, Gilles 24; Quebec, 1655 ***9221.17*** *p322*
Danken, Anna; New York, 1860 ***358.56*** *p6*
Dankes, John; New York, 1859 ***358.56*** *p100*
Danks, Samuel 35; Ontario, 1871 ***1823.21*** *p83*
Dankwerth, Otto; America, 1852 ***7420.1*** *p87*
With wife 3 sons & daughter
Danley, James; New Orleans, 1850 ***7242.30*** *p139*
Danley, John; New Orleans, 1850 ***7242.30*** *p139*
Dann, Frank 31; Ontario, 1871 ***1823.21*** *p83*
Dann, George 46; Ontario, 1871 ***1823.21*** *p83*
Dann, John 50; Ontario, 1871 ***1823.21*** *p83*
Dann, William 70; Ontario, 1871 ***1823.21*** *p83*
Dannemiller, Benedict; Ohio, 1809-1852 ***4511.35*** *p10*
Dannemiller, Henry; Ohio, 1809-1852 ***4511.35*** *p10*
Dannenhauer, Dorothea; Philadelphia, 1860 ***8513.31*** *p429*
Danner, Anton; Valdivia, Chile, 1852 ***1192.4*** *p55*
Dannesse, Esther; Quebec, 1668 ***4514.3*** *p296*
Danneville, Anne *SEE* Danneville, Gabrielle
Danneville, Anne *SEE* Danneville, Marguerite Roy

Danneville, Gabrielle; Quebec, 1665 ***4514.3*** *p296*
*Mother:*Marguerite Roy
*Sister:*Anne
With brother & nephew
Danneville, Gabrielle *SEE* Danneville, Marguerite Roy
Danneville, Marguerite Roy *SEE* Danneville, Gabrielle
Danneville, Marguerite; Quebec, 1665 ***4514.3*** *p368*
*Daughter:*Anne
*Daughter:*Gabrielle
With sister-in-law & 2 grandchildren
Dannewald, Adam; America, 1886 ***2526.43*** *p203*
Dannewald, Adam *SEE* Dannewald, Katharina
Dannewald, Adam *SEE* Dannewald, Katharina
Dannewald, Katharina; America, 1886 ***2526.43*** *p203*
Dannewald, Katharina; America, 1886 ***2526.43*** *p205*
*Brother:*Adam
Dannewald, Katharina; New York, 1886 ***2526.43*** *p206*
*Brother:*Adam
Dannins, Pat 23; St. Johns, N.F., 1811 ***1053.20*** *p20*
Dannuf, Max; New York, 1860 ***358.56*** *p149*
Danoy, A. W. 50; New Orleans, 1840 ***778.6*** *p82*
Dansac, B. 30; New Orleans, 1845 ***778.6*** *p82*
Danse-A-L'Ombre, Louis 15; Quebec, 1656 ***9221.17*** *p332*
Danstall, William 28; Ontario, 1871 ***1823.21*** *p83*
Dantagnan, Antoine 20; New Orleans, 1845 ***778.6*** *p82*
Dantagnan, D.; Louisiana, 1874-1875 ***4981.45*** *p298*
Dantzer, Louis 42; Port uncertain, 1848 ***778.6*** *p82*
Dantzer, Salome 38; Port uncertain, 1848 ***778.6*** *p82*
Danvoye, Jean Baptiste; Wisconsin, 1854-1858 ***1495.20*** *p50*
Danz, F.; Valparaiso, Chile, 1850 ***1192.4*** *p50*
Dapomel, Louis 27; America, 1845 ***778.6*** *p82*
Darach, Jenny; Brunswick, NC, 1767 ***1422.10*** *p61*
Daran, Adrien 31; Quebec, 1646 ***9221.17*** *p160*
Darbey, Ann 57; Ontario, 1871 ***1823.21*** *p83*
Darby, . . .; South Carolina, 1680 ***9228.50*** *p171*
Darby, James; America, 1881-1981 ***9228.50*** *p171*
Darby, James; North Carolina, 1850 ***1088.45*** *p7*
Darby, John; North Carolina, 1850 ***1088.45*** *p7*
Darby, John 40; North Carolina, 1774 ***1422.10*** *p55*
Darby, Joseph; Halifax, N.S., 1863 ***9228.50*** *p171*
Darby, Mary; Boston, 1757 ***9228.50*** *p366*
Darby, Mary Ann; Providence, RI, 1870-1927 ***9228.50*** *p413*
Darby, Roxanna 62; Ontario, 1871 ***1823.21*** *p83*
Darby, Teresah 23; Ontario, 1871 ***1823.21*** *p83*
Darby, William 60; Ontario, 1871 ***1823.21*** *p83*
Darbyson, Rose 70; Ontario, 1871 ***1823.17*** *p38*
Darcey, Dennis 64; Ontario, 1871 ***1823.21*** *p83*
Darch, James 32; Ontario, 1871 ***1823.21*** *p83*
Darch, James F. 49; Ontario, 1871 ***1823.21*** *p83*
Darch, Jane 34; Ontario, 1871 ***1823.21*** *p83*
Darch, John 75; Ontario, 1871 ***1823.21*** *p83*
Darch, Robert 50; Ontario, 1871 ***1823.21*** *p83*
Darche, L. D. 50; America, 1841 ***778.6*** *p82*
Darcy, John 45; Ontario, 1871 ***1823.21*** *p83*
Darcy, Martin 28; Ontario, 1871 ***1823.21*** *p83*
Darcy, Mary 16; Ontario, 1871 ***1823.17*** *p38*
Darcy, Patrick 53; Ontario, 1871 ***1823.17*** *p38*
Darcy, Thom; New Orleans, 1851 ***7242.30*** *p139*
Dard, Henri 49; Louisiana, 1848 ***778.6*** *p82*
Dard, Pernette 36; Louisiana, 1848 ***778.6*** *p82*
Dardenne, Marie 22; Montreal, 1659 ***9221.17*** *p416*
Dardenne, Marie 22; Montreal, 1659 ***9221.17*** *p416*
Dargelas, Raymond 34; Texas, 1848 ***778.6*** *p82*
Dargencour, Francois; Quebec, 1654 ***9221.17*** *p304*
Dargis, Elisabeth; Quebec, 1661 ***9221.17*** *p452*
Dargol, Jeanne 40; New Orleans, 1848 ***778.6*** *p82*
Dargon, Elizabeth 40; Ontario, 1871 ***1823.21*** *p83*
Darian, Thomas; Illinois, 1860 ***6079.1*** *p4*
Daricau, Miss 3; Texas, 1848 ***778.6*** *p82*
Daricau, Miss 35; Texas, 1848 ***778.6*** *p82*
Daricau, Arnaud 42; Texas, 1848 ***778.6*** *p82*
Darim, Andrew; Ohio, 1809-1852 ***4511.35*** *p10*
Daring, Benja.; Maryland, 1674-1675 ***1236.25*** *p51*
Dariot, P...re 26; New Orleans, 1840 ***778.6*** *p82*
Dark, Amelia; Ontario, 1871 ***1823.17*** *p38*
Dark, Benjamin 61; Ontario, 1871 ***1823.21*** *p83*
Dark, Henry 34; Ontario, 1871 ***1823.21*** *p83*
Dark, James 29; Ontario, 1871 ***1823.21*** *p83*
Dark, James 48; Ontario, 1871 ***1823.21*** *p83*
Dark, James 50; Ontario, 1871 ***1823.21*** *p83*
Dark, John; Ontario, 1871 ***1823.17*** *p38*
Dark, Mathew 47; Ontario, 1871 ***1823.21*** *p83*
Dark, Robert 50; Ontario, 1871 ***1823.17*** *p38*
Dark, William 36; Ontario, 1871 ***1823.21*** *p83*
Darkringer, Alois 21; America, 1846 ***778.6*** *p82*
Darley, Thomas 49; Ontario, 1871 ***1823.17*** *p38*
Darling, David; New York, NY, 1825 ***3274.55*** *p67*
Darling, George 24; New York, NY, 1835 ***5024.1*** *p136*
Darling, John 67; Ontario, 1871 ***1823.21*** *p83*
Darling, Robert 28; New York, NY, 1835 ***5024.1*** *p136*
Darlingson, William 19; Quebec, 1870 ***8364.32*** *p23*
Darloting, Marie 24; Port uncertain, 1843 ***778.6*** *p82*
Darmagnac, Jean 24; Port uncertain, 1846 ***778.6*** *p82*
Darmes, Dan; Louisiana, 1874-1875 ***4981.45*** *p298*
Darmoey, Jeremiah; New York, NY, 1837 ***3274.56*** *p98*
Darnajou, Francois; Quebec, 1654 ***9221.17*** *p306*
Darner, Johann; America, 1857 ***5475.1*** *p320*
Darner, Joseph 24; New Orleans, 1848 ***778.6*** *p83*
Darner, Margaretha 25; New Orleans, 1848 ***778.6*** *p83*
Darnstadt, Carl Friedrich August; America, 1867 ***7919.3*** *p529*
With family
Daron, C. J.; Louisiana, 1836-1840 ***4981.45*** *p212*
Darondeau, Pierre; Montreal, 1653 ***9221.17*** *p286*
Daroux, Bertrand 22; America, 1845 ***778.6*** *p83*
Daroux, J. M. 21; America, 1845 ***778.6*** *p83*
Darrach, Mary 46; Ontario, 1871 ***1823.21*** *p83*
Darragh, Daniel 23; New York, NY, 1825 ***6178.50*** *p78*
Darragh, James 37; Ontario, 1871 ***1823.21*** *p83*
Darragh, James 75; Ontario, 1871 ***1823.21*** *p83*
D'Arras, Marie-Catherine; Quebec, 1664 ***4514.3*** *p293*
Darrez, Jean; Louisiana, 1874 ***4981.45*** *p295*
Darrien, Patrick; North Carolina, 1860 ***1088.45*** *p7*
Darrou, Mr. 22; Port uncertain, 1844 ***778.6*** *p83*
Darroux, Guillaume 19; New Orleans, 1848 ***778.6*** *p83*
Darrouy, Bernard 23; New Orleans, 1845 ***778.6*** *p83*
Darssar, Narcisse Jean 17; Port uncertain, 1848 ***778.6*** *p83*
Dart, Agnus 34; Ontario, 1871 ***1823.21*** *p83*
Dart, George 26; Ontario, 1871 ***1823.21*** *p83*
Dart, John 33; Ontario, 1871 ***1823.21*** *p83*
Dart, John 50; Ontario, 1871 ***1823.17*** *p39*
Dart, Roger 38; Ontario, 1871 ***1823.21*** *p83*
Dartch, Richard 28; Ontario, 1871 ***1823.21*** *p83*
Dartch, Thomas 48; Ontario, 1871 ***1823.21*** *p83*
Darte, Jacques 32; New Orleans, 1848 ***778.6*** *p83*
Darte, Margaretha 35; New Orleans, 1848 ***778.6*** *p83*
Darthes, L. 25; Port uncertain, 1841 ***778.6*** *p83*
Dartier, P. 18; New Orleans, 1848 ***778.6*** *p83*
Dartigues, Mr. 29; Port uncertain, 1844 ***778.6*** *p83*
Dartigues, Jean 32; New Orleans, 1843 ***778.6*** *p83*
Darton, Mary; Maryland, 1672 ***1236.25*** *p47*
Darton, Robert; Ipswich, MA, 1675-1678 ***1642*** *p69*
Dartugere, Mr. 26; America, 1841 ***778.6*** *p83*
Darvell, William 50; Ontario, 1871 ***1823.17*** *p39*
Darvill, David 39; Ontario, 1871 ***1823.21*** *p83*
Daryman, William; Illinois, 1834-1900 ***6020.5*** *p131*
Das, J. 22; America, 1846 ***778.6*** *p83*
Dasbaugh, John; Ohio, 1809-1852 ***4511.35*** *p10*
Dascher, Eva Maria; Virginia, 1831 ***152.20*** *p61*
Dasko, John; Detroit, 1930 ***1640.60*** *p78*
Dasko, Tessie; Detroit, 1930 ***1640.60*** *p78*
Dassonville, Gabrielle 16; Quebec, 1654 ***9221.17*** *p316*
Dastageay, Louis; Quebec, 1643 ***9221.17*** *p130*
Dastague, Laurent 19; New Orleans, 1843 ***778.6*** *p83*
Dastat, Mr. 21; America, 1846 ***778.6*** *p83*
Dastellon, P. 21; America, 1848 ***778.6*** *p83*
Daster, Jacob; Ohio, 1809-1852 ***4511.35*** *p10*
Dastugue, G. 18; New Orleans, 1847 ***778.6*** *p83*
Dastugue, John 18; New Orleans, 1746 ***778.6*** *p83*
Dasuf, Joseph 8; Ohio, 1880 ***4879.40*** *p260*
Dasuf, Peter 13; Ohio, 1880 ***4879.40*** *p260*
Dasuf, William 15; Ohio, 1880 ***4879.40*** *p260*
Date, Thomas 61; Ontario, 1871 ***1823.17*** *p39*
Dater, Jacob; North Carolina, 1823-1827 ***1088.45*** *p7*
Dathie, Robert 31; Ontario, 1871 ***1823.21*** *p83*
Daton, Marg; Jamestown, VA, 1633 ***1658.20*** *p211*
Datuche, Florian 31; New Orleans, 1848 ***778.6*** *p83*
Datuche, Loiuis 1; New Orleans, 1848 ***778.6*** *p83*
Datuche, Zephire 11; New Orleans, 1848 ***778.6*** *p83*
Daub, John; Ohio, 1809-1852 ***4511.35*** *p10*
Daub, Nikolaus 28; Colorado, 1888 ***5475.1*** *p174*
Daubard, Annette Charlotte 14; America, 1845 ***778.6*** *p83*
Daubertshauser, Andreas *SEE* Daubertshauser, Elisabeth Margarethe
Daubertshauser, Elisabeth Margarethe *SEE* Daubertshauser, Elisabeth Margarethe
Daubertshauser, Elisabeth Margarethe; America, 1852 ***8115.12*** *p326*
*Child:*Elisabeth Margarethe
*Child:*Ludwig
*Child:*Helene
*Child:*Katharine
*Child:*Friedrich
*Child:*Jakob
*Child:*Andreas
*Child:*Regina Katharine
Daubertshauser, Friedrich *SEE* Daubertshauser, Elisabeth Margarethe
Daubertshauser, Georg; America, 1882 ***8115.12*** *p325*
Daubertshauser, Helene *SEE* Daubertshauser, Elisabeth Margarethe
Daubertshauser, Jakob *SEE* Daubertshauser, Elisabeth Margarethe
Daubertshauser, Katharine *SEE* Daubertshauser, Elisabeth Margarethe
Daubertshauser, Ludwig *SEE* Daubertshauser, Elisabeth Margarethe
Daubertshauser, Ludwig; America, 1881 ***8115.12*** *p325*
Daubertshauser, Regina Katharine *SEE* Daubertshauser, Elisabeth Margarethe
Daubigeon, Julien; Montreal, 1653 ***9221.17*** *p287*
*Wife:*Perrine Lemeusnier
Daubigeon, Perrine Lemeusnier 32 *SEE* Daubigeon, Julien
Daubigny, E. M. 35; America, 1847 ***778.6*** *p83*
Daubigny, Marguerite; Quebec, 1673 ***4514.3*** *p296*
Dauboin, Gustavus 21; New Orleans, 1844 ***778.6*** *p83*
D'Aubree, Mr. 16; Jackson, MS, 1845 ***778.6*** *p83*
Daubrespy deLa Farelle, Pierre-Philippe; Quebec, 1755-1757 ***2314.30*** *p170*
Daubrespy deLa Farelle, Pierre-Philippe; Quebec, 1755 ***2314.30*** *p180*
Daubrey, Barak 50; Ontario, 1871 ***1823.21*** *p83*
Daubrey, Henry 41; Ontario, 1871 ***1823.21*** *p83*
Daudt, Christoph Ludwig; Toledo, OH, 1859 ***2526.43*** *p138*
Daudt, Karl Ludwig; Toledo, OH, 1862 ***2526.43*** *p138*
Daue, Justus Wilhelm; America, 1866 ***7420.1*** *p241*
With son
Daue, Karl; Paraguay, 1906 ***7420.1*** *p380*
Dauenhauer, Charles 36; America, 1842 ***778.6*** *p83*
Dauerman, Laurent 38; America, 1846 ***778.6*** *p83*
Dauferies, Mr. 45; America, 1842 ***778.6*** *p83*
Daugherty, Mary; Massachusetts, 1765 ***1642*** *p66*
Daugropel, Sarah 66; Ontario, 1871 ***1823.21*** *p83*
Dauiel, Mr. 19; New Orleans, 1840 ***778.6*** *p84*
Daujean, Pierre Marie 21; Biloxi, MS,, 1845 ***778.6*** *p84*
Dauks, Isaiah 32; Ontario, 1871 ***1823.21*** *p83*
Daul, Antoin 24; America, 1847 ***778.6*** *p84*
Dauligney, Mr. 29; New Orleans, 1842 ***778.6*** *p84*
Dauligny, Mr. 35; America, 1848 ***778.6*** *p84*
Daulon, Laurent 24; New Orleans, 1844 ***778.6*** *p84*
Daum, Adam; America, 1892 ***2526.43*** *p122*
Daum, Adam Georg 59; America, 1853 ***2526.42*** *p149*
*Wife:*Eva Schuler 50
*Child:*Elisabetha 20
*Child:*Karoline 13
*Child:*Louise 6
*Child:*Philipp 23
Daum, Anna Elisabeth *SEE* Daum, Katharine
Daum, Anna Katharina *SEE* Daum, Mrs. Hiernoymus
Daum, Carl Ludwig; America, 1889 ***2526.43*** *p165*
Daum, Christine Margarethe *SEE* Daum, Katharine
Daum, Elisabeth *SEE* Daum, Mrs. Hiernoymus
Daum, Elisabetha 20 *SEE* Daum, Adam Georg
Daum, Elisabetha 32; America, 1858 ***2526.43*** *p144*
Daum, Eva Schuler 50 *SEE* Daum, Adam Georg
Daum, Eva Margaretha; America, 1853 ***2526.42*** *p149*
Daum, Friedrich; America, 1857 ***2526.43*** *p122*
Daum, Georg; America, 1856 ***2526.43*** *p190*
Daum, Georg; America, 1867 ***2526.43*** *p122*
With family
Daum, Georg 44; America, 1832 ***2526.43*** *p138*
Daum, Georg; Ohio, 1853 ***2526.42*** *p118*
With wife
*Child:*Ludwig
*Child:*Margaretha
*Child:*Leonhard
*Child:*Johannes
*Child:*Heinrich
Daum, Georg, III; America, 1865 ***2526.43*** *p122*
*Wife:*Sophie Kriegbaum
*Son:*Philipp
Daum, Georg Peter; Dayton, OH, 1883 ***2526.42*** *p149*
Daum, George Lewis; Ohio, 1809-1852 ***4511.35*** *p10*
Daum, Heinrich; America, 1885 ***2526.43*** *p190*
Daum, Heinrich 14 *SEE* Daum, Georg
Daum, Hiernoymus; America, 1855 ***2526.43*** *p125*
Daum, Mrs. Hiernoymus; America, 1861 ***2526.43*** *p125*
*Daughter:*Elisabeth
*Son:*Michael
*Daughter:*Anna Katharina
*Son:*Johann Adam
Daum, Johann Adam *SEE* Daum, Mrs. Hiernoymus
Daum, Johann Robert; America, 1891 ***2526.43*** *p165*
Daum, Johannes; America, 1841 ***2526.42*** *p119*
With wife & 5 children
Daum, Johannes 20; America, 1849 ***2526.43*** *p122*
Daum, Johannes 18 *SEE* Daum, Georg
Daum, John; Ohio, 1809-1852 ***4511.35*** *p10*
Daum, Karoline 13 *SEE* Daum, Adam Georg
Daum, Katharina 16; America, 1893 ***2526.43*** *p130*

Daum, Katharine; America, 1836 *8115.12 p326*
*Child:*Christine Margarethe
*Child:*Anna Elisabeth
Daum, Leonhard; America, 1854 *2526.43 p146*
Daum, Leonhard 8 *SEE* Daum, Georg
Daum, Louise 6 *SEE* Daum, Adam Georg
Daum, Ludwig 2 *SEE* Daum, Georg
Daum, Margaretha; America, 1881 *2526.43 p125*
Daum, Margaretha 11 *SEE* Daum, Georg
Daum, Michael *SEE* Daum, Mrs. Hiernoymus
Daum, Peter; America, 1852 *2526.43 p120*
Daum, Peter; America, 1887 *2526.43 p125*
Daum, Philipp *SEE* Daum, Georg, III
Daum, Philipp 23 *SEE* Daum, Adam Georg
Daum, Sophie Kriegbaum *SEE* Daum, Georg, III
Daumiller, Rosine 23; New York, NY, 1885 *1883.7 p45*
Daunapple, Chs. Victor; Louisiana, 1841-1844 *4981.45 p210*
Daunay, Antoine 23; Quebec, 1661 *9221.17 p453*
Daunerty, John 18; Quebec, 1870 *8364.32 p23*
Daunt, William 78; Ontario, 1871 *1823.21 p83*
Daupley, Mrs. 44; New Orleans, 1846 *778.6 p84*
Daure, Pierre 24; New Orleans, 1848 *778.6 p84*
Daurm, John; Louisiana, 1874-1875 *4981.45 p298*
Dausacq, Denis; Quebec, 1661 *9221.17 p453*
Daussat, Louis 19; America, 1843 *778.6 p84*
Dausse, Jean; Louisiana, 1874-1875 *4981.45 p298*
Dauth, Luise; America, 1845 *2526.43 p175*
Daveine, Jean-Baptiste; Montreal, 1642 *9221.17 p123*
Davenne, Francois; Montreal, 1650 *9221.17 p231*
Davern, James; Louisiana, 1836-1840 *4981.45 p212*
Davey, George 46; Ontario, 1871 *1823.21 p83*
Davey, Grace 22; Ontario, 1871 *1823.21 p83*
Davey, James 40; Ontario, 1871 *1823.21 p83*
Davey, John 72; Ontario, 1893 *9228.50 p172*
Davey, Louisa Rebecca 35; Ontario, 1871 *1823.21 p84*
Davey, Roger Richards 32; Ontario, 1871 *1823.21 p84*
David, Andre; Montreal, 1650 *9221.17 p231*
David, August; Illinois, 1857 *6079.1 p4*
David, Catha. 48; New York, NY, 1893 *1883.7 p44*
David, Christian 7; New York, NY, 1893 *1883.7 p44*
David, Claude 25; Quebec, 1646 *9221.17 p163*
David, Elisabeth 5; New York, NY, 1893 *1883.7 p44*
David, Eva 11; New York, NY, 1893 *1883.7 p44*
David, Georg 55; New York, NY, 1893 *1883.7 p44*
David, Guillaume 21; Quebec, 1657 *9221.17 p355*
*Wife:*Marie Armand 19
David, J. C.; Louisiana, 1836-1840 *4981.45 p212*
David, Jacob 37; New Orleans, 1840 *778.6 p84*
David, Jacques 26; Quebec, 1658 *9221.17 p378*
David, Jean; Quebec, 1642 *9221.17 p114*
David, Johann; America, 1868 *5475.1 p455*
David, John 40; Ontario, 1871 *1823.21 p84*
David, Johs. 15; New York, NY, 1893 *1883.7 p44*
David, Juan 39; America, 1846 *778.6 p84*
David, Kristan; Greenland, 1733 *2853.20 p18*
David, Laurent 27; New Orleans, 1840 *778.6 p84*
David, Luise 25; New Orleans, 1846 *778.6 p84*
David, Maria 3; New York, NY, 1893 *1883.7 p44*
David, Marie Armand 19 *SEE* David, Guillaume
David, Pierre; Montreal, 1652 *9221.17 p268*
David, Rose; Detroit, 1929-1930 *6214.5 p67*
David, Theod.re 24; America, 1843 *778.6 p84*
Davidsohn, Widow; America, 1859 *7420.1 p184*
With 2 sons & 2 daughters
Davidsohn, David; America, 1855 *7420.1 p135*
Davidsohn, Elise; America, 1855 *7420.1 p135*
Davidsohn, Jeanette; America, 1855 *7420.1 p135*
Davidson, Agnes 65; Ontario, 1871 *1823.21 p84*
Davidson, Andrew 45; Ontario, 1871 *1823.21 p84*
Davidson, Andrew 25; South Carolina, 1812 *3476.30 p11*
Davidson, Ang 39; Ontario, 1871 *1823.17 p39*
Davidson, Charles 70; Ontario, 1871 *1823.21 p84*
Davidson, Gavin 33; Ontario, 1871 *1823.21 p84*
Davidson, Gus; Louisiana, 1874-1875 *4981.45 p298*
Davidson, Hilda S.; Chicago, 1883-1885 *1865.50 p100*
Davidson, Isabella 33; New York, NY, 1835 *5024.1 p137*
Davidson, James; Iowa, 1873 *1211.15 p10*
Davidson, James; North Carolina, 1860 *1088.45 p7*
Davidson, James 37; Ontario, 1871 *1823.21 p84*
Davidson, James 56; Ontario, 1871 *1823.21 p84*
Davidson, Jennet 27; Ontario, 1871 *1823.21 p84*
Davidson, John 35; Ontario, 1871 *1823.17 p39*
Davidson, John 35; Ontario, 1871 *1823.21 p84*
Davidson, John 45; Ontario, 1871 *1823.17 p39*
Davidson, John 47; Ontario, 1871 *1823.17 p39*
Davidson, John 52; Ontario, 1871 *1823.17 p39*
Davidson, John 58; Ontario, 1871 *1823.17 p39*
Davidson, John; Toronto, 1844 *2910.35 p116*
Davidson, John; Wisconsin, 1899 *6795.8 p179*
Davidson, John M. 57; Ontario, 1871 *1823.17 p39*
Davidson, Jonathan; New York, 1776 *8529.30 p6*

Davidson, Mary 49; Ontario, 1871 *1823.21 p84*
Davidson, Nicholas; Washington, 1881 *2770.40 p135*
Davidson, Robert 54; Ontario, 1871 *1823.21 p84*
Davidson, Robert 62; Ontario, 1871 *1823.17 p39*
Davidson, Robert St 30; Ontario, 1871 *1823.21 p84*
Davidson, Rodrick 36; Ontario, 1871 *1823.21 p84*
Davidson, Thomas; North Carolina, 1823 *1088.45 p7*
Davidson, Thomas 41; Ontario, 1871 *1823.17 p39*
Davidson, Thomas 50; Ontario, 1871 *1823.21 p84*
Davidson, William 20; New York, NY, 1835 *5024.1 p136*
Davidson, William 61; Ontario, 1871 *1823.17 p39*
Davie, Christina; New York, NY, 1836 *5024.1 p138*
Davier, Jean 33; America, 1847 *778.6 p84*
Davies, Ann *SEE* Davies, Evan O.
Davies, Ann *SEE* Davies, John Lot
Davies, Catherine *SEE* Davies, John B.
Davies, Charles 16; Ontario, 1871 *1823.21 p84*
Davies, Daniel *SEE* Davies, John W.
Davies, Daniel; Ohio, 1864 *4022.20 p272*
*Wife:*Sarah
Davies, Daniel; Ohio, 1898 *1029.59 p20*
Davies, Daniel; Washington, 1889 *2770.40 p27*
Davies, David *SEE* Davies, Lewis
Davies, David; Ohio, 1837 *4022.20 p274*
*Wife:*Mary Jenkins
*Child:*Evan Ll.
*Child:*David S.
*Child:*Mary S.
*Child:*John S.
*Child:*Peter S.
With child
Davies, David *SEE* Davies, Evan O.
Davies, David; Ohio, 1840 *4022.20 p272*
With 4 daughters
Davies, David; Ohio, 1847 *4022.20 p272*
*Wife:*Sarah
*Child:*Mary
*Child:*Evan D.
Davies, David *SEE* Davies, John W.
Davies, David L.; Ohio, 1838 *4022.20 p272*
Davies, David S. *SEE* Davies, David
Davies, David T.; Ohio, 1839 *4022.20 p273*
Davies, David T. *SEE* Davies, Thomas
Davies, Eliza *SEE* Davies, Owen
Davies, Elizabeth *SEE* Davies, John C.
Davies, Elizabeth *SEE* Davies, Evan O.
Davies, Elizabeth D. *SEE* Davies, William
Davies, Evan *SEE* Davies, John C.
Davies, Evan; Ohio, 1855 *4022.20 p273*
*Wife:*Mary Pugh
Davies, Evan D. *SEE* Davies, David
Davies, Evan John; Illinois, 1930 *121.35 p100*
Davies, Evan Ll. *SEE* Davies, David
Davies, Evan O.; Ohio, 1838-1841 *4022.20 p273*
*Wife:*Mary Jenkins
*Child:*Elizabeth
*Child:*Thomas E.
*Child:*Ann
*Child:*David
Davies, Geo. W.; Colorado, 1862-1894 *1029.59 p20*
Davies, Hannah *SEE* Davies, Isaac
Davies, Isaac; Ohio, 1837 *4022.20 p273*
*Wife:*Hannah
Davies, James 58; Ontario, 1871 *1823.21 p84*
Davies, James 75; Ontario, 1871 *1823.21 p84*
Davies, Jane *SEE* Davies, John C.
Davies, Jane *SEE* Davies, Thomas
Davies, Jenkin; Ohio, 1838 *4022.20 p273*
Davies, Joel; Ohio, 1851 *4022.20 p273*
Davies, John; Ohio, 1814-1880 *4022.20 p273*
*Wife:*Mary
Davies, John *SEE* Davies, Lewis
Davies, John *SEE* Davies, Thomas
Davies, John; Ohio, 1837 *4022.20 p273*
Davies, John; Ohio, 1840 *4022.20 p273*
*Wife:*Margaret S.
*Child:*Mary S.
With 2 children
Davies, John B.; Ohio, 1838 *4022.20 p273*
*Wife:*Catherine
With 4 children
Davies, John C.; Ohio, 1817 *4022.20 p273*
*Wife:*Mary
*Child:*Elizabeth
*Child:*Jane
*Child:*Evan
Davies, John C.; Ohio, 1837-1838 *4022.20 p273*
*Wife:*Mary C.
*Child:*John J.
Davies, John D. *SEE* Davies, John Lot
Davies, John D.; Ohio, 1846 *4022.20 p273*
*Wife:*Mary

Davies, John J. 54; New York, NY, 1894 *6512.1 p186*
Davies, John J. *SEE* Davies, John C.
Davies, John K.; Ohio, 1842 *4022.20 p273*
With family
Davies, John Lot; Ohio, 1841 *4022.20 p274*
*Wife:*Ann
*Child:*John D.
*Child:*Lot
Davies, John S. *SEE* Davies, David
Davies, John W.; Ohio, 1849 *4022.20 p274*
*Wife:*Mary
*Child:*Stephen J.
*Child:*Daniel
*Child:*David
Davies, Lewis; Ohio, 1818 *4022.20 p274*
*Wife:*Mariah Evans
*Child:*John
*Child:*David
Davies, Lot *SEE* Davies, John Lot
Davies, Margaret; Ohio, 1837 *4022.20 p277*
Davies, Margaret *SEE* Davies, William
Davies, Margaret S. *SEE* Davies, John
Davies, Mariah Evans *SEE* Davies, Lewis
Davies, Mary *SEE* Davies, John
Davies, Mary *SEE* Davies, John C.
Davies, Mary Jenkins *SEE* Davies, David
Davies, Mary Jenkins *SEE* Davies, Evan O.
Davies, Mary; Ohio, 1839 *4022.20 p283*
Davies, Mary *SEE* Davies, John D.
Davies, Mary *SEE* Davies, Thomas
Davies, Mary *SEE* Davies, Thomas
Davies, Mary; Ohio, 1846 *4022.20 p277*
Davies, Mary *SEE* Davies, David
Davies, Mary *SEE* Davies, John W.
Davies, Mary Pugh *SEE* Davies, Evan
Davies, Mary Ann; Ohio, 1834 *4022.20 p272*
Davies, Mary C. *SEE* Davies, John C.
Davies, Mary S. *SEE* Davies, David
Davies, Mary S. *SEE* Davies, John
Davies, Morgan; Ohio, 1814-1880 *4022.20 p274*
Davies, Owen; Ohio, 1849 *4022.20 p274*
*Wife:*Eliza
With 4 children
Davies, Peter S. *SEE* Davies, David
Davies, Richard; Ohio, 1837-1841 *4022.20 p274*
Davies, Sarah 55; New York, NY, 1894 *6512.1 p186*
Davies, Sarah *SEE* Davies, David
Davies, Sarah *SEE* Davies, Daniel
Davies, Stephen J. *SEE* Davies, John W.
Davies, Thomas; Ohio, 1831 *4022.20 p274*
*Wife:*Jane
*Child:*John
Davies, Thomas; Ohio, 1846 *4022.20 p274*
*Wife:*Mary
*Child:*Mary
With 4 children
*Child:*David T.
Davies, Thomas E. *SEE* Davies, Evan O.
Davies, Thomas G.; Ohio, 1837 *4022.20 p274*
Davies, William; New York, 1776 *8529.30 p6*
Davies, William; Ohio, 1849 *4022.20 p274*
*Wife:*Margaret
*Child:*Elizabeth D.
Davignon, Blaise; Montreal, 1644 *9221.17 p147*
Davignon, Noel; Montreal, 1659 *9221.17 p420*
Daviland, Cornelius; North America, 1750 *1640.8 p233*
Davill, . . .; Ontario, 1871 *1823.21 p84*
Davis, Mr. 40; New Orleans, 1848 *778.6 p84*
Davis, Alfred 40; Ontario, 1871 *1823.21 p84*
Davis, Almore C. 51; Ontario, 1871 *1823.21 p84*
Davis, Ann; Ohio, 1849 *4022.20 p275*
*Father:*David
With 2 relatives
Davis, Annie 13; Quebec, 1870 *8364.32 p23*
Davis, Benj.; Quebec, 1823-1845 *9228.50 p407*
*Wife:*Julia Ann Leavitt
Davis, Benjamin; Marston's Wharf, 1782 *8529.30 p11*
Davis, Benjamin 71; Ontario, 1871 *1823.21 p84*
Davis, Catherine; America, 1744 *1220.12 p720*
Davis, Christopher; Ohio, 1809-1852 *4511.35 p10*
Davis, Daniel 54; Ontario, 1871 *1823.21 p84*
Davis, Daniel J. *SEE* Davis, John
Davis, Daniel W.; Colorado, 1881 *1029.59 p20*
Davis, Darriel W.; Colorado, 1881 *1029.59 p20*
Davis, David; Maine, 1640-1688 *9228.50 p172*
*Wife:*Susanna Smith
Davis, David; New York, 1776 *8529.30 p11*
Davis, David; Ohio, 1841 *2763.1 p9*
Davis, David; Ohio, 1841 *4022.20 p275*
*Wife:*Margaret
*Child:*John
*Child:*Jenkin
Davis, David *SEE* Davis, Ann

Davis, David; Ohio, 1858 ***4022.20*** *p275*
Davis, David 39; Ontario, 1871 ***1823.21*** *p84*
Davis, David 50; Ontario, 1871 ***1823.21*** *p84*
Davis, David J. B. *SEE* Davis, John
Davis, David T.; Washington, 1884 ***2770.40*** *p192*
Davis, Dennis; New York, 1775 ***9228.50*** *p172*
Davis, E. A.; Louisiana, 1836-1840 ***4981.45*** *p212*
Davis, Edward; Ohio, 1809-1852 ***4511.35*** *p10*
Davis, Eliza Lovilla; Quebec, 1874-1877 ***9228.50*** *p408*
Davis, Elizabeth Phillips *SEE* Davis, Thomas P.
Davis, Elizabeth 50; Ontario, 1871 ***1823.21*** *p84*
Davis, Emily 27; Ontario, 1871 ***1823.17*** *p39*
Davis, Evan 53; Indiana, 1888-1896 ***9076.20*** *p74*
Davis, Evan T.; Ohio, 1847 ***4022.20*** *p275*
*Wife:*Margaret
*Child:*Thomas
*Child:*Jane
Davis, Francis 41; Ontario, 1871 ***1823.21*** *p84*
Davis, Frederick 63; Ontario, 1871 ***1823.17*** *p39*
Davis, Fredric 43; Ontario, 1871 ***1823.17*** *p39*
Davis, Gabriel C.; North Carolina, 1853 ***1088.45*** *p7*
Davis, Geo.; California, 1868 ***1131.61*** *p89*
Davis, George; Colorado, 1873 ***1029.59*** *p20*
Davis, Hannah Maria; New York, 1845-1850 ***9228.50*** *p407*
Davis, Henry 67; Ontario, 1871 ***1823.21*** *p84*
Davis, Hugh 59; Ontario, 1871 ***1823.21*** *p84*
Davis, Isaac 38; Ontario, 1871 ***1823.17*** *p39*
Davis, Jacob; Ohio, 1809-1852 ***4511.35*** *p10*
Davis, James; North Carolina, 1823 ***1088.45*** *p7*
Davis, James 11; Ontario, 1871 ***1823.17*** *p39*
Davis, James 50; Ontario, 1871 ***1823.21*** *p84*
Davis, James, Jr. 43; Michigan, 1880 ***4491.39*** *p7*
Davis, James, Sr. 64; Michigan, 1880 ***4491.39*** *p7*
Davis, Jane *SEE* Davis, Evan T.
Davis, Jane *SEE* Davis, John
Davis, Jefferson 15; Santa Clara Co., CA, 1870 ***8704.1*** *p24*
Davis, Jenkin *SEE* Davis, David
Davis, Jenkin; Ohio, 1847 ***4022.20*** *p275*
Davis, Jeremiah; Boston, 1766 ***1642*** *p37*
Davis, Jno.; Ontario, 1787 ***1276.15*** *p230*
Davis, John; Boston, 1774 ***8529.30*** *p2A*
Davis, John; Jamestown, VA, 1633 ***1658.20*** *p211*
Davis, John; Ohio, 1814-1880 ***4022.20*** *p275*
Davis, John *SEE* Davis, Thomas P.
Davis, John *SEE* Davis, David
Davis, John; Ohio, 1847 ***4022.20*** *p275*
*Wife:*Mary
*Child:*Jane
*Child:*Daniel J.
*Child:*Stephen
*Child:*David J. B.
*Child:*Thomas
Davis, John; Ohio, 1847 ***4022.20*** *p275*
*Child:*John Davis
With wife
*Child:*Saer
Davis, John 36; Ontario, 1871 ***1823.21*** *p84*
Davis, John 39; Ontario, 1871 ***1823.21*** *p85*
Davis, John 45; Ontario, 1871 ***1823.17*** *p39*
Davis, John 60; Ontario, 1871 ***1823.21*** *p84*
Davis, John; Utah, 1860 ***9228.50*** *p396*
Davis, John Davis *SEE* Davis, John
Davis, John P. 47; Ontario, 1871 ***1823.21*** *p85*
Davis, Joseph; Ohio, 1809-1852 ***4511.35*** *p10*
Davis, Julia Ann Leavitt *SEE* Davis, Benj.
Davis, Lewis 65; Ontario, 1871 ***1823.21*** *p85*
Davis, Margaret *SEE* Davis, David
Davis, Margaret *SEE* Davis, Evan T.
Davis, Margaret Evans *SEE* Davis, Thomas
Davis, Martin; Louisiana, 1836-1841 ***4981.45*** *p208*
Davis, Mary; Maryland, 1674-1675 ***1236.25*** *p52*
Davis, Mary Albans *SEE* Davis, Stephen
Davis, Mary *SEE* Davis, John
Davis, Mary 48; Ontario, 1871 ***1823.21*** *p85*
Davis, Mary 69; Ontario, 1871 ***1823.21*** *p85*
Davis, Mary A. 67; Michigan, 1880 ***4491.39*** *p7*
Davis, Morgan; Ohio, 1847 ***4022.20*** *p275*
Davis, P. 36; New Orleans, 1844 ***778.6*** *p84*
Davis, Percy Leonard Edward; Miami, 1935 ***4984.12*** *p39*
Davis, Robert 67; Michigan, 1880 ***4491.39*** *p7*
Davis, Robert; New York, 1783 ***8529.30*** *p11*
Davis, Robert 60; Ontario, 1871 ***1823.17*** *p39*
Davis, Robert D. 67; Ontario, 1871 ***1823.17*** *p39*
Davis, Saer *SEE* Davis, John
Davis, Samuel; Boston, 1766 ***1642*** *p36*
Davis, Samuel 69; Ontario, 1871 ***1823.21*** *p85*
Davis, Sarah Lucinda; Quebec, 1876 ***9228.50*** *p408*
Davis, Stephen; Ohio, 1836 ***4022.20*** *p275*
*Wife:*Mary Albans
With 4 children
Davis, Stephen *SEE* Davis, John
Davis, Susanna Smith *SEE* Davis, David
Davis, Thomas; Marston's Wharf, 1782 ***8529.30*** *p11*
Davis, Thomas *SEE* Davis, Evan T.
Davis, Thomas *SEE* Davis, John
Davis, Thomas; Ohio, 1847 ***4022.20*** *p275*
*Wife:*Margaret Evans
With 5 children
Davis, Thomas 27; Ontario, 1871 ***1823.21*** *p85*
Davis, Thomas 31; Ontario, 1871 ***1823.21*** *p85*
Davis, Thomas 60; Ontario, 1871 ***1823.21*** *p85*
Davis, Thomas E. 55; Ontario, 1871 ***1823.17*** *p39*
Davis, Thomas P.; Ohio, 1840 ***4022.20*** *p275*
*Father:*John
*Mother:*Elizabeth Phillips
Davis, Timothy; Iowa, 1885 ***1211.15*** *p10*
Davis, Tom; New York, NY, 1884 ***8427.14*** *p45*
Davis, W. J.; Iowa, 1888 ***1211.15*** *p10*
Davis, William; New Jersey, 1777 ***8529.30*** *p6*
Davis, William 22; Ontario, 1871 ***1823.21*** *p85*
Davis, William 28; Ontario, 1871 ***1823.17*** *p39*
Davis, William 33; Ontario, 1871 ***1823.21*** *p85*
Davis, William 40; Ontario, 1871 ***1823.21*** *p85*
Davis, William 42; Ontario, 1871 ***1823.21*** *p85*
Davis, William 43; Ontario, 1871 ***1823.17*** *p39*
Davis, William 50; Ontario, 1871 ***1823.21*** *p85*
Davis, William 60; Ontario, 1871 ***1823.21*** *p85*
Davis, William; Philadelphia, 1777 ***8529.30*** *p7A*
Davis, William; Washington, 1883 ***2770.40*** *p136*
Davis, William G. 37; Ontario, 1871 ***1823.17*** *p39*
Davis, William M.; Iowa, 1884 ***1211.15*** *p10*
Davis, William R. 30; Indiana, 1879-1883 ***9076.20*** *p70*
Davis, Wm J. 19; Ontario, 1871 ***1823.21*** *p85*
Davison, Alexander 40; Ontario, 1871 ***1823.17*** *p39*
Davison, Alexander 57; Ontario, 1871 ***1823.21*** *p85*
Davison, Benjamin; Boston, 1764 ***1642*** *p33*
Davison, Crawford 5; Ontario, 1871 ***1823.17*** *p39*
Davison, Isaac 38; Ontario, 1871 ***1823.17*** *p39*
Davison, James; South Carolina, 1813 ***3208.30*** *p19*
Davison, James; South Carolina, 1813 ***3208.30*** *p31*
Davison, John 33; Ontario, 1871 ***1823.21*** *p85*
Davison, John 49; Ontario, 1871 ***1823.21*** *p85*
Davison, Joseph; Washington, 1884 ***2770.40*** *p192*
Davison, Thomas 40; Ontario, 1871 ***1823.21*** *p85*
Davison, William 50; Ontario, 1871 ***1823.21*** *p85*
Davisson, David; Maine, 1640-1688 ***9228.50*** *p172*
*Wife:*Susanna Smith
Davisson, Susanna Smith *SEE* Davisson, David
Davitt, Thomas 85; Ontario, 1871 ***1823.17*** *p39*
Davost, Ambroise; Quebec, 1632 ***9221.17*** *p27*
Davoust, Jean; Montreal, 1653 ***9221.17*** *p287*
Davuze, Etienne Victor 26; Port uncertain, 1848 ***778.6*** *p84*
Davy, John; Maryland, 1672 ***1236.25*** *p47*
Davy, Sarah 56; Ontario, 1871 ***1823.21*** *p85*
Davy, William 46; Ontario, 1871 ***1823.21*** *p85*
Daw, George 16; Ontario, 1871 ***1823.21*** *p85*
Daw, Susan 21; Ontario, 1871 ***1823.21*** *p85*
Dawby, Thomas; Massachusetts, 1675-1676 ***1642*** *p128*
Dawlins, James; Philadelphia, 1777 ***8529.30*** *p7A*
Dawson, Arthur; California, 1934-1983 ***9228.50*** *p394*
Dawson, Benjamin 68; Ontario, 1871 ***1823.21*** *p85*
Dawson, George; Ohio, 1809-1852 ***4511.35*** *p10*
Dawson, James 53; Ontario, 1871 ***1823.21*** *p85*
Dawson, John; North Carolina, 1827-1832 ***1088.45*** *p7*
Dawson, John 40; Ontario, 1871 ***1823.21*** *p85*
Dawson, Jonathan 59; Ontario, 1871 ***1823.21*** *p85*
Dawson, Joseph 44; Ontario, 1871 ***1823.21*** *p85*
Dawson, Margaret 42; Ontario, 1871 ***1823.17*** *p40*
Dawson, Martha 20; Ontario, 1871 ***1823.17*** *p40*
Dawson, Mary Jane; New Orleans, 1851 ***7242.30*** *p139*
Dawson, Mathew 60; Ontario, 1871 ***1823.17*** *p40*
Dawson, Peter 30; Ontario, 1871 ***1823.21*** *p85*
Dawson, Philip 58; Ontario, 1871 ***1823.21*** *p85*
Dawson, Richard 56; Ontario, 1871 ***1823.17*** *p40*
Dawson, Samuel; Ohio, 1809-1852 ***4511.35*** *p10*
Dawson, Thomas; Marston's Wharf, 1782 ***8529.30*** *p11*
Dawson, Thomas; New Orleans, 1851 ***7242.30*** *p139*
Dawson, Thomas 57; Ontario, 1871 ***1823.21*** *p85*
Dawson, W. F. 41; Ontario, 1871 ***1823.21*** *p85*
Dawson, Wm 40; Ontario, 1871 ***1823.21*** *p85*
Dawson, Wm. 32; Quebec, 1910 ***2897.7*** *p10*
Day, Abram 41; Ontario, 1871 ***1823.17*** *p40*
Day, Alicia 24; Ontario, 1871 ***1823.21*** *p86*
Day, Antony 37; Ontario, 1871 ***1823.21*** *p86*
Day, Flora 7; Ontario, 1871 ***1823.21*** *p86*
Day, George 36; Ontario, 1871 ***1823.17*** *p40*
Day, George 40; Ontario, 1871 ***1823.21*** *p86*
Day, James; New York, 1777 ***8529.30*** *p11*
Day, John 29; Ontario, 1871 ***1823.17*** *p40*
Day, Mary 10; Quebec, 1870 ***8364.32*** *p23*
Day, Michael; New York, NY, 1832 ***3274.55*** *p27*
Day, Patrick; Boston, 1763 ***1642*** *p32*
Day, William 43; Ontario, 1871 ***1823.21*** *p86*
Dayet, J. 19; America, 1843 ***778.6*** *p84*
Dayley, Michael 21; Ontario, 1871 ***1823.17*** *p40*
Daymares, Pierre 20; New Orleans, 1840 ***778.6*** *p84*
Dayre, Mr. 22; Port uncertain, 1844 ***778.6*** *p84*
Dayton, Aaron Ogden; Ohio, 1818 ***3580.20*** *p31*
Dayton, Aaron Ogden; Ohio, 1818 ***6020.12*** *p7*
Dayton, George; New York, 1860 ***358.56*** *p4*
Dazemard deLusignan, Paul-Louis; Quebec, 1683-1688 ***2314.30*** *p168*
Dazemard deLusignan, Paul-Louis; Quebec, 1685 ***2314.30*** *p180*
Dazemat, Joseph-Arnauld; Quebec, 1662 ***9221.17*** *p483*
Dazet, Mr. 40; Port uncertain, 1844 ***778.6*** *p84*
Dazet, Dominique; Louisiana, 1874 ***4981.45*** *p295*
Dazet, Francois 19; New Orleans, 1844 ***778.6*** *p84*
Dazete, Jean 18; America, 1845 ***778.6*** *p84*
Dazette, H. 26; America, 1848 ***778.6*** *p84*
Dazette, P. 22; America, 1848 ***778.6*** *p84*
Dazwell, Elizabeth; Maryland, 1672 ***1236.25*** *p48*
Dea, Alice 17; Ontario, 1871 ***1823.21*** *p86*
Dea, Henrietta 28; Ontario, 1871 ***1823.21*** *p86*
Deach, George 57; Ontario, 1871 ***1823.21*** *p86*
Deacon, Ann 84; Ontario, 1871 ***1823.21*** *p86*
Deacon, Georgina 12; Ontario, 1871 ***1823.21*** *p86*
Deacon, Heneretta 34; Ontario, 1871 ***1823.21*** *p86*
Deacon, John 50; Ontario, 1871 ***1823.21*** *p86*
Deacon, Joseph 69; Ontario, 1871 ***1823.21*** *p86*
Deacon, William 50; Ontario, 1871 ***1823.17*** *p40*
Deacons, Garrett 47; Ontario, 1871 ***1823.17*** *p40*
Deadman, Abdiel G. 50; Ontario, 1871 ***1823.21*** *p86*
Deadman, Henry 60; Ontario, 1871 ***1823.21*** *p86*
Deadman, J. D. 48; Ontario, 1871 ***1823.21*** *p86*
Deadman, Jane 51; Ontario, 1871 ***1823.21*** *p86*
Deadman, Tho.; Maryland, 1674 ***1236.25*** *p49*
Deadman, William 23; Ontario, 1871 ***1823.21*** *p86*
Deadman, William 38; Ontario, 1871 ***1823.21*** *p86*
Deady, Martin; Toronto, 1844 ***2910.35*** *p115*
Deady, Michael; Toronto, 1844 ***2910.35*** *p115*
Dealy, Patrick; Boston, 1763 ***1642*** *p48*
Dean, Edwin 42; Ontario, 1871 ***1823.21*** *p86*
Dean, Emma 15; Ontario, 1871 ***1823.17*** *p40*
Dean, John; Ohio, 1809-1852 ***4511.35*** *p10*
Dean, John 32; Ontario, 1871 ***1823.21*** *p86*
Dean, John 50; Ontario, 1871 ***1823.17*** *p40*
Dean, William 41; Ontario, 1871 ***1823.21*** *p86*
Dean, William; Philadelphia, 1777 ***8529.30*** *p2A*
Deane, James 18; Quebec, 1870 ***8364.32*** *p23*
Deaneois, Leke 26; New York, NY, 1884 ***8427.14*** *p45*
DeAnglis, Giovanni 20; New Orleans, 1748 ***778.6*** *p84*
Dear, Edward; Ipswich, MA, 1678 ***1642*** *p70*
Dearness, John 45; Ontario, 1871 ***1823.21*** *p86*
Death, Charles 21; Quebec, 1870 ***8364.32*** *p23*
Death, William 33; Ontario, 1871 ***1823.17*** *p40*
Deavenport, Peter; North Carolina, 1842 ***1088.45*** *p7*
Deaw, Andrew; Ohio, 1809-1852 ***4511.35*** *p10*
Debacher, Adam; New Castle, DE, 1817-1818 ***90.20*** *p150*
DeBaillon, Catherine; Quebec, 1669 ***4514.3*** *p297*
Debardon, Jacques 50; Port uncertain, 1842 ***778.6*** *p84*
De Bartone, . . .; New England, n.d. ***9228.50*** *p94*
De Bartone Family ; Newfoundland, 1500-1599 ***9228.50*** *p96*
De Bartram, Thomas; Ohio, 1810 ***9228.50*** *p95*
Debartson, Angelina 14; Mississippi, 1847 ***778.6*** *p84*
Debartson, Catherina 5; Mississippi, 1847 ***778.6*** *p84*
Debartson, Marie 19; Mississippi, 1847 ***778.6*** *p84*
Debartson, Marie 43; Mississippi, 1847 ***778.6*** *p84*
Debartson, Mathis 12; Mississippi, 1847 ***778.6*** *p85*
Debartson, Pierre 20; Mississippi, 1847 ***778.6*** *p85*
Debartson, Pierre 44; Mississippi, 1847 ***778.6*** *p85*
Debauche, Ollvier; Philadelphia, 1880 ***1494.20*** *p13*
Debauge, Eugene Etienne; Illinois, 1860 ***6079.1*** *p4*
De Bausset, A.; Louisiana, 1874 ***4981.45*** *p131*
De Bavee, Dr. 27; New York, NY, 1856 ***1766.1*** *p45*
De Beauchamp, James; Wisconsin, 1847 ***9228.50*** *p317*
*Wife:*Rachel Mahy
De Beauchamp, Rachel Mahy *SEE* De Beauchamp, James
DeBeaulieu, Pierre; Quebec, 1653 ***9221.17*** *p274*
DeBeaune, Joseph; Quebec, 1639 ***9221.17*** *p87*
Debeauregard, Marie; Canada, 1665 ***1142.10*** *p128*
DeBeauregard, Marie; Quebec, 1665 ***4514.3*** *p297*
De Beaurenom, Antoinette; Quebec, 1671 ***4514.3*** *p273*
DeBelleau, Catherine; Quebec, 1667 ***4514.3*** *p297*
deBelleborne, Jean; Quebec, 1619 ***9221.17*** *p20*
deBellecour, Guy 17; Quebec, 1647 ***9221.17*** *p188*
*Sister:*Marie-Madeleine 3
deBellecour, Marie-Madeleine 3 *SEE* deBellecour, Guy
Debello, Michele; Colorado, 1894 ***1029.59*** *p21*
De Bello, Michele; Colorado, 1894 ***1029.59*** *p22*
Debenham, . . .; California, 1890-1899 ***9228.50*** *p172*
Debenham, . . .; California, 1890 ***9228.50*** *p473*

Debergh, Gilbert F.; Ontario, 1787 *1276.15 p231*
  With child & 3 relatives
de Bernales, Lucy Maria; New York, 1845-1870 *9228.50 p271*
Debersold, Christian; Ohio, 1809-1852 *4511.35 p10*
DeBerunine, Marie; Quebec, 1671 *4514.3 p297*
DeBidequin, Marie-Madeleine; Quebec, 1673 *4514.3 p297*
Deblanc, Jean 35; America, 1845 *778.6 p85*
Deblois, Gregoire 23; Quebec, 1657 *9221.17 p355*
De Blois, Stephen; America, n.d. *9228.50 p172*
De Boer, Fred Wander; Indiana, 1919 *1029.59 p21*
  Wife:Klaska
  Child:Joseph A.
De Boer, Joseph A. 1 SEE De Boer, Fred Wander
De Boer, Klaska SEE De Boer, Fred Wander
DeBoisandre, Catherine; Quebec, 1663 *4514.3 p297*
DeBoisandre, Jeanne-Claude; Quebec, 1667 *4514.3 p297*
DeBonin, Nicole; Quebec, 1671 *4514.3 p298*
Debose, V...or 25; Port uncertain, 1842 *778.6 p85*
Debourase, Alexandre 43; America, 1841 *778.6 p85*
De Bourcier, . . .; Iowa, n.d. *9228.50 p172*
De Bourcier, Peter; Nova Scotia, 1767 *9228.50 p172*
DeBoza, M. 38; America, 1845 *778.6 p85*
DeBretigny, Marie; Quebec, 1667 *4514.3 p298*
Debrie, Joseph 22; Louisiana, 1848 *778.6 p85*
De Broder, Elise Marie Louise; Toronto, 1916 *9228.50 p173*
De Broder, Elise Marie Louise; Wisconsin, 1916-1990 *9228.50 p173*
De Broder, Frederick John; Chicago, 1893-1927 *9228.50 p173*
De Broder, George Philip; America, 1891-1972 *9228.50 p172*
De Broder, Lillian; Canada, 1964 *9228.50 p160*
De Broder, Lillian; Wisconsin, 1964 *9228.50 p160*
De Broder, Lillian Maud; Canada, 1895-1977 *9228.50 p174*
De Broder, Lillian Maud; Wisconsin, 1895-1977 *9228.50 p174*
De Broder, Linda Lucy; New York, 1947 *9228.50 p174*
De Broder, Philippa Georgina; Madison, WI, 1885-1965 *9228.50 p172*
De Broder, Philippa Georgina; Wisconsin, 1909-1933 *9228.50 p522*
De Broder, Wm. Coghlan; Canada, 1895-1977 *9228.50 p174*
De Broder, Wm. Coghlan; Wisconsin, 1895-1977 *9228.50 p174*
Debroux, Alphonse; New York, NY, 1855 *1494.20 p13*
Debroux, Anne Josephe Denis SEE Debroux, Hubert
Debroux, Clementine SEE Debroux, Hubert
Debroux, Ernest SEE Debroux, Hubert
Debroux, Hubert; Wisconsin, 1846-1856 *1495.20 p29*
  Wife:Anne Josephe Denis
  Child:Ernest
  Child:Clementine
Debroux, Isidore; Wisconsin, 1846-1856 *1495.20 p29*
Debure, Marie; Quebec, 1665 *4514.3 p298*
  Sister:Suzanne
  With brother-in-law & niece
Debure, Suzanne SEE Debure, Marie
Debure, Suzanne; Quebec, 1665 *4514.3 p298*
Debure, Suzanne; Quebec, 1665 *4514.3 p298*
Debus, Dorothea Friederike; America, 1882 *7420.1 p328*
Debus, Eberhardt; North Carolina, 1845 *1088.45 p7*
Debusmann, Christian; America, 1881 *5475.1 p120*
  Wife:Sophie Muller
Debusmann, Sophie Muller SEE Debusmann, Christian
De Caen, . . .; New England, n.d. *9228.50 p151*
De Caen, Ann; Newfoundland, 1845-1945 *9228.50 p174*
De Caen, Ann; Newfoundland, 1845-1945 *9228.50 p174*
De Caen, Ezechiel; Ohio, 1810 *9228.50 p18A*
  With wife
  With 12 sons & 5 daughters
De Caen, Frank; Canada, 1914 *9228.50 p175*
De Cain, . . .; New England, n.d. *9228.50 p151*
Decamp, Charles; Boston, 1871 *1494.20 p12*
Decamp, Charles Joseph; New York, NY, 1874 *1494.20 p12*
De Camp, Ezechiel; Ohio, 1810 *9228.50 p18A*
  With wife
  With 12 sons & 5 daughters
Decamp, Marie Therese; Wisconsin, 1855-1870 *1495.20 p8*
Decariau, Francois 44; Louisiana, 1848 *778.6 p85*
DeCarpenterie, Miss 43; America, 1843 *778.6 p85*
De Carteret, Charles; Boston, 1715 *9228.50 p155*
De Carteret, Clement; New England, 1776 *9228.50 p18A*
De Carteret, Clement; Newfoundland, 1776 *9228.50 p18A*
De Carteret, Clement; Ontario, 1880 *9228.50 p155*

De Carteret, John Alpheus SEE De Carteret, John Dumaresq
De Carteret, John Dumaresq; Massachusetts, 1873 *9228.50 p155*
  Son:John Alpheus
De Carteret, Peyton; West Indies, 1652 *9228.50 p156*
De Carteret, Philip; New York, 1665 *9228.50 p156*
DeCarteret, Philip; Virginia, 1665 *9228.50 p124*
De Carteret, Philippe; New Jersey, 1665 *9228.50 p51*
DeCastello, Richard M.; Chicago, 1870-1910 *2853.20 p460*
De Castello, Richard M.; Iowa, 1895 *2853.20 p227*
Decaux, A. 31; New Orleans, 1844 *778.6 p85*
Decaux, N. 25; New Orleans, 1844 *778.6 p85*
De Caux, Peter; Portsmouth, NH, 1735 *9228.50 p170*
Dechard, Jeanne; Quebec, 1667 *4514.3 p298*
DeCharmesnil, Francoise; Quebec, 1667 *4514.3 p298*
Dechaux, Francoise 39; Quebec, 1660 *9221.17 p432*
Dechaux, Francoise 39; Quebec, 1660 *9221.17 p432*
Decher, Joseph; Valdivia, Chile, 1850 *1192.4 p50*
  With wife & 7 children
  With child 2
  With child 26
DeChevrainville, Claude; Quebec, 1665 *4514.3 p298*
DeChevrainville, Marie-Madeleine; Quebec, 1663-1665 *4514.3 p298*
Deckelnick, Anna 1 SEE Deckelnick, Nik.
Deckelnick, Franz 3 SEE Deckelnick, Nik.
Deckelnick, Karl 5 SEE Deckelnick, Nik.
Deckelnick, Margarethe Wagner 40 SEE Deckelnick, Nik.
Deckelnick, Mathias 13 SEE Deckelnick, Nik.
Deckelnick, Nik. 36; America, 1864 *5475.1 p353*
  Wife:Margarethe Wagner 40
  Son:Franz 3
  Daughter:Anna 1
  Son:Karl 5
  Son:P. Otto 15
  Son:Nikolaus 10
  Son:Mathias 13
Deckelnick, Nikolaus 10 SEE Deckelnick, Nik.
Deckelnick, P. Otto 15 SEE Deckelnick, Nik.
Decker, Anna; America, 1876 *5475.1 p257*
Decker, Christ. 24; America, 1840 *778.6 p85*
Decker, Christian; New York, 1860 *358.56 p4*
Decker, David; Brazil, 1862 *5475.1 p515*
  Wife:Elisabeth Muller
  Son:Friedrich
  Daughter:Katharina
  Daughter:Karoline
  Son:Peter
  Son:Jakob
Decker, David Y. 75; Ontario, 1871 *1823.21 p86*
Decker, Elisabeth Muller 45 SEE Decker, David
Decker, Frederick; Ohio, 1844 *2763.1 p9*
Decker, Friedrich 11 SEE Decker, David
Decker, Gertrud SEE Decker, Peter
Decker, Jakob 16 SEE Decker, David
Decker, Johann; America, 1880 *5475.1 p219*
Decker, Karoline 9 SEE Decker, David
Decker, Katharina 7 SEE Decker, David
Decker, Margarethe Becker SEE Decker, Peter
Decker, Michel; America, 1880 *5475.1 p219*
Decker, Peter; America, 1880 *5475.1 p220*
  Wife:Margarethe Becker
  Daughter:Gertrud
Decker, Peter 17 SEE Decker, David
Deckert, Francis; Ohio, 1809-1852 *4511.35 p10*
Deckert, Johanne; America, 1867 *7919.3 p527*
Deckes, John; Ohio, 1809-1852 *4511.35 p10*
Deckmann, Johann Henrich; New England, 1850 *170.15 p22*
Deckmann, Johannes; Pennsylvania, 1809 *170.15 p22*
De Clarck, Bruno; New York, 1902 *1766.20 p18*
Declew, John; New York, NY, 1866 *1494.20 p12*
Decloux, John; New York, NY, 1866 *1494.20 p12*
Decobert, Eugene; Illinois, 1918 *6007.60 p9*
DeCognac, Jacques 22; Montreal, 1659 *9221.17 p417*
DeCoignac, Jean; Quebec, 1656 *9221.17 p337*
Decombe, August 40; St. Louis, 1847 *778.6 p85*
Decon, Catharine 64; Ontario, 1871 *1823.21 p86*
DeCoppequesne, Marie-Charlotte; Quebec, 1666 *4514.3 p299*
de Corne, Pierre; Virginia, 1700 *9230.15 p81*
Decoss, E. 13; America, 1847 *778.6 p85*
Decoss, M. 38; America, 1847 *778.6 p85*
De Costa, . . .; Plymouth, MA, 1623 *9228.50 p176*
De Coster, . . .; Annapolis, N.S., 1758 *9228.50 p175*
De Coster, . . .; Plymouth, MA, 1623 *9228.50 p176*
Decouenne, . . .; Quebec, 1667 *9221.17 p179*
Decour, Joseph Theodore 22; New Orleans, 1840 *778.6 p85*
De Coursey, . . .; Los Angeles, n.d. *9228.50 p176*

Decourt, Mr. 33; Port uncertain, 1845 *778.6 p85*
Decremer, Anne Marie SEE Decremer, Henri
Decremer, Charles Joseph SEE Decremer, Henri
Decremer, Floriant SEE Decremer, Henri
Decremer, Henri; Wisconsin, 1855 *1495.20 p40*
  Wife:Ursule Dupuis
  Child:Anne Marie
  Child:Jean Joseph
  Child:Floriant
  Child:Charles Joseph
  Child:Victor Joseph
  Child:Henri Joseph
  Child:Pierre
Decremer, Henri Joseph SEE Decremer, Henri
Decremer, Jean Joseph SEE Decremer, Henri
Decremer, Pierre SEE Decremer, Henri
Decremer, Ursule Dupuis SEE Decremer, Henri
Decremer, Victor Joseph SEE Decremer, Henri
Decrocq, Joseph 54; New Orleans, 1848 *778.6 p85*
Decrocq, Louise 48; New Orleans, 1848 *778.6 p85*
Decuille, Jacques I.; Illinois, 1852 *6079.1 p4*
Decuyes, Jules 22; America, 1848 *778.6 p85*
Dedeker, Charles Bernard; Wisconsin, 1880 *1495.20 p45*
  Wife:Jeanne Delligne
  Child:Jean Baptiste
  Child:Pierre Joseph
  With daughter-in-law
  Child:Olivier
Dedeker, Jean Baptiste SEE Dedeker, Charles Bernard
Dedeker, Jeanne Delligne SEE Dedeker, Charles Bernard
Dedeker, Olivier SEE Dedeker, Charles Bernard
Dedeker, Pierre Joseph SEE Dedeker, Charles Bernard
Dedera, Vojtech J.; America, 1882 *2853.20 p442*
  With parents
Dedinger, Barbara 18; Missouri, 1845 *778.6 p85*
Dedisse, Julius; Colorado, 1897 *1029.59 p21*
Dedisse, Julius C.; Colorado, 1861 *1029.59 p21*
Dee, Carl F.; Wisconsin, 1907 *6795.8 p160*
Dee, Julius; Wisconsin, 1912 *6795.8 p175*
Dee, Patrick; Ohio, 1840-1897 *8365.35 p15*
Dee, Robert 33; North Carolina, 1774 *1422.10 p56*
Deep, John; North Carolina, 1710 *3629.40 p8*
Deesby, Armand 49; Ontario, 1871 *1823.17 p40*
DeFer, Ed. 28; New Orleans, 1848 *778.6 p85*
Deffanday, Theodore; Illinois, 1852 *6079.1 p4*
Deffez, Alex. 28; New Orleans, 1843 *778.6 p85*
Deffis, P. 26; New Orleans, 1848 *778.6 p85*
Deffosse, F. 32; America, 1842 *778.6 p85*
DeFontenay, Catherine; Quebec, 1667 *4514.3 p299*
Deforest, Abram; Ontario, 1787 *1276.15 p230*
  With 2 relatives
Defrain, Eli 28; Ontario, 1871 *1823.17 p40*
Defranclieu, Marie; Quebec, 1667 *4514.3 p353*
Defrenne, Hector; Detroit, 1871 *1494.20 p11*
Defretat, Amable 32; Quebec, 1646 *5224.17 p160*
Defrul, Nicholas; Ontario, 1871 *1823.17 p40*
Degan, Terrence; Ohio, 1809-1852 *4511.35 p10*
De Garie, Charles; Wisconsin, 1819-1919 *9228.50 p176*
De Garie Family ; Florida, 1980-1989 *9228.50 p176*
De Garis, Charles; Wisconsin, 1819-1919 *9228.50 p176*
De Garis, George SEE De Garis, Thomas
De Garis, Thomas; Wisconsin, 1860 *9228.50 p176*
  Relative:George
Degasperi, Guiseppe 26; New York, NY, 1894 *6512.1 p182*
DeGasson, Mrs. 49; New Orleans, 1848 *778.6 p85*
Degel, Jacob; Ohio, 1809-1852 *4511.35 p10*
Degelow, W. F.; Valdivia, Chile, 1852 *1192.4 p54*
Degen, John; Colorado, 1897 *1029.59 p21*
Degener, Christian Friedrich; Wisconsin, 1859 *6795.8 p137*
Degenhard, Henrich; Port uncertain, 1896 *170.15 p22*
  With 3 children
Degenhard, Joseph; Ohio, 1809-1852 *4511.35 p10*
Degenhardt, Kaspar G. 20; New York, NY, 1864 *8425.62 p198*
Degenhart, Jan; Baltimore, 1872 *2853.20 p126*
Degenhart, Ralthaser 27; Louisiana, 1848 *778.6 p85*
Degeria, Cornelius 33; Ontario, 1871 *1823.17 p87*
Degermont, Claude; Quebec, 1643 *9221.17 p132*
DeGiacinto, Vittorio; Illinois, 1930 *121.35 p101*
DeGienet, Geo.; Louisiana, 1874 *4981.45 p295*
Deglise, Mr. 22; New Orleans, 1840 *778.6 p85*
De Grace, Geo.; Louisiana, 1874-1875 *4981.45 p298*
Degraf, Gottfried 17; Portland, ME, 1911 *970.38 p76*
Degraf, Heinrich Carl 26; Portland, ME, 1911 *970.38 p76*
Degrangagnage, Alexandre SEE Degrangagnage, Francois Jos.
Degrangagnage, Dieudonne Jean SEE Degrangagnage, Francois Jos.
Degrangagnage, Felicien SEE Degrangagnage, Francois Jos.

Degrangagnage, Francois A. *SEE* Degrangagnage, Francois Jos.
Degrangagnage, Francois Jos.; Wisconsin, 1856 ***1495.20*** *p28*
*Wife:*Marie Josephine Cheron
*Child:*Alexandre
*Child:*Pascal
*Child:*Jean Baptiste
*Child:*Francois A.
*Child:*Dieudonne Jean
*Child:*Felicien
*Child:*Victor
Degrangagnage, Jean Baptiste *SEE* Degrangagnage, Francois Jos.
Degrangagnage, Marie Josephine Cheron *SEE* Degrangagnage, Francois Jos.
Degrangagnage, Pascal *SEE* Degrangagnage, Francois Jos.
Degrangagnage, Victor *SEE* Degrangagnage, Francois Jos.
Degraw, Cornelius 60; Ontario, 1871 ***1823.21*** *p87*
Degraw, Cornelius 62; Ontario, 1871 ***1823.21*** *p87*
De Greaves, John; Honolulu, 1878 ***9228.50*** *p176*
De Grenier, Earnest; Colorado, 1878 ***1029.59*** *p21*
Degri, Dominique 32; America, 1840 ***778.6*** *p85*
Degri, Francoise 23; America, 1840 ***778.6*** *p85*
Degrot, Sarah 35; Ontario, 1871 ***1823.17*** *p40*
de Grote, Benjamin; New York, 1859 ***358.56*** *p54*
de Grouchy, Mr.; America, n.d. ***9228.50*** *p179*
De Gruchy, . . .; California, 1900-1983 ***9228.50*** *p180*
DeGruchy, Mr.; America, 1800-1817 ***9228.50*** *p179*
With wife
De Gruchy, Abraham; America, 1793-1893 ***9228.50*** *p179*
De Gruchy, Abraham; Canada, 1793-1893 ***9228.50*** *p179*
De Gruchy, Allan Garfield; Indiana, 1937 ***9228.50*** *p177*
DeGruchy, Alphonse; America, 1817 ***9228.50*** *p179*
De Gruchy, David *SEE* De Gruchy, Jeanne Marie
De Gruchy, David 18; Baltimore, 1872 ***9228.50*** *p178*
De Gruchy, David; Nova Scotia, 1836 ***9228.50*** *p176*
De Gruchy, E. Douglas; Chicago, 1850-1950 ***9228.50*** *p178*
De Gruchy, E.F.; New York, 1850-1950 ***9228.50*** *p178*
De Gruchy, Edward; Canada, n.d. ***9228.50*** *p178*
De Gruchy, Edward; Quebec, 1868-1876 ***9228.50*** *p178*
De Gruchy, Elias; New York, 1850-1859 ***9228.50*** *p81*
De Gruchy, Elias; New York, NY, 1852 ***9228.50*** *p177*
*Brother:*John
*Brother:*Thomas
De Gruchy, Elizabeth; America, 1850-1950 ***9228.50*** *p177*
De Gruchy, Francis; Canada, n.d. ***9228.50*** *p178*
De Gruchy, George John; Canada, 1870 ***9228.50*** *p178*
De Gruchy, Henry Eustace Sligh; Maine, 1920-1983 ***9228.50*** *p178*
De Gruchy, James; America, 1871-1971 ***9228.50*** *p178*
De Gruchy, James Gwyer; America, 1890-1899 ***9228.50*** *p177*
De Gruchy, Jean; America, 1795-1895 ***9228.50*** *p179*
De Gruchy, Jean; Canada, 1795-1895 ***9228.50*** *p179*
De Gruchy, Jeanne Marie; Baltimore, 1913 ***9228.50*** *p178*
De Gruchy, Jeanne Marie; Baltimore, 1913 ***9228.50*** *p284*
*Brother:*David
De Gruchy, John; America, n.d. ***9228.50*** *p178*
De Gruchy, John; New York, n.d. ***9228.50*** *p178*
De Gruchy, John *SEE* De Gruchy, Elias
De Gruchy, John; Newfoundland, n.d. ***9228.50*** *p178*
De Gruchy, John; St. Johns, N.F., n.d. ***9228.50*** *p178*
De Gruchy, John Walter; Montreal, 1900 ***9228.50*** *p178*
De Gruchy, Judith 71; Massachusetts, 1847 ***9228.50*** *p18A*
De Gruchy, Matthew; Virginia, 1825 ***9228.50*** *p178*
De Gruchy, Moses; America, 1791-1891 ***9228.50*** *p179*
De Gruchy, Moses; Canada, 1791-1891 ***9228.50*** *p179*
De Gruchy, Muriel; Baltimore, 1907 ***9228.50*** *p179*
De Gruchy, Philip; America, 1769 ***9228.50*** *p179*
De Gruchy, Philip; America, 1776 ***9228.50*** *p179*
De Gruchy, Philip; America, 1789-1889 ***9228.50*** *p179*
De Gruchy, Philip; America, 1798-1799 ***9228.50*** *p179*
De Gruchy, Philip; Canada, 1789-1889 ***9228.50*** *p179*
De Gruchy, Philip J.; America, 1798 ***9228.50*** *p179*
De Gruchy, Thomas; Canada, n.d. ***9228.50*** *p178*
De Gruchy, Thomas *SEE* De Gruchy, Elias
De Gruchy, Thomas James; Boston, 1741 ***9228.50*** *p179*
De Gruchy, Walter John; America, 1857-1944 ***9228.50*** *p177*
De Gruchy, William; Virginia, 1870-1879 ***9228.50*** *p179*
DeGruchy Family ; America, n.d. ***9228.50*** *p21A*
Degrysr, Camiel; New York, 1903 ***1766.20*** *p25*
Degu, Michel; Quebec, 1659 ***9221.17*** *p413*
De Guerneze, Guillaume; Canada, 1534 ***9228.50*** *p260*
De Guerre, George; Boston, 1720 ***9228.50*** *p244*
DeGuesnel, Jeanne-Marie; Quebec, 1671 ***4514.3*** *p299*
Degursie, Peter 45; Ontario, 1871 ***1823.17*** *p40*
Dehan, N. 43; New York, NY, 1856 ***1766.1*** *p45*
Deharde, Jean B. 34; America, 1844 ***778.6*** *p85*
Dehaughty, John; Dedham, MA, 1742 ***1642*** *p102*
Dehaux, Francois; Detroit, 1856 ***1494.21*** *p31*
De Havilland, . . .; New York, 1688 ***9228.50*** *p275*
Dehl, Fredericke; Wisconsin, 1883 ***6795.8*** *p46*
Dehm, Hermann; Valdivia, Chile, 1851 ***1192.4*** *p51*
With wife & 2 children
Dehn, Andrew; Ohio, 1809-1852 ***4511.35*** *p10*
Dehne, Mr.; America, 1873 ***7420.1*** *p299*
Dehne, Carl Friedrich; Port uncertain, 1880 ***7420.1*** *p315*
Dehne, Carl Friedrich Christian; America, 1867 ***7420.1*** *p255*
Dehne, Carl Friedrich Wilhelm; Port uncertain, 1835 ***7420.1*** *p8*
Dehne, Christian; America, 1887 ***7420.1*** *p399*
Dehne, Christoph; America, 1873 ***7420.1*** *p299*
With wife
*Daughter:*Hanna Sophie Louise
*Daughter:*Wilhelmine Karoline Marie
*Son:*Karl Friedrich Christoph
Dehne, Friedrich; America, 1852 ***7420.1*** *p87*
With family
Dehne, Friedrich Christian; America, 1835 ***7420.1*** *p8*
Dehne, Hanna Sophie Louise *SEE* Dehne, Christoph
Dehne, Heinrich; America, 1864 ***7420.1*** *p223*
With wife & child
Dehne, Heinrich; America, 1868 ***7420.1*** *p270*
Dehne, Heinrich Wilhelm; America, 1882 ***7420.1*** *p328*
Dehne, Karl Friedrich Christoph *SEE* Dehne, Christoph
Dehne, Wilhelmine Karoline Marie *SEE* Dehne, Christoph
de Houlme, Judith *SEE* de Houlme, Pierre
de Houlme, Pierre; Ohio, 1832-1836 ***9228.50*** *p278*
*Wife:*Judith
Dehut, Rosalie; Wisconsin, 1854-1858 ***1495.20*** *p50*
Deibert, Joseph 21; New York, NY, 1898 ***7951.13*** *p43*
Deibert, Magdalena 14; New York, NY, 1898 ***7951.13*** *p43*
Deich, Gustav Herman Hugo; Wisconsin, 1894 ***6795.8*** *p105*
Deichmann, Mrs.; America, 1900 ***7420.1*** *p376*
Deichmann, Carl Heinrich Ludwig; America, 1883 ***7420.1*** *p335*
Deichmann, Friedrich Wilhelm; Port uncertain, 1837 ***7420.1*** *p12*
Deichmann, Karl Christian August; America, 1887 ***7420.1*** *p353*
Deickman, Fred; Missouri, 1892 ***3276.1*** *p1*
Deidrick, Margaretha 40; America, 1747 ***778.6*** *p86*
Deidrick, Peter 9; America, 1747 ***778.6*** *p86*
Deidrick, Peter 59; America, 1747 ***778.6*** *p86*
Deihl, John; Louisiana, 1841-1844 ***4981.45*** *p210*
Deihl, Ludwig; Ohio, 1809-1852 ***4511.35*** *p10*
Deipt, John; North Carolina, 1710 ***3629.40*** *p8*
Deiss, Johannes; Nova Scotia, 1784 ***7105*** *p22*
Deitchler, Charles; Illinois, 1865 ***6079.1*** *p4*
Deiterding, August Heinrich Friedrich; America, 1846 ***7420.1*** *p43*
Deiterding, Caroline Wilh. Just.; America, 1883 ***7420.1*** *p341*
Deiters, Marie Louise; America, 1892 ***7420.1*** *p366*
Deiver, John; Louisiana, 1841-1844 ***4981.45*** *p210*
Deivis, Catha. 23; New York, NY, 1893 ***1883.7*** *p43*
Deivis, Georg 11 months; New York, NY, 1893 ***1883.7*** *p43*
Deivis, Heinr. 26; New York, NY, 1893 ***1883.7*** *p43*
De Jardin, John; New Jersey, 1665 ***9228.50*** *p180*
De Jardin, John; Virginia, 1665 ***9228.50*** *p53*
De Jean, Elizabeth; New York, 1713 ***9228.50*** *p180*
With sister
De Jersey, Arthur Francis; Charleston, SC, 1856-1956 ***9228.50*** *p181*
De Jersey, Elizabeth; New York, 1713 ***9228.50*** *p180*
With sister
DeJersey Family ; Prince Edward Island, 1806 ***9228.50*** *p128*
DeJonge, Marie Felicite 17; America, 1848 ***778.6*** *p86*
Dejoux, Jean 39; America, 1840 ***778.6*** *p86*
Deker, Edward; Colorado, 1862-1894 ***1029.59*** *p21*
Deker, Josephine 9; America, 1847 ***778.6*** *p86*
Dekiert, Emil M. 39; Michigan, 1880 ***4491.30*** *p8*
deLaBardilliere, Marie 36; Montreal, 1658 ***9221.17*** *p391*
Delabarre, Franz; Galveston, TX, 1855 ***571.7*** *p16*
Delaberge, Robert 20; Quebec, 1658 ***9221.17*** *p378*
Delabroy, Mr. 26; America, 1846 ***778.6*** *p86*
Delabroy, Josephine 2; America, 1846 ***778.6*** *p86*
Delachaussee, . . .; Quebec, 1647 ***9221.17*** *p179*
Delachaux, L. 37; Port uncertain, 1843 ***778.6*** *p86*
De La Cloche, John; New Jersey, 1665 ***9228.50*** *p159*
De La Cloche, Rachel; Salem, MA, 1600-1687 ***9228.50*** *p181*
De La Cloche, Rachel; Salem, MA, 1672 ***9228.50*** *p159*
De La Close, John; New Jersey, 1665 ***9228.50*** *p159*
De La Close, Rachel; Salem, MA, 1672 ***9228.50*** *p159*
DeLacour, Marie; Quebec, 1669 ***4514.3*** *p299*
deLacques, Jules 35; America, 1843 ***778.6*** *p86*
De La Croix, . . .; Massachusetts, n.d. ***9228.50*** *p170*
De La Croix, F.; San Francisco, 1852 ***9228.50*** *p181*
DeLacroix, Francoise; Quebec, 1669 ***4514.3*** *p299*
Delacroix, Peter; Maine, n.d. ***9228.50*** *p18A*
Delaet, Cecil 3; America, 1844 ***778.6*** *p86*
Delaet, Celestine; Ohio, 1840-1897 ***8365.35*** *p15*
Delaet, Emeline 1; America, 1844 ***778.6*** *p86*
Delaet, Henri 15; America, 1844 ***778.6*** *p86*
Delaet, Henry 51; America, 1844 ***778.6*** *p86*
Delaet, Louis 7; America, 1844 ***778.6*** *p86*
Delaet, Margaretha 28; America, 1844 ***778.6*** *p86*
Delaet, Marie 24; America, 1844 ***778.6*** *p86*
Delaet, Marie 46; America, 1844 ***778.6*** *p86*
Delaet, Meslin 4; America, 1844 ***778.6*** *p86*
Delaet, Pier 9; America, 1844 ***778.6*** *p86*
DeLafitte, Apolline; Quebec, 1673 ***4514.3*** *p299*
Delafond, Etienne 27; Quebec, 1642 ***9221.17*** *p114*
deLaFontaine, Maurice 29; Quebec, 1649 ***9221.17*** *p219*
Delafosse, Pierre; Quebec, 1648 ***9221.17*** *p197*
Delagarde, Francois; Quebec, 1654 ***9221.17*** *p306*
Delage, Jean; Illinois, 1852 ***6079.1*** *p4*
Delagrange, Constance 34; Port uncertain, 1843 ***778.6*** *p86*
Delagrange, Constant 11; Port uncertain, 1843 ***778.6*** *p86*
Delagrange, Jacques 57; Port uncertain, 1843 ***778.6*** *p86*
Delagrange, Joseph 15; Port uncertain, 1843 ***778.6*** *p86*
Delagrange, Marie 55; Port uncertain, 1843 ***778.6*** *p86*
DeLagueripiere, Elisabeth; Quebec, 1671 ***4514.3*** *p300*
Delahaie, Louis; Quebec, 1659 ***9221.17*** *p397*
De La Hay, John; Maine, 1706 ***9228.50*** *p182*
DeLaHaye, Miss; America, 1850-1900 ***9228.50*** *p182*
De La Haye, Mr.; Massachusetts, 1800-1850 ***9228.50*** *p182*
De La Haye, Abraham *SEE* De La Haye, Jane
De La Haye, Ada Michel *SEE* De La Haye, James
Delahaye, Andre 51; New Orleans, 1848 ***778.6*** *p86*
DelaHaye, Benjamin 24; New Orleans, 1848 ***778.6*** *p86*
De La Haye, Bertram James; America, 1898-1953 ***9228.50*** *p182*
De La Haye, Carole May Trachy *SEE* De La Haye, Lawrence
DeLahaye, Catherine; Quebec, 1669 ***4514.3*** *p300*
De La Haye, Elias; Massachusetts, 1896 ***9228.50*** *p514*
*Wife:*Louisa Pinel
With 2 sons & daughter
De La Haye, Elias Francis; Massachusetts, 1896 ***9228.50*** *p182*
De La Haye, Eliza; Quebec, 1822 ***9228.50*** *p182*
Delahaye, Francois 20; Quebec, 1632 ***9221.17*** *p20*
De La Haye, James; America, 1926 ***9228.50*** *p182*
De La Haye, James; Lexington, MA, 1926 ***9228.50*** *p465*
With 4 daughters
*Wife:*Ada Michel
De La Haye, Jane; Maine, 1713 ***9228.50*** *p317*
*Relative:*Abraham
DeLahaye, Jeanne; Quebec, 1666 ***4514.3*** *p300*
De La Haye, Jesse; Massachusetts, 1890 ***9228.50*** *p247*
With parents
De La Haye, Lawrence; Victoria, B.C., 1939-1983 ***9228.50*** *p635*
*Wife:*Carole May Trachy
De La Haye, Louisa Pinel *SEE* De La Haye, Elias
De La Haye, Margaret; Salt Lake City, 1868 ***9228.50*** *p287*
De La Haye, Margaret; Utah, 1828-1906 ***9228.50*** *p182*
DeLahaye, Michelle; Quebec, 1670 ***4514.3*** *p300*
De La Haye, Nancy; Utah, 1868 ***9228.50*** *p182*
Delahogue, Marie-Claire; Quebec, 1669 ***4514.3*** *p300*
Dela'Hook, Edward 28; Ontario, 1871 ***1823.21*** *p87*
Delahot, Jean 27; America, 1840 ***778.6*** *p86*
Delain, Anne Jandrain *SEE* Delain, Henri Joseph
Delain, Henri Joseph; Wisconsin, 1854-1858 ***1495.20*** *p50*
*Wife:*Anne Jandrain
*Child:*Marie Antoinette
*Child:*Virginie
*Child:*Philomene
*Child:*Marie-Josephe
*Child:*Joseph
Delain, Joseph; New York, NY, 1856 ***1494.21*** *p31*
Delain, Joseph *SEE* Delain, Henri Joseph
Delain, Joseph; Wisconsin, 1854-1858 ***1495.20*** *p50*
*Wife:*Marie Junion
Delain, Marie Junion *SEE* Delain, Joseph
Delain, Marie Antoinette *SEE* Delain, Henri Joseph
Delain, Marie-Josephe *SEE* Delain, Henri Joseph
Delain, Philomene *SEE* Delain, Henri Joseph
Delain, Virginie *SEE* Delain, Henri Joseph
DeLallande, Mr. 20; Mexico, 1840 ***778.6*** *p86*

DeLalore, Catherine; Quebec, 1671 ***4514.3*** *p300*
De La Mare, Alan *SEE* De La Mare, Edgar Naftel
DeLa Mare, Alpheus; New York, NY, 1870-1879 ***9228.50*** *p183*
De La Mare, Charlotte De Mouilpied *SEE* De La Mare, Francois
De La Mare, Edgar Naftel; New York, 1900-1940 ***9228.50*** *p183*
With wife & 2 sons
*Son:*Alan
De La Mare, Francois; Quebec, 1821-1869 ***9228.50*** *p183*
*Wife:*Charlotte De Mouilpied
Delamare, Francoise; Quebec, 1657 ***9221.17*** *p356*
Delamare, Francoise; Quebec, 1657 ***9221.17*** *p356*
Delamare, Jacques; Quebec, 1659 ***9221.17*** *p413*
De La Mare, Julia; Canada, 1800-1857 ***9228.50*** *p184*
Delamare, Louis; Quebec, 1658 ***9221.17*** *p378*
De La Mare, Mary Jane *SEE* De La Mare, Philip
De La Mare, Nita Louisa *SEE* De La Mare, Philip
De La Mare, Nita Louisa *SEE* De La Mare, Philip
De La Mare, Philip; British Columbia, 1912-1916 ***9228.50*** *p183*
*Child:*Philip Waddington
*Child:*Nita Louisa
*Child:*Winifred Eva
De La Mare, Philip; Los Angeles, 1912-1916 ***9228.50*** *p183*
*Child:*Nita Louisa
De La Mare, Philip; Utah, 1852-1855 ***9228.50*** *p183*
*Child:*Mary Jane
*Child:*Philip Francois
*Child:*Theophilus
De La Mare, Philip Francois *SEE* De La Mare, Philip
De La Mare, Philip Waddington *SEE* De La Mare, Philip
De La Mare, Theophilus *SEE* De La Mare, Philip
De La Mare, Thomas Naftel; Canada, 1800-1857 ***9228.50*** *p184*
De La Mare, Winifred Eva *SEE* De La Mare, Philip
Delamarre, Mr.; America, 1841 ***778.6*** *p86*
DeLamarre, Marie; Quebec, 1668 ***4514.3*** *p301*
DeLaMartiniere, Marie 41; Quebec, 1647 ***9221.17*** *p190*
Delambourg, Esther 18; Quebec, 1648 ***9221.17*** *p197*
Delambre, Amedee 26; New Orleans, 1848 ***778.6*** *p86*
Delambre, Juliana 16; New Orleans, 1848 ***778.6*** *p86*
Delameric, Mr. 27; America, 1841 ***778.6*** *p87*
De La Motte, Diane; Quebec, 1671 ***4514.3*** *p301*
DeLancletta, Juan; Louisiana, 1874-1875 ***4981.45*** *p298*
Delancy, Michael 21; North Carolina, 1774 ***1422.10*** *p55*
Delancy, William; Ohio, 1809-1852 ***4511.35*** *p10*
Deland, . . .; Portsmouth, NH, 1636 ***9228.50*** *p184*
Delandre, Mr. 42; America, 1842 ***778.6*** *p87*
Delaney, Mrs.; Salem, MA, 1774 ***1642*** *p81*
Delaney, Alice E. 42; Michigan, 1880 ***4491.39*** *p7*
Delaney, Bridget 27; Ontario, 1871 ***1823.21*** *p87*
Delaney, Bridget; Toronto, 1844 ***2910.35*** *p113*
Delaney, Catherine 25; Ontario, 1871 ***1823.21*** *p87*
Delaney, Catherine; Toronto, 1844 ***2910.35*** *p113*
Delaney, Dennis 20; Michigan, 1880 ***4491.39*** *p7*
Delaney, John; Boston, 1763 ***1642*** *p32*
Delaney, Margaret; Halifax, N.S., 1827 ***7009.9*** *p62*
Delaney, Margaret; Maine, 1929 ***9228.50*** *p404*
Delaney, Mary 34; Ontario, 1871 ***1823.17*** *p40*
Delaney, Michael 49; Michigan, 1880 ***4491.39*** *p8*
Delaney, Michael 36; Ontario, 1871 ***1823.21*** *p87*
Delaney, Patrick 45; Ontario, 1871 ***1823.21*** *p87*
Delaney, Patrick 65; Ontario, 1871 ***1823.21*** *p87*
Delaney, Patrick 71; Ontario, 1871 ***1823.21*** *p87*
Delaney, Patrick; Toronto, 1844 ***2910.35*** *p116*
Delang, William 40; Florida, 1824-1841 ***8481.1*** *p18*
Delanoe, Rene; Quebec, 1649 ***9221.17*** *p211*
Delany, John 23; Ontario, 1871 ***1823.21*** *p87*
DeLaParre, Pascal 33; Port uncertain, 1843 ***778.6*** *p87*
Delaplace, Anne; Quebec, 1669 ***4514.3*** *p319*
Delaplace, Jacques; Quebec, 1637 ***9221.17*** *p66*
DeLaplace, Marguerite; Quebec, 1671 ***4514.3*** *p301*
De La Place, Thomas; Boston, 1736 ***9228.50*** *p184*
Delaporte, Jacques 27; Montreal, 1653 ***9221.17*** *p287*
Delaporte, Louis; Montreal, 1661 ***9221.17*** *p472*
DeLaporte, Marie-Anne; Quebec, 1665 ***4514.3*** *p301*
Delaporte, Pierre; Quebec, 1636 ***9221.17*** *p55*
Delaporte, Robert; Quebec, 1657 ***9221.17*** *p355*
Delaree, James; America, 1817 ***9228.50*** *p18A*
*Relative:*Mary Eliz
Delaree, Mary Eliz *SEE* Delaree, James
Delarge, Martial; Quebec, 1648 ***9221.17*** *p197*
Delargy, Patrick 60; Ontario, 1871 ***1823.21*** *p87*
Delaroche, Eugene 22; America, 1746 ***778.6*** *p87*
Delaroche, Eugene 20; Port uncertain, 1843 ***778.6*** *p87*
Delaroche, Nomie 23; America, 1746 ***778.6*** *p87*
Delaroe, Anne Fosse 37 *SEE* Delaroe, Jacques
Delaroe, Francois 9 *SEE* Delaroe, Jacques
Delaroe, Jacques 38; Quebec, 1661 ***9221.17*** *p453*
*Wife:*Anne Fosse 37
*Son:*Francois 9
De La Rue, . . .; America, 1635 ***9228.50*** *p325*
DeLarue, Charlotte; Quebec, 1673 ***4514.3*** *p301*
De La Rue, Elias; Ohio, 1860 ***9228.50*** *p185*
Delarue, Francois; Quebec, 1659 ***9221.17*** *p413*
Delarue, Guillaume 26; Quebec, 1661 ***9221.17*** *p453*
Delarue, Jean-Baptiste 22; Quebec, 1656 ***9221.17*** *p334*
De La Rue, John; Ohio, 1800-1840 ***9228.50*** *p185*
De La Rue, John; Ohio, n.d. ***9228.50*** *p326*
Delarue, Pierre-Hector 30; Quebec, 1659 ***9221.17*** *p397*
De La Rue, Rachel; North America, n.d. ***9228.50*** *p326*
De La Rue, Rachel; Ohio, 1800-1840 ***9228.50*** *p185*
De La Rue, Rachel; Ohio, 1807 ***9228.50*** *p103*
Delaruelle, Florence *SEE* Delaruelle, Xavier
Delaruelle, Floribert *SEE* Delaruelle, Xavier
Delaruelle, Marie Antoinette *SEE* Delaruelle, Xavier
Delaruelle, Marie Appoline *SEE* Delaruelle, Xavier
Delaruelle, Marie Catherine Delhaze *SEE* Delaruelle, Xavier
Delaruelle, Pelagie Josephe *SEE* Delaruelle, Xavier
Delaruelle, Victor Joseph *SEE* Delaruelle, Xavier
Delaruelle, Xavier; Wisconsin, 1854-1858 ***1495.20*** *p66*
*Wife:*Marie Catherine Delhaze
*Child:*Pelagie Josephe
*Child:*Victor Joseph
*Child:*Marie Appoline
*Child:*Florence
*Child:*Marie Antoinette
*Child:*Floribert
Delas, Jean 23; New Orleans, 1844 ***778.6*** *p87*
Delasaudraye, Louis; Montreal, 1653 ***9221.17*** *p287*
Delaselle, Thomas; Quebec, 1659 ***9221.17*** *p413*
Delastre, Adrienne; Quebec, 1665 ***4514.3*** *p301*
Delathe, Mr. 36; America, 1841 ***778.6*** *p87*
Delathe, Mrs. 28; America, 1841 ***778.6*** *p87*
De La Tour Envoivre, Catherine; Quebec, 1671 ***4514.3*** *p301*
Delau, Aug. 37; New Orleans, 1843 ***778.6*** *p87*
Delauconte, C. 48; New Orleans, 1843 ***778.6*** *p87*
Delauconte, F. 24; New Orleans, 1843 ***778.6*** *p87*
Delauconte, N. 25; Port uncertain, 1841 ***778.6*** *p87*
Delaumone, Guillaume; Quebec, 1659 ***9221.17*** *p413*
Delaunay, Anne 26; Quebec, 1661 ***9221.17*** *p453*
Delaunay, Henri 12; New Orleans, 1848 ***778.6*** *p87*
Delaunay, Jacques 47; Quebec, 1643 ***9221.17*** *p130*
Delaunay, Jeanne 21; Quebec, 1662 ***9221.17*** *p483*
Delaunay, L. 43; America, 1841 ***778.6*** *p87*
Delaunay, Madeleine; Quebec, 1670 ***4514.3*** *p302*
Delaunay, Nicolas 20; Quebec, 1654 ***9221.17*** *p306*
Delaunay, Pierre; Quebec, 1635 ***9221.17*** *p46*
De Laune, . . .; California, n.d. ***9228.50*** *p185*
Delaune, Claude 21; Quebec, 1661 ***9221.17*** *p454*
Delaune, Eustache; Quebec, 1658 ***9221.17*** *p378*
Delauney, Pierre A.; New York, 1838 ***9228.50*** *p185*
Delaunie, Alex. 35; America, 1841 ***778.6*** *p87*
Delautal, Alexandre 28; Louisiana, 1848 ***778.6*** *p87*
Delautal, Elise 13; Louisiana, 1848 ***778.6*** *p87*
Delautal, Fois. 45; Louisiana, 1848 ***778.6*** *p87*
Delautal, Francoise 45; Louisiana, 1848 ***778.6*** *p87*
Delautal, Genevieve 15; Louisiana, 1848 ***778.6*** *p87*
Delautal, Melanie 17; Louisiana, 1848 ***778.6*** *p87*
Delautal, Xavier 8; Louisiana, 1848 ***778.6*** *p87*
De La Valley, John; Maryland, 1657 ***9228.50*** *p327*
*Relative:*Nicholas
De La Valley, Nicholas *SEE* De La Valley, John
Delavaux, Catherine 29; Montreal, 1650 ***9221.17*** *p231*
Delaville, Emelie 9; New Orleans, 1848 ***778.6*** *p87*
Delaville, George 41; New Orleans, 1848 ***778.6*** *p87*
Delaville, Henry 9; New Orleans, 1848 ***778.6*** *p87*
Delaville, Hyacinthe 34; New Orleans, 1848 ***778.6*** *p87*
Delaville, Jacques; Quebec, 1634 ***9221.17*** *p35*
Delaville, Jacques 22; Quebec, 1653 ***9221.17*** *p274*
Delaville, Napoleon 17; Louisiana, 1848 ***778.6*** *p87*
Delaville, P. A.; Louisiana, 1836-1841 ***4981.45*** *p208*
Delavoie, Rene 23; Quebec, 1655 ***9221.17*** *p322*
Delay, Donald 53; Ontario, 1871 ***1823.21*** *p87*
Delay, Josph; Washington, 1883 ***2770.40*** *p136*
Del Bondio, E. T.; Louisiana, 1874 ***4981.45*** *p295*
Delbreil, Raymond 41; New Orleans, 1843 ***778.6*** *p87*
Delcoming, Henry; Ohio, 1809-1852 ***4511.35*** *p10*
Delcommene, John Michael; Ohio, 1809-1852 ***4511.35*** *p10*
Delcourt, A. 38; America, 1844 ***778.6*** *p87*
Delcourt, D. 22; America, 1844 ***778.6*** *p87*
Delcourt, J.B. 31; America, 1844 ***778.6*** *p87*
Deleau, Felix 19; New Orleans, 1840 ***778.6*** *p88*
Deleblu, M. 24; New Orleans, 1841 ***778.6*** *p88*
DeLeenur, Mr.; British Columbia, 1910 ***2897.7*** *p8*
DeLeenur, Maria 32; Quebec, 1910 ***2897.7*** *p8*
Deleglis, Francois Augustin; Wisconsin, 1876 ***2853.20*** *p336*
*Wife:*Marie Borova
With children
Deleglis, Marie Borova *SEE* Deleglis, Francois Augustin
Delelis, Louis 38; New Orleans, 1848 ***778.6*** *p88*
Delelis, Louis 62; New Orleans, 1848 ***778.6*** *p88*
Delenler, Emile 29; New Orleans, 1848 ***778.6*** *p88*
Deleo, Rufus 13; Ontario, 1871 ***1823.21*** *p87*
Deleray, Mr. 25; New Orleans, 1848 ***778.6*** *p88*
DeLespanne, Louise 18; New Orleans, 1845 ***778.6*** *p88*
Delessart, Etienne 24; Quebec, 1645 ***9221.17*** *p153*
Delestre, Alonie 30; Montreal, 1659 ***9221.17*** *p420*
Delestre, Anne; Quebec, 1673 ***4514.3*** *p302*
Delestre, Thierry 28; Quebec, 1652 ***9221.17*** *p257*
Deleugre, Elisabeth; Quebec, 1647 ***9221.17*** *p177*
Deleugre, Jacques 19; Quebec, 1655 ***9221.17*** *p322*
Deleur, Madeleine; Quebec, 1667 ***4514.3*** *p310*
Delforge, Albert; Wisconsin, 1856 ***1495.20*** *p45*
*Wife:*Florence Sprimont
*Child:*Auguste
*Child:*Julienne
*Child:*Francois Joseph
Delforge, Auguste *SEE* Delforge, Albert
Delforge, Florence Sprimont *SEE* Delforge, Albert
Delforge, Francois Joseph *SEE* Delforge, Albert
Delforge, Julie Josephe; Wisconsin, 1854-1858 ***1495.20*** *p66*
Delforge, Julienne *SEE* Delforge, Albert
Delfosse, Augustin *SEE* Delfosse, Jean Baptiste
Delfosse, Eugene *SEE* Delfosse, Jean Baptiste
Delfosse, Jean Baptiste; Wisconsin, 1857 ***1495.20*** *p46*
*Wife:*Marie Therese Masset
*Son:*Noel Joseph
*Son:*Eugene
*Son:*Louis
*Son:*Augustin
Delfosse, Jean Joseph *SEE* Delfosse, Pierre Joseph
Delfosse, Louis *SEE* Delfosse, Jean Baptiste
Delfosse, Marie Dieudonnee *SEE* Delfosse, Pierre Joseph
Delfosse, Marie Therese Koekelberg *SEE* Delfosse, Pierre Joseph
Delfosse, Marie Therese Masset *SEE* Delfosse, Jean Baptiste
Delfosse, Noel Joseph *SEE* Delfosse, Jean Baptiste
Delfosse, Pierre Joseph; Wisconsin, 1857 ***1495.20*** *p46*
*Wife:*Marie Therese Koekelberg
*Child:*Marie Dieudonnee
*Child:*Jean Joseph
Delgado, Jesus; New Mexico, 1914 ***4812.1*** *p87*
Delhaze, Marie Catherine; Wisconsin, 1854-1858 ***1495.20*** *p66*
Delhom, L.; Louisiana, 1874 ***4981.45*** *p295*
Delhotal, F. Alexandre 39; America, 1847 ***778.6*** *p88*
Delhotal, Francois 19; America, 1847 ***778.6*** *p88*
Delhotal, Honore 13; America, 1847 ***778.6*** *p88*
Delhotal, Hypolite 11; America, 1847 ***778.6*** *p88*
Delhotal, Imbert 6 months; America, 1847 ***778.6*** *p88*
Delhotal, Joseph 6 months; America, 1847 ***778.6*** *p88*
Delhotal, Louis 9; America, 1847 ***778.6*** *p88*
Delhotal, Margaretha 39; America, 1847 ***778.6*** *p88*
Delhotal, Melanie 7; America, 1847 ***778.6*** *p88*
Delhotal, Pierre 15; America, 1847 ***778.6*** *p88*
Delhotal, Virginie 4; America, 1847 ***778.6*** *p88*
Delhotal, Xavier 17; America, 1847 ***778.6*** *p88*
Delhuile, Joseph; Illinois, 1852 ***6079.1*** *p4*
Delia, Francois 28; New Orleans, 1848 ***778.6*** *p88*
DeLicerace, Suzanne; Quebec, 1663 ***4514.3*** *p302*
Deliercourt, Antoinette 17; Quebec, 1650 ***9221.17*** *p225*
Deligny, Elisabeth 39; New Orleans, 1848 ***778.6*** *p88*
Deligny, Jeanne Baltide 9; New Orleans, 1848 ***778.6*** *p88*
Deligny, Jn. Bte. Joseph 39; New Orleans, 1848 ***778.6*** *p88*
Deligny, Marie 20; Quebec, 1655 ***9221.17*** *p322*
DeLimoges, Marie; Quebec, 1667 ***4514.3*** *p302*
Delimont, Antoine; Detroit, 1864 ***1494.21*** *p31*
Delimont, Gregoire; Detroit, 1864 ***1494.21*** *p31*
Delimont, Victor; Detroit, 1864 ***1494.21*** *p31*
Delin, N.; New York, NY, 1844 ***6412.40*** *p147*
Deliney, Mary; Massachusetts, 1759 ***1642*** *p102*
Delingen, Johann 19; New Orleans, 1848 ***778.6*** *p88*
Delingher, Mr. 2; America, 1843 ***778.6*** *p88*
Delingher, Mrs. 30; America, 1843 ***778.6*** *p88*
Delingher, G. 37; America, 1843 ***778.6*** *p88*
Delingher, Moshe 31; America, 1843 ***778.6*** *p88*
Delisle, Albert; Quebec, 1651 ***9221.17*** *p236*
De Lisle, Alfred Henry; California, 1892-1893 ***9228.50*** *p185*
*Wife:*Anna Young Fraser
De Lisle, Alfred Henry; Victoria, B.C., 1863-1892 ***9228.50*** *p185*
De Lisle, Anna Young Fraser *SEE* De Lisle, Alfred Henry

De Lisle, Daniel; America, 1800-1899 ***9228.50*** *p185*
Delisle, Etienne 25; Quebec, 1644 ***9221.17*** *p145*
De Lisle, Mary; Ohio, 1807 ***9228.50*** *p567*
De Lisle, Wilfrid; New York, NY, 1935 ***9228.50*** *p104*
Delitz, Kurt von; Chile, 1878 ***7420.1*** *p310*
Dell, Anton; Illinois, 1857 ***6079.1*** *p4*
Dell, Elsie; New York, 1860 ***358.56*** *p148*
Dell, Franklin 40; Ontario, 1871 ***1823.17*** *p40*
Dell, Mary Ann 15; Ontario, 1871 ***1823.17*** *p40*
Dellantoneo, Giao 35; New York, NY, 1894 ***6512.1*** *p230*
Delleac, Mr. 19; New Orleans, 1840 ***778.6*** *p88*
Delles, Eva 18; Port uncertain, 1843 ***778.6*** *p88*
Delleson, Jean; Quebec, 1656 ***9221.17*** *p334*
Delleware, Anna; Marblehead, MA, 1768 ***9228.50*** *p347*
Delligne, Anne Joseph Bauwin *SEE* Delligne, Francois
Delligne, Ferdinand; Wisconsin, 1855 ***1495.20*** *p45*
Delligne, Francois; Wisconsin, 1856 ***1495.20*** *p45*
*Wife:*Anne Joseph Bauwin
*Child:*Philomene
*Child:*Joseph
Delligne, Jeanne; Wisconsin, 1880 ***1495.20*** *p45*
Delligne, Joseph *SEE* Delligne, Francois
Delligne, Philomene *SEE* Delligne, Francois
Delligne, Seraphine; Wisconsin, 1856 ***1495.20*** *p45*
Dellilo, Nicola; Colorado, 1885 ***1029.59*** *p21*
Dellis, Charles Antoine *SEE* Dellis, Pierre
Dellis, Francoise Lamblot *SEE* Dellis, Pierre
Dellis, Jean Louis *SEE* Dellis, Pierre
Dellis, Jules *SEE* Dellis, Pierre
Dellis, Laurent *SEE* Dellis, Pierre
Dellis, Marie Victoire *SEE* Dellis, Pierre
Dellis, Philomene *SEE* Dellis, Pierre
Dellis, Pierre; Wisconsin, 1855 ***1495.20*** *p40*
*Wife:*Francoise Lamblot
*Child:*Victor Joseph
*Child:*Charles Antoine
*Child:*Jules
*Child:*Marie Victoire
*Child:*Pierre Joseph
*Child:*Jean Louis
*Child:*Laurent
*Child:*Philomene
Dellis, Pierre Joseph *SEE* Dellis, Pierre
Dellis, Victor Joseph *SEE* Dellis, Pierre
Dellisse, Adeline *SEE* Dellisse, Joseph
Dellisse, Auguste *SEE* Dellisse, Joseph
Dellisse, Joseph; Wisconsin, 1855 ***1495.20*** *p8*
*Child:*Xavier
*Child:*Marie Louise
*Child:*Adeline
*Child:*Julie
*Child:*Auguste
*Child:*Marie Catherine
*Wife:*Julie Gohir Lefebvre
With stepchild
Dellisse, Julie *SEE* Dellisse, Joseph
Dellisse, Julie Gohir Lefebvre *SEE* Dellisse, Joseph
Dellisse, Marie Catherine *SEE* Dellisse, Joseph
Dellisse, Marie Louise *SEE* Dellisse, Joseph
Dellisse, Xavier *SEE* Dellisse, Joseph
Dellson, Patrick 53; Ontario, 1871 ***1823.21*** *p88*
Delmac, Jean 30; America, 1841 ***778.6*** *p88*
Delmage, Eliza 49; Ontario, 1871 ***1823.17*** *p40*
Delmager, Arthur 56; Ontario, 1871 ***1823.17*** *p40*
Delmas, . . .; Port uncertain, 1840 ***778.6*** *p89*
Delmas, Mr. 18; America, 1841 ***778.6*** *p89*
Delmas, Mr. 42; Port uncertain, 1840 ***778.6*** *p88*
Deloche, Louis; Louisiana, 1836-1840 ***4981.45*** *p212*
Deloffre, Mrs. 36; New Orleans, 1848 ***778.6*** *p89*
Delome, Pierre; Virginia, 1700 ***9230.15*** *p80*
With wife
Delon, . . .; Portsmouth, NH, 1636 ***9228.50*** *p184*
De Londes, . . .; Portsmouth, NH, 1636 ***9228.50*** *p184*
DeLongchamps, Esther; Quebec, 1668 ***4514.3*** *p296*
Delongville, Hubert Jos.; New York, NY, 1855 ***1494.20*** *p12*
Delop, Mr.; Died enroute, 1725 ***1642*** *p84*
With wife 4 brothers & sisters
Delop, James 14; Massachusetts, 1725 ***1642*** *p84*
Delop, James; Nova Scotia, 1774 ***1642*** *p84*
With family
Delor, Mrs.; America, 1845 ***778.6*** *p89*
Delor, Bernard 29; America, 1845 ***778.6*** *p89*
Delord, P. 54; New Orleans, 1843 ***778.6*** *p89*
Delorme, Marguerite; Quebec, 1669 ***4514.3*** *p302*
Delory, Mr. 30; America, 1841 ***778.6*** *p89*
DeLostelneau, Catherine; Quebec, 1667 ***4514.3*** *p302*
De Louche, Joseph Charles; Newfoundland, 1846-1868 ***9228.50*** *p186*
De Louche, Joseph Charles; Quebec, 1827 ***9228.50*** *p185*
Delouise, S. 36; New Orleans, 1844 ***778.6*** *p89*
DeLouvre, J. 40; America, 1845 ***778.6*** *p89*
Deloynece, Mr. 32; New Orleans, 1845 ***778.6*** *p89*
Delpech, A. 17; America, 1848 ***778.6*** *p89*
Delpeuch, Pierre 36; New Orleans, 1848 ***778.6*** *p89*
Delphus, Francois 25; Mississippi, 1847 ***778.6*** *p89*
Delpierre, Antoine; Wisconsin, 1855-1867 ***1495.20*** *p67*
Delprat, Jean Francois 31; New Orleans, 1848 ***778.6*** *p89*
Delseit, Nikolaus; America, 1854 ***5475.1*** *p78*
Delsipee, Florence; Wisconsin, 1855 ***1495.20*** *p8*
Delugny, Elisabeth; Quebec, 1647 ***9221.17*** *p177*
Delun, Joseph 24; America, 1840 ***778.6*** *p89*
Deluzat, C. 23; America, 1840 ***778.6*** *p89*
Delvaux, Jean Joseph; Wisconsin, 1846-1856 ***1495.20*** *p29*
*Wife:*Marie Josephe Hoslet
*Daughter:*Marie Therese
Delvaux, Marie Josephe Hoslet *SEE* Delvaux, Jean Joseph
Delvaux, Marie Therese *SEE* Delvaux, Jean Joseph
Delve, Elizabeth 18; Ontario, 1871 ***1823.17*** *p40*
Delve, George 22; Ontario, 1871 ***1823.17*** *p40*
Delve, Robert 42; Ontario, 1871 ***1823.17*** *p40*
Delve, Sarah 14; Ontario, 1871 ***1823.17*** *p40*
Delwiche, Desire; Wisconsin, 1879 ***1495.20*** *p46*
*Wife:*Marie Joseph Dethy
Delwiche, J. Bte.; Detroit, 1855 ***1494.20*** *p12*
Delwiche, Marie Francoise; Wisconsin, 1856 ***1495.20*** *p8*
Delwiche, Marie Joseph Dethy *SEE* Delwiche, Desire
Delzaudy, Adam; Quebec, 1647 ***9221.17*** *p179*
Delzer, Barbara 38; New York, NY, 1874 ***6954.7*** *p39*
Delzer, Christian 6; New York, NY, 1874 ***6954.7*** *p39*
Delzer, Gottlieb 53; New York, NY, 1874 ***6954.7*** *p39*
Delzer, Michael 18; New York, NY, 1874 ***6954.7*** *p39*
De Maggio, Spiridonue; Louisiana, 1874 ***4981.45*** *p131*
DeMagnac, Jean; Montreal, 1654 ***9221.17*** *p318*
Demain, John; New York, NY, 1871 ***1494.21*** *p31*
Demange, J. B. Petit; Louisiana, 1874-1875 ***4981.45*** *p298*
Demange, Margaretha 30; Mississippi, 1847 ***778.6*** *p89*
DeMangeon, Claude; Quebec, 1664 ***4514.3*** *p302*
Demant, Pierre 27; Mississippi, 1847 ***778.6*** *p89*
DeMarcy, John; Roxbury, MA, 1685 ***1642*** *p107*
Demartini, G.; Louisiana, 1874 ***4981.45*** *p295*
DeMartino, Antonio; North Carolina, 1849 ***1088.45*** *p7*
De Matino, Pavla; Louisiana, 1874 ***4981.45*** *p131*
DeMatras, Jeanne-Judith; Quebec, 1669 ***4514.3*** *p302*
Dembinski, Anna 30; New York, NY, 1885 ***1883.7*** *p46*
Dembinski, Maria 30; New York, NY, 1885 ***1883.7*** *p46*
Demee, Mr. 28; New Orleans, 1848 ***778.6*** *p89*
Demeny, Gregoire Jos.; New York, NY, 1880 ***1494.20*** *p13*
Demer, Peter; Ohio, 1809-1852 ***4511.35*** *p10*
DeMerinne, Jeanne; Quebec, 1665 ***4514.3*** *p303*
De Merit, John; Boston, 1650-1750 ***9228.50*** *p189*
Demeritt, Charles; Boston, 1700 ***9228.50*** *p188*
Demeritt, Eli; New Hampshire, 1694 ***9228.50*** *p187*
Demers, Andre 16 *SEE* Demers, Jean
Demers, Etienne 20 *SEE* Demers, Jean
Demers, Jean; Quebec, 1644 ***9221.17*** *p141*
*Son:*Etienne
*Son:*Jean
*Wife:*Miotte Lecombe
*Son:*Andre
Demers, Jean 13 *SEE* Demers, Jean
Demers, Miotte Lecombe *SEE* Demers, Jean
Demery, Charles; Boston, 1700 ***9228.50*** *p188*
Demery, John; Boston, 1650-1750 ***9228.50*** *p189*
Demery, Sarah 81; Ontario, 1871 ***1823.21*** *p88*
Demery, William 65; Ontario, 1871 ***1823.17*** *p40*
Demeusnes, Simon; Quebec, 1649 ***9221.17*** *p212*
Demien, Rose 19; America, 1845 ***778.6*** *p89*
Demill, Marinda 36; Michigan, 1880 ***4491.36*** *p5*
Demille, John Charles; North Carolina, 1820-1825 ***1088.45*** *p7*
Demilly, John Lewis; North Carolina, 1820-1825 ***1088.45*** *p7*
Demme, Conrad; Valdivia, Chile, 1852 ***1192.4*** *p53*
Demme, Louis; New York, 1859 ***358.56*** *p100*
Demmer, Bertha *SEE* Demmer, Nikolaus
Demmer, Elisabeth 32; America, 1873 ***5475.1*** *p298*
*Daughter:*Elisabeth
*Daughter:*Gertrud
*Son:*Nikolaus
*Daughter:*Juliane
*Daughter:*Angela
Demmer, Katharina 6 *SEE* Demmer, Nikolaus
Demmer, Nikolaus 30; New York, 1892 ***5475.1*** *p79*
*Wife:*Bertha
*Daughter:*Katharina 6
Demmer, Peter; America, 1883 ***5475.1*** *p316*
Demmerer, Friedrich; Valdivia, Chile, 1852 ***1192.4*** *p53*
DeMonelpied, Francis A.; Washington, 1885 ***2770.40*** *p194*
Demonguichet, . . .; Quebec, 1653 ***9221.17*** *p271*
Demonts, Marie Depere 35 *SEE* Demonts, Pierre
Demonts, Pierre; Quebec, 1656 ***9221.17*** *p335*
*Wife:*Marie Depere
De Mouilpied, Amice; Manitoba, 1909 ***9228.50*** *p18A*
*Wife:*Sadie B. McClennan
De Mouilpied, Charlotte; Quebec, 1821-1869 ***9228.50*** *p183*
De Mouilpied, Nicholas; Wisconsin, 1840-1849 ***9228.50*** *p189*
De Mouilpied, Sadie B. McClennan *SEE* De Mouilpied, Amice
Demoulin, Marie Madelene Destenay; Wisconsin, 1870 ***1495.20*** *p56*
De Mount, . . .; Boston, 1729 ***9228.50*** *p189*
Demount, John; Boston, 1729 ***9228.50*** *p189*
Demousseaux, Jean; Quebec, 1659 ***9221.17*** *p413*
Dempflin, Albert; Valdivia, Chile, 1850 ***1192.4*** *p48*
Dempsey, Anne; St. Johns, N.F., 1825 ***1053.15*** *p6*
Dempsey, Honora; New Orleans, 1851 ***7242.30*** *p140*
Dempsey, Judith; St. Johns, N.F., 1825 ***1053.15*** *p6*
Dempsey, Louis; Louisiana, 1874-1875 ***4981.45*** *p298*
Dempsey, Margaret; Chicago, 1868-1958 ***9228.50*** *p515*
Dempsey, Margrett; Massachusetts, 1744 ***1642*** *p105*
Dempsey, Margt; St. Johns, N.F., 1825 ***1053.15*** *p6*
Dempsey, Maria W. 28; Ontario, 1871 ***1823.21*** *p88*
Dempsey, Robert; St. Johns, N.F., 1825 ***1053.15*** *p7*
Dempsey, Thomas; St. Johns, N.F., 1825 ***1053.15*** *p7*
Dempsey, William; St. Johns, N.F., 1825 ***1053.15*** *p7*
Dempster, Robert 39; Ontario, 1871 ***1823.21*** *p88*
Dempster, Robert 53; Ontario, 1871 ***1823.21*** *p88*
Dempster, William 34; Ontario, 1871 ***1823.21*** *p88*
Dempsy, John; Newfoundland, 1814 ***3476.10*** *p54*
Dempsy, John 62; Ontario, 1871 ***1823.21*** *p88*
Demsey, Jerimiah 45; Ontario, 1871 ***1823.21*** *p88*
Demusey, Francis; Ohio, 1809-1852 ***4511.35*** *p10*
Demuth, Andreas 19; America, 1846 ***778.6*** *p89*
Demuth, Georg; America, 1847 ***5475.1*** *p473*
Demuth, Johann; America, 1839 ***5475.1*** *p469*
Demuth, Johann; America, 1840 ***5475.1*** *p470*
Demuth, Katharina 42; America, 1859 ***5475.1*** *p522*
Demuth, Michel 21; America, 1836 ***5475.1*** *p468*
Demuth, Peter; America, 1837 ***5475.1*** *p468*
Demuth, Peter; America, 1839 ***5475.1*** *p469*
Demuth, Peter; America, 1840 ***5475.1*** *p470*
Demuth, Peter; America, 1848 ***5475.1*** *p475*
Denach, George 26; Port uncertain, 1840 ***778.6*** *p89*
Denaux, Charles 16; America, 1843 ***778.6*** *p89*
Denaux, Theodor 42; America, 1843 ***778.6*** *p89*
Denbel, Henry; Ohio, 1809-1852 ***4511.35*** *p10*
Dencate, Marie 33; America, 1840 ***778.6*** *p89*
Dencate, Nic. 37; America, 1840 ***778.6*** *p89*
Denechaud, Mr. 17; America, 1841 ***778.6*** *p89*
DeNevelet, Marguerite; Quebec, 1667 ***4514.3*** *p303*
Denevers, Etienne 22; Quebec, 1649 ***9221.17*** *p212*
Denger, Christian; North Carolina, 1835 ***1088.45*** *p7*
Dengert, John H.; New York, 1860 ***358.56*** *p148*
Denham, Mathew 42; Ontario, 1871 ***1823.17*** *p40*
Denhane, David A. 46; Ontario, 1871 ***1823.21*** *p88*
Denholm, Andrew 45; Ontario, 1871 ***1823.21*** *p88*
Deniau, Jean 23; Montreal, 1653 ***9221.17*** *p287*
Deniau, Marin 33; Montreal, 1653 ***9221.17*** *p288*
Deniau, Paul Louis; Illinois, 1852 ***6079.1*** *p4*
Denies, Amalia 4; New York, NY, 1893 ***1883.7*** *p43*
Denies, Friedr. 12; New York, NY, 1893 ***1883.7*** *p43*
Denies, Friedrich 42; New York, NY, 1893 ***1883.7*** *p43*
Denies, Heinrich 3 months; New York, NY, 1893 ***1883.7*** *p43*
Denies, Heinrich 7; New York, NY, 1893 ***1883.7*** *p43*
Denies, Jacob 3; New York, NY, 1893 ***1883.7*** *p43*
Denies, Magdalena 10; New York, NY, 1893 ***1883.7*** *p43*
Denies, Maria 23; New York, NY, 1893 ***1883.7*** *p43*
Denies, Maria 43; New York, NY, 1893 ***1883.7*** *p43*
Denig, Johann; America, 1862 ***5475.1*** *p521*
Denige, . . .; Quebec, 1662 ***9221.17*** *p484*
Denil, Antoine *SEE* Denil, Henri Joseph
Denil, Florent; Wisconsin, 1880 ***1495.20*** *p28*
Denil, Gustave Joseph *SEE* Denil, Henri Joseph
Denil, Henri Joseph; Wisconsin, 1880 ***1495.20*** *p55*
*Child:*Gustave Joseph
*Child:*Marie
*Child:*Louis
*Child:*Marie Esperance
*Child:*Antoine
Denil, Louis *SEE* Denil, Henri Joseph
Denil, Marie *SEE* Denil, Henri Joseph
Denil, Marie Esperance *SEE* Denil, Henri Joseph
Denis, Anne Josephe; Wisconsin, 1846-1856 ***1495.20*** *p29*
Denis, Antoine; Quebec, 1642 ***9221.17*** *p115*
Denis, Antoine; Quebec, 1649 ***9221.17*** *p212*
Denis, Augustine; Wisconsin, 1869 ***1495.20*** *p8*
Denis, Brigetta 69; New York, NY, 1893 ***1883.7*** *p44*
Denis, Conrad 8; New York, NY, 1893 ***1883.7*** *p44*
Denis, Francois; Quebec, 1650 ***9221.17*** *p225*
Denis, Franziska 2; New York, NY, 1893 ***1883.7*** *p44*

Denis, Jacob 1 months; New York, NY, 1893 ***1883.7*** *p44*
Denis, Jean; Quebec, 1646 ***9221.17*** *p163*
Denis, Jean Baptiste; Wisconsin, 1882 ***1495.20*** *p28*
*Brother:*Joseph
Denis, Joseph *SEE* Denis, Jean Baptiste
Denis, Laurent 23; Quebec, 1659 ***9221.17*** *p398*
Denis, St. Nicolas 26; America, 1845 ***778.6*** *p89*
Denis, Valentin 26; New York, NY, 1893 ***1883.7*** *p44*
Denis, Wendelin 1 months; New York, NY, 1893 ***1883.7*** *p44*
Denis, Xavier 25; Louisiana, 1848 ***778.6*** *p89*
Denisart, Franc. 44; Port uncertain, 1840 ***778.6*** *p89*
Denisol, Mr. 32; America, 1843 ***778.6*** *p90*
Denisot, Mr. 32; America, 1843 ***778.6*** *p90*
Denisot, Pierre; Quebec, 1642 ***9221.17*** *p115*
Denizre, Pierre 17; Port uncertain, 1841 ***778.6*** *p90*
Denk, Emanuel; St. Louis, 1848-1849 ***2853.20*** *p21*
Denker, Miss; America, 1851 ***7420.1*** *p79*
Denker, Mr.; America, 1878 ***7420.1*** *p310*
Denker, Carl Anton Heinrich; America, 1879 ***7420.1*** *p313*
Denker, Carl Friedrich; America, 1871 ***7420.1*** *p289*
Denker, Carl Friedrich; America, 1882 ***7420.1*** *p328*
*Wife:*Schakel Mesch
With 5 children
Denker, Christian Anton; America, 1881 ***7420.1*** *p320*
Denker, Christian Friedrich Wilhelm; America, 1883 ***7420.1*** *p335*
Denker, Christine *SEE* Denker, Leonore
Denker, Leonore; Fort Wayne, IN, 1872 ***7420.1*** *p294*
*Daughter:*Christine
Denker, Schakel Mesch *SEE* Denker, Carl Friedrich
Denley, John; Illinois, 1858 ***6079.1*** *p4*
Denley, William 17; Quebec, 1870 ***8364.32*** *p23*
Denly, Matilda 53; Ontario, 1871 ***1823.21*** *p88*
Denman, Tho.; Maryland, 1674 ***1236.25*** *p49*
Denman, Thomas; Maryland, 1680 ***1236.25*** *p53*
Denman, William Henry 31; Ontario, 1871 ***1823.17*** *p40*
Dennavan, Dennis; Boston, 1763 ***1642*** *p32*
Dennaven, Dennis; Boston, 1745 ***1642*** *p45*
Denne, E. Margarethe *SEE* Denne, Friedrich, III
Denne, Friedrich, III; Pittsburgh, 1880 ***5475.1*** *p434*
*Wife:*Katharina Busch
*Son:*J. Conrad
*Daughter:*E. Margarethe
*Son:*Joh. Peter
*Son:*Heinrich
*Son:*Joh. Friedrich
Denne, Heinrich *SEE* Denne, Friedrich, III
Denne, J. Conrad *SEE* Denne, Friedrich, III
Denne, Jean; Quebec, 1659 ***9221.17*** *p413*
Denne, Joh. Friedrich *SEE* Denne, Friedrich, III
Denne, Joh. Peter *SEE* Denne, Friedrich, III
Denne, Katharina Busch 37 *SEE* Denne, Friedrich, III
Denner, Mr. 24; America, 1847 ***778.6*** *p90*
Denner, Berthom. Louis 28; America, 1847 ***778.6*** *p90*
Denner, Godfrey; Ohio, 1809-1852 ***4511.35*** *p10*
Denner, Gregorit Hypolite 29; America, 1847 ***778.6*** *p90*
Dennet, James 50; Ontario, 1871 ***1823.17*** *p40*
Denni, Henry; Ohio, 1809-1852 ***4511.35*** *p10*
Denning, Henry; Illinois, 1861 ***4487.25*** *p55*
Denning, James 45; Ontario, 1871 ***1823.21*** *p88*
Denning, John 27; Ontario, 1871 ***1823.21*** *p88*
Denning, Mathew 46; Ontario, 1871 ***1823.21*** *p88*
Denning, William 23; Ontario, 1871 ***1823.21*** *p88*
Denninger, Magdalena 24; Port uncertain, 1848 ***778.6*** *p90*
Denninger, Michel 31; Port uncertain, 1848 ***778.6*** *p90*
Dennis, David 43; Michigan, 1880 ***4491.42*** *p10*
Dennis, Elizabeth 64; Ontario, 1871 ***1823.17*** *p40*
Dennis, Henry 30; Ontario, 1871 ***1823.21*** *p88*
Dennis, Henry 42; Ontario, 1871 ***1823.17*** *p41*
Dennis, James 30; Ontario, 1871 ***1823.17*** *p41*
Dennis, James 32; Ontario, 1871 ***1823.21*** *p88*
Dennis, James 61; Ontario, 1871 ***1823.17*** *p41*
Dennis, John 38; Ontario, 1871 ***1823.17*** *p41*
Dennis, John; Virginia, 1652 ***6254.4*** *p243*
Dennis, Joseph, Jr.; Colorado, 1891 ***1029.59*** *p21*
Dennis, Louis 21; America, 1843 ***778.6*** *p90*
Dennis, Mary; Ontario, 1835 ***3160.1*** *p150*
Dennis, Patrick; Ontario, 1835 ***3160.1*** *p150*
Dennis, Robert 44; Ontario, 1871 ***1823.21*** *p88*
Dennis, Robert E.; Colorado, 1900 ***1029.59*** *p21*
Dennis, Samuel 28; Ontario, 1871 ***1823.17*** *p41*
Dennis, Thomas 53; Ontario, 1871 ***1823.21*** *p88*
Dennis, William; North Carolina, 1825 ***1088.45*** *p7*
Dennis, William 33; Ontario, 1871 ***1823.17*** *p41*
Dennis, William 40; Ontario, 1871 ***1823.17*** *p41*
Dennis, William 64; Ontario, 1871 ***1823.17*** *p41*
Dennison, Ann; Ontario, 1835 ***3160.1*** *p150*
Dennison, Ann; Prescott, Ont., 1835 ***3289.1*** *p61*
Dennison, John 39; Ontario, 1871 ***1823.21*** *p88*
Denny, V.; Louisiana, 1874-1875 ***4981.45*** *p298*
Denny, William; America, 1756 ***1220.12*** *p731*
Denol, Aime 51; New Orleans, 1848 ***778.6*** *p90*
Denot, Jeanne; Quebec, 1666 ***4514.3*** *p303*
Denot, Marie 41; Quebec, 1647 ***9221.17*** *p190*
DeNoue, Anne; Quebec, 1626 ***9221.17*** *p23*
Denoue, Jacques; Quebec, 1640 ***9221.17*** *p95*
Denovan, John; Boston, 1749 ***1642*** *p46*
Denoyon, Jean 18; Quebec, 1653 ***9221.17*** *p271*
Denoyon, Marie; Quebec, 1670 ***4514.3*** *p303*
Denoyon, Suzanne 23; Quebec, 1649 ***9221.17*** *p212*
Denshan, William 42; Ontario, 1871 ***1823.21*** *p88*
Denslow, Nicholas; Dorchester, MA, 1632 ***117.5*** *p158*
Dent, William 56; Ontario, 1871 ***1823.21*** *p88*
Denton, Alice 26; Michigan, 1880 ***4491.33*** *p7*
Denton, J. M. 39; Ontario, 1871 ***1823.21*** *p88*
Dentsch, Paul; Louisiana, 1841-1844 ***4981.45*** *p210*
Dentz, Martin; Ohio, 1809-1852 ***4511.35*** *p10*
DeNul, Alphonse 20; Quebec, 1910 ***2897.7*** *p8*
Denys, Catherine 5 *SEE* Denys, Simon
Denys, Charles 7 *SEE* Denys, Simon
Denys, David F. 39; New Orleans, 1840 ***778.6*** *p90*
Denys, Francoise 7 *SEE* Denys, Simon
Denys, Francoise Dutertre 27 *SEE* Denys, Simon
Denys, Joseph 30; New Orleans, 1840 ***778.6*** *p90*
Denys, Marguerite *SEE* Denys, Simon
Denys, Marie 15; Quebec, 1659 ***9221.17*** *p398*
Denys, Paul 3 *SEE* Denys, Simon
Denys, Pierre 20 *SEE* Denys, Simon
Denys, Simon 52; Quebec, 1651 ***9221.17*** *p240*
*Wife:*Francoise Dutertre 27
*Daughter:*Marguerite
*Son:*Paul 3
*Son:*Charles 7
*Daughter:*Francoise 7
*Daughter:*Catherine 5
*Son:*Pierre 20
Denys DeLaRonde, Pierre 20; Quebec, 1651 ***9221.17*** *p240*
Denys DeLaTrinite, Catherine 5; Quebec, 1651 ***9221.17*** *p241*
Denys DeLaTrinite, Francoise 7; Quebec, 1651 ***9221.17*** *p240*
Denys DeLaTrinite, Marguerite; Quebec, 1651 ***9221.17*** *p241*
Denys deLa Trinite, Simon; Quebec, 1651 ***2314.30*** *p167*
Denys deLa Trinite, Simon; Quebec, 1668 ***2314.30*** *p180*
Denys DeLaTrinite, Simon 52; Quebec, 1651 ***9221.17*** *p240*
Denys DeSaint-Simon, Paul 3; Quebec, 1651 ***9221.17*** *p241*
Denys DeVitre, Charles 7; Quebec, 1651 ***9221.17*** *p240*
Denzin, Friedrich; Wisconsin, 1881 ***6795.8*** *p44*
Depacey, Alex. 28; America, 1841 ***778.6*** *p90*
Deparde, Charles; Quebec, 1660 ***9221.17*** *p433*
Deparis, Claire-Francoise 16; Quebec, 1661 ***9221.17*** *p454*
DeParis, Jean 20; Quebec, 1662 ***9221.17*** *p492*
Depas, Mr. 25; America, 1843 ***778.6*** *p90*
De Peerture, Erarist Victor; New York, 1903 ***1766.20*** *p23*
Depere, Marie 35; Quebec, 1656 ***9221.17*** *p335*
Depere, Suzanne; Quebec, 1659 ***9221.17*** *p398*
DePersan, Alexandre 26; America, 1842 ***778.6*** *p90*
DePersan, Henry Georges 28; America, 1842 ***778.6*** *p90*
Depew, Chas.; Ontario, 1787 ***1276.15*** *p230*
With child & 2 relatives
Depkin, Henry A.; North Carolina, 1854 ***1088.45*** *p7*
Deplaigne, Juan 30; America, 1841 ***778.6*** *p90*
Depner, Hans Heinrich; America, 1850 ***7420.1*** *p70*
*Brother:*Johann Otto
Depner, Johann Otto *SEE* Depner, Hans Heinrich
Depner, Philippine; America, 1857 ***7420.1*** *p160*
Depner Children, . . .; America, 1863 ***7420.1*** *p217*
Depoictiers, Marie-Charlotte 22; Quebec, 1659 ***9221.17*** *p398*
Depoiri, Hortense 18; New Orleans, 1848 ***778.6*** *p90*
Depoiri, Marie 46; New Orleans, 1848 ***778.6*** *p90*
DePoitiers, Jean-Baptiste; Quebec, 1600-1667 ***4514.3*** *p297*
*Relative:*Marie-Charlotte
DePoitiers, Marie-Charlotte *SEE* DePoitiers, Jean-Baptiste
Depoortes, Camiel; Detroit, 1901 ***1766.20*** *p25*
DePornasse, Jose 30; Port uncertain, 1842 ***778.6*** *p90*
DePortas, Marie-Angelique; Quebec, 1667 ***4514.3*** *p303*
Depouri, Adele 16; New Orleans, 1848 ***778.6*** *p90*
Depouri, Apolonia 11; New Orleans, 1848 ***778.6*** *p90*
Depouri, Emile 8; New Orleans, 1848 ***778.6*** *p90*
Depouri, Julie 5; New Orleans, 1848 ***778.6*** *p90*
Depouri, Justine 13; New Orleans, 1848 ***778.6*** *p90*
Depp, John; North Carolina, 1710 ***3629.40*** *p8*
Depper, Agustus 23; Ontario, 1871 ***1823.21*** *p89*
Deppmeier, Carl Friedrich Christian; America, 1884 ***7420.1*** *p342*
Deppmeier, Friedrich; America, 1885 ***7420.1*** *p347*
Deppmeier, Heinrich Friedrich Wilhelm; America, 1881 ***7420.1*** *p320*
Deprard, John; Marston's Wharf, 1782 ***8529.30*** *p11*
Depres, Xavier; Ohio, 1809-1852 ***4511.35*** *p10*
Deprez, Antoinette Barette *SEE* Deprez, Desire
Deprez, Desire; Wisconsin, 1854-1858 ***1495.20*** *p66*
*Wife:*Antoinette Barette
*Child:*Genevieve
*Child:*Jean Baptiste
Deprez, Genevieve *SEE* Deprez, Desire
Deprez, Gustave Joseph *SEE* Deprez, Jean Baptiste
Deprez, Jean Baptiste *SEE* Deprez, Desire
Deprez, Jean Baptiste; Wisconsin, 1854-1858 ***1495.20*** *p66*
*Wife:*Marie Natalie Louis
*Child:*Melanie Josephe
*Child:*Gustave Joseph
*Child:*Victor Antoine Joseph
*Child:*Jean Francois
*Child:*Jean Joseph
Deprez, Jean Francois *SEE* Deprez, Jean Baptiste
Deprez, Jean Joseph *SEE* Deprez, Jean Baptiste
Deprez, Jeanne; Wisconsin, 1854-1858 ***1495.20*** *p50*
Deprez, Marie Natalie Louis *SEE* Deprez, Jean Baptiste
Deprez, Melanie Josephe *SEE* Deprez, Jean Baptiste
Deprez, Victor Antoine Joseph *SEE* Deprez, Jean Baptiste
DeProvinlieu, Marie-Marguerite; Quebec, 1671 ***4514.3*** *p303*
Depruy, Samuel; Ohio, 1809-1852 ***4511.35*** *p10*
Dept, John; North Carolina, 1710 ***3629.40*** *p8*
Depta, J.; Galveston, TX, 1855 ***571.7*** *p18*
Depurgue, Felix 29; America, 1845 ***778.6*** *p90*
De Putron, Ann Carre *SEE* De Putron, Daniel
De Putron, Anne Carre *SEE* De Putron, Daniel
De Putron, Catherine; Ohio, 1850-1895 ***9228.50*** *p190*
De Putron, Daniel; America, n.d. ***9228.50*** *p191*
De Putron, Daniel; Cleveland, OH, 1822-1900 ***9228.50*** *p189*
*Wife:*Anne Carre
*Child:*Ann Carre
De Putron, John; Philadelphia, 1797-1863 ***9228.50*** *p89*
De Putron, John; Philadelphia, 1834 ***9228.50*** *p190*
De Putron, Percival Walter; Vancouver, B.C., 1920-1979 ***9228.50*** *p621*
Depuy, G. 30; New Orleans, 1841 ***778.6*** *p90*
Dequain, Anne; Quebec, 1669 ***4514.3*** *p303*
De Quedville, John; Cambridge, MA, 1860 ***9228.50*** *p531*
DeQuen, Jean 32; Quebec, 1635 ***9221.17*** *p41*
de Quetteville, Abraham; Marblehead, MA, 1681 ***9228.50*** *p312*
De Quetteville, Abraham; Massachusetts, 1600-1699 ***9228.50*** *p531*
De Quetteville, Edward; Massachusetts, 1748 ***9228.50*** *p286*
De Quetteville, John; Cambridge, MA, 1860 ***9228.50*** *p531*
Derahy, John 40; Ontario, 1871 ***1823.21*** *p89*
Derainville, Anne 6 *SEE* Derainville, Pauline Poete
Derainville, Charles 7 *SEE* Derainville, Pauline Poete
Derainville, Jean 20 *SEE* Derainville, Pauline Poete
Derainville, Marie 19 *SEE* Derainville, Pauline Poete
Derainville, Marthe 12 *SEE* Derainville, Pauline Poete
Derainville, Paul 39; Quebec, 1655 ***9221.17*** *p322*
Derainville, Pauline; Quebec, 1659 ***9221.17*** *p398*
*Son:*Jean
*Daughter:*Marie
*Daughter:*Marthe
*Son:*Charles
*Daughter:*Anne
Deramond, M. 35; New Orleans, 1848 ***778.6*** *p90*
Derandt, Cerceille; New York, 1903 ***1766.20*** *p3*
Derbes, A. L. M.; Louisiana, 1836-1840 ***4981.45*** *p212*
Derbey, Mary; Boston, 1757 ***9228.50*** *p366*
Derbut, Emilie 35; America, 1843 ***778.6*** *p90*
Derby, Chester 73; Ontario, 1871 ***1823.21*** *p89*
Derby, J. C. 40; Ontario, 1871 ***1823.21*** *p89*
Derdoussat, Dque. 22; New Orleans, 1848 ***778.6*** *p90*
Derenne, Edouard; Boston, 1871 ***1494.21*** *p31*
Derennes, Bertrand 25; Montreal, 1653 ***9221.17*** *p288*
Derennes, Valentin 25; Quebec, 1648 ***9221.17*** *p198*
Derepa, Vincent 30; Port uncertain, 1841 ***778.6*** *p90*
Derepas, Sivant 42; America, 1846 ***778.6*** *p90*
Dergenski, Andrew; Texas, 1892-1896 ***6015.15*** *p24*
Derham, . . .; Ontario, 1871 ***1823.21*** *p89*
Derich, Albert; America, 1882 ***5475.1*** *p228*
Derie, Gabriel 41; Montreal, 1659 ***9221.17*** *p420*
Deringer, Brigetta 2; Baltimore, 1889 ***8425.16*** *p35*
Deringer, Joh. 45; Baltimore, 1889 ***8425.16*** *p35*
Deringer, Lucie 30; Baltimore, 1889 ***8425.16*** *p35*

Deringer, Norpap; Ohio, 1809-1852 ***4511.35*** *p10*
Deringer, Xavier; Ohio, 1809-1852 ***4511.35*** *p10*
De Rivoire, Apollos; Boston, 1735 ***9228.50*** *p27*
Derivon deButmont, Pierre; Quebec, 1702 ***2314.30*** *p169*
Derivon deButmont, Pierre; Quebec, 1702 ***2314.30*** *p180*
Derk, Samuel 24; Ontario, 1871 ***1823.17*** *p41*
Derks, Peter; Illinois, 1852 ***6079.1*** *p4*
Derler, Christian; Ohio, 1809-1852 ***4511.35*** *p10*
Derlikiewicz, Alexander; Detroit, 1929 ***1640.55*** *p117*
Dernis, Claire 33; America, 1845 ***778.6*** *p91*
DeRoche, Clara *SEE* DeRoche, Daniel J.
DeRoche, Clara Remon *SEE* DeRoche, Daniel J.
DeRoche, Daniel J.; Maine, 1884-1888 ***9228.50*** *p534*
*Wife:*Clara Remon
*Daughter:*Clara
Deroissy, Nicolas 22; Quebec, 1662 ***9221.17*** *p484*
Derom, Michael 60; Ontario, 1871 ***1823.21*** *p89*
Derome, Denis 30; Quebec, 1653 ***9221.17*** *p271*
Deron, Miss 22; Louisiana, 1848 ***778.6*** *p91*
Deron, Mr. 24; Louisiana, 1848 ***778.6*** *p91*
De Ronde, . . .; New England, 1630-1670 ***9228.50*** *p555*
Derosny, Francois; Quebec, 1651 ***9221.17*** *p241*
Deroussy, Jeanne 22; Quebec, 1636 ***9221.17*** *p62*
DeRoybon D'Alonne, Madeleine; Quebec, 1671 ***4514.3*** *p304*
Deroye La Barre, Jean-Michel; Quebec, 1726 ***2314.30*** *p171*
Derr, Abraham 53; Halifax, N.S., 1902 ***1860.4*** *p42*
Derr, Jos.; Louisiana, 1874 ***4981.45*** *p295*
Derr, Katha 59; Halifax, N.S., 1902 ***1860.4*** *p42*
Derra, John; Wisconsin, 1892 ***6795.8*** *p69*
Derre, Charles; Quebec, 1640 ***9221.17*** *p95*
Derre DeGand, Francois; Quebec, 1628 ***9221.17*** *p27*
Derre DeGand, Jeanne; Quebec, 1638 ***9221.17*** *p76*
Derrez, Mrs. 32; Port uncertain, 1843 ***778.6*** *p91*
Derrez, J. B. 34; Port uncertain, 1843 ***778.6*** *p91*
Derrick, Mary 36; Ontario, 1871 ***1823.21*** *p89*
Derrick, Michael 43; Ontario, 1871 ***1823.21*** *p89*
Derry, Mrs. 32; Port uncertain, 1843 ***778.6*** *p91*
Derry, J. B. 34; Port uncertain, 1843 ***778.6*** *p91*
De Rue, Francis; Boston, 1715 ***9228.50*** *p196*
De Rue, Gilbert; America, 1732-1812 ***9228.50*** *p661*
De Rue, Townsend; America, 1848-1911 ***9228.50*** *p659*
Dervillers deLa Boissiere, Benjamin; Quebec, 1696 ***2314.30*** *p169*
Dervillers deLa Boissiere, Benjamin; Quebec, 1696 ***2314.30*** *p180*
Dervilliers, Benjamin; Quebec, 1670 ***4514.3*** *p311*
Derwing, Elisabeth; America, 1873 ***5475.1*** *p362*
Derwing, Elisabeth 34; America, 1873 ***5475.1*** *p363*
Derzensky, Andrew; Texas, 1892-1896 ***6015.15*** *p24*
Desache, Mr. 45; America, 1844 ***778.6*** *p91*
Desaigues, P. H. 24; America, 1840 ***778.6*** *p91*
Desainctes, Etienne 24; Montreal, 1662 ***9221.17*** *p497*
De Sainte Croix, . . .; Philadelphia, 1771-1773 ***9228.50*** *p485*
De Sainte Croix, Ann; Philadelphia, 1772 ***9228.50*** *p192*
De Sainte Croix, John *SEE* De Sainte Croix, Thomas
De Sainte Croix, Joshua Temple; Annapolis, N.S., 1783-1803 ***9228.50*** *p192*
De Sainte Croix, Joshua Temple; New York, 1734-1783 ***9228.50*** *p192*
De Sainte Croix, Marie Gaure *SEE* De Sainte Croix, Moyse
De Sainte Croix, Moyse; New York, 1751 ***9228.50*** *p192*
*Wife:*Marie Gaure
With son
De Sainte Croix, Nicholas France; Quebec, 1888 ***9228.50*** *p192*
De Sainte Croix, Philip; Boston, 1769 ***9228.50*** *p192*
De Sainte Croix, Sarah; Marblehead, MA, 1732 ***9228.50*** *p316*
De Sainte Croix, Thomas; New Brunswick, 1800-1840 ***9228.50*** *p193*
*Brother:*John
De Sainte Croix, William 26; Toronto, 1860 ***9228.50*** *p192*
De Saint Jeor, Eliza *SEE* De Saint Jeor, Francis F.
De Saint Jeor, Elizabeth Jena *SEE* De Saint Jeor, Francis F.
De Saint Jeor, Francis F.; Utah, 1855 ***9228.50*** *p193*
*Wife:*Elizabeth Jena
*Child:*Louisa
*Child:*Eliza
*Child:*Francis John
De Saint Jeor, Francis John *SEE* De Saint Jeor, Francis F.
De Saint Jeor, Louisa *SEE* De Saint Jeor, Francis F.
Desalm, Anton 22 *SEE* Desalm, Anton
Desalm, Anton 49; Galveston, TX, 1844 ***3967.10*** *p374*
*Son:*Anton 22
Desalm, Joseph 9; Galveston, TX, 1844 ***3967.10*** *p374*
Desalm, Katharina 12; Galveston, TX, 1844 ***3967.10*** *p374*
Desalm, Magdalena 14; Galveston, TX, 1844 ***3967.10*** *p374*
Desalm, Magdalena 43; Galveston, TX, 1844 ***3967.10*** *p374*
Desangles, Joseph 22; New Orleans, 1843 ***778.6*** *p91*
Desangles, Marie Louis G. 21; New Orleans, 1840 ***778.6*** *p91*
Desanis, Jean; Quebec, 1661 ***9221.17*** *p454*
Desautels, Etienne; Montreal, 1660 ***9221.17*** *p441*
Desautels, Pierre 20; Montreal, 1653 ***9221.17*** *p288*
Desbon, Mr. 19; Port uncertain, 1845 ***778.6*** *p91*
Desbons, Mr. 22; America, 1747 ***778.6*** *p91*
Desbordes, Jacob; Quebec, 1647 ***9221.17*** *p179*
Desbordes, Jean; Quebec, 1656 ***9221.17*** *p335*
Desbordes, Mathurine 25; Montreal, 1659 ***9221.17*** *p421*
*Daughter:*Jeanne 3
Desbornes, Maurice; Quebec, 1662 ***9221.17*** *p481*
Desborough, James; Massachusetts, 1700-1799 ***9228.50*** *p264*
Desborough, Jennet; Portsmouth, NH, 1676 ***9228.50*** *p194*
With child
Des Bross, James; Massachusetts, 1700-1799 ***9228.50*** *p191*
Desbross, James; Massachusetts, 1700-1799 ***9228.50*** *p264*
Descant, Mr. 27; America, 1846 ***778.6*** *p91*
Descant, Marie 24; America, 1846 ***778.6*** *p91*
Descaries, Jean 22; Montreal, 1643 ***9221.17*** *p136*
Descarreaux, Denis 30; Quebec, 1653 ***9221.17*** *p271*
Descartes DuMesnil, Auguste; Quebec, 1661 ***9221.17*** *p445*
Descelle Marbrelle, Francois; Quebec, 1694 ***2314.30*** *p169*
Descelle Marbrelle, Francois; Quebec, 1694 ***2314.30*** *p180*
Deschalets, Claude; Quebec, 1668 ***4514.3*** *p304*
*Sister:*Elisabeth
*Sister:*Madeleine
Deschalets, Elisabeth *SEE* Deschalets, Claude
Deschalets, Madeleine; Canada, 1668 ***1142.10*** *p128*
Deschalets, Madeleine *SEE* Deschalets, Claude
Deschamp, Benoit G.; Illinois, 1856 ***6079.1*** *p4*
Deschamp, Dominique 24; New Orleans, 1843 ***778.6*** *p91*
Deschamps, Anne; Quebec, 1668 ***4514.3*** *p304*
Deschamps, Anne 33; Quebec, 1643 ***9221.17*** *p128*
Des Champs, Arthur; America, 1900-1983 ***9228.50*** *p192*
With brother
Deschamps, Ezechiel; Quebec, 1638 ***9221.17*** *p76*
Deschamps, Jean; Quebec, 1642 ***9221.17*** *p115*
Deschamps, Marguerite; Quebec, 1647 ***9221.17*** *p188*
Deschamps, Marguerite; Quebec, 1647 ***9221.17*** *p188*
Deschamps, Marie; Quebec, 1667 ***4514.3*** *p304*
Deschamps, Marie; Quebec, 1669 ***4514.3*** *p304*
Deschamps, Marie; Quebec, 1672 ***4514.3*** *p304*
Deschamps, Marie-Madeleine; Quebec, 1670 ***4514.3*** *p304*
Deschamps, Pierre 19; Quebec, 1646 ***9221.17*** *p163*
Deschamps, Thomas; Nova Scotia, 1783 ***9228.50*** *p191*
Deschamps, Toussaint 27; Montreal, 1653 ***9221.17*** *p293*
Deschamps DeBeaulieu, Jean; Montreal, 1645 ***9221.17*** *p158*
Deschamps deLa Bouteillerie, Jean-Baptiste-Francois; Quebec, 1671 ***2314.30*** *p180*
Deschamps deLa Bouteillerie, Jean-Bte-Francois; Quebec, 1671 ***2314.30*** *p166*
Deschesnesverts, Guillaume 26; Quebec, 1659 ***9221.17*** *p406*
DesColombiers, Charles 19; Quebec, 1647 ***9221.17*** *p189*
Descolombiers, Marc-Antoine 24; Montreal, 1660 ***9221.17*** *p441*
Descorne, Jean 30; Port uncertain, 1841 ***778.6*** *p91*
Descouviere, Anatole 59; New Orleans, 1847 ***778.6*** *p91*
Descouviere, Jean 19; New Orleans, 1847 ***778.6*** *p91*
Descouviere, Jeanne Marie 62; New Orleans, 1847 ***778.6*** *p91*
Descouy, Jacques 27; Quebec, 1658 ***9221.17*** *p379*
Desenberg, Bernhard; New York, 1859 ***358.56*** *p55*
Deseniss, Engel Marie Sophie; America, 1860 ***7420.1*** *p192*
Deseniss, Hans Heinrich; America, 1845 ***7420.1*** *p35*
*Wife:*Marie Dorothea Meyer
With child 7
With child 3
With child 6 months
With child 5
With stepchild
Deseniss, Marie Dorothea Meyer *SEE* Deseniss, Hans Heinrich
Desenisse, Engel Marie Dorothea; America, 1882 ***7420.1*** *p332*
Desenle, Alex. 20; America, 1841 ***778.6*** *p91*
Desenne, Catherine; Quebec, 1672 ***4514.3*** *p305*
Deserre, Jean; Quebec, 1645 ***9221.17*** *p153*
Desfereaux, Paul 17; Missouri, 1845 ***778.6*** *p91*
Desfontaines, . . .; Quebec, 1648 ***9221.17*** *p198*
Desforges, Etienne 20; Montreal, 1653 ***9221.17*** *p300*
Desforges, H. 39; America, 1745 ***778.6*** *p91*
Desforges, Joseph 19; Quebec, 1646 ***9221.17*** *p162*
Desforges, Marcel; Quebec, 1649 ***9221.17*** *p217*
Desfosses, Francoise; Quebec, 1669 ***4514.3*** *p305*
Desfosses, Jacques; Quebec, 1647 ***9221.17*** *p179*
*Brother:*Simon
Desfosses, Simon *SEE* Desfosses, Jacques
Desfourneaux, Antoine; Quebec, 1661 ***9221.17*** *p451*
Desgranges, Jean-Baptiste; Quebec, 1652 ***9221.17*** *p257*
Desgranges, Louise; Quebec, 1669 ***4514.3*** *p305*
DesGroseilliers, Medard 23; Quebec, 1641 ***9221.17*** *p103*
Deshayes, Henri 49; New Orleans, 1844 ***778.6*** *p91*
Deshayes, Marguerite; Quebec, 1670 ***4514.3*** *p305*
Deshayes, Marie; Quebec, 1664 ***4514.3*** *p326*
Deshayes, Marie; Quebec, 1668 ***4514.3*** *p305*
DesHazards, Pierre 21; Quebec, 1651 ***9221.17*** *p248*
DeSilva, Francis; North Carolina, 1845 ***1088.45*** *p7*
Desiner, Frederick; Illinois, 1852 ***6079.1*** *p4*
Desiner, William; Illinois, 1852 ***6079.1*** *p4*
Desinglier, Emelie 10 months; New Orleans, 1848 ***778.6*** *p91*
Desinglier, Henri 27; New Orleans, 1848 ***778.6*** *p91*
Desinglier, Victorine 28; New Orleans, 1848 ***778.6*** *p91*
Desjardins, Christophe 25; Montreal, 1659 ***9221.17*** *p416*
Desjardins, Francoise; Quebec, 1665 ***4514.3*** *p305*
Desjardins, Guillaume; Quebec, 1653 ***9221.17*** *p277*
Desjardins, Jean; Montreal, 1660 ***9221.17*** *p441*
Desjardins, Michel; Montreal, 1653 ***9221.17*** *p296*
Desjardins Rupallais, Marc-Antoine; Quebec, 1693 ***2314.30*** *p172*
DesLandes, . . .; Portsmouth, NH, 1636 ***9228.50*** *p184*
Des Landes, Capt.; San Francisco, 1851 ***9228.50*** *p192*
Deslauriers, . . .; Quebec, 1642 ***9221.17*** *p115*
Deslauriers, . . .; Quebec, 1652 ***9221.17*** *p257*
Deslauriers, Benigne 23; Montreal, 1657 ***9221.17*** *p372*
Deslauriers, David; Quebec, 1639 ***9221.17*** *p87*
Deslauriers, Jean 24; Quebec, 1659 ***9221.17*** *p397*
Deslauriers, Pierre; Quebec, 1650 ***9221.17*** *p225*
Deslauriers, Robert 24; Montreal, 1650 ***9221.17*** *p230*
Desle, Caroline 20; Port uncertain, 1846 ***778.6*** *p91*
Deslin, Pierre Jean Alex; Louisiana, 1841-1844 ***4981.45*** *p210*
Desmaisons, Mrs. H. 50; New Orleans, 1848 ***778.6*** *p91*
Desmaisons, Marie; Quebec, 1600-1663 ***4514.3*** *p375*
Desmaisons, Marie; Quebec, 1650 ***9221.17*** *p228*
Desmarais, Catherine; Quebec, 1669 ***4514.3*** *p305*
Desmarais, Etiennette; Quebec, 1669 ***4514.3*** *p306*
Desmarais, Pierre 17; Montreal, 1660 ***9221.17*** *p441*
Desmarets, Gilles; Quebec, 1639 ***9221.17*** *p87*
Desmarets, Jean 38; Quebec, 1655 ***9221.17*** *p323*
Desmarquest, Eugenie 61; Ontario, 1871 ***1823.21*** *p89*
Desmas, Edouard 12; New Orleans, 1840 ***778.6*** *p91*
Desmond, And; St. John, N.B., 1847 ***2978.15*** *p40*
Desmond, Jeremiah 30; Ontario, 1871 ***1823.17*** *p41*
Desmond, Mary 26; Ontario, 1871 ***1823.17*** *p41*
Desmonde, Humphry; Toronto, 1844 ***2910.35*** *p113*
Des Monts, . . .; Boston, 1729 ***9228.50*** *p189*
Desmoulins, Antoine 14 *SEE* Desmoulins, Pierre
Desmoulins, Henri; Quebec, 1658 ***9221.17*** *p378*
Desmoulins, Jacques 41; Quebec, 1662 ***9221.17*** *p484*
Desmoulins, Jeanne Crespeau Regnault 43 *SEE* Desmoulins, Pierre
Desmoulins, Pierre 49; Montreal, 1659 ***9221.17*** *p424*
*Wife:*Jeanne Crespeau Regnault 43
*Son:*Antoine 14
Desmoulins, Pierre 26; Quebec, 1657 ***9221.17*** *p362*
Desmousseaux, Mr. 30; Port uncertain, 1848 ***778.6*** *p91*
Desmousseaux, Louise 21; Quebec, 1654 ***9221.17*** *p306*
Desmund, John 30; St. Johns, N.F., 1811 ***1053.20*** *p21*
Desnaguets, Catherine-Francoise; Quebec, 1647 ***9221.17*** *p186*
Desnaguets, Charlotte-Elisabeth; Quebec, 1659 ***9221.17*** *p399*
Desneux, Victoire; Wisconsin, 1855 ***1495.20*** *p8*
Desneux, Victoire; Wisconsin, 1855 ***1495.20*** *p8*
Desnonts, Francois 29; America, 1842 ***778.6*** *p91*
Desnoyers, Francois; Quebec, 1649 ***9221.17*** *p218*
Desnoyers, Noel; Quebec, 1640 ***9221.17*** *p96*
Desoine, Hector; Wisconsin, 1856 ***1494.21*** *p31*
Desorcy, Francoise Delamare *SEE* Desorcy, Michel
Desorcy, Michel 2 *SEE* Desorcy, Michel
Desorcy, Michel 31; Quebec, 1657 ***9221.17*** *p356*
*Wife:*Francoise Delamare
*Son:*Michel 2
Desormeaux, Rene; Quebec, 1643 ***9221.17*** *p130*
Desorson, Zacharie; Montreal, 1653 ***9221.17*** *p288*
De Souchet, John *SEE* De Souchet, Thomas

De Souchet, Nicholas *SEE* De Souchet, Thomas
De Souchet, Peter *SEE* De Souchet, Thomas
De Souchet, Peter *SEE* De Souchet, Thomas
De Souchet, Thomas; Ohio, 1807 ***9228.50*** *p566*
*Brother:*Peter
*Brother:*John
*Cousin:*Peter
*Brother:*Nicholas
Despagnet, Mr. 25; America, 1848 ***778.6*** *p92*
Despard, John; Marston's Wharf, 1782 ***8529.30*** *p11*
Despart, Henry; Lynn, MA, 1676 ***9228.50*** *p194*
Despatis, Nicolas 31; Quebec, 1652 ***9221.17*** *p258*
Despaux, Jean 24; New Orleans, 1848 ***778.6*** *p92*
Despaux, Joseph 22; New Orleans, 1840 ***778.6*** *p92*
Despeaux, Pierre 26; America, 1845 ***778.6*** *p92*
Desperques, Myra; Michigan, 1900-1950 ***9228.50*** *p192*
Desplats, Francois 26; New Orleans, 1840 ***778.6*** *p92*
Desponey, D. 60; New Orleans, 1843 ***778.6*** *p92*
Desportes, Francoise Langlois *SEE* Desportes, Pierre
Desportes, Francoise; Quebec, 1669 ***4514.3*** *p306*
Desportes, Pierre; Quebec, 1619 ***9221.17*** *p23*
*Wife:*Francoise Langlois
Desportes, Pierre; Quebec, 1659 ***9221.17*** *p413*
Desportes DuChemin, Al...; Quebec, 1662 ***9221.17*** *p484*
Despousy, Bernard 14; New Orleans, 1848 ***778.6*** *p92*
Despouys, Miss 25; New Orleans, 1848 ***778.6*** *p92*
Despras, Ms. 28; New Orleans, 1848 ***778.6*** *p92*
Despras, C. 27; New Orleans, 1848 ***778.6*** *p92*
Despreaux, Pre. Phil. 35; Missouri, 1848 ***778.6*** *p92*
Despres, Anne 23; Quebec, 1651 ***9221.17*** *p241*
*Sister:*Genevieve 13
*Brother:*Guillaume
Despres, Etiennette 24; Quebec, 1651 ***9221.17*** *p235*
Despres, Etiennette 24; Quebec, 1651 ***9221.17*** *p235*
DesPres, Francois 1; Quebec, 1636 ***9221.17*** *p57*
Despres, Genevieve 13 *SEE* Despres, Anne
Despres, Guillaume *SEE* Despres, Anne
Despres, Jennet; Portsmouth, NH, 1676 ***9228.50*** *p194*
With child
Despres, Madeleine; Quebec, 1670 ***4514.3*** *p306*
Despres, Simon; Montreal, 1653 ***9221.17*** *p288*
Despres, Vincente; Quebec, 1648 ***9221.17*** *p199*
Despres, Xavier; Ohio, 1809-1852 ***4511.35*** *p10*
Despres Family ; Michigan, 1905 ***9228.50*** *p192*
Despres Family ; Quebec, 1800-1905 ***9228.50*** *p192*
D'Esquincourt, Anne; Quebec, 1669 ***4514.3*** *p306*
DesRochers, Charles; Quebec, 1642 ***9221.17*** *p115*
Desrochers, Denis 25; Quebec, 1637 ***9221.17*** *p69*
Desrochers, Jean 24; Montreal, 1647 ***9221.17*** *p192*
Desroches, Jean 24; Montreal, 1647 ***9221.17*** *p192*
Desrosiers, Mr.; Quebec, 1659 ***9221.17*** *p399*
Desrosiers, Andre; Quebec, 1659 ***9221.17*** *p403*
Desrosiers, Antoine 22; Quebec, 1641 ***9221.17*** *p103*
Desrosiers, Francois 15; Quebec, 1654 ***9221.17*** *p308*
Dessalles, Emilie D. 21; Port uncertain, 1841 ***778.6*** *p92*
Dessan, Emil; Illinois, 1857 ***6079.1*** *p4*
Desselmann, Carl; Valdivia, Chile, 1852 ***1192.4*** *p55*
Dessen, Francois 49; America, 1847 ***778.6*** *p92*
Dessieux, Claude 16; America, 1843 ***778.6*** *p92*
Dessieux, Claude 44; America, 1843 ***778.6*** *p92*
Dessieux, Elise 8; America, 1843 ***778.6*** *p92*
Dessieux, Jean 15; America, 1843 ***778.6*** *p92*
Dessieux, Joseph 12; America, 1843 ***778.6*** *p92*
Dessieux, Marie 40; America, 1843 ***778.6*** *p92*
Dessler, George; Ohio, 1809-1852 ***4511.35*** *p10*
Dessu, Xavier 21; America, 1844 ***778.6*** *p92*
Destaillis, Marin 33; Montreal, 1653 ***9221.17*** *p288*
Desteche, Josephine Boucher *SEE* Desteche, Pierre Joseph
Desteche, Pierre Joseph; Wisconsin, 1856 ***1495.20*** *p41*
*Wife:*Josephine Boucher
*Daughter:*Rosalie
Desteche, Rosalie *SEE* Desteche, Pierre Joseph
de Ste. Croix, . . .; Boston, 1769 ***9228.50*** *p5*
De Ste. Croix, Philip; Boston, 1769 ***9228.50*** *p48*
Destenay, Marie Madelene; Wisconsin, 1870 ***1495.20*** *p56*
Destensky, Frantisek; Texas, 1856-1906 ***2853.20*** *p64*
Dester, Jacob; Ohio, 1809-1852 ***4511.35*** *p10*
Destes, Mr. 51; America, 1843 ***778.6*** *p92*
Destez, Louis C.; Louisiana, 1836-1840 ***4981.45*** *p212*
Destouches, Marie-Agnes; Quebec, 1669 ***4514.3*** *p306*
Destrac, William; North Carolina, 1827 ***1088.45*** *p7*
Destree, Frank J. J.; Detroit, 1873 ***1494.20*** *p12*
Destree, Jean-Baptiste; Detroit, 1870 ***1494.20*** *p12*
Destreme, Joseph 18; New Orleans, 1843 ***778.6*** *p92*
Desvarieux, Jean; Quebec, 1642 ***9221.17*** *p115*
*Son:*Vincente
Desvarieux, Vincente 19 *SEE* Desvarieux, Jean
Desvaux, Jacques Lewis; Illinois, 1856 ***6079.1*** *p4*
DesVerges, Joseph; Boston, 1755 ***9228.50*** *p21A*
DesVerges, Joseph; Nova Scotia, 1755-1800 ***9228.50*** *p21A*
*Wife:*Mary Blewett
DesVerges, Mary Blewett *SEE* DesVerges, Joseph
Desvignets, Jacques 19; Montreal, 1661 ***9221.17*** *p475*
Desvillettes, Pierre; Quebec, 1642 ***9221.17*** *p116*
Detamble, Ludwig; New York, 1886 ***5475.1*** *p69*
Detave, P.erre 24; New Orleans, 1848 ***778.6*** *p92*
Detein, Nicolas; Quebec, 1659 ***9221.17*** *p413*
Deterding, Friederike Charlotte Geweke *SEE* Deterding, Heinrich Conrad
Deterding, Friedrich Wilhelm Louis *SEE* Deterding, Heinrich Conrad
Deterding, Gottlieb; America, 1870 ***7420.1*** *p283*
Deterding, Heinrich; America, 1854 ***7420.1*** *p118*
Deterding, Heinrich Conrad; America, 1893 ***7420.1*** *p368*
*Wife:*Friederike Charlotte Geweke
*Son:*Friedrich Wilhelm Louis
*Son:*Heinrich Wilhelm
Deterding, Heinrich Wilhelm *SEE* Deterding, Heinrich Conrad
Detering, Federick; Washington, 1885 ***2770.40*** *p194*
Detering, William F.; Washington, 1885 ***2770.40*** *p194*
Dethy, Marie Joseph; Wisconsin, 1879 ***1495.20*** *p46*
Detienne, Josephine; Wisconsin, 1854 ***1495.20*** *p29*
Detier, Fredrick; North Carolina, 1848 ***1088.45*** *p7*
Detlaf, John 30; North Carolina, 1774 ***1422.10*** *p55*
Detlaf, Sarah 25; North Carolina, 1774 ***1422.10*** *p55*
Detlaff, Joseph; Detroit, 1890 ***9980.23*** *p97*
Detling, Anna 7; New York, NY, 1893 ***1883.7*** *p38*
Detling, Karl 32; New York, NY, 1893 ***1883.7*** *p38*
Detling, Marianna 32; New York, NY, 1893 ***1883.7*** *p38*
Detling, Martha 2; New York, NY, 1893 ***1883.7*** *p38*
Detling, Walburga 4; New York, NY, 1893 ***1883.7*** *p38*
Detman, Marianna 22; New York, NY, 1847 ***9176.15*** *p49*
Detmer, Heinrich Conrad; America, 1883 ***7420.1*** *p335*
deTorrier, Mr. 32; New Orleans, 1840 ***778.6*** *p92*
Detrepagny, Romain 28; Quebec, 1655 ***9221.17*** *p323*
Detrie, Mr. 26; America, 1841 ***778.6*** *p92*
Detrie, Mr. 28; America, 1841 ***778.6*** *p92*
Detrie, Ysid. 28; America, 1840 ***778.6*** *p92*
Dettinger, Gottleib; New York, 1860 ***358.56*** *p149*
Dettinger, Michael; New York, 1860 ***358.56*** *p149*
Dettmann, Johanne; Wisconsin, 1884 ***6795.8*** *p89*
Dettmer, Carl; America, 1846 ***7420.1*** *p43*
Dettmer, Engel Marie Dorothee; America, 1856 ***7420.1*** *p154*
Dettmer, Hans Heinrich; America, 1850 ***7420.1*** *p70*
*Brother:*Johann Otto
Dettmer, Johann Christoph; Port uncertain, 1837 ***7420.1*** *p13*
Dettmer, Johann Otto *SEE* Dettmer, Hans Heinrich
Detweiler, Boniface; Ohio, 1809-1852 ***4511.35*** *p10*
Detwiler, Ambrose; Ohio, 1809-1852 ***4511.35*** *p10*
Detzlaff, Daniel 6; New York, NY, 1893 ***1883.7*** *p42*
Detzlaff, Dorothea 41; New York, NY, 1893 ***1883.7*** *p42*
Detzlaff, Friedrich 14; New York, NY, 1893 ***1883.7*** *p42*
Detzlaff, Gustav 4; New York, NY, 1893 ***1883.7*** *p42*
Detzlaff, Jacob 39; New York, NY, 1893 ***1883.7*** *p42*
Detzlaff, Julianna 4 months; New York, NY, 1893 ***1883.7*** *p42*
Detzlaff, Maria 17; New York, NY, 1893 ***1883.7*** *p42*
Detzlaff, Rosina 2; New York, NY, 1893 ***1883.7*** *p42*
Detzlaff, Samuel 11; New York, NY, 1893 ***1883.7*** *p42*
Deubel, Antonio 24; America, 1847 ***778.6*** *p92*
Deuble, John F.; Ohio, 1809-1852 ***4511.35*** *p10*
Deuble, John Frederick; Ohio, 1809-1852 ***4511.35*** *p10*
Deudeville, Henri; Quebec, 1660 ***9221.17*** *p434*
Deusing, Caroline; Valdivia, Chile, 1851 ***1192.4*** *p50*
Deuter, Jakob; Wisconsin, 1901 ***6795.8*** *p233*
Deutras, Bertrand; Louisiana, 1874 ***4981.45*** *p131*
Deutsch, Adolph; Philadelphia, 1868 ***8513.31*** *p302*
*Wife:*Rosalie Kohn
Deutsch, Anna 22 *SEE* Deutsch, Matias
Deutsch, Jakob; America, 1800-1899 ***5475.1*** *p43*
Deutsch, M. Barbara; Chicago, 1889 ***5475.1*** *p197*
Deutsch, Magdalena; America, 1871 ***5475.1*** *p263*
Deutsch, Margarethe; America, 1856 ***5475.1*** *p365*
Deutsch, Mathias 25 *SEE* Deutsch, Matias
Deutsch, Matias; America, 1855 ***5475.1*** *p255*
With family
*Daughter:*Anna
*Son:*Mathias
Deutsch, Rosalie Kohn *SEE* Deutsch, Adolph
Deutsch, Uri 18; America, 1840 ***778.6*** *p92*
Deutscher, Georg 48; Portland, ME, 1906 ***970.38*** *p76*
Deutscher, Kata. 16; Portland, ME, 1906 ***970.38*** *p76*
Deutscher, Margareta 37; Portland, ME, 1906 ***970.38*** *p76*
Deutscher, Pauline 21; Portland, ME, 1906 ***970.38*** *p76*
Deutscher, Wilhelm 9; Portland, ME, 1906 ***970.38*** *p76*
Deutschmann, Magdalena 53; America, 1841 ***778.6*** *p92*
Deuve, Jean; Quebec, 1659 ***9221.17*** *p413*
DeValmont, Miss 24; Louisiana, 1848 ***778.6*** *p92*
Devalois, Catherine; Quebec, 1671 ***4514.3*** *p306*
Devanchy, Pierre 21; Montreal, 1661 ***9221.17*** *p472*
Devany, Michael 11; Quebec, 1870 ***8364.32*** *p23*
Devardt, Remi; New York, 1902 ***1766.20*** *p25*
Devaud, Marie 29; New Orleans, 1848 ***778.6*** *p92*
Devault, Marie; Quebec, 1667 ***4514.3*** *p306*
Devaux, Jeanne Pierrette 25; Texas, 1843 ***778.6*** *p93*
Devaux, Marie; Quebec, 1656 ***9221.17*** *p335*
Devaux, Servois 38; Texas, 1843 ***778.6*** *p93*
Develyn, Arthur; Philadelphia, 1778 ***8529.30*** *p2*
Devenish, Priscilla; Maryland, 1674-1675 ***1236.25*** *p52*
Devenish, Robert; Maryland, 1674 ***1236.25*** *p49*
Devennes, Gilles 24; Quebec, 1643 ***9221.17*** *p131*
Dever, James 22; Ontario, 1871 ***1823.21*** *p89*
Dever, Mary 52; Ontario, 1871 ***1823.21*** *p89*
Deveraux, John; North Carolina, 1813 ***1088.45*** *p7*
Devereaux, James 10; Ontario, 1871 ***1823.21*** *p89*
Devereux, Eliz. Matthews *SEE* Devereux, William
Devereux, John; Marblehead, MA, 1630 ***9228.50*** *p193*
Devereux, Sargent John *SEE* Devereux, William
Devereux, William; Maine, 1627-1669 ***9228.50*** *p197*
*Wife:*Eliz. Matthews
*Child:*Sargent John
Deverick, Mary 40; Ontario, 1871 ***1823.21*** *p89*
Devericks, Sarah 47; Ontario, 1871 ***1823.21*** *p89*
De Veulle, Henry 33; Quebec, 1881 ***9228.50*** *p194*
Devigne, James; Quebec, 1852-1900 ***9228.50*** *p129*
Deville Cenillon, Mr. 30; Louisiana, 1840 ***778.6*** *p93*
Devillers, Auguste; Wisconsin, 1857 ***1495.20*** *p28*
*Wife:*Felicitee Dore
*Son:*Emile Joseph
Devillers, Emile Joseph *SEE* Devillers, Auguste
Devillers, Felicitee Dore *SEE* Devillers, Auguste
Devilliers, Philipp 16; New Orleans, 1848 ***778.6*** *p93*
Devin, Andrew; Dedham, MA, 1652 ***1642*** *p102*
Devin, Georg 28; New Orleans, 1848 ***778.6*** *p93*
Devincent, Therda 55; Michigan, 1880 ***4491.42*** *p10*
de Vinchelez, Elizabeth; Marblehead, MA, 1705 ***9228.50*** *p165*
Devine, Biddy 4; St. John, N.B., 1834 ***6469.7*** *p4*
Devine, Biddy 40; St. John, N.B., 1834 ***6469.7*** *p4*
Devine, Charles 12; St. John, N.B., 1834 ***6469.7*** *p4*
Devine, Elizabeth; Maryland, 1673 ***1236.25*** *p48*
Devine, James; Massachusetts, 1771 ***1642*** *p104*
Devine, James 38; Michigan, 1880 ***4491.36*** *p5*
Devine, James 30; Ontario, 1871 ***1823.21*** *p89*
Devine, James; Quebec, 1852-1900 ***9228.50*** *p129*
Devine, James H.; Illinois, 1865 ***6079.1*** *p4*
Devine, John 9; Michigan, 1880 ***4491.36*** *p5*
Devine, John 18; St. John, N.B., 1834 ***6469.7*** *p4*
Devine, Julia E. 12; Michigan, 1880 ***4491.36*** *p5*
Devine, Lewis; Maryland, 1673 ***1236.25*** *p48*
Devine, Margaret 32; Michigan, 1880 ***4491.36*** *p5*
Devine, Margaret A. 15; Michigan, 1880 ***4491.36*** *p5*
Devine, Maria 57; Ontario, 1871 ***1823.21*** *p89*
Devine, Mary 20; St. John, N.B., 1834 ***6469.7*** *p4*
Devine, Mary A. 13; Michigan, 1880 ***4491.36*** *p5*
Devine, Patrick 2; St. John, N.B., 1834 ***6469.7*** *p4*
Devine, Robert; Ohio, 1840-1897 ***8365.35*** *p15*
Devine, Thomas; Ohio, 1809-1852 ***4511.35*** *p10*
Devine, Timothy; Louisiana, 1874 ***4981.45*** *p131*
Deviney, John; Philadelphia, 1855 ***5720.10*** *p377*
Devinney, Elizabeth *SEE* Devinney, Samuel
Devinney, Henry; Ohio, 1809-1852 ***4511.35*** *p10*
Devinney, Margaret Donaldson *SEE* Devinney, Samuel
Devinney, Samuel; New York, 1856 ***8513.31*** *p302*
*Wife:*Margaret Donaldson
*Daughter:*Elizabeth
Devit, John 47; Indiana, 1847-1876 ***9076.20*** *p69*
Devitt, Charles 30; Ontario, 1871 ***1823.17*** *p41*
Devitt, Patrick; Boston, 1830 ***3274.55*** *p68*
Devitt, Peter 39; Ontario, 1871 ***1823.17*** *p41*
Devlin, Barney; St. John, N.B., 1847 ***2978.15*** *p41*
Devlin, Bridget Keegan *SEE* Devlin, Louis
Devlin, Charles; St. John, N.B., 1847 ***2978.15*** *p41*
Devlin, Edward; St. John, N.B., 1847 ***2978.15*** *p41*
Devlin, Hugh; Louisiana, 1874 ***4981.45*** *p131*
Devlin, John; Louisiana, 1874 ***4981.45*** *p131*
Devlin, Louis; Philadelphia, 1850 ***8513.31*** *p303*
*Wife:*Bridget Keegan
Devlin, Patrick; St. John, N.B., 1847 ***2978.15*** *p41*
Devlin, Peter 38; Indiana, 1870-1872 ***9076.20*** *p67*
Devlin, William 65; Ontario, 1871 ***1823.21*** *p89*
Devney, Patrick 40; Ontario, 1871 ***1823.21*** *p89*
Devo, Peter; Ohio, 1809-1852 ***4511.35*** *p10*
Devoisy, Jeanne 22; Quebec, 1636 ***9221.17*** *p62*
Devosque, Mrs. 45; America, 1846 ***778.6*** *p93*
De Vouge, . . .; Quebec, 1800-1840 ***9228.50*** *p194*
Devoy, Mary 52; Ontario, 1871 ***1823.21*** *p89*
Devroye, Marie Joseph; Wisconsin, 1854-1858 ***1495.20*** *p66*
Devry, James; Ohio, 1809-1852 ***4511.35*** *p10*

DeVul, Alphonse 20; Quebec, 1910 *2897.7 p8*
Dew, John 53; Ontario, 1871 *1823.17 p41*
Dew, John; Virginia, 1652 *6254.4 p243*
Dew, Samuel 22; Ontario, 1871 *1823.17 p41*
Dewaar, Lancet 60; Ontario, 1871 *1823.21 p89*
Dewald, Jacob 24; New Orleans, 1834 *1002.51 p111*
Dewald, Johann 59; America, 1843 *5475.1 p309*
Dewalt, Charles; Ohio, 1809-1852 *4511.35 p11*
Dewalt, Nicholas; Ohio, 1809-1852 *4511.35 p11*
Dewalt, Peter; Ohio, 1809-1852 *4511.35 p11*
Dewan, Michael 66; Ontario, 1871 *1823.21 p89*
Dewan, Patrick 61; Ontario, 1871 *1823.21 p89*
Dewar, Alexander 64; Ontario, 1871 *1823.21 p89*
Dewar, Alexander 80; Ontario, 1871 *1823.17 p41*
Dewar, Archibald 42; Ontario, 1871 *1823.21 p89*
Dewar, Duncan 39; Ontario, 1871 *1823.21 p89*
Dewar, Duncan 40; Ontario, 1871 *1823.21 p89*
Dewar, Georgina 52; Ontario, 1871 *1823.21 p89*
Dewar, Hugh 53; Ontario, 1871 *1823.21 p89*
Dewar, James 58; Ontario, 1871 *1823.21 p89*
Dewar, John 51; Ontario, 1871 *1823.17 p41*
Dewar, John 75; Ontario, 1871 *1823.17 p41*
Dewar, John G. 26; Ontario, 1871 *1823.21 p89*
Dewar, Malcolm 33; Ontario, 1871 *1823.17 p41*
Dewar, Malcolm 54; Ontario, 1871 *1823.17 p41*
Dewar, Robert 66; Ontario, 1871 *1823.21 p90*
Dewar, William 18; Ontario, 1871 *1823.17 p41*
Dewe, Eliz. Mary 23; Quebec, 1910 *2897.7 p8*
DeWeaver, John; North Carolina, 1839 *1088.45 p7*
Dewer, Donald 74; Ontario, 1871 *1823.21 p90*
Dewes, Anna; America, 1834 *5475.1 p437*
Dewes, Anna SEE Dewes, Peter
Dewes, Anna Backes 27 SEE Dewes, Michel
Dewes, Barbara 6 SEE Dewes, Jakob
Dewes, Barbara 8 SEE Dewes, Michel
Dewes, Barbara 27; Brazil, 1872 *5475.1 p442*
Dewes, Elisabeth; America, 1833 *5475.1 p436*
Dewes, Elisabeth Lermen SEE Dewes, Jakob
Dewes, Elisabeth; Brazil, 1846 *5475.1 p438*
Dewes, Franz; Brazil, 1880 *5475.1 p444*
Dewes, Gertrud SEE Dewes, Katharina
Dewes, J. Peter SEE Dewes, Peter
Dewes, Jakob; America, 1834 *5475.1 p436*
  Wife:Elisabeth Lermen
  With 8 children
Dewes, Jakob; Brazil, 1857 *5475.1 p441*
  With wife & 7 children
Dewes, Jakob 36; Brazil, 1872 *5475.1 p443*
  Wife:Maria Spohn 36
  Daughter:Margarethe 2 months
  Daughter:Barbara 6
  Daughter:Magdalena 4
Dewes, Jakob SEE Dewes, Katharina
Dewes, Johann 2 SEE Dewes, Michel
Dewes, Johann 36; Brazil, 1872 *5475.1 p443*
Dewes, Johann August; Chicago, 1877 *5475.1 p298*
Dewes, Karl Johann; Chicago, 1882 *5475.1 p300*
Dewes, Karoline SEE Dewes, Peter
Dewes, Karoline Hoffmann SEE Dewes, Peter
Dewes, Katharina SEE Dewes, Katharina
Dewes, Katharina; Rio Grande do Sul, Brazil, 1883
  5475.1 p445
  Son:Jakob
  Daughter:Katharina
  Daughter:Gertrud
Dewes, Magdalena 4 SEE Dewes, Jakob
Dewes, Margarethe; America, 1834 *5475.1 p437*
Dewes, Margarethe 2 SEE Dewes, Jakob
Dewes, Margarethe 5 SEE Dewes, Michel
Dewes, Maria; America, 1833 *5475.1 p436*
Dewes, Maria; America, 1833 *5475.1 p436*
Dewes, Maria; America, 1834 *5475.1 p437*
Dewes, Maria 56; America, 1856 *5475.1 p358*
  Child:Susanna 23
  Child:Maria 21
Dewes, Maria; Brazil, 1872 *5475.1 p249*
Dewes, Maria SEE Dewes, Peter
Dewes, Maria Spohn 36 SEE Dewes, Jakob
Dewes, Maria 41; Brazil, 1863 *5475.1 p502*
Dewes, Mathias 21; Brazil, 1872 *5475.1 p443*
Dewes, Michel; America, 1882 *5475.1 p445*
Dewes, Michel 27; Brazil, 1872 *5475.1 p443*
Dewes, Michel 31; Brazil, 1872 *5475.1 p442*
  Wife:Anna Backes 27
  Son:Johann 2 months
  Daughter:Barbara 8
  Daughter:Margarethe 5
Dewes, Nikolaus; America, 1879 *5475.1 p382*
Dewes, Nikolaus SEE Dewes, Peter
Dewes, Peter; America, 1882 *5475.1 p445*
Dewes, Peter; Brazil, 1879 *5475.1 p444*
  Wife:Karoline Hoffmann
  Son:J. Peter

Son:Nikolaus
  Daughter:Anna
  Daughter:Maria
  Daughter:Karoline
Dewes, Susanna; Brazil, 1846 *5475.1 p439*
Dewey, Fredrick 41; Ontario, 1871 *1823.21 p90*
Dewey, William 69; Ontario, 1871 *1823.21 p90*
Dewhurst, George; Ohio, 1843 *2763.1 p9*
Dewhurst, George, Jr.; Ohio, 1843 *2763.1 p9*
Dewhurst, Miles; Ohio, 1843 *2763.1 p9*
Dewhurst, Thomas; Ohio, 1843 *2763.1 p9*
Dews, Thomas; North Carolina, 1825 *1088.45 p7*
Dews, Thomas, Jr.; North Carolina, 1808-1838 *9228.50
  p194*
Dey, Philipp 20; Missouri, 1845 *778.6 p93*
Deyhle, Gottlieb Charles; Wisconsin, 1901 *6795.8 p158*
De Young, Peter; Maryland, 1674-1675 *1236.25 p51*
Deys, John; Nova Scotia, 1784 *7105 p22*
Deysinger, Anna Magdalena 23; Pennsylvania, 1851
  170.15 p22
  With family
Deysinger, Friedrich 28; Pennsylvania, 1851 *170.15 p22*
  With family
Deysinger, Johann Friedr. 1; Pennsylvania, 1851 *170.15
  p22*
  With family
Dezac, P. H. 22; America, 1847 *778.6 p93*
Dezane, Gaspard; Quebec, 1638 *9221.17 p145*
Dezes, Margarethe; America, 1871 *5475.1 p139*
Dezesvaux, Desire 39; New Orleans, 1845 *778.6 p93*
Dezin, Catharine 28; New Orleans, 1847 *778.6 p93*
Dezin, Jane 66; Port uncertain, 1847 *778.6 p93*
Dezin, John 30; New Orleans, 1847 *778.6 p93*
Dezzy, David 13; Michigan, 1880 *4491.39 p8*
d'Heren, Gaspard; Quebec, 1638 *9221.17 p145*
DHerete, Mr. 19; Port uncertain, 1845 *778.6 p93*
DHerite, Mr. 19; Port uncertain, 1845 *778.6 p93*
DHerite-Cousine, Ignace 39; New Orleans, 1848 *778.6
  p93*
D'Hugues, Louis-Joseph-Francois; Quebec, 1757 *2314.30
  p170*
D'Hugues, Louis-Joseph-Francois; Quebec, 1757 *2314.30
  p180*
Diamond, John 75; Ontario, 1871 *1823.21 p90*
Diaz, A. 22; America, 1843 *778.6 p93*
Diaz, John; Louisiana, 1874 *4981.45 p295*
Dibb, Richard 56; Ontario, 1871 *1823.21 p90*
Dibb, William 45; Ontario, 1871 *1823.17 p41*
Dibble, Deborah M. 40; Michigan, 1880 *4491.42 p10*
Dibbs, William 59; Ontario, 1871 *1823.21 p90*
Dibeau, Maria Magdalena; Venezuela, 1843 *3899.5 p542*
Di Bello, Michele; Colorado, 1894 *1029.59 p22*
Di Bello, Ralph; Colorado, 1904 *1029.59 p21*
Diber, Elizabeth; Detroit, 1929 *1640.55 p115*
Diber, Theodore; Detroit, 1929 *1640.55 p115*
Dibold, Catharina 40; Port uncertain, 1847 *778.6 p93*
Dibold, Catherina 4; Port uncertain, 1847 *778.6 p93*
Dibold, Franz 23; New York, NY, 1847 *9176.15 p49*
Dibold, Joseph 40; Port uncertain, 1847 *778.6 p93*
Dicby, Charles 34; New Orleans, 1848 *778.6 p93*
Dichtli, . . .; North Carolina, 1710 *3629.40 p3*
Dichtli, Daniel; North Carolina, 1710 *3629.40 p7*
Dick, Amalie SEE Dick, Johann Karl
Dick, Carolina 20 SEE Dick, Georg Jakob
Dick, Elisabeth SEE Dick, Johann Karl
Dick, Georg Jakob 60; America, 1843 *5475.1 p528*
  With daughter 25
  Wife:Luise Reina 54
  Daughter:Carolina 20
  Daughter: 29
  With 2 grandchildren & sisters-in-law
Dick, Henry; Colorado, 1899 *1029.59 p22*
Dick, James; North Carolina, 1799 *1088.45 p8*
Dick, Johann Karl; America, 1863-1900 *5475.1 p499*
  Wife:M. Elisabeth Drumm
  Daughter:Elisabeth
  Daughter:Phillipine
  Daughter:Rosine
  Daughter:Amalie
  Daughter:Katharina
  Daughter:Luise
Dick, Johann Nikolaus; America, 1848 *5475.1 p538*
Dick, Joseph; Ohio, 1809-1852 *4511.35 p11*
Dick, Karolina; America, 1866 *5475.1 p498*
Dick, Katharina SEE Dick, Johann Karl
Dick, Katharina 21; America, 1836 *5475.1 p536*
Dick, Katharina 29; Ohio, 1800-1899 *5475.1 p528*
Dick, Louis Jacob; Missouri, 1903 *3276.1 p4*
Dick, Luise SEE Dick, Johann Karl
Dick, Luise Reina 54 SEE Dick, Georg Jakob
Dick, M. Elisabeth Drumm SEE Dick, Johann Karl
Dick, Phillipine SEE Dick, Johann Karl
Dick, Rosine SEE Dick, Johann Karl

Dick, William Henry 45; Ontario, 1871 *1823.21 p90*
Dickas, C. Henry; Ohio, 1840-1897 *8365.35 p15*
Dicken, Matthew; Louisiana, 1836-1841 *4981.45 p208*
Dickens, John; Marston's Wharf, 1782 *8529.30 p11*
Dickens, Willis 44; Ontario, 1871 *1823.21 p90*
Dickerson, Charles 47; Ontario, 1871 *1823.21 p90*
Dickey, Ann 78; Ontario, 1871 *1823.21 p90*
Dickey, English 37; Ontario, 1871 *1823.21 p90*
Dickey, James 30; Ontario, 1871 *1823.21 p90*
Dickey, Robert 52; Ontario, 1871 *1823.21 p90*
Dickey, Robert R. 38; Ontario, 1871 *1823.17 p41*
Dickfell, Andrew; New York, 1859 *358.56 p55*
Dickie, Jane; Boston, 1740 *1642 p26*
Dickie, John 57; Ontario, 1871 *1823.21 p90*
Dickings, John; Marston's Wharf, 1782 *8529.30 p11*
Dickins, John; Marston's Wharf, 1782 *8529.30 p11*
Dickinson, Alex 35; Ontario, 1871 *1823.17 p41*
Dickinson, Charles 71; Ontario, 1871 *1823.21 p90*
Dickinson, Craven; North Carolina, 1822 *1088.45 p8*
Dickinson, Margt 71; Ontario, 1871 *1823.21 p90*
Dickinson, Thomas 70; Ontario, 1871 *1823.21 p90*
Dicklan, Frederick 35; Ontario, 1871 *1823.17 p41*
Dickman, Henry; New York, 1778 *8529.30 p2A*
Dickmann, Carl August Leopold; America, 1856 *7420.1
  p146*
Dickmann, Christine; New York, 1859 *358.56 p55*
Dickmann, H.; New York, 1860 *358.56 p3*
Dickow, Fritz; Wisconsin, 1895 *6795.8 p162*
Dickson, George 31; Ontario, 1871 *1823.17 p41*
Dickson, George 45; Ontario, 1871 *1823.21 p90*
Dickson, James 38; Ontario, 1871 *1823.21 p90*
Dickson, James 105; Ontario, 1871 *1823.21 p90*
Dickson, James; South Carolina, 1813 *3208.30 p18*
Dickson, James; South Carolina, 1813 *3208.30 p31*
Dickson, James 52; South Carolina, 1812 *3476.30 p11*
Dickson, John; North Carolina, 1812 *1088.45 p8*
Dickson, Samuel; Boston, 1766 *1642 p36*
Dickson, Thomas 40; Ontario, 1871 *1823.21 p90*
Dickson, William; South Carolina, 1813 *3208.30 p19*
Dickson, William; South Carolina, 1813 *3208.30 p31*
Didas, Johann; America, 1872 *5475.1 p446*
Didenko, Anna; Halifax, N.S., 1902 *1860.4 p42*
Didenko, Conrad; Halifax, N.S., 1902 *1860.4 p42*
Didenko, Lina; Halifax, N.S., 1902 *1860.4 p42*
Didenko, Olga; Halifax, N.S., 1902 *1860.4 p42*
Diderle, George; New York, 1859 *358.56 p54*
Didert, Joseph 9 months; Missouri, 1846 *778.6 p93*
Didert, Marie 25; Missouri, 1846 *778.6 p93*
Didert, Nicolas 30; Missouri, 1846 *778.6 p93*
Didier, Francois 23; Louisiana, 1848 *778.6 p93*
Didier, Jean Babptise; Illinois, 1856 *6079.1 p4*
Didier, Joseph 32; America, 1847 *778.6 p93*
Didier, Pierre; Montreal, 1643 *9221.17 p137*
Didier, Victor; Ohio, 1840-1897 *8365.35 p15*
Didion, Jakob SEE Didion, Johann
Didion, Johann SEE Didion, Johann
Didion, Johann; America, 1881 *5475.1 p429*
  Wife:Maria Bechtel
  Daughter:Margarethe
  Daughter:Maria
  Son:Johann
  Son:Jakob
Didion, Katharina 28; America, 1881 *5475.1 p429*
Didion, Margarethe SEE Didion, Johann
Didion, Maria SEE Didion, Johann
Didion, Maria Bechtel 24 SEE Didion, Johann
Didiot, Nicholas; Boston, 1831 *3274.55 p71*
Didoit, Joseph 9 months; Missouri, 1846 *778.6 p93*
Didoit, Marie 25; Missouri, 1846 *778.6 p93*
Didoit, Nicolas 30; Missouri, 1846 *778.6 p93*
Didon, Lina; St. Paul, MN, 1894 *1865.50 p45*
Diebach, Johannes 39; America, 1835 *2526.43 p224*
Diebold, Ignatius; Ohio, 1809-1852 *4511.35 p11*
Dieckmann, Caroline Wilhelmine; America, 1862 *7420.1
  p211*
Dieckmann, Heinrich August; America, 1865 *7420.1
  p230*
  With wife
Dieckmann, Johanne Charlotte Sophie; America, 1868
  7420.1 p270
  With son
Diederich, Johann; Louisiana, 1836-1840 *4981.45 p212*
Diedler, Charles; Ohio, 1809-1852 *4511.35 p11*
Diedrich, Barbara 3 SEE Diedrich, Peter
Diedrich, Elisabeth 2 SEE Diedrich, Peter
Diedrich, Heinrich; Chicago, 1873 *5475.1 p361*
Diedrich, Hugo Robert 22; America, 1850 *5475.1 p478*
Diedrich, Katharina 2 SEE Diedrich, Peter
Diedrich, Ludwig; America, 1866 *7420.1 p241*
  With family
Diedrich, Maria Jager 28 SEE Diedrich, Peter

Diedrich, Peter; America, 1869 *5475.1 p361*
  *Wife:*Maria Jager
  *Daughter:*Elisabeth
  *Daughter:*Barbara
  *Daughter:*Katharina
Diegel, John G.; Ohio, 1809-1852 *4511.35 p11*
Diehhmer, Frederick; New York, 1859 *358.56 p53*
Diehl, Anna Maria 45; America, 1854 *2526.42 p202*
Diehl, Gustav 25; Argentina, 1914 *8023.44 p373*
Diehl, Heinrich; New York, NY, 1893 *3366.30 p70*
Diehl, Ludwick; Ohio, 1809-1852 *4511.35 p11*
Diehl, Maria; America, 1895 *5475.1 p387*
Diehl, Marie; America, 1864 *8115.12 p325*
Diehl, Michael 16; America, 1883 *2526.42 p135*
Diehl, Philipp Paul; New York, 1887 *5475.1 p53*
Diekmann, . . .; Port uncertain, 1837 *7420.1 p13*
Diekmann, Mr.; America, 1872 *7420.1 p294*
  With wife 4 sons & daughter
Diekmann, Arnold; America, 1857 *7420.1 p160*
Diekmann, Bernhard; America, 1889 *7420.1 p400*
Diekmann, Carl Anton Friedrich; America, 1882 *7420.1
  p328*
Diekmann, Carl Heinrich Wilhelm; America, 1871
  7420.1 p289
Diekmann, Charlotte; America, 1875 *7420.1 p305*
Diekmann, Christian Ludwig; Port uncertain, 1836
  7420.1 p10
Diekmann, Friedrich; America, 1854 *7420.1 p118*
Diekmann, Friedrich; America, 1860 *7420.1 p193*
  With wife & 2 sons
Diekmann, Friedrich Wilhelm Ludwig; America, 1882
  7420.1 p328
Diekmann, Georg Heinrich Ludwig; America, 1859
  7420.1 p184
Diekmann, Johann Friedrich; America, 1858 *7420.1 p177*
Diekmann, Wilhelmine; America, 1853 *7420.1 p104*
Diel, Hen'y.; Ontario, 1787 *1276.15 p230*
  With relative
Dielherm, Peter; Ohio, 1809-1852 *4511.35 p11*
Dielmann, Anna Katharina *SEE* Dielmann, Johann Peter
Dielmann, Elisabeth Margareth Boehm *SEE* Dielmann,
  Johann Peter
Dielmann, Johann Adam *SEE* Dielmann, Johann Peter
Dielmann, Johann Peter; Virginia, 1831 *152.20 p63*
  *Wife:*Elisabeth Margareth Boehm
  *Child:*Johann Adam
  *Child:*Anna Katharina
Diem, Albert 45; Ontario, 1871 *1823.21 p90*
Diem, Friedrich; America, 1884 *179.55 p19*
Diemer, George; Illinois, 1863 *6079.1 p4*
Diemer, Godfrey; Ohio, 1809-1852 *4511.35 p11*
Diems, Nicolas 3; America, 1847 *778.6 p93*
Diener, Charles 42; Ontario, 1871 *1823.21 p90*
Diener, Charlotte *SEE* Diener, Friedrich
Diener, Charlotte Rausen *SEE* Diener, Friedrich
Diener, Dorothea *SEE* Diener, Ludwig
Diener, Elisabeth *SEE* Diener, Ludwig
Diener, Friedrich *SEE* Diener, Friedrich
Diener, Friedrich; America, 1881 *5475.1 p24*
  *Wife:*Charlotte Rausen
  *Son:*Friedrich
  *Daughter:*Charlotte
Diener, Georg; America, 1843-1900 *5475.1 p22*
Diener, Heinrich *SEE* Diener, Heinrich
Diener, Heinrich; America, 1881 *5475.1 p55*
  *Wife:*Sophie Schampel
  *Daughter:*Karoline
  *Son:*Heinrich
Diener, Heinrich *SEE* Diener, Ludwig
Diener, Karl; America, 1881 *5475.1 p24*
Diener, Karl *SEE* Diener, Ludwig
Diener, Karoline *SEE* Diener, Heinrich
Diener, Karoline *SEE* Diener, Ludwig
Diener, Katharina *SEE* Diener, Ludwig
Diener, Ludwig; New York, NY, 1883 *5475.1 p26*
  *Wife:*Margarethe Martin
  *Daughter:*Katharina
  *Daughter:*Dorothea
  *Son:*Wilhelm
  *Son:*Heinrich
  *Daughter:*Elisabeth
  *Son:*Karl
  *Daughter:*Sophie
  *Daughter:*Karoline
Diener, Margarethe Martin *SEE* Diener, Ludwig
Diener, Sophie Schampel *SEE* Diener, Heinrich
Diener, Sophie *SEE* Diener, Ludwig
Diener, Wilhelm *SEE* Diener, Ludwig
Dienhart, Elisabeth Luxenburger *SEE* Dienhart, Friedr.
Dienhart, Friedr.; America, 1872 *5475.1 p172*
  *Wife:*Elisabeth Luxenburger
  *Son:*Nikolaus
Dienhart, Nikolaus *SEE* Dienhart, Friedr.

Dienstall, W. J.; Montreal, 1922 *4514.4 p32*
Dier, A. Maria 13 *SEE* Dier, Thomas
Dier, Anna 10 *SEE* Dier, Thomas
Dier, Elisabeth Ripplinger *SEE* Dier, Johann
Dier, Elisabeth Trierweiler 40 *SEE* Dier, Thomas
Dier, Elizabeth *SEE* Dier, George
Dier, George; Massachusetts, 1630 *117.5 p153*
  With wife
  *Daughter:*Mary
  *Daughter:*Elizabeth
Dier, Heinrich *SEE* Dier, Johann
Dier, Jakob *SEE* Dier, Johann
Dier, Johann; America, 1857 *5475.1 p266*
  *Wife:*Elisabeth Ripplinger
Dier, Johann; America, 1864 *5475.1 p338*
  *Wife:*Maria Schneider
  *Son:*Jakob
  *Son:*Heinrich
Dier, Johann 24; America, 1882 *5475.1 p339*
Dier, Maria Schneider 30 *SEE* Dier, Johann
Dier, Mary *SEE* Dier, George
Dier, Mathias; America, 1864 *5475.1 p338*
Dier, Mathias 5 *SEE* Dier, Thomas
Dier, Robert 45; Ontario, 1871 *1823.17 p41*
Dier, Thomas 46; America, 1885 *5475.1 p319*
  *Wife:*Elisabeth Trierweiler 40
  *Son:*Mathias 5
  With sister-in-law 42
  *Daughter:*Anna 10
  *Daughter:*A. Maria 13
Dierck, Charlotte; America, 1872 *7420.1 p396*
Dierkes, August; Louisiana, 1841-1844 *4981.45 p210*
Dierkes, Julius 22; New York, NY, 1864 *8425.62 p198*
Dierking, August Friedrich Heinrich; America, 1872
  7420.1 p294
Dierking, Hermann Louis Wilhelm; America, 1871
  7420.1 p289
Dierkott, Clement F.; Ohio, 1809-1852 *4511.35 p11*
Dierks, Caroline 24; Galveston, TX, 1844 *3967.10 p371*
Dierks, Johann Karl 29; Galveston, TX, 1844 *3967.10
  p371*
Dierstein, Berta *SEE* Dierstein, Heinrich
Dierstein, Christian 5 *SEE* Dierstein, Heinrich
Dierstein, Dorothea 8 *SEE* Dierstein, Heinrich
Dierstein, Elisabeth Ries *SEE* Dierstein, Heinrich
Dierstein, Friedrich *SEE* Dierstein, Heinrich
Dierstein, Heinrich 13 *SEE* Dierstein, Heinrich
Dierstein, Heinrich 40; America, 1871 *5475.1 p62*
  *Wife:*Sophie Reinhard 36
  *Daughter:*Katharina 11 months
  *Son:*Heinrich 13
  *Son:*Philipp 12
  *Daughter:*Dorothea 8
  *Son:*Christian 5
Dierstein, Heinrich; Pittsburgh, 1881 *5475.1 p60*
  *Wife:*Elisabeth Ries
  *Daughter:*Karoline
  *Daughter:*Sophie
  *Son:*Friedrich
  *Daughter:*Berta
Dierstein, Karoline *SEE* Dierstein, Heinrich
Dierstein, Katharina 11 *SEE* Dierstein, Heinrich
Dierstein, Philipp 12 *SEE* Dierstein, Heinrich
Dierstein, Sophie Reinhard 36 *SEE* Dierstein, Heinrich
Dierstein, Sophie *SEE* Dierstein, Heinrich
Diesel, John George; New York, 1860 *358.56 p5*
Diesel, Philipp; New York, 1875 *5475.1 p483*
Diesinger, Johann; America, 1847 *5475.1 p473*
Diesinger, Wendel; America, 1834 *5475.1 p467*
  With wife & 2 children
Diesmeier, Heinrich Gottlieb; America, 1861 *7420.1
  p204*
  With family
Diesonburg, Lem; Louisiana, 1874 *4981.45 p131*
Diesselhorst, Sophie Caroline; America, 1868 *7420.1
  p270*
Diestler, Conrad; Ohio, 1809-1852 *4511.35 p11*
Dieter, Georg; New Jersey, 1854 *2526.42 p118*
Dieter, Margaretha; America, 1852 *2526.42 p118*
Dieter, Peter; New Jersey, 1854 *2526.42 p118*
Dieterich, Anna Magdalena 11; Pennsylvania, 1851
  170.15 p22
  With family
Dieterich, Anna Margaretha; Pennsylvania, 1867 *170.15
  p22*
  With family
Dieterich, Anna Margaretha 3; Pennsylvania, 1851
  170.15 p22
  With family
Dieterich, Anna Margaretha 20; Pennsylvania, 1851
  170.15 p22
  With family

Dieterich, Anna Maria 15; Pennsylvania, 1851 *170.15
  p22*
  With family
Dieterich, Elisabeth 5; Pennsylvania, 1851 *170.15 p22*
  With family
Dieterich, Elisabeth 45; Pennsylvania, 1851 *170.15 p22*
  With family
Dieterich, Peter 51; Pennsylvania, 1851 *170.15 p22*
  With family
Dieterle, Johann 21; Galveston, TX, 1845 *3967.10 p377*
Dieters, Bernhard Heinrich 39; Galveston, TX, 1845
  3967.10 p376
Diether, Johann Stephan; Philadelphia, 1753 *2526.43
  p159*
  With wife & 7 daughters
Dietler, Franz Joseph 24; Galveston, TX, 1844 *3967.10
  p373*
Dietrich, Adam 26; America, 1881 *2526.42 p159*
Dietrich, Adam 28; New England, 1866 *170.15 p22*
  With family & daughter
Dietrich, Amalie Wilhelmine; Wisconsin, 1891 *6795.8
  p79*
Dietrich, Auguste Emilie; Wisconsin, 1881 *6795.8 p47*
Dietrich, Carl; Wisconsin, 1894 *6795.8 p29*
Dietrich, Daniel; America, 1868 *7919.3 p527*
Dietrich, Elisabeth; America, 1854 *2526.43 p146*
Dietrich, Eva 12 *SEE* Dietrich, Johann
Dietrich, Eva Elisabeth 28; New England, 1866 *170.15
  p22*
  With family
Dietrich, Fanny Phillipp *SEE* Dietrich, Jacob
Dietrich, Friedrich Karl; America, 1887 *179.55 p19*
Dietrich, Friedrich Michael 19; America, 1867 *2526.42
  p159*
  *Brother:*Leonhard
Dietrich, Georg; America, 1857 *2526.43 p146*
Dietrich, Jacob; Philadelphia, 1854 *8513.31 p303*
  *Wife:*Fanny Phillipp
Dietrich, Jakob; America, 1836 *2526.42 p107*
  With wife
  With son 8
  With daughter 4
Dietrich, Jakob; America, 1856 *179.55 p19*
Dietrich, Joh.Adam; New England, 1866 *170.15 p22*
Dietrich, Joh.Adam; New England, 1866 *170.15 p22*
Dietrich, Johann 49; America, 1882 *2526.43 p146*
  *Wife:*Rosina 53
  *Daughter:*Eva 12
  *Daughter:*Margaretha 22
  *Daughter:*Katharina 17
Dietrich, Johann Adam; New England, 1899 *170.15 p22*
  With wife & 2 daughters
Dietrich, Johann Adam; Port uncertain, 1866 *170.15 p22*
Dietrich, Johann Carl; America, 1870 *179.55 p19*
Dietrich, Johann Friedrich; America, 1785 *2526.42 p118*
  *Wife:*Maria Magdalena Grunewald
  With child 6 months
Dietrich, Joseph 23; Galveston, TX, 1844 *3967.10 p372*
Dietrich, Karl; America, 1866 *5475.1 p557*
Dietrich, Karl; America, 1868 *2526.43 p186*
Dietrich, Karl; America, 1871 *2526.43 p146*
Dietrich, Karl 14; America, 1847 *2526.43 p146*
Dietrich, Karl 17; America, 1874 *2526.43 p146*
Dietrich, Karl 21; America, 1880 *2526.43 p146*
Dietrich, Kaspar; Port uncertain, 1800-1899 *170.15 p22*
  With wife & 4 children
Dietrich, Katharina 17 *SEE* Dietrich, Johann
Dietrich, Leonhard *SEE* Dietrich, Friedrich Michaél
Dietrich, Ludwig Karl 37; America, 1865 *5475.1 p504*
Dietrich, Margaretha 22 *SEE* Dietrich, Johann
Dietrich, Maria Magdalena Grunewald *SEE* Dietrich,
  Johann Friedrich
Dietrich, Mathias 28; America, 1843 *778.6 p93*
Dietrich, Michel; America, 1869 *5475.1 p361*
Dietrich, Philipp 18; America, 1880 *2526.43 p146*
Dietrich, Rosina 53 *SEE* Dietrich, Johann
Dietrich, Wilhelm Robert; Wisconsin, 1893 *6795.8 p230*
Dietrick, Jacob; West Virginia, 1787 *1132.30 p146*
Dietrick, John; Ohio, 1809-1852 *4511.35 p11*
Dietrick, Nicholas; Ohio, 1809-1852 *4511.35 p11*
Diette, Alexandre 24; Missouri, 1848 *778.6 p93*
Diettrich, C. G.; Valdivia, Chile, 1852 *1192.4 p54*
  With son 7
Dietz, Conrath; South Dakota, 1887-1900 *3366.30 p70*
Dietz, Hermann; Colorado, 1895 *1029.59 p22*
Dietz, Hermann; Colorado, 1895 *1029.59 p54*
Dietz, Hermann; Colorado, 1895 *1029.59 p54*
Dietz, J. Francis; New York, 1860 *358.56 p3*
Dietz, Jacob 22; America, 1840 *778.6 p93*
Dietz, John; New York, 1859 *358.56 p54*
Dietz, Jonas; Pennsylvania, 1848 *170.15 p22*
Dietz, Jonas; Pennsylvania, 1848 *170.15 p23*
Dietz, Jonas; Pennsylvania, 1848 *170.15 p23*

Dietz, Jonas; Pennsylvania, 1848 ***170.15*** *p23*
Dietz, Jonas; Pennsylvania, 1848 ***170.15*** *p23*
Dietz, Jonas 58; Pennsylvania, 1848 ***170.15*** *p22*
Dietz, Ludwig; Ohio, 1809-1852 ***4511.35*** *p11*
Dietz, Michael; Pennsylvania, 1848 ***170.15*** *p23*
Dietz, Theodor; America, 1868 ***7919.3*** *p534*
With wife & 3 children
Dietzen, Anton; America, 1874 ***5475.1*** *p355*
Dietzen, Barbara *SEE* Dietzen, G. Josef
Dietzen, G. Josef; America, 1879 ***5475.1*** *p386*
*Wife:*Margarethe Zewe
*Daughter:*Katharina
*Son:*P. Mathias
*Son:*Johann
*Daughter:*Barbara
Dietzen, Johann *SEE* Dietzen, G. Josef
Dietzen, Johann; America, 1885 ***5475.1*** *p387*
Dietzen, Katharina *SEE* Dietzen, G. Josef
Dietzen, Margarethe Zewe *SEE* Dietzen, G. Josef
Dietzen, P. Mathias *SEE* Dietzen, G. Josef
Dietzler, Henry; Ohio, 1809-1852 ***4511.35*** *p11*
Dietzsch, Caspar; America, 1868 ***7919.3*** *p530*
With wife & children
Dieudonne, Bernhard 42; New Orleans, 1848 ***778.6*** *p93*
Dieudonne, Denis 44; Quebec, 1654 ***9221.17*** *p306*
Dieudonne, Magdalina 36; New Orleans, 1848 ***778.6*** *p93*
Dieudonne, Nicolas; New Orleans, 1840 ***778.6*** *p93*
Diez, Jonas; Pennsylvania, 1848 ***170.15*** *p23*
Diez, Jonas; Pennsylvania, 1848 ***170.15*** *p23*
Diez, Jonas; Pennsylvania, 1848 ***170.15*** *p23*
Diez, Jonas; Pennsylvania, 1848 ***170.15*** *p23*
Diez, Jonas; Pennsylvania, 1848 ***170.15*** *p23*
Diez, Jonas; Pennsylvania, 1848 ***170.15*** *p23*
Digel, Frederick; Washington, 1889 ***2770.40*** *p27*
Digges, Edward; Ohio, 1840-1897 ***8365.35*** *p16*
Diggins, Jurdon 61; Ontario, 1871 ***1823.21*** *p90*
Dight, Thomas 47; Ontario, 1871 ***1823.21*** *p90*
Dignam, Dean 40; Ontario, 1871 ***1823.21*** *p90*
Dignam, Hugh 55; Ontario, 1871 ***1823.21*** *p90*
Dignovity, Antonin M.; New York, NY, 1832 ***2853.20*** *p57*
Dihue, James; Boston, 1739 ***1642*** *p44*
Dilamothe, Francis Augustus; North Carolina, 1840 ***1088.45*** *p8*
Dilb, John 54; Ontario, 1871 ***1823.21*** *p90*
Dilbo, Joseph 30; America, 1840 ***778.6*** *p93*
Dilger, Casper; Ohio, 1809-1852 ***4511.35*** *p11*
Dill, Joh. Phil. 32; Louisiana, 1848 ***778.6*** *p94*
Dill, Sarah 50; Ontario, 1871 ***1823.21*** *p91*
Dillehay, Thomas; Boston, 1740 ***9228.50*** *p182*
Dillemann, Christina; America, 1892 ***170.15*** *p23*
With child
Dillen, Richard; Boston, 1739 ***1642*** *p44*
Dillen, Thomas; Ohio, 1840-1897 ***8365.35*** *p16*
Dillensburger, Mathias 25; Brazil, 1828 ***5475.1*** *p233*
Diller, Franz; America, n.d. ***8115.12*** *p326*
Diller, Gottlieb Jacob; America, 1868 ***7919.3*** *p532*
Dillilo, Nicola; Colorado, 1885 ***1029.59*** *p22*
Dilling, Mrs.; America, 1883 ***7420.1*** *p398*
*Son:*Heinrich
Dilling, Heinrich *SEE* Dilling, Mrs.
Dillinger, Johann; America, 1890 ***5475.1*** *p168*
Dillinger, Nikolaus; Chicago, 1888 ***5475.1*** *p168*
Dillion, Erek; Colorado, 1893 ***1029.59*** *p22*
Dillion, H. St J. 25; Ontario, 1871 ***1823.21*** *p91*
Dillmann, Margarethe 48; America, 1857 ***5475.1*** *p512*
Dillon, Annie; Colorado, 1897 ***1029.59*** *p22*
Dillon, Barrey; Boston, 1739 ***1642*** *p44*
Dillon, Bridget 20; Ontario, 1871 ***1823.21*** *p91*
Dillon, Catharine 38; Ontario, 1871 ***1823.21*** *p91*
Dillon, D.; New Orleans, 1850 ***7242.30*** *p140*
Dillon, Edward; St. Johns, N.F., 1825 ***1053.15*** *p7*
Dillon, Erek; Colorado, 1897 ***1029.59*** *p22*
Dillon, Erick; Colorado, 1893 ***1029.59*** *p22*
Dillon, Fred; Colorado, 1893 ***1029.59*** *p22*
Dillon, Jane; St. Johns, N.F., 1825 ***1053.15*** *p7*
Dillon, John; Boston, 1763 ***1642*** *p32*
Dillon, John; Colorado, 1891 ***1029.59*** *p22*
Dillon, John; Ohio, 1840-1897 ***8365.35*** *p16*
Dillon, John 49; Ontario, 1871 ***1823.21*** *p91*
Dillon, John J.; Colorado, 1895 ***1029.59*** *p22*
Dillon, Margaret; Boston, 1730 ***1642*** *p44*
Dillon, Martin; North Carolina, 1837 ***1088.45*** *p8*
Dillon, Michael; Ohio, 1840-1897 ***8365.35*** *p16*
Dillon, Michael 44; Ontario, 1871 ***1823.17*** *p42*
Dillon, Patrick; Ontario, 1871 ***1823.21*** *p91*
Dillon, Patrick; Toronto, 1844 ***2910.35*** *p114*
Dillon, Patrick; Toronto, 1844 ***2910.35*** *p114*
Dillon, Peter; Colorado, 1891 ***1029.59*** *p23*
Dillon, Thos; New Orleans, 1850 ***7242.30*** *p140*
Dillschneider, Anna *SEE* Dillschneider, Math.
Dillschneider, Heinrich *SEE* Dillschneider, Math.
Dillschneider, Johann *SEE* Dillschneider, Math.
Dillschneider, Magdalena *SEE* Dillschneider, Math.
Dillschneider, Margarethe *SEE* Dillschneider, Math.
Dillschneider, Margarethe Pathen *SEE* Dillschneider, Math.
Dillschneider, Maria *SEE* Dillschneider, Math.
Dillschneider, Maria 42; America, 1873 ***5475.1*** *p322*
Dillschneider, Math.; America, 1880 ***5475.1*** *p302*
*Wife:*Margarethe Pathen
*Son:*Nikolaus
*Daughter:*Magdalena
*Son:*Johann
*Daughter:*Anna
*Son:*Heinrich
*Daughter:*Margarethe
*Daughter:*Maria
Dillschneider, Nikolaus *SEE* Dillschneider, Math.
Dilly, J. 31; America, 1846 ***778.6*** *p94*
Dilly, William 14; Quebec, 1870 ***8364.32*** *p23*
Dimel, August; America, 1882 ***5475.1*** *p137*
Dimond, Alice; Canada, 1774 ***3036.5*** *p41*
Dimond, William 43; Ontario, 1871 ***1823.21*** *p91*
Dinahan, Richard 70; Ontario, 1871 ***1823.21*** *p91*
Dinan, Hugh 38; Ontario, 1871 ***1823.17*** *p42*
Dinau, Jules 23; New Orleans, 1840 ***778.6*** *p94*
Dinbel, Henry; Ohio, 1809-1852 ***4511.35*** *p11*
Dine, Josef; America, 1883 ***5475.1*** *p198*
Dinebier, Josef; Omaha, NE, 1878 ***2853.20*** *p512*
Dingeldein, Anna Elisabetha; Virginia, 1831 ***152.20*** *p68*
Dingeldein, Anna Maria; America, 1852 ***2526.43*** *p122*
Dingeldein, Elisabeth; America, 1881 ***2526.43*** *p124*
Dingeldein, Georg Wilhelm 31; America, 1852 ***2526.43*** *p217*
Dingeldein, Philipp 34; America, 1846 ***2526.43*** *p146*
With wife
Dingerkus, Rudolf; New York, NY, 1923 ***8023.44*** *p373*
Dingles, John 24; Ontario, 1871 ***1823.21*** *p91*
Dingley, Alfred 26; Ontario, 1871 ***1823.17*** *p42*
Dingley, Thomas; Marston's Wharf, 1782 ***8529.30*** *p11*
Dingman, James P. 34; Ontario, 1871 ***1823.21*** *p91*
Dingwell, Alexander 64; Ontario, 1871 ***1823.17*** *p42*
Dingwell, George 43; Ontario, 1871 ***1823.17*** *p42*
Dingwell, R. H. 39; Ontario, 1871 ***1823.17*** *p42*
Dingwell, Roderick 41; Ontario, 1871 ***1823.17*** *p42*
Dinnswell, Robert 50; Ontario, 1871 ***1823.21*** *p91*
Dins, John 19; Ontario, 1871 ***1823.21*** *p91*
Dinsmore, John 67; Ontario, 1871 ***1823.21*** *p91*
Dinsmore, Margaret; Philadelphia, 1855 ***8513.31*** *p429*
Dinsmore, Thomas 28; Ontario, 1871 ***1823.17*** *p42*
Dintillas, Auguste 24; Missouri, 1848 ***778.6*** *p94*
Dintzenberger, Catherine 1; Missouri, 1845 ***778.6*** *p94*
Dintzenberger, Catherine 37; Missouri, 1845 ***778.6*** *p94*
Dintzenberger, Jacques 43; Missouri, 1845 ***778.6*** *p94*
Dintzenberger, Madelaine 9; Missouri, 1845 ***778.6*** *p94*
Dintzenberger, Marie 6; Missouri, 1845 ***778.6*** *p94*
Dintzenberger, Martin 12; Missouri, 1845 ***778.6*** *p94*
Dintzenberger, Rose 4; Missouri, 1845 ***778.6*** *p94*
Diny, Josef; America, 1883 ***5475.1*** *p198*
Dioer, Stefan 19; Halifax, N.S., 1902 ***1860.4*** *p39*
Dionne, Jean; Quebec, 1661 ***9221.17*** *p454*
Diot, Jean; Montreal, 1658 ***9221.17*** *p388*
Dipes, Henry 20; Santa Clara Co., CA, 1860 ***8704.1*** *p23*
Dipirris, Jules 26; Port uncertain, 1840 ***778.6*** *p94*
Dippe, William; New York, 1860 ***358.56*** *p4*
Dippel, Georg Heinr.; Valdivia, Chile, 1852 ***1192.4*** *p55*
Diprose, Henry; Ontario, 1871 ***1823.21*** *p91*
Diprose, Robert 27; Ontario, 1871 ***1823.21*** *p91*
DiRago, Francisco; Louisiana, 1881-1886 ***7710.1*** *p159*
Dirick, Victor; Wisconsin, 1854-1858 ***1495.20*** *p66*
Disache, M.; Louisiana, 1836-1840 ***4981.45*** *p212*
Discher, Joseph 27; Galveston, TX, 1844 ***3967.10*** *p372*
Diselvy, John 22; Santa Clara Co., CA, 1852 ***8704.1*** *p22*
Dishart, Lizzie 27; Quebec, 1910 ***2897.7*** *p10*
*Husband:*Robert 27
Dishart, Robert 27 *SEE* Dishart, Lizzie
Disher, Elizabeth 64; Ontario, 1871 ***1823.21*** *p91*
Dislau, Christoph 43; America, 1847 ***778.6*** *p94*
Dislau, Elisabeth 9; America, 1847 ***778.6*** *p94*
Dislau, Jacques 11; America, 1847 ***778.6*** *p94*
Dislau, Marianne 9 months; America, 1847 ***778.6*** *p94*
Dislau, Marianne 45; America, 1847 ***778.6*** *p94*
Dislau, Marie 12; America, 1847 ***778.6*** *p94*
Dispaw, Henry; Lynn, MA, 1676 ***9228.50*** *p194*
Displand, John 28; Ontario, 1871 ***1823.17*** *p42*
Dispose, Jennet; Portsmouth, NH, 1676 ***9228.50*** *p194*
With child
Disque, Michel 21; America, 1840 ***778.6*** *p94*
Diss DeBar, Francis Joseph; Boston, 1842 ***1132.30*** *p147*
Disselhorst, Ludwig Wilhelm; America, 1867 ***7420.1*** *p255*
With family
Dissler, George; Ohio, 1809-1852 ***4511.35*** *p11*
Disteche, Clemence Josephe; Wisconsin, 1854-1858 ***1495.20*** *p50*
Distel, Louis; Colorado, 1873 ***1029.59*** *p23*
Disteldorf, Johann; America, 1880 ***5475.1*** *p375*
Distler, Conrad; Ohio, 1809-1852 ***4511.35*** *p11*
Distler, Franz; America, 1861 ***5475.1*** *p523*
*Wife:*Karoline Ruppenthal
*Son:*Karl
Distler, Karl *SEE* Distler, Franz
Distler, Karoline Ruppenthal *SEE* Distler, Franz
Distler, Wilhelm 2; America, 1846 ***778.6*** *p94*
Disy, Pierre 16; Quebec, 1653 ***9221.17*** *p272*
Ditehy, Daniel; North Carolina, 1710 ***3629.40*** *p7*
Ditfurth, Max von; America, 1881 ***7420.1*** *p320*
Diton, Clement; Maryland, 1674-1675 ***1236.25*** *p52*
Ditten, Elisabeth; America, 1881 ***5475.1*** *p15*
Ditter, Friedrich; America, 1886 ***2526.43*** *p217*
Ditter, Georg; America, 1888 ***2526.43*** *p217*
Ditter, Georg; America, 1894 ***2526.43*** *p159*
Ditter, Johann; Indiana, 1867 ***2526.43*** *p159*
*Wife:*Katharina Pfeifer
Ditter, Johann Georg; America, 1866 ***2526.43*** *p159*
Ditter, Johann Peter; America, 1883 ***2526.43*** *p217*
Ditter, Katharina; America, 1883 ***2526.43*** *p217*
Ditter, Katharina Pfeifer *SEE* Ditter, Johann
Ditter, Margaretha; America, 1856 ***2526.42*** *p115*
Ditter, Marie; America, 1886 ***2526.43*** *p217*
Ditter, Philipp; America, 1855 ***2526.43*** *p159*
Dittgen, Anna *SEE* Dittgen, Nikolaus
Dittgen, Barbara; America, 1864 ***5475.1*** *p264*
Dittgen, Elisabeth *SEE* Dittgen, Nikolaus
Dittgen, Heinrich *SEE* Dittgen, Nikolaus
Dittgen, Jakob *SEE* Dittgen, Nikolaus
Dittgen, Josef *SEE* Dittgen, Nikolaus
Dittgen, Karl *SEE* Dittgen, Nikolaus
Dittgen, Margarethe Schmitt *SEE* Dittgen, Nikolaus
Dittgen, Nikolaus *SEE* Dittgen, Nikolaus
Dittgen, Nikolaus; Brazil, 1887 ***5475.1*** *p42*
*Wife:*Margarethe Schmitt
With stepchild
*Daughter:*Elisabeth
*Son:*Jakob
*Son:*Heinrich
*Daughter:*Anna
*Son:*Karl
*Son:*Josef
*Son:*Nikolaus
Dittmar, Benjamin Gottfried; Port uncertain, 1880 ***7420.1*** *p397*
Dittmar, Johannes Thomas; America, 1868 ***7919.3*** *p529*
Diven, Ruth; Boston, 1718 ***1642*** *p24*
Divens, Patrick; North Carolina, 1828 ***1088.45*** *p8*
Divine, James; Louisiana, 1848 ***7710.1*** *p150*
Divine, James 40; Louisiana, 1832-1846 ***7710.1*** *p149*
Divine, John; Illinois, 1860 ***6079.1*** *p4*
Divine, John; Massachusetts, 1769 ***1642*** *p104*
Divine, Sarah; Massachusetts, 1770 ***1642*** *p104*
Divver, James; South Carolina, 1846 ***6155.4*** *p18*
Diwersi, Johann; America, 1860 ***5475.1*** *p412*
Diwersi, Kath. 35; America, 1826 ***5475.1*** *p409*
Dixius, A. Maria *SEE* Dixius, Nikolaus
Dixius, Angela *SEE* Dixius, Nikolaus
Dixius, Angela Jakobs *SEE* Dixius, Nikolaus
Dixius, Jakob *SEE* Dixius, Nikolaus
Dixius, Katharina *SEE* Dixius, Nikolaus
Dixius, Nikolaus; America, 1871 ***5475.1*** *p262*
*Wife:*Angela Jakobs
*Daughter:*A. Maria
*Daughter:*Angela
*Daughter:*Katharina
*Son:*Jakob
Dixon, Alley; St. Johns, N.F., 1825 ***1053.15*** *p6*
Dixon, Benjamin; Ohio, 1820 ***3580.20*** *p31*
Dixon, Benjamin; Ohio, 1820 ***6020.12*** *p7*
Dixon, Benjamin 29; Ontario, 1871 ***1823.21*** *p91*
Dixon, Christiana 19; Quebec, 1870 ***8364.32*** *p23*
Dixon, Ms. E. 21; Quebec, 1870 ***8364.32*** *p23*
Dixon, Elizabeth 61; Ontario, 1871 ***1823.21*** *p91*
Dixon, George 27; Ontario, 1871 ***1823.21*** *p91*
Dixon, James 32; Ontario, 1871 ***1823.21*** *p91*
Dixon, Jane 60; Ontario, 1871 ***1823.21*** *p91*
Dixon, John 35; Ontario, 1871 ***1823.21*** *p91*
Dixon, Joseph 60; Ontario, 1871 ***1823.21*** *p91*
Dixon, Maria 14; Quebec, 1870 ***8364.32*** *p23*
Dixon, Mary 48; Ontario, 1871 ***1823.17*** *p42*
Dixon, Mary Ann 35; Ontario, 1871 ***1823.21*** *p91*
Dixon, Patrick; Illinois, 1834-1900 ***6020.5*** *p131*
Dixon, Robert 49; Ontario, 1871 ***1823.21*** *p91*
Dixon, Robert 52; Ontario, 1871 ***1823.21*** *p91*
Dixon, Robert 57; Ontario, 1871 ***1823.21*** *p91*
Dixon, Thomas 36; Ontario, 1871 ***1823.21*** *p91*
Dixon, Thomas 59; Ontario, 1871 ***1823.21*** *p91*
Dixon, William 36; Ontario, 1871 ***1823.21*** *p91*
Dixon, William; St. Johns, N.F., 1825 ***1053.15*** *p6*
Dixon, William J. 26; Ontario, 1871 ***1823.21*** *p91*

Dizzard, Nancy 84; Ontario, 1871 1823.17 p42
Djurberg, N.; New York, NY, 1844 6412.40 p148
D'Liddg, John 65; Ontario, 1871 1823.17 p38
Dlugasch, F.; Galveston, TX, 1855 571.7 p18
Dlugosz, Antony 32; New York, NY, 1920 930.50 p49
D'Menga, Aug.; Louisiana, 1874 4981.45 p295
Doan, Silas 12; Ontario, 1871 1823.21 p91
Doaty, Deborah; Massachusetts, 1755 1642 p85
Dobatt, Christian; New York, 1860 358.56 p6
Dobbin, Edward; Newfoundland, 1814 3476.10 p54
Dobbin, John 41; Ontario, 1871 1823.17 p42
Dobbin, John 48; Ontario, 1871 1823.17 p42
Dobbin, Mary 70; Ontario, 1871 1823.17 p42
Dobbin, Robert 35; Ontario, 1871 1823.17 p42
Dobbins, John 29; Ontario, 1871 1823.17 p42
Dobbins, Joseph 28; Ontario, 1871 1823.17 p42
Dobbs, Charles 17; Quebec, 1870 8364.32 p23
Dobbs, Joseph 63; Ontario, 1871 1823.21 p92
Dobbs, William 50; Ontario, 1871 1823.21 p92
Dobell, Henry 20; Virginia, 1635 9228.50 p195
Dobelmann, William; Louisiana, 1841-1844 4981.45 p210
Dobias, Jaroslav; Minnesota, 1891 2853.20 p285
Dobias, Jaroslav; Omaha, NE, 1874-1903 2853.20 p153
Dobie, David 51; Ontario, 1871 1823.21 p92
Dobie, William 31; Ontario, 1871 1823.21 p92
Dobie, William 58; Ontario, 1871 1823.21 p92
Dobie, William C. 63; Ontario, 1871 1823.21 p92
Dobrindt, Otto; Mexico, 1902 7420.1 p378
Dobrinske, Friedrich; Wisconsin, 1883 6795.8 p147
Dobrinske, Herman; Wisconsin, 1892 6795.8 p171
Dobrinski, Hermann Leopold; Wisconsin, 1901 6795.8 p147
Dobrohlav, Jan; Iowa, 1845-1852 2853.20 p217
Dobrowolska, Clara; Detroit, 1890 9980.23 p97
Dobrowolski, Wincenty 35; New York, NY, 1911 6533.11 p10
Dobrowska, Jozefa 18; New York, NY, 1911 6533.11 p9
Dobson, Isaac; Washington, 1886 2770.40 p195
Dobson, John; Ohio, 1809-1852 4511.35 p11
Dobson, John; Washington, 1889 2770.40 p27
Dobson, Joseph; Utah, 1872 3687.1 p37
Dobson, Richard; Canada, 1774 3036.5 p41
Docharty, Rose; New York, 1738 8277.31 p117
Dochenaski, Sam; New Orleans, 1881 6015.15 p24
Dock, Catharina 51; America, 1846 778.6 p94
Dock, Frederic 8; America, 1846 778.6 p94
Dock, Frederic 52; America, 1846 778.6 p94
Dock, Frederick; Ohio, 1809-1852 4511.35 p11
Dock, Frederick; Ohio, 1809-1852 4511.35 p11
Dock, Magdalena 20; America, 1846 778.6 p94
Dock, Philip; Ohio, 1809-1852 4511.35 p11
Dock, Philipp 12; America, 1846 778.6 p94
Dockter, Caroline 42; New Orleans, 1848 778.6 p94
Dockter, Friederika 16; New Orleans, 1848 778.6 p94
Dockter, George 12; New Orleans, 1848 778.6 p94
Dockter, Jacuqes 42; New Orleans, 1848 778.6 p94
Dockter, Louis 3; New Orleans, 1848 778.6 p94
Docquier, Jean Lambert; Wisconsin, 1857 1495.20 p46
*Wife:*Marie Francois Hody
*Sister:*Veronique Joseph
Docquier, Marie Francois Hody *SEE* Docquier, Jean Lambert
Docquier, Veronique Joseph *SEE* Docquier, Jean Lambert
Docquir, Marie Virginie; Wisconsin, 1878 1495.20 p28
Docquir, Marie Virginie Pire; Wisconsin, 1878 1495.20 p28
Doctor, Jacob 2; New York, NY, 1886 8425.16 p33
Doctor, Jacob 26; New York, NY, 1886 8425.16 p33
Doctor, Marga 24; New York, NY, 1886 8425.16 p33
Dodanne, John B.; Ohio, 1809-1852 4511.35 p11
Dodd, George 62; Ontario, 1871 1823.21 p92
Dodd, H.R.F. 24; Quebec, 1910 2897.7 p9
Dodd, James 49; Ontario, 1871 1823.21 p92
Dodd, Jane 42; Ontario, 1871 1823.21 p92
Dodd, Jane 10; Quebec, 1870 8364.32 p23
Dodd, John; Ohio, 1809-1852 4511.35 p11
Dodd, John 56; Ontario, 1871 1823.21 p92
Dodd, John 80; Ontario, 1871 1823.21 p92
Dodd, Matilda 18; Ontario, 1871 1823.21 p92
Dodd, Thomas; Ohio, 1809-1852 4511.35 p11
Dodd, Thomas 18; Ontario, 1871 1823.21 p92
Dodd, Thomas 18; Ontario, 1871 1823.21 p92
Dodds, Andrew 60; Ontario, 1871 1823.21 p92
Dodds, Elizabeth 47; Ontario, 1871 1823.17 p42
Dodds, John; Toronto, 1844 2910.35 p112
Dodeman, Martial 40; Port uncertain, 1840 778.6 p94
Dodge, Richard 22; Ontario, 1871 1823.21 p92
Dodge, Thomas 36; Ontario, 1871 1823.17 p42
Dodge, Thomas 61; Ontario, 1871 1823.17 p42
Dodge, William 18; Ontario, 1871 1823.21 p92
Dodge, William 28; Ontario, 1871 1823.17 p42
Dodier, Catherine 8 *SEE* Dodier, Sebastien
Dodier, Jacques 19; Quebec, 1656 9221.17 p335
Dodier, Jeanne; Quebec, 1663 4514.3 p307
Dodier, Marie 1 *SEE* Dodier, Sebastien
Dodier, Marie Belhomme 34 *SEE* Dodier, Sebastien
Dodier, Pierre 32; Louisiana, 1848 778.6 p94
Dodier, Sebastien 7 *SEE* Dodier, Sebastien
Dodier, Sebastien 35; Quebec, 1644 9221.17 p140
*Wife:*Marie Belhomme 34
*Daughter:*Catherine 8
*Daughter:*Marie 1
*Son:*Sebastien 7
Dodin, Anne; Quebec, 1669 4514.3 p307
Dods, John 34; Ontario, 1871 1823.17 p43
Dods, William 67; Ontario, 1871 1823.17 p43
Dodson, William 37; Ontario, 1871 1823.21 p92
Dody, Thomas; Toronto, 1844 2910.35 p112
Doe, James 69; Ontario, 1871 1823.17 p43
Doe, Thomas 49; Ontario, 1871 1823.21 p92
Doe, William 41; Ontario, 1871 1823.17 p43
Doede, Emil Reinhard; Wisconsin, 1898 6795.8 p192
Doege, Emma; Wisconsin, 1891 6795.8 p149
Doell, Barbara 11; Pennsylvania, 1850 170.15 p23
With family
Doell, Christoph 16; Pennsylvania, 1850 170.15 p23
With family
Doell, Elisabeth 53; Pennsylvania, 1850 170.15 p23
With family
Doell, Gertraud 14; Pennsylvania, 1850 170.15 p23
With family
Doell, Johann Adam 26; Pennsylvania, 1850 170.15 p23
With family
Doell, Johann Henrich 49; Pennsylvania, 1850 170.15 p23
With family
Doell, Michael 19; Pennsylvania, 1850 170.15 p23
With family
Doell, Philipp 16; Pennsylvania, 1850 170.15 p23
Doelling, Hermann; Iowa, 1904 1211.15 p10
D'Oenagne, Bernard 47; America, 1843 778.6 p95
Doepke, Daniel; Wisconsin, 1907 6795.8 p177
Doerloff, Joseph 22; America, 1841 778.6 p95
Doerr, Adolf; America, 1880 5475.1 p406
Doerr, Anna 15; America, 1880 5475.1 p406
Doerr, Anna Caroline 18; America, 1880 5475.1 p406
Doerr, Katharina; America, 1830 5475.1 p449
Doerr, Nikolaus 25; America, 1896 5475.1 p25
Doerr, Peter 21; America, 1880 5475.1 p406
Doerring, Franz Herman Gustav; Wisconsin, 1897 6795.8 p71
Dogan, Richard; Massachusetts, 1633-1668 1642 p91
Dogerty, Wm 41; Ontario, 1871 1823.21 p92
Doggenweiler, Matth.; Chile, 1852 1192.4 p51
Dogharty, James; Boston, 1758 1642 p47
Dogherty, Mary 54; Ontario, 1871 1823.21 p92
Doguet, Jean; Quebec, 1642 9221.17 p116
Doguet, Louis; Montreal, 1653 9221.17 p288
Doharty, James 45; Ontario, 1871 1823.21 p92
Doharty, Judith; Boston, 1762 1642 p48
Doherty, Adam 18; St. John, N.B., 1834 6469.7 p5
Doherty, Catherine; New Orleans, 1850 7242.30 p140
Doherty, Charles; Toronto, 1844 2910.35 p115
Doherty, Jane 22; St. John, N.B., 1834 6469.7 p5
Doherty, John 26; Ontario, 1871 1823.21 p92
Doherty, Nancy 24; St. John, N.B., 1834 6469.7 p5
Doherty, Thomas 33; Ontario, 1871 1823.21 p92
Doherty, Tobias; New Orleans, 1850 7242.30 p140
Dohey, Thos; St. John, N.B., 1848 2978.15 p39
Dohl, Elisabeth; America, 1867 7919.3 p531
Dohler, Gotthelf; America, 1867 7919.3 p532
Dohler, Henriette; America, 1867 7919.3 p532
Dohles, Marie; America, 1868 7919.3 p529
With 2 children
Dohm, Mr.; America, 1853 7420.1 p104
With wife & 3 sons
Dohm, Mr.; Port uncertain, 1888 7420.1 p356
Dohm, Auguste; America, 1854 7420.1 p118
Dohm, Carl; America, 1852 7420.1 p87
With wife 6 sons & daughter
Dohm, Carl; America, 1854 7420.1 p118
With wife & 2 sons
Dohm, Carl August Ferdinand; America, 1893 7420.1 p368
Dohm, Carl Ferdinand; America, 1867 7420.1 p260
Dohm, Carl Friedrich Wilhelm; America, 1849 7420.1 p64
Dohm, Carl Ludwig; America, 1871 7420.1 p289
Dohm, Caroline Wilhelmine Charlotte *SEE* Dohm, Christina Wilhelmine Charlotte
Dohm, Christina Wilhelmine Charlotte; America, 1847 7420.1 p52
*Daughter:*Caroline Wilhelmine Charlotte
Dohm, Christina Wilhelmine Charlotte; America, 1847 7420.1 p55
Dohm, Christine Wilhemine; America, 1847 7420.1 p55
Dohm, Wilhelmine Christ. Charl.; America, 1884 7420.1 p342
Dohme, Carl Adolph *SEE* Dohme, Georg Ferdinand
Dohme, Ferdinand; America, 1852 7420.1 p87
Dohme, Georg Ferdinand; America, 1853 7420.1 p104
*Brother:*Gustav Heinrich
*Brother:*Carl Adolph
Dohme, Gustav Heinrich *SEE* Dohme, Georg Ferdinand
Dohme, Ludwig; America, 1843 7420.1 p28
With son 16
With daughter 10
With son 13
Dohmeier, Engel Marie Sophie; America, 1855 7420.1 p136
Dohmeier, Engel Sophia Dorothea; America, 1857 7420.1 p170
Dohmeier, Heinrich; South America, 1901 7420.1 p377
Dohmeier, Johann Philipp; America, 1854 7420.1 p118
Dohmeier, Justine; America, 1854 7420.1 p118
Dohmeier, Trine Engel; America, 1854 7420.1 p118
Dohmeyer, Engel Marie Sophie; America, 1866 7420.1 p241
Dohohue, Patt; New Orleans, 1850 7242.30 p140
Dohortz, Jeramiah; Ohio, 1809-1852 4511.35 p11
Dohortz, Julius; Ohio, 1809-1852 4511.35 p11
Dohrman, Charles; Ohio, 1809-1852 4511.35 p11
Dohrmann, Ferdinand; Valdivia, Chile, 1851 1192.4 p50
Dohrmann, Friedrich; Valdivia, Chile, 1851 1192.4 p50
Doidge, John 22; Ontario, 1871 1823.21 p92
Doig, Elen 16; Michigan, 1880 4491.30 p9
Doig, Robert 49; Ontario, 1871 1823.17 p43
Doig, Tena 20; Michigan, 1880 4491.30 p9
Doig, William 48; Ontario, 1871 1823.17 p43
Doigt, Ambroise; Quebec, 1669 4514.3 p307
Doije, John 28; Ontario, 1871 1823.17 p43
Doile, Benj'n; Ontario, 1787 1276.15 p230
With 2 children & 2 relatives
Dokler, Pancras; Kansas, 1917-1918 1826.15 p81
Dokupie, Fran; Galveston, TX, 1912 3331.4 p11
Dokupie, Frank; New York, NY, 1908 3331.4 p11
Dokupie, Jaroslov; Galveston, TX, 1906 3331.4 p12
Dolan, . . .; Ontario, 1871 1823.21 p92
Dolan, Ann; St. John, N.B., 1834 6469.7 p5
Dolan, Barnard 75; Michigan, 1880 4491.39 p8
Dolan, Bridgett 28; Michigan, 1880 4491.39 p8
Dolan, Frank 40; Michigan, 1880 4491.39 p8
Dolan, James 3; St. John, N.B., 1834 6469.7 p5
Dolan, Jane 35; St. John, N.B., 1834 6469.7 p5
Dolan, John 4; St. John, N.B., 1834 6469.7 p5
Dolan, Margarett 79; Ontario, 1871 1823.21 p92
Dolan, Mary 9 months; St. John, N.B., 1834 6469.7 p5
Dolan, Patrick 44; Michigan, 1880 4491.39 p8
Dolan, Patrick; Ohio, 1840-1897 8365.35 p16
Dolan, Sarah 80; Michigan, 1880 4491.39 p8
Dolan, William 40; St. John, N.B., 1834 6469.7 p5
Doland, Jerry; Ohio, 1840-1897 8365.35 p16
Dolatowska, Franciszka; Detroit, 1929-1930 6214.5 p61
Dolatowski, Stefan; Detroit, 1928 6214.5 p61
Dolbear, William 34; Ontario, 1871 1823.17 p43
Dolbeau, Jean; Montreal, 1653 9221.17 p288
Dolbel, Charles *SEE* Dolbel, Philip
Dolbel, Eliza A. *SEE* Dolbel, Philip
Dolbel, Elizabeth *SEE* Dolbel, Susan
Dolbel, Henry 20; Virginia, 1635 9228.50 p195
Dolbel, Jane *SEE* Dolbel, Philip
Dolbel, Jean *SEE* Dolbel, Philip
Dolbel, Joshua; Boston, 1763 9228.50 p195
Dolbel, Marie *SEE* Dolbel, Philip
Dolbel, Philip; Utah, 1840-1860 9228.50 p194
*Wife:*Susan Esnouf
*Child:*Marie
*Child:*Jane
With son
*Child:*Richard
*Child:*Eliza A.
*Child:*Philippe
*Child:*Jean
*Child:*Charles
Dolbel, Philippe *SEE* Dolbel, Philip
Dolbel, Richard *SEE* Dolbel, Philip
Dolbel, Susan Esnouf *SEE* Dolbel, Philip
Dolbel, Susan; Utah, 1855 9228.50 p195
*Relative:*Elizabeth
Dold, Anselm; Michigan, 1868 1029.59 p23
Doleac, Philippe 44; New Orleans, 1844 778.6 p95
Dolejs, Frantisek; Minnesota, 1857 2853.20 p259
Dolejs, Frantisek; North Dakota, 1872 2853.20 p251
Dolgner, Franz Ferdinand; Wisconsin, 1894 6795.8 p72
Dolgner, Gusta Emilie; Wisconsin, 1890 6795.8 p81
Dolhagarage, Bernard 28; New Orleans, 1848 778.6 p95

Dolibois, Johann; America, 1881 ***5475.1*** *p137*
Dolibois, Katharina; America, 1881 ***5475.1*** *p136*
Dolier, Jennie; California, 1868 ***1131.61*** *p89*
Dolinger, Catherine 23; America, 1846 ***778.6*** *p95*
Dolis, Jacques 30; New Orleans, 1848 ***778.6*** *p95*
Dolive, J. M. 24; New Orleans, 1848 ***778.6*** *p95*
Doll, Catharina; Valdivia, Chile, 1850 ***1192.4*** *p48*
Doll, Charles; Washington, 1889 ***2770.40*** *p27*
Doll, Ferdinand; Valdivia, Chile, 1850 ***1192.4*** *p48*
Dollard DesOrmeaux, Adam 23; Montreal, 1658 ***9221.17*** *p388*
Dolle, Mrs. 46; New Orleans, 1843 ***778.6*** *p95*
Dolle, Auguste 10; New Orleans, 1843 ***778.6*** *p95*
Dolle, Carl Friedrich Julius Christian; Port uncertain, 1880 ***7420.1*** *p397*
Dolle, Felix 18; New Orleans, 1843 ***778.6*** *p95*
Dolle, Joseph 45; New Orleans, 1843 ***778.6*** *p95*
Dolle, Josephine 7; New Orleans, 1843 ***778.6*** *p95*
Dolle, Therese 23; New Orleans, 1843 ***778.6*** *p95*
Dolle, Xavier 13; New Orleans, 1843 ***778.6*** *p95*
Dollen, Thomas 40; Ontario, 1871 ***1823.17*** *p43*
Dollingen, Christian; Illinois, 1855 ***6079.1*** *p4*
Dollinger, Antoine 31; Mississippi, 1845-1846 ***778.6*** *p95*
Dollinger, Catherine 21; Mississippi, 1845-1846 ***778.6*** *p95*
Dollinger, Catherine 25; Mississippi, 1845-1846 ***778.6*** *p95*
Dollinger, Mathias 24; America, 1746 ***778.6*** *p95*
Dollman, Andrew; North Carolina, 1835 ***1088.45*** *p8*
Dollman, William; Kansas, 1917-1918 ***2094.25*** *p50*
Dolls, Peter 38; Ontario, 1871 ***1823.17*** *p43*
Dolly, Caroline 16; Quebec, 1870 ***8364.32*** *p23*
Dolman, George 46; Ontario, 1871 ***1823.17*** *p43*
Dolp, Anna Christina; America, 1853 ***2526.43*** *p133*
Dolp, Ewald; America, 1860 ***2526.43*** *p188*
Dolp, Heinrich; America, n.d. ***2526.43*** *p138*
Dolp, Jakob; America, 1870 ***2526.43*** *p138*
Dolp, Jakob; America, 1884 ***2526.43*** *p138*
Dolp, Johann Adam; Pittsburgh, 1903 ***2526.43*** *p138*
Dolp, Karl; America, 1881 ***2526.43*** *p138*
Dolp, Leonhard; America, 1889 ***2526.43*** *p138*
Dolp, Nikolaus Heinrich; America, 1884 ***2526.43*** *p138*
Dolphin, Alexander 33; Ontario, 1871 ***1823.21*** *p92*
Dolz, August; America, 1867 ***7919.3*** *p525*
Dom, William; Louisiana, 1874 ***4981.45*** *p131*
Domachowska, Josephina; Wisconsin, 1882 ***6795.8*** *p55*
Domango, Eliza 24; Port uncertain, 1841 ***778.6*** *p95*
Domaszek, Anastasia; Wisconsin, 1898 ***6795.8*** *p57*
Dombroski, Francine 32; Missouri, 1845 ***778.6*** *p95*
Dombroski, Hermes 12; Missouri, 1845 ***778.6*** *p95*
Dombrovsky, Fel.; Texas, 1870 ***2853.20*** *p64*
Dombrowski, Adam; Detroit, 1929-1930 ***6214.5*** *p63*
Dombrowski, Alexander; Detroit, 1929-1930 ***6214.5*** *p60*
Dombrowski, Frank; Detroit, 1929-1930 ***6214.5*** *p65*
Dombrowski, John; Detroit, 1929 ***1640.55*** *p117*
Dombrowski, Walter 42; New York, NY, 1920 ***930.50*** *p49*
Domen, Charles 45; Ontario, 1871 ***1823.17*** *p43*
Domenek, Peter; New York, NY, 1896-1900 ***6015.15*** *p24*
Domeyer, Johann Otto; America, 1836 ***7420.1*** *p11*
Domineck, Emanuel 20; America, 1846 ***778.6*** *p95*
Dominek, John; Texas, 1900-1917 ***6015.15*** *p24*
Dominick, Frank; New York, NY, 1883 ***6015.15*** *p24*
Dominick, Vellus; New York, NY, 1886 ***6015.15*** *p24*
Dominik, Frank; New York, NY, 1883 ***6015.15*** *p24*
Dominik, John; Texas, 1900-1917 ***6015.15*** *p24*
Dominik, Peter; New York, NY, 1896-1900 ***6015.15*** *p24*
Dominique, H. 34; America, 1843 ***778.6*** *p95*
Dominique, J. 19; New Orleans, 1840 ***778.6*** *p95*
Dominique, Luc 26; New Orleans, 1843 ***778.6*** *p95*
Domler, Henry; North Carolina, 1857-1858 ***1088.45*** *p8*
Domm, Fredrick; New York, 1860 ***358.56*** *p148*
Donagher, Mr.; Boston, 1768 ***1642*** *p40*
Donagher, Peter; Jamaica, 1778 ***8529.30*** *p13A*
Donaghey, Catherine 45; Ontario, 1871 ***1823.21*** *p92*
Donaghy, . . . 40; Ontario, 1871 ***1823.17*** *p43*
Donaher, Peter; Jamaica, 1778 ***8529.30*** *p13A*
Donahew, Captain; Newburyport, MA, 1743 ***1642*** *p76*
Donahew, Abigail; Boston, 1746 ***1642*** *p46*
Donahew, David; Massachusetts, 1745 ***1642*** *p105*
Donahew, David; New England, 1745 ***1642*** *p28*
Donahew, Dennis; Massachusetts, 1745 ***1642*** *p66*
Donahew, Margaret; Boston, 1763 ***1642*** *p48*
Donahew, Nelle; Massachusetts, 1758 ***1642*** *p111*
Donahoe, James; Ohio, 1840-1897 ***8365.35*** *p16*
Donahoe, Thomas 40; Ontario, 1871 ***1823.21*** *p92*
Donahoughe, Cornelius; Boston, 1839 ***3274.56*** *p99*
Donahoughe, Daniel; Maine, 1839 ***3274.56*** *p97*
Donahue, Dennis 60; Ontario, 1871 ***1823.21*** *p92*
Donahue, John; Illinois, 1866 ***6079.1*** *p4*
Donahue, John; North Carolina, 1858 ***1088.45*** *p8*
Donahue, Kitty; St. John, N.B., 1842 ***2978.20*** *p7*
Donahue, Kitty, Jr.; St. John, N.B., 1842 ***2978.20*** *p7*
Donahue, Nelle; Massachusetts, 1758 ***1642*** *p102*
Donahue, Timothy; St. John, N.B., 1842 ***2978.20*** *p7*
Donal, George; Massachusetts, 1740 ***1642*** *p82*
Donald, David 41; Ontario, 1871 ***1823.17*** *p43*
Donald, Henry 31; Ontario, 1871 ***1823.21*** *p92*
Donald, John 59; Ontario, 1871 ***1823.17*** *p43*
Donald, Margaret 30; Ontario, 1871 ***1823.17*** *p43*
Donald, Robert; Jamaica, 1783 ***8529.30*** *p13A*
Donald, Thomas 19; St. John, N.B., 1834 ***6469.7*** *p5*
Donald, Thomas; Washington, 1881 ***2770.40*** *p135*
Donaldson, Ellen 36; Ontario, 1871 ***1823.21*** *p93*
Donaldson, George 42; Ontario, 1871 ***1823.17*** *p43*
Donaldson, James 44; Ontario, 1871 ***1823.21*** *p93*
Donaldson, Jane 26; Ontario, 1871 ***1823.17*** *p43*
Donaldson, Jas 45; Ontario, 1871 ***1823.21*** *p93*
Donaldson, John 30; Ontario, 1871 ***1823.21*** *p93*
Donaldson, John 34; Ontario, 1871 ***1823.21*** *p93*
Donaldson, John 56; Ontario, 1871 ***1823.21*** *p93*
Donaldson, John 57; Ontario, 1871 ***1823.21*** *p93*
Donaldson, Joseph; Jamaica, 1760 ***8529.30*** *p13A*
Donaldson, Margaret; New York, 1856 ***8513.31*** *p302*
Donaldson, Sarah 58; Ontario, 1871 ***1823.21*** *p93*
Donaldson, William; North Carolina, 1807-1817 ***1088.45*** *p8*
Donall, Michael; Massachusetts, 1677 ***1642*** *p81*
Donall, Robert; Jamaica, 1783 ***8529.30*** *p13A*
Donallen, Matthew; Boston, 1745 ***1642*** *p45*
Donalley, Henry 47; Ontario, 1871 ***1823.21*** *p93*
Donaly, Mary; Boston, 1744 ***1642*** *p45*
Donamette, Mr. 37; New Orleans, 1842 ***778.6*** *p95*
Donamiller, Benedict; Ohio, 1809-1852 ***4511.35*** *p11*
Donasher, William 29; Ontario, 1871 ***1823.17*** *p43*
Donat, John; Ohio, 1809-1852 ***4511.35*** *p11*
Donate, Johann Adam; America, 1873 ***5475.1*** *p136*
*Wife:*Katharina Gaspar
Donate, Katharina Gaspar *SEE* Donate, Johann Adam
Donavan, Jno.; Louisiana, 1874 ***4981.45*** *p295*
Donbat, John; Ohio, 1809-1852 ***4511.35*** *p11*
Doncaster, Hiram; Washington, 1881 ***2770.40*** *p135*
Donch, Heinrich; America, 1860 ***7420.1*** *p193*
Done, P. A. 41; America, 1846 ***778.6*** *p95*
Donell, Michall; Massachusetts, 1688 ***1642*** *p82*
Donelley, Margret 64; Ontario, 1871 ***1823.21*** *p93*
Donelley, Patrick 48; Ontario, 1871 ***1823.21*** *p93*
Donelly, Dan; St. John, N.B., 1847 ***2978.15*** *p37*
Donelly, Jas 45; Ontario, 1871 ***1823.21*** *p93*
Donelly, Michael 14; Quebec, 1870 ***8364.32*** *p23*
Donelly, Neil 60; Ontario, 1871 ***1823.21*** *p93*
Donelly, Patrick 28; Ontario, 1871 ***1823.21*** *p93*
Donelly, Peter; St. John, N.B., 1847 ***2978.15*** *p37*
Donelly, Samuel 50; Ontario, 1871 ***1823.21*** *p93*
Donelly, Thomas 14; Quebec, 1870 ***8364.32*** *p23*
Donelson, Annie; Salt Lake City, 1891 ***9228.50*** *p346*
Donelson, John 70; Ontario, 1871 ***1823.21*** *p93*
Donevan, James 2; St. Johns, N.F., 1811 ***1053.20*** *p20*
Donevan, Luke; Salem, MA, 1769 ***1642*** *p78*
Donevan, William; Ohio, 1809-1852 ***4511.35*** *p11*
Dongan, Hannah; Boston, 1695 ***1642*** *p16*
Dongan, Thomas; Massachusetts, 1683 ***1642*** *p88*
Dongan, Thomas; New York, 1684 ***1642*** *p14*
Donges, Andreas *SEE* Donges, Marie Katharine
Donges, Andreas; America, 1850 ***8115.12*** *p326*
Donges, Andreas; America, 1870 ***8115.12*** *p319*
Donges, Andreas; America, n.d. ***8115.12*** *p319*
Donges, Anna Elisabeth *SEE* Donges, Anna Elisabeth
Donges, Anna Elisabeth; America, 1834 ***8115.12*** *p323*
*Child:*Christoph Ludwig
*Child:*Anna Elisabeth
*Child:*Caspar Ludwig
Donges, Anna Elisabeth; America, 1840 ***8115.12*** *p326*
Donges, Anna Katharine; America, n.d. ***8115.12*** *p323*
*Child:*Johann Georg
Donges, Anna Magdalene; America, 1847 ***8115.12*** *p325*
*Child:*Anna Marie
*Child:*Johann Georg
Donges, Anna Marie *SEE* Donges, Anna Magdalene
Donges, Anna Marie; America, 1852 ***8115.12*** *p321*
*Child:*Johann Jakob
*Child:*Johann Georg
*Child:*Ludwig
*Child:*Georg Andreas
*Child:*Konrad
*Child:*Henrich
Donges, Caspar Ludwig *SEE* Donges, Anna Elisabeth
Donges, Christian; America, 1857 ***8115.12*** *p319*
Donges, Christoph Ludwig *SEE* Donges, Anna Elisabeth
Donges, Eleonore Margar.; America, 1858 ***8115.12*** *p319*
Donges, Elisabeth; America, 1840 ***8115.12*** *p325*
Donges, Elisabeth *SEE* Donges, Marie Katharine
Donges, Georg Andreas *SEE* Donges, Anna Marie
Donges, Helene *SEE* Donges, Marie Katharine
Donges, Henrich *SEE* Donges, Anna Marie
Donges, Johann Conrad *SEE* Donges, Marie Katharine
Donges, Johann Friedrich; America, n.d. ***8115.12*** *p319*
Donges, Johann Friedrich; America, n.d. ***8115.12*** *p326*
Donges, Johann Georg *SEE* Donges, Marie Katharine
Donges, Johann Georg *SEE* Donges, Anna Magdalene
Donges, Johann Georg *SEE* Donges, Marie Katharine
Donges, Johann Georg *SEE* Donges, Anna Marie
Donges, Johann Georg; America, 1858 ***8115.12*** *p319*
Donges, Johann Georg *SEE* Donges, Anna Katharine
Donges, Johann Jakob *SEE* Donges, Anna Marie
Donges, Johannes *SEE* Donges, Marie Katharine
Donges, Johannes; America, 1847 ***8115.12*** *p319*
Donges, Katharine *SEE* Donges, Marie Katharine
Donges, Katharine Margarethe *SEE* Donges, Marie Katharine
Donges, Konrad; America, 1811-1862 ***8115.12*** *p319*
Donges, Konrad *SEE* Donges, Anna Marie
Donges, Ludwig *SEE* Donges, Anna Marie
Donges, Ludwig; America, n.d. ***8115.12*** *p319*
*Father:*Wilhelm
Donges, Luise; America, 1865 ***8115.12*** *p319*
Donges, Magdalene; America, 1857 ***8115.12*** *p319*
Donges, Magdalene; America, n.d. ***8115.12*** *p325*
Donges, Marie Katharine; America, 1840 ***8115.12*** *p322*
*Child:*Andreas
*Child:*Katharine Margarethe
*Child:*Johannes
*Child:*Johann Georg
*Child:*Johann Conrad
Donges, Marie Katharine; America, 1852 ***8115.12*** *p320*
*Child:*Elisabeth
*Child:*Katharine
*Child:*Johann Georg
*Child:*Helene
Donges, Wilhelm *SEE* Donges, Ludwig
Dongiyer, John; Ohio, 1809-1852 ***4511.35*** *p11*
Dongres, Ludvik V.; Omaha, NE, 1891 ***2853.20*** *p420*
Donie, Johann; America, 1873 ***5475.1*** *p138*
Donie, Peter; America, 1881 ***5475.1*** *p227*
Donigan, M.; New Orleans, 1850 ***7242.30*** *p140*
Donigan, P.; New Orleans, 1850 ***7242.30*** *p140*
Donkel, Christina 45; America, 1874 ***5475.1*** *p378*
Donlevy, C.; Toronto, 1844 ***2910.35*** *p111*
Donlevy, Miss E.; Toronto, 1844 ***2910.35*** *p111*
Donley, Mary Ann 50; Ontario, 1871 ***1823.21*** *p93*
Donley, Matthew 18; Ontario, 1871 ***1823.21*** *p93*
Donley, Peter 60; Michigan, 1880 ***4491.30*** *p9*
Donlin, Michel; Louisiana, 1836-1840 ***4981.45*** *p212*
Donlon, Timothy; North Carolina, 1860 ***1088.45*** *p8*
Donnahew, Timothy; Massachusetts, 1746 ***1642*** *p105*
Donnahue, Dennis; New England, 1745 ***1642*** *p28*
Donnally, Elizabeth 80; Ontario, 1871 ***1823.17*** *p43*
Donnally, Hugh 64; Ontario, 1871 ***1823.17*** *p43*
Donnaly, Margret 50; Ontario, 1871 ***1823.17*** *p43*
Donnato, Antonin; America, 1880-1889 ***2853.20*** *p534*
Donnawen, Katharine; Boston, 1745 ***1642*** *p45*
Donnel, Captain; New England, 1745 ***1642*** *p27*
Donnel, Alex; Boston, 1765 ***1642*** *p35*
Donnel, James; New England, 1745 ***1642*** *p28*
Donnell, . . .; Massachusetts, 1692 ***1642*** *p138*
Donnell, Mr.; Massachusetts, 1692 ***1642*** *p16*
Donnell, Barnard M. 56; Ontario, 1871 ***1823.17*** *p43*
Donnell, Benjamin *SEE* Donnell, Elizabeth
Donnell, Elizabeth; Rowley, MA, 1714 ***1642*** *p77*
*Relative:*Benjamin
Donnell, Nathaniel; New England, 1745 ***1642*** *p28*
Donnell, William O.; Iowa, 1880 ***1211.15*** *p10*
Donnelly, Arthur; Ohio, 1855 ***3580.20*** *p31*
Donnelly, Arthur; Ohio, 1855 ***6020.12*** *p7*
Donnelly, James; Ontario, 1871 ***1823.21*** *p93*
Donnelly, James; Toronto, 1844 ***2910.35*** *p113*
Donnelly, John 69; Michigan, 1880 ***4491.39*** *p8*
Donnelly, John 60; Ontario, 1871 ***1823.17*** *p43*
Donnelly, John; Toronto, 1844 ***2910.35*** *p113*
Donnelly, Maria 85; Ontario, 1871 ***1823.17*** *p43*
Donnelly, May 35; Ontario, 1871 ***1823.21*** *p93*
Donnelly, Michael 76; Ontario, 1871 ***1823.21*** *p93*
Donnelly, Patrick 21; Ontario, 1871 ***1823.21*** *p93*
Donnelly, William 58; Ontario, 1871 ***1823.17*** *p43*
Donnemiller, Henry; Ohio, 1809-1852 ***4511.35*** *p11*
Donner, Anna 24; New York, NY, 1886 ***6954.7*** *p40*
Donner, Emilie Dorothea *SEE* Donner, Sarah Matthews
Donner, Gottlieb; Valdivia, Chile, 1851 ***1192.4*** *p50*
Donner, Heinrich 9 months; New York, NY, 1886 ***6954.7*** *p40*
Donner, Herman; North America, 1862 ***6410.15*** *p105*
Donner, Mia Hermanna *SEE* Donner, Sarah Matthews
Donner, Regine; New York, 1860 ***358.56*** *p150*
Donner, Sarah; America, 1904 ***6410.15*** *p108*
*Daughter:*Wendla Maria
*Daughter:*Mia Hermanna
*Daughter:*Emilie Dorothea
Donner, Theador 3; New York, NY, 1886 ***6954.7*** *p40*
Donner, Theador 32; New York, NY, 1886 ***6954.7*** *p40*

Donner, Wendla Maria *SEE* Donner, Sarah Matthews
Donnery, John; New Orleans, 1850 ***7242.30*** *p140*
Donnihie, Timothy; Massachusetts, 1769 ***1642*** *p66*
Donniker, Wm 26; Ontario, 1871 ***1823.21*** *p93*
Donnon, Thomas; Ohio, 1836 ***3580.20*** *p31*
Donnon, Thomas; Ohio, 1836 ***6020.12*** *p7*
Donnon, Thomas; Ohio, 1838 ***3580.20*** *p31*
Donnon, Thomas; Ohio, 1838 ***6020.12*** *p7*
Donnovan, Hugh; Salem, MA, 1755 ***1642*** *p78*
Donohaugh, Thomas; Louisiana, 1841-1844 ***4981.45*** *p210*
Donohoe, Daniel 40; Ontario, 1871 ***1823.21*** *p93*
Donohoe, Patrick 45; Ontario, 1871 ***1823.21*** *p93*
Donohoe, Patrick 65; Ontario, 1871 ***1823.21*** *p93*
Donohoy, William 26; Ontario, 1871 ***1823.21*** *p93*
Donohue, Andrew 25; Ontario, 1871 ***1823.21*** *p93*
Donohue, Bridget; New Orleans, 1850 ***7242.30*** *p140*
Donohue, Fred 28; Ontario, 1871 ***1823.21*** *p93*
Donohue, James; New Orleans, 1850 ***7242.30*** *p140*
Donohue, James; Ohio, 1840-1897 ***8365.35*** *p16*
Donohue, James 40; Ontario, 1871 ***1823.17*** *p43*
Donohue, John 11; Quebec, 1870 ***8364.32*** *p23*
Donohue, Maria 7; Ontario, 1871 ***1823.17*** *p43*
Donohue, Mary 10; Quebec, 1870 ***8364.32*** *p23*
Donohue, Michael 40; Ontario, 1871 ***1823.21*** *p93*
Donohue, Patt; New Orleans, 1850 ***7242.30*** *p140*
Donohue, Richard 77; Ontario, 1871 ***1823.21*** *p93*
Donohue, Susan 7; Quebec, 1870 ***8364.32*** *p23*
Donohue, William; Quebec, 1870 ***8364.32*** *p23*
Donoley, James 50; Ontario, 1871 ***1823.21*** *p93*
Donoly, P.; New Orleans, 1850 ***7242.30*** *p140*
Donon, Simon; North Carolina, 1854-1856 ***1088.45*** *p8*
Donoughe, Catherine 71; Ontario, 1871 ***1823.21*** *p93*
Donoughue, Michael 22; Ontario, 1871 ***1823.21*** *p93*
Donoughy, Richard 32; Ontario, 1871 ***1823.21*** *p93*
Donovan, Alex; St. John, N.B., 1848 ***2978.15*** *p40*
Donovan, Catharine; Boston, 1744 ***1642*** *p45*
Donovan, Cornelius 15; Quebec, 1870 ***8364.32*** *p23*
Donovan, Danl; St. John, N.B., 1847 ***2978.15*** *p35*
Donovan, John; Boston, 1747 ***1642*** *p29*
Donovan, John 62; Ontario, 1871 ***1823.21*** *p93*
Donovan, Mary 42; Ontario, 1871 ***1823.21*** *p93*
Donovan, Michael; Louisiana, 1874 ***4981.45*** *p131*
Donovan, Thomas 16; Quebec, 1870 ***8364.32*** *p23*
Donovan, William 28; Ontario, 1871 ***1823.21*** *p93*
Donovan, William 14; Quebec, 1870 ***8364.32*** *p23*
Donshin, William; Boston, 1766 ***1642*** *p37*
Donslman, J. F.; California, 1868 ***1131.61*** *p89*
Dontaille, Jacques-Philippe; Quebec, 1723 ***2314.30*** *p170*
Dontaille, Jacques-Philippe; Quebec, 1723 ***2314.30*** *p180*
Dontseisen, John; Ohio, 1809-1852 ***4511.35*** *p11*
Donzeisen, Frederick; Ohio, 1809-1852 ***4511.35*** *p11*
Donzelot, . . .; New Orleans, 1840 ***778.6*** *p95*
Donzelot, . . .; New Orleans, 1840 ***778.6*** *p96*
Donzelot, Prothose; New Orleans, 1840 ***778.6*** *p96*
Donziger, Lehman; Ohio, 1809-1852 ***4511.35*** *p11*
Doody, Edmond; Louisiana, 1836-1841 ***4981.45*** *p208*
Dooker, William 56; Ontario, 1871 ***1823.21*** *p94*
Doolan, Ann 70; Ontario, 1871 ***1823.21*** *p94*
Doolan, Annorah 46; Ontario, 1871 ***1823.17*** *p43*
Doolan, John 43; Ontario, 1871 ***1823.17*** *p43*
Dooley, John 40; Ontario, 1871 ***1823.17*** *p43*
Doozley, Samuel; New York, NY, 1778 ***8529.30*** *p2*
Dopat, Jakob 32; New York, NY, 1904 ***8355.1*** *p15*
Dopeler, Mr. 18; America, 1847 ***778.6*** *p96*
Dopeler, Magline 20; America, 1847 ***778.6*** *p96*
Dopke, Christian; America, 1854 ***7420.1*** *p118*
Dopke, Dorothea Caroline Auguste; America, 1868 ***7420.1*** *p270*
Dopke, Friedrich Wilhelm; Iowa, 1876 ***7420.1*** *p306*
Dopke, Johann Heinrich Ludwig; America, 1868 ***7420.1*** *p270*
Dopke, Joseph; Wisconsin, 1898 ***6795.8*** *p67*
Dopke, Thrine Engel Sophia; America, 1850 ***7420.1*** *p70*
Dopke, Wilhelm; America, 1876 ***7420.1*** *p306*
Dopking, Mrs.; America, 1888 ***7420.1*** *p356*
With son
Dopking, Sophie Eleonore; America, 1855 ***7420.1*** *p134*
Dopp, August Wilhelm Georg; America, 1860 ***7420.1*** *p193*
Doppe, August Wilhelm Georg; America, 1860 ***7420.1*** *p193*
Doppeler, Francoise 26; America, 1846 ***778.6*** *p96*
Dopper, Frederica 56; Ontario, 1871 ***1823.21*** *p94*
Dopping, Friedrich Wilhelm; America, 1856 ***7420.1*** *p146*
Dopping, Johann Friedrich; America, 1855 ***7420.1*** *p135*
Doppler, Jean 38; New Orleans, 1843 ***778.6*** *p96*
Doppler, Rudolfe 24; America, 1844 ***778.6*** *p96*
Doran, Ann; New Orleans, 1851 ***7242.30*** *p140*
Doran, Biddy; New Orleans, 1850 ***7242.30*** *p140*
Doran, Dolly; New Orleans, 1850 ***7242.30*** *p140*
Doran, George 48; Ontario, 1871 ***1823.17*** *p43*
Doran, James 15; Michigan, 1880 ***4491.30*** *p9*
Doran, James 36; Michigan, 1880 ***4491.30*** *p9*
Doran, John; North Carolina, 1857 ***1088.45*** *p8*
Doran, Lizza 36; Michigan, 1880 ***4491.30*** *p9*
Doran, Maggy 18; Michigan, 1880 ***4491.30*** *p9*
Doran, Miles; New Orleans, 1851 ***7242.30*** *p140*
Doran, William 37; Michigan, 1880 ***4491.30*** *p9*
Dorange, Barbe; Quebec, 1669 ***4514.3*** *p307*
Dorange, Cecile; Quebec, 1669 ***4514.3*** *p375*
Dorant, George 30; Ontario, 1871 ***1823.17*** *p43*
Dorbe, P. 21; New Orleans, 1842 ***778.6*** *p96*
Dorbochan, Pierre 38; Louisiana, 1848 ***778.6*** *p96*
Dorcey, Patrick 38; Ontario, 1871 ***1823.21*** *p94*
Dore, Caroline Ann; Massachusetts, 1836-1862 ***9228.50*** *p195*
Dore, Felicitee; Wisconsin, 1857 ***1495.20*** *p28*
Dore, Jacques; Quebec, 1649 ***9221.17*** *p212*
Dore, Philip; New Hampshire, 1715 ***9228.50*** *p196*
Dore, Philip; Nova Scotia, 1799-1863 ***9228.50*** *p195*
Dore, Roger; Quebec, 1657 ***9221.17*** *p356*
Dore de Berville, Mr.; New Orleans, 1840 ***778.6*** *p96*
Doretti, Gabriele Alfred; Illinois, 1930 ***121.35*** *p101*
Dorety, Jenne; Massachusetts, 1767 ***1642*** *p100*
Dorey, Addie *SEE* Dorey, John
Dorey, Addie; Iowa, 1880-1899 ***9228.50*** *p18A*
Dorey, Alice; Canada, 1920 ***9228.50*** *p621*
Dorey, Alice; Salt Lake City, 1920-1983 ***9228.50*** *p621*
Dorey, Caroline Ann; Massachusetts, 1836-1862 ***9228.50*** *p195*
Dorey, Harriet Winsey *SEE* Dorey, John
Dorey, Harriet Louise *SEE* Dorey, John
Dorey, Henriette Le Mesurier; New York, 1870 ***9228.50*** *p435*
Dorey, Johanna *SEE* Dorey, John
Dorey, John; America, n.d. ***9228.50*** *p18A*
Dorey, John; Bridgeport, CT, 1850-1851 ***9228.50*** *p195*
*Wife:*Harriet Winsey
*Child:*Addie
*Child:*Johanna
*Child:*Harriet Louise
Dorey, Mary; Ontario, 1920-1929 ***9228.50*** *p627*
Dorey, Philip; New Hampshire, 1715 ***9228.50*** *p196*
Dorey, Philip; Nova Scotia, 1799-1863 ***9228.50*** *p195*
Dorgemont, Hugues; Quebec, 1660 ***9221.17*** *p434*
Dorges, Henry W.; Ohio, 1809-1852 ***4511.35*** *p11*
Dorian, Brigid; Philadelphia, 1855 ***8513.31*** *p301*
Doriant, Simone; Quebec, 1665 ***4514.3*** *p307*
Doribeau, Catherine; Quebec, 1669 ***4514.3*** *p307*
Dorigan, John 31; Kansas, 1892 ***1447.20*** *p62*
Dorin, Mrs.; Boston, 1764 ***1642*** *p33*
With sons
Doringshoff, Friederike; America, 1892 ***7420.1*** *p365*
Doringshoff, Ludwig; America, 1899 ***7420.1*** *p375*
Doriot, Margaret; Philadelphia, 1847 ***8513.31*** *p306*
Dorival, Jean; Quebec, 1635 ***9221.17*** *p46*
Dorivau, Lawrence 25; America, 1840 ***778.6*** *p96*
Dork, Frederick; Ohio, 1809-1852 ***4511.35*** *p11*
Dorksen, Julius 23; New York, NY, 1893 ***1883.7*** *p40*
Dorksen, Katharina 18; New York, NY, 1893 ***1883.7*** *p40*
Dorle, Maria Anna; Venezuela, 1843 ***3899.5*** *p540*
Dorlerin, Maria Anna; Venezuela, 1843 ***3899.5*** *p540*
Dorlin, Eva Magdalena; Venezuela, 1843 ***3899.5*** *p543*
Dorlin, Joseph; Venezuela, 1843 ***3899.5*** *p540*
Dorlin, Maria Anna; Venezuela, 1843 ***3899.5*** *p540*
Dorman, Mr.; Roxbury, MA, 1681 ***1642*** *p107*
Dorman, Andreas; North Carolina, 1710 ***3629.40*** *p8*
Dorman, William 44; Ontario, 1871 ***1823.21*** *p94*
Dormann, Ernst Gottlieb; Port uncertain, 1869 ***7420.1*** *p279*
Dormayer, Henry 20; America, 1840 ***778.6*** *p96*
Dormer, Ann 43; Ontario, 1871 ***1823.21*** *p94*
Dormire, Christian; Ohio, 1840-1897 ***8365.35*** *p16*
Dorn, Ernst; Illinois, 1852 ***6079.1*** *p4*
Dorn, Ludwig; Ohio, 1840-1897 ***8365.35*** *p16*
Dornais, Francois; Quebec, 1640 ***9221.17*** *p96*
Dornais, Louis; Quebec, 1642 ***9221.17*** *p116*
Dornberger, Georg Leonhard; New York, 1855 ***2526.43*** *p193*
Dornberger, Johannes; America, 1882 ***2526.43*** *p193*
Dornbusch, Mr.; America, 1861 ***7420.1*** *p204*
With family
Dornfeld, Charlotte Friederike 45 *SEE* Dornfeld, Johannes
Dornfeld, Eva Katharina 12 *SEE* Dornfeld, Johannes
Dornfeld, Johann Philipp 6 *SEE* Dornfeld, Johannes
Dornfeld, Johann Wilhelm 13 *SEE* Dornfeld, Johannes
Dornfeld, Johannes 44; America, 1853 ***2526.43*** *p166*
*Wife:*Charlotte Friederike 45
*Daughter:*Eva Katharina 12
*Son:*Johann Philipp 6
*Daughter:*Margaretha Katharina 9
*Son:*Johann Wilhelm 13
Dornfeld, Katharina; America, 1854 ***2526.43*** *p119*
Dornfeld, Margaretha Katharina 9 *SEE* Dornfeld, Johannes
Dorogan, Timothy 45; Ontario, 1871 ***1823.17*** *p44*
Dorothy, Elizabeth; Boston, 1723 ***1642*** *p25*
Dorr, Andreas Georg 2; America, 1854 ***5475.1*** *p63*
Dorr, Friedrich 29; America, 1854 ***5475.1*** *p63*
*Wife:*Maria Katharina Dorr 29
*Daughter:*Kath. Luise 1 months
*Son:*Josef Friedrich 4
*Son:*Andreas Georg 2
Dorr, Jakob Christian; Pittsburgh, 1864 ***5475.1*** *p54*
Dorr, Johann; Brazil, 1887 ***5475.1*** *p432*
Dorr, Josef Friedrich 4; America, 1854 ***5475.1*** *p63*
Dorr, Kath. Luise 1 months; America, 1854 ***5475.1*** *p63*
Dorr, Louis 24; America, 1840 ***778.6*** *p96*
Dorr, Maria; America, 1847 ***5475.1*** *p21*
*Son:*Johann Friedrich
*Son:*Christian
*Daughter:*Magdalena
*Daughter:*Maria
Dorr, Maria Katharina 29; America, 1854 ***5475.1*** *p63*
Dorrenbacher, Barbara *SEE* Dorrenbacher, Jakob
Dorrenbacher, Elisabeth *SEE* Dorrenbacher, Jakob
Dorrenbacher, Jakob; America, 1860 ***5475.1*** *p493*
Dorrenbacher, Jakob *SEE* Dorrenbacher, Jakob
Dorrenbacher, Jakob; America, 1882 ***5475.1*** *p514*
With stepchild
*Son:*Johann
*Daughter:*Jakob
*Daughter:*Elisabeth
*Daughter:*Barbara
*Wife:*Katharina Findeis
*Daughter:*Katharina
Dorrenbacher, Johann *SEE* Dorrenbacher, Jakob
Dorrenbacher, Katharina *SEE* Dorrenbacher, Jakob
Dorrenbacher, Katharina Findeis *SEE* Dorrenbacher, Jakob
Dorrenbecher, Anna 57; America, 1854 ***5475.1*** *p53*
*Son:*Georg
Dorrenbecher, Georg *SEE* Dorrenbecher, Anna Ribofode
Dorritrey, John; Massachusetts, 1766 ***1642*** *p91*
Dorrothy, Elizabeth; Massachusetts, 1765 ***1642*** *p104*
D'Orsau LeBert, H. 18; America, 1842 ***778.6*** *p96*
Dorsay, John; New Orleans, 1850 ***7242.30*** *p140*
Dorsery, William 22; Ontario, 1871 ***1823.21*** *p94*
Dorsey, Jane 22; Ontario, 1871 ***1823.21*** *p94*
Dorson, Thomas; Marston's Wharf, 1782 ***8529.30*** *p11*
Dorson, Timothy; Boston, 1766 ***1642*** *p36*
With wife
Dorstewitz, Carl Julius; America, 1867 ***7919.3*** *p528*
Dorton, John; Newfoundland, 1814 ***3476.10*** *p54*
D'Orval, Claude 31; Quebec, 1643 ***9221.17*** *p129*
Dorvas, Dimitrios 23; New York, NY, 1894 ***6512.1*** *p186*
Dorwald, Louise; New York, NY, 1878 ***7420.1*** *p310*
Dorward, William 44; Michigan, 1880 ***4491.36*** *p6*
Dory, Victor; Illinois, 1854 ***6079.1*** *p4*
Dos, J. 22; America, 1846 ***778.6*** *p83*
Dosch, Dionis 25; New York, NY, 1893 ***1883.7*** *p44*
Dosch, Eva Margarethe; America, 1857 ***2526.43*** *p208*
Dosch, Katharina 1; New York, NY, 1893 ***1883.7*** *p44*
Dosch, Maria Elisabetha; America, 1853 ***2526.42*** *p140*
Dosch, Regina 3; New York, NY, 1893 ***1883.7*** *p44*
Dosch, Rochus 25; New York, NY, 1893 ***1883.7*** *p44*
Dosdat, P. G. 29; America, 1848 ***778.6*** *p96*
Doser, Jos..h 34; America, 1840 ***778.6*** *p96*
Dossen, George; Washington, 1882 ***2770.40*** *p135*
Dostal, Hynek; Iowa, 1898 ***2853.20*** *p29*
Dostal, Jan; Iowa, 1856 ***2853.20*** *p211*
*Father:*Jiri
Dostal, Jiri *SEE* Dostal, Jan
Dostal, Josef; Iowa, 1898 ***2853.20*** *p29*
Dostal, Josef; Nebraska, 1873 ***2853.20*** *p171*
Dostal, Josef; Omaha, NE, 1896 ***2853.20*** *p234*
Dostalova, Anna; America, 1899 ***2853.20*** *p512*
Doszen, George; Washington, 1886 ***2770.40*** *p195*
Doth, Hessian 29; America, 1848 ***778.6*** *p96*
Doty, Edward; Plymouth, MA, 1620 ***1920.45*** *p5*
Doty, Frank Henry 21; Ontario, 1871 ***1823.17*** *p44*
Douaire DeBondy, Thomas 19; Quebec, 1655 ***9221.17*** *p323*
Douart, Jacques 16; Quebec, 1642 ***9221.17*** *p116*
Douay, Auguste 22; America, 1845 ***778.6*** *p96*
Doubat, John; Ohio, 1809-1852 ***4511.35*** *p11*
Doublet, Francois; Quebec, 1637 ***9221.17*** *p69*
Doubravsky, Vaclav; Missouri, 1859-1860 ***2853.20*** *p53*
Doubre, Emile 27; Louisiana, 1848 ***778.6*** *p96*
Douce, Mr. 22; Louisiana, 1848 ***778.6*** *p96*
Doucet, Alexandre; Quebec, 1670 ***4514.3*** *p332*
Doucet, Jean; Quebec, 1646 ***9221.17*** *p163*
With son
Doucet, Marie-Madeleine; Quebec, 1662 ***9221.17*** *p484*
Doucet, Peter; Boston, 1718 ***9228.50*** *p87*
Doucher, Bridget 65; Ontario, 1871 ***1823.17*** *p44*

Doucinet, Elisabeth; Quebec, 1666 ***4514.3*** *p307*
Doucinet, Marguerite; Quebec, 1666 ***4514.3*** *p308*
Doucinet, Marguerite 21; Quebec, 1662 ***9221.17*** *p484*
Doud, John; Massachusetts, 1675-1676 ***1642*** *p128*
Douet, Sebastien; Quebec, 1657 ***9221.17*** *p356*
Douey, Samuel 22; Ontario, 1871 ***1823.17*** *p44*
Dougale, Anne; Boston, 1766 ***1642*** *p37*
Dougale, Jonas; Boston, 1766 ***1642*** *p37*
Dougale, Robert; Boston, 1766 ***1642*** *p37*
Dougale, Thomas; Boston, 1766 ***1642*** *p37*
Dougall, William; North Carolina, 1827-1832 ***1088.45*** *p8*
Dougharty, William; Boston, 1763 ***1642*** *p32*
Dougherty, Charles 51; Ontario, 1871 ***1823.17*** *p44*
Dougherty, George 30; New York, NY, 1825 ***6178.50*** *p148*
Dougherty, George; Philadelphia, 1858 ***8513.31*** *p303*
*Wife:*Rosanna O'Donnell
Dougherty, James; Ohio, 1809-1852 ***4511.35*** *p11*
Dougherty, John; Toronto, 1844 ***2910.35*** *p115*
Dougherty, Micah; Massachusetts, 1771 ***1642*** *p100*
Dougherty, Pat; St. John, N.B., 1847 ***2978.15*** *p37*
Dougherty, Robert; Ipswich, MA, 1753 ***1642*** *p71*
Dougherty, Rosanna O'Donnell *SEE* Dougherty, George
Dougherty, Rosean 38; St. John, N.B., 1834 ***6469.7*** *p5*
Dougherty, Walter; Boston, 1731 ***1642*** *p44*
Dougherty, William; Boston, 1734 ***1642*** *p44*
Doughety, David; New England, 1745 ***1642*** *p27*
Doughney, Brazill 64; Michigan, 1880 ***4491.36*** *p6*
Doughton, James 43; Ontario, 1871 ***1823.21*** *p94*
Douglas, Adam 28; Ontario, 1871 ***1823.21*** *p94*
Douglas, Alexander 22; North Carolina, 1774 ***1422.10*** *p56*
Douglas, Amelia 50; Ontario, 1871 ***1823.21*** *p94*
Douglas, And 74; Ontario, 1871 ***1823.21*** *p94*
Douglas, Crawford 73; Ontario, 1871 ***1823.21*** *p94*
Douglas, Edward; Toronto, 1844 ***2910.35*** *p114*
Douglas, Eliz.; Virginia, 1749 ***3675.1*** *p*
Douglas, Henry; North Carolina, 1828 ***1088.45*** *p8*
Douglas, James 31; Ontario, 1871 ***1823.17*** *p44*
Douglas, James 40; Ontario, 1871 ***1823.21*** *p94*
Douglas, James 69; Ontario, 1871 ***1823.21*** *p94*
Douglas, James; Toronto, 1844 ***2910.35*** *p112*
Douglas, Jessie G. MacLaren *SEE* Douglas, Otis King
Douglas, John; North Carolina, 1775 ***1422.10*** *p56*
Douglas, Marvin 72; Ontario, 1871 ***1823.21*** *p94*
Douglas, Oliver 36; Ontario, 1871 ***1823.17*** *p44*
Douglas, Otis King; Warren, RI, 1902 ***9228.50*** *p526*
*Wife:*Jessie G. MacLaren
Douglas, Richard; North Carolina, 1825 ***1088.45*** *p8*
Douglas, Thomas; North Carolina, 1792-1798 ***1088.45*** *p8*
Douglas, Thomas 30; Ontario, 1871 ***1823.21*** *p94*
Douglas, Thomas 36; Ontario, 1871 ***1823.21*** *p94*
Douglas, Thomas 46; Ontario, 1871 ***1823.21*** *p94*
Douglas, William 27; Ontario, 1871 ***1823.17*** *p44*
Douglas, William 35; Ontario, 1871 ***1823.21*** *p94*
Douglass, Ann 18; St. John, N.B., 1834 ***6469.7*** *p4*
Douglass, Ann 45; St. John, N.B., 1834 ***6469.7*** *p4*
Douglass, Chester H.; Port Huron, MI, 1891 ***3366.30*** *p70*
Douglass, Francois-Prosper; Quebec, 1755-1757 ***2314.30*** *p170*
Douglass, Francois-Prosper; Quebec, 1755 ***2314.30*** *p180*
Douglass, Hugh; Boston, 1747 ***1642*** *p29*
Douglass, James; Ohio, 1809-1852 ***4511.35*** *p11*
Douglass, James 59; Ontario, 1871 ***1823.21*** *p94*
Douglass, William; Washington, 1883 ***2770.40*** *p136*
Dougle, Ann; Boston, 1766 ***1642*** *p37*
Dougle, Mary; Boston, 1766 ***1642*** *p37*
Dougourt, Baptiste; Louisiana, 1836-1840 ***4981.45*** *p212*
Douhet deLa Riviere deLestang, Jean de; Quebec, 1683-1686 ***2314.30*** *p180*
Douhet deLa Riviere deLestang, Jean de; Quebec, 1683-1688 ***2314.30*** *p168*
Douily, . . .; America, 1846 ***778.6*** *p96*
Douily, Mrs. M. A. 25; America, 1846 ***778.6*** *p96*
Doulan, Timothy; North Carolina, 1857 ***1088.45*** *p8*
Douley, Terrence 45; Ontario, 1871 ***1823.17*** *p44*
Doulin, Hugh; Louisiana, 1841-1844 ***4981.45*** *p210*
Douney, Miss 15; New Orleans, 1844 ***778.6*** *p96*
Douney, Mrs. 32; New Orleans, 1844 ***778.6*** *p96*
Douney, J. B. 34; New Orleans, 1844 ***778.6*** *p96*
Dounnai, Clementine; Wisconsin, 1856 ***1495.20*** *p28*
Dour, Bertrand 17; America, 1841 ***778.6*** *p96*
Dourneau, Fco. 45; North America, 1841 ***778.6*** *p96*
Dours, J. 17; New Orleans, 1848 ***778.6*** *p96*
Dours, Jean Bernard 32; New Orleans, 1746 ***778.6*** *p96*
Dours, Paul 28; New Orleans, 1848 ***778.6*** *p96*
Douseman, Jacob; Ohio, 1809-1852 ***4511.35*** *p11*
Douson, Antoine 43; America, 1843 ***778.6*** *p96*
Dousset, Mathieu 23; Quebec, 1656 ***9221.17*** *p335*
Doussin, Rene 23; Montreal, 1653 ***9221.17*** *p289*
Doustin, Pierre 46; Texas, 1848 ***778.6*** *p97*
Douthwaite, Charles 55; Ontario, 1871 ***1823.21*** *p94*
Douville, Joseph; Nova Scotia, 1753 ***3051*** *p112*
*Wife:*Judith Guimin
Douville, Judith Guimin *SEE* Douville, Joseph
Douze, Marie 36; New Orleans, 1845 ***778.6*** *p97*
Dove, Charles; Boston, 1769 ***9228.50*** *p168*
Dove, Isaac; New York, 1860 ***358.56*** *p148*
Dove, James 50; Ontario, 1871 ***1823.21*** *p94*
Dove, John H.; Illinois, 1852 ***6079.1*** *p4*
Dover, S.; Louisiana, 1874 ***4981.45*** *p295*
Dow, Joseph 30; Michigan, 1880 ***4491.30*** *p9*
Dow, Robert 43; Ontario, 1871 ***1823.21*** *p94*
Dowd, Dennis; Toronto, 1844 ***2910.35*** *p112*
Dowd, John; Ohio, 1809-1852 ***4511.35*** *p11*
Dowdell, Bridgett 34; Michigan, 1880 ***4491.30*** *p9*
Dowdell, Charles E. 11; Michigan, 1880 ***4491.30*** *p9*
Dowdell, Patrick 40; Michigan, 1880 ***4491.30*** *p9*
Dowdell, William 40; Ontario, 1871 ***1823.21*** *p94*
Dowden, Thos. 38; Ontario, 1871 ***1823.17*** *p44*
Dowele, John; Long Island, 1781 ***8529.30*** *p9A*
Dowell, Arthur 22; Ontario, 1871 ***1823.21*** *p94*
Dowell, John; Long Island, 1780 ***8529.30*** *p9A*
Dower, John 25; St. Johns, N.F., 1811 ***1053.20*** *p19*
Dowerson, Jane; Maryland, 1670 ***1236.25*** *p46*
Dowey, Robert 53; Ontario, 1871 ***1823.21*** *p94*
Dowle, John; Boston, 1766 ***1642*** *p37*
Dowlen, Patrick 35; Ontario, 1871 ***1823.21*** *p94*
Dowles, John 25; Ontario, 1871 ***1823.17*** *p44*
Dowley, Thomas 22; Ontario, 1871 ***1823.17*** *p44*
Dowlin, Byron 37; Ontario, 1871 ***1823.21*** *p94*
Dowling, Eleanor Mulhall *SEE* Dowling, Eleanor
Dowling, Eleanor; Halifax, N.S., 1827 ***7009.9*** *p61*
*Father:*James
*Mother:*Eleanor Mulhall
Dowling, James *SEE* Dowling, Eleanor
Dowling, Jeremiah; New York, 1778 ***8529.30*** *p11*
Dowling, John; Colorado, 1900 ***1029.59*** *p23*
Dowling, Margaret 18; Ontario, 1871 ***1823.17*** *p44*
Dowling, Mary; Colorado, 1871 ***1029.59*** *p23*
Dowling, Mary; Colorado, 1881 ***1029.59*** *p23*
Dowling, Mary; Colorado, 1884 ***1029.59*** *p23*
Dowling, Mary; Colorado, 1885 ***1029.59*** *p23*
Dowling, Mathew; Colorado, 1871 ***1029.59*** *p23*
Dowling, Nicholas 65; Ontario, 1871 ***1823.21*** *p95*
Dowling, Pat; Louisiana, 1874 ***4981.45*** *p295*
Dowling, Patrick; Boston, 1766 ***1642*** *p36*
Dowling, Patrick; Colorado, 1899 ***1029.59*** *p23*
Dowling, Robert 55; Ontario, 1871 ***1823.21*** *p95*
Dowling, Samuel 43; Ontario, 1871 ***1823.21*** *p95*
Dowling, Thomas; Halifax, N.S., 1827 ***7009.9*** *p62*
Dowling, Thomas 15; Quebec, 1870 ***8364.32*** *p23*
Down, George 32; Ontario, 1871 ***1823.21*** *p95*
Down, Patrick 21; Ontario, 1871 ***1823.21*** *p95*
Down, Robert 50; Ontario, 1871 ***1823.21*** *p95*
Down, Samuel; Louisiana, 1836-1841 ***4981.45*** *p208*
Down, Susan 60; Ontario, 1871 ***1823.21*** *p95*
Downe, John; New York, NY, 1830 ***3274.55*** *p67*
Downeing, William; Ipswich, MA, 1661 ***1642*** *p69*
Downer, John 54; Ontario, 1871 ***1823.21*** *p95*
Downes, George C. 21; Indiana, 1884 ***9076.20*** *p70*
Downes, John; Ohio, 1846 ***3580.20*** *p31*
Downes, John; Ohio, 1846 ***6020.12*** *p7*
Downes, Robert L.; Colorado, 1889 ***1029.59*** *p23*
Downes, Robert L.; Colorado, 1898 ***1029.59*** *p23*
Downes, Thomas; Albany, NY, 1831 ***3274.55*** *p68*
Downes, Walter J. 23; Indiana, 1886-1888 ***9076.20*** *p72*
Downey, Edward; Toronto, 1844 ***2910.35*** *p115*
Downey, James; New York, 1836 ***471.10*** *p88*
Downey, John; St. John, N.B., 1847 ***2978.15*** *p39*
Downey, John; St. Johns, N.F., 1825 ***1053.15*** *p6*
Downey, Mary; New Orleans, 1850 ***7242.30*** *p140*
Downey, Pat; St. John, N.B., 1847 ***2978.15*** *p39*
Downey, Patrick; Louisiana, 1836-1841 ***4981.45*** *p208*
Downey, William; New Orleans, 1850 ***7242.30*** *p140*
Downey, William; New York, 1783 ***8529.30*** *p11*
Downie, Christn. 30; North Carolina, 1774 ***1422.10*** *p57*
Downie, James 36; Ontario, 1871 ***1823.21*** *p95*
Downie, Joseph; North Carolina, 1775 ***1422.10*** *p59*
Downie, Malcolm, Sr. 80; Ontario, 1871 ***1823.21*** *p95*
Downie, Mary 4; North Carolina, 1775 ***1422.10*** *p59*
Downie, Mary 35; North Carolina, 1774 ***1422.10*** *p57*
Downie, William 40; Ontario, 1871 ***1823.21*** *p95*
Downing, Emma 22; Michigan, 1880 ***4491.42*** *p10*
Downing, John; Ipswich, MA, 1661 ***1642*** *p69*
Downing, John; North Carolina, 1858 ***1088.45*** *p8*
Downing, John 63; Ontario, 1871 ***1823.21*** *p95*
Downing, Mackum; Lynn, MA, 1653 ***1642*** *p71*
Downing, William; Ipswich, MA, 1661 ***1642*** *p69*
Downs, Albert G.; Colorado, 1882 ***1029.59*** *p23*
Downs, James 37; Ontario, 1871 ***1823.21*** *p95*
Downs, Michael 56; Ontario, 1871 ***1823.17*** *p44*
Downs, Michael; Toronto, 1844 ***2910.35*** *p115*
Downs, Patrick 30; Ontario, 1871 ***1823.17*** *p44*
Downs, Patrick 50; Ontario, 1871 ***1823.17*** *p44*
Downy, Christian 25; North Carolina, 1775 ***1422.10*** *p59*
Doxtator, Baptist 44; Ontario, 1871 ***1823.21*** *p95*
Doxtator, Dolly 50; Ontario, 1871 ***1823.21*** *p95*
Doxtator, Isaac 56; Ontario, 1871 ***1823.21*** *p95*
Doxtator, Lucy 31; Ontario, 1871 ***1823.21*** *p95*
Doxtator, Thomas 59; Ontario, 1871 ***1823.21*** *p95*
Doxtator, William 65; Ontario, 1871 ***1823.21*** *p95*
Doyal, James; New York, NY, 1776 ***8529.30*** *p2*
Doyale, Patrick; Louisiana, 1874 ***4981.45*** *p131*
Doyel, Larance 27; Ontario, 1871 ***1823.21*** *p95*
Doyel, Michael; Boston, 1767 ***1642*** *p48*
Doyen, Friederika Piedt *SEE* Doyen, Theodor
Doyen, Jean 30; America, 1841 ***778.6*** *p97*
Doyen, Theodor; Dakota, 1887 ***554.30*** *p25*
*Wife:*Friederika Piedt
Doyl, Mary; Massachusetts, 1752 ***1642*** *p66*
Doyl, Michael; Boston, 1765 ***1642*** *p48*
Doyl, Sara; Massachusetts, 1769 ***1642*** *p66*
Doyle, Mr.; Boston, 1880-1980 ***9228.50*** *p507*
With brother
Doyle, Anty; New Orleans, 1850 ***7242.30*** *p140*
Doyle, Bess; New Orleans, 1850 ***7242.30*** *p140*
Doyle, Betty; New Orleans, 1850 ***7242.30*** *p140*
Doyle, Bridgett 59; Michigan, 1880 ***4491.33*** *p7*
Doyle, Catherine; New Orleans, 1850 ***7242.30*** *p140*
Doyle, E.; New Orleans, 1850 ***7242.30*** *p140*
Doyle, Edward; Ohio, 1838 ***3580.20*** *p31*
Doyle, Edward; Ohio, 1838 ***6020.12*** *p7*
Doyle, Ellen; New Orleans, 1850 ***7242.30*** *p140*
Doyle, Felix; Ipswich, MA, 1759 ***1642*** *p71*
Doyle, Francis 66; Ontario, 1871 ***1823.21*** *p95*
Doyle, George; North Carolina, 1812 ***1088.45*** *p8*
Doyle, Gerald; Toronto, 1844 ***2910.35*** *p115*
Doyle, James; Boston, 1766 ***1642*** *p35*
Doyle, James; New Orleans, 1850 ***7242.30*** *p140*
Doyle, James; Ohio, 1809-1852 ***4511.35*** *p12*
Doyle, James 32; Ontario, 1871 ***1823.21*** *p95*
Doyle, James 34; Ontario, 1871 ***1823.21*** *p95*
Doyle, James 36; Ontario, 1871 ***1823.21*** *p95*
Doyle, James 45; Ontario, 1871 ***1823.21*** *p95*
Doyle, James 73; Ontario, 1871 ***1823.21*** *p95*
Doyle, James; Toronto, 1844 ***2910.35*** *p115*
Doyle, James J.; Washington, 1889 ***2770.40*** *p27*
Doyle, John; Boston, 1770 ***1642*** *p49*
Doyle, John; Colorado, 1873 ***1029.59*** *p23*
Doyle, John 60; Michigan, 1880 ***4491.33*** *p7*
Doyle, John; New Orleans, 1850 ***7242.30*** *p140*
Doyle, John 30; New York, NY, 1826 ***6178.50*** *p150*
Doyle, John; Washington, 1888 ***2770.40*** *p25*
Doyle, Joseph 20; Ontario, 1871 ***1823.21*** *p95*
Doyle, Joseph 34; Ontario, 1871 ***1823.21*** *p95*
Doyle, Joseph B.; Ohio, 1870 ***3580.20*** *p31*
Doyle, Joseph B.; Ohio, 1870 ***6020.12*** *p7*
Doyle, Kate; New Orleans, 1850 ***7242.30*** *p140*
Doyle, Lawrence; St. Johns, N.F., 1825 ***1053.15*** *p7*
Doyle, Margaret; New Orleans, 1850 ***7242.30*** *p140*
Doyle, Margarett 30; Ontario, 1871 ***1823.21*** *p95*
Doyle, Martin 55; Ontario, 1871 ***1823.17*** *p44*
Doyle, Mary; Boston, 1772 ***1642*** *p49*
Doyle, Mary; Massachusetts, 1752 ***1642*** *p66*
Doyle, Mary 30; Michigan, 1880 ***4491.33*** *p7*
Doyle, Mary; New Orleans, 1850 ***7242.30*** *p140*
Doyle, Mary Ann; New Orleans, 1850 ***7242.30*** *p141*
Doyle, Mary Anne; New Orleans, 1851 ***7242.30*** *p141*
Doyle, Mary J. 50; Ontario, 1871 ***1823.21*** *p95*
Doyle, Michael; New Orleans, 1850 ***7242.30*** *p141*
Doyle, Michel 50; Ontario, 1871 ***1823.21*** *p95*
Doyle, Moses; St. Johns, N.F., 1825 ***1053.15*** *p6*
Doyle, Owen 72; Ontario, 1871 ***1823.21*** *p95*
Doyle, P.; New Orleans, 1850 ***7242.30*** *p141*
Doyle, Patrick; Albany, NY, 1840 ***3274.56*** *p101*
Doyle, Patrick; Toronto, 1844 ***2910.35*** *p112*
Doyle, Patrick J.; Washington, 1888 ***2770.40*** *p25*
Doyle, Patt; New Orleans, 1850 ***7242.30*** *p141*
Doyle, Peter; New Orleans, 1850 ***7242.30*** *p141*
Doyle, Peter; Newfoundland, 1814 ***3476.10*** *p54*
Doyle, Sarah; New Orleans, 1850 ***7242.30*** *p141*
Doyle, Terence; New Orleans, 1850 ***7242.30*** *p141*
Doyle, Thomas; Iowa, 1873 ***1211.15*** *p10*
Doyle, Thomas; New Orleans, 1850 ***7242.30*** *p141*
Doyle, William; New Orleans, 1850 ***7242.30*** *p141*
Doyle, William 35; Ontario, 1871 ***1823.21*** *p95*
Doyle, William 62; Ontario, 1871 ***1823.21*** *p95*
Doyle, William; Washington, 1889 ***2770.40*** *p27*
Doylone, Simon 29; New Orleans, 1848 ***778.6*** *p97*
Doyon, Jean 25; Quebec, 1644 ***9221.17*** *p140*
Dozung, Jacob 35; New Orleans, 1848 ***778.6*** *p97*
Drabecki, John; Detroit, 1930 ***1640.60*** *p77*
Drady, Jane; Massachusetts, 1733 ***1642*** *p66*
Draeger, Emma; Wisconsin, 1902 ***6795.8*** *p201*
Draeger, Rudolph; Wisconsin, 1895 ***6795.8*** *p72*
Draeseke, Frederick D.; Colorado, 1886 ***1029.59*** *p23*
Drager, Frederick; Illinois, 1860 ***6079.1*** *p4*

Drager, Gotleib; Iowa, 1884 ***1211.15*** *p10*
Drager, Mary T.; Wisconsin, 1895 ***6795.8*** *p36*
Drager, William; Iowa, 1884 ***1211.15*** *p10*
Drager, Wm. Frederick; Wisconsin, 1870 ***6795.8*** *p125*
D'Rago, Frank 20; New York, NY, 1869 ***7710.1*** *p157*
Dragoun, Karel; Kansas, 1885 ***2853.20*** *p201*
Dragutinovich, L.; Louisiana, 1874-1875 ***4981.45*** *p298*
Draize, Jean; Wisconsin, 1870 ***1495.20*** *p12*
*Wife:*Marie Catherine Kinet
*Son:*Jean Joseph
*Son:*Louis Joseph
Draize, Jean Joseph *SEE* Draize, Jean
Draize, Louis Joseph *SEE* Draize, Jean
Draize, Marie Catherine Kinet *SEE* Draize, Jean
Draize, Pauline; Wisconsin, 1887 ***1495.20*** *p12*
Drake, Bartholemew 39; Ontario, 1871 ***1823.21*** *p96*
Drake, Edwd J. 26; Ontario, 1871 ***1823.21*** *p96*
Drake, Edwin 32; Ontario, 1871 ***1823.21*** *p96*
Drake, James 32; Ontario, 1871 ***1823.21*** *p96*
Drake, John; New England, 1630 ***117.5*** *p159*
Drake, Phinea 74; Ontario, 1871 ***1823.21*** *p96*
Dralle, Mr.; America, 1868 ***7420.1*** *p270*
With family
Dralle, Conrad; America, 1857 ***7420.1*** *p160*
With wife 2 sons & daughter
Dralle, Ernst Wilhelm; Illinois, 1881 ***7420.1*** *p320*
Dralle, Heinrich Christoph; Port uncertain, 1837 ***7420.1*** *p13*
Dralle, Johann Heinrich Christoph; America, 1857 ***7420.1*** *p160*
With daughter wife & 2 sons
Dralle, Wilhelm, Sr.; America, 1880 ***7420.1*** *p398*
Dramger, Mary 30; Ontario, 1871 ***1823.21*** *p96*
Dranger, John 44; Ontario, 1871 ***1823.21*** *p96*
Draper, Mrs. F.; Montreal, 1922 ***4514.4*** *p32*
Draper, George; Washington, 1883 ***2770.40*** *p136*
Draper, John 39; Ontario, 1871 ***1823.21*** *p96*
Draper, John 55; Ontario, 1871 ***1823.21*** *p96*
Draper, S. H. 52; Ontario, 1871 ***1823.17*** *p44*
Draper, Thomas 77; Ontario, 1871 ***1823.21*** *p96*
Drapinski, Vincent; Detroit, 1929-1930 ***6214.5*** *p69*
Drasky, Josef; Nebraska, 1876 ***2853.20*** *p158*
Dratz, Jean 18; America, 1840 ***778.6*** *p97*
Draudine, Jean; Quebec, 1650 ***9221.17*** *p225*
Drauz, Anna; Philadelphia, 1854 ***8513.31*** *p425*
Drawford, Jean; Lynn, MA, 1732 ***1642*** *p71*
Draynum, Janet 42; Ontario, 1871 ***1823.21*** *p96*
Drayton, Henry 29; Ontario, 1871 ***1823.21*** *p96*
Drbal, Josef; Nebraska, 1905 ***2853.20*** *p184*
Dreachle, Gotlieb; Ohio, 1809-1852 ***4511.35*** *p12*
Dreany, Robert 50; Ontario, 1871 ***1823.21*** *p96*
Drechsler, C. W.; Louisiana, 1836-1840 ***4981.45*** *p212*
Drechsler, Katharine; America, 1894 ***179.55*** *p19*
Dredske, Fred William; Wisconsin, 1888 ***6795.8*** *p29*
Drees, Theodore; Texas, 1909 ***3435.45*** *p35*
Dreger, Alexander 14; Halifax, N.S., 1902 ***1860.4*** *p43*
Dreger, Arthur 2; Halifax, N.S., 1902 ***1860.4*** *p40*
Dreger, Emilie 49; Halifax, N.S., 1902 ***1860.4*** *p43*
Dreger, Emma 7; Halifax, N.S., 1902 ***1860.4*** *p43*
Dreger, Friedrich 7; Halifax, N.S., 1902 ***1860.4*** *p40*
Dreger, Gustav 36; Halifax, N.S., 1902 ***1860.4*** *p40*
Dreger, Gustov 54; Halifax, N.S., 1902 ***1860.4*** *p43*
Dreger, Helene 9; Halifax, N.S., 1902 ***1860.4*** *p43*
Dreger, Henrich 17; Halifax, N.S., 1902 ***1860.4*** *p43*
Dreger, Hermonne 11; Halifax, N.S., 1902 ***1860.4*** *p43*
Dreger, Leopold 17; Halifax, N.S., 1902 ***1860.4*** *p43*
Dreger, Martha 28; Halifax, N.S., 1902 ***1860.4*** *p40*
Dreger, Rudolph; Wisconsin, 1895 ***6795.8*** *p72*
Dreger, Wanda; Halifax, N.S., 1902 ***1860.4*** *p40*
Drehes, Wilh.; Valdivia, Chile, 1851 ***1192.4*** *p51*
Drehmer, Barbara 27; Ohio, 1843 ***5475.1*** *p546*
Drehmer, Barbara 11 *SEE* Drehmer, Heinrich
Drehmer, Charlotte 43 *SEE* Drehmer, Heinrich
Drehmer, Gertrud Bill 30 *SEE* Drehmer, Johann Georg
Drehmer, Heinrich 16 *SEE* Drehmer, Heinrich
Drehmer, Heinrich 47; Rio Grande do Sul, Brazil, 1854 ***5475.1*** *p532*
*Wife:*Charlotte 43
*Daughter:*Barbara 11
*Son:*Konrad 9
*Son:*Jakob 5
*Daughter:*Maria 14
*Son:*Heinrich 16
Drehmer, Jakob 4 *SEE* Drehmer, Johann Georg
Drehmer, Jakob 5 *SEE* Drehmer, Heinrich
Drehmer, Johann 4 *SEE* Drehmer, Johann Georg
Drehmer, Johann Georg 35; America, 1843 ***5475.1*** *p529*
With parents
*Wife:*Gertrud Bill 30
*Daughter:*Maria 1
*Daughter:*Maria 6 months
*Son:*Johann 4
*Daughter:*Sophie 6
*Son:*Jakob 4
Drehmer, Konrad 9 *SEE* Drehmer, Heinrich
Drehmer, Maria 1 *SEE* Drehmer, Johann Georg
Drehmer, Maria 6 *SEE* Drehmer, Johann Georg
Drehmer, Maria 14 *SEE* Drehmer, Heinrich
Drehmer, Sophie 6 *SEE* Drehmer, Johann Georg
Dreholder, Joseph 11 months; New York, NY, 1894 ***6512.1*** *p228*
Dreholer, Mrs. 28; New York, NY, 1894 ***6512.1*** *p228*
Dreholer, Adolph 33; New York, NY, 1894 ***6512.1*** *p228*
Dreholer, Golda 3; New York, NY, 1894 ***6512.1*** *p228*
Dreholer, Rosa 5; New York, NY, 1894 ***6512.1*** *p228*
Dreier, August; Port uncertain, 1840 ***7420.1*** *p18*
Dreier, Catharina Meier *SEE* Dreier, Jobst Heinrich
Dreier, Ernestine Sophie *SEE* Dreier, Ernst Heinrich Gottlieb
Dreier, Ernst Heinrich Gottlieb; America, 1872 ***7420.1*** *p294*
*Wife:*Sophie Wilhelmine Louise Koch
*Sister:*Ernestine Sophie
*Daughter:*Sophie Wilhelmine Christine
Dreier, Friedrich Christian; America, 1867 ***7420.1*** *p255*
With family
Dreier, Heinrich Christian *SEE* Dreier, Jobst Heinrich
Dreier, Heinrich Ferdinand *SEE* Dreier, Jobst Heinrich
Dreier, Jobst Heinrich; America, 1847 ***7420.1*** *p52*
*Wife:*Catharina Meier
With mother
*Son:*Heinrich Ferdinand
*Son:*Heinrich Christian
Dreier, Sophie Caroline Ernestine; America, 1861 ***7420.1*** *p204*
Dreier, Sophie Catharine; America, 1847 ***7420.1*** *p57*
Dreier, Sophie Wilhelmine; America, 1886 ***7420.1*** *p352*
*Son:*Christian Heinrich Wilhelm
With son
Dreier, Sophie Wilhelmine Christine *SEE* Dreier, Ernst Heinrich Gottlieb
Dreier, Sophie Wilhelmine Louise Koch *SEE* Dreier, Ernst Heinrich Gottlieb
Dreissigacker, Heinrich Christoph; America, 1868 ***7919.3*** *p534*
Dreistadt, Peter 26; America, 1889 ***5475.1*** *p152*
Dreize, August; America, 1872 ***1494.20*** *p12*
Dreize, J. B.; Wisconsin, 1871 ***1494.20*** *p11*
Dreize, Nicolas; America, 1872 ***1494.20*** *p12*
Drell, Henry; Louisiana, 1874 ***4981.45*** *p131*
Drennon, Robert; South Carolina, 1810 ***6155.4*** *p18*
Drescher, Augustus; Illinois, 1856 ***6079.1*** *p4*
Drescher, Johann Ludwig; America, 1836 ***8115.12*** *p319*
Dreschner, Carl Friedrich; Wisconsin, 1871 ***6795.8*** *p89*
Dresden, Mary; Boston, 1764 ***1642*** *p34*
Dresel, Otto; Ohio, 1809-1852 ***4511.35*** *p12*
Dreses, Joseph; Ohio, 1840-1897 ***8365.35*** *p16*
Dresmire, John; Long Island, 1778 ***8529.30*** *p9A*
Dresse, August; America, 1872 ***1494.20*** *p12*
Dresse, Christian 23 *SEE* Dresse, Maria Dorr
Dresse, Johann Friedrich 26 *SEE* Dresse, Maria Dorr
Dresse, Magdalena 21 *SEE* Dresse, Maria Dorr
Dresse, Maria; America, 1847 ***5475.1*** *p21*
*Son:*Johann Friedrich
*Son:*Christian
*Daughter:*Magdalena
*Daughter:*Maria
Dresse, Maria 18 *SEE* Dresse, Maria Dorr
Dresse, Nicolas; America, 1872 ***1494.20*** *p12*
Dressel, Christian; America, 1867 ***7919.3*** *p526*
Dressel, Elisabeth; America, 1868 ***7919.3*** *p527*
Dressel, Ernst August; America, 1867 ***7919.3*** *p526*
Dressel, Johannes Karl; America, 1867 ***7919.3*** *p533*
Dressel, Nicol Friedrich Ferdinand; America, 1867 ***7919.3*** *p525*
Dressler, Mr.; America, 1887 ***7420.1*** *p353*
Dressy, Anna Maria 22; New Orleans, 1848 ***778.6*** *p97*
Dressy, Carl 16; New Orleans, 1848 ***778.6*** *p97*
Dressy, Catharine 21; New Orleans, 1848 ***778.6*** *p97*
Dressy, Catharine 53; New Orleans, 1848 ***778.6*** *p97*
Dressy, Elisabeth 9; New Orleans, 1848 ***778.6*** *p97*
Dressy, Franz 56; New Orleans, 1848 ***778.6*** *p97*
Dressy, Jacob 8; New Orleans, 1848 ***778.6*** *p97*
Dressy, Johannis 24; New Orleans, 1848 ***778.6*** *p97*
Dressy, Magdalena 22; New Orleans, 1848 ***778.6*** *p97*
Dretske, Fred William; Wisconsin, 1888 ***6795.8*** *p29*
Dreuth, Ludwig; America, n.d. ***8115.12*** *p325*
Drevitz, Gottlieb; Wisconsin, 1899 ***6795.8*** *p177*
Drew, Alfred 25; Ontario, 1871 ***1823.21*** *p96*
Drew, Charles; New Hampshire, 1738 ***9228.50*** *p197*
Drew, Charles; Portsmouth, NH, 1738 ***9228.50*** *p661*
Drew, Clement; New Hampshire, 1790 ***9228.50*** *p197*
Drew, Eliz. Matthews *SEE* Drew, William
Drew, Francis; Boston, 1715 ***9228.50*** *p196*
Drew, Francis; New Hampshire, 1648 ***9228.50*** *p661*
Drew, Gilbert; America, 1732-1812 ***9228.50*** *p661*
Drew, James 43; Ontario, 1871 ***1823.17*** *p44*
Drew, James S.; Ohio, 1809-1852 ***4511.35*** *p12*
Drew, John; Ohio, 1809-1852 ***4511.35*** *p12*
Drew, John 48; Ontario, 1871 ***1823.17*** *p44*
Drew, Joshua; New Hampshire, 1790 ***9228.50*** *p197*
Drew, Sargent John *SEE* Drew, William
Drew, Townsend; America, 1848-1911 ***9228.50*** *p659*
Drew, William; Maine, 1627-1669 ***9228.50*** *p197*
*Wife:*Eliz. Matthews
*Child:*Sargent John
Drew, William; New Hampshire, 1648 ***9228.50*** *p197*
Drew, William 27; Ontario, 1871 ***1823.17*** *p44*
Drewes, Asmus; Valdivia, Chile, 1852 ***1192.4*** *p53*
Drewes, Ernst Karl Heinrich; America, 1887 ***7420.1*** *p353*
Drewes, Henery Christopher; Missouri, 1888 ***3276.1*** *p3*
Drewes, Wm.; Missouri, 1887 ***3276.1*** *p1*
Drewitz, Gottlieb; Wisconsin, 1873 ***6795.8*** *p120*
Drewitz, Gottlieb; Wisconsin, 1899 ***6795.8*** *p177*
Drews, Wm.; Missouri, 1894 ***3276.1*** *p1*
Drexler, H. W.; New York, 1859 ***358.56*** *p101*
Drey, John; Ohio, 1809-1852 ***4511.35*** *p12*
Drey, Nathan; North Carolina, 1846 ***1088.45*** *p8*
Dreyer, Anna Maria 18; Galveston, TX, 1844 ***3967.10*** *p373*
Dreyer, Dorette Wilhelmine; America, 1851 ***7420.1*** *p79*
Dreyer, Dorothee Aug. Charlotte; America, 1865 ***7420.1*** *p230*
Dreyer, Ernest; North Carolina, 1854 ***1088.45*** *p8*
Dreyer, Heinrich; America, 1857 ***7420.1*** *p160*
Dreyer, Heinrich 11; Galveston, TX, 1844 ***3967.10*** *p373*
Dreyer, Heinrich 18; New York, NY, 1864 ***8425.62*** *p199*
Dreyer, Heinrich Christian; America, 1866 ***7420.1*** *p241*
With family
Dreyer, Johann Friedrich; America, 1868 ***7420.1*** *p270*
Dreyer, Karoline 14; Galveston, TX, 1844 ***3967.10*** *p373*
Dreyer, Katharina 22; Galveston, TX, 1844 ***3967.10*** *p373*
Dreyer, Katharina 47; Galveston, TX, 1844 ***3967.10*** *p373*
Dreyer, Maria Anna 16; Galveston, TX, 1844 ***3967.10*** *p373*
Dreyer, Martin 48; Galveston, TX, 1844 ***3967.10*** *p373*
Dreyer, Therese 25; Galveston, TX, 1844 ***3967.10*** *p373*
Dreyer, Wilhelm; America, 1852 ***7420.1*** *p87*
Dreyer, Wilhelm; Port uncertain, 1883 ***7420.1*** *p335*
Dreyfus, Emanuel 28; Port uncertain, 1847 ***778.6*** *p97*
Dreyfus, Joseph 26; New Orleans, 1847 ***778.6*** *p97*
Dreyfus, Madeline 22; New Orleans, 1847 ***778.6*** *p97*
Dreyfus, Rosalie 24; Port uncertain, 1847 ***778.6*** *p97*
Dreyfuss, Barnet 18; New Orleans, 1848 ***778.6*** *p97*
Dreyfuss, Benoit 22; New Orleans, 1848 ***778.6*** *p97*
Dreyfuss, David, Jr.; Louisiana, 1883-1891 ***7710.1*** *p160*
Dreyfuss, Solomon 36; New Orleans, 1866 ***7710.1*** *p158*
Dreystadt, Elisabeth 22; America, 1866 ***5475.1*** *p150*
Dreze, Jean; Wisconsin, 1870 ***1495.20*** *p12*
*Wife:*Marie Catherine Kinet
*Son:*Louis Joseph
*Son:*Jean Joseph
Dreze, Jean Joseph *SEE* Dreze, Jean
Dreze, Louis Joseph *SEE* Dreze, Jean
Dreze, Marie Catherine Kinet *SEE* Dreze, Jean
Dreze, Pauline; Wisconsin, 1887 ***1495.20*** *p12*
Driem, Peter; Ohio, 1809-1852 ***4511.35*** *p12*
Dries, Elisabeth 22; America, 1865 ***5475.1*** *p534*
Driher, Vendel 23; America, 1847 ***778.6*** *p97*
Dris, Thomas 78; Ontario, 1871 ***1823.17*** *p44*
Driscall, Elias; Massachusetts, 1768 ***1642*** *p66*
Driscall, Susanna; Massachusetts, 1769 ***1642*** *p66*
Drischler, Franz Johann Peter Andreas; America, 1860 ***7420.1*** *p193*
Driscol, Dan; St. John, N.B., 1848 ***2978.15*** *p37*
Driscol, Mary; Quebec, 1870 ***8364.32*** *p23*
Driscoll, Mary; Boston, 1767 ***1642*** *p49*
Driscoll, Olive 16; Minnesota, 1923 ***2769.54*** *p1383*
Driscoll, Timothy; Ohio, 1840-1897 ***8365.35*** *p16*
Driscoll, William J.; Washington, 1881 ***2770.40*** *p135*
Driskell, Catharine; Boston, 1752 ***1642*** *p46*
Driskill, Mary; Boston, 1738 ***1642*** *p44*
Drisscal, Katharine; Boston, 1763 ***1642*** *p48*
Drivon, Domingne; Louisiana, 1841-1844 ***4981.45*** *p210*
Droescher, Elisabeth 27; America, 1857 ***5475.1*** *p551*
Droge, Mr.; America, 1837 ***7420.1*** *p13*
With wife
With 6 children
Droge, Frille; Port uncertain, 1836 ***7420.1*** *p11*
Drogemeier, Friedrich Wilhelm; Illinois, 1874 ***7420.1*** *p303*
Drogue, Louis 26; Missouri, 1848 ***778.6*** *p97*
Drogy, Mr. 24; New Orleans, 1841 ***778.6*** *p97*
Droham, Patrick; Boston, 1763 ***1642*** *p32*
Droit, Alexis 30; New Orleans, 1843 ***778.6*** *p97*
Droitcour, Maria; America, 1874 ***5475.1*** *p78*
Drolet, Christophe; Quebec, 1654 ***9221.17*** *p307*
*Wife:*Jeanne Levasseur

Drolet, Jeanne Levasseur *SEE* Drolet, Christophe
Drollmann, Therese; New York, 1860 ***358.56*** *p5*
Dromer, Louis 35; Port uncertain, 1846 ***778.6*** *p97*
Drompole, John 27; Ontario, 1871 ***1823.21*** *p96*
Droop, William 75; Ontario, 1871 ***1823.17*** *p44*
Drope, William; Jamaica, 1780 ***8529.30*** *p13A*
Drossart, Alexandre; Wisconsin, 1854-1858 ***1495.20*** *p66*
*Wife:*Julie Josephe Delforge
*Son:*Antoine Joseph
*Son:*Eugene Joseph
Drossart, Antoine Joseph *SEE* Drossart, Alexandre
Drossart, Eugene Joseph *SEE* Drossart, Alexandre
Drossart, Julie Josephe Delforge *SEE* Drossart, Alexandre
Droste, Franz; Argentina, 1826 ***8023.44*** *p373*
Droste, Hugo; Argentina, 1926 ***8023.44*** *p373*
Droste, J.; America, 1874 ***8023.44*** *p372*
Droste, Johann; America, 1874 ***8023.44*** *p373*
Drou, Etienne 28; America, 1847 ***778.6*** *p97*
Drouard, Elie 21; Texas, 1848 ***778.6*** *p97*
Drouart, Jacques 16; Quebec, 1642 ***9221.17*** *p116*
Drouart, Jean 22; Quebec, 1660 ***9221.17*** *p434*
Drouart, Louis; Quebec, 1646 ***9221.17*** *p163*
Drouet, Catherine; Quebec, 1671 ***4514.3*** *p308*
Drouet, Francois 22; Quebec, 1637 ***9221.17*** *p69*
Drouet, Francois 24; Quebec, 1661 ***9221.17*** *p454*
Drouet, Hilaire; Quebec, 1651 ***9221.17*** *p242*
Drouet, Jacques 31; Quebec, 1647 ***9221.17*** *p179*
Drouet, Louis 17; Port uncertain, 1843 ***778.6*** *p97*
Drouet, Pierre; Quebec, 1634 ***9221.17*** *p35*
Drouet, Pierre 24; Quebec, 1661 ***9221.17*** *p454*
Drouet deRicherville, Claude; Quebec, 1683-1688 ***2314.30*** *p168*
Drouet deRicherville, Claude; Quebec, 1687 ***2314.30*** *p180*
Droughady, Mary; Boston, 1739 ***1642*** *p45*
Drought, Henry Pigote 65; Ontario, 1871 ***1823.21*** *p96*
Drought, John 34; Ontario, 1871 ***1823.21*** *p96*
Drought, Thos 53; Ontario, 1871 ***1823.21*** *p96*
Drouhier, Wolf 31; Port uncertain, 1847 ***778.6*** *p97*
Drouillart, Charles; Quebec, 1646 ***9221.17*** *p163*
Drouillart, Marie 20; Quebec, 1657 ***9221.17*** *p356*
Drouillart, Simon; Quebec, 1646 ***9221.17*** *p163*
Drouin, Jean; Quebec, 1646 ***9221.17*** *p164*
Drouin, Robert 26; Quebec, 1633 ***9221.17*** *p28*
Droupe, William; Jamaica, 1780 ***8529.30*** *p13A*
Droussmer, John; Ohio, 1840-1897 ***8365.35*** *p16*
Drown, James Franklin 38; Ontario, 1871 ***1823.21*** *p96*
Drownilee, Brunell 47; Ontario, 1871 ***1823.21*** *p96*
Droxler, Ant. 25; America, 1840 ***778.6*** *p97*
Droz, Buscallien 37; Mississippi, 1847 ***778.6*** *p97*
Droz, Georges 11; Mississippi, 1847 ***778.6*** *p98*
Droz, Jean Pierre 44; Mississippi, 1847 ***778.6*** *p98*
Droz, Martin 9; Mississippi, 1847 ***778.6*** *p98*
Drucker, David; Texas, 1888 ***3435.45*** *p35*
Drue, William; New Hampshire, 1648 ***9228.50*** *p197*
Druez, Peter Joseph; North Carolina, 1805 ***1088.45*** *p8*
Drug, Christian; America, 1882 ***179.55*** *p19*
Drugeon, Elisabeth 20; Quebec, 1659 ***9221.17*** *p399*
Druillettes, Gabriel 33; Quebec, 1643 ***9221.17*** *p127*
Drulle, John; New York, 1859-1860 ***358.56*** *p102*
Drum, Anna; Philadelphia, 1864 ***8513.31*** *p422*
Drum, J.; New Orleans, 1850 ***7242.30*** *p141*
Drum, John; Massachusetts, 1751 ***1642*** *p104*
Drum, Joseph; Ohio, 1809-1852 ***4511.35*** *p12*
Drum, Reuben; Ohio, 1809-1852 ***4511.35*** *p12*
Drumel, Philip C.; Philadelphia, 1839 ***8513.31*** *p303*
Drumm, Adam; America, 1836 ***5475.1*** *p555*
With wife
*Son:*Nikolaus
*Son:*Adam
*Daughter:*Barbara
*Daughter:*Caroline
*Daughter:*Elisabeth
*Son:*Jakob
Drumm, Adam 7 *SEE* Drumm, Adam
Drumm, Barbara 4 *SEE* Drumm, Adam
Drumm, Caroline 3 *SEE* Drumm, Adam
Drumm, Elisabeth 11 *SEE* Drumm, Adam
Drumm, Jakob 16 *SEE* Drumm, Adam
Drumm, Katharina; America, 1839 ***5475.1*** *p555*
Drumm, Katharina 63; America, 1858 ***5475.1*** *p499*
Drumm, M. Elisabeth; America, 1863-1900 ***5475.1*** *p499*
Drumm, Nikolaus 13 *SEE* Drumm, Adam
Drumm, Philipp 23; New York, 1884 ***5475.1*** *p556*
Drummond, Duncan 45; Ontario, 1871 ***1823.21*** *p96*
Drummond, Janet 68; Ontario, 1871 ***1823.21*** *p96*
Drummond, John 45; Ontario, 1871 ***1823.21*** *p96*
Drummond, John 48; Ontario, 1871 ***1823.21*** *p96*
Drummond, William; Boston, 1737 ***1642*** *p26*
Drummond, William; Colorado, 1892 ***1029.59*** *p24*
Drummond, William; Ohio, 1832 ***3580.20*** *p31*
Drummond, William; Ohio, 1832 ***6020.12*** *p7*
Drummond, William 65; Ontario, 1871 ***1823.21*** *p96*
Drumond, James M. 40; Ontario, 1871 ***1823.21*** *p96*
Drury, Thomas 55; Ontario, 1871 ***1823.21*** *p96*
Drury, William; Illinois, 1860 ***6079.1*** *p4*
Drusch, Anna 47; America, 1857 ***5475.1*** *p374*
Drusch, Nikolaus; America, 1873 ***5475.1*** *p341*
Dryander, Max Paul Rich.; New York, 1886 ***5475.1*** *p37*
Dryman, William 34; Ontario, 1871 ***1823.21*** *p96*
Drywood, John 43; Ontario, 1871 ***1823.21*** *p96*
Dryzer, Louis; Tennessee, 1886-1893 ***3665.20*** *p111*
Drzewicki, John; Detroit, 1890 ***9980.23*** *p96*
Drzymalla, Johann; Texas, 1879-1886 ***9980.22*** *p16*
Dschak, Adaline 2; Halifax, N.S., 1902 ***1860.4*** *p43*
Dschak, August 4; Halifax, N.S., 1902 ***1860.4*** *p43*
Dschak, Barbara 7; Halifax, N.S., 1902 ***1860.4*** *p43*
Dschak, Barbara 26; Halifax, N.S., 1902 ***1860.4*** *p43*
Dschak, Christian 2; Halifax, N.S., 1902 ***1860.4*** *p43*
Dschak, Emil; Halifax, N.S., 1902 ***1860.4*** *p43*
Dschak, Emilie 3; Halifax, N.S., 1902 ***1860.4*** *p43*
Dschak, Heinrich 3; Halifax, N.S., 1902 ***1860.4*** *p43*
Dschak, Jocob 31; Halifax, N.S., 1902 ***1860.4*** *p43*
Dschak, Louise 28; Halifax, N.S., 1902 ***1860.4*** *p43*
Dschak, Peter 28; Halifax, N.S., 1902 ***1860.4*** *p43*
Duan, Thomas; Boston, 1766 ***1642*** *p36*
Duantoni, Felix 24; America, 1846 ***778.6*** *p98*
Duay, Stanislas 21; New Orleans, 1848 ***778.6*** *p98*
Duay, Virginie 30; America, 1840 ***778.6*** *p98*
Dubac, Juan Pedro 28; New Orleans, 1842 ***778.6*** *p98*
Dubach, John; Ohio, 1809-1852 ***4511.35*** *p12*
Dubail, Francois 36; America, 1844 ***778.6*** *p98*
Dubail, Valentin 44; America, 1843 ***778.6*** *p98*
Dubans, Jacques; Quebec, 1660 ***9221.17*** *p434*
Dubard, Francois; Louisiana, 1874 ***4981.45*** *p131*
Dubarry, Mr. 29; New Orleans, 1848 ***778.6*** *p98*
DuBarry, Mrs. 26; America, 1844 ***778.6*** *p98*
Dubarry, Mrs. 20; New Orleans, 1848 ***778.6*** *p98*
DuBataillon, Francois; Quebec, 1661 ***9221.17*** *p452*
Dubaus, Pierre; Quebec, 1659 ***9221.17*** *p413*
Dubeau, Galbriel 17; New Orleans, 1844 ***778.6*** *p98*
Dubeck, Adam; America, 1853 ***2526.42*** *p118*
Dubele, Henry 20; Virginia, 1635 ***9228.50*** *p195*
Dubent, Jean 23; New Orleans, 1845 ***778.6*** *p98*
Duber Carl, Mr. 33; America, 1847 ***778.6*** *p98*
Duberg, Georg 20; Port uncertain, 1847 ***778.6*** *p98*
Dubicourt, Jeanne; Quebec, 1669 ***4514.3*** *p308*
Dubie, Marie-Francoise; Quebec, 1671 ***4514.3*** *p308*
Dubiel, Szymon 30; New York, NY, 1911 ***6533.11*** *p9*
Dubina, Frantisek; Wisconsin, 1856-1910 ***2853.20*** *p345*
Duboc, Batiste 35; America, 1842 ***778.6*** *p98*
Duboc, George 32; America, 1842 ***778.6*** *p98*
Duboc, L. 30; America, 1842 ***778.6*** *p98*
Duboc, Michel 36; America, 1842 ***778.6*** *p98*
Dubоct, Laurent 23; Quebec, 1657 ***9221.17*** *p356*
Dubois, . . .; Montreal, 1658 ***9221.17*** *p389*
Dubois, Mr. 22; America, 1747 ***778.6*** *p91*
Dubois, Mr. 22; America, 1747 ***778.6*** *p98*
Dubois, Const. 30; America, 1845 ***778.6*** *p98*
Dubois, Desire; Detroit, 1873 ***1494.20*** *p12*
Dubois, Eugene; Chicago, 1873 ***1494.20*** *p13*
Dubois, Francois Jos.; Detroit, 1871 ***1494.20*** *p12*
Dubois, Gustave; New York, NY, 1857 ***1494.20*** *p13*
Dubois, Jean 28; Port uncertain, 1843 ***778.6*** *p98*
Dubois, Jean; Quebec, 1648 ***9221.17*** *p198*
Dubois, Julius; Detroit, 1871 ***1494.20*** *p12*
Dubois, Karl 15; Galveston, TX, 1844 ***3967.10*** *p372*
Dubois, Leonard; Wisconsin, 1854-1858 ***1495.20*** *p66*
*Wife:*Marie Joseph Devroye
Dubois, Madeleine 23; Quebec, 1661 ***9221.17*** *p454*
Dubois, Magdalena 57; America, 1843 ***778.6*** *p98*
Dubois, Marguerite; Quebec, 1669 ***4514.3*** *p345*
Dubois, Marie; Quebec, 1670 ***4514.3*** *p308*
Dubois, Marie 44; Quebec, 1659 ***9221.17*** *p399*
*Son:*Urbain 16
Dubois, Marie Joseph Devroye *SEE* Dubois, Leonard
Dubois, Martin; Quebec, 1657 ***9221.17*** *p356*
Dubois, P. 23; America, 1843 ***778.6*** *p98*
Dubois, Peter; Canada, 1850-1950 ***9228.50*** *p659*
Dubois, Pierre; Quebec, 1649 ***9221.17*** *p212*
Dubois, Rene 29; Quebec, 1658 ***9221.17*** *p378*
Dubois, Urbain 16 *SEE* Dubois, Marie Rouer
Dubois, Virg..ia 28; America, 1841 ***778.6*** *p98*
Dubois Berthelot deBeaucour, Josue; Quebec, 1683-1688 ***2314.30*** *p168*
Dubois Berthelot deBeaucour, Josue; Quebec, 1688 ***2314.30*** *p181*
DuBois D'Avaugour, Pierre; Quebec, 1661 ***9221.17*** *p445*
Dubois deLa Miltiere, Honore; Quebec, 1755-1757 ***2314.30*** *p170*
Dubois deLa Miltiere, Honore; Quebec, 1755-1757 ***2314.30*** *p181*
Dubois-Morel, Pierre 26; Quebec, 1650 ***9221.17*** *p225*
Dubok, . . .; Quebec, 1645 ***9221.17*** *p153*
Dubos, Jr. 19; America, 1747 ***778.6*** *p98*
Dubos, Mr. 29; America, 1747 ***778.6*** *p98*
Dubos, Alexandre 42; America, 1843 ***778.6*** *p98*
Dubos, Guillaume 34; Quebec, 1660 ***9221.17*** *p434*
Dubos, J.; Louisiana, 1874 ***4981.45*** *p295*
Dubos, Jean F. 24; New Orleans, 1848 ***778.6*** *p98*
Duboseq, Jeanne Varspoulier 27; New Orleans, 1840 ***778.6*** *p98*
Duboseq, Mathieu 35; New Orleans, 1840 ***778.6*** *p98*
Dubourg, Mrs. 46; America, 1843 ***778.6*** *p99*
Dubourg, Adolph 15; America, 1843 ***778.6*** *p99*
Dubourg, Celine 8; America, 1843 ***778.6*** *p99*
Dubourg, Emile L. 14; New Orleans, 1844 ***778.6*** *p99*
Dubourg, Eugene 17; New Orleans, 1844 ***778.6*** *p99*
Dubourg, P. 40; New Orleans, 1846 ***778.6*** *p99*
Dubozchat, Jules 27; New Orleans, 1840 ***778.6*** *p99*
Dubras, Maurice; Ontario, 1965 ***9228.50*** *p197*
Dubras, Wm.; America, 1600-1699 ***9228.50*** *p83*
Dubratz, Gust. Karl Eduard; Wisconsin, 1899 ***6795.8*** *p221*
Dubreuil, Anne; Quebec, 1673 ***4514.3*** *p277*
Dubreuil, Isabelle; Quebec, 1665 ***4514.3*** *p308*
Dubreuil, Louis; Quebec, 1647 ***9221.17*** *p179*
Dubry, Pierre 25; Quebec, 1655 ***9221.17*** *p323*
Dubuisson, Mrs. 32; America, 1842 ***778.6*** *p99*
Dubuisson, A. 7; America, 1842 ***778.6*** *p99*
Dubuisson, Ab. 5; America, 1842 ***778.6*** *p99*
Dubuisson, Ant. 7; America, 1842 ***778.6*** *p99*
Dubuisson, B. 50; New Orleans, 1842 ***778.6*** *p99*
Dubuisson, Etienne 28; Missouri, 1848 ***778.6*** *p99*
Dubuisson, Jacques; Quebec, 1658 ***9221.17*** *p378*
Dubuisson, Jean 15 *SEE* Dubuisson, Jean
Dubuisson, Jean 42; Quebec, 1634 ***9221.17*** *p36*
*Son:*Jean 15
Dubuisson, M. 8; America, 1842 ***778.6*** *p99*
Dubuisson, Pierre; Quebec, 1646 ***9221.17*** *p166*
Dubuisson, Rosalie 32; New Orleans, 1848 ***778.6*** *p99*
Dubuque, Nelson; Washington, 1885 ***2770.40*** *p194*
Dubuque, Sidney; Washington, 1883 ***2770.40*** *p136*
Duburg, Pierre 49; Texas, 1840 ***778.6*** *p99*
Duby, Philip; New Hampshire, 1665-1745 ***9228.50*** *p202*
Duc, John 30; America, 1843 ***778.6*** *p99*
Duc, John 42; New Orleans, 1843 ***778.6*** *p99*
Ducas, . . .; Quebec, 1660 ***9221.17*** *p434*
Ducas, Mr. 29; Port uncertain, 1845 ***778.6*** *p99*
Duccroc, Marie Joseph; Wisconsin, 1856 ***1495.20*** *p46*
Ducero, Johann; America, 1847 ***5475.1*** *p474*
Ducey, Hannah 55; Ontario, 1871 ***1823.17*** *p44*
Ducharme, Catherine; Quebec, 1671 ***4514.3*** *p308*
Ducharme, Pierre 21; Montreal, 1661 ***9221.17*** *p471*
Ducharne, Fiacre 26; Montreal, 1653 ***9221.17*** *p289*
Duchein, Jean 22; New Orleans, 1840 ***778.6*** *p99*
Duchemin, Daniel 69; Indiana, n.d. ***9228.50*** *p18A*
Duchemin, Jean; Quebec, 1659 ***9221.17*** *p413*
Duchemin, Marie-Anne; Quebec, 1673 ***4514.3*** *p308*
Duchemin, Pierre 35; New Orleans, 1848 ***778.6*** *p99*
Duchene, Mr. 19; Port uncertain, 1748 ***778.6*** *p99*
Duchene, B. 44; America, 1840 ***778.6*** *p99*
Duchene, B. 49; America, 1845 ***778.6*** *p99*
Duchene, John 22; New Orleans, 1840 ***778.6*** *p99*
Duchene, Marie-Louise; Wisconsin, 1886 ***1495.20*** *p56*
Duchesne, Mr. 24; Port uncertain, 1845 ***778.6*** *p99*
Duchesne, Adrien; Quebec, 1632 ***9221.17*** *p18*
Duchesne, Barbe; Quebec, 1671 ***4514.3*** *p308*
Duchesne, C. 22; Port uncertain, 1842 ***778.6*** *p99*
Duchesne, Chs. 21; America, 1843 ***778.6*** *p99*
Duchesne, Jacques 27; Quebec, 1659 ***9221.17*** *p399*
Duchesne, Joseph 20; Montreal, 1661 ***9221.17*** *p472*
Duchesne, Marc; Quebec, 1662 ***9221.17*** *p484*
Duchesne, Nicole 21; Montreal, 1657 ***9221.17*** *p372*
Duchesne D'Iberville, . . .; Montreal, 1662 ***9221.17*** *p497*
Ducheval, Estelle 31; America, 1843 ***778.6*** *p99*
Duchman, Margaretha 52; New Orleans, 1847 ***778.6*** *p99*
Duchman, Stephen; Ohio, 1809-1852 ***4511.35*** *p12*
Duchmann, Elisabeth 8; America, 1847 ***778.6*** *p99*
Duchmann, Friederick 7; America, 1847 ***778.6*** *p99*
Duchmann, George 14; America, 1847 ***778.6*** *p100*
Duchmann, George 55; New Orleans, 1847 ***778.6*** *p100*
Duchmann, Lana 12; America, 1847 ***778.6*** *p100*
Duchmann, Magretha 19; New Orleans, 1847 ***778.6*** *p100*
Duchmann, Salome 17; New Orleans, 1847 ***778.6*** *p100*
Duchoslav, Jan; New York, NY, 1848 ***2853.20*** *p100*
Duchoslav, Jan; New York, NY, 1850-1870 ***2853.20*** *p104*
Duchoslav, Josef; Wisconsin, 1853 ***2853.20*** *p312*
Duck, Patrick 40; Ontario, 1871 ***1823.17*** *p44*
Duck, Samuel 39; Ontario, 1871 ***1823.21*** *p96*
Duck, Thomas 38; Ontario, 1871 ***1823.17*** *p44*
Duckels, Mary 105; Ontario, 1871 ***1823.21*** *p96*
Ducker, Mary 74; Ontario, 1871 ***1823.21*** *p96*
Duckro, Barbara Marx *SEE* Duckro, Jakob
Duckro, Jakob 29; America, 1880 ***5475.1*** *p484*
*Wife:*Barbara Marx
Duckworth, Lawrence 44; Ontario, 1871 ***1823.21*** *p96*

Duclaun, Mr. 25; New Orleans, 1840 ***778.6*** *p100*
Duclos, Mr. 33; New Orleans, 1840 ***778.6*** *p100*
Duclos, Antoine 18; New Orleans, 1845 ***778.6*** *p100*
Duclos, Antoine 25; Port uncertain, 1841 ***778.6*** *p100*
Duclos, Auguste 16; America, 1845 ***778.6*** *p100*
Duclos, Francois 24; New Orleans, 1840 ***778.6*** *p100*
Duclos, Francois 27; Quebec, 1660 ***9221.17*** *p434*
Duclos, Jean 32; America, 1845 ***778.6*** *p100*
Duclos, Jean 32; Mississippi, 1847 ***778.6*** *p100*
Duclos, Leontine 21; America, 1845 ***778.6*** *p100*
Duclos, Martin; Quebec, 1644 ***9221.17*** *p141*
Duclos, V...or 27; New Orleans, 1840 ***778.6*** *p100*
Duco, J. 19; America, 1848 ***778.6*** *p100*
Duco-Lagarde, Jacques 22; New Orleans, 1848 ***778.6*** *p100*
Duco-Lagarde, P. A. 47; New Orleans, 1848 ***778.6*** *p100*
Ducorps, Jeanne; Quebec, 1666 ***4514.3*** *p309*
Ducos, Armand 35; New Orleans, 1842 ***778.6*** *p100*
Ducos, Michel 34; Port uncertain, 1841 ***778.6*** *p100*
Ducos-Clos, Adolphe 25; New Orleans, 1848 ***778.6*** *p100*
Ducoudray, Marie; Quebec, 1670 ***4514.3*** *p309*
Ducouran, Jean Baptiste 27; Port uncertain, 1847 ***778.6*** *p100*
Ducourau, Charles 30; Port uncertain, 1847 ***778.6*** *p100*
Ducournau, L. 34; New Orleans, 1845 ***778.6*** *p100*
Ducro, Josef; America, 1849 ***5475.1*** *p477*
Ducroq, Charles 34; Texas, 1843 ***778.6*** *p100*
Ducuron, H. 20; America, 1847 ***778.6*** *p100*
Duda, V. Antonin; Omaha, NE, 1895 ***2853.20*** *p241*
Duday, Moses; Massachusetts, 1660 ***9228.50*** *p203*
Duday, Philip; New Hampshire, 1665-1745 ***9228.50*** *p202*
Dudden, William; New York, 1775 ***8529.30*** *p11*
Dudek, Karoline; Detroit, 1929-1930 ***6214.5*** *p70*
Dudek, Mike; Texas, 1901 ***6015.15*** *p25*
Dudek, Walter; Detroit, 1929 ***1640.55*** *p112*
Dudenhofer, Andreas; America, 1857 ***8115.12*** *p319*
Dudenhofer, Anna Elisabeth; America, 1857 ***8115.12*** *p321*
*Child:*Luise
*Child:*Johann Georg
*Child:*Georg Andreas
Dudenhofer, Christian *SEE* Dudenhofer, Elisabeth
Dudenhofer, Elisabeth; America, 1871 ***8115.12*** *p324*
*Child:*Christian
*Child:*Marie
Dudenhofer, Elisabeth *SEE* Dudenhofer, Katharine Margarethe
Dudenhofer, Friedrich *SEE* Dudenhofer, Helene
Dudenhofer, Georg *SEE* Dudenhofer, Katharine Margarethe
Dudenhofer, Georg Andreas *SEE* Dudenhofer, Anna Elisabeth
Dudenhofer, Georg Caspar; America, n.d. ***8115.12*** *p326*
Dudenhofer, Georg Philipp; America, 1840 ***8115.12*** *p319*
Dudenhofer, Helene; America, 1846 ***8115.12*** *p321*
*Child:*Magdalene
*Child:*Ludwig
*Child:*Marie Katharine
*Child:*Katharine Elisabeth
*Child:*Katharine Margarethe
*Child:*Friedrich
Dudenhofer, Johann Georg; America, 1857 ***8115.12*** *p319*
Dudenhofer, Johann Georg *SEE* Dudenhofer, Anna Elisabeth
Dudenhofer, Johann Georg; America, n.d. ***8115.12*** *p319*
Dudenhofer, Karl *SEE* Dudenhofer, Katharine Margarethe
Dudenhofer, Katharine *SEE* Dudenhofer, Katharine Margarethe
Dudenhofer, Katharine Elisabeth; America, 1846 ***8115.12*** *p319*
Dudenhofer, Katharine Elisabeth *SEE* Dudenhofer, Helene
Dudenhofer, Katharine Margarethe *SEE* Dudenhofer, Helene
Dudenhofer, Katharine Margarethe; America, n.d. ***8115.12*** *p319*
*Child:*Konrad
*Child:*Margarethe
*Child:*Karl
*Child:*Katharine
*Child:*Georg
*Child:*Ludwig
*Child:*Elisabeth
Dudenhofer, Konrad; America, 1882 ***8115.12*** *p319*
Dudenhofer, Konrad *SEE* Dudenhofer, Katharine Margarethe
Dudenhofer, Ludwig *SEE* Dudenhofer, Helene
Dudenhofer, Ludwig *SEE* Dudenhofer, Katharine Margarethe
Dudenhofer, Luise *SEE* Dudenhofer, Anna Elisabeth
Dudenhofer, Luise *SEE* Dudenhofer, Magdalene
Dudenhofer, Luise Magdalene; America, 1857 ***8115.12*** *p319*
Dudenhofer, Magdalene *SEE* Dudenhofer, Helene
Dudenhofer, Magdalene; America, n.d. ***8115.12*** *p320*
*Child:*Luise
*Child:*Margarethe
Dudenhofer, Margarethe *SEE* Dudenhofer, Katharine Margarethe
Dudenhofer, Margarethe *SEE* Dudenhofer, Magdalene
Dudenhofer, Marie *SEE* Dudenhofer, Elisabeth
Dudenhofer, Marie Katharine *SEE* Dudenhofer, Helene
Dudey, Philip; New Hampshire, 1665-1745 ***9228.50*** *p202*
Dudgeon, John; Ohio, 1832 ***3580.20*** *p31*
Dudgeon, John; Ohio, 1832 ***6020.12*** *p7*
Dudley, Abig; Boston, 1766 ***1642*** *p37*
Dudley, Joseph; Ohio, 1843 ***2763.1*** *p9*
Dudley, Patrick 58; Ontario, 1871 ***1823.17*** *p44*
Dudouit, Pierre 32; New Orleans, 1848 ***778.6*** *p100*
Dudoussat, Mrs. 30; New Orleans, 1846 ***778.6*** *p100*
Dudouyt, Jean 34; Quebec, 1662 ***9221.17*** *p478*
Dudy, Philip; New Hampshire, 1665-1745 ***9228.50*** *p202*
Dudycha, Vaclav; Iowa, 1863-1892 ***2853.20*** *p461*
Dudziec, Stanislaw; Detroit, 1929 ***1640.55*** *p114*
Duehlen, H.; Galveston, TX, 1855 ***571.7*** *p18*
Duerenberger, Frederick; Ohio, 1809-1852 ***4511.35*** *p12*
Duermberger, Frederick; Ohio, 1809-1852 ***4511.35*** *p12*
Duerr, P. 32; America, 1846 ***778.6*** *p100*
Duerr, William; Washington, 1889 ***2770.40*** *p27*
Duesterhoeft, August; Wisconsin, 1913 ***6795.8*** *p168*
Duesterhoeft, Charles Robert; Wisconsin, 1910 ***6795.8*** *p165*
Duesterhoeft, Gustav Julius; Wisconsin, 1894 ***6795.8*** *p115*
Duesterhoeft, John Gottlieb; Wisconsin, 1882 ***6795.8*** *p165*
Duesterhoeft, Wilhelmine; Wisconsin, 1885 ***6795.8*** *p137*
Dueyrouze, S. 55; America, 1846 ***778.6*** *p100*
Dufahl, Frederick; Louisiana, 1874 ***4981.45*** *p131*
Dufale, Mr. 17; America, 1848 ***778.6*** *p100*
Dufan, Benoit; Louisiana, 1874-1875 ***4981.45*** *p298*
Dufau, Mr. 19; America, 1747 ***778.6*** *p100*
Dufau, C. 4 months; New Orleans, 1848 ***778.6*** *p101*
Dufau, C. 24; New Orleans, 1848 ***778.6*** *p101*
Dufau, J. 4; New Orleans, 1848 ***778.6*** *p101*
Dufau, L. A. 34; New Orleans, 1848 ***778.6*** *p101*
Dufaut, J. B.; Louisiana, 1874 ***4981.45*** *p131*
Dufaye, Francoise; Quebec, 1673 ***4514.3*** *p309*
Dufenil, Charlotte Proffit *SEE* Dufenil, Thomas
Dufenil, Thomas; Quebec, 1649 ***9221.17*** *p212*
*Wife:*Charlotte Proffit
Duff, Christopher; Boston, 1859 ***7710.1*** *p160*
Duff, Jane 44; Ontario, 1871 ***1823.17*** *p45*
Duff, John 20; North Carolina, 1775 ***1422.10*** *p57*
Duff, Robert 27; Ontario, 1871 ***1823.17*** *p45*
Duff, Robert 35; Ontario, 1871 ***1823.17*** *p45*
Duff, Thomas 28; Ontario, 1871 ***1823.21*** *p97*
Duffard, Dominique 30; New Orleans, 1848 ***778.6*** *p101*
Duffaud, Mr. 35; Port uncertain, 1844 ***778.6*** *p101*
Duffee, Frank 40; Ontario, 1871 ***1823.21*** *p97*
Duffee, William 40; Ontario, 1871 ***1823.21*** *p97*
Duffet, Babette *SEE* Duffet, Wm. Edmund
Duffet, Johanna Henrietta Barrett *SEE* Duffet, Wm. Edmund
Duffet, Rosie *SEE* Duffet, Wm. Edmund
Duffet, Wm. Edmund; Chicago, 1854-1868 ***9228.50*** *p197*
*Wife:*Johanna Henrietta Barrett
*Child:*Babette
*Child:*Rosie
Duffett, Mark 51; Indiana, 1879-1882 ***9076.20*** *p70*
Duffey, Patrick; New England, 1745 ***1642*** *p28*
Duffin, Isaac; Ohio, 1809-1852 ***4511.35*** *p12*
Duffin, James 61; Ontario, 1871 ***1823.21*** *p97*
Duffin, John 53; Ontario, 1871 ***1823.21*** *p97*
Duffin, John 80; Ontario, 1871 ***1823.21*** *p97*
Duffin, Robert 50; Ontario, 1871 ***1823.21*** *p97*
Duffin, Samuel 55; Ontario, 1871 ***1823.21*** *p97*
Duffo, Jn.-Bte. 32; New Orleans, 1840 ***778.6*** *p101*
Duffus, Adam 52; Ontario, 1871 ***1823.17*** *p45*
Duffy, Ann 25; Ontario, 1871 ***1823.21*** *p97*
Duffy, Anthony; St. John, N.B., 1847 ***2978.15*** *p37*
Duffy, Charles; North Carolina, 1850 ***1088.45*** *p8*
Duffy, Charles 43; Ontario, 1871 ***1823.17*** *p45*
Duffy, Dominick 36; Ontario, 1871 ***1823.17*** *p45*
Duffy, Edward; South Carolina, 1861 ***6155.4*** *p18*
Duffy, Frances 40; Ontario, 1871 ***1823.17*** *p45*
Duffy, Francis; North Carolina, 1846 ***1088.45*** *p8*
Duffy, J. Hugh 38; Indiana, 1844-1868 ***9076.20*** *p66*
Duffy, James; St. John, N.B., 1847 ***2978.15*** *p36*
Duffy, James E. S.; North Carolina, 1833 ***1088.45*** *p8*
Duffy, Jane 56; Ontario, 1871 ***1823.21*** *p97*
Duffy, John; Boston, 1767 ***1642*** *p38*
Duffy, John; North Carolina, 1855 ***1088.45*** *p8*
Duffy, John 53; Ontario, 1871 ***1823.17*** *p45*
Duffy, John; South Carolina, 1854 ***6155.4*** *p18*
Duffy, John; Toronto, 1844 ***2910.35*** *p114*
Duffy, Mary; Toronto, 1844 ***2910.35*** *p113*
Duffy, Patrick; Ohio, 1834 ***3580.20*** *p31*
Duffy, Patrick; Ohio, 1834 ***6020.12*** *p7*
Duffy, Richard N.; North Carolina, 1845 ***1088.45*** *p8*
Duffy, William; Washington, 1882 ***2770.40*** *p135*
Dufiguier, Helene; Quebec, 1663 ***4514.3*** *p309*
Dufille, Miss 14; America, 1844 ***778.6*** *p101*
Dufille, Miss 16; America, 1844 ***778.6*** *p101*
Dufille, Miss 45; America, 1844 ***778.6*** *p101*
Dufille, Mrs. 9; America, 1844 ***778.6*** *p101*
Dufont, J. B. 37; America, 1845 ***778.6*** *p101*
DuFore, Catherine; Pennsylvania, 1650-1765 ***9228.50*** *p251*
Dufosse, Jeanne; Quebec, 1669 ***4514.3*** *p309*
Dufour, Mr. 47; America, 1843 ***778.6*** *p101*
Du Four, Catherine; Pennsylvania, 1650-1765 ***9228.50*** *p251*
Dufour, Chs. Honore 76; America, 1845 ***778.6*** *p101*
Du Four, Elizabeth; Wisconsin, 1854 ***9228.50*** *p198*
With 3 sons & daughter
Du Four, Elizabeth; Wisconsin, 1855 ***9228.50*** *p247*
With 3 sons & daughter
Dufour, Hilary; Chicago, 1800-1899 ***9228.50*** *p18A*
DuFour, Hilary; Wisconsin, 1854-1857 ***9228.50*** *p198*
Dufour, Jean; Quebec, 1647 ***9221.17*** *p179*
DuFour, Joseph; New York, 1853-1854 ***9228.50*** *p198*
Du Four, Josephine; North America, 1875-1975 ***9228.50*** *p198*
DuFour, Mary; Wisconsin, 1839-1878 ***9228.50*** *p198*
Du Four, Peter; Wisconsin, 1844 ***9228.50*** *p198*
DuFour, Peter C.; Wisconsin, 1853 ***9228.50*** *p198*
Du Four Family ; New York, 1875-1930 ***9228.50*** *p198*
Dufour Sauvage, Mr. 18; America, 1848 ***778.6*** *p101*
Dufrasne, Enriqu 30; America, 1847 ***778.6*** *p101*
Dufrechau, Jean 25; New Orleans, 1843 ***778.6*** *p101*
Dufrechau, Louis 23; New Orleans, 1843 ***778.6*** *p101*
Dufresne, . . .; Quebec, 1657 ***9221.17*** *p357*
Du Fresne, Elizabeth I. *SEE* Du Fresne, Mary Remon
Dufresne, Eugenie; New Orleans, 1848 ***778.6*** *p101*
Dufresne, Jacques 27; Montreal, 1661 ***9221.17*** *p472*
Du Fresne, James Philip; Utah, 1800-1858 ***9228.50*** *p198*
Du Fresne, Jane Mary *SEE* Du Fresne, Mary Remon
Dufresne, Jeanne; Quebec, 1666 ***4514.3*** *p309*
Du Fresne, John P. *SEE* Du Fresne, Mary Remon
Du Fresne, Mary; Salt Lake City, 1854 ***9228.50*** *p198*
*Child:*Mary Ann
*Child:*Peter C.
*Child:*Jane Mary
*Child:*Elizabeth I.
*Child:*John P.
Du Fresne, Mary Ann *SEE* Du Fresne, Mary Remon
Du Fresne, Peter C. *SEE* Du Fresne, Mary Remon
Dufresne, Pierre; Quebec, 1654 ***9221.17*** *p307*
Dufresne, Pierre 33; Quebec, 1661 ***9221.17*** *p454*
Du Fresne, Samuel 43; Lancaster, PA, 1835 ***9228.50*** *p198*
Du Fresne Family ; Detroit, n.d. ***9228.50*** *p198*
Dufrost deLa Jemerais, Christophe; Quebec, 1683-1688 ***2314.30*** *p168*
Dufrost deLa Jemerais, Christophe; Quebec, 1687 ***2314.30*** *p181*
Dufton, E. T. 51; Ontario, 1871 ***1823.21*** *p97*
Dufton, John 46; Ontario, 1871 ***1823.21*** *p97*
Dufur, Hepzibeth; Quebec, 1775 ***9228.50*** *p198*
Dufva, Knut Oscar; Minneapolis, 1887-1895 ***1865.50*** *p45*
*Wife:*Mathilda F.
Dufva, Mathilda F. *SEE* Dufva, Knut Oscar
Dugal, Charles; Louisiana, 1836-1840 ***4981.45*** *p212*
Dugald, Mary 72; Ontario, 1871 ***1823.17*** *p45*
Dugale, Thomas; Boston, 1766 ***1642*** *p37*
Dugalley, Jean; Quebec, 1638 ***9221.17*** *p76*
Dugan, Arthur 48; Ontario, 1871 ***1823.17*** *p45*
Dugan, Cornelius; New York, NY, 1837 ***3274.55*** *p25*
Dugan, David 40; Ontario, 1871 ***1823.17*** *p45*
Dugan, Matthew; Ohio, 1840-1897 ***8365.35*** *p16*
Dugan, Michael 50; Ontario, 1871 ***1823.17*** *p45*
Dugan, Sarah; Nantucket, MA, 1773 ***1642*** *p89*
Dugan, Thomas; Boston, 1772 ***1642*** *p49*
Dugas, Andre 35; New York, NY, 1920 ***930.50*** *p49*
Dugen, Thomas; Boston, 1744 ***1642*** *p45*
Duggan, Dennis; Boston, 1836 ***3274.55*** *p75*
Duggan, Dennis 30; Ontario, 1871 ***1823.17*** *p45*
Duggan, Dub; Colorado, 1873 ***1029.59*** *p24*
Duggan, Jacob 28; Indiana, 1868-1880 ***9076.20*** *p69*
Duggan, John 40; Ontario, 1871 ***1823.17*** *p45*
Duggan, Michael 70; Ontario, 1871 ***1823.17*** *p45*
Duggan, Patrick 81; Ontario, 1871 ***1823.21*** *p97*
Duggen, Martin; Colorado, 1864 ***1029.59*** *p24*
Duggin, Juda; Boston, 1765 ***1642*** *p34*
Duglas, Andrew 65; Ontario, 1871 ***1823.21*** *p97*
Duglas, John 32; Ontario, 1871 ***1823.21*** *p97*

110 *FOR A COMPLETE EXPLANATION OF ENTRY, SEE "HOW TO READ A CITATION" SECTION*

Duglas, John 50; Ontario, 1871 *1823.21* p97
Duglas, Robert; Boston, 1722 *1642* p25
Duglass, Jean; Boston, 1743 *1642* p45
Dugler, Antony 41; Ontario, 1871 *1823.21* p97
Dugless, George 51; Ontario, 1871 *1823.21* p97
Dugmore, Josiah; New York, 1777 *8529.30* p11
Duguay, Jeanne 35; Quebec, 1651 *9221.17* p242
Dugue, . . .; New Orleans, 1848 *778.6* p101
Dugue deBoisbriand, Sidrac; Quebec, 1665 *2314.30* p167
Dugue de Boisbriand, Sidrac; Quebec, 1665 *2314.30* p181
Duguid, Alex 62; Ontario, 1871 *1823.21* p97
Duguid, William 67; Ontario, 1871 *1823.21* p97
Du Hamel, . . .; Ohio, 1800-1899 *9228.50* p198
Duhamel, Antoine; Quebec, 1769 *9221.17* p406
Du Hamel, John *SEE* Du Hamel, Mary Le Gresley
Du Hamel, John *SEE* Du Hamel, Mary Le Gresley
Du Hamel, Julia *SEE* Du Hamel, Mary Le Gresley
Du Hamel, Leah *SEE* Du Hamel, Mary Le Gresley
Duhamel, Marie 42; Quebec, 1651 *9221.17* p242
  Daughter: Marie-Clemence 22
Duhamel, Marie-Clemence 22 *SEE* Duhamel, Marie Grandin
Du Hamel, Mary *SEE* Du Hamel, Mary Le Gresley
Du Hamel, Mary; Utah, 1851 *9228.50* p198
  Child: John
  Child: Julia
  Child: Leah
  Relative: John
  Child: Mary
Duhart, Bautista 22; California, 1878 *3276.8* p18
Duhaux, Jean Marie; Illinois, 1852 *6079.1* p4
Du Heaume, Jane 24; Toronto, 1864 *9228.50* p350
Du Heaume, Judith *SEE* Du Heaume, Pierre
Du Heaume, Pierre; Ohio, 1832-1836 *9228.50* p278
  Wife: Judith
DuHerisson, Anne 4; Quebec, 1636 *9221.17* p61
Duhlmeier, Engel Marie Eleonore; America, 1855 *7420.1* p137
Duhlmeyer, Engel Dorothee Louise; America, 1856 *7420.1* p153
  Daughter: Ilse Marie Charlotte
  Son: Hans Heinrich Conrad
  Son: Johann Philipp
  Daughter: Catharine Marie Dorothee
Duhlmeyer, Hans Heinrich; Port uncertain, 1853 *7420.1* p104
  With son & daughter
Duhlmeyer, Otto; America, 1853 *7420.1* p104
Duhlmeyer, Thrine Marie Sophie; America, 1852 *7420.1* p94
  Son: Johann Philipp
Duhn, Elisabeth; Valparaiso, Chile, 1850 *1192.4* p50
Duhn, Margaretha; Valparaiso, Chile, 1850 *1192.4* p50
Duig, John; St. John, N.B., 1847 *2978.15* p40
Duig, Pat; St. John, N.B., 1847 *2978.15* p40
Duignan, Mrs.; Toronto, 1844 *2910.35* p112
  Son: Francis
  Son: Terence J.
  Son: Cornelius
Duignan, Cornelius *SEE* Duignan, Mrs.
Duignan, Francis *SEE* Duignan, Mrs.
Duignan, Terence; Toronto, 1844 *2910.35* p112
Duignan, Terence J. *SEE* Duignan, Mrs.
Dujardin, Zoe 27; Port uncertain, 1841 *778.6* p101
Dujay, F. L. A.; Louisiana, 1836-1841 *4981.45* p208
Duke, Frank; Louisiana, 1874-1875 *4981.45* p298
Duke, Jane Quail *SEE* Duke, Thomas
Duke, Thomas 30; Ontario, 1871 *1823.21* p97
Duke, Thomas; Philadelphia, 1853 *8513.31* p303
  Wife: Jane Quail
Dulac, A. 30; America, 1843 *778.6* p101
Dulak, Ludwika 15; New York, NY, 1904 *8355.1* p15
Dulay, J.E. 28; Indiana, 1859-1876 *9076.20* p69
Dulever, Dennis 40; Ontario, 1871 *1823.21* p97
Dulignon deLamirande, Jean; Quebec, 1670 *2314.30* p172
Dulin, Luke; Boston, 1766 *1642* p37
DuLion, A. 26; America, 1848 *778.6* p101
Dulka, Emilia; Detroit, 1930 *1640.60* p77
Dulka, Emilija; Detroit, 1930 *1640.60* p78
Dullaghan, William; Ohio, 1809-1852 *4511.35* p12
Dulm, Charles; Illinois, 1851 *6079.1* p4
Dulmage, Adam 30; Ontario, 1871 *1823.17* p45
Dulmage, Eliza 38; Ontario, 1871 *1823.21* p97
Dulmage, Jacob 40; Ontario, 1871 *1823.17* p45
Dulordyer, Jean 27; America, 1841 *778.6* p101
du Loy, Pierre; Virginia, 1700 *9230.15* p80
Dulreuil, Cath. 26; New Orleans, 1846 *778.6* p101
Duls, Jacob; North Carolina, 1853 *1088.45* p8
Duluc, Mr. 40; New Orleans, 1848 *778.6* p101
Dumain, Felix 23; America, 1842 *778.6* p101

Dumaine, Jean 26; Quebec, 1638 *9221.17* p79
Dumais, Andre 16 *SEE* Dumais, Jean
Dumais, Etienne 20 *SEE* Dumais, Jean
Dumais, Jean; Quebec, 1644 *9221.17* p141
  Son: Etienne
  Wife: Miotte Lecombe
  Son: Andre
  Son: Jean
Dumais, Jean 13 *SEE* Dumais, Jean
Dumais, Miotte Lecombe *SEE* Dumais, Jean
Duman, Mr. 16; New Orleans, 1848 *778.6* p101
Dumange, Peter 36; New Orleans, 1843 *778.6* p101
Dumany, C. 10; New Orleans, 1844 *778.6* p101
Dumar, Charles 30; America, 1841 *778.6* p101
Dumarche, Charles 33; Quebec, 1635 *9221.17* p42
Dumaresq, . . .; Boston, 1769 *9228.50* p5
Dumaresq, Edward; Boston, 1717 *9228.50* p200
Dumaresq, Edward; Boston, 1745 *9228.50* p652
Dumaresq, Geo.; America, 1649-1700 *9228.50* p18A
Dumaresq, John; Boston, 1769 *9228.50* p48
Dumaresq, John; Boston, 1769 *9228.50* p200
Dumaresq, John *SEE* Dumaresq, Thomas
Dumaresq, John; New York, 1914-1983 *9228.50* p200
Dumaresq, Marie Le Brocq *SEE* Dumaresq, Thomas
Dumaresq, Philip; Boston, 1695-1716 *9228.50* p16
Dumaresq, Philip; Boston, 1695-1716 *9228.50* p199
Dumaresq, Rachel; Boston, 1800-1900 *9228.50* p200
Dumaresq, Sarah; Boston, 1800-1900 *9228.50* p200
Dumaresq, Steven; Boston, 1769 *9228.50* p200
Dumaresq, Stevens; Boston, 1769 *9228.50* p48
Dumaresq, Thomas; New Brunswick, 1800-1840 *9228.50* p193
  Brother: John
Dumaresq, Thomas; New England, 1698 *9228.50* p335
  Wife: Marie Le Brocq
Dumaresq, Thomas; Salem, MA, 1685 *9228.50* p200
Dumaresq, Thomas; Yorktown, VA, 1781 *9228.50* p576
Dumarin, Christina; Trenton, NJ, 1853 *8513.31* p431
Dumas, Mr. 21; America, 1846 *778.6* p102
Dumas, Mr. 59; America, 1841 *778.6* p102
Dumas, Alexandre 42; New Orleans, 1844 *778.6* p102
Dumas, Felix 29; New Orleans, 1848 *778.6* p102
Dumas, Francois 25; Louisiana, 1848 *778.6* p102
Dumas, Jacque 25; America, 1841 *778.6* p102
Dumas, Jean 22; Port uncertain, 1843 *778.6* p102
Dumas, Jerome; Virginia, 1700 *9230.15* p80
Dumas, L. C. 40; America, 1848 *778.6* p102
Dumayre, Jean 20; Quebec, 1655 *9221.17* p323
Dumdey, Julius; Wisconsin, 1880 *6795.8* p41
Dumesnil, Marie 12; Montreal, 1654 *9221.17* p317
Dumesnil, Richard 23; Quebec, 1654 *9221.17* p307
Dumesnil Heurry deSt-Marc, Jacques; Quebec, 1668 *2314.30* p171
Dumestre, Pierre 15; New Orleans, 1848 *778.6* p102
Dumestre, R.; Louisiana, 1874 *4981.45* p295
Dumets, Andre 16 *SEE* Dumets, Jean
Dumets, Etienne 20 *SEE* Dumets, Jean
Dumets, Jean; Quebec, 1644 *9221.17* p141
  Son: Etienne
  Wife: Miotte Lecombe
  Son: Andre
  Son: Jean
Dumets, Jean 13 *SEE* Dumets, Jean
Dumets, Miotte Lecombe *SEE* Dumets, Jean
Duministre, Mr. 19; New Orleans, 1840 *778.6* p102
Dumis, Cotter 30; Ontario, 1871 *1823.21* p97
Dumke, Auguste E.; Wisconsin, 1885 *6795.8* p123
Dummack, Eliz.; Maryland, 1674-1675 *1236.25* p51
Du Mont, . . .; Boston, 1729 *9228.50* p199
Dumont, A. C.; Louisiana, 1836-1840 *4981.45* p212
Dumont, Anne 40; Port uncertain, 1843 *778.6* p102
Dumont, Anne-Julienne; Quebec, 1665 *4514.3* p309
Dumont, Auguste Joseph; Wisconsin, 1856 *1495.20* p55
  Wife: Marie-Therese Houyout
  Daughter: Marie Barbe
Dumont, Aurence 36; New Orleans, 1843 *778.6* p102
Dumont, Barbe; Quebec, 1668 *4514.3* p309
Dumont, Francis Louis; Ohio, 1809-1852 *4511.35* p12
Dumont, Francois; Quebec, 1660 *9221.17* p434
Dumont, John James L.; Ohio, 1809-1852 *4511.35* p12
Dumont, M. 59; New Orleans, 1840 *778.6* p102
Dumont, Margaretha 44; Port uncertain, 1843 *778.6* p102
Dumont, Marie Barbe *SEE* Dumont, Auguste Joseph
Dumont, Marie-Therese Houyout *SEE* Dumont, Auguste Joseph
Dumont, Pierre 27; Mississippi, 1847 *778.6* p89
Dumont, Pierre 18; New Orleans, 1848 *778.6* p102
Dumontel, Pierre; Quebec, 1642 *9221.17* p116
Dumontel, Alphonse 25; America, 1847 *778.6* p102
Dumontier, Antoinette; Quebec, 1669 *4514.3* p310
Dumontier, Guillaume; Montreal, 1661 *9221.17* p472
Dumortier, Madeleine; Quebec, 1667 *4514.3* p310
Dumoulin, Alfred 19; America, 1841 *778.6* p102

Du Moulin, Augustine; Died enroute, 1810 *9228.50* p200
Dumoulin, Joseph; New York, 1860 *358.56* p149
Dumoulin, Sylvestre 36; America, 1746 *778.6* p102
Dumpair, Ludwig; Louisiana, 1874-1875 *4981.45* p298
Dumphey, Patrick; Boston, 1763 *1642* p32
Dun, Dorothy; Massachusetts, 1743 *1642* p89
Dun, John; New England, 1745 *1642* p28
Dun, Margret; Massachusetts, 1747 *1642* p111
Dunam, James 68; Ontario, 1871 *1823.21* p97
Dunard, Eloise 37; America, 1848 *778.6* p102
Dunard, Prutine 10; America, 1848 *778.6* p102
Dunavan, John; Boston, 1747 *1642* p29
Dunavan, Martin; Boston, 1764 *1642* p34
Dunavan, Mary; Boston, 1764 *1642* p34
Dunavaz, William; Boston, 1764 *1642* p34
Dunbar, Alex 60; Ontario, 1871 *1823.21* p97
Dunbar, Elsie 27; Ontario, 1871 *1823.21* p97
Dunbar, James 20; Ontario, 1871 *1823.21* p97
Dunbar, James 59; Ontario, 1871 *1823.21* p97
Dunbar, Joseph; New York, NY, 1832 *3274.55* p70
Dunbar, William 31; Ontario, 1871 *1823.17* p45
Dunbar, William 52; Ontario, 1871 *1823.21* p97
Duncan, Adam 74; Ontario, 1871 *1823.21* p45
Duncan, Alx 58; Ontario, 1871 *1823.17* p45
Duncan, Anderson 75; Ontario, 1871 *1823.21* p97
Duncan, Andrew; North Carolina, 1820-1825 *1088.45* p8
Duncan, Charles S. 48; Ontario, 1871 *1823.17* p45
Duncan, James 27; North Carolina, 1774 *1422.10* p58
Duncan, James 42; Ontario, 1871 *1823.17* p45
Duncan, James 60; Ontario, 1871 *1823.17* p45
Duncan, James 61; Ontario, 1871 *1823.21* p97
Duncan, James K. 46; Ontario, 1871 *1823.17* p45
Duncan, John 39; Ontario, 1871 *1823.21* p97
Duncan, John 59; Ontario, 1871 *1823.17* p45
Duncan, John 65; Ontario, 1871 *1823.17* p45
Duncan, Keith; North Carolina, 1844 *1088.45* p8
Duncan, Lewis Henry 37; Ontario, 1871 *1823.21* p97
Duncan, Mary 46; Ontario, 1871 *1823.21* p97
Duncan, Park 62; Ontario, 1871 *1823.17* p45
Duncan, Peter 40; Ontario, 1871 *1823.17* p45
Duncan, Peter 43; Ontario, 1871 *1823.17* p45
Duncan, Richard 32; Ontario, 1871 *1823.17* p45
Duncan, Richard; Philadelphia, 1777 *8529.30* p7A
Duncan, Robert; Boston, 1737 *1642* p26
Duncan, Robert; Washington, 1886 *2770.40* p195
Duncan, Susan 40; Ontario, 1871 *1823.17* p45
Duncan, Thomas 60; Ontario, 1871 *1823.17* p45
Duncan, William 26; Ontario, 1871 *1823.21* p98
Duncan, William 55; Ontario, 1871 *1823.21* p97
Duncan, William 56; Ontario, 1871 *1823.17* p45
Duncey, Aron 56; Ontario, 1871 *1823.21* p98
Duncker, Martin; Chile, 1852 *1192.4* p51
Dunckling, Elizabeth 11; Quebec, 1870 *8364.32* p23
Duncun, Andrew 30; Ontario, 1871 *1823.21* p98
Dundas, Amelia Sophia; Ontario, 1862 *9228.50* p201
Dundas, Gustavis 61; Ontario, 1871 *1823.21* p98
Dundas, James H. 41; Ontario, 1871 *1823.21* p98
Dundas, Mary 41; Ontario, 1871 *1823.21* p98
Dundas, Robert 30; Ontario, 1871 *1823.21* p98
Dundass, Charles 47; Ontario, 1871 *1823.21* p98
Dundass, George 66; Ontario, 1871 *1823.21* p98
Dundass, John 56; Ontario, 1871 *1823.21* p98
Dundass, John 60; Ontario, 1871 *1823.21* p98
Dundei, Julius; Wisconsin, 1880 *6795.8* p41
Dunels, Thomas 44; Ontario, 1871 *1823.17* p45
Dunet, David; Quebec, 1639 *9221.17* p87
Dunewart, John; Ohio, 1809-1852 *4511.35* p12
Dunewort, John; Ohio, 1809-1852 *4511.35* p12
Dunfay, Wm 30; St. Johns, N.F., 1811 *1053.20* p21
Dunfister, George 21; Quebec, 1910 *2897.7* p10
Dunfy, Richard 47; Ontario, 1871 *1823.17* p45
Dunham, James 35; Ontario, 1871 *1823.21* p98
Duniette, D. 46; New Orleans, 1842 *778.6* p102
Dunk, Joseph 29; New Orleans, 1843 *778.6* p102
Dunk, Louisa 24; New Orleans, 1843 *778.6* p102
Dunk, Marans A. 3; New Orleans, 1843 *778.6* p102
Dunkel, Friedrich *SEE* Dunkel, Johann
Dunkel, Jakob *SEE* Dunkel, Johann
Dunkel, Johann; America, 1867 *5475.1* p545
  Wife: Luise Karol. Elisabeth Stieh
  Son: Jakob
  Son: Friedrich
  Son: Karl
  Son: Philipp
Dunkel, Karl *SEE* Dunkel, Johann
Dunkel, Luise Karol. Elisabeth Stieh *SEE* Dunkel, Johann
Dunkel, Philipp *SEE* Dunkel, Johann
Dunkelan, A. Mgt.; New York, 1860 *358.56* p6
Dunkerque, Claude 10; Quebec, 1642 *9221.17* p112
Dunkin, Archibald 78; Ontario, 1871 *1823.17* p46
Dunkin, George 44; Ontario, 1871 *1823.21* p98
Dunkin, James 50; Ontario, 1871 *1823.21* p98

Dunkinson, Cathrin 64; Ontario, 1871 *1823.21* p98
Dunkinson, Peter 42; Ontario, 1871 *1823.21* p98
Dunkinson, Peter 66; Ontario, 1871 *1823.21* p98
Dunlever, Dennis 40; Ontario, 1871 *1823.21* p98
Dunlevy, John C.; Ohio, 1848 *3580.20* p31
Dunlevy, John C.; Ohio, 1848 *6020.12* p7
Dunlop, Alexander; Ohio, 1826 *3580.20* p31
Dunlop, Alexander; Ohio, 1826 *6020.12* p7
Dunlop, Andrew; Boston, 1797 *1642* p26
Dunlop, Barbara 54; Ontario, 1871 *1823.17* p46
Dunlop, Dunkin 50; Ontario, 1871 *1823.17* p46
Dunlop, Hamilton 62; Ontario, 1871 *1823.21* p98
Dunlop, Henry 30; Ontario, 1871 *1823.21* p98
Dunlop, James 28; Ontario, 1871 *1823.21* p98
Dunlop, James C. 75; Ontario, 1871 *1823.21* p98
Dunlop, John 22; Ontario, 1871 *1823.21* p98
Dunlop, John 38; Ontario, 1871 *1823.21* p98
Dunlop, Samuel 50; Ontario, 1871 *1823.21* p98
Dunlop, Samuel 55; Ontario, 1871 *1823.21* p98
Dunlop, Thomas 17; Ontario, 1871 *1823.17* p46
Dunlop, William; Boston, 1713 *1642* p24
Dunmaid, Thomas; Philadelphia, 1777 *8529.30* p2A
Dunn, Mrs.; Boston, 1766 *1642* p37
Dunn, Agnus 41; Ontario, 1871 *1823.17* p46
Dunn, Alexander 55; Ontario, 1871 *1823.21* p98
Dunn, Andrew; Massachusetts, 1721 *1642* p109
  *Wife:*Elizabeth
Dunn, Andrew; New York, NY, 1776 *8529.30* p2
Dunn, Ann 31; Michigan, 1880 *4491.30* p9
Dunn, Ann W. 46; Ontario, 1871 *1823.21* p98
Dunn, Bridget; New Orleans, 1850 *7242.30* p141
Dunn, Carroll; New York, 1776 *8529.30* p6
Dunn, Charles; Boston, 1749 *1642* p46
Dunn, David; Boston, 1753 *1642* p21
Dunn, Edward 34; Michigan, 1880 *4491.30* p9
Dunn, Edward 20; Ontario, 1871 *1823.21* p98
Dunn, Edward 64; Ontario, 1871 *1823.21* p98
Dunn, Edward 65; Ontario, 1871 *1823.21* p98
Dunn, Elizabeth SEE Dunn, Andrew
Dunn, Emily; Ontario, 1871 *1823.17* p46
Dunn, Frederick 41; Ontario, 1871 *1823.17* p46
Dunn, Henry 40; Ontario, 1871 *1823.21* p98
Dunn, James; Boston, 1835 *3274.55* p23
Dunn, James; Massachusetts, 1737 *1642* p113
Dunn, James 32; Ontario, 1871 *1823.21* p98
Dunn, James 35; Ontario, 1871 *1823.21* p98
Dunn, Jane SEE Dunn, John
Dunn, John; Boston, 1767 *1642* p38
Dunn, John; Massachusetts, 1745 *1642* p111
  *Wife:*Jane
Dunn, John 35; Michigan, 1880 *4491.30* p9
Dunn, John; New England, 1745 *1642* p28
Dunn, John 38; Ontario, 1871 *1823.21* p99
Dunn, John 41; Ontario, 1871 *1823.17* p46
Dunn, John 45; Ontario, 1871 *1823.21* p98
Dunn, John 72; Ontario, 1871 *1823.21* p98
Dunn, John, Jr.; Massachusetts, 1751 *1642* p102
Dunn, Margaret 25; Ontario, 1871 *1823.21* p99
Dunn, Mary 74; Ontario, 1871 *1823.21* p99
Dunn, Patrick; Boston, 1772 *1642* p49
Dunn, Patrick 53; Michigan, 1880 *4491.33* p8
Dunn, Rachael 20; Ontario, 1871 *1823.21* p99
Dunn, Richard 24; Ontario, 1871 *1823.21* p99
Dunn, Sarah Neely SEE Dunn, Thomas
Dunn, Thomas; Boston, 1763 *1642* p32
Dunn, Thomas; New York, 1783 *8529.30* p11
Dunn, Thomas 28; Ontario, 1871 *1823.21* p99
Dunn, Thomas 61; Ontario, 1871 *1823.17* p46
Dunn, Thomas; Philadelphia, 1778 *8529.30* p2A
Dunn, Thomas; Philadelphia, 1853 *8513.31* p304
  *Wife:*Sarah Neely
Dunn, William; Massachusetts, 1758 *1642* p110
Dunn, William 31; Ontario, 1871 *1823.17* p46
Dunn, William 37; Ontario, 1871 *1823.21* p99
Dunn, William 39; Ontario, 1871 *1823.21* p99
Dunnavan, Grissel; Boston, 1756 *1642* p47
Dunnavan, Margaret; Boston, 1756 *1642* p47
Dunnaven, Anna; Boston, 1768 *1642* p49
Dunnaven, Sarah; Boston, 1774 *1642* p50
Dunne, Bryan 40; Ontario, 1871 *1823.21* p99
Dunne, Charles 30; Ontario, 1871 *1823.21* p99
Dunne, Gregory 35; Ontario, 1871 *1823.17* p46
Dunne, Patrick 38; Ontario, 1871 *1823.21* p99
Dunne, Stephen; New Orleans, 1850 *7242.30* p141
Dunnel, Joseph; Boston, 1736 *1642* p44
Dunnel, Sarah; Boston, 1714 *1642* p24
Dunnemann, Engel Marie Sophie Eleonore; America, 1857 *7420.1* p162
Dunnenswager, Em.a 1; Louisiana, 1847 *778.6* p102
Dunnenswager, Emile 3; Louisiana, 1847 *778.6* p102
Dunnenswager, G. 44; Louisiana, 1847 *778.6* p102
Dunnenswager, Henriette 34; Louisiana, 1847 *778.6* p102

Dunnenswager, Wilhelm 6; Louisiana, 1847 *778.6* p102
Dunnett, Charles 46; Ontario, 1871 *1823.21* p99
Dunnigan, Kate 60; Ontario, 1871 *1823.21* p99
Dunning, John; Canada, 1774 *3036.5* p41
Dunowho, Julian; Boston, 1739 *1642* p44
Dunoyer, . . .; Nova Scotia, 1753 *3051* p112
Dunphy, Martin 29; New York, NY, 1826 *6178.50* p150
Dunse, Engel Sophie Caroline SEE Dunse, Johann Friedr. Conrad
Dunse, Johann Friedr. Conrad; America, 1869 *7420.1* p279
  *Wife:*Sophie Dorothee Schermer
  *Son:*Johann Heinr. Christoph
  *Daughter:*Engel Sophie Caroline
Dunse, Johann Heinr. Christoph SEE Dunse, Johann Friedr. Conrad
Dunse, Johann Heinrich; America, 1868 *7420.1* p270
Dunse, Sophie Dorothee Schermer SEE Dunse, Johann Friedr. Conrad
Dunsheath, Margaret; Philadelphia, 1867 *8513.31* p310
Dunsmore, James 47; Ontario, 1871 *1823.17* p46
Dunstan, Wm.; Toronto, 1920 *9228.50* p201
Dunton, Daniel 24; Florida, 1839 *8481.1* p18
Dunz, Lorens 28; New Orleans, 1848 *778.6* p102
Duon, Conrad 20; New Orleans, 1846 *778.6* p102
Duor, Jean 12; New Orleans, 1848 *778.6* p102
Dououenne, C.C. 22; New York, NY, 1856 *1766.1* p45
Dupah, Ann; Marblehead, MA, 1834 *9228.50* p201
Dupan, Louis Alfred 30; Port uncertain, 1840 *778.6* p103
Dupassy, James 22; America, 1846 *778.6* p103
Dupaty, C. 17; New Orleans, 1848 *778.6* p103
Dupechoir, Jean 23; America, 1845 *778.6* p103
Duperon, Francois 28; Quebec, 1638 *9221.17* p74
Duperon, Joseph-Imbert; Quebec, 1640 *9221.17* p93
Duperon, Marguerite Duplessis; Quebec, 1664 *4514.3* p315
Duperon, Marguerite Gaillard; Quebec, 1664 *4514.3* p315
Duperron, L. 37; New Orleans, 1846 *778.6* p103
Dupeux, Jean 29; America, 1843 *778.6* p103
Dupez, Mr. 35; New Orleans, 1845 *778.6* p103
Dupez, Mrs.; New Orleans, 1845 *778.6* p103
Dupiat, J. J.; Louisiana, 1874 *4981.45* p131
Dupierris, Francois; Louisiana, 1874-1875 *4981.45* p298
Dupin deBelugard, Jean-Baptiste; Quebec, 1727 *2314.30* p170
Dupin deBelugard, Jean-Baptiste; Quebec, 1727 *2314.30* p181
Duplauti, Margarita; Puerto Rico, 1817 *3476.25* p112
Duplessis, . . .; Quebec, 1652 *9221.17* p257
Duplessis, Marguerite; Quebec, 1664 *4514.3* p315
Duplessis, Nicolas; Quebec, 1653 *9221.17* p272
Duplessis, Pierre; Quebec, 1661 *9221.17* p456
DuPlessis-Bochart, Theodore; Quebec, 1632 *9221.17* p23
Dupong, Ab. Elisabeth; New Castle, DE, 1817-1818 *90.20* p150
Dupont, Mr. 35; America, 1747 *778.6* p103
Dupont, Mr. 27; Port uncertain, 1845 *778.6* p103
Dupont, Ambrose 24; America, 1848 *778.6* p103
Dupont, Anna Maria Conrad SEE Dupont, Michel
Dupont, Auguste 25; Missouri, 1845 *778.6* p103
Dupont, Francois 22; Quebec, 1659 *9221.17* p400
Dupont, Gilles 24; Quebec, 1660 *9221.17* p434
Dupont, Jakob SEE Dupont, Michel
Dupont, Johann SEE Dupont, Michel
Dupont, Julie 23; New Orleans, 1848 *778.6* p103
Dupont, Marie 21; Missouri, 1845 *778.6* p103
Dupont, Marie; Quebec, 1651 *9221.17* p242
  *Daughter:*Marie-Madeleine
  *Son:*Nicolas-Joseph
Dupont, Marie-Madeleine 16 SEE Dupont, Marie Gaulchet
Dupont, Michel SEE Dupont, Michel
Dupont, Michel; Pittsburgh, 1866 *5475.1* p433
  *Wife:*Anna Maria Conrad
  *Son:*Michel
  *Son:*Johann
  *Son:*Jakob
Dupont, Nicolas-Joseph 11 SEE Dupont, Marie Gaulchet
Dupont, Xaintes 40; Quebec, 1636 *9221.17* p53
  *Son:*Jean 16
  *Daughter:*Louise 4
  *Son:*Charles 7
  *Daughter:*Anne 11
Dupont deChambon deVergor, Louis; Quebec, 1751 *2314.30* p170
Dupont deChambon deVergor, Louis; Quebec, 1751 *2314.30* p181
Dupont deNeuville, Nicolas; Quebec, 1651 *2314.30* p167
Dupont deNeuville, Nicolas; Quebec, 1669 *2314.30* p181
Duportal, Ms. 25; New Orleans, 1840 *778.6* p231
Duportal, Jeanne Obin 56; New Orleans, 1840 *778.6* p103

Dupper, Christina 1 month; New York, NY, 1893 *1883.7* p42
Dupper, Johanna 20; New York, NY, 1893 *1883.7* p42
Dupper, Johannes 23; New York, NY, 1893 *1883.7* p42
Dupper, Karl 11 months; New York, NY, 1893 *1883.7* p42
Duppre, Maria Junker 30 SEE Duppre, Peter
Duppre, Peter SEE Duppre, Peter
Duppre, Peter; America, 1871 *5475.1* p418
  *Wife:*Maria Junker
  *Son:*Peter
Duprat, Mr. 25; America, 1848 *778.6* p103
Duprat, Mr. 30; America, 1747 *778.6* p103
Duprat, Mr. 54; America, 1747 *778.6* p103
Duprat, Mrs. 20; America, 1848 *778.6* p103
Duprat, Claude 28; New Orleans, 1848 *778.6* p103
Duprat, Dominique 24; America, 1845 *778.6* p103
Duprateau, . . .; Montreal, 1662 *9221.17* p497
Dupre, Anna Marie 7; New Orleans, 1848 *778.6* p103
Du Pre, Charles; Massachusetts, 1713 *9228.50* p201
Dupre, Francois; Quebec, 1654 *9221.17* p307
Dupre, Francoise; Quebec, 1669 *4514.3* p310
Dupre, J. 30; America, 1847 *778.6* p103
Dupre, J. 35; New Orleans, 1844 *778.6* p103
Dupre, Jacob 9; New Orleans, 1848 *778.6* p103
Dupre, Johan 2; New Orleans, 1848 *778.6* p103
Dupre, Nicolas 1; New Orleans, 1848 *778.6* p103
Dupre, Rosina 5; New Orleans, 1848 *778.6* p103
Dupres, Maurice; Ohio, 1809-1852 *4511.35* p12
Duprez, Miss 3; America, 1841 *778.6* p103
Duprez, Miss 5; America, 1841 *778.6* p103
Duprez, Mr. 35; America, 1841 *778.6* p103
Duprez, Ms. 33; America, 1841 *778.6* p103
Dupuis, Miss 6; New Orleans, 1840 *778.6* p104
Dupuis, Mr. 9; New Orleans, 1840 *778.6* p104
Dupuis, Mr. 11; New Orleans, 1840 *778.6* p104
Dupuis, Mr. 40; New Orleans, 1840 *778.6* p104
Dupuis, Mrs. 26; New Orleans, 1840 *778.6* p104
Dupuis, Catherine; Quebec, 1663 *4514.3* p310
Dupuis, Jean; Quebec, 1654 *9221.17* p307
Dupuis, Louis 23; America, 1848 *778.6* p104
Dupuis, Nicolas 20; Quebec, 1662 *9221.17* p484
Dupuis, Paul; Quebec, 1665 *2314.30* p167
Dupuis, Paul; Quebec, 1665 *2314.30* p181
Dupuis, Pierre; Quebec, 1650 *9221.17* p223
Dupuis, Sebastien; Quebec, 1654 *9221.17* p307
Dupuis, Ursule; Wisconsin, 1855 *1495.20* p40
Dupuy, . . .; Canada, n.d. *9228.50* p18A
Dupuy, Mr. 35; Port uncertain, 1845 *778.6* p104
Dupuy, Adolphus; Louisiana, 1836-1840 *4981.45* p212
Dupuy, Anne; Quebec, 1642 *9221.17* p121
Dupuy, Bernard 21; America, 1845 *778.6* p104
Dupuy, Guillaume 24; New Orleans, 1848 *778.6* p104
Dupuy, Jean 45; Quebec, 1655 *9221.17* p323
Dupuy, Pascal 30; New Orleans, 1846 *778.6* p104
Dupuy, Zacharie 45; Quebec, 1655 *9221.17* p323
du Pyn, Loys; Virginia, 1700 *9230.15* p81
Duqueld Geige, Henri 25; Port uncertain, 1847 *778.6* p104
Duquemin, . . .; America, 1912 *9228.50* p18A
Duquesnay, A. L. 21; America, 1846 *778.6* p104
Duquet, Denis 25; Quebec, 1637 *9221.17* p69
Duquet, Marie Dugenia; California, 1886 *3276.8* p19
Durain, Antoine 25; New Orleans, 1848 *778.6* p104
Durain, Hypolithe 27; New Orleans, 1848 *778.6* p104
Duran, A. 19; New Orleans, 1848 *778.6* p104
Duran, J. 19; New Orleans, 1848 *778.6* p104
Durance, Dannial 48; Ontario, 1871 *1823.17* p46
Durand, . . .; Quebec, 1659 *9221.17* p400
Durand, Dr. 44; America, 1846 *778.6* p104
Durand, Mr. 38; Louisiana, 1848 *778.6* p104
Durand, A. 24; America, 1848 *778.6* p104
Durand, Anne Claude 23; Port uncertain, 1846 *778.6* p104
Durand, Anne-Antoinette 23; Quebec, 1659 *9221.17* p400
Durand, Benvenuto; Louisiana, 1836-1840 *4981.45* p212
Durand, Catherine; Quebec, 1665 *4514.3* p310
Durand, Claude 29; America, 1843 *778.6* p104
Durand, Claude Francois 18; Port uncertain, 1846 *778.6* p104
Durand, Donald 70; Ontario, 1871 *1823.21* p99
Durand, Elisabeth; Quebec, 1670 *4514.3* p310
Durand, Eugenie 20; Port uncertain, 1846 *778.6* p104
Durand, Francoise 24; Port uncertain, 1846 *778.6* p104
Durand, Francoise SEE Durand, Francoise Brunet
Durand, Francoise; Quebec, 1663 *4514.3* p284
  *Child:*Jeanne
  *Child:*Francoise
Durand, Francoise; Quebec, 1670 *4514.3* p310
Durand, George 30; Port uncertain, 1846 *778.6* p104
Durand, Guillaume; Quebec, 1653 *9221.17* p272
Durand, James 43; Ontario, 1871 *1823.21* p99

Durand, Jean; Quebec, 1652 ***9221.17*** *p257*
Durand, Jean 21; Quebec, 1657 ***9221.17*** *p357*
Durand, Jeanne *SEE* Durand, Francoise Brunet
Durand, John 59; Ontario, 1871 ***1823.21*** *p99*
Durand, Joseph 24; Missouri, 1845 ***778.6*** *p104*
Durand, Nelson; Louisiana, 1836-1841 ***4981.45*** *p208*
Durand, Nicolas 25; Quebec, 1658 ***9221.17*** *p379*
Durand, Rollin M. 46; Ontario, 1871 ***1823.17*** *p46*
Durand, Suzanne; Quebec, 1667 ***4514.3*** *p310*
Durand, William 45; Ontario, 1871 ***1823.21*** *p99*
Duran Solet, Juan; Puerto Rico, 1829 ***3476.25*** *p112*
Duras, Cenek; Chicago, 1846-1910 ***2853.20*** *p405*
Duras, Cenek; Chicago, 1872 ***2853.20*** *p158*
Duraue, August; Illinois, 1859 ***6079.1*** *p4*
Duraue, Julian; Illinois, 1859 ***6079.1*** *p4*
Durawa, August; Wisconsin, 1890 ***6795.8*** *p55*
Durawa, John; Wisconsin, 1878 ***6795.8*** *p47*
Durban, Jakob; Wisconsin, 1873 ***6795.8*** *p100*
Durbois, Sebastien 27; Quebec, 1654 ***9221.17*** *p313*
Durdin, Alexander 40; Ontario, 1871 ***1823.21*** *p99*
Dureau, Aime; Quebec, 1652 ***9221.17*** *p258*
Durege, Julio 23; Port uncertain, 1846 ***778.6*** *p104*
Durell, Francis; Boston, 1715 ***9228.50*** *p205*
Durell, Peter; Boston, 1700-1799 ***9228.50*** *p205*
Durell, Peter; Boston, 1740 ***9228.50*** *p5*
Durell, Philip; New Hampshire, 1665-1745 ***9228.50*** *p202*
*Sister:*Rachel
Durell, Philippe; Nova Scotia, 1745 ***9228.50*** *p201*
Durell, Rachel; America, 1700-1793 ***9228.50*** *p359*
Durell, Rachel *SEE* Durell, Susan
Durell, Rachel *SEE* Durell, Philip
Durell, Susan; Canada, 1703 ***9228.50*** *p202*
*Sister:*Rachel
Durell, Susanna; Salem, MA, 1670 ***9228.50*** *p201*
Duren, Elisabeth 8 *SEE* Duren, Johann
Duren, Helena 10 *SEE* Duren, Johann
Duren, Johann; America, 1874 ***5475.1*** *p256*
*Wife:*Maria Kohl
*Daughter:*Elisabeth
*Daughter:*Maria
*Daughter:*Helena
Duren, Maria 11 *SEE* Duren, Johann
Duren, Maria Kohl 36 *SEE* Duren, Johann
Durernberger, Frederick; Ohio, 1809-1852 ***4511.35*** *p12*
Durero, Charles 34; New Orleans, 1848 ***778.6*** *p104*
Durero, Pierre Joseph 25; New Orleans, 1848 ***778.6*** *p104*
Durham, Henry; Toronto, 1844 ***2910.35*** *p112*
Durham, Margaret 80; Ontario, 1871 ***1823.17*** *p46*
Duri, Maria 2; America, 1847 ***778.6*** *p104*
Duri, Maria 22; America, 1847 ***778.6*** *p104*
Duri, Wendel 44; America, 1847 ***778.6*** *p104*
Durian, John; North Carolina, 1710 ***3629.40*** *p8*
Durian, Mary; North Carolina, 1710 ***3629.40*** *p8*
Duriene, J.C. 24; New York, NY, 1856 ***1766.1*** *p45*
Durieu, Theodore 33; New Orleans, 1844 ***778.6*** *p105*
Durin, Moses; Massachusetts, 1660 ***9228.50*** *p203*
Durin, Philip; New Hampshire, 1665-1745 ***9228.50*** *p202*
Durin, Susanna; Salem, MA, 1670 ***9228.50*** *p201*
During, Marcel.n 33; Louisiana, 1848 ***778.6*** *p105*
Duringer, Balthasar; America, 1855 ***2526.42*** *p94*
Duringer, Balthasar *SEE* Duringer, Georg Adam
Duringer, Eva Margareta *SEE* Duringer, Georg Adam
Duringer, Georg Adam; America, 1858 ***2526.42*** *p94*
*Wife:*Eva Margareta
*Child:*Katharina
*Child:*Philipp
*Child:*Leonhard
*Child:*Balthasar
Duringer, Katharina *SEE* Duringer, Georg Adam
Duringer, Leonhard *SEE* Duringer, Georg Adam
Duringer, Philipp *SEE* Duringer, Georg Adam
Durken, Miles; Illinois, 1860 ***6079.1*** *p4*
Durkin, James 35; Ontario, 1871 ***1823.21*** *p99*
Durkin, Martin 47; Ontario, 1871 ***1823.21*** *p99*
Durkin, Michael 36; Ontario, 1871 ***1823.21*** *p99*
Durks, John 27; Boston, 1835 ***6424.55*** *p30*
Durlacher, Ferdinand Nathan; North Carolina, 1856 ***1088.45*** *p8*
Durler, Englebert; Kansas, 1917-1918 ***2094.25*** *p50*
Durler, Frank Joseph; Kansas, 1917-1918 ***2094.25*** *p50*
Durmmond, John; North Carolina, 1775 ***1422.10*** *p56*
Durnay, Arundal 12; Ontario, 1871 ***1823.17*** *p46*
Durob, Thomas 22; Ontario, 1871 ***1823.21*** *p99*
Duroisier, Philipp 30; New Orleans, 1848 ***778.6*** *p105*
Duroisin, Louis 13; New Orleans, 1848 ***778.6*** *p105*
Duroisin, Marie 35; New Orleans, 1848 ***778.6*** *p105*
Duroisin, Pier.e 14; New Orleans, 1848 ***778.6*** *p105*
Duros, John 39; America, 1843 ***778.6*** *p105*
Durosaire, Esperance; Quebec, 1668 ***4514.3*** *p311*
Durouthy, Jean 18; America, 1840 ***778.6*** *p105*
DuRouvray, Michel 2; Quebec, 1636 ***9221.17*** *p57*
Durr, Christiane; America, 1883 ***179.55*** *p19*
Durr, Karl August; Ohio, 1840-1897 ***8365.35*** *p16*
Durrell, Joseph; Quebec, 1769-1842 ***9228.50*** *p203*
Durrell, Moses; Massachusetts, 1660 ***9228.50*** *p203*
Durrell, Peter; Boston, 1700-1799 ***9228.50*** *p205*
Durrell, Philip; New Hampshire, 1665-1745 ***9228.50*** *p202*
Durrell, Philippe; Nova Scotia, 1745 ***9228.50*** *p201*
Durrell, Thomas; Boston, 1724 ***9228.50*** *p201*
Durrfeld, Ludwig; America, 1883 ***5475.1*** *p385*
Durringer, Ignace 5; Louisiana, 1848 ***778.6*** *p105*
Durringer, Ignace 43; Louisiana, 1848 ***778.6*** *p105*
Durringer, Louis 8; Louisiana, 1848 ***778.6*** *p105*
Durringer, Madelaine 10; Louisiana, 1848 ***778.6*** *p105*
Durringer, Madelaine 43; Louisiana, 1848 ***778.6*** *p105*
Durringer, Marie Rose 9; Louisiana, 1848 ***778.6*** *p105*
Durringer, Michel 3; Louisiana, 1848 ***778.6*** *p105*
Durroux, J. M. 20; New Orleans, 1848 ***778.6*** *p105*
Durrue, P. Jonsson; New York, NY, 1851 ***6412.40*** *p152*
Durst, Bertha Schickhardt *SEE* Durst, Conrad
Durst, Conrad; Philadelphia, 1857 ***8513.31*** *p304*
*Wife:*Bertha Schickhardt
Durst, Jakob; Iowa, 1913 ***1211.15*** *p10*
Durton, William 26; America, 1844 ***778.6*** *p105*
Duruau, Martine; Quebec, 1647 ***9221.17*** *p188*
Durudine, Jean; Quebec, 1650 ***9221.17*** *p225*
Dury, Gaspard; Boston, 1870 ***1494.20*** *p11*
Dusance, James 39; Ontario, 1871 ***1823.17*** *p46*
Dusante Delacroix, Mr. 35; America, 1846 ***778.6*** *p105*
Dusanter, Mrs. 37; America, 1843 ***778.6*** *p105*
Dusaucay, Marie-Anne; Quebec, 1670 ***4514.3*** *p311*
Dusault, Toussaint 23; Quebec, 1638 ***9221.17*** *p81*
Dusceau, Elie 27; Quebec, 1662 ***9221.17*** *p484*
Dusch, Jacques; Louisiana, 1874 ***4981.45*** *p131*
Dusee, Peter; Boston, 1718 ***9228.50*** *p87*
Dusee, Peter; Boston, 1718 ***9228.50*** *p197*
Dusek, Bartolomej; St. Louis, 1896 ***2853.20*** *p54*
Dusek, Josef; Chicago, 1857 ***2853.20*** *p389*
Dusel, Babette; Philadelphia, 1859 ***8513.31*** *p317*
Dusel, Frederick; Ohio, 1840-1897 ***8365.35*** *p16*
Dushinski, Anna; Wisconsin, 1903 ***6795.8*** *p164*
Dusne, V. 20; Mobile, AL, 1845 ***778.6*** *p105*
Du Souchet, Francis; Ohio, 1823 ***9228.50*** *p205*
Du Souchet, John *SEE* Du Souchet, Thomas
Du Souchet, Nicholas *SEE* Du Souchet, Thomas
Du Souchet, Peter *SEE* Du Souchet, Thomas
Du Souchet, Peter *SEE* Du Souchet, Thomas
Du Souchet, Thomas; Ohio, 1807 ***9228.50*** *p566*
*Brother:*Peter
*Cousin:*Peter
*Brother:*Nicholas
*Brother:*John
Dusram, Mr. 25; Port uncertain, 1840 ***778.6*** *p105*
Dussablon, Leonard C. 34; Port uncertain, 1848 ***778.6*** *p105*
Dussant, Jean 51; New Orleans, 1848 ***778.6*** *p105*
Dusseaud, Mr. 46; Port uncertain, 1844 ***778.6*** *p105*
Dusseaux, J. 47; New Orleans, 1843 ***778.6*** *p105*
Dusson, Marguerite; Quebec, 1670 ***4514.3*** *p311*
Duston, Amelia Beatrice Byam; Honduras, 1982 ***9228.50*** *p360*
Duszynski, Stanislaus; Texas, 1884 ***6015.15*** *p25*
Dutartre, Francois; Quebec, 1648 ***9221.17*** *p198*
du Tartre, Francois; Virginia, 1700 ***9230.15*** *p81*
Dutartre, Pierre; Quebec, 1654 ***9221.17*** *p308*
Dutasta, Jean 21; Quebec, 1659 ***9221.17*** *p400*
Dutaut, Charles 15 *SEE* Dutaut, Jeanne Perrin
Dutaut, Jeanne; Quebec, 1658 ***9221.17*** *p379*
*Daughter:*Marie-Michelle
*Son:*Charles
*Daughter:*Madeleine
Dutaut, Madeleine 9 *SEE* Dutaut, Jeanne Perrin
Dutaut, Marie-Michelle 22 *SEE* Dutaut, Jeanne Perrin
Dutchman, Charles; North Carolina, 1856 ***1088.45*** *p8*
Duteil, Rene; Quebec, 1647 ***9221.17*** *p180*
Dutel, Mr. 15; Port uncertain, 1844 ***778.6*** *p105*
Dutertre, Antoinette 20; Quebec, 1657 ***9221.17*** *p357*
Dutertre, Francoise 27; Quebec, 1651 ***9221.17*** *p240*
DuTertre, Francoise 27; Quebec, 1651 ***9221.17*** *p241*
Dutertre, J. J. 23; New Orleans, 1848 ***778.6*** *p105*
Dutertre, Jean; Quebec, 1657 ***9221.17*** *p357*
Dutertre, Rene 34; Quebec, 1661 ***9221.17*** *p462*
Duthorel, Nicolas; Quebec, 1645 ***9221.17*** *p153*
Duthy, Auguste 33; Missouri, 1848 ***778.6*** *p105*
Dutilloy, J. 32; America, 1842 ***778.6*** *p105*
Dutour, Louis; Louisiana, 1874-1875 ***4981.45*** *p298*
Dutrey, Mr. 26; Port uncertain, 1840 ***778.6*** *p105*
Dutt, Georg; America, 1875 ***5475.1*** *p226*
Dutt, Nikolaus; America, 1869 ***5475.1*** *p225*
Dutten, William; New York, 1776 ***8529.30*** *p11*
Dutter, Chs. 26; America, 1841 ***778.6*** *p105*
Duttlinger, Geo.; Ohio, 1840-1897 ***8365.35*** *p16*
Dutton, Benjamin; Ohio, 1844 ***2763.1*** *p9*
Dutton, Samuel Dalton 46; Ontario, 1871 ***1823.21*** *p99*
Dutton, William 45; Ontario, 1871 ***1823.21*** *p99*
Duttrie, Pierre; Louisiana, 1836-1840 ***4981.45*** *p212*
Dutuit, Felicite 39; Port uncertain, 1843 ***778.6*** *p106*
Duval, Capt.; Quebec, 1800-1840 ***9228.50*** *p206*
Duval, A. 30; America, 1843 ***778.6*** *p106*
Duval, Alexander; North Carolina, 1849 ***1088.45*** *p8*
Duval, Arsene 21; Louisiana, 1845 ***778.6*** *p106*
Duval, Augustus; Ohio, 1809-1852 ***4511.35*** *p12*
Duval, Caesar; South Carolina, 1833 ***6155.4*** *p18*
Duval, Charles 31; Louisiana, 1848 ***778.6*** *p106*
Duval, Francois; Quebec, n.d. ***9228.50*** *p206*
Duval, Francoise; Quebec, 1670 ***4514.3*** *p311*
Duval, Gabriel 30; America, 1847 ***778.6*** *p106*
Duval, Guillaume; Quebec, 1660 ***9221.17*** *p435*
Duval, Jeanne Labarbe 51 *SEE* Duval, Pierre
Duval, Julia 26; Port uncertain, 1840 ***778.6*** *p106*
Duval, Lezar; South Carolina, 1811 ***6155.4*** *p18*
Duval, Louis; Quebec, 1659 ***9221.17*** *p400*
Duval, Louise 20; Quebec, 1659 ***9221.17*** *p400*
Duval, Madeleine 16 *SEE* Duval, Pierre
Duval, Marie 23 *SEE* Duval, Pierre
Duval, Marie-Madeleine; Quebec, 1671 ***4514.3*** *p311*
Duval, Marin; Quebec, 1659 ***9221.17*** *p400*
Duval, Michelle; Quebec, 1670 ***4514.3*** *p311*
Duval, Nicolas; Montreal, 1653 ***9221.17*** *p289*
Duval, Nicolas *SEE* Duval, Pierre
Duval, Philippe; New Brunswick, 1771-1862 ***9228.50*** *p206*
Duval, Philippe; Quebec, 1861 ***9228.50*** *p205*
Duval, Pierre *SEE* Duval, Pierre
Duval, Pierre 51; Quebec, 1653 ***9221.17*** *p272*
*Wife:*Jeanne Labarbe 51
*Daughter:*Marie 23
*Son:*Pierre
*Daughter:*Madeleine 16
*Son:*Romain 11
*Son:*Nicolas
Duval, Romain 11 *SEE* Duval, Pierre
Duval, Suzanne 18; Quebec, 1657 ***9221.17*** *p357*
Duvallon, Charles; Quebec, 1654 ***9221.17*** *p308*
Duvar, Arthur 38; Ontario, 1871 ***1823.21*** *p99*
duVault, Anne 35; Quebec, 1649 ***9221.17*** *p213*
DuVaultpain, Martin; Quebec, 1638 ***9221.17*** *p76*
Duverdier, Francoise 21; Montreal, 1659 ***9221.17*** *p428*
DuVergee, Joseph; Boston, 1755 ***9228.50*** *p21A*
DuVergee, Joseph; Nova Scotia, 1755-1800 ***9228.50*** *p21A*
*Wife:*Mary Blewett
DuVergee, Mary Blewett *SEE* DuVergee, Joseph
Du Vergee Family ; Nova Scotia, n.d. ***9228.50*** *p650*
Duverger, Emma 4; America, 1843 ***778.6*** *p106*
Duverger, Francoise 17; Montreal, 1659 ***9221.17*** *p420*
*Sister:*Suzanne 17
Duverger, Maria 20; America, 1843 ***778.6*** *p106*
Duverger, Suzanne 17 *SEE* Duverger, Francoise
Duvernay, Jean; Quebec, 1638 ***9221.17*** *p76*
Duvie, Antoine 24; America, 1847 ***778.6*** *p106*
Duviez, Jos.; Louisiana, 1874 ***4981.45*** *p295*
Duvivier, Adrienne 21; Montreal, 1647 ***9221.17*** *p192*
Duvivier, Adrienne 21; Montreal, 1647 ***9221.17*** *p192*
Duvivier, Philippe; Virginia, 1700 ***9230.15*** *p80*
Duwel, Bernard; Ohio, 1840-1897 ***8365.35*** *p16*
Duwel, Henry; Ohio, 1840-1897 ***8365.35*** *p16*
Duwelshoft, Heinrich; America, 1867 ***7420.1*** *p255*
Duxin, Francois 33; America, 1842 ***778.6*** *p106*
Duyer, William 61; Ontario, 1871 ***1823.21*** *p99*
Duzban, Jean 19; New Orleans, 1848 ***778.6*** *p106*
Duzenski, Stanislaus; Texas, 1884 ***6015.15*** *p25*
Dvorak, Frantisek; Iowa, 1854 ***2853.20*** *p230*
Dvorak, Frantisek; Iowa, 1870 ***2853.20*** *p202*
Dvorak, Ignac; Nebraska, 1871-1872 ***2853.20*** *p176*
Dvorak, Ignac, Sr.; Nebraska, 1876-1877 ***2853.20*** *p172*
Dvorak, Josef; Illinois, 1853-1910 ***2853.20*** *p471*
Dvorak, Josef; Nebraska, 1850-1910 ***2853.20*** *p182*
Dvorak, Vaclav; South Dakota, 1886 ***2853.20*** *p248*
Dvorak, Vaclav; Wisconsin, 1865-1869 ***2853.20*** *p316*
Dvorak, Vojtech; Nebraska, 1874 ***2853.20*** *p171*
Dwire, Michael; Toronto, 1844 ***2910.35*** *p115*
Dwire, William 22; Michigan, 1880 ***4491.30*** *p10*
Dwyer, Cornelius; New Orleans, 1851 ***7242.30*** *p141*
Dwyer, John; Boston, 1832 ***3274.55*** *p69*
Dwyer, John; New Orleans, 1851 ***7242.30*** *p141*
Dwyer, John; Newport, RI, 1831 ***3274.55*** *p66*
Dwyer, Joseph 45; Ontario, 1871 ***1823.21*** *p99*
Dwyer, Mary; Ohio, 1860 ***8513.31*** *p311*
Dwyer, Saney; New Orleans, 1851 ***7242.30*** *p141*
Dwyer, Stephen 50; Ontario, 1871 ***1823.21*** *p99*
Dwyer, Timothy; Toronto, 1844 ***2910.35*** *p116*
Dwyer, William 60; Ontario, 1871 ***1823.21*** *p99*
Dwyre, John 22; Ontario, 1871 ***1823.21*** *p99*
Dyaon, P.; Montreal, 1922 ***4514.4*** *p32*
Dyas, John 63; Ontario, 1871 ***1823.21*** *p99*
Dyas, John T. 32; Ontario, 1871 ***1823.21*** *p99*
Dybus, John; Detroit, 1929-1930 ***6214.5*** *p69*

Dych, Michel; Wisconsin, 1885 *6795.8 p33*
Dyck, David 4; New York, NY, 1893 *1883.7 p45*
Dyck, Heinr. 2; New York, NY, 1893 *1883.7 p45*
Dyck, Johann 25; New York, NY, 1893 *1883.7 p45*
Dyck, Maria 22; New York, NY, 1893 *1883.7 p45*
Dyde, Charles 47; Ontario, 1871 *1823.21 p99*
Dye, William; Barbados or St. Christopher, 1780 *8529.30 p7A*
Dyer, Mr.; Massachusetts, 1754 *1642 p108*
Dyer, Alida 11; Quebec, 1870 *8364.32 p23*
Dyer, Anthony; North America, n.d. *9228.50 p206*
Dyer, Edward 35; Ontario, 1871 *1823.21 p99*
Dyer, Elizabeth *SEE* Dyer, George
Dyer, Emanuel 21; Ontario, 1871 *1823.21 p100*
Dyer, George; Massachusetts, 1630 *117.5 p153*
  With wife
  *Daughter:*Elizabeth
  *Daughter:*Mary
Dyer, James E. 42; Ontario, 1871 *1823.21 p100*
Dyer, John; North Carolina, 1856 *1088.45 p8*
Dyer, John 24; Ontario, 1871 *1823.21 p100*
Dyer, Joseph 21; North Carolina, 1774 *1422.10 p56*
Dyer, Luke 40; Ontario, 1871 *1823.21 p100*
Dyer, Luke 69; Ontario, 1871 *1823.21 p100*
Dyer, Mary *SEE* Dyer, George
Dyer, Phillip 35; Ontario, 1871 *1823.17 p46*
Dyer, Thomas 34; Ontario, 1871 *1823.21 p100*
Dyer, William 26; Ontario, 1871 *1823.21 p100*

Dyer, Wm.; West Indies, 1640-1660 *9228.50 p206*
Dygon, John; Detroit, 1929-1930 *6214.5 p65*
Dyhrkopp, Christian H. F.; Iowa, 1896 *1211.15 p10*
Dyk, Anna 16; New York, NY, 1893 *1883.7 p45*
Dyk, Heinr. 18; New York, NY, 1893 *1883.7 p45*
Dyk, Heinrich 51; New York, NY, 1893 *1883.7 p45*
Dyk, Jacob 7; New York, NY, 1893 *1883.7 p45*
Dyk, Marga. 51; New York, NY, 1893 *1883.7 p45*
Dyk, Peter 14; New York, NY, 1893 *1883.7 p45*
Dyk, Sara 13; New York, NY, 1893 *1883.7 p45*
Dyke, James 33; Ontario, 1871 *1823.21 p100*
Dyke, William 52; Ontario, 1871 *1823.21 p100*
Dykeman, Jas 26; Ontario, 1871 *1823.21 p100*
Dyken, Henry Van; Boston, 1899 *6212.1 p16*
Dykers, Thomas M.; Louisiana, 1836-1840 *4981.45 p212*
Dykes, John 60; Ontario, 1871 *1823.21 p100*
Dykowski, John; New York, NY, 1906 *6015.15 p9*
Dylla, Frank; Texas, 1855-1886 *9980.22 p16*
Dylla, Frank 22; Texas, 1886 *9980.22 p17*
Dylla, Frank 59; Texas, 1884 *9980.22 p17*
Dymock, William 39; Ontario, 1871 *1823.21 p100*
Dymott, Elizabeth 14; Quebec, 1870 *8364.32 p23*
Dymott, Sarah 15; Quebec, 1870 *8364.32 p23*
Dyne, Luke; Virginia, 1652 *6254.4 p243*
Dynes, Letitia 50; Ontario, 1871 *1823.17 p46*
Dypka, Jan; Detroit, 1930 *1640.60 p78*
Dypka, Teofila; Detroit, 1930 *1640.60 p77*
Dyre, Joseph; New England, 1745 *1642 p28*

Dyson, Arthur; Iowa, 1920 *1211.15 p10*
Dyson, Eli; New York, NY, 1841 *3274.56 p72*
Dyson, John 75; Ontario, 1871 *1823.21 p100*
Dyson, John W.; Ohio, 1809-1852 *4511.35 p12*
Dyson, Sarah 73; Ontario, 1871 *1823.21 p100*
Dyson, William 42; Ontario, 1871 *1823.21 p100*
Dystiniffe, Hiram 35; Ontario, 1871 *1823.17 p46*
Dzedzak, Piotr 18; New York, NY, 1911 *6533.11 p10*
Dzengloviez, Teodor; New York, NY, 1882 *6015.15 p25*
Dzenko, John; Detroit, 1930 *1640.60 p77*
  *Wife:*Karolina Kolasa
Dzenko, Karolina Kolasa *SEE* Dzenko, John
Dziadus, Aleksander 20; New York, NY, 1904 *8355.1 p15*
Dziedzic, Mary; Detroit, 1929 *1640.55 p113*
Dzieglewicz, Albert; Texas, 1879 *6015.15 p25*
Dzieglewicz, Alexander; New York, NY, 1881 *6015.15 p25*
Dzieglewicz, Louis; New York, NY, 1882 *6015.15 p25*
Dzieglewicz, Teodor; New York, NY, 1882 *6015.15 p25*
Dzieglewiez, Albert; Texas, 1879 *6015.15 p25*
Dzieglewiez, Alexander; New York, NY, 1881 *6015.15 p25*
Dzieglewiez, Louis; New York, NY, 1882 *6015.15 p25*
Dziminska, Elizabeth; Detroit, 1929 *1640.55 p115*
Dzschoschel, Julius 42; New York, NY, 1883 *8427.14 p44*

FOR A COMPLETE EXPLANATION OF ENTRY, SEE "HOW TO READ A CITATION" SECTION

E

Eace, Patrick 70; Ontario, 1871 *1823.21* p100
Eagan, Catharine 47; Ontario, 1871 *1823.17* p46
Eagan, M. H.; Louisiana, 1874-1875 *4981.45* p298
Eagane, Mary; Boston, 1745 *1642* p46
Eagen, Elizabeth; Roxbury, MA, 1743 *1642* p108
Eagen, James 45; Ontario, 1871 *1823.21* p100
Eagen, Mich 38; Ontario, 1871 *1823.21* p100
Eager, Charles; Ohio, 1809-1852 *4511.35* p12
Eager, John; Ohio, 1840 *2763.1* p9
Eagin, Esther; Boston, 1739 *1642* p45
Eagle, Edward; Marston's Wharf, 1782 *8529.30* p11
Eakin, Jane; Philadelphia, 1850 *8513.31* p299
Eakins, Samuel 35; Ontario, 1871 *1823.21* p100
Eames, Robert; Philadelphia, 1777 *8529.30* p2
Earekson, William; Colorado, 1890 *1029.59* p24
Earhardt, David 12; Ontario, 1871 *1823.21* p100
Earhart, Adolph; Kansas, 1903 *1447.20* p65
Earl, Alfcus 36; Ontario, 1871 *1823.17* p46
Earl, Alfred 25; Ontario, 1871 *1823.17* p46
Earl, George 59; Ontario, 1871 *1823.17* p46
Earl, James 21; Ontario, 1871 *1823.17* p46
Earl, Richard 16; Quebec, 1870 *8364.32* p23
Early, Buell 44; Ontario, 1871 *1823.21* p100
Early, James 56; Ontario, 1871 *1823.21* p100
Early, Samuel 48; Ontario, 1871 *1823.21* p100
Earns, John C.; New York, NY, 1840 *3274.56* p100
Earnsby, Jane A.; Pennsylvania, 1856 *8513.31* p416
Earth, Anton 22; Galveston, TX, 1844 *3967.10* p370
Easpery, Edward 14; Ontario, 1871 *1823.21* p100
East, Cornelius 23; Ontario, 1871 *1823.21* p100
East, William 60; Ontario, 1871 *1823.21* p100
Eastabrook, William 40; Ontario, 1871 *1823.21* p100
Eastham, George; New York, 1783 *8529.30* p11
Eastman, Cordelia 19; Ontario, 1871 *1823.21* p100
Eastman, Ellen 13; Ontario, 1871 *1823.17* p46
Eastman, George 37; Ontario, 1871 *1823.17* p46
Eastman, Lutia 47; Ontario, 1871 *1823.17* p46
Eastman, Nial 69; Ontario, 1871 *1823.17* p46
Eastman, T. F. 47; Ontario, 1871 *1823.17* p46
Eastman, William 38; Ontario, 1871 *1823.17* p46
Eastman, William 50; Ontario, 1871 *1823.21* p100
Easton, Wm 29; Ontario, 1871 *1823.21* p100
Eastwood, Sarah 16; North Carolina, 1774 *1422.10* p56
Eath, Moses; Ohio, 1809-1852 *4511.35* p12
Eaton, Francis; Plymouth, MA, 1620 *1920.45* p5
  *Wife:*Sarah
  *Son:*Samuell
Eaton, George; New York, 1782 *8529.30* p11
Eaton, James 29; Ontario, 1871 *1823.21* p101
Eaton, James 40; Ontario, 1871 *1823.21* p101
Eaton, James 52; Ontario, 1871 *1823.21* p101
Eaton, John 50; Ontario, 1871 *1823.21* p101
Eaton, Mary 17; Quebec, 1870 *8364.32* p23
Eaton, Philip 50; Ontario, 1871 *1823.21* p101
Eaton, Samuell *SEE* Eaton, Francis
Eaton, Sarah *SEE* Eaton, Francis
Eaves, G.; Montreal, 1922 *4514.4* p32
Eavins, George 48; Ontario, 1871 *1823.17* p46
Eavoy, James 60; Ontario, 1871 *1823.21* p101
Ebarias, Valeri 28; Port uncertain, 1841 *778.6* p106
Ebbert, Mary 30 *SEE* Ebbert, Peter
Ebbert, Peter 28; Ohio, 1880 *4879.40* p257
  *Wife:*Mary 30
Ebbinghaus, Charles; Washington, 1883 *2770.40* p136
Ebel, Francois 29; Mississippi, 1847 *778.6* p106
Ebeling, Mr.; America, 1853 *7420.1* p104
Ebeling, Carl; America, 1859 *7420.1* p184

Ebeling, Carl Friedrich August *SEE* Ebeling, Carl
  Friedrich Wilhelm
Ebeling, Carl Friedrich Wilhelm *SEE* Ebeling, Carl
  Friedrich Wilhelm
Ebeling, Carl Friedrich Wilhelm; America, 1892 *7420.1*
  p365
  *Wife:*Sophie Wilhelmine Charlotte Kromer
  *Son:*Carl Friedrich Wilhelm
  *Son:*Heinrich Wilhelm
  *Son:*Carl Friedrich August
  *Daughter:*Sophie Wilhelmine Charlotte
  *Daughter:*Caroline Sophie Louise
Ebeling, Carl Johann August; America, 1882 *7420.1*
  p328
  *Wife:*Caroline Wilhelmine Luise Prasun
  *Son:*Wilhelm Gottlieb Carl
  *Sister:*Caroline Wilhelmine Luise
Ebeling, Caroline Sophie Louise *SEE* Ebeling, Carl
  Friedrich Wilhelm
Ebeling, Caroline Wilhelmine Luise *SEE* Ebeling, Carl
  Johann August
Ebeling, Caroline Wilhelmine Luise Prasun *SEE* Ebeling,
  Carl Johann August
Ebeling, Christian; America, 1854 *7420.1* p118
  With wife
Ebeling, Friedrich Wilhelm; Port uncertain, 1855 *7420.1*
  p135
Ebeling, Heinrich; Port uncertain, 1861 *7420.1* p204
Ebeling, Heinrich Wilhelm *SEE* Ebeling, Carl Friedrich
  Wilhelm
Ebeling, Johann Friedrich; America, 1849 *7420.1* p64
Ebeling, Johann Heinrich Carl; America, 1870 *7420.1*
  p283
  With family
Ebeling, Johann Heinrich Christian; America, 1867
  7420.1 p255
  With family
Ebeling, Karl; America, 1882 *7420.1* p398
  With family
Ebeling, Sophie Wilhelmine Charlotte *SEE* Ebeling, Carl
  Friedrich Wilhelm
Ebeling, Sophie Wilhelmine Charlotte Kromer *SEE*
  Ebeling, Carl Friedrich Wilhelm
Ebeling, Wilhelm Carl Emil Heinrich; Port uncertain,
  1836 *7420.1* p11
Ebeling, Wilhelm Gottlieb Carl *SEE* Ebeling, Carl
  Johann August
Ebensberger, Jacob; Valdivia, Chile, 1852 *1192.4* p53
Eber, Georges 20; America, 1846 *778.6* p106
Eber, Henry; Baltimore, 1839 *471.10* p87
Eber, Jacob; Ohio, 1809-1852 *4511.35* p12
Eberhard, Adolph; New York, 1860 *358.56* p5
Eberhard, Carl Friedrich Christian; America, 1864
  7420.1 p223
Eberhard, Catherine 23; America, 1847 *778.6* p106
Eberhard, Damascus; Ohio, 1809-1852 *4511.35* p12
Eberhard, Dietrich Christian; America, 1860 *7420.1*
  p193
  *Sister:*Johanna Henriette Friederika
Eberhard, Georg; America, 1891 *179.55* p19
Eberhard, Jean-Baptiste 18; New Orleans, 1848 *778.6*
  p106
Eberhard, Johanna Henriette Friederika *SEE* Eberhard,
  Dietrich Christian
Eberhard, Louise 26; Port uncertain, 1847 *778.6* p106
Eberhard, Luise 37; America, 1836 *5475.1* p413
Eberhard, Simon 18; America, 1847 *778.6* p106

Eberhardt, Carl; America, 1852 *7420.1* p87
  With family
Eberhardt, Friedrich; America, 1858 *7420.1* p177
  With wife & child
Eberhardt, Johann; America, 1867 *5475.1* p170
Eberhardt, John D.; Louisiana, 1874 *4981.45* p131
Eberhardt, Jost; Pennsylvania, 1850 *170.15* p23
Eberhardt, Simon; Louisiana, 1874 *4981.45* p131
Eberhardt, Tobias; Louisiana, 1874-1875 *4981.45* p298
Eberhart, Catharina 8 months; New York, NY, 1874
  6954.7 p37
Eberhart, Elisabeth 22; New York, NY, 1874 *6954.7*
  p37
Eberhart, Friedrich 24; New York, NY, 1874 *6954.7*
  p37
Eberhart, Johann 1 months; New York, NY, 1874
  6954.7 p37
Eberhart, Johann 20; New York, NY, 1893 *1883.7* p41
Eberlein, Carl Friedrich Albrecht; America, 1868 *7420.1*
  p270
Eberlein, Carl Friedrich Wilhelm; America, 1870 *7420.1*
  p286
Eberlein, Carl Gustav Emil; America, 1868 *7420.1* p271
Eberlein, Emil Carl; Illinois, 1874 *7420.1* p303
Eberlein, Friedrich; America, 1883 *7420.1* p335
Eberlein, Hermann; America, 1868 *7919.3* p532
Eberlein, Ludwig Heinrich; Port uncertain, 1880 *7420.1*
  p398
Eberlein, Wilhelm; America, 1852 *7420.1* p87
Eberlein, Wilhelm; America, 1853 *7420.1* p104
  With wife 3 sons & 3 daughters
Eberlin, Jacob 7; Port uncertain, 1840 *778.6* p106
Eberlin, Jean 35; Port uncertain, 1840 *778.6* p106
Eberlin, Marguerite 7; Port uncertain, 1840 *778.6* p106
Eberlin, Marguerite 37; Port uncertain, 1840 *778.6* p106
Ebersohl, Heinrich; America, 1845 *5475.1* p28
  With family
Ebert, Adam; America, 1868 *7919.3* p534
Ebert, Andreas; America, 1868 *7919.3* p534
  With wife & 2 daughters
Ebert, Anton; Ohio, 1840-1897 *8365.35* p16
Ebert, August *SEE* Ebert, Georg Wilhelm
Ebert, Auguste; Wisconsin, 1896 *6795.8* p37
Ebert, Franz, Jr.; America, 1842 *2526.42* p188
Ebert, Franz 2; America, 1842 *2526.42* p188
Ebert, Georg Wilhelm; America, 1867 *7919.3* p534
  *Brother:*August
Ebert, Henry; Wisconsin, 1863 *6795.8* p225
Ebert, Jost; Pennsylvania, 1850 *170.15* p23
Ebert, Leonhard; America, 1834 *2526.42* p180
  With wife
Ebert, Nikolaus 25 *SEE* Ebert, Peter
Ebert, Peter; America, 1846 *2526.42* p140
  With wife
  *Child:*Peter
  *Child:*Nikolaus
Ebert, Peter 17 *SEE* Ebert, Peter
Ebert, Richard; Colorado, 1893 *1029.59* p24
Ebert, Richard; Colorado, 1893 *1029.59* p24
Ebery, Andrew 37; Ontario, 1871 *1823.21* p101
Ebinger, John; Illinois, 1852 *6079.1* p4
Ebner, Bernard 22; Missouri, 1845 *778.6* p106
Ebner, Lorenzo; Ohio, 1809-1852 *4511.35* p12
Ebreham, Pierre 54; Port uncertain, 1842 *778.6* p106
Eccles, Mrs.; Toronto, 1844 *2910.32* p112
Eccles, Hugh 71; Ontario, 1871 *1823.21* p101
Eccles, James 45; Ontario, 1871 *1823.21* p101
Eccles, John D. 55; Ontario, 1871 *1823.17* p47

Eccles, William 24; Ontario, 1871 *1823.21 p101*
Eccles, William 26; Ontario, 1871 *1823.21 p101*
Echappe, Pierre; Quebec, 1650 *9221.17 p225*
Echard, Miss 15; New Orleans, 1840 *778.6 p106*
Echezabal, Jos.; Louisiana, 1874 *4981.45 p295*
Echler, Peter; Ohio, 1809-1852 *4511.35 p12*
Echlerderfer, Ernst F.; Ohio, 1809-1852 *4511.35 p12*
Echroyd, Hargrave; Philadelphia, 1858 *8513.31 p304*
  *Wife:*Mary Lear
Echroyd, Mary Lear *SEE* Echroyd, Hargrave
Eck, Eleonore; New York, NY, 1881 *5475.1 p15*
Eck, Mathias; America, 1873 *5475.1 p346*
Eckard, Andreas 28; Port uncertain, 1843 *778.6 p106*
Eckardt, Wilh.; Valdivia, Chile, 1852 *1192.4 p55*
  With wife & child
Eckart, Karl; Iowa, 1883 *5475.1 p36*
Eckbaum, John F.; Illinois, 1866 *6079.1 p4*
Eckel, Adam 9 *SEE* Eckel, Peter, III
Eckel, Elisabetha Katharina 8 *SEE* Eckel, Peter, III
Eckel, Ernestine; America, 1854 *7420.1 p118*
Eckel, Friedrich *SEE* Eckel, Jakob
Eckel, Georg 5 *SEE* Eckel, Peter, III
Eckel, Herman; North Carolina, 1856 *1088.45 p8*
Eckel, Jakob; America, 1867 *5475.1 p521*
  *Brother:*Friedrich
Eckel, Johann Henrich 32; Pennsylvania, 1850 *170.15 p23*
  With child
Eckel, John; Ohio, 1809-1852 *4511.35 p12*
Eckel, John Benjamin; Ohio, 1809-1852 *4511.35 p12*
Eckel, Juliane; America, 1857 *5475.1 p520*
Eckel, Margarethe; America, 1856 *5475.1 p520*
Eckel, Michel 10; New Orleans, 1848 *778.6 p106*
Eckel, Peter, III 33; America, 1854 *2526.43 p159*
  With wife 30
  *Daughter:*Elisabetha Katharina 8
  *Daughter:*Salome 2
  *Son:*Georg 5
  *Son:*Adam 9
Eckel, Philipp; America, 1852 *2526.43 p159*
Eckel, Salome 2 *SEE* Eckel, Peter, III
Eckel, Valentin 48; New Orleans, 1848 *778.6 p106*
Eckeldorf, C. 28; America, 1841 *778.6 p106*
Eckeldorf, E. 4; America, 1841 *778.6 p106*
Eckell, John Benjamin; Ohio, 1809-1852 *4511.35 p12*
Ecker, Etienne 23; America, 1847 *778.6 p106*
Ecker, Martin; Illinois, 1858 *6079.1 p4*
Eckermann, Mr.; America, 1853 *7420.1 p104*
  With wife & 2 sons
Eckermann, August; America, 1860 *7420.1 p193*
Eckermann, Christoph Ernst; America, 1853 *7420.1 p104*
Eckermann, Conrad; America, 1857 *7420.1 p160*
Eckermann, Friedrich Christian; America, 1868 *7420.1 p273*
Eckermann, Louis; America, 1856 *7420.1 p146*
Eckermeier, Carl Heinrich Ferdinand; America, 1863 *7420.1 p218*
Eckert, Adam; America, 1847 *2526.42 p188*
  With wife
Eckert, Adam; America, 1853 *2526.43 p133*
Eckert, Adam 9 *SEE* Eckert, Christoph
Eckert, Adam, I; America, 1836 *2526.42 p180*
  With wife 2 sons & child
Eckert, Alfred; Texas, 1883 *2526.42 p188*
Eckert, Andreas; America, 1842 *2526.42 p188*
  With wife
  With child 6 months
  With child 3
Eckert, Anna Barbara 3 *SEE* Eckert, Konrad
Eckert, Anna Katharina 6 *SEE* Eckert, Christoph
Eckert, Anna Margaretha Bauer *SEE* Eckert, Friedrich
Eckert, Anna Walburgis 3 *SEE* Eckert, Christoph
Eckert, August 5 *SEE* Eckert, Friedrich
Eckert, Barbara; America, 1831 *2526.43 p208*
Eckert, Christoph; America, 1832 *2526.43 p133*
  With wife
  *Son:*Friedrich
  *Son:*Nikolaus
  *Son:*Christoph
  *Son:*Adam
  *Son:*Peter
  *Daughter:*Elisabtha
Eckert, Christoph; America, 1844 *2526.43 p133*
  With wife
  *Daughter:*Anna Katharina
  *Daughter:*Anna Walburgis
  *Son:*Philipp
Eckert, Christoph 4 *SEE* Eckert, Christoph
Eckert, Elisabeth; America, 1869 *2526.43 p224*
Eckert, Elisabetha; America, 1853 *2526.42 p140*
Eckert, Elisabtha 16 *SEE* Eckert, Christoph
Eckert, Eva Margaretha; America, 1853 *2526.42 p140*

Eckert, Friedrich 5 *SEE* Eckert, Konrad
Eckert, Friedrich 11 *SEE* Eckert, Christoph
Eckert, Friedrich 27; America, 1852 *2526.42 p188*
  *Wife:*Anna Margaretha Bauer
  *Son:*August 5
  *Daughter:*Luise 2
Eckert, Georg Konrad; America, 1831 *2526.43 p208*
Eckert, Gottlob; America, 1887 *179.55 p19*
Eckert, Heinrich 16 *SEE* Eckert, Konrad
Eckert, Ignatius; Ohio, 1809-1852 *4511.35 p12*
Eckert, Johann Nikolaus; America, 1840 *5475.1 p528*
Eckert, Johann Nikolaus; America, 1840 *5475.1 p536*
Eckert, Johanna; Philadelphia, 1859 *8513.31 p321*
Eckert, Johannes 6 *SEE* Eckert, Konrad
Eckert, Johannes 28; America, 1836 *2526.43 p208*
Eckert, Karl; America, 1881 *2526.43 p193*
Eckert, Katharina; America, 1845 *2526.42 p104*
Eckert, Katharina; Brazil, 1886 *5475.1 p432*
Eckert, Katharina 38; Dayton, OH, 1855 *2526.43 p135*
Eckert, Katharina Elisabetha 17 *SEE* Eckert, Konrad
Eckert, Konrad; America, 1846 *2526.42 p140*
  With wife
  *Child:*Konrad
  *Child:*Johannes
  *Child:*Anna Barbara
  *Child:*Friedrich
  *Child:*Katharina Elisabetha
  *Child:*Heinrich
Eckert, Konrad 11 *SEE* Eckert, Konrad
Eckert, Leonhard; America, 1856 *2526.43 p166*
Eckert, Luise 2 *SEE* Eckert, Friedrich
Eckert, Michael August 18; America, 1881 *2526.42 p188*
Eckert, N.; America, 1870 *2526.43 p159*
Eckert, Nikolaus; America, 1831 *2526.43 p208*
  With wife & 6 children
Eckert, Nikolaus 7 *SEE* Eckert, Christoph
Eckert, Peter 13 *SEE* Eckert, Christoph
Eckert, Peter, III; America, 1836 *2526.43 p133*
  With wife
  With daughter 11
  With daughter 19
  With son 22
  With son 16
  With son 14
  With son 9
Eckert, Philipp; America, 1831 *2526.43 p195*
  With wife & 4 children
Eckert, Philipp 9 *SEE* Eckert, Christoph
Eckert, Rosine; New York, 1860 *358.56 p3*
Eckert, Walburga; America, 1836 *2526.43 p134*
Eckhard, Adam; America, 1854 *2526.43 p224*
Eckhard, Christoph 12 *SEE* Eckhard, Georg
Eckhard, Eva 1 *SEE* Eckhard, Georg
Eckhard, Georg; America, 1847 *2526.42 p119*
  With wife
  *Child:*Michael
  *Child:*Eva
  *Child:*Christoph
  *Child:*Katharina
Eckhard, Katharina 7 *SEE* Eckhard, Georg
Eckhard, Michael 3 *SEE* Eckhard, Georg
Eckhardt, C. W.; Valdivia, Chile, 1852 *1192.4 p55*
Eckhardt, Christiane; America, 1867 *7919.3 p533*
Eckhardt, Maria; Valdivia, Chile, 1852 *1192.4 p55*
Eckhart, Friedrich 19; New York, NY, 1893 *1883.7 p42*
Eckland, Charles; Colorado, 1888 *1029.59 p24*
Eckles, John 12; North Carolina, 1775 *1422.10 p57*
Eckles, Martha 45; North Carolina, 1775 *1422.10 p57*
Eckles, Robert; South Carolina, 1808 *6155.4 p18*
Eckles, Wm. 40; North Carolina, 1775 *1422.10 p57*
Eckley, Henry K. 43; Ontario, 1871 *1823.21 p101*
Eckley, James 56; Michigan, 1842 *4491.42 p10*
Eckstein, Barbara; America, 1868 *7919.3 p533*
Eckstein, Georg; America, 1867 *7919.3 p533*
Eckstein, Margaretha Barbara; America, 1868 *7919.3 p533*
Eckstein, Michael; Ohio, 1809-1852 *4511.35 p12*
Eckstrom, A. A.; Valparaiso, Chile, 1850 *1192.4 p50*
Ecobichon, Edward; New Jersey, 1830 *9228.50 p206*
Ecreman, Augustus; Ohio, 1809-1852 *4511.35 p12*
Eddie, Alexander 52; Ontario, 1871 *1823.21 p101*
Eddie, George 25; Ontario, 1871 *1823.21 p101*
Eddie, James 46; Ontario, 1871 *1823.21 p101*
Eddie, William 52; Ontario, 1871 *1823.21 p101*
Eddings, John 52; Ontario, 1871 *1823.17 p47*
Eddy, Elizabeth J.; Colorado, 1902 *1029.59 p24*
Eddy, Richard; Colorado, 1902 *1029.59 p24*
Eddy, Richard 34; Colorado, 1902 *1029.59 p24*
Edel, Anna Elisabeth; Port uncertain, 1866 *170.15 p24*
Edelbrut, Felicite 25; New Orleans, 1843 *778.6 p106*
Edell, Mary; Philadelphia, 1855 *8513.31 p304*
Edell, Richd.; Maryland, 1674 *1236.25 p50*

Edelmann, Jacob; America, 1867 *7919.3 p532*
  With wife & 5 children
Edelstein, Alfred; South America, 1901 *7420.1 p377*
Edelstein, Moses; America, 1880 *7420.1 p315*
Eden, John 26; Ontario, 1871 *1823.21 p101*
Edervalle, Mr. 27; Port uncertain, 1842 *778.6 p107*
Edervalle, Mrs. 23; Port uncertain, 1842 *778.6 p107*
Edey, Joseph 55; Ontario, 1871 *1823.21 p101*
Edgar, John 74; Ontario, 1871 *1823.17 p47*
Edgar, Joseph 45; Ontario, 1871 *1823.21 p101*
Edgar, Margaret 9; Quebec, 1870 *8364.32 p23*
Edgar, Thomas 47; Ontario, 1871 *1823.17 p47*
Edgington, Thomas; Ohio, 1825 *3580.20 p31*
Edgington, Thomas; Ohio, 1825 *6020.12 p7*
Edgren, Herman C.; St. Paul, MN, 1882 *1865.50 p45*
Edholm, Charles J.T.; St. Paul, MN, 1894 *1865.50 p45*
Edinborogh, Thomas 58; Ontario, 1871 *1823.21 p101*
Edinger, Carl *SEE* Edinger, Johann
Edinger, Christian *SEE* Edinger, Joseph
Edinger, Daniel; Brazil, 1864 *5475.1 p524*
  *Daughter:*Luise
  *Daughter:*Karoline
Edinger, Dorothea *SEE* Edinger, Peter, III
Edinger, Elisabeth *SEE* Edinger, Peter, III
Edinger, Friedrich *SEE* Edinger, Friedrich
Edinger, Friedrich; Dakota, 1886 *554.30 p25*
  *Wife:*Susanna Piedt
  *Child:*Ludwig
  *Child:*Jakob
  *Child:*Friedrich
  *Child:*Joseph
  *Child:*Johann
  *Child:*Rosina
Edinger, Helene Adam *SEE* Edinger, Joseph
Edinger, Jacob *SEE* Edinger, Johann
Edinger, Jakob *SEE* Edinger, Peter, III
Edinger, Jakob *SEE* Edinger, Friedrich
Edinger, Johann *SEE* Edinger, Joseph
Edinger, Johann *SEE* Edinger, Friedrich
Edinger, Johann *SEE* Edinger, Johann
Edinger, Johann; North Dakota, 1887 *554.30 p26*
  *Wife:*Wilhelmina Rust
  *Child:*Johann
  *Child:*Carl
  *Child:*Jacob
Edinger, Joseph; Dakota, 1884-1918 *554.30 p25*
  *Wife:*Helene Adam
  *Child:*Christian
  *Child:*Johann
Edinger, Joseph *SEE* Edinger, Friedrich
Edinger, Karl *SEE* Edinger, Peter, III
Edinger, Karl; America, 1862 *5475.1 p523*
Edinger, Karoline *SEE* Edinger, Peter, III
Edinger, Karoline *SEE* Edinger, Daniel
Edinger, Katharina; Brazil, 1859 *5475.1 p523*
Edinger, Katharina; Dakota, 1883 *554.30 p25*
Edinger, Ludwig *SEE* Edinger, Friedrich
Edinger, Luise *SEE* Edinger, Daniel
Edinger, Magdalena *SEE* Edinger, Peter, III
Edinger, Magdalena Muller *SEE* Edinger, Peter, III
Edinger, Maria; Dakota, 1883-1918 *554.30 p25*
Edinger, Peter, III; America, 1862 *5475.1 p523*
  *Wife:*Magdalena Muller
  *Daughter:*Elisabeth
  *Daughter:*Philippine
  *Daughter:*Dorothea
  *Son:*Jakob
  *Daughter:*Karoline
  *Son:*Karl
  *Daughter:*Magdalena
Edinger, Philippine *SEE* Edinger, Peter, III
Edinger, Rosina *SEE* Edinger, Friedrich
Edinger, Susanna Piedt *SEE* Edinger, Friedrich
Edinger, Wilhelmina Rust *SEE* Edinger, Johann
Edler, Dietrich; America, 1856 *7420.1 p147*
Edleston, George 38; Ontario, 1871 *1823.21 p101*
Edling, Emma; St. Paul, MN, 1889 *1865.50 p45*
Edmands, Edward 41; Ontario, 1871 *1823.21 p101*
Edme, Richard 45; Missouri, 1845 *778.6 p107*
Edme, Sophie 34; Missouri, 1845 *778.6 p107*
Edmensar, Richsard 47; New Orleans, 1847 *778.6 p107*
Edmonds, Charles; Marston's Wharf, 1782 *8529.30 p11*
Edmonds, John; Philadelphia, 1778 *8529.30 p6*
Edmonds, Thomas; Philadelphia, 1778 *8529.30 p6*
Edmont, Mr. 35; America, 1843 *778.6 p107*
Edmont, Mrs. 28; America, 1843 *778.6 p107*
Edmont, Marguerite 3; America, 1843 *778.6 p107*
Edmunds, Martha 75; Ontario, 1871 *1823.21 p101*
Edmundson, William Graham; Illinois, 1852 *6079.1 p4*
Edstrom, N. Persson; Charleston, SC, 1851 *6412.40 p153*
Edvall, Olof S.; Missouri, 1861 *4487.25 p55*
Edward, James 49; Ontario, 1871 *1823.17 p47*

FOR A COMPLETE EXPLANATION OF ENTRY, SEE "HOW TO READ A CITATION" SECTION

Edward, Jane 27; North Carolina, 1774 *1422.10 p54*
Edward, John 26; North Carolina, 1774 *1422.10 p54*
Edward, Symon; Maryland, 1672 *1236.25 p47*
Edward, Whithook 36; Ontario, 1871 *1823.21 p101*
Edwards, Abraham, Sr.; Ohio, 1836 *4022.20 p275*
  *Wife:*Ann
Edwards, Ann *SEE* Edwards, Abraham, Sr.
Edwards, Ann *SEE* Edwards, Lewis
Edwards, Ann 56; Ontario, 1871 *1823.21 p101*
Edwards, Ann 64; Ontario, 1871 *1823.21 p101*
Edwards, Arthur 40; Ontario, 1871 *1823.17 p47*
Edwards, Catherine *SEE* Edwards, Thomas
Edwards, Catherine *SEE* Edwards, David
Edwards, Charles; Ontario, 1835 *3160.1 p150*
Edwards, Daniel; Ohio, 1834-1835 *4022.20 p276*
  *Wife:*Mary Hughes
  *Child:*Mary
  *Child:*Susan
  *Child:*John D.
  *Child:*Elizabeth
Edwards, Daniel *SEE* Edwards, Elizabeth
Edwards, David; Ohio, 1835 *4022.20 p276*
  *Brother:*Thomas
Edwards, David; Ohio, 1837 *4022.20 p276*
  *Wife:*Margaret
  *Child:*Elizabeth
Edwards, David; Ohio, 1838 *4022.20 p276*
  *Wife:*Catherine
  *Child:*Edward
  *Child:*Mary
  *Child:*Evan
Edwards, David 44; Ontario, 1871 *1823.17 p47*
Edwards, David C. *SEE* Edwards, Elizabeth
Edwards, David N.; Ohio, 1835 *4022.20 p276*
  *Wife:*Eleanor Jones Evans
  *Child:*Avarina
  With 5 children
Edwards, Deborah *SEE* Edwards, Jenkin
Edwards, Edward; Colorado, 1880 *1029.59 p24*
Edwards, Edward; Colorado, 1891 *1029.59 p24*
Edwards, Edward *SEE* Edwards, David
Edwards, Edward *SEE* Edwards, Evan W.
Edwards, Edward; Ohio, 1838 *4022.20 p276*
  *Wife:*Mary Lewis
Edwards, Edward *SEE* Edwards, Elizabeth
Edwards, Edward; Ohio, n.d. *4022.20 p276*
  *Wife:*Gaynor
  *Child:*Thomas E.
Edwards, Edward 54; Ontario, 1871 *1823.21 p101*
Edwards, Edward 69; Ontario, 1871 *1823.21 p101*
Edwards, Eleanor Jones Evans *SEE* Edwards, David N.
Edwards, Elizabeth *SEE* Edwards, Daniel
Edwards, Elizabeth *SEE* Edwards, David
Edwards, Elizabeth *SEE* Edwards, Evan W.
Edwards, Elizabeth *SEE* Edwards, Elizabeth
Edwards, Elizabeth; Ohio, 1865 *4022.20 p276*
  *Child:*Nathaniel
  *Child:*Elizabeth
  *Child:*Edward
  *Child:*Margaret
  *Child:*David C.
  *Child:*Daniel
  *Child:*Reese N.
Edwards, Evan *SEE* Edwards, David
Edwards, Evan *SEE* Edwards, Evan W.
Edwards, Evan T.; Ohio, 1838 *4022.20 p276*
  *Wife:*Margaret
Edwards, Evan W.; Ohio, 1838 *4022.20 p276*
  *Wife:*Susan Hughes
  *Child:*Evan
  *Child:*Sarah
  *Child:*Mary
  *Child:*Margaret
  *Child:*John
  *Child:*Jane
  *Child:*Edward
  *Child:*Elizabeth
  *Child:*Nathaniel
Edwards, Francis 55; Ontario, 1871 *1823.21 p101*
Edwards, Gaynor *SEE* Edwards, Edward
Edwards, George 32; Indiana, 1861-1880 *9076.20 p70*
Edwards, George 40; Ontario, 1871 *1823.21 p101*
Edwards, George 65; Ontario, 1871 *1823.21 p101*
Edwards, Harry 55; Ontario, 1871 *1823.21 p101*
Edwards, Henry 44; Ontario, 1871 *1823.21 p101*
Edwards, Henry T.; Colorado, 1876 *1029.59 p24*
Edwards, James 40; Ontario, 1871 *1823.17 p47*
Edwards, James 61; Ontario, 1871 *1823.17 p47*
Edwards, Jane *SEE* Edwards, Evan W.
Edwards, Jane; Ohio, 1840 *4022.20 p288*
Edwards, Jane 54; Ontario, 1871 *1823.21 p101*
Edwards, Jenkin; Colorado, 1873 *1029.59 p25*

Edwards, Jenkin; Colorado, 1884 *1029.59 p25*
Edwards, Jenkin; Ohio, 1844 *4022.20 p277*
  *Wife:*Mary
  *Child:*Deborah
Edwards, Jenkins; Colorado, 1884 *1029.59 p25*
Edwards, John; Cleveland, OH, 1868-1878 *9722.10 p118*
Edwards, John; Marston's Wharf, 1782 *8529.30 p11*
Edwards, John *SEE* Edwards, Evan W.
Edwards, John 30; Ontario, 1871 *1823.21 p102*
Edwards, John 34; Ontario, 1871 *1823.21 p102*
Edwards, John 34; Ontario, 1871 *1823.21 p102*
Edwards, John 68; Ontario, 1871 *1823.21 p102*
Edwards, John 74; Ontario, 1871 *1823.17 p47*
Edwards, John 18; Quebec, 1870 *8364.32 p23*
Edwards, John D. *SEE* Edwards, Daniel
Edwards, Letitia *SEE* Edwards, Reese
Edwards, Lewis; Ohio, 1849 *4022.20 p277*
  *Wife:*Ann
  With 3 children
Edwards, Margaret *SEE* Edwards, David
Edwards, Margaret *SEE* Edwards, Thomas
Edwards, Margaret *SEE* Edwards, Evan W.
Edwards, Margaret *SEE* Edwards, Evan T.
Edwards, Margaret; Ohio, 1838 *4022.20 p290*
Edwards, Margaret; Ohio, 1838 *4022.20 p290*
Edwards, Margaret *SEE* Edwards, Elizabeth
Edwards, Mary *SEE* Edwards, Daniel
Edwards, Mary Hughes *SEE* Edwards, Daniel
Edwards, Mary; Ohio, 1837-1838 *4022.20 p286*
Edwards, Mary *SEE* Edwards, David
Edwards, Mary *SEE* Edwards, Evan W.
Edwards, Mary Lewis *SEE* Edwards, Edward
Edwards, Mary *SEE* Edwards, Jenkin
Edwards, Nathaniel *SEE* Edwards, Evan W.
Edwards, Nathaniel *SEE* Edwards, Elizabeth
Edwards, Phillip 33; Ontario, 1871 *1823.21 p102*
Edwards, Reese; Ohio, 1841 *4022.20 p277*
  *Wife:*Letitia
  With children
Edwards, Reese N. *SEE* Edwards, Elizabeth
Edwards, Richard 70; Ontario, 1871 *1823.21 p102*
Edwards, Robert; Colorado, 1862-1894 *1029.59 p25*
Edwards, Robert 55; Ontario, 1871 *1823.17 p47*
Edwards, Sarah *SEE* Edwards, Evan W.
Edwards, Susan *SEE* Edwards, Daniel
Edwards, Susan Hughes *SEE* Edwards, Evan W.
Edwards, Susana 74; Ontario, 1871 *1823.17 p47*
Edwards, Thomas *SEE* Edwards, David
Edwards, Thomas; Ohio, 1837 *4022.20 p277*
  *Wife:*Catherine
  *Child:*Margaret
Edwards, Thomas; Ohio, 1837 *4022.20 p277*
Edwards, Thomas 52; Ontario, 1871 *1823.17 p47*
Edwards, Thomas 18; Quebec, 1870 *8364.32 p23*
Edwards, Thomas E. *SEE* Edwards, Edward
Edwards, Thomas Henry; Washington, 1889 *2770.40 p27*
Edwards, William 28; Ontario, 1871 *1823.17 p47*
Edwards, William 59; Ontario, 1871 *1823.21 p102*
Edwards, William Charles; Miami, 1935 *4984.12 p39*
Edwards, William L. 17; Louisiana, 1847-1853 *7710.1 p153*
Edy, John 51; Ontario, 1871 *1823.21 p102*
Eedy, Charles 60; Ontario, 1871 *1823.21 p102*
Eedy, Mariah 35; Ontario, 1871 *1823.21 p102*
Eedy, Richard 58; Ontario, 1871 *1823.21 p102*
Eeten, Enno; Iowa, 1917 *1211.15 p10*
Effard, Peter; Virginia, 1657 *9228.50 p206*
Efford, Abigail; Marblehead, MA, 1758 *9228.50 p206*
Efford, Peter; Virginia, 1657 *9228.50 p206*
Effron, William 25; Ontario, 1871 *1823.21 p102*
Efler, Jan 2; New York, NY, 1911 *6533.11 p9*
Efler, Paulina 23; New York, NY, 1911 *6533.11 p9*
Efner, Abraham 67; Ontario, 1871 *1823.21 p102*
Egan, Bridget Hickey *SEE* Egan, Elizabeth
Egan, Edward Joseph; North Carolina, 1853 *1088.45 p9*
Egan, Elizabeth; Halifax, N.S., 1827 *7009.9 p61*
  *Father:*William
  *Mother:*Bridget Hickey
Egan, James 41; Ontario, 1871 *1823.21 p102*
Egan, John 28; Ontario, 1871 *1823.17 p47*
Egan, John 70; Ontario, 1871 *1823.17 p47*
Egan, Julia 38; Ontario, 1871 *1823.21 p102*
Egan, Kate 16; Ontario, 1871 *1823.21 p102*
Egan, M. C. 31; Ontario, 1871 *1823.17 p47*
Egan, Mary 49; Ontario, 1871 *1823.21 p102*
Egan, Michael 53; Ontario, 1871 *1823.17 p47*
Egan, Patrick; Boston, 1718 *1642 p24*
Egan, Thomas; Ohio, 1836 *3580.20 p31*
Egan, Thomas; Ohio, 1836 *6020.12 p7*
Egan, William *SEE* Egan, Elizabeth
Egar, Jonathan 35; Ontario, 1871 *1823.21 p102*
Egart, Henry 55; Ontario, 1871 *1823.21 p102*
Egart, James; Boston, 1737 *1642 p26*

Egart, John 38; Ontario, 1871 *1823.21 p102*
Egbers, Charles; Illinois, 1859 *6079.1 p4*
Egelden, Daniell; Maryland, 1671-1672 *1236.25 p45*
Egelson, Axel; Colorado, 1893 *1029.59 p25*
Egelton, George 52; Ontario, 1871 *1823.21 p102*
Eger, George; Washington, 1889 *2770.40 p27*
Eger, William; Ohio, 1809-1852 *4511.35 p12*
Egere, Jean; Quebec, 1639 *9221.17 p87*
Egermajer, Josef V.; Iowa, 1870-1889 *2853.20 p223*
Egett, Christopher 30; Ontario, 1871 *1823.21 p102*
Egger, Laur. 37; America, 1840 *778.6 p107*
Eggerding, . . .; America, 1852 *7420.1 p87*
  With family
Eggerding, Carl; America, 1859 *7420.1 p184*
Eggerding, Carl Heinrich; America, 1857 *7420.1 p160*
  With family
Eggerding, Caroline Friedrike Amalie; America, 1884 *7420.1 p344*
  *Daughter:*Caroline Friederike Auguste
  *Daughter:*Louise Sophie
  *Daughter:*Johanne Friederike Amalie
  *Daughter:*Friederike Charlotte Amalie
  *Son:*Friedrich August
  *Son:*August Wilhelm
Eggerding, Caroline Wilhelmine Juliane; America, 1867 *7420.1 p255*
Eggerding, Ernst Heinrich Wilhelm; America, 1858 *7420.1 p177*
  With mother
Eggerding, Friedrich Heinrich; Port uncertain, 1859 *7420.1 p184*
Eggerding, Heinrich August Louis; America, 1859 *7420.1 p184*
Eggerstedt, Johann; Valdivia, Chile, 1852 *1192.4 p55*
Eggert, H.; New York, 1859 *358.56 p55*
Eggeth, John 32; Ontario, 1871 *1823.21 p102*
Eggett, John 32; Ontario, 1871 *1823.21 p102*
Eggleston, Bygod; Massachusetts, 1630 *117.5 p156*
  *Son:*James
  *Son:*Samuel
Eggleston, James *SEE* Eggleston, Bygod
Eggleston, Samuel *SEE* Eggleston, Bygod
Eggleton, Thomas; Philadelphia, 1778 *8529.30 p2*
Egin, Esther; Boston, 1747 *1642 p46*
Eglay, F. J.; Louisiana, 1874 *4981.45 p295*
Egle, Henry; Illinois, 1866 *6079.1 p4*
Egler, Johann; America, 1867 *5475.1 p49*
  *Wife:*Karolina Karb
  *Son:*Peter
  *Son:*Ludwig
Egler, Karolina Karb 26 *SEE* Egler, Johann
Egler, Ludwig 11 *SEE* Egler, Johann
Egler, Peter 22 *SEE* Egler, Johann
Egli, Jean 32; Missouri, 1845 *778.6 p107*
Eglin, Stephen 25; North Carolina, 1774 *1422.10 p56*
Eglin, Susanna; America, 1882 *5475.1 p229*
Egly, Konrad; America, 1852 *2526.43 p139*
Egry, Widow; America, 1854 *7420.1 p118*
Ehenberger, Samuel 40; Ontario, 1871 *1823.21 p102*
Ehinger, Ambrosius *SEE* Ehinger, Heinrich
Ehinger, Ambrosius; Venezuela, 1529 *3899.5 p538*
Ehinger, Georg *SEE* Ehinger, Heinrich
Ehinger, Georg; Venezuela, 1529 *3899.5 p538*
Ehinger, Hans *SEE* Ehinger, Ulrich
Ehinger, Heinrich; Venezuela, 1529 *3899.5 p538*
Ehinger, Heinrich; Venezuela, 1529 *3899.5 p538*
  *Brother:*Ambrosius
  *Brother:*Georg
Ehinger, Ulrich; Venezuela, 1529 *3899.5 p538*
  *Brother:*Hans
Ehl, Franz; Ohio, 1886 *5475.1 p181*
Ehl, Joh. Baptist; America, 1881 *5475.1 p181*
Ehl, Peter; Cincinnati, 1887 *5475.1 p181*
Ehlen, Katharina 49; America, 1868 *5475.1 p297*
Ehlen, Susanna; America, 1881 *5475.1 p359*
Ehler, George; Illinois, 1851 *6079.1 p4*
Ehlerding, Engel Marie Sophie Dorothee Latwesen *SEE* Ehlerding, Friedrich Wilhelm
Ehlerding, Friedrich Wilhelm; America, 1872 *7420.1 p294*
  *Wife:*Engel Marie Sophie Dorothee Latwesen
  *Son:*Johann Friedrich Wilhelm
Ehlerding, Johann Friedrich Wilhelm *SEE* Ehlerding, Friedrich Wilhelm
Ehlers, Fried; Galveston, TX, 1855 *571.7 p16*
Ehlers, Henry; North Carolina, 1849 *1088.45 p9*
Ehlers, J. Edv. Eggert; New Orleans, 1851 *6412.40 p153*
Ehlers, John; Ohio, 1840-1897 *8365.35 p16*
Ehlert, Caroline Hannah Charlotte; Wisconsin, 1895 *6795.8 p72*
Ehlert, Ernstine Mary Louise; Wisconsin, 1894 *6795.8 p92*

Ehlert, Gustav Emil Richard; Wisconsin, 1901 *6795.8 p152*
Ehly, Margarethe 22; Brazil, 1865 *5475.1 p506*
Ehmann, Jean; Louisiana, 1841-1844 *4981.45 p210*
Ehmke, William; Washington, 1884 *6015.10 p16*
Ehrenberg, Franz; America, 1880 *5475.1 p129*
   *Wife:*Maria Frey
Ehrenberg, Maria Frey *SEE* Ehrenberg, Franz
Ehrenberger, Frantisek; Iowa, 1881 *2853.20 p232*
Ehrenberger, Frantisek; Missouri, 1869 *2853.20 p54*
Ehret, Charles; Louisiana, 1874 *4981.45 p131*
Ehrhard, Adam 20; America, 1852 *2526.43 p146*
Ehrhard, Adam; Ohio, 1809-1852 *4511.35 p12*
Ehrhard, Adam Eberhard; America, 1865-1884 *2526.43 p139*
Ehrhard, Albert; America, 1872-1900 *5475.1 p37*
Ehrhard, Albert; Wisconsin, 1874 *6795.8 p41*
Ehrhard, Charlotte 32; America, 1881 *2526.43 p156*
Ehrhard, Elisabeth; America, 1867 *2526.43 p146*
Ehrhard, Friedrich; America, 1890 *2526.43 p139*
   With sister
Ehrhard, Friedrich; Baltimore, 1831 *2526.43 p139*
   With wife & 3 children
Ehrhard, Georg; America, 1836 *2526.42 p107*
   With wife & children
Ehrhard, Georg; America, 1885 *2526.43 p139*
Ehrhard, Jakob; America, 1888 *2526.43 p139*
Ehrhard, Karl; America, 1883 *5475.1 p36*
Ehrhard, Peter; America, 1854 *2526.43 p195*
Ehrhard, Peter; America, 1854 *2526.43 p203*
Ehrhard, Philipp; America, 1866 *2526.43 p188*
Ehrhardt, Amalie 20; Portland, ME, 1906 *970.38 p76*
Ehrhardt, Anna 11; Portland, ME, 1906 *970.38 p76*
Ehrhardt, Anna Elisabeth 2 *SEE* Ehrhardt, Valentin
Ehrhardt, Anna Margarethe; America, 1868 *7919.3 p527*
Ehrhardt, Charlotte 48; Portland, ME, 1906 *970.38 p76*
Ehrhardt, Dawid 3; Portland, ME, 1906 *970.38 p76*
Ehrhardt, Georg Ludwig; America, 1866 *2526.43 p166*
Ehrhardt, Joh. Georg 45; Portland, ME, 1906 *970.38 p76*
Ehrhardt, Johann; America, 1899 *2526.43 p224*
Ehrhardt, Johann Georg 4 *SEE* Ehrhardt, Valentin
Ehrhardt, Johann Leonhard 2 *SEE* Ehrhardt, Valentin
Ehrhardt, Margaretha Elisabetha 5 *SEE* Ehrhardt, Valentin
Ehrhardt, Maria Elisabetha Ruhl *SEE* Ehrhardt, Valentin
Ehrhardt, Marie; America, 1866 *2526.43 p166*
Ehrhardt, Marie 15; Portland, ME, 1906 *970.38 p76*
Ehrhardt, Peter; America, 1887 *2526.43 p224*
Ehrhardt, Valentin; America, 1752 *2526.42 p172*
   *Wife:*Maria Elisabetha Ruhl
   *Child:*Johann Leonhard
   *Child:*Margaretha Elisabetha
   *Child:*Anna Elisabeth
   *Child:*Johann Georg
Ehrmann, Babette; America, 1866 *2526.43 p146*
Ehrmann, Baruch; America, 1854 *2526.42 p119*
Ehrmann, Baruch; America, 1886 *2526.42 p119*
Ehrmann, Isaak; America, 1891 *2526.42 p119*
Ehrmann, Klara; America, 1855 *2526.43 p146*
Ehrmann, Moses; America, 1893 *2526.43 p146*
Ehrmann, Simon; America, 1891 *2526.42 p119*
Ehrsam, Barbara; America, 1867 *7919.3 p531*
   *Child:*Caroline Gruber
Ehrsam, Caroline Gruber *SEE* Ehrsam, Barbara
Ehrsam, Johann Nicol; America, 1867 *7919.3 p531*
Ehselen, Nikolaus; America, 1882 *5475.1 p134*
Eibach, Jacob; North Carolina, 1710 *3629.40 p3*
Eibel, Moritz Christian; Port uncertain, 1835 *7420.1 p8*
Eiberrpach, Johann 24; Halifax, N.S., 1902 *1860.4 p42*
Eiberrpach, Magdalena 23; Halifax, N.S., 1902 *1860.4 p42*
Eibling, Carl Heinrich Christoph *SEE* Eibling, Hans Heinrich
Eibling, Caroline Louise *SEE* Eibling, Hans Heinrich
Eibling, Engel Marie Dorothea *SEE* Eibling, Hans Heinrich
Eibling, Engel Sophie Dorothea Battermann *SEE* Eibling, Hans Heinrich
Eibling, Hans Heinrich; Illinois, 1880 *7420.1 p315*
   *Wife:*Engel Sophie Dorothea Battermann
   *Son:*Nicolaus Carl Wilhelm
   *Son:*Carl Heinrich Christoph
   *Daughter:*Caroline Louise
   *Daughter:*Engel Marie Dorothea
Eibling, Nicolaus Carl Wilhelm *SEE* Eibling, Hans Heinrich
Eich, Alfred; London, Eng., 1898 *5475.1 p107*
Eichacker, Emil 17; America, 1888 *5475.1 p38*
Eichacker, Ernst Karl; America, 1886 *5475.1 p37*
Eichel, Babette; America, 1868 *7919.3 p533*
Eichel, Catharina; America, 1867 *7919.3 p533*
Eichel, Friedrich Karl 16; America, 1853 *2526.43 p195*

Eichel, Herman; Ohio, 1840-1897 *8365.35 p16*
Eichel, Johann Heinrich; America, 1883 *2526.43 p195*
Eichel, Julius; Texas, 1897 *3435.45 p35*
Eichelberger, Anna Elisabeth; America, 1867 *7919.3 p535*
   With child
Eichele, Barbara; America, 1852 *179.55 p19*
   With child
Eichele, Barbara 22; Chile, 1852 *1192.4 p51*
Eichele, Christ.; Chile, 1852 *1192.4 p51*
   With child
Eichele, Gottl.; Chile, 1852 *1192.4 p51*
Eichele, Heinrich; America, 1853 *179.55 p19*
Eichele, Jacob; America, 1852 *179.55 p19* .
Eichele, Jakob; America, 1852 *179.55 p19*
Eichenlaub, Anton 19; New York, NY, 1898 *7951.13 p42*
Eicher, Jacob; Ohio, 1809-1852 *4511.35 p12*
Eichhorn, Anna Christine Therese; America, 1867 *7919.3 p530*
Eichhorn, Friederike; America, 1868 *7919.3 p530*
Eichhorn, Werner; America, 1868 *7919.3 p528*
Eichler, Juliane; Valdivia, Chile, 1850 *1192.4 p48*
Eichler, William; New Jersey, 1773-1774 *927.31 p3*
Eichmann, Adam 3 *SEE* Eichmann, Adam
Eichmann, Adam 37; America, 1850 *2526.42 p94*
   *Wife:*Anna Margareta Olt 35
   *Child:*Andreas 6
   *Child:*Adam 3
   *Child:*Eva Katharina 9
Eichmann, Andreas 6 *SEE* Eichmann, Adam
Eichmann, Anna Margareta Olt 35 *SEE* Eichmann, Adam
Eichmann, Eva Katharina; America, 1853 *2526.42 p94*
Eichmann, Eva Katharina 9 *SEE* Eichmann, Adam
Eichmann, Georg 5 *SEE* Eichmann, Leonhard
Eichmann, Johannes 2 *SEE* Eichmann, Leonhard
Eichmann, Joseph; Wisconsin, 1876 *6795.8 p69*
Eichmann, Julius Ferdinand; Wisconsin, 1882 *6795.8 p171*
Eichmann, Julius Ferdinand; Wisconsin, 1897 *6795.8 p69*
Eichmann, Katharina 7 *SEE* Eichmann, Leonhard
Eichmann, Leonhard 35; America, 1865 *2526.42 p140*
   *Wife:*Rosina 36
   *Child:*Johannes 2
   *Child:*Magdalena 1
   *Child:*Georg 5
   *Child:*Katharina 7
Eichmann, Magdalena 1 *SEE* Eichmann, Leonhard
Eichmann, Rosina 36 *SEE* Eichmann, Leonhard
Eichstedt, Gustav; Wisconsin, 1893 *6795.8 p144*
Eicke, Fritz v.; Valdivia, Chile, 1851 *1192.4 p51*
Eickhof, Johann Heinrich Ludwig; America, 1865 *7420.1 p230*
   *Wife:*Sophie Dorothee Ch. Gewecke
   *Daughter:*Sophie Dorothee Ch.
Eickhof, Sophie Dorothee Ch. *SEE* Eickhof, Johann Heinrich Ludwig
Eickhof, Sophie Dorothee Ch. Gewecke *SEE* Eickhof, Johann Heinrich Ludwig
Eickhof, Wilhelmine; Port uncertain, 1854 *7420.1 p118*
Eickhoff, August; America, 1892 *7420.1 p365*
   With child
Eickhoff, Johann Heinrich Ludwig; America, 1857 *7420.1 p160*
   With family
Eickhoff, Karl August; America, 1885 *7420.1 p347*
Eickmeier, August Friedrich Wilhelm *SEE* Eickmeier, Heinrich Gottlieb Wilhelm Christian Ludwig
Eickmeier, Caroline Wilhelmine Henriette; America, 1866 *7420.1 p244*
   *Daughter:*Wilhelmine Caroline Sophie Charlotte
   *Daughter:*Caroline Friede. Charl.
   *Daughter:*Louise Marie Charlotte
   *Daughter:*Caroline Sophie Charlotte
   *Son:*Ernst Aug. Ferd.
Eickmeier, Caroline Wilhelmine Louise Scheuermann *SEE* Eickmeier, Heinrich Gottlieb Wilhelm Christian Ludwig
Eickmeier, Charlotte Dorothe Wilhelmine *SEE* Eickmeier, Heinrich Gottlieb Wilhelm Christian Ludwig
Eickmeier, Heinrich; America, 1854 *7420.1 p118*
Eickmeier, Heinrich; America, 1888 *7420.1 p399*
   With family
Eickmeier, Heinrich Gottlieb Wilhelm Christian Ludwig; America, 1888 *7420.1 p356*
   *Wife:*Caroline Wilhelmine Louise Scheuermann
   *Daughter:*Charlotte Dorothe Wilhelmine
   *Son:*August Friedrich Wilhelm
Eickmeier, Wilhelm; America, 1854 *7420.1 p118*
Eidenmuler, Peter; America, 1882 *2526.43 p166*
Eidenmuller, Adam; America, 1882 *2526.43 p159*

Eidenmuller, Anna Maria 27 *SEE* Eidenmuller, Peter, I
Eidenmuller, Eva Katharina 13 *SEE* Eidenmuller, Peter, I
Eidenmuller, Georg; America, 1884 *2526.43 p139*
Eidenmuller, Georg 10 *SEE* Eidenmuller, Peter, I
Eidenmuller, Jakob; America, 1870 *2526.43 p139*
Eidenmuller, Johann Heinrich; America, 1871 *2526.43 p139*
Eidenmuller, Johannes; America, 1890 *2526.43 p139*
Eidenmuller, Katharina 25 *SEE* Eidenmuller, Peter, I
Eidenmuller, Leonhard 28; America, 1846 *2526.43 p160*
Eidenmuller, Magdalena 16 *SEE* Eidenmuller, Peter, I
Eidenmuller, Nikolaus 22 *SEE* Eidenmuller, Peter, I
Eidenmuller, Nikolaus 38; America, 1832 *2526.43 p166*
   With wife & 4 children
Eidenmuller, Peter; America, 1855 *2526.43 p139*
Eidenmuller, Peter, I; America, 1847 *2526.43 p139*
   With wife
   *Daughter:*Katharina
   *Daughter:*Magdalena
   *Son:*Georg
   *Daughter:*Eva Katharina
   *Son:*Nikolaus
   *Daughter:*Anna Maria
Eidmann, Elisabeth 16 *SEE* Eidmann, Mrs. Friedrich
Eidmann, Elisabetha; America, 1854 *2526.42 p140*
Eidmann, Mrs. Friedrich; America, 1847 *2526.42 p180*
   *Daughter:*Elisabeth
   *Son:*Johannes
Eidmann, Johannes 12 *SEE* Eidmann, Mrs. Friedrich
Eidmann, Ludwig; America, 1872 *2526.43 p166*
Eidmann, Maria Elisabetha; America, 1854 *2526.42 p140*
Eidmann, Maria Elisabetha; America, 1858 *2526.42 p140*
Eidmann, Wilhelm; America, 1891 *2526.42 p140*
Eie, Tonnes Christiansen; Philadelphia, 1895 *1766.20 p14*
Eier, Barbara 48; Missouri, 1846 *778.6 p107*
Eier, Dorothe 23; Missouri, 1846 *778.6 p107*
Eier, Dorothe 43; Missouri, 1846 *778.6 p107*
Eier, Eva 3; Missouri, 1846 *778.6 p107*
Eier, George 27; Missouri, 1846 *778.6 p107*
Eier, George 54; Missouri, 1846 *778.6 p107*
Eier, Helene 6 months; Missouri, 1846 *778.6 p107*
Eier, Henry 9; Missouri, 1846 *778.6 p107*
Eier, Louis 20; Missouri, 1846 *778.6 p107*
Eier, Michel 9; Missouri, 1846 *778.6 p107*
Eifler, Maria Luise; Brazil, 1863 *5475.1 p550*
Eignt, Engelburtus; Ohio, 1840-1897 *8365.35 p16*
Eikhoff, Friedrich Ludwig; America, 1870 *7420.1 p395*
Eikmann, . . .; America, 1847 *7420.1 p52*
   *Son:*Johann Heinrich Philipp
   *Son:*Friedrich
   With daughter
   *Son:*Johann Friedrich Conrad
Eikmann, Friedrich *SEE* Eikmann, . . .
Eikmann, Johann Friedrich Conrad *SEE* Eikmann, . . .
Eikmann, Johann Heinrich Philipp *SEE* Eikmann, . . .
Eiler, Herman B.; North Carolina, 1847 *1088.45 p9*
Eiler, Kellman B.; North Carolina, 1840-1849 *1088.45 p9*
Eilert, Franz Robert Theodor; Wisconsin, 1893 *6795.8 p81*
Eimer, Jacques H.; Louisiana, 1836-1841 *4981.45 p208*
Einamanti, O. 14; New York, NY, 1894 *6512.1 p182*
Einemann, Henry; Nebraska, 1905 *3004.30 p46*
Einger, Jacob; Ohio, 1809-1852 *4511.35 p12*
Eiondel, Laurent; Illinois, 1852 *6079.1 p4*
Eipert, Michael; Ohio, 1809-1852 *4511.35 p12*
Eirkson, Gust; Colorado, 1892 *1029.59 p25*
Eisel, Georg 32; Galveston, TX, 1844 *3967.10 p371*
Eisel, Karl; America, 1884 *5475.1 p422*
Eisel, Sophie 27; America, 1852 *5475.1 p555*
Eisele, Agnes 24; Chile, 1852 *1192.4 p51*
Eisele, Willibald; New York, 1859 *358.56 p54*
Eiselen, Maria M.; Philadelphia, 1846 *8513.31 p308*
Eiseman, Sabastian; Ohio, 1809-1852 *4511.35 p12*
Eiseman, Sebastian; Ohio, 1809-1852 *4511.35 p12*
Eisemann, Friedrich; America, 1890 *179.55 p19*
Eisemann, Rosina Katharina; America, 1700-1899 *179.55 p19*
Eisenbart, Barbara 23; America, 1868 *5475.1 p174*
Eisenbarth, Johann *SEE* Eisenbarth, Johann
Eisenbarth, Johann; America, 1876 *5475.1 p151*
   *Wife:*Katharina Reinstaedler
   *Son:*Johann
   *Daughter:*Margarethe
   *Son:*Nikolaus
   *Son:*Michel
Eisenbarth, Johann Michel; America, 1875 *5475.1 p151*
Eisenbarth, Katharina Reinstaedler *SEE* Eisenbarth, Johann
Eisenbarth, Margarethe *SEE* Eisenbarth, Johann

Eisenbarth, Michel *SEE* Eisenbarth, Johann
Eisenbarth, Nikolaus *SEE* Eisenbarth, Johann
Eisenbarth, Philipp; America, 1869 ***5475.1*** *p62*
Eisenbarth, Sophie; America, 1869 ***5475.1*** *p62*
Eisenbeis, Catherina 13; New York, NY, 1898 ***7951.13*** *p41*
Eisenbeis, Christina 9; New York, NY, 1898 ***7951.13*** *p41*
Eisenbeis, Jacob 16; New York, NY, 1898 ***7951.13*** *p41*
Eisenbeis, Jacob 26; New York, NY, 1898 ***7951.13*** *p41*
Eisenbeis, Jacob 36; New York, NY, 1898 ***7951.13*** *p41*
Eisenbeis, Johann 2; New York, NY, 1898 ***7951.13*** *p41*
Eisenbeis, Katherina 10 months; New York, NY, 1898 ***7951.13*** *p41*
Eisenbeis, Katherina 21; New York, NY, 1898 ***7951.13*** *p41*
Eisenbeis, Katherina 36; New York, NY, 1898 ***7951.13*** *p41*
Eisenbeis, Maria 6; New York, NY, 1898 ***7951.13*** *p41*
Eisenbeiss, Wilhelm; America, 1870 ***5475.1*** *p460*
Eisenberg, John; Louisiana, 1841-1844 ***4981.45*** *p210*
Eisenbrey, Jakob; New York, NY, 1889 ***3366.30*** *p70*
Eisenhauer, Adam; America, 1891 ***2526.43*** *p190*
*Wife:*Elise
*Daughter:*Anna
*Son:*Georg
Eisenhauer, Anna 2 *SEE* Eisenhauer, Adam
Eisenhauer, Elise 27 *SEE* Eisenhauer, Adam
Eisenhauer, Georg 3 *SEE* Eisenhauer, Adam
Eisenhauer, Jakob; America, 1887 ***2526.43*** *p190*
Eisenhauer, Leonhard; America, 1867 ***2526.43*** *p190*
Eisenhauer, Maria Margaretha; America, 1785 ***2526.42*** *p133*
Eisenhut, August; New York, 1860 ***358.56*** *p4*
Eisenhuth, Friedrich *SEE* Eisenhuth, Juliane Guckert
Eisenhuth, Juliane; Brazil, 1863 ***5475.1*** *p498*
*Daughter:*Phillippine
*Daughter:*Katharina
*Son:*Michel
*Son:*Friedrich
Eisenhuth, Katharina *SEE* Eisenhuth, Juliane Guckert
Eisenhuth, Michel *SEE* Eisenhuth, Juliane Guckert
Eisenhuth, Phillippine *SEE* Eisenhuth, Juliane Guckert
Eisenmann, Matthews; Louisiana, 1836-1841 ***4981.45*** *p208*
Eisenstein, Jacob; Ohio, 1840-1897 ***8365.35*** *p16*
Eisentrager, Charles 45; Michigan, 1880 ***4491.42*** *p10*
Eisenzimmer, Bartel 20; Philadelphia, 1912 ***8425.16*** *p34*
Eisenzimmer, Joseph 8; Philadelphia, 1912 ***8425.16*** *p34*
Eisenzimmer, Joseph 48; Philadelphia, 1912 ***8425.16*** *p34*
Eisenzimmer, Lambert 16; Philadelphia, 1912 ***8425.16*** *p34*
Eisenzimmer, Magdalena 18; Philadelphia, 1912 ***8425.16*** *p34*
Eisenzimmer, Margarota 42; Philadelphia, 1912 ***8425.16*** *p34*
Eisenzimmer, Michael; Ohio, 1809-1852 ***4511.35*** *p12*
Eisknut, August; New York, 1860 ***358.56*** *p4*
Eissel, Otto Friedrich Hugo; Ohio, 1874 ***7420.1*** *p303*
Eistertz, Martin N.; Illinois, 1860 ***6079.1*** *p4*
Eisvogel, Maria 65; America, 1867 ***5475.1*** *p211*
Eisvogel, Wilhelm; America, 1880 ***5475.1*** *p231*
Eiswarth, Geo.; Louisiana, 1874-1875 ***4981.45*** *p298*
Eitenmuller, Anna Margaretha 11 *SEE* Eitenmuller, Johannes
Eitenmuller, Christina 8 *SEE* Eitenmuller, Johannes
Eitenmuller, Johannes 33; America, 1853 ***2526.42*** *p180*
*Wife:*Maria Katharina 32
*Daughter:*Christina 8
*Daughter:*Maria Katharina 6
*Son:*Martin 3
*Daughter:*Anna Margaretha 11
Eitenmuller, Maria Katharina 6 *SEE* Eitenmuller, Johannes
Eitenmuller, Maria Katharina 32 *SEE* Eitenmuller, Johannes
Eitenmuller, Martin 3 *SEE* Eitenmuller, Johannes
Eitle, E. F.; North Carolina, 1842 ***1088.45*** *p9*
Eizenberger, Max; Washington, 1889 ***2770.40*** *p27*
Eizenmann, Fred.; Wisconsin, 1895 ***6795.8*** *p162*
Ejsmont, Waclaw 41; New York, NY, 1920 ***930.50*** *p49*
Ek, A.; Washington, 1889 ***2770.40*** *p27*
Ekberg, Anton; Nebraska, 1890 ***1029.59*** *p25*
Ekberg, C.G.; Charleston, SC, 1850 ***6412.40*** *p152*
Ekblad, Albert; Boston, 1901 ***1766.20*** *p18*
Ekblom, F.; New York, NY, 1848 ***6412.40*** *p151*
Ekegren, Sv. Adolf; New York, NY, 1847 ***6412.40*** *p150*
Ekenstedt, C.A.; New York, NY, 1848 ***6412.40*** *p151*
Ekensteen, A. L. von; Valparaiso, Chile, 1850 ***1192.4*** *p50*
Ekensteen, B. von; Valparaiso, Chile, 1850 ***1192.4*** *p50*
Eker, Frederick; Ohio, 1809-1852 ***4511.35*** *p12*
Ekermann, Caroline Wilhelmine Justine *SEE* Ekermann, Heinrich
Ekermann, Engel Louise Wilhelmine *SEE* Ekermann, Heinrich
Ekermann, Heinrich; America, 1860 ***7420.1*** *p193*
With wife
*Daughter:*Engel Louise Wilhelmine
*Daughter:*Sophie Caroline Louise
*Daughter:*Caroline Wilhelmine Justine
*Son:*Heinrich Friedrich August
*Daughter:*Leonore Wilhelmine Charlotte
Ekermann, Heinrich Friedrich August *SEE* Ekermann, Heinrich
Ekermann, Leonore Wilhelmine Charlotte *SEE* Ekermann, Heinrich
Ekermann, Sophie Caroline Louise *SEE* Ekermann, Heinrich
Ekert, Anna 27; New York, NY, 1847 ***9176.15*** *p51*
Ekert, Antoin 46; New York, NY, 1847 ***9176.15*** *p50*
Ekert, Carl 1; New York, NY, 1847 ***9176.15*** *p51*
Ekert, Fred. 28; New York, NY, 1847 ***9176.15*** *p51*
Ekert, Liboratha 6; New York, NY, 1847 ***9176.15*** *p51*
Eklof, Per Gustaf; Iowa, 1875 ***1211.15*** *p10*
Eklund, C.J.; New Orleans, 1843 ***6412.40*** *p147*
Eklund, John; Cleveland, OH, 1888-1896 ***9722.10*** *p118*
Eklund, Nils P.; Colorado, 1887 ***1029.59*** *p25*
Eklund, Peter; Colorado, 1892 ***1029.59*** *p25*
Ekman, Carl M.; Colorado, 1880 ***1029.59*** *p25*
Ekmann, August; Wisconsin, 1879 ***6795.8*** *p55*
Ekmann, John; Wisconsin, 1881 ***6795.8*** *p55*
Ekroos, H. J. 43; Minnesota, 1925 ***2769.54*** *p1382*
Ekroth, Nels; Colorado, 1893 ***1029.59*** *p25*
Ekroth, Nils; Colorado, 1893 ***1029.59*** *p25*
Ekroth, Nils; Colorado, 1903 ***1029.59*** *p25*
Ekroth, Olaf; Colorado, 1892 ***1029.59*** *p25*
Ekroth, Olof T.; Colorado, 1892 ***1029.59*** *p26*
Ekroth, Olof T.; Colorado, 1900 ***1029.59*** *p26*
Ekroth, S.P.; New York, NY, 1849 ***6412.40*** *p151*
Ekroth, Selma; Colorado, 1894 ***1029.59*** *p26*
Ekstrom, Anna Tornblom *SEE* Ekstrom, Peter A.
Ekstrom, Anna Katrina *SEE* Ekstrom, Peter A.
Ekstrom, Carl Natanael *SEE* Ekstrom, Peter A.
Ekstrom, Fred; New York, 1902 ***1766.20*** *p3*
Ekstrom, Gustaf; Cleveland, OH, 1906 ***9722.10*** *p118*
Ekstrom, Jacob; New York, NY, 1846 ***6412.40*** *p149*
Ekstrom, Peter A.; St. Paul, MN, 1887 ***1865.50*** *p45*
*Wife:*Anna Tornblom
*Child:*Anna Katrina
*Child:*Carl Natanael
Elacott, Charles 72; Ontario, 1871 ***1823.17*** *p47*
Elbling, Jiri; Nebraska, 1869 ***2853.20*** *p161*
Elbrecht, Frederick; Ohio, 1840-1897 ***8365.35*** *p16*
Eldebluth, Katharina; Chicago, 1889 ***5475.1*** *p155*
Elder, Eliza 70; Ontario, 1871 ***1823.21*** *p102*
Elder, James; Iowa, 1892 ***1211.15*** *p10*
Eldon, Kirkland; Miami, 1920 ***4984.15*** *p38*
Eldon, Thomas; Miami, 1920 ***4984.15*** *p38*
Eldred, Edwd 50; Ontario, 1871 ***1823.17*** *p47*
Eldridge, John 30; Ontario, 1871 ***1823.21*** *p102*
Eldridge, John 60; Ontario, 1871 ***1823.21*** *p102*
Eldridge, Rufis 35; Ontario, 1871 ***1823.21*** *p102*
Elehenger, Alios; Ohio, 1809-1852 ***4511.35*** *p12*
Elehenger, Alois; Ohio, 1809-1852 ***4511.35*** *p12*
Element, William 37; Ontario, 1871 ***1823.21*** *p103*
Elett, William; Jamaica, 1779 ***8529.30*** *p13A*
Elfgin, Henry; Illinois, 1859 ***6079.1*** *p5*
Elfstrom, Catharine; New York, 1849 ***9722.10*** *p113*
Elg, J.; Valparaiso, Chile, 1850 ***1192.4*** *p50*
Elget, Johann 39; New York, NY, 1893 ***1883.7*** *p38*
Elgie, Thomas 48; Ontario, 1871 ***1823.21*** *p103*
Elgin, Eliza 58; Ontario, 1871 ***1823.17*** *p47*
Elias, Elizabeth *SEE* Elias, John
Elias, F. 28; America, 1845 ***778.6*** *p107*
Elias, Jan *SEE* Elias, Jan
Elias, Jan; Wisconsin, 1854 ***2853.20*** *p304*
*Father:*Jan
Elias, John; Ohio, 1836 ***4022.20*** *p277*
*Wife:*Elizabeth
Eliason, Axel Emil; New York, 1887 ***1766.20*** *p36*
Eliason, Charley; Iowa, 1888 ***1211.15*** *p10*
Eliasson, Karin; St. Paul, MN, 1888 ***1865.50*** *p44*
Elich, V.; Louisiana, 1874 ***4981.45*** *p295*
Elie, Antoine 40; America, 1845 ***778.6*** *p107*
Elie, Francois; Nova Scotia, 1753 ***3051*** *p112*
Elie, Joseph 42; Port uncertain, 1843 ***778.6*** *p107*
Elie, Philipp 14; Port uncertain, 1843 ***778.6*** *p107*
Eliment, Harriet 67; Ontario, 1871 ***1823.21*** *p103*
Elinz, Jacques 24; America, 1847 ***778.6*** *p107*
Eliol, George; Louisiana, 1874 ***4981.45*** *p131*
Eliopoulos, Jean 33; New York, NY, 1894 ***6512.1*** *p185*
Eliopoulos, Nicolas 10; New York, NY, 1894 ***6512.1*** *p185*
Eliott, Gilbert 57; Ontario, 1871 ***1823.21*** *p103*
Eliott, James 50; Ontario, 1871 ***1823.21*** *p103*
Elis, Charles E. 36; Michigan, 1880 ***4491.42*** *p10*
Elison, Alfred; Cleveland, OH, 1888-1894 ***9722.10*** *p118*
Elitt, Thomas; Jamaica, 1779 ***8529.30*** *p13A*
Ella, Jacob; Louisiana, 1874-1875 ***4981.45*** *p298*
Ellebracht, Friedrich; Texas, 1845 ***7420.1*** *p35*
With family
With son 1
With son 11
With son 9
With son 3
With son 13
Ellemann, Johann 30; New Orleans, 1848 ***778.6*** *p107*
Ellenor, Henry 31; Ontario, 1871 ***1823.17*** *p47*
Ellenor, Samuel 64; Ontario, 1871 ***1823.17*** *p47*
Eller, Phillip; North Carolina, 1812 ***1088.45*** *p9*
Ellerly, Thomas C. 60; Ontario, 1871 ***1823.17*** *p47*
Ellermann, Jacob 24; New Orleans, 1848 ***778.6*** *p107*
Ellertsen, Ludwig; Iowa, 1875 ***1211.15*** *p10*
Elles, Rob 21; St. Johns, N.F., 1811 ***1053.20*** *p20*
Elles, William C. 21; Ontario, 1871 ***1823.21*** *p103*
Elleson, Ann 70; Ontario, 1871 ***1823.21*** *p103*
Ellet, Francis; Maryland, 1674-1675 ***1236.25*** *p52*
Ellett, Francis; Maryland, 1674-1675 ***1236.25*** *p52*
Elliason, Ole; Washington, 1886 ***6015.10*** *p16*
Ellice, William 54; Ontario, 1871 ***1823.21*** *p103*
Ellico, Charles 53; Ontario, 1871 ***1823.21*** *p103*
Elliker, Michael 40; Ontario, 1871 ***1823.17*** *p47*
Ellinger, Karl; America, 1885 ***179.55*** *p19*
Ellinger, Pauline; America, 1893 ***179.55*** *p19*
Ellinghen, Cefin; Ohio, 1809-1852 ***4511.35*** *p12*
Ellio, E.; Louisiana, 1874 ***4981.45*** *p295*
Elliot, Aaron; Ohio, 1809-1852 ***4511.35*** *p12*
Elliot, Adam 79; Ontario, 1871 ***1823.21*** *p103*
Elliot, Andrew 62; Ontario, 1871 ***1823.17*** *p47*
Elliot, Gabez; New York, 1776 ***8529.30*** *p3A*
Elliot, Helen 77; Ontario, 1871 ***1823.21*** *p103*
Elliot, Helen 83; Ontario, 1871 ***1823.17*** *p47*
Elliot, Jane 21; Ontario, 1871 ***1823.17*** *p47*
Elliot, John 24; Ontario, 1871 ***1823.21*** *p103*
Elliot, John 26; Ontario, 1871 ***1823.21*** *p103*
Elliot, John 32; Ontario, 1871 ***1823.17*** *p47*
Elliot, John 50; Ontario, 1871 ***1823.21*** *p103*
Elliot, John 56; Ontario, 1871 ***1823.17*** *p47*
Elliot, Margaret 14; Ontario, 1871 ***1823.17*** *p47*
Elliot, Ninian 72; Ontario, 1871 ***1823.21*** *p103*
Elliot, Samuel; Boston, 1757 ***1642*** *p26*
Elliot, Simon, Jr.; Boston, 1791 ***1642*** *p26*
Elliot, Thomas 48; Ontario, 1871 ***1823.21*** *p103*
Elliot, William 53; Ontario, 1871 ***1823.21*** *p103*
Elliot, William 60; Ontario, 1871 ***1823.21*** *p103*
Elliott, Alexander 25; Ontario, 1871 ***1823.21*** *p103*
Elliott, Anna 21; Michigan, 1880 ***4491.30*** *p10*
Elliott, Edward; Ohio, 1809-1852 ***4511.35*** *p12*
Elliott, Edward 25; Ontario, 1871 ***1823.21*** *p103*
Elliott, Edward 30; Ontario, 1871 ***1823.17*** *p47*
Elliott, Elizabeth 57; Ontario, 1871 ***1823.17*** *p47*
Elliott, Ellen 55; Ontario, 1871 ***1823.21*** *p103*
Elliott, Francis 36; Ontario, 1871 ***1823.21*** *p103*
Elliott, Gabez; New York, 1776 ***8529.30*** *p3A*
Elliott, George 23; Ontario, 1871 ***1823.21*** *p103*
Elliott, George 41; Ontario, 1871 ***1823.21*** *p103*
Elliott, George 43; Ontario, 1871 ***1823.21*** *p103*
Elliott, George M.; Ohio, 1859 ***3580.20*** *p31*
Elliott, George M.; Ohio, 1859 ***6020.12*** *p7*
Elliott, Gideon 40; Ontario, 1871 ***1823.21*** *p103*
Elliott, Hugh; Colorado, 1882 ***1029.59*** *p26*
Elliott, James 29; Ontario, 1871 ***1823.21*** *p103*
Elliott, James 44; Ontario, 1871 ***1823.17*** *p47*
Elliott, James 50; Ontario, 1871 ***1823.21*** *p103*
Elliott, James 68; Ontario, 1871 ***1823.21*** *p103*
Elliott, James 19; Quebec, 1870 ***8364.32*** *p23*
Elliott, James D. 36; Ontario, 1871 ***1823.21*** *p103*
Elliott, Jane 18; Michigan, 1880 ***4491.33*** *p8*
Elliott, Jane 84; Ontario, 1871 ***1823.21*** *p103*
Elliott, John 40; Ontario, 1871 ***1823.17*** *p48*
Elliott, John 43; Ontario, 1871 ***1823.17*** *p48*
Elliott, John 44; Ontario, 1871 ***1823.17*** *p48*
Elliott, John 49; Ontario, 1871 ***1823.21*** *p104*
Elliott, John 50; Ontario, 1871 ***1823.21*** *p104*
Elliott, John 51; Ontario, 1871 ***1823.21*** *p103*
Elliott, John 57; Ontario, 1871 ***1823.21*** *p104*
Elliott, John Forster 30; Ontario, 1871 ***1823.17*** *p48*
Elliott, John Foster 30; Ontario, 1871 ***1823.17*** *p48*
Elliott, Joseph H. 40; Ontario, 1871 ***1823.21*** *p104*
Elliott, M. J.; Louisiana, 1874 ***4981.45*** *p131*
Elliott, Mary 38; Michigan, 1880 ***4491.33*** *p8*
Elliott, Nelson 45; Ontario, 1871 ***1823.21*** *p104*
Elliott, Ralph 25; Indiana, 1854-1860 ***9076.20*** *p65*
Elliott, Richard 46; Ontario, 1871 ***1823.21*** *p104*
Elliott, Richard 73; Ontario, 1871 ***1823.17*** *p48*
Elliott, Robert 32; Ontario, 1871 ***1823.21*** *p104*
Elliott, Robert 81; Ontario, 1871 ***1823.21*** *p104*

Elliott, Robt. 30; Ontario, 1871 ***1823.17*** *p48*
Elliott, Samuel; Ontario, 1871 ***1823.21*** *p104*
Elliott, Samuel 38; Ontario, 1871 ***1823.17*** *p48*
Elliott, Samuel 56; Ontario, 1871 ***1823.21*** *p104*
Elliott, Samuel 56; Ontario, 1871 ***1823.21*** *p104*
Elliott, Sarah 34; Ontario, 1871 ***1823.21*** *p104*
Elliott, Stephen 78; Ontario, 1871 ***1823.21*** *p104*
Elliott, Thomas; Jamaica, 1779 ***8529.30*** *p13A*
Elliott, Thomas 42; Ontario, 1871 ***1823.21*** *p104*
Elliott, Thomas 59; Ontario, 1871 ***1823.17*** *p48*
Elliott, William; Jamaica, 1779 ***8529.30*** *p13A*
Elliott, William 46; Michigan, 1880 ***4491.33*** *p8*
Elliott, William 25; Ontario, 1871 ***1823.21*** *p104*
Elliott, William 27; Ontario, 1871 ***1823.21*** *p104*
Elliott, William 37; Ontario, 1871 ***1823.21*** *p104*
Elliott, William 60; Ontario, 1871 ***1823.21*** *p104*
Elliott, William; Philadelphia, 1869 ***7074.20*** *p132*
Elliott, Wm 78; Ontario, 1871 ***1823.21*** *p104*
Ellis, Miss; Salem, MA, n.d. ***9228.50*** *p207*
Ellis, Agnes; Colorado, 1862-1920 ***1029.59*** *p26*
Ellis, Agnes; Colorado, 1887 ***1029.59*** *p26*
Ellis, Agnes; Colorado, 1892 ***1029.59*** *p26*
Ellis, Andrew 60; Ontario, 1871 ***1823.21*** *p104*
Ellis, Charles 18; Ontario, 1871 ***1823.17*** *p48*
Ellis, David J. 66; Michigan, 1880 ***4491.36*** *p6*
Ellis, Edmond; Philadelphia, 1777 ***8529.30*** *p3A*
Ellis, Edward 22; Ontario, 1871 ***1823.17*** *p48*
Ellis, Eliza 17; Ontario, 1871 ***1823.21*** *p104*
Ellis, Eliza 60; Ontario, 1871 ***1823.21*** *p104*
Ellis, Elizabeth; Ohio, 1846 ***4022.20*** *p283*
Ellis, Harriett 25; Michigan, 1880 ***4491.36*** *p6*
Ellis, Henry 30; Ontario, 1871 ***1823.17*** *p48*
Ellis, Henry 57; Ontario, 1871 ***1823.17*** *p48*
Ellis, Henry B. 13; Michigan, 1880 ***4491.36*** *p6*
Ellis, Henry C.; Washington, 1886 ***2770.40*** *p195*
Ellis, James 61; Michigan, 1880 ***4491.42*** *p11*
Ellis, James; Ohio, 1844 ***2763.1*** *p9*
Ellis, James 27; Santa Clara Co., CA, 1852 ***8704.1*** *p22*
Ellis, Jane 60; Ontario, 1871 ***1823.21*** *p104*
Ellis, John; New Jersey, 1812 ***3845.2*** *p129*
Ellis, John 30; Ontario, 1871 ***1823.21*** *p104*
Ellis, John 15; Quebec, 1870 ***8364.32*** *p23*
Ellis, Jonathan 40; Ontario, 1871 ***1823.21*** *p104*
Ellis, Joseph 20; Ontario, 1871 ***1823.17*** *p48*
Ellis, Lazarus 69; Ontario, 1871 ***1823.17*** *p48*
Ellis, Margaret 17; Quebec, 1870 ***8364.32*** *p23*
Ellis, Patrick 30; Ontario, 1871 ***1823.21*** *p104*
Ellis, Richard; Boston, 1717 ***1642*** *p116*
Ellis, Richard; Massachusetts, 1745 ***1642*** *p116*
Ellis, Sarah 66; Michigan, 1880 ***4491.42*** *p11*
Ellis, Stephen 45; Ontario, 1871 ***1823.21*** *p104*
Ellis, Thomas 28; Ontario, 1871 ***1823.17*** *p48*
Ellis, Thomas 30; Ontario, 1871 ***1823.21*** *p104*
Ellis, Thomas 45; Ontario, 1871 ***1823.21*** *p104*
Ellis, Thomas 52; Ontario, 1871 ***1823.17*** *p48*
Ellis, Thomas 18; Quebec, 1870 ***8364.32*** *p23*
Ellis, William; Boston, 1775 ***8529.30*** *p3A*
Ellis, William 23; Ontario, 1871 ***1823.21*** *p104*
Ellis, William 24; Ontario, 1871 ***1823.17*** *p48*
Ellis, William 29; Ontario, 1871 ***1823.21*** *p104*
Ellis, William 54; Ontario, 1871 ***1823.17*** *p48*
Ellis, William 78; Ontario, 1871 ***1823.21*** *p104*
Ellise, Catharine 50; Ontario, 1871 ***1823.21*** *p104*
Ellise, Lawrence 24; Ontario, 1871 ***1823.21*** *p104*
Ellison, John; North Carolina, 1840 ***1088.45*** *p9*
Ellison, Thomas 43; Ontario, 1871 ***1823.17*** *p48*
Ellsbach, Michael; Ohio, 1809-1852 ***4511.35*** *p12*
Ellsbech, Michael; Ohio, 1809-1852 ***4511.35*** *p13*
Ellsbury, Charles E. *SEE* Ellsbury, John
Ellsbury, Elizabeth Gould *SEE* Ellsbury, John
Ellsbury, John; New York, 1832 ***9228.50*** *p207*
With 4 children
*Wife:*Elizabeth Gould
*Child:*Charles E.
Ellsler, L. 49; America, 1848 ***778.6*** *p107*
Ellstrom, Axel; Cleveland, OH, 1895-1897 ***9722.10*** *p118*
Ellwanger, Ad.; Valdivia, Chile, 1851 ***1192.4*** *p50*
With wife
With child 2
Ellwood, Gardner 63; Ontario, 1871 ***1823.21*** *p104*
Ellwood, Harvey 33; Ontario, 1871 ***1823.21*** *p104*
Ellwood, James; North Carolina, 1839 ***1088.45*** *p9*
Ellwood, Joseph 43; Ontario, 1871 ***1823.21*** *p104*
Ellwood, Joseph 71; Ontario, 1871 ***1823.17*** *p48*
Ellwood, Mark 48; Ontario, 1871 ***1823.21*** *p105*
Ellwood, Mathew 53; Ontario, 1871 ***1823.21*** *p105*
Ellwood, Richard; Louisiana, 1874 ***4981.45*** *p131*
Ellwood, William 58; Ontario, 1871 ***1823.21*** *p105*
Ellworthy, Francis 11; Ontario, 1871 ***1823.21*** *p105*
Elm, Jacob 35; Ontario, 1871 ***1823.21*** *p105*
Elm, Peter 46; Ontario, 1871 ***1823.21*** *p105*
Elmgren, John; Cleveland, OH, 1902-1904 ***9722.10*** *p118*
Elmore, James 24; Ontario, 1871 ***1823.21*** *p105*
Elms, George 50; Ontario, 1871 ***1823.21*** *p105*
Elms, Henry George 24; Ontario, 1871 ***1823.21*** *p105*
Elms, Valentine 41; Ontario, 1871 ***1823.21*** *p105*
Elmstrom, Johan; New York, NY, 1851 ***6412.40*** *p153*
Elnor, Daniel 53; Ontario, 1871 ***1823.17*** *p48*
Elofson, Herman; Cleveland, OH, 1902-1903 ***9722.10*** *p118*
Elofson, Nels; Washington, 1884 ***2770.40*** *p192*
Elofson, Victor; Cleveland, OH, 1906 ***9722.10*** *p118*
Eloy, Antoinette; Quebec, 1665 ***4514.3*** *p311*
Eloy, Marguerite; Quebec, 1667 ***4514.3*** *p312*
Elsass, Christian; Ohio, 1809-1852 ***4511.35*** *p13*
Elsbury, Charles E. *SEE* Elsbury, John
Elsbury, Elizabeth Gould *SEE* Elsbury, John
Elsbury, John; New York, 1832 ***9228.50*** *p207*
With 4 children
*Wife:*Elizabeth Gould
*Child:*Charles E.
Elsemore, Mary; Maryland, 1674 ***1236.25*** *p50*
Elser, Anastasia; America, 1853 ***179.55*** *p19*
Elser, Joseph; America, 1853 ***179.55*** *p19*
Elser, Victoria; America, 1700-1899 ***179.55*** *p19*
Elsfelder, Daniel; Ohio, 1809-1852 ***4511.35*** *p13*
Elsinger, Christopher; Ohio, 1809-1852 ***4511.35*** *p13*
Elsinger, John; Ohio, 1809-1852 ***4511.35*** *p13*
Elsmann, Max Eduard Valentin; America, 1867 ***7919.3*** *p529*
Elsmore, Mary; Maryland, 1674 ***1236.25*** *p50*
Elsner, Johann; Galveston, TX, 1855 ***571.7*** *p16*
Elsner, John; Wisconsin, 1885 ***6795.8*** *p128*
Elsner, Wilhelm; America, 1884 ***2526.43*** *p224*
Elsoff, H. H.; Ohio, 1840-1897 ***8365.35*** *p16*
Elsoff, Wm.; Ohio, 1840-1897 ***8365.35*** *p16*
Elson, Charles; Colorado, 1891 ***1029.59*** *p26*
Elson, John 36; Ontario, 1871 ***1823.21*** *p105*
Elson, John 48; Ontario, 1871 ***1823.21*** *p105*
Elson, John 64; Ontario, 1871 ***1823.21*** *p105*
Elson, Mary 63; Ontario, 1871 ***1823.21*** *p105*
Elteste, Fr. Heinr. Rud. Joh.; America, 1872 ***5475.1*** *p298*
Elvidge, Mark 44; Ontario, 1871 ***1823.21*** *p105*
Elvis, John; North Carolina, 1852 ***1088.45*** *p9*
Elward, William; Maryland, 1671 ***1236.25*** *p46*
Elwick, Simpson 38; Indiana, 1879-1881 ***9076.20*** *p70*
Elwood, Alice C. 55; Michigan, 1880 ***4491.39*** *p9*
Elwood, Asa 35; Ontario, 1871 ***1823.21*** *p105*
Elwood, Edwin 65; Michigan, 1880 ***4491.39*** *p9*
Elwood, Ephriam 45; Ontario, 1871 ***1823.21*** *p105*
Elwood, John 38; Ontario, 1871 ***1823.21*** *p105*
Elwood, Margret 67; Ontario, 1871 ***1823.21*** *p105*
Elwood, William; Maryland, 1671 ***1236.25*** *p46*
Elworthy, Richard 71; Ontario, 1871 ***1823.21*** *p105*
Ely, . . .; Plymouth, MA, 1620 ***1920.45*** *p5*
Ely, Philip 44; America, 1840 ***778.6*** *p107*
Emanuel, Albert; Louisiana, 1836-1841 ***4981.45*** *p208*
Emanuel, Berta Isenberg *SEE* Emanuel, Julius
Emanuel, Johann 20; America, 1867 ***5475.1*** *p175*
Emanuel, Johann Mathias; America, 1873 ***5475.1*** *p175*
Emanuel, Julius; Argentina, 1941 ***8023.44*** *p373*
*Wife:*Berta Isenberg
Emanuel, Peter; America, 1873 ***5475.1*** *p175*
Emart, Mary; Ontario, 1835 ***3160.1*** *p150*
Emberson, Alfred 18; Quebec, 1870 ***8364.32*** *p23*
Emblin, James 65; Ontario, 1871 ***1823.21*** *p105*
Embser, A. Maria; America, 1881 ***5475.1*** *p334*
Eme, Claire 32; America, 1846 ***778.6*** *p107*
Eme, Hubert 36; America, 1846 ***778.6*** *p107*
Emeq, Francois 25; Mississippi, 1847 ***778.6*** *p108*
Emerich, Michael; Louisiana, 1855 ***7710.1*** *p155*
Emerson, Alexr 50; Ontario, 1871 ***1823.21*** *p105*
Emerson, John 43; Ontario, 1871 ***1823.17*** *p48*
Emerson, Thomas; Washington, 1881 ***2770.40*** *p135*
Emery, A. S. 33; Ontario, 1871 ***1823.21*** *p105*
Emery, Daniel 36; Michigan, 1880 ***4491.42*** *p11*
Emery, Frank S.; Colorado, 1896 ***1029.59*** *p26*
Emery, George 43; Ontario, 1871 ***1823.21*** *p105*
Emery, John 32; Michigan, 1880 ***4491.30*** *p10*
Emery, Margaret R.; Colorado, 1896 ***1029.59*** *p26*
Emery, Mary Ann 29; Ontario, 1871 ***1823.21*** *p105*
Emery, Robert; North Carolina, 1837 ***1088.45*** *p9*
Emery, Thomas 32; Ontario, 1871 ***1823.17*** *p48*
Emhardt, J.; Chile, 1852 ***1192.4*** *p51*
With wife & 3 children
With child 12
With child 5
Emig, Friedrich; America, 1831 ***2526.42*** *p104*
With wife & 6 children
Emig, Johannes; America, 1884 ***2526.42*** *p168*
With mother
Emmans, Minor 46; Ontario, 1871 ***1823.21*** *p105*
Emmel, Gertrud *SEE* Emmel, Peter
Emmel, Gertrud Klein 42 *SEE* Emmel, Peter
Emmel, Jakob *SEE* Emmel, Peter
Emmel, Margarethe 20 *SEE* Emmel, Peter
Emmel, Peter 45; America, 1855 ***5475.1*** *p250*
*Wife:*Gertrud Klein 42
*Son:*Jakob
*Daughter:*Gertrud
*Son:*Philipp
*Daughter:*Margarethe 20
Emmel, Philipp *SEE* Emmel, Peter
Emmenacker, Franz 4; Galveston, TX, 1844 ***3967.10*** *p371*
Emmenacker, Franziska 32; Galveston, TX, 1844 ***3967.10*** *p371*
Emmenacker, Joseph 10; Galveston, TX, 1844 ***3967.10*** *p371*
Emmenacker, Joseph 32; Galveston, TX, 1844 ***3967.10*** *p371*
Emmenacker, Karl 2; Galveston, TX, 1844 ***3967.10*** *p371*
Emmenacker, Ludwig 9; Galveston, TX, 1844 ***3967.10*** *p371*
Emmenacker, Marianne 12; Galveston, TX, 1844 ***3967.10*** *p371*
Emmenaker, Franz 4; Galveston, TX, 1844 ***3967.10*** *p371*
Emmenaker, Franziska 32; Galveston, TX, 1844 ***3967.10*** *p371*
Emmenaker, Joseph 10; Galveston, TX, 1844 ***3967.10*** *p371*
Emmenaker, Joseph 32; Galveston, TX, 1844 ***3967.10*** *p371*
Emmenaker, Karl 2; Galveston, TX, 1844 ***3967.10*** *p371*
Emmenaker, Ludwig 9; Galveston, TX, 1844 ***3967.10*** *p371*
Emmenaker, Marianne 12; Galveston, TX, 1844 ***3967.10*** *p371*
Emmerich, Anna Maria; America, 1872 ***5475.1*** *p419*
*Son:*Peter
Emmerich, Johann Peter; America, 1846 ***5475.1*** *p234*
Emmerich, Mathias; America, 1843 ***5475.1*** *p330*
Emmerich, Peter *SEE* Emmerich, Anna Maria
Emmerson, Mary A. 42; Ontario, 1871 ***1823.21*** *p105*
Emmet, Margaret 21; Ontario, 1871 ***1823.21*** *p105*
Emmett, Augustus; North Carolina, 1830 ***1088.45*** *p9*
Emmett, James 54; Ontario, 1871 ***1823.17*** *p48*
Emmons, John 61; Ontario, 1871 ***1823.21*** *p105*
Emonet, Michael 22; New Orleans, 1843 ***778.6*** *p108*
Emont, Rene 25; Quebec, 1661 ***9221.17*** *p454*
Emourgeon, Felix 48; Missouri, 1845 ***778.6*** *p108*
Emrich, Michael; New Orleans, 1849 ***7710.1*** *p152*
Emrich, William 23; Louisiana, 1849 ***7710.1*** *p150*
Emrick, Francis 80; Ontario, 1871 ***1823.21*** *p105*
Emrick, J. H.; Illinois, 1856 ***6079.1*** *p5*
Emslie, Alex 53; Ontario, 1871 ***1823.21*** *p105*
Emuell, Martin 25; Texas, 1848 ***778.6*** *p108*
Enart, Jeanne 16; Quebec, 1639 ***9221.17*** *p86*
Enart, Jeanne 16; Quebec, 1639 ***9221.17*** *p86*
Enchelmaier, Friedr.; Valdivia, Chile, 1852 ***1192.4*** *p55*
Encloux, J. B.; Louisiana, 1874 ***4981.45*** *p131*
Endeldinger, Anna M.; America, 1873 ***5475.1*** *p318*
*Daughter:*Magdalena
*Son:*Peter
Endell, John; New York, 1783 ***8529.30*** *p11*
Ender, John; New York, 1860 ***358.56*** *p149*
Ender, Peter; North Carolina, 1710 ***3629.40*** *p4*
Ender, Philipp; America, 1868 ***7919.3*** *p531*
Enderle, G.; Louisiana, 1836-1840 ***4981.45*** *p212*
Enderlin, Elisa 45; Port uncertain, 1845 ***778.6*** *p108*
Enderlin, Henry 45; Port uncertain, 1845 ***778.6*** *p108*
Enderly, Peter; Ohio, 1809-1852 ***4511.35*** *p13*
Endle, John; New York, 1783 ***8529.30*** *p11*
Endorf, Carl; America, 1870 ***7420.1*** *p286*
Endorf, Friedrich; America, 1852 ***7420.1*** *p87*
With wife
Endres, Anna Maria; America, 1879 ***5475.1*** *p186*
Endres, Christian; New Jersey, 1773-1774 ***927.31*** *p3*
Endress, Christopher; Ohio, 1809-1852 ***4511.35*** *p13*
Enevoldsen, Clifford; New Jersey, 1928 ***9228.50*** *p207*
Enevoldsen, Peder; Iowa, 1895 ***1211.15*** *p10*
Enevoldson, Peter; Iowa, 1895 ***1211.15*** *p10*
Enfre, Francoise; Quebec, 1669 ***4514.3*** *p312*
Engberg, Frederick N.; St. Paul, MN, 1893 ***1865.50*** *p45*
Engberg, Maria; Wisconsin, 1880-1901 ***1865.50*** *p45*
Engbert, August 21; New York, NY, 1883 ***8427.14*** *p44*
Engbert, Carl 9; New York, NY, 1883 ***8427.14*** *p44*
Engbert, Johann 58; New York, NY, 1883 ***8427.14*** *p44*
Engbert, Mathe. 16; New York, NY, 1883 ***8427.14*** *p44*
Engbert, Wilhele. 55; New York, NY, 1883 ***8427.14*** *p44*
Engblad, Alfred; Cleveland, OH, 1894-1897 ***9722.10*** *p118*
Eng-Chang, . . .; North Carolina, 1839 ***1088.45*** *p9*
Engebretsen, Kristian; Washington, 1888 ***2770.40*** *p25*
Engel, Agethe 45; New York, NY, 1886 ***6954.7*** *p40*
Engel, Alfred; New York, 1874 ***5475.1*** *p496*
Engel, Angela Weyrich *SEE* Engel, Jakob, II

Engel, Angela Benn 47 *SEE* Engel, Mathias
Engel, Anna *SEE* Engel, Peter
Engel, Anna 11 *SEE* Engel, Johann
Engel, Anna 3; New York, NY, 1876 *6954.7 p39*
Engel, Anni; Died enroute, 1710 *3629.40 p4*
Engel, Antoine 3; Port uncertain, 1848 *778.6 p108*
Engel, August *SEE* Engel, Konrad
Engel, Carl 3; New York, NY, 1886 *6954.7 p40*
Engel, Carl 17; New York, NY, 1876 *6954.7 p39*
Engel, Catharina 26; America, 1844 *778.6 p108*
Engel, Catherina 19; New York, NY, 1886 *6954.7 p40*
Engel, Catherina 26; New York, NY, 1876 *6954.7 p39*
Engel, Christen; North Carolina, 1710 *3629.40 p4*
Engel, Dietrich; North Carolina, 1710 *3629.40 p4*
Engel, Elisabeth 2 *SEE* Engel, Johann
Engel, Elisabeth 18 *SEE* Engel, Mathias
Engel, Elisabeth 40; Port uncertain, 1848 *778.6 p108*
Engel, Emma *SEE* Engel, Konrad
Engel, Fanny 4; New Orleans, 1848 *778.6 p108*
Engel, Franz 5 *SEE* Engel, Johann
Engel, Fried. 20; America, 1840 *778.6 p108*
Engel, Friedrich 30; New York, NY, 1876 *6954.7 p39*
Engel, Georg *SEE* Engel, Jakob, II
Engel, Georg 33; Pennsylvania, 1850 *170.15 p24*
  With wife
Engel, Georg 25; Rio Grande do Sul, Brazil, 1854 *5475.1
  p532*
Engel, Heinrich 9; New York, NY, 1876 *6954.7 p39*
Engel, Helena; America, 1872 *5475.1 p304*
Engel, J.; New York, 1859 *358.56 p99*
Engel, Jacob 20; New York, NY, 1886 *6954.7 p40*
Engel, Jakob *SEE* Engel, Jakob, II
Engel, Jakob; America, 1882 *5475.1 p464*
  With wife
Engel, Jakob 7 *SEE* Engel, Mathias
Engel, Jakob, II; America, 1882 *5475.1 p464*
  Wife: Angela Weyrich
  Son: Peter
  Son: Georg
  Son: Jakob
  Son: Margarethe
  Son: Nikolaus
  Daughter: Maria
Engel, Johann *SEE* Engel, Peter
Engel, Johann; America, 1873 *5475.1 p256*
Engel, Johann; America, 1874 *5475.1 p256*
  Wife: M. Gliedner
  Daughter: Elisabeth
  Son: Mathias
  Daughter: Anna
  Son: Franz
  Son: Michel
  Son: Peter
Engel, Johann 6; New York, NY, 1876 *6954.7 p39*
Engel, Johann; Ohio, 1867 *5475.1 p487*
Engel, Johann Peter; Pennsylvania, 1848 *170.15 p24*
Engel, John 40; America, 1843 *778.6 p108*
Engel, Joseph 17; New York, NY, 1886 *6954.7 p40*
Engel, Joseph 46; New York, NY, 1886 *6954.7 p40*
Engel, Joseph 5; Port uncertain, 1848 *778.6 p108*
Engel, Kaspar; Pennsylvania, 1848 *170.15 p24*
Engel, Kaspar 54; Pennsylvania, 1850 *170.15 p24*
Engel, Katharina; America, 1852 *179.55 p19*
Engel, Katharina 22 *SEE* Engel, Mathias
Engel, Katharina Bauer *SEE* Engel, Konrad
Engel, Konrad; Rio Grande do Sul, Brazil, 1881 *5475.1
  p533*
  Wife: Katharina Bauer
  Son: Nikolaus
  Daughter: M. Johanna
  Daughter: Emma
  Son: Robert
  Daughter: M. Magdalena
  Son: August
Engel, Louis 10; Port uncertain, 1848 *778.6 p108*
Engel, M. Gliedner 45 *SEE* Engel, Johann
Engel, M. Johanna *SEE* Engel, Konrad
Engel, M. Magdalena *SEE* Engel, Konrad
Engel, Madgalena 12 *SEE* Engel, Mathias
Engel, Margaretha Katharina; America, 1885 *179.55 p19*
Engel, Margarethe *SEE* Engel, Jakob, II
Engel, Maria Simon *SEE* Engel, Peter
Engel, Maria *SEE* Engel, Jakob, II
Engel, Maria 15 *SEE* Engel, Mathias
Engel, Maria 20 *SEE* Engel, Mathias
Engel, Maria Theresa; Rio Grande do Sul, Brazil, 1881
  5475.1 p533
  Daughter: Rosa
Engel, Martin 22; America, 1840 *778.6 p108*
Engel, Mary 30; America, 1843 *778.6 p108*
Engel, Mathias 5 *SEE* Engel, Mathias
Engel, Mathias 15 *SEE* Engel, Johann

Engel, Mathias 47; America, 1846 *5475.1 p463*
  Wife: Angela Benn 47
  Daughter: Elisabeth 18
  Daughter: Madgalena 12
  Son: Mathias 5
  Son: Jakob 7
  Daughter: Maria 15
  Daughter: Katharina 22
  Daughter: Maria 20
Engel, Mathilda 2; New Orleans, 1848 *778.6 p108*
Engel, Mathilde; America, 1868 *7919.3 p527*
Engel, Michel 9 *SEE* Engel, Johann
Engel, Nikolaus *SEE* Engel, Jakob, II
Engel, Nikolaus *SEE* Engel, Konrad
Engel, Oswald 48; Port uncertain, 1848 *778.6 p108*
Engel, Peter; America, 1871 *5475.1 p304*
  Wife: Maria Simon
  Son: Johann
  Daughter: Anna
Engel, Peter *SEE* Engel, Jakob, II
Engel, Peter 17 *SEE* Engel, Johann
Engel, Peter 36; New Orleans, 1848 *778.6 p108*
Engel, Peter; North Carolina, 1710 *3629.40 p4*
Engel, Regina 34; New Orleans, 1848 *778.6 p108*
Engel, Robert *SEE* Engel, Konrad
Engel, Rosa *SEE* Engel, Maria Theresa
Engel, Rosina; America, 1871 *179.55 p19*
Engel, Theador 2; New York, NY, 1886 *6954.7 p40*
Engel, Wilhelm 7; New York, NY, 1886 *6954.7 p40*
Engelder, Georg Wilhelm 24; America, 1854 *2526.43
  p146*
Engeldinger, Anna *SEE* Engeldinger, Mathias
Engeldinger, Anna 4 *SEE* Engeldinger, Johann
Engeldinger, Anna 20 *SEE* Engeldinger, Johann
Engeldinger, Anna Maria Nittler 42 *SEE* Engeldinger,
  Johann
Engeldinger, Barbara Kiefer 35 *SEE* Engeldinger,
  Mathias
Engeldinger, Elisabeth; Wisconsin, 1877 *5475.1 p363*
Engeldinger, Johann 12 *SEE* Engeldinger, Johann
Engeldinger, Johann 46; America, 1885 *5475.1 p319*
  Wife: Anna Maria Nittler 42
  Son: Johann 12
  Daughter: Anna 4
  Son: Peter 8
  Daughter: Anna 20
  Son: Nikolaus 16
Engeldinger, Katharina *SEE* Engeldinger, Mathias
Engeldinger, Mathias; America, 1800-1899 *5475.1 p288*
Engeldinger, Mathias; America, 1871 *5475.1 p318*
  Wife: Barbara Kiefer
  Son: Peter
  Daughter: Katharina
  Daughter: Anna
  Son: Nikolaus
Engeldinger, Nikolaus *SEE* Engeldinger, Mathias
Engeldinger, Nikolaus 16 *SEE* Engeldinger, Johann
Engeldinger, Peter *SEE* Engeldinger, Mathias
Engeldinger, Peter 8 *SEE* Engeldinger, Johann
Engelhard, Heinrich; America, 1853 *7420.1 p104*
Engelhard, Wilhelm; America, 1853 *7420.1 p104*
Engelhardt, Heinr.; Valdivia, Chile, 1852 *1192.4 p55*
  With wife
Engelhardt, John M.; New York, 1860 *358.56 p150*
Engelhardt, Marg.; New York, 1860 *358.56 p4*
Engelke, Friedrich; America, 1893 *7420.1 p368*
Engelking, Mr.; America, 1850 *7420.1 p71*
Engelking, Mr.; America, 1870 *7420.1 p283*
  With brother & 2 sisters
Engelking, Albert; New York, NY, 1876 *7420.1 p306*
Engelking, Anna Sophie Dorothee *SEE* Engelking,
  Johann Heinrich Christian
Engelking, Anna Sophie Dorothee Rehling *SEE*
  Engelking, Johann Heinrich Christian
Engelking, Anne Sophie Dorothee; America, 1856
  7420.1 p147
Engelking, Catharina Sophia Richers *SEE* Engelking,
  Hans Heinrich
Engelking, Catharine Engel *SEE* Engelking, Hans
  Heinrich
Engelking, Christine; America, 1855 *7420.1 p136*
Engelking, Christoph; America, 1878 *7420.1 p310*
Engelking, Engel Dorothea; America, 1867 *7420.1 p255*
Engelking, Engel Dorothee Sophie *SEE* Engelking, Hans
  Heinrich
Engelking, Engel Elisabeth; America, 1854 *7420.1 p127*
Engelking, Engel Maria *SEE* Engelking, Hans Heinrich
Engelking, Engel Maria Sophia; America, 1850 *7420.1
  p72*
  Daughter: Engel Maria Sophia
  Daughter: Engel Maria
  Daughter: Engel Maria Dorothea
  Daughter: Catharina Sophia

Engelking, Engel Marie Sophie Dohmeier *SEE*
  Engelking, Hans Heinrich
Engelking, Ferdinand; America, 1876 *7420.1 p306*
  With wife
  Son: Friedrich Ferdinand
Engelking, Friedrich; America, 1852 *7420.1 p87*
Engelking, Friedrich Ferdinand *SEE* Engelking,
  Ferdinand
Engelking, Friedrich Wilhelm; America, 1867 *7420.1
  p256*
Engelking, Hans Heinrich; America, 1836 *7420.1 p11*
Engelking, Hans Heinrich; America, 1852 *7420.1 p87*
Engelking, Hans Heinrich; America, 1855 *7420.1 p136*
  Wife: Engel Marie Sophie Dohmeier
  Daughter: Catharine Engel
  Daughter: Engel Maria
  Son: Johann Heinrich
  Son: Johann Philipp
Engelking, Hans Heinrich; America, 1857 *7420.1 p160*
  Wife: Catharina Sophia Richers
  Daughter: Engel Dorothee Sophie
Engelking, Johann Heinrich *SEE* Engelking, Hans
  Heinrich
Engelking, Johann Heinrich Christian; America, 1855
  7420.1 p136
  Wife: Anna Sophie Dorothee Rehling
  Daughter: Anna Sophie Dorothee
Engelking, Johann Heinrich Gottlieb; America, 1844
  7420.1 p31
Engelking, Johann Otto; America, 1850 *7420.1 p71*
Engelking, Johann Philipp; America, 1853 *7420.1 p104*
Engelking, Johann Philipp *SEE* Engelking, Hans Heinrich
Engelking, Philipp; America, 1854 *7420.1 p118*
Engelking, Thrine Sophie; America, 1833 *7420.1 p7*
Engelking, W.; America, 1852 *7420.1 p87*
Engelmann, Jakob; America, 1854 *5475.1 p459*
Engelmann, Joh. Christ.; America, 1854 *5475.1 p459*
  Daughter: Sophie Margarethe
  Daughter: Luise
  Son: Johann Friedrich
  Son: Johann Nikolaus
Engelmann, Johann Friedrich *SEE* Engelmann, Joh.
  Christ.
Engelmann, Johann Nikolaus *SEE* Engelmann, Joh.
  Christ.
Engelmann, Luise *SEE* Engelmann, Joh. Christ.
Engelmann, Peter; Louisiana, 1841-1844 *4981.45 p210*
Engelmann, Sophie Margarethe *SEE* Engelmann, Joh.
  Christ.
Engels, David; Ohio, 1809-1852 *4511.35 p13*
Engels, Johann *SEE* Engels, Wilhelm
Engels, Johann; Arkansas, 1880 *5475.1 p245*
Engels, John; New York, 1859 *358.56 p101*
Engels, Michel; Chicago, 1888 *5475.1 p247*
Engels, Nikolaus; America, 1881 *5475.1 p245*
Engels, Susanna Meiers *SEE* Engels, Wilhelm
Engels, Wilhelm; America, 1881 *5475.1 p245*
Engels, Wilhelm; America, 1881 *5475.1 p299*
  Wife: Susanna Meiers
  Son: Johann
Engelson, Axel; Colorado, 1893 *1029.59 p26*
Engers, Jakob; America, 1872 *5475.1 p215*
Enggren, M.A.; New York, NY, 1844 *6412.40 p148*
Enghauser, Michel 24; Mississippi, 1848 *778.6 p108*
Engholm, Lina *SEE* Engholm, Olof A.
Engholm, Olof A.; St. Paul, MN, 1894 *1865.50 p45*
  Wife: Lina
Enginger, Catharine 24; America, 1843 *778.6 p108*
Enginger, Charles 30; America, 1843 *778.6 p108*
England, August F.; Washington, 1889 *2770.40 p27*
England, Charles 14; Quebec, 1870 *8364.32 p23*
England, Henry 45; Ontario, 1871 *1823.21 p105*
England, John 60; Ontario, 1871 *1823.21 p106*
England, Richard 36; Ontario, 1871 *1823.21 p106*
Engle, Francis; North Carolina, 1850 *1088.45 p9*
Engle, Jacob; Ohio, 1809-1852 *4511.35 p13*
Englebert, Joseph; New York, NY, 1856 *1494.20 p11*
Engler, Max; Kansas, 1917-1918 *2054.10 p48*
English, . . .; Ontario, 1871 *1823.21 p106*
English, Alexander 58; Ontario, 1871 *1823.17 p48*
English, Benjamin; New Haven, CT, 1620-1720 *9228.50
  p208*
English, Clement; Salem, MA, 1600-1699 *9228.50 p208*
English, Elizabeth 39; Ontario, 1871 *1823.21 p106*
English, George 56; Ontario, 1871 *1823.21 p106*
English, Hetty; New Orleans, 1850 *7242.30 p141*
English, James 52; Ontario, 1871 *1823.17 p48*
English, James 62; Ontario, 1871 *1823.21 p106*
English, Jno. 23; South Carolina, 1812 *3476.30 p11*
English, John 50; Ontario, 1871 *1823.21 p106*
English, Noble 74; Ontario, 1871 *1823.21 p106*
English, Philip; Massachusetts, 1651-1734 *9228.50 p207*
English, Philip; Massachusetts, n.d. *9228.50 p207*

English, Philip; Salem, MA, 1640-1660 *9228.50 p618*
English, Philip; Salem, MA, 1670 *9228.50 p5*
English, Philippe; Salem, MA, 1670 *9228.50 p24*
English, Rachel; Ohio, 1764-1846 *9228.50 p209*
English, Thomas; Boston, 1791 *1642 p26*
English, Thomas 51; Ontario, 1871 *1823.21 p106*
English, Thomas; Plymouth, MA, 1620 *1920.45 p5*
Englund, Mrs. Alfred; Minnesota, 1925 *2769.54 p1382*
Englund, Emil E.; St. Paul, MN, 1894 *1865.50 p45*
Engmann, Simon; Louisiana, 1874 *4981.45 p131*
Engnell, Peter J.; America, 1844 *4487.25 p55*
  With parents
Engquist, Cathrina; Minnesota, 1900-1901 *1865.50 p45*
Engqvist, C.; Valparaiso, Chile, 1850 *1192.4 p50*
Engqvist, Cathrina; Minnesota, 1900-1901 *1865.50 p45*
Engstler, Jakob; America, 1876 *5475.1 p141*
  *Wife:*Katharina Staudt
  *Son:*Stephan
Engstler, Kath.; America, 1873 *5475.1 p140*
Engstler, Katharina Staudt *SEE* Engstler, Jakob
Engstler, Margarethe; America, 1877 *5475.1 p134*
Engstler, Stephan *SEE* Engstler, Jakob
Engstrom, A. N.; America, 1852 *6410.15 p104*
Engstrom, Alma Sophia *SEE* Engstrom, Erick A.
Engstrom, Andrew; America, 1853 *4487.25 p56*
  With parents
Engstrom, Anna S. Andersdotter *SEE* Engstrom, Erick A.
Engstrom, August Alf. *SEE* Engstrom, Erick A.
Engstrom, Charles A.; St. Paul, MN, 1884 *1865.50 p45*
Engstrom, Christian A.; St. Paul, MN, 1881 *1865.50 p46*
Engstrom, Christina E.; St. Paul, MN, 1884 *1865.50 p45*
Engstrom, Erick A.; Kansas, 1870 *777.40 p13*
  *Wife:*Anna S. Andersdotter
  *Daughter:*Alma Sophia
  *Son:*August Alf.
Engstrom, Fr.; Philadelphia, 1847 *6412.40 p150*
Engstrom, Fredrik; America, 1852 *6410.15 p104*
Engstrom, Hannah; St. Paul, MN, 1894 *1865.50 p46*
Engstrom, Henric Fredr.; New York, NY, 1856 *6412.40 p154*
Engstrom, N.; New York, NY, 1843 *6412.40 p147*
Enhart, Caroline 24; New Orleans, 1846 *778.6 p108*
Enimen, Amena 21; Ontario, 1871 *1823.21 p106*
Enjouis, Pierre; Quebec, 1648 *9221.17 p198*
Ennis, Jane 45; Ontario, 1871 *1823.17 p48*
Ennis, Laurence; Colorado, 1873 *1029.59 p26*
Ennis, Lawrence 39; Ontario, 1871 *1823.17 p48*
Ennis, Peter 67; Michigan, 1880 *4491.30 p10*
Ennis, Thomas; Long Island, 1778 *8529.30 p9A*
Enright, Denis 56; Ontario, 1871 *1823.17 p49*
Enright, Thomas 47; Ontario, 1871 *1823.17 p49*
Ensenat, M.; Louisiana, 1874 *4981.45 p295*
Ensign, Hannah A. 48; Michigan, 1880 *4491.36 p6*
Ensinger, Philipp; America, 1831 *2526.43 p166*
  With wife 46
  With stepchild 23
  With child 10
  With child 6
  With child 3
  With child 8
Ensley, William 60; Ontario, 1871 *1823.21 p106*
Enslin, Karl 25; Galveston, TX, 1844 *3967.10 p370*
Ensserger, Lorenz; Colorado, 1882 *1029.59 p26*
Enticknap, A. D. 33; Ontario, 1871 *1823.21 p106*
Entinger, Joh. Baptist; Chicago, 1885 *5475.1 p331*
Entinger, Katharina Schangel *SEE* Entinger, Peter
Entinger, Margarethe *SEE* Entinger, Peter
Entinger, Maria; America, 1881 *5475.1 p308*
Entinger, Mathias *SEE* Entinger, Peter
Entinger, Michel; America, 1881 *5475.1 p247*
Entinger, Peter *SEE* Entinger, Peter
Entinger, Peter; Chicago, 1880 *5475.1 p335*
  *Son:*Mathias
  *Daughter:*Susanna
  *Wife:*Katharina Schangel
  *Daughter:*Margarethe
  *Son:*Peter
Entinger, Susanna *SEE* Entinger, Peter
Entner, Louis 41; New Orleans, 1848 *778.6 p108*
Entriss, Catharina; Wisconsin, 1904 *6795.8 p236*
Enz, David; Louisiana, 1841-1844 *4981.45 p210*
Enzeroth, Justus; Illinois, 1864 *6079.1 p5*
Enzi, Andreas 12; New York, NY, 1898 *7951.13 p42*
Enzi, Christian 16; New York, NY, 1898 *7951.13 p42*
Enzi, Friedricka 46; New York, NY, 1898 *7951.13 p42*
Enzi, Jacob 14; New York, NY, 1898 *7951.13 p42*
Enzi, Johann 4; New York, NY, 1898 *7951.13 p42*
Enzi, Johann 56; New York, NY, 1898 *7951.13 p42*
Enzi, Karl 3; New York, NY, 1898 *7951.13 p42*
Enzweiler, A. Maria *SEE* Enzweiler, Johann
Enzweiler, J. Nikolaus *SEE* Enzweiler, Johann
Enzweiler, Joh. Peter *SEE* Enzweiler, Johann

Enzweiler, Johann *SEE* Enzweiler, Johann
Enzweiler, Johann; Brazil, 1879 *5475.1 p265*
  *Wife:*Katharina Naumann
  *Son:*J. Nikolaus
  *Son:*Johann
  *Daughter:*Maria
  *Daughter:*A. Maria
  *Son:*Joh. Peter
  *Daughter:*Margarethe
  *Son:*Wendel
  *Son:*Nikolaus
  *Son:*Peter
Enzweiler, Katharina Naumann *SEE* Enzweiler, Johann
Enzweiler, Margarethe *SEE* Enzweiler, Johann
Enzweiler, Maria *SEE* Enzweiler, Johann
Enzweiler, Michael 38; America, 1843 *5475.1 p280*
Enzweiler, Nikolaus; America, 1881 *5475.1 p245*
Enzweiler, Nikolaus *SEE* Enzweiler, Johann
Enzweiler, Peter *SEE* Enzweiler, Johann
Enzweiler, Wendel *SEE* Enzweiler, Johann
Eon, Pre. Paul 32; Missouri, 1848 *778.6 p108*
Epbinder, Robert; Port uncertain, 1899 *7420.1 p375*
Epenin, Th. 22; America, 1847 *778.6 p108*
Eper, Henry; Baltimore, 1839 *471.10 p86*
Eperson, Nelson 57; Ontario, 1871 *1823.21 p106*
Epinhern, Peter 55; Port uncertain, 1843 *778.6 p108*
Epple, Conrad; Valdivia, Chile, 1852 *1192.4 p53*
  With wife
  With child 3 months
  With child 4
Epple, David 63; Kansas, 1895 *1447.20 p62*
Epple, Georg; Valdivia, Chile, 1852 *1192.4 p53*
  With wife & child
  With child 3 months
  With child 6
Eppler, Carl Ferdinand; America, 1868 *7919.3 p529*
Eppler, David; Kansas, 1895 *1447.20 p64*
Eppler, Michael Leopold; America, 1867 *7919.3 p527*
Eppstein, Anna *SEE* Eppstein, David
Eppstein, David; America, 1867 *5475.1 p207*
  *Wife:*Henriette Haas
  *Daughter:*Mathilde
  *Daughter:*Anna
Eppstein, Henriette Haas *SEE* Eppstein, David
Eppstein, Mathilde *SEE* Eppstein, David
Eranet, Odile 24; New Orleans, 1848 *778.6 p108*
Erasmus, Barbara 7; America, 1847 *778.6 p108*
Erb, Albert Edmund; America, 1867 *7919.3 p535*
Erb, Babette 15 *SEE* Erb, Johannes
Erb, Bernard; New Castle, DE, 1817-1818 *90.20 p150*
Erb, Johannes 52; America, 1855 *2526.43 p166*
  *Wife:*Margaretha Schneider 48
  *Son:*Philipp 22
  *Daughter:*Katharina 18
  *Daughter:*Babette 15
Erb, Katharina 18 *SEE* Erb, Johannes
Erb, Louis; America, 1867 *7919.3 p534*
Erb, Margaretha Schneider 48 *SEE* Erb, Johannes
Erb, Philipp 22 *SEE* Erb, Johannes
Erben, Jan Bolemil; St. Louis, 1860 *2853.20 p47*
Erck, Valtin; America, 1867 *7919.3 p531*
  With family
Erdmann, Emil; Wisconsin, 1896 *6795.8 p115*
Erdmann, Georg; America, 1868 *7919.3 p529*
  With wife & 7 children
Erdmann, Gustav; Wisconsin, 1894 *6795.8 p188*
Erdmann, Thedor Julius; Wisconsin, 1896 *6795.8 p38*
Ereaut, Lemuel; Montreal, n.d. *9228.50 p209*
Erhard, Chretien 18; America, 1846 *778.6 p108*
Erhard, Nikolaus; America, 1833 *5475.1 p467*
Erhardt, Friedrich *SEE* Erhardt, Mrs. Friedrich
Erhardt, Friedrich 7 *SEE* Erhardt, Mrs. Friedrich
Erhardt, Mrs. Friedrich; New York, NY, 1897 *5475.1 p26*
  *Son:*Friedrich
  *Son:*Karl
Erhardt, Mrs. Friedrich 33; New York, NY, 1898 *5475.1 p19*
  *Son:*Friedrich 7
  *Son:*Karl 5
Erhardt, Karl *SEE* Erhardt, Mrs. Friedrich
Erhardt, Karl 5 *SEE* Erhardt, Mrs. Friedrich
Erhart, Charles; North Carolina, 1842 *1088.45 p9*
Erhart, Frederick; Philadelphia, 1778 *8529.30 p6*
Erhart, John; New York, 1778 *8529.30 p6*
Erickson, Andrew; Colorado, 1875 *1029.59 p26*
Erickson, Andrew; St. Paul, MN, 1894 *1865.50 p46*
Erickson, Andrew Algoth *SEE* Erickson, Brita M.
Erickson, Andrew John; Boston, 1903 *1766.20 p23*
Erickson, Andrew P.; St. Paul, MN, 1881 *1865.50 p46*
Erickson, Anna; Illinois, 1864 *6529.11 p24*
Erickson, Anna; Illinois, 1869 *777.40 p12*
Erickson, Anna Betty; St. Paul, MN, 1888 *1865.50 p94*

Erickson, Anna Sophia; Illinois, 1880-1881 *1865.50 p46*
Erickson, Anton; Colorado, 1893 *1029.59 p26*
Erickson, Arthur; Cleveland, OH, 1887-1893 *9722.10 p118*
Erickson, Augusta; St. Paul, MN, 1894 *1865.50 p46*
Erickson, Augusta *SEE* Erickson, Louis M.
Erickson, Benn; Colorado, 1887 *1029.59 p27*
Erickson, Betze; Kansas, 1876 *777.40 p14*
Erickson, Brita Andersdotter *SEE* Erickson, Olof
Erickson, Brita; Kansas, 1876 *777.40 p14*
Erickson, Brita M.; St. Paul, MN, 1881-1883 *1865.50 p46*
  *Son:*Andrew Algoth
  *Son:*Per Alfred
Erickson, Catherine Ersdotter *SEE* Erickson, John
Erickson, Charles E.; St. Paul, MN, 1889-1890 *1865.50 p46*
  *Wife:*Stina K.
Erickson, Charlotta Johnson *SEE* Erickson, Theodore
Erickson, Christina C.; St. Paul, MN, 1882 *1865.50 p36*
Erickson, E. W.; Colorado, 1899 *1029.59 p27*
Erickson, Emma; St. Paul, MN, 1874-1905 *1865.50 p46*
Erickson, Erick; Kansas, 1876 *777.40 p8*
  *Wife:*Karin Ersdotter
  *Son:*Erick, Jr.
  *Son:*Peter D.
  *Daughter:*Mary
  *Son:*Jacob
Erickson, Erick, Jr. *SEE* Erickson, Erick
Erickson, Fredrika; St. Paul, MN, 1894 *1865.50 p46*
Erickson, Gerhs; Washington, 1887 *2770.40 p24*
Erickson, Gustaf; Minnesota, 1885-1888 *1865.50 p46*
Erickson, Gustaf A.; St. Paul, MN, 1889-1890 *1865.50 p46*
Erickson, Gustav W.; Illinois, 1861 *4487.25 p56*
Erickson, Henry *SEE* Erickson, John
Erickson, Henry; St. Paul, MN, 1889 *1865.50 p47*
Erickson, Jacob *SEE* Erickson, Erick
Erickson, John; Cleveland, OH, 1879-1888 *9722.10 p118*
Erickson, John; Illinois, 1869 *777.40 p13*
  *Wife:*Catherine Ersdotter
  *Son:*Olof J.
  *Son:*Henry
  *Daughter:*Lina
Erickson, John A.; Illinois, 1861 *4487.25 p56*
Erickson, John Adolf Mauris; New York, 1903 *1766.20 p34*
Erickson, John Alfred; New York, 1903 *1766.20 p36*
Erickson, John J.; Kansas, 1869 *777.40 p15*
  With parents
Erickson, John W.; Illinois, 1861 *4487.25 p56*
Erickson, Justaf; Colorado, 1875 *1029.59 p27*
Erickson, Karin Ersdotter *SEE* Erickson, Erick
Erickson, Lina *SEE* Erickson, John
Erickson, Louis M.; St. Paul, MN, 1894 *1865.50 p47*
  *Wife:*Augusta
Erickson, Margareta C.; Chicago, 1880 *1865.50 p113*
Erickson, Margareta C.; Chicago, 1880 *1865.50 p113*
Erickson, Mary *SEE* Erickson, Erick
Erickson, Minnie Fredrika; St. Paul, MN, 1887 *1865.50 p47*
Erickson, Ole; Washington, 1884 *2770.40 p192*
Erickson, Olof; Iowa, 1866-1869 *777.40 p8*
  *Wife:*Brita Andersdotter
Erickson, Olof J. *SEE* Erickson, John
Erickson, Per Alfred *SEE* Erickson, Brita M.
Erickson, Peter; America, 1869 *777.40 p12*
  With parents
Erickson, Peter D. *SEE* Erickson, Erick
Erickson, Peter G.; Colorado, 1887 *1029.59 p27*
Erickson, Simon E.; Colorado, 1905 *1029.59 p27*
Erickson, Simon E. 31; Colorado, 1905 *1029.59 p27*
Erickson, Stina K. *SEE* Erickson, Charles E.
Erickson, Storker A.; Washington, 1883 *2770.40 p136*
Erickson, Theodore; St. Paul, MN, 1879-1880 *1865.50 p47*
  *Wife:*Charlotta Johnson
Ericksson, John; Cleveland, OH, 1890-1892 *9722.10 p118*
Ericson, John 43; Minnesota, 1925 *2769.54 p1383*
Ericson, Segre; Colorado, 1895 *1029.59 p27*
Ericsson, Lars Carl; North America, 1855 *6410.15 p105*
Ericsson, William; Cleveland, OH, 1896-1903 *9722.10 p118*
Erikeson, Axel 24; New York, NY, 1894 *6512.1 p230*
Erikson, Anna Louisa 20; New York, NY, 1894 *6512.1 p184*
Erikson, Charles; Washington, 1888 *2770.40 p25*
Erikson, E. W.; Colorado, 1899 *1029.59 p27*
Erikson, Gust; Cleveland, OH, 1892-1895 *9722.10 p118*
Erikson, Gust; Colorado, 1892 *1029.59 p27*
Erikson, Hjalman Eamanuul; Philadelphia, 1902 *1766.20 p36*

Erikson, John; Cleveland, OH, 1883-1893 *9722.10* p118
Erikson, John; Cleveland, OH, 1895-1901 *9722.10* p119
Erikson, Soren Kristian; Iowa, 1920 *1211.15* p10
Eriksson, . . .; Colorado, 1882 *1029.59* p27
Eriksson, C.E.; New Orleans, 1851 *6412.40* p152
Eriksson, Carl J.K.; Cleveland, OH, 1901-1903 *9722.10* p119
Eriksson, Caroline 41; New York, NY, 1894 *6512.1* p185
Eriksson, Jon 24; New York, 1856 *6529.11* p22
Eringer, Marguerite 38; Port uncertain, 1840 *778.6* p108
Erington, Fredrick 47; Ontario, 1871 *1823.21* p106
Erise, Lewis; Ohio, 1809-1852 *4511.35* p13
Erk, Bernhard; America, 1867 *7919.3* p534
    With wife & 3 children
Erk, Caspar; America, 1868 *7919.3* p529
Erk, Elisabeth Bernhardine; America, 1868 *7919.3* p534
Erk, Joseph 27; New York, NY, 1893 *1883.7* p38
Erk, Julianna 19; New York, NY, 1893 *1883.7* p38
Erk, Stephana 54; New York, NY, 1898 *7951.13* p43
Erk, Valtin; America, 1867 *7919.3* p534
    With wife & 3 children
Erkehr, Alois 21; Mississippi, 1847 *778.6* p109
Erkkila, John 20; Minnesota, 1923 *2769.54* p1381
Erl, Wilson 20; Ontario, 1871 *1823.17* p49
Erlandson, Peter F.; Colorado, 1880 *1029.59* p27
Ermann, Jacob; Ohio, 1844 *2763.1* p9
Ermel, John; Ohio, 1809-1852 *4511.35* p13
Erne, Sebastian 22; New Castle, DE, 1817-1818 *90.20* p150
Ernest, Pierre 25; Louisiana, 1848 *778.6* p109
Ernesti, Charles; Nebraska, 1905 *3004.30* p46
Ernesti, Ferd; Nebraska, 1905 *3004.30* p46
Ernig, Sebastian 22; New Castle, DE, 1817-1818 *90.20* p150
Ernst, Adam; Illinois, 1856 *6079.1* p5
Ernst, Adolph; America, 1854 *2526.42* p160
Ernst, Agnes SEE Ernst, Ida Frese
Ernst, Anton 22; Galveston, TX, 1844 *3967.10* p370
Ernst, C.J.; Galveston, TX, 1855 *571.7* p16
Ernst, Carl Ludwig; Wisconsin, 1873 *6795.8* p201
Ernst, Dorothea; America, 1867 *7919.3* p533
    With child
Ernst, Frieda SEE Ernst, Ida Frese
Ernst, Friedrich Theodor Hermann; America, 1852 *7420.1* p87
Ernst, Ida; Pittsburgh, 1908 *7420.1* p383
    Grandchild:Frieda
    Grandchild:Agnes
    Grandchild:Paul
Ernst, Jakob 39; Galveston, TX, 1844 *3967.10* p370
Ernst, Louis 37; Ontario, 1871 *1823.17* p49
Ernst, Otto; New York, NY, 1856 *7420.1* p147
Ernst, Paul SEE Ernst, Ida Frese
Ernst, Susanna; America, 1883 *5475.1* p377
Ernstmeyer, Reinhard; Illinois, 1930 *121.35* p101
Erny, Sebastian 22; New Castle, DE, 1817-1818 *90.20* p150
Err, Ja's; Ontario, 1787 *1276.15* p230
Erramuspe, Grace Etcheverria SEE Erramuspe, John
Erramuspe, Grace Etcheverria SEE Erramuspe, John
Erramuspe, John; California, 1870 *3276.8* p
    Wife:Grace Etcheverria
Erramuspe, John; South America, 1864-1870 *3276.8* p19
    Wife:Grace Etcheverria
Erreca, Miguel 19; California, 1873 *3276.8* p19
Errett, Letticia 58; Ontario, 1871 *1823.21* p106
Errington, Robert; North Carolina, 1843 *1088.45* p9
Errocarte, Francisco; California, 1860-1890 *3276.8* p19
Errunt, Sigumund W.; North Carolina, 1852 *1088.45* p9
Ersdotter, Carin; Illinois, 1869 *777.40* p13
Ersdotter, Carin 24; New York, 1856 *6529.11* p22
Ersdotter, Catherine; Illinois, 1869 *777.40* p13
Ersdotter, Karin; Kansas, 1876 *777.40* p8
Ersdotter, Margareta; New York, 1857 *6529.11* p24
Ersdotter, Martha; Kansas, 1869-1871 *777.40* p9
Ersdotter, Martha; Kansas, 1869-1871 *777.40* p9
Ersdotter, Martha; Kansas, 1869-1871 *777.40* p9
Ersdotter, Martha; Kansas, 1876 *777.40* p14
Erskin, Christopher; Massachusetts, 1729 *1642* p86
Erskine, Andrew 59; Ontario, 1871 *1823.21* p106
Erskine, David 68; Ontario, 1871 *1823.21* p106
Erskine, Emmett E.; Ohio, 1879 *3580.20* p31
Erskine, Emmett E.; Ohio, 1879 *6020.12* p7
Erskine, John 59; Ontario, 1871 *1823.21* p106
Erskine, Mary 15; Ontario, 1871 *1823.21* p106
Erskine, Thomas 45; Ontario, 1871 *1823.21* p106
Ersson, Anders 36; New York, 1856 *6529.11* p19
    Wife:Carin Persdotter 34
    Son:Per August 4 months
    Daughter:Carin 10
    Son:Eric 5
Ersson, Anna SEE Ersson, Lars

Ersson, Anna 12 SEE Ersson, Anna
Ersson, Anna 55; New York, 1856 *6529.11* p22
    Daughter:Anna 12
Ersson, Brita Hansdotter SEE Ersson, Olof E.
Ersson, Carin Ersdotter SEE Ersson, Jon
Ersson, Carin 10 SEE Ersson, Anders
Ersson, Carin Persdotter 34 SEE Ersson, Anders
Ersson, Christina Pehrsdotter SEE Ersson, Lars
Ersson, Eric 5 SEE Ersson, Anders
Ersson, Eric 34; New York, 1856 *6529.11* p21
Ersson, Henry SEE Ersson, Jon
Ersson, Joh 29; New York, 1856 *6529.11* p19
    Wife:Lisa Andersdotter 30
Ersson, Jon; Illinois, 1869 *777.40* p13
    Wife:Carin Ersdotter
    Son:Henry
    Daughter:Lina
    Son:Olof J.
Ersson, Jons; America, 1864 *6529.11* p26
    With wife
    With child 5
    With child 14
Ersson, Lars; Kansas, 1870 *777.40* p14
    Wife:Christina Pehrsdotter
    Son:Peter L.
    Daughter:Anna
Ersson, Lars 31; New York, 1856 *6529.11* p21
Ersson, Lina SEE Ersson, Jon
Ersson, Lisa Andersdotter 30 SEE Ersson, Joh
Ersson, Olof E.; Kansas, 1868-1869 *777.40* p8
    Wife:Brita Hansdotter
Ersson, Olof J. SEE Ersson, Jon
Ersson, Pehr; America, 1854 *777.40* p15
Ersson, Per August 4 SEE Ersson, Anders
Ersson, Peter L. SEE Ersson, Lars
Erst, Adolf; Chicago, 1891 *2853.20* p465
Erstgaard, Karl Magnuson; Oregon, 1941 *9157.47* p2
Ertel, Heinrich 35; Portland, ME, 1911 *970.38* p76
Erter, Baltzer; Ohio, 1809-1852 *4511.35* p13
Ertler, Frederick; Ohio, 1809-1852 *4511.35* p13
Erusting, Henry; Missouri, 1886 *3276.1* p1
Ervens, Julien 27; America, 1847 *778.6* p109
Ervin, John 31; South Carolina, 1812 *3476.30* p11
Ervine, Edward 39; Ontario, 1871 *1823.21* p106
Erving, John; South Carolina, 1813 *3208.30* p18
Erving, John; South Carolina, 1813 *3208.30* p31
Erwin, Andrew 39; Ontario, 1871 *1823.21* p106
Erwin, George 50; Ontario, 1871 *1823.21* p106
Erwin, George 73; Ontario, 1871 *1823.21* p106
Erwin, John; Ohio, 1818 *3580.20* p31
Erwin, John; Ohio, 1818 *6020.12* p7
Erwin, John 87; Ontario, 1871 *1823.21* p106
Esabe, Bernard 14; America, 1846 *778.6* p109
Esabe, J. 18; America, 1846 *778.6* p109
Esabe, Mary Carolina 24; America, 1846 *778.6* p109
Esala, Anselm 32; Minnesota, 1925 *2769.54* p1383
Escaig, Bertrand 18; New Orleans, 1845 *778.6* p109
Escaig, Francois 18; New Orleans, 1845 *778.6* p109
Escat, Jean Jacques; Louisiana, 1874 *4981.45* p131
Escayrac de Lautheur de Veau, Pierre d'; Quebec, 1683-1687 *2314.30* p182
Escayrac deLautheur deVeau, Pierre d'; Quebec, 1683-1688 *2314.30* p168
Escelmont, William 25; Ontario, 1871 *1823.17* p49
Esch, Johann; America, 1844 *5475.1* p555
Esch, Madalaine 42; Louisiana, 1848 *778.6* p109
Eschart, Samuel; Salem, MA, 1577-1652 *9228.50* p75
Escher, Anna; America, 1881 *5475.1* p23
Escher, Katharina 38; America, 1853 *5475.1* p53
Eschiberman, Barbara 3; America, 1745 *778.6* p109
Eschiberman, Barbara 39; America, 1745 *778.6* p109
Eschiberman, Elisa 20; America, 1745 *778.6* p109
Eschiberman, Gaspard 12; America, 1745 *778.6* p109
Eschiberman, Georg 14; America, 1745 *778.6* p109
Eschiberman, Georg 42; America, 1745 *778.6* p109
Eschiberman, Jacob 7; America, 1745 *778.6* p109
Eschiberman, Philippe 9; America, 1745 *778.6* p109
Eschmann, August Reinhard; America, 1877 *7420.1* p308
Eschmann, Johann Gerhard Ludwig Clemens; America, 1870 *7420.1* p283
Eschmann, Rudolph; America, 1871 *7420.1* p289
Eschoffier, John 30; Port uncertain, 1848 *778.6* p109
Eschrich, August; America, 1867 *7919.3* p531
Eschrich, Johann; America, 1840 *5475.1* p471
Esclemont, James 50; Ontario, 1871 *1823.17* p49
Escoffier, Pierre 19; America, 1841 *778.6* p109
Escola Acosta, Jose; Puerto Rico, 1896 *3476.25* p112
Escole, Mr. 24; America, 1848 *778.6* p109
Escorcia, Raymond; New York, 1880-1980 *9228.50* p603
Escoubas, Jean Baptiste 28; New Orleans, 1746 *778.6* p109
Escudero, Gregorio; Louisiana, 1836-1840 *4981.45* p212

Escudie, . . .; Quebec, 1662 *9221.17* p485
Eseler, John Gottfried; New York, 1860 *358.56* p5
Esemann, Carl August Otto; America, 1868 *7420.1* p271
Esemann, Gustav Heinrich Friedrich; America, 1866 *7420.1* p242
Eseverri, Ysidoro; California, 1901 *3276.8* p20
Eshmyer, Henry; Ohio, 1840-1897 *8365.35* p16
Esler, Christian; North Carolina, 1710 *3629.40* p4
Eslick, Albert; Colorado, 1878 *1029.59* p27
Eslick, Albert; Colorado, 1888 *1029.59* p27
Eslinger, Christopher; Ohio, 1809-1852 *4511.35* p13
Eslinger, John; Ohio, 1809-1852 *4511.35* p13
Esmard, Anne 21; Quebec, 1648 *9221.17* p198
    Sister:Madeleine
Esmard, Barbe; Quebec, 1648 *9221.17* p200
Esmard, Madeleine SEE Esmard, Anne
Esmard, Madeleine 22; Quebec, 1648 *9221.17* p197
Esmond, James Wiseman SEE Esmond, John
Esmond, John; Toronto, 1844 *2910.35* p111
    Son:James Wiseman
    Son:John Patrick
    Son:Wm George
Esmond, John Patrick SEE Esmond, John
Esmond, Sarah; New Orleans, 1850 *7242.30* p141
Esmond, Wm George SEE Esmond, John
Esnard, Gilles 10; Quebec, 1646 *9221.17* p164
Esnard, Jean; Quebec, 1659 *9221.17* p400
Esnault, Jacques; Quebec, 1659 *9221.17* p413
Esnault, Martin; Illinois, 1852 *6079.1* p5
Esnault, Michel 24; Quebec, 1659 *9221.17* p400
Esner, Theobald; Ohio, 1809-1852 *4511.35* p13
Esnouf, Abraham; Utah, 1855 *9228.50* p209
    Relative:Elizabeth
    Relative:Thomas
Esnouf, Elizabeth SEE Esnouf, Abraham
Esnouf, Susan; Utah, 1800-1900 *9228.50* p209
Esnouf, Susan; Utah, 1840-1860 *9228.50* p194
Esnouf, Thomas SEE Esnouf, Abraham
Espareicad, Johan 27; America, 1842 *778.6* p109
Espenin, Chs. 20; America, 1847 *778.6* p109
Esperros, Martial; Louisiana, 1874-1875 *4981.45* p298
Espinal, Juanita; California, 1860-1890 *3276.8* p19
Esping, Axel; Illinois, 1864 *4487.25* p57
Esping, Julius L.; Chicago, 1864 *4487.25* p57
Esprit, Alfred 19; New Orleans, 1844 *778.6* p109
Esselburn, Michael; Ohio, 1809-1852 *4511.35* p13
Essency, Joseph; Washington, 1889 *2770.40* p27
Essery, Mathew 49; Ontario, 1871 *1823.21* p107
Essery, Peter 40; Ontario, 1871 *1823.21* p107
Essery, Thomas 42; Ontario, 1871 *1823.21* p107
Essery, William 57; Ontario, 1871 *1823.21* p107
Essex, John; Virginia, 1652 *6254.4* p243
Essex, Theodore J. 30; Ontario, 1871 *1823.17* p49
Essig, Christian 19; New York, NY, 1893 *1883.7* p40
Essig, Georg 26; New York, NY, 1893 *1883.7* p40
Essig, George; Long Island, 1781 *8529.30* p10A
Essinger, Charles; Ohio, 1809-1852 *4511.35* p13
Essinger, Jacob; Ohio, 1809-1852 *4511.35* p13
Essinger, Philip; Ohio, 1809-1852 *4511.35* p13
Esslebun, Henry; Ohio, 1809-1852 *4511.35* p13
Essmann, Heinrich Christoph; Port uncertain, 1835 *7420.1* p9
Essmann, Louis; America, 1872 *7420.1* p294
Essner, Theobold; Ohio, 1809-1852 *4511.35* p13
Esson, William 50; Ontario, 1871 *1823.17* p49
Essot, John; Port uncertain, 1842 *778.6* p109
Estabrook, Charles W.; Washington, 1889 *2770.40* p27
Estar, Laurent 30; Texas, 1843 *778.6* p109
Estel, Conrad 7; America, 1893 *1883.7* p38
Estel, Gottlieb 4; America, 1893 *1883.7* p38
Estel, Johann 6; America, 1893 *1883.7* p38
Estel, Johannes 35; America, 1893 *1883.7* p38
Estel, Johannes; New York, NY, 1893 *1883.7* p39
Estel, Sophia 2; America, 1893 *1883.7* p38
Estel, Sophia 32; America, 1893 *1883.7* p38
Estep, . . .; West Virginia, 1850-1860 *1132.30* p149
Esteves, Peter 30; America, 1847 *778.6* p109
Estienne, Claude; Quebec, 1637 *9221.17* p69
Estienne, Guillaume 31; Montreal, 1656 *9221.17* p348
Estienne, Philippe 24; Quebec, 1653 *9221.17* p273
Estienne deClerin duBourguet, Denis d'; Quebec, 1683-1688 *2314.30* p168
Estienne de Clerin du Bourguet, Denis d'; Quebec, 1685 *2314.30* p182
Estienne DeMontgalley, Jacques; Quebec, 1657 *9221.17* p357
Estish, Frank; Louisiana, 1874 *4981.45* p295
Estlemont, Alexander 42; Ontario, 1871 *1823.21* p107
Estourneau, David 19 SEE Estourneau, David
Estourneau, David 45; Quebec, 1660 *9221.17* p435
    Son:David 19
    Son:Jean 18
Estourneau, Jean 18 SEE Estourneau, David

Estrees, Jacques; Quebec, 1660 *9221.17 p435*
Estur, Terence 35; Ontario, 1871 *1823.21 p107*
Etabli, Louis 30; New Orleans, 1841 *778.6 p109*
Etchell, John Robert; Illinois, 1930 *121.35 p100*
Etcheverria, Grace; California, 1870 *3276.8 p19*
Etcheverria, Grace; California, 1870 *3276.8 p*
Etcheverria, Grace; South America, 1864-1870 *3276.8 p19*
Etcheverria, Marie; California, 1877-1890 *3276.8 p19*
Eternel, Claude 29; America, 1847 *778.6 p109*
Etienne, Antoine 38; New Orleans, 1848 *778.6 p109*
Etienne, Antoine Marie 12; New Orleans, 1848 *778.6 p110*
Etienne, Auguste 47; New Orleans, 1847 *778.6 p110*
Etienne, Baptiste Marie 10; New Orleans, 1848 *778.6 p110*
Etienne, Georges 43; America, 1846 *778.6 p110*
Etienne, Joseph; Ohio, 1809-1852 *4511.35 p13*
Etienne, Marie 32; New Orleans, 1848 *778.6 p110*
Etienne, Peter F.; Ohio, 1809-1852 *4511.35 p13*
Etiveaud, Benoit 29; New Orleans, 1846 *778.6 p110*
Etlemis, Casimer 25; New York, NY, 1893 *1883.7 p38*
Etling, Fred August; Kansas, 1917-1918 *2094.25 p50*
Etne, Joseph 56; Michigan, 1880 *4491.30 p10*
Etne, Olive 55; Michigan, 1880 *4491.30 p10*
Etne, Oliver 22; Michigan, 1880 *4491.30 p10*
Etrick, Amelia A.; Illinois, 1885 *1447.20 p63*
Etrick, Fredericka; Illinois, 1885 *1447.20 p63*
Etringer, Elisabeth Scheffler 25 *SEE* Etringer, Heinrich
Etringer, Heinrich *SEE* Etringer, Heinrich
Etringer, Heinrich; America, 1882 *5475.1 p241*
  *Wife:*Elisabeth Scheffler
  *Son:*Heinrich
  *Son:*Johann
Etringer, Johann *SEE* Etringer, Heinrich
Etringer, Nikolaus; America, 1872 *5475.1 p239*
Ettlinger, Margarethe; America, 1867 *7919.3 p531*
Etton, Jane 75; Ontario, 1871 *1823.21 p107*
Ettstrom, J.G.; Cleveland, OH, 1891-1892 *9722.10 p119*
Etzell, John; New York, 1778 *8529.30 p6*
Eubank, Alice Charlotte; Shreveport, LA, 1948 *9228.50 p476*
Eubank, Edna Ruby; Kansas, 1921-1934 *9228.50 p476*
Eubank, Lola Esther; Texas, 1903-1983 *9228.50 p475*
Eudemare, Georges 53; Quebec, 1642 *9221.17 p111*
Eudey, John; North Carolina, 1850 *1088.45 p9*
Euget, Anne Claude 48; Louisiana, 1848 *778.6 p110*
Euget, Delphine 10; Louisiana, 1848 *778.6 p110*
Euget, Elise 20; Louisiana, 1848 *778.6 p110*
Euget, Jn. Bte. 50; Louisiana, 1848 *778.6 p110*
Euget, Laide 15; Louisiana, 1848 *778.6 p110*
Euget, Leonie 8; Louisiana, 1848 *778.6 p110*
Euget, Louise 22; Louisiana, 1848 *778.6 p110*
Euhring, Heinrich Wilhelm; America, 1869 *7420.1 p279*
Euron, Jacques; Quebec, 1638 *9221.17 p76*
Eusby, Stephn.; Maryland, 1674 *1236.25 p50*
Eustache, Francis; Ohio, 1840-1897 *8365.35 p16*
Eustis, Rosanna; Bridgeport, CT, 1856 *8513.31 p421*
Eutzminger, Philip; Louisiana, 1874 *4981.45 p295*
Evan, Thomas 56; Ontario, 1871 *1823.17 p49*
Evans, Ann *SEE* Evans, William
Evans, Ann *SEE* Evans, David
Evans, Ann; Ohio, 1839 *4022.20 p282*
Evans, Ann *SEE* Evans, Evan J.
Evans, Ann 53; Ontario, 1871 *1823.21 p107*
Evans, Ann 70; Ontario, 1871 *1823.21 p107*
Evans, Ann G. *SEE* Evans, David
Evans, Annie 3; New York, NY, 1894 *6512.1 p186*
Evans, Arnold 56; Ontario, 1871 *1823.17 p49*
Evans, Bazilla 35; Ontario, 1871 *1823.17 p49*
Evans, Benjamin 22; North Carolina, 1774 *1422.10 p55*
Evans, Benjamin; Ohio, 1846 *4022.20 p277*
  *Wife:*Mary Davies
Evans, Catherine; Died enroute, 1839 *4022.20 p279*
Evans, Chas; St. John, N.B., 1847 *2978.15 p40*
Evans, Dafydd; Ohio, 1844 *4022.20 p277*
  *Wife:*Mary
  *Child:*Jane
Evans, Daniel *SEE* Evans, David
Evans, David *SEE* Evans, Evan
Evans, David *SEE* Evans, Thomas
Evans, David *SEE* Evans, David
Evans, David; Ohio, 1837 *4022.20 p277*
  *Child:*Daniel
  *Child:*Thomas
  *Child:*Margaret
  *Child:*Evan
  *Child:*Joshua
  *Child:*David
  *Wife:*Margaret Davies
  With relatives
  *Child:*Eleanor
  *Child:*Mary

Evans, David *SEE* Evans, David
Evans, David; Ohio, 1839 *4022.20 p277*
  *Wife:*Ann
  *Child:*Richard D.
  *Child:*Jenkin
  *Child:*David
Evans, David; Ohio, 1839 *4022.20 p277*
  *Wife:*Margaret
  With children
Evans, David; Ohio, 1847-1850 *4022.20 p277*
  *Wife:*Hannah Williams
  *Child:*Ann G.
  *Child:*Mary
Evans, David; Ohio, 1847 *4022.20 p277*
Evans, David *SEE* Evans, Isaac
Evans, David; Ohio, 1837 *4022.20 p288*
Evans, David 55; Ontario, 1871 *1823.21 p107*
Evans, David; Washington, 1889 *2770.40 p27*
Evans, David G.; Ohio, 1840 *4022.20 p277*
  *Wife:*Jane
  *Child:*Francis
  *Child:*Evan
Evans, David J.; Ohio, 1841 *4022.20 p277*
  *Wife:*Margaret
  With 3 children
Evans, David O. *SEE* Evans, Owen
Evans, David S.; Washington, 1889 *2770.40 p27*
Evans, Edith 10 months; New York, NY, 1894 *6512.1 p186*
Evans, Edward; Iowa, 1879 *1211.15 p10*
Evans, Edward *SEE* Evans, Evan J.
Evans, Edward 63; Ontario, 1871 *1823.21 p107*
Evans, Edward D.; Ohio, 1849 *4022.20 p278*
  *Wife:*Rachel Phillips
  *Child:*Rachel
  *Child:*Mary
  *Child:*Kate
Evans, Edward Price 42; Ontario, 1871 *1823.21 p107*
Evans, Eleanor *SEE* Evans, John
Evans, Eleanor *SEE* Evans, David
Evans, Eleanor; Ohio, 1837 *4022.20 p288*
Evans, Eleanor James *SEE* Evans, Owen
Evans, Eleanor Jones; Ohio, 1835 *4022.20 p276*
Evans, Elenor; Ohio, 1837-1840 *4022.20 p293*
Evans, Elenor *SEE* Evans, John R.
Evans, Elizabeth *SEE* Evans, Evan
Evans, Elizabeth *SEE* Evans, John
Evans, Elizabeth *SEE* Evans, Evan J.
Evans, Elizabeth *SEE* Evans, John D.
Evans, Elj. 35; Ontario, 1871 *1823.17 p49*
Evans, Ellen 11; Quebec, 1870 *8364.32 p23*
Evans, Eva; Chicago, 1882-1904 *9228.50 p237*
Evans, Evan *SEE* Evans, Evan
Evans, Evan; Ohio, 1818 *4022.20 p278*
  *Wife:*Susanna Jones
  *Sister:*Elizabeth
  *Child:*Evan
  *Child:*David
Evans, Evan; Ohio, 1835 *4022.20 p285*
Evans, Evan *SEE* Evans, David
Evans, Evan *SEE* Evans, David G.
Evans, Evan *SEE* Evans, Evan J.
Evans, Evan; Ohio, 1840 *4022.20 p278*
  *Wife:*Margaret
  *Child:*Margaret
Evans, Evan; Ohio, 1840 *4022.20 p278*
  *Wife:*Margaret Richards
  With children
Evans, Evan; Ohio, 1842 *4022.20 p278*
  *Wife:*Mary
  With 6 children
Evans, Evan; Ohio, 1818 *4022.20 p285*
  *Wife:*Susanna Jones
  *Child:*Timothy
  *Child:*Jane
Evans, Evan E.; Ohio, 1853 *4022.20 p278*
Evans, Evan J.; Ohio, 1840 *4022.20 p278*
  *Wife:*Mary
  *Child:*John E.
  *Child:*Edward
  *Child:*Evan
  *Child:*James
  *Child:*Margaret
  *Child:*Jane
  *Child:*Ann
  *Child:*Mary
  *Child:*Elizabeth
Evans, Evan P.; Ohio, 1840 *4022.20 p279*
  *Wife:*Mary P.
Evans, Evan T. 30; Indiana, 1865-1872 *9076.20 p68*
Evans, Evans D.; Washington, 1889 *2770.40 p27*
Evans, Francis *SEE* Evans, David G.
Evans, Francis 50; Ontario, 1871 *1823.21 p107*

Evans, George; Ontario, 1871 *1823.17 p49*
Evans, George 53; Ontario, 1871 *1823.21 p107*
Evans, Hannah Williams *SEE* Evans, David
Evans, Henry 38; Ontario, 1871 *1823.21 p107*
Evans, Henry I. 28; Ontario, 1871 *1823.21 p107*
Evans, Hugh G.; Tennessee, 1876 *3665.20 p111*
Evans, Isaac; Ohio, 1850 *4022.20 p278*
  *Wife:*Mary
  *Child:*David
  With 4 children
Evans, James *SEE* Evans, Evan J.
Evans, James 28; Ontario, 1871 *1823.21 p107*
Evans, James 50; Ontario, 1871 *1823.21 p107*
Evans, James 60; Ontario, 1871 *1823.21 p107*
Evans, Jane *SEE* Evans, Evan
Evans, Jane *SEE* Evans, Owen
Evans, Jane *SEE* Evans, David G.
Evans, Jane *SEE* Evans, Evan J.
Evans, Jane; Ohio, 1841 *4022.20 p289*
Evans, Jane *SEE* Evans, Dafydd
Evans, Jane; Philadelphia, 1868 *8513.31 p417*
Evans, Jane Morgan; Ohio, 1849 *4022.20 p278*
  With children
Evans, Jenkin *SEE* Evans, David
Evans, John; Iowa, 1919 *1211.15 p10*
Evans, John; Ohio, 1818 *4022.20 p279*
  *Wife:*Mary Jones
  *Child:*John J.
  *Child:*Mary
  *Child:*William
  *Child:*Eleanor
Evans, John *SEE* Evans, Thomas
Evans, John; Ohio, 1838-1841 *4022.20 p278*
Evans, John; Ohio, 1839 *4022.20 p278*
  *Wife:*Elizabeth
Evans, John *SEE* Evans, John J.
Evans, John; Ohio, 1818 *4022.20 p285*
  *Wife:*Mary Jones
Evans, John 25; Ontario, 1871 *1823.21 p107*
Evans, John 31; Ontario, 1871 *1823.21 p107*
Evans, John 35; Ontario, 1871 *1823.21 p107*
Evans, John 39; Ontario, 1871 *1823.17 p49*
Evans, John 40; Ontario, 1871 *1823.17 p49*
Evans, John 44; Ontario, 1871 *1823.21 p107*
Evans, John 50; Ontario, 1871 *1823.21 p107*
Evans, John 66; Ontario, 1871 *1823.21 p107*
Evans, John; Philadelphia, 1778 *8529.30 p3A*
Evans, John D.; Ohio, 1850 *4022.20 p278*
  *Wife:*Mary Jones
  *Child:*Elizabeth
Evans, John E.; Ohio, 1834-1835 *4022.20 p279*
  *Wife:*Mary
Evans, John E. *SEE* Evans, Evan J.
Evans, John Edward 32; Ontario, 1871 *1823.21 p107*
Evans, John J. *SEE* Evans, John
Evans, John J.; Ohio, 1849 *4022.20 p279*
  *Father:*John
  *Mother:*Mary
Evans, John L. W. *SEE* Evans, Lewis L.
Evans, John R.; Ohio, 1838 *4022.20 p279*
  *Wife:*Elenor
  With relatives
  *Child:*Rowland H.
Evans, John W.; Ohio, 1841 *4022.20 p279*
  *Wife:*Mary Williams
  *Brother:*Morgan
  With parents
Evans, Joshua *SEE* Evans, David
Evans, Joshua; Ohio, 1837 *4022.20 p279*
  *Wife:*Margaret
  *Child:*Mary
Evans, Kate *SEE* Evans, Edward D.
Evans, Lewis L.; Ohio, 1839 *4022.20 p279*
  *Wife:*Sarah Jenkins
  *Child:*Owen L.
  *Child:*John L. W.
  With sister & brother-in-law
Evans, Louesa L.; Colorado, 1891 *1029.59 p27*
Evans, Madalaine *SEE* Evans, Thomas
Evans, Margaret 5; New York, NY, 1894 *6512.1 p186*
Evans, Margaret *SEE* Evans, William
Evans, Margaret *SEE* Evans, Thomas
Evans, Margaret *SEE* Evans, Thomas
Evans, Margaret *SEE* Evans, Thomas
Evans, Margaret *SEE* Evans, David
Evans, Margaret Davies *SEE* Evans, David
Evans, Margaret *SEE* Evans, Joshua
Evans, Margaret; Ohio, 1837 *4022.20 p291*
Evans, Margaret *SEE* Evans, David
Evans, Margaret *SEE* Evans, Evan
Evans, Margaret *SEE* Evans, Evan J.
Evans, Margaret *SEE* Evans, Evan
Evans, Margaret Richards *SEE* Evans, Evan

Evans, Margaret *SEE* Evans, David J.
Evans, Margaret; Ohio, 1847 *4022.20 p275*
Evans, Margaret; Ohio, 1840 *4022.20 p290*
Evans, Mariah; Ohio, 1818 *4022.20 p274*
Evans, Mary 30; New York, NY, 1894 *6512.1 p186*
Evans, Mary *SEE* Evans, John
Evans, Mary Jones *SEE* Evans, John
Evans, Mary Jones *SEE* Evans, John
Evans, Mary *SEE* Evans, John E.
Evans, Mary *SEE* Evans, David
Evans, Mary *SEE* Evans, Joshua
Evans, Mary *SEE* Evans, Evan J.
Evans, Mary *SEE* Evans, Evan J.
Evans, Mary; Ohio, 1840 *4022.20 p287*
Evans, Mary Williams *SEE* Evans, John W.
Evans, Mary *SEE* Evans, Evan
Evans, Mary *SEE* Evans, Dafydd
Evans, Mary Davies *SEE* Evans, Benjamin
Evans, Mary *SEE* Evans, David
Evans, Mary *SEE* Evans, Edward D.
Evans, Mary *SEE* Evans, John J.
Evans, Mary *SEE* Evans, Isaac
Evans, Mary Jones *SEE* Evans, John D.
Evans, Mary *SEE* Evans, Moses
Evans, Mary 11; Quebec, 1870 *8364.32 p23*
Evans, Mary P. *SEE* Evans, Evan P.
Evans, Mathew; South Carolina, 1808 *6155.4 p18*
Evans, Morgan *SEE* Evans, John W.
Evans, Moses; Ohio, 1850 *4022.20 p279*
  *Wife:*Mary
Evans, Noah 30; Ontario, 1871 *1823.21 p107*
Evans, Owen; Ohio, 1839-1842 *4022.20 p279*
  *Wife:*Eleanor James
  *Child:*William
  *Child:*Jane
  *Child:*David O.
Evans, Owen L. *SEE* Evans, Lewis L.
Evans, Rachel *SEE* Evans, Richard
Evans, Rachel *SEE* Evans, Edward D.
Evans, Rachel Phillips *SEE* Evans, Edward D.
Evans, Rebecca; Ohio, 1843 *4022.20 p279*
  With husband
Evans, Rees; Colorado, 1883 *1029.59 p27*
Evans, Richard; Illinois, 1834-1900 *6020.5 p131*
Evans, Richard; Iowa, 1910 *1211.15 p10*
Evans, Richard; Ohio, 1846 *4022.20 p279*
  *Wife:*Rachel
Evans, Richard 39; Ontario, 1871 *1823.21 p107*
Evans, Richard D. *SEE* Evans, David
Evans, Richard G. 42; Ontario, 1871 *1823.21 p107*
Evans, Richard J. 46; Ontario, 1871 *1823.21 p107*
Evans, Richd.; Maryland, 1674 *1236.25 p50*
Evans, Rowland H. *SEE* Evans, John R.
Evans, Sarah Jenkins *SEE* Evans, Lewis L.
Evans, Sarah 40; Ontario, 1871 *1823.21 p107*
Evans, Susan 52; Ontario, 1871 *1823.21 p107*
Evans, Susanna Jones *SEE* Evans, Evan
Evans, Susanna Jones *SEE* Evans, Evan
Evans, Thomas; Ohio, 1818 *4022.20 p280*
  *Wife:*Margaret
  *Child:*Madalaine
  *Child:*Margaret
  *Child:*John
  *Child:*David
Evans, Thomas; Ohio, 1833-1834 *4022.20 p280*
  *Wife:*Margaret
Evans, Thomas *SEE* Evans, David
Evans, Thomas 40; Ontario, 1871 *1823.21 p107*
Evans, Thomas 54; Ontario, 1871 *1823.21 p107*
Evans, Thomas; Washington, 1888 *2770.40 p25*
Evans, Timothy *SEE* Evans, Evan
Evans, William; Ohio, 1814-1815 *4022.20 p280*
  *Wife:*Ann
  With children
Evans, William; Ohio, 1814-1880 *4022.20 p280*
  *Wife:*Margaret
Evans, William *SEE* Evans, John
Evans, William *SEE* Evans, Owen
Evans, William 70; Ontario, 1871 *1823.21 p107*
Evans, William 80; Ontario, 1871 *1823.21 p107*
Evans, William J.; Illinois, 1834-1900 *6020.5 p131*
Eve, Mary; Quebec, 1816-1825 *9228.50 p637*
Eve, Nicolas 21; America, 1847 *778.6 p110*
Evedall, Richd.; Maryland, 1674 *1236.25 p50*
Eveland, John 53; Ontario, 1871 *1823.17 p49*
Eveland, Joshua 49; Ontario, 1871 *1823.17 p49*
Eveleigh, Louisa 16; Ontario, 1871 *1823.17 p49*
Eveleigh, William; Marston's Wharf, 1780 *8529.30 p11*
Evens, John 40; Ontario, 1871 *1823.17 p49*

Everding, . . .; America, 1847 *7420.1 p52*
  *Son:*Johann Philipp
  *Son:*Friedrich Christian
Everding, . . .; America, 1865 *7420.1 p230*
Everding, Miss; America, 1855 *7420.1 p136*
  *Stepfather:*Carl
  With mother & 2 brothers
Everding, Mr.; America, 1867 *7420.1 p256*
  With wife
  With son 3
  *Brother:*Johann Heinrich
  *Sister:*Caroline
  *Sister:*Sophie
  With son 9
  With daughter 6
Everding, Carl *SEE* Everding, Miss
Everding, Caroline *SEE* Everding, Mr.
Everding, Ernst; America, 1873 *7420.1 p299*
Everding, Ernst Heinrich Wilhelm; America, 1869 *7420.1 p279*
Everding, Ernst Wilhelm Louis; America, 1886 *7420.1 p350*
Everding, Friedrich Christian *SEE* Everding, . . .
Everding, Friedrich Christian; Illinois, 1852 *7420.1 p88*
Everding, Friedrich Wilhelm; Port uncertain, 1888 *7420.1 p356*
Everding, Heinrich; America, 1854 *7420.1 p118*
  With wife 2 sons & 4 daughters
Everding, Heinrich Christoph; America, 1850 *7420.1 p71*
Everding, Heinrich Wilhelm Christian; America, 1891 *7420.1 p362*
Everding, Johann Heinrich *SEE* Everding, Mr.
Everding, Johann Philipp *SEE* Everding, . . .
Everding, Sophie *SEE* Everding, Mr.
Everest, George 62; Ontario, 1871 *1823.17 p49*
Everette, John; Louisiana, 1874-1875 *4981.45 p298*
Everingham, George G. 55; Ontario, 1871 *1823.21 p108*
Everingham, John 31; Ontario, 1871 *1823.17 p49*
Evers, Ernst; Valdivia, Chile, 1852 *1192.4 p55*
Everson, James H.; Ohio, 1878 *3580.20 p31*
Everson, James H.; Ohio, 1878 *6020.12 p7*
Evin, Marguerite; Quebec, 1670 *4514.3 p312*
Evins, Richard 65; Ontario, 1871 *1823.17 p49*
Evoy, Thomas 60; Ontario, 1871 *1823.21 p108*
Evrard, Alphonse *SEE* Evrard, Pierre Joseph
Evrard, Charles Joseph; Wisconsin, 1856 *1495.20 p41*
Evrard, Eugene Clement; Wisconsin, 1880 *1495.20 p55*
Evrard, Fulvie Leloux *SEE* Evrard, Jean Baptiste
Evrard, Jean Baptiste; New York, NY, 1880 *1494.20 p13*
Evrard, Jean Baptiste; Wisconsin, 1880 *1495.20 p55*
  *Wife:*Fulvie Leloux
  *Child:*Louis Joseph
  *Child:*Marie
Evrard, Joseph *SEE* Evrard, Pierre Joseph
Evrard, Louis Joseph *SEE* Evrard, Jean Baptiste
Evrard, Marie *SEE* Evrard, Jean Baptiste
Evrard, Marie Therese Baye *SEE* Evrard, Pierre Joseph
Evrard, Marie Therese; Wisconsin, 1856 *1495.20 p41*
Evrard, Pierre Joseph; Wisconsin, 1856 *1495.20 p41*
  *Wife:*Marie Therese Baye
  *Child:*Alphonse
  *Child:*Victor
  *Child:*Joseph
Evrard, Victor; Buffalo, NY, 1856 *1494.20 p12*
Evrard, Victor *SEE* Evrard, Pierre Joseph
Evras, Etienne; Wisconsin, 1854 *1495.20 p29*
  *Wife:*Sophie Vandorslaer
  *Child:*Petronille
  *Child:*Jean Baptiste
Evras, Jean Baptiste *SEE* Evras, Etienne
Evras, Petronille *SEE* Evras, Etienne
Evras, Sophie Vandorslaer *SEE* Evras, Etienne
Ewald, August Johann; Wisconsin, 1893 *6795.8 p69*
Ewald, N.P.; New York, NY, 1843 *6412.40 p147*
Ewall, Olaf Emanuel; Cleveland, OH, 1898-1904 *9722.10 p119*
Ewalt, Ingry; Illinois, 1828-1851 *777.40 p6*
Ewalt, Julius 34; Ontario, 1871 *1823.17 p49*
Ewart, James C. 40; Ontario, 1871 *1823.21 p108*
Ewart, Thomas 35; Ontario, 1871 *1823.21 p108*
Ewdall, Richard; Barbados, 1673 *1220.12 p820*
Ewdall, Richd.; Maryland, 1674 *1236.25 p50*
Ewen, Andreas *SEE* Ewen, Peter
Ewen, Barbara *SEE* Ewen, Johann
Ewen, Charles 67; Ontario, 1871 *1823.21 p108*
Ewen, George 20; Ontario, 1871 *1823.21 p108*
Ewen, Jakob *SEE* Ewen, Peter
Ewen, Johann *SEE* Ewen, Peter

Ewen, Johann 45; America, 1867 *5475.1 p201*
  *Wife:*Margarethe Wein 34
  *Son:*Nikolaus
  *Son:*Peter
  *Son:*Philipp
  *Daughter:*Barbara
Ewen, Johanna Kuhn *SEE* Ewen, Peter
Ewen, Katharina *SEE* Ewen, Peter
Ewen, Margarethe Wein 34 *SEE* Ewen, Johann
Ewen, Nikolaus *SEE* Ewen, Johann
Ewen, Nikolaus *SEE* Ewen, Peter
Ewen, Peter *SEE* Ewen, Johann
Ewen, Peter *SEE* Ewen, Peter
Ewen, Peter; America, 1880 *5475.1 p272*
  *Wife:*Johanna Kuhn
  *Son:*Peter
  *Son:*Nikolaus
  *Son:*Jakob
  *Son:*Andreas
  *Daughter:*Katharina
  *Son:*Johann
Ewen, Peter; America, 1881 *5475.1 p227*
Ewen, Peter; America, 1881 *5475.1 p333*
Ewen, Philipp *SEE* Ewen, Johann
Ewensohn, Moses 17; New York, NY, 1878 *9253.2 p45*
Ewer, William; Marston's Wharf, 1782 *8529.30 p11*
Ewer, Wm Henry 40; Ontario, 1871 *1823.21 p108*
Ewerhardy, Joh. Jak.; America, 1881 *3476.30 p263*
Ewerling, Barbara 14 *SEE* Ewerling, Mathias
Ewerling, Johann 2 *SEE* Ewerling, Mathias
Ewerling, Maria 9 *SEE* Ewerling, Mathias
Ewerling, Maria Seimetz 42 *SEE* Ewerling, Mathias
Ewerling, Mathias 13 *SEE* Ewerling, Mathias
Ewerling, Mathias 40; Brazil, 1857 *5475.1 p356*
  *Wife:*Maria Seimetz 42
  *Son:*Nikolaus 1
  *Son:*Johann 2
  *Son:*Mathias 13
  *Daughter:*Maria 9
  *Son:*Peter 6
  *Daughter:*Barbara 14
Ewerling, Nikolaus 1 *SEE* Ewerling, Mathias
Ewerling, Peter 6 *SEE* Ewerling, Mathias
Ewert, Andreas 25; Portland, ME, 1906 *970.38 p76*
Ewert, Edward 1 months; Portland, ME, 1906 *970.38 p76*
Ewert, Olga 22; Portland, ME, 1906 *970.38 p76*
Ewin, James 61; Ontario, 1871 *1823.21 p108*
Ewing, Hannah 56; Ontario, 1871 *1823.17 p49*
Ewing, John 36; South Carolina, 1812 *3476.30 p11*
Ewre, William; Marston's Wharf, 1782 *8529.30 p11*
Excoffee, Mr. 40; Port uncertain, 1842 *778.6 p110*
Expert, Miss; New Orleans, 1845 *778.6 p110*
Expert, Mr. 38; New Orleans, 1845 *778.6 p110*
Expert, Mrs.; New Orleans, 1845 *778.6 p110*
Exss, Heinrich; Valdivia, Chile, 1850 *1192.4 p49*
  With wife
  With daughter 19
  With daughter 24
Exss, Hugo; Valdivia, Chile, 1850 *1192.4 p49*
Ey, George; Nova Scotia, 1784 *7105 p22*
Eydt, Johann; America, 1852 *5475.1 p439*
  *Wife:*Maria Steimer
  With 4 children
Eydt, Maria Steimer *SEE* Eydt, Johann
Eyeller, Nicholas; New York, 1846 *471.10 p88*
Eymam, Christian; Illinois, 1851 *6079.1 p5*
Eymann, John; Illinois, 1853 *6079.1 p5*
Eymess, Johann; America, 1867 *7919.3 p530*
Eymier, Jacque 34; America, 1848 *778.6 p110*
Eyre, John James 52; Ontario, 1871 *1823.17 p49*
Eyre, Thomas George 25; Ontario, 1871 *1823.17 p49*
Eyring, Lisette; America, 1868 *7919.3 p527*
Eysell, Carl Georg August; America, 1866 *7420.1 p242*
Eysell, Wilhelm; America, 1887 *7420.1 p353*
Eyssel, Daniel Emil; America, 1882 *7420.1 p328*
  *Brother:*Friedrich August
Eyssel, Emil; Kansas, 1879 *7420.1 p313*
Eyssel, Friedrich August *SEE* Eyssel, Daniel Emil
Eyssel, Johann Friedrich Otto; America, 1879 *7420.1 p313*
  *Brother:*Moritz E.
Eyssel, Johann Georg; America, 1872 *7420.1 p294*
Eyssel, Moritz E. *SEE* Eyssel, Johann Friedrich Otto
Eyssell, Friedrich Adolph; Kansas, 1875 *7420.1 p305*
Eyssell, Otto Friedrich Hugo; Ohio, 1874 *7420.1 p303*
Eyssert, Georg 32; New Orleans, 1847 *778.6 p110*
Ezekeil, E.; Louisiana, 1874-1875 *4981.45 p298*

F

Faatz, Johann Georg; America, 1889 *2526.43 p166*
Faatz, Karl Georg Heinrich; America, 1888 *2526.43 p166*
Fabaron, Eug.; Louisiana, 1874 *4981.45 p295*
Fabel, Fridrich; Wisconsin, 1869 *6795.8 p103*
Faber, Carl Julius; America, 1867 *7919.3 p527*
Faber, Charles; Ohio, 1841 *2763.1 p9*
Faber, David; New York, 1860 *358.56 p4*
Faber, Michael Heinrich; America, 1867 *7919.3 p526*
Faber Children, . . .; America, 1861 *7420.1 p204*
Fabertas, Jean; Quebec, 1661 *9221.17 p455*
Fabian, Eduard; America, 1868 *7919.3 p530*
Fabian, Frantisek; Texas, 1880 *2853.20 p75*
Fabian, Josef; Texas, 1884 *2853.20 p70*
Fabicuis, Alexander 20; New York, NY, 1893 *1883.7 p43*
Fabicuis, Elisabeth 9 months; New York, NY, 1893 *1883.7 p43*
Fabicuis, Maria 21; New York, NY, 1893 *1883.7 p43*
Fabisz, Anne; Wisconsin, 1893 *6795.8 p57*
Fabre, Maurice 18; Port uncertain, 1843 *778.6 p110*
Fabrecque, Madeleine 23; Montreal, 1659 *9221.17 p420*
Fabrice, Hanne Caroline Wilhelmine; America, 1883 *7420.1 p341*
Fabrizak, Mary; Wisconsin, 1893 *6795.8 p57*
Fabry, Patrick; Louisiana, 1874 *4981.45 p132*
Facey, Edmund 58; Ontario, 1871 *1823.21 p108*
Facey, Robert 29; Ontario, 1871 *1823.21 p108*
Fach, Regina; America, 1872 *179.55 p19*
Fachan, Jacques; Louisiana, 1874-1875 *4981.45 p298*
Fache, August; Ohio, 1809-1852 *4511.35 p13*
Fachs, Balthazar; Ohio, 1809-1852 *4511.35 p13*
Fachs, Nicolas 20; Port uncertain, 1847 *778.6 p127*
Facius, Charles 20; America, 1846 *778.6 p110*
Fadden, Mary; Boston, 1728 *1642 p25*
Fadicia, Vincent 28; New York, NY, 1881 *7710.1 p159*
Fadlspail, Augustin 20; Indiana, 1840 *778.6 p110*
Faegger, Cath. 22; New Orleans, 1840 *778.6 p110*
Faegole, Antoine; Illinois, 1852 *6079.1 p5*
Faes, Adam 17; Port uncertain, 1847 *778.6 p110*
Faess, Peter 57; Port uncertain, 1847 *778.6 p110*
Faess, Philipp 15; Port uncertain, 1847 *778.6 p110*
Fafard, Bertrand 18; Quebec, 1637 *9221.17 p69*
Fafard, Francois 20; Quebec, 1650 *9221.17 p225*
Fafard, Francoise 26; Montreal, 1647 *9221.17 p192*
Fagan, Thomas 55; Michigan, 1880 *8364.32 p9*
Fagan, William; Vermont, 1827 *3274.56 p70*
Fagen, Barnabas; Boston, 1766 *1642 p36*
   With wife & child
Fagen, John; Boston, 1710 *1642 p24*
Fageol, Louis; Illinois, 1852 *6079.1 p5*
Fager, Eva Sophia *SEE* Fager, Johannes
Fager, Johannes; St. Paul, MN, 1900 *1865.50 p47*
   *Wife:*Eva Sophia
Fagerberg, Andrew J.; Washington, 1884 *2770.40 p192*
Fagerstrom, Gustaf; Cleveland, OH, 1902-1906 *9722.10 p119*
Faget, J. B. 38; America, 1841 *778.6 p110*
Fagin, John; Boston, 1710 *1642 p24*
Fagot, Barbara 42; New Orleans, 1847 *778.6 p110*
Fagot, Catharine 28; New Orleans, 1847 *778.6 p110*
Fagot, Claude 10; New Orleans, 1847 *778.6 p110*
Fagot, Francois 1; New Orleans, 1847 *778.6 p110*
Fagot, Francois 4; New Orleans, 1847 *778.6 p111*
Fagot, Franz 29; New Orleans, 1847 *778.6 p111*
Fagot, J. B. 28; America, 1841 *778.6 p111*
Fagot, Jacque 7; New Orleans, 1847 *778.6 p111*
Fagot, Je.nne 10; New Orleans, 1847 *778.6 p111*

Fagot, Jean 8; New Orleans, 1847 *778.6 p111*
Fagot, Joseph 42; New Orleans, 1847 *778.6 p111*
Fagot, Marie 3 months; New Orleans, 1847 *778.6 p111*
Fagot, Marie 6; New Orleans, 1847 *778.6 p111*
Fagot, Mathias 5; New Orleans, 1847 *778.6 p111*
Fagris, Alexander V.; Illinois, 1852 *6079.1 p5*
Faha, Veronika; America, 1880 *5475.1 p336*
Faherty, Patk; St. John, N.B., 1847 *2978.15 p36*
Fahey, John 60; Ontario, 1871 *1823.17 p49*
Fahey, Pat; St. John, N.B., 1848 *2978.15 p39*
Fahey, Patrick 40; Ontario, 1871 *1823.17 p49*
Fahiner, Anton 32; Mississippi, 1846 *778.6 p111*
Fahiner, Francois 6 months; Mississippi, 1846 *778.6 p111*
Fahiner, J. Michel 2; Mississippi, 1846 *778.6 p111*
Fahiner, Joseph 1; Mississippi, 1846 *778.6 p111*
Fahiner, Marie 2; Mississippi, 1846 *778.6 p111*
Fahiner, Marie 28; Mississippi, 1846 *778.6 p111*
Fahiner, Michel 35; Mississippi, 1846 *778.6 p111*
Fahlquist, John; St. Paul, MN, 1882 *1865.50 p47*
Fahlquist, Maria *SEE* Fahlquist, Sophia Johanson
Fahlquist, Olof Anton *SEE* Fahlquist, Sophia Johanson
Fahlquist, Sophia; St. Paul, MN, 1880 *1865.50 p47*
   *Child:*Olof Anton
   *Child:*Maria
Fahlqvist, John; St. Paul, MN, 1882 *1865.50 p47*
Fahlqvist, Maria *SEE* Fahlqvist, Sophia Johanson
Fahlqvist, Olof Anton *SEE* Fahlqvist, Sophia Johanson
Fahlqvist, Sophia; St. Paul, MN, 1880 *1865.50 p47*
   *Child:*Olof Anton
   *Child:*Maria
Fahlsten, C.E.; New York, NY, 1846 *6412.40 p149*
Fahlsten, Carl Johan Eric; New York, NY, 1846 *6410.15 p104*
Fahly, Daniel; Ohio, 1809-1852 *4511.35 p13*
Fahnderich, Johann Bernhard; America, 1854 *2526.43 p203*
Fahndrich, Christina; Dakota, 1875-1918 *554.30 p25*
Fahndrich, Philipp; America, 1854 *2526.43 p203*
Fahrenschon, Max; Colorado, 1894 *1029.59 p28*
Fahringer, Charles; Louisiana, 1874-1875 *4981.45 p298*
Fahrion, Lewis, Sr.; West Virginia, 1865 *1132.30 p150*
Fahsing, Christian Wilhelm; Port uncertain, 1887 *7420.1 p353*
Faierbother, Nathaniell 21; Virginia, 1635 *1183.3 p30*
Faine, James 15; Quebec, 1880 *8364.32 p23*
Fainot, Frederick; Ohio, 1809-1852 *4511.35 p13*
Fair, Claracy; Ontario, 1871 *1823.17 p49*
Fair, Francis 45; Ontario, 1871 *1823.17 p49*
Fair, John Charles 26; Ontario, 1871 *1823.17 p49*
Fair, Josias 35; Ontario, 1871 *1823.17 p49*
Fairall, Frederick 43; Ontario, 1871 *1823.21 p108*
Fairbairn, George; Illinois, 1860 *6079.1 p5*
Fairbairn, James 43; Ontario, 1871 *1823.21 p108*
Fairbairn, Walter 37; Ontario, 1871 *1823.21 p108*
Fairbairn, Walter 49; Ontario, 1871 *1823.21 p108*
Fairbank, John H. 39; Ontario, 1871 *1823.17 p49*
Fairbank, Mary 84; Ontario, 1871 *1823.17 p50*
Fairbrother, Edward 33; Ontario, 1871 *1823.21 p108*
Fairbrother, Sarah 58; Ontario, 1871 *1823.21 p108*
Fairburn, William; Illinois, 1860 *6079.1 p5*
Faircloth, George 56; Ontario, 1871 *1823.21 p108*
Faircloth, William 51; Ontario, 1871 *1823.21 p108*
Fairdan, Thomas; North Carolina, 1843 *1088.45 p9*
Faire, Martha; Boston, 1734 *1642 p26*
Fairhall, Henry 42; Ontario, 1871 *1823.21 p108*
Fairley, James; New York, 1777 *8529.30 p3A*
Fairservice, John; Boston, 1766 *1642 p36*

Fairu, Auustus 28; New Orleans, 1843 *778.6 p111*
Fairweather, William 57; Ontario, 1871 *1823.21 p108*
Faisluypeur, Charles; Montreal, 1660 *9221.17 p443*
Faitch, Abigail; Boston, 1746 *1642 p46*
Faithfull, William; Philadelphia, 1777 *8529.30 p2*
Faithorne, Robert 61; Ontario, 1871 *1823.17 p50*
Faiver, Lewis; Ohio, 1809-1852 *4511.35 p13*
Faiver, Louis; Ohio, 1809-1852 *4511.35 p13*
Faivre, Mrs. 40; Texas, 1843 *778.6 p111*
Faivre, Edouard 2; America, 1843 *778.6 p111*
Faivre, Felicie 6; America, 1843 *778.6 p111*
Faivre, Francois 22; America, 1843 *778.6 p111*
Faivre, Francois 4; Texas, 1843 *778.6 p111*
Faivre, Francoise 8; Texas, 1843 *778.6 p111*
Faivre, Henri 6; Texas, 1843 *778.6 p111*
Faivre, Ignace 35; Texas, 1843 *778.6 p111*
Faivre, Marie 34; America, 1843 *778.6 p111*
Faivre, Nestor; Louisiana, 1874-1875 *4981.45 p298*
Faivre, Pierre; Louisiana, 1836-1841 *4981.45 p208*
Faivre, Sophie 9; America, 1843 *778.6 p111*
Faivre, Suzanne 2; Texas, 1843 *778.6 p111*
Faivre, Theodore 46; America, 1843 *778.6 p111*
Faivre, Virginie 12; America, 1843 *778.6 p111*
Fajala, Johan 17; Halifax, N.S., 1902 *1860.4 p44*
Fajtlik, Benedikt; St. Louis, 1895-1900 *2853.20 p32*
Faktor, Jan; Iowa, 1854 *2853.20 p259*
Falaise, Judith; Ohio, 1806 *9228.50 p209*
Falaise, Judith; Ohio, 1806 *9228.50 p572*
Falbach, Bernh. 20; America, 1840 *778.6 p112*
Falby, Patrick 45; Ontario, 1871 *1823.21 p108*
Falconbridge, John 20; New York, NY, 1884 *8427.14 p45*
Falconer, Charles; North Carolina, 1837 *1088.45 p9*
Falconer, James 48; Ontario, 1871 *1823.21 p108*
Faldtz, Franz W.; Cleveland, OH, 1872-1884 *9722.10 p119*
Falen, M. L.; California, 1868 *1131.61 p89*
Fales, Stephen; Ohio, 1819 *3580.20 p31*
Fales, Stephen; Ohio, 1819 *6020.12 p7*
Falk, Anna *SEE* Falk, Peter
Falk, Annie P. Resser; Washington, 1889 *2770.40 p27*
Falk, Augusta; St. Paul, MN, 1893 *1865.50 p104*
Falk, Christian; Louisiana, 1841-1844 *4981.45 p210*
Falk, Clara Clossner *SEE* Falk, John
Falk, Eduard; Wisconsin, 1886 *6795.8 p29*
Falk, Edward; Wisconsin, 1887 *6795.8 p175*
Falk, Elise *SEE* Falk, Peter
Falk, J.P.; New York, NY, 1845 *6412.40 p149*
Falk, John; Baltimore, 1853 *8513.31 p305*
   *Wife:*Clara Clossner
Falk, Karl; Pittsburgh, 1889 *5475.1 p131*
Falk, M. Barbara Deutsch *SEE* Falk, Peter
Falk, Margareta; St. Paul, MN, 1885 *1865.50 p106*
Falk, Peter; Chicago, 1889 *5475.1 p197*
   *Wife:*M. Barbara Deutsch
   *Daughter:*Anna
   *Daughter:*Elise
Falk, Peter; Washington, 1889 *2770.40 p27*
Falke, Dorothee Louise; America, 1847 *7420.1 p54*
Falke, Johann Ernst; America, 1859 *7420.1 p184*
   With wife son & 3 daughters
Falkenberg, Frederick 21; Portland, ME, 1911 *970.38 p76*
Falkenhagen, Carl 16 *SEE* Falkenhagen, Joachim
Falkenhagen, Joachim; Valdivia, Chile, 1850 *1192.4 p49*
   *Son:*Carl

Falkenstein, Christian, I 47; America, 1856 2526.43 p166
Wife:Margaretha
Daughter:Margaretha 15
Son:Georg Heinrich 10
Daughter:Katharina 12
Son:Georg 19
Falkenstein, Georg 19 SEE Falkenstein, Christian, I
Falkenstein, Georg Heinrich 10 SEE Falkenstein, Christian, I
Falkenstein, Georg Michael; America, 1865 2526.43 p166
Falkenstein, Katharina 12 SEE Falkenstein, Christian, I
Falkenstein, Margaretha SEE Falkenstein, Christian, I
Falkenstein, Margaretha 15 SEE Falkenstein, Christian, I
Falkingham, George; Illinois, 1834-1900 6020.5 p131
Falkner, William; Ohio, 1844 2763.1 p9
Falkson, Margarete; New York, NY, 1912 7420.1 p389
Fall, Francis; New York, 1776 8529.30 p2
Fall, Jane; Boston, 1697 9228.50 p213
Fall, Matthew; Boston, 1715 9228.50 p213
Fall, Philip; Portsmouth, NH, 1669-1670 9228.50 p210
Falla, Albin; Maine, 1896-1918 9228.50 p210
Falla, Daisy Harriet; Massachusetts, 1889-1962 9228.50 p210
Falla, Emile Albin; Massachusetts, 1905 9228.50 p209
Falla, Harriet Ann Renouf SEE Falla, Nicholas
Falla, Hedley; New Hampshire, 1887-1912 9228.50 p210
Falla, Judith; Wisconsin, 1809-1874 9228.50 p391
Falla, Judith; Wisconsin, 1809-1909 9228.50 p210
Falla, Nicholas; Weymouth, MA, 1908 9228.50 p209
Wife:Harriet Ann Renouf
Fallaize, Judith; Ohio, 1806 9228.50 p209
Fallan, Patrick; North Carolina, 1846 1088.45 p9
Fallas, Jeanne 42; America, 1843 778.6 p112
Fallas, Joseph 7; America, 1843 778.6 p112
Fallas, Louis 46; America, 1843 778.6 p112
Fallas, Marie 9; America, 1843 778.6 p112
Fallas, Pierre 12; America, 1843 778.6 p112
Falle, Annie H. SEE Falle, Susan Jane Le Sueur
Falle, Clement; Wisconsin, n.d. 9228.50 p348
Falle, Elias SEE Falle, Susan Jane Le Sueur
Falle, Elias; New York, 1853-1910 9228.50 p157
Wife:Mary Ann Champion
With children
Falle, Elias Thomas Marche SEE Falle, Susan Jane Le Sueur
Falle, Elinora R.M. SEE Falle, Susan Jane Le Sueur
Falle, Helen Ellnora Le Febvre SEE Falle, Susan Jane Le Sueur
Falle, Jane; Montreal, n.d. 9228.50 p289
Falle, Jane; Ontario, 1837-1937 9228.50 p213
Falle, Joshua; Maine, 1787 9228.50 p213
Falle, Joshua; Quebec, 1840 9228.50 p213
Falle, Mary Ann SEE Falle, Susan Jane Le Sueur
Falle, Mary Ann Champion SEE Falle, Susan Jane Le Sueur
Falle, Mary Ann Champion SEE Falle, Elias
Falle, Rachel; Canada, 1841-1865 9228.50 p213
Falle, Rachel; New York, 1865-1870 9228.50 p213
Falle, Richard; Maine, 1672-1772 9228.50 p212
Falle, Richard; Newfoundland, 1672-1772 9228.50 p212
Falle, Susan Jane; New York, 1843-1871 9228.50 p213
Grandson:Thomas
Granddaughter:Elinora R.M.
Daughter-In-Law:Helen Ellnora Le Febvre
Son:Thomas
Daughter:Mary Ann
Son:Elias
Grandson:Elias Thomas Marche
Daughter:Annie H.
Daughter-In-Law:Mary Ann Champion
Falle, Thomas; New England, 1699 9228.50 p214
Falle, Thomas SEE Falle, Susan Jane Le Sueur
Falle, Thomas SEE Falle, Susan Jane Le Sueur
Falledin, Pierre 32; New Orleans, 1746 778.6 p112
Fallen, Michael 30; Ontario, 1871 1823.21 p108
Faller, Lukas; New York, 1860 358.56 p4
Fallewey, Patrick 30; Ontario, 1871 1823.21 p108
Falley, Mr.; New London, CT, 1670-1699 9228.50 p591
Fallo, Francisco; Louisiana, 1874-1875 4981.45 p298
Fallon, Christopher; Ohio, 1859 3580.20 p31
Fallon, Christopher; Ohio, 1859 6020.12 p7
Fallon, Patrick; Iowa, 1918 1211.15 p10
Fallon, Patrick 27; Ontario, 1871 1823.21 p108
Falloon, Rosanna 81; Ontario, 1871 1823.17 p50
Falls, F.A.W.; Quebec, 1885 1937.10 p52
Fallu, Abraham; Maine, 1658 9228.50 p214
Fallu, Irene; Edmonton, Alberta, 1888-1919 9228.50 p368
Sister:Monica Maude
Fallu, Irene Gladys; Edmonton, Alberta, 1888-1983 9228.50 p214
Fallu, Monica Maude; California, n.d. 9228.50 p214
Fallu, Monica Maude; Canada, n.d. 9228.50 p214
Fallu, Monica Maude SEE Fallu, Irene
Fallydown, Patience; Canada, 1775 3036.5 p68
Falombier, Marcelin 39; New Orleans, 1848 778.6 p112
Falter, Katharina; America, 1882 2526.43 p140
Falzilia, Elisabeth 40; Port uncertain, 1848 778.6 p112
Famagalli, E. 26; America, 1845 778.6 p112
Famden, John; Philadelphia, 1777 8529.30 p2
Fammeree, Alphonse Joseph SEE Fammeree, Jean Baptiste
Fammeree, Anne Josephe Stuter SEE Fammeree, Jean Baptiste
Fammeree, Honore Joseph SEE Fammeree, Jean Baptiste
Fammeree, Jean Baptiste; Wisconsin, 1854-1858 1495.20 p50
Wife:Anne Josephe Stuter
Child:Marie-Josephe
Child:Alphonse Joseph
Child:Honore Joseph
Fammeree, Marie-Josephe SEE Fammeree, Jean Baptiste
Fanaty, Patrick; North Carolina, 1836 1088.45 p9
Fanborg, Charles P.; Colorado, 1886 1029.59 p28
Fancy, Edward 43; Ontario, 1871 1823.17 p50
Fandray, Christian; Wisconsin, 1881 6795.8 p201
Fanet, M. 28; America, 1846 778.6 p112
Fanet, Sophia 33; America, 1846 778.6 p112
Fanis, Adolphe 29; Louisiana, 1848 778.6 p112
Fanis, Ferdinand 43; America, 1843 778.6 p112
Fanis, Louis 31; Louisiana, 1848 778.6 p112
Fannen, Morice 48; Michigan, 1880 4491.30 p11
Fannen, Sarah 35; Michigan, 1880 4491.30 p11
Fannin, John; Louisiana, 1874 4981.45 p131
Fanning, Edward; Ohio, 1834 3580.20 p31
Fanning, Edward; Ohio, 1834 6020.12 p7
Fanning, Timothy; Ohio, 1834 3580.20 p31
Fanning, Timothy; Ohio, 1834 6020.12 p7
Fanning, William; North Carolina, 1845 1088.45 p9
Fannis, R. D. 45; America, 1845 778.6 p112
Fanse, Jacob; Ohio, 1809-1852 4511.35 p13
Fansher, Frederick 73; Ontario, 1871 1823.17 p50
Fansher, John 64; Ontario, 1871 1823.17 p50
Fansher, Richard 67; Ontario, 1871 1823.17 p50
Fantin, Joseph 32; Port uncertain, 1848 778.6 p112
Faragaher, John; Ohio, 1844 2763.1 p9
Farah, Dean Khalil; Miami, 1935 4984.12 p39
Farber, Hinde 17; New York, NY, 1894 6512.1 p232
Fare, Jessie; Ontario, 1871 1823.17 p50
Farer, Thomas 74; Ontario, 1871 1823.21 p108
Farewell, Noah 63; Ontario, 1871 1823.17 p50
Fargue, Guillaume 28; Port uncertain, 1841 778.6 p112
Fargues, Mr. 26; America, 1841 778.6 p112
Farguharson, Alexander 40; Ontario, 1871 1823.17 p50
Faride, Guillaume; Quebec, 1659 9221.17 p413
Faride, Louis; Quebec, 1659 9221.17 p413
Faries, Janet 69; Ontario, 1871 1823.21 p108
Faries, Samuel W.; South Carolina, 1813 3208.30 p18
Faries, Samuel W.; South Carolina, 1813 3208.30 p31
Farish, And 47; Ontario, 1871 1823.21 p108
Farlam, Joseph 50; Ontario, 1871 1823.21 p108
Farland, Joseph 30; America, 1842 778.6 p112
Farland, Lawrence 28; America, 1842 778.6 p112
Farland, Philomele 1; America, 1842 778.6 p112
Farlane, George Mc 65; Ontario, 1871 1823.17 p50
Farlas, Anne 40; New Orleans, 1848 778.6 p112
Farlas, Pierre 37; New Orleans, 1848 778.6 p112
Farley, Ebenezer; Massachusetts, 1758 1642 p102
Wife:Hipsebeth
Farley, Hipsebeth SEE Farley, Ebenezer
Farley, M.; Toronto, 1844 2910.35 p114
Farley, Mary; Massachusetts, 1734 1642 p100
Farley, Mary SEE Farley, Timothy
Farley, Mary; Massachusetts, 1766 1642 p117
Farley, Phillip; Ohio, 1840-1897 8365.35 p16
Farley, Sarah; Massachusetts, 1741 1642 p102
Farley, Thomas B. 37; Ontario, 1871 1823.17 p50
Farley, Timothy; Massachusetts, 1761 1642 p100
Wife:Mary
Farlman, Georg 17; New Orleans, 1840 778.6 p112
Farly, Timothy; Massachusetts, 1700 1642 p105
Farly, Timothy; Massachusetts, 1764 1642 p99
Farmades, Elinor; Maryland, 1674 1236.25 p50
Farmer, Elinor; Maryland, 1674 1236.25 p50
Farmer, Henry 34; Ontario, 1871 1823.21 p108
Farmer, James 46; Ontario, 1871 1823.21 p108
Farmer, James 51; Ontario, 1871 1823.21 p108
Farmer, Jane E. 34; Michigan, 1880 4491.33 p9
Farmer, John; Boston, 1837 3274.55 p27
Farmer, Richard 60; Ontario, 1871 1823.21 p109
Farmer, Thomas 34; Michigan, 1880 4491.33 p9
Farmer, William; Philadelphia, 1778 8529.30 p3A
Farmin, Thomas 62; Ontario, 1871 1823.21 p109
Farmworth, George 31; Ontario, 1871 1823.21 p109
Farncomb, Thomas 47; Ontario, 1871 1823.21 p109
Farnechau, Jules 24; Texas, 1848 778.6 p112
Farney, Patrick; Colorado, 1882 1029.59 p28
Farnik, Matej; Chicago, 1891 2853.20 p440
Farnowsky, Albert; Galveston, TX, 1896 6015.15 p9
Farnsworth, Mary 34; Michigan, 1880 4491.39 p9
Farnsworth, Robert 49; Michigan, 1880 4491.39 p9
Farnum, Agnes 40; Ontario, 1871 1823.21 p109
Farnworth, Samuel 32; Ontario, 1871 1823.17 p50
Farquaher, James 40; Ontario, 1871 1823.21 p109
Farquhar, Ellen 55; Ontario, 1871 1823.21 p109
Farquhar, John 47; Ontario, 1871 1823.21 p109
Farquharson, John 58; Michigan, 1880 4491.36 p7
Farr, Allace 14; Michigan, 1880 4491.36 p7
Farr, Bismark 8; Michigan, 1880 4491.36 p7
Farr, Charles Allen 33; Ontario, 1871 1823.17 p50
Farr, Charlotte 29; Ontario, 1871 1823.17 p50
Farr, Eugene 37; Michigan, 1880 4491.36 p7
Farr, Florence Matilda; Tucson, AZ, 1921 9228.50 p311
Farr, G. W. 40; Ontario, 1871 1823.21 p109
Farr, Ida M. 9; Michigan, 1880 4491.36 p7
Farr, Josh 40; Ontario, 1871 1823.21 p109
Farr, Kitta 16; Michigan, 1880 4491.36 p7
Farr, Lessie 12; Michigan, 1880 4491.36 p7
Farr, Lucy 37; Michigan, 1880 4491.36 p7
Farr, Samual 69; Ontario, 1871 1823.21 p109
Farr, Sara; New Orleans, 1853-1855 9228.50 p337
Child:Elizabeth
Child:Peter
Child:Osmond
Child:Edmond
Child:Agnes
Farr, W. P.; South Carolina, 1854 6155.4 p18
Farr, William 43; Ontario, 1871 1823.17 p50
Farr, William 74; Ontario, 1871 1823.21 p109
Farran, Pierre 30; New Orleans, 1845 778.6 p112
Farrane, Edmond 28; America, 1842 778.6 p112
Farrar, Elspet 43; Ontario, 1871 1823.21 p109
Farrar, Rachel 82; Ontario, 1871 1823.21 p109
Farrara, Savario; Louisiana, 1874-1875 4981.45 p298
Farrel, Isaac; Palmer, MA, 1762 1642 p119
Farrel, John; California, 1868 1131.61 p89
Farrel, John; St. John, N.B., 1847 2978.15 p41
Farrel, Joseph; Palmer, MA, 1768 1642 p119
Farrel, Robert 12; Ontario, 1871 1823.21 p109
Farrel, Sarah; Palmer, MA, 1762 1642 p119
Farrel, W. 14; Quebec, 1870 8364.32 p23
Farrell, Andrew; Washington, 1886 2770.40 p195
Farrell, Andrew R.; North Carolina, 1848 1088.45 p9
Farrell, Bartholomew; Toronto, 1844 2910.35 p115
Farrell, Bridget 40; Ontario, 1871 1823.17 p50
Farrell, Charles; North Carolina, 1844 1088.45 p9
Farrell, Edward; North Carolina, 1844 1088.45 p9
Farrell, Edward; North Carolina, 1851 1088.45 p9
Farrell, Eliza 48; Ontario, 1871 1823.21 p109
Farrell, Elizabeth J. 40; Ontario, 1871 1823.17 p50
Farrell, Eric; Washington, 1886 2770.40 p195
Farrell, John 62; Ontario, 1871 1823.17 p50
Farrell, Mina 31; Ontario, 1871 1823.17 p50
Farrell, Patrick; Boston, 1834 3274.55 p44
Farrell, Patrick 40; Ontario, 1871 1823.21 p109
Farrell, Patrick 67; Ontario, 1871 1823.21 p109
Farrell, Peter; New Orleans, 1850 7242.30 p141
Farrell, Richard; Barbados or St. Christopher, 1780 8529.30 p7A
Farrell, Thomas; Louisiana, 1874 4981.45 p131
Farrell, Thomas; New Orleans, 1850 7242.30 p141
Farrell, Thomas 47; Ontario, 1871 1823.21 p109
Farrell, Timothy; Palmer, MA, 1760 1642 p119
Farrent, Wm.; Illinois, 1834-1900 6020.5 p131
Farrie, Elizabeth; New York, 1713 9228.50 p180
With sister
Farrier, Felix 25; America, 1846 778.6 p112
Farrin, Patrick; Boston, 1721 1642 p25
Farrin, Susanna; Ipswich, MA, 1764 1642 p71
Farris, Elizabeth 18; Ontario, 1871 1823.21 p109
Farris, Elizabeth 58; Ontario, 1871 1823.21 p109
Farris, R. 36; New Orleans, 1834 1002.51 p113
Farron, Mary Regina; Detroit, 1929-1930 6214.5 p61
Farrow, Charles; Washington, 1889 2770.40 p27
Farrow, Robert 53; Ontario, 1871 1823.21 p109
Farrow, Robert Stephen 29; Minnesota, 1913 1029.59 p28
Farrow, Thomas 45; Ontario, 1871 1823.17 p50
Farry, Jean; Virginia, 1700 9230.15 p80
Farsky, Hanus; Chicago, 1864-1910 2853.20 p406
Farthings, William 56; Ontario, 1871 1823.21 p109
Fartingue, Louis 26; Louisiana, 1840 778.6 p112
Fase, Fanne; New Orleans, 1851 7242.30 p141
Faski, Ms. 30; New Orleans, 1841 778.6 p112
Fasky, Matilde 5; New Orleans, 1841 778.6 p112
Fass, Menasze; Detroit, 1929 1640.55 p116
Fass, Nathan; Louisiana, 1874-1875 4981.45 p298

Fassbender, Philip; New Jersey, 1710-1774 ***927.31*** *p3*
Fasse, Friedrich Christoph *SEE* Fasse, Heinrich Friedrich
Fasse, Hanna Sophie Caroline Wenthe *SEE* Fasse, Heinrich Friedrich
Fasse, Heinrich Christoph *SEE* Fasse, Heinrich Friedrich
Fasse, Heinrich Christoph Gottlieb; America, 1861 ***7420.1*** *p204*
Fasse, Heinrich Friedrich; Iowa, 1871 ***7420.1*** *p289*
*Wife:*Hanna Sophie Caroline Wenthe
*Daughter:*Johanne Caroline Wilhelmine Charlotte
*Son:*Heinrich Christoph
*Son:*Friedrich Christoph
Fasse, Johann Heinrich Christoph; America, 1851 ***7420.1*** *p79*
Fasse, Johanne Caroline Wilhelmine Charlotte *SEE* Fasse, Heinrich Friedrich
Fassmeyer, J. F.; Valdivia, Chile, 1852 ***1192.4*** *p53*
Fassy, Emile 27; Louisiana, 1848 ***778.6*** *p113*
Fastbender, Philip; New Jersey, 1710-1774 ***927.31*** *p3*
Fastlett, James 53; Ontario, 1871 ***1823.21*** *p109*
Fath, Philip; Ohio, 1809-1852 ***4511.35*** *p13*
Fatho, Wilhela Theodore; Philadelphia, 1856 ***5720.10*** *p381*
Fatin, Jacques 27; Quebec, 1658 ***9221.17*** *p379*
Fatteux, Mr. 37; America, 1843 ***778.6*** *p113*
Fauche, Anne Margarethe 5; Galveston, TX, 1845 ***3967.10*** *p376*
Fauche, Elisabeth 44; Galveston, TX, 1845 ***3967.10*** *p376*
Fauche, Francois-Nicole 47; Galveston, TX, 1845 ***3967.10*** *p376*
Fauche, Marie 8; Galveston, TX, 1845 ***3967.10*** *p376*
Faucheux, Jeanne; Quebec, 1671 ***4514.3*** *p312*
Faucon, Marie; Quebec, 1663 ***4514.3*** *p312*
Fauconnier, Marie-Jeanne; Quebec, 1668 ***4514.3*** *p312*
Faucques, Jean 21; Quebec, 1649 ***9221.17*** *p213*
Faugeas, Charles E.; Philadelphia, 1858 ***8513.31*** *p305*
*Wife:*Virginia Bouillon
Faugeas, Virginia Bouillon *SEE* Faugeas, Charles E.
Faugue, Mr. 28; America, 1841 ***778.6*** *p113*
Faul, Barbara 3; New York, NY, 1885 ***1883.7*** *p46*
Faul, Carl 32; New York, NY, 1885 ***1883.7*** *p46*
Faul, Katha. 7; New York, NY, 1885 ***1883.7*** *p46*
Faul, Katha. 28; New York, NY, 1885 ***1883.7*** *p46*
Faul, Rosine 4; New York, NY, 1885 ***1883.7*** *p46*
Faulconnier, Anne 33; Quebec, 1654 ***9221.17*** *p310*
Faulkes, John; Louisiana, 1841-1844 ***4981.45*** *p210*
Faulkins, B. 16; Quebec, 1870 ***8364.32*** *p23*
Faulkner, Arthur 70; South Carolina, 1812 ***3476.30*** *p11*
Faulkner, C. 16; Quebec, 1870 ***8364.32*** *p23*
Faulkner, James 38; Ontario, 1871 ***1823.17*** *p50*
Faulkner, Micheal 71; Ontario, 1871 ***1823.21*** *p109*
Faulstich, Julie; Virginia, 1831 ***152.20*** *p63*
Faulx, Antoine; Quebec, 1641 ***9221.17*** *p100*
Faunnier, Ferdinand 27; Ohio, 1880 ***4879.40*** *p258*
Faunt, Henry 49; Ontario, 1871 ***1823.21*** *p109*
Faure, Mr. 29; New Orleans, 1848 ***778.6*** *p113*
Faure, Adolph; Louisiana, 1874 ***4981.45*** *p131*
Faure, Alphonse 25; New Orleans, 1848 ***778.6*** *p113*
Faure, Jean 23; New Orleans, 1840 ***778.6*** *p113*
Faure, Jean; Quebec, 1656 ***9221.17*** *p335*
Faure, Louise; Quebec, 1668 ***4514.3*** *p313*
Faurnier, Mr. 29; America, 1842 ***778.6*** *p113*
Fauroux, Mathieu 16; Port uncertain, 1843 ***778.6*** *p113*
Fausan, Louis 22; America, 1841 ***778.6*** *p113*
Fause, Jacob; Ohio, 1809-1852 ***4511.35*** *p13*
Fausel, Christian; Illinois, 1857 ***6079.1*** *p5*
Faust, Carl Daniel Georg; America, 1859 ***7420.1*** *p184*
Faust, Carl Friedrich Eduard; America, 1865 ***7420.1*** *p230*
Faust, Carl Wilhelm Eduard; Chicago, 1879 ***7420.1*** *p313*
Faust, Jean 25; Port uncertain, 1843 ***778.6*** *p113*
Faust, Josef; Oklahoma City, 1929 ***8023.44*** *p373*
Faustus, Baptist; Ohio, 1809-1852 ***4511.35*** *p13*
Fauth, John Jacob; Washington, 1888 ***2770.40*** *p25*
Fautz, Jacob 21; Mississippi, 1847 ***778.6*** *p113*
Fauvati, Augustin 34; America, 1846 ***778.6*** *p113*
Fauvati, Francoise 3; America, 1846 ***778.6*** *p113*
Fauvati, Joseph 31; America, 1846 ***778.6*** *p113*
Fauvati, Justine 5; America, 1846 ***778.6*** *p113*
Fauvati, Louis 26; America, 1846 ***778.6*** *p113*
Fauvault, Jeanne; Quebec, 1669 ***4514.3*** *p313*
Fauvel, John; Massachusetts, n.d. ***9228.50*** *p214*
Fauvel, Mary; Massachusetts, 1706 ***9228.50*** *p171*
Fauvel, Mathieu; Quebec, 1643 ***9221.17*** *p131*
Fauvel, Nicolas; Quebec, 1637 ***9221.17*** *p69*
Faux, Cassaline 17; Iowa, 1860 ***9228.50*** *p214*
Favard, Pierre 31; Missouri, 1848 ***778.6*** *p113*
Favard, Pierre Joseph; Illinois, 1852 ***6079.1*** *p5*
Favarello, Joseph 25; Port uncertain, 1846 ***778.6*** *p113*
Favereau, Pierre; Illinois, 1852 ***6079.1*** *p5*
Faveron, Francois 24; New Orleans, 1845 ***778.6*** *p113*
Favery, Marie 20; Quebec, 1636 ***9221.17*** *p58*
Favier, Luke; Ohio, 1809-1852 ***4511.35*** *p13*
Favier, Venice; Ohio, 1809-1852 ***4511.35*** *p13*
Favill, John; Massachusetts, n.d. ***9228.50*** *p214*
Favol, Mary; Massachusetts, 1706 ***9228.50*** *p171*
Favor, Philippe 26; Missouri, 1845 ***778.6*** *p113*
Favor, William; Boston, 1717 ***9228.50*** *p348*
Favor, Wm.; Boston, 1717 ***9228.50*** *p197*
Favre, Antoine 28; New Orleans, 1843 ***778.6*** *p113*
Favre, Antoine 45; New Orleans, 1846 ***778.6*** *p113*
Favre, Claude 42; America, 1842 ***778.6*** *p113*
Favre, Elisabeth 39; New Orleans, 1843 ***778.6*** *p113*
Favre, Eugene 25; America, 1840 ***778.6*** *p113*
Favre, Joseph 26; America, 1840 ***778.6*** *p113*
Favre, Joseph 40; America, 1842 ***778.6*** *p113*
Favre, Maria 26; Port uncertain, 1847 ***778.6*** *p113*
Favre, Mary E. 40; New Orleans, 1846 ***778.6*** *p113*
Favre, Pedro 35; Port uncertain, 1840 ***778.6*** *p113*
Favre, Pierre 28; America, 1840 ***778.6*** *p113*
Favre, Simeon; Ohio, 1809-1852 ***4511.35*** *p13*
Favre, Sophia 27; Port uncertain, 1847 ***778.6*** *p114*
Favreau, Francoise; Quebec, 1671 ***4514.3*** *p313*
Favret, Jean Bertrand 27; New Orleans, 1845 ***778.6*** *p114*
Fawcett, George 33; Ontario, 1871 ***1823.17*** *p50*
Fawcett, Mary; Philadelphia, 1867 ***8513.31*** *p324*
Fawcett, Simon Wesley 37; Ontario, 1871 ***1823.21*** *p109*
Fawcett, Thomas 29; Ontario, 1871 ***1823.21*** *p109*
Fawkes, George 66; Ontario, 1871 ***1823.21*** *p109*
Fawlden, John 52; Ontario, 1871 ***1823.21*** *p109*
Fawles, Andrew 60; Ontario, 1871 ***1823.21*** *p109*
Fawne, George 10; Jamaica, 1685 ***9228.50*** *p214*
Fax, John B.; New York, NY, 1857 ***1494.21*** *p31*
Fax, John Peter; New York, NY, 1873 ***1494.21*** *p31*
Fax, Jos. H.; New York, NY, 1873 ***1494.21*** *p31*
Fay, Jacob; Louisiana, 1841-1844 ***4981.45*** *p210*
Fay, Joseph 35; New York, NY, 1894 ***6512.1*** *p228*
Fay, Stephen; Ontario, 1871 ***1823.21*** *p109*
Fayard, Jean 11; America, 1844 ***778.6*** *p114*
Fayard, Jean 50; America, 1844 ***778.6*** *p114*
Fayard, Victorine 35; America, 1844 ***778.6*** *p114*
Fayet, Anne; Quebec, 1670 ***4514.3*** *p313*
Fayet, John 31; America, 1843 ***778.6*** *p114*
Fayette, John F. Ds 61; Ontario, 1871 ***1823.21*** *p109*
Fayette, Marie 17; Quebec, 1661 ***9221.17*** *p455*
Fayiol, Antoine 29; America, 1841 ***778.6*** *p114*
Fayiol, Guillaume 41; America, 1841 ***778.6*** *p114*
Fayot, Jacq. 40; America, 1841 ***778.6*** *p114*
Fazoldt, Carl Gottl.; Valdivia, Chile, 1852 ***1192.4*** *p54*
With wife
With child 6
With child 7
Fazzio, Salvadore; Louisiana, 1874-1875 ***4981.45*** *p298*
Fe, Mr. 35; America, 1846 ***778.6*** *p114*
Feagin, Patrick; Louisiana, 1836-1841 ***4981.45*** *p208*
Feaman, L.; Louisiana, 1874 ***4981.45*** *p131*
Fearsdos, Charles; Ohio, 1809-1852 ***4511.35*** *p13*
Featherston, William 86; Ontario, 1871 ***1823.17*** *p50*
Featherstone, Mary 42; Ontario, 1871 ***1823.17*** *p50*
Feaute, Pierre; Quebec, 1635 ***9221.17*** *p42*
Febrier, Attelie 6 months; America, 1843 ***778.6*** *p114*
Febrier, Claude 40; America, 1843 ***778.6*** *p114*
Febrier, Felicien 6; America, 1843 ***778.6*** *p114*
Febrier, Francois 62; America, 1843 ***778.6*** *p114*
Febrier, Germain 58; America, 1843 ***778.6*** *p114*
Febrier, Marie 62; America, 1843 ***778.6*** *p114*
Febrier, Severin 4; America, 1843 ***778.6*** *p114*
Febrier, Therese 33; America, 1843 ***778.6*** *p114*
February, Edward; Boston, 1664 ***9228.50*** *p217*
Febvre, Pierre; Quebec, 1656 ***9221.17*** *p335*
Febvrier, Christophe; Quebec, 1661 ***9221.17*** *p455*
Febvris, Christophe; Quebec, 1661 ***9221.17*** *p455*
Feddis, James 37; Ontario, 1871 ***1823.17*** *p50*
Federer, John; Colorado, 1884 ***1029.59*** *p28*
Federmann, Nikolaus; Venezuela, 1529 ***3899.5*** *p538*
Federmeier, Nikolaus 29; America, 1880 ***5475.1*** *p280*
Federspiel, Nik.; America, 1881 ***5475.1*** *p279*
Fedet, Andrew 15; New Orleans, 1846 ***778.6*** *p114*
Feducia, Frank 42; New Orleans, 1882 ***7710.1*** *p159*
Fee, David 40; Ontario, 1871 ***1823.21*** *p109*
Fee, James; Louisiana, 1874-1875 ***4981.45*** *p298*
Feehely, Michael 52; Ontario, 1871 ***1823.21*** *p109*
Feekings, John 45; Ontario, 1871 ***1823.21*** *p110*
Feeney, Catharine; Pittsburgh, 1854 ***8513.31*** *p413*
Feeney, Martin; Louisiana, 1874 ***4981.45*** *p295*
Feeney, Mic; St. John, N.B., 1847 ***2978.15*** *p37*
Feeny, James; Toronto, 1844 ***2910.35*** *p113*
Feeny, Michael; Ohio, 1840-1897 ***8365.35*** *p16*
Fees, Anastasia; Venezuela, 1843 ***3899.5*** *p544*
Fees, Johann Georg Gottlieb; America, 1866 ***2526.43*** *p167*
Fees, Maria Anna; Venezuela, 1843 ***3899.5*** *p545*
Fehder, Clemenz 18; New Orleans, 1848 ***778.6*** *p114*
Fehling, Heinrich Wilhelm Christoph; America, 1866 ***7420.1*** *p242*
Fehr, Johannetta; America, 1873 ***5475.1*** *p312*
Fehr, Rosa; Venezuela, 1843 ***3899.5*** *p545*
Fehre, Rosa; Venezuela, 1843 ***3899.5*** *p545*
Fehrenbach, Edward; Louisiana, 1874 ***4981.45*** *p131*
Fehrenberg, Christ.; Valdivia, Chile, 1852 ***1192.4*** *p55*
Fehrenberg, Heinr.; Valdivia, Chile, 1852 ***1192.4*** *p55*
Fehrenberg, Jean; Valdivia, Chile, 1852 ***1192.4*** *p55*
Fehrence, John; Ohio, 1809-1852 ***4511.35*** *p13*
Fehring, Heinrich Carl Christian; America, 1903 ***7420.1*** *p379*
Fehser, Julius Frederick; Wisconsin, 1890 ***6795.8*** *p236*
Fei, Maria Katharina; Venezuela, 1843 ***3899.5*** *p543*
Feiber, Augustus; Louisiana, 1853-1856 ***7710.1*** *p156*
Feid, Nikolaus 24; America, 1881 ***5475.1*** *p491*
Feidt, Jean 35; America, 1846 ***778.6*** *p114*
Feieberg, Raechel; Miami, 1935 ***4984.12*** *p39*
Feierstein, Edna; Detroit, 1930 ***1640.60*** *p78*
Feierstein, Joseph; Detroit, 1930 ***1640.60*** *p78*
Feige, Emil; Kansas, 1917-1918 ***2094.25*** *p50*
Feige, Martha; Kansas, 1917-1918 ***2094.25*** *p50*
Feigeler, . . .; Port uncertain, 1846 ***7420.1*** *p44*
Feigert, Peter; Ohio, 1809-1852 ***4511.35*** *p13*
Feild, Walter; Maryland, 1674-1675 ***1236.25*** *p52*
Feilen, Eva 62; Brazil, 1862 ***5475.1*** *p369*
*Daughter:*Angela
Feilen, Johann; New York, 1885 ***5475.1*** *p357*
Feilen, Margarethe; Brazil, 1873 ***5475.1*** *p371*
Fein, Georg Philipp 30; America, 1832 ***5475.1*** *p27*
Fein, Johann Georg 42; America, 1832 ***5475.1*** *p27*
With 6 children
Fein, Konrad; America, 1800-1899 ***5475.1*** *p27*
With child 25
With child 27
Feinberg, Rose; Miami, 1935 ***4984.12*** *p39*
Feinebein, Ilse Marie Caroline; America, 1850 ***7420.1*** *p71*
Feinioull, Jean; Quebec, 1654 ***9221.17*** *p308*
Feinman, Gertrude; Detroit, 1930 ***1640.60*** *p82*
Feintel, Nicholas; Ohio, 1809-1852 ***4511.35*** *p13*
Feis, Meyer; America, 1878 ***5475.1*** *p433*
Feishand, Elisabeth 46; America, 1846 ***778.6*** *p114*
Feishand, Joseph 23; America, 1846 ***778.6*** *p114*
Feist, Alexander 6 months; New York, NY, 1898 ***7951.13*** *p44*
Feist, Anton 2; New York, NY, 1898 ***7951.13*** *p44*
Feist, Anton 42; New York, NY, 1898 ***7951.13*** *p44*
Feist, Barbara 12; New York, NY, 1898 ***7951.13*** *p43*
Feist, Benedikt 4; New York, NY, 1898 ***7951.13*** *p44*
Feist, David 24; America, 1847 ***778.6*** *p114*
Feist, Eva 14; New York, NY, 1898 ***7951.13*** *p44*
Feist, Franz 3; New York, NY, 1898 ***7951.13*** *p44*
Feist, Helen 39; New York, NY, 1898 ***7951.13*** *p44*
Feist, Johanna 17; New York, NY, 1898 ***7951.13*** *p44*
Feist, Joseph 38; New York, NY, 1898 ***7951.13*** *p43*
Feist, Magdalena 5; New York, NY, 1898 ***7951.13*** *p44*
Feist, Maria Anna 1; New York, NY, 1898 ***7951.13*** *p43*
Feist, Maria Anna 35; New York, NY, 1898 ***7951.13*** *p43*
Feist, Regina 7; New York, NY, 1898 ***7951.13*** *p43*
Feist, Regina 58; New York, NY, 1898 ***7951.13*** *p43*
Feist, Sophia 8; New York, NY, 1898 ***7951.13*** *p44*
Feist, Theresia 9; New York, NY, 1898 ***7951.13*** *p43*
Feist, Valentine 19; Halifax, N.S., 1902 ***1860.4*** *p40*
Feit, A. Maria *SEE* Feit, Johann
Feit, Barbara *SEE* Feit, Johann
Feit, Franz; Illinois, 1891 ***5475.1*** *p218*
Feit, Johann; America, 1881 ***5475.1*** *p427*
*Daughter:*Maria
*Son:*Josef
*Daughter:*A. Maria
*Daughter:*Barbara
*Son:*Mathias
Feit, Josef *SEE* Feit, Johann
Feit, Maria *SEE* Feit, Johann
Feit, Mathias *SEE* Feit, Johann
Feith, Anna 2 *SEE* Feith, Peter
Feith, Anne 8; America, 1840 ***778.6*** *p114*
Feith, Anne Fey 36; America, 1840 ***778.6*** *p114*
Feith, Elisabeth Wirtz 23 *SEE* Feith, Peter
Feith, Marie 11; America, 1840 ***778.6*** *p114*
Feith, Peter 2 *SEE* Feith, Peter
Feith, Peter 28; America, 1864 ***5475.1*** *p370*
*Wife:*Elisabeth Wirtz 23
*Son:*Peter 2 months
*Daughter:*Anna 2
Feitmuller, John; New York, 1859 ***358.56*** *p100*
Fejfar, Frantisek; South Dakota, 1850-1910 ***2853.20*** *p246*
Felan, Andrew 34; Ontario, 1871 ***1823.21*** *p110*
Feld, Friedrich 3 *SEE* Feld, Mathias
Feld, Henriette Munig 32 *SEE* Feld, Mathias
Feld, Jakob 23; America, 1882 ***5475.1*** *p452*
Feld, Johann Ludwig; America, 1854 ***5475.1*** *p451*

Feld, Mathias; America, 1864 ***5475.1*** *p41*
*Wife:*Henriette Munig
*Son:*Mathias
*Son:*Friedrich
Feld, Mathias 9 *SEE* Feld, Mathias
Feldbrugge, Geo; Nebraska, 1905 ***3004.30*** *p46*
Felde, Emma vom; America, 1900 ***7420.1*** *p400*
Felder, Abraham; Illinois, 1858 ***6079.1*** *p5*
Feldman, Mrs. 25; New York, NY, 1894 ***6512.1*** *p229*
Feldman, Frederick; Iowa, 1869 ***1211.15*** *p10*
Feldman, Harrie 2; New York, NY, 1894 ***6512.1*** *p229*
Feldman, Joe 5; New York, NY, 1894 ***6512.1*** *p229*
Feldman, Martin 26; New York, NY, 1885 ***1883.7*** *p45*
Feldman, Rebecca 6 months; New York, NY, 1894 ***6512.1*** *p229*
Feldman, Simon 27; New York, NY, 1894 ***6512.1*** *p229*
Feldmann, Barth.; Chicago, 1944 ***8023.44*** *p373*
Feldmann, Carl Friedrich August; America, 1883 ***7420.1*** *p335*
Feldmann, Christoph; America, 1848 ***7420.1*** *p59*
With child 29
With child 27
Feldmann, Georg 32; America, 1846 ***778.6*** *p114*
Feldmann, Georges 28; Port uncertain, 1843 ***778.6*** *p114*
Feldmann, Herman Albert; Missouri, 1878 ***3276.1*** *p4*
Feldmann, Ludwig; America, 1884 ***7420.1*** *p342*
Feldstein, Olga 17; New York, NY, 1893 ***1883.7*** *p37*
Feldt, Ernestine Wilhelmine; Wisconsin, 1900 ***6795.8*** *p72*
Feleisch, Barbara 24; Louisiana, 1848 ***778.6*** *p114*
Feleisch, Henry 25; Louisiana, 1848 ***778.6*** *p114*
Feleon, Theodore 44; Michigan, 1880 ***4491.30*** *p11*
Felger, Anthony; Ohio, 1809-1852 ***4511.35*** *p13*
Felhmer, Paul; New York, NY, 1886 ***6212.1*** *p15*
Felix, Franc. 36; America, 1840 ***778.6*** *p114*
Felix, John; New York, 1860 ***358.56*** *p148*
Felix, Mathias 28; New Orleans, 1848 ***778.6*** *p115*
Felix, Paul Ceasar; Tennessee, 1904 ***3665.20*** *p111*
Fell, Barbara *SEE* Fell, Peter
Fell, Barbara Helena; America, 1882 ***5475.1*** *p203*
Fell, Jesse W.; Ohio, 1832 ***3580.20*** *p31*
Fell, Jesse W.; Ohio, 1832 ***6020.12*** *p7*
Fell, Katharina Hoffmann 29 *SEE* Fell, Peter
Fell, Mathias; America, 1882 ***5475.1*** *p203*
Fell, Mathias *SEE* Fell, Peter
Fell, Peter 30; America, 1883 ***5475.1*** *p203*
*Wife:*Katharina Hoffmann 29
*Daughter:*Barbara
*Son:*Mathias
Fell, Susanna; America, 1882 ***5475.1*** *p203*
Feller, Nicholas; Ohio, 1809-1852 ***4511.35*** *p13*
Fellerath, Franz 27; Missouri, 1845 ***778.6*** *p115*
Fellerath, Louis 24; Missouri, 1845 ***778.6*** *p115*
Fellew, Charles 40; Ontario, 1871 ***1823.21*** *p110*
Fellew, Henry 67; Ontario, 1871 ***1823.21*** *p110*
Felloon, Mr. 64; New Orleans, 1848 ***778.6*** *p115*
Fellow, Abraham; Maine, 1658 ***9228.50*** *p214*
Fellows, Joseph 32; Ontario, 1871 ***1823.21*** *p110*
Fellrath, Caroline 3 months; Mississippi, 1845-1846 ***778.6*** *p115*
Fellrath, Catherine 10; Mississippi, 1845-1846 ***778.6*** *p115*
Fellrath, Francois 14; Mississippi, 1845-1846 ***778.6*** *p115*
Fellrath, Jean 5 months; Mississippi, 1845-1846 ***778.6*** *p115*
Fellrath, Joseph 12; Mississippi, 1845-1846 ***778.6*** *p115*
Fellrath, Joseph 43; Mississippi, 1845-1846 ***778.6*** *p115*
Fellrath, Josephine 7; Mississippi, 1845-1846 ***778.6*** *p115*
Fellrath, Rekina 38; Mississippi, 1845-1846 ***778.6*** *p115*
Fellrath, Therese 8; Mississippi, 1845-1846 ***778.6*** *p115*
Fells, William; Illinois, 1855 ***6079.1*** *p5*
Feloic, Joseph 14; New Orleans, 1847 ***778.6*** *p115*
Felow, K.; New York, 1859 ***358.56*** *p101*
Fels, Mr. 25; America, 1843 ***778.6*** *p115*
Fels, Mrs. 22; America, 1843 ***778.6*** *p115*
Fels, Lazarus; North Carolina, 1851 ***1088.45*** *p9*
Felsenthal, William; America, 1882 ***5475.1*** *p242*
Felsinger, Loiuis 34; New Orleans, 1847 ***778.6*** *p115*
Felten, Angela *SEE* Felten, Peter
Felten, Angela; America, 1879 ***5475.1*** *p376*
Felten, Anna Gill *SEE* Felten, Peter
Felten, Johann *SEE* Felten, Peter
Felten, Johann; Ohio, 1886 ***5475.1*** *p375*
Felten, Margarethe *SEE* Felten, Peter
Felten, Maria *SEE* Felten, Peter
Felten, Michel; America, 1870 ***5475.1*** *p345*
Felten, Michel *SEE* Felten, Peter
Felten, Nikolaus *SEE* Felten, Peter
Felten, Nikolaus; Milwaukee, 1863 ***5475.1*** *p345*
Felten, Peter *SEE* Felten, Peter
Felten, Peter; America, 1879 ***5475.1*** *p376*
*Wife:*Anna Gill
*Daughter:*Angela
*Daughter:*Maria
*Son:*Michel
*Son:*Johann
*Daughter:*Margarethe
*Son:*Nikolaus
*Son:*Peter
Felter, Gotleib; Ohio, 1809-1852 ***4511.35*** *p13*
Feltes, Jacob; Illinois, 1920 ***1029.59*** *p28*
*Wife:*Lena Koke
Feltes, Katharina 37; Brazil, 1857 ***5475.1*** *p248*
Feltes, Lena Koke *SEE* Feltes, Jacob
Felton, Lafayette 36; Ontario, 1871 ***1823.17*** *p50*
Felyps, Frederick *SEE* Felyps, Vrederych
Felyps, Vrederych; New York, 1647-1653 ***2853.20*** *p14*
*Son:*Frederick
Felypsen, Frederick *SEE* Felypsen, Vrederych
Felypsen, Vrederych; New York, 1647-1653 ***2853.20*** *p14*
*Son:*Frederick
Felz, Anna; America, 1882 ***5475.1*** *p339*
Felz, Anna; Chicago, 1882 ***5475.1*** *p350*
With mother
Felz, Anna Maria 47; America, 1867 ***5475.1*** *p376*
Felz, Anton; America, 1863 ***5475.1*** *p349*
Felz, Mrs. Ludwig; Chicago, 1882 ***5475.1*** *p350*
Felz, Nikolaus; Chicago, 1891 ***5475.1*** *p351*
Fenchant, Joseph 21; New Orleans, 1848 ***778.6*** *p115*
Fenck, Karl; America, 1882 ***5475.1*** *p381*
Fender, John; Ohio, 1809-1852 ***4511.35*** *p13*
Fendt, Elizabeth Law *SEE* Fendt, Rudolf
Fendt, Rudolf; Philadelphia, 1851 ***8513.31*** *p305*
*Wife:*Elizabeth Law
Fenell, Marget; New Orleans, 1851 ***7242.30*** *p141*
Fenell, Mary; New Orleans, 1851 ***7242.30*** *p141*
Feneyer, Philip; North Carolina, 1710 ***3629.40*** *p4*
Fenigan, Hugh; Illinois, 1860 ***6079.1*** *p5*
Fenimore, Humphrey; Boston, 1774 ***8529.30*** *p2*
Feniou, Guillaume 25; Quebec, 1647 ***9221.17*** *p336*
Fenn, W. A. 33; Ontario, 1871 ***1823.21*** *p110*
Fennacey, William; Boston, 1759 ***1642*** *p47*
Fennan, George; Illinois, 1856 ***6079.1*** *p5*
Fennant, Charles; Iowa, 1879 ***1211.15*** *p10*
Fennecy, Bartholomew; Boston, 1742 ***1642*** *p45*
Fennel, Amos 35; Ontario, 1871 ***1823.21*** *p110*
Fennell, Jane 11; Quebec, 1870 ***8364.32*** *p23*
Fennell, John; St. Johns, N.F., 1825 ***1053.15*** *p7*
Fennell, Mary; New Orleans, 1850 ***7242.30*** *p141*
Fennell, Mary 76; Ontario, 1871 ***1823.21*** *p110*
Fennell, Mary; St. Johns, N.F., 1825 ***1053.15*** *p7*
Fennell, Robert 86; Ontario, 1871 ***1823.21*** *p110*
Fenner, Caroline 37; Michigan, 1880 ***4491.30*** *p11*
Fenner, Johann Ludwig; Wisconsin, 1893 ***6795.8*** *p117*
Fenner, John 63; Ontario, 1871 ***1823.17*** *p50*
Fenner, Julius; Wisconsin, 1876 ***6795.8*** *p36*
Fenner, Mary 50; Ontario, 1871 ***1823.21*** *p110*
Fenner, Theophiles 72; Ontario, 1871 ***1823.17*** *p50*
Fennese, James; Boston, 1748 ***1642*** *p46*
Fennesey, James; Boston, 1755 ***1642*** *p47*
Fenske, Daniel 36; Portland, ME, 1911 ***970.38*** *p76*
Fenske, Theodor; Wisconsin, 1880 ***6795.8*** *p47*
Fenstin, Emma 12; Quebec, 1870 ***8364.32*** *p23*
Fentenheim, Jacob; Ohio, 1809-1852 ***4511.35*** *p13*
Fenton, Mr.; Canada, 1775 ***3036.5*** *p68*
Fenton, Catherine 55; Ontario, 1871 ***1823.21*** *p110*
Fenton, George; North America, 1750 ***1640.8*** *p233*
Fenton, Mary *SEE* Fenton, Sarah
Fenton, Sarah; Canada, 1775 ***3036.5*** *p68*
*Sister:*Mary
Fenton, William 59; Ontario, 1871 ***1823.21*** *p110*
Fenwick, Edward; Canada, 1774 ***3036.5*** *p41*
Fenwick, Eliza 46; Ontario, 1871 ***1823.21*** *p110*
Fenwick, James 64; Ontario, 1871 ***1823.21*** *p110*
Fenwick, John 55; Ontario, 1871 ***1823.21*** *p110*
Fenwick, Mathew; Canada, 1774 ***3036.5*** *p42*
Fenzerich, Anna 8; America, 1840 ***778.6*** *p115*
Fenzerich, Barbara 37; America, 1840 ***778.6*** *p115*
Fenzerich, Ch...an 6; America, 1840 ***778.6*** *p115*
Fenzerich, Ch...an 16; America, 1840 ***778.6*** *p115*
Fenzerich, Jean 39; America, 1840 ***778.6*** *p115*
Fenzerich, Maria 12; America, 1840 ***778.6*** *p115*
Fenzerich, Peter 14; America, 1840 ***778.6*** *p115*
Fer, Rosa; Venezuela, 1843 ***3899.5*** *p545*
Feragalo, Jose; Louisiana, 1836-1840 ***4981.45*** *p212*
Ferand, B. 29; America, 1843 ***778.6*** *p115*
Ferarty, Michael; Toronto, 1844 ***2910.35*** *p115*
Ferber, Margarethe; Brazil, 1857 ***5475.1*** *p517*
Ferbrache, Andrew N. *SEE* Ferbrache, Daniel P.
Ferbrache, Daniel; America, 1776-1792 ***9228.50*** *p18A*
Ferbrache, Daniel; Died enroute, 1806 ***9228.50*** *p215*
Ferbrache, Daniel; Norfolk, VA, 1806 ***9228.50*** *p56*
*Wife:*Judith Sarchet
With children
Ferbrache, Daniel; Ohio, 1806 ***9228.50*** *p215*
*Wife:*Judith Sarchet
*Child:*John
*Child:*Thomas
*Child:*Judith
*Child:*Mary
Ferbrache, Daniel D. *SEE* Ferbrache, Daniel P.
Ferbrache, Daniel P.; Ohio, 1802 ***9228.50*** *p214*
With wife
*Child:*Nathaniel
*Child:*Solomon T.
*Child:*Susan M.
*Child:*Andrew N.
*Child:*Daniel D.
*Child:*Thomas R.
*Child:*Peter T.
Ferbrache, John *SEE* Ferbrache, Daniel
Ferbrache, Judith Sarchet *SEE* Ferbrache, Daniel
Ferbrache, Judith *SEE* Ferbrache, Daniel
Ferbrache, Judith Sarchet *SEE* Ferbrache, Daniel
Ferbrache, Mary *SEE* Ferbrache, Daniel
Ferbrache, Nathaniel *SEE* Ferbrache, Daniel P.
Ferbrache, Peter T. *SEE* Ferbrache, Daniel P.
Ferbrache, Solomon T. *SEE* Ferbrache, Daniel P.
Ferbrache, Susan M. *SEE* Ferbrache, Daniel P.
Ferbrache, Thomas *SEE* Ferbrache, Daniel
Ferbrache, Thomas R. *SEE* Ferbrache, Daniel P.
Ferch, Christian Friedrich Hermann; Wisconsin, 1866 ***6795.8*** *p72*
Ferch, J.; New York, 1859 ***358.56*** *p55*
Ferch, Johann Charles August; Wisconsin, 1880 ***6795.8*** *p72*
Ferdinand, Filip *SEE* Ferdinand, Josef
Ferdinand, Jenny 15; America, 1848 ***778.6*** *p115*
Ferdinand, Josef; Chicago, 1855 ***2853.20*** *p388*
*Brother:*Filip
Ferdinand, Levis Louis 33; America, 1843 ***778.6*** *p115*
Ferdinand, Louis 44; America, 1848 ***778.6*** *p115*
Fere, Francois 34; America, 1845 ***778.6*** *p115*
Ferg, Eduard; Wisconsin, 1882 ***6795.8*** *p72*
Ferge, Christoph; Wisconsin, 1888 ***6795.8*** *p97*
Ferge, Eduard; Wisconsin, 1882 ***6795.8*** *p72*
Fergeson, Margaret 69; Michigan, 1880 ***4491.30*** *p11*
Fergeson, Robert 67; Michigan, 1880 ***4491.30*** *p11*
Fergus, Victor 28; America, 1845 ***778.6*** *p115*
Ferguson, Mr. 32; America, 1745 ***778.6*** *p115*
Ferguson, A. J.; Iowa, 1892 ***1211.15*** *p10*
Ferguson, Alexander 45; Ontario, 1871 ***1823.21*** *p110*
Ferguson, Alexander 53; Ontario, 1871 ***1823.21*** *p110*
Ferguson, Alexander 62; Ontario, 1871 ***1823.17*** *p51*
Ferguson, Alexander; Philadelphia, 1844-1846 ***7074.20*** *p132*
Ferguson, Andrew; North Carolina, 1837 ***1088.45*** *p9*
Ferguson, Christiena 76; Ontario, 1871 ***1823.21*** *p110*
Ferguson, Christine 80; Ontario, 1871 ***1823.17*** *p51*
Ferguson, Colin 57; Ontario, 1871 ***1823.21*** *p110*
Ferguson, David 49; Ontario, 1871 ***1823.17*** *p51*
Ferguson, Dugald 51; Ontario, 1871 ***1823.17*** *p51*
Ferguson, Duncan 45; Ontario, 1871 ***1823.21*** *p110*
Ferguson, Duncan 54; Ontario, 1871 ***1823.17*** *p51*
Ferguson, E.T.; Washington, 1886 ***2770.40*** *p195*
Ferguson, Ellen 80; Ontario, 1871 ***1823.17*** *p51*
Ferguson, Henry 63; Ontario, 1871 ***1823.21*** *p110*
Ferguson, Hugh 75; Ontario, 1871 ***1823.21*** *p110*
Ferguson, Jacob 47; Ontario, 1871 ***1823.21*** *p110*
Ferguson, James 40; Ontario, 1871 ***1823.21*** *p110*
Ferguson, James 50; Ontario, 1871 ***1823.21*** *p110*
Ferguson, James 60; Ontario, 1871 ***1823.21*** *p110*
Ferguson, James 60; Ontario, 1871 ***1823.21*** *p110*
Ferguson, James; Salt Lake City, 1863 ***3687.1*** *p34*
Ferguson, Janet; New York, 1738 ***8277.31*** *p115*
With son
Ferguson, Jennie 46; Ontario, 1871 ***1823.21*** *p110*
Ferguson, John; North Carolina, 1821 ***1088.45*** *p9*
Ferguson, John 19; North Carolina, 1774 ***1422.10*** *p58*
Ferguson, John 19; North Carolina, 1774 ***1422.10*** *p62*
Ferguson, John 37; Ontario, 1871 ***1823.21*** *p110*
Ferguson, John 49; Ontario, 1871 ***1823.21*** *p110*
Ferguson, John 56; Ontario, 1871 ***1823.21*** *p110*
Ferguson, John 62; Ontario, 1871 ***1823.21*** *p110*
Ferguson, John 68; Ontario, 1871 ***1823.21*** *p110*
Ferguson, Kate 17; Ontario, 1871 ***1823.17*** *p51*
Ferguson, Margaret 24; Ontario, 1871 ***1823.21*** *p111*
Ferguson, Margaret 66; Ontario, 1871 ***1823.21*** *p111*
Ferguson, Marshal 35; Ontario, 1871 ***1823.21*** *p111*
Ferguson, Peter 72; Ontario, 1871 ***1823.21*** *p111*
Ferguson, Robert 30; Ontario, 1871 ***1823.21*** *p111*
Ferguson, Robert 50; Ontario, 1871 ***1823.21*** *p111*
Ferguson, Robert 58; Ontario, 1871 ***1823.21*** *p111*
Ferguson, Roderick 41; Ontario, 1871 ***1823.17*** *p51*
Ferguson, Samuel; Iowa, 1890 ***1211.15*** *p10*
Ferguson, Thomas 65; Ontario, 1871 ***1823.21*** *p111*
Ferguson, William 50; Ontario, 1871 ***1823.17*** *p51*

Fergusson, Bernard; Toronto, 1844 *2910.35 p115*
Fergusson, John 37; Ontario, 1871 *1823.21 p111*
Fergusson, Thomas 14; Quebec, 1870 *8364.32 p23*
Ferguys, William; North Carolina, 1836 *1088.45 p9*
Ferhman, John; Louisiana, 1836-1840 *4981.45 p212*
Ferine, Lewis 30; Port uncertain, 1845 *778.6 p116*
Ferino, Monzio; Louisiana, 1874-1875 *4981.45 p298*
Feris, Jacque 62; America, 1843 *778.6 p116*
Ferld, John; Boston, 1766 *1642 p36*
Ferlitz, Paul; Colorado, 1882 *1029.59 p28*
Fermant, Georg 30; America, 1846 *778.6 p116*
Fermer, Theolus 72; Ontario, 1871 *1823.17 p51*
Fermimich, John; Louisiana, 1874 *4981.45 p295*
Fermong, George; Ohio, 1809-1852 *4511.35 p13*
Fermony, George; Ohio, 1809-1852 *4511.35 p14*
Fermyn, Jane 43; Ontario, 1871 *1823.21 p111*
Fernan, Jahn; Ohio, 1809-1852 *4511.35 p14*
Fernandez, Christopher; Louisiana, 1874 *4981.45 p131*
Fernandez, Jean 35; America, 1841 *778.6 p116*
Fernandez, Jose; Louisiana, 1836-1840 *4981.45 p212*
Fernandez, Macario Romulo; Miami, 1935 *4984.12 p39*
Fernandez, Manuel; Louisiana, 1836-1840 *4981.45 p212*
Fernandez, S. 19; New York, NY, 1894 *6512.1 p181*
Fernandez y Valdes, Macario Romulo; Miami, 1935 *4984.12 p39*
Fernatize, C. 35; America, 1846 *778.6 p116*
Fernatize, Catherine 1; America, 1846 *778.6 p116*
Fernatize, Francois 3; America, 1846 *778.6 p116*
Fernau, Jahn; Ohio, 1809-1852 *4511.35 p14*
Fernby, William 62; Ontario, 1871 *1823.17 p51*
Ferne, John 48; Ontario, 1871 *1823.21 p111*
Fernet, Mr. 30; America, 1844 *778.6 p116*
Ferneyhough, Albert 6 *SEE* Ferneyhough, Jane
Ferneyhough, Alice 6 *SEE* Ferneyhough, Jane
Ferneyhough, Amos 9 *SEE* Ferneyhough, Jane
Ferneyhough, George 2 *SEE* Ferneyhough, Jane
Ferneyhough, Jane 38; Halifax, N.S., n.d. *1833.5 p7*
Ferneyhough, Jane 38; Halifax, N.S., n.d. *8445.10 p7*
  *Relative:*Mary 16
  *Relative:*Albert 6 months
  *Relative:*Martha Ann 7
  *Relative:*Alice 6
  *Relative:*George 2
  *Relative:*William 4
  *Relative:*Amos 9
Ferneyhough, Martha Ann 7 *SEE* Ferneyhough, Jane
Ferneyhough, Mary 16 *SEE* Ferneyhough, Jane
Ferneyhough, William 4 *SEE* Ferneyhough, Jane
Fernholz Family ; America, n.d. *8023.44 p373*
Fernley, George 60; Ontario, 1871 *1823.21 p111*
Ferns, William 70; Ontario, 1871 *1823.17 p51*
Fernsner, Ludwig; America, 1863 *5475.1 p72*
  *Wife:*Sophie Schnerring
Fernsner, Sophie Schnerring 27 *SEE* Fernsner, Ludwig
Feron, Francois Joseph, Jr. *SEE* Feron, Francois Joseph, Sr.
Feron, Francois Joseph, Sr.; Wisconsin, 1855 *1495.20 p8*
  *Wife:*Julienne Barbier
  *Son:*Francois Joseph, Jr.
Feron, Julienne Barbier *SEE* Feron, Francois Joseph, Sr.
Ferra, Marie 13; Quebec, 1658 *9221.17 p380*
Ferrall, Thomas; North Carolina, 1834 *1088.45 p9*
Ferran, Guillaume 19; New Orleans, 1845 *778.6 p116*
Ferran, Jean Louis 26; New Orleans, 1848 *778.6 p116*
Ferrand, Mr. 7; New Orleans, 1848 *778.6 p116*
Ferrand, Pierre 42; New Orleans, 1848 *778.6 p116*
Ferrand, Pierre Athanaze 17; America, 1845 *778.6 p116*
Ferranden, Charles 33; New Orleans, 1848 *778.6 p116*
Ferrandon, Charles; Illinois, 1852 *6079.1 p5*
Ferraquet, Louis; Quebec, 1657 *9221.17 p357*
Ferrau, Bertrand 40; New Orleans, 1848 *778.6 p116*
Ferraud, Michel; Quebec, 1653 *9221.17 p273*
Ferre, Catherine; Quebec, 1668 *4514.3 p313*
Ferre, Jean; Quebec, 1641 *9221.17 p103*
Ferreaud, Ls. 19; America, 1746 *778.6 p116*
Ferree, Elizabeth; New York, 1713 *9228.50 p180*
  With sister
Ferrell, Christopher; Harrisburg, PA, 1854 *5720.10 p381*
Ferrell, Joanna *SEE* Ferrell, Partrick
Ferrell, Partrick; Ipswich, MA, 1732 *1642 p71*
  *Wife:*Joanna
Ferrell, Patrick; North Carolina, 1840 *1088.45 p9*
Ferren, Abigail *SEE* Ferren, Patrick
Ferren, Patrick; Ipswich, MA, 1735 *1642 p71*
  *Wife:*Abigail
Ferrer, Edouard 34; America, 1848 *778.6 p116*
Ferrer, Elisabeth; America, 1856 *5475.1 p259*
Ferrer, John 35; New Orleans, 1847 *778.6 p116*
Ferrera, Andrew; Louisiana, 1874-1875 *4981.45 p298*
Ferri, Emilie *SEE* Ferri, Paul Joseph
Ferri, Leopold *SEE* Ferri, Paul Joseph

Ferri, Paul Joseph; Wisconsin, 1855 *1495.20 p8*
  *Wife:*Victoire Desneux
  *Child:*Emilie
  *Child:*Theodore
  *Child:*Leopold
Ferri, Theodore *SEE* Ferri, Paul Joseph
Ferri, Victoire Desneux *SEE* Ferri, Paul Joseph
Ferriene, Mr. 26; Texas, 1840 *778.6 p116*
Ferrier, A. 50; New Orleans, 1843 *778.6 p116*
Ferrier, Hilla.re 40; New Orleans, 1845 *778.6 p116*
Ferrier, L. 21; New Orleans, 1840 *778.6 p116*
Ferrier, Pierre; Virginia, 1700 *9230.15 p81*
  With wife & child
Ferrier, Suzanne; Quebec, 1661 *9221.17 p470*
  *Relative:*Simon
Ferriere, Georg Carl Christian Otto; America, 1868 *7919.3 p527*
Ferriere, Jacques 29; Port uncertain, 1847 *778.6 p116*
Ferries, George 49; Ontario, 1871 *1823.21 p111*
Ferrion, Simon 57; New Orleans, 1848 *778.6 p116*
Ferris, Elijah 77; Ontario, 1871 *1823.21 p111*
Ferris, Wm Y. 60; Ontario, 1871 *1823.21 p111*
Ferron, Marguerite; Quebec, 1671 *4514.3 p313*
Ferry, Daniel; Charleston, SC, 1718 *9228.50 p14*
Ferry, Daniel 28; Louisiana, 1848 *778.6 p116*
Ferry, Emilie *SEE* Ferry, Paul Joseph
Ferry, Henri; Boston, 1716 *9228.50 p199*
Ferry, Jacob 24; Louisiana, 1848 *778.6 p116*
Ferry, John 30; Ontario, 1871 *1823.21 p111*
Ferry, Leopold *SEE* Ferry, Paul Joseph
Ferry, Louisa 17; Quebec, 1870 *8364.32 p23*
Ferry, Marie 35; Louisiana, 1848 *778.6 p116*
Ferry, Paul Joseph; Wisconsin, 1855 *1495.20 p8*
  *Wife:*Victoire Desneux
  *Child:*Leopold
  *Child:*Emilie
  *Child:*Theodore
Ferry, Susanna; Boston, 1716 *9228.50 p217*
Ferry, Theodore *SEE* Ferry, Paul Joseph
Ferry, Victoire Desneux *SEE* Ferry, Paul Joseph
Fersing, Anna *SEE* Fersing, Philipp
Fersing, Georg *SEE* Fersing, Philipp
Fersing, Jakob *SEE* Fersing, Philipp
Fersing, Nikolaus *SEE* Fersing, Philipp
Fersing, Philipp; New Orleans, 1873 *5475.1 p31*
  *Son:*Jakob
  *Daughter:*Anna
  *Son:*Georg
  *Son:*Nikolaus
Ferth, Thomas 38; Ontario, 1871 *1823.21 p111*
Fertig, Adam Michael; America, 1836 *2526.42 p104*
Fertig, Barbara; Philadelphia, 1843 *8513.31 p423*
Fertig, Michael Adam; America, 1836 *2526.42 p189*
  With wife & 3 children
Fery, Adeline 12; Louisiana, 1848 *778.6 p116*
Fery, Benjamin 6 months; Louisiana, 1848 *778.6 p116*
Fery, Francoise 34; Louisiana, 1848 *778.6 p116*
Fery, Johann; Ohio, 1893 *5475.1 p215*
Fery, Joseph 37; Louisiana, 1848 *778.6 p116*
Fery, Josephe 9; Louisiana, 1848 *778.6 p116*
Fery, Leonie 4; Louisiana, 1848 *778.6 p117*
Fery, Marie 7; Louisiana, 1848 *778.6 p117*
Fery, Michel; America, 1871 *5475.1 p219*
Fesel, Philipp; America, 1881 *2526.43 p188*
Fest, Simon 20; Galveston, TX, 1846 *3967.10 p377*
Fesvey, Eugenie 28; America, 1843 *778.6 p117*
Fethirston, Joseph 49; Ontario, 1871 *1823.17 p51*
Fetine, Jeanne; Quebec, 1662 *9221.17 p481*
Fetsch, Anna Maria; Venezuela, 1843 *3899.5 p544*
Fetsch, Blasius; Venezuela, 1843 *3899.5 p541*
Fetsch, Franz Joseph *SEE* Fetsch, Theresia
Fetsch, Johann; Venezuela, 1843 *3899.5 p541*
Fetsch, Johann; Venezuela, 1843 *3899.5 p541*
Fetsch, Johann; Venezuela, 1843 *3899.5 p543*
Fetsch, Johann *SEE* Fetsch, Theresia
Fetsch, Johann; Venezuela, 1843 *3899.5 p545*
Fetsch, Johann Kaspar; Venezuela, 1843 *3899.5 p543*
Fetsch, Johannes; Venezuela, 1843 *3899.5 p541*
Fetsch, Josef 29; New York, NY, 1893 *1883.7 p42*
Fetsch, Luitgard; Venezuela, 1843 *3899.5 p542*
Fetsch, Maria Anna *SEE* Fetsch, Theresia
Fetsch, Rosina 27; New York, NY, 1893 *1883.7 p42*
Fetsch, Theresia; Venezuela, 1843 *3899.5 p545*
  *Child:*Franz Joseph
  *Child:*Maria Anna
  *Child:*Johann
Fetsch Children, . . .; Venezuela, 1843 *3899.5 p541*
Fett, Johann 30; America, 1845 *5475.1 p366*
Fette, . . .; America, 1846 *7420.1 p44*
Fetters, Jacob; Ohio, 1809-1852 *4511.35 p14*
Fetters, Lucas; Ohio, 1809-1852 *4511.35 p14*
Fettich, Catha 27; New York, NY, 1886 *8425.16 p33*

Fettich, Lippold 11 months; New York, NY, 1886 *8425.16 p33*
Fettich, Wendelin 37; New York, NY, 1886 *8425.16 p33*
Fettig, Barbara 25; New York, NY, 1898 *7951.13 p44*
Fettig, Elisabeth 25; New York, NY, 1898 *7951.13 p44*
Fettig, Emilia 1; New York, NY, 1898 *7951.13 p44*
Fettig, Eva 2; New York, NY, 1898 *7951.13 p44*
Fettig, Josef 9 months; New York, NY, 1898 *7951.13 p44*
Fettig, Joseph 19; New York, NY, 1898 *7951.13 p44*
Fettig, Joseph 26; New York, NY, 1898 *7951.13 p44*
Fettig, Ludwina 26; New York, NY, 1898 *7951.13 p44*
Fettig, Peter 25; New York, NY, 1898 *7951.13 p44*
Fettig, Phillip 3; New York, NY, 1898 *7951.13 p44*
Fettig, Valantine 30; New York, NY, 1898 *7951.13 p44*
Fetzer, Adalbert; America, 1885 *179.55 p19*
Fetzer, Albert; America, 1864 *179.55 p19*
Fetzer, Anton F.; America, 1880 *179.55 p19*
Fetzer, Cazilia; America, 1880 *179.55 p19*
Fetzer, Emma; America, 1880 *179.55 p19*
Fetzer, Fridolin; America, 1880 *179.55 p19*
Fetzer, Friedrich *SEE* Fetzer, Jakob
Fetzer, Jacob; America, 1864 *179.55 p19*
Fetzer, Jakob *SEE* Fetzer, Jakob
Fetzer, Jakob; Brazil, 1862 *5475.1 p506*
  *Wife:*Maria Kath. Reichardt
  *Son:*Friedrich
  *Daughter:*Karoline
  *Son:*Jakob
Fetzer, Johann Michael; America, 1885 *179.55 p19*
Fetzer, Josefa Barbara; America, 1880 *179.55 p19*
Fetzer, Joseph; America, 1853 *179.55 p19*
Fetzer, Karl; America, 1885 *179.55 p19*
Fetzer, Karoline *SEE* Fetzer, Jakob
Fetzer, Leonhard; America, 1860 *179.55 p19*
Fetzer, Maria Kath. Reichardt 32 *SEE* Fetzer, Jakob
Fetzlaf, Bertha Emilie; Wisconsin, 1898 *6795.8 p122*
Feucht, Jakob; America, 1893 *179.55 p19*
Feudner, John; Ohio, 1809-1852 *4511.35 p14*
Feuerbrand, Hy. 21; America, 1840 *778.6 p117*
Feuerpfeil, Friedrich; America, 1868 *7919.3 p532*
Feuerrohr, Malwine; America, 1901 *7420.1 p377*
Feuerstein, Johannes; New Jersey, 1750-1774 *927.31 p3*
Feuillade, Clarice 10; Port uncertain, 1843 *778.6 p117*
Feuillade, Eucharis 9; Port uncertain, 1843 *778.6 p117*
Feuillade, Marie 27; Port uncertain, 1843 *778.6 p117*
Feuillade, Pierre 35; Port uncertain, 1843 *778.6 p117*
Feuillard, Mr. 32; America, 1847 *778.6 p117*
Feuille, A. 30; Mobile, AL, 1840 *778.6 p117*
Feuille, Jean 20; America, 1844 *778.6 p117*
Feuilliay, Michel 31; Quebec, 1661 *9221.17 p455*
Feuschter, John Jacob David; Ohio, 1809-1852 *4511.35 p14*
Feuville, Jean 49; Quebec, 1649 *9221.17 p208*
Feveryear, Edward; Boston, 1664 *9228.50 p217*
Fevre, Francois 21; Missouri, 1846 *778.6 p117*
Fevrier, Edward; Boston, 1664 *9228.50 p217*
Fewings, George 41; Ontario, 1871 *1823.21 p111*
Fey, Jakob; Venezuela, 1843 *3899.5 p543*
Fey, Johann; America, 1881 *5475.1 p344*
  *Wife:*Katharina Klein
  *Daughter:*Katharina
Fey, Johann Jakob; Venezuela, 1843 *3899.5 p543*
Fey, Katharina *SEE* Fey, Johann
Fey, Katharina Klein *SEE* Fey, Johann
Fey, Magdalena; Venezuela, 1843 *3899.5 p541*
Fey, Maria Katharina; Venezuela, 1843 *3899.5 p543*
Fey, Martin; Venezuela, 1843 *3899.5 p543*
Feymi, Michel 31; Quebec, 1661 *9221.17 p455*
Feyette, Michel 9; America, 1846 *778.6 p117*
Feyette, Pierre 19; America, 1846 *778.6 p117*
Fezeret, Claude; Quebec, 1663 *4514.3 p349*
  *Wife:*Suzanne Guilbaut
  *Child:*Rene
  *Child:*Jacques
Fezeret, Claude 42; Quebec, 1647 *9221.17 p180*
  *Wife:*Simone Guilebaut 34
  *Son:*Rene 5
  *Son:*Jacques 3
Fezeret, Jacques *SEE* Fezeret, Claude
Fezeret, Jacques 3 *SEE* Fezeret, Claude
Fezeret, Rene *SEE* Fezeret, Claude
Fezeret, Rene 5 *SEE* Fezeret, Claude
Fezeret, Simone Guilebaut 34 *SEE* Fezeret, Claude
Fezeret, Suzanne Guilbaut *SEE* Fezeret, Claude
Ffersick, Frederick C.; Ohio, 1809-1852 *4511.35 p14*
Ffienel, Anne 45; Ontario, 1871 *1823.21 p111*
FfitzGerald, Mr.; Massachusetts, 1727 *1642 p82*
Ffulford, Humfry; Virginia, 1652 *6254.4 p243*
Fiacco, Arky; New York, 1926 *1173.1 p2*
Fiala, Frantisek, Sr.; Nebraska, 1871-1872 *2853.20 p176*
Fiala, Josef; Cleveland, OH, 1852 *2853.20 p216*
Ficca, Libert A.; Colorado, 1902 *1029.59 p28*

Ficca, Libert A. 26; Colorado, 1902 ***1029.59*** *p28*
Fichet, Claude; Quebec, 1641 ***9221.17*** *p103*
Ficht, Carl; Colorado, 1893 ***1029.59*** *p28*
Ficht, Carl; Colorado, 1901 ***1029.59*** *p28*
Ficht, Franz; Colorado, 1890 ***1029.59*** *p28*
Ficht, Franz; Colorado, 1896 ***1029.59*** *p28*
Ficht, Paul; Colorado, 1887 ***1029.59*** *p28*
Ficht, Paul; Colorado, 1890 ***1029.59*** *p28*
Fichter, Andrew; Ohio, 1809-1852 ***4511.35*** *p14*
Fichtner, Oswin; Colorado, 1882 ***1029.59*** *p28*
Fick, Christain; North Carolina, 1853 ***1088.45*** *p9*
Fickeis, Elisabeth; Brazil, 1863 ***5475.1*** *p550*
Ficker, Charlotte; America, 1852 ***7420.1*** *p88*
Fickett, John; Maine, 1645-1745 ***9228.50*** *p217*
Ficquet, Marguerite 23; Quebec, 1657 ***9221.17*** *p350*
Fiddes, Thomas 37; Ontario, 1871 ***1823.21*** *p111*
Fiddy, William; North Carolina, 1855 ***1088.45*** *p9*
Fide, Jacob; Long Island, 1778 ***8529.30*** *p9A*
Fiedeke, Wilhelmine; Wisconsin, 1904 ***6795.8*** *p176*
Fiedler, Barbara Spinnweber 20 *SEE* Fiedler, Johann
Fiedler, Catharine F. Bantte *SEE* Fiedler, Wilhelm F.
Fiedler, Johann 30; America, 1849 ***5475.1*** *p415*
  *Wife:*Barbara Spinnweber 20
  *Daughter:*Maria 3 months
Fiedler, Maria 3 *SEE* Fiedler, Johann
Fiedler, Martin; Ohio, 1809-1852 ***4511.35*** *p14*
Fiedler, Nikolaus; America, 1853 ***2526.43*** *p167*
Fiedler, Wilhelm F.; Philadelphia, 1855 ***8513.31*** *p305*
  *Wife:*Catharine F. Bantte
Fieker, Miss; America, 1888 ***7420.1*** *p356*
  *Son:*Friedrich
Fieker, Friedrich *SEE* Fieker, Miss
Field, Antonie 42; New Orleans, 1844 ***778.6*** *p117*
Field, Darby; Massachusetts, 1642 ***1642*** *p7*
Field, James; Ohio, 1840 ***2763.1*** *p9*
Field, Joseph 45; Ontario, 1871 ***1823.21*** *p111*
Field, Malsh; Boston, 1764 ***1642*** *p34*
Field, Mary 45; Ontario, 1871 ***1823.21*** *p111*
Field, Rose 11; Quebec, 1870 ***8364.32*** *p23*
Field, William 48; Ontario, 1871 ***1823.21*** *p111*
Fielder, Herman; North Carolina, 1849 ***1088.45*** *p9*
Fieldhouse, Benjamin 55; Ontario, 1871 ***1823.21*** *p111*
Fielding, John 18; Ontario, 1871 ***1823.21*** *p111*
Fields, Gilbert; Ontario, 1787 ***1276.15*** *p230*
  With 2 relatives
Fields, Henry 37; Ontario, 1871 ***1823.21*** *p111*
Fields, Michael; Louisiana, 1874-1875 ***4981.45*** *p298*
Fields, Nathan; Ontario, 1787 ***1276.15*** *p230*
Fields, Samuel; Ohio, 1838 ***3580.20*** *p31*
Fields, Samuel; Ohio, 1838 ***6020.12*** *p7*
Fields, Samuel; Ohio, 1840 ***3580.20*** *p31*
Fields, Samuel; Ohio, 1840 ***6020.12*** *p7*
Fieler, Berta 4; Portland, ME, 1906 ***970.38*** *p76*
Fieler, Imanuel 11 months; Portland, ME, 1906 ***970.38*** *p76*
Fieler, Jacob 16; Portland, ME, 1906 ***970.38*** *p76*
Fieler, Johann 43; Portland, ME, 1906 ***970.38*** *p77*
Fieler, Johannes 19; Portland, ME, 1906 ***970.38*** *p77*
Fieler, Katarina 9; Portland, ME, 1906 ***970.38*** *p77*
Fieler, Lydia 14; Portland, ME, 1906 ***970.38*** *p77*
Fieler, Margareta 17; Portland, ME, 1906 ***970.38*** *p77*
Fieler, Marie 40; Portland, ME, 1906 ***970.38*** *p77*
Fieler, Reinhold 10; Portland, ME, 1906 ***970.38*** *p77*
Fiene, Fred; Missouri, 1894 ***3276.1*** *p1*
Fierabras, Martin; Montreal, 1661 ***9221.17*** *p473*
Fierke, Friedrich; Wisconsin, 1885 ***6795.8*** *p130*
Fierke, Friedrich; Wisconsin, 1897 ***6795.8*** *p162*
Fieser, Christian; Colorado, 1897 ***1029.59*** *p29*
Fiestle, Gotlieb; Ohio, 1809-1852 ***4511.35*** *p14*
Fietz, Theodor Carl; Port uncertain, 1884 ***7420.1*** *p342*
Fievre, Catherine; Quebec, 1663 ***4514.3*** *p313*
Fife, John; Utah, 1825-1847 ***1211.45*** *p132*
Fifield, Hiram 55; Ontario, 1871 ***1823.21*** *p111*
Figeux, Jacques; Quebec, 1646 ***9221.17*** *p164*
Fight, Daniel; New Jersey, 1773-1774 ***927.31*** *p3*
Fight, John; New Jersey, 1773-1774 ***927.31*** *p3*
Fightlin, Jane; Maryland, 1900-1940 ***9228.50*** *p217*
Figner, Michael; Ohio, 1809-1852 ***4511.35*** *p14*
Fignera, Joseph 23; New Orleans, 1847 ***778.6*** *p117*
Figolist, . . .; Chile, 1852 ***1192.4*** *p52*
  With child
Figu, Jacques; Quebec, 1646 ***9221.17*** *p164*
Figuery, Etienne-Guillaume de; Quebec, 1755-1757 ***2314.30*** *p170*
Figuery, Etienne-Guillaume de; Quebec, 1755 ***2314.30*** *p182*
Figuier, Jean; Quebec, 1642 ***9221.17*** *p116*
Fike, Conrad; Ohio, 1809-1852 ***4511.35*** *p14*
Fike, Daniel 74; Ontario, 1871 ***1823.21*** *p111*
Filbert, Christian 11 *SEE* Filbert, Johann Andreas
Filbert, Dorothea 8 *SEE* Filbert, Johann Andreas
Filbert, Emma 5 *SEE* Filbert, Johann Andreas
Filbert, Jakob 3 *SEE* Filbert, Johann Andreas
Filbert, Johann Andreas; Minneapolis, 1880 ***2526.43*** *p167*
  *Wife:*Marie Gottwald
  *Daughter:*Dorothea
  *Son:*Christian
  *Daughter:*Maria
  *Son:*Ludwig
  *Son:*Jakob
  *Daughter:*Emma
Filbert, Ludwig 7 *SEE* Filbert, Johann Andreas
Filbert, Maria 9 *SEE* Filbert, Johann Andreas
Filbert, Marie Gottwald *SEE* Filbert, Johann Andreas
Fildpauche, Conrad; Philadelphia, 1847 ***8513.31*** *p306*
  *Wife:*Margaret Doriot
Fildpauche, Margaret Doriot *SEE* Fildpauche, Conrad
Filetti, Joseph; Louisiana, 1836-1840 ***4981.45*** *p212*
Filgeano, Theophelas; Toronto, 1844 ***2910.35*** *p112*
Filiastre, Pierre; Quebec, 1639 ***9221.17*** *p88*
Filing, Peter; Marston's Wharf, 1782 ***8529.30*** *p11*
Filion, Antoine; Quebec, 1665 ***4514.3*** *p296*
  *Mother:*Marguerite Roy
  *Son:*Pierre
  With 2 sisters
Filion, Antoine; Quebec, 1665 ***4514.3*** *p368*
  With wife
  *Child:*Jeanne
  *Child:*Pierre
Filion, Jeanne *SEE* Filion, Antoine
Filion, Marguerite Roy *SEE* Filion, Antoine
Filion, Michel; Quebec, 1622-1665 ***4514.3*** *p368*
Filion, Pierre *SEE* Filion, Antoine
Filion, Pierre *SEE* Filion, Antoine
Filip, Bedrich; New York, 1647-1653 ***2853.20*** *p14*
  *Son:*Frederick
Filip, Frederick *SEE* Filip, Bedrich
Filipek, Frantisek; St. Paul, MN, 1860 ***2853.20*** *p277*
Filipi, Josef; Iowa, 1859 ***2853.20*** *p228*
Filipi, Josef; Nebraska, 1863-1910 ***2853.20*** *p182*
Filipowitz, Maria 43; America, 1865 ***5475.1*** *p70*
  *Son:*Jakob
  *Daughter:*Barbara 13
  *Daughter:*Margarethe 15
Filipowska, Maryanna; Detroit, 1890 ***9980.23*** *p97*
Fillastreau, Rene 23; Quebec, 1654 ***9221.17*** *p308*
Filler, Hiob; America, 1868 ***7919.3*** *p527*
Fillete, J. 34; America, 1841 ***778.6*** *p117*
Filleul, Abraham; Maine, 1658 ***9228.50*** *p214*
Filley, Frank 7; Quebec, 1870 ***8364.32*** *p23*
Filliatre, Samuel; Newfoundland, n.d. ***9228.50*** *p18A*
Filling, Peter; Marston's Wharf, 1782 ***8529.30*** *p11*
Fillion, Michel 20; Quebec, 1653 ***9221.17*** *p273*
Fillman, James 36; Ontario, 1871 ***1823.21*** *p111*
Fillo, Adam 5; New York, NY, 1864 ***8425.62*** *p195*
Fillo, Eva 24; New York, NY, 1864 ***8425.62*** *p195*
Fillo, Georg 29; New York, NY, 1864 ***8425.62*** *p195*
Fillo, Joseph 3; New York, NY, 1864 ***8425.62*** *p195*
Fillo, Stephan; New York, NY, 1864 ***8425.62*** *p196*
Fillye, Pierre; Quebec, 1661 ***9221.17*** *p455*
Filsche, Manuel 22; Port uncertain, 1840 ***778.6*** *p117*
Filson, Alexander; South Carolina, 1808 ***6155.4*** *p18*
Filson, Thomas; North Carolina, 1795 ***1088.45*** *p9*
Filtz, Catharine 24; Louisiana, 1848 ***778.6*** *p117*
Filtz, Marguerite 2; Louisiana, 1848 ***778.6*** *p117*
Filtz, Wilham 28; Louisiana, 1848 ***778.6*** *p117*
Fily, Michel; Quebec, 1698 ***2314.30*** *p169*
Fily, Michel; Quebec, 1698 ***2314.30*** *p182*
Finaly, Mary 20; Ontario, 1871 ***1823.21*** *p111*
Finause, Eulalie 24; America, 1843 ***778.6*** *p117*
Finch, Hugh; South Carolina, 1813 ***3208.30*** *p18*
Finch, Hugh; South Carolina, 1813 ***3208.30*** *p31*
Finch, Hugh 40; South Carolina, 1812 ***3476.30*** *p11*
Finch, Isaac 29; Ontario, 1871 ***1823.21*** *p112*
Finch, Jane 40; Ontario, 1871 ***1823.21*** *p112*
Finch, John; Virginia, 1652 ***6254.4*** *p243*
Finch, Mary 9; Quebec, 1870 ***8364.32*** *p23*
Finch, Sam.; Maryland, 1672 ***1236.25*** *p47*
Finch, Susan 14; Ontario, 1871 ***1823.17*** *p51*
Finch, William H.; Washington, 1884 ***2770.40*** *p192*
Finchamp, John G.A. 36; Ontario, 1871 ***1823.21*** *p112*
Finck, Anton 50; Mississippi, 1846 ***778.6*** *p117*
Finck, Catharine 55; Mississippi, 1846 ***778.6*** *p117*
Finck, Eva; Pennsylvania, 1848 ***170.15*** *p24*
Finck, Katharina; Pennsylvania, 1848 ***170.15*** *p24*
Findeis, Katharina; America, 1882 ***5475.1*** *p514*
Findeis, Nikolaus; America, 1882 ***5475.1*** *p514*
Findlater, Robert; North Carolina, 1837 ***1088.45*** *p10*
Findlater, S.W.; Quebec, 1885 ***1937.10*** *p52*
Findlater, Thos 65; Ontario, 1871 ***1823.21*** *p112*
Findlay, Allan 29; Ontario, 1871 ***1823.21*** *p112*
Findlay, Ann Maria; Ontario, 1858 ***9228.50*** *p218*
Findlay, Thomas 25; Ontario, 1871 ***1823.17*** *p51*
Findley, Thomas B.; Ohio, 1863 ***3580.20*** *p31*
Findley, Thomas B.; Ohio, 1863 ***6020.12*** *p7*
Findt, Henry L.; North Carolina, 1856 ***1088.45*** *p10*
Fine, Johann; America, 1878 ***5475.1*** *p128*
Finegan, Phalane 51; Ontario, 1871 ***1823.17*** *p51*
Finely, Thomas 60; Ontario, 1871 ***1823.17*** *p51*
Finen, Michal; Louisiana, 1874 ***4981.45*** *p131*
Fingards, Charles 24; Missouri, 1845 ***778.6*** *p117*
Finger, Henry 29; Indiana, 1892-1894 ***9076.20*** *p74*
Fingerson, Erick; Iowa, 1900 ***1211.15*** *p10*
Fingerson, Thomas; Iowa, 1888 ***1211.15*** *p10*
Finhold, Adolph Hermann Christian; America, 1870 ***7420.1*** *p283*
Finigan, Charles; St. John, N.B., 1842 ***2978.20*** *p7*
Finigan, Ellen; St. John, N.B., 1842 ***2978.20*** *p7*
Finigan, Julia; St. John, N.B., 1842 ***2978.20*** *p7*
Finigan, Timothy; Ohio, 1809-1852 ***4511.35*** *p14*
Finigau, James 55; Ontario, 1871 ***1823.21*** *p112*
Fining, James 35; Ontario, 1871 ***1823.21*** *p112*
Finisee, John; Massachusetts, 1753 ***1642*** *p66*
Fink, Auguste Emilie Hanel *SEE* Fink, Heinr. Aug
Fink, Heinr. Aug; America, 1865 ***5475.1*** *p49*
  *Wife:*Auguste Emilie Hanel
  *Son:*Robert Wilhelm
Fink, Henry; Missouri, 1890 ***3276.1*** *p1*
Fink, Jacob; Missouri, 1880 ***3276.1*** *p3*
Fink, Jacob 24; Portland, ME, 1911 ***970.38*** *p77*
Fink, Robert Wilhelm *SEE* Fink, Heinr. Aug
Fink, Wilhelm Hermann; America, 1887 ***7420.1*** *p353*
Fink, William 40; Ontario, 1871 ***1823.21*** *p112*
Finkbein, Conr.; New York, 1860 ***358.56*** *p150*
Finkeldey, Carl; America, 1854 ***7420.1*** *p119*
Finken, Frederick; Washington, 1884 ***2770.40*** *p192*
Finkler, A. Maria *SEE* Finkler, Jakob
Finkler, Anna; Brazil, 1881 ***5475.1*** *p390*
Finkler, Barbara *SEE* Finkler, Jakob
Finkler, Eva 36; America, 1857 ***5475.1*** *p352*
Finkler, Franz *SEE* Finkler, Jakob
Finkler, Franz; America, 1887 ***5475.1*** *p314*
Finkler, Jakob *SEE* Finkler, Jakob
Finkler, Jakob; America, 1882 ***5475.1*** *p313*
  *Son:*Jakob
  *Wife:*Maria Weber
  *Son:*Johann
  *Son:*Franz
  *Daughter:*A. Maria
  *Daughter:*Maria
  *Daughter:*Barbara
Finkler, James; Barbados or St. Christopher, 1780 ***8529.30*** *p7A*
Finkler, Johanetta Lorsong *SEE* Finkler, Philipp
Finkler, Johann; America, 1880 ***5475.1*** *p416*
Finkler, Johann *SEE* Finkler, Jakob
Finkler, Katharina 4 *SEE* Finkler, Mathias
Finkler, Katharina; Brazil, 1879 ***5475.1*** *p390*
Finkler, Margarethe Ferber *SEE* Finkler, Peter
Finkler, Maria *SEE* Finkler, Jakob
Finkler, Maria Weber *SEE* Finkler, Jakob
Finkler, Maria Backes 28 *SEE* Finkler, Mathias
Finkler, Mathias 6 *SEE* Finkler, Mathias
Finkler, Mathias 34; America, 1873 ***5475.1*** *p389*
  *Wife:*Maria Backes 28
  *Son:*Mathias 6 months
  *Daughter:*Katharina 4
Finkler, Nikolaus; America, 1880 ***5475.1*** *p416*
Finkler, Nikolaus; America, 1881 ***5475.1*** *p313*
Finkler, Peter; America, 1860 ***5475.1*** *p248*
Finkler, Peter; America, 1881 ***5475.1*** *p313*
Finkler, Peter; Brazil, 1857 ***5475.1*** *p517*
  *Wife:*Margarethe Ferber
Finkler, Peter 36; Brazil, 1856 ***5475.1*** *p290*
Finkler, Philipp; America, 1852 ***5475.1*** *p62*
  *Wife:*Johanetta Lorsong
Finkler, William 73; Ontario, 1871 ***1823.21*** *p112*
Finlan, Elenn; St. Johns, N.F., 1825 ***1053.15*** *p7*
Finlan, Timothy; St. Johns, N.F., 1825 ***1053.15*** *p7*
Finlay, Alexander 59; Ontario, 1871 ***1823.21*** *p112*
Finlay, Janet; Prince Edward Island, 1771 ***3799.30*** *p41*
Finlayson, Alexander 33; Ontario, 1871 ***1823.17*** *p51*
Finlayson, Catherine 80; Ontario, 1871 ***1823.17*** *p51*
Finlayson, Donald 36; Ontario, 1871 ***1823.17*** *p51*
Finlayson, Jesse 36; Ontario, 1871 ***1823.17*** *p51*
Finlayson, John 41; Ontario, 1871 ***1823.17*** *p51*
Finlayson, John 46; Ontario, 1871 ***1823.17*** *p51*
Finlayson, Roderick 38; Ontario, 1871 ***1823.17*** *p51*
Finleson, Alexander 60; Ontario, 1871 ***1823.21*** *p112*
Finley, Ann 38; Ontario, 1871 ***1823.21*** *p112*
Finley, George Laurence; Washington, 1887 ***6015.10*** *p16*
Finley, Louisa 50; Ontario, 1871 ***1823.21*** *p112*
Finley, Mary 59; Ontario, 1871 ***1823.21*** *p112*
Finley, Patrick; Ohio, 1833 ***3580.20*** *p31*
Finley, Patrick; Ohio, 1833 ***6020.12*** *p7*
Finley, Robert; Ohio, 1832 ***3580.20*** *p31*
Finley, Robert; Ohio, 1832 ***6020.12*** *p7*
Finlof, Casper; St. Paul, MN, 1888 ***1865.50*** *p47*

132
FOR A COMPLETE EXPLANATION OF ENTRY, SEE "HOW TO READ A CITATION" SECTION

Finly, William 37; Ontario, 1871 ***1823.21*** *p112*
Finlyson, Hugh 54; Ontario, 1871 ***1823.21*** *p112*
Finn, Miss; Quebec, 1870 ***8364.32*** *p23*
Finn, Daniel; New Orleans, 1850 ***7242.30*** *p141*
Finn, Hannah; Boston, 1744 ***1642*** *p45*
Finn, Hannah; Boston, 1744 ***1642*** *p45*
Finn, Henry 62; Michigan, 1880 ***4491.39*** *p9*
Finn, Honora 38; Michigan, 1880 ***4491.39*** *p9*
Finn, Hugh 49; Michigan, 1880 ***4491.39*** *p9*
Finn, Hugh, Jr. 34; Michigan, 1880 ***4491.39*** *p9*
Finn, Margarett 14; Michigan, 1880 ***4491.39*** *p10*
Finn, Margarett 28; Michigan, 1880 ***4491.39*** *p9*
Finn, Margarett 64; Michigan, 1880 ***4491.39*** *p9*
Finn, Mary; St. Johns, N.F., 1825 ***1053.15*** *p6*
Finn, Michael; Louisiana, 1848-1850 ***7710.1*** *p151*
Finn, Michael 19; Quebec, 1870 ***8364.32*** *p23*
Finn, Patrick; Boston, 1739 ***1642*** *p45*
Finnamore, William Henry 17; Ontario, 1871 ***1823.21*** *p112*
Finnarty, Patrick 46; Ontario, 1871 ***1823.21*** *p112*
Finney, Martin 35; Ontario, 1871 ***1823.21*** *p112*
Finney, S. J.; California, 1868 ***1131.61*** *p89*
With son
Finnicey, Neley; Boston, 1742 ***1642*** *p45*
Finnigan, Charles; Washington, 1885 ***2770.40*** *p194*
Finnigan, John 52; Ontario, 1871 ***1823.17*** *p51*
Finnigan, Pat; St. John, N.B., 1847 ***2978.15*** *p36*
Finnighan, Ann 20; Ontario, 1871 ***1823.21*** *p112*
Finnighan, Thomas 30; Ontario, 1871 ***1823.21*** *p112*
Finster, . . .; West Virginia, 1850-1860 ***1132.30*** *p147*
Finton, Margaret; New Brunswick, 1842 ***2978.20*** *p8*
Finton, Mary; New Brunswick, 1842 ***2978.20*** *p8*
Finton, Owen; New Brunswick, 1842 ***2978.20*** *p8*
Finton, William; New Brunswick, 1842 ***2978.20*** *p8*
Finzel, Carl; Valdivia, Chile, 1851 ***1192.4*** *p50*
Fiodquist, Anna Marie *SEE* Fiodquist, Ernest
Fiodquist, Carl Johan *SEE* Fiodquist, Ernest
Fiodquist, Ernest; Colorado, 1916 ***1029.59*** *p29*
*Wife:*Marie
*Child:*Anna Marie
*Child:*Carl Johan
Fiodquist, Marie *SEE* Fiodquist, Ernest
Fiott, Elizabeth; America, 1850-1950 ***9228.50*** *p177*
Fippe, Jacob 20; Halifax, N.S., 1902 ***1860.4*** *p42*
Firestone, John; New Jersey, 1750-1774 ***927.31*** *p3*
Firestoss, Joseph; Ohio, 1809-1852 ***4511.35*** *p14*
Firman, Marie-Anne; Quebec, 1667 ***4514.3*** *p313*
Firmen, Dennis 37; Ontario, 1871 ***1823.21*** *p112*
Firmin, Theophile 25; Ontario, 1871 ***1823.17*** *p51*
Firmuga, Michael 40; New York, NY, 1920 ***930.50*** *p48*
First, Madeleine 28; America, 1844 ***778.6*** *p117*
Firstoss, Joseph; Ohio, 1809-1852 ***4511.35*** *p14*
Firth, Abraham; New York, NY, 1827 ***3274.55*** *p66*
Firth, George; Illinois, 1918 ***6007.60*** *p9*
Firth, Joseph 41; Quebec, 1870 ***8364.32*** *p23*
Firth, Thomas 41; Ontario, 1871 ***1823.21*** *p112*
Fisch, Margarethe; America, 1883 ***5475.1*** *p275*
Fischbach, Dennis; Boston, 1774 ***8529.30*** *p2*
Fischer, . . .; West Virginia, 1850-1860 ***1132.30*** *p147*
Fischer, Widow; America, 1868 ***7420.1*** *p271*
*Daughter:*Dorothea Helene Auguste
*Son:*Ernst Heinrich Wilhelm
*Son:*Wilhelm Hermann August
*Son:*Heinrich Wilhelm Louis
Fischer, Adam 9; New York, NY, 1893 ***1883.7*** *p37*
Fischer, Adam Ernst; America, 1868 ***7919.3*** *p528*
Fischer, Andreas 32; New York, NY, 1893 ***1883.7*** *p41*
Fischer, Anna 59; New York, NY, 1892 ***8425.16*** *p34*
Fischer, Anna Maria 37; Pennsylvania, 1850 ***170.15*** *p24*
Fischer, Anton; America, 1882 ***5475.1*** *p147*
Fischer, Anton 32; Mississippi, 1846 ***778.6*** *p117*
Fischer, Anton 28; New York, NY, 1885 ***8425.16*** *p32*
Fischer, Anton 34; New York, NY, 1893 ***1883.7*** *p37*
Fischer, Barbara 25; America, 1847 ***778.6*** *p117*
Fischer, Barbara 26; America, 1866 ***5475.1*** *p170*
Fischer, Barbara 13; New York, NY, 1847 ***9176.15*** *p51*
Fischer, Barbara 33; New York, NY, 1893 ***1883.7*** *p37*
Fischer, C. A.; Louisiana, 1836-1841 ***4981.45*** *p208*
Fischer, Carolina 21; New York, NY, 1893 ***1883.7*** *p41*
Fischer, Carolina 25; Port uncertain, 1840 ***778.6*** *p117*
Fischer, Cath. 34; New York, NY, 1847 ***9176.15*** *p51*
Fischer, Catharina Barbara; America, 1867 ***7919.3*** *p531*
Fischer, Charles 27; Port uncertain, 1840 ***778.6*** *p117*
Fischer, Christiane; America, 1867 ***7919.3*** *p535*
Fischer, Christina 14; New York, NY, 1898 ***7951.13*** *p41*
Fischer, Christine Bleses *SEE* Fischer, Peter
Fischer, Christine 16; New York, NY, 1892 ***8425.16*** *p34*
Fischer, Conrad; America, 1868 ***7919.3*** *p535*
Fischer, Dorothea 57; New York, NY, 1885 ***1883.7*** *p45*
Fischer, Dorothea Helene Auguste *SEE* Fischer, Widow
Fischer, Eduard *SEE* Fischer, Johann
Fischer, Elisabeth *SEE* Fischer, Peter
Fischer, Elisabeth 9; New York, NY, 1898 ***7951.13*** *p41*
Fischer, Elisabethe; America, 1867 ***2526.42*** *p160*
With brother 24
Fischer, Emilie Clara Bahnle *SEE* Fischer, Friederike
Fischer, Engel Marie; America, 1854 ***7420.1*** *p119*
Fischer, Ernst Heinrich; Port uncertain, 1892 ***7420.1*** *p365*
Fischer, Ernst Heinrich Wilhelm *SEE* Fischer, Widow
Fischer, Eva Caroline; America, 1867 ***7919.3*** *p524*
Fischer, Francois 21; America, 1846 ***778.6*** *p117*
Fischer, Frank Seraph; Miami, 1935 ***4984.12*** *p39*
Fischer, Fredrick; New York, 1860 ***358.56*** *p149*
Fischer, Friederike; America, 1867 ***7919.3*** *p530*
*Child:*Emilie Clara Bahnle
With daughter
Fischer, Friedrich 54; New York, NY, 1898 ***7951.13*** *p41*
Fischer, Friedrich 2; Pennsylvania, 1850 ***170.15*** *p24*
Fischer, Friedrich August; America, 1868 ***7919.3*** *p535*
With wife & 3 children
Fischer, Friedrich Gerhard; Port uncertain, 1837 ***7420.1*** *p13*
Fischer, Georg Adam; America, 1868 ***7919.3*** *p524*
With wife & 5 children
Fischer, Gerdrad 9; New York, NY, 1847 ***9176.15*** *p51*
Fischer, Gotthard Andreas; America, 1867 ***7919.3*** *p535*
Fischer, Gregoir 63; New York, NY, 1847 ***9176.15*** *p51*
Fischer, Heinrich; America, 1866 ***7420.1*** *p242*
Fischer, Heinrich Hermann; America, 1881 ***7420.1*** *p320*
Fischer, Heinrich Wilhelm Louis *SEE* Fischer, Widow
Fischer, Helene; America, 1867 ***7919.3*** *p529*
Fischer, Hermann; Valdivia, Chile, 1851 ***1192.4*** *p51*
With wife & 2 children
Fischer, J. Wilhelm *SEE* Fischer, Johann
Fischer, Jacob; Louisiana, 1874-1875 ***4981.45*** *p298*
Fischer, Jacob 20; New York, NY, 1898 ***7951.13*** *p41*
Fischer, Jacqs. 29; New Orleans, 1840 ***778.6*** *p117*
Fischer, Johann; America, 1867 ***5475.1*** *p224*
*Wife:*Margarethe Wagner
*Son:*Eduard
*Daughter:*Maria
*Son:*Peter
*Son:*J. Wilhelm
*Son:*Nikolaus
Fischer, Johann *SEE* Fischer, Peter
Fischer, Johann 3 months; New York, NY, 1893 ***1883.7*** *p41*
Fischer, Johann 6; New York, NY, 1898 ***7951.13*** *p41*
Fischer, Johann 25; New York, NY, 1893 ***1883.7*** *p41*
Fischer, Johann Conrad; America, 1852 ***7420.1*** *p88*
Fischer, Johann David; America, 1867 ***7919.3*** *p530*
Fischer, Johann Heinrich Christian; New York, NY, 1879 ***7420.1*** *p313*
*Wife:*Sophie Dorothea Bake
Fischer, Johann Heinrich Conrad; America, 1866 ***7420.1*** *p242*
Fischer, Johannes; Nova Scotia, 1784 ***7105*** *p22*
Fischer, Johs. 57; New York, NY, 1885 ***1883.7*** *p45*
Fischer, Josef 1; New York, NY, 1893 ***1883.7*** *p37*
Fischer, Josef 4; New York, NY, 1893 ***1883.7*** *p41*
Fischer, Josefa; America, 1923 ***8023.44*** *p373*
Fischer, Joseph 19; America, 1847 ***778.6*** *p118*
Fischer, Joseph; Philadelphia, 1878 ***8513.31*** *p306*
*Wife:*Mary Roeser
Fischer, Katharina 26; America, 1853 ***2526.42*** *p160*
Fischer, Katharina 32; New York, NY, 1893 ***1883.7*** *p41*
Fischer, Klara 6; New York, NY, 1893 ***1883.7*** *p37*
Fischer, Lisbeth 4; New York, NY, 1885 ***8425.16*** *p32*
Fischer, Lisbeth 28; New York, NY, 1885 ***8425.16*** *p32*
Fischer, Louisa 3 months; Port uncertain, 1840 ***778.6*** *p118*
Fischer, Louise; America, 1867 ***7919.3*** *p527*
Fischer, Marcellinia 8; New York, NY, 1893 ***1883.7*** *p41*
Fischer, Margaret 43; New York, NY, 1898 ***7951.13*** *p41*
Fischer, Margaretha 60; America, 1846 ***778.6*** *p118*
Fischer, Margaretha 4; New York, NY, 1893 ***1883.7*** *p37*
Fischer, Margaretha 5; Pennsylvania, 1850 ***170.15*** *p24*
Fischer, Margarethe Wagner *SEE* Fischer, Johann
Fischer, Margarethe *SEE* Fischer, Peter
Fischer, Margarethe Zang *SEE* Fischer, Peter
Fischer, Maria *SEE* Fischer, Johann
Fischer, Maria *SEE* Fischer, Peter
Fischer, Maria *SEE* Fischer, Peter
Fischer, Maria 6; New York, NY, 1893 ***1883.7*** *p41*
Fischer, Mary Roeser *SEE* Fischer, Joseph
Fischer, Matthias; America, 1867 ***7919.3*** *p528*
Fischer, Matthias Johannes; America, 1867 ***7420.1*** *p256*
Fischer, Michael 22; New York, NY, 1885 ***8425.16*** *p32*
Fischer, Michael 37; Pennsylvania, 1850 ***170.15*** *p24*
Fischer, Michel *SEE* Fischer, Peter
Fischer, Michel; Louisiana, 1836-1841 ***4981.45*** *p208*
Fischer, Minna; America, 1870 ***7420.1*** *p395*
Fischer, Nikolaus *SEE* Fischer, Johann
Fischer, Nikolaus; America, 1877 ***5475.1*** *p151*
Fischer, O.R.; New York, NY, 1845 ***6412.40*** *p148*
Fischer, Peter *SEE* Fischer, Johann
Fischer, Peter *SEE* Fischer, Peter
Fischer, Peter; America, 1870 ***5475.1*** *p211*
*Son:*Peter
*Son:*Johann
*Daughter:*Margarethe
*Daughter:*Elisabeth
*Daughter:*Maria
*Wife:*Margarethe Zang
*Son:*Michel
Fischer, Peter 25; America, 1882 ***5475.1*** *p206*
*Wife:*Christine Bleses
*Daughter:*Maria
Fischer, Peter 11; New York, NY, 1893 ***1883.7*** *p37*
Fischer, Peter 11 months; New York, NY, 1893 ***1883.7*** *p41*
Fischer, Philipp 59; New York, NY, 1892 ***8425.16*** *p34*
Fischer, Philipp; Wisconsin, 1874 ***6795.8*** *p101*
Fischer, Reinhard Friedr; Pennsylvania, 1854 ***170.15*** *p25*
With wife & 2 children
Fischer, Sophie Dorothea Bake *SEE* Fischer, Johann Heinrich Christian
Fischer, Therese Marie Mathilde; Wisconsin, 1900 ***6795.8*** *p220*
Fischer, Thinoria 11; New York, NY, 1847 ***9176.15*** *p51*
Fischer, Urban 42; New York, NY, 1847 ***9176.15*** *p51*
Fischer, Valentin 26; America, 1846 ***778.6*** *p118*
Fischer, Veit; Valdivia, Chile, 1852 ***1192.4*** *p53*
With wife & 4 children
With child 8
With child 23
Fischer, Wilhelm; Wisconsin, 1879 ***6795.8*** *p225*
Fischer, Wilhelm Hermann August *SEE* Fischer, Widow
Fischhaupt, Friedrich; America, 1854 ***7420.1*** *p119*
With wife 2 sons & 2 daughters
Fischinger, Vitisia 28; New York, NY, 1847 ***9176.15*** *p51*
Fischke, Catharine 2; New York, NY, 1885 ***1883.7*** *p46*
Fischke, Johann 4; New York, NY, 1885 ***1883.7*** *p46*
Fischke, Ludwig 6; New York, NY, 1885 ***1883.7*** *p46*
Fischke, Magdal. 30; New York, NY, 1885 ***1883.7*** *p46*
Fischke, Magdalina 8 months; New York, NY, 1885 ***1883.7*** *p46*
Fischke, Margar. 8; New York, NY, 1885 ***1883.7*** *p46*
Fischke, Wilhelm 34; New York, NY, 1885 ***1883.7*** *p46*
Fischler, Bernard 24; New Castle, DE, 1817-1818 ***90.20*** *p150*
Fischoff, Rubin; Detroit, 1929-1930 ***6214.5*** *p71*
Fiser, Frantisek; Milwaukee, 1849 ***2853.20*** *p312*
With parents
Fiser, Frantisek; Milwaukee, 1851 ***2853.20*** *p308*
With mother
*Father:*Josef
Fiser, Frantisek; Wisconsin, 1855 ***2853.20*** *p333*
*Brother:*Josef
Fiser, Josef *SEE* Fiser, Frantisek
Fiser, Josef; New York, NY, 1851 ***2853.20*** *p100*
Fiser, Josef; New York, NY, 1851 ***2853.20*** *p387*
Fiser, Josef *SEE* Fiser, Frantisek
Fisera, Frantisek; Wisconsin, 1855 ***2853.20*** *p333*
*Brother:*Josef
Fisera, Frantisek J.; Chicago, 1888 ***2853.20*** *p420*
Fisera, Josef *SEE* Fisera, Frantisek
Fiset, Abraham 18; Quebec, 1653 ***9221.17*** *p273*
Fish, John 60; Ontario, 1871 ***1823.21*** *p112*
Fish, Norman 56; Ontario, 1871 ***1823.21*** *p112*
Fish, Robert 46; Ontario, 1871 ***1823.21*** *p112*
Fish, Simon; Jamaica, 1777 ***8529.30*** *p13A*
Fishback, Dennis; Philadelphia, 1777 ***8529.30*** *p2*
Fishback, Francis; Marston's Wharf, 1782 ***8529.30*** *p11*
Fishburn, Henry 70; Ontario, 1871 ***1823.21*** *p112*
Fishel, Joseph 33; New Orleans, 1848 ***778.6*** *p118*
Fisher, Adam C. 42; Ontario, 1871 ***1823.17*** *p51*
Fisher, Albert 20; Ontario, 1871 ***1823.17*** *p51*
Fisher, Alexander; Ohio, 1840-1897 ***8365.35*** *p16*
Fisher, Alfred 50; Ontario, 1871 ***1823.17*** *p52*
Fisher, Alice 9; Quebec, 1870 ***8364.32*** *p23*
Fisher, Andrew; Ohio, 1809-1852 ***4511.35*** *p14*
Fisher, Archibald 57; Ontario, 1871 ***1823.17*** *p52*
Fisher, Balth. 27; America, 1845 ***778.6*** *p118*
Fisher, Miss C. 40; New Orleans, 1834 ***1002.51*** *p112*
Fisher, Charles 23; Ontario, 1871 ***1823.17*** *p52*
Fisher, Clement 50; Ontario, 1871 ***1823.21*** *p112*
Fisher, Davis Y.; North Carolina, 1844 ***1088.45*** *p10*
Fisher, Donald 45; Ontario, 1871 ***1823.21*** *p112*
Fisher, Eliza 34; Ontario, 1871 ***1823.17*** *p52*
Fisher, Elizabeth 50; Ontario, 1871 ***1823.17*** *p52*
Fisher, Elizabeth 11; Quebec, 1870 ***8364.32*** *p23*
Fisher, F.W.; Montreal, 1922 ***4514.4*** *p32*
Fisher, Ferdenand 20; Ontario, 1871 ***1823.17*** *p52*
Fisher, Francis; Ohio, 1840-1897 ***8365.35*** *p16*
Fisher, Frantisek; Milwaukee, 1849 ***2853.20*** *p312*
With parents

Fisher, Frederick 27; Ontario, 1871 ***1823.21*** *p112*
Fisher, Friedrich 24; America, 1845 ***778.6*** *p118*
Fisher, George; Ohio, 1840-1897 ***8365.35*** *p16*
Fisher, George 36; Ontario, 1871 ***1823.17*** *p52*
Fisher, George Michael; Ohio, 1809-1852 ***4511.35*** *p14*
Fisher, Henry; Louisiana, 1874 ***4981.45*** *p131*
Fisher, Henry; Ohio, 1809-1852 ***4511.35*** *p14*
Fisher, Isacc 32; Ontario, 1871 ***1823.17*** *p52*
Fisher, Jacob; Colorado, 1871 ***1029.59*** *p29*
Fisher, James; Louisiana, 1836-1840 ***4981.45*** *p212*
Fisher, James; Ohio, 1809-1852 ***4511.35*** *p14*
Fisher, James 40; Ontario, 1871 ***1823.21*** *p113*
Fisher, James 44; Ontario, 1871 ***1823.21*** *p113*
Fisher, James 49; Ontario, 1871 ***1823.17*** *p52*
Fisher, John; Colorado, 1862-1894 ***1029.59*** *p29*
Fisher, John; Nova Scotia, 1784 ***7105*** *p22*
Fisher, John 39; Ontario, 1871 ***1823.21*** *p113*
Fisher, John 46; Ontario, 1871 ***1823.21*** *p113*
Fisher, John 63; Ontario, 1871 ***1823.21*** *p113*
Fisher, John, Sr. 70; Ontario, 1871 ***1823.17*** *p52*
Fisher, John Jacob; Missouri, 1895 ***3276.1*** *p3*
Fisher, Joseph 34; Ontario, 1871 ***1823.21*** *p113*
Fisher, Malcolm 34; Ontario, 1871 ***1823.17*** *p52*
Fisher, Margaret Emily; America, 1857-1902 ***9228.50*** *p218*
Fisher, Martha 11; Quebec, 1870 ***8364.32*** *p23*
Fisher, Mary; Maryland, 1674-1675 ***1236.25*** *p52*
Fisher, Mary; Philadelphia, 1863 ***8513.31*** *p427*
Fisher, Michael; Illinois, 1852 ***6079.1*** *p5*
Fisher, Michael; Ohio, 1809-1852 ***4511.35*** *p14*
Fisher, Nicolas 22; America, 1845 ***778.6*** *p118*
Fisher, Peter; Illinois, 1854 ***6079.1*** *p5*
Fisher, Peter; Illinois, 1856 ***6079.1*** *p5*
Fisher, Peter; Ohio, 1809-1852 ***4511.35*** *p14*
Fisher, Phillip; Louisiana, 1874-1875 ***4981.45*** *p298*
Fisher, R. 50; New Orleans, 1834 ***1002.51*** *p112*
Fisher, Robert 50; Ontario, 1871 ***1823.21*** *p113*
Fisher, Samuel 22; Ontario, 1871 ***1823.21*** *p113*
Fisher, Sarah 67; Ontario, 1871 ***1823.21*** *p113*
Fisher, Thomas; Washington, 1885 ***2770.40*** *p194*
Fisher, Valentine 40; Ontario, 1871 ***1823.17*** *p52*
Fisher, Vicais 61; Ontario, 1871 ***1823.21*** *p113*
Fisher, Wilhelm; Wisconsin, 1879 ***6795.8*** *p225*
Fisher, William 27; Ontario, 1871 ***1823.21*** *p113*
Fisher, William 46; Ontario, 1871 ***1823.17*** *p52*
Fisher, William 46; Ontario, 1871 ***1823.21*** *p113*
Fisher, Wm 60; Ontario, 1871 ***1823.21*** *p113*
Fishman, Philip; Detroit, 1929-1930 ***6214.5*** *p69*
Fisk, Robert; Iowa, 1888 ***1211.15*** *p10*
Fisk, Romanzo 31; Ontario, 1871 ***1823.21*** *p113*
Fismer, Arnold H.; Illinois, 1855 ***6079.1*** *p5*
Fisne, P. 35; America, 1848 ***778.6*** *p118*
Fison, Henry; America, 1751 ***1220.12*** *p819*
Fispatrick, Michael 39; Ontario, 1871 ***1823.17*** *p52*
Fissene, Anna *SEE* Fissene, Sebastian
Fissene, Anna *SEE* Fissene, Nikolaus
Fissene, Jakob; Pennsylvania, 1881 ***5475.1*** *p78*
Fissene, Katharina *SEE* Fissene, Nikolaus
Fissene, Maria *SEE* Fissene, Sebastian
Fissene, Maria Kiefer *SEE* Fissene, Sebastian
Fissene, Maria *SEE* Fissene, Nikolaus
Fissene, Maria Kiefer *SEE* Fissene, Nikolaus
Fissene, Michel *SEE* Fissene, Sebastian
Fissene, Nikolaus *SEE* Fissene, Sebastian
Fissene, Nikolaus; New York, 1884 ***5475.1*** *p221*
*Wife:*Maria Kiefer
*Daughter:*Maria
*Son:*Philipp
*Daughter:*Katharina
*Daughter:*Anna
Fissene, Philipp *SEE* Fissene, Nikolaus
Fissene, Sebastian; America, 1881 ***5475.1*** *p214*
*Wife:*Maria Kiefer
*Son:*Simon
*Wife:*Maria
*Daughter:*Anna
*Son:*Michel
*Son:*Nikolaus
Fissene, Simon *SEE* Fissene, Sebastian
Fisteren, Mr. 23; Port uncertain, 1841 ***778.6*** *p118*
Fitch, John, Jr.; Ohio, 1819 ***3580.20*** *p31*
Fitch, John, Jr.; Ohio, 1819 ***6020.12*** *p7*
Fitch, Timothy; Boston, 1746 ***1642*** *p46*
Fitcha, Hilda Carolina; Oregon, 1941 ***9157.47*** *p2*
Fitchgeral, William; Boston, 1767 ***1642*** *p38*
Fitchgerel, John; Boston, 1731 ***1642*** *p44*
Fitchler, Bernard 24; New Castle, DE, 1817-1818 ***90.20*** *p150*
Fitchpatrick, James; Boston, 1767 ***1642*** *p38*
Fitsbibbous, John 44; Ontario, 1871 ***1823.17*** *p52*
Fitsgerald, Edward; Beverly, MA, 1740 ***1642*** *p64*
Fitsgerald, Mary; Boston, 1759 ***1642*** *p47*
Fitspatrick, Elizabeth; Boston, 1722 ***1642*** *p25*
Fitspatrick, William 50; Ontario, 1871 ***1823.21*** *p113*
FitsSymmonds, James; Boston, 1754 ***1642*** *p47*
Fitterman, Ethel; Detroit, 1929-1930 ***6214.5*** *p71*
Fitton, James; America, 1873 ***9076.20*** *p68*
Fitzallen, John 48; Ontario, 1871 ***1823.21*** *p113*
Fitze, Louis; Illinois, 1858 ***6079.1*** *p5*
Fitzgaret, Garrt.; Maryland, 1672 ***1236.25*** *p47*
FitzGarril, Lewis; Boston, 1766 ***1642*** *p48*
Fitzgarrold, William; Marston's Wharf, 1780 ***8529.30*** *p11*
Fitzgearld, Fredrick 67; Ontario, 1871 ***1823.21*** *p113*
Fitzgearld, Thomas; Boston, 1753 ***1642*** *p31*
Fitzgearld, William 74; Ontario, 1871 ***1823.21*** *p113*
Fitzgeral, George; Boston, 1766 ***1642*** *p36*
Fitzgerald, . . .; Nantucket, MA, 1752 ***1642*** *p89*
Fitzgerald, Andrew; Boston, 1744 ***1642*** *p45*
Fitzgerald, Bridget; St. Johns, N.F., 1825 ***1053.15*** *p7*
Fitzgerald, Catharine; Boston, 1752 ***1642*** *p46*
Fitzgerald, Deborah; Nantucket, MA, 1761 ***1642*** *p89*
Fitzgerald, Frederic; North Carolina, 1849 ***1088.45*** *p10*
Fitzgerald, Garritt; St. John, N.B., 1842 ***2978.20*** *p9*
Fitzgerald, Gerald 46; Ontario, 1871 ***1823.21*** *p113*
Fitzgerald, Hanna 81; Ontario, 1871 ***1823.21*** *p113*
Fitzgerald, James; Boston, 1773 ***1642*** *p49*
Fitzgerald, James; Ipswich, MA, 1727 ***1642*** *p71*
Fitzgerald, James; New Orleans, 1850 ***7242.30*** *p141*
Fitzgerald, James; New Orleans, 1850 ***7242.30*** *p141*
Fitzgerald, James 27; Ontario, 1871 ***1823.21*** *p113*
Fitzgerald, James; St. Johns, N.F., 1825 ***1053.15*** *p7*
Fitzgerald, James 29; St. Johns, N.F., 1811 ***1053.20*** *p20*
Fitzgerald, James; Toronto, 1844 ***2910.35*** *p112*
Fitzgerald, Jane; Newbury, MA, 1736 ***1642*** *p75*
Fitzgerald, Johanna 67; Ontario, 1871 ***1823.21*** *p113*
Fitzgerald, John; Boston, 1708 ***1642*** *p24*
Fitzgerald, John; Boston, 1763 ***1642*** *p48*
Fitzgerald, John; Colorado, 1862-1894 ***1029.59*** *p29*
Fitzgerald, John; North Carolina, 1860 ***1088.45*** *p10*
Fitzgerald, John; Ohio, 1809-1852 ***4511.35*** *p14*
Fitzgerald, John 44; Ontario, 1871 ***1823.21*** *p113*
Fitzgerald, John 69; Ontario, 1871 ***1823.21*** *p113*
Fitzgerald, John; St. Johns, N.F., 1825 ***1053.15*** *p7*
Fitzgerald, John 22; St. Johns, N.F., 1811 ***1053.20*** *p21*
Fitzgerald, John 38; St. Johns, N.F., 1811 ***1053.20*** *p20*
Fitzgerald, John H.; Washington, 1889 ***2770.40*** *p27*
Fitzgerald, Kitty; St. Johns, N.F., 1825 ***1053.15*** *p7*
Fitzgerald, Margaret; Boston, 1760 ***1642*** *p48*
Fitzgerald, Margaret; Boston, 1771 ***1642*** *p49*
Fitzgerald, Margaret; Nantucket, MA, 1765 ***1642*** *p89*
Fitzgerald, Margaret 55; Ontario, 1871 ***1823.21*** *p113*
Fitzgerald, Martha; Boston, 1770 ***1642*** *p49*
Fitzgerald, Mary; Boston, 1749 ***1642*** *p46*
Fitzgerald, Mary; Boston, 1754 ***1642*** *p47*
Fitzgerald, Mary; Boston, 1755 ***1642*** *p47*
Fitzgerald, Mary 25; Ontario, 1871 ***1823.21*** *p114*
Fitzgerald, Mary 52; Ontario, 1871 ***1823.21*** *p114*
Fitzgerald, Mary; St. Johns, N.F., 1825 ***1053.15*** *p7*
Fitzgerald, Maurice; New Orleans, 1850 ***7242.30*** *p141*
FitzGerald, Michael; Boston, 1748 ***1642*** *p46*
Fitzgerald, Michael; Boston, 1753 ***1642*** *p47*
Fitzgerald, Michael; Boston, 1762 ***1642*** *p48*
Fitzgerald, Michael; Massachusetts, 1772 ***1642*** *p91*
Fitzgerald, Michael 31; Ontario, 1871 ***1823.17*** *p52*
Fitzgerald, Nancy; St. Johns, N.F., 1825 ***1053.15*** *p7*
Fitzgerald, Nicholas; Boston, 1762 ***1642*** *p48*
Fitzgerald, Pat; St. Johns, N.F., 1825 ***1053.15*** *p7*
Fitzgerald, Patrick; Boston, 1709 ***1642*** *p24*
Fitzgerald, Patrick; New Orleans, 1850 ***7242.30*** *p141*
FitzGerald, Patrick; Salem, MA, 1750 ***1642*** *p78*
Fitzgerald, Richard; Massachusetts, 1620-1775 ***1642*** *p138*
Fitzgerald, Richard; Massachusetts, 1729 ***1642*** *p91*
Fitzgerald, Richard; New England, 1745 ***1642*** *p28*
Fitzgerald, Sally; New Orleans, 1850 ***7242.30*** *p141*
Fitzgerald, Thomas; Boston, 1717 ***1642*** *p24*
Fitzgerald, William; Boston, 1745 ***1642*** *p46*
Fitzgerald, William; Boston, 1751 ***1642*** *p46*
Fitzgerald, William; Boston, 1766 ***1642*** *p37*
Fitzgerald, William 85; Indiana, 1847-1864 ***9076.20*** *p65*
Fitzgerald, William; Marston's Wharf, 1780 ***8529.30*** *p11*
Fitzgerald, William 27; Ontario, 1871 ***1823.21*** *p114*
Fitzgerald, Wm.; Louisiana, 1874 ***4981.45*** *p295*
Fitzgerld, James 35; Ontario, 1871 ***1823.21*** *p114*
Fitzgerrald, James; Boston, 1767 ***1642*** *p38*
Fitzgibbon, David 32; Ontario, 1871 ***1823.17*** *p52*
Fitzgibbon, James 45; Ontario, 1871 ***1823.21*** *p114*
Fitzgibbon, Michael; Ohio, 1809-1852 ***4511.35*** *p14*
Fitzgibbons, Ann 41; Ontario, 1871 ***1823.21*** *p114*
Fitzgibbons, James 66; Michigan, 1880 ***4491.30*** *p12*
Fitzgibbons, Mary 58; Michigan, 1880 ***4491.30*** *p12*
Fitzhenry, Mr.; Massachusetts, 1754 ***1642*** *p108*
Fitzhenry, Joseph 45; Ontario, 1871 ***1823.21*** *p114*
Fitzimons, Hedley 46; Ontario, 1871 ***1823.21*** *p114*
Fitzimons, Thomas 52; Ontario, 1871 ***1823.21*** *p114*
FitzJerald, Katherine; Roxbury, MA, 1757 ***1642*** *p107*
Fitzke, Emilie; Wisconsin, 1904 ***6795.8*** *p159*
Fitzke, Henry Chr.; Wisconsin, 1896 ***6795.8*** *p106*
Fitzloff, Julius; Iowa, 1896 ***1211.15*** *p10*
Fitzman, William; Illinois, 1834-1900 ***6020.5*** *p131*
Fitznichols, Mary; Boston, 1678-1679 ***1642*** *p11*
Fitzpatrick, Catharine; Boston, 1757 ***1642*** *p47*
Fitzpatrick, Daniel; Ohio, 1809-1852 ***4511.35*** *p14*
Fitzpatrick, Darby; Boston, 1746 ***1642*** *p46*
Fitzpatrick, Donald 50; Ontario, 1871 ***1823.21*** *p114*
Fitzpatrick, Francis 30; Ontario, 1871 ***1823.21*** *p114*
Fitzpatrick, George; Boston, 1765 ***1642*** *p35*
FitzPatrick, H.; Toronto, 1844 ***2910.35*** *p115*
Fitzpatrick, James; Boston, 1763 ***1642*** *p32*
Fitzpatrick, James; Boston, 1825 ***3274.56*** *p69*
Fitzpatrick, James 56; Ontario, 1871 ***1823.21*** *p114*
Fitzpatrick, James; Toronto, 1844 ***2910.35*** *p113*
Fitzpatrick, John; Ipswich, MA, 1754-1763 ***1642*** *p70*
Fitz-Patrick, John 15; Ipswich, MA, 1753 ***1642*** *p70*
Fitzpatrick, John; Ohio, 1809-1852 ***4511.35*** *p14*
Fitzpatrick, Matthew; Illinois, 1834-1900 ***6020.5*** *p131*
Fitzpatrick, Peter D.; Ohio, 1840-1897 ***8365.35*** *p16*
Fitzpatrick, Selia 17; Ontario, 1871 ***1823.21*** *p114*
FitzPatrick, Thomas; Boston, 1748 ***1642*** *p46*
Fitzpatrick, Thomas; New York, NY, 1834 ***3274.56*** *p97*
Fitzpatrick, Thomas 28; Ontario, 1871 ***1823.21*** *p114*
Fitzpatrick, Thomas 45; Ontario, 1871 ***1823.21*** *p114*
Fitzpatrick, William 14; Ontario, 1871 ***1823.17*** *p52*
Fitzsimmons, John; Ohio, 1809-1852 ***4511.35*** *p14*
Fitzsimmons, Mary 40; Ontario, 1871 ***1823.21*** *p114*
Fitzsimmons, Robert; Jamaica, 1783 ***8529.30*** *p13A*
Fitzsimmons, William; Ohio, 1809-1852 ***4511.35*** *p14*
Fitzsimons, George 46; Ontario, 1871 ***1823.21*** *p114*
Fitzsimons, Henry 44; Ontario, 1871 ***1823.21*** *p114*
Fitzwilliam, Patrick; New Orleans, 1850 ***7242.30*** *p141*
Fitzwilliams, Mary Ann 16; Ontario, 1871 ***1823.21*** *p114*
Fitzwilliams, Mary Ellen 17; Ontario, 1871 ***1823.21*** *p114*
Fiut, Emilia Dulka *SEE* Fiut, John
Fiut, Emilija Dulka *SEE* Fiut, John
Fiut, John; Detroit, 1930 ***1640.60*** *p77*
*Wife:*Emilia Dulka
Fiut, John; Detroit, 1930 ***1640.60*** *p78*
*Wife:*Emilija Dulka
Fivideveur, Jacques; Wisconsin, 1855 ***1495.20*** *p41*
Fix, Adam; New Jersey, 1750-1774 ***927.31*** *p2*
Fix, Anna 30; New York, NY, 1893 ***1883.7*** *p44*
Fix, Edward 4; New York, NY, 1893 ***1883.7*** *p44*
Fix, Joseph 30; Michigan, 1880 ***4491.39*** *p10*
Fixe, Adam; New Jersey, 1750-1774 ***927.31*** *p2*
Fixter, George 38; Ontario, 1871 ***1823.21*** *p114*
Fixter, Thomas 52; Ontario, 1871 ***1823.21*** *p114*
Fizjarrell, Margaret; Boston, 1764 ***1642*** *p48*
Fjellstedt, Swan J.; Illinois, 1861 ***4487.25*** *p57*
Flaccus, Friedrich; Pittsburgh, 1890 ***5475.1*** *p38*
Flace, Lorenz 28; America, 1747 ***778.6*** *p118*
Flach, Christoph; Texas, 1847 ***2526.43*** *p185*
Flach, J. A.; Chile, 1852 ***1192.4*** *p52*
With wife & child
Flach, Johannes; Port uncertain, 1866 ***170.15*** *p25*
Flach, John; Nova Scotia, 1784 ***7105*** *p23*
Flach, Matthias; America, 1773 ***2526.42*** *p172*
Flachart, Catherine Antonie 47; New Orleans, 1848 ***778.6*** *p118*
Flachart, Jean Marie Aug. 50; New Orleans, 1848 ***778.6*** *p118*
Flachart, Julie Clotilde 12; New Orleans, 1848 ***778.6*** *p118*
Flachmann, Carl Heinrich Otto; America, 1861 ***7420.1*** *p204*
Flachmann, Friedrich; America, 1861 ***7420.1*** *p204*
Flachsenhar, Elisabeth; America, 1866 ***2526.43*** *p224*
Flack, Andrew; Long Island, 1778 ***8529.30*** *p9A*
Flacke, Richard Carl; America, 1888 ***7420.1*** *p356*
Fladmark, Evan; Minnesota, 1893 ***1447.20*** *p64*
Flagg, Cornelius 30; Ontario, 1871 ***1823.17*** *p52*
Flagg, Thomas W.; Ohio, 1831 ***3580.20*** *p32*
Flagg, Thomas W.; Ohio, 1841 ***6020.12*** *p7*
Flagnigan, Patrick; Boston, 1723 ***1642*** *p25*
Flaharty, Timothy; Boston, 1767 ***1642*** *p39*
Flahaux, J. B.; New York, NY, 1881 ***1494.20*** *p13*
Flaherty, Mary 23; Ontario, 1871 ***1823.21*** *p114*
Flaherty, Methias 32; Ontario, 1871 ***1823.21*** *p114*
Flaherty, Patrick 59; Ontario, 1871 ***1823.21*** *p114*
Flaherty, Peter; New Orleans, 1850 ***7242.30*** *p141*
Flaherty, William; Marblehead, MA, 1764 ***1642*** *p73*
Flaicher, Joseph 31; New Orleans, 1848 ***778.6*** *p118*
Flaig, Jacob 3; Halifax, N.S., 1902 ***1860.4*** *p42*
Flaig, Johann 4; Halifax, N.S., 1902 ***1860.4*** *p42*
Flaig, Justine 32; Halifax, N.S., 1902 ***1860.4*** *p42*
Flaig, Katha 9; Halifax, N.S., 1902 ***1860.4*** *p42*
Flaig, Kristian 34; Halifax, N.S., 1902 ***1860.4*** *p42*
Flaig, Magda 1; Halifax, N.S., 1902 ***1860.4*** *p42*
Flaig, Maria 7; Halifax, N.S., 1902 ***1860.4*** *p42*

Flake, August Wilhelm Ludwig; America, 1882 *7420.1 p328*
  *Brother:*Heinrich August
Flake, Auguste; America, 1861 *7420.1 p204*
Flake, Charlotte; Chicago, 1891 *7420.1 p363*
Flake, Heinrich; Chicago, 1884 *7420.1 p342*
Flake, Heinrich August *SEE* Flake, August Wilhelm Ludwig
Flake, Louise; Ohio, 1879 *7420.1 p313*
  *Granddaughter:*Marie
Flake, Ludwig; Chicago, 1884 *7420.1 p342*
Flake, Marie *SEE* Flake, Louise Wilhelm
Flamand, Nicole; Quebec, 1668 *4514.3 p313*
Flamand, Robert 23; Montreal, 1660 *9221.17 p443*
Flamant, Leopold; Wisconsin, 1856 *1495.20 p41*
Flamen, Elizabeth; Lynn, MA, 1775 *1642 p71*
Flammang, Jennit; Massachusetts, 1732 *1642 p66*
Flammer, Anna Maria Meier *SEE* Flammer, Thomas
Flammer, Thomas; Pennsylvania, 1852 *8513.31 p306*
  *Wife:*Anna Maria Meier
Flanagan, Bridgett 44; Michigan, 1880 *4491.39 p10*
Flanagan, Dominick; St. John, N.B., 1847 *2978.15 p36*
Flanagan, Hugh 34; Ontario, 1871 *1823.17 p52*
Flanagan, James S.; Boston, 1826 *3274.55 p25*
Flanagan, John; Toronto, 1844 *2910.35 p113*
Flanagan, Michael; North Carolina, 1814-1820 *1088.45 p10*
Flanagan, Michael 50; Ontario, 1871 *1823.17 p52*
Flanagan, Patrick 53; Michigan, 1880 *4491.39 p10*
Flanagan, Peter; North Carolina, 1814-1820 *1088.45 p10*
Flanagan, Rebecca; Boston, 1759 *1642 p47*
Flanagan, Rebecca; Boston, 1762 *1642 p48*
Flanagan, Richard; Ohio, 1809-1852 *4511.35 p14*
Flanagan, Sarah; Boston, 1771 *1642 p49*
Flanary, Edward 10; Ontario, 1871 *1823.21 p114*
Flander, Anna *SEE* Flander, Johann
Flander, Elisabeth *SEE* Flander, Johann
Flander, Johann *SEE* Flander, Johann
Flander, Johann; America, 1873 *5475.1 p341*
  *Wife:*Kath. Theobald
  *Daughter:*Elisabeth
  *Daughter:*Katharina
  *Son:*Peter
  *Son:*Nikolaus
  *Son:*Michel
  *Son:*Johann
  *Daughter:*Anna
Flander, Kath. Theobald *SEE* Flander, Johann
Flander, Katharina *SEE* Flander, Johann
Flander, Michel *SEE* Flander, Johann
Flander, Nikolaus *SEE* Flander, Johann
Flander, Peter *SEE* Flander, Johann
Flandrin, Mr. 27; America, 1842 *778.6 p118*
Flanegan, Mary; Marblehead, MA, 1752 *1642 p73*
Flanegin, Michael; Boston, 1765 *1642 p35*
Flanekin, Eleanor; Boston, 1756 *1642 p47*
Flanigan, Andrew 40; Ontario, 1871 *1823.21 p114*
Flanigan, Hiram 44; Ontario, 1871 *1823.21 p114*
Flanigan, John 67; Ontario, 1871 *1823.21 p114*
Flanigan, William 36; Ontario, 1871 *1823.21 p114*
Flannagan, Bernard; Louisiana, 1848 *4981.45 p131*
Flannagan, John; Louisiana, 1874 *4981.45 p131*
Flannagan, Laughlin; Boston, 1753 *1642 p47*
Flannagan, Lawrence; North Carolina, 1859-1860 *1088.45 p10*
Flannaghan, John; Marblehead, MA, 1749 *1642 p73*
Flannaghan, Michael; Massachusetts, 1769 *1642 p66*
Flannagin, John; Boston, 1765 *1642 p35*
Flannakin, Mary; Boston, 1756 *1642 p47*
Flannelly, Maria; Philadelphia, 1853 *8513.31 p420*
Flannery, Edward 34; Ontario, 1871 *1823.21 p114*
Flannery, Jerimiah 54; Ontario, 1871 *1823.21 p114*
Flannery, Saml 40; Ontario, 1871 *1823.21 p115*
Flannery, William 29; Ontario, 1871 *1823.21 p115*
Flannigan, James 62; Ontario, 1871 *1823.21 p115*
Flannigan, Thos 35; Ontario, 1871 *1823.17 p52*
Flannighan, D. 39; Ontario, 1871 *1823.21 p115*
Flartee, Mary; Salisbury, MA, 1727 *1642 p61*
Flash, Wm.; Louisiana, 1874-1875 *4981.45 p298*
Flat, Jeramiah; Ohio, 1809-1852 *4511.35 p14*
Flaten, Ove; Missouri, 1868 *3276.1 p3*
Flath, Adam; America, 1852 *2526.42 p135*
Flath, Adam; America, 1852 *2526.43 p160*
Flath, Adam; America, 1868 *2526.43 p125*
Flath, Adam 16 *SEE* Flath, Peter, I
Flath, Balthasar 18 *SEE* Flath, Balthasar, I
Flath, Balthasar, I 56; America, 1853 *2526.42 p149*
  *Wife:*Marie Katharina Kissebert 52
  *Child:*Balthasar 18
  *Child:*Leonhard 24
  *Child:*Katharina Elisabeth 22
Flath, Barbara 15 *SEE* Flath, Georg
Flath, Elise *SEE* Flath, Peter

Flath, Georg; America, 1869 *2526.42 p150*
Flath, Georg 1 *SEE* Flath, Georg
Flath, Georg 19 *SEE* Flath, Margaretha
Flath, Georg 19; America, 1852 *2526.42 p150*
Flath, Georg 36; America, 1846 *2526.42 p199*
  With wife
  *Son:*Philipp 12
  *Son:*Peter 12
  *Son:*Georg 1
  *Daughter:*Barbara 15
Flath, Johannes 18; America, 1852 *2526.42 p102*
Flath, Karl *SEE* Flath, Peter
Flath, Katharina; America, 1871 *2526.42 p150*
Flath, Katharina *SEE* Flath, Peter
Flath, Katharina 24 *SEE* Flath, Peter, I
Flath, Katharina Elisabeth 22 *SEE* Flath, Balthasar, I
Flath, Leonhard; America, 1881 *2526.42 p166*
Flath, Leonhard 17; America, 1881 *2526.42 p135*
Flath, Leonhard 24 *SEE* Flath, Balthasar, I
Flath, Margaretha; America, 1856 *2526.42 p113*
Flath, Margaretha *SEE* Flath, Peter
Flath, Margaretha 1 *SEE* Flath, Wilhelm
Flath, Margaretha 16; America, 1852 *2526.42 p150*
  *Brother:*Georg 19
Flath, Maria Elisabetha 26; America, 1853 *2526.42 p120*
Flath, Marie Katharina Kissebert 52 *SEE* Flath, Balthasar, I
Flath, Peter; America, 1854 *2526.42 p102*
Flath, Peter; America, 1865 *2526.42 p166*
Flath, Peter; America, 1884 *2526.42 p166*
Flath, Peter; America, 1887 *2526.42 p166*
  *Wife:*Katharina
  *Child:*Karl
  *Child:*Margaretha
  *Child:*Elise
Flath, Peter 12 *SEE* Flath, Georg
Flath, Peter 12 *SEE* Flath, Peter, I
Flath, Peter, I; America, 1854 *2526.42 p199*
  With wife
  *Son:*Peter
  *Daughter:*Katharina
  *Son:*Adam
Flath, Philipp 3 *SEE* Flath, Wilhelm
Flath, Philipp 12 *SEE* Flath, Georg
Flath, Wilhelm 32; America, 1853 *2526.43 p160*
  With wife 23
  *Son:*Philipp 3
  *Daughter:*Margaretha 1
Flathman, J. H.; Louisiana, 1836-1840 *4981.45 p212*
Flatt, James 25; North Carolina, 1774 *1422.10 p56*
Flecelles DeBregy, Marguerite 26; Quebec, 1640 *9221.17 p94*
Flechet, Anne; Quebec, 1673 *4514.3 p314*
Flechibus, Leon 21; America, 1848 *778.6 p118*
Flechner, Auguste 36; Louisiana, 1848 *778.6 p118*
Flechner, Babette 30; Louisiana, 1848 *778.6 p118*
Flechsenhar, Elisabeth Margaretha; America, 1853 *2526.43 p224*
Flechsenhar, Georg Adam, II; America, 1855 *2526.43 p224*
Flechsenhar, Georg Martin *SEE* Flechsenhar, Johannes
Flechsenhar, Georg Michael; America, 1855 *2526.43 p224*
Flechsenhar, Georg Wilhelm; America, 1855 *2526.43 p224*
Flechsenhar, Johannes; America, 1888 *2526.43 p167*
  *Uncle:*Georg Martin
Flechsenhar, Karl; America, 1854 *2526.43 p167*
Flechsenhar, Margaretha Elisabetha 13; America, 1855 *2526.43 p224*
Fleck, Mr.; Died enroute, 1839-1854 *9228.50 p265*
  With wife
Fleck, Augusta Caroline; Ohio, 1839-1854 *9228.50 p265*
Fleck, Friedrich; America, 1858 *2526.42 p107*
Fleck, Georg Peter 4 *SEE* Fleck, Georg Wilhelm
Fleck, Georg Wilhelm; America, 1846 *2526.43 p139*
  With wife
  *Son:*Georg Peter
Fleck, George H. 33; Ontario, 1871 *1823.21 p115*
Fleck, J.N.; America, 1869 *2526.43 p190*
Fleck, James 52; Ontario, 1871 *1823.17 p52*
Fleck, James; South Carolina, 1844 *6155.4 p18*
Fleck, John; Ohio, 1809-1852 *4511.35 p14*
Fleck, John 56; Ontario, 1871 *1823.17 p52*
Fleck, John A. 39; Indiana, 1872-1876 *9076.20 p68*
Fleck, Joseph 19; New Orleans, 1847 *778.6 p118*
Fleck, Katharina; America, 1881 *2526.42 p135*
  With 4 children
Fleck, Peter; America, 1881 *2526.42 p135*
Fleck, Phil. 28; America, 1840 *778.6 p118*
Fleckenshaar, Peter; America, 1846 *2526.43 p195*
Fleckenstein, Anton; New York, 1913 *1029.59 p29*
Fleckenstein, Barbara 9 *SEE* Fleckenstein, Peter

Fleckenstein, Barbara Jochheim 34 *SEE* Fleckenstein, Peter
Fleckenstein, Elisabeth; America, 1855 *2526.43 p146*
Fleckenstein, Elisabetha 2 *SEE* Fleckenstein, Peter
Fleckenstein, Eva Elisabeth; America, 1854 *2526.43 p147*
Fleckenstein, Friedrich Hermann; America, 1854 *7420.1 p119*
Fleckenstein, Heinrich; America, 1854 *2526.43 p147*
Fleckenstein, Heinrich 7 *SEE* Fleckenstein, Peter
Fleckenstein, Jakob; America, 1903 *2526.43 p167*
Fleckenstein, Katharina 12 *SEE* Fleckenstein, Peter
Fleckenstein, Peter; America, 1854 *2526.42 p119*
Fleckenstein, Peter; America, 1854 *2526.42 p123*
Fleckenstein, Peter 40; America, 1854 *2526.42 p119*
  *Wife:*Barbara Jochheim 34
  *Child:*Barbara 9
  *Child:*Philipp 5
  *Child:*Elisabetha 2
  *Child:*Heinrich 7
  *Child:*Katharina 12
Fleckenstein, Philipp 5 *SEE* Fleckenstein, Peter
Fleckenstein, Wilhelm; America, 1852 *7420.1 p88*
Fleckenstein, Wilhelm; America, 1883 *2526.43 p147*
Fleestein, Alexander 23; Missouri, 1845 *778.6 p118*
Fleet, Sarah A.; Long Island, 1853 *8513.31 p306*
Flegel, Wilhelm; Wisconsin, 1881 *6795.8 p96*
Flehmer, Jerome Herman; New York, NY, 1902 *6212.1 p16*
Flehmer, Jerome Herman; New York, NY, 1904 *6212.1 p15*
Flehmer, Paul; New York, NY, 1902 *6212.1 p16*
Fleig, Agatha 8; Port uncertain, 1847 *778.6 p118*
Fleig, Agatha 39; Port uncertain, 1847 *778.6 p118*
Fleig, Anton 42; Port uncertain, 1847 *778.6 p118*
Fleig, Eugene 5; Port uncertain, 1847 *778.6 p118*
Fleig, Joseph 11; Port uncertain, 1847 *778.6 p118*
Fleig, Victor 10; Port uncertain, 1847 *778.6 p118*
Fleischhauer, Georg; America, 1867 *7919.3 p528*
  With wife & daughter
Fleischhauer, Heinrich Christian; America, 1868 *7919.3 p532*
  With daughter
Fleischman, Johanne Regine; America, 1867 *7919.3 p532*
Fleischmann, Carl Friedrich; America, 1867 *7919.3 p528*
  With wife & 5 children
Flemal, J. F.; New York, NY, 1864 *1494.20 p11*
Fleming, Abraham; Massachusetts, 1770 *1642 p116*
  *Wife:*Mary
Fleming, Andrew; Massachusetts, 1738 *1642 p102*
Fleming, Ann; New Orleans, 1851 *7242.30 p142*
Fleming, Ann 36; Ontario, 1871 *1823.21 p115*
Fleming, Arthur; Boston, 1745 *1642 p28*
Fleming, Catherine; New Brunswick, 1842 *2978.20 p9*
Fleming, David; Palmer, MA, 1766 *1642 p119*
  *Wife:*Sarah
Fleming, Ellen; New Orleans, 1851 *7242.30 p142*
Fleming, James; New Orleans, 1851 *7242.30 p142*
Fleming, James 52; Ontario, 1871 *1823.17 p52*
Fleming, Jane Thompson *SEE* Fleming, John
Fleming, John; Massachusetts, 1770 *1642 p85*
Fleming, John; Massachusetts, 1771 *1642 p106*
Fleming, John 64; Ontario, 1871 *1823.21 p115*
Fleming, John; Pennsylvania, 1859 *8513.31 p306*
  *Wife:*Jane Thompson
Fleming, Margaret; Boston, 1767 *1642 p39*
Fleming, Mary; Boston, 1761 *1642 p48*
Fleming, Mary *SEE* Fleming, Abraham
Fleming, Mary; New Orleans, 1851 *7242.30 p142*
Fleming, Michael 29; Ontario, 1871 *1823.17 p52*
Fleming, Michael 81; Ontario, 1871 *1823.21 p115*
Fleming, Pat 20; St. Johns, N.F., 1811 *1053.20 p21*
Fleming, Pat'k; Ontario, 1787 *1276.15 p30*
Fleming, Patrick; New Orleans, 1851 *7242.30 p142*
Fleming, Patrick 50; Ontario, 1871 *1823.17 p52*
Fleming, Richard; Boston, 1763 *1642 p32*
Fleming, Robert 28; Ontario, 1871 *1823.21 p115*
Fleming, Robert 61; Ontario, 1871 *1823.21 p115*
Fleming, Sarah *SEE* Fleming, David
Fleming, Thomas 58; Ontario, 1871 *1823.21 p115*
Fleming, Walter 58; Ontario, 1871 *1823.17 p52*
Fleming, William; Colorado, 1891 *1029.59 p29*
Fleming, William 47; Ontario, 1871 *1823.21 p115*
Fleming, William 53; Ontario, 1871 *1823.21 p115*
Flemming, Andrew; New York, NY, 1778 *8529.30 p2*
Flemming, Andrew 53; Ontario, 1871 *1823.21 p115*
Flemming, Ann. 30; Ontario, 1871 *1823.21 p115*
Flemming, August; Wisconsin, 1898 *6795.8 p132*
Flemming, Edmund; Boston, 1756 *1642 p47*
Flemming, James; Louisiana, 1874 *4981.45 p131*

Flemming, James Edward; Philadelphia, 1840 ***7074.20*** *p132*
Flemming, John 36; Ontario, 1871 ***1823.21*** *p115*
Flemming, Joseph; Detroit, 1890 ***9980.23*** *p97*
Flemming, Mary; Massachusetts, 1743 ***1642*** *p111*
Flemming, Richard 45; Ontario, 1871 ***1823.21*** *p115*
Flemming, William 27; Ontario, 1871 ***1823.21*** *p115*
Flems, Francois 23; America, 1846 ***778.6*** *p118*
Flenter, Helene; America, 1854 ***7420.1*** *p119*
With daughter
Flentge, Engel Dorothee; America, 1853 ***7420.1*** *p113*
Flentge, Engel Marie Dorothee; America, 1845 ***7420.1*** *p38*
Flentge, Friedrich; America, 1858 ***7420.1*** *p177*
Flentge, Friedrich Wilhelm; America, 1852 ***7420.1*** *p88*
Flentge, Heinrich; America, 1855 ***7420.1*** *p136*
With wife
Flentge, Louis Borries; America, 1868 ***7420.1*** *p271*
Flentje, Widow; America, 1870 ***7420.1*** *p286*
*Son:*Heinrich Friedrich Wilhelm
*Daughter:*Sophie Wilhelmine Charlotte
Flentje, Anton Ludwig Christoph *SEE* Flentje, Johann Heinrich Wilhelm
Flentje, Heinrich Friedrich Wilhelm *SEE* Flentje, Widow
Flentje, Johann Heinrich Wilhelm; America, 1857 ***7420.1*** *p160*
*Brother:*Anton Ludwig Christoph
Flentje, Sophie Wilhelmine Charlotte *SEE* Flentje, Widow
Flera, Vincent; Detroit, 1929-1930 ***6214.5*** *p67*
Flerchinger, J. Nikolaus *SEE* Flerchinger, Johann
Flerchinger, Jakob; America, 1882 ***5475.1*** *p257*
Flerchinger, Johann 41; America, 1890 ***5475.1*** *p257*
*Wife:*Magdalena Legill
*Son:*J. Nikolaus
*Daughter:*M. Magdalena
Flerchinger, M. Magdalena *SEE* Flerchinger, Johann
Flerchinger, Magdalena Legill *SEE* Flerchinger, Johann
Flerchinger, Michel; America, 1873 ***5475.1*** *p256*
Flerchinger, Nikolaus; America, 1872 ***5475.1*** *p255*
Flerchinger, Peter; America, 1873 ***5475.1*** *p256*
Flesch, Margarethe; America, 1872 ***5475.1*** *p153*
Fletcher, Alfred 40; Ontario, 1871 ***1823.21*** *p115*
Fletcher, Angus 40; North Carolina, 1774 ***1422.10*** *p57*
Fletcher, Angus 60; Ontario, 1871 ***1823.21*** *p115*
Fletcher, Archibald 63; Ontario, 1871 ***1823.21*** *p115*
Fletcher, C.; Louisiana, 1874 ***4981.45*** *p295*
Fletcher, Caleb 70; Ontario, 1871 ***1823.21*** *p115*
Fletcher, Christie 46; Ontario, 1871 ***1823.21*** *p115*
Fletcher, Donald 53; Ontario, 1871 ***1823.21*** *p115*
Fletcher, Duncan 30; Ontario, 1871 ***1823.21*** *p115*
Fletcher, Edwin 30; Ontario, 1871 ***1823.17*** *p52*
Fletcher, Elen 50; Ontario, 1871 ***1823.21*** *p115*
Fletcher, Elizabeth 36; Michigan, 1880 ***4491.30*** *p12*
Fletcher, Elizabeth 48; Ontario, 1871 ***1823.21*** *p115*
Fletcher, Euphame 10; North Carolina, 1774 ***1422.10*** *p57*
Fletcher, Fanny 10; Quebec, 1870 ***8364.32*** *p23*
Fletcher, Henry 40; Ontario, 1871 ***1823.21*** *p115*
Fletcher, Hugh 51; Ontario, 1871 ***1823.21*** *p115*
Fletcher, Hugh 60; Ontario, 1871 ***1823.21*** *p115*
Fletcher, James 63; Ontario, 1871 ***1823.21*** *p115*
Fletcher, James; Philadelphia, 1854 ***8513.31*** *p307*
*Wife:*Susanah Matson
Fletcher, John; Illinois, 1834-1900 ***6020.5*** *p131*
Fletcher, John 34; Michigan, 1880 ***4491.30*** *p12*
Fletcher, John 30; Ontario, 1871 ***1823.21*** *p115*
Fletcher, John 31; Ontario, 1871 ***1823.21*** *p115*
Fletcher, John 46; Ontario, 1871 ***1823.21*** *p115*
Fletcher, John 56; Ontario, 1871 ***1823.21*** *p115*
Fletcher, John 60; Ontario, 1871 ***1823.21*** *p115*
Fletcher, Joseph 29; Ontario, 1871 ***1823.21*** *p115*
Fletcher, Kathrine 40; North Carolina, 1774 ***1422.10*** *p57*
Fletcher, Lucy 11; Quebec, 1870 ***8364.32*** *p23*
Fletcher, Mary 6; North Carolina, 1774 ***1422.10*** *p57*
Fletcher, Nancy 3; North Carolina, 1774 ***1422.10*** *p57*
Fletcher, Nancy 17; Ontario, 1871 ***1823.21*** *p116*
Fletcher, Robert 25; Michigan, 1880 ***4491.30*** *p12*
Fletcher, Robt 40; Ontario, 1871 ***1823.17*** *p52*
Fletcher, Stephen 67; Ontario, 1871 ***1823.21*** *p116*
Fletcher, Susanah Matson *SEE* Fletcher, James
Fletcher, Thomas 42; Ontario, 1871 ***1823.21*** *p116*
Fletcher, William 28; Ontario, 1871 ***1823.21*** *p116*
Fletcher, William 45; Ontario, 1871 ***1823.21*** *p116*
Fletcher, Wm 25; Ontario, 1871 ***1823.21*** *p116*
Flett, John H. 32; Ontario, 1871 ***1823.17*** *p53*
Fleurant, Jean 25; Quebec, 1656 ***9221.17*** *p336*
Fleure, Marie-Anne; Quebec, 1673 ***4514.3*** *p314*
Fleure, Martha V.; Wisconsin, 1856-1865 ***9228.50*** *p592*
Fleureau, Marie; Quebec, 1669 ***4514.3*** *p314*
Fleurot, Theophile 35; America, 1845 ***778.6*** *p118*
Fleurus, L. 40; New York, NY, 1856 ***1766.1*** *p45*
Fleury, . . . 1; New Orleans, 1848 ***778.6*** *p118*
Fleury, . . .; Quebec, 1534 ***9228.50*** *p3*
Fleury, Mr. 55; America, 1842 ***778.6*** *p119*
Fleury, Mr. 28; New Orleans, 1848 ***778.6*** *p118*
Fleury, Mrs. 30; New Orleans, 1848 ***778.6*** *p119*
Fleury, A. 3; New Orleans, 1848 ***778.6*** *p119*
Fleury, Charles; Marblehead, MA, 1725 ***9228.50*** *p218*
Fleury, Elizabet; Virginia, 1700 ***9230.15*** *p81*
Fleury, Ferdinand 10 months; Louisiana, 1848 ***778.6*** *p119*
Fleury, Francois 31; Quebec, 1659 ***9221.17*** *p401*
Fleury, Francoise; Montreal, 1679 ***4514.3*** *p286*
Fleury, Gabriel; Quebec, 1659 ***9221.17*** *p401*
Fleury, Henri 70; New Orleans, 1848 ***778.6*** *p119*
Fleury, Jean 33; Louisiana, 1848 ***778.6*** *p119*
Fleury, Jean; Quebec, 1646 ***9221.17*** *p164*
Fleury, Paul; Quebec, 1659 ***9221.17*** *p413*
Fleury, Rose 19; Louisiana, 1848 ***778.6*** *p119*
Fleury, Th. 25; America, 1840 ***778.6*** *p119*
Fleury, Theodor 25; America, 1840 ***778.6*** *p119*
Fleury Deschambault, Jacques-Alexis; Quebec, 1671 ***2314.30*** *p166*
Fleury Deschambault, Jacques-Alexis; Quebec, 1671 ***2314.30*** *p182*
Flick, Danil; Illinois, 1856 ***6079.1*** *p5*
Flick, Elizabeth 39; Port uncertain, 1846 ***778.6*** *p119*
Flick, Georg 40; Port uncertain, 1846 ***778.6*** *p119*
Flick, Jacob; Louisiana, 1874 ***4981.45*** *p295*
Flick, John; Louisiana, 1874-1875 ***4981.45*** *p298*
Fliegauf, Franz Joseph 55; New Castle, DE, 1817-1818 ***90.20*** *p151*
Fliegauf, Stephan; New Castle, DE, 1817-1818 ***90.20*** *p151*
Flies, Elisabeth Ferrer *SEE* Flies, Johann
Flies, Johann; America, 1856 ***5475.1*** *p259*
*Wife:*Elisabeth Ferrer
Fligl, Ladislav; Chicago, 1863-1910 ***2853.20*** *p405*
Fligl, Ladislav; Illinois, 1879-1902 ***2853.20*** *p513*
Fliguier, Jean; Quebec, 1642 ***9221.17*** *p116*
Fliming, Hannah; Palmer, MA, 1772 ***1642*** *p119*
Fliming, Sarah *SEE* Fliming, William
Fliming, William; Palmer, MA, 1770 ***1642*** *p119*
*Wife:*Sarah
Flin, Dennis; Boston, 1774 ***1642*** *p50*
Flin, John; Boston, 1728 ***1642*** *p25*
Flin, John; Boston, 1753 ***1642*** *p47*
Flin, Joshua; Massachusetts, 1753 ***1642*** *p105*
Flin, Mary; Lynn, MA, 1773 ***1642*** *p72*
Flin, William 54; Ontario, 1871 ***1823.21*** *p116*
Fling, John; Boston, 1728 ***1642*** *p25*
Fling, Patrick; Boston, 1713 ***1642*** *p24*
Fling, Thomas; Boston, 1766 ***1642*** *p38*
With wife
Fling, Thomas 17; Ontario, 1871 ***1823.17*** *p53*
Flinn, George; Jamaica, 1777 ***8529.30*** *p13A*
Flinn, James; Boston, 1769 ***1642*** *p40*
Flinn, Mary; Boston, 1772 ***1642*** *p49*
Flinn, Mary; Massachusetts, 1720 ***1642*** *p66*
Flinn, Mary; Massachusetts, 1739 ***1642*** *p66*
Flinn, Maurice; Newfoundland, 1814 ***3476.10*** *p54*
Flinn, Michael; Boston, 1774 ***1642*** *p50*
Flinn, Patrick; Newfoundland, 1814 ***3476.10*** *p54*
Flinn, Steven 70; Ontario, 1871 ***1823.21*** *p116*
Flinn, Thomas; Boston, 1773 ***1642*** *p49*
Flinn, Thomas; Ohio, 1840-1897 ***8365.35*** *p16*
Flinn, Thomas 30; Ontario, 1871 ***1823.21*** *p116*
Flinn, William; Newfoundland, 1814 ***3476.10*** *p54*
Flint, A.; New York, 1859 ***358.56*** *p100*
Flint, Perney 45; Ontario, 1871 ***1823.21*** *p116*
Flintoff, William 23; Ontario, 1871 ***1823.21*** *p116*
Flintoft, James 67; Ontario, 1871 ***1823.17*** *p53*
Flinton, William 58; Ontario, 1871 ***1823.21*** *p116*
Flipsey, Peter I.; Iowa, 1896 ***1211.15*** *p10*
Flirk, Ferdinand 28; America, 1846 ***778.6*** *p119*
Flodine, Caroline 63 *SEE* Flodine, John
Flodine, Emma 17 *SEE* Flodine, John
Flodine, John 29; Kansas, 1880 ***777.40*** *p19*
*Father:*Peter 67
*Sister:*Emma 17
*Brother:*Peter 34
*Mother:*Caroline 63
Flodine, Peter 34 *SEE* Flodine, John
Flodine, Peter 67 *SEE* Flodine, John
Floeter, Adolf. Rudolf; Wisconsin, 1887 ***6795.8*** *p123*
Floeter, August; Wisconsin, 1869 ***6795.8*** *p123*
Floeter, August; Wisconsin, 1906 ***6795.8*** *p177*
Floeter, Ernestine; Wisconsin, 1899 ***6795.8*** *p120*
Floeter, Louise Henriette; Wisconsin, 1884 ***6795.8*** *p120*
Floeter, Wilhelm; Wisconsin, 1888 ***6795.8*** *p120*
Floeter, Wilhelmine; Wisconsin, 1887 ***6795.8*** *p120*
Flohr, A. D. A.; Chile, 1852 ***1192.4*** *p52*
Flohr, Daniel; New Jersey, 1858 ***8513.31*** *p307*
*Wife:*Josephine Gutheinz
Flohr, Josephine Gutheinz *SEE* Flohr, Daniel
Flood, Barney 55; Ontario, 1871 ***1823.21*** *p116*
Flood, Bernard; Ohio, 1809-1852 ***4511.35*** *p14*
Flood, Danual 54; Ontario, 1871 ***1823.21*** *p116*
Flood, James 60; Ontario, 1871 ***1823.21*** *p116*
Flood, John 56; Ontario, 1871 ***1823.17*** *p53*
Flood, John 64; Ontario, 1871 ***1823.21*** *p116*
Flood, Lawrence; Ohio, 1809-1852 ***4511.35*** *p14*
Flood, Michael; Louisiana, 1841-1844 ***4981.45*** *p210*
Flood, Philip; New Jersey, 1665 ***9228.50*** *p218*
Flood, Richard; Ipswich, MA, 1729 ***1642*** *p71*
Flood, Thomas 57; Ontario, 1871 ***1823.21*** *p116*
Flood, William 33; Ontario, 1871 ***1823.21*** *p116*
Flood, Worley 16; Quebec, 1870 ***8364.32*** *p23*
Floom, Charles; Ohio, 1809-1852 ***4511.35*** *p14*
Floom, Francis; Ohio, 1809-1852 ***4511.35*** *p14*
Floom, John; Ohio, 1809-1852 ***4511.35*** *p14*
Flora, Charles H. 28; Ontario, 1871 ***1823.17*** *p53*
Florath, Theresia; America, 1927 ***8023.44*** *p373*
Florence, Louis 44; Ontario, 1871 ***1823.21*** *p116*
Florent, Alex. 19; America, 1840 ***778.6*** *p119*
Florent, Ant. 15; America, 1840 ***778.6*** *p119*
Florent, Florenz 30; America, 1840 ***778.6*** *p119*
Florent, Fritz 57; America, 1840 ***778.6*** *p119*
Florent, Guillaume 20; Quebec, 1662 ***9221.17*** *p485*
Florent, Magd. 17; America, 1840 ***778.6*** *p119*
Florent, Roman 26; America, 1840 ***778.6*** *p119*
Florent, Sophie 52; America, 1840 ***778.6*** *p119*
Flores, E.; California, 1868 ***1131.61*** *p89*
Flores, Narcisse; Louisiana, 1874 ***4981.45*** *p131*
Flori, Barbara 30; America, 1845 ***2526.42*** *p189*
Flori, Mrs. Joseph 67; America, 1845 ***2526.42*** *p189*
With son-in-law
Florian, Tomas; St. Louis, 1854 ***2853.20*** *p21*
Floriat, J. A. B.; Louisiana, 1836-1840 ***4981.45*** *p212*
Floriot, John 26; America, 1843 ***778.6*** *p119*
Florke, Heinrich Johann Wilhelm; New York, NY, 1873 ***7420.1*** *p299*
Florke, Ludwig; America, 1852 ***7420.1*** *p88*
With wife & 3 daughters
Florschutz, Gottlob; America, 1867 ***7919.3*** *p533*
Flory, . . . 48; Port uncertain, 1843 ***778.6*** *p119*
Flory, Emile 24; America, 1841 ***778.6*** *p119*
Flory, Samuel 38; Ontario, 1871 ***1823.21*** *p116*
Flosinger, Katharina 54; America, 1800-1899 ***5475.1*** *p453*
With 3 children
Flot, Michelle 11; Quebec, 1652 ***9221.17*** *p261*
Flour, Louis Ant. 31; New Orleans, 1844 ***778.6*** *p119*
Floure, Caleb 47; Ontario, 1871 ***1823.21*** *p116*
Flourthy, Timothy; Boston, 1770 ***1642*** *p49*
Flower, John; New York, 1776 ***8529.30*** *p11*
Flowers, Andrew 33; Ontario, 1871 ***1823.21*** *p116*
Flowers, Charles; Salem, MA, 1832 ***9228.50*** *p449*
Flowers, Edward 18; Quebec, 1870 ***8364.32*** *p23*
Flowers, Elizabeth 56; Ontario, 1871 ***1823.21*** *p116*
Flowers, George; Colorado, 1881 ***1029.59*** *p29*
Flowers, James 20; Ontario, 1871 ***1823.21*** *p116*
Flowers, John 39; Ontario, 1871 ***1823.21*** *p116*
Flowers-Fleury, Charles; Salem, MA, 1832 ***9228.50*** *p449*
Floyd, John; New Jersey, 1777 ***8529.30*** *p6*
Floyd, Philip; New Jersey, 1665 ***9228.50*** *p218*
Floyd, Tho.; Maryland, 1672 ***1236.25*** *p48*
Fltecher, Moyses; Plymouth, MA, 1620 ***1920.45*** *p5*
Fluchman, Henry; North Carolina, 1849 ***1088.45*** *p10*
Fluck, William; Marston's Wharf, 1782 ***8529.30*** *p11*
Flude, Arthur 21; Ontario, 1871 ***1823.17*** *p53*
Flugge, Caroline Wilhelmine Rosenbaum *SEE* Flugge, Christian Friedrich
Flugge, Christian Friedrich; Port uncertain, 1834 ***7420.1*** *p7*
*Wife:*Caroline Wilhelmine Rosenbaum
Flugrad, Julius Heinrich; Wisconsin, 1894 ***6795.8*** *p230*
Fluharty, John; Boston, 1748 ***1642*** *p46*
Fluhr, Anna Maria 4; New Orleans, 1848 ***778.6*** *p119*
Fluhr, Antoinette 7; New Orleans, 1848 ***778.6*** *p119*
Fluhr, Margaretha 36; New Orleans, 1848 ***778.6*** *p119*
Fluhr, Martin 52; New Orleans, 1848 ***778.6*** *p119*
Fluhr, Pratie 40; New Orleans, 1848 ***778.6*** *p119*
Fluhr, Rosina 12; New Orleans, 1848 ***778.6*** *p119*
Flum, Hannah; St. Paul, MN, 1889-1890 ***1865.50*** *p47*
Flume, Francis; Ohio, 1809-1852 ***4511.35*** *p14*
Flurey, M. 38; Port uncertain, 1848 ***778.6*** *p119*
Flurschutz, Andreas; America, 1867 ***7919.3*** *p527*
Fluster, Julius; Valdivia, Chile, 1850 ***1192.4*** *p49*
Flut, Thomas 25; America, 1841 ***778.6*** *p119*
Fluter, August; Wisconsin, 1906 ***6795.8*** *p177*
Flygelholm, Fred; Cleveland, OH, 1905-1906 ***9722.10*** *p119*
Flyn, Patrick; Boston, 1721 ***1642*** *p25*
Flynn, Catherine S. 45; Michigan, 1880 ***4491.39*** *p10*
Flynn, Edward 50; Michigan, 1880 ***4491.39*** *p10*
Flynn, George; Jamaica, 1777 ***8529.30*** *p13A*

136 *FOR A COMPLETE EXPLANATION OF ENTRY, SEE "HOW TO READ A CITATION" SECTION*

Flynn, James 32; Ontario, 1871 *1823.21* p116
Flynn, James; Toronto, 1844 *2910.35* p113
Flynn, James Neville 30; Ontario, 1871 *1823.17* p53
Flynn, John 45; Indiana, 1866-1879 *9076.20* p69
Flynn, John 35; Ontario, 1871 *1823.21* p116
Flynn, John 76; Ontario, 1871 *1823.21* p116
Flynn, Maggie 48; Michigan, 1880 *4491.39* p10
Flynn, Maud 21; Ontario, 1871 *1823.21* p116
Flynn, Michael; Nantucket, MA, 1767 *1642* p89
Flynn, Nathaniel; New England, 1745 *1642* p28
Flynn, Owen 35; Ontario, 1871 *1823.21* p116
Flynn, Patrick 45; Michigan, 1880 *4491.39* p10
Flynn, Peter 50; Michigan, 1880 *4491.39* p10
Flynn, Robert 50; Ontario, 1871 *1823.21* p116
Flynn, Robert; Washington, 1882 *2770.40* p136
Flynn, Thomas; Boston, 1766 *1642* p38
    With wife
Flynn, Thomas; Massachusetts, 1639 *1642* p109
Flynn, Thomas; Ohio, 1842 *2763.1* p9
Flynn, William 58; Ontario, 1871 *1823.21* p116
Flynne, Cath; New Orleans, 1851 *7242.30* p142
Flynne, Owen; New Orleans, 1851 *7242.30* p142
Flynt, Ri; Virginia, 1652 *6254.4* p243
Flypson, Frederick SEE Flypson, Vrederych
Flypson, Vrederych; New York, 1647-1653 *2853.20* p14
    Son:Frederick
Focke, Louis Carl Heinrich; Port uncertain, 1895 *7420.1* p372
Fockey, John; Ohio, 1809-1852 *4511.35* p14
Foden, Oakes B.F. 53; Ontario, 1871 *1823.21* p116
Foechter, Francis J.; Ohio, 1809-1852 *4511.35* p14
Foegtling, John; Ohio, 1809-1852 *4511.35* p14
Foegtling, Joseph; Ohio, 1809-1852 *4511.35* p14
Foell, Charles; Missouri, 1890 *3276.1* p1
Foerster, Emil SEE Foerster, Johann Martin
Foerster, Johann Martin; Virginia, 1831 *152.20* p63
    Wife:Julie Faulstich
    Child:Emil
Foerster, Julie Faulstich SEE Foerster, Johann Martin
Foerster, Louis 20; Missouri, 1847 *778.6* p119
Foerster, Wilhelm; Wisconsin, 1868 *6795.8* p104
Foerter, Kaspar; Port uncertain, 1851 *170.15* p25
Fogal, Fred; Washington, 1884 *2770.40* p192
Fogarty, Edwd; St. John, N.B., 1848 *2978.15* p39
Fogarty, Ellen; New Orleans, 1851 *7242.30* p142
Fogarty, Ellen 48; Ontario, 1871 *1823.21* p117
Fogarty, John; New Orleans, 1851 *7242.30* p142
Fogarty, Martin 38; Ontario, 1871 *1823.21* p117
Fogarty, Patrick 22; Ontario, 1871 *1823.21* p117
Fogarty, Patrick 54; Ontario, 1871 *1823.21* p117
Fogel, F.L.; Cleveland, OH, 1882-1896 *9722.10* p119
Fogelgesang, Frederick; Ohio, 1809-1852 *4511.35* p14
Fogelstrom, Fredrika Caroline; North America, 1868 *6410.15* p105
Fogere, E. 45; New Orleans, 1846 *778.6* p120
Fogerty, Micah; New Jersey, 1837 *3274.56* p98
Fogerty, Timothy 25; Ontario, 1871 *1823.21* p117
Fogg, William 40; Ontario, 1871 *1823.21* p117
Foglegesong, Charles; Ohio, 1809-1852 *4511.35* p14
Foglegesong, Isaac; Ohio, 1809-1852 *4511.35* p14
Foglesong, Christian; Ohio, 1809-1852 *4511.35* p14
Fogt, Anthony; Ohio, 1809-1852 *4511.35* p14
Fogt, Michael; Ohio, 1840-1897 *8365.35* p16
Fohnar, May 9; Quebec, 1870 *8364.32* p23
Fohrman, S.; Louisiana, 1874-1875 *4981.45* p298
Foin, Francois 23; Missouri, 1846 *778.6* p120
Foirellard, Jean 29; Missouri, 1848 *778.6* p120
Foisane, S. 35; New Orleans, 1845 *778.6* p120
Foisy, Martin 18; Quebec, 1661 *9221.17* p455
Folan, Bridget; New Orleans, 1851 *7242.30* p142
Folan, Mary; New Orleans, 1851 *7242.30* p142
Foland, . . .; West Virginia, 1850-1860 *1132.30* p149
Folb, Lewis; North Carolina, 1888 *1088.45* p10
Folda, Frantisek SEE Folda, Martin
Folda, Jan SEE Folda, Martin
Folda, Josef SEE Folda, Martin
Folda, Martin; Wisconsin, 1857 *2853.20* p181
    With wife
    Son:Frantisek
    Son:Josef
    Son:Jan
Foldo, Martin; Ohio, 1809-1852 *4511.35* p15
Folendorf, Wilhelm Friedrick Gottfried; Wisconsin, 1889 *6795.8* p221
Foley, Catherine; Boston, 1772 *1642* p49
Foley, Daniel; Ohio, 1809-1852 *4511.35* p15
Foley, Jas 23; St. Johns, N.F., 1811 *1053.20* p21
Foley, Kathryn Irene; Montreal, 1944 *9228.50* p455
Foley, Margaret; New Orleans, 1850 *7242.30* p142
Foley, Martin; St. John, N.B., 1848 *2978.15* p36
Foley, Mathew; New Orleans, 1850 *7242.30* p142
Foley, Michael 20; St. Johns, N.F., 1811 *1053.20* p20

Foley, Pat; St. John, N.B., 1848 *2978.15* p39
Foley, Patrick; Illinois, 1856 *6079.1* p5
Foley, Patrick 50; Ontario, 1871 *1823.17* p53
Foley, Thomas; New Orleans, 1850 *7242.30* p142
Foley, Thomas 61; Ontario, 1871 *1823.17* p53
Folgate, Valentine; Ohio, 1844 *2763.1* p9
Folik, Anna 23; Portland, ME, 1910 *970.38* p77
Folin, Pierre; Quebec, 1661 *9221.17* p456
Folkenbach, Joseph; Ohio, 1809-1852 *4511.35* p15
Folks, William 46; Ontario, 1871 *1823.17* p53
Folland, Thomas; Massachusetts, 1675-1676 *1642* p130
    *Relative:*William
Folland, William SEE Folland, Thomas
Follard, Tobias; New York, 1783 *8529.30* p11
Follendorf, Hermann; Wisconsin, 1877 *6795.8* p225
Follet, Philip; Marblehead, MA, 1752 *9228.50* p226
Follett, Johanna; Maine, 1762 *9228.50* p226
Follett, Thomas; Portsmouth, NH, 1730 *9228.50* p226
Folleville, Charles 20; Montreal, 1660 *9221.17* p443
Folley, Jeremiah; Boston, 1765 *1642* p35
Folly, Eliza; Ontario, 1871 *1823.21* p117
Folmer, Christian; Ohio, 1809-1852 *4511.35* p15
Folmond, Mr. 21; America, 1848 *778.6* p120
Folon, Marie Catherine; Wisconsin, 1856 *1495.20* p45
Folske, Bertha; Wisconsin, 1893 *6795.8* p132
Folsome, Lewis 62; Ontario, 1871 *1823.17* p53
Folson, William 36; Ontario, 1871 *1823.21* p117
Foltz, Jacob; Ohio, 1809-1852 *4511.35* p15
Foltz, Jacob; Valdivia, Chile, 1850 *1192.4* p50
Foltz, John; Ohio, 1809-1852 *4511.35* p15
Foltz, Valentine; Ohio, 1809-1852 *4511.35* p15
Folz, Anna SEE Folz, Johann
Folz, Anna Maria; Wisconsin, 1891 *5475.1* p326
Folz, Elisabeth Weller 28 SEE Folz, Michel
Folz, Elisabeth Fuhs 43 SEE Folz, Johann
Folz, Franz SEE Folz, Johann
Folz, Henry; Louisiana, 1874 *4981.45* p131
Folz, Jakob; Wisconsin, 1890 *5475.1* p325
    *Wife:*Margarethe Fox
    *Son:*Michel
    *Daughter:*Margarethe
    *Son:*Peter
    *Son:*Johann
Folz, Joh. Franz; Kentucky, 1884 *5475.1* p286
    *Son:*Nikolaus
    *Son:*Joh. Peter
Folz, Joh. Peter SEE Folz, Joh. Franz
Folz, Johann; America, 1857 *5475.1* p375
    *Wife:*Maria Carl
    *Son:*Mathias
    *Son:*Franz
    With 2 stepchildren
Folz, Johann SEE Folz, Johann
Folz, Johann; America, 1864 *5475.1* p266
    *Son:*Mathias
    *Wife:*Elisabeth Fuhs
    *Daughter:*Anna
    *Son:*Johann
    *Daughter:*Katharina
Folz, Johann SEE Folz, Jakob
Folz, Katharina; America, 1800-1899 *5475.1* p342
Folz, Katharina; America, 1856 *5475.1* p342
Folz, Katharina SEE Folz, Johann
Folz, Katharina 63; America, 1854 *5475.1* p268
Folz, Margarethe SEE Folz, Jakob
Folz, Margarethe Fox SEE Folz, Jakob
Folz, Maria Carl SEE Folz, Johann
Folz, Maria 8 SEE Folz, Michel
Folz, Mathias SEE Folz, Johann
Folz, Mathias SEE Folz, Johann
Folz, Michel 32; America, 1856 *5475.1* p348
    *Wife:*Elisabeth Weller 28
    *Daughter:*Maria 8 months
Folz, Michel SEE Folz, Jakob
Folz, Nikolaus SEE Folz, Joh. Franz
Folz, Peter SEE Folz, Jakob
Folz, Peter; Wisconsin, 1891 *5475.1* p326
Fomemoy, Mr.; Toronto, 1844 *2910.35* p111
Fomie, Jacob; Ohio, 1809-1852 *4511.35* p15
Fonasse, Jean; Virginia, 1700 *9230.15* p81
Fondan, Pierre; New England, 1686 *9228.50* p226
Fonderhide, John; Ohio, 1840-1897 *8365.35* p16
Fonfara, Edward 6 months; New York, NY, 1912 *8355.1* p16
Fonfara, Maria 7; New York, NY, 1912 *8355.1* p16
Fonfara, Wiktoria 36; New York, NY, 1912 *8355.1* p16
Fongerat, August 29; St. Louis, 1847 *778.6* p120
Fonley, Gerard; Louisiana, 1841-1844 *4981.45* p210
Font, William 38; Ontario, 1871 *1823.17* p53
Fontaine, Andre 24; Louisiana, 1840 *778.6* p120
Fontaine, Johann; America, 1882 *5475.1* p137
Fontaine, Katharina 49; America, 1881 *5475.1* p196

Fontaine, Louis 37; Montreal, 1653 *9221.17* p289
Fontaine, Louis 20; Quebec, 1651 *9221.17* p243
Fontaine, N. Joseph; New York, NY, 1874 *1494.20* p12
Fontaine, Peter; America, 1882 *5475.1* p137
Fontaine, Pierre; New England, 1686 *9228.50* p226
Fontan, Louis 19; Port uncertain, 1844 *778.6* p120
Fontarabie, Pierre; Quebec, 1645 *9221.17* p155
Fontas, Bertrand 17; Havana, 1845 *778.6* p120
Fontelieu, J. 33; New Orleans, 1848 *778.6* p120
Fontenay, Jane; Boston, 1769 *9228.50* p48
Fontenay, Jane; Boston, n.d. *9228.50* p226
Fonteneau, . . .; Montreal, 1659 *9221.17* p421
Fonteneau, Marie 28; Montreal, 1659 *9221.17* p416
Fonteneau, Marie 28; Montreal, 1659 *9221.17* p416
Fonzen, Joseph 52; New York, NY, 1856 *1766.1* p45
Fooke, John 49; Ontario, 1871 *1823.17* p53
Foot, Jobe 44; Ontario, 1871 *1823.17* p53
Footed, James 41; Ontario, 1871 *1823.21* p117
For, Christopher; Louisiana, 1841-1844 *4981.45* p210
Forbes, Alex 24; New York, NY, 1835 *5024.1* p136
Forbes, Alexander; Colorado, 1883 *1029.59* p29
Forbes, Alexander 40; Ontario, 1871 *1823.17* p53
Forbes, Andrew 33; Indiana, 1885-1894 *9076.20* p74
Forbes, Bill 9; New York, NY, 1835 *5024.1* p136
Forbes, Bill 50; New York, NY, 1835 *5024.1* p136
Forbes, Charles 11; New York, NY, 1835 *5024.1* p136
Forbes, David 50; Ontario, 1871 *1823.17* p53
Forbes, Duncan 65; Ontario, 1871 *1823.21* p117
Forbes, George 45; Ontario, 1871 *1823.17* p53
Forbes, Harry 38; Ontario, 1871 *1823.17* p53
Forbes, Henry; New York, 1778 *8529.30* p11
Forbes, Henry; New York, 1911 *1029.59* p29
Forbes, Henry Fraser; Colorado, 1926 *1029.59* p29
    *Wife:*Mary
Forbes, J. M. 21; Ontario, 1871 *1823.21* p117
Forbes, James 24; Ontario, 1871 *1823.17* p53
Forbes, James 72; Ontario, 1871 *1823.17* p53
Forbes, John 7; New York, NY, 1835 *5024.1* p136
Forbes, John 41; Ontario, 1871 *1823.21* p117
Forbes, John 53; Ontario, 1871 *1823.21* p117
Forbes, John 77; Ontario, 1871 *1823.21* p117
Forbes, Mary SEE Forbes, Henry Fraser
Forbes, Peter; North Carolina, 1852 *1088.45* p10
Forbes, Sarah E. 25; Ontario, 1871 *1823.21* p117
Forbes, Thomas 30; Ontario, 1871 *1823.21* p117
Forbes, Thomas 65; Ontario, 1871 *1823.21* p117
Forbes, Thomas H.; Washington, 1883 *2770.40* p136
Forbes, William 26; Ontario, 1871 *1823.17* p53
Forbes, William 49; Ontario, 1871 *1823.21* p117
Forbis, Duncan 36; Ontario, 1871 *1823.21* p117
Forbs, Mary 11; Ontario, 1871 *1823.21* p117
Ford, Mrs. 50; Ontario, 1871 *1823.21* p117
Ford, Abigail SEE Ford, Thomas
Ford, Albert 27; Ontario, 1871 *1823.21* p117
Ford, Alexander 61; Ontario, 1871 *1823.17* p53
Ford, Celia 40; Ontario, 1871 *1823.21* p117
Ford, Daniel 54; Ontario, 1871 *1823.17* p53
Ford, David 30; Ontario, 1871 *1823.21* p117
Ford, Dennis 30; Ontario, 1871 *1823.17* p53
Ford, Edward J. 73; Ontario, 1871 *1823.21* p117
Ford, Elizabeth SEE Ford, Thomas
Ford, Frederick 16; Quebec, 1870 *8364.32* p23
Ford, G. Henry; Ontario, 1871 *1823.21* p117
Ford, George 34; Ontario, 1871 *1823.17* p53
Ford, Hannah SEE Ford, Thomas
Ford, Hepzibah SEE Ford, Thomas
Ford, Jesse 28; Ontario, 1871 *1823.21* p117
Ford, Jesse 65; Ontario, 1871 *1823.21* p117
Ford, Joanna SEE Ford, Thomas
Ford, John 27; Ontario, 1871 *1823.21* p117
Ford, John 36; Ontario, 1871 *1823.21* p117
Ford, John 53; Ontario, 1871 *1823.21* p117
Ford, John 60; Ontario, 1871 *1823.17* p53
Ford, John; Washington, 1884 *2770.40* p192
Ford, Maria 26; Ontario, 1871 *1823.21* p117
Ford, Mary 53; Michigan, 1880 *4491.33* p9
Ford, Patrick 35; Ontario, 1871 *1823.17* p53
Ford, Susan 38; Ontario, 1871 *1823.17* p53
Ford, Thomas; Massachusetts, 1630 *117.5* p154
    *Wife:*Elizabeth
    *Daughter:*Hannah
    With stepchild
    *Daughter:*Joanna
    *Daughter:*Abigail
    *Daughter:*Hepzibah
Ford, William 53; Michigan, 1880 *4491.33* p9
Ford, William 24; Ontario, 1871 *1823.21* p117
Ford, William 30; Ontario, 1871 *1823.17* p53
Ford, William 39; Ontario, 1871 *1823.17* p53
Ford, William 43; Ontario, 1871 *1823.17* p53
Ford, William 47; Ontario, 1871 *1823.21* p117
Ford, William 73; Ontario, 1871 *1823.17* p53
Forde, Elizabeth 30; Ontario, 1871 *1823.21* p117

Forde, James; New Orleans, 1851 ***7242.30*** *p142*
Forde, Thomas 70; Ontario, 1871 ***1823.21*** *p118*
Forderer, C. P.; Louisiana, 1874 ***4981.45*** *p295*
Fordet, Isaac; Virginia, 1700 ***9230.15*** *p81*
Fordham, John 30; Ontario, 1871 ***1823.21*** *p118*
Fordham, Samuel 71; Ontario, 1871 ***1823.17*** *p53*
Fordham, Susan 35; Ontario, 1871 ***1823.17*** *p53*
Fordyce, George 58; Ontario, 1871 ***1823.21*** *p118*
Foreman, . . .; Ontario, 1871 ***1823.21*** *p118*
Foreman, Jeptha 32; Ontario, 1871 ***1823.21*** *p118*
Foreman, Joseph 45; Ontario, 1871 ***1823.21*** *p118*
Foreman, S. W.; California, 1868 ***1131.61*** *p90*
Forest, Adelaide 12; America, 1847 ***778.6*** *p120*
Forest, Aime 5; America, 1847 ***778.6*** *p120*
Forest, Constance 7; America, 1847 ***778.6*** *p120*
Forest, James 66; Ontario, 1871 ***1823.21*** *p118*
Forest, Joseph 4; America, 1847 ***778.6*** *p120*
Forest, Josephine 13; America, 1847 ***778.6*** *p120*
Forest, Leroy 36; America, 1847 ***778.6*** *p120*
Forest, Rosalie 36; America, 1847 ***778.6*** *p120*
Forestier, Catherine 22; Quebec, 1657 ***9221.17*** *p358*
Forestier, Marie 22; Quebec, 1639 ***9221.17*** *p84*
Forestier, Noel 45; Quebec, 1662 ***9221.17*** *p485*
Forestier, Pierre; Quebec, 1658 ***9221.17*** *p380*
Forge, Achille *SEE* Forge, Jean Baptiste
Forge, Andree *SEE* Forge, Jean Baptiste
Forge, Florian *SEE* Forge, Jean Baptiste
Forge, Jean Baptiste; Wisconsin, 1880 ***1495.20*** *p46*
*Wife:*Leocadie Hody
*Child:*Andree
*Child:*Florian
*Child:*Achille
Forge, Leocadie Hody *SEE* Forge, Jean Baptiste
Forgeat, Charles; Washington, 1885 ***2770.40*** *p194*
Forger, Cevile 35; Ohio, 1880 ***4879.40*** *p260*
Forgerat, Jean 30; Quebec, 1656 ***9221.17*** *p336*
Forgeron, Joseph 28; America, 1846 ***778.6*** *p120*
Forget, . . .; Texas, 1848 ***778.6*** *p120*
Forget, Miss; Texas, 1848 ***778.6*** *p120*
Forget, Charles; Washington, 1885 ***2770.40*** *p194*
Forget, Francoise *SEE* Forget, Renee Guillocheau
Forget, Philippe 22; Texas, 1848 ***778.6*** *p120*
Forget, Renee Guillocheau; Quebec, 1667 ***4514.3*** *p353*
Forget, Renee Guillocheau; Quebec, 1667 ***4514.3*** *p353*
*Daughter:*Francoise
Forgue, Mr. 27; Port uncertain, 1845 ***778.6*** *p120*
Forgus, Mr. 34; America, 1841 ***778.6*** *p120*
Forgy, Joseph; Ohio, 1809-1852 ***4511.35*** *p15*
Forimann, Jacque; New York, 1859 ***358.56*** *p54*
Forissier, Claude 46; New Orleans, 1848 ***778.6*** *p120*
Forke, John; Philadelphia, 1778 ***8529.30*** *p3A*
Forkey, John; Philadelphia, 1778 ***8529.30*** *p3A*
Forknell, Robert 51; Ontario, 1871 ***1823.21*** *p118*
Form, Mary 51; Ontario, 1871 ***1823.21*** *p118*
Formage DesTroymontz, Nicolas; Quebec, 1642 ***9221.17*** *p116*
Forman, Ann 17; Ontario, 1871 ***1823.21*** *p118*
Forman, Elizabeth 60; Ontario, 1871 ***1823.21*** *p118*
Forman, Frank 35; Ontario, 1871 ***1823.21*** *p118*
Forman, Margaret 55; Ontario, 1871 ***1823.17*** *p53*
Forman, Richard J. 40; Ontario, 1871 ***1823.21*** *p118*
Formanek, Vojtech; North Dakota, 1872 ***2853.20*** *p251*
Formanek, Vojtech; Wisconsin, 1857-1861 ***2853.20*** *p334*
Formel, Miss 12; America, 1848 ***778.6*** *p120*
Formel, Mrs. 32; America, 1848 ***778.6*** *p120*
Formel, Jacques 35; New Orleans, 1848 ***778.6*** *p120*
Formerois, Mr. 30; America, 1841 ***778.6*** *p120*
Formerois, Mrs. 25; America, 1841 ***778.6*** *p120*
Formmholz, Emil Friedrich; America, 1883 ***5475.1*** *p37*
Fornander, Carl Victor; Cleveland, OH, 1891-1893 ***9722.10*** *p119*
Fornander, Oscar; Cleveland, OH, 1888-1892 ***9722.10*** *p119*
Fornier, A. 27; New Orleans, 1840 ***778.6*** *p120*
Fornoff, Ludwig; America, 1836 ***2526.42*** *p189*
With wife
With child 8
With child 3
With child 10
Fornoff, Ludwig 19; America, 1851 ***2526.43*** *p221*
Fornoff, Peter; America, 1853 ***2526.43*** *p122*
Fornoff, Peter; Pennsylvania, 1831 ***2526.43*** *p141*
Fornoff, Wilhelm; America, 1841 ***2526.42*** *p135*
With wife 5 sons & child
Foroyce, William 63; Ontario, 1871 ***1823.21*** *p118*
Forrest, Alexander; New York, 1776 ***8529.30*** *p11*
Forrest, Bella 27; Ontario, 1871 ***1823.21*** *p118*
Forrest, James 6; St. John, N.B., 1834 ***6469.7*** *p5*
Forrest, Jane 30; St. John, N.B., 1834 ***6469.7*** *p5*
Forrest, Mary Ann 4; St. John, N.B., 1834 ***6469.7*** *p5*
Forrest, William 1; St. John, N.B., 1834 ***6469.7*** *p5*
Forrestier, E. 23; New Orleans, 1848 ***778.6*** *p120*
Forsander, Arvid; Miami, 1920 ***4984.15*** *p38*
Forsberg, Andrew G.; Kansas, 1879 ***777.40*** *p15*
Forsberg, Erik; St. Paul, MN, 1885-1901 ***1865.50*** *p47*
Forsberg, J.O.; New York, NY, 1855 ***6412.40*** *p153*
Forsberg, John Richard; Colorado, 1891 ***1029.59*** *p29*
Forsberg, P.G.; New York, NY, 1847 ***6412.40*** *p150*
Forsblade, John; Washington, 1888 ***2770.40*** *p25*
Forsburg, John O.; Colorado, 1891 ***1029.59*** *p29*
Forshay, Charles 32; Ontario, 1871 ***1823.17*** *p53*
Forshea, Eleanor; America, 1762 ***1220.12*** *p749*
Forslund, Anna Erickson *SEE* Forslund, Olof
Forslund, Christine C. *SEE* Forslund, Olof
Forslund, Gustav Joel; Cleveland, OH, 1900-1902 ***9722.10*** *p119*
Forslund, Olof; Illinois, 1869 ***777.40*** *p12*
*Wife:*Anna Erickson
*Daughter:*Christine C.
Forslund, Peter 34; Kansas, 1880 ***777.40*** *p20*
Forsman, Ida F.; St. Paul, MN, 1867 ***1865.50*** *p44*
Forssest, James 32; New Orleans, 1848 ***778.6*** *p120*
Forsstrom, G.W.; New York, NY, 1847 ***6412.40*** *p149*
Forstedt, Alfrid; St. Paul, MN, 1874-1905 ***1865.50*** *p47*
*Wife:*Tilda
Forstedt, Tilda *SEE* Forstedt, Alfrid
Forster, Mrs.; Brazil, 1865 ***5475.1*** *p506*
Forster, A. Maria von Ehr 28 *SEE* Forster, Wilhelm
Forster, Anna 47; America, 1846 ***5475.1*** *p401*
Forster, Dorothea 32; Brazil, 1865 ***5475.1*** *p506*
*Son:*Karl
*Daughter:*Dorothea
*Son:*Wilhelm
Forster, Elisabeth; Pittsburgh, 1880 ***5475.1*** *p23*
Forster, Johann, II; Brazil, 1865 ***5475.1*** *p501*
*Son:*Michel
*Son:*Peter
*Daughter:*Maria
Forster, Johann Jakob; Brazil, 1865 ***5475.1*** *p506*
*Wife:*Margarethe Ehly
Forster, John; New Jersey, 1777 ***8529.30*** *p7A*
Forster, John 24; North Carolina, 1774 ***1422.10*** *p55*
Forster, Karl 24; Brazil, 1863 ***5475.1*** *p506*
Forster, Margarethe Ehly 22 *SEE* Forster, Johann Jakob
Forster, Maria *SEE* Forster, Johann, II
Forster, Michel *SEE* Forster, Johann, II
Forster, Nicolaus Friedrich; America, 1868 ***7919.3*** *p525*
Forster, Otto Heinrich Daniel; Port uncertain, 1883 ***7420.1*** *p335*
Forster, Peter *SEE* Forster, Johann, II
Forster, Wilhelm; Brazil, 1864 ***5475.1*** *p501*
*Wife:*A. Maria von Ehr
Forstmann, Christina; America, 1859 ***2526.43*** *p167*
Forstmann, Christina 48; America, 1857 ***2526.43*** *p169*
Forstner, Gottlieb; America, 1892 ***179.55*** *p19*
Forsyth, Alexander 30; Ontario, 1871 ***1823.17*** *p53*
Forsyth, Annie; Colorado, 1884 ***1029.59*** *p29*
Forsyth, Annie 52; Ontario, 1871 ***1823.21*** *p118*
Forsyth, Archibald 50; Ontario, 1871 ***1823.21*** *p118*
Forsyth, Betsey 29; Ontario, 1871 ***1823.21*** *p118*
Forsyth, Bezabeer 22; North Carolina, 1774 ***1422.10*** *p56*
Forsyth, James 70; Ontario, 1871 ***1823.17*** *p53*
Forsyth, Joseph 25; Ontario, 1871 ***1823.17*** *p53*
Forsyth, Margaret 18; Ontario, 1871 ***1823.21*** *p118*
Forsyth, Richmond; Colorado, 1871 ***1029.59*** *p29*
Forsyth, Robert 63; Ontario, 1871 ***1823.21*** *p118*
Forsyth, Samuel A.; Colorado, 1882 ***1029.59*** *p29*
Forsyth, William 20; Ontario, 1871 ***1823.21*** *p118*
Forsyth, William 55; Ontario, 1871 ***1823.21*** *p118*
Forsythe, Bridget McCauley *SEE* Forsythe, Thomas
Forsythe, Gilbert; Nova Scotia, 1741-1800 ***9228.50*** *p108*
*Wife:*Mary Bishop
Forsythe, Mary Bishop *SEE* Forsythe, Gilbert
Forsythe, Mary 22; Ontario, 1871 ***1823.21*** *p118*
Forsythe, Thomas; Pennsylvania, 1858 ***8513.31*** *p307*
*Wife:*Bridget McCauley
Fort, Auguste 43; New York, NY, 1893 ***1883.7*** *p37*
Fort, Emilie 6; New York, NY, 1893 ***1883.7*** *p37*
Fort, Gustav 9; New York, NY, 1893 ***1883.7*** *p37*
Fort, Julius 2; New York, NY, 1893 ***1883.7*** *p37*
Fort, Karl 20; New York, NY, 1893 ***1883.7*** *p37*
Fort, Leo 10; New York, NY, 1893 ***1883.7*** *p37*
Fort, Wilhelm 53; New York, NY, 1893 ***1883.7*** *p37*
Fortanere, Laurent 30; New Orleans, 1848 ***778.6*** *p121*
Fortemps, Marie Anastasie; Wisconsin, 1855 ***1495.20*** *p8*
Fortemps, Marie Josephe Justine; Wisconsin, 1855-1870 ***1495.20*** *p8*
Fortes, A.; New York, 1859 ***358.56*** *p55*
Fortescue, John; New Orleans, 1851 ***7242.30*** *p142*
Forth, William 53; Ontario, 1871 ***1823.21*** *p118*
Fortia DeLafresnaye, Charles; Quebec, 1646 ***9221.17*** *p164*
Fortier, Catherine 22; Quebec, 1657 ***9221.17*** *p358*
Fortin, Francois 15; Quebec, 1654 ***9221.17*** *p308*
Fortin, Jacques; Quebec, 1656 ***9221.17*** *p336*
Fortin, Julien 29; Quebec, 1650 ***9221.17*** *p225*
Fortman, Henry; Ohio, 1840-1897 ***8365.35*** *p16*
Fortmann, George 17; Port uncertain, 1848 ***778.6*** *p121*
Fortmann, Joseph 9; Port uncertain, 1848 ***778.6*** *p121*
Fortmann, Louis 18; Port uncertain, 1848 ***778.6*** *p121*
Fortmann, Magdalena 15; Port uncertain, 1848 ***778.6*** *p121*
Fortmann, Magdalena 45; Port uncertain, 1848 ***778.6*** *p121*
Fortmann, Michel 13; Port uncertain, 1848 ***778.6*** *p121*
Fortmann, Michel 44; Port uncertain, 1848 ***778.6*** *p121*
Fortmiller, Jacob; Ohio, 1809-1852 ***4511.35*** *p15*
Fortner, David 26; Ontario, 1871 ***1823.21*** *p118*
Fortner, James 27; Ontario, 1871 ***1823.21*** *p118*
Fortoul, Henri 18; New Orleans, 1848 ***778.6*** *p121*
Fortune, George 38; Ontario, 1871 ***1823.21*** *p118*
Fortune, Mary 71; Ontario, 1871 ***1823.21*** *p118*
Fortune, Thomas Jim 30; Ontario, 1871 ***1823.21*** *p118*
Foryseski, Felyks; Galveston, TX, 1900 ***6015.15*** *p9*
Forysht, Peter 50; Ontario, 1871 ***1823.21*** *p118*
Foryszewski, Albert; Galveston, TX, 1896 ***6015.15*** *p9*
Foryszewski, Felyks; Galveston, TX, 1900 ***6015.15*** *p9*
Fos, Mr.; New Orleans, 1845 ***778.6*** *p121*
Fos, Bertrand 47; New Orleans, 1845 ***778.6*** *p121*
Fos, Clement; Louisiana, 1874 ***4981.45*** *p295*
Fos, George 14; Ontario, 1871 ***1823.17*** *p54*
Fos, Jacques 69; New Orleans, 1845 ***778.6*** *p121*
Fos, Jean 25; Havana, 1848 ***778.6*** *p121*
Fos, Paul 38; New Orleans, 1845 ***778.6*** *p121*
Fosenbach, Joseph 23; New Orleans, 1847 ***778.6*** *p121*
Foset, Joseph 35; America, 1843 ***778.6*** *p121*
Fosiche, Wm. A.; Louisiana, 1874 ***4981.45*** *p295*
Foss, Maria; America, 1886 ***5475.1*** *p161*
Fosse, Anne 37; Quebec, 1661 ***9221.17*** *p453*
Fosse, Jean; Quebec, 1659 ***9221.17*** *p413*
Fossett, Elis; New Orleans, 1851 ***7242.30*** *p142*
Fossier, Theodule 23; America, 1843 ***778.6*** *p121*
Fossy, G. F. 42; Port uncertain, 1843 ***778.6*** *p121*
Foster, . . .; Charlestown, MA, 1733 ***1642*** *p105*
Foster, Mrs.; Toronto, 1844 ***2910.35*** *p114*
Foster, Alice; Maryland, 1673 ***1236.25*** *p49*
Foster, Caroline 50; Ontario, 1871 ***1823.21*** *p118*
Foster, Charles 30; Ontario, 1871 ***1823.21*** *p119*
Foster, Charles 44; Ontario, 1871 ***1823.17*** *p54*
Foster, Charles J.B. 61; Ontario, 1871 ***1823.21*** *p119*
Foster, Charlote 47; Ontario, 1871 ***1823.17*** *p54*
Foster, Chas 34; Ontario, 1871 ***1823.21*** *p119*
Foster, David 45; Ontario, 1871 ***1823.21*** *p119*
Foster, David 60; Ontario, 1871 ***1823.21*** *p119*
Foster, Edward 38; Ontario, 1871 ***1823.21*** *p119*
Foster, Edward 40; Ontario, 1871 ***1823.21*** *p119*
Foster, Eliza 18; St. John, N.B., 1834 ***6469.7*** *p5*
Foster, Elizabeth 44; Michigan, 1880 ***4491.39*** *p10*
Foster, Ellen 20; Ontario, 1871 ***1823.21*** *p119*
Foster, George 52; Ontario, 1871 ***1823.21*** *p119*
Foster, George, Sr. 63; Ontario, 1871 ***1823.21*** *p119*
Foster, George W.; North Carolina, 1852 ***1088.45*** *p10*
Foster, George W. 32; Ontario, 1871 ***1823.21*** *p119*
Foster, John; Ohio, 1809-1852 ***4511.35*** *p15*
Foster, John 30; Ontario, 1871 ***1823.21*** *p119*
Foster, John 43; Ontario, 1871 ***1823.17*** *p54*
Foster, John 50; Ontario, 1871 ***1823.17*** *p54*
Foster, John 54; Ontario, 1871 ***1823.21*** *p119*
Foster, John 61; Ontario, 1871 ***1823.17*** *p54*
Foster, John; Philadelphia, 1777 ***8529.30*** *p7A*
Foster, John C. 31; Ontario, 1871 ***1823.17*** *p54*
Foster, Joseph 25; Ontario, 1871 ***1823.21*** *p119*
Foster, Joseph 30; Ontario, 1871 ***1823.21*** *p119*
Foster, Joseph 50; Ontario, 1871 ***1823.17*** *p54*
Foster, Joseph 60; Ontario, 1871 ***1823.21*** *p119*
Foster, Michael; Louisiana, 1874-1875 ***4981.45*** *p298*
Foster, Milton 52; Ontario, 1871 ***1823.17*** *p54*
Foster, Patrick; Louisiana, 1874 ***4981.45*** *p295*
Foster, Robert 30; Ontario, 1871 ***1823.21*** *p119*
Foster, Robson 35; Ontario, 1871 ***1823.21*** *p119*
Foster, Samuel; Ohio, 1809-1852 ***4511.35*** *p15*
Foster, Sarah 66; Ontario, 1871 ***1823.21*** *p119*
Foster, Thomas 50; Ontario, 1871 ***1823.21*** *p119*
Foster, Thomas 65; Ontario, 1871 ***1823.21*** *p119*
Foster, William 58; Michigan, 1880 ***4491.30*** *p12*
Foster, Wm.; Louisiana, 1874 ***4981.45*** *p295*
Fostiker, Susanna; Maryland, 1674 ***1236.25*** *p50*
Fotsch, Johann Kaspar; Venezuela, 1843 ***3899.5*** *p543*
Fotsch, Luitgard; Venezuela, 1843 ***3899.5*** *p542*
Foubert, Anne; Quebec, 1670 ***4514.3*** *p314*
Foubert, Marguerite 54; Quebec, 1656 ***9221.17*** *p336*
Foubert, Marie 16 *SEE* Foubert, Marie-Jeffine Riviere
Foubert, Marie-Jeffine 45; Quebec, 1656 ***9221.17*** *p336*
*Daughter:*Marie 16
Foubert, Philippe; Quebec, 1649 ***9221.17*** *p213*
Foubert, Robert 52; Quebec, 1651 ***9221.17*** *p243*
Foucard, Charles Joseph 58; New Orleans, 1848 ***778.6*** *p121*
Foucault, Andre; Quebec, 1659 ***9221.17*** *p401*

Foucault, Etienne; Montreal, 1653 ***9221.17*** *p289*
Foucault, Francois; Montreal, 1653 ***9221.17*** *p289*
Foucault, Francois 30; Quebec, 1661 ***9221.17*** *p456*
Foucek, Karel; Chicago, 1868 ***2853.20*** *p393*
Fouchar, Joseph 48; New Orleans, 1848 ***778.6*** *p121*
Fouchard, Jules 6; America, 1844 ***778.6*** *p121*
Fouchard, Marie 47; America, 1844 ***778.6*** *p121*
Fouchard, Zacharie 52; Quebec, 1655 ***9221.17*** *p324*
Foucher, Jean 31; Quebec, 1657 ***9221.17*** *p358*
Foucherat, Charlotte 24; Quebec, 1662 ***9221.17*** *p485*
Fouchereau, Jean; Montreal, 1644 ***9221.17*** *p146*
Fouchie, Jean; Virginia, 1700 ***9230.15*** *p80*
Fougerat, Mr. 30; Louisiana, 1848 ***778.6*** *p121*
Fougerat, Jules 24; Louisiana, 1848 ***778.6*** *p121*
Fouillade, John 32; America, 1748 ***778.6*** *p121*
Fouilleau, Jacques 23; Quebec, 1657 ***9221.17*** *p358*
Fouin, Eugene 19; New Orleans, 1848 ***778.6*** *p121*
Fouin, Nicolas; Quebec, 1638 ***9221.17*** *p76*
Foulard, Joseph P.; Illinois, 1856 ***6079.1*** *p5*
Foulds, James 40; Ontario, 1871 ***1823.17*** *p54*
Fountain, Charles 48; Ontario, 1871 ***1823.21*** *p119*
Fountaine, Aaron; Maryland, 1671-1672 ***1236.25*** *p45*
Fouquet, Leonarde; Quebec, 1653 ***9221.17*** *p277*
Fouquet, Leonarde; Quebec, 1653 ***9221.17*** *p277*
Fouquet, Marc; Quebec, 1642 ***9221.17*** *p116*
Fouquet, Marie; Quebec, 1671 ***4514.3*** *p314*
Fouquet, Marie Duvall 40; Port uncertain, 1841 ***778.6*** *p121*
Fourcade, Mr. 22; New Orleans, 1840 ***778.6*** *p121*
Fourchet, Josephine 38; Louisiana, 1848 ***778.6*** *p121*
Fourgerel, Frederic 4; New Orleans, 1848 ***778.6*** *p121*
Fourgerel, Louis 32; New Orleans, 1848 ***778.6*** *p121*
Fourgerel, Sophie 27; New Orleans, 1848 ***778.6*** *p121*
Fourman, Charles 51; Ontario, 1871 ***1823.21*** *p119*
Fourman, George 40; Ontario, 1871 ***1823.21*** *p119*
Fourmentin, David; Quebec, 1655 ***9221.17*** *p324*
Fournie, Jean Louis Auguste; Illinois, 1852 ***6079.1*** *p5*
Fournier, Mr. 30; New Orleans, 1848 ***778.6*** *p122*
Fournier, Constant 19; Mississippi, 1847 ***778.6*** *p122*
Fournier, Francois 34; America, 1848 ***778.6*** *p122*
Fournier, Francois; Quebec, 1660 ***9221.17*** *p435*
Fournier, Guillaume 25; Quebec, 1651 ***9221.17*** *p243*
Fournier, Jacques 22; Quebec, 1653 ***9221.17*** *p274*
Fournier, Jean 34; Montreal, 1661 ***9221.17*** *p473*
Fournier, Julie 20; New Orleans, 1848 ***778.6*** *p122*
Fournier, Marie 25; New Orleans, 1848 ***778.6*** *p122*
Fournier, Philippe; Quebec, 1646 ***9221.17*** *p164*
Fournier, Prosper 35; America, 1846 ***778.6*** *p122*
Fournier, Robert; Montreal, 1661 ***9221.17*** *p473*
Fournier deBelleval, Pierre; Quebec, 1688 ***2314.30*** *p172*
Fourniot, Ann 30; New Orleans, 1840 ***778.6*** *p122*
Fourouge, Paul; Louisiana, 1836-1840 ***4981.45*** *p212*
Fourrier, Mr. 22; New Orleans, 1848 ***778.6*** *p122*
Fourrier, Catherine; Quebec, 1670 ***4514.3*** *p314*
Fourrier, Jeanne; Quebec, 1667 ***4514.3*** *p314*
Foust, John 43; Ontario, 1871 ***1823.21*** *p119*
Foustus, Baptist; Ohio, 1809-1852 ***4511.35*** *p15*
Foutcheur, Marie 26; America, 1840 ***778.6*** *p122*
Foutcheur, Pierre 55; America, 1840 ***778.6*** *p122*
Foutos, Elizabeth 75; Ontario, 1871 ***1823.17*** *p54*
Foutrel, Denis 31; Texas, 1843 ***778.6*** *p122*
Fouvreau, Jean; Quebec, 1647 ***9221.17*** *p180*
Fower, Louisa 50; Michigan, 1880 ***4491.30*** *p12*
Fowl, Godfrey; Ohio, 1844 ***2763.1*** *p9*
Fowl, Henry; Ohio, 1842 ***2763.1*** *p9*
Fowle, Isaac; Boston, 1760 ***1642*** *p48*
Fowler, Aseneth 62; OOntario, 1871 ***1823.17*** *p54*
Fowler, Charles 20; Ontario, 1871 ***1823.21*** *p119*
Fowler, Elizabeth 11; Quebec, 1870 ***8364.32*** *p23*
Fowler, Johnson 40; Ontario, 1871 ***1823.17*** *p54*
Fowler, Mary 41; Ontario, 1871 ***1823.17*** *p54*
Fowler, Nathan; Ontario, 1787 ***1276.15*** *p231*
Fowler, Rebecca; Philadelphia, 1874 ***8513.31*** *p301*
Fowler, Robert 27; Ontario, 1871 ***1823.17*** *p54*
Fowler, Robert; Philadelphia, 1778 ***8529.30*** *p3A*
Fowler, Rosanna 20; Ontario, 1871 ***1823.17*** *p54*
Fowler, Sam.; Maryland, 1672 ***1236.25*** *p47*
Fowler, Samuel 42; Ontario, 1871 ***1823.17*** *p54*
Fowler, Wm 60; Ontario, 1871 ***1823.21*** *p119*
Fowles, William; Boston, 1832 ***3274.55*** *p44*
Fowley, Anne Daniel *SEE* Fowley, John
Fowley, John; Ohio, 1832 ***4022.20*** *p280*
*Wife:*Anne Daniel
Fowlks, Louisa 6; Quebec, 1870 ***8364.32*** *p23*
Fox, Adam 50; America, 1853 ***5475.1*** *p277*
*Wife:*Susanna Gaudi
Fox, Allin 63; Ontario, 1871 ***1823.21*** *p119*
Fox, Ann 46; Ontario, 1871 ***1823.21*** *p119*
Fox, Anthony; Ohio, 1809-1852 ***4511.35*** *p15*
Fox, Charles James 36; Ontario, 1871 ***1823.21*** *p119*
Fox, Cornelius; Boston, 1766 ***1642*** *p37*
Fox, Daniel; Detroit, 1930 ***1640.60*** *p76*
Fox, Eli A. 47; Ontario, 1871 ***1823.21*** *p119*
Fox, Eliza 52; Ontario, 1871 ***1823.21*** *p120*
Fox, Ellen 40; Ontario, 1871 ***1823.21*** *p120*
Fox, Esther 60; Ontario, 1871 ***1823.21*** *p120*
Fox, Felix; America, 1864 ***5475.1*** *p237*
Fox, Fred; Kansas, 1917-1918 ***2094.25*** *p50*
Fox, George 46; Ontario, 1871 ***1823.21*** *p120*
Fox, Heinrich 18; New York, 1854 ***5475.1*** *p236*
Fox, James; Marston's Wharf, 1782 ***8529.30*** *p11*
Fox, James 45; Ontario, 1871 ***1823.21*** *p120*
Fox, James 50; Ontario, 1871 ***1823.21*** *p120*
Fox, Jean A.; Louisiana, 1836-1840 ***4981.45*** *p212*
Fox, Johann 27; America, 1856 ***5475.1*** *p323*
Fox, Johann; Wisconsin, 1891 ***5475.1*** *p326*
Fox, John 27; Ontario, 1871 ***1823.21*** *p120*
Fox, John 28; Ontario, 1871 ***1823.21*** *p120*
Fox, Margarethe; America, 1873 ***5475.1*** *p324*
Fox, Margarethe; America, 1880 ***5475.1*** *p240*
Fox, Margarethe 19; America, 1868 ***5475.1*** *p239*
Fox, Margarethe; Wisconsin, 1890 ***5475.1*** *p325*
Fox, Michael 60; Ontario, 1871 ***1823.21*** *p120*
Fox, Patrick; North Carolina, 1824 ***1088.45*** *p10*
Fox, Robert 28; Michigan, 1880 ***4491.30*** *p13*
Fox, Robert 49; Ontario, 1871 ***1823.21*** *p120*
Fox, Susanna Gaudi *SEE* Fox, Adam
Fox, Tabitha 39; Ontario, 1871 ***1823.21*** *p120*
Fox, Thomas; Marston's Wharf, 1782 ***8529.30*** *p11*
Foxton, Robert 41; Ontario, 1871 ***1823.21*** *p120*
Foxworthy, Samuel 22; Ontario, 1871 ***1823.21*** *p120*
Foy, James; Toronto, 1844 ***2910.35*** *p112*
Foy, Jeffery; Boston, 1676 ***9228.50*** *p228*
Foy, John; Boston, 1671 ***9228.50*** *p228*
Foy, Marguerite; Quebec, 1667 ***4514.3*** *p314*
Foy, Mrs. P.; Toronto, 1844 ***2910.35*** *p114*
Foye, Elizabeth; Boston, 1748 ***1642*** *p46*
Foye, Susannah; America, 1775 ***9228.50*** *p227*
Foye, William; Salem, MA, 1745-1776 ***9228.50*** *p227*
Foyere, Giovani 50; Port uncertain, 1841 ***778.6*** *p122*
Foyle, Judith Sally *SEE* Foyle, Thomas
Foyle, Thomas; Halifax, N.S., 1827 ***7009.9*** *p62*
*Wife:*Judith Sally
Foylings, Peter; Marston's Wharf, 1782 ***8529.30*** *p11*
Foynton, Anna 61; Michigan, 1880 ***4491.33*** *p9*
Foynton, George 67; Michigan, 1880 ***4491.33*** *p9*
Fra, Adelaide 35; America, 1847 ***778.6*** *p122*
Fracer, Ewald; Illinois, 1854 ***6079.1*** *p5*
Fracsch, Anton 37; America, 1841 ***778.6*** *p122*
Frain, Richo 23; Ontario, 1871 ***1823.17*** *p54*
Fraise, Pierre 20; America, 1848 ***778.6*** *p122*
Fraizer, B. 27; New Orleans, 1845 ***778.6*** *p122*
Fraley, Thos; New Orleans, 1850 ***7242.30*** *p142*
Fralrey, Thos; New Orleans, 1850 ***7242.30*** *p142*
Fram, William 68; Ontario, 1871 ***1823.21*** *p120*
Frame, Alex 27; Ontario, 1871 ***1823.17*** *p54*
Frame, David 31; Ontario, 1871 ***1823.17*** *p54*
Frampton, William; America, 1773 ***1220.12*** *p630*
Franc, Eliza 30; America, 1848 ***778.6*** *p122*
France, Edward; Boston, 1767 ***1642*** *p39*
France, Jacob; Ohio, 1809-1852 ***4511.35*** *p15*
France, John; Ohio, 1809-1852 ***4511.35*** *p15*
France, Lewis; Ohio, 1809-1852 ***4511.35*** *p15*
France, Maria 10; Quebec, 1870 ***8364.32*** *p23*
France, Meniquette 30; New Orleans, 1845 ***778.6*** *p122*
Frances, Henry; Philadelphia, 1777 ***8529.30*** *p7A*
Franceschi, B. 40; America, 1846 ***778.6*** *p122*
Franceschi, M. 18; America, 1846 ***778.6*** *p122*
Francez, Jacques 25; Missouri, 1845 ***778.6*** *p122*
Francez, Joseph 24; Port uncertain, 1842 ***778.6*** *p122*
Franch, Mr. 24; America, 1847 ***778.6*** *p122*
Francheteau, Jean; Quebec, 1642 ***9221.17*** *p116*
Franchetot, Mathurin; Quebec, 1650 ***9221.17*** *p225*
Franchomte, Moise G.; New Castle, DE, 1817-1818 ***90.20*** *p151*
Francis, . . . 33; Ontario, 1871 ***1823.21*** *p120*
Francis, Abraham 56; Ontario, 1871 ***1823.21*** *p120*
Francis, Alex. 26; America, 1841 ***778.6*** *p122*
Francis, Alexander Thomas *SEE* Francis, Daniel
Francis, Daniel *SEE* Francis, Daniel
Francis, Daniel; Baltimore, 1799-1806 ***9228.50*** *p228*
*Wife:*Rachel Le Messurier
*Child:*Alexander Thomas
*Child:*Peter
*Child:*Daniel
*Child:*Nicholas
*Child:*Elizabeth
*Child:*Judith
*Child:*Jean
*Child:*Susanna
Francis, Daniel; Ohio, 1800-1817 ***9228.50*** *p31*
*Son:*Nicholas
Francis, Daniel de; Norfolk, VA, 1806 ***9228.50*** *p56*
With family
Francis, Ebenezer *SEE* Francis, Judith
Francis, Edward 30; Ontario, 1871 ***1823.21*** *p120*
Francis, Elisabeth 5; Missouri, 1845 ***778.6*** *p122*
Francis, Elisabeth 37; Missouri, 1845 ***778.6*** *p122*
Francis, Elizabeth *SEE* Francis, Daniel
Francis, George 3; Missouri, 1845 ***778.6*** *p122*
Francis, George 45; Missouri, 1845 ***778.6*** *p122*
Francis, Jane 35; America, 1848 ***778.6*** *p122*
Francis, Jean *SEE* Francis, Daniel
Francis, John 17; America, 1848 ***778.6*** *p122*
Francis, John Glan; Ohio, 1840-1897 ***8365.35*** *p16*
Francis, John J. 37; Ontario, 1871 ***1823.17*** *p54*
Francis, Judith *SEE* Francis, Daniel
Francis, Judith; Massachusetts, 1700-1799 ***9228.50*** *p231*
*Relative:*Ebenezer
Francis, Nicholas *SEE* Francis, Daniel
Francis, Nicholas *SEE* Francis, Daniel
Francis, Peter *SEE* Francis, Daniel
Francis, Rachel Le Messurier *SEE* Francis, Daniel
Francis, Robt 36; Ontario, 1871 ***1823.21*** *p120*
Francis, Stephen; Ohio, 1809-1852 ***4511.35*** *p15*
Francis, Susanna *SEE* Francis, Daniel
Francis, Thomas 9; America, n.d. ***9228.50*** *p228*
With parents brothers & sisters
Francis, Wm.; Ohio, 1798-1881 ***9228.50*** *p231*
Francisco, Alexis; Louisiana, 1874 ***4981.45*** *p131*
Francisco, Joseph; Washington, 1882 ***2770.40*** *p135*
Franck, Elisabetha 25 *SEE* Franck, Georg Wilhelm
Franck, Georg 23 *SEE* Franck, Georg Wilhelm
Franck, Georg Wilhelm 54; America, 1854 ***2526.43*** *p147*
*Wife:*Katharina Elisabetha Hubner 55
*Daughter:*Margaretha 28
*Son:*Georg 23
*Daughter:*Sophie 18
*Daughter:*Elisabetha 25
Franck, John Martin; North Carolina, 1710 ***3629.40*** *p4*
Franck, Katharina Elisabetha Hubner 55 *SEE* Franck, Georg Wilhelm
Franck, Margaretha 28 *SEE* Franck, Georg Wilhelm
Franck, Sophie 18 *SEE* Franck, Georg Wilhelm
Franck, Therese 26; Mississippi, 1848 ***778.6*** *p122*
Franck, Xavier 25; Mississippi, 1848 ***778.6*** *p123*
Francke, Arthur; Valdivia, Chile, 1852 ***1192.4*** *p53*
Francke, Richard; Valdivia, Chile, 1852 ***1192.4*** *p53*
Francoeur, Claude 20; Quebec, 1646 ***9221.17*** *p162*
Francois, . . .; Quebec, 1642 ***9221.17*** *p121*
Francois, Mr. 24; America, 1846 ***778.6*** *p123*
Francois, Mr. 24; New Orleans, 1840 ***778.6*** *p123*
Francois, Antoine 28; America, 1842 ***778.6*** *p123*
Francois, Barbaaria 28; America, 1847 ***778.6*** *p123*
Francois, Claude 35; America, 1847 ***778.6*** *p123*
Francois, Claude 30; New Orleans, 1848 ***778.6*** *p123*
Francois, Guillaume Eugene 23; America, 1747 ***778.6*** *p123*
Francois, Henriette 6; America, 1847 ***778.6*** *p123*
Francois, Hyacinthe 20; America, 1846 ***778.6*** *p123*
Francois, J. D. 55; America, 1847 ***778.6*** *p123*
Francois, Jean Claude 38; America, 1847 ***778.6*** *p123*
Francois, Joseph 31; America, 1847 ***778.6*** *p123*
Francois, Joseph 45; Port uncertain, 1843 ***778.6*** *p124*
Francois, Laurent 8; America, 1847 ***778.6*** *p123*
Francois, Leonie 2; America, 1842 ***778.6*** *p123*
Francois, Margarette 5; America, 1847 ***778.6*** *p123*
Francois, Marie 31; New Orleans, 1848 ***778.6*** *p123*
Francois, Marie 45; Port uncertain, 1843 ***778.6*** *p124*
Francois, Marieanne 25; America, 1842 ***778.6*** *p123*
Francois, Martin 25; New Orleans, 1848 ***778.6*** *p123*
Francois, Pe.er 3; America, 1847 ***778.6*** *p123*
Francois, Theophile 18; America, 1846 ***778.6*** *p123*
Francoisse, Moise G.; New Castle, DE, 1817-1818 ***90.20*** *p151*
Francy, Wm.; Ohio, 1798-1881 ***9228.50*** *p231*
Franczak, Piotr 29; New York, NY, 1920 ***930.50*** *p48*
Franer, Adele 9; America, 1847 ***778.6*** *p123*
Franer, Alexandre 8; America, 1847 ***778.6*** *p123*
Franer, Jeanne 45; America, 1847 ***778.6*** *p123*
Franer, Josephine 3; America, 1847 ***778.6*** *p123*
Franer, Marie 4; America, 1847 ***778.6*** *p123*
Franey, Bridget; New Orleans, 1850 ***7242.30*** *p142*
Franey, Bridget; New Orleans, 1850 ***7242.30*** *p142*
Franey, Catherine; New Orleans, 1850 ***7242.30*** *p142*
Franey, Joseph; New Orleans, 1850 ***7242.30*** *p142*
Franey, Patrick; New Orleans, 1850 ***7242.30*** *p142*
Franey, Patt; New Orleans, 1850 ***7242.30*** *p142*
Franey, Stephen; New Orleans, 1850 ***7242.30*** *p142*
Frank, Abraham; America, 1887 ***2526.43*** *p167*
Frank, Anna 16; America, 1855 ***5475.1*** *p352*
*Brother:*Augustin 13
Frank, August; Wisconsin, 1869 ***6795.8*** *p123*
Frank, Augustin 13 *SEE* Frank, Anna
Frank, Carl A.; Wisconsin, 1871 ***6795.8*** *p154*
Frank, Carl August; Wisconsin, 1895 ***6795.8*** *p217*
Frank, Christian; Ohio, 1809-1852 ***4511.35*** *p15*
Frank, Dawid 26; Portland, ME, 1906 ***970.38*** *p77*
Frank, Ferdinand; Wisconsin, 1876 ***6795.8*** *p167*

Frank, Franz 23; New York, NY, 1905 *8425.16 p34*
Frank, Frederick 63; Ontario, 1871 *1823.17 p54*
Frank, George 22; Ontario, 1871 *1823.21 p120*
Frank, George; Quebec, 1870 *8364.32 p23*
Frank, Harriette 21; Ontario, 1871 *1823.21 p120*
Frank, Herman; Wisconsin, 1884 *6795.8 p89*
Frank, Isaac 18; America, 1846 *778.6 p123*
Frank, Jacob; Ohio, 1809-1852 *4511.35 p15*
Frank, Jakob; America, 1880 *179.55 p19*
Frank, James; Chicago, 1930 *121.35 p100*
Frank, John; Ohio, 1809-1852 *4511.35 p15*
Frank, Josef; America, 1882 *5475.1 p148*
Frank, L.; Louisiana, 1841-1844 *4981.45 p210*
Frank, Ladislav; New York, NY, 1889 *2853.20 p116*
Frank, Madeleine 16; America, 1846 *778.6 p123*
Frank, Maria 20; Portland, ME, 1906 *970.38 p77*
Frank, Mathis; America, 1868 *5475.1 p297*
Frank, Meier; America, 1868 *7919.3 p525*
Frank, Michal 18; America, 1843 *778.6 p123*
Frank, Peter 18; America, 1854 *5475.1 p352*
Frank, Richard 69; Ontario, 1871 *1823.21 p120*
Frank, Ricke; America, 1867 *7919.3 p534*
Frank, Robert 70; Ontario, 1871 *1823.21 p120*
Frank, Rosalie; America, 1868 *7919.3 p525*
Frank, Sarah 65; Ontario, 1871 *1823.21 p120*
Frank, Sophie; America, 1867 *7919.3 p525*
Frank, Th.; New York, 1860 *358.56 p5*
Frank, Theodor; America, 1893 *2526.43 p167*
Frank, Therese; America, 1858 *2526.43 p147*
Frank, Urban 26; New Orleans, 1847 *778.6 p123*
Frank, William; North Carolina, 1710 *3629.40 p4*
Franke, . . .; Port uncertain, 1839 *7420.1 p16*
Franke, Andrew Christian; Ohio, 1809-1852 *4511.35 p15*
Franke, Barbara SEE Franke, Herm. Leopold
Franke, Barbara Schleich SEE Franke, Herm. Leopold
Franke, C.; America, 1856 *7420.1 p147*
Franke, Carl Friedrich Wilhelm; America, 1885 *7420.1 p399*
Franke, Christian Wilhelm; America, 1864 *7420.1 p223*
Franke, Engel Sophie Caroline; America, 1864 *7420.1 p223*
Franke, Friedrich August Isidor Udo; America, 1868 *7919.3 p531*
Franke, Georg SEE Franke, Herm. Leopold
Franke, Gottlieb; Wisconsin, 1875 *6795.8 p38*
Franke, Heinrich Conrad; America, 1852 *7420.1 p88*
  With son & 2 daughters
Franke, Heinrich Gottlieb; America, 1888 *7420.1 p356*
Franke, Henry; Galveston, TX, 1855 *571.7 p16*
Franke, Herm. Leopold; America, 1873 *5475.1 p161*
  *Wife:*Barbara Schleich
  *Son:*Jakob
  *Daughter:*Barbara
  *Son:*Georg
  *Son:*Nikolaus
Franke, Jakob SEE Franke, Herm. Leopold
Franke, Lawrence 23; Ontario, 1871 *1823.17 p54*
Franke, Max; America, 1868 *7420.1 p271*
Franke, Nikolaus SEE Franke, Herm. Leopold
Franke, Sophie Louise Caroline; America, 1865 *7420.1 p231*
Franken, Joseph 11; Galveston, TX, 1844 *3967.10 p375*
Franken, Kaspar 45; Galveston, TX, 1844 *3967.10 p375*
Franken, Katharina 13; Galveston, TX, 1844 *3967.10 p375*
Franken, Philipp 9; Galveston, TX, 1844 *3967.10 p375*
Frankenstein, Babette; America, 1858 *2526.43 p167*
Frankenthall, Henry; North Carolina, 1856 *1088.45 p10*
Frankfort, Moses; North Carolina, 1853 *1088.45 p10*
Frankfourt, Ben; Texas, 1903 *3435.45 p35*
Frankhanel, Arthur Paul; Wisconsin, 1902 *6795.8 p157*
Franklin, Dominic 58; Ontario, 1871 *1823.21 p121*
Franklin, Isaac 19; Ontario, 1871 *1823.21 p121*
Franklin, Joseph 35; Ontario, 1871 *1823.21 p121*
Franklin, Scott 21; Ontario, 1871 *1823.21 p121*
Franklin, William; Boston, 1739 *8529.30 p6*
Franklin, William 17; Quebec, 1870 *8364.32 p23*
Franks, Charles 19; Quebec, 1870 *8364.32 p23*
Franks, James 23; Indiana, 1855-1860 *9076.20 p65*
Franks, John 27; Ontario, 1871 *1823.21 p121*
Franks, Peter; Philadelphia, 1778 *8529.30 p3A*
Franks, Thomas; North America, 1750 *1640.8 p233*
Franquet, Jeanne 27; America, 1843 *778.6 p123*
Frantz, Anna; America, 1882 *5475.1 p214*
Frantz, Eleonore SEE Frantz, Georg Heinrich
Frantz, Eleonore Eck SEE Frantz, Georg Heinrich
Frantz, Elisabeth; America, 1886 *5475.1 p423*
Frantz, Friedrich; New York, NY, 1882 *5475.1 p15*
Frantz, Georg Heinrich; New York, NY, 1881 *5475.1 p15*
  *Wife:*Eleonore Eck
  *Son:*Heinrich
  *Daughter:*Eleonore

Frantz, Heinrich SEE Frantz, Georg Heinrich
Frantz, Joseph; Ohio, 1809-1852 *4511.35 p15*
Franz, Anna Maria; America, 1873 *5475.1 p249*
Franz, Anna Minnie Emilie; Wisconsin, 1884 *6795.8 p72*
Franz, Barbara; New York, 1859 *358.56 p54*
Franz, Bernhard; New York, 1859 *358.56 p100*
Franz, Elizabeth 18; America, 1845 *778.6 p123*
Franz, Friedr. Ernst Adolf; New York, 1865 *5475.1 p120*
Franz, Hermann; Wisconsin, 1886 *6795.8 p72*
Franz, Hermon; North Carolina, 1854 *1088.45 p10*
Franz, Jacob; Ohio, 1809-1852 *4511.35 p15*
Franz, Margarethe; Chicago, 1892 *5475.1 p77*
Franz, Nikolaus; New York, 1887 *5475.1 p131*
Franzel, Caroline Pauline; Indianapolis, 1858 *7420.1 p177*
Franzen, Anna Maria 27 SEE Franzen, Peter
Franzen, Barbara 22 SEE Franzen, Peter
Franzen, Elisabeth SEE Franzen, Johann
Franzen, Elisabeth Zeimet SEE Franzen, Johann
Franzen, Johann; America, 1871 *5475.1 p262*
  *Wife:*Elisabeth Zeimet
  *Son:*Peter
  *Son:*M. Josef
  *Daughter:*Elisabeth
  *Son:*Mathias
Franzen, Johann 60; America, 1843 *5475.1 p247*
Franzen, Karl; Cleveland, OH, 1901-1903 *9722.10 p119*
Franzen, M. Josef SEE Franzen, Johann
Franzen, Mathias SEE Franzen, Johann
Franzen, Peter; America, 1857 *5475.1 p258*
  *Sister:*Anna Maria
  *Sister:*Barbara
Franzen, Peter SEE Franzen, Johann
Franzlau, . . .; America, 1853 *7420.1 p104*
  With family
Franzmann, Christian SEE Franzmann, Jakob Karl
Franzmann, Ernst SEE Franzmann, Jakob Karl
Franzmann, Jakob Karl; Brazil, 1865 *5475.1 p507*
  *Wife:*Maria Margarethe Mohr
  *Son:*Ernst
  *Son:*Christian
  *Son:*Rudolph
  *Son:*Philipp
Franzmann, Johann Wilhelm; America, 1864 *5475.1 p503*
Franzmann, Maria Margarethe Mohr SEE Franzmann, Jakob Karl
Franzmann, Philipp SEE Franzmann, Jakob Karl
Franzmann, Rudolph SEE Franzmann, Jakob Karl
Frappin, Sebast. 18; America, 1847 *778.6 p124*
Frapwell, William; Philadelphia, 1777 *8529.30 p3A*
Fraser, Alexander 46; Ontario, 1871 *1823.21 p121*
Fraser, Alexander 52; Ontario, 1871 *1823.21 p121*
Fraser, Alexander 55; Ontario, 1871 *1823.21 p121*
Fraser, Alexander; Washington, 1887 *2770.40 p24*
Fraser, Alexander U. 17; Ontario, 1871 *1823.21 p121*
Fraser, Angus 47; Ontario, 1871 *1823.21 p121*
Fraser, Angus 55; Ontario, 1871 *1823.21 p121*
Fraser, Ann 62; Ontario, 1871 *1823.17 p54*
Fraser, Ann 75; Ontario, 1871 *1823.21 p121*
Fraser, Anna Young; California, 1892-1893 *9228.50 p185*
Fraser, Anna Young; Victoria, B.C., 1873-1892 *9228.50 p185*
Fraser, Catharine; New York, 1738 *8277.31 p115*
Fraser, Catharine SEE Fraser, Robert
Fraser, Charles SEE Fraser, Robert
Fraser, Christine; Alabama, 1846-1876 *9228.50 p341*
Fraser, Colin; Quebec, 1786 *1416.15 p8*
Fraser, Dal. 60; Ontario, 1871 *1823.17 p54*
Fraser, Daniel; Washington, 1881 *2770.40 p135*
Fraser, Daniel; Washington, 1889 *2770.40 p27*
Fraser, David 28; Ontario, 1871 *1823.21 p121*
Fraser, David 43; Ontario, 1871 *1823.21 p121*
Fraser, Donald; North Carolina, 1854 *1088.45 p10*
Fraser, Donald 26; Ontario, 1871 *1823.17 p54*
Fraser, Donald 28; Ontario, 1871 *1823.21 p121*
Fraser, Donald 51; Ontario, 1871 *1823.17 p54*
Fraser, Donald 65; Ontario, 1871 *1823.21 p121*
Fraser, Donald 68; Ontario, 1871 *1823.21 p121*
Fraser, Duncan 50; New York, NY, 1894 *6512.1 p229*
Fraser, Finlay 60; Ontario, 1871 *1823.21 p121*
Fraser, Grace 78; Ontario, 1871 *1823.21 p121*
Fraser, Hugh 63; Ontario, 1871 *1823.21 p121*
Fraser, Hugh 83; Ontario, 1871 *1823.21 p121*
Fraser, Isabel SEE Fraser, Robert
Fraser, James 24; Ontario, 1871 *1823.21 p121*
Fraser, James 50; Ontario, 1871 *1823.21 p121*
Fraser, Jane 35; Ontario, 1871 *1823.21 p121*
Fraser, Jane 61; Ontario, 1871 *1823.21 p121*
Fraser, Janet 70; Ontario, 1871 *1823.21 p121*
Fraser, John 21; Ontario, 1871 *1823.21 p121*
Fraser, John 24; Ontario, 1871 *1823.21 p121*

Fraser, John 63; Ontario, 1871 *1823.21 p121*
Fraser, John 66; Ontario, 1871 *1823.21 p121*
Fraser, John; Philadelphia, 1778 *8529.30 p7A*
Fraser, John R. 22; Ontario, 1871 *1823.21 p121*
Fraser, Joseph; North Carolina, 1838 *1088.45 p10*
Fraser, Maggie 28; New York, NY, 1894 *6512.1 p229*
Fraser, Margaret 71; Ontario, 1871 *1823.21 p121*
Fraser, Mary SEE Fraser, Robert
Fraser, Mary McLean SEE Fraser, Robert
Fraser, Robert; New York, 1739 *8277.31 p115*
  *Wife:*Mary McLean
  *Child:*Catharine
  *Child:*Mary
  *Child:*Isabel
  *Child:*Sarah
  *Child:*Charles
Fraser, S. M. 40; Ontario, 1871 *1823.21 p121*
Fraser, Sara; New York, 1739 *8277.31 p114*
Fraser, Sarah SEE Fraser, Robert
Fraser, Sarah 70; Ontario, 1871 *1823.21 p121*
Fraser, Simon 44; Ontario, 1871 *1823.17 p54*
Fraser, Simon 50; Ontario, 1871 *1823.21 p121*
Fraser, Thomas 23; Ontario, 1871 *1823.21 p121*
Fraser, Thomas 54; Ontario, 1871 *1823.21 p121*
Fraser, William 12; Ontario, 1871 *1823.17 p54*
Fraser, William 34; Ontario, 1871 *1823.21 p121*
Fraser, William 36; Ontario, 1871 *1823.21 p121*
Fraser, William 37; Ontario, 1871 *1823.17 p54*
Fraser, William 42; Ontario, 1871 *1823.21 p122*
Fraser, William 55; Ontario, 1871 *1823.17 p55*
Fraser, William 79; Ontario, 1871 *1823.21 p122*
Fraser, William G. 30; Ontario, 1871 *1823.17 p55*
Fraser, William George 39; Ontario, 1871 *1823.17 p55*
Fraser, William W.; Colorado, 1896 *1029.59 p30*
Frasier, Robert 40; Ontario, 1871 *1823.17 p55*
Fraso, Michael; Ohio, 1809-1852 *4511.35 p15*
Frauenheim, Otto; Colorado, 1894 *1029.59 p30*
Frawinska, Julianna; Detroit, 1890 *9980.23 p96*
Frawley, Ellen 34; Michigan, 1880 *4491.30 p13*
Frawley, Martin 43; Michigan, 1880 *4491.30 p13*
Frawley, Sarah 80; Michigan, 1880 *4491.30 p13*
Fray, Armand; Wisconsin, 1854-1858 *1495.20 p66*
  *Wife:*Josephine Albert
  *Daughter:*Marie Genevieve
  With stepchild
Fray, Emily 7; Ontario, 1871 *1823.17 p55*
Fray, Josephine Albert SEE Fray, Armand
Fray, Marie Genevieve SEE Fray, Armand
Fray, Ruben 63; Ontario, 1871 *1823.21 p122*
Frayn, Richard 46; Ontario, 1871 *1823.17 p55*
Frayne, Samuel 36; Ontario, 1871 *1823.21 p122*
Frayney, John; Newfoundland, 1814 *3476.10 p54*
Frayzer, Robert; Jamaica, 1777 *8529.30 p13A*
Frazer, Alex 56; Ontario, 1871 *1823.17 p55*
Frazer, Alexander 66; Ontario, 1871 *1823.21 p122*
Frazer, Caroline 21; Toronto, 1865 *9228.50 p231*
Frazer, George 33; Ontario, 1871 *1823.21 p122*
Frazer, Isabella 65; Ontario, 1871 *1823.21 p122*
Frazer, James; Philadelphia, 1778 *8529.30 p2*
Frazer, Philip 45; Ontario, 1871 *1823.17 p55*
Frazer, Robert; Jamaica, 1777 *8529.30 p13A*
Frazier, Catherine 67; Ontario, 1871 *1823.21 p122*
Frazier, George; Washington, 1886 *2770.40 p195*
Frazier, Thomas 32; Ontario, 1871 *1823.21 p122*
Frazier, William 39; Ontario, 1871 *1823.21 p122*
Freakley, John S.; North Carolina, 1840 *1088.45 p10*
Freapleton, Charles 28; Ontario, 1871 *1823.21 p122*
Frearly, William 61; Ontario, 1871 *1823.21 p122*
Frebart, Ernst; Wisconsin, 1900 *6795.8 p201*
Frebel, Ludwig; America, 1868 *7919.3 p526*
Freberg, Gustav; Iowa, 1889 *1211.15 p10*
Frechard, Jean 22; America, 1843 *778.6 p124*
Freche, Jean Louis 20; New Orleans, 1845 *778.6 p124*
Frechon, Eulalie Rose 25; America, 1847 *778.6 p124*
Frechon, Philippe 33; America, 1847 *778.6 p124*
Frechou, Mr. 21; America, 1747 *778.6 p124*
Freckenstein, A.; Nebraska, 1905 *3004.30 p46*
Frecker, George; New York, 1850-1934 *9228.50 p232*
  *Wife:*Harriet Norman
  With daughter
Frecker, Harriet Norman SEE Frecker, George
Freckmann, Heinrich; Chile, 1852 *1192.4 p52*
Fredberg, Ellen; St. Paul, MN, 1887 *1865.50 p47*
Fredberg, Olof J.; St. Paul, MN, 1883 *1865.50 p47*
Fredeking, Heinrich Wilhelm; America, 1882 *7420.1 p328*
Fredell, Alfred; Minneapolis, 1882-1884 *1865.50 p47*
Fredell, Kerstin; Minnesota, 1882-1883 *1865.50 p47*
Frederic, Antonio; Louisiana, 1836-1840 *4981.45 p212*
Frederic, Johann 23; Galveston, TX, 1844 *3967.10 p372*
Frederick, John 27; New Orleans, 1842 *778.6 p124*
Frederickson, Christina SEE Frederickson, George C.

Frederickson, Elizabeth 5 *SEE* Frederickson, George C.
Frederickson, George C.; Denver, CO, 1918 *1029.59 p30*
  *Wife:*Christina
  *Child:*Elizabeth
  *Child:*Harold
Frederickson, Harold 2 *SEE* Frederickson, George C.
Frederickson, James C.; Colorado, 1882 *1029.59 p30*
Fredine, Andrew; Washington, 1888 *2770.40 p25*
Frediver, Havier 28; New York, NY, 1847 *9176.15 p51*
Fredman, Perry; New York, NY, 1894 *3665.20 p111*
Fredrich, Albert; Wisconsin, 1884 *6795.8 p225*
Fredrich, Auguste Wilhelmine Bertha; Wisconsin, 1893 *6795.8 p148*
Fredrich, Julius; Wisconsin, 1883 *6795.8 p193*
Free, George; Ohio, 1809-1852 *4511.35 p15*
Free, Martin; Louisiana, 1874-1875 *4981.45 p298*
Freed, James; Washington, 1886 *2770.40 p195*
Freedburg, Ellen; St. Paul, MN, 1887 *1865.50 p47*
Freedburg, Olof J.; St. Paul, MN, 1883 *1865.50 p47*
Freedlund, Carl Magnus; Illinois, 1871-1880 *1865.50 p48*
Freedman, Joseph; Ohio, 1809-1852 *4511.35 p15*
Freedman, Mathias; Ohio, 1809-1852 *4511.35 p15*
Freedman, Saul; Illinois, 1930 *121.35 p100*
Freek, Johann Carl Wilhelm; America, 1868 *7420.1 p271*
Freel, Edward; Toronto, 1844 *2910.35 p115*
Freel, Patrick; Toronto, 1844 *2910.35 p115*
Freeland, James; Lexington, MA, 1740 *1642 p107*
Freeland, William; Boston, 1737 *1642 p26*
Freeland, William I. 32; Ontario, 1871 *1823.21 p122*
Freele, Hugh 37; Ontario, 1871 *1823.21 p122*
Freele, William 62; Ontario, 1871 *1823.21 p122*
Freeman, . . .; Ontario, n.d. *9228.50 p232*
Freeman, Dorothea May; Ontario, 1957 *9228.50 p270*
Freeman, George 50; Ontario, 1871 *1823.21 p122*
Freeman, Henry 21; Ontario, 1871 *1823.21 p122*
Freeman, J. 45; Ontario, 1871 *1823.21 p122*
Freeman, James; Lexington, MA, 1740 *1642 p106*
Freeman, James 38; Ontario, 1871 *1823.21 p122*
Freeman, John; Ontario, 1871 *1823.21 p122*
Freeman, William; Marston's Wharf, 1782 *8529.30 p11*
Freeman, William 51; Ontario, 1871 *1823.21 p122*
Frees, William; Iowa, 1876 *1211.15 p10*
Freeser, John; Ohio, 1809-1852 *4511.35 p15*
Freeto, . . .; Marblehead, MA, n.d. *9228.50 p232*
Freeto, John; North America, 1807 *9228.50 p233*
Freeto, Manuel; Marblehead, MA, 1776 *9228.50 p233*
Frehe, Heinrich Wilhelm; America, 1881 *7420.1 p398*
Frehe, Sophie Marie; America, 1890 *7420.1 p400*
Frei, Charles; New York, 1860 *358.56 p150*
Frei, Daniel 25; Chicago, 1800-1899 *5475.1 p380*
Frei, Ferdinand; Wisconsin, 1858 *6795.8 p100*
Frei, Margarethe 51; Brazil, 1862 *5475.1 p369*
Frei, Yorick 20; New York, NY, 1874 *6954.7 p37*
Freiberger, Jakob *SEE* Freiberger, Mathias
Freiberger, Johann; Brazil, 1853 *5475.1 p439*
Freiberger, Johann *SEE* Freiberger, Mathias
Freiberger, Katharina *SEE* Freiberger, Mathias
Freiberger, Katharina Backes 43 *SEE* Freiberger, Mathias
Freiberger, Maria *SEE* Freiberger, Mathias
Freiberger, Mathias *SEE* Freiberger, Mathias
Freiberger, Mathias; Brazil, 1879 *5475.1 p444*
  *Wife:*Katharina Backes
  *Son:*Mathias
  *Son:*Jakob
  *Son:*Nikolaus
  *Son:*Michel
  *Daughter:*Maria
  *Son:*Johann
  *Daughter:*Katharina
Freiberger, Michel *SEE* Freiberger, Mathias
Freiberger, Nikolaus *SEE* Freiberger, Mathias
Freichel, Anna Maria; Chicago, 1894 *5475.1 p156*
Freid, Levi 43; Ontario, 1871 *1823.21 p122*
Freidmeyer, Charles; Ohio, 1809-1852 *4511.35 p15*
Freiheit, Wilhelm; Wisconsin, 1887 *6795.8 p128*
Freimuth, Ernst 20; New York, NY, 1864 *8425.62 p197*
Freimuth, Louise 26; New York, NY, 1864 *8425.62 p197*
Freir, Leon 21; New York, NY, 1893 *1883.7 p40*
Freise, Carl Friedrich Christian; America, 1892 *7420.1 p365*
Freise, Dorothee Caroline Wilhelmine *SEE* Freise, Friedrich Ludwig
Freise, Dorothee Eleonore *SEE* Freise, Friedrich Ludwig
Freise, Friedrich Ludwig; America, 1857 *7420.1 p161*
  With wife
  *Daughter:*Sophie Louise Charlotte
  *Daughter:*Dorothee Caroline Wilhelmine
  *Granddaughter:*Sophie Charlotte
  *Daughter:*Dorothee Eleonore

Freise, Johann Heinrich; America, 1870 *7420.1 p283*
Freise, Sophie Charlotte *SEE* Freise, Friedrich Ludwig
Freise, Sophie Louise Charlotte *SEE* Freise, Friedrich Ludwig
Freise, Wilhelm; America, 1882 *7420.1 p328*
Freistroffer, Jakob; America, 1881 *5475.1 p227*
Freitag, Anton 26; New York, NY, 1893 *1883.7 p41*
Freitag, Charlotte; America, 1853 *7420.1 p104*
Freitag, Heinrich August; Wisconsin, 1896 *6795.8 p192*
Freitag, Heinrich August; Wisconsin, 1910 *6795.8 p167*
Freitag, Johann; Wisconsin, 1881 *6795.8 p201*
Freitag, Johann Conrad; America, 1855 *7420.1 p136*
Frejd, Charley; Colorado, 1887 *1029.59 p30*
Frelick, John 37; Ontario, 1871 *1823.17 p55*
Frelick, Nancy 54; Ontario, 1871 *1823.21 p122*
Fremaux, G. M. 35; Port uncertain, 1840 *778.6 p124*
Fremel, Bernard 30; America, 1841 *778.6 p124*
Fremel, Franc. 33; America, 1841 *778.6 p124*
Fremin, Jacques 27; Quebec, 1655 *9221.17 p320*
Fremont, Honore 22; New Orleans, 1848 *778.6 p124*
Frenais, L. 20; New Orleans, 1844 *778.6 p124*
French, Christian; Illinois, 1834-1900 *6020.5 p131*
French, Harriet 22; Ontario, 1871 *1823.21 p122*
French, James 45; Ontario, 1871 *1823.17 p55*
French, Thomas 59; Ontario, 1871 *1823.21 p122*
French, William 56; Ontario, 1871 *1823.21 p123*
Frencham, Alice 67; Ontario, 1871 *1823.21 p123*
Frendelmann, Mr.; America, 1865 *7420.1 p231*
  With family
Frene, Friedrich; America, 1883 *7420.1 p336*
Freney, Peggy; New Orleans, 1850 *7242.30 p142*
Frenia, Louis 24; New Orleans, 1843 *778.6 p128*
Frenier, Pierre 32; America, 1840 *778.6 p124*
Frenly, George 60; Ontario, 1871 *1823.21 p123*
Frenul, Marable 20; America, 1843 *778.6 p328*
Frenz, Peter; America, 1879 *5475.1 p186*
Frenzel, Emil; Ohio, 1809-1852 *4511.35 p15*
Frenzler, Elias; New York, 1859 *358.56 p55*
Frereck, Heinrich Ludwig Christ.; America, 1867 *7420.1 p256*
  With father
Freres, Angela Mersch *SEE* Freres, Peter
Freres, Helena *SEE* Freres, Peter
Freres, Katharina *SEE* Freres, Peter
Freres, Nikolaus *SEE* Freres, Peter
Freres, Peter *SEE* Freres, Peter
Freres, Peter; America, 1875 *5475.1 p257*
  *Wife:*Angela Mersch
  *Son:*Nikolaus
  *Daughter:*Katharina
  *Daughter:*Susanna
  *Daughter:*Helena
  *Son:*Peter
Freres, Susanna *SEE* Freres, Peter
Freret, Richard; Louisiana, 1874 *4981.45 p132*
Frerichs, W. C. A.; North Carolina, 1856 *1088.45 p10*
Freron, Mrs. 45; New Orleans, 1848 *778.6 p124*
Fresco, Antonio; Louisiana, 1874-1875 *4981.45 p298*
Frese, Ida; Pittsburgh, 1908 *7420.1 p383*
  *Grandchild:*Frieda
  *Grandchild:*Agnes
  *Grandchild:*Paul
Freshney, Samuel H. 24; Ontario, 1871 *1823.21 p123*
Freskley, Sarah 65; Ontario, 1871 *1823.21 p123*
Freslon, Jacqueline 24; Quebec, 1662 *9221.17 p485*
Fresnel deLa Pipardiere, Joseph-Antoine de; Quebec, 1691 *2314.30 p169*
Fresnel deLa Pipardiere, Joseph-Antoine de; Quebec, 1691 *2314.30 p182*
Fresnier, Joseph 19; America, 1846 *778.6 p124*
Fresnot, Jean; Montreal, 1653 *9221.17 p290*
Fressel, Isabelle; Quebec, 1671 *4514.3 p315*
Fressel, Jeanne; Quebec, 1670 *4514.3 p315*
Fresson, Therese; Wisconsin, 1855 *1495.20 p41*
Fretelliere, August 20; Galveston, TX, 1844 *3967.10 p371*
Fretter, . . .; America, n.d. *8023.44 p373*
Fretter, Thomas; Ohio, 1840 *2763.1 p9*
Freude, Carl; Chile, 1852 *1192.4 p52*
Freudenberg, Aloine; New York, 1859 *358.56 p101*
Freudenberger, Adam; America, 1839 *2526.42 p104*
  With daughter 17
Freudenberger, Georg; America, 1854 *2526.42 p140*
Freudenberger, Johannes 18; America, 1895 *2526.42 p140*
Freudenberger, Katharina; America, 1853 *2526.42 p141*
Freudenberger, Marie; Virginia, 1831 *152.20 p63*
Freudenfels, Sigmund 26; Ontario, 1871 *1823.21 p123*
Freudenhammer, Anna Reimsbach *SEE* Freudenhammer, Joh. Heinr.
Freudenhammer, Joh. Heinr.; Peru, 1877 *5475.1 p205*
  *Mother:*Anna Reimsbach

Freudenhammer, Philipp Albert; Peru, 1872 *5475.1 p205*
Frevel, Miss; America, 1870 *7420.1 p283*
Freville, Charles 26; New Orleans, 1848 *778.6 p124*
Freville, Jean 49; Quebec, 1649 *9221.17 p208*
Frevot, August 18; New Orleans, 1845 *778.6 p124*
Frewert, Christian Gottlieb; Port uncertain, 1856 *7420.1 p147*
Frewert, Friedrich; America, 1854 *7420.1 p119*
Frewert, Heinrich; Port uncertain, 1840 *7420.1 p18*
Frey, Miss A. 17; New Orleans, 1834 *1002.51 p112*
Frey, Miss A. 45; New Orleans, 1834 *1002.51 p112*
Frey, Angela Meiers 59 *SEE* Frey, Mathias
Frey, Anna Maria Thome 26 *SEE* Frey, Mathias
Frey, Antoine 29; America, 1844 *778.6 p124*
Frey, Bernard; Ontario, 1787 *1276.15 p230*
  With child & 7 relatives
Frey, C. 46; New Orleans, 1834 *1002.51 p112*
Frey, Miss C. 3; New Orleans, 1834 *1002.51 p112*
Frey, Catha. 33; America, 1847 *778.6 p124*
Frey, Charles 22; America, 1847 *778.6 p124*
Frey, Chretien 28; Louisiana, 1848 *778.6 p124*
Frey, Else *SEE* Frey, Otto
Frey, Emma 8 months; Portland, ME, 1911 *970.38 p77*
Frey, Famille; New Castle, DE, 1817-1818 *90.20 p151*
Frey, Frank; Wisconsin, 1885 *6795.8 p100*
Frey, Fredrik 16; Portland, ME, 1911 *970.38 p77*
Frey, Frida 14; Portland, ME, 1911 *970.38 p77*
Frey, Friedrich; New York, NY, 1888 *3366.30 p70*
Frey, G. 15; New Orleans, 1834 *1002.51 p112*
Frey, George; Colorado, 1871 *1029.59 p30*
Frey, George; Ohio, 1809-1852 *4511.35 p15*
Frey, Gottfried; New York, NY, 1893 *3366.30 p70*
Frey, H. 8; New Orleans, 1834 *1002.51 p112*
Frey, Miss H. 6; New Orleans, 1834 *1002.51 p112*
Frey, Henry; Ohio, 1809-1852 *4511.35 p15*
Frey, Hilda 10; Portland, ME, 1911 *970.38 p77*
Frey, Jacq. 31; America, 1840 *778.6 p124*
Frey, Jakob; America, 1883 *179.55 p19*
Frey, Jakob 8; Portland, ME, 1911 *970.38 p77*
Frey, Johann; America, 1882 *5475.1 p130*
Frey, Johann 12; Portland, ME, 1911 *970.38 p77*
Frey, Joseph 26; New Castle, DE, 1817-1818 *90.20 p151*
Frey, Katharina; America, 1854 *5475.1 p459*
Frey, Margaret 11; Ontario, 1871 *1823.17 p55*
Frey, Maria; America, 1880 *5475.1 p129*
Frey, Mathias; Brazil, 1857 *5475.1 p368*
  *Wife:*Anna Maria Thome
Frey, Mathias; Brazil, 1857 *5475.1 p368*
  *Wife:*Angela Meiers
  *Son:*Peter
Frey, Otilia 13; Portland, ME, 1911 *970.38 p77*
Frey, Otilia 36; Portland, ME, 1911 *970.38 p77*
Frey, Otto; America, 1906 *8023.44 p373*
  With children
  *Sister:*Else
Frey, Peter 28; America, 1843 *5475.1 p366*
Frey, Peter 22 *SEE* Frey, Mathias
Frey, Philip R.; Ontario, 1787 *1276.15 p230*
  With child & 2 relatives
Frey, Miss S. 12; New Orleans, 1834 *1002.51 p112*
Frey, S. Ulrich 25; New Castle, DE, 1817-1818 *90.20 p151*
Frey, Wilhelm 22; Louisiana, 1848 *778.6 p124*
Freyberger, Katharina Bard *SEE* Freyberger, Michel
Freyberger, Michel; Brazil, 1846 *5475.1 p438*
  *Wife:*Katharina Bard
  With 5 children
Freyberger, Peter; Brazil, 1846 *5475.1 p438*
Freyburger, Paul; Ohio, 1840-1897 *8365.35 p16*
Freyenmuth, Florian 2; America, 1846 *778.6 p124*
Freyenmuth, Ja.ques 34; America, 1846 *778.6 p124*
Freyenmuth, Marg. 32; America, 1846 *778.6 p124*
Freyenmuth, Mgad. 1; America, 1846 *778.6 p124*
Freygang, Julius; Ohio, 1809-1852 *4511.35 p15*
Freyre Gros, Juan Ramon; Puerto Rico, 1830 *3476.25 p112*
Freytag, Heinrich; Valdivia, Chile, 1851 *1192.4 p50*
Freytag, Johann 21; New York, NY, 1864 *8425.62 p199*
Frezard, Miss 1; New Orleans, 1843 *778.6 p125*
Frezard, Bd. 45; New Orleans, 1843 *778.6 p125*
Frezard, Marie 33; New Orleans, 1843 *778.6 p125*
Frezarde, A. 58; New Orleans, 1844 *778.6 p125*
Frezell, Daniel; South Carolina, 1671 *9228.50 p233*
Fri, Charles 18; New Orleans, 1847 *778.6 p125*
Frianch, Catherine 46; Port uncertain, 1841 *778.6 p125*
Frianch, Magdelin 48; Port uncertain, 1841 *778.6 p125*
Fribel, Caroline 21; America, 1846 *778.6 p125*
Friberg, Frans Aug.; New Orleans, 1851 *6412.40 p153*
Friberg, L.P.; New York, NY, 1842 *6412.40 p146*
Friberg, R.L.J.; New York, NY, 1846 *6412.40 p149*
Fribourg, Carolina 19; America, 1847 *778.6 p125*
Fribourg, David 19; Mississippi, 1845 *778.6 p125*

Fribourg, Fanny 30; America, 1847 ***778.6*** *p125*
Fribourg, Felix 52; America, 1847 ***778.6*** *p125*
Fribourg, Henriette 17; America, 1847 ***778.6*** *p125*
Fribourg, Minette 35; America, 1847 ***778.6*** *p125*
Fribourg, Pauline 10; America, 1847 ***778.6*** *p125*
Fribourg, Rose 35; America, 1847 ***778.6*** *p125*
Fribourg, Serf 16; America, 1847 ***778.6*** *p125*
Fribourg, Sophie 12; America, 1847 ***778.6*** *p125*
Frich, C. Martin 39; America, 1847 ***778.6*** *p125*
Frich, Jean Christophe 36; America, 1847 ***778.6*** *p125*
Frich, Sebastien 37; America, 1847 ***778.6*** *p125*
Frichet, Pierre 18; Quebec, 1658 ***9221.17*** *p380*
Frichley, John; Ohio, 1809-1852 ***4511.35*** *p15*
Frick, George 47; Ontario, 1871 ***1823.21*** *p123*
Frick, Peter 26; America, 1857 ***5475.1*** *p489*
Fricke, Miss; America, 1872 ***7420.1*** *p298*
Fricke, A. August; Valdivia, Chile, 1852 ***1192.4*** *p54*
With wife
With child 4
With baby
Fricke, H.; America, 1884 ***7420.1*** *p342*
Fricke, Heinrich; America, 1883 ***7420.1*** *p398*
Fricke, Otto; Valdivia, Chile, 1852 ***1192.4*** *p54*
Frickel, Christine 23; Halifax, N.S., 1902 ***1860.4*** *p41*
Frickel, Herman; Halifax, N.S., 1902 ***1860.4*** *p41*
Frickel, Johann 25; Halifax, N.S., 1902 ***1860.4*** *p41*
Frickenstein, Henry; Ohio, 1840-1897 ***8365.35*** *p16*
Frickenstein, J.; Nebraska, 1905 ***3004.30*** *p46*
Fricker, Joseph 20; Died enroute, 1817-1818 ***90.20*** *p151*
Frickert, Francois Joseph; Ohio, 1809-1852 ***4511.35*** *p15*
Frickett, Japh; Marston's Wharf, 1782 ***8529.30*** *p11*
Frickley, John; Ohio, 1809-1852 ***4511.35*** *p15*
Fricon, J. 35; Port uncertain, 1840 ***778.6*** *p125*
Fridan, William; New York, 1859-1860 ***358.56*** *p102*
Fridberg, Ellen; St. Paul, MN, 1887 ***1865.50*** *p47*
Fridberg, Olof J.; St. Paul, MN, 1883 ***1865.50*** *p47*
Fridd, Jacob; Ohio, 1809-1852 ***4511.35*** *p15*
Fridlund, Carl Magnus; Illinois, 1871-1880 ***1865.50*** *p48*
Fridrich, Herman; Long Island, 1700-1799 ***2853.20*** *p18*
Frie, Marie 37; Montreal, 1658 ***9221.17*** *p389*
Frieber, Johann; New Castle, DE, 1817-1818 ***90.20*** *p151*
Friechlier, Joseph 60; New Orleans, 1847 ***778.6*** *p125*
Fried, Elisabeth; Brazil, 1846 ***5475.1*** *p438*
Friedenreich, Louis; North Carolina, 1855 ***1088.45*** *p10*
Friederich, Christine 17; Valdivia, Chile, 1852 ***1192.4*** *p53*
Friederich, J. P.; Valdivia, Chile, 1852 ***1192.4*** *p53*
Friederich, Jean 33; Mississippi, 1847 ***778.6*** *p125*
Friederich, Nicolas 27; Mississippi, 1847 ***778.6*** *p125*
Friederich, Pauline; Miami, 1935 ***4984.12*** *p39*
Friederich, Philip J.; Louisiana, 1874 ***4981.45*** *p132*
Friedlein, Friedrich Wilhelm August; America, 1883 ***2526.43*** *p205*
Friedlein, Margaretha; America, 1865 ***2526.43*** *p167*
Friedling, Peter *SEE* Friedling, Peter
Friedling, Peter; Pittsburgh, 1882 ***5475.1*** *p130*
*Son:*Peter
With family
Friedlund, Carl Magnus; Illinois, 1871-1880 ***1865.50*** *p48*
Friedman, Nioritz; Louisiana, 1874 ***4981.45*** *p131*
Friedman, Tillie; Oregon, 1941 ***9157.47*** *p2*
Friedmann, A. Marie 1; Mississippi, 1847 ***778.6*** *p125*
Friedmann, Agathe 11; Mississippi, 1847 ***778.6*** *p125*
Friedmann, Caroline 3; Mississippi, 1847 ***778.6*** *p125*
Friedmann, Catherine 15; Mississippi, 1847 ***778.6*** *p125*
Friedmann, Eleonore 16; Mississippi, 1847 ***778.6*** *p125*
Friedmann, Elisabeth 13; Mississippi, 1847 ***778.6*** *p125*
Friedmann, G.; Galveston, TX, 1855 ***571.7*** *p18*
Friedmann, Johann 7; Mississippi, 1847 ***778.6*** *p125*
Friedmann, Joseph 40; Mississippi, 1847 ***778.6*** *p126*
Friedmann, Leonhard 5; Mississippi, 1847 ***778.6*** *p126*
Friedmann, Regine 9; Mississippi, 1847 ***778.6*** *p126*
Friedmann, Rosa 38; Mississippi, 1847 ***778.6*** *p126*
Friedmann, Sophie 18; Mississippi, 1847 ***778.6*** *p126*
Friedrich, Adam; America, 1856 ***2526.42*** *p94*
With wife
*Child:*Eva Marie
*Child:*Philipp
Friedrich, Adam 3 *SEE* Friedrich, Michael
Friedrich, Adam 19; America, 1867 ***2526.43*** *p125*
Friedrich, Adam 68; America, 1853 ***2526.42*** *p120*
*Wife:*Anna Katharina Vetter 52
*Granddaughter:*Anna Katharina 6
Friedrich, Anna Katharina 6 *SEE* Friedrich, Adam
Friedrich, Anna Katharina Vetter 52 *SEE* Friedrich, Adam
Friedrich, Anna Margaretha 24 *SEE* Friedrich, Wilhelm
Friedrich, Anna Maria; America, 1867 ***2526.43*** *p191*
Friedrich, Anna Maria; America, 1880 ***2526.42*** *p135*
Friedrich, Anna Rosina; Dayton, OH, 1862-1906 ***2526.42*** *p172*
Friedrich, Balthasar; America, 1854 ***2526.42*** *p135*
Friedrich, Barbara 25; America, 1853 ***2526.42*** *p120*
Friedrich, Barbara 51; America, 1857 ***5475.1*** *p266*
*Son:*Johann
*Daughter:*Margarethe
Friedrich, Barbara 48; New York, NY, 1885 ***6954.7*** *p40*
Friedrich, C. G.; Valdivia, Chile, 1850 ***1192.4*** *p49*
With wife & 5 children
With child 27
With child 11
Friedrich, Christian; America, 1831 ***2526.42*** *p180*
With wife & 3 children
Friedrich, Christian; America, 1846 ***2526.43*** *p188*
With wife
*Daughter:*Katharina
*Daughter:*Eva Elisabetha
Friedrich, Christian *SEE* Friedrich, Leonhard
Friedrich, Dorothea *SEE* Friedrich, Leonhard
Friedrich, Elisabeth *SEE* Friedrich, Leonhard
Friedrich, Elisabeth 2 weeks months *SEE* Friedrich, Wilhelm
Friedrich, Eva Elisabetha 2 *SEE* Friedrich, Christian
Friedrich, Eva Margareta 11 *SEE* Friedrich, Georg
Friedrich, Eva Marie 6 *SEE* Friedrich, Adam
Friedrich, Franz Heinrich; Wisconsin, 1889 ***6795.8*** *p88*
Friedrich, Friedrich 37 *SEE* Friedrich, Jakob
Friedrich, Georg; America, 1840 ***5475.1*** *p27*
With family
Friedrich, Georg; America, 1853 ***2526.42*** *p140*
Friedrich, Georg 46; America, 1856 ***2526.42*** *p94*
*Child:*Eva Margareta 11
Friedrich, Georg Christoph; America, 1868 ***7919.3*** *p533*
With wife & 5 children
Friedrich, Heinrich Ludwig; America, 1886 ***7420.1*** *p399*
Friedrich, Helena *SEE* Friedrich, Leonhard
Friedrich, Hieronymus 11 *SEE* Friedrich, Michael
Friedrich, Jakob 61; America, 1867 ***2526.43*** *p190*
*Son:*Friedrich 37
*Son:*Konrad 23
*Son:*Leonhard 21
*Daughter:*Margaretha Elisabetha 34
*Daughter:*Katharina 13
Friedrich, Johann; America, 1852 ***5475.1*** *p480*
Friedrich, Johann; America, 1852 ***5475.1*** *p547*
Friedrich, Johann Georg; America, 1884 ***2526.42*** *p166*
Friedrich, Johann Wilhelm; America, 1890 ***2526.43*** *p224*
Friedrich, Johannes; America, 1832 ***2526.42*** *p173*
With wife & 2 children
Friedrich, Johannes 17; America, 1866 ***2526.42*** *p166*
Friedrich, Johannn 23; Galveston, TX, 1844 ***3967.10*** *p372*
Friedrich, John; Louisiana, 1841-1844 ***4981.45*** *p210*
Friedrich, Karl August Friedrich; Wisconsin, 1904 ***6795.8*** *p152*
Friedrich, Kaspar; America, 1857 ***2526.43*** *p208*
Friedrich, Katharina 4 *SEE* Friedrich, Christian
Friedrich, Katharina 6 *SEE* Friedrich, Michael
Friedrich, Katharina 13 *SEE* Friedrich, Jakob
Friedrich, Katharina 32; America, 1857 ***5475.1*** *p328*
Friedrich, Katharina 40; America, 1880 ***5475.1*** *p362*
Friedrich, Konrad; America, 1859 ***2526.43*** *p190*
Friedrich, Konrad 23 *SEE* Friedrich, Jakob
Friedrich, Leonhard; America, 1836 ***2526.42*** *p173*
With wife
With child 9 months
Friedrich, Leonhard; America, 1852 ***2526.42*** *p136*
Friedrich, Leonhard 21 *SEE* Friedrich, Jakob
Friedrich, Leonhard 52; America, 1853 ***2526.42*** *p180*
With wife
*Son:*Matthaus
*Daughter:*Elisabeth
*Son:*Christian
*Daughter:*Helena
*Daughter:*Dorothea
Friedrich, Louis Carl; America, 1853 ***179.55*** *p19*
Friedrich, Ludwig; America, 1867 ***2526.42*** *p173*
Friedrich, Ludwig; America, 1891 ***7420.1*** *p362*
Friedrich, Luzia; America, 1881 ***5475.1*** *p276*
Friedrich, Magdalena 34; Port uncertain, 1843 ***778.6*** *p126*
Friedrich, Margaretha; America, 1867 ***2526.42*** *p136*
Friedrich, Margaretha; America, 1885 ***2526.42*** *p136*
Friedrich, Margaretha Elisabetha 34 *SEE* Friedrich, Jakob
Friedrich, Margarethe; America, 1873 ***5475.1*** *p269*
Friedrich, Maria; America, 1882 ***5475.1*** *p276*
Friedrich, Maria 18; New York, NY, 1885 ***6954.7*** *p40*
Friedrich, Maria Elisabetha Flath 26 *SEE* Friedrich, Michael
Friedrich, Matthaus *SEE* Friedrich, Leonhard
Friedrich, Michael; America, 1868 ***2526.42*** *p180*
Friedrich, Michael 31; America, 1853 ***2526.42*** *p120*
*Wife:*Maria Elisabetha Flath 26
*Child:*Adam 3
*Child:*Hieronymus 11
*Child:*Katharina 6
Friedrich, Michael 42; New York, NY, 1885 ***6954.7*** *p40*
Friedrich, Nikolaus Friedrich; America, 1857 ***2526.43*** *p190*
Friedrich, Peter; America, 1865 ***2526.42*** *p166*
Friedrich, Philipp 1 *SEE* Friedrich, Adam
Friedrich, Sebastian; America, 1852 ***5475.1*** *p548*
Friedrich, Wilhelm; America, 1892 ***7420.1*** *p365*
Friedrich, Wilhelm 28; America, 1883 ***2526.42*** *p120*
*Wife:*Anna Margaretha 24
*Child:*Elisabeth 2 weeks
With mother-in-law 64
Friedrichs, Eleonore; America, 1857 ***7420.1*** *p161*
With daughter
Friedrichs, Friedrich; America, 1854 ***7420.1*** *p119*
Friedrichs, Ludwig Minna; Galveston, TX, 1855 ***571.7*** *p16*
Friedrichs, Maria; America, 1881 ***5475.1*** *p276*
Friedrichs, Minna; Galveston, TX, 1855 ***571.7*** *p16*
Friedrick, Gottfried; Wisconsin, 1887 ***6795.8*** *p188*
Friel, Bridget; Philadelphia, 1868 ***8513.31*** *p308*
Friel, J.G.; Toronto, 1844 ***2910.35*** *p116*
Frieling, Frederick; Missouri, 1887 ***3276.1*** *p1*
Friem, Peter; Ohio, 1809-1852 ***4511.35*** *p15*
Friend, Anthony 60; Ontario, 1871 ***1823.21*** *p123*
Friend, Joseph 28; Louisiana, 1840 ***778.6*** *p126*
Friend, Maria 19; Ontario, 1871 ***1823.17*** *p55*
Friend, William 70; Ontario, 1871 ***1823.21*** *p123*
Friendship, Samuel 33; Ontario, 1871 ***1823.21*** *p123*
Friendship, Thomas 48; Ontario, 1871 ***1823.21*** *p123*
Frier, Abraham; Louisiana, 1836-1841 ***4981.45*** *p208*
Friers, Charles 60; Ontario, 1871 ***1823.21*** *p123*
Fries, Anton B.; Colorado, 1873 ***1029.59*** *p30*
Fries, Christian 15; New York, NY, 1894 ***6512.1*** *p185*
Fries, Franz *SEE* Fries, Nikolaus
Fries, Georg; America, 1880 ***5475.1*** *p23*
*Wife:*Katharina Hartmann
*Son:*Jakob
*Son:*Karl Georg
*Daughter:*Maria
Fries, Henry 28; America, 1846 ***778.6*** *p126*
Fries, Jakob *SEE* Fries, Georg
Fries, Johann *SEE* Fries, Nikolaus
Fries, Karl Georg *SEE* Fries, Georg
Fries, Katharina *SEE* Fries, Nikolaus
Fries, Katharina Kramer *SEE* Fries, Nikolaus
Fries, Katharina Hartmann *SEE* Fries, Georg
Fries, Margaretha 24; America, 1846 ***778.6*** *p126*
Fries, Maria; America, 1873 ***5475.1*** *p140*
Fries, Maria *SEE* Fries, Georg
Fries, Nikolaus *SEE* Fries, Nikolaus
Fries, Nikolaus; America, 1872 ***5475.1*** *p168*
*Wife:*Katharina Kramer
*Daughter:*Katharina
*Son:*Nikolaus
*Son:*Franz
*Son:*Johann
*Daughter:*Susanna
Fries, Soren Peter; Chile, 1852 ***1192.4*** *p52*
Fries, Susanna *SEE* Fries, Nikolaus
Fries, Thomas; Iowa, 1887 ***1211.15*** *p10*
Fries, Ulrick Engelhard; Washington, 1887 ***6015.10*** *p16*
Fries, William; North Carolina, 1816 ***1088.45*** *p10*
Friesen, Abraham 1; New York, NY, 1893 ***1883.7*** *p40*
Friesen, Ann 4; New York, NY, 1893 ***1883.7*** *p40*
Friesen, Cornelia 2; New York, NY, 1893 ***1883.7*** *p40*
Friesen, Cornelia 35; New York, NY, 1893 ***1883.7*** *p40*
Friesen, Cornelius 5; New York, NY, 1893 ***1883.7*** *p40*
Friesen, Jacob 9; New York, NY, 1893 ***1883.7*** *p40*
Friesen, Jacob 34; New York, NY, 1893 ***1883.7*** *p40*
Friesen, Johann 27; New York, NY, 1893 ***1883.7*** *p45*
Friesen, Katharina 7; New York, NY, 1893 ***1883.7*** *p40*
Friesen, Maria 10; New York, NY, 1893 ***1883.7*** *p40*
Friess, Fred; Louisiana, 1874 ***4981.45*** *p131*
Friess, Jacob 17; America, 1840 ***778.6*** *p126*
Friess, Joseph 16; America, 1840 ***778.6*** *p126*
Friesson, Marie 55; America, 1841 ***778.6*** *p126*
Frietsch, Joseph 50; New Orleans, 1847 ***778.6*** *p126*
Frietsch, Magdalena 28; New Orleans, 1847 ***778.6*** *p126*
Frietsch, Marianna 17; New Orleans, 1847 ***778.6*** *p126*
Frietsch, Mathias 19; New Orleans, 1847 ***778.6*** *p126*
Frig, Mathias 22; America, 1845 ***778.6*** *p126*
Frigen, Catha 23; New York, NY, 1890 ***1883.7*** *p47*
Frigen, Jacob 6 months; New York, NY, 1890 ***1883.7*** *p47*
Frigen, Jacob 23; New York, NY, 1890 ***1883.7*** *p47*
Frigiere, C. D. J.; Louisiana, 1836-1840 ***4981.45*** *p212*
Frimaire, Valentin 30; New Orleans, 1843 ***778.6*** *p126*
Frink, Ambrose 49; Ontario, 1871 ***1823.17*** *p55*
Frink, Sarah Ann 38; Ontario, 1871 ***1823.17*** *p55*
Frinquart, Nicolas 40; Port uncertain, 1840 ***778.6*** *p126*

Frinson, Marie Francoise 62; Wisconsin, 1855-1858 ***1495.20*** *p67*
Fririn, Mrs. 45; New Orleans, 1848 ***778.6*** *p126*
Frisch, Friedrich; America, 1847 ***5475.1*** *p234*
Frisch, John; New York, 1859 ***358.56*** *p54*
Frisch, Josef; Wisconsin, 1856 ***2853.20*** *p345*
Frische, George; New York, 1860 ***358.56*** *p148*
Frischknecht, John M.; Philadelphia, 1846 ***8513.31*** *p308*
*Wife:*Maria M. Eiselen
Frischknecht, Maria M. Eiselen *SEE* Frischknecht, John M.
Frise, William 45; Ontario, 1871 ***1823.21*** *p123*
Frishly, John; Newfoundland, 1814 ***3476.10*** *p54*
Frisk, Andrew August; St. Paul, MN, 1896 ***1865.50*** *p48*
Frisk, Carrie; St. Paul, MN, 1885 ***1865.50*** *p48*
Friskin, George; Marston's Wharf, 1782 ***8529.30*** *p11*
Frison, Franz 19; New York, NY, 1893 ***1883.7*** *p42*
Frisque, Antoinette Gueunick *SEE* Frisque, Edouard
Frisque, David; New York, NY, 1855 ***1494.21*** *p31*
Frisque, David Joseph; Wisconsin, 1854-1858 ***1495.20*** *p49*
Frisque, Edouard; Wisconsin, 1846-1856 ***1495.20*** *p29*
*Wife:*Antoinette Gueunick
Frisque, Hubert Henri; Wisconsin, 1854-1858 ***1495.20*** *p49*
Frisque, Isidore *SEE* Frisque, Pierre Joseph, Sr.
Frisque, Josephine *SEE* Frisque, Pierre Joseph, Sr.
Frisque, Marie Laure Catherine Le Brun *SEE* Frisque, Pierre Joseph, Sr.
Frisque, Pierre Joseph *SEE* Frisque, Pierre Joseph, Sr.
Frisque, Pierre Joseph, Sr.; Wisconsin, 1854-1858 ***1495.20*** *p49*
*Wife:*Marie Laure Catherine Le Brun
*Child:*Pierre Joseph
*Child:*Josephine
*Child:*Isidore
Frisse, Karl; Louisiana, 1874 ***4981.45*** *p131*
Fristrom, Joh. Erik; New York, NY, 1851 ***6412.40*** *p152*
Fritche, Ferdinand; Ohio, 1854 ***3580.20*** *p32*
Fritche, Ferdinand; Ohio, 1854 ***6020.12*** *p7*
Fritche, Jacob; Ohio, 1809-1852 ***4511.35*** *p15*
Fritel, Caroline 21; America, 1846 ***778.6*** *p125*
Frithjoff, Peter J.; America, 1852 ***4487.25*** *p57*
With parents
Fritot, . . .; America, 1803 ***9228.50*** *p232*
Fritsch, Ferdinand; Philadelphia, 1856 ***8513.31*** *p308*
*Wife:*Mary Kluge
Fritsch, Gottfried; New York, 1860 ***358.56*** *p6*
Fritsch, Josef Heinrich; America, 1879 ***5475.1*** *p483*
Fritsch, Mary Kluge *SEE* Fritsch, Ferdinand
Fritschack, Gottfried; Washington, 1886 ***2770.40*** *p195*
Fritter, Jean 74; America, 1846 ***778.6*** *p126*
Fritz, . . . 4 months; Port uncertain, 1843 ***778.6*** *p126*
Fritz, Andrew; Ohio, 1809-1852 ***4511.35*** *p15*
Fritz, Andrew 28; Port uncertain, 1843 ***778.6*** *p126*
Fritz, Anna; Wisconsin, 1888 ***6795.8*** *p81*
Fritz, Anna; Wisconsin, 1898 ***6795.8*** *p234*
Fritz, Auguste 3; Port uncertain, 1843 ***778.6*** *p126*
Fritz, Auguste 20; Port uncertain, 1843 ***778.6*** *p126*
Fritz, Carl; America, 1882 ***179.55*** *p19*
Fritz, Charles 36; Port uncertain, 1847 ***778.6*** *p126*
Fritz, Charles Ludwic; Wisconsin, 1891 ***6795.8*** *p72*
Fritz, Emil; Wisconsin, 1889 ***6795.8*** *p138*
Fritz, Ernst Heinrich; Wisconsin, 1885 ***6795.8*** *p201*
Fritz, Fredrick Bathos; North Carolina, 1832 ***1088.45*** *p10*
Fritz, Gustav Gottlieb; Wisconsin, 1896 ***6795.8*** *p72*
Fritz, Gustav Gottlieb; Wisconsin, 1896 ***6795.8*** *p73*
Fritz, Jac.; New York, 1859 ***358.56*** *p55*
Fritz, Jacob; Ohio, 1840-1897 ***8365.35*** *p16*
Fritz, Johann; Dakota, 1888 ***5475.1*** *p340*
Fritz, Johanna Lorson *SEE* Fritz, Peter
Fritz, John G.; Illinois, 1857 ***6079.1*** *p5*
Fritz, Karl Friedrich; America, 1882 ***179.55*** *p19*
Fritz, Katharina Neu *SEE* Fritz, Peter
Fritz, Lorenz 25; New Orleans, 1848 ***778.6*** *p126*
Fritz, Ludwig *SEE* Fritz, Sophie
Fritz, Ludwig; Valdivia, Chile, 1852 ***1192.4*** *p55*
With wife
With child 8
With child 13
Fritz, Margaret 22; Port uncertain, 1843 ***778.6*** *p126*
Fritz, Margarethe *SEE* Fritz, Peter
Fritz, Maria Auguste Louise; Wisconsin, 1898 ***6795.8*** *p85*
Fritz, Marie 18; Port uncertain, 1843 ***778.6*** *p126*
Fritz, Marie 23; Port uncertain, 1843 ***778.6*** *p126*
Fritz, Marie 56; Port uncertain, 1843 ***778.6*** *p126*
Fritz, Michael; Washington, 1885 ***2770.40*** *p194*
Fritz, Ottilie Amelia Theresa; Wisconsin, 1893 ***6795.8*** *p73*
Fritz, Otto Paul; Wisconsin, 1896 ***6795.8*** *p231*
Fritz, Peter; America, 1869 ***5475.1*** *p289*
*Wife:*Katharina Neu
*Daughter:*Margarethe
Fritz, Peter; America, 1880 ***5475.1*** *p220*
*Wife:*Johanna Lorson
Fritz, Peter; Illinois, 1851 ***6079.1*** *p5*
Fritz, Robert Gottlob; America, 1873 ***179.55*** *p19*
Fritz, Sophie; Milwaukee, 1882 ***5475.1*** *p460*
*Brother:*Ludwig
Fritzch, Franziska; Galveston, TX, 1855 ***571.7*** *p16*
Fritze, Emilie; America, 1867 ***7919.3*** *p533*
Fritze, Johann Christian Friedrich Wilhelm; America, 1867 ***7919.3*** *p527*
Fritze, Julie; America, 1868 ***7919.3*** *p533*
Fritze, Reinhard; America, 1868 ***7919.3*** *p525*
Fritze, Selma; America, 1867 ***7919.3*** *p533*
Fritzsche, Carl Christoph Gottlieb; Port uncertain, 1881 ***7420.1*** *p320*
Frizell, Daniel; South Carolina, 1671 ***9228.50*** *p233*
Fro, Louise; Quebec, 1670 ***4514.3*** *p315*
Frochlicher, Joseph; Louisiana, 1836-1840 ***4981.45*** *p212*
Frodyma, Anna 17; New York, NY, 1911 ***6533.11*** *p10*
Froehlich, Amelia 4; New York, NY, 1893 ***1883.7*** *p42*
Froehlich, Catherina 27; New York, NY, 1893 ***1883.7*** *p42*
Froehlich, Dionn 28; New York, NY, 1893 ***1883.7*** *p42*
Froehlich, Franziska; Venezuela, 1843 ***3899.5*** *p540*
Froehlich, Michael; Wisconsin, 1876 ***6795.8*** *p42*
Froehlich, Rosa Arnold 10 months; New York, NY, 1893 ***1883.7*** *p42*
Froelich, Catharine 2; New Orleans, 1846 ***778.6*** *p127*
Froelich, Catharine 26; New Orleans, 1846 ***778.6*** *p126*
Froelich, Elizabeth 6 months; New Orleans, 1846 ***778.6*** *p127*
Froelich, Franziska; Venezuela, 1843 ***3899.5*** *p540*
Froelich, Jacob 31; New Orleans, 1846 ***778.6*** *p127*
Froelich, Jan; Chicago, 1859-1910 ***2853.20*** *p406*
Froelich, Louis 20; New York, NY, 1894 ***6512.1*** *p182*
Froetele, Catherine 22; New Orleans, 1848 ***778.6*** *p127*
Froetele, Jacob 17; New Orleans, 1848 ***778.6*** *p127*
Frog, Barbara 32; New Orleans, 1848 ***778.6*** *p127*
Frog, Henri 3; New Orleans, 1848 ***778.6*** *p127*
Frog, Henri 33; New Orleans, 1848 ***778.6*** *p127*
Frogeau, Pierre; Montreal, 1653 ***9221.17*** *p290*
Froget, Nicolas 31; Quebec, 1652 ***9221.17*** *p258*
Frohlich, Balthasar, III; America, 1870 ***2526.42*** *p120*
Frohlich, Elisabeth; America, 1870 ***2526.42*** *p141*
Frohlich, Eva Katharina Ruhl *SEE* Frohlich, Nikolaus
Frohlich, Friedrich *SEE* Frohlich, Nikolaus
Frohlich, J. H.; Valdivia, Chile, 1852 ***1192.4*** *p55*
Frohlich, Jean 36; America, 1843 ***778.6*** *p127*
Frohlich, Johann Michael; Venezuela, 1843 ***3899.5*** *p544*
Frohlich, Karl; London, Eng., 1887 ***2526.43*** *p167*
Frohlich, Maria Theresia; Venezuela, 1843 ***3899.5*** *p543*
Frohlich, Nikolaus; America, 1883 ***2526.42*** *p120*
*Wife:*Eva Katharina Ruhl
*Child:*Peter
*Child:*Friedrich
Frohlich, Peter *SEE* Frohlich, Nikolaus
Frohling, Meint Andressen; Iowa, 1917 ***1211.15*** *p10*
Frohnapfel, . . .; West Virginia, 1850-1860 ***1132.30*** *p149*
Frohner, J.; Galveston, TX, 1855 ***571.7*** *p18*
Froldemont, Adele 17; New Orleans, 1848 ***778.6*** *p127*
Froldemont, Adeline 13; New Orleans, 1848 ***778.6*** *p127*
Froldemont, Auguste 9; New Orleans, 1848 ***778.6*** *p127*
Froldemont, Augustine C. 21; New Orleans, 1848 ***778.6*** *p127*
Froldemont, Emilie 15; New Orleans, 1848 ***778.6*** *p127*
Froldemont, Jean 51; New Orleans, 1848 ***778.6*** *p127*
Froldemont, Mariane 47; New Orleans, 1848 ***778.6*** *p127*
Froldemont, Rosine 20; New Orleans, 1848 ***778.6*** *p127*
Frolich, Johann Michael; Venezuela, 1843 ***3899.5*** *p544*
Froliger, Jacob 24; America, 1847 ***778.6*** *p127*
Fromald, Louis 33; Missouri, 1845 ***778.6*** *p127*
Fromel, Jean 23; America, 1847 ***778.6*** *p127*
Froment, Marie 22; America, 1846 ***778.6*** *p127*
Fromentin, Jacques; Quebec, 1661 ***9221.17*** *p456*
Fromme, Dorothea; America, 1854 ***7420.1*** *p119*
Fromme, Friedrich; America, 1853 ***7420.1*** *p104*
Frondiere, Raoullin; Quebec, 1647 ***9221.17*** *p180*
Frone, Constance 21; New Orleans, 1848 ***778.6*** *p127*
Frone, Francois 26; New Orleans, 1848 ***778.6*** *p127*
Fronehafer, Michael; Ohio, 1809-1852 ***4511.35*** *p15*
Fronehafer, Peter; Ohio, 1809-1852 ***4511.35*** *p15*
Fronhaffer, Michael; Ohio, 1809-1852 ***4511.35*** *p15*
Frontin, Francois; Quebec, 1659 ***9221.17*** *p413*
Fronville, Albertine; Illinois, 1856 ***1495.20*** *p8*
Fronville, Albertine *SEE* Fronville, Joseph
Fronville, Florent *SEE* Fronville, Joseph
Fronville, Jean Louis *SEE* Fronville, Joseph
Fronville, Joseph; Illinois, 1856 ***1495.20*** *p28*
*Wife:*Marie Catherine Thiry
*Child:*Jean Louis
*Child:*Marie Therese
*Child:*Florent
*Child:*Albertine
Fronville, Marie Catherine Thiry *SEE* Fronville, Joseph
Fronville, Marie Therese *SEE* Fronville, Joseph
Frost, John 14; Quebec, 1870 ***8364.32*** *p23*
Frothen, Wm 60; Ontario, 1871 ***1823.21*** *p123*
Froues, C. 25; America, 1846 ***778.6*** *p127*
Froues, Josephine 2 months; America, 1846 ***778.6*** *p127*
Froues, Maria 4; America, 1846 ***778.6*** *p127*
Frouin, Jean; Quebec, 1646 ***9221.17*** *p164*
Fruelles, J. 39; America, 1848 ***778.6*** *p127*
Fruhling, Frederich; Illinois, 1864 ***6079.1*** *p5*
Fruitier, Jean; Montreal, 1653 ***9221.17*** *p290*
Frusher, Phebe 20; Michigan, 1880 ***4491.33*** *p9*
Fry, Alfred 35; Ontario, 1871 ***1823.21*** *p123*
Fry, Clara 12; Quebec, 1870 ***8364.32*** *p23*
Fry, George 45; Ontario, 1871 ***1823.21*** *p123*
Fry, Henry; Ohio, 1809-1852 ***4511.35*** *p15*
Fry, John; Ohio, 1809-1852 ***4511.35*** *p15*
Fry, John 22; Ontario, 1871 ***1823.21*** *p123*
Fry, Louis; Illinois, 1834-1900 ***6020.5*** *p131*
Fry, Teresa 52; Ontario, 1871 ***1823.21*** *p123*
Fry, William 29; Ontario, 1871 ***1823.21*** *p123*
Fryberger, Frederick; Ohio, 1809-1852 ***4511.35*** *p15*
Fryberger, Frederick; Ohio, 1809-1852 ***4511.35*** *p16*
Fryckberg, Christina C.; St. Paul, MN, 1884-1885 ***1865.50*** *p48*
Fryckholm, August; Chicago, 1880-1883 ***1865.50*** *p48*
*Wife:*Charlotta
*Child:*Mary
*Child:*Evan
Fryckholm, Charlotta *SEE* Fryckholm, August
Fryckholm, Evan *SEE* Fryckholm, August
Fryckholm, Mary *SEE* Fryckholm, August
Frycz, Stanislaw; Detroit, 1929 ***1640.55*** *p113*
Frydenborg, Peter; Iowa, 1897 ***1211.15*** *p10*
Fryer, Augustin; Louisiana, 1836-1841 ***4981.45*** *p208*
Fryer, Charles 53; Ontario, 1871 ***1823.17*** *p55*
Fryer, F. 41; New Orleans, 1845 ***778.6*** *p127*
Fryer, Fanny 40; America, 1843 ***778.6*** *p127*
Fryer, Francis L.; South Carolina, 1853 ***6155.4*** *p18*
Fryer, John 32; Ontario, 1871 ***1823.21*** *p123*
Fryers, John; Toronto, 1844 ***2910.35*** *p113*
Frykholm, August; Chicago, 1880-1883 ***1865.50*** *p48*
*Wife:*Charlotta
*Child:*Evan
*Child:*Mary
Frykholm, Charlotta *SEE* Frykholm, August
Frykholm, Evan *SEE* Frykholm, August
Frykholm, Mary *SEE* Frykholm, August
Fuchens, Jno. J.; Louisiana, 1874 ***4981.45*** *p295*
Fuchs, Abraham 40; Missouri, 1846 ***778.6*** *p127*
Fuchs, Adam 1; America, 1848 ***778.6*** *p127*
Fuchs, Andreas 34; America, 1847 ***5475.1*** *p393*
*Wife:*Margarethe Spaniol
*Son:*Johann Jakob
Fuchs, Anna Maria; Wisconsin, 1887 ***5475.1*** *p534*
Fuchs, Anna Marie; America, 1853 ***2526.42*** *p141*
Fuchs, Anton 29; Galveston, TX, 1846 ***3967.10*** *p378*
Fuchs, August Theodor Hermann; America, 1888 ***2526.43*** *p147*
Fuchs, August Theodor Hermann; England, 1888 ***2526.43*** *p147*
Fuchs, Catharina 21; America, 1848 ***778.6*** *p128*
Fuchs, Catherine 32; Missouri, 1847 ***778.6*** *p128*
Fuchs, Christine Hach *SEE* Fuchs, Gottleb
Fuchs, Daniel; Detroit, 1930 ***1640.60*** *p76*
Fuchs, Elisabeth Schaefer *SEE* Fuchs, Peter
Fuchs, Ernst 26; Philadelphia, 1881 ***5475.1*** *p154*
Fuchs, Franziska 25; Galveston, TX, 1846 ***3967.10*** *p378*
Fuchs, Georg Jakob; America, 1846 ***5475.1*** *p531*
Fuchs, Georg Jakob, II; America, 1846 ***5475.1*** *p531*
Fuchs, Gertrud Meiser *SEE* Fuchs, Peter
Fuchs, Gertrud 8 *SEE* Fuchs, Peter
Fuchs, Gottleb; Philadelphia, 1867 ***8513.31*** *p308*
*Wife:*Christine Hach
Fuchs, Heinrich 34; America, 1836 ***5475.1*** *p513*
*Brother:*Nikolaus 17
Fuchs, Heinrich 19; New York, 1854 ***5475.1*** *p236*
Fuchs, Jakob; America, 1847 ***5475.1*** *p547*
Fuchs, Jakob 5 *SEE* Fuchs, Peter
Fuchs, Jakob 12 *SEE* Fuchs, Nikolaus
Fuchs, Jakob; Indiana, 1885 ***5475.1*** *p246*
Fuchs, Johann; America, 1842 ***5475.1*** *p397*
Fuchs, Johann; America, 1860 ***5475.1*** *p397*
Fuchs, Johann 18 *SEE* Fuchs, Nikolaus
Fuchs, Johann 46; America, 1846 ***5475.1*** *p397*
With family
Fuchs, Johann Georg; America, 1846 ***5475.1*** *p547*

Fuchs, Johann Jakob *SEE* Fuchs, Andreas
Fuchs, Joseph 35; America, 1847 *778.6 p128*
Fuchs, Kaspar; America, 1753 *2526.42 p181*
  With wife & 6 children
Fuchs, Kath. Juliana; America, 1864 *5475.1 p237*
Fuchs, Katharina *SEE* Fuchs, Michel
Fuchs, Katharina Schwaz *SEE* Fuchs, Wilh. Aug.
Fuchs, Katharina 1 *SEE* Fuchs, Peter
Fuchs, Katharina 44; America, 1846 *5475.1 p451*
Fuchs, Luise Katharina *SEE* Fuchs, Wilh. Aug.
Fuchs, Margarethe Andler *SEE* Fuchs, Nikolaus
Fuchs, Margarethe Spaniol *SEE* Fuchs, Andreas
Fuchs, Margarethe 38; America, 1854 *5475.1 p539*
  *Son:*Jakob 8
Fuchs, Margarethe 39; America, 1847 *5475.1 p408*
Fuchs, Maria 13 *SEE* Fuchs, Peter
Fuchs, Maria Arnold; America, 1862 *5475.1 p296*
Fuchs, Mathias; America, 1843 *5475.1 p294*
  With wife
Fuchs, Michel; America, 1836 *5475.1 p462*
  *Sister:*Katharina
Fuchs, Nickel; America, 1834-1899 *5475.1 p453*
Fuchs, Nicolas 28; America, 1848 *778.6 p128*
Fuchs, Nicolas 20; Port uncertain, 1847 *778.6 p127*
Fuchs, Nikolaus; America, 1838 *5475.1 p463*
Fuchs, Nikolaus 17 *SEE* Fuchs, Heinrich
Fuchs, Nikolaus 51; America, 1843 *5475.1 p453*
  *Wife:*Margarethe Andler
  *Child:*Johann 18
  *Child:*Jakob 12
  *Child:*Wilhelm 7
Fuchs, Nikolaus 54; America, 1800-1899 *5475.1 p453*
Fuchs, Peter; America, 1842 *5475.1 p397*
  *Wife:*Gertrud Meiser
  *Daughter:*Maria
  *Daughter:*Gertrud
Fuchs, Peter; America, 1845 *5475.1 p28*
  With family
Fuchs, Peter; America, 1847 *5475.1 p485*
Fuchs, Peter; America, 1882 *5475.1 p184*
Fuchs, Peter 4 *SEE* Fuchs, Peter
Fuchs, Peter 27; America, 1886 *5475.1 p539*
Fuchs, Peter 42; America, 1847 *5475.1 p408*
  *Wife:*Elisabeth Schaefer
  *Daughter:*Katharina 1
  *Son:*Jakob 5
  *Son:*Peter 4
Fuchs, Wilh. Aug.; America, 1881 *5475.1 p33*
  *Wife:*Katharina Schwaz
  *Daughter:*Luise Katharina
Fuchs, Wilhelm 7 *SEE* Fuchs, Nikolaus
Fuchs, Wilhelm 21; America, 1880 *5475.1 p398*
Fuchs Family ; America, 1856 *7420.1 p147*
Fuchslocher, J. F.; Chile, 1852 *1192.4 p52*
  With wife & 4 children
  With child 4
  With child 22
Fuchte, Heinrich 21; New York, NY, 1897 *5475.1 p19*
Fucik, Frantisek; Chicago, 1867 *2853.20 p391*
Fud, Andr. 37; America, 1840 *778.6 p128*
Fud, Catha. 1; America, 1840 *778.6 p128*
Fud, Dorothe 6; America, 1840 *778.6 p128*
Fud, Eva 35; America, 1840 *778.6 p128*
Fud, Francs. 28; America, 1840 *778.6 p128*
Fud, Georg. 1; America, 1840 *778.6 p128*
Fud, Georg. 26; America, 1840 *778.6 p128*
Fud, Sophie 3; America, 1840 *778.6 p128*
Fudge, James 36; Ontario, 1871 *1823.21 p123*
Fuengling, John; Ohio, 1809-1852 *4511.35 p16*
Fuety, Giovian 24; New Orleans, 1844 *778.6 p128*
Fugere, Thomas; Quebec, 1659 *9221.17 p413*
Fugler, Bartholomaus 21; Galveston, TX, 1846 *3967.10 p377*
Fuguard, Thomas; Jamaica, 1783 *8529.30 p13A*
Fuhde, Emilie; Wisconsin, 1892 *6795.8 p69*
Fuhlen, Herman; Illinois, 1806 *6079.1 p5*
Fuhler, Michel 22; America, 1847 *778.6 p128*
Fuhr, Juliane; Pennsylvania, 1878-1900 *5475.1 p35*
Fuhrer, Adam 6 *SEE* Fuhrer, Johannes, II
Fuhrer, Amelie 8; New York, NY, 1874 *6954.7 p38*
Fuhrer, Anna Maria 14 *SEE* Fuhrer, Johannes, II
Fuhrer, Caroline 5; New York, NY, 1874 *6954.7 p37*
Fuhrer, Catharina 10; New York, NY, 1874 *6954.7 p37*
Fuhrer, Catherina 36; New York, NY, 1874 *6954.7 p37*
Fuhrer, Elisabeth 3; New York, NY, 1874 *6954.7 p38*
Fuhrer, Elisabeth 7; New York, NY, 1874 *6954.7 p37*
Fuhrer, Elisabetha 8 *SEE* Fuhrer, Johannes, II
Fuhrer, Georg 4 *SEE* Fuhrer, Johannes, II
Fuhrer, Georg 15; New York, NY, 1874 *6954.7 p37*
Fuhrer, Georg 40; New York, NY, 1874 *6954.7 p37*
Fuhrer, Jacob 6; New York, NY, 1874 *6954.7 p38*
Fuhrer, Jacob 9; New York, NY, 1874 *6954.7 p37*
Fuhrer, Johann 20; New York, NY, 1874 *6954.7 p38*

Fuhrer, Johanna 1; New York, NY, 1874 *6954.7 p38*
Fuhrer, Johannes, II 38; America, 1846 *2526.42 p141*
  With wife
  *Child:*Philipp 1
  *Child:*Georg 4
  *Child:*Michael 11
  *Child:*Elisabetha 8
  *Child:*Adam 6
  *Child:*Anna Maria 14
Fuhrer, Michael 11 *SEE* Fuhrer, Johannes, II
Fuhrer, Michael 3 months; New York, NY, 1874 *6954.7 p37*
Fuhrer, Pauline 10; New York, NY, 1874 *6954.7 p38*
Fuhrer, Philipp 1 *SEE* Fuhrer, Johannes, II
Fuhrer, Philipp 20; New York, NY, 1874 *6954.7 p37*
Fuhring, Christine Dorothee Amalie; America, 1851 *7420.1 p78*
Fuhs, Elisabeth 43; America, 1864 *5475.1 p266*
Fuhs, Joh. Josef; Chicago, 1885 *5475.1 p435*
Fuhter, Michel 22; America, 1847 *778.6 p128*
Fuidy, Joseph 36; New Orleans, 1848 *778.6 p128*
Fuke, S. Henry 33; Ontario, 1871 *1823.21 p123*
Fulbrook, James 14; Quebec, 1870 *8364.32 p23*
Fulch, Daniel; North Carolina, 1710 *3629.40 p4*
Fulch, Jacob; North Carolina, 1710 *3629.40 p4*
Fulcher, Joseph 50; Ontario, 1871 *1823.21 p123*
Fulda, Bernhard; North Carolina, 1840 *1088.45 p10*
Fulda, Julius; Louisiana, 1836-1841 *4981.45 p208*
Fullarton, John 67; Ontario, 1871 *1823.17 p55*
Fullarton, Mary 14; Quebec, 1870 *8364.32 p23*
Fullberth, Wilhelm; America, 1851 *2526.42 p160*
Fullberth, Wilhelm; America, 1881 *2526.42 p160*
Fuller, Edward; Plymouth, MA, 1620 *1920.45 p5*
  With wife
  *Son:*Samuell
Fuller, Frederick; Nebraska, 1853-1953 *9228.50 p233*
Fuller, Frederick; Vancouver, B.C., 1853-1953 *9228.50 p233*
Fuller, George 51; Ontario, 1871 *1823.17 p55*
Fuller, Isaac 67; Ontario, 1871 *1823.17 p55*
Fuller, Isabella 17; Quebec, 1870 *8364.32 p23*
Fuller, James 18; Quebec, 1870 *8364.32 p23*
Fuller, John P. 60; Ontario, 1871 *1823.21 p123*
Fuller, Samuel; Plymouth, MA, 1620 *1920.45 p5*
Fuller, Samuell *SEE* Fuller, Edward
Fuller, William 59; Ontario, 1871 *1823.21 p123*
Fuller, William J. 53; Ontario, 1871 *1823.21 p123*
Fuller, Wm. H.; Colorado, 1880 *1029.59 p30*
Fullerton, Fulton, Sr.; Illinois, 1918 *6007.60 p9*
Fulling, Georg Christian; America, 1866 *7420.1 p242*
  With family
Fullmer, Jacob; Ohio, 1809-1852 *4511.35 p16*
Fullock, John 38; Ontario, 1871 *1823.17 p55*
Fullon, James 70; Ontario, 1871 *1823.21 p123*
Fulmer, Christian; Ohio, 1809-1852 *4511.35 p16*
Fulmer, Daniel; Ohio, 1809-1852 *4511.35 p16*
Fulmer, Frederick; Ohio, 1809-1852 *4511.35 p16*
Fulmer, Jacob; Ohio, 1809-1852 *4511.35 p16*
Fulmer, Martin; Ohio, 1809-1852 *4511.35 p16*
Fulmer, Martin; Ohio, 1844 *2763.1 p9*
Fulsome, Allen 25; Ontario, 1871 *1823.17 p55*
Fulsome, Samuel 57; Ontario, 1871 *1823.17 p55*
Fultman, Adam; Ohio, 1809-1852 *4511.35 p16*
Fultner, Adam; Ohio, 1809-1852 *4511.35 p16*
Fulton, David; North Carolina, 1840 *1088.45 p10*
Fulton, James; Ohio, 1836 *3580.20 p32*
Fulton, James; Ohio, 1836 *6020.12 p7*
Fulton, Thomas 25; Ontario, 1871 *1823.21 p123*
Fulton, William 30; Ontario, 1871 *1823.21 p123*
Fultz, Magil; Ohio, 1809-1852 *4511.35 p16*
Fumell, George; North Carolina, 1820-1825 *1088.45 p10*
Fumichon, Nicolas; Quebec, 1661 *9221.17 p456*
Fumwal, Martha 9; Quebec, 1870 *8364.32 p23*
Funcher, Sister 3; Boston, 1835 *6424.55 p30*
Funcher, Frances 6; Boston, 1835 *6424.55 p30*
Funcher, Jane 36; Boston, 1835 *6424.55 p30*
Funck, Anna 20; New York, NY, 1893 *1883.7 p43*
Funck, Anne 40; Mississippi, 1846 *778.6 p128*
Funck, Conrad 7; New York, NY, 1893 *1883.7 p43*
Funck, Georg 21; New York, NY, 1893 *1883.7 p43*
Funck, Georg 40; New York, NY, 1893 *1883.7 p43*
Funck, Henry 34; Mississippi, 1846 *778.6 p128*
Funck, Jacob 6; New York, NY, 1893 *1883.7 p43*
Funck, Joh. 11 months; New York, NY, 1893 *1883.7 p43*
Funck, Lisbeth 4; New York, NY, 1893 *1883.7 p43*
Funck, Maria 17; New York, NY, 1893 *1883.7 p43*
Funck, Maria 29; New York, NY, 1893 *1883.7 p43*
Funck, Marie 9; Mississippi, 1846 *778.6 p128*
Funck, Michel 56; Mississippi, 1846 *778.6 p128*
Funck, Philipp 11 months; New York, NY, 1893 *1883.7 p43*
Funcke, Fritz; New York, 1860 *358.56 p3*

Funde, Gustave F.; Wisconsin, 1890 *6795.8 p189*
Funfack, Joh. Carl; Valdivia, Chile, 1852 *1192.4 p54*
  With wife & baby
  With child 3
Fung, Adam 27; New Orleans, 1840 *778.6 p128*
Fung, Caroline 23; New Orleans, 1840 *778.6 p128*
Fung, Salome 44; New Orleans, 1840 *778.6 p128*
Funia, Louis 24; New Orleans, 1843 *778.6 p128*
Funk, Adam Friedrich; America, 1866 *2526.43 p147*
Funk, Adolf Ehrhardt; America, 1867 *7919.3 p528*
Funk, Caroline; America, 1867 *7919.3 p530*
Funk, G. Jacob; Kansas, 1894 *1447.20 p65*
Funk, George; Kansas, 1896 *1447.20 p65*
Funk, Heinrich; Kansas, 1893 *1447.20 p65*
Funk, Jacob 22; Kansas, 1906 *1447.20 p62*
Funk, Katharina 9 *SEE* Funk, Katharina
Funk, Katharina 30; New York, 1872 *5475.1 p533*
  *Daughter:*Katharina 9
Funk, Margarethe; Brazil, 1864 *5475.1 p500*
  *Son:*Peter
  *Daughter:*Margarethe
  *Son:*Johann
  *Son:*Nikolaus
Funk, Mathias; America, 1860 *5475.1 p261*
Funk, Peter; America, 1871 *5475.1 p263*
Funk, Reinhold 21; Halifax, N.S., 1902 *1860.4 p41*
Funk, Wilhelm; Mexico, 1902 *7420.1 p378*
Funke, Anna; America, 1923 *8023.44 p373*
Funsch, George 42; Michigan, 1880 *4491.39 p10*
Funsch, Jane 40; Michigan, 1880 *4491.39 p10*
Funsch, John 56; Michigan, 1880 *4491.39 p10*
Funte, Bernard; Ohio, 1840-1897 *8365.35 p16*
Furatte, Gaston 31; Port uncertain, 1845 *778.6 p128*
Furber, William 43; Ontario, 1871 *1823.21 p124*
Furbrush, Andrew N. *SEE* Furbrush, Daniel P.
Furbrush, Daniel D. *SEE* Furbrush, Daniel P.
Furbrush, Daniel P.; Ohio, 1802 *9228.50 p214*
  With wife
  *Child:*Nathaniel
  *Child:*Solomon T.
  *Child:*Susan M.
  *Child:*Andrew N.
  *Child:*Daniel D.
  *Child:*Thomas R.
  *Child:*Peter T.
Furbrush, Nathaniel *SEE* Furbrush, Daniel P.
Furbrush, Peter T. *SEE* Furbrush, Daniel P.
Furbrush, Solomon T. *SEE* Furbrush, Daniel P.
Furbrush, Susan M. *SEE* Furbrush, Daniel P.
Furbrush, Thomas R. *SEE* Furbrush, Daniel P.
Furbrushe, Andrew N. *SEE* Furbrushe, Daniel P.
Furbrushe, Daniel D. *SEE* Furbrushe, Daniel P.
Furbrushe, Daniel P.; Ohio, 1802 *9228.50 p214*
  With wife
  *Child:*Nathaniel
  *Child:*Solomon T.
  *Child:*Susan M.
  *Child:*Andrew N.
  *Child:*Daniel D.
  *Child:*Thomas R.
  *Child:*Peter T.
Furbrushe, Nathaniel *SEE* Furbrushe, Daniel P.
Furbrushe, Peter T. *SEE* Furbrushe, Daniel P.
Furbrushe, Solomon T. *SEE* Furbrushe, Daniel P.
Furbrushe, Susan M. *SEE* Furbrushe, Daniel P.
Furbrushe, Thomas R. *SEE* Furbrushe, Daniel P.
Furbush, Andrew N. *SEE* Furbush, Daniel P.
Furbush, Daniel D. *SEE* Furbush, Daniel P.
Furbush, Daniel P.; Ohio, 1802 *9228.50 p214*
  With wife
  *Child:*Nathaniel
  *Child:*Solomon T.
  *Child:*Susan M.
  *Child:*Andrew N.
  *Child:*Daniel D.
  *Child:*Thomas R.
  *Child:*Peter T.
Furbush, Nathaniel *SEE* Furbush, Daniel P.
Furbush, Peter T. *SEE* Furbush, Daniel P.
Furbush, Solomon T. *SEE* Furbush, Daniel P.
Furbush, Susan M. *SEE* Furbush, Daniel P.
Furbush, Thomas R. *SEE* Furbush, Daniel P.
Furch, John; Boston, 1767 *1642 p38*
Furdek, Stepan; Cleveland, OH, 1882 *2853.20 p490*
Furet, Gilles; Quebec, 1661 *9221.17 p456*
Furey Family ; Newfoundland, 1750 *9228.50 p233*
Furfaro, Frank; New York, 1926 *1173.1 p2*
Furgison, George F. 12; Michigan, 1880 *4491.30 p13*
Furgison, John C. 48; Michigan, 1880 *4491.30 p13*
Furlong, James; Boston, 1764 *1642 p33*
Furnace, Lewis; Ohio, 1809-1852 *4511.35 p16*
Furnas, Lewis; Ohio, 1809-1852 *4511.35 p16*
Furnas, Lewis, Jr.; Ohio, 1809-1852 *4511.35 p16*

Furness, John 72; Ontario, 1871 *1823.21 p124*
Furness, John; Washington, 1885 *2770.40 p194*
Fursa, James 39; Ontario, 1871 *1823.21 p124*
Fursey, John 20; Ontario, 1871 *1823.21 p124*
Furst, August Wilh.; Chicago, 1889 *5475.1 p381*
Furst, Barbara; America, 1867 *179.55 p19*
Furst, Catharina 26; America, 1843 *778.6 p128*
Furst, Heinrich; America, 1883 *5475.1 p37*
Furstenau, Friedrich Ludwig; America, 1834 *7420.1 p7*

Fusbert, Antoine 23; America, 1841 *778.6 p128*
Fusch, Anton 25; America, 1848 *778.6 p128*
Fuss, Anna 27; America, 1867 *5475.1 p349*
Fuss, Anna Maria 40; America, 1837 *5475.1 p385*
Fuss, John 16; Port uncertain, 1847 *778.6 p128*
Fuss, Kaspar; Port uncertain, 1866 *170.15 p25*
   With sister
Fuss, Nicolas 24; Port uncertain, 1847 *778.6 p128*
Futch, Jacob; North Carolina, 1710 *3629.40 p8*

Futch, Onesimus; North Carolina, 1710 *3629.40 p8*
Futl, Jehine 66; America, 1840 *778.6 p128*
Futscher, Maria 47; America, 1881 *5475.1 p198*
Fuxa, Jakub; Nebraska, 1871-1872 *2853.20 p176*
Fyfe, James; North Carolina, 1799 *1088.45 p10*
Fyling, Peter; Marston's Wharf, 1782 *8529.30 p11*
Fyoh, Hewett 46; Ontario, 1871 *1823.21 p124*
Fysh, Henry 49; Ontario, 1871 *1823.21 p124*

G

Gaave, John Emile; Louisiana, 1874 *4981.45 p295*
Gabachuler, John U.; Colorado, 1890 *1029.59 p30*
Gabathulen, John U.; Colorado, 1890 *1029.59 p30*
Gabby, Wm.; Maryland, 1672 *1236.25 p47*
Gabe, Elizabeth 62; Ontario, 1871 *1823.21 p124*
Gabel, Jacob 35; Missouri, 1845 *778.6 p128*
Gabel, Moses 25; New York, NY, 1894 *6512.1 p229*
Gabel, Osias 16; New York, NY, 1894 *6512.1 p229*
Gabenisch, Christof 38; New Orleans, 1848 *778.6 p128*
Gabers, Elsie 17; New York, NY, 1885 *1883.7 p45*
Gabers, Minna 17; New York, NY, 1885 *1883.7 p45*
Gabert, Gustav 27; New York, NY, 1885 *1883.7 p45*
Gabidel, Louis F. 60; New Orleans, 1840 *778.6 p129*
Gabin, Charles; Quebec, 1646 *9221.17 p164*
Gabiul, Martin; Ohio, 1809-1852 *4511.35 p16*
Gabler, Balthasar 19; America, 1852 *5475.1 p532*
Gabley, Samuel Jacob; North Carolina, 1710 *3629.40 p4*
Gabory, Louis 22; Quebec, 1661 *9221.17 p456*
Gabory, Simon; Quebec, 1646 *9221.17 p164*
Gaboury, Antoine 18; Quebec, 1659 *9221.17 p401*
Gaboury, Catherine; Quebec, 1663 *4514.3 p363*
Gabrel, Viktor; Detroit, 1930 *1640.60 p82*
Gabriel, . . .; Baltimore, 1889 *8425.16 p35*
Gabriel, Barbaria 17; America, 1847 *778.6 p129*
Gabriel, Catherina 9; America, 1847 *778.6 p129*
Gabriel, Elisabeth Hohlweck SEE Gabriel, Franz Josef
Gabriel, Franz 20; Baltimore, 1889 *8425.16 p36*
Gabriel, Franz Josef; America, 1867 *5475.1 p379*
   *Wife:*Elisabeth Hohlweck
Gabriel, Gilbert; Georgia, 1795 *1451.56 p118*
Gabriel, Johann 32; Baltimore, 1889 *8425.16 p35*
Gabriel, Joseph; America, 1847 *778.6 p129*
Gabriel, Magdalina 15; America, 1847 *778.6 p129*
Gabriel, Maria 44; America, 1847 *778.6 p129*
Gabriel, Marie 27; Baltimore, 1889 *8425.16 p35*
Gabriel, Martin; Ohio, 1809-1852 *4511.35 p16*
Gabriel, Susana 8; America, 1847 *778.6 p129*
Gabriel, Suzanne de 36; Montreal, 1659 *9221.17 p427*
Gabriel, Wilhelm; America, 1881 *5475.1 p145*
Gabrio, Widow; America, 1854 *7420.1 p119*
   With daughter
Gabrio, Charlotte; America, 1854 *7420.1 p119*
Gabrio, Friedrich; America, 1853 *7420.1 p105*
Gabrio, Mrs. Friedrich G.; America, 1854 *7420.1 p119*
   With 2 sons
Gabrio, Mrs. G.; America, 1854 *7420.1 p119*
   With 3 sons
Gabrio, Heinrich; America, 1853 *7420.1 p105*
Gabrysewski, Julyian; Detroit, 1929-1930 *6214.5 p69*
Gachatte, Joseph; Ohio, 1809-1852 *4511.35 p16*
Gachter, Francis J.; Ohio, 1809-1852 *4511.35 p16*
Gadal, Alphonse; Louisiana, 1874-1875 *4981.45 p298*
Gadda, Robert; Cleveland, OH, 1903-1906 *9722.10 p119*
Gadlemann, Conrad; Illinois, 1859 *6079.1 p5*
Gadois, Francoise 50; Montreal, 1641 *9221.17 p107*
Gadois, Louise Mauger 36 SEE Gadois, Pierre
Gadois, Pierre 4 SEE Gadois, Pierre
Gadois, Pierre 38; Quebec, 1636 *9221.17 p55*
   *Wife:*Louise Mauger 36
   *Son:*Pierre 4
   *Son:*Roberte 8
Gadois, Roberte 8 SEE Gadois, Pierre
Gadomsky, Anna SEE Gadomsky, Anna Winkel
Gadomsky, Anna; America, 1882 *5475.1 p167*
   *Daughter:*Anna
   *Son:*Anstreicher
   *Daughter:*Elisabeth
   *Son:*Jakob

Gadomsky, Anstreicher SEE Gadomsky, Anna Winkel
Gadomsky, Elisabeth SEE Gadomsky, Anna Winkel
Gadomsky, Ferdinand Rudolf; St. Louis, 1880 *5475.1 p32*
Gadomsky, Jakob SEE Gadomsky, Anna Winkel
Gadomsky, Maria; America, 1882 *5475.1 p228*
Gadsby, Charles 39; Ontario, 1871 *1823.21 p124*
Gadsby, George; North Carolina, 1860 *1088.45 p10*
Gadsby, Thomas; Iowa, 1907 *1211.15 p10*
Gadsly, Elizabeth; North Carolina, 1850 *1088.45 p10*
Gadzinski, Joseph; Detroit, 1929-1930 *6214.5 p65*
Gaede, John J.F.; Illinois, 1834-1900 *6020.5 p131*
Gaegan, Joseph 45; Ontario, 1871 *1823.21 p124*
Gaehiz, John; Illinois, 1865 *6079.1 p5*
Gaelcow, Emielie; Wisconsin, 1894 *6795.8 p152*
Gaerner, Adolf; New York, NY, 1899 *5475.1 p19*
Gaertner, Franz Heinrich SEE Gaertner, Franz Heinrich
Gaertner, Franz Heinrich; America, 1847 *7420.1 p53*
   *Wife:*Friedericke Henriette Requardt
   *Daughter:*Wilhelmine Charlotte
   *Son:*Franz Heinrich
Gaertner, Friedericke Henriette Requardt SEE Gaertner, Franz Heinrich
Gaertner, Maria Anna; Venezuela, 1843 *3899.5 p544*
Gaertner, Wilhelmine Charlotte SEE Gaertner, Franz Heinrich
Gaffiero, James; North Carolina, 1842 *1088.45 p10*
Gaffney, Dennis; New Orleans, 1851 *7242.30 p142*
Gaffney, James; Boston, 1832 *3274.55 p67*
Gaffy, Jean; Quebec, 1642 *9221.17 p117*
Gagan, Ann 46; Ontario, 1871 *1823.21 p124*
Gagan, Betsy 24; Ontario, 1871 *1823.21 p124*
Gagan, James 30; Ontario, 1871 *1823.21 p124*
Gagan, Thomas 71; Ontario, 1871 *1823.21 p124*
Gage, A. 30; America, 1848 *778.6 p129*
Gage, John 33; Ontario, 1871 *1823.17 p55*
Gagerfeldt, August; Cleveland, OH, 1886-1889 *9722.10 p119*
Gagneier, Joseph 38; Louisiana, 1848 *778.6 p129*
Gagnelin, Francois 50; New Orleans, 1847 *778.6 p129*
Gagnelin, Jacques 16; New Orleans, 1847 *778.6 p129*
Gagneret, Jacques; Quebec, 1649 *9221.17 p213*
Gagnon, Jean 30 SEE Gagnon, Mathurin
Gagnon, Marguerite 45; Quebec, 1664 *9221.17 p135*
Gagnon, Marthe 5 SEE Gagnon, Mathurin
Gagnon, Mathurin 34; Quebec, 1640 *9221.17 p96*
   *Daughter:*Marthe 5
   *Brother:*Jean 30
   *Brother:*Pierre 28
Gagnon, Pierre 28 SEE Gagnon, Mathurin
Gagnon, Renee; Quebec, 1647 *9221.17 p181*
Gagnon, Robert 27; Quebec, 1655 *9221.17 p324*
Gahaie, Mr. 22; Port uncertain, 1842 *778.6 p129*
Gahan, James 48; Michigan, 1880 *4491.39 p10*
Gahan, Mary 47; Michigan, 1880 *4491.39 p11*
Gahe, Thomas; New York, 1776 *8529.30 p11*
Gaherty, Owen; Toronto, 1844 *2910.35 p115*
Gaherty, Patrick; Toronto, 1844 *2910.35 p115*
Gaherty, Patrick, Jr.; Toronto, 1844 *2910.35 p115*
Gahm, Knut A. E.; Colorado, 1903 *1029.59 p30*
Gahn, Knut A. E.; Colorado, 1903 *1029.59 p30*
Gahnberg, C.N.; New York, NY, 1852 *6412.40 p153*
Gahviller, Jakob 26; Galveston, TX, 1846 *3967.10 p379*
Gahwiler, Jakob 26; Galveston, TX, 1846 *3967.10 p379*
Gai, Johann Claudius 31; Galveston, TX, 1844 *3967.10 p374*
Gai, Joseph 5; Galveston, TX, 1844 *3967.10 p374*
Gai, Katharina 36; Galveston, TX, 1844 *3967.10 p374*

Gai, Theobald 3; Galveston, TX, 1844 *3967.10 p374*
Gaidt, Katharina; America, 1884 *5475.1 p333*
Gaig, Anna Caroline; Wisconsin, 1882 *6795.8 p47*
Gaignard, Anna 9; Louisiana, 1848 *778.6 p129*
Gaignard, Jn. Marie 26; Louisiana, 1848 *778.6 p129*
Gaillarbois, Jean; Quebec, 1647 *9221.17 p182*
   *Wife:*Marie Heude
Gaillarbois, Marie Heude 20 SEE Gaillarbois, Jean
Gaillard, Miss 2; Texas, 1848 *778.6 p129*
Gaillard, Miss 25; Texas, 1848 *778.6 p129*
Gaillard, Mr. 40; America, 1841 *778.6 p129*
Gaillard, August 18; New Orleans, 1848 *778.6 p129*
Gaillard, Bernard 18; New Orleans, 1746 *778.6 p129*
Gaillard, Christophe 21; Montreal, 1653 *9221.17 p290*
Gaillard, Etienne 22; New Orleans, 1848 *778.6 p129*
Gaillard, Francois; Quebec, 1643 *9221.17 p131*
Gaillard, Gerard 37; Texas, 1848 *778.6 p129*
Gaillard, Jean 45; Montreal, 1662 *9221.17 p497*
Gaillard, Jean; Virginia, 1700 *9230.15 p81*
   With sons
Gaillard, Jean Augte. 35; Texas, 1848 *778.6 p129*
Gaillard, Marguerite; Quebec, 1664 *4514.3 p315*
Gaillard, Marie; Quebec, 1669 *4514.3 p315*
Gaillardet, F. 32; New York, 1842 *778.6 p129*
Gaillet, Francois 18; America, 1843 *778.6 p129*
Gaillou, Jean 2 SEE Gaillou, Nicolas
Gaillou, Nicolas 29; Quebec, 1644 *9221.17 p141*
   *Wife:*Vivienne Godeur 24
   *Son:*Pierre
   *Son:*Jean 2
Gaillou, Pierre SEE Gaillou, Nicolas
Gaillou, Vivienne Godeur 24 SEE Gaillou, Nicolas
Gaine, Pierre Antoine; Illinois, 1852 *6079.1 p5*
Gainey, John 51; Michigan, 1880 *4491.33 p9*
Gainforth, Jane 38; Ontario, 1871 *1823.21 p124*
Gair, Henry 15; Ohio, 1880 *4879.40 p257*
Gairard, Jacques 35; New Orleans, 1843 *778.6 p129*
Gaiser, C.; Louisiana, 1874 *4981.45 p296*
Gait, David 60; Ontario, 1871 *1823.17 p55*
Gaitan, . . . 42; Galveston, TX, 1844 *3967.10 p376*
Gal, Francois 50; Louisiana, 1848 *778.6 p129*
Gal, Rosalie 50; Louisiana, 1848 *778.6 p129*
Gala, John; Detroit, 1929-1930 *6214.5 p70*
   *Wife:*Salomeia
   *Son:*Joseph
Gala, Joseph SEE Gala, John
Gala, Salomeia SEE Gala, John
Galabert, F. M. 39; New Orleans, 1848 *778.6 p129*
Galabie, Bartolomio; Louisiana, 1836-1840 *4981.45 p212*
Galagani, Ursula 22; Louisiana, 1840 *778.6 p129*
Galagher, James 22; Indiana, 1860 *9076.20 p66*
Galant, Jan; Detroit, 1929-1930 *6214.5 p70*
Galba, Franz 23; New York, NY, 1894 *6512.1 p232*
Galbenia, James; Toronto, 1844 *2910.35 p116*
Galbes, Michael; Texas, 1906 *3435.45 p35*
Galbraith, Angus 34; Ontario, 1871 *1823.21 p124*
Galbraith, Cathrin 66; Ontario, 1871 *1823.21 p124*
Galbraith, Donald 53; Ontario, 1871 *1823.17 p55*
Galbraith, James; Ohio, 1823 *3580.20 p32*
Galbraith, James; Ohio, 1823 *6020.12 p7*
Galbraith, James 58; Ontario, 1871 *1823.21 p124*
Galbraith, John 33; Ontario, 1871 *1823.21 p124*
Galbraith, John 61; Ontario, 1871 *1823.21 p124*
Galbraith, Joseph 34; Ontario, 1871 *1823.21 p124*
Galbraith, Malcolm 31; Ontario, 1871 *1823.21 p124*
Galbraith, Margaret 40; Ontario, 1871 *1823.21 p124*
Galbraith, Mary 30; Ontario, 1871 *1823.21 p124*
Galbraith, Peter; Missouri, 1892 *3276.1 p1*

Galbraith, Robert 29; Ontario, 1871 ***1823.21*** *p124*
Galbraith, Robt 60; Ontario, 1871 ***1823.21*** *p124*
Galbreath, Angus 30; North Carolina, 1774 ***1422.10*** *p57*
Galbreath, Katrine 26; North Carolina, 1774 ***1422.10*** *p57*
Galbreth, Cathrine 18; Ontario, 1871 ***1823.21*** *p124*
Galbrun, Simon 18; Montreal, 1653 ***9221.17*** *p290*
Galdon, Rene 27; America, 1843 ***778.6*** *p129*
Galdware, Cahn 24; America, 1843 ***778.6*** *p129*
Galdware, Phillip 22; America, 1843 ***778.6*** *p129*
Gale, Miss; Ontario, 1800-1899 ***9228.50*** *p327*
Gale, Ann; Detroit, 1850-1935 ***9228.50*** *p233*
Gale, Ann; Toronto, 1850-1935 ***9228.50*** *p233*
Gale, Anne; Detroit, 1772-1884 ***9228.50*** *p488*
Gale, Anne; Ontario, 1872-1884 ***9228.50*** *p488*
Gale, Benj.; Marblehead, MA, 1650-1750 ***9228.50*** *p233*
Gale, Charles 23; Ontario, 1871 ***1823.21*** *p124*
Gale, Charles 28; Ontario, 1871 ***1823.21*** *p124*
Gale, Enoch 50; Ontario, 1871 ***1823.21*** *p124*
Gale, James 16; Ontario, 1871 ***1823.21*** *p124*
Gale, James 45; Ontario, 1871 ***1823.21*** *p124*
Gale, Robert 61; Ontario, 1871 ***1823.21*** *p124*
Gale, Sarah; Massachusetts, 1756 ***9228.50*** *p233*
Galegar, James; Maine, 1833 ***3274.56*** *p69*
Galere, Humbert 30; America, 1840 ***778.6*** *p130*
Galerneau, Jacques 19; Quebec, 1660 ***9221.17*** *p435*
Galerneau, Pierre 41; Quebec, 1651 ***9221.17*** *p243*
Gales, Johannetta 55; America, 1854 ***5475.1*** *p255*
Galessaux, Etienne 47; New Orleans, 1848 ***778.6*** *p130*
Galet, Anne; Quebec, 1670 ***4514.3*** *p316*
Galeucia, Daniel; Montreal, 1706 ***9228.50*** *p239*
Galeucia, Daniel 8; Plymouth, MA, 1630 ***9228.50*** *p239*
With parents
Galeucia, Elijah; Maine, 1800 ***9228.50*** *p239*
With 7 brothers
Galey, Bertrand 21; New Orleans, 1848 ***778.6*** *p130*
Galey, Pierre 36; New Orleans, 1845 ***778.6*** *p130*
Galgallon, Thomas 50; Ontario, 1871 ***1823.21*** *p124*
Galibert, Marc-Antoine 24; Montreal, 1660 ***9221.17*** *p441*
Galichet, . . .; North America, n.d. ***9228.50*** *p239*
Galichon, . . .; North America, n.d. ***9228.50*** *p239*
Galien, Mr. 3 months; New Orleans, 1842 ***778.6*** *p130*
Galien, F. Marguerite 45; New Orleans, 1842 ***778.6*** *p130*
Galien, Louise Charlotte 22; New Orleans, 1842 ***778.6*** *p130*
Galien, Marie-Therese; Quebec, 1665 ***4514.3*** *p316*
Galien, P. C. 22; New Orleans, 1842 ***778.6*** *p130*
Galiffet deCaffin, Francois; Quebec, 1697 ***2314.30*** *p171*
Galiko, Hugh; Massachusetts, 1675-1676 ***1642*** *p128*
Galimard deChamplain, Augustin de; Quebec, 1699 ***2314.30*** *p169*
Galimard deChamplain, Augustin de; Quebec, 1699 ***2314.30*** *p182*
Galinier, Dominique 41; Montreal, 1657 ***9221.17*** *p371*
Galison, Philip; Boston, 1725 ***1642*** *p25*
Galissaux, Reine 43; New Orleans, 1848 ***778.6*** *p130*
Galiton, Mrs. 27; New Orleans, 1841 ***778.6*** *p130*
Galiton, Pierre 43; New Orleans, 1841 ***778.6*** *p130*
Galka, John; Detroit, 1929 ***1640.55*** *p114*
Galkowski, John; Detroit, 1929-1930 ***6214.5*** *p63*
Gall, Balthasar 9 months; New York, NY, 1874 ***6954.7*** *p38*
Gall, Balthasar 27; New York, NY, 1874 ***6954.7*** *p38*
Gall, Barbara 5; New York, NY, 1874 ***6954.7*** *p38*
Gall, Barbara 21; New York, NY, 1874 ***6954.7*** *p38*
Gall, Christine 1 month; New York, NY, 1874 ***6954.7*** *p38*
Gall, George; Ohio, 1809-1852 ***4511.35*** *p16*
Gall, Johann; America, 1881 ***5475.1*** *p155*
*Wife:*Maria Kratz
*Daughter:*Maria
*Son:*Nikolaus
Gall, John; Ohio, 1809-1852 ***4511.35*** *p16*
Gall, Margarethe 4; New York, NY, 1874 ***6954.7*** *p38*
Gall, Maria *SEE* Gall, Johann
Gall, Maria Kratz 29 *SEE* Gall, Johann
Gall, Michel 19; New Orleans, 1848 ***778.6*** *p130*
Gall, Nikolaus *SEE* Gall, Johann
Gall, Peter; Chicago, 1872 ***5475.1*** *p153*
Gall, William 25; Ontario, 1871 ***1823.17*** *p56*
Gallagher, Alex 60; Ontario, 1871 ***1823.21*** *p124*
Gallagher, Diven; Illinois, 1918 ***6007.60*** *p9*
Gallagher, Dominick; St. John, N.B., 1847 ***2978.15*** *p37*
Gallagher, Ellen; Philadelphia, 1854 ***8513.31*** *p298*
Gallagher, Gerald; St. John, N.B., 1847 ***2978.15*** *p38*
Gallagher, Henry 9; St. John, N.B., 1834 ***6469.7*** *p4*
Gallagher, Hugh; Ontario, 1787 ***1276.15*** *p230*
With child & relative
Gallagher, J.; California, 1868 ***1131.61*** *p89*
Gallagher, Jno; St. John, N.B., 1847 ***2978.15*** *p36*
Gallagher, John 44; Ontario, 1871 ***1823.21*** *p124*
Gallagher, John; St. John, N.B., 1847 ***2978.15*** *p41*
Gallagher, John; Toronto, 1844 ***2910.35*** *p116*
Gallagher, Margaret; Ontario, 1835 ***3160.1*** *p150*
Gallagher, Margaret; Prescott, Ont., 1835 ***3289.1*** *p61*
Gallagher, Mary 40; St. John, N.B., 1834 ***6469.7*** *p4*
Gallagher, Mary 40; St. John, N.B., 1834 ***6469.7*** *p6*
Gallagher, Mic; St. John, N.B., 1847 ***2978.15*** *p38*
Gallagher, Michael 57; Ontario, 1871 ***1823.17*** *p56*
Gallagher, Michael; Pennsylvania, 1856 ***5720.10*** *p111*
Gallagher, Micl; St. John, N.B., 1848 ***2978.15*** *p41*
Gallagher, Owen 40; Ontario, 1871 ***1823.21*** *p124*
Gallagher, Owen 6; St. John, N.B., 1834 ***6469.7*** *p4*
Gallagher, P.; Louisiana, 1874 ***4981.45*** *p296*
Gallagher, Patrick; Ohio, 1809-1852 ***4511.35*** *p16*
Gallagher, Patrick 4; St. John, N.B., 1834 ***6469.7*** *p4*
Gallagher, Peter; Washington, 1889 ***2770.40*** *p27*
Gallagher, Samuel; Philadelphia Co., PA, 1850 ***5720.10*** *p111*
Gallagher, William; Quebec, 1870 ***8364.32*** *p23*
Gallaher, J. P.; Louisiana, 1874 ***4981.45*** *p296*
Gallaher, Jane 49; Ontario, 1871 ***1823.21*** *p125*
Gallaher, John 60; Ontario, 1871 ***1823.21*** *p125*
Gallaiher, Patrick; New York, 1778 ***8529.30*** *p11*
Gallant, Catherine 35; Missouri, 1845 ***778.6*** *p130*
Gallant, Louis 36; Missouri, 1845 ***778.6*** *p130*
Gallant, Marie 1; Missouri, 1845 ***778.6*** *p130*
Gallatin, John; Ohio, 1809-1852 ***4511.35*** *p16*
Gallaup, Francois 29; Quebec, 1660 ***9221.17*** *p436*
Galle, Friedrich; America, 1853 ***7420.1*** *p105*
Galle, Gabriel; Ohio, 1809-1852 ***4511.35*** *p16*
Gallee, John 78; Massachusetts, 1683 ***9228.50*** *p234*
Gallen, Bridget Friel *SEE* Gallen, Patrick
Gallen, James *SEE* Gallen, Patrick
Gallen, Patrick; Philadelphia, 1868 ***8513.31*** *p308*
*Wife:*Bridget Friel
*Son:*James
Gallene, Francis 42; Ontario, 1871 ***1823.21*** *p125*
Galler, Francis; Ohio, 1809-1852 ***4511.35*** *p16*
Galler, Mathias; New Castle, DE, 1817-1818 ***90.20*** *p151*
Gallet, Francois; Quebec, 1637 ***9221.17*** *p69*
Gallet, Pierre; Quebec, 1649 ***9221.17*** *p213*
Gallevet, Francis 27; New Orleans, 1843 ***778.6*** *p130*
Galley, John 78; Massachusetts, 1683 ***9228.50*** *p234*
Galley, John; Salem, MA, 1635 ***9228.50*** *p18A*
Galley, Thomas; Salem, MA, 1790 ***9228.50*** *p350*
Gallez, John 78; Massachusetts, 1683 ***9228.50*** *p234*
Gallez, Thomas; Salem, MA, 1790 ***9228.50*** *p350*
Gallia, Ondrej; Texas, 1860-1865 ***2853.20*** *p67*
Gallichan, Abigail; Massachusetts, 1766 ***1642*** *p66*
Gallichan, Alice 9; Ontario, 1871 ***1823.21*** *p125*
Gallichan, Hannah; New Brunswick, 1773-1822 ***9228.50*** *p234*
Gallichan, John; Boston, 1769 ***9228.50*** *p48*
Gallichan, John; Boston, 1769 ***9228.50*** *p234*
Gallichan, John; Massachusetts, 1650-1700 ***9228.50*** *p238*
Gallichan, Joseph; Marblehead, MA, 1698 ***9228.50*** *p238*
Gallichan, Vincent; Massachusetts, 1678 ***9228.50*** *p238*
Gallie, Anna Maria Scott *SEE* Gallie, Francis
Gallie, David 50; Ontario, 1871 ***1823.21*** *p125*
Gallie, Elizabeth Law *SEE* Gallie, Francis
Gallie, Francis; Michigan, 1888-1906 ***9228.50*** *p235*
*Wife:*Elizabeth Law
Gallie, Francis; Quebec, 1768-1924 ***9228.50*** *p236*
Gallie, Francis; Quebec, 1790-1819 ***9228.50*** *p234*
*Son:*John Francis
*Daughter-In-Law:*Anna Maria Scott
*Granddaughter:*Joanna
Gallie, Frederick James; Michigan, 1887 ***9228.50*** *p235*
Gallie, Joanna *SEE* Gallie, Francis
Gallie, John; Quebec, 1789-1874 ***9228.50*** *p236*
Gallie, John Francis *SEE* Gallie, Francis
Galliehan, John 49; Ontario, 1871 ***1823.21*** *p125*
Gallien, Abraham; New York, NY, 1812-1850 ***9228.50*** *p237*
Gallien, Auguste 35; America, 1842 ***778.6*** *p130*
Gallien, Christian Peter *SEE* Gallien, Nicholas
Gallien, Jane; New York, 1844 ***9228.50*** *p239*
Gallien, John *SEE* Gallien, John
Gallien, John; Ohio, 1840 ***9228.50*** *p236*
*Wife:*Rachel
*Son:*John
Gallien, Martha *SEE* Gallien, Nicholas
Gallien, Mary *SEE* Gallien, Nicholas
Gallien, Maud *SEE* Gallien, Nicholas
Gallien, Nettie; Wisconsin, 1808-1870 ***9228.50*** *p237*
Gallien, Nicholas; America, 1877-1950 ***9228.50*** *p238*
*Relative:*Christian Peter
*Relative:*Maud
With relative
*Relative:*Mary
*Relative:*Martha
Gallien, Nicholas; Wisconsin, 1808-1900 ***9228.50*** *p237*
Gallien, Rachel *SEE* Gallien, John
Gallien, W.D.; Ohio, 1860 ***9228.50*** *p237*
Gallienne, Eva; Canada, 1900-1983 ***9228.50*** *p236*
Gallier, James; Louisiana, 1836-1840 ***4981.45*** *p212*
Gallier, Mary; Cincinnati, 1827 ***9228.50*** *p333*
Galligher, John 50; Ontario, 1871 ***1823.21*** *p125*
Gallikan, . . .; Boston, 1769 ***9228.50*** *p5*
Gallishon, John; Massachusetts, 1650-1700 ***9228.50*** *p238*
Gallishon, Joseph; Marblehead, MA, 1698 ***9228.50*** *p238*
Gallishon, Vincent; Massachusetts, 1678 ***9228.50*** *p238*
Gallison, John; Massachusetts, 1650-1700 ***9228.50*** *p238*
Gallison, Joseph; Marblehead, MA, 1698 ***9228.50*** *p238*
Gallison, Vincent; Massachusetts, 1678 ***9228.50*** *p238*
Gallison, Vincent; Massachusetts, 1678 ***9228.50*** *p238*
Gallogly, Peter 29; Ontario, 1871 ***1823.17*** *p56*
Gallon, Jane; New York, 1844 ***9228.50*** *p239*
Gallop, John; Dorchester, MA, 1633 ***117.5*** *p159*
Galloppe, John; Dorchester, MA, 1633 ***117.5*** *p159*
Galloway, Andrew 34; New York, NY, 1835 ***5024.1*** *p136*
Galloway, Ann 17 *SEE* Galloway, John
Galloway, Elizabeth 10 *SEE* Galloway, John
Galloway, Elizabeth 44 *SEE* Galloway, John
Galloway, Henry 33; Ontario, 1871 ***1823.17*** *p56*
Galloway, Isabella 7 *SEE* Galloway, John
Galloway, Jane 13 *SEE* Galloway, John
Galloway, Jessie 14; Ontario, 1871 ***1823.17*** *p56*
Galloway, John; New England, 1747 ***1642*** *p29*
Galloway, John 44; New York, NY, 1821 ***6178.50*** *p76*
*Relative:*Elizabeth 44
*Relative:*Thomas 4
*Relative:*Isabella 7
*Relative:*Mary 18
*Relative:*John, Jr. 15
*Relative:*Jane 13
*Relative:*Elizabeth 10
*Relative:*Ann 17
Galloway, John, Jr. 15 *SEE* Galloway, John
Galloway, Mary 18 *SEE* Galloway, John
Galloway, Mary 50; Ontario, 1871 ***1823.17*** *p56*
Galloway, Shallo 51; Ontario, 1871 ***1823.21*** *p125*
Galloway, Thomas 4 *SEE* Galloway, John
Galloway, William 40; Ontario, 1871 ***1823.21*** *p125*
Galluccia, Daniel; Montreal, 1706 ***9228.50*** *p239*
Galluccia, Daniel 8; Plymouth, MA, 1630 ***9228.50*** *p239*
With parents
Galluccia, Elijah; Maine, 1800 ***9228.50*** *p239*
With 7 brothers
Galluccio, . . .; North America, n.d. ***9228.50*** *p239*
Gallucia, . . .; North America, n.d. ***9228.50*** *p239*
Galluno, Mr. 35; America, 1843 ***778.6*** *p130*
Gallwitz, Charles Christian William; Ohio, 1809-1852 ***4511.35*** *p16*
Gally, William 49; Ontario, 1871 ***1823.17*** *p56*
Galm, Amalie; Iowa, 1931 ***1211.15*** *p10*
Galm, John; Iowa, 1930 ***1211.15*** *p10*
Galmor, Alois; Galveston, TX, 1914 ***3331.4*** *p12*
Galonka, Agnes; Detroit, 1929-1930 ***6214.5*** *p63*
Galpin, Edward 45; Ontario, 1871 ***1823.21*** *p125*
Galpin, John; Boston, 1774 ***8529.30*** *p3A*
Galpin, Richard 41; Ontario, 1871 ***1823.21*** *p125*
Galsworthy, John M. 34; Ontario, 1871 ***1823.21*** *p125*
Galtier, Mr. 36; America, 1746 ***778.6*** *p130*
Galuschka, . . .; North America, n.d. ***9228.50*** *p239*
Galusha, Daniel; Massachusetts, 1676 ***9228.50*** *p239*
Galusha, Daniel; Montreal, 1706 ***9228.50*** *p239*
Galusha, Daniel 8; Plymouth, MA, 1630 ***9228.50*** *p239*
With parents
Galusha, Elijah; Maine, 1800 ***9228.50*** *p239*
With 7 brothers
Galuszka, John; Detroit, 1930 ***1640.60*** *p76*
Galvin, Ann 40; Michigan, 1880 ***4491.39*** *p11*
Galvin, John 30; Michigan, 1880 ***4491.39*** *p11*
Galvin, John; North Carolina, 1821 ***1088.45*** *p10*
Galvin, John 60; Ontario, 1871 ***1823.17*** *p56*
Galvin, John J. 4; Michigan, 1880 ***4491.39*** *p11*
Galvin, Margaret I. 3; Ontario, 1871 ***1823.17*** *p56*
Galvin, Mary 6; Michigan, 1880 ***4491.39*** *p11*
Galvin, Mary 35; Ontario, 1871 ***1823.21*** *p125*
Galway, . . .; Toronto, 1844 ***2910.35*** *p114*
Galwitz, Charles Christian William; Ohio, 1809-1852 ***4511.35*** *p16*
Galy, Jean 33; New Orleans, 1848 ***778.6*** *p130*
Gamache, Genevieve 16 *SEE* Gamache, Nicolas
Gamache, Jacques 26 *SEE* Gamache, Nicolas
Gamache, Nicolas *SEE* Gamache, Nicolas
Gamache, Nicolas; Quebec, 1652 ***9221.17*** *p258*
*Son:*Jacques
*Daughter:*Genevieve
*Son:*Nicolas
Gambier, Marguerite; Quebec, 1664 ***4514.3*** *p316*
Gambin, Wm.; Illinois, 1834-1900 ***6020.5*** *p131*
Gamble, James 31; Ontario, 1871 ***1823.21*** *p125*
Gamble, Matilda 16; St. John, N.B., 1834 ***6469.7*** *p5*
Gamble, Thomas; North Carolina, 1839 ***1088.45*** *p10*

Gamble, William 37; Ontario, 1871 ***1823.21*** *p125*
Gambol, Andrew; North Carolina, 1837 ***1088.45*** *p10*
Gamelin, Michel 20; Quebec, 1660 ***9221.17*** *p436*
Gammack, James 27; Ontario, 1871 ***1823.21*** *p125*
Gammage, James 63; Ontario, 1871 ***1823.21*** *p125*
Gammey, John; North Carolina, 1814 ***1088.45*** *p10*
Gammock, Ann 60; Ontario, 1871 ***1823.21*** *p125*
Gammon, George 70; Ontario, 1871 ***1823.17*** *p56*
Gammon, James 40; Ontario, 1871 ***1823.17*** *p56*
Gammon, John 42; Ontario, 1871 ***1823.17*** *p56*
Gammon, Thomas 30; Ontario, 1871 ***1823.17*** *p56*
Gammon, William 43; Ontario, 1871 ***1823.17*** *p56*
Gamney, Charlotte 26; Ontario, 1871 ***1823.21*** *p125*
Gamol, Gaspard; Quebec, 1642 ***9221.17*** *p117*
Gamp, George; New Castle, DE, 1817-1818 ***90.20*** *p151*
Gamshaw, Joseph 31; Ontario, 1871 ***1823.21*** *p125*
Gancer, Joseph; Detroit, 1930 ***1640.60*** *p81*
Ganczarczyk, Joseph; Detroit, 1930 ***1640.60*** *p81*
Ganderie, Marie 17; Quebec, 1662 ***9221.17*** *p486*
Gandner, Nikolaus; North America, 1840 ***5475.1*** *p204*
Gandoulf, Pierre Jacques 22; New Orleans, 1848 ***778.6*** *p130*
Ganer, Frederick; Ohio, 1809-1852 ***4511.35*** *p16*
Ganet, Henry 26; America, 1848 ***778.6*** *p130*
Ganfer, Christian 15; Port uncertain, 1846 ***778.6*** *p130*
Ganfer, Elisabeth 35; Port uncertain, 1846 ***778.6*** *p130*
Ganfer, Philipp 74; Port uncertain, 1846 ***778.6*** *p130*
Gange, Samuel; Wisconsin, 1875 ***6795.8*** *p201*
Ganger, Bertha Minnie Augusta; Wisconsin, 1895 ***6795.8*** *p106*
Gangloff, Carolina 30; America, 1847 ***778.6*** *p130*
Gania, G. 50; America, 1848 ***778.6*** *p130*
Ganje, Catharina 3; New York, NY, 1893 ***1883.7*** *p38*
Ganje, Christian 13; New York, NY, 1893 ***1883.7*** *p38*
Ganje, Franz 5; New York, NY, 1893 ***1883.7*** *p38*
Ganje, Josef 4 months; New York, NY, 1893 ***1883.7*** *p38*
Ganje, Magda 1 months; New York, NY, 1893 ***1883.7*** *p38*
Ganje, Peter 35; New York, NY, 1893 ***1883.7*** *p38*
Ganje, Regina 33; New York, NY, 1893 ***1883.7*** *p38*
Ganje, Scholastika 2; New York, NY, 1893 ***1883.7*** *p38*
Gann, John; Ohio, 1840 ***2763.1*** *p9*
Ganner, Augustus; North Carolina, 1853 ***1088.45*** *p10*
Gannes, Georges de; Quebec, 1732 ***2314.30*** *p170*
Gannes, Georges de; Quebec, 1732 ***2314.30*** *p182*
Gannes, Jean-Baptiste de; Quebec, 1737 ***2314.30*** *p170*
Gannes, Jean-Baptiste de; Quebec, 1737 ***2314.30*** *p182*
Gannes deFalaise, Louis de; Quebec, 1683-1688 ***2314.30*** *p168*
Gannes deFalaise, Louis de; Quebec, 1687 ***2314.30*** *p183*
Gannes deFalaize, Francois de; Quebec, 1715 ***2314.30*** *p169*
Gannes deFalaize, Francois de; Quebec, 1715 ***2314.30*** *p182*
Gannon, William; Louisiana, 1874-1875 ***4981.45*** *p298*
Gannon, William 36; Ontario, 1871 ***1823.21*** *p125*
Gano Family ; New York, 1661 ***9228.50*** *p242*
Gans, Joseph; Philadelphia, 1850 ***5720.10*** *p377*
Gans, Maria Margarethe 36; America, 1872 ***5475.1*** *p41*
Gansjager, . . .; West Virginia, 1850-1860 ***1132.30*** *p147*
Ganss, Carl; America, 1867 ***7919.3*** *p527*
Ganster, Anna 12 *SEE* Ganster, Johann
Ganster, Elisabeth 2 *SEE* Ganster, Johann
Ganster, Georg *SEE* Ganster, Karl, II
Ganster, Georg 4 *SEE* Ganster, Johann
Ganster, Johann 7 *SEE* Ganster, Johann
Ganster, Johann 39; America, 1853 ***5475.1*** *p53*
*Wife:*Katharina Escher 38
*Son:*Georg 4
*Daughter:*Elisabeth 2
*Son:*Johann 7
*Daughter:*Margarethe 14
*Daughter:*Anna 12
*Daughter:*Katharina 9
Ganster, Karl *SEE* Ganster, Karl, II
Ganster, Karl, II; America, 1880 ***5475.1*** *p55*
*Wife:*Maria Kern
*Son:*Karl
*Son:*Georg
*Son:*Wilhelm
Ganster, Katharina 9 *SEE* Ganster, Johann
Ganster, Katharina Escher 38 *SEE* Ganster, Johann
Ganster, Margarethe 14 *SEE* Ganster, Johann
Ganster, Maria Kern *SEE* Ganster, Karl, II
Ganster, Regina 28; America, 1875 ***5475.1*** *p420*
Ganster, Wilhelm *SEE* Ganster, Karl, II
Ganter, Christian; North Carolina, 1710 ***3629.40*** *p4*
Ganter, Joseph; Venezuela, 1843 ***3899.5*** *p541*
Ganter, Margaretha; Venezuela, 1843 ***3899.5*** *p542*
Ganter, Nicholas; Long Island, 1780 ***8529.30*** *p9A*
Gantes, John; North Carolina, 1857 ***1088.45*** *p10*
Ganther, Anna Maria; Venezuela, 1843 ***3899.5*** *p541*
Ganther, Margaretha; Venezuela, 1843 ***3899.5*** *p542*
Gantz, Louise; America, 1868 ***7919.3*** *p527*
Ganzert, Susanna; America, 1851 ***2526.43*** *p145*
Gar, John 48; Indiana, 1883-1888 ***9076.20*** *p71*
Garbaille, Phillip 26; America, 1841 ***778.6*** *p130*
Garbarino, Louis; Colorado, 1868 ***1029.59*** *p30*
Garber, Friedrich Johann; Wisconsin, 1875 ***6795.8*** *p90*
Garber, John W.; Ohio, 1809-1852 ***4511.35*** *p16*
Garberding, Heinrich Dietrich Wilhelm *SEE* Garberding, Marie Dorothee
Garberding, Marie Dorothee; America, 1873 ***7420.1*** *p299*
*Son:*Heinrich Dietrich Wilhelm
Garbolino, Louis; Illinois, 1918 ***6007.60*** *p9*
Garburton, John 18; Ontario, 1871 ***1823.21*** *p125*
Garbutt, William 75; Ontario, 1871 ***1823.21*** *p125*
Garcelon, Mark; Maine, 1776 ***9228.50*** *p242*
Garchan, Andrew; North Carolina, 1844 ***1088.45*** *p11*
Garcia, Pedro; Louisiana, 1841-1844 ***4981.45*** *p210*
Garczyk, Antonina; Detroit, 1890 ***9980.23*** *p96*
Gard, Anna; America, 1850-1899 ***6442.17*** *p65*
Gard, Patrick; Washington, 1885 ***2770.40*** *p194*
Gardebled, James 28; New Orleans, 1844 ***778.6*** *p130*
Gardeen, Oscar S.; St. Paul, MN, 1888 ***1865.50*** *p48*
Gardell, Jacob Niclas; North America, 1866 ***6410.15*** *p105*
Gardell, Johan Rudolf; New York, NY, 1850 ***6410.15*** *p104*
Gardellar, P. 46; America, 1848 ***778.6*** *p130*
Garden, Robert 70; Ontario, 1871 ***1823.21*** *p125*
Gardener, Frederick 5; Quebec, 1870 ***8364.32*** *p23*
Gardener, John; Marston's Wharf, 1782 ***8529.30*** *p11*
Gardener, John S. 45; Ontario, 1871 ***1823.21*** *p125*
Gardener, Robert 53; Ontario, 1871 ***1823.21*** *p125*
Gardener, Thomas 6; Quebec, 1870 ***8364.32*** *p23*
Gardener, William 47; Ontario, 1871 ***1823.21*** *p125*
Gardere, J. P. 20; New Orleans, 1843 ***778.6*** *p130*
Gardet, A. P. 27; America, 1845 ***778.6*** *p130*
Gardin, Jacquette; Quebec, 1668 ***4514.3*** *p348*
Gardine, Isaac D.; Illinois, 1856 ***6079.1*** *p5*
Gardiner, Elisabeth 48; Ontario, 1871 ***1823.21*** *p125*
Gardiner, John; Boston, 1774 ***8529.30*** *p2*
Gardiner, John; Marston's Wharf, 1782 ***8529.30*** *p11*
Gardiner, Maria 24; Ontario, 1871 ***1823.21*** *p125*
Gardiner, Peter 88; Ontario, 1871 ***1823.21*** *p125*
Gardiner, Rebecca 46; Ontario, 1871 ***1823.21*** *p125*
Gardiner, Richard; Plymouth, MA, 1620 ***1920.45*** *p5*
Gardiner, Robert 45; Ontario, 1871 ***1823.21*** *p125*
Gardiner, Robert 56; Ontario, 1871 ***1823.17*** *p56*
Gardiner, Sylvester; Bahamas, 1700-1800 ***9228.50*** *p199*
Gardiner, Sylvester; Halifax, N.S., 1700-1800 ***9228.50*** *p199*
Gardiner, Thomas; Boston, 1775 ***8529.30*** *p3A*
Gardiner, Thomas 44; Ontario, 1871 ***1823.21*** *p125*
Gardiner, William 39; Ontario, 1871 ***1823.21*** *p125*
Gardiner, William Timbs; Washington, 1889 ***2770.40*** *p27*
Gardner, George 24; Ontario, 1871 ***1823.17*** *p56*
Gardner, Henry 17; Quebec, 1870 ***8364.32*** *p23*
Gardner, Isaac; Boston, 1827 ***3274.55*** *p66*
Gardner, James; New York, NY, 1828 ***3274.55*** *p66*
Gardner, James; Ohio, 1809-1852 ***4511.35*** *p16*
Gardner, James 49; Ontario, 1871 ***1823.21*** *p125*
Gardner, Johanna 26; Ontario, 1871 ***1823.21*** *p125*
Gardner, John; America, 1715 ***9228.50*** *p195*
Gardner, John; Marston's Wharf, 1782 ***8529.30*** *p11*
Gardner, John, Sr. 62; Ontario, 1871 ***1823.21*** *p125*
Gardner, Robert 64; Ontario, 1871 ***1823.21*** *p125*
Gardner, Samuel 21; Ontario, 1871 ***1823.21*** *p125*
Gardner, Thom; New Orleans, 1851 ***7242.30*** *p142*
Gardner, Thomas; New York, 1859 ***358.56*** *p99*
Gardon, Mr. 60; Port uncertain, 1841 ***778.6*** *p131*
Gardow, Alfred; Wisconsin, 1910 ***6795.8*** *p167*
Gardow, Emil; Wisconsin, 1898 ***6795.8*** *p123*
Gardro, Marianna 18; New York, NY, 1911 ***6533.11*** *p10*
Gareis, Kunigunde 20; New York, NY, 1864 ***8425.62*** *p198*
Garelle, Suzanne 23; Quebec, 1662 ***9221.17*** *p485*
Gareman, Florence 10 *SEE* Gareman, Pierre
Gareman, Madeleine Charlot *SEE* Gareman, Pierre
Gareman, Nicole-Madeleine 9 *SEE* Gareman, Pierre
Gareman, Pierre; Quebec, 1639 ***9221.17*** *p88*
*Wife:*Madeleine Charlot
*Daughter:*Florence
*Daughter:*Nicole-Madeleine
Garenback, Adam 36; Ontario, 1871 ***1823.21*** *p126*
Garey, Thomas; Marston's Wharf, 1782 ***8529.30*** *p11*
Garf, Lewis 35; America, 1848 ***778.6*** *p131*
Gargottin, Louise; Quebec, 1663 ***4514.3*** *p316*
Gargy, Jean 28; America, 1840 ***778.6*** *p131*
Gariepy, Francois 27; Quebec, 1656 ***9221.17*** *p336*
Garigue, Emile 36; America, 1841 ***778.6*** *p131*
Garin, Edmond; Ohio, 1809-1852 ***4511.35*** *p16*
Garland, Francis 35; Ontario, 1871 ***1823.21*** *p126*
Garland, George 3; Ontario, 1871 ***1823.21*** *p126*
Garland, Georgina 8; Quebec, 1870 ***8364.32*** *p23*
Garland, James 45; Ontario, 1871 ***1823.21*** *p126*
Garland, Susan 13; Quebec, 1870 ***8364.32*** *p23*
Garland, William; Philadelphia, 1858 ***5720.10*** *p378*
Garlej, Franciszka 19; New York, NY, 1911 ***6533.11*** *p10*
Garlick, Robert 61; Ontario, 1871 ***1823.21*** *p126*
Garman, Frederick; Ohio, 1809-1852 ***4511.35*** *p16*
Garman, John; Ohio, 1809-1852 ***4511.35*** *p16*
Garmell, Sebastian 34; Port uncertain, 1841 ***778.6*** *p131*
Garmony, John; South Carolina, 1808 ***6155.4*** *p18*
Garms, Elsie Sophia; Iowa, 1925 ***1211.15*** *p10*
Garms, Henry Nickolas; Iowa, 1925 ***1211.15*** *p10*
Garms, Otto Carl; Iowa, 1928 ***1211.15*** *p10*
Garn, Gustavis; Illinois, 1834-1900 ***6020.5*** *p131*
Garnauld, Louis 21; Quebec, 1656 ***9221.17*** *p338*
Garner, Fannie; Philadelphia, 1846 ***8513.31*** *p412*
Garner, John 24; Ontario, 1871 ***1823.21*** *p126*
Garner, Joseph Stokes 32; Ontario, 1871 ***1823.17*** *p56*
Garnett, Rothwell 60; Ontario, 1871 ***1823.21*** *p126*
Garnett, Saml. 45; Ontario, 1871 ***1823.17*** *p56*
Garney, Mary 25; Ontario, 1871 ***1823.21*** *p126*
Garnien, Joseph 27; New Orleans, 1848 ***778.6*** *p131*
Garnien, Josephine 21; New Orleans, 1848 ***778.6*** *p131*
Garnier, Mr.; New Orleans, 1840 ***778.6*** *p131*
Garnier, Anne-Michelle 26; Montreal, 1659 ***9221.17*** *p418*
Garnier, Charles 25; Quebec, 1661 ***9221.17*** *p456*
Garnier, Charles 30; Quebec, 1636 ***9221.17*** *p50*
Garnier, Francois 24; Quebec, 1662 ***9221.17*** *p485*
Garnier, Francoise; Quebec, 1634 ***9221.17*** *p35*
Garnier, Francoise 25; Quebec, 1662 ***9221.17*** *p480*
Garnier, Jean; Quebec, 1647 ***9221.17*** *p181*
Garnier, Jean 23; Quebec, 1656 ***9221.17*** *p337*
Garnier, Jean 23; Quebec, 1656 ***9221.17*** *p343*
Garnier, Jeanne 21; Quebec, 1657 ***9221.17*** *p358*
Garnier, Julien 19; Quebec, 1662 ***9221.17*** *p478*
Garnier, Louise 22; Montreal, 1658 ***9221.17*** *p389*
Garnier, Marie 27; Montreal, 1659 ***9221.17*** *p421*
Garnier, Marie 34; Montreal, 1659 ***9221.17*** *p419*
Garnier, Nicolas; Quebec, 1642 ***9221.17*** *p117*
Garnot, Jean; Quebec, 1662 ***9221.17*** *p485*
Garnsey, Guillaume; Canada, 1534 ***9228.50*** *p260*
Garnsey, Guillaume; Canada, 1534 ***9228.50*** *p260*
Garramone, John 24; Colorado, 1924 ***1029.59*** *p30*
Garratt, Andrew; New York, 1783 ***8529.30*** *p11*
Garratt, Micheal 51; Ontario, 1871 ***1823.17*** *p56*
Garratt, William; Marston's Wharf, 1782 ***8529.30*** *p11*
Garraty, John 65; Ontario, 1871 ***1823.21*** *p126*
Garreau, . . .; America, 1841 ***778.6*** *p131*
Garreau, Mr. 24; America, 1841 ***778.6*** *p131*
Garreau, Mrs. 22; America, 1841 ***778.6*** *p131*
Garreau, Ms. 29; America, 1747 ***778.6*** *p131*
Garreau, Leonard 34; Quebec, 1643 ***9221.17*** *p127*
Garrett, Bruff; Quebec, 1885 ***1937.10*** *p52*
Garrett, E. V.; Montreal, 1922 ***4514.4*** *p32*
Garrett, Hugh 28; Ontario, 1871 ***1823.17*** *p56*
Garrett, James 33; Ontario, 1871 ***1823.17*** *p56*
Garrett, John J.; Missouri, 1888 ***3276.1*** *p1*
Garrett, Mark 44; Ontario, 1871 ***1823.21*** *p126*
Garrett, Sarah 18; Quebec, 1870 ***8364.32*** *p23*
Garrett, Thomas 80; Ontario, 1871 ***1823.17*** *p56*
Garrett, William 74; Ontario, 1871 ***1823.21*** *p126*
Garrety, Mary; New Orleans, 1851 ***7242.30*** *p142*
Garride, Jean 21; New Orleans, 1845 ***778.6*** *p131*
Garrier, Jean 24; Montreal, 1660 ***9221.17*** *p441*
Garrigan, Matthew; Louisiana, 1874-1875 ***4981.45*** *p298*
Garris, Sarah A. 37; Michigan, 1880 ***4491.36*** *p8*
Garrity, P. B.; California, 1868 ***1131.61*** *p89*
Garroch, John 39; Ontario, 1871 ***1823.17*** *p56*
Garrow, Alexander; Illinois, 1858 ***6079.1*** *p5*
Garry, Jean Bte. 44; America, 1746 ***778.6*** *p131*
Garry, Michael; North Carolina, 1856 ***1088.45*** *p11*
Garry, Michael M. 54; Ontario, 1871 ***1823.21*** *p126*
Garsed, Alfred 24; Quebec, 1870 ***8364.32*** *p23*
Garside, James 49; Ontario, 1871 ***1823.21*** *p126*
Garside, Joshua; Massachusetts, 1831 ***3274.55*** *p67*
Garside, Thos 41; Ontario, 1871 ***1823.21*** *p126*
Garso, Jose; Louisiana, 1874-1875 ***4981.45*** *p29*
Gartland, James; Toronto, 1844 ***2910.35*** *p114*
Gartner, Angela *SEE* Gartner, Jakob
Gartner, Angela *SEE* Gartner, Nikolaus
Gartner, Anna *SEE* Gartner, Jakob
Gartner, Barbara *SEE* Gartner, Jakob
Gartner, Engel Marie; America, 1864 ***7420.1*** *p223*
With 2 children
Gartner, Franziska Mayer *SEE* Gartner, Jakob
Gartner, Friedrich; America, 1852 ***2526.43*** *p139*
Gartner, Jakob; America, 1872 ***5475.1*** *p160*
*Wife:*Franziska Mayer
*Daughter:*Anna
*Daughter:*Angela

*Son:*Peter
*Daughter:*Barbara
*Daughter:*Maria
Gartner, Jakob *SEE* Gartner, Nikolaus
Gartner, Jakob 20; America, 1847 ***2526.43*** *p139*
Gartner, Johann *SEE* Gartner, Nikolaus
Gartner, Johann Christian; America, 1854 ***7420.1*** *p119*
Gartner, Josef; Milwaukee, 1871 ***2853.20*** *p310*
Gartner, Katharina *SEE* Gartner, Nikolaus
Gartner, Margarethe Hauch 41 *SEE* Gartner, Nikolaus
Gartner, Maria *SEE* Gartner, Peter
Gartner, Maria *SEE* Gartner, Jakob
Gartner, Maria; America, 1881 ***5475.1*** *p161*
Gartner, Maria Klein 56 *SEE* Gartner, Peter
Gartner, Nikolaus *SEE* Gartner, Nikolaus
Gartner, Nikolaus 46; America, 1881 ***5475.1*** *p196*
*Wife:*Margarethe Hauch 41
*Son:*Johann
*Son:*Nikolaus
*Son:*Peter
*Daughter:*Katharina
*Daughter:*Angela
*Son:*Jakob
Gartner, Peter *SEE* Gartner, Jakob
Gartner, Peter *SEE* Gartner, Nikolaus
Gartner, Peter 56; America, 1855 ***5475.1*** *p272*
*Wife:*Maria Klein 56
*Daughter:*Maria
Gartner Family ; America, 1858 ***7420.1*** *p177*
Garton, Alfred; Washington, 1880 ***2770.40*** *p134*
Garton, Arthur; North Carolina, 1811 ***1088.45*** *p11*
Gartsen, Christian; Washington, 1886 ***2770.40*** *p195*
Gartz, Rudolph; America, 1867 ***7919.3*** *p529*
Garvey, John 36; Ontario, 1871 ***1823.17*** *p56*
Garvey, Michael; Illinois, 1834-1900 ***6020.5*** *p131*
Garvey, William; New York, 1777 ***8529.30*** *p3A*
Garvin, John 34; Ontario, 1871 ***1823.17*** *p56*
Garvin, W. H.; California, 1868 ***1131.61*** *p89*
Garvin, William; Boston, 1833 ***3274.56*** *p97*
Gary, Mr. 45; America, 1846 ***778.6*** *p131*
Gary, Daniel B.; Ohio, 1858 ***3580.20*** *p32*
Gary, Daniel B.; Ohio, 1858 ***6020.12*** *p7*
Gary, E. 26; New Orleans, 1844 ***778.6*** *p131*
Gary, Thomas; Marston's Wharf, 1782 ***8529.30*** *p11*
Gary, William; Maryland, 1671 ***1236.25*** *p46*
Gasch, F.; Galveston, TX, 1855 ***571.7*** *p18*
Gaschet, Marie 30; Quebec, 1649 ***9221.17*** *p213*
Gascoine, John 66; Ontario, 1871 ***1823.17*** *p56*
Gascomb, Thomas; Marston's Wharf, 1782 ***8529.30*** *p12*
Gasden, Edward 60; Ontario, 1871 ***1823.21*** *p126*
Gasden, Elizabeth 95; Ontario, 1871 ***1823.21*** *p126*
Gasiewski, Antoni 40; New York, NY, 1911 ***6533.11*** *p9*
Gasinski, Joseph Stefan; Detroit, 1930 ***1640.60*** *p77*
Gaskins, Jno; Virginia, 1652 ***6254.4*** *p243*
Gaskins, Thomas; Virginia, 1652 ***6254.4*** *p243*
Gasnier, Anne 35; Quebec, 1649 ***9221.17*** *p213*
Gasnier, Louis 10 *SEE* Gasnier, Pierre
Gasnier, Louis 32; Quebec, 1644 ***9221.17*** *p142*
*Wife:*Marie Michel 22
*Daughter:*Louise 2
Gasnier, Louise 2 *SEE* Gasnier, Louis
Gasnier, Marguerite Roset 38 *SEE* Gasnier, Pierre
Gasnier, Marie Michel 22 *SEE* Gasnier, Louis
Gasnier, Nicolas 2 *SEE* Gasnier, Pierre
Gasnier, Pierre 8 *SEE* Gasnier, Pierre
Gasnier, Pierre 43; Quebec, 1653 ***9221.17*** *p274*
*Wife:*Marguerite Roset 38
*Son:*Louis 10
*Son:*Pierre 8
*Son:*Nicolas 2
Gaspar, Anna Maria Felz 47 *SEE* Gaspar, Mathias
Gaspar, Celestine 22; America, 1841 ***778.6*** *p131*
Gaspar, Johann; America, 1889 ***5475.1*** *p351*
Gaspar, Katharina; America, 1873 ***5475.1*** *p136*
Gaspar, Mathias *SEE* Gaspar, Mathias
Gaspar, Mathias 47; America, 1867 ***5475.1*** *p376*
*Wife:*Anna Maria Felz 47
*Son:*Mathias
*Son:*Peter
Gaspar, Nicolas 20; Mississippi, 1847 ***778.6*** *p131*
Gaspar, Peter *SEE* Gaspar, Mathias
Gaspard, Alexandre; New York, NY, 1855 ***1494.21*** *p31*
Gaspard, J. Charles; New York, NY, 1869 ***1494.21*** *p31*
Gaspard, Johann Adam; America, 1882 ***5475.1*** *p197*
Gaspard, Joseph; New York, NY, 1855 ***1494.21*** *p31*
Gaspard, Seraphin; New York, NY, 1855 ***1494.21*** *p31*
Gaspe, Amy; Los Angeles, 1895-1950 ***9228.50*** *p244*
Gaspe, Violet; San Francisco, 1901-1950 ***9228.50*** *p244*
Gasper, Angela *SEE* Gasper, Nikolaus
Gasper, Barbara *SEE* Gasper, Nikolaus
Gasper, Elisabeth *SEE* Gasper, Nikolaus
Gasper, Helena *SEE* Gasper, Nikolaus
Gasper, Maria *SEE* Gasper, Nikolaus
Gasper, Mathias *SEE* Gasper, Nikolaus
Gasper, Nikolaus *SEE* Gasper, Nikolaus
Gasper, Nikolaus; America, 1881 ***5475.1*** *p334*
*Daughter:*Helena
*Daughter:*Elisabeth
*Son:*Mathias
*Daughter:*Angela
*Daughter:*Barbara
*Son:*Nikolaus
*Daughter:*Maria
Gasper, Nikolaus; Iowa, 1883 ***5475.1*** *p257*
Gasquet, Louis 38; New Orleans, 1848 ***778.6*** *p131*
Gass, Frank; Colorado, 1873 ***1029.59*** *p30*
Gass, John C. 61; Ontario, 1871 ***1823.21*** *p126*
Gass, Martin; Ohio, 1809-1852 ***4511.35*** *p16*
Gassard, Francois 20; America, 1845 ***778.6*** *p131*
Gassenheimer, Josef, Jr.; America, 1868 ***7919.3*** *p525*
Gassenheimer, Simon; America, 1867 ***7919.3*** *p525*
Gassenheimer, Therese; America, 1867 ***7919.3*** *p525*
Gasser, Jacob 53; Died enroute, 1817-1818 ***90.20*** *p151*
Gasser, Victor; Ohio, 1809-1852 ***4511.35*** *p16*
Gassion, Louis; Quebec, 1658 ***9221.17*** *p378*
Gassis, Guiseppe; Louisiana, 1874-1875 ***4981.45*** *p29*
Gassman, Anna Margarethe Preiss *SEE* Gassman, Johann Adam
Gassman, Conrad *SEE* Gassman, Johann Adam
Gassman, Johann Adam; Virginia, 1831 ***152.20*** *p63*
*Wife:*Anna Margarethe Preiss
*Child:*Conrad
Gast, George; Ohio, 1840-1897 ***8365.35*** *p16*
Gast, Michel 20; America, 1746 ***778.6*** *p131*
Gastaud, Honore 29; New York, NY, 1894 ***6512.1*** *p182*
Gastauer, Barbara; America, 1864 ***5475.1*** *p264*
Gastauer, Nikolaus; America, 1871 ***5475.1*** *p262*
Gasteau, Jean 20; Montreal, 1653 ***9221.17*** *p290*
Gasteau, Louis; Quebec, 1655 ***9221.17*** *p324*
Gastier, Theodore 21; Kansas, 1887 ***1447.20*** *p62*
Gastineau-Duplessis, Nicolas 22; Quebec, 1650 ***9221.17*** *p226*
Gastreich, Jos.; America, 1926 ***8023.44*** *p373*
Gastrel, Mrs. 46; America, 1848 ***778.6*** *p131*
Gate, Thomas; New York, 1776 ***8529.30*** *p11*
Gateau, Catherine; Quebec, 1671 ***4514.3*** *p316*
Gatecliff, George 23; Ontario, 1871 ***1823.21*** *p126*
Gatecliff, Henry 20; Ontario, 1871 ***1823.21*** *p126*
Gateley, Thomas 56; Ontario, 1871 ***1823.21*** *p126*
Gatello, Andrew 45; New Orleans, 1843 ***778.6*** *p131*
Gatello, Frederick 40; New Orleans, 1843 ***778.6*** *p131*
Gates, Alfred 35; Ohio, 1874 ***9722.10*** *p115*
Gates, Charles 44; Ontario, 1871 ***1823.17*** *p56*
Gates, Francis; Ohio, 1809-1852 ***4511.35*** *p16*
Gates, Henry 24; Ontario, 1871 ***1823.21*** *p126*
Gates, Henry 24; Ontario, 1871 ***1823.21*** *p126*
Gates, Jerome; Ohio, 1809-1852 ***4511.35*** *p16*
Gates, John; Ohio, 1809-1852 ***4511.35*** *p16*
Gates, John 34; Ontario, 1871 ***1823.17*** *p56*
Gates, Martin 40; America, 1848 ***778.6*** *p131*
Gates, Matthais; Ohio, 1809-1852 ***4511.35*** *p16*
Gates, Matthias; Ohio, 1809-1852 ***4511.35*** *p16*
Gates, William 54; Ontario, 1871 ***1823.21*** *p126*
Gathy, Xavier; New York, NY, 1870 ***1494.20*** *p13*
Gatineau, L. Victor; Louisiana, 1841-1844 ***4981.45*** *p210*
Gatinelli, Louis 29; New Orleans, 1848 ***778.6*** *p131*
Gatlery, William 27; Ontario, 1871 ***1823.21*** *p126*
Gaton, Alexander 49; New York, NY, 1885 ***1883.7*** *p45*
Gaton, Ernst 19; New York, NY, 1885 ***1883.7*** *p45*
Gaton, Lydia 18; New York, NY, 1885 ***1883.7*** *p45*
Gaton, Patrick; North Carolina, 1838 ***1088.45*** *p11*
Gattchur, Caroline 65; Ontario, 1871 ***1823.21*** *p126*
Gattie, Xavier; New York, NY, 1870 ***1494.20*** *p13*
Gattis, William 36; Ontario, 1871 ***1823.17*** *p56*
Gatz, Jean 28; America, 1840 ***778.6*** *p131*
Gau, Wilhelm 22; Louisiana, 1848 ***778.6*** *p131*
Gaub, Christina 25; New York, NY, 1898 ***7951.13*** *p41*
Gaub, Jacob 25; New York, NY, 1898 ***7951.13*** *p41*
Gaubault, . . .; Galveston, TX, 1844 ***3967.10*** *p376*
Gaubert, Louis 26; Quebec, 1633 ***9221.17*** *p29*
Gauchiron, Michel 29; America, 1843 ***778.6*** *p131*
Gaudefroy, Mrs. 35; New Orleans, 1843 ***778.6*** *p132*
Gaudefroy, Arile 4; New Orleans, 1843 ***778.6*** *p131*
Gaudefroy, Auguste 2; New Orleans, 1843 ***778.6*** *p131*
Gaudefroy, Jean Florin 32; New Orleans, 1843 ***778.6*** *p132*
Gaudel, Mrs. 26; New Orleans, 1843 ***778.6*** *p132*
Gaudel, Joseph 27; New Orleans, 1843 ***778.6*** *p132*
Gauden, Henry; Massachusetts, 1628 ***9228.50*** *p243*
Gaudens, Estrade 28; Havana, 1848 ***778.6*** *p132*
Gaudi, Susanna; America, 1853 ***5475.1*** *p277*
Gaudin, Anne 15 *SEE* Gaudin, Elie
Gaudin, Barthelemy 29; Quebec, 1643 ***9221.17*** *p131*
Gaudin, Charles 26; Quebec, 1656 ***9221.17*** *p337*
Gaudin, Dorcas Jessup Thoumine *SEE* Gaudin, George Henry
Gaudin, Elie 35; Quębec, 1654 ***9221.17*** *p308*
*Wife:*Esther-Marie Ramage 31
*Daughter:*Anne 15
*Son:*Pierre 4
Gaudin, Esdale Little *SEE* Gaudin, Lizzie Breen
Gaudin, Esther-Marie Ramage 31 *SEE* Gaudin, Elie
Gaudin, George Augustus *SEE* Gaudin, George Henry
Gaudin, George Henry; New York, NY, 1907 ***9228.50*** *p249*
*Wife:*Dorcas Jessup Thoumine
*Child:*George Augustus
*Child:*William Alfred
Gaudin, Lizzie Breen; Portsmouth, NH, 1899-1926 ***9228.50*** *p243*
*Daughter:*Esdale Little
Gaudin, Marthe 42; Quebec, 1648 ***9221.17*** *p198*
Gaudin, Nicolas; Quebec, 1659 ***9221.17*** *p413*
Gaudin, Philip; Salem, MA, 1675 ***9228.50*** *p243*
Gaudin, Pierre 23; Montreal, 1653 ***9221.17*** *p290*
Gaudin, Pierre 4 *SEE* Gaudin, Elie
Gaudin, William Alfred *SEE* Gaudin, George Henry
Gaudin, Yves 45; Quebec, 1656 ***9221.17*** *p337*
Gaudin Family ; Canada, 1826-1926 ***9228.50*** *p243*
Gaudion, Emily; Pennsylvania, 1886 ***9228.50*** *p382*
Gaudion, Louise; Detroit, 1910 ***9228.50*** *p315*
Gaudion, Wm. Thomas; Detroit, 1906 ***9228.50*** *p243*
Gaudron, Jean B. 24; Texas, 1848 ***778.6*** *p132*
Gaudry, Charlotte 46; Quebec, 1647 ***9221.17*** *p181*
*Son:*Nicolas 27
*Son:*Jacques 10
Gaudry, Jacques 10 *SEE* Gaudry, Charlotte Chevalier
Gaudry, Mathurin; Quebec, 1642 ***9221.17*** *p117*
Gaudry, Nicolas 27 *SEE* Gaudry, Charlotte Chevalier
Gaudry, Rene; Montreal, 1658 ***9221.17*** *p389*
Gauer, Frederick; Ohio, 1809-1852 ***4511.35*** *p16*
Gaufroy, Jean-baptiste 19; Texas, 1843 ***778.6*** *p132*
Gaugel, Georg; America, 1886 ***179.55*** *p19*
Gaugel, Karl; America, 1700-1899 ***179.55*** *p19*
Gauger, Louis 29; Louisiana, 1848 ***778.6*** *p132*
Gaulchet, Marie; Quebec, 1651 ***9221.17*** *p242*
*Daughter:*Marie-Madeleine
*Son:*Nicolas-Joseph
Gaulchet DeBelleville, Catherine 15; Montreal, 1659 ***9221.17*** *p421*
Gauld, Alex 53; Ontario, 1871 ***1823.21*** *p126*
Gauld, George 62; Ontario, 1871 ***1823.21*** *p126*
Gauld, James 58; Ontario, 1871 ***1823.21*** *p126*
Gauld, William 29; Ontario, 1871 ***1823.21*** *p126*
Gaule, John; Louisiana, 1874 ***4981.45*** *p295*
Gaulin, Francois 22; Quebec, 1652 ***9221.17*** *p258*
Gaulin, Marguerite 27; Quebec, 1654 ***9221.17*** *p309*
Gaulin, Pierre 29; Quebec, 1657 ***9221.17*** *p358*
Gaulion, Charles 36; America, 1842 ***778.6*** *p132*
Gaulion, Claudine 35; America, 1842 ***778.6*** *p132*
Gaulon, Phillip 37; New Orleans, 1846 ***778.6*** *p132*
Gault, Isaac 49; Michigan, 1880 ***4491.39*** *p11*
Gaultier, Catherine 11 *SEE* Gaultier, Marie Pichon
Gaultier, Charles 11 *SEE* Gaultier, Marie Pichon
Gaultier, Denise 40; Quebec, 1662 ***9221.17*** *p491*
*Daughter:*Marguerite 7
*Son:*Jean 6
Gaultier, Elie-Joseph 33; Quebec, 1659 ***9221.17*** *p401*
Gaultier, Guillaume *SEE* Gaultier, Marie Pichon
Gaultier, Jacques *SEE* Gaultier, Marie Pichon
Gaultier, Jean; Quebec, 1662 ***9221.17*** *p486*
Gaultier, Marie Pichon; Quebec, 1636 ***9221.17*** *p63*
*Daughter:*Catherine
*Son:*Charles
*Son:*Guillaume
*Son:*Jacques
Gaultier deComporte, Philippe; Quebec, 1665 ***2314.30*** *p167*
Gaultier deComporte, Philippe; Quebec, 1665 ***2314.30*** *p183*
Gaultier deVarennes, Rene; Quebec, 1665 ***2314.30*** *p167*
Gaultier deVarennes, Rene; Quebec, 1665 ***2314.30*** *p183*
Gaumond, Madeleine; Quebec, 1668 ***4514.3*** *p316*
Gauney, Mary 35; Ontario, 1871 ***1823.21*** *p126*
Gaure, Marie; New York, 1751 ***9228.50*** *p192*
Gauret, Celestin 25; Louisiana, 1848 ***778.6*** *p132*
Gauret, Constance 50; Louisiana, 1848 ***778.6*** *p132*
Gauret, Pierre 50; Louisiana, 1848 ***778.6*** *p132*
Gaurin, Ernest; New York, 1926 ***1173.1*** *p2*
Gaury, Jean; Virginia, 1700 ***9230.15*** *p80*
With wife & child
Gaury, Pierre; Virginia, 1700 ***9230.15*** *p80*
With wife & child
Gaus, Magdalena; America, 1859 ***179.55*** *p19*
Gauss, Anna Friedericke; America, 1700-1899 ***179.55*** *p19*
With child
Gauss, Christiana Margaretha; America, 1852 ***179.55*** *p19*
Gausse, Francoise 24; Quebec, 1661 ***9221.17*** *p457*

Gausse, Nicolas; Quebec, 1659 *9221.17 p401*
Gautal, Mr. 21; America, 1848 *778.6 p132*
Gauthe, Theod. 27; America, 1840 *778.6 p132*
Gautherin, Mr. 21; New Orleans, 1846 *778.6 p132*
Gautherin, Mr. 58; New Orleans, 1846 *778.6 p132*
Gauthier, C. E.; Louisiana, 1874 *4981.45 p296*
Gauthier, Marie; Quebec, 1669 *4514.3 p317*
Gauthier, Marie-Jeanne; Quebec, 1668 *4514.3 p317*
Gautie, Simon; Nova Scotia, 1753 *3051 p112*
Gautier, Ms. 22; New Orleans, 1748 *778.6 p132*
Gautier, Clement; Nova Scotia, 1753 *3051 p112*
Gautier, Louis 26; New Orleans, 1748 *778.6 p132*
Gautier, Michael 26; America, 1840 *778.6 p132*
Gautier, P. 35; America, 1846 *778.6 p132*
Gautier, Victour 30; Port uncertain, 1846 *778.6 p132*
Gauvain, Anthony; Illinois, 1856 *6079.1 p5*
Gauvin, Jean 23; Quebec, 1662 *9221.17 p486*
Gauvreau, Nicolas 24; Quebec, 1661 *9221.17 p457*
Gauvreau, O.E.; Quebec, 1885 *1937.10 p52*
Gauvreau, Pierre; Quebec, 1653 *9221.17 p274*
Gavet, Philip; Salem, MA, 1631-1655 *9228.50 p243*
Gavet, Thomas; Salem, MA, 1700 *9228.50 p157*
Gavett, Hannah; Boston, 1740 *9228.50 p182*
Gavey, John; Quebec, 1819-1869 *9228.50 p244*
Gavey, Philip; Salem, MA, 1631-1655 *9228.50 p243*
Gavigan, Rosanna 50; Ontario, 1871 *1823.17 p56*
Gavin, J.; Quebec, 1870 *8364.32 p23*
Gavin, Lawrence; Toronto, 1844 *2910.35 p115*
Gaw, John 54; Ontario, 1871 *1823.17 p56*
Gawel, John; Detroit, 1930 *1640.60 p78*
Gawron, Edward 31; New York, NY, 1911 *6533.11 p10*
Gay, Mr. 26; America, 1747 *778.6 p132*
Gay, Carl; Wisconsin, 1882 *6795.8 p165*
Gay, Claude 36; America, 1840 *778.6 p132*
Gay, Elizabeth 15; America, 1843 *778.6 p132*
Gay, John 38; Ontario, 1871 *1823.21 p126*
Gay, Josiah D.; Colorado, 1892 *1029.59 p30*
Gay, Munroe 54; Ontario, 1871 *1823.17 p56*
Gay, Richard 29; Ontario, 1871 *1823.21 p126*
Gay, Susanna 34; America, 1843 *778.6 p132*
Gayard, Charles; New Orleans, 1840 *778.6 p132*
Gayde, Antoine 22; America, 1846 *778.6 p132*
Gayde, Hipolite 33; New Orleans, 1848 *778.6 p132*
Gaydousek, Josef; Kansas, 1886-1888 *2853.20 p199*
Gaydusek, Josef; America, 1886 *2853.20 p233*
Gayer, Friedrich; St. Louis, 1885 *5475.1 p243*
  *Wife:*Sophie Paul
Gayer, Sophie Paul *SEE* Gayer, Friedrich
Gayet, Jean 21; America, 1840 *778.6 p132*
Gaylord, Elizabeth *SEE* Gaylord, William
Gaylord, John *SEE* Gaylord, William
Gaylord, Joseph *SEE* Gaylord, William
Gaylord, Samuel *SEE* Gaylord, William
Gaylord, Walter *SEE* Gaylord, William
Gaylord, William *SEE* Gaylord, William
Gaylord, William; Massachusetts, 1630 *117.5 p154*
  With wife
  *Son:*Walter
  *Daughter:*Elizabeth
  *Son:*Joseph
  *Son:*William
  *Son:*Samuel
  *Son:*John
Gaynor, Geo 42; Ontario, 1871 *1823.21 p126*
Gazaley, Joseph; New York, 1926 *1173.1 p2*
Gazave, Mr. 22; America, 1841 *778.6 p132*
Gaze, Elizabeth 33; Ontario, 1871 *1823.21 p126*
Gazon deLa Chataignerays, Charles-Etienne; Quebec, 1694 *2314.30 p171*
Gazor, Stephen; Boston, 1767 *1642 p38*
Gazzera, Frances; North Carolina, 1860 *1088.45 p11*
Geach, John 18; Ontario, 1871 *1823.21 p126*
Geagan, Prudence; Boston, 1749 *1642 p46*
Geain, Delphos 35; Ohio, 1880 *4879.40 p258*
  *Wife:*Eliza 31
Geain, Eliza 31 *SEE* Geain, Delphos
Gear, . . . 28; Ontario, 1871 *1823.21 p126*
Gear, Alexander 19; Ontario, 1871 *1823.21 p126*
Gear, George; Boston, 1720 *9228.50 p244*
Gear, Loftus; Colorado, 1880 *1029.59 p31*
Gearhard, Julian; Ohio, 1809-1852 *4511.35 p16*
Gearharst, Michael; Ohio, 1809-1852 *4511.35 p16*
Gearhart, Michael; Ohio, 1809-1852 *4511.35 p16*
Gearns, Edward 64; Ontario, 1871 *1823.17 p56*
Geary, Annie 17; Quebec, 1870 *8364.32 p23*
Geary, Catherine 11; Quebec, 1870 *8364.32 p23*
Geary, Charles 61; Ontario, 1871 *1823.21 p126*
Geary, Eliza 40; Ontario, 1871 *1823.21 p126*
Geary, John 30; Ontario, 1871 *1823.21 p127*
Geary, Richard 40; Ontario, 1871 *1823.21 p127*
Geary, Sarah 48; Ontario, 1871 *1823.21 p127*
Geary, William 29; Ontario, 1871 *1823.21 p127*
Geaume, Anastasie 4; New Orleans, 1843 *778.6 p133*

Geaume, Anne 12; New Orleans, 1843 *778.6 p133*
Geaume, Charles 15; New Orleans, 1843 *778.6 p133*
Geaume, Joseph 43; New Orleans, 1843 *778.6 p133*
Geaume, Philomene 7; New Orleans, 1843 *778.6 p133*
Geaume, Victor 9; New Orleans, 1843 *778.6 p133*
Geaume, Victorine 34; New Orleans, 1843 *778.6 p133*
Gebauer, Joseph; Chile, 1852 *1192.4 p52*
  With wife & 5 children
  With child 3
  With child 18
Gebel, Barbara Hans *SEE* Gebel, Michel
Gebel, Joseph 19; Port uncertain, 1847 *778.6 p133*
Gebel, Maria Lermen *SEE* Gebel, Peter
Gebel, Michel; America, 1834 *5475.1 p436*
  *Wife:*Barbara Hans
  With 8 children
Gebel, Peter; America, 1800-1899 *5475.1 p436*
  *Wife:*Maria Lermen
  With 8 children
Gebert, Aug. 25; New York, NY, 1864 *8425.62 p197*
Gebert, Chat. Charlotte 26; New York, NY, 1864 *8425.62 p197*
Gebert, Georg; America, 1880 *5475.1 p213*
Gebert, Gustay Fr. 11 months; New York, NY, 1864 *8425.62 p197*
Gebert, Joh. H. 28; New York, NY, 1864 *8425.62 p197*
Gebhard, Adam 17 *SEE* Gebhard, Mrs. Adam
Gebhard, Mrs. Adam; America, 1846 *2526.43 p122*
  *Son:*Adam
  *Son:*Peter
Gebhard, Anna Barbara *SEE* Gebhard, Johann Peter
Gebhard, August Friedrich Wilhelm; America, 1910 *7420.1 p387*
Gebhard, C. 71; New Orleans, 1834 *1002.51 p113*
Gebhard, Miss C. 28; New Orleans, 1834 *1002.51 p113*
Gebhard, Elisabetha *SEE* Gebhard, Johann Peter
Gebhard, Eva Margaretha *SEE* Gebhard, Johann Peter
Gebhard, Franz 18; America, 1853 *2526.43 p208*
Gebhard, Georg Heinrich *SEE* Gebhard, Karl Heinrich Christian
Gebhard, J. 8; New Orleans, 1834 *1002.51 p113*
Gebhard, Johann Balthasar *SEE* Gebhard, Johann Peter
Gebhard, Johann Georg; Pennsylvania, 1785 *2526.42 p120*
  With wife
Gebhard, Johann Nikolaus *SEE* Gebhard, Johann Peter
Gebhard, Johann Peter; Nova Scotia, 1751 *2526.43 p208*
  *Wife:*Maria Eva Zettelmeyer von Furstenau
  *Daughter:*Anna Barbara
  *Daughter:*Maria Eva
  *Son:*Johann Nikolaus
  *Daughter:*Elisabetha
  *Daughter:*Eva Margaretha
  *Son:*Johann Balthasar
Gebhard, Karl August Wilhelm *SEE* Gebhard, Karl Heinrich Christian
Gebhard, Karl Heinrich Christian; America, 1913 *7420.1 p391*
  *Wife:*Marie Karoline Mohme
  *Son:*Karl August Wilhelm
  *Son:*Georg Heinrich
  *Son:*Konrad Friedrich Wilhelm
Gebhard, Konrad Friedrich Wilhelm *SEE* Gebhard, Karl Heinrich Christian
Gebhard, Miss M. 6 months; New Orleans, 1834 *1002.51 p113*
Gebhard, Miss M. 11; New Orleans, 1834 *1002.51 p113*
Gebhard, Maria Eva *SEE* Gebhard, Johann Peter
Gebhard, Maria Eva Zettelmeyer von Furstenau *SEE* Gebhard, Johann Peter
Gebhard, Marie Karoline Mohme *SEE* Gebhard, Karl Heinrich Christian
Gebhard, P. 3; New Orleans, 1834 *1002.51 p113*
Gebhard, P. 5; New Orleans, 1834 *1002.51 p113*
Gebhard, P. 28; New Orleans, 1834 *1002.51 p113*
Gebhard, Peter 8 *SEE* Gebhard, Mrs. Adam
Gebhardt, Albert; Missouri, 1896 *3276.1 p1*
Gebhardt, Christian; Chicago, 1893 *5475.1 p425*
Gebhardt, Emil; Chile, 1852 *1192.4 p54*
Gebhardt, Ernst; Chile, 1852 *1192.4 p54*
Gebhardt, Franz Michael Helmuth; Wisconsin, 1896 *6795.8 p73*
Gebhardt, Friedrich August; America, 1868 *7420.1 p268*
Gebhardt, Gustav; Chile, 1852 *1192.4 p54*
Gebhardt, Hermann; Missouri, 1887 *3276.1 p1*
Gebhardt, Johannes; America, 1854 *2526.43 p195*
Gebhardt, Karl; America, 1912 *7420.1 p402*
Gebhardt, Nikolaus 51; New Jersey, 1903 *2526.43 p203*
Gebhardt, Wilhelmine; America, 1867 *7919.3 p530*
  With 4 children
Gebhart, Jno.; Louisiana, 1874 *4981.45 p296*
Gebler, Joseph; Wisconsin, 1913 *6795.8 p174*
Gebner, Marguerite 27; Louisiana, 1848 *778.6 p133*

Gebs, Matthew; Louisiana, 1874-1875 *4981.45 p29*
Geck, Franz; America, 1896 *7420.1 p372*
Geddes, Arthur 40; Ontario, 1871 *1823.21 p127*
Geddes, Patrick 56; Ontario, 1871 *1823.21 p127*
Geddes, Robert 55; Ontario, 1871 *1823.21 p127*
Geddes, William 56; Ontario, 1871 *1823.21 p127*
Geddis, James 31; Ontario, 1871 *1823.21 p127*
Geddis, Martha 64; Ontario, 1871 *1823.21 p127*
Geddis, Robert 70; Ontario, 1871 *1823.21 p127*
Gee, Daniel 35; Ontario, 1871 *1823.21 p127*
Gee, Fred'k; Ontario, 1787 *1276.15 p231*
  With 5 children & 3 relatives
Gee, George; Maryland, 1674 *1236.25 p49*
Gee, James 31; Ontario, 1871 *1823.21 p127*
Gee, Michael T.; Washington, 1883 *2770.40 p136*
Gee, Peter; Maine, 1653 *9228.50 p244*
Gee, Susanna; Boston, 1746 *1642 p46*
Gee, William 50; Ontario, 1871 *1823.21 p127*
Geel, Heinr.; Valdivia, Chile, 1852 *1192.4 p55*
Geele, Franz; Milwaukee, n.d. *8023.44 p373*
Geer, Thomas; Connecticut, 1700-1740 *9228.50 p244*
Geertz, C.; Venezuela, 1843 *3899.5 p546*
Geffery, Samuel; Philadelphia, 1778 *8529.30 p3A*
Geffroy, Edouard 30; New Orleans, 1848 *778.6 p133*
Gehecz, George 41; New York, NY, 1920 *930.50 p49*
Gehl, A. Maria *SEE* Gehl, Maria Theobald
Gehl, Andreas *SEE* Gehl, Maria Theobald
Gehl, Andreas 32; America, 1872 *5475.1 p202*
Gehl, Anna *SEE* Gehl, Maria Theobald
Gehl, Joh. Peter *SEE* Gehl, Maria Theobald
Gehl, Maria; America, 1883 *5475.1 p204*
  *Son:*Andreas
  *Son:*Joh. Peter
  *Daughter:*A. Maria
  *Daughter:*Anna
Gehl, Mathias; America, 1883 *5475.1 p203*
Gehl, Pierre 25; America, 1847 *778.6 p133*
Gehlbach, Phillippe; Louisiana, 1841-1844 *4981.45 p210*
Gehlen, Katharina; Brazil, 1879 *5475.1 p444*
Gehler, Philippine; Brazil, 1859 *5475.1 p523*
Gehlhaar, Anna Elizabeth; Wisconsin, 1897 *6795.8 p176*
Gehlhaar, Ferdinand; Wisconsin, 1899 *6795.8 p44*
Gehlhaar, Gustav Adolf; Wisconsin, 1891 *6795.8 p43*
Gehlhaar, Gustav Adolf; Wisconsin, 1896 *6795.8 p47*
Gehres, Albert; New York, 1894 *5475.1 p543*
Gehres, Georg; Brazil, 1861 *5475.1 p557*
Gehres, Karl 33; America, 1843 *5475.1 p557*
Gehret, John; Ohio, 1840-1897 *8365.35 p16*
Gehrhardt, C.; Venezuela, 1843 *3899.5 p546*
Gehrig, Anna Margaretha 49; America, 1851 *2526.43 p221*
  *Son:*Heinrich 20
Gehrig, Heinrich 20 *SEE* Gehrig, Anna Margaretha Straus
Gehrig, Joseph 21; New Orleans, 1848 *778.6 p133*
Gehring, Godfried; Wisconsin, 1855 *6795.8 p24*
Gehringer, Catharina 14; Port uncertain, 1843 *778.6 p133*
Gehringer, Eva 23; Port uncertain, 1843 *778.6 p133*
Gehringer, Eva Margaretha; America, 1869 *2526.43 p208*
Gehringer, Friedrich 21; Port uncertain, 1843 *778.6 p133*
Gehringer, Katharina; America, 1869 *2526.43 p208*
Gehringer, Pierre 50; Port uncertain, 1843 *778.6 p133*
Gehris, Peter; Ohio, 1809-1852 *4511.35 p16*
Gehrke, Heinrich; Wisconsin, 1875 *6795.8 p216*
Gehrke, Mathilde; America, 1881 *6795.8 p90*
Gehroldt, Gustav Adolph; Port uncertain, 1883 *7420.1 p336*
Gehse, August 18; New York, NY, 1893 *1883.7 p38*
Gehsner, Michel; America, 1846 *5475.1 p546*
Geib, Frederick Wm.; Missouri, 1895 *3276.1 p3*
Geib, Henry; Ohio, 1809-1852 *4511.35 p16*
Geib, Henry Wm. Neklaus; Missouri, 1894 *3276.1 p3*
Geibel, Joh. Nikolaus; America, 1867 *5475.1 p499*
Geibel, Theodore; Ohio, 1853 *3580.20 p32*
Geibel, Theodore; Ohio, 1853 *6020.12 p7*
Geiber, Christian; Ohio, 1809-1852 *4511.35 p17*
Geidecker, Jacob; Ohio, 1809-1852 *4511.35 p16*
Geidel, Anna Barbara 3 *SEE* Geidel, Jakob
Geidel, Anna Elisabetha Lang 38 *SEE* Geidel, Johann Adam, II
Geidel, Eva Katharina 42; America, 1855 *2526.43 p128*
Geidel, Eva Margaretha 4 *SEE* Geidel, Jakob
Geidel, Georg Muller 7 *SEE* Geidel, Jakob
Geidel, Jakob 33; America, 1831 *2526.43 p195*
  *Wife:*Margaretha 32
  *Son:*Georg Muller 7
  *Daughter:*Anna Barbara 3 months
  *Daughter:*Eva Margaretha 4
Geidel, Johann 1 *SEE* Geidel, Johann Adam, II

Geidel, Johann Adam, II 34; America, 1864 *2526.43 p147*
*Wife:*Anna Elisabetha Lang 38
*Son:*Johann 1
With mother-in-law 64
Geidel, Johannes 40; America, 1844 *2526.43 p208*
With sister 31
With child 11
Geidel, Margaretha 32 *SEE* Geidel, Jakob
Geidel, Susanna 57; America, 1882 *2526.43 p158*
*Son:*Heinrich 18
Geier, Eva; America, 1881 *5475.1 p342*
Geier, Mrs. Johannes; America, 1853 *2526.42 p163*
Geier, Mrs. Johannes 61; America, 1853 *2526.42 p160*
With son-in-law
Geiger, Christian; Ohio, 1809-1852 *4511.35 p16*
Geiger, Christian; Ohio, 1809-1852 *4511.35 p17*
Geiger, Conrad; Ohio, 1809-1852 *4511.35 p17*
Geiger, Jacob; Ohio, 1809-1852 *4511.35 p17*
Geiger, Jacob; Ohio, 1840-1897 *8365.35 p16*
Geiger, Leon Georges 40; Louisiana, 1848 *778.6 p133*
Geiger, Wilhelmine 60; Portland, ME, 1911 *970.38 p77*
Geihsler, Peter; America, 1869 *5475.1 p183*
Geiler, Francois 3; America, 1847 *778.6 p133*
Geiler, Helena 9; America, 1847 *778.6 p133*
Geiler, Jacob 15; America, 1847 *778.6 p133*
Geiler, Joseph 20; America, 1847 *778.6 p133*
Geiler, Michel 12; America, 1847 *778.6 p133*
Geiler, Michel 53; America, 1847 *778.6 p133*
Geiler, Philipp 8; America, 1847 *778.6 p133*
Geiler, Pierre 5; America, 1847 *778.6 p133*
Geiler, Theresia 42; America, 1847 *778.6 p133*
Geilet, H. 28; New Orleans, 1843 *778.6 p133*
Geillard, Pauline 30; Ontario, 1871 *1823.21 p127*
Geir, J. R. 22; Ontario, 1871 *1823.21 p127*
Geir, Jean 30; America, 1845 *778.6 p133*
Geir, Phillip 20; Ontario, 1871 *1823.21 p127*
Geirer, Jacob; Ohio, 1809-1852 *4511.35 p17*
Geis, Henry; Ohio, 1809-1852 *4511.35 p17*
Geis, John; Ohio, 1809-1852 *4511.35 p17*
Geisdorf, Henriette; New York, 1860 *358.56 p149*
Geise, Anton; Ohio, 1840-1897 *8365.35 p16*
Geise, Friedr.; Valdivia, Chile, 1852 *1192.4 p55*
With wife & 5 children
With child 6
With child 22
Geise, Philipp; Valdivia, Chile, 1852 *1192.4 p55*
Geise, Wilh. Heinr.; Valdivia, Chile, 1852 *1192.4 p55*
With wife & 3 children
With child 22
With child 5
Geisen, Mathias 36; America, 1843 *5475.1 p330*
Geisert, Friedrich Robert 12 *SEE* Geisert, Katharina
Geisert, Katharina; America, 1854 *2526.43 p167*
*Son:*Friedrich Robert
*Daughter:*Margaretha
Geisert, Margaretha 6 *SEE* Geisert, Katharina
Geishirt, August; America, 1868 *7919.3 p524*
*Son:*Johannes
Geishirt, Johannes *SEE* Geishirt, August
Geishirt, Johannes; America, 1868 *7919.3 p524*
With wife & 2 children
Geisler, Adam 11 months; New York, NY, 1893 *1883.7 p44*
Geisler, Christe. 30; New York, NY, 1893 *1883.7 p44*
Geisler, Christine; Philadelphia, 1835 *8513.31 p309*
Geisler, Eva 3; New York, NY, 1893 *1883.7 p44*
Geiss, Franz D.; Wisconsin, 1876 *6795.8 p98*
Geiss, Georg Carl Heinrch; America, 1881 *2526.42 p160*
Geiss, Henry; Ohio, 1809-1852 *4511.35 p17*
Geiss, Karl; America, 1889 *2526.42 p160*
Geiss, Michel 24; America, 1852 *5475.1 p538*
Geisse, Justus H.; Valdivia, Chile, 1852 *1192.4 p55*
With wife & 5 children
Geist, Anna Margaretha; America, 1883 *2526.42 p168*
Geist, Jakob; America, 1831 *2526.43 p195*
With wife & 2 children
Geist, Johannes 14; America, 1852 *2526.43 p147*
Geist, Margaretha 5; America, 1883 *2526.42 p168*
Geistfeld, Engel Marie Charlotte; America, 1851 *7420.1 p79*
Geistfeld, Heinrich; America, 1867 *7420.1 p256*
Geistfeld, Thrine Engel Marie Doroth.; America, 1857 *7420.1 p161*
Geitz, Simon; Illinois, 1856 *6079.1 p5*
Geiwitz, S. J.; Chile, 1852 *1192.4 p52*
With wife & child
With child 1
With child 8
Gejorski, Peter; Texas, 1900 *6015.15 p25*
Geldart, Henry 37; Ontario, 1871 *1823.21 p127*
Gelee, Louise 43; Quebec, 1659 *9221.17 p401*
Gelei, Alexandre 18; New Orleans, 1847 *778.6 p133*

Gelhar, Gustav Adolf; Wisconsin, 1891 *6795.8 p43*
Gelhart, Ferdinand; Wisconsin, 1899 *6795.8 p44*
Geli, John; Washington, 1887 *2770.40 p24*
Gelin, Alex. 39; America, 1841 *778.6 p133*
Gelinat, Etienne 34; Quebec, 1658 *9221.17 p380*
*Son:*Jean 12
Gelinat, Jean 12 *SEE* Gelinat, Etienne
Gelineau, Etienne 34; Quebec, 1658 *9221.17 p380*
*Son:*Jean 12
Gelineau, Jean 12 *SEE* Gelineau, Etienne
Gelinne, Alphonse *SEE* Gelinne, Xavier
Gelinne, Amelie; Wisconsin, 1854-1858 *1495.20 p50*
Gelinne, Francois Joseph; Wisconsin, 1880 *1495.20 p56*
Gelinne, Julienne; Wisconsin, 1880 *1495.20 p56*
Gelinne, Louis *SEE* Gelinne, Louis Joseph
Gelinne, Louis Francois *SEE* Gelinne, Xavier
Gelinne, Louis Joseph; Wisconsin, 1885 *1495.20 p56*
*Wife:*Rosalie Piedfort
*Child:*Louis
*Child:*Marie Julie
Gelinne, Marie Joseph; Wisconsin, 1880 *1495.20 p56*
Gelinne, Marie Julie *SEE* Gelinne, Louis Joseph
Gelinne, Marie Louise *SEE* Gelinne, Xavier
Gelinne, Marie Madelene Destenay Demoulin *SEE* Gelinne, Xavier
Gelinne, Rosalie Piedfort *SEE* Gelinne, Louis Joseph
Gelinne, Xavier; New York, NY, 1870 *1494.21 p31*
Gelinne, Xavier; Wisconsin, 1870 *1495.20 p56*
*Wife:*Marie Madelene Destenay Demoulin
*Stepchild:*Marie Louise
*Child:*Louis Francois
*Child:*Alphonse
Gelis, Carl Wilhelm Christian; America, 1868 *7420.1 p271*
Gellermann, Widow; America, 1853 *7420.1 p105*
With son
Gellermann, Engel Marie Phil.; America, 1851 *7420.1 p80*
Gellermann, Heinrich Friedrich Wilhelm *SEE* Gellermann, Heinrich Ludwig
Gellermann, Heinrich Ludwig; Chicago, 1873 *7420.1 p299*
With wife
*Son:*Heinrich Friedrich Wilhelm
Gellermann, Johann Heinrich Gottlieb; Texas, 1845 *7420.1 p36*
With family 5 sons & 2 daughters
Gellis, Katherine Kulpa *SEE* Gellis, Luke
Gellis, Luke; Detroit, 1930 *1640.60 p78*
*Wife:*Katherine Kulpa
Gellman, Phillip; Detroit, 1929-1930 *6214.5 p70*
Gellowlus, Robert 50; New York, NY, 1835 *5024.1 p136*
Gelpi, Jerome; Louisiana, 1836-1840 *4981.45 p212*
Gelpi, Pablo; Louisiana, 1836-1840 *4981.45 p212*
Gely, Louise 43; Quebec, 1659 *9221.17 p401*
Gelz, Jacob F.; Ohio, 1809-1852 *4511.35 p17*
Gelz, Peter; America, 1873 *5475.1 p328*
Gemmel, Maria Rosina 38; America, 1865 *5475.1 p511*
Gemmell, John 62; Ontario, 1871 *1823.17 p56*
Gemmill, Francis 27; Ontario, 1871 *1823.21 p127*
Gemmill, Duncan 36; Ontario, 1871 *1823.17 p56*
Gemming, Henriette 9; New York, NY, 1864 *8425.62 p198*
Gemming, Joh. H. 68; New York, NY, 1864 *8425.62 p198*
Gemming, Wilhelmine 56; New York, NY, 1864 *8425.62 p198*
Gendenen, William 36; Ontario, 1871 *1823.21 p127*
Gendre, Marie 45; Quebec, 1652 *9221.17 p254*
Gendreau, Anne; Quebec, 1663 *4514.3 p317*
Gendreau, Joseph-Daniel 27; Quebec, 1659 *9221.17 p402*
Gendreau, Nicolas 18; Quebec, 1652 *9221.17 p259*
Gendreau, Pierre 25; Quebec, 1656 *9221.17 p337*
Gendron, Francois; America, 1643 *9221.17 p131*
Gendron, Guillaume 23; Montreal, 1653 *9221.17 p291*
Gendron, Guillaume; Quebec, 1646 *9221.17 p165*
Gendron, Louise; Quebec, 1666 *4514.3 p291*
Gendron, Nicolas 18; Quebec, 1652 *9221.17 p259*
Geneiss, J. Joseph; Iowa, 1903 *1211.15 p10*
Generch, Antoine 20; Mississippi, 1846 *778.6 p133*
Generch, Therese 12; Mississippi, 1846 *778.6 p134*
Generch, Therese 48; Mississippi, 1846 *778.6 p133*
Generio, Janos 17; New York, NY, 1894 *6512.1 p183*
Generio, Maria 45; New York, NY, 1894 *6512.1 p183*
Genest, Jeanne-Leonarde; Quebec, 1669 *4514.3 p317*
Genet, Mater 60; America, 1847 *778.6 p134*
Gengler, Margarethe; America, 1867 *5475.1 p321*
Gengler, Mathias; America, 1866 *5475.1 p321*
Geniesse, Eleonore Felicie *SEE* Geniesse, Jean Baptiste
Geniesse, Gillain *SEE* Geniesse, Jean Baptiste
Geniesse, Gillain Eugene *SEE* Geniesse, Jean Baptiste

Geniesse, Henriette Josephine *SEE* Geniesse, Jean Baptiste
Geniesse, Honorine *SEE* Geniesse, Jean Baptiste
Geniesse, Jean Baptiste; Wisconsin, 1871 *1495.20 p12*
*Wife:*Marie Agnes Josephe Calonne
*Child:*Honorine
*Child:*Gillain
*Child:*Marie Barbe
*Child:*Gillain Eugene
*Child:*Henriette Josephine
*Child:*Eleonore Felicie
*Child:*Valerie Desiree
Geniesse, Marie Agnes Josephe Calonne *SEE* Geniesse, Jean Baptiste
Geniesse, Marie Barbe *SEE* Geniesse, Jean Baptiste
Geniesse, Valerie Desiree *SEE* Geniesse, Jean Baptiste
Genillet, Aglae 20; America, 1843 *778.6 p134*
Genillet, Loiuis 26; America, 1843 *778.6 p134*
Genin, Louis Joseph; New York, NY, 1871 *1494.20 p12*
Gennrich, Gustave F.E.; Wisconsin, 1890 *6795.8 p209*
Genois, Anna 1; America, 1847 *778.6 p134*
Genois, Hans 4; America, 1847 *778.6 p134*
Genois, Jan 36; America, 1847 *778.6 p134*
Genois, Jan Peter 6; America, 1847 *778.6 p134*
Genois, Jean 8; America, 1847 *778.6 p134*
Genois, Margarethe 36; America, 1847 *778.6 p134*
Genorel, L.; Mississippi, 1848 *778.6 p134*
Genrich, Gottlieb Frederich; Wisconsin, 1881 *6795.8 p47*
Genser, Boniface 35; Indiana, 1840 *778.6 p134*
Genser, Margaret 34; Indiana, 1840 *778.6 p134*
Genser, Otilla 8; Indiana, 1840 *778.6 p134*
Gensert, Julius; Chile, 1852 *1192.4 p52*
With wife
Genssler, August Gottlieb; America, 1867 *7919.3 p534*
Gentil, Jean-Louis-Theodore 24; Galveston, TX, 1844 *3967.10 p374*
Gentle, Edward; New York, 1782 *8529.30 p11*
Gentleman, Annie 19; Quebec, 1870 *8364.32 p23*
Gentleman, David 62; Ontario, 1871 *1823.21 p127*
Gentner, George; New York, 1859 *358.56 p54*
Genty, Joseph 28; Mississippi, 1847 *778.6 p134*
Genz, Karl Ludwig; New Jersey, 1887 *5475.1 p230*
Genz, Reinhard; New Jersey, 1884 *5475.1 p229*
Genzbudel, Franziska 35; America, 1846 *778.6 p134*
Genzbudel, Heracius 9 months; America, 1846 *778.6 p134*
Geoffrey, E.; Missouri, 1903 *3276.1 p1*
Geoffroy, Anne; Quebec, 1670 *4514.3 p317*
Geoffroy, Marie-Marthe; Quebec, 1673 *4514.3 p317*
Geogan, James 36; Ontario, 1871 *1823.21 p127*
Geoghagan, Thomas 42; Ontario, 1871 *1823.21 p127*
Geoghan, Henry D. 25; Ontario, 1871 *1823.21 p127*
Geoghan, John 46; Ontario, 1871 *1823.21 p127*
Geoghean, Ann; Boston, 1762 *1642 p44*
Geoghegan, Michael; Boston, 1737 *1642 p44*
Geoghegan, Michael; Boston, 1743 *1642 p45*
Geogrog, Amedus 5 *SEE* Geogrog, Amedus
Geogrog, Amedus 28; Ohio, 1880 *4879.40 p260*
*Wife:*Matilda 24
*Son:*George 9 months
*Son:*Amedus 5
*Son:*Tabelia 8
Geogrog, George 9 *SEE* Geogrog, Amedus
Geogrog, Matilda 24 *SEE* Geogrog, Amedus
Geogrog, Tabelia 8 *SEE* Geogrog, Amedus
Geohagen, Michael; Massachusetts, 1744 *1642 p99*
Geometre, Albert 27; America, 1844 *778.6 p134*
Georg, Christophe 20; Port uncertain, 1841 *778.6 p134*
Georg, Georg *SEE* Georg, Jakob
Georg, Georg Bareis; America, 1854 *179.55 p19*
Georg, Jakob; America, 1833 *5475.1 p62*
Georg, Jakob *SEE* Georg, Jakob
Georg, Jakob 62; America, 1833 *5475.1 p70*
With wife
With daughter son-in-law daughter-in-law & 7 grandchildren
With daughter 16
*Son:*Jakob
*Son:*Georg
With daughter 13
*Son:*Johann
Georg, Johann; America, 1833 *5475.1 p62*
Georg, Johann *SEE* Georg, Jakob
Georg, Konrad; America, 1847 *2526.42 p121*
Georg, Lewis 33; Port uncertain, 1841 *778.6 p134*
Georg, Mary 18; Port uncertain, 1841 *778.6 p134*
Georg, Walter 29; America, 1847 *778.6 p134*
George, Mr. 46; Port uncertain, 1847 *778.6 p134*
George, Mrs. 42; America, 1846 *778.6 p134*
George, Mrs. 35; Port uncertain, 1847 *778.6 p134*
George, Annie 30; Michigan, 1880 *4491.42 p11*
George, Baptist 33; Ontario, 1871 *1823.21 p127*
George, Benjamin 35; Ontario, 1871 *1823.21 p127*

FOR A COMPLETE EXPLANATION OF ENTRY, SEE "HOW TO READ A CITATION" SECTION

George, Carlia 52; Michigan, 1880 *4491.42 p11*
George, Caroline 47; Ontario, 1871 *1823.21 p127*
George, Catherine 38; Missouri, 1845 *778.6 p134*
George, Cezar B. 21; Michigan, 1880 *4491.42 p11*
George, Constant 48; Michigan, 1880 *4491.42 p11*
George, Emma 5; Michigan, 1880 *4491.42 p11*
George, Emma 25; Toronto, 1859 *9228.50 p558*
George, Eugene 3; Michigan, 1880 *4491.42 p11*
George, Eugene 50; Michigan, 1880 *4491.42 p11*
George, Eugenie 9; Missouri, 1845 *778.6 p134*
George, George 44; Michigan, 1880 *4491.42 p11*
George, Gunder 34; Ontario, 1871 *1823.21 p127*
George, Hannah 40; Michigan, 1880 *4491.42 p11*
George, Henry; Ohio, 1809-1852 *4511.35 p17*
George, Henry 34; Ontario, 1871 *1823.21 p127*
George, Henry 59; Ontario, 1871 *1823.21 p127*
George, Jacob; New Jersey, 1777 *8529.30 p6*
George, Jacob; Ohio, 1809-1852 *4511.35 p17*
George, James 60; Ontario, 1871 *1823.21 p127*
George, Jean-Claude; Quebec, 1638 *9221.17 p76*
George, John; Ohio, 1809-1852 *4511.35 p17*
George, John 68; Ontario, 1871 *1823.21 p127*
George, Joseph; Colorado, 1905 *1029.59 p31*
George, Joseph 53; Michigan, 1880 *4491.42 p11*
George, Maggie 6; Michigan, 1880 *4491.42 p11*
George, Margret 36; Ontario, 1871 *1823.21 p127*
George, Mary 40; Ontario, 1871 *1823.21 p127*
George, Nicholas; Washington, 1886 *2770.40 p195*
George, Pheba 47; Ontario, 1871 *1823.21 p127*
George, Pnilip; Louisiana, 1874 *4981.45 p296*
George, Richard 35; Ontario, 1871 *1823.21 p127*
George, Samuel 32; Ontario, 1871 *1823.17 p57*
George, William 33; Ontario, 1871 *1823.21 p127*
Georgea, Early 55; Ontario, 1871 *1823.21 p127*
Georgeff, Stayn; Illinois, 1930 *121.35 p100*
Georges, J. A.; Louisiana, 1836-1841 *4981.45 p208*
Georgeson, George; Iowa, 1888 *1211.15 p11*
Georgi, Henrich; Pennsylvania, 1867 *170.15 p26*
Geppert, Anna Maria; Venezuela, 1843 *3899.5 p542*
Geppinger, Ferdinand; Missouri, 1886 *3276.1 p1*
Gera, Christian; Long Island, 1778 *8529.30 p9A*
Gerame, Pauline 34; New Orleans, 1748 *778.6 p134*
Gerard, Mr.; America, 1847 *778.6 p134*
Gerard, Mrs. 35; New Orleans, 1847 *778.6 p135*
Gerard, Mrs. Alex 43; New Orleans, 1845 *778.6 p135*
Gerard, Anton 23; America, 1866 *5475.1 p180*
Gerard, Antonio 36; America, 1848 *778.6 p134*
Gerard, Cath. 56; New Orleans, 1846 *778.6 p134*
Gerard, Charles 50; Ontario, 1871 *1823.21 p128*
Gerard, Jean 3 months; America, 1843 *778.6 p135*
Gerard, Jean 18; America, 1843 *778.6 p135*
Gerard, Jean 44; America, 1843 *778.6 p134*
Gerard, Jean B.; Illinois, 1852 *6079.1 p5*
Gerard, Jean Bapt. 30; New Orleans, 1845 *778.6 p135*
Gerard, Joseph 10; America, 1843 *778.6 p135*
Gerard, Joseph 14; Ontario, 1871 *1823.21 p128*
Gerard, Joseph 34; Ontario, 1871 *1823.21 p128*
Gerard, Katharina 2; America, 1843 *778.6 p135*
Gerard, Louise 28; Port uncertain, 1845 *778.6 p135*
Gerard, Margaretha 13; America, 1843 *778.6 p135*
Gerard, Maria 47; America, 1868 *5475.1 p146*
  *Daughter:*Elisabeth
  *Daughter:*Maria
  *Daughter:*Anna Maria
  *Son:*J. Kaspar
  *Son:*Jos. Mathias
Gerard, Martin 5; America, 1843 *778.6 p135*
Gerard, Nicolas 16; America, 1843 *778.6 p135*
Gerard, Nicolas 19; Mississippi, 1846 *778.6 p135*
Gerard, Pauline 3; America, 1843 *778.6 p135*
Gerard, Rosalia 17; America, 1843 *778.6 p135*
Gerard, Mrs. Uranea 40; New Orleans, 1845 *778.6 p135*
Gerard, Ursule 38; America, 1843 *778.6 p135*
Gerardy, Hubert *SEE* Gerardy, Johann Peter
Gerardy, Johann Peter; America, 1873 *5475.1 p346*
  *Wife:*Maria Berg
  *Son:*Mathias
  *Daughter:*Margarethe
  *Son:*Hubert
  *Daughter:*Maria
Gerardy, Kath.; America, 1881 *5475.1 p195*
Gerardy, Margarethe *SEE* Gerardy, Johann Peter
Gerardy, Maria *SEE* Gerardy, Johann Peter
Gerardy, Maria Berg *SEE* Gerardy, Johann Peter
Gerardy, Mathias *SEE* Gerardy, Johann Peter
Gerau, Tabeda 23; America, 1848 *778.6 p135*
Gerbach, Amalia 9; Halifax, N.S., 1902 *1860.4 p43*
Gerbach, Amalie 19; Halifax, N.S., 1902 *1860.4 p43*
Gerbach, Elisabeth 53; Halifax, N.S., 1902 *1860.4 p43*
Gerbach, Johanna 15; Halifax, N.S., 1902 *1860.4 p43*
Gerbach, Konrad 55; Halifax, N.S., 1902 *1860.4 p43*
Gerbach, Stefan 12; Halifax, N.S., 1902 *1860.4 p43*

Gerbault DeBellegarde, Christophe 18; Quebec, 1661 *9221.17 p457*
Gerber, A. Maria *SEE* Gerber, Peter
Gerber, Anna 15 *SEE* Gerber, Barbara
Gerber, Barbara *SEE* Gerber, Peter
Gerber, Barbara 21; New York, 1849 *5475.1 p465*
  *Sister:*Anna 15
Gerber, Catherina 40; America, 1847 *778.6 p135*
Gerber, Christian; Ohio, 1809-1852 *4511.35 p17*
Gerber, Christine 11; Missouri, 1847 *778.6 p135*
Gerber, Elisabeth 30; Missouri, 1846 *778.6 p135*
Gerber, Friedrich; America, 1867 *7420.1 p256*
  With wife & daughter
Gerber, Heinrich; America, 1866 *7420.1 p240*
Gerber, Heinrich; America, 1869 *7420.1 p279*
  With wife
  With daughter 13
Gerber, Jakob 38; America, 1846 *5475.1 p385*
  *Wife:*Katharina Kleer 34
  With 4 children
Gerber, Johann 30; Missouri, 1846 *778.6 p135*
Gerber, Katharina Maurer *SEE* Gerber, Peter
Gerber, Katharina Kleer 34 *SEE* Gerber, Jakob
Gerber, Louisa 1; Missouri, 1846 *778.6 p135*
Gerber, Louise 29; America, 1841 *778.6 p135*
Gerber, Ludwig *SEE* Gerber, Peter
Gerber, Maria *SEE* Gerber, Peter
Gerber, Mathias; America, 1855 *5475.1 p484*
Gerber, Nikolaus *SEE* Gerber, Peter
Gerber, Peter; America, 1883 *5475.1 p413*
  *Wife:*Katharina Maurer
  *Daughter:*Barbara
  *Daughter:*Maria
  *Daughter:*A. Maria
  *Son:*Nikolaus
  *Son:*Ludwig
Gerber, Peter; Illinois, 1834-1900 *6020.5 p131*
Gerbet, Mathurin 25; Quebec, 1659 *9221.17 p402*
Gerbig, Anna Katharina; America, 1846 *2526.43 p122*
  *Daughter:*Maria Katharina
Gerbig, Anna Margaretha 18 *SEE* Gerbig, Konrad
Gerbig, August 22; New York, NY, 1864 *8425.62 p195*
Gerbig, Elisabeth 8 *SEE* Gerbig, Konrad
Gerbig, Elisabetha Katharina 33; America, 1855 *2526.43 p123*
  *Son:*Johannes 12
  *Son:*Georg 10
  *Son:*Heinrich 2
  *Son:*Jakob 7
Gerbig, Eva Katharina; New York, 1886 *2526.43 p206*
Gerbig, Georg; America, 1831 *2526.43 p167*
  With wife 54
Gerbig, Georg 10 *SEE* Gerbig, Elisabetha Katharina Vogel
Gerbig, Heinrich; America, 1872 *2526.43 p122*
Gerbig, Heinrich 2 *SEE* Gerbig, Elisabetha Katharina Vogel
Gerbig, Jakob 7 *SEE* Gerbig, Elisabetha Katharina Vogel
Gerbig, Jakob 35; Trinidad, 1843 *2526.43 p221*
  With wife
  With child 11
Gerbig, Johann; America, 1880 *2526.43 p205*
Gerbig, Johann Ludwig; Texas, 1882 *2526.43 p205*
Gerbig, Johannes; America, 1880 *2526.43 p205*
Gerbig, Johannes 12 *SEE* Gerbig, Elisabetha Katharina Vogel
Gerbig, Katharina 23 *SEE* Gerbig, Konrad
Gerbig, Katharina Kumpf 52 *SEE* Gerbig, Konrad
Gerbig, Katharina Elisabetha 13 *SEE* Gerbig, Konrad
Gerbig, Konrad 50; America, 1872 *2526.43 p122*
  *Wife:*Katharina Kumpf 52
  *Daughter:*Katharina Elisabetha 13
  *Daughter:*Elisabeth 8
  *Son:*Leonhard
  *Daughter:*Anna Margaretha 18
  *Daughter:*Katharina 23
Gerbig, Leonhard *SEE* Gerbig, Konrad
Gerbig, Maria Katharina 16 *SEE* Gerbig, Anna Katharina
Gerbig, Nikolaus; America, 1852 *2526.43 p122*
Gerbitz, Wilhelm Franz; Wisconsin, 1888 *6795.8 p175*
Gerblich, Christian; New York, 1859 *358.56 p99*
Gerbracht, Ernst Wilhelm; America, 1871 *7420.1 p290*
Gerbracht, Friedrich Franz; America, 1906 *7420.1 p380*
Gerbracht, Georg Friedrich; America, 1869 *7420.1 p279*
Gerbracht, Wilhelm; America, 1897 *7420.1 p373*
Gerbrandt, Anna 3; Portland, ME, 1911 *970.38 p77*
Gerbrandt, Anna M. 34; Portland, ME, 1911 *970.38 p77*
Gerbrandt, Derk 42; Portland, ME, 1911 *970.38 p77*
Gerbrandt, Dieltrich 9; Portland, ME, 1911 *970.38 p77*
Gerbrandt, Helene 10; Portland, ME, 1911 *970.38 p77*
Gerbrandt, Jacob 11; Portland, ME, 1911 *970.38 p77*
Gerbrandt, Johan 19; Portland, ME, 1911 *970.38 p77*
Gerbrandt, Martin 8; Portland, ME, 1911 *970.38 p77*

Gerbrandt, Peter 4; Portland, ME, 1911 *970.38 p77*
Gerdes, Anna 29; Galveston, TX, 1845 *3967.10 p376*
Gerdes, Henry; Kansas, 1917-1918 *2094.25 p50*
Gerdes, Henry; Missouri, 1891 *3276.1 p1*
Gerdes, Hermann 3; Galveston, TX, 1845 *3967.10 p376*
Gerdes, Johann Heinrich 36; Galveston, TX, 1845 *3967.10 p376*
Gerdes, Johanna; Kansas, 1917-1918 *2094.25 p50*
Gerdes, John Gerhard; Kansas, 1917-1918 *2094.25 p50*
Gerdes, Maria 9; Galveston, TX, 1845 *3967.10 p376*
Gerdlatine, Robert 58; Ontario, 1871 *1823.17 p57*
Gerell, John W.; Cleveland, OH, 1890-1893 *9722.10 p119*
Gerenger, Georg 33; America, 1747 *778.6 p135*
Geres, Philippine; Brazil, 1859 *5475.1 p523*
Gerhard, Jacob 26; New Orleans, 1848 *778.6 p135*
Gerhard, Magdalena 19; New York, NY, 1898 *7951.13 p44*
Gerhardi, Adam; New York, 1860 *358.56 p148*
Gerhardt, John; Illinois, 1852 *6079.1 p5*
Gerhardt, Max; Nebraska, 1905 *3004.30 p46*
Gerhart, John; Ohio, 1809-1852 *4511.35 p17*
Gerheirt, Ignatz; Ohio, 1840-1897 *8365.35 p16*
Gerhold, Berta 32; America, 1914 *8023.44 p374*
Gerhold, John; Ohio, 1809-1852 *4511.35 p17*
Gerholt, Christian; Ohio, 1809-1852 *4511.35 p17*
Geringer, August; Chicago, 1869 *2853.20 p394*
Geringer, Jan; Chicago, 1870 *2853.20 p425*
Gerke, Anton; Washington, 1884 *2770.40 p192*
Gerke, Heinrick; Wisconsin, 1875 *6795.8 p216*
Gerl, Leonard; Pennsylvania, 1881 *2853.20 p438*
Gerl, Linhart; Chicago, 1910 *2853.20 p433*
Gerla, Piotr 26; New York, NY, 1920 *930.50 p49*
Gerlach, A. 3; New Orleans, 1834 *1002.51 p111*
Gerlach, Adolf; New Jersey, 1773-1774 *927.31 p2*
Gerlach, Albert Julius; Wisconsin, 1889 *6795.8 p44*
Gerlach, Andreas *SEE* Gerlach, Anna Elisabeth
Gerlach, Anna Elisabeth; America, 1846 *8115.12 p323*
  *Child:*Elisabeth
  *Child:*Johann Georg
  *Child:*Andreas
  *Child:*Katharine
  *Child:*Heinrich
Gerlach, Miss C. 5; New Orleans, 1834 *1002.51 p111*
Gerlach, Miss C. 17; New Orleans, 1834 *1002.51 p110*
Gerlach, Miss C. 37; New Orleans, 1834 *1002.51 p110*
Gerlach, Miss E. 13; New Orleans, 1834 *1002.51 p110*
Gerlach, Elisabeth *SEE* Gerlach, Anna Elisabeth
Gerlach, Elisabeth Margarethe; America, 1840 *8115.12 p319*
Gerlach, Emilie; Wisconsin, 1889 *6795.8 p36*
Gerlach, George; Ohio, 1809-1852 *4511.35 p17*
Gerlach, Miss H. 1; New Orleans, 1834 *1002.51 p111*
Gerlach, Heinrich *SEE* Gerlach, Anna Elisabeth
Gerlach, J. 8; New Orleans, 1834 *1002.51 p110*
Gerlach, J. 41; New Orleans, 1834 *1002.51 p110*
Gerlach, Miss J. 12; New Orleans, 1834 *1002.51 p110*
Gerlach, Johann Georg *SEE* Gerlach, Anna Elisabeth
Gerlach, Johann Georg; America, 1880 *8115.12 p319*
Gerlach, Johann Georg; America, n.d. *8115.12 p319*
Gerlach, John; New Jersey, 1773-1774 *927.31 p2*
Gerlach, Katharine *SEE* Gerlach, Anna Elisabeth
Gerlach, Miss L. 6; New Orleans, 1834 *1002.51 p110*
Gerlach, Ludwig; America, 1870 *8115.12 p326*
Gerlach, Miss M. 16; New Orleans, 1834 *1002.51 p110*
Gerlach, Miss M. 19; New Orleans, 1834 *1002.51 p110*
Gerlach, Marie; America, 1889 *8115.12 p319*
Gerlach, P. 20; New Orleans, 1834 *1002.51 p111*
Gerlach, Miss P. 11; New Orleans, 1834 *1002.51 p110*
Gerlach, Joh. Aug. Freederick; Wisconsin, 1868 *6795.8 p233*
Gerland, Anne Sophie Marie Charlotte; America, 1849 *7420.1 p64*
Gerland, Engel Marie Sophie Charlotte; America, 1871 *7420.1 p396*
  With 2 children
Gerland, Hans Heinrich; America, 1867 *7420.1 p256*
Gerland, Heinrich Conrad; America, 1887 *7420.1 p353*
Gerler, Anna 12; America, 1840 *778.6 p135*
Gerler, Cathal. 10; America, 1840 *778.6 p135*
Gerler, Ch...an 27; America, 1840 *778.6 p135*
Gerler, Cisl. 8; America, 1840 *778.6 p135*
Gerler, H...ch 3; America, 1840 *778.6 p135*
Gerler, Joh. 18; America, 1840 *778.6 p135*
Gerler, Joseph 23; America, 1840 *778.6 p135*
Gerler, Magd. 17; America, 1840 *778.6 p136*
Gerler, Magd. 44; America, 1840 *778.6 p136*
Gerler, Magd. 61; America, 1840 *778.6 p136*
Gerler, Peter 20; America, 1840 *778.6 p136*
Gerler, Peter 46; America, 1840 *778.6 p136*
Gerler, Vic. 68; America, 1840 *778.6 p136*
Gerlier, . . .; New Orleans, 1848 *778.6 p136*
Gerlier, P. 43; America, 1848 *778.6 p136*

Gerling, Bernhard; Ohio, 1840-1897 8365.35 p16
Gerling, Catharine 21; New York, NY, 1864 8425.62 p197
Gerling, Fr. August 9 months; New York, NY, 1864 8425.62 p197
Gerling, Heinr. 24; New York, NY, 1864 8425.62 p197
Gerling, John; Ohio, 1840-1897 8365.35 p16
Gerlinger, Friedrich 17; New Orleans, 1848 778.6 p136
Gerlinger, J.; Louisiana, 1874 4981.45 p296
Gerlinger, Louisa 24; New Orleans, 1848 778.6 p136
Gerlitzki, August William; Iowa, 1916 1211.15 p10
Germain, Mr. 26; America, 1747 778.6 p136
Germain, Joseph; Quebec, 1755 2314.30 p183
Germain, Lewis; Nova Scotia, 1784 7105 p23
Germain, Mary; New England, 1650-1750 9228.50 p604
Germain, U. 31; New Orleans, 1840 778.6 p136
German, . . .; Salem, MA, 1692 9228.50 p308
German, Daniel 29; Ontario, 1871 1823.17 p57
German, John; Ohio, 1809-1852 4511.35 p17
German, Joseph; Quebec, 1755-1757 2314.30 p170
German, Louis; Nova Scotia, 1784 7105 p23
Germann, Adam, II; America, 1854 2526.43 p203
 *Wife:*Kath. Lisabeth Heilmann
 *Son:*Leonhard
 *Daughter:*Barbara
Germann, Aloirie 14; Halifax, N.S., 1902 1860.4 p41
Germann, Anna; America, 1881 5475.1 p190
Germann, Anna 24; Halifax, N.S., 1902 1860.4 p41
Germann, Barbara 3 *SEE* Germann, Adam, II
Germann, Elisabetha; America, 1854 2526.43 p203
Germann, Elisabetha 9 *SEE* Germann, Peter
Germann, Franziska 18; Halifax, N.S., 1902 1860.4 p41
Germann, Franziska 50; Halifax, N.S., 1902 1860.4 p41
Germann, Georg; America, 1895 2526.43 p190
 With wife & 2 children
Germann, Georg Peter; America, 1854 2526.43 p203
 *Brother:*Michael
Germann, Ignatz 51; Halifax, N.S., 1902 1860.4 p41
Germann, Jacob 20; Halifax, N.S., 1902 1860.4 p41
Germann, Jakob; America, 1853 2526.43 p221
 With wife & 9 children
Germann, Johann 49; America, 1881 5475.1 p190
Germann, Johann Georg; America, 1854 2526.43 p203
Germann, Johann Nikolaus; America, 1867 2526.43 p120
Germann, Kath. Lisabeth Heilmann 25 *SEE* Germann, Adam, II
Germann, Konrad; America, 1857 2526.43 p120
Germann, Leonhard; America, 1856 2526.43 p203
 *Brother:*Wilhelm
Germann, Leonhard 1 *SEE* Germann, Adam, II
Germann, Ludwig; America, 1887 2526.43 p190
Germann, Ludwig; Nova Scotia, 1784 7105 p23
Germann, Magdalena 22; Halifax, N.S., 1902 1860.4 p41
Germann, Michael *SEE* Germann, Georg Peter
Germann, Michael 9; Halifax, N.S., 1902 1860.4 p41
Germann, Peter; America, 1867 2526.43 p120
 With wife 52
 *Daughter:*Elisabetha
 *Son:*Valentin
Germann, Regina 3; Halifax, N.S., 1902 1860.4 p41
Germann, Valentin 8 *SEE* Germann, Peter
Germann, Wilhelm *SEE* Germann, Leonhard
Germeien, Phil. 31; New Orleans, 1846 778.6 p136
Germiat, Agnes *SEE* Germiat, Francois Joseph
Germiat, Charles Louis *SEE* Germiat, Francois Joseph
Germiat, Francois Joseph; Wisconsin, 1872 1495.20 p12
 With wife
 *Child:*Louis
 *Child:*Joseph Albert
 *Child:*Charles Louis
 *Child:*Agnes
Germiat, Joseph Albert *SEE* Germiat, Francois Joseph
Germiat, Louis *SEE* Germiat, Francois Joseph
Gerndt, Wilhelm; Valdivia, Chile, 1851 1192.4 p50
Gerneau, Clement; Boston, 1769 9228.50 p267
Gerneaux Family ; New York, 1661 9228.50 p242
Gerner, Elisabeth Welsch *SEE* Gerner, Nikolaus Karl
Gerner, Eugen; America, 1881 5475.1 p75
Gerner, Nikolaus *SEE* Gerner, Nikolaus Karl
Gerner, Nikolaus Karl; America, 1881 5475.1 p213
 *Wife:*Elisabeth Welsch
 *Son:*Nikolaus
Gerney, Alexander; Ohio, 1809-1852 4511.35 p17
Geroux, Laurent 26; Louisiana, 1840 778.6 p136
Geroux, Matilde 22; Louisiana, 1840 778.6 p136
Gerrits, William; Wisconsin, 1873 6795.8 p106
Gerritsen, Herman; Washington, 1884 2770.40 p192
Gerritzen, Herman; Washington, 1884 2770.40 p192
Gerson, C. 21; America, 1846 778.6 p136
Gerson, Rene; Quebec, 1661 9221.17 p457
Gerssin, Guillaume *SEE* Gerssin, Hugo
Gerssin, Hugo; Wisconsin, 1854-1858 1495.20 p66
 *Wife:*Marie Barbe Barette
 *Son:*Guillaume
Gerssin, Marie Barbe Barette *SEE* Gerssin, Hugo
Gerstenegger, Charles 19; Port uncertain, 1843 778.6 p136
Gerster, Paul; Valdivia, Chile, 1850 1192.4 p49
Gerstner, Jakob 39; America, 1840 5475.1 p50
 *Wife:*Katharina Kraemer 36
 With child 6
 With child 3
 With child 1
Gerstner, Katharina Kraemer 36 *SEE* Gerstner, Jakob
Gertbleu, Antoine 35; New York, NY, 1856 1766.1 p45
Gerth, August; Iowa, 1891 1211.15 p10
Gerts, Wm. T.; North America, 1836 9228.50 p366
Gertt, Louis 24; Louisiana, 1848 778.6 p151
Gertt, Simon 29; Louisiana, 1848 778.6 p151
Gervais, Amelie Tordeur *SEE* Gervais, Prosper
Gervais, Elisa *SEE* Gervais, Prosper
Gervais, Justine *SEE* Gervais, Prosper
Gervais, Marie-Andre; Quebec, 1665 4514.3 p292
Gervais, Marin 24; Quebec, 1661 9221.17 p457
Gervais, Prosper; Wisconsin, 1869 1495.20 p56
 *Wife:*Amelie Tordeur
 *Child:*Elisa
 *Child:*Justine
Gervaise, Elizabeth; Columbus, OH, 1852 9228.50 p158
Gervaise, Jean 40; Montreal, 1653 9221.17 p291
Gervin, Robert; Ohio, 1840 3580.20 p32
Gervin, Robert; Ohio, 1840 6020.12 p7
Gerwatowski, Stanley; Detroit, 1930 1640.60 p81
Gerwiatowski, Julian; Detroit, 1930 1640.60 p78
Gery, Miss 42; New Orleans, 1845 778.6 p136
Gesabin, Jame; Louisiana, 1836-1840 4981.45 p212
Gesang, Carl; Philadelphia, 1865 8513.31 p309
 *Wife:*Sabine Bindel
Gesang, Sabine Bindel *SEE* Gesang, Carl
Gesbacher, Conrad; Ohio, 1809-1852 4511.35 p17
Geschke, August 34; New York, NY, 1885 1883.7 p46
Geschke, Emilie 6; New York, NY, 1885 1883.7 p46
Geschke, Emilie 38; New York, NY, 1885 1883.7 p46
Geschke, Johannes 1; New York, NY, 1885 1883.7 p46
Geschke, Paul 9; New York, NY, 1885 1883.7 p46
Geschwind, Melchior; Ohio, 1809-1852 4511.35 p17
Gesdart, Ludwig; New Orleans, 1851 7242.30 p142
Geseller, Jules 25; America, 1847 778.6 p136
Gesener, John George; New York, 1859 358.56 p54
Geser, Jacob 52; Ontario, 1871 1823.21 p128
Gesibel, Michael; North Carolina, 1710 3629.40 p4
Geske, Franz; Port uncertain, 1897 7420.1 p373
Gesle, Jacques; Quebec, 1650 9221.17 p226
Gesper, Charles; Louisiana, 1836-1841 4981.45 p208
Gesser, Franklin; Ohio, 1809-1852 4511.35 p17
Gesseron, Louis 16; Quebec, 1659 9221.17 p402
Gestbacher, Conrad; Ohio, 1809-1852 4511.35 p17
Gestner, George; Ohio, 1840-1897 8365.35 p16
Getard, E. 30; America, 1847 778.6 p136
Gethins, Thomas; Colorado, 1876 1029.59 p31
Gettis, William; Ohio, 1832 3580.20 p32
Gettis, William; Ohio, 1832 6020.12 p7
Gettner, Emma 1; Halifax, N.S., 1902 1860.4 p40
Gettner, Franz 30; Halifax, N.S., 1902 1860.4 p40
Gettner, Karoline 4; Halifax, N.S., 1902 1860.4 p40
Gettner, Marie 24; Halifax, N.S., 1902 1860.4 p40
Getty, Mary 91; Ontario, 1871 1823.21 p128
Getz, Bernard; Ohio, 1809-1852 4511.35 p17
Getz, Jacob; Ohio, 1809-1852 4511.35 p17
Geubel, Gertrude 82; Port uncertain, 1843 778.6 p136
Geubel, Josephe 24; Port uncertain, 1843 778.6 p136
Geubel, Louis 1; Port uncertain, 1843 778.6 p136
Geubel, Marie 4; Port uncertain, 1843 778.6 p136
Geubel, Michel 6; Port uncertain, 1843 778.6 p136
Geumann, Elisabeth; America, 1864 5475.1 p503
Geurcien, Marie 22; America, 1846 778.6 p136
Geuren, G. 25; New Orleans, 1834 1002.51 p114
Geveke, Heinrich Friedrich Conrad; America, 1850 7420.1 p71
Gevers, Aproline 26; New York, NY, 1864 8425.62 p196
Gevers, Eliese 1; New York, NY, 1864 8425.62 p196
Gevers, Hermann 25; New York, NY, 1864 8425.62 p196
Gewecke, Anne Catherine Sophie Tecklenburg *SEE* Gewecke, Johann Heinrich Friedrich Conrad
Gewecke, Catharine Sophie; New York, NY, 1856 7420.1 p154
Gewecke, Cord Henrich G. *SEE* Gewecke, Johann Heinrich
Gewecke, Engel Marie Dorothee Tatge *SEE* Gewecke, Johann Heinrich
Gewecke, Engel Sophie *SEE* Gewecke, Johann Heinrich
Gewecke, Hans Heinrich Christoph; America, 1867 7420.1 p256
 *Brother:*Johann Heinrich Wilhelm
Gewecke, Heinrich Conrad G. *SEE* Gewecke, Johann Heinrich Conrad
Gewecke, Heinrich Wilhelm; America, 1857 7420.1 p161
Gewecke, Johann Friedrich Wilh.; America, 1857 7420.1 p161
Gewecke, Johann Heinrich; America, 1857 7420.1 p161
 *Wife:*Engel Marie Dorothee Tatge
 *Mother:*Sophie Dorothee Charlotte Henriette
 *Daughter:*Engel Sophie
 *Father:*Cord Henrich G.
Gewecke, Johann Heinrich Conrad; America, 1851 7420.1 p79
 *Brother:*Heinrich Conrad G.
Gewecke, Johann Heinrich Friedrich Conrad; America, 1851 7420.1 p80
 *Mother:*Anne Catherine Sophie Tecklenburg
 *Brother:*Johann Heinrich Wilhelm
Gewecke, Johann Heinrich Wilhelm *SEE* Gewecke, Johann Heinrich Friedrich Conrad
Gewecke, Johann Heinrich Wilhelm *SEE* Gewecke, Hans Heinrich Christoph
Gewecke, Sophie Charlotte; America, 1857 7420.1 p161
Gewecke, Sophie Dorothee Ch.; America, 1865 7420.1 p230
Gewecke, Sophie Dorothee Charlotte Henriette *SEE* Gewecke, Johann Heinrich
Geweke, . . .; America, 1846 7420.1 p44
 With family
Geweke, Anne Sophie Caroline *SEE* Geweke, Engel Marie Sophie
Geweke, Engel Marie Dorothee *SEE* Geweke, Engel Marie Sophie
Geweke, Engel Marie Sophie; America, 1846 7420.1 p44
 *Sister:*Anne Sophie Caroline
 *Sister:*Engel Marie Dorothee
Geweke, Friederike Charlotte; America, 1893 7420.1 p368
Geweke, Friedrich; America, 1857 7420.1 p161
Geweke, Hans Heinrich; America, 1856 7420.1 p147
Geweke, Heinrich; America, 1857 7420.1 p161
 With wife & daughter
Gewike, Ernst; America, 1852 7420.1 p88
Gey, Francois 27; America, 1847 778.6 p136
Gey, Lucien 22; America, 1842 778.6 p136
Geyger, Elisabeth 7; Pennsylvania, 1899 170.15 p26
 With family
Geyger, Gertraud 33; Pennsylvania, 1851 170.15 p26
 With family
Geyger, Johann Adam 9; Pennsylvania, 1851 170.15 p26
 With family
Geyger, Johann Peter 45; Pennsylvania, 1851 170.15 p26
 With family
Geyger, Julianna; Wisconsin, 1883 6795.8 p57
Geziski, Josef 31; New York, NY, 1890 1883.7 p47
Gezycki, Marcin; Detroit, 1929 1640.55 p115
G.F., Johann Philip; America, 1882 179.55 p19
Ghiglione, Vincenzo; Washington, 1888 2770.40 p25
Giacomo, Sabbatino; Colorado, 1886 1029.59 p31
Giamente, C.; Louisiana, 1874-1875 4981.45 p29
Gian, Antoin 10; America, 1847 778.6 p136
Gianazzie, Emilio 16; America, 1846 778.6 p136
Giard, Nicolas 20; Quebec, 1658 9221.17 p380
Giard, Peirre C. P.; North Carolina, 1848 1088.45 p11
Gibault, Jean 24; Quebec, 1661 9221.17 p457
Gibaut, Abraham; Boston, 1739 9228.50 p246
 *Wife:*Mary
Gibaut, Edward; Salem, MA, 1728-1803 9228.50 p245
Gibaut, Jourdain; New York, 1822 9228.50 p146
Gibaut, Mary *SEE* Gibaut, Abraham
Gibaut, Sophia; Ohio, 1840 9228.50 p244
Gibb, Archibald 43; Ontario, 1871 1823.17 p57
Gibb, James 52; Ontario, 1871 1823.21 p128
Gibb, John 39; Ontario, 1871 1823.17 p57
Gibb, John 83; Ontario, 1871 1823.21 p128
Gibb, Robert 66; Ontario, 1871 1823.17 p57
Gibbings, Thomas 54; Ontario, 1871 1823.21 p128
Gibbins, Patrick; New England, 1745 1642 p28
Gibbley, William 19; Ontario, 1871 1823.21 p128
Gibbon, Anne Maria 40; Ontario, 1871 1823.17 p57
Gibbon, Charles H. 33; Ontario, 1871 1823.17 p57
Gibbon, John 41; Michigan, 1880 4491.30 p13
Gibbons, . . .; Boston, 1630-1644 1642 p3
Gibbons, Joseph 21; Ontario, 1871 1823.21 p128
Gibbons, Joseph 33; Ontario, 1871 1823.21 p128
Gibbons, Mary; Barbados or Jamaica, 1697 1220.12 p844
Gibbons, Michael; Toronto, 1844 2910.35 p116
Gibbons, Sarah A. 59; Ontario, 1871 1823.21 p128
Gibbons, William 61; Ontario, 1871 1823.17 p57
Gibbs, Aron 86; Ontario, 1871 1823.21 p128

Gibbs, Daniel; Boston, 1737 ***1642*** *p26*
Gibbs, Ellis 25; Ontario, 1871 ***1823.21*** *p128*
Gibbs, Giles; Dorchester, MA, 1632 ***117.5*** *p158*
Gibbs, Isaac 29; Ontario, 1871 ***1823.21*** *p128*
Gibbs, John 27; Ontario, 1871 ***1823.21*** *p128*
Gibbs, John 31; Ontario, 1871 ***1823.21*** *p128*
Gibbs, John 33; Ontario, 1871 ***1823.21*** *p128*
Gibbs, John 45; Ontario, 1871 ***1823.21*** *p128*
Gibbs, Thomas Farmer 52; Ontario, 1871 ***1823.21*** *p128*
Gibbs, William H.; Washington, 1885 ***2770.40*** *p194*
Gibbson, Richard 49; Ontario, 1871 ***1823.21*** *p128*
Gibeaut, Joseph; Ohio, 1800-1858 ***9228.50*** *p245*
Gibeaut, Jourdain; New York, 1800-1850 ***9228.50*** *p246*
Gibeaut, Rachel; Ohio, 1806 ***9228.50*** *p246*
Gibling, William 32; Ontario, 1871 ***1823.21*** *p128*
Gibouin, Pierre 21; Quebec, 1648 ***9221.17*** *p199*
Gibs, John; Jamaica, 1783 ***8529.30*** *p13A*
Gibson, . . .; Ontario, 1871 ***1823.21*** *p128*
Gibson, Ann; Maryland, 1673 ***1236.25*** *p48*
Gibson, Ann 40; Ontario, 1871 ***1823.21*** *p128*
Gibson, Anna 34; Michigan, 1880 ***4491.33*** *p10*
Gibson, Anne Josephe *SEE* Gibson, Henri
Gibson, Charles 38; Ontario, 1871 ***1823.21*** *p128*
Gibson, Christopher; Massachusetts, 1630 ***117.5*** *p156*
*Wife:*Sarah
Gibson, Cristopher 46; Ontario, 1871 ***1823.21*** *p128*
Gibson, David 30; Ontario, 1871 ***1823.17*** *p57*
Gibson, Edward 56; Ontario, 1871 ***1823.17*** *p57*
Gibson, Elisa 15; Ontario, 1871 ***1823.21*** *p128*
Gibson, George; Canada, 1774 ***3036.5*** *p42*
Gibson, George 31; Ontario, 1871 ***1823.21*** *p129*
Gibson, George 32; Ontario, 1871 ***1823.21*** *p129*
Gibson, George 34; Ontario, 1871 ***1823.21*** *p129*
Gibson, George 55; Ontario, 1871 ***1823.17*** *p57*
Gibson, George 60; Ontario, 1871 ***1823.21*** *p129*
Gibson, Henri; Wisconsin, 1854-1858 ***1495.20*** *p66*
*Wife:*Anne Josephe
Gibson, James; North Carolina, 1838 ***1088.45*** *p11*
Gibson, James 39; Ontario, 1871 ***1823.17*** *p57*
Gibson, James 51; Ontario, 1871 ***1823.21*** *p129*
Gibson, James 72; Ontario, 1871 ***1823.17*** *p57*
Gibson, John; Boston, 1766 ***1642*** *p37*
Gibson, John 30; New York, NY, 1894 ***6512.1*** *p228*
Gibson, John 29; Ontario, 1871 ***1823.17*** *p57*
Gibson, John 35; Ontario, 1871 ***1823.21*** *p129*
Gibson, John 49; Ontario, 1871 ***1823.21*** *p129*
Gibson, John 63; Ontario, 1871 ***1823.21*** *p129*
Gibson, John 65; Ontario, 1871 ***1823.21*** *p129*
Gibson, John W. 28; Ontario, 1871 ***1823.21*** *p129*
Gibson, Joseph C. 41; Ontario, 1871 ***1823.21*** *p129*
Gibson, Lawrence 34; Ontario, 1871 ***1823.21*** *p129*
Gibson, Michael 33; Ontario, 1871 ***1823.21*** *p129*
Gibson, Robert 33; Ontario, 1871 ***1823.21*** *p129*
Gibson, Robert 36; Ontario, 1871 ***1823.21*** *p129*
Gibson, Samuel 40; Ontario, 1871 ***1823.21*** *p129*
Gibson, Samuel 44; Ontario, 1871 ***1823.21*** *p129*
Gibson, Sarah; Manitoba, 1908 ***9228.50*** *p549*
Gibson, Sarah *SEE* Gibson, Christopher
Gibson, Thomas 25; Ontario, 1871 ***1823.17*** *p57*
Gibson, William 63; Ontario, 1871 ***1823.21*** *p129*
Gibson, William 65; Ontario, 1871 ***1823.21*** *p129*
Gibson, William J. 25; Ontario, 1871 ***1823.21*** *p129*
Gibson, William K. 30; Ontario, 1871 ***1823.17*** *p57*
Gibson, Wm; Louisiana, 1874-1875 ***4981.45*** *p29*
Gichs, Marguerite 27; Port uncertain, 1840 ***778.6*** *p136*
Giddings, Elizabeth; Ipswich, MA, 1737 ***1642*** *p70*
Giddings, William; New York, 1860 ***358.56*** *p4*
Gidien, F. 40; America, 1840 ***778.6*** *p137*
Gidon, Elisabeth 21; New York, NY, 1893 ***1883.7*** *p44*
Giedd, Anna 6 months; New York, NY, 1876 ***6954.7*** *p39*
Giedd, Emmanuel 8; New York, NY, 1876 ***6954.7*** *p39*
Giedd, Heinrich 9; New York, NY, 1876 ***6954.7*** *p39*
Giedd, Heinrich 39; New York, NY, 1876 ***6954.7*** *p39*
Giedd, Johann 3; New York, NY, 1876 ***6954.7*** *p39*
Giedd, Johann 35; New York, NY, 1876 ***6954.7*** *p39*
Giedd, Johann 59; New York, NY, 1876 ***6954.7*** *p39*
Giedd, Katherina 2; New York, NY, 1876 ***6954.7*** *p39*
Giedd, Katherina 5; New York, NY, 1876 ***6954.7*** *p39*
Giedd, Katherina 54; New York, NY, 1876 ***6954.7*** *p39*
Giedd, Margaretha 28; New York, NY, 1876 ***6954.7*** *p39*
Giedd, Michael 20; New York, NY, 1876 ***6954.7*** *p39*
Giedd, Peter 9; New York, NY, 1876 ***6954.7*** *p39*
Giedd, Suzanna 30; New York, NY, 1876 ***6954.7*** *p39*
Giedd, Theador 5; New York, NY, 1876 ***6954.7*** *p39*
Giedd, Theador 14; New York, NY, 1876 ***6954.7*** *p39*
Giedd, Veronica 20; New York, NY, 1876 ***6954.7*** *p39*
Giedd, Wilhelm 29; New York, NY, 1876 ***6954.7*** *p39*
Giedelmann, Xavier 33; Port uncertain, 1847 ***778.6*** *p137*
Giedeman, Edward; Iowa, 1897 ***1211.15*** *p10*
Giedeman, Wendelin; Iowa, 1905 ***1211.15*** *p10*
Giedt, Anna 7; New York, NY, 1886 ***6954.7*** *p41*
Giedt, Anna 8; New York, NY, 1886 ***6954.7*** *p41*
Giedt, Anna 8; New York, NY, 1886 ***6954.7*** *p41*
Giedt, Christina 7; New York, NY, 1886 ***6954.7*** *p41*
Giedt, Christina 7; New York, NY, 1886 ***6954.7*** *p41*
Giedt, Christina 46; New York, NY, 1886 ***6954.7*** *p41*
Giedt, Dorothea 9; New York, NY, 1886 ***6954.7*** *p41*
Giedt, Dorothea 9; New York, NY, 1886 ***6954.7*** *p41*
Giedt, Dorothea 33; New York, NY, 1886 ***6954.7*** *p41*
Giedt, Elisabeth 37; New York, NY, 1886 ***6954.7*** *p41*
Giedt, Emelia 3; New York, NY, 1886 ***6954.7*** *p41*
Giedt, Emelia 3; New York, NY, 1886 ***6954.7*** *p41*
Giedt, Emelia 6; New York, NY, 1886 ***6954.7*** *p40*
Giedt, Emelia 8; New York, NY, 1886 ***6954.7*** *p41*
Giedt, Emelia 39; New York, NY, 1886 ***6954.7*** *p41*
Giedt, Emmanuel 6 months; New York, NY, 1886 ***6954.7*** *p41*
Giedt, Emmanuel 6 months; New York, NY, 1886 ***6954.7*** *p41*
Giedt, Ephriam 20; New York, NY, 1886 ***6954.7*** *p40*
Giedt, Fedor 4; New York, NY, 1886 ***6954.7*** *p41*
Giedt, Georg 43; New York, NY, 1886 ***6954.7*** *p41*
Giedt, Heinrich 9; New York, NY, 1886 ***6954.7*** *p41*
Giedt, Heinrich 14; New York, NY, 1886 ***6954.7*** *p41*
Giedt, Heinrich 14; New York, NY, 1886 ***6954.7*** *p41*
Giedt, Heinrich 18; New York, NY, 1886 ***6954.7*** *p40*
Giedt, Johann 6 months; New York, NY, 1886 ***6954.7*** *p41*
Giedt, Johann 18; New York, NY, 1886 ***6954.7*** *p41*
Giedt, Johann 34; New York, NY, 1886 ***6954.7*** *p41*
Giedt, Johann 38; New York, NY, 1886 ***6954.7*** *p41*
Giedt, Johann 47; New York, NY, 1886 ***6954.7*** *p41*
Giedt, Johannes 14; New York, NY, 1886 ***6954.7*** *p41*
Giedt, Katharina 2; New York, NY, 1886 ***6954.7*** *p41*
Giedt, Katherina 2; New York, NY, 1886 ***6954.7*** *p41*
Giedt, Lydia 9 months; New York, NY, 1886 ***6954.7*** *p41*
Giedt, Marie 42; New York, NY, 1886 ***6954.7*** *p40*
Giedt, Mathilda 2; New York, NY, 1886 ***6954.7*** *p41*
Giedt, Sophia 20; New York, NY, 1886 ***6954.7*** *p41*
Giedt, Theador 4; New York, NY, 1886 ***6954.7*** *p41*
Giedt, Theador 8; New York, NY, 1886 ***6954.7*** *p41*
Giedt, Theador 9; New York, NY, 1886 ***6954.7*** *p41*
Giedt, Wilhelm 6; New York, NY, 1886 ***6954.7*** *p41*
Giedt, Wilhelm 20; New York, NY, 1886 ***6954.7*** *p40*
Gieg, Adam; America, 1754 ***2526.42*** *p120*
*Wife:*Juliane Schuchert
*Child:*Johann Adam
*Child:*Johann Ludwig
*Child:*Johann Jakob
*Child:*Maria Katharina
*Child:*Hieronymus
*Child:*Johann Michael
Gieg, Anna Margaretha 42 *SEE* Gieg, Wilhelm, I
Gieg, Eva Katharina 15 *SEE* Gieg, Wilhelm, I
Gieg, Georg; Pennsylvania, 1754 ***2526.42*** *p120*
With wife
Gieg, Hieronymus 20 *SEE* Gieg, Adam
Gieg, Johann Adam 16 *SEE* Gieg, Adam
Gieg, Johann Jakob 2 *SEE* Gieg, Adam
Gieg, Johann Ludwig 7 *SEE* Gieg, Adam
Gieg, Johann Michael 17 *SEE* Gieg, Adam
Gieg, Johannes; America, 1837 ***2526.42*** *p150*
With family
Gieg, Johannes; America, 1853 ***2526.42*** *p150*
Gieg, Juliane Schuchert *SEE* Gieg, Adam
Gieg, Katharina 29 *SEE* Gieg, Wilhelm, I
Gieg, Leonhard; America, 1883 ***2526.43*** *p139*
Gieg, Margaretha 3 *SEE* Gieg, Wilhelm, I
Gieg, Maria Katharina 12 *SEE* Gieg, Adam
Gieg, Wilhelm; America, 1836 ***2526.42*** *p150*
With wife
With son 8
With son 4
With daughter 12
With daughter 16
Gieg, Wilhelm; America, 1865-1884 ***2526.43*** *p139*
Gieg, Wilhelm 20 *SEE* Gieg, Wilhelm, I
Gieg, Wilhelm, I 69; America, 1867 ***2526.42*** *p150*
*Daughter:*Katharina 29
*Grandchild:*Wilhelm 20
*Grandchild:*Eva Katharina 15
*Grandchild:*Margaretha 3
*Daughter:*Anna Margaretha 42
Giegeler, John; New York, 1860 ***358.56*** *p4*
Giegerich, Adam; America, 1876 ***2526.43*** *p123*
Giehl, Anton *SEE* Giehl, Mathias
Giehl, Katharina *SEE* Giehl, Mathias
Giehl, Katharina *SEE* Giehl, Mathias
Giehl, Margarethe Kolling 21 *SEE* Giehl, Mathias
Giehl, Mathias 29; Brazil, 1862 ***5475.1*** *p369*
*Wife:*Margarethe Kolling 21
*Brother:*Anton
*Sister:*Katharina
*Daughter:*Katharina
Gier, Barbara *SEE* Gier, Nikolaus
Gier, Charles; North Carolina, 1848 ***1088.45*** *p11*
Gier, Katharina *SEE* Gier, Nikolaus
Gier, Katharina 47; America, 1858 ***5475.1*** *p251*
*Son:*Peter 20
*Son:*Philipp 17
*Daughter:*Katharina 15
Gier, Margarethe *SEE* Gier, Nikolaus
Gier, Nikolaus *SEE* Gier, Nikolaus
Gier, Nikolaus 40; America, 1872 ***5475.1*** *p153*
*Wife:*Susanna Burger
*Daughter:*Barbara
*Daughter:*Katharina
*Son:*Nikolaus
*Daughter:*Margarethe
Gier, Susanna Burger *SEE* Gier, Nikolaus
Gierend, Kath.; America, 1882 ***5475.1*** *p436*
Gierend, Margaretha; America, 1864-1899 ***6442.17*** *p65*
Giering, Margarethe; America, 1834 ***5475.1*** *p437*
Giernues, Jean 25; America, 1847 ***778.6*** *p137*
Gierszewski, Frank; Wisconsin, 1898 ***6795.8*** *p57*
Giertier, Gottlieb; Colorado, 1889 ***1029.59*** *p31*
Gierty, William; Louisiana, 1841-1844 ***4981.45*** *p210*
Giese, John; Wisconsin, 1886 ***6795.8*** *p168*
Giese, William Fred; Wisconsin, 1892 ***6795.8*** *p85*
Giesecke, Johann Conrad; America, 1868 ***7420.1*** *p271*
Gieseke, . . .; America, 1846 ***7420.1*** *p44*
With family
Gieseke, Hans Heinrich; America, 1860 ***7420.1*** *p193*
Gieseke, Johann Heinrich; South America, 1842 ***7420.1*** *p24*
Gieseking, Mr.; America, 1860 ***7420.1*** *p193*
Gieseler, Carl August; America, 1859 ***7420.1*** *p184*
Gieseler, Johann Christoph Wilhelm; America, 1853 ***7420.1*** *p105*
Giesemann, Clemens; Carolina, 1841 ***170.15*** *p26*
With wife & 4 children
Giesen, William; Illinois, 1851 ***6079.1*** *p5*
Gieser, John; Wisconsin, 1893 ***6795.8*** *p138*
Giesewelle, Engel Marie; America, 1847 ***7420.1*** *p53*
Giesler, Dorothee; America, 1854 ***7420.1*** *p119*
Giesler, Wilhelm 32; New York, NY, 1893 ***1883.7*** *p39*
Giesmann, George; Illinois, 1855 ***6079.1*** *p5*
Giess, Edward; New York, 1859 ***358.56*** *p55*
Giess, Michel 64; America, 1846 ***778.6*** *p137*
Giessen, Carl; Valdivia, Chile, 1850 ***1192.4*** *p49*
Giessman, Eva; Virginia, 1831 ***152.20*** *p65*
Gietzel, Daniel 25; Portland, ME, 1911 ***970.38*** *p77*
Gietzel, Emilie 23; Portland, ME, 1911 ***970.38*** *p77*
Gietzel, Olga 3; Portland, ME, 1911 ***970.38*** *p77*
Gietzen, Jakob; South America, 1846 ***5475.1*** *p531*
Gietzen, Johann; South America, 1846 ***5475.1*** *p531*
Gietzen, Johann Peter; South America, 1846 ***5475.1*** *p531*
Gieves, Mary Walburga; Kansas, 1917-1918 ***2094.25*** *p50*
Giff, Thomas 60; Ontario, 1871 ***1823.17*** *p57*
Giffard, Charles 3 *SEE* Giffard, Marie Regnouard
Giffard, Florence Mary; Ottawa, 1934 ***9228.50*** *p246*
Giffard, John; Salem, MA, 1650-1750 ***9228.50*** *p307*
Giffard, Louis; Quebec, 1653 ***9221.17*** *p274*
Giffard, Marie 6 *SEE* Giffard, Marie Regnouard
Giffard, Marie 35; Quebec, 1634 ***9221.17*** *p36*
*Daughter:*Marie 6
*Son:*Charles 3
Giffard, Nicolas; Quebec, 1641 ***9221.17*** *p104*
Giffard, Robert; Quebec, 1634 ***2314.30*** *p167*
Giffard, Robert; Quebec, 1658 ***2314.30*** *p184*
Giffard, Walter; Honolulu, 1875 ***9228.50*** *p247*
Giffard DuMoncel, Robert; Quebec, 1621-1622 ***9221.17*** *p35*
Giffels, William 37; Ontario, 1871 ***1823.17*** *p57*
Giffin, William 50; Ontario, 1871 ***1823.21*** *p129*
Gifford, Francis Thos.; Colorado, 1880 ***1029.59*** *p31*
Gifford, Gerono 49; Ontario, 1871 ***1823.17*** *p57*
Gigandet, Francis N.; Ohio, 1840-1897 ***8365.35*** *p16*
Gigandet, John J.; Ohio, 1840-1897 ***8365.35*** *p16*
Gigandet, Joseph; Ohio, 1840-1897 ***8365.35*** *p16*
Gignard, Elisabeth Sorin 25 *SEE* Gignard, Laurent
Gignard, Laurent 22; Quebec, 1657 ***9221.17*** *p358*
*Wife:*Elisabeth Sorin 25
Gignous, Michel; Louisiana, 1836-1840 ***4981.45*** *p212*
Gignoux, B...d 25; America, 1841 ***778.6*** *p137*
Gigos, Bless 4; Indiana, 1840 ***778.6*** *p137*
Gigos, Bless 42; Indiana, 1840 ***778.6*** *p137*
Gigos, Mary Ann 25; Indiana, 1840 ***778.6*** *p137*
Gigot, Felix; New York, NY, 1855 ***1494.20*** *p12*
Gigou, Magdelain; Virginia, 1700 ***9230.15*** *p81*
Giguere, Jean; Quebec, 1650 ***9221.17*** *p226*
Giguiere, Robert 28; Quebec, 1644 ***9221.17*** *p142*
Gilarek, Albina 18; New York, NY, 1912 ***8355.1*** *p16*
Gilberg, Ellen C.; St. Paul, MN, 1894 ***1865.50*** *p48*
Gilberg, Mathilda; St. Paul, MN, 1884 ***1865.50*** *p107*
Gilbert, Aloise 8; Missouri, 1846 ***778.6*** *p137*
Gilbert, Bolenber 52; Missouri, 1846 ***778.6*** *p137*
Gilbert, Charles 19; Missouri, 1846 ***778.6*** *p137*
Gilbert, Daniel 57; Ontario, 1871 ***1823.21*** *p129*

Gilbert, David 24; Ontario, 1871 ***1823.17*** *p57*
Gilbert, David 64; Ontario, 1871 ***1823.21*** *p129*
Gilbert, Dorah 69; Ontario, 1871 ***1823.21*** *p129*
Gilbert, Elizabeth; Wisconsin, 1854 ***9228.50*** *p198*
With 3 sons & daughter
Gilbert, Elizabeth; Wisconsin, 1855 ***9228.50*** *p247*
With 3 sons & daughter
Gilbert, George 29; Ontario, 1871 ***1823.21*** *p129*
Gilbert, Ira 34; Ontario, 1871 ***1823.21*** *p129*
Gilbert, Isabell 58; Michigan, 1880 ***4491.30*** *p13*
Gilbert, Jane 40; Ontario, 1871 ***1823.21*** *p129*
Gilbert, Jean; Quebec, 1651 ***9221.17*** *p243*
Gilbert, John 33; Ontario, 1871 ***1823.21*** *p129*
Gilbert, John; Washington, 1889 ***2770.40*** *p27*
Gilbert, John Felix; North Carolina, 1855 ***1088.45*** *p11*
Gilbert, Louis 14; Missouri, 1846 ***778.6*** *p137*
Gilbert, Madeleine 48; Missouri, 1846 ***778.6*** *p137*
Gilbert, Margaret 53; Michigan, 1880 ***4491.39*** *p11*
Gilbert, Marie 17; Missouri, 1846 ***778.6*** *p137*
Gilbert, Mary 60; Ontario, 1871 ***1823.17*** *p57*
Gilbert, Oskar; Cleveland, OH, 1893-1894 ***9722.10*** *p119*
Gilbert, Pearce Wm.; Colorado, 1888 ***1029.59*** *p31*
Gilbert, Pearce Wm.; Colorado, 1894 ***1029.59*** *p31*
Gilbert, Pearce Wm. 54; Colorado, 1889 ***1029.59*** *p31*
Gilbert, Philippe 9; Missouri, 1846 ***778.6*** *p137*
Gilbert, Pierre 35; Quebec, 1658 ***9221.17*** *p380*
Gilbert, Roger 31; Ontario, 1871 ***1823.21*** *p129*
Gilbert, Sarah 84; Ontario, 1871 ***1823.21*** *p129*
Gilbert, Sophia 44; Michigan, 1880 ***4491.36*** *p8*
Gilbert, Sophia; New York, 1829-1900 ***9228.50*** *p468*
Gilbert, Valentine; Ohio, 1809-1852 ***4511.35*** *p17*
Gilbert, William 31; Ontario, 1871 ***1823.17*** *p57*
Gilbert, William 36; Ontario, 1871 ***1823.17*** *p57*
Gilbert, William 43; Ontario, 1871 ***1823.21*** *p129*
Gilbral, Antoine; South Carolina, 1831 ***6155.4*** *p18*
Gilchrist, Alexander; New York, 1738 ***8277.31*** *p115*
Gilchrist, Duncan; New York, 1738 ***8277.31*** *p115*
*Wife:*Florence McAllister
*Daughter:*Mary
Gilchrist, Florence McAllister *SEE* Gilchrist, Duncan
Gilchrist, Isabella 64; Ontario, 1871 ***1823.21*** *p129*
Gilchrist, John; New York, 1738 ***8277.31*** *p115*
Gilchrist, John 25; North Carolina, 1774 ***1422.10*** *p58*
Gilchrist, John 25; North Carolina, 1774 ***1422.10*** *p62*
Gilchrist, John 40; Ontario, 1871 ***1823.21*** *p129*
Gilchrist, John 70; Ontario, 1871 ***1823.21*** *p129*
Gilchrist, Margaret; New York, 1740 ***8277.31*** *p115*
Gilchrist, Margaret; Philadelphia, 1850 ***8513.31*** *p428*
Gilchrist, Marion 21; North Carolina, 1774 ***1422.10*** *p58*
Gilchrist, Marion 21; North Carolina, 1774 ***1422.10*** *p62*
Gilchrist, Mary *SEE* Gilchrist, Duncan
Gilchrist, Mary 70; Ontario, 1871 ***1823.21*** *p129*
Gilchrist, William; Ohio, 1839 ***2763.1*** *p9*
Gildart, John; Canada, 1774 ***3036.5*** *p41*
Gildart, Joshua; Canada, 1774 ***3036.5*** *p41*
Gildemeister, Anna 28; New York, NY, 1893 ***1883.7*** *p37*
Gildemeister, Auguste 4; New York, NY, 1893 ***1883.7*** *p37*
Gildemeister, Emilie 10 months; New York, NY, 1893 ***1883.7*** *p37*
Gildemeister, Emilie 11 months; New York, NY, 1893 ***1883.7*** *p37*
Gildemeister, Gustav 4; New York, NY, 1893 ***1883.7*** *p37*
Gildemeister, Hanne 10; New York, NY, 1893 ***1883.7*** *p37*
Gildemeister, Heinrich 3; New York, NY, 1893 ***1883.7*** *p37*
Gildemeister, Leo 25; New York, NY, 1893 ***1883.7*** *p37*
Gildemeister, Paul 15; New York, NY, 1893 ***1883.7*** *p37*
Gildemeister, Pauline 7; New York, NY, 1893 ***1883.7*** *p37*
Gildemeister, Pauline 9; New York, NY, 1893 ***1883.7*** *p37*
Gildemeister, Theresa 28; New York, NY, 1893 ***1883.7*** *p37*
Gildenlaw, J. 20; Quebec, 1870 ***8364.32*** *p23*
Gile, Mr. 22; America, 1841 ***778.6*** *p137*
Gile, Ann 20 *SEE* Gile, John
Gile, Ann; Massachusetts, 1772 ***1642*** *p68*
Gile, John 18; Dedham, MA, 1636 ***9228.50*** *p264*
*Brother:*Samuel 16
*Sister:*Ann 20
Gile, Noah; Boston, 1650-1712 ***9228.50*** *p266*
Gile, Samuel 16 *SEE* Gile, John
Giles, Alfred 36; Ontario, 1871 ***1823.17*** *p57*
Giles, Eli; Salem, MA, 1600-1699 ***9228.50*** *p247*
Giles, John 33; Ontario, 1871 ***1823.17*** *p57*
Giles, Mathew; Maine, 1653 ***9228.50*** *p270*
Giles, Noah; Boston, 1650-1712 ***9228.50*** *p266*
Giles, Robert 28; Ontario, 1871 ***1823.21*** *p130*
Giles, Walter Newell; Nebraska, 1866-1895 ***9228.50*** *p381*
Giles, William; New York, 1783 ***8529.30*** *p11*
Giles, William; Ohio, 1851 ***3580.20*** *p32*
Giles, William; Ohio, 1851 ***6020.12*** *p7*
Giles, William B. 45; Ontario, 1871 ***1823.21*** *p130*
Giles, Willison; North Carolina, 1792-1862 ***1088.45*** *p11*
Gilfoy, John 74; Ontario, 1871 ***1823.21*** *p130*
Gilfoyle, Anna 20; Ontario, 1871 ***1823.21*** *p130*
Gilfoyle, Henry 34; Ontario, 1871 ***1823.21*** *p130*
Gilgan, John Jacob; Wisconsin, 1874 ***6795.8*** *p128*
Gilgann, John Jacob; Wisconsin, 1874 ***6795.8*** *p128*
Gilgate, Jo. 22; Virginia, 1635 ***1183.3*** *p30*
Gilges, Anna Maria; America, 1868 ***5475.1*** *p388*
Gilges, Johann; America, 1870 ***5475.1*** *p393*
Gilgingen, M. 26; Louisiana, 1840 ***778.6*** *p137*
Gilins, Francois 33; America, 1848 ***778.6*** *p137*
Gilisse, Jean Baptiste *SEE* Gilisse, Jean Baptiste
Gilisse, Jean Baptiste; Wisconsin, 1855 ***1495.20*** *p56*
*Wife:*Rosalie Thirion
*Child:*Jean Baptiste
*Son:*Leopold F.
*Son:*Maximilien
*Child:*Seraphine
Gilisse, Leopold F. *SEE* Gilisse, Jean Baptiste
Gilisse, Maximilien *SEE* Gilisse, Jean Baptiste
Gilisse, Rosalie Thirion *SEE* Gilisse, Jean Baptiste
Gilisse, Seraphine *SEE* Gilisse, Jean Baptiste
Gilks, Edward 22; North Carolina, 1774 ***1422.10*** *p55*
Gill, Andrew; Ohio, 1809-1852 ***4511.35*** *p17*
Gill, Anna; America, 1879 ***5475.1*** *p376*
Gill, Benjamin; Miami, 1920 ***4984.15*** *p38*
Gill, John; Louisiana, 1874 ***4981.45*** *p132*
Gill, Joseph; Ohio, 1809-1852 ***4511.35*** *p17*
Gill, Joseph J.; Ohio, 1868 ***3580.20*** *p32*
Gill, Joseph J.; Ohio, 1868 ***6020.12*** *p7*
Gill, Mary 81; Ontario, 1871 ***1823.21*** *p130*
Gill, Michael 48; Ontario, 1871 ***1823.21*** *p130*
Gill, Thomas; North Carolina, 1804 ***1088.45*** *p11*
Gill, Thomas; Toronto, 1844 ***2910.35*** *p115*
Gill, William; Colorado, 1869 ***1029.59*** *p31*
Gill, William 25; Ontario, 1871 ***1823.21*** *p130*
Gill, William C.L. 45; Ontario, 1871 ***1823.21*** *p130*
Gill, Wm 23; Ontario, 1871 ***1823.21*** *p130*
Gillam, Ann; Massachusetts, 1635 ***9228.50*** *p247*
*Son:*Benjamin
With 4 children
Gillam, Benjamin *SEE* Gillam, Ann
Gillam, Carteret; Connecticut, 1690 ***9228.50*** *p265*
Gillam, Charles; Connecticut, 1690 ***9228.50*** *p265*
Gillam, Charles 53; Ontario, 1871 ***1823.21*** *p130*
Gillam, Hiram 24; Ontario, 1871 ***1823.21*** *p130*
Gillam, Zachariah; Massachusetts, 1663 ***9228.50*** *p247*
Gillan, William; Ohio, 1840 ***2763.1*** *p9*
Gillard, Mr. 38; Port uncertain, 1848 ***778.6*** *p137*
Gillard, H.; Quebec, 1885 ***1937.10*** *p52*
Gillard, John 24; Ontario, 1871 ***1823.17*** *p57*
Gillas, Jane 48; Ontario, 1871 ***1823.21*** *p130*
Gillaspie, Angus *SEE* Gillaspie, Neil
Gillaspie, Gilbert *SEE* Gillaspie, Neil
Gillaspie, Mary McIlepheder *SEE* Gillaspie, Neil
Gillaspie, Neil; New York, 1739 ***8277.31*** *p115*
*Wife:*Mary McIlepheder
*Son:*Angus
*Son:*Gilbert
Gillatry, Alexander 29; Ontario, 1871 ***1823.17*** *p57*
Gillatry, David 27; Ontario, 1871 ***1823.17*** *p58*
Gillatry, John 32; Ontario, 1871 ***1823.17*** *p58*
Gillatry, John 57; Ontario, 1871 ***1823.17*** *p58*
Gillberg, Ellen C.; St. Paul, MN, 1894 ***1865.50*** *p48*
Gillberg, The.dor; Cleveland, OH, 1898-1902 ***9722.10*** *p119*
Gillcer, Henry; Ohio, 1809-1852 ***4511.35*** *p17*
Gille, J. 19; America, 1848 ***778.6*** *p137*
Gille, Noah; Boston, 1650-1712 ***9228.50*** *p266*
Gillean, James 46; Ontario, 1871 ***1823.21*** *p130*
Gillearvosse, Robert 30; Ontario, 1871 ***1823.21*** *p130*
Gilles, Anne; Quebec, 1663 ***4514.3*** *p329*
Gilles, Donald 60; Ontario, 1871 ***1823.21*** *p130*
Gilles, Duncan 62; Ontario, 1871 ***1823.21*** *p130*
Gilles, Jeanne; Quebec, 1670 ***4514.3*** *p317*
Gilles, Jesse 68; Ontario, 1871 ***1823.21*** *p130*
Gilles, Laulan; Quebec, 1786 ***1416.15*** *p8*
Gilles, Michel 19; Montreal, 1653 ***9221.17*** *p301*
Gilles, William; Quebec, 1786 ***1416.15*** *p8*
Gillespie, Cornelius 30; Ontario, 1871 ***1823.17*** *p58*
Gillespie, Ralph 21; Ontario, 1871 ***1823.21*** *p130*
Gillespie, Robert; Ohio, 1809-1852 ***4511.35*** *p17*
Gillet, Jean; Quebec, 1639 ***9221.17*** *p88*
Gillet, Jean; Quebec, 1658 ***9221.17*** *p381*
Gillet, Jonathan; New England, 1634 ***117.5*** *p159*
Gillet, Mathew; Salem, MA, 1641 ***9228.50*** *p248*
Gillet, Nathan; New England, 1634 ***117.5*** *p159*
Gillet, Noel; Montreal, 1653 ***9221.17*** *p291*
Gillett, Armund; North Carolina, 1841 ***1088.45*** *p11*
Gillett, Elizabeth 56; Michigan, 1880 ***4491.42*** *p12*
Gillett, Jonathan; New England, 1634 ***117.5*** *p159*
Gillett, Nathan; New England, 1634 ***117.5*** *p159*
Gilley, Mr.; America, 1706-1806 ***9228.50*** *p248*
Gilley, John 24; Ontario, 1871 ***1823.21*** *p130*
Gilley, John 35; Ontario, 1871 ***1823.21*** *p130*
Gilley, Wm.; America, 1807 ***9228.50*** *p341*
Gillhar, Anna Elizabeth; Wisconsin, 1897 ***6795.8*** *p176*
Gillhofer, George; Illinois, 1858 ***6079.1*** *p5*
Gillich, Andrew; Ohio, 1809-1852 ***4511.35*** *p17*
Gillich, Martin; Ohio, 1809-1852 ***4511.35*** *p17*
Gillick, Andrew; Ohio, 1809-1852 ***4511.35*** *p17*
Gillier, Henry; Ohio, 1809-1852 ***4511.35*** *p17*
Gillies, Catharine; New York, 1739 ***8277.31*** *p116*
Gillies, Donald 35; Ontario, 1871 ***1823.21*** *p130*
Gillies, Dugald 40; Ontario, 1871 ***1823.21*** *p130*
Gillies, Duncan 41; Ontario, 1871 ***1823.21*** *p130*
Gillies, Elizabeth 28; Ontario, 1871 ***1823.17*** *p58*
Gillies, Janet; New York, 1739 ***8277.31*** *p118*
Gillies, Janet; New York, 1739 ***8277.31*** *p118*
Gillies, Margaret 55; Ontario, 1871 ***1823.17*** *p58*
Gillies, Mary; New York, 1738 ***8277.31*** *p119*
Gillies, Matthew 29; Ontario, 1871 ***1823.21*** *p130*
Gillies, Neil 53; Ontario, 1871 ***1823.21*** *p130*
Gillies, William 27; Ontario, 1871 ***1823.17*** *p58*
Gillig, Annie 13; Ontario, 1871 ***1823.17*** *p58*
Gillig, Caroline 6; Ontario, 1871 ***1823.17*** *p58*
Gilligan, Michael 35; Ontario, 1871 ***1823.21*** *p130*
Gilligan, Patrick; Illinois, 1866 ***6079.1*** *p5*
Gilliland, David 44; Ontario, 1871 ***1823.17*** *p58*
Gilliland, James 55; Ontario, 1871 ***1823.17*** *p58*
Gilliland, John 53; Ontario, 1871 ***1823.17*** *p58*
Gilliland, Robert 66; Ontario, 1871 ***1823.17*** *p58*
Gilliland, William; Ohio, 1842 ***2763.1*** *p9*
Gilliland, William 46; Ontario, 1871 ***1823.17*** *p58*
Gillilande, Stewart 52; Ontario, 1871 ***1823.17*** *p58*
Gillin, James; St. John, N.B., 1847 ***2978.15*** *p36*
Gillis, Archibald 26; Ontario, 1871 ***1823.21*** *p130*
Gillis, Archibald 62; Ontario, 1871 ***1823.17*** *p58*
Gillis, Catharin 22; Ontario, 1871 ***1823.21*** *p130*
Gillis, Donald 38; Ontario, 1871 ***1823.21*** *p130*
Gillis, Duncan 50; Ontario, 1871 ***1823.17*** *p58*
Gillis, Malcolm 60; Ontario, 1871 ***1823.21*** *p130*
Gillis, Marcelin 18; America, 1843 ***778.6*** *p137*
Gillis, Robert 42; Ontario, 1871 ***1823.17*** *p58*
Gillispie, Christina 63; Ontario, 1871 ***1823.21*** *p131*
Gillman, Francis; Marston's Wharf, 1782 ***8529.30*** *p11*
Gillmann, Karoline; Brazil, 1862 ***5475.1*** *p561*
Gillmore, James 29; Ontario, 1871 ***1823.21*** *p131*
Gillmore, Jane 58; Ontario, 1871 ***1823.21*** *p131*
Gillmore, Mary; Massachusetts, 1767 ***1642*** *p120*
Gillo, Maria; America, 1873 ***5475.1*** *p226*
Gillooly, Michael 45; Ontario, 1871 ***1823.21*** *p131*
Gillot, Charles; Ohio, 1809-1852 ***4511.35*** *p17*
Gillroy, John; New York, 1776 ***8529.30*** *p3A*
Gilly, Henry G. 20; Ontario, 1871 ***1823.21*** *p131*
Gillyard, Peter; Portsmouth, NH, 1733 ***9228.50*** *p248*
Gilman, Francis; Marston's Wharf, 1782 ***8529.30*** *p11*
Gilman, Lewes; Virginia, 1652 ***6254.4*** *p243*
Gilmann, Anna Elis.; Valdivia, Chile, 1852 ***1192.4*** *p55*
Gilmartin, Patrick; Newfoundland, 1814 ***3476.10*** *p54*
Gilmond, David W.; New York, NY, 1877 ***7710.1*** *p159*
Gilmore, Ann Moore *SEE* Gilmore, Archibald
Gilmore, Archibald; Philadelphia, 1856 ***8513.31*** *p309*
*Wife:*Ann Moore
Gilmore, Charles B.; Ohio, 1876 ***3580.20*** *p32*
Gilmore, Charles B.; Ohio, 1876 ***6020.12*** *p7*
Gilmore, Edward; New England, 1745 ***1642*** *p28*
Gilmore, Ellen; Ohio, 1853 ***8513.31*** *p322*
Gilmore, James *SEE* Gilmore, William
Gilmore, Margaret; Massachusetts, 1733 ***1642*** *p85*
Gilmore, Owen 29; New York, NY, 1849 ***6178.50*** *p152*
Gilmore, Robert *SEE* Gilmore, William
Gilmore, William; Massachusetts, 1741 ***1642*** *p67*
*Relative:*James
*Relative:*Robert
Gilot, Francois; New York, NY, 1871 ***1494.20*** *p12*
Gilpin, John; Boston, 1774 ***8529.30*** *p3A*
Gilpin, John W. 33; Ontario, 1871 ***1823.17*** *p58*
Gilroy, John; New York, 1776 ***8529.30*** *p3A*
Gils, Edward C. 48; Ontario, 1871 ***1823.21*** *p131*
Gilson, Alexander *SEE* Gilson, Jean Baptiste
Gilson, Charles *SEE* Gilson, Jean Baptiste
Gilson, Clementine *SEE* Gilson, Jean Baptiste
Gilson, Desiree *SEE* Gilson, Jean Baptiste
Gilson, Isidore *SEE* Gilson, Jean Baptiste
Gilson, Jean Baptiste *SEE* Gilson, Jean Baptiste
Gilson, Jean Baptiste; Wisconsin, 1854-1858 ***1495.20*** *p50*
*Wife:*Rosalie Dehut
*Child:*Isidore
*Child:*Alexander
*Child:*Clementine
*Child:*Jean Baptiste

*Child:*Jean Francois
*Child:*Desiree
*Child:*Charles
Gilson, Jean Francois *SEE* Gilson, Jean Baptiste
Gilson, Rosalie Dehut *SEE* Gilson, Jean Baptiste
Gilsoul, Ferdinand; Wisconsin, 1800-1857 ***1495.20*** *p56*
*Wife:*Virginie Corroy
*Child:*Irma
*Child:*Mathilde
*Child:*Louis
Gilsoul, Irma *SEE* Gilsoul, Ferdinand
Gilsoul, Louis *SEE* Gilsoul, Ferdinand
Gilsoul, Mathilde *SEE* Gilsoul, Ferdinand
Gilsoul, Virginie Corroy *SEE* Gilsoul, Ferdinand
Giltzinger, Johann Georg; Pennsylvania, 1854 ***170.15*** *p26*
With wife & 2 children
Gimbel, Frederick; Ohio, 1809-1852 ***4511.35*** *p17*
Gimler, Elisabeth; New York, 1880 ***5475.1*** *p378*
Gimler, Katharina; America, 1881 ***5475.1*** *p344*
Gimmler, Nikolaus; America, 1881 ***5475.1*** *p511*
Gimpsin, Elizabeth 13; Quebec, 1870 ***8364.32*** *p23*
Ginard, Elisabeth Sorin 25 *SEE* Ginard, Laurent
Ginard, Laurent 22; Quebec, 1657 ***9221.17*** *p358*
*Wife:*Elisabeth Sorin 25
Ginas, Andreas; New York, 1860 ***358.56*** *p150*
Gindler, Hermine; Philadelphia, 1856 ***8513.31*** *p431*
Gingerich, Daniel; Ohio, 1809-1852 ***4511.35*** *p17*
Gingerick, Daniel; Ohio, 1809-1852 ***4511.35*** *p17*
Gingras, Sebastien 19; Quebec, 1659 ***9221.17*** *p402*
Ginity, Patrick 22; Ontario, 1871 ***1823.21*** *p131*
Ginn, John; Indiana, 1837 ***471.10*** *p86*
Ginn, John 39; Ontario, 1871 ***1823.17*** *p58*
Ginn, Lancelot; Indiana, 1840-1847 ***471.10*** *p87*
Ginn, William; Indiana, 1850 ***471.10*** *p87*
Ginnings, Mr. 25; North Carolina, 1774 ***1422.10*** *p55*
Ginoska, Barbara 42; New York, NY, 1879 ***6954.7*** *p40*
Ginoska, Friedrich 11 months; New York, NY, 1879 ***6954.7*** *p40*
Ginoska, Johannes 17; New York, NY, 1879 ***6954.7*** *p40*
Ginoska, Leonore 15; New York, NY, 1879 ***6954.7*** *p40*
Ginsbach, Anna Hohn 47 *SEE* Ginsbach, Nikolaus
Ginsbach, Johann; America, 1874 ***5475.1*** *p341*
*Wife:*Magdalena Hild
With child
*Son:*Mathias
Ginsbach, Katharina 37; America, 1868 ***5475.1*** *p323*
Ginsbach, Magdalena Hild 46 *SEE* Ginsbach, Johann
Ginsbach, Mathias *SEE* Ginsbach, Johann
Ginsbach, Nikolaus 47; America, 1872 ***5475.1*** *p147*
*Wife:*Anna Hohn 47
Ginther, Gottlieb; Colorado, 1894 ***1029.59*** *p31*
Ginton, Victoire 30; Louisiana, 1848 ***778.6*** *p137*
Ginzburg, Mr. 17; New York, NY, 1885 ***1883.7*** *p46*
Gion, Catharina 19; America, 1847 ***778.6*** *p137*
Gion, Joseph 45; America, 1847 ***778.6*** *p137*
Gion, Marian 13; America, 1847 ***778.6*** *p137*
Gion, Nicolas 17; America, 1847 ***778.6*** *p137*
Giorgano, Luka; Louisiana, 1874 ***4981.45*** *p132*
Giorgi, Olga; Illinois, 1930 ***121.35*** *p101*
Giot, Adele 26; America, 1847 ***778.6*** *p137*
Giot, Hippolite 17; America, 1847 ***778.6*** *p137*
Gipson, William 52; Ontario, 1871 ***1823.21*** *p131*
Giradot, Alexis; Ohio, 1809-1852 ***4511.35*** *p17*
Giradot, Anthony; Ohio, 1809-1852 ***4511.35*** *p17*
Giragi, Phil.; Louisiana, 1874 ***4981.45*** *p295*
Giral, Miss; New Orleans, 1845 ***778.6*** *p137*
Giral, Antoin 20; New Orleans, 1845 ***778.6*** *p137*
Girard, Miss 17; New Orleans, 1841 ***778.6*** *p138*
Girard, Mr. 31; America, 1846 ***778.6*** *p137*
Girard, Anne; Quebec, 1665 ***4514.3*** *p318*
Girard, Antoine 2; America, 1848 ***778.6*** *p138*
Girard, Antoine 35; America, 1848 ***778.6*** *p137*
Girard, Apoline 28; New Orleans, 1845 ***778.6*** *p138*
Girard, Catherine 5; America, 1848 ***778.6*** *p138*
Girard, Catherine 39; America, 1848 ***778.6*** *p138*
Girard, Elizabeth; Quebec, 1889 ***9228.50*** *p359*
Girard, Etienne 34; América, 1841 ***778.6*** *p138*
Girard, Francis 48; St. Louis, 1843 ***778.6*** *p138*
Girard, Henrietta Eliz.; Maryland, 1879-1966 ***9228.50*** *p289*
Girard, Isabelle 22; Quebec, 1662 ***9221.17*** *p486*
Girard, Joachim 20; Quebec, 1659 ***9221.17*** *p402*
Girard, Joseph 8; America, 1848 ***778.6*** *p138*
Girard, Joseph 38; America, 1840 ***778.6*** *p138*
Girard, Margarite 36; America, 1848 ***778.6*** *p138*
Girard, Marguerite; Quebec, 1673 ***4514.3*** *p318*
Girard, Marianne 23; New Orleans, 1845 ***778.6*** *p138*
Girard, Marie; Quebec, 1667 ***4514.3*** *p318*
Girard, Marie 18; Quebec, 1652 ***9221.17*** *p259*
Girard, Marie 35; Quebec, 1651 ***9221.17*** *p244*
Girard, Me. 43; New Orleans, 1841 ***778.6*** *p138*
Girard, Michel 25; New Orleans, 1845 ***778.6*** *p138*
Girard, Olivier; Quebec, 1648 ***9221.17*** *p199*
Girard, Phil. Chs. 17; New Orleans, 1844 ***778.6*** *p138*
Girard, Pierre; Quebec, 1642 ***9221.17*** *p117*
Girard, Pierre 18; Quebec, 1661 ***9221.17*** *p458*
Girard, Rosalie 6 months; New Orleans, 1845 ***778.6*** *p138*
Girard, Syvret; Toronto, 1970-1979 ***9228.50*** *p248*
Girard DuFoy, Francois 28; Quebec, 1658 ***9221.17*** *p381*
Girardeau, Noel; Quebec, 1641 ***9221.17*** *p104*
Girard Family ; Sacramento, CA, n.d. ***9228.50*** *p248*
Girardin, Jean-Baptiste 28; New Orleans, 1843 ***778.6*** *p138*
Girardy, Deriole 1; America, 1840 ***778.6*** *p138*
Girardy, Francoise 28; America, 1840 ***778.6*** *p138*
Girardy, Nicolas 30; America, 1840 ***778.6*** *p138*
Girart, George 24; Louisiana, 1848 ***778.6*** *p138*
Giraud, Anne; Quebec, 1669 ***4514.3*** *p318*
Giraud, Auguste 31; America, 1844 ***778.6*** *p138*
Giraud, Certes 27; Port uncertain, 1848 ***778.6*** *p138*
Giraud, Isabelle 22; Quebec, 1662 ***9221.17*** *p486*
Giraud, Jean 18; New York, NY, 1894 ***6512.1*** *p182*
Giraud, Mathurin; Quebec, 1658 ***9221.17*** *p381*
Giraud, Robin 25; Port uncertain, 1841 ***778.6*** *p138*
Giraudon, James 32; America, 1846 ***778.6*** *p138*
Girault, Jean; Quebec, 1662 ***9221.17*** *p486*
Girdler, Richard; Marblehead, MA, n.d. ***9228.50*** *p577*
Girdlestone, Christana 42; Ontario, 1871 ***1823.21*** *p131*
Girinouithon, J. 54; America, 1843 ***778.6*** *p138*
Girod, Miss 36; New Orleans, 1845 ***778.6*** *p138*
Giron, Francois 18; Quebec, 1657 ***9221.17*** *p359*
Girosset, Laurent 28; Port uncertain, 1840 ***778.6*** *p138*
Girot, Mr. 38; America, 1841 ***778.6*** *p138*
Giroust, Rene; Quebec, 1654 ***9221.17*** *p309*
Giroust, Thomas; Quebec, 1635 ***9221.17*** *p46*
With wife
Giroux, C. 21; America, 1840 ***778.6*** *p138*
Giroux, Toussaint 20; Quebec, 1653 ***9221.17*** *p274*
Girt, Jane; Ontario, 1871 ***1823.17*** *p58*
Gisecke, Florentine Wilhelmine *SEE* Gisecke, Johann Christoph
Gisecke, Friedr. Aug. Christoph *SEE* Gisecke, Johann Christoph
Gisecke, Joh. Henr. Wilhelm *SEE* Gisecke, Johann Christoph
Gisecke, Johann Christoph; America, 1847 ***7420.1*** *p53*
*Wife:*Wilhelmine Charlotte Bense
*Son:*Friedr. Aug. Christoph
*Daughter:*Florentine Wilhelmine
*Son:*Joh. Henr. Wilhelm
Gisecke, Wilhelmine Charlotte Bense *SEE* Gisecke, Johann Christoph
Giseke, Christine Wilhelmine; America, 1852 ***7420.1*** *p101*
Giseke, Engel Marie Sophie Wilhelmine; America, 1845 ***7420.1*** *p36*
*Sister:*Sophie Wilhelmine Louise
Giseke, Friedrich; America, 1847 ***7420.1*** *p53*
Giseke, Sophie Wilhelmine Louise *SEE* Giseke, Engel Marie Sophie Wilhelmine
Giseke, Wilhelmine Dorothee Louise; America, 1845 ***7420.1*** *p41*
Gisenhard, Charles 25; New Orleans, 1848 ***778.6*** *p138*
Gissel, Rasmus; Iowa, 1895 ***1211.15*** *p11*
Gisselmann, Wilhelmine; America, 1857 ***7420.1*** *p161*
Gissot, Ren Pier.e 43; Port uncertain, 1841 ***778.6*** *p138*
Gitton, Jean; Quebec, 1658 ***9221.17*** *p381*
Gitzinger, Anna M.; America, 1873 ***5475.1*** *p318*
*Daughter:*Magdalena
*Son:*Peter
Gitzinger, Kath.; America, 1880 ***5475.1*** *p277*
Gitzinger, Magdalena *SEE* Gitzinger, Anna M. Endeldinger
Gitzinger, Mathias; America, 1888 ***5475.1*** *p343*
Gitzinger, Peter; America, 1868 ***5475.1*** *p277*
Gitzinger, Peter *SEE* Gitzinger, Anna M. Endeldinger
Giveaut, Rachel; Ohio, 1806 ***9228.50*** *p246*
Given, Andrew 42; Ontario, 1871 ***1823.21*** *p131*
Given, William 41; Ontario, 1871 ***1823.17*** *p58*
Giza, Antoni; Detroit, 1929-1930 ***6214.5*** *p71*
Gizela, Bertha; Wisconsin, 1893 ***6795.8*** *p57*
Gizella, Andreas; Wisconsin, 1898 ***6795.8*** *p67*
Gizella, Matilda; Wisconsin, 1898 ***6795.8*** *p102*
Gizynski, Wlodzimierz; Detroit, 1890 ***9980.23*** *p96*
Glaback, John; Missouri, 1892 ***3276.1*** *p1*
Glabille, Guillaume; Quebec, 1642 ***9221.17*** *p117*
Glackemeyer, Heinrich August; America, 1866 ***7420.1*** *p242*
With family
Glad, Greta 39; New York, 1856 ***6529.11*** *p22*
*Daughter:*Kajsa 13
Glad, Kajsa 13 *SEE* Glad, Greta
Glade, Engel Marie; America, 1855 ***7420.1*** *p141*
Glade, Engel Sophie; America, 1858 ***7420.1*** *p177*
Glade, Johann Conrad; America, 1852 ***7420.1*** *p88*
*Wife:*Marie Sophie Eleonore
*Son:*Johann Heinrich
With son
*Son:*Johann Heinrich Christoph
Glade, Johann Heinrich *SEE* Glade, Johann Conrad
Glade, Johann Heinrich Christoph *SEE* Glade, Johann Conrad
Glade, Marie Sophie Eleonore *SEE* Glade, Johann Conrad
Gladel, Nikolaus; America, 1871 ***5475.1*** *p159*
Gladieux, John Peter; Ohio, 1809-1852 ***4511.35*** *p17*
Gladieux, Joseph; Ohio, 1809-1852 ***4511.35*** *p17*
Gladieux, Victor; Ohio, 1809-1852 ***4511.35*** *p17*
Gladu, Jean; Quebec, 1656 ***9221.17*** *p337*
Glaeser, Augustus H.; Philadelphia, 1835 ***8513.31*** *p309*
*Wife:*Christine Geisler
Glaeser, Christine Geisler *SEE* Glaeser, Augustus H.
Glakossky, Edouard 30; Louisiana, 1848 ***778.6*** *p138*
Glamm, Carl Friedrich Hermann; Wisconsin, 1885 ***6795.8*** *p90*
Glan, Austin; North Carolina, 1856 ***1088.45*** *p11*
Glanz, Mina 36; Ontario, 1871 ***1823.21*** *p131*
Glardere, Delphine 8; America, 1845 ***778.6*** *p139*
Glardere, Louise 10; America, 1845 ***778.6*** *p139*
Glardere, Pierre 47; America, 1845 ***778.6*** *p139*
Glardere, Susan 18; America, 1845 ***778.6*** *p139*
Glas, Catherine; Quebec, 1671 ***4514.3*** *p306*
Glas, Elisabeth 18; New York, NY, 1898 ***7951.13*** *p43*
Glaser, Anna; America, 1868 ***7919.3*** *p532*
Glaser, Marg. Klahsen *SEE* Glaser, Peter
Glaser, Mathias *SEE* Glaser, Peter
Glaser, Mathias; Ohio, 1809-1852 ***4511.35*** *p17*
Glaser, Nicolas 17; Port uncertain, 1840 ***778.6*** *p139*
Glaser, Nikolaus; America, 1871 ***5475.1*** *p247*
Glaser, Peter; America, 1881 ***5475.1*** *p359*
*Wife:*Marg. Klahsen
*Son:*Mathias
Glasgow, Ezekiel; Maryland, 1713 ***9228.50*** *p249*
Glasgow, James; North America, 1770 ***9228.50*** *p249*
*Wife:*Mary
With children
Glasgow, Mary *SEE* Glasgow, James
Glaske, Auguste Julia; Wisconsin, 1893 ***6795.8*** *p134*
Glaske, Emil; Wisconsin, 1906 ***6795.8*** *p236*
Glaske, Hermann; Wisconsin, 1898 ***6795.8*** *p213*
Glass, Archibald 49; Ontario, 1871 ***1823.17*** *p58*
Glass, Auguste; Illinois, 1856 ***6079.1*** *p5*
Glass, Georg Anton; America, 1894 ***5475.1*** *p18*
Glass, George 34; Ontario, 1871 ***1823.21*** *p131*
Glass, Graham 41; Ontario, 1871 ***1823.21*** *p131*
Glass, James 32; Ontario, 1871 ***1823.17*** *p58*
Glass, James 35; Ontario, 1871 ***1823.17*** *p58*
Glass, John; Ohio, 1809-1852 ***4511.35*** *p17*
Glass, Matthew 45; Ontario, 1871 ***1823.21*** *p131*
Glass, Samuel 71; Ontario, 1871 ***1823.21*** *p131*
Glasser, Mathias; Ohio, 1809-1852 ***4511.35*** *p17*
Glasses, T. 41; America, 1846 ***778.6*** *p139*
Glassing, Elisabeth *SEE* Glassing, Karl
Glassing, Georg; America, 1880 ***2526.43*** *p195*
Glassing, Karl; America, 1853 ***2526.43*** *p168*
*Wife:*Elisabeth
Glassing, Karl; America, 1853 ***2526.43*** *p179*
Glassner, George 33; Louisiana, 1848 ***778.6*** *p139*
Glaub, Nikolaus; America, 1843 ***5475.1*** *p294*
Glaubrecht, Friedrich; America, 1867 ***7919.3*** *p531*
With wife & 2 children
Glaughlin, Donald M. 50; Ontario, 1871 ***1823.17*** *p58*
Glaus, Catherine 16; Missouri, 1845 ***778.6*** *p139*
Glaus, Elisabeth 9; Missouri, 1845 ***778.6*** *p139*
Glaus, Frederic 14; Missouri, 1845 ***778.6*** *p139*
Glaus, George 26; Missouri, 1845 ***778.6*** *p139*
Glaus, Jacob 51; Missouri, 1845 ***778.6*** *p139*
Glaus, Madeleine 20; Missouri, 1845 ***778.6*** *p139*
Glaus, Michel 23; Missouri, 1845 ***778.6*** *p139*
Glaus, Rosine 12; Missouri, 1845 ***778.6*** *p139*
Glaus, Rosine 51; Missouri, 1845 ***778.6*** *p139*
Glauser, Ferdinand; Missouri, 1885 ***3276.1*** *p3*
Glavati, Paul 32; New York, NY, 1894 ***6512.1*** *p184*
Glaven, Mary 86; Ontario, 1871 ***1823.21*** *p131*
Glavin, Edward 60; Ontario, 1871 ***1823.21*** *p131*
Glavin, John 62; Ontario, 1871 ***1823.21*** *p131*
Glavin, Michael 32; Ontario, 1871 ***1823.21*** *p131*
Glaydon, Michael; New Orleans, 1851 ***7242.30*** *p142*
Gleason, Cornelious 77; Ontario, 1871 ***1823.21*** *p131*
Gleason, David; Louisiana, 1874 ***4981.45*** *p132*
Gleason, Matthew; North Carolina, 1805 ***1088.45*** *p11*
Gleason, Richard 55; Ontario, 1871 ***1823.21*** *p131*
Gleason, Thomas 35; Ontario, 1871 ***1823.21*** *p131*
Gleason, William 60; Ontario, 1871 ***1823.21*** *p131*
Gleeb, Joseph; Venezuela, 1843 ***3899.5*** *p541*
Gleed, James 17; Quebec, 1870 ***8364.32*** *p23*
Gleeson, Catherine 55; Ontario, 1871 ***1823.17*** *p58*

Gleeson, Edward 51; Ontario, 1871 ***1823.21*** *p131*
Gleeson, Eliza 49; Ontario, 1871 ***1823.21*** *p131*
Gleeson, Ellen 48; Ontario, 1871 ***1823.21*** *p131*
Gleeson, James 48; Ontario, 1871 ***1823.21*** *p131*
Gleeson, James 48; Ontario, 1871 ***1823.21*** *p131*
Gleeson, John 89; Ontario, 1871 ***1823.17*** *p58*
Gleeson, Martin 30; Ontario, 1871 ***1823.17*** *p58*
Gleeson, Martin; Washington, 1879 ***2770.40*** *p134*
Gleeson, Mary 60; Ontario, 1871 ***1823.21*** *p131*
Gleeson, Michael 60; Ontario, 1871 ***1823.21*** *p131*
Gleeson, Patrick 29; Ontario, 1871 ***1823.17*** *p58*
Gleeson, Patrick 40; Ontario, 1871 ***1823.21*** *p131*
Gleeson, Timothy 57; Ontario, 1871 ***1823.17*** *p58*
Gleich, Christian; America, 1856-1882 ***179.55*** *p19*
Gleich, Christian; America, 1880 ***179.55*** *p19*
Gleich, Eva M.; America, 1880 ***179.55*** *p19*
Gleich, Tobias; America, 1700-1899 ***179.55*** *p19*
Gleichmann, Ludwig; America, 1882 ***5475.1*** *p16*
Gleichmann, Sophie 22; America, 1882 ***5475.1*** *p16*
Gleim, August Ludwig Otto; America, 1866 ***7420.1*** *p242*
Gleissner, Auguste 24; Valdivia, Chile, 1852 ***1192.4*** *p53*
Gleissner, Caroline; America, 1868 ***7919.3*** *p526*
With 2 children
Gleissner, Moritz; Valdivia, Chile, 1852 ***1192.4*** *p53*
Glemaker, Swan Pearson; Minneapolis, 1891-1894 ***1865.50*** *p48*
Glemier, Alexandre; New York, NY, 1872 ***1494.20*** *p11*
Glen, Eleanor 52; Ontario, 1871 ***1823.21*** *p132*
Glen, George; Boston, 1737 ***1642*** *p26*
Glen, James 42; Ontario, 1871 ***1823.21*** *p132*
Glen, James 54; Ontario, 1871 ***1823.21*** *p132*
Glendenen, Adam 26; Ontario, 1871 ***1823.21*** *p132*
Glendenen, Thomas 74; Ontario, 1871 ***1823.21*** *p132*
Glendennen, John 35; Ontario, 1871 ***1823.21*** *p132*
Glendenning, Alexr 63; Ontario, 1871 ***1823.21*** *p132*
Glendenning, William 81; Ontario, 1871 ***1823.21*** *p132*
Glendinning, John 68; Ontario, 1871 ***1823.21*** *p132*
Glenister, Henry 18; Quebec, 1870 ***8364.32*** *p23*
Glenn, John; Philadelphia, 1778 ***8529.30*** *p3A*
Glenn, Mary 60; Ontario, 1871 ***1823.21*** *p132*
Glenn, Michael 39; Ontario, 1871 ***1823.21*** *p132*
Glenn, Walter 46; Ontario, 1871 ***1823.21*** *p132*
Glenn, William 27; Ontario, 1871 ***1823.21*** *p132*
Glenn, William 65; Ontario, 1871 ***1823.21*** *p132*
Glennon, Matilda 40; Ontario, 1871 ***1823.21*** *p132*
Glenz, Adolf; America, 1887 ***2526.43*** *p147*
Glenz, Albrecht; America, 1880 ***2526.43*** *p168*
Glenz, August; Wisconsin, 1873 ***6795.8*** *p125*
Glenz, Christian; Chicago, 1896 ***2526.43*** *p168*
Glenz, Friedrich; America, 1856 ***2526.43*** *p168*
Glenz, Georg; America, 1885 ***2526.43*** *p147*
Glenz, Georg Albrecht; America, 1877 ***2526.43*** *p168*
Glenz, Georg Friedrich Karl; America, 1877 ***2526.43*** *p168*
Glenz, Georg Karl Tobias; America, 1882 ***2526.43*** *p168*
Glenz, Johann Gottlieb; Wisconsin, 1859 ***6795.8*** *p24*
Glew, Thomas; Ohio, 1854 ***3580.20*** *p32*
Glew, Thomas; Ohio, 1854 ***6020.12*** *p7*
Gley, John Theo. Fred.; Wisconsin, 1892 ***6795.8*** *p155*
Gley, Nicolas 27; New Orleans, 1848 ***778.6*** *p139*
Glick, Jack; Detroit, 1929 ***1640.55*** *p113*
Glick, Ludwick; Ohio, 1809-1852 ***4511.35*** *p17*
Gliedner, M. 45; America, 1874 ***5475.1*** *p256*
Glime, Alexandre; New York, NY, 1872 ***1494.20*** *p11*
Glinn, John; Philadelphia, 1778 ***8529.30*** *p3A*
Glissner, Robert; New York, 1859 ***358.56*** *p102*
Glody, Thomas; Boston, 1753 ***1642*** *p31*
Gloff, Emilie; Wisconsin, 1898 ***6795.8*** *p201*
Glog, Henri 37; America, 1846 ***778.6*** *p139*
Gloner, Michael; Colorado, 1880 ***1029.59*** *p31*
Glonier, Mrs. 25; America, 1844 ***778.6*** *p139*
Glorel, Leonne-Louise; Pennsylvania, 1921 ***9228.50*** *p432*
Gloria, Jean 19; Quebec, 1649 ***9221.17*** *p213*
Gloria, Pierre; Quebec, 1657 ***9221.17*** *p359*
Glory, Laurent 19; Montreal, 1658 ***9221.17*** *p389*
Glos, Michael; Chile, 1852 ***1192.4*** *p52*
Glose, Adolph; Massachusetts, 1854 ***8513.31*** *p309*
*Wife:*Elise Koch
Glose, Elise Koch *SEE* Glose, Adolph
Gloss, Christopher; Ohio, 1809-1852 ***4511.35*** *p17*
Gloss, Jacob; Ohio, 1809-1852 ***4511.35*** *p17*
Glosser, Gottleib; Ohio, 1809-1852 ***4511.35*** *p18*
Glotius, Danais; Washington, 1882 ***2770.40*** *p135*
Glott, Arthur 5; New Orleans, 1848 ***778.6*** *p139*
Glott, Catherine 40; New Orleans, 1848 ***778.6*** *p139*
Glott, Marie 7; New Orleans, 1848 ***778.6*** *p139*
Glour, A. 27; New Orleans, 1841 ***778.6*** *p139*
Glouser, Gottfried; Iowa, 1905 ***1211.15*** *p10*
Glover, Goody; Boston, 1688 ***1642*** *p16*
Glover, Eliz.; Maryland, 1674-1675 ***1236.25*** *p51*
Glover, James 38; Ontario, 1871 ***1823.21*** *p132*
Glover, Michael; Colorado, 1885 ***1029.59*** *p31*
Glover, Richard; New York, 1782 ***8529.30*** *p11*
Glover, Thomas; Ohio, 1840 ***2763.1*** *p9*
Glover, William 32; Ontario, 1871 ***1823.21*** *p132*
Glover, William 52; Ontario, 1871 ***1823.21*** *p132*
Glover, William 89; Ontario, 1871 ***1823.21*** *p132*
Gluck, August 27; New York, NY, 1893 ***1883.7*** *p37*
Gluck, Nicholas; Ohio, 1809-1852 ***4511.35*** *p18*
Gluck, Ottilie 18; New York, NY, 1893 ***1883.7*** *p37*
Glückselig, Joseph; Illinois, 1834-1900 ***6020.5*** *p131*
Glueck, Elisabeth 1; Pennsylvania, 1851 ***170.15*** *p26*
With family
Glueck, Elisabeth 13; Pennsylvania, 1851 ***170.15*** *p26*
With family
Glueck, Johann Eeorg 10; Pennsylvania, 1851 ***170.15*** *p26*
With family
Glueck, Johann Georg 10; Pennsylvania, 1851 ***170.15*** *p26*
With family
Glueck, Katharina 30; Pennsylvania, 1851 ***170.15*** *p26*
With family
Glueck, Nicholas; Ohio, 1809-1852 ***4511.35*** *p18*
Glueck, Nikolaus 46; Pennsylvania, 1851 ***170.15*** *p26*
With family
Glueck, Peter; Ohio, 1809-1852 ***4511.35*** *p18*
Glueek, Peter; Ohio, 1809-1852 ***4511.35*** *p18*
Gluntz, Anne Josephine 4; New Orleans, 1848 ***778.6*** *p139*
Gluntz, Jeanne Marie 38; New Orleans, 1848 ***778.6*** *p139*
Glusner, Daniel; Illinois, 1852 ***6079.1*** *p5*
Gluyas, John; North Carolina, 1838 ***1088.45*** *p11*
Glynn, Edward; Iowa, 1892 ***1211.15*** *p10*
Glynn, George; Iowa, 1892 ***1211.15*** *p10*
Glynn, Llewelyn; Iowa, 1895 ***1211.15*** *p10*
Glynn, Mic; St. John, N.B., 1848 ***2978.15*** *p38*
Glynn, Richard 28; Ontario, 1871 ***1823.17*** *p58*
Glynn, William 26; Ontario, 1871 ***1823.17*** *p58*
Gmunder, Frederic; Illinois, 1852 ***6079.1*** *p5*
Gnam, Theodore 45; Ontario, 1871 ***1823.17*** *p58*
Gnigel, Heinrich 33; Galveston, TX, 1855 ***571.7*** *p16*
Gnigel, Sophia 28; Galveston, TX, 1855 ***571.7*** *p16*
Goadbroth, Ludvick; New York, 1778 ***8529.30*** *p3A*
Goard, Mathurine; Quebec, 1666 ***4514.3*** *p318*
Goaticke, August; Iowa, 1884 ***1211.15*** *p10*
Gobbe, P.; Quebec, 1635 ***9221.17*** *p46*
Gobe, Sophie Dorothea Justine; America, 1861 ***7420.1*** *p205*
Gobel, George; Illinois, 1852 ***6079.1*** *p5*
Gobel, Johannes; America, 1854 ***7420.1*** *p119*
Gobel, Louis; America, 1868 ***7919.3*** *p526*
With 3 children
Gobel, Maria Sara; America, 1834 ***5475.1*** *p457*
Gobeli, Jacob; North Carolina, 1710 ***3629.40*** *p4*
Gobeli, Samuel Jacob; North Carolina, 1710 ***3629.40*** *p4*
Gobert, Marie-Madeleine; Quebec, 1670 ***4514.3*** *p318*
Gobineau, Marie 26; Quebec, 1662 ***9221.17*** *p486*
Gobinet, Elisabeth 17; Montreal, 1658 ***9221.17*** *p389*
Goble, Elen 35; Ontario, 1871 ***1823.21*** *p132*
Goble, Gideon 46; Ontario, 1871 ***1823.21*** *p132*
Goble, Thomas 25; Ontario, 1871 ***1823.21*** *p132*
Goblet, P.; Quebec, 1635 ***9221.17*** *p46*
Gobley, Jacob; North Carolina, 1710 ***3629.40*** *p4*
Gobley, Samuel Jacob; North Carolina, 1710 ***3629.40*** *p4*
Gobtel, . . .; Maine, n.d. ***9228.50*** *p268*
Gobtel, . . .; New Brunswick, n.d. ***9228.50*** *p268*
Goche, Isaac 35; Ohio, 1880 ***4879.40*** *p259*
Gockel, Wilhelm; America, 1854 ***2526.42*** *p199*
Godard, Godard 25; New Orleans, 1848 ***778.6*** *p139*
Godard, Marie 14; Quebec, 1654 ***9221.17*** *p309*
Godart, Jeanne 20; Montreal, 1658 ***9221.17*** *p389*
Godbold, James 47; Ontario, 1871 ***1823.21*** *p132*
Godbold, John 69; Ontario, 1871 ***1823.21*** *p132*
Godchaux, Adolphe 21; Port uncertain, 1842 ***778.6*** *p139*
Godchaux, Lazare 17; America, 1843 ***778.6*** *p139*
Goddard, Charles; North Carolina, 1853 ***1088.45*** *p11*
Goddard, Edward; Maryland, 1674-1675 ***1236.25*** *p52*
Goddard, Elias; Maryland, 1672 ***1236.25*** *p47*
Goddard, Elizabeth; America, 1757 ***1220.12*** *p624*
Godden, Dorcas Jessup Thoumine *SEE* Godden, George Henry
Godden, George Augustus *SEE* Godden, George Henry
Godden, George Henry; New York, NY, 1907 ***9228.50*** *p249*
*Wife:*Dorcas Jessup Thoumine
*Child:*William Alfred
*Child:*George Augustus
Godden, William Alfred *SEE* Godden, George Henry
Goddery, Charles; Illinois, 1834-1900 ***6020.5*** *p131*
Gode, Francois 20 *SEE* Gode, Nicolas
Gode, Francoise 5 *SEE* Gode, Nicolas
Gode, Francoise Gadois 50 *SEE* Gode, Nicolas
Gode, Mathurine 2 *SEE* Gode, Nicolas
Gode, Nicolas 12 *SEE* Gode, Nicolas
Gode, Nicolas 52; Montreal, 1641 ***9221.17*** *p107*
*Wife:*Francoise Gadois 50
*Son:*Francois 20
*Son:*Nicolas 12
*Daughter:*Francoise 5
*Daughter:*Mathurine 2
Godeau, Marie 15; Quebec, 1658 ***9221.17*** *p381*
Godebout, Nicolas 19; Quebec, 1654 ***9221.17*** *p309*
Godebout, Robert; Montreal, 1654 ***9221.17*** *p317*
Godeby, Anne; Quebec, 1669 ***4514.3*** *p318*
Godechot, Fanchory 13; America, 1846 ***778.6*** *p139*
Godechot, Florette 22; America, 1846 ***778.6*** *p139*
Godechot, Minette 56; America, 1846 ***778.6*** *p139*
Godechot, Pauline 8; America, 1846 ***778.6*** *p140*
Godefroid, Pierre 16; America, 1847 ***778.6*** *p140*
Godefroy, Jean-Paul; Quebec, 1629 ***9221.17*** *p55*
Godefroy, Jean-Paul; Quebec, 1646 ***2314.30*** *p171*
Godefroy, Nicolas; Quebec, 1651 ***9221.17*** *p243*
Godefroy deLinctot, Jean; Quebec, 1626 ***2314.30*** *p167*
Godefroy deLinctot, Jean; Quebec, 1668 ***2314.30*** *p184*
Godefroy DeLintot, Jean; Quebec, 1626 ***9221.17*** *p18*
Godefroy DeNormanville, Thomas; Quebec, 1626 ***9221.17*** *p18*
Godek, Andrzej 48; New York, NY, 1911 ***6533.11*** *p10*
Godek, Stefania 17; New York, NY, 1911 ***6533.11*** *p10*
Godel, Barbara 38; America, 1843 ***778.6*** *p140*
Godel, Etienne 1; America, 1843 ***778.6*** *p140*
Godel, Georges 10; America, 1843 ***778.6*** *p140*
Godel, Jean 4; America, 1843 ***778.6*** *p140*
Godel, Jean 14; America, 1843 ***778.6*** *p140*
Godel, Magdalena 12; America, 1843 ***778.6*** *p140*
Godel, Nicolas 6; America, 1843 ***778.6*** *p140*
Godel, Nicolas 36; America, 1843 ***778.6*** *p140*
Godequin, Jeanne; Quebec, 1669 ***4514.3*** *p319*
Godet, Rolland; Quebec, 1651 ***9221.17*** *p243*
Godeur, Vivienne 24; Quebec, 1644 ***9221.17*** *p141*
Godeur, Vivienne 24; Quebec, 1644 ***9221.17*** *p141*
Godfrey, Annie 7; Quebec, 1870 ***8364.32*** *p23*
Godfrey, Eliza.; Maryland, 1672 ***1236.25*** *p47*
Godfrey, Elizabeth; Nova Scotia, 1776 ***9228.50*** *p602*
Godfrey, George 61; Ontario, 1871 ***1823.21*** *p132*
Godfrey, Michael; Massachusetts, 1832 ***3274.55*** *p42*
Godfrey, P. D.; Louisiana, 1874 ***4981.45*** *p132*
Godfrind, Alphonse Dieudonne *SEE* Godfrind, Constant
Godfrind, Clementine Dounnai *SEE* Godfrind, Constant
Godfrind, Constant; Wisconsin, 1856 ***1495.20*** *p28*
*Wife:*Clementine Dounnai
*Child:*Alphonse Dieudonne
*Child:*Theodule
*Child:*Francois
Godfrind, Francois *SEE* Godfrind, Constant
Godfrind, Theodule *SEE* Godfrind, Constant
Godfroy, Mr. 36; Port uncertain, 1840 ***778.6*** *p140*
Godfroy, Mr. 39; Port uncertain, 1840 ***778.6*** *p140*
Godillon, Elisabeth; Quebec, 1670 ***4514.3*** *p319*
Godin, Mr. 30; Louisiana, 1848 ***778.6*** *p140*
Godin, Mrs. 30; America, 1846 ***778.6*** *p140*
Godin, Chs. 8; America, 1846 ***778.6*** *p140*
Godin, Jeanne; Quebec, 1661 ***9221.17*** *p458*
Godin, Joseph 6; America, 1846 ***778.6*** *p140*
Godin, Noel; Quebec, 1650 ***9221.17*** *p226*
Godin, Perrine 20; Quebec, 1637 ***9221.17*** *p70*
Godington, Aaron 65; Ontario, 1871 ***1823.21*** *p132*
Godion, Louis; Quebec, 1659 ***9221.17*** *p413*
Godkin, Thomas 72; Ontario, 1871 ***1823.21*** *p132*
Godna, Fannie; Detroit, 1930 ***1640.60*** *p77*
Godolphe, Anne 33; Missouri, 1847 ***778.6*** *p140*
Godolphe, Georg 20; Missouri, 1847 ***778.6*** *p140*
Godolphe, Margareth 25; Missouri, 1847 ***778.6*** *p140*
Godolphe, Mathias 27; Missouri, 1847 ***778.6*** *p140*
Godolphe, Nicolas 31; Missouri, 1847 ***778.6*** *p140*
Godsave, Thomas 44; Ontario, 1871 ***1823.21*** *p132*
Godwal, Catharine; Virginia, 1700 ***9230.15*** *p81*
Godwalt, Bernard; Ohio, 1809-1852 ***4511.35*** *p18*
Godwin, Sydney 29; Ontario, 1871 ***1823.21*** *p132*
Goe, Peter; Maine, 1653 ***9228.50*** *p244*
Goebel, Edward 7; Portland, ME, 1906 ***970.38*** *p77*
Goebel, Elizabeth 14; Portland, ME, 1906 ***970.38*** *p77*
Goebel, Heinrich 18; Portland, ME, 1906 ***970.38*** *p77*
Goebel, Jakob; America, 1840 ***5475.1*** *p458*
Goebel, Josephine 42; Portland, ME, 1906 ***970.38*** *p77*
Goechter, Francis J.; Ohio, 1809-1852 ***4511.35*** *p14*
Goedick, Ernest; Iowa, 1888 ***1211.15*** *p11*
Goedicke, Henry; Iowa, 1890 ***1211.15*** *p11*
Goehl, Helena; America, 1880 ***5475.1*** *p194*
Goehrke, August; Wisconsin, 1878 ***6795.8*** *p201*
Goeken, E.; Louisiana, 1836-1841 ***4981.45*** *p208*
Goeken, John B.; Louisiana, 1836-1841 ***4981.45*** *p208*
Goelte, Jacob; Louisiana, 1841-1844 ***4981.45*** *p210*
Goentzel, D.; Galveston, TX, 1855 ***571.7*** *p18*
Goergen, A. Maria 71; America, 1876 ***5475.1*** *p175*
Goergen, Josef; America, 1843 ***5475.1*** *p416*
With wife & son

Goergens, Kasper; America, 1863 ***5475.1*** *p289*
Goerick, Gottlob; New York, 1859 ***358.56*** *p55*
Goerz, Andreas; North Dakota, 1895 ***554.30*** *p26*
*Wife:*Emilie
Goerz, Emilie *SEE* Goerz, Andreas
Goetsch, Frederick; New York, 1859 ***358.56*** *p54*
Goetschberger, Andrew; New York, 1860 ***358.56*** *p3*
Goette, Fred; Colorado, 1904 ***1029.59*** *p31*
Goettert, Angela *SEE* Goettert, Johann
Goettert, Anna *SEE* Goettert, Johann
Goettert, Barbara; America, 1855 ***5475.1*** *p343*
*Son:*Mathias
*Son:*Peter
*Son:*Johann
*Daughter:*Magdalena
Goettert, Johann; Brazil, 1874 ***5475.1*** *p371*
*Wife:*Maria Kuhn
*Daughter:*Maria
*Son:*Karl
*Daughter:*Angela
*Daughter:*Anna
*Son:*Nikolaus
Goettert, Karl *SEE* Goettert, Johann
Goettert, Maria *SEE* Goettert, Johann
Goettert, Maria Kuhn *SEE* Goettert, Johann
Goettert, Nikolaus *SEE* Goettert, Johann
Goettgen, Jakob 17; America, 1857 ***5475.1*** *p496*
Goettmann, Johannes; Virginia, 1831 ***152.20*** *p64*
Goetz, Anna Barbara; Virginia, 1831 ***152.20*** *p62*
Goetz, Appolonia; Virginia, 1831 ***152.20*** *p67*
Goetz, Edward; Louisiana, 1874-1875 ***4981.45*** *p298*
Goetz, Heinrich Georg Friedrich; America, 1881 ***7420.1*** *p320*
*Son:*Heinrich Hermann Ferdinand
Goetz, Heinrich Hermann Ferdinand *SEE* Goetz, Heinrich Georg Friedrich
Goetz, Ida; Colorado, 1903 ***1029.59*** *p32*
Goetz, John Julius; Wisconsin, 1874 ***6795.8*** *p24*
Goetze, Heinrich Georg Friedrich; America, 1881 ***7420.1*** *p320*
*Son:*Heinrich Hermann Ferdinand
Goetze, Heinrich Hermann Ferdinand *SEE* Goetze, Heinrich Georg Friedrich
Goetze, Ida; Colorado, 1903 ***1029.59*** *p32*
Goetzschka, J.; New York, 1860 ***358.56*** *p148*
Goff, David 69; Ontario, 1871 ***1823.21*** *p132*
Goff, Eilzabeth 27; Michigan, 1880 ***4491.33*** *p10*
Goff, John 33; Ontario, 1871 ***1823.21*** *p132*
Goff, John; Tennessee, 1886-1892 ***3665.20*** *p111*
Goff, Pat 24; St. Johns, N.F., 1811 ***1053.20*** *p21*
Goffe, Edward; Maryland, 1671-1672 ***1236.25*** *p45*
Goffga, Maria 23; New York, NY, 1882 ***5475.1*** *p15*
Goffinet, Euphrasie; Wisconsin, 1855 ***1495.20*** *p45*
Gogarty, Thomas; North Carolina, 1853 ***1088.45*** *p11*
Goggel, Anna Maria; Venezuela, 1843 ***3899.5*** *p545*
Goggin, David; St. John, N.B., 1847 ***2978.15*** *p36*
Gohen, K. A. E.; Colorado, 1903 ***1029.59*** *p32*
Gohey, Aglaie 29; New Orleans, 1848 ***778.6*** *p140*
Gohey, Aime 10; New Orleans, 1848 ***778.6*** *p140*
Gohey, Alexis 28; New Orleans, 1848 ***778.6*** *p140*
Gohey, Eugenie 15; New Orleans, 1848 ***778.6*** *p140*
Gohir, Julie; Wisconsin, 1855 ***1495.20*** *p8*
Gohl, Jacob; Ohio, 1809-1852 ***4511.35*** *p18*
Gohner, Christof 7; Halifax, N.S., 1902 ***1860.4*** *p43*
Gohner, Emannel; Halifax, N.S., 1902 ***1860.4*** *p43*
Gohner, Friedrich 3; Halifax, N.S., 1902 ***1860.4*** *p43*
Gohner, Jacob 10; Halifax, N.S., 1902 ***1860.4*** *p43*
Gohner, Jacob 34; Halifax, N.S., 1902 ***1860.4*** *p43*
Gohner, Johann 11; Halifax, N.S., 1902 ***1860.4*** *p43*
Gohner, Maria 4; Halifax, N.S., 1902 ***1860.4*** *p43*
Gohner, Rosina 37; Halifax, N.S., 1902 ***1860.4*** *p43*
Gohre, Gustav Reinhard; America, 1867 ***7919.3*** *p532*
Gohring, Georg Gottfried; America, 1867 ***7919.3*** *p532*
Gohring, Jacob Heinrich; America, 1868 ***7919.3*** *p526*
Gohring, Martin 78; America, 1841 ***778.6*** *p140*
Gohrke, Anna Louise; Wisconsin, 1892 ***6795.8*** *p120*
Goidin, Jacques 30; Quebec, 1661 ***9221.17*** *p458*
Goidin, Jean 30; Quebec, 1661 ***9221.17*** *p458*
Goik, Antom; Wisconsin, 1885 ***6795.8*** *p57*
Going, Conrad; Port uncertain, 1841 ***7420.1*** *p22*
Going, Harriett 41; Ontario, 1871 ***1823.21*** *p132*
Going, Henry 53; Ontario, 1871 ***1823.21*** *p132*
Goiset, Anne; Quebec, 1669 ***4514.3*** *p319*
Goka, Benjamin 30; Ohio, 1880 ***4879.40*** *p257*
Goka, Francis 25; Ohio, 1880 ***4879.40*** *p257*
Goksch, Hulda 23; New York, NY, 1885 ***1883.7*** *p45*
Gola, Helena 19; New York, NY, 1911 ***6533.11*** *p10*
Golakorona, Miss 26; New York, NY, 1894 ***6512.1*** *p232*
Goland, Emma Ida; Wisconsin, 1897 ***6795.8*** *p94*
Goland, George; Ohio, 1843 ***2763.1*** *p9*
Goland, George; Ohio, 1844 ***2763.1*** *p9*
Goland, Thomas; Ohio, 1842 ***2763.1*** *p9*
Gold, Abrahm *SEE* Gold, Louis
Gold, Beatrice *SEE* Gold, Louis
Gold, Fannie *SEE* Gold, Louis
Gold, Louis; Denver, CO, 1914 ***1029.59*** *p32*
*Wife:*Fannie
*Child:*Abrahm
*Child:*Beatrice
*Child:*Meldon
*Child:*Robt
Gold, Louis; Montreal, 1906 ***1029.59*** *p1A*
Gold, Mary; Boston, 1734-1766 ***9228.50*** *p325*
Gold, Meldon *SEE* Gold, Louis
Gold, Michael; Long Island, 1781 ***8529.30*** *p9A*
Gold, Robt *SEE* Gold, Louis
Goldade, Sebastian 18; New York, NY, 1898 ***7951.13*** *p43*
Goldberg, Christiane; Valdivia, Chile, 1850 ***1192.4*** *p49*
With daughter 5
Goldberg, Johanna Jul. 28; Valdivia, Chile, 1852 ***1192.4*** *p54*
With 2 children
With child 7
With child 3 months
Goldberg, Leah; Detroit, 1930 ***1640.60*** *p77*
Goldberg, T. E.; Valdivia, Chile, 1852 ***1192.4*** *p54*
Goldberg, Trudel Baer 35; New York, NY, 1894 ***6512.1*** *p230*
Goldblat, Isaac 29; New York, NY, 1894 ***6512.1*** *p229*
Goldbrand, Emil; Cleveland, OH, 1903-1906 ***9722.10*** *p119*
Golde, Jacob Samuel; New Jersey, 1771-1774 ***927.31*** *p3*
Golde, Niclaus Samuel; New Jersey, 1771-1774 ***927.31*** *p3*
Goldenberg, Solomon 36; New York, NY, 1894 ***6512.1*** *p228*
Goldenstein, Henrich Johnson; Iowa, 1900-1901 ***1211.15*** *p10*
Goldflam, Ronia; Detroit, 1929-1930 ***6214.5*** *p63*
Goldie, John 37; Ontario, 1871 ***1823.21*** *p132*
Golding, Edward 46; Ontario, 1871 ***1823.21*** *p132*
Golding, Fredk 46; Ontario, 1871 ***1823.21*** *p132*
Golding, Isabella 18; Ontario, 1871 ***1823.21*** *p132*
Goldmann, Karl; America, 1862 ***2526.43*** *p168*
Goldner, Abraham 26; New York, NY, 1894 ***6512.1*** *p232*
Goldner, Joseph 37; Ontario, 1871 ***1823.21*** *p132*
Goldner, Rebecca 21; New York, NY, 1894 ***6512.1*** *p232*
Goldrick, Edward 56; Ontario, 1871 ***1823.21*** *p133*
Goldschmidt, August C.; Wisconsin, 1907 ***6795.8*** *p179*
Goldschmidt, August Carl; Wisconsin, 1902 ***6795.8*** *p162*
Goldschmidt, Auguste Hulda; Wisconsin, 1893 ***6795.8*** *p162*
Goldschmidt, Emma; America, 1866 ***7420.1*** *p242*
Goldschmidt, Johann Georg; America, 1867 ***7919.3*** *p534*
Goldschmidt, Julie 23; New Orleans, 1848 ***778.6*** *p140*
Goldschmidt, Peter; Chicago, 1890 ***5475.1*** *p325*
Goldschmitt, Peter; Wisconsin, 1855 ***5475.1*** *p323*
Goldsmith, Alfred 23; Ontario, 1871 ***1823.21*** *p133*
Goldsmith, August C.; Wisconsin, 1907 ***6795.8*** *p179*
Goldsmith, Benjamin; North Carolina, 1859 ***1088.45*** *p11*
Goldsmith, George 42; Ontario, 1871 ***1823.21*** *p133*
Goldsmith, Joseph; Ohio, 1809-1852 ***4511.35*** *p18*
Goldsmith, Mordica; Detroit, 1929-1930 ***6214.5*** *p71*
Goldsmith, William; Ohio, 1809-1852 ***4511.35*** *p18*
Goldstein, Charles; Washington, 1886 ***2770.40*** *p195*
Goldstein, Isaac 23; New York, NY, 1894 ***6512.1*** *p186*
Goldstiche, Michael 26; America, 1847 ***778.6*** *p140*
Goldstine, Charles; Philadelphia, 1856 ***8513.31*** *p310*
Goldstone, Joseph; Texas, 1884 ***3435.45*** *p35*
Goldsworthy, Geo.; Colorado, 1873 ***1029.59*** *p32*
Goldsworthy, George; Colorado, 1903 ***1029.59*** *p32*
Goldsworthy, James; Colorado, 1873 ***1029.59*** *p32*
Goldwasser, Meyer 9; New York, NY, 1878 ***9253.2*** *p45*
Goldy, Daniel; New Jersey, 1771-1774 ***927.31*** *p3*
Goldy, John; New Jersey, 1771-1774 ***927.31*** *p3*
Goldy, Samuel, Jr.; New Jersey, 1771-1774 ***927.31*** *p3*
Goldy, Samuel, Sr.; New Jersey, 1771-1774 ***927.31*** *p3*
Golemin, Benjamin 17; New Orleans, 1845 ***778.6*** *p140*
Golemin, Louis 19; New Orleans, 1845 ***778.6*** *p140*
Golemin, Louis 36; New Orleans, 1845 ***778.6*** *p140*
Golen, Jan 26; New York, NY, 1911 ***6533.11*** *p9*
Golett, Henry; Louisiana, 1836-1840 ***4981.45*** *p212*
Golewin, James 29; Ontario, 1871 ***1823.17*** *p59*
Golhaar, Gustav Adolf; Wisconsin, 1896 ***6795.8*** *p47*
Golightly, George C.; Colorado, 1891 ***1029.59*** *p32*
Golightly, George G.; Colorado, 1891 ***1029.59*** *p32*
Golightly, William; Colorado, 1891 ***1029.59*** *p32*
Golightly, Wm.; Illinois, 1862-1920 ***1029.59*** *p32*
Golitzer, Friedrich; America, 1868 ***7919.3*** *p529*
Golke, Christieb; New York, NY, 1893 ***3366.30*** *p70*
Golke, Johann; New York, NY, 1893 ***3366.30*** *p70*
Goll, William 50; Ontario, 1871 ***1823.21*** *p133*
Gollan, Brooke 18; Quebec, 1870 ***8364.32*** *p23*
Gollay, Phoeby 76; Ontario, 1871 ***1823.21*** *p133*
Gollnick, Johan; Wisconsin, 1882 ***6795.8*** *p234*
Gollogly, Owen 33; Ontario, 1871 ***1823.17*** *p59*
Gollop, William 50; Ontario, 1871 ***1823.21*** *p133*
Golnik, Francis; Wisconsin, 1899 ***6795.8*** *p232*
Golsleichter, Jakob 29; America, 1883 ***5475.1*** *p422*
Golsmith, Mr. 26; New Orleans, 1848 ***778.6*** *p141*
Golsmith, Mrs. 49; New Orleans, 1848 ***778.6*** *p141*
Golub, Nathan; Texas, 1910 ***3435.45*** *p35*
Golz, Adalbert 6 *SEE* Golz, Leonhard
Golz, Adam 3 *SEE* Golz, Leonhard
Golz, Anna Christina *SEE* Golz, Konrad
Golz, Anna Margaretha 6 *SEE* Golz, Leonhard
Golz, Anna Margaretha 31 *SEE* Golz, Leonhard
Golz, Christian 16 *SEE* Golz, Konrad
Golz, Eva Dorothea Rapp *SEE* Golz, Konrad
Golz, Georg Wilhelm 60; America, 1872 ***2526.43*** *p217*
*Wife:*Marie Elisabetha Berres 49
*Son:*Kaspar Friedrich 18
*Son:*Wilhelm 13
Golz, Johann Adam; America, 1884 ***2526.43*** *p205*
Golz, Kaspar Friedrich 18 *SEE* Golz, Georg Wilhelm
Golz, Konrad; America, 1854 ***2526.43*** *p217*
*Wife:*Eva Dorothea Rapp
*Son:*Christian
*Daughter:*Anna Christina
*Son:*Leonhard
With mother
*Daughter:*Maria Elisabetha
Golz, Konrad 9 *SEE* Golz, Leonhard
Golz, Leonhard; America, 1884 ***2526.43*** *p195*
Golz, Leonhard 1 *SEE* Golz, Konrad
Golz, Leonhard; New York, 1854 ***2526.43*** *p217*
*Wife:*Anna Margaretha
*Son:*Konrad
*Daughter:*Anna Margaretha
*Son:*Adalbert
*Son:*Adam
Golz, Maria Elisabetha *SEE* Golz, Konrad
Golz, Marie Elisabetha Berres 49 *SEE* Golz, Georg Wilhelm
Golz, Wilhelm 13 *SEE* Golz, Georg Wilhelm
Gomaner, George 6 months; America, 1846 ***778.6*** *p141*
Gomaner, Madeline 6; America, 1846 ***778.6*** *p141*
Gomaner, Nicolas 4; America, 1846 ***778.6*** *p141*
Gomaner, Pierre 60; America, 1846 ***778.6*** *p141*
Gombeaud, Mr. 35; Mexico, 1846 ***778.6*** *p141*
Gombo, P. 38; New Orleans, 1848 ***778.6*** *p141*
Gome, Francis; Ohio, 1809-1852 ***4511.35*** *p18*
Gomes, Sabino 31; America, 1846 ***778.6*** *p141*
Gomez, Bicente; Louisiana, 1874-1875 ***4981.45*** *p29*
Gomolowicz, Michael; Detroit, 1929-1930 ***6214.5*** *p65*
*Wife:*Violette Valeria
Gomolowicz, Violette Valeria *SEE* Gomolowicz, Michael
Gomski, John 33; Indiana, 1881-1896 ***9076.20*** *p74*
Gonder, Andreas; America, 1872 ***5475.1*** *p151*
Gonder, Joseph; Ohio, 1809-1852 ***4511.35*** *p18*
Gondey, Mr. 31; America, 1841 ***778.6*** *p141*
Gondoin, Nicolas; Quebec, 1637 ***9221.17*** *p67*
Gondret, P. 27; America, 1841 ***778.6*** *p141*
Gonel, P. 30; America, 1840 ***778.6*** *p141*
Gonet L'Henne, Ms. 34; Port uncertain, 1846 ***778.6*** *p141*
Gongiovanni, Gieuseppe; Miami, 1935 ***4984.12*** *p39*
Gongloff, Philip Jacob; Ohio, 1809-1852 ***4511.35*** *p18*
Gonhenarch, Adolphe 42; Texas, 1848 ***778.6*** *p141*
Gonse, John; Ohio, 1809-1852 ***4511.35*** *p18*
Gonsillon, Louis 30; New Orleans, 1840 ***778.6*** *p141*
Gonthier, Pierre; Quebec, 1641 ***9221.17*** *p104*
Gontier, Gottlieb; Colorado, 1889 ***1029.59*** *p32*
Gonvay, Gustave 29; New Orleans, 1848 ***778.6*** *p141*
Gony, Jean 33; America, 1846 ***778.6*** *p141*
Gonzales, Jose M.; Louisiana, 1874-1875 ***4981.45*** *p29*
Gonzalez, E. 23; New York, NY, 1894 ***6512.1*** *p181*
Good, Arthur; Boston, 1774 ***8529.30*** *p2*
Good, Charles; Ohio, 1809-1852 ***4511.35*** *p18*
Good, Jacob; Ohio, 1809-1852 ***4511.35*** *p18*
Good, John 29; Ontario, 1871 ***1823.21*** *p133*
Good, Sydney; Quebec, 1910 ***2897.7*** *p7*
Goodacre, Albert 35; Ontario, 1871 ***1823.21*** *p133*
Goodacre, Edwin 26; Ontario, 1871 ***1823.21*** *p133*
Goodacre, George 52; Ontario, 1871 ***1823.21*** *p133*
Goodall, Charles 62; Ontario, 1871 ***1823.17*** *p59*
Goodall, Peter 36; Michigan, 1880 ***4491.33*** *p10*
Goodard, Robert 58; Ontario, 1871 ***1823.21*** *p133*
Goodboy, Jacob; Ohio, 1809-1852 ***4511.35*** *p18*
Goodenough, James; Colorado, 1890 ***1029.59*** *p32*
Gooderham, James 45; Ontario, 1871 ***1823.21*** *p133*
Gooderham, James 59; Ontario, 1871 ***1823.21*** *p133*
Gooderich, James 43; Ontario, 1871 ***1823.17*** *p59*
Goodhande, Joseph 70; Ontario, 1871 ***1823.17*** *p59*
Goodhill, David 55; Ontario, 1871 ***1823.17*** *p59*
Goodhue, Louisa 66; Ontario, 1871 ***1823.21*** *p133*
Goodison, John 22; Ontario, 1871 ***1823.21*** *p133*

Goodman, Abraham 22; New York, NY, 1894 ***6512.1*** *p229*
Goodman, Alvi 39; Ontario, 1871 ***1823.21*** *p133*
Goodman, Dewalt; Ohio, 1809-1852 ***4511.35*** *p18*
Goodman, George 36; Ontario, 1871 ***1823.21*** *p133*
Goodman, Gustav 33; Indiana, 1877-1886 ***9076.20*** *p71*
Goodman, Harry; Detroit, 1929-1930 ***6214.5*** *p63*
Goodman, Isaac D.; North Carolina, 1856 ***1088.45*** *p11*
Goodman, John; Plymouth, MA, 1620 ***1920.45*** *p5*
Goodman, Marcus; Ohio, 1809-1852 ***4511.35*** *p18*
Goodman, Samuel 22; Indiana, 1881-1885 ***9076.20*** *p71*
Goodrich, William 50; Ontario, 1871 ***1823.17*** *p59*
Goodridge, George 30; Ontario, 1871 ***1823.21*** *p133*
Goods, James 43; Ontario, 1871 ***1823.21*** *p133*
Goodson, George 60; Ontario, 1871 ***1823.21*** *p133*
Goodson, Irving; Detroit, 1929-1930 ***6214.5*** *p65*
Goodstein, Irving; Detroit, 1929-1930 ***6214.5*** *p65*
Goodwill, Thomas 43; Ontario, 1871 ***1823.21*** *p133*
Goodwin, Abraham 42; Ontario, 1871 ***1823.21*** *p133*
Goodwin, Dan'l 23; Ontario, 1871 ***1823.17*** *p59*
Goodwin, James 30; Ontario, 1871 ***1823.17*** *p59*
Goodwin, Jane 16; Quebec, 1870 ***8364.32*** *p23*
Goodwin, John; Kansas, 1878 ***777.40*** *p6*
Goodwin, Mary 65; Ontario, 1871 ***1823.17*** *p59*
Goodwin, Patrick 35; Ontario, 1871 ***1823.21*** *p133*
Goodyear, Albert; Colorado, 1893 ***1029.59*** *p33*
Goodyear, Nathaniel 32; Michigan, 1880 ***4491.36*** *p8*
Googan, Simon; St. Johns, N.F., 1825 ***1053.15*** *p7*
Gook, Wilhelm; Wisconsin, 1878 ***6795.8*** *p233*
Goomley, Andrew; North Carolina, 1824 ***1088.45*** *p11*
Goos, William; Illinois, 1852 ***6079.1*** *p5*
Goot, Robert; Ontario, 1871 ***1823.17*** *p59*
Goour, Charles 16; Quebec, 1870 ***8364.32*** *p23*
Goran, Gheodor 43; Port uncertain, 1847 ***778.6*** *p141*
Goran, Margareth 28; Port uncertain, 1847 ***778.6*** *p141*
Goranson, Anna Elisabeth; St. Paul, MN, 1890 ***1865.50*** *p48*
Goranson, Leonard; Wisconsin, 1887-1889 ***1865.50*** *p48*
Goransson, Batel Johannes; Kansas, 1869 ***777.40*** *p7*
Goransson, Lars; New York, NY, 1848 ***6412.40*** *p151*
Gorble, James 60; Ontario, 1871 ***1823.21*** *p133*
Gorczyca, Anthony; Detroit, 1930 ***1640.60*** *p77*
Gorden, George W. 32; Ontario, 1871 ***1823.21*** *p133*
Gordin, John, Sr. 63; Ontario, 1871 ***1823.21*** *p133*
Gordon, Mrs.; Montreal, 1922 ***4514.4*** *p32*
Gordon, Alexander; North Carolina, 1774 ***1422.10*** *p58*
Gordon, Alfred John 37; Ontario, 1871 ***1823.17*** *p59*
Gordon, Angus 55; Ontario, 1871 ***1823.21*** *p133*
Gordon, Bertha; Detroit, 1929 ***1640.55*** *p114*
Gordon, C.; Montreal, 1922 ***4514.4*** *p32*
Gordon, Miss C.; Montreal, 1922 ***4514.4*** *p32*
Gordon, Charles 60; Ontario, 1871 ***1823.17*** *p59*
Gordon, Charles 68; Ontario, 1871 ***1823.21*** *p133*
Gordon, Miss D.; Montreal, 1922 ***4514.4*** *p32*
Gordon, F.; Louisiana, 1836-1840 ***4981.45*** *p212*
Gordon, George; North Carolina, 1848 ***1088.45*** *p11*
Gordon, George 46; Ontario, 1871 ***1823.21*** *p133*
Gordon, Hannah 40; Ontario, 1871 ***1823.21*** *p133*
Gordon, Harriet 5; Quebec, 1870 ***8364.32*** *p23*
Gordon, Isabella 65; Ontario, 1871 ***1823.21*** *p133*
Gordon, J.; Montreal, 1922 ***4514.4*** *p32*
Gordon, J. B. 40; Ontario, 1871 ***1823.21*** *p133*
Gordon, J. S.; Montreal, 1922 ***4514.4*** *p32*
Gordon, James 44; Ontario, 1871 ***1823.21*** *p133*
Gordon, James 50; Ontario, 1871 ***1823.17*** *p59*
Gordon, James 51; Ontario, 1871 ***1823.21*** *p133*
Gordon, Jane 35; Ontario, 1871 ***1823.21*** *p133*
Gordon, John; New York, 1783 ***8529.30*** *p12*
Gordon, John; North Carolina, 1774 ***1422.10*** *p58*
Gordon, John 29; Ontario, 1871 ***1823.21*** *p133*
Gordon, John 44; Ontario, 1871 ***1823.17*** *p59*
Gordon, Joseph 46; Ontario, 1871 ***1823.21*** *p134*
Gordon, Marg. 39; North Carolina, 1775 ***1422.10*** *p57*
Gordon, Massie 21; Ohio, 1880 ***4879.40*** *p258*
Gordon, Michal; Detroit, 1930 ***1640.60*** *p82*
Gordon, Peter 19; New York, NY, 1835 ***5024.1*** *p136*
Gordon, Peter 38; Ontario, 1871 ***1823.21*** *p134*
Gordon, Peter 60; Ontario, 1871 ***1823.21*** *p134*
Gordon, Robert 22; Ontario, 1871 ***1823.21*** *p134*
Gordon, Robert 30; Ontario, 1871 ***1823.17*** *p59*
Gordon, Robert B. 34; Ontario, 1871 ***1823.21*** *p134*
Gordon, Thomas 45; Ontario, 1871 ***1823.21*** *p134*
Gordon, Thomas 69; Ontario, 1871 ***1823.21*** *p134*
Gordon, Thomas; Wyoming, 1884 ***1447.20*** *p63*
Gordon, William 60; North Carolina, 1774 ***1422.10*** *p58*
Gordon, William 49; Ontario, 1871 ***1823.17*** *p59*
Gordon, William 54; Ontario, 1871 ***1823.21*** *p134*
Gordon, William 17; Quebec, 1870 ***8364.32*** *p23*
Gordon, William Alex 45; Ontario, 1871 ***1823.21*** *p134*
Gore, H. H. 30; Ontario, 1871 ***1823.21*** *p134*
Gore, Mercy; Nova Scotia, 1743-1817 ***9228.50*** *p107*
Gorecka, Johanna 19; New York, NY, 1911 ***6533.11*** *p10*
Gorg, Nikolaus; America, 1882 ***5475.1*** *p147*
Gorg, Nikolaus; Indiana, 1896 ***5475.1*** *p207*
Gorg, Peter; Indiana, 1883 ***5475.1*** *p252*
Gorgen, Anna; America, 1881 ***5475.1*** *p344*
Gorgen, Anna Maria Nilles *SEE* Gorgen, Mathias
Gorgen, Auguste 4 *SEE* Gorgen, Nikolaus
Gorgen, Elisabeth *SEE* Gorgen, Peter
Gorgen, Elisabeth; America, 1881 ***5475.1*** *p344*
Gorgen, J. Peter *SEE* Gorgen, Mathias
Gorgen, Johann 7 *SEE* Gorgen, Nikolaus
Gorgen, Katharina *SEE* Gorgen, Peter
Gorgen, Katharina Gimler *SEE* Gorgen, Peter
Gorgen, Mathias *SEE* Gorgen, Mathias
Gorgen, Mathias; America, 1880 ***5475.1*** *p287*
*Daughter:*Anna Maria Nilles
*Son:*J. Peter
*Son:*Nikolaus
*Son:*Peter
*Son:*Mathias
Gorgen, Michel *SEE* Gorgen, Peter
Gorgen, Nik.; America, 1882 ***5475.1*** *p290*
Gorgen, Nikolaus *SEE* Gorgen, Mathias
Gorgen, Nikolaus 43; America, 1857 ***5475.1*** *p279*
*Son:*Johann 7
*Son:*Auguste 4
With child 7
Gorgen, Peter *SEE* Gorgen, Mathias
Gorgen, Peter *SEE* Gorgen, Peter
Gorgen, Peter; America, 1881 ***5475.1*** *p344*
*Wife:*Katharina Gimler
*Daughter:*Katharina
*Child:*Michel
*Son:*Peter
*Daughter:*Elisabeth
Gorgen, Peter; America, 1883 ***5475.1*** *p344*
Gorgen-Waschbusch, Elisabeth Gorgen *SEE* Gorgen-Waschbusch, Math.
Gorgen-Waschbusch, Franz *SEE* Gorgen-Waschbusch, Math.
Gorgen-Waschbusch, Johann *SEE* Gorgen-Waschbusch, Math.
Gorgen-Waschbusch, Math.; America, 1881 ***5475.1*** *p344*
*Wife:*Elisabeth Gorgen
*Son:*Peter
*Son:*Franz
*Son:*Mathias
*Son:*Johann
Gorgen-Waschbusch, Mathias *SEE* Gorgen-Waschbusch, Math.
Gorgen-Waschbusch, Peter *SEE* Gorgen-Waschbusch, Math.
Gorges, M.; New York, 1860 ***358.56*** *p5*
Gorie, Isabella 38; Ontario, 1871 ***1823.17*** *p59*
Goritz, Heinrich; America, 1854 ***7420.1*** *p120*
Goritz, Johann Hermann Friedrich; America, 1854 ***7420.1*** *p120*
Gorius, Joseph 42; America, 1846 ***778.6*** *p141*
Gorius, Marie 36; America, 1846 ***778.6*** *p141*
Gorius, Therese 32; America, 1846 ***778.6*** *p141*
Gorkowska, Mary; Wisconsin, 1894 ***6795.8*** *p57*
Gorley, George 48; Ontario, 1871 ***1823.17*** *p59*
Gorma, T. H.; Louisiana, 1836-1841 ***4981.45*** *p208*
Gorman, . . . 32; Colorado, 1902 ***1029.59*** *p33*
Gorman, Catherine; Halifax, N.S., 1827 ***7009.9*** *p61*
*Husband:*Denis
Gorman, Cornelius 71; Ontario, 1871 ***1823.21*** *p134*
Gorman, Daniel 35; Ontario, 1871 ***1823.21*** *p134*
Gorman, David; Toronto, 1844 ***2910.35*** *p114*
Gorman, Denis *SEE* Gorman, Catherine Parker
Gorman, Edward 15; Quebec, 1870 ***8364.32*** *p23*
Gorman, Elen 26; Ontario, 1871 ***1823.21*** *p134*
Gorman, James 39; Ontario, 1871 ***1823.21*** *p134*
Gorman, Joanne; Boston, 1753 ***1642*** *p47*
Gorman, John; Colorado, 1891 ***1029.59*** *p33*
Gorman, John; Colorado, 1891 ***1029.59*** *p33*
Gorman, John; Colorado, 1900 ***1029.59*** *p33*
Gorman, John; Louisiana, 1874 ***4981.45*** *p132*
Gorman, John; New Orleans, 1850 ***7242.30*** *p142*
Gorman, John J.; North Carolina, 1824 ***1088.45*** *p11*
Gorman, Lawrence; Colorado, 1902 ***1029.59*** *p33*
Gorman, Lewis; Nova Scotia, 1784 ***7105*** *p23*
Gorman, Michael; Washington, 1884 ***2770.40*** *p192*
Gorman, Patrick; Louisiana, 1836-1840 ***4981.45*** *p212*
Gorman, Patrick; Louisiana, 1836-1841 ***4981.45*** *p208*
Gorman, William; Boston, 1766 ***1642*** *p36*
Gormelly, John; Philadelphia, 1852 ***8513.31*** *p310*
*Wife:*Margaret Wilson
Gormelly, Margaret Wilson *SEE* Gormelly, John
Gormely, Michael 50; Ontario, 1871 ***1823.21*** *p134*
Gormely, Patrick 50; Ontario, 1871 ***1823.21*** *p134*
Gormley, John; Delaware, 1854 ***5720.10*** *p111*
Gormley, John; Philadelphia, 1852 ***8513.31*** *p310*
*Wife:*Margaret Wilson
Gormley, Margaret Wilson *SEE* Gormley, John
Gormly, James; Ohio, 1809-1852 ***4511.35*** *p18*
Gormon, Michel 35; Ontario, 1871 ***1823.21*** *p134*
Gornich, Anna 21; America, 1864 ***5475.1*** *p284*
Gorny, Michel; Wisconsin, 1886 ***6795.8*** *p38*
Gorre, Charles; Quebec, 1647 ***9221.17*** *p181*
Gorrie, John; North Carolina, 1817 ***1088.45*** *p11*
Gorschiel, Mary; Iowa, 1870-1879 ***9228.50*** *p249*
Gorshowitz, Anna; Detroit, 1929-1930 ***6214.5*** *p61*
Gorsline, R. P. 41; Ontario, 1871 ***1823.17*** *p59*
Gortland, John; New Orleans, 1850 ***7242.30*** *p142*
Gortsch, Eduard Carl Friedrich; Wisconsin, 1896 ***6795.8*** *p231*
Gory, Jean 28; Quebec, 1639 ***9221.17*** *p88*
Gory, Sarah; Boston, 1700 ***9228.50*** *p578*
Gorz, F. Wilhelm; Dakota, 1884-1918 ***554.30*** *p26*
*Wife:*Maria
Gorz, Maria *SEE* Gorz, F. Wilhelm
Gorzal, Frank; Texas, 1855-1886 ***9980.22*** *p16*
Gorzycki, Jacob Andrew; New York, NY, 1881 ***6015.15*** *p25*
Gorzycki, Valeria; New York, NY, 1883 ***6015.15*** *p25*
Gosar, Anton; Illinois, 1930 ***121.35*** *p100*
Gosch, John; Illinois, 1864 ***6079.1*** *p5*
Goscomb, Thomas; Marston's Wharf, 1782 ***8529.30*** *p12*
Gosevitch, Harry; Detroit, 1929-1930 ***6214.5*** *p63*
Gosewicz, Aron; Detroit, 1929-1930 ***6214.5*** *p63*
Gosh, Anna; Wisconsin, 1898 ***6795.8*** *p36*
Goshe, Henry; Ohio, 1809-1852 ***4511.35*** *p18*
Goshelaar, Harm Wilbur; Iowa, 1894 ***1211.15*** *p10*
Gosin, Amelie Joseph *SEE* Gosin, Dieudonne
Gosin, Amelie Joseph Ramoisy *SEE* Gosin, Dieudonne
Gosin, Augustin *SEE* Gosin, Dieudonne
Gosin, Dieudonne; Wisconsin, 1855-1858 ***1495.20*** *p67*
*Wife:*Amelie Joseph Ramoisy
*Child:*Augustin
*Child:*Virginie Joseph
*Child:*Jean Baptiste
*Child:*Amelie Joseph
*Child:*Francois Xavier
Gosin, Francois Xavier *SEE* Gosin, Dieudonne
Gosin, Jean Baptiste *SEE* Gosin, Dieudonne
Gosin, Virginie Joseph *SEE* Gosin, Dieudonne
Goslar, Heinrich Adolf; New York, NY, 1878 ***7420.1*** *p310*
Gosler, Joseph; Ohio, 1809-1852 ***4511.35*** *p18*
Goslin, Eliza; New Orleans, 1850 ***7242.30*** *p142*
Goslin, James; New Orleans, 1850 ***7242.30*** *p142*
Goslin, Mary; New Orleans, 1850 ***7242.30*** *p142*
Goslin, Mary; New Orleans, 1850 ***7242.30*** *p143*
Gosling, Palmer; Louisiana, 1836-1841 ***4981.45*** *p208*
Gosman, A.; Louisiana, 1874 ***4981.45*** *p296*
Goss, P.; New Orleans, 1850 ***7242.30*** *p143*
Goss, William G. 58; Kansas, 1903 ***1447.20*** *p62*
Gossard, Noelle; Quebec, 1671 ***4514.3*** *p319*
Gosselin, Charles; Trinidad, 1780-1803 ***9228.50*** *p250*
Gosselin, Frank G.; Rochester, NY, 1851-1876 ***9228.50*** *p250*
Gosselin, Gabriel 24; Quebec, 1650 ***9221.17*** *p226*
Gosselin, Jane K.; New York, 1871-1874 ***9228.50*** *p250*
*Child:*May Jane
*Child:*William F.
Gosselin, Jane K.; Rochester, NY, n.d. ***9228.50*** *p537*
*Child:*May Jane
*Child:*William F.
Gosselin, John T., Jr.; Rochester, NY, 1839-1862 ***9228.50*** *p250*
Gosselin, John T., Sr.; New York, 1864-1880 ***9228.50*** *p250*
*Wife:*Mary Mulley
Gosselin, Mary Mulley *SEE* Gosselin, John T., Sr.
Gosselin, Nicolas 20; Quebec, 1654 ***9221.17*** *p309*
Gosselin, Philippe 35; Quebec, 1648 ***9221.17*** *p199*
*Wife:*Vincente Despres
Gosselin, Vincente Despres *SEE* Gosselin, Philippe
Gosset, Achil 32; Port uncertain, 1840 ***778.6*** *p141*
Gossett, Catherine Du Four *SEE* Gossett, Peter
Gossett, Esther *SEE* Gossett, Peter
Gossett, Gabriel; South Carolina, 1779-1835 ***9228.50*** *p252*
Gossett, Jane *SEE* Gossett, Peter
Gossett, John *SEE* Gossett, Peter
Gossett, John; Pennsylvania, 1699-1735 ***9228.50*** *p251*
Gossett, John; Virginia, 1766-1816 ***9228.50*** *p251*
Gossett, Major; South Carolina, 1768-1862 ***9228.50*** *p251*
Gossett, Martha; America, 1752-1775 ***9228.50*** *p251*
Gossett, Mary *SEE* Gossett, Peter
Gossett, Matthew *SEE* Gossett, Peter
Gossett, Peter; Pennsylvania, 1650-1765 ***9228.50*** *p251*
*Wife:*Catherine Du Four
*Child:*Matthew
*Child:*Esther
*Child:*Mary

*Child:*Jane
*Child:*John
Gossett, Richard; Ontario, n.d. ***9228.50*** *p18A*
With wife
Gossett Family ; Ohio, 1770-1830 ***9228.50*** *p252*
Gossfeldt, Carl Friedrick Wilhelm; Wisconsin, 1898 ***6795.8*** *p96*
Gossfeldt, Marie Emilie Auguste; Wisconsin, 1898 ***6795.8*** *p81*
Gossman, Frances; Detroit, 1929 ***1640.55*** *p113*
Gosson, Jean 27; America, 1848 ***778.6*** *p141*
Gosz, Veronica; Detroit, 1890 ***9980.23*** *p97*
Got, Joseph 18; America, 1845 ***778.6*** *p141*
Gotchauz, Mariz 35; America, 1844 ***778.6*** *p141*
Goth, Elisabeth 30; New Orleans, 1848 ***778.6*** *p141*
Goth, Johannis 32; New Orleans, 1848 ***778.6*** *p141*
Goth, Marie 3; New Orleans, 1848 ***778.6*** *p141*
Gotier, Jacob 26; America, 1843 ***778.6*** *p141*
Gotland, John; New Orleans, 1850 ***7242.30*** *p143*
Gotland, L.; New Orleans, 1850 ***7242.30*** *p143*
Gotlieb, Jacob 23; Missouri, 1848 ***778.6*** *p141*
Gotschi, Johan Jacob; North Carolina, 1710 ***3629.40*** *p3*
Gott, Benjamin 37; Ontario, 1871 ***1823.17*** *p59*
Gott, George 60; Ontario, 1871 ***1823.21*** *p134*
Gott, Robert 36; Ontario, 1871 ***1823.17*** *p59*
Gott, William 33; Ontario, 1871 ***1823.21*** *p134*
Gottberg, Anna Olivia; America, 1899 ***6410.15*** *p109*
*Child:*Carl Wilhelm
*Child:*Carl August
*Child:*Carl Robert
*Child:*Emmy
*Child:*Tekla Olivia
*Child:*Anna Lilly Sophia
Gottchaux, Samuel 35; Port uncertain, 1847 ***778.6*** *p142*
Gotte, Rudolf; St. Louis, 1876 ***7420.1*** *p306*
Gottelmann, Johann Baptist 30; Galveston, TX, 1844 ***3967.10*** *p371*
Gottelmann, Karl 1; Galveston, TX, 1844 ***3967.10*** *p371*
Gottelmann, Therese 30; Galveston, TX, 1844 ***3967.10*** *p371*
Gottfred, Albert A.; Washington, 1885 ***2770.40*** *p194*
Gottfried, Friedrich Gustav; America, 1867 ***7919.3*** *p528*
Gottfried, Heinrich; America, 1847 ***5475.1*** *p28*
With parents
Gottfrois, Anna; America, 1881 ***5475.1*** *p300*
Gottgen, Johann Jakob; America, 1866 ***5475.1*** *p515*
Gottgen, Peter; America, 1843 ***5475.1*** *p515*
Gottinger, Elisabeth 4; Missouri, 1846 ***778.6*** *p142*
Gottinger, Elisabeth 34; Missouri, 1846 ***778.6*** *p142*
Gottinger, Michel 2; Missouri, 1846 ***778.6*** *p142*
Gottinger, Michel 34; Missouri, 1846 ***778.6*** *p142*
Gottlieb, George; Nova Scotia, 1784 ***7105*** *p23*
Gottmann, Anna Margaretha Scholl von Hochst *SEE* Gottmann, Leonhard
Gottmann, Barbara; America, 1856 ***2526.43*** *p123*
Gottmann, Elisabetha Margaretha; America, 1858 ***2526.43*** *p188*
Gottmann, Elisabethe *SEE* Gottmann, Jakob
Gottmann, Eva Katharina *SEE* Gottmann, Leonhard
Gottmann, Georg; America, 1884 ***2526.42*** *p121*
Gottmann, Jakob; America, 1885 ***2526.42*** *p136*
*Wife:*Margaretha Friedrich
*Child:*Wilhelm
*Child:*Sophie
*Child:*Elisabethe
*Child:*Maria
Gottmann, Johann Adam *SEE* Gottmann, Leonhard
Gottmann, Johann Peter; America, 1785 ***2526.42*** *p121*
*Wife:*Maria Katharina Jung
Gottmann, Johannes; America, 1852 ***2526.43*** *p189*
Gottmann, Leonhard; America, 1773 ***2526.43*** *p140*
*Wife:*Anna Margaretha Scholl von Hochst
*Daughter:*Eva Katharina
*Son:*Johann Adam
Gottmann, Ludwig; America, 1867 ***2526.42*** *p121*
Gottmann, Margaretha Friedrich *SEE* Gottmann, Jakob
Gottmann, Maria *SEE* Gottmann, Jakob
Gottmann, Maria Katharina Jung *SEE* Gottmann, Johann Peter
Gottmann, Sophie *SEE* Gottmann, Jakob
Gottmann, Wilhelm *SEE* Gottmann, Jakob
Gottschalk, Barbara 47; Halifax, N.S., 1902 ***1860.4*** *p42*
Gottschalk, Caroline; America, 1868 ***7420.1*** *p271*
Gottschalk, Caroline 53; Halifax, N.S., 1902 ***1860.4*** *p42*
Gottschalk, Elisabeth 15; Halifax, N.S., 1902 ***1860.4*** *p42*
Gottschalk, Ferdinand Ludwig August; America, 1893 ***7420.1*** *p368*
Gottschalk, Geo.; Louisiana, 1874 ***4981.45*** *p132*
Gottschalk, Heinrich; America, 1868 ***7420.1*** *p271*
Gottschalk, Heinrich 56; Halifax, N.S., 1902 ***1860.4*** *p42*
Gottschalk, Heinrich; Port uncertain, 1827 ***7420.1*** *p3*
Gottschalk, Jacob 7; Halifax, N.S., 1902 ***1860.4*** *p42*
Gottschalk, Johann 17; Halifax, N.S., 1902 ***1860.4*** *p42*
Gottschalk, Johann 49; Halifax, N.S., 1902 ***1860.4*** *p42*
Gottschalk, Juliana 12; Halifax, N.S., 1902 ***1860.4*** *p42*
Gottschalk, Rosina 9; Halifax, N.S., 1902 ***1860.4*** *p42*
Gottschall, Gustav; America, 1893 ***2526.43*** *p168*
Gottschimmer, John; Illinois, 1852 ***6079.1*** *p6*
Gottshaw, John F.; South Carolina, 1850 ***6155.4*** *p18*
Gottwald, Adam 19; America, 1849 ***2526.43*** *p168*
Gottwald, Adam Konrad 19 *SEE* Gottwald, Michael, II
Gottwald, Caroline; America, 1857 ***2526.43*** *p168*
Gottwald, Elisabeth 12 *SEE* Gottwald, Michael, II
Gottwald, Georg Konrad 17 *SEE* Gottwald, Michael, II
Gottwald, John; Ohio, 1809-1852 ***4511.35*** *p18*
Gottwald, Katharina Steiger *SEE* Gottwald, Michael, II
Gottwald, Katharine Margarethe 22 *SEE* Gottwald, Michael, II
Gottwald, Marie 27 *SEE* Gottwald, Michael, II
Gottwald, Marie; Minneapolis, 1880 ***2526.43*** *p167*
Gottwald, Michael, II; America, 1879 ***2526.43*** *p168*
*Wife:*Katharina Steiger
*Son:*Adam Konrad
*Daughter:*Elisabeth
*Son:*Georg Konrad
*Daughter:*Katharine Margarethe
*Daughter:*Marie
Gotuon, Peter; Port uncertain, 1842 ***778.6*** *p142*
Gotz, Adolph 28; Halifax, N.S., 1902 ***1860.4*** *p44*
Gotz, Albina 2; Halifax, N.S., 1902 ***1860.4*** *p44*
Gotz, Andreas; Venezuela, 1843 ***3899.5*** *p541*
Gotz, Anna; America, 1891 ***179.55*** *p19*
Gotz, Anna Maria 42; America, 1853 ***2526.42*** *p114*
Gotz, Chris; Halifax, N.S., 1902 ***1860.4*** *p44*
Gotz, Johann Friedrich; America, 1867 ***7919.3*** *p529*
Gotz, Johann Leonhard; America, 1880 ***2526.43*** *p160*
Gotz, Johann Nicolaus Bernhard; America, 1868 ***7919.3*** *p525*
Gotz, Johannes; America, 1911 ***7420.1*** *p388*
Gotz, Leonhard; America, 1842 ***2526.43*** *p123*
With wife
With child 10
With child 7
Gotz, Louisa 25; Halifax, N.S., 1902 ***1860.4*** *p44*
Gotz, Ludwig; America, 1900 ***2526.43*** *p160*
Gotz, Lydia 3; Halifax, N.S., 1902 ***1860.4*** *p44*
Gotz, Margaretha; America, 1870 ***2526.43*** *p160*
Gotz, Rosina 35; New York, NY, 1910 ***8425.16*** *p34*
Gotz, Theresia; Venezuela, 1843 ***3899.5*** *p541*
Gotz, Wilhelm; America, 1867 ***2526.43*** *p160*
Gouaut, Gaspard; Quebec, 1646 ***9221.17*** *p165*
Goubilleau, Francoise; Quebec, 1670 ***4514.3*** *p319*
*Son:*Pierre
Goubot, Jacques Noel 40; Louisiana, 1848 ***778.6*** *p142*
Goucher, Gotleib; Ohio, 1809-1852 ***4511.35*** *p18*
Goudall, James 30; Ontario, 1871 ***1823.21*** *p134*
Goude, John; Maryland, 1672 ***1236.25*** *p47*
Goudeau, Francoise 14; Quebec, 1647 ***9221.17*** *p177*
Goudeau, Louis; Montreal, 1647 ***9221.17*** *p192*
Gouder, Joseph; Ohio, 1809-1852 ***4511.35*** *p18*
Goudrault, Daniel; Quebec, 1656 ***9221.17*** *p337*
Goudse, Francois 35; America, 1840 ***778.6*** *p142*
Gough, John 51; Ontario, 1871 ***1823.21*** *p134*
Gough, John 71; Ontario, 1871 ***1823.21*** *p134*
Gough, Mary 13; Quebec, 1870 ***8364.32*** *p23*
Gough, Richard 65; Ontario, 1871 ***1823.21*** *p134*
Gough, Richard Alexander 37; Ontario, 1871 ***1823.21*** *p134*
Gough, William 34; Ontario, 1871 ***1823.21*** *p134*
Gouilhard, J. 14; America, 1846 ***778.6*** *p142*
Gouin, Jean 18; Quebec, 1659 ***9221.17*** *p402*
Gouin, Laurent 20; Quebec, 1657 ***9221.17*** *p359*
*Relative:*Mathurin 20
Gouin, Mathurin 20 *SEE* Gouin, Laurent
Goujet, Catherine 23; Quebec, 1640 ***9221.17*** *p96*
Goulard, Antoine 55; America, 1842 ***778.6*** *p142*
Gould, Charlous 37; Ontario, 1871 ***1823.21*** *p134*
Gould, Elizabeth; New York, 1832 ***9228.50*** *p207*
Gould, Elizabeth; New York, 1832 ***9228.50*** *p207*
Gould, Emily 21; Ontario, 1871 ***1823.21*** *p134*
Gould, Frances 17; Ontario, 1871 ***1823.21*** *p134*
Gould, George; Colorado, 1920 ***1029.59*** *p33*
Gould, George 58; New York, NY, 1911 ***1029.59*** *p33*
Gould, George 41; Ontario, 1871 ***1823.17*** *p59*
Gould, Mary; Boston, 1734-1766 ***9228.50*** *p325*
Gould, Michael; Long Island, 1781 ***8529.30*** *p9A*
Gould, Peter 32; Ontario, 1871 ***1823.17*** *p59*
Gould, Richard 48; Ontario, 1871 ***1823.21*** *p134*
Gould, Richard 52; Ontario, 1871 ***1823.21*** *p134*
Gould, Samuel 49; Ontario, 1871 ***1823.21*** *p134*
Gould, Thomas 34; Ontario, 1871 ***1823.21*** *p134*
Gould, William 42; Ontario, 1871 ***1823.17*** *p59*
Gould, Wordey 25; Ontario, 1871 ***1823.21*** *p134*
Goulder, James; Quebec, 1870 ***8364.32*** *p23*
Goulding, Ann 68; Ontario, 1871 ***1823.21*** *p134*
Goulding, John; North Carolina, 1795 ***1088.45*** *p11*
Goulding, Thomas; Ohio, 1809-1852 ***4511.35*** *p18*
Goulding, Thomas 55; Ontario, 1871 ***1823.21*** *p134*
Goulds, Martin 50; Ontario, 1871 ***1823.21*** *p134*
Gouldy, John 41; Ontario, 1871 ***1823.17*** *p59*
Goule, Madeleine; Quebec, 1638 ***9221.17*** *p77*
Goulet, Jacques 31; Quebec, 1646 ***9221.17*** *p165*
*Wife:*Marguerite Mullier 17
Goulet, Marguerite Mullier 17 *SEE* Goulet, Jacques
Goulet, Vincent 24; New Orleans, 1848 ***778.6*** *p142*
Goulty, James; Illinois, 1860 ***6079.1*** *p6*
Goumin, Annet; Quebec, 1661 ***9221.17*** *p458*
Goupil, Nicolas; Quebec, 1642 ***9221.17*** *p117*
Goupil, Rene 32; Quebec, 1640 ***9221.17*** *p97*
Goupil dela Pequeliere, Chs. 17; America, 1840 ***778.6*** *p142*
Goupteille, . . .; Maine, n.d. ***9228.50*** *p268*
Goupteille, . . .; New Brunswick, n.d. ***9228.50*** *p268*
Gourbin, Pierre 27; Mississippi, 1847 ***778.6*** *p142*
Gourd, Thomas 33; Ontario, 1871 ***1823.21*** *p134*
Gourdais, Miss 7; Texas, 1848 ***778.6*** *p142*
Gourdais, Miss 22; Texas, 1848 ***778.6*** *p142*
Gourdais, Pierrent 28; Texas, 1848 ***778.6*** *p142*
Gourdeau, Nicolas; Quebec, 1657 ***9221.17*** *p359*
Gourdeau DeBeaulieu, Jacques; Quebec, 1651 ***9221.17*** *p244*
Gourdin, Alizon; Quebec, 1636 ***9221.17*** *p52*
Gourdon, Jules; Louisiana, 1874-1875 ***4981.45*** *p298*
Gourdon, Pierre 35; Quebec, 1657 ***9221.17*** *p359*
Gourdon, Mrs. Victorine 19; America, 1842 ***778.6*** *p142*
Gourey, Sarah; Boston, 1700 ***9228.50*** *p578*
Gourgues, Armand 20; America, 1845 ***778.6*** *p142*
Gourgues, Pierre 18; America, 1845 ***778.6*** *p142*
Gourie, Joseph; North Carolina, 1827-1832 ***1088.45*** *p11*
Gourlay, Alexander 50; Ontario, 1871 ***1823.21*** *p135*
Gourlay, Andrew 60; Ontario, 1871 ***1823.21*** *p135*
Gourlay, Geo.; Louisiana, 1874 ***4981.45*** *p295*
Gourlay, John 42; Ontario, 1871 ***1823.21*** *p135*
Gourlay, John 43; Ontario, 1871 ***1823.21*** *p135*
Gourlay, Robert; Washington, 1889 ***2770.40*** *p27*
Gourley, John 23; Ontario, 1871 ***1823.17*** *p59*
Gourniez, Eugenie 31; America, 1848 ***778.6*** *p142*
Gourrayer, Jean; Montreal, 1644 ***9221.17*** *p146*
Goury, Elizabeth 78; Ontario, 1871 ***1823.21*** *p135*
Gouse, John; Ohio, 1809-1852 ***4511.35*** *p18*
Gousse, Nicolas; Quebec, 1659 ***9221.17*** *p401*
Gousserat, Pierre 24; Havana, 1848 ***778.6*** *p142*
Gouthier, Philibert 24; Mississippi, 1845 ***778.6*** *p142*
Gouvy, Charles; Quebec, 1646 ***9221.17*** *p165*
Goux, Ja.ques 43; Mississippi, 1846 ***778.6*** *p142*
Gouzard, Jean 18; New Orleans, 1846 ***778.6*** *p142*
Gouzon, F. 31; America, 1842 ***778.6*** *p142*
Gouzy, Claudius 7; New Orleans, 1844 ***778.6*** *p142*
Gouzy, Julius 3; New Orleans, 1844 ***778.6*** *p142*
Gouzy, Peter 40; New Orleans, 1844 ***778.6*** *p142*
Govan, Robert 44; Ontario, 1871 ***1823.21*** *p135*
Gove, William 54; Ontario, 1871 ***1823.17*** *p59*
Govenlock, Andrew 45; Ontario, 1871 ***1823.21*** *p135*
Govenlock, Thos 40; Ontario, 1871 ***1823.17*** *p59*
Govern, Margaret 20; Ontario, 1871 ***1823.21*** *p135*
Governor, Hattie 10; Ontario, 1871 ***1823.21*** *p135*
Govin, Antoine; Quebec, 1649 ***9221.17*** *p214*
Gow, George 42; Ontario, 1871 ***1823.21*** *p135*
Gow, George; Philadelphia, 1854 ***7074.20*** *p132*
Gowan, Susan 32; Ontario, 1871 ***1823.21*** *p135*
Gowan, William 24; Ontario, 1871 ***1823.17*** *p59*
Gowanlock, James 62; Ontario, 1871 ***1823.21*** *p135*
Gowans, James 28; Ontario, 1871 ***1823.17*** *p59*
Gowans, Margaret 70; Ontario, 1871 ***1823.17*** *p59*
Gowans, Mary 67; New York, NY, 1835 ***5024.1*** *p137*
Gowas, James 50; Ontario, 1871 ***1823.21*** *p135*
Gowe, William 44; Ontario, 1871 ***1823.21*** *p135*
Gowen, Charles 46; Ontario, 1871 ***1823.21*** *p135*
Gowen, Jennie 20; Ontario, 1871 ***1823.21*** *p135*
Gower, George 50; Ontario, 1871 ***1823.21*** *p135*
Gower, Steven 60; Ontario, 1871 ***1823.21*** *p135*
Gowing, John; North Carolina, 1827 ***1088.45*** *p11*
Gowinlock, John 45; Ontario, 1871 ***1823.21*** *p135*
Gowling, Thomas 57; Ontario, 1871 ***1823.17*** *p59*
Gowman, Thomas; Ohio, 1840 ***2763.1*** *p9*
Gowman, Thomas 46; Ontario, 1871 ***1823.21*** *p135*
Gowrie, John 54; Ontario, 1871 ***1823.21*** *p135*
Goy, Virg. 29; New Orleans, 1840 ***778.6*** *p142*
Goye, J. 35; America, 1840 ***778.6*** *p142*
Goyeatte, Michel; Louisiana, 1874 ***4981.45*** *p132*
Goyen, J. 35; Port uncertain, 1848 ***778.6*** *p142*
Goyer, Marie Garnier 27 *SEE* Goyer, Pierre
Goyer, Marie-Anne 2 *SEE* Goyer, Pierre
Goyer, Mathurin 26; Quebec, 1648 ***9221.17*** *p199*
Goyer, Pierre 40; Montreal, 1659 ***9221.17*** *p421*
*Wife:*Marie Garnier 27
*Daughter:*Marie-Anne 2
Gozdznik, Michal 44; New York, NY, 1911 ***6533.11*** *p10*
Gozumplik, Anton 43; Minnesota, 1925 ***2769.54*** *p1384*

Grabarkewith, Stanislaus; Galveston, TX, 1889 ***6015.15*** *p9*
Grabarkiewicz, Peter; Galveston, TX, 1898 ***6015.15*** *p12*
Grabarkiewicz, Stanislaus; Galveston, TX, 1889 ***6015.15*** *p9*
Grabarkiewitz, Peter; Galveston, TX, 1898 ***6015.15*** *p12*
Grabau, Theodore; Louisiana, 1836-1841 ***4981.45*** *p208*
Grabe, Dorothea; America, 1870 ***7420.1*** *p395*
Grabe, Frederick; Philadelphia, 1837 ***5720.10*** *p382*
Grabe, Lewis; Philadelphia, 1837 ***5720.10*** *p382*
Grabe, Wilhelm; America, 1856 ***7420.1*** *p147*
Grabenorst, Clara 21; New York, NY, 1864 ***8425.62*** *p196*
Graber, John; Colorado, 1904 ***1029.59*** *p33*
Graber, John; New York, 1875 ***1029.59*** *p33*
Grabill, Joseph; Ohio, 1809-1852 ***4511.35*** *p18*
Grable, C. E.; California, 1868 ***1131.61*** *p89*
With sister
Grabow, August; New York, 1859 ***358.56*** *p101*
Grabowski, Aleksander 19; New York, NY, 1911 ***6533.11*** *p9*
Grabowsky, Wolf; New York, 1860 ***358.56*** *p150*
Grace, Annie Louisa 18; Ontario, 1871 ***1823.21*** *p135*
Grace, Bridget 70; Ontario, 1871 ***1823.21*** *p135*
Grace, John 55; Ontario, 1871 ***1823.21*** *p135*
Grace, John 66; Ontario, 1871 ***1823.21*** *p135*
Grace, John; St. Johns, N.F., 1825 ***1053.15*** *p7*
Grace, Micheal 30; Ontario, 1871 ***1823.21*** *p135*
Grace, Sarah 7; Quebec, 1870 ***8364.32*** *p23*
Grace, Simon 58; Ontario, 1871 ***1823.17*** *p60*
Grace, Thomas; Louisiana, 1836-1840 ***4981.45*** *p212*
Grace, Thomas; Marston's Wharf, 1782 ***8529.30*** *p12*
Grace, William; New York, 1783 ***8529.30*** *p12*
Gracianot, Pierce; Louisiana, 1874-1875 ***4981.45*** *p298*
Graciette, J. 24; New Orleans, 1842 ***778.6*** *p142*
Gracy, Alexander; Toronto, 1844 ***2910.35*** *p115*
Grad, Catherina 1; New York, NY, 1898 ***7951.13*** *p43*
Grad, George 8; New York, NY, 1898 ***7951.13*** *p43*
Grad, Johann 24; New York, NY, 1898 ***7951.13*** *p43*
Grad, Joseph 17; New York, NY, 1898 ***7951.13*** *p43*
Grad, Magdalena 19; New York, NY, 1898 ***7951.13*** *p43*
Grad, Nicholas 10; New York, NY, 1898 ***7951.13*** *p43*
Grad, Peter 48; New York, NY, 1898 ***7951.13*** *p43*
Grad, Theresia 45; New York, NY, 1898 ***7951.13*** *p43*
Grade, James O.; Ohio, 1840-1897 ***8365.35*** *p16*
Grade, Martin 24; Louisiana, 1848 ***778.6*** *p143*
Gradler, Johann Ernst; America, 1868 ***7919.3*** *p530*
Grady, Alley; St. Johns, N.F., 1825 ***1053.15*** *p6*
Grady, James 22; New York, NY, 1826 ***6178.50*** *p150*
Grady, John; Boston, 1739 ***1642*** *p44*
Grady, John 21; St. Johns, N.F., 1811 ***1053.20*** *p21*
Grady, Martin; Boston, 1763 ***1642*** *p32*
Grady, Pat 23; St. Johns, N.F., 1811 ***1053.20*** *p21*
Grady, T.; New Orleans, 1850 ***7242.30*** *p143*
Grady, Thomas; Louisiana, 1848-1850 ***7710.1*** *p152*
Gradziel, P.; Galveston, TX, 1855 ***571.7*** *p18*
Graeber, Gottfried 21; America, 1847 ***778.6*** *p143*
Graeble, Thomas 20; New Orleans, 1847 ***778.6*** *p143*
Graepler, Friderich August; Wisconsin, 1884 ***6795.8*** *p81*
Graessle, Jacob; Ohio, 1840-1897 ***8365.35*** *p16*
Graeulick, Jacque; New York, 1860 ***358.56*** *p149*
Graf, Anton; Louisiana, 1874 ***4981.45*** *p295*
Graf, Auguste; America, 1868 ***7919.3*** *p535*
Graf, Bernhard; Colorado, 1894 ***1029.59*** *p33*
Graf, Bernhard; Wyoming, 1884 ***1029.59*** *p33*
Graf, Christian; Ohio, 1840-1897 ***8365.35*** *p16*
Graf, Deter 37; America, 1846 ***778.6*** *p143*
Graf, Dorothea Henriette; America, 1866 ***7420.1*** *p242*
Graf, Edward 9; Halifax, N.S., 1902 ***1860.4*** *p43*
Graf, Ferdinand; Long Island, 1781 ***8529.30*** *p9A*
Graf, Ferdinand 17; New York, NY, 1893 ***1883.7*** *p39*
Graf, Ferdinand 17; New York, NY, 1893 ***1883.7*** *p47*
Graf, Frank E.; Colorado, 1874 ***1029.59*** *p33*
Graf, Jacob 18; Halifax, N.S., 1902 ***1860.4*** *p43*
Graf, Jakob; America, 1882 ***5475.1*** *p316*
Graf, Johanne 15; Halifax, N.S., 1902 ***1860.4*** *p43*
Graf, John; Washington, 1889 ***2770.40*** *p27*
Graf, John U.; Georgia, 1902 ***1029.59*** *p33*
Graf, Karl 11; Halifax, N.S., 1902 ***1860.4*** *p43*
Graf, Katharina 44; Halifax, N.S., 1902 ***1860.4*** *p43*
Graf, Ludwig 18; Galveston, TX, 1844 ***3967.10*** *p370*
Graf, Lydia 4; Halifax, N.S., 1902 ***1860.4*** *p43*
Graf, M. 40; America, 1875 ***5475.1*** *p331*
Graf, Maria 14; Halifax, N.S., 1902 ***1860.4*** *p43*
Graf, Martha 3; Halifax, N.S., 1902 ***1860.4*** *p43*
Graf, Martin 42; Halifax, N.S., 1902 ***1860.4*** *p43*
Graf, Mathilde 2; Halifax, N.S., 1902 ***1860.4*** *p43*
Graf, Peter; America, 1879 ***5475.1*** *p186*
Graf, Peter; America, 1882 ***5475.1*** *p203*
Graff, Gustav; Wisconsin, 1884 ***6795.8*** *p69*
Graff, Henry; New York, NY, 1842 ***3274.56*** *p101*
Graff, Jacob; Louisiana, 1874-1875 ***4981.45*** *p298*
Graff, John 24; America, 1841 ***778.6*** *p143*
Graff, Lewis G.; Ohio, 1809-1852 ***4511.35*** *p18*
Graff, Tilman; Ohio, 1809-1852 ***4511.35*** *p18*
Grafs, Heinrich 21; New York, NY, 1874 ***6954.7*** *p37*
Grafs, Johann 14; New York, NY, 1874 ***6954.7*** *p37*
Grafs, Philipp 16; New York, NY, 1874 ***6954.7*** *p37*
Grafton, Francis J. 33; Ontario, 1871 ***1823.21*** *p135*
Grafton, John 25; North Carolina, 1774 ***1422.10*** *p55*
Grager, Frank; Washington, 1887 ***6015.10*** *p16*
Graham, Mrs.; Toronto, 1844 ***2910.35*** *p114*
Graham, Alexander; New York, 1738 ***8277.31*** *p115*
Graham, Alexander; North Carolina, 1823 ***1088.45*** *p11*
Graham, Alexander; North Carolina, 1835 ***1088.45*** *p11*
Graham, Alexander 39; Ontario, 1871 ***1823.21*** *p135*
Graham, Alexander 52; Ontario, 1871 ***1823.21*** *p135*
Graham, Andrew 77; Ontario, 1871 ***1823.17*** *p60*
Graham, Angus; New York, 1740 ***8277.31*** *p115*
Graham, Angus 55; Ontario, 1871 ***1823.21*** *p135*
Graham, Ann 24; New York, NY, 1835 ***5024.1*** *p137*
Graham, Archabald 60; Ontario, 1871 ***1823.21*** *p135*
Graham, Archd 45; Ontario, 1871 ***1823.21*** *p135*
Graham, Archy 48; Ontario, 1871 ***1823.21*** *p135*
Graham, Arthur 22; New York, NY, 1835 ***5024.1*** *p137*
Graham, Catharine; New York, 1738 ***8277.31*** *p116*
Graham, Catherine 47; Ontario, 1871 ***1823.21*** *p135*
Graham, Charles 50; Ontario, 1871 ***1823.17*** *p60*
Graham, Christian 53; Ontario, 1871 ***1823.21*** *p135*
Graham, Christopher 38; Ontario, 1871 ***1823.21*** *p135*
Graham, Crawford 24; Ontario, 1871 ***1823.21*** *p135*
Graham, D.; Quebec, 1870 ***8364.32*** *p23*
Graham, Daniel 20; Ontario, 1871 ***1823.21*** *p135*
Graham, David 21; Ontario, 1871 ***1823.17*** *p60*
Graham, David 38; Ontario, 1871 ***1823.21*** *p135*
Graham, David 45; Ontario, 1871 ***1823.21*** *p135*
Graham, Donald 44; Ontario, 1871 ***1823.21*** *p135*
Graham, Donald 51; Ontario, 1871 ***1823.21*** *p136*
Graham, Donald 59; Ontario, 1871 ***1823.21*** *p136*
Graham, Donald 60; Ontario, 1871 ***1823.21*** *p136*
Graham, Dugald 45; Ontario, 1871 ***1823.21*** *p136*
Graham, Dugald 65; Ontario, 1871 ***1823.21*** *p136*
Graham, Duncan 39; Ontario, 1871 ***1823.21*** *p136*
Graham, Duncan 49; Ontario, 1871 ***1823.21*** *p136*
Graham, Duncan 54; Ontario, 1871 ***1823.21*** *p136*
Graham, Duncan 56; Ontario, 1871 ***1823.21*** *p136*
Graham, Duncan 63; Ontario, 1871 ***1823.21*** *p136*
Graham, Elizabeth; New York, 1738 ***8277.31*** *p116*
Graham, Elizabeth 52; Ontario, 1871 ***1823.21*** *p136*
Graham, Fergus 35; Ontario, 1871 ***1823.17*** *p60*
Graham, Francis 36; Ontario, 1871 ***1823.17*** *p60*
Graham, Frederick; Wisconsin, 1854 ***9228.50*** *p253*
Graham, George 35; Ontario, 1871 ***1823.21*** *p136*
Graham, George 45; Ontario, 1871 ***1823.17*** *p60*
Graham, Hugh 35; Michigan, 1880 ***4491.33*** *p10*
Graham, Isabella 5; Ontario, 1871 ***1823.17*** *p60*
Graham, James 1; New York, NY, 1835 ***5024.1*** *p137*
Graham, James 34; Ontario, 1871 ***1823.17*** *p60*
Graham, James 38; Ontario, 1871 ***1823.21*** *p136*
Graham, James 38; Ontario, 1871 ***1823.21*** *p136*
Graham, James 50; Ontario, 1871 ***1823.21*** *p136*
Graham, James 56; Ontario, 1871 ***1823.17*** *p60*
Graham, James 66; Ontario, 1871 ***1823.21*** *p136*
Graham, James 70; Ontario, 1871 ***1823.21*** *p136*
Graham, James C.; North Carolina, 1866 ***1088.45*** *p11*
Graham, Jane 45; Ontario, 1871 ***1823.21*** *p136*
Graham, Jane 52; Ontario, 1871 ***1823.17*** *p60*
Graham, Jenet 57; Ontario, 1871 ***1823.21*** *p136*
Graham, John; New York, NY, 1823 ***3274.55*** *p67*
Graham, John; New York, NY, 1837 ***3274.55*** *p42*
Graham, John 28; Ontario, 1871 ***1823.21*** *p136*
Graham, John 45; Ontario, 1871 ***1823.21*** *p136*
Graham, John 48; Ontario, 1871 ***1823.21*** *p136*
Graham, John 50; Ontario, 1871 ***1823.21*** *p136*
Graham, John 60; Ontario, 1871 ***1823.21*** *p136*
Graham, John 63; Ontario, 1871 ***1823.21*** *p136*
Graham, John 67; Ontario, 1871 ***1823.21*** *p136*
Graham, Joseph 59; Ontario, 1871 ***1823.17*** *p60*
Graham, Martha 19; Michigan, 1880 ***4491.39*** *p11*
Graham, Mary; New York, 1738 ***8277.31*** *p115*
Graham, Mary 30; Ontario, 1871 ***1823.21*** *p136*
Graham, Mathew 49; Ontario, 1871 ***1823.21*** *p136*
Graham, Matthew; Toronto, 1844 ***2910.35*** *p115*
Graham, Miles; New Orleans, 1850 ***7242.30*** *p143*
Graham, Murdoc 70; Ontario, 1871 ***1823.17*** *p60*
Graham, Nancy 27; Ontario, 1871 ***1823.21*** *p136*
Graham, Nathaniel 49; Ontario, 1871 ***1823.21*** *p136*
Graham, Neil 50; Ontario, 1871 ***1823.21*** *p136*
Graham, Normom 39; Ontario, 1871 ***1823.21*** *p136*
Graham, Patrick; Toronto, 1844 ***2910.35*** *p113*
Graham, Patrick; Washington, 1882 ***2770.40*** *p135*
Graham, Peter 44; Ontario, 1871 ***1823.21*** *p136*
Graham, Peter 50; Ontario, 1871 ***1823.17*** *p60*
Graham, Robert; Boston, 1839 ***3274.55*** *p26*
Graham, Thomas 1; Michigan, 1880 ***4491.39*** *p11*
Graham, Thomas 23; Michigan, 1880 ***4491.39*** *p11*
Graham, Thomas; Ohio, 1843 ***2763.1*** *p9*
Graham, Thomas 51; Ontario, 1871 ***1823.17*** *p60*
Graham, Thomas 66; Ontario, 1871 ***1823.21*** *p136*
Graham, Thomas; Toronto, 1844 ***2910.35*** *p115*
Graham, W. F. 29; Ontario, 1871 ***1823.21*** *p136*
Graham, William 29; Ontario, 1871 ***1823.17*** *p60*
Graham, William 32; Ontario, 1871 ***1823.21*** *p136*
Graham, William 35; Ontario, 1871 ***1823.21*** *p136*
Graham, William 40; Ontario, 1871 ***1823.21*** *p136*
Graham, William 50; Ontario, 1871 ***1823.21*** *p136*
Graham, William 60; Ontario, 1871 ***1823.17*** *p60*
Graham, William 84; Ontario, 1871 ***1823.17*** *p60*
Graham, William; Philadelphia, 1883 ***8513.31*** *p310*
Graham, Wm.; St. John, N.B., 1848 ***2978.15*** *p41*
Grahame, Abigail 55; Ontario, 1871 ***1823.21*** *p137*
Grahame, Duncan 54; Ontario, 1871 ***1823.21*** *p137*
Grahams, Daniel; South Carolina, 1813 ***3208.30*** *p18*
Grahams, Daniel; South Carolina, 1813 ***3208.30*** *p31*
Grahn, . . .; America, 1832 ***7420.1*** *p6*
Grahn, Gustav Wilhelm; Wisconsin, 1895 ***6795.8*** *p138*
Grahser, Katharina; Ohio, 1884 ***5475.1*** *p316*
Graig, John 50; Ontario, 1871 ***1823.21*** *p137*
Grain, Mathurin 32; Quebec, 1662 ***9221.17*** *p486*
Graineau, Frederick 22; Louisiana, 1842 ***778.6*** *p143*
Grainger, Richard; North Carolina, 1852 ***1088.45*** *p11*
Grainshiells, Charles 26; Ontario, 1871 ***1823.17*** *p60*
Graithe, . . . 3; America, 1843 ***778.6*** *p143*
Graithe, . . . 4; America, 1843 ***778.6*** *p143*
Graithe, Mrs. 30; America, 1843 ***778.6*** *p143*
Graithe, Alexandre 32; America, 1843 ***778.6*** *p143*
Grajewski, Michael; Detroit, 1890 ***9980.23*** *p97*
Grajper, Andrzej 45; New York, NY, 1920 ***930.50*** *p49*
Grall, Louise; America, 1928 ***8023.44*** *p374*
Grambo, Franz; America, 1871 ***5475.1*** *p171*
Grames, Nancy; Ontario, 1835 ***3160.1*** *p150*
Grames, Nancy; Prescott, Ont., 1835 ***3289.1*** *p61*
Gramm, Adam 3 months; New York, NY, 1893 ***1883.7*** *p42*
Gramm, Adam 24; New York, NY, 1893 ***1883.7*** *p42*
Gramm, Adam 51; New York, NY, 1893 ***1883.7*** *p42*
Gramm, Christina 24; New York, NY, 1893 ***1883.7*** *p42*
Gramm, Christina 61; New York, NY, 1893 ***1883.7*** *p42*
Gramm, Friedrich 27; New York, NY, 1893 ***1883.7*** *p42*
Gramm, Georg Jakob; New York, NY, 1889 ***3366.30*** *p70*
Gramm, Jacob 19; New York, NY, 1893 ***1883.7*** *p42*
Grammond, Elisa 12; Missouri, 1845 ***778.6*** *p143*
Grammond, Jean 43; Missouri, 1845 ***778.6*** *p143*
Grammond, Jeanette 40; Missouri, 1845 ***778.6*** *p143*
Grammond, Joseph 4; Missouri, 1845 ***778.6*** *p143*
Gramon, Patrick 55; Ontario, 1871 ***1823.21*** *p137*
Grams, August; Wisconsin, 1870 ***6795.8*** *p130*
Grams, Gusta Lena; Wisconsin, 1897 ***6795.8*** *p81*
Grams, Ottilie Amelia Theresa; Wisconsin, 1893 ***6795.8*** *p73*
Gramse, Augusta; Wisconsin, 1896 ***6795.8*** *p130*
Gramse, Reinhold; Wisconsin, 1898 ***6795.8*** *p197*
Gramse, Rosina; Wisconsin, 1904 ***6795.8*** *p177*
Granade, John; North Carolina, 1710 ***3629.40*** *p4*
Granade, Joseph; North Carolina, 1710 ***3629.40*** *p4*
Granahan, James; Philadelphia, 1867 ***8513.31*** *p310*
*Wife:*Margaret Dunsheath
Granahan, Margaret Dunsheath *SEE* Granahan, James
Granajean, Marie 35; America, 1843 ***778.6*** *p143*
Granback, Gustaf; Chicago, 1879-1886 ***1865.50*** *p48*
Granback, Josephina; Chicago, 1883-1886 ***1865.50*** *p48*
Granbeck, Gustaf; Chicago, 1879-1886 ***1865.50*** *p48*
Granbeck, Josephina; Chicago, 1883-1886 ***1865.50*** *p48*
Granberg, Carolina; St. Paul, MN, 1896 ***1865.50*** *p48*
Granberg, Rudolph; Cleveland, OH, 1894-1898 ***9722.10*** *p119*
Grand, Joseph 23; Louisiana, 1845 ***778.6*** *p143*
Grandchamp, Jean; Quebec, 1654 ***9221.17*** *p305*
Grandel, Jean Jacques; Illinois, 1856 ***6079.1*** *p6*
Grandelaudins, Jean 38; America, 1842 ***778.6*** *p143*
Granderye, Marie 17; Quebec, 1662 ***9221.17*** *p486*
Grandin, . . .; Boston, 1769 ***9228.50*** *p5*
Grandin, . . .; Fargo, ND,, 1800-1899 ***9228.50*** *p254*
Grandin, Amice; Boston, 1769 ***9228.50*** *p48*
Grandin, Amice; Boston, 1769 ***9228.50*** *p253*
*Relative:*Eliz.
Grandin, Daniel; New Jersey, 1695-1742 ***9228.50*** *p253*
Grandin, Eliz. *SEE* Grandin, Amice
Grandin, Helen; America, 1825 ***9228.50*** *p253*
Grandin, Jeanne; Quebec, 1671 ***4514.3*** *p319*
Grandin, Marie; Quebec, 1668 ***4514.3*** *p319*
Grandin, Marie; Quebec, 1670 ***4514.3*** *p319*
Grandin, Marie 42; Quebec, 1651 ***9221.17*** *p242*
*Daughter:*Marie-Clemence 22
Grandiniere, Jacques 28; Quebec, 1647 ***9221.17*** *p184*
Grandjean, Adrienne; Quebec, 1665 ***4514.3*** *p320*
Grandjean, Alexis 5; Illinois, 1845 ***778.6*** *p143*
Grand-Jean, Catherine Mercier *SEE* Grand-Jean, Jean

Grandjean, Celine 2; Illinois, 1845 ***778.6*** *p143*
Grandjean, Felicite 10; Illinois, 1845 ***778.6*** *p143*
Grandjean, Francoise 36; Illinois, 1845 ***778.6*** *p143*
Grandjean, Jean 30; Mississippi, 1845-1846 ***778.6*** *p143*
Grand-Jean, Jean; Montreal, 1649 ***9221.17*** *p221*
*Wife:*Catherine Mercier
Grandjean, Jean Louis 32; Illinois, 1845 ***778.6*** *p143*
Grandlemire, Peter; New Jersey, 1735-1774 ***927.31*** *p3*
Grandmaison, Eleonore de 22; Quebec, 1641 ***9221.17*** *p102*
Grandmaison, Laurent 24; Montreal, 1662 ***9221.17*** *p496*
Grandmesnil, Jean; Quebec, 1645 ***9221.17*** *p158*
Grandmont, Rene 22; Montreal, 1653 ***9221.17*** *p292*
Grandmontagne, Christine Schneider 26 *SEE* Grandmontagne, Nik.
Grandmontagne, Nik.; America, 1865 ***5475.1*** *p152*
*Wife:*Christine Schneider
*Son:*Rudolf
*Son:*Otto
Grandmontagne, Otto *SEE* Grandmontagne, Nik.
Grandmontagne, Rudolf *SEE* Grandmontagne, Nik.
Grandpra, Ms. 17; Cuba, 1840 ***778.6*** *p143*
Grandval, Charles; Quebec, 1644 ***9221.17*** *p139*
Grandy, John; Washington, 1885 ***2770.40*** *p194*
Grandy, Marie 17; Quebec, 1662 ***9221.17*** *p486*
Grane, John; Toronto, 1844 ***2910.35*** *p115*
Granen, James; Louisiana, 1874-1875 ***4981.45*** *p29*
Graner, Charles 21; America, 1847 ***778.6*** *p143*
Granet, B. 45; New Orleans, 1840 ***778.6*** *p143*
Graney, Bridget; New Orleans, 1851 ***7242.30*** *p143*
Graney, Thomas 40; Ontario, 1871 ***1823.17*** *p60*
Grangeon, Marie-Madeleine; Quebec, 1667 ***4514.3*** *p320*
Granger, Augustus 46; Ontario, 1871 ***1823.21*** *p137*
Granger, Catherine; Quebec, 1673 ***4514.3*** *p320*
Granger, Edward 44; Ontario, 1871 ***1823.21*** *p137*
Granger, Harriet 13; Quebec, 1870 ***8364.32*** *p23*
Granger, Louis 32; Missouri, 1845 ***778.6*** *p143*
Granger, William 18; Ontario, 1871 ***1823.21*** *p137*
Granier, Wilhelm; Louisiana, 1874 ***4981.45*** *p132*
Grannan, William 61; Ontario, 1871 ***1823.21*** *p137*
Granpoirier, Emanuel 61; New Orleans, 1847 ***778.6*** *p143*
Granpoirier, Hortense 18; New Orleans, 1847 ***778.6*** *p143*
Granpoirier, Julie 30; New Orleans, 1847 ***778.6*** *p143*
Granpoirier, Justine 22; New Orleans, 1847 ***778.6*** *p143*
Granpoirier, Louis 26; New Orleans, 1847 ***778.6*** *p143*
Granpoirier, Pierre 19; New Orleans, 1847 ***778.6*** *p144*
Granqvist, S.P.; New York, NY, 1843 ***6412.40*** *p147*
Granschow, Friedrich; Wisconsin, 1896 ***6795.8*** *p106*
Grant, Alexander 63; Ontario, 1871 ***1823.21*** *p137*
Grant, Angus 28; New York, NY, 1835 ***5024.1*** *p136*
Grant, Beeney 27; Ontario, 1871 ***1823.21*** *p137*
Grant, Betsey 28 *SEE* Grant, John
Grant, Charles 44; Ontario, 1871 ***1823.21*** *p137*
Grant, Charles 65; Ontario, 1871 ***1823.21*** *p137*
Grant, Christina 55; Ontario, 1871 ***1823.21*** *p137*
Grant, David 24; Ontario, 1871 ***1823.21*** *p137*
Grant, Elizabeth 45; Ontario, 1871 ***1823.21*** *p137*
Grant, Frederick; Jamaica, 1782 ***8529.30*** *p13A*
Grant, George 20; North Carolina, 1774 ***1422.10*** *p59*
Grant, George 29; Ontario, 1871 ***1823.21*** *p137*
Grant, George 31; Ontario, 1871 ***1823.21*** *p137*
Grant, Gregor 60; Ontario, 1871 ***1823.21*** *p137*
Grant, James 29; Michigan, 1880 ***4491.36*** *p8*
Grant, James; New York, NY, 1841 ***3274.56*** *p100*
Grant, James 23; Ontario, 1871 ***1823.21*** *p137*
Grant, James 38; Ontario, 1871 ***1823.17*** *p60*
Grant, James 48; Ontario, 1871 ***1823.21*** *p137*
Grant, James 53; Ontario, 1871 ***1823.21*** *p137*
Grant, James 15; Quebec, 1870 ***8364.32*** *p23*
Grant, James W.; New Brunswick, 1855-1955 ***9228.50*** *p315*
Grant, Jane 38; Ontario, 1871 ***1823.17*** *p60*
Grant, Janet 19; New York, NY, 1835 ***5024.1*** *p136*
Grant, John 45; Ohio, 1880 ***4879.40*** *p257*
Grant, John 45; Ohio, 1880 ***4879.40*** *p259*
*Sister:*Betsey 28
*Brother:*Phillip 28
Grant, John 22; Ontario, 1871 ***1823.21*** *p137*
Grant, John 23; Ontario, 1871 ***1823.21*** *p137*
Grant, John 33; Ontario, 1871 ***1823.17*** *p60*
Grant, John 39; Ontario, 1871 ***1823.17*** *p60*
Grant, John 46; Ontario, 1871 ***1823.17*** *p60*
Grant, John; Quebec, 1786 ***1416.15*** *p8*
Grant, John; Quebec, 1786 ***1416.15*** *p9*
Grant, Lawrence 30; Ontario, 1871 ***1823.21*** *p137*
Grant, Marcus 60; Ontario, 1871 ***1823.21*** *p137*
Grant, Margaret 30; Ontario, 1871 ***1823.21*** *p137*
Grant, Margeret 70; Ontario, 1871 ***1823.21*** *p137*
Grant, Matthew; Massachusetts, 1630 ***117.5*** *p157*
*Wife:*Priscilla
*Daughter:*Priscilla
Grant, Patrick; Jamaica, 1783 ***8529.30*** *p13A*
Grant, Peter; Boston, 1774 ***8529.30*** *p3A*
Grant, Peter; Quebec, 1786 ***1416.15*** *p8*
Grant, Phillip 28 *SEE* Grant, John
Grant, Priscilla *SEE* Grant, Matthew
Grant, Priscilla *SEE* Grant, Matthew
Grant, Sarah 49; Ontario, 1871 ***1823.21*** *p137*
Grant, William 25; Ontario, 1871 ***1823.21*** *p137*
Grant, William 28; Ontario, 1871 ***1823.21*** *p137*
Grant, William 34; Ontario, 1871 ***1823.21*** *p137*
Grant, William 38; Ontario, 1871 ***1823.21*** *p137*
Grant, William 40; Ontario, 1871 ***1823.21*** *p137*
Grant, William 48; Ontario, 1871 ***1823.21*** *p137*
Grant, William 55; Ontario, 1871 ***1823.21*** *p137*
Grant, William 61; Ontario, 1871 ***1823.21*** *p137*
Grant, William 70; Ontario, 1871 ***1823.21*** *p137*
Grant, William R.; Philadelphia, 1834 ***7074.20*** *p132*
Grante, Charles; Quebec, 1659 ***9221.17*** *p413*
Granthims, Catherine 67; Ontario, 1871 ***1823.21*** *p137*
Granville, . . .; North Carolina, 1700-1799 ***9228.50*** *p55*
Granville, Mr.; New Hampshire, n.d. ***9228.50*** *p254*
Granville, Mr.; Newbury, MA, 1762 ***9228.50*** *p254*
Gras, Mr. 27; America, 1745 ***778.6*** *p144*
Gras, Mr. 20; Port uncertain, 1843 ***778.6*** *p144*
Gras, Gertrud 26; Galveston, TX, 1844 ***3967.10*** *p375*
Graser, A. Margarethe; America, 1854 ***5475.1*** *p459*
Graser, Friedrich *SEE* Graser, Kath. Kramer
Graser, Heinrich *SEE* Graser, Kath. Kramer
Graser, Karl *SEE* Graser, Kath. Kramer
Graser, Kath. 38; America, 1890 ***5475.1*** *p52*
*Son:*Friedrich
*Son:*Heinrich
*Son:*Karl
*Son:*Ludw. Hermann
*Daughter:*Katharina
Graser, Katharina *SEE* Graser, Kath. Kramer
Graser, Ludw. Hermann *SEE* Graser, Kath. Kramer
Grasieux, Eugenie 29; America, 1843 ***778.6*** *p144*
Grasieux, Francois 27; America, 1843 ***778.6*** *p144*
Grasieux, Fransine 3; America, 1843 ***778.6*** *p144*
Grasieux, Jean 32; America, 1843 ***778.6*** *p144*
Grasmuck, Adam 6 *SEE* Grasmuck, Mrs. Franz
Grasmuck, Franz; America, 1852 ***2526.43*** *p147*
Grasmuck, Mrs. Franz; America, 1853 ***2526.43*** *p147*
*Daughter:*Magdalena
*Son:*Wilhelm
*Son:*Adam
Grasmuck, Magdalena 8 *SEE* Grasmuck, Mrs. Franz
Grasmuck, Wilhelm 4 *SEE* Grasmuck, Mrs. Franz
Grason, Susan 42; Ontario, 1871 ***1823.21*** *p138*
Grass, Mr. 24; America, 1843 ***778.6*** *p144*
Grass, Christian; Ohio, 1809-1852 ***4511.35*** *p18*
Grass, Henry; Ohio, 1809-1852 ***4511.35*** *p18*
Grass, John; Ohio, 1809-1852 ***4511.35*** *p18*
Grass, Lewis; Ohio, 1809-1852 ***4511.35*** *p18*
Grass, Margarethe 48; America, 1862 ***5475.1*** *p500*
Grasser, Joseph 18; New Orleans, 1848 ***778.6*** *p144*
Grassien, Henry 31; America, 1843 ***778.6*** *p144*
Grassin, R. Vi.cent 31; Port uncertain, 1846 ***778.6*** *p144*
Grassiot, . . . 27; Quebec, 1660 ***9221.17*** *p436*
*Wife:*Madeleine Michaud
Grassiot, Jacques 25; Quebec, 1656 ***9221.17*** *p337*
Grassiot, Madeleine Michaud *SEE* Grassiot, . . .
Grassmann, Katharina Elisabetha 48; New York, 1859 ***2526.43*** *p127*
Grasza, Andrew; Detroit, 1929 ***1640.55*** *p117*
Grataloupayabruf, Js. 48; America, 1842 ***778.6*** *p144*
Grater, John George; Ohio, 1809-1852 ***4511.35*** *p18*
Grathwohl, Gottlieb; New York, 1860 ***358.56*** *p4*
Graton, Claude *SEE* Graton, Mathurine
Graton, Helene *SEE* Graton, Mathurine
Graton, Marguerite Moncion *SEE* Graton, Mathurine
Graton, Mathurine; Quebec, 1670 ***4514.3*** *p320*
*Brother:*Claude
*Niece:*Rene
*Sister-In-Law:*Marguerite Moncion
*Niece:*Helene
Graton, Rene *SEE* Graton, Mathurine
Gratz, Johann; America, 1860 ***5475.1*** *p273*
Gratz, Johann Jakob; America, 1874 ***5475.1*** *p285*
Grau, Gottleib; Ohio, 1840-1897 ***8365.35*** *p16*
Grau, Gottlieb; America, 1883 ***179.55*** *p19*
Grau, Jakob Friedrich; America, 1867 ***179.55*** *p19*
Grau, Johann Gottlieb; America, 1871 ***179.55*** *p19*
Grau, Karl Wilhelm; America, 1867 ***179.55*** *p19*
Grau, Wilhelm Jakob; America, 1883 ***179.55*** *p19*
Graubner, Elise; America, 1868 ***7919.3*** *p529*
With child
Grau Family ; America, 1852 ***5475.1*** *p52*
Grault, Babett 6; Missouri, 1846 ***778.6*** *p144*
Grault, Francois 4; Missouri, 1846 ***778.6*** *p144*
Grault, J. Pierre 42; Missouri, 1846 ***778.6*** *p144*
Grault, Jean 15; Missouri, 1846 ***778.6*** *p144*
Grault, Joseph 16; Missouri, 1846 ***778.6*** *p144*
Grault, Marquerite 46; Missouri, 1846 ***778.6*** *p144*
Grault, Philip; Boston, 1769 ***9228.50*** *p256*
Graus, Charley A.; Iowa, 1896 ***1211.15*** *p10*
Grausman, Mores; North Carolina, 1857 ***1088.45*** *p11*
Grautt, . . .; Boston, 1769 ***9228.50*** *p5*
Grautt, Philip; Boston, 1769 ***9228.50*** *p48*
Grautt, Philip; Boston, 1769 ***9228.50*** *p256*
Grave, J.H.; New York, NY, 1847 ***6412.40*** *p151*
Gravel, George; Philadelphia, 1837 ***5720.10*** *p382*
Gravel, Masse 26; Quebec, 1641 ***9221.17*** *p104*
Graveline, Urbain 20; Montreal, 1653 ***9221.17*** *p281*
Gravell, Frank 32; Ohio, 1880 ***4879.40*** *p260*
Gravelle, Frank 32; Ohio, 1880 ***4879.40*** *p260*
Graves, Mrs.; California, 1868 ***1131.61*** *p89*
With sister
Graves, Daniel 59; Ontario, 1871 ***1823.21*** *p138*
Graves, Elinor; Maryland, 1671-1672 ***1236.25*** *p45*
Graves, James 40; Ontario, 1871 ***1823.21*** *p138*
Graves, John W. 38; Michigan, 1880 ***4491.36*** *p8*
Graves, Otto B. 42; Ontario, 1871 ***1823.21*** *p138*
Graves, Simon; Colorado, 1900 ***1029.59*** *p33*
Graves, Simon; Portland, ME, 1868 ***1029.59*** *p34*
Gravier, Ms. 22; New Orleans, 1748 ***778.6*** *p144*
Gravois, Marie; Quebec, 1667 ***4514.3*** *p320*
Gray, Mr. 30; America, 1847 ***778.6*** *p144*
Gray, Allen 39; Ontario, 1871 ***1823.17*** *p60*
Gray, Anthony 68; Ontario, 1871 ***1823.21*** *p138*
Gray, Archibald 40; Ontario, 1871 ***1823.21*** *p138*
Gray, Archibald 42; Ontario, 1871 ***1823.17*** *p60*
Gray, Archibald 60; Ontario, 1871 ***1823.17*** *p60*
Gray, Bartholew 25; Michigan, 1880 ***4491.30*** *p14*
Gray, Bridget 43; Ontario, 1871 ***1823.21*** *p138*
Gray, Daniel 46; Ontario, 1871 ***1823.21*** *p138*
Gray, David 62; Ontario, 1871 ***1823.17*** *p60*
Gray, Donald 35; Ontario, 1871 ***1823.17*** *p60*
Gray, Elinor; Maryland, 1671-1672 ***1236.25*** *p45*
Gray, Elizabeth; New York, 1835-1866 ***9228.50*** *p374*
Gray, George; Boston, 1720 ***9228.50*** *p254*
Gray, George; Boston, 1767 ***1642*** *p38*
With wife
Gray, George 28; Ontario, 1871 ***1823.21*** *p138*
Gray, George 29; Ontario, 1871 ***1823.17*** *p60*
Gray, George 36; Ontario, 1871 ***1823.21*** *p138*
Gray, George 40; Ontario, 1871 ***1823.17*** *p61*
Gray, George Duncan; Ohio, 1840-1897 ***8365.35*** *p16*
Gray, Henrey 50; Ontario, 1871 ***1823.17*** *p61*
Gray, Herbert 60; Ontario, 1871 ***1823.21*** *p138*
Gray, James; Marston's Wharf, 1782 ***8529.30*** *p12*
Gray, James 44; Ontario, 1871 ***1823.21*** *p138*
Gray, James 50; Ontario, 1871 ***1823.21*** *p138*
Gray, James 65; Ontario, 1871 ***1823.21*** *p138*
Gray, Jane 55; Ontario, 1871 ***1823.21*** *p138*
Gray, Johanna 65; Ontario, 1871 ***1823.21*** *p138*
Gray, John; Boston, 1766 ***1642*** *p36*
Gray, John 28; Ontario, 1871 ***1823.17*** *p61*
Gray, John 29; Ontario, 1871 ***1823.21*** *p138*
Gray, John 30; Ontario, 1871 ***1823.21*** *p138*
Gray, John 40; Ontario, 1871 ***1823.21*** *p138*
Gray, John 73; Ontario, 1871 ***1823.21*** *p138*
Gray, John Jay 46; Ontario, 1871 ***1823.17*** *p61*
Gray, Joseph B. 41; Ontario, 1871 ***1823.21*** *p138*
Gray, Margaret 64; Ontario, 1871 ***1823.17*** *p61*
Gray, Mathew 50; Ontario, 1871 ***1823.21*** *p138*
Gray, Michael 25; Ontario, 1871 ***1823.21*** *p138*
Gray, Niel 59; Ontario, 1871 ***1823.21*** *p138*
Gray, Richard K.; Ohio, 1809-1852 ***4511.35*** *p18*
Gray, Robert 24; Ohio, 1880 ***4879.40*** *p259*
Gray, Robert 38; Ontario, 1871 ***1823.21*** *p138*
Gray, Robert 40; Ontario, 1871 ***1823.17*** *p61*
Gray, Robert 60; Ontario, 1871 ***1823.21*** *p138*
Gray, Robert 63; Ontario, 1871 ***1823.17*** *p61*
Gray, Sidney R.S.; Washington, 1889 ***2770.40*** *p27*
Gray, Thomas; Marston's Wharf, 1782 ***8529.30*** *p12*
Gray, Thomas; Massachusetts, 1730 ***1642*** *p91*
Gray, Thomas 50; Ontario, 1871 ***1823.21*** *p138*
Gray, William; Illinois, 1855 ***6079.1*** *p6*
Gray, William; North Carolina, 1812 ***1088.45*** *p11*
Gray, William 48; Ontario, 1871 ***1823.17*** *p61*
Gray, William 57; Ontario, 1871 ***1823.21*** *p138*
Gray, William Wall 56; Ontario, 1871 ***1823.21*** *p138*
Graybill, Christian; Ohio, 1809-1852 ***4511.35*** *p18*
Graydon, Alexander 40; Ontario, 1871 ***1823.21*** *p138*
Graydon, S. H. 49; Ontario, 1871 ***1823.21*** *p138*
Grayham, John; Virginia, 1652 ***6254.4*** *p243*
Grayson, Alice 29; Ontario, 1871 ***1823.21*** *p138*
Grayson, John 17; Ontario, 1871 ***1823.21*** *p138*
Grayson, Michael 50; Ontario, 1871 ***1823.21*** *p139*
Grayson, William 59; Ontario, 1871 ***1823.21*** *p139*
Grazer, Peter; Ohio, 1809-1852 ***4511.35*** *p18*
Grazier, Daniel; Ipswich, MA, 1661 ***1642*** *p70*
Gready, John; Boston, 1749 ***1642*** *p46*
Greason, Walter 58; Ontario, 1871 ***1823.21*** *p139*

Greaves, Eddison 30; Ontario, 1871 ***1823.21*** *p139*
Greay, John; California, 1868 ***1131.61*** *p89*
Greay, M. H.; California, 1868 ***1131.61*** *p89*
Grebe, Mr.; New Orleans, 1850 ***7420.1*** *p73*
With wife
With child 4
With son 9
With son 7
With daughter 5
With son 12
Grebe, Heinrich; Venezuela, 1843 ***3899.5*** *p546*
Grece, Frances 61; Ontario, 1871 ***1823.21*** *p139*
Grece, Horato 68; Ontario, 1871 ***1823.21*** *p139*
Greeley, Andrew; Massachusetts, 1638-1669 ***9228.50*** *p255*
Greeley, Thomas; Portsmouth, NH, 1723 ***9228.50*** *p255*
Green, A. P.; Washington, 1889 ***2770.40*** *p27*
Green, Ann 13; Quebec, 1870 ***8364.32*** *p23*
Green, Anna 22; Michigan, 1880 ***4491.36*** *p9*
Green, Borni; Boston, 1763 ***1642*** *p32*
Green, C.; Louisiana, 1874 ***4981.45*** *p295*
Green, Clem; Marston's Wharf, 1782 ***8529.30*** *p12*
Green, Daniel; New York, 1782 ***8529.30*** *p12*
Green, Dennis; New York, 1776 ***8529.30*** *p6*
Green, Edward; America, 1780 ***8529.30*** *p12*
Green, Edward; North Carolina, 1860 ***1088.45*** *p11*
Green, Edward 32; Ontario, 1871 ***1823.17*** *p61*
Green, Edward 55; Ontario, 1871 ***1823.21*** *p139*
Green, Eliza 48; Ontario, 1871 ***1823.21*** *p139*
Green, Elizabeth 34; Michigan, 1880 ***4491.39*** *p12*
Green, Elizabeth 74; Michigan, 1880 ***4491.33*** *p10*
Green, Frank; Colorado, 1873 ***1029.59*** *p34*
Green, George 38; Ontario, 1871 ***1823.17*** *p61*
Green, Gus; Colorado, 1894 ***1029.59*** *p34*
Green, Gus; New York, NY, 1888 ***1029.59*** *p1A*
Green, Henry 27; Ontario, 1871 ***1823.17*** *p61*
Green, Henry 33; Ontario, 1871 ***1823.21*** *p139*
Green, Henry 15; Quebec, 1870 ***8364.32*** *p23*
Green, Isaac; Ohio, 1840-1897 ***8365.35*** *p16*
Green, James; North Carolina, 1820-1825 ***1088.45*** *p11*
Green, James 65; Ontario, 1871 ***1823.17*** *p61*
Green, Jamison 25; New York, NY, 1878 ***9253.2*** *p44*
Green, Jane E. 37; Ontario, 1871 ***1823.21*** *p139*
Green, Jno.; Maryland, 1674 ***1236.25*** *p50*
Green, John 46; Ontario, 1871 ***1823.17*** *p61*
Green, John 48; Ontario, 1871 ***1823.17*** *p61*
Green, John H.; Washington, 1889 ***2770.40*** *p27*
Green, Joseph 85; Ontario, 1871 ***1823.21*** *p139*
Green, Leander; Washington, 1883 ***2770.40*** *p136*
Green, Maria 11; Quebec, 1870 ***8364.32*** *p23*
Green, Maria 31; Quebec, 1870 ***8364.32*** *p23*
Green, Mary 45; Ontario, 1871 ***1823.21*** *p139*
Green, Mary 67; Ontario, 1871 ***1823.21*** *p139*
Green, Mary Ann 52; Ontario, 1871 ***1823.21*** *p139*
Green, Michael; Colorado, 1869 ***1029.59*** *p34*
Green, Pat; St. John, N.B., 1847 ***2978.15*** *p38*
Green, Richard; North Carolina, 1842 ***1088.45*** *p11*
Green, Samuel; New York, 1782 ***8529.30*** *p12*
Green, Samuel 40; Ontario, 1871 ***1823.21*** *p139*
Green, William; New York, 1776 ***8529.30*** *p6*
Green, William 27; Ontario, 1871 ***1823.21*** *p139*
Green, William 32; Ontario, 1871 ***1823.17*** *p61*
Green, William 34; Ontario, 1871 ***1823.21*** *p139*
Green, William 36; Ontario, 1871 ***1823.21*** *p139*
Greenacre, John 70; Ontario, 1871 ***1823.21*** *p139*
Greenaway, Charles 45; Ontario, 1871 ***1823.21*** *p139*
Greenberg, Bere 11; New York, NY, 1894 ***6512.1*** *p184*
Greenberg, David 14; New York, NY, 1894 ***6512.1*** *p184*
Greenberg, Raphael; North Carolina, 1860 ***1088.45*** *p12*
Greenberg, W.; California, 1868 ***1131.61*** *p90*
Greenblat, Morris 23; New York, NY, 1894 ***6512.1*** *p229*
Greene, David; New York, NY, 1841 ***3274.56*** *p100*
Greene, Tho.; Maryland, 1672 ***1236.25*** *p46*
Greene, Tho. 24; Virginia, 1635 ***1183.3*** *p31*
Greene, Thomas 33; Ontario, 1871 ***1823.21*** *p139*
Greenfield, David 28; Michigan, 1880 ***4491.30*** *p14*
Greenhough, John 44; Ontario, 1871 ***1823.17*** *p61*
Greening, George 38; Ontario, 1871 ***1823.17*** *p61*
Greenlee, Alex 47; Ontario, 1871 ***1823.21*** *p139*
Greenlees, Alx 57; Ontario, 1871 ***1823.17*** *p61*
Greenlees, Angus 38; Ontario, 1871 ***1823.17*** *p61*
Greenlees, David 43; Ontario, 1871 ***1823.17*** *p61*
Greenlees, Donald 30; Ontario, 1871 ***1823.17*** *p61*
Greenlees, John 25; North Carolina, 1774 ***1422.10*** *p57*
Greenlees, John 25; North Carolina, 1774 ***1422.10*** *p62*
Greenlees, Mary 25; North Carolina, 1774 ***1422.10*** *p57*
Greenlees, Mary 25; North Carolina, 1774 ***1422.10*** *p62*
Greenless, Robert 24; Ontario, 1871 ***1823.21*** *p139*
Greenly, Hellen 63; Michigan, 1880 ***4491.39*** *p12*
Greensalde, James; Salem, MA, 1711 ***9228.50*** *p255*
Greenslade, Ann; Salem, MA, 1677 ***9228.50*** *p523*
Greenslade, George 69; Ontario, 1871 ***1823.21*** *p139*
Greenslade, James 37; Ontario, 1871 ***1823.21*** *p139*
Greenslet, James; Salem, MA, 1711 ***9228.50*** *p255*
Greenspoon, Anna *SEE* Greenspoon, Louis I.
Greenspoon, Anna 36; Colorado, 1923 ***1029.59*** *p34*
Greenspoon, Gertrude M. 8 *SEE* Greenspoon, Louis I.
Greenspoon, Louis I.; Boston, 1894 ***1029.59*** *p34*
Greenspoon, Louis I.; Colorado, 1920 ***1029.59*** *p34*
*Wife:*Anna
*Child:*Morris A.
*Child:*Gertrude M.
Greenspoon, Morris A. 12 *SEE* Greenspoon, Louis I.
Greenwalt, Michael; Ohio, 1809-1852 ***4511.35*** *p18*
Greenway, Elizabeth *SEE* Greenway, John
Greenway, James 30; Ontario, 1871 ***1823.21*** *p139*
Greenway, John; Massachusetts, 1630 ***117.5*** *p157*
*Wife:*Mary
*Daughter:*Elizabeth
*Daughter:*Susanna
*Daughter:*Katherine
Greenway, Katherine *SEE* Greenway, John
Greenway, Mary *SEE* Greenway, John
Greenway, Mary; Massachusetts, 1635 ***117.5*** *p157*
Greenway, Susanna *SEE* Greenway, John
Greenway, Ursula; Massachusetts, 1635 ***117.5*** *p157*
Greenway, William W. 33; Ontario, 1871 ***1823.21*** *p139*
Greenwood, George; Washington, 1878 ***2770.40*** *p134*
Greenwood, George; Washington, 1883 ***2770.40*** *p136*
Greenwood, Richard 38; Ontario, 1871 ***1823.21*** *p139*
Greenwood, William; North Carolina, 1844 ***1088.45*** *p12*
Greer, Clarinda 66; Ontario, 1871 ***1823.21*** *p139*
Greer, John; Louisiana, 1874-1875 ***4981.45*** *p29*
Greer, Mary 28; Ontario, 1871 ***1823.17*** *p61*
Greer, William 65; Ontario, 1871 ***1823.17*** *p61*
Greer, William H.; Ohio, 1809-1852 ***4511.35*** *p18*
Greff, Antoinette; America, 1883 ***5475.1*** *p131*
Greff, Dorothea 41; America, 1854 ***5475.1*** *p53*
Greff, Francoise 27; Missouri, 1848 ***778.6*** *p144*
Greff, Magdalena 59; America, 1854 ***5475.1*** *p53*
Greff, Peter; America, 1853 ***5475.1*** *p53*
Greffard, Joseph Josue; Yamaska, Que., 1786 ***9228.50*** *p255*
Greg, John 38; Ontario, 1871 ***1823.17*** *p61*
Greg, Margart 22; New York, NY, 1835 ***5024.1*** *p137*
Gregart, Charles 30; New Orleans, 1847 ***778.6*** *p144*
Greger, Albertina; Wisconsin, 1894 ***6795.8*** *p57*
Greger, Karl; New York, NY, 1889 ***3366.30*** *p70*
Greger, Martin; New York, NY, 1889 ***3366.30*** *p70*
Greger, Martin; Wisconsin, 1890 ***6795.8*** *p57*
Gregg, Ephraim L.; North Carolina, 1857 ***1088.45*** *p12*
Gregg, William 29; Ontario, 1871 ***1823.21*** *p139*
Gregier, August; Wisconsin, 1885 ***6795.8*** *p57*
Gregoire, . . .; Port uncertain, 1844 ***778.6*** *p144*
Gregoire, Mr. 45; America, 1846 ***778.6*** *p144*
Gregoire, Mrs. 32; America, 1848 ***778.6*** *p144*
Gregoire, Mrs. 36; Port uncertain, 1844 ***778.6*** *p144*
Gregoire, J. B. 35; America, 1848 ***778.6*** *p144*
Gregoire, Louis; Montreal, 1653 ***9221.17*** *p291*
Gregoire, Pascal 34; America, 1842 ***778.6*** *p144*
Gregoire DuCriel, Jacques; Quebec, 1644 ***9221.17*** *p142*
Gregor, Jan; Wisconsin, 1853 ***2853.20*** *p303*
Gregor, Vaclav; Kansas, 1869-1910 ***2853.20*** *p201*
Gregoris, P. 22; Port uncertain, 1846 ***778.6*** *p144*
Gregorius, A. Maria 40; Brazil, 1864 ***5475.1*** *p501*
Gregorius, Barbara; Pittsburgh, 1893 ***5475.1*** *p409*
Gregorius, Jakob 20; America, 1849 ***5475.1*** *p486*
Gregorius, Johann; America, 1847 ***5475.1*** *p485*
Gregorius, Johann; Brazil, 1853 ***5475.1*** *p439*
Gregorius, Karl 19; America, 1849 ***5475.1*** *p476*
Gregorius, Kath.; America, 1867 ***5475.1*** *p487*
Gregorius, Nikolaus 27; America, 1800-1899 ***5475.1*** *p419*
Gregorova, Frantiska; Wisconsin, 1854 ***2853.20*** *p513*
With parents
Gregory, Alfred 29; Ontario, 1871 ***1823.21*** *p139*
Gregory, Annie 15; Quebec, 1870 ***8364.32*** *p23*
Gregory, Daniel; New York, NY, 1830 ***3274.55*** *p42*
Gregory, Elijah 67; Ontario, 1871 ***1823.21*** *p139*
Gregory, Henry 22; Ontario, 1871 ***1823.17*** *p61*
Gregory, Jeremiah; New York, NY, 1830 ***3274.55*** *p43*
Gregory, John 37; Quebec, 1858 ***9228.50*** *p255*
Gregory, Joseph; Marblehead, MA, 1790 ***9228.50*** *p593*
Gregory, Joseph; Ohio, 1836 ***3580.20*** *p32*
Gregory, Joseph; Ohio, 1836 ***6020.12*** *p7*
Gregory, Margaret; Philadelphia, 1867 ***8513.31*** *p417*
Gregory, Martha 17; Quebec, 1870 ***8364.32*** *p23*
Gregory, Matilda 12; Quebec, 1870 ***8364.32*** *p23*
Gregory, Patrick 63; Rutland, MA, 1756 ***1642*** *p108*
Gregory, Paul 18; Quebec, 1870 ***8364.32*** *p23*
Gregory, Philip; New York, 1775 ***8529.30*** *p12*
Gregory, Richard 30; Ontario, 1871 ***1823.17*** *p61*
Gregory, Thomas 31; Ontario, 1871 ***1823.21*** *p140*
Gregory, William 29; Ontario, 1871 ***1823.17*** *p61*
Gregory, William 60; Ontario, 1871 ***1823.17*** *p61*
Gregory, William 15; Quebec, 1870 ***8364.32*** *p23*
Gregsten, Ellen 38; Ontario, 1871 ***1823.21*** *p140*
Greh, Friedrich Wilhelm; Wisconsin, 1900 ***6795.8*** *p159*
Greif, Adam; America, 1834 ***5475.1*** *p468*
With wife & 6 children
Greif, Albin Daniel; America, 1868 ***7919.3*** *p526*
Greif, Franz; America, 1839 ***5475.1*** *p470*
Greif, Johann; America, 1839 ***5475.1*** *p470*
Greif, Johann Georg; Port uncertain, 1894 ***170.15*** *p26*
With 2 children
Greig, Mr.; British Columbia, 1910 ***2897.7*** *p9*
Greig, Arthur W. 7; Quebec, 1910 ***2897.7*** *p9*
Greig, Eliz. 37; Quebec, 1910 ***2897.7*** *p9*
Greig, Lawrence 11; Quebec, 1910 ***2897.7*** *p9*
Greig, Olive E. 9; Quebec, 1910 ***2897.7*** *p9*
Greille, Nicholas 31; Ontario, 1871 ***1823.21*** *p140*
Greilund, Gust. Ad.; New York, NY, 1843 ***6412.40*** *p147*
Greim, Johann Peter; America, 1884 ***2526.42*** *p189*
Greim, Johannes; America, 1868 ***2526.42*** *p168*
Greineisen, Johann Peter; Ohio, 1857 ***5475.1*** *p346*
Greineisen, Peter; Ohio, 1857 ***5475.1*** *p346*
Greiner, Carl; America, 1868 ***7919.3*** *p531*
Greiner, Emma Rosalie Louise; America, 1867 ***7919.3*** *p528*
Greiner, Georg Max; America, 1868 ***7919.3*** *p531*
Greiner, Gotthelf; America, 1867 ***7919.3*** *p529*
Greiner, Martin; America, 1867 ***7919.3*** *p528*
With wife & 4 children
Greiner, Nicol Gottlieb; America, 1867 ***7919.3*** *p531*
Greisinger, Frederick; Ohio, 1809-1852 ***4511.35*** *p19*
Greive, Thomas 59; Ontario, 1871 ***1823.21*** *p140*
Greives, Andrew 52; Ontario, 1871 ***1823.21*** *p140*
Greives, Thomas 59; Ontario, 1871 ***1823.21*** *p140*
Greiweldinger, Marg. 37; America, 1857 ***5475.1*** *p362*
Grela, Marie 20; America, 1843 ***778.6*** *p144*
Grelet, Caspar 22; New Orleans, 1848 ***778.6*** *p144*
Grelet, Pierre; Virginia, 1700 ***9230.15*** *p81*
Grell, Jakob; New York, NY, 1883 ***5475.1*** *p16*
Grell, Julia; New York, NY, 1883 ***5475.1*** *p16*
Grell, Katharina 29; New York, NY, 1883 ***5475.1*** *p16*
Grell, Wilhelmine; America, 1878 ***7420.1*** *p397*
Grell, Willi; New York, NY, 1883 ***5475.1*** *p16*
Grellen, Augustin 18; Missouri, 1845 ***778.6*** *p144*
Grenault, Isaac 21; Quebec, 1661 ***9221.17*** *p458*
Grendelmeyer, Ursula 27; New Jersey, 1735-1774 ***927.31*** *p3*
Grending, Carl Christian Ludwig; America, 1884 ***7420.1*** *p342*
Grenet, Guillaume 22; Quebec, 1656 ***9221.17*** *p338*
*Cousin:*Simon 20
Grenet, Simon 20 *SEE* Grenet, Guillaume
Grenfell, John 23; Ontario, 1871 ***1823.17*** *p61*
Grenier, Antoinette 19; Quebec, 1656 ***9221.17*** *p338*
Grenier, Auguste 23; Missouri, 1847 ***778.6*** *p145*
Greniuk, Andrew; Detroit, 1929-1930 ***6214.5*** *p69*
Grennay, Abraham 28; Michigan, 1880 ***4491.36*** *p9*
Grennay, Allen 60; Michigan, 1880 ***4491.36*** *p9*
Grennay, Caroline 51; Michigan, 1880 ***4491.36*** *p9*
Grenner, Johannes 26; Port uncertain, 1848 ***778.6*** *p145*
Grenner, Magdalena 20; Port uncertain, 1848 ***778.6*** *p145*
Grentz, Katharina; America, 1881 ***5475.1*** *p72*
Grenz, Caroline 69; New York, NY, 1893 ***1883.7*** *p42*
Grenz, Catharina 9; New York, NY, 1893 ***1883.7*** *p42*
Grenz, Ferdinand 4 months; New York, NY, 1893 ***1883.7*** *p42*
Grenz, Georg Adam; America, 1854 ***2526.43*** *p140*
Grenz, Gottfried 38; New York, NY, 1893 ***1883.7*** *p42*
Grenz, Katharina 37; New York, NY, 1893 ***1883.7*** *p42*
Grenz, Philipp 11; New York, NY, 1893 ***1883.7*** *p42*
Grenzler, Barbara 33; New York, NY, 1885 ***8425.16*** *p32*
Grenzler, Bernhd. 5; New York, NY, 1885 ***8425.16*** *p32*
Grenzler, Christ. 10 months; New York, NY, 1885 ***8425.16*** *p32*
Grenzler, Gottl. 3; New York, NY, 1885 ***8425.16*** *p32*
Grenzler, Joh. 36; New York, NY, 1885 ***8425.16*** *p32*
Grenzler, Johann 7; New York, NY, 1885 ***8425.16*** *p32*
Grenzler, Rosina 8; New York, NY, 1885 ***8425.16*** *p32*
Gresich, Louis; Louisiana, 1874-1875 ***4981.45*** *p29*
Greslon, Adrien 31; Quebec, 1647 ***9221.17*** *p172*
Greslon, Jacques 25; Quebec, 1650 ***9221.17*** *p226*
Gress, Anton; Colorado, 1894 ***1029.59*** *p34*
Gress, Anton; Kansas City, 1890 ***1029.59*** *p34*
Gressel, Johann Ludwig; America, 1856 ***7420.1*** *p147*
Gresser, Andreas 28; Mississippi, 1846 ***778.6*** *p145*
Gressinger, Adam; Ohio, 1840-1897 ***8365.35*** *p16*
Gressy, Charlotte 19; America, 1843 ***778.6*** *p145*
Gresthbach, Henry; Illinois, 1860 ***6079.1*** *p6*
Grether, Michael; Ohio, 1809-1852 ***4511.35*** *p19*
Greuel, Ernst Ludwig; America, 1853 ***7420.1*** *p105*
Greulick, Charles; North Carolina, 1857 ***1088.45*** *p12*
Greuling, Robert; America, 1867 ***7919.3*** *p529*
Greult, Philip; Boston, 1769 ***9228.50*** *p256*
Greve, August; America, 1855 ***7420.1*** *p136*
Greve, Hermann; Chile, 1852 ***1192.4*** *p54*

Greve, Wilhelmine 32; Chile, 1852 ***1192.4*** *p54*
Grevel, Jean; Quebec, 1651 ***9221.17*** *p244*
Grew, Bridget 20; Ohio, 1880 ***4879.40*** *p258*
Grey, . . .; America, 1600-1695 ***9228.50*** *p354*
Grey, George 64; Ontario, 1871 ***1823.17*** *p61*
Grey, James 29; Ontario, 1871 ***1823.21*** *p140*
Grey, James 31; Ontario, 1871 ***1823.21*** *p140*
Grey, James 47; Ontario, 1871 ***1823.17*** *p61*
Grey, James 50; Ontario, 1871 ***1823.21*** *p140*
Grey, Juan; Puerto Rico, 1835 ***3476.25*** *p112*
Grey, Martha 64; Ontario, 1871 ***1823.21*** *p140*
Grey, Mary Jane 21; Toronto, 1867 ***9228.50*** *p255*
Grey, William; America, 1757 ***1220.12*** *p562*
Greysolon Dulhut, Daniel; Quebec, 1675 ***2314.30*** *p166*
Greysolon Dulhut, Daniel; Quebec, 1675 ***2314.30*** *p184*
Gribbe, Elisabeth 22; America, 1847 ***778.6*** *p145*
Gribbe, Marga. 24; America, 1847 ***778.6*** *p145*
Gribben, Peter; Toronto, 1844 ***2910.35*** *p112*
Gribble, John; North Carolina, 1850 ***1088.45*** *p12*
Gribble, William; North Carolina, 1852 ***1088.45*** *p12*
Grieb, Elizabeth; Philadelphia, 1867 ***8513.31*** *p321*
Griebel, Michael; America, 1868 ***7919.3*** *p527*
Griebel, Reinhard Heinrich; America, 1867 ***7919.3*** *p532*
Grieger, Johan Julius; Wisconsin, 1882 ***6795.8*** *p24*
Griencourt, Wilhelm 18; Port uncertain, 1846 ***778.6*** *p145*
Grienke, Michael 19; Halifax, N.S., 1902 ***1860.4*** *p41*
Grier, Adele 27; America, 1846 ***778.6*** *p145*
Grier, Francois 36; America, 1846 ***778.6*** *p145*
Grier, Jacob; Ohio, 1809-1852 ***4511.35*** *p19*
Grier, Joseph 5; America, 1846 ***778.6*** *p145*
Grier, Thomas; North Carolina, 1855 ***1088.45*** *p12*
Grierson, John 50; Ontario, 1871 ***1823.21*** *p140*
Gries, Caroline 7; New York, NY, 1874 ***6954.7*** *p38*
Gries, Catherine 15; New York, NY, 1874 ***6954.7*** *p38*
Gries, Christian 9 months; New York, NY, 1874 ***6954.7*** *p38*
Gries, Christian 9; New York, NY, 1874 ***6954.7*** *p38*
Gries, Christine 9 months; New York, NY, 1874 ***6954.7*** *p38*
Gries, Christine 25; New York, NY, 1874 ***6954.7*** *p38*
Gries, Elisabeth 13; New York, NY, 1874 ***6954.7*** *p38*
Gries, Elisabeth 19; New York, NY, 1874 ***6954.7*** *p38*
Gries, Eva 3; New York, NY, 1874 ***6954.7*** *p38*
Gries, Eva 34; New York, NY, 1874 ***6954.7*** *p38*
Gries, Heinrich 1 months; New York, NY, 1874 ***6954.7*** *p38*
Gries, Heinrich 7; New York, NY, 1874 ***6954.7*** *p38*
Gries, Heinrich 26; New York, NY, 1874 ***6954.7*** *p38*
Gries, Heinrich 34; New York, NY, 1874 ***6954.7*** *p38*
Gries, Jacob 6 months; New York, NY, 1874 ***6954.7*** *p38*
Gries, Johann 15; New York, NY, 1874 ***6954.7*** *p38*
Gries, Johann 39; New York, NY, 1874 ***6954.7*** *p38*
Gries, Magdalena 5; New York, NY, 1874 ***6954.7*** *p38*
Gries, Margarethe 10; New York, NY, 1874 ***6954.7*** *p38*
Gries, Margarethe 12; New York, NY, 1874 ***6954.7*** *p38*
Gries, Margarethe 39; New York, NY, 1874 ***6954.7*** *p38*
Gries, Peter 3; New York, NY, 1874 ***6954.7*** *p38*
Gries, Peter 17; New York, NY, 1874 ***6954.7*** *p38*
Griese, Engel Marie Sophie; America, 1859 ***7420.1*** *p184*
Griese, Friedrich Wilhelm; Wisconsin, 1869 ***6795.8*** *p41*
Griese, Herman Wilhelm; Wisconsin, 1884 ***6795.8*** *p85*
Griese, Johann Conrad; America, 1852 ***7420.1*** *p88*
*Wife:*Sophie Dorothee Charlotte Hunerberg
*Son:*Johann Friedrich Conrad
With son
Griese, Johann Friedrich Conrad *SEE* Griese, Johann Conrad
Griese, Johann Ludwig; Wisconsin, 1858 ***6795.8*** *p138*
Griese, Sophie Dorothee Charlotte Hunerberg *SEE* Griese, Johann Conrad
Griesenbeck, Maria; Wisconsin, 1881 ***5475.1*** *p308*
Griesinger, Frederick; Ohio, 1809-1852 ***4511.35*** *p19*
Griess, Julius 24; New York, NY, 1883 ***8427.14*** *p44*
Grieve, Elliott 87; Ontario, 1871 ***1823.21*** *p140*
Grieve, William 61; Ontario, 1871 ***1823.21*** *p140*
Grieves, Elizabeth 24; Ontario, 1871 ***1823.21*** *p140*
Grieves, William 35; Ontario, 1871 ***1823.17*** *p61*
Griffen, Adonirum; Boston, 1745 ***1642*** *p28*
Griffen, Edward; Boston, 1766 ***1642*** *p37*
Griffen, John; Maryland, 1672 ***1236.25*** *p48*
Griffen, John 51; Ontario, 1871 ***1823.17*** *p61*
Griffen, Joseph 55; Ontario, 1871 ***1823.17*** *p61*
Griffen, Samuel; Massachusetts, 1675-1676 ***1642*** *p128*
Griffeth, Richard; Massachusetts, 1675-1676 ***1642*** *p129*
Griffin, Mr.; Massachusetts, 1754 ***1642*** *p108*
Griffin, Alonson 55; Ontario, 1871 ***1823.17*** *p62*
Griffin, Anthony; St. John, N.B., 1848 ***2978.15*** *p38*
Griffin, Daniel 30; Ontario, 1871 ***1823.21*** *p140*
Griffin, David 42; Ontario, 1871 ***1823.17*** *p62*
Griffin, Edmund; Dorchester, MA, 1770 ***1642*** *p102*
Griffin, Fanny 47; Ontario, 1871 ***1823.17*** *p62*
Griffin, Frank; Washington, 1889 ***2770.40*** *p27*
Griffin, Gilbert E. 50; Ontario, 1871 ***1823.21*** *p140*
Griffin, Hugh; Massachusetts, 1639 ***1642*** *p109*
Griffin, Isaac; Massachusetts, 1675-1676 ***1642*** *p129*
Griffin, James; New England, 1745 ***1642*** *p28*
Griffin, James; New England, 1745 ***1642*** *p28*
Griffin, James 67; Ontario, 1871 ***1823.21*** *p140*
Griffin, John; America, 1780 ***8529.30*** *p12*
Griffin, John; Massachusetts, 1675-1676 ***1642*** *p129*
Griffin, John; St. John, N.B., 1847 ***2978.15*** *p38*
Griffin, John; St. John, N.B., 1848 ***2978.15*** *p41*
Griffin, Joseph; Massachusetts, 1675-1676 ***1642*** *p128*
Griffin, Joseph; Massachusetts, 1675-1676 ***1642*** *p128*
Griffin, Joseph; Massachusetts, 1675-1676 ***1642*** *p129*
Griffin, L. Nathan 26; Ontario, 1871 ***1823.17*** *p62*
Griffin, Matthew; Massachusetts, 1675-1676 ***1642*** *p127*
Griffin, Michael; Washington, 1889 ***2770.40*** *p27*
Griffin, Peggy; Massachusetts, 1733 ***1642*** *p66*
Griffin, Peter F.; Illinois, 1855 ***6079.1*** *p6*
Griffin, Richard; Massachusetts, 1675-1676 ***1642*** *p128*
Griffin, Richard 62; Ontario, 1871 ***1823.21*** *p140*
Griffin, Thomas 26; Ontario, 1871 ***1823.21*** *p140*
Griffin, Timothy; Alexandria, VA, 1778 ***8529.30*** *p12*
Griffin, Tun.; St. John, N.B., 1848 ***2978.15*** *p41*
Griffin, William 40; Ontario, 1871 ***1823.21*** *p140*
Griffin, Wynfred Arnold; Miami, 1935 ***4984.12*** *p39*
Griffins, Patrick; Massachusetts, 1745 ***1642*** *p28*
Griffith, Briget 50; Ontario, 1871 ***1823.17*** *p62*
Griffith, D. J. 21; Indiana, 1881-1892 ***9076.20*** *p73*
Griffith, David; South Carolina, 1800-1899 ***6155.4*** *p18*
Griffith, David T.; Colorado, 1891 ***1029.59*** *p34*
Griffith, David T.; Colorado, 1906 ***1029.59*** *p34*
Griffith, Eli 65; Ontario, 1871 ***1823.21*** *p140*
Griffith, Ezra 80; Ontario, 1871 ***1823.21*** *p140*
Griffith, Henry 72; Ontario, 1871 ***1823.21*** *p140*
Griffith, James 57; Ontario, 1871 ***1823.21*** *p140*
Griffith, James J.; Ohio, 1840 ***2763.1*** *p9*
Griffith, John; Boston, 1745 ***1642*** *p28*
Griffith, John 56; Ontario, 1871 ***1823.17*** *p62*
Griffith, Mary; Maryland, 1674 ***1236.25*** *p50*
Griffith, Peter; Iowa, 1883 ***1211.15*** *p10*
Griffith, Robert 34; Ontario, 1871 ***1823.21*** *p140*
Griffith, Thomas; Boston, 1745 ***1642*** *p28*
Griffith, Thomas 25; Halifax, N.S., n.d. ***1833.5*** *p7*
Griffith, Thomas 25; Halifax, N.S., n.d. ***8445.10*** *p7*
Griffith, Thomas J. 25; Louisiana, 1845-1847 ***7710.1*** *p150*
Griffith, Tunis 37; Ontario, 1871 ***1823.21*** *p140*
Griffith, William; Louisiana, 1874 ***4981.45*** *p132*
Griffiths, David; Colorado, 1891 ***1029.59*** *p34*
Griffiths, David; Ohio, 1838 ***4022.20*** *p280*
*Wife:*Elizabeth Hugh
*Child:*Jane
Griffiths, Elizabeth Hugh *SEE* Griffiths, David
Griffiths, Evan; Ohio, 1837 ***4022.20*** *p280*
*Wife:*Jane
*Child:*Mary
*Child:*Margaret
Griffiths, Griffith 40; Ontario, 1871 ***1823.21*** *p140*
Griffiths, Jane *SEE* Griffiths, Evan
Griffiths, Jane *SEE* Griffiths, David
Griffiths, John 43; Ontario, 1871 ***1823.21*** *p141*
Griffiths, Margaret *SEE* Griffiths, Evan
Griffiths, Mary *SEE* Griffiths, Evan
Griffiths, Morgan; Boston, 1767 ***1642*** *p38*
Griffiths, Parry; Ohio, 1836 ***4022.20*** *p293*
Griffiths, Richard 45; Ontario, 1871 ***1823.21*** *p141*
Griffiths, Thomas 22; Ontario, 1871 ***1823.21*** *p141*
Griffiths, William; Ohio, 1836 ***4022.20*** *p293*
Griffittis, Steph F. 35; Ontario, 1871 ***1823.17*** *p62*
Griffknecht, August 3; Halifax, N.S., 1902 ***1860.4*** *p42*
Griffknecht, Edward 20; Halifax, N.S., 1902 ***1860.4*** *p42*
Griffknecht, Elisabeth 24; Halifax, N.S., 1902 ***1860.4*** *p42*
Griffknecht, Jacob 32; Halifax, N.S., 1902 ***1860.4*** *p42*
Griffknecht, Ludwig 11; Halifax, N.S., 1902 ***1860.4*** *p42*
Griffknecht, Maria 57; Halifax, N.S., 1902 ***1860.4*** *p42*
Griffknecht, Wilh. 58; Halifax, N.S., 1902 ***1860.4*** *p42*
Griffknecht, Wilhelm 17; Halifax, N.S., 1902 ***1860.4*** *p42*
Griffon, Louis 19; Montreal, 1660 ***9221.17*** *p441*
Grigg, John 41; Ontario, 1871 ***1823.21*** *p141*
Grigg, Mary Ann 47; Ontario, 1871 ***1823.21*** *p141*
Grigg, William 29; Ontario, 1871 ***1823.21*** *p141*
Grigg, William 45; Ontario, 1871 ***1823.21*** *p141*
Grignault, Marie 26; Quebec, 1662 ***9221.17*** *p486*
Grignon, Antoine; Quebec, 1658 ***9221.17*** *p381*
*Son:*Jean
Grignon, Jean 22 *SEE* Grignon, Antoine
Grigor, John R.; Colorado, 1887 ***1029.59*** *p34*
Grigor, William; Colorado, 1880 ***1029.59*** *p34*
Grill, Gudmund E. S.; Iowa, 1900 ***1211.15*** *p10*
Grill, Josef 30; Halifax, N.S., 1902 ***1860.4*** *p40*
Grill, Katharina 57; America, 1866 ***5475.1*** *p490*
Grille, A. 22; America, 1846 ***778.6*** *p145*
Grillet, Mrs. 36; Port uncertain, 1843 ***778.6*** *p145*
Grillet, Jean 10; Port uncertain, 1843 ***778.6*** *p145*
Grillet, Josephine 9; Port uncertain, 1843 ***778.6*** *p145*
Grillot, Charles 4; Missouri, 1845 ***778.6*** *p145*
Grillot, Francois 34; Missouri, 1845 ***778.6*** *p145*
Grillot, Joseph 3; Missouri, 1845 ***778.6*** *p145*
Grillot, Marie 26; Missouri, 1845 ***778.6*** *p145*
Grillot, Xavier 1; Missouri, 1845 ***778.6*** *p145*
Grills, James 52; Ontario, 1871 ***1823.21*** *p141*
Grim, A. Barbara Thome 57 *SEE* Grim, Nikolaus
Grim, Edmund; America, 1881 ***5475.1*** *p129*
Grim, Elisabeth 33 *SEE* Grim, Nikolaus
Grim, Jakob *SEE* Grim, Nikolaus
Grim, Katharina 26 *SEE* Grim, Nikolaus
Grim, Mathias Eugen; Cincinnati, 1889 ***5475.1*** *p131*
Grim, Nikolaus; America, 1882 ***5475.1*** *p129*
Grim, Nikolaus 24; America, 1872 ***5475.1*** *p446*
Grim, Nikolaus 58; America, 1878 ***5475.1*** *p447*
*Wife:*A. Barbara Thome 57
*Daughter:*Katharina 26
*Son:*Jakob
*Daughter:*Elisabeth 33
Grim, Valentine 45; Ontario, 1871 ***1823.21*** *p141*
Grimard, Anne 38; Quebec, 1647 ***9221.17*** *p182*
*Son:*Jean 11
Grimard, Elie 51; Quebec, 1642 ***9221.17*** *p118*
Grimard, Jean 11 *SEE* Grimard, Anne Perrin
Grimault, Jacques 22; Quebec, 1659 ***9221.17*** *p402*
Grimaux, Alfred 22; America, 1843 ***778.6*** *p145*
Grimbault, Anne; Quebec, 1670 ***4514.3*** *p320*
Grimber, Mathias 43; America, 1746 ***778.6*** *p145*
Grimber, Rolland 14; America, 1746 ***778.6*** *p145*
Grime, Alexis; Ohio, 1809-1852 ***4511.35*** *p19*
Grimes, Henry; North Carolina, 1853 ***1088.45*** *p12*
Grimes, James; Marston's Wharf, 1780 ***8529.30*** *p12*
Grimes, John 32; Ontario, 1871 ***1823.21*** *p141*
Grimm, Dionys; Colorado, 1879 ***1029.59*** *p34*
Grimm, Diouys; Colorado, 1879 ***1029.59*** *p35*
Grimm, F. A.; Valdivia, Chile, 1850 ***1192.4*** *p48*
Grimm, Ferdinand 59; New York, NY, 1894 ***6512.1*** *p232*
Grimm, Frederick; Wisconsin, 1894 ***6795.8*** *p236*
Grimm, George; New York, 1860 ***358.56*** *p5*
Grimm, Gustav; America, 1868 ***5475.1*** *p417*
Grimm, Jacob; Ohio, 1809-1852 ***4511.35*** *p19*
Grimm, Jakob; America, 1858 ***5475.1*** *p489*
Grimm, Katharina; America, 1857 ***5475.1*** *p490*
Grimm, Katharina Grill 57 *SEE* Grimm, Philipp
Grimm, Ludwig; America, 1856 ***5475.1*** *p489*
Grimm, Mathilde; America, 1867 ***7919.3*** *p534*
Grimm, Philipp 58; America, 1866 ***5475.1*** *p490*
*Wife:*Katharina Grill 57
Grimme, August Heinrich; Port uncertain, 1883 ***7420.1*** *p336*
Grimme, Friedrich; America, 1834 ***7420.1*** *p7*
Grimmin, Marget 21; Ontario, 1871 ***1823.17*** *p62*
Grimne, Ernest C. M. J.; North Carolina, 1847-1854 ***1088.45*** *p12*
Grimont, Claire 18; New Orleans, 1848 ***778.6*** *p145*
Grimont, Jean-Baptist 20; New Orleans, 1848 ***778.6*** *p145*
Grimont, Margarethe 22; New Orleans, 1848 ***778.6*** *p145*
Grimont, Margarethe 48; New Orleans, 1848 ***778.6*** *p145*
Grimont, Nicolas 48; New Orleans, 1848 ***778.6*** *p145*
Grimoult, Marie 30; Quebec, 1637 ***9221.17*** *p73*
Grimoult, Olive; Quebec, 1637 ***9221.17*** *p73*
Grimoult, Pierre; Quebec, 1638 ***9221.17*** *p76*
Grimpe, Sophie Marie Friederike Dorothea; America, 1866 ***7420.1*** *p242*
Grimsby, Charles 40; Ontario, 1871 ***1823.21*** *p141*
Grimwood, Charles 58; Ontario, 1871 ***1823.21*** *p141*
Grinaud, Auguste 4; America, 1847 ***778.6*** *p145*
Grinaud, Elise 1; America, 1847 ***778.6*** *p145*
Grinaud, F. 38; America, 1847 ***778.6*** *p145*
Grinaud, Marie 8; America, 1847 ***778.6*** *p145*
Grinaud, Queine 5; America, 1847 ***778.6*** *p146*
Grinaud, Ursule 34; America, 1847 ***778.6*** *p146*
Grinder, John Jacob; North Carolina, 1710 ***3629.40*** *p8*
Grinnin, Margaret 48; Ontario, 1871 ***1823.17*** *p62*
Grinslett, James; Salem, MA, 1711 ***9228.50*** *p255*
Griolin, Jean 29; America, 1846 ***778.6*** *p146*
Grip, Carle Arvid; Cleveland, OH, 1891-1896 ***9722.10*** *p119*
Grip, John August; Cleveland, OH, 1902-1903 ***9722.10*** *p119*
Grip, Per Gustaf; Cleveland, OH, 1880-1892 ***9722.10*** *p119*
Gripp, Carle Arvid; Cleveland, OH, 1891-1896 ***9722.10*** *p119*
Gripp, John August; Cleveland, OH, 1902-1903 ***9722.10*** *p119*
Grippe, Marin; Quebec, 1661 ***9221.17*** *p458*
Gripton, Henry 43; Ontario, 1871 ***1823.21*** *p141*

Grisard, Louise 27; Montreal, 1660 *9221.17 p440*
   *Son:*Louis 9
Grisard, Louise 27; Montreal, 1660 *9221.17 p440*
   *Son:*Louis 9
Grisbrook, Edward 36; Ontario, 1871 *1823.17 p62*
Grises, James 45; America, 1847 *778.6 p146*
Grismond, James 48; Ontario, 1871 *1823.21 p141*
Grissen, Clem; Marston's Wharf, 1782 *8529.30 p12*
Grisseth, Pierre 21; America, 1846 *778.6 p146*
Grisson, Charles 21; Missouri, 1848 *778.6 p146*
Grist, Charles 25; Ontario, 1871 *1823.21 p141*
Grist, Henry; North Carolina, 1710 *3629.40 p4*
Grist, Henry 20; Ontario, 1871 *1823.21 p141*
Grister, Theodore; New York, 1859 *358.56 p101*
Grith, John; Ohio, 1809-1852 *4511.35 p19*
Griver, Mangin; Louisiana, 1836-1840 *4981.45 p212*
Griveran, Guillaume; Quebec, 1648 *9221.17 p199*
Grives, James 30; Ontario, 1871 *1823.21 p141*
Grix, Marin; Quebec, 1661 *9221.17 p458*
Groat, James 21; Ontario, 1871 *1823.17 p62*
Grob, A. Maria *SEE* Grob, Katharina
Grob, Elisabeth *SEE* Grob, Katharina
Grob, Friedrich; Valdivia, Chile, 1852 *1192.4 p53*
Grob, Johann *SEE* Grob, Katharina
Grob, Katharina; America, 1853 *5475.1 p539*
   *Son:*Johann
   *Daughter:*A. Maria
   *Daughter:*M. Barbara
   *Son:*Peter
   *Daughter:*Elisabeth
   *Son:*Konrad
Grob, Konrad *SEE* Grob, Katharina
Grob, M. Barbara *SEE* Grob, Katharina
Grob, Nikolaus 25; America, 1867 *5475.1 p558*
Grob, Peter *SEE* Grob, Katharina
Groce, William; Marston's Wharf, 1782 *8529.30 p12*
Groenvelt, Edward; Louisiana, 1874 *4981.45 p132*
Groezinger, Christian F.; Ohio, 1840-1897 *8365.35 p16*
Grof, John V.; Georgia, 1900 *1029.59 p35*
Groff, Ferdinand; Long Island, 1781 *8529.30 p9A*
Groffer, Rene 31; New Orleans, 1848 *778.6 p146*
Groffmiller, Andrew; Ohio, 1809-1852 *4511.35 p19*
Groffmiller, Matthias; Ohio, 1809-1852 *4511.35 p19*
Groh, Adam; America, 1881 *2526.42 p105*
Groh, Adam; America, 1885 *2526.42 p104*
Groh, Elisabeth Droescher 27 *SEE* Groh, Jakob, II
Groh, Georg Adam; Argentina, 1855 *2526.43 p208*
   With family of 8
Groh, Jakob *SEE* Groh, Jakob, II
Groh, Jakob, II 30; America, 1857 *5475.1 p551*
   *Wife:*Elisabeth Droescher 27
   *Son:*Peter
   *Son:*Jakob
Groh, Michael Otto; America, 1863 *2526.42 p121*
Groh, Otto; America, 1887 *2526.43 p209*
Groh, Peter *SEE* Groh, Jakob, II
Groh, Peter; America, 1881 *2526.42 p104*
   With family
Grohn, Anna; America, 1882 *5475.1 p276*
Grohne, Friederike Auguste; Baltimore, 1850 *7420.1 p71*
Grohne, Juliane Theodora Adelaide; America, 1865 *7420.1 p231*
Grohs, Jakob; America, 1881 *5475.1 p398*
Grohs, Mathias; America, 1881 *5475.1 p358*
Groisard, Jeanne; Quebec, 1665 *4514.3 p321*
Groleau, Madeleine; Quebec, 1669 *4514.3 p321*
Groll, Anna Margaretha 24 *SEE* Groll, Johannes, III
Groll, Christine 7 *SEE* Groll, Johannes, III
Groll, Elisabeth; America, 1854 *2526.43 p221*
Groll, Friedrich Jakob *SEE* Groll, Johannes, III
Groll, Johannes 16; America, 1854 *2526.43 p221*
   *Brother:*Philipp
Groll, Johannes, III; America, 1852 *2526.43 p221*
   *Wife:*Sophie Elisabetha
   *Daughter:*Anna Margaretha
   *Son:*Konrad
   *Daughter:*Christine
   *Son:*Philipp
   *Son:*Friedrich Jakob
Groll, Konrad 15 *SEE* Groll, Johannes, III
Groll, Margaretha; America, 1881 *2526.43 p139*
Groll, Philipp *SEE* Groll, Johannes
Groll, Philipp 12 *SEE* Groll, Johannes, III
Groll, Sophie Elisabetha 43 *SEE* Groll, Johannes, III
Grolleau, Pierre; Quebec, 1649 *9221.17 p214*
Grolot, Const. 28; New Orleans, 1847 *778.6 p146*
Grolott, J. Pierre 24; Missouri, 1847 *778.6 p146*
Gronan, Alexander 18; New York, NY, 1893 *1883.7 p38*
Gronbeck, Hans B.; Iowa, 1893 *1211.15 p11*
Grondahl, Wilhelm; Cleveland, OH, 1887-1893 *9722.10 p119*
Grondelle, Anna Julie 50; Louisiana, 1848 *778.6 p146*
Grondelle, Jean 17; Louisiana, 1848 *778.6 p146*

Grondelle, Jean 45; Louisiana, 1848 *778.6 p146*
Grondelle, Julie 20; Louisiana, 1848 *778.6 p146*
Grondelle, Mary 18; Louisiana, 1848 *778.6 p146*
Grondin, Michel; Quebec, 1654 *9221.17 p309*
Grone, Mr.; America, 1867 *7420.1 p256*
Grone, Carl Friedrich *SEE* Grone, Fr.
Grone, Carl Heinrich Wilhelm *SEE* Grone, Fr.
Grone, Engel Sophie Wilhelmine *SEE* Grone, Fr.
Grone, Ernst Heinrich Wilhelm *SEE* Grone, Fr.
Grone, Fr.; America, 1868 *7420.1 p271*
   With wife
   *Son:*Carl Heinrich Wilhelm
   *Son:*Carl Friedrich
   *Daughter:*Engel Sophie Wilhelmine
   *Son:*Ernst Heinrich Wilhelm
   *Son:*Heinrich Friedrich Wilhelm
Grone, Heinrich Friedrich Wilhelm *SEE* Grone, Fr.
Gronen, G. G.; Louisiana, 1874 *4981.45 p296*
Gronlund, Jonas; New York, NY, 1844 *6412.40 p148*
Gronosky, H.; California, 1868 *1131.61 p89*
Gronoslalski, Michael; Detroit, 1929 *1640.55 p115*
Gronwald, Maria 18; New York, NY, 1893 *1883.7 p43*
Gronwald, Reinhold Eduard; Port uncertain, 1880 *7420.1 p316*
Gronwald, Wilhelm 16; New York, NY, 1893 *1883.7 p43*
Gronwaldt, Franz; America, 1872 *7420.1 p295*
Gronwaldt, Friedrich Carl Richard; Cincinnati, 1879 *7420.1 p313*
Groom, Martha; America, 1752-1775 *9228.50 p251*
Groom, William; Jamaica, 1783 *8529.30 p13A*
Groos, Hedwig; Galveston, TX, 1855 *571.7 p16*
Grope, Heinrich Friedrich August; America, 1857 *7420.1 p161*
Groper, Friedrich August Christian; America, 1861 *7420.1 p205*
Groper, Friedrich August Christian; America, 1866 *7420.1 p242*
Groper, Johann; America, 1858 *7420.1 p177*
Gropper, Johann Henrich Christoph; America, 1858 *7420.1 p177*
Gros, Anne 52; Missouri, 1845 *778.6 p146*
Gros, Appoline 26; New Orleans, 1847 *778.6 p146*
Gros, Catharina 57; New Orleans, 1847 *778.6 p146*
Gros, Clementine 24; New Orleans, 1847 *778.6 p146*
Gros, Elisa 17; New Orleans, 1847 *778.6 p146*
Gros, Eloi 28; New Orleans, 1847 *778.6 p146*
Gros, F...cois 37; Port uncertain, 1842 *778.6 p146*
Gros, Felicienne 13; New Orleans, 1847 *778.6 p146*
Gros, Jacques 28; Missouri, 1848 *778.6 p146*
Gros, Johann; Brazil, 1885 *5475.1 p432*
   *Wife:*Kath. Scheid
   *Daughter:*Katharina
Gros, Joseph 34; Mississippi, 1846 *778.6 p146*
Gros, Joseph 67; Missouri, 1845 *778.6 p146*
Gros, Joseph 27; New Orleans, 1847 *778.6 p146*
Gros, Joseph 62; New Orleans, 1847 *778.6 p146*
Gros, Kath. Scheid *SEE* Gros, Johann
Gros, Katharina *SEE* Gros, Johann
Gros, Maria; America, 1857 *5475.1 p548*
Gros, Marie Claude 28; New Orleans, 1847 *778.6 p146*
Grosch, Ludwig; Chile, 1852 *1192.4 p52*
Groschowsky, Bernhd 19; New York, NY, 1886 *8425.16 p33*
Grose, F. W.; Ohio, 1809-1852 *4511.35 p19*
Grose, Henry; New Jersey, 1811 *3845.2 p129*
Grose, Nicholas 47; Ontario, 1871 *1823.17 p62*
Grosebacher, Henry; Ohio, 1809-1852 *4511.35 p19*
Grosenbacher, Henry; Ohio, 1809-1852 *4511.35 p19*
Gros Family ; Marblehead, MA, 1684 *9228.50 p255*
Grosgean, Constant; Ohio, 1809-1852 *4511.35 p19*
Grosgean, John C.; Ohio, 1809-1852 *4511.35 p19*
Grosider, John 39; Ontario, 1871 *1823.17 p62*
Gross, Andreas 37; Baltimore, 1889 *8425.16 p36*
Gross, Anna *SEE* Gross, Nikolaus
Gross, Anna Schneider 47 *SEE* Gross, Nikolaus
Gross, Barbara; America, 1871 *5475.1 p139*
Gross, Barbara *SEE* Gross, Nikolaus
Gross, Caroline; America, 1867 *7919.3 p529*
Gross, Christian *SEE* Gross, Joh. Christian
Gross, Christian; Missouri, 1886 *3276.1 p1*
Gross, Christian Georg; America, n.d. *8115.12 p320*
Gross, Christiana; Philadelphia, 1852 *8513.31 p312*
Gross, Daniel 8; America, 1846 *778.6 p146*
Gross, Elisabeth *SEE* Gross, Peter
Gross, Elisabeth 31; America, 1843 *5475.1 p546*
Gross, Ellis H.; Washington, 1883 *2770.40 p136*
Gross, Erasmus; Illinois, 1864 *6079.1 p6*
Gross, Ernst 13 *SEE* Gross, Georg
Gross, Eva *SEE* Gross, Nikolaus
Gross, Eva Streit *SEE* Gross, Nikolaus
Gross, Franz 5; Baltimore, 1889 *8425.16 p36*
Gross, Friedrich *SEE* Gross, Joh. Christian

Gross, Georg; America, 1836 *5475.1 p546*
   *Daughter:*Katharina
   *Son:*Johann
   *Son:*Ernst
   *Son:*Georg
Gross, Georg 18 *SEE* Gross, Georg
Gross, Georg 28; America, 1846 *778.6 p146*
Gross, Georg; Baltimore, 1889 *8425.16 p36*
Gross, George 23; America, 1846 *778.6 p146*
Gross, George; Ohio, 1809-1852 *4511.35 p19*
Gross, Heinrich; America, 1888 *5475.1 p141*
Gross, Helena 4; America, 1846 *778.6 p146*
Gross, Isidor; America, 1874 *5475.1 p134*
Gross, Jacob; America, n.d. *9228.50 p256*
Gross, Jacob 35; America, 1846 *778.6 p147*
Gross, Jacob 3; Baltimore, 1889 *8425.16 p36*
Gross, Jacob; Ohio, 1809-1852 *4511.35 p19*
Gross, Jakob *SEE* Gross, Peter
Gross, Joh. Christian; America, 1836 *5475.1 p457*
   *Wife:*Philippine Friederike Schwarz
   *Son:*Friedrich
   *Son:*Christian
   *Son:*Karl
Gross, Johann; America, 1846 *5475.1 p455*
Gross, Johann *SEE* Gross, Nikolaus
Gross, Johann *SEE* Gross, Peter
Gross, Johann 16 *SEE* Gross, Georg
Gross, Johann J.; Missouri, 1892 *3276.1 p1*
Gross, Johann Jacob; Missouri, 1886 *3276.1 p1*
Gross, John; Marblehead, MA, 1700-1736 *9228.50 p256*
Gross, John; Ohio, 1809-1852 *4511.35 p19*
Gross, Juliana *SEE* Gross, Peter
Gross, Karl *SEE* Gross, Joh. Christian
Gross, Karoline; America, 1833 *5475.1 p394*
Gross, Katharina *SEE* Gross, Peter
Gross, Katharina *SEE* Gross, Nikolaus
Gross, Katharina *SEE* Gross, Peter
Gross, Katharina Bies 25 *SEE* Gross, Peter
Gross, Katharina 26 *SEE* Gross, Georg
Gross, Katharina Demuth 42 *SEE* Gross, Peter
Gross, Katharina Fontaine 49 *SEE* Gross, Peter
Gross, Luise 21; America, 1843 *5475.1 p546*
   *Sister:*Maria 19
Gross, Marg. 32; America, 1846 *778.6 p147*
Gross, Maria *SEE* Gross, Nikolaus
Gross, Maria Jung *SEE* Gross, Peter
Gross, Maria 19 *SEE* Gross, Luise
Gross, Maria 30; Baltimore, 1889 *8425.16 p36*
Gross, Maria; Cincinnati, 1888 *5475.1 p168*
Gross, Michael 23; New Orleans, 1848 *778.6 p147*
Gross, Nicholas; Ohio, 1809-1852 *4511.35 p19*
Gross, Nikolaus; America, 1872 *5475.1 p195*
Gross, Nikolaus *SEE* Gross, Nikolaus
Gross, Nikolaus *SEE* Gross, Nikolaus
Gross, Nikolaus; America, 1879 *5475.1 p267*
   *Wife:*Eva Streit
   *Daughter:*Eva
   *Son:*Nikolaus
Gross, Nikolaus *SEE* Gross, Peter
Gross, Nikolaus; America, 1892 *5475.1 p157*
Gross, Nikolaus 51; America, 1876 *5475.1 p351*
   *Wife:*Anna Schneider 47
   *Daughter:*Anna
   *Daughter:*Maria
   *Son:*Nikolaus
   *Son:*Johann
   *Daughter:*Katharina
   *Son:*Peter
   *Daughter:*Barbara
   *Daughter:*Susanna
Gross, Peter *SEE* Gross, Peter
Gross, Peter; America, 1859 *5475.1 p522*
   *Wife:*Katharina Demuth
   *Daughter:*Elisabeth
   *Son:*Peter
   *Son:*Jakob
   *Daughter:*Juliana
   *Daughter:*Katharina
Gross, Peter; America, 1869 *5475.1 p47*
Gross, Peter *SEE* Gross, Nikolaus
Gross, Peter *SEE* Gross, Peter
Gross, Peter; America, 1881 *5475.1 p241*
   *Wife:*Maria Jung
   *Son:*Wendel
Gross, Peter 27; America, 1860 *5475.1 p266*
   *Wife:*Katharina Bies 25
Gross, Peter 37; America, 1869 *5475.1 p195*
Gross, Peter 58; America, 1881 *5475.1 p196*
   *Wife:*Katharina Fontaine 49
   *Son:*Johann
   *Son:*Peter
   *Son:*Nikolaus
   *Daughter:*Katharina

            FOR A COMPLETE EXPLANATION OF ENTRY, SEE "HOW TO READ A CITATION" SECTION

Gross, Philipp; America, 1856 *5475.1 p343*
Gross, Philippine Friederike Schwarz SEE Gross, Joh. Christian
Gross, Sophia 29; America, 1833 *5475.1 p393*
Gross, Susanna SEE Gross, Nikolaus
Gross, Wendel SEE Gross, Peter
Gross, Wilhelmina 6; America, 1846 *778.6 p147*
Grossberg, Charles Isaac; Detroit, 1929-1930 *6214.5 p63*
Grossclaus, John; Ohio, 1809-1852 *4511.35 p19*
Grossclous, Christian; Ohio, 1809-1852 *4511.35 p19*
Grossclous, John; Ohio, 1809-1852 *4511.35 p19*
Grosse, Isaac; Salem, MA, 1637 *9228.50 p256*
Grossee, John; Marblehead, MA, 1700-1736 *9228.50 p256*
Grosse Family ; Marblehead, MA, 1684 *9228.50 p255*
Grossejambe, Francoise; Quebec, 1671 *4514.3 p321*
Grossembach, Anna 6; Galveston, TX, 1846 *3967.10 p379*
Grossembach, Anna 9 months; Galveston, TX, 1846 *3967.10 p379*
Grossembach, Barbara 9; Galveston, TX, 1846 *3967.10 p379*
Grossembach, Benedikt 2; Galveston, TX, 1846 *3967.10 p379*
Grossembach, Elisabeth 8; Galveston, TX, 1846 *3967.10 p379*
Grossembach, Elisabeth 38; Galveston, TX, 1846 *3967.10 p379*
Grossembach, Johann 18; Galveston, TX, 1846 *3967.10 p379*
Grossembach, Johann 44; Galveston, TX, 1846 *3967.10 p379*
Grossembach, Rosine 4; Galveston, TX, 1846 *3967.10 p379*
Grossen, Friedr.; Valdivia, Chile, 1852 *1192.4 p55*
  With wife & 2 children
Grosset, Jean 35; New Orleans, 1848 *778.6 p147*
Grossin, Jacques; Quebec, 1655 *9221.17 p324*
Grosskop, August; England, 1885 *7420.1 p347*
Grosskopf, Auguste; New York, 1859 *358.56 p99*
Grosskopf, Ernestine Wilhelmine Caroline Schottelndreyer SEE Grosskopf, Johann Heinrich Christoph
Grosskopf, Johann Heinrich Christoph; America, 1847 *7420.1 p53*
  *Wife:*Ernestine Wilhelmine Caroline Schottelndreyer
  With son 3
  With daughter 1
Grosskurth, Caroline Pauline; Indianapolis, 1858 *7420.1 p177*
Grossman, Lesbeth 12; America, 1841 *778.6 p147*
Grossmann, Adolph Carl Louis August; America, 1866 *7420.1 p243*
Grossmann, Georg Gideon Heinrich; America, 1866 *7420.1 p243*
Grossmann, Georges 25; Port uncertain, 1844 *778.6 p147*
Grossmann, Johann Carl Heinrich; America, 1859 *7420.1 p184*
Grossmann, Salomonn 22; New York, NY, 1878 *9253.2 p45*
  *Child:*Sara 9
Grossmann, Sara 9 SEE Grossmann, Salomonn
Grossonneau, Jeanne; Quebec, 1670 *4514.3 p365*
Grossy, A. 38; Port uncertain, 1843 *778.6 p147*
Grota, Albert; Wisconsin, 1882 *6795.8 p57*
Grota, Anastasia; Wisconsin, 1898 *6795.8 p57*
Grota, Joseph; Wisconsin, 1899 *6795.8 p57*
Grote, August; San Francisco, 1924 *8023.44 p374*
Grote, Heinrich Friedrich Wilhelm; America, 1867 *7420.1 p256*
Grote, Hermine; America, 1897 *7420.1 p373*
Grote, Louise; America, 1856 *7420.1 p147*
Grote, Marie; America, 1895 *7420.1 p372*
Grote, Philipp; America, 1846 *7420.1 p44*
  With wife & 4 children
Grotgen, George; North Carolina, 1854-1856 *1088.45 p12*
Grotgin, John H.; North Carolina, 1835 *1088.45 p12*
Groth, Christ; Nebraska, 1905 *3004.30 p46*
Groth, Franz; Iowa, 1906 *1211.15 p11*
Groth, Fred Henry; Iowa, 1929 *1211.15 p10*
Groth, Gottlieb; Iowa, 1882 *1211.15 p10*
Grothe, . . .; America, 1854 *7420.1 p120*
  With son & daughter
Grothe, C.; America, 1847 *7420.1 p53*
  With wife & 7 children
Grothe, C.; America, 1849 *7420.1 p64*
  With family
Grothe, Juliane Sophie Dorothe; America, 1861 *7420.1 p205*
Groton, Jean 18; Quebec, 1655 *9221.17 p324*
Grouard, Richard; Quebec, 1656 *9221.17 p338*

Grouchy, Matthew; Iowa, 1870-1879 *9228.50 p179*
Grough, William 46; Ontario, 1871 *1823.17 p62*
Grouse, Charles 33; Ontario, 1871 *1823.21 p141*
Grousman, Moris; North Carolina, 1857 *1088.45 p12*
Groussin, Jacques; Quebec, 1655 *9221.17 p324*
Groussin, Jean; Quebec, 1645 *9221.17 p153*
Grout, Philip; Boston, 1769 *9228.50 p256*
Grouvel, Martin; Quebec, 1635 *9221.17 p46*
Grove, John 46; Ontario, 1871 *1823.21 p141*
Grove, Nicholas 49; North Carolina, 1702 *9228.50 p257*
Grovemiller, Andrew; Ohio, 1809-1852 *4511.35 p19*
Grover, Hannah 32; Michigan, 1880 *4491.30 p14*
Grover, May; Atlanta, GA, 1830 *9228.50 p256*
Groves, Fredrick 51; Ontario, 1871 *1823.21 p141*
Groves, Henry 64; Ontario, 1871 *1823.21 p141*
Groves, James 44; Ontario, 1871 *1823.21 p141*
Groves, Mary 68; Ontario, 1871 *1823.21 p142*
Groves, Nicholas; Salem, MA, 1668 *9228.50 p257*
Groves, Richard 40; Ontario, 1871 *1823.21 p142*
Groves, Walter 9; Quebec, 1870 *8364.32 p23*
Groves, William; Maryland, 1674-1675 *1236.25 p51*
Groves Family ; Marblehead, MA, 1684 *9228.50 p256*
Grow, William; Marston's Wharf, 1782 *8529.30 p12*
Growley, John 31; Ontario, 1871 *1823.21 p142*
Gruaux, Jeanne; Quebec, 1670 *4514.3 p321*
Grub, Abraham; America, 1857 *5475.1 p556*
  *Wife:*Margarethe Schneider
  *Daughter:*Elisabeth
  *Daughter:*Charlotte
  *Son:*Gustav Adolph
  *Son:*Friedrich Philipp
  *Daughter:*Julia
  *Son:*Georg Wilhelm
Grub, Charlotte SEE Grub, Abraham
Grub, Elisabeth SEE Grub, Abraham
Grub, Friedrich Philipp SEE Grub, Abraham
Grub, Georg Wilhelm SEE Grub, Abraham
Grub, Gustav Adolph SEE Grub, Abraham
Grub, Julia SEE Grub, Abraham
Grub, Margarethe Schneider SEE Grub, Abraham
Grubb, Frank; Wisconsin, 1905 *6795.8 p175*
Grubb, George; Illinois, 1856 *6079.1 p6*
Grubb, George 25; Ontario, 1871 *1823.17 p62*
Grubb, Peter; Ohio, 1809-1852 *4511.35 p19*
Grubb, Peter; Washington, 1889 *2770.40 p27*
Gruber, Alfred; Pittsburgh, 1892 *2526.42 p160*
Gruber, F. 34; America, 1846 *778.6 p147*
Gruber, Johann Michael; America, 1867 *7919.3 p531*
Gruber, Madeline 19; America, 1847 *778.6 p147*
Gruber, Philip; Illinois, 1854 *6079.1 p6*
Gruber, Rosalia 21; America, 1847 *778.6 p147*
Gruber, Sebast. 20; Halifax, N.S., 1902 *1860.4 p43*
Gruber, Wilhelm Alois; Pittsburgh, 1888 *2526.42 p160*
Grubert, Claude Antoin; Illinois, 1852 *6079.1 p6*
Grubka, Rozalia; Detroit, 1929 *1640.55 p116*
Gruchac, John 38; New York, NY, 1920 *930.50 p49*
Gruche, John; Marblehead, MA, 1700-1729 *9228.50 p258*
Gruchie, John; Marblehead, MA, 1700-1729 *9228.50 p258*
Gruchy, . . .; Boston, 1769 *9228.50 p5*
Gruchy, Philip; Boston, 1769 *9228.50 p48*
Gruchy, Thomas James De; Boston, 1719-1741 *9228.50 p17*
Gruchy, Walter John; America, 1857-1944 *9228.50 p177*
Grudzin, Adam; Detroit, 1929-1930 *6214.5 p67*
Gruebill, Henry; Ohio, 1809-1852 *4511.35 p19*
Gruen, James 42; Ontario, 1871 *1823.17 p62*
Gruener, Philipp; Virginia, 1831 *152.20 p64*
Gruenig, Ludwig; Illinois, 1852 *6079.1 p6*
Gruenmeyer, Johann 67; New Orleans, 1847 *778.6 p147*
Gruenmeyer, Joseph 29; New Orleans, 1847 *778.6 p147*
Gruenmeyer, Marianne 22; New Orleans, 1847 *778.6 p147*
Gruenmeyer, Marianne 66; New Orleans, 1847 *778.6 p147*
Gruetzner, Alvine; Wisconsin, 1888 *6795.8 p90*
Grukow, Johann; Iowa, 1896 *1211.15 p10*
Grum, Herman; North Carolina, 1710 *3629.40 p4*
Grun, Barbara Altmeyer SEE Grun, Hubert
Grun, Dorothea 8; New York, NY, 1885 *6954.7 p40*
Grun, Dorothea 32; New York, NY, 1885 *6954.7 p40*
Grun, Elisabeth 8 SEE Grun, Mathias
Grun, Elisabeth Becker 22 SEE Grun, Wilhelm
Grun, Emelia 11 months; New York, NY, 1885 *6954.7 p40*
Grun, Friedrich SEE Grun, Wilhelm
Grun, Hubert; America, 1836 *5475.1 p65*
  *Wife:*Barbara Altmeyer
  With 7 children
Grun, Johann 9; New York, NY, 1885 *6954.7 p40*
Grun, Katharina Lorig 33 SEE Grun, Mathias

Grun, Mathias 32; America, 1857 *5475.1 p362*
  *Wife:*Katharina Lorig 33
  *Son:*Nikolaus 3
  *Daughter:*Elisabeth 8
Grun, Nikolaus 3 SEE Grun, Mathias
Grun, Peter 36; New York, NY, 1885 *6954.7 p40*
Grun, Wilhelm; America, 1837 *5475.1 p63*
  *Wife:*Elisabeth Becker
  *Son:*Friedrich
Grunbaum, Rosette; America, 1867 *7919.3 p525*
Grund, Joseph; Iowa, 1917 *1211.15 p10*
Grund, Wilhelm Heinrich; America, 1873 *5475.1 p71*
Grunder, Jacob; Ohio, 1809-1852 *4511.35 p19*
Grunder, Michael; Wisconsin, 1893 *6795.8 p102*
Grundler, Anton; Iowa, 1893 *1211.15 p10*
Grundler, Joseph; Iowa, 1896 *1211.15 p10*
Grundman, Fred.; Wisconsin, 1905 *6795.8 p233*
Grundmeier, Heinrich; Port uncertain, 1853 *7420.1 p105*
Grundmeier, Johann Carl Ludwig; America, 1857 *7420.1 p161*
  With wife & 2 daughters
Grundmeyer, Caroline Sophia Louise Schrader SEE Grundmeyer, Johann Christian Ludwig
Grundmeyer, Johann Christian Ludwig; America, 1857 *7420.1 p161*
  *Wife:*Caroline Sophia Louise Schrader
Grundy, George Henry 26; Ontario, 1871 *1823.17 p62*
Grundy, Henry; North Carolina, 1843 *1088.45 p12*
Grundy, John 54; Ontario, 1871 *1823.21 p142*
Gruneisen, George; New York, 1860 *358.56 p149*
Grunenwald, Angela SEE Grunenwald, Jakob
Grunenwald, Christine; America, 1883 *5475.1 p377*
Grunenwald, Jakob SEE Grunenwald, Jakob
Grunenwald, Jakob; Wisconsin, 1883 *5475.1 p360*
  *Son:*Jakob
  *Daughter:*Angela
Grunenwald, Margarethe; America, 1883 *5475.1 p377*
Grunenwald, Nikolaus; America, 1883 *5475.1 p377*
  *Wife:*Susanna Ernst
  *Son:*Peter
Grunenwald, Peter SEE Grunenwald, Nikolaus
Grunenwald, Susanna Ernst SEE Grunenwald, Nikolaus
Grunerts, Theodor; America, 1890 *5475.1 p424*
Grunewald, Adam 17; America, 1881 *2526.42 p190*
Grunewald, Anna Margaretha; America, 1832 *2526.42 p178*
Grunewald, Barbara; America, 1855 *2526.42 p136*
  With 3 children
Grunewald, Barbara 55; America, 1891 *2526.43 p120*
Grunewald, Elisabeth 29; America, 1844 *2526.42 p190*
  With child 2
  With child 1
Grunewald, Elisabeth Margarethe; America, 1840 *8115.12 p325*
Grunewald, Franz 30; Galveston, TX, 1844 *3967.10 p372*
Grunewald, Friedrich 14; America, 1865 *2526.42 p141*
Grunewald, Georg; America, 1889 *2526.42 p130*
Grunewald, Georg 7 SEE Grunewald, Johannes
Grunewald, Helena; America, 1881 *5475.1 p263*
Grunewald, Jakob; America, 1855 *2526.42 p141*
Grunewald, Jakob 58; America, 1866 *2526.42 p141*
Grunewald, Johann Michael; America, 1766 *2526.43 p130*
Grunewald, Johannes 17; America, 1858 *2526.42 p141*
Grunewald, Johannes 45; America, 1855 *2526.42 p190*
  *Wife:*Maria
  *Daughter:*Katharine 11
  *Son:*Georg 7
  *Son:*Philipp 14
Grunewald, Katharine 11 SEE Grunewald, Johannes
Grunewald, Maria SEE Grunewald, Johannes
Grunewald, Maria Magdalena; America, 1785 *2526.42 p118*
Grunewald, Michael; America, 1853 *2526.42 p190*
Grunewald, Nikolaus; Pennsylvania, 1771 *2526.43 p130*
Grunewald, Peter; America, 1871 *2526.42 p199*
Grunewald, Peter 16; America, 1854 *2526.43 p130*
Grunewald, Philipp; America, 1883 *2526.42 p181*
Grunewald, Philipp 14 SEE Grunewald, Johannes
Grunewald, Philipp 30; America, 1873 *2526.43 p130*
Grunger, Wilhelmina; Dakota, 1885 *554.30 p25*
Grunhagen, Heinrich; Valdivia, Chile, 1851 *1192.4 p51*
Grunheiser, Johann; America, 1847 *5475.1 p345*
Gruning, Christoph Johann; Wisconsin, 1875 *6795.8 p201*
Gruning, Friedresh Wilhelm; Wisconsin, 1864 *6795.8 p231*
Gruninger, Francis; New York, 1859 *358.56 p100*
Grunwald, Daniel 31; New York, NY, 1885 *1883.7 p46*
Grunwald, Emilie 3; New York, NY, 1893 *1883.7 p39*
Grunwald, Emilie 3; New York, NY, 1893 *1883.7 p47*

Grunwald, Gottl.; Valdivia, Chile, 1850 ***1192.4*** *p49*
With wife
With child 18
With child 10
Grunwald, Helena 10; New York, NY, 1893 ***1883.7*** *p39*
Grunwald, Helena 10; New York, NY, 1893 ***1883.7*** *p47*
Grunwald, Johann; New York, NY, 1893 ***1883.7*** *p39*
Grunwald, Johann 4; New York, NY, 1893 ***1883.7*** *p47*
Grunwald, Johann 36; New York, NY, 1893 ***1883.7*** *p39*
Grunwald, Julia 36; New York, NY, 1893 ***1883.7*** *p47*
Grunwald, Maria 11; New York, NY, 1893 ***1883.7*** *p39*
Grunwald, Maria 11; New York, NY, 1893 ***1883.7*** *p47*
Grunwald, Martha 6 months; New York, NY, 1893 ***1883.7*** *p39*
Grunwald, Martha 6 months; New York, NY, 1893 ***1883.7*** *p47*
Grunwald, Pauline 1; New York, NY, 1893 ***1883.7*** *p39*
Grunwald, Pauline 1; New York, NY, 1893 ***1883.7*** *p47*
Grunwald, Wilhelm 5; New York, NY, 1893 ***1883.7*** *p39*
Grunwald, Wilhelm 5; New York, NY, 1893 ***1883.7*** *p47*
Grupe, Anne Sophie Wilhelmine *SEE* Grupe, Justine Wilhelmine Eleonore
Grupe, Carl Christian; America, 1857 ***7420.1*** *p162*
Grupe, Christian; America, 1854 ***7420.1*** *p120*
Grupe, Johann Heinrich Christoph; America, 1858 ***7420.1*** *p177*
Grupe, Justine Wilhelmine Eleonore; New York, NY, 1856 ***7420.1*** *p147*
*Sister:*Anne Sophie Wilhelmine
Grupe, Ludwig; America, 1857 ***7420.1*** *p162*
Grupe, Peter; Ohio, 1809-1852 ***4511.35*** *p19*
Grupe, Wilhelm; America, 1859 ***7420.1*** *p185*
Gruse, Emilie; Wisconsin, 1885 ***6795.8*** *p81*
Grush, Elizabeth; Illinois, 1847 ***9228.50*** *p259*
Grush, John; Marblehead, MA, 1700-1729 ***9228.50*** *p258*
Grush, Judith 71; Massachusetts, 1847 ***9228.50*** *p18A*
Grush, Philip; Beverly, MA, 1800-1846 ***9228.50*** *p259*
Grush, Philip; Massachusetts, 1769 ***9228.50*** *p257*
Grusseau, Marie; Quebec, 1667 ***4514.3*** *p321*
Grute Family ; Windsor, Ont., n.d. ***9228.50*** *p259*
Grutschky, A.; Galveston, TX, 1855 ***571.7*** *p18*
Grut Sheppard, Wm.; Quebec, 1820 ***9228.50*** *p129*
Grutt, Benjamin; Illinois, 1820 ***9228.50*** *p259*
Gry, Mathias; America, 1883 ***5475.1*** *p204*
Gryc, Alois F.; Kansas, 1909 ***2853.20*** *p210*
Grygo, Joseph; Chicago, 1930 ***121.35*** *p100*
Gryzen, L. 36; America, 1843 ***778.6*** *p147*
Grzemia, Joseph; Wisconsin, 1881 ***6795.8*** *p58*
Grzenkowska, Martha; Detroit, 1890 ***9980.23*** *p97*
Grzesik, Wiktoria 22; New York, NY, 1912 ***8355.1*** *p15*
Grzeszczeszyn, Mike; Detroit, 1929-1930 ***6214.5*** *p70*
Grzybala, Franciszek 38; New York, NY, 1920 ***930.50*** *p48*
Grzybowska, Aniela 17; New York, NY, 1911 ***6533.11*** *p10*
Gschwind, Frederick; Nova Scotia, 1784 ***7105*** *p23*
Gsell, Andreas 1; Galveston, TX, 1844 ***3967.10*** *p375*
Gsell, Anna Maria 9; Galveston, TX, 1844 ***3967.10*** *p375*
Gsell, Michael 37; Galveston, TX, 1844 ***3967.10*** *p375*
Gsell, Therese 3; Galveston, TX, 1844 ***3967.10*** *p375*
Gsell, Xaver 10; Galveston, TX, 1844 ***3967.10*** *p375*
Gual, Paul; Louisiana, 1874 ***4981.45*** *p132*
Gualliardo, G.; Louisiana, 1874-1875 ***4981.45*** *p29*
Gualliardo, L.; Louisiana, 1874-1875 ***4981.45*** *p29*
Guardheffner, Andrew; Ohio, 1809-1852 ***4511.35*** *p19*
Guay, Frank 50; Ontario, 1871 ***1823.21*** *p142*
Guay, Jean 22; Quebec, 1646 ***9221.17*** *p165*
Gubbins, Robert 40; Ontario, 1871 ***1823.17*** *p62*
Gubert, Ernst Heinr. *SEE* Gubert, Johann Dieder. Christ.
Gubert, Friedrich Christian *SEE* Gubert, Johann Dieder. Christ.
Gubert, Friedrich Wilh. *SEE* Gubert, Johann Dieder. Christ.
Gubert, Johann Dieder. Christ.; America, 1854 ***7420.1*** *p120*
*Wife:*Sophie Eleonore Kempker
*Son:*Ernst Heinr.
*Son:*Friedrich Wilh.
*Son:*Friedrich Christian
Gubert, Sophie Eleonore Kempker *SEE* Gubert, Johann Dieder. Christ.
Gubin, Josef; New York, NY, 1848 ***2853.20*** *p100*
Guch, Friedrich Wilhelm; Wisconsin, 1900 ***6795.8*** *p159*
Guckeisen, Christina Schreier *SEE* Guckeisen, Johann
Guckeisen, Johann; Chicago, 1852 ***5475.1*** *p263*
With wife & child
Guckeisen, Johann; Chicago, 1880 ***5475.1*** *p241*
*Wife:*Christina Schreier
Guckeisen, Nikolaus; Wisconsin, 1891 ***5475.1*** *p326*
Guckenmuhs, Gustav; America, 1873 ***5475.1*** *p355*
Guckert, Friedrich; Brazil, 1862 ***5475.1*** *p497*
*Wife:*Katharina Scharf
*Daughter:*Katharina
Guckert, Juliane; Brazil, 1863 ***5475.1*** *p498*
*Daughter:*Phillippine
*Daughter:*Katharina
*Son:*Michel
*Son:*Friedrich
Guckert, Katharina *SEE* Guckert, Friedrich
Guckert, Katharina Scharf *SEE* Guckert, Friedrich
Gudaitis, Anna 7; New York, NY, 1890 ***1883.7*** *p48*
Gudaitis, Ozib 40; New York, NY, 1890 ***1883.7*** *p48*
Gudarian, Gustav; Wisconsin, 1880 ***6795.8*** *p47*
Gudel, Anne 8; America, 1846 ***778.6*** *p147*
Gudel, Catherine 16; America, 1846 ***778.6*** *p147*
Gudel, Louis 2; America, 1846 ***778.6*** *p147*
Gudel, Louis 40; America, 1846 ***778.6*** *p147*
Gudel, Marie 12; America, 1846 ***778.6*** *p147*
Gudel, Marie 38; America, 1846 ***778.6*** *p147*
Gudenkauf, Anton; Ohio, 1840-1897 ***8365.35*** *p16*
Guderian, Gustav; Wisconsin, 1880 ***6795.8*** *p47*
Gudgeon, William 65; Ontario, 1871 ***1823.21*** *p142*
Gudlestone, Mary Ann 55; Ontario, 1871 ***1823.21*** *p142*
Gudmundsen, Gilbert; Washington, 1884 ***2770.40*** *p192*
Guedon, Mrs. 26; Louisiana, 1848 ***778.6*** *p147*
Guedon, Ad. 40; Louisiana, 1848 ***778.6*** *p147*
Guedon, George; Louisiana, 1874 ***4981.45*** *p132*
Guedon, Marie-Anne; Quebec, 1665 ***4514.3*** *p321*
Guedon, Pierre 19; New Orleans, 1848 ***778.6*** *p147*
Guedon, Theodore 38; America, 1843 ***778.6*** *p147*
Guege, John Frederick William; Wisconsin, 1871 ***6795.8*** *p152*
Guehne, Carl; Galveston, TX, 1855 ***571.7*** *p16*
Guel, Urbain Jean 20; New Orleans, 1848 ***778.6*** *p147*
Guelzow, Emielie; Wisconsin, 1894 ***6795.8*** *p152*
Guelzow, Pauline; Wisconsin, 1893 ***6795.8*** *p220*
Guenard, Andres; Puerto Rico, 1815-1915 ***3476.25*** *p112*
Guenard Merand, Andres; Puerto Rico, 1815 ***3476.25*** *p112*
Guenaud, Francois 33; Mississippi, 1845 ***778.6*** *p147*
Guender, John; Ohio, 1809-1852 ***4511.35*** *p19*
Guener, Charles 34; New Orleans, 1848 ***778.6*** *p147*
Guenet, Marie 29; Quebec, 1639 ***9221.17*** *p84*
Gueneville, Jeanne; Quebec, 1671 ***4514.3*** *p321*
Guennec, O. M.; Louisiana, 1836-1840 ***4981.45*** *p212*
Guenther, John George; New York, 1859 ***358.56*** *p101*
Guenther, Karl Friedrich; Wisconsin, 1898 ***6795.8*** *p157*
Guerante, Nicolas; Quebec, 1658 ***9221.17*** *p382*
Guerard, Catherine; Quebec, 1669 ***4514.3*** *p322*
Guerard, Francois 28; America, 1846 ***778.6*** *p147*
Guerard, Francois; Quebec, 1659 ***9221.17*** *p413*
Guerard, Martin 25; Quebec, 1658 ***9221.17*** *p382*
Gueretin, Louis 20; Montreal, 1653 ***9221.17*** *p291*
Guerin, Ann 70; Ontario, 1871 ***1823.21*** *p142*
Guerin, Emilie 20; New Orleans, 1848 ***778.6*** *p147*
Guerin, Eugenie 27; New Orleans, 1848 ***778.6*** *p148*
Guerin, Francois; Illinois, 1852 ***6079.1*** *p6*
Guerin, Jean; Quebec, 1641 ***9221.17*** *p104*
Guerin, Jean-Edmond 28; Galveston, TX, 1845 ***3967.10*** *p376*
Guerin, Louis; Quebec, 1644 ***9221.17*** *p143*
Guerin, Madeleine; Quebec, 1665 ***4514.3*** *p322*
Guerin, Marie; Canada, 1681 ***1142.10*** *p128*
With family
Guerin, Marie 23; New Orleans, 1845 ***778.6*** *p148*
Guerin, Marie-Jeanne; Quebec, 1667 ***4514.3*** *p322*
Guerin, Melanie 20; America, 1843 ***778.6*** *p148*
Guerin, Pierre 26; New Orleans, 1848 ***778.6*** *p148*
Guerin, Susannah; Boston, 1808 ***9228.50*** *p260*
Guerin, Toussaint; Quebec, 1652 ***9221.17*** *p259*
Guerineau, Mr. 36; America, 1844 ***778.6*** *p148*
Guerineau, Louis 21; Quebec, 1656 ***9221.17*** *p338*
Gueritil, Antoine 19; Quebec, 1661 ***9221.17*** *p459*
Guerne, Claude 34; Texas, 1848 ***778.6*** *p148*
Guerneze, Guillaume de; Quebec, 1534 ***9228.50*** *p3*
Guernsey, Guillaume; Canada, 1534 ***9228.50*** *p260*
Guernsey, Joseph G.; Connecticut, 1730 ***9228.50*** *p260*
*Wife:*Rachel Marchant
Guernsey, Lydia 71; Ontario, 1871 ***1823.21*** *p142*
Guernsey, Rachel Marchant *SEE* Guernsey, Joseph G.
Guerrd, Lewis; Louisiana, 1836-1840 ***4981.45*** *p212*
Guerre, Francois 48; New Orleans, 1847 ***778.6*** *p148*
Guerri, Angelo; Illinois, 1930 ***121.35*** *p101*
Guerrier, Bonne; Quebec, 1665 ***4514.3*** *p322*
Guerrier, Jean 24; Montreal, 1660 ***9221.17*** *p441*
Guerrineau, M. 33; America, 1840 ***778.6*** *p148*
Guersaut, Gabriel 21; Quebec, 1662 ***9221.17*** *p486*
Guest, James 59; Ontario, 1871 ***1823.21*** *p142*
Guest, John; Colorado, 1894 ***1029.59*** *p35*
Guest, Polly A. 28; Michigan, 1880 ***4491.42*** *p12*
Guest, Robert 56; Ontario, 1871 ***1823.21*** *p142*
Guest, Thomas 60; Ontario, 1871 ***1823.21*** *p142*
Guest, William 63; Michigan, 1880 ***4491.42*** *p12*
Guest, William W. 49; Ontario, 1871 ***1823.21*** *p142*
Guester, Anna; New Orleans, 1851 ***7242.30*** *p143*
Gueth, Johann Adam; Venezuela, 1843 ***3899.5*** *p541*
Gueunick, Antoinette; Wisconsin, 1846-1856 ***1495.20*** *p29*
Guevin, Etienne; Virginia, 1700 ***9230.15*** *p81*
Gueydin, Mrs. 30; America, 1844 ***778.6*** *p148*
Gueyriaux, Chas. 50; Texas, 1843 ***778.6*** *p148*
Gueyron, C. E. 35; New Orleans, 1848 ***778.6*** *p148*
Gueyron, W. 11; New Orleans, 1848 ***778.6*** *p148*
Gugelman, Jacob; Ohio, 1809-1852 ***4511.35*** *p19*
Gugenmiller, Henry; New York, NY, 1843 ***471.10*** *p86*
Guggenheim, Barbara Meyers *SEE* Guggenheim, Meyer
Guggenheim, Meyer; Philadelphia, 1858 ***8513.31*** *p311*
*Wife:*Barbara Meyers
Guhan, William 49; Ontario, 1871 ***1823.17*** *p62*
Guiberge, Jeanne 3 *SEE* Guiberge, Mathurine Desbordes
Guiberge, Mathurine 25; Montreal, 1659 ***9221.17*** *p421*
*Daughter:*Jeanne 3
Guibert, . . .; Maryland, 1600-1699 ***9228.50*** *p260*
Guibert, Michel 11; Montreal, 1659 ***9221.17*** *p422*
Guiberteau, Baptiste 20; America, 1845 ***778.6*** *p148*
Guibertot, Felicie 28; Louisiana, 1848 ***778.6*** *p148*
Guibertot, Michel 18; Louisiana, 1848 ***778.6*** *p148*
Guichard, Francois 35; America, 1843 ***778.6*** *p148*
Guichart, Mathurin 40; Quebec, 1658 ***9221.17*** *p382*
Guichelin, Catherine; Quebec, 1669 ***4514.3*** *p322*
Guiender, N.; Louisiana, 1841-1844 ***4981.45*** *p210*
Guignard, Pierre 32; Quebec, 1657 ***9221.17*** *p359*
Guignion, Harriet Mary Rose *SEE* Guignion, Nicholas, Sr.
Guignion, Mary Ann; Massachusetts, 1700-1799 ***9228.50*** *p191*
Guignion, Mary Ann; Massachusetts, 1700-1799 ***9228.50*** *p264*
Guignion, Nicholas, Sr.; Quebec, 1842 ***9228.50*** *p260*
*Wife:*Harriet Mary Rose
Guignion, Simon; Quebec, 1800-1840 ***9228.50*** *p264*
Guigod, Mr. 30; Port uncertain, 1842 ***778.6*** *p148*
Guilani, Jean Andre 27; Mexico, 1848 ***778.6*** *p148*
Guilbaut, Suzanne; Quebec, 1663 ***4514.3*** *p349*
Guilbert, . . .; Maryland, 1600-1699 ***9228.50*** *p260*
Guilbert, James; Wisconsin, 1850 ***9228.50*** *p264*
Guilbert, Judith; Ohio, 1800-1840 ***9228.50*** *p264*
Guilbert, Marguerite; Ohio, 1800-1840 ***9228.50*** *p264*
Guilbert, Martha; Ohio, n.d. ***9228.50*** *p264*
Guilbert, Rachel; Ohio, n.d. ***9228.50*** *p264*
Guild, Alexander; Illinois, 1918 ***6007.60*** *p9*
Guild, Ann 20 *SEE* Guild, John
Guild, John 18; Dedham, MA, 1636 ***9228.50*** *p264*
*Brother:*Samuel 16
*Sister:*Ann 20
Guild, Mathew; Maine, 1653 ***9228.50*** *p270*
Guild, Samuel 16 *SEE* Guild, John
Guilde, Ann 20 *SEE* Guilde, John
Guilde, John 18; Dedham, MA, 1636 ***9228.50*** *p264*
*Sister:*Ann 20
*Brother:*Samuel 16
Guilde, Samuel 16 *SEE* Guilde, John
Guile, Ann 20 *SEE* Guile, John
Guile, John 18; Dedham, MA, 1636 ***9228.50*** *p264*
*Sister:*Ann 20
*Brother:*Samuel 16
Guile, Samuel 16 *SEE* Guile, John
Guilebaut, Simone 34; Quebec, 1647 ***9221.17*** *p180*
Guilfoye, John 37; Ontario, 1871 ***1823.21*** *p142*
Guilfoyl, Edward 60; Ontario, 1871 ***1823.21*** *p142*
Guiline, Philipine 24; America, 1847 ***778.6*** *p148*
Guill, Ann 20 *SEE* Guill, John
Guill, John 18; Dedham, MA, 1636 ***9228.50*** *p264*
*Brother:*Samuel 16
*Sister:*Ann 20
Guill, Samuel 16 *SEE* Guill, John
Guillard, Peter; Portsmouth, NH, 1733 ***9228.50*** *p248*
Guillas, Pierre 47; Texas, 1848 ***778.6*** *p148*
Guillaume, Mr. 21; America, 1847 ***778.6*** *p148*
Guillaume, A.; Louisiana, 1874 ***4981.45*** *p295*
Guillaume, Alexis 28; America, 1840 ***778.6*** *p148*
Guillaume, Anne; Quebec, 1671 ***4514.3*** *p322*
Guillaume, Carteret; Connecticut, 1690 ***9228.50*** *p265*
Guillaume, Charles; Connecticut, 1690 ***9228.50*** *p265*
Guillaume, Flor..t 50; America, 1840 ***778.6*** *p148*
Guillaume, Jacques, Son; America, 1677-1827 ***9228.50*** *p265*
With brother
Guillaume, Jeanette 39; America, 1840 ***778.6*** *p148*
Guillaume, Marie; Quebec, 1670 ***4514.3*** *p323*
Guillaumet, . . .; Quebec, 1652 ***9221.17*** *p259*
Guillaumi, George; Ohio, 1809-1852 ***4511.35*** *p19*
Guille, . . .; New York, NY, 1834 ***9228.50*** *p449*
Guille, Andrew; Ohio, 1860 ***9228.50*** *p266*
Guille, Ann 20 *SEE* Guille, John
Guille, Arthur *SEE* Guille, James Philippe
Guille, James Philippe; Virginia, 1900-1940 ***9228.50*** *p266*
*Son:*Arthur

Guille, John 18; Dedham, MA, 1636 ***9228.50*** *p264*
*Sister:*Ann 20
*Brother:*Samuel 16
Guille, Joseph Francis Nicholas; Philadelphia, 1810 ***9228.50*** *p265*
Guille, Julie Marie; America, n.d. ***9228.50*** *p266*
Guille, Mathew; Maine, 1653 ***9228.50*** *p270*
Guille, Noah; Boston, 1650-1712 ***9228.50*** *p266*
Guille, Samuel 16 *SEE* Guille, John
Guille, Thomas; New York, NY, 1834 ***9228.50*** *p266*
Guille, Walter Peter; America, 1865-1900 ***9228.50*** *p266*
Guilleaume, Adele 2; New Orleans, 1843 ***778.6*** *p148*
Guilleaume, Jean-Baptiste 25; New Orleans, 1843 ***778.6*** *p148*
Guilleaume, Josephine 22; New Orleans, 1843 ***778.6*** *p148*
Guilleaume, Leonor 1; New Orleans, 1843 ***778.6*** *p148*
Guilleaume, Leonor 54; New Orleans, 1843 ***778.6*** *p148*
Guilleaume, Lucene 1; New Orleans, 1843 ***778.6*** *p148*
Guilleaume, Madelaine 33; New Orleans, 1843 ***778.6*** *p148*
Guilleaume, Marcelin 54; New Orleans, 1843 ***778.6*** *p148*
Guilleaume, Victoire 24; New Orleans, 1843 ***778.6*** *p149*
Guilleaume, Victor 16; New Orleans, 1843 ***778.6*** *p149*
Guilleaume, Xavier 14; New Orleans, 1843 ***778.6*** *p149*
Guillebert, Pierre; Quebec, 1650 ***9221.17*** *p227*
Guilleboeuf, Marie-Madeleine; Quebec, 1668 ***4514.3*** *p323*
Guillebourday, Marguerite; Quebec, 1650 ***9221.17*** *p227*
Guillebourg, Charles; Quebec, 1646 ***9221.17*** *p165*
Guilleman, A. 35; America, 1843 ***778.6*** *p149*
Guillemol, Louis Marie 35; New Orleans, 1848 ***778.6*** *p149*
Guillemot Duplessis, Anne 2 *SEE* Guillemot Duplessis, Guillaume
Guillemot Duplessis, Dominique *SEE* Guillemot Duplessis, Guillaume
Guillemot Duplessis, Etiennette Despres 24 *SEE* Guillemot Duplessis, Guillaume
Guillemot Duplessis, Francois *SEE* Guillemot Duplessis, Guillaume
Guillemot Duplessis, Guillaume; Quebec, 1651 ***2314.30*** *p166*
Guillemot Duplessis, Guillaume; Quebec, 1651 ***2314.30*** *p184*
Guillemot Duplessis, Guillaume 43; Quebec, 1651 ***9221.17*** *p235*
*Wife:*Etiennette Despres 24
*Daughter:*Dominique
*Daughter:*Anne 2
*Son:*Francois
Guillemot Duplessis-Kerbodot, Anne 2 *SEE* Guillemot Duplessis-Kerbodot, Guillaume
Guillemot Duplessis-Kerbodot, Dominique *SEE* Guillemot Duplessis-Kerbodot, Guillaume
Guillemot Duplessis-Kerbodot, Etiennette Despres 24 *SEE* Guillemot Duplessis-Kerbodot, Guillaume
Guillemot Duplessis-Kerbodot, Francois *SEE* Guillemot Duplessis-Kerbodot, Guillaume
Guillemot Duplessis-Kerbodot, Guillaume 43; Quebec, 1651 ***9221.17*** *p235*
*Wife:*Etiennette Despres 24
*Son:*Francois
*Daughter:*Dominique
*Daughter:*Anne 2
Guillenone, Nicola; New Orleans, 1851 ***7242.30*** *p143*
Guillet, Abraham 36; Ohio, 1847 ***778.6*** *p149*
Guillet, Ant. 30; America, 1840 ***778.6*** *p149*
Guillet, Edouard 28; Missouri, 1845 ***778.6*** *p149*
Guillet, Fanny 7; Ohio, 1847 ***778.6*** *p149*
Guillet, Francois; Quebec, 1658 ***9221.17*** *p382*
Guillet, Joseph 5; Ohio, 1847 ***778.6*** *p149*
Guillet, Mary 1; Ohio, 1847 ***778.6*** *p149*
Guillet, Mathew; Salem, MA, 1641 ***9228.50*** *p248*
Guillet, Mathurin; Quebec, 1646 ***9221.17*** *p166*
Guillet, Peter; Maine, 1636 ***9228.50*** *p267*
Guillet, Pierre 15; Quebec, 1642 ***9221.17*** *p118*
Guillet, Walter John; Brazil, 1850 ***9228.50*** *p266*
Guillet, Wm.; America, 1807 ***9228.50*** *p341*
Guillet Family ; Akron, OH, n.d. ***9228.50*** *p267*
Guilliard, Peter; Portsmouth, NH, 1733 ***9228.50*** *p248*
Guilliem, George 25; New Orleans, 1845 ***778.6*** *p149*
Guillin, Francoise; Quebec, 1668 ***4514.3*** *p323*
Guillin, Guillaume; Montreal, 1642 ***9221.17*** *p123*
Guillnau, Louiis 31; New Orleans, 1841 ***778.6*** *p149*
Guillocheau, Renee; Quebec, 1667 ***4514.3*** *p353*
Guillodeau, Madeleine; Quebec, 1669 ***4514.3*** *p323*
Guillon, Delphine 26; America, 1840 ***778.6*** *p149*
Guillot, Adrien; Quebec, 1661 ***9221.17*** *p459*
Guillot, Baptiste 47; America, 1846 ***778.6*** *p149*
Guillot, Catherine; Quebec, 1663 ***4514.3*** *p323*
Guillot, Claude 8; America, 1846 ***778.6*** *p149*
Guillot, Emerentine 9; America, 1846 ***778.6*** *p149*
Guillot, Francois 5; America, 1846 ***778.6*** *p149*
Guillot, Francoise 40; America, 1846 ***778.6*** *p149*
Guillot, Geoffroy; Quebec, 1649 ***9221.17*** *p214*
Guillot, Guillaume 45; Texas, 1848 ***778.6*** *p149*
Guillot, Jean; Quebec, 1644 ***9221.17*** *p143*
Guillot, L. M. 19; America, 1841 ***778.6*** *p149*
Guillot, Marie 13; America, 1846 ***778.6*** *p149*
Guillot, Marie; Quebec, 1662 ***9221.17*** *p482*
Guillot, Pierre 4; America, 1846 ***778.6*** *p149*
Guilloteau, Pierre; Quebec, 1661 ***9221.17*** *p459*
Guilmour, John 33; Ontario, 1871 ***1823.21*** *p142*
Guimin, Judith; Nova Scotia, 1753 ***3051*** *p112*
Guimont, Louis; Quebec, 1647 ***9221.17*** *p182*
Guinet, Georg 23; America, 1847 ***778.6*** *p149*
Guinet, Nicolas 27; America, 1847 ***778.6*** *p149*
Guinle, Joseph 18; New Orleans, 1845 ***778.6*** *p149*
Guinner, Fredrick; New York, 1860 ***358.56*** *p5*
Guinot, Francois; Quebec, 1646 ***9221.17*** *p166*
Guion, Barbe 35; Quebec, 1652 ***9221.17*** *p263*
Guion, Claude 7 *SEE* Guion, Mathurine Robin
Guion, Denis 5 *SEE* Guion, Mathurine Robin
Guion, Francois 1 *SEE* Guion, Mathurine Robin
Guion, Gabriel 29; Quebec, 1659 ***9221.17*** *p403*
Guion, Jean; Quebec, 1638 ***9221.17*** *p77*
*Wife:*Madeleine Goule
Guion, Jean 15 *SEE* Guion, Jean
Guion, Jean 42; Quebec, 1634 ***9221.17*** *p36*
*Son:*Jean 15
Guion, Madeleine Goule *SEE* Guion, Jean
Guion, Marie 12 *SEE* Guion, Mathurine Robin
Guion, Mathurine; Quebec, 1636 ***9221.17*** *p56*
*Son:*Simon
*Daughter:*Marie
*Son:*Claude
*Son:*Michel
*Son:*Denis
*Son:*Francois
Guion, Michel 2 *SEE* Guion, Mathurine Robin
Guion, Simon 15 *SEE* Guion, Mathurine Robin
Guionow, Mary Ann; Massachusetts, 1700-1799 ***9228.50*** *p191*
Guionow, Mary Ann; Massachusetts, 1700-1799 ***9228.50*** *p264*
Guiot, Jean; Quebec, 1634 ***9221.17*** *p37*
Guiraud, L. M.; Louisiana, 1836-1841 ***4981.45*** *p208*
Guise, Jeannette; Ontario, 1967 ***9228.50*** *p267*
Guiseppe, G. 24; America, 1847 ***778.6*** *p150*
Guisselin, Catherine; Quebec, 1669-1675 ***1142.10*** *p128*
Guisson, Charles 33; Texas, 1848 ***778.6*** *p150*
Guitanny, Mr.; America, 1844 ***778.6*** *p150*
Guitar, John 28; America, 1848 ***778.6*** *p150*
Guitet, Jean; Quebec, 1637 ***9221.17*** *p70*
Guivelt, Etienne 33; America, 1847 ***778.6*** *p150*
Gujor, John R.; Colorado, 1887 ***1029.59*** *p35*
Guldner, Katharina; America, 1854 ***5475.1*** *p57*
Guletia, . . .; North America, n.d. ***9228.50*** *p239*
Gulich, Amalia 2; New York, NY, 1893 ***1883.7*** *p39*
Gulich, Elisabeth 24; New York, NY, 1893 ***1883.7*** *p39*
Gulich, Joh. 25; New York, NY, 1893 ***1883.7*** *p39*
Gullas, Pierre; Illinois, 1852 ***6079.1*** *p6*
Gullet, Peter; Maine, 1636 ***9228.50*** *p267*
Gullian, Ann; Ohio, 1875-1907 ***9228.50*** *p238*
Gulliksen, Christian; Colorado, 1883 ***1029.59*** *p35*
Gulliksen, Jens; Colorado, 1880 ***1029.59*** *p35*
Gulliksen, Jens; Colorado, 1895 ***1029.59*** *p35*
Gulling, Louis; Ohio, 1809-1852 ***4511.35*** *p19*
Gulling, Theobald; Ohio, 1809-1852 ***4511.35*** *p19*
Gulliver, Anthony; Boston, 1619-1659 ***1642*** *p3*
Gullock, Thomas; Maryland, 1673 ***1236.25*** *p48*
Gully, Katharina 22; Galveston, TX, 1844 ***3967.10*** *p373*
Gulpin, John; Boston, 1774 ***8529.30*** *p3A*
Gulzow, Emilie; Wisconsin, 1894 ***6795.8*** *p152*
Gumaer, Benjamin 70; Ontario, 1871 ***1823.21*** *p142*
Gumb, Lewis; North Carolina, 1858 ***1088.45*** *p12*
Gumela, George 40; New York, NY, 1920 ***930.50*** *p49*
Gummer, Miss; America, 1890 ***7420.1*** *p360*
Gummer, Anne Sophie Hinze *SEE* Gummer, Hans Heinrich Christoph
Gummer, Engel Dorothee Friederike *SEE* Gummer, Hans Heinrich Christoph
Gummer, Engel Marie; America, 1871 ***7420.1*** *p396*
Gummer, Engel Marie Sophie *SEE* Gummer, Hans Heinrich Christoph
Gummer, Friedrich Wilhelm *SEE* Gummer, Hans Heinrich Christoph
Gummer, Hans Heinrich Christoph; America, 1848 ***7420.1*** *p59*
*Wife:*Anne Sophie Hinze
*Daughter:*Engel Dorothee Friederike
*Son:*Friedrich Wilhelm
*Daughter:*Engel Marie Sophie
Gummer, Hans Heinrich Christoph; America, 1866 ***7420.1*** *p243*
Gummer, Hans Heinrich Otto; America, 1882 ***7420.1*** *p329*
Gummer, Heinrich Christoph Gottlieb; America, 1868 ***7420.1*** *p271*
With family
Gummer, Maria Dorothea; America, 1845 ***7420.1*** *p37*
Gumowski, John; Detroit, 1929-1930 ***6214.5*** *p67*
Gumpel, Abraham; America, 1849 ***7420.1*** *p64*
*Wife:*Henriette Bing
Gumpel, Henriette Bing *SEE* Gumpel, Abraham
Gumper, Maria Anna; Venezuela, 1843 ***3899.5*** *p542*
Gumpper, Maria Anna; Venezuela, 1843 ***3899.5*** *p542*
Gumz, Richard August Heinrich; Iowa, 1929 ***1211.15*** *p10*
Gun, Donald 33; North Carolina, 1774 ***1422.10*** *p59*
Gun, Thomas 41; Ontario, 1871 ***1823.21*** *p142*
Gunder, Elisabeth; America, 1881 ***5475.1*** *p151*
Gunderson, Ole; Washington, 1885 ***2770.40*** *p194*
Gundlach, Carl Wilhelm; America, 1882 ***7420.1*** *p329*
Gundlach, Jacob; Valparaiso, Chile, 1850 ***1192.4*** *p50*
Gundlach, Wilhelm; Port uncertain, 1911 ***7420.1*** *p402*
Gundry, Charles 38; Michigan, 1880 ***4491.42*** *p12*
Gundry, Hannah 59; Michigan, 1880 ***4491.33*** *p11*
Gundry, John 23; Michigan, 1880 ***4491.33*** *p11*
Gundry, Thomas 57; Michigan, 1880 ***4491.33*** *p11*
Gundy, David 45; Ontario, 1871 ***1823.21*** *p142*
Gunguat, P. 29; New Orleans, 1848 ***778.6*** *p150*
Gunkel, Anna Maria 27 *SEE* Gunkel, Mrs. Georg
Gunkel, Franz 18 *SEE* Gunkel, Mrs. Georg
Gunkel, Mrs. Georg; America, 1848 ***2526.42*** *p115*
*Child:*Anna Maria
*Child:*Franz
Gunloff, Lorenz 19; Missouri, 1845 ***778.6*** *p150*
Gunn, Alexander 52; Ontario, 1871 ***1823.21*** *p142*
Gunn, Ann 40; Michigan, 1880 ***4491.30*** *p14*
Gunn, Daniel 38; Ontario, 1871 ***1823.21*** *p142*
Gunn, David; Washington, 1883 ***2770.40*** *p136*
Gunn, G. M. 49; Ontario, 1871 ***1823.21*** *p142*
Gunn, Hugh 26; Ontario, 1871 ***1823.21*** *p142*
Gunn, Hugh 50; Ontario, 1871 ***1823.21*** *p142*
Gunn, John 65; Ontario, 1871 ***1823.17*** *p62*
Gunn, Marcus 70; Ontario, 1871 ***1823.21*** *p142*
Gunn, Robert 54; Ontario, 1871 ***1823.21*** *p142*
Gunn, Thomas 80; Michigan, 1880 ***4491.30*** *p14*
Gunn, William 40; Ontario, 1871 ***1823.17*** *p62*
Gunnarsen, Carl; Iowa, 1898 ***1211.15*** *p10*
Gunnarson, Victor; Iowa, 1922 ***1211.15*** *p10*
Gunne, John 56; Ontario, 1871 ***1823.17*** *p62*
Gunne, Robert 48; Ontario, 1871 ***1823.17*** *p62*
Gunnel, Clement; Boston, 1769 ***9228.50*** *p267*
Gunnerson, Kris; Washington, 1887 ***2770.40*** *p24*
Gunnert, Minna 21; New York, NY, 1894 ***6512.1*** *p183*
Gunniel, Clement; Boston, 1769 ***9228.50*** *p267*
Gunnin, John; St. John, N.B., 1847 ***2978.15*** *p35*
Gunnll, Clement; Boston, 1769 ***9228.50*** *p48*
Gunnll, Clement; Boston, 1769 ***9228.50*** *p267*
Gunpler, Johann Heinrich; America, 1868 ***7919.3*** *p528*
With wife & child
Gunrel, Sal. 24; America, 1840 ***778.6*** *p150*
Gunsch, Ernestine *SEE* Gunsch, Margarete
Gunsch, Margarete; America, 1867 ***7919.3*** *p534*
*Daughter:*Ernestine
Gunson, Henry 30; Ontario, 1871 ***1823.21*** *p142*
Gunter, Fidel 23; New Castle, DE, 1817-1818 ***90.20*** *p151*
Gunter, Johann Ch. 23; Portland, ME, 1911 ***970.38*** *p77*
Gunter, John W.; North Carolina, 1857 ***1088.45*** *p12*
Gunter, Joseph 40; New Castle, DE, 1817-1818 ***90.20*** *p151*
Gunter, William 49; Ontario, 1871 ***1823.21*** *p142*
Gunterblum, George; New York, 1860 ***358.56*** *p148*
Guntermann, Johann Christian; America, 1871 ***2526.43*** *p140*
Gunther, Adam 30; New York, NY, 1893 ***1883.7*** *p44*
Gunther, August; America, 1846 ***7420.1*** *p44*
With wife
With daughter 2
With daughter 14
With daughter 7
Gunther, Auguste; North Carolina, 1849 ***1088.45*** *p12*
Gunther, Carole. 4; New York, NY, 1893 ***1883.7*** *p44*
Gunther, Catha. 6; New York, NY, 1893 ***1883.7*** *p44*
Gunther, Charles; Louisiana, 1836-1841 ***4981.45*** *p208*
Gunther, Ernest; Colorado, 1892 ***1029.59*** *p35*
Gunther, Franz; America, 1834 ***5475.1*** *p467*
With family
Gunther, Georg 8; New York, NY, 1893 ***1883.7*** *p44*
Gunther, Heinrich; America, 1842 ***2526.42*** *p190*
With wife & child
Gunther, Jean 22; Port uncertain, 1847 ***778.6*** *p150*
Gunther, Johann; America, 1840 ***5475.1*** *p470*
Gunther, Joseph 40; New Castle, DE, 1817-1818 ***90.20*** *p151*

Gunther, Louis; Texas, 1852 ***3435.45*** *p35*
Gunther, Sebastian; America, 1868 ***7919.3*** *p535*
Gunther, Tobias 2; New York, NY, 1893 ***1883.7*** *p44*
Gunther, Wilh. 32; New York, NY, 1893 ***1883.7*** *p44*
Gunton, Ernest; Ontario, 1860 ***9228.50*** *p267*
Gunton, John Russell; Ontario, 1839-1859 ***9228.50*** *p267*
Gunton, Joseph Robert; Ontario, 1842-1919 ***9228.50*** *p267*
Guntz, John 28; America, 1846 ***778.6*** *p150*
Guntzenhouser, John; Ohio, 1809-1852 ***4511.35*** *p19*
Guoth, Johann Adam; Venezuela, 1843 ***3899.5*** *p541*
Guott, Johann Adam; Venezuela, 1843 ***3899.5*** *p541*
Guphill, . . .; Maine, n.d. ***9228.50*** *p268*
Guphill, . . .; New Brunswick, n.d. ***9228.50*** *p268*
Guppy, William 39; Ontario, 1871 ***1823.21*** *p142*
Guptil, . . .; Maine, n.d. ***9228.50*** *p268*
Guptil, . . .; New Brunswick, n.d. ***9228.50*** *p268*
Gurd, John 58; Ontario, 1871 ***1823.21*** *p142*
Gurd, William 31; Ontario, 1871 ***1823.21*** *p142*
Gurd, William 63; Ontario, 1871 ***1823.17*** *p62*
Gurden, Dick 28; Michigan, 1880 ***4491.30*** *p14*
Gurer, Jacob; Ohio, 1809-1852 ***4511.35*** *p19*
Gurger, Lewis; New York, 1859 ***358.56*** *p54*
Gurgon, Fcs. 28; America, 1841 ***778.6*** *p150*
Guriee, Louis Marie 23; New Orleans, 1848 ***778.6*** *p150*
Gurin, Patrick 35; Ontario, 1871 ***1823.21*** *p142*
Gurnett, William 42; Ontario, 1871 ***1823.17*** *p62*
Gurpson, Artha 25; Ontario, 1871 ***1823.21*** *p142*
Gurrin, Mary *SEE* Gurrin, William
Gurrin, William; Boston, 1714 ***9228.50*** *p260*
*Wife:*Mary
Gurski, Anna 8; New York, NY, 1894 ***6512.1*** *p184*
Gurski, Franz 24; New York, NY, 1894 ***6512.1*** *p184*
Gurski, Johanna 20; New York, NY, 1894 ***6512.1*** *p184*
Gurski, Josef 48; New York, NY, 1894 ***6512.1*** *p184*
Gurski, Maria 18; New York, NY, 1894 ***6512.1*** *p184*
Gurski, Veromika 48; New York, NY, 1894 ***6512.1*** *p184*
Gurten, Baptiste 20; America, 1847 ***778.6*** *p150*
Gurten, Baptiste 58; America, 1847 ***778.6*** *p150*
Gurten, Barbara 9; America, 1847 ***778.6*** *p150*
Gurten, Catharine 47; America, 1747 ***778.6*** *p150*
Gurten, Catherine 14; America, 1847 ***778.6*** *p150*
Gurten, Chretien 15; America, 1847 ***778.6*** *p150*
Gurten, Jacques 8; America, 1847 ***778.6*** *p150*
Gurten, Jean 7; America, 1847 ***778.6*** *p150*
Gurten, Madeline 6; America, 1847 ***778.6*** *p150*
Gurten, Michel 9; America, 1847 ***778.6*** *p150*
Gurten, Nanette 5; America, 1847 ***778.6*** *p150*
Gurten, Pierre 4; America, 1847 ***778.6*** *p150*
Gurten, Pierre 28; America, 1847 ***778.6*** *p150*
Gurtner, Michel 20; America, 1840 ***778.6*** *p150*
Gurzentaner, Sebast. 32; Louisiana, 1847 ***778.6*** *p150*
Gusching, Alphonse 5; America, 1847 ***778.6*** *p150*
Gusching, Anna 27; America, 1847 ***778.6*** *p150*
Gusching, Edouard 9 months; America, 1847 ***778.6*** *p150*
Gusching, Georg 27; America, 1847 ***778.6*** *p151*
Gusenburger, Elise *SEE* Gusenburger, Johann
Gusenburger, Johann; America, 1882 ***5475.1*** *p34*
*Sister:*Elise
Gusenburger, Johann; America, 1882 ***5475.1*** *p242*
Gusenburger, Niklaus; New York, 1883 ***5475.1*** *p242*
With mother & sister
Gusewelle, Mr.; America, 1850 ***7420.1*** *p71*
With wife & 3 children
Gusewelle, Mr.; America, 1861 ***7420.1*** *p205*
With family
Gusewelle, Ernestine Dorothee; America, 1861 ***7420.1*** *p205*
Gusewelle, Ernst; Port uncertain, 1842 ***7420.1*** *p26*
With brother-in-law
Gusewelle, Ernst Mittelbrink; America, 1842 ***7420.1*** *p24*
With wife 5 children & brother-in-law
Gushman, Alexis; Ohio, 1809-1852 ***4511.35*** *p19*
Gusmann, George; North Carolina, 1792-1862 ***1088.45*** *p12*
Guss, Anna *SEE* Guss, Georg
Guss, Georg; America, 1873 ***5475.1*** *p226*
*Wife:*Maria Gillo
*Daughter:*Margarethe
*Son:*Nikolaus
*Daughter:*Anna
*Son:*Josef
Guss, Josef *SEE* Guss, Georg
Guss, Margarethe *SEE* Guss, Georg
Guss, Maria Gillo *SEE* Guss, Georg
Guss, Nikolaus *SEE* Guss, Georg
Guss, Sarah 68; Ontario, 1871 ***1823.21*** *p142*
Gust, Gertrud; America, 1872 ***5475.1*** *p153*
Gust, Gustav Emil; Wisconsin, 1902 ***6795.8*** *p133*
Gustafson, Albin; Cleveland, OH, 1903-1906 ***9722.10*** *p119*
Gustafson, Alfred A.; Illinois, 1887-1901 ***1865.50*** *p48*
Gustafson, Andrew; St. Paul, MN, 1871 ***1865.50*** *p48*
Gustafson, Carl Emil; Cleveland, OH, 1881-1894 ***9722.10*** *p119*
Gustafson, Carl Gustaf; St. Paul, MN, 1903 ***1865.50*** *p49*
Gustafson, Charles; Indiana, 1881 ***1865.50*** *p49*
*Wife:*Johanna Johnson
Gustafson, Christina; St. Paul, MN, 1880-1885 ***1865.50*** *p49*
Gustafson, Christina; St. Paul, MN, 1883 ***1865.50*** *p52*
Gustafson, Clara; St. Paul, MN, 1882 ***1865.50*** *p114*
Gustafson, Clara; St. Paul, MN, 1889 ***1865.50*** *p94*
Gustafson, Erik Anton; Colorado, 1892 ***1029.59*** *p35*
Gustafson, Gustaf Adolph; Cleveland, OH, 1891-1898 ***9722.10*** *p119*
Gustafson, Gustaf Adolph; Iowa, 1908 ***1211.15*** *p10*
Gustafson, Gustav 22; Minnesota, 1925 ***2769.54*** *p1382*
Gustafson, Johanna Johnson *SEE* Gustafson, Charles
Gustafson, Johanna; St. Paul, MN, 1880 ***1865.50*** *p105*
Gustafson, John; Colorado, 1897 ***1029.59*** *p35*
Gustafson, John; Iowa, 1915 ***1211.15*** *p10*
Gustafson, John Albert; Colorado, 1897 ***1029.59*** *p35*
Gustafson, John G.; Cleveland, OH, 1890-1905 ***9722.10*** *p119*
Gustafson, Mathilda; St. Paul, MN, 1880 ***1865.50*** *p102*
Gustafson, Olivia A.; St. Paul, MN, 1881-1889 ***1865.50*** *p49*
Gustafsson, A.; Savannah, GA, 1849 ***6412.40*** *p152*
Gustafsson, Anders W.; Cleveland, OH, 1887-1897 ***9722.10*** *p119*
Gustave, Jacob 23; Mississippi, 1846 ***778.6*** *p151*
Gusterson, William 16; Quebec, 1870 ***8364.32*** *p23*
Gusti, Georges 20; New Orleans, 1847 ***778.6*** *p151*
Gustin, Henry 24; Ontario, 1871 ***1823.21*** *p143*
Gustin, John 28; New England, 1675-1676 ***9228.50*** *p268*
Gustofson, Charles E.; Washington, 1887 ***2770.40*** *p24*
Gustorson, John L.; Michigan, 1872 ***1029.59*** *p35*
Gustovson, John N.; Colorado, 1888 ***1029.59*** *p35*
Gut, Emilia 18; New York, NY, 1911 ***6533.11*** *p9*
Gut, Johann Jakob; Venezuela, 1843 ***3899.5*** *p541*
Gut, Johann Michael; Venezuela, 1843 ***3899.5*** *p541*
Gut, Michael; Venezuela, 1843 ***3899.5*** *p541*
Gutbrot, Ludvick; New York, 1778 ***8529.30*** *p3A*
Gutcher, Francis; Ohio, 1809-1852 ***4511.35*** *p19*
Gutfried, Elisabeth 1; Missouri, 1845 ***778.6*** *p151*
Gutfried, George 4; Missouri, 1845 ***778.6*** *p151*
Gutfried, Jacob 8; Missouri, 1845 ***778.6*** *p151*
Gutfried, Jacob 36; Missouri, 1845 ***778.6*** *p151*
Gutfried, Madeleine 10; Missouri, 1845 ***778.6*** *p151*
Gutfried, Marguerite 27; Missouri, 1845 ***778.6*** *p151*
Gutfried, Salome 6; Missouri, 1845 ***778.6*** *p151*
Guth, Christian; America, 1867 ***7919.3*** *p531*
Guth, Heinrich; America, 1889 ***5475.1*** *p424*
Guth, Johann Michael; Venezuela, 1843 ***3899.5*** *p541*
Guth, John; Ohio, 1840-1897 ***8365.35*** *p16*
Guth, Juliane Friederike; America, 1867 ***7919.3*** *p529*
With child
Guth, Michael; Venezuela, 1843 ***3899.5*** *p541*
Guth Children, . . .; Venezuela, 1843 ***3899.5*** *p541*
Gutheinz, Josephine; New Jersey, 1858 ***8513.31*** *p307*
Guthmann, Salomon 24; Indiana, 1866-1869 ***9076.20*** *p66*
Guthmuller, Christine 24; New York, NY, 1874 ***6954.7*** *p37*
Guthmuller, Friedrich 28; New York, NY, 1874 ***6954.7*** *p37*
Guthmuller, Johann 9 months; New York, NY, 1874 ***6954.7*** *p37*
Guthorl, Valentin; America, 1880 ***5475.1*** *p464*
Guthorl, Wilhelm; America, 1880 ***5475.1*** *p464*
Guthrie, Andrew D.; Washington, 1887 ***2770.40*** *p24*
Guthrie, Ann 58; Ontario, 1871 ***1823.21*** *p143*
Guthwasser, Claude 23; New York, NY, 1894 ***6512.1*** *p182*
Gutjahr, Eva 25; Baltimore, 1893 ***1883.7*** *p38*
Gutjahr, Friederika 18; Baltimore, 1893 ***1883.7*** *p38*
Gutjahr, Jacob 3; Baltimore, 1893 ***1883.7*** *p38*
Gutjahr, Jacob 26; Baltimore, 1893 ***1883.7*** *p38*
Gutjahr, Karolina 16; Baltimore, 1893 ***1883.7*** *p38*
Gutjahr, Magdalena 10 months; Baltimore, 1893 ***1883.7*** *p38*
Gutknecht, Aug. Wilh.; Philadelphia, 1891 ***5475.1*** *p76*
*Wife:*Luise Sohlinger
*Son:*Hermann
Gutknecht, Hermann *SEE* Gutknecht, Aug. Wilh.
Gutknecht, Luise Sohlinger *SEE* Gutknecht, Aug. Wilh.
Gutkowski, Alexander; Detroit, 1929-1930 ***6214.5*** *p67*
Gutmann, Christian; New York, 1860 ***358.56*** *p148*
Gutmann, Jacob 39; New York, NY, 1893 ***1883.7*** *p43*
Gutmann, Joseph; Colorado, 1881 ***1029.59*** *p36*
Gutowska, Euphemia; Wisconsin, 1890 ***6795.8*** *p58*
Gutowski, Euphemia; Wisconsin, 1890 ***6795.8*** *p58*
Gutowski, Joseph; Detroit, 1930 ***1640.60*** *p82*
Gutrich, Helena 22; Baltimore, 1889 ***8425.16*** *p35*
Gutrich, Peter 25; Baltimore, 1889 ***8425.16*** *p35*
Gutrich, Theador 6 months; Baltimore, 1889 ***8425.16*** *p35*
Gutridge, James 52; Ontario, 1871 ***1823.21*** *p143*
Gutridge, Mary 63; Ontario, 1871 ***1823.21*** *p143*
Gutsch, Julius; Wisconsin, 1892 ***6795.8*** *p117*
Gutsche, Emil; Wisconsin, 1885 ***6795.8*** *p117*
Gutsche, Julius; Wisconsin, 1892 ***6795.8*** *p117*
Gutt, Louis 24; Louisiana, 1848 ***778.6*** *p151*
Gutt, Simon 29; Louisiana, 1848 ***778.6*** *p151*
Gutteben, Antoine 27; America, 1842 ***778.6*** *p151*
Gutter, Reinhold; America, 1867 ***7919.3*** *p525*
With family
Guttermann, Babette; America, 1867 ***7919.3*** *p527*
Guttierez, Vincent; Louisiana, 1874 ***4981.45*** *p132*
Gutwich, Ferdinand 24; America, 1841 ***778.6*** *p151*
Gutwich, Heland 13; America, 1841 ***778.6*** *p151*
Gutwich, Hubert 8; America, 1841 ***778.6*** *p151*
Gutwich, Maria 22; America, 1841 ***778.6*** *p151*
Gutwich, Mary 17; America, 1841 ***778.6*** *p151*
Gutwich, Michel 49; America, 1841 ***778.6*** *p151*
Gutwin, Alexander 3; Portland, ME, 1912 ***970.38*** *p77*
Gutwin, Elizabeth 35; Portland, ME, 1912 ***970.38*** *p77*
Gutwin, Helena 15; Portland, ME, 1912 ***970.38*** *p77*
Gutwin, Johann 10; Portland, ME, 1912 ***970.38*** *p77*
Gutwin, Margaretha 4; Portland, ME, 1912 ***970.38*** *p77*
Gutwin, Nicolaus 9; Portland, ME, 1912 ***970.38*** *p77*
Gutwin, Titus 37; Portland, ME, 1912 ***970.38*** *p77*
Gutz, Christian; New York, 1860 ***358.56*** *p4*
Gutz, Emil 23; New York, NY, 1890 ***1883.7*** *p47*
Guy, . . .; Ontario, 1871 ***1823.21*** *p143*
Guy, Benjamin 40; Ontario, 1871 ***1823.21*** *p143*
Guy, Charles 27; New Orleans, 1847 ***778.6*** *p151*
Guy, Dorothea May Freeman *SEE* Guy, Leonard Frank
Guy, Eugenie 26; New Orleans, 1847 ***778.6*** *p151*
Guy, Farmer 25; Ontario, 1871 ***1823.17*** *p62*
Guy, Francois; Quebec, 1662 ***9221.17*** *p486*
Guy, Gillian Dawn *SEE* Guy, Leonard Frank
Guy, John 37; Ontario, 1871 ***1823.21*** *p143*
Guy, Leonard Frank; Ontario, 1957 ***9228.50*** *p270*
*Wife:*Dorothea May Freeman
*Child:*Gillian Dawn
Guy, William; New England, 1634 ***9228.50*** *p270*
Guyard, Catherine; Quebec, 1665 ***4514.3*** *p323*
Guyard, Claud Francois 33; America, 1848 ***778.6*** *p151*
Guyart, Marie 40; Quebec, 1639 ***9221.17*** *p84*
Guye, Thomas; Boston, 1774 ***8529.30*** *p2*
Guyet, Jean; Montreal, 1653 ***9221.17*** *p292*
Guyet, Jean 22; Quebec, 1646 ***9221.17*** *p165*
Guyet, Marie; Quebec, 1668 ***4514.3*** *p324*
Guyon, Felix 26; New Orleans, 1846 ***778.6*** *p151*
Guyon, Jean-Baptiste; Quebec, 1740 ***2314.30*** *p170*
Guyon, Jean-Baptiste; Quebec, 1740 ***2314.30*** *p184*
Guyon, M. 30; New Orleans, 1846 ***778.6*** *p151*
Guyot, Mr. 31; Port uncertain, 1840 ***778.6*** *p151*
Guyot, Mrs. 23; Port uncertain, 1840 ***778.6*** *p151*
Guyot, August 26; America, 1848 ***778.6*** *p151*
Guyot, Guillaume 19; Quebec, 1662 ***9221.17*** *p487*
Guzik, Jozefa 19; New York, NY, 1904 ***8355.1*** *p15*
Guzler, Josephine 24; Missouri, 1845 ***778.6*** *p151*
Guzman, Frances; Detroit, 1929 ***1640.55*** *p113*
Gwiazdzinski, Victoria; Detroit, 1929-1930 ***6214.5*** *p67*
Gwitt, Nicolaus; Wisconsin, 1885 ***6795.8*** *p42*
Gy, Francois; Quebec, 1659 ***9221.17*** *p413*
Gyberg, Gustaf Harald; Cleveland, OH, 1888-1892 ***9722.10*** *p119*
Gyde, Emma 27; Ontario, 1871 ***1823.21*** *p143*
Gyde, Thomas 56; Ontario, 1871 ***1823.21*** *p143*
Gyette, Francis 34; Ontario, 1871 ***1823.17*** *p62*
Gyles, Jane; Boston, 1752 ***1642*** *p46*
Gyles, John; Massachusetts, 1679 ***9228.50*** *p270*
Gyles, Mathew; Maine, 1653 ***9228.50*** *p270*
Gyllensten, Peter; Colorado, 1887 ***1029.59*** *p36*
Gynan, Ed Francis 33; Ontario, 1871 ***1823.21*** *p143*
Gyrion, Casimir; Wisconsin, 1878 ***1495.20*** *p12*
*Child:*Gustave Ferdinand
*Wife:*Desiree Calonne
*Child:*Oscar
*Child:*Desire George
*Child:*Florimond
*Child:*Henri
*Child:*Nicolas Joseph
Gyrion, Desire George *SEE* Gyrion, Casimir
Gyrion, Desiree Calonne *SEE* Gyrion, Casimir
Gyrion, Florimond *SEE* Gyrion, Casimir
Gyrion, Gustave Ferdinand *SEE* Gyrion, Casimir
Gyrion, Henri *SEE* Gyrion, Casimir
Gyrion, Nicolas Joseph *SEE* Gyrion, Casimir
Gyrion, Oscar *SEE* Gyrion, Casimir
Gysksonicz, Franziska 22; New York, NY, 1894 ***6512.1*** *p184*

H

Haab, Johann; Brazil, 1867 *5475.1 p505*
  *Wife:*Margarethe Wobedo
  *Daughter:*Katharina
  *Daughter:*Susanna
Haab, Katharina *SEE* Haab, Johann
Haab, Margarethe Wobedo *SEE* Haab, Johann
Haab, Susanna *SEE* Haab, Johann
Haacke, Albert; England, 1881 *7420.1 p320*
Haag, Agathe *SEE* Haag, Anna Katharina
Haag, Alexander 18; Mississippi, 1847 *778.6 p151*
Haag, Anna Katharina; Venezuela, 1843 *3899.5 p543*
  *Child:*Maria Anna
  *Child:*Johannes
  *Child:*Judith
  *Child:*Maria Anna
  *Child:*Agathe
Haag, Babette 8; Mississippi, 1847 *778.6 p151*
Haag, Catherina 47; Mississippi, 1847 *778.6 p151*
Haag, Franz Anton; Venezuela, 1843 *3899.5 p544*
Haag, G.; Louisiana, 1874 *4981.45 p296*
Haag, Henriett 22; Mississippi, 1847 *778.6 p151*
Haag, Henry 12; Mississippi, 1847 *778.6 p152*
Haag, Henry 51; Mississippi, 1847 *778.6 p152*
Haag, Jacob F., Jr.; Ohio, 1809-1852 *4511.35 p19*
Haag, Johannes *SEE* Haag, Anna Katharina
Haag, Judith *SEE* Haag, Anna Katharina
Haag, Karl Leonhard; America, 1892 *2526.43 p169*
Haag, Laurent 18; Mississippi, 1847 *778.6 p152*
Haag, Madelaine 5; Mississippi, 1847 *778.6 p152*
Haag, Maria Anna *SEE* Haag, Anna Katharina
Haag, Peter; Ohio, 1809-1852 *4511.35 p19*
Haag, Philip; Ohio, 1809-1852 *4511.35 p19*
Haag, Pippin 15; Mississippi, 1847 *778.6 p152*
Haag, Wilhelm; America, 1832 *2526.42 p173*
  With wife & child
Haak, Carl; Wisconsin, 1897 *6795.8 p33*
Haak, Friederike; New York, 1860 *358.56 p5*
Haak, Philip; Ohio, 1809-1852 *4511.35 p19*
Haaland, Marselius; Iowa, 1897 *1211.15 p11*
Haaland, Thor; Iowa, 1890 *1211.15 p11*
Haan, Barbara; Kansas, 1882 *5475.1 p196*
Haan, Jakob; Kansas, 1882 *5475.1 p196*
Haan, Johann; Kansas, 1882 *5475.1 p196*
Haas, A. Barbara Koch 35 *SEE* Haas, Jakob
Haas, Adam; America, 1866 *2526.43 p209*
Haas, Adam *SEE* Haas, Jakob
Haas, Albert; America, 1891 *2526.43 p169*
Haas, Ana Maria; America, 1852 *179.55 p19*
Haas, Andreas 53; America, 1865 *5475.1 p417*
  *Wife:*Eva Bloch 48
  *Son:*Isaak
  *Son:*Felix
  *Daughter:*Friederike
  *Son:*Simon
  *Daughter:*Karoline
Haas, Aron 21; Louisiana, 1848 *778.6 p152*
Haas, Augustinus; Wisconsin, 1891 *6795.8 p58*
Haas, Barbara; America, 1852 *179.55 p19*
Haas, Barbara; America, 1858 *2526.43 p209*
Haas, Catharina; America, 1852 *179.55 p19*
Haas, Charles 3; America, 1845 *778.6 p152*
Haas, Constant 1; America, 1845 *778.6 p152*
Haas, Emil; America, 1888 *2526.43 p169*
Haas, Eugene 8; America, 1845 *778.6 p152*
Haas, Eva Bloch 48 *SEE* Haas, Andreas
Haas, Eva Catharina; America, 1852 *179.55 p19*
Haas, Felix *SEE* Haas, Andreas
Haas, Franz *SEE* Haas, Jakob

Haas, Friederike *SEE* Haas, Andreas
Haas, Friedrich; America, 1884 *2526.43 p169*
Haas, Friedrich 18; America, 1853 *2526.43 p209*
Haas, Georg; America, 1852 *179.55 p19*
  With wife
Haas, Georg; America, 1887 *2526.43 p169*
Haas, Gustav; Colorado, 1879 *1029.59 p36*
Haas, Henriette; America, 1867 *5475.1 p207*
Haas, Isaak *SEE* Haas, Andreas
Haas, Isidor; America, 1886 *2526.43 p169*
Haas, Jakob; America, 1866 *5475.1 p550*
  *Wife:*M. E. Christine Schmidt
  *Daughter:*Katharina
Haas, Jakob 33; America, 1868 *5475.1 p312*
  *Wife:*A. Barbara Koch 35
  *Son:*Adam
  *Son:*Josef
  *Son:*Franz
Haas, Jakob; New York, 1885 *5475.1 p364*
Haas, Johann Georg; America, 1852 *179.55 p19*
Haas, Johannes; America, 1882 *179.55 p19*
Haas, Josef *SEE* Haas, Jakob
Haas, Josef; America, 1871 *5475.1 p363*
Haas, Josef 20; America, 1882 *5475.1 p421*
Haas, Josef; Pennsylvania, 1880 *5475.1 p331*
  *Brother:*Nikolaus
Haas, Joseph 9; America, 1845 *778.6 p152*
Haas, Joseph 40; America, 1845 *778.6 p152*
Haas, Julius; America, 1881 *2526.43 p169*
Haas, Karoline *SEE* Haas, Andreas
Haas, Katharina *SEE* Haas, Jakob
Haas, Konrad; America, 1869 *2526.43 p209*
Haas, Konrad, III; America, 1868 *2526.43 p209*
Haas, Ludwig; Dayton, OH, 1859 *2526.43 p209*
Haas, Ludwig; Ohio, 1882 *5475.1 p380*
Haas, M. E. Christine Schmidt *SEE* Haas, Jakob
Haas, Margaretha; America, 1852 *179.55 p19*
Haas, Maria; America, 1868 *2526.43 p209*
Haas, Maria Marg.; America, 1872 *5475.1 p384*
Haas, Marie 35; America, 1845 *778.6 p152*
Haas, Mathias; America, 1874 *5475.1 p363*
  *Brother:*Peter
Haas, Max; London, Eng., 1890 *2526.43 p169*
Haas, Michael; America, 1856 *2526.43 p209*
Haas, Michael; Dayton, OH, 1888 *2526.43 p169*
Haas, Michael Ludwig; America, 1885 *2526.43 p169*
Haas, Nikolaus; America, 1868 *5475.1 p363*
Haas, Nikolaus *SEE* Haas, Josef
Haas, Peter *SEE* Haas, Mathias
Haas, Philip M.; Ohio, 1809-1852 *4511.35 p19*
Haas, Philipp; America, 1858 *2526.43 p209*
Haas, Philipp 16; America, 1852 *2526.43 p209*
Haas, Rosine; America, 1852 *179.55 p19*
Haas, Salomon; America, 1865 *5475.1 p416*
Haas, Simon *SEE* Haas, Andreas
Haas, Wilhelm; America, 1889 *2526.43 p169*
Haas, William; New York, 1860 *358.56 p3*
Haase, Conrad; Illinois, 1861 *6079.1 p6*
Haase, Emilie Auguste; Wisconsin, 1897 *6795.8 p24*
Haase, Frederick W.; Wisconsin, 1888 *6795.8 p220*
Haase, K.; New York, 1859 *358.56 p54*
Haase, Rudolph; Wisconsin, 1906 *6795.8 p165*
Haase, Rudolph Herman; Wisconsin, 1911 *6795.8 p165*
Haaser, Angelika 7 *SEE* Haaser, Heinrich
Haaser, Dorothea Greff 41 *SEE* Haaser, Heinrich
Haaser, Heinrich 9 *SEE* Haaser, Heinrich

Haaser, Heinrich 41; America, 1854 *5475.1 p53*
  *Wife:*Dorothea Greff 41
  *Daughter:*Angelika 7
  *Daughter:*Maria 2
  *Daughter:*Katharina 6
  *Son:*Heinrich 9
  *Son:*Sebastian 16
  *Daughter:*Magdalena 14
  *Son:*Johann 12
Haaser, Johann 12 *SEE* Haaser, Heinrich
Haaser, Katharina 6 *SEE* Haaser, Heinrich
Haaser, Magdalena 14 *SEE* Haaser, Heinrich
Haaser, Maria 2 *SEE* Haaser, Heinrich
Haaser, Sebastian 16 *SEE* Haaser, Heinrich
Haass, Friedrich; New York, 1859 *358.56 p101*
Hab, Ad. 29; America, 1840 *778.6 p152*
Habel, Guillaume; Quebec, 1648 *9221.17 p199*
Haben, Mathias 42; America, 1843 *5475.1 p305*
Habenicht, Hans Heinrich; America, 1867 *7420.1 p256*
  With family
Habenicht, Johann Heinrich Conrad; Illinois, 1873
  7420.1 p299
Habentish, . . .; North Carolina, 1710 *3629.40 p4*
Haber, Paul 29; New Orleans, 1848 *778.6 p152*
Haberbosch, Scholastica 25; Chile, 1852 *1192.4 p52*
Haberkern, Henry 26; Louisiana, 1848 *778.6 p152*
Haberland, Dorothee; America, 1854 *7420.1 p120*
Haberle, Georg; Valdivia, Chile, 1850 *1192.4 p48*
Haberle, Wilhelm August; America, 1879 *179.55 p19*
Habermann, Anna 24; America, 1840 *778.6 p152*
Habermann, Anne Catharine; America, 1867 *7919.3*
  p527
  With child
Habermann, Ernst; America, 1868 *7919.3 p528*
Habermann, Johanne; America, 1867 *7919.3 p528*
Habermann, Suzanne 60; Missouri, 1845 *778.6 p152*
Haberstich, . . .; North Carolina, 1710 *3629.40 p4*
Haberstock, Francois 27; Louisiana, 1848 *778.6 p152*
Haberstroh, Jacob; Valdivia, Chile, 1852 *1192.4 p55*
Habertheur, Nicholas; Ohio, 1809-1852 *4511.35 p19*
Habertheus, Nicholas; Ohio, 1809-1852 *4511.35 p19*
Habits, Eugene 27; Port uncertain, 1841 *778.6 p152*
Haby, Andreas 20; Galveston, TX, 1846 *3967.10 p377*
Haby, Catharina 38; Galveston, TX, 1844 *3967.10 p375*
Haby, Jakob 10; Galveston, TX, 1844 *3967.10 p375*
Haby, Jakob 48; Galveston, TX, 1844 *3967.10 p375*
Haby, Joseph 30; Galveston, TX, 1844 *3967.10 p373*
Haby, Ludwig Philipp 1; Galveston, TX, 1844 *3967.10*
  p375
Haby, Nikolaus 26; Galveston, TX, 1844 *3967.10 p373*
Haby, Therese 5; Galveston, TX, 1844 *3967.10 p375*
Hach, Christine; Philadelphia, 1867 *8513.31 p308*
Hachard, Amedee 32; New Orleans, 1845 *778.6 p152*
Hachaud, Jean 27; America, 1841 *778.6 p152*
Hache, Fanny 20; America, 1844 *778.6 p152*
Hache, Henry 13; America, 1844 *778.6 p152*
Hache, Pierre; Nova Scotia, 1753 *3051 p112*
Hache, Robert; Quebec, 1633 *9221.17 p29*
Hacher, William 49; Ontario, 1871 *1823.21 p143*
Hachmeister, Caroline Aug. Charl. *SEE* Hachmeister,
  Heinrich Friedrich August
Hachmeister, Friedrich Aug. *SEE* Hachmeister, Heinrich
  Friedrich August
Hachmeister, Hanne Wilh. Charl. *SEE* Hachmeister,
  Heinrich Friedrich August
Hachmeister, Heinr. Friedr. Wilh. *SEE* Hachmeister,
  Heinrich Friedrich August

Hachmeister, Heinr. Wilh. Ludw. *SEE* Hachmeister, Heinrich Friedrich August
Hachmeister, Heinrich; America, 1884 ***7420.1*** *p342*
With family
Hachmeister, Heinrich Ferd. Aug. *SEE* Hachmeister, Heinrich Friedrich August
Hachmeister, Heinrich Friedr. Wilh. *SEE* Hachmeister, Heinrich Friedrich August
Hachmeister, Heinrich Friedrich August; America, 1884 ***7420.1*** *p342*
*Wife:*Wilhelmine Christ. Charl. Dohm
*Daughter:*Caroline Aug. Charl.
*Son:*Heinrich Ferd. Aug.
*Son:*Friedrich Aug.
*Son:*Heinrich Friedr. Wilh.
*Daughter:*Wilhelmine Carol. Charl.
*Son:*Heinr. Friedr. Wilh.
*Daughter:*Hanne Wilh. Charl.
*Son:*Heinr. Wilh. Ludw.
Hachmeister, Wilhelm; America, 1883 ***7420.1*** *p336*
Hachmeister, Wilhelmine Carol. Charl. *SEE* Hachmeister, Heinrich Friedrich August
Hachmeister, Wilhelmine Christ. Charl. Dohm *SEE* Hachmeister, Heinrich Friedrich August
Hachowicz, Katarynia 21; New York, NY, 1894 ***6512.1*** *p232*
Hacicky, Frantisek; South Dakota, 1871-1910 ***2853.20*** *p247*
Hack, Christian; Pennsylvania, 1848 ***170.15*** *p26*
Hacke, Marg.; America, 1886 ***8023.44*** *p379*
*Daughter:*Elis. Maria
*Son:*Friedrich
Hacket, William; South Carolina, 1798 ***3208.30*** *p18*
Hacket, William; South Carolina, 1798 ***3208.30*** *p31*
Hacket, William 57; South Carolina, 1812 ***3476.30*** *p11*
Hacket, Willis; Ontario, 1835 ***3160.1*** *p150*
Hacket, Wm. 20; South Carolina, 1812 ***3476.30*** *p11*
Hackett, Rosa; Philadelphia, 1860 ***8513.31*** *p431*
Hackett, Thomas; Illinois, 1860 ***6079.1*** *p6*
Hackett, William; South Carolina, 1798 ***3208.30*** *p18*
Hackett, William; South Carolina, 1798 ***3208.30*** *p31*
Hacking, John Thomas; Marblehead, MA, 1792 ***9228.50*** *p270*
Hacking, Mary; America, 1841-1941 ***9228.50*** *p270*
Hackney, George 40; Michigan, 1880 ***4491.39*** *p12*
Hackney, James 43; Michigan, 1880 ***4491.39*** *p12*
Hackney, Jonathon 44; Michigan, 1880 ***4491.39*** *p12*
Hackney, Joseph 32; Michigan, 1880 ***4491.39*** *p12*
Hackney, Mary 42; Michigan, 1880 ***4491.39*** *p12*
Hackney, William 45; Ontario, 1871 ***1823.17*** *p62*
Hackny, Robert 28; Ontario, 1871 ***1823.17*** *p62*
Hackstein, Carl Friedrich *SEE* Hackstein, Caroline
Hackstein, Caroline; America, 1851 ***7420.1*** *p80*
*Son:*Carl Friedrich
*Son:*Friedrich Gottlieb.
Hackstein, Friedrich Gottlieb. *SEE* Hackstein, Caroline
Hacquoil, James Clement; Newfoundland, n.d. ***9228.50*** *p273*
Hacquoil, Oswald Xavier; Canada, 1805-1806 ***9228.50*** *p270*
Hadden, John 55; Ontario, 1871 ***1823.17*** *p62*
Hadden, Joseph 42; Ontario, 1871 ***1823.21*** *p143*
Hadden, Mary 80; Ontario, 1871 ***1823.17*** *p62*
Hadel, Heinrich; Wisconsin, 1889 ***6795.8*** *p24*
Hadfield, Joseph; Colorado, 1873 ***1029.59*** *p36*
Hadnett, Francis; Boston, 1767 ***1642*** *p38*
Hadon, Elvina; Wisconsin, 1884 ***6795.8*** *p138*
Hadow, John; Wisconsin, 1881 ***6795.8*** *p168*
Hadwen, Thomas 50; Ontario, 1871 ***1823.21*** *p143*
Hadwin, Francis; Kingston, Jamaica, 1776 ***8529.30*** *p13A*
Haebler, C. Benjam; Valdivia, Chile, 1850 ***1192.4*** *p49*
Haebler, Carl Gottl.; Valdivia, Chile, 1850 ***1192.4*** *p49*
Haeder, David; Long Island, 1781 ***8529.30*** *p9A*
Haeffer, Joseph; Illinois, 1856 ***6079.1*** *p6*
Haeflui, Maria 38; Ontario, 1871 ***1823.21*** *p143*
Haegel, Maurice 34; Missouri, 1845 ***778.6*** *p152*
Haegerling, Anton Henrich; America, 1842 ***7420.1*** *p25*
Haegry, Michel 47; New Orleans, 1848 ***778.6*** *p152*
Haegry, Xavier 28; New Orleans, 1848 ***778.6*** *p152*
Haehn, Adam 38; Ontario, 1871 ***1823.21*** *p143*
Haeker, Applonia 20; America, 1847 ***778.6*** *p152*
Haemling, August 2; Ohio, 1847 ***778.6*** *p152*
Haemling, Marie 6; Ohio, 1847 ***778.6*** *p152*
Haemling, Marie 33; Ohio, 1847 ***778.6*** *p152*
Haemling, Peter 35; Ohio, 1847 ***778.6*** *p152*
Haemling, Sophie 8; Ohio, 1847 ***778.6*** *p152*
Haemling, Susanne 3 months; Ohio, 1847 ***778.6*** *p153*
Haemling, Veronica 10; Ohio, 1847 ***778.6*** *p153*
Haemling, Victor 4; Ohio, 1847 ***778.6*** *p153*
Haen, Johann; America, 1852 ***5475.1*** *p78*
With wife
With 4 children
Haen, Johann Peter; America, 1852 ***5475.1*** *p78*
Haen, Sebastian; America, 1846-1847 ***5475.1*** *p77*
Haendchen, John; Ohio, 1809-1852 ***4511.35*** *p19*
Haensch, Carl W.; Valdivia, Chile, 1852 ***1192.4*** *p54*
Haensel, Minnie; Wisconsin, 1894 ***6795.8*** *p197*
Haentschel, F. August; Valdivia, Chile, 1850 ***1192.4*** *p49*
Haerter, Johannes; New York, NY, 1892 ***3366.30*** *p70*
Haes, Mary; Massachusetts, 1668 ***1642*** *p101*
Haesloop, Michael; North Carolina, 1848 ***1088.45*** *p12*
Haeuser, Konrad; Pennsylvania, 1854 ***170.15*** *p27*
With wife & 2 children
Haeusser, Heinrich 21; New Orleans, 1847 ***778.6*** *p153*
Haevers, Ferdinand; New York, NY, 1855 ***1494.21*** *p31*
Hafeman, Albert; Wisconsin, 1892 ***6795.8*** *p173*
Hafeman, Karl Friedrich Albert; Wisconsin, 1894 ***6795.8*** *p152*
Hafemann, Karl Friedrich Albert; Wisconsin, 1894 ***6795.8*** *p152*
Haff, Bernhard; Wisconsin, 1885 ***6795.8*** *p201*
Haffenden, William 38; Ontario, 1871 ***1823.21*** *p143*
Haffner, Thomas 18; America, 1847 ***778.6*** *p153*
Haflin, Maria; Ontario, 1871 ***1823.21*** *p143*
Hafner, Johann Christian; America, 1885 ***179.55*** *p19*
Hafner, Johannes; America, 1887 ***2526.42*** *p166*
Hafner, Leonhard; New York, 1860 ***358.56*** *p148*
Hag, Agathe *SEE* Hag, Anna Katharina
Hag, Anna Katharina; Venezuela, 1843 ***3899.5*** *p543*
*Child:*Maria Anna
*Child:*Judith
*Child:*Maria Anna
*Child:*Johannes
*Child:*Agathe
Hag, Franz Anton; Venezuela, 1843 ***3899.5*** *p544*
Hag, Jacob; Ohio, 1809-1852 ***4511.35*** *p19*
Hag, Johannes *SEE* Hag, Anna Katharina
Hag, Johannes; Venezuela, 1843 ***3899.5*** *p544*
Hag, Judith *SEE* Hag, Anna Katharina
Hag, Maria Anna *SEE* Hag, Anna Katharina
Hagale, Fridrick; Colorado, 1873 ***1029.59*** *p36*
Hagan, Bryan 61; Ontario, 1871 ***1823.17*** *p62*
Hagan, Ellen 54; Ontario, 1871 ***1823.17*** *p62*
Hagan, Henry 26; Ontario, 1871 ***1823.21*** *p143*
Hagan, James 55; Ontario, 1871 ***1823.17*** *p62*
Hagan, James 16; Quebec, 1870 ***8364.32*** *p23*
Hagan, Mary 40; Ontario, 1871 ***1823.17*** *p62*
Hagan, Mary 41; Ontario, 1871 ***1823.17*** *p62*
Hagan, Michael 46; Ontario, 1871 ***1823.17*** *p62*
Hagans, Mary 76; Ontario, 1871 ***1823.17*** *p62*
Hagarty, Cornelius; Boston, 1766 ***1642*** *p37*
Hagberg, Brita 60; Kansas, 1879-1880 ***777.40*** *p19*
Hagberg, Carl 27; Kansas, 1879-1880 ***777.40*** *p19*
Hagberg, Pehr Adolf; New York, NY, 1845 ***6412.40*** *p149*
Hage, Anna Sophie Dorothea; America, 1868 ***7420.1*** *p271*
Hage, Engel Dorothea; America, 1864 ***7420.1*** *p223*
Hage, Engel Marie Dorothea; America, 1882 ***7420.1*** *p332*
Hage, Engel Marie Sophie Dorothea; America, 1868 ***7420.1*** *p271*
Hage, Heinrich Christoph Conrad; America, 1864 ***7420.1*** *p223*
Hage, Mrs. Horsten; America, 1881 ***7420.1*** *p320*
Hage, Jans; Iowa, 1889 ***1211.15*** *p11*
Hage, Johann Otto; America, 1864 ***7420.1*** *p223*
Hage, Sigurd; Iowa, 1919 ***1211.15*** *p11*
Hagedorn, Carl; America, 1853 ***7420.1*** *p105*
With wife & daughter
Hagedorn, Caroline Wilhelmine; Illinois, 1845 ***7420.1*** *p37*
Hagedorn, Ferdinand August; Texas, 1854 ***7420.1*** *p120*
Hagedorn, Heinrich Conrad; America, 1844 ***7420.1*** *p31*
*Wife:*Wilhelmine Heidorn
Hagedorn, Wilhelm; America, 1855 ***7420.1*** *p136*
With wife & 5 children
Hagedorn, Wilhelm; America, 1871 ***7420.1*** *p290*
Hagedorn, Wilhelmine Heidorn *SEE* Hagedorn, Heinrich Conrad
Hagel, Jakob; America, 1882 ***179.55*** *p19*
Hagel, Johannes 20; New York, NY, 1893 ***1883.7*** *p41*
Hagele, Barbara 3; New York, NY, 1893 ***1883.7*** *p40*
Hagele, Brigita 1; New York, NY, 1893 ***1883.7*** *p40*
Hagele, Elisabeth 6 months; New York, NY, 1893 ***1883.7*** *p40*
Hagele, Emanuel 31; New York, NY, 1893 ***1883.7*** *p40*
Hagele, Gottlieb Heinrich; America, 1882 ***179.55*** *p19*
Hagele, Helena 29; New York, NY, 1893 ***1883.7*** *p40*
Hagele, Jakob; America, 1885 ***179.55*** *p19*
Hagele, Johann 6; New York, NY, 1893 ***1883.7*** *p40*
Hagele, Josef 27; New York, NY, 1893 ***1883.7*** *p41*
Hagele, Karl Friedrich; America, 1884 ***179.55*** *p19*
With wife
Hagele, Karl Friedrich; America, 1884 ***179.55*** *p19*
Hagele, Maria Rosa; America, 1884 ***179.55*** *p19*
Hagele, Martha 20; New York, NY, 1893 ***1883.7*** *p41*
Hagele, Wilhelm; America, 1870 ***179.55*** *p19*
Hagelin, Jakob 13; Galveston, TX, 1844 ***3967.10*** *p370*
Hagelin, Joseph 24; Galveston, TX, 1844 ***3967.10*** *p370*
Hagelin, Therese 20; Galveston, TX, 1844 ***3967.10*** *p370*
Hagelin, Tilma; Minneapolis, 1876-1881 ***1865.50*** *p52*
Hagelqvist, Samuel; Valparaiso, Chile, 1850 ***1192.4*** *p50*
Hagelsiebs, Maria; Valdivia, Chile, 1852 ***1192.4*** *p55*
Hagelstein, John; Washington, 1889 ***2770.40*** *p27*
Hageltrein, Georges 31; Missouri, 1848 ***778.6*** *p153*
Hageltrein, Marie 24; Missouri, 1848 ***778.6*** *p153*
Hageltrein, Marie 28; Missouri, 1848 ***778.6*** *p153*
Hagemann, Christian; America, 1867 ***7420.1*** *p257*
Hagemann, Christian Wilhelm; America, 1845 ***7420.1*** *p36*
With daughter 10
Hagemann, Friederike; America, 1867 ***7420.1*** *p257*
Hagemann, Friedrich; America, 1884 ***7420.1*** *p343*
Hagemann, Friedrich Conrad; America, 1890 ***7420.1*** *p360*
Hagemann, Hermann; America, 1854 ***7420.1*** *p120*
Hagemann, Hermann Heinrich Wilhelm; America, 1870 ***7420.1*** *p286*
Hagemeier, Friedrich; America, 1867 ***7420.1*** *p257*
Hagen, Aaden P.; Iowa, 1889 ***1211.15*** *p11*
Hagen, Agnes; America, 1868 ***7919.3*** *p530*
Hagen, Anne 1; America, 1842 ***778.6*** *p153*
Hagen, Anne Marie 32; Missouri, 1845 ***778.6*** *p153*
Hagen, Anton 42; America, 1842 ***778.6*** *p153*
Hagen, Barbara 44; Port uncertain, 1843 ***778.6*** *p153*
Hagen, Catharina 12; Port uncertain, 1843 ***778.6*** *p153*
Hagen, Catherine 4; Missouri, 1845 ***778.6*** *p153*
Hagen, Christoph 6; Port uncertain, 1843 ***778.6*** *p153*
Hagen, Elisabetha 3; Port uncertain, 1843 ***778.6*** *p153*
Hagen, Etienne 38; Missouri, 1845 ***778.6*** *p153*
Hagen, Francois 46; Port uncertain, 1843 ***778.6*** *p153*
Hagen, Franz Anton; Venezuela, 1843 ***3899.5*** *p544*
Hagen, Henry; Kansas, 1917-1918 ***2094.25*** *p50*
Hagen, Jean; Illinois, 1852 ***6079.1*** *p6*
Hagen, Jean; Illinois, 1856 ***6079.1*** *p6*
Hagen, Jeannette 8; America, 1842 ***778.6*** *p153*
Hagen, Johanne; America, 1868 ***7919.3*** *p530*
Hagen, Johannes; Venezuela, 1843 ***3899.5*** *p544*
Hagen, John Javelin; North Carolina, 1823 ***1088.45*** *p12*
Hagen, Louis 8; Port uncertain, 1843 ***778.6*** *p153*
Hagen, Madelaine 9; Missouri, 1845 ***778.6*** *p153*
Hagen, Magdalena 10; Port uncertain, 1843 ***778.6*** *p153*
Hagen, Margaretha 9; Port uncertain, 1843 ***778.6*** *p153*
Hagen, Marie 11; America, 1842 ***778.6*** *p153*
Hagen, Marie 42; America, 1842 ***778.6*** *p153*
Hagen, Nicolas 1; Missouri, 1845 ***778.6*** *p153*
Hagen, Victor 6; Missouri, 1845 ***778.6*** *p153*
Hagen, Vigan 23; Port uncertain, 1843 ***778.6*** *p153*
Hagenmuller, Johann 28; Galveston, TX, 1846 ***3967.10*** *p377*
Hagens, George 19; Michigan, 1880 ***4491.39*** *p12*
Hager, Ambrose; Ohio, 1809-1852 ***4511.35*** *p19*
Hager, Ambrose; Ohio, 1809-1852 ***4511.35*** *p20*
Hager, Conrad; Wisconsin, 1855 ***6795.8*** *p99*
Hager, Joh. 24; America, 1840 ***778.6*** *p153*
Hager, Louisa 26; America, 1840 ***778.6*** *p153*
Hagerdorn, Thomson; Iowa, 1887 ***1211.15*** *p11*
Hagerling, Mr.; America, 1853 ***7420.1*** *p105*
With wife son & daughter
Hagerman, Andrew 40; Kansas, 1880 ***777.40*** *p21*
Hagerman, Oliver 58; Ontario, 1871 ***1823.17*** *p62*
Hagermann, H. W.; Valdivia, Chile, 1852 ***1192.4*** *p53*
Hagerty, Caroline 60; Ontario, 1871 ***1823.21*** *p143*
Hagerty, James; New York, NY, 1834 ***3274.56*** *p72*
Hagerty, John 32; Ontario, 1871 ***1823.21*** *p143*
Hagerty, John 55; Ontario, 1871 ***1823.21*** *p143*
Hagewalt, Wilhelm; Washington, 1885 ***2770.40*** *p194*
Hagg, Heinrich; America, 1881 ***5475.1*** *p241*
Hagg, Philip M.; Ohio, 1809-1852 ***4511.35*** *p20*
Haggamon, Geo.; California, 1868 ***1131.61*** *p89*
Haggan, Joseph; Ohio, 1809-1852 ***4511.35*** *p20*
Haggard, John; New York, NY, 1866 ***1029.59*** *p42*
Haggarty, William 60; Ontario, 1871 ***1823.21*** *p143*
Haggerman, Nancy; Ontario, 1871 ***1823.21*** *p143*
Haggerty, Dinnes 55; Ontario, 1871 ***1823.17*** *p62*
Haggerty, Eliz.; Regina, Sask., 1917 ***9228.50*** *p507*
Haggerty, Hannah; Massachusetts, 1666 ***1642*** *p82*
Haggerty, Jeremiah 44; Ontario, 1871 ***1823.17*** *p62*
Haggerty, John 29; Ontario, 1871 ***1823.17*** *p63*
Haggett, Abraham 40; Ontario, 1871 ***1823.21*** *p143*
Haggith, Thomas 40; Ontario, 1871 ***1823.21*** *p143*
Haggqvist, N.J.; New Orleans, 1851 ***6412.40*** *p152*
Haglund, Maria; St. Paul, MN, 1887-1892 ***1865.50*** *p49*
Haglund, Olof; St. Paul, MN, 1887 ***1865.50*** *p49*
Hagman, Albert E.; St. Paul, MN, 1887-1894 ***1865.50*** *p49*
Hagman, Alma Maria *SEE* Hagman, Carl

Hagman, Carl; St. Paul, MN, 1887 *1865.50 p49*
*Wife:*Alma Maria
Hagman, Johanna Maria SEE Hagman, John L.
Hagman, John L.; St. Paul, MN, 1886 *1865.50 p49*
*Wife:*Johanna Maria
Hagny, Adam; America, 1865 *2526.42 p161*
Hagny, Mrs. Balthasar; America, 1836 *2526.42 p161*
Hagny, Ernst Ludwig; America, 1836 *2526.42 p161*
With wife mother & sister
With child 9
With child 6
With child 3
With child 12
Hagny, Friedrich; America, 1836 *2526.42 p161*
Hagny, Georg 22; America, 1865 *2526.42 p107*
With wife 32
*Father:*Martin 60
With child 3 months
Hagny, Georg, II; America, 1836 *2526.42 p161*
With wife
With child 9
Hagny, Maria; America, 1836 *2526.42 p161*
Hagny, Martin 60 SEE Hagny, Georg
Hagon, Amos; Colorado, 1862-1920 *1029.59 p36*
Hagstrom, Anders Wilhelm 3 SEE Hagstrom, Reinhold Anders
Hagstrom, Carin Jonsdotter 28 SEE Hagstrom, Reinhold Anders
Hagstrom, Carl Zachrisson; North America, 1854 *6410.15 p104*
Hagstrom, Johan A.; Cleveland, OH, 1888-1889 *9722.10 p119*
Hagstrom, Magnus; Cleveland, OH, 1885-1890 *9722.10 p120*
Hagstrom, Reinhold Anders 26; New York, 1856 *6529.11 p20*
*Wife:*Carin Jonsdotter 28
*Son:*Anders Wilhelm 3
Hague, Richard 44; Ontario, 1871 *1823.17 p63*
Haguenier, Leger 27; Montreal, 1651 *9221.17 p251*
Haguin, Elisabeth 16; Montreal, 1662 *9221.17 p497*
Hahn, Mr. 27; America, 1844 *778.6 p153*
Hahn, A. Margarethe; Brazil, 1862 *5475.1 p519*
Hahn, Alfons; America, 1908 *7420.1 p402*
Hahn, Andrew; Ohio, 1809-1852 *4511.35 p20*
Hahn, Anna; America, 1865 *5475.1 p509*
Hahn, Anne Marie 33; Louisiana, 1848 *778.6 p153*
Hahn, Anthony; Ohio, 1809-1852 *4511.35 p20*
Hahn, August; New York, 1859 *358.56 p53*
Hahn, Barbara SEE Hahn, Ph
Hahn, Barbara 35; America, 1881 *5475.1 p196*
Hahn, Carl Friedrich Wilhelm; America, 1861 *7420.1 p205*
Hahn, Caroline Philippine Ernestine; America, 1861 *7420.1 p205*
Hahn, Dorothea; Brazil, 1859 *5475.1 p522*
Hahn, Elisabeth SEE Hahn, Ph
Hahn, Elisabeth Helfen SEE Hahn, Ph
Hahn, Elisabeth; Brazil, 1862 *5475.1 p519*
Hahn, F. J.; Chile, 1852 *1192.4 p52*
With wife
With daughter 10
Hahn, Gertrud Leinen 45 SEE Hahn, Jakob
Hahn, Heinrich SEE Hahn, Ph
Hahn, Heinrich Carl; America, 1854 *7420.1 p120*
Hahn, Herman; Galveston, TX, 1855 *571.7 p16*
Hahn, Jakob SEE Hahn, Ph
Hahn, Jakob 8 SEE Hahn, Jakob
Hahn, Jakob 49; America, 1863 *5475.1 p314*
*Wife:*Gertrud Leinen 45
*Daughter:*Susanna 14
*Son:*Nikolaus 10
*Son:*Jakob 8
*Daughter:*Maria 3
*Daughter:*Margarethe 12
*Son:*Peter 16
Hahn, Jakob; Brazil, 1878 *5475.1 p446*
Hahn, Jean; Louisiana, 1836-1841 *4981.45 p208*
Hahn, Joh.; Iowa, 1885 *5475.1 p319*
*Daughter:*Katharina
With father-in-law
*Son:*Josef
*Daughter:*Maria
Hahn, Johann; America, 1871 *5475.1 p311*
Hahn, Johann SEE Hahn, Mathias
Hahn, Johann Friedrich Anton; America, 1846 *7420.1 p44*
Hahn, Johann Friedrich Christian; America, 1847 *7420.1 p53*
Hahn, Johanna SEE Hahn, Ph
Hahn, Josef SEE Hahn, Ph
Hahn, Josef SEE Hahn, Joh.
Hahn, Josephine 23; New Orleans, 1847 *778.6 p154*

Hahn, Karl; America, 1866 *5475.1 p542*
Hahn, Katharina SEE Hahn, Joh.
Hahn, Margarethe 12 SEE Hahn, Jakob
Hahn, Margarethe Schutz SEE Hahn, Mathias
Hahn, Margarethe 65; Brazil, 1862 *5475.1 p519*
With son-in-law
Hahn, Maria 3 SEE Hahn, Jakob
Hahn, Maria SEE Hahn, Joh.
Hahn, Maria Juliana; Brazil, 1862 *5475.1 p519*
Hahn, Mathias; Brazil, 1881 *5475.1 p445*
*Wife:*Margarethe Schutz
*Son:*Johann
*Son:*Peter
Hahn, Michel SEE Hahn, Ph
Hahn, Nicolaus; Chile, 1852 *1192.4 p54*
With wife
Hahn, Nikolaus SEE Hahn, Ph
Hahn, Nikolaus 10 SEE Hahn, Jakob
Hahn, Peter; America, 1882 *5475.1 p315*
Hahn, Peter 16 SEE Hahn, Ph
Hahn, Peter SEE Hahn, Mathias
Hahn, Peter; Ohio, 1844 *2763.1 p8*
Hahn, Ph; America, 1882 *5475.1 p315*
*Wife:*Elisabeth Helfen
*Son:*Michel
*Son:*Josef
*Daughter:*Barbara
*Son:*Heinrich
*Son:*Nikolaus
*Son:*Jakob
*Daughter:*Elisabeth
*Daughter:*Johanna
Hahn, Philippine; America, 1866 *5475.1 p542*
Hahn, Susanna 14 SEE Hahn, Jakob
Hahn, Wendel; America, 1847 *5475.1 p473*
Hahn, Wendel; America, 1852 *5475.1 p480*
Hahn, Wilhelm; America, 1860 *7420.1 p194*
Hahn, Wilhelmina; Philadelphia, 1854 *8513.31 p319*
Hahne, Christoph SEE Hahne, Heinrich August Wilhelm
Hahne, Heinrich August Wilhelm; America, 1871 *7420.1 p290*
*Father:*Christoph
With mother
Hahne, Heinrich Wilhelm August; America, 1870 *7420.1 p395*
Hahnenfeld, Brunn; America, 1889 *7420.1 p358*
Hahnenfeld, Bruno SEE Hahnenfeld, Heinrich
Hahnenfeld, Heinrich; America, 1889 *7420.1 p358*
*Brother:*Bruno
Hahnenfeld, Karl Johann; America, 1891 *7420.1 p362*
Hahr, Carolina; North America, 1854 *6410.15 p104*
With daughter
Hahr, Nicholas; Ohio, 1809-1852 *4511.35 p20*
Hahsdenteufel, Katharina 42; America, 1858 *5475.1 p501*
Haiding, Mary 49; Ontario, 1871 *1823.21 p143*
Haidt, Otto L.; Ohio, 1809-1852 *4511.35 p20*
Haidusek, Augustin; Texas, 1856 *2853.20 p72*
*Father:*Valentin
Haidusek, Valentin; Galveston, TX, 1856 *2853.20 p63*
Haidusek, Valentin SEE Haidusek, Augustin
Haies, Silvester; Massachusetts, 1675-1676 *1642 p129*
Haig, William; Ohio, 1840-1897 *8365.35 p16*
Haigele, A. Marie 4; Louisiana, 1848 *778.6 p154*
Haigele, F. Pierre 7; Louisiana, 1848 *778.6 p154*
Haigele, Joseph 43; Louisiana, 1848 *778.6 p154*
Haigele, Leo 16; Louisiana, 1848 *778.6 p154*
Haigele, Marie 42; Louisiana, 1848 *778.6 p154*
Haigele, Therese 14; Louisiana, 1848 *778.6 p154*
Haigh, Annie; Salt Lake City, 1891 *9228.50 p346*
Haigh, Benjamin; Ohio, 1809-1852 *4511.35 p20*
Haigh, Joseph; Ohio, 1809-1852 *4511.35 p20*
Haigh, Richard; Ohio, 1824 *3580.20 p32*
Haigh, Richard; Ohio, 1824 *6020.12 p12*
Haigh, Thomas 35; Ontario, 1871 *1823.21 p143*
Haight, Benjamin B. 30; Ontario, 1871 *1823.21 p143*
Haile, Tho; Virginia, 1652 *6254.4 p243*
Hails, John; Philadelphia, 1778 *8529.30 p3A*
Haimann, Ester 37; America, 1860 *5475.1 p561*
Haime, Abraham 18; Died enroute, 1846 *778.6 p154*
Hain, Georg 25; Port uncertain, 1846 *778.6 p154*
Haina, Domingo 42; New York, NY, 1894 *6512.1 p181*
Haina, Graciano 15; New York, NY, 1894 *6512.1 p181*
Haine, Anthony; Burlington, VT, 1844 *471.10 p88*
Hainmuller, Johann Werner; Port uncertain, 1853 *7420.1 p105*
Hains, Ezekial Smith; Ohio, 1818 *3580.20 p32*
Hains, Ezekial Smith; Ohio, 1818 *6020.12 p12*
Hains, John 62; Ontario, 1871 *1823.17 p63*
Hains, Martin; Ohio, 1809-1852 *4511.35 p20*
Hains, Nancy 63; Ontario, 1871 *1823.17 p63*
Hair, Archie 40; Ontario, 1871 *1823.21 p143*
Hair, Henry James 7; Ontario, 1871 *1823.17 p63*

Hair, Jacob 38; Ontario, 1871 *1823.17 p63*
Hair, William 11; Ontario, 1871 *1823.17 p63*
Haire, Rachael; Massachusetts, 1775 *1642 p100*
Haisch, John; Ohio, 1809-1852 *4511.35 p20*
Haise, Mary; Salisbury, MA, 1724 *1642 p81*
Haisman, Jan; New Orleans, 1848 *2853.20 p390*
Haite, J. H.; Louisiana, 1874 *4981.45 p132*
Haith, James; Philadelphia, 1777 *8529.30 p7A*
Hajek, Antonin; Nebraska, 1860-1910 *2853.20 p168*
Hajek, Frantisek; Wisconsin, 1865 *2853.20 p290*
Hajek, Jindrich; Chicago, 1867 *2853.20 p405*
Hajek, Marie SEE Hajek, Vaclav
Hajek, Vaclav; Nebraska, 1892 *2853.20 p168*
*Wife:*Marie
Hakala, Esther 25; Minnesota, 1923 *2769.54 p1383*
Hakansdotter, Anna Catharina; North America, 1858 *6410.15 p105*
Hakanson, Hilda 21; New York, NY, 1894 *6512.1 p185*
Hakanson, Nels; Colorado, 1886 *1029.59 p36*
Hakansson, Johan Otto; Cleveland, OH, 1903-1904 *9722.10 p120*
Hake, Dietrich Wilhelm SEE Hake, Dietrich Wilhelm
Hake, Dietrich Wilhelm; America, 1856 *7420.1 p147*
*Wife:*Engel Marie Sophie Brandes
*Daughter:*Thrine Sophie Marie
*Son:*Hans Heinrich Christoph
*Son:*Dietrich Wilhelm
Hake, Engel Marie Sophie Brandes SEE Hake, Dietrich Wilhelm
Hake, Gustav Heinrich; America, 1881 *7420.1 p321*
Hake, Hans Heinrich Christoph SEE Hake, Dietrich Wilhelm
Hake, Philip; Illinois, 1858 *6079.1 p6*
Hake, Thrine Sophie Marie SEE Hake, Dietrich Wilhelm
Hakl, Jan; South Dakota, 1871-1910 *2853.20 p247*
Halack, Jakim 30; New York, NY, 1912 *8355.1 p16*
Halamicek, Josef; Chicago, 1882 *2853.20 p465*
Halamuda, Anton; Texas, 1855-1886 *9980.22 p16*
Halander, Anders; New York, NY, 1848 *6412.40 p151*
Halaska, Jan; Wisconsin, 1856 *2853.20 p345*
Halay, Barbe 12 SEE Halay, Mathurine Valet
Halay, Elisabeth 10 SEE Halay, Mathurine Valet
Halay, Jean-Baptiste 48; Quebec, 1655 *9221.17 p325*
Halay, Marie; Quebec, 1670 *4514.3 p324*
Halay, Marie; Quebec, 1671 *4514.3 p324*
Halay, Marie 18 SEE Halay, Mathurine Valet
Halay, Mathurine; Quebec, 1659 *9221.17 p403*
*Daughter:*Marie
*Daughter:*Barbe
*Daughter:*Elisabeth
Halberding, Minna; America, 1868 *7420.1 p271*
Halberg, Gustaf; Iowa, 1896 *1211.15 p11*
Halberstadt, Charlotte SEE Halberstadt, Karl
Halberstadt, Fritz Georg Ludwig; America, 1853 *7420.1 p105*
Halberstadt, Johann; Brazil, 1862 *5475.1 p506*
Halberstadt, Julius Christian Franz; America, 1866 *7420.1 p243*
Halberstadt, Karl; Brazil, 1861 *5475.1 p506*
*Wife:*Sophie Mohr
*Daughter:*Charlotte
*Son:*Wilhelm
Halberstadt, Ludwig; America, 1855 *7420.1 p136*
Halberstadt, Sophie Mohr SEE Halberstadt, Karl
Halberstadt, Wilhelm SEE Halberstadt, Karl
Halberstatt, Anthony; New Jersey, 1784-1786 *927.31 p3*
Halbert, Louis; Missouri, 1896 *3276.1 p1*
Halbert, William 74; Ontario, 1871 *1823.21 p143*
Halcombe, William 17; Quebec, 1870 *8364.32 p23*
Haldane, James 77; Ontario, 1871 *1823.21 p143*
Haldane, Joseph 40; Ontario, 1871 *1823.21 p143*
Haldane, Robert 37; Ontario, 1871 *1823.21 p143*
Haldane, Susan 24; Ontario, 1871 *1823.21 p143*
Halder, . . .; West Virginia, n.d. *1132.30 p151*
Halder, Jacob; West Virginia, 1869 *1132.30 p151*
Halderson, Hannah 11; Quebec, 1870 *8364.32 p23*
Haldon, William; New York, 1776 *8529.30 p3A*
Haldy, Benjamin 4; Galveston, TX, 1846 *3967.10 p378*
Haldy, Joseph 40; Galveston, TX, 1846 *3967.10 p378*
Haldy, Katharina 7; Galveston, TX, 1846 *3967.10 p378*
Haldy, Katharina 39; Galveston, TX, 1846 *3967.10 p378*
Haldy, Maria 27; Galveston, TX, 1846 *3967.10 p378*
Haldy, Maria Josephine 11 months; Galveston, TX, 1846 *3967.10 p378*
Hale, Caroline; New York, 1855 *9228.50 p271*
Hale, Caroline; New York, 1858 *9228.50 p636*
Hale, Geo; Virginia, 1652 *6254.4 p243*
Hale, George 15; Quebec, 1870 *8364.32 p23*
Hale, John H.; North Carolina, 1842 *1088.45 p12*
Hale, Mary 44; Ontario, 1871 *1823.21 p144*
Hale, Mary 68; Ontario, 1871 *1823.21 p144*
Hale, Richard 60; Ontario, 1871 *1823.21 p144*
Hale, Thomas; Boston, 1832 *3274.55 p24*

Hale, Thomas 67; Ontario, 1871 ***1823.17*** *p63*
Halengreen, William; Colorado, 1873 ***1029.59*** *p36*
Halenstein, Catharine; New York, 1849 ***9722.10*** *p113*
Hales, John; Philadelphia, 1778 ***8529.30*** *p3A*
Hales, Tho; Virginia, 1652 ***6254.4*** *p243*
Haleut, Louis; Quebec, 1652 ***9221.17*** *p259*
Haley, Annie 12; Quebec, 1870 ***8364.32*** *p23*
Haley, Charles 35; Ontario, 1871 ***1823.21*** *p144*
Haley, Elizabeth; Boston, 1744 ***1642*** *p45*
Haley, George 46; Ontario, 1871 ***1823.17*** *p63*
Haley, James 32; Ontario, 1871 ***1823.21*** *p144*
Haley, Jane 15; St. John, N.B., 1834 ***6469.7*** *p5*
Haley, Jeremiah; Boston, 1765 ***1642*** *p35*
Haley, John; Ohio, 1809-1852 ***4511.35*** *p20*
Haley, John 39; Ontario, 1871 ***1823.21*** *p144*
Haley, Olliver 27; Ontario, 1871 ***1823.21*** *p144*
Haley, Patrick; Louisiana, 1857 ***7710.1*** *p156*
Haley, Robert 39; Ontario, 1871 ***1823.21*** *p144*
Haley, Thomas 45; Ontario, 1871 ***1823.21*** *p144*
Haley, William 37; Ontario, 1871 ***1823.21*** *p144*
Haley, William 64; Ontario, 1871 ***1823.21*** *p144*
Halfeldt, . . .; America, 1853 ***7420.1*** *p105*
With family
Halier, Perrette; Quebec, 1669 ***4514.3*** *p324*
Haligan, Denis; Toronto, 1844 ***2910.35*** *p115*
Haliwell, William 60; Ontario, 1871 ***1823.21*** *p144*
Hall, Ann; Quebec, 1865 ***9228.50*** *p307*
Hall, Ann Eliza 45; Ontario, 1871 ***1823.17*** *p63*
Hall, Catherine 35; Ontario, 1871 ***1823.21*** *p144*
Hall, Charles; Ohio, 1809-1852 ***4511.35*** *p20*
Hall, Charles 33; Ontario, 1871 ***1823.17*** *p63*
Hall, Charles 36; Ontario, 1871 ***1823.17*** *p63*
Hall, Charles 48; Ontario, 1871 ***1823.17*** *p63*
Hall, Charles 60; Ontario, 1871 ***1823.21*** *p144*
Hall, Charles G.; Colorado, 1881 ***1029.59*** *p36*
Hall, Diana Baker; California, 1867-1937 ***9228.50*** *p320*
Hall, Diana Baker; California, 1867-1937 ***9228.50*** *p320*
Hall, Eliza 22; Ontario, 1871 ***1823.21*** *p144*
Hall, Frank 23; Ontario, 1871 ***1823.21*** *p144*
Hall, Frank 41; Ontario, 1871 ***1823.21*** *p144*
Hall, G. A. 39; Ontario, 1871 ***1823.21*** *p144*
Hall, George 21; New York, NY, 1825 ***6178.50*** *p76*
Hall, George; Ohio, 1809-1852 ***4511.35*** *p20*
Hall, George 44; Ontario, 1871 ***1823.21*** *p144*
Hall, George 52; Ontario, 1871 ***1823.17*** *p63*
Hall, Gust; Colorado, 1883 ***1029.59*** *p36*
Hall, Gustaf; America, 1853 ***4487.25*** *p57*
With family
Hall, Harvey 52; Ontario, 1871 ***1823.21*** *p144*
Hall, Henry 19; Ontario, 1871 ***1823.21*** *p144*
Hall, Henry 41; Ontario, 1871 ***1823.17*** *p63*
Hall, Hilma A.; Minnesota, 1880-1887 ***1865.50*** *p49*
Hall, James; Colorado, 1894 ***1029.59*** *p36*
Hall, James; Colorado, 1903 ***1029.59*** *p36*
Hall, James; New Orleans, 1850 ***7242.30*** *p143*
Hall, James 37; Ontario, 1871 ***1823.17*** *p63*
Hall, James E.; Washington, 1889 ***2770.40*** *p79*
Hall, Jean 34; New Orleans, 1848 ***778.6*** *p154*
Hall, John; Colorado, 1880 ***1029.59*** *p41*
Hall, John; Colorado, 1883 ***1029.59*** *p36*
Hall, John; North Carolina, 1842 ***1088.45*** *p12*
Hall, John 33; Ontario, 1871 ***1823.17*** *p63*
Hall, John 52; Ontario, 1871 ***1823.21*** *p144*
Hall, John 54; Ontario, 1871 ***1823.21*** *p144*
Hall, John 60; Ontario, 1871 ***1823.17*** *p63*
Hall, John 65; Ontario, 1871 ***1823.21*** *p144*
Hall, John; Washington, 1889 ***2770.40*** *p27*
Hall, John Wesley 40; Ontario, 1871 ***1823.17*** *p63*
Hall, Joseph 7; New Orleans, 1848 ***778.6*** *p154*
Hall, Joseph 47; Ontario, 1871 ***1823.17*** *p63*
Hall, Marianne 33; Ontario, 1871 ***1823.21*** *p144*
Hall, Mary; Ohio, 1860 ***8513.31*** *p311*
Hall, Morrison 38; Ontario, 1871 ***1823.17*** *p63*
Hall, Nebuch...r; Philadelphia, 1778 ***8529.30*** *p3A*
Hall, Nickolas 35; Ontario, 1871 ***1823.17*** *p63*
Hall, Peter 52; Ontario, 1871 ***1823.21*** *p144*
Hall, Richard; Ontario, 1871 ***1823.17*** *p63*
Hall, Richard 43; Ontario, 1871 ***1823.17*** *p63*
Hall, Richard 44; Ontario, 1871 ***1823.21*** *p144*
Hall, Robert 40; Ontario, 1871 ***1823.21*** *p144*
Hall, Stephen 70; Ontario, 1871 ***1823.21*** *p144*
Hall, Thomas; Marston's Wharf, 1782 ***8529.30*** *p12*
Hall, Thomas 36; Ontario, 1871 ***1823.21*** *p144*
Hall, Thomas 47; Ontario, 1871 ***1823.21*** *p144*
Hall, Thomas 64; Ontario, 1871 ***1823.17*** *p63*
Hall, Thomas A. 49; Ontario, 1871 ***1823.21*** *p144*
Hall, William; Boston, 1737 ***1642*** *p26*
Hall, William 18; Ontario, 1871 ***1823.21*** *p144*
Hall, William 21; Ontario, 1871 ***1823.21*** *p144*
Hall, William 22; Ontario, 1871 ***1823.21*** *p144*
Hall, William 28; Ontario, 1871 ***1823.21*** *p144*
Hall, William 40; Ontario, 1871 ***1823.17*** *p63*
Hall, William 19; Quebec, 1870 ***8364.32*** *p23*
Hall, Wilson 30; Ontario, 1871 ***1823.21*** *p144*
Hallais, Marie Jeanne Francoise; Nova Scotia, 1753 ***3051*** *p112*
Hallam, Thomas A.; Illinois, 1861 ***6079.1*** *p6*
Hallamby, Mrs.; Montreal, 1922 ***4514.4*** *p32*
With baby
Hallamby, H. J.; Montreal, 1922 ***4514.4*** *p32*
Hallauer, Franz; America, 1847 ***5475.1*** *p474*
Hallauer, Johann; America, 1839 ***5475.1*** *p469*
Hallauer, Johann; America, 1839 ***5475.1*** *p470*
Hallauer, Johann; America, 1847 ***5475.1*** *p473*
*Brother:*Josef
With sister
Hallauer, Johann; America, 1851 ***5475.1*** *p479*
*Brother:*Peter
*Brother:*Wendel
Hallauer, Josef; America, 1837 ***5475.1*** *p469*
Hallauer, Josef *SEE* Hallauer, Johann
Hallauer, Peter *SEE* Hallauer, Johann
Hallauer, Wendel *SEE* Hallauer, Johann
Hallaway, Henry; Illinois, 1858 ***6079.1*** *p6*
Hallberg, Carl Fr.; New York, NY, 1848 ***6412.40*** *p151*
Hallberg, Lars Petter; North America, 1854 ***6410.15*** *p104*
Halle, Constantine; Louisiana, 1874-1875 ***4981.45*** *p29*
Halleck, Catherine 13; Ontario, 1871 ***1823.17*** *p63*
Halleday, Mary 60; Ontario, 1871 ***1823.21*** *p144*
Hallenberg, Edward; Cleveland, OH, 1902-1905 ***9722.10*** *p120*
Hallenden, William; Ontario, 1871 ***1823.21*** *p144*
Haller, A.; Louisiana, 1874-1875 ***4981.45*** *p29*
Haller, Augustin 1; Galveston, TX, 1844 ***3967.10*** *p374*
Haller, C. W.; Louisiana, 1874 ***4981.45*** *p296*
Haller, Charles 15; New Orleans, 1848 ***778.6*** *p154*
Haller, Christiane 5; Galveston, TX, 1844 ***3967.10*** *p374*
Haller, Christoph 24; Galveston, TX, 1846 ***3967.10*** *p378*
Haller, Elizabeth; Miami, 1935 ***4984.12*** *p39*
Haller, Emilie 9; Galveston, TX, 1846 ***3967.10*** *p378*
Haller, Franziska 50; Galveston, TX, 1846 ***3967.10*** *p378*
Haller, Jacob; Long Island, 1778 ***8529.30*** *p9A*
Haller, Johann 38; Galveston, TX, 1844 ***3967.10*** *p374*
Haller, Joseph 31; Galveston, TX, 1844 ***3967.10*** *p372*
Haller, Josephine 3; Galveston, TX, 1844 ***3967.10*** *p374*
Haller, Louis 1; America, 1840 ***778.6*** *p154*
Haller, Maria Anna 10; Galveston, TX, 1844 ***3967.10*** *p374*
Haller, Maria Anna 35; Galveston, TX, 1844 ***3967.10*** *p374*
Haller, Marie 17; Mississippi, 1845-1846 ***778.6*** *p154*
Haller, Michel 23; America, 1842 ***778.6*** *p154*
Haller, Paul 12; Galveston, TX, 1844 ***3967.10*** *p374*
Haller, Regina 14; Galveston, TX, 1844 ***3967.10*** *p374*
Haller, Sophia 27; America, 1840 ***778.6*** *p154*
Haller, Valentin 48; Galveston, TX, 1846 ***3967.10*** *p378*
Halleron, Michael; Toronto, 1844 ***2910.35*** *p113*
Halles, John; Philadelphia, 1778 ***8529.30*** *p3A*
Hallesy, Hanora 16; Ontario, 1871 ***1823.17*** *p64*
Hallesy, Patrick 45; Ontario, 1871 ***1823.17*** *p64*
Hallet, Eugene; New Orleans, 1871 ***1494.21*** *p31*
Hallet, Victor; New Orleans, 1871 ***1494.21*** *p31*
Hallett, Miss; Ontario, 1820-1900 ***9228.50*** *p271*
With sister
Hallett, Jane; Ontario, 1866-1869 ***9228.50*** *p139*
Halley, Robert 45; Ontario, 1871 ***1823.21*** *p144*
Halley, William 41; Ontario, 1871 ***1823.21*** *p145*
Hallfast, Olof A.; Illinois, 1861 ***4487.25*** *p58*
Hallfeldt, Engel Marie; America, 1868 ***7420.1*** *p271*
*Daughter:*Ernestine
*Son:*Heinrich Conrad Wilhelm
Hallfeldt, Ernestine *SEE* Hallfeldt, Engel Marie Brands
Hallfeldt, Heinrich Conrad Wilhelm *SEE* Hallfeldt, Engel Marie Brands
Hallgren, Nels N.; Illinois, 1861 ***4487.25*** *p58*
Hallgren, Niclas August; North America, 1887 ***6410.15*** *p106*
Hallicey, Michael 35; Ontario, 1871 ***1823.17*** *p64*
Halliday, James; North Carolina, 1822-1824 ***1088.45*** *p12*
Halliday, James 67; Ontario, 1871 ***1823.21*** *p145*
Halliday, Thomas 52; Ontario, 1871 ***1823.17*** *p64*
Halligan, John 31; Ontario, 1871 ***1823.21*** *p145*
Halligan, William 18; Quebec, 1870 ***8364.32*** *p23*
Hallimi..., Jacques; Quebec, 1648 ***9221.17*** *p199*
Hallin, Jacques; Quebec, 1648 ***9221.17*** *p199*
Hallisey, John 37; Ontario, 1871 ***1823.21*** *p145*
Hallman, Amelia; Wisconsin, 1892 ***6795.8*** *p179*
Hallman, H.J.; Wisconsin, 1895 ***6795.8*** *p123*
Hallman, Herman Julius; Wisconsin, 1913 ***6795.8*** *p167*
Hallman, Jane 45; Ontario, 1871 ***1823.21*** *p145*
Hallman, Thomas 33; Ontario, 1871 ***1823.21*** *p145*
Hallnam, Agnes 5; New York, NY, 1835 ***5024.1*** *p136*
Hallnam, Buddie 3; New York, NY, 1835 ***5024.1*** *p136*
Hallnam, Catherine 15; New York, NY, 1835 ***5024.1*** *p136*
Hallnam, Dailey 16; New York, NY, 1835 ***5024.1*** *p136*
Hallnam, Elizabeth 40; New York, NY, 1835 ***5024.1*** *p136*
Hallnam, John 11; New York, NY, 1835 ***5024.1*** *p136*
Hallnam, Michael 7; New York, NY, 1835 ***5024.1*** *p136*
Hallnam, Peter 9; New York, NY, 1835 ***5024.1*** *p136*
Hallnam, William 17; New York, NY, 1835 ***5024.1*** *p136*
Halloran, Catherine; New Orleans, 1851 ***7242.30*** *p143*
Hallorand, Elizabeth; New Orleans, 1851 ***7242.30*** *p143*
Halloren, Martin 34; Ontario, 1871 ***1823.21*** *p145*
Hallowell, Joseph; New York, NY, 1827 ***3274.55*** *p68*
Halls, John; Colorado, 1880 ***1029.59*** *p36*
Halls, John 65; Ontario, 1871 ***1823.21*** *p145*
Halls, Thomas 53; Ontario, 1871 ***1823.21*** *p145*
Halls, William 27; Ontario, 1871 ***1823.21*** *p145*
Hallstein, Adam; America, 1841 ***2526.42*** *p173*
With wife
With child 12
With child 18
Hallstein, Adam, VII; America, 1906 ***2526.42*** *p173*
Hallstein, Anna Eva 3 *SEE* Hallstein, Johannes
Hallstein, Anna Eva Hartmann 72 *SEE* Hallstein, Leonhard
Hallstein, Anna Margaretha *SEE* Hallstein, Georg, IV
Hallstein, Anna Margaretha 13 *SEE* Hallstein, Johannes
Hallstein, Anna Margaretha Nickel 36 *SEE* Hallstein, Johannes
Hallstein, Anna Margaretha; Illinois, 1853 ***2526.43*** *p124*
Hallstein, Barbara; America, 1869 ***2526.42*** *p107*
Hallstein, Friedrich; America, 1833 ***2526.42*** *p121*
With wife & 2 children
Hallstein, Georg; America, 1836 ***2526.42*** *p107*
With wife
With son 3 months
With son 4
With daughter 11
With son 8
Hallstein, Georg *SEE* Hallstein, Georg, IV
Hallstein, Georg, IV; America, 1869 ***2526.42*** *p107*
*Wife:*Anna Margaretha
*Child:*Georg
Hallstein, Georg Adam; America, 1831 ***2526.42*** *p199*
With wife & child
Hallstein, Johann Georg 2 *SEE* Hallstein, Johannes
Hallstein, Johann Philipp 6 *SEE* Hallstein, Johannes
Hallstein, Johannes; America, 1832 ***2526.42*** *p173*
With wife & 2 children
Hallstein, Johannes; America, 1836 ***2526.42*** *p107*
With wife
With daughter 4
With daughter 1
Hallstein, Johannes 5 *SEE* Hallstein, Johannes
Hallstein, Johannes 43; America, 1856 ***2526.42*** *p181*
*Wife:*Anna Margaretha Nickel 36
*Son:*Johann Georg 2
*Son:*Johann Philipp 6 months
*Daughter:*Anna Eva 3
*Daughter:*Anna Margaretha 13
*Daughter:*Maria Magdalena 9
*Son:*Johannes 5
*Son:*Leonhard 15
Hallstein, Johannes, IV; America, 1852 ***2526.42*** *p173*
Hallstein, Leonhard; America, 1838 ***2526.42*** *p121*
With wife & 8 children
Hallstein, Leonhard; America, 1854 ***2526.42*** *p102*
Hallstein, Leonhard; America, 1869 ***2526.42*** *p108*
Hallstein, Leonhard 15 *SEE* Hallstein, Johannes
Hallstein, Leonhard 70; America, 1856 ***2526.42*** *p181*
*Wife:*Anna Eva Hartmann 72
Hallstein, Margaretha; America, 1867 ***2526.42*** *p108*
Hallstein, Maria Magdalena 9 *SEE* Hallstein, Johannes
Hallstein, Michael; America, 1867 ***2526.42*** *p121*
Hallstein, Wilhelm; America, 1866 ***2526.42*** *p121*
Hallstrand, Axel Gedcon; Boston, 1904 ***1766.20*** *p34*
Hallstrohm, Egon Nathanael; Iowa, 1932 ***1211.15*** *p11*
Hallu, Eugene; Kansas, 1917-1918 ***2094.25*** *p50*
Halman, Frank; Wisconsin, 1891 ***6795.8*** *p58*
Halminen, Eino 33; Minnesota, 1926 ***2769.54*** *p1383*
Halminen, Ida 27; Minnesota, 1926 ***2769.54*** *p1383*
Halpin, James; Ohio, 1840-1897 ***8365.35*** *p16*
Halpin, John 43; Ontario, 1871 ***1823.21*** *p145*
Halpin, M. H.; Washington, 1881 ***2770.40*** *p135*
Halpin, Mathew; Ohio, 1840-1897 ***8365.35*** *p16*
Halpin, Patrick 49; Ontario, 1871 ***1823.21*** *p145*
Halpin, Philip; Ohio, 1840-1897 ***8365.35*** *p16*
Halpin, William Henry 46; Ontario, 1871 ***1823.21*** *p145*
Halsall, Robert 21; Quebec, 1870 ***8364.32*** *p23*
Halse, John; New Jersey, 1885 ***9228.50*** *p466*
*Wife:*Mary Jane Mitchell
Halse, Mary Jane Mitchell *SEE* Halse, John
Halsindine, George; Philadelphia, 1778 ***8529.30*** *p3A*
Halsteen, C.; Louisiana, 1874 ***4981.45*** *p296*

Haltendorff, Christiane 20; Valdivia, Chile, 1852 *1192.4 p53*
Haltendorff, Eduard 13; Valdivia, Chile, 1852 *1192.4 p53*
Haltendorff, Gust.; Valdivia, Chile, 1852 *1192.4 p53*
Haltendorff, Pauline 20; Valdivia, Chile, 1852 *1192.4 p53*
Halter, Anthony; Ohio, 1809-1852 *4511.35 p20*
Halter, Benedict; Ohio, 1809-1852 *4511.35 p20*
Halter, Christian; Ohio, 1809-1852 *4511.35 p20*
Halter, George; Ohio, 1809-1852 *4511.35 p20*
Halter, Joseph; Ohio, 1809-1852 *4511.35 p20*
Halter, Lewis; Ohio, 1809-1852 *4511.35 p20*
Halter, Lorantz; Ohio, 1809-1852 *4511.35 p20*
Halter, Matthias; Ohio, 1809-1852 *4511.35 p20*
Halter, Mottice; Ohio, 1809-1852 *4511.35 p20*
Halterman, Harvey 27; Ontario, 1871 *1823.17 p64*
Halvarson, Charlotta; St. Paul, MN, 1888 *1865.50 p50*
Halverhout, Frederick; Colorado, 1882 *1029.59 p36*
Halverhout, Frederick; Colorado, 1891 *1029.59 p36*
Halverhout, Fredick A.; Colorado, 1882 *1029.59 p37*
Halverson, Charles; Washington, 1882 *2770.40 p135*
Halverson, Hans; Washington, 1886 *2770.40 p195*
Halvorson, Halvor; Massachusetts, 1836 *3274.56 p72*
Ham, Daniel; Illinois, 1860 *6079.1 p6*
Ham, Daniel 34; Missouri, 1847 *778.6 p154*
Ham, Henry 24; Ontario, 1871 *1823.21 p145*
Ham, Henry 25; Ontario, 1871 *1823.21 p145*
Hamahon, Michel; North Carolina, 1809-1814 *1088.45 p12*
Hamahon, John; North Carolina, 1809-1814 *1088.45 p12*
Haman, Adam 39; New York, NY, 1898 *7951.13 p44*
Haman, Anton 7; New York, NY, 1898 *7951.13 p44*
Haman, Franz 2; New York, NY, 1898 *7951.13 p44*
Haman, Johanna 9 months; New York, NY, 1898 *7951.13 p44*
Haman, Johanna 37; New York, NY, 1898 *7951.13 p44*
Haman, Lorentz 3; New York, NY, 1898 *7951.13 p44*
Haman, Michael 14; New York, NY, 1898 *7951.13 p44*
Haman, Peter 5; New York, NY, 1898 *7951.13 p44*
Haman, Wendelin 8; New York, NY, 1898 *7951.13 p44*
Haman, Wendelin 10; New York, NY, 1898 *7951.13 p44*
Hamann, Adam 33; America, 1854 *2526.43 p134*
  With wife 33
  *Daughter:*Elisabeth 6 months
  *Son:*Michael 8
  *Son:*Peter 4
Hamann, Elisabeth 6 *SEE* Hamann, Adam
Hamann, Georg; America, 1866 *2526.43 p209*
Hamann, Michael; America, 1868 *2526.43 p209*
Hamann, Michael 8 *SEE* Hamann, Adam
Hamann, Peter 4 *SEE* Hamann, Adam
Hamare, Jean; Montreal, 1651 *9221.17 p251*
Hamberg, Gust; Iowa, 1887 *1211.15 p11*
Hamberg, J.C.; New York, NY, 1842 *6412.40 p146*
Hamberger, Daniel; Ohio, 1809-1852 *4511.35 p20*
Hambert, Jean 30; America, 1747 *778.6 p154*
Hambley, John 55; Ontario, 1871 *1823.21 p145*
Hambon, Pierre 33; New Orleans, 1848 *778.6 p154*
Hambrecht, Paul; New Jersey, 1778-1780 *927.31 p3*
Hambrick, Paul; New Jersey, 1778-1780 *927.31 p3*
Hambry, Marie 3; New Orleans, 1848 *778.6 p154*
Hamburger, Johann Georg; America, 1871 *2526.43 p205*
Hamburger, Johann Georg; America, 1888 *2526.43 p205*
Hamel, . . . 23; Quebec, 1660 *9221.17 p436*
  *Wife:*Marie Auvray
Hamel, Catherine Lemaistre 39 *SEE* Hamel, Charles
Hamel, Charles 3 *SEE* Hamel, Charles
Hamel, Charles 37; Quebec, 1662 *9221.17 p487*
  *Wife:*Catherine Lemaistre 39
  *Son:*Jean 10
  *Son:*Charles 3
Hamel, Jean 10 *SEE* Hamel, Charles
Hamel, Jean 19; Quebec, 1653 *9221.17 p275*
Hamel, Jeanne 49; Quebec, 1651 *9221.17 p245*
Hamel, Maria Anna; Venezuela, 1843 *3899.5 p540*
Hamel, Marie Auvray *SEE* Hamel, . . .
Hamel, Virginie 26; New Orleans, 1848 *778.6 p154*
Hamel, Wilhelm; Port uncertain, 1854 *7420.1 p120*
Hameley, William; New York, NY, 1846 *7710.1 p153*
Hamelin, Mr. 32; America, 1845 *778.6 p154*
Hamelin, Julia; Utah, n.d. *9228.50 p317*
Hamelin deBourgchemin, Jean-Francois; Quebec, 1687 *2314.30 p171*
Hamer, Pierre 33; America, 1848 *778.6 p154*
Hamerschold, Charles J.; North Carolina, 1854 *1088.45 p12*
Hamill, George 67; Ontario, 1871 *1823.21 p145*
Hamilton, Alexander; North Carolina, 1813 *1088.45 p12*
Hamilton, Alexr 69; Ontario, 1871 *1823.17 p64*
Hamilton, Alice 60; Ontario, 1871 *1823.21 p145*
Hamilton, Andrew; Louisiana, 1874 *4981.45 p132*
Hamilton, Ann 53; Ontario, 1871 *1823.17 p64*

Hamilton, Arch 75; Ontario, 1871 *1823.17 p64*
Hamilton, Bell 12 *SEE* Hamilton, Ida
Hamilton, Courtland 48; Ontario, 1871 *1823.17 p64*
Hamilton, D. 47; Ontario, 1871 *1823.17 p64*
Hamilton, Dennis; New Orleans, 1850 *7242.30 p143*
Hamilton, Duncan 67; Ontario, 1871 *1823.21 p145*
Hamilton, Eliza 37; Ontario, 1871 *1823.21 p145*
Hamilton, Ellen; New Orleans, 1850 *7242.30 p143*
Hamilton, Erskine B.; Ohio, 1863 *3580.20 p32*
Hamilton, Erskine B.; Ohio, 1863 *6020.12 p12*
Hamilton, Gustavus 42; Ontario, 1871 *1823.21 p145*
Hamilton, Gustavus G. 56; Ontario, 1871 *1823.21 p145*
Hamilton, Ida 60; Ohio, 1880 *4879.40 p260*
  *Son:*John 16
  *Daughter:*Seton 14
  *Daughter:*Bell 12
Hamilton, Isaac; Philadelphia, 1851 *7074.20 p132*
Hamilton, James; Boston, 1775 *8529.30 p2*
Hamilton, James; North Carolina, 1802 *1088.45 p12*
Hamilton, James 32; Ontario, 1871 *1823.17 p64*
Hamilton, James 50; Ontario, 1871 *1823.17 p64*
Hamilton, James 62; Ontario, 1871 *1823.21 p145*
Hamilton, James; Worcester, MA, 1718 *1642 p118*
Hamilton, John; Baton Rouge, LA, 1781 *8529.30 p9A*
Hamilton, John 62; Michigan, 1880 *4491.33 p11*
Hamilton, John; New York, 1778 *8529.30 p12*
Hamilton, John 16 *SEE* Hamilton, Ida
Hamilton, John 30; Ontario, 1871 *1823.21 p145*
Hamilton, John 46; Ontario, 1871 *1823.21 p145*
Hamilton, John 48; Ontario, 1871 *1823.21 p145*
Hamilton, John 52; Ontario, 1871 *1823.21 p145*
Hamilton, John 60; Ontario, 1871 *1823.17 p64*
Hamilton, John 60; Ontario, 1871 *1823.21 p145*
Hamilton, John 60; Ontario, 1871 *1823.21 p145*
Hamilton, John 14; Quebec, 1870 *8364.32 p23*
Hamilton, John 17; Quebec, 1870 *8364.32 p23*
Hamilton, John Henry 57; Ontario, 1871 *1823.17 p64*
Hamilton, Joseph; Nova Scotia, 1839 *7078 p80*
Hamilton, Mary 70; Ontario, 1871 *1823.21 p145*
Hamilton, May B. 24; Michigan, 1880 *4491.33 p11*
Hamilton, Patrick; North Carolina, 1807-1811 *1088.45 p12*
Hamilton, R. J. 47; Ontario, 1871 *1823.21 p145*
Hamilton, R. R.; Louisiana, 1836-1841 *4981.45 p208*
Hamilton, Robert; Massachusetts, 1775 *1642 p116*
Hamilton, Robert; North Carolina, 1813 *1088.45 p12*
Hamilton, Robert 46; Ontario, 1871 *1823.17 p64*
Hamilton, Seton 14 *SEE* Hamilton, Ida
Hamilton, Thomas; Ohio, 1818 *6020.12 p12*
Hamilton, Thomas 47; Ontario, 1871 *1823.21 p145*
Hamilton, William; Louisiana, 1874 *4981.45 p132*
Hamilton, William; New York, NY, 1778 *8529.30 p2*
Hamilton, William; North Carolina, 1817 *1088.45 p12*
Hamker, Engel M. D. Salge *SEE* Hamker, Heinrich Ernst Gottlieb
Hamker, Engel M. S. *SEE* Hamker, Heinrich Ernst Gottlieb
Hamker, Engel M. S. C. *SEE* Hamker, Heinrich Ernst Gottlieb
Hamker, Ernst F. G. *SEE* Hamker, Heinrich Ernst Gottlieb
Hamker, Ernst H. W. *SEE* Hamker, Heinrich Ernst Gottlieb
Hamker, Friedrich W. *SEE* Hamker, Heinrich Ernst Gottlieb
Hamker, Heinrich Ernst Gottlieb; America, 1867 *7420.1 p256*
  *Wife:*Engel M. D. Salge
  *Daughter:*Engel M. S. C.
  *Son:*Friedrich W.
  *Daughter:*Engel M. S.
  *Son:*Ernst F. G.
  *Son:*Ernst H. W.
Hamler, August Wilhem; Wisconsin, 1870 *6795.8 p63*
Hamlett, Lambert; Illinois, 1858 *6079.1 p6*
Hamlett, William; Illinois, 1858 *6079.1 p6*
Hamley, Wm. Jas. Cole 26; Quebec, 1910 *2897.7 p8*
Hamlyn, Henry 22; Ontario, 1871 *1823.21 p145*
Hamlyn, Thomas 57; Ontario, 1871 *1823.21 p145*
Hamm, Alexius; Venezuela, 1843 *3899.5 p541*
Hamm, Anna Lorsong *SEE* Hamm, Peter
Hamm, Anton; Venezuela, 1843 *3899.5 p541*
Hamm, Antonius; Venezuela, 1843 *3899.5 p540*
Hamm, Daniel 34; Mississippi, 1847 *778.6 p154*
Hamm, Florent 21; America, 1844 *778.6 p154*
Hamm, Franz Anton; Venezuela, 1843 *3899.5 p541*
Hamm, Jakob; Venezuela, 1843 *3899.5 p542*
Hamm, Jean 1; Port uncertain, 1843 *778.6 p154*
Hamm, Johann 22; America, 1846 *5475.1 p61*
Hamm, Maria Anna; Venezuela, 1843 *3899.5 p540*
Hamm, Peter 31; America, 1846 *5475.1 p61*
  *Wife:*Anna Lorsong
Hammann, F.; Venezuela, 1843 *3899.5 p546*

Hammann, Georg 12 *SEE* Hammann, Peter
Hammann, Georg; Dayton, OH, 1835-1906 *2526.42 p173*
Hammann, Heinrich 17; America, 1883 *2526.42 p161*
Hammann, Johannes; America, 1883 *2526.42 p161*
Hammann, Konrad; America, 1846-1906 *2526.42 p173*
  *Mother:*Margaretha
Hammann, Leonhard; America, 1845-1906 *2526.42 p173*
Hammann, Leonhard 2 *SEE* Hammann, Peter
Hammann, Margaretha *SEE* Hammann, Konrad
Hammann, Maria Magdalena; America, 1753 *2526.42 p145*
Hammann, Marie Elisabeth 8 *SEE* Hammann, Peter
Hammann, Marie Elisabetha; America, 1839-1906 *2526.42 p173*
Hammann, Michael 17 *SEE* Hammann, Peter
Hammann, Peter; America, 1848 *2526.42 p174*
  With wife
  *Daughter:*Marie Elisabeth
  *Son:*Leonhard
  *Son:*Michael
  *Son:*Georg
Hammar, Henry; Chicago, 1864 *4487.25 p58*
Hammarberg, Martin A.; Cleveland, OH, 1895 *9722.10 p120*
Hammarstrand, F.W.; New Orleans, 1843 *6412.40 p147*
Hammarstrand, M. W.; Valparaiso, Chile, 1850 *1192.4 p50*
Hammarstrom, A. Lars; New Orleans, 1851 *6412.40 p153*
Hamm Children, . . .; Venezuela, 1843 *3899.5 p541*
Hammel, Jordan; Kansas, 1917-1918 *1826.15 p81*
Hammel, Mary; New York, 1740 *8277.31 p115*
Hammell, Adam; Illinois, 1865 *6079.1 p6*
Hammen, Anna 39; Iowa, 1863 *5475.1 p340*
Hammen, Jakob; America, 1875 *5475.1 p341*
  *Wife:*Susanna Hammes
  *Son:*Peter
  *Son:*Karl
  *Son:*Nikolaus
  *Son:*Johann
Hammen, Johann *SEE* Hammen, Jakob
Hammen, Karl *SEE* Hammen, Jakob
Hammen, Nikolaus *SEE* Hammen, Jakob
Hammen, Peter; America, 1831-1900 *5475.1 p340*
Hammen, Peter *SEE* Hammen, Jakob
Hammen, Susanna Hammes 47 *SEE* Hammen, Jakob
Hammer, Adam; Louisiana, 1874-1875 *4981.45 p29*
Hammer, Dominic; Ohio, 1809-1852 *4511.35 p20*
Hammer, Dominick; Ohio, 1809-1852 *4511.35 p20*
Hammer, George; Ohio, 1844 *2763.1 p8*
Hammer, Gustav; Wisconsin, 1874 *6795.8 p173*
Hammer, Gustav Wilhelm Ernst; Wisconsin, 1882 *6795.8 p92*
Hammer, John Adam; Ohio, 1809-1852 *4511.35 p20*
Hammer, Lawrence; Ohio, 1809-1852 *4511.35 p20*
Hammerberg, Martin A.; Cleveland, OH, 1895 *9722.10 p120*
Hammerschmitt, Eva *SEE* Hammerschmitt, Johann
Hammerschmitt, Johann *SEE* Hammerschmitt, Johann
Hammerschmitt, Johann; Brazil, 1873 *5475.1 p371*
  *Wife:*Margarethe Feilen
  *Daughter:*Eva
  *Son:*Nikolaus
  *Son:*Peter
  *Son:*Mathias
  *Son:*Johann
Hammerschmitt, Margarethe Feilen *SEE* Hammerschmitt, Johann
Hammerschmitt, Mathias *SEE* Hammerschmitt, Johann
Hammerschmitt, Nikolaus *SEE* Hammerschmitt, Johann
Hammerschmitt, Peter *SEE* Hammerschmitt, Johann
Hammerskold, Charles William; North Carolina, 1855 *1088.45 p12*
Hammersmark, John; Washington, 1886 *2770.40 p195*
Hammersmith, Adam; Ohio, 1809-1852 *4511.35 p20*
Hammes, Angela *SEE* Hammes, Johann
Hammes, Elisabeth *SEE* Hammes, Johann
Hammes, Elisabeth Vonbanck *SEE* Hammes, Johann
Hammes, Friedrich *SEE* Hammes, Johann
Hammes, Johann *SEE* Hammes, Johann
Hammes, Johann 57; America, 1855 *5475.1 p327*
  *Wife:*Elisabeth Vonbanck
  *Daughter:*Elisabeth
  *Son:*Friedrich
  *Son:*Johann
  *Daughter:*Margarethe
  *Daughter:*Angela
Hammes, Joseph 13; Quebec, 1870 *8364.32 p23*
Hammes, Margarethe *SEE* Hammes, Johann
Hammes, Peter; America, 1882 *5475.1 p322*
Hammes, Susanna 47; America, 1875 *5475.1 p341*
Hammett, William 39; Ontario, 1871 *1823.21 p145*

Hammon, . . .; Boston, 1769 *9228.50 p5*
Hammon, George; Boston, 1769 *9228.50 p48*
Hammon, Henry; Halifax, N.S., 1827 *7009.9 p62*
Hammon, John; North Carolina, 1849 *1088.45 p12*
Hammon, Patrick; Boston, 1768 *1642 p39*
Hammon, Philip; Beverly, MA, 1750-1850 *9228.50 p272*
Hammond, Charles 23; Ontario, 1871 *1823.21 p145*
Hammond, Chas 30; Ontario, 1871 *1823.21 p145*
Hammond, D. Sarre; St. John, N.B., n.d. *9228.50 p272*
Hammond, Edmund; Maine, 1707 *9228.50 p367*
  Wife: Jane Le Montais
Hammond, Eliza 42; Ontario, 1871 *1823.17 p64*
Hammond, Elizabeth 84; Ontario, 1871 *1823.17 p64*
Hammond, G. E. 16; Quebec, 1870 *8364.32 p23*
Hammond, George; Boston, 1769 *9228.50 p272*
Hammond, Henry *SEE* Hammond, Henry
Hammond, Henry; Canada, 1774 *3036.5 p41*
  Wife: Margaret
  Child: Henry
  Child: Jane
  Child: Margaret
Hammond, Henry 31; Ontario, 1871 *1823.21 p145*
Hammond, Jane *SEE* Hammond, Henry
Hammond, Jane Le Montais *SEE* Hammond, Edmund
Hammond, John; Annapolis, MD, 1685 *9228.50 p272*
Hammond, John 50; Ontario, 1871 *1823.17 p64*
Hammond, Margaret *SEE* Hammond, Henry
Hammond, Margaret *SEE* Hammond, Henry
Hammond, Marie Francoise; Quebec, 1688-1707 *9228.50 p467*
Hammond, Randle C. 47; Ontario, 1871 *1823.21 p146*
Hammond, William H. 33; Ontario, 1871 *1823.17 p64*
Hammonds, Edward 40; Indiana, 1866-1888 *9076.20 p72*
Hammons, James; Boston, 1768 *1642 p39*
Hammons, Richard 62; Ontario, 1871 *1823.21 p146*
Hammy, George; Illinois, 1855 *6079.1 p6*
Hammy, George; Ohio, 1840-1897 *8365.35 p16*
Hamon, Edmund; Maine, 1707 *9228.50 p367*
  Wife: Jane Le Montais
Hamon, Elie; Marblehead, MA, 1730 *9228.50 p272*
Hamon, Elizabeth Susan; Iowa, 1833-1905 *9228.50 p355*
Hamon, Elizabeth Susan; Quebec, 1833 *9228.50 p355*
Hamon, Jane Le Montais *SEE* Hamon, Edmund
Hamon, Joseph 30; Louisiana, 1848 *778.6 p154*
Hamon, Mathurin; Nova Scotia, 1753 *3051 p112*
Hampe, August; New Jersey, 1910 *1029.59 p37*
Hampel, Gust. Freidr. Wilh.; Wisconsin, 1898 *6795.8 p209*
Hampshire, Mr. 15; Quebec, 1870 *8364.32 p23*
Hampson, Thomas 52; Ontario, 1871 *1823.17 p64*
Hampton, Gertrude *SEE* Hampton, William Chas.
Hampton, Gertrude *SEE* Hampton, Lily
Hampton, Joseph *SEE* Hampton, William Chas.
Hampton, Joseph *SEE* Hampton, Lily
Hampton, Lily *SEE* Hampton, William Chas.
Hampton, Lily; Colorado, 1925 *1029.59 p37*
  Husband: William Charles
  Child: Gertrude
  Child: Joseph
  Child: Mella M.
Hampton, Margaret *SEE* Hampton, William Chas.
Hampton, Mella M. *SEE* Hampton, Lily
Hampton, William Charles *SEE* Hampton, Lily
Hampton, William Chas.; Colorado, 1920 *1029.59 p37*
  Wife: Lily
  Child: Gertrude
  Child: Joseph
  Child: Margaret
Hampton, William Chas.; New York, NY, 1900-1920 *1029.59 p37*
Hamrlik, Jan; Iowa, 1856-1858 *2853.20 p211*
Hamstrom, J.G.; Boston, 1855 *6412.40 p153*
Hanafin, Timothy 60; Ontario, 1871 *1823.21 p146*
Hanan, J. N., Jr. 45; America, 1846 *778.6 p154*
Hanan, M. 30; America, 1846 *778.6 p154*
Hanan, Madeline 21; America, 1846 *778.6 p154*
Hanau, Lion; New York, 1882 *5475.1 p129*
Hanau, Max; America, 1867 *5475.1 p136*
Hanau, Seligmann; America, 1867 *5475.1 p238*
Hanauer, Anna Maria 6 *SEE* Hanauer, Peter
Hanauer, Anton 25; Galveston, TX, 1844 *3967.10 p371*
Hanauer, Jakob; America, 1832 *5475.1 p379*
  With family
Hanauer, Maria 23; Galveston, TX, 1844 *3967.10 p371*
Hanauer, Nanette 1; Galveston, TX, 1844 *3967.10 p371*
Hanauer, Peter; America, 1836 *5475.1 p527*
  With wife
  Daughter: Anna Maria
Hanauer, Theresa 23; New Orleans, 1848 *778.6 p154*
Hanbottle, James; New York, NY, 1826 *3274.55 p74*
Hance, John 22; Ontario, 1871 *1823.21 p146*
Hanck, Adolphe 5; Missouri, 1845 *778.6 p154*
Hanck, Clemence 9; Missouri, 1845 *778.6 p155*

Hanck, Edouard 7; Missouri, 1845 *778.6 p155*
Hanck, Elisabeth 28; Halifax, N.S., 1902 *1860.4 p41*
Hanck, Hortence 6; Missouri, 1845 *778.6 p155*
Hanck, Katharina 2; Halifax, N.S., 1902 *1860.4 p41*
Hanck, Leon 13; Missouri, 1845 *778.6 p155*
Hanck, Michel 15; Missouri, 1845 *778.6 p155*
Hanck, Michel 41; Missouri, 1845 *778.6 p155*
Hanck, Nicolaus; Halifax, N.S., 1902 *1860.4 p41*
Hanck, Nicolaus 30; Halifax, N.S., 1902 *1860.4 p41*
Hanck, Salome 38; Missouri, 1845 *778.6 p155*
Hancock, Anthony; Boston, 1681 *1642 p20*
Hancock, Edward 22; Indiana, 1868-1874 *9076.20 p68*
Hancock, Emma Eliza; America, 1876-1902 *9228.50 p636*
Hancock, Ernest H. 37; Quebec, 1910 *2897.7 p9*
Hancock, George 22; Ontario, 1871 *1823.21 p146*
Hancock, James 11; Quebec, 1870 *8364.32 p23*
Hancock, John; Massachusetts, 1700-1799 *1642 p138*
Hancock, John; New York, NY, 1835 *3274.55 p24*
Hancock, John 23; Ontario, 1858 *9228.50 p218*
Hancock, John 50; Ontario, 1871 *1823.21 p146*
Hancox, John 40; Ontario, 1871 *1823.21 p146*
Hand, Fancy; Bermuda, 1851 *8513.31 p421*
Hand, Fancy; Philadelphia, 1868 *8513.31 p421*
Hand, Heinrich *SEE* Hand, Johann
Hand, Johann 63; America, 1864 *5475.1 p353*
  Son: Heinrich
  Son: Peter
Hand, John 48; Ontario, 1871 *1823.17 p64*
Hand, Peter *SEE* Hand, Johann
Hand, Thomas 55; Ontario, 1871 *1823.21 p146*
Handel, Frederick 30; Louisiana, 1840 *778.6 p155*
Handel, Gottlieb; America, 1867 *7919.3 p526*
Handel, Julius Karl; America, 1866 *5475.1 p504*
Handel, Paul; America, 1867 *7919.3 p526*
Handford, Joseph; America, 1869 *9076.20 p69*
Handin, B. 22; New York, NY, 1893 *1883.7 p43*
Handl, Vojta; St. Paul, MN, 1860 *2853.20 p277*
Handley, John; North America, 1750 *1640.8 p233*
Handlon, Edward 61; Ontario, 1871 *1823.17 p64*
Handrich, Wilhelm; Wisconsin, 1878 *6795.8 p226*
Handrin, William; Newfoundland, 1814 *3476.10 p54*
Hands, James; Boston, 1774 *8529.30 p3A*
Hands, James 61; Ontario, 1871 *1823.17 p64*
Handshah, Frederick; Ohio, 1809-1852 *4511.35 p20*
Handwick, Elizabeth *SEE* Handwick, James
Handwick, James; Canada, 1774 *3036.5 p41*
  Wife: Elizabeth
Handy, Alicia 48; Ontario, 1871 *1823.21 p146*
Handy, Edward 48; Ontario, 1871 *1823.21 p146*
Hane, John; North Carolina, 1842 *1088.45 p12*
Haneally, Patrick 39; Ontario, 1871 *1823.21 p146*
Hanel, Auguste Emilie; America, 1865 *5475.1 p49*
Hanel, Jiri; Iowa, 1870 *2853.20 p202*
Hanely, Peter 30; Ontario, 1871 *1823.21 p146*
Haneton, Madeleine; Quebec, 1668 *4514.3 p324*
Haney, John 79; Ontario, 1871 *1823.17 p64*
Haney, Louis 32; New Orleans, 1845 *778.6 p155*
Hanf, . . .; North Carolina, 1710 *3629.40 p4*
Hanff, Elisabeth; America, 1868 *7919.3 p525*
Hanff, John Ferdinand; North Carolina, 1848 *1088.45 p12*
Hanfin, Michael; Ohio, 1840-1897 *8365.35 p16*
Hanford, John 30; Ontario, 1871 *1823.21 p146*
Hanibal, Carl Heinrich Ferdinand; Port uncertain, 1853 *7420.1 p105*
Haniford, Ephraim; New York, 1778 *8529.30 p3A*
Hanig, Frederick; Ohio, 1809-1852 *4511.35 p20*
Hanka, Alex 35; Minnesota, 1923 *2769.54 p1381*
Hankel, Katharine Elisabeth; America, 1854 *8115.12 p320*
Hankel, Wilhelm; America, n.d. *8115.12 p320*
Hankey, Richard; Philadelphia, 1778 *8529.30 p3A*
Hanks, Antony 49; Ontario, 1871 *1823.17 p64*
Hanks, Barney; Ohio, 1809-1852 *4511.35 p20*
Hanks, George; Ohio, 1809-1852 *4511.35 p20*
Hanks, Joseph; Ohio, 1809-1852 *4511.35 p20*
Hanlen, Joseph; Ohio, 1818 *3580.20 p32*
Hanlen, Joseph; Ohio, 1818 *6020.12 p12*
Hanley, James; Louisiana, 1874 *4981.45 p132*
Hanley, John 37; Ontario, 1871 *1823.21 p146*
Hanley, John; Virginia, 1652 *6254.4 p243*
Hanley, John W. 71; Ontario, 1871 *1823.21 p146*
Hanley, Lawrence; Toronto, 1844 *2910.35 p114*
Hanline, Michael; Ohio, 1809-1852 *4511.35 p20*
Hanlon, Bryan; New Orleans, 1851 *7242.30 p143*
Hanlon, James; Newfoundland, 1814 *3476.10 p54*
Hanlon, John; Ohio, 1832 *3580.20 p32*
Hanlon, John; Ohio, 1832 *6020.12 p12*
Hanlon, Moses; Ohio, 1832 *3580.20 p32*
Hanlon, Moses; Ohio, 1832 *6020.12 p12*
Hanlon, Thomas T. 59; Ontario, 1871 *1823.21 p146*
Hanlon, William; Newfoundland, 1814 *3476.10 p54*

Hann, Anna; New York, 1859 *358.56 p101*
Hanna, A. W.; California, 1868 *1131.61 p89*
Hanna, Alex 56; Ontario, 1871 *1823.17 p64*
Hanna, Michal 42; Ontario, 1871 *1823.17 p64*
Hanna, Nicholas; Washington, 1886 *2770.40 p195*
Hanna, Robert 30; Ontario, 1871 *1823.17 p64*
Hannah, George 46; Ontario, 1871 *1823.21 p146*
Hannah, Jane; Ohio, 1819 *9228.50 p272*
Hannah, John 30; Ontario, 1871 *1823.21 p146*
Hannah, Martha 24; Ontario, 1871 *1823.21 p146*
Hannah, Mary; Ohio, 1816 *9228.50 p272*
Hannah, Mary 25; Ontario, 1871 *1823.21 p146*
Hannahan, Simon; Boston, 1763 *1642 p32*
Hannan, Bernard; Ohio, 1854 *3580.20 p32*
Hannan, Bernard; Ohio, 1854 *6020.12 p12*
Hannan, John; Boston, 1764 *1642 p34*
Hannan, John; Massachusetts, 1620-1775 *1642 p138*
Hannan, John 72; Ontario, 1871 *1823.17 p65*
Hannard, Auguste *SEE* Hannard, Thomas Francois
Hannard, Jean Joseph *SEE* Hannard, Thomas Francois
Hannard, Marie Philippine *SEE* Hannard, Thomas Francois
Hannard, Thomas Francois; Wisconsin, 1856 *1495.20 p56*
  Child: Jean Joseph
  Child: Auguste
  Child: Marie Philippine
Hannaway, Caroline Elizabeth; Quebec, 1890-1940 *9228.50 p261*
Hannegan, Mathew; Barbados or St. Christopher, 1780 *8529.30 p7A*
Hannekin, Anna Marie 46; America, 1847 *778.6 p155*
Hannekin, Francois 47; America, 1847 *778.6 p155*
Hannemann, August; Wisconsin, 1882 *6795.8 p226*
Hannenburger, Daniel; Ohio, 1809-1852 *4511.35 p20*
Hannessy, Richard; Boston, 1756 *1642 p47*
Hannet, Jeanne 54; Quebec, 1659 *9221.17 p393*
Hannet, John 30; Ontario, 1871 *1823.21 p146*
Hanniford, Ephraim; New York, 1778 *8529.30 p3A*
Hannigan, John 34; Ontario, 1871 *1823.17 p65*
Hannigan, Michael 43; Ontario, 1871 *1823.17 p65*
Hannon, Adele *SEE* Hannon, Jean Francois
Hannon, Anna 72; Michigan, 1880 *4491.36 p9*
Hannon, Antoine Jean Francois *SEE* Hannon, Jean Francois
Hannon, Gaspard David *SEE* Hannon, Jean Francois
Hannon, Jean Francois; Wisconsin, 1846-1856 *1495.20 p29*
  Wife: Melanie Boucher
  Child: Gaspard David
  Child: Antoine Jean Francois
  Child: Jean Joseph
  Child: Adele
Hannon, Jean Joseph *SEE* Hannon, Jean Francois
Hannon, Melanie Boucher *SEE* Hannon, Jean Francois
Hannon, Thomas 74; Michigan, 1880 *4491.36 p9*
Hannon, William; Boston, 1765 *1642 p35*
Hannon, William 45; Ontario, 1871 *1823.17 p65*
Hannus, Josef W.; Colorado, 1887 *1029.59 p37*
Hanold, Georg Friedrich; America, 1888 *179.55 p19*
Hanon, Bridget 37; Michigan, 1880 *4491.39 p13*
Hanon, Daniel 17; Michigan, 1880 *4491.39 p13*
Hanon, Morris 37; Michigan, 1880 *4491.39 p13*
Hanotaint, Jean 50; New Orleans, 1848 *778.6 p155*
Hanousek, A.; Cleveland, OH, 1863 *2853.20 p477*
Hanratty, James D. 32; Ontario, 1871 *1823.21 p146*
Hanriot, Mrs. 42; Texas, 1843 *778.6 p155*
Hanriot, Be.jamin 8; Texas, 1843 *778.6 p155*
Hanriot, Charles 16; Texas, 1843 *778.6 p155*
Hanriot, Felicien 10; Texas, 1843 *778.6 p155*
Hanriot, Francois 5; Texas, 1843 *778.6 p155*
Hanriot, Marie Julie 14; Texas, 1843 *778.6 p155*
Hanriot, Nestor 1; Texas, 1843 *778.6 p155*
Hanriot, Theodore 40; Texas, 1843 *778.6 p155*
Hanrum, Meds Hansen; Iowa, 1887 *1211.15 p11*
Hanry, George; Salem, MA, 1694 *1642 p77*
  Wife: Sarah
Hanry, Samuel; Boston, 1766 *1642 p36*
Hanry, Sarah *SEE* Hanry, George
Hans, Barbara; America, 1834 *5475.1 p436*
Hans, Barbara Conrath *SEE* Hans, Peter
Hans, Elisabeth; America, 1881 *5475.1 p435*
Hans, Elisabeth 2; Galveston, TX, 1844 *3967.10 p372*
Hans, Elisabeth 31; Galveston, TX, 1844 *3967.10 p372*
Hans, Ernst; America, 1867 *7919.3 p534*
Hans, Hillmar; America, 1867 *7919.3 p534*
Hans, Johann; America, 1850-1899 *6442.17 p65*
Hans, Johanna; America, 1852 *5475.1 p439*
Hans, Justinus 6 months; Galveston, TX, 1844 *3967.10 p372*
Hans, Leonhard 30; Galveston, TX, 1844 *3967.10 p372*
Hans, Margaretha; America, 1887-1899 *6442.17 p69*
Hans, Matthias; America, 1845-1899 *6442.17 p65*

Hans, Peter; Brazil, 1846 ***5475.1*** *p438*
*Wife:*Barbara Conrath
With child
Hansan, Peter; Colorado, 1862-1894 ***1029.59*** *p37*
Hanschu, Johannes 27; Portland, ME, 1906 ***970.38*** *p77*
Hanschu, Kata 25; Portland, ME, 1906 ***970.38*** *p77*
Hansdotter, Anna 38; New York, 1856 ***6529.11*** *p22*
Hansdotter, Betse; Kansas, 1868-1869 ***777.40*** *p8*
Hansdotter, Brita; Kansas, 1868-1869 ***777.40*** *p8*
Hansdotter, Elisabeth; Iowa, 1865-1870 ***777.40*** *p8*
Hansdotter, Ingrid 43; New York, 1856 ***6529.11*** *p21*
Hansdotter, Johanna Maria; Kansas, 1868-1869 ***777.40*** *p7*
Hansdotter, Lisa 33; New York, 1856 ***6529.11*** *p22*
Hanse, Engel Marie Sophie; America, 1868 ***7420.1*** *p272*
Hansel, Jacob; Ohio, 1840-1897 ***8365.35*** *p16*
Hansen, Anna 16; New York, NY, 1894 ***6512.1*** *p182*
Hansen, Antone; Iowa, 1890 ***1211.15*** *p11*
Hansen, Carl Peter; Iowa, 1930 ***1211.15*** *p11*
Hansen, Christen; Louisiana, 1874 ***4981.45*** *p132*
Hansen, Christian; Iowa, 1880 ***1211.15*** *p11*
Hansen, Christian; Iowa, 1905 ***1211.15*** *p11*
Hansen, Christian A.F.; Colorado, 1892 ***1029.59*** *p37*
Hansen, Elna I.N.; Arizona, 1913-1915 ***9228.50*** *p398*
Hansen, Frederick J.; Kansas, 1888 ***1447.20*** *p64*
Hansen, George; Colorado, 1903 ***1029.59*** *p37*
Hansen, George; Kansas, 1891 ***1029.59*** *p37*
Hansen, H.P.; New York, 1860 ***358.56*** *p150*
Hansen, Halven; New York, 1903 ***1766.20*** *p3*
Hansen, Hand J.; Washington, 1887 ***2770.40*** *p24*
Hansen, Hans; New York, 1880 ***1766.20*** *p23*
Hansen, James P.; Missouri, 1895 ***3276.1*** *p1*
Hansen, Jeorgen; Iowa, 1877 ***1211.15*** *p11*
Hansen, Jorgen; Iowa, 1892 ***1211.15*** *p11*
Hansen, Niels; New York, 1860 ***358.56*** *p150*
Hansen, Ole; Colorado, 1883 ***1029.59*** *p37*
Hansen, Ole; Colorado, 1904 ***1029.59*** *p37*
Hansen, Pete; Colorado, 1898 ***1029.59*** *p37*
Hansen, Tage Edward; Iowa, 1932 ***1211.15*** *p11*
Hansen, William; Ohio, 1809-1852 ***4511.35*** *p20*
Hansford, William 31; Ontario, 1871 ***1823.17*** *p65*
Hansing, Adolph; America, 1869 ***7420.1*** *p279*
Hansing, Adolph Ernst; America, 1871 ***7420.1*** *p290*
*Brother:*Gustav Friedrich H.
Hansing, Engel Dorothee; Port uncertain, 1854 ***7420.1*** *p120*
Hansing, Ferdinand Louis Friedrich Dietrich Wilhelm; Missouri, 1892 ***7420.1*** *p365*
Hansing, Friedrich Wilhelm; America, 1874 ***7420.1*** *p303*
Hansing, Gustav Friedrich H. *SEE* Hansing, Adolph Ernst
Hansing, Heinrich Dietrich Christian; Wisconsin, 1887 ***7420.1*** *p353*
With wife 5 children
Hansing, Johann Heinrich Ludwig Conrad; Port uncertain, 1854 ***7420.1*** *p120*
Hansing, Ludwig; America, 1852 ***7420.1*** *p89*
With wife
Hansing, Wilhelm; New York, NY, 1867 ***7420.1*** *p257*
Hansler, Christian; Ohio, 1840-1897 ***8365.35*** *p16*
Hanson, Adelia; Kansas, 1871 ***777.40*** *p17*
Hanson, Andrew; Iowa, 1911 ***1211.15*** *p11*
Hanson, Andrew M.; Illinois, 1864 ***4487.25*** *p58*
Hanson, Charles; Kansas, 1869-1870 ***777.40*** *p7*
Hanson, Charles *SEE* Hanson, Maria Bolin
Hanson, Charles 52; Ontario, 1871 ***1823.21*** *p146*
Hanson, Christian; Iowa, 1892 ***1211.15*** *p11*
Hanson, Christian F.; New York, NY, 1855 ***8513.31*** *p312*
*Wife:*Frederika Amelia
Hanson, Daisy 16; Minnesota, 1923 ***2769.54*** *p1378*
Hanson, Dina *SEE* Hanson, Maria Bolin
Hanson, Emil Reinhold; Iowa, 1915 ***1211.15*** *p11*
Hanson, Ferid Peter; Washington, 1889 ***2770.40*** *p27*
Hanson, Frank; Cleveland, OH, 1889-1891 ***9722.10*** *p120*
Hanson, Frederick J. 27; Kansas, 1888 ***1447.20*** *p62*
Hanson, Frederika Amelia *SEE* Hanson, Christian F.
Hanson, Hans B.; Washington, 1883 ***2770.40*** *p136*
Hanson, Hans Ferdinand; Iowa, 1918 ***1211.15*** *p11*
Hanson, Henry; Iowa, 1879 ***1211.15*** *p11*
Hanson, Henry; North Carolina, 1855 ***1088.45*** *p12*
Hanson, Henry 47; Ontario, 1871 ***1823.21*** *p146*
Hanson, Herman; Iowa, 1877 ***1211.15*** *p11*
Hanson, Jacob; Iowa, 1914 ***1211.15*** *p11*
Hanson, James; Iowa, 1908 ***1211.15*** *p11*
Hanson, John; Cleveland, OH, 1902-1903 ***9722.10*** *p120*
Hanson, John; Iowa, 1868 ***1211.15*** *p11*
Hanson, John; Washington, 1885 ***2770.40*** *p194*
Hanson, Lars; Kansas, 1869-1871 ***777.40*** *p15*
Hanson, Maria; Kansas, 1871 ***777.40*** *p15*
*Daughter:*Dina
*Son:*Charles
Hanson, Mathias 23; Ontario, 1871 ***1823.17*** *p65*
Hanson, Matilda A.; Kansas, 1853-1875 ***777.40*** *p7*
Hanson, Ole John; Iowa, 1917 ***1211.15*** *p11*
Hanson, Pete; Colorado, 1898 ***1029.59*** *p37*
Hanson, Peter; Colorado, 1900 ***1029.59*** *p37*
Hanson, Robert; Iowa, 1895 ***1211.15*** *p11*
Hanson, Susan C.; America, 1848 ***9228.50*** *p586*
Hansson, Anna 44; New York, 1856 ***6529.11*** *p22*
*Daughter:*Brita 16
Hansson, Bengt Johnas; Cleveland, OH, 1901-1903 ***9722.10*** *p120*
Hansson, Brita 10 *SEE* Hansson, Pehr
Hansson, Brita 16 *SEE* Hansson, Anna Olsdotter
Hansson, C.C.; San Francisco, 1855 ***6412.40*** *p153*
Hansson, Cherstin Jonsdotter 42 *SEE* Hansson, Pehr
Hansson, E.M.; New York, NY, 1849 ***6412.40*** *p151*
Hansson, Hans 14 *SEE* Hansson, Pehr
Hansson, Hans 25; New York, 1856 ***6529.11*** *p21*
Hansson, J.A.; Philadelphia, 1847 ***6412.40*** *p150*
Hansson, Karin 17 *SEE* Hansson, Pehr
Hansson, Kjerstin 7 *SEE* Hansson, Pehr
Hansson, Lars; America, 1855 ***6529.11*** *p26*
Hansson, Lars; Kansas, 1869-1871 ***777.40*** *p15*
Hansson, Nils; New York, NY, 1844 ***6412.40*** *p148*
Hansson, Pehr 45; New York, 1856 ***6529.11*** *p20*
*Wife:*Cherstin Jonsdotter 42
*Daughter:*Kjerstin 7
*Daughter:*Brita 10
*Daughter:*Karin 17
*Son:*Hans 14
Hansson, S.; New York, NY, 1847 ***6412.40*** *p150*
Hanster, August Wilhelm; Wisconsin, 1870 ***6795.8*** *p63*
Hanting, Henry 54; Boston, 1835 ***6424.55*** *p31*
Hanton, Jane; St. Johns, N.F., 1825 ***1053.15*** *p6*
Hanton, Richard; St. Johns, N.F., 1825 ***1053.15*** *p6*
Hantzelmann, George; Ohio, 1809-1852 ***4511.35*** *p20*
Hanum, Elijah 45; Ontario, 1871 ***1823.21*** *p146*
Hanvill, Mary C. 50; Ohio, 1880 ***4879.40*** *p259*
Hanwood, Robert 23; Quebec, 1910 ***2897.7*** *p8*
Hanzl, J.; St. Paul, MN, 1856 ***2853.20*** *p258*
Happe, Friederike; Port uncertain, 1854 ***7420.1*** *p120*
Happel, Emilie; America, 1868 ***7919.3*** *p535*
Happer, Robert 45; Ontario, 1871 ***1823.21*** *p146*
Harahan, Mark; Louisiana, 1874 ***4981.45*** *p132*
Haraldsen, O.; Iowa, 1899 ***1211.15*** *p11*
Harambours, T. H. 18; America, 1746 ***778.6*** *p155*
Harang, Charles 25; Port uncertain, 1840 ***778.6*** *p155*
Harbach, Barbe 19; Port uncertain, 1843 ***778.6*** *p155*
Harbert, Johannes; Illinois, 1855 ***6079.1*** *p6*
Harbige, John; Marston's Wharf, 1782 ***8529.30*** *p12*
Harbord, B.; America, 1852 ***7420.1*** *p89*
Harbord, Justine Louise; America, 1850 ***7420.1*** *p71*
Harborne, Jeffery 21; Ontario, 1871 ***1823.21*** *p146*
Harbour, Mr. 24; Port uncertain, 1841 ***778.6*** *p155*
Harbridge, John; Marston's Wharf, 1782 ***8529.30*** *p12*
Harbridge, John; Maryland, 1674-1675 ***1236.25*** *p52*
Harbrige, John; Marston's Wharf, 1782 ***8529.30*** *p12*
Harbron, William 60; Ontario, 1871 ***1823.21*** *p146*
Harbrook, Peter; Ohio, 1809-1852 ***4511.35*** *p20*
Harbrook, Philip; Ohio, 1809-1852 ***4511.35*** *p20*
Harck, Julius; Wisconsin, 1899 ***6795.8*** *p132*
Harczyk, Adolphe; Louisiana, 1860 ***7710.1*** *p157*
Hardaker, James 44; Ontario, 1871 ***1823.17*** *p65*
Hardekopf, Mr.; America, 1873 ***7420.1*** *p300*
With sister
Hardekopf, Johann Heinrich Ludwig *SEE* Hardekopf, Johann Ludwig
Hardekopf, Johann Heinrich Ludwig; Chicago, 1870 ***7420.1*** *p283*
Hardekopf, Johann Ludwig; America, 1872 ***7420.1*** *p295*
*Son:*Johann Heinrich Ludwig
Hardekopf Brothers, . . .; America, 1865 ***7420.1*** *p231*
Hardel, Eliza 35; America, 1846 ***778.6*** *p155*
Hardel, Suzanna 25; America, 1846 ***778.6*** *p155*
Harden, Mic; St. John, N.B., 1848 ***2978.15*** *p39*
Harden, Patrick; Boston, 1764 ***1642*** *p33*
Harden, Richd; St. John, N.B., 1848 ***2978.15*** *p39*
Harden, Thomas; Philadelphia, 1778 ***8529.30*** *p3A*
Harden, Wm.; St. John, N.B., 1848 ***2978.15*** *p39*
Hardenberger, Georg 22; New Orleans, 1848 ***778.6*** *p155*
Harder, Arnold; Missouri, 1898 ***3276.1*** *p2*
Harder, Arnold; Missouri, 1900 ***3276.1*** *p2*
Harder, Fritz; New York, NY, 1873 ***1494.20*** *p13*
Harder, Johann August; Wisconsin, 1871 ***6795.8*** *p123*
Hardi, Jacob 20; Died enroute, 1817-1818 ***90.20*** *p151*
Hardil, Henry; North Carolina, 1816-1819 ***1088.45*** *p12*
Hardin, Thomas; Philadelphia, 1778 ***8529.30*** *p3A*
Harding, Blanche; America, 1892 ***9228.50*** *p281*
Harding, Hannah 60; Ontario, 1871 ***1823.21*** *p146*
Harding, Henry 46; Ontario, 1871 ***1823.21*** *p147*
Harding, Hiawatha Montressa; Charlestown, MA, 1883 ***9228.50*** *p641*
Harding, Jacob; Washington, 1887 ***2770.40*** *p24*
Harding, John; New York, 1776 ***8529.30*** *p12*
Harding, John 55; Ontario, 1871 ***1823.21*** *p147*
Harding, John 62; Ontario, 1871 ***1823.17*** *p65*
Harding, Philip; Boston, 1659 ***9228.50*** *p272*
Harding, Robert 50; Ontario, 1871 ***1823.21*** *p147*
Harding, Robt 55; Ontario, 1871 ***1823.21*** *p147*
Harding, Sarah Abigail; Massachusetts, 1845-1929 ***9228.50*** *p641*
Harding, William 32; Ontario, 1871 ***1823.21*** *p147*
Harding, William 35; Ontario, 1871 ***1823.21*** *p147*
Harding, William J. 42; Ontario, 1871 ***1823.21*** *p147*
Harding, Winifred 21; Quebec, 1910 ***2897.7*** *p9*
Hardisse, Rich. 16; America, 1845 ***778.6*** *p155*
Hardle, John 22; Ontario, 1871 ***1823.21*** *p147*
Hardon, Thomas; Philadelphia, 1778 ***8529.30*** *p3A*
Hardouin, Albert 26; America, 1840 ***778.6*** *p155*
Hardouin, Anne 32; Quebec, 1647 ***9221.17*** *p175*
Hardouin, Etienne 18; Montreal, 1659 ***9221.17*** *p422*
Hardt, Heinrich 17; New York, NY, 1893 ***1883.7*** *p40*
Hardt, Heinrich 17; New York, NY, 1893 ***1883.7*** *p47*
Hardway, Edward 44; Ontario, 1871 ***1823.17*** *p65*
Hardwick, John; Ohio, 1836 ***2763.1*** *p8*
Hardwin, Jules; Louisiana, 1874-1875 ***4981.45*** *p29*
Hardwin, Thomas; Jamaica, 1783 ***8529.30*** *p13A*
Hardy, . . .; Quebec, 1651 ***9221.17*** *p244*
Hardy, Alexander 40; Ontario, 1871 ***1823.21*** *p147*
Hardy, Anne *SEE* Hardy, Elizabeth
Hardy, Ariet 11; Ontario, 1871 ***1823.21*** *p147*
Hardy, Charles 60; Ontario, 1871 ***1823.21*** *p147*
Hardy, David 35; Ontario, 1871 ***1823.21*** *p147*
Hardy, Edward 36; Ontario, 1871 ***1823.21*** *p147*
Hardy, Elizabeth; Utah, 1855 ***9228.50*** *p272*
*Relative:*Anne
*Relative:*William
Hardy, Francis 51; Ontario, 1871 ***1823.21*** *p147*
Hardy, George; Marston's Wharf, 1782 ***8529.30*** *p12*
Hardy, Henery 45; Ontario, 1871 ***1823.21*** *p147*
Hardy, Henry 9; Ontario, 1871 ***1823.21*** *p147*
Hardy, James 29; Ontario, 1871 ***1823.21*** *p147*
Hardy, James 55; Ontario, 1871 ***1823.21*** *p147*
Hardy, James 60; Ontario, 1871 ***1823.21*** *p147*
Hardy, Jane 16; Ontario, 1871 ***1823.21*** *p147*
Hardy, Jean 19; Montreal, 1661 ***9221.17*** *p473*
Hardy, Jeanne; Quebec, 1668 ***4514.3*** *p324*
Hardy, John 7; Ontario, 1871 ***1823.21*** *p147*
Hardy, John 40; Ontario, 1871 ***1823.21*** *p147*
Hardy, Joseph 62; Ontario, 1871 ***1823.21*** *p147*
Hardy, Joseph; Salem, MA, 1700 ***9228.50*** *p272*
Hardy, Joseph Lanse 5; Ontario, 1871 ***1823.21*** *p147*
Hardy, Marie-Anne 28; Montreal, 1662 ***9221.17*** *p498*
Hardy, Mickeal 57; Ontario, 1871 ***1823.21*** *p147*
Hardy, Pierre 37; Montreal, 1653 ***9221.17*** *p292*
Hardy, Robert 54; Ontario, 1871 ***1823.21*** *p147*
Hardy, Thomas 45; Ontario, 1871 ***1823.21*** *p147*
Hardy, Thomas 66; Ontario, 1871 ***1823.21*** *p147*
Hardy, William 71; Ontario, 1871 ***1823.21*** *p147*
Hardy, William *SEE* Hardy, Elizabeth
Hare, Ann 45; Ontario, 1871 ***1823.21*** *p147*
Hare, Ebenezer 52; Ontario, 1871 ***1823.17*** *p65*
Hare, Elizabeth 18; Ontario, 1871 ***1823.17*** *p65*
Hare, George 48; Ontario, 1871 ***1823.17*** *p65*
Hare, H. R.; Ohio, 1840-1897 ***8365.35*** *p16*
Hare, James 55; Ontario, 1871 ***1823.17*** *p65*
Hare, Jane 18; Ontario, 1871 ***1823.21*** *p147*
Hare, Peter; Ontario, 1787 ***1276.15*** *p230*
With 3 relatives
Hare, Peter, Jr.; Ontario, 1787 ***1276.15*** *p230*
Hare, Robert 27; Ontario, 1871 ***1823.17*** *p65*
Hare, Thomas 35; Ontario, 1871 ***1823.21*** *p147*
Harelet, George 58; Ontario, 1871 ***1823.21*** *p147*
Harenburg, Thias; North Carolina, 1807 ***1088.45*** *p13*
Harenc, Thomas; Quebec, 1641 ***9221.17*** *p104*
Harene, Thomas; Quebec, 1641 ***9221.17*** *p104*
Hargarten, Barbara 49; America, 1873 ***5475.1*** *p307*
Hargarter, Mathias 29; America, 1846 ***5475.1*** *p280*
Hargreaves, John 40; Ontario, 1871 ***1823.21*** *p147*
Hargreaves, John; Texas, 1854 ***3435.45*** *p35*
Hargreaves, William; New York, NY, 1832 ***3274.55*** *p68*
Hargrove, Christopher; Marston's Wharf, 1782 ***8529.30*** *p12*
Hargrove, James 73; Ontario, 1871 ***1823.17*** *p65*
Hargrove, Michael; Louisiana, 1836-1841 ***4981.45*** *p208*
Harig, Johann; America, 1838 ***5475.1*** *p458*
*Wife:*Maria Volz
Harig, Ludwig; America, 1872 ***5475.1*** *p460*
Harig, Maria Volz *SEE* Harig, Johann
Harig, Maria 50; America, 1867 ***5475.1*** *p344*
Harig, Nikolaus Georg; America, 1880 ***5475.1*** *p460*
Harigan, Eliza 45; Michigan, 1880 ***4491.39*** *p13*
Harigan, James 19; Michigan, 1880 ***4491.39*** *p13*
Harigan, John 12; Michigan, 1880 ***4491.39*** *p13*
Harigan, John 47; Michigan, 1880 ***4491.39*** *p13*

Harigel, Ludwig; Chile, 1852 1192.4 p52
With wife
With child 3
With child 1
Haring, Maria Anna; Venezuela, 1843 3899.5 p540
Haring, Michael; Venezuela, 1843 3899.5 p540
Haring, Patrick; Boston, 1767 1642 p48
Haring, Philip; Ohio, 1809-1852 4511.35 p20
Haringer, John; Dakota, 1893 554.30 p25
*Wife:*Ludwige
Haringer, Ludwige *SEE* Haringer, John
Harise, George; Jamaica, 1783 8529.30 p13A
Harison, Edwin 45; Ontario, 1871 1823.21 p148
Harispe, Charles 19; New Orleans, 1840 778.6 p155
Harjamaki, Jack 52; Minnesota, 1925 2769.54 p1380
Hark, Bertha; Wisconsin, 1890 6795.8 p138
Hark, Bertha; Wisconsin, 1895 6795.8 p132
Hark, Emilie; Wisconsin, 1894 6795.8 p193
Hark, Lina; Wisconsin, 1907 6795.8 p128
Harke, Louise; Wisconsin, 1899 6795.8 p179
Harker, Joseph 61; Ontario, 1871 1823.21 p148
Harker, Kesiah; New Jersey, 1722 9228.50 p18A
Harkes, George 46; Ontario, 1871 1823.21 p148
Harkett, Caleb 33; Ontario, 1871 1823.21 p148
Harkins, Charles; Boston, 1774 8529.30 p6
Harkins, James 44; Ontario, 1871 1823.21 p148
Harkins, Pat; St. John, N.B., 1847 2978.15 p36
Harkness, Alex 52; Ontario, 1871 1823.21 p148
Harkness, Andrew 36; Ontario, 1871 1823.17 p65
Harkness, David 50; Ontario, 1871 1823.17 p65
Harkness, Hamilton 48; Ontario, 1871 1823.17 p65
Harkness, Hariette 19; Ontario, 1871 1823.21 p148
Harkness, Isabella 59; Ontario, 1871 1823.21 p148
Harkness, James 24; Ontario, 1871 1823.17 p65
Harkness, Perula 40; Ontario, 1871 1823.21 p148
Harknip, Adam 70; Ontario, 1871 1823.21 p148
Harknip, Alexander S. 21; Ontario, 1871 1823.21 p148
Harknss, Anthony 45; Ontario, 1871 1823.17 p65
Harkonen, Matt 39; Minnesota, 1926 2769.54 p1383
Harkopf, Mr.; America, 1859 7420.1 p185
Harkopf, Friedrich Wilhelm; America, 1860 7420.1 p194
With wife & daughter
Harland, William; Canada, 1774 3036.5 p40
Harley, Francois 3; Port uncertain, 1841 778.6 p155
Harley, Josephine 2; Port uncertain, 1841 778.6 p155
Harley, Marie 28; Port uncertain, 1841 778.6 p156
Harley, Robert; Boston, 1738 1642 p44
Harley, Thomas A. 30; Ontario, 1871 1823.21 p148
Harlferl, A. 26; Halifax, N.S., 1902 1860.4 p44
Harlig, Mrs. 42; America, 1844 778.6 p156
Harlin, John; Toronto, 1844 2910.35 p115
Harlington, William 50; Ontario, 1871 1823.21 p148
Harliston, . . .; South Carolina, 1669 9228.50 p272
Harliston Family ; Carolina, n.d. 9228.50 p55
Harlocker, Jacob; Texas, 1851 3435.45 p35
Harlter, Sophie 24; Valdivia, Chile, 1852 1192.4 p53
Harlter, Wilhelm; Valdivia, Chile, 1852 1192.4 p53
With wife
Harlton, Thomas 45; Ontario, 1871 1823.21 p148
Harlton, Thomas 50; Ontario, 1871 1823.21 p148
Harlum, George 47; Ontario, 1871 1823.21 p148
Harlund, G.A.; New York, NY, 1842 6412.40 p146
Harman, Anthony; Ohio, 1809-1852 4511.35 p20
Harman, Dennis 24; St. Johns, N.F., 1811 1053.20 p21
Harman, Fra; Jamestown, VA, 1633 1658.20 p211
With wife
Harman, Frederick; Ohio, 1809-1852 4511.35 p20
Harman, Frederick, Jr.; Ohio, 1809-1852 4511.35 p21
Harman, George; Ohio, 1809-1852 4511.35 p21
Harman, Jacob; Ohio, 1809-1852 4511.35 p21
Harman, Joseph; Ohio, 1809-1852 4511.35 p21
Harman, Mary 45; America, 1745 778.6 p156
Harman, Wm.; Jamestown, VA, 1633 1658.20 p211
Harmanet, Louis 35; America, 1848 778.6 p156
Harmel, Hermann; Wisconsin, 1886 6795.8 p47
Harmening, . . .; America, 1847 7420.1 p53
With wife & 4 children
Harmening, Mr.; America, 1855 7420.1 p136
*Son:*Heinrich
*Daughter:*Caroline
*Daughter:*Auguste
With wife
*Daughter:*Friederike
*Son:*Wilhelm
Harmening, Mr.; America, 1876 7420.1 p307
*Son:*Johann Christian Wilhelm
Harmening, Auguste *SEE* Harmening, Mr.
Harmening, Carl Friedrich Ferdinand; America, 1872 7420.1 p295
Harmening, Caroline *SEE* Harmening, Mr.
Harmening, Catharine Marie Mensching *SEE* Harmening, Heinrich Christoph
Harmening, Christian *SEE* Harmening, Johann Heinrich
Harmening, Christian; Port uncertain, 1854 7420.1 p121
Harmening, Christian Friedrich Ferdinand; America, 1870 7420.1 p284
Harmening, Christian Gottlieb; America, 1853 7420.1 p105
*Wife:*Christine Louise Aumann
*Son:*Hermann Heinrich Christian
Harmening, Christine Louise Aumann *SEE* Harmening, Christian Gottlieb
Harmening, Dorothee Caroline *SEE* Harmening, Johann Friedrich Conrad
Harmening, Engel Doroth. *SEE* Harmening, Johann Otto
Harmening, Engel Marie Doroth. *SEE* Harmening, Johann Otto
Harmening, Engel Marie Dorothea Pfingsten *SEE* Harmening, Friedrich Wilhelm Christoph
Harmening, Engel Marie Phil. Gellermann *SEE* Harmening, Johann Otto
Harmening, Engel Marie Soph. *SEE* Harmening, Johann Conrad
Harmening, Engel Marie Soph. *SEE* Harmening, Johann Otto
Harmening, Engel Marie Sophie Charlotte *SEE* Harmening, Johann Conrad
Harmening, Ernestine Dorothee Gusewelle *SEE* Harmening, Johann Friedrich Conrad
Harmening, Ernst Gottlieb Wilhelm; America, 1881 7420.1 p321
Harmening, Friederike *SEE* Harmening, Mr.
Harmening, Friedrich Wilhelm Christoph; Ohio, 1879 7420.1 p313
*Wife:*Engel Marie Dorothea Pfingsten
Harmening, Hans Heinr. Christ. *SEE* Harmening, Heinrich Christoph
Harmening, Hans Heinr. Conrad *SEE* Harmening, Heinrich Christoph
Harmening, Heinrich *SEE* Harmening, Mr.
Harmening, Heinrich; Port uncertain, 1854 7420.1 p121
Harmening, Heinrich Christoph; America, 1850 7420.1 p71
*Wife:*Catharine Marie Mensching
*Daughter:*Marie Doroth.
*Son:*Hans Heinr. Christ.
*Son:*Hans Heinr. Conrad
*Daughter:*Thrine Engel Marie
Harmening, Heinrich Otto *SEE* Harmening, Johann Otto
Harmening, Hermann Heinrich Christian *SEE* Harmening, Christian Gottlieb
Harmening, Johann Christian Wilhelm *SEE* Harmening, Mr.
Harmening, Johann Conrad *SEE* Harmening, Johann Conrad
Harmening, Johann Conrad; America, 1848 7420.1 p59
*Wife:*Thrine Marie Charl Busche
*Daughter:*Engel Marie Sophie Charlotte
*Son:*Johann Herm.
*Son:*Johann Conrad
*Daughter:*Engel Marie Soph.
*Daughter:*Thrine Marie Soph.
Harmening, Johann Friedrich; America, 1857 7420.1 p162
Harmening, Johann Friedrich Conrad; America, 1861 7420.1 p205
*Wife:*Ernestine Dorothee Gusewelle
With children
*Daughter:*Dorothee Caroline
Harmening, Johann Heinrich; America, 1866 7420.1 p243
*Grandson:*Christian
Harmening, Johann Herm. *SEE* Harmening, Johann Conrad
Harmening, Johann Otto; America, 1851 7420.1 p80
*Wife:*Engel Marie Phil. Gellermann
*Son:*Heinrich Otto
*Daughter:*Engel Marie Doroth.
*Daughter:*Marie Doroth.
*Daughter:*Engel Marie Soph.
*Daughter:*Engel Doroth.
Harmening, Louise; America, 1857 7420.1 p162
Harmening, Louise; America, 1857 7420.1 p175
Harmening, Marie Doroth. *SEE* Harmening, Heinrich Christoph
Harmening, Marie Doroth. *SEE* Harmening, Johann Otto
Harmening, Thrine Engel Marie *SEE* Harmening, Heinrich Christoph
Harmening, Thrine Marie Charl Busche *SEE* Harmening, Johann Conrad
Harmening, Thrine Marie Soph. *SEE* Harmening, Johann Conrad
Harmening, Wilhelm *SEE* Harmening, Mr.
Harmer, Charles 52; Ontario, 1871 1823.21 p148
Harmes, William; Massachusetts, 1654-1684 9228.50 p84
Harmon, John; South Carolina, 1808 6155.4 p18
Harmon, Naomi; Boston, 1696 1642 p17
Harmon, Wm.; Jamestown, VA, 1633 1658.20 p211
Harmons, John R. 66; Ontario, 1871 1823.21 p148
Harms, Johann Heinrich Conrad; America, 1870 7420.1 p286
Harmsen, Heinrich Dietrich Wilhelm; America, 1884 7420.1 p343
Harmssen, . . .; America, 1849 7420.1 p64
With wife & 2 children
Harmssen, Dietrich; America, 1851 7420.1 p80
With wife & 4 children
Harndout, Florentin 40; New Orleans, 1848 778.6 p156
Harnecker, Otto 7; Chile, 1852 1192.4 p52
Harnecker, Reinhard 8; Chile, 1852 1192.4 p52
Harnet, William 61; Ontario, 1871 1823.21 p148
Harney, Anne; New Orleans, 1850 7242.30 p143
Harney, Arthur; New Orleans, 1850 7242.30 p143
Harney, Bessy; New Orleans, 1850 7242.30 p143
Harney, John; New Orleans, 1850 7242.30 p143
Harney, M. J.; Louisiana, 1874 4981.45 p132
Harney, Mary; New Orleans, 1850 7242.30 p143
Harney, Michael; New Orleans, 1850 7242.30 p143
Harney, Patrick; Ohio, 1809-1852 4511.35 p21
Harney, Philip; New Orleans, 1850 7242.30 p143
Harnisch, Juliane; Valdivia, Chile, 1850 1192.4 p48
Harnois, Isaac 20; Quebec, 1661 9221.17 p459
Harnott, John; New York, NY, 1778 8529.30 p2
Harodel, Anna 19; New Orleans, 1848 778.6 p156
Harodel, Caspar 27; New Orleans, 1848 778.6 p156
Harodel, Dorothea 30; New Orleans, 1848 778.6 p156
Harodel, Margaretha 47; New Orleans, 1848 778.6 p156
Harodel, Wilhelmina 7; New Orleans, 1848 778.6 p156
Harold, Barbara 22; Port uncertain, 1847 778.6 p156
Harold, Mary 27; Ontario, 1871 1823.21 p148
Harper, Alfred 61; Ontario, 1871 1823.21 p148
Harper, Benjamin 55; Ontario, 1871 1823.21 p148
Harper, Catharine *SEE* Harper, Chistopher
Harper, Charlotte *SEE* Harper, Chistopher
Harper, Chistopher; Canada, 1775 3036.5 p67
*Child:*John
*Wife:*Elizabeth
*Child:*Elizabeth
*Child:*Thomas
*Child:*Charlotte
*Child:*William
*Child:*Catharine
*Child:*Hannah
Harper, David 38; Ontario, 1871 1823.21 p148
Harper, David; St. John, N.B., 1847 2978.15 p40
Harper, Dring 66; Ontario, 1871 1823.17 p65
Harper, Elizabeth *SEE* Harper, Chistopher
Harper, Elizabeth *SEE* Harper, Chistopher
Harper, Gerhard; North Carolina, 1857 1088.45 p13
Harper, Hannah *SEE* Harper, Chistopher
Harper, Henry; North Carolina, 1833 1088.45 p13
Harper, James C.; New York, NY, 1832 3274.55 p26
Harper, John *SEE* Harper, Chistopher
Harper, John; New Jersey, 1777 8529.30 p7A
Harper, John 57; Ontario, 1871 1823.21 p148
Harper, John 57; Ontario, 1871 1823.21 p148
Harper, Jonathan; Washington, 1882 2770.40 p135
Harper, Mary 48; Ontario, 1871 1823.17 p65
Harper, Matthew; South Carolina, 1813 3208.30 p18
Harper, Matthew; South Carolina, 1813 3208.30 p31
Harper, Secky; Ohio, 1838 3580.20 p32
Harper, Secky; Ohio, 1838 6020.12 p12
Harper, Thomas *SEE* Harper, Chistopher
Harper, Truman; Washington, 1888 2770.40 p25
Harper, William *SEE* Harper, Chistopher
Harper, William 37; Ontario, 1871 1823.21 p148
Harper, William 65; Ontario, 1871 1823.17 p65
Harper, Wm F. 48; Ontario, 1871 1823.21 p148
Harpman, William; Illinois, 1861 4487.25 p58
Harpprecht, Emma; America, 1855 179.55 p19
Harpprecht, Friederike-W.; America, 1855 179.55 p19
Harpprecht, Ottilie; America, 1855 179.55 p19
Harquail, G.M.; Ontario, 1900-1983 9228.50 p273
Harquail, John Albert; Maine, 1875-1904 9228.50 p273
Harratt, William 40; Ontario, 1871 1823.21 p148
Harre, Karl August; America, 1890 7420.1 p360
Harrendorf, Miss; America, 1849 7420.1 p65
Harrigan, John 75; Ontario, 1871 1823.21 p148
Harrigan, Michael; Toronto, 1844 2910.35 p115
Harrington, Mrs.; Toronto, 1844 2910.35 p114
Harrington, Darby 22; St. Johns, N.F., 1811 1053.20 p21
Harrington, Edgar 39; Ontario, 1871 1823.21 p148
Harrington, Fanny; Pennsylvania, 1858 8513.31 p312
Harrington, Henry 17; Quebec, 1870 8364.32 p23
Harrington, James 55; Ontario, 1871 1823.21 p148
Harrington, John; New Orleans, 1851 7242.30 p143
Harrington, John 58; Ontario, 1871 1823.21 p148
Harrington, Joshua 29; Ontario, 1871 1823.21 p148

Harrington, Judson; Ohio, 1844 ***2763.1*** *p8*
Harrington, Maurice; New Orleans, 1851 ***7242.30*** *p143*
Harrington, Michl 2; St. Johns, N.F., 1811 ***1053.20*** *p22*
Harrington, Patrick 19; Ontario, 1871 ***1823.21*** *p148*
Harrington, Patt; New Orleans, 1851 ***7242.30*** *p143*
Harrington, Phillip 20; St. Johns, N.F., 1811 ***1053.20*** *p22*
Harrington, Timothy; Toronto, 1844 ***2910.35*** *p113*
Harrington, Timothy; Toronto, 1844 ***2910.35*** *p114*
Harriott, Edward John; Miami, 1935 ***4984.12*** *p39*
Harris, Abraham; South Carolina, 1860 ***6155.4*** *p18*
Harris, Adam 50; Ontario, 1871 ***1823.21*** *p148*
Harris, Albert Arthur; Illinois, 1930 ***121.35*** *p101*
Harris, Ann 46; New York, NY, 1894 ***6512.1*** *p229*
Harris, Arthur C.; New York, NY, 1865 ***1029.59*** *p38*
Harris, Blodwin 6; New York, NY, 1894 ***6512.1*** *p229*
Harris, Catherine 78; Ontario, 1871 ***1823.21*** *p149*
Harris, Charles; North Carolina, 1839 ***1088.45*** *p13*
Harris, Charles 30; Ontario, 1871 ***1823.21*** *p149*
Harris, Charles H. 31; Ontario, 1871 ***1823.17*** *p65*
Harris, David; Washington, 1870 ***2770.40*** *p134*
Harris, David; Washington, 1883 ***2770.40*** *p136*
Harris, Eleanor 58; Michigan, 1880 ***4491.33*** *p11*
Harris, Eliz.; Maryland, 1674-1675 ***1236.25*** *p52*
Harris, Elizabeth 42; Michigan, 1880 ***4491.33*** *p11*
Harris, Elizabeth 70; Ontario, 1871 ***1823.21*** *p149*
Harris, Ellen 16; Ontario, 1871 ***1823.21*** *p149*
Harris, Emma 24; Michigan, 1880 ***4491.33*** *p11*
Harris, Francis; New Jersey, 1777 ***8529.30*** *p6*
Harris, Frederick 46; Ontario, 1871 ***1823.21*** *p149*
Harris, Frederick 16; Quebec, 1870 ***8364.32*** *p24*
Harris, George 31; Ontario, 1871 ***1823.21*** *p149*
Harris, George 40; Ontario, 1871 ***1823.21*** *p149*
Harris, Henery 48; Ontario, 1871 ***1823.21*** *p149*
Harris, Henry 27; Ontario, 1871 ***1823.21*** *p149*
Harris, Henry 29; Ontario, 1871 ***1823.21*** *p149*
Harris, Henry 49; Ontario, 1871 ***1823.17*** *p65*
Harris, Henry 17; Quebec, 1870 ***8364.32*** *p24*
Harris, James; North Carolina, 1858-1859 ***1088.45*** *p13*
Harris, James 23; Ontario, 1871 ***1823.21*** *p149*
Harris, James 37; Ontario, 1871 ***1823.21*** *p149*
Harris, James 43; Ontario, 1871 ***1823.21*** *p149*
Harris, James; Washington, 1886 ***2770.40*** *p195*
Harris, James, Sr. 50; Ontario, 1871 ***1823.21*** *p149*
Harris, Jane 34; Ontario, 1871 ***1823.21*** *p149*
Harris, Jane 47; Ontario, 1871 ***1823.21*** *p149*
Harris, Jane 70; Ontario, 1871 ***1823.21*** *p149*
Harris, Jo. 20; Virginia, 1635 ***1183.3*** *p30*
Harris, John; Marston's Wharf, 1782 ***8529.30*** *p12*
Harris, John; North Carolina, 1854 ***1088.45*** *p13*
Harris, John; North Carolina, 1858-1859 ***1088.45*** *p13*
Harris, John; Ohio, 1840 ***2763.1*** *p8*
Harris, John 20; Ontario, 1871 ***1823.17*** *p65*
Harris, John 34; Ontario, 1871 ***1823.21*** *p149*
Harris, John 45; Ontario, 1871 ***1823.21*** *p149*
Harris, John 50; Ontario, 1871 ***1823.21*** *p149*
Harris, John 71; Ontario, 1871 ***1823.21*** *p149*
Harris, John D. 55; Ontario, 1871 ***1823.21*** *p149*
Harris, Joseph 15; Ontario, 1871 ***1823.17*** *p65*
Harris, Joseph 27; Ontario, 1871 ***1823.21*** *p149*
Harris, Joseph; Philadelphia, 1777 ***8529.30*** *p7A*
Harris, Joshua 48; Ontario, 1871 ***1823.21*** *p149*
Harris, Julia 36; Ontario, 1871 ***1823.21*** *p149*
Harris, Lewis 12; Quebec, 1870 ***8364.32*** *p24*
Harris, Mary 56; Ontario, 1871 ***1823.21*** *p149*
Harris, Mary Ann 22; Ontario, 1871 ***1823.21*** *p149*
Harris, Mary I. 31; Ontario, 1871 ***1823.21*** *p149*
Harris, Nath 54; Ontario, 1871 ***1823.21*** *p149*
Harris, Noah; North Carolina, 1840 ***1088.45*** *p13*
Harris, Peter; Ohio, 1809-1852 ***4511.35*** *p21*
Harris, Richard 56; Michigan, 1880 ***4491.33*** *p11*
Harris, Richard 42; Ontario, 1871 ***1823.21*** *p150*
Harris, Richard 52; Ontario, 1871 ***1823.21*** *p149*
Harris, Richard H.; Colorado, 1869 ***1029.59*** *p38*
Harris, Ruth 24; Michigan, 1880 ***4491.33*** *p11*
Harris, Salathel; North Carolina, 1843 ***1088.45*** *p13*
Harris, Sam 21; Ontario, 1871 ***1823.21*** *p150*
Harris, Tho.; Maryland, 1674 ***1236.25*** *p50*
Harris, Thomas 28; Ontario, 1871 ***1823.21*** *p150*
Harris, Thomas 28; Ontario, 1871 ***1823.21*** *p150*
Harris, Thomas 43; Ontario, 1871 ***1823.17*** *p66*
Harris, Thomas 60; Ontario, 1871 ***1823.21*** *p150*
Harris, Thomas L.; Ohio, 1840 ***2763.1*** *p8*
Harris, William 47; Michigan, 1880 ***4491.33*** *p11*
Harris, William; New York, 1778 ***8529.30*** *p12*
Harris, William 35; Ontario, 1871 ***1823.17*** *p66*
Harris, William 52; Ontario, 1871 ***1823.21*** *p150*
Harris, William 54; Ontario, 1871 ***1823.17*** *p66*
Harris, Wm 18; Ontario, 1871 ***1823.21*** *p150*
Harris, Wm 58; Ontario, 1871 ***1823.21*** *p150*
Harrison, Mr.; British Columbia, 1910 ***2897.7*** *p8*
Harrison, Anne 77; Ontario, 1871 ***1823.21*** *p150*
Harrison, Caroline 44; Ontario, 1871 ***1823.17*** *p66*
Harrison, Duncan E.; Colorado, 1891 ***1029.59*** *p38*
Harrison, Ed. 18; Quebec, 1870 ***8364.32*** *p24*
Harrison, Eleanor; Canada, 1774 ***3036.5*** *p41*
Harrison, Eliz.; Maryland, 1674-1675 ***1236.25*** *p52*
Harrison, Eliza 40; Ontario, 1871 ***1823.17*** *p66*
Harrison, Eliza 50; Ontario, 1871 ***1823.21*** *p150*
Harrison, Elizabeth; Carolina, 1724 ***1220.12*** *p677*
Harrison, Elizabeth 60; Ontario, 1871 ***1823.21*** *p150*
Harrison, Fra; Jamestown, VA, 1633 ***1658.20*** *p211*
With wife
Harrison, Harvey 25; Ontario, 1871 ***1823.17*** *p66*
Harrison, Henry; South Carolina, 1813 ***3208.30*** *p18*
Harrison, Henry; South Carolina, 1813 ***3208.30*** *p31*
Harrison, James 35; Ontario, 1871 ***1823.21*** *p150*
Harrison, John; Illinois, 1854 ***6079.1*** *p6*
Harrison, John; New York, 1783 ***8529.30*** *p12*
Harrison, John 19; Ontario, 1871 ***1823.21*** *p150*
Harrison, John 30; Ontario, 1871 ***1823.17*** *p66*
Harrison, John 45; Ontario, 1871 ***1823.21*** *p150*
Harrison, John 46; Ontario, 1871 ***1823.21*** *p150*
Harrison, John 51; Ontario, 1871 ***1823.21*** *p150*
Harrison, John 55; Ontario, 1871 ***1823.21*** *p150*
Harrison, Joseph; Marston's Wharf, 1782 ***8529.30*** *p12*
Harrison, Joshua; Marston's Wharf, 1782 ***8529.30*** *p12*
Harrison, Martha; Philadelphia, 1852 ***8513.31*** *p319*
Harrison, Mary; Canada, 1774 ***3036.5*** *p40*
Harrison, Mary 48; Ontario, 1871 ***1823.21*** *p150*
Harrison, Pat; St. John, N.B., 1847 ***2978.15*** *p37*
Harrison, Robert 45; Ontario, 1871 ***1823.21*** *p150*
Harrison, Sarah A. 43; Quebec, 1910 ***2897.7*** *p8*
Harrison, Thomas; Canada, 1774 ***3036.5*** *p41*
Harrison, Thomas 45; Ontario, 1871 ***1823.21*** *p150*
Harrison, Thomas 53; Ontario, 1871 ***1823.21*** *p150*
Harrison, Thomas 61; Ontario, 1871 ***1823.21*** *p150*
Harrison, William; North Carolina, 1838 ***1088.45*** *p13*
Harrison, William 26; Ontario, 1871 ***1823.21*** *p150*
Harrison, Wm. J. 4; Quebec, 1910 ***2897.7*** *p8*
Harriss, Francis; New Jersey, 1777 ***8529.30*** *p6*
Harriss, John; Marston's Wharf, 1782 ***8529.30*** *p12*
Harrold, Allen 60; Michigan, 1880 ***4491.33*** *p11*
Harrold, Michael 47; Michigan, 1880 ***4491.33*** *p11*
Harrold, Rose 60; Michigan, 1880 ***4491.33*** *p11*
Harrold, William 50; Ontario, 1871 ***1823.17*** *p66*
Harroon, Hannah; Massachusetts, 1755 ***1642*** *p117*
Harroon, Mary; Massachusetts, 1761 ***1642*** *p117*
Harroughey, Mrs.; Toronto, 1844 ***2910.35*** *p114*
Harroughey, John; Toronto, 1844 ***2910.35*** *p112*
Harrower, Andrew 63; Ontario, 1871 ***1823.17*** *p66*
Harrower, George 65; Ontario, 1871 ***1823.17*** *p66*
Harry, Mrs. E. O.; Montreal, 1922 ***4514.4*** *p32*
Harry, John; Colorado, 1884 ***1029.59*** *p38*
Harry, John; Colorado, 1899 ***1029.59*** *p38*
Harsch, Christian 4; New York, NY, 1898 ***7951.13*** *p42*
Harsch, Emma 4; New York, NY, 1898 ***7951.13*** *p42*
Harsch, Friedrich 11; New York, NY, 1898 ***7951.13*** *p42*
Harsch, Friedrich 34; New York, NY, 1898 ***7951.13*** *p42*
Harsch, Friedricka 35; New York, NY, 1898 ***7951.13*** *p42*
Harsch, Johannes 2; New York, NY, 1898 ***7951.13*** *p42*
Harshaw, John 28; Ontario, 1871 ***1823.21*** *p150*
Harske, Johann; Wisconsin, 1871 ***6795.8*** *p42*
Harste, Ferdinand Friedrich Wilhelm; America, 1882 ***7420.1*** *p329*
Harste, Otto Heinrich; America, 1884 ***7420.1*** *p343*
Harstedt, G.T.; New York, NY, 1844 ***6412.40*** *p148*
Hart, Andrew; North Carolina, 1830 ***1088.45*** *p13*
Hart, Anne; Worcester, MA, 1774 ***1642*** *p114*
Hart, David; Washington, 1881 ***2770.40*** *p135*
Hart, Elizabeth 63; Ontario, 1871 ***1823.21*** *p150*
Hart, Emily *SEE* Hart, James H.
Hart, Friedrich 38; America, 1856 ***5475.1*** *p488*
*Wife:*Katharina Muller 36
*Daughter:*Karoline 1
*Daughter:*Katharina 6
Hart, George 59; Ontario, 1871 ***1823.17*** *p66*
Hart, Hugh 31; Ontario, 1871 ***1823.21*** *p150*
Hart, Isaac; Louisiana, 1836-1840 ***4981.45*** *p212*
Hart, James; North Carolina, 1822 ***1088.45*** *p13*
Hart, James 37; Ontario, 1871 ***1823.21*** *p150*
Hart, James 43; Ontario, 1871 ***1823.21*** *p150*
Hart, James H.; Utah, 1854 ***9228.50*** *p272*
*Relative:*Emily
Hart, Jeremiah 52; Ontario, 1871 ***1823.17*** *p66*
Hart, John 31; Ontario, 1871 ***1823.21*** *p150*
Hart, John 55; Ontario, 1871 ***1823.21*** *p151*
Hart, Joseph 20; Ontario, 1871 ***1823.21*** *p151*
Hart, Karoline 1 *SEE* Hart, Friedrich
Hart, Katharina 6 *SEE* Hart, Friedrich
Hart, Katharina Muller 36 *SEE* Hart, Friedrich
Hart, Margaret 55; Ontario, 1871 ***1823.21*** *p151*
Hart, Maria 73; Ontario, 1871 ***1823.21*** *p151*
Hart, Michael; Boston, 1832 ***3274.55*** *p72*
Hart, Michael 66; Ontario, 1871 ***1823.17*** *p66*
Hart, Rich'd 20; Ontario, 1871 ***1823.21*** *p151*
Hart, Rich'd 50; Ontario, 1871 ***1823.21*** *p151*
Hart, Richard 48; Ontario, 1871 ***1823.21*** *p151*
Hart, William; Marston's Wharf, 1782 ***8529.30*** *p12*
Hart, William; Ohio, 1809-1852 ***4511.35*** *p21*
Hart, William 31; Ontario, 1871 ***1823.21*** *p151*
Hart, William 34; Ontario, 1871 ***1823.17*** *p66*
Hartefan, Tom 30; Ontario, 1871 ***1823.17*** *p66*
Hartegan, James; Boston, 1770 ***1642*** *p43*
Hartenberger, Katharina *SEE* Hartenberger, Nik.
Hartenberger, Maria Diehl *SEE* Hartenberger, Nik.
Hartenberger, Nik.; America, 1895 ***5475.1*** *p387*
*Wife:*Maria Diehl
*Son:*Nikolaus
*Daughter:*Katharina
Hartenberger, Nikolaus *SEE* Hartenberger, Nik.
Harter, Johannes; New York, NY, 1892 ***3366.30*** *p70*
Harterich, Nikolaus; America, 1892 ***170.15*** *p27*
Hartfiel, Emilie; Wisconsin, 1885 ***6795.8*** *p44*
Hartful, A. 26; Halifax, N.S., 1902 ***1860.4*** *p44*
Hartfuss, Heinrich; America, 1846 ***5475.1*** *p233*
Hartfuss, Johann; America, 1854 ***5475.1*** *p235*
Hartgerbeld, Jacq. 28; America, 1841 ***778.6*** *p156*
Harth, Albert; America, 1882 ***5475.1*** *p380*
Harthmann, Magdalena; America, 1866 ***5475.1*** *p503*
Harthof, vom, Miss; America, 1839 ***2526.42*** *p110*
Hartigan, Catherine 55; Ontario, 1871 ***1823.17*** *p66*
Hartigan, James; Boston, 1769 ***1642*** *p49*
Hartigan, Julia; Philadelphia, 1854 ***8513.31*** *p422*
Hartin, Eliza 58; Ontario, 1871 ***1823.21*** *p151*
Hartinam, Alfred 22; Portland, ME, 1910 ***970.38*** *p77*
Harting, . . .; America, 1845 ***7420.1*** *p36*
Harting, Mr.; Port uncertain, 1854 ***7420.1*** *p121*
With family
Harting, Carl; America, 1857 ***7420.1*** *p162*
Harting, Carl Friedrich Wilhelm; America, 1852 ***7420.1*** *p89*
Harting, Carl Ludwig; Port uncertain, 1837 ***7420.1*** *p13*
Harting, Friedrich Christian; America, 1857 ***7420.1*** *p162*
With wife
Harting, Friedrich Wilhelm; America, 1852 ***7420.1*** *p89*
Harting, Friedrich Wilhelm; America, 1856 ***7420.1*** *p148*
Harting, Heinrich; America, 1857 ***7420.1*** *p162*
Hartinger, Joseph; Illinois, 1856 ***6079.1*** *p6*
Hartle, Charles 29; America, 1747 ***778.6*** *p156*
Hartley, George 29; Ontario, 1871 ***1823.17*** *p66*
Hartley, George 31; Ontario, 1871 ***1823.17*** *p66*
Hartley, George 37; Ontario, 1871 ***1823.21*** *p151*
Hartley, George 45; Ontario, 1871 ***1823.17*** *p66*
Hartley, George 68; Ontario, 1871 ***1823.17*** *p66*
Hartley, James 48; Ontario, 1871 ***1823.17*** *p66*
Hartley, John 25; Ontario, 1871 ***1823.17*** *p66*
Hartley, Joseph 21; Ontario, 1871 ***1823.17*** *p66*
Hartley, Martha 24; Ontario, 1871 ***1823.21*** *p151*
Hartley, W. B.; California, 1868 ***1131.61*** *p90*
Hartley, William 63; Ontario, 1871 ***1823.17*** *p66*
Hartman, . . .; West Virginia, 1865-1879 ***1132.30*** *p150*
Hartman, Jacob; Ohio, 1809-1852 ***4511.35*** *p21*
Hartman, Katharine 24; Portland, ME, 1911 ***970.38*** *p77*
Hartman, L.; Louisiana, 1874 ***4981.45*** *p296*
Hartman, Martin; Louisiana, 1874-1875 ***4981.45*** *p29*
Hartman, Philip; Louisiana, 1874 ***4981.45*** *p296*
Hartman, Salomon 6 months; Portland, ME, 1911 ***970.38*** *p77*
Hartman, Salomon 26; Portland, ME, 1911 ***970.38*** *p77*
Hartmann, Miss; America, 1866 ***7420.1*** *p243*
Hartmann, Adam 4 *SEE* Hartmann, Adam
Hartmann, Adam 9 *SEE* Hartmann, Jakob
Hartmann, Adam 16 *SEE* Hartmann, Michael
Hartmann, Adam 38; America, 1853 ***2526.43*** *p127*
*Wife:*Eva Weber 29
*Daughter:*Elisabetha 6 months
*Sister:*Maria Elisabetha 19
*Brother:*Heinrich
*Mother:*Marie Elisabetha Stein 56
*Father:*Adam 65
*Daughter:*Marie Elisabetha 2
*Son:*Johannes 8
*Daughter:*Anna Margaretha 6
*Son:*Adam 4
Hartmann, Adam 65 *SEE* Hartmann, Adam
Hartmann, Adolph; America, 1852 ***7420.1*** *p89*
Hartmann, Adolph; America, 1881 ***7420.1*** *p321*
Hartmann, Anna 6 *SEE* Hartmann, Jakob
Hartmann, Anna Eva 72; America, 1856 ***2526.42*** *p181*
Hartmann, Anna Katharina 14 *SEE* Hartmann, Michael
Hartmann, Anna Margaretha 6 *SEE* Hartmann, Adam
Hartmann, Anna Marie 33 *SEE* Hartmann, Jakob
Hartmann, Anna Regina; Pennsylvania, 1899 ***170.15*** *p27*
Hartmann, Anton Friedrich; America, 1879 ***7420.1*** *p313*
Hartmann, August; America, 1861 ***7420.1*** *p205*
With family
Hartmann, August; America, 1883 ***7420.1*** *p336*

Hartmann, Auguste; Chile, 1909 *7420.1 p385*
Hartmann, Carl Friedrich Anton; America, 1857 *7420.1 p162*
  *Wife:*Christine Marie Leonore Reising
  *Brother:*Christian Friedrich
  *Sister-In-Law:*Sophie
Hartmann, Carl Friedrich Christian; America, 1883 *7420.1 p336*
Hartmann, Carl Friedrich Wilhelm *SEE* Hartmann, Carl Friedrich Wilhelm
Hartmann, Carl Friedrich Wilhelm; America, 1870 *7420.1 p286*
  *Son:*Carl Friedrich Wilhelm
  With wife
Hartmann, Caroline Wilhelmine; America, 1857 *7420.1 p172*
Hartmann, Caspar; Illinois, 1851 *6079.1 p6*
Hartmann, Catharine Elisabeth; America, 1868 *7919.3 p527*
Hartmann, Christian; America, 1868 *7919.3 p527*
  With sister
Hartmann, Christian; America, 1869 *7420.1 p280*
  With wife & 2 daughters
Hartmann, Christian Friedrich *SEE* Hartmann, Carl Friedrich Anton
Hartmann, Christian Friedrich; America, 1883 *7420.1 p336*
Hartmann, Christian Heinrich; America, 1851 *7420.1 p80*
  With brother
Hartmann, Christine Marie Leonore Reising *SEE* Hartmann, Carl Friedrich Anton
Hartmann, Dorothee Louise Wilhelmine Rotermund *SEE* Hartmann, Johann Friedrich Wilhelm
Hartmann, Elisabetha 6 *SEE* Hartmann, Adam
Hartmann, Engel Marie Charlotte; America, 1870 *7420.1 p287*
Hartmann, Ernst; America, 1858 *7420.1 p178*
  With family
Hartmann, Eva Weber 29 *SEE* Hartmann, Adam
Hartmann, Eva Maria *SEE* Hartmann, Maria Katharina
Hartmann, Eva Maria 6 *SEE* Hartmann, Michael
Hartmann, Friedrich; Port uncertain, 1854 *7420.1 p121*
  With family
Hartmann, Friedrich Jakob; America, 1886 *2526.43 p217*
Hartmann, Friedrich Otto; America, 1866 *7420.1 p243*
Hartmann, Friedrich Wilhelm; America, 1841 *7420.1 p22*
Hartmann, Friedrich Wilhelm; America, 1875 *7420.1 p305*
Hartmann, Friedrich Wilhelm August; America, 1870 *7420.1 p287*
Hartmann, Geneva 2; Halifax, N.S., 1902 *1860.4 p43*
Hartmann, Georg *SEE* Hartmann, Maria Katharina
Hartmann, Georg; America, 1882 *2526.43 p186*
Hartmann, Georg 6 *SEE* Hartmann, Michael
Hartmann, Hans Heinrich; America, 1855 *7420.1 p137*
Hartmann, Hans Heinrich C.; America, 1859 *7420.1 p185*
Hartmann, Hans Heinrich Christian; America, 1863 *7420.1 p218*
Hartmann, Hans Heinrich Conrad; America, 1859 *7420.1 p185*
Hartmann, Hans Heinrich Wilhelm; Illinois, 1873 *7420.1 p300*
Hartmann, Harwara; Halifax, N.S., 1902 *1860.4 p43*
Hartmann, Heinrich *SEE* Hartmann, Adam
Hartmann, Heinrich; America, 1868 *7420.1 p272*
  With family
Hartmann, Heinrich Christian Ludwig; America, 1867 *7420.1 p257*
Hartmann, Heinrich Conrad *SEE* Hartmann, Ilse Marie Sophie
Hartmann, Heinrich Friedrich Wilhelm; America, 1891 *7420.1 p362*
Hartmann, Heinrich Tonnies Daniel; America, 1867 *7420.1 p257*
Hartmann, Heinrich Wilhelm; America, 1888 *7420.1 p356*
Hartmann, Henriette; Valdivia, Chile, 1852 *1192.4 p54*
  With child 8
Hartmann, Ilse Marie Sophie; America, 1866 *7420.1 p243*
  *Son:*Heinrich Conrad
Hartmann, Ilse Marie Sophie; America, 1866 *7420.1 p248*
Hartmann, Ilse Marie Sophie; America, 1866 *7420.1 p248*
Hartmann, Jakob 7 *SEE* Hartmann, Jakob
Hartmann, Jakob 41; America, 1881 *2526.42 p168*
  *Wife:*Anna Marie 33
  *Child:*Jakob 7

  *Child:*Anna 6
  *Child:*Magdalena 2
  *Child:*Adam 9
Hartmann, Johann 4; Halifax, N.S., 1902 *1860.4 p43*
Hartmann, Johann Friedrich; America, 1864 *7420.1 p224*
Hartmann, Johann Friedrich Wilhelm; America, 1845 *7420.1 p36*
  *Wife:*Dorothee Louise Wilhelmine Rotermund
  With children
Hartmann, Johann Heinrich; America, 1852 *7420.1 p89*
Hartmann, Johann Peter; America, 1885 *2526.43 p203*
Hartmann, Johannes; America, 1866 *2526.42 p169*
Hartmann, Johannes 8 *SEE* Hartmann, Adam
Hartmann, Johannes 13 *SEE* Hartmann, Michael
Hartmann, Johannes 17; America, 1854 *2526.43 p209*
Hartmann, Kaspar; Pennsylvania, 1850 *170.15 p27*
  With family
Hartmann, Katharina; America, 1880 *5475.1 p23*
Hartmann, Leonhard; America, 1853 *2526.42 p181*
Hartmann, Luise Sophie Eleonore; America, 1888 *7420.1 p356*
Hartmann, Magdalena 2 *SEE* Hartmann, Jakob
Hartmann, Margaretha; New York, 1853 *2526.43 p125*
Hartmann, Margaretha; New York, 1860 *358.56 p4*
Hartmann, Margaretha 31; Pennsylvania, 1850 *170.15 p27*
  With family
Hartmann, Maria Elisabetha 19 *SEE* Hartmann, Adam
Hartmann, Maria Katharina; America, 1857 *2526.42 p166*
  *Child:*Georg
  *Child:*Eva Maria
Hartmann, Maria Katharina Hertel 39 *SEE* Hartmann, Michael
Hartmann, Marie Elisabetha 2 *SEE* Hartmann, Adam
Hartmann, Marie Elisabetha Stein 56 *SEE* Hartmann, Adam
Hartmann, Michael; America, 1852 *2526.42 p136*
Hartmann, Michael 44; America, 1855 *2526.42 p167*
  *Wife:*Maria Katharina Hertel 39
  *Child:*Anna Katharina 14
  *Child:*Georg 6 months
  *Child:*Eva Maria 6 months
  *Child:*Johannes 13
  *Child:*Adam 16
Hartmann, Nicolas 36; America, 1841 *778.6 p156*
Hartmann, Peter; America, 1831 *2526.43 p218*
Hartmann, Peter 35; Pennsylvania, 1850 *170.15 p27*
Hartmann, Philip 4; Halifax, N.S., 1902 *1860.4 p43*
Hartmann, Philip 34; Halifax, N.S., 1902 *1860.4 p43*
Hartmann, Philipp; Pennsylvania, 1850 *170.15 p27*
Hartmann, Sophie *SEE* Hartmann, Carl Friedrich Anton
Hartmann, Sophie Wilhelmine Caroline; America, 1857 *7420.1 p162*
  With mother
Hartmann, Theresa 31; Halifax, N.S., 1902 *1860.4 p43*
Hartmann, Valentin; Port uncertain, 1866 *170.15 p27*
  With wife & 2 children
Hartmann, Wilhelmine; America, 1869 *7420.1 p280*
Hartmeyer, Franz Joseph 30; New Castle, DE, 1817-1818 *90.20 p151*
Hartmuller, Joseph; New York, 1860 *358.56 p5*
Hartnagel, Anton 29; Mississippi, 1847 *778.6 p156*
Hartnagel, Joseph 22; Mississippi, 1847 *778.6 p156*
Hartnell, James 50; Ontario, 1871 *1823.21 p151*
Hartner Family ; Uruguay, 1900-1904 *609.10 p14*
Hartness, W. G. 46; Ontario, 1871 *1823.17 p66*
Hartnett, Albert 37; Michigan, 1880 *4491.30 p15*
Hartnett, Eva 32; Michigan, 1880 *4491.30 p15*
Hartnett, Hellena M. 2; Michigan, 1880 *4491.30 p15*
Hartnett, Hurbert 4; Michigan, 1880 *4491.30 p15*
Hartquist, Charles Aron; St. Paul, MN, 1882 *1865.50 p49*
Hartquist, Ida Maria; St. Paul, MN, 1883 *1865.50 p49*
Hartqvist, Charles Aron; St. Paul, MN, 1882 *1865.50 p49*
Hartqvist, Ida Maria; St. Paul, MN, 1883 *1865.50 p49*
Hartry, Alfred 45; Ontario, 1871 *1823.17 p66*
Hartry, William; Toronto, 1844 *2910.35 p114*
Hartshorn, Daniel 35; Michigan, 1880 *4491.36 p9*
Hartshorn, Delilah 61; Michigan, 1880 *4491.36 p9*
Hartshorn, Martha 46; Michigan, 1880 *4491.36 p9*
Hartshue, John; Ohio, 1809-1852 *4511.35 p21*
Hartson, Aaron 64; Ontario, 1871 *1823.21 p151*
Hartsook, Frederick; Ohio, 1809-1852 *4511.35 p21*
Hartsyok, Frederick; Cleveland, OH, 1854-1858 *9722.10 p120*
Hartung, August; America, 1867 *7919.3 p528*
Hartung, August; Halifax, N.S., 1902 *1860.4 p40*
Hartung, August 47; Halifax, N.S., 1902 *1860.4 p40*
Hartung, Dorothea; America, 1835 *7420.1 p10*
Hartung, Georg; America, 1867 *7919.3 p525*

Hartung, Georg Caspar; America, 1867 *7919.3 p529*
Hartung, Heinrich Gottlieb Emil; America, 1873 *7420.1 p300*
Hartung, Henriette; America, 1868 *7919.3 p533*
Hartung, Jonny 16; Halifax, N.S., 1902 *1860.4 p40*
Hartung, Louise 40; Halifax, N.S., 1902 *1860.4 p40*
Hartung, Marie Elisabeth; America, 1867 *7919.3 p531*
Hartung, Phil. Joh. Baptist Christian; America, 1882 *5475.1 p161*
Hartwick, Sarah 40; Ontario, 1871 *1823.21 p151*
Hartwig, Albin; America, 1867 *7919.3 p526*
Hartwig, August; Texas, 1865 *7420.1 p231*
Hartwig, Auguste Bertha; America, 1868 *7919.3 p530*
Hartwig, Friedrich; Chile, 1852 *1192.4 p52*
Hartwig, Friedrich Wm. F.; Wisconsin, 1890 *6795.8 p152*
Hartwig, Johann 32; New York, NY, 1885 *1883.7 p46*
Hartwig, Louise Sophie Dorothee Charlotte; New York, NY, 1897 *7420.1 p373*
Harty, James; North Carolina, 1824 *1088.45 p13*
Harty, Michael 58; Ontario, 1871 *1823.21 p151*
Harty, Patrick; North Carolina, 1824 *1088.45 p13*
Hartzell, Adam; Ohio, 1809-1851 *4511.35 p21*
Harvey, . . .; South Carolina, 1680 *9228.50 p273*
Harvey, Alexander; North Carolina, 1857 *1088.45 p13*
Harvey, Andrew J. 21; Indiana, 1890-1896 *9076.20 p74*
Harvey, Donald 52; Ontario, 1871 *1823.21 p151*
Harvey, Duncan 55; Ontario, 1871 *1823.21 p151*
Harvey, George 43; Ontario, 1871 *1823.21 p151*
Harvey, Henry; Colorado, 1886 *1029.59 p38*
Harvey, Henry; Colorado, 1894 *1029.59 p38*
Harvey, Hugh 38; Ontario, 1871 *1823.17 p66*
Harvey, James 49; Ontario, 1871 *1823.21 p151*
Harvey, James 50; Ontario, 1871 *1823.21 p151*
Harvey, John 34; New York, NY, 1835 *5024.1 p137*
Harvey, Joseph 40; Ontario, 1871 *1823.17 p66*
Harvey, Robert; Maryland, 1673 *1236.25 p49*
Harvey, Robert; North Carolina, 1859 *1088.45 p13*
Harvey, Robert; Ohio, 1801-1835 *5024.1 p139*
  With parents
Harvey, Roger; North America, 1750 *1640.8 p234*
Harvey, Samuel 52; Ontario, 1871 *1823.21 p151*
Harvey, Thomas 33; Ontario, 1871 *1823.21 p151*
Harvey, William; Baltimore, 1818 *9228.50 p273*
Harvey, William; Louisiana, 1855 *7710.1 p155*
Harvey, William; Marston's Wharf, 1782 *8529.30 p12*
Harvey, William 70; Ontario, 1871 *1823.21 p151*
Harvie, Clement; New Hampshire, n.d. *9228.50 p273*
Harvy, Adelaid 15; Ontario, 1871 *1823.21 p151*
Harvy, Michal 50; Ontario, 1871 *1823.21 p151*
Harvy, Richard 32; Virginia, 1635 *1183.3 p31*
Harvy, William 50; Ontario, 1871 *1823.21 p151*
Harward, Charles; Louisiana, 1841-1844 *4981.45 p210*
Harwood, Jabez 45; Ontario, 1871 *1823.21 p151*
Harwood, Sarah 39; Ontario, 1871 *1823.21 p151*
Harwood, Thomas 29; Ontario, 1871 *1823.21 p151*
Harwood, William 37; Ontario, 1871 *1823.21 p151*
Harwood, William 46; Ontario, 1871 *1823.17 p66*
Hary, Elisabeth Lorenz 25 *SEE* Hary, Jakob
Hary, Jakob; America, 1864 *5475.1 p45*
  *Wife:*Elisabeth Lorenz
  *Son:*Jakob
  *Son:*Philipp
Hary, Jakob 3 *SEE* Hary, Jakob
Hary, Philipp 9 *SEE* Hary, Jakob
Harz, Barthel; America, 1846 *5475.1 p322*
Hasbach, Eckhard; America, 1843 *5475.1 p551*
Haschert, Adam; America, 1836 *2526.42 p151*
Haschert, Anton 8 *SEE* Haschert, Kaspar
Haschert, Kaspar; America, 1841 *2526.42 p151*
  With wife
  *Child:*Ludwig
  *Child:*Anton
  *Child:*Magdalena
  *Child:*Leonhard
  *Child:*Philipp
  *Stepchild:*Konrad Heinrich
  *Child:*Margaretha
Haschert, Konrad Heinrich 20 *SEE* Haschert, Kaspar
Haschert, Leonhard 2 *SEE* Haschert, Kaspar
Haschert, Ludwig 12 *SEE* Haschert, Kaspar
Haschert, Magdalena 1 *SEE* Haschert, Kaspar
Haschert, Margaretha 17 *SEE* Haschert, Kaspar
Haschert, Peter; America, 1853 *2526.42 p151*
Haschert, Philipp; America, 1836 *2526.42 p151*
  With wife
  With child 6 months
  With child 6
  With child 3
Haschert, Philipp 10 *SEE* Haschert, Kaspar
Hascoul, John; Boston, 1741 *9228.50 p273*
Hascoul, Philip; Boston, 1716 *9228.50 p273*
Hase, Thomas; Boston, 1762 *1642 p48*

Hasek, Frantisek; Iowa, 1867 *2853.20 p218*
Haselin, Catherine 38; America, 1842 *778.6 p156*
Hasemann, Engel Marie Dorothee *SEE* Hasemann, Johann Heinrich Christoph
Hasemann, Engel Marie Sophie *SEE* Hasemann, Heinrich Conrad Christian
Hasemann, Heinr. Christian *SEE* Hasemann, Heinrich Conrad Christian
Hasemann, Heinrich Conrad *SEE* Hasemann, Heinrich Conrad Christian
Hasemann, Heinrich Conrad Christian; America, 1847 *7420.1 p53*
  *Wife:*Thrine Marie Sophie Hinze
  *Son:*Heinr. Christian
  *Daughter:*Engel Marie Sophie
  *Son:*Heinrich Conrad
Hasemann, Heinrich Friedrich Christoph; America, 1872 *7420.1 p295*
Hasemann, Johann Christ.; America, 1861 *7420.1 p205*
  With wife & 5 daughters & 2 sons
Hasemann, Johann Heinrich; America, 1857 *7420.1 p162*
Hasemann, Johann Heinrich Christoph; America, 1872 *7420.1 p295*
  *Daughter:*Engel Marie Dorothee
Hasemann, Johann Heinrich Gottlieb; America, 1867 *7420.1 p257*
Hasemann, Sophie Marie Dorothee; America, 1846 *7420.1 p44*
Hasemann, Thrine Marie Sophie Hinze *SEE* Hasemann, Heinrich Conrad Christian
Hasemann Brothers, . . .; America, 1881 *7420.1 p321*
Hasenfraz, Therese 26; Ohio, 1847 *778.6 p156*
Hasenjaeger, Anne Sophie Marie Charlotte Gerland *SEE* Hasenjaeger, Johann Philipp
Hasenjaeger, Engel Marie Louise *SEE* Hasenjaeger, Engel Marie Sophie Charlotte
Hasenjaeger, Engel Marie Sophie Charlotte; America, 1847 *7420.1 p54*
Hasenjaeger, Engel Marie Sophie Charlotte; America, 1849 *7420.1 p64*
  *Daughter:*Engel Marie Louise
Hasenjaeger, Johann Philipp; America, 1849 *7420.1 p64*
  *Wife:*Anne Sophie Marie Charlotte Gerland
Hasenjager, Engel Marie Sophie Charlotte *SEE* Hasenjager, Johann Christoph
Hasenjager, Engel Marie Sophie Charlotte Lohmann *SEE* Hasenjager, Johann Christoph
Hasenjager, Friedrich Philipp; America, 1846 *7420.1 p44*
Hasenjager, Heinrich Conrad Christoph *SEE* Hasenjager, Johann Christoph
Hasenjager, Johann Christoph; America, 1853 *7420.1 p106*
  *Wife:*Engel Marie Sophie Charlotte Lohmann
  *Daughter:*Engel Marie Sophie Charlotte
  *Son:*Heinrich Conrad Christoph
  *Son:*Johann Christoph
Hasenjager, Johann Heinrich Christoph *SEE* Hasenjager, Johann Christoph
Hasenpflug, Anton; Ohio, 1844 *2763.1 p8*
Hasenpflug, Henry; Ohio, 1843 *2763.1 p8*
Haser, Anna Konig *SEE* Haser, Peter
Haser, Anna Maria Buchleitner *SEE* Haser, Johann
Haser, Elisabeth *SEE* Haser, Johann
Haser, Franziska *SEE* Haser, Susanna Prediger
Haser, Johann; America, 1854 *5475.1 p57*
  *Wife:*Anna Maria Buchleitner
  *Daughter:*Elisabeth
Haser, Josef; America, 1884 *5475.1 p119*
Haser, Josef; Illinois, 1888 *5475.1 p58*
Haser, Magdalena; America, 1853 *5475.1 p56*
Haser, Magdalena *SEE* Haser, Susanna Prediger
Haser, Peter; America, 1841 *5475.1 p56*
  *Wife:*Anna Konig
  With 4 children
Haser, Peter *SEE* Haser, Susanna Prediger
Haser, Susanna 46; America, 1854 *5475.1 p57*
  *Son:*Peter
  *Daughter:*Magdalena
  *Daughter:*Franziska
Hashagan, Henry G.; North Carolina, 1856 *1088.45 p13*
Hashagen, Diedrick; North Carolina, 1844 *1088.45 p13*
Hasket, John 70; Ontario, 1871 *1823.21 p151*
Hasket, Mitchel 56; Ontario, 1871 *1823.21 p151*
Hasket, Thomas 60; Ontario, 1871 *1823.21 p152*
Haskett, Catherine 22; Ontario, 1871 *1823.21 p152*
Haskett, Eliza 57; Ontario, 1871 *1823.21 p152*
Haskett, Eliza 66; Ontario, 1871 *1823.21 p152*
Haskett, Henry 34; Ontario, 1871 *1823.21 p152*
Haskett, James 36; Ontario, 1871 *1823.21 p152*
Haskett, Maria 38; Ontario, 1871 *1823.21 p152*
Haskett, Thomas 54; Ontario, 1871 *1823.21 p152*
Haskey, Joseph 53; Ontario, 1871 *1823.21 p152*
Haskindine, George; Philadelphia, 1778 *8529.30 p3A*

Hasking, John; North Carolina, 1853 *1088.45 p13*
Haskins, Eli; Illinois, 1865 *6079.1 p6*
Haskins, Thomas; North Carolina, 1858 *1088.45 p13*
Haslebacher, . . .; West Virginia, 1865-1879 *1132.30 p150*
Haslett, James 28; Ontario, 1871 *1823.21 p152*
Hason, Ellen; Maryland, 1672 *1236.25 p47*
Haspe, John; North Carolina, 1855 *1088.45 p13*
Hasper, Gerhard Frederick; North Carolina, 1857 *1088.45 p13*
Hasper, Wm; North Carolina, 1849 *1088.45 p13*
Hass, August; America, 1868 *7919.3 p526*
Hass, Francis; Ohio, 1809-1852 *4511.35 p21*
Hass, Gustav Emil; Wisconsin, 1886 *6795.8 p41*
Hass, Jakob; Venezuela, 1843 *3899.5 p542*
Hassa, Herman; Illinois, 1855 *6079.1 p6*
Hasse, Engel Marie; America, 1852 *7420.1 p89*
Hasse, Ernestine; Wisconsin, 1885 *6795.8 p29*
Hasse, Frederic; Illinois, 1858 *6079.1 p6*
Hasse, George; Jamaica, 1780 *8529.30 p13A*
Hasse, George; Jamaica, 1783 *8529.30 p13A*
Hassel, Christian; America, 1854 *5475.1 p11*
Hasselberg, Jens; New York, NY, 1844 *6412.40 p147*
Hasselin, Mr. 10; America, 1842 *778.6 p156*
Hasselin, Laurianne 1; America, 1842 *778.6 p156*
Hasselta, James 35; Ontario, 1871 *1823.21 p66*
Hassenauer, Jacob; Philadelphia, 1851 *8513.31 p312*
Hassencamp, August Friedrich Theodor; America, 1850 *7420.1 p71*
Hassett, Patrick C.; New York, NY, 1893 *3366.30 p70*
Hassey, Henry 29; Ontario, 1871 *1823.21 p152*
Hassler, Georg Jakob 27; America, 1885 *2526.43 p221*
Hassler, Jacob; Ohio, 1840-1897 *8365.35 p16*
Hassler, Wilhelm 17; America, 1866 *2526.43 p186*
Hassly, Philippe; New Castle, DE, 1817-1818 *90.20 p151*
Hassman, Ottilia; Philadelphia, 1853 *8513.31 p320*
Hassoldt, William; Ohio, 1809-1852 *4511.35 p21*
Hasson, Bridget 43; Ontario, 1871 *1823.21 p152*
Hastang, Jno; Jamestown, VA, 1633 *1658.20 p211*
Haste, Jean 24; Montreal, 1661 *9221.17 p473*
Haste, Mary 13; Quebec, 1870 *8364.32 p24*
Hastenteufel, Johann; America, 1847 *5475.1 p547*
Haster, Fred; North Carolina, 1852 *1088.45 p13*
Hastie, John 35; Ontario, 1871 *1823.17 p66*
Hastie, Joseph 36; Ontario, 1871 *1823.17 p66*
Hastie, William 34; Ontario, 1871 *1823.17 p66*
Hastie, William 64; Ontario, 1871 *1823.17 p66*
Hasting, Adam Lawrence; Louisiana, 1841-1844 *4981.45 p210*
Hasting, George 22; Ontario, 1871 *1823.21 p152*
Hasting, Jno; Jamestown, VA, 1633 *1658.20 p211*
Hastings, Elizabeth 55; Ontario, 1871 *1823.21 p152*
Hastings, James 40; Ontario, 1871 *1823.21 p152*
Hastrel deRivedoux, Jean-Baptiste-Christophe d'; Quebec, 1755 *2314.30 p185*
Hastrel deRivedoux, Jean-Bte-Christophe d'; Quebec, 1755-1757 *2314.30 p170*
Hasty, Betsy 70; Ontario, 1871 *1823.17 p66*
Haszczak, Olga; Detroit, 1930 *1640.60 p78*
Haszczyn, Joseph; Detroit, 1929-1930 *6214.5 p65*
Haszerer, Nicholas; Ohio, 1809-1852 *4511.35 p21*
Hatalewicz, Stefan 34; New York, NY, 1903 *8355.1 p15*
Hatanville, Marie; Quebec, 1669 *4514.3 p324*
Hatch, John; Louisiana, 1874 *4981.45 p132*
Hatch, John; New Orleans, 1850 *7242.30 p143*
Hatch, John; Portsmouth, NH, 1684 *9228.50 p273*
Hatfield, John 59; Ontario, 1871 *1823.21 p152*
Hatfield, John; Philadelphia, 1777 *8529.30 p2*
Hatham, Thomas 40; Ontario, 1871 *1823.17 p67*
Hathley, Rufus 38; Michigan, 1880 *4491.30 p15*
Hatlie, George 70; Ontario, 1871 *1823.21 p152*
Haton, Francis Martin; Louisiana, 1836-1840 *4981.45 p212*
Hatrel, Jacques Auguste 36; New Orleans, 1848 *778.6 p156*
Hatrel, Louise Felicite 31; New Orleans, 1848 *778.6 p156*
Hatry, Julius 23; Indiana, 1882-1886 *9076.20 p71*
Hatry, Leopold; Louisiana, 1836-1841 *4981.45 p208*
Hatson, Robert 36; Ontario, 1871 *1823.21 p152*
Hatt, Jean 28; Port uncertain, 1843 *778.6 p156*
Hatte, Gilles 24; Missouri, 1848 *778.6 p156*
Hattendorf, Miss; America, 1849 *7420.1 p65*
Hattendorf, Mr.; America, 1857 *7420.1 p162*
  With 2 sons 2 daughters & wife
Hattendorf, Adolf Heinrich Rudolf; America, 1883 *7420.1 p336*
Hattendorf, Anna Engel Marie *SEE* Hattendorf, Johann Heinrich Conrad
Hattendorf, Anna Engel Marie; America, 1844 *7420.1 p31*
Hattendorf, Anne Sophie Marie; America, 1850 *7420.1 p73*

Hattendorf, Anton Heinrich Friedrich; America, 1890 *7420.1 p360*
Hattendorf, Catharine Sophie *SEE* Hattendorf, Johann Heinrich Wilhelm
Hattendorf, Christian Friedrich; America, 1889 *7420.1 p358*
  *Brother:*Heinrich Friedrich Gottlieb
Hattendorf, Christine Louise; America, 1852 *7420.1 p89*
Hattendorf, Christine Louise Charlotte; America, 1851 *7420.1 p80*
Hattendorf, Engel Marie Schweer *SEE* Hattendorf, Johann Heinrich Wilhelm
Hattendorf, Engel Marie Charl. *SEE* Hattendorf, Johann Heinrich Wilhelm
Hattendorf, Engel Sophie *SEE* Hattendorf, Hans Heinrich Otto
Hattendorf, Hans Heinr. Wilh. *SEE* Hattendorf, Johann Heinrich Wilhelm
Hattendorf, Hans Heinrich; America, 1867 *7420.1 p257*
  With family
Hattendorf, Hans Heinrich *SEE* Hattendorf, Hans Heinrich Otto
Hattendorf, Hans Heinrich Otto; America, 1868 *7420.1 p272*
  *Wife:*Marie Dorothee Sophie Oltrogge
  *Son:*Hans Heinrich
  *Son:*Johann Heinrich
  *Daughter:*Engel Sophie
Hattendorf, Heinrich; Indianapolis, 1884 *7420.1 p343*
Hattendorf, Heinrich Friedrich Gottlieb *SEE* Hattendorf, Christian Friedrich
Hattendorf, Heinrich Wilhelm; America, 1852 *7420.1 p89*
Hattendorf, Johann Conrad; Port uncertain, 1838 *7420.1 p14*
Hattendorf, Johann Heinrich; America, 1867 *7420.1 p257*
Hattendorf, Johann Heinrich *SEE* Hattendorf, Hans Heinrich Otto
Hattendorf, Johann Heinrich Christian; Chicago, 1888 *7420.1 p356*
Hattendorf, Johann Heinrich Christoph; America, 1850 *7420.1 p71*
  With sister
Hattendorf, Johann Heinrich Christoph; America, 1853 *7420.1 p106*
Hattendorf, Johann Heinrich Conrad; America, 1844 *7420.1 p31*
  *Sister:*Anna Engel Marie
Hattendorf, Johann Heinrich Conrad *SEE* Hattendorf, Johann Heinrich Wilhelm
Hattendorf, Johann Heinrich Wilhelm; America, 1848 *7420.1 p59*
  *Wife:*Engel Marie Schweer
  *Son:*Johann Heinrich Conrad
  *Daughter:*Catharine Sophie
  *Daughter:*Engel Marie Charl.
  *Son:*Hans Heinr. Wilh.
Hattendorf, Johanne Sophie Eleonore; America, 1857 *7420.1 p164*
  With 2 sons & daughter
Hattendorf, Marie Dorothee Sophie Oltrogge *SEE* Hattendorf, Hans Heinrich Otto
Hattendorf, Philipp; Port uncertain, 1854 *7420.1 p121*
Hattendorf, Sophie; America, 1868 *7420.1 p272*
Hatterer, Joseph F. 39; New Orleans, 1848 *778.6 p156*
Hatterich, Conrad; Venezuela, 1843 *3899.5 p546*
Hatton, John 15; Quebec, 1870 *8364.32 p24*
Hattridge, Alexander; North Carolina, 1814-1820 *1088.45 p13*
Hatzfeld, Hermann 16; America, 1897 *5475.1 p25*
Hatzfeld, Nikolaus; Pittsburgh, 1896 *5475.1 p25*
Haubert, Elisabeth 29; America, 1855 *5475.1 p270*
Haubert, Michael; America, 1880 *5475.1 p245*
Haubert, Nikolaus; America, 1880 *5475.1 p246*
Haubli, Karl; New Castle, DE, 1817-1818 *90.20 p151*
Haubli, Nicobus 49; New Castle, DE, 1817-1818 *90.20 p151*
Haubrich, Katharina; America, 1866 *5475.1 p542*
Hauch, Margarethe 41; America, 1881 *5475.1 p196*
Hauck, Adam *SEE* Hauck, Adam
Hauck, Adam; America, 1881 *5475.1 p409*
  *Wife:*Henriette Henkel
  *Son:*Michel
  *Daughter:*Luise
  *Son:*Adam
Hauck, Mrs. Adam Karl; America, 1888 *5475.1 p77*
  With 4 children
Hauck, Balthasar 58; New York, NY, 1874 *6954.7 p38*
Hauck, Christina 9; New York, NY, 1874 *6954.7 p38*
Hauck, Edward; Ohio, 1809-1852 *4511.35 p21*
Hauck, Elisabeth 17; New York, NY, 1874 *6954.7 p39*
Hauck, Friedricke 60; New York, NY, 1874 *6954.7 p38*

Hauck, Gottlieb 18; New York, NY, 1874 ***6954.7*** *p38*
Hauck, Henriette Henkel *SEE* Hauck, Adam
Hauck, Henriette 40; America, 1854 ***5475.1*** *p78*
Hauck, Jac. J.; Louisiana, 1874-1875 ***4981.45*** *p29*
Hauck, Jacob; Louisiana, 1874 ***4981.45*** *p296*
Hauck, Jacob 3; New York, NY, 1874 ***6954.7*** *p39*
Hauck, Johann 5; New York, NY, 1874 ***6954.7*** *p39*
Hauck, Johann 36; New York, NY, 1874 ***6954.7*** *p39*
Hauck, Luise *SEE* Hauck, Adam
Hauck, Michel *SEE* Hauck, Adam
Hauck, Therese 28; America, 1846 ***778.6*** *p156*
Hauck, Valentin 28; Louisiana, 1848 ***778.6*** *p156*
Haud, Eliza Frances 30; Ontario, 1871 ***1823.21*** *p152*
Haud, Johann 39; America, 1843 ***5475.1*** *p252*
Haudebert, Jacques; Montreal, 1642 ***9221.17*** *p123*
Hauer, George Joseph; Oregon, 1941 ***9157.47*** *p2*
Hauer, Maria 2; New York, NY, 1893 ***1883.7*** *p44*
Hauer, Richarte 26; New York, NY, 1893 ***1883.7*** *p44*
Hauer, Rochus 28; New York, NY, 1893 ***1883.7*** *p44*
Haufs, Wenda; Chicago, 1900 ***5475.1*** *p427*
Haug, Carl Friedrich; America, 1865 ***179.55*** *p19*
Haug, Catharina; America, 1885 ***179.55*** *p19*
Haug, Gottfried Robert; America, 1861 ***179.55*** *p19*
Haug, Miss H. 22; New Orleans, 1834 ***1002.51*** *p112*
Haugen, Amund; Colorado, 1903 ***1029.59*** *p38*
Haugen, Amund; Detroit, 1877 ***1029.59*** *p38*
Haugen, Nels 29; Minnesota, 1923 ***2769.54*** *p1378*
Haugh, Alexander; Colorado, 1893 ***1029.59*** *p38*
Haugh, Philip; Ohio, 1809-1852 ***4511.35*** *p21*
Haughans, Micheal 52; Ontario, 1871 ***1823.17*** *p67*
Haughn, Helen; Massachusetts, 1930 ***9228.50*** *p417*
Haughton, Martha; Maryland, 1674 ***1236.25*** *p50*
Hauhs, Elisabeth; New York, 1864 ***5475.1*** *p490*
Hauk, Michael; Ohio, 1809-1852 ***4511.35*** *p21*
Hauk, Paul; Ohio, 1809-1852 ***4511.35*** *p21*
Hauknecht, Catharine 10; Louisiana, 1847 ***778.6*** *p156*
Hauknecht, Jean 23; Louisiana, 1847 ***778.6*** *p156*
Hauknecht, Julie 22; Louisiana, 1847 ***778.6*** *p156*
Hauknecht, Pierre 28; Louisiana, 1847 ***778.6*** *p156*
Haulin, Francoise; Quebec, 1656 ***9221.17*** *p341*
Haulin, Francoise; Quebec, 1656 ***9221.17*** *p341*
Haulotte, Clemence *SEE* Haulotte, Stanislas J.
Haulotte, Edouard *SEE* Haulotte, Stanislas J.
Haulotte, Eugene *SEE* Haulotte, Stanislas J.
Haulotte, Leon *SEE* Haulotte, Stanislas J.
Haulotte, Marie Victoire Coulon *SEE* Haulotte, Stanislas J.
Haulotte, Stanislas J.; Wisconsin, 1846-1856 ***1495.20*** *p29*
*Wife:*Marie Victoire Coulon
*Child:*Clemence
*Child:*Leon
*Child:*Eugene
*Child:*Edouard
Haunin, Adele 7; America, 1847 ***778.6*** *p156*
Haunin, Conrad 8; America, 1847 ***778.6*** *p157*
Haunin, Conrad 34; America, 1847 ***778.6*** *p157*
Haunin, Jean 41; America, 1847 ***778.6*** *p157*
Haunin, Joseph 6 months; America, 1847 ***778.6*** *p157*
Haunin, Marie Catherine 9; America, 1847 ***778.6*** *p157*
Haunin, Marie Catherine 44; America, 1847 ***778.6*** *p157*
Haunin, Marie Francoise 14; America, 1847 ***778.6*** *p157*
Haunin, Marie Louise 28; America, 1847 ***778.6*** *p157*
Haunin, Nicolas 12; America, 1847 ***778.6*** *p157*
Haupental, Barbara 44; Brazil, 1865 ***5475.1*** *p521*
Haupenthal, Anna Maria Hoffmann *SEE* Haupenthal, Peter
Haupenthal, Elisabeth; Brazil, 1867 ***5475.1*** *p505*
Haupenthal, Josef; America, 1886 ***5475.1*** *p293*
Haupenthal, Maria; America, 1872 ***6442.17*** *p65*
Haupenthal, Matthias; America, 1870 ***6442.17*** *p65*
Haupenthal, Peter; America, 1836-1899 ***6442.17*** *p65*
*Wife:*Anna Maria Hoffmann
With 4 children
Haupert, Mr.; America, 1843 ***5475.1*** *p540*
With 2 daughters
Haupert, Anna Dewes *SEE* Haupert, Jakob
Haupert, Franz; America, 1874 ***5475.1*** *p362*
*Wife:*Katharina Neusius
*Daughter:*Maria
Haupert, Friedrich Peter; America, 1843 ***5475.1*** *p540*
Haupert, Jakob; America, 1834 ***5475.1*** *p437*
*Wife:*Anna Dewes
With 2 children
Haupert, Jakob 37; America, 1843 ***5475.1*** *p257*
Haupert, Johann; America, 1874 ***5475.1*** *p362*
Haupert, Johann 50; America, 1843 ***5475.1*** *p430*
With wife
With 6 children
Haupert, Katharina Neusius *SEE* Haupert, Franz
Haupert, Katharina Wallerius *SEE* Haupert, Peter
Haupert, M. Elisabeth 35; America, 1865 ***5475.1*** *p562*
Haupert, Maria *SEE* Haupert, Franz
Haupert, Mathias; America, 1867 ***5475.1*** *p321*
Haupert, Michel; America, 1843 ***5475.1*** *p551*
Haupert, Nikolaus 24; America, 1855 ***5475.1*** *p318*
Haupert, Peter; America, 1871 ***5475.1*** *p267*
Haupert, Peter; America, 1880 ***5475.1*** *p240*
*Wife:*Katharina Wallerius
Haupt, Mr.; Port uncertain, 1854 ***7420.1*** *p121*
Haupt, Adolf 4; Halifax, N.S., 1902 ***1860.4*** *p42*
Haupt, Linn 6; Halifax, N.S., 1902 ***1860.4*** *p42*
Haupt, Mroine 27; Halifax, N.S., 1902 ***1860.4*** *p42*
Haupt, Wolf 28; Halifax, N.S., 1902 ***1860.4*** *p42*
Hauptly, Jacob; Washington, 1882 ***2770.40*** *p135*
Hauptman, Alexander; Louisiana, 1874 ***4981.45*** *p132*
Hauptmann, Henriette 6; Louisiana, 1848 ***778.6*** *p157*
Hauptmann, Jacob; Colorado, 1880 ***1029.59*** *p38*
Hauptmann, Jakob; America, 1865-1870 ***5475.1*** *p405*
Hauptmann, Joh.; America, 1872 ***5475.1*** *p405*
Hauptmann, John; Colorado, 1880 ***1029.59*** *p38*
Hauptmann, Joseph 28; Port uncertain, 1848 ***778.6*** *p157*
Hauptmann, Peter 38; America, 1855 ***5475.1*** *p250*
Haurut, Mr. 30; New Orleans, 1843 ***778.6*** *p157*
Haus, Barbera 32; Missouri, 1848 ***778.6*** *p157*
Haus, Grete 49; America, 1845 ***778.6*** *p157*
Haus, Helena 5; Missouri, 1848 ***778.6*** *p157*
Haus, Jacob 29; Missouri, 1848 ***778.6*** *p157*
Haus, Nicolas 31; Missouri, 1848 ***778.6*** *p157*
Hausch, Louis; Louisiana, 1874-1875 ***4981.45*** *p29*
Householder, Jacob; Ohio, 1809-1852 ***4511.35*** *p21*
Hausel, Anna Margaretha; Iowa, 1883 ***2526.42*** *p121*
With 2 sons
*Child:*Philipp
Hausel, Babette Mohr *SEE* Hausel, Leonhard
Hausel, Johann Leonhard; America, 1885 ***2526.43*** *p169*
Hausel, Leonhard; America, 1883 ***2526.42*** *p161*
*Wife:*Babette Mohr
Hausel, Philipp *SEE* Hausel, Anna Margaretha Schafer
Hausen, William; Ohio, 1809-1852 ***4511.35*** *p21*
Hauser, Andreas 34; America, 1847 ***778.6*** *p157*
Hauser, Friedrich; Died enroute, 1817-1818 ***90.20*** *p151*
Hauser, Gustav; Valdivia, Chile, 1851 ***1192.4*** *p50*
Hauser, John; Louisiana, 1836-1840 ***4981.45*** *p212*
Hauser, Maria Barbara 40; America, 1847 ***778.6*** *p157*
Hauser, Xavvier; Ohio, 1809-1852 ***4511.35*** *p21*
Hauser, Xavvier, Jr.; Ohio, 1809-1852 ***4511.35*** *p21*
Hauserer, Anna 37; New Orleans, 1847 ***778.6*** *p157*
Hauserer, Antoine 37; New Orleans, 1847 ***778.6*** *p157*
Hauserer, Barbara 4; New Orleans, 1847 ***778.6*** *p157*
Hauserer, Charles 9 months; New Orleans, 1847 ***778.6*** *p157*
Hauserer, Clemens 2; New Orleans, 1847 ***778.6*** *p157*
Hauserer, Jean 7; New Orleans, 1847 ***778.6*** *p157*
Hauserer, Regina 9; New Orleans, 1847 ***778.6*** *p157*
Hauserer, Simon 5; New Orleans, 1847 ***778.6*** *p157*
Hauserer, Urizenz 8; New Orleans, 1847 ***778.6*** *p157*
Hausler, Paul 27; Mississippi, 1846 ***778.6*** *p157*
Hausler, Rosa 21; Mississippi, 1846 ***778.6*** *p157*
Hausler, Sebastian 9; Mississippi, 1846 ***778.6*** *p157*
Hausley, Margaret 34; Ontario, 1871 ***1823.21*** *p152*
Hausley, William 1; Ontario, 1871 ***1823.21*** *p152*
Hausman, G.F.; Valdivia, Chile, 1852 ***1192.4*** *p53*
Hausmann, Conrad; Port uncertain, 1839 ***7420.1*** *p16*
Hausmann, David; Galveston, TX, 1844 ***3967.10*** *p374*
Hausner, Adam 30; New York, NY, 1920 ***930.50*** *p49*
Hausner, Sophie 24; America, 1854 ***2526.43*** *p205*
Haussler, Johann Jakob 28; America, 1880 ***2526.43*** *p195*
Haussner, Jakob 8 months; America, 1881 ***2526.43*** *p196*
Haustadt, Peter Philip; Illinois, 1852 ***6079.1*** *p6*
Haut, Jacob; Ohio, 1809-1852 ***4511.35*** *p21*
Hautas, Mr. 14; New Orleans, 1848 ***778.6*** *p157*
Hautau, Carl Ludwig *SEE* Hautau, Friedrich
Hautau, Carl Ludwig; America, 1871 ***7420.1*** *p290*
Hautau, Friedrich; America, 1871 ***7420.1*** *p290*
*Brother:*Carl Ludwig
With family
Hautau, Mrs. H.; America, 1857 ***7420.1*** *p162*
Hauter, Margarethe 34; America, 1873 ***5475.1*** *p138*
Hautman, Gregoria 31; New York, NY, 1847 ***9176.15*** *p49*
Hautreux, Marthe 15; Montreal, 1658 ***9221.17*** *p387*
Hauvet, Victor; Louisiana, 1841-1844 ***4981.45*** *p210*
Havelka, Frantisek S.; Idaho, 1900 ***2853.20*** *p205*
Havemeier, Ernst Friedrich Wilhelm; America, 1873 ***7420.1*** *p299*
Havemeier, Heinrich Christian; New York, NY, 1877 ***7420.1*** *p309*
Haven, Silas 45; Ontario, 1871 ***1823.21*** *p152*
Haver, Eliz.; Maryland, 1674-1675 ***1236.25*** *p51*
Havercroft, Thomas 63; Ontario, 1871 ***1823.21*** *p152*
Haverin, Bridget; Ontario, 1835 ***3160.1*** *p150*
Haverkamp, August; Washington, 1886 ***2770.40*** *p195*
Havers, Cole 51; Ontario, 1871 ***1823.17*** *p67*
Havers, George 30; Ontario, 1871 ***1823.17*** *p67*
Havers, John 56; Ontario, 1871 ***1823.17*** *p67*
Havey, Louis 32; New Orleans, 1845 ***778.6*** *p155*
Havilland, . . .; Newport, RI, 1653 ***9228.50*** *p275*
Havlasa, Jan; St. Louis, 1904 ***2853.20*** *p513*
Havlicek, Jan; Cleveland, OH, 1852 ***2853.20*** *p475*
Havlicek, Jan; Cleveland, OH, 1854 ***2853.20*** *p497*
Havlicek, Josef; Omaha, NE, 1866-1910 ***2853.20*** *p144*
Havlik, Vaclav; Iowa, 1855-1856 ***2853.20*** *p237*
Havlovic, Valerian; Pennsylvania, 1887 ***2853.20*** *p433*
Havranek, Alb. Jar.; America, 1810-1910 ***2853.20*** *p513*
Havranek, Jar. Alb.; Chicago, 1906 ***2853.20*** *p514*
Hawer, George; Ohio, 1809-1852 ***4511.35*** *p21*
Hawes, Robert; Boston, 1714 ***1642*** *p24*
Hawes, Wolf; Boston, 1838 ***3274.56*** *p101*
Hawk, Gustaf; Cleveland, OH, 1888-1897 ***9722.10*** *p120*
Hawke, Robert; Ohio, 1809-1852 ***4511.35*** *p21*
Hawken, Henry 45; Ontario, 1871 ***1823.21*** *p152*
Hawken, Joseph 63; Ontario, 1871 ***1823.21*** *p152*
Hawken, Maria 69; Ontario, 1871 ***1823.21*** *p152*
Hawkens, Thomas; New York, 1779 ***8529.30*** *p12*
Hawker, James 40; Ontario, 1871 ***1823.21*** *p152*
Hawkey, John 45; Ontario, 1871 ***1823.21*** *p152*
Hawkin, David 27; Ontario, 1871 ***1823.21*** *p152*
Hawkin, Joseph 33; Ontario, 1871 ***1823.21*** *p152*
Hawkin, William 17; Ontario, 1871 ***1823.21*** *p153*
Hawkin, William 50; Ontario, 1871 ***1823.21*** *p152*
Hawkin, William 65; Ontario, 1871 ***1823.21*** *p153*
Hawkins, Agatha 49; Ontario, 1871 ***1823.21*** *p153*
Hawkins, Charlotte; Boston, 1800-1875 ***9228.50*** *p277*
Hawkins, Charlotte; Providence, RI, 1849-1900 ***9228.50*** *p276*
Hawkins, David 27; Ontario, 1871 ***1823.21*** *p153*
Hawkins, Elisha M.; New York, NY, 1849-1900 ***9228.50*** *p276*
Hawkins, Eliza M.; Providence, RI, 1849-1900 ***9228.50*** *p276*
Hawkins, George 54; Ontario, 1871 ***1823.21*** *p153*
Hawkins, Giles; Prince Edward Island, 1799-1839 ***9228.50*** *p275*
*Wife:*Susannah Chessell
*Child:*Giles Nicholas
Hawkins, Giles Nicholas *SEE* Hawkins, Giles
Hawkins, Jacob 27; Ontario, 1871 ***1823.21*** *p153*
Hawkins, James 23; Ontario, 1871 ***1823.21*** *p153*
Hawkins, James 38; Ontario, 1871 ***1823.21*** *p153*
Hawkins, James 58; Ontario, 1871 ***1823.17*** *p67*
Hawkins, Joel; Boston, 1901 ***1766.20*** *p23*
Hawkins, John 32; Ontario, 1871 ***1823.17*** *p67*
Hawkins, Joseph 40; Ontario, 1871 ***1823.21*** *p153*
Hawkins, Lewis; Iowa, 1896 ***1211.15*** *p11*
Hawkins, Margret 50; Ontario, 1871 ***1823.21*** *p153*
Hawkins, Maria A.; Boston, 1800-1875 ***9228.50*** *p277*
Hawkins, Matthias; Prince Edward Island, 1804-1850 ***9228.50*** *p276*
Hawkins, Richard 40; Ontario, 1871 ***1823.17*** *p67*
Hawkins, Sarah 20; Ontario, 1871 ***1823.21*** *p153*
Hawkins, Susannah Chessell *SEE* Hawkins, Giles
Hawkins, Thomas 15; Ontario, 1871 ***1823.21*** *p153*
Hawkins, Thomas 50; Ontario, 1871 ***1823.21*** *p153*
Hawkins, Thomas 58; Ontario, 1871 ***1823.21*** *p153*
Hawkins, William 45; Ontario, 1871 ***1823.17*** *p67*
Hawkins Family ; Prince Edward Island, 1806 ***9228.50*** *p128*
Hawks, John; Massachusetts, n.d. ***9228.50*** *p84*
Hawksford, Samuel; Havana, 1782 ***8529.30*** *p9A*
Hawkshaw, Elizabeth 70; Ontario, 1871 ***1823.21*** *p153*
Hawkshaw, John 34; Ontario, 1871 ***1823.21*** *p153*
Hawkshaw, John 37; Ontario, 1871 ***1823.21*** *p153*
Hawkshaw, William 34; Michigan, 1880 ***4491.39*** *p13*
Hawksworth, Jane 50; Ontario, 1871 ***1823.21*** *p153*
Hawksworth, Jno.; Maryland, 1674 ***1236.25*** *p50*
Hawley, Martha 45; Ontario, 1871 ***1823.21*** *p153*
Hawlings, Joseph 30; Ontario, 1871 ***1823.21*** *p153*
Hawman, Ann 58; Ontario, 1871 ***1823.21*** *p153*
Hawn, Phillip; Ontario, 1871 ***1823.17*** *p67*
Haworth, James; Marston's Wharf, 1782 ***8529.30*** *p12*
Hawsworth, Jno.; Maryland, 1674 ***1236.25*** *p50*
Hawthorn, Andrew 57; Ontario, 1871 ***1823.21*** *p153*
Hawthorn, John; North Carolina, 1829 ***1088.45*** *p13*
Hawthorn, Joseph 45; Ontario, 1871 ***1823.21*** *p153*
Hawthorn, Marico Maria 16; Ontario, 1871 ***1823.21*** *p153*
Hawthorne, Ann 80; Ontario, 1871 ***1823.21*** *p153*
Hawthorne, Mariah 16; Ontario, 1871 ***1823.21*** *p153*
Hay, Adam; Ohio, 1809-1852 ***4511.35*** *p21*
Hay, Alexander 78; Ontario, 1871 ***1823.17*** *p67*
Hay, Christian 28; America, 1843 ***778.6*** *p158*
Hay, Christian; Boston, 1760 ***1642*** *p48*
Hay, Daniel 70; Ontario, 1871 ***1823.17*** *p67*
Hay, Frederick; Washington, 1884 ***2770.40*** *p192*
Hay, Henry 23; Ontario, 1871 ***1823.21*** *p153*
Hay, Jane 48; Ontario, 1871 ***1823.21*** *p153*
Hay, Jane 60; Ontario, 1871 ***1823.17*** *p67*
Hay, John; Colorado, 1893 ***1029.59*** *p38*

Hay, John 86; Ontario, 1871 ***1823.21*** *p153*
Hay, Patrick; Lynn, MA, 1690 ***1642*** *p71*
Hay, Robert 54; Ontario, 1871 ***1823.17*** *p67*
Hay, Thomas; Marblehead, MA, 1755 ***1642*** *p73*
Hay, Thomas 29; Ontario, 1871 ***1823.21*** *p153*
Hay, Thomas 62; Ontario, 1871 ***1823.21*** *p153*
Hay, Thomas 68; Ontario, 1871 ***1823.17*** *p67*
Hay, Walter 39; Ontario, 1871 ***1823.21*** *p153*
Hay, Walter 47; Ontario, 1871 ***1823.17*** *p67*
Hay, William B.; Colorado, 1891 ***1029.59*** *p38*
Hayden, Anne 45; Ontario, 1871 ***1823.17*** *p67*
Hayden, Charles 35; Ontario, 1871 ***1823.17*** *p67*
Hayden, Daniel 67; Ontario, 1871 ***1823.17*** *p67*
Hayden, James 52; Ontario, 1871 ***1823.17*** *p67*
Hayden, Mathew; New Orleans, 1850 ***7242.30*** *p143*
Hayden, Sarah 50; Michigan, 1880 ***4491.42*** *p13*
Hayden, Thomas; New Orleans, 1850 ***7242.30*** *p143*
Hayden, Thos T. 40; Ontario, 1871 ***1823.21*** *p153*
Hayden, William 57; Michigan, 1880 ***4491.42*** *p13*
Hayden, William 27; Ontario, 1871 ***1823.21*** *p153*
Haye, John; Massachusetts, 1718 ***1642*** *p110*
Haye, Nancy Le Marchant De la; New York, 1868 ***9228.50*** *p33*
Haye, Robert; North Carolina, 1813 ***1088.45*** *p13*
Hayem, Moise; New Orleans, 1840 ***778.6*** *p158*
Hayer, Antoine 25; America, 1840 ***778.6*** *p158*
Hayer, Ignace 3; America, 1840 ***778.6*** *p158*
Hayer, Madelaine 28; America, 1840 ***778.6*** *p158*
Hayer, Marguerite 3 months; America, 1840 ***778.6*** *p158*
Hayes, Daniel 59; Ontario, 1871 ***1823.21*** *p153*
Hayes, Daniel 66; Ontario, 1871 ***1823.21*** *p153*
Hayes, Edmund 57; Ontario, 1871 ***1823.21*** *p153*
Hayes, Elisabeth; Newbury, MA, 1730 ***1642*** *p75*
Hayes, Elizabeth; Salisbury, MA, 1729 ***1642*** *p81*
Hayes, Eloner; Newbury, MA, 1696 ***1642*** *p74*
Hayes, Francis; Washington, 1883 ***2770.40*** *p136*
Hayes, George; Jamaica, 1780 ***8529.30*** *p13A*
Hayes, George 21; Ontario, 1871 ***1823.21*** *p153*
Hayes, George 55; Ontario, 1871 ***1823.21*** *p153*
Hayes, George; Wisconsin, 1906 ***6795.8*** *p173*
Hayes, Hannah; Boston, 1761 ***1642*** *p48*
Hayes, Isaac 65; Ontario, 1871 ***1823.21*** *p153*
Hayes, J.; California, 1868 ***1131.61*** *p89*
Hayes, James; Massachusetts, 1730 ***1642*** *p89*
Hayes, James; Newbury, MA, 1757 ***1642*** *p75*
Hayes, James 40; Ontario, 1871 ***1823.21*** *p153*
Hayes, James 16; Quebec, 1870 ***8364.32*** *p24*
Hayes, John; Boston, 1739 ***1642*** *p44*
Hayes, John; Boston, 1766 ***1642*** *p37*
Hayes, John; Massachusetts, 1754 ***1642*** *p63*
Hayes, John 28; Ontario, 1871 ***1823.21*** *p153*
Hayes, Joseph 58; Ontario, 1871 ***1823.21*** *p153*
Hayes, L. 28; Quebec, 1910 ***2897.7*** *p9*
Hayes, Margarett; Massachusetts, 1718 ***1642*** *p105*
Hayes, Mary 28; Ontario, 1871 ***1823.21*** *p154*
Hayes, Mathew 55; Ontario, 1871 ***1823.21*** *p154*
Hayes, Michael; Toronto, 1844 ***2910.35*** *p112*
Hayes, Patrick; Toronto, 1844 ***2910.35*** *p115*
Hayes, Phillip 67; Ontario, 1871 ***1823.21*** *p154*
Hayes, Richard 84; Ontario, 1871 ***1823.21*** *p154*
Hayes, Silas 45; Ontario, 1871 ***1823.17*** *p67*
Hayes, Stephen; Boston, 1765 ***1642*** *p48*
Hayes, Thomas 38; Ontario, 1871 ***1823.21*** *p154*
Hayet, Francoise 10; Quebec, 1646 ***9221.17*** *p166*
*Sister:*Marguerite 16
Hayet, Marguerite 16 *SEE* Hayet, Francoise
Haygarth, Thomas; Iowa, 1894 ***1211.15*** *p11*
Hayman, John 26; Ontario, 1871 ***1823.21*** *p154*
Hayman, William 29; Ontario, 1871 ***1823.21*** *p154*
Haymann, Rebekka 46; America, 1857 ***5475.1*** *p560*
Hayne, Edward H. 28; Ontario, 1871 ***1823.21*** *p154*
Hayne, Ellen 25; Ontario, 1871 ***1823.21*** *p154*
Hayne, George 22; Ontario, 1871 ***1823.21*** *p154*
Haynes, Cornelius; Colorado, 1900 ***1029.59*** *p38*
Haynes, Cornelius H.; New York, 1895 ***1029.59*** *p39*
Haynes, Mary 12; Quebec, 1870 ***8364.32*** *p24*
Haynie, John; Virginia, 1652 ***6254.4*** *p243*
Hayo, Anna Maria 48; America, 1873 ***5475.1*** *p58*
Hayo, Johann; America, 1837 ***5475.1*** *p56*
Hayot, Genevieve 8 *SEE* Hayot, Thomas
Hayot, Jean 2 *SEE* Hayot, Thomas
Hayot, Jeanne Boucher 31 *SEE* Hayot, Thomas
Hayot, Rodolphe 4 *SEE* Hayot, Thomas
Hayot, Thomas 29; Quebec, 1638 ***9221.17*** *p77*
*Wife:*Jeanne Boucher 31
*Son:*Jean 2
*Daughter:*Genevieve 8
*Son:*Rodolphe 4
Hays, Alas *SEE* Hays, William
Hays, Barbara; Philadelphia, 1853 ***8513.31*** *p312*
Hays, Charles *SEE* Hays, William
Hays, Daniel 30; Ontario, 1871 ***1823.17*** *p67*
Hays, Elizabeth A. 12; Ontario, 1871 ***1823.17*** *p67*
Hays, Honest E. 70; Ontario, 1871 ***1823.21*** *p154*
Hays, James; New York, 1782 ***8529.30*** *p12*
Hays, James 19; Ontario, 1871 ***1823.21*** *p154*
Hays, James 49; Ontario, 1871 ***1823.21*** *p154*
Hays, Jean; Boston, 1769 ***1642*** *p49*
Hays, John 52; Ontario, 1871 ***1823.21*** *p154*
Hays, Lawrence 77; Ontario, 1871 ***]1823.17*** *p67*
Hays, Margaret; Boston, 1750 ***1642*** *p46*
Hays, Mary *SEE* Hays, William
Hays, Patrick; Illinois, 1834-1900 ***6020.5*** *p131*
Hays, Sarah *SEE* Hays, William
Hays, Susanna; Newburyport, MA, 1766 ***1642*** *p76*
Hays, Thos 23; St. Johns, N.F., 1811 ***1053.20*** *p20*
Hays, Timothy 30; Ontario, 1871 ***1823.21*** *p154*
Hays, William; Massachusetts, 1753 ***1642*** *p108*
*Wife:*Alas
Hays, William; Massachusetts, 1766 ***1642*** *p118*
*Wife:*Mary
*Child:*Charles
*Child:*Sarah
Hays, William 33; Ontario, 1871 ***1823.21*** *p154*
Hays, Wm 35; Ontario, 1871 ***1823.21*** *p154*
Haysor, Cornelius 54; Ontario, 1871 ***1823.17*** *p67*
Haystead, David 49; Ontario, 1871 ***1823.21*** *p154*
Hayter, James 37; Ontario, 1871 ***1823.17*** *p67*
Hayto, Jacob 44; Ontario, 1871 ***1823.17*** *p67*
Hayton, John; Ontario, 1871 ***1823.21*** *p154*
Hayward, Charles 58; Ontario, 1871 ***1823.17*** *p67*
Hayward, Isaac 28; Ontario, 1871 ***1823.21*** *p154*
Hayward, James 46; Ontario, 1871 ***1823.21*** *p154*
Hayward, John 48; Ontario, 1871 ***1823.21*** *p154*
Hayward, John; Virginia, 1652 ***6254.4*** *p243*
Hayward, William 50; Ontario, 1871 ***1823.21*** *p154*
Haywood, Allen 33; Ontario, 1871 ***1823.17*** *p67*
Haywood, James; North Carolina, 1829 ***1088.45*** *p13*
Haywood, Joseph 42; Ontario, 1871 ***1823.17*** *p67*
Haywood, Martha 30; New York, NY, 1884 ***8427.14*** *p45*
Haywood, Thomas 25; Ontario, 1871 ***1823.21*** *p154*
Haywood, William 48; Ontario, 1871 ***1823.17*** *p67*
Haywood, William 67; Ontario, 1871 ***1823.17*** *p67*
Hayword, Martha 30; New York, NY, 1884 ***8427.14*** *p45*
Hazardee, H.in...ch 22; America, 1842 ***778.6*** *p158*
Hazday, Joseph; New York, NY, 1909 ***3331.4*** *p12*
Haze, Abigail; Massachusetts, 1759 ***1642*** *p111*
Haze, Hezkiah; Massachusetts, 1748 ***1642*** *p111*
Haze, James 45; Ontario, 1871 ***1823.21*** *p154*
Haze, Walter 75; Ontario, 1871 ***1823.21*** *p154*
Hazel, Benjamin; Marston's Wharf, 1782 ***8529.30*** *p12*
Hazel, John 38; Ontario, 1871 ***1823.17*** *p67*
Hazel, William 32; Ontario, 1871 ***1823.17*** *p68*
Hazen, Joseph; Detroit, 1929-1930 ***6214.5*** *p65*
Hazinski, Anna; Wisconsin, 1907 ***6795.8*** *p132*
Hazle, Benjamin; Marston's Wharf, 1782 ***8529.30*** *p12*
Hazle, John Alexander; North Carolina, 1857 ***1088.45*** *p13*
Hazlegrove, W. F. 30; Ontario, 1871 ***1823.21*** *p154*
Hazlehurst, John; New York, NY, 1778 ***8529.30*** *p2*
Hazlett, James; Ohio, 1809-1852 ***4511.35*** *p21*
Hazlett, Mathew 70; Ontario, 1871 ***1823.21*** *p154*
Hazlewood, John 35; Ontario, 1871 ***1823.21*** *p154*
Heach, Edmund 18; Portland, ME, 1911 ***970.38*** *p77*
Head, John 45; Ontario, 1871 ***1823.17*** *p68*
Head, Rachel 74; Ontario, 1871 ***1823.21*** *p154*
Head, William 18; Quebec, 1870 ***8364.32*** *p24*
Headech, William; Colorado, 1906 ***1029.59*** *p39*
Headin, James; Toronto, 1844 ***2910.35*** *p115*
Headley, John; Ohio, 1808-1873 ***9228.50*** *p278*
Headley, Robert; Portland, ME, 1885 ***9228.50*** *p404*
Headley, Susan; Boston, 1902 ***9228.50*** *p278*
Headrick, Peter 51; Ontario, 1871 ***1823.21*** *p154*
Headstrom, Lewis 22; New York, 1856 ***6529.11*** *p20*
Heague, Anthony; Philadelphia, 1777 ***8529.30*** *p3A*
Heal, James 64; Ontario, 1871 ***1823.17*** *p68*
Heal, John 29; Ontario, 1871 ***1823.17*** *p68*
Heal, Mary 50; Ontario, 1871 ***1823.21*** *p154*
Heal, Robert 43; Ontario, 1871 ***1823.17*** *p68*
Healey, Anthony; St. John, N.B., 1847 ***2978.15*** *p37*
Healey, Eliz 2; St. John, N.B., 1834 ***6469.7*** *p4*
Healey, H. P. 35; Ontario, 1871 ***1823.21*** *p154*
Healey, James; New Orleans, 1850 ***7242.30*** *p143*
Healey, John 23; Ontario, 1871 ***1823.21*** *p154*
Healey, John; St. John, N.B., 1847 ***2978.15*** *p37*
Healey, John 3 months; St. John, N.B., 1834 ***6469.7*** *p4*
Healey, Mary 17; Ontario, 1871 ***1823.21*** *p154*
Healey, Mary 25; St. John, N.B., 1834 ***6469.7*** *p4*
Healey, Mary Ann 3; St. John, N.B., 1834 ***6469.7*** *p4*
Healey, Neal 25; St. John, N.B., 1834 ***6469.7*** *p4*
Healey, Peter J. 42; Ontario, 1871 ***1823.21*** *p154*
Healey, Tim; St. John, N.B., 1847 ***2978.15*** *p36*
Healy, Henry 70; Ontario, 1871 ***1823.17*** *p68*
Healy, James; New Orleans, 1850 ***7242.30*** *p143*
Healy, John; Toronto, 1844 ***2910.35*** *p114*
Healy, Margaret 24; Ontario, 1871 ***1823.21*** *p155*
Healy, Patrick 57; Ontario, 1871 ***1823.17*** *p68*
Healy, Rosanna 57; Ontario, 1871 ***1823.21*** *p155*
Healy, Thomas 29; Ontario, 1871 ***1823.17*** *p68*
Healy, William; Boston, 1718 ***1642*** *p24*
Heamel, Daniel; Illinois, 1856 ***6079.1*** *p6*
Heaney, Jno.; St. John, N.B., 1847 ***2978.15*** *p35*
Heanry, Robert; Boston, 1766 ***1642*** *p36*
Heaps, John 38; Ontario, 1871 ***1823.21*** *p155*
Heard, Ann 24; Quebec, 1705-1706 ***9228.50*** *p278*
Heard, Anthony; North Carolina, 1817 ***1088.45*** *p13*
Heard, Benj.; New Jersey, 1690 ***9228.50*** *p278*
Heard, George 44; Ontario, 1871 ***1823.21*** *p155*
Heard, John; Maine, 1660-1669 ***9228.50*** *p278*
Heard, John; New York, 1783 ***8529.30*** *p12*
Heard, John 49; Ontario, 1871 ***1823.21*** *p155*
Heard, John; Salem, MA, 1633 ***9228.50*** *p278*
Heard, Robert 36; Ontario, 1871 ***1823.21*** *p155*
Heard, Thos, Jr. 52; Ontario, 1871 ***1823.21*** *p155*
Heard, Thos, Sr. 75; Ontario, 1871 ***1823.21*** *p155*
Heard, William; New York, 1783 ***8529.30*** *p12*
Heargarty, Thomas; Boston, 1750 ***1642*** *p46*
Hearl, Wm.; America, 1638 ***9228.50*** *p278*
Hearn, Mrs. 50; New Orleans, 1840 ***778.6*** *p158*
Hearn, Edmund; Boston, 1763 ***1642*** *p32*
Hearn, Joseph 15; Quebec, 1870 ***8364.32*** *p24*
Hearne, Michl; St. John, N.B., 1847 ***2978.15*** *p35*
Hearne, Patk; St. John, N.B., 1847 ***2978.15*** *p35*
Hearnes, Margaret; Boston, 1772 ***1642*** *p49*
Heart, James 26; Ontario, 1871 ***1823.17*** *p68*
Heartley, Mary 75; Ontario, 1871 ***1823.17*** *p68*
Heas, Elizabeth; Massachusetts, 1770 ***1642*** *p120*
Hease, Cath; New Orleans, 1851 ***7242.30*** *p143*
Heaslip, S. F.; Louisiana, 1874 ***4981.45*** *p132*
Heater, David; Long Island, 1781 ***8529.30*** *p9A*
Heath, Ann 81; Ontario, 1871 ***1823.17*** *p68*
Heath, C. H.; California, 1868 ***1131.61*** *p90*
Heath, Clement 35; Ontario, 1871 ***1823.17*** *p68*
Heath, George 49; Ontario, 1871 ***1823.21*** *p155*
Heath, Henry; New York, 1777 ***8529.30*** *p12*
Heath, Thomas 40; Ontario, 1871 ***1823.21*** *p155*
Heath, W. B. 41; Ontario, 1871 ***1823.21*** *p155*
Heathen, Andrew; North Carolina, 1837 ***1088.45*** *p13*
Heatherly, Thomas; Boston, 1774 ***8529.30*** *p2*
Heatherton, William 60; Ontario, 1871 ***1823.21*** *p155*
Heathfield, Mathew 45; Ontario, 1871 ***1823.21*** *p155*
Heatley, Abraham; New Orleans, 1850 ***7242.30*** *p143*
Heatley, Christina; New Orleans, 1850 ***7242.30*** *p143*
Heatley, Daniel; New Orleans, 1850 ***7242.30*** *p143*
Heatley, Edward; New Orleans, 1850 ***7242.30*** *p143*
Heatley, Eliza; New Orleans, 1850 ***7242.30*** *p143*
Heatley, Eliza; New Orleans, 1850 ***7242.30*** *p144*
Heatley, Fanny; New Orleans, 1850 ***7242.30*** *p144*
Heatley, Lucy; New Orleans, 1850 ***7242.30*** *p144*
Heatley, William; New Orleans, 1850 ***7242.30*** *p144*
Heaton, Elizabeth 67; Ontario, 1871 ***1823.21*** *p155*
Heaton, James; Louisiana, 1836-1840 ***4981.45*** *p212*
Heaume, Ann; Ohio, 1795-1866 ***9228.50*** *p280*
Heaume, Betsy *SEE* Heaume, Pierre, Jr.
Heaume, Charlotte *SEE* Heaume, Pierre, Jr.
Heaume, Daniel *SEE* Heaume, Pierre, Jr.
Heaume, John; Ohio, 1750-1836 ***9228.50*** *p280*
Heaume, John *SEE* Heaume, Pierre, Jr.
Heaume, Judith; Ohio, 1792-1852 ***9228.50*** *p280*
Heaume, Judith *SEE* Heaume, Pierre, Jr.
Heaume, Judith *SEE* Heaume, Pierre, Jr.
Heaume, Judith *SEE* Heaume, Pierre
Heaume, Nicholas; Ohio, 1750-1836 ***9228.50*** *p280*
Heaume, Nicholas *SEE* Heaume, Pierre, Jr.
Heaume, Pierre *SEE* Heaume, Pierre, Jr.
Heaume, Pierre; Ohio, 1832-1836 ***9228.50*** *p278*
*Wife:*Judith
Heaume, Pierre, Jr.; Ohio, 1831-1852 ***9228.50*** *p279*
*Wife:*Judith
*Child:*Nicholas
*Child:*Betsy
*Child:*Daniel
*Child:*Charlotte
*Child:*Judith
*Child:*Pierre
*Child:*John
Heavenor, William 67; Ontario, 1871 ***1823.21*** *p155*
Heazel, Benjamin; Marston's Wharf, 1782 ***8529.30*** *p12*
Hebb, William; West Virginia, 1787 ***1132.30*** *p146*
Hebbe, Julius; Wisconsin, 1897 ***6795.8*** *p133*
Hebblewaite, Alfred 45; Ontario, 1871 ***1823.21*** *p155*
Hebderig, Pierre 19; America, 1747 ***778.6*** *p158*
Hebenstreit, Max; Valdivia, Chile, 1852 ***1192.4*** *p55*
Heber, Carl Friedrich; America, 1867 ***7919.3*** *p526*
Heberer, Adam; Illinois, 1856 ***6079.1*** *p6*
Heberle, Anna Elisabetha 31; America, 1882 ***2526.43*** *p141*
Heberle, Georg 6; America, 1882 ***2526.43*** *p140*
Heberlein, H.; America, 1886 ***5475.1*** *p423*

Hebert, Adrienne 21; Montreal, 1647 *9221.17 p192*
Hebert, Anne Faulconnier 33 *SEE* Hebert, Francois
Hebert, Augustin 17; Quebec, 1637 *9221.17 p70*
Hebert, Elisabeth 22; America, 1846 *778.6 p158*
Hebert, Francois 32; Quebec, 1654 *9221.17 p310*
  *Wife:*Anne Faulconnier 33
  *Son:*Nicolas 5
Hebert, Francoise; Quebec, 1667 *4514.3 p325*
Hebert, Guillaume; Quebec, 1617 *9221.17 p19*
  With parents
Hebert, Guillemette; Quebec, 1617 *9221.17 p18*
  *Father:*Louis
  *Mother:*Marie Rollet
Hebert, Jean; Montreal, 1650 *9221.17 p231*
Hebert, Jean; Nova Scotia, 1753 *3051 p112*
  *Wife:*Veronique Sirre
Hebert, Kaffie 41; New York, NY, 1894 *6512.1 p231*
Hebert, Laurent 23; Quebec, 1655 *9221.17 p325*
Hebert, Louis; Colorado, 1884 *1029.59 p39*
Hebert, Louis 30; Missouri, 1845 *778.6 p158*
Hebert, Louis *SEE* Hebert, Guillemette
Hebert, Louis *SEE* Hebert, Marie Rollet
Hebert, Maria 11 months; America, 1846 *778.6 p158*
Hebert, Marie; Nova Scotia, 1753 *3051 p112*
Hebert, Marie; Nova Scotia, 1753 *3051 p112*
Hebert, Marie Rollet *SEE* Hebert, Guillemette
Hebert, Marie; Quebec, 1617 *9221.17 p19*
  *Husband:*Louis
Hebert, Marie-Madeleine; Quebec, 1670 *4514.3 p325*
Hebert, Nicolas 5 *SEE* Hebert, Francois
Hebert, Philippe 23; America, 1846 *778.6 p158*
Hebert, Pierre; Quebec, 1645 *9221.17 p153*
Hebert, Veronique Sirre *SEE* Hebert, Jean
Hebert, Wilfred; Colorado, 1888 *1029.59 p39*
Hebert DeBelle-Isle, Robert; Quebec, 1652 *9221.17 p259*
Hebery, John; Marston's Wharf, 1782 *8529.30 p12*
Heblethwaite, Charles 35; Ontario, 1871 *1823.21 p155*
Hebuiard, Hanna 17; America, 1848 *778.6 p158*
Hechler, Carle; Illinois, 1855 *6079.1 p6*
Hecht, Miss; America, 1875 *7420.1 p304*
Hecht, Mr.; Port uncertain, 1854 *7420.1 p121*
  With wife & 2 sons
Hecht, Anna Engel Marie Hattendorf *SEE* Hecht, Johann
  Friedrich
Hecht, August Friedrich; America, 1870 *7420.1 p395*
Hecht, Carl; America, 1858 *7420.1 p178*
  With 2 daughters wife & 3 sons
Hecht, Caroline Sophie Wilhelmine; America, 1864
  7420.1 p224
Hecht, Christian Wilhelm Conrad; America, 1864 *7420.1
  p224*
Hecht, Christine Louise Charlotte Hattendorf *SEE* Hecht,
  Heinrich Conrad
Hecht, Conrad; America, 1858 *7420.1 p178*
Hecht, Engel Maria Dorothea; America, 1859 *7420.1
  p185*
Hecht, Engel Marie; America, 1850 *7420.1 p69*
Hecht, Engel Marie Dorothea; America, 1882 *7420.1
  p329*
Hecht, Engel Marie Dorothee; America, 1866 *7420.1
  p243*
Hecht, Engel Marie Sophie Eleonore Dunnemann *SEE*
  Hecht, Johann Friedrich Christian
Hecht, Friedrich; America, 1867 *7420.1 p257*
  With family
Hecht, Friedrich Ludwig *SEE* Hecht, Johann Friedrich
Hecht, Georg Heinrich; America, 1864 *7420.1 p224*
Hecht, Georg Wilhelm; America, 1872 *7420.1 p295*
Hecht, Heinrich; America, 1859 *7420.1 p185*
Hecht, Heinrich Conrad; America, 1851 *7420.1 p80*
  *Wife:*Christine Louise Charlotte Hattendorf
  *Daughter:*Sophie Charlotte
Hecht, Heinrich Conrad Otto; America, 1882 *7420.1
  p329*
Hecht, Heinrich Friedrich Conrad *SEE* Hecht, Johann
  Friedrich
Hecht, Heinrich Friedrich Wilhelm; America, 1866
  7420.1 p243
Hecht, Johann Friedrich; America, 1844 *7420.1 p31*
  *Wife:*Anna Engel Marie Hattendorf
  *Son:*Heinrich Friedrich Conrad
  *Son:*Friedrich Ludwig
Hecht, Johann Friedrich Christ; America, 1868 *7420.1
  p272*
  With family
Hecht, Johann Friedrich Christian; America, 1857 *7420.1
  p162*
  *Wife:*Engel Marie Sophie Eleonore Dunnemann
  With daughter
  With son 10
  With son 16
Hecht, Johann Heinrich Conrad; America, 1872 *7420.1
  p295*

Hecht, Johann Heinrich Philipp; Chicago, 1883 *7420.1
  p336*
  *Wife:*Karoline Charlotte Struckmeier
Hecht, Karoline Charlotte Struckmeier *SEE* Hecht,
  Johann Heinrich Philipp
Hecht, Lewis; North Carolina, 1852 *1088.45 p13*
Hecht, Philipp; America, 1883 *7420.1 p336*
Hecht, Sophie Charlotte *SEE* Hecht, Heinrich Conrad
Hecht, Sophie Dorothee; America, 1866 *7420.1 p243*
Hecht, Sophie Louise; America, 1864 *7420.1 p224*
Hecht, Sophie Wilhelmine; America, 1867 *7420.1 p257*
Hecht, Wilhelm; Port uncertain, 1854 *7420.1 p121*
Heck, Anna 18 *SEE* Heck, Mathias
Heck, Antoine 45; Mississippi, 1846 *778.6 p158*
Heck, Christian Wilhelm 53; America, 1857 *2526.43
  p169*
  *Wife:*Christina Forstmann 48
  *Son:*Peter 13
  *Son:*Wilhelm 7
  *Son:*Jakob 10
Heck, Christina Forstmann 48 *SEE* Heck, Christian
  Wilhelm
Heck, Elisabeth Will 44 *SEE* Heck, Mathias
Heck, Ernst 19; America, 1853 *2526.43 p169*
Heck, Friederika 4; New Orleans, 1848 *778.6 p158*
Heck, Friederika 22; New Orleans, 1848 *778.6 p158*
Heck, Friedrich; America, 1845 *7420.1 p36*
  With 5 sons
Heck, Jakob 10 *SEE* Heck, Christian Wilhelm
Heck, Jakob 20 *SEE* Heck, Mathias
Heck, Joh. Georg; Chile, 1852 *1192.4 p52*
Heck, Joh. Peter 42; America, 1843 *5475.1 p261*
Heck, Marianne 42; New Orleans, 1848 *778.6 p158*
Heck, Mathias; America, 1864 *5475.1 p544*
  *Wife:*Elisabeth Will
  *Daughter:*Anna
  *Son:*Jakob
Heck, Peter 13 *SEE* Heck, Christian Wilhelm
Heck, Peter; New York, 1882 *5475.1 p517*
Heck, Pierre 1; New Orleans, 1848 *778.6 p158*
Heck, Pierre 32; New Orleans, 1848 *778.6 p158*
Heck, Rosina; America, 1752 *2526.42 p179*
Heck, Wilhelm 7 *SEE* Heck, Christian Wilhelm
Heckel, Karl; America, 1848 *5475.1 p28*
Heckelbach, Jsoeph 28; America, 1846 *778.6 p158*
Heckelbach, Madeleine 28; America, 1846 *778.6 p158*
Heckelback, Joseph 2; America, 1846 *778.6 p158*
Heckermann, Wilhelm; America, 1861 *7420.1 p205*
Heckes, Hermann; Wisconsin, 1859 *6795.8 p102*
Heckew, John; Boston, 1741 *9228.50 p273*
Heckling, Joseph; Ohio, 1809-1852 *4511.35 p21*
Hecksamer, Jacob; Ohio, 1809-1852 *4511.35 p21*
Hecot, Emile; Louisiana, 1874-1875 *4981.45 p29*
Hector, A.F.; New York, NY, 1848 *6412.40 p151*
Hector, Jakob; America, 1886 *5475.1 p197*
Hed, Isaac; Kansas, 1870-1876 *777.40 p14*
  *Son:*Jonas
Hed, Jonas *SEE* Hed, Isaac
Hed, Martha; Kansas, 1876 *777.40 p14*
Hedberg, Bernhard; St. Paul, MN, 1888 *1865.50 p49*
  *Wife:*Hilma Person
Hedberg, Gustaf; St. Paul, MN, 1887 *1865.50 p49*
Hedberg, Hilma Person *SEE* Hedberg, Bernhard
Hedblom, Jan 31; New York, 1856 *6529.11 p21*
Hedblom, Jan Marche; New York, 1857 *6529.11 p25*
  *Wife:*Kerstin Andersdotter
  With 3 sisters
Hedblom, Kerstin Andersdotter *SEE* Hedblom, Jan
  Marche
Hedde, Francis; North Carolina, 1853 *1088.45 p13*
Hedely, Vitus; Illinois, 1855 *6079.1 p6*
Hederich, Johannes; America, 1863 *8115.12 p320*
Hedges, Agustus 26; Ontario, 1871 *1823.21 p155*
Hedges, Isaac 20; Quebec, 1870 *8364.32 p24*
Hedges, Rensaler 45; Ontario, 1871 *1823.21 p155*
Hedges, Richard 45; Ontario, 1871 *1823.21 p155*
Hedin, Charlotta Halvarson *SEE* Hedin, John J.
Hedin, John J.; St. Paul, MN, 1888 *1865.50 p50*
  *Wife:*Charlotta Halvarson
Hedin, Lars Erik; Cleveland, OH, 1892-1897 *9722.10
  p120*
Hedisheimer, John; Ohio, 1809-1852 *4511.35 p21*
Hedke, Gustav; Wisconsin, 1878 *6795.8 p201*
Hedley, Mark 36; Indiana, 1886-1892 *9076.20 p73*
Hedlund, Anna 15 *SEE* Hedlund, Olof
Hedlund, Anna 45 *SEE* Hedlund, Olof
Hedlund, Christina; St. Paul, MN, 1880 *1865.50 p43*
Hedlund, Eric; Oregon, 1941 *9157.47 p2*
Hedlund, Louis 17 *SEE* Hedlund, Olof
Hedlund, Olof 45; Kansas, 1880 *777.40 p10*
  *Wife:*Anna 45
  *Son:*Louis 17
  *Daughter:*Anna 15

Hedlund, Olof 35; New York, 1856 *6529.11 p22*
Hedman, An 36; New York, 1856 *6529.11 p22*
  *Wife:*Anna Hansdotter 38
  *Daughter:*Christina Juliana 4
  *Daughter:*Anna Brita 2
Hedman, Anna Hansdotter 38 *SEE* Hedman, An
Hedman, Anna Brita 2 *SEE* Hedman, An
Hedman, Charles 53; Ontario, 1871 *1823.21 p155*
Hedman, Charley; Cleveland, OH, 1890-1893 *9722.10
  p120*
Hedman, Christina Juliana 4 *SEE* Hedman, An
Hedman, Margareta; America, 1867 *6529.11 p24*
Hedman, Mathias; St. Paul, MN, 1894 *1865.50 p50*
Hedman, Nels; Minnesota, 1880-1883 *1865.50 p50*
Hedony, Charles 24; Texas, 1848 *778.6 p158*
Hedouin, Jacques 25; Quebec, 1652 *9221.17 p259*
Hedouin, Marguerite; Quebec, 1671 *4514.3 p325*
Heeman, Thomas 45; Ontario, 1871 *1823.21 p155*
Heenan, Anthoney 48; Ontario, 1871 *1823.21 p155*
Heenan, Antoney 49; Ontario, 1871 *1823.21 p155*
Heenan, Denis 80; Ontario, 1871 *1823.21 p155*
Heenan, John 76; Ontario, 1871 *1823.21 p155*
Heer, Ewald; Canada, 1930 *8023.44 p374*
Heering, Maria Anna; Venezuela, 1843 *3899.5 p540*
Heermann, F. W.; America, 1838 *7420.1 p14*
Heermeyer, Martha; America, 1894 *7420.1 p370*
Heese, Chas; Nebraska, 1905 *3004.30 p46*
Heesemann, Chat. Eliese 52; New York, NY, 1864
  8425.62 p196
Heesemann, Chatarina Friedr. 18; New York, NY, 1864
  8425.62 p196
Heesemann, Fr. Wilhelm 9; New York, NY, 1864
  8425.62 p196
Heesemann, Fr. Wm. 52; New York, NY, 1864 *8425.62
  p196*
Heesemann, Franziska Henr. 21; New York, NY, 1864
  8425.62 p196
Heess, Sebastian; Venezuela, 1843 *3899.5 p541*
Hefchac, Ant. 24; America, 1841 *778.6 p158*
Hefener, Johann Georg; Nova Scotia, 1784 *7105 p23*
Heff, Louis 41; Ohio, 1847 *778.6 p158*
Heffel, Jacob 18; Texas, 1913 *8425.16 p31*
Heffelfinger, Bernard; Ohio, 1809-1852 *4511.35 p21*
Heffernan, Dennis; Toronto, 1844 *2910.35 p112*
Heffernan, John 25; St. Johns, N.F., 1811 *1053.20 p22*
Heffinger, Nikolaus; California, 1890 *5475.1 p195*
Hefflefinger, Bernard; Ohio, 1809-1852 *4511.35 p21*
Heffne, Alexander; Portland, ME, 1911 *970.38 p77*
Heffner, Fredrik 29; Portland, ME, 1911 *970.38 p77*
Heffner, John; Nova Scotia, 1784 *7105 p23*
Heffner, Mary 27; Portland, ME, 1911 *970.38 p77*
Hefke, Ernst; Ohio, 1840-1897 *8365.35 p16*
Hefling, George; New York, 1778 *8529.30 p6*
Hefner, . . .; West Virginia, 1865-1879 *1132.30 p150*
Hefner, Daniel; West Virginia, 1868 *1132.30 p149*
Hefner, James; West Virginia, 1868 *1132.30 p149*
Hefs, Charles F.; Washington, 1874 *2770.40 p134*
Hegan, John; St. John, N.B., 1847 *2978.15 p37*
Hegan, Mary; Boston, 1746 *1642 p46*
Hegel, Rosimmur; Halifax, N.S., 1902 *1860.4 p40*
Hegele, Anton 1; New York, NY, 1886 *8425.16 p33*
Hegele, Emanuel 37; New York, NY, 1886 *8425.16 p33*
Hegele, Emil 7; New York, NY, 1886 *8425.16 p33*
Hegele, Franz 2; New York, NY, 1886 *8425.16 p33*
Hegele, Franz Josef 4; New York, NY, 1886 *8425.16 p33*
Hegele, Jacob 8; New York, NY, 1886 *8425.16 p33*
Hegele, Janatz 10; New York, NY, 1886 *8425.16 p33*
Hegele, Margarethe 36; New York, NY, 1886 *8425.16
  p33*
Hegele, Peter 3 months; New York, NY, 1886 *8425.16
  p33*
Hegele, Thomas 5; New York, NY, 1886 *8425.16 p33*
Hegener, . . .; America, n.d. *8023.44 p374*
Hegerhorst, . . .; America, 1841 *7420.1 p22*
Heggele, Christiana Gross *SEE* Heggele, Frederick
Heggele, Frederick; Philadelphia, 1852 *8513.31 p312*
  *Wife:*Christiana Gross
Heggen, Rasmus S.; Iowa, 1888 *1211.15 p11*
Heggi, Theophile I.; Illinois, 1852 *6079.1 p6*
Hegi, J. 27; New Orleans, 1834 *1002.51 p112*
Hegman, Albert E.; St. Paul, MN, 1887-1894 *1865.50
  p49*
Hegman, Alma Maria *SEE* Hegman, Carl
Hegman, Carl; St. Paul, MN, 1887 *1865.50 p49*
  *Wife:*Alma Maria
Hegman, Johanna Maria *SEE* Hegman, John L.
Hegman, John L.; St. Paul, MN, 1886 *1865.50 p49*
  *Wife:*Johanna Maria
Hehl, Richard 19; New York, 1899 *5475.1 p40*
Hehner, Heinrich; America, 1890 *2526.42 p151*
Hehner, Johann Georg; America, 1859 *2526.42 p151*
Hehr, Nicholas; Ohio, 1809-1852 *4511.35 p20*
Hehse, Hugo; Chicago, 1885 *5475.1 p131*

Heibler, Maria Magdalena; Venezuela, 1843 *3899.5 p540*
Heick, John Fred; Iowa, 1895 *1211.15 p11*
Heid, Adam; America, 1883 *2526.43 p190*
Heidacker, Ferdinand 16; America, 1851 *5475.1 p479*
Heidacker, Josef; America, 1839 *5475.1 p470*
Heidacker, Karl; America, 1847 *5475.1 p474*
Heidecke, Fredrick; New York, 1860 *358.56 p150*
Heidemann, Caroline; America, 1861 *7420.1 p205*
Heidemann, Friedrich; America, 1861 *7420.1 p206*
  With wife & son & 3 daughters
Heidemann, Friedrich; America, 1888 *7420.1 p356*
  With wife
  *Brother:*Wilhelm
Heidemann, Heinrich Dietrich; Port uncertain, 1887
  7420.1 p353
Heidemann, Heinrich Friedrich; Port uncertain, 1882
  7420.1 p329
Heidemann, Wilhelm *SEE* Heidemann, Friedrich
Heiden, H.; New York, 1860 *358.56 p6*
Heidenreich, Adam; America, 1883 *2526.43 p123*
Heidenreich, Jakob; America, 1884 *2526.43 p123*
Heidenreich, Johann Leonhard; America, 1882 *2526.43*
  p123
Heidenreich, Johannes; America, 1880 *2526.43 p123*
Heidenreich, Peter; America, 1884 *2526.43 p123*
Heidenrich, Henry; Ohio, 1844 *2763.1 p8*
Heider, Caroline 22; New Orleans, 1847 *778.6 p158*
Heider, Jacob 26; New Orleans, 1847 *778.6 p158*
Heider, Valentin 1; New Orleans, 1847 *778.6 p158*
Heiderich, Christian 26; Brazil, 1859 *5475.1 p545*
Heidet, Anna 25; Galveston, TX, 1844 *3967.10 p373*
Heidet, Johann Klaudius Franz 32; Galveston, TX, 1844
  3967.10 p373
Heidle, Hans Jerg, Jr.; New Jersey, 1754-1774 *927.31 p3*
Heidle, Hans Jerg, Sr.; New Jersey, 1754-1774 *927.31 p3*
Heidley, George; New Jersey, 1754-1774 *927.31 p3*
Heidmann, Carl; America, 1862 *7420.1 p212*
  With family
Heidmann, Friedrich; America, 1861 *7420.1 p206*
Heidorn, Miss; Port uncertain, 1880 *7420.1 p316*
Heidorn, Mr.; America, 1882 *7420.1 p329*
Heidorn, Friedrich August Christian; America, 1849
  7420.1 p65
Heidorn, Heinrich Dietrich Friedrich; America, 1883
  7420.1 p336
Heidorn, Heinrich Dietrich Friedrich; America, 1888
  7420.1 p356
Heidorn, Wilhelmine; America, 1844 *7420.1 p31*
Heier, Anna Auguste; Wisconsin, 1884 *6795.8 p81*
Heier, Friedrich Karl; America, 1870 *2526.43 p169*
Heier, Markus Maximilian; America, 1868 *2526.43 p169*
Heierberg, Johann Hermann Friedrich; America, 1860
  7420.1 p194
Heierding, Friedrich Ernst; America, 1894 *7420.1 p370*
Heig, Antoine 26; America, 1847 *778.6 p158*
Heighton, John 36; Ontario, 1871 *1823.17 p68*
Heighway, Thomas 34; Ontario, 1871 *1823.21 p155*
Heikkila, John 42; Minnesota, 1925 *2769.54 p1378*
Heil, Adam 29; Portland, ME, 1911 *970.38 p77*
Heil, Amelia 1; Portland, ME, 1911 *970.38 p77*
Heil, Anna; America, 1892 *170.15 p27*
Heil, Anna 26; Portland, ME, 1911 *970.38 p77*
Heil, Antoine 19; Port uncertain, 1844 *778.6 p158*
Heil, Barbara *SEE* Heil, Mathias
Heil, Barbara Hockert *SEE* Heil, Mathias
Heil, Barbara 2; America, 1847 *778.6 p158*
Heil, Catherine; New Orleans, 1847 *778.6 p159*
Heil, Elisabeth 28; America, 1847 *778.6 p159*
Heil, Fr. 55; New York, NY, 1893 *1883.7 p39*
Heil, Francois 35; America, 1847 *778.6 p159*
Heil, Franz 25; America, 1871 *5475.1 p202*
Heil, Frederick; New Orleans, 1844 *778.6 p159*
Heil, Friedrich 26; New York, NY, 1893 *1883.7 p39*
Heil, Jacob 3; New York, NY, 1893 *1883.7 p39*
Heil, Jacob 16; New York, NY, 1893 *1883.7 p39*
Heil, Johann *SEE* Heil, Mathias
Heil, Johann 16; America, 1863 *5475.1 p338*
Heil, Karl Franz 27; America, 1881 *2526.43 p170*
Heil, Katha. 19; New York, NY, 1893 *1883.7 p39*
Heil, Louise 67; New York, NY, 1893 *1883.7 p39*
Heil, Marga. 9; New York, NY, 1893 *1883.7 p39*
Heil, Marga. 9; New York, NY, 1893 *1883.7 p39*
Heil, Margethe *SEE* Heil, Mathias
Heil, Margtha 1 months; New York, NY, 1893 *1883.7
  p39*
Heil, Margtha. 26; New York, NY, 1893 *1883.7 p39*
Heil, Mathias *SEE* Heil, Mathias
Heil, Mathias 48; America, 1864 *5475.1 p338*
  *Wife:*Barbara Hockert
  *Daughter:*Barbara
  With daughter
  *Daughter:*Margarethe

*Son:*Mathias
*Son:*Johann
Heil, Peter 59; New York, NY, 1893 *1883.7 p39*
Heil, Theresia 43; New York, NY, 1893 *1883.7 p39*
Heilbrouner, Lazarus; North Carolina, 1855 *1088.45 p13*
Heilich, Johann 33; Louisiana, 1848 *778.6 p159*
Heilig, Peter; America, 1867 *5475.1 p120*
Heilmann, Andreas; America, 1867 *2526.43 p147*
  *Uncle:*Georg Heinrich
Heilmann, Georg Heinrich *SEE* Heilmann, Andreas
Heilmann, Kath. Lisabeth 25; America, 1854 *2526.43
  p203*
Heilmann, Michael; America, 1836 *2526.42 p105*
  With wife
  With child 5
  With child 9
Heily, Henry; Massachusetts, 1771 *1642 p100*
Heim, Basil; Kansas, 1917-1918 *1826.15 p81*
Heim, Christina 20; New York, 1856 *2526.43 p205*
Heim, Christine Kocher *SEE* Heim, John Frederick
Heim, Franz Anton *SEE* Heim, Franz Leopold
Heim, Franz Leopold; Venezuela, 1843 *3899.5 p545*
  *Wife:*Maria Anna Fees
  *Brother:*Franz Anton
  *Brother:*Johann Georg Anton
Heim, Hans Jorg; New Jersey, 1751-1774 *927.31 p3*
Heim, Johann Georg Anton *SEE* Heim, Franz Leopold
Heim, John Frederick; Philadelphia, 1839 *8513.31 p313*
  *Wife:*Christine Kocher
Heim, Maria Anna Fees *SEE* Heim, Franz Leopold
Heiman, Frank; Nebraska, 1905 *3004.30 p46*
Heimann, Anna Maas *SEE* Heimann, Richard
Heimann, Christian 22; Philadelphia, 1880 *5475.1 p14*
Heimann, Katharina *SEE* Heimann, Richard
Heimann, Maria Anna; Ohio, 1891 *5475.1 p162*
Heimann, Richard; America, 1882 *5475.1 p229*
  *Wife:*Anna Maas
  *Daughter:*Katharina
Heimann, Samuel 17; Louisiana, 1848 *778.6 p159*
Heimb, Anna Maria Goggel *SEE* Heimb, Anton
Heimb, Anton; Venezuela, 1843 *3899.5 p545*
  *Wife:*Anna Maria Goggel
Heimbach, Anna Maria Oswald 25 *SEE* Heimbach, Josef
Heimbach, Johann; America, 1843 *5475.1 p305*
  With wife & son
Heimbach, Johann; America, 1881 *5475.1 p300*
Heimbach, Josef 32; America, 1867 *5475.1 p296*
  *Wife:*Anna Maria Oswald 25
  *Son:*Nikolaus
Heimbach, Nikolaus *SEE* Heimbach, Josef
Heimberger, . . .; North Carolina, 1710 *3629.40 p4*
Heimberger, Elisabt. 26; America, 1847 *778.6 p159*
Heimbold, Paul; America, 1867 *7919.3 p526*
Heime, Frantz 18; New Orleans, 1846 *778.6 p159*
Heimert, Georg Caspar; America, 1867 *7919.3 p524*
  With wife & 2 children
Heimpel, Christian; New York, 1778 *8529.30 p3A*
Heimrod, Georg; America, 1865 *7420.1 p231*
Heimrod, Joachim Ludwig; America, 1868 *7420.1 p272*
Heimsot, Friedrich Heinrich Christian; Wisconsin, 1847
  7420.1 p53
  With 2 daughters
  *Wife:*Sophie Wilhelmine Louise Prasuhn
Heimsot, Sophie Wilhelmine Louise Prasuhn *SEE*
  Heimsot, Friedrich Heinrich Christian
Hein, A.; New York, 1860 *358.56 p3*
Hein, August; Iowa, 1888 *1211.15 p11*
Hein, August; Wisconsin, 1894 *6795.8 p90*
Hein, Charle 38; New Orleans, 1848 *778.6 p159*
Hein, Emma 20; Portland, ME, 1911 *970.38 p77*
Hein, Emma; Wisconsin, 1897 *6795.8 p92*
Hein, Hermann; Wisconsin, 1908 *1822.55 p10*
Hein, J.; Port uncertain, 1844 *778.6 p159*
Hein, Jacob; Colorado, 1898 *1029.59 p39*
Hein, Johann 24; America, 1855 *5475.1 p317*
  *Sister:*Magdalena 21
Hein, Johann 27; America, 1864 *5475.1 p311*
Hein, Joseph 24; Louisiana, 1848 *778.6 p159*
Hein, Julius; Iowa, 1896 *1211.15 p11*
Hein, Louisa; Wisconsin, 1891 *6795.8 p33*
Hein, Magdalena 21 *SEE* Hein, Johann
Hein, Margarethe; America, 1867 *7919.3 p532*
  With daughter & 3 children
Hein, Michel 31; Missouri, 1848 *778.6 p159*
Hein, Nikolaus 29; America, 1885 *5475.1 p319*
Hein, Paul; Ohio, 1809-1852 *4511.35 p21*
Hein, Reimer Jacob; Iowa, 1913 *1211.15 p11*
Heinbuch, Christe. 17; New York, NY, 1885 *1883.7 p46*
Heinbuch, Christe. 20; New York, NY, 1885 *1883.7 p46*
Heinbuch, Johannes 23; New York, NY, 1885 *1883.7
  p46*
Heindl, Ernst; Chile, 1852 *1192.4 p54*
Heine, . . .; America, 1844 *7420.1 p31*

Heine, Armand; Louisiana, 1841-1844 *4981.45 p210*
Heine, Carl Adolf Friedrich; Missouri, 1882 *7420.1 p329*
Heine, Charles; New York, 1860 *358.56 p150*
Heine, Christian; America, 1848 *7420.1 p60*
  With wife & 2 children
  With son 13
Heine, Christian; America, 1857 *7420.1 p163*
  With wife son & daughter
Heine, Engel Marie; America, 1855 *7420.1 p137*
Heine, Engel Marie; Port uncertain, 1854 *7420.1 p121*
Heine, Engel Marie Eleonore Kromer *SEE* Heine,
  Friedrich Wilhelm
Heine, Engel Marie Philippine; America, 1845 *7420.1
  p36*
  *Sister:*Ernestine Philippine
Heine, Ernestine Philippine *SEE* Heine, Engel Marie
  Philippine
Heine, Ernst Friedrich Gottlieb; America, 1861 *7420.1
  p206*
Heine, Friedrich Wilhelm; America, 1862 *7420.1 p212*
  *Wife:*Engel Marie Eleonore Kromer
  With 2 daughters & 2 sons
Heine, Georg Friedrich; America, 1884 *7420.1 p343*
Heine, Hans Heinrich; America, 1850 *7420.1 p72*
Heine, Heinrich; Baltimore, 1914 *7420.1 p394*
Heine, Heinrich Christoph; America, 1852 *7420.1 p89*
Heine, Heinrich Friedrich Gottlieb; America, 1860 *7420.1
  p194*
Heine, Hermann *SEE* Heine, Leopold
Heine, Joseph; America, 1869 *7420.1 p280*
Heine, Leopold; America, 1870 *7420.1 p284*
  *Brother:*Hermann
Heine, Margarete; Baltimore, 1914 *7420.1 p394*
Heine, Maria; Baltimore, 1908 *7420.1 p384*
Heine, Michel; Louisiana, 1841-1844 *4981.45 p210*
Heine, Sophie; America, 1855 *7420.1 p137*
Heine, Sophie; America, 1903 *7420.1 p379*
  *Son:*Ernst Friedrich Wilhelm
  *Daughter:*Caroline
Heine, Therese; Baltimore, 1914 *7420.1 p394*
Heine, W.; America, 1852 *7420.1 p89*
  With wife & son
Heine, Wilhelm; America, 1857 *7420.1 p163*
Heine, Wilhelmine Auguste Dorothea; America, 1862
  7420.1 p212
Heineman, Frederick; Ohio, 1809-1852 *4511.35 p21*
Heinemann, Otto; Cincinnati, 1852 *7420.1 p89*
Heinemann, Pauline; New York, 1859 *358.56 p55*
Heinemeyer, Carl August Eduard; Dakota, 1885 *7420.1
  p347*
Heinemeyer, Carl Heinrich Ludwig Eduard August
  Christian; Dakota, 1885 *7420.1 p343*
  *Wife:*Dorothea Sophie Anna Strobel
Heinemeyer, Dorothea Sophie Anna Strobel *SEE*
  Heinemeyer, Carl Heinrich Ludwig Eduard August
  Christian
Heinemeyer, Ernst August; America, 1868 *7420.1 p272*
Heinemeyer, Georg Wilhelm; America, 1870 *7420.1
  p284*
Heinen, Anna Gertrud 10 *SEE* Heinen, Josef
Heinen, Heinrich; Brazil, 1862 *5475.1 p518*
Heinen, Johann; Brazil, 1862 *5475.1 p518*
Heinen, Josef 31; America, 1867 *5475.1 p49*
  *Wife:*Maria Muller 36
  *Daughter:*Anna Gertrud 10 months
  *Daughter:*Katharina 3
Heinen, Karl; Brazil, 1862 *5475.1 p518*
Heinen, Katharina 3 *SEE* Heinen, Josef
Heinen, Margarethe 47; Brazil, 1862 *5475.1 p518*
Heinen, Maria Muller 36 *SEE* Heinen, Josef
Heinen, Maria; Pittsburgh, 1882 *5475.1 p35*
Heinen, P. Jakob; Brazil, 1862 *5475.1 p518*
Heinen, Peter; Brazil, 1862 *5475.1 p518*
Heinen, Peter Jakob 46; Brazil, 1862 *5475.1 p518*
  *Wife:*Margarethe Heinen 47
  *Son:*Peter
  *Son:*Heinrich
  *Son:*Karl
  *Son:*Johann
  *Son:*P. Jakob
Heinerich, Maria Anna; Venezuela, 1843 *3899.5 p542*
Heinert, Valentin; America, 1868 *7919.3 p533*
Heines, Miss 19; Cuba, 1840 *778.6 p159*
Heinfeltz, Johan 30; America, 1842 *778.6 p159*
Heinichen, Ernst Wilhelm Arnold; Port uncertain, 1876
  7420.1 p307
Heinick, Carl Friedrich Reinhold; America, 1867 *7919.3
  p531*
Heinicke, Carl Friedrich Gottlieb; America, 1868 *7919.3
  p529*
Heinicke, Wilhelm; America, 1867 *7919.3 p529*
  With wife
Heinis, Franz 18; America, 1843 *778.6 p159*

Heinlein, John; New York, 1860 *358.56 p5*
Heinlicht, Emilie 5; New York, NY, 1894 *6512.1 p231*
Heinlicht, Henriette 38; New York, NY, 1894 *6512.1 p231*
Heinlicht, Julianna 16; New York, NY, 1894 *6512.1 p231*
Heinlicht, Karl 2; New York, NY, 1894 *6512.1 p231*
Heinlicht, Ludwig 14; New York, NY, 1894 *6512.1 p231*
Heinlicht, Mathilde 10; New York, NY, 1894 *6512.1 p231*
Heinrich, Ms.; New York, NY, 1909 *7420.1 p385*
Heinrich, Benedikt; Venezuela, 1843 *3899.5 p541*
Heinrich, Elisabeth 35; America, 1866 *5475.1 p535*
Heinrich, Heribert; Venezuela, 1843 *3899.5 p541*
Heinrich, J.; North America, 1840 *5475.1 p204*
Heinrich, Jakob *SEE* Heinrich, Johann Peter
Heinrich, Joh. Peter *SEE* Heinrich, Johann Peter
Heinrich, Johan Otto; Illinois, 1860 *6079.1 p6*
Heinrich, Johann 12 *SEE* Heinrich, Margarethe Funk
Heinrich, Johann Peter; Brazil, 1862 *5475.1 p519*
  *Wife:*Maria Juliana Hahn
  *Daughter:*Margarethe
  *Son:*Jakob
  *Son:*Joh. Peter
Heinrich, L.; Valdivia, Chile, 1850 *1192.4 p50*
Heinrich, Margarethe *SEE* Heinrich, Johann Peter
Heinrich, Margarethe; Brazil, 1864 *5475.1 p500*
  *Son:*Peter
  *Daughter:*Margarethe
  *Son:*Johann
  *Son:*Nikolaus
Heinrich, Margarethe 6 *SEE* Heinrich, Margarethe Funk
Heinrich, Maria Anna; Venezuela, 1843 *3899.5 p541*
Heinrich, Maria Anna; Venezuela, 1843 *3899.5 p542*
Heinrich, Maria Juliana Hahn *SEE* Heinrich, Johann Peter
Heinrich, Martin; Illinois, 1851 *6079.1 p6*
Heinrich, Michael; Venezuela, 1843 *3899.5 p541*
Heinrich, Nikolaus 10 *SEE* Heinrich, Margarethe Funk
Heinrich, Otto; Illinois, 1930 *121.35 p100*
Heinrich, Peter 18 *SEE* Heinrich, Margarethe Funk
Heinrichsohn, Christina 65; New York, NY, 1886 *6954.7 p41*
Heinrichsohn, Dorothea 16; New York, NY, 1886 *6954.7 p41*
Heinrichsohn, Theador 18; New York, NY, 1886 *6954.7 p41*
Heins, Eva 34; Texas, 1913 *8425.16 p31*
Heins, John F.; North Carolina, 1854-1856 *1088.45 p13*
Heinsberger, Phillip; North Carolina, 1855 *1088.45 p13*
Heinsch, Robert; Washington, 1880 *2770.40 p134*
Heinsohn, Carl; Valdivia, Chile, 1851 *1192.4 p51*
Heintz, Christian; America, 1880 *5475.1 p396*
Heintz, Friedrich 16 *SEE* Heintz, Valentin
Heintz, Louise 19 *SEE* Heintz, Valentin
Heintz, Philip; Ohio, 1840-1897 *8365.35 p16*
Heintz, Valentin; America, 1880 *5475.1 p464*
  *Daughter:*Louise
  *Son:*Friedrich
Heintze, Johan August; Cleveland, OH, 1894-1896 *9722.10 p120*
Heinz, Anna Maria 35; America, 1856 *5475.1 p289*
Heinz, Anthony; Long Island, 1781 *8529.30 p9A*
Heinz, Anton; America, 1872 *5475.1 p265*
Heinz, Daniel; America, 1861 *5475.1 p521*
Heinz, Elisabeth 56; Brazil, 1862 *5475.1 p561*
Heinz, Friedrich; America, 1882 *179.55 p19*
Heinz, Friedrike Arnold *SEE* Heinz, Johann Jakob
Heinz, Jacob; Colorado, 1895 *1029.59 p39*
Heinz, Jacob; Colorado, 1898 *1029.59 p39*
Heinz, Jakob; America, 1861 *5475.1 p521*
Heinz, Jakob *SEE* Heinz, Johann Jakob
Heinz, Johann Jakob 26; Brazil, 1862 *5475.1 p561*
  *Wife:*Friedrike Arnold
  *Son:*Jakob
Heinz, Johann Philipp; Brazil, 1862 *5475.1 p561*
  *Wife:*Karoline Gillmann
Heinz, Joseph 30; New York, NY, 1893 *1883.7 p41*
Heinz, Julianna 10; Portland, ME, 1906 *970.38 p77*
Heinz, Karoline Gillmann *SEE* Heinz, Johann Philipp
Heinz, Leopolde 2; New York, NY, 1893 *1883.7 p41*
Heinz, Ludwig; America, 1881 *5475.1 p117*
  *Wife:*Margarethe Kirsch
Heinz, Margaretha 24; New York, NY, 1893 *1883.7 p41*
Heinz, Margarethe Kirsch *SEE* Heinz, Ludwig
Heinz, Maria; Brazil, 1862 *5475.1 p561*
Heinz, Mathias 34; America, 1869 *5475.1 p298*
Heinz, Philip; Ohio, 1809-1852 *4511.35 p21*
Heinz, Regina 11 months; New York, NY, 1893 *1883.7 p41*
Heinz, Susanna; America, 1869 *5475.1 p139*
Heinze, Marie 40; Portland, ME, 1906 *970.38 p77*
Heinzelmann, John; New York, 1859 *358.56 p54*

Heinzenberger, Amanda; Valdivia, Chile, 1851 *1192.4 p51*
  With 2 children
Heinzmann, Anna 28; Baltimore, 1889 *8425.16 p35*
Heinzmann, Emelia 6 months; Baltimore, 1889 *8425.16 p35*
Heinzmann, Franz 29; Baltimore, 1889 *8425.16 p35*
Heiring, George; Ohio, 1809-1852 *4511.35 p21*
Heisdorf, Anna Klein *SEE* Heisdorf, Valentin
Heisdorf, Johann *SEE* Heisdorf, Valentin
Heisdorf, Katharina *SEE* Heisdorf, Valentin
Heisdorf, Nikolaus *SEE* Heisdorf, Valentin
Heisdorf, Peter *SEE* Heisdorf, Valentin
Heisdorf, Valentin; America, 1867 *5475.1 p343*
  *Wife:*Anna Klein
  *Daughter:*Katharina
  *Son:*Johann
  *Son:*Peter
  *Son:*Nikolaus
Heise, Carl; Valdivia, Chile, 1852 *1192.4 p55*
Heise, Friedr.; Valdivia, Chile, 1852 *1192.4 p55*
Heisel, A. Margarethe 18 *SEE* Heisel, Peter
Heisel, Anna Speicher *SEE* Heisel, Jakob
Heisel, Eva Buss *SEE* Heisel, Peter
Heisel, Jakob; America, 1836 *5475.1 p65*
  *Wife:*Anna Speicher
  *Son:*Jakob
  *Son:*Johann
Heisel, Jakob 1 *SEE* Heisel, Jakob
Heisel, Johann; America, 1838 *5475.1 p67*
Heisel, Johann 3 *SEE* Heisel, Jakob
Heisel, Josef; America, 1869 *5475.1 p361*
Heisel, Magdalena 22 *SEE* Heisel, Peter
Heisel, Margarethe 20 *SEE* Heisel, Peter
Heisel, Maria 6 *SEE* Heisel, Peter
Heisel, Peter; America, 1873 *5475.1 p361*
  *Wife:*Eva Buss
  *Daughter:*Margarethe
  *Daughter:*A. Margarethe
  *Daughter:*Maria
  *Daughter:*Magdalena
Heisen, Philip; Ohio, 1809-1852 *4511.35 p21*
Heiser, Anna Breit 50 *SEE* Heiser, Peter
Heiser, Anna Maria 12 *SEE* Heiser, Peter
Heiser, Elisabeth 40; America, 1855 *5475.1 p317*
Heiser, Friderika; Wisconsin, 1898 *6795.8 p47*
Heiser, George; Ohio, 1809-1852 *4511.35 p21*
Heiser, Johannetta 20 *SEE* Heiser, Peter
Heiser, Peter 50; America, 1855 *5475.1 p318*
  *Wife:*Anna Breit 50
  *Daughter:*Johannetta 20
  *Daughter:*Anna Maria 12
Heisermann, Christian; New York, 1859 *358.56 p54*
Heisser, Amelie 5; Mississippi, 1845-1846 *778.6 p159*
Heisser, Catherine 30; Mississippi, 1845-1846 *778.6 p159*
Heist, Ernst Georg; America, 1883 *2526.43 p170*
Heist, Margaretha; America, 1867 *2526.43 p170*
Heist, Sophie; America, 1867 *2526.43 p170*
Heisterberg, Hans Heinr. Christ. *SEE* Heisterberg, Johann Heinrich Christoph
Heisterberg, Hans Heinrich; America, 1848 *7420.1 p60*
Heisterberg, Johann Heinrich Christoph; America, 1845 *7420.1 p37*
  *Wife:*Maria Dorothea Gummer
  *Daughter:*Sophia Doroth.
  *Son:*Wilhelm Christoph
  *Son:*Hans Heinr. Christ.
  *Son:*Johann Otto
Heisterberg, Johann Otto *SEE* Heisterberg, Johann Heinrich Christoph
Heisterberg, Maria Dorothea Gummer *SEE* Heisterberg, Johann Heinrich Christoph
Heisterberg, Sophia Doroth. *SEE* Heisterberg, Johann Heinrich Christoph
Heisterberg, Wilhelm Christoph *SEE* Heisterberg, Johann Heinrich Christoph
Heisterhagen, Friedrich Wilhelm Adolph; America, 1874 *7420.1 p303*
Heisterhagen, Heinrich Friedrich Hugo; America, 1878 *7420.1 p310*
Heisterhagen, Helene; America, 1883 *7420.1 p336*
Heisterhagen, Louis; America, NY, 1876 *7420.1 p307*
Heisterhagen, Louis Heinrich August *SEE* Heisterhagen, Viktor Louis
Heisterhagen, Viktor Louis; America, 1870 *7420.1 p287*
  *Brother:*Louis Heinrich August
Heisterhagen, Wilhelmine; America, 1858 *7420.1 p178*
Heiter, John 30; Ontario, 1871 *1823.17 p68*
Heith, Jean 24; America, 1845 *778.6 p159*
Heitmann, H.; Venezuela, 1843 *3899.5 p546*
Heitsmann, Florence; Ohio, 1809-1852 *4511.35 p21*
Heitz, Berthold; Louisiana, 1874-1875 *4981.45 p29*

Heitz, Jean 26; New Orleans, 1848 *778.6 p159*
Heitz, Margarethe; Illinois, 1885 *5475.1 p147*
Heitzelmann, . . . 20; New Castle, DE, 1817-1818 *90.20 p151*
Heitzelmann, Magdalena *SEE* Heitzelmann, Mathaus
Heitzelmann, Mathaus; North Dakota, 1885-1887 *554.30 p26*
  *Wife:*Magdalena
Heitzmann, Xavier 28; Port uncertain, 1848 *778.6 p159*
Heizelman, Catharina 20; America, 1847 *778.6 p159*
Heizelman, Clara 56; America, 1847 *778.6 p159*
Heizelman, Jacob 17; America, 1847 *778.6 p159*
Heizelman, Valentin 14; America, 1847 *778.6 p159*
Heizer, David; Long Island, 1781 *8529.30 p9A*
Hejl, Josef; South Dakota, 1869-1871 *2853.20 p246*
Hel, Johann 43; New Castle, DE, 1817-1818 *90.20 p151*
Helander, C.W.; New York, NY, 1845 *6412.40 p149*
Helard, Jean; Quebec, 1650 *9221.17 p227*
Helbig, Maria; America, 1868 *7919.3 p533*
Helbing, Babette; America, 1868 *7919.3 p533*
Helble, Cassimer; Ohio, 1809-1852 *4511.35 p21*
Helchinger, Johannes; Venezuela, 1843 *3899.5 p544*
Helchinger, Magdalena; Venezuela, 1843 *3899.5 p544*
Helchlinger, Johannes; Venezuela, 1843 *3899.5 p544*
Helchlinger, Magdalena; Venezuela, 1843 *3899.5 p544*
Helchowska, Klementyna; Detroit, 1929 *1640.55 p117*
Held, Carl Gottfried; Port uncertain, 1850 *7420.1 p72*
Held, Carl Ludwig; Wisconsin, 1854 *6795.8 p47*
Held, Friedrich; England, 1907 *7420.1 p382*
Held, Gottfd.; Valdivia, Chile, 1852 *1192.4 p54*
  With wife & child
  With child 6
  With child 14
Held, Hermann 28; Wisconsin, 1926 *1822.55 p10*
Held, Karl Wilhelm Ludwig; America, 1882 *7420.1 p329*
Held, Philip; Ohio, 1809-1852 *4511.35 p21*
Held, Pierre 24; New York, NY, 1847 *9176.15 p51*
Held, Sophie Wilhelmine Justine Charlotte; America, 1870 *7420.1 p395*
Heldebront, Cristophel; New Jersey, 1740-1774 *927.31 p3*
Heldt, Alois; Ohio, 1809-1852 *4511.35 p21*
Heldt, Alois; Ohio, 1809-1852 *4511.35 p22*
Heldt, John A.; Iowa, 1888 *1211.15 p11*
Hele, Jacques; Quebec, 1659 *9221.17 p413*
Heleles, Andres 27; Louisiana, 1848 *778.6 p159*
Helerigel, Benedict 24; America, 1845 *778.6 p159*
Helf, Peter; Boston, 1832 *3274.55 p72*
Helfen, Elisabeth; America, 1882 *5475.1 p315*
Helfer, Peter; Ohio, 1809-1852 *4511.35 p22*
Helfers, Henry; Missouri, 1869 *3276.1 p4*
Helgen, Anton 36; Galveston, TX, 1844 *3967.10 p371*
Helgeson, Charles G.; St. Paul, MN, 1874-1900 *1865.50 p50*
Helgeson, Jenny Kristina; St. Paul, MN, 1900 *1865.50 p50*
Helier, Rachel Judith; Nova Scotia, 1852 *9228.50 p357*
Helix, Louis H.; Illinois, 1852 *6079.1 p6*
Heljeson, Nils; New York, NY, 1848 *6412.40 p151*
Helk, Eva Margarethe Christiane; America, 1868 *7919.3 p525*
  With 2 children
Hell, Charles 17; Quebec, 1870 *8364.32 p24*
Hell, Christoph; Wisconsin, 1886 *6795.8 p168*
Hell, Friedrich; America, 1881 *5475.1 p460*
Hell, Maria; America, 1882 *5475.1 p460*
Hella, Rosalia; Wisconsin, 1900 *6795.8 p36*
Hellbruck, Anna 33; America, 1846 *5475.1 p410*
Helle, Charlotte Johanne; America, 1865 *7420.1 p231*
Helle, Engel Sophie Dorothea Charlotte; America, 1867 *7420.1 p257*
Helle, Heinrich Christian; America, 1857 *7420.1 p163*
Helle, Heinrich Ludwig Christoph; Port uncertain, 1854 *7420.1 p121*
Helle, Johann Georg; America, 1859 *7420.1 p185*
  With family
Helle, Maggry 26; Ontario, 1871 *1823.21 p155*
Helleman, John M.; Ohio, 1836 *3580.20 p32*
Helleman, John Michael; Ohio, 1836 *6020.12 p12*
Hellenbrand, Ambrosius; America, 1883 *5475.1 p155*
Heller, A.; Wisconsin, 1869-1877 *2853.20 p346*
Heller, Albert *SEE* Heller, Jos.
Heller, Alois; Baltimore, 1876 *2853.20 p128*
Heller, Arnold *SEE* Heller, Jos.
Heller, August; America, 1867 *7919.3 p533*
Heller, Auguste Friedericke Louise; Wisconsin, 1899 *6795.8 p76*
Heller, Christian 27; New Castle, DE, 1817-1818 *90.20 p151*
Heller, Edward; Marblehead, MA, 1736 *9228.50 p284*
Heller, Emil Heinrich; Wisconsin, 1889 *6795.8 p33*
Heller, Friedrich; America, 1884 *5475.1 p422*
Heller, Georg Ernst; America, 1867 *7919.3 p526*

Heller, Hynek; Milwaukee, 1848-1849 ***2853.20*** *p308*
Heller, Jacq. 22; America, 1840 ***778.6*** *p159*
Heller, Jos.; America, 1888 ***8023.44*** *p374*
With wife
*Daughter:*Maria
*Son:*Arnold
*Son:*Wilhelm
*Son:*Albert
Heller, Maria *SEE* Heller, Jos.
Heller, Martin 40; Died enroute, 1817-1818 ***90.20*** *p151*
Heller, Nicolaus; America, 1867 ***7919.3*** *p533*
With wife 2 daughters & granddaughter
Heller, Rosina; America, 1824-1866 ***179.55*** *p19*
Heller, Wilhelm *SEE* Heller, Jos.
Helles, Edward; Marblehead, MA, 1736 ***9228.50*** *p284*
Helleur, Edward; Marblehead, MA, 1736 ***9228.50*** *p284*
Helleur, Stanley; British Columbia, n.d. ***9228.50*** *p280*
Hellman, C.E.; Baltimore, 1852 ***6412.40*** *p153*
Hellmann, Frederick; New York, 1859-1860 ***358.56*** *p102*
Hellmer, Anna 15; New York, NY, 1885 ***1883.7*** *p45*
Hellmers, G.; Louisiana, 1874-1875 ***4981.45*** *p29*
Hellmuth, Isaac 53; Ontario, 1871 ***1823.21*** *p155*
Hellstern, C. A.; Louisiana, 1874 ***4981.45*** *p296*
Hellstrom, Carl Emil; Cleveland, OH, 1903-1906 ***9722.10*** *p120*
Hellstrom, Corine; Cleveland, OH, 1893-1899 ***9722.10*** *p120*
Hellstrom, Hilda; Cleveland, OH, 1889-1899 ***9722.10*** *p120*
Hellstrom, J.L.; Philadelphia, 1848 ***6412.40*** *p150*
Hellstrom, Joh.; New York, NY, 1846 ***6412.40*** *p149*
Hellstrom, Joseph; St. Paul, MN, 1885 ***1865.50*** *p50*
Hellweger, Catha. 26; New York, NY, 1885 ***8425.16*** *p32*
Hellweger, Christ. 11 months; New York, NY, 1885 ***8425.16*** *p32*
Hellweger, Friedr. 8; New York, NY, 1885 ***8425.16*** *p32*
Hellweger, Jacob 2; New York, NY, 1885 ***8425.16*** *p32*
Hellweger, Jacob 32; New York, NY, 1885 ***8425.16*** *p32*
Hellweger, Johann 5; New York, NY, 1885 ***8425.16*** *p32*
Hellwig, Alexander; Washington, 1889 ***2770.40*** *p27*
Hellwig, Eduard Adolph; America, 1846 ***7420.1*** *p45*
Hellwig, Hermann Heinrich 49; New York, NY, 1864 ***8425.62*** *p195*
Hellyer, Bernard; Philadelphia, 1700-1799 ***9228.50*** *p280*
Hellyer, Robert; Virginia, 1750-1850 ***9228.50*** *p280*
Helm, Friedrich *SEE* Helm, Jakob
Helm, Jakob *SEE* Helm, Jakob
Helm, Jakob; Dakota, 1886 ***554.30*** *p25*
*Wife:*Katharina Spiesz
*Child:*Jakob
*Child:*Philipp
*Child:*Peter
*Child:*Johannes
*Child:*Friedrich
*Child:*Louise
Helm, James Joseph Henry 61; Ontario, 1871 ***1823.21*** *p155*
Helm, Johannes *SEE* Helm, Jakob
Helm, John 47; Ontario, 1871 ***1823.21*** *p155*
Helm, Katharina Spiesz *SEE* Helm, Jakob
Helm, Louise *SEE* Helm, Jakob
Helm, Peter *SEE* Helm, Jakob
Helm, Philipp *SEE* Helm, Jakob
Helman, George; Ohio, 1809-1852 ***4511.35*** *p22*
Helmann, Chas.; Louisiana, 1874-1875 ***4981.45*** *p29*
Helmann, George; North Carolina, 1840 ***1088.45*** *p14*
Helmer, Anataise 18; New Orleans, 1848 ***778.6*** *p159*
Helmer, August Ferdinand; Wisconsin, 1886 ***6795.8*** *p106*
Helmer, Catharina 8; New Orleans, 1848 ***778.6*** *p159*
Helmer, Herman August; Wisconsin, 1886 ***6795.8*** *p73*
Helmer, Joseph 19; America, 1847 ***778.6*** *p159*
Helmer, Joseph 48; New Orleans, 1848 ***778.6*** *p159*
Helmer, Therese 45; New Orleans, 1848 ***778.6*** *p159*
Helmer, Theresia 11; New Orleans, 1848 ***778.6*** *p160*
Helmke, Johann; Venezuela, 1843 ***3899.5*** *p546*
Helmrich, Julius; Chile, 1852 ***1192.4*** *p52*
Helms, Henrich; Illinois, 1855 ***6079.1*** *p6*
Helms, Oscar; Iowa, 1901 ***1211.15*** *p11*
Helmsmeier, Anna; America, 1891 ***7420.1*** *p362*
Helmstadter, Adam; America, 1854 ***2526.43*** *p127*
Helmstadter, Adam; America, 1883 ***2526.43*** *p127*
Helmstadter, Adam 7 *SEE* Helmstadter, Jakob
Helmstadter, Adam; New Jersey, 1873 ***2526.43*** *p127*
Helmstadter, Adam, I 53; America, 1854 ***2526.43*** *p127*
With wife
Helmstadter, Babette 9 *SEE* Helmstadter, Jakob
Helmstadter, Benedikt; America, 1867 ***2526.43*** *p127*
Helmstadter, Eva Margaretha 38; America, 1857 ***2526.43*** *p192*
*Son:*Egidius 15
*Daughter:*Anna Elisabetha 4
*Daughter:*Elisabetha 8
*Son:*Johannes 5
*Son:*Philipp 6
Helmstadter, Georg 20; America, 1854 ***2526.43*** *p127*
Helmstadter, Georg Adam 13 *SEE* Helmstadter, Peter
Helmstadter, Jakob *SEE* Helmstadter, Jakob
Helmstadter, Jakob; America, 1882 ***2526.43*** *p186*
*Wife:*Katharina Horn
*Son:*Adam
*Son:*Johann
*Son:*Jakob
*Son:*Philipp
*Daughter:*Babette
Helmstadter, Johann *SEE* Helmstadter, Jakob
Helmstadter, Johannes; America, 1855 ***2526.43*** *p127*
Helmstadter, Katharina Horn *SEE* Helmstadter, Jakob
Helmstadter, Katharina 9 *SEE* Helmstadter, Peter
Helmstadter, Katharina 34; America, 1867 ***2526.43*** *p225*
Helmstadter, Katharina 60; America, 1866 ***2526.43*** *p155*
Helmstadter, Maria Elisabetha; America, 1855 ***2526.43*** *p127*
Helmstadter, Michael 12 *SEE* Helmstadter, Peter
Helmstadter, Peter; America, 1865 ***2526.42*** *p167*
Helmstadter, Peter 5 *SEE* Helmstadter, Peter
Helmstadter, Peter 35; America, 1846 ***2526.43*** *p127*
With wife
*Son:*Georg Adam 13
*Son:*Michael 12
*Daughter:*Katharina 9
*Son:*Peter 5
Helmstadter, Philipp *SEE* Helmstadter, Jakob
Helmstadter, Philipp 29; America, 1865 ***2526.42*** *p174*
Helot, Philip; Ohio, 1809-1852 ***4511.35*** *p22*
Helouin, Catherine; Nova Scotia, 1753 ***3051*** *p112*
Helper, Friedrich Christian; America, 1867 ***7420.1*** *p257*
Helper, Heinrich Wilhelm; America, 1871 ***7420.1*** *p290*
Helps, Henry 64; Ontario, 1871 ***1823.17*** *p68*
Helps, John 34; Ontario, 1871 ***1823.17*** *p68*
Helps, William 39; Ontario, 1871 ***1823.17*** *p68*
Hels, A. H.; New York, 1859 ***358.56*** *p100*
Helsendegn, George; New York, 1778 ***8529.30*** *p3A*
Helt, Emilie; Valdivia, Chile, 1850 ***1192.4*** *p49*
Helt, Jacob; Ohio, 1809-1852 ***4511.35*** *p22*
Helzer, Eliza. 30; Portland, ME, 1906 ***970.38*** *p77*
Helzer, Henry 2; Portland, ME, 1906 ***970.38*** *p78*
Helzer, Jacob 5; Portland, ME, 1906 ***970.38*** *p78*
Helzer, Lena 18; Portland, ME, 1906 ***970.38*** *p78*
Helzer, Phillip 16; Portland, ME, 1906 ***970.38*** *p78*
Hemalaski, Peter; New Orleans, 1872 ***6015.15*** *p24*
Hemel, Mrs. Friedrich; America, 1836 ***2526.42*** *p161*
Hemhardt, Jacob; Louisiana, 1874 ***4981.45*** *p296*
Hemingway, Robert; North Carolina, 1850 ***1088.45*** *p14*
Hemler, Jean 27; Port uncertain, 1848 ***778.6*** *p160*
Hemm, Frank; Ohio, 1840-1897 ***8365.35*** *p16*
Hemman, Jacob; Ohio, 1809-1852 ***4511.35*** *p22*
Hemman, John; Ohio, 1809-1852 ***4511.35*** *p22*
Hemmer, Barbara *SEE* Hemmer, Maria Buhl
Hemmer, Maria; America, 1871 ***5475.1*** *p139*
*Daughter:*Barbara
Hemmer, Nicolas 32; Missouri, 1846 ***778.6*** *p160*
Hemmes, Anna 19; Port uncertain, 1843 ***778.6*** *p160*
Hemmes, Barbara 42; Port uncertain, 1843 ***778.6*** *p160*
Hemmes, Jean 18; Port uncertain, 1843 ***778.6*** *p160*
Hemmes, Maria 16; Port uncertain, 1843 ***778.6*** *p160*
Hemmes, Martin 48; Port uncertain, 1843 ***778.6*** *p160*
Hemmes, Peter 14; Port uncertain, 1843 ***778.6*** *p160*
Hempel, Auguste Ernestine; Wisconsin, 1896 ***6795.8*** *p66*
Hempel, Wilhelmine Auguste; Wisconsin, 1893 ***6795.8*** *p230*
Hemphill, David; Philadelphia, 1854 ***8513.31*** *p313*
*Wife:*Margaret McGorman
Hemphill, Margaret McGorman *SEE* Hemphill, David
Hemphill, Robert; Ohio, 1857 ***3580.20*** *p32*
Hemphill, Robert; Ohio, 1857 ***6020.12*** *p12*
Hemphill, W. N.; Washington, 1888 ***2770.40*** *p25*
Hempstead, Anna 32; Michigan, 1880 ***4491.36*** *p9*
Hemsing, Anna 49; Galveston, TX, 1845 ***3967.10*** *p376*
Hemsing, Anna Maria 22; Galveston, TX, 1845 ***3967.10*** *p376*
Hemsing, Bernhard 8; Galveston, TX, 1845 ***3967.10*** *p376*
Hemsing, Bernhard 51; Galveston, TX, 1845 ***3967.10*** *p376*
Hen, Adam; Ohio, 1809-1852 ***4511.35*** *p22*
Hen, Eduard Wendel; America, 1838 ***5475.1*** *p469*
Hen, Ferdinand Adolf; America, 1846 ***5475.1*** *p472*
Henault, Jacques; Quebec, 1659 ***9221.17*** *p413*
Henault, Leo Jospeph; Iowa, 1922 ***1211.15*** *p11*
Henaut, Julien 54; New Orleans, 1848 ***778.6*** *p160*
Henaut, Marie 53; New Orleans, 1848 ***778.6*** *p160*
Henbarger, Philip; Ohio, 1809-1852 ***4511.35*** *p22*
Henberry, Nicholas; Louisiana, 1874 ***4981.45*** *p132*
Hencke, Wilhelm; Valdivia, Chile, 1851 ***1192.4*** *p51*
Henckel, Andres 28; Louisiana, 1848 ***778.6*** *p160*
Henckelmann, Johann Heinrich; Nova Scotia, 1784 ***7105*** *p23*
Hender, Thomas; New Orleans, 1850 ***7242.30*** *p144*
Henderson, Mr.; Quebec, 1885 ***1937.10*** *p52*
Henderson, Abel J.G. 45; Ontario, 1871 ***1823.21*** *p156*
Henderson, Alex 53; Ontario, 1871 ***1823.21*** *p156*
Henderson, Alexander 29; Ontario, 1871 ***1823.21*** *p156*
Henderson, Alexander 63; Ontario, 1871 ***1823.21*** *p156*
Henderson, Alexander 70; Ontario, 1871 ***1823.21*** *p156*
Henderson, Andrew 54; Ontario, 1871 ***1823.21*** *p156*
Henderson, Ann 60; Ontario, 1871 ***1823.21*** *p156*
Henderson, Archy 86; Ontario, 1871 ***1823.21*** *p156*
Henderson, Blemyre; Pennsylvania, 1863 ***8513.31*** *p427*
Henderson, Charles 30; Ontario, 1871 ***1823.21*** *p156*
Henderson, Christopher 25; Ontario, 1871 ***1823.21*** *p156*
Henderson, David R.; Washington, 1882 ***2770.40*** *p135*
Henderson, Donald 40; Ontario, 1871 ***1823.21*** *p156*
Henderson, Donald 74; Ontario, 1871 ***1823.21*** *p156*
Henderson, Elisabeth 80; Ontario, 1871 ***1823.21*** *p156*
Henderson, Eliza 14; Ontario, 1871 ***1823.21*** *p156*
Henderson, George 56; Ontario, 1871 ***1823.21*** *p156*
Henderson, Henry 46; Ontario, 1871 ***1823.21*** *p156*
Henderson, Isabella 27; Ontario, 1871 ***1823.21*** *p156*
Henderson, Issabella 50; Ontario, 1871 ***1823.21*** *p156*
Henderson, James; Ohio, 1818 ***3580.20*** *p32*
Henderson, James; Ohio, 1818 ***6020.12*** *p12*
Henderson, James 24; Ontario, 1871 ***1823.21*** *p156*
Henderson, James 26; Ontario, 1871 ***1823.17*** *p68*
Henderson, James 32; Ontario, 1871 ***1823.17*** *p68*
Henderson, James 38; Ontario, 1871 ***1823.21*** *p156*
Henderson, James 50; Ontario, 1871 ***1823.21*** *p156*
Henderson, James 58; Ontario, 1871 ***1823.21*** *p156*
Henderson, James 65; Ontario, 1871 ***1823.21*** *p156*
Henderson, Jno M. 41; Ontario, 1871 ***1823.17*** *p68*
Henderson, John; Boston, 1766 ***1642*** *p37*
Henderson, John 33; Indiana, 1853-1871 ***9076.20*** *p67*
Henderson, John; Louisiana, 1874-1875 ***4981.45*** *p29*
Henderson, John 28; Ontario, 1871 ***1823.21*** *p156*
Henderson, John 30; Ontario, 1871 ***1823.21*** *p156*
Henderson, John 60; Ontario, 1871 ***1823.21*** *p156*
Henderson, John 66; Ontario, 1871 ***1823.17*** *p68*
Henderson, John 66; Ontario, 1871 ***1823.21*** *p156*
Henderson, Mrs. John; Toronto, 1844 ***2910.35*** *p114*
Henderson, John Ritchie; North Carolina, 1852 ***1088.45*** *p14*
Henderson, Joseph 40; Ontario, 1871 ***1823.21*** *p156*
Henderson, Margaret 40; Ontario, 1871 ***1823.21*** *p156*
Henderson, Mary 16; Ontario, 1871 ***1823.21*** *p156*
Henderson, Robert 36; Ontario, 1871 ***1823.17*** *p68*
Henderson, Ronald 40; Ontario, 1871 ***1823.17*** *p68*
Henderson, Samuel 22; Ontario, 1871 ***1823.21*** *p156*
Henderson, W. 17; Quebec, 1870 ***8364.32*** *p24*
Henderson, William 66; Ontario, 1871 ***1823.17*** *p68*
Henderson, Wm 21; Ontario, 1871 ***1823.21*** *p156*
Henderson, Mrs. Wm.; Toronto, 1844 ***2910.35*** *p114*
Hendia, Thomas 75; Ontario, 1871 ***1823.17*** *p68*
Hendley, James 53; Ontario, 1871 ***1823.21*** *p156*
Hendra, John 42; Ontario, 1871 ***1823.21*** *p156*
Hendra, William 59; Ontario, 1871 ***1823.21*** *p156*
Hendre, Nichs 76; Ontario, 1871 ***1823.21*** *p156*
Hendrick, Andrew; New Orleans, 1850 ***7242.30*** *p144*
Hendrick, Carl; Wisconsin, 1880 ***6795.8*** *p226*
Hendrick, Desire; Wisconsin, 1854-1858 ***1495.20*** *p66*
*Wife:*Jeanne Van Malderen
*Son:*Toussaint
Hendrick, Jeanne Van Malderen *SEE* Hendrick, Desire
Hendrick, John; Ontario, 1871 ***1823.21*** *p156*
Hendrick, Michael 82; Ontario, 1871 ***1823.21*** *p156*
Hendrick, Toussaint *SEE* Hendrick, Desire
Hendrickson, Carl; New York, 1900 ***1766.20*** *p16*
Hendrickson, Hans; Iowa, 1876 ***1211.15*** *p11*
Hendrie, James 45; Ontario, 1871 ***1823.21*** *p156*
Hendrie, William 40; Ontario, 1871 ***1823.21*** *p156*
Hendriks, Aug.; Iowa, 1874 ***8023.44*** *p374*
Hendriks, J. Franz Anton; Iowa, 1874 ***8023.44*** *p374*
Hendry, Alexander; North Carolina, 1837 ***1088.45*** *p14*
Hendry, Catherine 35; North Carolina, 1774 ***1422.10*** *p60*
Hendry, Catherine 35; North Carolina, 1774 ***1422.10*** *p62*
Hendry, James; North Carolina, 1856 ***1088.45*** *p14*
Hendry, Jane 23; Quebec, 1870 ***8364.32*** *p24*
Hendry, Neil 27; North Carolina, 1774 ***1422.10*** *p61*
Hendry, Neil 27; North Carolina, 1774 ***1422.10*** *p63*
Hendt, Johannes; Pennsylvania, 1809 ***170.15*** *p28*
Hendy, Nicholas 51; Ontario, 1871 ***1823.17*** *p68*
Henebery, James 29; Ontario, 1871 ***1823.21*** *p156*
Heneisen, Philip E.; Ohio, 1840-1897 ***8365.35*** *p16*
Henery, Agnes 50; Ontario, 1871 ***1823.21*** *p156*
Henery, Elizabeth 70; Ontario, 1871 ***1823.21*** *p156*
Henery, William 22; Ontario, 1871 ***1823.21*** *p157*
Henesey, Charles; Boston, 1738 ***1642*** *p44*
Henessey, John; Jamaica, 1778 ***8529.30*** *p13A*
Henessy, Many 11; Ontario, 1871 ***1823.21*** *p157*
Henesy, James 35; Ontario, 1871 ***1823.21*** *p157*

Henesy, John 59; Ontario, 1871 ***1823.21*** *p157*
Henesy, Patrick 40; Ontario, 1871 ***1823.21*** *p157*
Henesy, Sarah; Boston, 1762 ***1642*** *p48*
Heney, Nicholas 60; Ontario, 1871 ***1823.17*** *p68*
Hengesch, Pierre 45; New Orleans, 1845 ***778.6*** *p160*
Henig, Madelaine 28; Ohio, 1847 ***778.6*** *p160*
Henke, August Ferdinand; Wisconsin, 1913 ***6795.8*** *p167*
Henke, Carl; Wisconsin, 1903 ***6795.8*** *p120*
Henke, Charles Ludwig; Wisconsin, 1913 ***6795.8*** *p167*
Henke, Emil; Wisconsin, 1897 ***6795.8*** *p134*
Henke, Frederick Wm.; Wisconsin, 1869 ***6795.8*** *p123*
Henke, Louise Bertha; Wisconsin, 1894 ***6795.8*** *p120*
Henke, Wm.; Ohio, 1840-1897 ***8365.35*** *p16*
Henkel, Adam; America, 1885 ***2526.43*** *p130*
Henkel, Adam; America, 1885 ***2526.43*** *p131*
Henkel, Adam; America, 1885 ***2526.43*** *p190*
Henkel, Elsie; New York, 1859 ***358.56*** *p100*
Henkel, Henriette; America, 1881 ***5475.1*** *p409*
Henkel, Peter; America, 1864 ***2526.43*** *p130*
Henkelman, J. Henry; Nova Scotia, 1784 ***7105*** *p23*
Henker, George 37; New Orleans, 1843 ***778.6*** *p160*
Henkes, Adam *SEE* Henkes, Jakob
Henkes, Anna Maria *SEE* Henkes, Johann
Henkes, Jakob *SEE* Henkes, Jakob
Henkes, Jakob 43; South America, 1857 ***5475.1*** *p512*
*Wife:*Maria Scheid 44
*Daughter:*Maria
*Son:*Mathias
*Son:*Adam
*Daughter:*Magdalena
*Son:*Peter
*Son:*Jakob
Henkes, Johann *SEE* Henkes, Johann
Henkes, Johann 38; America, 1857 ***5475.1*** *p492*
*Wife:*Maria Thome 34
*Daughter:*Anna Maria
*Son:*Johann
Henkes, Katharina 34; America, 1857 ***5475.1*** *p492*
Henkes, Magdalena *SEE* Henkes, Jakob
Henkes, Maria Thome 34 *SEE* Henkes, Johann
Henkes, Maria *SEE* Henkes, Jakob
Henkes, Maria Scheid 44 *SEE* Henkes, Jakob
Henkes, Mathias *SEE* Henkes, Jakob
Henkes, Peter 23; Brazil, 1862 ***5475.1*** *p544*
Henkes, Peter *SEE* Henkes, Jakob
Henlean, Amelia; Philadelphia, 1863 ***8513.31*** *p411*
Henley, Honor; St. Johns, N.F., 1825 ***1053.15*** *p6*
Henley, William; St. Johns, N.F., 1825 ***1053.15*** *p6*
Henley, William Joseph James; Miami, 1935 ***4984.12*** *p39*
Henly, Edw; Virginia, 1652 ***6254.4*** *p243*
Henly, James; Philadelphia, 1778 ***8529.30*** *p2*
Henly, John 80; Ontario, 1871 ***1823.21*** *p157*
Henly, Wm.; Toronto, 1844 ***2910.35*** *p112*
Henman, Jno; Jamestown, VA, 1633 ***1658.20*** *p211*
Henn, Catharina Caroline; America, 1867 ***7919.3*** *p530*
Henn, Ernst Friedrich Max Carl; America, 1867 ***7919.3*** *p532*
Henn, Karl 21; Philadelphia, 1899 ***5475.1*** *p40*
Henn, Katharina; Brazil, 1863 ***5475.1*** *p498*
Henn, Margrethe; America, 1860 ***5475.1*** *p519*
Henn, Maria Elisabeth; Brazil, 1863 ***5475.1*** *p498*
Hennaford, Jane 40; Ontario, 1871 ***1823.21*** *p157*
Hennchen, Elisabeth Niklas *SEE* Hennchen, Heinrich
Hennchen, Georg; America, 1857 ***5475.1*** *p520*
Hennchen, Heinrich; America, 1859 ***54475.1*** *p522*
*Wife:*Elisabeth Niklas
*Son:*J. Heinrich
*Son:*Jakob
*Daughter:*Philippine
Hennchen, J. Heinrich *SEE* Hennchen, Heinrich
Hennchen, Jakob *SEE* Hennchen, Heinrich
Hennchen, Peter; America, 1857 ***5475.1*** *p520*
Hennchen, Philippine *SEE* Hennchen, Heinrich
Henne, Aug. Heinrich Christian; Wisconsin, 1871 ***6795.8*** *p158*
Henneberry, Peter; North Carolina, 1850-1854 ***1088.45*** *p14*
Henneisen, Anna Arbenz *SEE* Henneisen, Frederick
Henneisen, Frederick; Philadelphia, 1861 ***8513.31*** *p313*
*Wife:*Anna Arbenz
Hennekson, Robert; Iowa, 1890 ***1211.15*** *p11*
Hennelly, Patrick J.; Washington, 1883 ***2770.40*** *p136*
Hennemann, Franz 23; New York, NY, 1864 ***8425.62*** *p198*
Hennemann, Heinrich 60; New York, NY, 1864 ***8425.62*** *p198*
Hennemann, Justa 20; New York, NY, 1864 ***8425.62*** *p198*
Hennemann, Minna 16; New York, NY, 1864 ***8425.62*** *p198*
Hennemann, Minna 54; New York, NY, 1864 ***8425.62*** *p198*
Hennemann, Wilhelm 9; New York, NY, 1864 ***8425.62*** *p198*
Hennen, Elisabeth Petto 49 *SEE* Hennen, Johann
Hennen, Johann; Chicago, 1885 ***5475.1*** *p555*
*Wife:*Elisabeth Petto
*Son:*Nikolaus
Hennen, Nikolaus *SEE* Hennen, Johann
Hennersdorf, August; Galveston, TX, 1855 ***571.7*** *p16*
Hennes, . . .; America, 1846 ***5475.1*** *p531*
Hennes, Christian 2 *SEE* Hennes, Jakob
Hennes, Jakob; America, 1843 ***5475.1*** *p528*
*Son:*Jakob
*Son:*Jakob
*Son:*Christian
*Daughter:*Katharina
Hennes, Jakob 6 *SEE* Hennes, Jakob
Hennes, Jakob 27 *SEE* Hennes, Jakob
Hennes, Jakob; Wheeling, WV, 1885 ***5475.1*** *p388*
Hennes, Katharina 3 *SEE* Hennes, Jakob
Hennesey, James; Boston, 1755 ***1642*** *p47*
Hennesey, Josephine 19; Ontario, 1871 ***1823.21*** *p157*
Hennesey, Robert J. 31; Ontario, 1871 ***1823.21*** *p157*
Hennessey, Elizabeth 50; Ontario, 1871 ***1823.21*** *p157*
Hennessey, James; Ohio, 1840-1897 ***8365.35*** *p16*
Hennessey, Nicholas 55; Ontario, 1871 ***1823.21*** *p157*
Hennessy, Dennis; Toronto, 1844 ***2910.35*** *p112*
Hennesy, Jno; St. John, N.B., 1847 ***2978.15*** *p41*
Hennesy, Mary; Boston, 1769 ***1642*** *p49*
Hennesy, Peter; Boston, 1756 ***1642*** *p47*
Hennet, Louise 3; Missouri, 1848 ***778.6*** *p160*
Hennet, Margte. 24; Missouri, 1848 ***778.6*** *p160*
Hennet, Marie 2 months; Missouri, 1848 ***778.6*** *p160*
Hennet, Pierre 24; Missouri, 1848 ***778.6*** *p160*
Henney, P.; New Orleans, 1850 ***7242.30*** *p144*
Hennig, John Ernest; Wisconsin, 1870 ***6795.8*** *p138*
Hennin, Marie 22; Port uncertain, 1843 ***778.6*** *p160*
Henning, Georg; Valdivia, Chile, 1852 ***1192.4*** *p53*
Henning, Heinrich; America, 1854 ***7420.1*** *p121*
Henning, Heinrich; America, 1860 ***7420.1*** *p194*
With wife & daughter
Henning, John; New York, 1859 ***358.56*** *p55*
Henning, John; New York, 1860 ***358.56*** *p150*
Henning, John Frederick; Ohio, 1809-1852 ***4511.35*** *p22*
Henning, Joseph; Iowa, 1914 ***1211.15*** *p11*
Henning, Karl; America, 1881 ***2526.43*** *p170*
Henning, Robert; North Carolina, 1854 ***1088.45*** *p14*
Henning, William; Ohio, 1840-1897 ***8365.35*** *p16*
Hennings, Paul Heinrich; Illinois, 1855 ***6079.1*** *p6*
Hennrich, Elisabetha 3 *SEE* Hennrich, Franz, II
Hennrich, Eva 9 *SEE* Hennrich, Franz, II
Hennrich, Franz 8 *SEE* Hennrich, Franz, II
Hennrich, Franz, II; America, 1842 ***2526.42*** *p191*
With wife
*Son:*Franz
*Daughter:*Elisabetha
*Daughter:*Margaretha
*Son:*Peter
*Daughter:*Eva
Hennrich, Margaretha 5 *SEE* Hennrich, Franz, II
Hennrich, Peter 11 *SEE* Hennrich, Franz, II
Henny, Francois 29; Missouri, 1846 ***778.6*** *p160*
Henny, Henry; Washington, 1883 ***2770.40*** *p136*
Henquinet, A. Desire; America, 1870 ***1494.20*** *p11*
Henri, . . .; Montreal, 1642 ***9221.17*** *p123*
Henrich, George; Ohio, 1809-1852 ***4511.35*** *p22*
Henrich, Joseph; Ohio, 1809-1852 ***4511.35*** *p22*
Henrich, Maria Anna; Venezuela, 1843 ***3899.5*** *p542*
Henrickson, H. P.; Iowa, 1876 ***1211.15*** *p11*
Henrickson, H. Peter; Iowa, 1884 ***1211.15*** *p11*
Henriette, Fanny 33; Missouri, 1846 ***778.6*** *p160*
Henriette, Gustave 5; Missouri, 1846 ***778.6*** *p160*
Henriette, Jeanne 27; Missouri, 1846 ***778.6*** *p160*
Henriette, Xavier 38; Missouri, 1846 ***778.6*** *p160*
Henright, John 45; Ontario, 1871 ***1823.21*** *p157*
Henrikson, A. F.; Washington, 1885 ***2770.40*** *p194*
Henriod, Napoleon 49; Ontario, 1871 ***1823.17*** *p68*
Henrion, Amelie *SEE* Henrion, Jean Francois
Henrion, Jean Francois; Wisconsin, 1854 ***1495.20*** *p29*
*Wife:*Josephine Detienne
*Daughter:*Julie
*Daughter:*Amelie
Henrion, Josephine Detienne *SEE* Henrion, Jean Francois
Henrion, Julie *SEE* Henrion, Jean Francois
Henriot, Jean 74; Port uncertain, 1843 ***778.6*** *p160*
Henriot, Theodore 42; Port uncertain, 1843 ***778.6*** *p160*
Henroid, Leah Rose; Utah, 1862 ***9228.50*** *p280*
Henry, Bertram H. 18; Ontario, 1871 ***1823.21*** *p157*
Henry, Blair 12; Ontario, 1871 ***1823.17*** *p68*
Henry, Charlotte 59; Ontario, 1871 ***1823.17*** *p68*
Henry, Chester; Massachusetts, 1889-1962 ***9228.50*** *p281*
Henry, Christian; Ohio, 1809-1852 ***4511.35*** *p22*
Henry, Christman; Louisiana, 1874 ***4981.45*** *p132*
Henry, David 55; Ontario, 1871 ***1823.21*** *p157*
Henry, Dorothy Frances; Montreal, 1942 ***9228.50*** *p455*
Henry, Elizabeth; Massachusetts, 1716-1750 ***9228.50*** *p113*
Henry, Elizabeth 75; Ontario, 1871 ***1823.21*** *p157*
Henry, Elizabeth; Utah, 1783-1855 ***9228.50*** *p282*
Henry, Elsie Louise; Massachusetts, 1892-1914 ***9228.50*** *p281*
Henry, Ezra Matthew; Boston, 1862-1950 ***9228.50*** *p281*
Henry, Ezra Matthew; Boston, 1869-1919 ***9228.50*** *p277*
Henry, Francois; Illinois, 1852 ***6079.1*** *p6*
Henry, Frank Irving; Boston, 1913 ***9228.50*** *p281*
Henry, Henry; Washington, 1883 ***2770.40*** *p136*
Henry, Jacob; Ohio, 1809-1852 ***4511.35*** *p22*
Henry, James 35; America, 1846 ***778.6*** *p160*
Henry, James; Philadelphia, 1854 ***8513.31*** *p313*
*Wife:*Margaret McGrogan
*Son:*William
Henry, Jane 19; Ontario, 1871 ***1823.21*** *p157*
Henry, Jane E. 27; Ontario, 1871 ***1823.21*** *p157*
Henry, Johan Ott; Illinois, 1860 ***6079.1*** *p6*
Henry, John; Canada, 1775-1776 ***1642*** *p85*
Henry, John 30; Ontario, 1871 ***1823.17*** *p68*
Henry, John 38; Ontario, 1871 ***1823.21*** *p157*
Henry, John 41; Ontario, 1871 ***1823.21*** *p157*
Henry, John 50; Ontario, 1871 ***1823.21*** *p157*
Henry, Jonas 48; Ontario, 1871 ***1823.17*** *p68*
Henry, Joseph 47; Ontario, 1871 ***1823.21*** *p157*
Henry, Julien; New York, NY, 1872 ***1494.20*** *p13*
Henry, Lizzie 40; Ontario, 1871 ***1823.21*** *p157*
Henry, Louis; Illinois, 1852 ***6079.1*** *p6*
Henry, Louis 30; New Orleans, 1847 ***778.6*** *p160*
Henry, Louise 13; Port uncertain, 1840 ***778.6*** *p160*
Henry, Margaret McGrogan *SEE* Henry, James
Henry, Mary J. 21; Ontario, 1871 ***1823.21*** *p157*
Henry, Nickolas 59; Port uncertain, 1840 ***778.6*** *p160*
Henry, Patric 73; Ontario, 1871 ***1823.21*** *p157*
Henry, Patrick; Boston, 1836 ***3274.55*** *p26*
Henry, Paul 42; New Orleans, 1847 ***778.6*** *p160*
Henry, Peter; Louisiana, 1874 ***4981.45*** *p296*
Henry, Peter; Washington, 1886 ***2770.40*** *p195*
Henry, R. J. 40; Ontario, 1871 ***1823.21*** *p157*
Henry, Robert 28; Ontario, 1871 ***1823.17*** *p69*
Henry, S. 20; America, 1846 ***778.6*** *p161*
Henry, Sarah; Ontario, 1835 ***3160.1*** *p150*
Henry, Sarah 59; Ontario, 1871 ***1823.21*** *p157*
Henry, Sarah; Prescott, Ont., 1835 ***3289.1*** *p61*
Henry, Smith; Ohio, 1809-1852 ***4511.35*** *p22*
Henry, Theobald 21; Ontario, 1871 ***1823.21*** *p157*
Henry, Thomas; Massachusetts, 1740 ***1642*** *p85*
Henry, Thomas; Ohio, 1809-1852 ***4511.35*** *p22*
Henry, Thomas Arthur Herdman; Beverly, MA, 1898-1923 ***9228.50*** *p281*
Henry, Thomas S.; Prince Edward Island, 1842 ***9228.50*** *p280*
Henry, William 64; Ontario, 1871 ***1823.21*** *p157*
Henry, William 71; Ontario, 1871 ***1823.21*** *p157*
Henry, William *SEE* Henry, James
Henry DuChasterie, Edmond; Quebec, 1662 ***9221.17*** *p487*
Henrypierre, Joseph 34; Missouri, 1845 ***778.6*** *p161*
Henscheidt, Henry; Illinois, 1834-1900 ***6020.5*** *p132*
Hensel, August; Galveston, TX, 1855 ***571.7*** *p16*
Hensey, Sarah; Boston, 1750 ***1642*** *p46*
Hensgen, Johann; America, 1882 ***5475.1*** *p261*
Hensgen, Johann *SEE* Hensgen, Johann
Hensgen, Johann 51; Wisconsin, 1858 ***5475.1*** *p260*
*Wife:*Katharina Scherer 49
*Daughter:*Margarethe
*Daughter:*Magdalena
*Son:*Michel
*Son:*Johann
Hensgen, Katharina; America, 1882 ***5475.1*** *p261*
Hensgen, Katharina Scherer 49 *SEE* Hensgen, Johann
Hensgen, Magdalena *SEE* Hensgen, Johann
Hensgen, Margarethe *SEE* Hensgen, Johann
Hensgen, Mathias; Wisconsin, 1857 ***5475.1*** *p260*
Hensgen, Michel *SEE* Hensgen, Johann
Hensgen, Peter 23; America, 1863 ***5475.1*** *p375*
Henshaw, George 52; Ontario, 1871 ***1823.21*** *p158*
Henshaw, Samuel 71; Ontario, 1871 ***1823.21*** *p158*
Henshaw, W.; California, 1868 ***1131.61*** *p89*
Hensick, George; Ohio, 1809-1852 ***4511.35*** *p22*
Hensler, John; Ohio, 1840-1897 ***8365.35*** *p16*
Hensler, Mathieu; New Castle, DE, 1817-1818 ***90.20*** *p151*
Henson, Martin; Washington, 1879 ***2770.40*** *p134*
Henss, Anna Regina 26; New England, 1866 ***170.15*** *p28*
With family
Henss, Johann Georg 2; New England, 1866 ***170.15*** *p28*
With family
Henss, Johannes 31; New England, 1866 ***170.15*** *p28*
With family
Hensworth, John 50; Ontario, 1871 ***1823.21*** *p158*

Hentage, William 30; Ontario, 1871 *1823.21 p158*
Hentzler, Cath. 54; New Orleans, 1846 *778.6 p161*
Hentzler, Jacob 53; New Orleans, 1846 *778.6 p161*
Hentzler, Marie 19; New Orleans, 1846 *778.6 p161*
Hentzler, Pauline 5; New Orleans, 1846 *778.6 p161*
Hentzler, Philipp 15; New Orleans, 1846 *778.6 p161*
Henville, Jamison T. 51; Ontario, 1871 *1823.21 p158*
Henwood, Mary Ann; Massachusetts, 1910 *9228.50 p127*
Henwood, Mary Ann; Massachusetts, n.d. *9228.50 p282*
Henwood, William 49; Ontario, 1871 *1823.21 p158*
Henz, Nikolaus 43; America, 1843 *5475.1 p347*
Henz, Wendel; America, 1843 *5475.1 p347*
Heoffman, Seligman; North Carolina, 1850 *1088.45 p14*
Heoft, Anthony; Wisconsin, 1883 *6795.8 p117*
Heon, Simon; Quebec, 1642 *9221.17 p118*
Hepburn, John Ross; Oregon, 1941 *9157.47 p2*
Hepke, Auguste; America, 1867 *7420.1 p267*
  *Daughter:*Emma
Heplen, George 69; Ontario, 1871 *1823.21 p158*
Hepp, John George; Ohio, 1809-1852 *4511.35 p22*
Hepp, John Jacob; Ohio, 1809-1852 *4511.35 p22*
Hepper, Anthony; North Carolina, 1837 *1088.45 p14*
Heppn, Anthony; North Carolina, 1835 *1088.45 p14*
Heppner, Joh. C. A.; Valdivia, Chile, 1852 *1192.4 p54*
  With wife
  With child 6
Heraly, Michel; New York, NY, 1855 *1494.21 p31*
Herauf, Tomas; St. Paul, MN, 1858-1859 *2853.20 p277*
Herault, Henry; New England, 1679 *9228.50 p19A*
Herault, Jeanne 28; Montreal, 1658 *9221.17 p389*
Herault deSaint-Michel, Francois; Quebec, 1713
  2314.30 p169
Herault deSaint-Michel, Francois; Quebec, 1713
  2314.30 p185
Herbault, A.J.J.E.; Louisiana, 1836-1840 *4981.45 p212*
Herbeck, Carl; Valdivia, Chile, 1852 *1192.4 p55*
Herbelet, Mr. 33; America, 1840 *778.6 p161*
Herber, Anthony; Detroit, 1890 *9980.23 p96*
Herber, Carl Christoph Heinrich Julius; America, 1860
  7420.1 p194
Herber, Nicolas 34; America, 1846 *778.6 p161*
Herber, Peter; Iowa, 1855 *5475.1 p377*
Herber, William Julius; Colorado, 1891 *1029.59 p39*
Herbert, Jane *SEE* Herbert, John
Herbert, Jessie 21; Ontario, 1871 *1823.21 p158*
Herbert, John; Ohio, 1838 *4022.20 p280*
  *Wife:*Jane
  With 5 children
Herbert, L.; Louisiana, 1874 *4981.45 p132*
Herbert, L. 37; South Carolina, 1812 *3476.30 p11*
Herbert, Philip 62; Ontario, 1871 *1823.21 p158*
Herbert, Rebecca; Virginia, 1671 *1236.25 p44*
Herbert, Robert 44; Ontario, 1871 *1823.17 p69*
Herbert, Sarah 64; Ontario, 1871 *1823.21 p158*
Herbert, Thomas; Illinois, 1861 *6079.1 p6*
Herbert, William; New York, NY, 1778 *8529.30 p2*
Herbet, Robert 30; Ontario, 1871 *1823.21 p158*
Herbez, Juan; Louisiana, 1874 *4981.45 p132*
Herbig, Michael; Nova Scotia, 1784 *7105 p23*
Herbin, Frederic-Louis; Quebec, 1698 *2314.30 p169*
Herbin, Frederic-Louis; Quebec, 1698 *2314.30 p185*
Herblin, Joseph Francois 28; New Orleans, 1848 *778.6*
  p161
Herbot, Suzanne 26; Louisiana, 1848 *778.6 p161*
Herbot, Wendelin 21; Louisiana, 1848 *778.6 p161*
Herbruck, Peter; Ohio, 1809-1852 *4511.35 p22*
Herbst, Adam; Illinois, 1852 *6079.1 p6*
Herbst, Adolph; Valdivia, Chile, 1850 *1192.4 p50*
Herbst, Carl 9; Louisiana, 1847 *778.6 p161*
Herbst, Caroline 8; Louisiana, 1847 *778.6 p161*
Herbst, Christine 3; Louisiana, 1847 *778.6 p161*
Herbst, Frank; Colorado, 1904 *1029.59 p39*
Herbst, Friedrich; America, 1868 *7420.1 p272*
  With family
Herbst, Henry; North Carolina, 1828 *1088.45 p14*
Herbst, Jacob 35; Louisiana, 1847 *778.6 p161*
Herbst, Johann 10; Louisiana, 1847 *778.6 p161*
Herbst, Louis 1; Louisiana, 1847 *778.6 p161*
Herbst, Maria 50; Halifax, N.S., 1902 *1860.4 p42*
Herbst, Marie 29; Louisiana, 1847 *778.6 p161*
Herbst, Martin 54; Halifax, N.S., 1902 *1860.4 p42*
Herbst, Sophia 5; Louisiana, 1847 *778.6 p161*
Herbst, Wilhelmina 6; Louisiana, 1847 *778.6 p161*
Herch, Marcus 37; New York, NY, 1878 *9253.2 p45*
Herchenhahn, Christoph; America, 1867 *7919.3 p532*
Hercht, George 27; America, 1847 *778.6 p161*
Hercke, Konrad; America, 1838 *170.15 p28*
Herd, Jonas; Washington, 1889 *2770.40 p27*
Herda, Frantisek; Wisconsin, 1856-1910 *2853.20 p345*
Herda, Joseph 28; America, 1847 *778.6 p161*
Herdahl, Sara; St. Paul, MN, 1896 *1865.50 p99*
Hereau, Mr. 48; America, 1842 *778.6 p161*
Herefordshire, Thos. P.; Ohio, 1840-1897 *8365.35 p16*

Hergel, Guillaume 36; Missouri, 1845 *778.6 p161*
Hergerling, Heinrich Wilhelm Albert; Port uncertain,
  1842 *7420.1 p25*
  With son 29
  With son 20
  With son 2
  With daughter 6
  With daughter 11
  With son 5
  With son 26
  With son 23
Hergert, Benedict; Illinois, 1834-1900 *6020.5 p132*
Heric, Louis 26; New Orleans, 1848 *778.6 p161*
Heric, Marie 18; New Orleans, 1848 *778.6 p161*
Herichon, Nicolas; Quebec, 1640 *9221.17 p97*
Hering, Adam; America, 1836 *2526.42 p181*
Hering, Georg Ernst; America, 1883 *2526.43 p170*
Hering, James 38; Ontario, 1871 *1823.17 p69*
Hering, Ludwig; America, 1836 *2526.42 p163*
Heringer, Johann; Dakota, 1892-1918 *554.30 p26*
  *Wife:*Ludwige Massier
Heringer, Ludwige Massier *SEE* Heringer, Johann
Heringer, Sophia; Dakota, 1881-1918 *554.30 p25*
Herington, Alanson 52; Ontario, 1871 *1823.21 p158*
Heripel, Marie 17; Quebec, 1639 *9221.17 p86*
Herisse, Francois; Montreal, 1653 *9221.17 p292*
Herisson, Jean 27; Quebec, 1660 *9221.17 p436*
Herisson, Nicolas 17; Quebec, 1638 *9221.17 p80*
Heritesova, Marie; St. Louis, 1904 *2853.20 p514*
Herivel, Mr.; Detroit, 1913 *9228.50 p282*
  With 2 brothers
Herivel, Richard; Detroit, 1895-1975 *9228.50 p282*
Herivel Family ; Ohio, n.d. *9228.50 p282*
Herker, George; Ohio, 1809-1852 *4511.35 p22*
Herkert, Fredolin; Iowa, 1920 *1211.15 p11*
Herlache, August; New York, NY, 1856 *1494.20 p11*
Herlache, Clement; New York, NY, 1856 *1494.20 p12*
Herlin, Anne; Quebec, 1662 *9221.17 p487*
Herlin, Claude 13; Quebec, 1639 *9221.17 p89*
Herlitz, Anton; North America, 1860 *6410.15 p105*
Herlitz, Carl Ludvig Lorens; North America, 1886
  6410.15 p106
Herlitz, Nils Elias; Argentina, 1889 *6410.15 p106*
Herman, Augustin; New Netherland, 1633 *2853.20 p11*
Herman, Bastian 36; America, 1843 *778.6 p161*
Herman, Francis Joseph; Ohio, 1809-1852 *4511.35 p22*
Herman, Frederick; Ohio, 1809-1852 *4511.35 p22*
Herman, Jan; Wisconsin, 1853 *2853.20 p312*
Herman, Jno; Jamestown, VA, 1633 *1658.20 p211*
Herman, Josef; South Dakota, 1869-1871 *2853.20 p246*
Herman, Laurent 20; Quebec, 1661 *9221.17 p459*
Herman, Lewis; Washington, 1887 *6015.10 p16*
Herman, Roy; Detroit, 1929-1930 *6214.5 p63*
Hermani, Elisabeth 13 *SEE* Hermani, Peter
Hermani, Johann 19 *SEE* Hermani, Peter
Hermani, Karoline 3 *SEE* Hermani, Peter
Hermani, Margarethe 8 *SEE* Hermani, Peter
Hermani, Margarethe Dillmann 48 *SEE* Hermani, Peter
Hermani, Peter 52; America, 1857 *5475.1 p512*
  *Wife:*Margarethe Dillmann 48
  *Daughter:*Margarethe 8
  *Daughter:*Karoline 3
  *Son:*Johann 19
  *Daughter:*Elisabeth 13
Hermann, A. Maria; America, 1883 *5475.1 p135*
Hermann, Adolf 18; New York, NY, 1893 *1883.7 p43*
Hermann, Angela; Iowa, 1886 *5475.1 p141*
Hermann, Anton 30; Louisiana, 1847 *778.6 p161*
Hermann, August; Valdivia, Chile, 1850 *1192.4 p48*
Hermann, Carl; Chile, 1852 *1192.4 p52*
Hermann, Carolina 1 months; New York, NY, 1893
  1883.7 p42
Hermann, Catharina 67; New York, NY, 1893 *1883.7*
  p42
Hermann, Friederike 4; New York, NY, 1893 *1883.7*
  p42
Hermann, Friedrich 43; New York, NY, 1893 *1883.7*
  p41
Hermann, George 24; Louisiana, 1848 *778.6 p161*
Hermann, George; Ohio, 1809-1852 *4511.35 p22*
Hermann, Georges 25; Louisiana, 1848 *778.6 p161*
Hermann, Gertrud *SEE* Hermann, Johann
Hermann, Jacob; Halifax, N.S., 1902 *1860.4 p39*
Hermann, Jacob 2; New York, NY, 1893 *1883.7 p42*
Hermann, Jacob 27; New York, NY, 1893 *1883.7 p42*
Hermann, Johann *SEE* Hermann, Johann
Hermann, Johann; America, 1879 *5475.1 p186*
  *Daughter:*Gertrud
  *Son:*Nikolaus
  *Daughter:*Maria
  *Daughter:*Johann
  *Daughter:*Peter
Hermann, Johann 20; America, 1893 *1883.7 p38*

Hermann, Johann 11 months; New York, NY, 1893
  1883.7 p42
Hermann, Johann Heinrich; America, 1852 *2526.43 p222*
Hermann, Joseph W.; Missouri, 1889 *3276.1 p1*
Hermann, Karolina 25; New York, NY, 1893 *1883.7*
  p42
Hermann, Katherine 34; Halifax, N.S., 1902 *1860.4 p39*
Hermann, Leopold; America, 1868 *7919.3 p534*
Hermann, Ludwig; New York, 1866 *5475.1 p417*
Hermann, Margarethe; America, 1870 *5475.1 p134*
Hermann, Maria; America, 1872 *5475.1 p134*
Hermann, Maria *SEE* Hermann, Johann
Hermann, Michael; Illinois, 1834-1900 *6020.5 p132*
Hermann, Michel; America, 1882 *5475.1 p169*
Hermann, Nikolaus *SEE* Hermann, Johann
Hermann, Ottilia; Wisconsin, 1897 *6795.8 p95*
Hermann, Peter *SEE* Hermann, Johann
Hermann, Susanna; America, 1800-1899 *5475.1 p135*
Hermann, Wilhelm; Wisconsin, 1885 *6795.8 p67*
Hermann-Mauer, Magdalene; America, 1882 *5475.1*
  p141
Hermany, Elisabeth Hahn *SEE* Hermany, Joh. Friedr.
Hermany, Heinrich *SEE* Hermany, Joh. Friedr.
Hermany, Joh. Friedr.; Brazil, 1862 *5475.1 p519*
  *Wife:*Elisabeth Hahn
  *Son:*Heinrich
  *Son:*Wilhelm
  *Daughter:*Karoline
  *Daughter:*M. Elisabeth
Hermany, Johann Friedrich; Brazil, 1862 *5475.1 p519*
Hermany, Karoline *SEE* Hermany, Joh. Friedr.
Hermany, M. Elisabeth *SEE* Hermany, Joh. Friedr.
Hermany, Wilhelm *SEE* Hermany, Joh. Friedr.
Hermes, Heinrich Conrad; America, 1866 *7420.1 p243*
Hermes, Maria 15; Ontario, 1871 *1823.17 p69*
Hermes, William; New York, 1860 *358.56 p4*
Hermitage, Andrew; Louisiana, 1874 *4981.45 p132*
Hermon, Charles; Ontario, 1871 *1823.21 p158*
Hermstad, Arthur; Iowa, 1921 *1211.15 p11*
Hern, David; Louisiana, 1874-1875 *4981.45 p29*
Hernard, Charles 12; Texas, 1843 *778.6 p161*
Hernard, Franconia 1; Texas, 1843 *778.6 p162*
Hernard, J. B. 34; Texas, 1843 *778.6 p162*
Hernard, Margaret 34; Texas, 1843 *778.6 p162*
Hernard, Mary Ann 6; Texas, 1843 *778.6 p162*
Hernard, Nicolas 10; Texas, 1843 *778.6 p162*
Hernard, Virginia 9; Texas, 1843 *778.6 p162*
Herndobler, Mary; Wisconsin, 1897 *6795.8 p158*
Herne, E. A. 22; New Orleans, 1844 *778.6 p162*
Herner, Louise; Philadelphia, 1858 *8513.31 p293*
Hernkind, August; Wisconsin, 1878 *6795.8 p12*
Hernrine, John; North Carolina, 1839 *1088.45 p14*
Hero, Johann; America, 1872 *5475.1 p370*
  *Wife:*Katharina Burke
  *Daughter:*Katharina
  *Daughter:*Margarethe
  *Daughter:*Maria
Hero, Katharina *SEE* Hero, Johann
Hero, Katharina Burke *SEE* Hero, Johann
Hero, Margarethe *SEE* Hero, Johann
Hero, Maria *SEE* Hero, Johann
Heroat, Gustave 22; New Orleans, 1848 *778.6 p162*
Herod, Helena; Detroit, 1929-1930 *6214.5 p61*
Heroi, A. 55; New Orleans, 1840 *778.6 p162*
Herold, Anthony 22; New Orleans, 1848 *778.6 p162*
Herold, Catharina Bertha; America, 1868 *7919.3 p526*
Herold, Christian Frederick; Illinois, 1854 *6079.1 p6*
Herold, Peter M.; Ohio, 1868 *3580.20 p32*
Herold, Peter M.; Ohio, 1868 *6020.12 p12*
Herold, Thomas 36; Ontario, 1871 *1823.21 p158*
Heron, Eugene 28; America, 1846 *778.6 p162*
Heron, Jacqueline; Quebec, 1665 *4514.3 p325*
Heron, James 52; Ontario, 1871 *1823.21 p158*
Heron, Jeannette 59; Ontario, 1871 *1823.21 p158*
Heron, Robert 43; Ontario, 1871 *1823.21 p158*
Herons, James 16; Quebec, 1870 *8364.32 p24*
Heronshaw, Eliza 64; Ontario, 1871 *1823.21 p158*
Herosme, . . .; Quebec, 1658 *9221.17 p382*
Herpin, Charles; Nova Scotia, 1753 *3051 p112*
  *Wife:*Jeanne Philippon
Herpin, Isabelle; Nova Scotia, 1753 *3051 p112*
Herpin, Jean; Quebec, 1669 *3051 p112*
Herpin, Jeanne Philippon *SEE* Herpin, Charles
Herpin, Marie-Josephe; Nova Scotia, 1753 *3051 p113*
Herque, Carolina 1; Texas, 1848 *778.6 p162*
Herque, Chathefrine 20; Texas, 1848 *778.6 p162*
Herque, Pierre Paul 31; Texas, 1848 *778.6 p162*
Herr, Anna Margaretha 28; Pennsylvania, 1850 *170.15*
  p28
  With family
Herr, John; Ohio, 1809-1852 *4511.35 p22*
Herr, Katharina 2; Pennsylvania, 1850 *170.15 p28*
  With family

Herr, Magdalena 4; Pennsylvania, 1850 ***170.15*** *p28*
With family
Herr, Peter 35; Pennsylvania, 1850 ***170.15*** *p28*
With family
Herrenbauer, Rosine; America, 1850 ***179.55*** *p19*
Herres, Friedrich; America, 1867 ***5475.1*** *p123*
Herrguth, Franz; Valdivia, Chile, 1851 ***1192.4*** *p51*
Herrick, . . .; West Virginia, 1850-1860 ***1132.30*** *p149*
Herrin, Patrick; Boston, 1772 ***1642*** *p49*
Herring, Francis 50; Ontario, 1871 ***1823.21*** *p158*
Herring, Hugh 56; Ontario, 1871 ***1823.17*** *p69*
Herring, James 39; Ontario, 1871 ***1823.17*** *p69*
Herrington, Theodore 34; Ontario, 1871 ***1823.17*** *p69*
Herrmann, Adam; New York, NY, 1889 ***3366.30*** *p70*
Herrmann, Anna 22; Louisiana, 1847 ***778.6*** *p162*
Herrmann, Anna Maria *SEE* Herrmann, Peter
Herrmann, Christian; America, 1868 ***7919.3*** *p535*
Herrmann, Friedrich; South Dakota, 1887-1900 ***3366.30*** *p70*
Herrmann, Georg; America, 1868 ***7919.3*** *p535*
*Brother:*Simon
*Brother:*Quirinus Reinhold
Herrmann, Georg Wilhelm; America, 1884 ***2526.43*** *p205*
Herrmann, Hermann; America, 1889 ***2526.42*** *p122*
Herrmann, Isaak; America, 1882 ***2526.42*** *p122*
Herrmann, Jakob; America, 1843 ***5475.1*** *p252*
Herrmann, Johann; America, 1843 ***5475.1*** *p280*
Herrmann, Johann 4; Louisiana, 1847 ***778.6*** *p162*
Herrmann, Johann 25; Louisiana, 1847 ***778.6*** *p162*
Herrmann, Johann Adam; America, 1891 ***2526.43*** *p205*
Herrmann, Johannette; America, 1867 ***7919.3*** *p534*
Herrmann, Karl; New York, NY, 1893 ***3366.30*** *p70*
Herrmann, Magdalena *SEE* Herrmann, Peter
Herrmann, Maria Elisabeth *SEE* Herrmann, Peter
Herrmann, Maria Gertrud *SEE* Herrmann, Peter
Herrmann, Marx 17; America, 1875 ***2526.42*** *p122*
Herrmann, Mathias 25; America, 1843 ***5475.1*** *p252*
Herrmann, Moritz; Valdivia, Chile, 1852 ***1192.4*** *p54*
Herrmann, Nicolas 32; America, 1841 ***778.6*** *p162*
Herrmann, Peter; America, 1870 ***5475.1*** *p171*
Herrmann, Peter; Pittsburgh, 1879 ***5475.1*** *p60*
*Son:*Peter Heinrich
*Daughter:*Magdalena
*Daughter:*Maria Elisabeth
*Daughter:*Anna Maria
*Daughter:*Maria Gertrud
Herrmann, Peter Heinrich *SEE* Herrmann, Peter
Herrmann, Quirinus Reinhold *SEE* Herrmann, Georg
Herrmann, Samuel; America, 1893 ***2526.43*** *p170*
Herrmann, Simon *SEE* Herrmann, Georg
Herron, Frank 35; Ontario, 1871 ***1823.21*** *p158*
Herrschaft, Adam; America, 1846 ***2526.42*** *p141*
With wife & 3 children
Hersh, Frederick; West Virginia, 1787 ***1132.30*** *p146*
Hershey, Gertrude; Miami, 1935 ***4984.12*** *p39*
Hershog, J. 27; America, 1848 ***778.6*** *p162*
Herson, Edme 6; America, 1848 ***778.6*** *p162*
Herson, J.B. 53; America, 1848 ***778.6*** *p162*
Herson, Mrs. J.B. 48; America, 1848 ***778.6*** *p162*
Herson, Mathias 55; Ontario, 1871 ***1823.17*** *p69*
Herstrom, John; Cleveland, OH, 1895-1898 ***9722.10*** *p120*
Hert, Louis 28; Kentucky, 1846 ***778.6*** *p162*
Hertel, Aug.; Valdivia, Chile, 1852 ***1192.4*** *p55*
Hertel, Elisabeth Straub *SEE* Hertel, Georg Philipp
Hertel, Francois; Quebec, 1716 ***2314.30*** *p185*
Hertel, Fredric William; North Carolina, 1809 ***1088.45*** *p14*
Hertel, Georg Philipp; America, 1752 ***2526.42*** *p174*
*Wife:*Elisabeth Straub
*Son:*Johannes
*Son:*Johann Leonhard
*Daughter:*Katharina Elisabetha
Hertel, George Adam; Ohio, 1809-1852 ***4511.35*** *p22*
Hertel, Jacques; Quebec, 1635 ***9221.17*** *p46*
Hertel, Johann Leonhard 2 *SEE* Hertel, Georg Philipp
Hertel, Johannes 5 *SEE* Hertel, Georg Philipp
Hertel, Katharina Elisabetha 8 *SEE* Hertel, Georg Philipp
Hertel, Maria Katharina 39; America, 1855 ***2526.42*** *p167*
Hertel, Nicolas; Quebec, 1637 ***9221.17*** *p70*
Hertel DeLaFresniere, Jacques; Quebec, 1626 ***9221.17*** *p19*
Hertfelder, Mary; Philadelphia, 1858 ***8513.31*** *p316*
Herth, Elisabeth 2; America, 1846 ***778.6*** *p162*
Herth, Joseph Lenze; New Castle, DE, 1817-1818 ***90.20*** *p151*
Herth, Madeleine 5; America, 1846 ***778.6*** *p162*
Herth, Madeleine 30; America, 1846 ***778.6*** *p162*
Hertschuch, Sebastian; Illinois, 1834-1900 ***6020.5*** *p132*
Hertz, Jno.; Louisiana, 1874 ***4981.45*** *p296*
Hertz, Ludwig Jacobus; Kansas, 1880 ***7420.1*** *p316*
Hertz, Philip; Ohio, 1809-1852 ***4511.35*** *p22*
Hertzhog, Peter; Ohio, 1809-1852 ***4511.35*** *p22*
Herve, Jean 39; America, 1843 ***778.6*** *p162*
Herve, Renee 25; Quebec, 1660 ***9221.17*** *p469*
Hervey, John 55; Ontario, 1871 ***1823.17*** *p69*
Hervieu, Martin; Quebec, 1639 ***9221.17*** *p89*
Hervy, Sarah 54; Ontario, 1871 ***1823.17*** *p69*
Herwahn, Yngwar; New York, NY, 1843 ***6412.40*** *p147*
Herwig, Jacob; Ohio, 1844 ***2763.1*** *p8*
Herynk, Frantisek; Ohio, 1881-1889 ***2853.20*** *p505*
Herz, Bernhard; America, 1867 ***5475.1*** *p284*
Herz, David; America, 1864 ***5475.1*** *p510*
Herz, David; Chile, 1852 ***1192.4*** *p52*
Herz, Frederick William; Wisconsin, 1890 ***6795.8*** *p174*
Herz, Henriette Klein 63 *SEE* Herz, Joseph
Herz, Hermann; America, 1874 ***5475.1*** *p284*
Herz, Jakob; America, 1874 ***5475.1*** *p284*
Herz, Josef; America, 1882 ***5475.1*** *p286*
Herz, Joseph 65; America, 1865 ***5475.1*** *p511*
*Wife:*Henriette Klein 63
*Daughter:*Wilhelmine
*Son:*Moses
Herz, Mathilde; Milwaukee, 1923 ***8023.44*** *p375*
Herz, Moses *SEE* Herz, Joseph
Herz, Stephanie; America, 1860 ***5475.1*** *p510*
Herz, Wilhelmine *SEE* Herz, Joseph
Herzberger, Margarethe 46; America, 1855 ***5475.1*** *p318*
Herzfeld, August; Wisconsin, 1886 ***6795.8*** *p92*
Herzfeld, Carl; Wisconsin, 1884 ***6795.8*** *p226*
Herzfeld, Friedr. J.W.; Wisconsin, 1898 ***6795.8*** *p224*
Herzfeld, Gustav Wilhelm; Wisconsin, 1896 ***6795.8*** *p221*
Herzfeld, Herrmann; America, 1892 ***2526.43*** *p147*
Herzfeld, Herz; America, 1895 ***2526.43*** *p148*
Herzfeld, Hugo; America, 1898 ***2526.43*** *p148*
Herzfeld, Joseph; America, 1892 ***2526.43*** *p148*
Herzfeldt, Ernest Friedrich Christian; Wisconsin, 1893 ***6795.8*** *p226*
Herzig, Benedikt; New Castle, DE, 1817-1818 ***90.20*** *p151*
Herzig, Johann 25; New Castle, DE, 1817-1818 ***90.20*** *p151*
Herzing, Henry; Illinois, 1930 ***121.35*** *p101*
Herzman, August; Colorado, 1904 ***1029.59*** *p39*
Herzman, Charles; Colorado, 1904 ***1029.59*** *p39*
Herzog, Benedikt; New Castle, DE, 1817-1818 ***90.20*** *p151*
Herzog, Helene; America, 1864 ***5475.1*** *p21*
Herzog, Jerome; Illinois, 1852 ***6079.1*** *p6*
Herzog, Johann 25; New Castle, DE, 1817-1818 ***90.20*** *p151*
Herzog, Johann Wilhelm; America, 1872 ***7420.1*** *p295*
Herzog, Joseph 33; New Castle, DE, 1817-1818 ***90.20*** *p151*
Herzog, Lambert; New Castle, DE, 1817-1818 ***90.20*** *p151*
Herzog, Melchior; America, 1844 ***7420.1*** *p31*
With son 22
With daughter 3
With son 17
With daughter 11
Herzog, Michael 25; New Castle, DE, 1817-1818 ***90.20*** *p151*
Herzog, Paul 47; Kansas, 1887 ***1447.20*** *p62*
Hes, Georg Ludwig; Pennsylvania, 1864 ***2526.43*** *p218*
Hes, Johannes Carl; Cincinnati, 1869 ***2526.43*** *p218*
Hesch, Elisabeth; America, 1867 ***5475.1*** *p543*
Hesche, Karl; America, 1867 ***7919.3*** *p526*
Heschler, Catharin 28; America, 1846 ***778.6*** *p162*
Hescler, Jack 60; Ontario, 1871 ***1823.17*** *p69*
Hesden, George; Ontario, 1871 ***1823.21*** *p158*
Hesener, Wilhelm 19; America, 1926 ***8023.44*** *p374*
Heskett, Mr.; Virginia, 1750 ***9228.50*** *p283*
With 2 brothers
Heskew, Philip; Boston, 1716 ***9228.50*** *p273*
Hesler, Cath. 21; America, 1846 ***778.6*** *p162*
Hesler, Magdalena 24; America, 1846 ***778.6*** *p162*
Heslip, Wm 56; Ontario, 1871 ***1823.21*** *p158*
Hesly, Catherine 26; Missouri, 1848 ***778.6*** *p162*
Hesly, Jacob 23; Missouri, 1848 ***778.6*** *p162*
Hespe, C. P.; Valdivia, Chile, 1850 ***1192.4*** *p50*
Hespe, John; North Carolina, 1849 ***1088.45*** *p14*
Hess, Adam; America, 1836 ***2526.42*** *p105*
Hess, Adam; America, 1836 ***2526.42*** *p191*
With wife
With child 17
With child 12
With child 9
With child 20
With child 22
Hess, Adam; Illinois, 1834-1900 ***6020.5*** *p132*
Hess, Anna Margaretha; America, 1837 ***2526.42*** *p191*
Hess, Anna Margaretha 14 *SEE* Hess, Daniel
Hess, Ant. 34; America, 1840 ***778.6*** *p163*
Hess, August; New York, 1860 ***358.56*** *p148*
Hess, August; New York, 1860 ***358.56*** *p150*
Hess, Caspar Ernst; America, 1867 ***7919.3*** *p524*
Hess, Christian; Ohio, 1809-1852 ***4511.35*** *p22*
Hess, Christina Margarethe; America, 1867 ***7919.3*** *p524*
Hess, Daniel; America, 1858 ***2526.42*** *p95*
*Wife:*Elisabetha
*Child:*Eva Margareta
Hess, Daniel 32; America, 1858 ***2526.42*** *p191*
*Wife:*Elisabetha Roth 35
*Daughter:*Anna Margaretha 14
Hess, Edouard 19; America, 1746 ***778.6*** *p163*
Hess, Elisabeth; America, 1856 ***2526.43*** *p222*
Hess, Elisabeth; America, 1865 ***5475.1*** *p541*
Hess, Elisabetha *SEE* Hess, Daniel
Hess, Elisabetha Roth 35 *SEE* Hess, Daniel
Hess, Emil Friedrich; America, 1868 ***7919.3*** *p527*
With wife & 2 children
Hess, Eva Margareta *SEE* Hess, Daniel
Hess, Ferdinand; Chile, 1852 ***1192.4*** *p52*
With wife
Hess, Francois 38; Missouri, 1847 ***778.6*** *p163*
Hess, Fred. 49; America, 1845 ***778.6*** *p163*
Hess, Jakob; America, 1859 ***2526.43*** *p222*
Hess, Jakob; America, 1889 ***179.55*** *p19*
Hess, Jakob; Venezuela, 1843 ***3899.5*** *p542*
Hess, Jette; America, 1868 ***7919.3*** *p525*
Hess, Johann 27; America, 1867 ***5475.1*** *p169*
Hess, Johann Adam; America, 1868 ***7919.3*** *p524*
Hess, Johannes; Pennsylvania, 1809 ***170.15*** *p28*
Hess, John; Ohio, 1809-1852 ***4511.35*** *p22*
Hess, Joseph; Venezuela, 1843 ***3899.5*** *p541*
Hess, Julien 22; America, 1845 ***778.6*** *p163*
Hess, Katharina; Venezuela, 1843 ***3899.5*** *p540*
Hess, Konrad; America, 1875-1890 ***179.55*** *p19*
Hess, Margarethe 40; America, 1867 ***5475.1*** *p224*
Hess, Peter; America, 1837 ***2526.42*** *p105*
Hess, Peter; America, 1837 ***2526.42*** *p192*
With wife
With child 9 months
With child 3
Hess, Philip M.; Ohio, 1809-1852 ***4511.35*** *p22*
Hess, Sebastian; Venezuela, 1843 ***3899.5*** *p541*
Hess, Sophia Regina; America, 1868 ***7919.3*** *p524*
Hess, Theresia; Venezuela, 1843 ***3899.5*** *p541*
Hess, Woolrick; North Carolina, 1710 ***3629.40*** *p8*
Hess, Woolruk; North Carolina, 1710 ***3629.40*** *p4*
Hessberg, Daniel; America, 1867 ***7919.3*** *p525*
Hesse, Carl Gottlieb; North Carolina, 1848 ***1088.45*** *p14*
Hesse, Caspar 24; Mississippi, 1847 ***778.6*** *p163*
Hesse, Ehregott; Ohio, 1809-1852 ***4511.35*** *p22*
Hesse, Friedrich; America, 1849 ***5475.1*** *p29*
Hesse, Friedrich 50; New York, NY, 1883 ***8427.14*** *p44*
Hesse, Georg 28; Mississippi, 1847 ***778.6*** *p163*
Hesse, Jakob Remigius; New York, 1875 ***5475.1*** *p127*
Hesse, Johann Heinrich; America, 1867 ***7420.1*** *p257*
With family
Hesse, M. Maria Philippa 76; Brazil, n.d. ***8023.44*** *p374*
Hesse, Maria; America, 1888 ***8023.44*** *p374*
Hesse, Nanette 48; Port uncertain, 1842 ***778.6*** *p163*
Hesse, Peter; America, 1867 ***5475.1*** *p123*
Hesse, Sarah 18; Port uncertain, 1842 ***778.6*** *p163*
Hesse, Sarah 28; Port uncertain, 1842 ***778.6*** *p163*
Hesse, Wilhelmine; America, 1858 ***7420.1*** *p178*
Hessedenz, Maria Becker *SEE* Hessedenz, Mathias
Hessedenz, Mathias; America, 1871 ***5475.1*** *p212*
*Wife:*Maria Becker
Hessel, Andrew; Colorado, 1889 ***1029.59*** *p39*
Hessel, Lewis 63; Ontario, 1871 ***1823.21*** *p158*
Hessel, Simon; America, 1857 ***5475.1*** *p522*
Hesselin, J.; New York, NY, 1845 ***6412.40*** *p148*
Hessell, Andrew; Illinois, 1869 ***1029.59*** *p40*
Hesseltreet, Zacharias; Valdivia, Chile, 1851 ***1192.4*** *p50*
Hessenthaler, Johann; America, 1892 ***179.55*** *p19*
Hesser, Andre 21; Louisiana, 1848 ***778.6*** *p163*
Hesser, Charles; New York, 1859 ***358.56*** *p53*
Hesser, Eugene 20; Louisiana, 1848 ***778.6*** *p163*
Hesser, Eugenie 25; Louisiana, 1848 ***778.6*** *p163*
Hesser, Philippine 43; Louisiana, 1848 ***778.6*** *p163*
Hessey, James 40; Ontario, 1871 ***1823.17*** *p69*
Hessig, Luise; Texas, 1848 ***2526.43*** *p184*
Hessoun, Josef; St. Louis, 1865 ***2853.20*** *p25*
Hessoun, Josef; St. Louis, 1865 ***2853.20*** *p514*
Hester, Stengrime Enderson; Iowa, 1868 ***1211.15*** *p11*
Hesterberg, . . .; America, 1852 ***7420.1*** *p90*
*Daughter:*Christine
Hesterberg, . . .; America, 1852 ***7420.1*** *p90*
With family
Hesterberg, Caroline Christ. *SEE* Hesterberg, Ernst Friedrich Wilhelm
Hesterberg, Christine *SEE* Hesterberg, . . .
Hesterberg, Engel Eleonore Kerkhof *SEE* Hesterberg, Ernst Friedrich Wilhelm

Hesterberg, Ernst Friedrich Wilhelm; America, 1852 ***7420.1*** *p90*
*Wife:*Sophie Wilhelmine Korff
*Niece:*Caroline Christ.
*Brother:*Friedrich Gottlieb
*Sister-In-Law:*Engel Eleonore Kerkhof
Hesterberg, Friedrich Gottlieb *SEE* Hesterberg, Ernst Friedrich Wilhelm
Hesterberg, Hans Heinrich; America, 1852 ***7420.1*** *p90*
With family
Hesterberg, Sophie Wilhelmine Korff *SEE* Hesterberg, Ernst Friedrich Wilhelm
Het, Johann 43; New Castle, DE, 1817-1818 ***90.20*** *p151*
Heter, Helen 56; Michigan, 1880 ***4491.30*** *p15*
Hetherington, Aurthur 55; Ontario, 1871 ***1823.21*** *p158*
Hetherington, Christopher; New York, NY, 1840 ***3274.56*** *p69*
Hetherington, John; Boston, 1841 ***3274.56*** *p97*
Hetherington, Simon 49; Ontario, 1871 ***1823.17*** *p69*
Hetherington, William 52; Ontario, 1871 ***1823.21*** *p158*
Hetley, John 40; Ontario, 1871 ***1823.21*** *p158*
Hettich, Andreas; Venezuela, 1843 ***3899.5*** *p540*
Hettich, Andreas; Venezuela, 1843 ***3899.5*** *p540*
Hettich, C. G.; Valdivia, Chile, 1850 ***1192.4*** *p48*
Hettich, G. S.; Valdivia, Chile, 1850 ***1192.4*** *p48*
Hettich, Joh. Martin; Venezuela, 1843 ***3899.5*** *p540*
Hettich, Maria Josepha; Venezuela, 1843 ***3899.5*** *p540*
Hettler, Christopher; Nova Scotia, 1784 ***7105*** *p23*
Hettrich, Georg Daniel; America, 1872 ***5475.1*** *p71*
Hettrich, Peter; America, 1868 ***5475.1*** *p71*
Hetzel, Miss C. 27; New Orleans, 1834 ***1002.51*** *p113*
Hetzel, F. 3; New Orleans, 1834 ***1002.51*** *p113*
Hetzel, H. 30; New Orleans, 1834 ***1002.51*** *p113*
Hetzel, Miss M. 50; New Orleans, 1834 ***1002.51*** *p113*
Hetzel, S. 1; New Orleans, 1834 ***1002.51*** *p113*
Hetzler, Nikolaus; America, 1882 ***5475.1*** *p229*
Heubach, Barbara; America, 1868 ***7919.3*** *p531*
With 3 children
Heubach, Hugo; America, 1867 ***7919.3*** *p531*
Heuberger, John; New York, 1859 ***358.56*** *p54*
Heubler, Maria Magdalena; Venezuela, 1843 ***3899.5*** *p540*
Heude, Francois; Quebec, 1657 ***9221.17*** *p359*
Heude, Marie 20; Quebec, 1647 ***9221.17*** *p182*
Heude, Marie 20; Quebec, 1647 ***9221.17*** *p182*
Heuel, Peter; America, 1905-1907 ***8023.44*** *p375*
Heuer, Friederike; America, 1858 ***7420.1*** *p178*
Heuer, Marie Luise; America, 1872 ***7420.1*** *p295*
Heuerberg, Johann Hermann Friedrich; America, 1860 ***7420.1*** *p194*
Heufemann, Wilhelm; Chile, 1852 ***1192.4*** *p52*
Heugs, Bernank 23; New York, NY, 1847 ***9176.15*** *p49*
Heulard, Charles 20; America, 1846 ***778.6*** *p163*
Heulard, Dominique 55; America, 1846 ***778.6*** *p163*
Heuly, George 55; New Orleans, 1848 ***778.6*** *p163*
Heumann, August Heinrich Wilhelm; America, 1865 ***7420.1*** *p231*
Heumann, Ernst Friedrich Wilhelm; America, 1868 ***7420.1*** *p272*
Heumann, Ferdinand Hermann Wilhelm; America, 1871 ***7420.1*** *p290*
Heumann, Fr.; America, 1857 ***7420.1*** *p163*
Heumann, Heinrich; America, 1871 ***7420.1*** *p290*
With family
Heunton, J. B. 20; New Orleans, 1842 ***778.6*** *p163*
Heurich, Adolph Theodor; America, 1868 ***7919.3*** *p528*
Heurtebise, Andre 23; Montreal, 1653 ***9221.17*** *p292*
*Brother:*Marin 21
Heurtebise, Marin 21 *SEE* Heurtebise, Andre
Heusel, Adam, II; America, 1847 ***2526.42*** *p122*
With wife
Heusel, Anna Margaretha 12 *SEE* Heusel, Johann Friedrich
Heusel, Elisabeth; America, 1853 ***2526.42*** *p152*
Heusel, Eva Elisabetha Steiger *SEE* Heusel, Johann Friedrich
Heusel, Eva Maria 18 *SEE* Heusel, Johann Friedrich
Heusel, Friedrich; America, 1860 ***2526.42*** *p181*
Heusel, Johann Dieter 21; America, 1853 ***2526.42*** *p122*
Heusel, Johann Dieter 15 *SEE* Heusel, Johann Friedrich
Heusel, Johann Friedrich; Cincinnati, 1854 ***2526.42*** *p174*
*Wife:*Eva Elisabetha Steiger
*Daughter:*Anna Margaretha
*Son:*Johannes
*Son:*Johann Dieter
*Daughter:*Marg. Elisabetha
*Daughter:*Eva Maria
Heusel, Johannes 2 *SEE* Heusel, Johann Friedrich
Heusel, Marg. Elisabetha 21 *SEE* Heusel, Johann Friedrich
Heusel, Martin; America, 1837 ***2526.42*** *p192*
With wife
Heusel, Martin; America, 1837 ***2526.42*** *p193*
With daughter & mother-in-law
Heusel, Nikolaus 17; America, 1841 ***2526.42*** *p182*
Heusel, Philipp, III; America, 1841 ***2526.42*** *p182*
With wife & child
Heuser, Caroline 27; America, 1840 ***778.6*** *p163*
Heuser, Conrad 54; Kansas, 1892 ***1447.20*** *p62*
Heuser, Ernst Louis Valentin; Chile, 1886 ***7420.1*** *p350*
Heuser, Lazave 9; America, 1840 ***778.6*** *p163*
Heuser, Rosine 32; America, 1840 ***778.6*** *p163*
Heuser, Theodore Charlotte Johannette; America, 1858 ***7420.1*** *p178*
Heushler, Jacob; Ohio, 1809-1852 ***4511.35*** *p22*
Heusing, Carl Friedrich Wilhelm; America, 1864 ***7420.1*** *p224*
Heusing, Friedrich; Port uncertain, 1854 ***7420.1*** *p121*
Heusing, Wilhelmine; America, 1867 ***7420.1*** *p266*
With daughters
Heusinger, Anton; America, 1868 ***7919.3*** *p528*
With family
Heusinger, August; America, 1867 ***7919.3*** *p528*
Heusinger, Friedrich Ernst; America, 1867 ***7919.3*** *p528*
Heusler, Mathieu; New Castle, DE, 1817-1818 ***90.20*** *p151*
Heusner, Carl; America, 1857 ***7420.1*** *p163*
Heusser, Anna Katharina; Pennsylvania, 1866 ***170.15*** *p28*
Heusser, Henrich; Pennsylvania, 1866 ***170.15*** *p28*
With wife
Heussi, Jacob 26; America, 1844 ***778.6*** *p163*
Heuston, George 55; Ontario, 1871 ***1823.21*** *p158*
Heuzler, Franz 18; Port uncertain, 1840 ***778.6*** *p163*
Hevey, James 60; Ontario, 1871 ***1823.21*** *p158*
Hevia, Antonio; Miami, 1935 ***4984.12*** *p39*
Hevia y Gutierrez, Jose Antonio; Miami, 1935 ***4984.12*** *p39*
Hewes, George; Massachusetts, 1675-1676 ***1642*** *p128*
Hewett, Charles; Boston, 1766 ***1642*** *p37*
Hewett, John T.; Philadelphia, 1859 ***5720.10*** *p378*
Hewiston, Edward J.; Colorado, 1893 ***1029.59*** *p40*
Hewit, James 34; Ontario, 1871 ***1823.21*** *p158*
Hewit, Simon 46; Ontario, 1871 ***1823.17*** *p69*
Hewitt, . . .; South Carolina, 1680 ***9228.50*** *p283*
Hewitt, Alexander; Baltimore, 1831 ***471.10*** *p87*
Hewitt, Allen 38; Ontario, 1871 ***1823.21*** *p158*
Hewitt, Christina 15; Ontario, 1871 ***1823.17*** *p69*
Hewitt, John T.; Philadelphia, 1859 ***5720.10*** *p378*
Hewitt, Louise 75; Ontario, 1871 ***1823.17*** *p69*
Hewitt, Nancy 32; Michigan, 1880 ***4491.36*** *p10*
Hewitt, Rich; Jamestown, VA, 1633 ***1658.20*** *p211*
Hewitt, Richard 38; Ontario, 1871 ***1823.21*** *p158*
Hewitt, Sarah 60; Michigan, 1880 ***4491.42*** *p13*
Hewlet, George 40; Ontario, 1871 ***1823.21*** *p158*
Hewlette, Mr. 8; America, 1847 ***778.6*** *p163*
Hewlette, Mrs. 28; America, 1847 ***778.6*** *p163*
Hewson, Ann 46; Ontario, 1871 ***1823.21*** *p158*
Hexamer, David; Ohio, 1809-1852 ***4511.35*** *p22*
Hexamer, Jacob; Ohio, 1809-1852 ***4511.35*** *p22*
Hexton, James 50; Ontario, 1871 ***1823.17*** *p69*
Hey, Shackleton 36; Ontario, 1871 ***1823.21*** *p158*
Heyabrandt, Edmond; New York, 1903 ***1766.20*** *p3*
Heyd, Maria; America, 1888 ***8023.44*** *p374*
Heyde, James; Ohio, 1809-1852 ***4511.35*** *p22*
Heyde, Nicolas 30; America, 1840 ***778.6*** *p163*
Heyden, L. 27; America, 1872 ***5475.1*** *p419*
Heydon, Henry 64; Ontario, 1871 ***1823.21*** *p158*
Heyer, Frederick Wm; North Carolina, 1850 ***1088.45*** *p14*
Heyer, Helena Auguste Pauline; Wisconsin, 1892 ***6795.8*** *p149*
Heyer, John C.; North Carolina, 1856 ***1088.45*** *p14*
Heyer, William A.; North Carolina, 1856 ***1088.45*** *p14*
Heyfron, Daniel; New Orleans, 1850 ***7242.30*** *p144*
Heyfron, Esther; New Orleans, 1850 ***7242.30*** *p144*
Heyfron, Martin; New Orleans, 1850 ***7242.30*** *p144*
Heyfron, Mary; New Orleans, 1850 ***7242.30*** *p144*
Heyfron, Mary Anne; New Orleans, 1850 ***7242.30*** *p144*
Heyfron, Michael; New Orleans, 1850 ***7242.30*** *p144*
Heyl, Christoph, II; America, 1832 ***2526.43*** *p170*
With wife & 4 children
Heyl, Friedrich Karl; America, 1883 ***2526.43*** *p170*
Heyl, Johann Georg; America, n.d. ***2526.43*** *p170*
Heyl, Karl Franz; America, 1881 ***2526.43*** *p170*
Heyl, Wendel; America, 1847 ***5475.1*** *p475*
Heylmann, Marie 17; Port uncertain, 1846 ***778.6*** *p163*
Heymann, . . .; America, 1837 ***7420.1*** *p13*
Heymel, Ant. 28; Louisiana, 1840 ***778.6*** *p163*
Heywood, Thomas 28; Ontario, 1871 ***1823.21*** *p158*
Heywood, William 55; Ontario, 1871 ***1823.21*** *p158*
Hiardin, Marguerite; Quebec, 1665 ***4514.3*** *p325*
Hibbard, . . .; Ontario, 1871 ***1823.21*** *p158*
Hibbard, Johanna; Canada, 1689-1695 ***9228.50*** *p617*
*Child:*Mary
*Child:*Jasper
Hibbard, Johanna; Canada, 1689-1695 ***9228.50*** *p617*
*Child:*Mary
*Child:*Jasper
Hibberd, Emma; Philadelphia, 1860 ***8513.31*** *p316*
Hibbert, Emily 12; Quebec, 1870 ***8364.32*** *p24*
Hibbins, William; Boston, 1620-1775 ***1642*** *p138*
Hibbins, William; Boston, 1634 ***1642*** *p5*
Hibbs, James; Louisiana, 1874-1875 ***4981.45*** *p29*
Hiberney, William; Plymouth, MA, 1661 ***1642*** *p2*
Hibery, John; Marston's Wharf, 1782 ***8529.30*** *p12*
Hibler, Anna Maria; Venezuela, 1843 ***3899.5*** *p544*
Hibler, Maria Magdalena; Venezuela, 1843 ***3899.5*** *p540*
Hibschen, Mathias 30; America, 1843 ***5475.1*** *p305*
Hibzinger, John; North Carolina, 1856 ***1088.45*** *p14*
Hick, Charles Peter; Colorado, 1881 ***1029.59*** *p40*
Hick, Grim 36; Ontario, 1871 ***1823.21*** *p158*
Hick, Henry 64; Ontario, 1871 ***1823.21*** *p158*
Hick, John 18; Ontario, 1871 ***1823.21*** *p158*
Hick, William 70; Ontario, 1871 ***1823.17*** *p69*
Hickard, John 40; Ontario, 1871 ***1823.21*** *p159*
Hickery, Robert 37; Ontario, 1871 ***1823.21*** *p159*
Hickes, Margret 26; Ontario, 1871 ***1823.21*** *p159*
Hickey, Arden 24; New York, NY, 1844 ***6178.50*** *p151*
Hickey, Bridget; Halifax, N.S., 1827 ***7009.9*** *p61*
Hickey, C. M.; Louisiana, 1874 ***4981.45*** *p296*
Hickey, Catherine 70; Ontario, 1871 ***1823.21*** *p159*
Hickey, Charles; Boston, 1776 ***8529.30*** *p3A*
Hickey, Daniel; Boston, 1773 ***1642*** *p49*
Hickey, Eleanor; Marblehead, MA, 1761 ***1642*** *p73*
Hickey, James; Boston, 1768 ***1642*** *p39*
Hickey, James; Burlington, VT, 1830 ***3274.55*** *p24*
Hickey, John; Boston, 1759 ***1642*** *p47*
Hickey, John; Colorado, 1884 ***1029.59*** *p40*
Hickey, John; Toronto, 1844 ***2910.35*** *p114*
Hickey, Margaret; Halifax, N.S., 1827 ***7009.9*** *p62*
Hickey, Margrett 45; Ontario, 1871 ***1823.17*** *p69*
Hickey, Michael; New York, 1778 ***8529.30*** *p3A*
Hickey, Michael 33; New York, NY, 1844 ***6178.50*** *p151*
Hickey, Patrick; Marblehead, MA, 1726 ***1642*** *p73*
Hickey, Patrick 40; New York, NY, 1844 ***6178.50*** *p151*
Hickey, Patrick; Salem, MA, 1726 ***1642*** *p78*
Hickey, Thomas; New Jersey, 1777 ***8529.30*** *p6*
Hickey, Thomas 35; Ontario, 1871 ***1823.21*** *p159*
Hickling, William 50; Ontario, 1871 ***1823.21*** *p159*
Hickman, Ann 10; Ontario, 1871 ***1823.21*** *p159*
Hickman, Nath; Virginia, 1652 ***6254.4*** *p243*
Hickmotte, George 42; Ontario, 1871 ***1823.17*** *p69*
Hicknbotham, George 32; Ontario, 1871 ***1823.17*** *p69*
Hicks, Andrew 38; Ontario, 1871 ***1823.21*** *p159*
Hicks, Charles 53; Ontario, 1871 ***1823.21*** *p159*
Hicks, Henry 16; Quebec, 1870 ***8364.32*** *p24*
Hicks, James 36; Ontario, 1871 ***1823.21*** *p159*
Hicks, John 30; Ontario, 1871 ***1823.21*** *p159*
Hicks, Joseph 32; Ontario, 1871 ***1823.21*** *p159*
Hicks, Richard 28; Ontario, 1871 ***1823.21*** *p159*
Hicks, Samuel 24; Michigan, 1880 ***4491.36*** *p10*
Hicks, Samuel 37; Ontario, 1871 ***1823.21*** *p159*
Hicks, Sarah 21; Michigan, 1880 ***4491.36*** *p10*
Hicks, Thomas; Marston's Wharf, 1782 ***8529.30*** *p12*
Hickson, Mary Jordan *SEE* Hickson, Thomas
Hickson, Samuel 54; Ontario, 1871 ***1823.21*** *p159*
Hickson, Thomas; Maryland, 1860 ***8513.31*** *p314*
*Wife:*Mary Jordan
Hickson, William 48; Ontario, 1871 ***1823.21*** *p159*
Hicky, Edward 28; Ontario, 1871 ***1823.21*** *p159*
Hidelee, George; New Jersey, 1754-1774 ***927.31*** *p3*
Hidinge, Christina; St. Paul, MN, 1888 ***1865.50*** *p98*
*Daughter:*Anna Alfrida
*Daughter:*Frida Elisabeth
*Son:*Fritz Gerhard
Hidinge, Christina; St. Paul, MN, 1888 ***1865.50*** *p98*
*Daughter:*Anna Alfrida
*Son:*Fritz Gerhard
*Daughter:*Frida Elisabeth
Hidou, Francois Pierre 45; Texas, 1848 ***778.6*** *p163*
Hier, Johan 48; America, 1848 ***778.6*** *p163*
Hieronymus, August; America, 1865 ***2526.43*** *p170*
Hiery, Catharine McKernan *SEE* Hiery, Patrick
Hiery, Patrick; Philadelphia, 1851 ***8513.31*** *p314*
*Wife:*Catharine McKernan
Hiess, Clemens; New York, 1859 ***358.56*** *p54*
Hietala, Hilda 38; Minnesota, 1925 ***2769.54*** *p1380*
Hiettanen, John 36; Minnesota, 1923 ***2769.54*** *p1381*
Hiff, Miss 16; Quebec, 1870 ***8364.32*** *p24*
Higason, Stewart; Jamaica, 1776 ***8529.30*** *p13A*
Higgan, Mic; St. John, N.B., 1847 ***2978.15*** *p40*
Higgenbotham, Mark; Ohio, 1809-1852 ***4511.35*** *p22*
Higgenbotham, Robert; Ohio, 1809-1852 ***4511.35*** *p22*
Higges, Samuel 17; Quebec, 1870 ***8364.32*** *p24*
Higginbotham, Mark; Ohio, 1809-1852 ***4511.35*** *p22*
Higgins, Mr.; Plymouth, MA, 1606-1621 ***1642*** *p1*
Higgins, Ben, Sr. 63; Ontario, 1871 ***1823.21*** *p159*

Higgins, Bernard; Philadelphia, 1857 ***8513.31*** *p314*
*Wife:*Sarah Cole
Higgins, David 34; Ontario, 1871 ***1823.17*** *p69*
Higgins, Ebenezer 55; Ontario, 1871 ***1823.21*** *p159*
Higgins, Elenor; Boston, 1765 ***1642*** *p48*
Higgins, Florence Mable; Miami, 1920 ***4984.15*** *p38*
Higgins, Henry 25; Ontario, 1871 ***1823.21*** *p159*
Higgins, James; Ohio, 1809-1852 ***4511.35*** *p22*
Higgins, James 35; Ontario, 1871 ***1823.17*** *p69*
Higgins, John; North Carolina, 1792-1862 ***1088.45*** *p14*
Higgins, John; Ohio, 1809-1852 ***4511.35*** *p22*
Higgins, John 46; Ontario, 1871 ***1823.17*** *p69*
Higgins, John G. 4; Florida, 1818-1843 ***8481.1*** *p18*
Higgins, Mary; Boston, 1754 ***1642*** *p47*
Higgins, Mary 40; Ontario, 1871 ***1823.17*** *p69*
Higgins, Pat; St. John, N.B., 1847 ***2978.15*** *p38*
Higgins, Patrick; Maine, 1837 ***3274.56*** *p99*
Higgins, Robert 25; Ontario, 1871 ***1823.21*** *p159*
Higgins, Sarah Cole *SEE* Higgins, Bernard
Higgins, Thomas 31; Ontario, 1871 ***1823.17*** *p69*
Higgins, Thomas 40; Ontario, 1871 ***1823.17*** *p69*
Higgins, Thomas 72; Ontario, 1871 ***1823.17*** *p69*
Higgins, Thomas; Philadelphia, 1777 ***8529.30*** *p6*
Higgins, William 45; Ontario, 1871 ***1823.17*** *p69*
Higgins, Wm; Louisiana, 1874-1875 ***4981.45*** *p29*
Higgison, Arthur 31; Ontario, 1871 ***1823.17*** *p69*
Higgison, Stewart; Jamaica, 1776 ***8529.30*** *p13A*
Higgs, Harold James; Miami, 1935 ***4984.12*** *p39*
Higgs, Mary 48; Ontario, 1871 ***1823.21*** *p159*
Higgs, William 27; Ontario, 1871 ***1823.21*** *p159*
High, John; America, 1772 ***1220.12*** *p548*
High, John; Marblehead, MA, 1700-1799 ***9228.50*** *p451*
High, Thomas 12; Quebec, 1870 ***8364.32*** *p24*
Higham, Enoch 40; Ontario, 1871 ***1823.21*** *p159*
Highfield, Christopher 34; Ontario, 1871 ***1823.17*** *p69*
Highfield, Eliza 53; Ontario, 1871 ***1823.21*** *p159*
Highman, John 26; Ontario, 1871 ***1823.17*** *p69*
Highwarden, Simeon 40; Ontario, 1871 ***1823.17*** *p70*
Higman, James 31; Ontario, 1871 ***1823.21*** *p159*
Higoneul, Jean Pierre 32; New Orleans, 1847 ***778.6*** *p163*
Higson, Willoughby; North Carolina, 1792-1862 ***1088.45*** *p14*
Higuet, Mrs. 21; Port uncertain, 1842 ***778.6*** *p163*
Hilaire, Mrs. 23; New Orleans, 1844 ***778.6*** *p164*
Hilbeck, George 32; Ontario, 1871 ***1823.21*** *p159*
Hilbert, Adam; Ohio, 1809-1852 ***4511.35*** *p22*
Hilbert, Catherine 24; New Orleans, 1844 ***778.6*** *p164*
Hilbert, Mrs. Philipp; America, 1847 ***2526.42*** *p152*
Hilborn, Joseph 37; Ontario, 1871 ***1823.17*** *p70*
Hilbourne, Charles H. 34; Ontario, 1871 ***1823.21*** *p159*
Hild, Adam 5 *SEE* Hild, Mrs. Heinrich
Hild, Anna 57; America, 1875 ***5475.1*** *p256*
Hild, Anna Eva; America, 1856 ***2526.43*** *p130*
Hild, Anna Katharina; America, 1856 ***2526.43*** *p130*
Hild, Anna Margaretha 18 *SEE* Hild, Mrs. Heinrich
Hild, Anna Maria 16 *SEE* Hild, Mrs. Heinrich
Hild, Elisabetha; America, 1860 ***2526.42*** *p169*
Hild, Eva Margaretha 12 *SEE* Hild, Mrs. Heinrich
Hild, Friedrich 31; America, 1882 ***2526.42*** *p169*
Hild, Georg; America, 1860 ***2526.42*** *p169*
Hild, Georg; America, 1882 ***2526.43*** *p148*
Hild, George; Ohio, 1809-1852 ***4511.35*** *p22*
Hild, Mrs. Heinrich; America, 1845 ***2526.42*** *p142*
*Child:*Anna Margaretha
*Child:*Eva Margaretha
*Child:*Johann Michael
*Child:*Adam
*Child:*Anna Maria
Hild, Johann Dieter; America, 1856 ***2526.43*** *p130*
Hild, Johann Georg 32; America, 1882 ***2526.42*** *p174*
Hild, Johann Michael 9 *SEE* Hild, Mrs. Heinrich
Hild, Josef; New York, 1865 ***5475.1*** *p12*
*Brother:*Karl Emmerich
Hild, Karl Emmerich *SEE* Hild, Josef
Hild, Magdalena 46; America, 1874 ***5475.1*** *p341*
Hild, Margaretha; America, 1853 ***2526.42*** *p199*
Hild, Philipp; America, 1893 ***2526.42*** *p108*
Hild, Philipp 27; America, 1882 ***2526.42*** *p169*
Hild, Xavier 25; America, 1846 ***778.6*** *p164*
Hildabrandt, Jurgen; Iowa, 1889 ***1211.15*** *p11*
Hildebrand, Ernst; America, 1867 ***7919.3*** *p527*
With wife & 8 children
Hildebrand, Francis J.; Colorado, 1892 ***1029.59*** *p40*
Hildebrand, Henry; Ohio, 1842 ***2763.1*** *p8*
Hildebrand, John; Ohio, 1844 ***2763.1*** *p8*
Hildebrand, John, Jr.; Ohio, 1844 ***2763.1*** *p8*
Hildebrandt, Joh. 24; America, 1893 ***1883.7*** *p38*
Hilderbrand, Francis; Colorado, 1892 ***1029.59*** *p40*
Hilderbrant, Ernast; Ohio, 1840-1897 ***8365.35*** *p16*
Hilderman, David 40; Portland, ME, 1911 ***970.38*** *p78*
Hilderman, Friedrick 22; Portland, ME, 1911 ***970.38*** *p78*
Hilderman, Gottfried 18; Portland, ME, 1911 ***970.38*** *p78*
Hildermann, Anna 19; Portland, ME, 1912 ***970.38*** *p78*
Hildermann, David 20; Portland, ME, 1912 ***970.38*** *p78*
Hildermann, Johann Georg 17; Portland, ME, 1912 ***970.38*** *p78*
Hildner, John Gottleib; New York, 1859 ***358.56*** *p101*
Hildpold, Henry; Ohio, 1809-1852 ***4511.35*** *p22*
Hildy, William 60; Ontario, 1871 ***1823.17*** *p70*
Hile, John 50; Ontario, 1871 ***1823.17*** *p70*
Hile, John 60; Ontario, 1871 ***1823.21*** *p159*
Hilgen, Phillip; Illinois, 1865 ***6079.1*** *p6*
Hilgers, Jane; Philadelphia, 1861 ***8513.31*** *p323*
Hilke, Emilie 7; New York, NY, 1893 ***1883.7*** *p37*
Hilke, Ferdinand 38; New York, NY, 1893 ***1883.7*** *p37*
Hilke, Julius 15; New York, NY, 1893 ***1883.7*** *p37*
Hilke, Justine 48; New York, NY, 1893 ***1883.7*** *p37*
Hilke, Mathilde 17; New York, NY, 1893 ***1883.7*** *p37*
Hilker, Heinrich; Port uncertain, 1837 ***7420.1*** *p13*
Hill, Mr. 17; Halifax, N.S., 1902 ***1860.4*** *p39*
Hill, A. E.; California, 1868 ***1131.61*** *p89*
Hill, Alexander 30; Halifax, N.S., 1902 ***1860.4*** *p39*
Hill, Alexr. 23; South Carolina, 1812 ***3476.30*** *p12*
Hill, Alexr. 45; South Carolina, 1812 ***3476.30*** *p11*
Hill, Alfred 6; Quebec, 1870 ***8364.32*** *p24*
Hill, Andrew; Ohio, 1809-1852 ***4511.35*** *p22*
Hill, Ann; Boston, 1767 ***1642*** *p39*
Hill, Ann 59; Michigan, 1880 ***4491.42*** *p13*
Hill, Ann 50; Ontario, 1871 ***1823.21*** *p159*
Hill, Anna 34; Halifax, N.S., 1902 ***1860.4*** *p39*
Hill, Anna 39; Michigan, 1880 ***4491.33*** *p12*
Hill, Annie 11; Quebec, 1870 ***8364.32*** *p24*
Hill, Barbara 53; Halifax, N.S., 1902 ***1860.4*** *p39*
Hill, Cantwell 54; Ontario, 1871 ***1823.17*** *p70*
Hill, Charles 48; Ontario, 1871 ***1823.17*** *p70*
Hill, Charlotta 4; Halifax, N.S., 1902 ***1860.4*** *p39*
Hill, Clement; Maryland, 1662 ***9228.50*** *p283*
Hill, Daniel 68; Ontario, 1871 ***1823.21*** *p159*
Hill, Edward 36; Ontario, 1871 ***1823.21*** *p159*
Hill, Edward; South Carolina, 1808 ***6155.4*** *p18*
Hill, Elisabeth; America, 1881 ***5475.1*** *p23*
Hill, Elizabeth *SEE* Hill, John
Hill, Elizabeth Moon *SEE* Hill, Emanuel
Hill, Emanuel; New London, CT, 1850-1854 ***9228.50*** *p283*
Hill, Emanuel; New London, CT, 1850 ***9228.50*** *p468*
*Wife:*Elizabeth Moon
*Child:*John Moon
*Child:*Emanuel, Jr.
*Child:*Rosalia Mary
Hill, Emanuel, Jr. *SEE* Hill, Emanuel
Hill, Eva; America, 1867 ***2526.42*** *p122*
Hill, Frank; Minnesota, 1925 ***2769.54*** *p1383*
Hill, Frederick 7; Quebec, 1870 ***8364.32*** *p24*
Hill, Friedrich 8; Halifax, N.S., 1902 ***1860.4*** *p39*
Hill, Friedrich 54; Halifax, N.S., 1902 ***1860.4*** *p39*
Hill, George; New York, 1779 ***8529.30*** *p12*
Hill, George 40; Ontario, 1871 ***1823.21*** *p159*
Hill, George 53; Ontario, 1871 ***1823.21*** *p159*
Hill, Grace 14; Quebec, 1870 ***8364.32*** *p24*
Hill, Hannah; America, 1722 ***1220.12*** *p635*
Hill, Heinrich; Halifax, N.S., 1902 ***1860.4*** *p39*
Hill, Heinrich 32; Halifax, N.S., 1902 ***1860.4*** *p39*
Hill, Henry *SEE* Hill, William
Hill, Henry; Virginia, 1665 ***9228.50*** *p53*
Hill, Hilma 32; Minnesota, 1925 ***2769.54*** *p1381*
Hill, J. Robert; St. Paul, MN, 1874-1905 ***1865.50*** *p50*
Hill, Jack 32; Minnesota, 1925 ***2769.54*** *p1379*
Hill, James; Newfoundland, 1814 ***3476.10*** *p54*
Hill, James 33; Ontario, 1871 ***1823.21*** *p159*
Hill, James 41; Ontario, 1871 ***1823.21*** *p160*
Hill, James 53; Ontario, 1871 ***1823.21*** *p160*
Hill, James 58; Ontario, 1871 ***1823.17*** *p70*
Hill, James 62; Ontario, 1871 ***1823.21*** *p160*
Hill, Jane *SEE* Hill, John
Hill, Jane 30; Ontario, 1871 ***1823.21*** *p160*
Hill, John; Boston, 1774 ***8529.30*** *p2*
Hill, John; Canada, 1774 ***3036.5*** *p41*
*Wife:*Jane
*Child:*Elizabeth
*Child:*Mary
*Child:*Thomas
Hill, John 33; Michigan, 1880 ***4491.42*** *p14*
Hill, John 62; Michigan, 1880 ***4491.42*** *p14*
Hill, John 17; Minnesota, 1925 ***2769.54*** *p1378*
Hill, John 26; Ontario, 1871 ***1823.21*** *p160*
Hill, John 46; Ontario, 1871 ***1823.21*** *p160*
Hill, John 61; Ontario, 1871 ***1823.17*** *p70*
Hill, John; Washington, 1884 ***2770.40*** *p192*
Hill, John E. 30; Ontario, 1871 ***1823.21*** *p160*
Hill, John Moon *SEE* Hill, Emanuel
Hill, Joseph 60; Ontario, 1871 ***1823.21*** *p160*
Hill, Katarina 12; Halifax, N.S., 1902 ***1860.4*** *p39*
Hill, Katherina 3; Halifax, N.S., 1902 ***1860.4*** *p39*
Hill, Lydia 8; Halifax, N.S., 1902 ***1860.4*** *p39*
Hill, Maria; Halifax, N.S., 1902 ***1860.4*** *p39*
Hill, Maria 11; Halifax, N.S., 1902 ***1860.4*** *p39*
Hill, Maria 30; Halifax, N.S., 1902 ***1860.4*** *p39*
Hill, Mary *SEE* Hill, John
Hill, Mary 32; Michigan, 1880 ***4491.42*** *p14*
Hill, Mary 29; Ontario, 1871 ***1823.21*** *p160*
Hill, Mary A. 61; Michigan, 1880 ***4491.30*** *p15*
Hill, Maud 3; Ontario, 1871 ***1823.21*** *p160*
Hill, Milward 63; Ontario, 1871 ***1823.17*** *p70*
Hill, Papline 1; Halifax, N.S., 1902 ***1860.4*** *p39*
Hill, Peter; Boston, 1827 ***3274.56*** *p71*
Hill, Peter J. 45; Michigan, 1880 ***4491.33*** *p12*
Hill, Miss R. E.; Montreal, 1922 ***4514.4*** *p32*
Hill, Richard; Louisiana, 1874-1875 ***4981.45*** *p29*
Hill, Richard; Massachusetts, 1830 ***3274.55*** *p23*
Hill, Richard; New Jersey, 1777 ***8529.30*** *p6*
Hill, Richard 30; Ontario, 1871 ***1823.21*** *p160*
Hill, Richard 32; Ontario, 1871 ***1823.21*** *p160*
Hill, Robert 29; Michigan, 1880 ***4491.30*** *p15*
Hill, Robert; South Carolina, 1808 ***6155.4*** *p18*
Hill, Rosalia Mary *SEE* Hill, Emanuel
Hill, Saml.; California, 1868 ***1131.61*** *p89*
Hill, Samuel; Maine, 1653 ***9228.50*** *p283*
Hill, Sarah; Iowa, 1844 ***9228.50*** *p331*
Hill, Sarah 35; Ontario, 1871 ***1823.21*** *p160*
Hill, Sarah 67; Ontario, 1871 ***1823.21*** *p160*
Hill, Sarah 16; Quebec, 1870 ***8364.32*** *p24*
Hill, Stacy 40; Ontario, 1871 ***1823.21*** *p160*
Hill, Thersa 30; Michigan, 1880 ***4491.42*** *p14*
Hill, Thomas *SEE* Hill, John
Hill, Thomas; Marston's Wharf, 1782 ***8529.30*** *p12*
Hill, Thomas 26; Michigan, 1880 ***4491.42*** *p14*
Hill, Thomas; North Carolina, 1775 ***1422.10*** *p57*
Hill, Thomas 16; Ontario, 1871 ***1823.21*** *p160*
Hill, Thomas 51; Ontario, 1871 ***1823.21*** *p160*
Hill, Thomas 64; Ontario, 1871 ***1823.21*** *p160*
Hill, Thomas 65; Ontario, 1871 ***1823.17*** *p70*
Hill, Thomas 69; Ontario, 1871 ***1823.21*** *p160*
Hill, Thomas R. 62; Michigan, 1880 ***4491.30*** *p15*
Hill, Weikko 19; Minnesota, 1925 ***2769.54*** *p1378*
Hill, William; Dorchester, MA, 1633 ***117.5*** *p158*
Hill, William 36; Michigan, 1880 ***4491.42*** *p14*
Hill, William; New Jersey, 1665 ***9228.50*** *p283*
*Relative:*Henry
Hill, William 25; Ontario, 1871 ***1823.21*** *p160*
Hill, William 35; Ontario, 1871 ***1823.17*** *p70*
Hill, William 48; Ontario, 1871 ***1823.21*** *p160*
Hill, William 49; Ontario, 1871 ***1823.21*** *p160*
Hill, William 61; Ontario, 1871 ***1823.21*** *p160*
Hill, William; Virginia, 1665 ***9228.50*** *p53*
Hillard, Isaac F. 41; Michigan, 1880 ***4491.36*** *p10*
Hillard, James G. 13; Michigan, 1880 ***4491.36*** *p10*
Hillard, John 56; Ontario, 1871 ***1823.21*** *p160*
Hillard, Robert W. 43; Michigan, 1880 ***4491.36*** *p10*
Hillard, Solomon G. 11; Michigan, 1880 ***4491.36*** *p10*
Hillay, Ambrose 19; Quebec, 1870 ***8364.32*** *p24*
Hille, Josef; America, 1924 ***8023.44*** *p375*
Hillebrandt, Christoffel; New Jersey, 1740-1774 ***927.31*** *p3*
Hillebrecht, Hermann Gustav Ferdinand; New York, NY, 1870 ***7420.1*** *p284*
*Wife:*Nanny Friederike Wilhelmine Ernestine Rinne
With child
Hillebrecht, Nanny Friederike Wilhelmine Ernestine Rinne *SEE* Hillebrecht, Hermann Gustav Ferdinand
Hiller, Christian 47; Port uncertain, 1846 ***778.6*** *p164*
Hiller, Christiana 2; Portland, ME, 1910 ***970.38*** *p78*
Hiller, Christoph 34; New York, NY, 1893 ***1883.7*** *p39*
Hiller, Christoph 34; New York, NY, 1893 ***1883.7*** *p47*
Hiller, Edward; Marblehead, MA, 1736 ***9228.50*** *p284*
Hiller, Friedrich Ernst *SEE* Hiller, Fritz
Hiller, Fritz; America, 1868 ***7420.1*** *p272*
With wife & 3 daughters
*Son:*Heinrich Conrad
*Son:*Friedrich Ernst
*Son:*Ludolph Heinrich Carl
Hiller, Gustav 11 months; New York, NY, 1893 ***1883.7*** *p39*
Hiller, Gustav 11 months; New York, NY, 1893 ***1883.7*** *p47*
Hiller, Gustav 1; Portland, ME, 1910 ***970.38*** *p78*
Hiller, Heinrich Conrad *SEE* Hiller, Fritz
Hiller, Jacob; Missouri, 1894 ***3276.1*** *p1*
Hiller, Louise 30; New York, NY, 1893 ***1883.7*** *p39*
Hiller, Louise 30; New York, NY, 1893 ***1883.7*** *p47*
Hiller, Louise 16; Portland, ME, 1910 ***970.38*** *p78*
Hiller, Ludolph Heinrich Carl *SEE* Hiller, Fritz
Hiller, Madaleine 22; Port uncertain, 1846 ***778.6*** *p164*
Hiller, Magdalena 47; Port uncertain, 1846 ***778.6*** *p164*
Hiller, Mathilda 35; Portland, ME, 1910 ***970.38*** *p78*
Hiller, Rosine 4; New York, NY, 1893 ***1883.7*** *p39*
Hiller, Rosine 4; New York, NY, 1893 ***1883.7*** *p47*
Hiller, Thophila; Portland, ME, 1910 ***970.38*** *p78*
Hiller, Wilhelm 1; Portland, ME, 1910 ***970.38*** *p78*

Hiller, Wilhelmina 2; Portland, ME, 1910 970.38 p78
Hillerich, Adam; America, 1852 2526.42 p192
Hillerich, August 1 *SEE* Hillerich, Leonhard
Hillerich, Casimir 14 *SEE* Hillerich, Leonhard
Hillerich, Friedrich; America, 1842 2526.42 p192
With family
Hillerich, Friedrich 27; America, 1842 2526.42 p192
Hillerich, Johannes; America, 1887 2526.42 p192
Hillerich, Johannes 18; America, 1883 2526.42 p192
Hillerich, Kaspar 19 *SEE* Hillerich, Leonhard
Hillerich, Leonhard; America, 1853 2526.42 p192
Hillerich, Leonhard 49; America, 1853 2526.42 p105
With wife 48
*Grandchild:*August 1
*Child:*Maria 5
*Child:*Theres 22
*Child:*Casimir 14
*Child:*Kaspar 19
Hillerich, Maria 5 *SEE* Hillerich, Leonhard
Hillerich, Michael; America, 1842 2526.42 p192
With wife & 6 children
With 2 sons 12
Hillerich, Theres 22 *SEE* Hillerich, Leonhard
Hilliar, Maria 41; Ontario, 1871 1823.21 p160
Hilliar, Nicholas; Boston, 1712 9228.50 p284
Hilliar, Sophia 35; Ontario, 1871 1823.21 p160
Hilliard, David; Massachusetts, 1689 9228.50 p284
Hilliard, Edward; Marblehead, MA, 1736 9228.50 p284
Hilliard, Philip; Massachusetts, 1670-1699 9228.50 p284
Hilliard, Thomas 60; Ontario, 1871 1823.21 p160
Hilliard, Thomas 62; Ontario, 1871 1823.21 p160
Hillier, Edward; Marblehead, MA, 1736 9228.50 p284
Hillier, George 28; Ontario, 1871 1823.17 p70
Hillier, George 60; Ontario, 1871 1823.17 p70
Hillier, Lydia; Boston, 1698 9228.50 p284
Hilliker, Mary E.; Utah, 1852 9228.50 p284
Hillis, F. 45; America, 1847 778.6 p164
Hillis, Francis 33; Ontario, 1871 1823.17 p70
Hillis, James 48; Ontario, 1871 1823.17 p70
Hillis, James F. 9; Ontario, 1871 1823.21 p160
Hillis, John 39; Ontario, 1871 1823.17 p70
Hillis, Joseph 40; Ontario, 1871 1823.17 p70
Hillis, Margaret 62; Ontario, 1871 1823.21 p160
Hillman, . . .; America, 1830-1930 9228.50 p436
With sibling
Hillman, Margaret; Virginia, 1671 1236.25 p44
Hillman, Thomas 31; Ontario, 1871 1823.21 p160
Hillmer, John; Wisconsin, 1890 6795.8 p174
Hillmer, Martha Maria Christine; Wisconsin, 1901 6795.8 p158
Hillock, James 48; Ontario, 1871 1823.17 p70
Hills, George 37; Ontario, 1871 1823.21 p160
Hills, George 54; Ontario, 1871 1823.21 p160
Hills, Henry; Louisiana, 1874 4981.45 p132
Hills, John 35; Ontario, 1871 1823.21 p160
Hills, John 36; Ontario, 1871 1823.21 p160
Hills, Robert 35; Ontario, 1871 1823.21 p160
Hillse, John H.; North Carolina, 1792-1862 1088.45 p14
Hillstrom, Joseph; St. Paul, MN, 1885 1865.50 p50
Hillyard, Charles 21; Ontario, 1871 1823.21 p160
Hillyard, Edward; Marblehead, MA, 1736 9228.50 p284
Hillyer, Lydia; Boston, 1698 9228.50 p284
Hilman, George 40; Ontario, 1871 1823.21 p160
Hilman, John 44; Ontario, 1871 1823.21 p160
Hilman, Reuben 40; Ontario, 1871 1823.21 p160
Hilmer, Ferdinand; America, 1867 7420.1 p258
Hilmer, Friedrich; America, 1852 7420.1 p90
Hilmer, Heinrich; America, 1871 7420.1 p290
Hilmer, Johann Heinrich Wilhelm; America, 1870 7420.1 p284
With wife 2 daughters & son
Hilmer, Wilhelm; America, 1870 7420.1 p284
With wife
Hilpert, Oskar Wilhelm; America, 1867 7919.3 p534
Hilpret, H. A.; Nebraska, 1905 3004.30 p46
Hilsdorf, Miss C. 5; New Orleans, 1834 1002.51 p113
Hilsdorf, Miss C. 9; New Orleans, 1834 1002.51 p113
Hilsdorf, H. 22; New Orleans, 1834 1002.51 p112
Hilsdorf, Miss J. 2; New Orleans, 1834 1002.51 p113
Hilsdorf, Miss J. 34; New Orleans, 1834 1002.51 p113
Hilsdorf, P. 34; New Orleans, 1834 1002.51 p113
Hilsenbeck, Charles; Missouri, 1893 3276.1 p1
Hilsenbeck, Charles W.; Missouri, 1892 3276.1 p2
Hilsenbeck, Frederick; Missouri, 1897 3276.1 p2
Hilsenbeck, Jacob; Missouri, 1869 3276.1 p4
Hilsenbek, Maria; America, 1867 179.55 p19
Hilsenkopf, Barbara 42; Port uncertain, 1843 778.6 p164
Hilson, John; Marston's Wharf, 1782 8529.30 p12
Hilson, Richard 59; Ontario, 1871 1823.21 p160
Hilt, Edward; Wisconsin, 1908 1822.55 p10
Hilt, Gustav; Wisconsin, 1908 1822.55 p10
Hilt, Johann; Illinois, 1885 5475.1 p147
*Wife:*Margarethe Heitz
*Daughter:*Maria
*Son:*Nikolaus
*Son:*Peter
Hilt, Margarethe Heitz *SEE* Hilt, Johann
Hilt, Maria *SEE* Hilt, Johann
Hilt, Nikolaus *SEE* Hilt, Johann
Hilt, Peter *SEE* Hilt, Johann
Hilton, Alexander 55; Ontario, 1871 1823.21 p160
Hilton, David; New York, NY, 1842 3274.56 p100
Hilton, Friend 46; Ontario, 1871 1823.21 p160
Hilton, Henry 65; Ontario, 1871 1823.21 p160
Hilton, John; Marston's Wharf, 1782 8529.30 p12
Hilton, John; Washington, 1889 2770.40 p27
Hilyard, Edward; Marblehead, MA, 1736 9228.50 p284
Himes, George; New Jersey, 1751-1774 927.31 p3
Himler, Jacob; North Carolina, 1710 3629.40 p4
Himmel, Georg; America, 1867 7919.3 p531
Himmelbach, Herman 5 *SEE* Himmelbach, Rosa
Himmelbach, Jenny 11 *SEE* Himmelbach, Rosa
Himmelbach, Moses 1 *SEE* Himmelbach, Rosa
Himmelbach, Rosa 30; New York, NY, 1878 9253.2 p45
*Son:*Herman 5
*Child:*Moses 1 month
*Child:*Jenny 11 months
Himmeler, Ms. 19; America, 1847 778.6 p172
Himmelheber, Katharina; America, 1841 2526.42 p113
Himmelman, Asaph Simeon; Massachusetts, 1930 9228.50 p417
*Wife:*Helen Haughn
Himmelman, Helen Haughn *SEE* Himmelman, Asaph Simeon
Himmelreich, Max; New York, 1860 358.56 p149
Himples, Christian; New York, 1778 8529.30 p3A
Hinard, Jean; Quebec, 1657 9221.17 p360
Hinca, Frank; Wisconsin, 1880 6795.8 p47
Hinchcliff, George 36; Ontario, 1871 1823.21 p161
Hincum, David 28; Boston, 1835 6424.55 p30
Hincum, Fred K. 35; Boston, 1835 6424.55 p30
Hind, Edward 12; Quebec, 1870 8364.32 p24
Hind, T.S.; Washington, 1884 2770.40 p192
Hind, William 30; Ontario, 1871 1823.21 p161
Hinder, Henry; Ohio, 1809-1852 4511.35 p22
Hinderer, Agustus; Ohio, 1809-1852 4511.35 p23
Hinderer, Augustus; Ohio, 1809-1852 4511.35 p23
Hinderer, Henry; Ohio, 1809-1852 4511.35 p23
Hinderer, John; Ohio, 1809-1852 4511.35 p23
Hinderer, Louise; Pittsburgh, 1850 8513.31 p432
Hindley, Joseph; Illinois, 1930 121.35 p100
Hindman, James; Ohio, 1825 3580.20 p32
Hindman, James; Ohio, 1825 6020.12 p12
Hindman, Mary 18; North Carolina, 1774 1422.10 p58
Hindman, William; Ohio, 1825 3580.20 p32
Hindman, William; Ohio, 1825 6020.12 p12
Hindmarch, John 50; Ontario, 1871 1823.21 p161
Hindmarsh, Isaack 22; Ontario, 1871 1823.21 p161
Hindrichsson, Sven; North America, 1850 6410.15 p104
Hindry, Alexnader; North Carolina, 1792-1862 1088.45 p14
Hinds, Hugh; Ohio, 1836 3580.20 p32
Hinds, Hugh; Ohio, 1836 6020.12 p12
Hinds, Walter 63; Ontario, 1871 1823.21 p161
Hine, Geo. A.; Toronto, 1852 9228.50 p284
Hine, Hannah; Marblehead, MA, 1760-1823 9228.50 p284
Hine, Henry; Ohio, 1809-1852 4511.35 p23
Hine, Jeanne Marie; Baltimore, 1913 9228.50 p178
Hine, Jeanne Marie De Gruchy *SEE* Hine, John Bromfield
Hine, John Bromfield; Baltimore, 1913 9228.50 p284
*Wife:*Jeanne Marie De Gruchy
Hineline, Frederick; Baltimore, 1839 471.10 p62
Hineline, Frederick; New York, 1844 471.10 p88
Hineline, Henry; New York, 1844 471.10 p62
Hinemarsh, Thomas 66; Ontario, 1871 1823.21 p161
Hines, Abel 44; Ontario, 1871 1823.21 p161
Hines, Dominick; Ohio, 1809-1852 4511.35 p23
Hines, John; Louisiana, 1874 4981.45 p132
Hines, John; North Carolina, 1792-1862 1088.45 p14
Hines, Philip; North Carolina, 1792-1862 1088.45 p14
Hinessy, James; Ontario, 1787 1276.15 p231
With relative
Hinet, B.; Nova Scotia, n.d. 9228.50 p284
Hingre Puygibault, Louis; Quebec, 1701 2314.30 p169
Hingre Puygibault, Louis; Quebec, 1701 2314.30 p185
Hinkel, A. Maria Krein *SEE* Hinkel, Peter
Hinkel, Johann Peter *SEE* Hinkel, Peter
Hinkel, Peter; America, 1882 5475.1 p242
*Wife:*A. Maria Krein
*Son:*Johann Peter
Hinneman, Leopold; Colorado, 1888 1029.59 p40
Hinneman, Leopold; Colorado, 1897 1029.59 p40
Hins, Nathanael; New York, NY, 1878 3366.30 p70
Hinsch, Richard; Valdivia, Chile, 1850 1192.4 p49
Hinter, . . .; West Virginia, 1850-1860 1132.30 p147
Hinter, H. 27; America, 1840 778.6 p164
Hinterer, . . .; West Virginia, 1850-1860 1132.30 p147
Hinterholz, Anton; Brazil, 1880 5475.1 p372
*Wife:*Maria Behles
*Daughter:*Maria
*Daughter:*Katharina
*Son:*Peter
*Daughter:*Barbara
Hinterholz, Barbara *SEE* Hinterholz, Anton
Hinterholz, Katharina *SEE* Hinterholz, Anton
Hinterholz, Maria *SEE* Hinterholz, Anton
Hinterholz, Maria Behles *SEE* Hinterholz, Anton
Hinterholz, Peter *SEE* Hinterholz, Anton
Hintermeyer, Jean-Baptiste 36; New Orleans, 1848 778.6 p164
Hinton, William 27; Ontario, 1871 1823.21 p161
Hintz, Daniel; New York, NY, 1887 3366.30 p70
Hinz, Anna 44; New York, NY, 1886 8425.16 p32
Hinz, Carl 43; New York, NY, 1886 8425.16 p32
Hinz, Caroline 16; New York, NY, 1886 8425.16 p32
Hinz, Catharina 7; New York, NY, 1886 8425.16 p32
Hinz, Christina 6; New York, NY, 1886 8425.16 p32
Hinz, Georg 19; New York, NY, 1886 8425.16 p32
Hinz, Louise 18; New York, NY, 1886 8425.16 p32
Hinz, Manuel 1; New York, NY, 1886 8425.16 p32
Hinz, Mary Poline; Wisconsin, 1882 6795.8 p47
Hinz, Regina 10; New York, NY, 1886 8425.16 p32
Hinz, Wilhelm; Wisconsin, 1876 6795.8 p201
Hinze, Widow; America, 1854 7420.1 p121
With daughter
Hinze, Catharina Sophia *SEE* Hinze, Engel Maria Sophia Engelking
Hinze, Charles; Colorado, 1882 1029.59 p40
Hinze, Dorothee Louise Falke *SEE* Hinze, Johann Friedrich Wilhelm
Hinze, Engel Maria *SEE* Hinze, Engel Maria Sophia Engelking
Hinze, Engel Maria Dorothea *SEE* Hinze, Engel Maria Sophia Engelking
Hinze, Engel Maria Sophia *SEE* Hinze, Engel Maria Sophia Engelking
Hinze, Engel Maria Sophia; America, 1850 7420.1 p72
*Daughter:*Engel Maria Sophia
*Daughter:*Engel Maria
*Daughter:*Engel Maria Dorothea
*Daughter:*Catharina Sophia
Hinze, Engel Marie Dorothee Charlotte *SEE* Hinze, Johann Friedrich Wilhelm
Hinze, Friedrich Wilhelm; America, 1862 7420.1 p212
Hinze, Johann Friedrich Wilhelm; America, 1847 7420.1 p54
*Wife:*Dorothee Louise Falke
*Daughter:*Engel Marie Dorothee Charlotte
Hinze, Johann Philipp; New York, NY, 1856 7420.1 p148
With family
Hinze, Thrine Marie Sophie; America, 1847 7420.1 p53
Hinzmann, Alexander 3; New York, NY, 1877 6954.7 p40
Hinzmann, Alexander 11 months; New York, NY, 1886 6954.7 p40
Hinzmann, Andreas 32; New York, NY, 1877 6954.7 p40
Hinzmann, Carl 4; New York, NY, 1885 6954.7 p40
Hinzmann, Carolina 36; New York, NY, 1885 6954.7 p40
Hinzmann, Catherina 5; New York, NY, 1877 6954.7 p40
Hinzmann, Catherina 28; New York, NY, 1877 6954.7 p40
Hinzmann, Christina 13; New York, NY, 1886 6954.7 p41
Hinzmann, Christina 20; New York, NY, 1886 6954.7 p40
Hinzmann, Christina 42; New York, NY, 1886 6954.7 p41
Hinzmann, Dorothea 9; New York, NY, 1886 6954.7 p40
Hinzmann, Elisabeth 8; New York, NY, 1885 6954.7 p40
Hinzmann, Elisabeth 70; New York, NY, 1886 6954.7 p40
Hinzmann, Emelia 2; New York, NY, 1877 6954.7 p40
Hinzmann, Emelia 6 months; New York, NY, 1877 6954.7 p40
Hinzmann, Emelia 8; New York, NY, 1886 6954.7 p41
Hinzmann, Emmanuel 3; New York, NY, 1886 6954.7 p40
Hinzmann, Friedrich 19; New York, NY, 1887 6954.7 p41

Hinzmann, Heinrich 5; New York, NY, 1877 ***6954.7*** *p40*
Hinzmann, Heinrich 5; New York, NY, 1886 ***6954.7*** *p41*
Hinzmann, Heinrich 7; New York, NY, 1886 ***6954.7*** *p40*
Hinzmann, Johann 2; New York, NY, 1885 ***6954.7*** *p40*
Hinzmann, Johann 9; New York, NY, 1886 ***6954.7*** *p41*
Hinzmann, Johann 52; New York, NY, 1886 ***6954.7*** *p41*
Hinzmann, Johannes 23; New York, NY, 1886 ***6954.7*** *p40*
Hinzmann, Katherina 17; New York, NY, 1886 ***6954.7*** *p40*
Hinzmann, Katherina 38; New York, NY, 1886 ***6954.7*** *p40*
Hinzmann, Leonora 8; New York, NY, 1877 ***6954.7*** *p40*
Hinzmann, Lydia 1 months; New York, NY, 1886 ***6954.7*** *p40*
Hinzmann, Lydia 3; New York, NY, 1886 ***6954.7*** *p41*
Hinzmann, Maria 9; New York, NY, 1885 ***6954.7*** *p40*
Hinzmann, Maria 31; New York, NY, 1886 ***6954.7*** *p41*
Hinzmann, Martin 45; New York, NY, 1885 ***6954.7*** *p40*
Hinzmann, Martin 48; New York, NY, 1886 ***6954.7*** *p40*
Hinzmann, Mathilda 4 months; New York, NY, 1877 ***6954.7*** *p40*
Hinzmann, Rachel 26; New York, NY, 1877 ***6954.7*** *p40*
Hinzmann, Theador 5; New York, NY, 1886 ***6954.7*** *p40*
Hinzmann, Wilhelm 8; New York, NY, 1886 ***6954.7*** *p40*
Hinzmann, Wilhelm 30; New York, NY, 1877 ***6954.7*** *p40*
Hip, John Jacob; Ohio, 1809-1852 ***4511.35*** *p23*
Hipkin, Thomas H. 58; Ontario, 1871 ***1823.21*** *p161*
Hipkins, Edward 37; Ontario, 1871 ***1823.17*** *p70*
Hipkins, Richard 63; Ontario, 1871 ***1823.17*** *p70*
Hipp, Frederick; Ohio, 1809-1852 ***4511.35*** *p23*
Hipp, George; Ohio, 1809-1852 ***4511.35*** *p23*
Hipp, Peter; Ohio, 1809-1852 ***4511.35*** *p23*
Hippchen, A. Margarethe *SEE* Hippchen, Anton
Hippchen, Anton; America, 1881 ***5475.1*** *p534*
*Wife:*Margarethe Johann
*Daughter:*A. Margarethe
*Daughter:*Maria
Hippchen, Margarethe Johann *SEE* Hippchen, Anton
Hippchen, Maria *SEE* Hippchen, Anton
Hipsley, Luke; Boston, 1831 ***3274.55*** *p75*
Hirchlergen, Elisabeth 29; Mississippi, 1847 ***778.6*** *p164*
Hire, James; Toronto, 1844 ***2910.35*** *p115*
Hireling, George; Ohio, 1809-1852 ***4511.35*** *p23*
Hirley, Anne 40; Ontario, 1871 ***1823.21*** *p161*
Hirmes, Barbara 28; New York, NY, 1847 ***9176.15*** *p49*
Hirmes, Havier 24; New York, NY, 1847 ***9176.15*** *p49*
Hirmes, Theresa 2; New York, NY, 1847 ***9176.15*** *p49*
Hirsch, Aaron 26; America, 1846 ***778.6*** *p164*
Hirsch, Abraham; Louisiana, 1874-1875 ***4981.45*** *p29*
Hirsch, Anna Maria; America, 1854 ***179.55*** *p19*
Hirsch, Ehrmann; America, 1885 ***2526.42*** *p122*
Hirsch, George; Illinois, 1855 ***6079.1*** *p6*
Hirsch, Henry; North Carolina, 1792-1862 ***1088.45*** *p14*
Hirsch, Hermann; North Carolina, 1792-1862 ***1088.45*** *p14*
Hirsch, Isaac 32; New Orleans, 1847 ***778.6*** *p164*
Hirsch, Jonas; America, 1866 ***5475.1*** *p238*
Hirsch, Josef; Texas, 1852 ***2853.20*** *p59*
Hirsch, Joseph; Chicago, 1870 ***2526.42*** *p122*
Hirsch, Joseph 50; New Orleans, 1848 ***778.6*** *p164*
Hirsch, Leopold; America, 1882 ***2526.42*** *p122*
Hirsch, Margaret; Philadelphia, 1866 ***8513.31*** *p424*
Hirsch, Max 28; New Orleans, 1847 ***778.6*** *p164*
Hirsch, Seligmann 28; Chicago, 1870 ***2526.42*** *p123*
Hirschauer, Viktor E.; Baltimore, 1872 ***2853.20*** *p125*
Hirschberg, Emma 28; New York, NY, 1878 ***9253.2*** *p45*
*Child:*Selig 11 months
Hirschberg, Selig 11 *SEE* Hirschberg, Emma
Hirschberger, Katharina Scheib *SEE* Hirschberger, Nikolaus
Hirschberger, Nikolaus; Brazil, 1846 ***5475.1*** *p438*
*Wife:*Katharina Scheib
With 2 children
Hirschbrunner, Frederrik; Texas, 1851 ***3435.45*** *p35*
Hirschfeld, Hans Heinrich Christoph; America, 1856 ***7420.1*** *p148*
Hirschfeld, Johann Friedrich; Port uncertain, 1838 ***7420.1*** *p14*
Hirschfeldt, John; New York, 1859 ***358.56*** *p55*
Hirschiff, Samuel; Illinois, 1860 ***6079.1*** *p6*
Hirschkoru, John; New York, NY, 1890 ***3366.30*** *p70*
Hirson, Stewart 70; Ontario, 1871 ***1823.21*** *p161*
Hirst, Florence 15; Ontario, 1871 ***1823.21*** *p161*
Hirth, Antoine 49; New Castle, DE, 1817-1818 ***90.20*** *p151*
Hirth, S. Lonzi 40; New Castle, DE, 1817-1818 ***90.20*** *p151*
Hirth, William; Boston, 1774 ***8529.30*** *p3A*
Hirtz, Anna 59; America, 1880 ***5475.1*** *p227*
*Son:*Wilhelm
With 2 grandchildren
*Daughter:*Maria
*Son:*Heinrich
Hirtz, Barbara 29; America, 1880 ***5475.1*** *p227*
Hirtz, Heinrich *SEE* Hirtz, Anna Milde
Hirtz, Heinrich; America, 1881 ***5475.1*** *p227*
Hirtz, Joh. Nikolaus; America, 1878 ***5475.1*** *p147*
*Mother:*Katharina Adam
Hirtz, Katharina Adam 62 *SEE* Hirtz, Joh. Nikolaus
Hirtz, Magdalena 36; America, 1880 ***5475.1*** *p227*
Hirtz, Maria *SEE* Hirtz, Anna Milde
Hirtz, Maria 76; America, 1855 ***5475.1*** *p317*
Hirtz, Mathias; America, 1882 ***5475.1*** *p228*
Hirtz, Wilhelm *SEE* Hirtz, Anna Milde
Hiry, Johann; America, 1882 ***5475.1*** *p205*
Hirz, Heinrich; America, 1871 ***2526.42*** *p174*
Hirz, Joseph; Nebraska, 1904 ***2526.43*** *p190*
Hirz, Maria Katharina; America, 1832 ***2526.42*** *p177*
Hirz, Philipp 14; America, 1879 ***2526.42*** *p174*
Hirz, Wilhelm; America, 1832 ***2526.42*** *p174*
Hirz, Wilhelmine; America, 1868 ***2526.42*** *p175*
Hirzig, Josephine 25; America, 1877 ***5475.1*** *p309*
Hiscott, John 57; Ontario, 1871 ***1823.17*** *p70*
Hiscox, James 58; Ontario, 1871 ***1823.21*** *p161*
Hiser, Emanuel Frederick; Ohio, 1809-1852 ***4511.35*** *p23*
Hiser, John; Ohio, 1809-1852 ***4511.35*** *p23*
Hishon, Patrick; Toronto, 1844 ***2910.35*** *p115*
Hiskey, Thomas; Massachusetts, 1755 ***1642*** *p84*
Hislop, Adam 55; Ontario, 1871 ***1823.21*** *p161*
Hislop, Janet; Quebec, 1885 ***1937.10*** *p52*
Hislop, John 55; Ontario, 1871 ***1823.21*** *p161*
Hislop, Mary 15; Ontario, 1871 ***1823.21*** *p161*
Hislop, Robert 46; Ontario, 1871 ***1823.21*** *p161*
Hisse, Anne; Quebec, 1665 ***4514.3*** *p364*
Hitch, Elizabeth 73; Ontario, 1871 ***1823.21*** *p161*
Hitchcock, Miles; Ontario, 1787 ***1276.15*** *p231*
With 3 children & 8 relatives
Hitchcock, Samuel 58; Ontario, 1871 ***1823.17*** *p70*
Hitchcock, Thomas; Jamaica, 1783 ***8529.30*** *p13A*
Hitchen, Joseph 52; Ontario, 1871 ***1823.21*** *p161*
Hitchler, A. H.; Louisiana, 1874 ***4981.45*** *p296*
Hitschcock, Caroline 45; Ontario, 1871 ***1823.21*** *p161*
Hittle, Leo; America, 1880-1910 ***2853.20*** *p339*
With parents
Hitton, George 46; Ontario, 1871 ***1823.21*** *p161*
Hituhler, Michel; New Orleans, 1840 ***778.6*** *p164*
Hitz, Joseph 52; New Castle, DE, 1817-1818 ***90.20*** *p151*
Hitzemann, Mr.; America, 1857 ***7420.1*** *p163*
With wife
With son 10
With daughter
With son 16
Hitzemann, Anne Marie Reese *SEE* Hitzemann, Heinrich Christoph
Hitzemann, Carl Heinrich Friedrich; America, 1883 ***7420.1*** *p336*
Hitzemann, Caroline; America, 1857 ***7420.1*** *p163*
Hitzemann, Caroline; America, 1857 ***7420.1*** *p169*
Hitzemann, Engel Maria H. *SEE* Hitzemann, Ernst
Hitzemann, Engel Marie Sophie; New York, NY, 1856 ***7420.1*** *p148*
Hitzemann, Ernst; America, 1852 ***7420.1*** *p90*
*Sister:*Engel Maria H.
Hitzemann, Friedrich Christian; America, 1860 ***7420.1*** *p194*
Hitzemann, Gottlieb; Wisconsin, 1857 ***7420.1*** *p163*
With wife
With son 10
With daughter 8
With son 17
With son 15
Hitzemann, Heinrich; Port uncertain, 1858 ***7420.1*** *p178*
Hitzemann, Heinrich Christoph; Chicago, 1857 ***7420.1*** *p163*
*Wife:*Anne Marie Reese
With child 14
*Son:*Johann Heinrich Christoph
With child 18
With child 10
With child 7
With child 23
With child 27
With child 4
Hitzemann, Johann Heinrich Christoph *SEE* Hitzemann, Heinrich Christoph
Hitzemann, Marie Sophie; Illinois, 1884 ***7420.1*** *p343*
Hitzemann, Philipp Conrad; America, 1854 ***7420.1*** *p121*
Hitzemann, Sophie; America, 1858 ***7420.1*** *p178*
Hitzerkapl, Hubert 35; America, 1840 ***778.6*** *p164*
Hizeau, L. F.; Louisiana, 1836-1841 ***4981.45*** *p208*
Hjalmer, Oberg; Minnesota, 1925-1926 ***2769.54*** *p1382*
Hjelm, Jens; Iowa, 1900 ***1211.15*** *p11*
Hjelm, Louie J.; Iowa, 1898 ***1211.15*** *p11*
Hjerpe, Charley; Cleveland, OH, 1887-1893 ***9722.10*** *p120*
Hjert, Per; Colorado, 1887 ***1029.59*** *p40*
Hjertberg, Fredrik A.; Illinois, 1864 ***4487.25*** *p58*
Hjorth, Eskild Anton; Iowa, 1900 ***1211.15*** *p11*
Hladik, Jindrich; Cleveland, OH, 1845-1849 ***2853.20*** *p475*
Hladky, Frantisek; Chicago, 1867-1910 ***2853.20*** *p465*
Hlavacek, . . .; Pennsylvania, 1750-1799 ***2853.20*** *p17*
Hlavacek, Frantisek; Chicago, 1896 ***2853.20*** *p419*
Hlavacek, Josef; Chicago, 1893-1910 ***2853.20*** *p469*
Hlavaty, Vaclav; Iowa, 1891 ***2853.20*** *p227*
Hlinsky, Frantisek; Minnesota, 1858-1860 ***2853.20*** *p259*
Hoagland, Alfred; Cleveland, OH, 1897-1898 ***9722.10*** *p120*
Hoar, C. S. 26; Ontario, 1871 ***1823.21*** *p161*
Hoar, Catharine; Boston, 1765 ***1642*** *p48*
Hoar, Katharine; Boston, 1757 ***1642*** *p47*
Hoar, Sarah; Massachusetts, n.d. ***9228.50*** *p464*
Hoare, John 63; Ontario, 1871 ***1823.21*** *p161*
Hoasz, Anthony; Ohio, 1809-1852 ***4511.35*** *p23*
Hoban, Ellen 54; Ontario, 1871 ***1823.21*** *p161*
Hoban, William; Boston, 1767 ***1642*** *p38*
Hobane, Mary; Boston, 1755 ***1642*** *p47*
Hobane, Patrick; Boston, 1755 ***1642*** *p47*
Hobbart, Mary 15; Ontario, 1871 ***1823.21*** *p161*
Hobbings, Jacob; Boston, 1775 ***8529.30*** *p2*
Hobbins, Daniel 75; Ontario, 1871 ***1823.21*** *p161*
Hobbins, James 39; Ontario, 1871 ***1823.21*** *p161*
Hobbins, James 40; Ontario, 1871 ***1823.21*** *p161*
Hobbins, James 40; Ontario, 1871 ***1823.21*** *p161*
Hobbins, Patrick 33; Ontario, 1871 ***1823.21*** *p161*
Hobbs, James 30; Ontario, 1871 ***1823.17*** *p70*
Hobbs, James 43; Ontario, 1871 ***1823.21*** *p161*
Hobbs, James 64; Ontario, 1871 ***1823.21*** *p161*
Hobbs, Robert 48; Ontario, 1871 ***1823.21*** *p161*
Hobbs, Robert 60; Ontario, 1871 ***1823.21*** *p161*
Hobbs, William R. 24; Ontario, 1871 ***1823.21*** *p161*
Hobday, John 39; Ontario, 1871 ***1823.21*** *p162*
Hober, Michael; New Jersey, 1773-1774 ***927.31*** *p2*
Hoberty, John Nicholas; Ohio, 1809-1852 ***4511.35*** *p23*
Hoberty, Michael; Ohio, 1809-1852 ***4511.35*** *p23*
Hobin, Arnould; Wisconsin, 1880 ***1495.20*** *p56*
*Wife:*Julienne Gelinne
*Child:*Josephine
*Child:*Clemence Marie
Hobin, Clemence Marie *SEE* Hobin, Arnould
Hobin, Francois 24; America, 1845 ***778.6*** *p164*
Hobin, Josephine *SEE* Hobin, Arnould
Hobin, Julienne Gelinne *SEE* Hobin, Arnould
Hoblitcel, Jacob; Ohio, 1809-1852 ***4511.35*** *p23*
Hobson, Mary 66; Ontario, 1871 ***1823.21*** *p162*
Hobson, R. W. 27; Ontario, 1871 ***1823.21*** *p162*
Hobson, William 46; Ontario, 1871 ***1823.17*** *p70*
Hoburne, Mary; Boston, 1761 ***1642*** *p48*
Hocamp, Frederick William; Illinois, 1861 ***6079.1*** *p7*
Hoch, A.; Galveston, TX, 1855 ***571.7*** *p18*
Hoch, F.; Galveston, TX, 1855 ***571.7*** *p18*
Hoch, Jean 47; New Orleans, 1847 ***778.6*** *p190*
Hoch, Joseph 16; New Orleans, 1847 ***778.6*** *p190*
Hoch, Joseph 47; New Orleans, 1847 ***778.6*** *p190*
Hochatter, Henry; Illinois, 1852 ***6079.1*** *p7*
Hochdofer, Antoine 7; America, 1747 ***778.6*** *p164*
Hochdofer, Carl 2; America, 1747 ***778.6*** *p164*
Hochdofer, Catharina 16; America, 1747 ***778.6*** *p164*
Hochdofer, Franz 6; America, 1747 ***778.6*** *p164*
Hochdofer, Georg 4; America, 1747 ***778.6*** *p164*
Hochdofer, Jean 14; America, 1747 ***778.6*** *p164*
Hochdofer, Jean 42; America, 1747 ***778.6*** *p164*
Hochdofer, Michel 8; America, 1747 ***778.6*** *p164*
Hochdofer, Rosina 9; America, 1747 ***778.6*** *p164*
Hochdum, Simiche 18; New York, NY, 1878 ***9253.2*** *p45*
Hochgenug, Margarethe Elisabeth; Virginia, 1831 ***152.20*** *p60*
Hochmeier, George; New Jersey, 1777 ***8529.30*** *p6*
Hochschulte, Margaret 30; Michigan, 1880 ***4491.39*** *p14*
Hochstadt, Marg.; New York, 1860 ***358.56*** *p5*
Hochstater, Barbara 13; New York, NY, 1885 ***1883.7*** *p46*
Hochstater, Jacob 13; New York, NY, 1885 ***1883.7*** *p46*
Hochstater, Jacob 60; New York, NY, 1885 ***1883.7*** *p46*
Hochstater, Johannes 7; New York, NY, 1885 ***1883.7*** *p46*
Hochstater, Katharine 22; New York, NY, 1885 ***1883.7*** *p46*
Hochstater, Louise 13; New York, NY, 1885 ***1883.7*** *p46*
Hochstater, Louise 48; New York, NY, 1885 ***1883.7*** *p46*
Hochstater, Magda. 4; New York, NY, 1885 ***1883.7*** *p46*
Hochstrasser, Emil 38; America, 1897 ***5475.1*** *p73*
Hochstrasser, Nicolas 19; America, 1841 ***778.6*** *p164*
Hock, . . .; America, 1892 ***170.15*** *p28*
With family

Hock, Child; America, 1892 ***170.15*** *p28*
With family
Hock, Mrs.; America, 1892 ***170.15*** *p28*
With family
Hock, Friedrich; America, 1845 ***7420.1*** *p37*
Hock, Joseph; Illinois, 1858 ***6079.1*** *p7*
Hock, Peter 19; America, 1881 ***2526.42*** *p192*
Hocker, Hermann; America, 1852 ***7420.1*** *p90*
With family
Hocker, Philipp Heinrich Friedrich Eduard; England, 1867 ***7420.1*** *p258*
Hocker, Wilhelm; Port uncertain, 1853 ***7420.1*** *p106*
Hockert, Barbara; America, 1864 ***5475.1*** *p338*
Hockert, Nikolaus 24; America, 1878 ***5475.1*** *p339*
Hockert, Peter; America, 1862 ***5475.1*** *p337*
Hockert, V.; New York, NY, 1844 ***6412.40*** *p148*
Hockin, Joseph W. 33; Ontario, 1871 ***1823.21*** *p162*
Hockin, Saml 42; Ontario, 1871 ***1823.17*** *p70*
Hockin, Samuel 27; Ontario, 1871 ***1823.21*** *p162*
Hockin, William 51; Ontario, 1871 ***1823.21*** *p162*
Hocking, Simon; Colorado, 1880 ***1029.59*** *p40*
Hocking, Simon; Colorado, 1894 ***1029.59*** *p40*
Hockomb, Magnus; Illinois, 1864 ***4487.25*** *p59*
Hockridge, Thos 40; Ontario, 1871 ***1823.17*** *p70*
Hockshasser, Henri 19; New Orleans, 1848 ***778.6*** *p164*
Hocquard, Charles *SEE* Hocquard, Francis
Hocquard, Elizabeth *SEE* Hocquard, Francis
Hocquard, Elizabeth Jeune *SEE* Hocquard, Francis
Hocquard, Frances Sophia *SEE* Hocquard, Francis
Hocquard, Francis *SEE* Hocquard, Francis
Hocquard, Francis; Utah, 1831-1865 ***9228.50*** *p284*
*Wife:*Elizabeth Jeune
*Child:*Charles
*Child:*John
*Child:*Philip
*Child:*Frances Sophia
*Child:*Elizabeth
*Child:*Francis
Hocquard, John *SEE* Hocquard, Francis
Hocquard, Philip *SEE* Hocquard, Francis
Hodann, Albrecht; America, 1846 ***7420.1*** *p45*
With wife & 3 children
Hodann, Marie; America, 1889 ***7420.1*** *p360*
*Daughter:*Sophie Dorothee Louise
Hodder, Albert 24; Ontario, 1871 ***1823.21*** *p162*
Hodder, John 52; Ontario, 1871 ***1823.21*** *p162*
Hode, Jean 23; Missouri, 1848 ***778.6*** *p164*
Hode, Mathurin 29; Missouri, 1848 ***778.6*** *p164*
Hodge, Elizabeth 11; Quebec, 1870 ***8364.32*** *p24*
Hodge, Robert; North Carolina, 1792-1862 ***1088.45*** *p14*
Hodges, . . .; Ontario, 1835 ***3160.1*** *p150*
Hodges, Arthur; North Carolina, 1792-1862 ***1088.45*** *p14*
Hodges, Caroline 7; Quebec, 1870 ***8364.32*** *p24*
Hodges, Charles; Louisiana, 1874 ***4981.45*** *p132*
Hodges, George 19; Ontario, 1871 ***1823.21*** *p162*
Hodges, Hiram A. 33; Michigan, 1880 ***4491.33*** *p12*
Hodges, Robert; North Carolina, 1792-1862 ***1088.45*** *p14*
Hodges, Thomas; Marston's Wharf, 1782 ***8529.30*** *p12*
Hodges, William; North Carolina, 1792-1862 ***1088.45*** *p14*
Hodgett, Jane 82; Ontario, 1871 ***1823.21*** *p162*
Hodging, Edward 34; Ontario, 1871 ***1823.17*** *p70*
Hodgins, . . .; Ontario, 1871 ***1823.21*** *p162*
Hodgins, Adam 50; Ontario, 1871 ***1823.21*** *p162*
Hodgins, Adam 70; Ontario, 1871 ***1823.21*** *p162*
Hodgins, Catharine 50; Ontario, 1871 ***1823.21*** *p162*
Hodgins, Catherine 58; Ontario, 1871 ***1823.21*** *p162*
Hodgins, Edward 60; Ontario, 1871 ***1823.21*** *p162*
Hodgins, Edward 67; Ontario, 1871 ***1823.21*** *p162*
Hodgins, Elizabeth 32; Ontario, 1871 ***1823.17*** *p71*
Hodgins, Elizabeth 35; Ontario, 1871 ***1823.17*** *p70*
Hodgins, Elizabeth 55; Ontario, 1871 ***1823.21*** *p162*
Hodgins, Ellen 39; Ontario, 1871 ***1823.21*** *p162*
Hodgins, Ellen 100; Ontario, 1871 ***1823.21*** *p162*
Hodgins, George 40; Ontario, 1871 ***1823.17*** *p71*
Hodgins, George 44; Ontario, 1871 ***1823.21*** *p162*
Hodgins, George 65; Ontario, 1871 ***1823.21*** *p162*
Hodgins, Henery 47; Ontario, 1871 ***1823.21*** *p162*
Hodgins, Henry 60; Ontario, 1871 ***1823.21*** *p162*
Hodgins, James 45; Ontario, 1871 ***1823.21*** *p162*
Hodgins, James 55; Ontario, 1871 ***1823.21*** *p162*
Hodgins, Jane 40; Ontario, 1871 ***1823.21*** *p162*
Hodgins, John 26; Ontario, 1871 ***1823.21*** *p163*
Hodgins, John 32; Ontario, 1871 ***1823.21*** *p163*
Hodgins, John 34; Ontario, 1871 ***1823.21*** *p163*
Hodgins, John 45; Ontario, 1871 ***1823.21*** *p163*
Hodgins, John 50; Ontario, 1871 ***1823.21*** *p163*
Hodgins, John 50; Ontario, 1871 ***1823.21*** *p163*
Hodgins, John 55; Ontario, 1871 ***1823.21*** *p163*
Hodgins, John 59; Ontario, 1871 ***1823.21*** *p163*
Hodgins, John 65; Ontario, 1871 ***1823.21*** *p163*
Hodgins, John 70; Ontario, 1871 ***1823.21*** *p163*
Hodgins, John 78; Ontario, 1871 ***1823.21*** *p163*
Hodgins, John D. 69; Ontario, 1871 ***1823.21*** *p163*
Hodgins, Margaret 67; Ontario, 1871 ***1823.21*** *p163*
Hodgins, Mary 60; Ontario, 1871 ***1823.21*** *p163*
Hodgins, Mary 80; Ontario, 1871 ***1823.21*** *p163*
Hodgins, Moses 37; Ontario, 1871 ***1823.21*** *p163*
Hodgins, Nathan 48; Ontario, 1871 ***1823.21*** *p163*
Hodgins, Rich'd 31; Ontario, 1871 ***1823.21*** *p163*
Hodgins, Richard 22; Ontario, 1871 ***1823.21*** *p163*
Hodgins, Robert; Ontario, 1871 ***1823.21*** *p163*
Hodgins, Thomas 47; Ontario, 1871 ***1823.21*** *p163*
Hodgins, Thomas 73; Ontario, 1871 ***1823.21*** *p163*
Hodgins, Thomas, Sr. 64; Ontario, 1871 ***1823.21*** *p163*
Hodgins, William 25; Ontario, 1871 ***1823.21*** *p163*
Hodgins, William 29; Ontario, 1871 ***1823.21*** *p163*
Hodgins, William 31; Ontario, 1871 ***1823.21*** *p163*
Hodgins, William 50; Ontario, 1871 ***1823.21*** *p163*
Hodgins, William 65; Ontario, 1871 ***1823.21*** *p163*
Hodgins, William 70; Ontario, 1871 ***1823.21*** *p163*
Hodgson, . . . 73; Ontario, 1871 ***1823.17*** *p71*
Hodgson, David 78; Ontario, 1871 ***1823.17*** *p71*
Hodgson, George 43; Ontario, 1871 ***1823.21*** *p164*
Hodgson, John 45; Ontario, 1871 ***1823.21*** *p164*
Hodgson, John 47; Ontario, 1871 ***1823.21*** *p164*
Hodgson, Joseph 35; Ontario, 1871 ***1823.21*** *p164*
Hodgson, Robert 49; Ontario, 1871 ***1823.21*** *p164*
Hodgson, T. P.; Washington, 1888 ***2770.40*** *p25*
Hodgson, T.E.; Quebec, 1885 ***1937.10*** *p52*
Hodgson, William 40; Ontario, 1871 ***1823.21*** *p164*
Hodgson, William 74; Ontario, 1871 ***1823.21*** *p164*
Hodiau, Marie 44; Montreal, 1659 ***9221.17*** *p422*
*Daughter:*Urbaine 14
Hodiau, Sebastien 34; Montreal, 1650 ***9221.17*** *p231*
Hodiau, Urbaine 14 *SEE* Hodiau, Marie Mousnier
Hodjins, Thos 62; Ontario, 1871 ***1823.21*** *p164*
Hodjson, Thomas D. 32; Ontario, 1871 ***1823.21*** *p164*
Hodson, Charity 86; Ontario, 1871 ***1823.21*** *p164*
Hodson, Thomas 49; Ontario, 1871 ***1823.21*** *p164*
Hodsworth, Thomas 40; Ontario, 1871 ***1823.17*** *p71*
Hody, Leocadie; Wisconsin, 1880 ***1495.20*** *p46*
Hody, Marie Francois; Wisconsin, 1857 ***1495.20*** *p46*
Hodyc, Jan; Nebraska, 1889 ***2853.20*** *p152*
Hodyc, Jan; Omaha, NE, 1889 ***2853.20*** *p449*
Hodzen, Anthony; Detroit, 1930 ***1640.60*** *p82*
Hoeck, Friedrich; Pennsylvania, 1848 ***170.15*** *p28*
Hoeck, Friedrich 48; Pennsylvania, 1848 ***170.15*** *p28*
With wife & 4 children
Hoeffner, Fred; Louisiana, 1874-1875 ***4981.45*** *p29*
Hoefling, George; New York, 1778 ***8529.30*** *p6*
Hoefner, Frantisek; Cleveland, OH, 1868 ***2853.20*** *p498*
Hoeft, Anthony; Wisconsin, 1883 ***6795.8*** *p117*
Hoeft, Emma Bertha; Wisconsin, 1888 ***6795.8*** *p29*
Hoeft, Maria Louise; Wisconsin, 1892 ***6795.8*** *p88*
Hoege, Henry; Washington, 1888 ***2770.40*** *p25*
Hoegel, Friedrich; America, 1881 ***5475.1*** *p386*
Hoeglander, Emil; Cleveland, OH, 1891-1895 ***9722.10*** *p120*
Hoeler, Aberham 23; America, 1846 ***778.6*** *p165*
Hoell, Anton; Illinois, 1864 ***6079.1*** *p7*
Hoell, John G.; Washington, 1889 ***2770.40*** *p27*
Hoeller, Wilhelmina; Kansas, 1917-1918 ***1826.15*** *p81*
Hoellinger, Adelgunde 1; America, 1848 ***778.6*** *p165*
Hoellinger, Anton 6; America, 1848 ***778.6*** *p165*
Hoellinger, Anton 47; America, 1848 ***778.6*** *p165*
Hoellinger, Elisabeth 4; America, 1848 ***778.6*** *p165*
Hoellinger, Elisabeth 37; America, 1848 ***778.6*** *p165*
Hoellinger, Euphromea 19; America, 1848 ***778.6*** *p165*
Hoellinger, Victoria 17; America, 1848 ***778.6*** *p165*
Hoellinger, Wilhelm 14; America, 1848 ***778.6*** *p165*
Hoen, Elisabeth Katharina; Indiana, 1882 ***5475.1*** *p191*
*Son:*Johann
*Daughter:*Maria
Hoen, Johann; America, 1882 ***5475.1*** *p191*
Hoen, Johann; America, 1882 ***5475.1*** *p198*
Hoen, Johann Adam; America, 1882 ***5475.1*** *p198*
Hoen, Nicolas 55; Port uncertain, 1843 ***778.6*** *p165*
Hoen, Peter *SEE* Hoen, Peter
Hoen, Peter; America, 1887 ***5475.1*** *p230*
*Son:*Peter
Hoerner, Barbara 1; Port uncertain, 1843 ***778.6*** *p165*
Hoerner, Barbara 12; Port uncertain, 1843 ***778.6*** *p165*
Hoerner, Franziska 43; Port uncertain, 1843 ***778.6*** *p165*
Hoerner, Jean 43; Port uncertain, 1843 ***778.6*** *p165*
Hoerner, Michel 8; Port uncertain, 1843 ***778.6*** *p165*
Hoerner, Nicolas 3; Port uncertain, 1843 ***778.6*** *p165*
Hoerner, Peter 5; Port uncertain, 1843 ***778.6*** *p165*
Hoerner, Philipp; Colorado, 1900 ***1029.59*** *p40*
Hoerner, Philipp; Illinois, 1889 ***1029.59*** *p40*
Hoerr, Philipp; America, 1841 ***5475.1*** *p396*
Hoeshield, Adam; New Jersey, 1736-1744 ***927.31*** *p3*
Hoestermann, Ludwig Paul Wilh. Gustav; America, 1863 ***5475.1*** *p12*
Hoey, Mrs. 45; Quebec, 1870 ***8364.32*** *p24*
Hoey, Alfred 14; Quebec, 1870 ***8364.32*** *p24*
Hoey, Edward 7; Quebec, 1870 ***8364.32*** *p24*
Hoey, Jane 17; Quebec, 1870 ***8364.32*** *p24*
Hoey, Joseph 15; Quebec, 1870 ***8364.32*** *p24*
Hof, Charles; Louisiana, 1841-1844 ***4981.45*** *p210*
Hofelmyer, Christian; Ohio, 1840-1897 ***8365.35*** *p16*
Hofer, Anna Maria 26; Valdivia, Chile, 1852 ***1192.4*** *p53*
Hofer, Friedrich 54; New Castle, DE, 1817-1818 ***90.20*** *p151*
Hofer, Joseph 36; Galveston, TX, 1846 ***3967.10*** *p378*
Hoff, . . .; America, 1844 ***7420.1*** *p32*
Hoff, Angela *SEE* Hoff, Eva Feilen
Hoff, Eva 62; Brazil, 1862 ***5475.1*** *p369*
*Daughter:*Angela
Hoff, Jacob Solomon; Detroit, 1930 ***1640.60*** *p78*
Hoff, Johann; Brazil, 1862 ***5475.1*** *p370*
Hoff, Margarethe 36; Brazil, 1862 ***5475.1*** *p369*
Hoff, Maria; America, 1868 ***5475.1*** *p378*
Hoff, Mathias; America, 1874 ***5475.1*** *p281*
Hoff, Peter; America, 1872 ***5475.1*** *p331*
Hoff, Theodore; Ohio, 1840-1897 ***8365.35*** *p16*
Hoffabert, Anna 2; Halifax, N.S., 1902 ***1860.4*** *p44*
Hoffabert, Ignauz; Halifax, N.S., 1902 ***1860.4*** *p44*
Hoffabert, Joseph 28; Halifax, N.S., 1902 ***1860.4*** *p44*
Hoffabert, Rosa 28; Halifax, N.S., 1902 ***1860.4*** *p44*
Hoffahrt, Benedict 1 months; New York, NY, 1893 ***1883.7*** *p38*
Hoffahrt, Christina 2; New York, NY, 1893 ***1883.7*** *p38*
Hoffahrt, Jacob 37; New York, NY, 1893 ***1883.7*** *p38*
Hoffahrt, Kaspar 4; New York, NY, 1893 ***1883.7*** *p38*
Hoffahrt, Theresia 32; New York, NY, 1893 ***1883.7*** *p38*
Hoffahrt, Vincenz 9; New York, NY, 1893 ***1883.7*** *p38*
Hoffart, Adam; America, 1866 ***2526.43*** *p148*
Hoffart, Agatha 24; New York, NY, 1893 ***1883.7*** *p41*
Hoffart, Anna Maria; America, 1853 ***2526.42*** *p182*
Hoffart, Anton 31; New York, NY, 1893 ***1883.7*** *p41*
Hoffart, August; America, 1893 ***2526.43*** *p148*
Hoffart, Dorothea; America, 1856 ***2526.43*** *p148*
Hoffart, Elisabeth *SEE* Hoffart, Heinrich
Hoffart, Eva Margarethe; America, 1869 ***2526.43*** *p148*
Hoffart, Franz 9 months; New York, NY, 1893 ***1883.7*** *p41*
Hoffart, Georg; America, 1871 ***2526.43*** *p148*
Hoffart, Georg Heinrich; America, 1880 ***2526.43*** *p140*
Hoffart, Gottlieb; America, 1866 ***2526.43*** *p148*
Hoffart, Heinrich; America, 1882 ***2526.43*** *p140*
*Wife:*Katharina Falter
*Son:*Jakob
*Daughter:*Elisabeth
*Daughter:*Maria
*Daughter:*Margaretha
*Son:*Ludwig
Hoffart, Heinrich Ludwig; America, 1880 ***2526.43*** *p148*
Hoffart, Jakob; America, 1855 ***2526.43*** *p148*
With family
Hoffart, Jakob; America, 1869 ***2526.43*** *p148*
Hoffart, Jakob *SEE* Hoffart, Heinrich
Hoffart, Katharina; America, 1866 ***2526.43*** *p148*
Hoffart, Katharina Falter *SEE* Hoffart, Heinrich
Hoffart, Ludwig *SEE* Hoffart, Heinrich
Hoffart, Margaretha *SEE* Hoffart, Heinrich
Hoffart, Margaretha 26; New York, NY, 1893 ***1883.7*** *p41*
Hoffart, Maria *SEE* Hoffart, Heinrich
Hoffart, Michael; America, 1881 ***2526.43*** *p140*
Hoffart, Michael; America, 1890 ***2526.43*** *p148*
Hoffart, Paul 26; New York, NY, 1893 ***1883.7*** *p41*
Hoffart, Wilhelm; America, 1892 ***2526.43*** *p148*
Hoffbour, Dominique 5; Missouri, 1845 ***778.6*** *p165*
Hoffbour, Elisabeth 39; Missouri, 1845 ***778.6*** *p165*
Hoffbour, Marie 16; Missouri, 1845 ***778.6*** *p165*
Hoffbour, Michel 45; Missouri, 1845 ***778.6*** *p165*
Hoffbour, Nicolas 11; Missouri, 1845 ***778.6*** *p165*
Hoffedietz, Christian Ludewig; Illinois, 1858 ***6079.1*** *p7*
Hoffemann, Y. Frederic; Illinois, 1852 ***6079.1*** *p7*
Hofferbert, Adam 25; America, 1847 ***2526.42*** *p108*
With wife
*Child:*Michael 2
*Child:*Wilhelm 4
Hofferbert, Eva Katharina 40; America, 1868 ***2526.43*** *p157*
Hofferbert, Michael 2 *SEE* Hofferbert, Adam
Hofferbert, Wilhelm 4 *SEE* Hofferbert, Adam
Hofferberth, Adam; America, 1881 ***2526.42*** *p108*
Hofferberth, Anna Eva 11 *SEE* Hofferberth, Philipp, II
Hofferberth, Anna Margaretha 6 *SEE* Hofferberth, Wilhelm
Hofferberth, Barbara; America, 1881 ***2526.42*** *p152*
Hofferberth, Elisabeth; America, 1871 ***2526.42*** *p182*
Hofferberth, Elise Margaretha 6 *SEE* Hofferberth, Wilhelm
Hofferberth, Eva Elisabetha; America, 1867 ***2526.42*** *p152*

Hofferberth, Eva Katharina; America, 1883 *2526.42 p129*
Hofferberth, Georg; America, 1850 *2526.42 p175*
Hofferberth, Georg; America, 1853 *2526.42 p95*
  *Uncle:*Georg
Hofferberth, Georg; America, 1865 *2526.43 p125*
Hofferberth, Georg; America, 1868 *2526.43 p148*
Hofferberth, Georg; America, 1868 *2526.43 p186*
Hofferberth, Georg 8 *SEE* Hofferberth, Wilhelm
Hofferberth, Georg 14 *SEE* Hofferberth, Georg
Hofferberth, Heinrich 24; America, 1883 *2526.43 p148*
Hofferberth, Heinrich 24; America, 1883 *2526.43 p148*
Hofferberth, Johann Michael; America, 1895 *2526.43 p148*
Hofferberth, Johann Philipp 19; America, 1852 *2526.43 p148*
Hofferberth, Karl Friedrich Theodor; America, 1883 *2526.42 p123*
Hofferberth, Katharina Elisabetha; America, 1867 *2526.42 p152*
Hofferberth, Leonhard; America, 1852 *2526.42 p153*
Hofferberth, Leonhard 16; America, 1853 *2526.43 p148*
Hofferberth, Leonhard 16; America, 1871 *2526.42 p153*
Hofferberth, Ludwig; America, 1867 *2526.42 p153*
Hofferberth, Marie Elisabethe 22; America, 1853 *2526.43 p186*
Hofferberth, Michael; America, 1836 *2526.42 p153*
  With wife & 5 children
Hofferberth, Michael; America, 1871 *2526.42 p153*
Hofferberth, Peter; America, 1881 *2526.42 p153*
Hofferberth, Peter 18; America, 1852 *2526.43 p148*
Hofferberth, Philipp; America, 1883 *2526.43 p148*
Hofferberth, Philipp 2 *SEE* Hofferberth, Philipp, II
Hofferberth, Philipp 35; America, 1882 *2526.43 p125*
Hofferberth, Philipp, II 38; America, 1855 *2526.43 p149*
  With wife 29
  *Daughter:*Anna Eva 11
  *Son:*Philipp 2
Hofferberth, Philipp Jakob, II 18; America, 1850 *2526.43 p149*
Hofferberth, Sophie 3 *SEE* Hofferberth, Wilhelm
Hofferberth, Wilhelm; America, 1845 *2526.43 p188*
  With wife
  *Son:*Georg
  *Daughter:*Anna Margaretha
  *Daughter:*Elise Margaretha
  *Daughter:*Sophie
Hoffler, Andreas 5; America, 1846 *778.6 p165*
Hoffler, Anna Maria 42; America, 1846 *778.6 p165*
Hoffler, Elisabeth 8; America, 1846 *778.6 p165*
Hoffler, Lorenz 13; America, 1846 *778.6 p165*
Hoffler, Lorenz 45; America, 1846 *778.6 p165*
Hoffler, Magdelena 7; America, 1846 *778.6 p165*
Hofflund, Alexander; America, 1850 *4487.25 p59*
  With family
Hoffman, Mrs. 35; America, 1841 *778.6 p165*
Hoffman, Adam; Ohio, 1809-1852 *4511.35 p23*
Hoffman, Albert Beuno; Ohio, 1809-1852 *4511.35 p23*
Hoffman, Anna 21; Portland, ME, 1906 *970.38 p78*
Hoffman, Cal.; Louisiana, 1874-1875 *4981.45 p29*
Hoffman, Caroline; Galveston, TX, 1855 *571.7 p16*
Hoffman, Charles G.; Cleveland, OH, 1888-1891 *9722.10 p120*
Hoffman, Daniel; Ohio, 1809-1852 *4511.35 p23*
Hoffman, Daniel, Jr.; Ohio, 1809-1852 *4511.35 p23*
Hoffman, Elisabeth 8; New York, NY, 1898 *7951.13 p41*
Hoffman, Franz Wilhelm Herman; Wisconsin, 1866 *6795.8 p73*
Hoffman, Frederick; Ohio, 1809-1852 *4511.35 p23*
Hoffman, Friedrich 2; New York, NY, 1898 *7951.13 p41*
Hoffman, Geo.; Louisiana, 1874-1875 *4981.45 p29*
Hoffman, Gertrude; Miami, 1935 *4984.12 p39*
Hoffman, H.H.; New Mexico, 1914 *4812.1 p87*
Hoffman, Henry; Washington, 1889 *2770.40 p27*
Hoffman, J.C. Gottlieb; Wisconsin, 1885 *6795.8 p62*
Hoffman, Jacob; Baltimore, 1894 *1766.20 p3*
Hoffman, Jacob; Ohio, 1809-1852 *4511.35 p23*
Hoffman, Johann 40; New York, NY, 1898 *7951.13 p41*
Hoffman, John; Colorado, 1893 *1029.59 p41*
Hoffman, John; Ohio, 1840-1897 *8365.35 p16*
Hoffman, John A.; Washington, 1884 *2770.40 p192*
Hoffman, Joseph 4; New York, NY, 1898 *7951.13 p41*
Hoffman, Justine; Wisconsin, 1901 *6795.8 p176*
Hoffman, Lydia 10; New York, NY, 1898 *7951.13 p41*
Hoffman, Maria 12; New York, NY, 1898 *7951.13 p41*
Hoffman, Marie 58; America, 1845 *778.6 p165*
Hoffman, Martin; Ohio, 1809-1852 *4511.35 p23*
Hoffman, Michael 15; New York, NY, 1898 *7951.13 p41*
Hoffman, Michael; Ohio, 1809-1852 *4511.35 p23*
Hoffman, Nicolas; Washington, 1887 *2770.40 p24*
Hoffman, Peter; Ohio, 1809-1852 *4511.35 p23*
Hoffman, Rosina 37; New York, NY, 1898 *7951.13 p41*

Hoffman, Samuel 14; New York, NY, 1898 *7951.13 p41*
Hoffman, Sebastian; Ohio, 1809-1852 *4511.35 p23*
Hoffman, Siligman; North Carolina, 1850 *1088.45 p14*
Hoffman, William; Ohio, 1809-1852 *4511.35 p23*
Hoffmann, Miss; America, 1873 *7420.1 p300*
Hoffmann, A. Maria *SEE* Hoffmann, Nikolaus
Hoffmann, Angela *SEE* Hoffmann, Mathias
Hoffmann, Angelika 33; America, 1858 *5475.1 p328*
Hoffmann, Anna; America, 1881 *5475.1 p445*
  *Son:*Jakob
  *Daughter:*Magdalena
Hoffmann, Anna *SEE* Hoffmann, Peter
Hoffmann, Anna 17 *SEE* Hoffmann, Peter
Hoffmann, Anna Katharina; Port uncertain, 1865 *170.15 p29*
  With family
Hoffmann, Anna Maria; America, 1836-1899 *6442.17 p65*
Hoffmann, Anton 46; America, 1873 *5475.1 p307*
  *Wife:*Elisabeth Schwarz
  *Son:*Peter 7
  *Daughter:*Katharina 8
Hoffmann, August; America, 1853 *2526.43 p140*
Hoffmann, Aurelie; Valdivia, Chile, 1850 *1192.4 p49*
Hoffmann, Barbara *SEE* Hoffmann, Johann
Hoffmann, Barbara *SEE* Hoffmann, Mathias
Hoffmann, Barbara 24; America, 1800-1899 *5475.1 p41*
Hoffmann, Barbara Helena Fell *SEE* Hoffmann, Michel
Hoffmann, Beltchen; America, 1867 *7919.3 p525*
Hoffmann, Carl; Valdivia, Chile, 1850 *1192.4 p49*
Hoffmann, Carl Gregor; San Francisco, 1889 *7420.1 p359*
Hoffmann, Christian; New York, 1859 *358.56 p55*
Hoffmann, Elisabeth Schwarz *SEE* Hoffmann, Anton
Hoffmann, Elisabeth 19 *SEE* Hoffmann, Peter
Hoffmann, Elisabeth; Brazil, 1870 *5475.1 p441*
Hoffmann, Elisabeth; New York, NY, 1868 *5475.1 p26*
Hoffmann, Elisabeth Becker Jager; America, 1881 *5475.1 p336*
  With 5 children
Hoffmann, Friedrich; America, 1868 *7919.3 p527*
Hoffmann, Friedrich 24; Brazil, 1872 *5475.1 p443*
Hoffmann, Gertrude *SEE* Hoffmann, Johannes, II
Hoffmann, Gottl.; Valdivia, Chile, 1852 *1192.4 p54*
  With wife & child
  With child 8
  With child 1
Hoffmann, J. Baptist *SEE* Hoffmann, Nikolaus
Hoffmann, J. Nikolaus 7 *SEE* Hoffmann, Peter
Hoffmann, Jakob *SEE* Hoffmann, Johann
Hoffmann, Jakob *SEE* Hoffmann, Mathias
Hoffmann, Jakob 3 *SEE* Hoffmann, Peter
Hoffmann, Jakob Christian; America, 1841 *5475.1 p458*
  *Wife:*Margarethe Schutz
  *Daughter:*Sophie
Hoffmann, Johann; America, 1869 *5475.1 p276*
Hoffmann, Johann *SEE* Hoffmann, Johann
Hoffmann, Johann; America, 1871 *5475.1 p442*
  *Wife:*Nathalie Zehler
  *Daughter:*Johannetta
  *Son:*Jakob
  *Son:*Johann
  *Daughter:*Barbara
  *Daughter:*Maria
  *Daughter:*Margarethe
Hoffmann, Johann; America, 1873 *5475.1 p351*
  *Wife:*Margarethe Veauthier
Hoffmann, Johann *SEE* Hoffmann, Mathias
Hoffmann, Johann 15 *SEE* Hoffmann, Peter
Hoffmann, Johann; Brazil, 1880 *5475.1 p444*
  With wife
  With 7 children
Hoffmann, Johannes *SEE* Hoffmann, Johannes, II
Hoffmann, Johannes; Port uncertain, 1865 *170.15 p29*
Hoffmann, Johannes, I; America, 1853 *2526.43 p123*
  With wife & 2 sons
Hoffmann, Johannes, II; America, 1853 *2526.43 p123*
  *Wife:*Gertrude
  *Son:*Johannes
  *Son:*Wilhelm
  *Son:*Peter
Hoffmann, Johannetta *SEE* Hoffmann, Johann
Hoffmann, Josef *SEE* Hoffmann, Nikolaus
Hoffmann, Karl; America, 1843 *5475.1 p505*
Hoffmann, Karl; America, 1863 *5475.1 p237*
Hoffmann, Karl Jos. Edmund; America, 1871 *5475.1 p13*
Hoffmann, Karoline; Brazil, 1879 *5475.1 p444*
Hoffmann, Katharina *SEE* Hoffmann, Mathias
Hoffmann, Katharina *SEE* Hoffmann, Nikolaus
Hoffmann, Katharina Martin *SEE* Hoffmann, Nikolaus
Hoffmann, Katharina 8 *SEE* Hoffmann, Anton
Hoffmann, Katharina 29; America, 1883 *5475.1 p203*
Hoffmann, Louise; America, 1867 *7919.3 p525*

Hoffmann, Ludw. Albert; America, 1880 *5475.1 p48*
Hoffmann, Ludwig Anton; America, 1853 *5475.1 p30*
Hoffmann, M. Jakob *SEE* Hoffmann, Mathias
Hoffmann, Margarethe Schutz *SEE* Hoffmann, Jakob Christian
Hoffmann, Margarethe *SEE* Hoffmann, Margarethe
Hoffmann, Margarethe *SEE* Hoffmann, Johann
Hoffmann, Margarethe Veauthier *SEE* Hoffmann, Johann
Hoffmann, Margarethe 31; America, 1861 *5475.1 p13*
  *Daughter:*Margarethe
Hoffmann, Maria *SEE* Hoffmann, Johann
Hoffmann, Maria Sauer *SEE* Hoffmann, Peter
Hoffmann, Maria *SEE* Hoffmann, Nikolaus
Hoffmann, Maria Nittler 45 *SEE* Hoffmann, Peter
Hoffmann, Maria Siersdorfer 61 *SEE* Hoffmann, Peter
Hoffmann, Maria Magdalena *SEE* Hoffmann, Peter
Hoffmann, Marie; New York, 1860 *358.56 p4*
Hoffmann, Mathias *SEE* Hoffmann, Mathias
Hoffmann, Mathias; America, 1874 *5475.1 p339*
  *Wife:*Susanna Weiten
  *Daughter:*Katharina
  *Son:*Johann
  *Son:*Mathias
  *Son:*M. Jakob
  *Daughter:*Barbara
  *Son:*Nikolaus
  *Son:*Jakob
  *Daughter:*Angela
Hoffmann, Mathias; America, 1883 *5475.1 p203*
Hoffmann, Mathias; New Jersey, 1885 *5475.1 p149*
Hoffmann, Mathilde Emilie; Wisconsin, 1896 *6795.8 p213*
Hoffmann, Max; America, 1899 *5475.1 p77*
Hoffmann, Michael; America, 1884 *2526.43 p149*
Hoffmann, Michael; Port uncertain, 1865 *170.15 p29*
  With family
Hoffmann, Michal 21; Portland, ME, 1906 *970.38 p78*
Hoffmann, Michel; America, 1882 *5475.1 p203*
  *Wife:*Barbara Helena Fell
Hoffmann, Michel 25; South America, 1857 *5475.1 p*
Hoffmann, Nathalie Zehler 45 *SEE* Hoffmann, Johann
Hoffmann, Nikolaus; America, 1866 *2526.43 p186*
Hoffmann, Nikolaus *SEE* Hoffmann, Mathias
Hoffmann, Nikolaus; America, 1882 *5475.1 p330*
  *Wife:*Katharina Martin
  *Daughter:*Maria
  *Daughter:*Katharina
  *Daughter:*A. Maria
  *Son:*Josef
  *Son:*J. Baptist
Hoffmann, Nikolaus; America, 1885 *5475.1 p330*
Hoffmann, Nikolaus 10 *SEE* Hoffmann, Peter
Hoffmann, Pauline, Child 9; Baltimore, 1889 *8425.16 p35*
Hoffmann, Pet. Jak.; America, 1869 *5475.1 p62*
  *Wife:*Sophie Eisenbarth
Hoffmann, Peter; America, 1849 *5475.1 p386*
Hoffmann, Peter *SEE* Hoffmann, Johannes, II
Hoffmann, Peter *SEE* Hoffmann, Peter
Hoffmann, Peter; America, 1881 *5475.1 p315*
  *Wife:*Maria Sauer
  *Son:*Peter
Hoffmann, Peter; America, 1882 *5475.1 p149*
Hoffmann, Peter; America, 1882 *5475.1 p215*
Hoffmann, Peter; America, 1882 *5475.1 p203*
  *Wife:*Maria Siersdorfer
  *Daughter:*Anna
  *Daughter:*Maria Magdalena
Hoffmann, Peter; America, 1887 *2526.43 p149*
Hoffmann, Peter 7 *SEE* Hoffmann, Anton
Hoffmann, Peter 13 *SEE* Hoffmann, Peter
Hoffmann, Peter 47; America, 1855 *5475.1 p317*
  *Wife:*Maria Nittler 45
  *Son:*Johann 15
  *Son:*Nikolaus 10
  *Son:*Jakob 3
  With mother-in-law 76
  *Son:*J. Nikolaus 7
  *Son:*Peter 13
  *Daughter:*Elisabeth 19
  *Daughter:*Anna 17
Hoffmann, Peter 32; New York, 1854 *5475.1 p235*
Hoffmann, Philipp, II; America, 1853 *2526.43 p149*
Hoffmann, Sophie *SEE* Hoffmann, Jakob Christian
Hoffmann, Sophie Eisenbarth *SEE* Hoffmann, Pet. Jak.
Hoffmann, Sophie Katharina; America, 1854 *5475.1 p459*
  *Son:*Jakob
  *Son:*Johannes
  *Son:*Friedrich
  *Son:*Christian
Hoffmann, Susanna Weiten *SEE* Hoffmann, Mathias

Hoffmann, Syprian; New Castle, DE, 1817-1818 ***90.20*** *p151*
Hoffmann, Wilh. Julius; Wisconsin, 1902 ***6795.8*** *p213*
Hoffmann, Wilhelm *SEE* Hoffmann, Johannes, II
Hoffmann, Wilhelm; America, 1889 ***2526.42*** *p108*
Hoffmeyer, Henry Albert; Louisiana, 1841-1844 ***4981.45*** *p210*
Hoffmeyer, Johannes Heinrich Wilhelm; South America, 1892 ***7420.1*** *p365*
Hoffner, Anthony; Ohio, 1844 ***2763.1*** *p8*
Hoffner, Fredrich 26; Portland, ME, 1911 ***970.38*** *p78*
Hoffner, Maria 22; Portland, ME, 1911 ***970.38*** *p78*
Hoffohrt, Gertrude 48; Halifax, N.S., 1902 ***1860.4*** *p44*
Hoffohrt, Melchior 55; Halifax, N.S., 1902 ***1860.4*** *p44*
Hoffort, Barbara 47; Halifax, N.S., 1902 ***1860.4*** *p42*
Hoffort, Christine 19; Halifax, N.S., 1902 ***1860.4*** *p42*
Hoffort, Elisabeth 11; Halifax, N.S., 1902 ***1860.4*** *p42*
Hoffort, Johann 17; Halifax, N.S., 1902 ***1860.4*** *p42*
Hoffort, Johann 50; Halifax, N.S., 1902 ***1860.4*** *p42*
Hoffort, Pauline 6; Halifax, N.S., 1902 ***1860.4*** *p42*
Hoffsancess, John 26; America, 1842 ***778.6*** *p165*
Hoffstadt, Jakob 57; America, 1837 ***2526.43*** *p171*
With wife & daughter
With grandson 3
With son 19
Hoffstetter, B. 27; New Orleans, 1834 ***1002.51*** *p112*
Hoffstetter, G. 20; New Orleans, 1834 ***1002.51*** *p112*
Hofman, George; Washington, 1885 ***2770.40*** *p194*
Hofmann, Adam 7 *SEE* Hofmann, Philipp Jakob, I
Hofmann, Anna Elisabetha 33; America, 1841 ***2526.43*** *p144*
Hofmann, Anna Eva; America, 1861 ***2526.43*** *p186*
With 3 children
*Son:*Johannes
*Daughter:*Sophie
*Daughter:*Anna Margaretha
*Son:*Wilhelm
Hofmann, Anna Katharina; Virginia, 1831 ***152.20*** *p60*
Hofmann, Anna Margaretha; America, 1785 ***2526.42*** *p155*
Hofmann, Anna Margarethe; Virginia, 1831 ***152.20*** *p60*
Hofmann, August; Illinois, 1930 ***121.35*** *p101*
Hofmann, Balthasar 3 *SEE* Hofmann, Johannes
Hofmann, Carl; America, 1867 ***7919.3*** *p534*
Hofmann, Ch. 40; America, 1846 ***778.6*** *p165*
Hofmann, Charles 9; America, 1846 ***778.6*** *p166*
Hofmann, Eduard; America, 1867 ***7919.3*** *p534*
Hofmann, Elisabetha; America, 1868 ***2526.43*** *p140*
Hofmann, Engel Sophie Louise Wilhelmine; America, 1867 ***7420.1*** *p258*
Hofmann, Eva Maria; America, 1871 ***2526.43*** *p210*
Hofmann, Eva Maria Allmanritter 37 *SEE* Hofmann, Philipp Jakob, I
Hofmann, Friedrich; America, 1858 ***2526.43*** *p149*
Hofmann, Friedrich Jakob 13 *SEE* Hofmann, Johannes
Hofmann, Georg; America, 1867 ***7919.3*** *p527*
Hofmann, Georgine; America, 1867 ***7919.3*** *p533*
Hofmann, Jacob 25; Portland, ME, 1906 ***970.38*** *p78*
Hofmann, Jakob; America, 1868-1895 ***179.55*** *p19*
Hofmann, Jakob; America, 1879 ***2526.43*** *p210*
Hofmann, Jeanne 3; America, 1846 ***778.6*** *p166*
Hofmann, Johannes; America, 1900 ***2526.43*** *p210*
Hofmann, Johannes 10 *SEE* Hofmann, Philipp Jakob, I
Hofmann, Johannes 42; America, 1839 ***2526.43*** *p140*
With wife 41
With stepchild 16
*Son:*Balthasar 3
*Daughter:*Margaretha 9
*Son:*Friedrich Jakob 13
Hofmann, Katharina 5 *SEE* Hofmann, Philipp Jakob, I
Hofmann, Leonhard; America, 1867 ***2526.43*** *p186*
Hofmann, Ludwig 5; America, 1846 ***778.6*** *p166*
Hofmann, Marg. 28; America, 1846 ***778.6*** *p166*
Hofmann, Margaretha; America, 1868 ***2526.43*** *p140*
Hofmann, Margaretha 2 *SEE* Hofmann, Philipp Jakob, I
Hofmann, Margaretha 9 *SEE* Hofmann, Johannes
Hofmann, Margarethe Dewes *SEE* Hofmann, Michel
Hofmann, Maria; America, 1836 ***5475.1*** *p437*
Hofmann, Maria Elisabetha; America, 1854 ***2526.43*** *p149*
Hofmann, Max; America, 1868 ***7919.3*** *p534*
Hofmann, Michel; America, 1834 ***5475.1*** *p437*
*Wife:*Margarethe Dewes
With 2 children
Hofmann, Nicolas 6; America, 1846 ***778.6*** *p166*
Hofmann, Otto; America, 1850 ***2526.43*** *p140*
Hofmann, Peter; Brazil, 1855 ***5475.1*** *p440*
With family of 5
Hofmann, Philipp; America, 1873 ***2526.43*** *p186*
Hofmann, Philipp Jakob, I 37; America, 1854 ***2526.43*** *p149*
*Wife:*Eva Maria Allmanritter 37
*Son:*Wilhelm 14
*Son:*Adam 7
*Daughter:*Margaretha 2
*Daughter:*Katharina 5
*Son:*Johannes 10
Hofmann, Wilhelm 14 *SEE* Hofmann, Philipp Jakob, I
Hofmeister, Caroline; America, 1854 ***7420.1*** *p121*
Hofmeister, Friedrich; America, 1854 ***7420.1*** *p121*
With wife & son
Hofmeister, Heinrich Gerhard; Port uncertain, 1836 ***7420.1*** *p11*
Hofmeister, Kasper; Colorado, 1880 ***1029.59*** *p41*
Hofmeister, Kasper; Colorado, 1891 ***1029.59*** *p41*
Hofmeyer, Carl Heinrich Wilhelm; America, 1866 ***7420.1*** *p243*
Hofmeyer, Catharina 14; New Orleans, 1847 ***778.6*** *p166*
Hofmeyer, Joseph 42; New Orleans, 1847 ***778.6*** *p166*
Hofmeyer, Katharina 16; New Orleans, 1847 ***778.6*** *p166*
Hofmeyer, Marianna 5; New Orleans, 1847 ***778.6*** *p166*
Hofmeyer, Martha 9; New Orleans, 1847 ***778.6*** *p166*
Hofner, Ernst Wilhelm Gottlieb; America, 1868 ***7919.3*** *p526*
Hofner, Joseph 44; Ontario, 1871 ***1823.17*** *p71*
Hofner, Michael Christian Wilhelm Adolph; America, 1868 ***7919.3*** *p526*
Hofstadt, Johannes; America, 1885 ***2526.42*** *p123*
Hoft, Matilda Emilie; Wisconsin, 1897 ***6795.8*** *p30*
Hog, Jacob; Ohio, 1809-1852 ***4511.35*** *p19*
Hogain, Hannah; Boston, 1754 ***1642*** *p47*
Hogan, Alice; New Orleans, 1850 ***7242.30*** *p144*
Hogan, Anne; New Orleans, 1850 ***7242.30*** *p144*
Hogan, Anne; St. Johns, N.F., 1825 ***1053.15*** *p7*
Hogan, Annie 22; Ontario, 1871 ***1823.17*** *p71*
Hogan, Bridget; New York, 1909 ***9228.50*** *p603*
Hogan, Dan; Boston, 1768 ***1642*** *p39*
Hogan, Denis; Louisiana, 1836-1841 ***4981.45*** *p208*
Hogan, Edward; St. John, N.B., 1847 ***2978.15*** *p37*
Hogan, Eliza; St. Johns, N.F., 1825 ***1053.15*** *p7*
Hogan, Elizabeth; Boston, 1758 ***1642*** *p47*
Hogan, Elizabeth; Ipswich, MA, 1747 ***1642*** *p71*
Hogan, Ellen 40; Ontario, 1871 ***1823.21*** *p164*
Hogan, Felix; Boston, 1747 ***1642*** *p46*
Hogan, Henry 29; Ontario, 1871 ***1823.17*** *p71*
Hogan, James; New Orleans, 1850 ***7242.30*** *p144*
Hogan, James 70; Ontario, 1871 ***1823.21*** *p164*
Hogan, John; Boston, 1741 ***1642*** *p45*
Hogan, John; Boston, 1742 ***1642*** *p45*
Hogan, John; Boston, 1748 ***1642*** *p46*
Hogan, John; Toronto, 1844 ***2910.35*** *p116*
Hogan, Kitty; St. Johns, N.F., 1825 ***1053.15*** *p7*
Hogan, Martin; St. Johns, N.F., 1825 ***1053.15*** *p6*
Hogan, Mary; Boston, 1766 ***1642*** *p48*
Hogan, Mary; New Orleans, 1850 ***7242.30*** *p144*
Hogan, Mary 28; Ontario, 1871 ***1823.21*** *p164*
Hogan, Mary 65; Ontario, 1871 ***1823.21*** *p164*
Hogan, Matthew; Indiana, 1880 ***9076.20*** *p70*
Hogan, Michael; Marston's Wharf, 1782 ***8529.30*** *p12*
Hogan, Michael 35; Ontario, 1871 ***1823.21*** *p164*
Hogan, Michael 55; Ontario, 1871 ***1823.21*** *p164*
Hogan, Michl 26; St. Johns, N.F., 1811 ***1053.20*** *p22*
Hogan, Pat 3; St. Johns, N.F., 1811 ***1053.20*** *p20*
Hogan, Patrick; Boston, 1744 ***1642*** *p45*
Hogan, Patrick; Massachusetts, 1766 ***1642*** *p66*
Hogan, Stephen 25; New York, NY, 1826 ***6178.50*** *p150*
Hogan, Thomas; Marblehead, MA, 1751 ***1642*** *p73*
Hogan, Thomas; Salem, MA, 1751 ***1642*** *p78*
Hogan, William; Boston, 1737 ***1642*** *p44*
Hogan, William; New Orleans, 1850 ***7242.30*** *p144*
Hogan, William; Vermont, 1827 ***3274.55*** *p44*
Hogdgs, Thomas 74; Ontario, 1871 ***1823.21*** *p164*
Hoge, Joseph P.; Ohio, 1832 ***3580.20*** *p32*
Hoge, Joseph P.; Ohio, 1832 ***6020.12*** *p12*
Hogel, Friedrich; America, 1882 ***5475.1*** *p406*
With wife
Hogele, Andreas 7; New York, NY, 1893 ***1883.7*** *p44*
Hogele, Christina 1; New York, NY, 1893 ***1883.7*** *p44*
Hogele, Christina 29; New York, NY, 1893 ***1883.7*** *p44*
Hogele, Fiane 4; New York, NY, 1893 ***1883.7*** *p44*
Hogele, Jacob 27; New York, NY, 1893 ***1883.7*** *p44*
Hogen, Daniel; Boston, 1714 ***1642*** *p24*
Hogen, John; Boston, 1761 ***1642*** *p48*
Hogg, Ann 65; Ontario, 1871 ***1823.21*** *p164*
Hogg, Eliza 30; Ontario, 1871 ***1823.21*** *p164*
Hogg, Francis; North Carolina, 1792-1862 ***1088.45*** *p14*
Hogg, Issac 37; Ontario, 1871 ***1823.21*** *p164*
Hogg, John; Philadelphia, 1778 ***8529.30*** *p7A*
Hogg, Mary 52; Ontario, 1871 ***1823.21*** *p164*
Hogg, Walter 50; Ontario, 1871 ***1823.21*** *p164*
Hogg, William 24; New York, NY, 1894 ***6512.1*** *p183*
Hoggan, Joseph; Ohio, 1809-1852 ***4511.35*** *p23*
Hoggen, Matthew; Boston, 1765 ***1642*** *p48*
Hogh, Johannes Carl; America, 1868 ***7919.3*** *p535*
Hogin, Elisabeth; Newbury, MA, 1748 ***1642*** *p75*
Hogins, Thomas 62; Ontario, 1871 ***1823.21*** *p164*
Hogland, John; Cleveland, OH, 1892-1906 ***9722.10*** *p120*
Hoglund, Anton; Colorado, 1887 ***1029.59*** *p41*
Hoglund, Arvid Samuel; Cleveland, OH, 1899-1901 ***9722.10*** *p120*
Hoglund, C.P.; New York, NY, 1845 ***6412.40*** *p149*
Hogmire, Mr.; West Virginia, 1787 ***1132.30*** *p146*
Hogner, Wilhelm; New Jersey, 1812 ***3845.2*** *p129*
Hogrefe, Catharine; America, 1866 ***7420.1*** *p240*
Hogvall, Anna Sophia Christina; North America, 1886 ***6410.15*** *p106*
Hohenberger, Ferd.; Galveston, TX, 1855 ***571.7*** *p16*
Hohenschilt, Johann Adam; New Jersey, 1736-1744 ***927.31*** *p2*
Hohenstein, Louis; Louisiana, 1874 ***4981.45*** *p132*
Hohermuth, Georg; Venezuela, 1529 ***3899.5*** *p538*
Hohl, Ida Ritter *SEE* Hohl, Philip
Hohl, Johanne; Philadelphia, 1856 ***8513.31*** *p428*
Hohl, Philip; Allegheny Co., PA, 1852 ***8513.31*** *p315*
*Wife:*Ida Ritter
Hohle, Frederic 19; America, 1846 ***778.6*** *p166*
Hohle, Goerge 27; America, 1846 ***778.6*** *p166*
Hohlt, Anna Maria Caroline Henriette *SEE* Hohlt, Otto
Hohlt, Elise Henriette Louise *SEE* Hohlt, Otto
Hohlt, Friederike Lisette Caroline Franzisca *SEE* Hohlt, Otto
Hohlt, Friedr. Wilh. Adolf *SEE* Hohlt, Otto
Hohlt, Otto; America, 1870 ***7420.1*** *p287*
With wife
*Daughter:*Anna Maria Caroline Henriette
*Daughter:*Friederike Lisette Caroline Franzisca
*Son:*Friedr. Wilh. Adolf
*Daughter:*Elise Henriette Louise
Hohlweck, Elisabeth; America, 1867 ***5475.1*** *p379*
Hohman, . . .; West Virginia, 1850-1860 ***1132.30*** *p149*
Hohmann, Heinrich; Valdivia, Chile, 1852 ***1192.4*** *p53*
With wife
Hohmeier, George; New Jersey, 1777 ***8529.30*** *p6*
Hohmeier, Johann Heinrich; America, 1872 ***7420.1*** *p295*
Hohn, Anna 47; America, 1872 ***5475.1*** *p147*
Hohn, Barbara 40; America, 1846 ***778.6*** *p166*
Hohn, Chretien 23; America, 1846 ***778.6*** *p166*
Hohn, Frederic 22; America, 1746 ***778.6*** *p166*
Hohn, Frederique 21; America, 1846 ***778.6*** *p166*
Hohn, Jacob; America, 1867 ***7919.3*** *p526*
Hohn, Philipp; America, 1867 ***7919.3*** *p526*
Hohn, Thomas; Colorado, 1901 ***1029.59*** *p41*
Hohn, Thomas; Philadelphia, 1886 ***1029.59*** *p41*
Hohn, Valentin 17; America, 1746 ***778.6*** *p166*
Hohnborst, Johann Otto; Port uncertain, 1835 ***7420.1*** *p9*
Hohne, Richard; America, 1881 ***7420.1*** *p321*
Hoie, Ellen Gunhilda; Illinois, 1930 ***121.35*** *p101*
Hoie, Lara; Illinois, 1930 ***121.35*** *p101*
Hoijer, Fr. Wilhelm; New York, NY, 1851 ***6412.40*** *p153*
Hoil, David 56; Ontario, 1871 ***1823.17*** *p71*
Hoile, . . .; Marblehead, MA, 1669-1687 ***9228.50*** *p289*
Hoiles, James; Chicago, 1845-1880 ***9228.50*** *p289*
Hojda, Jan; Baltimore, 1872-1879 ***2853.20*** *p128*
Hojrup, Martin Aksel Hansel; Iowa, 1930 ***1211.15*** *p11*
Hokanson, Nels; Colorado, 1862-1920 ***1029.59*** *p41*
Hokanson, Nils; Colorado, 1888 ***1029.59*** *p41*
Hoke, George; Ohio, 1809-1852 ***4511.35*** *p23*
Hokenson, Gust; Iowa, 1904 ***1211.15*** *p11*
Hokenson, Martin; Washington, 1883 ***2770.40*** *p136*
Hokuf, Matej; Nebraska, 1875 ***2853.20*** *p157*
Holbeck, William; Plymouth, MA, 1620 ***1920.45*** *p5*
Holben, James 35; Ontario, 1871 ***1823.21*** *p164*
Holberton, Lina 21; Ontario, 1871 ***1823.21*** *p164*
Holbrock, John; Philadelphia, 1778 ***8529.30*** *p3A*
Holbrook, Edwin 46; Ontario, 1871 ***1823.17*** *p71*
Holbrook, John; Philadelphia, 1778 ***8529.30*** *p3A*
Holbrook, John S.; Washington, 1880 ***2770.40*** *p134*
Holbrook, Thomas 49; Ontario, 1871 ***1823.17*** *p71*
Holbrook, William 28; Ontario, 1871 ***1823.17*** *p71*
Holbrook, William 40; Ontario, 1871 ***1823.17*** *p71*
Holbysan, John; Ohio, 1809-1852 ***4511.35*** *p23*
Hold, Joseph 65; Ontario, 1871 ***1823.21*** *p164*
Hold, Margret 61; Ontario, 1871 ***1823.21*** *p164*
Holdaway, John 63; Ontario, 1871 ***1823.21*** *p164*
Holden, Bartholomew; Washington, 1888 ***2770.40*** *p25*
Holden, John; Boston, 1775 ***8529.30*** *p2*
Holden, John 57; Ontario, 1871 ***1823.21*** *p164*
Holden, John; St. Johns, N.F., 1825 ***1053.15*** *p6*
Holden, Patrick; New York, NY, 1836 ***3274.55*** *p25*
Holden, Rich; Virginia, 1652 ***6254.4*** *p243*
Holden, Thomas; Illinois, 1858 ***6079.1*** *p7*
Holden, William; New York, 1781 ***8529.30*** *p12*
Holden, William 56; Ontario, 1871 ***1823.17*** *p71*
Holder, James 41; Ontario, 1871 ***1823.17*** *p71*
Holderbaum, C. P.; America, 1848 ***5475.1*** *p28*
Holderer, John; North Carolina, 1792-1862 ***1088.45*** *p14*
Holderith, Daniel; Louisiana, 1841-1844 ***4981.45*** *p210*
Holderness, Edward P.G.; Illinois, 1834-1900 ***6020.5*** *p132*

Holdernesse, Henry James; Philadelphia, 1807 ***7074.20*** *p133*
Holderrieth, Franz 28; Port uncertain, 1843 ***778.6*** *p166*
Holdin, James 44; Ontario, 1871 ***1823.21*** *p164*
Holdinnoe, John 58; Ontario, 1871 ***1823.21*** *p164*
Holdsworth, Robert; Colorado, 1862-1920 ***1029.59*** *p41*
Holecek, Frantisek; Chicago, 1891 ***2853.20*** *p417*
Holecek, Jan; Nebraska, 1869 ***2853.20*** *p193*
Holender, Catherine 5; Missouri, 1846 ***778.6*** *p166*
Holender, Maria 34; Missouri, 1846 ***778.6*** *p166*
Holes, John; Colorado, 1880 ***1029.59*** *p36*
Holes, John; Colorado, 1880 ***1029.59*** *p41*
Holgate, William 28; Ontario, 1871 ***1823.21*** *p164*
Holier, Guillaume-Simon; Montreal, 1661 ***9221.17*** *p473*
Holiway, John 25; Ontario, 1871 ***1823.21*** *p164*
Holl, Josef; America, 1875 ***179.55*** *p19*
Holla, Klara; Galveston, TX, 1854 ***2853.20*** *p61*
Hollam, John; North America, 1750 ***1640.8*** *p234*
Holland, Anna 28; Michigan, 1880 ***4491.33*** *p12*
Holland, Anne; St. Johns, N.F., 1825 ***1053.15*** *p7*
Holland, Anty; St. Johns, N.F., 1825 ***1053.15*** *p7*
Holland, Catherine; St. Johns, N.F., 1825 ***1053.15*** *p6*
Holland, Clara Mary Ann; Illinois, 1930 ***121.35*** *p101*
Holland, Edward 37; Ontario, 1871 ***1823.21*** *p164*
Holland, Elizabeth *SEE* Holland, Patrick F.
Holland, Ellen 7; Quebec, 1870 ***8364.32*** *p24*
Holland, Henry; Boston, 1833 ***3274.55*** *p25*
Holland, Mrs. Henry; New York, 1926 ***1173.1*** *p2*
Holland, John 38; Michigan, 1880 ***4491.33*** *p12*
Holland, John; North Carolina, 1792-1862 ***1088.45*** *p14*
Holland, John 69; Ontario, 1871 ***1823.17*** *p71*
Holland, John; Philadelphia, 1778 ***8529.30*** *p2*
Holland, John 14; St. Johns, N.F., 1811 ***1053.20*** *p20*
Holland, Lars; Iowa, 1890 ***1211.15*** *p11*
Holland, Lucey; Massachusetts, 1754 ***1642*** *p100*
Holland, Maria 24; Ontario, 1871 ***1823.21*** *p164*
Holland, Martyn 29; Ontario, 1871 ***1823.21*** *p164*
Holland, Mary Riley *SEE* Holland, Patrick F.
Holland, Patrick 45; Ontario, 1871 ***1823.17*** *p71*
Holland, Patrick F.; New York, 1855 ***8513.31*** *p315*
*Wife:*Mary Riley
*Daughter:*Elizabeth
Holland, Richard; St. Johns, N.F., 1825 ***1053.15*** *p6*
Holland, Thomas; Louisiana, 1836-1840 ***4981.45*** *p212*
Holland, Thomas 45; Ontario, 1871 ***1823.17*** *p71*
Holland, Thomas 60; Ontario, 1871 ***1823.17*** *p71*
Holland, William 16; Quebec, 1870 ***8364.32*** *p24*
Hollander, Gustav T.; Wisconsin, 1871 ***6795.8*** *p145*
Hollander, Johann; Missouri, 1883 ***3276.1*** *p3*
Hollander, Moritz; America, 1867 ***7919.3*** *p525*
Holle, Mr.; America, 1880 ***7420.1*** *p316*
Holle, Engel Dorothea; America, 1867 ***7420.1*** *p258*
With 5 sons & 2 daughters
Holle, Friedrich Gottlieb; America, 1881 ***7420.1*** *p321*
Holle, Johann Friedrich Christoph; America, 1846 ***7420.1*** *p45*
With family
Holle, Johann Heinrich; America, 1854 ***7420.1*** *p122*
Holleane, William; Colorado, 1873 ***1029.59*** *p36*
Hollender, Anna Stena; Wisconsin, 1911 ***6795.8*** *p177*
Hollendorf, J. Charles; Nova Scotia, 1784 ***7105*** *p25*
Holler, George; Ohio, 1840-1897 ***8365.35*** *p16*
Holler, Johannes; America, 1883 ***2526.42*** *p169*
Holleran, John 50; Ontario, 1871 ***1823.17*** *p71*
Holliday, Charles 32; Ontario, 1871 ***1823.21*** *p165*
Holliday, John 28; Indiana, 1878-1888 ***9076.20*** *p71*
Hollidge, George; Washington, 1886 ***2770.40*** *p195*
Hollihan, Con 22; St. Johns, N.F., 1811 ***1053.20*** *p19*
Hollin, Charles 15; America, 1846 ***778.6*** *p166*
Holling, John 46; Ontario, 1871 ***1823.17*** *p71*
Holling, John 71; Ontario, 1871 ***1823.17*** *p71*
Holling, William; Colorado, 1873 ***1029.59*** *p36*
Hollingsworth, Antony 38; Ontario, 1871 ***1823.17*** *p71*
Hollingsworth, David; America, 1870 ***9076.20*** *p67*
Hollingsworth, John 34; Ontario, 1871 ***1823.21*** *p165*
Hollington, Mr. 5; Quebec, 1870 ***8364.32*** *p24*
Hollington, Ann 36; Quebec, 1870 ***8364.32*** *p24*
Hollingworth, Jabez; New York, NY, 1826 ***3274.55*** *p67*
Hollingworth, Joseph; New York, NY, 1827 ***3274.56*** *p70*
Hollman, August W.; Wisconsin, 1906 ***6795.8*** *p177*
Hollman, Peter Albert; North Carolina, 1792-1862 ***1088.45*** *p15*
Holloran, Francis 55; Ontario, 1871 ***1823.17*** *p71*
Holloran, William 48; Ontario, 1871 ***1823.21*** *p165*
Holloway, Alfred 36; Ontario, 1871 ***1823.21*** *p165*
Holloway, Alfred 70; Ontario, 1871 ***1823.21*** *p165*
Holloway, John; Virginia, 1652 ***6254.4*** *p243*
Holloway, Thomas; New York, 1782 ***8529.30*** *p12*
Holloway, Wm.; Maryland, 1673 ***1236.25*** *p49*
Holm, Andrew; St. Paul, MN, 1883 ***1865.50*** *p50*
Holm, Carl August; Cleveland, OH, 1904-1905 ***9722.10*** *p120*
Holm, Eli.; Maryland, 1672 ***1236.25*** *p48*
Holm, Emil; Washington, 1889 ***2770.40*** *p27*
Holm, Johan Ferdinand; Cleveland, OH, 1905 ***9722.10*** *p120*
Holm, John; Washington, 1889 ***2770.40*** *p27*
Holm, Oskar; Cleveland, OH, 1903 ***9722.10*** *p120*
Holman, Francis 38; Ontario, 1871 ***1823.21*** *p165*
Holman, Hulda; St. Paul, MN, 1894 ***1865.50*** *p50*
Holman, Jacob 40; Ontario, 1871 ***1823.21*** *p165*
Holman, Jane 22; Ontario, 1871 ***1823.17*** *p71*
Holman, John; Massachusetts, 1630 ***117.5*** *p154*
Holman, Samuel 27; Ontario, 1871 ***1823.21*** *p165*
Holman, William 53; Ontario, 1871 ***1823.17*** *p71*
Holmberg, Carl Victor; New York, NY, 1851 ***6412.40*** *p153*
Holmberg, John A.; Chicago, 1879-1882 ***1865.50*** *p50*
Holmberg, Olaf M. 24; New York, NY, 1894 ***6512.1*** *p184*
Holmberg, Swan; Cleveland, OH, 1880-1882 ***9722.10*** *p120*
Holmburg, Andrew B.; Iowa, 1903 ***1211.15*** *p11*
Holme, Elizabeth; America, 1732 ***1220.12*** *p520*
Holme, Robert 66; Ontario, 1871 ***1823.17*** *p71*
Holmen, Augusta *SEE* Holmen, Frank
Holmen, Frank; St. Paul, MN, 1894 ***1865.50*** *p50*
*Wife:*Augusta
Holmen, Hulda; St. Paul, MN, 1894 ***1865.50*** *p50*
Holmer, Christina *SEE* Holmer, Olof A.
Holmer, Olof A.; St. Paul, MN, 1894 ***1865.50*** *p50*
*Wife:*Christina
Holmes, Andrew 35; Ontario, 1871 ***1823.17*** *p72*
Holmes, Anne 5; Ontario, 1871 ***1823.21*** *p165*
Holmes, Benjamin; Philadelphia, 1778 ***8529.30*** *p3A*
Holmes, Christopher 17; Quebec, 1870 ***8364.32*** *p24*
Holmes, David 40; Ontario, 1871 ***1823.17*** *p72*
Holmes, George 18; Ontario, 1871 ***1823.21*** *p165*
Holmes, George 21; Ontario, 1871 ***1823.21*** *p165*
Holmes, George 17; Quebec, 1870 ***8364.32*** *p24*
Holmes, Henry 24; Ontario, 1871 ***1823.21*** *p165*
Holmes, Jacob 49; Ontario, 1871 ***1823.21*** *p165*
Holmes, James; Louisiana, 1874 ***4981.45*** *p132*
Holmes, Jane 38; Ontario, 1871 ***1823.21*** *p165*
Holmes, Jane 76; Ontario, 1871 ***1823.17*** *p72*
Holmes, John; Ohio, 1824 ***3580.20*** *p32*
Holmes, John; Ohio, 1824 ***6020.12*** *p12*
Holmes, John 2; Ontario, 1871 ***1823.21*** *p165*
Holmes, John 31; Ontario, 1871 ***1823.21*** *p165*
Holmes, John 45; Ontario, 1871 ***1823.17*** *p72*
Holmes, John William; North Carolina, 1792-1862 ***1088.45*** *p15*
Holmes, Joseph 38; Ontario, 1871 ***1823.17*** *p72*
Holmes, Mark 65; Ontario, 1871 ***1823.21*** *p165*
Holmes, Samuel 73; Ontario, 1871 ***1823.21*** *p165*
Holmes, Samuell 20; Virginia, 1635 ***1183.3*** *p31*
Holmes, Thomas 38; Ontario, 1871 ***1823.21*** *p165*
Holmes, Thomas 56; Ontario, 1871 ***1823.21*** *p165*
Holmes, William 31; Ontario, 1871 ***1823.21*** *p165*
Holmes, William 40; Ontario, 1871 ***1823.17*** *p72*
Holmqvist, N.; New York, NY, 1846 ***6412.40*** *p149*
Holms, Marie 20; New York, NY, 1885 ***1883.7*** *p45*
Holmstead, Frederick W. 26; Ontario, 1871 ***1823.17*** *p72*
Holowecki, Michal; Detroit, 1930 ***1640.60*** *p76*
Hols, William 27; Ontario, 1871 ***1823.21*** *p165*
Holscher, Carl August Wilhelm; America, 1881 ***7420.1*** *p321*
Holscher, Heinrich Wilhelm; America, 1872 ***7420.1*** *p295*
Holscher, Wilhelm; America, 1881 ***7420.1*** *p321*
Holste, Ernst August Heinrich; New York, NY, 1892 ***7420.1*** *p366*
Holste, Heinrich Carl; America, 1888 ***7420.1*** *p357*
Holste, Heinrich Wilhelm; Port uncertain, 1856 ***7420.1*** *p148*
Holstead, Edward 40; Ontario, 1871 ***1823.21*** *p165*
Holstein, Katha 4; Halifax, N.S., 1903 ***1860.4*** *p44*
Holstein, Lisbet; Halifax, N.S., 1903 ***1860.4*** *p44*
Holstein, Maria 38; Halifax, N.S., 1903 ***1860.4*** *p44*
Holstein, Pauline 3; Halifax, N.S., 1903 ***1860.4*** *p44*
Holstein, Philippine; America, 1867 ***7420.1*** *p258*
Holster, Christian; Ohio, 1809-1852 ***4511.35*** *p23*
Holt, Ann 59; Ontario, 1871 ***1823.21*** *p165*
Holt, Ann *SEE* Holt, Joseph
Holt, Emma Hibberd *SEE* Holt, James
Holt, George S. 27; Ontario, 1871 ***1823.17*** *p72*
Holt, James; Philadelphia, 1860 ***8513.31*** *p316*
*Wife:*Emma Hibberd
Holt, Jason 65; Ontario, 1871 ***1823.17*** *p72*
Holt, Jason S. 34; Ontario, 1871 ***1823.17*** *p72*
Holt, John *SEE* Holt, Joseph
Holt, Joseph; Philadelphia, 1861 ***8513.31*** *p315*
*Wife:*Mary Connelly
*Daughter:*Ann
*Son:*John
Holt, Magnus M.; Illinois, 1861 ***4487.25*** *p59*
Holt, Mary; New Orleans, 1851 ***7242.30*** *p144*
Holt, Mary Connelly *SEE* Holt, Joseph
Holt, William; New Orleans, 1851 ***7242.30*** *p144*
Holt, William; New York, NY, 1834 ***3274.55*** *p24*
Holter, Oscar 32; Minnesota, 1925 ***2769.54*** *p1383*
Holtermann, Eller; Valdivia, Chile, 1850 ***1192.4*** *p49*
Holtge, Friedrich Christian *SEE* Holtge, Sophie
Holtge, Heinrich *SEE* Holtge, Sophie
Holtge, Sophie; America, 1852 ***7420.1*** *p90*
*Son:*Friedrich Christian
With daughter
*Son:*Wilhelm
*Son:*Heinrich
Holtge, Wilhelm *SEE* Holtge, Sophie
Holthower, Henry; Washington, 1881 ***2770.40*** *p135*
Holthusen, Augusta S. S.; North Carolina, 1792-1862 ***1088.45*** *p15*
Holton, Ann 75; Ontario, 1871 ***1823.21*** *p165*
Holton, Frances Josepline 26; Ontario, 1871 ***1823.21*** *p165*
Holton, Henry 43; Ontario, 1871 ***1823.21*** *p165*
Holton, Lucy A. 37; Michigan, 1880 ***4491.33*** *p12*
Holton, Margaret 56; Michigan, 1880 ***4491.39*** *p14*
Holton, Thos.; Louisiana, 1874-1875 ***4981.45*** *p29*
Holton, Wm 74; Michigan, 1880 ***4491.39*** *p14*
Holtorf, Albert; Ohio, 1840-1897 ***8365.35*** *p16*
Holtsman, Michael; Philadelphia, 1777 ***8529.30*** *p6*
Holtsmann, Jacob; New York, NY, 1871 ***1029.59*** *p41*
Holtz, Joh. W. Ludw.; Chile, 1852 ***1192.4*** *p54*
Holtz, Lewis; New York, 1859 ***358.56*** *p100*
Holtz, Mary; Wisconsin, 1906 ***6795.8*** *p179*
Holtzman, Hyman; Detroit, 1929-1930 ***6214.5*** *p61*
Holtzmann, Michael; Philadelphia, 1777 ***8529.30*** *p6*
Holtzschuter, Julius; North Carolina, 1792-1862 ***1088.45*** *p15*
Holtzweg, . . .; West Virginia, n.d. ***1132.30*** *p151*
Holtzweg, Xavior; West Virginia, 1869 ***1132.30*** *p151*
Holub, Bohumil; Chicago, 1853-1910 ***2853.20*** *p466*
Holub, Frantisek; Ohio, 1881-1889 ***2853.20*** *p505*
Holub, Valentin; Galveston, TX, 1856 ***2853.20*** *p63*
Holubar, Josef; Iowa, 1856-1858 ***2853.20*** *p211*
Holverstot, Anthony; New Jersey, 1784-1786 ***927.31*** *p3*
Holway, Charlotte 37; Ontario, 1871 ***1823.21*** *p165*
Holwell, George 34; Ontario, 1871 ***1823.17*** *p72*
Holyoke, Aaron Bradbury; Washington, 1889 ***2770.40*** *p27*
Holz, Barbara; Brazil, 1883 ***5475.1*** *p445*
Holz, Bernard 62; America, 1843 ***5475.1*** *p280*
Holz, Ferdinand; Wisconsin, 1855 ***6795.8*** *p50*
Holz, H.; New York, 1860 ***358.56*** *p3*
Holz, Joh. Karl; America, 1867 ***5475.1*** *p42*
Holz, Katharina 26; Brazil, 1879 ***5475.1*** *p390*
Holz, Nikolaus 24; Brazil, 1876 ***5475.1*** *p389*
Holzapfel, Juliane; London, Eng., 1850 ***7420.1*** *p78*
Holzaxle, Wilhelm 10; New York, NY, 1874 ***6954.7*** *p38*
Holzer, August; America, 1867 ***7919.3*** *p525*
Holzer, Christian 30; America, 1852 ***5475.1*** *p555*
*Wife:*Sophie Eisel 27
Holzer, Lorenz; America, 1867 ***7919.3*** *p534*
With wife & child
Holzer, Margarethe; St. Louis, 1893 ***5475.1*** *p409*
Holzer, Sophie Eisel 27 *SEE* Holzer, Christian
Holzhausen, Carl Wilhelm Friedrich; America, 1881 ***7420.1*** *p321*
Holzhausen, Hugo; America, 1867 ***7919.3*** *p528*
Holzinger, Anton 24; Mississippi, 1846 ***778.6*** *p166*
Holzinger, Regine; America, 1867 ***7919.3*** *p532*
Holzmann, Auguste; America, 1867 ***7919.3*** *p534*
Holzmann, Christian Ludwig; America, 1859 ***7420.1*** *p185*
Holzner, A. 25; Port uncertain, 1842 ***778.6*** *p166*
Holzschuh, Anna Eva; America, 1861 ***2526.43*** *p186*
With 3 children
*Son:*Johannes
*Daughter:*Sophie
*Daughter:*Anna Margaretha
*Son:*Wilhelm
Holzschuh, Anna Margaretha 8 *SEE* Holzschuh, Anna Eva Hofmann
Holzschuh, Johannes 15 *SEE* Holzschuh, Anna Eva Hofmann
Holzschuh, Sophie 17 *SEE* Holzschuh, Anna Eva Hofmann
Holzschuh, Wilhelm 4 *SEE* Holzschuh, Anna Eva Hofmann
Homad, Frederick; Washington, 1888 ***2770.40*** *p25*
Homann, Engel Marie Sophie Tegtmeier *SEE* Homann, Heinrich Wilhelm
Homann, Friedrich Wilhelm *SEE* Homann, Heinrich Wilhelm
Homann, Georg 4; New York, NY, 1885 ***1883.7*** *p46*
Homann, Gg. 28; New York, NY, 1885 ***1883.7*** *p46*
Homann, Heinrich Wilhelm *SEE* Homann, Heinrich Wilhelm

Homann, Heinrich Wilhelm; America, 1891 ***7420.1*** *p362*
*Wife:*Engel Marie Sophie Tegtmeier
*Daughter:*Marie Dorothea
*Son:*Friedrich Wilhelm
*Son:*Heinrich Wilhelm
Homann, Jacob 6 months; New York, NY, 1885 ***1883.7*** *p46*
Homann, Marie 25; New York, NY, 1885 ***1883.7*** *p46*
Homann, Marie Dorothea *SEE* Homann, Heinrich Wilhelm
Homann, Rosina 3; New York, NY, 1885 ***1883.7*** *p46*
Homberg, Philipp; America, 1846 ***5475.1*** *p472*
Homeier, Anna Kathar. Marie; America, 1845 ***7420.1*** *p34*
Homeier, Anne Marie Henriette; America, 1846 ***7420.1*** *p49*
Homeier, Catharina Engel Sophia; America, 1848 ***7420.1*** *p62*
Homeier, Engel Cathar. Margr.; America, 1855 ***7420.1*** *p140*
Homeier, Wilhelm; America, 1852 ***7420.1*** *p90*
With wife & son
Homer, Lucy 67; Ontario, 1871 ***1823.21*** *p165*
Homer, Thomas 46; Ontario, 1871 ***1823.21*** *p165*
Homes, William; Massachusetts, 1620-1775 ***1642*** *p138*
Homes, William; Massachusetts, 1620-1775 ***1642*** *p139*
Homes, William; Massachusetts, 1686 ***1642*** *p88*
Homes, William; Massachusetts, 1700-1799 ***1642*** *p85*
With wife
Homeyer, Johann Heinrich; America, 1850 ***7420.1*** *p72*
Homeyer, Sophie Charlotte; Port uncertain, 1850 ***7420.1*** *p76*
Homister, Christian 73; Ontario, 1871 ***1823.21*** *p165*
Homister, Frederic 36; Ontario, 1871 ***1823.21*** *p165*
Homolka, Frantisek; Iowa, 1870 ***2853.20*** *p202*
Homsster, Charles 48; Ontario, 1871 ***1823.21*** *p165*
Homyer, George; New Jersey, 1777 ***8529.30*** *p6*
Hone, Charles 38; Ontario, 1871 ***1823.21*** *p165*
Honecker, Margarethe; Chicago, 1881 ***5475.1*** *p344*
Honecker, Nikolaus 32; America, 1865 ***5475.1*** *p264*
Honecker, Sophie; America, 1854 ***5475.1*** *p459*
Honel, Mayer 43; New Orleans, 1848 ***778.6*** *p166*
Honell, Aceath 71; Ontario, 1871 ***1823.17*** *p72*
Honer, Linhart; South Dakota, 1869-1871 ***2853.20*** *p246*
Honfleur, Pierre 21; Quebec, 1652 ***9221.17*** *p262*
Hong, Gum 21; Kansas, 1887 ***1447.20*** *p62*
Honig, Balthasar 42; America, 1833 ***2526.43*** *p170*
Honnore, Pierre 35; America, 1843 ***778.6*** *p166*
Honore, Andre 23; Port uncertain, 1846 ***778.6*** *p166*
Honteux, Barbara 36; America, 1747 ***778.6*** *p166*
Honteux, Dominique; America, 1747 ***778.6*** *p166*
Honuse, Joseph 40; Ontario, 1871 ***1823.21*** *p165*
Hony, Nikolaus; America, 1882 ***5475.1*** *p457*
With wife
With 7 children
Hood, Charles 26; Ontario, 1871 ***1823.17*** *p72*
Hood, David 34; Ontario, 1871 ***1823.17*** *p72*
Hood, David 63; Ontario, 1871 ***1823.17*** *p72*
Hoods, Thomas; New York, NY, 1837 ***3274.55*** *p23*
Hoofer, Feellese; New Jersey, 1738-1739 ***927.31*** *p3*
Hoofver, Feellese; New Jersey, 1738-1739 ***927.31*** *p3*
Hoofver, Henry; New Jersey, 1773-1774 ***927.31*** *p3*
Hoofver, Joseph; New Jersey, 1773-1774 ***927.31*** *p3*
Hoofver, Michael; New Jersey, 1773-1774 ***927.31*** *p3*
Hoofver, Peter; New Jersey, 1773-1774 ***927.31*** *p3*
Hook, Fried.; Galveston, TX, 1855 ***571.7*** *p17*
Hook, Michael; South Carolina, 1839 ***6155.4*** *p18*
Hooke, John; Plymouth, MA, 1620 ***1920.45*** *p5*
Hooker, Henry; Marston's Wharf, 1781 ***8529.30*** *p12*
Hooker, Henry 15; Quebec, 1870 ***8364.32*** *p24*
Hookway, Frederick; Ohio, 1809-1852 ***4511.35*** *p23*
Hookway, Robert 27; Ontario, 1871 ***1823.21*** *p165*
Hoolehan, Luse; New Orleans, 1851 ***7242.30*** *p144*
Hooley, John; St. John, N.B., 1847 ***2978.15*** *p40*
Hooley, Mic; St. John, N.B., 1847 ***2978.15*** *p40*
Hooley, Wm; St. John, N.B., 1847 ***2978.15*** *p40*
Hooleymen, Mary 65; Ontario, 1871 ***1823.21*** *p165*
Hooper, . . .; Maine, 1642 ***9228.50*** *p285*
Hooper, Arthur 29; Ontario, 1871 ***1823.21*** *p165*
Hooper, Charles 38; Ontario, 1871 ***1823.21*** *p166*
Hooper, Edouard; Chicago, 1871-1971 ***9228.50*** *p287*
Hooper, Frank; Newfoundland, 1771-1871 ***9228.50*** *p287*
Hooper, Isaac 40; Ontario, 1871 ***1823.17*** *p72*
Hooper, James 41; Ontario, 1871 ***1823.21*** *p166*
Hooper, John 38; Ontario, 1871 ***1823.21*** *p166*
Hooper, John 50; Ontario, 1871 ***1823.21*** *p166*
Hooper, Richard 45; Ontario, 1871 ***1823.17*** *p72*
Hooper, Samuel; Marston's Wharf, 1782 ***8529.30*** *p12*
Hooper, Samuel 30; Ontario, 1871 ***1823.21*** *p166*
Hooper, Thomas 14; Ontario, 1871 ***1823.21*** *p166*
Hooper, William 35; Ontario, 1871 ***1823.21*** *p166*
Hoopert, Antoine; Louisiana, 1874 ***4981.45*** *p132*
Hoore, George 29; Ontario, 1871 ***1823.17*** *p72*
Hoot, Mary 13; Quebec, 1870 ***8364.32*** *p24*
Hoothner, Jos; New Orleans, 1851 ***7242.30*** *p144*
Hoover, Engelbert; Ohio, 1840-1897 ***8365.35*** *p16*
Hoover, Jacob; North Carolina, 1710 ***3629.40*** *p4*
Hoover, Jacob; Ohio, 1809-1852 ***4511.35*** *p23*
Hoover, Matthias; Ohio, 1809-1852 ***4511.35*** *p23*
Hoowee, John 61; Ontario, 1871 ***1823.21*** *p166*
Hope, Edgar 65; Ontario, 1871 ***1823.21*** *p166*
Hope, George N.; North Carolina, 1792-1862 ***1088.45*** *p15*
Hopf, . . .; North Carolina, 1710 ***3629.40*** *p4*
Hopf, Caspar; America, 1867 ***7919.3*** *p531*
Hopf, Christian; America, 1867 ***7919.3*** *p531*
Hopf, Felix Reinhold; America, 1912 ***7420.1*** *p390*
Hopf, Georg Peter; America, 1868 ***7919.3*** *p530*
Hopf, Johann Gotthelf; America, 1867 ***7919.3*** *p528*
Hopf, Karl Franklin; America, 1868 ***7919.3*** *p527*
Hopf, Margarethe Mathilde; America, 1867 ***7919.3*** *p526*
Hopf, Mathias; America, 1867 ***7919.3*** *p531*
With wife & 2 children
Hopf, Richard; America, 1897 ***7420.1*** *p373*
Hopie, James 70; Ontario, 1871 ***1823.17*** *p72*
Hopie, Janet 40; Ontario, 1871 ***1823.17*** *p72*
Hopkins, Bridget; New Orleans, 1851 ***7242.30*** *p144*
Hopkins, Constanta *SEE* Hopkins, Steven
Hopkins, Damaris *SEE* Hopkins, Steven
Hopkins, E. 50; Ontario, 1871 ***1823.21*** *p166*
Hopkins, Elizabeth *SEE* Hopkins, Steven
Hopkins, George W. 38; Ontario, 1871 ***1823.21*** *p166*
Hopkins, Giles *SEE* Hopkins, Steven
Hopkins, H. P. 53; Ontario, 1871 ***1823.21*** *p166*
Hopkins, John; North Carolina, 1792-1862 ***1088.45*** *p15*
Hopkins, John; Ohio, 1843 ***2763.1*** *p8*
Hopkins, John 48; Ontario, 1871 ***1823.21*** *p166*
Hopkins, John 47; South Carolina, 1812 ***3476.30*** *p12*
Hopkins, Joseph; South Carolina, 1813 ***3208.30*** *p18*
Hopkins, Joseph; South Carolina, 1813 ***3208.30*** *p31*
Hopkins, Oceanus *SEE* Hopkins, Steven
Hopkins, Owen; Ohio, 1832 ***4022.20*** *p280*
Hopkins, Steven; Plymouth, MA, 1620 ***1920.45*** *p5*
*Relative:*Elizabeth
*Relative:*Damaris
*Relative:*Oceanus
*Relative:*Giles
*Relative:*Constanta
Hopkins, Thomas; Philadelphia, 1835 ***5720.10*** *p378*
Hopkins, William; North Carolina, 1843 ***1088.45*** *p15*
Hopkinson, James; Ohio, 1843 ***2763.1*** *p8*
Hopp, Christian 7; Mississippi, 1847 ***778.6*** *p166*
Hopp, Jean 14; Mississippi, 1847 ***778.6*** *p166*
Hopp, Marie 5; Mississippi, 1847 ***778.6*** *p166*
Hopp, Marie 44; Mississippi, 1847 ***778.6*** *p166*
Hopp, Marie Ann 1; Mississippi, 1847 ***778.6*** *p167*
Hopp, Michel 9; Mississippi, 1847 ***778.6*** *p167*
Hopp, Nicolas 46; Mississippi, 1847 ***778.6*** *p167*
Hoppa, Anthony; Wisconsin, 1887 ***6795.8*** *p50*
Hoppe, Carl; America, 1884 ***7420.1*** *p399*
With son
Hoppe, Carl Friedrich August; America, 1874 ***7420.1*** *p303*
Hoppe, Carl Friedrich Gottlieb; America, 1872 ***7420.1*** *p397*
Hoppe, Charles C.; Illinois, 1856 ***6079.1*** *p7*
Hoppe, Charlotte; America, 1853 ***7420.1*** *p106*
Hoppe, Conrad Anton; America, 1851 ***7420.1*** *p80*
With wife 3 sons & daughter
Hoppe, Dorothee Louise Mayer *SEE* Hoppe, Johann Heinrich Christian Ludwig
Hoppe, Friedrich; America, 1875 ***7420.1*** *p397*
Hoppe, Friedrich Wilhelm; America, 1836 ***7420.1*** *p11*
Hoppe, Friedrich Wilhelm; Port uncertain, 1858 ***7420.1*** *p178*
Hoppe, Heinrich; America, 1853 ***7420.1*** *p106*
Hoppe, Heinrich Christian Ludwig *SEE* Hoppe, Johann Heinrich Christian Ludwig
Hoppe, Heinrich Friedrich Wilh.; America, 1900 ***7420.1*** *p376*
Hoppe, Hermann; America, 1877 ***7420.1*** *p309*
Hoppe, Johann Heinrich Christian Ludwig; America, 1868 ***7420.1*** *p272*
*Wife:*Dorothee Louise Mayer
*Son:*Heinrich Christian Ludwig
*Daughter:*Sophie Dorothee Louise
Hoppe, John Didrich Arnhold; Kansas, 1917-1918 ***2054.10*** *p48*
Hoppe, Louis Ernst Heinrich; St. Louis, 1878 ***7420.1*** *p310*
Hoppe, Louise; America, 1877 ***7420.1*** *p309*
Hoppe, Sophie Dorothee Louise *SEE* Hoppe, Johann Heinrich Christian Ludwig
Hoppenstock, Sophie; America, 1852 ***7420.1*** *p90*
Hoppenstock, Wilhelm; America, 1860 ***7420.1*** *p194*
Hopper, George 30; Ontario, 1871 ***1823.21*** *p166*
Hopper, Hugh; South Carolina, 1808 ***6155.4*** *p18*
Hopper, John; New York, 1859 ***358.56*** *p100*
Hopper, Maria 26; Michigan, 1880 ***4491.42*** *p14*
Hopper, Robert 32; Ontario, 1871 ***1823.21*** *p166*
Hoppner, Heinrich; Wisconsin, 1865 ***6795.8*** *p155*
Hopps, Mathias; Ohio, 1809-1852 ***4511.35*** *p23*
Hopps, Matthias; Ohio, 1809-1852 ***4511.35*** *p23*
Hoppstatter, Mrs. Johann; America, 1899 ***5475.1*** *p26*
Hopwood, Thomas 35; Ontario, 1871 ***1823.21*** *p166*
Hor, Andreas *SEE* Hor, Karl
Hor, Karl *SEE* Hor, Karl
Hor, Karl; America, 1871 ***5475.1*** *p418*
*Wife:*Maria Stummbillig
*Daughter:*Luise
*Daughter:*Lina
*Son:*Karl
*Daughter:*Magdalena
*Son:*Ludwig
*Son:*Andreas
*Daughter:*Maria
Hor, Lina *SEE* Hor, Karl
Hor, Ludwig *SEE* Hor, Karl
Hor, Luise *SEE* Hor, Karl
Hor, Magdalena *SEE* Hor, Karl
Hor, Maria *SEE* Hor, Karl
Hor, Maria Stummbillig *SEE* Hor, Karl
Hora, Johann Adam 21; Pennsylvania, 1863 ***170.15*** *p29*
Horak, Josef; Texas, 1856 ***2853.20*** *p67*
Horak, Josef; Texas, 1889-1909 ***2853.20*** *p74*
Horan, . . .; New Orleans, 1851 ***7242.30*** *p144*
Horan, Cath; New Orleans, 1851 ***7242.30*** *p144*
Horan, Ellen 11; Quebec, 1870 ***8364.32*** *p24*
Horan, Judy 60; Ontario, 1871 ***1823.21*** *p166*
Horan, Michael; Louisiana, 1874 ***4981.45*** *p132*
Horbach, Charlotte *SEE* Horbach, Peter
Horbach, Karoline *SEE* Horbach, Peter
Horbach, Katharina *SEE* Horbach, Peter
Horbach, Peter; America, 1859 ***5475.1*** *p522*
*Wife:*Sophie Muller
*Daughter:*Karoline
*Daughter:*Charlotte
*Daughter:*Katharina
Horbach, Sophie Muller *SEE* Horbach, Peter
Horbacher, Jacob 29; Missouri, 1845 ***778.6*** *p167*
Horbert, Eva Elisabeth; America, 1881 ***2526.43*** *p124*
Hord, G. Henry 32; Ontario, 1871 ***1823.21*** *p166*
Hord, Mark 60; Ontario, 1871 ***1823.21*** *p166*
Hordequin, Jacques 20; Montreal, 1662 ***9221.17*** *p498*
Hore, Thomas; New Orleans, 1850 ***7242.30*** *p144*
Horguard, Eliz; America, 1855 ***9228.50*** *p285*
Horie, Joseph; Quebec, 1857 ***9228.50*** *p533*
Horkola, Hilda 42; Minnesota, 1925 ***2769.54*** *p1380*
Horlacher, Heinrich; America, 1854 ***179.55*** *p19*
With wife
Horlebein, Jakob; America, 1857 ***2526.43*** *p171*
Horles, Carl 22; Louisiana, 1848 ***778.6*** *p167*
Horlick, Thomas; Detroit, 1877 ***1766.20*** *p14*
Horlivy, Frantisek; Chicago, 1893-1910 ***2853.20*** *p469*
Horlop, Mary Ann 46; Ontario, 1871 ***1823.21*** *p166*
Horman, . . .; Detroit, n.d. ***9228.50*** *p288*
Horman, Alfred *SEE* Horman, Charles
Horman, Ann *SEE* Horman, Charles
Horman, Anthony; Ohio, 1809-1852 ***4511.35*** *p23*
Horman, Charles *SEE* Horman, Charles
Horman, Charles; Salt Lake City, 1868 ***9228.50*** *p287*
*Wife:*Margaret De La Haye
*Child:*Ann
*Child:*Alfred
*Child:*Francis
*Child:*Mary
*Child:*George
*Child:*Edmund D.
*Child:*Charles
Horman, Edmund D. *SEE* Horman, Charles
Horman, Francis *SEE* Horman, Charles
Horman, Francis De la Haye; New York, 1868 ***9228.50*** *p33*
*Brother:*Thomas
With parents grandmother & 5 siblings
Horman, George *SEE* Horman, Charles
Horman, Margaret De La Haye *SEE* Horman, Charles
Horman, Mary *SEE* Horman, Charles
Horman, Thomas *SEE* Horman, Francis De la Haye
Horman Family ; Ohio, 1860 ***9228.50*** *p288*
Hormann, Anna Sophie Dorothea *SEE* Hormann, Heinrich Christoph
Hormann, Clement; Ohio, 1840-1897 ***8365.35*** *p16*
Hormann, Dorothe 39; America, 1840 ***778.6*** *p167*
Hormann, Engel Sophie Charlotte *SEE* Hormann, Heinrich Christoph
Hormann, Gust. A.; Valdivia, Chile, 1852 ***1192.4*** *p55*
Hormann, Heinrich; America, 1881 ***7420.1*** *p321*
With family

Hormann, Heinrich Christoph; America, 1881 *7420.1 p321*
  *Wife:*Engel Sophie Charlotte
  *Daughter:*Anna Sophie Dorothea
  *Son:*Johann Heinrich
  *Daughter:*Wilhelmine Sophie Dorothea
  *Son:*Heinrich Christoph Wilhelm
  *Son:*Otto Heinrich Georg
  *Son:*Heinrich Friedrich
Hormann, Heinrich Christoph Wilhelm *SEE* Hormann, Heinrich Christoph
Hormann, Heinrich Friedrich *SEE* Hormann, Heinrich Christoph
Hormann, Herman; Ohio, 1840-1897 *8365.35 p16*
Hormann, Johann Heinrich *SEE* Hormann, Heinrich Christoph
Hormann, Otto Heinrich Georg *SEE* Hormann, Heinrich Christoph
Hormann, Wilhelmine Sophie Dorothea *SEE* Hormann, Heinrich Christoph
Horn, A.; America, 1848 *7420.1 p60*
Horn, Adam; America, 1853 *2526.42 p153*
Horn, Adam 2 *SEE* Horn, Philipp
Horn, Adam 9 *SEE* Horn, Georg Michael
Horn, Adam 29; America, 1867 *2526.43 p149*
  With wife
Horn, Anna Barbara *SEE* Horn, Jakob, III
Horn, Anna Barbara Schaller *SEE* Horn, Georg Peter
Horn, Anna Elisabeth Koch 47 *SEE* Horn, Georg Michael
Horn, Anna Eva; America, n.d. *2526.43 p186*
  *Son:*Benedikt
  *Son:*Leonard
  *Son:*Philipp
Horn, Anna Eva Mark 41 *SEE* Horn, Philipp
Horn, Anna Katharina; America, 1854 *2526.43 p224*
Horn, Anna Katharine 15 *SEE* Horn, Georg Michael
Horn, Anna Margaretha; America, 1881 *2526.43 p126*
Horn, Anna Regina 18 *SEE* Horn, Georg Michael
Horn, Anton; America, 1859 *2526.42 p153*
Horn, Balthasar 6 *SEE* Horn, Jakob, III
Horn, Benedikt 23 *SEE* Horn, Anna Eva
Horn, Charlotte; America, 1871 *2526.43 p149*
Horn, Christian; Long Island, 1779 *8529.30 p9A*
Horn, Christian; Ohio, 1809-1852 *4511.35 p23*
Horn, Dawid 40; Portland, ME, 1911 *970.38 p78*
Horn, Dieter; America, 1858 *2526.43 p149*
Horn, E. 23; Port uncertain, 1844 *778.6 p167*
Horn, Ekaterina 6; Portland, ME, 1911 *970.38 p78*
Horn, Elisabeth 39; America, 1889 *2526.43 p140*
Horn, Elisabeth Margarethe *SEE* Horn, Georg Peter
Horn, Elisabetha 18 *SEE* Horn, Philipp
Horn, Elisabethe; America, 1844 *2526.42 p192*
  *Son:*Johannes
  *Daughter:*Eva
Horn, Eva 13 *SEE* Horn, Elisabethe
Horn, Eva Katharina; America, 1857 *2526.43 p149*
Horn, Eva Katharina 15; America, 1853 *2526.43 p225*
  With sister
Horn, Eva Maria; America, 1855 *2526.43 p227*
Horn, Eva Marie 11 *SEE* Horn, Georg Michael
Horn, Francis; Louisiana, 1841-1844 *4981.45 p210*
Horn, Friedrich Jakob; Wisconsin, 1875 *5475.1 p54*
Horn, Georg; America, 1883 *2526.43 p149*
Horn, Georg, III; America, 1832 *2526.43 p225*
  With family
Horn, Georg Adam 1 *SEE* Horn, Jakob, III
Horn, Georg Ludwig; America, 1880 *2526.43 p171*
Horn, Georg Michael; America, 1857 *2526.43 p225*
Horn, Georg Michael; America, 1885 *2526.43 p225*
Horn, Georg Michael 47; America, 1860 *2526.43 p196*
  *Wife:*Anna Elisabeth Koch 47
  *Daughter:*Magdalena 22
  *Daughter:*Anna Katharine 15
  *Son:*Adam 9
  *Daughter:*Eva Marie 11
  *Daughter:*Anna Regina 18
  *Daughter:*Marie Katharine 25
Horn, Georg Peter; Virginia, 1831 *152.20 p64*
  *Wife:*Anna Barbara Schaller
  *Child:*Elisabeth Margarethe
Horn, Georg Philipp 22; America, 1855 *2526.43 p225*
Horn, Georg Wilhelm; America, 1885 *2526.43 p225*
Horn, Heinrich; America, 1867 *7420.1 p258*
Horn, Heinrich; America, 1884 *2526.42 p192*
Horn, Heinrich 3; New York, NY, 1893 *1883.7 p39*
Horn, Hyroniemus 10 *SEE* Horn, Wendel
Horn, J.F.H.; Venezuela, 1843 *3899.5 p546*
Horn, Jakob; America, 1883 *2526.42 p192*
Horn, Jakob; America, 1893 *2526.43 p149*
Horn, Jakob 16; America, 1839 *2526.43 p140*
Horn, Jakob; Chicago, 1894 *5475.1 p156*

Horn, Jakob, III 34; America, 1835 *2526.43 p225*
  *Wife:*Anna Barbara
  *Son:*Georg Adam 1
  *Son:*Balthasar 6
  *Daughter:*Regina Margaretha 5
  *Daughter:*Maria Elisabetha 3
Horn, Johann Heinrich; America, 1883 *2526.43 p218*
Horn, Johann Michael; America, 1882 *2526.43 p225*
Horn, Johann Nikolaus; America, 1880 *2526.43 p149*
Horn, Johann Peter; America, 1883 *2526.43 p225*
Horn, Johanna 40; New York, NY, 1893 *1883.7 p39*
Horn, Johannes; America, 1753 *2526.42 p142*
Horn, Johannes; America, 1867 *2526.43 p149*
Horn, Johannes; America, 1904 *2526.43 p225*
  With brother
Horn, Johannes 23 *SEE* Horn, Elisabethe
Horn, John 75; Michigan, 1880 *4491.36 p10*
Horn, John 30; Ontario, 1871 *1823.21 p166*
Horn, John 31; Ontario, 1871 *1823.21 p166*
Horn, John 33; Ontario, 1871 *1823.21 p166*
Horn, Katharina; America, 1882 *2526.43 p186*
Horn, Konrad; America, 1892 *2526.43 p225*
Horn, Leonard 21 *SEE* Horn, Anna Eva
Horn, Leonhard; America, 1831 *2526.43 p218*
Horn, Magdalena 22 *SEE* Horn, Georg Michael
Horn, Margaretha; America, 1871 *2526.43 p149*
Horn, Margaretha 15 *SEE* Horn, Wendel
Horn, Margaretha 16 *SEE* Horn, Philipp
Horn, Maria; America, 1856 *2526.43 p196*
Horn, Maria 33; Portland, ME, 1911 *970.38 p78*
Horn, Maria Elisabetha 3 *SEE* Horn, Jakob, III
Horn, Maria Katharina; America, 1856 *2526.43 p218*
Horn, Marie Katharine 25 *SEE* Horn, Georg Michael
Horn, Martin; America, 1853 *2526.43 p225*
Horn, Matthaeus; Port uncertain, 1865 *170.15 p29*
Horn, Michael; America, 1882 *2526.42 p108*
Horn, Michael 13 *SEE* Horn, Philipp
Horn, Otto 12 *SEE* Horn, Wendel
Horn, Otto; Valdivia, Chile, 1852 *1192.4 p54*
  With wife
Horn, Peter; America, 1852 *2526.43 p225*
  With daughter
Horn, Philipp; America, 1852 *2526.43 p149*
Horn, Philipp; America, 1871 *2526.43 p149*
Horn, Philipp 19 *SEE* Horn, Anna Eva
Horn, Philipp 39; America, 1854 *2526.42 p200*
  *Wife:*Anna Eva Mark 41
  *Daughter:*Margaretha 16
  *Son:*Adam 2
  *Son:*Michael 13
  *Daughter:*Elisabetha 18
Horn, Philipp Jakob; America, 1895 *2526.43 p225*
Horn, Regina Margaretha 5 *SEE* Horn, Jakob, III
Horn, Sophie; America, 1857 *2526.43 p149*
Horn, Theodor Emil; America, 1884 *2526.42 p192*
Horn, Thomas 57; Ontario, 1871 *1823.17 p72*
Horn, Wendel; America, 1847 *2526.43 p149*
  With wife
  *Daughter:*Margaretha
  *Son:*Otto
  *Son:*Wilhelm
  *Daughter:*Wilhelmine
  *Son:*Hyroniemus
Horn, Wilhelm; America, 1854 *2526.42 p142*
Horn, Wilhelm 5 *SEE* Horn, Wendel
Horn, Wilhelm 7; New York, NY, 1893 *1883.7 p39*
Horn, Wilhelmine 2 *SEE* Horn, Wendel
Hornbacker, Otto 33; Portland, ME, 1911 *970.38 p78*
Hornberger, Elisabeth; America, 1883 *5475.1 p422*
Hornburg, Pauline; Wisconsin, 1903 *6795.8 p147*
Hornby, Thomas 50; Ontario, 1871 *1823.21 p166*
Horndebat, August; Louisiana, 1874 *4981.45 p132*
Horne, Adam 35; Ontario, 1871 *1823.21 p166*
Hornemann, Carl Heinrich Elias; Port uncertain, 1892 *7420.1 p366*
Horner, Beatrice 21; Ontario, 1871 *1823.21 p166*
Horner, George 46; Ontario, 1871 *1823.21 p166*
Horner, Joseph; New York, 1779 *8529.30 p12*
Horner, Lilie J. 17; Ontario, 1871 *1823.21 p166*
Horner, Mahatable 24; Ontario, 1871 *1823.21 p166*
Horner, William 26; Ontario, 1871 *1823.21 p166*
Horner, William 32; Ontario, 1871 *1823.21 p166*
Horner, William 50; Ontario, 1871 *1823.17 p72*
Hornetz, Maria 55; South America, 1856 *5475.1 p492*
  *Son:*Mathias
Horning, A. 23; Ontario, 1871 *1823.21 p166*
Horning, Abraham 36; Michigan, 1880 *4491.36 p10*
Horning, Anna M. 15; Michigan, 1880 *4491.36 p11*
Horning, James 32; Michigan, 1880 *4491.36 p10*
Horning, Luca; Louisiana, 1874 *4981.45 p132*
Horning, Margaret 70; Michigan, 1880 *4491.36 p10*
Hornung, Eduard J.; New York, NY, 1870-1910 *2853.20 p110*

Hornung, Friedrich; America, 1868 *7919.3 p535*
  With family
Hornung, Magdalena 26; America, 1865 *5475.1 p510*
Horodecki, Roman; Detroit, 1929-1930 *6214.5 p70*
Horr, Adam 17; America, 1882 *2526.43 p203*
Horr, Eduard Christian; America, 1892 *2526.43 p203*
Horr, Elisabeth; America, 1847 *5475.1 p21*
Horr, Eva Elisabetha 7 *SEE* Horr, Peter
Horr, Joachim; America, 1848 *2526.43 p203*
  With family
Horr, Johann Nikolaus; America, 1885 *2526.43 p203*
Horr, Johannes; America, 1883 *2526.43 p140*
Horr, John; Illinois, 1856 *6079.1 p7*
Horr, Katharina; America, 1853 *2526.43 p224*
  With relative
Horr, Magdalena 6 *SEE* Horr, Peter
Horr, Maria Barbara 2 *SEE* Horr, Peter
Horr, Peter 4 *SEE* Horr, Peter
Horr, Peter 29; America, 1841 *2526.43 p140*
  With wife 31
  *Son:*Peter 4
  *Daughter:*Eva Elisabetha 7
  *Daughter:*Magdalena 6
  *Daughter:*Maria Barbara 2
Horras, Johann *SEE* Horras, Peter
Horras, Kath. Jochum *SEE* Horras, Peter
Horras, Katharina *SEE* Horras, Peter
Horras, Maria *SEE* Horras, Peter
Horras, Peter *SEE* Horras, Peter
Horras, Peter; America, 1882 *5475.1 p429*
  *Wife:*Kath. Jochum
  *Son:*Peter
  *Daughter:*Katharina
  *Son:*Johann
  *Daughter:*Maria
Horrman, Jacob 18; America, 1840 *778.6 p167*
Horrmann, . . .; America, 1840 *778.6 p167*
Horrmann, Georges 10; America, 1840 *778.6 p167*
Horrmann, Hen..k 5; America, 1840 *778.6 p167*
Horrmann, Jac. 41; America, 1840 *778.6 p167*
Horsch, Catharine 24; New York, NY, 1885 *1883.7 p45*
Horsch, Heinrich 27; New York, NY, 1885 *1883.7 p45*
Horsch, Jacob 1; New York, NY, 1885 *1883.7 p45*
Horseman, Mary 64; Ontario, 1871 *1823.17 p72*
Horsky, Josef; Iowa, 1857 *2853.20 p143*
Horsky, Joseph; Texas, 1888 *6015.15 p25*
Horslsy, Ralph; Virginia, 1652 *6254.4 p244*
Horsman, Christopher; Canada, 1775 *3036.5 p67*
Horsman, John 40; Ontario, 1871 *1823.21 p166*
Horst, Catharine 14; New York, NY, 1874 *6954.7 p37*
Horst, Catharine 41; New York, NY, 1874 *6954.7 p37*
Horst, Christina 7; New York, NY, 1874 *6954.7 p37*
Horst, Friedrich 3; New York, NY, 1874 *6954.7 p37*
Horst, Jacob 9 months; New York, NY, 1874 *6954.7 p37*
Horst, Johann 39; New York, NY, 1874 *6954.7 p37*
Horst, Louise 18; New York, NY, 1874 *6954.7 p37*
Horst, Margaretha 8; New York, NY, 1874 *6954.7 p37*
Horsten, William; Iowa, 1891 *1211.15 p11*
Horstmeyer, Carl *SEE* Horstmeyer, Ludwig
Horstmeyer, Ludwig; America, 1857 *7420.1 p163*
  *Son:*Carl
  With wife & 2 daughters
Hort, Christafus 23; New Castle, DE, 1817-1818 *90.20 p151*
Hort, Louis 36; America, 1845 *778.6 p167*
Hort, Mathias; America, 1883 *5475.1 p130*
Horten, Isaac; Ontario, 1787 *1276.15 p231*
  With child & 3 relatives
Horth, Christafus 23; New Castle, DE, 1817-1818 *90.20 p151*
Horth, Jacob 30; America, 1846 *778.6 p167*
Hortich, Tice; New Jersey, 1773-1774 *927.31 p3*
Hortig, Tice; New Jersey, 1773-1774 *927.31 p3*
Horton, George; Marston's Wharf, 1782 *8529.30 p12*
Horton, James 48; Ontario, 1871 *1823.17 p72*
Horton, James 18; Quebec, 1870 *8364.32 p24*
Horvey, George 30; Ontario, 1871 *1823.21 p166*
Horvey, Paul 31; Ontario, 1871 *1823.21 p166*
Horzebski, Michael 39; New York, NY, 1920 *930.50 p49*
Hosay, Lawrence; New York, NY, 1841 *3274.56 p100*
Hose, Friedrich August; America, 1867 *7919.3 p525*
Hosey, James; Boston, 1827 *3274.55 p42*
Hosey, Patrick; New York, NY, 1837 *3274.56 p72*
Hoshell, Adam; New Jersey, 1736-1744 *927.31 p2*
Hoshell, Adam; New Jersey, 1736-1744 *927.31 p3*
Hoshur, William; New Jersey, 1773-1774 *927.31 p3*
Hosie, James 32; Ontario, 1871 *1823.21 p166*
Hoskin, Philip 20; Ontario, 1871 *1823.17 p72*
Hoskin, William 29; Ontario, 1871 *1823.17 p72*
Hoskin, William 47; Ontario, 1871 *1823.17 p72*
Hosking, Mary Ann; Utah, 1856 *9228.50 p530*
Hoskins, Ann *SEE* Hoskins, John

Hoskins, Ann 55; Ontario, 1871 ***1823.17*** *p72*
Hoskins, Benjamin 47; Ontario, 1871 ***1823.17*** *p72*
Hoskins, Gilbert 30; Ontario, 1871 ***1823.21*** *p166*
Hoskins, John *SEE* Hoskins, John
Hoskins, John; Massachusetts, 1630 ***117.5*** *p157*
*Wife:*Ann
*Son:*John
*Son:*Thomas
*Daughter:*Katherine
Hoskins, John 44; Ontario, 1871 ***1823.17*** *p72*
Hoskins, John 45; Ontario, 1871 ***1823.17*** *p72*
Hoskins, John B. 69; Michigan, 1880 ***4491.36*** *p11*
Hoskins, Katherine *SEE* Hoskins, John
Hoskins, Lucy 67; Michigan, 1880 ***4491.36*** *p11*
Hoskins, Richard 61; Ontario, 1871 ***1823.21*** *p166*
Hoskins, Thomas *SEE* Hoskins, John
Hoskins, William 60; Ontario, 1871 ***1823.21*** *p166*
Hoslet, Marie Josephe; Wisconsin, 1846-1856 ***1495.20*** *p29*
Hosmer, Mary 24; Ontario, 1871 ***1823.21*** *p167*
Hospodsky, Josef; Cleveland, OH, 1879 ***2853.20*** *p146*
Hospodsky, Josef; Cleveland, OH, 1879 ***2853.20*** *p498*
Hospos, Margaretha; Valdivia, Chile, 1852 ***1192.4*** *p55*
Hosser, Geo; New Orleans, 1851 ***7242.30*** *p144*
Hossfeld, Friederike; America, 1867 ***7919.3*** *p533*
Hossfeld, Otto; America, 1890 ***7420.1*** *p361*
Hossick, John Paul; Missouri, 1875 ***3276.1*** *p3*
Hossick, Wm. Alexander; Missouri, 1880 ***3276.1*** *p3*
Hossie, David 48; Ontario, 1871 ***1823.17*** *p72*
Hossie, Janet 75; Ontario, 1871 ***1823.17*** *p72*
Hossie, William 40; Ontario, 1871 ***1823.17*** *p72*
Host, Jacob; Ohio, 1809-1852 ***4511.35*** *p23*
Hostedt, Wilhelm; Valdivia, Chile, 1850 ***1192.4*** *p49*
Hostell, George 25; Ontario, 1871 ***1823.21*** *p167*
Hotham, Abraham 46; Ontario, 1871 ***1823.21*** *p167*
Hothan, Widow; America, 1865 ***7420.1*** *p232*
Hothan, Caroline; America, 1857 ***7420.1*** *p163*
Hothan, Christian; America, 1857 ***7420.1*** *p164*
Hothan, Engel Sophie Louise; America, 1864 ***7420.1*** *p224*
Hothan, Friedrich Heinrich Christ.; America, 1881 ***7420.1*** *p321*
Hothan, Hanne Sophie Wilhelmine; America, 1865 ***7420.1*** *p232*
Hothan, Heinrich Wilhelm; America, 1856 ***7420.1*** *p148*
Hothan, Johann Friedrich Wilhelm; America, 1853 ***7420.1*** *p106*
Hotinger, Johannes; Venezuela, 1843 ***3899.5*** *p544*
Hotop, E.; New York, 1859 ***358.56*** *p99*
Hotra, Katherine; Detroit, 1929-1930 ***6214.5*** *p63*
Hotsch, Christafus 23; New Castle, DE, 1817-1818 ***90.20*** *p151*
Hotson, Alex 48; Ontario, 1871 ***1823.21*** *p167*
Hottinger, Jakob; Venezuela, 1843 ***3899.5*** *p544*
Hottinger, Johann Michael; Venezuela, 1843 ***3899.5*** *p542*
Hottinger, Johann Michael, Sr.; Venezuela, 1843 ***3899.5*** *p542*
Hottinger, Johannes; Venezuela, 1843 ***3899.5*** *p544*
Hottinger, Maria Elisabeth; Venezuela, 1843 ***3899.5*** *p544*
Hottinger, Maria Theresia; Venezuela, 1843 ***3899.5*** *p541*
Hotton, Daphne Henrietta; Maryland, 1912-1983 ***9228.50*** *p289*
Hotton, Percy Philip; Maryland, 1903-1958 ***9228.50*** *p289*
Hotton, William Philip; British Columbia, 1909 ***9228.50*** *p289*
Hotton, William Philip; Maryland, 1921 ***9228.50*** *p289*
Hottot, Jacques 25; Quebec, 1652 ***9221.17*** *p259*
Hotz, Adam; America, 1831 ***2526.42*** *p95*
With wife & 4 children
Hotz, Adam; America, 1881 ***2526.43*** *p140*
Hotz, Adam 8 *SEE* Hotz, Peter
Hotz, Anna Elisabeth; America, 1753 ***2526.42*** *p139*
Hotz, Anna Eva Leiss *SEE* Hotz, Johannes
Hotz, Anna Margaretha; America, 1856 ***2526.43*** *p123*
Hotz, Anna Margaretha 13 *SEE* Hotz, Peter
Hotz, Barbara Marquard *SEE* Hotz, Konrad
Hotz, Ernst Gottlieb 7 *SEE* Hotz, Johannes
Hotz, Eva Elisabetha Lannert *SEE* Hotz, Peter
Hotz, Eva Maria 30; America, 1857 ***2526.42*** *p142*
Hotz, Friedrich; America, 1853 ***2526.42*** *p142*
Hotz, Georg Peter; America, 1892 ***2526.43*** *p218*
Hotz, Heinrich 43; America, 1867 ***2526.42*** *p142*
Hotz, Jakob; America, 1887 ***2526.43*** *p218*
Hotz, Johannes; America, 1832 ***2526.43*** *p210*
With wife & 2 children
Hotz, Johannes; America, 1847 ***2526.42*** *p175*
*Wife:*Anna Eva Leiss
*Daughter:*Maria Elisabetha
*Son:*Ernst Gottlieb
Hotz, Johannes 18; America, 1853 ***2526.43*** *p134*
Hotz, Konrad; America, 1854 ***2526.43*** *p134*
*Wife:*Barbara Marquard
With daughter 7
With daughter 5
Hotz, Margaretha; America, 1880 ***2526.43*** *p226*
Hotz, Maria Elisabetha; America, 1856 ***2526.43*** *p123*
Hotz, Maria Elisabetha 9 *SEE* Hotz, Johannes
Hotz, Nikolaus; America, 1854 ***2526.43*** *p134*
Hotz, Peter; America, 1857 ***2526.43*** *p123*
*Wife:*Eva Elisabetha Lannert
*Daughter:*Anna Margaretha
*Son:*Adam
Hotz, Philipp; America, 1856 ***2526.43*** *p123*
Hotz, Philipp; America, 1897 ***2526.43*** *p203*
With wife & 2 children
Houart, Catherine 24; Quebec, 1662 ***9221.17*** *p487*
Houck, Edward; Ohio, 1809-1852 ***4511.35*** *p23*
Houdan, Jean; Quebec, 1647 ***9221.17*** *p182*
*Wife:*Marie Heude
Houdan, Marie Heude 20 *SEE* Houdan, Jean
Houdan, Pierre; Quebec, 1653 ***9221.17*** *p275*
Houde, Louis 31; Quebec, 1647 ***9221.17*** *p182*
Houdek, Jan; Iowa, 1870 ***2853.20*** *p202*
Houdek, Jan; Wisconsin, 1852 ***2853.20*** *p303*
Houdek, Jan; Wisconsin, 1854 ***2853.20*** *p304*
Houdin, Jean 20; Quebec, 1655 ***9221.17*** *p325*
Houdin, Marie 18; Quebec, 1657 ***9221.17*** *p360*
Houdin, Rene 18; Quebec, 1661 ***9221.17*** *p459*
Houdinan, Nicolas; Quebec, 1642 ***9221.17*** *p118*
Houdon, Pierre; Quebec, 1660 ***9221.17*** *p436*
Houel, Charles; Quebec, 1640 ***9221.17*** *p97*
Houel, Louis 24; Quebec, 1640 ***9221.17*** *p97*
Houellion, Ja.que 37; Missouri, 1846 ***778.6*** *p167*
Hougardy, Fulvie Joseph *SEE* Hougardy, Joseph
Hougardy, Hortense Joseph *SEE* Hougardy, Joseph
Hougardy, Joseph; Wisconsin, 1856 ***1495.20*** *p41*
*Daughter:*Fulvie Joseph
*Daughter:*Marie Antoinette
*Daughter:*Hortense Joseph
Hougardy, Marie Antoinette *SEE* Hougardy, Joseph
Hougaret, Mr. 30; America, 1846 ***778.6*** *p167*
Hough, Isaac 55; Ontario, 1871 ***1823.17*** *p72*
Houghton, Elizabeth D. 52; Ontario, 1871 ***1823.21*** *p167*
Houghton, Martha; Maryland, 1674 ***1236.25*** *p50*
Houghton, Maxwell 36; Ontario, 1871 ***1823.17*** *p73*
Houghton, Nehm'a; Ontario, 1787 ***1276.15*** *p231*
Houjer, Michael; Wisconsin, 1858 ***6795.8*** *p44*
Houk, Michael; Ohio, 1809-1852 ***4511.35*** *p24*
Houlbrooke, John 66; Ontario, 1871 ***1823.17*** *p73*
Hould, Marie 26; New Orleans, 1848 ***778.6*** *p167*
Houlehan, P.; Louisiana, 1874 ***4981.45*** *p296*
Houlett, James 45; Ontario, 1871 ***1823.21*** *p167*
Houmard, David Louis 36; Galveston, TX, 1844 ***3967.10*** *p374*
Houray, Rene 22; Montreal, 1653 ***9221.17*** *p292*
Hourcade, C. 19; America, 1848 ***778.6*** *p167*
Hourcade, J. 19; America, 1848 ***778.6*** *p167*
Hourd, Arthur 14; Quebec, 1870 ***8364.32*** *p24*
Hourd, Charles 13; Quebec, 1870 ***8364.32*** *p24*
Hourd, Richard 45; Ontario, 1871 ***1823.21*** *p167*
Hourq, Germain 25; New Orleans, 1848 ***778.6*** *p167*
House, Erasmus; New Jersey, 1655 ***9228.50*** *p289*
House, Erasmus; Virginia, 1665 ***9228.50*** *p53*
House, George 52; Ontario, 1871 ***1823.17*** *p73*
House, Jacob 43; Ontario, 1871 ***1823.21*** *p167*
House, Thomas 35; Ontario, 1871 ***1823.21*** *p167*
House, Walter K. 66; Ontario, 1871 ***1823.21*** *p167*
House, William 61; Ontario, 1871 ***1823.21*** *p167*
Householder, Lewis; Ohio, 1809-1852 ***4511.35*** *p24*
Householder, Louis; Ohio, 1809-1852 ***4511.35*** *p24*
Houseman, George; Ohio, 1809-1852 ***4511.35*** *p24*
Houseman, Henry 35; North Carolina, 1774 ***1422.10*** *p56*
Houser, Daniel 60; Ontario, 1871 ***1823.21*** *p167*
Houser, Dorothea; Miami, 1935 ***4984.12*** *p39*
Houserman, John; Philadelphia, 1858 ***8513.31*** *p316*
*Wife:*Mary Hertfelder
Houserman, Mary Hertfelder *SEE* Houserman, John
Houshilt, Matthias; New Jersey, 1736-1744 ***927.31*** *p3*
Housi, Samuel; Illinois, 1858 ***6079.1*** *p7*
Houska, Frantisek; St. Paul, MN, 1864 ***2853.20*** *p277*
Houska, Jan; South Dakota, 1863 ***2853.20*** *p250*
Houska, Jan; Wisconsin, 1856 ***2853.20*** *p344*
Housman, J. M.; Illinois, 1865 ***6079.1*** *p7*
Houson, John 45; Ontario, 1871 ***1823.21*** *p167*
Houssard, Claude, Le Petit 26; Quebec, 1642 ***9221.17*** *p118*
Housseau, Marguerite; Quebec, 1670 ***4514.3*** *p325*
Houssoy, Adelaide *SEE* Houssoy, Joseph
Houssoy, Dieudonnee *SEE* Houssoy, Joseph
Houssoy, Heloise Anne Marie *SEE* Houssoy, Joseph
Houssoy, Joseph; Wisconsin, 1856 ***1495.20*** *p56*
*Wife:*Marie Therese Tordeur
*Child:*Heloise Anne Marie
*Child:*Adelaide
*Child:*Rosalie
*Child:*Maximilien
*Child:*Dieudonnee
*Child:*Marie Louise
Houssoy, Marie Louise *SEE* Houssoy, Joseph
Houssoy, Marie Therese Tordeur *SEE* Houssoy, Joseph
Houssoy, Maximilien *SEE* Houssoy, Joseph
Houssoy, Rosalie *SEE* Houssoy, Joseph
Houst, Antonin Petr; Louisville, KY, 1882 ***2853.20*** *p31*
Housta, Pierre; Quebec, 1646 ***9221.17*** *p166*
Houston, George, Jr.; North Carolina, 1833 ***1088.45*** *p15*
Houston, Isabella 49; Ontario, 1871 ***1823.21*** *p167*
Houston, James 54; Ontario, 1871 ***1823.17*** *p73*
Houston, John 45; Ontario, 1871 ***1823.21*** *p167*
Houston, Robert 45; Ontario, 1871 ***1823.17*** *p73*
Houston, William 24; Ontario, 1871 ***1823.17*** *p73*
Houston, William 71; Ontario, 1871 ***1823.17*** *p73*
Houszknecht, Adam; Ohio, 1809-1852 ***4511.35*** *p24*
Hout, Jacob; Ohio, 1809-1852 ***4511.35*** *p24*
Houy, Andreas *SEE* Houy, Andreas
Houy, Andreas; America, 1881 ***5475.1*** *p428*
*Wife:*Maria Rectenwald
*Daughter:*Andreas
*Daughter:*Maria
Houy, Anna; Chicago, 1887 ***5475.1*** *p17*
*Daughter:*Emma
*Son:*Karl
*Son:*Ludwig
Houy, Margarethe 52; Pittsburgh, 1871 ***5475.1*** *p418*
*Son:*Josef
*Son:*Georg
*Son:*Peter
*Son:*Wilhelm
*Daughter:*Luise
Houy, Maria *SEE* Houy, Andreas
Houy, Maria Rectenwald *SEE* Houy, Andreas
Houyout, Marie-Therese; Wisconsin, 1856 ***1495.20*** *p55*
Hover, Jacob; North Carolina, 1710 ***3629.40*** *p4*
Hover, Jermiah 37; Ontario, 1871 ***1823.17*** *p73*
Hovila, Eino 19; Minnesota, 1925 ***2769.54*** *p1378*
Hovinga, S. S.; Iowa, 1893 ***1211.15*** *p11*
Hovora, Frantisek; Lincoln, NE, 1888-1889 ***2853.20*** *p161*
Hovorka, Josef; Nebraska, 1877 ***2853.20*** *p169*
Hovorka, Tomas *SEE* Hovorka, Tomas
Hovorka, Tomas; Minnesota, 1871 ***2853.20*** *p265*
With family
*Son:*Tomas
How, Samour 38; Ontario, 1871 ***1823.17*** *p73*
How, William; Boston, 1766 ***1642*** *p37*
Howald, Jeremiah; Ohio, 1809-1852 ***4511.35*** *p24*
Howalt, Jacob; Ohio, 1809-1852 ***4511.35*** *p24*
Howard, Daniel; North America, 1750 ***1640.8*** *p233*
Howard, Dennis K.; Washington, 1881 ***2770.40*** *p135*
Howard, Edward 20; Ontario, 1871 ***1823.21*** *p167*
Howard, Edward 71; Ontario, 1871 ***1823.21*** *p167*
Howard, Elizabeth 38; Ontario, 1871 ***1823.21*** *p167*
Howard, Elizabeth 57; Ontario, 1871 ***1823.21*** *p167*
Howard, Franklin 30; Ontario, 1871 ***1823.17*** *p73*
Howard, George 53; Ontario, 1871 ***1823.21*** *p167*
Howard, Henry 66; Ontario, 1871 ***1823.21*** *p167*
Howard, James; Colorado, 1905 ***1029.59*** *p41*
Howard, James; Louisiana, 1874 ***4981.45*** *p132*
Howard, James 21; Ontario, 1871 ***1823.21*** *p167*
Howard, James 55; Ontario, 1871 ***1823.21*** *p167*
Howard, Jn; Louisiana, 1874 ***4981.45*** *p132*
Howard, John 59; Ontario, 1871 ***1823.21*** *p167*
Howard, John 60; Ontario, 1871 ***1823.21*** *p167*
Howard, John A.; Colorado, 1882 ***1029.59*** *p41*
Howard, Levi 36; Ontario, 1871 ***1823.21*** *p167*
Howard, Margaret 75; Ontario, 1871 ***1823.21*** *p167*
Howard, Mary; Boston, 1767 ***1642*** *p38*
Howard, Mary 50; Ontario, 1871 ***1823.21*** *p167*
Howard, Mary 70; Ontario, 1871 ***1823.21*** *p167*
Howard, Mary Ann 48; Ontario, 1871 ***1823.21*** *p167*
Howard, Mathew; Boston, 1766 ***1642*** *p37*
Howard, Patrick 33; Ontario, 1871 ***1823.21*** *p167*
Howard, Robert; Kansas, 1886 ***1447.20*** *p64*
Howard, Sarah 50; Ontario, 1871 ***1823.21*** *p167*
Howard, Thomas 14; Ontario, 1871 ***1823.17*** *p73*
Howard, Thomas 31; Ontario, 1871 ***1823.21*** *p167*
Howard, Thomas 39; Ontario, 1871 ***1823.21*** *p167*
Howard, Thomas 68; Ontario, 1871 ***1823.21*** *p167*
Howard, William; Iowa, 1874 ***1211.15*** *p11*
Howard, William 35; Ontario, 1871 ***1823.17*** *p73*
Howard, William 36; Ontario, 1871 ***1823.21*** *p167*
Howard, William 48; Ontario, 1871 ***1823.21*** *p167*
Howarth, George; Marston's Wharf, 1780 ***8529.30*** *p12*
Howarth, James; Marston's Wharf, 1782 ***8529.30*** *p12*
Howarth, Peter 85; Michigan, 1880 ***4491.42*** *p14*
Howatson, Alex 45; New York, NY, 1835 ***5024.1*** *p136*
Howden, John 43; Ontario, 1871 ***1823.17*** *p73*

Howden, Margert 48; Ontario, 1871 ***1823.17*** *p73*
Howden, Richard; Louisiana, 1849 ***7710.1*** *p151*
Howden, Samuel 54; Ontario, 1871 ***1823.17*** *p73*
Howe, Armgier; Boston, 1764 ***1642*** *p34*
Howe, Catharine 50; Ontario, 1871 ***1823.21*** *p168*
Howe, Catherine 82; Ontario, 1871 ***1823.21*** *p168*
Howe, David; Boston, 1764 ***1642*** *p34*
Howe, Frances 25; Ontario, 1871 ***1823.21*** *p168*
Howe, Frederick 26; Ontario, 1871 ***1823.21*** *p168*
Howe, Hamilton 38; Ontario, 1871 ***1823.17*** *p73*
Howe, Hamilton 58; Ontario, 1871 ***1823.21*** *p168*
Howe, Hattie; Los Angeles, 1830-1920 ***9228.50*** *p416*
Howe, James 35; Ontario, 1871 ***1823.21*** *p168*
Howe, James 36; Ontario, 1871 ***1823.21*** *p168*
Howe, John 46; Ontario, 1871 ***1823.21*** *p168*
Howe, John H. 20; Ontario, 1871 ***1823.21*** *p168*
Howe, Mary 45; Ontario, 1871 ***1823.21*** *p168*
Howe, Michael 66; Ontario, 1871 ***1823.21*** *p168*
Howe, Otis 48; Ontario, 1871 ***1823.21*** *p168*
Howe, Patrick 56; Ontario, 1871 ***1823.21*** *p168*
Howe, Richard; Boston, 1764 ***1642*** *p33*
Howe, Timothy 50; Ontario, 1871 ***1823.21*** *p168*
Howe, William 62; Ontario, 1871 ***1823.21*** *p168*
Howeld, Jeremiah; Ohio, 1809-1852 ***4511.35*** *p24*
Howell, Ada 3; Quebec, 1870 ***8364.32*** *p24*
Howell, Agnes 11; Quebec, 1870 ***8364.32*** *p24*
Howell, Daniell; Maryland, 1672 ***1236.25*** *p47*
Howell, Elizabeth 35; Ontario, 1871 ***1823.21*** *p168*
Howell, Jame; North Carolina, 1840 ***1088.45*** *p15*
Howell, John 73; Ontario, 1871 ***1823.21*** *p168*
Howell, Ms. M.J. 17; Quebec, 1870 ***8364.32*** *p24*
Howell, Maggie 14; Michigan, 1880 ***4491.36*** *p11*
Howell, Sarah 45; Michigan, 1880 ***4491.36*** *p11*
Howell, William Fay 30; Ontario, 1871 ***1823.21*** *p168*
Hower, George; Ohio, 1809-1852 ***4511.35*** *p24*
Hower, Nikolaus 23; America, 1865 ***5475.1*** *p511*
Howes, Erasmus; New Jersey, 1655 ***9228.50*** *p289*
Howes, Erasmus; Virginia, 1665 ***9228.50*** *p53*
Howes, John 17; Quebec, 1870 ***8364.32*** *p24*
However, Jacob; North Carolina, 1710 ***3629.40*** *p4*
Howey, Robert; Ohio, 1866 ***3580.20*** *p32*
Howey, Robert H.; Ohio, 1866 ***6020.12*** *p12*
Howie, James 21; Ontario, 1871 ***1823.21*** *p168*
Howie, James 57; Ontario, 1871 ***1823.21*** *p168*
Howie, Mary 25; North Carolina, 1774 ***1422.10*** *p57*
Howie, Mary 25; North Carolina, 1774 ***1422.10*** *p62*
Howie, Robt. 18; North Carolina, 1774 ***1422.10*** *p57*
Howie, William 30; Ontario, 1871 ***1823.21*** *p168*
Howieson, Robert 38; Ontario, 1871 ***1823.17*** *p73*
Howit, Mary 50; Ontario, 1871 ***1823.21*** *p168*
Howland, John; Plymouth, MA, 1620 ***1920.45*** *p5*
Howlet, Richd 24; Ontario, 1871 ***1823.21*** *p168*
Howlett, George; New Jersey, 1665 ***9228.50*** *p298*
Howlett, John 55; Ontario, 1871 ***1823.21*** *p168*
Howlett, John; St. Johns, N.F., 1825 ***1053.15*** *p6*
Howley, Amy; Miami, 1935 ***4984.12*** *p39*
Howman, John; Massachusetts, 1630 ***117.5*** *p154*
Howorth, James; Marston's Wharf, 1782 ***8529.30*** *p12*
Howragin, Patrick; Ohio, 1809-1852 ***4511.35*** *p24*
Hows, Celia 20; Ontario, 1871 ***1823.21*** *p168*
Hows, Harriet 24; Ontario, 1871 ***1823.21*** *p168*
Howse, Erasmus; New Jersey, 1655 ***9228.50*** *p289*
Howse, Erasmus; Virginia, 1665 ***9228.50*** *p53*
Hoxey, Andrew 40; Ontario, 1871 ***1823.17*** *p73*
Hoyd, John; New Jersey, 1777 ***8529.30*** *p6*
Hoyde, John; New Jersey, 1777 ***8529.30*** *p6*
Hoyer, Adolf G.W.; Wisconsin, 1881 ***6795.8*** *p104*
Hoyer, Mary E. 4; Ontario, 1871 ***1823.21*** *p168*
Hoyl, Mary 82; Ontario, 1871 ***1823.21*** *p168*
Hoyle, . . .; Marblehead, MA, 1669-1687 ***9228.50*** *p289*
Hoyle, David; Ontario, 1871 ***1823.17*** *p73*
Hoyle, John; Ohio, 1836 ***3580.20*** *p32*
Hoyle, John; Ohio, 1836 ***6020.12*** *p12*
Hoyle, John Alexander; North Carolina, 1839 ***1088.45*** *p15*
Hoyles, Eliz.; Montreal, n.d. ***9228.50*** *p289*
Hoyles, James; Chicago, 1845-1880 ***9228.50*** *p289*
Hoyles, Jane; Montreal, n.d. ***9228.50*** *p289*
Hoyles, Mary Ann; Michigan, 1860 ***9228.50*** *p339*
Hoyles, Mary Ann; Michigan, n.d. ***9228.50*** *p289*
Hoyles, Mary Ann; Quebec, n.d. ***9228.50*** *p289*
Hoyles, Nancy Ann; Ontario, n.d. ***9228.50*** *p289*
Hoynat, Jean; Quebec, 1661 ***9221.17*** *p459*
Hoyt, Daniel Y. 48; Ontario, 1871 ***1823.21*** *p168*
Hoyten, William 50; Ontario, 1871 ***1823.21*** *p168*
Hrabe, Jan; Oklahoma, 1890 ***2853.20*** *p372*
Hrabe, Matej; South Dakota, 1881 ***2853.20*** *p250*
Hrachovsky, Frantisek; St. Paul, MN, 1892 ***2853.20*** *p283*
Hradowsky, Andrew; Detroit, 1929-1930 ***6214.5*** *p63*
Hrbek, Frantisek; Wisconsin, 1857-1860 ***2853.20*** *p324*
Hrdlicka, Josef; South Dakota, 1850-1910 ***2853.20*** *p246*
Hrejsa, Frantisek J.; Chicago, 1868-1884 ***2853.20*** *p460*
Hrille, Oscar; Washington, 1884 ***2770.40*** *p192*
Hrissikopoulos, Vasileaos K.; Texas, 1911 ***3435.45*** *p35*
Hrncirova, Kristina; New York, NY, 1893 ***2853.20*** *p469*
Hroch, Frantisek J.; Cleveland, OH, 1870 ***2853.20*** *p495*
With parents
Hromada, Franz; Valdivia, Chile, 1852 ***1192.4*** *p54*
Hromadka, Antonin V.; Milwaukee, 1839-1910 ***2853.20*** *p309*
Hrub, Georg.s 48; America, 1840 ***778.6*** *p167*
Hrub, Jacob 2; America, 1840 ***778.6*** *p167*
Hrub, Jean 4; America, 1840 ***778.6*** *p167*
Hrub, Marie 8; America, 1840 ***778.6*** *p167*
Hrub, Marie 40; America, 1840 ***778.6*** *p167*
Hrub, Michel 11; America, 1840 ***778.6*** *p167*
Hruby, Karel Martin; St. Louis, 1870 ***2853.20*** *p22*
With wife
Hruska, Jan; South Dakota, 1869-1871 ***2853.20*** *p246*
Hruska, Jan; Texas, 1856 ***2853.20*** *p64*
Hruska, Josef; South Dakota, 1869-1871 ***2853.20*** *p246*
Huan, Martin 40; Quebec, 1647 ***9221.17*** *p183*
Huart, Hubert Joseph 14; Wisconsin, 1854-1858 ***1495.20*** *p66*
Huart, Jean 25; Quebec, 1662 ***9221.17*** *p487*
Huart, Jean Francois 56; Wisconsin, 1854-1858 ***1495.20*** *p66*
Huart, Joseph; Wisconsin, 1855-1867 ***1495.20*** *p67*
Huault DeMontmagny, Charles 50; Quebec, 1636 ***9221.17*** *p49*
Hub, Friedrich 22; Brazil, 1856 ***5475.1*** *p510*
Hub, H. Peter *SEE* Hub, Maria Dorothea Retzler
Hub, Karl; America, 1870 ***5475.1*** *p522*
Hub, Ludwig *SEE* Hub, Maria Dorothea Retzler
Hub, Maria Dorothea; America, 1867 ***5475.1*** *p561*
*Son:*Ludwig
*Son:*H. Peter
Hubacek, Josef; San Francisco, 1836-1901 ***2853.20*** *p101*
Hubacek, Ondrej; New York, NY, 1836-1901 ***2853.20*** *p101*
Hubacek, Ondrej 36; New York, NY, 1848 ***2853.20*** *p100*
Hubbach, Christian; North Carolina, 1710 ***3629.40*** *p7*
Hubball, Richard; Virginia, 1652 ***6254.4*** *p243*
Hubband, Parmelia 67; Ontario, 1871 ***1823.17*** *p73*
Hubbard, . . .; Maine, 1642 ***9228.50*** *p285*
Hubbard, Elizabeth 63; Ontario, 1871 ***1823.17*** *p73*
Hubbard, Grace Eliz.; Texas, 1898 ***9228.50*** *p476*
Hubbard, James; New York, 1637 ***9228.50*** *p289*
Hubbard, James 30; Ontario, 1871 ***1823.17*** *p73*
Hubbard, Jane 47; Ontario, 1871 ***1823.21*** *p168*
Hubbard, Michael 53; Ontario, 1871 ***1823.21*** *p168*
Hubbard, Philip; Berwick, ME, 1692 ***9228.50*** *p290*
Hubbard, Philip; Maine, 1787-1850 ***9228.50*** *p295*
Hubbard, Philippe; Berwick, ME, 1692 ***9228.50*** *p19A*
Hubbard, Sarah 27; Michigan, 1880 ***4491.30*** *p17*
Hubbard, Sarah 28; Ontario, 1871 ***1823.17*** *p73*
Hubele, Anna 29; Louisiana, 1848 ***778.6*** *p167*
Hubenthal, Jacob; Valdivia, Chile, 1852 ***1192.4*** *p53*
Huber, Anne 40; New Orleans, 1848 ***778.6*** *p167*
Huber, Barbara 28; New York, NY, 1847 ***9176.15*** *p50*
Huber, Catherine 34; New Orleans, 1848 ***778.6*** *p167*
Huber, Christian 7; New York, NY, 1910 ***8425.16*** *p34*
Huber, Christian 62; Ontario, 1871 ***1823.17*** *p73*
Huber, Elisabeth 30; New Orleans, 1848 ***778.6*** *p167*
Huber, Elizabeth 4; New York, NY, 1910 ***8425.16*** *p34*
Huber, Felix 38; New Jersey, 1738-1739 ***927.31*** *p3*
Huber, Fr.; New York, 1859 ***358.56*** *p54*
Huber, Franz; Ohio, 1840-1897 ***8365.35*** *p16*
Huber, Fredrika 16; New York, NY, 1910 ***8425.16*** *p34*
Huber, Gottlieb 3; New York, NY, 1910 ***8425.16*** *p34*
Huber, Jacob 9 months; New York, NY, 1910 ***8425.16*** *p34*
Huber, Jacob; North Carolina, 1710 ***3629.40*** *p4*
Huber, Jacob; North Carolina, 1710 ***3629.40*** *p4*
Huber, John; New York, 1859 ***358.56*** *p99*
Huber, Joseph; Philadelphia, 1832 ***5720.10*** *p378*
Huber, Kristina 9; New York, NY, 1910 ***8425.16*** *p34*
Huber, Magdelena 19; America, 1844 ***778.6*** *p167*
Huber, Maria 11; New York, NY, 1910 ***8425.16*** *p34*
Huber, Martin; Illinois, 1852 ***6079.1*** *p7*
Huber, Michael; New Jersey, 1773-1774 ***927.31*** *p2*
Huber, Rosina 14; New York, NY, 1910 ***8425.16*** *p34*
Huber, Rosina 35; New York, NY, 1910 ***8425.16*** *p34*
Huber, Simon 38; New York, NY, 1910 ***8425.16*** *p34*
Hubert, . . .; Maine, 1642 ***9228.50*** *p285*
Hubert, A. 38; New Orleans, 1840 ***778.6*** *p167*
Hubert, Andrew; Ohio, 1860 ***9228.50*** *p296*
Hubert, Antoine 30; Missouri, 1845 ***778.6*** *p168*
Hubert, Carterette; Ohio, 1788-1878 ***9228.50*** *p376*
Hubert, Catherine; Ohio, 1812 ***9228.50*** *p297*
Hubert, Daniel; Ohio, 1824 ***9228.50*** *p297*
Hubert, Daniel; Philadelphia, 1741 ***9228.50*** *p296*
*Relative:*George
Hubert, Elisabeth; Quebec, 1667 ***4514.3*** *p326*
Hubert, Eva; Edmonton, Alberta, 1888-1964 ***9228.50*** *p214*
Hubert, George *SEE* Hubert, Daniel
Hubert, Henri 22; America, 1847 ***778.6*** *p168*
Hubert, Jane; Ohio, 1830 ***9228.50*** *p297*
With 4 daughters
Hubert, Jane; Ohio, 1860 ***9228.50*** *p297*
Hubert, Jean 30; America, 1843 ***778.6*** *p168*
Hubert, Jean 42; America, 1843 ***778.6*** *p168*
Hubert, Josef; New York, NY, 1910 ***2853.20*** *p116*
Hubert, Lorenz 26; America, 1840 ***778.6*** *p168*
Hubert, Marguerite 29; Montreal, 1654 ***9221.17*** *p317*
Hubert, Marie; Quebec, 1670 ***4514.3*** *p326*
Hubert, Marie-Marthe 14; Quebec, 1655 ***9221.17*** *p325*
Hubert, Mary; Ohio, 1787-1814 ***9228.50*** *p544*
Hubert, Mary; Ohio, 1787-1845 ***9228.50*** *p297*
Hubert, Mary; Ohio, 1807 ***9228.50*** *p57*
With family
Hubert, Michael; New York, 1777 ***8529.30*** *p6*
Hubert, Nicolas 48; Quebec, 1649 ***9221.17*** *p214*
Hubert, Philip; Berwick, ME, 1692 ***9228.50*** *p290*
Hubert, Philippe; Berwick, ME, 1692 ***9228.50*** *p19A*
Hubert, Thomas; Ohio, 1830 ***9228.50*** *p19A*
Hubertaud, Charles 28; New Orleans, 1848 ***778.6*** *p168*
Hubert Family ; California, 1800-1899 ***9228.50*** *p297*
Huberty, John; Ohio, 1809-1852 ***4511.35*** *p24*
Huberty, John Nicholas; Ohio, 1809-1852 ***4511.35*** *p24*
Huberty, Michael; Ohio, 1809-1852 ***4511.35*** *p24*
Huberty, Nicholas; Ohio, 1809-1852 ***4511.35*** *p24*
Hubex, Michael; New Jersey, 1773-1774 ***927.31*** *p2*
Hubin, Barbe 25; Port uncertain, 1840 ***778.6*** *p168*
Hubin, Henry 30; Port uncertain, 1840 ***778.6*** *p168*
Hubinet, Louise; Quebec, 1671 ***4514.3*** *p326*
Hubka, Josef; South Dakota, 1850-1910 ***2853.20*** *p246*
Hubler, Maria Magdalena; Venezuela, 1843 ***3899.5*** *p540*
Hublin, Nicolas; Quebec, 1651 ***9221.17*** *p244*
Hublinger, Melchior; Ohio, 1809-1852 ***4511.35*** *p24*
Hubner, Miss 11 months; New York, NY, 1886 ***6954.7*** *p40*
Hubner, Adam; America, 1873 ***2526.42*** *p123*
Hubner, Andreas; New York, NY, 1886 ***6954.7*** *p40*
With family
Hubner, Andreas 33; New York, NY, 1886 ***6954.7*** *p41*
Hubner, Andreas 66; New York, NY, 1885 ***6954.7*** *p40*
Hubner, Anna 11 months; New York, NY, 1886 ***6954.7*** *p41*
Hubner, Anna 26; New York, NY, 1886 ***6954.7*** *p41*
Hubner, Anna 33; New York, NY, 1886 ***6954.7*** *p41*
Hubner, Anna 45; New York, NY, 1886 ***6954.7*** *p41*
Hubner, Appolonia 5 *SEE* Hubner, Balthasar Ludwig Albrecht
Hubner, Appolonia 21 *SEE* Hubner, Balthasar Ludwig Albrecht
Hubner, Babette 17 *SEE* Hubner, Georg
Hubner, Balthasar Ludwig Albrecht; America, 1854 ***2526.42*** *p123*
With wife
*Child:*Eva Maria
*Child:*Appolonia
*Grandchild:*Appolonia
*Child:*Leonhard
*Child:*Margaretha Elisabetha
Hubner, Barbara Margaretha *SEE* Hubner, Georg
Hubner, Christina 25; New York, NY, 1886 ***6954.7*** *p40*
Hubner, Daniel 1 months; New York, NY, 1886 ***6954.7*** *p40*
Hubner, Elenora 40; New York, NY, 1886 ***6954.7*** *p40*
Hubner, Elisabeth Horn 39 *SEE* Hubner, Georg
Hubner, Elisabethe 1 *SEE* Hubner, Georg
Hubner, Emanuel 1 months; New York, NY, 1886 ***6954.7*** *p41*
Hubner, Emelia 18; New York, NY, 1885 ***6954.7*** *p40*
Hubner, Emmanuel 11 months; New York, NY, 1886 ***6954.7*** *p41*
Hubner, Eva Maria 27 *SEE* Hubner, Balthasar Ludwig Albrecht
Hubner, Friedrich 9; New York, NY, 1886 ***6954.7*** *p41*
Hubner, Friedrich 55; New York, NY, 1886 ***6954.7*** *p41*
Hubner, Georg; America, 1887 ***2526.42*** *p136*
*Wife:*Regina Karg
*Child:*Barbara Margaretha
Hubner, Georg; America, 1887 ***2526.43*** *p140*
Hubner, Georg 41; America, 1889 ***2526.43*** *p140*
*Wife:*Elisabeth Horn 39
*Daughter:*Babette 17
*Daughter:*Marie 15
*Daughter:*Katharine 3
*Daughter:*Elisabethe 1
Hubner, Heinrich; America, 1867 ***2526.43*** *p188*
Hubner, Johann 6 months; New York, NY, 1885 ***6954.7*** *p40*
Hubner, Johann 9; New York, NY, 1886 ***6954.7*** *p40*
Hubner, Johann Philipp; America, 1887 ***2526.43*** *p140*

Hubner, Joseph; America, 1882 ***2526.43*** *p141*
Hubner, Katharina Elisabetha 55; America, 1854 ***2526.43*** *p147*
Hubner, Katharine 3 *SEE* Hubner, Georg
Hubner, Leonhard 29 *SEE* Hubner, Balthasar Ludwig Albrecht
Hubner, Louisa 54; New York, NY, 1886 ***6954.7*** *p40*
Hubner, Margaretha Elisabetha 32 *SEE* Hubner, Balthasar Ludwig Albrecht
Hubner, Maria Elisabetha 30; America, 1865 ***2526.43*** *p218*
Hubner, Marie 15 *SEE* Hubner, Georg
Hubner, Martin 57; New York, NY, 1886 ***6954.7*** *p40*
Hubner, Maryanna; Detroit, 1890 ***9980.23*** *p97*
Hubner, Michael 6 months; New York, NY, 1886 ***6954.7*** *p41*
Hubner, Paul 3; New York, NY, 1886 ***6954.7*** *p41*
Hubner, Paulina 15; New York, NY, 1886 ***6954.7*** *p40*
Hubner, Peter 15; New York, NY, 1886 ***6954.7*** *p40*
Hubner, Peter 39; New York, NY, 1886 ***6954.7*** *p40*
Hubner, Regina Karg *SEE* Hubner, Georg
Hubner, Theador 8; New York, NY, 1886 ***6954.7*** *p40*
Hubner, Theador 11 months; New York, NY, 1886 ***6954.7*** *p40*
Hubner, Theador 26; New York, NY, 1886 ***6954.7*** *p40*
Hubner, Wilhelm 5; New York, NY, 1886 ***6954.7*** *p40*
Hubner, Wilhelm 5; New York, NY, 1886 ***6954.7*** *p41*
Hubner, Wilhelmine; Wisconsin, 1895 ***6795.8*** *p106*
Huboust, Barbe; Quebec, 1639 ***9221.17*** *p89*
Huboust, Francoise 24; Quebec, 1662 ***9221.17*** *p488*
Huboust, Guillaume; Quebec, 1629 ***9221.17*** *p19*
Huboust DesLongschamps, Mathieu 14; Quebec, 1641 ***9221.17*** *p104*
Hubsch, Adam; America, 1882 ***5475.1*** *p24*
*Wife:*Margarethe Kohnen
*Son:*Johann
*Daughter:*Anna
Hubsch, Anna *SEE* Hubsch, Adam
Hubsch, Jacob 28; America, 1844 ***778.6*** *p168*
Hubsch, Johann *SEE* Hubsch, Adam
Hubsch, Margarethe Kohnen *SEE* Hubsch, Adam
Hubschen, Katharina 21; America, 1843 ***5475.1*** *p330*
Hubusch, Maximilion; Louisiana, 1836-1841 ***4981.45*** *p208*
Huch, Ludwick; Ohio, 1809-1852 ***4511.35*** *p24*
Huche, Francoise; Quebec, 1664 ***4514.3*** *p326*
With aunt & uncle
Huchel, Alexandre 25; Missouri, 1845 ***778.6*** *p168*
Huchro, Stanley; Detroit, 1929-1930 ***6214.5*** *p65*
Huck, . . .; America, 1852 ***7420.1*** *p90*
With family
Huck, Jacob 3; New York, NY, 1898 ***7951.13*** *p42*
Huck, Joseph 6 months; New York, NY, 1898 ***7951.13*** *p42*
Huck, Josephine 6; New York, NY, 1898 ***7951.13*** *p42*
Huck, Magdalena 30; New York, NY, 1898 ***7951.13*** *p42*
Huck, Otto; America, 1867 ***7919.3*** *p524*
Huck, Valintine 31; New York, NY, 1898 ***7951.13*** *p42*
Hucke, Ernest; Washington, 1887 ***2770.40*** *p24*
Huckemeier, Justine; America, 1854 ***7420.1*** *p122*
Huckemeier, Katharine; America, 1854 ***7420.1*** *p122*
Huckemeier, Sophie Friedericke Marie Dorothea; America, 1881 ***7420.1*** *p321*
Huckemeier, Sophie Marie Dorothea; America, 1882 ***7420.1*** *p333*
Huckemeier, Sophie Marie Dorothea; America, 1897 ***7420.1*** *p374*
Huckemeyer, Wilhelm; New York, NY, 1888 ***7420.1*** *p357*
Hucker, Caroline Wilhelmine; America, 1867 ***7420.1*** *p262*
Hucker, Friedrich Wilhelm *SEE* Hucker, Karl Heinrich
Hucker, Heinrich Ferdinand; America, 1890 ***7420.1*** *p361*
Hucker, Karl Heinrich; America, 1886 ***7420.1*** *p350*
*Wife:*Wilhelmine Auguste Clavey
*Son:*Friedrich Wilhelm
*Son:*Karl Heinrich Christian
Hucker, Karl Heinrich Christian *SEE* Hucker, Karl Heinrich
Hucker, Karl Heinrich Christian; America, 1900 ***7420.1*** *p376*
Hucker, Wilhelmine Auguste Clavey *SEE* Hucker, Karl Heinrich
Hucos, A. 35; America, 1841 ***778.6*** *p168*
Hudecek, Josef; Texas, 1888 ***2853.20*** *p74*
Hudek, Prokop; Chicago, 1855 ***2853.20*** *p388*
Huderle, Jan; Wisconsin, 1854 ***2853.20*** *p304*
Hudin, Francois; Montreal, 1653 ***9221.17*** *p293*
Hudritz, Antoine 19; New Orleans, 1847 ***778.6*** *p168*
Hudritz, Margarethe 42; New Orleans, 1847 ***778.6*** *p168*
Hudritz, Marianna 16; New Orleans, 1847 ***778.6*** *p168*
Hudritz, Roman 11; New Orleans, 1847 ***778.6*** *p168*
Hudritz, Salome 3; New Orleans, 1847 ***778.6*** *p168*
Hudry, Jane; Canada, 1775 ***3036.5*** *p67*
Hudson, A. J.; California, 1868 ***1131.61*** *p89*
With wife
Hudson, Edw; Virginia, 1652 ***6254.4*** *p243*
Hudson, Elizabeth 58; Ontario, 1871 ***1823.21*** *p168*
Hudson, Grissell; Maryland, 1674-1675 ***1236.25*** *p52*
Hudson, Henry 62; Ontario, 1871 ***1823.17*** *p73*
Hudson, James 29; Ontario, 1871 ***1823.21*** *p169*
Hudson, John; New York, 1782 ***8529.30*** *p12*
Hudson, John 67; Ontario, 1871 ***1823.21*** *p169*
Hudson, Robert; Ohio, 1809-1852 ***4511.35*** *p24*
Hudson, Samuel 65; Ontario, 1871 ***1823.17*** *p73*
Hudson, William; New York, NY, 1820 ***3274.55*** *p74*
Hudson, William 18; Ontario, 1871 ***1823.17*** *p73*
Hudson, William 33; Ontario, 1871 ***1823.21*** *p169*
Hue, Mrs.; America, 1867 ***7420.1*** *p258*
Hue, Anna Catharine *SEE* Hue, Heinrich August
Hue, Anna Sophie Dorothea; America, 1868 ***7420.1*** *p272*
Hue, Anna Sophie Marie *SEE* Hue, Heinrich August
Hue, Carl Ludwig Hermann; America, 1859 ***7420.1*** *p185*
Hue, Catharine Engel Steuber *SEE* Hue, Heinrich August
Hue, Heinrich; America, 1852 ***7420.1*** *p90*
With wife & 3 daughters
Hue, Heinrich August; America, 1868 ***7420.1*** *p272*
*Wife:*Catharine Engel Steuber
*Daughter:*Anna Sophie Marie
*Daughter:*Sophie Dorothea
*Daughter:*Anna Catharine
Hue, Heinrich Wilhelm *SEE* Hue, Heinrich Wilhelm
Hue, Heinrich Wilhelm; America, 1868 ***7420.1*** *p273*
*Son:*Heinrich Wilhelm
Hue, Johann Heinrich Wilhelm; America, 1862 ***7420.1*** *p212*
Hue, Marie; Quebec, 1667 ***4514.3*** *p326*
Hue, Sophie Dorothea *SEE* Hue, Heinrich August
Hue, Sophie Dorothea Louise; America, 1867 ***7420.1*** *p258*
Huebner, Auguste Alvine; Wisconsin, 1889 ***6795.8*** *p44*
Huebner, Frank Wm.; Wisconsin, 1901 ***6795.8*** *p226*
Huebner, Jonathan; Manitoba, 1886-1908 ***1822.55*** *p10*
Huebner, Jonathan; Wisconsin, 1908 ***1822.55*** *p10*
Huebner, Karl; Wisconsin, 1896 ***6795.8*** *p162*
Huebner, Reinhard; Wisconsin, 1874 ***6795.8*** *p204*
Huelin, Alice; Massachusetts, 1883 ***9228.50*** *p512*
Huelin, Elias; Marblehead, MA, 1751 ***9228.50*** *p297*
Huelin, Ellen; Massachusetts, 1874 ***9228.50*** *p512*
Huelle, Leopold 26; Port uncertain, 1843 ***778.6*** *p168*
Huelsebusch, August; Colorado, 1894 ***1029.59*** *p41*
Huer, William; Iowa, 1889 ***1211.15*** *p11*
Hues, John; Massachusetts, 1675-1676 ***1642*** *p128*
Hues, Mary; Boston, 1720 ***9228.50*** *p298*
Hueston, John 31; Ontario, 1871 ***1823.21*** *p169*
Hueston, Mary 49; Ontario, 1871 ***1823.21*** *p169*
Hueston, Sam 35; Ontario, 1871 ***1823.21*** *p169*
Hueston, William 31; Ontario, 1871 ***1823.21*** *p169*
Hueston, William 50; Ontario, 1871 ***1823.21*** *p169*
Hueston, Wm 50; Ontario, 1871 ***1823.21*** *p169*
Huet, Mr. 35; America, 1844 ***778.6*** *p168*
Huet, Ms. 23; America, 1745 ***778.6*** *p168*
Huet, Antoine; Montreal, 1659 ***9221.17*** *p422*
Huet, C. 34; America, 1845 ***778.6*** *p168*
Huet, Jean 23; Missouri, 1848 ***778.6*** *p168*
Huet, Laurent 27; Quebec, 1661 ***9221.17*** *p459*
Huet, Mat; Louisiana, 1874 ***4981.45*** *p296*
Huffer, Joseph; Philadelphia, 1778 ***8529.30*** *p3A*
Huffman, Christofer 56; Ontario, 1871 ***1823.21*** *p169*
Huffman, Lydia 70; Ontario, 1871 ***1823.21*** *p169*
Huffman, Peter; Ohio, 1809-1852 ***4511.35*** *p24*
Huffnagel, Johannes 38; Nova Scotia, 1852 ***170.15*** *p29*
With wife & 4 children
Hufnagel, Christoph; America, 1892 ***170.15*** *p29*
Hufnagel, Joseph; New York, NY, 1883 ***6212.1*** *p13*
Hufner, Johann Adam; America, 1894 ***2526.43*** *p203*
Hufner, Johann Georg Jakob; America, 1887 ***2526.43*** *p204*
Hufner, Johann Jakob; America, 1885 ***2526.43*** *p204*
Hufner, Konrad; America, 1883 ***2526.43*** *p204*
Hug, John Joseph; Ohio, 1809-1852 ***4511.35*** *p24*
Hugel, Andreas 50; Port uncertain, 1847 ***778.6*** *p168*
Hugel, Catherine 5; Port uncertain, 1847 ***778.6*** *p168*
Hugel, Eva 44; Port uncertain, 1847 ***778.6*** *p168*
Hugel, Georg 7; Port uncertain, 1847 ***778.6*** *p168*
Hugel, Jacob 2; Port uncertain, 1847 ***778.6*** *p168*
Hugel, Jacob 28; Port uncertain, 1847 ***778.6*** *p168*
Hugel, Marie 9; Port uncertain, 1847 ***778.6*** *p168*
Hugel, Michel 22; New Orleans, 1848 ***778.6*** *p168*
Huges, Hannah; Beverly, MA, 1728 ***1642*** *p64*
Huggard, John; Colorado, 1894 ***1029.59*** *p41*
Huggard, John; New York, NY, 1866 ***1029.59*** *p42*
Huggard, Thomas J.; Colorado, 1894 ***1029.59*** *p42*
Huggin, William 23; Ontario, 1871 ***1823.21*** *p169*
Huggins, Edward; Missouri, 1888 ***3276.1*** *p1*
Huggins, George 18; Michigan, 1880 ***4491.36*** *p11*
Huggins, James 40; Michigan, 1880 ***4491.36*** *p11*
Huggins, Jane 66; Ontario, 1871 ***1823.21*** *p169*
Huggins, Sarah 39; Michigan, 1880 ***4491.36*** *p11*
Hughes, Alexander 21; Ontario, 1871 ***1823.21*** *p169*
Hughes, Ann 43; Michigan, 1880 ***4491.39*** *p14*
Hughes, Anne *SEE* Hughes, John
Hughes, Anne *SEE* Hughes, William
Hughes, Anne *SEE* Hughes, William
Hughes, Anne *SEE* Hughes, Evan
Hughes, Biddy; New Orleans, 1850 ***7242.30*** *p144*
Hughes, Charles; Marston's Wharf, 1782 ***8529.30*** *p12*
Hughes, Christopher 74; Michigan, 1880 ***4491.30*** *p17*
Hughes, Clement; Portsmouth, NH, 1720 ***9228.50*** *p298*
Hughes, Daniel; Washington, 1886 ***2770.40*** *p195*
Hughes, David *SEE* Hughes, John
Hughes, David *SEE* Hughes, William
Hughes, David; Philadelphia, 1778 ***8529.30*** *p3A*
Hughes, Edward 57; Michigan, 1880 ***4491.39*** *p14*
Hughes, Edward 30; New York, NY, 1844 ***6178.50*** *p151*
Hughes, Eliza 35; Ontario, 1871 ***1823.21*** *p169*
Hughes, Elizabeth *SEE* Hughes, Evan
Hughes, Elizabeth; Ohio, n.d. ***4022.20*** *p286*
Hughes, Evan *SEE* Hughes, William
Hughes, Evan; Ohio, 1839 ***4022.20*** *p280*
*Wife:*Elizabeth
*Child:*Anne
Hughes, Frank 24; Ontario, 1871 ***1823.21*** *p169*
Hughes, Henry; Toronto, 1844 ***2910.35*** *p112*
Hughes, Isabella 11; Quebec, 1870 ***8364.32*** *p24*
Hughes, James; Massachusetts, 1675-1676 ***1642*** *p127*
*Relative:*Joshuah
Hughes, James; Ohio, 1855 ***3580.20*** *p32*
Hughes, James; Ohio, 1855 ***6020.12*** *p12*
Hughes, James 34; Ontario, 1871 ***1823.17*** *p74*
Hughes, James 14; Quebec, 1870 ***8364.32*** *p24*
Hughes, Jane 16; Quebec, 1870 ***8364.32*** *p24*
Hughes, John; Illinois, 1860 ***6079.1*** *p7*
Hughes, John; Louisiana, 1874 ***4981.45*** *p132*
Hughes, John; Marston's Wharf, 1782 ***8529.30*** *p12*
Hughes, John; Massachusetts, 1675-1676 ***1642*** *p128*
Hughes, John 50; Michigan, 1880 ***4491.30*** *p17*
Hughes, John *SEE* Hughes, John
Hughes, John; Ohio, 1838 ***4022.20*** *p280*
*Wife:*Anne
*Child:*David
*Child:*Winnie
*Child:*Thomas J.
*Child:*John
*Child:*Lewis
Hughes, John *SEE* Hughes, William
Hughes, John; Ohio, 1844 ***2763.1*** *p8*
Hughes, John 36; Ontario, 1871 ***1823.21*** *p169*
Hughes, John 40; Ontario, 1871 ***1823.21*** *p169*
Hughes, John, Jr.; Ohio, 1844 ***2763.1*** *p8*
Hughes, Johnson; New York, 1782 ***8529.30*** *p12*
Hughes, Joshuah *SEE* Hughes, James
Hughes, Lewis *SEE* Hughes, John
Hughes, Margaret *SEE* Hughes, William
Hughes, Mary 39; Michigan, 1880 ***4491.30*** *p17*
Hughes, Mary 48; Michigan, 1880 ***4491.30*** *p17*
Hughes, Mary 48; Michigan, 1880 ***4491.39*** *p15*
Hughes, Mary 74; Michigan, 1880 ***4491.30*** *p17*
Hughes, Mary; Ohio, 1834-1835 ***4022.20*** *p276*
Hughes, Mary *SEE* Hughes, William
Hughes, Mary *SEE* Hughes, Thomas
Hughes, Mary 36; Ontario, 1871 ***1823.21*** *p169*
Hughes, Mary Roddy *SEE* Hughes, Thomas
Hughes, Mary 10; Quebec, 1870 ***8364.32*** *p24*
Hughes, Mary 22; Quebec, 1870 ***8364.32*** *p24*
Hughes, Michael 54; Michigan, 1880 ***4491.39*** *p15*
Hughes, Michael; Ohio, 1844 ***2763.1*** *p8*
Hughes, Nathan 45; Ontario, 1871 ***1823.21*** *p169*
Hughes, Owen; New Orleans, 1849 ***7710.1*** *p155*
Hughes, Patrick 39; Indiana, 1871-1880 ***9076.20*** *p67*
Hughes, Patrick; Ohio, 1855 ***3580.20*** *p32*
Hughes, Patrick; Ohio, 1855 ***6020.12*** *p12*
Hughes, Peter J.; New York, NY, 1840 ***3274.56*** *p98*
Hughes, Richard 46; Ontario, 1871 ***1823.21*** *p169*
Hughes, Richard 11; Quebec, 1870 ***8364.32*** *p24*
Hughes, Richd 42; Ontario, 1871 ***1823.21*** *p169*
Hughes, Robert H.; Ohio, 1839 ***4022.20*** *p281*
Hughes, Robert T.; Iowa, 1896 ***1211.15*** *p11*
Hughes, Rose A. 32; Michigan, 1880 ***4491.30*** *p17*
Hughes, Sarah 12; Quebec, 1870 ***8364.32*** *p24*
Hughes, Stephen R. 35; Michigan, 1880 ***4491.30*** *p17*
Hughes, Susan; Ohio, 1838 ***4022.20*** *p276*
Hughes, Thomas; New Orleans, 1850 ***7242.30*** *p144*
Hughes, Thomas; Ohio, 1844 ***2763.1*** *p8*
Hughes, Thomas; Ohio, 1846 ***4022.20*** *p281*
*Wife:*Mary
Hughes, Thomas; Philadelphia, 1856 ***8513.31*** *p317*
*Wife:*Mary Roddy
Hughes, Thomas J. *SEE* Hughes, John

Hughes, Thomas Llewelyn; Ohio, 1840 ***4022.20*** *p281*
Hughes, Thomas R.; Washington, 1887 ***2770.40*** *p24*
Hughes, Thos 51; Ontario, 1871 ***1823.21*** *p169*
Hughes, William; New England, 1745 ***1642*** *p28*
Hughes, William; Ohio, 1838 ***4022.20*** *p281*
*Wife:*Anne
*Child:*Anne
*Child:*John
*Child:*Evan
*Mother:*Margaret
*Father:*David
*Child:*Mary
Hughes, William 62; Ontario, 1871 ***1823.21*** *p169*
Hughes, William 64; Ontario, 1871 ***1823.21*** *p169*
Hughes, Winnie *SEE* Hughes, John
Hughey, John C.; North Carolina, 1826 ***1088.45*** *p15*
Hughs, Andrew; Philadelphia, 1777 ***8529.30*** *p2*
Hughs, Cath; New Orleans, 1851 ***7242.30*** *p144*
Hughs, Charles; Marston's Wharf, 1782 ***8529.30*** *p12*
Hughs, David 65; Ontario, 1871 ***1823.21*** *p169*
Hughs, Frederick 33; Ontario, 1871 ***1823.21*** *p169*
Hughs, Jane E.I. 35; Ontario, 1871 ***1823.21*** *p170*
Hughs, John 46; Ontario, 1871 ***1823.21*** *p170*
Hughs, Joseph, Sr. 78; Ontario, 1871 ***1823.21*** *p170*
Hughston, David 79; Ontario, 1871 ***1823.17*** *p74*
Hughston, Samuel 62; Ontario, 1871 ***1823.17*** *p74*
Hugo, William; New Orleans, 1850 ***7242.30*** *p144*
Hugol, Louis 31; Port uncertain, 1848 ***778.6*** *p168*
Huguenard, Mr. 50; America, 1847 ***778.6*** *p168*
Huguenard, Alexandre 28; America, 1847 ***778.6*** *p168*
Huguenard, Auguste 12; America, 1847 ***778.6*** *p169*
Huguenard, George 28; America, 1847 ***778.6*** *p169*
Huguenard, Gerard 34; America, 1847 ***778.6*** *p169*
Huguenard, Jean.e Marie 45; America, 1847 ***778.6*** *p169*
Huguenard, Jeanne 53; America, 1847 ***778.6*** *p169*
Huguenard, Josephine 9; America, 1847 ***778.6*** *p169*
Huguenard, Louisse 22; America, 1847 ***778.6*** *p169*
Huguenard, Marie 6; America, 1847 ***778.6*** *p169*
Huguenard, Moses 22; America, 1847 ***778.6*** *p169*
Huguenard, Victorine 10; America, 1847 ***778.6*** *p169*
Huguenel, Louis; Louisiana, 1874-1875 ***4981.45*** *p29*
Huguenot Family ; Carolina, n.d. ***9228.50*** *p55*
Huguet, Catherine 6; America, 1843 ***778.6*** *p169*
Huguet, Jean 5; America, 1843 ***778.6*** *p169*
Huguet, Jean 26; America, 1843 ***778.6*** *p169*
Huguet, Margaretha 36; America, 1843 ***778.6*** *p169*
Huhn, Elisabeth *SEE* Huhn, Georg
Huhn, Georg; America, 1868 ***7919.3*** *p528*
*Sister:*Elisabeth
Huhn, Georgine; America, 1867 ***7919.3*** *p529*
Huhne, Maria 23; Valdivia, Chile, 1852 ***1192.4*** *p55*
Huhnerberg, Heinrich; America, 1883 ***7420.1*** *p336*
Huhta, Charles 38; Minnesota, 1925 ***2769.54*** *p1382*
Huhydi, James 50; Ontario, 1871 ***1823.21*** *p170*
Huie, Jean 23; North Carolina, 1774 ***1422.10*** *p58*
Huie, Jean 23; North Carolina, 1774 ***1422.10*** *p62*
Huie, Martha 26; North Carolina, 1774 ***1422.10*** *p57*
Huilier, Lewis; New York, 1860 ***358.56*** *p3*
Huille, Zacharie 24; America, 1842 ***778.6*** *p169*
Huins, John 40; Ontario, 1871 ***1823.21*** *p170*
Huish, Ruth; Canada, 1968 ***9228.50*** *p355*
Huker, Conrad 23; Louisiana, 1848 ***778.6*** *p169*
Huker, Maria 27; New York, NY, 1847 ***9176.15*** *p50*
Hulbird, William; Massachusetts, 1630 ***117.5*** *p157*
Huldeen, Andrew P.; St. Paul, MN, 1882 ***1865.50*** *p51*
Hulden, Andrew P.; St. Paul, MN, 1882 ***1865.50*** *p51*
Huldin, Andrew P.; St. Paul, MN, 1882 ***1865.50*** *p51*
Hulen, Elias; Marblehead, MA, 1751 ***9228.50*** *p297*
Hulen, Francis; New York, 1696 ***9228.50*** *p297*
Hulet, George; New Jersey, 1665 ***9228.50*** *p298*
Hulier, Jacques 28; America, 1747 ***778.6*** *p169*
Hulin, Leonarde Lepoigneux *SEE* Hulin, Philippe
Hulin, Philippe 38; Quebec, 1658 ***9221.17*** *p382*
*Wife:*Leonarde Lepoigneux
Hull, Ann 35; Ontario, 1871 ***1823.17*** *p74*
Hull, David 49; Ontario, 1871 ***1823.21*** *p170*
Hull, Franciz 44; Ontario, 1871 ***1823.21*** *p170*
Hull, George; Dorchester, MA, 1632 ***117.5*** *p158*
Hull, George 42; Ontario, 1871 ***1823.21*** *p170*
Hull, Henry 30; Ontario, 1871 ***1823.21*** *p170*
Hull, Henry 47; Ontario, 1871 ***1823.21*** *p170*
Hull, John 35; Ontario, 1871 ***1823.21*** *p170*
Hull, Joseph; Weymouth, MA, 1635 ***117.5*** *p158*
Hull, Richard; Marston's Wharf, 1776 ***8529.30*** *p13*
Hull, William 46; Ontario, 1871 ***1823.21*** *p170*
Hullagaard, John Otto; Iowa, 1888 ***1211.15*** *p11*
Huller, Fidel; Texas, 1851 ***3435.45*** *p35*
Hullett, George; New Jersey, 1665 ***9228.50*** *p298*
Hullmann, John 23; Port uncertain, 1843 ***778.6*** *p169*
Hulm, Annette 2; Portland, ME, 1906 ***970.38*** *p78*
Hulm, Magdalena 24; Portland, ME, 1906 ***970.38*** *p78*
Hulm, Marie 11; Portland, ME, 1906 ***970.38*** *p78*
Hulm, Michael 28; Portland, ME, 1906 ***970.38*** *p78*
Hulme, Thos.; Louisiana, 1874-1875 ***4981.45*** *p29*
Hulne, Mr. 30; America, 1843 ***778.6*** *p169*
Hulony, Francois 14; America, 1841 ***778.6*** *p169*
Hulony, Francoise 37; America, 1841 ***778.6*** *p169*
Hulony, Paul 20; America, 1841 ***778.6*** *p169*
Hulse, Sarah 21; Ontario, 1871 ***1823.21*** *p170*
Hulse, Sarah 22; Ontario, 1871 ***1823.21*** *p170*
Hult, Emma Carolina; North Dakota, 1891-1892 ***1865.50*** *p51*
Hult, John O.; New York, NY, 1893 ***1865.50*** *p51*
Hultberg, Carl Daniel; North America, 1854 ***6410.15*** *p104*
Hultberg, Samuel P.; Illinois, 1862-1864 ***4487.25*** *p59*
Hulter, Valentine; Ohio, 1809-1852 ***4511.35*** *p24*
Hultgren, Andrew G.; St. Paul, MN, 1899 ***1865.50*** *p51*
With wife
Hultgren, Charles A.; Minnesota, 1871-1881 ***1865.50*** *p51*
Hultgren, Johan Oscar; California, 1888 ***6410.15*** *p106*
Hultgren, John A.; Minnesota, 1871-1889 ***1865.50*** *p51*
Hulthin, B.; New York, NY, 1843 ***6412.40*** *p147*
Hulthin, Magnus; North Carolina, 1805 ***1088.45*** *p15*
Hultin, A.; New York, NY, 1848 ***6412.40*** *p151*
Hultman, August; Colorado, 1871 ***1029.59*** *p42*
Hultman, C.P.O.; New York, NY, 1843 ***6412.40*** *p146*
Hultman, Nils A.; Colorado, 1893 ***1029.59*** *p42*
Hultmon, Nels A.; Colorado, 1893 ***1029.59*** *p42*
Hulton, James; Canada, 1775 ***3036.5*** *p68*
Hultquist, Andrew M.; St. Paul, MN, 1884 ***1865.50*** *p51*
Hultqvist, Anders; St. Paul, MN, 1884 ***1865.50*** *p51*
Huly, Adele 19; New Orleans, 1848 ***778.6*** *p169*
Hulyre, Jaques; Virginia, 1700 ***9230.15*** *p80*
With wife & 4 children
Human, Mrs.; California, 1868 ***1131.61*** *p89*
With child
Humard, Hortense 10; New Orleans, 1848 ***778.6*** *p169*
Humard, Marguerite 44; New Orleans, 1848 ***778.6*** *p169*
Humard, Marie 26; New Orleans, 1848 ***778.6*** *p169*
Humbere, Lise 30; America, 1847 ***778.6*** *p169*
Humbert, Mr. 35; America, 1840 ***778.6*** *p169*
Humbert, Anna *SEE* Humbert, Mathias
Humbert, Ant. 30; America, 1840 ***778.6*** *p169*
Humbert, Augustin 1; America, 1840 ***778.6*** *p169*
Humbert, Francois 39; America, 1842 ***778.6*** *p169*
Humbert, Jn. Baptiste 26; Port uncertain, 1847 ***778.6*** *p169*
Humbert, Leon Hubert; Illinois, 1857 ***6079.1*** *p7*
Humbert, Louisa 19; America, 1846 ***778.6*** *p170*
Humbert, Marg. 27; America, 1840 ***778.6*** *p170*
Humbert, Marguerite 37; America, 1842 ***778.6*** *p170*
Humbert, Marie 4; America, 1840 ***778.6*** *p170*
Humbert, Mathias; America, 1880 ***5475.1*** *p227*
*Sister:*Anna
Humbert, Victor 9; America, 1842 ***778.6*** *p170*
Humble, Ann 57; Ontario, 1871 ***1823.21*** *p170*
Humble, John 40; Ontario, 1871 ***1823.21*** *p170*
Humbly, Leslie 18; Quebec, 1910 ***2897.7*** *p7*
Humbracht, Friedrich; America, 1852 ***7420.1*** *p90*
With wife & son
Humbracht, Justine; America, 1852 ***7420.1*** *p91*
With son & daughter
Humbrecht, D.; Louisiana, 1836-1841 ***4981.45*** *p208*
Humburg, J.C.; Venezuela, 1843 ***3899.5*** *p546*
Hume, Betsy *SEE* Hume, Pierre
Hume, Cassie May; Massachusetts, 1910-1912 ***9228.50*** *p277*
Hume, Charlotte *SEE* Hume, Pierre
Hume, Daniel *SEE* Hume, Pierre
Hume, Henry 61; Ontario, 1871 ***1823.17*** *p74*
Hume, James 73; Ontario, 1871 ***1823.17*** *p74*
Hume, John *SEE* Hume, Pierre
Hume, John 68; Ontario, 1871 ***1823.17*** *p74*
Hume, Joseph W. 28; Ontario, 1871 ***1823.17*** *p74*
Hume, Judith *SEE* Hume, Pierre
Hume, Judith *SEE* Hume, Pierre
Hume, Nicholas *SEE* Hume, Pierre
Hume, Pierre *SEE* Hume, Pierre
Hume, Pierre; Ohio, 1831-1852 ***9228.50*** *p279*
*Wife:*Judith
*Child:*Nicholas
*Child:*Betsy
*Child:*Daniel
*Child:*Charlotte
*Child:*Judith
*Child:*Pierre
*Child:*John
Hume, Robert 57; Ontario, 1871 ***1823.21*** *p170*
Hume, William 34; Ontario, 1871 ***1823.17*** *p74*
Hume, William 50; Ontario, 1871 ***1823.21*** *p170*
Humeau, Jean; Quebec, 1646 ***9221.17*** *p166*
Humelot, Catherine; Quebec, 1670 ***4514.3*** *p326*
Humes, John 60; Ontario, 1871 ***1823.17*** *p74*
Humfridge, Fredrick 29; Ontario, 1871 ***1823.21*** *p170*
Hummel, Catharine 27; Missouri, 1848 ***778.6*** *p170*
Hummel, Christ. 26; Missouri, 1848 ***778.6*** *p170*
Hummel, Christian; Illinois, 1852 ***6079.1*** *p7*
Hummel, Frantz 6; Missouri, 1848 ***778.6*** *p170*
Hummel, Joseph; Ohio, 1809-1852 ***4511.35*** *p24*
Hummel, Marie 5; Missouri, 1848 ***778.6*** *p170*
Hummel, Philip; Illinois, 1855 ***6079.1*** *p7*
Hummel, Stefan 23; Missouri, 1848 ***778.6*** *p170*
Hummer, Mathias; Illinois, 1858 ***6079.1*** *p7*
Humpage, Samuel; Jamaica, 1783 ***8529.30*** *p13A*
Humpalova-Zemanova, Josefina; Chicago, 1873 ***2853.20*** *p418*
With parents
Humph..., J. 17; Quebec, 1870 ***8364.32*** *p24*
Humphrey, Arthur 18; Ontario, 1871 ***1823.21*** *p170*
Humphrey, Clark 27; Ontario, 1871 ***1823.21*** *p170*
Humphrey, Edward; Colorado, 1891 ***1029.59*** *p42*
Humphrey, Henry 60; Ontario, 1871 ***1823.21*** *p170*
Humphrey, Mary; Massachusetts, 1765 ***1642*** *p100*
Humphrey, Matthew 47; Ontario, 1871 ***1823.17*** *p74*
Humphries, Humphrey 32; Ontario, 1871 ***1823.21*** *p170*
Humphries, James 17; Quebec, 1870 ***8364.32*** *p24*
Humphries, Joseph 71; Ontario, 1871 ***1823.17*** *p74*
Humphries, Ralph 73; Ontario, 1871 ***1823.21*** *p170*
Humphries, Samuel; Colorado, 1883 ***1029.59*** *p42*
Humphry, Robert 51; Ontario, 1871 ***1823.21*** *p170*
Humpidge, Martha 50; Ontario, 1871 ***1823.21*** *p170*
Huna, Jan; St. Paul, MN, 1886-1892 ***2853.20*** *p205*
Hunan, Antony 32; Ontario, 1871 ***1823.21*** *p170*
Hunault, Toussaint 27; Montreal, 1653 ***9221.17*** *p293*
Hund, Friedr.; Valdivia, Chile, 1852 ***1192.4*** *p55*
Hund, Wilhelm; Wisconsin, 1883 ***6795.8*** *p44*
Hundshamer, Francine C. 55; Michigan, 1880 ***4491.36*** *p11*
Hundshamer, Sebastian 55; Michigan, 1880 ***4491.36*** *p11*
Hunerberg, Engel Marie; America, 1853 ***7420.1*** *p106*
Hunerberg, Johann Friedrich Wilh. *SEE* Hunerberg, Johann Henrich Christoph
Hunerberg, Johann Friedrich Wilhelm *SEE* Hunerberg, Johann Henrich Christoph
Hunerberg, Johann Henrich *SEE* Hunerberg, Johann Henrich Christoph
Hunerberg, Johann Henrich Christoph; America, 1846 ***7420.1*** *p45*
*Wife:*Sophie Eleonore Wilkening
*Son:*Johann Friedrich Wilhelm
*Son:*Johann Henrich
*Son:*Johann Friedrich Wilh.
Hunerberg, Johann Henrich Wilhelm; America, 1855 ***7420.1*** *p137*
Hunerberg, Sophie Dorothee Charlotte; America, 1852 ***7420.1*** *p88*
Hunerberg, Sophie Eleonore Wilkening *SEE* Hunerberg, Johann Henrich Christoph
Hunerfauth, Peter; Louisiana, 1841-1844 ***4981.45*** *p210*
Hunger, Christiane 51; Valdivia, Chile, 1852 ***1192.4*** *p54*
Hungerford, Becher 60; Ontario, 1871 ***1823.21*** *p170*
Hungerford, Richard 26; Ontario, 1871 ***1823.21*** *p170*
Hunier, Catherine 12; Louisiana, 1848 ***778.6*** *p170*
Hunier, Elisabeth 38; Louisiana, 1848 ***778.6*** *p170*
Hunier, Georges 39; Louisiana, 1848 ***778.6*** *p170*
Hunier, Jacob 8; Louisiana, 1848 ***778.6*** *p170*
Hunier, Jn. Gges. 29; Louisiana, 1848 ***778.6*** *p170*
Hunier, Margte. 10; Louisiana, 1848 ***778.6*** *p170*
Hunier, Michel 5; Louisiana, 1848 ***778.6*** *p170*
Hunkele, Gregor 30; New York, NY, 1898 ***7951.13*** *p43*
Hunkele, Helen 28; New York, NY, 1898 ***7951.13*** *p43*
Hunkele, Karla 4; New York, NY, 1898 ***7951.13*** *p43*
Hunkele, Katherine 2; New York, NY, 1898 ***7951.13*** *p43*
Hunley, Martha 18; Ontario, 1871 ***1823.21*** *p170*
Hunn, Catherine 41; Ontario, 1871 ***1823.21*** *p170*
Hunot, Jean 26; Quebec, 1637 ***9221.17*** *p70*
Hunpriage, William 54; Ontario, 1871 ***1823.21*** *p170*
Hunsberger, Phillipp; North Carolina, 1853 ***1088.45*** *p15*
Hunsicker, Jacob; Ohio, 1809-1852 ***4511.35*** *p24*
Hunslyn, J.U.; Quebec, 1870 ***8364.32*** *p24*
Hunt, Bernard Austin; Iowa, 1911 ***1211.15*** *p11*
Hunt, Charles 52; Ontario, 1871 ***1823.21*** *p171*
Hunt, David P.; North Carolina, 1821 ***1088.45*** *p15*
Hunt, Edmund; America, 1782 ***8529.30*** *p13*
Hunt, Elisha 48; Ontario, 1871 ***1823.21*** *p171*
Hunt, George 45; Ontario, 1871 ***1823.21*** *p171*
Hunt, James 41; Ontario, 1871 ***1823.21*** *p171*
Hunt, John; Colorado, 1886 ***1029.59*** *p42*
Hunt, John 36; Ontario, 1871 ***1823.21*** *p171*
Hunt, John 80; Ontario, 1871 ***1823.21*** *p171*
Hunt, Nancy A. 30; Michigan, 1880 ***4491.42*** *p15*
Hunt, Patrick 28; Ontario, 1871 ***1823.21*** *p171*
Hunt, Sophie Charlotte; America, 1857 ***7420.1*** *p161*
Hunt, Sophie Charlotte; America, 1857 ***7420.1*** *p161*
Hunt, William 35; Ontario, 1871 ***1823.21*** *p171*
Hunt, William 47; Ontario, 1871 ***1823.21*** *p171*
Hunt, William; Vermont, 1834 ***3274.56*** *p96*

Hunt, William Henry 37; Ontario, 1871 ***1823.21*** *p171*
Hunter, Abram 28; North Carolina, 1774 ***1422.10*** *p57*
Hunter, Cathrine 33; Ontario, 1871 ***1823.21*** *p171*
Hunter, Charles 38; Ontario, 1871 ***1823.21*** *p171*
Hunter, Daniel; Toronto, 1844 ***2910.35*** *p115*
Hunter, Eliga 65; Ontario, 1871 ***1823.17*** *p74*
Hunter, Fred; North Carolina, 1792-1862 ***1088.45*** *p15*
Hunter, George; Canada, 1774 ***3036.5*** *p41*
Hunter, George 38; Ontario, 1871 ***1823.21*** *p171*
Hunter, George 56; Ontario, 1871 ***1823.21*** *p171*
Hunter, George; South Carolina, 1800-1899 ***6155.4*** *p18*
Hunter, Hamilton 32; Ontario, 1871 ***1823.17*** *p74*
Hunter, Hamilton 60; Ontario, 1871 ***1823.21*** *p171*
Hunter, Hugh 69; Ontario, 1871 ***1823.17*** *p74*
Hunter, James; Illinois, 1834-1900 ***6020.5*** *p132*
Hunter, James; North Carolina, 1834 ***1088.45*** *p15*
Hunter, James 40; Ontario, 1871 ***1823.17*** *p74*
Hunter, James; South Carolina, 1812 ***6155.4*** *p18*
Hunter, Jean *SEE* Hunter, Patricia
Hunter, John 10; Ontario, 1871 ***1823.21*** *p171*
Hunter, John 26; Ontario, 1871 ***1823.21*** *p171*
Hunter, John 27; Ontario, n.d. ***9228.50*** *p298*
Hunter, John 50; Ontario, 1871 ***1823.21*** *p171*
Hunter, Joseph; South Carolina, 1800-1899 ***6155.4*** *p18*
Hunter, Josth 42; Ontario, 1871 ***1823.21*** *p171*
Hunter, Mathew; Washington, 1889 ***2770.40*** *p27*
Hunter, Nathan; South Carolina, 1800-1899 ***6155.4*** *p18*
Hunter, Nathan, Jr.; South Carolina, 1800-1899 ***6155.4*** *p18*
Hunter, Patricia; Toronto, 1900-1983 ***9228.50*** *p298*
*Sister:*Jean
Hunter, Patrick 20; Ontario, 1871 ***1823.21*** *p171*
Hunter, Paul 58; Ontario, 1871 ***1823.21*** *p171*
Hunter, Peter, Sr. 68; Ontario, 1871 ***1823.21*** *p171*
Hunter, Robert 28; Ontario, 1871 ***1823.17*** *p74*
Hunter, Robert 80; Ontario, 1871 ***1823.21*** *p171*
Hunter, Thomas; North Carolina, 1807 ***1088.45*** *p15*
Hunter, Thomas; North Carolina, 1811-1812 ***1088.45*** *p15*
Hunter, Thomas 30; Ontario, 1871 ***1823.21*** *p171*
Hunter, Thomas 34; Ontario, 1871 ***1823.21*** *p171*
Hunter, Thomas 60; Ontario, 1871 ***1823.17*** *p74*
Hunter, William; Jamaica, 1778 ***8529.30*** *p13A*
Hunter, William; North Carolina, 1792-1862 ***1088.45*** *p15*
Hunter, William; North Carolina, 1821 ***1088.45*** *p15*
Hunter, William; North Carolina, 1852 ***1088.45*** *p15*
Hunter, William 40; Ontario, 1871 ***1823.21*** *p171*
Hunter, William 45; Ontario, 1871 ***1823.21*** *p171*
Hunter, William; South Carolina, 1800-1899 ***6155.4*** *p18*
Hunter, William A. 5; Ontario, 1871 ***1823.21*** *p171*
Hunter, Wm.; Ohio, 1840-1897 ***8365.35*** *p16*
Huntley, Arthur 33; Ontario, 1871 ***1823.21*** *p171*
Huntley, Eliza 70; Ontario, 1871 ***1823.21*** *p171*
Huntley, Hathmira 68; Ontario, 1871 ***1823.21*** *p171*
Huntley, James 69; Ontario, 1871 ***1823.21*** *p172*
Huntley, Joseph P.; Washington, 1887 ***2770.40*** *p24*
Huntley, William 36; Ontario, 1871 ***1823.21*** *p172*
Hunton, Samuell; Maryland, 1671-1672 ***1236.25*** *p45*
Huntoon, Philip; New Hampshire, 1664-1689 ***9228.50*** *p298*
Hunty, Cath; New Orleans, 1851 ***7242.30*** *p144*
Hunty, Daniel; New Orleans, 1851 ***7242.30*** *p144*
Hunty, Dennis; New Orleans, 1851 ***7242.30*** *p144*
Hunty, Jeremiah; New Orleans, 1851 ***7242.30*** *p144*
Hunty, Johanna; New Orleans, 1851 ***7242.30*** *p145*
Hunty, John; New Orleans, 1851 ***7242.30*** *p145*
Huntziger, Rudy; North Carolina, 1710 ***3629.40*** *p4*
Huntziger, Samuel; North Carolina, 1710 ***3629.40*** *p4*
Hunziger, Robert; Missouri, 1900 ***3276.1*** *p2*
Hunziger, Robert; Missouri, 1902 ***3276.1*** *p2*
Hunziker, Rudy; North Carolina, 1710 ***3629.40*** *p4*
Hunziker, Samuel; North Carolina, 1710 ***3629.40*** *p4*
Huoerland, Mary 18; Quebec, 1870 ***8364.32*** *p24*
Huot, Alexis 54; America, 1843 ***778.6*** *p170*
Huot, Charles 37; New Orleans, 1843 ***778.6*** *p170*
Huot, Jean-Baptiste 42; Texas, 1843 ***778.6*** *p170*
Huot, Joseph 29; New Orleans, 1843 ***778.6*** *p170*
Huot, Nicolas 30; Quebec, 1657 ***9221.17*** *p360*
Huot, Timothee 27; New Orleans, 1843 ***778.6*** *p170*
Huot, Victor 21; Texas, 1843 ***778.6*** *p170*
Hup, Rosalie 19; New York, NY, 1884 ***8427.14*** *p45*
Hupakka, Aino 16; Minnesota, 1923 ***2769.54*** *p1383*
Hupakka, Eva 14; Minnesota, 1923 ***2769.54*** *p1383*
Hupakka, George 18; Minnesota, 1923 ***2769.54*** *p1383*
Hupe, Mr.; America, 1854 ***7420.1*** *p122*
With wife son & daughter
Hupe, Anton Friedrich Wilhelm; America, 1854 ***7420.1*** *p122*
Hupe, Carl; America, 1853 ***7420.1*** *p106*
Hupe, Carl; Port uncertain, 1854 ***7420.1*** *p122*
With family
Hupe, Carl Friedrich Ferdinand; America, 1884 ***7420.1*** *p343*
*Wife:*Justine Louise Loehle
*Daughter:*Wilhelmine Auguste
*Daughter:*Caroline Auguste
*Son:*Hermann Friedrich August
Hupe, Carl Ludwig; Port uncertain, 1854 ***7420.1*** *p122*
Hupe, Caroline Tegtmeier *SEE* Hupe, Christian Ludwig
Hupe, Caroline; America, 1883 ***7420.1*** *p337*
Hupe, Caroline Auguste *SEE* Hupe, Carl Friedrich Ferdinand
Hupe, Christian Ludwig; America, 1842 ***7420.1*** *p25*
*Wife:*Caroline Tegtmeier
With son 15
With son 5
Hupe, Ernst Carl; America, 1884 ***7420.1*** *p344*
Hupe, Friedrich; America, 1851 ***7420.1*** *p80*
Hupe, Friedrich; America, 1882 ***7420.1*** *p329*
Hupe, Fritz; America, 1883 ***7420.1*** *p337*
Hupe, Hermann Friedrich August *SEE* Hupe, Carl Friedrich Ferdinand
Hupe, Justine Louise Loehle *SEE* Hupe, Carl Friedrich Ferdinand
Hupe, Louis; America, 1865 ***7420.1*** *p232*
Hupe, Wilhelm; America, 1857 ***7420.1*** *p164*
Hupe, Wilhelm; America, 1882 ***7420.1*** *p329*
Hupe, Wilhelmine Auguste *SEE* Hupe, Carl Friedrich Ferdinand
Huper, Laurence; Illinois, 1851 ***6079.1*** *p7*
Hupert, Henry; Ohio, 1809-1852 ***4511.35*** *p24*
Hupertz, Alex; America, 1926 ***8023.44*** *p375*
Hupgen, Arnold 19; Galveston, TX, 1846 ***3967.10*** *p378*
Hupgen, Helene 48; Galveston, TX, 1846 ***3967.10*** *p378*
Hupgen, Johann Hubert 61; Galveston, TX, 1846 ***3967.10*** *p378*
Hupgen, Marie 21; Galveston, TX, 1846 ***3967.10*** *p378*
Hupgen, Nikolaus 23; Galveston, TX, 1846 ***3967.10*** *p378*
Huppe, Michel 29; Quebec, 1645 ***9221.17*** *p153*
Huppentaum, Joh. Christ.; Valdivia, Chile, 1852 ***1192.4*** *p53*
Huppenthal, Mathias 42; America, 1843 ***5475.1*** *p294*
Hupper, . . .; Maine, 1642 ***9228.50*** *p285*
Huppert, Eduard 20; America, 1899 ***5475.1*** *p47*
Huppert, Georg Peter; America, 1807-1835 ***5475.1*** *p50*
Huppert, Karl *SEE* Huppert, Wilhelm
Huppert, Ludwig; America, 1854 ***5475.1*** *p30*
With wife & 3 children
Huppert, Sophie Klein *SEE* Huppert, Wilhelm
Huppert, Wilhelm *SEE* Huppert, Wilhelm
Huppert, Wilhelm; America, 1881 ***5475.1*** *p48*
*Son:*Wilhelm
*Daughter:*Wilhelmine
*Son:*Karl
*Wife:*Sophie Klein
Huppert, Wilhelmine *SEE* Huppert, Wilhelm
Huquet, Claude; Boston, 1800 ***9228.50*** *p299*
Hurd, Emeline 28; Ontario, 1871 ***1823.21*** *p172*
Hurd, Thomas 33; Ontario, 1871 ***1823.21*** *p172*
Hurdle, John 50; Ontario, 1871 ***1823.21*** *p172*
Hureas, Louis Francois 50; New Orleans, 1848 ***778.6*** *p170*
Hureau, Catherine 15; Montreal, 1654 ***9221.17*** *p317*
Hurel, . . .; Ohio, 1840-1860 ***9228.50*** *p299*
Hurel, Mr. 35; New Orleans, 1848 ***778.6*** *p170*
Hurley, Barthol 65; Ontario, 1871 ***1823.17*** *p74*
Hurley, Bridget 68; Ontario, 1871 ***1823.17*** *p74*
Hurley, Daniel; Ohio, 1857 ***3580.20*** *p32*
Hurley, Daniel; Ohio, 1857 ***6020.12*** *p12*
Hurley, Edward 44; Ontario, 1871 ***1823.21*** *p172*
Hurley, James; Beverly, MA, 1763 ***1642*** *p64*
Hurley, James 45; Ontario, 1871 ***1823.21*** *p172*
Hurley, Jeremiah; Boston, 1772 ***1642*** *p49*
Hurley, John; Boston, 1757 ***1642*** *p47*
Hurley, John; Massachusetts, 1745 ***1642*** *p74*
Hurley, Josiah; Boston, 1773 ***1642*** *p49*
Hurley, Lydia; Boston, 1774 ***1642*** *p50*
Hurley, Martin 35; Ontario, 1871 ***1823.21*** *p172*
Hurley, Mary; Boston, 1765 ***1642*** *p48*
Hurley, Oliver J.; New York, NY, 1882 ***7710.1*** *p160*
Hurley, William; Boston, 1766 ***1642*** *p36*
Hurley, William; Boston, 1773 ***1642*** *p49*
Huron, Bishop 68; Ontario, 1871 ***1823.21*** *p172*
Hurrel, . . .; Ohio, 1840-1860 ***9228.50*** *p299*
Hurst, Alexander 3; America, 1841 ***778.6*** *p170*
Hurst, Andrew; Maryland, 1673 ***1236.25*** *p49*
Hurst, Barbe 29; America, 1841 ***778.6*** *p170*
Hurst, Frederick; Ohio, 1842 ***2763.1*** *p8*
Hurst, Fuslering 1; America, 1841 ***778.6*** *p170*
Hurst, George 43; Ontario, 1871 ***1823.17*** *p74*
Hurst, Henry; Virginia, 1652 ***6254.4*** *p243*
Hurst, Isac 25; Ontario, 1871 ***1823.17*** *p74*
Hurst, Jacob; Iowa, 1909 ***1211.15*** *p11*
Hurst, Jacob; Ohio, 1809-1852 ***4511.35*** *p24*
Hurst, John; Ohio, 1809-1852 ***4511.35*** *p24*
Hurst, John 45; Ontario, 1871 ***1823.17*** *p75*
Hurst, Joseph; Ohio, 1836 ***2763.1*** *p8*
Hurst, Josiah; Ohio, 1836 ***2763.1*** *p8*
Hurst, Stephan 28; America, 1841 ***778.6*** *p170*
Hurst, Thomas; Ohio, 1836 ***2763.1*** *p8*
Hurst, Trwan 47; Ontario, 1871 ***1823.17*** *p75*
Hurst, William; Ohio, 1836 ***2763.1*** *p8*
Hurst, William 35; Ontario, 1871 ***1823.21*** *p172*
Hurst, William 52; Ontario, 1871 ***1823.17*** *p75*
Hurth, Johann 27; America, 1860 ***5475.1*** *p375*
*Wife:*Katharina Nilles
Hurth, Johann; Iowa, 1882 ***5475.1*** *p269*
Hurth, Katharina Nilles *SEE* Hurth, Johann
Hurtigan, James 29; Ontario, 1871 ***1823.17*** *p75*
Hurtle, Elizabeth 36; America, 1747 ***778.6*** *p170*
Hurtle, George 3; America, 1747 ***778.6*** *p170*
Hurtle, Michel 2; America, 1747 ***778.6*** *p171*
Hurtle, Michel 34; America, 1747 ***778.6*** *p170*
Hurtly, Joseph 9; America, 1747 ***778.6*** *p171*
Hurtly, Louis 50; America, 1747 ***778.6*** *p171*
Hurtly, Magdalena 20; America, 1747 ***778.6*** *p171*
Hurtly, Magdalena 52; America, 1747 ***778.6*** *p171*
Hurtly, Marian 18; America, 1747 ***778.6*** *p171*
Husband, Charles; Marston's Wharf, 1780 ***8529.30*** *p13*
Husband, John 41; Ontario, 1871 ***1823.17*** *p75*
Husbands, Charles; Marston's Wharf, 1780 ***8529.30*** *p13*
Huschar, Nikolaus; America, 1846 ***5475.1*** *p485*
Huser, Andreas; Venezuela, 1843 ***3899.5*** *p544*
Huser, Ignaz; Venezuela, 1843 ***3899.5*** *p544*
Huser, Johann Georg; Venezuela, 1843 ***3899.5*** *p544*
Huser, Johann Kaspar; Venezuela, 1843 ***3899.5*** *p544*
Husermann, Marx 35; New Castle, DE, 1817-1818 ***90.20*** *p152*
Husey, Edward 45; Ontario, 1871 ***1823.21*** *p172*
Huslelow, John 45; Ontario, 1871 ***1823.21*** *p172*
Husler, John; North Carolina, 1829 ***1088.45*** *p15*
Huss, Alexandre 2; Missouri, 1846 ***778.6*** *p171*
Huss, Anselm 8; Missouri, 1846 ***778.6*** *p171*
Huss, Bernhard 42; Missouri, 1846 ***778.6*** *p171*
Huss, Engillhart 9; Missouri, 1846 ***778.6*** *p171*
Huss, Fiht 2; Missouri, 1846 ***778.6*** *p171*
Huss, Francois 13; Missouri, 1846 ***778.6*** *p171*
Huss, Isidore 6 months; Missouri, 1846 ***778.6*** *p171*
Huss, Philippine 38; Missouri, 1846 ***778.6*** *p171*
Hussar, William 30; Ontario, 1871 ***1823.21*** *p172*
Husser, Frederick 43; Ontario, 1871 ***1823.21*** *p172*
Hussey, Bridget 19; Quebec, 1870 ***8364.32*** *p24*
Hussey, Henry 23; St. Johns, N.F., 1811 ***1053.20*** *p21*
Hussey, John 29; Ontario, 1871 ***1823.21*** *p172*
Hussey, John 54; Ontario, 1871 ***1823.21*** *p172*
Hussey, William 16; Quebec, 1870 ***8364.32*** *p24*
Hussin, Joseph; New York, NY, 1856 ***1494.20*** *p11*
Husson, Annette 14; Mississippi, 1845 ***778.6*** *p171*
Husson, Antoine 31; Louisiana, 1848 ***778.6*** *p171*
Husson, Augustin 34; America, 1847 ***778.6*** *p171*
Husson, Catherine 8; Louisiana, 1848 ***778.6*** *p171*
Husson, Charles 7; Louisiana, 1848 ***778.6*** *p171*
Husson, Christine 20; Louisiana, 1848 ***778.6*** *p171*
Husson, Dominique 23; America, 1847 ***778.6*** *p171*
Husson, Elisabeth 19; Louisiana, 1848 ***778.6*** *p171*
Husson, Francois 3; Louisiana, 1848 ***778.6*** *p171*
Husson, Francoise 11; Mississippi, 1845 ***778.6*** *p171*
Husson, Francoise 40; Mississippi, 1845 ***778.6*** *p171*
Husson, Jean 10; Louisiana, 1848 ***778.6*** *p171*
Husson, Jean 47; Louisiana, 1848 ***778.6*** *p171*
Husson, Jules 9; Louisiana, 1848 ***778.6*** *p171*
Husson, Marianne 43; Louisiana, 1848 ***778.6*** *p171*
Husson, Marie 18; Louisiana, 1848 ***778.6*** *p171*
Husson, Petronie 2; Louisiana, 1848 ***778.6*** *p171*
Husson, Samuel T.; Colorado, 1903 ***1029.59*** *p42*
Husson, Samuel T.; Michigan, 1886 ***1029.59*** *p42*
Husson, Victor 10; Mississippi, 1845 ***778.6*** *p171*
Hussong, Elias 79; Philadelphia, 1899 ***5475.1*** *p40*
Hussy, Annie 5; Quebec, 1870 ***8364.32*** *p24*
Hussy, Mary 9; Quebec, 1870 ***8364.32*** *p24*
Huster, Frederick; North Carolina, 1850-1853 ***1088.45*** *p15*
Huston, James 20; Ontario, 1871 ***1823.17*** *p75*
Huston, Thomas 51; Ontario, 1871 ***1823.17*** *p75*
Husy, Catharina 40; Port uncertain, 1848 ***778.6*** *p172*
Husy, Felix 33; Port uncertain, 1848 ***778.6*** *p172*
Husy, Fritz 1; Port uncertain, 1848 ***778.6*** *p172*
Husy, Louis 3; Port uncertain, 1848 ***778.6*** *p172*
Husy, Marianne 7; Port uncertain, 1848 ***778.6*** *p172*
Hutcheson, Emely 43; Ontario, 1871 ***1823.21*** *p172*
Hutchins, Walter 19; Quebec, 1870 ***8364.32*** *p24*
Hutchinson, Alexander 55; Ontario, 1871 ***1823.21*** *p172*
Hutchinson, Charles; Boston, 1774 ***8529.30*** *p3A*
Hutchinson, Charles 44; Ontario, 1871 ***1823.21*** *p172*
Hutchinson, Charles 70; Ontario, 1871 ***1823.21*** *p172*
Hutchinson, James 50; Ontario, 1871 ***1823.21*** *p172*

Hutchinson, James 68; Ontario, 1871 *1823.17 p75*
Hutchinson, James Edw.; Boston, 1887 *1029.59 p42*
Hutchinson, James Edw.; Massachusetts, 1891 *1029.59 p42*
Hutchinson, John; North Carolina, 1822 *1088.45 p15*
Hutchinson, Joseph 71; Ontario, 1871 *1823.21 p172*
Hutchinson, Robert 40; Ontario, 1871 *1823.21 p172*
Hutchinson, William 28; Ontario, 1871 *1823.17 p75*
Hutchinson, William 45; Ontario, 1871 *1823.21 p172*
Hutchison, John 48; Ontario, 1871 *1823.21 p172*
Huth, Albert 24; Galveston, TX, 1846 *3967.10 p377*
Huth, Anna Elisabeth, Sr. 11; Pennsylvania, 1851 *170.15 p30*
With family
Huth, Anna Katharina; Pennsylvania, 1850 *170.15 p29*
With family
Huth, Christina 20; Pennsylvania, 1851 *170.15 p29*
With family
Huth, Daniel 57; Pennsylvania, 1851 *170.15 p29*
With family
Huth, Friedrich; Valdivia, Chile, 1852 *1192.4 p53*
Huth, Gottlieb; Wisconsin, 1897 *6795.8 p24*
Huth, Gustav; Wisconsin, 1887 *6795.8 p25*
Huth, Johann Adam, Sr. 14; Pennsylvania, 1851 *170.15 p30*
With family
Huth, Johann Michael; Pennsylvania, 1850 *170.15 p29*
With family
Huth, Johannes 41; Pennsylvania, 1850 *170.15 p29*
With family
Huth, Johannes; Venezuela, 1843 *3899.5 p546*
Huth, Katharina 36; Pennsylvania, 1850 *170.15 p29*
With family
Huth, Katharina 60; Pennsylvania, 1851 *170.15 p29*
With family
Huth, Lorenz, Sr. 8; Pennsylvania, 1851 *170.15 p30*
With family
Huth, Ludwig 30; Galveston, TX, 1844 *3967.10 p370*
Huth, Magdalena; Pennsylvania, 1850 *170.15 p30*
With family
Huth, Magdalena, Sr. 37; Pennsylvania, 1851 *170.15 p30*
With family
Huth, Margaretha; Pennsylvania, 1850 *170.15 p30*
With family
Huth, Michael, Sr. 17; Pennsylvania, 1851 *170.15 p30*
With family
Huth, Peter 25; Port uncertain, 1850 *170.15 p30*
Huth, Valentin, Sr. 43; Pennsylvania, 1851 *170.15 p30*
With family
Hution, John; Ontario, 1871 *1823.17 p75*
Hutkins, John 21; Ontario, 1871 *1823.21 p172*
Hutru, Perrine; Quebec, 1669 *4514.3 p326*
Hutson, Benjamin 48; Ontario, 1871 *1823.17 p75*
Hutson, William 51; Ontario, 1871 *1823.21 p172*

Hutt, Friedrich; Valdivia, Chile, 1852 *1192.4 p53*
Hutt, Friedrich; Valdivia, Chile, 1852 *1192.4 p53*
With wife & child
With child 7
With child 3 months
Huttenrauch, Carl Friedrich Ludwig; America, 1868 *7919.3 p532*
Hutter, C. 26; America, 1847 *778.6 p172*
Hutter, Catherine 23; America, 1846 *778.6 p172*
Hutter, Friederich 29; America, 1844 *778.6 p172*
Hutter, Friedrich; America, 1869 *2526.43 p171*
Hutter, Margaretha; America, 1866 *2526.43 p171*
Huttig, Eduard; America, 1867 *7919.3 p530*
With family
Huttmann, Thresia; America, 1925 *8023.44 p375*
Huttner, Henrica; Kansas, 1917-1918 *1826.15 p81*
Hutton, Alexander 39; Ontario, 1871 *1823.21 p172*
Hutton, Fred Augustus 76; Ontario, 1871 *1823.21 p172*
Hutton, James 26; Ontario, 1871 *1823.21 p172*
Hutton, James 32; Ontario, 1871 *1823.17 p75*
Hutton, John; Ontario, 1871 *1823.17 p75*
Hutton, John 47; Ontario, 1871 *1823.21 p172*
Hutton, Peter 62; Ontario, 1871 *1823.21 p172*
Hutts, John 30; Ontario, 1871 *1823.21 p172*
Hutty, Peter 52; Ontario, 1871 *1823.21 p172*
Hutz, Jean; New Castle, DE, 1817-1818 *90.20 p152*
Hutz, Lonzi; New Castle, DE, 1817-1818 *90.20 p152*
Hutzin, Marianne; New Castle, DE, 1817-1818 *90.20 p152*
Huwer, Elisabeth 22; America, 1872 *5475.1 p231*
Huwer, Franz; America, 1870 *5475.1 p230*
Huwer, Joh. Franz; America, 1871 *5475.1 p153*
*Wife:*Therese Berberich
*Daughter:*Maria
Huwer, Katharina; America, 1867 *5475.1 p225*
Huwer, Maria 4 SEE Huwer, Joh. Franz
Huwer, Mathias; America, 1843 *5475.1 p247*
Huwer, Therese Berberich 24 SEE Huwer, Joh. Franz
Huxold, Conrad; America, 1855 *7420.1 p137*
Huxold, Friedrich Wilhelm; America, 1868 *7420.1 p273*
Huxold, Johann Conrad; America, 1857 *7420.1 p164*
With wife son & 2 daughters
Huxold, Johann Conrad; America, 1857 *7420.1 p164*
*Wife:*Sophie Charlotte Steuber
With 2 sons & 2 daughters
Huxold, Sophie Charlotte Steuber SEE Huxold, Johann Conrad
Huxter, . . .; New Jersey, 1862 *9228.50 p299*
Huxter, Elizabeth Stonelake SEE Huxter, William
Huxter, William; New Jersey, 1862 *9228.50 p615*
*Wife:*Elizabeth Stonelake
Huzel, Anthony 52; Ontario, 1871 *1823.21 p172*
Huzen, George; New Castle, DE, 1817-1818 *90.20 p152*
Hyam, Isaac; North Carolina, 1811-1812 *1088.45 p15*

Hyams, Daniel; North Carolina, 1811-1812 *1088.45 p15*
Hyat, Charles 10; Ontario, 1871 *1823.21 p172*
Hyat, George 12; Ontario, 1871 *1823.21 p173*
Hyat, James 24; Ontario, 1871 *1823.21 p173*
Hyat, John 19; Ontario, 1871 *1823.21 p173*
Hyat, Sarah 53; Ontario, 1871 *1823.21 p173*
Hyat, William H. 26; Ontario, 1871 *1823.21 p173*
Hyatt, Jane 48; Ontario, 1871 *1823.21 p173*
Hyatt, John 31; Ontario, 1871 *1823.21 p173*
Hybler, Anna Maria; Venezuela, 1843 *3899.5 p544*
Hybler, Maria Magdalena; Venezuela, 1843 *3899.5 p540*
Hyde, Annie 35; Ontario, 1871 *1823.21 p173*
Hyde, John Church 60; Ontario, 1871 *1823.17 p75*
Hyde, Joseph; North Carolina, 1853 *1088.45 p15*
Hyde, Mary 11; Quebec, 1870 *8364.32 p24*
Hyde, Robert 33; Ontario, 1871 *1823.17 p75*
Hyer, Helena Auguste Pauline; Wisconsin, 1892 *6795.8 p149*
Hyllested, Rasmus; Iowa, 1892 *1211.15 p11*
Hyman, Mr. 22; America, 1843 *778.6 p172*
Hyman, Ellis W. 57; Ontario, 1871 *1823.21 p173*
Hyman, Joseph; Louisiana, 1880 *7710.1 p157*
Hyman, Mary; New York, 1739 *8277.31 p119*
Hyman, Peter 60; Ontario, 1871 *1823.21 p173*
Hyndman, Andw 46; North Carolina, 1774 *1422.10 p62*
Hyndman, Andw. 46; North Carolina, 1774 *1422.10 p58*
Hyndman, Angus; North Carolina, 1774 *1422.10 p62*
Hyndman, Angus Gilchrist 25; North Carolina, 1774 *1422.10 p58*
Hyndman, Cathn 46; North Carolina, 1774 *1422.10 p62*
Hyndman, Cathn. 46; North Carolina, 1774 *1422.10 p58*
Hyndman, Gilbert 50; Ontario, 1871 *1823.21 p173*
Hyndman, Margt; North Carolina, 1774 *1422.10 p62*
Hyndman, Margt. 14; North Carolina, 1774 *1422.10 p58*
Hyndman, Mary; North Carolina, 1774 *1422.10 p62*
Hyndman, Neil 48; Ontario, 1871 *1823.21 p173*
Hynek, Antonin; Pennsylvania, 1871 *2853.20 p478*
Hynek, Matej; Iowa, 1855 *2853.20 p217*
Hynek, Methodej; Missouri, 1891-1910 *2853.20 p54*
Hynes, Anthony; Long Island, 1781 *8529.30 p9A*
Hynes, Frances 48; Ontario, 1871 *1823.21 p173*
Hynes, John; Philadelphia, 1867 *8513.31 p317*
*Wife:*Julia McDermott
*Son:*Joseph
Hynes, Joseph SEE Hynes, John
Hynes, Julia McDermott SEE Hynes, John
Hynes, Vojtech; Nebraska, 1873 *2853.20 p171*
Hynes, William; Marston's Wharf, 1780 *8529.30 p13*
Hynton, Wm. 25; Virginia, 1635 *1183.3 p30*
Hyslop, John 40; Ontario, 1871 *1823.17 p75*
Hyttenrach, St. John E. 38; Ontario, 1871 *1823.21 p173*
Hytwiler, John 28; America, 1841 *778.6 p172*

I

Iacchen, Pompeo; North Carolina, 1856 *1088.45 p15*
Iages, Ed. 17; Quebec, 1870 *8364.32 p24*
Ibach, Adam 3; New York, NY, 1898 *7951.13 p43*
Ibach, Andreas 9 months; New York, NY, 1898 *7951.13 p43*
Ibach, Helen 40; New York, NY, 1898 *7951.13 p43*
Ibach, Joseph 43; New York, NY, 1898 *7951.13 p43*
Ibach, Maria 9; New York, NY, 1898 *7951.13 p43*
Ibach, Paul 6; New York, NY, 1898 *7951.13 p43*
Iback, Jacob; North Carolina, 1710 *3629.40 p3*
Iback, Vallentine; North Carolina, 1710 *3629.40 p4*
Ibaquez, Sebastien 21; America, 1844 *778.6 p172*
Ibberson, Elizabeth; Wisconsin, 1846 *9228.50 p299*
Ibberson, George *SEE* Ibberson, George
Ibberson, George; Wisconsin, 1841-1844 *9228.50 p299*
   *Wife:*Mary Ann Storor
   *Child:*George
Ibberson, Mary Ann Storor *SEE* Ibberson, George
Ibbison, James; Colorado, 1884 *1029.59 p42*
Ibbison, James S.; Colorado, 1893 *1029.59 p42*
Ibbitson, Elizebeth 23; Ontario, 1871 *1823.21 p173*
Ibbitson, George *SEE* Ibbitson, George
Ibbitson, George; Wisconsin, 1841-1844 *9228.50 p299*
   *Wife:*Mary Ann Storor
   *Child:*George
Ibbitson, Mary Ann Storor *SEE* Ibbitson, George
Ibershoff, Charles; Denver, CO, 1888 *1029.59 p43*
Iberson, David; St. John, N.B., 1848 *2978.15 p41*
Iberson, John; St. John, N.B., 1848 *2978.15 p41*
Iberson, Thomas; St. John, N.B., 1848 *2978.15 p41*
Iberville, Mr. 28; America, 1841 *778.6 p172*
Icaac, Erscott 41; Ontario, 1871 *1823.21 p173*
Ickus, . . .; Pennsylvania, 1838 *170.15 p30*
   With 6 siblings
Ickus, Mrs. Johann; Pennsylvania, 1838 *170.15 p30*
Ickus, Johann Friedr.; Pennsylvania, 1865 *170.15 p30*
Ickus, Martin; Pennsylvania, 1854 *170.15 p30*
   With wife & 2 children
Idecker, Frederick; Missouri, 1889 *3276.1 p2*
Iden, George 41; Ontario, 1871 *1823.17 p75*
Idesheim, Anna Decker *SEE* Idesheim, Michel
Idesheim, Michel; America, 1876 *5475.1 p257*
   *Wife:*Anna Decker
Idout, Jean Louis 41; America, 1746 *778.6 p172*
Idoux, Caspar 17; Port uncertain, 1845 *778.6 p172*
Idoux, Cather. 13; Port uncertain, 1845 *778.6 p172*
Idoux, Franc. Jos. 24; Port uncertain, 1845 *778.6 p172*
Idoux, Franc. Jos. 48; Port uncertain, 1845 *778.6 p172*
Idoux, Franz Joseph 23; Galveston, TX, 1844 *3967.10 p370*
Idoux, Franz Joseph 46; Galveston, TX, 1844 *3967.10 p370*
   *Wife:*Marie 46
   *Son:*Johann 21
Idoux, Johann 21 *SEE* Idoux, Franz Joseph
Idoux, John 22; Port uncertain, 1845 *778.6 p172*
Idoux, Joseph 38; America, 1845 *778.6 p172*
Idoux, Joseph Karl 13; Galveston, TX, 1844 *3967.10 p370*
Idoux, Kaspar 15; Galveston, TX, 1844 *3967.10 p370*
Idoux, Katharina 11; Galveston, TX, 1844 *3967.10 p370*
Idoux, Maria Eve 48; Port uncertain, 1845 *778.6 p172*
Idoux, Marie 46 *SEE* Idoux, Franz Joseph
Ietzer, Johann 36; New Castle, DE, 1817-1818 *90.20 p152*
Iezer, Johann 36; New Castle, DE, 1817-1818 *90.20 p152*
Iffrig, Joseph 2; America, 1847 *778.6 p172*

Iffrig, Marguerite 6; America, 1847 *778.6 p172*
Iffrig, Rosine 7; America, 1847 *778.6 p172*
Iffrig, Sophie 30; America, 1847 *778.6 p172*
Ifkowitsch, Konrad; Chicago, 1891 *5475.1 p156*
Igler, William; New Jersey, 1773-1774 *927.31 p3*
Ignaseck, Kazmier; New York, NY, 1881 *6015.15 p25*
Ignasik, Kazmier; New York, NY, 1881 *6015.15 p25*
Ignatius, Paul Emel Franz; Iowa, 1892 *1211.15 p11*
Ignatovich, Elena; Detroit, 1929-1930 *6214.5 p70*
Ihahns, Herm.; Valdivia, Chile, 1852 *1192.4 p55*
Ihling, Anna Catharina; America, 1868 *7919.3 p529*
   *Son:*Elias
Ihling, Barbara Rosina; America, 1868 *7919.3 p529*
Ihling, Elias *SEE* Ihling, Anna Catharina
Ihnling, Martha Elisabeth; America, 1867 *7919.3 p528*
   With child
Ihrig, Mr.; Texas, 1847 *2526.43 p222*
   With wife
   With son 17
   With son 16
Ihrig, Adam; America, 1848 *2526.43 p160*
Ihrig, Adam; America, 1867 *2526.43 p225*
   *Wife:*Katharina Helmstadter
   *Son:*Adam
   *Daughter:*Margarethe
   *Son:*Jakob
   *Son:*Michael
   *Daughter:*Elisabeth
Ihrig, Adam 6 *SEE* Ihrig, Adam
Ihrig, Adolf; America, 1887 *2526.43 p149*
Ihrig, Elisabeth 6 *SEE* Ihrig, Adam
Ihrig, Jakob 2 *SEE* Ihrig, Adam
Ihrig, Johann Balthasar Theodor; America, 1854 *2526.43 p225*
Ihrig, Johann Jakob; America, 1880 *2526.43 p225*
Ihrig, Johannes; America, 1881 *2526.43 p225*
Ihrig, Katharina Helmstadter 34 *SEE* Ihrig, Adam
Ihrig, Margarethe 6 *SEE* Ihrig, Adam
Ihrig, Michael 11 *SEE* Ihrig, Adam
Ihry, Antoine; Iowa, 1918 *1211.15 p11*
Ihry, Jean Baptiste, Sr.; Iowa, 1915 *1211.15 p11*
Ihry, Jean Henri; Iowa, 1915 *1211.15 p11*
Ikus, Friedrich; Port uncertain, 1865 *170.15 p30*
Ildis, Franziska 22; New Orleans, 1847 *778.6 p172*
Iles, Andrew 60; Ontario, 1871 *1823.17 p75*
Ilg, Katharina; Venezuela, 1843 *3899.5 p540*
Illimus, Minna; Chicago, 1891 *7420.1 p362*
Illy, Ruppert 28; America, 1846 *778.6 p172*
Ilsemann, Mr.; New York, NY, 1850 *7420.1 p72*
Ilsemann, Heinrich; Port uncertain, 1850 *7420.1 p72*
Imbere, Isador 42; Baltimore, 1889 *8425.16 p35*
Imbere, Margaretha 40; Baltimore, 1889 *8425.16 p35*
Imbere, Maria 17; Baltimore, 1889 *8425.16 p35*
Imbere, Markus 9; Baltimore, 1889 *8425.16 p35*
Imbere, Peter 2; Baltimore, 1889 *8425.16 p35*
Imbere, Sigfried 6; Baltimore, 1889 *8425.16 p35*
Imbert, J.; Montreal, 1659 *9221.17 p422*
Imbert, Jean; Virginia, 1700 *9230.15 p81*
   With wife
Imblo, Heinrich; Colorado, 1903 *1029.59 p43*
Imblo, Heinrich; New York, NY, 1878 *1029.59 p43*
Imblo, Kasper; Colorado, 1862-1920 *1029.59 p43*
Imblo, Kasper; New York, 1886 *1029.59 p43*
Imboden, Christ; Missouri, 1898 *3276.1 p2*
Imboden, Christ; Missouri, 1898 *3276.1 p2*
Imbouf, Melenie 25; America, 1844 *778.6 p172*
Imhof, Fred; Missouri, 1896 *3276.1 p2*
Imholz, Johann; New Castle, DE, 1817-1818 *90.20 p152*

Immeler, Ms. 19; America, 1847 *778.6 p172*
Immergluck, Jonas; New York, NY, 1875 *7710.1 p160*
Immroth, Gustav; Kansas, 1892 *1447.20 p65*
Immroth, Heinrich; Kansas, 1890-1897 *1447.20 p65*
Impet, Isaac 77; Ontario, 1871 *1823.17 p75*
Impett, Stephen 30; Ontario, 1871 *1823.21 p173*
Imsland, Nels J.; Iowa, 1892 *1211.15 p11*
Inan, Patrick; Hingham, MA, 1685 *1642 p15*
Incarnation, Mere de l' 40; Quebec, 1639 *9221.17 p84*
Inch, Elizabeth A. 22; Ontario, 1871 *1823.21 p173*
Inch, Richard 18; Ontario, 1871 *1823.21 p173*
Inch, Richard 46; Ontario, 1871 *1823.21 p173*
Inches, John 40; Ontario, 1871 *1823.21 p173*
Inches, Thomas 39; Ontario, 1871 *1823.21 p173*
Indian, Bemahkodoonce 60; Ontario, 1871 *1823.17 p75*
Indian, Kahshuch 39; Ontario, 1871 *1823.17 p75*
Indian, Kaligajewon 110; Ontario, 1871 *1823.17 p75*
Indian, Kewakotigua 75; Ontario, 1871 *1823.17 p75*
Indian, Kewayough 45; Ontario, 1871 *1823.17 p75*
Indian, Kewhtah 90; Ontario, 1871 *1823.17 p75*
Indian, Kicknosway 66; Ontario, 1871 *1823.17 p75*
Indian, Kojeawo 24; Ontario, 1871 *1823.17 p76*
Indian, Macoonse 27; Ontario, 1871 *1823.17 p76*
Indian, Mahkomese 42; Ontario, 1871 *1823.17 p76*
Indian, Mejekenawa 42; Ontario, 1871 *1823.17 p76*
Indian, Mekesegua 32; Ontario, 1871 *1823.17 p76*
Indian, Menaguat 66; Ontario, 1871 *1823.17 p76*
Indian, Mesquhunquat 22; Ontario, 1871 *1823.17 p76*
Indian, Moonish 28; Ontario, 1871 *1823.17 p76*
Indian, Nanobegua 40; Ontario, 1871 *1823.17 p76*
Indian, Negahnekezhik 40; Ontario, 1871 *1823.17 p76*
Indian, Nimkeence 41; Ontario, 1871 *1823.17 p76*
Indian, Nowgishuk 42; Ontario, 1871 *1823.17 p76*
Indian, Oshabau 60; Ontario, 1871 *1823.17 p76*
Indian, Pandegashewa 47; Ontario, 1871 *1823.17 p76*
Indian, Penesequa 43; Ontario, 1871 *1823.17 p76*
Indian, Pewaymoo 60; Ontario, 1871 *1823.17 p76*
Indian, Pungeshinoqua 56; Ontario, 1871 *1823.17 p76*
Indian, Quaaasong 62; Ontario, 1871 *1823.17 p76*
Indian, Saugautch 42; Ontario, 1871 *1823.17 p76*
Indian, Seaah 49; Ontario, 1871 *1823.17 p76*
Indian, Shanee 69; Ontario, 1871 *1823.17 p76*
Indian, Shawahnose 44; Ontario, 1871 *1823.17 p76*
Indian, Shenaish 62; Ontario, 1871 *1823.17 p76*
Indian, Songoqua 30; Ontario, 1871 *1823.17 p77*
Indian, Tagwahjewon 46; Ontario, 1871 *1823.17 p77*
Indian, Tahyaguam 53; Ontario, 1871 *1823.17 p77*
Indian, Takoose 80; Ontario, 1871 *1823.17 p77*
Indian, Waulegosheenle 66; Ontario, 1871 *1823.17 p77*
Indian, We Show 45; Ontario, 1871 *1823.17 p77*
Indian, Weejeseyah 29; Ontario, 1871 *1823.17 p77*
Indyka, Karolina 18; New York, NY, 1911 *6533.11 p10*
Ineman, Rudolf; New York, NY, 1893 *2853.20 p469*
Inemanova, Lud.; New York, NY, 1893 *2853.20 p469*
Ingall, William; Ohio, 1843 *2763.1 p8*
Ingamalls, James B. 39; Ontario, 1871 *1823.21 p173*
Inge, Thomas 25; Ontario, 1871 *1823.21 p173*
Ingeman, H. 23; America, 1848 *778.6 p172*
Ingerom, John; Virginia, 1652 *6254.4 p243*
Ingle, Whilten 20; Port uncertain, 1841 *778.6 p172*
Ingledew, R.; Quebec, 1870 *8364.32 p24*
Inglis, George 39; Ontario, 1871 *1823.21 p173*
Inglis, John 48; Ontario, 1871 *1823.21 p173*
Ingoldsby, Thomas; Toronto, 1844 *2910.35 p115*
Ingraham, Charles 24; Ontario, 1871 *1823.21 p173*
Ingraham, Jane 34; Ontario, 1871 *1823.21 p173*
Ingraham, John 44; Ontario, 1871 *1823.17 p77*

Ingraham, Richard 62; South Carolina, 1812 *3476.30 p12*
Ingraham, Thomas 24; South Carolina, 1812 *3476.30 p12*
Ingram, Alexander 36; Ontario, 1871 *1823.17 p77*
Ingram, Francis; Philadelphia, 1778 *8529.30 p3A*
Ingram, Henry; Marston's Wharf, 1782 *8529.30 p13*
Ingram, Henry 62; Ontario, 1871 *1823.21 p173*
Ingram, James 46; Ontario, 1871 *1823.21 p173*
Ingram, James 60; Ontario, 1871 *1823.17 p77*
Ingram, Jas. 40; Ontario, 1871 *1823.17 p77*
Ingram, Jno. 26; South Carolina, 1812 *3476.30 p12*
Ingram, John 30; Ontario, 1871 *1823.21 p173*
Ingram, Margt 20; St. John, N.B., 1834 *6469.7 p4*
Ingram, Sarah; Maryland, 1674-1675 *1236.25 p51*
Ingram Family ; Detroit, 1900 *9228.50 p299*
Ingrouille, Harriet; New York, 1911-1914 *9228.50 p548*
Ingrum, John 46; Ontario, 1871 *1823.21 p173*
Ingulf, Eugene 20; America, 1848 *778.6 p172*
Ingulf, Selestine 18; America, 1848 *778.6 p172*
Inman, James; Philadelphia, 1856 *5720.10 p382*
Inman, John; New Orleans, 1850 *7242.30 p145*
Inman, Thomas 30; Ontario, 1871 *1823.17 p77*
Innes, Canon 45; Ontario, 1871 *1823.21 p173*
Innes, David 32; Ontario, 1871 *1823.17 p77*
Innes, William 28; New York, NY, 1835 *5024.1 p136*
Innes, William 45; Ontario, 1871 *1823.21 p173*
Innis, Donald 40; Ontario, 1871 *1823.21 p173*
Innis, James 33; Ontario, 1871 *1823.17 p77*
Innis, Jane 45; Ontario, 1871 *1823.21 p173*
Innis, Jennet 78; Ontario, 1871 *1823.21 p173*
Innison, Joseph E. 65; Ontario, 1871 *1823.21 p173*
Inoraell, Xavier 18; America, 1847 *778.6 p173*
Insell, Emma 49; Ontario, 1871 *1823.21 p173*
Insgood, Harry 14; Quebec, 1870 *8364.32 p24*
Insulin, W.E.; New York, NY, 1845 *6412.40 p149*
Intchaffer, Adolph 2 months; America, 1846 *778.6 p173*
Intchaffer, M. 26; America, 1846 *778.6 p173*
Intchaffer, Maria 30; America, 1846 *778.6 p173*
Intrest, Christian; New Jersey, 1773-1774 *927.31 p3*
Iou, Anne 17; Montreal, 1659 *9221.17 p415*
Ioya, Giacamo; Louisiana, 1874 *4981.45 p132*
Ipock, Jacob; North Carolina, 1710 *3629.40 p3*
Ipsen, Anders P.; Colorado, 1878 *1029.59 p43*
Iquain, Madeleine; Nova Scotia, 1753 *3051 p113*
Iralle, Miss; America, 1846 *7420.1 p44*
Ireland, Ann; Boston, 1739 *1642 p44*
Ireland, David 33; Ontario, 1871 *1823.21 p173*
Ireland, Deborah 10; Quebec, 1870 *8364.32 p24*
Ireland, George 46; Ontario, 1871 *1823.21 p173*
Ireland, Gilbert E. 41; Indiana, 1882-1892 *9076.20 p73*
Ireland, James 68; Ontario, 1871 *1823.21 p173*
Ireland, Jane 57; Ontario, 1871 *1823.21 p173*
Ireland, Mary; Maryland, 1674-1675 *1236.25 p52*
Ireland, Walter 70; Ontario, 1871 *1823.21 p173*
Ireland, William 32; Ontario, 1871 *1823.21 p174*
Ireland, William 40; Ontario, 1871 *1823.17 p77*
Ireland, Willm.; Maryland, 1674 *1236.25 p50*
Irinbefott, J. 24; New Orleans, 1840 *778.6 p173*
Irish, James; Massachusetts, 1855 *5720.10 p382*
Irle, Jean; Louisiana, 1874 *4981.45 p132*
Irlinger, Georg 9; America, 1842 *778.6 p173*
Irlinger, Joseph 4; America, 1842 *778.6 p173*
Irlinger, Joseph 44; America, 1842 *778.6 p173*
Irlinger, Lisabetha 14; America, 1842 *778.6 p173*
Irlinger, Marie 12; America, 1842 *778.6 p173*
Irlinger, Marie 44; America, 1842 *778.6 p173*
Irlinger, Nicolas 6; America, 1842 *778.6 p173*
Irman, James; Louisiana, 1874 *4981.45 p132*
Irninger, Franz Heinrich 33; New Castle, DE, 1817-1818 *90.20 p152*
Irons, John 36; Ontario, 1871 *1823.21 p174*
Irons, Oliver 18; Quebec, 1870 *8364.32 p24*

Ironside, William 39; Ontario, 1871 *1823.21 p174*
Ironside, William 55; Ontario, 1871 *1823.21 p174*
Ironsides, James 40; Ontario, 1871 *1823.17 p77*
Ironsides, John 45; Ontario, 1871 *1823.17 p77*
Irr, Joseph; Washington, 1887 *2770.40 p24*
Irsch, Josef; America, 1882 *5475.1 p16*
Irschermann, Gottlieb; New York, 1860 *358.56 p149*
Irveson, Andes; Iowa, 1875 *1211.15 p11*
Irvin, John; New York, NY, 1853 *5720.10 p382*
Irvin, Thomas; North Carolina, 1822-1828 *1088.45 p15*
Irvin, Thompson; Philadelphia, 1858 *5720.10 p382*
Irvine, Cherry 45; Ontario, 1871 *1823.17 p77*
Irvine, David 47; Ontario, 1871 *1823.17 p77*
Irvine, George; Ohio, 1809-1852 *4511.35 p24*
Irvine, James 30; Ontario, 1871 *1823.21 p174*
Irvine, Richard 46; Ontario, 1871 *1823.21 p174*
Irvine, Robert 39; Ontario, 1871 *1823.21 p174*
Irvine, Thomas 61; Indiana, 1870-1880 *9076.20 p70*
Irvine, Thomas 45; Ontario, 1871 *1823.17 p77*
Irvine, Thomas 52; Ontario, 1871 *1823.17 p77*
Irvine, Thomas; Philadelphia, 1859 *5720.10 p382*
Irvine, Walter 36; Indiana, 1869-1880 *9076.20 p70*
Irvine, William 40; Ontario, 1871 *1823.21 p174*
Irvine, William 69; Ontario, 1871 *1823.21 p174*
Irving, George; North Carolina, 1832 *1088.45 p15*
Irving, George 69; Ontario, 1871 *1823.21 p174*
Irving, George C. 42; Ontario, 1871 *1823.17 p77*
Irving, James 31; Ontario, 1871 *1823.21 p174*
Irving, Jane; North Carolina, 1834 *1088.45 p15*
Irving, Margaret 45; Ontario, 1871 *1823.21 p174*
Irving, Thomas 39; Ontario, 1871 *1823.21 p174*
Irving, Thomas T. 36; Ontario, 1871 *1823.21 p174*
Irwin, Alexander 52; Ontario, 1871 *1823.17 p77*
Irwin, Ann 64; Ontario, 1871 *1823.21 p174*
Irwin, Christopher; America, 1779 *8529.30 p13*
Irwin, Edward 40; Ontario, 1871 *1823.21 p174*
Irwin, Edward 50; Ontario, 1871 *1823.21 p174*
Irwin, Francis 50; Ontario, 1871 *1823.21 p174*
Irwin, Henry J. 49; Ontario, 1871 *1823.21 p174*
Irwin, James 22; Ontario, 1871 *1823.17 p77*
Irwin, James 30; Ontario, 1871 *1823.21 p174*
Irwin, James 34; Ontario, 1871 *1823.17 p77*
Irwin, John; Harrisburg, PA, 1855 *5720.10 p382*
Irwin, John; North Carolina, 1851 *1088.45 p15*
Irwin, John 47; Ontario, 1871 *1823.17 p77*
Irwin, John 48; Ontario, 1871 *1823.21 p174*
Irwin, Joseph; Ohio, 1809-1852 *4511.35 p24*
Irwin, Marie 31; Quebec, 1657 *9221.17 p350*
Irwin, Michael; Louisiana, 1874-1875 *4981.45 p29*
Irwin, Samuel 35; Ontario, 1871 *1823.17 p77*
Irwin, Thomas 43; Ontario, 1871 *1823.21 p174*
Irwin, William 38; Ontario, 1871 *1823.17 p77*
Irwin, William 42; Ontario, 1871 *1823.17 p78*
Irwin, Wm 45; Ontario, 1871 *1823.21 p174*
Isaac, Ann *SEE* Isaac, Evan
Isaac, Ann *SEE* Isaac, Evan
Isaac, Catherine; Ohio, n.d. *4022.20 p287*
  With mother
  With father
Isaac, Elizabeth *SEE* Isaac, Evan
Isaac, Elizabeth; Ohio, 1838 *4022.20 p281*
Isaac, Elizebeth 70; Ontario, 1871 *1823.21 p174*
Isaac, Emanuel 53; Ontario, 1871 *1823.21 p174*
Isaac, Evan; Ohio, 1838 *4022.20 p281*
  *Wife:*Ann
  With grandson
  With son-in-law & daughter
  With granddaughter
  *Child:*Thomas
  *Child:*Margaret
  *Child:*Ann
  *Child:*Elizabeth
  *Child:*Morgan

Isaac, Gustavis; North Carolina, 1850 *1088.45 p15*
Isaac, Isaac; Ohio, 1814-1880 *4022.20 p287*
  *Wife:*Margaret
Isaac, James 27; Ontario, 1871 *1823.21 p174*
Isaac, Jane; Ohio, 1847-1848 *4022.20 p285*
Isaac, John; Ohio, 1844 *4022.20 p281*
  *Wife:*Mary
  With child
Isaac, John 50; Ontario, 1871 *1823.21 p174*
Isaac, Margaret *SEE* Isaac, Isaac
Isaac, Margaret *SEE* Isaac, Evan
Isaac, Mary *SEE* Isaac, John
Isaac, Mcouen 21; Ontario, 1871 *1823.21 p174*
Isaac, Morgan *SEE* Isaac, Evan
Isaac, Siegmund; New York, 1887 *5475.1 p193*
Isaac, Thomas *SEE* Isaac, Evan
Isaacson, Huldah; Baltimore, 1877 *1766.20 p14*
Isaacson, Issac Ferdinand; Washington, 1883 *2770.40 p136*
Isaacson, Jennie N.; St. Paul, MN, 1889-1890 *1865.50 p51*
Isaacson, John A.; Washington, 1883 *2770.40 p136*
Isaacson, Peter; Colorado, 1885 *1029.59 p43*
Isaak, Adolf; New York, 1892 *5475.1 p448*
Isaak, Hermann; Louisville, KY, 1888 *5475.1 p447*
Isabelle, Guillaume; Quebec, 1636 *9221.17 p57*
Isabet, Cyprien 26; Port uncertain, 1842 *778.6 p173*
Isakson, Jakob; Cleveland, OH, 1892-1895 *9722.10 p120*
Isambert, Adele 27; America, 1846 *778.6 p173*
Isambert, Catherine; Quebec, 1673 *4514.3 p327*
Isberg, Carl; Cleveland, OH, 1891-1895 *9722.10 p120*
Isberg, Emelie; Cleveland, OH, 1892-1898 *9722.10 p120*
Isbister, Adam 25; Ontario, 1871 *1823.17 p78*
Isch, Jean 29; America, 1843 *778.6 p173*
Isch, Joseph 24; America, 1843 *778.6 p173*
Ischi, John; Philadelphia, 1856 *5720.10 p382*
Isebeli, Jean 41; Port uncertain, 1843 *778.6 p173*
Iseh, Margaret 24; Mississippi, 1846 *778.6 p173*
Isenberg, Berta; Argentina, 1941 *8023.44 p373*
Isenbuehl, L.; Galveston, TX, 1855 *571.7 p18*
Isenman, Jacob; Ohio, 1809-1852 *4511.35 p24*
Isherie, C. 33; America, 1848 *778.6 p173*
Isherwood, Thomas 40; Ontario, 1871 *1823.21 p174*
Ishipp, Mary; Maryland, 1674 *1236.25 p50*
Iska, Frantisek; America, 1810-1910 *2853.20 p513*
Iska, Frantisek; Chicago, 1902 *2853.20 p400*
Island, Baptist 59; Ontario, 1871 *1823.21 p174*
Island, Cornelius 78; Ontario, 1871 *1823.21 p174*
Isle, Ludwig 24; New Orleans, 1848 *778.6 p173*
Isler, Mr.; West Virginia, 1860-1870 *1132.30 p150*
Isler, Christian; North Carolina, 1710 *3629.40 p4*
Isler, Nicholas; North Carolina, 1710 *3629.40 p5*
Isolara, D.; California, 1868 *1131.61 p89*
Isom, Julius 28; Port uncertain, 1842 *778.6 p173*
Isonburg, Jacob 30; Ontario, 1871 *1823.21 p174*
Isooja, Jaako; Oregon, 1941 *9157.47 p2*
Israel, Albert 30; New York, 1855 *5475.1 p403*
Israel, C. B.; Valdivia, Chile, 1850 *1192.4 p49*
  With wife
  With child 1
Israel, Gotan 17; New Orleans, 1848 *778.6 p173*
Israel, Mark 23; Port uncertain, 1846 *778.6 p173*
Israel, Raphael 22; New Orleans, 1848 *778.6 p173*
Israel, Rose 21; New Orleans, 1848 *778.6 p173*
Issenbrand, Magd. 28; Port uncertain, 1840 *778.6 p173*
Issenbrand, Wilh. 33; Port uncertain, 1840 *778.6 p173*
Itas, Marguerite; Quebec, 1667 *4514.3 p327*
Itzkowitz, Yassel; New York, NY, 1907 *3331.4 p11*
Iungbluth, John; Ohio, 1809-1852 *4511.35 p24*
Ivanicz, Mary; Detroit, 1929 *1640.55 p112*
Ivy, Ellen 45; Ontario, 1871 *1823.21 p174*

J

Jabbusch, Herman; Wisconsin, 1880 *6795.8 p25*
Jabbush, Herman; Wisconsin, 1880 *6795.8 p25*
Jabert, . . .; America, 1840 *778.6 p173*
Jabert, Mrs. 33; America, 1840 *778.6 p173*
Jabert, Jacques 46; America, 1840 *778.6 p173*
Jabes, East 24; Ontario, 1871 *1823.21 p174*
Jabionski, Anton; Chicago, 1930 *121.35 p100*
Jabionski, Maryan; Chicago, 1930 *121.35 p100*
Jablonski, Frank; Galveston, TX, 1901 *6015.15 p11*
Jacek, Frances; Detroit, 1930 *1640.60 p77*
Jachnes, Samuel 22; New York, NY, 1878 *9253.2 p45*
Jack, James 35; Ontario, 1871 *1823.21 p174*
Jackel, Josef; America, 1855 *5475.1 p258*
Jacker, Francis; New York, 1859 *358.56 p101*
Jacker, William; New York, 1859 *358.56 p101*
Jackisch, Albert Friedrich Louis; America, 1867 *7919.3 p527*
Jackle, Christiana Marg.; America, 1865 *179.55 p19*
Jackle, Christina Jacobine; America, 1865 *179.55 p19*
Jackle, Johann Christoph; America, 1865 *179.55 p19*
   With wife
Jackle, Maria Carolina; America, 1865 *179.55 p19*
Jackman, Edward 14; Ontario, 1871 *1823.17 p78*
Jackman, John W.; Ohio, 1878 *3580.20 p32*
Jackman, John W.; Ohio, 1878 *6020.12 p12*
Jackman, Patt; New Orleans, 1850 *7242.30 p145*
Jackowski, Casimir; Wisconsin, 1876 *6795.8 p33*
Jackson, Miss; Quebec, 1885 *1937.10 p52*
Jackson, Mrs.; Quebec, 1885 *1937.10 p52*
Jackson, Abraham 39; Ontario, 1871 *1823.21 p174*
Jackson, Adam; St. Johns, N.F., 1825 *1053.15 p7*
Jackson, Alexander 15; Quebec, 1870 *8364.32 p24*
Jackson, Amelia 37; Ontario, 1871 *1823.21 p174*
Jackson, Amelia 44; Ontario, 1871 *1823.21 p174*
Jackson, Amelia 21; Quebec, 1870 *8364.32 p24*
Jackson, Amos 36; Ontario, 1871 *1823.17 p78*
Jackson, Archibald 17; Quebec, 1870 *8364.32 p24*
Jackson, Charles 18; Ontario, 1871 *1823.21 p175*
Jackson, Charles 35; Ontario, 1871 *1823.21 p175*
Jackson, Charles 44; Ontario, 1871 *1823.21 p175*
Jackson, D.; Quebec, 1885 *1937.10 p52*
Jackson, David 44; Ontario, 1871 *1823.21 p175*
Jackson, David 69; Ontario, 1871 *1823.21 p175*
Jackson, Edmund 53; Ontario, 1871 *1823.21 p175*
Jackson, Eliza 11; Quebec, 1870 *8364.32 p24*
Jackson, Ephrim 65; Ontario, 1871 *1823.21 p175*
Jackson, George; New York, 1778 *8529.30 p3A*
Jackson, George; Ontario, 1871 *1823.21 p175*
Jackson, George 18; Ontario, 1871 *1823.21 p175*
Jackson, George 27; Ontario, 1871 *1823.17 p78*
Jackson, George 45; Ontario, 1871 *1823.21 p175*
Jackson, George 45; Ontario, 1871 *1823.21 p175*
Jackson, George 49; Ontario, 1871 *1823.17 p78*
Jackson, George A. 39; Ontario, 1871 *1823.17 p78*
Jackson, Gustaf A.; Cleveland, OH, 1892-1897 *9722.10 p120*
Jackson, Harvey C. 44; Ontario, 1871 *1823.21 p175*
Jackson, Henry 33; Ontario, 1871 *1823.21 p175*
Jackson, Henry 40; Ontario, 1871 *1823.17 p78*
Jackson, Henry 79; Ontario, 1871 *1823.21 p175*
Jackson, J. J.; Louisiana, 1874 *4981.45 p296*
Jackson, James; Illinois, 1859 *6079.1 p7*
Jackson, James 36; Ontario, 1871 *1823.21 p175*
Jackson, James 37; Ontario, 1871 *1823.21 p175*
Jackson, James 55; Ontario, 1871 *1823.21 p175*
Jackson, James 65; Ontario, 1871 *1823.21 p175*
Jackson, Jane 21; Ontario, 1871 *1823.17 p78*
Jackson, Jno.; Maryland, 1674 *1236.25 p50*

Jackson, John; Boston, 1767 *1642 p39*
Jackson, John; Colorado, 1886 *1029.59 p43*
Jackson, John 24; Ontario, 1871 *1823.17 p78*
Jackson, John 32; Ontario, 1871 *1823.17 p78*
Jackson, John 39; Ontario, 1871 *1823.21 p175*
Jackson, John 42; Ontario, 1871 *1823.17 p78*
Jackson, John 45; Ontario, 1871 *1823.21 p175*
Jackson, John 46; Ontario, 1871 *1823.21 p175*
Jackson, John 61; Ontario, 1871 *1823.21 p175*
Jackson, John 92; Ontario, 1871 *1823.17 p78*
Jackson, John 13; Quebec, 1870 *8364.32 p24*
Jackson, John; Salem, MA, 1634-1700 *9228.50 p300*
Jackson, Josiah; Colorado, 1872 *1029.59 p43*
Jackson, Luke; Illinois, 1857 *6079.1 p7*
Jackson, Mary Ann 38; Ontario, 1871 *1823.17 p78*
Jackson, Michael 40; Ontario, 1871 *1823.21 p175*
Jackson, Mincin 59; Ontario, 1871 *1823.21 p175*
Jackson, Richard 52; Ontario, 1871 *1823.21 p175*
Jackson, Robert 20; Ontario, 1871 *1823.21 p175*
Jackson, Samuel 29; Ontario, 1871 *1823.21 p175*
Jackson, Samuel 16; Quebec, 1870 *8364.32 p24*
Jackson, Thomas 44; Ontario, 1871 *1823.21 p175*
Jackson, Thomas 57; Ontario, 1871 *1823.21 p175*
Jackson, Thomas 62; Ontario, 1871 *1823.17 p78*
Jackson, Thomas; Toronto, 1844 *2910.35 p113*
Jackson, Thomas G. 28; Ontario, 1871 *1823.17 p78*
Jackson, William; Illinois, 1857 *6079.1 p7*
Jackson, William 20; Ontario, 1871 *1823.21 p176*
Jackson, William 28; Ontario, 1871 *1823.21 p176*
Jackson, William 30; Ontario, 1871 *1823.21 p176*
Jackson, William 47; Ontario, 1871 *1823.21 p176*
Jackson, William 48; Ontario, 1871 *1823.21 p176*
Jackson, William 62; Ontario, 1871 *1823.21 p176*
Jackson, William 68; Ontario, 1871 *1823.21 p176*
Jackson, William 77; Ontario, 1871 *1823.21 p176*
Jackson, Wm. H. 50; Ontario, 1871 *1823.17 p78*
Jackson Caleen, Anna Jacobsdotter *SEE* Jackson Caleen, Peter
Jackson Caleen, Betze C. *SEE* Jackson Caleen, Peter
Jackson Caleen, Jacob E. *SEE* Jackson Caleen, Peter
Jackson Caleen, Peter; Kansas, 1868 *777.40 p12*
   *Wife:*Anna Jacobsdotter
   *Son:*Jacob E.
   *Daughter:*Betze C.
Jacob, Bartholomaus *SEE* Jacob, Jakob
Jacob, Claude 34; Port uncertain, 1843 *778.6 p173*
Jacob, Clemence 12; New Orleans, 1848 *778.6 p173*
Jacob, D. 35; New Orleans, 1834 *1002.51 p112*
Jacob, Emmanuel 14; America, 1746 *778.6 p174*
Jacob, Etienne; Quebec, 1653 *9221.17 p275*
Jacob, George; New York, 1859 *358.56 p99*
Jacob, Henry 30; America, 1845 *778.6 p174*
Jacob, Henry; Wisconsin, 1905 *6795.8 p179*
Jacob, Jacob 16; Missouri, 1845 *778.6 p174*
Jacob, Jakob *SEE* Jacob, Jakob
Jacob, Jakob; America, 1881 *5475.1 p44*
   *Wife:*Magdalena Briam
   *Son:*Jakob
   *Son:*Bartholomaus
Jacob, John; Illinois, 1851 *6079.1 p7*
Jacob, Joseph; Ohio, 1809-1852 *4511.35 p24*
Jacob, Magdalena Briam *SEE* Jacob, Jakob
Jacob, Margarethe 73; New York, NY, 1898 *7951.13 p42*
Jacob, Mathias; Ohio, 1809-1852 *4511.35 p24*
Jacob, Therese 28; New Orleans, 1848 *778.6 p174*
Jacob, Victor 21; America, 1846 *778.6 p174*

Jacobs, Alexander Edward; North Carolina, 1855 *1088.45 p15*
Jacobs, Anna Maria 23; Port uncertain, 1848 *778.6 p174*
Jacobs, Catrina 50; St. Louis, 1844 *778.6 p174*
Jacobs, Daniel 22; Port uncertain, 1840 *778.6 p174*
Jacobs, Francis; Ohio, 1809-1852 *4511.35 p24*
Jacobs, Frank; Detroit, 1929 *1640.55 p114*
Jacobs, Gustaf; Washington, 1884 *2770.40 p192*
Jacobs, Henry; Illinois, 1860 *6079.1 p7*
Jacobs, J. H. W.; Valdivia, Chile, 1852 *1192.4 p53*
Jacobs, John B.; Illinois, 1860 *6079.1 p7*
Jacobs, Joseph 22; St. Louis, 1844 *778.6 p174*
Jacobs, Justin; Ohio, 1844 *2763.1 p8*
Jacobs, Louis; Washington, 1882 *2770.40 p135*
Jacobs, Magdeline 74; St. Louis, 1844 *778.6 p174*
Jacobs, Matthias; Ohio, 1809-1852 *4511.35 p24*
Jacobs, Peter; New York, NY, 1902 *6212.1 p15*
Jacobs, Peter 46; Ontario, 1871 *1823.17 p78*
Jacobsdotter, Anna; Kansas, 1868 *777.40 p12*
Jacobsdotter, Anna; Kansas, 1868 *777.40 p12*
Jacobsdotter, Betse; Iowa, 1866-1870 *777.40 p9*
Jacobsen, Jess; Valdivia, Chile, 1852 *1192.4 p55*
Jacobsen, Lars; Iowa, 1894 *1211.15 p15*
Jacobsohn, Pauline; America, 1858 *7420.1 p178*
Jacobson, Carl; Cleveland, OH, 1891-1900 *9722.10 p120*
Jacobson, Carolina; New York, NY, 1887-1888 *1865.50 p51*
Jacobson, Elisabeth Hansdotter *SEE* Jacobson, Jacob
Jacobson, Henry; North Carolina, 1835 *1088.45 p15*
Jacobson, Jacob *SEE* Jacobson, Jacob
Jacobson, Jacob; Iowa, 1865-1870 *777.40 p8*
   *Wife:*Elisabeth Hansdotter
   *Son:*Jacob
Jacobson, Jacob; Iowa, 1906 *1211.15 p15*
Jacobson, Jacob; St. Paul, MN, 1887 *1865.50 p51*
Jacobson, John; Illinois, 1864 *4487.25 p60*
Jacobson, Lars; Iowa, 1877 *1211.15 p15*
Jacobson, Lars Peter; Cleveland, OH, 1893-1900 *9722.10 p120*
Jacobson, Oscar; Cleveland, OH, 1888-1893 *9722.10 p120*
Jacobson, Peter; Iowa, 1877 *1211.15 p15*
Jacobson, Soran; Colorado, 1896 *1029.59 p43*
Jacobson, William; North Carolina, 1857 *1088.45 p15*
Jacobssohn, Mr.; America, 1854 *7420.1 p122*
Jacobsson, Anna Jacobsdotter *SEE* Jacobsson, Pehr
Jacobsson, Betze C. *SEE* Jacobsson, Pehr
Jacobsson, Erik 22; New York, 1856 *6529.11 p22*
Jacobsson, Fr. Niclas; Savannah, GA, 1851 *6412.40 p153*
Jacobsson, J.; New York, NY, 1851 *6412.40 p153*
Jacobsson, Jacob E. *SEE* Jacobsson, Pehr
Jacobsson, L.; New York, NY, 1846 *6412.40 p149*
Jacobsson, L.P.; New York, NY, 1848 *6412.40 p151*
Jacobsson, Martha Ersdotter *SEE* Jacobsson, Olof
Jacobsson, Olof; Kansas, 1869-1871 *777.40 p9*
   *Wife:*Martha Ersdotter
Jacobsson, P.Z.; New York, NY, 1844 *6412.40 p148*
Jacobsson, Pehr; Kansas, 1868 *777.40 p12*
   *Wife:*Anna Jacobsdotter
   *Son:*Jacob E.
   *Daughter:*Betze C.
Jacobsson, Thomas Petter; North America, 1868 *6410.15 p105*
Jacoby, Francis; Ohio, 1809-1852 *4511.35 p24*
Jacoby, Peter; America, 1876 *5475.1 p343*
Jacomet, P. 23; New Orleans, 1842 *778.6 p174*
Jacou, Edouard 19; America, 1840 *778.6 p174*

Jacquait, Catharina 21; New Orleans, 1847 *778.6 p174*
Jacquart, Theophile; New York, NY, 1870 *1494.20 p13*
Jacquelin, Henry; Louisiana, 1836-1840 *4981.45 p212*
Jacquemard, August 22; New Orleans, 1847 *778.6 p174*
Jacquemard, Rosalie 22; New Orleans, 1847 *778.6 p174*
Jacquereau, Jean 27; Quebec, 1658 *9221.17 p382*
Jacques, Catherine 16; America, 1845 *778.6 p174*
Jacques, Elenor *SEE* Jacques, Joseph
Jacques, Eliza 37; America, 1845 *778.6 p174*
Jacques, Henry; Newbury, MA, 1620-1687 *9228.50 p300*
Jacques, Joseph; Canada, 1774 *3036.5 p41*
   *Wife:*Elenor
Jacques, Pierre 42; America, 1845 *778.6 p174*
Jacquet, Cecana 26; New Orleans, 1847 *778.6 p174*
Jacquet, Elie; Quebec, 1660 *9221.17 p436*
Jacquet, Ellen Roy; New Orleans, 1847 *778.6 p174*
Jacquet, Euphrosine 35; New Orleans, 1847 *778.6 p174*
Jacquet, Jean Charles; Louisiana, 1874 *4981.45 p132*
Jacquet, Jean Marie 27; America, 1845 *778.6 p174*
Jacquet, Paul 2; New Orleans, 1848 *778.6 p174*
Jacquet, Pierre 32; New Orleans, 1848 *778.6 p174*
Jacquet, Prre Joseph 4 months; New Orleans, 1848 *778.6 p174*
Jacquetan, Paul 38; New Orleans, 1848 *778.6 p174*
Jacqueuin, Frederic J. M.; Illinois, 1856 *6079.1 p7*
Jacquey, Vict. 29; America, 1840 *778.6 p174*
Jacquier, Louise; Quebec, 1670 *4514.3 p327*
Jacquinet, Denis 13; New Orleans, 1848 *778.6 p174*
Jacquinet, Ferdinand 41; New Orleans, 1848 *778.6 p174*
Jacquot, Barbe 27; Mississippi, 1845 *778.6 p174*
Jacquot, Joseph 35; Mississippi, 1845 *778.6 p174*
Jacquot, Victoire 29; Mississippi, 1845 *778.6 p175*
Jader, Hans 30; Kansas, 1880 *777.40 p13*
Jaderberg, Jon 25; New York, 1856 *6529.11 p22*
Jaderborg, Louis; Kansas, 1855-1858 *777.40 p11*
Jaderbourg Olson, Louis; Kansas, 1855-1858 *777.40 p11*
Jaderholm, Claes Johan; Boston, 1855 *6412.40 p154*
Jaderholm, Eric; Washington, 1884 *2770.40 p192*
Jaderholm, Mary B.; Washington, 1884 *2770.40 p192*
Jaderstrom, Jons 30; New York, 1856 *6529.11 p22*
Jadin, Auguste Joseph; Wisconsin, 1854-1858 *1495.20 p66*
   *Wife:*Eleonore Josephe Paris
   *Child:*Rosalie Josephe
   *Child:*Maximilien
   *Child:*Jean Baptiste
   *Child:*Jean Joseph
   *Child:*Marie Therese
Jadin, Desiree *SEE* Jadin, Pierre Joseph
Jadin, Eleonore Josephe Paris *SEE* Jadin, Auguste Joseph
Jadin, Jean Baptiste *SEE* Jadin, Auguste Joseph
Jadin, Jean Joseph *SEE* Jadin, Auguste Joseph
Jadin, John B.; New York, NY, 1870 *1494.20 p12*
Jadin, Josephine Wautlet *SEE* Jadin, Pierre Joseph
Jadin, Julien Joseph *SEE* Jadin, Pierre Joseph
Jadin, Marie Catherine *SEE* Jadin, Pierre Joseph
Jadin, Marie Therese *SEE* Jadin, Auguste Joseph
Jadin, Maximilien *SEE* Jadin, Auguste Joseph
Jadin, Maximilien Joseph 21; Wisconsin, 1854-1858 *1495.20 p66*
Jadin, Maximillien; New York, NY, 1855 *1494.21 p31*
Jadin, Pierre Joseph; Wisconsin, 1854-1858 *1495.20 p66*
   *Wife:*Josephine Wautlet
   *Child:*Marie Catherine
   *Child:*Julien Joseph
   *Child:*Desiree
Jadin, Rosalie Josephe *SEE* Jadin, Auguste Joseph
Jadot, Eleonore *SEE* Jadot, Louis
Jadot, Emerance *SEE* Jadot, Louis
Jadot, Josephine Tombal *SEE* Jadot, Louis
Jadot, Louis; Wisconsin, 1869 *1495.20 p56*
   *Wife:*Josephine Tombal
   *Daughter:*Eleonore
   *Daughter:*Emerance
Jaeger, Catharina 31; Port uncertain, 1847 *778.6 p175*
Jaeger, Elisabeth; America, 1866 *5475.1 p490*
Jaeger, Georg 30; Port uncertain, 1847 *778.6 p175*
Jaeger, Helen 18; New York, NY, 1898 *7951.13 p44*
Jaeger, Helena 72; Port uncertain, 1847 *778.6 p175*
Jaeger, Jan Nepomuk; New York, NY, 1852 *2853.20 p430*
   With parents
Jaeger, Johann 2; New York, NY, 1898 *7951.13 p44*
Jaeger, John; New Jersey, 1879 *554.30 p26*
   *Wife:*Louise
Jaeger, Katherina 1; New York, NY, 1898 *7951.13 p44*
Jaeger, Lorentz 8; New York, NY, 1898 *7951.13 p44*
Jaeger, Louis 6 months; America, 1847 *778.6 p175*
Jaeger, Louise *SEE* Jaeger, John
Jaeger, Ludwig 35; New York, NY, 1898 *7951.13 p44*
Jaeger, Magdalena 30; New York, NY, 1898 *7951.13 p44*

Jaeger, Marie 6; America, 1847 *778.6 p175*
Jaeger, Marie 41; America, 1847 *778.6 p175*
Jaeger, Mathias 35; America, 1847 *778.6 p175*
Jaeger, Melchior 48; America, 1847 *778.6 p175*
Jaeger, Melchior 3; New York, NY, 1898 *7951.13 p44*
Jaeger, Melichor 22; New York, NY, 1898 *7951.13 p44*
Jaeger, Pierre 9; America, 1847 *778.6 p175*
Jaeger, Valentin; Wisconsin, 1895 *6795.8 p158*
Jaeger, Vincent 5; New York, NY, 1898 *7951.13 p44*
Jaeger, Voltz Jacob 22; America, 1847 *778.6 p175*
Jaeggi, Jean 28; America, 1840 *778.6 p175*
Jaeker, Therese; Galveston, TX, 1855 *571.7 p17*
Jaendel, Joseph 28; America, 1841 *778.6 p175*
Jaenke, Carl; Galveston, TX, 1855 *571.7 p17*
Jaensch, Robert; Miami, 1935 *4984.12 p39*
Jager, Anna *SEE* Jager, Elisabeth Kronenberger
Jager, Anton *SEE* Jager, Elisabeth Becker
Jager, Barbara *SEE* Jager, Jakob
Jager, Barbara *SEE* Jager, Elisabeth Kronenberger
Jager, Benedikt; America, 1885 *2526.43 p149*
Jager, Bernhard; Venezuela, 1843 *3899.5 p546*
Jager, Charles; Illinois, 1855 *6079.1 p7*
Jager, Christian; America, 1868 *7919.3 p528*
Jager, Christine Klopper *SEE* Jager, Friedrich
Jager, Christine *SEE* Jager, Elisabeth Becker
Jager, Christoph; America, 1847-1900 *5475.1 p193*
Jager, Claude; Quebec, 1639 *9221.17 p83*
Jager, Dorothea *SEE* Jager, Jakob
Jager, Elisabeth; Philadelphia, 1884 *5475.1 p229*
   *Daughter:*Barbara
   *Daughter:*Anna
   *Daughter:*Katharina
   *Son:*Johann
   *Son:*Georg
Jager, Elisabeth Becker; America, 1881 *5475.1 p336*
   *Son:*Heinrich
   *Son:*Anton
   *Daughter:*Christine
   *Son:*Nikolaus
   *Son:*Wilhelm
Jager, Friedrich; America, 1856 *7420.1 p148*
   *Wife:*Christine Klopper
   *Daughter:*Philippine
Jager, Georg *SEE* Jager, Elisabeth Kronenberger
Jager, Hedwig *SEE* Jager, Jakob
Jager, Heinrich *SEE* Jager, Elisabeth Becker
Jager, Jakob; America, 1879 *5475.1 p372*
   *Wife:*Maria Meier
   *Daughter:*Hedwig
   *Daughter:*Dorothea
   With stepchild
   *Daughter:*Barbara
   *Son:*Peter
   *Daughter:*Maria
Jager, Johann *SEE* Jager, Elisabeth Kronenberger
Jager, Katharina; America, 1881 *5475.1 p336*
Jager, Katharina *SEE* Jager, Elisabeth Kronenberger
Jager, Maria; America, 1879 *5475.1 p267*
Jager, Maria *SEE* Jager, Jakob
Jager, Maria Meier *SEE* Jager, Jakob
Jager, Maria 28; America, 1869 *5475.1 p361*
Jager, Nikolaus *SEE* Jager, Elisabeth Becker
Jager, Peter; America, 1870 *5475.1 p336*
Jager, Peter *SEE* Jager, Jakob
Jager, Philipp; Chicago, 1887 *5475.1 p243*
Jager, Philippine *SEE* Jager, Friedrich
Jager, Wilhelm *SEE* Jager, Elisabeth Becker
Jaggar, Abraham; New York, 1778 *8529.30 p3A*
Jagger, Abraham; New York, 1778 *8529.30 p3A*
Jagielski, Feliks 28; New York, NY, 1911 *6533.11 p9*
Jagnot, Marie 6 months; New Orleans, 1846 *778.6 p175*
Jagnot, Marie 33; New Orleans, 1846 *778.6 p175*
Jagodzinska, Theophila; Wisconsin, 1899 *6795.8 p58*
Jagodzinski, Theophila; Wisconsin, 1899 *6795.8 p58*
Jagoel, Wilhelmine; Wisconsin, 1899 *6795.8 p42*
Jagon, Henry; Louisiana, 1874 *4981.45 p132*
Jahan, Jacques 22; Quebec, 1658 *9221.17 p382*
Jahan, Jeanne 49; Quebec, 1651 *9221.17 p246*
Jahan, Laurent 18; America, 1846 *778.6 p175*
Jahn, August Karl Friedrich; America, n.d. *8115.12 p320*
Jahn, Fernau; Ohio, 1809-1852 *4511.35 p24*
Jahne, Dorothea 22 *SEE* Jahne, Philipp
Jahne, Philipp 27; America, 1854 *5475.1 p74*
   *Sister:*Dorothea 22
Jahnke, Giitlieb; Wisconsin, 1859 *6795.8 p138*
Jahnke, Johann Friedrich; Wisconsin, 1873 *6795.8 p154*
Jahnke, Ludwig; Wisconsin, 1874 *6795.8 p25*
Jahns, August; Wisconsin, 1874 *6795.8 p25*
Jahns, Auguste Bolter; Wisconsin, 1897 *6795.8 p186*
Jahns, Eduard; Wisconsin, 1875 *6795.8 p36*
Jahns, Samuel; Wisconsin, 1869 *6795.8 p138*
Jailes, John 55; Ontario, 1871 *1823.21 p176*
Jakes, George 22; Ontario, 1871 *1823.21 p176*

Jakes, Mary 8; Ontario, 1871 *1823.17 p78*
Jakkobson, Hans; Iowa, 1876 *1211.15 p15*
Jakman, Eliza B. 12; Ontario, 1871 *1823.21 p176*
Jakob, Anna; America, 1872 *5475.1 p321*
Jakob, Johann 66; America, 1843 *5475.1 p529*
   *Wife:*Luise Becker 70
Jakob, Luise Becker 70 *SEE* Jakob, Johann
Jakobi, Barbara *SEE* Jakobi, Heinrich
Jakobi, Heinrich; America, 1881-1900 *5475.1 p228*
   *Wife:*Katharina Belles
   *Daughter:*Maria
   *Daughter:*Barbara
   *Son:*J. Heinrich
Jakobi, J. Heinrich *SEE* Jakobi, Heinrich
Jakobi, Katharina Belles *SEE* Jakobi, Heinrich
Jakobi, Maria *SEE* Jakobi, Heinrich
Jakobik, Tomasz 17; New York, NY, 1903 *8355.1 p15*
Jakobs, Adam *SEE* Jakobs, Wendel
Jakobs, Angela; America, 1871 *5475.1 p262*
Jakobs, Angela; America, 1879 *5475.1 p376*
   *Daughter:*Elisabeth
   *Son:*Peter
Jakobs, Elisabeth Muller 33 *SEE* Jakobs, Jakob
Jakobs, Franz *SEE* Jakobs, Peter
Jakobs, Friedrich *SEE* Jakobs, Jakob
Jakobs, Gottfried *SEE* Jakobs, Peter
Jakobs, Jakob *SEE* Jakobs, Jakob
Jakobs, Jakob 32; Brazil, 1862 *5475.1 p519*
   *Wife:*Elisabeth Muller 33
   *Son:*Peter
   *Son:*Karl
   *Son:*Friedrich
   *Son:*Philipp
   *Son:*Jakob
Jakobs, Johann *SEE* Jakobs, Peter
Jakobs, Johannetta Kettenhofen *SEE* Jakobs, Wendel
Jakobs, Josef; America, 1872 *5475.1 p337*
Jakobs, Karl *SEE* Jakobs, Jakob
Jakobs, Katharina *SEE* Jakobs, Peter
Jakobs, Margarethe *SEE* Jakobs, Wendel
Jakobs, Maria 58 *SEE* Jakobs, Peter Josef
Jakobs, Maria *SEE* Jakobs, Peter
Jakobs, Maria *SEE* Jakobs, Wendel
Jakobs, Mathias; New York, 1880 *5475.1 p299*
Jakobs, Nikolaus; America, 1872 *5475.1 p306*
Jakobs, Nikolaus *SEE* Jakobs, Peter
Jakobs, Peter *SEE* Jakobs, Jakob
Jakobs, Peter *SEE* Jakobs, Peter
Jakobs, Peter; Illinois, 1880 *5475.1 p373*
   *Wife:*Therese Schonart
   *Daughter:*Maria
   *Son:*Johann
   *Son:*Gottfried
   *Daughter:*Susanna
   *Son:*Peter
   *Son:*Franz
   *Daughter:*Katharina
   *Son:*Nikolaus
Jakobs, Peter Josef 61; America, 1897 *5475.1 p25*
   *Wife:*Maria 58
Jakobs, Philipp *SEE* Jakobs, Jakob
Jakobs, Susanna *SEE* Jakobs, Peter
Jakobs, Therese Schonart *SEE* Jakobs, Peter
Jakobs, Wendel; New York, 1884 *5475.1 p167*
   *Wife:*Johannetta Kettenhofen
   *Daughter:*Margarethe
   *Son:*Adam
   *Daughter:*Maria
Jakobson, Lars; Iowa, 1875 *1211.15 p15*
Jakoby, Margarethe 41; America, 1856 *5475.1 p323*
   *Daughter:*Margarethe 19
   *Daughter:*Angela 10
   *Son:*Nikolaus 8
   *Son:*Caspar 17
Jakub, Josef, Sr.; Nebraska, 1876-1877 *2853.20 p172*
Jakubiec, Andrej 39; New York, NY, 1920 *930.50 p48*
Jakubisek, Frantisek; Texas, 1873 *2853.20 p75*
Jakubik, John; Detroit, 1929-1930 *6214.5 p69*
Jakubiszyn, Franciszek; Detroit, 1929 *1640.55 p114*
Jalageas, Philibert; Illinois, 1852 *6079.1 p7*
Jalais, Marie; Quebec, 1669 *4514.3 p327*
Jalaux, Jeanne 22; Quebec, 1646 *9221.17 p166*
Jalhr, Vincent 19; New Orleans, 1848 *778.6 p175*
Jallet, Hortense; Wisconsin, 1854-1858 *1495.20 p50*
Jalvetat, P. J. 50; New Orleans, 1840 *778.6 p175*
Jamaison, James; North Carolina, 1775 *1422.10 p57*
Jamare, Marie 20; Quebec, 1656 *9221.17 p338*
Jambel, Marie Barbe 27; Port uncertain, 1843 *778.6 p175*
Jamcotchain, M. 21; New York, NY, 1894 *6512.1 p181*
Jame, Feiska 49; Halifax, N.S., 1902 *1860.4 p43*
Jame, George 15; Halifax, N.S., 1902 *1860.4 p43*
Jame, Jean; Quebec, 1653 *9221.17 p275*

Jame, Johanne 52; Halifax, N.S., 1902 ***1860.4*** *p43*
Jame, Maria 11; Halifax, N.S., 1902 ***1860.4*** *p43*
Jame, Mary 18; Halifax, N.S., 1902 ***1860.4*** *p43*
Jame, Pauline 8; Halifax, N.S., 1902 ***1860.4*** *p43*
Jameison, Alexander 36; Ontario, 1871 ***1823.21*** *p176*
Jameison, Charles 19; Ontario, 1871 ***1823.21*** *p176*
Jameison, Mary 74; Ontario, 1871 ***1823.21*** *p176*
Jameison, Peter 67; Ontario, 1871 ***1823.21*** *p176*
James, Alfred; Wisconsin, 1800-1899 ***9228.50*** *p19A*
With wife
James, Benjamin 42; Ontario, 1871 ***1823.21*** *p176*
James, Catherine Mary; Illinois, 1930 ***121.35*** *p101*
James, Charles; Ohio, 1809-1852 ***4511.35*** *p24*
James, Charlotte 8; Quebec, 1870 ***8364.32*** *p24*
James, David 27; Ontario, 1871 ***1823.21*** *p176*
James, David L. 42; Indiana, 1880-1888 ***9076.20*** *p72*
James, Edward 32; Ontario, 1871 ***1823.21*** *p176*
James, Eleanor; Ohio, 1839-1842 ***4022.20*** *p279*
James, Ephraim; Ohio, 1809-1852 ***4511.35*** *p24*
James, Francis; Hampton, NH, 1670 ***9228.50*** *p300*
James, George 46; Ontario, 1871 ***1823.21*** *p176*
James, Henry 40; Ontario, 1871 ***1823.17*** *p78*
James, Henry 52; Ontario, 1871 ***1823.21*** *p176*
James, Henry 65; Ontario, 1871 ***1823.21*** *p176*
James, James 24; Ontario, 1871 ***1823.21*** *p176*
James, James 53; Ontario, 1871 ***1823.21*** *p176*
James, John; New York, 1778 ***8529.30*** *p6*
James, John 26; Ontario, 1871 ***1823.21*** *p176*
James, John 36; Ontario, 1871 ***1823.21*** *p176*
James, John 53; Ontario, 1871 ***1823.17*** *p78*
James, John 75; Ontario, 1871 ***1823.17*** *p78*
James, John 80; Ontario, 1871 ***1823.17*** *p78*
James, Jonathan; Colorado, 1891 ***1029.59*** *p43*
James, Joseph; Ohio, 1809-1852 ***4511.35*** *p24*
James, Joseph 36; Ontario, 1871 ***1823.21*** *p176*
James, Joseph 38; Ontario, 1871 ***1823.17*** *p78*
James, Joseph 49; Ontario, 1871 ***1823.21*** *p176*
James, Mary 40; Ontario, 1871 ***1823.21*** *p176*
James, Mary 14; Quebec, 1870 ***8364.32*** *p24*
James, Mary A. 20; Ontario, 1871 ***1823.21*** *p177*
James, McIntosh 70; Ontario, 1871 ***1823.17*** *p78*
James, Philip; New York, NY, 1899 ***1029.59*** *p43*
James, Richard 42; Ontario, 1871 ***1823.17*** *p78*
James, Tabitha 63; Ontario, 1871 ***1823.21*** *p177*
James, Thomas; Louisiana, 1850 ***7710.1*** *p151*
James, Thomas; Louisiana, 1854 ***7710.1*** *p154*
James, Thomas; Ohio, 1809-1852 ***4511.35*** *p24*
James, Thomas 38; Ontario, 1871 ***1823.17*** *p78*
James, Thomas 47; Ontario, 1871 ***1823.21*** *p177*
James, Thos 38; Ontario, 1871 ***1823.21*** *p177*
James, Titus R.; North Carolina, 1855 ***1088.45*** *p16*
James, William 52; Indiana, 1880-1888 ***9076.20*** *p72*
James, William; Ohio, 1809-1852 ***4511.35*** *p24*
James, William 15; Ontario, 1871 ***1823.21*** *p177*
James, William 28; Ontario, 1871 ***1823.21*** *p177*
James, William 47; Ontario, 1871 ***1823.21*** *p177*
James, William 64; Ontario, 1871 ***1823.21*** *p177*
James, William; Philadelphia, 1777 ***8529.30*** *p7A*
James, William E.M.; Washington, 1886 ***2770.40*** *p195*
Jameson, Hugh 44; Ontario, 1871 ***1823.17*** *p79*
Jamieson, Agnes 68; Ontario, 1871 ***1823.17*** *p79*
Jamieson, Alexander 36; Ontario, 1871 ***1823.21*** *p177*
Jamieson, Andrew 70; Ontario, 1871 ***1823.21*** *p177*
Jamieson, Anne 30; Ontario, 1871 ***1823.21*** *p177*
Jamieson, Archibald 69; Ontario, 1871 ***1823.17*** *p79*
Jamieson, Catherine 21; Ontario, 1871 ***1823.21*** *p177*
Jamieson, James 33; Ontario, 1871 ***1823.17*** *p79*
Jamieson, Robert 10; Ontario, 1871 ***1823.21*** *p177*
Jamieson, Robert 30; Ontario, 1871 ***1823.21*** *p177*
Jamieson, Sarah Lewis; Chicago, 1830-1900 ***9228.50*** *p145*
Jamieson, Thomas 43; Ontario, 1871 ***1823.17*** *p79*
Jamieson, Wm 32; Ontario, 1871 ***1823.21*** *p177*
Jamieson, Wm 39; Ontario, 1871 ***1823.21*** *p177*
Jamison, Edmund 26; Ontario, 1871 ***1823.17*** *p79*
Jamison, Elizabeth 41; Michigan, 1880 ***4491.30*** *p17*
Jamison, Harry; Colorado, 1884 ***1029.59*** *p43*
Jamison, Henry; Colorado, 1876 ***1029.59*** *p44*
Jamison, Henry 62; Ontario, 1871 ***1823.17*** *p79*
Jamison, James; North Carolina, 1834 ***1088.45*** *p16*
Jamison, James W.; Colorado, 1887 ***1029.59*** *p44*
Jamison, John 40; Ontario, 1871 ***1823.21*** *p177*
Jamison, Joseph; New York, 1776 ***8529.30*** *p2*
Jamison, Tomas 35; Michigan, 1880 ***4491.30*** *p17*
Jamison, William; Ohio, 1809-1852 ***4511.35*** *p24*
Jamison, William 30; Ontario, 1871 ***1823.21*** *p177*
Jammision, James 39; Ontario, 1871 ***1823.21*** *p177*
Jamrosz, Frank 37; New York, NY, 1920 ***930.50*** *p49*
Jamroz, Chester; Detroit, 1930 ***1640.60*** *p78*
Jams, Consant 17; America, 1846 ***778.6*** *p175*
Jams, Elise 42; America, 1846 ***778.6*** *p175*
Janacek, . . .; Pennsylvania, 1750-1799 ***2853.20*** *p17*
Janacek Family ; Iowa, 1870 ***2853.20*** *p202*
Janak, Frantisek; Nebraska, 1876 ***2853.20*** *p172*
Janak, Jan; Nebraska, 1875 ***2853.20*** *p172*
Janak, Jan; Nebraska, 1898 ***2853.20*** *p145*
Janda, Alois; Chicago, 1869-1910 ***2853.20*** *p517*
Janda, Jan; Texas, 1860 ***2853.20*** *p68*
*Brother:*Karel
Janda, Jan; Wisconsin, 1856 ***2853.20*** *p345*
Janda, Josef; Galveston, TX, 1856 ***2853.20*** *p63*
Janda, Josef; Texas, 1856 ***2853.20*** *p68*
Janda, Karel *SEE* Janda, Jan
Janda, Vaclav; South Dakota, 1869-1871 ***2853.20*** *p246*
Jandova, Karolina; Nebraska, 1860-1910 ***2853.20*** *p168*
Jandrain, Alexis *SEE* Jandrain, Francois
Jandrain, Anne; Wisconsin, 1854-1858 ***1495.20*** *p50*
Jandrain, Anne-Joseph Lecocq *SEE* Jandrain, Francois
Jandrain, Francois; Wisconsin, 1856 ***1495.20*** *p12*
*Wife:*Anne-Joseph Lecocq
*Son:*Alexis
Jandron, . . .; South Carolina, n.d. ***9228.50*** *p300*
Jandron, Francis Lyster; Detroit, 1850-1921 ***9228.50*** *p300*
Jandron, Francis Lyster; Quebec, 1850-1921 ***9228.50*** *p300*
Janecek, Jan; Nebraska, 1850-1910 ***2853.20*** *p182*
Janecek, Josef; Detroit, 1889 ***2853.20*** *p360*
Janecek, Josef; Milwaukee, 1854 ***2853.20*** *p308*
Janes, Charles M. 46; Ontario, 1871 ***1823.17*** *p79*
Janes, John; New York, 1783 ***8529.30*** *p13*
Janes, Samuel 75; Ontario, 1871 ***1823.17*** *p79*
Janes, William 51; Ontario, 1871 ***1823.21*** *p177*
Janes, William 15; Quebec, 1870 ***8364.32*** *p24*
Janet, James 25; Ontario, 1871 ***1823.17*** *p79*
Janeway, John; Louisiana, 1874 ***4981.45*** *p296*
Janfret, J. 37; America, 1842 ***778.6*** *p175*
Jangester, Mr. 35; Louisiana, 1840 ***778.6*** *p175*
Janghen, Cath. 33; New York, NY, 1847 ***9176.15*** *p51*
Janghen, Conrad 33; New York, NY, 1847 ***9176.15*** *p50*
Janghen, Richard 3; New York, NY, 1847 ***9176.15*** *p51*
Janich, N. 28; New Orleans, 1844 ***778.6*** *p175*
Janicka, Elisabeth; Wisconsin, 1885 ***6795.8*** *p58*
Janicke, Mr.; America, 1852 ***7420.1*** *p91*
With wife
With daughter sister-in-law & brother-in-law
Janicke, Kolon; America, 1852 ***7420.1*** *p96*
With family
Janicki, Anton; Wisconsin, 1893 ***6795.8*** *p58*
Janicki, Elisabeth; Wisconsin, 1885 ***6795.8*** *p58*
Janin, Dr. 45; America, 1840 ***778.6*** *p175*
Janin, Mr. 44; America, 1844 ***778.6*** *p175*
Janin, Aline 16; New Orleans, 1848 ***778.6*** *p175*
Janin, Lazare 33; America, 1843 ***778.6*** *p175*
Janiszewska, Josephine; Detroit, 1890 ***9980.23*** *p97*
Janiszewski, Marian; Galveston, TX, 1885 ***6015.15*** *p11*
Janitzki, John; Wisconsin, 1889 ***6795.8*** *p69*
Janius, Nicolas 31; New Orleans, 1841 ***778.6*** *p175*
Jankard, Charles; New York, NY, 1870 ***1494.20*** *p11*
Janke, Christine *SEE* Janke, Gottfried
Janke, Friedrich; South Dakota, 1887 ***554.30*** *p26*
*Wife:*Salome
Janke, Gottfried; Dakota, 1889 ***554.30*** *p26*
*Wife:*Christine
Janke, Henriette; Wisconsin, 1907 ***6795.8*** *p177*
Janke, Louis Martin; Wisconsin, 1884 ***6795.8*** *p165*
Janke, Salome *SEE* Janke, Friedrich
Janko, Jan; Iowa, 1859 ***2853.20*** *p228*
Jankowska, Anne; Wisconsin, 1891 ***6795.8*** *p58*
Jankowski, Michal 33; New York, NY, 1920 ***930.50*** *p48*
Jankowski, Wm.; Wisconsin, 1878 ***6795.8*** *p50*
Janne, Joseph 25; Mississippi, 1845 ***778.6*** *p175*
Jannery, John; New York, 1782 ***8529.30*** *p13*
Jannin, Claude 37; Missouri, 1845 ***778.6*** *p175*
Jannin, Victor; Ohio, 1809-1852 ***4511.35*** *p24*
Jannsen, William; Iowa, 1875 ***1211.15*** *p15*
Janoski, Frederick; Wisconsin, 1908 ***1822.55*** *p10*
Janot, Antoine; Quebec, 1662 ***9221.17*** *p488*
Janot, Jacques; Quebec, 1659 ***9221.17*** *p414*
Janot, Marin 26; Montreal, 1653 ***9221.17*** *p293*
Janouch, Frantisek; Wisconsin, 1856-1910 ***2853.20*** *p345*
Janousek, Frantisek; Nebraska, 1869-1910 ***2853.20*** *p193*
Janovsky, Josef; St. Louis, 1896 ***2853.20*** *p54*
Jansdotter, Anna 36; Kansas, 1880 ***777.40*** *p4*
Jansdotter, Anna 36; Kansas, 1880 ***777.40*** *p4*
Jansdotter, Anna 12 *SEE* Jansdotter, Anna
Jansdotter, Anna 22; New York, 1856 ***6529.11*** *p21*
Jansdotter, Anna 55; New York, 1856 ***6529.11*** *p22*
*Daughter:*Anna 12
Jansdotter, Brita; Iowa, 1867-1869 ***777.40*** *p9*
Jansdotter, Lena; Iowa, 1842-1868 ***777.40*** *p10*
Jansdotter, Martha; Iowa, 1865-1878 ***777.40*** *p4*
Jansen, Andrew; Iowa, 1875 ***1211.15*** *p15*
Jansen, Anna; Colorado, 1881 ***1029.59*** *p44*
Jansen, Frank Jacob; New York, 1888 ***1766.20*** *p36*
Jansen, Heinrich; America, 1862 ***5475.1*** *p504*
Jansen, Jakob 28; America, 1865 ***5475.1*** *p504*
Jansen, Jan; Colorado, 1883 ***1029.59*** *p44*
Jansing, Amalie 35; New York, NY, 1864 ***8425.62*** *p198*
Jansing, Heinr. 54; New York, NY, 1864 ***8425.62*** *p198*
Janska, Miss; America, 1874 ***2853.20*** *p168*
Janson, Bernhard; Cleveland, OH, 1890-1897 ***9722.10*** *p121*
Janson, John Adrian; Cleveland, OH, 1906 ***9722.10*** *p121*
Janssen, Bernhard; Iowa, 1915 ***1211.15*** *p15*
Janssen, Frans Oscar; Cleveland, OH, 1902-1904 ***9722.10*** *p121*
Janssen, Heinr 10 months; New York, NY, 1864 ***8425.62*** *p196*
Janssen, Hermann 41; New York, NY, 1864 ***8425.62*** *p196*
Janssen, Margaretha 28; New York, NY, 1864 ***8425.62*** *p196*
Jansson, Anders *SEE* Jansson, Anders Johan
Jansson, Anders Johan; America, 1869 ***777.40*** *p27*
*Wife:*Maria Lisa Andersdotter
*Stepchild:*Anders
Jansson, Aron; Cleveland, OH, 1888 ***9722.10*** *p121*
Jansson, C. Aug.; New Orleans, 1856 ***6412.40*** *p154*
Jansson, J.F.; New York, NY, 1847 ***6412.40*** *p150*
Jansson, L.; New York, NY, 1846 ***6412.40*** *p149*
Jansson, Maria Lisa Andersdotter *SEE* Jansson, Anders Johan
Jansson, Petter; New York, NY, 1845 ***6412.40*** *p148*
Jansson, Svante; Philadelphia, 1847 ***6412.40*** *p150*
Jansson, Sven Fredrik; North America, 1854 ***6410.15*** *p104*
Jantz, Christen; North Carolina, 1710 ***3629.40*** *p5*
Jantz, Dichtli Benedicta; North Carolina, 1710 ***3629.40*** *p5*
Jantz, Zioria; North Carolina, 1710 ***3629.40*** *p5*
Janverin, Richard; Salem, MA, 1699 ***9228.50*** *p19A*
Janvrin, Mr.; New England, 1800-1840 ***9228.50*** *p300*
With 2 brothers
Janvrin, Daniel; New England, 1681 ***9228.50*** *p306*
Janvrin, Florence; Ottawa, 1800-1899 ***9228.50*** *p306*
Janvrin, George; Boston, 1600-1699 ***9228.50*** *p300*
Janvrin, George; Boston, 1719 ***9228.50*** *p304*
Janvrin, Jean; Portsmouth, NH, 1670-1699 ***9228.50*** *p300*
Janvrin, John; Boston, 1715 ***9228.50*** *p306*
Janvrin, John; New Hampshire, 1769-1801 ***9228.50*** *p303*
Janvrin, John; New York, 1600-1699 ***9228.50*** *p300*
Janvrin, Richard; Salem, MA, 1700 ***9228.50*** *p18A*
Janvrin, Thomas; Maine, 1648 ***9228.50*** *p306*
Janz, Hermann Albert; Wisconsin, 1892 ***6795.8*** *p63*
Japes, Henry 34; Ontario, 1871 ***1823.17*** *p79*
Jaque, Eugene; New York, NY, 1856 ***1494.21*** *p31*
Jaquen, Rosalie 62; New Orleans, 1848 ***778.6*** *p175*
Jaques, Alexandre 1; Missouri, 1846 ***778.6*** *p176*
Jaques, Baptiste 2; Missouri, 1846 ***778.6*** *p176*
Jaques, Baptiste 32; Missouri, 1846 ***778.6*** *p176*
Jaques, Francoise 37; Missouri, 1846 ***778.6*** *p176*
Jaques, Frederic 30; Missouri, 1848 ***778.6*** *p176*
Jaques, Nigles 60; Ontario, 1871 ***1823.21*** *p177*
Jaques, Veuve 58; Missouri, 1848 ***778.6*** *p176*
Jaquet, John; Louisiana, 1874-1875 ***4981.45*** *p29*
Jaquet, Julian; Ohio, 1809-1852 ***4511.35*** *p24*
Jaqus, John 80; Ontario, 1871 ***1823.21*** *p177*
Jarabere, Mr. 20; Louisiana, 1848 ***778.6*** *p176*
Jardin, Erquel 22; America, 1846 ***778.6*** *p176*
Jardin, Sebastien 20; St. Louis, 1847 ***778.6*** *p176*
Jardine, John; New Jersey, 1665 ***9228.50*** *p180*
Jardine, Joseph 43; Ontario, 1871 ***1823.17*** *p79*
Jardine, Robert 68; Ontario, 1871 ***1823.17*** *p79*
Jardinel, Claude 28; New Orleans, 1848 ***778.6*** *p176*
Jarensslas, Constance 28; Missouri, 1845 ***778.6*** *p176*
Jarmain, Henry 50; Ontario, 1871 ***1823.21*** *p177*
Jarman, Benjamin 65; Ontario, 1871 ***1823.21*** *p177*
Jarman, Daniel; Philadelphia, 1777 ***8529.30*** *p2*
Jarmin, William 52; Ontario, 1871 ***1823.21*** *p177*
Jarninais, Francois 20; America, 1847 ***778.6*** *p176*
Jarno, Jean Pierre 28; New Orleans, 1848 ***778.6*** *p176*
Jarosz, Maryanna 18; New York, NY, 1911 ***6533.11*** *p10*
Jarousseau, Jacquette 41; Quebec, 1653 ***9221.17*** *p275*
*Daughter:*Suzanne 10
Jarousseau, Suzanne 10 *SEE* Jarousseau, Jacquette Tourault
Jaroussel, Jacquette 41; Quebec, 1653 ***9221.17*** *p275*
*Daughter:*Suzanne 10
Jaroussel, Suzanne 10 *SEE* Jaroussel, Jacquette Tourault
Jarratt, Andrew; New York, 1783 ***8529.30*** *p13*
Jarret deVercheres, Francois; Quebec, 1665 ***2314.30*** *p167*
Jarret deVercheres, Francois; Quebec, 1665 ***2314.30*** *p185*
Jarrett, James 36; Ontario, 1871 ***1823.17*** *p79*
Jarrith, Elijah 39; Ontario, 1871 ***1823.21*** *p177*
Jarry, Andre; Quebec, 1659 ***9221.17*** *p403*
Jarry, Eloi; Montreal, 1653 ***9221.17*** *p293*

Jarry, Pierre 32; Quebec, 1658 ***9221.17*** *p383*
Jarves, Deming *SEE* Jarves, John Jackson
Jarves, Hannah Seabury *SEE* Jarves, John
Jarves, Hannah Seabury *SEE* Jarves, John Jackson
Jarves, John; Boston, 1787 ***9228.50*** *p25*
*Wife:*Hannah Seabury
Jarves, John Jackson; Boston, 1787 ***9228.50*** *p306*
*Wife:*Hannah Seabury
*Son:*Deming
Jarvi, Peter 52; Minnesota, 1925 ***2769.54*** *p1383*
Jarvinpaa, John 35; Minnesota, 1925 ***2769.54*** *p1381*
Jarvis, Deming *SEE* Jarvis, John Jackson
Jarvis, Elizabeth; Columbus, OH, 1852 ***9228.50*** *p158*
Jarvis, George; America, 1874 ***9076.20*** *p69*
Jarvis, Hannah Seabury *SEE* Jarvis, John Jackson
Jarvis, John Jackson; Boston, 1787 ***9228.50*** *p306*
*Wife:*Hannah Seabury
*Son:*Deming
Jarvis, Saney 65; Ontario, 1871 ***1823.21*** *p177*
Jarvs, Thomas 49; Ontario, 1871 ***1823.21*** *p177*
Jarwice, Paul 48; Ontario, 1871 ***1823.17*** *p79*
Jary, William; Maryland, 1671 ***1236.25*** *p46*
Jarzyna, Catharina; Wisconsin, 1886 ***6795.8*** *p38*
Jasek, Frantisek; Wisconsin, 1857-1861 ***2853.20*** *p334*
Jasel, Ohlila 23; America, 1845 ***778.6*** *p176*
Jasper, Rose; Colorado, 1903 ***1029.59*** *p44*
Jasselin, Marguerite; Quebec, 1670 ***4514.3*** *p327*
Jaszezyk, Mary; Wisconsin, 1900 ***6795.8*** *p67*
Jatha, Friedr.; Valdivia, Chile, 1852 ***1192.4*** *p55*
Jauillard, John; Ohio, 1809-1852 ***4511.35*** *p24*
Jaulliard, John; Ohio, 1809-1852 ***4511.35*** *p24*
Jaumain, Emile; Boston, 1883 ***1494.20*** *p13*
Jauquet, Nicolas J.; Boston, 1870 ***1494.20*** *p12*
Javelot, Anne; Quebec, 1666 ***4514.3*** *p327*
Javet, Hypolithe 18; New Orleans, 1848 ***778.6*** *p176*
Javorsky, Antonin; Iowa, 1856-1858 ***2853.20*** *p211*
Javorsky, Josef; Iowa, 1856-1858 ***2853.20*** *p211*
Jawarski, Andrew; Texas, 1915-1920 ***6015.15*** *p26*
Jaworski, Andrew; Texas, 1915-1920 ***6015.15*** *p26*
Jaworski, Clemens; Wisconsin, 1886 ***6795.8*** *p44*
Jaworski, Mary; New York, NY, 1891 ***6015.15*** *p29*
Jazdzewski, Anne; Wisconsin, 1891 ***6795.8*** *p58*
Jeach, William; Marston's Wharf, 1782 ***8529.30*** *p13*
Jean, . . .; Canada, 1700-1799 ***9228.50*** *p307*
Jean, Mr. 38; New Orleans, 1847 ***778.6*** *p176*
Jean, Augustine 28; New England, 1675-1676 ***9228.50*** *p268*
Jean, Denis 22; Quebec, 1654 ***9221.17*** *p310*
Jean, Estienne; Quebec, 1659 ***9221.17*** *p414*
Jean, Francois 27; Missouri, 1846 ***778.6*** *p176*
Jean, J. B. 20; America, 1845 ***778.6*** *p176*
Jean, Jean 30; New Orleans, 1840 ***778.6*** *p176*
Jeandebot, Adolphe 9; Louisiana, 1848 ***778.6*** *p176*
Jeandebot, Alexis 18; Louisiana, 1848 ***778.6*** *p176*
Jeandebot, Auguste 12; Louisiana, 1848 ***778.6*** *p176*
Jeandebot, Charles 25; Louisiana, 1848 ***778.6*** *p176*
Jeandebot, Dorothee 34; Louisiana, 1848 ***778.6*** *p176*
Jeandebot, Elisab. 30; Louisiana, 1848 ***778.6*** *p176*
Jeandebot, Fois. 7; Louisiana, 1848 ***778.6*** *p176*
Jeandebot, Honore 10; Louisiana, 1848 ***778.6*** *p176*
Jeandebot, Honore 17; Louisiana, 1848 ***778.6*** *p176*
Jeandebot, Jonpierre 13; Louisiana, 1848 ***778.6*** *p176*
Jeandebot, Joseph 26; Louisiana, 1848 ***778.6*** *p176*
Jeandebot, Julie 50; Louisiana, 1848 ***778.6*** *p176*
Jeandebot, Leonore 5; Louisiana, 1848 ***778.6*** *p176*
Jeandebot, Leonore 5; Louisiana, 1848 ***778.6*** *p177*
Jeandebot, Napoleon 37; Louisiana, 1848 ***778.6*** *p177*
Jeandebot, Odile 44; Louisiana, 1848 ***778.6*** *p177*
Jeandebot, Xavier 6; Louisiana, 1848 ***778.6*** *p177*
Jean DeParis, Jacques 16; Quebec, 1652 ***9221.17*** *p254*
Jeandron, Jean; Louisiana, 1874 ***4981.45*** *p132*
Jeandron, John Edward; Quebec, 1865 ***9228.50*** *p307*
Jeandron, William John; New Jersey, 1866-1930 ***9228.50*** *p307*
Jeanes, John; Port uncertain, n.d. ***8529.30*** *p13*
Jeannin, Aime 17; America, 1843 ***778.6*** *p177*
Jeannin, Auguste 19; America, 1843 ***778.6*** *p177*
Jeannin, Augustine 15; America, 1843 ***778.6*** *p177*
Jeannin, Jacques 18; America, 1843 ***778.6*** *p177*
Jeannin, Jean 64; America, 1843 ***778.6*** *p177*
Jeannin, Josephine 28; America, 1843 ***778.6*** *p177*
Jeannin, Marie 10; America, 1843 ***778.6*** *p177*
Jeannin, Marie 57; America, 1843 ***778.6*** *p177*
Jeannin, Victor; Ohio, 1809-1852 ***4511.35*** *p24*
Jeanquart, Charles; New York, NY, 1870 ***1494.20*** *p11*
Jeanquart, Emil; New York, NY, 1870 ***1494.20*** *p11*
Jeans, John; Port uncertain, n.d. ***8529.30*** *p13*
Jeantee, Jean 21; Port uncertain, 1843 ***778.6*** *p177*
Jeantrit, Francois 21; America, 1840 ***778.6*** *p177*
Jeay, Jan 36; America, 1843 ***778.6*** *p177*
Jebaser, Francis 10; Port uncertain, 1841 ***778.6*** *p177*
Jebaser, Jean 41; Port uncertain, 1841 ***778.6*** *p177*
Jebaser, Mary 40; Port uncertain, 1841 ***778.6*** *p177*
Jebaser, Nicolas 3; Port uncertain, 1841 ***778.6*** *p177*
Jebaser, Paulean 1; Port uncertain, 1841 ***778.6*** *p177*
Jebenne, J. J. 24; America, 1843 ***778.6*** *p177*
Jecker, Christian 19; America, 1880 ***5475.1*** *p456*
Jecmenek, Josef; Texas, 1856 ***2853.20*** *p64*
*Brother:*Pavel
Jecmenek, Pavel *SEE* Jecmenek, Josef
Jederberg, Jon 25; New York, 1856 ***6529.11*** *p22*
Jederstrom, Jons 30; New York, 1856 ***6529.11*** *p22*
Jedurin, Mr. 35; America, 1842 ***778.6*** *p177*
Jeeves, John 20; Quebec, 1870 ***8364.32*** *p24*
Jeffard, Jacques; Quebec, 1637 ***9221.17*** *p70*
Jefferds, John; Salem, MA, 1650-1750 ***9228.50*** *p307*
Jefferies, William 29; Ontario, 1871 ***1823.21*** *p178*
Jefferson, John 71; Ontario, 1871 ***1823.21*** *p178*
Jeffery, Ann 48; Michigan, 1880 ***4491.33*** *p12*
Jeffery, Anna 7; Michigan, 1880 ***4491.33*** *p12*
Jeffery, Arthur 10; Michigan, 1880 ***4491.33*** *p12*
Jeffery, Clara 14; Michigan, 1880 ***4491.33*** *p12*
Jeffery, Elizabeth 45; Ontario, 1871 ***1823.21*** *p178*
Jeffery, John; Ohio, 1833 ***5024.1*** *p138*
Jeffery, Joseph 42; Ontario, 1871 ***1823.21*** *p178*
Jeffery, Richard 57; Ontario, 1871 ***1823.21*** *p178*
Jeffery, Robert; Marston's Wharf, 1782 ***8529.30*** *p13*
Jeffery, Robert 46; Michigan, 1880 ***4491.33*** *p12*
Jeffery, Samuel; Philadelphia, 1778 ***8529.30*** *p3A*
Jeffery, Thomas 18; Michigan, 1880 ***4491.33*** *p12*
Jeffery, William 50; Ontario, 1871 ***1823.21*** *p178*
Jefferys, Ambrose G.; Washington, 1882 ***2770.40*** *p135*
Jefferys, Arthur 31; Ontario, 1871 ***1823.21*** *p178*
Jeffrey, Henry 36; Ontario, 1871 ***1823.21*** *p178*
Jeffrey, James 35; Ontario, 1871 ***1823.21*** *p178*
Jeffrey, James 46; Ontario, 1871 ***1823.21*** *p178*
Jeffrey, John 30; Ontario, 1871 ***1823.21*** *p178*
Jeffrey, John 52; Ontario, 1871 ***1823.21*** *p178*
Jeffries, James; North Carolina, 1821 ***1088.45*** *p16*
Jeffries, Stephen 51; Ontario, 1871 ***1823.21*** *p178*
Jeffries, W. 15; Quebec, 1870 ***8364.32*** *p24*
Jeffry, William 41; Ontario, 1871 ***1823.17*** *p79*
Jegarski, Peter; New York, NY, 1881 ***6015.15*** *p30*
Jegarski, Peter; Texas, 1900 ***6015.15*** *p25*
Jegg, Carl 13; Halifax, N.S., 1902 ***1860.4*** *p40*
Jegg, Carl 49; Halifax, N.S., 1902 ***1860.4*** *p40*
Jegg, Friederika 6; Halifax, N.S., 1902 ***1860.4*** *p40*
Jegg, Jacob 16; Halifax, N.S., 1902 ***1860.4*** *p40*
Jegg, Jacob 35; Halifax, N.S., 1902 ***1860.4*** *p40*
Jegg, Johannes 4; Halifax, N.S., 1902 ***1860.4*** *p40*
Jegg, Magdalene 8; Halifax, N.S., 1902 ***1860.4*** *p40*
Jegg, Margaretha 11; Halifax, N.S., 1902 ***1860.4*** *p40*
Jegg, Margaretha 41; Halifax, N.S., 1902 ***1860.4*** *p40*
Jegle, Ph.; New York, 1859 ***358.56*** *p55*
Jehan, Lucy; Ohio, 1846 ***9228.50*** *p307*
With sister
Jehanne, Gregoire; Quebec, 1654 ***9221.17*** *p310*
Jehl, Anna 13; America, 1847 ***778.6*** *p177*
Jehl, Jacques 15; America, 1847 ***778.6*** *p177*
Jehl, Jean 45; America, 1847 ***778.6*** *p177*
Jehl, Maria 11; America, 1847 ***778.6*** *p177*
Jehl, Maria 35; America, 1847 ***778.6*** *p177*
Jehl, Pierre 1; America, 1847 ***778.6*** *p177*
Jehle, Babette Dusel *SEE* Jehle, Jacob
Jehle, Jacob; Philadelphia, 1859 ***8513.31*** *p317*
*Wife:*Babette Dusel
Jehli, Jos Anton; Washington, 1887 ***2770.40*** *p24*
Jeis, Conrad; New Orleans, 1840 ***778.6*** *p177*
Jelden, John; Iowa, 1895 ***1211.15*** *p15*
Jelen, John; Colorado, 1891 ***1029.59*** *p44*
Jelh, J. 30; America, 1843 ***778.6*** *p177*
Jelinek, Frantisek *SEE* Jelinek, Vaclav
Jelinek, Jan; Chicago, 1910 ***2853.20*** *p421*
Jelinek, Jan; Minnesota, 1857 ***2853.20*** *p259*
Jelinek, Josef *SEE* Jelinek, Vaclav
Jelinek, Matej; St. Paul, MN, 1868 ***2853.20*** *p277*
Jelinek, Vaclav; Wisconsin, 1854 ***2853.20*** *p155*
*Son:*Frantisek
*Son:*Vit
*Son:*Josef
Jelinek, Vit *SEE* Jelinek, Vaclav
Jell, Horatis 44; Ontario, 1871 ***1823.21*** *p178*
Jelly, Henry 16; Ontario, 1871 ***1823.21*** *p178*
Jelly, Jane E. 18; Ontario, 1871 ***1823.21*** *p178*
Jelly, Mabella 20; Ontario, 1871 ***1823.21*** *p178*
Jelly, Mary H. 16; Ontario, 1871 ***1823.21*** *p178*
Jelly, William 62; Ontario, 1871 ***1823.21*** *p178*
Jelonek, Ludwicka; Philadelphia, 1850 ***8513.31*** *p323*
Jeltz, Mr. 37; Port uncertain, 1840 ***778.6*** *p177*
Jemison, Patrick 71; Ontario, 1871 ***1823.21*** *p178*
Jemmes, Martin; Quebec, 1651 ***9221.17*** *p244*
Jemmison, Joseph; New York, 1776 ***8529.30*** *p2*
Jena, Elizabeth; Utah, 1855 ***9228.50*** *p193*
Jena, Elizabeth; Utah, 1855 ***9228.50*** *p193*
Jenander, Charles; Galveston, TX, 1855 ***571.7*** *p17*
Jenc, F.; New York, NY, 1888 ***2853.20*** *p109*
Jenc, Jan; Baltimore, 1882 ***2853.20*** *p129*
Jenc, Jan; New York, NY, 1888 ***2853.20*** *p110*
Jenck, John; Colorado, 1891 ***1029.59*** *p44*
Jene, Dorothea 22 *SEE* Jene, Philipp
Jene, Johann; America, 1847 ***5475.1*** *p537*
Jene, Philipp 27; America, 1854 ***5475.1*** *p74*
*Sister:*Dorothea 22
Jenesse, Anne 38; Missouri, 1845 ***778.6*** *p177*
Jenesse, Benjamin 3 months; Missouri, 1845 ***778.6*** *p178*
Jenesse, Etienne 11; Missouri, 1845 ***778.6*** *p178*
Jenesse, Felix 2; Missouri, 1845 ***778.6*** *p178*
Jenesse, Francois 8; Missouri, 1845 ***778.6*** *p178*
Jenesse, Jean 38; Missouri, 1845 ***778.6*** *p178*
Jenesse, Remy 5; Missouri, 1845 ***778.6*** *p178*
Jenesse, Virginie 9; Missouri, 1845 ***778.6*** *p178*
Jeneto, Mr. 50; America, 1846 ***778.6*** *p178*
Jeneto, Mrs. 42; America, 1846 ***778.6*** *p178*
Jenewe, Elisabeth *SEE* Jenewe, Peter
Jenewe, Elisabeth Keip *SEE* Jenewe, Peter
Jenewe, Jakob *SEE* Jenewe, Peter
Jenewe, Johann; America, 1846 ***5475.1*** *p514*
Jenewe, Katharina *SEE* Jenewe, Peter
Jenewe, Maria *SEE* Jenewe, Peter
Jenewe, Peter *SEE* Jenewe, Peter
Jenewe, Peter; America, 1857 ***5475.1*** *p514*
*Wife:*Elisabeth Keip
*Daughter:*Maria
*Son:*Jakob
*Daughter:*Katharina
*Daughter:*Elisabeth
*Son:*Peter
Jenewe, Wendel; America, 1846 ***5475.1*** *p514*
Jenewein, Christian *SEE* Jenewein, Nikolaus
Jenewein, J. Jakob *SEE* Jenewein, Nikolaus
Jenewein, Joh. Nikolaus *SEE* Jenewein, Joh. Philipp
Jenewein, Joh. Philipp; America, 1835 ***5475.1*** *p457*
*Wife:*Magdalena Wolfanger
*Daughter:*M. Karoline
*Daughter:*Sophie
*Daughter:*M. Katharina
*Son:*Joh. Nikolaus
*Daughter:*Margarethe
Jenewein, Johann; America, 1846 ***5475.1*** *p514*
Jenewein, Karl; America, 1841 ***5475.1*** *p458*
Jenewein, Kath. Leibenguth *SEE* Jenewein, Nikolaus
Jenewein, L. Katharina *SEE* Jenewein, Nikolaus
Jenewein, M. Karoline *SEE* Jenewein, Joh. Philipp
Jenewein, M. Katharina *SEE* Jenewein, Joh. Philipp
Jenewein, Magdalena Wolfanger *SEE* Jenewein, Joh. Philipp
Jenewein, Margarethe *SEE* Jenewein, Joh. Philipp
Jenewein, Nikolaus; America, 1836 ***5475.1*** *p458*
*Wife:*Kath. Leibenguth
*Daughter:*L. Katharina
*Son:*J. Jakob
*Son:*Christian
Jenewein, Sophie *SEE* Jenewein, Joh. Philipp
Jenior, John; Ohio, 1809-1852 ***4511.35*** *p25*
Jenista, Jan *SEE* Jenista, Jan
Jenista, Jan; Wisconsin, 1854 ***2853.20*** *p304*
*Son:*Jan
*Son:*Matej
*Son:*Josef
Jenista, Josef *SEE* Jenista, Jan
Jenista, Matej *SEE* Jenista, Jan
Jenken, John 40; Ontario, 1871 ***1823.17*** *p79*
Jenkens, Pierre Joseph; New York, NY, 1866 ***1494.20*** *p12*
Jenkin, Alex 48; Ontario, 1871 ***1823.17*** *p79*
Jenkins, Ann *SEE* Jenkins, David
Jenkins, Benjamin 40; Ontario, 1871 ***1823.21*** *p178*
Jenkins, Catherine *SEE* Jenkins, James
Jenkins, Charles 31; Ontario, 1871 ***1823.17*** *p79*
Jenkins, D. J. *SEE* Jenkins, Evan
Jenkins, David *SEE* Jenkins, Moses
Jenkins, David; Ohio, 1846 ***4022.20*** *p281*
*Wife:*Mary
*Child:*Ann
Jenkins, David J. *SEE* Jenkins, James
Jenkins, David T.; Ohio, 1836 ***4022.20*** *p281*
Jenkins, Edward J. *SEE* Jenkins, Evan
Jenkins, Elizabeth *SEE* Jenkins, Evan
Jenkins, Elizabeth *SEE* Jenkins, Moses
Jenkins, Elizabeth 18; Ontario, 1871 ***1823.21*** *p178*
Jenkins, Elizabeth 87; Ontario, 1871 ***1823.21*** *p178*
Jenkins, Evan; Ohio, 1837 ***4022.20*** *p281*
*Wife:*Elizabeth
*Child:*D. J.
*Child:*John
*Child:*Edward J.
Jenkins, George 24; Ontario, 1871 ***1823.21*** *p178*
Jenkins, Hannah *SEE* Jenkins, Moses
Jenkins, Henry; North Carolina, 1811 ***1088.45*** *p16*

Jenkins, James; Ohio, 1837 4022.20 p281
Wife:Jane
Child:David J.
Child:Catherine
Jenkins, Jane SEE Jenkins, James
Jenkins, John; Boston, 1766 1642 p36
Jenkins, John; Marston's Wharf, 1782 8529.30 p13
Jenkins, John SEE Jenkins, Evan
Jenkins, John; Ohio, 1849 4022.20 p281
With wife
With children
Child:Margaret
Jenkins, John 62; Ontario, 1871 1823.21 p178
Jenkins, Margaret SEE Jenkins, Moses
Jenkins, Margaret SEE Jenkins, John
Jenkins, Mary; Ohio, 1837 4022.20 p274
Jenkins, Mary; Ohio, 1838-1841 4022.20 p273
Jenkins, Mary SEE Jenkins, David
Jenkins, Mary 16; Ontario, 1871 1823.21 p178
Jenkins, Mary 20; Ontario, 1871 1823.17 p79
Jenkins, Masting 63; Ontario, 1871 1823.21 p178
Jenkins, Moses; Ohio, 1839 4022.20 p281
Wife:Elizabeth
Child:Margaret
Child:Hannah
Child:David
Child:Stephen
Child:Thomas
Jenkins, Pierre Joseph; New York, NY, 1866 1494.20 p12
Jenkins, Sarah; Ohio, 1839 4022.20 p279
Jenkins, Stephen SEE Jenkins, Moses
Jenkins, Thomas; New York, 1777 8529.30 p3A
Jenkins, Thomas 25; New York, NY, 1825 6178.50 p78
Jenkins, Thomas SEE Jenkins, Moses
Jenkins, William 31; Ontario, 1871 1823.21 p178
Jenkins, William 35; Ontario, 1871 1823.21 p178
Jenkins, Wm 45; Ontario, 1871 1823.21 p178
Jenkinson, George 45; Ontario, 1871 1823.17 p79
Jenkinson, William 60; Ontario, 1871 1823.17 p79
Jenks, Thomas; Louisiana, 1836-1840 4981.45 p212
Jenne, . . .; Boston, 1769 9228.50 p5
Jenne, Andreas; Louisiana, 1841-1844 4981.45 p210
Jenne, John; Boston, 1769 9228.50 p48
Jenne, John; Boston, 1769 9228.50 p308
Jennee, . . .; Vermont, n.d. 9228.50 p308
Jenner, Anna Maria; New York, 1884 5475.1 p71
Jenner, Barbara Steffen SEE Jenner, Paul
Jenner, Emilie; America, 1868 7919.3 p529
Jenner, Kaspar SEE Jenner, Paul
Jenner, Paul; America, 1800-1899 5475.1 p148
Wife:Barbara Steffen
Son:Kaspar
Jennerman, Christoph; Wisconsin, 1874 6795.8 p117
Jennes, Nicholas; Massachusetts, n.d. 9228.50 p308
Jennes, Samuel SEE Jennes, Simon
Jennes, Simon; Maine, 1700-1799 9228.50 p308
Relative:Samuel
Jenness, Nicholas; Massachusetts, n.d. 9228.50 p308
Jennet, Georg SEE Jennet, Peter
Jennet, Johann SEE Jennet, Peter
Jennet, Josef SEE Jennet, Peter
Jennet, Josef; America, 1882 5475.1 p242
Jennet, Peter SEE Jennet, Peter
Jennet, Peter; Akron, OH, 1880 5475.1 p240
Son:Georg
Son:Peter
Son:Wilhelm
Son:Josef
Son:Johann
Jennet, Wilhelm SEE Jennet, Peter
Jennewein, Leondina; America, 1869 5475.1 p428
Jennez, Joseph; Ohio, 1809-1852 4511.35 p25
Jennings, Ellen 46; Ontario, 1871 1823.21 p178
Jennings, Francis 50; Ontario, 1871 1823.21 p178
Jennings, George; North Carolina, 1811 1088.45 p16
Jennings, Heneretta 63; Ontario, 1871 1823.21 p178
Jennings, Hugh 50; Ontario, 1871 1823.21 p178
Jennings, Jane 49; Michigan, 1880 4491.30 p18
Jennings, John 38; Indiana, 1855-1892 9076.20 p73
Jennings, John 33; Ontario, 1871 1823.21 p178
Jennings, Nicholas; Massachusetts, n.d. 9228.50 p308
Jennings, Richard; North Carolina, 1809 1088.45 p16
Jennings, Wm 55; Ontario, 1871 1823.17 p79
Jennison, John 24; Ontario, 1871 1823.21 p179
Jenny, Ms. 25; New Orleans, 1844 778.6 p178
Jenny, George 45; Ontario, 1871 1823.21 p179
Jenquinne, Pierre Joseph; New York, NY, 1866 1494.20 p12
Jenry, Elizabeth; Massachusetts, 1716-1750 9228.50 p113
Jenry, Elizabeth; Massachusetts, 1716-1750 9228.50 p113
Jenry, Elizabeth; Massachusetts, 1716-1750 9228.50 p113
Jensen, Alfred W.; Iowa, 1898 1211.15 p15
Jensen, Anton; Iowa, 1896 1211.15 p15
Jensen, Christ M.; Iowa, 1900 1211.15 p15
Jensen, Christian; Chile, 1852 1192.4 p54
Jensen, Christian; Iowa, 1896 1211.15 p15
Jensen, Erik; Iowa, 1896 1211.15 p15
Jensen, Fred; Iowa, 1911 1211.15 p15
Jensen, Hans 21; New York, NY, 1894 6512.1 p185
Jensen, Hans Christan; Iowa, 1892 1211.15 p15
Jensen, J.; Valparaiso, Chile, 1850 1192.4 p50
Jensen, Jens; Iowa, 1891 1211.15 p15
Jensen, Jens; Iowa, 1920 1211.15 p15
Jensen, Jens 37; New York, NY, 1883 8427.14 p43
Jensen, Jens C.; Iowa, 1904 1211.15 p15
Jensen, Jens Co.; Iowa, 1904 1211.15 p15
Jensen, Jens Erik; Iowa, 1923 1211.15 p15
Jensen, Jens Hansen; Iowa, 1915 1211.15 p15
Jensen, Jens Kristian Peter; Iowa, 1914 1211.15 p15
Jensen, Jens R. 16; New York, NY, 1883 8427.14 p44
Jensen, Jensine 6; New York, NY, 1883 8427.14 p43
Jensen, Johann 4; New York, NY, 1883 8427.14 p43
Jensen, Johanne 3; New York, NY, 1883 8427.14 p43
Jensen, Karen Kristine 19; New York, NY, 1894 6512.1 p185
Jensen, Kresten 20; New York, NY, 1883 8427.14 p44
Jensen, Lars 42; New York, NY, 1883 8427.14 p43
Jensen, Marie 9 months; New York, NY, 1883 8427.14 p43
Jensen, Marie 37; New York, NY, 1883 8427.14 p43
Jensen, Nels; North Carolina, 1859 1088.45 p16
Jensen, Nilsine 5; New York, NY, 1883 8427.14 p43
Jensen, Ole; Washington, 1888 2770.40 p25
Jensen, Ole; Washington, 1889 2770.40 p27
Jensen, Paul; Iowa, 1920 1211.15 p15
Jensen, Peter Hanssinins; Washington, 1886 6015.10 p16
Jensen, Thomas; Washington, 1884 2770.40 p192
Jenson, Fredrick; Washington, 1880 2770.40 p134
Jenson, Martin; Iowa, 1896 1211.15 p15
Jenson, Paul; Iowa, 1878 1211.15 p15
Jentes, Elisabeth 47; America, 1857 5475.1 p497
Jephson, William 11; Quebec, 1870 8364.32 p24
Jepperson, Carrie; Iowa, 1880 1211.15 p15
Jeppeson, George; Iowa, 1880 1211.15 p15
Jepsen, Thomas; Valdivia, Chile, 1850 1192.4 p49
Jepson, Miss E.; Montreal, 1922 4514.4 p32
Jepson, John 45; Ontario, 1871 1823.21 p179
Jepson, Sarah E.; Maine, 1893 9228.50 p492
Jepson, William 28; Ontario, 1871 1823.21 p179
Jerabek, Cenek; Chicago, 1864-1910 2853.20 p405
Jeree, Peter; Boston, 1716 9228.50 p309
Jeremie, Noel 26; Quebec, 1654 9221.17 p310
Jerger, Phillip; Louisiana, 1874 4981.45 p132
Jerick, Emelie Amelia; Wisconsin, 1901 6795.8 p186
Jerk, Carl; Wisconsin, 1869 6795.8 p73
Jerman, . . .; Salem, MA, 1692 9228.50 p308
Jerman, John; Ohio, 1809-1852 4511.35 p25
Jerman, John 62; Ontario, 1871 1823.21 p179
Jermel, Pierre 33; Port uncertain, 1840 778.6 p178
Jermyn, John 44; Ontario, 1871 1823.21 p179
Jermyn, Mary 70; Ontario, 1871 1823.21 p179
Jernholm, Gust. Leonard; New York, NY, 1849 6412.40 p152
Jerome, Mrs. 30; America, 1846 778.6 p178
Jerome, Jeanne; Quebec, 1639 9221.17 p85
Jertson, Robert H.; Washington, 1888 2770.40 p25
Jervois, Benjamin; Buffalo, NY, 1835 9228.50 p309
With wife & 3 children
Jervois, Elizabeth; Columbus, OH, 1852 9228.50 p158
Jerzak, Peter; Detroit, 1929-1930 6214.5 p65
Jespersen, Anton; Iowa, 1898 1211.15 p15
Jespersen, Hans Aucher Daniel; Iowa, 1921 1211.15 p15
Jessan, J. Micaise 29; New Orleans, 1842 778.6 p178
Jessen, George; Iowa, 1889 1211.15 p15
Jessen, Johannes J.; Iowa, 1903 1211.15 p15
Jessia, Francis 50; America, 1848 778.6 p178
Jessup, Dorcas Fannie; New York, 1854-1922 9228.50 p309
Jessup, Dorcas Fannie; New York, 1886-1907 9228.50 p624
Child:Augustus
Child:Dorcas
Child:Florence
Jessy, Auguste 22; America, 1841 778.6 p178
Jest, John 40; Ontario, 1871 1823.21 p179
Jester, Simon 32; Louisiana, 1848 778.6 p178
Jetschmann, F. W.; Valdivia, Chile, 1850 1192.4 p50
Jette, Urbain 26; Montreal, 1653 9221.17 p293
Jetter, Jacob; Valparaiso, Chile, 1850 1192.4 p50
Jeumelot, Jules 19; America, 1844 778.6 p178
Jeun, Rachel; Utah, 1851 9228.50 p309
Jeune, Mr.; British Columbia, 1886 9228.50 p309
With 2 brothers
Jeune, Elizabeth; Utah, 1793-1864 9228.50 p309
Jeune, Elizabeth; Utah, 1831-1865 9228.50 p284
Jeune, Fabi.n L. 30; New Orleans, 1841 778.6 p178
Jeune, Fanny SEE Jeune, Philip
Jeune, Fanny E. SEE Jeune, Philip
Jeune, Francois; Grenada, n.d. 9228.50 p309
With wife
Jeune, John; Salem, MA, 1713 9228.50 p335
Jeune, Julia; Utah, 1855 9228.50 p309
Jeune, Julia M. SEE Jeune, Philip
Jeune, Philip SEE Jeune, Philip
Jeune, Philip; Utah, 1852 9228.50 p309
Wife:Fanny
Child:Fanny E.
Relative:Julia M.
Child:Philip
Jeune, William; Boston, 1850-1950 9228.50 p309
Jeune Family ; Carolina, n.d. 9228.50 p19A
Jeune Le Vavasseur, Peter; Boston, 1700-1799 9228.50 p205
Jeurmes, J. E.; Louisiana, 1874 4981.45 p132
Jevardeaux, August 6; New Orleans, 1847 778.6 p178
Jevardeaux, Ettine 6 months; New Orleans, 1847 778.6 p178
Jevardeaux, Maria 40; New Orleans, 1847 778.6 p178
Jevardeaux, Victorin 40; New Orleans, 1847 778.6 p178
Jeveeney, Richard 13; Quebec, 1870 8364.32 p24
Jewell, George F. 34; Ontario, 1871 1823.21 p179
Jewell, John 20; Ontario, 1871 1823.21 p179
Jewell, Walter 14; Michigan, 1880 4491.36 p11
Jey, Eddison 46; Ontario, 1871 1823.17 p79
Jezek, Josef; Texas, 1854 2853.20 p78
Jicha, Antonin; Wisconsin, 1880-1889 2853.20 p339
Jidou, Jean Marie 18; New Orleans, 1848 778.6 p178
Jiffard, Jacques; Quebec, 1637 9221.17 p70
Jilek, Josef; Iowa, 1859 2853.20 p228
Jilek, Josef Fr.; Pennsylvania, 1849 2853.20 p119
Jilek, Vaclav; Iowa, 1855 2853.20 p239
Jimison, John 30; Ontario, 1871 1823.21 p179
Jindra, Josef; Nebraska, 1866 2853.20 p156
Jindra, Josef; St. Louis, 1852 2853.20 p21
Jindra, Vaclav; St. Paul, MN, 1863 2853.20 p277
Jinkens, John 42; Ontario, 1871 1823.21 p179
Jinkinson, Joseph 28; Ontario, 1871 1823.21 p179
Jiranek, Frantisek; Minnesota, 1871-1910 2853.20 p272
Jirasek, Jan; Chicago, 1857 2853.20 p389
Jirasek, Josef; New York, NY, 1857 2853.20 p100
Jirauch, Vaclav; St. Louis, 1852 2853.20 p21
Jirka, Frantisek J.; Chicago, 1867 2853.20 p391
Jirka, Josef; Wisconsin, 1856 2853.20 p345
Jirsa, Antonin; Wisconsin, 1856 2853.20 p345
Joa, Philipp 35; Galveston, TX, 1844 3967.10 p374
Joabe, John; Philadelphia, 1777 8529.30 p7A
Joachim, Ambroise Gerard SEE Joachim, Hubert Joseph
Joachim, Hubert Joseph; Wisconsin, 1880 1495.20 p56
Wife:Marie Joseph Gelinne
Child:Jean Baptiste
Child:Ambroise Gerard
Child:Josephine
Joachim, Jean Baptiste SEE Joachim, Hubert Joseph
Joachim, Josephine SEE Joachim, Hubert Joseph
Joachim, Louis 35; America, 1843 778.6 p178
Joachim, Marie Joseph Gelinne SEE Joachim, Hubert Joseph
Joanes, William 41; Ontario, 1871 1823.21 p179
Joanis, Lucas; Louisiana, 1874 4981.45 p132
Joanlong, Mr. 26; America, 1841 778.6 p178
Joannes, Francois-Augustin de; Quebec, 1705 2314.30 p169
Joannes, Francois-Augustin de; Quebec, 1705 2314.30 p185
Job, Benoit 40; New Orleans, 1846 778.6 p178
Job, Hermann 20; America, 1846 778.6 p178
Job, Isidor 22; St. Louis, 1847 778.6 p178
Job, Joseph; Detroit, 1929 1640.55 p113
Jobard, Claude-Antoine; Montreal, 1657 9221.17 p372
Jobbins, Peter; Burlington, VT, 1832 3274.55 p75
Jobert, Mr. 9; America, 1844 778.6 p178
Jobert, Jean Baptiste 24; New Orleans, 1748 778.6 p178
Jobidon, Louis 24; Quebec, 1655 9221.17 p325
Jobin, Francoise 18; Quebec, 1652 9221.17 p260
Jobin, Jean 37; Quebec, 1651 9221.17 p244
Wife:Marie Girard 35
Jobin, Marie Girard 35 SEE Jobin, Jean
Jobling, Joseph 16; Quebec, 1870 8364.32 p24
Joblonski, Frank; Galveston, TX, 1901 6015.15 p11
Jobson, Frances; Virginia, 1671 1236.25 p44
Jobst, Elise; America, 1867 7919.3 p532
Jobst, Frank; Washington, 1889 2770.40 p27
Jobst, Frank; Washington, 1889 2770.40 p79
Jobst, Henriette; America, 1868 7919.3 p532

Joch, August 2 *SEE* Joch, Peter Christian
Joch, Bernhardine; America, 1867 *7919.3 p528*
Joch, Friedrich 6 *SEE* Joch, Peter Christian
Joch, Helene Herzog *SEE* Joch, Peter Christian
Joch, Katharina 5 *SEE* Joch, Peter Christian
Joch, Peter 10 *SEE* Joch, Peter Christian
Joch, Peter Christian 33; America, 1864 *5475.1 p21*
  Wife: Helene Herzog
  Son: Peter 10
  Son: Wilhelm 3
  Son: Friedrich 6 months
  Son: August 2
  Daughter: Katharina 5
Joch, Wilhelm 3 *SEE* Joch, Peter Christian
Jochheims, Barbara 34; America, 1854 *2526.42 p119*
Jochheims, Adam 7 *SEE* Jochheims, Eva Maria
Jochheims, Mrs. Adam; America, 1847 *2526.42 p123*
  Child: Katharina
  Child: Anton
Jochheims, Mrs. Adam 56; America, 1854 *2526.42 p123*
  With son-in-law
  Child: Susanna 23
Jochheims, Anton 20 *SEE* Jochheims, Mrs. Adam
Jochheims, Appolonia 9 *SEE* Jochheims, Eva Maria
Jochheims, Eva Maria; America, 1865 *2526.42 p124*
  Child: Michael
  Child: Appolonia
  Child: Adam
Jochheims, Katharina 25 *SEE* Jochheims, Mrs. Adam
Jochheims, Michael 11 *SEE* Jochheims, Eva Maria
Jochheims, Susanna 23 *SEE* Jochheims, Mrs. Adam
Jochs, Jacob 9; America, 1846 *778.6 p178*
Jochs, Lucie 5; America, 1846 *778.6 p178*
Jochs, M. 41; America, 1846 *778.6 p179*
Jochs, Marguerita 36; America, 1846 *778.6 p179*
Jochum, Anna Maria Jost *SEE* Jochum, Ferdinand
Jochum, Christian *SEE* Jochum, Johann
Jochum, Christina Nau *SEE* Jochum, Nikolaus
Jochum, Dorothea *SEE* Jochum, Johann
Jochum, Dorothea Bost *SEE* Jochum, Johann
Jochum, Elisabeth Blatt *SEE* Jochum, Ferdinand
Jochum, Elisabeth *SEE* Jochum, Jakob
Jochum, Ferdinand *SEE* Jochum, Ferdinand
Jochum, Ferdinand; America, 1880 *5475.1 p398*
  Wife: Elisabeth Blatt
  Son: Ferdinand
  Daughter: Susanna
  Son-In-Law: Jakob
Jochum, Ferdinand 40; America, 1847 *5475.1 p427*
  Wife: Anna Maria Jost
  Daughter: Margarethe 5
  Daughter: Maria 1
  Son: Jakob 2
  Daughter: Katharina 9
  Son: Nikolaus 7
Jochum, Franz *SEE* Jochum, Jakob
Jochum, Georg *SEE* Jochum, Johann
Jochum, Jakob; America, 1846 *5475.1 p411*
Jochum, Jakob; America, 1857 *5475.1 p548*
  Wife: Katharina Kob
  Daughter: Maria
  Daughter: Katharina
  Son: Nikolaus
Jochum, Jakob *SEE* Jochum, Ferdinand
Jochum, Jakob; America, 1881 *5475.1 p429*
  Wife: Margarethe Strauss
  Daughter: Elisabeth
  Son: Johann
  Son: Franz
Jochum, Jakob 2 *SEE* Jochum, Ferdinand
Jochum, Jakob 24 *SEE* Jochum, Nikolaus
Jochum, Johann *SEE* Jochum, Jakob
Jochum, Johann; America, 1881 *5475.1 p429*
  Wife: Dorothea Bost
  Daughter: Katharina
  Daughter: Dorothea
  Son: Peter
  Son: Georg
  Daughter: Margarethe
  Son: Christian
Jochum, Johann Baptist; America, 1854 *5475.1 p57*
Jochum, Kath.; America, 1882 *5475.1 p429*
Jochum, Katharina *SEE* Jochum, Maria
Jochum, Katharina *SEE* Jochum, Nikolaus
Jochum, Katharina *SEE* Jochum, Johann
Jochum, Katharina 7 *SEE* Jochum, Jakob
Jochum, Katharina 9 *SEE* Jochum, Ferdinand
Jochum, Katharina 27; America, 1846 *5475.1 p411*
Jochum, Katharina Didion 28 *SEE* Jochum, Nikolaus
Jochum, Katharina Kob 32 *SEE* Jochum, Jakob

Jochum, Margarethe; America, 1854 *5475.1 p57*
  Son: Nikolaus
  Daughter: Sus. Veronika
  Son: Joh. Eduard
Jochum, Margarethe; America, 1877 *5475.1 p408*
Jochum, Margarethe; America, 1881 *5475.1 p50*
Jochum, Margarethe *SEE* Jochum, Johann
Jochum, Margarethe Strauss *SEE* Jochum, Jakob
Jochum, Margarethe 5 *SEE* Jochum, Ferdinand
Jochum, Margarethe 27; America, 1837 *5475.1 p399*
Jochum, Margarethe; Pittsburgh, 1891 *5475.1 p393*
Jochum, Maria; America, 1877 *5475.1 p452*
  Daughter: Katharina
  With 5 stepchildren
Jochum, Maria 1 *SEE* Jochum, Ferdinand
Jochum, Maria 1 *SEE* Jochum, Jakob
Jochum, Mathias; America, 1836 *5475.1 p462*
Jochum, Nikolaus; America, 1846 *5475.1 p411*
  Wife: Christina Nau
  With daughter
Jochum, Nikolaus *SEE* Jochum, Nikolaus
Jochum, Nikolaus; America, 1881 *5475.1 p429*
  Wife: Katharina Didion
  Child: Katharina
  Child: Jakob
  Child: Nikolaus
Jochum, Nikolaus 4 *SEE* Jochum, Jakob
Jochum, Nikolaus 7 *SEE* Jochum, Ferdinand
Jochum, Peter *SEE* Jochum, Johann
Jochum, Peter; America, 1883 *5475.1 p407*
Jochum, Susanna *SEE* Jochum, Ferdinand
Jock, Peter 32; Louisiana, 1848 *778.6 p179*
Jockel, Eva Maria 10 *SEE* Jockel, Martin
Jockel, Heinrich 1 *SEE* Jockel, Martin
Jockel, Jakob; America, 1854 *2526.42 p161*
Jockel, Johannes; America, 1836 *2526.42 p162*
Jockel, Katharina Elisabetha 6 *SEE* Jockel, Martin
Jockel, Martin 4 *SEE* Jockel, Martin
Jockel, Martin 29; America, 1846 *2526.42 p200*
  With wife
  Son: Heinrich 1
  Daughter: Eva Maria 10
  Son: Martin 4
  Daughter: Katharina Elisabetha 6
Jockel, Wilhelm; America, 1866 *2526.42 p162*
Jodon, Marie; Quebec, 1669 *4514.3 p328*
Jodwelkis, Casimir 24; New York, NY, 1893 *1883.7 p37*
Joelsson, Erik 22; New York, 1856 *6529.11 p22*
Joensson, Wilhelm Gustav Otto; Miami, 1935 *4984.12 p39*
Joerg, Maternus; America, 1846 *5475.1 p472*
Joergenson, Christain; Washington, 1885 *2770.40 p194*
Joerger, Xavier 21; Mississippi, 1847 *778.6 p179*
Joester, Adolf 22; Portland, ME, 1906 *970.38 p78*
Joester, Pauline 20; Portland, ME, 1906 *970.38 p78*
Joester, Wilhelm; Portland, ME, 1906 *970.38 p78*
Jogues, Isaac 28; Quebec, 1636 *9221.17 p50*
Joguet, Peter; Boston, 1650-1750 *9228.50 p309*
  Relative: Rebecca
Joguet, Rebecca *SEE* Joguet, Peter
Johaendgen, Margarethe; America, 1846 *5475.1 p401*
Johann, Anna *SEE* Johann, Peter
Johann, Anna; America, 1879 *5475.1 p372*
Johann, Barbara *SEE* Johann, Peter
Johann, Franz 46; America, 1843 *5475.1 p343*
Johann, Katharina Reiter *SEE* Johann, Philipp
Johann, Katharina *SEE* Johann, Peter
Johann, Magdalena Kieffer *SEE* Johann, Peter
Johann, Margarethe; America, 1881 *5475.1 p534*
Johann, Nikl.; America, 1833 *5475.1 p70*
  With wife & 4 children
Johann, Nikolaus; America, 1833 *5475.1 p63*
  With child 7
  With child 6 months
  With child 5
  With child 3
Johann, Nikolaus *SEE* Johann, Peter
Johann, Peter; America, 1873 *5475.1 p249*
  Wife: Magdalena Kieffer
  Son: Nikolaus
  Daughter: Katharina
  Daughter: Anna
  Daughter: Barbara
Johann, Philipp; America, 1833 *5475.1 p436*
  Wife: Katharina Reiter
  With 5 children
Johannbraer, Antoine; Colorado, 1884 *1029.59 p44*
Johannbraer, Helena; Colorado, 1883 *1029.59 p44*
Johannbroer, Anton; Wyoming, 1880 *1029.59 p44*
Johannbroer, Helena; Wyoming, 1880 *1029.59 p44*
Johanne, S. 18; America, 1846 *778.6 p179*
Johannes, A. Margarethe; America, 1858 *5475.1 p283*
Johannes, Adolph; America, 1883 *7420.1 p337*

Johannes, Johann Michel; Wisconsin, 1857 *5475.1 p260*
Johannes, Maria; America, 1859 *5475.1 p278*
Johannes, Mathias; America, 1855 *5475.1 p259*
Johannes, Michel; New York, 1857 *5475.1 p260*
Johannes, Nikolaus 66; America, 1859 *5475.1 p278*
Johannes, Wilhelmine Louise Charlotte; America, 1881 *7420.1 p322*
Johannesdotter, Christina Catharina; Buffalo, NY, 1852 *777.40 p11*
Johannesson, Johan Peter; Kansas, 1875-1879 *777.40 p12*
Johannette, J. 29; America, 1846 *778.6 p179*
Johannette, S. 18; America, 1846 *778.6 p179*
Johannsen, John; New York, 1859-1860 *358.56 p102*
Johansdotter, Christina; North America, 1854 *6410.15 p104*
Johansdotter, Margareta Christina; North America, 1858 *6410.15 p105*
Johansdotter, Sarah M.; Kansas, 1880 *777.40 p17*
Johansen, Carl Adolph; Iowa, 1900 *1211.15 p15*
Johansen, Johannes 27; New York, NY, 1894 *6512.1 p185*
Johansen, Laust; Iowa, 1903 *1211.15 p15*
Johanson, A.F.; Cleveland, OH, 1880-1884 *9722.10 p121*
Johanson, Ada C.; St. Paul, MN, 1887-1902 *1865.50 p51*
Johanson, Anna Lisa; St. Paul, MN, 1890-1901 *1865.50 p51*
Johanson, Augusta 16; New York, NY, 1894 *6512.1 p184*
Johanson, C.; New York, NY, 1845 *6412.40 p148*
Johanson, C. J.; Valparaiso, Chile, 1850 *1192.4 p50*
Johanson, Christ Emil; Iowa, 1918 *1211.15 p15*
Johanson, Enock; Cleveland, OH, 1888-1891 *9722.10 p121*
Johanson, Gerda Sophia; St. Paul, MN, 1901 *1865.50 p51*
Johanson, Gottfried 18; New York, NY, 1894 *6512.1 p185*
Johanson, Hartvig; Cleveland, OH, 1886-1896 *9722.10 p121*
Johanson, J.; Valparaiso, Chile, 1850 *1192.4 p50*
Johanson, Johanna; St. Paul, MN, 1887 *1865.50 p106*
Johanson, Martin; Washington, 1883 *2770.40 p136*
Johanson, Mathilda; St. Paul, MN, 1894-1904 *1865.50 p51*
Johanson, Per. A.; St. Paul, MN, 1882 *1865.50 p51*
Johanson, Sigrid M. 26; New York, NY, 1894 *6512.1 p184*
Johanson, Sophia; St. Paul, MN, 1880 *1865.50 p47*
  Child: Olof Anton
  Child: Maria
Johanson, Sophia; St. Paul, MN, 1880 *1865.50 p47*
  Child: Olof Anton
  Child: Maria
Johanson, Swen August; Cleveland, OH, 1901-1904 *9722.10 p121*
Johanson Hult, Frans August; Illinois, 1852-1861 *4487.25 p61*
Johanssen, Sonick 19; Quebec, 1910 *2897.7 p10*
Johansson, A.; New York, NY, 1845 *6412.40 p148*
Johansson, Adolph; Cleveland, OH, 1902 *9722.10 p121*
Johansson, Anders; New York, NY, 1849 *6412.40 p151*
Johansson, Beda; Minneapolis, 1892 *1865.50 p111*
Johansson, Carl Johan; Cleveland, OH, 1903 *9722.10 p121*
Johansson, Edvin Oscar; North America, 1887 *6410.15 p106*
Johansson, Emma J.; Iowa, 1870-1872 *1865.50 p98*
Johansson, G.; New York, NY, 1847 *6412.40 p150*
Johansson, Gerda Victoria 2; New York, NY, 1894 *6512.1 p185*
Johansson, Lars Johan; North America, 1858 *6410.15 p105*
Johansson, Niclas August; North America, 1855 *6410.15 p104*
Johansson, Nils Osc.; New York, NY, 1856 *6412.40 p154*
Johansson, Olof Emil; North America, 1880 *6410.15 p106*
Johansson, Oscar Wilhelm; Cleveland, OH, 1903 *9722.10 p121*
Johansson Hult, Wilhelm; Illinois, 1852-1861 *4487.25 p62*
Johantgen, Angela *SEE* Johantgen, Math.
Johantgen, Anneliese *SEE* Johantgen, Math.
Johantgen, Christina Muller *SEE* Johantgen, Math.
Johantgen, Christine *SEE* Johantgen, Math.
Johantgen, Ferdinand; America, 1865-1870 *5475.1 p405*
Johantgen, Josephine *SEE* Johantgen, Math.
Johantgen, Katharina *SEE* Johantgen, Math.
Johantgen, Math.; Arkansas, 1880 *5475.1 p358*
  Daughter: Josephine
  Daughter: Angela

*Daughter:*Anneliese
*Son:*Stephan
*Daughter:*Katharina
*Wife:*Christina Muller
*Daughter:*Christine
*Son:*Nikolaus
Johantgen, Nikolaus *SEE* Johantgen, Math.
Johantgen, Stephan *SEE* Johantgen, Math.
Johes, Charles 17; Quebec, 1870 ***8364.32*** *p24*
Johler, Ellen 52; Michigan, 1880 ***4491.39*** *p15*
Johler, Liberath 59; Michigan, 1880 ***4491.39*** *p15*
John, Mr. 19; America, 1846 ***778.6*** *p179*
John, Abraham 35; Ontario, 1871 ***1823.21*** *p179*
John, Alex 18; Ontario, 1871 ***1823.17*** *p79*
John, Andrew 34; America, 1846 ***778.6*** *p179*
John, Augustine 28; New England, 1675-1676 ***9228.50*** *p268*
John, Christopher; Barbados or St. Christopher, 1780 ***8529.30*** *p7A*
John, Friedrich *SEE* John, Ludwig Wilhelm
John, Hutton 63; Ontario, 1871 ***1823.17*** *p79*
John, Jakob *SEE* John, Nikolaus
John, Jean 32; America, 1846 ***778.6*** *p179*
John, Jerusha 37; Ontario, 1871 ***1823.21*** *p179*
John, Johann; Louisiana, 1874-1875 ***4981.45*** *p29*
John, Johns 19; Ontario, 1871 ***1823.21*** *p179*
John, Kath. Gregorius *SEE* John, Nikolaus
John, Lewis 26; Ontario, 1871 ***1823.17*** *p79*
John, Ludwig Wilhelm *SEE* John, Ludwig Wilhelm
John, Ludwig Wilhelm; Chicago, 1893 ***5475.1*** *p72*
*Wife:*Maria Eva Rothlander
*Daughter:*Mar. Katharina
*Son:*Wilhelm Karl
*Son:*Ludwig Wilhelm
*Daughter:*Margarethe
*Son:*Friedrich
*Daughter:*Maria Klara
*Daughter:*Sophie
*Daughter:*Susanna
John, Mar. Katharina *SEE* John, Ludwig Wilhelm
John, Margaret 70; Ontario, 1871 ***1823.17*** *p79*
John, Margarethe *SEE* John, Ludwig Wilhelm
John, Maria Eva Rothlander *SEE* John, Ludwig Wilhelm
John, Maria Klara *SEE* John, Ludwig Wilhelm
John, Nikolaus; America, 1867 ***5475.1*** *p487*
*Wife:*Kath. Gregorius
*Son:*Jakob
John, Sophie *SEE* John, Ludwig Wilhelm
John, Susanna *SEE* John, Ludwig Wilhelm
John, Wilhelm Karl *SEE* John, Ludwig Wilhelm
John, William; New York, 1859 ***358.56*** *p55*
John, William 31; Ontario, 1871 ***1823.21*** *p179*
Johnes, David 28; Ontario, 1871 ***1823.21*** *p179*
Johnke, August Friedrich; Wisconsin, 1893 ***6795.8*** *p186*
Johnke, Frederick; Wisconsin, 1869 ***6795.8*** *p138*
Johns, Alex 19; Ontario, 1871 ***1823.21*** *p179*
Johns, Amelia; Colorado, 1903 ***1029.59*** *p44*
Johns, Amelia; Colorado, 1903 ***1029.59*** *p45*
Johns, Benjamin 75; Ontario, 1871 ***1823.21*** *p179*
Johns, Francis R. 33; Ontario, 1871 ***1823.17*** *p79*
Johns, Mary Ann; Colorado, 1903 ***1029.59*** *p45*
Johns, Solomon 42; Ontario, 1871 ***1823.21*** *p179*
Johnson, A.O.; Cleveland, OH, 1891-1893 ***9722.10*** *p121*
Johnson, Adolf O.; Washington, 1889 ***2770.40*** *p27*
Johnson, Adolphina A. 25; Kansas, 1880 ***777.40*** *p17*
Johnson, Agnes 54; Ontario, 1871 ***1823.21*** *p179*
Johnson, Albert; Iowa, 1894 ***1211.15*** *p15*
Johnson, Albert 54; Minnesota, 1925 ***2769.54*** *p1378*
Johnson, Albin; New York, NY, 1906 ***6212.1*** *p15*
Johnson, Albin; St. Paul, MN, 1880 ***1865.50*** *p52*
*Father:*August
*Mother:*Mary Johnson
Johnson, Alex 69; Ontario, 1871 ***1823.21*** *p179*
Johnson, Alexander 76; Ontario, 1871 ***1823.21*** *p179*
Johnson, Alfred; Iowa, 1886 ***1211.15*** *p15*
Johnson, Alfred 40; Ontario, 1871 ***1823.21*** *p179*
Johnson, Alfred E.; Colorado, 1887 ***1029.59*** *p45*
Johnson, Alfred E.; Colorado, 1891 ***1029.59*** *p45*
Johnson, Alfred S.; Washington, 1884 ***2770.40*** *p192*
Johnson, Allice 26; Michigan, 1880 ***4491.36*** *p11*
Johnson, Alma Mathilda *SEE* Johnson, John P.
Johnson, Amanda; Ohio, 1890 ***9722.10*** *p131*
Johnson, Anders; St. Paul, MN, 1894 ***1865.50*** *p52*
Johnson, Andrew; Cleveland, OH, 1881-1890 ***9722.10*** *p121*
Johnson, Andrew; Cleveland, OH, 1901-1903 ***9722.10*** *p121*
Johnson, Andrew; Illinois, 1861 ***4487.25*** *p60*
Johnson, Andrew; Iowa, 1892 ***1211.15*** *p15*
Johnson, Andrew; Iowa, 1913 ***1211.15*** *p15*
Johnson, Andrew; Washington, 1888 ***2770.40*** *p25*
Johnson, Andrew Gust; Iowa, 1908 ***1211.15*** *p15*
Johnson, Andrew H.; St. Paul, MN, 1883 ***1865.50*** *p52*
Johnson, Andrew N.; St. Paul, MN, 1854-1883 ***1865.50*** *p52*
Johnson, Andrew S.; Iowa, 1892 ***1211.15*** *p15*
Johnson, Anna; St. Paul, MN, 1874-1905 ***1865.50*** *p52*
Johnson, Anna; St. Paul, MN, 1888 ***1865.50*** *p52*
Johnson, Anna *SEE* Johnson, Olof
Johnson, Anna; St. Paul, MN, 1894 ***1865.50*** *p52*
Johnson, Anna C. *SEE* Johnson, Sven
Johnson, Anna Maria *SEE* Johnson, Johanna
Johnson, Annie L. Samuelsdotter 67 *SEE* Johnson, Olof
Johnson, Anton; Boston, 1901 ***1766.20*** *p23*
Johnson, Anton; St. Paul, MN, 1880 ***1865.50*** *p52*
Johnson, Aron; Colorado, 1897 ***1029.59*** *p45*
Johnson, Arthur 32; Minnesota, 1925 ***2769.54*** *p1384*
Johnson, Arthur 36; Ontario, 1871 ***1823.21*** *p179*
Johnson, August; Cleveland, OH, 1887-1894 ***9722.10*** *p121*
Johnson, August; Cleveland, OH, 1905-1906 ***9722.10*** *p121*
Johnson, August; Iowa, 1887 ***1211.15*** *p15*
Johnson, August; St. Paul, MN, 1880 ***1865.50*** *p52*
Johnson, August; St. Paul, MN, 1880 ***1865.50*** *p52*
*Wife:*Mary
Johnson, Augusta; Colorado, 1894 ***1029.59*** *p45*
Johnson, Axel; St. Paul, MN, 1880 ***1865.50*** *p52*
Johnson, Axel T.; Cleveland, OH, 1896-1899 ***9722.10*** *p121*
Johnson, Axel V.; Cleveland, OH, 1896-1902 ***9722.10*** *p121*
Johnson, Betsy; St. Paul, MN, 1882 ***1865.50*** *p52*
Johnson, Betsy; St. Paul, MN, 1894 ***1865.50*** *p52*
Johnson, Betty; St. Paul, MN, 1891 ***1865.50*** *p44*
Johnson, Betty; St. Paul, MN, 1891 ***1865.50*** *p44*
Johnson, Brita Stina; St. Paul, MN, 1892 ***1865.50*** *p108*
Johnson, Brodin; St. Paul, MN, 1894 ***1865.50*** *p91*
Johnson, C.; Cleveland, OH, 1899-1903 ***9722.10*** *p121*
Johnson, C. H.; California, 1868 ***1131.61*** *p89*
Johnson, C.F.; Iowa, 1893 ***1211.15*** *p15*
Johnson, Carl; Cleveland, OH, 1903-1905 ***9722.10*** *p121*
Johnson, Carl Herman; Iowa, 1908 ***1211.15*** *p15*
Johnson, Carl Johan *SEE* Johnson, Johanna
Johnson, Carl L.; Cleveland, OH, 1897-1901 ***9722.10*** *p121*
Johnson, Carolina; St. Paul, MN, 1884 ***1865.50*** *p95*
Johnson, Caroline 34 *SEE* Johnson, Magnus
Johnson, Catherine 50; Ontario, 1871 ***1823.17*** *p79*
Johnson, Charles; Cleveland, OH, 1892-1896 ***9722.10*** *p121*
Johnson, Charles; Colorado, 1882 ***1029.59*** *p45*
Johnson, Charles; Colorado, 1888 ***1029.59*** *p45*
Johnson, Charles; Colorado, 1891 ***1029.59*** *p45*
Johnson, Charles; Illinois, 1861 ***4487.25*** *p60*
Johnson, Charles; Illinois, 1864 ***4487.25*** *p60*
Johnson, Charles; Iowa, 1888 ***1211.15*** *p15*
Johnson, Charles; Toronto, 1844 ***2910.35*** *p114*
Johnson, Charles; Washington, 1880 ***2770.40*** *p134*
Johnson, Charles A.; Colorado, 1888 ***1029.59*** *p45*
Johnson, Charles A.; Illinois, 1864 ***4487.25*** *p60*
Johnson, Charles A.; Michigan, 1886-1887 ***1865.50*** *p91*
Johnson, Charles Erick; St. Paul, MN, 1868 ***1865.50*** *p91*
Johnson, Charles N.; Illinois, 1861 ***4487.25*** *p60*
Johnson, Charles O.; Washington, 1883 ***2770.40*** *p136*
Johnson, Charles P.; Illinois, 1857-1861 ***4487.25*** *p61*
Johnson, Charles W.; Illinois, 1861 ***4487.25*** *p61*
Johnson, Charlotta; St. Paul, MN, 1879-1880 ***1865.50*** *p47*
Johnson, Christiana 34 *SEE* Johnson, Oscar
Johnson, Christina *SEE* Johnson, Gustaf W.
Johnson, Christina; St. Paul, MN, 1894 ***1865.50*** *p91*
Johnson, Christine I.; Iowa, 1840-1870 ***777.40*** *p10*
Johnson, Clara Wilhelmina; St. Paul, MN, 1902 ***1865.50*** *p91*
Johnson, Claus; Cleveland, OH, 1895-1898 ***9722.10*** *p121*
Johnson, Curtis G.; Ohio, 1860 ***3580.20*** *p32*
Johnson, Curtis G.; Ohio, 1860 ***6020.12*** *p12*
Johnson, Dan 46; Ontario, 1871 ***1823.17*** *p79*
Johnson, Dan. 34; Ontario, 1871 ***1823.17*** *p79*
Johnson, Dave August; Colorado, 1873 ***1029.59*** *p45*
Johnson, David; Cleveland, OH, 1901-1904 ***9722.10*** *p121*
Johnson, David; Cleveland, OH, 1903-1904 ***9722.10*** *p121*
Johnson, David 16; Ontario, 1871 ***1823.17*** *p80*
Johnson, David 40; Ontario, 1871 ***1823.17*** *p79*
Johnson, Davy; Massachusetts, 1630 ***117.5*** *p157*
With wife
Johnson, Donald 71; Ontario, 1871 ***1823.21*** *p179*
Johnson, Ed.; Colorado, 1893 ***1029.59*** *p45*
Johnson, Ed.; Colorado, 1893 ***1029.59*** *p46*
Johnson, Edmond 47; Michigan, 1880 ***4491.30*** *p18*
Johnson, Edwin 5 *SEE* Johnson, Oscar
Johnson, Ella 16; Ontario, 1871 ***1823.21*** *p179*
Johnson, Ellen; St. Paul, MN, 1874-1905 ***1865.50*** *p91*
Johnson, Elmer Algott; Boston, 1902 ***1766.20*** *p25*
Johnson, Emanuel *SEE* Johnson, William
Johnson, Emil 38; New York, NY, 1904 ***1029.59*** *p46*
Johnson, Emile; Galveston, TX, 1894 ***1029.59*** *p46*
Johnson, Emma; Minnesota, 1893-1895 ***1865.50*** *p91*
Johnson, Emma; St. Paul, MN, 1881 ***1865.50*** *p103*
Johnson, Emma; St. Paul, MN, 1887 ***1865.50*** *p91*
Johnson, Emma A.; Cleveland, OH, 1905 ***9722.10*** *p132*
Johnson, Emma A.; St. Paul, MN, 1889 ***1865.50*** *p113*
Johnson, Emma S.; St. Paul, MN, 1887 ***1865.50*** *p42*
Johnson, Eric; Washington, 1871 ***2770.40*** *p134*
Johnson, Erik; Minnesota, 1882-1883 ***1865.50*** *p92*
Johnson, Esaias Lambert; Cleveland, OH, 1889-1891 ***9722.10*** *p121*
Johnson, Eva Mathilda; St. Paul, MN, 1886 ***1865.50*** *p92*
Johnson, Felix 31; Ontario, 1871 ***1823.17*** *p80*
Johnson, Ferdinand 3 *SEE* Johnson, Oscar
Johnson, Francis; Illinois, 1852-1861 ***4487.25*** *p61*
Johnson, Francis; North Carolina, 1830 ***1088.45*** *p16*
Johnson, Francis 22; Ontario, 1871 ***1823.21*** *p179*
Johnson, Francis 53; Ontario, 1871 ***1823.17*** *p80*
Johnson, Frank; Iowa, 1883 ***1211.15*** *p15*
Johnson, Frank J.; St. Paul, MN, 1882 ***1865.50*** *p92*
Johnson, Frederick 29; Ontario, 1871 ***1823.21*** *p179*
Johnson, Fridolf; Cleveland, OH, 1904-1905 ***9722.10*** *p121*
Johnson, George; Canada, 1775 ***3036.5*** *p68*
Johnson, George 24; Ontario, 1871 ***1823.21*** *p179*
Johnson, George 28; Ontario, 1871 ***1823.21*** *p180*
Johnson, George 50; Ontario, 1871 ***1823.21*** *p179*
Johnson, George; Quebec, 1870 ***8364.32*** *p24*
Johnson, George; Washington, 1886 ***2770.40*** *p195*
Johnson, Gus; Washington, 1886 ***2770.40*** *p195*
Johnson, Gust; Cleveland, OH, 1882-1888 ***9722.10*** *p121*
Johnson, Gust; Cleveland, OH, 1891-1892 ***9722.10*** *p121*
Johnson, Gust; Washington, 1889 ***2770.40*** *p27*
Johnson, Gustaf; St. Paul, MN, 1884 ***1865.50*** *p92*
Johnson, Gustaf Adolf; Cleveland, OH, 1879-1892 ***9722.10*** *p121*
Johnson, Gustaf W.; St. Paul, MN, 1880 ***1865.50*** *p92*
*Wife:*Christina
Johnson, Gustav; Washington, 1888 ***2770.40*** *p26*
Johnson, H. 16; Quebec, 1870 ***8364.32*** *p24*
Johnson, Hanna Pernilla *SEE* Johnson, Karin
Johnson, Hannah 49; Michigan, 1880 ***4491.39*** *p15*
Johnson, Hannah; St. Paul, MN, 1882 ***1865.50*** *p37*
Johnson, Hannah Mathilda; St. Paul, MN, 1888 ***1865.50*** *p92*
Johnson, Hans; Iowa, 1892 ***1211.15*** *p15*
Johnson, Hattie L.; St. Paul, MN, 1880-1894 ***1865.50*** *p92*
Johnson, Henry; Colorado, 1888 ***1029.59*** *p46*
Johnson, Henry; Iowa, 1910 ***1211.15*** *p15*
Johnson, Henry 35; New York, NY, 1846 ***6178.50*** *p152*
Johnson, Henry; Ontario, 1871 ***1823.21*** *p180*
Johnson, Henry 30; Ontario, 1871 ***1823.21*** *p180*
Johnson, Henry 34; Ontario, 1871 ***1823.21*** *p180*
Johnson, Hilma 1 *SEE* Johnson, Oscar
Johnson, Hilma 34; Minnesota, 1925 ***2769.54*** *p1380*
Johnson, Hugh 50; Ontario, 1871 ***1823.17*** *p80*
Johnson, Irene 27; Minnesota, 1925 ***2769.54*** *p1379*
Johnson, Isaac; Louisiana, 1874 ***4981.45*** *p132*
Johnson, Isaac 57; Ontario, 1871 ***1823.21*** *p180*
Johnson, J.W. 16; Quebec, 1870 ***8364.32*** *p24*
Johnson, Jacob; Washington, 1889 ***2770.40*** *p27*
Johnson, James; Cleveland, OH, 1887-1892 ***9722.10*** *p121*
Johnson, James; Colorado, 1871 ***1029.59*** *p46*
Johnson, James; Ohio, 1843 ***2763.1*** *p8*
Johnson, James 39; Ontario, 1871 ***1823.17*** *p80*
Johnson, James 53; Ontario, 1871 ***1823.17*** *p80*
Johnson, James 59; Ontario, 1871 ***1823.21*** *p180*
Johnson, James 19; Quebec, 1870 ***8364.32*** *p24*
Johnson, James; Washington, 1881 ***2770.40*** *p135*
Johnson, James C.; Iowa, 1896 ***1211.15*** *p15*
Johnson, James C.; Ohio, 1868 ***3580.20*** *p32*
Johnson, James C.; Ohio, 1868 ***6020.12*** *p12*
Johnson, James Henry; Iowa, 1888 ***1211.15*** *p15*
Johnson, Jane; Philadelphia, 1854 ***8513.31*** *p318*
Johnson, Jane J. 56; Ontario, 1871 ***1823.21*** *p180*
Johnson, Jarl Albert; Cleveland, OH, 1894-1904 ***9722.10*** *p121*
Johnson, Johanna; Indiana, 1881 ***1865.50*** *p49*
Johnson, Johanna; Minneapolis, 1893-1896 ***1865.50*** *p93*
Johnson, Johanna; St. Paul, MN, 1883 ***1865.50*** *p92*
*Child:*Anna Maria
*Child:*Carl Johan
*Child:*Mina Johanna
Johnson, John; Canada, 1774 ***3036.5*** *p41*
*Wife:*Martha
*Son:*William
Johnson, John; Cleveland, OH, 1887-1893 ***9722.10*** *p121*
Johnson, John; Cleveland, OH, 1887-1898 ***9722.10*** *p121*

Johnson, John; Cleveland, OH, 1891-1894 ***9722.10*** *p121*
Johnson, John; Colorado, 1874 ***1029.59*** *p46*
Johnson, John; Colorado, 1885 ***1029.59*** *p46*
Johnson, John; Illinois, 1861 ***4487.25*** *p61*
Johnson, John; Illinois, 1864 ***4487.25*** *p61*
Johnson, John; Iowa, 1887 ***1211.15*** *p15*
Johnson, John; Iowa, 1890 ***1211.15*** *p15*
Johnson, John; Maine, 1826 ***3274.55*** *p24*
Johnson, John; Missouri, 1896 ***3276.1*** *p2*
Johnson, John; New York, 1905 ***1766.20*** *p34*
Johnson, John 35; New York, NY, 1825 ***6178.50*** *p149*
Johnson, John; North Carolina, 1792-1862 ***1088.45*** *p16*
Johnson, John; North Carolina, 1843 ***1088.45*** *p16*
Johnson, John; North Carolina, 1846 ***1088.45*** *p16*
Johnson, John; Ohio, 1842 ***2763.1*** *p8*
Johnson, John 24; Ontario, 1871 ***1823.21*** *p180*
Johnson, John 40; Ontario, 1871 ***1823.21*** *p180*
Johnson, John 44; Ontario, 1871 ***1823.17*** *p80*
Johnson, John 48; Ontario, 1871 ***1823.17*** *p80*
Johnson, John 52; Ontario, 1871 ***1823.17*** *p80*
Johnson, John 54; Ontario, 1871 ***1823.17*** *p80*
Johnson, John 65; Ontario, 1871 ***1823.21*** *p180*
Johnson, John; Washington, 1889 ***2770.40*** *p27*
Johnson, John; Washington, 1889 ***2770.40*** *p27*
Johnson, John; Washington, 1889 ***2770.40*** *p79*
Johnson, John A.; Cleveland, OH, 1891-1893 ***9722.10*** *p121*
Johnson, John A. 30; Minnesota, 1925 ***2769.54*** *p1379*
Johnson, John Adrian; New York, 1901 ***1766.20*** *p27*
Johnson, John Alfred; Illinois, 1886-1893 ***1865.50*** *p92*
Johnson, John Efraim; New York, 1902 ***1766.20*** *p14*
Johnson, John Efraim; New York, 1902 ***1766.20*** *p14*
Johnson, John Gust; Boston, 1902 ***1766.20*** *p16*
Johnson, John M.; Washington, 1885 ***2770.40*** *p194*
Johnson, John P.; Cleveland, OH, 1883-1892 ***9722.10*** *p121*
Johnson, John P.; Wisconsin, 1881-1890 ***1865.50*** *p92*
*Wife:*Mathilda
*Daughter:*Alma Mathilda
Johnson, John Peter; Colorado, 1891 ***1029.59*** *p46*
Johnson, John R.; Colorado, 1887 ***1029.59*** *p46*
Johnson, John S.H.; Washington, 1885 ***2770.40*** *p194*
Johnson, John W.; Chicago, 1864 ***4487.25*** *p62*
Johnson, Joseph *SEE* Johnson, William
Johnson, Joseph; Marston's Wharf, 1782 ***8529.30*** *p13*
Johnson, Joseph; Ohio, 1809-1852 ***4511.35*** *p25*
Johnson, Joseph 18; Ontario, 1871 ***1823.17*** *p80*
Johnson, Joseph 18; Quebec, 1870 ***8364.32*** *p24*
Johnson, Joseph Wm. R.; Washington, 1887 ***2770.40*** *p24*
Johnson, Joshua; Minneapolis, 1886-1888 ***1865.50*** *p92*
Johnson, Julius; Cleveland, OH, 1889-1892 ***9722.10*** *p121*
Johnson, Karin; St. Paul, MN, 1871 ***1865.50*** *p91*
*Child:*Minna Christina
*Child:*Hanna Pernilla
Johnson, Karl Emil; New York, 1897 ***1766.20*** *p25*
Johnson, Karl M.; St. Paul, MN, 1894 ***1865.50*** *p92*
Johnson, Krist; Iowa, 1895 ***1211.15*** *p15*
Johnson, Lars; Iowa, 1893 ***1211.15*** *p15*
Johnson, Lars; Washington, 1889 ***2770.40*** *p27*
Johnson, Lars Christian; Washington, 1881 ***2770.40*** *p134*
Johnson, Lars Gus; Colorado, 1893 ***1029.59*** *p46*
Johnson, Lawrence 36; Ontario, 1871 ***1823.17*** *p80*
Johnson, Lellah 16; Minnesota, 1923 ***2769.54*** *p1378*
Johnson, Lewis; Iowa, 1887 ***1211.15*** *p15*
Johnson, Lovisa *SEE* Johnson, Olof
Johnson, Ludwig Julius; Cleveland, OH, 1902-1906 ***9722.10*** *p121*
Johnson, Magnus 39; Kansas, 1880 ***777.40*** *p18*
*Wife:*Caroline 34
Johnson, Margaret; Canada, 1775 ***3036.5*** *p68*
Johnson, Margaret 17; Ontario, 1871 ***1823.21*** *p180*
Johnson, Mari; Colorado, 1895 ***1029.59*** *p46*
Johnson, Maria; Duluth, MN, 1882-1886 ***1865.50*** *p100*
Johnson, Maria; St. Paul, MN, 1882 ***1865.50*** *p115*
Johnson, Martha *SEE* Johnson, John
Johnson, Martha; St. Paul, MN, 1887 ***1865.50*** *p107*
Johnson, Martin; Iowa, 1876 ***1211.15*** *p15*
Johnson, Martin; New York, 1903 ***1766.20*** *p34*
Johnson, Martin; St. Paul, MN, 1887 ***1865.50*** *p92*
Johnson, Mary 4; Ontario, 1871 ***1823.17*** *p80*
Johnson, Mary 31; Ontario, 1871 ***1823.21*** *p180*
Johnson, Mary; St. Paul, MN, 1880 ***1865.50*** *p52*
Johnson, Mary *SEE* Johnson, August
Johnson, Mathilda; St. Paul, MN, 1881 ***1865.50*** *p95*
Johnson, Mathilda *SEE* Johnson, John P.
Johnson, Mathilda J.; St. Paul, MN, 1882 ***1865.50*** *p100*
Johnson, Mina; St. Paul, MN, 1874-1905 ***1865.50*** *p93*
Johnson, Mina Johanna *SEE* Johnson, Johanna
Johnson, Minfred; New York, 1901 ***1766.20*** *p34*
Johnson, Minna Christina *SEE* Johnson, Karin
Johnson, Moore 47; Ontario, 1871 ***1823.21*** *p180*
Johnson, Murdok 63; Ontario, 1871 ***1823.21*** *p180*
Johnson, N. John; Cleveland, OH, 1897-1902 ***9722.10*** *p122*
Johnson, Nellie; Pittsburgh, 1884-1886 ***1865.50*** *p91*
Johnson, Nels; Iowa, 1875 ***1211.15*** *p15*
Johnson, Nels Elmer; New York, 1902 ***1766.20*** *p3*
Johnson, Nels Gustaf; Wisconsin, 1880-1882 ***1865.50*** *p93*
Johnson, Nels Peter; Iowa, 1892 ***1211.15*** *p15*
Johnson, Nicholas; Colorado, 1888 ***1029.59*** *p46*
Johnson, Nickolas; Colorado, 1888 ***1029.59*** *p46*
Johnson, Niklas; Colorado, 1892 ***1029.59*** *p47*
Johnson, Nils E.; Colorado, 1862-1894 ***1029.59*** *p47*
Johnson, Ole; Washington, 1889 ***2770.40*** *p27*
Johnson, Olof; Illinois, 1861 ***4487.25*** *p62*
Johnson, Olof 68; Kansas, 1875-1880 ***777.40*** *p19*
*Wife:*Annie L. Samuelsdotter 67
Johnson, Olof; St. Paul, MN, 1880 ***1865.50*** *p93*
Johnson, Olof; St. Paul, MN, 1892 ***1865.50*** *p93*
*Wife:*Anna
*Child:*Lovisa
Johnson, Oscar; Cleveland, OH, 1887-1896 ***9722.10*** *p122*
Johnson, Oscar; Cleveland, OH, 1902-1905 ***9722.10*** *p122*
Johnson, Oscar; Colorado, 1884 ***1029.59*** *p47*
Johnson, Oscar; Colorado, 1891 ***1029.59*** *p47*
Johnson, Oscar 33; Kansas, 1871-1880 ***777.40*** *p18*
*Wife:*Sigrid Dahlstrom 37
Johnson, Oscar 35; Kansas, 1880 ***777.40*** *p19*
*Wife:*Christiana 34
*Nephew:*Ferdinand 3
*Niece:*Hilma 1
*Nephew:*Edwin 5
*Brother:*Otto 30
*Niece:*Selma 7
*Sister-In-Law:*Stare 31
Johnson, Oscar Walford; New York, 1902 ***1766.20*** *p36*
Johnson, Otto 30 *SEE* Johnson, Oscar
Johnson, P.W.; Cleveland, OH, 1883-1893 ***9722.10*** *p122*
Johnson, Pat; Louisiana, 1874 ***4981.45*** *p296*
Johnson, Patrick 40; Ontario, 1871 ***1823.21*** *p180*
Johnson, Pete; Cleveland, OH, 1901-1903 ***9722.10*** *p122*
Johnson, Peter; Colorado, 1873 ***1029.59*** *p47*
Johnson, Peter; Iowa, 1877 ***1211.15*** *p15*
Johnson, Peter 20; Kansas, 1880 ***777.40*** *p7*
Johnson, Peter 38; Ontario, 1871 ***1823.17*** *p80*
Johnson, Peter D.; St. Paul, MN, 1894 ***1865.50*** *p93*
Johnson, Peter E. 38; New York, NY, 1894 ***6512.1*** *p184*
Johnson, Peter Magnus; Iowa, 1917 ***1211.15*** *p15*
Johnson, Peter Martin; Iowa, 1892 ***1211.15*** *p15*
Johnson, Richard; Cleveland, OH, 1895-1900 ***9722.10*** *p122*
Johnson, Richard 45; Ontario, 1871 ***1823.17*** *p80*
Johnson, Robert; Cleveland, OH, 1906 ***9722.10*** *p122*
Johnson, Robert; Maryland, 1674-1675 ***1236.25*** *p52*
Johnson, Robert; North Carolina, 1795 ***1088.45*** *p16*
Johnson, Robert; Washington, 1889 ***2770.40*** *p27*
Johnson, Sam Sorenson; Iowa, 1912 ***1211.15*** *p15*
Johnson, Samuel; Toronto, 1844 ***2910.35*** *p113*
Johnson, Samuel August; Montreal, 1869-1896 ***1865.50*** *p93*
Johnson, Selma 7 *SEE* Johnson, Oscar
Johnson, Selma; St. Paul, MN, 1889 ***1865.50*** *p93*
Johnson, Sigrid Dahlstrom 37 *SEE* Johnson, Oscar
Johnson, Stare 31 *SEE* Johnson, Oscar
Johnson, Steward 50; Ontario, 1871 ***1823.17*** *p80*
Johnson, Susan 17; Ontario, 1871 ***1823.21*** *p180*
Johnson, Sven; St. Paul, MN, 1897 ***1865.50*** *p93*
*Wife:*Anna C.
Johnson, Swan; Colorado, 1887 ***1029.59*** *p47*
Johnson, Swan; Colorado, 1888 ***1029.59*** *p47*
Johnson, Swan; Colorado, 1892 ***1029.59*** *p47*
Johnson, Swen; Iowa, 1894 ***1211.15*** *p15*
Johnson, Theodor; Cleveland, OH, 1891-1903 ***9722.10*** *p122*
Johnson, Thomas 26; Ontario, 1871 ***1823.21*** *p180*
Johnson, Thomas 44; Ontario, 1871 ***1823.21*** *p180*
Johnson, Thomas F.; Louisiana, 1841-1844 ***4981.45*** *p210*
Johnson, Victor Fredrik; Cleveland, OH, 1889-1902 ***9722.10*** *p122*
Johnson, Victor William; Cleveland, OH, 1897-1903 ***9722.10*** *p122*
Johnson, William *SEE* Johnson, John
Johnson, William; Canada, 1775 ***3036.5*** *p67*
Johnson, William; Canada, 1775 ***3036.5*** *p68*
*Brother:*Emanuel
*Brother:*Joseph
Johnson, William; Canada, 1775 ***3036.5*** *p68*
Johnson, William; Cleveland, OH, 1893-1898 ***9722.10*** *p122*
Johnson, William; Illinois, 1852-1861 ***4487.25*** *p62*
Johnson, William; Illinois, 1864 ***4487.25*** *p62*
Johnson, William; Miami, 1935 ***4984.12*** *p39*
Johnson, William 58; Michigan, 1880 ***4491.30*** *p18*
Johnson, William; Ohio, 1809-1852 ***4511.35*** *p25*
Johnson, William 26; Ontario, 1871 ***1823.21*** *p180*
Johnson, William 50; Ontario, 1871 ***1823.17*** *p80*
Johnson, William 51; Ontario, 1871 ***1823.21*** *p180*
Johnson, William; Washington, 1883 ***2770.40*** *p136*
Johnson, William C.; Ohio, 1809-1852 ***4511.35*** *p25*
Johnson, William Clark; Ohio, 1809-1852 ***4511.35*** *p25*
Johnson, Wm 27; Ontario, 1871 ***1823.21*** *p180*
Johnson, Wm 30; Ontario, 1871 ***1823.21*** *p180*
Johnsson, Andrew; New York, 1902 ***1766.20*** *p18*
Johnsson, Elias; New York, NY, 1851 ***6412.40*** *p152*
Johnsson, Erik Arthur; Cleveland, OH, 1902-1903 ***9722.10*** *p122*
Johnsson, Gustaf Alfred; Cleveland, OH, 1903 ***9722.10*** *p122*
Johnsson, Johannes; New York, NY, 1849 ***6412.40*** *p151*
Johnsson, John 26; Ontario, 1871 ***1823.21*** *p180*
Johnsson, Jonas; New Orleans, 1851 ***6412.40*** *p153*
Johnsson, Niclas; New York, NY, 1851 ***6412.40*** *p152*
Johnsson, Olaus; New Orleans, 1851 ***6412.40*** *p153*
Johnsson, P.; New York, NY, 1843 ***6412.40*** *p147*
Johnsson, Sven; Charleston, SC, 1853 ***6412.40*** *p153*
Johnsson, Sven; Philadelphia, 1847 ***6412.40*** *p150*
Johnston, Adam; St. John, N.B., 1847 ***2978.15*** *p35*
Johnston, Alex 26; Ontario, 1871 ***1823.21*** *p180*
Johnston, Alex 49; Ontario, 1871 ***1823.17*** *p80*
Johnston, Alex 59; Ontario, 1871 ***1823.21*** *p180*
Johnston, Alexander; North Carolina, 1839 ***1088.45*** *p16*
Johnston, Alexander 24; Ontario, 1871 ***1823.21*** *p180*
Johnston, Alexander 44; Ontario, 1871 ***1823.21*** *p180*
Johnston, Alexander 53; Ontario, 1871 ***1823.21*** *p180*
Johnston, Ann; New Orleans, 1851 ***7242.30*** *p145*
Johnston, Anna; New York, 1739 ***8277.31*** *p117*
Johnston, Archibald 40; Ontario, 1871 ***1823.21*** *p180*
Johnston, Archibald 52; Ontario, 1871 ***1823.21*** *p180*
Johnston, Benjamin 32; Ontario, 1871 ***1823.21*** *p180*
Johnston, Benjamin 48; Ontario, 1871 ***1823.21*** *p180*
Johnston, Bezaleel W.; Ohio, 1846 ***6020.12*** *p12*
Johnston, Catharine 37; Ontario, 1871 ***1823.21*** *p180*
Johnston, Charles 55; Ontario, 1871 ***1823.17*** *p80*
Johnston, Elisabeth 22; Ontario, 1871 ***1823.21*** *p180*
Johnston, Eliza D. 76; Kansas, 1893 ***1447.20*** *p62*
Johnston, Elizabeth C.; Philadelphia, 1858 ***8513.31*** *p300*
Johnston, Ezibella 63; Ontario, 1871 ***1823.21*** *p180*
Johnston, Fergus 77; Ontario, 1871 ***1823.21*** *p180*
Johnston, George 16; Michigan, 1880 ***4491.36*** *p12*
Johnston, George 36; Ontario, 1871 ***1823.21*** *p181*
Johnston, George 38; Ontario, 1871 ***1823.17*** *p80*
Johnston, George 41; Ontario, 1871 ***1823.21*** *p181*
Johnston, George 44; Ontario, 1871 ***1823.17*** *p80*
Johnston, George B. 53; Ontario, 1871 ***1823.17*** *p80*
Johnston, Hannah 83; Ontario, 1871 ***1823.21*** *p181*
Johnston, Hannah 83; Ontario, 1871 ***1823.21*** *p181*
Johnston, Hardy 34; Ontario, 1871 ***1823.21*** *p181*
Johnston, Henry; Ontario, 1787 ***1276.15*** *p230*
With 3 children & 4 relatives
Johnston, Henry 26; Ontario, 1871 ***1823.17*** *p80*
Johnston, Henry 35; Ontario, 1871 ***1823.21*** *p181*
Johnston, Hugh; Ohio, 1809-1852 ***4511.35*** *p25*
Johnston, J. B. 61; Ontario, 1871 ***1823.21*** *p181*
Johnston, James; Ohio, 1832 ***3580.20*** *p32*
Johnston, James; Ohio, 1832 ***6020.12*** *p12*
Johnston, James 28; Ontario, 1871 ***1823.17*** *p80*
Johnston, James 30; Ontario, 1871 ***1823.21*** *p181*
Johnston, James 35; Ontario, 1871 ***1823.17*** *p80*
Johnston, James 35; Ontario, 1871 ***1823.17*** *p80*
Johnston, James 40; Ontario, 1871 ***1823.21*** *p181*
Johnston, James 41; Ontario, 1871 ***1823.21*** *p181*
Johnston, James 45; Ontario, 1871 ***1823.21*** *p181*
Johnston, James 50; Ontario, 1871 ***1823.21*** *p181*
Johnston, James 60; Ontario, 1871 ***1823.21*** *p181*
Johnston, James 65; Ontario, 1871 ***1823.17*** *p80*
Johnston, James 77; Ontario, 1871 ***1823.21*** *p181*
Johnston, James Ferguson; Iowa, 1910 ***1211.15*** *p15*
Johnston, James H. 28; Ontario, 1871 ***1823.17*** *p80*
Johnston, Jane 35; Ontario, 1871 ***1823.17*** *p80*
Johnston, Janice D. 42; Kansas, 1893 ***1447.20*** *p62*
Johnston, John 18; Michigan, 1880 ***4491.36*** *p12*
Johnston, John; Ohio, 1840 ***3580.20*** *p32*
Johnston, John; Ohio, 1840 ***6020.12*** *p12*
Johnston, John; Ohio, 1843 ***2763.1*** *p8*
Johnston, John 26; Ontario, 1871 ***1823.21*** *p181*
Johnston, John 29; Ontario, 1871 ***1823.21*** *p181*
Johnston, John 30; Ontario, 1871 ***1823.17*** *p81*
Johnston, John 32; Ontario, 1871 ***1823.17*** *p81*
Johnston, John 35; Ontario, 1871 ***1823.21*** *p181*
Johnston, John 39; Ontario, 1871 ***1823.17*** *p81*
Johnston, John 39; Ontario, 1871 ***1823.21*** *p181*
Johnston, John 40; Ontario, 1871 ***1823.17*** *p81*
Johnston, John 41; Ontario, 1871 ***1823.17*** *p81*
Johnston, John 42; Ontario, 1871 ***1823.17*** *p81*
Johnston, John 43; Ontario, 1871 ***1823.17*** *p81*

Johnston, John 48; Ontario, 1871 *1823.21 p181*
Johnston, John 48; Ontario, 1871 *1823.21 p181*
Johnston, John 49; Ontario, 1871 *1823.21 p181*
Johnston, John 55; Ontario, 1871 *1823.17 p81*
Johnston, John 58; Ontario, 1871 *1823.17 p81*
Johnston, John 60; Ontario, 1871 *1823.21 p181*
Johnston, John 60; Ontario, 1871 *1823.21 p181*
Johnston, John; St. John, N.B., 1847 *2978.15 p35*
Johnston, John; Toronto, 1844 *2910.35 p114*
Johnston, John P.; Illinois, 1864 *6079.1 p7*
Johnston, Johnathan 30; Ontario, 1871 *1823.21 p181*
Johnston, Joseph 33; Ontario, 1871 *1823.17 p81*
Johnston, Joseph 62; Ontario, 1871 *1823.21 p181*
Johnston, Joseph 79; Ontario, 1871 *1823.21 p181*
Johnston, Joshua 64; Ontario, 1871 *1823.21 p181*
Johnston, Margaret 44; Ontario, 1871 *1823.21 p181*
Johnston, Margret 44; Ontario, 1871 *1823.21 p181*
Johnston, Margt 51; Ontario, 1871 *1823.21 p181*
Johnston, Mary 11; Michigan, 1880 *4491.36 p12*
Johnston, Mary; New Orleans, 1851 *7242.30 p145*
Johnston, Mary 15; Ontario, 1871 *1823.21 p181*
Johnston, Mary 38; Ontario, 1871 *1823.21 p181*
Johnston, Mary 68; Ontario, 1871 *1823.21 p181*
Johnston, Nancy 38; Michigan, 1880 *4491.36 p12*
Johnston, Neil 50; Ontario, 1871 *1823.21 p181*
Johnston, Parson; New England, 1758 *1642 p120*
Johnston, Peter 75; Ontario, 1871 *1823.21 p181*
Johnston, Peter H. 28; Ontario, 1871 *1823.21 p181*
Johnston, Richard 36; Ontario, 1871 *1823.17 p81*
Johnston, Robert 48; Ontario, 1871 *1823.17 p81*
Johnston, Robert 50; Ontario, 1871 *1823.17 p81*
Johnston, Robert; Washington, 1887 *2770.40 p24*
Johnston, Roderick 69; Ontario, 1871 *1823.17 p81*
Johnston, Samuel 34; Ontario, 1871 *1823.17 p81*
Johnston, Samuel; South Carolina, 1800-1899 *6155.4 p18*
Johnston, Samuel M.; North Carolina, 1792-1862 *1088.45 p16*
Johnston, Simon 29; Ontario, 1871 *1823.21 p181*
Johnston, Stephen 38; Ontario, 1871 *1823.21 p181*
Johnston, Thomas; Colorado, 1873 *1029.59 p47*
Johnston, Thomas; Ohio, 1809-1852 *4511.35 p25*
Johnston, Thomas 46; Ontario, 1871 *1823.17 p81*
Johnston, Thomas 47; Ontario, 1871 *1823.21 p182*
Johnston, Thomas 48; Ontario, 1871 *1823.17 p81*
Johnston, Thomas 56; Ontario, 1871 *1823.21 p182*
Johnston, Thomas 70; Ontario, 1871 *1823.21 p182*
Johnston, Thomas Henry; Iowa, 1908 *1211.15 p15*
Johnston, Thomas W. 57; Ontario, 1871 *1823.17 p81*
Johnston, Timothy 32; Ontario, 1871 *1823.17 p81*
Johnston, William; Maine, 1827 *3274.55 p44*
Johnston, William 42; Michigan, 1880 *4491.36 p12*
Johnston, William; North Carolina, 1841 *1088.45 p16*
Johnston, William; Ohio, 1831 *3580.20 p32*
Johnston, William; Ohio, 1831 *6020.12 p12*
Johnston, William; Ohio, 1840 *3580.20 p32*
Johnston, William; Ohio, 1840 *6020.12 p12*
Johnston, William 28; Ontario, 1871 *1823.17 p81*
Johnston, William 29; Ontario, 1871 *1823.17 p81*
Johnston, William 29; Ontario, 1871 *1823.21 p182*
Johnston, William 34; Ontario, 1871 *1823.21 p182*
Johnston, William 36; Ontario, 1871 *1823.17 p81*
Johnston, William 44; Ontario, 1871 *1823.17 p81*
Johnston, William 47; Ontario, 1871 *1823.21 p182*
Johnston, William 59; Ontario, 1871 *1823.17 p81*
Johnston, William H.; Iowa, 1906 *1211.15 p15*
Johnston, William M. 51; Ontario, 1871 *1823.21 p182*
Johnstone, Alex 54; Ontario, 1871 *1823.21 p182*
Johnstone, David 65; Ontario, 1871 *1823.21 p182*
Johnstone, George 70; Ontario, 1871 *1823.17 p81*
Johnstone, Henry 55; Ontario, 1871 *1823.21 p182*
Johnstone, Henry 70; Ontario, 1871 *1823.21 p182*
Johnstone, James 35; Ontario, 1871 *1823.17 p81*
Johnstone, James 59; Ontario, 1871 *1823.21 p182*
Johnstone, James L. 44; Ontario, 1871 *1823.21 p182*
Johnstone, John 45; Ontario, 1871 *1823.21 p182*
Johnstone, John 73; Ontario, 1871 *1823.21 p182*
Johnstone, Joseph 42; Ontario, 1871 *1823.21 p182*
Johnstone, Joseph 44; Ontario, 1871 *1823.17 p81*
Johnstone, Lesslie 48; Ontario, 1871 *1823.21 p182*
Johnstone, Robert; Long Island, 1778 *8529.30 p9A*
Johnstone, Sarah 53; Ontario, 1871 *1823.21 p182*
Johnton, John 41; Ontario, 1871 *1823.21 p182*
Johny, Andre 22; Louisiana, 1848 *778.6 p179*
Johson, Lars J. 23; Kansas, 1906 *1447.20 p62*
Johson, Percy 23; Kansas, 1888 *1447.20 p62*
Joidann, John; Illinois, 1852 *6079.1 p7*
Joiner, Edward; Massachusetts, 1740 *9228.50 p309*
Joiner, Robert 36; Ontario, 1871 *1823.21 p182*
Joint, Jane 41; Ontario, 1871 *1823.21 p182*
Joint, Robert 62; Ontario, 1871 *1823.17 p81*
Jokes, Francis K. 32; Michigan, 1880 *4491.30 p18*
Jolaff, John 29; Ontario, 1871 *1823.21 p182*

Jolaff, Richard 48; Ontario, 1871 *1823.21 p182*
Jolicart, Anna 40; New Orleans, 1847 *778.6 p179*
Jolicart, Ba.tist 35; New Orleans, 1847 *778.6 p179*
Jolicart, Elise 5; New Orleans, 1847 *778.6 p179*
Jolicart, Henrietta 4; New Orleans, 1847 *778.6 p179*
Jolicart, Lena 10; New Orleans, 1847 *778.6 p179*
Jolidon, Francis; Illinois, 1856 *6079.1 p7*
Jolidon, Francis Joseph; Illinois, 1856 *6079.1 p7*
Joliet, Louis; Chicago, 1673 *2853.20 p382*
Joliffe, William J. 29; Ontario, 1871 *1823.21 p182*
Jolivet, Charlotte-Catherine; Quebec, 1671 *4514.3 p328*
Jolleys, Henry; Indiana, 1894 *9076.20 p73*
Jolliet, Jean; Quebec, 1626 *9221.17 p77*
Jollifee, William 45; Ontario, 1871 *1823.21 p182*
Jolly, George N.; New York, 1859 *358.56 p54*
Jolly, Jasinthe; Port uncertain, 1844 *778.6 p179*
Jolly, William; Colorado, 1900 *1029.59 p47*
Jolopp, Mary; Maryland, 1674 *1236.25 p50*
Joly, Charlotte; Quebec, 1669 *4514.3 p328*
Joly, Claude 45; Louisiana, 1848 *778.6 p179*
Joly, Jean; Quebec, 1638 *9221.17 p78*
Joly, Marie 42; Louisiana, 1848 *778.6 p179*
Joly, Marie; Quebec, 1639 *9221.17 p89*
Jolycauste, Anthony; America, 1842 *778.6 p179*
Jolycoeur, Adrienne 21; Montreal, 1647 *9221.17 p192*
Jolycoeur, Antoine 18; Montreal, 1659 *9221.17 p419*
Jolycoeur, Augustin 17; Quebec, 1637 *9221.17 p70*
Jombert, Mr. 44; America, 1841 *778.6 p179*
Jombert, Cammilla 8; America, 1841 *778.6 p179*
Jombert, Eugenie 5; America, 1841 *778.6 p179*
Jombert, Louis 12; America, 1841 *778.6 p179*
Jombert, Rose 5; America, 1841 *778.6 p179*
Jombert, Susan 42; America, 1841 *778.6 p179*
Jonas, Bedrich; Wisconsin, 1865 *2853.20 p299*
Jonas, Hans; Miami, 1935 *4984.12 p39*
Jonas, Jacob; America, 1872 *7420.1 p295*
Jonas, Jonas; America, 1873 *5475.1 p239*
Jonas, Karel; Wisconsin, 1863 *2853.20 p292*
Jonas, Leopold; America, 1867 *5475.1 p238*
Jonasson, Christina Catharina Johannesdotter *SEE* Jonasson, Peter Daniel
Jonasson, Peter Daniel; Buffalo, NY, 1852 *777.40 p11*
   *Wife:*Christina Catharina Johannesdotter
Jonathon, John 46; Ontario, 1871 *1823.21 p182*
Joncaire, Louis-Thomas de; Quebec, 1690 *2314.30 p169*
Joncaire, Louis-Thomas de; Quebec, 1690 *2314.30 p185*
Jone, Abraham 86; Ontario, 1871 *1823.17 p81*
Jones, . . .; Died enroute, 1840 *4022.20 p286*
   With 4 sisters
Jones, Abraham; Washington, 1888 *2770.40 p26*
Jones, Agnes 20; Ontario, 1871 *1823.21 p182*
Jones, Agnes 45; Ontario, 1871 *1823.21 p182*
Jones, Agness 22; Ontario, 1871 *1823.21 p182*
Jones, Ann *SEE* Jones, David
Jones, Ann *SEE* Jones, Thomas T.
Jones, Ann *SEE* Jones, David
Jones, Ann; Ohio, 1838 *4022.20 p292*
Jones, Ann *SEE* Jones, David
Jones, Ann *SEE* Jones, Thomas
Jones, Ann Evans *SEE* Jones, Daniel
Jones, Ann *SEE* Jones, Evan
Jones, Ann *SEE* Jones, David E.
Jones, Ann Thomas *SEE* Jones, David E.
Jones, Ann *SEE* Jones, William
Jones, Ann Lewis *SEE* Jones, John P.
Jones, Ann *SEE* Jones, David E.
Jones, Ann 20; Ontario, 1871 *1823.21 p182*
Jones, Ann 44; Ontario, 1871 *1823.21 p182*
Jones, Ann 96; Ontario, 1871 *1823.17 p81*
Jones, Anne *SEE* Jones, David
Jones, Anne *SEE* Jones, Thomas Y.
Jones, Anne *SEE* Jones, Richard
Jones, Annie 9; Quebec, 1874 *8364.32 p24*
Jones, Antony 80; Ontario, 1871 *1823.21 p182*
Jones, Augustus; Ontario, 1787 *1276.15 p231*
Jones, Barbara; Nebraska, 1927 *9228.50 p136*
Jones, Benjamin 33; Ontario, 1871 *1823.21 p182*
Jones, Benjamin 36; Ontario, 1871 *1823.17 p81*
Jones, Betsy 60; Ontario, 1871 *1823.21 p182*
Jones, Catherine Richards *SEE* Jones, Jenkin
Jones, Catherine; Ohio, 1840 *4022.20 p290*
Jones, Catherine T. Jenkins; Ohio, 1847 *4022.20 p281*
   With parents
Jones, Charles; Louisiana, 1874-1875 *4981.45 p29*
Jones, Charles; Maryland, 1673 *1236.25 p48*
Jones, Charles 56; Ontario, 1871 *1823.21 p182*
Jones, Daniel *SEE* Jones, David
Jones, Daniel; Ohio, 1839 *4022.20 p282*
   *Wife:*Ann Evans
   With children
Jones, Daniel *SEE* Jones, Isaac
Jones, Daniel *SEE* Jones, John D.
Jones, Daniel 73; Ontario, 1871 *1823.21 p182*

Jones, Daniel; South Carolina, 1858 *6155.4 p18*
Jones, Daniel O. *SEE* Jones, Thomas O.
Jones, Daniel W.; Ohio, 1847 *4022.20 p282*
   *Wife:*Jane Roderick
   With children
   *Child:*Thomas D.
Jones, Daniel William; North Carolina, 1833 *1088.45 p16*
Jones, David; North Carolina, 1833 *1088.45 p16*
Jones, David; Ohio, 1836-1837 *4022.20 p282*
   *Wife:*Ann
   *Child:*John
   *Child:*Mary
   *Child:*Eleanor
   *Child:*Daniel
Jones, David *SEE* Jones, David
Jones, David; Ohio, 1838 *4022.20 p282*
   *Wife:*Anne
   *Child:*John D.W.
   *Child:*W.
   *Child:*Mary
   *Child:*David
   *Sister:*Ann
   *Child:*Margaret
Jones, David; Ohio, 1838 *4022.20 p282*
   *Wife:*Margaret
   *Child:*Sarah
   *Child:*Mary
   *Child:*Elizabeth
Jones, David; Ohio, 1839 *4022.20 p279*
   *Wife:*Ann
   With 2 children
Jones, David *SEE* Jones, David
Jones, David; Ohio, 1839 *4022.20 p282*
   *Child:*Ann
   *Child:*David
Jones, David; Ohio, 1842 *4022.20 p282*
   *Wife:*Mary
Jones, David 20; Ontario, 1871 *1823.21 p182*
Jones, David D.; Ohio, 1820 *4022.20 p282*
Jones, David D. *SEE* Jones, David E.
Jones, David D. *SEE* Jones, David E.
Jones, David E.; Ohio, 1841 *4022.20 p282*
   *Wife:*Elizabeth
   *Child:*William E.
   *Child:*David D.
Jones, David E.; Ohio, 1847 *4022.20 p282*
   *Wife:*Ann Thomas
   *Child:*Mary
   *Child:*Ann
Jones, David E.; Ohio, 1852 *4022.20 p282*
   *Wife:*Ann
   *Child:*David D.
   With children
Jones, David G. *SEE* Jones, Isaac
Jones, David H.; Colorado, 1886 *1029.59 p47*
Jones, David H.; Washington, 1879 *2770.40 p134*
Jones, David Henry; Colorado, 1891 *1029.59 p47*
Jones, David T. *SEE* Jones, Thomas T.
Jones, Ebenezer *SEE* Jones, Thomas T.
Jones, Ebenezer; Ohio, 1842 *2763.1 p8*
Jones, Ebenezer; Ontario, 1787 *1276.15 p231*
Jones, Ebenezer E.; Ohio, 1844 *4022.20 p283*
   With 2 children
   *Child:*Jane
Jones, Edward *SEE* Jones, Isaac
Jones, Edward E. *SEE* Jones, J. Edward
Jones, Edward R. 53; Ontario, 1871 *1823.17 p81*
Jones, Edwin; America, 1873 *9076.20 p68*
Jones, Eleanor *SEE* Jones, John
Jones, Eleanor; Ohio, 1830 *4022.20 p291*
Jones, Eleanor *SEE* Jones, David
Jones, Eleanor; Ohio, 1835 *4022.20 p276*
Jones, Elinor *SEE* Jones, Thomas J.
Jones, Eliz.; Maryland, 1671-1672 *1236.25 p45*
Jones, Elizabeth *SEE* Jones, John
Jones, Elizabeth; Ohio, 1818 *4022.20 p291*
   With father
   With mother
Jones, Elizabeth; Ohio, 1829-1837 *4022.20 p288*
Jones, Elizabeth *SEE* Jones, J. Edward
Jones, Elizabeth *SEE* Jones, David
Jones, Elizabeth *SEE* Jones, Evan C.
Jones, Elizabeth *SEE* Jones, Margaret E.
Jones, Elizabeth Samuel *SEE* Jones, John
Jones, Elizabeth *SEE* Jones, Evan
Jones, Elizabeth *SEE* Jones, Isaac T.
Jones, Elizabeth *SEE* Jones, Isaac T.
Jones, Elizabeth *SEE* Jones, David E.
Jones, Elizabeth Ellis *SEE* Jones, Evan T.
Jones, Elizabeth *SEE* Jones, Richard
Jones, Elizabeth 60; Ontario, 1871 *1823.17 p81*
Jones, Elizabeth; Utah, 1855 *9228.50 p193*

Jones, Esther *SEE* Jones, William
Jones, Esther 66; Ontario, 1871 *1823.17 p81*
Jones, Evan; Colorado, 1884 *1029.59 p47*
Jones, Evan; Ohio, 1839 *4022.20 p283*
Jones, Evan; Ohio, 1840 *4022.20 p283*
  *Wife:*Jane
  *Child:*Elizabeth
  *Child:*Ann
Jones, Evan; Ohio, 1840 *4022.20 p283*
  *Wife:*Jane
  *Child:*John
Jones, Evan *SEE* Jones, Morgan
Jones, Evan 50; Ontario, 1871 *1823.17 p81*
Jones, Evan C.; Ohio, 1838 *4022.20 p283*
  *Wife:*Elizabeth
Jones, Evan D.; Iowa, 1877 *1211.15 p15*
Jones, Evan S.; Ohio, 1839 *4022.20 p283*
  *Wife:*Mary Davies
  *Child:*Mary
Jones, Evan T.; Ohio, 1846 *4022.20 p283*
  *Wife:*Elizabeth Ellis
Jones, Evans; Colorado, 1884 *1029.59 p47*
Jones, Francis 59; Ontario, 1871 *1823.21 p182*
Jones, Fredrick 24; Indiana, 1864-1870 *9076.20 p66*
Jones, Mrs. G.; Montreal, 1922 *4514.4 p32*
Jones, George 20; Ontario, 1871 *1823.21 p183*
Jones, George 37; Ontario, 1871 *1823.21 p182*
Jones, George 14; Quebec, 1870 *8364.32 p24*
Jones, George William 35; Ontario, 1871 *1823.21 p183*
Jones, Gwenllian *SEE* Jones, Isaac
Jones, Henry; Iowa, 1905 *1211.15 p15*
Jones, Henry 44; Ontario, 1871 *1823.21 p183*
Jones, Henry 18; Quebec, 1870 *8364.32 p24*
Jones, Henry S. 27; New York, NY, 1869 *7710.1 p157*
Jones, Henry Stephens; Colorado, 1891 *1029.59 p48*
Jones, Hiram 63; Ontario, 1871 *1823.21 p183*
Jones, Hugh; Ohio, 1838 *4022.20 p283*
  *Wife:*Mary
Jones, Humphrey; Washington, 1888 *2770.40 p26*
Jones, Isaac *SEE* Jones, John
Jones, Isaac; Ohio, 1839 *4022.20 p283*
  *Wife:*Gwenllian
  *Child:*Daniel
  *Child:*Edward
  *Child:*John
  *Child:*William
  *Child:*Thomas I.
  *Child:*David G.
Jones, Isaac T.; Ohio, 1840 *4022.20 p283*
  *Wife:*Elizabeth
  With children
Jones, Isaac T.; Ohio, 1840 *4022.20 p283*
  *Wife:*Elizabeth
Jones, Isaack 46; Ontario, 1871 *1823.21 p183*
Jones, Isabella 68; Ontario, 1871 *1823.21 p183*
Jones, J. Edward; Ohio, 1831 *4022.20 p284*
  *Father:*Edward E.
  With siblings
  *Mother:*Elizabeth
Jones, James 39; Indiana, 1862-1872 *9076.20 p67*
Jones, James; Iowa, 1888 *1211.15 p15*
Jones, James; Marston's Wharf, 1782 *8529.30 p13*
Jones, James; North Carolina, 1833 *1088.45 p16*
Jones, James 24; Ontario, 1871 *1823.21 p183*
Jones, James 29; Ontario, 1871 *1823.21 p183*
Jones, James 49; Ontario, 1871 *1823.21 p183*
Jones, James 52; Ontario, 1871 *1823.17 p82*
Jones, James; Philadelphia, 1777 *8529.30 p7A*
Jones, James B. 33; Ontario, 1871 *1823.21 p183*
Jones, Jane *SEE* Jones, John
Jones, Jane *SEE* Jones, William
Jones, Jane *SEE* Jones, Evan
Jones, Jane *SEE* Jones, Evan
Jones, Jane *SEE* Jones, Ebenezer E.
Jones, Jane Isaac *SEE* Jones, Thomas L.
Jones, Jane Roderick *SEE* Jones, Daniel W.
Jones, Jane *SEE* Jones, Thomas M.
Jones, Jane A. *SEE* Jones, John P.
Jones, Jemima *SEE* Jones, Thomas M.
Jones, Jenkin; Ohio, 1840 *4022.20 p284*
  *Wife:*Catherine Richards
Jones, Jessie 10; Quebec, 1870 *8364.32 p24*
Jones, John; America, 1718 *1220.12 p877*
Jones, John; Marston's Wharf, 1782 *8529.30 p13*
Jones, John; Maryland, 1672 *1236.25 p47*
Jones, John; Maryland, 1674-1675 *1236.25 p52*
Jones, John 24; New York, NY, 1884 *8427.14 p45*
Jones, John; North Carolina, 1821 *1088.45 p16*
Jones, John; Ohio, 1818 *4022.20 p285*
  With 2 grandchildren
  *Wife:*Eleanor
  *Daughter:*Susanna
  *Child:*Timothy

  *Child:*Jane
  With son-in-law
  With son-in-law
  *Daughter:*Mary
Jones, John; Ohio, 1818 *4022.20 p291*
  *Daughter:*Elizabeth
  *Wife:*Mary
Jones, John *SEE* Jones, David
Jones, John; Ohio, 1838 *4022.20 p285*
  *Wife:*Elizabeth Samuel
  *Child:*Isaac
  *Child:*John J.
Jones, John *SEE* Jones, Isaac
Jones, John *SEE* Jones, Evan
Jones, John; Ohio, 1847 *4022.20 p284*
  With wife
Jones, John 30; Ontario, 1871 *1823.21 p183*
Jones, John 58; Ontario, 1871 *1823.17 p82*
Jones, John 67; Ontario, 1871 *1823.21 p183*
Jones, John 69; Ontario, 1871 *1823.17 p82*
Jones, John; South Carolina, 1800-1899 *6155.4 p18*
Jones, John; Washington, 1889 *2770.40 p79*
Jones, John D. *SEE* Jones, William
Jones, John D.; Ohio, 1846 *4022.20 p284*
  With mother
  *Father:*Daniel
Jones, John D.W. *SEE* Jones, David
Jones, John Daniel; Washington, 1889 *2770.40 p79*
Jones, John E.; Ohio, 1837 *4022.20 p284*
Jones, John G.; Iowa, 1872 *1211.15 p15*
Jones, John H.; Ohio, 1837 *4022.20 p284*
Jones, John I.; Ohio, 1836-1837 *4022.20 p284*
Jones, John J. *SEE* Jones, John
Jones, John L.; Colorado, 1888 *1029.59 p48*
Jones, John P.; Ohio, 1850 *4022.20 p284*
  *Wife:*Ann Lewis
  *Child:*Jane A.
Jones, John P.; Washington, 1883 *2770.40 p136*
Jones, John P.; Washington, 1888 *2770.40 p26*
Jones, John R. 35; Ontario, 1871 *1823.17 p82*
Jones, John R. 55; Ontario, 1871 *1823.17 p82*
Jones, John Sisyllt; Ohio, 1879 *4022.20 p284*
  *Wife:*Margaret Morgan
Jones, John T.; Ohio, 1841 *4022.20 p284*
Jones, John W. 21; Indiana, 1881-1892 *9076.20 p73*
Jones, Joseph 25; Indiana, 1851-1865 *9076.20 p66*
Jones, Joseph; New York, 1778 *8529.30 p6*
Jones, Joseph; Ohio, n.d. *4022.20 p285*
Jones, Joseph 27; Ontario, 1871 *1823.21 p183*
Jones, Joseph W. 41; Ontario, 1871 *1823.21 p183*
Jones, Lewis; Ohio, 1809-1852 *4511.35 p25*
Jones, Lewis B.; North Carolina, 1858 *1088.45 p16*
Jones, Margaret; Ohio, 1835 *4022.20 p285*
Jones, Margaret *SEE* Jones, Thomas T.
Jones, Margaret *SEE* Jones, David
Jones, Margaret *SEE* Jones, David
Jones, Margaret Williams *SEE* Jones, Thomas S.
Jones, Margaret *SEE* Jones, Thomas S.
Jones, Margaret *SEE* Jones, Thomas O.
Jones, Margaret Morgan *SEE* Jones, John Sisyllt
Jones, Margaret E.; Ohio, 1838 *4022.20 p285*
  *Child:*Mary
  *Child:*Elizabeth
Jones, Margret 87; Ontario, 1871 *1823.21 p183*
Jones, Mary; Ohio, 1818 *4022.20 p279*
Jones, Mary *SEE* Jones, John
Jones, Mary; Ohio, 1818 *4022.20 p285*
Jones, Mary *SEE* Jones, John
Jones, Mary; Ohio, 1820 *4022.20 p289*
Jones, Mary *SEE* Jones, David
Jones, Mary; Ohio, 1836 *4022.20 p293*
Jones, Mary Edwards *SEE* Jones, Thomas T.
Jones, Mary *SEE* Jones, William
Jones, Mary *SEE* Jones, David
Jones, Mary *SEE* Jones, Hugh
Jones, Mary *SEE* Jones, Margaret E.
Jones, Mary *SEE* Jones, Evan S.
Jones, Mary Davies *SEE* Jones, Evan S.
Jones, Mary *SEE* Jones, Thomas O.
Jones, Mary *SEE* Jones, David
Jones, Mary *SEE* Jones, David E.
Jones, Mary *SEE* Jones, William
Jones, Mary; Ohio, 1850 *4022.20 p278*
Jones, Mary 6; Ontario, 1871 *1823.21 p183*
Jones, Mary 25; Ontario, 1871 *1823.21 p183*
Jones, Maurice; Colorado, 1883 *1029.59 p48*
Jones, Maurice; Colorado, 1903 *1029.59 p48*
Jones, Michael 40; Ontario, 1871 *1823.21 p183*
Jones, Morgan; Ohio, 1847 *4022.20 p285*
  *Wife:*Winifred
  *Child:*Evan
  With 3 children

Jones, Nancy 52; Ontario, 1871 *1823.21 p183*
Jones, Orlando 42; Ontario, 1871 *1823.17 p82*
Jones, Rachel; Ohio, 1854 *4022.20 p285*
Jones, Richard; Colorado, 1885 *1029.59 p48*
Jones, Richard; New York, 1783 *8529.30 p13*
Jones, Richard; Ohio, 1847 *4022.20 p283*
  *Wife:*Elizabeth
  *Child:*Anne
Jones, Richard 40; Ontario, 1871 *1823.21 p183*
Jones, Robert; America, 1742 *1220.12 p501*
Jones, Robert; Boston, 1775 *8529.30 p2*
Jones, Robert; Iowa, 1873 *1211.15 p15*
Jones, Robert 50; Ontario, 1871 *1823.21 p183*
Jones, Robert 57; Ontario, 1871 *1823.21 p183*
Jones, Robert; Philadelphia, 1777 *8529.30 p2*
Jones, Robert H.; North Carolina, 1817 *1088.45 p16*
Jones, Sally 48; Ontario, 1871 *1823.21 p183*
Jones, Samuel 41; Ontario, 1871 *1823.21 p183*
Jones, Sandy 44; Ontario, 1871 *1823.21 p183*
Jones, Sarah *SEE* Jones, David
Jones, Sarah; Ohio, 1866 *4022.20 p293*
Jones, Sarah 36; Ontario, 1871 *1823.21 p183*
Jones, Sarah 61; Ontario, 1871 *1823.21 p183*
Jones, Sarah 11; Quebec, 1870 *8364.32 p24*
Jones, Scott; Washington, 1889 *2770.40 p79*
Jones, Shaun 50; Ontario, 1871 *1823.17 p82*
Jones, Shederick 102; Ontario, 1871 *1823.21 p183*
Jones, Susanna; Ohio, 1818 *4022.20 p278*
Jones, Susanna *SEE* Jones, John
Jones, Susanna; Ohio, 1818 *4022.20 p285*
Jones, Thomas; New York, 1776 *8529.30 p13*
Jones, Thomas; North Carolina, 1842 *1088.45 p16*
Jones, Thomas *SEE* Jones, Thomas T.
Jones, Thomas 17; Ontario, 1871 *1823.21 p183*
Jones, Thomas 30; Ontario, 1871 *1823.17 p82*
Jones, Thomas 34; Ontario, 1871 *1823.21 p183*
Jones, Thomas 37; Ontario, 1871 *1823.17 p82*
Jones, Thomas 55; Ontario, 1871 *1823.21 p183*
Jones, Thomas 60; Ontario, 1871 *1823.21 p183*
Jones, Thomas 73; Ontario, 1871 *1823.17 p82*
Jones, Thomas 14; Quebec, 1870 *8364.32 p24*
Jones, Thomas D. *SEE* Jones, Daniel W.
Jones, Thomas I. *SEE* Jones, Isaac
Jones, Thomas J. *SEE* Jones, Thomas J.
Jones, Thomas J.; Ohio, 1847-1848 *4022.20 p285*
  *Child:*Thomas J.
  With 2 children
  *Wife:*Elinor
Jones, Thomas L.; Ohio, 1847-1848 *4022.20 p285*
  *Wife:*Jane Isaac
Jones, Thomas M.; Ohio, 1852 *4022.20 p286*
  *Wife:*Jemima
Jones, Thomas M.; Ohio, n.d. *4022.20 p285*
  *Wife:*Jane
Jones, Thomas O.; Ohio, 1840 *4022.20 p286*
  *Wife:*Margaret
  *Child:*Mary
  *Child:*Daniel O.
Jones, Thomas S.; Ohio, 1838 *4022.20 p285*
  *Wife:*Margaret Williams
Jones, Thomas S.; Ohio, 1838 *4022.20 p286*
  *Wife:*Margaret
Jones, Thomas T.; Ohio, 1837-1838 *4022.20 p286*
  *Wife:*Mary Edwards
  *Child:*Ebenezer
  *Child:*Margaret
  *Child:*David T.
  *Child:*Ann
  *Child:*Thomas
Jones, Thomas Y.; Ohio, 1840 *4022.20 p286*
  *Wife:*Anne
  With 6 children
Jones, Thos 56; Ontario, 1871 *1823.21 p183*
Jones, Timothy *SEE* Jones, John
Jones, Vanny 10; Quebec, 1870 *8364.32 p24*
Jones, W. *SEE* Jones, David
Jones, W. 15; Quebec, 1870 *8364.32 p24*
Jones, Walter 33; Ontario, 1871 *1823.17 p82*
Jones, William; New Jersey, 1795-1804 *3845.2 p129*
Jones, William; New York, 1778 *8529.30 p13*
Jones, William; North Carolina, 1855 *1088.45 p16*
Jones, William; North Carolina, 1857 *1088.45 p16*
Jones, William; Ohio, 1837 *4022.20 p286*
  *Wife:*Mary
  *Child:*Esther
  *Child:*John D.
  *Child:*William D.
  *Child:*Jane
Jones, William *SEE* Jones, Isaac
Jones, William; Ohio, 1849 *4022.20 p286*
  *Wife:*Ann
  *Child:*Mary
Jones, William 23; Ontario, 1871 *1823.21 p184*

Jones, William 36; Ontario, 1871 ***1823.21*** *p183*
Jones, William 42; Ontario, 1871 ***1823.21*** *p184*
Jones, William 46; Ontario, 1871 ***1823.17*** *p82*
Jones, William 80; Ontario, 1871 ***1823.21*** *p183*
Jones, William 17; Quebec, 1870 ***8364.32*** *p24*
Jones, William D. *SEE* Jones, William
Jones, William E. *SEE* Jones, David E.
Jones, William R. 50; Ontario, 1871 ***1823.21*** *p184*
Jones, Winifred *SEE* Jones, Morgan
Jongnell, Franz; New York, 1873 ***5475.1*** *p380*
Jongnell, Nik. Franz Jos. Gust.; New York, 1867 ***5475.1*** *p417*
Jonhnson, Peter; Colorado, 1887 ***1029.59*** *p48*
Jonsdotter, Anna 12 *SEE* Jonsdotter, Anna
Jonsdotter, Anna 19; New York, 1856 ***6529.11*** *p22*
Jonsdotter, Anna 22; New York, 1856 ***6529.11*** *p21*
Jonsdotter, Anna 55; New York, 1856 ***6529.11*** *p22*
*Daughter:*Anna 12
Jonsdotter, Brita 40; New York, 1856 ***6529.11*** *p21*
Jonsdotter, Carin 28; New York, 1856 ***6529.11*** *p20*
Jonsdotter, Carolina 40; Kansas, 1880 ***777.40*** *p13*
Jonsdotter, Caroline 40; Kansas, 1880 ***777.40*** *p13*
Jonsdotter, Cherstin 42; New York, 1856 ***6529.11*** *p20*
Jonsdotter, Golin 24; New York, 1856 ***6529.11*** *p22*
Jonsdotter, Great Lisa 27; New York, 1856 ***6529.11*** *p22*
Jonsdotter, Great Lisa 27; New York, 1856 ***6529.11*** *p22*
Jonsdotter, Kerstin; New York, 1857 ***6529.11*** *p25*
*Daughter:*Anna Christina
Jonsdotter, Kerstin; New York, 1857 ***6529.11*** *p25*
*Daughter:*Anna Christina
Jonsdotter, Kjerstin; New York, 1856 ***6529.11*** *p20*
Jonsdotter, Martha 34; New York, 1856 ***6529.11*** *p19*
Jonsdotter, Martha 34; New York, 1856 ***6529.11*** *p19*
Jonsdotter, Martha 34; New York, 1856 ***6529.11*** *p19*
Jonson, John August; Cleveland, OH, 1887-1889 ***9722.10*** *p122*
Jonsson, A.; New York, NY, 1845 ***6412.40*** *p148*
Jonsson, Anna Brita 10 *SEE* Jonsson, Ol
Jonsson, Anna Catharina Hakansdotter *SEE* Jonsson, Carl Petter
Jonsson, Anna Lena Samuelsdotter 67 *SEE* Jonsson, Olof
Jonsson, Brita 6 *SEE* Jonsson, Jon
Jonsson, Brita Jonsdotter 40 *SEE* Jonsson, Ol
Jonsson, C.; Boston, 1847 ***6412.40*** *p150*
Jonsson, Cajsa 3 *SEE* Jonsson, Jon
Jonsson, Cajsa 11 *SEE* Jonsson, Ol
Jonsson, Carl Gustaf Victor *SEE* Jonsson, Johan Erik
Jonsson, Carl Petter; North America, 1858 ***6410.15*** *p105*
*Wife:*Anna Catharina Hakansdotter
Jonsson, Christina 6 *SEE* Jonsson, Ol
Jonsson, Hans 19; New York, 1856 ***6529.11*** *p21*
Jonsson, J.P.; New York, NY, 1843 ***6412.40*** *p147*
Jonsson, Jan Olof 4 *SEE* Jonsson, Ol
Jonsson, Johan; New York, NY, 1844 ***6412.40*** *p148*
Jonsson, Johan Erik; North America, 1857 ***6410.15*** *p105*
*Wife:*Maria Christina Pehrsdotter
*Child:*Carl Gustaf Victor
*Child:*Johan Petter
Jonsson, Johan Petter; North America, 1854 ***6410.15*** *p104*
Jonsson, Johan Petter *SEE* Jonsson, Johan Erik
Jonsson, Jon 15; New York, 1856 ***6529.11*** *p21*
Jonsson, Jon 46; New York, 1856 ***6529.11*** *p22*
*Wife:*Maria Danielsdotter 32
*Daughter:*Brita 6
*Daughter:*Cajsa 3
*Son:*Jonas 9
Jonsson, Jonas 9 *SEE* Jonsson, Jon
Jonsson, Jonas 13 *SEE* Jonsson, Ol
Jonsson, Jonas 18; New York, 1856 ***6529.11*** *p21*
Jonsson, L.; New York, NY, 1843 ***6412.40*** *p147*
Jonsson, Lars 22; New York, 1856 ***6529.11*** *p20*
Jonsson, Magn.; New York, NY, 1844 ***6412.40*** *p148*
Jonsson, Margareta 2 *SEE* Jonsson, Ol
Jonsson, Maria 7 *SEE* Jonsson, Ol
Jonsson, Maria Danielsdotter 32 *SEE* Jonsson, Jon
Jonsson, Maria Christina Pehrsdotter *SEE* Jonsson, Johan Erik
Jonsson, N.M.; New York, NY, 1846 ***6412.40*** *p149*
Jonsson, Nils; New York, NY, 1853 ***6412.40*** *p153*
Jonsson, Ol 39; New York, 1856 ***6529.11*** *p21*
*Wife:*Brita Jonsdotter 40
*Daughter:*Christina 6 months
*Daughter:*Margareta 2
*Daughter:*Cajsa 11
*Daughter:*Anna Brita 10
*Son:*Jan Olof 4
*Daughter:*Maria 7
*Son:*Jonas 13
Jonsson, Olof 68; Kansas, 1875-1880 ***777.40*** *p19*
*Wife:*Anna Lena Samuelsdotter 67
Jonsson, Per; Iowa, 1920 ***1211.15*** *p15*
Jonsson, Petter; New York, NY, 1849 ***6412.40*** *p151*
Jonsson, Petter; Philadelphia, 1847 ***6412.40*** *p150*
Jonsson, Sven; New York, NY, 1846 ***6412.40*** *p149*
Jonsson, Sven; New York, NY, 1849 ***6412.40*** *p151*
Jontson, Henry 47; Ontario, 1871 ***1823.21*** *p184*
Jontson, William 53; Ontario, 1871 ***1823.21*** *p184*
Jonvau, Antoine Aime; Illinois, 1852 ***6079.1*** *p7*
Jonvaux, Aime 35; New Orleans, 1848 ***778.6*** *p179*
Jonvaux, Catherine 32; New Orleans, 1848 ***778.6*** *p179*
Jonvaux, Jeanne 10; New Orleans, 1848 ***778.6*** *p179*
Jonvaux, Loiuise 5; New Orleans, 1848 ***778.6*** *p179*
Jonville, J.; Louisiana, 1874 ***4981.45*** *p296*
Joos, Friedrich; America, 1893 ***179.55*** *p19*
Joos, Jakob; America, 1889 ***179.55*** *p19*
Joos, Jakob Friedrich; America, 1883 ***179.55*** *p19*
Joos, Karl Heinrich; America, 1867 ***179.55*** *p19*
Joosen, Joseph 25; Louisiana, 1848 ***778.6*** *p179*
Jopie, Anne 32; Quebec, 1657 ***9221.17*** *p360*
Jorda, Gernimo; Louisiana, 1836-1840 ***4981.45*** *p212*
Jordahl, Anton; Iowa, 1900 ***1211.15*** *p15*
Jordan, Mrs.; Toronto, 1844 ***2910.35*** *p114*
Jordan, Adam 10; New York, NY, 1898 ***7951.13*** *p44*
Jordan, Anton; America, 1872 ***5475.1*** *p14*
*Wife:*Luise Meyer
*Son:*Franz
Jordan, August Friedrich Louis; America, 1856 ***7420.1*** *p148*
Jordan, Carl August Wilhelm; America, 1854 ***7420.1*** *p122*
Jordan, Carl Hermann August Wilhelm; America, 1858 ***7420.1*** *p178*
Jordan, Carl Wilh. Aug. Hermann; Havre de Grace, MD, 1857 ***7420.1*** *p164*
Jordan, Charley; Cleveland, OH, 1901-1903 ***9722.10*** *p122*
Jordan, Della Beatrice; Florida, 1918-1974 ***9228.50*** *p277*
Jordan, Franz *SEE* Jordan, Anton
Jordan, Georg Wilhelm; Port uncertain, 1854 ***7420.1*** *p122*
Jordan, Herman 21; Santa Clara Co., CA, 1852 ***8704.1*** *p22*
Jordan, Jacob 38; New York, NY, 1898 ***7951.13*** *p44*
Jordan, James; Michigan, 1857 ***1447.20*** *p64*
Jordan, James 20; Quebec, 1870 ***8364.32*** *p24*
Jordan, Johann Carl Adolph; America, 1858 ***7420.1*** *p178*
Jordan, John 40; Ontario, 1871 ***1823.21*** *p184*
Jordan, Joseph 19; Quebec, 1870 ***8364.32*** *p24*
Jordan, Joseph W.; Ohio, 1871 ***3580.20*** *p32*
Jordan, Joseph W.; Ohio, 1871 ***6020.12*** *p12*
Jordan, Julianna 9 months; New York, NY, 1898 ***7951.13*** *p44*
Jordan, Julianna 37; New York, NY, 1898 ***7951.13*** *p44*
Jordan, Luise Meyer *SEE* Jordan, Anton
Jordan, Mary; Maryland, 1860 ***8513.31*** *p314*
Jordan, Mary 40; Ontario, 1871 ***1823.21*** *p184*
Jordan, William 35; Ontario, 1871 ***1823.17*** *p82*
Jordan, Wm.; Louisiana, 1874-1875 ***4981.45*** *p29*
Jordening, Johann Philipp; America, 1854 ***7420.1*** *p122*
With wife 4 sons & 5 daughters
Jordison, John; Washington, 1883 ***2770.40*** *p136*
Jordon, Edward; Toronto, 1844 ***2910.35*** *p113*
Jordon, Peter 45; Havana, 1848 ***778.6*** *p179*
Jordon, Simon; Toronto, 1844 ***2910.35*** *p112*
Jordy, Francois de; Quebec, 1683-1688 ***2314.30*** *p168*
Jordy, Francois de; Quebec, 1685 ***2314.30*** *p186*
Jordy deCabanac, Joseph des; Quebec, 1683-1688 ***2314.30*** *p168*
Jordy deCabanac, Joseph des; Quebec, 1685 ***2314.30*** *p186*
Jorg, Johann; America, 1891 ***2526.43*** *p150*
Jorgen, Bernhart 4; New York, NY, 1847 ***9176.15*** *p49*
Jorgen, F. A. 30; New York, NY, 1847 ***9176.15*** *p49*
Jorgen, Lous 1; New York, NY, 1847 ***9176.15*** *p49*
Jorgen, Maria 31; New York, NY, 1847 ***9176.15*** *p49*
Jorgen, Marianna 4 months; New York, NY, 1847 ***9176.15*** *p49*
Jorgen, Zenach 3; New York, NY, 1847 ***9176.15*** *p49*
Jorgensen, Jens Oluf; Iowa, 1928 ***1211.15*** *p15*
Jorgensen, Johan; Washington, 1889 ***2770.40*** *p79*
Jorgenson, Hans Johan; Iowa, 1910 ***1211.15*** *p15*
Jors, Elisabeth 24; America, 1847 ***778.6*** *p179*
Jortenat, Henriette 40; New Orleans, 1844 ***778.6*** *p180*
Jortlund, Erik; Iowa, 1898 ***1211.15*** *p15*
Joseau, Philippe 25; Port uncertain, 1842 ***778.6*** *p180*
Joselsen, Andrew J.; Washington, 1889 ***2770.40*** *p79*
Joseph, Mrs. 33; America, 1848 ***778.6*** *p180*
Joseph, Aaron 20; New York, NY, 1882 ***7710.1*** *p159*
Joseph, Amy 29; America, 1848 ***778.6*** *p180*
Joseph, Anna 31; America, 1847 ***778.6*** *p180*
Joseph, Cesar 38; America, 1848 ***778.6*** *p180*
Joseph, Clement 19; America, 1848 ***778.6*** *p180*
Joseph, Emanuel; America, 1862 ***2526.43*** *p171*
Joseph, Ferga 47; New York, NY, 1894 ***6512.1*** *p228*
Joseph, Georg 6 months; America, 1847 ***778.6*** *p180*
Joseph, Georg 38; Port uncertain, 1841 ***778.6*** *p180*
Joseph, Henry 27; Santa Clara Co., CA, 1870 ***8704.1*** *p25*
Joseph, Isaak; America, 1860 ***5475.1*** *p519*
Joseph, Isaak; America, 1865 ***2526.43*** *p171*
Joseph, Jakob; America, 1864 ***2526.43*** *p171*
Joseph, Jakob; America, 1873 ***5475.1*** *p446*
Joseph, Jakob 16; America, 1856 ***5475.1*** *p518*
Joseph, Jakob; Tennessee, 1885 ***5475.1*** *p447*
Joseph, Jean; Louisiana, 1874 ***4981.45*** *p132*
Joseph, Jesel 19; America, 1849 ***2526.43*** *p196*
Joseph, Johann; America, 1909 ***2526.43*** *p150*
Joseph, John 22; St. Louis, 1844 ***778.6*** *p180*
Joseph, Joseph; America, 1860 ***2526.43*** *p171*
Joseph, Julius; America, 1866 ***5475.1*** *p520*
Joseph, Julius; Louisiana, 1874 ***4981.45*** *p132*
Joseph, Louis; America, 1882 ***2526.43*** *p171*
Joseph, Ludwig; America, 1906 ***2526.43*** *p171*
Joseph, Maix; Ohio, 1809-1852 ***4511.35*** *p25*
Joseph, Manuel; Louisiana, 1836-1841 ***4981.45*** *p208*
Joseph, Margaret 26; Port uncertain, 1841 ***778.6*** *p180*
Joseph, Mary 28; Ontario, 1871 ***1823.21*** *p184*
Joseph, Mary 40; Port uncertain, 1841 ***778.6*** *p180*
Joseph, Max 25; New York, NY, 1894 ***6512.1*** *p228*
Joseph, Meier; America, 1866 ***2526.43*** *p172*
Joseph, Michel T. 30; America, 1847 ***778.6*** *p180*
Joseph, Nicolas 27; New Orleans, 1848 ***778.6*** *p180*
Joseph, Oskar; America, 1892 ***2526.43*** *p172*
Joseph, Simon; Ohio, 1809-1852 ***4511.35*** *p25*
Joseph, Stinson 37; Ontario, 1871 ***1823.21*** *p184*
Josephsson, Zach.; New York, NY, 1856 ***6412.40*** *p154*
Joshel, Henry Julius; New York, 1904 ***1766.20*** *p34*
Jossard, Elisabeth; Quebec, 1670 ***4514.3*** *p328*
Jossart, Jean Joseph *SEE* Jossart, Pierre Joseph
Jossart, Jeanne Joseph *SEE* Jossart, Pierre Joseph
Jossart, Pierre Joseph; Wisconsin, 1855 ***1495.20*** *p46*
*Child:*Jeanne Joseph
*Child:*Jean Joseph
*Child:*Rosalie Joseph
Jossart, Rosalie Joseph *SEE* Jossart, Pierre Joseph
Josselin, Nicolas 22; Montreal, 1653 ***9221.17*** *p293*
Jost, A. Maria *SEE* Jost, Mathias
Jost, Adam; Brazil, 1858 ***2526.43*** *p127*
Jost, Anna *SEE* Jost, Mathias
Jost, Anna Hahn *SEE* Jost, Mathias
Jost, Anna; Minnesota, 1884 ***5475.1*** *p142*
Jost, Anna Maria; America, 1847 ***5475.1*** *p427*
Jost, Anna Maria Schmitt *SEE* Jost, Mathias
Jost, August W.; Wisconsin, 1906 ***6795.8*** *p179*
Jost, Barbara 15 *SEE* Jost, Mrs. Johann
Jost, Daniel 32; America, 1847 ***778.6*** *p180*
Jost, Elisabeth 34; America, 1847 ***778.6*** *p180*
Jost, Elisabethe 66 *SEE* Jost, Margaretha
Jost, Elizabeth 9; America, 1847 ***778.6*** *p180*
Jost, Franz 9 *SEE* Jost, Mrs. Johann
Jost, Friedrich 26; New York, 1887 ***5475.1*** *p75*
Jost, Georg; America, 1887 ***2526.42*** *p124*
Jost, Georg; America, 1887 ***2526.43*** *p127*
Jost, Gertrud 1 *SEE* Jost, Peter
Jost, Gertrud Klassen 36 *SEE* Jost, Peter
Jost, Jakob 9 *SEE* Jost, Margaretha
Jost, Johann *SEE* Jost, Mathias
Jost, Johann *SEE* Jost, Mathias
Jost, Johann; America, 1889 ***2526.42*** *p192*
Jost, Johann; America, 1889 ***2526.43*** *p127*
Jost, Mrs. Johann 38; New York, 1854 ***5475.1*** *p493*
*Daughter:*Barbara 15
*Son:*Franz 9
Jost, Johann Konrad 25; America, 1881 ***2526.43*** *p196*
Jost, Katharina 7 *SEE* Jost, Peter
Jost, Margaretha 26; America, 1859 ***2526.43*** *p127*
*Son:*Jakob 9 months
*Mother:*Elisabethe 66
Jost, Maria *SEE* Jost, Mathias
Jost, Maria 4 *SEE* Jost, Peter
Jost, Maria; Iowa, 1878 ***5475.1*** *p334*
Jost, Mathias *SEE* Jost, Mathias
Jost, Mathias; America, 1865 ***5475.1*** *p509*
*Wife:*Anna Hahn
*Daughter:*Anna
*Son:*Peter
*Son:*Johann
*Son:*Mathias
Jost, Mathias; America, 1876 ***5475.1*** *p157*
*Wife:*Anna Maria Schmitt
*Daughter:*Maria
*Son:*Johann
*Daughter:*A. Maria
Jost, Peter *SEE* Jost, Mathias
Jost, Peter; Brazil, 1857 ***5475.1*** *p319*
*Wife:*Gertrud Klassen
*Daughter:*Maria
*Daughter:*Gertrud
*Daughter:*Katharina

Jost, Peter; Ohio, 1840-1897 ***8365.35*** *p16*
Jost, Phillippe 3; America, 1847 ***778.6*** *p180*
Josten, Barbara; America, 1887 ***5475.1*** *p243*
Josten, Margarethe; America, 1862 ***5475.1*** *p524*
Josufson, Carl Adolf; New York, 1901 ***1766.20*** *p16*
Joszko, Stanislaw 17; New York, NY, 1912 ***8355.1*** *p15*
Jots, Franc.s 8; America, 1847 ***778.6*** *p180*
Jots, Johann 45; America, 1847 ***778.6*** *p180*
Jots, Nicolas 27; America, 1847 ***778.6*** *p180*
Jouan, B. 35; Cuba, 1841 ***778.6*** *p180*
Jouanier, Jean 23; Port uncertain, 1840 ***778.6*** *p180*
Jouanneau, Mathurin 36; Montreal, 1653 ***9221.17*** *p294*
Jouansan, Widow 44; Texas, 1848 ***778.6*** *p180*
Jouanson, Mr. 20; Texas, 1848 ***778.6*** *p180*
Jouanson, Ms. 11; Texas, 1848 ***778.6*** *p180*
Joubert, Mr. 37; America, 1846 ***778.6*** *p180*
Jouet, Alfred 22; New Orleans, 1848 ***778.6*** *p180*
Jouet, Louis; Quebec, 1645 ***9221.17*** *p153*
Jouhanau, P. J. 20; New Orleans, 1848 ***778.6*** *p180*
Jouiel, Jacques 18; Quebec, 1656 ***9221.17*** *p339*
Jouin, Jacques; Quebec, 1656 ***9221.17*** *p339*
Jouineau, Edouarde; Quebec, 1647 ***9221.17*** *p185*
Jouineau, Edouarde; Quebec, 1647 ***9221.17*** *p185*
Jouineau, Jean 36; Quebec, 1649 ***9221.17*** *p215*
*Wife:*Marie Billaud
*Relative:*Pierre
Jouineau, Marie Billaud *SEE* Jouineau, Jean
Jouineau, Pierre *SEE* Jouineau, Jean
Joulie, Joseph 33; America, 1847 ***778.6*** *p180*
Jourdain, Abraham; Quebec, 1649 ***9221.17*** *p214*
Jourdain, Alexandre; Quebec, 1650 ***9221.17*** *p227*
Jourdain, Joh John; Plymouth, MA, 1643 ***9228.50*** *p310*
Jourdain, Marguerite; Quebec, 1667 ***4514.3*** *p328*
Jourdain, Pierre; Quebec, 1661 ***9221.17*** *p459*
Jourdan, Philippe 18; Missouri, 1845 ***778.6*** *p180*
Jourdon, Marie; Virginia, 1700 ***9230.15*** *p81*
Jourdon, Symon; Virginia, 1700 ***9230.15*** *p81*
Jouserre, Lucien 36; New Orleans, 1848 ***778.6*** *p180*
Jousin, Francois 18; Port uncertain, 1846 ***778.6*** *p181*
Joussalyn, Raymond 1; America, 1848 ***778.6*** *p181*
Joussef, Abib 25; New York, NY, 1894 ***6512.1*** *p232*
Joussef, Rachisk 18; New York, NY, 1894 ***6512.1*** *p232*
Jousset, Mathurin 24; Montreal, 1653 ***9221.17*** *p294*
Jouver, Peter; America, 1882 ***5475.1*** *p421*
Jouy, Mr. 41; Louisiana, 1848 ***778.6*** *p181*
Jouy, Jean 33; Quebec, 1651 ***9221.17*** *p245*
Jovany, Jean; Virginia, 1700 ***9230.15*** *p81*
With wife & 2 children
Joven, Jacob; North Carolina, 1710 ***3629.40*** *p8*
Joy, Melzar; Boston, 1800-1899 ***9228.50*** *p310*
Joy, Thomas 35; Ontario, 1871 ***1823.17*** *p82*
Joybert deSoulanges et deMarson, Pierre de; Quebec, 1665 ***2314.30*** *p167*
Joybert deSoulanges et deMarson, Pierre de; Quebec, 1665 ***2314.30*** *p186*
Joyce, John 56; Ontario, 1871 ***1823.21*** *p184*
Joyce, Joseph 63; Ontario, 1871 ***1823.17*** *p82*
Joyce, Patrick; Louisiana, 1841-1844 ***4981.45*** *p210*
Joyce, Thomas 28; Ontario, 1871 ***1823.21*** *p184*
Joyce, Thomas 39; Ontario, 1871 ***1823.17*** *p82*
Joyce, Ulick 61; Ontario, 1871 ***1823.21*** *p184*
Joyes, Daniel 36; Ontario, 1871 ***1823.21*** *p184*
Joyner, Edward; Massachusetts, 1740 ***9228.50*** *p309*
Jrupnick, Israel 18; New York, NY, 1878 ***9253.2*** *p44*
Juby, Helen M.; America, 1946 ***9228.50*** *p539*
Jucha, Agnes; Detroit, 1929-1930 ***6214.5*** *p63*
Jucha, Sebastian; Detroit, 1927 ***6214.5*** *p63*
Juchereau, Genevieve 2 *SEE* Juchereau, Jean
Juchereau, Jean 11 *SEE* Juchereau, Jean
Juchereau, Jean 42; Quebec, 1634 ***9221.17*** *p37*
*Wife:*Marie Langlois
*Son:*Jean 11
*Daughter:*Genevieve 2
*Son:*Nicolas
*Son:*Noel
Juchereau, Marie Langlois *SEE* Juchereau, Jean
Juchereau, Nicolas *SEE* Juchereau, Jean
Juchereau, Noel *SEE* Juchereau, Jean
Juchereau DeLaFerte, Jean; Quebec, 1634 ***9221.17*** *p37*
Juchereau DeMaure, Jean; Quebec, 1634 ***9221.17*** *p37*
Juchereau DeSaint-Denys, Nicolas; Quebec, 1634 ***9221.17*** *p37*
Juchereau DesChastelets, Noel; Quebec, 1634 ***9221.17*** *p57*
Juchereau deSt-Denis, Nicolas; Quebec, 1634 ***2314.30*** *p167*
Juchereau deSt-Denis, Nicolas; Quebec, 1692 ***2314.30*** *p186*
Juda, Mrs. Gabriel; America, 1839 ***2526.42*** *p124*
With family
Juda, Herz; America, 1836 ***2526.42*** *p124*
Juda, Isidor; California, 1889 ***5475.1*** *p206*
Juda, Lion; Chicago, 1884 ***5475.1*** *p206*
Juda, Simon; America, 1867 ***5475.1*** *p205*
Juda, Simon; America, 1882 ***5475.1*** *p161*
Judas, Auguste 22; Port uncertain, 1840 ***778.6*** *p181*
Judas, Carl; New York, 1903 ***1766.20*** *p36*
Judas, Johann Friedrich Christoph; America, 1864 ***7420.1*** *p224*
Judas, Simon 20; America, 1746 ***778.6*** *p181*
Judd, Henry; Ohio, 1809-1852 ***4511.35*** *p25*
Judd, Henry 30; Ontario, 1871 ***1823.21*** *p184*
Judd, John 35; Ontario, 1871 ***1823.21*** *p184*
Judd, Michel 8; Ontario, 1871 ***1823.21*** *p184*
Judd, Thomas 28; Ontario, 1871 ***1823.21*** *p184*
Judd, William; Ohio, 1809-1852 ***4511.35*** *p25*
Jude, Benjamin; Quebec, 1870 ***8364.32*** *p24*
Judge, Amelia Beatrice Byam; Honduras, 1982 ***9228.50*** *p360*
Judge, Annie 20; Ontario, 1871 ***1823.17*** *p82*
Judge, James 65; Ontario, 1871 ***1823.21*** *p184*
Judge, James, Jr.; Toronto, 1844 ***2910.35*** *p112*
Judge, James, Sr.; Toronto, 1844 ***2910.35*** *p112*
Judge, John 35; Ontario, 1871 ***1823.21*** *p184*
Judge, Patrick; Toronto, 1844 ***2910.35*** *p113*
Judge, William; America, 1863 ***9076.20*** *p68*
Judycki, Joseph; Detroit, 1929 ***1640.55*** *p113*
Juengling, Fr.; Cleveland, OH, 1836-1910 ***2853.20*** *p476*
Juge, Henry 16; Port uncertain, 1846 ***778.6*** *p181*
Juge, Jean Baptiste 52; America, 1848 ***778.6*** *p181*
Juhl, William A.; Colorado, 1872 ***1029.59*** *p48*
Juif, . . . 7; New Orleans, 1842 ***778.6*** *p181*
Juif, . . . 10; New Orleans, 1842 ***778.6*** *p181*
Juif, Mrs. 23; New Orleans, 1842 ***778.6*** *p181*
Juif, Ms. 22; New Orleans, 1842 ***778.6*** *p181*
Juif, Gabriel 25; New Orleans, 1842 ***778.6*** *p181*
Juillard, Louis 23; Missouri, 1846 ***778.6*** *p181*
Juillet, Blaise; Montreal, 1644 ***9221.17*** *p147*
Juin, Jeanne; Quebec, 1672 ***4514.3*** *p328*
Julia, Mr. 17; America, 1848 ***778.6*** *p196*
Julian, Caroline 22 *SEE* Julian, Frank
Julian, Emeline 15; Ontario, 1871 ***1823.17*** *p82*
Julian, Frank 33; Ohio, 1880 ***4879.40*** *p258*
*Wife:*Caroline 22
Julian, Johannah 50; Ontario, 1871 ***1823.21*** *p184*
Julian, John 16; Ontario, 1871 ***1823.17*** *p82*
Julian, William 24; Ontario, 1871 ***1823.17*** *p82*
Julien, Mr. 20; America, 1842 ***778.6*** *p181*
Julien, Andre; Montreal, 1644 ***9221.17*** *p147*
Julien, Anne; Quebec, 1668 ***4514.3*** *p328*
Julien, Hortense 24; Port uncertain, 1841 ***778.6*** *p181*
Julien, Hypolite 26; Port uncertain, 1841 ***778.6*** *p181*
Julien, Jean 19; Quebec, 1659 ***9221.17*** *p403*
Julien, Josephine 26; New Orleans, 1847 ***778.6*** *p181*
Julien, Marie; Quebec, 1639 ***9221.17*** *p89*
Julis, Clovis 35; Port uncertain, 1846 ***778.6*** *p181*
Juliusberg, Samuel; Valdivia, Chile, 1852 ***1192.4*** *p53*
Jullian, Frank 35; Ohio, 1880 ***4879.40*** *p258*
Jullien, Armandine 25; America, 1840 ***778.6*** *p181*
Jullien, Lapatiere 35; America, 1840 ***778.6*** *p181*
Jumonville d'Onville, Mr. 37; America, 1842 ***778.6*** *p181*
Junck, Anna 11; New York, NY, 1893 ***1883.7*** *p41*
Junck, Anna 45; New York, NY, 1893 ***1883.7*** *p41*
Junck, Catharina 19; New York, NY, 1893 ***1883.7*** *p41*
Junck, Franz 22; New York, NY, 1893 ***1883.7*** *p41*
Junck, Georg 17; New York, NY, 1893 ***1883.7*** *p41*
Junck, Josef 9; New York, NY, 1893 ***1883.7*** *p41*
Junck, Michael 15; New York, NY, 1893 ***1883.7*** *p41*
Junck, Michael 47; New York, NY, 1893 ***1883.7*** *p41*
Jund, Magdelene 27; New Orleans, 1847 ***778.6*** *p181*
Jund, Philipp 2; New Orleans, 1847 ***778.6*** *p181*
Jundt, Alfred Daniel; Ohio, 1840-1897 ***8365.35*** *p16*
June, George 32; Ontario, 1871 ***1823.17*** *p82*
Juneau, Jean 26; Quebec, 1637 ***9221.17*** *p70*
Juneau, Jean 36; Quebec, 1649 ***9221.17*** *p215*
*Wife:*Marie Billaud
*Relative:*Pierre
Juneau, Marie Billaud *SEE* Juneau, Jean
Juneau, Pierre *SEE* Juneau, Jean
June Family ; Carolina, n.d. ***9228.50*** *p19A*
Jung, A. Maria Klein 30 *SEE* Jung, Mathias
Jung, Adolph; America, 1867 ***7919.3*** *p535*
Jung, Anna 19; Mississippi, 1847 ***778.6*** *p181*
Jung, Anton 28; New York, NY, 1893 ***1883.7*** *p42*
Jung, August; America, 1867 ***7919.3*** *p535*
With wife & child
Jung, Aurel Michael; Wisconsin, 1870 ***6795.8*** *p81*
Jung, Baptist *SEE* Jung, Peter
Jung, Carl 22; America, 1846 ***778.6*** *p181*
Jung, Carl 18; New York, NY, 1893 ***1883.7*** *p47*
Jung, Caroline; America, 1868 ***7919.3*** *p535*
Jung, Catharina 3; New York, NY, 1893 ***1883.7*** *p37*
Jung, Catherine 31; Louisiana, 1848 ***778.6*** *p181*
Jung, Catherine 20; Mississippi, 1845-1846 ***778.6*** *p181*
Jung, Charlotte 24 *SEE* Jung, Katharina Schmelzer
Jung, Christian 20; America, 1850 ***5475.1*** *p479*
Jung, Christian 2; New York, NY, 1893 ***1883.7*** *p37*
Jung, Christiana Margaretha; America, 1863 ***179.55*** *p19*
Jung, Dorothea; America, 1866 ***5475.1*** *p504*
Jung, Dorothea 26; New York, NY, 1893 ***1883.7*** *p42*
Jung, Dorothea Friederike; America, 1867 ***7919.3*** *p535*
Jung, Elisabeth *SEE* Jung, Mathias
Jung, Elisabeth; America, 1873 ***5475.1*** *p140*
*Son:*Johann
*Daughter:*Eva
*Son:*Peter
*Mother-In-Law:*Kath. Engstler
Jung, Elisabeth *SEE* Jung, Marie Elisabeth
Jung, Elisabeth *SEE* Jung, Nikolaus
Jung, Elisabeth Margarethe; America, 1846 ***8115.12*** *p320*
Jung, Ferdinand; America, 1867 ***7919.3*** *p535*
Jung, Franz 2; New York, NY, 1893 ***1883.7*** *p42*
Jung, Frederic 7; America, 1848 ***778.6*** *p181*
Jung, Frederic 21; Louisiana, 1848 ***778.6*** *p181*
Jung, Fried.; America, 1924 ***8023.44*** *p375*
Jung, Friedrich *SEE* Jung, Nikolaus
Jung, Friedrich Bruno; America, 1867 ***7919.3*** *p535*
Jung, Friedrich Oskar; America, 1867 ***7919.3*** *p535*
Jung, Frnacois 6; America, 1848 ***778.6*** *p181*
Jung, Georg; America, 1868 ***7919.3*** *p533*
With wife & 2 children
Jung, Georg 24; America, 1847 ***778.6*** *p181*
Jung, Georg Friedrich; America, 1868 ***7919.3*** *p535*
With wife & 2 children
Jung, Gertrud 27; America, 1856 ***5475.1*** *p295*
Jung, Gertrud 2 months; New York, NY, 1893 ***1883.7*** *p37*
Jung, Gustav; America, 1867 ***7919.3*** *p535*
Jung, Heinrich; America, 1849 ***5475.1*** *p476*
Jung, Jacob 30; New York, NY, 1893 ***1883.7*** *p37*
Jung, Jakob 15; America, 1890 ***5475.1*** *p424*
Jung, Jakob 70; America, 1865 ***5475.1*** *p534*
Jung, Johann; America, 1833 ***5475.1*** *p466*
With family
Jung, Johann *SEE* Jung, Peter
Jung, Johann 23 *SEE* Jung, Katharina Schmelzer
Jung, Johann; Chicago, 1881 ***5475.1*** *p167*
Jung, Johann; Illinois, 1854 ***6079.1*** *p7*
Jung, Johann 20; Montgomery, AL, 1850 ***5475.1*** *p478*
Jung, Johann Georg; America, n.d. ***8115.12*** *p320*
Jung, Johann Leonhard; America, 1785 ***2526.42*** *p124*
With wife & 2 children
Jung, Johannes 3; New York, NY, 1893 ***1883.7*** *p42*
Jung, Josephine 36; Galveston, TX, 1844 ***3967.10*** *p371*
Jung, Karl *SEE* Jung, Peter
Jung, Karl; America, 1891 ***5475.1*** *p424*
Jung, Karl 18; New York, NY, 1893 ***1883.7*** *p39*
Jung, Katharina Raschel *SEE* Jung, Peter
Jung, Katharina 54; America, 1843 ***5475.1*** *p528*
*Daughter:*Charlotte 24
*Son:*Johann 23
Jung, Konrad *SEE* Jung, Nikolaus
Jung, Konrad; America, n.d. ***8115.12*** *p320*
Jung, Ludwig; America, 1868 ***7919.3*** *p535*
Jung, Ludwig *SEE* Jung, Marie Elisabeth
Jung, Luise *SEE* Jung, Marie Elisabeth
Jung, Luise *SEE* Jung, Nikolaus
Jung, Luise Schwingel *SEE* Jung, Nikolaus
Jung, Margarethe; America, 1868 ***7919.3*** *p535*
With child
Jung, Maria *SEE* Jung, Mathias
Jung, Maria *SEE* Jung, Peter
Jung, Maria; America, 1881 ***5475.1*** *p241*
Jung, Maria Katharina; America, 1785 ***2526.42*** *p121*
Jung, Maria Sara; America, 1834 ***5475.1*** *p457*
Jung, Marie 11; America, 1848 ***778.6*** *p181*
Jung, Marie Catharine 31; America, 1848 ***778.6*** *p182*
Jung, Marie Elisabeth; America, 1880 ***8115.12*** *p324*
*Child:*Ludwig
*Child:*Elisabeth
*Child:*Wilhelm
*Child:*Luise
Jung, Marie Katharine; America, 1869 ***8115.12*** *p320*
Jung, Martha 8 months; New York, NY, 1893 ***1883.7*** *p42*
Jung, Mathias 33; America, 1867 ***5475.1*** *p558*
*Wife:*A. Maria Klein 30
*Daughter:*Elisabeth
*Daughter:*Maria
Jung, Mathias 34; America, 1845 ***778.6*** *p182*
Jung, Michael; America, 1856 ***2526.42*** *p162*
Jung, Nicholas; New York, 1777 ***8529.30*** *p5A*
Jung, Nicolas 8; America, 1848 ***778.6*** *p182*
Jung, Nikolaus; America, 1847 ***5475.1*** *p473*
Jung, Nikolaus; America, 1874 ***5475.1*** *p226*
Jung, Nikolaus *SEE* Jung, Peter

Jung, Nikolaus; America, 1881 *5475.1 p539*
  *Wife:*Luise Schwingel
  *Son:*Konrad
  *Daughter:*Luise
  *Son:*Friedrich
  *Daughter:*Elisabeth
Jung, Peter *SEE* Jung, Peter
Jung, Peter; America, 1879 *5475.1 p141*
  *Wife:*Katharina Raschel
  *Son:*Karl
  *Son:*Peter
  *Daughter:*Maria
  *Son:*Nikolaus
  *Son:*Johann
  *Son:*Baptist
Jung, Pierre 5; America, 1848 *778.6 p182*
Jung, Regina 22; America, 1846 *778.6 p182*
Jung, Sostmann; America, 1866 *7420.1 p243*
Jung, Theresia 33; New York, NY, 1893 *1883.7 p37*
Jung, Vaclav A.; Omaha, NE, 1882 *2853.20 p158*
Jung, Wilh. Jak. Peter; America, 1867 *5475.1 p505*
Jung, Wilhelm *SEE* Jung, Marie Elisabeth
Jung, Wilhelm; Illinois, 1854 *6079.1 p7*
Jung, Wilhelmine; America, 1867 *7919.3 p535*
Jung, Xaver 40; Galveston, TX, 1844 *3967.10 p371*
Jungblut, Kath. 36; America, 1856 *5475.1 p352*
Jungbluth, Barbara *SEE* Jungbluth, Jakob
Jungbluth, El. Margarethe 17 *SEE* Jungbluth, Margarethe
  Steinmetz
Jungbluth, Jakob 13 *SEE* Jungbluth, Margarethe
  Steinmetz
Jungbluth, Jakob *SEE* Jungbluth, Jakob
Jungbluth, Jakob; Brazil, 1879 *5475.1 p444*
  *Wife:*Katharina Gehlen
  *Daughter:*Katharina
  *Daughter:*Barbara
  *Son:*Jakob
  *Daughter:*Karoline
  *Daughter:*Maria
Jungbluth, Joh. Peter 20 *SEE* Jungbluth, Margarethe
  Steinmetz
Jungbluth, John; Ohio, 1809-1852 *4511.35 p25*
Jungbluth, Karoline 11 *SEE* Jungbluth, Margarethe
  Steinmetz
Jungbluth, Karoline *SEE* Jungbluth, Jakob
Jungbluth, Kath.; America, 1865 *5475.1 p498*
Jungbluth, Katharina *SEE* Jungbluth, Jakob
Jungbluth, Katharina Gehlen *SEE* Jungbluth, Jakob
Jungbluth, Luise 8 *SEE* Jungbluth, Margarethe Steinmetz
Jungbluth, Margarethe 43; America, 1856 *5475.1 p491*
  *Daughter:*El. Margarethe 17
  *Son:*Joh. Peter 20
  *Son:*Jakob 13
  *Daughter:*Karoline 11
  *Daughter:*Luise 8
Jungbluth, Margarethe; New York, 1867 *5475.1 p499*
Jungbluth, Maria *SEE* Jungbluth, Jakob
Junge, Aug.; Valdivia, Chile, 1852 *1192.4 p54*
  With wife
Junge, J. G.; Valdivia, Chile, 1852 *1192.4 p54*
  With wife & 2 children
  With child 3 months
  With child 8
Junger, Elisabeth; America, 1868 *7919.3 p525*
Jungfleisch, Joh. Nikolaus; America, 1868 *5475.1 p71*
Jungfleisch, Sophie; Pennsylvania, 1888 *5475.1 p55*

Junghans, Carl Ludwig Emil; America, 1882 *7420.1 p329*
Jungk, Charlotte; America, 1857 *7420.1 p164*
Jungk, Friedrich Wilhelm; America, 1857 *7420.1 p164*
Jungk, Sarah; America, 1867 *7420.1 p258*
Jungkeit, Anna *SEE* Jungkeit, August
Jungkeit, August; Dakota, 1833-1918 *554.30 p26*
  *Wife:*Anna
Jungkuns, Carl 23; New York, NY, 1885 *1883.7 p45*
Jungling, Ida; America, 1860 *7420.1 p194*
Jungmann, Anna *SEE* Jungmann, Johann
Jungmann, Barbara *SEE* Jungmann, Johann
Jungmann, Berta *SEE* Jungmann, Johann
Jungmann, Dorothea Zahe *SEE* Jungmann, Johann
Jungmann, Johann; America, 1881 *5475.1 p332*
  *Wife:*Dorothea Zahe
  *Daughter:*Berta
  *Son:*Mathias
  *Daughter:*Barbara
  *Daughter:*Anna
Jungmann, Johann; Port uncertain, 1881 *5475.1 p332*
Jungmann, Maria 36; America, 1857 *5475.1 p250*
Jungmann, Mathias *SEE* Jungmann, Johann
Jungwall, Axel; Colorado, 1883 *1029.59 p48*
Jungwall, Axel; Colorado, 1883 *1029.59 p55*
Junier, Jacques; Quebec, 1632 *9221.17 p19*
Junion, Francois Xavier *SEE* Junion, Jean Lambert
Junion, Jean Joseph *SEE* Junion, Jean Lambert
Junion, Jean Lambert; Wisconsin, 1854-1858 *1495.20 p50*
  *Wife:*Marie Julienne Raison
  *Child:*Francois Xavier
  *Child:*Jean Joseph
  *Child:*Josephine
  *Child:*Pierre Joseph
  *Child:*Philippe
Junion, Josephine *SEE* Junion, Jean Lambert
Junion, Marie; Wisconsin, 1854-1858 *1495.20 p50*
Junion, Marie Julienne Raison *SEE* Junion, Jean Lambert
Junion, P. J.; New York, NY, 1856 *1494.21 p31*
Junion, Philippe *SEE* Junion, Jean Lambert
Junion, Pierre Joseph *SEE* Junion, Jean Lambert
Junis, George 45; Ontario, 1871 *1823.21 p184*
Junk, Anna Maria *SEE* Junk, Maria Becker
Junk, Christoph *SEE* Junk, Maria Becker
Junk, Elisabeth *SEE* Junk, Maria Becker
Junk, Gerhard; America, 1882 *5475.1 p35*
Junk, Heinrich; England, 1878 *5475.1 p94*
Junk, Helena *SEE* Junk, Maria Becker
Junk, Johann 27; America, 1866 *5475.1 p323*
  *Wife:*Katharina Lackas 24
Junk, Karl; New York, 1889 *5475.1 p38*
Junk, Katharina *SEE* Junk, Maria Becker
Junk, Katharina Lackas 24 *SEE* Junk, Johann
Junk, Maria; America, 1861 *5475.1 p482*
  *Daughter:*Katharina
  *Daughter:*Anna Maria
  *Daughter:*Elisabeth
  *Daughter:*Helena
  *Son:*Christoph
Junker, Jeannette 3; America, 1842 *778.6 p182*
Junker, Karl; Nashville, TN, 1846 *8023.44 p375*
Junker, Marguueritte 30; America, 1842 *778.6 p182*
Junker, Maria 30; America, 1871 *5475.1 p418*
Junker, Marie 50; America, 1842 *778.6 p182*
Junker, Marie Anne 38; America, 1840 *778.6 p182*

Junker, Therese 11; America, 1842 *778.6 p182*
Junker, Victo.re 7; America, 1842 *778.6 p182*
Junkova, Anna; New York, NY, 1893 *2853.20 p469*
Junl, Neils; Iowa, 1897 *1211.15 p15*
Junod, Miss R. 28; New York, NY, 1894 *6512.1 p181*
Junt, Andreas 44; Port uncertain, 1848 *778.6 p182*
Junt, Johann 18; Port uncertain, 1848 *778.6 p182*
Junt, Louis 1; Port uncertain, 1848 *778.6 p182*
Junt, Regina 27; Port uncertain, 1848 *778.6 p182*
Junt, Theresia 21; Port uncertain, 1848 *778.6 p182*
Juntunen, Henry 37; Minnesota, 1923 *2769.54 p1384*
Juntunen, Minnie 38; Minnesota, 1923 *2769.54 p1384*
Jupier, Claude 34; New Orleans, 1848 *778.6 p182*
Jupier, Louise 20; New Orleans, 1848 *778.6 p182*
Jupp, Spencer 43; Ontario, 1871 *1823.17 p82*
Juranek, Tomas; America, 1849 *2853.20 p519*
Juranek, Tomas; Wisconsin, 1810-1910 *2853.20 p317*
Jure, John 47; New Orleans, 1848 *778.6 p182*
Juren, Jindrich; Texas, 1876 *2853.20 p65*
Juren, Jindrich; Texas, 1876 *2853.20 p79*
Jurgens, Carl Friedrich Wilhelm; America, 1882 *7420.1 p329*
Jurgens, Carl Wilhelm; America, 1854 *7420.1 p122*
Jurgens, Egon; Milwaukee, 1923 *8023.44 p375*
  *Wife:*Mathilde Herz
Jurgens, Mathilde Herz *SEE* Jurgens, Egon
Jurgensen, Reinhold 19; New York, NY, 1885 *1883.7 p46*
Jurguen, Girard 37; New Orleans, 1842 *778.6 p182*
Juringius, Carl; New York, NY, 1845 *6412.40 p148*
Jurka, Antonin; Chicago, 1810-1910 *2853.20 p404*
Jurka, Antonin; Chicago, 1866 *2853.20 p277*
Jurka, Josef; Chicago, 1866 *2853.20 p405*
Juron, Louis 37; Montreal, 1653 *9221.17 p289*
Jury, James 25; Ontario, 1871 *1823.21 p184*
Jury, John 38; Ontario, 1871 *1823.21 p184*
Jury, Robert 23; Montreal, 1659 *9221.17 p422*
Jury, William 35; Ontario, 1871 *1823.21 p184*
Jury, William 49; Ontario, 1871 *1823.21 p184*
Jury, William 61; Ontario, 1871 *1823.17 p82*
Jus, Antoine 21; New Orleans, 1848 *778.6 p182*
Jusaquet, R. 30; Mexico, 1846 *778.6 p182*
Juschnowitz, Anna 20; New York, NY, 1893 *1883.7 p41*
Juschnowitz, Winzens 36; New York, NY, 1893 *1883.7 p41*
Jusik, Martinus; Wisconsin, 1893 *6795.8 p58*
Jusik, Mary; Wisconsin, 1894 *6795.8 p58*
Jussigny, J. 25; New Orleans, 1844 *778.6 p182*
Just, August Karl; Wisconsin, 1889 *6795.8 p167*
Just, Franklin 76; Ontario, 1871 *1823.21 p184*
Just, Frantisek J.; San Antonio, TX, 1892 *2853.20 p253*
Just, Frantisek J.; San Antonio, TX, 1893 *2853.20 p320*
Just, Frederick 30; Ontario, 1871 *1823.21 p184*
Just, Lawrence; Ohio, 1809-1852 *4511.35 p25*
Justi, Ernst Reinhard Ferdinand; America, 1866 *7420.1 p244*
Justi, Louis Philipp; America, 1859 *7420.1 p186*
Justi, Wilhelm Adolph; America, 1858 *7420.1 p178*
Jutras, Claude 26; Quebec, 1654 *9221.17 p310*
Jutte, Christian; Galveston, TX, 1855 *571.7 p17*
Jutz, Carl; Valdivia, Chile, 1851 *1192.4 p51*
  With wife
Juvenneton, Joseph; Louisiana, 1841-1844 *4981.45 p210*
Juz, Philip 19; America, 1844 *778.6 p182*

K

Kaakinen, Helen Esther; Oregon, 1941 *9157.47 p2*
Kaas, Johann; America, 1880 *5475.1 p267*
Kaas, Peter; Iowa, 1884 *5475.1 p268*
Kaatz, Friedrich Herman; Wisconsin, 1883 *6795.8 p120*
Kaatz, Gottlob; Wisconsin, 1874 *6795.8 p122*
Kaatz, Reinhold A.; Wisconsin, 1902 *6795.8 p231*
Kabat, Jan; Wisconsin, 1856 *2853.20 p345*
Kabel, Georg; America, 1856 *2526.42 p95*
Kabel, Georg 16 *SEE* Kabel, Leonhard
Kabel, Heinrich; America, 1871 *2526.42 p95*
Kabel, Johannes; America, 1860 *2526.42 p162*
Kabel, Johannes; America, 1869 *2526.42 p95*
Kabel, Konrad; New York, 1813-1913 *2526.43 p127*
Kabel, Leonhard; America, 1856 *2526.42 p95*
  *Child:*Georg
  *Child:*Philipp
  *Child:*Leonhard
Kabel, Leonhard 6 *SEE* Kabel, Leonhard
Kabel, Maria Elisabetha; America, 1856 *2526.43 p120*
Kabel, Nikolaus; America, 1836 *2526.42 p108*
Kabel, Philipp 9 *SEE* Kabel, Leonhard
Kabeldey, Fredrick; Washington, 1889 *2770.40 p79*
Kabelka, Frantisek; Milwaukee, 1897 *2853.20 p311*
Kabeoh, John 56; Ontario, 1871 *1823.17 p82*
Kable, Daniel; America, 1849 *5475.1 p28*
Kabourek, Matej; Nebraska, 1871-1872 *2853.20 p176*
Kabourek, Matej; Wisconsin, 1876-1877 *2853.20 p172*
Kabourek, Vaclav; Wisconsin, 1856 *2853.20 p344*
Kabs, Stephan 22; America, 1844 *778.6 p182*
Kacer, Kaspar Fr.; Texas, 1895 *2853.20 p85*
Kacer, Martin 12; St. Louis, 1853 *2853.20 p50*
  With parents
Kachel, H.; New York, 1859 *358.56 p54*
Kachele, Christ.; Valdivia, Chile, 1852 *1192.4 p53*
Kachler, Edward; Ohio, 1809-1852 *4511.35 p25*
Kaczmarek, Paul; Texas, 1845-1872 *9980.22 p16*
Kaczocha, Julianna 19; New York, NY, 1911 *6533.11 p10*
Kaczocha, Wincenty 11 months; New York, NY, 1911 *6533.11 p10*
Kaderly, Jacques 21; Galveston, TX, 1844 *3967.10 p374*
Kaderly, Jean 18; Galveston, TX, 1844 *3967.10 p374*
Kadlec, Anton; Nebraska, 1905 *3004.30 p46*
Kadlec, Antonin; St. Louis, 1896 *2853.20 p54*
Kadlec, Vavrinec; Chicago, 1873 *2853.20 p397*
Kadrowski, Stanislas 42; New York, NY, 1920 *930.50 p49*
Kaehler, Edward; Ohio, 1809-1852 *4511.35 p25*
Kaemff, Fred; Missouri, 1902 *3276.1 p2*
Kaemichon, Anna 28; New York, NY, 1894 *6512.1 p182*
Kaempf, Agatha 15; Mississippi, 1846 *778.6 p182*
Kaempf, Johann 17; Mississippi, 1846 *778.6 p182*
Kaerton, John Hilton; New York, NY, 1892 *3366.30 p70*
Kaessel, Vincenzo 32; America, 1847 *778.6 p182*
Kaewske, Michael; Wisconsin, 1889 *6795.8 p138*
Kafer, Christian 17; New York, NY, 1893 *1883.7 p41*
Kafer, Christian 47; New York, NY, 1893 *1883.7 p41*
Kafer, Christian; Ohio, 1809-1852 *4511.35 p25*
Kafer, Elisabeth 23; Missouri, 1848 *778.6 p182*
Kafer, Elisabeth 1; New York, NY, 1893 *1883.7 p41*
Kafer, Friedrich 16; New York, NY, 1893 *1883.7 p41*
Kafer, Georg 8; New York, NY, 1893 *1883.7 p41*
Kafer, Johannes 4; New York, NY, 1893 *1883.7 p41*
Kafer, Karl 7; New York, NY, 1893 *1883.7 p41*
Kafer, Katharina 11; New York, NY, 1893 *1883.7 p41*
Kafer, Katharina 44; New York, NY, 1893 *1883.7 p41*
Kaffenbenberger, Anna Eva; Virginia, 1831 *152.20 p65*

Kaffenbenberger, Anna Katharina *SEE* Kaffenbenberger, Johannes
Kaffenbenberger, Anna Margarethe Arras *SEE* Kaffenbenberger, Johannes
Kaffenbenberger, Elisabeth Katharina *SEE* Kaffenbenberger, Johannes
Kaffenbenberger, Johannes; Virginia, 1831 *152.20 p64*
  *Wife:*Anna Margarethe Arras
  *Child:*Anna Katharina
  *Child:*Elisabeth Katharina
  *Child:*Margarethe Elisabeth
Kaffenbenberger, Margarethe Elisabeth *SEE* Kaffenbenberger, Johannes
Kaffenberger, Adam; America, 1866 *2526.43 p191*
Kaffenberger, Anna Eva; Virginia, 1831 *152.20 p65*
Kaffenberger, Georg Adam; America, 1880 *2526.42 p136*
Kaffenberger, Georg Konrad; America, 1896 *2526.43 p172*
Kaffenberger, Heinrich; America, 1866 *2526.43 p172*
Kaffenberger, Johann Philipp; America, 1881 *2526.43 p196*
Kaffenberger, Johann Philipp; America, 1895 *2526.43 p196*
Kaffenberger, Johannes; America, 1880 *2526.43 p191*
Kaffenberger, Magdalena; America, 1853 *2526.43 p196*
Kaffenberger, Michael; America, 1866 *2526.43 p172*
Kaffenberger, Peter; America, 1882 *2526.43 p160*
Kaffenberger, Wilhelm; America, 1870 *2526.43 p160*
Kaffenberger, Wilhelm 17; America, 1866 *2526.43 p172*
Kaffer, Christian; Ohio, 1809-1852 *4511.35 p25*
Kafle, A.V.; New York, NY, 1843 *6412.40 p147*
Kager, John; New York, 1860 *358.56 p4*
Kah, Charles; Ohio, 1840-1897 *8365.35 p16*
Kah, Crist; Ohio, 1840-1897 *8365.35 p16*
Kahanek, Josef; Texas, 1860 *2853.20 p74*
Kahaven, William; Boston, 1766 *1642 p37*
Kahes, Henry W. 25; Ontario, 1871 *1823.21 p184*
Kahl, Anna Barbara; Nova Scotia, 1750 *2526.42 p167*
Kahl, Katharina Elisabeth; America, 1752 *2526.42 p167*
Kahle, Heinrich Friedrich Conrad; America, 1858 *7420.1 p179*
Kahle, John; Ohio, 1809-1852 *4511.35 p25*
Kahler, Christian 37; Portland, ME, 1906 *970.38 p78*
Kahler, Franz Carl; Port uncertain, 1880 *7420.1 p398*
Kahler, Johannes Ludwig Philipp; Port uncertain, 1856 *7420.1 p148*
Kahler, Max Ludwig; America, 1873 *7420.1 p300*
Kahn, Mr. 50; America, 1843 *778.6 p182*
Kahn, B.; Louisiana, 1874 *4981.45 p132*
Kahn, Daniel; America, 1875 *5475.1 p128*
Kahn, Eduard; America, 1882 *5475.1 p447*
Kahn, Esther 20; Cincinnati, 1846 *778.6 p182*
Kahn, Ferdinand; America, 1892 *2526.42 p153*
Kahn, Ferdinand; America, 1896 *5475.1 p448*
Kahn, Heyum; America, 1881 *2526.42 p172*
Kahn, Heyum; America, 1891 *2526.42 p153*
Kahn, Hirsch 21; New Orleans, 1848 *778.6 p182*
Kahn, Jakob; America, 1889 *2526.42 p124*
Kahn, Johannetta; America, 1896 *5475.1 p448*
Kahn, Julius; America, 1895 *5475.1 p448*
Kahn, Leopold 20; America, 1846 *778.6 p183*
Kahn, Mathias 23; America, 1845 *778.6 p183*
Kahn, Max; Michigan, 1890 *5475.1 p448*
Kahn, Samuel; Indiana, 1892 *5475.1 p448*
Kahn, Simon 19; Louisiana, 1848 *778.6 p183*
Kahn, Simon; North Carolina, 1844 *1088.45 p16*
Kahn, Veist; America, 1864 *2526.42 p153*

Kahnweiler, David; North Carolina, 1852 *1088.45 p16*
Kahnwiler, John; Ohio, 1809-1852 *4511.35 p25*
Kahshgrance, William 68; Ontario, 1871 *1823.17 p82*
Kaihsling, Philipp 19; America, 1849 *5475.1 p476*
Kail, Konrad; Iowa, 1921 *1211.15 p16*
Kain, John 70; Ontario, 1871 *1823.21 p184*
Kain, Maria; New York, 1860 *358.56 p5*
Kains, Edmond 41; Ontario, 1871 *1823.21 p184*
Kaiser, Andreas; America, 1868 *7919.3 p528*
Kaiser, Anne Marie 22; Missouri, 1845 *778.6 p183*
Kaiser, August; New York, 1860 *358.56 p150*
Kaiser, Bernhard; America, 1868 *7919.3 p528*
  With wife & 2 children
Kaiser, Christine 23; Missouri, 1845 *778.6 p183*
Kaiser, Christine Ohmberger *SEE* Kaiser, Johan George
Kaiser, Christoph; America, 1868 *7919.3 p528*
  With wife & 5 children
Kaiser, Elisabeth 36; America, 1856 *5475.1 p277*
Kaiser, Ernestine Maria; America, 1868 *7919.3 p527*
Kaiser, Friedrich; Wisconsin, 1873 *6795.8 p100*
Kaiser, Johan George; Philadelphia, 1859 *8513.31 p318*
  *Wife:*Christine Ohmberger
Kaiser, John 29; Ontario, 1871 *1823.21 p184*
Kaiser, Maria; America, 1867 *7919.3 p528*
Kaiser, Paul; Iowa, 1910 *1211.15 p16*
Kaisling, Michel; America, 1846 *5475.1 p472*
Kaisling, Peter; America, 1852 *5475.1 p481*
Kajewske, John; Wisconsin, 1902 *6795.8 p138*
Kakalec, Jan 33; New York, NY, 1920 *930.50 p49*
Kakeldy, Charles; Washington, 1882 *2770.40 p135*
Kalaitzakis, Andro Agopitos; New York, NY, 1908 *3331.4 p12*
Kalal, Frantisek; Chicago, 1854 *2853.20 p387*
  With family
Kalamaves, Anastasia 38; New York, NY, 1894 *6512.1 p185*
Kalamaves, Antoino 13; New York, NY, 1894 *6512.1 p185*
Kalamaves, Atina 15; New York, NY, 1894 *6512.1 p185*
Kalamaves, Constantin 7; New York, NY, 1894 *6512.1 p185*
Kalamaves, George 48; New York, NY, 1894 *6512.1 p185*
Kalamaves, Nema 2; New York, NY, 1894 *6512.1 p185*
Kalas, Jan; Chicago, 1888-1910 *2853.20 p466*
Kalas, Wenzeslaus; Wisconsin, 1898 *6795.8 p58*
Kalasansky-Schuessler, Josef; Milwaukee, 1864 *2853.20 p159*
Kalb, Erasmus; America, 1868 *7919.3 p528*
  With family
Kalb, Hermann Ernst; America, 1849 *7420.1 p65*
Kalber, Heinrich Christian; America, 1867 *7919.3 p527*
Kalcik, Mikulas; Wisconsin, 1857 *2853.20 p323*
Kalert, Jean; Louisiana, 1841-1844 *4981.45 p210*
Kali, Anna 55; Halifax, N.S., 1902 *1860.4 p42*
Kali, Elise 8; Halifax, N.S., 1902 *1860.4 p42*
Kali, Joh. 55; Halifax, N.S., 1902 *1860.4 p42*
Kalin, Thomas; Canada, 1775 *3036.5 p68*
Kalina, Josef; Illinois, 1853-1910 *2853.20 p471*
Kalinowski, Albert; Texas, 1900 *6015.15 p9*
Kalinowski, Anton; Galveston, TX, 1900 *6015.15 p9*
  *Wife:*Ewa
Kalinowski, Ewa *SEE* Kalinowski, Anton
Kalinowski, F. C.; New York, NY, 1888 *6015.15 p10*
Kalinowski, George; Detroit, 1930 *1640.60 p77*
Kalinowski, John; Texas, 1902 *6015.15 p10*
Kalinowski, Simon; Texas, 1892-1900 *6015.15 p10*
Kalinowski, Voicich; Texas, 1892 *6015.15 p10*

Kalinski, Christoph; Wisconsin, 1895 ***6795.8*** *p125*
Kaliszewska, Anna; Detroit, 1890 ***9980.23*** *p97*
Kaliszewski, Jacob; Detroit, 1929-1930 ***6214.5*** *p69*
Kalivoda, Josef, Sr.; Iowa, 1870 ***2853.20*** *p202*
Kalkmann, Magdalena *SEE* Kalkmann, Peter
Kalkmann, Maria Heinz *SEE* Kalkmann, Peter
Kalkmann, Peter 30; Brazil, 1862 ***5475.1*** *p561*
*Wife:*Maria Heinz
*Daughter:*Magdalena
Kallenbach, Barbara; New York, 1860 ***358.56*** *p149*
Kallenbach, Christian; America, 1867 ***7919.3*** *p531*
With wife & 3 children
Kallenbach, Emil; America, 1881 ***5475.1*** *p421*
With wife & 2 children
Kallenbach, Wilhelm; America, 1867 ***7919.3*** *p535*
Kallenborn, Kat.; America, 1881 ***5475.1*** *p273*
Kalley, Judith; Boston, 1754 ***1642*** *p47*
Kallgren, Anna Elisabeth *SEE* Kallgren, Hedvig Lovisa
Kallgren, Gustaf F.; St. Paul, MN, 1887 ***1865.50*** *p44*
Kallgren, Hedvig Lovisa; St. Paul, MN, 1889 ***1865.50*** *p44*
*Daughter:*Anna Elisabeth
Kallin, Martha Ersdotter *SEE* Kallin, Olof
Kallin, Olof; Kansas, 1869-1871 ***777.40*** *p9*
*Wife:*Martha Ersdotter
Kallinack, Philip; Boston, n.d. ***9228.50*** *p392*
Kalling, Johann 18; New York, NY, 1893 ***1883.7*** *p43*
Kallio, Annie 33; Minnesota, 1925 ***2769.54*** *p1384*
Kallio, Matt 43; Minnesota, 1925 ***2769.54*** *p1380*
Kallmeier, Friederike Christine; America, 1883 ***7420.1*** *p337*
Kallmeyer, Johann Friedrich Wilhelm; America, 1872 ***7420.1*** *p295*
Kallstrom, O.; New York, NY, 1845 ***6412.40*** *p149*
Kallum, Thomas S. 29; Ontario, 1871 ***1823.21*** *p185*
Kaltenbach, Christine 10 *SEE* Kaltenbach, Wilhelm
Kaltenbach, Friedrich 8 *SEE* Kaltenbach, Wilhelm
Kaltenbach, Geo. 24; New York, NY, 1847 ***9176.15*** *p51*
Kaltenbach, Georg 17 *SEE* Kaltenbach, Wilhelm
Kaltenbach, Heinrich 1 *SEE* Kaltenbach, Wilhelm
Kaltenbach, Karoline 5 *SEE* Kaltenbach, Wilhelm
Kaltenbach, Katharina 13 *SEE* Kaltenbach, Wilhelm
Kaltenbach, Luise 16 *SEE* Kaltenbach, Wilhelm
Kaltenbach, Luise Eberhard 37 *SEE* Kaltenbach, Wilhelm
Kaltenbach, Michel 22; New York, NY, 1847 ***9176.15*** *p51*
Kaltenbach, Wilhelm 19 *SEE* Kaltenbach, Wilhelm
Kaltenbach, Wilhelm 42; America, 1836 ***5475.1*** *p413*
*Son:*Friedrich 8
*Daughter:*Christine 10
*Daughter:*Katharina 13
*Daughter:*Luise 16
*Son:*Georg 17
*Son:*Wilhelm 19
*Wife:*Luise Eberhard 37
*Daughter:*Karoline 5
*Daughter:*Wilhelmine 3
*Son:*Heinrich 1
Kaltenbach, Wilhelmine 3 *SEE* Kaltenbach, Wilhelm
Kalynowski, Anton; Galveston, TX, 1900 ***6015.15*** *p9*
*Wife:*Ewa
Kalynowski, Ewa *SEE* Kalynowski, Anton
Kalynowski, John; Texas, 1902 ***6015.15*** *p10*
Kalynowski, Simon; Texas, 1892-1900 ***6015.15*** *p10*
Kalynowski, Voicich; Texas, 1892 ***6015.15*** *p10*
Kamerer, Jacob; Washington, 1888 ***2770.40*** *p26*
Kamerer, Stanislas 35; America, 1746 ***778.6*** *p183*
Kamery, Samuel 42; Michigan, 1880 ***4491.30*** *p18*
Kaminek, Jan; St. Louis, 1848 ***2853.20*** *p21*
Kaminska, Anny; Wisconsin, 1881 ***6795.8*** *p58*
Kaminska, Julia; Wisconsin, 1893 ***6795.8*** *p58*
Kaminski, A. 19; Quebec, 1870 ***8364.32*** *p24*
Kaminski, Anny; Wisconsin, 1881 ***6795.8*** *p58*
Kaminski, Bronislaw; Detroit, 1930 ***1640.60*** *p81*
Kamker, Philippine; America, 1854 ***7420.1*** *p122*
Kamloth, Engel Marie Sophie; America, 1868 ***7420.1*** *p273*
Kammer, Konrad; America, 1849 ***8115.12*** *p321*
Kammer, Wilhelm; America, 1849 ***8115.12*** *p321*
Kamp, Friedrich; Wisconsin, 1897 ***6795.8*** *p149*
Kamper, Joseph 19; Minnesota, 1925 ***2769.54*** *p1384*
Kampermann, Max Robert Emil; Port uncertain, 1892 ***7420.1*** *p366*
Kampf, Auguste; America, 1867 ***7919.3*** *p534*
Kampf, Dorothea; America, 1861 ***5475.1*** *p542*
Kampner, Harry; Texas, 1903 ***3435.45*** *p36*
Kanaday, John Henry; North Carolina, 1852 ***1088.45*** *p16*
Kanast, John 39; America, 1843 ***778.6*** *p183*
Kanay, James; Louisiana, 1874 ***4981.45*** *p296*
Kane, Bridget; New Orleans, 1851 ***7242.30*** *p145*
Kane, Charles 60; Ontario, 1871 ***1823.17*** *p82*
Kane, Dennis 40; Ontario, 1871 ***1823.17*** *p82*
Kane, Emma M.; Philadelphia, 1851 ***8513.31*** *p318*
Kane, Francis 66; Michigan, 1880 ***4491.33*** *p12*
Kane, John 29; Indiana, 1887-1888 ***9076.20*** *p71*
Kane, John; North Carolina, 1840 ***1088.45*** *p16*
Kane, M. J.; Louisiana, 1874 ***4981.45*** *p132*
Kane, Margaret; New Orleans, 1850 ***7242.30*** *p145*
Kane, Mary 26; Ontario, 1871 ***1823.17*** *p82*
Kane, Mary Jane 34; Ontario, 1871 ***1823.21*** *p185*
Kane, Mattie 29; Michigan, 1880 ***4491.33*** *p13*
Kane, Patrick 31; Indiana, 1884-1888 ***9076.20*** *p71*
Kane, Patrick; New Orleans, 1850 ***7242.30*** *p145*
Kane, Patrick 56; Ontario, 1871 ***1823.21*** *p185*
Kane, Patt; New Orleans, 1851 ***7242.30*** *p145*
Kane, Richard; New Orleans, 1851 ***7242.30*** *p145*
Kane, Robert; Ohio, 1840-1897 ***8365.35*** *p16*
Kane, William 23; Ontario, 1871 ***1823.17*** *p82*
Kane, William 48; Ontario, 1871 ***1823.17*** *p82*
Kania, Julia 17; New York, NY, 1904 ***8355.1*** *p15*
Kanigowski, Stanislaw; Detroit, 1930 ***1640.60*** *p77*
Kanitz, Sebastian; Philadelphia, 1778 ***8529.30*** *p2A*
Kannengiesser, Jakob 21; America, 1883 ***5475.1*** *p496*
Kanner, Audie; Louisiana, 1874 ***4981.45*** *p132*
Kanney, James; Boston, 1743 ***1642*** *p45*
Kanney, Ruth; Boston, 1747 ***1642*** *p46*
Kanningusser, Otto 19; Ontario, 1871 ***1823.21*** *p185*
Kanny, Daniel 77; Ontario, 1871 ***1823.17*** *p82*
Kanowski, Albert; Detroit, 1930 ***1640.60*** *p81*
Kanter, Max; New York, 1860 ***358.56*** *p148*
Kantonen, Selma 31; Minnesota, 1925 ***2769.54*** *p1379*
Kantonen, Sulo 36; Minnesota, 1925 ***2769.54*** *p1379*
Kanz, David 23; Ohio, 1847 ***778.6*** *p183*
Kanzer, Jacques 27; Port uncertain, 1843 ***778.6*** *p183*
Kapcensky, Felix; Galveston, TX, 1870 ***6015.15*** *p26*
Kapczynski, Felix; Galveston, TX, 1870 ***6015.15*** *p26*
Kapczynski, Wm.; Texas, 1887-1890 ***6015.15*** *p26*
Kapen, Chas F. 30; Ontario, 1871 ***1823.21*** *p185*
Kapezynski, Wm.; Texas, 1887-1890 ***6015.15*** *p26*
Kapf, Adelaide; Chile, 1852 ***1192.4*** *p54*
With child
Kapf, Catharina 7; New Orleans, 1848 ***778.6*** *p183*
Kapf, Catharina 36; New Orleans, 1848 ***778.6*** *p183*
Kapf, Franzcois 9 months; New Orleans, 1848 ***778.6*** *p183*
Kapf, Georg 9; New Orleans, 1848 ***778.6*** *p183*
Kapf, George 49; New Orleans, 1848 ***778.6*** *p183*
Kapf, Joseph 14; New Orleans, 1848 ***778.6*** *p183*
Kapf, Josephine 3; New Orleans, 1848 ***778.6*** *p183*
Kapf, Magdalena 4; New Orleans, 1848 ***778.6*** *p183*
Kapf, Marianne 12; New Orleans, 1848 ***778.6*** *p183*
Kapfer, Anne 1; America, 1840 ***778.6*** *p183*
Kapfer, Catherine 5; America, 1840 ***778.6*** *p183*
Kapfer, George 3; America, 1840 ***778.6*** *p183*
Kapfer, Marie 34; America, 1840 ***778.6*** *p183*
Kapfer, Matis 35; America, 1840 ***778.6*** *p183*
Kaplan, Julia 6 months; New York, NY, 1894 ***6512.1*** *p230*
Kaplan, Mary 3; New York, NY, 1894 ***6512.1*** *p230*
Kaplan, Minnie 25; New York, NY, 1894 ***6512.1*** *p230*
Kaplan, Sarah 6; New York, NY, 1894 ***6512.1*** *p230*
Kapmeier, Daniel; America, 1856 ***7420.1*** *p148*
With wife & 5 daughters
Kapp, Antone; Colorado, 1901 ***1029.59*** *p48*
Kapp, Carl; Wisconsin, 1897 ***6795.8*** *p236*
Kapp, Conrad; Ohio, 1809-1852 ***4511.35*** *p25*
Kappel, Adam; Louisiana, 1836-1841 ***4981.45*** *p209*
Kappel, Dorothea; America, 1867 ***5475.1*** *p522*
Kappel, Jacob; Ohio, 1809-1852 ***4511.35*** *p25*
Kapper, F. 7; New Orleans, 1834 ***1002.51*** *p113*
Kapper, John; Ohio, 1809-1852 ***4511.35*** *p25*
Kapper, Miss M. 30; New Orleans, 1834 ***1002.51*** *p113*
Kapper, Martin; Ohio, 1809-1852 ***4511.35*** *p25*
Kapper, P. 5; New Orleans, 1834 ***1002.51*** *p113*
Kappes, Anna Katharina 37; America, 1863 ***5475.1*** *p482*
Kappes, Marie Margaretha; America, 1867 ***2526.43*** *p172*
Kappeser, Miss A. 16; New Orleans, 1834 ***1002.51*** *p112*
Kappeser, C. 13; New Orleans, 1834 ***1002.51*** *p112*
Kappeser, Miss C. 35; New Orleans, 1834 ***1002.51*** *p112*
Kappeser, F. 7; New Orleans, 1834 ***1002.51*** *p113*
Kappeser, F. 42; New Orleans, 1834 ***1002.51*** *p112*
Kappeser, H. 5; New Orleans, 1834 ***1002.51*** *p112*
Kappeser, J. 32; New Orleans, 1834 ***1002.51*** *p113*
Kappeser, Miss M. 4 months; New Orleans, 1834 ***1002.51*** *p112*
Kappeser, Miss M. 30; New Orleans, 1834 ***1002.51*** *p113*
Kappeser, P. 5; New Orleans, 1834 ***1002.51*** *p113*
Kappler, Catharina 20; America, 1747 ***778.6*** *p183*
Kappler, Louis 34; America, 1747 ***778.6*** *p183*
Kappmeyer, Friedrich Wilhelm; America, 1865 ***7420.1*** *p232*
With family
Kaps, Wilhelm; America, 1854 ***2526.42*** *p200*
Kara, Simon; South Carolina, 1808 ***6155.4*** *p18*
Karas, Josef; Baltimore, 1872 ***2853.20*** *p125*
Karas, Marcin; Detroit, 1929 ***1640.55*** *p116*
Karasek, Jan; New York, NY, 1860-1869 ***2853.20*** *p100*
Karb, Karolina 26; America, 1867 ***5475.1*** *p49*
Karberg, J.; Venezuela, 1843 ***3899.5*** *p546*
Karch, Anna Margarethe; Virginia, 1831 ***152.20*** *p65*
Karcher, Ludwig; Ohio, 1809-1852 ***4511.35*** *p25*
Kardel, Wilhelm; Iowa, 1889 ***1211.15*** *p15*
Kardener, Elizabeth 38; America, 1846 ***778.6*** *p183*
Kardener, Henry 2; America, 1846 ***778.6*** *p183*
Kardener, Jean 7; America, 1846 ***778.6*** *p183*
Kardener, Maria 4; America, 1846 ***778.6*** *p183*
Kardener, Nanette 6 months; America, 1846 ***778.6*** *p183*
Kardener, Octavia 6; America, 1846 ***778.6*** *p183*
Kardener, P. 36; America, 1846 ***778.6*** *p183*
Kardinal, Mr.; America, 1854 ***7420.1*** *p122*
Kardon, Joseph; Ohio, 1809-1852 ***4511.35*** *p25*
Karel, Jan; Wisconsin, 1868 ***2853.20*** *p325*
Karg, Adam 25; America, 1846 ***2526.42*** *p200*
With wife
Karg, Anna Margaretha 23 *SEE* Karg, Elisabetha
Karg, Bernhard; America, 1853 ***2526.43*** *p160*
Karg, Elisabetha; America, 1866 ***2526.43*** *p188*
*Daughter:*Anna Margaretha
*Daughter:*Margaretha
*Son:*Michael
*Son:*Nikolaus
Karg, Heinrich; America, 1881 ***2526.43*** *p150*
Karg, Jakob 16 *SEE* Karg, Johann Leonhard
Karg, Jakob 17 *SEE* Karg, Peter
Karg, Johann Leonhard; America, 1752 ***2526.42*** *p175*
*Wife:*Maria Elisabetha Stockum
*Child:*Peter
*Child:*Jakob
Karg, Leonhard; America, 1832 ***2526.42*** *p175*
With wife & 2 children
Karg, Leonhard 14 *SEE* Karg, Peter
Karg, Margaretha 20 *SEE* Karg, Elisabetha
Karg, Margaretha 29 *SEE* Karg, Peter
Karg, Maria Elisabetha Stockum *SEE* Karg, Johann Leonhard
Karg, Michael; America, 1832 ***2526.43*** *p172*
Karg, Michael 10 *SEE* Karg, Elisabetha
Karg, Nikolaus 17 *SEE* Karg, Elisabetha
Karg, Peter; America, 1846 ***2526.42*** *p200*
With wife
*Son:*Peter
*Son:*Philipp
*Son:*Leonhard
*Daughter:*Margaretha
*Son:*Jakob
Karg, Peter 14 *SEE* Karg, Peter
Karg, Peter 18 *SEE* Karg, Johann Leonhard
Karg, Philipp; America, 1836 ***2526.42*** *p109*
With wife
With child 7
With child 5
With child 2
With child 10
With child 12
Karg, Philipp 7 *SEE* Karg, Peter
Karg, Regina; America, 1887 ***2526.42*** *p136*
Kari, Andrew; Minnesota, 1925 ***2769.54*** *p1381*
Kari, Andrew 33; Minnesota, 1923 ***2769.54*** *p1381*
Karkainen, Matt 33; Minnesota, 1925 ***2769.54*** *p1381*
Karkiewicz, Maryanna 26; New York, NY, 1894 ***6512.1*** *p230*
Karl, Karl; America, 1889 ***5475.1*** *p206*
Karl, Leonard 44; Ontario, 1871 ***1823.21*** *p185*
Karl, Susanna; Iowa, 1874 ***5475.1*** *p318*
Karl, Victor; Chicago, 1889 ***5475.1*** *p206*
Karlestine, Cottile 46; America, 1840 ***778.6*** *p184*
Karlestine, Michael 36; America, 1840 ***778.6*** *p184*
Karlson, John E.; Colorado, 1888 ***1029.59*** *p48*
Karlson, Kerstin Charlotta; St. Paul, MN, 1893 ***1865.50*** *p93*
Karlson, Ruth Ada; St. Paul, MN, 1903 ***1865.50*** *p93*
Karlson, William; Iowa, 1888 ***1211.15*** *p16*
Karlsson, Karl G.; Cleveland, OH, 1900 ***9722.10*** *p122*
Karlsson, Karl Johan; Cleveland, OH, 1902 ***9722.10*** *p122*
Karlzan, Karl Gustaf; New York, 1903 ***1766.20*** *p36*
Karnas, Joseph; Detroit, 1930 ***1640.60*** *p77*
Karnath, Gustav F.; Wisconsin, 1888 ***6795.8*** *p147*
Karney, Denis 37; Ontario, 1871 ***1823.17*** *p82*
Karnohan, David 61; Ontario, 1871 ***1823.17*** *p82*
Karo, Mary 32; Minnesota, 1925 ***2769.54*** *p1379*
Karot, Rosine; New York, 1860 ***358.56*** *p5*
Karowczyk, Michal; Detroit, 1929-1930 ***6214.5*** *p71*
Karp, William; Illinois, 1860 ***6079.1*** *p7*
Karpinski, Johan 40; Portland, ME, 1911 ***970.38*** *p78*
Karpinski, Olga 19; Portland, ME, 1911 ***970.38*** *p78*
Karppe, Anchelle; Louisiana, 1851 ***7710.1*** *p152*
Karppers, Philip G.; Ohio, 1840-1897 ***8365.35*** *p16*

Karr, James; North Carolina, 1829 *1088.45 p16*
Karr, William; Toronto, 1844 *2910.35 p114*
Karrenbauer, Anna SEE Karrenbauer, Johann
Karrenbauer, Barbara; America, 1836 *5475.1 p64*
Karrenbauer, Barbara SEE Karrenbauer, Johann
Karrenbauer, Johann; America, 1836 *5475.1 p65*
  With wife & 5 children
Karrenbauer, Johann; America, 1880 *5475.1 p173*
  *Daughter:*Anna
  *Daughter:*Barbara
Karrenbauer, Kaspar; America, 1800-1899 *5475.1 p73*
  With wife
  With child 9
  With child 4
  With child 1
  With sister-in-law
  With child 6
Karrenbauer, Maria; America, 1880 *5475.1 p173*
Karrenbauer, Michel; America, 1846 *5475.1 p67*
Karrenbauer, Michel; America, 1872 *5475.1 p171*
Karrer, Cresens 12; Missouri, 1845 *778.6 p184*
Karrer, Ernest 13; Missouri, 1845 *778.6 p184*
Karrer, Johann 43; Missouri, 1845 *778.6 p184*
Karrer, Joseph 15; Missouri, 1845 *778.6 p184*
Karrer, Marie 39; Missouri, 1845 *778.6 p184*
Karrivan, Martin 45; Ontario, 1871 *1823.17 p82*
Karshner, Gotleib; Ohio, 1809-1852 *4511.35 p25*
Karst, Karl Ludwig Walter Paul; America, 1889 *7420.1 p359*
Karstine, John; Colorado, 1900 *1029.59 p48*
Kartak, Michal; St. Paul, MN, 1862 *2853.20 p277*
Karthaus, Adolf Eduard Ernst; America, 1870 *5475.1 p380*
Kartner, Jakob; America, 1837 *5475.1 p462*
Kartner, Nikolaus; America, 1837 *5475.1 p462*
Kartte, Paul R.H.; Colorado, 1883 *1029.59 p48*
Kartz, Henry; North Carolina, 1860 *1088.45 p16*
Karwood, Mary; America, 1772 *1220.12 p462*
Karwowska, Maryanna 20; New York, NY, 1911 *6533.11 p10*
Kas, Karl 24; Halifax, N.S., 1902 *1860.4 p40*
Kas, Mathilde 22; Halifax, N.S., 1902 *1860.4 p40*
Kasak, . . .; Pennsylvania, 1750-1799 *2853.20 p17*
Kasenmann, Gustav Johann; Wisconsin, 1897 *6795.8 p36*
Kaser, Mr. 50; America, 1847 *778.6 p184*
Kasey, Thomas; Boston, 1766 *1642 p37*
Kash, Joseph; Galveston, TX, 1881 *6015.15 p26*
Kaskel, F. J. M.; Valdivia, Chile, 1850 *1192.4 p48*
Kasnicki, Adam; Detroit, 1929 *1640.55 p114*
Kaspar, Frantisek J.; Omaha, NE, 1866-1910 *2853.20 p144*
Kaspar, Jan; Minnesota, 1865 *2853.20 p271*
Kaspar, Jan; Nebraska, 1870 *2853.20 p161*
Kaspar, Mrs. Jan; Minnesota, 1865 *2853.20 p271*
Kaspar, Josef; Colorado, 1896 *1029.59 p48*
Kaspar, Josef; Nebraska, 1866-1867 *2853.20 p161*
Kaspar, Maria Birtel SEE Kaspar, Peter
Kaspar, Nikolaus; America, 1883 *5475.1 p206*
Kaspar, Peter SEE Kaspar, Peter
Kaspar, Peter; America, 1872 *5475.1 p292*
  *Wife:*Maria Birtel
  *Son:*Peter
Kaspar, Vaclav; Nebraska, 1868 *2853.20 p161*
Kaspar, Vaclav; New York, NY, 1835-1864 *2853.20 p100*
Kaspar, Vaclav; New York, NY, 1853 *2853.20 p391*
Kaspar Family ; Wisconsin, 1854 *2853.20 p271*
Kasper, Johann; America, 1880 *5475.1 p427*
Kasper, Joseph; Colorado, 1886 *1029.59 p48*
Kasperek, Adam; Detroit, 1930 *1640.60 p78*
  *Wife:*Mary Sling
Kasperek, Mary Sling SEE Kasperek, Adam
Kasprowicz, Martinus; Wisconsin, 1894 *6795.8 p58*
Kasprzak, Franciszek 39; New York, NY, 1920 *930.50 p49*
Kassel, Philippe 45; America, 1847 *778.6 p184*
Kassell, Adam; Ohio, 1809-1852 *4511.35 p25*
Kassell, Jacob; Ohio, 1809-1852 *4511.35 p25*
Kast, Antoine 38; Mississippi, 1847 *778.6 p184*
Kast, Anton Yev; New York, 1902 *1766.20 p3*
Kast, Josephine 2; Mississippi, 1847 *778.6 p184*
Kast, Lena 19; Halifax, N.S., 1903 *1860.4 p44*
Kast, Marie 20; Mississippi, 1847 *778.6 p184*
Kast, Philibert 9 months; Mississippi, 1847 *778.6 p184*
Kast, Virginie 9 months; Mississippi, 1847 *778.6 p184*
Kasten, Karl August Heinrich Wilhelm SEE Kasten, Konrad Heinrich Friedrich
Kasten, Karoline Philippine Bertha SEE Kasten, Konrad Heinrich Friedrich

Kasten, Konrad Heinrich Friedrich; America, 1890 *7420.1 p361*
  *Wife:*Wihelmine Justine Charlotte Rugge
  *Daughter:*Karoline Philippine Bertha
  *Son:*Karl August Heinrich Wilhelm
Kasten, Robert; America, 1912 *7420.1 p390*
Kasten, Wihelmine Justine Charlotte Rugge SEE Kasten, Konrad Heinrich Friedrich
Kastengren, C.M.; New York, NY, 1847 *6412.40 p150*
Kastening, Heinrich Wilhelm Christoph; America, 1867 *7420.1 p258*
Kastening, Sophie; America, 1859 *7420.1 p186*
Kaster, A. Maria Hermann SEE Kaster, Peter
Kaster, Peter; America, 1883 *5475.1 p135*
  *Wife:*A. Maria Hermann
Kastieau, Michel 21; New Orleans, 1847 *778.6 p184*
Kastl, Petr; Nebraska, 1866 *2853.20 p161*
Kastler, Heinrich SEE Kastler, Nikolaus
Kastler, Katharina SEE Kastler, Nikolaus
Kastler, Maria SEE Kastler, Nikolaus
Kastler, Nikolaus 46; America, 1867 *5475.1 p281*
  *Wife:*Susanna Reinert 32
  *Daughter:*Katharina
  *Son:*Heinrich
  *Daughter:*Maria
Kastler, Peter; Missouri, 1884 *5475.1 p194*
Kastler, Susanna Reinert 32 SEE Kastler, Nikolaus
Kastorff, John C.; Illinois, 1834-1900 *6020.5 p132*
Kastrup, Konrad; New York, 1881 *1766.20 p34*
Kasyjanczyk, Fryderyk 26; New York, NY, 1911 *6533.11 p9*
Kaszubowski, Leo; Wisconsin, 1899 *6795.8 p50*
Kates, Francis; America, 1726 *1220.12 p462*
Kates, Jane; America, 1675 *1220.12 p462*
Kates, John; America, 1749 *1220.12 p462*
Kath, Ida Wilhelmine Ernestine; Wisconsin, 1897 *6795.8 p90*
Katherines, Edward; Annapolis, MD, 1722 *1220.12 p462*
Kathmann, James; Louisiana, 1836-1840 *4981.45 p212*
Kathmann, Justine Friederike; America, 1848 *7420.1 p61*
Katholi, Elisabeth; America, 1839 *5475.1 p469*
  With 2 children
Katoli, Johann; America, 1847 *5475.1 p486*
Kattenhorn, George; Washington, 1883 *2770.40 p136*
Katterer, Johann; Venezuela, 1843 *3899.5 p544*
Katterton, Robert; America, 1735 *1220.12 p462*
Kattmann, August; Iowa, 1850 *2526.43 p141*
Kattree, Friedrich; America, 1867 *7420.1 p258*
  With wife
  With son 9
  With son 7
  With son 15
Katz, Carl; Wisconsin, 1870 *6795.8 p125*
Katz, David 7 SEE Katz, Salomon
Katz, Engel Mar. Carol. SEE Katz, Johann Friedrich Christian
Katz, Engel Marie; America, 1856 *7420.1 p148*
Katz, Engel Wilhelm. Charl. SEE Katz, Johann Friedrich Christian
Katz, Ernst Friedr. SEE Katz, Johann Friedrich Christian
Katz, Freide 15 SEE Katz, Salomon
Katz, H. 21; New York, NY, 1894 *6512.1 p181*
Katz, Hanne Sophie Charl. Nerge SEE Katz, Johann Friedrich Christian
Katz, Heinr. Wilh. SEE Katz, Johann Friedrich Christian
Katz, Heinrich Christoph; America, 1856 *7420.1 p148*
Katz, Heinrich Christoph; America, 1857 *7420.1 p164*
  With wife 4 sons & 3 daughters
Katz, Johann Friedr. Wilh. K. SEE Katz, Johann Friedrich Christian
Katz, Johann Friedrich Christian; America, 1851 *7420.1 p81*
  *Wife:*Hanne Sophie Charl. Nerge
  *Brother:*Johann Friedr. Wilh. K.
  With mother
  *Brother:*Wilhelm. K.
  *Daughter:*Engel Wilhelm. Charl.
  *Daughter:*Soph. Carol. Wilhelm. Charl.
  *Sister:*Engel Mar. Carol.
  *Son:*Heinr. Wilh.
  *Son:*Ernst Friedr.
Katz, Joseph; Louisiana, 1874 *4981.45 p296*
Katz, Louise; America, 1852 *7420.1 p91*
  With daughter
Katz, Ludwig; America, 1859 *7420.1 p186*
  With wife 2 sons & daughter
Katz, Pirsch 9 SEE Katz, Salomon
Katz, Rebecca; Detroit, 1929 *1640.55 p117*
Katz, Roche 9 SEE Katz, Salomon
Katz, Salomon 40; New York, NY, 1878 *9253.2 p44*
  *Child:*Freide 15
  *Child:*David 7

  *Child:*Roche 9
  *Child:*Pirsch 9
Katz, Soph. Carol. Wilhelm. Charl. SEE Katz, Johann Friedrich Christian
Katz, Wilhelm. K. SEE Katz, Johann Friedrich Christian
Katze, Anne Sophie Catharine; America, 1857 *7420.1 p167*
Katze, Engel Mar. Carol. SEE Katze, Johann Friedrich Christian
Katze, Engel Marie Dorothee SEE Katze, Heinrich Christoph
Katze, Engel Marie Dorothee Wille SEE Katze, Heinrich Christoph
Katze, Engel Marie Soph. Eleon.; America, 1857 *7420.1 p175*
Katze, Engel Wilhelm. Charl. SEE Katze, Johann Friedrich Christian
Katze, Ernst Friedr. SEE Katze, Johann Friedrich Christian
Katze, Hanne Sophie Charl. Nerge SEE Katze, Johann Friedrich Christian
Katze, Heinr. Friedr. Phil. SEE Katze, Heinrich Christoph
Katze, Heinr. Wilh. SEE Katze, Johann Friedrich Christian
Katze, Heinrich Christoph SEE Katze, Heinrich Christoph
Katze, Heinrich Christoph; America, 1857 *7420.1 p164*
  *Wife:*Engel Marie Dorothee Wille
  *Daughter:*Thrine Sophie Dorothee
  *Son:*Johann Heinrich Otto
  *Daughter:*Engel Marie Dorothee
  *Son:*Heinr. Friedr. Phil.
  *Son:*Heinrich Christoph
Katze, Johann Friedr. Wilh. K. SEE Katze, Johann Friedrich Christian
Katze, Johann Friedrich Christian; America, 1851 *7420.1 p81*
  *Wife:*Hanne Sophie Charl. Nerge
  *Son:*Ernst Friedr.
  *Son:*Engel Wilhelm. Charl.
  *Daughter:*Soph. Carol. Wilhelm. Charl
  *Son:*Heinr. Wilh.
  *Sister:*Engel Mar. Carol.
  *Brother:*Wilhelm K.
  *Brother:*Johann Friedr. Wilh. K.
  With mother
Katze, Johann Friedrich Conrad; Port uncertain, 1838 *7420.1 p14*
Katze, Johann Heinrich Friedr. Christian; America, 1840 *7420.1 p18*
Katze, Johann Heinrich Otto SEE Katze, Heinrich Christoph
Katze, Johann Heinrich Wilhelm SEE Katze, Marie Sophie
Katze, Johanna Maria Dorothea SEE Katze, Marie Sophie
Katze, Johanne Sophie Eleonore; America, 1857 *7420.1 p164*
  With 2 sons & daughter
Katze, Marie Sophie; America, 1872 *7420.1 p295*
  *Son:*Johann Heinrich Wilhelm
  *Daughter:*Johanna Maria Dorothea
Katze, Soph. Carol. Wilhelm. Charl SEE Katze, Johann Friedrich Christian
Katze, Thrine Sophie Dorothee SEE Katze, Heinrich Christoph
Katze, Wilhelm K. SEE Katze, Johann Friedrich Christian
Katzenstein, Eduard; New York, NY, 1876 *7420.1 p307*
Katzenstein, Hugo; New York, NY, 1879 *7420.1 p313*
Katzenstein, Ida; America, 1884 *7420.1 p344*
Katzenstein, Marc 24; Port uncertain, 1840 *778.6 p184*
Katzenstein, Moritz; America, 1883 *7420.1 p337*
Katzman, Esther; Detroit, 1929-1930 *6214.5 p70*
Kaucke, Hans Heinrich Christian; Chicago, 1850 *7420.1 p72*
Kauffeld, Alfred; Mexico, 1903 *7420.1 p379*
Kauffman, Christopher; Nova Scotia, 1784 *7105 p23*
Kauffman, Jean 16; America, 1846 *778.6 p184*
Kauffman, John; Ohio, 1809-1852 *4511.35 p25*
Kauffman, M. 40; America, 1846 *778.6 p184*
Kauffman, Nicholas; Ohio, 1809-1852 *4511.35 p25*
Kauffman, Nicholus; Ohio, 1809-1852 *4511.35 p25*
Kauffman, Pierre 18; America, 1846 *778.6 p184*
Kauffmann, Mr. 9; America, 1847 *778.6 p184*
Kauffmann, Mr. 26; America, 1847 *778.6 p184*
Kauffmann, Louis; Louisiana, 1874-1875 *4981.45 p29*
Kaufman, David; Louisiana, 1874 *4981.45 p132*
Kaufman, David; Washington, 1881 *2770.40 p135*
Kaufman, Jakob 30; Galveston, TX, 1846 *3967.10 p377*
Kaufman, John; Ohio, 1809-1852 *4511.35 p25*
Kaufman, Louis 30; America, 1844 *778.6 p184*
Kaufman, Mr.; America, 1860 *7420.1 p195*
Kaufmann, Angela Simon SEE Kaufmann, Johann

Kaufmann, Benjamin 18; New York, NY, 1878 *9253.2 p45*
Kaufmann, Cath. 3 months; America, 1840 *778.6 p184*
Kaufmann, Elis. 21; New Orleans, 1840 *778.6 p184*
Kaufmann, Elisabeth 3 *SEE* Kaufmann, Paul
Kaufmann, Elisabeth 30; America, 1840 *778.6 p184*
Kaufmann, Friedrich 5 *SEE* Kaufmann, Paul
Kaufmann, Fritz 28; Halifax, N.S., 1902 *1860.4 p42*
Kaufmann, Heinrich Wilhelm Eduard; America, 1872 *7420.1 p296*
Kaufmann, Jacob; Philadelphia, 1870 *8513.31 p319*
  *Wife:*Sophie Loeb
Kaufmann, Jakob 30; Galveston, TX, 1846 *3967.10 p377*
Kaufmann, Johann; America, 1881 *5475.1 p311*
  *Wife:*Angela Simon
  *Son:*Ludwig
Kaufmann, Julius; America, 1866 *7420.1 p244*
Kaufmann, Katharina 44; Pennsylvania, 1867 *2526.43 p137*
Kaufmann, Ludwig *SEE* Kaufmann, Johann
Kaufmann, Maria; America, 1882 *5475.1 p35*
Kaufmann, Maria Wagner 28 *SEE* Kaufmann, Paul
Kaufmann, Paul 37; America, 1871 *5475.1 p62*
  *Wife:*Maria Wagner 28
  *Daughter:*Elisabeth 3
  *Son:*Peter 1
  *Son:*Friedrich 5
Kaufmann, Peter 1 *SEE* Kaufmann, Paul
Kaufmann, Peter 30; America, 1840 *778.6 p184*
Kaufmann, Peter; New York, 1882 *5475.1 p511*
Kaufmann, Sophie Loeb *SEE* Kaufmann, Jacob
Kauke, Widow; America, 1852 *7420.1 p91*
Kauke, Caroline Marie Dorothee *SEE* Kauke, Johann Friedrich Christian
Kauke, Dorothee Wilhelmine; America, 1889 *7420.1 p400*
Kauke, Engel Marie Eleonore Duhlmeier *SEE* Kauke, Johann Christian Ludolph
Kauke, Engel Marie Sophie Charlotte Hasenjaeger *SEE* Kauke, Johann Friedrich Christian
Kauke, Johann Christian Ludolph; America, 1855 *7420.1 p137*
  *Wife:*Engel Marie Eleonore Duhlmeier
  *Son:*Johann Heinrich Christian
Kauke, Johann Friedrich Christian; America, 1847 *7420.1 p54*
  *Wife:*Engel Marie Sophie Charlotte Hasenjaeger
  *Daughter:*Caroline Marie Dorothee
Kauke, Johann Heinrich Christian *SEE* Kauke, Johann Christian Ludolph
Kauke, Louise; America, 1859 *7420.1 p186*
  With son & 2 daughters
Kauke, W.; America, 1853 *7420.1 p106*
Kaukenmoller, Engel Maria Dorothea; America, 1860 *7420.1 p199*
Kaukenmoller, Hans Heinrich; America, 1866 *7420.1 p244*
Kaul, Christian 9 months; New York, NY, 1874 *6954.7 p37*
Kaul, Christian 33; New York, NY, 1874 *6954.7 p37*
Kaul, Karl Heinrich 29; America, 1889 *5475.1 p18*
Kaul, Rosina 22; New York, NY, 1874 *6954.7 p37*
Kaup, Carl Heinrich August *SEE* Kaup, Carl Heinrich Wilhelm
Kaup, Carl Heinrich Wilhelm *SEE* Kaup, Carl Heinrich Wilhelm
Kaup, Carl Heinrich Wilhelm; America, 1862 *7420.1 p212*
  *Son:*Carl Heinrich Wilhelm
  With wife & 2 daughters
  *Son:*Friedrich Wilhelm August
  *Son:*Georg Conrad Ludwig
  *Son:*Carl Heinrich August
  *Son:*Carl Wilhelm August
Kaup, Carl Wilhelm August *SEE* Kaup, Carl Heinrich Wilhelm
Kaup, Caroline; America, 1861 *7420.1 p206*
Kaup, Friedrich; America, 1882 *7420.1 p329*
Kaup, Friedrich Wilhelm August *SEE* Kaup, Carl Heinrich Wilhelm
Kaup, Georg Conrad Ludwig *SEE* Kaup, Carl Heinrich Wilhelm
Kaup, Heinrich Friedrich Wilhelm; America, 1895 *7420.1 p372*
Kaup, Henriette; America, 1861 *7420.1 p206*
Kaup, Herman; Nebraska, 1905 *3004.30 p46*
Kaup, Lawrence 24; Ontario, 1871 *1823.17 p82*
Kaupila, George 38; Minnesota, 1923 *2769.54 p1381*
Kauss, Anna Margarethe Catharine; America, 1864 *7420.1 p224*
Kauss, Wilhelm; America, 1823 *2526.43 p172*
Kausteniche, Jacques 25; America, 1840 *778.6 p184*

Kautenburger, A. Maria *SEE* Kautenburger, Nik.
Kautenburger, Kat. Kallenborn *SEE* Kautenburger, Nik.
Kautenburger, Katharina *SEE* Kautenburger, Nik.
Kautenburger, Nik.; America, 1881 *5475.1 p273*
  *Wife:*Kat. Kallenborn
  *Daughter:*Katharina
  *Daughter:*A. Maria
Kautz, August *SEE* Kautz, Jakob
Kautz, Friedrich Richard; Nicaragua, 1880 *5475.1 p37*
Kautz, Georg; America, 1865 *5475.1 p31*
Kautz, Jakob *SEE* Kautz, Jakob
Kautz, Jakob; America, 1866 *5475.1 p43*
  *Wife:*Magdalene Karoline Schmeer
  *Son:*Johann
  *Daughter:*Katharina
  *Son:*Philipp
  *Son:*August
  *Son:*Jakob
  *Daughter:*Luise
  *Daughter:*Sophie
  *Daughter:*Magdalena
Kautz, Johann *SEE* Kautz, Jakob
Kautz, Katharina *SEE* Kautz, Jakob
Kautz, Luise *SEE* Kautz, Jakob
Kautz, Magdalena *SEE* Kautz, Jakob
Kautz, Magdalene Karoline Schmeer *SEE* Kautz, Jakob
Kautz, Philipp *SEE* Kautz, Jakob
Kautz, Sophie *SEE* Kautz, Jakob
Kauz, Mr.; Philadelphia, 1800-1899 *170.15 p31*
Kauz, Christian 61; Pennsylvania, 1853 *170.15 p31*
  With wife
Kauz, Joh.Chrp; Nova Scotia, 1852 *170.15 p31*
Kauzar, Johann Heinrich 20 *SEE* Kauzar, Sophie
Kauzar, Lorenz 14 *SEE* Kauzar, Sophie
Kauzar, Margaretha 18 *SEE* Kauzar, Sophie
Kauzar, Sophie 39; America, 1881 *2526.43 p196*
  *Son:*Johann Heinrich 20
  *Daughter:*Margaretha 18
  With son 8 months
  *Son:*Lorenz 14
Kavanagh, Anne; New Orleans, 1850 *7242.30 p145*
Kavanagh, Biddy; New Orleans, 1850 *7242.30 p145*
Kavanagh, Charles; St. Johns, N.F., 1825 *1053.15 p6*
Kavanagh, Edward; New Orleans, 1850 *7242.30 p145*
Kavanagh, Elen; St. Johns, N.F., 1825 *1053.15 p6*
Kavanagh, Laurence; New Orleans, 1850 *7242.30 p145*
Kavanagh, Mary; New Orleans, 1850 *7242.30 p145*
Kavanagh, Michl 36; St. Johns, N.F., 1811 *1053.20 p21*
Kavanagh, Peter; New Orleans, 1850 *7242.30 p145*
Kavanagh, Richard; New Orleans, 1850 *7242.30 p145*
Kavanagh, Thomas 54; Ontario, 1871 *1823.21 p185*
Kavanah, Andy; New Orleans, 1851 *7242.30 p145*
Kavanah, Ann; New Orleans, 1851 *7242.30 p145*
Kavanah, Ellen; New Orleans, 1851 *7242.30 p145*
Kavanah, Julia; New Orleans, 1851 *7242.30 p145*
Kavanah, Margaret; New Orleans, 1851 *7242.30 p145*
Kavanah, Thomas; New Orleans, 1851 *7242.30 p145*
Kavanaugh, John; Boston, 1765 *1642 p35*
Kavanaugh, Thomas; Louisiana, 1874 *4981.45 p296*
Kavannah, James; New Orleans, 1850 *7242.30 p145*
Kavenaugh, Thomas; Philadelphia, 1777 *8529.30 p2*
Kawczynski, Stanley; Detroit, 1930 *1640.60 p83*
Kawecki, John; Detroit, 1929-1930 *6214.5 p71*
Kay, Abraham; America, 1730 *1220.12 p462*
Kay, Aleck 49; Ontario, 1871 *1823.21 p185*
Kay, Ann *SEE* Kay, Byran
Kay, Anthony Jan; Detroit, 1929-1930 *6214.5 p67*
Kay, Arthur; America, 1743 *1220.12 p462*
Kay, Brian; Canada, 1774 *3036.5 p41*
Kay, Byran; Canada, 1774 *3036.5 p40*
  *Wife:*Dorothy
  *Child:*Hannah
  *Child:*Ann
  *Child:*Jane
  *Child:*Sarah
  *Child:*Elizabeth
  *Brother:*Robert
Kay, Dorothy *SEE* Kay, Byran
Kay, Elizabeth; America, 1757 *1220.12 p462*
Kay, Elizabeth *SEE* Kay, Byran
Kay, Francis; America, 1750 *1220.12 p462*
Kay, Hannah; America, 1771 *1220.12 p462*
Kay, Hannah *SEE* Kay, Byran
Kay, James; America, 1765 *1220.12 p462*
Kay, James; America, 1767 *1220.12 p462*
Kay, James; Kingston, Jamaica, 1774 *8529.30 p13A*
Kay, James; North Carolina, 1819-1827 *1088.45 p16*
Kay, James 68; Ontario, 1871 *1823.21 p185*
Kay, Jane *SEE* Kay, Byran
Kay, John; America, 1759 *1220.12 p462*
Kay, Michael; America, 1753 *1220.12 p462*
Kay, Robert *SEE* Kay, Byran
Kay, Robert; North Carolina, 1822-1828 *1088.45 p16*

Kay, Sarah *SEE* Kay, Byran
Kay, Silvester; Maryland, 1671 *1236.25 p46*
Kay, Thomas; America, 1743 *1220.12 p462*
Kay, William; Canada, 1774 *3036.5 p40*
Kayberry, Thomas; America, 1735 *1220.12 p462*
Kaye, Abraham; America, 1769 *1220.12 p462*
Kayes, Henery 53; Ontario, 1871 *1823.21 p185*
Kaylor, Conrad; Ohio, 1809-1852 *4511.35 p25*
Kaylor, John; Ohio, 1809-1852 *4511.35 p25*
Kays, John 34; Ontario, 1871 *1823.17 p82*
Kayser, Anton, Jr.; Ohio, 1840-1897 *8365.35 p16*
Kayser, Anton, Sr.; Ohio, 1840-1897 *8365.35 p16*
Kayser, Conrad 34; Louisiana, 1847 *778.6 p184*
Kayser, Emil; Colorado, 1889 *1029.59 p49*
Kayser, Johannes 26; New England, 1867 *170.15 p31*
Kayser, Johannes; Pennsylvania, 1867 *170.15 p31*
Kayser, Joseph; Colorado, 1886 *1029.59 p49*
Kayser, M. Sara 28; Louisiana, 1847 *778.6 p184*
Kaysser, Velten 54; Pennsylvania, 1850 *170.15 p31*
  With wife & 3 children
Kazamais, Pascalos Polychroni; New York, NY, 1909 *3331.4 p12*
Kazimierowski, John; Texas, 1878 *6015.15 p26*
Keable, Henry; Barbados or Jamaica, 1676 *1220.12 p462*
Keach, Thomas; Barbados, 1665 *1220.12 p463*
Keach, Timothy; America, 1755 *1220.12 p463*
Keacy, Robert; Philadelphia, 1777 *8529.30 p3A*
Keag, Thomas W. 25; Ontario, 1871 *1823.17 p82*
Keakquet, Robert; America, 1754 *1220.12 p462*
Keal, Charles David; North Carolina, 1824 *1088.45 p16*
Keal, Michael; America, 1753 *1220.12 p463*
Kealey, William; St. Johns, N.F., 1825 *1053.15 p7*
Kealley, John; Boston, 1749 *1642 p46*
Kealshon, John; Boston, 1766 *1642 p36*
Kealty, William; America, 1765 *1220.12 p462*
Kealy, Cathe; St. Johns, N.F., 1825 *1053.15 p7*
Keamer, Jacob Gottlieb; Missouri, 1881 *3276.1 p3*
Kean, John 65; Ontario, 1871 *1823.21 p185*
Keanan, Michael; Boston, 1766 *1642 p36*
Kearn, Edward 81; Ontario, 1871 *1823.21 p185*
Kearnen, Francis; Toronto, 1844 *2910.35 p112*
Kearney, Gideon E.; Kansas, 1878 *1029.59 p49*
Kearney, Jos.; Louisiana, 1874-1875 *4981.45 p29*
Kearney, Thomas; Toronto, 1844 *2910.35 p116*
Kearney, William 26; New York, NY, 1825 *6178.50 p78*
Kearns, Brian 50; Ontario, 1871 *1823.17 p82*
Kearns, John 59; Ontario, 1871 *1823.21 p185*
Kearns, Michael 20; Ontario, 1871 *1823.17 p83*
Kearns, Patrick; Toronto, 1844 *2910.35 p112*
Kearns, Thomas 50; Ontario, 1871 *1823.17 p83*
Kearny, Michael 27; New York, NY, 1825 *6178.50 p77*
Kearny, William 26; New York, NY, 1825 *6178.50 p78*
Keary, John 32; Ontario, 1871 *1823.21 p185*
Keary, Mary 67; Ontario, 1871 *1823.21 p185*
Keast, Samuel 36; Ontario, 1871 *1823.21 p185*
Keate, Thomas; America, 1744 *1220.12 p462*
Keating, Anna; New Orleans, 1851 *7242.30 p145*
Keating, Anne; New Orleans, 1850 *7242.30 p145*
Keating, James; New Orleans, 1850 *7242.30 p145*
Keating, John; America, 1752 *1220.12 p462*
Keating, Laurence; New Orleans, 1850 *7242.30 p145*
Keating, Mary; New Orleans, 1850 *7242.30 p145*
Keating, Michael; Boston, 1763 *1642 p32*
Keating, Patt; New Orleans, 1850 *7242.30 p145*
Keating, William; Boston, 1763 *1642 p32*
Keating, William; Halifax, N.S., 1827 *7009.9 p62*
Keating, William 45; Ontario, 1871 *1823.17 p83*
Keatler, Stephen; America, 1753 *1220.12 p462*
Keatly, Thomas; America, 1773 *1220.12 p463*
Keaton, Michael; America, 1751 *1220.12 p462*
Keaton, Robert; North Carolina, 1810 *1088.45 p16*
Keay, Joseph; America, 1685 *1220.12 p462*
Keays, Mary Ann 61; Ontario, 1871 *1823.21 p185*
Kebbe, Franz; New York, 1850 *358.56 p101*
Kebbeck, Albert 13; Quebec, 1870 *8364.32 p24*
Kebbeck, Francis 16; Quebec, 1870 *8364.32 p24*
Kebble, Richard; America, 1758 *1220.12 p462*
Kechlen, Thomas; Ohio, 1809-1852 *4511.35 p25*
Kechler, Andrew; Illinois, 1852 *6079.1 p7*
Keck, Lores Jane; California, 1900-1970 *9228.50 p134*
Keck, Peter 35; Ontario, 1871 *1823.17 p83*
Kecke, Laurence; Barbados or Jamaica, 1686 *1220.12 p462*
Keckery, Joseph; Ohio, 1809-1852 *4511.35 p25*
Kecklen, Thomas; Ohio, 1809-1852 *4511.35 p25*
Keclik, Mr.; America, 1878-1910 *2853.20 p433*
  With wife
Keclik, Alois; Chicago, 1904 *2853.20 p433*
Keclik, Viktorin; Chicago, 1880 *2853.20 p416*
Keclik, Viktorin; Chicago, 1906 *2853.20 p406*
Kedanee, John P.; Wisconsin, 1897 *6795.8 p97*
Kedey, Mrs. 47; Texas, 1843 *778.6 p185*
Kedey, Angelique 17; Texas, 1843 *778.6 p184*

FOR A COMPLETE EXPLANATION OF ENTRY, SEE "HOW TO READ A CITATION" SECTION

Kedey, Charles Emeric 5; Texas, 1843 ***778.6*** *p184*
Kedey, Jean Baptiste 52; Texas, 1843 ***778.6*** *p184*
Kedinger, A. Maria 15 *SEE* Kedinger, Nikolaus
Kedinger, Anna 2 *SEE* Kedinger, Nikolaus
Kedinger, Anna 11 *SEE* Kedinger, Mathias
Kedinger, Anna Rhein 47 *SEE* Kedinger, Nikolaus
Kedinger, Christina Donkel 45 *SEE* Kedinger, Mathias
Kedinger, Franz 4 *SEE* Kedinger, Nikolaus
Kedinger, Katharina *SEE* Kedinger, Mathias
Kedinger, Maria 13 *SEE* Kedinger, Nikolaus
Kedinger, Mathias; America, 1874 ***5475.1*** *p378*
*Wife:*Christina Donkel
*Son:*Peter
*Daughter:*Anna
*Daughter:*Katharina
*Son:*Mathias
Kedinger, Mathias 19 *SEE* Kedinger, Mathias
Kedinger, Michel 11 *SEE* Kedinger, Nikolaus
Kedinger, Nikolaus; America, 1874 ***5475.1*** *p378*
*Wife:*Anna Rhein
*Son:*Franz
*Daughter:*Anna
*Son:*Michel
*Son:*Nikolaus
*Daughter:*Maria
*Daughter:*A. Maria
Kedinger, Nikolaus 19 *SEE* Kedinger, Nikolaus
Kedinger, Nikolaus; Minnesota, 1887 ***5475.1*** *p261*
Kedinger, Peter 8 *SEE* Kedinger, Mathias
Kedwell, William 39; Ontario, 1871 ***1823.17*** *p83*
Kedzierski, Josef 55; New York, NY, 1920 ***930.50*** *p48*
Kee, Harold Ernest; Miami, 1935 ***4984.12*** *p39*
Kee, Silvester; Maryland, 1671 ***1236.25*** *p46*
Keeble, Eleanor; Virginia, 1735 ***1220.12*** *p462*
Keeble, John; Nevis or Jamaica, 1722 ***1220.12*** *p462*
Keeble, Martin E. 30; Ontario, 1871 ***1823.21*** *p185*
Keeble, Richard; America, 1737 ***1220.12*** *p462*
Keeble, Richard; Virginia, 1739 ***1220.12*** *p462*
Keeble, Robert; Maryland, 1736 ***1220.12*** *p462*
Keeble, William; Annapolis, MD, 1726 ***1220.12*** *p462*
Keech, Richard; America, 1685 ***1220.12*** *p462*
Keed, William; America, 1740 ***1220.12*** *p463*
Keedy, William; America, 1740 ***1220.12*** *p463*
Keef, John; New England, 1745 ***1642*** *p28*
Keefe, . . .; New Orleans, 1851 ***7242.30*** *p145*
Keefe, Andrew 43; Ontario, 1871 ***1823.21*** *p185*
Keefe, Bryan; New Orleans, 1850 ***7242.30*** *p145*
Keefe, Daniel; Boston, 1766 ***1642*** *p37*
Keefe, David; America, 1737 ***1220.12*** *p463*
Keefe, Henry; Annapolis, MD, 1719 ***1220.12*** *p463*
Keefe, Honora; New Orleans, 1851 ***7242.30*** *p145*
Keefe, James 60; Ontario, 1871 ***1823.21*** *p185*
Keefe, John; New Orleans, 1850 ***7242.30*** *p145*
Keefe, John 14; Quebec, 1870 ***8364.32*** *p24*
Keefe, Martha 70; Ontario, 1871 ***1823.21*** *p185*
Keefe, Mary; Boston, 1693 ***1642*** *p16*
Keefe, Mary; Boston, 1754 ***1642*** *p47*
Keefe, Mary; New Orleans, 1850 ***7242.30*** *p145*
Keefe, Matthew 70; Ontario, 1871 ***1823.21*** *p185*
Keefe, Robert 45; Ontario, 1871 ***1823.21*** *p185*
Keefe, Timothy; New Orleans, 1851 ***7242.30*** *p146*
Keefer, Edward; Ohio, 1809-1852 ***4511.35*** *p25*
Keefer, George; Ohio, 1809-1852 ***4511.35*** *p25*
Keefer, Jacob; Ohio, 1809-1852 ***4511.35*** *p25*
Keefer, John; Ohio, 1809-1852 ***4511.35*** *p25*
Keefer, Lewis; Ohio, 1809-1852 ***4511.35*** *p25*
Keefer, Nicholas; Ohio, 1809-1852 ***4511.35*** *p25*
Keefer, Nicholas; Ohio, 1809-1852 ***4511.35*** *p26*
Keefer, Peter; Ohio, 1809-1852 ***4511.35*** *p26*
Keeffe, Thomas; Boston, 1765 ***1642*** *p35*
Keefh, Jacob; Massachusetts, 1731 ***1642*** *p87*
Keefs, Rose; America, 1772 ***1220.12*** *p463*
Keegan, Bridget; Philadelphia, 1850 ***8513.31*** *p303*
Keegan, James; Boston, 1833 ***3274.55*** *p75*
Keegan, John; Louisiana, 1841-1844 ***4981.45*** *p210*
Keeger, Margaret *SEE* Keeger, William
Keeger, William; Massachusetts, 1774 ***1642*** *p120*
*Wife:*Margaret
Keehn, Gust W.; Wisconsin, 1898 ***6795.8*** *p63*
Keel, George; America, 1685 ***1220.12*** *p463*
Keele, Robert; America, 1687 ***1220.12*** *p463*
Keeley, William; America, 1765 ***1220.12*** *p463*
Keeling, Andrew; America, 1770 ***1220.12*** *p463*
Keeling, Katherine; Barbados, 1674 ***1220.12*** *p463*
Keeling, Katherine; Maryland, 1674-1675 ***1236.25*** *p52*
Keelog, Julius Caeser; Toronto, 1844 ***2910.35*** *p116*
Keelson, Mary; America, 1721 ***1220.12*** *p465*
Keely, Patrick; Toronto, 1844 ***2910.35*** *p112*
Keemer, Matthias; Ohio, 1809-1852 ***4511.35*** *p26*
Keen, Daniel; America, 1740 ***1220.12*** *p463*
Keen, George 15; Quebec, 1870 ***8364.32*** *p24*
Keen, Henry; America, 1872 ***9076.20*** *p69*
Keen, Hugh; Boston, 1753 ***1642*** *p31*
Keen, James M.; Colorado, 1873 ***1029.59*** *p49*
Keen, John; America, 1745 ***1220.12*** *p463*
Keen, John; America, 1755 ***1220.12*** *p463*
Keen, John; America, 1759 ***1220.12*** *p463*
Keen, John; America, 1775 ***1220.12*** *p463*
Keen, Joseph Lewis; North Carolina, 1839 ***1088.45*** *p16*
Keen, Julius; Wisconsin, 1867 ***6795.8*** *p138*
Keen, Richard; America, 1772 ***1220.12*** *p463*
Keen, Tho; Virginia, 1652 ***6254.4*** *p243*
Keena, Patrick; Toronto, 1844 ***2910.35*** *p115*
Keenan, John; Washington, 1880 ***2770.40*** *p134*
Keenan, Patrick; Colorado, 1878 ***1029.59*** *p49*
Keenan, Patrick; Colorado, 1884 ***1029.59*** *p49*
Keenan, Paul 63; Ontario, 1871 ***1823.21*** *p185*
Keenaw, Patrick; Colorado, 1878 ***1029.59*** *p49*
Keene, John; America, 1751 ***1220.12*** *p463*
Keene, John; America, 1767 ***1220.12*** *p463*
Keene, Ralph; Barbados, 1688 ***1220.12*** *p463*
Keene, Richard; America, 1721 ***1220.12*** *p463*
Keene, Richard; America, 1763 ***1220.12*** *p463*
Keenleside, Richard; America, 1716 ***1220.12*** *p463*
Keenleyside, Anthony 45; Ontario, 1871 ***1823.21*** *p185*
Keep, Andrew; America, 1731 ***1220.12*** *p463*
Keeping, Philip; America, 1685 ***1220.12*** *p463*
Keerl, John; Washington, 1886 ***2770.40*** *p195*
Keesable, Michaell; North Carolina, 1710 ***3629.40*** *p5*
Keester, Charles; North Carolina, 1856 ***1088.45*** *p16*
Keffler, E. G.; Chile, 1852 ***1192.4*** *p52*
Kegan, Robert; America, 1760 ***1220.12*** *p463*
Kegel, Ch. A.; New York, 1860 ***358.56*** *p148*
Kegler, Andrew; Ohio, 1809-1852 ***4511.35*** *p26*
Kegler, Conrad; Ohio, 1809-1852 ***4511.35*** *p26*
Kegler, Thomas; Ohio, 1809-1852 ***4511.35*** *p26*
Kehae, Philip; Illinois, 1858 ***6079.1*** *p7*
Kehe, Caroline Charlotte; America, 1850 ***7420.1*** *p72*
*Brother:*Johann Christian Ludwig
Kehe, Christoph; America, 1852 ***7420.1*** *p91*
Kehe, Heinrich Ferdinand; America, 1853 ***7420.1*** *p106*
With wife
Kehe, Johann Christian Ludwig *SEE* Kehe, Caroline Charlotte
Kehe, Johann Friedrich Christoph; America, 1850 ***7420.1*** *p72*
Kehl, Chr.; Buffalo, NY, 1883 ***5475.1*** *p422*
Kehl, Elisabeth 7 *SEE* Kehl, Jakob
Kehl, Jakob 64; America, 1858 ***5475.1*** *p499*
*Wife:*Katharina Drumm 63
*Granddaughter:*Elisabeth 7
Kehl, Katharina Drumm 63 *SEE* Kehl, Jakob
Kehl, Martin 27; Louisiana, 1848 ***778.6*** *p185*
Kehl, Michael 39; Michigan, 1880 ***4491.30*** *p18*
Kehler, Jacob; Ohio, 1809-1852 ***4511.35*** *p26*
Kehler, Simon; North Carolina, 1710 ***3629.40*** *p5*
Kehlmeier, Carl Friedrich; America, 1894 ***7420.1*** *p370*
Kehlmeyer, Ernst August; America, 1881 ***7420.1*** *p322*
Kehmeier, Caroline Wilhelmine Auguste; America, 1880 ***7420.1*** *p316*
Kehn, Peter; Ohio, 1809-1852 ***4511.35*** *p26*
Kehoe, James; New Orleans, 1850 ***7242.30*** *p146*
Kehoe, James; St. Johns, N.F., 1825 ***1053.15*** *p6*
Kehoe, M.; New Orleans, 1850 ***7242.30*** *p146*
Kehoe, Michael; Washington, 1886 ***2770.40*** *p195*
Kehoe, Thos; St. Johns, N.F., 1825 ***1053.15*** *p7*
Kehoe, William R.; Illinois, 1834-1900 ***6020.5*** *p132*
Kehoye, Henry; North Carolina, 1848 ***1088.45*** *p17*
Kehr, Christian; America, 1868 ***7919.3*** *p533*
Kehr, Johannes; America, 1868 ***7919.3*** *p531*
With wife & 4 children
Kehrein, Reinhard; America, 1869 ***5475.1*** *p160*
Kehrer, Friedrich; America, 1894 ***2526.43*** *p172*
Kehri, Michel 30; Louisiana, 1848 ***778.6*** *p185*
Kehs, Joh. Philipp 26; America, 1880 ***5475.1*** *p339*
Keifaber, Michael; Ohio, 1809-1852 ***4511.35*** *p26*
Keife, Michael; Newfoundland, 1814 ***3476.10*** *p54*
Keifer, Jacob; Ohio, 1809-1852 ***4511.35*** *p26*
Keifer, Nicholas; Ohio, 1809-1852 ***4511.35*** *p26*
Keig, Robert 24; Ontario, 1871 ***1823.17*** *p83*
Keighley, Thomas; America, 1747 ***1220.12*** *p463*
Keightley, Christopher; Virginia, 1734 ***1220.12*** *p463*
Keightley, Robert 28; Ontario, 1871 ***1823.21*** *p185*
Keightley, William; Jamaica, 1661 ***1220.12*** *p463*
Keihn, Catherine 29; New Orleans, 1843 ***778.6*** *p185*
Keihn, Jacques 26; New Orleans, 1843 ***778.6*** *p185*
Keil, Adam 49; America, 1852 ***2526.43*** *p123*
*Wife:*Elisabetha 44
*Daughter:*Elisabetha 15
*Son:*Johannes 13
*Sister:*Magdalena 52
Keil, Anna Katharina; Illinois, 1846 ***2526.43*** *p132*
Keil, Balthasar; America, 1852 ***2526.43*** *p150*
Keil, Christian *SEE* Keil, Georg
Keil, Christian; North America, 1840 ***5475.1*** *p204*
Keil, Elisabetha 15 *SEE* Keil, Adam
Keil, Elisabetha 44 *SEE* Keil, Adam
Keil, Eva Maria; America, 1852 ***2526.43*** *p150*
Keil, Georg *SEE* Keil, Georg
Keil, Georg; America, 1883 ***2526.43*** *p132*
With wife
*Son:*Heinrich
*Son:*Christian
*Son:*Wilhelm
*Son:*Georg
Keil, Georg 19; New Orleans, 1848 ***778.6*** *p185*
Keil, Heinrich *SEE* Keil, Georg
Keil, Johann Philipp; America, 1860 ***2526.42*** *p169*
Keil, Johannes 13 *SEE* Keil, Adam
Keil, Kartharina; America, 1881 ***2526.42*** *p130*
Keil, Katharina; America, 1853 ***2526.43*** *p150*
Keil, Magdalena 52 *SEE* Keil, Adam
Keil, Michael; America, 1852 ***2526.43*** *p150*
Keil, Wilhelm *SEE* Keil, Georg
Keiley, David; Newbury, MA, 1707 ***1642*** *p75*
Keiling, James; America, 1752 ***1220.12*** *p463*
Keily, John; Massachusetts, 1768 ***1642*** *p66*
Keim, Franz 60; New Castle, DE, 1817-1818 ***90.20*** *p152*
Keim, Hermann; Valdivia, Chile, 1852 ***1192.4*** *p53*
With wife
Keimmery, Albirta 19; Michigan, 1880 ***4491.30*** *p18*
Keinckel, Johann Michael; London, Eng., 1866 ***170.15*** *p34*
Keip, Elisabeth; America, 1857 ***5475.1*** *p514*
Keip, Otto; Port uncertain, 1892 ***7420.1*** *p366*
Keir, John 45; Ontario, 1871 ***1823.17*** *p83*
Keirns, Michael; Toronto, 1844 ***2910.35*** *p115*
Keiser, Felix; Ohio, 1809-1852 ***4511.35*** *p26*
Keiser, Henry 3; Tennessee, 1845 ***778.6*** *p185*
Keiser, Jean 47; New Castle, DE, 1817-1818 ***90.20*** *p152*
Keiser, Johann Ulric; New Castle, DE, 1817-1818 ***90.20*** *p152*
Keiser, Louis 22; Tennessee, 1845 ***778.6*** *p185*
Keiser, Madelanie 20; Tennessee, 1845 ***778.6*** *p185*
Keisser, Jos. 27; America, 1845 ***778.6*** *p185*
Keister, Anton 44; New Castle, DE, 1817-1818 ***90.20*** *p152*
Keith, Alexander; America, 1764 ***1220.12*** *p463*
Keith, Alexander; America, 1773 ***1220.12*** *p463*
Keith, Effie; New York, 1739 ***8277.31*** *p116*
Keith, Eleanor; America, 1746 ***1220.12*** *p463*
Keith, John; America, 1751 ***1220.12*** *p463*
Keith, John; America, 1765 ***1220.12*** *p463*
Keith, John; Hartford, CT, 1719-1800 ***9228.50*** *p327*
Keith, Jonathon 51; Ontario, 1871 ***1823.17*** *p83*
Keith, Joseph; America, 1756 ***1220.12*** *p463*
Keith, Thomas; America, 1764 ***1220.12*** *p463*
Keithly, Elizabeth; America, 1766 ***1220.12*** *p463*
Keitle, Sophia; New York, 1860 ***358.56*** *p148*
Kejr, Jan; Chicago, 1891 ***2853.20*** *p461*
Kek, Mathias 46; America, 1847 ***778.6*** *p185*
Kelay, Thomas 41; Ontario, 1871 ***1823.17*** *p83*
Kelb, Heinrich; America, 1853 ***7420.1*** *p106*
Kelch, Lucas 24; Ontario, 1871 ***1823.17*** *p83*
Kelcy, Alexander; Massachusetts, 1741 ***1642*** *p67*
Keley, Jane; America, 1768 ***1220.12*** *p463*
Kelford, Nicholas; America, 1685 ***1220.12*** *p463*
Kelh, Joseph 23; Louisiana, 1848 ***778.6*** *p185*
Kelham, W. C.; California, 1868 ***1131.61*** *p89*
Kelineck, Hannah; Boston, 1719 ***9228.50*** *p310*
Kell, Johann; America, 1880 ***5475.1*** *p484*
With family
Kelland, Wm 40; Ontario, 1871 ***1823.21*** *p185*
Kellas, John; America, 1713 ***1220.12*** *p463*
Kellaway, Josiah; America, 1764 ***1220.12*** *p464*
Kellberg, Severin; Cleveland, OH, 1888-1893 ***9722.10*** *p122*
Kellby, Joseph; America, 1721 ***1220.12*** *p463*
Kelle, Sarah; Rowley, MA, 1659 ***1642*** *p77*
Kellenbach, Conrad 23; Mississippi, 1845-1846 ***778.6*** *p185*
Kellend, Thos 22; St. Johns, N.F., 1811 ***1053.20*** *p20*
Kellens, Samuel 27; Ohio, 1880 ***4879.40*** *p260*
Kelleo, Louis 21; America, 1840 ***778.6*** *p185*
Keller, Adam; America, 1891 ***2526.43*** *p120*
*Wife:*Barbara Grunewald
*Son:*Adam
Keller, Adam 15 *SEE* Keller, Adam
Keller, Alexander 16; America, 1856 ***5475.1*** *p560*
Keller, Amalia *SEE* Keller, Karl
Keller, Andreas 24; Galveston, TX, 1844 ***3967.10*** *p373*
Keller, Anna; America, 1897 ***5475.1*** *p25*
Keller, Anton 23; Halifax, N.S., 1902 ***1860.4*** *p43*
Keller, Barbara; America, 1867 ***7919.3*** *p534*
Keller, Barbara Grunewald 55 *SEE* Keller, Adam
Keller, Catharina; Valdivia, Chile, 1850 ***1192.4*** *p48*
Keller, Conrad; New York, 1778 ***8529.30*** *p3A*
Keller, Dan; Louisiana, 1874-1875 ***4981.45*** *p29*
Keller, David *SEE* Keller, Karl

Keller, Eduard 20; America, 1889 ***5475.1*** *p42*
Keller, Ferdinand 23; New York, NY, 1905 ***8425.16*** *p34*
Keller, Francois 5; America, 1844 ***778.6*** *p185*
Keller, Friederick 18; America, 1847 ***778.6*** *p185*
Keller, Friedrich; America, 1865 ***5475.1*** *p520*
Keller, Friedrich August; Wisconsin, 1888 ***6795.8*** *p189*
Keller, Friedrich Eduard 21; South America, 1890 ***5475.1*** *p42*
Keller, Georg; America, 1868 ***7919.3*** *p531*
With wife & child
Keller, Georg 18 *SEE* Keller, Mrs. Georg
Keller, Mrs. Georg; America, 1855 ***2526.43*** *p172*
*Daughter:*Mine
*Son:*Georg
*Daughter:*Josephine
Keller, George; Ohio, 1844 ***2763.1*** *p8*
Keller, Gustave 29; America, 1844 ***778.6*** *p185*
Keller, J. J.; Valdivia, Chile, 1850 ***1192.4*** *p48*
Keller, Jacob; Ohio, 1844 ***2763.1*** *p8*
Keller, Johann Jakob; America, 1863 ***5475.1*** *p519*
Keller, Josef; America, 1833 ***5475.1*** *p466*
Keller, Josef; America, 1833 ***5475.1*** *p467*
Keller, Joseph 9; New Orleans, 1848 ***778.6*** *p185*
Keller, Josephine 12 *SEE* Keller, Mrs. Georg
Keller, Karl 57; America, 1857 ***5475.1*** *p560*
*Wife:*Rebekka Haymann 46
*Son:*David
*Daughter:*Amalia
Keller, Karl Nikolaus; America, 1879 ***5475.1*** *p483*
Keller, Katharina 21; Halifax, N.S., 1902 ***1860.4*** *p43*
Keller, Lambert 2; Halifax, N.S., 1902 ***1860.4*** *p43*
Keller, Lawrence; Louisiana, 1874-1875 ***4981.45*** *p29*
Keller, Lorenz 7; New Orleans, 1848 ***778.6*** *p185*
Keller, Lorenz 45; New Orleans, 1848 ***778.6*** *p185*
Keller, Louise 41; New Orleans, 1847 ***778.6*** *p185*
Keller, Ludw. Aug. Emil; New York, 1885 ***5475.1*** *p41*
Keller, Ludwig 18; America, 1889 ***5475.1*** *p42*
Keller, Magdalena 15; New Orleans, 1848 ***778.6*** *p185*
Keller, Magdeline 29; America, 1844 ***778.6*** *p185*
Keller, Margaretha 44; America, 1847 ***778.6*** *p185*
Keller, Maria 47; New Orleans, 1848 ***778.6*** *p185*
Keller, Marianne 21; Galveston, TX, 1846 ***3967.10*** *p377*
Keller, Michel 41; America, 1847 ***778.6*** *p185*
Keller, Mine 15 *SEE* Keller, Mrs. Georg
Keller, Peter; America, 1852 ***5475.1*** *p480*
Keller, Peter; America, 1857 ***5475.1*** *p541*
Keller, Peter; Ohio, 1809-1852 ***4511.35*** *p26*
Keller, Philipp; America, 1884 ***2526.43*** *p120*
Keller, Philippine; America, 1847 ***5475.1*** *p474*
Keller, Rebekka Haymann 46 *SEE* Keller, Karl
Keller, Terefil; Wisconsin, 1902 ***6795.8*** *p213*
Keller, Theodor; America, 1856 ***5475.1*** *p560*
Keller, Theresa 16; New Orleans, 1848 ***778.6*** *p185*
Keller, Wilhelm Frederick; Wisconsin, 1901 ***6795.8*** *p179*
Keller, William; Wisconsin, 1894 ***6795.8*** *p229*
Kellermann, Mr.; America, 1853 ***7420.1*** *p107*
With wife & son
Kellestine, George 49; Ontario, 1871 ***1823.21*** *p186*
Kellet, George; America, 1733 ***1220.12*** *p463*
Kellett, Charles; America, 1752 ***1220.12*** *p463*
Kellett, Jane; America, 1754 ***1220.12*** *p463*
Kellett, John 35; Indiana, 1871-1878 ***9076.20*** *p69*
Kelley, Captain; Massachusetts, 1774 ***1642*** *p90*
Kelley, Abigail; Rowley, MA, 1726 ***1642*** *p77*
Kelley, Abigall; Massachusetts, 1736 ***1642*** *p74*
Kelley, Alexander; North Carolina, 1852 ***1088.45*** *p17*
Kelley, Alexander 60; Ontario, 1871 ***1823.17*** *p83*
Kelley, Ann; America, 1746 ***1220.12*** *p464*
Kelley, Ann; Marblehead, MA, 1750 ***1642*** *p73*
Kelley, Ann Maria; North Carolina, 1824 ***1088.45*** *p17*
Kelley, Anthony; Salisbury, MA, 1773 ***1642*** *p81*
Kelley, Cathrine 47; Ontario, 1871 ***1823.21*** *p186*
Kelley, Daniel; Marston's Wharf, 1780 ***8529.30*** *p13*
Kelley, Daniel; New England, 1745 ***1642*** *p28*
Kelley, Dunken; Edgartown, MA, 1735 ***1642*** *p86*
*Wife:*Jean
Kelley, Edward; Boston, 1730 ***1642*** *p44*
Kelley, Edward; Boston, 1762 ***1642*** *p48*
Kelley, Edward; Maine, 1832 ***3274.55*** *p26*
Kelley, Eleanor; Virginia, 1735 ***1220.12*** *p464*
Kelley, Elisabeth; Boston, 1737 ***1642*** *p44*
Kelley, Ellen; New Orleans, 1851 ***7242.30*** *p146*
Kelley, Faylam; Boston, 1726 ***1642*** *p25*
Kelley, Grace; Massachusetts, 1751 ***1642*** *p102*
Kelley, Grace; Massachusetts, 1751 ***1642*** *p105*
Kelley, Hannah; Boston, 1758 ***1642*** *p47*
Kelley, Henry; New York, NY, 1822 ***3274.56*** *p72*
Kelley, Henry P.; New York, NY, 1832 ***3274.55*** *p22*
Kelley, Hugh; Annapolis, MD, 1721 ***1220.12*** *p464*
Kelley, Hugh; Illinois, 1863 ***6079.1*** *p7*
Kelley, Isaac; Massachusetts, 1750 ***1642*** *p85*
Kelley, James; Boston, 1731 ***1642*** *p44*
Kelley, James; Boston, 1749 ***1642*** *p46*
Kelley, James; New York, 1776 ***8529.30*** *p13*
Kelley, James 41; Ontario, 1871 ***1823.17*** *p83*
Kelley, James; Worcester, MA, 1774 ***1642*** *p114*
Kelley, Jean *SEE* Kelley, Dunken
Kelley, John; America, 1742 ***1220.12*** *p464*
Kelley, John; Boston, 1719 ***1642*** *p25*
Kelley, John; Boston, 1756 ***1642*** *p47*
Kelley, John; Boston, 1765 ***1642*** *p34*
Kelley, John; Massachusetts, 1715 ***1642*** *p64*
Kelley, John; North Carolina, 1879 ***1088.45*** *p17*
Kelley, John 65; Ontario, 1871 ***1823.21*** *p186*
Kelley, John; Rowley, MA, 1725 ***1642*** *p77*
Kelley, John; Vermont, 1832 ***3274.55*** *p74*
Kelley, John, Jr.; Newbury, MA, 1691 ***1642*** *p74*
Kelley, John, Sr.; Newbury, MA, 1691 ***1642*** *p74*
Kelley, June; New Orleans, 1851 ***7242.30*** *p146*
Kelley, Lawrence; Illinois, 1858 ***6079.1*** *p7*
Kelley, Lawrence; Worcester, MA, 1770 ***1642*** *p114*
Kelley, Martin; Boston, 1739 ***1642*** *p45*
Kelley, Mary; Boston, 1693 ***1642*** *p16*
Kelley, Mary; Boston, 1752 ***1642*** *p46*
Kelley, Mary; Boston, 1760 ***1642*** *p48*
Kelley, Mary; Died enroute, 1851 ***7242.30*** *p146*
Kelley, Mary; Marblehead, MA, 1737 ***1642*** *p73*
Kelley, Mary 37; Ontario, 1871 ***1823.21*** *p186*
Kelley, Mary; Rowley, MA, 1771 ***1642*** *p77*
Kelley, Mathew; Boston, 1765 ***1642*** *p35*
Kelley, Matthew; Illinois, 1918 ***6007.60*** *p9*
Kelley, Michael 64; Ontario, 1871 ***1823.21*** *p186*
Kelley, Patrick; Boston, 1754 ***1642*** *p47*
Kelley, Patrick; Boston, 1757 ***1642*** *p47*
Kelley, Peter; New Orleans, 1851 ***7242.30*** *p146*
Kelley, Richard; America, 1768 ***1220.12*** *p465*
Kelley, Richard; Annapolis, MD, 1725 ***1220.12*** *p465*
Kelley, Richard; Newbury, MA, 1691 ***1642*** *p74*
Kelley, Richard; Newbury, MA, 1711 ***1642*** *p75*
Kelley, Robert; Charlestown, MA, 1759 ***1642*** *p100*
Kelley, Robert; Massachusetts, 1771 ***1642*** *p112*
Kelley, Robert; North Carolina, 1824 ***1088.45*** *p17*
Kelley, Robert; Ohio, 1809-1852 ***4511.35*** *p26*
Kelley, Ruth; Massachusetts, 1737 ***1642*** *p74*
Kelley, Samuel; Lynn, MA, 1731 ***1642*** *p71*
Kelley, Seth; Massachusetts, 1726 ***1642*** *p85*
Kelley, Susannah; Boston, 1746 ***1642*** *p46*
Kelley, Terence; America, 1750 ***1220.12*** *p465*
Kelley, Theodore; New York, 1778 ***8529.30*** *p3A*
Kelley, Thomas 40; Ontario, 1871 ***1823.21*** *p186*
Kelley, Thomas 50; Ontario, 1871 ***1823.21*** *p186*
Kelley, Thomas; Philadelphia, 1777 ***8529.30*** *p7A*
Kelley, William; Boston, 1754 ***1642*** *p47*
Kelley, William; Boston, 1759 ***1642*** *p47*
Kelley, William; Boston, 1763 ***1642*** *p32*
Kelley, William; Nantucket, MA, 1769 ***1642*** *p89*
Kelley, William 51; Ontario, 1871 ***1823.21*** *p186*
Kelley, William; Shrewsbury, MA, 1772 ***1642*** *p108*
Kelley, Wing; Massachusetts, 1774 ***1642*** *p111*
Kelley, Wm.; Utah, 1899 ***3687.1*** *p38*
Kellgren, Carl Peter; Washington, 1889 ***2770.40*** *p79*
Kellick, Charles 32; Ontario, 1871 ***1823.21*** *p186*
Kellick, John; America, 1765 ***1220.12*** *p463*
Kellick, Mary; America, 1758 ***1220.12*** *p464*
Kellihorn, John; America, 1770 ***1220.12*** *p464*
Kellin, Thomas; Ipswich, MA, 1678 ***1642*** *p70*
Kelling, James; Massachusetts, 1675-1676 ***1642*** *p127*
Kelling, James; Massachusetts, 1675-1676 ***1642*** *p129*
Kelling, Roy Thomas; Ontario, 1955-1983 ***9228.50*** *p310*
Kellinghaus, J. W.; Nebraska, 1905 ***3004.30*** *p46*
Kellner, Michal; Wisconsin, 1851 ***2853.20*** *p312*
Kellock, Andrew 47; Ontario, 1871 ***1823.21*** *p186*
Kellogg, Thomas; Boston, 1817 ***3274.55*** *p72*
Kellon, James; Massachusetts, 1675-1676 ***1642*** *p128*
Kelloway, Edward; Barbados or Jamaica, 1693 ***1220.12*** *p464*
Kells, Sarah 57; Ontario, 1871 ***1823.17*** *p83*
Kells, William 45; Ontario, 1871 ***1823.17*** *p83*
Kellsall, Samuel; America, 1750 ***1220.12*** *p464*
Kellsey, Alexander 39; Ohio, 1880 ***4879.40*** *p259*
Kellvie, Mary 10; Quebec, 1870 ***8364.32*** *p24*
Kelly, Abel; Salem, MA, 1643 ***1642*** *p78*
Kelly, Abigail; Massachusetts, 1715 ***1642*** *p68*
Kelly, Abner 36; Ontario, 1871 ***1823.21*** *p186*
Kelly, Andrew; America, 1763 ***1220.12*** *p464*
Kelly, Andrew 28; Ontario, 1871 ***1823.21*** *p186*
Kelly, Ann; America, 1761 ***1220.12*** *p464*
Kelly, Ann; America, 1774 ***1220.12*** *p464*
Kelly, Ann M. 60; Ontario, 1871 ***1823.17*** *p83*
Kelly, Anne; Massachusetts, 1751 ***1642*** *p68*
Kelly, Anthony 63; Ontario, 1871 ***1823.21*** *p186*
Kelly, Barbary; Boston, 1766 ***1642*** *p37*
Kelly, Betty; New Orleans, 1850 ***7242.30*** *p146*
Kelly, Biddy; New Orleans, 1850 ***7242.30*** *p146*
Kelly, Catherine; America, 1770 ***1220.12*** *p464*
Kelly, Catherine 62; Ontario, 1871 ***1823.21*** *p186*
Kelly, Catherine; Potomac, 1743 ***1220.12*** *p464*
Kelly, Catherine 13; Quebec, 1870 ***8364.32*** *p24*
Kelly, Cecilly; America, 1758 ***1220.12*** *p464*
Kelly, Charles; Barbados, 1679 ***1220.12*** *p464*
Kelly, Charles; Boston, 1727 ***1642*** *p25*
Kelly, Charles; New Jersey, 1834 ***3274.56*** *p70*
Kelly, Charles 22; Ontario, 1871 ***1823.17*** *p83*
Kelly, Charles 36; Ontario, 1871 ***1823.21*** *p186*
Kelly, Daniel; America, 1739 ***1220.12*** *p464*
Kelly, Daniel; Kansas, 1884 ***1447.20*** *p63*
Kelly, Daniel; Marston's Wharf, 1780 ***8529.30*** *p13*
Kelly, David; Washington, 1869 ***2770.40*** *p134*
Kelly, David; Washington, 1884 ***2770.40*** *p192*
Kelly, Duncan 70; Edgartown, MA, 1761 ***1642*** *p86*
Kelly, E.; New Orleans, 1850 ***7242.30*** *p146*
Kelly, Edmond 45; Ontario, 1871 ***1823.17*** *p83*
Kelly, Edmund; America, 1754 ***1220.12*** *p464*
Kelly, Edmund; Illinois, 1860 ***6079.1*** *p7*
Kelly, Elenor 23; St. John, N.B., 1834 ***6469.7*** *p4*
Kelly, Eliza; Boston, 1715 ***1642*** *p24*
Kelly, Elizabeth; Boston, 1709 ***1642*** *p24*
Kelly, Elizabeth; Boston, 1738 ***1642*** *p44*
Kelly, Elizabeth *SEE* Kelly, James
Kelly, Ellen McAvoy *SEE* Kelly, Michael
Kelly, Ellen N. 35; Michigan, 1880 ***4491.39*** *p16*
Kelly, Emm; Boston, 1700 ***1642*** *p24*
Kelly, Esther 55; Ontario, 1871 ***1823.17*** *p83*
Kelly, Francis; America, 1775 ***1220.12*** *p464*
Kelly, Georg; Boston, 1708 ***1642*** *p24*
Kelly, George; America, 1764 ***1220.12*** *p464*
Kelly, George; America, 1770 ***1220.12*** *p464*
Kelly, George; New Orleans, 1850 ***7242.30*** *p146*
Kelly, George 43; Ontario, 1871 ***1823.21*** *p186*
Kelly, George; Virginia, 1744 ***1220.12*** *p464*
Kelly, Grace *SEE* Kelly, John
Kelly, Grifsey; America, 1749 ***1220.12*** *p464*
Kelly, Hannah; Massachusetts, 1732 ***1642*** *p74*
Kelly, Hannora 36; Michigan, 1880 ***4491.30*** *p18*
Kelly, Henry; Boston, 1707 ***1642*** *p24*
Kelly, Henry 30; Michigan, 1880 ***4491.39*** *p16*
Kelly, Henry; Ohio, 1842 ***3580.20*** *p32*
Kelly, Henry; Ohio, 1842 ***6020.12*** *p12*
Kelly, Henry 33; Ontario, 1871 ***1823.21*** *p186*
Kelly, Hugh; America, 1767 ***1220.12*** *p464*
Kelly, Hugh 37; Ontario, 1871 ***1823.17*** *p83*
Kelly, James; America, 1742 ***1220.12*** *p464*
Kelly, James; America, 1763 ***1220.12*** *p464*
Kelly, James; America, 1773 ***1220.12*** *p464*
Kelly, James; Boston, 1767 ***1642*** *p39*
Kelly, James; Lexington, MA, 1733 ***1642*** *p105*
*Wife:*Elizabeth
Kelly, James; New Orleans, 1850 ***7242.30*** *p146*
Kelly, James 21; Ontario, 1871 ***1823.21*** *p186*
Kelly, James 30; Ontario, 1871 ***1823.17*** *p83*
Kelly, James 31; Ontario, 1871 ***1823.21*** *p186*
Kelly, James 34; Ontario, 1871 ***1823.21*** *p186*
Kelly, James 53; Ontario, 1871 ***1823.17*** *p83*
Kelly, James 56; Ontario, 1871 ***1823.21*** *p186*
Kelly, James 56; Ontario, 1871 ***1823.21*** *p186*
Kelly, James 60; Ontario, 1871 ***1823.21*** *p186*
Kelly, James *SEE* Kelly, Michael
Kelly, James 20; St. John, N.B., 1834 ***6469.7*** *p4*
Kelly, Jane; America, 1736 ***1220.12*** *p464*
Kelly, Jane; Boston, 1737 ***1642*** *p44*
Kelly, Jane; Boston, 1741 ***1642*** *p45*
Kelly, Jane; Boston, 1763 ***1642*** *p32*
Kelly, Jane; Massachusetts, 1737 ***1642*** *p68*
Kelly, Jane; Massachusetts, 1748 ***1642*** *p104*
Kelly, Jessie 50; Ontario, 1871 ***1823.17*** *p83*
Kelly, John; America, 1743 ***1220.12*** *p464*
Kelly, John; Annapolis, MD, 1735 ***1220.12*** *p464*
Kelly, John; Boston, 1741 ***1642*** *p45*
Kelly, John; Boston, 1743 ***1642*** *p45*
Kelly, John; Boston, 1743 ***1642*** *p45*
Kelly, John; Boston, 1764 ***1642*** *p33*
Kelly, John; Boston, 1766 ***1642*** *p37*
Kelly, John; Boston, 1769 ***1642*** *p49*
Kelly, John; Illinois, 1860 ***6079.1*** *p7*
Kelly, John; Iowa, 1871 ***1211.15*** *p15*
Kelly, John; Louisiana, 1853 ***7710.1*** *p154*
Kelly, John; Marblehead, MA, 1688 ***1642*** *p72*
*Wife:*Grace
Kelly, John; Marblehead, MA, 1723 ***1642*** *p73*
Kelly, John; Massachusetts, 1759 ***1642*** *p63*
Kelly, John; Massachusetts, 1759 ***1642*** *p68*
Kelly, John; New England, 1745 ***1642*** *p28*
Kelly, John; New Orleans, 1850 ***7242.30*** *p146*
Kelly, John; New Orleans, 1851 ***7242.30*** *p146*
Kelly, John; Newburyport, MA, 1635 ***1642*** *p76*
Kelly, John; Ontario, 1835 ***3160.1*** *p150*
Kelly, John 25; Ontario, 1871 ***1823.21*** *p187*
Kelly, John 30; Ontario, 1871 ***1823.21*** *p187*
Kelly, John 30; Ontario, 1871 ***1823.21*** *p187*

Kelly, John 35; Ontario, 1871 ***1823.21*** *p186*
Kelly, John 52; Ontario, 1871 ***1823.21*** *p187*
Kelly, John 58; Ontario, 1871 ***1823.21*** *p187*
Kelly, John 67; Ontario, 1871 ***1823.17*** *p83*
Kelly, John; Salem, MA, 1679 ***1642*** *p79*
Kelly, John; Virginia, 1719 ***1220.12*** *p464*
Kelly, John; Virginia, 1768 ***1220.12*** *p464*
Kelly, John; Washington, 1883 ***2770.40*** *p136*
Kelly, Joseph; Boston, 1839 ***3274.56*** *p69*
Kelly, Joseph; Massachusetts, 1741 ***1642*** *p67*
Kelly, Joseph; Massachusetts, 1798 ***1642*** *p67*
Kelly, Joseph, Jr.; Massachusetts, 1741 ***1642*** *p67*
Kelly, Joseph B. 33; Ontario, 1871 ***1823.21*** *p187*
Kelly, Judith; Massachusetts, 1747 ***1642*** *p68*
Kelly, Lang 18; Ontario, 1871 ***1823.21*** *p187*
Kelly, Lewis 37; Ontario, 1871 ***1823.17*** *p83*
Kelly, Lothary; America, 1753 ***1220.12*** *p464*
Kelly, Margaret; America, 1731 ***1220.12*** *p464*
Kelly, Martha; Massachusetts, 1769 ***1642*** *p104*
Kelly, Mary; America, 1748 ***1220.12*** *p464*
Kelly, Mary; America, 1749 ***1220.12*** *p464*
Kelly, Mary; America, 1750 ***1220.12*** *p464*
Kelly, Mary; America, 1754 ***1220.12*** *p464*
Kelly, Mary; Marblehead, MA, 1737 ***1642*** *p73*
Kelly, Mary; Massachusetts, 1731 ***1642*** *p74*
Kelly, Mary; New Orleans, 1850 ***7242.30*** *p146*
Kelly, Mary 17; Ontario, 1871 ***1823.21*** *p187*
Kelly, Mary; Philadelphia, 1860 ***8513.31*** *p319*
Kelly, Mary; Philadelphia, 1862 ***8513.31*** *p418*
Kelly, Mary 9; Quebec, 1870 ***8364.32*** *p24*
Kelly, Mary 17; Quebec, 1870 ***8364.32*** *p24*
Kelly, Mary *SEE* Kelly, Samuel
Kelly, Mary; Salisbury, MA, 1731 ***1642*** *p81*
Kelly, Mary Ann *SEE* Kelly, Michael
Kelly, Mary Colee; Massachusetts, 1700 ***1642*** *p68*
Kelly, Matthew; America, 1754 ***1220.12*** *p464*
Kelly, Matthew; America, 1761 ***1220.12*** *p464*
Kelly, Matthias; America, 1763 ***1220.12*** *p464*
Kelly, Mehatiball; Massachusetts, 1738 ***1642*** *p74*
Kelly, Merte; Boston, 1741 ***1642*** *p45*
Kelly, Michael; America, 1753 ***1220.12*** *p464*
Kelly, Michael; Louisiana, 1874 ***4981.45*** *p132*
Kelly, Michael 37; Michigan, 1880 ***4491.30*** *p18*
Kelly, Michael 64; Ontario, 1871 ***1823.21*** *p187*
Kelly, Michael; Philadelphia, 1851 ***8513.31*** *p319*
*Wife:*Ellen McAvoy
*Son:*James
*Daughter:*Mary Ann
Kelly, Miles; America, 1757 ***1220.12*** *p464*
Kelly, Nicholas; New Orleans, 1850 ***7242.30*** *p146*
Kelly, Patk; St. John, N.B., 1847 ***2978.15*** *p35*
Kelly, Patrick; America, 1750 ***1220.12*** *p464*
Kelly, Patrick; America, 1767 ***1220.12*** *p464*
Kelly, Patrick; America, 1774 ***1220.12*** *p464*
Kelly, Patrick; Burlington, VT, 1833 ***3274.56*** *p97*
Kelly, Patrick; Colorado, 1867 ***1029.59*** *p49*
Kelly, Patrick 30; Indiana, 1866-1868 ***9076.20*** *p66*
Kelly, Patrick 42; Ontario, 1871 ***1823.21*** *p187*
Kelly, Peter; America, 1755 ***1220.12*** *p464*
Kelly, Peter 28; Ontario, 1871 ***1823.21*** *p187*
Kelly, Peter 35; Ontario, 1871 ***1823.17*** *p83*
Kelly, Philip; Boston, 1747 ***1642*** *p29*
Kelly, Rachel; New London, CT, 1852-1952 ***9228.50*** *p310*
Kelly, Rebekah; Massachusetts, 1757 ***1642*** *p68*
Kelly, Richard; Boston, 1765 ***1642*** *p34*
Kelly, Richard; Massachusetts, 1753 ***1642*** *p68*
Kelly, Richard 15; Ontario, 1871 ***1823.21*** *p187*
Kelly, Richard 22; Ontario, 1871 ***1823.21*** *p187*
Kelly, Robert 32; Ontario, 1871 ***1823.21*** *p187*
Kelly, Robert 52; Ontario, 1871 ***1823.17*** *p83*
Kelly, Robert 75; Ontario, 1871 ***1823.21*** *p187*
Kelly, Roger; Maryland, 1672 ***1236.25*** *p47*
Kelly, Sally 21; St. John, N.B., 1834 ***6469.7*** *p4*
Kelly, Samuel; Newbury, MA, 1686 ***1642*** *p74*
Kelly, Samuel; Rowley, MA, 1724 ***1642*** *p77*
*Wife:*Mary
Kelly, Samuel; Rowley, MA, 1724 ***1642*** *p77*
Kelly, Samuel; Virginia, 1728 ***1220.12*** *p465*
Kelly, Samuell; Ipswich, MA, 1772 ***1642*** *p71*
Kelly, Sarah; Massachusetts, 1751 ***1642*** *p72*
Kelly, Susannah; Boston, 1727 ***1642*** *p25*
Kelly, Terence; Boston, 1734 ***1642*** *p44*
Kelly, Theodore; New York, 1778 ***8529.30*** *p3A*
Kelly, Thomas; America, 1733 ***1220.12*** *p465*
Kelly, Thomas; America, 1767 ***1220.12*** *p465*
Kelly, Thomas; America, 1768 ***1220.12*** *p465*
Kelly, Thomas; Boston, 1830 ***3274.56*** *p101*
Kelly, Thomas; Louisiana, 1841-1844 ***4981.45*** *p210*
Kelly, Thomas 18; Ontario, 1871 ***1823.21*** *p187*
Kelly, Thomas 19; Ontario, 1871 ***1823.21*** *p187*
Kelly, Thomas 35; Ontario, 1871 ***1823.21*** *p187*
Kelly, Thomas 40; Ontario, 1871 ***1823.17*** *p83*
Kelly, Thomas; Philadelphia, 1778 ***8529.30*** *p4A*
Kelly, Tobias; New Orleans, 1850 ***7242.30*** *p146*
Kelly, Valentine; Maryland or Virginia, 1738 ***1220.12*** *p465*
Kelly, William; America, 1738 ***1220.12*** *p465*
Kelly, William; America, 1771 ***1220.12*** *p465*
Kelly, William; Boston, 1755 ***1642*** *p47*
Kelly, William; New Orleans, 1850 ***7242.30*** *p146*
Kelly, William 25; Ontario, 1871 ***1823.17*** *p83*
Kelly, William 30; Ontario, 1871 ***1823.21*** *p187*
Kelly, William 37; Ontario, 1871 ***1823.21*** *p187*
Kelly, William 46; Ontario, 1871 ***1823.21*** *p187*
Kelly, William 46; Ontario, 1871 ***1823.21*** *p187*
Kelly, William 60; Ontario, 1871 ***1823.17*** *p83*
Kelly, William 17; Quebec, 1870 ***8364.32*** *p24*
Kelm, Julius Hermann; Wisconsin, 1873 ***6795.8*** *p33*
Kelp Family ; America, 1858 ***7420.1*** *p179*
Kelsch, Andreas 21; New York, NY, 1898 ***7951.13*** *p41*
Kelsey, J.; California, 1868 ***1131.61*** *p89*
With family
Kelsey, John; America, 1756 ***1220.12*** *p465*
Kelsey, John; America, 1766 ***1220.12*** *p465*
Kelsey, Richard, Sr.; Barbados, 1668 ***1220.12*** *p465*
Kelsey, Thomas; Barbados or Jamaica, 1689 ***1220.12*** *p465*
Kelso, Elizabeth 50; North Carolina, 1774 ***1422.10*** *p61*
Kelso, Elizabeth 50; North Carolina, 1774 ***1422.10*** *p63*
Kelson, Ann; America, 1772 ***1220.12*** *p465*
Kelson, George, Jr.; America, 1774 ***1220.12*** *p465*
Kelson, John; Iowa, 1901 ***1211.15*** *p16*
Kelsworth, John; America, 1770 ***1220.12*** *p465*
Kelsy, William; America, 1752 ***1220.12*** *p465*
Kem, George; America, 1772 ***1220.12*** *p465*
Kemeike, Nikols 21; New York, NY, 1893 ***1883.7*** *p41*
Kemenau, Heinrich; America, 1861 ***7420.1*** *p206*
With family
Kemeys, John; America, 1767 ***1220.12*** *p466*
Keminett, Hannah; Maryland, 1744 ***1220.12*** *p465*
Kemis, John; America, 1754 ***1220.12*** *p466*
Kemner, N.G.; New York, NY, 1843 ***6412.40*** *p147*
Kemp, Benjamin; America, 1731 ***1220.12*** *p465*
Kemp, Benjamin; America, 1738 ***1220.12*** *p465*
Kemp, Cornelius; America, 1766 ***1220.12*** *p465*
Kemp, Edward; America, 1685 ***1220.12*** *p465*
Kemp, Edward; America, 1687 ***1220.12*** *p465*
Kemp, Edward; America, 1767 ***1220.12*** *p465*
Kemp, Edward; America, 1770 ***1220.12*** *p465*
Kemp, Edward; Virginia, 1756 ***1220.12*** *p465*
Kemp, Elizabeth; America, 1729 ***1220.12*** *p465*
Kemp, George; America, 1752 ***1220.12*** *p465*
Kemp, George; America, 1753 ***1220.12*** *p465*
Kemp, George; America, 1773 ***1220.12*** *p465*
Kemp, Hannah; America, 1774 ***1220.12*** *p465*
Kemp, Henry; America, 1738 ***1220.12*** *p465*
Kemp, James 34; Ontario, 1871 ***1823.17*** *p83*
Kemp, James, Jr.; America, 1775 ***1220.12*** *p465*
Kemp, John; America, 1737 ***1220.12*** *p465*
Kemp, John; America, 1753 ***1220.12*** *p465*
Kemp, John; America, 1756 ***1220.12*** *p465*
Kemp, John; America, 1763 ***1220.12*** *p465*
Kemp, John; America, 1767 ***1220.12*** *p465*
Kemp, John 54; Ontario, 1871 ***1823.21*** *p187*
Kemp, Joseph; Barbados, 1664 ***1220.12*** *p465*
Kemp, Mary; Annapolis, MD, 1729 ***1220.12*** *p465*
Kemp, Thomas; America, 1766 ***1220.12*** *p465*
Kemp, Thomas; Potomac, 1729 ***1220.12*** *p465*
Kemp, William 57; Ontario, 1871 ***1823.17*** *p83*
Kempe, Amey; Virginia, 1730 ***1220.12*** *p465*
Kempe, William; America, 1775 ***1220.12*** *p465*
Kemper, Anna; New Jersey, 1913 ***5475.1*** *p73*
Kemper, Franz; Galveston, TX, 1855 ***571.7*** *p17*
Kempf, Alois; New York, 1859 ***358.56*** *p100*
Kempf, Anne Marie 5; Louisiana, 1848 ***778.6*** *p185*
Kempf, Anton 36; Galveston, TX, 1844 ***3967.10*** *p373*
Kempf, Barbara 10 *SEE* Kempf, Konrad
Kempf, Caroline 40; America, 1840 ***778.6*** *p185*
Kempf, Catherine 8; Louisiana, 1848 ***778.6*** *p185*
Kempf, Catherine 43; Louisiana, 1848 ***778.6*** *p185*
Kempf, Christine 6; Louisiana, 1848 ***778.6*** *p185*
Kempf, Elisabetha 3 *SEE* Kempf, Konrad
Kempf, Friedrich *SEE* Kempf, Heinrich
Kempf, Heinrich; America, 1882 ***5475.1*** *p16*
*Brother:*Friedrich
Kempf, Joseph 6 months; Galveston, TX, 1844 ***3967.10*** *p373*
Kempf, Joseph 34; Galveston, TX, 1844 ***3967.10*** *p373*
Kempf, Julie 7; America, 1840 ***778.6*** *p186*
Kempf, Konrad; America, 1883 ***2526.42*** *p153*
With wife
*Child:*Elisabetha
*Child:*Barbara
Kempf, Leonard 44; Louisiana, 1848 ***778.6*** *p186*
Kempf, Manuel 26; America, 1847 ***778.6*** *p186*
Kempf, Martha 39; Galveston, TX, 1844 ***3967.10*** *p375*
Kempf, Michael; America, 1881 ***2526.42*** *p154*
Kempf, Michel 19; America, 1847 ***778.6*** *p186*
Kempf, Philip.e 42; America, 1840 ***778.6*** *p186*
Kempf, Therese 2; Galveston, TX, 1844 ***3967.10*** *p373*
Kempf, Therese 20; Galveston, TX, 1844 ***3967.10*** *p373*
Kempf, Therese 10; Louisiana, 1848 ***778.6*** *p186*
Kempf, Victorine 1; Louisiana, 1848 ***778.6*** *p186*
Kempker, Heinrich Christian; America, 1840 ***7420.1*** *p18*
With wife
Kempker, Sophie Eleonore; America, 1854 ***7420.1*** *p120*
Kemplin, John; America, 1685 ***1220.12*** *p465*
Kempson, John; Virginia, 1734 ***1220.12*** *p466*
Kempster, Albert Enslin; Port uncertain, 1926 ***9228.50*** *p311*
*Wife:*Winifred Norah Buesnel
Kempster, Constance Winifred; California, 1934-1983 ***9228.50*** *p311*
Kempster, Elizabeth; America, 1754 ***1220.12*** *p466*
Kempster, John; America, 1751 ***1220.12*** *p466*
Kempster, John; America, 1774 ***1220.12*** *p466*
Kempster, Susanna; America, 1725 ***1220.12*** *p466*
Kempster, Winifred Norah Buesnel *SEE* Kempster, Albert Enslin
Kempstock, John; Virginia, 1726 ***1220.12*** *p466*
Kempton, Agnes 26; Ontario, 1871 ***1823.17*** *p83*
Kempton, Christopher; Virginia, 1761 ***1220.12*** *p466*
Kempton, Mary; Maryland, 1737 ***1220.12*** *p466*
Kempton, Samuel; America, 1717 ***1220.12*** *p466*
Kempton, Thomas; America, 1749 ***1220.12*** *p466*
Kempton, Thomas; America, 1775 ***1220.12*** *p466*
Kemsley, Thomas 51; Ontario, 1871 ***1823.17*** *p83*
Kemster, Willm.; Maryland, 1674 ***1236.25*** *p50*
Kenadey, John; Boston, 1774 ***8529.30*** *p6*
Kenady, Henry 45; Ontario, 1871 ***1823.21*** *p187*
Kenady, James; New England, 1745 ***1642*** *p28*
Kenady, James; New England, 1745 ***1642*** *p28*
Kenady, Thomas; Boston, 1766 ***1642*** *p37*
Kenady, Thomas; Boston, 1775 ***8529.30*** *p4A*
Kenan, Ann 28; Ontario, 1871 ***1823.17*** *p83*
Kenaud, . . .; America, 1843 ***778.6*** *p186*
Kenaud, Aglae 28; America, 1843 ***778.6*** *p186*
Kenaud, Alfred 4; America, 1843 ***778.6*** *p186*
Kenaud, Aristide 8; America, 1843 ***778.6*** *p186*
Kenaud, Prosper 38; America, 1843 ***778.6*** *p186*
Kendal, Samuel; America, 1753 ***1220.12*** *p466*
Kendal, Samuel; South Carolina, 1811 ***6155.4*** *p18*
Kendal, Thomas 52; Ontario, 1871 ***1823.17*** *p83*
Kendall, Ann; America, 1759 ***1220.12*** *p466*
Kendall, George; Rappahannock, VA, 1741 ***1220.12*** *p466*
Kendall, Isaac; America, 1738 ***1220.12*** *p466*
Kendall, James; America, 1700 ***1220.12*** *p466*
Kendall, Jane; America, 1755 ***1220.12*** *p466*
Kendall, John; Barbados or Jamaica, 1692 ***1220.12*** *p466*
Kendall, Mary; America, 1747 ***1220.12*** *p466*
Kendall, Thomas; America, 1759 ***1220.12*** *p466*
Kendall, Thomas; America, 1764 ***1220.12*** *p466*
Kendall, Thomas; America, 1774 ***1220.12*** *p466*
Kendall, William; America, 1745 ***1220.12*** *p466*
Kendall, William; America, 1750 ***1220.12*** *p466*
Kendel, Barbara 21; Portland, ME, 1906 ***970.38*** *p78*
Kendel, Georg 2; Portland, ME, 1906 ***970.38*** *p78*
Kendel, Heinrich 25; Portland, ME, 1906 ***970.38*** *p78*
Kendell, Thomas; America, 1760 ***1220.12*** *p466*
Kender, John; New York, 1859 ***358.56*** *p100*
Kenderdine, Thomas; Iowa, 1876 ***1211.15*** *p15*
Kenderdine, William; Iowa, 1890 ***1211.15*** *p16*
Kendrick, Ann; America, 1752 ***1220.12*** *p466*
Kendrick, James; America, 1772 ***1220.12*** *p466*
Kendrick, John 56; Ontario, 1871 ***1823.21*** *p187*
Kendrick, William; America, 1749 ***1220.12*** *p466*
Kenear, David; Virginia, 1724 ***1220.12*** *p473*
Kenedy, Donald 59; Ontario, 1871 ***1823.21*** *p187*
Kenedy, Edward 28; Ontario, 1871 ***1823.17*** *p84*
Kenedy, Elizabeth; Plymouth, MA, 1688 ***1642*** *p2*
Kenedy, John; Quebec, 1786 ***1416.15*** *p8*
Kenedy, Michael 58; Ontario, 1871 ***1823.17*** *p84*
Kenedy, Timmothy 56; Ontario, 1871 ***1823.21*** *p187*
Kenege, George; North Carolina, 1710 ***3629.40*** *p5*
Kenelum, Mary; New Orleans, 1851 ***7242.30*** *p146*
Kenery, Richard; New England, 1745 ***1642*** *p28*
Keney, Nathan; New England, 1745 ***1642*** *p28*
Kenhenbacker, Hermann; Wisconsin, 1898 ***6795.8*** *p226*
Kenhow, William 35; Ontario, 1871 ***1823.17*** *p84*
Keniday, Daniel; Massachusetts, 1675-1676 ***1642*** *p127*
Keniff, James 60; Michigan, 1880 ***4491.39*** *p16*
Keniff, Sarah 33; Michigan, 1880 ***4491.39*** *p16*
Kenilous, J.; New Orleans, 1850 ***7242.30*** *p146*
Kenilous, James; New Orleans, 1850 ***7242.30*** *p146*
Kenilous, John; New Orleans, 1850 ***7242.30*** *p146*
Kenilous, Thomas; New Orleans, 1850 ***7242.30*** *p146*
Kenilous, William; New Orleans, 1850 ***7242.30*** *p146*

Kenison, Joseph; Colorado, 1878 ***1029.59*** *p49*
Kenly, Arthur; Annapolis, MD, 1725 ***1220.12*** *p466*
Kenmore, Mary; America, 1740 ***1220.12*** *p466*
Kenna, Cornielus 47; Ontario, 1871 ***1823.21*** *p187*
Kennady, John 60; Ontario, 1871 ***1823.21*** *p187*
Kennady, John Henry; North Carolina, 1854 ***1088.45*** *p17*
Kennady, Nathaniel; Philadelphia, 1777 ***8529.30*** *p2*
Kennady, Robert; New England, 1745 ***1642*** *p28*
Kennan, Adam 35; Ontario, 1871 ***1823.17*** *p84*
Kennan, William H.; Ohio, 1853 ***3580.20*** *p32*
Kennan, William H.; Ohio, 1853 ***6020.12*** *p12*
Kennard, Evelyn; America, 1729 ***1220.12*** *p466*
Kennard, George; America, 1710 ***1220.12*** *p466*
Kennard, Samuel; America, 1758 ***1220.12*** *p466*
Kennaty, William; America, 1774 ***1220.12*** *p467*
Kenne, Catherine; America, 1759 ***1220.12*** *p466*
Kenne, John; New England, 1745 ***1642*** *p27*
Kenne, John; New England, 1745 ***1642*** *p28*
Kenne, Thomas; America, 1749 ***1220.12*** *p466*
Kenned, Duch; Boston, 1764 ***1642*** *p33*
Kenneday, Bartholomew; America, 1749 ***1220.12*** *p466*
Kenneday, Mary 21; North Carolina, 1774 ***1422.10*** *p55*
Kenneday, William 25; North Carolina, 1774 ***1422.10*** *p56*
Kennedy, Alexander 26; Ontario, 1871 ***1823.21*** *p187*
Kennedy, Andrew 80; Ontario, 1871 ***1823.21*** *p187*
Kennedy, Bartholeman A.; North Carolina, 1852 ***1088.45*** *p17*
Kennedy, Bridget 50; Ontario, 1871 ***1823.17*** *p84*
Kennedy, Catherine 66; Ontario, 1871 ***1823.21*** *p187*
Kennedy, Charles 50; Ontario, 1871 ***1823.21*** *p187*
Kennedy, Charles 20; St. John, N.B., 1834 ***6469.7*** *p5*
Kennedy, Christopher; Boston, 1765 ***1642*** *p34*
Kennedy, Cornelius 60; Ontario, 1871 ***1823.21*** *p187*
Kennedy, Daniel; Toronto, 1844 ***2910.35*** *p113*
Kennedy, David 60; Ontario, 1871 ***1823.21*** *p187*
Kennedy, David M. 40; Ontario, 1871 ***1823.17*** *p84*
Kennedy, Dennis; Ohio, 1840-1897 ***8365.35*** *p16*
Kennedy, Dennis 25; Ontario, 1871 ***1823.21*** *p187*
Kennedy, Donald; Quebec, 1786 ***1416.15*** *p8*
Kennedy, Dunn; Quebec, 1786 ***1416.15*** *p8*
Kennedy, Edward; America, 1769 ***1220.12*** *p466*
Kennedy, Edward 60; Ontario, 1871 ***1823.21*** *p187*
Kennedy, Edward 70; Ontario, 1871 ***1823.21*** *p187*
Kennedy, Elizabeth 70; Ontario, 1871 ***1823.21*** *p187*
Kennedy, Francis; Toronto, 1844 ***2910.35*** *p114*
Kennedy, George 60; Ontario, 1871 ***1823.21*** *p187*
Kennedy, Hannah 36; Ontario, 1871 ***1823.21*** *p187*
Kennedy, Hiram 15; Michigan, 1880 ***4491.39*** *p16*
Kennedy, Honora 22; Ontario, 1859 ***9228.50*** *p382*
Kennedy, Hugh; Illinois, 1860 ***6079.1*** *p7*
Kennedy, Isabel; America, 1760 ***1220.12*** *p466*
Kennedy, James; America, 1773 ***1220.12*** *p466*
Kennedy, James; Boston, 1763 ***1642*** *p32*
Kennedy, James; New York, NY, 1832 ***3274.55*** *p24*
Kennedy, James 26; Ontario, 1871 ***1823.21*** *p187*
Kennedy, James 37; Ontario, 1871 ***1823.21*** *p187*
Kennedy, James 37; Ontario, 1871 ***1823.21*** *p187*
Kennedy, James 41; Ontario, 1871 ***1823.21*** *p188*
Kennedy, James 42; Ontario, 1871 ***1823.21*** *p188*
Kennedy, James 45; Ontario, 1871 ***1823.21*** *p187*
Kennedy, James; Washington, 1889 ***2770.40*** *p79*
Kennedy, Jane 52; Ontario, 1871 ***1823.21*** *p188*
Kennedy, Jermiah 30; Ontario, 1871 ***1823.21*** *p188*
Kennedy, John; Annapolis, MD, 1726 ***1220.12*** *p466*
Kennedy, John; Iowa, 1884 ***1211.15*** *p15*
Kennedy, John; New Orleans, 1850 ***7242.30*** *p146*
Kennedy, John; North Carolina, 1840 ***1088.45*** *p17*
Kennedy, John 23; Ontario, 1871 ***1823.21*** *p188*
Kennedy, John 39; Ontario, 1871 ***1823.21*** *p188*
Kennedy, John 48; Ontario, 1871 ***1823.21*** *p188*
Kennedy, John 73; Ontario, 1871 ***1823.17*** *p84*
Kennedy, John 19; St. Johns, N.F., 1811 ***1053.20*** *p20*
Kennedy, Joseph; Colorado, 1873 ***1029.59*** *p49*
Kennedy, Joseph 54; Ontario, 1871 ***1823.17*** *p84*
Kennedy, Joseph 55; Ontario, 1871 ***1823.21*** *p188*
Kennedy, Lawrence; America, 1774 ***1220.12*** *p466*
Kennedy, Lawrence; America, 1775 ***1220.12*** *p466*
Kennedy, Lenien 25; St. Johns, N.F., 1811 ***1053.20*** *p20*
Kennedy, Louisa 13; Michigan, 1880 ***4491.39*** *p16*
Kennedy, Martha Harrison *SEE* Kennedy, Robert
Kennedy, Martin; America, 1755 ***1220.12*** *p467*
Kennedy, Mary 32; Ontario, 1871 ***1823.21*** *p188*
Kennedy, Mary 24; St. John, N.B., 1834 ***6469.7*** *p5*
Kennedy, Mary A. 38; Michigan, 1880 ***4491.39*** *p16*
Kennedy, Mathew; America, 1770 ***1220.12*** *p467*
Kennedy, Matthew; America, 1771 ***1220.12*** *p467*
Kennedy, Matthew 38; Ontario, 1871 ***1823.17*** *p84*
Kennedy, Michael; America, 1764 ***1220.12*** *p467*
Kennedy, Michael; America, 1771 ***1220.12*** *p467*
Kennedy, Michael; Toronto, 1844 ***2910.35*** *p116*
Kennedy, Micheal 44; Ontario, 1871 ***1823.17*** *p84*
Kennedy, Michel; Louisiana, 1874-1875 ***4981.45*** *p29*
Kennedy, Morris 76; Ontario, 1871 ***1823.17*** *p84*
Kennedy, Patrick; America, 1771 ***1220.12*** *p467*
Kennedy, Peter; America, 1774 ***1220.12*** *p467*
Kennedy, Philip; America, 1764 ***1220.12*** *p467*
Kennedy, Philip 20; St. Johns, N.F., 1811 ***1053.20*** *p21*
Kennedy, Robert; America, 1770 ***1220.12*** *p467*
Kennedy, Robert 43; Ontario, 1871 ***1823.21*** *p188*
Kennedy, Robert 53; Ontario, 1871 ***1823.21*** *p188*
Kennedy, Robert 56; Ontario, 1871 ***1823.21*** *p188*
Kennedy, Robert; Philadelphia, 1852 ***8513.31*** *p319*
*Wife:*Martha Harrison
Kennedy, Thima; North Carolina, 1837 ***1088.45*** *p17*
Kennedy, Thomas 39; Michigan, 1880 ***4491.39*** *p16*
Kennedy, Thomas; Newfoundland, 1814 ***3476.10*** *p54*
Kennedy, Thomas 41; Ontario, 1871 ***1823.17*** *p84*
Kennedy, Thomas 50; Ontario, 1871 ***1823.21*** *p188*
Kennedy, Timothy; America, 1767 ***1220.12*** *p467*
Kennedy, William; Iowa, 1890 ***1211.15*** *p16*
Kennedy, William; New York, 1782 ***8529.30*** *p13*
Kennedy, William; North Carolina, 1853 ***1088.45*** *p17*
Kennedy, William 21; Ontario, 1871 ***1823.21*** *p188*
Kennedys, John; Massachusetts, 1675-1676 ***1642*** *p127*
Kennefick, Edwd 28; St. Johns, N.F., 1811 ***1053.20*** *p19*
Kennells, Robert; Portsmouth, NH, 1671 ***9228.50*** *p311*
Kenner, Jacob; Chile, 1852 ***1192.4*** *p52*
Kenner, Samuel 16; Ontario, 1871 ***1823.21*** *p188*
Kennett, George; Virginia, 1727 ***1220.12*** *p467*
Kennett, Richard; Barbados, 1715 ***1220.12*** *p467*
Kennewall, Charles; America, 1745 ***1220.12*** *p467*
Kenney, Daniel; Boston, 1763 ***1642*** *p32*
Kenney, John; Boston, 1747 ***1642*** *p29*
Kenney, John; Jamaica, 1783 ***8529.30*** *p13A*
Kenney, John 50; Ontario, 1871 ***1823.21*** *p188*
Kenney, Joseph 30; Ontario, 1871 ***1823.21*** *p188*
Kenney, Margaret; Philadelphia, 1856 ***8513.31*** *p301*
Kenney, Mary A. 2; Ontario, 1871 ***1823.21*** *p188*
Kenney, Michael 39; Ontario, 1871 ***1823.21*** *p188*
Kenney, Nathan; New England, 1745 ***1642*** *p28*
Kenney, Peter; New York, NY, 1838 ***3274.56*** *p99*
Kenney, Thomas 28; Indiana, 1862-1880 ***9076.20*** *p70*
Kenney, Thomas; Massachusetts, 1675-1676 ***1642*** *p128*
Kennick, John; America, 1763 ***1220.12*** *p467*
Kennick, William; Barbados, 1695 ***1220.12*** *p467*
Kennish, John; Missouri, 1885 ***3276.1*** *p2*
Kennolds, Thomas; Maryland, 1719 ***1220.12*** *p467*
Kennon, Samuel S. 30; Ontario, 1871 ***1823.21*** *p188*
Kenny, Catherine; Halifax, N.S., 1827 ***7009.9*** *p62*
*Husband:*Nicholas
Kenny, Catherine 12; Quebec, 1870 ***8364.32*** *p24*
Kenny, Dennis; New Orleans, 1850 ***7242.30*** *p146*
Kenny, Edwd 40; St. Johns, N.F., 1811 ***1053.20*** *p20*
Kenny, Elisha; New England, 1747 ***1642*** *p29*
Kenny, Frederick H. 42; Ontario, 1871 ***1823.21*** *p188*
Kenny, Henry; Massachusetts, 1675-1676 ***1642*** *p127*
Kenny, Henry; Massachusetts, 1675-1676 ***1642*** *p128*
Kenny, Henry; Massachusetts, 1675-1676 ***1642*** *p129*
Kenny, James; New Orleans, 1850 ***7242.30*** *p146*
Kenny, James; New York, 1826 ***3274.55*** *p73*
Kenny, James W.; America, 1756 ***1220.12*** *p467*
Kenny, Jane 80; Ontario, 1871 ***1823.21*** *p188*
Kenny, John; Havana, 1782 ***8529.30*** *p9A*
Kenny, John; New Orleans, 1850 ***7242.30*** *p146*
Kenny, Julia; New Orleans, 1850 ***7242.30*** *p146*
Kenny, Luke; America, 1758 ***1220.12*** *p467*
Kenny, Mary; America, 1770 ***1220.12*** *p467*
Kenny, Mary; New Orleans, 1850 ***7242.30*** *p146*
Kenny, Nicholas *SEE* Kenny, Catherine Brennan
Kenny, Patrick; America, 1771 ***1220.12*** *p467*
Kenny, Patrick 60; Ontario, 1871 ***1823.21*** *p188*
Kenny, Robert 40; Ontario, 1871 ***1823.21*** *p188*
Kenny, William; America, 1771 ***1220.12*** *p467*
Kenrell, John; New Orleans, 1850 ***7242.30*** *p146*
Kensey, John; North Carolina, 1710 ***3629.40*** *p5*
Kensington, Martha; Barbados or Jamaica, 1710 ***1220.12*** *p467*
Kenstbach, Georg; America, 1877 ***5475.1*** *p154*
Kenstephens, Morgan; America, 1738 ***1220.12*** *p467*
Kent, Ann; America, 1744 ***1220.12*** *p467*
Kent, Cartwright 66; Ontario, 1871 ***1823.21*** *p188*
Kent, Charles 20; Quebec, 1870 ***8364.32*** *p24*
Kent, David 56; Ontario, 1871 ***1823.21*** *p188*
Kent, Edward; America, 1685 ***1220.12*** *p467*
Kent, Edward; Rappahannock, VA, 1729 ***1220.12*** *p467*
Kent, Francis 33; Ontario, 1871 ***1823.17*** *p84*
Kent, George; Barbados, 1673 ***1220.12*** *p467*
Kent, Grace; America, 1771 ***1220.12*** *p467*
Kent, Henry 28; Ontario, 1871 ***1823.21*** *p188*
Kent, Humphrey; Virginia, 1726 ***1220.12*** *p467*
Kent, James 35; Ontario, 1871 ***1823.21*** *p188*
Kent, Jo; Virginia, 1652 ***6254.4*** *p243*
Kent, John; America, 1736 ***1220.12*** *p467*
Kent, John; America, 1744 ***1220.12*** *p467*
Kent, John; America, 1747 ***1220.12*** *p467*
Kent, John; America, 1754 ***1220.12*** *p467*
Kent, John; Died enroute, 1731 ***1220.12*** *p467*
Kent, John; Maryland, 1742 ***1220.12*** *p467*
Kent, John 61; Ontario, 1871 ***1823.21*** *p188*
Kent, Mary J. 35; Ontario, 1871 ***1823.21*** *p188*
Kent, Patt; St. Augustine, FL, 1778 ***8529.30*** *p9A*
Kent, Peter; America, 1685 ***1220.12*** *p467*
Kent, Richard; America, 1752 ***1220.12*** *p467*
Kent, Richard; America, 1766 ***1220.12*** *p467*
Kent, Richard; America, 1772 ***1220.12*** *p467*
Kent, Sarah; America, 1740 ***1220.12*** *p467*
Kent, Saxtos 50; Ontario, 1871 ***1823.21*** *p188*
Kent, Stephen; America, 1772 ***1220.12*** *p467*
Kent, Thomas; Carolina, 1724 ***1220.12*** *p467*
Kent, Thomas 62; Ontario, 1871 ***1823.21*** *p188*
Kent, William 50; Ontario, 1871 ***1823.21*** *p188*
Kent, William 54; Ontario, 1871 ***1823.21*** *p188*
Kentroses, Frederick 26; Port uncertain, 1840 ***778.6*** *p186*
Kentroses, Jean 27; Port uncertain, 1840 ***778.6*** *p186*
Kentsbeare, Sarah; America, 1766 ***1220.12*** *p467*
Kentt, John; America, 1750 ***1220.12*** *p467*
Kenvin, Evan; America, 1773 ***1220.12*** *p468*
Kenwark, Jesse 54; Ontario, 1871 ***1823.17*** *p84*
Kenwell, Elizabeth 38; Michigan, 1880 ***4491.39*** *p16*
Kenwell, John 36; Michigan, 1880 ***4491.39*** *p16*
Kenword, Thomas 42; Ontario, 1871 ***1823.17*** *p84*
Keny, John; Toronto, 1844 ***2910.35*** *p115*
Kenyon, Joseph; New York, NY, 1826 ***3274.55*** *p74*
Kenzer, John; America, 1763 ***1220.12*** *p468*
Kenzie, Mary; America, 1775 ***1220.12*** *p468*
Keoffe, Jas; St. John, N.B., 1847 ***2978.15*** *p41*
Keoffe, Patk; St. John, N.B., 1847 ***2978.15*** *p41*
Keogh, Catherine; New Orleans, 1850 ***7242.30*** *p146*
Keogh, Christopher; New Orleans, 1850 ***7242.30*** *p146*
Keogh, Elizabeth 58; Ontario, 1871 ***1823.21*** *p189*
Keogh, Ellen; New Orleans, 1850 ***7242.30*** *p146*
Keogh, John; New Orleans, 1850 ***7242.30*** *p147*
Keogh, Mary; New Orleans, 1850 ***7242.30*** *p147*
Keogh, Michael; New Orleans, 1850 ***7242.30*** *p147*
Keogh, Miles; New Orleans, 1850 ***7242.30*** *p147*
Keogh, Patt; New Orleans, 1850 ***7242.30*** *p147*
Keogh, Sarah; New Orleans, 1850 ***7242.30*** *p147*
Keogh, Thomas; New Orleans, 1850 ***7242.30*** *p147*
Keoho, Thomas; Boston, 1765 ***1642*** *p35*
Keon, James 41; Ontario, 1871 ***1823.17*** *p84*
Keough, Augustin; Toronto, 1844 ***2910.35*** *p113*
Keough, James; Newfoundland, 1814 ***3476.10*** *p54*
Keough, Jane 24; Ontario, 1871 ***1823.21*** *p189*
Keough, John; Toronto, 1844 ***2910.35*** *p113*
Keown, John 54; Ontario, 1871 ***1823.21*** *p189*
Keppinger, Frederick; New York, 1859 ***358.56*** *p55*
Keppler, Josephine; America, 1865-1900 ***5475.1*** *p46*
Keppner, Anton; Venezuela, 1843 ***3899.5*** *p542*
Keppner, Franz Anton; Venezuela, 1843 ***3899.5*** *p542*
Keppner, Georg Anton; Venezuela, 1843 ***3899.5*** *p542*
Keppner, Gottfried; New York, 1859 ***358.56*** *p101*
Keppner, Theresia; Venezuela, 1843 ***3899.5*** *p542*
Kepshu, Jeremiah; Louisiana, 1874 ***4981.45*** *p132*
Ker, George; North Carolina, 1792-1862 ***1088.45*** *p17*
Ker, George 49; Ontario, 1871 ***1823.21*** *p189*
Kerans, Mathew 32; Ontario, 1871 ***1823.17*** *p84*
Kerber, A. Maria *SEE* Kerber, Nikolaus
Kerber, Adam 50; America, 1844 ***2526.43*** *p210*
Kerber, Jakob *SEE* Kerber, Nikolaus
Kerber, Joh. Peter *SEE* Kerber, Nikolaus
Kerber, Johannes; Argentina, 1855 ***2526.43*** *p210*
With family of 8
Kerber, Josef; America, 1873 ***5475.1*** *p163*
Kerber, Katharina *SEE* Kerber, Nikolaus
Kerber, Katharina Lorig *SEE* Kerber, Nikolaus
Kerber, Mathias *SEE* Kerber, Nikolaus
Kerber, Nikolaus *SEE* Kerber, Nikolaus
Kerber, Nikolaus 59; America, 1875 ***5475.1*** *p285*
*Wife:*Katharina Lorig
*Daughter:*Katharina
*Son:*Nikolaus
*Son:*Wilhelm
*Son:*Jakob
*Son:*Joh. Peter
*Son:*Mathias
*Daughter:*A. Maria
Kerber, Wilhelm *SEE* Kerber, Nikolaus
Kerberloh, Christian August Bernhard; America, 1881 ***7420.1*** *p322*
Kerby, Francis, Jr.; America, 1850 ***9228.50*** *p311*
*Wife:*Mary Le Cornu
*Child:*Mary Jane
Kerby, Martha; America, 1745 ***1220.12*** *p473*
Kerby, Mary Le Cornu *SEE* Kerby, Francis, Jr.
Kerby, Mary Jane *SEE* Kerby, Francis, Jr.
Kerby, Robert; Barbados, 1675 ***1220.12*** *p473*
Kerchner, Christopher; Ohio, 1809-1852 ***4511.35*** *p26*
Kerchoff, Ernest; Iowa, 1896 ***1211.15*** *p16*

Kerealowski, John; North Carolina, 1835 ***1088.45*** *p17*
Kerfaber, Jacob 22; America, 1847 ***778.6*** *p186*
Kerfoot, William 55; Ontario, 1871 ***1823.17*** *p84*
Kergall, Frank; Washington, 1885 ***2770.40*** *p194*
Keriecke, Gerar; Louisiana, 1874 ***4981.45*** *p132*
Kerigan, Thomas 40; Ontario, 1871 ***1823.21*** *p189*
Kerkhof, Mr.; America, 1865 ***7420.1*** *p232*
Kerkhof, Mr.; America, 1870 ***7420.1*** *p284*
With family
Kerkhof, Engel Eleonore; America, 1852 ***7420.1*** *p90*
Kerkhof, Friedrich; America, 1854 ***7420.1*** *p122*
Kerkmann, Caroline Wilhelmine Hagedorn *SEE* Kerkmann, Johann Heinrich Christian
Kerkmann, Engel Sophie; America, 1870 ***7420.1*** *p284*
Kerkmann, Heinrich Friedrich Christoph; America, 1865 ***7420.1*** *p232*
Kerkmann, Johann Heinrich Christian; Illinois, 1845 ***7420.1*** *p37*
*Wife:*Caroline Wilhelmine Hagedorn
With daughter 21
With son 19
Kerkmann, Johann Heinrich Christoph; America, 1865 ***7420.1*** *p232*
Kerl, Anna Maria Louise; Wisconsin, 1897 ***6795.8*** *p83*
Kerl, Bertha Emilie Auguste; Wisconsin, 1897 ***6795.8*** *p83*
Kerl, Maria Ida; Wisconsin, 1898 ***6795.8*** *p83*
Kerland, James 48; Ontario, 1871 ***1823.17*** *p84*
Kerle, John; America, 1685 ***1220.12*** *p468*
Kerle, Richard; Barbados, 1714 ***1220.12*** *p468*
Kerley, George; America, 1737 ***1220.12*** *p468*
Kerley, Tim; St. John, N.B., 1847 ***2978.15*** *p40*
Kerman, Ed; Louisiana, 1874 ***4981.45*** *p296*
Kermath, William 42; Ontario, 1871 ***1823.21*** *p189*
Kermele, Peter; Ohio, 1809-1852 ***4511.35*** *p29*
Kermott, J.W.; Toronto, 1844 ***2910.35*** *p116*
Kern, . . .; West Virginia, n.d. ***1132.30*** *p151*
Kern, . . .; West Virginia, n.d. ***1132.30*** *p151*
Kern, Adam; Ohio, 1809-1852 ***4511.35*** *p26*
Kern, Andrew; West Virginia, 1873 ***1132.30*** *p151*
Kern, Anna Marie; America, 1836 ***8115.12*** *p328*
*Child:*Katharine
*Child:*Elisabeth
Kern, Barbara; Venezuela, 1843 ***3899.5*** *p543*
Kern, Barbara; Venezuela, 1843 ***3899.5*** *p544*
Kern, Catherine; New York, 1860 ***358.56*** *p149*
Kern, Elisabeth *SEE* Kern, Anna Marie
Kern, Famille 33; New Castle, DE, 1817-1818 ***90.20*** *p152*
Kern, George; America, 1769 ***1220.12*** *p468*
Kern, George; New Orleans, 1840 ***778.6*** *p186*
Kern, Henry 48; Ontario, 1871 ***1823.21*** *p189*
Kern, Jacob; Ohio, 1809-1852 ***4511.35*** *p26*
Kern, John W. 49; Ontario, 1871 ***1823.21*** *p189*
Kern, Katharine *SEE* Kern, Anna Marie
Kern, Margaretha; New York, 1860 ***358.56*** *p150*
Kern, Maria; America, 1880 ***5475.1*** *p55*
Kern, Michel; Louisiana, 1874-1875 ***4981.45*** *p29*
Kern, Theresia; Venezuela, 1843 ***3899.5*** *p541*
Kernaghan, George 19; Ontario, 1871 ***1823.17*** *p84*
Kernahan, Andrew 34; Ontario, 1871 ***1823.17*** *p84*
Kernahan, James 35; Ontario, 1871 ***1823.17*** *p84*
Kernahan, William 46; Ontario, 1871 ***1823.21*** *p189*
Kernchan, John 34; Ontario, 1871 ***1823.21*** *p189*
Kerner, Bernh. 28; America, 1840 ***778.6*** *p186*
Kerner, Hermann; America, 1868 ***7919.3*** *p533*
Kerner, Josef; Chicago, 1872 ***2853.20*** *p406*
Kerner, Mathias; America, 1846 ***5475.1*** *p302*
Kerney, Michael 47; Ontario, 1871 ***1823.17*** *p84*
Kerney, Patrick 44; Ontario, 1871 ***1823.17*** *p84*
Kernick, James 37; Ontario, 1871 ***1823.21*** *p189*
Kernick, Thomas 21; Ontario, 1871 ***1823.21*** *p189*
Kernohan, Hugh 45; Ontario, 1871 ***1823.21*** *p189*
Kernohan, Hugh 56; Ontario, 1871 ***1823.21*** *p189*
Kernohan, James 30; Ontario, 1871 ***1823.21*** *p189*
Kernohan, John 35; Ontario, 1871 ***1823.21*** *p189*
Kernohan, John 59; Ontario, 1871 ***1823.21*** *p189*
Kernohan, Sam 30; Ontario, 1871 ***1823.21*** *p189*
Kernoman, David 20; Ontario, 1871 ***1823.21*** *p189*
Kernoman, Joseph 49; Ontario, 1871 ***1823.21*** *p189*
Kerns, John W. 39; Ontario, 1871 ***1823.21*** *p189*
Kero, Mary 32; Minnesota, 1925 ***2769.54*** *p1379*
Kerohl, Ann 19; New York, NY, 1894 ***6512.1*** *p182*
Kerol, Joseph; Louisiana, 1841-1844 ***4981.45*** *p210*
Kerr, Adam 31; Ontario, 1871 ***1823.21*** *p189*
Kerr, Alexander; America, 1744 ***1220.12*** *p468*
Kerr, Alexander 30; Ontario, 1871 ***1823.17*** *p84*
Kerr, Alexander 41; Ontario, 1871 ***1823.21*** *p189*
Kerr, Alexander 65; Ontario, 1871 ***1823.21*** *p189*
Kerr, Andrew; America, 1734 ***1220.12*** *p468*
Kerr, Ann Jane 18; St. John, N.B., 1834 ***6469.7*** *p5*
Kerr, Benjamin 52; Ontario, 1871 ***1823.17*** *p84*
Kerr, Catherine 46; Ontario, 1871 ***1823.21*** *p189*
Kerr, Cornelius 36; Ontario, 1871 ***1823.21*** *p189*
Kerr, Daniel 31; Ontario, 1871 ***1823.21*** *p189*
Kerr, Daniel; South Carolina, 1813 ***3208.30*** *p18*
Kerr, Daniel; South Carolina, 1813 ***3208.30*** *p31*
Kerr, Daniel 52; South Carolina, 1812 ***3476.30*** *p12*
Kerr, David 45; Ontario, 1871 ***1823.21*** *p189*
Kerr, Elizabeth; America, 1748 ***1220.12*** *p468*
Kerr, Elizabeth 16; Ontario, 1871 ***1823.17*** *p84*
Kerr, Fanny; St. John, N.B., 1842 ***2978.20*** *p6*
Kerr, George; North Carolina, 1821-1825 ***1088.45*** *p17*
Kerr, George 35; Ontario, 1871 ***1823.17*** *p84*
Kerr, Henery 43; Ontario, 1871 ***1823.17*** *p84*
Kerr, Henry 40; Ontario, 1871 ***1823.17*** *p84*
Kerr, James; America, 1740 ***1220.12*** *p468*
Kerr, James; North Carolina, 1837 ***1088.45*** *p17*
Kerr, James 30; Ontario, 1871 ***1823.17*** *p84*
Kerr, James 40; Ontario, 1871 ***1823.17*** *p84*
Kerr, James 40; Ontario, 1871 ***1823.21*** *p189*
Kerr, John 18; St. John, N.B., 1834 ***6469.7*** *p5*
Kerr, Lawrence; St. John, N.B., 1842 ***2978.20*** *p6*
Kerr, Moses; North Carolina, 1811-1812 ***1088.45*** *p17*
Kerr, Murdoch 44; Ontario, 1871 ***1823.21*** *p189*
Kerr, Peter 60; Ontario, 1871 ***1823.17*** *p85*
Kerr, Thomas 57; Ontario, 1871 ***1823.17*** *p85*
Kerr, William 37; Ontario, 1871 ***1823.21*** *p189*
Kerr, William 57; Ontario, 1871 ***1823.17*** *p85*
Kerr, William 86; Ontario, 1871 ***1823.17*** *p85*
Kerrigan, Martin; Ontario, 1871 ***1823.21*** *p189*
Kerril, Mary; America, 1734 ***1220.12*** *p468*
Kerrivan, Edward; America, 1766 ***1220.12*** *p468*
Kersey, Edward 69; Ontario, 1871 ***1823.17*** *p85*
Kershaw, Charles 32; Ontario, 1871 ***1823.21*** *p190*
Kershaw, Robert J.; North Carolina, 1853 ***1088.45*** *p17*
Kershaw, Thomas; America, 1730 ***1220.12*** *p468*
Kerskgen, Gottfried; Illinois, 1857 ***6079.1*** *p7*
Kerslake, Robert; America, 1773 ***1220.12*** *p468*
Kerslake, Thomas 44; Ontario, 1871 ***1823.21*** *p190*
Kerslake, William; America, 1742 ***1220.12*** *p468*
Kersley, William; America, 1774 ***1220.12*** *p468*
Kersly, John; America, 1770 ***1220.12*** *p468*
Kersten, Dorothea Sophie Louise; America, 1893 ***7420.1*** *p368*
Kersting, Anna 36; Galveston, TX, 1845 ***3967.10*** *p376*
Kersting, Heinrich 1; Galveston, TX, 1845 ***3967.10*** *p376*
Kersting, Heinrich 36; Galveston, TX, 1845 ***3967.10*** *p376*
Kersting, Hermann 8; Galveston, TX, 1845 ***3967.10*** *p376*
Kerston, Emily 39; Ontario, 1871 ***1823.21*** *p190*
Kersulich, Autmes; Louisiana, 1874 ***4981.45*** *p132*
Kerszewicz, Kazimira 2; New York, NY, 1894 ***6512.1*** *p231*
Kerszewicz, Teofila 46; New York, NY, 1894 ***6512.1*** *p231*
Kert, Louis 28; Kentucky, 1846 ***778.6*** *p162*
Kerton, Thomas; Barbados or Jamaica, 1694 ***1220.12*** *p474*
Kerton, Thomas, Jr.; Barbados, 1688 ***1220.12*** *p474*
Kerton, Willm.; Maryland, 1674 ***1236.25*** *p50*
Kertz, Ludwig Jacobus; Kansas, 1881 ***7420.1*** *p322*
Kertz, Wilhelm; America, 1882 ***7420.1*** *p329*
Kerubitz, Joseph 24; New York, NY, 1898 ***7951.13*** *p44*
Kerubitz, Magdalena 24; New York, NY, 1898 ***7951.13*** *p44*
Kervinen, Leo 16; Minnesota, 1925 ***2769.54*** *p1378*
Kerwer, Barbara 13 *SEE* Kerwer, Johann
Kerwer, Gertrud 4 *SEE* Kerwer, Johann
Kerwer, Jakob; America, 1882 ***5475.1*** *p259*
Kerwer, Johann 1 *SEE* Kerwer, Johann
Kerwer, Johann 39; America, 1857 ***5475.1*** *p250*
*Wife:*Maria Jungmann 36
*Son:*Johann 1
*Son:*Nikolaus 9
*Son:*Peter 7
*Daughter:*Gertrud 4
*Daughter:*Barbara 13
Kerwer, Maria Jungmann 36 *SEE* Kerwer, Johann
Kerwer, Nikolaus 9 *SEE* Kerwer, Johann
Kerwer, Peter 7 *SEE* Kerwer, Johann
Kerwin, Catherine; New Orleans, 1850 ***7242.30*** *p147*
Kerwin, James; New Orleans, 1850 ***7242.30*** *p147*
Kerwin, John; New Orleans, 1850 ***7242.30*** *p147*
Kerwin, Thomas; Halifax, N.S., 1827 ***7009.9*** *p61*
Kerwin, Winnefred; New Orleans, 1850 ***7242.30*** *p147*
Kesel, Jean Pierre 4; America, 1847 ***778.6*** *p186*
Kesel, Marie 9; America, 1847 ***778.6*** *p186*
Kesel, Marie 36; America, 1847 ***778.6*** *p186*
Kesel, Nicola 46; America, 1847 ***778.6*** *p186*
Kesel, Nicola, I 8; America, 1847 ***778.6*** *p186*
Kesel, Nicola, II 6; America, 1847 ***778.6*** *p186*
Kesel, Pierre 25; America, 1847 ***778.6*** *p186*
Keso, Herman; Wisconsin, 1868 ***6795.8*** *p59*
Kesow, Herman; Wisconsin, 1868 ***6795.8*** *p59*
Kessack, Jane 57; Ontario, 1871 ***1823.21*** *p190*
Kessel, Anna 2; New York, NY, 1898 ***7951.13*** *p44*
Kessel, Anna 38; New York, NY, 1898 ***7951.13*** *p44*
Kessel, Elisabeth 5; New York, NY, 1898 ***7951.13*** *p44*
Kessel, Franz 17; New York, NY, 1898 ***7951.13*** *p44*
Kessel, Henri 30; Louisiana, 1848 ***778.6*** *p186*
Kessel, Joseph 10; New York, NY, 1898 ***7951.13*** *p44*
Kessel, Katherina 12; New York, NY, 1898 ***7951.13*** *p44*
Kessel, Maria 1 months; New York, NY, 1898 ***7951.13*** *p44*
Kessel, Michael 47; New York, NY, 1898 ***7951.13*** *p44*
Kessel, Phillip 3; New York, NY, 1898 ***7951.13*** *p44*
Kessel, Salomea 8; New York, NY, 1898 ***7951.13*** *p44*
Kessel, Stephan 19; New York, NY, 1898 ***7951.13*** *p44*
Kessler, Anton 14; America, 1840 ***778.6*** *p186*
Kessler, Boas 68; America, 1840 ***778.6*** *p186*
Kessler, Charles; Ohio, 1809-1852 ***4511.35*** *p26*
Kessler, Dorothea; America, 1867 ***7919.3*** *p533*
With child
Kessler, Elisabeth Weyrich *SEE* Kessler, Franz
Kessler, Elisabeth Scherschel 36 *SEE* Kessler, Johann
Kessler, Franz; America, 1837 ***5475.1*** *p395*
*Mother:*Elisabeth Weyrich
Kessler, George 11; America, 1840 ***778.6*** *p186*
Kessler, Ignatius; Ohio, 1809-1852 ***4511.35*** *p26*
Kessler, Jacob; Ohio, 1809-1852 ***4511.35*** *p26*
Kessler, Jacques 28; America, 1844 ***778.6*** *p186*
Kessler, Jakob *SEE* Kessler, Jakob Heinrich
Kessler, Jakob; America, 1850 ***5475.1*** *p411*
Kessler, Jakob 4 *SEE* Kessler, Johann
Kessler, Jakob 4 *SEE* Kessler, Jakob
Kessler, Jakob 35; America, 1849 ***5475.1*** *p415*
*Wife:*Margarethe Bohrmann 35
*Son:*Jakob 4
*Daughter:*Sophia 11 months
*Son:*Josef 11
Kessler, Jakob Heinrich; America, 1836 ***5475.1*** *p457*
*Wife:*M. Elisabeth Backer
*Son:*Jakob
*Daughter:*Kath. Elisabeth
Kessler, Johann; America, 1837 ***5475.1*** *p454*
With wife
With sister 14
With child 6 months
With child 8
With child 2
Kessler, Johann 3 *SEE* Kessler, Nikolaus
Kessler, Johann 38; America, 1846 ***5475.1*** *p408*
*Wife:*Katharina Meiser 46
*Son:*Jakob 4
Kessler, Johann 53; America, 1836 ***5475.1*** *p399*
*Wife:*Elisabeth Scherschel 36
With 3 children
Kessler, Johannes 7; America, 1840 ***778.6*** *p186*
Kessler, John; Illinois, 1855 ***6079.1*** *p7*
Kessler, John; Ohio, 1809-1852 ***4511.35*** *p26*
Kessler, Josef; America, 1860 ***5475.1*** *p412*
Kessler, Josef 11 *SEE* Kessler, Jakob
Kessler, Kaspar 1 *SEE* Kessler, Nikolaus
Kessler, Kath. Elisabeth *SEE* Kessler, Jakob Heinrich
Kessler, Katharina Meiser 46 *SEE* Kessler, Johann
Kessler, M. Elisabeth Backer *SEE* Kessler, Jakob Heinrich
Kessler, Margarethe Bohrmann 35 *SEE* Kessler, Jakob
Kessler, Maria Blasius *SEE* Kessler, Nikolaus
Kessler, Maria 2 *SEE* Kessler, Nikolaus
Kessler, Marie 17; Mississippi, 1846 ***778.6*** *p186*
Kessler, Michael 18; New York, NY, 1893 ***1883.7*** *p44*
Kessler, Michael; Pennsylvania, 1865 ***170.15*** *p31*
Kessler, Nicolas 19; Mississippi, 1846 ***778.6*** *p186*
Kessler, Nikolaus; America, 1837 ***5475.1*** *p395*
*Wife:*Maria Blasius
*Son:*Kaspar
*Daughter:*Maria
*Son:*Johann
Kessler, Nikolaus 62; America, 1846 ***5475.1*** *p386*
Kessler, Peter; America, 1847 ***5475.1*** *p408*
Kessler, Sophia 11 *SEE* Kessler, Jakob
Kessler, Victori 41; America, 1840 ***778.6*** *p187*
Kessock, Elizabeth 20; Ontario, 1871 ***1823.21*** *p190*
Kesten, Ferdinand; Brazil, 1825 ***5475.1*** *p461*
With daughter 11
With son 9
With son 6
With daughter 2
Kester, Bewley 78; Ontario, 1871 ***1823.21*** *p190*
Kester, Cedbiad 19; Ontario, 1871 ***1823.21*** *p190*
Kesting, William; Illinois, 1859 ***6079.1*** *p7*
Kestl, Innocenc; Cleveland, OH, 1906 ***2853.20*** *p444*
Kestler, Charles; Illinois, 1856 ***6079.1*** *p7*
Kestler, E.; California, 1868 ***1131.61*** *p90*
Kestner, Henry; Washington, 1887 ***2770.40*** *p24*
Kestorer, Elisabeth 25; America, 1846 ***778.6*** *p187*
Ketch, Margaret; America, 1665 ***1220.12*** *p468*

Ketch, Susan; America, 1665 *1220.12 p468*
Ketcher, Mary; Virginia, 1732 *1220.12 p468*
Ketcher, Samuel; Annapolis, MD, 1725 *1220.12 p468*
Ketchum, H.G.C.; Quebec, 1885 *1937.10 p52*
Ketling, John; Barbados or Jamaica, 1698 *1220.12 p468*
Ketola, John 32; Minnesota, 1925 *2769.54 p1378*
Kett, Richard; America, 1771 *1220.12 p468*
Kettel, Peter; Ohio, 1809-1852 *4511.35 p26*
Kettelhake, . . .; America, 1854 *7420.1 p122*
　With family
Kettenhofen, Angela 28; America, 1855 *5475.1 p317*
Kettenhofen, Angela Schuhmacher 30 *SEE* Kettenhofen, Peter
Kettenhofen, Elisabeth *SEE* Kettenhofen, Josef
Kettenhofen, Elisabeth Becker *SEE* Kettenhofen, Josef
Kettenhofen, Johann; America, 1871 *5475.1 p324*
Kettenhofen, Johannetta; New York, 1884 *5475.1 p167*
Kettenhofen, Josef; America, 1881 *5475.1 p307*
　*Wife:*Elisabeth Becker
　*Daughter:*Elisabeth
　*Son:*Mathias
Kettenhofen, Katharina 20; America, 1871 *5475.1 p324*
Kettenhofen, Margarethe; Wisconsin, 1891 *5475.1 p326*
Kettenhofen, Mathias *SEE* Kettenhofen, Josef
Kettenhofen, Nikolaus; America, 1867 *5475.1 p323*
Kettenhofen, Peter *SEE* Kettenhofen, Peter
Kettenhofen, Peter 32; America, 1869 *5475.1 p307*
　*Wife:*Angela Schuhmacher 30
　*Son:*Peter
Ketterer, Johann; Venezuela, 1843 *3899.5 p544*
Ketterer, Johannes; Venezuela, 1843 *3899.5 p544*
Ketterlein, Elisabeth 17; Baltimore, 1893 *1883.7 p38*
Ketterling, Elisabeth 17; Baltimore, 1893 *1883.7 p38*
Ketting, Daniel; Illinois, 1855 *6079.1 p7*
Kettle, Bartholomew; Barbados, 1688 *1220.12 p468*
Kettle, James; Died enroute, 1719 *1220.12 p468*
Kettle, John; America, 1751 *1220.12 p468*
Kettle, Peter; Ohio, 1809-1852 *4511.35 p26*
Kettle, William; America, 1775 *1220.12 p468*
Kettleburne, Thomas; America, 1707 *1220.12 p468*
Kettler, Heinrich von; Wisconsin, 1888 *6795.8 p158*
Kettles, Richard; America, 1715 *1220.12 p468*
Kettlestrings, James; America, 1751 *1220.12 p468*
Kettlewell, George 42; Ontario, 1871 *1823.21 p190*
Kettlewell, Mary; America, 1735 *1220.12 p468*
Kettlewell, Richard 48; Ontario, 1871 *1823.21 p190*
Kettlewell, Richard 51; Ontario, 1871 *1823.21 p190*
Kettlewell, William 39; Ontario, 1871 *1823.21 p190*
Ketville, Abraham; Marblehead, MA, 1681 *9228.50 p312*
Ketville, Abraham; Massachusetts, 1600-1699 *9228.50 p531*
Keum, Philip; Ohio, 1809-1852 *4511.35 p43*
Keury, Edwd 40; St. Johns, N.F., 1811 *1053.20 p20*
Keuthan, Jno. H.; Louisiana, 1874-1875 *4981.45 p29*
Kew, John 22; Ontario, 1871 *1823.21 p190*
Kew, Sarah; America, 1755 *1220.12 p468*
Kew, William; Colorado, 1873 *1029.59 p49*
Kew, William 30; Ontario, 1871 *1823.21 p190*
Kewe, Charlotte Louise; St. Louis, 1886 *7420.1 p350*
Kewerkopp, Peter; America, 1846 *5475.1 p234*
Kewin, Edman; Missouri, 1889 *3276.1 p2*
Kewley, Edmund 44; Ontario, 1871 *1823.17 p85*
Key, Abraham; America, 1724 *1220.12 p468*
Key, Anthony; Virginia, 1732 *1220.12 p468*
Key, John; America, 1685 *1220.12 p468*
Key, John; America, 1746 *1220.12 p468*
Key, John; Barbados, 1671 *1220.12 p468*
Key, John; Boston, 1774 *8529.30 p2*
Key, Joseph; Barbados or Jamaica, 1685 *1220.12 p468*
Key, Richard; America, 1742 *1220.12 p468*
Key, Silvester; Barbados, 1671 *1220.12 p468*
Key, Thomas; America, 1753 *1220.12 p468*
Key, Thomas; America, 1764 *1220.12 p469*
Key, William; America, 1685 *1220.12 p469*
Key, William; Maryland, 1723 *1220.12 p469*
Key, Wood 39; Ontario, 1871 *1823.21 p190*
Keyer, Elias 25; New Orleans, 1846 *778.6 p187*
Keyler, Simon; North Carolina, 1710 *3629.40 p5*
Keys, Elizabeth; America, 1756 *1220.12 p469*
Keys, Elsie Ann; Michigan, 1929 *9228.50 p247*
　*Brother:*William Henry
Keys, George; Barbados, 1668 *1220.12 p469*
Keys, James 55; Ontario, 1871 *1823.21 p190*
Keys, James C.; Ohio, 1870 *3580.20 p32*
Keys, James C.; Ohio, 1870 *6020.12 p12*
Keys, John; America, 1748 *1220.12 p469*
Keys, John 51; Ontario, 1871 *1823.21 p190*
Keys, Miriam; Annapolis, MD, 1726 *1220.12 p469*
Keys, Patrick 47; Ontario, 1871 *1823.21 p190*
Keys, Stephen 77; Ontario, 1871 *1823.21 p190*
Keys, Thomas; America, 1771 *1220.12 p469*
Keys, Thomas 40; Ontario, 1871 *1823.21 p190*
Keys, Thomas 48; Ontario, 1871 *1823.21 p190*

Keys, Thomas; Potomac, 1729 *1220.12 p469*
Keys, Thomas; Rappahannock, VA, 1741 *1220.12 p469*
Keys, William; Annapolis, MD, 1723 *1220.12 p469*
Keys, William Henry *SEE* Keys, Elsie Ann
Keys, William Henry; Ottawa, 1908-1934 *9228.50 p247*
Keyse, William 34; Ontario, 1871 *1823.21 p190*
Keysell, George; America, 1769 *1220.12 p469*
Keyser, Adolph Albrecht; America, 1860 *7420.1 p195*
Keyser, Felix; Ohio, 1809-1852 *4511.35 p26*
Keyser, Jacob; Ohio, 1809-1852 *4511.35 p26*
Keyser, Jno W. 32; Ontario, 1871 *1823.21 p190*
Keyser, John 63; Ontario, 1871 *1823.21 p190*
Keysser, Carl Emil Ludwig; America, 1856 *7420.1 p149*
Keysser, Michel Paul Julius Emil; America, 1857 *7420.1 p164*
Keyte, James; America, 1719 *1220.12 p469*
Keyte, John; America, 1687 *1220.12 p469*
Keywood, Edward; America, 1773 *1220.12 p469*
Keywood, Robert; America, 1688 *1220.12 p469*
Keyworth, John, Jr.; New Jersey, 1807 *3845.2 p129*
Khip, J. 1; New Orleans, 1834 *1002.51 p113*
Kibble, John; Virginia, 1736 *1220.12 p462*
Kibum, Sarah 84; Ontario, 1871 *1823.21 p190*
Kichhofel, Ernst; America, 1846 *5475.1 p28*
　With family
Kichle, John; North Carolina, 1856 *1088.45 p17*
Kick, Carl Heinrich Wilhelm; America, 1887 *7420.1 p354*
Kick, Carl Wilhelm; America, 1891 *7420.1 p362*
Kickens, Leopold 40; Quebec, 1910 *2897.7 p8*
Kickham, Thom; New Orleans, 1851 *7242.30 p147*
Kid, William; America, 1740 *1220.12 p469*
Kidd, Ann; Potomac, 1731 *1220.12 p469*
Kidd, Arthur E.; Iowa, 1890 *1211.15 p16*
Kidd, Benjamin *SEE* Kidd, Charles
Kidd, Charles; Massachusetts, 1775 *1642 p116*
　*Relative:*Benjamin
Kidd, John; America, 1741 *1220.12 p469*
Kidd, John; America, 1772 *1220.12 p469*
Kidd, Margaret 60; Ontario, 1871 *1823.17 p85*
Kidd, Mary 78; Ontario, 1871 *1823.21 p190*
Kidd, Richard; America, 1744 *1220.12 p469*
Kidd, Thomas 50; Ontario, 1871 *1823.21 p190*
Kidder, Ann; America, 1769 *1220.12 p469*
Kidder, Edward; America, 1757 *1220.12 p469*
Kiddy, Anthony; America, 1766 *1220.12 p469*
Kiddy, George; America, 1731 *1220.12 p469*
Kidgell, Jane; America, 1720 *1220.12 p469*
Kidman, John; America, 1730 *1220.12 p469*
Kidman, William; America, 1716 *1220.12 p469*
Kidner, John 52; Ontario, 1871 *1823.21 p190*
Kidner, Robert; Barbados, 1686 *1220.12 p469*
Kidwell, Dorothy; Barbados or Jamaica, 1698 *1220.12 p469*
Kiebel, Johann 26; America, 1864 *5475.1 p501*
Kiebel, Nikolaus; America, 1863 *5475.1 p508*
Kiebel, Peter; America, 1863 *5475.1 p501*
Kiefaber, Charles; Ohio, 1809-1852 *4511.35 p26*
Kiefaber, Lawrence; Ohio, 1809-1852 *4511.35 p26*
Kiefaber, Michael; Ohio, 1809-1852 *4511.35 p26*
Kiefaber, Peter; Ohio, 1809-1852 *4511.35 p26*
Kiefer, Adam; America, 1837 *5475.1 p536*
Kiefer, Amalie *SEE* Kiefer, Jakob
Kiefer, Andreas *SEE* Kiefer, Johann Adam
Kiefer, Andreas 26; America, 1833 *5475.1 p461*
Kiefer, Angela Schul *SEE* Kiefer, Johann
Kiefer, Anna; America, 1881 *5475.1 p325*
Kiefer, Anna Maria 2 *SEE* Kiefer, Nikolaus
Kiefer, Barbara *SEE* Kiefer, Wilhelm
Kiefer, Barbara *SEE* Kiefer, Franz
Kiefer, Barbara 35; America, 1871 *5475.1 p318*
Kiefer, Catharina 14; America, 1847 *778.6 p187*
Kiefer, Charlotte Sophie; America, 1881 *5475.1 p14*
Kiefer, Christian *SEE* Kiefer, Johann
Kiefer, Christina 44; America, 1847 *778.6 p187*
Kiefer, Clara 21; America, 1847 *778.6 p187*
Kiefer, Daniel; America, 1838 *5475.1 p67*
　With wife & 6 children
Kiefer, Elisabeth *SEE* Kiefer, Wilhelm
Kiefer, Elisabeth 42; America, 1880 *5475.1 p325*
Kiefer, Francois 31; America, 1847 *778.6 p187*
Kiefer, Francois 27; New York, NY, 1894 *6512.1 p182*
Kiefer, Franz; America, 1880 *5475.1 p272*
　*Wife:*Maria Naumann
　*Daughter:*Maria
　*Daughter:*Katharina
　*Son:*Jakob
　*Daughter:*Barbara
Kiefer, Georg *SEE* Kiefer, Georg
Kiefer, Georg; America, 1881 *5475.1 p46*
　*Wife:*Maria Pitz
　*Son:*Karl
　*Son:*Heinrich

　*Daughter:*Magdalena
　*Son:*Wilhelm
　*Son:*Peter
　*Son:*Georg
　*Daughter:*Katharina
Kiefer, Georg, IV; America, 1866 *5475.1 p68*
　*Wife:*Maria Pistorius
　*Son:*Johann
　*Son:*Peter
Kiefer, Heinrich *SEE* Kiefer, Georg
Kiefer, Jakob; America, 1848 *5475.1 p475*
Kiefer, Jakob; America, 1868 *5475.1 p323*
Kiefer, Jakob *SEE* Kiefer, Franz
Kiefer, Jakob; America, 1896 *5475.1 p230*
　*Son:*Peter
　*Daughter:*Maria
　*Daughter:*Amalie
Kiefer, Jakob 36; New York, NY, 1882 *5475.1 p15*
Kiefer, Joh. Jakob *SEE* Kiefer, Johann
Kiefer, Johann *SEE* Kiefer, Georg, IV
Kiefer, Johann; America, 1868 *5475.1 p239*
Kiefer, Johann; America, 1870 *5475.1 p324*
　*Son:*Mathias
Kiefer, Johann; America, 1871 *5475.1 p324*
Kiefer, Johann *SEE* Kiefer, Mrs. Michel
Kiefer, Johann *SEE* Kiefer, Wilhelm
Kiefer, Johann 9 *SEE* Kiefer, Nikolaus
Kiefer, Johann 23; America, 1882 *5475.1 p206*
Kiefer, Johann; Pennsylvania, 1884 *5475.1 p465*
　*Wife:*Angela Schul
　*Son:*Christian
　*Son:*Joh. Jakob
Kiefer, Johann Adam; America, 1833 *5475.1 p454*
　*Brother:*Andreas
Kiefer, Johann Adam 29; America, 1833 *5475.1 p461*
Kiefer, Johann Josef; America, 1869 *5475.1 p178*
Kiefer, Johann Nikolaus; America, 1847 *5475.1 p538*
Kiefer, Karl *SEE* Kiefer, Georg
Kiefer, Katharina *SEE* Kiefer, Franz
Kiefer, Katharina *SEE* Kiefer, Georg
Kiefer, Katharina Kettenhofen 20 *SEE* Kiefer, Nikolaus
Kiefer, Klara *SEE* Kiefer, Mrs. Michel
Kiefer, Konrad; America, 1852 *5475.1 p538*
Kiefer, Magdalena *SEE* Kiefer, Georg
Kiefer, Margarethe; America, 1881 *5475.1 p48*
Kiefer, Margarethe 34; America, 1867 *5475.1 p195*
Kiefer, Maria Pistorius *SEE* Kiefer, Georg, IV
Kiefer, Maria; America, 1872 *5475.1 p153*
Kiefer, Maria Weber *SEE* Kiefer, Wilhelm
Kiefer, Maria *SEE* Kiefer, Franz
Kiefer, Maria Naumann *SEE* Kiefer, Franz
Kiefer, Maria Pitz *SEE* Kiefer, Georg
Kiefer, Maria; America, 1881 *5475.1 p214*
Kiefer, Maria *SEE* Kiefer, Jakob
Kiefer, Maria; New York, 1884 *5475.1 p221*
Kiefer, Maria; Pennsylvania, 1886 *5475.1 p265*
Kiefer, Mathias *SEE* Kiefer, Johann
Kiefer, Mathias 18; America, 1871 *5475.1 p378*
Kiefer, Michel; America, 1846 *5475.1 p322*
Kiefer, Michel; America, 1867 *5475.1 p376*
Kiefer, Michel; America, 1875 *5475.1 p213*
Kiefer, Mrs. Michel 51; America, 1877 *5475.1 p179*
　*Son:*Nikolaus
　*Daughter:*Klara
　*Son:*Johann
Kiefer, Michel Georg; Buffalo, NY, 1867 *5475.1 p178*
Kiefer, Nicholas; Ohio, 1809-1852 *4511.35 p26*
Kiefer, Nicolas 26; America, 1847 *778.6 p187*
Kiefer, Nicolas 56; America, 1847 *778.6 p187*
Kiefer, Nikolaus; America, 1852 *5475.1 p538*
Kiefer, Nikolaus; America, 1871 *5475.1 p324*
　*Wife:*Katharina Kettenhofen
　*Daughter:*Anna Maria
　*Son:*Johann
Kiefer, Nikolaus *SEE* Kiefer, Mrs. Michel
Kiefer, Nikolaus 27; America, 1866 *5475.1 p157*
Kiefer, Peter *SEE* Kiefer, Georg, IV
Kiefer, Peter *SEE* Kiefer, Wilhelm
Kiefer, Peter *SEE* Kiefer, Georg
Kiefer, Peter; America, 1884 *5475.1 p413*
Kiefer, Peter *SEE* Kiefer, Jakob
Kiefer, Peter; Chicago, 1890 *5475.1 p206*
Kiefer, Peter; Pittsburgh, 1885 *5475.1 p206*
Kiefer, Philip; Philadelphia, 1854 *8513.31 p319*
　*Wife:*Wilhelmina Hahn
Kiefer, Wendel 24; America, 1849 *5475.1 p477*
Kiefer, Wilhelm *SEE* Kiefer, Wilhelm
Kiefer, Wilhelm; America, 1879 *5475.1 p157*
　*Wife:*Maria Weber
　*Daughter:*Barbara
　*Daughter:*Elisabeth
　*Son:*Wilhelm

*Son:*Johann
*Son:*Peter
Kiefer, Wilhelm *SEE* Kiefer, Georg
Kiefer, Wilhelmina Hahn *SEE* Kiefer, Philip
Kiefer, Xavier 24; Louisiana, 1848 ***778.6*** *p187*
Kieff, John 63; Ontario, 1871 ***1823.21*** *p190*
Kieffe, Maurice; Boston, 1761 ***1642*** *p48*
Kieffer, Andreas *SEE* Kieffer, Andreas
Kieffer, Andreas; America, 1876 ***5475.1*** *p271*
*Wife:*Susanna Ving
*Daughter:*Anna
*Son:*Jakob
*Father:*Johann
*Daughter:*Maria
*Daughter:*Pauline
*Son:*Andreas
Kieffer, Anna *SEE* Kieffer, Andreas
Kieffer, Catha. 3; America, 1840 ***778.6*** *p187*
Kieffer, Catha. 28; America, 1840 ***778.6*** *p187*
Kieffer, Jakob *SEE* Kieffer, Andreas
Kieffer, Joh. 35; America, 1840 ***778.6*** *p187*
Kieffer, Johann *SEE* Kieffer, Andreas
Kieffer, Lorenzo; Louisiana, 1874-1875 ***4981.45*** *p29*
Kieffer, Magd. 14; America, 1840 ***778.6*** *p187*
Kieffer, Magdalena; America, 1873 ***5475.1*** *p249*
Kieffer, Marg. 20; America, 1846 ***778.6*** *p187*
Kieffer, Maria *SEE* Kieffer, Andreas
Kieffer, Pauline *SEE* Kieffer, Andreas
Kieffer, Susanna Ving *SEE* Kieffer, Andreas
Kiefner, Jiri; St. Vincent, PA, 1881 ***2853.20*** *p342*
Kiehl, Adam *SEE* Kiehl, Eva Katharina
Kiehl, Adam 3 *SEE* Kiehl, Eva Katharina
Kiehl, August; America, 1847 ***2526.43*** *p160*
Kiehl, Carl Albert Christian; America, 1882 ***7420.1*** *p329*
Kiehl, Elisabetha 14 *SEE* Kiehl, Eva Katharina
Kiehl, Eva Katharina; America, 1848 ***2526.43*** *p160*
*Son:*Adam
*Son:*Leonhard
*Daughter:*Salome
*Son:*Adam
*Daughter:*Katharina
*Son:*Wilhelm
*Daughter:*Elisabetha
Kiehl, Katharina 6 *SEE* Kiehl, Eva Katharina
Kiehl, Leonhard 2 *SEE* Kiehl, Eva Katharina
Kiehl, Ludwig; America, 1896 ***7420.1*** *p372*
Kiehl, Salome 5 *SEE* Kiehl, Eva Katharina
Kiehl, Wilhelm 13 *SEE* Kiehl, Eva Katharina
Kiel, Carl Albert Christian; America, 1882 ***7420.1*** *p329*
Kiel, Friedrich Christian; America, 1853 ***7420.1*** *p107*
Kiel, Heinrich; Port uncertain, 1853 ***7420.1*** *p107*
Kielgas, Wilhelm; Mexico, 1903 ***7420.1*** *p379*
Kiellerstedt, C.M.; Oregon, 1845 ***6412.40*** *p147*
Kielmann, Georg; America, 1853 ***7420.1*** *p107*
Kielwasser, Carolina; Wisconsin, 1897 ***6795.8*** *p102*
Kiely, John 2; St. Johns, N.F., 1811 ***1053.20*** *p20*
Kiemele, Edward 6; New York, NY, 1898 ***7951.13*** *p42*
Kiemele, Elisabeth 16; New York, NY, 1898 ***7951.13*** *p42*
Kiemele, Friedrich 8; New York, NY, 1898 ***7951.13*** *p42*
Kiemele, Jacob 53; New York, NY, 1898 ***7951.13*** *p42*
Kiemele, Johann 11; New York, NY, 1898 ***7951.13*** *p42*
Kiemele, Johanna 18; New York, NY, 1898 ***7951.13*** *p42*
Kiemele, Julianna 48; New York, NY, 1898 ***7951.13*** *p42*
Kiemele, Karoline 13; New York, NY, 1898 ***7951.13*** *p42*
Kiemele, Katherina 17; New York, NY, 1898 ***7951.13*** *p42*
Kiemele, Lydia 4; New York, NY, 1898 ***7951.13*** *p42*
Kiemele, Rosina 22; New York, NY, 1898 ***7951.13*** *p42*
Kienapfel, Johann Heinrich Gottlieb; America, 1852 ***7420.1*** *p91*
Kiener, Michel 24; America, 1843 ***778.6*** *p187*
Kienert, Joh. Aug.; Wisconsin, 1897 ***6795.8*** *p231*
Kienitz, Christoph Ludwig; Wisconsin, 1887 ***6795.8*** *p186*
Kienitz, Friedrich; Wisconsin, 1885 ***6795.8*** *p139*
Kienzle, Friedel 26; Galveston, TX, 1844 ***3967.10*** *p370*
Kienzle, Gustav Adolph; America, 1857-1871 ***179.55*** *p19*
Kieran, Bernard 17; Louisiana, 1853-1855 ***7710.1*** *p155*
Kieras, Stanley; Detroit, 1929-1930 ***6214.5*** *p69*
Kierman, John; Washington, 1882 ***2770.40*** *p135*
Kierski, John Joseph; Wisconsin, 1907 ***6795.8*** *p159*
Kierski, Walter; Wisconsin, 1906 ***6795.8*** *p154*
Kiesewetter, Friedrich; America, 1868 ***7919.3*** *p530*
Kiesseberth, Georg Friedrich, I; America, 1842 ***2526.43*** *p188*
With wife
With son 26
With son 23
Kiesseberth, Georg Friedrich, II; America, 1842 ***2526.43*** *p188*
With wife
With daughter 16
With son 9
With son 11
Kiessinger, Catherine 16; Port uncertain, 1841 ***778.6*** *p187*
Kiessinger, Catherine 45; Port uncertain, 1841 ***778.6*** *p187*
Kiessinger, Jacob 20; Port uncertain, 1841 ***778.6*** *p187*
Kiessinger, Jeanne 14; Port uncertain, 1841 ***778.6*** *p187*
Kiessling, Joh.Chrp; Nova Scotia, 1852 ***170.15*** *p31*
Kiessling, Johann Christph 38; Nova Scotia, 1852 ***170.15*** *p31*
Kiessling, Ludwig; America, 1888 ***179.55*** *p19*
Kiessling, Moritz; Valdivia, Chile, 1850 ***1192.4*** *p49*
Kieth, James; New York, 1778 ***8529.30*** *p6*
Kietzmann, Gustav; Wisconsin, 1898 ***6795.8*** *p204*
Kietzmann, Michael; Wisconsin, 1862 ***6795.8*** *p154*
Kiewicz, John; Wisconsin, 1891 ***6795.8*** *p59*
Kiewicz, Mary; Wisconsin, 1885 ***6795.8*** *p59*
Kiffe, Robert; Rappahannock, VA, 1726 ***1220.12*** *p463*
Kifner, Henry L. 39; Ontario, 1871 ***1823.21*** *p190*
Kightley, Mary; America, 1679 ***1220.12*** *p469*
Kikkelson, Anna 15; New York, NY, 1894 ***6512.1*** *p185*
Kilbert, John; America, 1772 ***1220.12*** *p469*
Kilbourne, Thomas; Virginia, 1773 ***1220.12*** *p469*
Kilbrath, Charles 23; Michigan, 1880 ***4491.42*** *p16*
Kilbride, John; St. John, N.B., 1847 ***2978.15*** *p37*
Kilbride, John; St. John, N.B., 1847 ***2978.15*** *p38*
Kilbride, John; St. John, N.B., 1847 ***2978.15*** *p41*
Kilbride, Mary 66; Ontario, 1871 ***1823.21*** *p190*
Kilbride, Mary 73; Ontario, 1871 ***1823.21*** *p190*
Kilbride, Pat; St. John, N.B., 1847 ***2978.15*** *p38*
Kilbride, Pat; St. John, N.B., 1847 ***2978.15*** *p41*
Kilbride, Patrick 45; Ontario, 1871 ***1823.21*** *p190*
Kilburn, Jeremiah; America, 1764 ***1220.12*** *p469*
Kilburn, Matthew; America, 1769 ***1220.12*** *p469*
Kilburn, Reuben; Maryland, 1742 ***1220.12*** *p469*
Kilburne, Richard; Virginia, 1730 ***1220.12*** *p469*
Kilby, Elizabeth; America, 1722 ***1220.12*** *p469*
Kilcolin, James; St. John, N.B., 1847 ***2978.15*** *p36*
Kilcup, Thomas; Maryland, 1737 ***1220.12*** *p469*
Kilellea, James; New York, NY, 1839 ***3274.56*** *p101*
Kilets, George 19; Ontario, 1871 ***1823.17*** *p85*
Kilets, George 19; Ontario, 1871 ***1823.21*** *p190*
Kilets, Ledolie A. 17; Ontario, 1871 ***1823.21*** *p191*
Kiley, Catharine; Philadelphia, 1868 ***8513.31*** *p418*
Kiley, James 42; Ontario, 1871 ***1823.21*** *p191*
Kilford, Thomas; America, 1693 ***1220.12*** *p469*
Kilfoyle, John; Illinois, 1834-1900 ***6020.5*** *p132*
Kilgallian, Ellanor 27; Ontario, 1871 ***1823.17*** *p85*
Kilgour, Alexander; America, 1760 ***1220.12*** *p469*
Kilgour, Thomas 42; Ontario, 1871 ***1823.21*** *p191*
Kilgren, C.G.; St. Paul, MN, 1874-1905 ***1865.50*** *p93*
Kilian, Elisabeth 26; America, 1846 ***778.6*** *p187*
Kilian, Jan; Nebraska, 1868 ***2853.20*** *p162*
*Brother:*Tomas
Kilian, John; Chicago, 1930 ***121.35*** *p100*
Kilian, K.; New York, 1860 ***358.56*** *p148*
Kilian, Laurent 25; America, 1846 ***778.6*** *p187*
Kilian, Lorenz 1; America, 1846 ***778.6*** *p187*
Kilian, Marianne 8; America, 1846 ***778.6*** *p187*
Kilian, Tomas *SEE* Kilian, Jan
Kilijan, Tomas; Nebraska, 1860-1910 ***2853.20*** *p168*
Kilke, Esther; America, 1772 ***1220.12*** *p469*
Kilkey, John; Braintree, MA, 1724 ***1642*** *p84*
*Wife:*Mary
Kilkey, Mary *SEE* Kilkey, John
Killam, Eliza D.; Montreal, 1870-1885 ***9228.50*** *p513*
Killam, William; Barbados, 1667 ***1220.12*** *p469*
Killberg, Severin; Cleveland, OH, 1888-1893 ***9722.10*** *p122*
Kille, Hannah; Massachusetts, 1745 ***1642*** *p90*
Kille, Jeremiah; Massachusetts, 1753 ***1642*** *p90*
Killean, Peter; Louisiana, 1874 ***4981.45*** *p132*
Killee, Deliverance; Massachusetts, 1748 ***1642*** *p91*
Killeen, James; Toronto, 1844 ***2910.35*** *p115*
Killeen, Michael; New York, 1841-1941 ***9228.50*** *p656*
Killegrew, Hannah; America, 1747 ***1220.12*** *p470*
Killen, James 34; Ontario, 1871 ***1823.21*** *p191*
Killey, Anna; Massachusetts, 1768 ***1642*** *p90*
Killey, Benjamin; Massachusetts, 1767 ***1642*** *p106*
Killey, Elisha; Massachusetts, 1767 ***1642*** *p90*
Killey, Hattil; Massachusetts, 1745 ***1642*** *p90*
Killey, John; Massachusetts, 1771 ***1642*** *p89*
Killey, John; New England, 1745 ***1642*** *p28*
Killey, Mary; Worcester, MA, 1757 ***1642*** *p114*
Killey, Patrick; Boston, 1763 ***1642*** *p32*
Killey, Robert; Boston, 1745 ***1642*** *p28*
Killey, Samuel; Edgartown, MA, 1757 ***1642*** *p86*
Killey Family ; Massachusetts, 1766 ***1642*** *p99*
Killgallon, Patrick 37; Ontario, 1871 ***1823.21*** *p191*
Killian, Elisabeth; Brazil, 1859 ***5475.1*** *p523*
Killicrees, William; America, 1751 ***1220.12*** *p469*
Killigrew, Cornelius; America, 1774 ***1220.12*** *p469*
Killigrew, Elizabeth; America, 1749 ***1220.12*** *p470*
Killinger, Gotleib; Ohio, 1809-1852 ***4511.35*** *p26*
Killiowe, May Christopher; Boston, 1693 ***1642*** *p16*
Killkelly, Maria 18; Ontario, 1871 ***1823.21*** *p191*
Killmister, Mary; America, 1724 ***1220.12*** *p470*
Killom, Thomas; Ipswich, MA, 1675-1676 ***1642*** *p130*
Killpatrick, John; Barbados or Jamaica, 1692 ***1220.12*** *p470*
Killy, Joseph; Watertown, MA, 1745 ***1642*** *p112*
Killyng, James; Boston, 1721 ***1642*** *p25*
Kilman, Joseph; America, 1773 ***1220.12*** *p470*
Kilmartin, Mic; St. John, N.B., 1847 ***2978.15*** *p36*
Kilmartin, Pat; St. John, N.B., 1847 ***2978.15*** *p37*
Kilmartin, Patk; St. John, N.B., 1847 ***2978.15*** *p36*
Kilmartin, Thos; St. John, N.B., 1847 ***2978.15*** *p36*
Kilmaster, Agnus 17; Ontario, 1871 ***1823.21*** *p191*
Kilner, Edmund; Kansas City, 1869-1916 ***9228.50*** *p311*
Kilner, Edmund; Kansas City, 1869-1969 ***9228.50*** *p536*
Kilner, Fred 19; Kansas City, n.d. ***9228.50*** *p312*
Kilner, Frederick Arthur; Kansas, 1875-1974 ***9228.50*** *p536*
Kilner, Ralph; Jamaica, 1864-1964 ***9228.50*** *p535*
Kilpateric, Thomas 45; Ontario, 1871 ***1823.17*** *p85*
Kilpatrick, Eliza 21; Ontario, 1871 ***1823.21*** *p191*
Kilpatrick, James; Virginia, 1752 ***1220.12*** *p470*
Kilpatrick, John; America, 1726 ***1220.12*** *p470*
Kilroy, Bernard; America, 1773 ***1220.12*** *p470*
Kilroy, Matthew; Boston, 1770 ***1642*** *p43*
Kilsten, Mathilda C.; Wisconsin, 1881-1882 ***1865.50*** *p96*
Kilty, Henry 45; Ontario, 1871 ***1823.17*** *p85*
Kilworth, William 38; Ontario, 1871 ***1823.21*** *p191*
Kim, Franz 60; New Castle, DE, 1817-1818 ***90.20*** *p152*
Kimball, Henry; Washington, 1889 ***2770.40*** *p79*
Kimball, Isaac 57; Michigan, 1880 ***4491.42*** *p16*
Kimball, Joanna; Quebec, 1823-1841 ***9228.50*** *p407*
Kimball, Richard H. 38; Ontario, 1871 ***1823.17*** *p85*
Kimball, Robert; America, 1729 ***1220.12*** *p470*
Kimball, William 80; Ontario, 1871 ***1823.21*** *p191*
Kimber, Edward; Virginia, 1750 ***1220.12*** *p470*
Kimber, George 38; Ontario, 1871 ***1823.21*** *p191*
Kimber, John; Virginia, 1766 ***1220.12*** *p470*
Kimber, Joseph; America, 1766 ***1220.12*** *p470*
Kimber, Lillian; Wisconsin, n.d. ***9228.50*** *p197*
Kimber, Mary; America, 1762 ***1220.12*** *p470*
Kimber, Mary; America, 1767 ***1220.12*** *p470*
Kimber, Richard; America, 1752 ***1220.12*** *p470*
Kimber, William; America, 1739 ***1220.12*** *p470*
Kimberly, John; America, 1737 ***1220.12*** *p470*
Kimble, Richard; America, 1766 ***1220.12*** *p470*
Kimel, Roman; Minnesota, 1875 ***2853.20*** *p262*
Kimmal, Conrad; North Carolina, 1855 ***1088.45*** *p17*
Kimmell, Conrad; Louisiana, 1874 ***4981.45*** *p132*
Kimmis, Thomas 47; Ontario, 1871 ***1823.17*** *p85*
Kimmlinger, Katharina; America, 1881 ***5475.1*** *p517*
Kimpinsky, Johann Anton Ludwig; America, 1889 ***7420.1*** *p359*
Kimpinsky, Marie; America, 1883 ***7420.1*** *p337*
Kinardy, Frances; America, 1743 ***1220.12*** *p466*
Kincade, Robert 40; Ontario, 1871 ***1823.21*** *p191*
Kincaid, Joseph 45; Ontario, 1871 ***1823.21*** *p191*
Kincella, Anne; New Orleans, 1850 ***7242.30*** *p147*
Kincella, Arthur; New Orleans, 1850 ***7242.30*** *p147*
Kincella, Betty; New Orleans, 1850 ***7242.30*** *p147*
Kincella, Dennis; New Orleans, 1850 ***7242.30*** *p147*
Kincella, Edward; New Orleans, 1850 ***7242.30*** *p147*
Kincella, James; New Orleans, 1850 ***7242.30*** *p147*
Kincella, John; New Orleans, 1850 ***7242.30*** *p147*
Kincella, Mary; New Orleans, 1850 ***7242.30*** *p147*
Kincella, Michael; New Orleans, 1850 ***7242.30*** *p147*
Kincella, Miles; New Orleans, 1850 ***7242.30*** *p147*
Kincella, Patrick; New Orleans, 1850 ***7242.30*** *p147*
Kinch, Peter 40; Ontario, 1871 ***1823.21*** *p191*
Kinchley, Peter; America, 1770 ***1220.12*** *p470*
Kind, A. M.; New York, 1859 ***358.56*** *p100*
Kind, Fried; Nebraska, 1905 ***3004.30*** *p46*
Kind, Thomas; Virginia, 1726 ***1220.12*** *p470*
Kindahl, A.J.; New York, NY, 1844 ***6412.40*** *p148*
Kindar, Samuel; America, 1768 ***1220.12*** *p470*
Kindberg, A.; Iowa, 1890 ***1211.15*** *p16*
Kinder, John; America, 1774 ***1220.12*** *p470*
Kinder, Ralph; America, 1747 ***1220.12*** *p470*
Kindermann, W. M.; Valdivia, Chile, 1850 ***1192.4*** *p48*
Kinders, Alexander; Burlington, VT, 1835 ***3274.55*** *p44*
Kindgren, Charles J.; St. Paul, MN, 1888 ***1865.50*** *p93*
Kindler, George; Ohio, 1809-1852 ***4511.35*** *p26*
Kindler, Joseph; Ohio, 1809-1852 ***4511.35*** *p26*
Kindling, Frederick; Washington, 1888 ***2770.40*** *p26*
Kindlund, Helena Christina; Sioux Falls, SD, 1884-1888 ***1865.50*** *p94*
Kindon, Ann 64; Ontario, 1871 ***1823.21*** *p191*
Kindschuh, Louise; America, 1867 ***7919.3*** *p527*
Kindsvogel, T.; Louisiana, 1874-1875 ***4981.45*** *p29*
Kindt, Andreas; North America, 1840 ***5475.1*** *p204*

Kindt, Johann; America, 1864 ***5475.1*** *p264*
Kinelski, Joseph; Detroit, 1929-1930 ***6214.5*** *p61*
Kinet, Marie Catherine; Wisconsin, 1870 ***1495.20*** *p12*
Kinet, Marie Catherine; Wisconsin, 1870 ***1495.20*** *p12*
Kinet, Martin; Ohio, 1809-1852 ***4511.35*** *p26*
King, Alexander 50; Ontario, 1871 ***1823.21*** *p191*
King, Andrew; America, 1763 ***1220.12*** *p470*
King, Ann; America, 1741 ***1220.12*** *p470*
King, Ann; America, 1757 ***1220.12*** *p470*
King, Ann; America, 1764 ***1220.12*** *p470*
King, Ann J.; Philadelphia, 1857 ***8513.31*** *p298*
King, Anna 34; Halifax, N.S., 1902 ***1860.4*** *p41*
King, Anthony 46; Ohio, 1880 ***4879.40*** *p257*
King, Bernard; Toronto, 1844 ***2910.35*** *p112*
King, Bernard Lipscomb; America, 1734 ***1220.12*** *p470*
King, Betty 26; Ontario, 1871 ***1823.17*** *p85*
King, Brian; St. John, N.B., 1848 ***2978.15*** *p37*
King, Bridget; America, 1767 ***1220.12*** *p470*
King, Cassandra; America, 1704 ***1220.12*** *p470*
King, Catherine 57; Ontario, 1871 ***1823.21*** *p191*
King, Chaje 53; New York, NY, 1894 ***6512.1*** *p230*
King, Charles; America, 1738 ***1220.12*** *p470*
King, Charles; America, 1775 ***1220.12*** *p470*
King, Charles; Annapolis, MD, 1733 ***1220.12*** *p470*
King, Charles; Maryland, 1725 ***1220.12*** *p470*
King, Charles 28; Ontario, 1871 ***1823.21*** *p191*
King, Charles 45; Ontario, 1871 ***1823.21*** *p191*
King, Charles 48; Ontario, 1871 ***1823.21*** *p191*
King, Daniel; America, 1761 ***1220.12*** *p470*
King, David; America, 1692 ***1220.12*** *p470*
King, David; America, 1745 ***1220.12*** *p470*
King, David; Barbados or Jamaica, 1694 ***1220.12*** *p470*
King, David; Halifax, N.S., 1902 ***1860.4*** *p41*
King, David 33; Halifax, N.S., 1902 ***1860.4*** *p41*
King, Deborah; America, 1752 ***1220.12*** *p470*
King, Donald 62; Ontario, 1871 ***1823.21*** *p191*
King, Edward; America, 1773 ***1220.12*** *p470*
King, Edward; Barbados, 1663 ***1220.12*** *p470*
King, Edward; Barbados, 1671 ***1220.12*** *p470*
King, Eleanor; America, 1744 ***1220.12*** *p470*
King, Eleanor; America, 1761 ***1220.12*** *p470*
King, Elise 2; Halifax, N.S., 1902 ***1860.4*** *p41*
King, Elizabeth; America, 1720 ***1220.12*** *p470*
King, Elizabeth; America, 1757 ***1220.12*** *p471*
King, Elizabeth; America, 1769 ***1220.12*** *p471*
King, Elizabeth; America, 1772 ***1220.12*** *p471*
King, Elizabeth; Virginia, 1739 ***1220.12*** *p471*
King, Eva 18; Halifax, N.S., 1902 ***1860.4*** *p41*
King, Francis; America, 1700 ***1220.12*** *p471*
King, Francis 30; New York, NY, 1825 ***6178.50*** *p78*
King, George; America, 1743 ***1220.12*** *p471*
King, George; America, 1767 ***1220.12*** *p471*
King, George; America, 1769 ***1220.12*** *p471*
King, George; America, 1771 ***1220.12*** *p471*
King, George; Ohio, 1809-1852 ***4511.35*** *p26*
King, George 21; Ontario, 1871 ***1823.21*** *p191*
King, George 61; Ontario, 1871 ***1823.21*** *p191*
King, Henry; America, 1682 ***1220.12*** *p471*
King, Henry; Colorado, 1873 ***1029.59*** *p49*
King, Henry; Ohio, 1840 ***2763.1*** *p8*
King, Hester; Barbados or Jamaica, 1693 ***1220.12*** *p471*
King, Hugh; America, 1741 ***1220.12*** *p471*
King, Isaac; America, 1768 ***1220.12*** *p471*
King, Mrs. J. R.; Montreal, 1922 ***4514.4*** *p32*
King, Jacob; America, 1685 ***1220.12*** *p471*
King, Jacob 34; Halifax, N.S., 1902 ***1860.4*** *p41*
King, James; America, 1737 ***1220.12*** *p471*
King, James; America, 1743 ***1220.12*** *p471*
King, James; America, 1752 ***1220.12*** *p471*
King, James; America, 1765 ***1220.12*** *p471*
King, James; America, 1769 ***1220.12*** *p471*
King, James 31; Ontario, 1871 ***1823.17*** *p85*
King, James 57; Ontario, 1871 ***1823.17*** *p85*
King, James; Virginia, 1727 ***1220.12*** *p471*
King, Jane; America, 1746 ***1220.12*** *p471*
King, Jane 40; Ontario, 1871 ***1823.21*** *p191*
King, Job; America, 1769 ***1220.12*** *p471*
King, John; America, 1682 ***1220.12*** *p471*
King, John; America, 1721 ***1220.12*** *p471*
King, John; America, 1732 ***1220.12*** *p471*
King, John; America, 1737 ***1220.12*** *p471*
King, John; America, 1745 ***1220.12*** *p471*
King, John; America, 1747 ***1220.12*** *p471*
King, John; America, 1749 ***1220.12*** *p471*
King, John; America, 1751 ***1220.12*** *p471*
King, John; America, 1753 ***1220.12*** *p471*
King, John; America, 1754 ***1220.12*** *p471*
King, John; America, 1756 ***1220.12*** *p471*
King, John; America, 1770 ***1220.12*** *p471*
King, John; America, 1773 ***1220.12*** *p471*
King, John; America, 1774 ***1220.12*** *p471*
King, John; Boston, 1766 ***1642*** *p37*
King, John; Died enroute, 1729 ***1220.12*** *p471*
King, John; North Carolina, 1851 ***1088.45*** *p17*
King, John; Ohio, 1844 ***3580.20*** *p32*
King, John; Ohio, 1844 ***6020.12*** *p12*
King, John 11; Ontario, 1871 ***1823.17*** *p85*
King, John 36; Ontario, 1871 ***1823.17*** *p85*
King, John 40; Ontario, 1871 ***1823.17*** *p85*
King, John 50; Ontario, 1871 ***1823.17*** *p85*
King, John 65; Ontario, 1871 ***1823.21*** *p191*
King, John; Philadelphia, 1778 ***8529.30*** *p7A*
King, John; Virginia, 1739 ***1220.12*** *p471*
King, John; Virginia, 1760 ***1220.12*** *p471*
King, John Charles 44; New York, NY, 1894 ***6512.1*** *p183*
King, Joseph; America, 1730 ***1220.12*** *p471*
King, Joseph; America, 1749 ***1220.12*** *p471*
King, Joseph; Boston, 1767 ***1642*** *p38*
King, Joseph; Long Island, 1778 ***8529.30*** *p9A*
King, Joseph; North Carolina, 1826 ***1088.45*** *p17*
King, Joseph 47; Ontario, 1871 ***1823.21*** *p191*
King, Katha 6; Halifax, N.S., 1902 ***1860.4*** *p41*
King, Katherine; Jamaica, 1717 ***1220.12*** *p470*
King, Katia 4; Halifax, N.S., 1902 ***1860.4*** *p41*
King, Laurence; Barbados or Jamaica, 1686 ***1220.12*** *p471*
King, Lisbet; Halifax, N.S., 1902 ***1860.4*** *p41*
King, Margaret; America, 1752 ***1220.12*** *p471*
King, Margaret; America, 1760 ***1220.12*** *p471*
King, Margaret 7; Quebec, 1870 ***8364.32*** *p24*
King, Margaret; Virginia, 1727 ***1220.12*** *p471*
King, Mary; America, 1715 ***1220.12*** *p471*
King, Mary; America, 1746 ***1220.12*** *p472*
King, Mary; America, 1748 ***1220.12*** *p472*
King, Mary; America, 1755 ***1220.12*** *p472*
King, Mary; America, 1762 ***1220.12*** *p472*
King, Mary; Annapolis, MD, 1723 ***1220.12*** *p471*
King, Mary; Annapolis, MD, 1731 ***1220.12*** *p471*
King, Mary; Virginia, 1734 ***1220.12*** *p472*
King, Matilda 71; Ontario, 1871 ***1823.21*** *p191*
King, Matilda Kate 20; Ontario, 1871 ***1823.21*** *p191*
King, Michael; America, 1767 ***1220.12*** *p472*
King, Millicent; Montreal, 1922 ***4514.4*** *p32*
King, Mona 6; Halifax, N.S., 1902 ***1860.4*** *p41*
King, Mona 34; Halifax, N.S., 1902 ***1860.4*** *p41*
King, Muriel; Montreal, 1922 ***4514.4*** *p32*
King, Nathan; Ohio, 1843 ***2763.1*** *p8*
King, Nicholas; Illinois, 1834-1900 ***6020.5*** *p132*
King, Pat; St. John, N.B., 1848 ***2978.15*** *p38*
King, Paul; America, 1741 ***1220.12*** *p472*
King, Peter 60; Ontario, 1871 ***1823.21*** *p191*
King, Richard; America, 1685 ***1220.12*** *p472*
King, Richard; America, 1746 ***1220.12*** *p472*
King, Richard; America, 1759 ***1220.12*** *p472*
King, Richard; America, 1773 ***1220.12*** *p472*
King, Robert; America, 1697 ***1220.12*** *p472*
King, Robert; America, 1739 ***1220.12*** *p472*
King, Robert; Maryland, 1736 ***1220.12*** *p472*
King, Robert 47; Ontario, 1871 ***1823.17*** *p86*
King, Robert 54; Ontario, 1871 ***1823.17*** *p86*
King, Sarah; America, 1774 ***1220.12*** *p472*
King, Susan; Virginia, 1736 ***1220.12*** *p472*
King, Terrance 30; Ontario, 1871 ***1823.21*** *p191*
King, Thomas; America, 1741 ***1220.12*** *p472*
King, Thomas; America, 1752 ***1220.12*** *p472*
King, Thomas; America, 1755 ***1220.12*** *p472*
King, Thomas; America, 1758 ***1220.12*** *p472*
King, Thomas; America, 1768 ***1220.12*** *p472*
King, Thomas; America, 1775 ***1220.12*** *p472*
King, Thomas; Annapolis, MD, 1733 ***1220.12*** *p472*
King, Thomas; Canada, 1775 ***3036.5*** *p67*
King, Thomas 27; Ontario, 1871 ***1823.17*** *p86*
King, Thomas 42; Ontario, 1871 ***1823.17*** *p86*
King, Thomas 56; Ontario, 1871 ***1823.21*** *p191*
King, Thomas 62; Ontario, 1871 ***1823.21*** *p191*
King, Thomas 65; Ontario, 1871 ***1823.21*** *p191*
King, Thomas; Virginia, 1761 ***1220.12*** *p472*
King, Thos 50; Ontario, 1871 ***1823.17*** *p86*
King, Valentine; Ohio, 1809-1852 ***4511.35*** *p26*
King, William; America, 1727 ***1220.12*** *p472*
King, William; America, 1736 ***1220.12*** *p472*
King, William; America, 1742 ***1220.12*** *p472*
King, William; America, 1750 ***1220.12*** *p472*
King, William; America, 1757 ***1220.12*** *p472*
King, William; America, 1758 ***1220.12*** *p472*
King, William; America, 1761 ***1220.12*** *p472*
King, William; America, 1765 ***1220.12*** *p472*
King, William; Ohio, 1809-1852 ***4511.35*** *p26*
King, William 28; Ontario, 1871 ***1823.21*** *p192*
King, William J. 42; Ontario, 1871 ***1823.21*** *p192*
Kingan, John; Barbados or Jamaica, 1699 ***1220.12*** *p472*
Kingden, James; Maryland, 1742 ***1220.12*** *p472*
Kingdom, Arthur; America, 1744 ***1220.12*** *p472*
Kingdon, John 49; Ontario, 1871 ***1823.21*** *p192*
Kinge, Edward; Barbados, 1671 ***1220.12*** *p470*
Kingham, James; Texas, 1892 ***3435.45*** *p36*
Kingham, John; America, 1767 ***1220.12*** *p472*
Kingham, Thomas; Annapolis, MD, 1722 ***1220.12*** *p472*
Kingham, Thomas; Port uncertain, 1720 ***1220.12*** *p472*
Kingham, William; Barbados, 1674 ***1220.12*** *p472*
Kinghorn, James; America, 1771 ***1220.12*** *p472*
Kingked, Alexander; America, 1720 ***1220.12*** *p472*
Kinglis, Elizabeth; America, 1708 ***1220.12*** *p472*
Kingman, Sarah; America, 1740 ***1220.12*** *p472*
Kingsberry, Thomas; Died enroute, 1729 ***1220.12*** *p472*
Kingsbury, Sara; Annapolis, MD, 1720 ***1220.12*** *p472*
Kingscote, William 15; Quebec, 1870 ***8364.32*** *p24*
Kingsland, David; America, 1742 ***1220.12*** *p472*
Kingsland, John; America, 1741 ***1220.12*** *p472*
Kingsland, Rowland 27; Ontario, 1871 ***1823.21*** *p192*
Kingsland, Thomas; America, 1741 ***1220.12*** *p472*
Kingsland, William; America, 1767 ***1220.12*** *p473*
Kingsmill, Thomas F. 32; Ontario, 1871 ***1823.21*** *p192*
Kingsnorth, William 27; Ontario, 1871 ***1823.21*** *p192*
Kingston, Charles; Maryland, 1725 ***1220.12*** *p473*
Kingston, Elizabeth 43; Ontario, 1871 ***1823.21*** *p192*
Kingston, George; America, 1764 ***1220.12*** *p473*
Kingston, George; America, 1768 ***1220.12*** *p473*
Kingston, Isaac; America, 1685 ***1220.12*** *p473*
Kingston, John; America, 1750 ***1220.12*** *p473*
Kingston, John P. 55; Ontario, 1871 ***1823.17*** *p86*
Kingston, Margaret 43; Ontario, 1871 ***1823.21*** *p192*
Kingston, Mary; America, 1756 ***1220.12*** *p473*
Kingston, Paul 55; Ontario, 1871 ***1823.17*** *p86*
Kingston, Robert 28; Ontario, 1871 ***1823.17*** *p86*
Kingstone, Charles J. 39; Ontario, 1871 ***1823.17*** *p86*
Kingstone, Thomas; Annapolis, MD, 1733 ***1220.12*** *p473*
Kingswell, Anthony; Jamestown, VA, 1633 ***1658.20*** *p211*
Kingswell, Edward; Jamestown, VA, 1633 ***1658.20*** *p211*
*Wife:*Jane Clifton
Kingswell, Jane Clifton *SEE* Kingswell, Edward
Kingswood, Isaac 32; Ontario, 1871 ***1823.21*** *p192*
Kingswood, Samuel; Barbados or Jamaica, 1710 ***1220.12*** *p473*
Kingwell, Tho; Virginia, 1652 ***6254.4*** *p243*
Kinkad, Wm 83; Ontario, 1871 ***1823.21*** *p192*
Kinkade, John 50; Ontario, 1871 ***1823.21*** *p192*
Kinkeldei, Carl Heinrich August; America, 1847 ***7420.1*** *p54*
Kinkeldey, Erich; America, 1904 ***7420.1*** *p401*
Kinkeldey, Friedrich Gottlieb; Minnesota, 1878 ***7420.1*** *p310*
Kinman, John; America, 1741 ***1220.12*** *p473*
Kinnearine, John; Ohio, 1844 ***2763.1*** *p8*
Kinnelly, Wm.; Toronto, 1844 ***2910.35*** *p112*
Kinner, Thomas; America, 1771 ***1220.12*** *p473*
Kinnett, Benjamin; Annapolis, MD, 1729 ***1220.12*** *p467*
Kinney, Mr.; Boston, 1768 ***1642*** *p40*
Kinney, Jerry 64; Ontario, 1871 ***1823.17*** *p86*
Kinney, John; Boston, 1767 ***1642*** *p38*
Kinney, Patrick; Boston, 1773 ***1642*** *p49*
Kinney, S. S.; California, 1868 ***1131.61*** *p89*
Kinney, Thomas 26; Ontario, 1871 ***1823.17*** *p86*
Kinningham, John; Watertown, MA, 1699 ***1642*** *p112*
Kinnister, James 36; Ontario, 1871 ***1823.17*** *p86*
Kinnon, John 38; Ontario, 1871 ***1823.17*** *p86*
Kinoth, Martin; Ohio, 1809-1852 ***4511.35*** *p26*
Kinse, Peter; North Carolina, 1710 ***3629.40*** *p5*
Kinsett, Roger; America, 1752 ***1220.12*** *p473*
Kinsey, John; America, 1751 ***1220.12*** *p473*
Kinsey, John; North Carolina, 1710 ***3629.40*** *p5*
Kinshellow, Anne; St. Johns, N.F., 1825 ***1053.15*** *p7*
Kinshellow, Eliza; St. Johns, N.F., 1825 ***1053.15*** *p7*
Kinshellow, James; St. Johns, N.F., 1825 ***1053.15*** *p7*
Kinshellow, John; St. Johns, N.F., 1825 ***1053.15*** *p7*
Kinshellow, Peter; St. Johns, N.F., 1825 ***1053.15*** *p7*
Kinshellow, Walter; St. Johns, N.F., 1825 ***1053.15*** *p7*
Kinsinger, Katharina 38; America, 1854 ***5475.1*** *p53*
Kinsley, Catherine 44; Ontario, 1871 ***1823.21*** *p192*
Kinsley, James 47; Ontario, 1871 ***1823.17*** *p86*
Kinsley, William; Newfoundland, 1814 ***3476.10*** *p54*
Kinsman, Henry 39; Ontario, 1871 ***1823.21*** *p192*
Kinsman, John; America, 1729 ***1220.12*** *p473*
Kinsner, Adam; Ohio, 1843 ***2763.1*** *p8*
Kinsvater, Jacob 22; New York, NY, 1893 ***1883.7*** *p43*
Kinyer, Mary 39; Michigan, 1880 ***4491.36*** *p12*
Kinzie, William M. 61; Ontario, 1871 ***1823.17*** *p86*
Kinzinger, Katharina 50; America, 1840 ***5475.1*** *p50*
*Son:*Nikolaus
Kiolbassa, Bernard; Texas, 1871 ***9980.22*** *p17*
Kiolbassa, Thomas 39; Texas, 1881 ***9980.22*** *p17*
Kip, Alice; America, 1680 ***1220.12*** *p473*
Kip, John Jacob; Ohio, 1809-1852 ***4511.35*** *p26*
Kipling, Charles; America, 1749 ***1220.12*** *p473*
Kipling, Robert; America, 1773 ***1220.12*** *p473*
Kipling, William; America, 1774 ***1220.12*** *p473*
Kipp, Franz; America, 1881 ***5475.1*** *p214*
Kipp, Wilhelm; Chicago, 1889 ***5475.1*** *p155*

234 *FOR A COMPLETE EXPLANATION OF ENTRY, SEE "HOW TO READ A CITATION" SECTION*

Kipp, William; Ohio, 1840-1897 ***8365.35*** *p16*
Kipper, Peter; America, 1883 ***5475.1*** *p51*
Kippert, Jean 25; Port uncertain, 1847 ***778.6*** *p187*
Kippert, Nicolas 27; Port uncertain, 1847 ***778.6*** *p187*
Kippi, Andrew 56; Ontario, 1871 ***1823.21*** *p192*
Kipping, Mary; America, 1746 ***1220.12*** *p473*
Kipps, William; Maryland, 1740 ***1220.12*** *p473*
Kirbee, Anthony; America, 1756 ***1220.12*** *p473*
Kirbee, William; America, 1756 ***1220.12*** *p473*
Kirby, Alex 65; Ontario, 1871 ***1823.17*** *p86*
Kirby, Bartley 30; Michigan, 1880 ***4491.39*** *p17*
Kirby, Benjamin; Maryland, 1741 ***1220.12*** *p473*
Kirby, Benjamin 1; Ontario, 1871 ***1823.21*** *p192*
Kirby, Elizabeth; America, 1773 ***1220.12*** *p473*
Kirby, John; America, 1751 ***1220.12*** *p473*
Kirby, John; America, 1764 ***1220.12*** *p473*
Kirby, John; Barbados, 1683 ***1220.12*** *p473*
Kirby, John; Barbados or Jamaica, 1691 ***1220.12*** *p473*
Kirby, John 26; Toronto, 1860 ***9228.50*** *p311*
Kirby, Margaret; America, 1745 ***1220.12*** *p473*
Kirby, Margaret; America, 1768 ***1220.12*** *p473*
Kirby, Mary; America, 1766 ***1220.12*** *p473*
Kirby, Mary; Maryland, 1719 ***1220.12*** *p473*
Kirby, Rebecca; Barbados, 1671 ***1220.12*** *p473*
Kirby, Richard; America, 1750 ***1220.12*** *p473*
Kirby, Robert; America, 1755 ***1220.12*** *p473*
Kirby, Samuel; America, 1761 ***1220.12*** *p473*
Kirby, Thomas; America, 1773 ***1220.12*** *p473*
Kirby, Thomas; Long Island, 1778 ***8529.30*** *p13*
Kirby, William; America, 1765 ***1220.12*** *p473*
Kirch, Barbara Bard 27 *SEE* Kirch, Johann
Kirch, Christian; America, n.d. ***8115.12*** *p320*
Kirch, Elisabeth Dewes *SEE* Kirch, Johann Adam
Kirch, Helene; America, n.d. ***8115.12*** *p320*
Kirch, Jakob; America, 1840 ***5475.1*** *p437*
With wife & 3 children
Kirch, Johann 1 *SEE* Kirch, Johann
Kirch, Johann 35; America, 1837 ***5475.1*** *p66*
*Wife:*Margarethe Speicher 35
*Son:*Peter 4
*Son:*Johann 1
Kirch, Johann 26; Brazil, 1872 ***5475.1*** *p442*
Kirch, Johann 27; Brazil, 1872 ***5475.1*** *p443*
*Wife:*Barbara Bard 27
Kirch, Johann Adam; Brazil, 1846 ***5475.1*** *p438*
*Wife:*Elisabeth Dewes
With 4 children
Kirch, Johann Georg; America, n.d. ***8115.12*** *p320*
Kirch, Johann Jakob; America, 1857 ***8115.12*** *p320*
Kirch, Josef; Brazil, 1879 ***5475.1*** *p447*
Kirch, Katharina Becker *SEE* Kirch, Peter
Kirch, Katharine Margar.; America, 1880 ***8115.12*** *p324*
Kirch, Konrad; America, 1858 ***8115.12*** *p320*
Kirch, Magdalena Scheid *SEE* Kirch, Nikolaus
Kirch, Margarethe Speicher 35 *SEE* Kirch, Johann
Kirch, Nikolaus; Brazil, 1854 ***5475.1*** *p440*
*Wife:*Magdalena Scheid
With 4 children
Kirch, Peter 4 *SEE* Kirch, Johann
Kirch, Peter 44; America, 1837 ***5475.1*** *p66*
*Wife:*Katharina Becker
With 3 children
Kirchberg, Friedr.; America, 1880 ***5475.1*** *p45*
Kirch-Brombach, Friedrich Ehrhard von; Baltimore, 1831 ***2526.43*** *p206*
Kirchen, Nicolas 20; New York, NY, 1856 ***1766.1*** *p45*
Kirchenheiter, Michael; Ohio, 1809-1852 ***4511.35*** *p26*
Kirchgasinek, Valentin 30; Portland, ME, 1906 ***970.38*** *p78*
Kirchman, Vaclav; Pennsylvania, 1860-1869 ***2853.20*** *p119*
Kirchmann, Vaclav; Nebraska, 1878 ***2853.20*** *p167*
Kirchner, Mr.; America, 1853 ***7420.1*** *p107*
With daughter
Kirchner, Auguste; America, 1867 ***7919.3*** *p529*
Kirchner, Betti; America, 1853 ***7420.1*** *p107*
Kirchner, Carl Friedrich Wilhelm *SEE* Kirchner, Heinrich Wilhelm
Kirchner, Heinrich; America, 1868 ***7919.3*** *p530*
Kirchner, Heinrich August Wilhelm *SEE* Kirchner, Heinrich Wilhelm
Kirchner, Heinrich Wilhelm; Nevada, 1873 ***7420.1*** *p300*
*Daughter:*Wilhelmine Louise Henriette
*Son:*Carl Friedrich Wilhelm
*Sister:*Louise Pauline Sophie
*Son:*Heinrich August Wilhelm
With wife
Kirchner, Heinrich Wilhelm; Nevada, 1873 ***7420.1*** *p301*
Kirchner, Johann Georg; America, 1867 ***7919.3*** *p531*
Kirchner, Johann Heinrich; America, 1868 ***7919.3*** *p531*
Kirchner, John W.; Kansas, 1876 ***777.40*** *p11*
Kirchner, Karel Frantisek; Iowa, 1870-1889 ***2853.20*** *p223*
Kirchner, Louise Pauline Sophie *SEE* Kirchner, Heinrich Wilhelm
Kirchner, Wilhelm; Valdivia, Chile, 1852 ***1192.4*** *p53*
Kirchner, Wilhelmine Louise Henriette *SEE* Kirchner, Heinrich Wilhelm
Kirchoeff, August; Illinois, 1857 ***6079.1*** *p7*
Kirk, Benjamin 21; Indiana, 1905-1906 ***9076.20*** *p75*
Kirk, Grafton; Maryland or Virginia, 1738 ***1220.12*** *p473*
Kirk, John; America, 1762 ***1220.12*** *p473*
Kirk, John; America, 1772 ***1220.12*** *p474*
Kirk, John; America, 1773 ***1220.12*** *p474*
Kirk, Joseph R. 36; Indiana, 1892-1894 ***9076.20*** *p73*
Kirk, Katherine; America, 1715 ***1220.12*** *p473*
Kirk, Peter; Colorado, 1883 ***1029.59*** *p50*
Kirk, Richard; America, 1725 ***1220.12*** *p474*
Kirk, Samuel; America, 1768 ***1220.12*** *p474*
Kirk, Sarah; America, 1727 ***1220.12*** *p474*
Kirk, Sarah; America, 1768 ***1220.12*** *p474*
Kirk, Thomas; America, 1745 ***1220.12*** *p474*
Kirk, Thomas; America, 1765 ***1220.12*** *p474*
Kirk, Thomas; America, 1766 ***1220.12*** *p474*
Kirk, Thomas 45; Ontario, 1871 ***1823.21*** *p192*
Kirk, William 54; Ontario, 1871 ***1823.17*** *p86*
Kirk, William 63; Ontario, 1871 ***1823.21*** *p192*
Kirkbride, David; Ohio, 1844 ***2763.1*** *p8*
Kirke, Thomas; America, 1772 ***1220.12*** *p474*
Kirke, Ursula; Barbados, 1668 ***1220.12*** *p474*
Kirkham, Maria 8; Quebec, 1870 ***8364.32*** *p24*
Kirkham, Mary; America, 1757 ***1220.12*** *p474*
Kirkland, George 48; Ontario, 1871 ***1823.21*** *p192*
Kirklin, Mary; America, 1763 ***1220.12*** *p474*
Kirkman, Charles Robt.; Colorado, 1899 ***1029.59*** *p50*
Kirkman, Charles Robt.; Colorado, 1903 ***1029.59*** *p50*
Kirkman, Elizabeth; America, 1775 ***1220.12*** *p474*
Kirkman, Sarah; America, 1772 ***1220.12*** *p474*
Kirkman, Zachariah; Ohio, 1851 ***3580.20*** *p32*
Kirkman, Zachariah; Ohio, 1851 ***6020.12*** *p12*
Kirkmann, Mr. 16; Port uncertain, 1844 ***778.6*** *p187*
Kirkon, Jean 10 weeks; New York, NY, 1835 ***5024.1*** *p137*
Kirkon, Jean 22; New York, NY, 1835 ***5024.1*** *p137*
Kirkon, William 31; New York, NY, 1835 ***5024.1*** *p137*
Kirkpatrick, Catherine 48; Ontario, 1871 ***1823.17*** *p86*
Kirkpatrick, Hiram 90; Ontario, 1871 ***1823.21*** *p192*
Kirkpatrick, J. 13; Ontario, 1871 ***1823.21*** *p192*
Kirkpatrick, Jas 48; Ontario, 1871 ***1823.21*** *p192*
Kirkpatrick, John; North Carolina, 1827 ***1088.45*** *p17*
Kirkpatrick, Robert 39; Ontario, 1871 ***1823.21*** *p192*
Kirkpatrick, Thomas; Ohio, 1809-1852 ***4511.35*** *p26*
Kirkpatrick, Thomas 60; Ontario, 1871 ***1823.17*** *p86*
Kirkpatrick, William 45; Ontario, 1871 ***1823.17*** *p86*
Kirkpatrick, William 45; Ontario, 1871 ***1823.21*** *p192*
Kirkton, Jean 10 weeks; New York, NY, 1835 ***5024.1*** *p137*
Kirkton, Jean 22; New York, NY, 1835 ***5024.1*** *p137*
Kirkton, William 31; New York, NY, 1835 ***5024.1*** *p137*
Kirkup, Mary; America, 1763 ***1220.12*** *p474*
Kirkwood, Charles 35; Ontario, 1871 ***1823.21*** *p192*
Kirkwood, John; America, 1753 ***1220.12*** *p474*
Kirner, Elisabeth; Venezuela, 1843 ***3899.5*** *p541*
Kirpal, Josef; Wisconsin, 1888 ***2853.20*** *p322*
Kirpal, Josef; Wisconsin, 1888 ***2853.20*** *p326*
Kirsch, Agnes *SEE* Kirsch, Mathias
Kirsch, Andreas *SEE* Kirsch, Mathias
Kirsch, Anna 25; America, 1856 ***5475.1*** *p374*
Kirsch, Anna Maria Schann *SEE* Kirsch, Mathias
Kirsch, Barbara *SEE* Kirsch, Mathias
Kirsch, Barbara 3 *SEE* Kirsch, Peter
Kirsch, Charlotte 15 *SEE* Kirsch, Kath. Kuhn
Kirsch, Christine Kraemer 27 *SEE* Kirsch, Peter
Kirsch, Elisabeth; America, 1866 ***5475.1*** *p490*
Kirsch, Elisabeth *SEE* Kirsch, Konrad
Kirsch, Elise 6 *SEE* Kirsch, Peter
Kirsch, Franz; America, 1880 ***5475.1*** *p169*
Kirsch, Jakob *SEE* Kirsch, Kath. Kuhn
Kirsch, Jakob 25; America, 1836 ***5475.1*** *p65*
Kirsch, Johann; America, 1871 ***5475.1*** *p274*
Kirsch, Karoline; Brazil, 1859 ***5475.1*** *p523*
Kirsch, Kath. 57; America, 1866 ***5475.1*** *p490*
*Son:*Jakob
*Daughter:*Charlotte 15
Kirsch, Katharina; America, 1866 ***5475.1*** *p490*
Kirsch, Konrad; America, 1881 ***5475.1*** *p429*
*Wife:*Magdalene Strauss
*Daughter:*Elisabeth
Kirsch, Luzia *SEE* Kirsch, Mathias
Kirsch, Magdalene Strauss *SEE* Kirsch, Konrad
Kirsch, Margarethe; America, 1881 ***5475.1*** *p117*
Kirsch, Mathias *SEE* Kirsch, Mathias
Kirsch, Mathias; Brazil, 1857 ***5475.1*** *p509*
*Daughter:*Barbara
*Son:*Mathias
*Daughter:*Luzia
*Wife:*Anna Maria Schann
*Daughter:*Agnes
*Son:*Michel
*Son:*Andreas
Kirsch, Mathias; Wisconsin, 1847 ***5475.1*** *p254*
Kirsch, Michel; America, 1852 ***5475.1*** *p480*
Kirsch, Michel; America, 1880 ***5475.1*** *p453*
Kirsch, Michel *SEE* Kirsch, Mathias
Kirsch, Peter; Brazil, 1870 ***5475.1*** *p441*
*Wife:*Christine Kraemer
*Daughter:*Elise
With mother-in-law
*Son:*Peter
*Daughter:*Barbara
Kirsch, Peter 1 *SEE* Kirsch, Peter
Kirschbaum, Julius; Wisconsin, 1887 ***6795.8*** *p50*
Kirschbaum, Reinhold; Wisconsin, 1889 ***6795.8*** *p189*
Kirschenmann, Christina 6 months; New York, NY, 1874 ***6954.7*** *p37*
Kirschenmann, Christina 18; New York, NY, 1874 ***6954.7*** *p37*
Kirschenmann, Eva 26; New York, NY, 1874 ***6954.7*** *p37*
Kirschenmann, Jacob 1 months; New York, NY, 1874 ***6954.7*** *p37*
Kirschenmann, Jacob 28; New York, NY, 1874 ***6954.7*** *p37*
Kirschenmann, Johann 21; New York, NY, 1874 ***6954.7*** *p37*
Kirschenmann, Ludwig 5; New York, NY, 1874 ***6954.7*** *p37*
Kirschenmann, Ludwig 44; New York, NY, 1874 ***6954.7*** *p37*
Kirschenmann, Magdalena 15; New York, NY, 1874 ***6954.7*** *p37*
Kirschenmann, Margaretha 6; New York, NY, 1874 ***6954.7*** *p37*
Kirschenmann, Margaretha 18; New York, NY, 1874 ***6954.7*** *p37*
Kirschenmann, Margarethe 42; New York, NY, 1874 ***6954.7*** *p37*
Kirschmer, Jacob; Louisiana, 1874-1875 ***4981.45*** *p29*
Kirschmeyer, M.; Louisiana, 1874 ***4981.45*** *p296*
Kirschner, Alexander; New York, 1783 ***8529.30*** *p10*
Kirschner, Franz 12; New York, NY, 1893 ***1883.7*** *p40*
Kirschner, Joh 18; New York, NY, 1893 ***1883.7*** *p40*
Kirschner, Magdel 21; New York, NY, 1893 ***1883.7*** *p40*
Kirschner, Marg 53; New York, NY, 1893 ***1883.7*** *p40*
Kirschner, Mich 20; New York, NY, 1893 ***1883.7*** *p40*
Kirschner, Paul 59; New York, NY, 1893 ***1883.7*** *p40*
Kirschner, Philip; Philadelphia, 1778 ***8529.30*** *p6*
Kirschner, Thomas 27; New York, NY, 1893 ***1883.7*** *p40*
Kirshner, Philip; Philadelphia, 1778 ***8529.30*** *p6*
Kirst, Emilie; Wisconsin, 1895 ***6795.8*** *p125*
Kirstenpfad, Ernestine; America, 1867 ***7919.3*** *p534*
Kirton, Anthony; America, 1766 ***1220.12*** *p474*
Kirton, James; America, 1770 ***1220.12*** *p474*
Kirton, Mary; Barbados, 1670 ***1220.12*** *p474*
Kirton, Sara; Barbados, 1667 ***1220.12*** *p474*
Kirton, William; Barbados, 1673 ***1220.12*** *p474*
Kirton, Willm.; Maryland, 1674 ***1236.25*** *p50*
Kirwood, Edward; America, 1722 ***1220.12*** *p474*
Kisby, Levi 58; Ontario, 1871 ***1823.21*** *p192*
Kiselbach, August Ferdinand Louis; America, 1863 ***7420.1*** *p218*
Kiseleff, Edgar 30; New York, NY, 1893 ***1883.7*** *p44*
Kiser, Michael; North Carolina, 1710 ***3629.40*** *p6*
Kisielewski, Adam; Wisconsin, 1897 ***6795.8*** *p59*
Kisker, Catarine 24; New York, NY, 1864 ***8425.62*** *p197*
Kisker, Chat. Wilhelm. 35; New York, NY, 1864 ***8425.62*** *p197*
Kisker, Chatar. Wilhm. 11 months; New York, NY, 1864 ***8425.62*** *p197*
Kisker, Henriette 18; New York, NY, 1864 ***8425.62*** *p197*
Kisker, Joh. Hein. 25; New York, NY, 1864 ***8425.62*** *p197*
Kisle, Sixlis 35; America, 1746 ***778.6*** *p187*
Kisler, George; Ohio, 1809-1852 ***4511.35*** *p26*
Kiss, John; America, 1747 ***1220.12*** *p474*
Kissebert, Marie Katharina 52; America, 1853 ***2526.42*** *p149*
Kisseberth, Georg Emil; England, 1900 ***2526.43*** *p172*
Kissler, Ignatius; Ohio, 1809-1852 ***4511.35*** *p26*
Kissler, Sebastian; Ohio, 1809-1852 ***4511.35*** *p26*
Kisslng, Johann Christph 38; Nova Scotia, 1852 ***170.15*** *p31*
Kissner, Adolph; America, 1867 ***7919.3*** *p526*
Kissner, Frederick; Ohio, 1809-1852 ***4511.35*** *p27*
Kissner, Ludwig; America, 1867 ***7919.3*** *p529*
Kister, George; Ohio, 1809-1852 ***4511.35*** *p27*
Kister, Louis 22; Port uncertain, 1843 ***778.6*** *p187*
Kistler, Rudy; North Carolina, 1710 ***3629.40*** *p6*

Kistner, Ferdinand; Ohio, 1840-1897 *8365.35 p16*
Kistner, Jean 30; Port uncertain, 1840 *778.6 p187*
Kitchen, Jane; America, 1721 *1220.12 p474*
Kitchen, John; America, 1746 *1220.12 p474*
Kitchen, John; America, 1753 *1220.12 p474*
Kitchen, John; America, 1769 *1220.12 p474*
Kitchen, Serah 38; Ontario, 1871 *1823.17 p86*
Kitchen, Thomas; America, 1770 *1220.12 p474*
Kitchener, James; America, 1774 *1220.12 p474*
Kitchener, John; America, 1769 *1220.12 p474*
Kitchener, Mary; America, 1767 *1220.12 p474*
Kitchenside, Abraham; America, 1773 *1220.12 p474*
Kitchin, Elizabeth; America, 1751 *1220.12 p474*
Kitchin, Hugh; New York, NY, 1821 *3274.55 p71*
Kitchin, John; America, 1770 *1220.12 p474*
Kitchin, John, Jr.; America, 1748 *1220.12 p474*
Kitching, John; America, 1741 *1220.12 p474*
Kitching, John 51; Ontario, 1871 *1823.21 p192*
Kitching, Mary; America, 1762 *1220.12 p474*
Kitching, Sarah 49; Ontario, 1871 *1823.21 p192*
Kitchinman, William; Virginia, 1738 *1220.12 p474*
Kite, John; America, 1757 *1220.12 p474*
Kite, Patience; Charles Town, SC, 1718 *1220.12 p474*
Kite, Richard; America, 1760 *1220.12 p474*
Kite, Robert; America, 1768 *1220.12 p474*
Kiteley, Benjamin; America, 1751 *1220.12 p474*
Kitfield, Abraham; Marblehead, MA, 1681 *9228.50 p312*
Kitfield, Edward; Massachusetts, 1748 *9228.50 p286*
Kithcart, John A.; Ohio, 1873 *3580.20 p32*
Kithcart, John A.; Ohio, 1873 *6020.12 p12*
Kitling, John; America, 1699 *1220.12 p474*
Kitratt, William; America, 1740 *1220.12 p474*
Kitson, James; America, 1759 *1220.12 p475*
Kitson, Joseph; Ohio, 1809-1852 *4511.35 p27*
Kitson, Mary; America, 1767 *1220.12 p475*
Kitt, William 55; Ontario, 1871 *1823.21 p192*
Kittbridge, Frank B. 20; Ontario, 1871 *1823.17 p86*
Kitte, Charles; Colorado, 1886 *1029.59 p50*
Kittel, John Michael; Illinois, 1854 *6079.1 p7*
Kittermaster, Albert 40; Ontario, 1871 *1823.17 p86*
Kittermaster, Anthony 41; Ontario, 1871 *1823.17 p86*
Kittle, Herbert; Illinois, 1834-1900 *6020.5 p132*
Kittle, Mary 13; Ontario, 1871 *1823.21 p192*
Kittleson, Olares; Iowa, 1875 *1211.15 p15*
Kitto, John; America, 1748 *1220.12 p475*
Kittoe, Grace; America, 1757 *1220.12 p475*
Kitz, Christoph; Valdivia, Chile, 1851 *1192.4 p50*
Kitz, Emma; Valdivia, Chile, 1851 *1192.4 p50*
Kivers, Jane 82; Ontario, 1871 *1823.21 p193*
Kiyoshk, Thomas 25; Ontario, 1871 *1823.17 p86*
Kizner, Mary; Detroit, 1929-1930 *6214.5 p63*
Kjellberg, Gustaf Adolph; Cleveland, OH, 1902-1903 *9722.10 p122*
Kjellgren, Anna Elisabeth *SEE* Kjellgren, Hedvig Lovisa
Kjellgren, Gustaf F.; St. Paul, MN, 1887 *1865.50 p44*
Kjellgren, Hedvig Lovisa; St. Paul, MN, 1889 *1865.50 p44*
  *Daughter:*Anna Elisabeth
Kjellman, Anders; New York, NY, 1849 *6412.40 p151*
Kjellman, J.P.; New York, NY, 1849 *6412.40 p151*
Klabunde, Herman Frederick; Wisconsin, 1890-1915 *6795.8 p16*
Klabzuba, . . .; Iowa, 1870 *2853.20 p202*
Klacel, Frantisek; Iowa, 1869 *2853.20 p213*
Klack, George 20; America, 1840 *778.6 p187*
Klaehs, A. Maria Meiers *SEE* Klaehs, Math. Jos.
Klaehs, Barbara *SEE* Klaehs, Math. Jos.
Klaehs, Johann *SEE* Klaehs, Math. Jos.
Klaehs, Karl *SEE* Klaehs, Math. Jos.
Klaehs, M. Josef *SEE* Klaehs, Math. Jos.
Klaehs, Math. Jos.; America, 1881 *5475.1 p299*
  *Wife:*A. Maria Meiers
  *Son:*Johann
  *Daughter:*Barbara
  *Son:*Karl
  *Daughter:*Susanna
  *Son:*M. Josef
  *Son:*Peter
Klaehs, Peter *SEE* Klaehs, Math. Jos.
Klaehs, Susanna *SEE* Klaehs, Math. Jos.
Klaes, Joh. Jak. Friedrich; America, 1869 *5475.1 p47*
Klaeser, Johannetta Fehr *SEE* Klaeser, Peter
Klaeser, Magdalena *SEE* Klaeser, Peter
Klaeser, Mathias 33; America, 1843 *5475.1 p309*
Klaeser, Nikolaus; America, 1871 *5475.1 p247*
Klaeser, Peter; America, 1873 *5475.1 p312*
  *Wife:*Johannetta Fehr
  *Daughter:*Magdalena
Klages, Johann Friedrich; America, 1866 *7420.1 p244*
  With family
Klagges, Francisca; Valdivia, Chile, 1851 *1192.4 p50*
Klagges, Friedrich; Valdivia, Chile, 1851 *1192.4 p50*
Klahm, Maria; America, 1890 *5475.1 p76*

Klahsen, Marg.; America, 1881 *5475.1 p359*
Klaiber, Paul 30; Louisiana, 1848 *778.6 p187*
Klaisner, Vaclav; St. Louis, 1848 *2853.20 p21*
Klanduck, John; Louisiana, 1874 *4981.45 p296*
Klane, George; Philadelphia, 1777 *8529.30 p4A*
Klapka, Alois; Chicago, 1893-1910 *2853.20 p469*
Klapoetke, August; Wisconsin, 1906 *6795.8 p170*
Klapoetke, Christoph; Wisconsin, 1882 *6795.8 p170*
Klare, Friedrich Wilhelm; America, 1852 *7420.1 p91*
Klare, Friedrich Wilhelm; America, 1860 *7420.1 p195*
  With wife
Klare, Friedrich Wilhelm; America, 1880 *7420.1 p316*
Klare, Wilhelm; Port uncertain, 1856 *7420.1 p149*
Klarstrom, John Ludwig; Iowa, 1921 *1211.15 p16*
Klasen, Angela; America, 1843 *5475.1 p366*
Klasen, Anna *SEE* Klasen, Nikolaus
Klasen, Elisabeth *SEE* Klasen, Nikolaus
Klasen, Elisabeth Derwing 34 *SEE* Klasen, Nikolaus
Klasen, Michel; America, 1883 *5475.1 p290*
Klasen, Nikolaus; America, 1873 *5475.1 p363*
  *Wife:*Elisabeth Derwing
  *Daughter:*Anna
  *Daughter:*Elisabeth
Klaser, Nikolaus; America, 1871 *5475.1 p247*
Klaser, Peter; America, 1880 *5475.1 p293*
Klasing, Mr.; America, 1868 *7420.1 p273*
Klason, Gustaf Emil; New York, NY, 1900-1915 *6212.1 p15*
Klassen, Gertrud 36; Brazil, 1857 *5475.1 p319*
Klatt, Frank Ferd; Wisconsin, 1893 *6795.8 p73*
Klatt, Gustav; Wisconsin, 1895 *6795.8 p25*
Klatt, Wilhelm; Wisconsin, 1879 *6795.8 p73*
Klauck, Anna *SEE* Klauck, Mathias
Klauck, Anna Maria Mergen *SEE* Klauck, Christoph
Klauck, Christoph *SEE* Klauck, Christoph
Klauck, Christoph; Brazil, 1874 *5475.1 p372*
  *Son:*Johann
  *Wife:*Anna Maria Mergen
  *Son:*Mathias
  *Son:*Peter
  *Son:*Christoph
  *Son:*Josef
  *Daughter:*Katharina
Klauck, Georg; America, 1883 *5475.1 p141*
Klauck, J. Adam 36; America, 1843 *5475.1 p366*
Klauck, Jakob *SEE* Klauck, Mathias
Klauck, Johann *SEE* Klauck, Christoph
Klauck, Josef *SEE* Klauck, Christoph
Klauck, Kath.; America, 1855 *5475.1 p352*
  *Daughter:*Susanna
  With child 13
  With child 16
  *Son:*Peter
Klauck, Katharina *SEE* Klauck, Christoph
Klauck, Katharina; Brazil, 1881 *5475.1 p374*
Klauck, Margarethe Behles *SEE* Klauck, Mathias
Klauck, Mathias *SEE* Klauck, Mathias
Klauck, Mathias; Brazil, 1874 *5475.1 p371*
  *Wife:*Margarethe Behles
  *Daughter:*Anna
  *Son:*Mathias
  *Son:*Jakob
  *Daughter:*Susanna
  With son
Klauck, Mathias *SEE* Klauck, Christoph
Klauck, Peter; America, 1843 *5475.1 p358*
Klauck, Peter *SEE* Klauck, Christoph
Klauck, Susanna *SEE* Klauck, Mathias
Klauk, Elisabeth Atz *SEE* Klauk, Mathias
Klauk, Katharina 45; Brazil, 1862 *5475.1 p369*
Klauk, Margarethe Behles 22 *SEE* Klauk, Mathias
Klauk, Mathias; Brazil, 1846 *5475.1 p438*
  *Wife:*Elisabeth Atz
  With 4 children
Klauk, Mathias 24; Brazil, 1862 *5475.1 p370*
  *Wife:*Margarethe Behles 22
Klaus, Christian; New York, 1860 *358.56 p150*
Klaus, K.; New York, 1860 *358.56 p148*
Klaus, Mae Schwartz; Detroit, 1930 *1640.60 p82*
Klausing, Christoph; America, 1855 *7420.1 p137*
Klausing, Ludwig; America, 1854 *7420.1 p122*
Klaussen, John; New York, 1860 *358.56 p149*
Klawikowski, Pauline; Wisconsin, 1900 *6795.8 p44*
Klawiter, Frank; Wisconsin, 1900 *6795.8 p37*
Klawitter, Albert Gustav; Wisconsin, 1898 *6795.8 p171*
Klawitter, Albert Gustav; Wisconsin, 1899 *6795.8 p145*
Klawitter, August; Wisconsin, 1888 *6795.8 p145*
Klawitter, Emil Edward; Wisconsin, 1896 *6795.8 p139*
Klawitter, Emil Ludwig; Wisconsin, 1900 *6795.8 p134*
Klawitter, Gustav Theodore; Wisconsin, 1892 *6795.8 p139*
Kleb, Barbara; Venezuela, 1843 *3899.5 p541*
Kleben, K.; Galveston, TX, 1855 *571.7 p18*

Klecan, Josef; Baltimore, 1850 *2853.20 p125*
Klecanda, Jan; St. Louis, 1904 *2853.20 p513*
Kleczynski, Andrew; Detroit, 1929-1930 *6214.5 p61*
Klee, Christiane Maria; America, 1868 *7919.3 p535*
Klee, Johann Jakob; America, 1864 *5475.1 p545*
Kleeb, Barbara; Venezuela, 1843 *3899.5 p541*
Kleeb, Joseph; Venezuela, 1843 *3899.5 p541*
Kleemann, Karl 26; America, 1897 *5475.1 p42*
Kleemann, Michel; America, 1880 *5475.1 p434*
Kleer, Anna 4 *SEE* Kleer, Nikolaus
Kleer, Anna Schu 32 *SEE* Kleer, Nikolaus
Kleer, Anna 45; America, 1846 *5475.1 p401*
Kleer, Anna Maria 6 *SEE* Kleer, Nikolaus
Kleer, Elisabeth 12 *SEE* Kleer, Nikolaus
Kleer, Elisabeth Simmet 43 *SEE* Kleer, Franz
Kleer, Franz 21 *SEE* Kleer, Franz
Kleer, Franz 44; America, 1837 *5475.1 p407*
  *Wife:*Elisabeth Simmet 43
  *Son:*Jakob 2
  *Daughter:*Katharina 6
  *Daughter:*Maria 19
  *Son:*Johann 15
  *Daughter:*Elisabeth 12
  *Son:*Peter 8
  *Son:*Jakob 17
  *Son:*Franz 21
Kleer, Jakob 2 *SEE* Kleer, Franz
Kleer, Jakob 17 *SEE* Kleer, Franz
Kleer, Johann; America, 1882 *5475.1 p457*
  With wife
Kleer, Johann 15 *SEE* Kleer, Franz
Kleer, Johann 39; America, 1882 *5475.1 p386*
  *Sister:*Maria 27
Kleer, Katharina 2 *SEE* Kleer, Nikolaus
Kleer, Katharina 5 weeks months *SEE* Kleer, Nikolaus
Kleer, Katharina 6 *SEE* Kleer, Franz
Kleer, Katharina 34; America, 1846 *5475.1 p385*
Kleer, Maria 19 *SEE* Kleer, Franz
Kleer, Maria 27 *SEE* Kleer, Johann
Kleer, Nikolaus 33; America, 1846 *5475.1 p401*
  *Wife:*Anna Schu 32
  *Daughter:*Anna 4
  *Daughter:*Katharina 2
  *Daughter:*Katharina 5 weeks
  *Daughter:*Anna Maria 6
Kleer, Peter 8 *SEE* Kleer, Franz
Kleff, Jos.; America, 1929 *8023.44 p375*
Kleiber, Alois 8; Galveston, TX, 1844 *3967.10 p373*
Kleiber, Alphons 6; Galveston, TX, 1844 *3967.10 p373*
Kleiber, Emil 4; Galveston, TX, 1844 *3967.10 p373*
Kleiber, Gabriel; Wisconsin, 1892 *6795.8 p100*
Kleiber, Georg; New Jersey, 1767-1774 *927.31 p2*
Kleiber, Henrich; New Jersey, 1767-1774 *927.31 p2*
Kleiber, Johann Georg 42; Galveston, TX, 1844 *3967.10 p373*
Kleiber, Joseph 10; Galveston, TX, 1844 *3967.10 p373*
Kleiber, Katharina 2; Galveston, TX, 1844 *3967.10 p373*
Kleiber, Therese 40; Galveston, TX, 1844 *3967.10 p373*
Kleidsman, Frederick; Ohio, 1809-1852 *4511.35 p27*
Klein, A. Maria Bruck 20 *SEE* Klein, Konrad
Klein, A. Maria 30; America, 1867 *5475.1 p558*
Klein, Adam; America, 1871 *2526.42 p154*
Klein, Adam *SEE* Klein, Mathias
Klein, Adam; America, 1886 *2526.43 p196*
Klein, Adam 49; Halifax, N.S., 1902 *1860.4 p44*
Klein, Adelheide 19; America, 1848 *778.6 p188*
Klein, Adolph 15; America, 1848 *778.6 p188*
Klein, Alicia 27; Halifax, N.S., 1902 *1860.4 p44*
Klein, Alois J.; Lincoln, NE, 1839 *2853.20 p179*
Klein, Amalie *SEE* Klein, Wilhelm
Klein, Andre 4; America, 1846 *778.6 p188*
Klein, Andreas 11 months; New York, NY, 1893 *1883.7 p38*
Klein, Andreas *SEE* Klein, Wilhelm
Klein, Anna; America, 1867 *5475.1 p343*
Klein, Anna *SEE* Klein, Johann
Klein, Anna Leichtweiss *SEE* Klein, Sebastian
Klein, Anna 26; America, 1865 *5475.1 p388*
Klein, Anna; Chicago, 1852 *5475.1 p264*
Klein, Anna Leichtweiss *SEE* Klein, Sebastian
Klein, Anna Eva; America, 1837 *5475.1 p527*
Klein, Anna Maria 65; America, 1800-1899 *5475.1 p453*
  With 2 daughters
Klein, Anton; Colorado, 1884 *1029.59 p50*
Klein, August 27; America, 1847 *778.6 p188*
Klein, Barbara *SEE* Klein, Nikolaus
Klein, Barbara *SEE* Klein, Franz
Klein, Barbara 29; America, 1860 *5475.1 p310*
Klein, Barbara Hahn 35 *SEE* Klein, Peter
Klein, Barbara Haan *SEE* Klein, Peter
Klein, Carolina 6 months; New Orleans, 1847 *778.6 p188*
Klein, Catherina 25; New York, NY, 1893 *1883.7 p38*

Klein, Catherine 5; America, 1846 *778.6 p188*
Klein, Chatherine 9; America, 1846 *778.6 p188*
Klein, Christian 67; New Orleans, 1847 *778.6 p188*
Klein, Christian 1 months; New York, NY, 1874 *6954.7 p37*
Klein, Christian Wilhelm *SEE* Klein, Mrs. Georg
Klein, Christine 4; New York, NY, 1893 *1883.7 p38*
Klein, Christine 6; New York, NY, 1874 *6954.7 p37*
Klein, Christine 1 *SEE* Klein, Kanrad
Klein, Christine Sophie *SEE* Klein, Jakob
Klein, Clemence 24; America, 1848 *778.6 p188*
Klein, Conrad Sebastian *SEE* Klein, Jakob
Klein, Dominek 24; Halifax, N.S., 1902 *1860.4 p41*
Klein, Dorothea Schmidt *SEE* Klein, Jakob
Klein, Dorothea *SEE* Klein, Jakob
Klein, Dorothea Sophie *SEE* Klein, Jakob
Klein, E. Diana 29; America, 1846 *778.6 p188*
Klein, Elisabeth *SEE* Klein, Jakob
Klein, Elisabeth; America, 1881 *5475.1 p33*
Klein, Elisabeth *SEE* Klein, Franz
Klein, Elisabeth Becker 29 *SEE* Klein, Peter
Klein, Elisabeth 37; America, 1846 *5475.1 p408*
Klein, Ernst Friedr.; Illinois, 1874 *5475.1 p32*
Klein, Eva *SEE* Klein, Johann
Klein, Eva Schleinz 40 *SEE* Klein, Johann
Klein, Fanny *SEE* Klein, Sebastian
Klein, Fanny *SEE* Klein, Sebastian
Klein, Franz *SEE* Klein, Nikolaus
Klein, Franz; America, 1882 *5475.1 p429*
  *Wife:*Barbara
  *Daughter:*Maria
  *Daughter:*Gertrud
  *Daughter:*Elisabeth
  *Daughter:*Barbara
  *Daughter:*Margarethe
  *Daughter:*Katharina
  *Son:*Jakob
Klein, Franziska 4; Halifax, N.S., 1902 *1860.4 p41*
Klein, Friedrich *SEE* Klein, Jakob
Klein, Friedrich; America, 1882 *5475.1 p464*
Klein, Friedrich Jakob *SEE* Klein, Jakob
Klein, G. J.; Valdivia, Chile, 1850 *1192.4 p48*
Klein, Georg 6; New Orleans, 1847 *778.6 p188*
Klein, Georg 34; New Orleans, 1847 *778.6 p188*
Klein, Georg 44; New Orleans, 1847 *778.6 p188*
Klein, Georg 26; New York, 1872 *5475.1 p539*
Klein, Georg; Valdivia, Chile, 1852 *1192.4 p55*
  With wife
Klein, Mrs. Georg; Wisconsin, 1868 *5475.1 p59*
  *Son:*Georg Christian
  *Daughter:*Katharina Sophie
  *Daughter:*L. Charlotte
  *Son:*Christian Wilhelm
Klein, Georg Christian *SEE* Klein, Mrs. Georg
Klein, George 3; America, 1846 *778.6 p188*
Klein, George H. 1; Michigan, 1880 *4491.42 p16*
Klein, Georges 7; America, 1846 *778.6 p188*
Klein, Gerhard; America, 1882 *5475.1 p464*
Klein, Gertrud *SEE* Klein, Franz
Klein, Gertrud 42; America, 1855 *5475.1 p250*
Klein, Helehne *SEE* Klein, Wilhelm
Klein, Helena *SEE* Klein, Maria
Klein, Helene 23; Halifax, N.S., 1902 *1860.4 p41*
Klein, Henriette 63; America, 1865 *5475.1 p511*
Klein, Henry; Louisiana, 1874-1875 *4981.45 p29*
Klein, J. Nikolaus *SEE* Klein, Jakob
Klein, Jakob; America, 1833 *5475.1 p20*
  *Son:*Jakob Martin
  *Daughter:*Dorothea Sophie
  *Son:*Friedrich Jakob
  *Son:*Conrad Sebastian
  *Son:*Peter Conrad
  *Daughter:*Christine Sophie
  *Daughter:*Kath. Dorothea
Klein, Jakob; America, 1836 *5475.1 p527*
  *Wife:*Dorothea Schmidt
  *Daughter:*Katharina
  *Son:*Jakob
Klein, Jakob; America, 1848 *5475.1 p402*
Klein, Jakob *SEE* Klein, Jakob
Klein, Jakob; America, 1854 *5475.1 p458*
  *Wife:*K. Dorothea
  *Daughter:*Katharina
  *Son:*J. Nikolaus
  *Daughter:*Dorothea
  *Daughter:*Elisabeth
  *Son:*Friedrich
  *Son:*Konrad
  *Daughter:*Wilhelmine
  *Son:*Jakob
Klein, Jakob; America, 1875 *5475.1 p151*
Klein, Jakob *SEE* Klein, Franz
Klein, Jakob; America, 1882 *5475.1 p464*

Klein, Jakob 2 *SEE* Klein, Peter
Klein, Jakob 5 *SEE* Klein, Jakob
Klein, Jakob 34; America, 1864 *5475.1 p535*
  *Wife:*Katharina Muller 33
  *Son:*Peter 4
  *Daughter:*Katharina 2 months
Klein, Jakob Martin *SEE* Klein, Jakob
Klein, Jan; Kansas, 1881 *2853.20 p520*
Klein, Jean 50; America, 1847 *778.6 p188*
Klein, Jean 41; New Orleans, 1847 *778.6 p188*
Klein, Johann; America, 1852 *5475.1 p52*
Klein, Johann *SEE* Klein, Johann
Klein, Johann *SEE* Klein, Peter
Klein, Johann *SEE* Klein, Sebastian
Klein, Johann *SEE* Klein, Mathias
Klein, Johann; America, 1883 *5475.1 p196*
Klein, Johann 25; America, 1869 *5475.1 p320*
Klein, Johann 40; America, 1872 *5475.1 p267*
  *Wife:*Eva Schleinz 40
  *Son:*Nikolaus
  *Son:*Michel
  *Daughter:*Anna
  *Son:*Johann
  *Daughter:*Eva
  With son
Klein, Johann 53; America, 1846 *778.6 p188*
Klein, Johann *SEE* Klein, Peter
Klein, Johann 3; New York, NY, 1893 *1883.7 p38*
Klein, Johann; Port uncertain, 1897 *5475.1 p485*
Klein, Johann *SEE* Klein, Sebastian
Klein, Johann Nikolaus 33; America, 1872 *5475.1 p41*
  *Wife:*Katharina Maes 22
Klein, John; Nova Scotia, 1784 *7105 p23*
Klein, John H.; Minnesota, 1867-1868 *1029.59 p50*
Klein, John H.; Minnesota, 1868 *1029.59 p50*
Klein, Josepf; Halifax, N.S., 1902 *1860.4 p41*
Klein, Joseph; Argentina, 1923 *8023.44 p375*
  With wife
Klein, Jost. 25; America, 1840 *778.6 p188*
Klein, Julius; America, 1884 *2526.42 p162*
Klein, K. Dorothea *SEE* Klein, Jakob
Klein, Kanrad 31; Ohio, 1800-1899 *5475.1 p528*
  *Wife:*Katharina Dick 29
  *Child:*Konrad 4
  *Child:*Christine 1
Klein, Karl; America, 1864 *5475.1 p119*
Klein, Karl Georg; Uruguay, 1883 *5475.1 p119*
Klein, Kath. Schneider *SEE* Klein, Mathias
Klein, Kath. Dorothea *SEE* Klein, Jakob
Klein, Katha 2; Halifax, N.S., 1902 *1860.4 p41*
Klein, Katharina *SEE* Klein, Jakob
Klein, Katharina; America, 1864 *5475.1 p508*
Klein, Katharina *SEE* Klein, Nikolaus
Klein, Katharina; America, 1881 *5475.1 p344*
Klein, Katharina; America, 1882 *5475.1 p316*
Klein, Katharina *SEE* Klein, Franz
Klein, Katharina *SEE* Klein, Maria
Klein, Katharina 2 *SEE* Klein, Jakob
Klein, Katharina 6 *SEE* Klein, Jakob
Klein, Katharina 22; America, 1846 *5475.1 p401*
Klein, Katharina Maes 22 *SEE* Klein, Johann Nikolaus
Klein, Katharina Muller 33 *SEE* Klein, Jakob
Klein, Katharina 60; America, 1800-1899 *5475.1 p558*
Klein, Katharina; Illinois, 1887 *5475.1 p75*
Klein, Katharina *SEE* Klein, Wilhelm
Klein, Katharina Dick 29 *SEE* Klein, Kanrad
Klein, Katharina Sophie *SEE* Klein, Mrs. Georg
Klein, Konrad *SEE* Klein, Jakob
Klein, Konrad 6 *SEE* Klein, Peter
Klein, Konrad 29; America, 1847 *5475.1 p393*
  *Wife:*A. Maria Bruck 20
  With niece 11
  *Daughter:*Margarethe 2 months
Klein, Konrad 30; America, 1843 *5475.1 p528*
Klein, Konrad 4 *SEE* Klein, Kanrad
Klein, L. Charlotte *SEE* Klein, Mrs. Georg
Klein, Loiuise 4; New Orleans, 1847 *778.6 p188*
Klein, Louis 34; America, 1840 *778.6 p188*
Klein, Louis 4; New Orleans, 1847 *778.6 p188*
Klein, Luise Meth *SEE* Klein, Wilhelm
Klein, M. 29; America, 1846 *778.6 p188*
Klein, Magdalena 7 *SEE* Klein, Peter
Klein, Magdalena 2; New Orleans, 1847 *778.6 p188*
Klein, Magdalena 21; New York, NY, 1898 *7951.13 p43*
Klein, Magdalene 20; America, 1846 *5475.1 p401*
  *Brother:*Peter 18
Klein, Margaretha 3; New Orleans, 1847 *778.6 p188*
Klein, Margaretha 7; New Orleans, 1847 *778.6 p188*
Klein, Margaretha 32; New Orleans, 1847 *778.6 p188*
Klein, Margaretha 28; New York, NY, 1874 *6954.7 p37*
Klein, Margarethe *SEE* Klein, Peter
Klein, Margarethe *SEE* Klein, Franz
Klein, Margarethe 2 *SEE* Klein, Konrad

Klein, Margarethe *SEE* Klein, Peter
Klein, Margarethe *SEE* Klein, Sebastian
Klein, Marguerite 8; America, 1846 *778.6 p188*
Klein, Marguerite 42; America, 1846 *778.6 p188*
Klein, Maria *SEE* Klein, Nikolaus
Klein, Maria *SEE* Klein, Peter
Klein, Maria *SEE* Klein, Franz
Klein, Maria; America, 1882 *5475.1 p493*
Klein, Maria; America, 1882 *5475.1 p512*
  *Sister:*Helena
  *Sister:*Katharina
Klein, Maria 1 *SEE* Klein, Valentin
Klein, Maria 32; America, 1865 *5475.1 p388*
Klein, Maria Schmitt 32 *SEE* Klein, Nikolaus
Klein, Maria 56; America, 1855 *5475.1 p272*
Klein, Maria *SEE* Klein, Peter
Klein, Maria 5; New Orleans, 1847 *778.6 p188*
Klein, Maria; Ohio, 1884 *5475.1 p316*
Klein, Maria; South America, 1856 *5475.1 p492*
Klein, Maria 55; South America, 1856 *5475.1 p492*
  *Son:*Mathias
Klein, Maria Anna 48; America, 1860 *5475.1 p552*
Klein, Maria Katharina 57; America, 1865 *5475.1 p518*
Klein, Marianna 34; New Orleans, 1847 *778.6 p188*
Klein, Marie 52; America, 1848 *778.6 p189*
Klein, Marie 21; Missouri, 1845 *778.6 p189*
Klein, Marie 65; Missouri, 1845 *778.6 p188*
Klein, Mary Boniface; Kansas, 1917-1918 *2094.25 p50*
Klein, Mathias; America, 1854 *5475.1 p440*
Klein, Mathias *SEE* Klein, Mathias
Klein, Mathias; America, 1881 *5475.1 p494*
  *Wife:*Kath. Schneider
  *Son:*Adam
  *Son:*Johann
  *Son:*Peter
  *Son:*Mathias
Klein, Mathias *SEE* Klein, Maria Hornetz
Klein, Mathias; St. Louis, 1885 *5475.1 p75*
Klein, Mathilde *SEE* Klein, Wilhelm
Klein, Michael 19; New York, NY, 1898 *7951.13 p43*
Klein, Michel; America, 1865 *5475.1 p340*
Klein, Michel *SEE* Klein, Johann
Klein, Michel 14; America, 1846 *778.6 p189*
Klein, Nicolas 18; America, 1840 *778.6 p189*
Klein, Nicolus 3; Halifax, N.S., 1902 *1860.4 p44*
Klein, Nikolaus; America, 1852 *5475.1 p486*
Klein, Nikolaus *SEE* Klein, Nikolaus
Klein, Nikolaus *SEE* Klein, Johann
Klein, Nikolaus *SEE* Klein, Nikolaus
Klein, Nikolaus; America, 1873 *5475.1 p271*
  *Wife:*Barbara
  *Son:*Nikolaus
Klein, Nikolaus *SEE* Klein, Peter
Klein, Nikolaus 38; America, 1865 *5475.1 p388*
  *Wife:*Maria Schmitt 32
  *Son:*Franz
  *Daughter:*Katharina
  *Son:*Peter
  *Son:*Nikolaus
  *Daughter:*Maria
Klein, Nikolaus *SEE* Klein, Peter
Klein, Peter *SEE* Klein, Nikolaus
Klein, Peter; America, 1880 *5475.1 p428*
Klein, Peter *SEE* Klein, Peter
Klein, Peter *SEE* Klein, Mathias
Klein, Peter; America, 1881 *5475.1 p494*
Klein, Peter; America, 1892 *5475.1 p141*
Klein, Peter 4 *SEE* Klein, Jakob
Klein, Peter 18 *SEE* Klein, Magdalene
Klein, Peter 30; America, 1843 *5475.1 p270*
Klein, Peter 33; America, 1837 *5475.1 p63*
  *Wife:*Elisabeth Becker 29
  *Son:*Konrad 6 months
  *Daughter:*Magdalena 7
  *Son:*Jakob 2
Klein, Peter 36; America, 1843 *5475.1 p558*
Klein, Peter 41; America, 1881 *5475.1 p196*
  *Wife:*Barbara Hahn 35
  *Son:*Nikolaus
  *Son:*Johann
  *Daughter:*Margarethe
  *Daughter:*Maria
  *Son:*Peter
Klein, Peter *SEE* Klein, Peter
Klein, Peter; Kansas, 1882 *5475.1 p196*
  *Wife:*Barbara Haan
  *Daughter:*Maria
  *Son:*Johann
  *Daughter:*Margarethe
  *Son:*Peter
  *Son:*Nikolaus
Klein, Peter 30; New York, NY, 1874 *6954.7 p37*
Klein, Peter; Ohio, 1809-1852 *4511.35 p27*

Klein, Peter Conrad *SEE* Klein, Jakob
Klein, Pierre 23; America, 1846 *778.6 p189*
Klein, Pierre 19; Louisiana, 1848 *778.6 p189*
Klein, Sebastian; America, 1881 *5475.1 p221*
  Wife: Anna Leichtweiss
  Son: Johann
  Daughter: Fanny
Klein, Sebastian 32; New York, NY, 1893 *1883.7 p38*
Klein, Sebastian; Scranton, PA, 1884 *5475.1 p221*
  Wife: Anna Leichtweiss
  Daughter: Margarethe
  Daughter: Fanny
  Son: Johann
Klein, Simon; America, 1881 *5475.1 p492*
Klein, Simon 7; America, 1846 *778.6 p189*
Klein, Sophia 12; America, 1846 *778.6 p189*
Klein, Sophia 9 months; New York, NY, 1874 *6954.7 p37*
Klein, Sophie; America, 1881 *5475.1 p48*
Klein, Sophie; St. Louis, 1880 *5475.1 p33*
  Daughter: Sophie
  Daughter: Charlotte
  Son: Karl
  Son: Adolph
  Daughter: Emilie
Klein, Susanna; America, 1883 *5475.1 p316*
Klein, Theodor 21; America, 1848 *778.6 p189*
Klein, Therese 32; New Orleans, 1847 *778.6 p189*
Klein, Valentin; America, 1836 *5475.1 p536*
  With wife
  Daughter: Maria
Klein, Valentine 1; Halifax, N.S., 1902 *1860.4 p44*
Klein, W. 26; America, 1846 *778.6 p189*
Klein, Wilhelm; North Dakota, 1908 *554.30 p26*
  Wife: Luise Meth
  Child: Amalie
  Child: Katharina
  Child: Andreas
  Child: Mathilde
  Child: Helehne
Klein, Wilhelmine *SEE* Klein, Jakob
Klein, William; Nova Scotia, 1784 *7105 p24*
Kleine, Mina; Chicago, 1926 *8023.44 p372*
  Daughter: Agnes
  Son: Otto
  Son: Eugen
Kleiner, David; Detroit, 1929 *1640.55 p116*
Kleiner, Jacob 40; New Castle, DE, 1817-1818 *90.20 p152*
Kleinfelder, . . .; Port uncertain, 1866 *170.15 p31*
Kleinfelder, Johannes; Pennsylvania, 1866 *170.15 p31*
  With wife & son
Kleinfeller, Anna Margaretha 35; Pennsylvania, 1851 *170.15 p31*
  With family
Kleinfeller, Elisabeth 19; Pennsylvania, 1851 *170.15 p31*
  With family
Kleinfeller, Elisabeth 25; Pennsylvania, 1851 *170.15 p31*
  With family
Kleinfeller, Elisabeth 48; Pennsylvania, 1851 *170.15 p31*
  With family
Kleinfeller, Georg 26; Pennsylvania, 1851 *170.15 p31*
  With family
Kleinfeller, Johann Albert 15; Pennsylvania, 1851 *170.15 p31*
  With family
Kleinfeller, Johann Peter 49; Pennsylvania, 1851 *170.15 p31*
  With family
Kleinfeller, Johannes; Pennsylvania, 1865 *170.15 p31*
  With family
Kleinfeller, Johannes 12; Pennsylvania, 1851 *170.15 p31*
  With family
Kleinfeller, Johannes 60; Pennsylvania, 1851 *170.15 p31*
  With family
Kleinfeller, Mrs. Johannes; Pennsylvania, 1865 *170.15 p31*
  With family
Kleinfeller, Melchior 23; Pennsylvania, 1851 *170.15 p31*
  With family
Kleinfeller, Michael 16; Pennsylvania, 1851 *170.15 p31*
  With family
Kleinglaus, Georg 29; America, 1845 *778.6 p189*
Kleinknecht, Jakob Adam; America, 1889 *179.55 p19*
Kleis, Anna; Pennsylvania, 1851 *170.15 p18*
  With family
Kleis, Engel; America, 1866 *7420.1 p244*
Kleis, Heinrich; America, 1865 *7420.1 p232*
Kleis, Wilhelm; America, 1867 *7420.1 p258*
  With wife
Kleis, Wilhelm; America, 1870 *7420.1 p284*
  With family
Kleist, Albert; Wisconsin, 1875 *6795.8 p226*

Kleist, August; Wisconsin, 1882 *6795.8 p226*
Kleist, Friedrich; Wisconsin, 1876 *6795.8 p226*
Kleist, Nikolaus; America, 1846 *5475.1 p455*
Kleitz, Jacob; Ohio, 1809-1852 *4511.35 p27*
Kleman, Kelly; Detroit, 1929-1930 *6214.5 p61*
Klemens, Elisabeth *SEE* Klemens, Jakob
Klemens, Jakob; Chicago, 1881 *5475.1 p344*
  Wife: Margarethe Honecker
  Son: Peter
  Daughter: Elisabeth
  Daughter: Margarethe
Klemens, Margarethe *SEE* Klemens, Jakob
Klemens, Margarethe Honecker *SEE* Klemens, Jakob
Klemens, Maria *SEE* Klemens, Susanna Klinkner
Klemens, Peter *SEE* Klemens, Jakob
Klemens, Susanna *SEE* Klemens, Susanna Klinkner
Klemens, Susanna; America, 1874 *5475.1 p331*
  Daughter: Maria
  Daughter: Susanna
Klemkow, J.; Venezuela, 1843 *3899.5 p546*
Klemm, Lorentz 20; America, 1840 *778.6 p189*
Klemm, Philip 41; Ontario, 1871 *1823.21 p193*
Klenche, Jean 57; Louisiana, 1848 *778.6 p189*
Kleng, John; Cleveland, OH, 1880-1884 *9722.10 p122*
Klenk, Ernst; America, 1858 *179.55 p19*
Klenk, Friedrich Michael; America, 1872 *179.55 p19*
Klenk, Gottlieb; America, 1856 *179.55 p19*
Klenk, Heinrich; America, 1887 *179.55 p19*
Klenk, Michael; America, 1853 *179.55 p19*
Klens, Franz; America, 1924 *8023.44 p376*
Klens, Joh.; America, 1909 *8023.44 p375*
Kleps, August; Wisconsin, 1880 *6795.8 p204*
Klerring, Richard 27; Ontario, 1871 *1823.17 p86*
Klesen, Angela; Brazil, 1883 *5475.1 p416*
Kleser, Nikolaus; America, 1871 *5475.1 p247*
Kleser, Susanna; America, 1872 *5475.1 p306*
Kletke, Frederick Martin; Wisconsin, 1869 *6795.8 p125*
Klett, John; New York, 1859 *358.56 p55*
Kley, Barbara 39; America, 1837 *5475.1 p408*
Kleyensteuber, Carl August Otto; America, 1867 *7420.1 p258*
Kleyensteuber, Ferdinand Arnold; America, 1862 *7420.1 p212*
Klicker, Helene *SEE* Klicker, Peter
Klicker, Margarethe Franz *SEE* Klicker, Peter
Klicker, Maria *SEE* Klicker, Peter
Klicker, Peter *SEE* Klicker, Peter
Klicker, Peter; Chicago, 1892 *5475.1 p77*
  Wife: Margarethe Franz
  Son: Peter
  Daughter: Maria
  Daughter: Helene
Klidrce, Auguste 21; Portland, ME, 1906 *970.38 p78*
Klidrce, Christian 27; Portland, ME, 1906 *970.38 p78*
Kliebenstein, Ludwig; America, 1847 *5475.1 p11*
Klien, Pet.; New York, 1860 *358.56 p4*
Klima, M.; Cleveland, OH, 1854 *2853.20 p340*
  Son: Josef
  With 2 daughters
Klima, Josef *SEE* Klima, Mr.
Klima, Matej; Wisconsin, 1855 *2853.20 p304*
Klimes, Jan; Iowa, 1854 *2853.20 p230*
Klimicek, Alois; Texas, 1856 *2853.20 p74*
Klimke, Albert Hermann; Wisconsin, 1888 *6795.8 p175*
Klimkowski, Petro; Detroit, 1929 *1640.55 p117*
Klimt, Bedrich; Chicago, 1847-1910 *2853.20 p404*
Klimt, Bedrich; Chicago, 1861 *2853.20 p388*
Klimt, Frantisek Antonin; Chicago, 1854 *2853.20 p388*
Kline, Adam; Illinois, 1856 *6079.1 p7*
Kline, Conrad; Ohio, 1809-1852 *4511.35 p27*
Kline, Jacob; Ohio, 1809-1852 *4511.35 p27*
Kline, Nicholas; Ohio, 1809-1852 *4511.35 p27*
Kline, Stephen; Ohio, 1809-1852 *4511.35 p27*
Klineshrode, Leonard; Ohio, 1809-1852 *4511.35 p27*
Klinet, Michael; Illinois, 1856 *6079.1 p7*
Kling, Adam 30; America, 1840 *2526.43 p150*
Kling, Anna Margaretha; Pennsylvania, 1850 *170.15 p31*
Kling, Anna Maria; America, 1847 *2526.43 p150*
Kling, August 26; New Jersey, 1847 *2526.43 p150*
Kling, Catharina; America, 1867 *7919.3 p530*
Kling, Charles John; New York, 1873 *1766.20 p23*
Kling, Elisabeth 17 *SEE* Kling, Wilhelm
Kling, John G.; Ohio, 1809-1852 *4511.35 p27*
Kling, Louis 24; America, 1840 *778.6 p189*
Kling, Marg. 36; America, 1840 *778.6 p189*
Kling, Wilhelm 20; America, 1845 *2526.43 p150*
  Sister: Elisabeth 17
Klingabiel, Charles; Illinois, 1855 *6079.1 p7*
Klingbeil, Carl; Wisconsin, 1884 *6795.8 p172*
Klingbeil, Emma Wilhelmine; Wisconsin, 1891 *6795.8 p95*
Klingbeil, Frank Otto; Wisconsin, 1911 *6795.8 p173*

Klingbeil, Ottilie Louise Antonia; Wisconsin, 1893 *6795.8 p73*
Klinge, Ernestine Wilhelmine; America, 1871 *7420.1 p290*
  Son: Leopold August Heinrich Carl Wilhelm
Klinge, Johann Paul August; Port uncertain, 1882 *7420.1 p329*
Klinge, Leopold August Heinrich Carl Wilhelm *SEE* Klinge, Ernestine Wilhelmine
Klingenberg, August; America, 1904 *7420.1 p401*
Klingenberg, August Wilhelm *SEE* Klingenberg, Caroline Friedrike Amalie Eggerding
Klingenberg, Carl; America, 1852 *7420.1 p91*
Klingenberg, Carl August; America, 1884 *7420.1 p344*
Klingenberg, Carl Gottlieb; Port uncertain, 1862 *7420.1 p212*
Klingenberg, Caroline Friederike Auguste *SEE* Klingenberg, Caroline Friedrike Amalie Eggerding
Klingenberg, Caroline Friedrike Amalie; America, 1884 *7420.1 p344*
  Daughter: Caroline Friederike Auguste
  Daughter: Louise Sophie
  Daughter: Johanne Friederike Amalie
  Daughter: Friederike Charlotte Amalie
  Son: Friedrich August
  Son: August Wilhelm
Klingenberg, Caroline Wilhelmine; America, 1881 *7420.1 p322*
Klingenberg, Friederike Charlotte Amalie *SEE* Klingenberg, Caroline Friedrike Amalie Eggerding
Klingenberg, Friedrich August *SEE* Klingenberg, Caroline Friedrike Amalie Eggerding
Klingenberg, Johanne Friederike Amalie *SEE* Klingenberg, Caroline Friedrike Amalie Eggerding
Klingenberg, Justine Karoline Henriette; America, 1882 *7420.1 p330*
Klingenberg, Justine Wilhelmine Caroline; America, 1862 *7420.1 p212*
Klingenberg, Louise Sophie *SEE* Klingenberg, Caroline Friedrike Amalie Eggerding
Klingenberg, Marie; America, 1891 *7420.1 p363*
Klingenberg, Wilhelm; America, 1852 *7420.1 p91*
  With family
Klingenberg, Wilhelm; America, 1864 *7420.1 p224*
  With family
Klinger, Ernst Ludwig; America, 1866 *2526.43 p150*
Klinger, Georg *SEE* Klinger, Johann Georg
Klinger, Johann Friedrich; Iowa, 1883 *2526.42 p121*
  Brother: Johannes
Klinger, Johann Georg; America, 1885 *2526.43 p225*
  Wife: Sophie
  Daughter: Sophie
  Son: Georg
Klinger, Johannes *SEE* Klinger, Johann Friedrich
Klinger, Margarethe; America, 1855 *2526.43 p160*
Klinger, Peter; America, 1841 *2526.42 p115*
  With wife & 3 children
Klinger, Sophie *SEE* Klinger, Johann Georg
Klinger, Sophie *SEE* Klinger, Johann Georg
Klinger, Wilhelm; America, 1893 *2526.43 p150*
Klinglemiller, Wolfgang; Illinois, 1854 *6079.1 p7*
Klingmann, Steffen; New York, 1860 *358.56 p5*
Klink, Johann Peter; Syracuse, NY, 1860 *5475.1 p497*
Klink, Karl 24; America, 1857 *5475.1 p497*
Klink, Peter 28; America, 1857 *5475.1 p497*
Klinke, Anna 10 *SEE* Klinke, Magrethe
Klinke, Josef 4 *SEE* Klinke, Magrethe
Klinke, Karl 8 *SEE* Klinke, Magrethe
Klinke, Magrethe 36; New York, 1900 *5475.1 p487*
  Daughter: Anna 10
  Son: Karl 8
  Son: Josef 4
  Son: Wilhelm 6
Klinke, Wilhelm 6 *SEE* Klinke, Magrethe
Klinkner, Anna Maria *SEE* Klinkner, Wilhelm
Klinkner, Barbara *SEE* Klinkner, Wilhelm
Klinkner, Katharina *SEE* Klinkner, Wilhelm
Klinkner, Katharina Lehnhoff 44 *SEE* Klinkner, Wilhelm
Klinkner, Margarethe *SEE* Klinkner, Wilhelm
Klinkner, Margarethe; America, 1872 *5475.1 p289*
  Child: Barbara
  Child: Margaretha
  Child: Johann
Klinkner, Maria *SEE* Klinkner, Wilhelm
Klinkner, Mathias *SEE* Klinkner, Wilhelm
Klinkner, Nikolaus *SEE* Klinkner, Wilhelm
Klinkner, Susanna; America, 1874 *5475.1 p331*
  Daughter: Maria
  Daughter: Susanna
Klinkner, Wilhelm 44; America, 1872 *5475.1 p271*
  Wife: Katharina Lehnhoff 44
  Daughter: Katharina
  Daughter: Barbara

FOR A COMPLETE EXPLANATION OF ENTRY, SEE "HOW TO READ A CITATION" SECTION

*Daughter:*Margarethe
With daughter
*Daughter:*Anna Maria
*Son:*Nikolaus
*Son:*Mathias
*Daughter:*Maria
Klinksieck, Ludwig August; Port uncertain, 1855 ***7420.1*** *p137*
Klinsbrook, Leonhart; Ohio, 1809-1852 ***4511.35*** *p27*
Klinshrode, Leonhart; Ohio, 1809-1852 ***4511.35*** *p27*
Klinsmith, Lawrence; America, 1728 ***1220.12*** *p475*
Klintberg, L.; New York, NY, 1845 ***6412.40*** *p149*
Klintberg, N.F.; New York, NY, 1847 ***6412.40*** *p149*
Klintbom, Anna Sophia Christina Hogvall *SEE* Klintbom, Olof Abraham Edvard
Klintbom, Olof Abraham Edvard; North America, 1886 ***6410.15*** *p106*
*Wife:*Anna Sophia Christina Hogvall
*Son:*Olof Anton Rudolf
Klintbom, Olof Anton Rudolf *SEE* Klintbom, Olof Abraham Edvard
Klipfel, Anthony; Ohio, 1809-1852 ***4511.35*** *p27*
Klipful, Anthony; Ohio, 1809-1852 ***4511.35*** *p27*
Klisewicz, Rozalia 18; New York, NY, 1911 ***6533.11*** *p10*
Klobasa, Antonin *SEE* Klobasa, Antonin
Klobasa, Antonin; Wisconsin, 1855 ***2853.20*** *p22*
*Father:*Antonin
Klock, Johann; America, 1852 ***5475.1*** *p480*
Klockebring, August; America, 1852 ***7420.1*** *p91*
Klockenbring, Carl; America, 1854 ***7420.1*** *p123*
Klockner, Peter; New Jersey, 1773-1774 ***927.31*** *p2*
Klocks, Chris; Louisiana, 1874-1875 ***4981.45*** *p29*
Kloeckner, A. Maria *SEE* Kloeckner, Johann
Kloeckner, Johann; Washington, 1855 ***5475.1*** *p255*
*Sister:*A. Maria
*Sister:*Katharina
Kloeckner, Katharina *SEE* Kloeckner, Johann
Klofac, V.; Chicago, 1909 ***2853.20*** *p410*
Klofandova, Katerina; Wisconsin, 1852 ***2853.20*** *p303*
With 2 sons
Klopfel, Michael; Ohio, 1809-1852 ***4511.35*** *p27*
Klopfenstein, Abraham; Ohio, 1809-1852 ***4511.35*** *p27*
Klopfenstein, Christian; Ohio, 1809-1852 ***4511.35*** *p27*
Klopfenstein, Jacob; Ohio, 1809-1852 ***4511.35*** *p27*
Klopfenstein, John; Ohio, 1809-1852 ***4511.35*** *p27*
Klopfinstein, Christian; Ohio, 1809-1852 ***4511.35*** *p27*
Klopper, Christine; America, 1856 ***7420.1*** *p148*
Klopper, Friedrich; America, 1854 ***7420.1*** *p123*
*Sister:*Philippine
With wife
Klopper, Philippine *SEE* Klopper, Friedrich
Klorenski, Mr.; Detroit, 1930 ***1640.60*** *p82*
Klose, Joseph Anthony; Detroit, 1930 ***1640.60*** *p82*
Klose, Victor; New York, 1908 ***5475.1*** *p191*
Klosen, Josef 24; America, 1857 ***5475.1*** *p290*
Klosen, Nikolaus 17; America, 1857 ***5475.1*** *p290*
Kloss, Friedrich; Wisconsin, 1904 ***6795.8*** *p175*
Kloss, Petr; Kansas, 1887 ***2853.20*** *p239*
Klossowksi, Wilhelm; Wisconsin, 1876 ***6795.8*** *p92*
Kloster, Catherine 35; Missouri, 1847 ***778.6*** *p189*
Kloster, Marie 3; Missouri, 1847 ***778.6*** *p189*
Kloster, Marie 12; Missouri, 1847 ***778.6*** *p189*
Kloster, Nicolas 2; Missouri, 1847 ***778.6*** *p189*
Kloster, Pierre 40; Missouri, 1847 ***778.6*** *p189*
Klostermann, Ferdinand Gustav August; America, 1889 ***7420.1*** *p400*
Klostermann, John. Fr. 48; New York, NY, 1864 ***8425.62*** *p196*
Klostermann, Marie Eleonore 19; New York, NY, 1864 ***8425.62*** *p196*
Klostermann, Marie Elisabeth 9; New York, NY, 1864 ***8425.62*** *p196*
Kloth, Julius; Wisconsin, 1874 ***6795.8*** *p25*
Klots, Henry 18; New Orleans, 1846 ***778.6*** *p189*
Klotz, Estelle 22; Port uncertain, 1847 ***778.6*** *p189*
Klotz, Frederick; Ohio, 1809-1852 ***4511.35*** *p27*
Klotz, Genofeva 18; Valdivia, Chile, 1852 ***1192.4*** *p53*
Klotz, Jos; Valdivia, Chile, 1852 ***1192.4*** *p53*
Klotz, Maria 19; Port uncertain, 1847 ***778.6*** *p189*
Klotz, Martin; Valdivia, Chile, 1850 ***1192.4*** *p49*
Kloucek, Ladislav; Wisconsin, 1900 ***2853.20*** *p323*
Klouss, William; North Carolina, 1855 ***1088.45*** *p17*
Klower, Elisabeth; Iowa, 1924 ***8023.44*** *p372*
Klozer, August; Wisconsin, 1908 ***1822.55*** *p10*
Klucak, Hynek V.; New York, NY, 1890 ***2853.20*** *p521*
Kluck, George 22; Mississippi, 1845 ***778.6*** *p189*
Klug, . . .; West Virginia, 1850-1860 ***1132.30*** *p149*
Kluge, Mary; Philadelphia, 1856 ***8513.31*** *p308*
Kluizer, Ana 32; America, 1847 ***778.6*** *p189*
Kluizer, Christina 65; America, 1847 ***778.6*** *p189*
Kluizer, Franz 22; America, 1847 ***778.6*** *p189*
Kluizer, Jean 28; America, 1847 ***778.6*** *p189*
Kluizer, Jean Georg 65; America, 1847 ***778.6*** *p189*
Kluizer, Magd. 24; America, 1847 ***778.6*** *p189*
Klumb, Gabriel 26; Mississippi, 1847 ***778.6*** *p189*
Klumb, Joseph 66; Mississippi, 1847 ***778.6*** *p190*
Klumker, Luilf; Colorado, 1894 ***1029.59*** *p50*
Klumker, Luilf; Nebraska, 1883 ***1029.59*** *p50*
Klumph, William 32; Ontario, 1871 ***1823.17*** *p86*
Klunder, Carl August; America, 1855 ***7420.1*** *p137*
Kluny, Bryan 25; Ontario, 1871 ***1823.21*** *p193*
Klunzinger, Eva Rosine; America, 1867 ***179.55*** *p19*
Klunzinger, Frederike Rosine; America, 1867 ***179.55*** *p19*
Klunzinger, Rosine; America, 1867 ***179.55*** *p19*
Kluppel, Adolph; Valdivia, Chile, 1852 ***1192.4*** *p55*
Klutz, Marie 17; Ontario, 1871 ***1823.21*** *p193*
Kluzinska, Maryanna; Detroit, 1929 ***1640.55*** *p115*
Kmoch, . . .; Pennsylvania, 1750-1799 ***2853.20*** *p17*
Knaack, H.; Venezuela, 1843 ***3899.5*** *p547*
Knaack, Wilhelmine; Wisconsin, 1873 ***6795.8*** *p16*
Knab, Mrs. 32; America, 1841 ***778.6*** *p190*
Knack, . . . 4; Texas, 1913 ***8425.16*** *p31*
Knack, . . . 8; Texas, 1913 ***8425.16*** *p31*
Knack, Heinrich 18; Texas, 1913 ***8425.16*** *p31*
Knack, Maria Elisabeth 45; Texas, 1913 ***8425.16*** *p31*
Knack, Peter 42; Texas, 1913 ***8425.16*** *p31*
Knacke, Catharine Marie Dorothea; America, 1868 ***7420.1*** *p273*
Knacke, Conrad; America, 1868 ***7420.1*** *p273*
Knafft, Jacob; Nova Scotia, 1784 ***7105*** *p24*
Knafton, Francis; America, 1739 ***1220.12*** *p475*
Knafts, Jacob; Nova Scotia, 1784 ***7105*** *p24*
Knaggs, George 48; Ontario, 1871 ***1823.17*** *p86*
Knakal, Alois; Kansas, 1866-1910 ***2853.20*** *p201*
Knake, Carl Heinrich Wilhelm; America, 1876 ***7420.1*** *p307*
Knap, Thomas; America, 1721 ***1220.12*** *p475*
Knap, Thomas, Jr.; America, 1739 ***1220.12*** *p475*
Knapp, Anna Maria; America, 1872 ***5475.1*** *p320*
Knapp, Chas 33; Ontario, 1871 ***1823.21*** *p193*
Knapp, Christoph 20; America, 1847 ***778.6*** *p190*
Knapp, Dorothea *SEE* Knapp, Dorothea Forster
Knapp, Dorothea 32; Brazil, 1865 ***5475.1*** *p506*
*Son:*Karl
*Daughter:*Dorothea
*Son:*Wilhelm
Knapp, Elisabeth; America, 1856 ***5475.1*** *p562*
Knapp, Elisabeth Haubert 29 *SEE* Knapp, Johann
Knapp, Elisabeth 31; America, 1847 ***778.6*** *p190*
Knapp, Elizabeth 6 months; America, 1847 ***778.6*** *p190*
Knapp, Emilie 5; New York, NY, 1893 ***1883.7*** *p40*
Knapp, Emilie 5; New York, NY, 1893 ***1883.7*** *p47*
Knapp, Georg 25; America, 1835 ***2526.43*** *p173*
Knapp, Jacob 31; America, 1847 ***778.6*** *p190*
Knapp, Jakob; America, 1885 ***2526.43*** *p222*
Knapp, Jakob 1 *SEE* Knapp, Johann
Knapp, James; America, 1754 ***1220.12*** *p475*
Knapp, Johann 34; America, 1855 ***5475.1*** *p270*
*Wife:*Elisabeth Haubert 29
*Son:*Thielmann 4
*Son:*Jakob 1 months
*Daughter:*Maria 8
Knapp, John; America, 1755 ***1220.12*** *p475*
Knapp, John; America, 1757 ***1220.12*** *p475*
Knapp, Karl *SEE* Knapp, Dorothea Forster
Knapp, Kath. 39; America, 1857 ***5475.1*** *p279*
*Son:*Johann 12
Knapp, Louisa 36; Michigan, 1880 ***4491.30*** *p18*
Knapp, Margarethe 38; America, 1873 ***5475.1*** *p509*
Knapp, Margarethe 44; Brazil, 1857 ***5475.1*** *p291*
Knapp, Maria 8 *SEE* Knapp, Johann
Knapp, Michael 30; New York, NY, 1893 ***1883.7*** *p40*
Knapp, Michael 30; New York, NY, 1893 ***1883.7*** *p47*
Knapp, Nikolaus 7; America, 1857 ***5475.1*** *p279*
Knapp, Nikolaus; Chicago, 1881 ***5475.1*** *p320*
Knapp, Ottilie 26; New York, NY, 1893 ***1883.7*** *p40*
Knapp, Ottilie 26; New York, NY, 1893 ***1883.7*** *p47*
Knapp, Peter Josef; America, 1857 ***5475.1*** *p509*
Knapp, Philippine 2; America, 1847 ***778.6*** *p190*
Knapp, Rudolph; Died enroute, 1893 ***1883.7*** *p40*
Knapp, Rudolph; Died enroute, 1893 ***1883.7*** *p47*
Knapp, Thielmann 4 *SEE* Knapp, Johann
Knapp, Thomas; Virginia, 1750 ***1220.12*** *p475*
Knapp, Wilhelm *SEE* Knapp, Dorothea Forster
Knappwurst, Friederike Elise Dorette; Chicago, 1856 ***7420.1*** *p149*
Knapton, Robert; America, 1754 ***1220.12*** *p475*
Knapton, Thomas 58; Ontario, 1871 ***1823.21*** *p193*
Knapwurst, Ferdinand; America, 1855 ***7420.1*** *p137*
Knash, Richard; America, 1741 ***1220.12*** *p575*
Knatchbull-Huggeson, R. A. 38; Ontario, 1871 ***1823.21*** *p193*
Knatzer, Ignatz; New York, 1859 ***358.56*** *p100*
Knauber, Heinr. Jak.; America, 1863 ***5475.1*** *p45*
Knauer, Anna Sibilla; America, 1868 ***7919.3*** *p530*
Knauer, Bernhard Louis Julius; America, 1867 ***7919.3*** *p532*
Knauer, Ferdinand; America, 1849 ***5475.1*** *p477*
Knauer, Theodor 19; America, 1849 ***5475.1*** *p477*
Knauf, Justus; Valdivia, Chile, 1852 ***1192.4*** *p55*
Knauf, Maria Anna; America, 1872 ***5475.1*** *p205*
Knauss, Heinrich Albert Gottfried; America, 1884 ***179.55*** *p19*
Knecht, Edward 14; Halifax, N.S., 1902 ***1860.4*** *p42*
Knecht, Emanuel 18; Halifax, N.S., 1902 ***1860.4*** *p42*
Knecht, Ferdinand 29; Louisiana, 1848 ***778.6*** *p190*
Knecht, Heinrich 14; Halifax, N.S., 1902 ***1860.4*** *p42*
Knecht, John; Missouri, 1892 ***3276.1*** *p2*
Knecht, Louis 26; New York, NY, 1894 ***6512.1*** *p232*
Knecht, Lydia 40; Halifax, N.S., 1902 ***1860.4*** *p42*
Knecht, Martha 16; Halifax, N.S., 1902 ***1860.4*** *p42*
Knecht, Simon 20; Halifax, N.S., 1902 ***1860.4*** *p42*
Knecht, Theodor 3; Halifax, N.S., 1902 ***1860.4*** *p42*
Knecht, Wilhelm 57; Halifax, N.S., 1902 ***1860.4*** *p42*
Knechtl, Frantisek; Cleveland, OH, 1852 ***2853.20*** *p475*
Kneebone, Joseph; Barbados, 1684 ***1220.12*** *p475*
Kneebone, Robert; America, 1753 ***1220.12*** *p475*
Knees, Wilhelm; America, 1853 ***7420.1*** *p107*
Kneib, Frederick; Louisiana, 1841-1844 ***4981.45*** *p210*
Kneip, Ferdinand; America, 1867 ***5475.1*** *p189*
Kneip, Franz; America, 1853 ***5475.1*** *p56*
*Wife:*Magdalena Haser
*Daughter:*Gertr. Magdalena
*Son:*Valentin
*Son:*Nikolaus
Kneip, Gertr. Magdalena 15 *SEE* Kneip, Franz
Kneip, Johann Josef 28; New York, 1887 ***5475.1*** *p75*
Kneip, Magdalena Haser *SEE* Kneip, Franz
Kneip, Nikolaus 6 *SEE* Kneip, Franz
Kneip, Valentin 4 *SEE* Kneip, Franz
Kneireman, Peter; Ohio, 1809-1852 ***4511.35*** *p27*
Knejsar, Vojtech; Illinois, 1851-1910 ***2853.20*** *p471*
Kneller, William; Virginia, 1764 ***1220.12*** *p475*
Knese, Ferdinand; America, 1845 ***7420.1*** *p37*
With son 27
With son 22
With daughter 12
Knetzing, Francis; Wisconsin, 1873 ***6795.8*** *p101*
Kneubuhler, Joseph 51; New Castle, DE, 1817-1818 ***90.20*** *p152*
Kneuler, George; Nova Scotia, 1784 ***7105*** *p25*
Kneuttel, John George; Illinois, 1852 ***6079.1*** *p8*
Knickrehm, Friedrich Wilhelm Eduard; America, 1879 ***7420.1*** *p313*
Knickriem, Carl Friedrich Wilhelm *SEE* Knickriem, Carl Heinrich Christian
Knickriem, Carl Heinrich *SEE* Knickriem, Carl Heinrich Christian
Knickriem, Carl Heinrich Christian; America, 1871 ***7420.1*** *p290*
*Wife:*Caroline Sophie Ernestine Meier
*Son:*Carl Heinrich
*Daughter:*Sophie Caroline Charlotte
*Son:*Carl Friedrich Wilhelm
*Daughter:*Wilhelmine Caroline Justine
Knickriem, Caroline Sophie Ernestine Meier *SEE* Knickriem, Carl Heinrich Christian
Knickriem, Sophie Caroline Charlotte *SEE* Knickriem, Carl Heinrich Christian
Knickriem, Wilhelmine Caroline Justine *SEE* Knickriem, Carl Heinrich Christian
Kniebel, Christian; New York, 1778 ***8529.30*** *p7*
Knief, Auguste; America, 1857 ***7420.1*** *p164*
Knief, Catharine Engel Oltrogge *SEE* Knief, Georg Wilhelm
Knief, Engel Anne Sophie *SEE* Knief, Heinrich Conrad
Knief, Engel Marie Charlotte Sandmeyer *SEE* Knief, Heinrich Conrad
Knief, Engel Marie Dorothea; America, 1867 ***7420.1*** *p258*
Knief, Engel Marie Sophie; America, 1849 ***7420.1*** *p65*
Knief, Engel Marie Sophie Charlotte *SEE* Knief, Heinrich Conrad
Knief, Engel Marie Wilhelmine *SEE* Knief, Georg Wilhelm
Knief, Georg Friedrich; America, 1856 ***7420.1*** *p149*
Knief, Georg Wilhelm; America, 1855 ***7420.1*** *p138*
*Wife:*Catharine Engel Oltrogge
*Daughter:*Engel Marie Wilhelmine
With 2 daughters son & grandchild
Knief, Hans Heinrich; America, 1857 ***7420.1*** *p165*
With family
Knief, Heinrich Conrad; America, 1857 ***7420.1*** *p165*
*Wife:*Engel Marie Charlotte Sandmeyer
*Daughter:*Thrine Engel Soph.
*Daughter:*Engel Marie Sophie Charlotte
*Daughter:*Engel Anne Sophie
*Son:*Johann Heinr. Christ.

Knief, Heinrich Friedrich; America, 1868 ***7420.1*** *p273*
Knief, Johann Christoph; America, 1852 ***7420.1*** *p91*
With family
Knief, Johann Heinr. Christ. *SEE* Knief, Heinrich Conrad
Knief, Thrine Engel Soph. *SEE* Knief, Heinrich Conrad
Knieling, Louis August; America, 1868 ***7919.3*** *p533*
Knieriem, Chr.; Venezuela, 1843 ***3899.5*** *p547*
Knieriem, Katharina Eva; New Jersey, 1836-1864 ***2526.42*** *p175*
Knierim, Paul; Philadelphia, 1866 ***8513.31*** *p319*
Kniermen, Peter; Ohio, 1809-1852 ***4511.35*** *p27*
Knigel, George 17; New Orleans, 1846 ***778.6*** *p190*
Knight, Alexander; America, 1743 ***1220.12*** *p475*
Knight, Ann 23; Annapolis, MD, 1721 ***1220.12*** *p475*
Knight, Ann 64; Ontario, 1871 ***1823.21*** *p193*
Knight, Ann; Virginia, 1735 ***1220.12*** *p475*
Knight, Barnabas 52; Ontario, 1871 ***1823.21*** *p193*
Knight, Benjamin; America, 1726 ***1220.12*** *p475*
Knight, Charles; America, 1768 ***1220.12*** *p475*
Knight, Charles 39; Ontario, 1871 ***1823.21*** *p193*
Knight, Charles D.; Washington, 1888 ***2770.40*** *p26*
Knight, Christopher; America, 1685 ***1220.12*** *p475*
Knight, Deborah; Annapolis, MD, 1732 ***1220.12*** *p475*
Knight, Edward; America, 1725 ***1220.12*** *p475*
Knight, Edward; America, 1730 ***1220.12*** *p475*
Knight, Elizabeth; America, 1740 ***1220.12*** *p475*
Knight, Elizabeth; Died enroute, 1723 ***1220.12*** *p475*
Knight, Fracis 74; Ontario, 1871 ***1823.21*** *p193*
Knight, Frances Mary; Florida, 1857-1910 ***9228.50*** *p315*
Knight, Fred Albert; Colorado, 1917 ***1029.59*** *p50*
*Wife:*Isadora
*Child:*Pauline
Knight, Fred Albert; New York, NY, 1892 ***1029.59*** *p1A*
Knight, Fred Albert 42; New York, NY, 1892 ***1029.59*** *p50*
Knight, George; America, 1748 ***1220.12*** *p475*
Knight, George; America, 1754 ***1220.12*** *p475*
Knight, George; America, 1761 ***1220.12*** *p475*
Knight, George 15; Ontario, 1871 ***1823.17*** *p87*
Knight, George 26; Ontario, 1871 ***1823.17*** *p87*
Knight, Henry 50; Ontario, 1871 ***1823.17*** *p87*
Knight, Humphrey; Barbados, 1665 ***1220.12*** *p475*
Knight, Isaac; America, 1737 ***1220.12*** *p475*
Knight, Isadora *SEE* Knight, Fred Albert
Knight, James; America, 1735 ***1220.12*** *p475*
Knight, James; America, 1743 ***1220.12*** *p475*
Knight, James; America, 1770 ***1220.12*** *p475*
Knight, James; America, 1771 ***1220.12*** *p475*
Knight, James; America, 1775 ***1220.12*** *p475*
Knight, James 44; Ontario, 1871 ***1823.21*** *p193*
Knight, John; America, 1673 ***1220.12*** *p475*
Knight, John; America, 1685 ***1220.12*** *p475*
Knight, John; America, 1721 ***1220.12*** *p475*
Knight, John; America, 1732 ***1220.12*** *p475*
Knight, John; America, 1744 ***1220.12*** *p475*
Knight, John; America, 1752 ***1220.12*** *p476*
Knight, John; America, 1763 ***1220.12*** *p476*
Knight, John; America, 1765 ***1220.12*** *p476*
Knight, John; America, 1769 ***1220.12*** *p476*
Knight, John; America, 1770 ***1220.12*** *p476*
Knight, John; America, 1772 ***1220.12*** *p476*
Knight, John; America, 1773 ***1220.12*** *p476*
Knight, John; Annapolis, MD, 1731 ***1220.12*** *p475*
Knight, John; Barbados, 1663 ***1220.12*** *p475*
Knight, John; Barbados, 1679 ***1220.12*** *p475*
Knight, John; Barbados, 1683 ***1220.12*** *p475*
Knight, John; Maryland, 1728 ***1220.12*** *p475*
Knight, John; New Hampshire, 1770 ***9228.50*** *p348*
Knight, John; Portsmouth, NH, 1684 ***9228.50*** *p313*
Knight, John; Virginia, 1736 ***1220.12*** *p475*
Knight, John; Virginia, 1766 ***1220.12*** *p476*
Knight, John; Virginia, 1771 ***1220.12*** *p476*
Knight, Jonathan; America, 1734 ***1220.12*** *p476*
Knight, Jonathan; America, 1748 ***1220.12*** *p476*
Knight, Joseph; America, 1769 ***1220.12*** *p476*
Knight, Joseph; America, 1775 ***1220.12*** *p476*
Knight, Louise; Detroit, 1858-1910 ***9228.50*** *p315*
Knight, Louise Gaudion *SEE* Knight, William Edward
Knight, Mary; America, 1766 ***1220.12*** *p476*
Knight, Mary; America, 1768 ***1220.12*** *p476*
Knight, Mary; America, 1772 ***1220.12*** *p476*
Knight, Mary 22; Ontario, 1871 ***1823.21*** *p193*
Knight, Mary; Virginia, 1734 ***1220.12*** *p476*
Knight, Nicholas; Barbados, 1676 ***1220.12*** *p476*
Knight, Pauline *SEE* Knight, Fred Albert
Knight, Peter; America, 1772 ***1220.12*** *p476*
Knight, Peter; America, 1775 ***1220.12*** *p476*
Knight, Peter 37; Ontario, 1871 ***1823.17*** *p87*
Knight, Peter 41; Ontario, 1871 ***1823.17*** *p87*
Knight, Peter; Virginia, 1652 ***6254.4*** *p243*
Knight, Philip 38; Ontario, 1871 ***1823.21*** *p193*
Knight, Richard; Barbados, 1679 ***1220.12*** *p476*
Knight, Richard; New England, 1650-1706 ***9228.50*** *p300*
Knight, Robert; Barbados, 1670 ***1220.12*** *p476*
Knight, Robert 80; Ontario, 1871 ***1823.17*** *p87*
Knight, Robt. 26; North Carolina, 1774 ***1422.10*** *p54*
Knight, Rose; Annapolis, MD, 1720 ***1220.12*** *p476*
Knight, Ruth; America, 1690 ***1220.12*** *p476*
Knight, Samuel; America, 1685 ***1220.12*** *p476*
Knight, Sarah; Annapolis, MD, 1725 ***1220.12*** *p476*
Knight, Thomas; America, 1736 ***1220.12*** *p476*
Knight, Thomas; America, 1752 ***1220.12*** *p476*
Knight, Thomas; America, 1753 ***1220.12*** *p476*
Knight, Thomas; America, 1761 ***1220.12*** *p476*
Knight, Thomas; America, 1775 ***1220.12*** *p476*
Knight, Thomas; Barbados or Jamaica, 1687 ***1220.12*** *p476*
Knight, Thomas 30; Colorado, 1901 ***1029.59*** *p50*
Knight, Thomas 43; Ontario, 1871 ***1823.21*** *p193*
Knight, Thomas H.; Colorado, 1901 ***1029.59*** *p50*
Knight, Walter; America, 1754 ***1220.12*** *p476*
Knight, Walter; America, 1768 ***1220.12*** *p476*
Knight, William; America, 1726 ***1220.12*** *p476*
Knight, William; America, 1750 ***1220.12*** *p476*
Knight, William; America, 1763 ***1220.12*** *p476*
Knight, William; America, 1768 ***1220.12*** *p477*
Knight, William; Annapolis, MD, 1722 ***1220.12*** *p476*
Knight, William; Barbados, 1669 ***1220.12*** *p476*
Knight, William 48; Ontario, 1871 ***1823.17*** *p87*
Knight, William; Virginia, 1738 ***1220.12*** *p476*
Knight, William Edward; Detroit, 1910 ***9228.50*** *p315*
*Wife:*Louise Gaudion
Knight, William John; Detroit, 1857-1910 ***9228.50*** *p315*
Knight, Wm 40; Ontario, 1871 ***1823.21*** *p193*
Knight, Wm.; New England, 1635 ***9228.50*** *p313*
Knighting, Louisa 18; Ontario, 1871 ***1823.21*** *p193*
Knightley, Thomas; America, 1759 ***1220.12*** *p477*
Knightley, Walter; Barbados or Jamaica, 1683 ***1220.12*** *p477*
Knightly, Winifred; Pennsylvania, 1905-1946 ***9228.50*** *p399*
Knighton, William; America, 1775 ***1220.12*** *p477*
Knights, Emanuel; America, 1764 ***1220.12*** *p477*
Knights, James; America, 1764 ***1220.12*** *p477*
Knights, Sarah; America, 1761 ***1220.12*** *p477*
Knights, Thomas; America, 1757 ***1220.12*** *p477*
Kniling, France 24; America, 1847 ***778.6*** *p190*
Kniling, Lorenet 29; America, 1847 ***778.6*** *p190*
Knipe, Samuel; America, 1699 ***1220.12*** *p478*
Knipper, Adolf; New Orleans, 1872 ***5475.1*** *p14*
Knipping, Hermann Ferdinand August; America, 1845 ***7420.1*** *p37*
Knipping, Karl Heinrich; America, 1845 ***7420.1*** *p37*
Knipping, Louis Emil August; America, 1853 ***7420.1*** *p107*
Knisley, John 39; Ontario, 1871 ***1823.17*** *p87*
Knitt, Johann Friedrich; Wisconsin, 1874 ***6795.8*** *p90*
Kniveton, John; America, 1738 ***1220.12*** *p477*
Kniviston, John; America, 1738 ***1220.12*** *p477*
Knneppel, Wilh.; Wisconsin, 1898 ***6795.8*** *p226*
Knobe, Barbara; America, 1879 ***5475.1*** *p175*
Knoblauch, G.; New York, 1860 ***358.56*** *p5*
Knobloch, Frederick; Ohio, 1809-1852 ***4511.35*** *p27*
Knobloch, George; Ohio, 1809-1852 ***4511.35*** *p27*
Knobloch, Henry; Ohio, 1809-1852 ***4511.35*** *p27*
Knobloch, Jacob; Ohio, 1809-1852 ***4511.35*** *p27*
Knobloch, Sophie 24; Valdivia, Chile, 1852 ***1192.4*** *p53*
Knoblock, Frederick; Ohio, 1809-1852 ***4511.35*** *p27*
Knoche, Caroline Friede. Charl. *SEE* Knoche, Caroline Wilhelmine Henriette Eickmeier
Knoche, Caroline Sophie Charlotte *SEE* Knoche, Caroline Wilhelmine Henriette Eickmeier
Knoche, Caroline Wilhelmine Henriette; America, 1866 ***7420.1*** *p244*
*Daughter:*Wilhelmine Caroline Sophie Charlotte
*Daughter:*Caroline Friede. Charl.
*Daughter:*Louise Marie Charlotte
*Daughter:*Caroline Sophie Charlotte
*Son:*Ernst Aug. Ferd.
Knoche, Engel Marie Dorothea; America, 1865 ***7420.1*** *p232*
*Son:*Hans Heinrich Otto
Knoche, Ernst Aug. Ferd. *SEE* Knoche, Caroline Wilhelmine Henriette Eickmeier
Knoche, Hans Heinrich Christoph; America, 1855 ***7420.1*** *p138*
Knoche, Hans Heinrich Otto *SEE* Knoche, Engel Marie Dorothea
Knoche, Louise Marie Charlotte *SEE* Knoche, Caroline Wilhelmine Henriette Eickmeier
Knoche, Wilhelmine Caroline Sophie Charlotte *SEE* Knoche, Caroline Wilhelmine Henriette Eickmeier
Knochenhauer, Carl; Valdivia, Chile, 1850 ***1192.4*** *p49*
Knock, Thomas; America, 1745 ***1220.12*** *p477*
Knocky, Sarah; America, 1750 ***1220.12*** *p477*
Knodel, Christian 16; New York, NY, 1874 ***6954.7*** *p37*
Knodel, Christina 36; New York, NY, 1874 ***6954.7*** *p37*
Knodel, Elisabeth 9 months; New York, NY, 1874 ***6954.7*** *p37*
Knodel, Friedrich 18; New York, NY, 1874 ***6954.7*** *p37*
Knodel, Friedrich 41; New York, NY, 1874 ***6954.7*** *p37*
Knodel, Jacob 10; New York, NY, 1874 ***6954.7*** *p37*
Knodel, Johannes 13; New York, NY, 1874 ***6954.7*** *p37*
Knodt, Carl Hermann Wilhelm; Port uncertain, 1887 ***7420.1*** *p354*
Knoebel, Christian; New York, 1778 ***8529.30*** *p7*
Knoechel, Herman; Ohio, 1840-1897 ***8365.35*** *p16*
Knoell, Balthasar; Virginia, 1831 ***152.20*** *p64*
Knoepfli, Jean 17; New Orleans, 1848 ***778.6*** *p190*
Knoepfli, Jean 50; New Orleans, 1848 ***778.6*** *p190*
Knoepp, Matthaeus; Pennsylvania, 1848 ***170.15*** *p32*
With wife & 2 children
Knoepp, Matthaeus 48; Pennsylvania, 1848 ***170.15*** *p32*
With wife
With child 6
With child 9
Knolke, Johann Heinrich Conrad; America, 1861 ***7420.1*** *p206*
Knolke, Sophie; America, 1860 ***7420.1*** *p195*
Knolke, Sophie Caroline; America, 1865 ***7420.1*** *p232*
Knolke, Stats Heinrich Anton; America, 1835 ***7420.1*** *p9*
Knoll, Ludwig; America, 1882 ***2526.42*** *p109*
Knoll, Martin; Ohio, 1809-1852 ***4511.35*** *p27*
Knoll, Philipp; America, 1882 ***2526.42*** *p109*
Knolle, Engel Sophie Reese *SEE* Knolle, Hans Heinrich
Knolle, Hans Heinrich; America, 1854 ***7420.1*** *p123*
*Wife:*Engel Sophie Reese
*Son:*Hans Heinrich Christoph
*Daughter:*Trine Engel Sophie
Knolle, Hans Heinrich Christoph *SEE* Knolle, Hans Heinrich
Knolle, Triene Sophia Charlotte; America, 1857 ***7420.1*** *p165*
Knolle, Trine Engel Sophie *SEE* Knolle, Hans Heinrich
Knolton, Marvin 30; Ontario, 1871 ***1823.21*** *p193*
Knoop, Georg Wilhelm Friedrich; America, 1883 ***7420.1*** *p337*
Knoop, Karl Wilhelm Gottfried; Indianapolis, 1903 ***7420.1*** *p379*
Knoop, Marga; Valdivia, Chile, 1851 ***1192.4*** *p50*
Knoop, Otto; Valdivia, Chile, 1851 ***1192.4*** *p50*
Knope, George; America, 1769 ***1220.12*** *p477*
Knope, Hannah; America, 1769 ***1220.12*** *p477*
Knopfler, Michel 32; Mississippi, 1847 ***778.6*** *p190*
Knoph, Elisabeth 31; America, 1847 ***778.6*** *p190*
Knoph, Jacob 31; America, 1847 ***778.6*** *p190*
Knoph, Philippine 2; America, 1847 ***778.6*** *p190*
Knopp, Jacob; Ohio, 1809-1852 ***4511.35*** *p27*
Knorr, Fredrieka Them *SEE* Knorr, Theodore
Knorr, Joseph 19; New Orleans, 1848 ***778.6*** *p190*
Knorr, Theodore; Philadelphia, 1854 ***8513.31*** *p320*
*Wife:*Fredrieka Them
Knorst, Barbara 30; Brazil, 1857 ***5475.1*** *p368*
Knorst, Franz *SEE* Knorst, Jakob
Knorst, Jakob *SEE* Knorst, Jakob
Knorst, Jakob; America, 1868 ***5475.1*** *p378*
*Wife:*Maria Hoff
*Son:*Peter
*Daughter:*K. Anna
*Son:*Johann
*Son:*Jakob
*Son:*Mathias
*Son:*Franz
*Daughter:*Katharina
Knorst, Johann *SEE* Knorst, Jakob
Knorst, Johann 27; America, 1843 ***5475.1*** *p280*
Knorst, K. Anna *SEE* Knorst, Jakob
Knorst, Katharina *SEE* Knorst, Jakob
Knorst, Maria Hoff *SEE* Knorst, Jakob
Knorst, Mathias *SEE* Knorst, Jakob
Knorst, Peter *SEE* Knorst, Jakob
Knorzer, Charlotte; America, 1833 ***5475.1*** *p118*
Knos, John; North Carolina, 1850 ***1088.45*** *p17*
Knot, Casper Fredrick; New York, 1860 ***358.56*** *p148*
Knoth, Jacob; America, 1867 ***7919.3*** *p525*
Knoth, Wilhelmine Justine; America, 1866 ***7420.1*** *p248*
Knotsmell, Elizabeth; America, 1757 ***1220.12*** *p477*
Knott, Andrew; America, 1773 ***1220.12*** *p477*
Knott, George Wilmott; America, 1774 ***1220.12*** *p477*
Knott, James; America, 1765 ***1220.12*** *p477*
Knott, James 37; Ontario, 1871 ***1823.21*** *p193*
Knott, John; America, 1683 ***1220.12*** *p477*
Knott, John; America, 1771 ***1220.12*** *p477*
Knott, John; Maryland, 1740 ***1220.12*** *p477*
Knott, Mary; America, 1756 ***1220.12*** *p477*
Knott, Thomas; America, 1756 ***1220.12*** *p477*
Knott, William 40; Ontario, 1871 ***1823.21*** *p193*
Knottge, Otto Carl Anastasius Victor; Port uncertain, 1873 ***7420.1*** *p300*

Know, John, Jr.; America, 1765 *1220.12 p477*
Knowland, Catherine; America, 1757 *1220.12 p585*
Knowland, Eleanor; America, 1774 *1220.12 p585*
Knowland, James; America, 1764 *1220.12 p585*
Knowland, James; Virginia, 1750 *1220.12 p585*
Knowland, Katherine; America, 1770 *1220.12 p585*
Knowland, William; America, 1762 *1220.12 p585*
Knowler, Shelwin; America, 1727 *1220.12 p477*
Knowles, Alice; America, 1763 *1220.12 p477*
Knowles, Clement; America, 1772 *1220.12 p477*
Knowles, Daniel 36; Ontario, 1871 *1823.21 p193*
Knowles, Eliza N. 39; Ontario, 1871 *1823.17 p87*
Knowles, Elizabeth; America, 1745 *1220.12 p477*
Knowles, Elizabeth; Jamaica, 1717 *1220.12 p477*
Knowles, Henry 34; Ontario, 1871 *1823.21 p193*
Knowles, Herbert; Missouri, 1880 *3276.1 p3*
Knowles, James; Marston's Wharf, 1782 *8529.30 p13*
Knowles, John; America, 1733 *1220.12 p477*
Knowles, John 50; Ontario, 1871 *1823.21 p193*
Knowles, Joseph; America, 1773 *1220.12 p477*
Knowles, Ralph Christopher; Miami, 1935 *4984.12 p39*
Knowles, Stephen; Portsmouth, NH, 1716-1717 *9228.50 p195*
Knowles, Thomas; America, 1771 *1220.12 p477*
Knowles, Thomas; Barbados or Jamaica, 1688 *1220.12 p477*
Knowles, William; America, 1728 *1220.12 p478*
Knowles, William; Barbados, 1683 *1220.12 p478*
Knowles, William K. 21; Indiana, 1882-1884 *9076.20 p71*
Knowling, John; Virginia, 1750 *1220.12 p478*
Knowling, Mary; America, 1764 *1220.12 p478*
Knowls, Samuel; America, 1765 *1220.12 p477*
Knows, Andrew 27; New York, NY, 1867 *7710.1 p157*
Knox, Mrs. 19; America, 1840 *778.6 p190*
Knox, Alexander 88; Ontario, 1871 *1823.21 p193*
Knox, Andrew; Boston, 1737 *1642 p26*
Knox, Charles; Philadelphia, 1778 *8529.30 p7A*
Knox, Harvey 50; Ontario, 1871 *1823.17 p87*
Knox, Mathew; Ohio, 1809-1852 *4511.35 p27*
Knox, Robert 34; Ontario, 1871 *1823.21 p193*
Knox, Sarah; America, 1750 *1220.12 p478*
Knox, Tobias; Ohio, 1809-1852 *4511.35 p27*
Knox, William 34; New York, NY, 1825 *6178.50 p78*
Knox, William 27; Ontario, 1871 *1823.17 p87*
Knox, William 38; Ontario, 1871 *1823.21 p193*
Knox, William 70; Ontario, 1871 *1823.21 p193*
Kns, Karl 24; Halifax, N.S., 1902 *1860.4 p40*
Kns, Mathilde 22; Halifax, N.S., 1902 *1860.4 p40*
Knudsen, Hans Jorgen; Colorado, 1873 *1029.59 p50*
Knudson, Anders; Colorado, 1893 *1029.59 p50*
Knudson, Anders; Colorado, 1893 *1029.59 p51*
Knudson, Martin; Colorado, 1893 *1029.59 p51*
Knueppel, Wilh.; Wisconsin, 1898 *6795.8 p226*
Knuth, Simon 31; New Orleans, 1847 *778.6 p190*
Knutson, Hans; America, 1767 *1220.12 p478*
Knutson, Nels; Illinois, 1853-1861 *4487.25 p62*
Knutson, Ole; Iowa, 1869 *1211.15 p15*
Knutson, Oscar; Washington, 1884 *2770.40 p192*
Knutson, Sigvald Andreas; Oregon, 1941 *9157.47 p2*
Knutsson, W.; New York, NY, 1843 *6412.40 p147*
Knuttel, Sylvester; Kansas, 1885-1887 *1029.59 p51*
Knuttel, Sylvester; Kansas, 1887 *1029.59 p51*
Knuz, Louise 21; Halifax, N.S., 1902 *1860.4 p41*
Knype, Samuel; America, 1699 *1220.12 p478*
Kob, Anna Maria Weynard 54 *SEE* Kob, Michel
Kob, Elisabeth *SEE* Kob, Michel
Kob, Johann *SEE* Kob, Michel
Kob, Katharina *SEE* Kob, Michel
Kob, Katharina 32; America, 1857 *5475.1 p548*
Kob, Michel *SEE* Kob, Michel
Kob, Michel 56; America, 1857 *5475.1 p548*
 Wife:Anna Maria Weynand 54
 Son:Johann
 Son:Michel
 Daughter:Katharina
 Daughter:Elisabeth
Kobel, Vitus Martin Blasius; America, 1868 *7420.1 p273*
Koberg, Heinrich Wilhelm Gottlieb; America, 1858 *7420.1 p179*
Kobiski, Johann Julius; Wisconsin, 1877 *6795.8 p216*
Koble, Jakob; Pennsylvania, 1888 *5475.1 p424*
Koble, Karl 17; America, 1890 *5475.1 p424*
Kobler, Jakob; America, 1831 *2526.43 p173*
 With 3 children
Kobloth, Xavier 36; New Orleans, 1841 *778.6 p190*
Kobs, Ottilie Emily; Wisconsin, 1898 *6795.8 p30*
Kobus, Nicolas 23; America, 1844 *778.6 p190*
Kobusz, Joseph 27; New York, NY, 1920 *930.50 p48*
Kobyliniak, Karol 33; New York, NY, 1911 *6533.11 p10*
Kocar, Frantisek; Wisconsin, 1856 *2853.20 p345*
Kocarnik, Vaclav; New York, NY, 1845-1866 *2853.20 p149*

Kocarnik, Vaclav; Westmoreland Co., PA, 1874 *2853.20 p430*
Kocer, Jan; South Dakota, 1871-1910 *2853.20 p247*
Koch, A. Barbara 35; America, 1868 *5475.1 p312*
Koch, Adam; America, 1866 *2526.43 p150*
Koch, Adam; America, 1882 *2526.43 p150*
Koch, Adam 6 *SEE* Koch, Ernst
Koch, Adam; Ohio, 1844 *2763.1 p8*
Koch, Amalie 2; Portland, ME, 1906 *970.38 p78*
Koch, Anna *SEE* Koch, Ernst
Koch, Anna Elisabeth 47; America, 1860 *2526.43 p196*
Koch, Anna Katharina; America, 1853 *2526.43 p150*
Koch, Anna Maria *SEE* Koch, Johann
Koch, Anna Maria *SEE* Koch, Johann
Koch, Anton; America, 1851 *7420.1 p81*
 With wife & 5 children
Koch, Arnold Wilhelm; America, 1861 *7420.1 p206*
Koch, Balthasar; America, 1882 *2526.43 p204*
Koch, Barbara *SEE* Koch, Johann
Koch, Barbara *SEE* Koch, Johann
Koch, Carl 25; Mississippi, 1847 *778.6 p190*
Koch, Carl; Port uncertain, 1854 *7420.1 p123*
Koch, Carl Ernst Friedrich Wilhelm *SEE* Koch, Ernst
Koch, Carl Friedrich; America, 1850 *7420.1 p72*
Koch, Carl Heiinrich Wilhelm; America, 1867 *7420.1 p258*
Koch, Carl Theodor; America, 1849 *7420.1 p65*
Koch, Caroline; Port uncertain, 1854 *7420.1 p123*
Koch, Caroline Wilhelmine; America, 1867 *7919.3 p527*
Koch, Catharine; Philadelphia, 1874 *7420.1 p303*
Koch, Ch.; New York, 1859 *358.56 p99*
Koch, Christi.n 56; America, 1847 *778.6 p190*
Koch, Christoph; America, 1847 *2526.43 p150*
 With wife
 Son:Philipp
Koch, Elisabeth *SEE* Koch, Johann
Koch, Elisabeth Katharina Trumpfheller *SEE* Koch, Jakob
Koch, Elise; Massachusetts, 1854 *8513.31 p309*
Koch, Elise 22; Valdivia, Chile, 1852 *1192.4 p53*
Koch, Emilie 6 months; Portland, ME, 1906 *970.38 p78*
Koch, Ernestine; America, 1867 *7919.3 p534*
Koch, Ernst; America, 1871 *7420.1 p291*
 Daughter:Wilhelmine
 With wife
 Son:Ferdinand Ernst Adolf Ludwig
 Daughter:Anna
 Daughter:Friederike
 Son:Carl Ernst Friedrich Wilhelm
Koch, Eva 36; Portland, ME, 1906 *970.38 p78*
Koch, Ferdinand Ernst Adolf Ludwig *SEE* Koch, Ernst
Koch, Franz; America, 1880 *5475.1 p355*
 Sister:Magdalena
Koch, Frederick W.; Washington, 1884 *2770.40 p192*
Koch, Friederike *SEE* Koch, Ernst
Koch, Friedrich; America, 1851 *7420.1 p81*
 With wife 2 children & 2 stepchildren
Koch, Friedrich; America, 1867 *7420.1 p259*
 With family
Koch, Friedrich; America, 1891 *5475.1 p424*
Koch, Friedrich; Chicago, 1895 *5475.1 p426*
Koch, Friedrich; Indianapolis, 1867 *7420.1 p219*
Koch, Friedrich 53; New Orleans, 1848 *778.6 p190*
Koch, Friedrich Wilhelm; America, 1867 *7420.1 p259*
 With wife
 With daughter 3
 With son 10
 With son 6
 With daughter 13
 With son 19
Koch, Friedrich Wilhelm Hermann; America, 1859 *7420.1 p186*
Koch, Georg; America, 1866 *5475.1 p123*
Koch, Georg Adam 12 *SEE* Koch, Leonhard, I
Koch, Georg Christian; America, 1867 *7919.3 p524*
 With mother
Koch, Georg Friedrich 13 *SEE* Koch, Jakob
Koch, Georg Simon; America, 1868 *7919.3 p532*
Koch, George; New York, 1859 *358.56 p54*
Koch, Heinrich, IV; America, 1885 *2526.43 p150*
 Wife:Julie Lust
 Daughter:Margaretha
 Son:Philipp
Koch, Heinrich Gottfried Christian; Port uncertain, 1854 *7420.1 p123*
Koch, Heinrich Otto Ludwig; America, 1865 *7420.1 p232*
Koch, Heinrich Theodor; America, 1860 *7420.1 p195*
Koch, Henry; Colorado, 1886 *1029.59 p51*
Koch, Henry; New York, NY, 1872 *1029.59 p51*
Koch, Herrmann; America, 1853 *7420.1 p107*
Koch, Jacob 8; Portland, ME, 1906 *970.38 p78*
Koch, Jacob 29; Portland, ME, 1906 *970.38 p78*

Koch, Jakob; America, 1854 *2526.43 p119*
 Wife:Elisabeth Katharina Trumpfheller
 Son:Johannes
 Son:Georg Friedrich
Koch, Jean 42; New Castle, DE, 1817-1818 *90.20 p152*
Koch, Jean 47; New Orleans, 1847 *778.6 p190*
Koch, Jeinle; America, 1859 *2526.43 p150*
Koch, Johann; America, 1858 *2526.43 p186*
Koch, Johann *SEE* Koch, Johann
Koch, Johann; America, 1880 *5475.1 p187*
 Son:Johann
 Daughter:Barbara
 Daughter:Anna Maria
 Daughter:Margarethe
 Son:Nikolaus
 Son:Peter
 Daughter:Maria
Koch, Johann; America, 1883 *5475.1 p188*
 Son:Nikolaus
 Daughter:Elisabeth
 Daughter:Anna Maria
 Daughter:Margarethe
 Daughter:Barbara
Koch, Johann 43; Portland, ME, 1906 *970.38 p78*
Koch, Johann Peter; New England, 1867 *170.15 p32*
 With wife & child
Koch, Johanna Sophia 44; Galveston, TX, 1844 *3967.10 p375*
Koch, Johannes; America, 1854 *2526.43 p119*
 Wife:Katharina Dornfeld
 Son:Adam
Koch, Johannes 20 *SEE* Koch, Jakob
Koch, Johannes; Venezuela, 1843 *3899.5 p543*
Koch, Johannes; Venezuela, 1843 *3899.5 p544*
Koch, John Adam; Illinois, 1855 *6079.1 p8*
Koch, Joseph 16; New Orleans, 1847 *778.6 p190*
Koch, Joseph 47; New Orleans, 1847 *778.6 p190*
Koch, Julie Lust *SEE* Koch, Heinrich, IV
Koch, Katharina Dornfeld *SEE* Koch, Johannes
Koch, Katharina 13; America, 1854 *5475.1 p64*
Koch, Katharina; Venezuela, 1843 *3899.5 p543*
Koch, Katharina Elisabetha Grassmann 48 *SEE* Koch, Leonhard, I
Koch, Leonhard; America, 1867 *2526.43 p150*
Koch, Leonhard 16 *SEE* Koch, Leonhard, I
Koch, Leonhard, I 49; New York, 1859 *2526.43 p127*
 Wife:Katharina Elisabetha Grassmann 48
 Daughter:Maria 25
 Son:Philipp 23
 Son:Leonhard 16
 Son:Georg Adam 12
Koch, Lewis; Ohio, 1809-1852 *4511.35 p27*
Koch, Louis; Ohio, 1809-1852 *4511.35 p27*
Koch, Magdalena *SEE* Koch, Franz
Koch, Margaretha *SEE* Koch, Heinrich, IV
Koch, Margarethe; America, 1873 *5475.1 p355*
 Son:Nikolaus
Koch, Margarethe *SEE* Koch, Johann
Koch, Margarethe *SEE* Koch, Johann
Koch, Maria *SEE* Koch, Johann
Koch, Maria; America, 1882 *179.55 p19*
Koch, Maria 24; Brazil, 1864 *5475.1 p501*
Koch, Maria 25 *SEE* Koch, Leonhard, I
Koch, Maria Anna; Venezuela, 1843 *3899.5 p542*
Koch, Maria Katharina; Venezuela, 1843 *3899.5 p544*
Koch, Maria Magdalena; America, 1836 *5475.1 p457*
Koch, Marie 4; Portland, ME, 1906 *970.38 p78*
Koch, Martin; Venezuela, 1843 *3899.5 p542*
Koch, Mathias; America, 1873 *5475.1 p340*
Koch, Mathias; New York, 1887 *5475.1 p355*
Koch, Michel; America, 1875 *5475.1 p341*
Koch, Michel; Chicago, 1881 *5475.1 p312*
Koch, Michel Victor; Indiana, 1881 *5475.1 p143*
Koch, Nikolaus; America, 1854 *2526.43 p127*
Koch, Nikolaus; America, 1872 *5475.1 p255*
Koch, Nikolaus; America, 1873 *5475.1 p354*
Koch, Nikolaus *SEE* Koch, Margarethe
Koch, Nikolaus; America, 1879 *5475.1 p187*
Koch, Nikolaus *SEE* Koch, Johann
Koch, Nikolaus *SEE* Koch, Johann
Koch, Nikolaus; Arkansas, 1884 *5475.1 p188*
Koch, Nikolaus Johann; America, 1880 *2526.43 p193*
Koch, Otto; New York, NY, 1909 *7420.1 p385*
 With wife & baby
Koch, Paul Albrecht; America, 1856 *7420.1 p149*
Koch, Peter *SEE* Koch, Johann
Koch, Philipp; America, 1854 *2526.43 p128*
Koch, Philipp; America, 1857 *2526.43 p128*
Koch, Philipp *SEE* Koch, Heinrich, IV
Koch, Philipp 2 *SEE* Koch, Christoph
Koch, Philipp 23 *SEE* Koch, Leonhard, I
Koch, Philipp Jakob 19; America, 1852 *2526.43 p150*
Koch, Rosina; Venezuela, 1843 *3899.5 p542*

Koch, Rosine; America, 1853 ***7420.1*** *p107*
Koch, Sophie *SEE* Koch, Wilhelm
Koch, Sophie Wilhelmine Louise; America, 1872 ***7420.1*** *p294*
Koch, Ursula; Venezuela, 1843 ***3899.5*** *p542*
Koch, Wilhelm; America, 1867 ***7919.3*** *p534*
*Sister:*Sophie
Koch, Wilhelm; America, 1867 ***7919.3*** *p534*
With 2 sisters
Koch, Wilhelm Heinrich Karl Otto; America, 1900 ***7420.1*** *p376*
Koch, Wilhelmine *SEE* Koch, Ernst
Koch, William; Nova Scotia, 1784 ***7105*** *p24*
Koch, William; Washington, 1886 ***2770.40*** *p195*
Kochanowski, Wladyslaw; Detroit, 1929 ***1640.55*** *p113*
Kochanski, John 44; New York, NY, 1920 ***930.50*** *p48*
Kochems, Hugo; North America, 1840 ***5475.1*** *p204*
Kochems, Nikolaus; America, 1873 ***5475.1*** *p554*
Kocher, Christine; Philadelphia, 1839 ***8513.31*** *p313*
Kochler, Ernst 32; New York, NY, 1883 ***8427.14*** *p44*
Kochler, Maria 32; New York, NY, 1883 ***8427.14*** *p44*
Kochler, Martha 9; New York, NY, 1883 ***8427.14*** *p44*
Kochler, Philip Jacob; Ohio, 1809-1852 ***4511.35*** *p27*
Kochman, Leo Leopold; New York, NY, 1882 ***2853.20*** *p115*
Kochs, Henry; New York, 1860 ***358.56*** *p150*
Kocian, Jan; St. Louis, 1855 ***2853.20*** *p334*
Kock, G.W.; New York, NY, 1849 ***6412.40*** *p151*
Kock, Jean 42; New Castle, DE, 1817-1818 ***90.20*** *p152*
Kockanch, Adolf 18; Halifax, N.S., 1902 ***1860.4*** *p40*
Kockanch, Bocallia 37; Halifax, N.S., 1902 ***1860.4*** *p40*
Kockanch, Emil 7; Halifax, N.S., 1902 ***1860.4*** *p40*
Kockanch, Hebert 9; Halifax, N.S., 1902 ***1860.4*** *p40*
Kockanch, Karl 58; Halifax, N.S., 1902 ***1860.4*** *p40*
Kockanch, Pauline 19; Halifax, N.S., 1902 ***1860.4*** *p40*
Kockenberger, Mary 34; Michigan, 1880 ***4491.42*** *p16*
Kockenberger, Rudolph 42; Michigan, 1880 ***4491.42*** *p16*
Kocker, Annie; Wisconsin, 1907 ***6795.8*** *p179*
Kockey, John; America, 1771 ***1220.12*** *p478*
Kockler, Franz 27; America, 1880 ***5475.1*** *p484*
Kockler, Johann 29; America, 1881 ***5475.1*** *p195*
Kockler, Mathias; America, 1872 ***5475.1*** *p195*
Kockler, Nikolaus; America, 1847 ***5475.1*** *p475*
Kockler, Nikolaus; Chicago, 1882 ***5475.1*** *p196*
Kockler, Philipp; America, 1847 ***5475.1*** *p473*
Kocley, Adam; Ohio, 1809-1852 ***4511.35*** *p27*
Kocourek, Jan; Chicago, 1881 ***2853.20*** *p376*
Kocurek, Jan; Texas, 1856 ***2853.20*** *p64*
Kodey, Adam; Ohio, 1809-1852 ***4511.35*** *p27*
Koebel, Carl 31; America, 1893 ***1883.7*** *p38*
Koebernik, William; Wisconsin, 1877 ***6795.8*** *p50*
Koeghly, Felix; Ohio, 1809-1852 ***4511.35*** *p27*
Koehl, Anna Maria; America, 1865 ***5475.1*** *p511*
*Son:*Nikolaus
Koehl, John; Long Island, 1778 ***8529.30*** *p9A*
Koehl, Nikolaus *SEE* Koehl, Anna Maria Loch
Koehler, Child; Pennsylvania, 1866 ***170.15*** *p32*
With family
Koehler, Anna Margaretha; New England, 1867 ***170.15*** *p32*
Koehler, Christoph; Nova Scotia, 1784 ***7105*** *p24*
Koehler, Conrad; Illinois, 1855 ***6079.1*** *p8*
Koehler, F.; Galveston, TX, 1855 ***571.7*** *p18*
Koehler, Frederick; Long Island, 1778 ***8529.30*** *p9A*
Koehler, Henry; Illinois, 1857 ***6079.1*** *p8*
Koehler, Johann Peter; Pennsylvania, 1848 ***170.15*** *p32*
Koehler, Johann Peter 42; Pennsylvania, 1848 ***170.15*** *p32*
Koehler, Johannes; Pennsylvania, 1867 ***170.15*** *p32*
Koehler, Johannes 20; Pennsylvania, 1867 ***170.15*** *p32*
With family & 4 sisters
Koehler, Joseph; Louisiana, 1874 ***4981.45*** *p132*
Koehler, Margaretha; Pennsylvania, 1866 ***170.15*** *p32*
With family
Koehler, Matthaeus 15; America, 1867 ***170.15*** *p32*
Koehler, Matthias; Port uncertain, 1867 ***170.15*** *p32*
Koehler, Michael; Pennsylvania, 1866 ***170.15*** *p32*
With wife & 2 children
Koehnk, Otto; Iowa, 1913 ***1211.15*** *p16*
Koekelberg, Marie Therese; Wisconsin, 1857 ***1495.20*** *p46*
Koeley, Adam; Ohio, 1809-1852 ***4511.35*** *p27*
Koella, Ernest; Tennessee, 1893-1903 ***3665.20*** *p112*
Koelle, Miss; Minnesota, 1873 ***7420.1*** *p301*
Koelle, Carl Heinrich Wilhelm *SEE* Koelle, Marie Sophie Charlotte
Koelle, Marie Sophie Charlotte; America, 1885 ***7420.1*** *p347*
*Brother:*Carl Heinrich Wilhelm
Koeller, Anna Barbara 28; Pennsylvania, 1850 ***170.15*** *p32*
With family
Koeller, Joh.Balthasar 6; Pennsylvania, 1850 ***170.15*** *p32*
With family
Koeller, Johann Adam 36; Pennsylvania, 1850 ***170.15*** *p32*
With family
Koeller, Susanna 3; Pennsylvania, 1850 ***170.15*** *p32*
With family
Koeller, Wm.; Wisconsin, 1899 ***6795.8*** *p230*
Koenck, John Theodore; Iowa, 1920 ***1211.15*** *p16*
Koeneke, Engel Marie Sophie; America, 1866 ***7420.1*** *p239*
Koeneman, Herman; Colorado, 1882 ***1029.59*** *p51*
Koenemann, Herman; Colorado, 1888 ***1029.59*** *p51*
Koenig, Alfred 22; New York, NY, 1886 ***8425.16*** *p32*
Koenig, Anton 38; Mississippi, 1846 ***778.6*** *p190*
Koenig, Arthur 5; New York, NY, 1886 ***8425.16*** *p32*
Koenig, Caroline 41; New York, NY, 1886 ***8425.16*** *p32*
Koenig, Emilie 18; New York, NY, 1886 ***8425.16*** *p32*
Koenig, Fides 29; Port uncertain, 1848 ***778.6*** *p190*
Koenig, Franz...a 40; America, 1840 ***778.6*** *p190*
Koenig, George 30; Port uncertain, 1848 ***778.6*** *p190*
Koenig, Henri 35; New Orleans, 1847 ***778.6*** *p191*
Koenig, Henrich 79; Pennsylvania, 1848 ***170.15*** *p32*
With family & 2 children
Koenig, Ignace 5; America, 1840 ***778.6*** *p191*
Koenig, Ilse Marie Sophie; America, 1847 ***7420.1*** *p54*
Koenig, Jac; Louisiana, 1874 ***4981.45*** *p296*
Koenig, Jacq. 7; America, 1840 ***778.6*** *p191*
Koenig, Jacq. 41; America, 1840 ***778.6*** *p191*
Koenig, Johann Henrich; Pennsylvania, 1848 ***170.15*** *p32*
With family & 2 children
Koenig, Johann Henrich; Pennsylvania, 1848 ***170.15*** *p32*
Koenig, Johann Henrich 79; Pennsylvania, 1848 ***170.15*** *p32*
With family
Koenig, Johannes 4; New York, NY, 1886 ***8425.16*** *p32*
Koenig, Josef; America, 1840 ***5475.1*** *p470*
Koenig, Magdalena 7; Port uncertain, 1848 ***778.6*** *p191*
Koenig, Marie 20; New York, NY, 1886 ***8425.16*** *p32*
Koenig, Otto 15; New York, NY, 1886 ***8425.16*** *p32*
Koenig, Peter 44; New York, NY, 1886 ***8425.16*** *p32*
Koenig, Robert 9 months; New York, NY, 1886 ***8425.16*** *p32*
Koenig, Rudolf 6; New York, NY, 1886 ***8425.16*** *p32*
Koenig, Wilhelm 7; New York, NY, 1886 ***8425.16*** *p32*
Koeniman, Herman; Colorado, 1888 ***1029.59*** *p51*
Koepke, Frank; Wisconsin, 1884 ***6795.8*** *p73*
Koepke, Leopold Frederick August; Wisconsin, 1898 ***6795.8*** *p94*
Koepp, August; Wisconsin, 1895 ***6795.8*** *p186*
Koepp, Augustus; Wisconsin, 1855 ***6795.8*** *p50*
Koeppeler, Mathias 18; Louisiana, 1848 ***778.6*** *p191*
Koeppeler, Mathias 25; Louisiana, 1848 ***778.6*** *p191*
Koerber, Frederick; Ohio, 1809-1852 ***4511.35*** *p27*
Koerner, Catharina 17; New York, NY, 1874 ***6954.7*** *p38*
Koerner, Elisabeth 9 months; New York, NY, 1874 ***6954.7*** *p38*
Koerner, Jacob 19; New York, NY, 1874 ***6954.7*** *p38*
Koerner, Johann 14; New York, NY, 1874 ***6954.7*** *p38*
Koerner, Johann 42; New York, NY, 1874 ***6954.7*** *p38*
Koerner, Rosina 30; New York, NY, 1874 ***6954.7*** *p38*
Koerner, Vaclav; Wisconsin, 1883 ***2853.20*** *p93*
Koerner, Vaclav Vilem; Wisconsin, 1883 ***2853.20*** *p320*
Koetz, Bartholomaus; Pennsylvania, 1878-1900 ***5475.1*** *p35*
*Wife:*Juliane Fuhr
*Son:*Peter
*Daughter:*Katharina
Koetz, Juliane Fuhr *SEE* Koetz, Bartholomaus
Koetz, Katharina *SEE* Koetz, Bartholomaus
Koetz, Peter *SEE* Koetz, Bartholomaus
Koetzsch, Charles; Illinois, 1861 ***6079.1*** *p8*
Koffman, Lucas 25; America, 1845 ***778.6*** *p191*
Kogler, Carl Heinr.; Valdivia, Chile, 1852 ***1192.4*** *p55*
With wife & baby
Kohl, Abraham; America, 1867 ***5475.1*** *p498*
Kohl, Friedrich; America, 1866 ***5475.1*** *p508*
Kohl, George; Illinois, 1858 ***6079.1*** *p8*
Kohl, Jakob 38; America, 1843 ***5475.1*** *p309*
Kohl, Louis 41; Ontario, 1871 ***1823.17*** *p87*
Kohl, Ludwig; America, 1833 ***5475.1*** *p118*
With wife
With child
Kohl, Margarethe; America, 1880 ***5475.1*** *p59*
Kohl, Maria 36; America, 1874 ***5475.1*** *p256*
Kohl, Nicholas; Ohio, 1809-1852 ***4511.35*** *p27*
Kohl, Pet.; New York, 1859 ***358.56*** *p55*
Kohl, Philipp Ludwig 29; America, 1833 ***5475.1*** *p27*
Kohl, Regina 53; America, 1865 ***5475.1*** *p498*
Kohlar, Joseph; Ohio, 1809-1852 ***4511.35*** *p27*
Kohlbacher, Dieter; America, 1882 ***2526.42*** *p154*
Kohlbacher, Georg; America, 1848 ***2526.42*** *p124*
With wife
*Child:*Georg
*Child:*Georg Adam
*Child:*Nikolaus
*Child:*Leonhard
With stepchild 11
Kohlbacher, Georg 6 *SEE* Kohlbacher, Georg
Kohlbacher, Georg Adam 4 *SEE* Kohlbacher, Georg
Kohlbacher, Jakob; America, 1869 ***2526.42*** *p93*
Kohlbacher, Leonhard 9 *SEE* Kohlbacher, Georg
Kohlbacher, Nikolaus 2 *SEE* Kohlbacher, Georg
Kohlbacher, Peter; America, 1851 ***2526.43*** *p189*
Kohlbacher, Philipp; America, 1846 ***2526.42*** *p200*
Kohlbacher, Regina 27; America, 1854 ***2526.42*** *p199*
Kohlbeck, Valentin; Pennsylvania, 1887 ***2853.20*** *p433*
Kohle, Andrew; Illinois, 1852 ***6079.1*** *p8*
Kohler, Andrew; Ohio, 1840-1897 ***8365.35*** *p16*
Kohler, Anna Maria; America, 1883 ***179.55*** *p19*
Kohler, Anton; America, n.d. ***8023.44*** *p376*
Kohler, Bernhard; New York, 1860 ***358.56*** *p148*
Kohler, Chaie 30; New York, NY, 1878 ***9253.2*** *p45*
*Child:*Chone 11 months
Kohler, Chone 11 *SEE* Kohler, Chaie
Kohler, Christopher; Nova Scotia, 1784 ***7105*** *p24*
Kohler, Daniel 3; New York, NY, 1898 ***7951.13*** *p41*
Kohler, Dorothea 4; New York, NY, 1898 ***7951.13*** *p41*
Kohler, Frederic 22; Louisiana, 1848 ***778.6*** *p191*
Kohler, Georg 36; America, 1874 ***5475.1*** *p78*
*Wife:*Maria Droitcour
*Son:*Heinrich 2
*Daughter:*Maria 6 months
*Daughter:*Selina 3
Kohler, George 29; New York, NY, 1898 ***7951.13*** *p41*
Kohler, Heinrich 2 *SEE* Kohler, Georg
Kohler, J. N.; Valdivia, Chile, 1850 ***1192.4*** *p49*
Kohler, Johann; America, 1872 ***5475.1*** *p171*
Kohler, Johann; America, 1888 ***5475.1*** *p435*
Kohler, John B.; Philadelphia, 1853 ***8513.31*** *p320*
Kohler, K.; New York, 1860 ***358.56*** *p5*
Kohler, Katherina 15 months; New York, NY, 1898 ***7951.13*** *p41*
Kohler, Maria Droitcour *SEE* Kohler, Georg
Kohler, Maria 6 *SEE* Kohler, Georg
Kohler, Nicolaus; America, 1868 ***7919.3*** *p532*
Kohler, Nikolaus 35; America, 1866 ***2526.42*** *p142*
*Wife:*Sophie 30
*Child:*Wilhelm 1
Kohler, Ottomar; America, 1868 ***7919.3*** *p525*
Kohler, Philip Jacob; Ohio, 1809-1852 ***4511.35*** *p27*
Kohler, Selina 3 *SEE* Kohler, Georg
Kohler, Sophie 30 *SEE* Kohler, Nikolaus
Kohler, Wilhelm 1 *SEE* Kohler, Nikolaus
Kohler, Wilhelmina 25; New York, NY, 1898 ***7951.13*** *p41*
Kohles, Elias; America, 1867 ***7919.3*** *p524*
Kohlhoff, J.; Venezuela, 1843 ***3899.5*** *p546*
Kohlmeier, Caroline; America, 1853 ***7420.1*** *p107*
Kohlmeier, Ernst Heinrich; Dakota, 1883 ***7420.1*** *p337*
Kohlmeier, Ferdinand; America, 1866 ***7420.1*** *p244*
Kohlmeyer, Widow; America, 1854 ***7420.1*** *p123*
*Son:*Ernst Heinrich
Kohlmeyer, Ernst Heinrich *SEE* Kohlmeyer, Widow
Kohmann, Philipp 20; America, 1846 ***778.6*** *p191*
Kohn, A. H.; Philadelphia, 1796 ***5720.10*** *p378*
Kohn, Eugenie 3; New Orleans, 1848 ***778.6*** *p191*
Kohn, Joseph; Louisiana, 1874-1875 ***4981.45*** *p29*
Kohn, Katharina; America, 1881 ***5475.1*** *p33*
Kohn, Maria 22; New York, NY, 1893 ***1883.7*** *p44*
Kohn, Michel; America, 1882 ***5475.1*** *p242*
Kohn, Philiippe 7; Louisiana, 1848 ***778.6*** *p191*
Kohn, Rosalie; Philadelphia, 1868 ***8513.31*** *p302*
Kohn, Soloman; Louisiana, 1836-1841 ***4981.45*** *p209*
Kohnaker, Christopher; Ohio, 1809-1852 ***4511.35*** *p27*
Kohnen, Margarethe; America, 1882 ***5475.1*** *p24*
Kohnert, Friedrich Wilhelm; America, 1882 ***7420.1*** *p330*
Kohntopp, . . .; Port uncertain, 1853 ***7420.1*** *p107*
Kohnweiler, Daniel; North Carolina, 1836 ***1088.45*** *p17*
Kohout, Frantisek; New York, NY, 1851 ***2853.20*** *p390*
Kohout, J.A.; Madison, WI, 1894 ***2853.20*** *p203*
Kohout, Jan; New York, NY, 1850-1870 ***2853.20*** *p104*
Kohout, Jan; New York, NY, 1851 ***2853.20*** *p100*
Kohr, Michel; America, 1843 ***5475.1*** *p330*
With wife 3 sons & daughter
Kohser, Michael; Ohio, 1809-1852 ***4511.35*** *p27*
Koivisto, Nick 48; Minnesota, 1925 ***2769.54*** *p1380*
Kok, Christ Jensen; Iowa, 1896 ***1211.15*** *p16*
Kok, Jacob; Illinois, 1856 ***6079.1*** *p8*
Koke, Erich Arnold; America, 1866 ***7420.1*** *p244*
Koke, Mrs. H. K.; America, 1867 ***7420.1*** *p259*
With children
Koke, Henriette Sophie Christiane; New York, NY, 1878 ***7420.1*** *p311*

Koke, Lena; Illinois, 1920 *1029.59 p28*
Kokes, . . .; Pennsylvania, 1750-1799 *2853.20 p17*
Kolacny, Bohumil; Texas, 1854 *2853.20 p60*
Kolar, Frantisek; Milwaukee, 1889 *2853.20 p311*
Kolar, Frantisek; Minnesota, 1858-1860 *2853.20 p259*
Kolar, Jan; Wisconsin, 1857-1861 *2853.20 p334*
Kolar, Josef; New York, NY, 1853 *2853.20 p387*
Kolasa, Eugenia 23; New York, NY, 1911 *6533.11 p9*
Kolasa, Karolina; Detroit, 1930 *1640.60 p77*
Kolb, Catherine; New York, 1859 *358.56 p102*
Kolb, Johann; Wisconsin, 1881 *6795.8 p106*
Kolb, John; New Jersey, 1773-1774 *927.31 p3*
Kolbeck, Balthasar; Colorado, 1903 *1029.59 p51*
Kolbeck, Balthasar 37; Colorado, 1903 *1029.59 p51*
Kolbring, Sophie; America, 1854 *7420.1 p123*
  With daughter
Kolcon, John; Detroit, 1929 *1640.55 p114*
Koldschne, Jacob; Ohio, 1809-1852 *4511.35 p28*
Kolenberger, John; Ohio, 1809-1852 *4511.35 p28*
Koleng, Philippe 21; Missouri, 1848 *778.6 p19*
Kolibal, Valentin; Galveston, TX, 1856 *2853.20 p63*
Kolibal, Valentin; Texas, 1856 *2853.20 p68*
Kolin, Karel; Milwaukee, 1884-1888 *2853.20 p87*
Kolitz, Albert George Ludwig; Wisconsin, 1898 *6795.8 p81*
Kolitz, Carl 29; New York, NY, 1885 *1883.7 p45*
Kolke, Emil 20; Halifax, N.S., 1902 *1860.4 p41*
Koll, Francis 35; America, 1843 *778.6 p19*
Koll, Laurent 29; America, 1840 *778.6 p191*
Kolle, Christian Carl August; America, 1881 *7420.1 p322*
  *Sister:*Marie Sophie Charlotte
Kolle, Engel Marie Dorothee; America, 1855 *7420.1 p138*
Kolle, Hanne Sophie Louise Charlotte; America, 1867 *7420.1 p259*
Kolle, Jean-Baptiste 23; New Orleans, 1843 *778.6 p191*
Kolle, Marie Sophie Charlotte *SEE* Kolle, Christian Carl August
Koller, Miss; Port uncertain, 1873 *7420.1 p299*
Koller, Anne Sophie Dorothee *SEE* Koller, Johann Friedrich Wilhelm
Koller, Engel Maria Sophia *SEE* Koller, Johann Tonjes Christoph
Koller, Engel Marie Sophie Caroline Wahlmann *SEE* Koller, Johann Friedrich Wilhelm
Koller, Ernestine *SEE* Koller, Sophie
Koller, Friedrich Wilhelm *SEE* Koller, Johann Friedrich Wilhelm
Koller, Friedrich Wilhelm; America, 1872 *7420.1 p296*
  *Son:*Heinrich Friedrich Wilhelm
Koller, Heinrich; America, 1846 *7420.1 p45*
Koller, Heinrich Friedrich Wilhelm *SEE* Koller, Friedrich Wilhelm
Koller, Johann Friedrich Wilhelm; America, 1872 *7420.1 p296*
  *Wife:*Engel Marie Sophie Caroline Wahlmann
  *Daughter:*Anne Sophie Dorothee
  *Son:*Friedrich Wilhelm
Koller, Johann Heinrich *SEE* Koller, Johann Tonjes Christoph
Koller, Johann Heinrich; Port uncertain, 1882 *7420.1 p330*
Koller, Johann Tonjes Christoph; America, 1862 *7420.1 p212*
  *Wife:*Thrine Sophia Moller
  *Daughter:*Engel Maria Sophia
  *Son:*Johann Heinrich
Koller, Joseph; Ohio, 1809-1852 *4511.35 p28*
Koller, Katharina; Port uncertain, 1887 *170.15 p33*
Koller, Melchior; New England, 1869 *170.15 p33*
  With wife & child
Koller, Nikolaus; Port uncertain, 1886 *170.15 p33*
Koller, Sophie; America, 1860 *7420.1 p195*
  *Sister:*Ernestine
Koller, Sophie Dorothee Charlotte; America, 1869 *7420.1 p280*
Koller, Thrine Sophia Moller *SEE* Koller, Johann Tonjes Christoph
Kollet, Elisabeth; Brazil, 1873 *5475.1 p517*
Kolling, Mr.; America, 1867 *7420.1 p259*
  With wife
  With son 5
  With daughter 16
  With son 14
Kolling, Mr.; America, 1871 *7420.1 p291*
  *Daughter:*Christiane Sophie
  With wife
  *Son:*Carl Friedrich
Kolling, Angela *SEE* Kolling, Nikolaus
Kolling, Anna *SEE* Kolling, Nikolaus
Kolling, Anna 28; Brazil, 1864 *5475.1 p370*
Kolling, Anton Friedrich 3 *SEE* Kolling, Johann
Kolling, Barbara; America, 1872 *5475.1 p320*

Kolling, Carl Friedrich *SEE* Kolling, Mr.
Kolling, Catharina Maria Louise Charlotte; America, 1840 *7420.1 p20*
Kolling, Charlotte; America, 1857 *7420.1 p165*
Kolling, Christiane Sophie *SEE* Kolling, Mr.
Kolling, Elisabeth *SEE* Kolling, Mathias
Kolling, Engel Marie; America, 1856 *7420.1 p153*
Kolling, Franz *SEE* Kolling, Michel
Kolling, Friedrich; America, 1852 *7420.1 p91*
Kolling, Friedrich Wilhelm; America, 1858 *7420.1 p179*
  With wife 7 sons & 2 daughters
Kolling, Heinrich C.; Ohio, 1876 *7420.1 p307*
Kolling, Heinrich Wilhelm; America, 1857 *7420.1 p165*
Kolling, Johann; America, 1864 *5475.1 p41*
  *Wife:*Maria Stuber
  *Son:*Peter Mathias
  *Son:*Anton Friedrich
  *Daughter:*Maria
Kolling, Johann *SEE* Kolling, Mathias
Kolling, Johann *SEE* Kolling, Michel
Kolling, Johann *SEE* Kolling, Nikolaus
Kolling, Johann Christoph; America, 1866 *7420.1 p244*
Kolling, Johann Friedrich Wilhelm; America, 1856 *7420.1 p149*
Kolling, Johann Heinr. Friedr.; America, 1852 *7420.1 p91*
Kolling, Katharina *SEE* Kolling, Mathias
Kolling, Katharina *SEE* Kolling, Nikolaus
Kolling, Katharina Klauk 45 *SEE* Kolling, Nikolaus
Kolling, Margarethe Backes *SEE* Kolling, Mathias
Kolling, Margarethe 21; Brazil, 1862 *5475.1 p369*
Kolling, Maria 10 *SEE* Kolling, Johann
Kolling, Maria Stuber 30 *SEE* Kolling, Johann
Kolling, Maria *SEE* Kolling, Nikolaus
Kolling, Maria *SEE* Kolling, Nikolaus
Kolling, Maria Margarethe Gans 36 *SEE* Kolling, Mathias
Kolling, Mathias; America, 1872 *5475.1 p41*
  *Wife:*Maria Margarethe Gans
  *Son:*Nikolaus
  *Daughter:*Susanna
  *Son:*Johann
  *Daughter:*Katharina
  *Daughter:*Elisabeth
Kolling, Mathias *SEE* Kolling, Michel
Kolling, Mathias *SEE* Kolling, Mathias
Kolling, Mathias; Brazil, 1873 *5475.1 p371*
  *Wife:*Margarethe Backes
  *Son:*Mathias
  *Son:*Peter
  *Son:*Nikolaus
  *Daughter:*Maria
Kolling, Mathias; Brazil, 1873 *5475.1 p371*
Kolling, Michel *SEE* Kolling, Michel
Kolling, Michel; Brazil, 1857 *5475.1 p368*
  *Son:*Peter
  *Son:*Michel
  *Son:*Franz
  *Son:*Mathias
  *Son:*Johann
Kolling, Nikolaus; America, 1871 *5475.1 p41*
Kolling, Nikolaus *SEE* Kolling, Mathias
Kolling, Nikolaus *SEE* Kolling, Mathias
Kolling, Nikolaus 46; Brazil, 1862 *5475.1 p369*
  *Wife:*Katharina Klauk 45
  *Daughter:*Maria
  *Daughter:*Angela
  *Son:*Johann
  *Daughter:*Katharina
  *Daughter:*Anna
Kolling, Peter 31; America, 1843 *5475.1 p366*
Kolling, Peter *SEE* Kolling, Michel
Kolling, Peter *SEE* Kolling, Mathias
Kolling, Peter Mathias 5 *SEE* Kolling, Johann
Kolling, Susanna *SEE* Kolling, Mathias
Kollmann, Barbara 13 *SEE* Kollmann, Maria Filipowitz
Kollmann, Jakob *SEE* Kollmann, Maria Filipowitz
Kollmann, Johann *SEE* Kollmann, Peter
Kollmann, Margarethe 15 *SEE* Kollmann, Maria Filipowitz
Kollmann, Maria *SEE* Kollmann, Peter
Kollmann, Maria 43; America, 1865 *5475.1 p70*
  *Son:*Jakob
  *Daughter:*Barbara 13
  *Daughter:*Margarethe 15
Kollmann, Maria Zang 49 *SEE* Kollmann, Peter
Kollmann, Peter; America, 1861-1900 *5475.1 p71*
  *Wife:*Maria Zang
  *Daughter:*Sophie
  *Son:*Johann
  *Daughter:*Maria
Kollmann, Sophie *SEE* Kollmann, Peter

Kollmer, Anna Barbara Seeger 44 *SEE* Kollmer, Wilhelm
Kollmer, Heinrich 21 *SEE* Kollmer, Wilhelm
Kollmer, Johann Adam 18 *SEE* Kollmer, Wilhelm
Kollmer, Katharina Barbara 13 *SEE* Kollmer, Wilhelm
Kollmer, Marie 10 *SEE* Kollmer, Wilhelm
Kollmer, Marie Magdalena 20 *SEE* Kollmer, Wilhelm
Kollmer, Wilhelm 51; America, 1851 *2526.43 p222*
  *Wife:*Anna Barbara Seeger 44
  *Son:*Johann Adam 18
  *Daughter:*Marie 10
  *Daughter:*Katharina Barbara 13
  *Daughter:*Marie Magdalena 20
  *Son:*Heinrich 21
Kolm, Ludwig; Wisconsin, 1903 *6795.8 p209*
Kolman, Antonin; Milwaukee, 1867 *2853.20 p309*
Kolman, Matej; Wisconsin, 1857-1861 *2853.20 p334*
Kolmer, Anson 20; Mississippi, 1847 *778.6 p191*
Kolmer, Baden 48; Mississippi, 1847 *778.6 p191*
Kolmer, Barbara 17; Mississippi, 1847 *778.6 p191*
Kolmer, Batiste 1; Mississippi, 1847 *778.6 p191*
Kolmer, Catherina 12; Mississippi, 1847 *778.6 p191*
Kolmer, Francois 7; Mississippi, 1847 *778.6 p191*
Kolmer, Joseph 9; Mississippi, 1847 *778.6 p191*
Kolmer, Maria 18; Mississippi, 1847 *778.6 p191*
Kolmer, Maria 40; Mississippi, 1847 *778.6 p191*
Kolmer, Wilhelm 3; Mississippi, 1847 *778.6 p191*
Kolmodin, Anna Lilly Sophia *SEE* Kolmodin, Anna Olivia Gottberg
Kolmodin, Anna Olivia; America, 1899 *6410.15 p109*
  *Child:*Carl Wilhelm
  *Child:*Carl August
  *Child:*Carl Robert
  *Child:*Emmy
  *Child:*Tekla Olivia
  *Child:*Anna Lilly Sophia
Kolmodin, Carl Anton; North America, 1888 *6410.15 p106*
Kolmodin, Carl August *SEE* Kolmodin, Anna Olivia Gottberg
Kolmodin, Carl Robert *SEE* Kolmodin, Anna Olivia Gottberg
Kolmodin, Carl Wilhelm *SEE* Kolmodin, Anna Olivia Gottberg
Kolmodin, Emmy *SEE* Kolmodin, Anna Olivia Gottberg
Kolmodin, Tekla Olivia *SEE* Kolmodin, Anna Olivia Gottberg
Kolock, John; New York, 1926 *1173.1 p2*
Kolodey, Katherine; Detroit, 1929 *1640.55 p114*
Kolodziej, Andrew; Detroit, 1929 *6214.5 p65*
Kolodziej, Mary; Detroit, 1929-1930 *6214.5 p63*
Kolonko, Frank; Texas, 1886 *9980.22 p16*
Kolowicz, John; Detroit, 1929-1930 *6214.5 p63*
Kolp, Louis; Ohio, 1809-1852 *4511.35 p28*
Kolp, Nicholas; Ohio, 1809-1852 *4511.35 p28*
Kolpin, William; Wisconsin, 1889 *6795.8 p82*
Kolsch, Jakob; America, 1880 *5475.1 p265*
Kolschner, Jacob; Ohio, 1809-1852 *4511.35 p28*
Koltes, John A.; Philadelphia, 1855 *8513.31 p320*
Kolthoff, Charles; Ohio, 1840-1897 *8365.35 p17*
Koltyka, Peter; Detroit, 1929-1930 *6214.5 p63*
Koluch, Julius; Detroit, 1929 *1640.55 p116*
Kolz, Peter; West Virginia, 1854 *1132.30 p148*
Kolzan, August 26; New York, NY, 1883 *8427.14 p44*
Kolzan, Dora 27; New York, NY, 1883 *8427.14 p44*
Kolzan, Heinrich 3 months; New York, NY, 1883 *8427.14 p44*
Kolzan, Ludwig 5; New York, NY, 1883 *8427.14 p44*
Kolzan, Wilhelm 3; New York, NY, 1883 *8427.14 p44*
Komar, Harry; Detroit, 1929 *1640.55 p116*
Komedulsan, Tosefo; Wisconsin, 1895 *6795.8 p59*
Kominski, William 28; Ontario, 1871 *1823.21 p193*
Komorous, Frantisek; St. Louis, 1852 *2853.20 p21*
Komorowski, Thomas; Detroit, 1929-1930 *6214.5 p65*
Komrs, Josef; St. Louis, 1855 *2853.20 p334*
Konczak, Anthony; Detroit, 1930 *1640.60 p78*
Konczal, Stanley; Detroit, 1890 *9980.23 p96*
Konecke, Johann Heinrich Christoph; America, 1868 *7420.1 p273*
  With family
Konecke, Johann Philipp; America, 1857 *7420.1 p165*
Koneke, Hans Heinrich; America, 1858 *7420.1 p179*
Konen, Anna Roeder *SEE* Konen, Johann
Konen, Johann; America, 1882 *5475.1 p24*
  *Wife:*Anna Roeder
  *Son:*Josef
Konen, Josef *SEE* Konen, Johann
Konhstamm, M. R.; North Carolina, 1860 *1088.45 p17*
Konicek, Jan N.; Virginia, 1905 *2853.20 p139*
Konick, Stefan 27; New York, NY, 1920 *930.50 p48*
Konieczna, Rosalia; Detroit, 1890 *9980.23 p97*
Konig, Andreas *SEE* Konig, Andreas

Konig, Andreas; America, 1881 *5475.1 p74*
*Wife:*Anna Raspiller
*Daughter:*Victoria
*Son:*August
With stepchild
*Son:*Andreas
*Daughter:*Anna
Konig, Andreas; America, 1886 *5475.1 p423*
*Wife:*Elisabeth Frantz
With 3 children
Konig, Anna; America, 1841 *5475.1 p56*
Konig, Anna *SEE* Konig, Andreas
Konig, Anna Raspiller *SEE* Konig, Andreas
Konig, Anna *SEE* Konig, Leonhard
Konig, Anna Katharina 1 *SEE* Konig, Johannes, II
Konig, Anna Maria *SEE* Konig, Leonhard
Konig, August *SEE* Konig, Andreas
Konig, August; Washington, 1882 *5475.1 p34*
Konig, Barbara 7 *SEE* Konig, Nikolaus
Konig, Christian 51; Halifax, N.S., 1902 *1860.4 p40*
Konig, Dorothea; America, 1880 *5475.1 p48*
Konig, Elisabeth; America, 1866 *2526.42 p105*
Konig, Elisabeth Frantz *SEE* Konig, Andreas
Konig, Elisabetha *SEE* Konig, Leonhard
Konig, Emanuel 9; Halifax, N.S., 1902 *1860.4 p40*
Konig, Emma 13; Halifax, N.S., 1902 *1860.4 p40*
Konig, Ernst 27; America, 1897 *5475.1 p77*
Konig, Eva Katharina 4 *SEE* Konig, Johannes, II
Konig, Friedrich; America, 1840 *2526.43 p125*
With wife
With child 1
Konig, Friedrich; America, 1847 *2526.42 p175*
Konig, Friedrich 27; America, 1838 *2526.42 p113*
With wife & 4 children
Konig, Friedrich 22; Halifax, N.S., 1902 *1860.4 p40*
Konig, Georg; America, 1895 *2526.43 p191*
With wife & 3 children
Konig, Georg 32; America, 1842 *2526.42 p154*
Konig, Georg Peter; America, 1887 *2526.43 p188*
Konig, Gottlieb 11; Halifax, N.S., 1902 *1860.4 p40*
Konig, Heinrich; America, 1881 *5475.1 p61*
Konig, Heinrich; America, 1882 *2526.42 p154*
Konig, Heinrich; Valdivia, Chile, 1852 *1192.4 p55*
With wife baby & child
With child 6
Konig, Henrich; Louisiana, 1874 *4981.45 p132*
Konig, Jacob 18; Halifax, N.S., 1902 *1860.4 p40*
Konig, Jakob; America, 1849 *5475.1 p477*
Konig, Jakob 18; America, 1852 *2526.42 p102*
Konig, Johann; Wisconsin, 1855 *6795.8 p25*
Konig, Johann Nikolaus; America, 1883 *2526.43 p188*
Konig, Johannes; America, 1853 *2526.42 p154*
Konig, Johannes, II; America, 1845 *2526.42 p154*
With wife
*Child:*Eva Katharina
*Child:*Anna Katharina
Konig, Katharina 5 *SEE* Konig, Nikolaus
Konig, Katharina 9 *SEE* Konig, Nikolaus
Konig, Konrad; America, 1836 *2526.43 p191*
With wife
With son 6
With daughter 16
With daughter 3
With daughter 11
Konig, Konrad 27; America, 1836 *2526.43 p126*
Konig, Leonhard; America, 1851 *2526.43 p126*
Konig, Leonhard; America, 1888 *2526.43 p188*
*Daughter:*Anna Maria
*Daughter:*Elisabetha
*Daughter:*Anna
Konig, Maria Elisabetha; America, 1854 *2526.42 p137*
Konig, Maria Elisabetha Hubner 30 *SEE* Konig, Nikolaus
Konig, Mathilde 16; Halifax, N.S., 1902 *1860.4 p40*
Konig, Nikolaus 1 *SEE* Konig, Nikolaus
Konig, Nikolaus 36; America, 1865 *2526.43 p218*
*Wife:*Maria Elisabetha Hubner 30
*Daughter:*Katharina 9
*Daughter:*Barbara 7
*Daughter:*Katharina 5
*Son:*Nikolaus 1
Konig, Paul 36; America, 1849 *5475.1 p455*
Konig, Peter; America, 1883 *5475.1 p384*
Konig, Peter; America, 1887 *2526.43 p188*
Konig, Peter von Balsbach; America, 1860 *2526.43 p141*
Konig, Philipp; New York, 1825-1898 *2526.43 p189*
Konig, Regina 52; Halifax, N.S., 1902 *1860.4 p40*
Konig, Simon; America, 1832 *2526.43 p128*
With wife & child
Konig, Victoria *SEE* Konig, Andreas
Konighof, Carl; America, 1867 *7919.3 p526*
Konigsfeld, Anna *SEE* Konigsfeld, Johann
Konigsfeld, Johann *SEE* Konigsfeld, Johann

Konigsfeld, Johann; America, 1879 *5475.1 p148*
*Wife:*Margarethe Schmitt
*Son:*Johann
*Son:*Peter
With son
*Daughter:*Anna
Konigsfeld, Margarethe Schmitt *SEE* Konigsfeld, Johann
Konigsfeld, Peter *SEE* Konigsfeld, Johann
Konigshof, Eduard; America, 1868 *7919.3 p527*
Konigshof, Johanne; America, 1868 *7919.3 p527*
Konitz, Sebastian; Philadelphia, 1778 *8529.30 p2A*
Konner, August 10 months; New York, NY, 1893 *1883.7 p41*
Konner, Lene 6; New York, NY, 1893 *1883.7 p41*
Konner, Ludwig 8; New York, NY, 1893 *1883.7 p41*
Konner, Michael 2; New York, NY, 1893 *1883.7 p41*
Konner, Stanislaw 34; New York, NY, 1893 *1883.7 p41*
Konner, Wilhelmina 32; New York, NY, 1893 *1883.7 p41*
Konnly, Conrad 21; America, 1847 *778.6 p191*
Konrad, Maria Dewes *SEE* Konrad, Nikolaus
Konrad, Nikolaus; America, 1834 *5475.1 p437*
*Wife:*Maria Dewes
With 5 children
Konrad, Nikolaus; North America, 1840 *5475.1 p204*
Konrath, Barbara Prinz *SEE* Konrath, Peter
Konrath, Peter; America, 1834 *5475.1 p437*
*Wife:*Barbara Prinz
Konred, Heinrich *SEE* Konred, Philipp
Konred, Jakob *SEE* Konred, Philipp
Konred, Karoline *SEE* Konred, Philipp
Konred, Karoline Pfeifer *SEE* Konred, Philipp
Konred, Peter *SEE* Konred, Philipp
Konred, Philipp *SEE* Konred, Philipp
Konred, Philipp; America, 1867 *5475.1 p491*
*Wife:*Karoline Pfeifer
*Daughter:*Karoline
*Son:*Heinrich
*Son:*Peter
*Son:*Philipp
*Son:*Jakob
Konstantynowicz, Jan 27; New York, NY, 1903 *8355.1 p15*
Konter, Maria Schmal *SEE* Konter, Peter
Konter, Mathias *SEE* Konter, Peter
Konter, Nikolaus *SEE* Konter, Peter
Konter, Peter *SEE* Konter, Peter
Konter, Peter; America, 1871 *5475.1 p263*
*Wife:*Maria Schmal
*Son:*Nikolaus
*Son:*Peter ·
*Son:*Mathias
Kontropp, Anton; America, 1852 *7420.1 p92*
Kontz, Jacob; Ohio, 1809-1852 *4511.35 p28*
Konvalinka, Jan; New York, NY, 1890 *2853.20 p98*
Konvalinka, Josef; Iowa, 1854 *2853.20 p211*
Konz, Katharina 24; America, 1847 *5475.1 p259*
Koons, Peter; Ohio, 1809-1852 *4511.35 p28*
Koontz, Jacob; Ohio, 1809-1852 *4511.35 p28*
Koontz, Paul; Ohio, 1809-1852 *4511.35 p28*
Koonz, Peter; Ohio, 1809-1852 *4511.35 p28*
Koop, Hermann Johann Friedrich; Wisconsin, 1889 *6795.8 p233*
Koop, Ida Friedericka Caroline; Wisconsin, 1891 *6795.8 p233*
Koopmann, Joh.; Valdivia, Chile, 1852 *1192.4 p53*
Kopacz, Ferdynand 45; New York, NY, 1912 *8355.1 p16*
Kopacz, Henryk 17; New York, NY, 1912 *8355.1 p15*
Kopecek, Antonin; Nebraska, 1874 *2853.20 p172*
Kopecky, Frantisek; Iowa, 1850-1860 *2853.20 p217*
Kopecky, Frantisek; Iowa, 1891 *2853.20 p224*
Kopelove, Bertha; Detroit, 1929 *1640.55 p114*
Kopenen, Ida 36; Minnesota, 1923 *2769.54 p1384*
Kopf, Michael; Ohio, 1840-1897 *8365.35 p17*
Kopfstein, Jan; Cleveland, OH, 1854 *2853.20 p475*
Kopiske, Julius Rudolf; Wisconsin, 1895 *6795.8 p204*
Koplin, Friedrich Wilhelm; Wisconsin, 1868 *6795.8 p74*
Koponen, Sam 31; Minnesota, 1926 *2769.54 p1381*
Kopp, A.; Galveston, TX, 1855 *571.7 p18*
Kopp, Ad.; Galvèston, TX, 1855 *571.7 p18*
Kopp, Gottlieb August Julius; Wisconsin, 1874 *6795.8 p83*
Kopp, Gottlob; Wisconsin, 1873 *6795.8 p37*
Kopp, Henry; Ohio, 1809-1852 *4511.35 p28*
Kopp, Philipp; America, 1880 *5475.1 p220*
Kopp, Theteleo 24; Mississippi, 1847 *778.6 p191*
Koppen, Karl Christoph Ernst; New York, NY, 1890 *7420.1 p361*
Kopple, Anna 4; Halifax, N.S., 1902 *1860.4 p40*
Kopple, Antonia 11; Halifax, N.S., 1902 *1860.4 p40*
Kopple, Jacob 39; Halifax, N.S., 1902 *1860.4 p40*
Kopple, Lucarda 38; Halifax, N.S., 1902 *1860.4 p40*
Kopple, Michael 9; Halifax, N.S., 1902 *1860.4 p40*

Kopple, Peter; Halifax, N.S., 1902 *1860.4 p40*
Kopplin, Julius; Wisconsin, 1874 *6795.8 p103*
Kopriva, Karel; St. Paul, MN, 1860 *2853.20 p277*
Koracker, Jean Baptiste 25; New Orleans, 1847 *778.6 p191*
Koraleska, Martin; Wisconsin, 1893 *6795.8 p204*
Korbel, Antonin; America, 1888 *2853.20 p497*
Korbel, Frantisek; New York, NY, 1850 *2853.20 p100*
Korbel, Frantisek; San Francisco, 1862 *2853.20 p104*
Korbel, Jan; Nebraska, 1803-1897 *2853.20 p157*
Korber, Elisabeth; America, 1856 *2526.43 p210*
Korber, Engel Marie Dorothea; America, 1864 *7420.1 p225*
Korber, Johann Adam; America, 1785 *2526.43 p141*
With wife
Korbholz, Philip W.; Missouri, 1888 *3276.1 p2*
Korbholz, Philip W.; Missouri, 1890 *3276.1 p2*
Kordela, Zofia 17; New York, NY, 1912 *8355.1 p16*
Kordmann, Alvine; Wisconsin, 1895 *6795.8 p95*
Kordner, Christian; Illinois, 1857 *6079.1 p8*
Korecki, Nicholas; Detroit, 1929-1930 *6214.5 p70*
Korf, Widow; Port uncertain, 1853 *7420.1 p107*
Korf, Carl; Port uncertain, 1853 *7420.1 p107*
With wife 4 sons & daughter
Korf, Carl Heinrich; America, 1859 *7420.1 p186*
Korf, Doris; America, 1854 *7420.1 p123*
Korf, Dorothea Wilhelmine; America, 1870 *7420.1 p288*
Korf, Friederike Sophie Louise; America, 1865 *7420.1 p232*
With child
Korf, Sophie; America, 1852 *7420.1 p92*
Korf, Wilhelm; America, 1854 *7420.1 p123*
Korff, Louis; Port uncertain, 1849 *7420.1 p65*
Korff, Sophie Wilhelmine; America, 1852 *7420.1 p90*
Korig, Bartholemew; Ohio, 1809-1852 *4511.35 p28*
Korin, Nicholas; Detroit, 1929-1930 *6214.5 p70*
Korinek, Dominik Tomas; Chicago, 1857 *2853.20 p389*
Koritz, M.; Chicago, 1880 *7420.1 p316*
With wife
Koritz, Catharine Marie Dorothea; America, 1864 *7420.1 p225*
Koritz, Christoph; Port uncertain, 1856 *7420.1 p149*
Koritz, Hans Heinrich; America, 1844 *7420.1 p32*
Koritz, Heinrich; America, 1858 *7420.1 p179*
Koritz, Heinrich Christoph Gottlieb; America, 1884 *7420.1 p344*
Korizek, Frantisek; Boston, 1854 *2853.20 p213*
Korizek, Frantisek; Boston, 1854 *2853.20 p291*
Korkery, Daniel 64; Ontario, 1871 *1823.21 p193*
Kormanyos, George; New York, 1926 *1173.1 p2*
Korn, Friedrich; London, Eng., 1868 *5475.1 p92*
Korn, Friedrich Karl; America, 1868 *5475.1 p32*
Korn, Henry 40; Ontario, 1871 *1823.21 p193*
Korn, Karl; America, 1847 *5475.1 p28*
Korn, Rudolf Georg; America, 1868 *5475.1 p119*
Korna, Frantisek V.; Nebraska, 1865-1869 *2853.20 p187*
Kornacki, Peter; Detroit, 1929-1930 *6214.5 p70*
Kornegay, George; North Carolina, 1710 *3629.40 p5*
Kornenbold, M.; America, 1866 *2526.43 p134*
Korner, Friedrich; America, 1888 *2526.43 p150*
Korner, Johannes; America, 1865 *2526.43 p150*
Korner, Theodor; Valdivia, Chile, 1860 *1192.4 p48*
Kornyk, Charles; Detroit, 1929 *1640.55 p113*
Korolewski, Vincent; Detroit, 1890 *9980.23 p97*
Korosin, Franz; Philadelphia, 1853 *8513.31 p320*
*Wife:*Ottilia Hassman
Korosin, Ottilia Hassman *SEE* Korosin, Franz
Korpela, Henry; Minnesota, 1925 *2769.54 p1383*
Korpi, William 55; Minnesota, 1923 *2769.54 p1379*
Korpman, Bernard; North Carolina, 1835 *1088.45 p17*
Korsell, Julia; St. Paul, MN, 1893 *1865.50 p94*
Korsell, Mary; Minnesota, 1891 *1865.50 p94*
Korseman, Lewis; Kansas, 1865-1897 *1447.20 p65*
Korsmeier, August; America, 1904 *7420.1 p380*
Korsmeier, Rudolf; New York, NY, 1907 *7420.1 p382*
Korte, Carl Theodor; America, 1867 *7919.3 p525*
Kortejohann, Hr. Chr. 23; New York, NY, 1864 *8425.62 p196*
Kortels, Joh.; Pittsburgh, 1880 *5475.1 p22*
Korth, Auguste; Wisconsin, 1905 *6795.8 p224*
Korth, Ernestine; Galveston, TX, 1855 *571.7 p17*
Korth, P.E.; Cleveland, OH, 1892-1893 *9722.10 p122*
Korthauer, . . .; America, 1853 *7420.1 p107*
With son
Korthauer, Hans Heinrich *SEE* Korthauer, Johann Heinrich Christoph
Korthauer, Heinrich; America, 1848 *7420.1 p60*
Korthauer, Heinrich Dietrich Wilhelm Conrad; America, 1849 *7420.1 p65*
Korthauer, Johann Heinrich Christoph; America, 1859 *7420.1 p186*
*Son:*Johann Otto Christoph
*Son:*Hans Heinrich

Korthauer, Johann Otto Christoph *SEE* Korthauer, Johann Heinrich Christoph
Kortmann, Ottilia; Wisconsin, 1897 ***6795.8*** *p95*
Korzeniecki, Stanley; Detroit, 1930 ***1640.60*** *p81*
Korzeniewski, Stanislaus; Detroit, 1930 ***1640.60*** *p82*
Kos, Frank; Texas, 1886-1890 ***6015.15*** *p26*
Kos, Josef; Iowa, 1857 ***2853.20*** *p237*
Kosak, Frantisek; Chicago, 1893 ***2853.20*** *p405*
Kosch, Frank; Texas, 1886-1890 ***6015.15*** *p26*
Koscielniak, Jozefa; Detroit, 1929 ***1640.55*** *p113*
Koseh, K. Fredrick; New York, 1860 ***358.56*** *p150*
Koser, Mr. 28; America, 1847 ***778.6*** *p191*
Kosh, John; Galveston, TX, 1900 ***6015.15*** *p26*
Kosh, Joseph; Galveston, TX, 1881 ***6015.15*** *p26*
Koshans, Amalie; Halifax, N.S., 1902 ***1860.4*** *p43*
Koshans, Emelie 2; Halifax, N.S., 1902 ***1860.4*** *p43*
Koshans, Natalie 25; Halifax, N.S., 1902 ***1860.4*** *p43*
Koshans, Peter 29; Halifax, N.S., 1902 ***1860.4*** *p43*
Kosiorek, Julia; Detroit, 1929 ***1640.55*** *p115*
Koskela, Olaf 19; Minnesota, 1925 ***2769.54*** *p1378*
Koski, David 39; Minnesota, 1925 ***2769.54*** *p1380*
Koski, Fred 48; Minnesota, 1925 ***2769.54*** *p1379*
Koski, John 38; Minnesota, 1923 ***2769.54*** *p1381*
Koski, Kaleb 31; Minnesota, 1925 ***2769.54*** *p1383*
Koski, Katie 44; Minnesota, 1925 ***2769.54*** *p1379*
Koski, Martha 36; Minnesota, 1925 ***2769.54*** *p1380*
Koski, Sandra 50; Minnesota, 1925 ***2769.54*** *p1380*
Kosling, Hermann August; Port uncertain, 1905 ***7420.1*** *p380*
Koslowske, Gustav Carl; Wisconsin, 1888 ***6795.8*** *p139*
Koslowske, Gustav Karl; Wisconsin, 1888 ***6795.8*** *p192*
Koslowsky, August H.; Wisconsin, 1888 ***6795.8*** *p117*
Kosnar, Vaclav; Chicago, 1854 ***2853.20*** *p388*
Kost, Catharine 1 months; New York, NY, 1874 ***6954.7*** *p38*
Kost, Christina 9 months; New York, NY, 1874 ***6954.7*** *p38*
Kost, Christina 43; New York, NY, 1874 ***6954.7*** *p38*
Kost, Christine 10; New York, NY, 1874 ***6954.7*** *p38*
Kost, David 6; New York, NY, 1874 ***6954.7*** *p38*
Kost, David 16; New York, NY, 1874 ***6954.7*** *p38*
Kost, Elisabeth 13; New York, NY, 1874 ***6954.7*** *p38*
Kost, Eva 1 months; New York, NY, 1874 ***6954.7*** *p38*
Kost, Georg 20; New York, NY, 1874 ***6954.7*** *p38*
Kost, Jacob 5; New York, NY, 1874 ***6954.7*** *p38*
Kost, Jacob 8; New York, NY, 1874 ***6954.7*** *p38*
Kost, Jacob 46; New York, NY, 1874 ***6954.7*** *p38*
Kost, Magdalena 43; New York, NY, 1874 ***6954.7*** *p38*
Kost, Margarethe 8; New York, NY, 1874 ***6954.7*** *p38*
Kost, Nicolaus 45; New York, NY, 1874 ***6954.7*** *p38*
Kost, Otto; St. Louis, 1924 ***8023.44*** *p376*
Kost, Philipp; New York, NY, 1887 ***3366.30*** *p70*
Kost, Sophie 6 months; New York, NY, 1874 ***6954.7*** *p38*
Koster, Mr.; America, 1854 ***7420.1*** *p123*
Koster, Gottlieb; America, 1868 ***7420.1*** *p273*
Koster, Heinrich; America, 1852 ***7420.1*** *p92*
With wife & daughter
With mother brother & sister
*Father:*Heinrich, Sr.
Koster, Heinrich, Sr. *SEE* Koster, Heinrich
Koster, Johann 28; America, 1843 ***5475.1*** *p347*
Koster, Johann Jacob; America, 1858 ***7420.1*** *p179*
With wife 2 sons & 2 daughters
Koster, Justina Carolina; America, 1847 ***7420.1*** *p55*
Koster, Ludwig; America, 1856 ***7420.1*** *p149*
With family
Koster, Peter 27; America, 1843 ***5475.1*** *p347*
Koster, Wilhelm; Valdivia, Chile, 1850 ***1192.4*** *p50*
Kostermann, C. G. 46; New York, NY, 1864 ***8425.62*** *p196*
Kostermann, Dorothea 57; Died enroute, 1864 ***8425.62*** *p196*
Kosters, Paul; America, 1926 ***8023.44*** *p376*
Kosths, Nicholus; Washington, 1887 ***2770.40*** *p24*
Kostlivy, Karel; Chicago, 1854 ***2853.20*** *p388*
Kostlivy, Petr Antonin; Wisconsin, 1851 ***2853.20*** *p312*
Kostner, Josef; Chicago, 1877 ***2853.20*** *p405*
Kostohryz, Jan; North Dakota, 1879-1881 ***2853.20*** *p252*
Kostomlatsky, Frantisek; Wisconsin, 1852 ***2853.20*** *p312*
Kostoryz, Stanislav; Omaha, NE, 1886-1898 ***2853.20*** *p147*
Kosub, Frank; Texas, 1855-1878 ***9980.22*** *p16*
Kosub, Joseph; Texas, 1855-1887 ***9980.22*** *p16*
Kosub, Lucas 24; Texas, 1872 ***9980.22*** *p17*
Kosub, Peter 35; Texas, 1884 ***9980.22*** *p17*
Kosub, Simon; Texas, 1855-1871 ***9980.22*** *p16*
Kosub, Simon; Texas, 1855-1886 ***9980.22*** *p16*
Kosub, Tom; Texas, 1855-1871 ***9980.22*** *p16*
Kotchemarasky, John; Texas, 1878 ***6015.15*** *p26*
Koth, Andreas 8 months; New York, NY, 1876 ***6954.7*** *p39*
Koth, Barbara 23; New York, NY, 1876 ***6954.7*** *p39*
Koth, Barbara 40; New York, NY, 1886 ***6954.7*** *p41*
Koth, Carl 17; New York, NY, 1876 ***6954.7*** *p39*
Koth, Christina 17; New York, NY, 1886 ***6954.7*** *p41*
Koth, Elisabeth 19; New York, NY, 1876 ***6954.7*** *p39*
Koth, Emelia 8; New York, NY, 1886 ***6954.7*** *p41*
Koth, Emmanuel 17; New York, NY, 1886 ***6954.7*** *p40*
Koth, Heinrich 27; New York, NY, 1876 ***6954.7*** *p39*
Koth, Heinrich 31; New York, NY, 1886 ***6954.7*** *p40*
Koth, Heinrich 49; New York, NY, 1876 ***6954.7*** *p39*
Koth, Johann 5; New York, NY, 1886 ***6954.7*** *p41*
Koth, Johann 20; New York, NY, 1876 ***6954.7*** *p39*
Koth, Johann Georg; America, n.d. ***8115.12*** *p320*
Koth, Katherina 3; New York, NY, 1886 ***6954.7*** *p40*
Koth, Katherina 6; New York, NY, 1876 ***6954.7*** *p39*
Koth, Katherina 28; New York, NY, 1886 ***6954.7*** *p40*
Koth, Ludwig; America, n.d. ***8115.12*** *p321*
Koth, Lydia 9 months; New York, NY, 1886 ***6954.7*** *p41*
Koth, Maria 49; New York, NY, 1876 ***6954.7*** *p39*
Koth, Michael 14; New York, NY, 1886 ***6954.7*** *p41*
Koth, Paulina 2; New York, NY, 1886 ***6954.7*** *p41*
Koth, Wilhelm 38; New York, NY, 1886 ***6954.7*** *p41*
Kother, J. G.; Valdivia, Chile, 1850 ***1192.4*** *p49*
With wife & 2 children
With child 3 months
With child 8
Kotlowska, Augusta; Wisconsin, 1884 ***6795.8*** *p59*
Kotlowski, Augusta; Wisconsin, 1884 ***6795.8*** *p59*
Kotouc, Alfons; Kansas, 1890 ***2853.20*** *p266*
Kotthoff, Josef 10 months; New York, NY, 1864 ***8425.62*** *p198*
Kotthoff, Marie 27; New York, NY, 1864 ***8425.62*** *p198*
Kotthoff, Tinna 9; New York, NY, 1864 ***8425.62*** *p198*
Kotthoff, Wilhelm 3; New York, NY, 1864 ***8425.62*** *p198*
Kotthoff, Wilhelm 29; New York, NY, 1864 ***8425.62*** *p198*
Kotula, Karolina 22; New York, NY, 1912 ***8355.1*** *p15*
Kotzenberg, Fritz August Gustav; St. Louis, 1877 ***7420.1*** *p309*
Kouba, Antonin V.; Nebraska, 1882 ***2853.20*** *p192*
Koudela, Frantisek; Nebraska, 1875 ***2853.20*** *p162*
Koudelka, Josef Maria; Wisconsin, 1868 ***2853.20*** *p483*
With parents
Kouen, Peter Andreas; America, 1873 ***5475.1*** *p55*
Koukol, Alois Bohuslav; New York, NY, 1891 ***2853.20*** *p80*
Koula, Josef; New York, 1856 ***2853.20*** *p118*
Kourbeight, J. C. 11; New Orleans, 1848 ***778.6*** *p191*
Kourbeight, P. L. 9; New Orleans, 1848 ***778.6*** *p191*
Koutek, Josef; Omaha, NE, 1889 ***2853.20*** *p169*
Koutz, Jacob; Ohio, 1809-1852 ***4511.35*** *p28*
Kovar, Frantisek; Nebraska, 1874 ***2853.20*** *p172*
Kovar, Ignac; Nebraska, 1873 ***2853.20*** *p171*
Kovar, Jindrich; New York, NY, 1893 ***2853.20*** *p469*
Kovar, Josef; Wisconsin, 1855 ***2853.20*** *p304*
Kovarik, J.J.; Iowa, 1868 ***2853.20*** *p234*
With parents
Kovarik, Matej *SEE* Kovarik, Tomas
Kovarik, Tomas; Nebraska, 1879 ***2853.20*** *p156*
*Brother:*Matej
Kowalchi, Antony 30; New York, NY, 1920 ***930.50*** *p48*
Kowalczewski, Anthony Jan; Detroit, 1929-1930 ***6214.5*** *p67*
Kowalczuk, Stanislaw; Detroit, 1929 ***1640.55*** *p117*
Kowalczyk, Frank; Detroit, 1930 ***1640.60*** *p81*
Kowald, Helne; Wisconsin, 1893 ***6795.8*** *p82*
Kowalec, Szymon; Detroit, 1930 ***1640.60*** *p78*
Kowalewski, Anthony; Detroit, 1930 ***1640.60*** *p81*
Kowalski, Frank; Detroit, 1929-1930 ***6214.5*** *p63*
*Wife:*Helen Kowalski
Kowalski, Helen Kowalski *SEE* Kowalski, Frank Kurczewska
Kowalski, Michael 40; New York, NY, 1920 ***930.50*** *p48*
Kowman, Thomas; New Orleans, 1850 ***7242.30*** *p147*
Kowolowski, Gustav; Wisconsin, 1891 ***6795.8*** *p25*
Koza, Frantisek; Texas, 1856 ***2853.20*** *p68*
Koza, Tomas; North Dakota, 1872 ***2853.20*** *p251*
Kozakowski, Kazimer; Detroit, 1930 ***1640.60*** *p81*
Kozarski, S.; Louisiana, 1874 ***4981.45*** *p296*
Kozdras, Jozef 42; New York, NY, 1904 ***8355.1*** *p15*
Kozelka, Vaclav Zigmund; Wisconsin, 1887 ***2853.20*** *p330*
Koziel, Wojciech 40; New York, NY, 1920 ***930.50*** *p48*
Kozikowski, Stanley; Detroit, 1929-1930 ***6214.5*** *p67*
Kozinko, Anna; Detroit, 1929 ***1640.55*** *p112*
Kozisek, Frantisek; Nebraska, 1873 ***2853.20*** *p171*
Kozlanska, Betty; New York, NY, 1893 ***2853.20*** *p469*
Kozlovsky, Vaclav Jan; New York, NY, 1849 ***2853.20*** *p218*
With parents
Kozlowska, Petronela 17; New York, NY, 1911 ***6533.11*** *p9*
Kozlowski, Felix; New York, NY, 1912 ***6214.5*** *p69*
Kozlowski, Jons 30; New York, NY, 1890 ***1883.7*** *p48*
Kozlowski, Jurgis 32; New York, NY, 1911 ***6533.11*** *p10*
Kozlowski, Kasimir 23; New York, NY, 1890 ***1883.7*** *p48*
Kozlowski, Roman; Detroit, 1930 ***1640.60*** *p81*
Kraas, Dorothee; New York, NY, 1845 ***7420.1*** *p41*
Kraas, Martha; New York, 1860 ***358.56*** *p5*
Krabs, Johann 30; New Orleans, 1847 ***778.6*** *p192*
Krach, Georges 31; Port uncertain, 1840 ***778.6*** *p192*
Kracht, Yorkeim; Washington, 1883 ***2770.40*** *p136*
Kraemer, Mrs.; Milwaukee, 1860 ***2853.20*** *p321*
Kraemer, Anna 8 *SEE* Kraemer, Johann
Kraemer, Barbara Kley 39 *SEE* Kraemer, Peter
Kraemer, Barbara *SEE* Kraemer, Jakob
Kraemer, Barbara Scherer *SEE* Kraemer, Jakob
Kraemer, Bohdan; Chicago, 1870-1918 ***2853.20*** *p466*
Kraemer, Christine 27; Brazil, 1870 ***5475.1*** *p441*
Kraemer, Elisabeth *SEE* Kraemer, Peter
Kraemer, Elisabeth; Brazil, 1870 ***5475.1*** *p441*
Kraemer, Franz 3 *SEE* Kraemer, Peter
Kraemer, Franz 25; America, 1837 ***5475.1*** *p450*
*Wife:*Henriette 21
Kraemer, Franz *SEE* Kraemer, Peter
Kraemer, Georg *SEE* Kraemer, Jakob
Kraemer, Henriette 21 *SEE* Kraemer, Franz
Kraemer, Jacob; Ohio, 1809-1852 ***4511.35*** *p28*
Kraemer, Jakob *SEE* Kraemer, Peter
Kraemer, Jakob 7 *SEE* Kraemer, Peter
Kraemer, Jakob *SEE* Kraemer, Jakob
Kraemer, Jakob; Washington, 1886 ***5475.1*** *p45*
*Wife:*Barbara Scherer
*Son:*Peter
*Daughter:*Barbara
*Son:*Karl
*Son:*Jakob
*Son:*Georg
Kraemer, Joh. 25; New Orleans, 1840 ***778.6*** *p192*
Kraemer, Johann; America, 1842 ***5475.1*** *p453*
Kraemer, Johann 31; America, 1871 ***5475.1*** *p446*
*Wife:*Katharina Langerle 29
*Daughter:*Katharina 4
*Daughter:*Margarethe 4 months
*Daughter:*Anna 8
*Son:*Nikolaus 5
Kraemer, Johann; Buffalo, NY, 1856 ***5475.1*** *p509*
Kraemer, Karl *SEE* Kraemer, Jakob
Kraemer, Katharina 4 *SEE* Kraemer, Johann
Kraemer, Katharina 12 *SEE* Kraemer, Peter
Kraemer, Katharina Langerle 29 *SEE* Kraemer, Johann
Kraemer, Katharina 36; America, 1840 ***5475.1*** *p50*
Kraemer, Katharina 50; America, 1840 ***5475.1*** *p50*
*Son:*Nikolaus
Kraemer, Klara 14 *SEE* Kraemer, Peter
Kraemer, Margarethe 4 *SEE* Kraemer, Johann
Kraemer, Margarethe Biel 47 *SEE* Kraemer, Peter
Kraemer, Maria *SEE* Kraemer, Peter
Kraemer, Mathias *SEE* Kraemer, Peter
Kraemer, Matthew; Ohio, 1809-1852 ***4511.35*** *p28*
Kraemer, Nikolaus *SEE* Kraemer, Katharina Kinzinger
Kraemer, Nikolaus 5 *SEE* Kraemer, Johann
Kraemer, P. Josef *SEE* Kraemeer, Peter
Kraemer, Peter; America, 1837 ***5475.1*** *p408*
*Wife:*Barbara Kley
*Daughter:*Katharina
*Son:*Jakob
*Son:*Franz
*Son:*Peter
*Daughter:*Klara
Kraemer, Peter *SEE* Kraemer, Peter
Kraemer, Peter; America, 1863 ***5475.1*** *p281*
*Father:*Peter
Kraemer, Peter 9 *SEE* Kraemer, Peter
Kraemer, Peter; America, 1877 ***5475.1*** *p452*
*Sibling:*Maria
*Sibling:*P. Josef
*Sibling:*Jakob
*Sibling:*Elisabeth
Kraemer, Peter 49; Cincinnati, 1863 ***5475.1*** *p281*
*Wife:*Margarethe Biel 47
*Son:*Mathias
*Son:*Franz
*Son:*Mathias
Kraemer, Peter *SEE* Kraemer, Jakob
Kraetze, Appolonia; Galveston, TX, 1855 ***571.7*** *p17*
Krafkzak, Katie; Wisconsin, 1902 ***6795.8*** *p130*
Kraft, Adam; America, 1854 ***2526.43*** *p151*
Kraft, Adam *SEE* Kraft, Heinrich
Kraft, Andre 25; Halifax, N.S., 1902 ***1860.4*** *p44*
Kraft, Barbara 23; New York, NY, 1893 ***1883.7*** *p44*
Kraft, Carl Martin; Boston, 1902 ***1766.20*** *p16*
Kraft, Conrad; America, 1853 ***7420.1*** *p107*
Kraft, Elisabeth Muller *SEE* Kraft, Heinrich
Kraft, Emil; New York, 1903 ***1766.20*** *p23*
Kraft, Frank; Illinois, 1834-1900 ***6020.5*** *p132*

Kraft, Franz 29; New York, NY, 1893 *1883.7 p44*
Kraft, Friedrich; America, 1862 *2526.43 p151*
Kraft, Friedrich 17; America, 1854 *2526.43 p151*
Kraft, Georg; America, 1859 *2526.43 p151*
Kraft, Georg 9; New York, NY, 1893 *1883.7 p44*
Kraft, Georg Adam; America, 1874 *2526.43 p141*
Kraft, Georg Karl; America, 1880 *2526.43 p141*
Kraft, Heinrich *SEE* Kraft, Heinrich
Kraft, Heinrich 55; America, 1866 *2526.43 p151*
  *Wife:*Elisabeth Muller
  *Son:*Adam
  *Son:*Heinrich
  *Daughter:*Margaretha 23
  *Son:*Wilhelm
Kraft, Herman Friedrich; Wisconsin, 1903 *6795.8 p236*
Kraft, J.; South Carolina, 1849 *6155.4 p18*
Kraft, Johann Ernst; America, n.d. *8115.12 p321*
Kraft, Joseph 26; New York, NY, 1898 *7951.13 p43*
Kraft, Kath 28; Halifax, N.S., 1902 *1860.4 p44*
Kraft, Katherina 19; New York, NY, 1898 *7951.13 p43*
Kraft, Leonhard; America, 1884 *2526.43 p141*
Kraft, Margaretha 23 *SEE* Kraft, Heinrich
Kraft, Mathilda 19; Halifax, N.S., 1902 *1860.4 p44*
Kraft, Michael 19; New York, NY, 1874 *6954.7 p38*
Kraft, Regina 28; America, 1866 *2526.42 p175*
Kraft, Richarda 11 months; Halifax, N.S., 1902 *1860.4 p44*
Kraft, Richarda 69; Halifax, N.S., 1902 *1860.4 p44*
Kraft, Sebastian 24; Halifax, N.S., 1902 *1860.4 p44*
Kraft, Wilhelm *SEE* Kraft, Heinrich
Kraft, Wilhelmina 2; Halifax, N.S., 1902 *1860.4 p44*
Kraftczak, Katie; Wisconsin, 1902 *6795.8 p130*
Krager, Adam *SEE* Krager, Leonhard
Krager, Adam 25 *SEE* Krager, Mrs. Johannes
Krager, Christoph *SEE* Krager, Leonhard
Krager, Elisabeth 42 *SEE* Krager, Leonhard
Krager, Georg 9 *SEE* Krager, Heinrich
Krager, Georg Karl *SEE* Krager, Leonhard
Krager, Heinrich *SEE* Krager, Leonhard
Krager, Heinrich 47; America, 1854 *2526.43 p151*
  With wife 44
  *Daughter:*Margaretha 18
  *Son:*Karl 11
  *Son:*Georg 9
Krager, Johann Nikolaus; America, 1864 *2526.43 p151*
Krager, Johannes; America, 1853 *2526.42 p182*
Krager, Johannes 20 *SEE* Krager, Mrs. Johannes
Krager, Mrs. Johannes 50; Illinois, 1864 *2526.42 p182*
  *Son:*Adam 25
  *Son:*Johannes 20
Krager, Karl 11 *SEE* Krager, Heinrich
Krager, Leonhard *SEE* Krager, Leonhard
Krager, Leonhard 42; America, 1866 *2526.43 p151*
  *Wife:*Elisabeth 42
  *Daughter:*Margaretha 17
  *Son:*Heinrich
  *Son:*Christoph
  *Son:*Adam
  *Son:*Georg Karl
  *Daughter:*Marie 8
  *Son:*Leonhard
Krager, Margaretha 17 *SEE* Krager, Leonhard
Krager, Margaretha 18 *SEE* Krager, Heinrich
Krager, Marie 8 *SEE* Krager, Leonhard
Kragler, Nicholas; Ohio, 1809-1852 *4511.35 p28*
Krahl, Friedrich August; America, 1871 *7420.1 p396*
Krahmer, Joh. C.; Valdivia, Chile, 1852 *1192.4 p55*
  With wife & 2 children
  With child 5
  With child 12
Krahn, Katharina 39; Brazil, 1862 *5475.1 p540*
Krahn, Theresia; New York, 1896 *5475.1 p426*
Krain, Jacob 2 months; New York, NY, 1885 *1883.7 p46*
Krain, Lisbeth 23; New York, NY, 1885 *1883.7 p46*
Krain, Michael 25; New York, NY, 1885 *1883.7 p46*
Krajavski, Jan 30; New York, NY, 1890 *1883.7 p47*
Krajewski, Walenty 25; New York, NY, 1920 *930.50 p48*
Krakan, Ernst M.; Ohio, 1809-1852 *4511.35 p28*
Krakau, Ernst N.; Ohio, 1809-1852 *4511.35 p28*
Krakora, Josef; Illinois, 1853-1910 *2853.20 p471*
Krakowski, John; Detroit, 1929-1930 *6214.5 p61*
Kral, . . .; Pennsylvania, 1750-1799 *2853.20 p17*
Kral, Josef Jiri; Chicago, 1889 *2853.20 p300*
Kralicek, Vaclav; Chicago, 1900 *2853.20 p461*
Krall, A.M.; America, 1869 *2526.42 p95*
Krall, Adam; America, 1886 *2526.43 p141*
Krall, Barbara Uhrig *SEE* Krall, Philipp, III
Krall, E. Margareta; America, 1869 *2526.42 p96*
Krall, Eva Margaretha 6 *SEE* Krall, Philipp
Krall, Eva Margaretha Staab 31 *SEE* Krall, Philipp
Krall, Katharina 3 *SEE* Krall, Philipp

Krall, Ludwig *SEE* Krall, Philipp
Krall, Ludwig; America, 1882 *2526.43 p141*
Krall, Magdalena; America, 1856 *2526.43 p120*
Krall, Maria Schantz *SEE* Krall, Philipp
Krall, Maria Ablona 9 *SEE* Krall, Philipp
Krall, Maria Elisabetha 8 *SEE* Krall, Philipp
Krall, Philipp; America, 1854 *2526.42 p96*
  *Wife:*Maria Schantz
  *Child:*Ludwig
Krall, Philipp; America, 1867 *2526.42 p96*
Krall, Philipp; America, 1870 *2526.42 p143*
Krall, Philipp 40; America, 1864 *2526.43 p151*
  *Wife:*Eva Margaretha Staab 31
  *Daughter:*Maria Elisabetha 8
  *Daughter:*Eva Margaretha 6
  *Daughter:*Katharina 3
  *Daughter:*Maria Ablona 9 months
Krall, Philipp, III; Ohio, 1864 *2526.42 p96*
  *Wife:*Barbara Uhrig
  With sister
Kralovec, Jan; Chicago, 1868 *2853.20 p393*
Kram, Georg. 19; New Orleans, 1840 *778.6 p192*
Kramar, William; Detroit, 1929-1930 *6214.5 p70*
Kramarsz, Blazej; Detroit, 1929-1930 *6214.5 p70*
Kramaz, Blazej; Detroit, 1929-1930 *6214.5 p70*
Krambeck, Johannes; Iowa, 1884 *1211.15 p15*
Kramer, A. Katharina *SEE* Kramer, Peter
Kramer, A. Maria *SEE* Kramer, Mathias
Kramer, Adam 9 *SEE* Kramer, Philipp, II
Kramer, Anna Schweitzer *SEE* Kramer, Peter
Kramer, Anna Maria Lehnhof *SEE* Kramer, Mathias
Kramer, Antonie; America, 1868 *7919.3 p535*
  *Daughter:*Ernestine
  *Daughter:*Caroline
Kramer, August 24; New York, 1889 *5475.1 p75*
Kramer, Carl 3; Halifax, N.S., 1902 *1860.4 p44*
Kramer, Caroline *SEE* Kramer, Antonie
Kramer, Caroline 2; Halifax, N.S., 1902 *1860.4 p44*
Kramer, Charles F.; Missouri, 1889 *3276.1 p2*
Kramer, Christine 2 months; Halifax, N.S., 1902 *1860.4 p44*
Kramer, Christine 23; Halifax, N.S., 1902 *1860.4 p44*
Kramer, Daniel; America, 1854 *5475.1 p30*
Kramer, Elisabeth; America, 1867 *7919.3 p531*
Kramer, Ernestine *SEE* Kramer, Antonie
Kramer, Fred; Missouri, 1886 *3276.1 p2*
Kramer, Fred; Missouri, 1889 *3276.1 p2*
Kramer, Friedrich Christian; America, 1854 *7420.1 p123*
  With wife 1 son & 2 daughters
Kramer, Friedrich Christian; America, 1868 *7420.1 p273*
Kramer, Georg; America, 1867 *7919.3 p525*
Kramer, Georg 34; Halifax, N.S., 1902 *1860.4 p44*
Kramer, Georg Ernst; America, 1864 *7420.1 p225*
Kramer, Georg Jakob; America, 1854 *2526.43 p193*
Kramer, George; Illinois, 1852 *6079.1 p8*
Kramer, George; Ohio, 1840-1897 *8365.35 p17*
Kramer, Gottfried; Galveston, TX, 1855 *571.7 p17*
Kramer, Gottlab W.; Missouri, 1889 *3276.1 p2*
Kramer, Hans Heinrich; America, 1857 *7420.1 p165*
Kramer, Hermann; America, 1895 *2526.42 p124*
Kramer, Hermann; Galveston, TX, 1855 *571.7 p17*
Kramer, Jacob 24; America, 1847 *778.6 p192*
Kramer, Jakob; America, 1840 *5475.1 p169*
Kramer, Johann; America, 1847 *5475.1 p486*
Kramer, Johann *SEE* Kramer, Mathias
Kramer, Johann *SEE* Kramer, Peter
Kramer, Johann 12 *SEE* Kramer, Kath. Knapp
Kramer, Karoline 26; America, 1896 *5475.1 p46*
Kramer, Kath.; America, 1874 *5475.1 p175*
Kramer, Kath. 38; America, 1890 *5475.1 p52*
  *Son:*Friedrich
  *Son:*Heinrich
  *Son:*Karl
  *Son:*Ludw. Hermann
  *Daughter:*Katharina
Kramer, Kath. 39; America, 1857 *5475.1 p279*
  *Son:*Johann 12
Kramer, Katharina *SEE* Kramer, Mathias
Kramer, Katharina; America, 1872 *5475.1 p168*
Kramer, Katharina Albert *SEE* Kramer, Peter
Kramer, Lewis; Ohio, 1840-1897 *8365.35 p17*
Kramer, Ludwig 14 *SEE* Kramer, Philipp, II
Kramer, Magdalena 24; New York, 1889 *5475.1 p75*
Kramer, Margarethe *SEE* Kramer, Peter
Kramer, Margarethe 21; America, 1897 *5475.1 p46*
Kramer, Maria *SEE* Kramer, Mathias
Kramer, Mathew; Ohio, 1809-1852 *4511.35 p28*
Kramer, Mathias; America, 1868 *5475.1 p139*
  *Wife:*Anna Maria Lehnhof
  *Daughter:*Maria
  *Son:*Johann
  *Daughter:*Katharina
  *Daughter:*A. Maria

Kramer, Mathias 43; America, 1843 *5475.1 p280*
Kramer, Mathilde Adelheid; America, 1868 *7919.3 p525*
  With 3 children & grandchild
Kramer, Michael 20; America, 1880 *2526.43 p123*
Kramer, Michel Peter; America, 1852-1862 *5475.1 p404*
Kramer, Nathan; North Carolina, 1856 *1088.45 p17*
Kramer, Peter; America, 1883 *5475.1 p176*
  *Wife:*Katharina Albert
  *Son:*Johann
Kramer, Peter; America, 1883 *5475.1 p176*
  *Wife:*Anna Schweitzer
  With mother-in-law
  *Daughter:*A. Katharina
  *Daughter:*Margarethe
Kramer, Philipp, II; America, 1844 *2526.43 p134*
  With wife
  *Son:*Ludwig
  *Son:*Adam
Kramer, Ulrich; Brazil, 1904 *7420.1 p401*
Kramer, Wendel; America, 1870 *2526.43 p197*
Kramer, Wilhelm; America, 1835 *2526.43 p173*
  With wife & 3 children
Kramer, Wilhelm; England, 1898 *5475.1 p430*
Krampert, John; New York, 1859 *358.56 p54*
Kranc, Wm.; Wisconsin, 1877 *6795.8 p82*
Krank, Wm.; Wisconsin, 1877 *6795.8 p82*
Krano, Johann 25; Portland, ME, 1906 *970.38 p78*
Krano, Marie 22; Portland, ME, 1906 *970.38 p78*
Kranskoff, Leopold; Ohio, 1856 *3580.20 p32*
Kranskoff, Leopold; Ohio, 1856 *6020.12 p12*
Krantz, Catharine 29; America, 1846 *778.6 p192*
Krantz, Michel 35; America, 1846 *778.6 p192*
Kranz, Carl Heinrich Ferdinand; America, 1865 *7420.1 p233*
Kranz, Juls. 19; New York, NY, 1893 *1883.7 p43*
Kranz, Wm.; Wisconsin, 1877 *6795.8 p82*
Kranza, Theophil; Wisconsin, 1885 *6795.8 p59*
Kranzer, Johannes 9 *SEE* Kranzer, Sebastian
Kranzer, Lorenz 4 *SEE* Kranzer, Sebastian
Kranzer, Maria 22 *SEE* Kranzer, Sebastian
Kranzer, Sebastian; America, 1848 *2526.43 p204*
  With wife
  *Son:*Johannes
  *Son:*Lorenz
  *Daughter:*Maria
Krapf, Valentine; Ohio, 1809-1852 *4511.35 p28*
Krase, Fr.; New York, 1860 *358.56 p3*
Krasny, Antonin; Cleveland, OH, 1857 *2853.20 p477*
Kratochvil, Frantisek; Milwaukee, 1858-1887 *2853.20 p309*
Kratochvil, Jan; New York, 1856 *2853.20 p118*
Kratochvil, Josef; Wisconsin, 1857-1861 *2853.20 p334*
Kratt, Elisabeth; Philadelphia, 1870 *8513.31 p422*
Kratz, Barbara *SEE* Kratz, Josef
Kratz, Ferdinand; Wisconsin, 1910 *6795.8 p175*
Kratz, John; Ohio, 1809-1852 *4511.35 p28*
Kratz, Josef 51; America, 1868 *5475.1 p297*
  *Wife:*Katharina Ehlen 49
  *Daughter:*Barbara
  *Daughter:*Margarethe
  *Daughter:*Maria
Kratz, Katharina Ehlen 49 *SEE* Kratz, Josef
Kratz, Margarethe *SEE* Kratz, Josef
Kratz, Maria *SEE* Kratz, Josef
Kratz, Maria 29; America, 1881 *5475.1 p155*
Kratzke, August; Wisconsin, 1889 *6795.8 p87*
Krau, Adam 24; Missouri, 1847 *778.6 p192*
Kraulik, Jan; Texas, 1854 *2853.20 p60*
Krault, Francois 38; America, 1843 *778.6 p192*
Kraup, Joseph 38; Ontario, 1871 *1823.17 p87*
Kraus, Adolf; Chicago, 1872 *2853.20 p397*
Kraus, Angela; America, 1867 *5475.1 p238*
Kraus, Angela; America, 1867 *5475.1 p265*
Kraus, David 19; Portland, ME, 1911 *970.38 p78*
Kraus, Heins 19; Baltimore, 1889 *8425.16 p35*
Kraus, Jakob; America, 1854 *2526.42 p116*
Kraus, Jakob; America, 1863 *5475.1 p264*
Kraus, Tomas; Chicago, 1893 *2853.20 p418*
Krausbauer, Carl Christian Otto Leo; Illinois, 1861 *7420.1 p206*
Krause, Anna; Wisconsin, 1895 *6795.8 p130*
Krause, Anton; Valdivia, Chile, 1852 *1192.4 p55*
Krause, Auguste; Valdivia, Chile, 1850 *1192.4 p49*
Krause, Auguste Mathilde; Wisconsin, 1892 *6795.8 p216*
Krause, Bernhard; Galveston, TX, 1855 *571.7 p17*
Krause, Carl; Chile, 1852 *1192.4 p52*
Krause, Carl; New York, 1889 *1766.20 p25*
Krause, Emil Eduard; America, 1869 *5475.1 p303*
Krause, Emma; Wisconsin, 1887 *6795.8 p117*
Krause, Franz; America, 1881 *5475.1 p23*
Krause, Friedr. 23; New York, NY, 1893 *1883.7 p43*
Krause, H.; Iowa, 1884 *1211.15 p15*
Krause, Hermann; Valdivia, Chile, 1850 *1192.4 p49*

Krause, Hermann; Wisconsin, 1880 *6795.8 p226*
Krause, Justus; Chile, 1852 *1192.4 p52*
Krause, Theodore; Iowa, 1888 *1211.15 p16*
Krause, Willy Carl; Chile, 1900 *7420.1 p376*
Krausin, Louisa; New Castle, DE, 1817-1818 *90.20 p152*
Krauskopf, Johann Philipp; America, n.d. *8115.12 p326*
Krauskopf, Katharine; America, n.d. *8115.12 p325*
Krauskopf, Luise; America, 1869 *8115.12 p325*
Krauss, Adam 9 months; America, 1847 *778.6 p192*
Krauss, Barbara 23; America, 1847 *778.6 p192*
Krauss, Barbara 64; America, 1847 *778.6 p192*
Krauss, Christian; America, 1868 *7919.3 p531*
Krauss, Conrad 3; America, 1847 *778.6 p192*
Krauss, Elisa; America, 1867 *7919.3 p528*
Krauss, Fd.; America, 1840 *778.6 p192*
Krauss, Georg; America, 1886 *2526.43 p218*
Krauss, Heinrich Christian; America, 1846 *7420.1 p45*
Krauss, Henriette Sophie Christiane; New York, NY, 1878 *7420.1 p311*
Krauss, Johann Jakob; America, 1892 *2526.43 p218*
Krauss, Nicolas 36; America, 1847 *778.6 p192*
Kraut, Christian; New York, 1860 *358.56 p148*
Krauter, Katharina; Pennsylvania, 1887 *5475.1 p17*
Kravetz, Rose; Detroit, 1929-1930 *6214.5 p70*
Krawczyk, Katie; Wisconsin, 1902 *6795.8 p130*
Krawczyk, Walenty; Detroit, 1929 *1640.55 p115*
Krawiec, Rose; Detroit, 1929-1930 *6214.5 p70*
Krawiec, Sam; Texas, 1855-1872 *9980.22 p16*
Krawitz, A.A. 60; Texas, 1906 *9980.22 p17*
Krayer, Christian Frederick; Ohio, 1809-1852 *4511.35 p28*
Krazmeyer, Ignaz 8; New Orleans, 1847 *778.6 p192*
Krazmeyer, Joseph 9; New Orleans, 1847 *778.6 p192*
Krazmeyer, Maria 34; New Orleans, 1847 *778.6 p192*
Krazmeyer, Michel 2; New Orleans, 1847 *778.6 p192*
Krc, Martin; Texas, 1876 *2853.20 p82*
Krc, Rudolf Martin; Texas, 1876 *2853.20 p64*
Krch, Frantisek; Iowa, 1856 *2853.20 p277*
Kreamer, Jacob; Ohio, 1809-1852 *4511.35 p28*
Krebast, Conrad; Ohio, 1809-1852 *4511.35 p28*
Kreber, Ignace 29; Louisiana, 1848 *778.6 p192*
Krebi, Frederic 1; New Orleans, 1848 *778.6 p192*
Krebi, Hariete 5; New Orleans, 1848 *778.6 p192*
Krebi, Jacob 3; New Orleans, 1848 *778.6 p192*
Krebi, Marie 34; New Orleans, 1848 *778.6 p192*
Krebs, Mr.; Pennsylvania, 1865 *170.15 p33*
  With wife
Krebs, Conrad Wilhelm Friedrich; America, 1865 *7420.1 p233*
Krebs, Ferdinand; New York, 1859 *358.56 p54*
Krebs, Friedrich; America, 1867 *7919.3 p530*
Krebs, Georg Erwin Oskar; America, 1887 *7420.1 p354*
Krebs, George; New York, 1860 *358.56 p3*
Krebs, H.; New York, 1859 *358.56 p101*
Krebs, Heinrich Wilhelm; America, 1870 *7420.1 p287*
Krebs, Henry Otto Albert; Wisconsin, 1889 *6795.8 p74*
Krebs, Jakob SEE Krebs, Margarethe
Krebs, Margarethe 33; America, 1867 *5475.1 p558*
  Son:Jakob
Krebs, Otto; New York, 1860 *358.56 p3*
Krebs, Sophie; New York, NY, 1870 *7420.1 p395*
Krebsbach, Nikolaus; America, 1848 *5475.1 p476*
Krech, Andreas; America, 1867 *7919.3 p535*
Krech, Dorothea Laurette; America, 1867 *7919.3 p527*
Krech, Georg Adam; America, 1867 *7919.3 p535*
Krech, Georg Richard; America, 1867 *7919.3 p535*
Krech, Johannes; America, 1868 *7919.3 p532*
Krech, Sebastian; America, 1868 *7919.3 p535*
  With wife daughter & 2 children
Krechel, Anton; Illinois, 1857 *6079.1 p8*
Kreck, Agenie 7; New York, NY, 1893 *1883.7 p44*
Kreck, Alexander 22; New York, NY, 1893 *1883.7 p44*
Kreck, Amalie 15; New York, NY, 1893 *1883.7 p44*
Kreck, Catha. 10; New York, NY, 1893 *1883.7 p44*
Kreck, Maria 3; New York, NY, 1893 *1883.7 p44*
Kreck, Maria 22; New York, NY, 1893 *1883.7 p44*
Kreck, Sofie 45; New York, NY, 1893 *1883.7 p44*
Kreckel, Adam; Pennsylvania, 1848 *170.15 p33*
  With wife & child
Kreckel, Elisabetha 26; Pennsylvania, 1848 *170.15 p33*
  With family
Kreckel, Johann Adam 30; Pennsylvania, 1848 *170.15 p33*
  With family
Kreckel, Johann Peter 1; Pennsylvania, 1848 *170.15 p33*
  With family
Kreckel, Johannes 4; Pennsylvania, 1848 *170.15 p33*
  With family
Kredel, Adam 19; America, 1852 *2526.43 p191*
Kredel, Anna Margaretha; America, 1854 *2526.43 p191*
Kredel, Charlotte; America, 1854 *2526.43 p132*
  With 4 children
Kredel, Jakob; America, 1854 *2526.43 p191*

Kredel, Katharina Luise; America, 1858 *2526.43 p141*
Kredel, Peter; America, 1854 *2526.43 p191*
Kredel, Peter; America, 1854 *2526.43 p204*
Kredell, Gustav; America, 1852 *2526.43 p173*
Kredo, August Wilhelm Louis; America, 1881 *7420.1 p322*
Kredo, Caroline Wilhelmine Charlotte SEE Kredo, Heinrich Friedrich
Kredo, Caroline Wilhelmine Charlotte; America, 1880 *7420.1 p316*
Kredo, Heinrich Friedrich; America, 1867 *7420.1 p259*
  Sister:Caroline Wilhelmine Charlotte
Kreegar, Christ; Washington, 1889 *2770.40 p79*
Kreft, Mr.; America, 1872 *7420.1 p296*
  With sister
Kreft, Ernst; America, 1858 *7420.1 p179*
Kreft, Heinrich Wilhelm Conrad; America, 1882 *7420.1 p330*
Kregier, Pauline; Wisconsin, 1881 *6795.8 p59*
Krehmeier, Earnest; Baltimore, 1880 *6212.1 p15*
Kreibill, John; Ohio, 1809-1852 *4511.35 p28*
Kreichy, Godfrey; Ohio, 1809-1852 *4511.35 p28*
Kreig, Frederic 33; Louisiana, 1848 *778.6 p192*
Kreig, Judith 35; Louisiana, 1848 *778.6 p192*
Kreimer, Philipp 20; America, 1846 *778.6 p192*
Krein, A. Maria; America, 1882 *5475.1 p242*
Krein, Anna Maria; America, 1837 *5475.1 p468*
Kreindels, Laser 20; New York, NY, 1878 *9253.2 p45*
Kreinders, John; Colorado, 1887 *1029.59 p51*
Kreis, Heinrich; America, 1846-1847 *5475.1 p51*
Kreisher, Philip; Ohio, 1809-1852 *4511.35 p28*
Kreitz, Charles; Ohio, 1809-1852 *4511.35 p28*
Kreitz, Philip; Ohio, 1809-1852 *4511.35 p28*
Krejar, August; Kansas, 1881 *1447.20 p64*
Krejca, Tomas SEE Krejca, Tomas
Krejca, Tomas; Texas, 1855 *2853.20 p63*
  Son:Tomas
Krejca, Vaclav; Chicago, 1863 *2853.20 p405*
Krejci, Frantisek; Iowa, 1854 *2853.20 p230*
Krejci, Martin; Cleveland, OH, 1854 *2853.20 p475*
Krekeler, Thomas; New York, NY, 1873 *7420.1 p300*
Krel, Pierre 30; America, 1847 *778.6 p192*
Krelis, Mr. 36; America, 1847 *778.6 p192*
Krelis, Jeanne 25; America, 1847 *778.6 p192*
Krelis, Marie 25; America, 1847 *778.6 p192*
Krell, Kaspar Julius; Philadelphia, 1866 *5475.1 p123*
Krell, Maria; America, 1867 *7919.3 p532*
Kremer, Anton; Port uncertain, 1852-1853 *5475.1 p287*
Kremer, David 36; New York, NY, 1890 *1883.7 p47*
Kremer, Henry; Ohio, 1809-1852 *4511.35 p28*
Kremer, Nikola; Louisiana, 1874 *4981.45 p209*
Kremer, Nikolaus; Wisconsin, 1882 *5475.1 p269*
Kremers, Pierre 24; New York, NY, 1856 *1766.1 p45*
Kremmer, Georg Wilhelm; America, 1868 *7919.3 p535*
Krempa, Theodorus; Wisconsin, 1893 *6795.8 p59*
Krems, Katharina; America, 1894 *5475.1 p425*
Krenek, Ignac; Texas, 1856-1906 *2853.20 p64*
Krenrick, Adam; Ohio, 1809-1852 *4511.35 p28*
Krentler, Eleonore; America, 1862 *7420.1 p213*
  Daughter:Wilhelmine
Krentler, Hermann W.; America, 1866 *7420.1 p244*
Krentler, Wilhelmine SEE Krentler, Eleonore
Krentler, Wilhelmine; America, 1863 *7420.1 p219*
Krentz, Albert Wilhelm; Wisconsin, 1895 *6795.8 p139*
Krentz, Alexander Fritz; Wisconsin, 1911 *6795.8 p168*
Krentz, Edmund; Wisconsin, 1908 *1822.55 p10*
Krentz, Emma; Wisconsin, 1892 *6795.8 p106*
Krentz, Jacques 1; New Orleans, 1848 *778.6 p192*
Krentz, William F.; Wisconsin, 1905 *6795.8 p178*
Krenz, Carl; Washington, 1881 *2770.40 p135*
Krenz, Robert Carl; Wisconsin, 1887 *6795.8 p33*
Krenzler, Adam 2; Baltimore, 1893 *1883.7 p38*
Krenzler, Barbara 32; Baltimore, 1893 *1883.7 p38*
Krenzler, Bernhard 5; Baltimore, 1893 *1883.7 p38*
Krenzler, Christine 3; Baltimore, 1893 *1883.7 p38*
Krenzler, Jacob 5; Baltimore, 1893 *1883.7 p38*
Krenzler, Jacob 30; Baltimore, 1893 *1883.7 p38*
Krenzler, Karoline 8; Baltimore, 1893 *1883.7 p38*
Krenzler, Marga 2 months; Baltimore, 1893 *1883.7 p38*
Krenzler, Rosine 4; Baltimore, 1893 *1883.7 p38*
Kreps, Samuel; Ohio, 1809-1852 *4511.35 p28*
Kresbeck, Barbara; New York, 1860 *358.56 p5*
Kresiensky, Anton; New Orleans, 1872 *6015.15 p26*
Kresin, Carl Wilhelm; Wisconsin, 1892 *6795.8 p221*
Kress, Ganese; America, 1867 *7919.3 p528*
Kretowicz, Zygmunt; Detroit, 1930 *1640.60 p81*
Kretsch, Mathias 22; America, 1856 *5475.1 p248*
Kretschmar, A.; New York, 1860 *358.56 p4*
Kretschmer, Henry; Illinois, 1860 *6079.1 p4*
Kreuschen, Elisa 28; America, 1841 *778.6 p193*
Kreuschen, Joseph 6; America, 1841 *778.6 p193*
Kreuschen, Laurent 2; America, 1841 *778.6 p193*
Kreuscher, Elisabeth 3 SEE Kreuscher, Peter

Kreuscher, Elisabeth Spielmann 28 SEE Kreuscher, Peter
Kreuscher, Jakob 4 SEE Kreuscher, Peter
Kreuscher, Karl 6 SEE Kreuscher, Peter
Kreuscher, Peter 9 SEE Kreuscher, Peter
Kreuscher, Peter 36; America, 1867 *5475.1 p508*
  Wife:Elisabeth Spielmann 28
  Son:Wilhelm 2
  Son:Karl 6
  Son:Jakob 4
  Daughter:Elisabeth 3
  Son:Peter 9
Kreuscher, Wilhelm 2 SEE Kreuscher, Peter
Kreutz, A. Maria SEE Kreutz, Peter
Kreutz, Barbara SEE Kreutz, Peter
Kreutz, J. 18; New Orleans, 1834 *1002.51 p111*
Kreutz, Katharina SEE Kreutz, Peter
Kreutz, M. Luzia SEE Kreutz, Peter
Kreutz, Magdalena Moritz SEE Kreutz, Peter
Kreutz, Maria SEE Kreutz, Peter
Kreutz, Peter; America, 1881 *5475.1 p285*
  Wife:Magdalena Moritz
  Daughter:A. Maria
  Daughter:M. Luzia
  Daughter:Katharina
  Daughter:Maria
  Daughter:Barbara
Kreuz, Albert; America, 1883 *5475.1 p37*
Kreuz, Charlotte SEE Kreuz, Philippine
Kreuz, Elise SEE Kreuz, Philippine
Kreuz, Heinrich SEE Kreuz, Philippine
Kreuz, Michael SEE Kreuz, Philippine
Kreuz, Philippine; America, 1857 *2526.43 p141*
  Daughter:Charlotte
  Son:Michael
  Son:Heinrich
  Daughter:Elise
Kreuzberger, Charles; New York, 1859 *358.56 p53*
Krichbaum, Johanna Elisabeth; Virginia, 1831 *152.20 p67*
Krichle, Frederic 28; America, 1847 *778.6 p193*
Krider, Jacob; Ohio, 1809-1852 *4511.35 p28*
Kriechbaum, Anna Elisabeth SEE Kriechbaum, Heinrich
Kriechbaum, Anna Eva 39 SEE Kriechbaum, Philipp
Kriechbaum, Anna Katharina SEE Kriechbaum, Heinrich
Kriechbaum, Elisabetha 15 SEE Kriechbaum, Philipp
Kriechbaum, Eva Katharina Seibert SEE Kriechbaum, Heinrich
Kriechbaum, Heinrich 17 SEE Kriechbaum, Philipp
Kriechbaum, Heinrich; Virginia, 1831 *152.20 p65*
  Wife:Eva Katharina Seibert
  Child:Anna Katharina
  Child:Johann Georg
  Child:Anna Elisabeth
Kriechbaum, Johann Georg SEE Kriechbaum, Heinrich
Kriechbaum, Margaretha 4 SEE Kriechbaum, Philipp
Kriechbaum, Maria 7 SEE Kriechbaum, Philipp
Kriechbaum, Philipp 3 SEE Kriechbaum, Philipp
Kriechbaum, Philipp 20 SEE Kriechbaum, Philipp
Kriechbaum, Philipp 52; America, 1882 *2526.43 p210*
  Wife:Anna Eva 39
  Son:Heinrich 17
  Son:Philipp 20
  Daughter:Elisabetha 15
  Daughter:Margaretha 4
  Son:Philipp 3
  Daughter:Maria 7
Kriegbaum, Anna Maria; Virginia, 1831 *152.20 p70*
Kriegbaum, Sophie; America, 1865 *2526.43 p122*
Krieger, Anna 9; New York, NY, 1893 *1883.7 p43*
Krieger, Augusta 35; New York, NY, 1893 *1883.7 p43*
Krieger, Carl Wilhelm Otto; America, 1883 *7420.1 p337*
Krieger, Charles; South Carolina, 1855 *6155.4 p18*
Krieger, Charles H.; Washington, 1888 *2770.40 p26*
Krieger, John; Ohio, 1809-1852 *4511.35 p28*
Kriehderfer, Andreas 20; America, 1846 *778.6 p193*
Kriehderfer, Carl 21; America, 1846 *778.6 p193*
Krienders, Johan; Iowa, 1870 *1029.59 p51*
Kriener, Felix 40; Louisiana, 1848 *778.6 p193*
Krienke, Edward; Wisconsin, 1870 *6795.8 p139*
Krier, Peter; Iowa, 1880 *5475.1 p275*
Kriete, John F.; North Carolina, 1852 *1088.45 p17*
Krikavova, Bozena; New York, NY, 1893 *2853.20 p469*
Krimmer, Christian; New York, 1859 *358.56 p55*
Krinkel, Ernst; Ohio, 1809-1852 *4511.35 p28*
Krinkie, Fred; Wisconsin, 1895 *6795.8 p128*
Krinkil, Charles; Ohio, 1809-1852 *4511.35 p28*
Krippers, Peter; Iowa, 1911 *1211.15 p16*
Krips, Samuel; Ohio, 1809-1852 *4511.35 p28*
Krisam, Jakob; America, 1880 *5475.1 p58*
Krise, Ludwig 45; Portland, ME, 1911 *970.38 p78*
Krisner, Louisa 25; America, 1843 *778.6 p193*
Kriss, Adam; Louisiana, 1874-1875 *4981.45 p29*
Krisser, Dominique 27; Louisiana, 1848 *778.6 p193*

Kristan, Vojtech; Wisconsin, 1879-1881 *2853.20 p328*
Kristenson, Charles Albin; Cleveland, OH, 1892-1903 *9722.10 p122*
Kristofferson, Soren Chris.; Washington, 1888 *2770.40 p26*
Kristufek, Jan; Chicago, 1854 *2853.20 p387*
Krivak, Anton 54; Minnesota, 1925 *2769.54 p1384*
Kriz, Frantisek; Chicago, 1854 *2853.20 p387*
Kriz, Frantisek; Milwaukee, 1854 *2853.20 p308*
  *Brother:*Hynek
  *Brother:*Jan
  *Sister:*Marie
Kriz, Frantisek; Wisconsin, 1856 *2853.20 p345*
Kriz, Hynek *SEE* Kriz, Frantisek
Kriz, Jan *SEE* Kriz, Frantisek
Kriz, Josef; Cleveland, OH, 1852 *2853.20 p475*
Kriz, Josef; Wisconsin, 1856 *2853.20 p345*
Kriz, Marie *SEE* Kriz, Frantisek
Krizek, Josef; South Dakota, 1876 *2853.20 p247*
Kriz Family ; Nebraska, 1874 *2853.20 p171*
Krob, Johann; America, 1842 *5475.1 p453*
Kroc, Josef; Iowa, 1855-1856 *2853.20 p237*
Krockenberger, Johann; America, 1871 *179.55 p19*
Krockenberger, Johann Gottfried B.; America, 1871 *179.55 p19*
Kroehnke, Augustus F.G.; Wisconsin, 1883 *6795.8 p220*
Kroenke, Fred; Wisconsin, 1895 *6795.8 p128*
Krofft, Cretien; Louisiana, 1841-1844 *4981.45 p210*
Kroger, C.; Venezuela, 1843 *3899.5 p546*
Kroger, J.; Venezuela, 1843 *3899.5 p546*
Kroger, Louise 30; New York, NY, 1864 *8425.62 p196*
Kroh, Johannes; America, 1852 *2526.43 p151*
Krohn, Frederick; Ohio, 1809-1852 *4511.35 p28*
Krojanke, John; Detroit, 1890 *9980.23 p96*
Kroke, Wilhelm; Valdivia, Chile, 1850 *1192.4 p49*
Krolczyk, John; Texas, 1917-1922 *6015.15 p26*
Kroll, August; Wisconsin, 1883 *6795.8 p197*
Kroll, Gustaf; Wisconsin, 1876 *6795.8 p175*
Kroll, Jakob; America, 1872 *2526.43 p191*
Kroll, John; New York, 1859 *358.56 p55*
Krolm, Frederick; Ohio, 1809-1852 *4511.35 p28*
Kroman, Niels; New York, 1860 *358.56 p150*
Kromberg, Heinrich; America, 1852 *7420.1 p92*
  With wife 3 daughters & 3 sons
Krome, Mr.; America, 1867 *7420.1 p259*
  With wife
  With child 5
  With child 12
  With child 9
Krome, Heinrich; Louisville, KY, 1847 *7420.1 p56*
Kromer, . . .; America, 1848 *7420.1 p60*
Kromer, August Gottlieb Anton *SEE* Kromer, Friedrich Wilhelm Ferdinand
Kromer, Carl Heinrich Ernst; America, 1890 *7420.1 p400*
Kromer, Dorothea; Philadelphia, 1904 *7420.1 p401*
Kromer, Engel Marie Eleonore; America, 1862 *7420.1 p212*
Kromer, Engel Marie Ernestine; America, 1870 *7420.1 p282*
Kromer, Ernst; America, 1841 *7420.1 p22*
Kromer, Ernst Friedrich Wilhelm; America, 1868 *7420.1 p273*
Kromer, Ernst Ludwig *SEE* Kromer, Friedrich Wilhelm Ferdinand
Kromer, Friedrich Christian; America, 1845 *7420.1 p37*
  *Wife:*Sophie Wilhelmine Witte
  With 6 children
Kromer, Friedrich Christian; Fort Wayne, IN, 1845 *7420.1 p37*
  *Wife:*Wilhelmine Christ. Meier
Kromer, Friedrich Wilhelm; Ohio, 1846 *7420.1 p45*
  With son 12
  With daughter
  With daughter 26
  With daughter 21
  With daughter 16
  With son 10
Kromer, Friedrich Wilhelm Ferdinand *SEE* Kromer, Friedrich Wilhelm Ferdinand
Kromer, Friedrich Wilhelm Ferdinand; America, 1869 *7420.1 p280*
  *Wife:*Sophie Dorothee Charlotte Koller
  *Son:*Heinrich August
  *Son:*August Gottlieb Anton
  *Son:*Friedrich Wilhelm Ferdinand
  *Son:*Ernst Ludwig
Kromer, Heinrich August *SEE* Kromer, Friedrich Wilhelm Ferdinand
Kromer, Heinrich Ludwig Ferdinand; America, 1869 *7420.1 p280*
Kromer, Johann Ernst Friedrich; America, 1845 *7420.1 p38*

Kromer, Johann Friedrich Andreas; America, 1845 *7420.1 p37*
  With son 3
  With daughter 14
  With daughter 12
  With daughter 10
  With daughter 16
  With daughter 17
Kromer, Ludwig; America, 1863 *7420.1 p219*
  With family
Kromer, Mois 19; America, 1844 *778.6 p193*
Kromer, Sophie Dorothee Charlotte Koller *SEE* Kromer, Friedrich Wilhelm Ferdinand
Kromer, Sophie Philippine; America, 1870 *7420.1 p284*
Kromer, Sophie Wilhelmine Witte *SEE* Kromer, Friedrich Christian
Kromer, Sophie Wilhelmine Charlotte; America, 1892 *7420.1 p365*
Kromer, W.; America, 1867 *7420.1 p259*
  With mother
Kromer, Wilhelmine Christ. Meier *SEE* Kromer, Friedrich Christian
Kromer, Wilhelmine Sophie Louise; America, 1893 *7420.1 p368*
Kromer Brothers, . . .; America, 1857 *7420.1 p165*
Kromin, Alexander 3; Portland, ME, 1911 *970.38 p78*
Kromin, Anna Maria 24; Portland, ME, 1911 *970.38 p78*
Kromin, Conrad 39; Portland, ME, 1911 *970.38 p78*
Kromin, Heinrich 25; Portland, ME, 1911 *970.38 p78*
Kromin, Heinrich 26; Portland, ME, 1911 *970.38 p78*
Kromin, Johannes 2; Portland, ME, 1911 *970.38 p79*
Kromin, Katarina E. 23; Portland, ME, 1911 *970.38 p79*
Kromin, Maria 1; Portland, ME, 1911 *970.38 p79*
Kromin, Maria K. 21; Portland, ME, 1911 *970.38 p79*
Kromin, Paulina 11; Portland, ME, 1911 *970.38 p79*
Kromm, Adam 29; Portland, ME, 1911 *970.38 p79*
Kromm, Elisabetha 24; Portland, ME, 1911 *970.38 p79*
Kromm, Maria 2; Portland, ME, 1911 *970.38 p79*
Kron, Barbara *SEE* Kron, Nikolaus
Kron, Barbara Becker 30 *SEE* Kron, Nikolaus
Kron, Casper; New York, 1860 *358.56 p149*
Kron, Charles; Colorado, 1893 *1029.59 p51*
Kron, Christine 6 months; Missouri, 1845 *778.6 p193*
Kron, Francis Joseph; North Carolina, 1844 *1088.45 p17*
Kron, Georg 26; Halifax, N.S., 1902 *1860.4 p44*
Kron, Gertrud *SEE* Kron, Nikolaus
Kron, Katharina *SEE* Kron, Nikolaus
Kron, Marie 26; Halifax, N.S., 1902 *1860.4 p44*
Kron, Nikolaus; America, 1800-1899 *5475.1 p314*
  *Wife:*Barbara Becker
  *Child:*Gertrud
  *Child:*Barbara
  *Child:*Katharina
Kron, Pierre 24; Missouri, 1845 *778.6 p193*
Kron, Sophie 29; Missouri, 1845 *778.6 p193*
Krone, Ann; New York, 1860 *358.56 p150*
Kronenberger, Bernhard; Chicago, 1884 *5475.1 p137*
Kronenberger, Elisabeth; Philadelphia, 1884 *5475.1 p229*
  *Daughter:*Barbara
  *Daughter:*Anna
  *Daughter:*Katharina
  *Son:*Johann
  *Son:*Georg
Kronenberger, Gertrud; America, 1873 *5475.1 p158*
Kronenberger, Katharina; New York, 1893 *5475.1 p391*
  *Daughter:*Rosa
  *Daughter:*Margarethe
  *Son:*Nikolaus
  *Son:*Jakob
  *Son:*Karl
  *Son:*Rudolph
Kronenberger, Moise 46; Louisiana, 1848 *778.6 p193*
Kronenbold, Elisabeth; America, 1869 *2526.43 p134*
Kronhert, John F.; Louisiana, 1836-1840 *4981.45 p212*
Kronmuller, Johann Georg; America, 1883 *179.55 p19*
Kronsberg, Louise Sophie Dorothee Charlotte; New York, NY, 1897 *7420.1 p373*
Krook, Gust. Georg; Charleston, SC, n.d. *6412.40 p152*
Krook, Otto W.; New York, NY, 1844 *6412.40 p147*
Krop, Wilhelm; Port uncertain, 1853 *7420.1 p107*
Krop, Wilhelmine Christine Friederike; America, 1894 *7420.1 p371*
  *Daughter:*Anna Wilhelmine Sophie
Kropf, Peter; America, 1882 *5475.1 p331*
Kropidlowska, Julianna; Detroit, 1890 *9980.23 p96*
Kropornicki, Adam; Detroit, 1929 *1640.55 p116*
Kropp, Dorothee; America, 1853 *7420.1 p107*
Kropp, Georg 48; America, 1836 *2526.43 p218*
  With wife & 4 children
Kropp, Hermann Eduard; Wisconsin, 1905 *6795.8 p154*
Kropp, Johannes; America, 1891 *2526.43 p219*

Kropp, Leonhard; America, 1836 *2526.43 p134*
  *Wife:*Walburga Eckert
  With child
  With child 4
Kropp, Walburga Eckert *SEE* Kropp, Leonhard
Kropp, Wilhelm; Port uncertain, 1853 *7420.1 p107*
Kroschell, Albertine; America, 1883 *7420.1 p337*
Kross, John N.; North Carolina, 1845 *1088.45 p17*
Krotz, Charles; Ohio, 1809-1852 *4511.35 p28*
Krotz, Jean 26; Port uncertain, 1847 *778.6 p193*
Krotz, Katharina; America, 1700-1899 *179.55 p19*
Kroulik, Vaclav; Wisconsin, 1852 *2853.20 p303*
Kroupa, Antonin; America, 1845-1849 *2853.20 p217*
Kroupa, Antonin; Cleveland, OH, 1888 *2853.20 p290*
Krouse, Alvina; Wisconsin, 1907 *6795.8 p232*
Krouz, John; Louisiana, 1836-1841 *4981.45 p209*
Krow, Charles; Colorado, 1893 *1029.59 p51*
Krozumska, Antone; Texas, 1870-1936 *6015.15 p27*
Krten, Frantisek; Milwaukee, 1857 *2853.20 p155*
Kruananman, Frederick; Ohio, 1809-1852 *4511.35 p28*
Krubeck, Ottilie Pauline; Wisconsin, 1893 *6795.8 p30*
Kruckeberg, Widow; America, 1856 *7420.1 p149*
  With son
Kruckeberg, Carl; America, 1852 *7420.1 p92*
  With wife 3 sons & daughter
Kruckeberg, Conrad; America, 1854 *7420.1 p123*
Kruckeberg, Ernst; Port uncertain, 1837 *7420.1 p13*
Kruckeberg, Friederike Charlotte Henriette; America, 1861 *7420.1 p206*
Kruckeberg, Friedrich; America, 1852 *7420.1 p92*
  With wife son & 3 daughters
Kruckeberg, Friedrich Wilhelm; America, 1881 *7420.1 p322*
Kruckeberg, Heinrich; America, 1852 *7420.1 p92*
Kruckeberg, Louis; America, 1885 *7420.1 p347*
Kruckeberg, Wilhelm; America, 1894 *7420.1 p370*
Krudop, Carl Friedrich Wilhelm; America, 1875 *7420.1 p305*
Krueger, Alvine Wilhelmine Henriette; Wisconsin, 1896 *6795.8 p74*
Krueger, August; Wisconsin, 1858 *6795.8 p154*
Krueger, August; Wisconsin, 1881 *6795.8 p226*
Krueger, August Frederick; Wisconsin, 1884 *6795.8 p165*
Krueger, August Friedrich; Wisconsin, 1896 *6795.8 p117*
Krueger, Bernhard; Wisconsin, 1893 *6795.8 p152*
Krueger, Bertha Albertine; Wisconsin, 1899 *6795.8 p217*
Krueger, Carl Julius; Wisconsin, 1887 *6795.8 p128*
Krueger, Emil; Wisconsin, 1886 *6795.8 p69*
Krueger, Emma Bertha; Wisconsin, 1907 *6795.8 p162*
Krueger, Ernst Ludwig; Wisconsin, 1890 *6795.8 p25*
Krueger, Herman August; Wisconsin, 1887 *6795.8 p117*
Krueger, Ida Auguste; Wisconsin, 1903 *6795.8 p162*
Krueger, Joachim; New York, 1859 *358.56 p101*
Krueger, Julius; Wisconsin, 1896 *6795.8 p212*
Krueger, Julius August; Wisconsin, 1885 *6795.8 p128*
Krueger, Karl Wilhelm; Wisconsin, 1868 *6795.8 p74*
Krueger, Mathilda Johanna Maria; Wisconsin, 1897 *6795.8 p87*
Krueger, Otto William; Wisconsin, 1910 *6795.8 p165*
Krueger, Wilhelm; Wisconsin, 1869 *6795.8 p41*
Krueger, Wilhelm Friedr.; Wisconsin, 1887 *6795.8 p50*
Krueger, Wilhelmine; Wisconsin, 1883 *6795.8 p85*
Krueger, William; Wisconsin, 1908 *1822.55 p10*
Kruesel, Wilhelm; Wisconsin, 1871 *6795.8 p122*
Krug, Adolph; Washington, 1889 *2770.40 p79*
Krug, Carl Friedrich Wilhelm; America, 1866 *7420.1 p245*
Krug, Frederick, Jr. 2; Louisiana, 1848 *778.6 p193*
Krug, Heinrich; Valdivia, Chile, 1850 *1192.4 p49*
Krug, Lisette; America, 1856 *7420.1 p149*
Kruger, Adolph Friedrich; America, 1881 *7420.1 p322*
Kruger, August; Wisconsin, 1888 *6795.8 p166*
Kruger, Carl; Wisconsin, 1899 *6795.8 p224*
Kruger, Eduard; Wisconsin, 1890 *6795.8 p147*
Kruger, Engel; America, 1854 *7420.1 p123*
Kruger, Ernst Christoph Friedrich; America, 1865 *7420.1 p233*
Kruger, Fred; Iowa, 1923 *1211.15 p16*
Kruger, Frederick; Iowa, 1884 *1211.15 p15*
Kruger, Fredrick; Wisconsin, 1871 *6795.8 p125*
Kruger, Friedrich; St. Louis, 1891 *7420.1 p363*
Kruger, Gusta Maria; Wisconsin, 1892 *6795.8 p85*
Kruger, Gustav Adolph; Wisconsin, 1888 *6795.8 p193*
Kruger, Herrmann; America, 1855 *7420.1 p138*
  With wife & son
Kruger, J.; Venezuela, 1843 *3899.5 p546*
Kruger, John; Illinois, 1851 *6079.1 p8*
Kruger, Melusine Auguste Justine Sophie; America, 1884 *7420.1 p345*
Kruger, Rhynie; Wisconsin, 1913 *6795.8 p168*
Kruger, Rosana; Wisconsin, 1895 *6795.8 p139*
Kruger, Vinzenz; America, 1892 *179.55 p19*

Kruger, Wilhalm; Washington, 1889 ***2770.40*** *p79*
Krugi, Johann; New Castle, DE, 1817-1818 ***90.20*** *p152*
Krugler, Nicholas; Ohio, 1809-1852 ***4511.35*** *p28*
Krugler, Nicholas; Ohio, 1809-1852 ***4511.35*** *p28*
Kruiser, Conrad; North Carolina, 1812 ***1088.45*** *p17*
Krulis, Josef; New York, NY, 1866 ***2853.20*** *p100*
Krull, Ernst Friedrich; Port uncertain, 1836 ***7420.1*** *p11*
Krull, Sophie Eleonore; Port uncertain, 1850 ***7420.1*** *p76*
Krum, Christian; Ohio, 1809-1852 ***4511.35*** *p28*
Krum, Garret; Louisiana, 1874 ***4981.45*** *p132*
Krumfuss, Carl Friedrich Wilhelm Conrad; America, 1881 ***7420.1*** *p322*
Krumholz, Susanna 22; America, 1846 ***778.6*** *p193*
Krumme, . . .; America, 1843 ***7420.1*** *p28*
Krumme, Gustav; America, 1882 ***5475.1*** *p130*
Krummfuss, Carl Heinrich Wilhelm; America, 1868 ***7420.1*** *p273*
Krummfuss, Friedrich Ludwig Christian; America, 1861 ***7420.1*** *p206*
Krummfuss, Ludwig August; America, 1867 ***7420.1*** *p259*
Krumrai, Emil 21; Portland, ME, 1912 ***970.38*** *p79*
Krumrei, George Francis; Ohio, 1809-1852 ***4511.35*** *p28*
Krumrei, Philip Jacob; Ohio, 1809-1852 ***4511.35*** *p28*
Krumrey, George Francis; Ohio, 1809-1852 ***4511.35*** *p28*
Krumrie, Philip Jacob; Ohio, 1809-1852 ***4511.35*** *p29*
Krumsiek, Sophie; America, 1852 ***7420.1*** *p92*
Krunn, Ottilie Auguste; Wisconsin, 1898 ***6795.8*** *p25*
Krupp, Eugene Frederick; Louisiana, 1874 ***4981.45*** *p132*
Krupp, John; New York, 1859 ***358.56*** *p54*
Krus, Andrew; New York, NY, 1885 ***6015.15*** *p27*
Krusa, Hermann; North Carolina, 1847 ***1088.45*** *p17*
Kruse, Miss; Montreal, 1922 ***4514.4*** *p32*
Kruse, Francis; Ohio, 1840-1897 ***8365.35*** *p17*
Kruse, Hans; Iowa, 1923 ***1211.15*** *p16*
Kruse, Hans Heinrich; America, 1857 ***7420.1*** *p165*
With wife
Kruse, Harm; Iowa, 1890 ***1211.15*** *p16*
Kruse, Heinrich; America, 1865 ***7420.1*** *p233*
With family
Kruse, Heinrich Conrad; America, 1850 ***7420.1*** *p73*
*Sister:*Sophie Charlotte
Kruse, Henry; Ohio, 1840-1897 ***8365.35*** *p17*
Kruse, Joach; New York, 1859 ***358.56*** *p101*
Kruse, Louis Julius; Wisconsin, 1880 ***6795.8*** *p50*
Kruse, Nibke 73; Kansas, 1888 ***1447.20*** *p62*
Kruse, Peter H.; Iowa, 1898 ***1211.15*** *p16*
Kruse, Peter Nielson; Iowa, 1911 ***1211.15*** *p16*
Kruse, Sophie Charlotte *SEE* Kruse, Heinrich Conrad
Krusell, Charles; Cleveland, OH, 1880-1889 ***9722.10*** *p122*
Krusitsh, Ralph; Louisiana, 1874 ***4981.45*** *p132*
Kruslock, Fr.; Philadelphia, 1848 ***6412.40*** *p150*
Kruszewski, Jennie Helen; Detroit, 1929-1930 ***6214.5*** *p60*
Kruten, Elisabeth Stephani 47 *SEE* Kruten, Peter
Kruten, Jakob *SEE* Kruten, Peter
Kruten, Mathias *SEE* Kruten, Peter
Kruten, Michel *SEE* Kruten, Peter
Kruten, Peter *SEE* Kruten, Peter
Kruten, Peter 48; America, 1859 ***5475.1*** *p332*
*Wife:*Elisabeth Stephani 47
*Son:*Peter
*Son:*Michel
*Son:*Jakob
*Son:*Mathias
Krutnor, Rebecca 54; Ontario, 1871 ***1823.17*** *p87*
Kryder, Jacob; Ohio, 1809-1852 ***4511.35*** *p29*
Kryder, John; Ohio, 1809-1852 ***4511.35*** *p29*
Kryl, Bohumir; Chicago, 1875-1910 ***2853.20*** *p466*
Krysiak, Agnieszka 17; New York, NY, 1912 ***8355.1*** *p15*
Kryzan, Anthony; Detroit, 1890 ***9980.23*** *p96*
Krzeczkowski, Michael; Detroit, 1930 ***1640.60*** *p78*
Krzeszynski, Anton; New Orleans, 1872 ***6015.15*** *p26*
Krzywicki, Jan 39; New York, NY, 1920 ***930.50*** *p49*
Krzywosinski, Frank; Galveston, TX, 1900 ***6015.15*** *p10*
Krzywosinski, John; Galveston, TX, 1901 ***6015.15*** *p10*
Kschinka, Christian; Valdivia, Chile, 1850 ***1192.4*** *p48*
Kuaf, G. A.; Louisiana, 1874 ***4981.45*** *p296*
Kuba, Gelasius; Milwaukee, 1871-1875 ***2853.20*** *p310*
Kubal, Frantisek; Wisconsin, 1855 ***2853.20*** *p344*
Kubalek, Jan; Nebraska, 1868 ***2853.20*** *p161*
Kuban, Carl; Iowa, 1896 ***1211.15*** *p16*
Kuban, Carl, Jr.; Iowa, 1906 ***1211.15*** *p16*
Kubasiak, Antoni; Detroit, 1929-1930 ***6214.5*** *p63*
Kubat, Frantisek; Illinois, 1853-1910 ***2853.20*** *p471*
Kubecki, John; Detroit, 1929 ***1640.55*** *p116*
Kuber, Marg. A. 21; New York, NY, 1847 ***9176.15*** *p49*
Kuber, Nicolaus 23; New York, NY, 1847 ***9176.15*** *p49*
Kubik, Frantisek; Wisconsin, 1854 ***2853.20*** *p304*
Kubin, Martin; Chicago, 1871 ***2853.20*** *p425*
Kubin, Otto; Chicago, 1867 ***2853.20*** *p391*
Kubischta, Franz 2; Halifax, N.S., 1902 ***1860.4*** *p43*
Kubischta, Franz 25; Halifax, N.S., 1902 ***1860.4*** *p43*
Kubischta, Josefine; Halifax, N.S., 1902 ***1860.4*** *p43*
Kubischta, Josefine 24; Halifax, N.S., 1902 ***1860.4*** *p43*
Kubischta, Julius 23; Halifax, N.S., 1902 ***1860.4*** *p43*
Kubitz, August; Galveston, TX, 1855 ***571.7*** *p17*
Kubler, Georg; America, 1884 ***179.55*** *p19*
Kubler, Mrs. Jakob; America, 1841 ***2526.42*** *p175*
With son-in-law
Kubler, Mrs. Jakob; America, 1841 ***2526.42*** *p176*
Kubler, M. Elisabeth; America, 1846 ***6442.17*** *p65*
Kubolton, George 36; Ontario, 1871 ***1823.21*** *p193*
Kubos, Vaclav; Texas, 1860 ***2853.20*** *p74*
Kubricht, Bohumil Ondrej; Texas, 1896 ***2853.20*** *p80*
Kucab, Stanislaw; Detroit, 1929 ***1640.55*** *p114*
Kucera, Vaclav; Cleveland, OH, 1866 ***2853.20*** *p144*
Kuchariski, Frank; Texas, 1915-1920 ***6015.15*** *p27*
Kuchenmeister, John; New York, 1860 ***358.56*** *p150*
Kuchler, Charlotte; America, 1857 ***2526.43*** *p173*
Kuchler, Katharina; America, 1857 ***2526.43*** *p173*
Kuchoriski, John; Galveston, TX, 1902 ***6015.15*** *p27*
Kuchta, Victorya; Detroit, 1929-1930 ***6214.5*** *p67*
Kuck, Wm.; Ohio, 1840-1897 ***8365.35*** *p17*
Kucker, Friedrich August Ludwig; America, 1866 ***7420.1*** *p245*
Kucker, Friedrich Wilhelm August; America, 1867 ***7420.1*** *p259*
With family
Kucker, Wilhelm; America, 1843 ***7420.1*** *p28*
With son 2
Kuckuck, Johann Christian; America, 1855 ***7420.1*** *p138*
With wife 2 sons & 2 daughters
Kudec, Chas; Nebraska, 1905 ***3004.30*** *p46*
Kuderle, Jakub; Detroit, 1854 ***2853.20*** *p356*
Kudrna, Jan; South Dakota, 1871-1910 ***2853.20*** *p247*
Kudrna, Ludvik J.; Nebraska, 1883 ***2853.20*** *p162*
Kuebel, Alois 50; New York, NY, 1847 ***9176.15*** *p50*
Kuebel, Amalia 8; New York, NY, 1847 ***9176.15*** *p50*
Kuebel, Cath.a 22; New York, NY, 1847 ***9176.15*** *p50*
Kuebel, Heazenith 19; New York, NY, 1847 ***9176.15*** *p50*
Kuebel, Magrinis 15; New York, NY, 1847 ***9176.15*** *p50*
Kuebel, Rosins 52; New York, NY, 1847 ***9176.15*** *p50*
Kuebel, Xavier 21; New York, NY, 1847 ***9176.15*** *p50*
Kuebler, John; New York, 1778 ***8529.30*** *p6*
Kuehle, Louis 48; Mississippi, 1846 ***778.6*** *p193*
Kuehn, Christoph; Wisconsin, 1868 ***6795.8*** *p123*
Kuehn, Gust W.; Wisconsin, 1898 ***6795.8*** *p63*
Kuehn, Julius; Wisconsin, 1867 ***6795.8*** *p138*
Kuehn, Lena Louise; Wisconsin, 1893 ***6795.8*** *p63*
Kuehnle, B.; Galveston, TX, 1855 ***571.7*** *p18*
Kuehnle, Fritz; Colorado, 1890 ***1029.59*** *p52*
Kuehnle, Fritz; Colorado, 1895 ***1029.59*** *p52*
Kuehnle, J.; Galveston, TX, 1855 ***571.7*** *p18*
Kuencke, H.; Galveston, TX, 1855 ***571.7*** *p18*
Kuenkel, Johann; Galveston, TX, 1855 ***571.7*** *p17*
Kuenzel, Louise; New York, NY, 1855 ***8513.31*** *p297*
Kuenzer, Anna Maria; Venezuela, 1843 ***3899.5*** *p543*
Kuenzer, Leonhard; Venezuela, 1843 ***3899.5*** *p543*
Kuenzer, Leonhard, Sr.; Venezuela, 1843 ***3899.5*** *p543*
Kuenzer, Maria Magdalena; Venezuela, 1843 ***3899.5*** *p543*
Kuester, Charles; North Carolina, 1836 ***1088.45*** *p17*
Kuetfield, Abraham; Marblehead, MA, 1681 ***9228.50*** *p312*
Kuetzing, Frances F.A.; Wisconsin, 1882 ***6795.8*** *p234*
Kufer, Carl Emile 25; Port uncertain, 1848 ***778.6*** *p193*
Kufer, Johann Wilhelm 17; America, 1854 ***2526.43*** *p151*
Kufer, Philipp; New York, 1831-1931 ***2526.43*** *p151*
Kuffer, Cath. 46; America, 1840 ***778.6*** *p193*
Kuffer, Nic. 42; America, 1840 ***778.6*** *p193*
Kuffneck, Hubert 20; Louisiana, 1840 ***778.6*** *p193*
Kuffneck, Michael 22; Port uncertain, 1840 ***778.6*** *p193*
Kugal, Martin; Ohio, 1809-1852 ***4511.35*** *p29*
Kugel, Albert; Ohio, 1809-1852 ***4511.35*** *p29*
Kugh, Martin; Ohio, 1809-1852 ***4511.35*** *p29*
Kugle, Martin; Ohio, 1809-1852 ***4511.35*** *p29*
Kugler, Christian; America, 1892 ***179.55*** *p19*
Kugler, Martin 23; Missouri, 1845 ***778.6*** *p193*
Kuhfuss, Adolf Eduard; America, 1909 ***7420.1*** *p386*
Kuhfuss, Fritz; Missouri, 1914 ***7420.1*** *p394*
Kuhfuss, Heinrich August; Port uncertain, 1856 ***7420.1*** *p149*
Kuhfuss, Johann Heinrich; America, 1891 ***7420.1*** *p363*
Kuhl, Elise; New York, 1859 ***358.56*** *p99*
Kuhl, Franz 21; America, 1854 ***2526.43*** *p174*
Kuhl, Kath.; New York, 1897 ***5475.1*** *p40*
Kuhlmann, Widow; America, 1861 ***7420.1*** *p207*
Kuhlmann, Carl August; America, 1857 ***7420.1*** *p166*
Kuhlmann, Carl Heinrich; America, 1868 ***7420.1*** *p274*
Kuhlmann, Christine Wilhelmine Charlotte; Minnesota, 1882 ***7420.1*** *p330*
*Son:*Friedrich Wilhelm Christian Ludwig
*Daughter:*Wilhelmine Sophie Luise
*Son:*Christoph Friedrich Wilhelm
With mother
*Son:*Friedrich Christian
*Daughter:*Sophie Caroline Charlotte
Kuhlmann, Ernst Wilhelm; America, 1848 ***7420.1*** *p60*
Kuhlmann, Friedrich Wilhelm; America, 1869 ***7420.1*** *p280*
*Sister:*Justine Wilhelmine Eleonore
Kuhlmann, Friedrich Wilhelm August; America, 1865 ***7420.1*** *p233*
With family
Kuhlmann, Georg Wilhelm; America, 1839 ***7420.1*** *p16*
Kuhlmann, H. D.; Nebraska, 1905 ***3004.30*** *p46*
Kuhlmann, Hans Heinrich; America, 1840 ***7420.1*** *p19*
With 6 children
Kuhlmann, Heinrich Eduard; America, 1857 ***7420.1*** *p166*
Kuhlmann, Heinrich Gottlieb; America, 1865 ***7420.1*** *p233*
With family
Kuhlmann, Heinrich Wilhelm; America, 1865 ***7420.1*** *p233*
Kuhlmann, Heinrich Wilhelm; America, 1866 ***7420.1*** *p245*
Kuhlmann, Johann Heinrich; Port uncertain, 1840 ***7420.1*** *p19*
Kuhlmann, Justine Wilhelmine Eleonore *SEE* Kuhlmann, Friedrich Wilhelm
Kuhlmann, Wilhelm; America, 1867 ***7420.1*** *p259*
With family
Kuhn, A. 24; New York, NY, 1856 ***1766.1*** *p45*
Kuhn, A. Maria Ludwig 48 *SEE* Kuhn, Michel
Kuhn, Adam *SEE* Kuhn, Nikolaus
Kuhn, Anna *SEE* Kuhn, Johann
Kuhn, Anna *SEE* Kuhn, Nikolaus
Kuhn, Anna *SEE* Kuhn, Michel
Kuhn, Anna Elisabetha Heberle 31 *SEE* Kuhn, Kaspar Joseph
Kuhn, Barbara Minniger 43 *SEE* Kuhn, Johann
Kuhn, Barbara *SEE* Kuhn, Michel
Kuhn, Barbara; Brazil, 1874 ***5475.1*** *p372*
Kuhn, Carl; America, 1867 ***7919.3*** *p528*
Kuhn, Carl; America, 1867 ***7919.3*** *p528*
Kuhn, George 30; New Orleans, 1847 ***778.6*** *p193*
Kuhn, Heinrich *SEE* Kuhn, Michel
Kuhn, J. Peter *SEE* Kuhn, Michel
Kuhn, Jakob; America, 1852-1862 ***5475.1*** *p404*
Kuhn, Jakob *SEE* Kuhn, Michel
Kuhn, Jean 29; New York, NY, 1856 ***1766.1*** *p45*
Kuhn, Joh. Peter *SEE* Kuhn, Nikolaus
Kuhn, Johann *SEE* Kuhn, Johann
Kuhn, Johann 42; America, 1868 ***5475.1*** *p253*
*Wife:*Barbara Minniger 43
*Son:*Nikolaus
*Daughter:*Katharina
*Daughter:*Anna
*Son:*Mathias
*Son:*Peter
*Son:*Johann
Kuhn, Johann *SEE* Kuhn, Nikolaus
Kuhn, Johann 18; New York, NY, 1899 ***6406.6*** *p47*
Kuhn, Johanna; America, 1880 ***5475.1*** *p272*
Kuhn, John M.; North Carolina, 1850-1853 ***1088.45*** *p17*
Kuhn, Josef; America, 1873 ***5475.1*** *p354*
Kuhn, Josef *SEE* Kuhn, Michel
Kuhn, Kaspar Joseph; America, 1882 ***2526.43*** *p141*
*Wife:*Anna Elisabetha Heberle
*Son:*Peter
Kuhn, Kath. 57; America, 1866 ***5475.1*** *p490*
*Son:*Jakob
*Daughter:*Charlotte 15
Kuhn, Kath. Schuhmacher *SEE* Kuhn, Nikolaus
Kuhn, Katharina *SEE* Kuhn, Johann
Kuhn, Katharina; America, 1880 ***5475.1*** *p355*
With nephew & niece
Kuhn, Katharina; America, 1881 ***5475.1*** *p456*
Kuhn, Katharina *SEE* Kuhn, Nikolaus
Kuhn, Katharina Elisabetha *SEE* Kuhn, Leonhard
Kuhn, Leonhard; America, 1881 ***2526.42*** *p105*
*Wife:*Katharina Elisabetha
With son
Kuhn, Ludwig; America, 1885 ***2526.43*** *p123*
Kuhn, M.; Louisiana, 1874 ***4981.45*** *p132*
Kuhn, Magdalena Berg *SEE* Kuhn, Nikolaus
Kuhn, Margarethe *SEE* Kuhn, Michel
Kuhn, Margarethe Frei 51 *SEE* Kuhn, Michel
Kuhn, Maria; America, 1869 ***179.55*** *p19*
Kuhn, Maria Dewes *SEE* Kuhn, Mathias
Kuhn, Maria; Brazil, 1874 ***5475.1*** *p371*

Kuhn, Maria 51; Brazil, 1862 *5475.1 p369*
Kuhn, Maria 54; Brazil, 1873 *5475.1 p389*
Kuhn, Maria *SEE* Kuhn, Michel
Kuhn, Mathias *SEE* Kuhn, Johann
Kuhn, Mathias *SEE* Kuhn, Michel
Kuhn, Mathias; Brazil, 1872 *5475.1 p249*
  *Wife:*Maria Dewes
Kuhn, Mathias *SEE* Kuhn, Nikolaus
Kuhn, Mathias *SEE* Kuhn, Nikolaus
Kuhn, Michael August; Wisconsin, 1866 *6795.8 p38*
Kuhn, Michel *SEE* Kuhn, Nikolaus
Kuhn, Michel 24; Brazil, 1872 *5475.1 p389*
Kuhn, Michel 53; Brazil, 1862 *5475.1 p369*
  *Wife:*Margarethe Frei 51
  *Daughter:*Mathias
  *Daughter:*Margarethe
  With daughter
  *Daughter:*Barbara
  *Son:*Josef
Kuhn, Michel *SEE* Kuhn, Michel
Kuhn, Michel 53; Rio Grande do Sul, Brazil, 1872
  5475.1 p249
  *Wife:*A. Maria Ludwig 48
  *Daughter:*Anna
  *Son:*Heinrich
  *Son:*Jakob
  *Son:*Nikolaus
  *Son:*Michel
  *Son:*J. Peter
  *Daughter:*Maria
  *Son:*Peter
Kuhn, Nikolaus *SEE* Kuhn, Johann
Kuhn, Nikolaus; Brazil, 1881 *5475.1 p391*
Kuhn, Nikolaus; Brazil, 1882 *5475.1 p391*
  *Wife:*Magdalena Berg
  *Son:*Michel
  *Son:*Mathias
  *Son:*Joh. Peter
  *Son:*Johann
  *Son:*Peter
Kuhn, Nikolaus; Ohio, 1886 *5475.1 p230*
  *Wife:*Kath. Schuhmacher
  *Daughter:*Katharina
  *Daughter:*Anna
  *Son:*Mathias
  *Son:*Adam
Kuhn, Nikolaus *SEE* Kuhn, Michel
Kuhn, Peter *SEE* Kuhn, Johann
Kuhn, Peter *SEE* Kuhn, Kaspar Joseph
Kuhn, Peter; America, 1883 *2526.43 p123*
Kuhn, Peter *SEE* Kuhn, Nikolaus
Kuhn, Peter 56; Brazil, 1828 *5475.1 p233*
Kuhn, Peter *SEE* Kuhn, Michel
Kuhn, Peter Josef; America, 1873 *5475.1 p354*
Kuhn, Raimund; America, 1883 *2526.42 p193*
Kuhn, Theresa; America, 1869 *2526.43 p211*
Kuhn, Ulrich; Illinois, 1853 *6079.1 p8*
Kuhn, Wilhelm; America, 1888 *179.55 p19*
Kuhne, Christian; Illinois, 1863 *6079.1 p8*
Kuhne, Heinrich; Port uncertain, 1855 *7420.1 p138*
Kuhner, Karl Christian; America, 1892 *5475.1 p425*
  *Wife:*Katharina Schmidt
Kuhner, Katharina Schmidt *SEE* Kuhner, Karl Christian
Kuhnholz, Andreas; America, n.d. *8115.12 p327*
Kuhnholz, Johann Ludwig; America, n.d. *8115.12 p327*
  With brother
Kuhnle, Anna Maria; America, 1883 *179.55 p19*
Kuhnle, Catharina; America, 1863-1883 *179.55 p19*
Kuhnle, Christina; America, 1882 *179.55 p19*
Kuhnle, Christine Catharine; America, 1883 *179.55 p19*
Kuhnle, Jakob; America, 1861-1883 *179.55 p19*
Kuhnle, Jakob; America, 1882 *179.55 p19*
  With wife
Kuhnle, Johann; Philadelphia, 1860 *8513.31 p320*
  *Wife:*Maria Scheuermann
Kuhnle, Johann F.; America, 1883 *179.55 p19*
Kuhnle, Johann Friedrich; America, 1883 *179.55 p19*
Kuhnle, Johann Georg; America, 1883 *179.55 p19*
Kuhnle, Louise Matthilde; America, 1883 *179.55 p19*
Kuhnle, Maria Scheuermann *SEE* Kuhnle, Johann
Kuhnle, Rosine; America, 1855-1883 *179.55 p19*
Kuhnle, Wilhelm Christian; America, 1882 *179.55 p19*
Kuhnwellen, David; North Carolina, 1852 *1088.45 p17*
Kuhr, Maria Elisabeth; America, 1845-1899 *6442.17 p65*
Kuhstadt, Heinrich; Chile, 1852 *1192.4 p52*
Kuithan, Frederick; Illinois, 1857 *6079.1 p8*
Kujat, Eleonora; Wisconsin; 1889 *6795.8 p50*
Kujath, Eleonora; Wisconsin, 1889 *6795.8 p50*
Kujath, Emil Robert; Wisconsin, 1892 *6795.8 p166*
Kukari, Isak 46; Minnesota, 1926 *2769.54 p1381*
Kukawski, Alexander; Detroit, 1929 *1640.55 p117*
Kukko, Arne 18; Minnesota, 1923 *2769.54 p1381*
Kukla, Anna 17; New York, NY, 1904 *8355.1 p15*

Kukol, Filipina 29; New York, NY, 1911 *6533.11 p9*
Kukol, Johann 35; New York, NY, 1911 *6533.11 p9*
Kukulka, Katarzyna 18; New York, NY, 1911 *6533.11 p9*
Kukutzis, Constantinos 30; New York, NY, 1894 *6512.1 p186*
Kula, Michal 30; New York, NY, 1904 *8355.1 p15*
Kulaga, Joseph; Detroit, 1930 *1640.60 p77*
Kulas, Pawel 22; New York, NY, 1920 *930.50 p49*
Kulcycka, Katherine; Detroit, 1929 *1640.55 p115*
Kuley, D.; Louisiana, 1874 *4981.45 p296*
Kulff, Heinrich 4; Portland, ME, 1906 *970.38 p79*
Kulff, Louise 2 months; Portland, ME, 1906 *970.38 p79*
Kulff, Marie 28; Portland, ME, 1906 *970.38 p79*
Kuliala, Jerry 39; Minnesota, 1925 *2769.54 p1379*
Kulisek, Frantisek; Kansas, 1885 *2853.20 p199*
Kullberg, Borje; Colorado, 1887 *1029.59 p52*
Kulle, Carl Heinrich *SEE* Kulle, Justus Heinrich
Kulle, Justus Heinrich; America, 1866 *7420.1 p245*
  *Son:*Carl Heinrich
Kullerstrand, Emil; Colorado, 1893 *1029.59 p52*
Kullerstrand, Emil; Colorado, 1903 *1029.59 p52*
Kullman, J.F.; New York, NY, 1848 *6412.40 p151*
Kulp, Joseph 19; America, 1845 *778.6 p193*
Kulp, Joseph 62; America, 1845 *778.6 p193*
Kulp, Maria 50; America, 1845 *778.6 p193*
Kulpa, Katherine; Detroit, 1930 *1640.60 p78*
Kultala, Andrew 33; Minnesota, 1925 *2769.54 p1380*
Kultala, Eino 28; Minnesota, 1925 *2769.54 p1380*
Kultala, Helga 27; Minnesota, 1925 *2769.54 p1380*
Kultala, Selma 47; Minnesota, 1925 *2769.54 p1380*
Kultala, Waino 30; Minnesota, 1925 *2769.54 p1380*
Kulu, Frantisek; Iowa, 1853 *2853.20 p217*
Kumele, Peter; Ohio, 1809-1852 *4511.35 p29*
Kumhera, Josef; Wisconsin, 1857-1861 *2853.20 p334*
Kummel, Auguste Henry; Louisiana, 1841-1844 *4981.45 p210*
Kummerle, Jeremias; America, 1848 *179.55 p19*
Kummert, Andreas; Valdivia, Chile, 1852 *1192.4 p53*
Kump, Mathias; Washington, 1886 *2770.40 p195*
Kumpel, Christoph Friedrich; America, 1867 *7919.3 p524*
Kumpf, Anna Katharina; Illinois, 1846 *2526.43 p124*
Kumpf, Katharina 52; America, 1872 *2526.43 p122*
Kumpf, Katharina Elisabetha; Pennsylvania, 1831 *2526.43 p141*
Kumpf, Konrad; America, 1883 *2526.43 p141*
Kumpf, Wilhelm; America, 1890 *2526.43 p142*
Kun, Frantisek; Iowa, 1856 *2853.20 p228*
Kunckel, Eberhard; Pennsylvania, 1848 *170.15 p33*
Kunckel, Georg; Pennsylvania, 1850 *170.15 p33*
  With family
  With son 5
  With son 10
  With son 7
Kunckel, Johann Michael; London, Eng., 1866 *170.15 p34*
Kunes, Josef; Michigan, 1888 *2853.20 p371*
Kunio, Franciszek 39; New York, NY, 1920 *930.50 p49*
Kunkel, . . .; Port uncertain, 1866 *170.15 p34*
Kunkel, Eberhard 26; Pennsylvania, 1848 *170.15 p34*
Kunkel, Elisabeth *SEE* Kunkel, Ferdinand
Kunkel, Ferdinand; America, 1887 *5475.1 p25*
  *Wife:*Katharina Mayer
  *Son:*Wilhelm
  *Daughter:*Elisabeth
Kunkel, Gottfried; Cleveland, OH, 1875 *7420.1 p305*
Kunkel, Johannes; Pennsylvania, 1849 *170.15 p34*
Kunkel, Katharina Mayer *SEE* Kunkel, Ferdinand
Kunkel, Wilhelm *SEE* Kunkel, Ferdinand
Kunkelmann, Adam 2 *SEE* Kunkelmann, Philipp Jakob, II
Kunkelmann, Balthasar 21; America, 1857 *2526.43 p151*
Kunkelmann, Balthasar 21; America, 1857 *2526.43 p156*
Kunkelmann, Balthasar 46; America, 1882 *2526.43 p151*
  *Wife:*Margaretha Dorothea 40
  *Son:*Michael 5
  *Daughter:*Elisabetha 9
  *Son:*Jakob 12
Kunkelmann, Dorothea; America, 1852 *2526.43 p151*
Kunkelmann, Elisabetha; America, 1857 *2526.43 p151*
Kunkelmann, Elisabetha 9 *SEE* Kunkelmann, Balthasar
Kunkelmann, Elisabetha Margaretha 17; America, 1857 *2526.43 p151*
Kunkelmann, Jakob 12 *SEE* Kunkelmann, Balthasar
Kunkelmann, Joseph; America, 1857 *2526.43 p151*
Kunkelmann, Katharina; America, 1858 *2526.43 p151*
Kunkelmann, Margaretha; America, 1857 *2526.43 p152*
Kunkelmann, Margaretha Dorothea 40 *SEE* Kunkelmann, Balthasar
Kunkelmann, Maria; America, 1858 *2526.43 p152*
Kunkelmann, Michael 5 *SEE* Kunkelmann, Balthasar

Kunkelmann, Philipp Jakob, II; America, 1847 *2526.43 p152*
  With wife
  *Son:*Adam
Kunnecke, Johann Christian; America, 1867 *7420.1 p259*
  With family
Kunolt, Ludwig; Texas, 1854 *3435.45 p36*
Kunrath, Franz; Brazil, 1857 *5475.1 p441*
  With wife & 7 children
Kuns, Henry 79; Ontario, 1871 *1823.17 p87*
Kunselman, Frank; Illinois, 1863 *6079.1 p8*
Kunstler, Michael; America, 1880 *2526.42 p169*
Kunstmann, . . .; Valdivia, Chile, 1852 *1192.4 p55*
  With wife
  With child 20
  With child 23
Kunstmann, H. H.; Valdivia, Chile, 1850 *1192.4 p48*
Kuntz, Adam 23; Louisiana, 1848 *778.6 p193*
Kuntz, Antoine 21; Mississippi, 1845 *778.6 p193*
Kuntz, Cathne. 24; Louisiana, 1848 *778.6 p193*
Kuntz, Christian; Ohio, 1809-1852 *4511.35 p29*
Kuntz, Danl. 33; America, 1848 *778.6 p193*
Kuntz, Danl., Jr. 6; America, 1848 *778.6 p194*
Kuntz, Eliz. 33; America, 1848 *778.6 p194*
Kuntz, Eliz...th 7; America, 1848 *778.6 p194*
Kuntz, F. 22; Port uncertain, 1842 *778.6 p194*
Kuntz, Francois 28; Missouri, 1848 *778.6 p194*
Kuntz, Frederick; Ohio, 1809-1852 *4511.35 p29*
Kuntz, Jacob; Ohio, 1809-1852 *4511.35 p29*
Kuntz, Jean 18; America, 1847 *778.6 p194*
Kuntz, Laurent 27; Mississippi, 1845 *778.6 p194*
Kuntz, Lewis; Ohio, 1809-1852 *4511.35 p29*
Kuntz, Louisa 1; America, 1848 *778.6 p194*
Kuntz, Madeleine 23; Mississippi, 1845 *778.6 p194*
Kuntz, Margte. 19; Louisiana, 1848 *778.6 p194*
Kuntz, Marie 30; Louisiana, 1848 *778.6 p194*
Kuntz, Marie 18; Missouri, 1848 *778.6 p194*
Kuntz, Walerja; Detroit, 1930 *1640.60 p83*
Kuntz, William 36; Louisiana, 1848 *778.6 p194*
Kuntzle, Wm.; Ohio, 1840-1897 *8365.35 p17*
Kuntzler, Chretien 24; Louisiana, 1848 *778.6 p194*
Kuntzler, Faerlier 24; Louisiana, 1848 *778.6 p194*
Kuntzli, Christen; North Carolina, 1710 *3629.40 p5*
  With wife & 6 children
Kuntzli, George; North Carolina, 1710 *3629.40 p3*
Kuntzmann, George; Illinois, 1865 *6079.1 p8*
Kuny, Frank 30; Ontario, 1871 *1823.21 p19*
Kunz, Adolf Karel; America, 1845-1849 *2853.20 p217*
Kunz, Anna Maria; America, 1882 *179.55 p19*
Kunz, Bettchen 5 *SEE* Kunz, Mrs. Ludwig
Kunz, Christina; America, 1882 *179.55 p19*
Kunz, Daniel; America, 1700-1899 *179.55 p19*
  With wife
Kunz, Daniel; America, 1882 *179.55 p19*
Kunz, Elisabeth Dewes *SEE* Kunz, Josef
Kunz, Friedrich 17; America, 1869 *5475.1 p418*
Kunz, Gottlieb; America, 1882 *179.55 p19*
Kunz, Jakob; America, 1882 *179.55 p19*
Kunz, Johannes; America, 1882 *179.55 p19*
Kunz, Josef; America, 1833 *5475.1 p436*
  *Wife:*Elisabeth Dewes
  With 7 children
Kunz, Karl *SEE* Kunz, Mrs. Ludwig
Kunz, Louis *SEE* Kunz, Mrs. Ludwig
Kunz, Mrs. Ludwig; America, 1855 *2526.43 p174*
  *Daughter:*Bettchen
  *Son:*Louis
  *Son:*Karl
Kunz, Rosina; America, 1882 *179.55 p19*
Kunz, Walerja; Detroit, 1930 *1640.60 p83*
Kunze, Charles; Ohio, 1809-1852 *4511.35 p29*
Kunze, Joseph; New York, 1860 *358.56 p4*
Kunzel, Christian; America, 1849 *2526.43 p173*
Kunzel, Georg Adam; America, 1883 *2526.43 p173*
Kunzel, Johann Georg Jakob; America, 1885 *2526.43 p173*
Kunzer, Anna Maria; Venezuela, 1843 *3899.5 p543*
Kunzer, Anton; Venezuela, 1843 *3899.5 p545*
Kunzer, Franz Anton; Venezuela, 1843 *3899.5 p543*
Kunzer, Ignaz; Venezuela, 1843 *3899.5 p545*
Kunzer, Leonhard; Venezuela, 1843 *3899.5 p543*
Kunzer, Maria Magdalena; Venezuela, 1843 *3899.5 p543*
Kunzler, Nikolaus; America, 1882 *5475.1 p130*
Kunzmann, Laurent 28; New Orleans, 1848 *778.6 p194*
Kuonzer, Leonhard; Venezuela, 1843 *3899.5 p543*
Kupecki, Antoni; Detroit, 1929-1930 *6214.5 p67*
Kupel, Anastas; Wisconsin, 1893 *6795.8 p59*
Kuper, Carl; America, 1887 *7420.1 p354*
Kuper, Heiji Jensen; Iowa, 1890 *1211.15 p16*
Kupfer, Caspar Martin; America, 1867 *7919.3 p526*
  With wife & 2 children
Kupfer, Maria Christiana; America, 1882 *179.55 p19*

Kupferschmeid, Benedicht; North Carolina, 1710 *3629.40 p5*
    With son & wife
Kupferstein, Reszi 16; New York, NY, 1894 *6512.1 p232*
Kupfner, Joseph; Colorado, 1896 *1029.59 p52*
Kupfour, Joseph; Colorado, 1891 *1029.59 p52*
Kupper, Joseph; Colorado, 1891 *1029.59 p52*
Kuppmeyer, Ignatz 30; America, 1746 *778.6 p194*
Kuppner, Joseph; Colorado, 1891 *1029.59 p52*
Kups, Samuel; Ohio, 1809-1852 *4511.35 p29*
Kurant, Mary; Detroit, 1929-1930 *6214.5 p61*
Kurant, Mary; Detroit, 1929 *1640.55 p114*
Kurant, Onufry; Detroit, 1927 *6214.5 p63*
Kurczewska, Frank; Detroit, 1929-1930 *6214.5 p63*
    *Wife:*Helen Kowalski
Kurczewski, Stanley; Detroit, 1890 *9980.23 p97*
Kurdelfinke, Marie Louise 15; New York, NY, 1864 *8425.62 p197*
Kurek, Josef 27; New York, NY, 1920 *930.50 p48*
Kuriger, Johann Albert; America, 1875 *179.55 p19*
Kurilik, Anthony; Detroit, 1930 *1640.60 p82*
Kuriluk, Anthony; Detroit, 1930 *1640.60 p82*
Kurkowski, John; Wisconsin, 1891 *6795.8 p59*
Kurscher, Philip; Ohio, 1809-1852 *4511.35 p29*
Kurschner, Elisabeth Auguste; America, 1868 *7919.3 p533*
    With child
Kurt, Pierre 22; Missouri, 1848 *778.6 p194*
Kurth, Otto F.; Colorado, 1890 *1029.59 p52*
Kurth, Otto F.; Colorado, 1891 *1029.59 p52*
Kurts, Philip; Ohio, 1809-1852 *4511.35 p29*
Kurtz, A. Maria 9 *SEE* Kurtz, Peter
Kurtz, Anne 10; Missouri, 1845 *778.6 p194*
Kurtz, Catharine 3; Missouri, 1845 *778.6 p194*
Kurtz, Christian *SEE* Kurtz, Gottfried
Kurtz, Christina Mehr *SEE* Kurtz, Gottfried
Kurtz, Christopher 1; Missouri, 1845 *778.6 p194*
Kurtz, Daniel *SEE* Kurtz, Gottfried
Kurtz, Elisabeth 4 *SEE* Kurtz, Peter
Kurtz, Friedrich 10 *SEE* Kurtz, Heinrich
Kurtz, Georg Konrad; America, 1880 *5475.1 p74*
Kurtz, Gottfried; Dakota, 1877-1918 *554.30 p25*
    *Wife:*Christina Mehr
    *Child:*Christian
    *Child:*Daniel
Kurtz, Heinrich 2 *SEE* Kurtz, Peter
Kurtz, Heinrich 52; America, 1880 *5475.1 p74*
    *Son:*Ph. Jakob 19
    *Son:*Friedrich 10
    *Son:*Karl 6
    *Daughter:*Sophie 15
Kurtz, Ja.ques 6; Missouri, 1845 *778.6 p194*
Kurtz, Jakob 7 *SEE* Kurtz, Peter
Kurtz, Johann 20 *SEE* Kurtz, Peter
Kurtz, Karl 6 *SEE* Kurtz, Heinrich
Kurtz, Karl 15 *SEE* Kurtz, Peter
Kurtz, Katharina 16 *SEE* Kurtz, Peter
Kurtz, Ludwig 13 *SEE* Kurtz, Peter
Kurtz, Luzia 10 *SEE* Kurtz, Peter
Kurtz, Madalain 8; Missouri, 1845 *778.6 p194*
Kurtz, Maria 6 *SEE* Kurtz, Peter
Kurtz, Marie 40; Missouri, 1845 *778.6 p194*
Kurtz, Michael; Illinois, 1834-1900 *6020.5 p132*
Kurtz, Michael; Illinois, 1854 *6079.1 p8*
Kurtz, Michel 39; Missouri, 1845 *778.6 p194*
Kurtz, Peter 12 *SEE* Kurtz, Peter
Kurtz, Peter 49; America, 1854 *5475.1 p74*
    *Wife:*Katharina Menges 43
    *Daughter:*A. Maria 9
    *Daughter:*Luzia 10
    *Daughter:*Maria 6 months
    *Son:*Heinrich 2
    *Daughter:*Elisabeth 4
    *Son:*Jakob 7

    *Son:*Johann 20
    *Son:*Karl 15
    *Son:*Ludwig 13
    *Son:*Peter 12
    *Daughter:*Katharina 16
Kurtz, Ph. Jakob 19 *SEE* Kurtz, Heinrich
Kurtz, Philip; Ohio, 1809-1852 *4511.35 p29*
Kurtz, Sophie 15 *SEE* Kurtz, Heinrich
Kurtzmann, Eric 18; America, 1840 *778.6 p194*
Kurz, Anna Kemper *SEE* Kurz, Hermann
Kurz, Christian *SEE* Kurz, Johann Jakob
Kurz, Fredrick; New York, 1860 *358.56 p6*
Kurz, Friedrich *SEE* Kurz, Johann Jakob
Kurz, Hermann; New Jersey, 1913 *5475.1 p73*
    *Wife:*Anna Kemper
Kurz, Jakob *SEE* Kurz, Johann Jakob
Kurz, Joh. Christian *SEE* Kurz, Johann Christian
Kurz, Johann Christian; America, 1836 *5475.1 p457*
    *Wife:*Kath. Elisabeth Trautmann
    *Son:*Joh. Christian
    *Daughter:*Katharina
Kurz, Johann Jakob; America, 1836 *5475.1 p457*
    *Wife:*Maria Schutz
    *Son:*Christian
    *Son:*Friedrich
    *Son:*Jakob
Kurz, Jul. Dorothea; America, 1853 *5475.1 p458*
Kurz, Kath. Elisabeth Trautmann *SEE* Kurz, Johann Christian
Kurz, Katharina *SEE* Kurz, Johann Christian
Kurz, Katharina; America, 1838 *5475.1 p458*
Kurz, Maria Schutz *SEE* Kurz, Johann Jakob
Kurz, Philipp; America, 1836 *2526.42 p105*
    With wife & 5 children
Kurzatowski, Adam; Detroit, 1929-1930 *6214.5 p70*
Kurzbein, Julius Edward; Wisconsin, 1870 *6795.8 p149*
Kurzmaull, C.; Louisiana, 1851 *4981.45 p296*
Kuschaus, Friedrich 2; Portland, ME, 1911 *970.38 p79*
Kuschaus, Katerina 10; Portland, ME, 1911 *970.38 p79*
Kuschaus, Konrad 30; Portland, ME, 1911 *970.38 p79*
Kuschaus, Maria 29; Portland, ME, 1911 *970.38 p79*
Kusenberg, Alfred; Philadelphia, 1862 *8513.31 p320*
Kush, Charles; Detroit, 1929-1930 *6214.5 p65*
Kusia, Francis 7; Quebec, 1870 *8364.32 p24*
Kusler, Christiane 15; New York, NY, 1874 *6954.7 p37*
Kusler, Dorothea 20; New York, NY, 1874 *6954.7 p37*
Kusler, Friedrich 11; New York, NY, 1874 *6954.7 p37*
Kusler, Jacob 8; New York, NY, 1874 *6954.7 p37*
Kusler, Johann 17; New York, NY, 1874 *6954.7 p37*
Kusler, Johannes 46; New York, NY, 1874 *6954.7 p37*
Kusler, Susanna 5; New York, NY, 1874 *6954.7 p37*
Kusler, Susanna 46; New York, NY, 1874 *6954.7 p37*
Kusmierz, Walenty; Detroit, 1930 *1640.60 p77*
Kusnack, Francis; Ohio, 1840-1897 *8365.35 p17*
Kuss, Emilie; Wisconsin, 1899 *6795.8 p106*
Kusse, William; New York, 1860 *358.56 p149*
Kussner, Elisabetha *SEE* Kussner, Philipp
Kussner, Friedrich *SEE* Kussner, Philipp
Kussner, Heinrich; America, 1863 *2526.43 p210*
Kussner, Jakob; America, 1851 *2526.42 p162*
Kussner, Johann Eduard; America, 1855 *2526.43 p210*
    *Brother:*Leonhard
Kussner, Leonhard *SEE* Kussner, Johann Eduard
Kussner, Leonhard *SEE* Kussner, Philipp
Kussner, Lorenz; America, 1852 *2526.43 p210*
Kussner, Magdalena *SEE* Kussner, Philipp
Kussner, Maria Barbara *SEE* Kussner, Philipp
Kussner, Philipp; America, 1868 *2526.42 p162*
    *Wife:*Maria Barbara
    *Child:*Leonhard
    *Child:*Elisabetha
    *Child:*Friedrich
    *Child:*Magdalena
Kuster, Albrecht Heinrich Wilhelm; America, 1868 *7420.1 p273*
Kuster, Carl Ludwig; Port uncertain, 1857 *7420.1 p165*

Kuster, Christiane; America, 1870 *7420.1 p395*
Kuster, Friedrich Wilhelm; Port uncertain, 1835 *7420.1 p9*
Kuster, Johann 37; New Castle, DE, 1817-1818 *90.20 p152*
Kuster, Johann Jacob; America, 1858 *7420.1 p179*
    With wife 2 sons & 2 daughters
Kusterer, Theresia; Venezuela, 1843 *3899.5 p541*
Kustner, Georg Christian; America, 1860 *179.55 p19*
Kutac, Josef; Texas, 1860 *2853.20 p74*
Kutak, Frantisek Jaroslav; Chicago, 1887 *2853.20 p147*
Kutemann, Heinrich; America, 1883 *7420.1 p337*
Kutemann, Heinrich Wilhelm; America, 1886 *7420.1 p351*
Kutemeier, Carl; Indianapolis, 1871 *7420.1 p291*
Kutemeier, Friederike Wilhelmine; America, 1860 *7420.1 p195*
Kutemeier, Heinrich Wilhelm; Port uncertain, 1835 *7420.1 p9*
Kutemeier, Mrs. Johann Otto; America, 1870 *7420.1 p395*
    With family
Kutemeier, Johannes Otto; America, 1850 *7420.1 p73*
Kutemeier, Sophie Marie; America, 1861 *7420.1 p206*
Kutemeyer, Carl Ludwig Christian; America, 1867 *7420.1 p259*
Kutter, Ferdinand 32; Missouri, 1845 *778.6 p194*
Kuyr, Margrat 46; New Orleans, 1843 *778.6 p194*
Kuzel, Josef; Cleveland, OH, 1865 *2853.20 p476*
    With parents
Kuzel, Josef; Cleveland, OH, 1865 *2853.20 p498*
    With parents
Kuzin, Peter 30; New York, NY, 1890 *1883.7 p48*
Kvetensky, Jaromil; Nebraska, 1887 *2853.20 p223*
Kvitek, Bartolomej; Chicago, 1892 *2853.20 p438*
Kwapniewski, Andrew; Detroit, 1930 *1640.60 p82*
Kwart, Irving; Miami, 1935 *4984.12 p39*
Kwart, Isak; Miami, 1935 *4984.12 p39*
Kwiatkowska, Marcela 19; New York, NY, 1911 *6533.11 p9*
Kwiatkowska, Mary; Detroit, 1929-1930 *6214.5 p69*
Kwiatkowski, John; North Carolina, 1835 *1088.45 p18*
Kwidzinsky, Eva; Wisconsin, 1897 *6795.8 p213*
Kwieceyriske, Lucie; Wisconsin, 1902 *6795.8 p236*
Kwiecien, Antoni; Detroit, 1929 *1640.55 p114*
Kwiller, Mrs.; New Orleans, 1840 *778.6 p194*
Kwiller, Pierre; New Orleans, 1840 *778.6 p194*
Kybutz, John; Illinois, 1860 *6079.1 p8*
Kyle, David; North Carolina, 1828 *1088.45 p18*
Kyle, Haglett; North Carolina, 1827 *1088.45 p18*
Kyle, James; North Carolina, 1834 *1088.45 p18*
Kyle, John; North Carolina, 1792-1862 *1088.45 p18*
Kyle, Rebecca; Philadelphia, 1860 *8513.31 p429*
Kym, Franz 60; New Castle, DE, 1817-1818 *90.20 p152*
Kynaston, Elizabeth; America, 1766 *1220.12 p478*
Kynaston, Mary; America, 1769 *1220.12 p478*
Kyrie, Robert; Marston's Wharf, 1782 *8529.30 p15*
Kysela, Frantisek; New York, NY, 1868 *2853.20 p498*
    With son
Kysela, Rudolf; St. Louis, 1863 *2853.20 p22*
Kystardt, Daniel *SEE* Kystardt, Johann
Kystardt, Friedrich *SEE* Kystardt, Johann
Kystardt, Jakob *SEE* Kystardt, Johann
Kystardt, Johann; America, 1854 *5475.1 p459*
    *Wife:*Katharina Frey
    *Son:*Jakob
    *Son:*Karl
    *Daughter:*Katharina
    *Son:*Friedrich
    *Son:*Daniel
Kystardt, Karl *SEE* Kystardt, Johann
Kystardt, Katharina *SEE* Kystardt, Johann
Kystardt, Katharina Frey *SEE* Kystardt, Johann
Kyte, Dorothy; Barbados, 1678 *1220.12 p474*
Kzsywosinski, Frank; Galveston, TX, 1900 *6015.15 p10*
Kzsywoswski, John; Galveston, TX, 1901 *6015.15 p10*

L

Laabs, August Bernhardt; Wisconsin, 1889 *6795.8 p217*
Laaksonen, John 52; Minnesota, 1923 *2769.54 p1379*
Laaksonen, Rosa 48; Minnesota, 1923 *2769.54 p1379*
Laaksonen, Urho 26; Minnesota, 1925 *2769.54 p1379*
Labadie, Mr. 48; New Orleans, 1846 *778.6 p194*
Labadie, A. L. 14; America, 1845 *778.6 p194*
Labadie, Ernesse 7; New Orleans, 1846 *778.6 p195*
Labadie, J. L. 42; America, 1845 *778.6 p195*
Labadie, Ls. Theodore 16; America, 1845 *778.6 p195*
Labadie, Marie Angel. Sus. 4; New Orleans, 1846 *778.6 p195*
Labaie, Vincent; Quebec, 1655 *9221.17 p325*
La Balister, Elizabeth 18; Toronto, 1868 *9228.50 p328*
Laban, Catherine; Annapolis, MD, 1719 *1220.12 p479*
Laban, George; Maryland, 1742 *1220.12 p479*
Labansot, Bernard; Louisiana, 1874-1875 *4981.45 p29*
La Bar, Pierre; America, 1752 *1220.12 p479*
Labarbe, Jeanne 51; Quebec, 1653 *9221.17 p272*
Labarche, Jacques; Quebec, 1654 *9221.17 p310*
Labarre, . . .; Montreal, 1644 *9221.17 p147*
La Barre, Augustin-Antoine de; Quebec, 1741 *2314.30 p171*
Labarre, Claude Camus 23 *SEE* Labarre, Claude
Labarre, Claude 26; Quebec, 1652 *9221.17 p256*
  *Wife:*Claude Camus 23
Labarre, J. 40; America, 1847 *778.6 p195*
Labarre, Jean Baptiste; Illinois, 1860 *6079.1 p8*
Labarte, Eugene 18; Port uncertain, 1843 *778.6 p195*
Labarte, P. 61; Philadelphia, 1841 *778.6 p195*
LaBarte, Walter 15; Quebec, 1870 *8364.32 p24*
Labarthe, Jean 35; New Orleans, 1848 *778.6 p195*
Labasse, Honore 18; New Orleans, 1846 *778.6 p195*
Labasse, J. 16; Louisiana, 1848 *778.6 p195*
Labasse, Jean; Louisiana, 1874-1875 *4981.45 p29*
Labastille, Renee; Quebec, 1668 *4514.3 p329*
Labat, Miss 14; New Orleans, 1844 *778.6 p195*
Labat, Charles 22; New Orleans, 1848 *778.6 p195*
Labat, Jean 20; New Orleans, 1840 *778.6 p195*
Labat, Leon 48; Texas, 1848 *778.6 p195*
Labat, Martin; California, 1870-1875 *3276.8 p20*
Labat, Mathieu 43; Quebec, 1647 *9221.17 p183*
Labat, Peter; California, 1883 *3276.8 p20*
Labat, Pierre 46; New Orleans, 1844 *778.6 p195*
Labat, Rose 21; Port uncertain, 1843 *778.6 p195*
Labat, Salvador 18; California, 1883 *3276.8 p20*
Labath deSivrac, Louis-Simon; Quebec, 1750 *2314.30 p170*
Labath deSivrac, Louis-Simon; Quebec, 1750 *2314.30 p186*
Labatt, Mrs. 30; Ontario, 1871 *1823.21 p193*
Labatt, Eliza 53; Ontario, 1871 *1823.21 p193*
Labatt, Louisa 55; Ontario, 1871 *1823.21 p193*
Labatut, J. Oscar 42; New Orleans, 1848 *778.6 p195*
Labbe, Anne; Quebec, 1663 *4514.3 p329*
Labbe, Francois 19; Quebec, 1660 *9221.17 p436*
Labbe, Jacqueline; Quebec, 1668 *4514.3 p329*
Labbe, Jeanne; Quebec, 1669 *4514.3 p329*
Labbe, Joseph 20; America, 1847 *778.6 p195*
Labbe, Leon 22; New Orleans, 1847 *778.6 p195*
Labbe, Nicolas 38; Quebec, 1661 *9221.17 p460*
Labe, Auguste; Illinois, 1852 *6079.1 p8*
Labe, P. 28; Mexico, 1841 *778.6 p195*
Labendz, Jozef 32; New York, NY, 1920 *930.50 p48*
Labenne, Joseph; Illinois, 1852 *6079.1 p8*
Labes, Pierre 12; New Orleans, 1848 *778.6 p195*
Labeur, Francis; America, 1771 *1220.12 p479*
Labey, Mary *SEE* Labey, Philip

Labey, Philip; Utah, 1854 *9228.50 p316*
  *Relative:*Mary
Labiere, Laurent 19; Montreal, 1658 *9221.17 p389*
Labiner, Fannie Godna *SEE* Labiner, Mathias
Labiner, Mathias; Detroit, 1930 *1640.60 p77*
  *Wife:*Fannie Godna
Labisch, Barbara 7; Galveston, TX, 1855 *571.7 p16*
Labisch, Florentine 1; Galveston, TX, 1855 *571.7 p16*
Labisch, Franziska 17; Galveston, TX, 1855 *571.7 p16*
Labisch, Johann 37; Galveston, TX, 1855 *571.7 p16*
Labisch, Maria 39; Galveston, TX, 1855 *571.7 p16*
Labisch, Mariane 6 months; Galveston, TX, 1855 *571.7 p16*
Labissonniere, Francois 19; Quebec, 1660 *9221.17 p436*
La Blanc, L. A.; Louisiana, 1836-1840 *4981.45 p213*
Laboissiere DuQuesnoy, Jean de; Quebec, 1657 *9221.17 p360*
Labondy, L. 40; New Orleans, 1840 *778.6 p195*
Labord, Mr.; Port uncertain, 1842 *778.6 p195*
Labord, D. 20; New Orleans, 1847 *778.6 p195*
Laborde, Mr. 26; New Orleans, 1840 *778.6 p195*
Laborde, J. D. 31; America, 1846 *778.6 p195*
Laborde, Jean Doassans 20; America, 1845 *778.6 p195*
Laborde, Jean de; Quebec, 1644 *9221.17 p143*
Laborde, John 17; America, 1848 *778.6 p195*
Laborde, V. F. Doassans 17; America, 1845 *778.6 p195*
Labordenave Charrieu, Mr. 22; America, 1848 *778.6 p195*
Labory, P. 22; New Orleans, 1842 *778.6 p196*
Laboule, Attile 24; America, 1843 *778.6 p196*
Laboule, Jean 35; America, 1843 *778.6 p196*
Labourdette, Mr. 22; Port uncertain, 1840 *778.6 p196*
Laboursso, Bernard 23; New Orleans, 1848 *778.6 p196*
Labouvie, Eduard *SEE* Labouvie, Peter
Labouvie, Katharina Eldebluth *SEE* Labouvie, Peter
Labouvie, Nikolaus *SEE* Labouvie, Peter
Labouvie, Peter *SEE* Labouvie, Peter
Labouvie, Peter; Chicago, 1889 *5475.1 p155*
  *Wife:*Katharina Eldebluth
  *Son:*Peter
  *Son:*Nikolaus
  *Son:*Eduard
Labreche, . . .; Montreal, 1653 *9221.17 p294*
Labrecque, Jean 20; Quebec, 1659 *9221.17 p404*
Labrecque, Pierre 32; Quebec, 1657 *9221.17 p360*
Labree, Cecily; America, 1704 *1220.12 p479*
Labree, Cecily; Barbados or Jamaica, 1700 *1220.12 p479*
Labrel, Pierre 37; New Orleans, 1843 *778.6 p196*
Labrenz, Gust; Wisconsin, 1886 *6795.8 p168*
Labrenz, Johann Gustav; Wisconsin, 1893 *6795.8 p139*
Labrie, . . .; Quebec, 1662 *9221.17 p488*
Labrie, Jacques 21; Quebec, 1643 *9221.17 p134*
Labrie, Nicolas 24; Quebec, 1661 *9221.17 p460*
Labrie, Philippe 29; Quebec, 1662 *9221.17 p490*
Labriere, Denis 25; Quebec, 1657 *9221.17 p353*
Labriere, Pierre 20; Quebec, 1657 *9221.17 p365*
Labro, Peter Camille; New Orleans, 1875 *5475.1 p127*
Labrosse, Benoit 53; New York, NY, 1894 *6512.1 p181*
Labrosse, Jean; Quebec, 1638 *9221.17 p75*
Labrunerie, Adolph; Illinois, 1852 *6079.1 p8*
Labruyere, Jno.; Louisiana, 1874 *4981.45 p296*
Labruyere, John; Louisiana, 1874 *4981.45 p132*
Labuwe, Maria; America, 1881 *5475.1 p325*
Lacabe, St. Julien 19; New Orleans, 1848 *778.6 p196*
Lacaille, Adrien; Quebec, 1635 *9221.17 p45*
  *Wife:*Simone Orville
  *Daughter:*Marie
Lacaille, Marie 17 *SEE* Lacaille, Adrien

Lacaille, Simone Orville *SEE* Lacaille, Adrien
Lacailly, Alex...r 32; New Orleans, 1841 *778.6 p196*
LaCarteniere, Monsieur de; Quebec, 1651 *9221.17 p245*
Lacassagne, I.; Louisiana, 1874 *4981.45 p296*
Lacasse, Mr. 17; America, 1848 *778.6 p196*
LaCasse, Edmond 49; America, 1843 *778.6 p196*
Lacasse, Pierre 17; America, 1845 *778.6 p196*
Lacast, Mrs. 50; America, 1846 *778.6 p196*
Lacaze, Mr. 35; New Orleans, 1840 *778.6 p196*
Lacaze, Barna.din 23; New Orleans, 1746 *778.6 p196*
Lacaze, Jean Marie 21; New Orleans, 1845 *778.6 p196*
Lacaze, John 41; New Orleans, 1841 *778.6 p196*
Lacaze, John Peter 23; New Orleans, 1746 *778.6 p196*
Lace, Augustus; New Orleans, 1851 *7242.30 p147*
Lace, Mary 12; Quebec, 1870 *8364.32 p24*
Lacey, Benjamin; America, 1719 *1220.12 p479*
Lacey, Daniel; Boston, 1758 *1642 p47*
Lacey, Frederick 25; Ontario, 1871 *1823.21 p194*
Lacey, James; America, 1758 *1220.12 p479*
Lacey, James 43; Ontario, 1871 *1823.21 p194*
Lacey, James; Virginia, 1721 *1220.12 p479*
Lacey, John; America, 1739 *1220.12 p479*
Lacey, John; America, 1760 *1220.12 p479*
Lacey, Joseph; America, 1685 *1220.12 p479*
Lacey, Joseph; America, 1752 *1220.12 p479*
Lacey, Joseph 25; Ontario, 1871 *1823.21 p194*
Lacey, Joseph 41; Ontario, 1871 *1823.21 p194*
Lacey, Martin; America, 1749 *1220.12 p479*
Lacey, Michael; America, 1774 *1220.12 p479*
Lacey, Philip; America, 1685 *1220.12 p479*
Lacey, Richard; America, 1767 *1220.12 p479*
Lacey, Robert; Virginia, 1759 *1220.12 p479*
Lacey, Thomas; America, 1769 *1220.12 p479*
Lacey, Walter P. 46; Ontario, 1871 *1823.21 p194*
Lacey, William; America, 1685 *1220.12 p479*
Lacey, William; America, 1730 *1220.12 p479*
Lacey, William; America, 1754 *1220.12 p479*
Lacey, William; America, 1771 *1220.12 p479*
Lachainee, Claude; Quebec, 1638 *9221.17 p78*
Lachaire, . . .; Quebec, 1661 *9221.17 p460*
Lachaise, Bernard 35; America, 1848 *778.6 p196*
Lachance, Antoine 16; Quebec, 1652 *9221.17 p264*
Lachapelle, Francois; Quebec, 1641 *9221.17 p105*
Lachapelle, Francoise Haulin *SEE* Lachapelle, Pierre
Lachapelle, Honore 19; Quebec, 1651 *9221.17 p245*
Lachapelle, Jean; Quebec, 1643 *9221.17 p133*
Lachapelle, Marin 26; Montreal, 1653 *9221.17 p293*
Lachapelle, Pierre 28; Quebec, 1656 *9221.17 p341*
  *Wife:*Francoise Haulin
Lachapelle, Prosper 22; New Orleans, 1845 *778.6 p196*
Lachapelle, Victor 18; New Orleans, 1845 *778.6 p196*
Lachat, Marie 31; Louisiana, 1848 *778.6 p196*
Lachaume, Geoffroy; Quebec, 1649 *9221.17 p214*
Lachaussee, Jean 23; Quebec, 1657 *9221.17 p351*
Lachaussee, Pierre; Quebec, 1650 *9221.17 p214*
Lachenay, Jean Julian; Virginia, 1766 *1220.12 p479*
Lacher, Elsie 23; New York, NY, 1885 *1883.7 p45*
Lachesnaie, Jean; Quebec, 1665 *9221.17 p157*
Lachesnaye, Catherine 11 *SEE* Lachesnaye, Marie Pichon
Lachesnaye, Charles 11 *SEE* Lachesnaye, Marie Pichon
Lachesnaye, Guillaume *SEE* Lachesnaye, Marie Pichon
Lachesnaye, Jacques *SEE* Lachesnaye, Marie Pichon
Lachesnaye, Marie Pichon; Quebec, 1636 *9221.17 p63*
  *Daughter:*Catherine
  *Son:*Charles
  *Son:*Jacques
  *Son:*Guillaume

Lachesnaye, Pierre; Quebec, 1661 9221.17 p449
Lachesnee, Antoine; Quebec, 1649 9221.17 p214
Lachise, Mr. 37; Port uncertain, 1840 778.6 p196
Lachte, Frederick; Philadelphia, 1859 8513.31 p321
*Wife:*Johanna Eckert
*Daughter:*Wilhelmina
Lachte, Johanna Eckert *SEE* Lachte, Frederick
Lachte, Wilhelmina *SEE* Lachte, Frederick
Lack, Francis; America, 1731 1220.12 p479
Lack, John; America, 1774 1220.12 p479
Lackas, Katharina 24; America, 1866 5475.1 p323
Lackas, Nikolaus; America, 1874 5475.1 p311
Lacke, William; New York, 1783 8529.30 p13
Lackey, Catherine; Charles Town, SC, 1719 1220.12 p479
Lackey, Charles 64; Ontario, 1871 1823.21 p194
Lackey, James; North Carolina, 1813 1088.45 p18
Lackey, James 35; Ontario, 1871 1823.21 p194
Lackey, John; America, 1735 1220.12 p479
Lackey, John 40; Ontario, 1871 1823.17 p87
Lackey, Matthew; Massachusetts, 1735 1642 p110
Lackie, Alexander 73; Ontario, 1871 1823.21 p194
Lackie, David 53; Ontario, 1871 1823.21 p194
Lackie, James 35; Ontario, 1871 1823.21 p194
Lackie, James 36; Ontario, 1871 1823.21 p194
Lackie, John 35; Ontario, 1871 1823.21 p194
Lackie, John 65; Ontario, 1871 1823.21 p194
Lackington, James; America, 1737 1220.12 p479
Lackman, David 11 months; Portland, ME, 1906 970.38 p79
Lackman, Elizabeth 4; Portland, ME, 1906 970.38 p79
Lackman, Elizabeth 18; Portland, ME, 1906 970.38 p79
Lackman, Heinrich 24; Portland, ME, 1906 970.38 p79
Lackman, Heinrich 48; Portland, ME, 1906 970.38 p79
Lackman, Jacob 2; Portland, ME, 1906 970.38 p79
Lackman, Jacob 6; Portland, ME, 1906 970.38 p79
Lackman, Jacob 21; Portland, ME, 1906 970.38 p79
Lackman, Johann 11; Portland, ME, 1906 970.38 p79
Lackman, Katarina 15; Portland, ME, 1906 970.38 p79
Lackman, Marie 6 months; Portland, ME, 1906 970.38 p79
Lackman, Marie 21; Portland, ME, 1906 970.38 p79
Lackman, Marie 42; Portland, ME, 1906 970.38 p79
Lackman, Sophie 29; Portland, ME, 1906 970.38 p79
Lackrow, John; Barbados or Jamaica, 1690 1220.12 p479
Lacks, Mary; Annapolis, MD, 1725 1220.12 p479
Laclair-Cambot, G. B. 28; Port uncertain, 1846 778.6 p196
Laclede, Aug.; St. Louis, 1764 2853.20 p20
La Cloche, John; New Jersey, 1665 9228.50 p159
La Cloche, John; Virginia, 1665 9228.50 p53
Lacny, John; Detroit, 1929 1640.55 p113
Lacombe, Henry 33; Port uncertain, 1843 778.6 p196
Lacomby, John 26; New Orleans, 1847 778.6 p196
Lacon, Edward; America, 1719 1220.12 p479
Lacon, Sarah; America, 1755 1220.12 p479
La Cooter, John; Boston, 1700-1713 9228.50 p340
Lacooter, John; Boston, 1707 9228.50 p424
Lacore, Mary; America, 1768 1220.12 p479
Lacorne deChaptes, Jean-Louis de; Quebec, 1683-1688 2314.30 p168
Lacorne deChaptes, Jean-Louis de; Quebec, 1685 2314.30 p186
La Corney, John 48; Iowa, 1870 9228.50 p339
Lacoste, Mr. 26; America, 1843 778.6 p196
Lacoste, Mr. 26; America, 1846 778.6 p196
Lacoste, Bernard 18; New Orleans, 1746 778.6 p196
Lacoste, Estelle 27; Port uncertain, 1846 778.6 p196
Lacoste, F. 33; New Orleans, 1848 778.6 p196
Lacoste, Francois 30; Port uncertain, 1846 778.6 p196
Lacoste, J. 30; America, 1843 778.6 p196
Lacoste, L. V. 17; America, 1846 778.6 p197
Lacoste, Numa 23; Port uncertain, 1846 778.6 p197
Lacoste, P. 58; New Orleans, 1848 778.6 p197
Lacoste, Paul 2; Port uncertain, 1846 778.6 p197
Lacoume, Mr. 26; America, 1846 778.6 p197
Lacour, . . .; Montreal, 1661 9221.17 p473
Lacour, Etienne 47; New Orleans, 1847 778.6 p197
Lacour, Josephine 30; Louisiana, 1840 778.6 p197
Lacour, M. 51; Louisiana, 1840 778.6 p197
Lacour, Marin 66; Port uncertain, 1847 778.6 p197
Lacour, Peter 20; America, 1846 778.6 p197
Lacour, Peter 46; Port uncertain, 1847 778.6 p197
Lacour, Pierre 48; New Orleans, 1848 778.6 p197
Lacour, Wilhelm 11; Port uncertain, 1847 778.6 p197
la Courru, Pierre; Virginia, 1700 9230.15 p81
Lacourt, Charles; Detroit, 1871 1494.21 p31
Lacourt, Joseph; Wisconsin, 1856 1494.20 p13
Lacousne, Mr. 26; America, 1846 778.6 p197
La Couteur, John; Boston, 1700-1713 9228.50 p340
Lacouture, Mr. 18; America, 1840 778.6 p197
Lacouture, Mr. 40; America, 1840 778.6 p197
Lacouture, Catherine 35; New Orleans, 1842 778.6 p197
Lacq, Pierre 20; Quebec, 1656 9221.17 p340
LaCrapaudiere, Jacques; Quebec, 1645 9221.17 p157
Lacrois, Prosper 27; New Orleans, 1843 778.6 p197
La Croix, . . .; Massachusetts, n.d. 9228.50 p170
Lacroix, . . .; Quebec, 1662 9221.17 p489
La Croix, Mr.; Massachusetts, 1850-1930 9228.50 p316
Lacroix, Mr. 32; New Orleans, 1840 778.6 p197
Lacroix, Mr. 55; Port uncertain, 1844 778.6 p197
Lacroix, Mrs. 50; Port uncertain, 1844 778.6 p197
Lacroix, Barbe; Quebec, 1668 4514.3 p337
Lacroix, Caroline 6 months; Missouri, 1845 778.6 p197
Lacroix, Caroline 30; Missouri, 1845 778.6 p197
Lacroix, Christophe; Quebec, 1648 9221.17 p200
Lacroix, Christophe; Quebec, 1661 9221.17 p455
Lacroix, Clotilde 10; New Orleans, 1848 778.6 p197
Lacroix, Ernestine 14; Port uncertain, 1844 778.6 p197
Lacroix, F. 35; New Orleans, 1844 778.6 p197
Lacroix, Jacob 35; Missouri, 1845 778.6 p197
Lacroix, Jane 33; America, 1848 778.6 p197
Lacroix, Jean 18; America, 1848 778.6 p197
Lacroix, Jean 20; Montreal, 1662 9221.17 p499
La Croix, John; Marblehead, MA, 1700-1741 9228.50 p170
Lacroix, Julie 18; Port uncertain, 1844 778.6 p197
Lacroix, Louis 17; Quebec, 1645 9221.17 p154
Lacroix, Mathurin 21; Montreal, 1653 9221.17 p294
Lacroix, Nicolas 48; Quebec, 1649 9221.17 p214
Lacroix, Olivier; Quebec, 1649 9221.17 p219
La Croix, Pierre; Maine, 1659 9228.50 p316
Lacroix, Robert 52; Quebec, 1651 9221.17 p243
La Croix, Sarah; Marblehead, MA, 1732 9228.50 p316
La Croix, Sarah; Marblehead, MA, 1732 9228.50 p593
Lacroix, Suzanne; Quebec, 1669 4514.3 p329
Lacroix, Theodore; Louisiana, 1836-1840 4981.45 p213
Lacroux, Jacob; Illinois, 1858 6079.1 p8
LaCrovois, Pierre 57; Port uncertain, 1842 778.6 p197
Lacruce, John; America, 1763 1220.12 p479
Lacy, Edw.; Maryland, 1672 1236.25 p47
Lacy, Edward; Annapolis, MD, 1730 1220.12 p479
Lacy, Elizabeth; America, 1755 1220.12 p479
Lacy, John; America, 1720 1220.12 p479
Lacy, Robert; America, 1694 1220.12 p479
Lacy, Robert, Sr.; America, 1742 1220.12 p479
Lacy, Thomas; America, 1734 1220.12 p479
Ladage, Gerhard Conrad; Port uncertain, 1840 7420.1 p19
Ladage, Heinrich; America, 1866 7420.1 p245
With wife & children
Ladage, Johann Friedrich August; America, 1853 7420.1 p108
Ladd, Calvin J. 50; Ontario, 1871 1823.21 p194
Ladd, Elizabeth; America, 1767 1220.12 p479
Ladd, James; Virginia, 1751 1220.12 p479
Ladd, John; America, 1698 1220.12 p480
Ladd, John; America, 1773 1220.12 p480
Ladd, Lucius J. 23; Ontario, 1871 1823.21 p194
Ladd, William C.; Ohio, 1839 2763.1 p20
Laddin, Michael; Ohio, 1840-1897 8365.35 p17
Lade, Edward; America, 1773 1220.12 p480
Ladewig, Johann Wilhelm Gottfried; Wisconsin, 1870 6795.8 p90
Ladle, Michael; America, 1772 1220.12 p480
Ladlow, John; America, 1768 1220.12 p513
Ladly, William; America, 1774 1220.12 p480
L'Adminirault, Jean 30; America, 1843 778.6 p197
Ladmore, Thomas; America, 1731 1220.12 p480
Ladner, Morris; Detroit, 1929 1640.55 p116
Ladomitz, Charles; New Castle, DE, 1817-1818 90.20 p152
Ladouceur, Pierre 33; Quebec, 1655 9221.17 p326
Ladowsky, Rubin 25; New York, NY, 1894 6512.1 p183
Ladrach, Suzanne 2; New York, NY, 1883 8427.14 p43
Ladrock, John; Ohio, 1809-1852 4511.35 p29
Lads, Joseph; America, 1752 1220.12 p480
Ladson, Michael 28; Indiana, 1874 9076.20 p68
LaDuk, Francis 18; Ohio, 1880 4879.40 p257
LaDuke, Moses 25; Ohio, 1880 4879.40 p257
Laduron, Julie; Wisconsin, 1855-1858 1495.20 p67
Ladwein, A. Maria *SEE* Ladwein, Mathias
Ladwein, Andreas *SEE* Ladwein, Mathias
Ladwein, Angela *SEE* Ladwein, Mathias
Ladwein, Barbara; America, 1867 5475.1 p281
With father
Ladwein, Johann *SEE* Ladwein, Mathias
Ladwein, Johann; America, 1889 5475.1 p197
Ladwein, Katharina *SEE* Ladwein, Mathias
Ladwein, Mathias; America, 1867 5475.1 p281
*Wife:*Susanna Spiedler
*Daughter:*Katharina
*Daughter:*A. Maria
*Daughter:*Angela
*Son:*Andreas
*Son:*Johann
Ladwein, Susanna Spiedler *SEE* Ladwein, Mathias
Ladwicke, William; America, 1768 1220.12 p480
Ladwig, Charles; Wisconsin, 1885 6795.8 p106
Lae, Thomas; Washington, 1877 2770.40 p134
Laehr, Michael; Ohio, 1809-1852 4511.35 p29
La Emanuel, . . .; North Carolina, 1841 1088.45 p18
Laemgruber, Mottice; Ohio, 1809-1852 4511.35 p29
Laeng, Phillip; Louisiana, 1874 4981.45 p132
Laengele, Balthazard 1; Mississippi, 1845 778.6 p198
Laengele, Balthazard 34; Mississippi, 1845 778.6 p198
Laengele, Catherine 25; Mississippi, 1845 778.6 p198
Laersas, Chiraco; Louisiana, 1874 4981.45 p296
Laeseke, Ilse Marie Justine; America, 1859 7420.1 p186
Laeseke, Ilse Marie Justine; America, 1859 7420.1 p186
Laeth, Charles; Illinois, 1834-1900 6020.5 p132
Lafaneade, Henry; Louisiana, 1874 4981.45 p132
Lafantaisie, Etienne 18; Montreal, 1659 9221.17 p422
Lafantaisie, Jean; Quebec, 1648 9221.17 p198
Lafarge, Etienne 38; Missouri, 1845 778.6 p198
Lafaurest, Jean 25; Quebec, 1656 9221.17 p339
LaFave, John 77; Michigan, 1880 4491.30 p19
Lafaveur, Marie; Quebec, 1668 4514.3 p285
Lafavie, Nicolas; Quebec, 1651 9221.17 p238
Lafaye, Jean; Quebec, 1662 9221.17 p488
Lafaye, Marie; Quebec, 1663 4514.3 p329
LaFee, Charles 18; New Orleans, 1846 778.6 p198
LaFee, Henry 19; New Orleans, 1846 778.6 p198
Laferty, John 87; Ontario, 1871 1823.21 p194
La Fetra, . . .; New York, 1640 9228.50 p317
La Fetra, Edmond; Salem, MA, 1666 9228.50 p316
Laffant, Jean; Louisiana, 1874 4981.45 p296
Laffargue, Jean Antoine 18; New Orleans, 1848 778.6 p198
Lafferanderie, Jean-Marie 18; America, 1845 778.6 p198
Lafferty, Arthur; Colorado, 1878 1029.59 p52
Laffey, Stephen; Illinois, 1860 6079.1 p8
Laffield, Thomas; America, 1741 1220.12 p480
Laffite, J. B. 22; New Orleans, 1843 778.6 p198
Laffiton, Mr. 37; New Orleans, 1843 778.6 p198
Laffitte, Gus; Louisiana, 1874-1875 4981.45 p29
Laffoley, . . .; New Brunswick, n.d. 9228.50 p317
Laffoley, . . .; New Jersey, n.d. 9228.50 p19A
Laffoley, Philip; Boston, 1812-1900 9228.50 p317
Laffoley, Philip; Quebec, 1812 9228.50 p317
Laffolley, James; Portsmouth, NH, 1667 9228.50 p317
Laffont, Mrs. 43; New Orleans, 1848 778.6 p198
LaFitte, Mr.; Canada, n.d. 9228.50 p369
Lafitte, Mr. 32; Louisiana, 1848 778.6 p198
LaFitte, Mr.; New Orleans, n.d. 9228.50 p369
LaFitte, Mr.; New York, n.d. 9228.50 p369
Lafitte, Antoine 8 months; St. Louis, 1844 778.6 p198
Lafitte, Emile 32; America, 1848 778.6 p198
Lafitte, G. A. 15; America, 1845 778.6 p198
Lafleche, Sebastien 34; Montreal, 1650 9221.17 p231
Lafleur, Elie 27; Quebec, 1662 9221.17 p484
Lafleur, Francois 32; Montreal, 1659 9221.17 p416
*Wife:*Marie Fonteneau 28
Lafleur, Francois; Quebec, 1649 9221.17 p221
Lafleur, Jean 18; Quebec, 1655 9221.17 p324
Lafleur, Jean 21; Quebec, 1656 9221.17 p333
Lafleur, Jean 21; Quebec, 1657 9221.17 p357
Lafleur, Joachine; Quebec, 1663 4514.3 p329
Lafleur, Marie Fonteneau 28 *SEE* Lafleur, Francois
Lafleur, Pierre 24; Quebec, 1651 9221.17 p239
Lafleur, Raymond; Quebec, 1660 9221.17 p438
Lafleur, Richard; Quebec, 1645 9221.17 p157
Laflotte, Louis; Montreal, 1652 9221.17 p267
Lafly, James; Portsmouth, NH, 1667 9228.50 p317
Lafollette, . . .; New Jersey, n.d. 9228.50 p19A
Lafon, Mr. 27; New Orleans, 1840 778.6 p198
Lafon, Charles 26; Texas, 1848 778.6 p198
Lafon, John B. 32; Port uncertain, 1842 778.6 p198
Lafons, Francois; Quebec, 1652 9221.17 p260
Lafontaine, . . .; Quebec, 1645 9221.17 p154
Lafontaine, . . .; Quebec, 1652 9221.17 p260
Lafontaine, Antoine 18; Montreal, 1662 9221.17 p498
Lafontaine, Claude; Quebec, 1665 4514.3 p298
Lafontaine, Fiacre 26; Montreal, 1653 9221.17 p289
Lafontaine, Jacques; Quebec, 1646 9221.17 p163
Lafontaine, Jacques 15; Quebec, 1643 9221.17 p133
Lafontaine, Jean; Quebec, 1645 9221.17 p153
Lafontaine, Jean; Quebec, 1652 9221.17 p266
Lafontaine, Jean 26; Quebec, 1661 9221.17 p463
Lafontaine, Joseph; Quebec, 1654 9221.17 p304
*Wife:*Marie-Madeleine Breman
Lafontaine, Laurent 22; Quebec, 1661 9221.17 p464
Lafontaine, Leger 27; Montreal, 1651 9221.17 p251
Lafontaine, Marie-Anne; Quebec, 1670 4514.3 p329
Lafontaine, Marie-Madeleine Breman *SEE* Lafontaine, Joseph
Lafontaine, Marie-Madeleine; Quebec, 1663-1665 4514.3 p298
Lafontaine, Mathurin 25; Quebec, 1659 9221.17 p402

Lafontaine, Michel; Quebec, 1645 ***9221.17*** *p151*
Lafontaine, Michel 20; Quebec, 1660 ***9221.17*** *p436*
Lafontaine, Nicolas 18; Quebec, 1652 ***9221.17*** *p259*
Lafontaine, Nicolas 27; Quebec, 1655 ***9221.17*** *p328*
Lafontaine, Pierre 40; Montreal, 1659 ***9221.17*** *p426*
Lafontaine, Pierre 5; Quebec, 1636 ***9221.17*** *p54*
Lafontan, . . . 23; America, 1747 ***778.6*** *p198*
Laforest, Abel 23; Quebec, 1650 ***9221.17*** *p223*
Laforest, Andre 20; Quebec, 1661 ***9221.17*** *p446*
Laforest, Catherine; Quebec, 1667 ***4514.3*** *p299*
La Forest, Francois de; Quebec, 1675 ***2314.30*** *p166*
La Forest, Francois de; Quebec, 1675 ***2314.30*** *p187*
Laforest, Gabriel 26; Quebec, 1662 ***9221.17*** *p479*
Laforest, Jean 21; Montreal, 1653 ***9221.17*** *p301*
Laforest, Jean 29; Quebec, 1659 ***9221.17*** *p411*
Laforest, Pierre; Montreal, 1642 ***9221.17*** *p123*
Laforge, Abel 23; Quebec, 1662 ***9221.17*** *p492*
Laforge, Bridget 10; Ontario, 1871 ***1823.17*** *p87*
Laforge, Jacques 25; Quebec, 1652 ***9221.17*** *p259*
Laforge, Jean de; Quebec, 1660 ***9221.17*** *p437*
Laforge, John 52; Ontario, 1871 ***1823.17*** *p87*
Laforgue, Blaize 29; New Orleans, 1845 ***778.6*** *p198*
Laforgue, Joseph 25; New Orleans, 1845 ***778.6*** *p198*
Lafortune, Francois; Quebec, 1645 ***9221.17*** *p157*
Lafortune, Hugues 31; Montreal, 1653 ***9221.17*** *p298*
Lafortune, Jean; Quebec, 1646 ***9221.17*** *p161*
*Wife:*Jeanne Richer
Lafortune, Jean 21; Quebec, 1657 ***9221.17*** *p357*
Lafortune, Jeanne Richer 45 *SEE* Lafortune, Jean
Lafortune, Marin; Quebec, 1648 ***9221.17*** *p196*
Lafortune, Paul; Quebec, 1642 ***9221.17*** *p113*
Lafosse, Pierre de; Quebec, 1650 ***9221.17*** *p227*
Lafougere, Adrien 54; Quebec, 1658 ***9221.17*** *p376*
Lafougere, Pierre; Quebec, 1649 ***9221.17*** *p218*
Lafous, Laura 25; Mississippi, 1847 ***778.6*** *p198*
Lafous, Pierre 40; Mississippi, 1847 ***778.6*** *p198*
Lafraicheur, Louis 27; Quebec, 1645 ***9221.17*** *p152*
Laframboise, Bertrand 18; Quebec, 1637 ***9221.17*** *p69*
Lafrance, Emile; Louisiana, 1874 ***4981.45*** *p132*
Lafrance, Francois; Quebec, 1659 ***9221.17*** *p404*
Lafranchise, Nicolas; Quebec, 1649 ***9221.17*** *p210*
La Frenaye deBrucy, Antoine de; Quebec, 1665 ***2314.30*** *p167*
La Frenaye deBrucy, Antoine de; Quebec, 1665 ***2314.30*** *p187*
Lafrenz, Hans; Valdivia, Chile, 1852 ***1192.4*** *p55*
Lafronde, Louis 38; Quebec, 1654 ***9221.17*** *p315*
Lagan, Thomas; Louisiana, 1836-1840 ***4981.45*** *p213*
LaGarde, Mr. 23; America, 1841 ***778.6*** *p198*
Lagarde, Jean; Quebec, 1652 ***9221.17*** *p254*
Lagardere, Henry; Louisiana, 1874 ***4981.45*** *p132*
Lagarenne, Bertrand 31; Quebec, 1656 ***9221.17*** *p333*
Lagarenne, Jean 24; Montreal, 1662 ***9221.17*** *p497*
Lagarere, Mr. 45; Mexico, 1845 ***778.6*** *p198*
Lagdell, George; Barbados or Jamaica, 1697 ***1220.12*** *p480*
Lagden, George; America, 1695 ***1220.12*** *p480*
Lagden, Robert; America, 1769 ***1220.12*** *p480*
Lage, August; Iowa, 1904 ***1211.15*** *p16*
Lagedy, Martha Le Brocq *SEE* Lagedy, Philip
Lagedy, Philip; Beverly, MA, 1698 ***9228.50*** *p159*
*Wife:*Martha Le Brocq
La Gerche, Wm. T.; North America, 1836 ***9228.50*** *p366*
Lagerre, Vautie 26; America, 1842 ***778.6*** *p198*
Lagerstrom, O.H.; Philadelphia, 1848 ***6412.40*** *p151*
Lages, Johann Christoph; New York, NY, 1856 ***7420.1*** *p149*
Lages, Johann Conrad; America, 1855 ***7420.1*** *p138*
Lages, Johann Conrad; America, 1868 ***7420.1*** *p274*
With family
Lagillie, Jacques; Quebec, 1660 ***9221.17*** *p437*
Laging, Dorothea Louise Friederike Lucke *SEE* Laging, Johann Friedrich Christian David
Laging, Engel Dorothea Justine Eleonore; America, 1850 ***7420.1*** *p77*
Laging, Heinrich Friedrich Gottlieb *SEE* Laging, Johann Friedrich Christian David
Laging, Johann Friedrich Christian David; America, 1857 ***7420.1*** *p166*
*Wife:*Dorothea Louise Friederike Lucke
*Daughter:*Louise Johanne
*Son:*Heinrich Friedrich Gottlieb
Laging, Louise Johanne *SEE* Laging, Johann Friedrich Christian David
LaGlardiere, Pierre 3; Quebec, 1634 ***9221.17*** *p40*
Lagnel, Etienne 32; Quebec, 1656 ***9221.17*** *p339*
Lagnier, Pierre 22; America, 1842 ***778.6*** *p198*
Lagody, Philip, Family; America, 1600-1699 ***9228.50*** *p337*
Lagogue, Pierre 14; Montreal, 1653 ***9221.17*** *p281*
Lagou, Anne; Quebec, 1670 ***4514.3*** *p330*
Lagourdette, Miss 25; New Orleans, 1848 ***778.6*** *p198*
Lagourdette, Jean 35; New Orleans, 1848 ***778.6*** *p198*
Lagracerie, Mr. 30; New Orleans, 1842 ***778.6*** *p198*
LaGrane, J. B. 25; America, 1848 ***778.6*** *p198*
Lagrange, Jacqueline 19; Montreal, 1658 ***9221.17*** *p389*
Lagrange, Jacques 26; Quebec, 1661 ***9221.17*** *p447*
Lagrange, Jean 26; Quebec, 1661 ***9221.17*** *p463*
Lagrange, Toussaint; Quebec, 1643 ***9221.17*** *p135*
Lagrave, Jean; Quebec, 1651 ***9221.17*** *p248*
Lagrisonniere, . . .; Quebec, 1654 ***9221.17*** *p311*
Lagroix, Louis 17; Quebec, 1645 ***9221.17*** *p154*
Lagronde, P. 28; America, 1841 ***778.6*** *p198*
Lagrouais, Louis 17; Quebec, 1645 ***9221.17*** *p154*
Lagrove, Celina 10 *SEE* Lagrove, Daniel
Lagrove, Daniel 42; Ohio, 1880 ***4879.40*** *p260*
*Wife:*Gurtie 32
*Son:*Joseph 2
*Son:*Delphos 4
*Son:*Fillanda 12
*Daughter:*Louisa 8
*Daughter:*Celina 10
Lagrove, Delphos 4 *SEE* Lagrove, Daniel
Lagrove, Fillanda 12 *SEE* Lagrove, Daniel
Lagrove, Gurtie 32 *SEE* Lagrove, Daniel
Lagrove, Joseph 2 *SEE* Lagrove, Daniel
Lagrove, Louisa 8 *SEE* Lagrove, Daniel
La Grove, Nicholas; Salem, MA, 1668 ***9228.50*** *p257*
La Groves, Nicholas; Salem, MA, 1668 ***9228.50*** *p317*
La Groves Family ; Marblehead, MA, 1684 ***9228.50*** *p256*
Lagroye, Michel 29; Quebec, 1645 ***9221.17*** *p153*
Lagud, Frank; Detroit, 1930 ***1640.60*** *p83*
Laguerenne, John T.; Louisiana, 1836-1840 ***4981.45*** *p213*
La Guerre deMorville, Claude-Dorothee; Quebec, 1717 ***2314.30*** *p169*
La Guerre deMorville, Claude-Dorothee; Quebec, 1717 ***2314.30*** *p187*
Laguet, Etienne 32; Quebec, 1656 ***9221.17*** *p339*
Laguide, Jean 33; America, 1842 ***778.6*** *p199*
Laguillermo, J. Louis 48; New Orleans, 1848 ***778.6*** *p199*
La Hah, Abraham *SEE* La Hah, Jane
La Hah, Jane; Maine, 1713 ***9228.50*** *p317*
*Relative:*Abraham
Lahaie, Jean 13; Quebec, 1659 ***9221.17*** *p405*
Lahaie, Pierre 25; Quebec, 1652 ***9221.17*** *p262*
Lahargouette, J. P. 18; New Orleans, 1848 ***778.6*** *p199*
Lahargouette, Jean 20; America, 1845 ***778.6*** *p199*
LaHarpiniere, Jean; Quebec, 1642 ***9221.17*** *p118*
Lahay, John; Canada, 1697 ***9228.50*** *p617*
Lahaye, Eloi; Montreal, 1653 ***9221.17*** *p293*
Lahey, Margaret 49; Ontario, 1871 ***1823.21*** *p194*
Lahin, Thomas 27; Ontario, 1871 ***1823.21*** *p194*
Lahman, Michael; Ohio, 1809-1852 ***4511.35*** *p29*
Lahman, Nicholas; Ohio, 1809-1852 ***4511.35*** *p29*
Lahmann, Friedrich; America, 1855 ***7420.1*** *p138*
Lahonette, R. 30; New Orleans, 1848 ***778.6*** *p199*
Lahourcade, Jean 29; New Orleans, 1848 ***778.6*** *p199*
Lahr, Anna; America, 1873 ***5475.1*** *p322*
Lahr, Anna; America, 1873 ***5475.1*** *p328*
Lahr, Jakob 22; America, 1871 ***5475.1*** *p327*
Lahr, Mathias; America, 1846 ***5475.1*** *p322*
Lahre, Artero 23; New Orleans, 1845 ***778.6*** *p199*
Lahtonen, Joseph 39; Minnesota, 1925 ***2769.54*** *p1378*
Lai, Johann 22; New York, NY, 1886 ***8425.16*** *p33*
Laib, Solomond; North Carolina, 1850 ***1088.45*** *p18*
Laicher, Barbara; Venezuela, 1843 ***3899.5*** *p541*
Laicher, Joseph; Venezuela, 1843 ***3899.5*** *p540*
Laicher, Maria Anna; Venezuela, 1843 ***3899.5*** *p540*
Laicher, Maria Anna; Venezuela, 1843 ***3899.5*** *p542*
Laick, Katharina Bruck *SEE* Laick, Mathias
Laick, Maria *SEE* Laick, Mathias
Laick, Mathias; Brazil, 1881 ***5475.1*** *p42*
*Wife:*Katharina Bruck
*Daughter:*Sophie
*Daughter:*Maria
Laick, Sophie *SEE* Laick, Mathias
Laidlaw, David; America, 1750 ***1220.12*** *p480*
Laidlaw, George 65; Ontario, 1871 ***1823.21*** *p194*
Laidlaw, Walter 56; Ontario, 1871 ***1823.21*** *p194*
Laidler, Adam; America, 1734 ***1220.12*** *p480*
Laidler, Thomas; America, 1767 ***1220.12*** *p480*
Laieh, Caroline; New York, 1859 ***358.56*** *p100*
Laighley, John 80; Ontario, 1871 ***1823.21*** *p194*
Laimery, Pierre 35; Quebec, 1641 ***9221.17*** *p105*
Lain, John 45; Ontario, 1871 ***1823.21*** *p194*
Laine, Alfred; America, 1840 ***9228.50*** *p317*
Laine, Alfred; Utah, 1830-1930 ***9228.50*** *p317*
Laine, Anna 48; Minnesota, 1926 ***2769.54*** *p1383*
Laine, Anne; Quebec, 1669 ***4514.3*** *p330*
Laine, Catherine; Quebec, 1671 ***4514.3*** *p330*
Laine, Charles 41; Minnesota, 1925 ***2769.54*** *p1381*
Laine, Genevieve; Quebec, 1667 ***4514.3*** *p330*
Laine, James; New York, NY, 1847 ***9228.50*** *p317*
*Wife:*Rachel Massey
Laine, James; Wisconsin, 1847 ***9228.50*** *p317*
*Wife:*Rachel Mahy
Laine, Julia; Utah, n.d. ***9228.50*** *p317*
Laine, Marie 34; America, 1845 ***778.6*** *p199*
Laine, Marie; Memphis, TN, 1830-1930 ***9228.50*** *p318*
Laine, Marion 33; Minnesota, 1925 ***2769.54*** *p1381*
Laine, Rachel Massey *SEE* Laine, James
Laine, Rachel Mahy *SEE* Laine, James
Laine, William John; Memphis, TN, n.d. ***9228.50*** *p317*
Laing, Alexander 36; Ontario, 1871 ***1823.17*** *p87*
Laing, Francis 4; Ontario, 1871 ***1823.17*** *p87*
Laing, George 31; Ontario, 1871 ***1823.21*** *p194*
Laing, James 32; Ontario, 1871 ***1823.17*** *p87*
Laing, John 19; Ontario, 1871 ***1823.21*** *p194*
Laing, John B. 33; Ontario, 1871 ***1823.21*** *p194*
Laing, Joseph 36; Ontario, 1871 ***1823.21*** *p194*
Laing, Thomas 65; Ontario, 1871 ***1823.17*** *p87*
Laird, Christopher; America, 1767 ***1220.12*** *p480*
Laird, Francis 47; Ontario, 1871 ***1823.17*** *p87*
Laird, George 74; Ontario, 1871 ***1823.17*** *p87*
Laird, Hugh 53; Ontario, 1871 ***1823.21*** *p194*
Laird, James 42; Ontario, 1871 ***1823.21*** *p194*
Laird, James 59; Ontario, 1871 ***1823.21*** *p194*
Laird, Jane 54; Ontario, 1871 ***1823.21*** *p194*
Laird, John; North Carolina, 1789 ***1088.45*** *p18*
Laird, John 45; Ontario, 1871 ***1823.21*** *p194*
Laird, Richd 36; Ontario, 1871 ***1823.17*** *p87*
Laird, Robert 50; Ontario, 1871 ***1823.17*** *p87*
Laird, Robert 51; Ontario, 1871 ***1823.21*** *p194*
Laird, Robert 61; Ontario, 1871 ***1823.17*** *p87*
Laird, Sarah 41; Ontario, 1871 ***1823.17*** *p87*
Laird, William 6; Ontario, 1871 ***1823.17*** *p87*
Lairgru, Basilae; Louisiana, 1874 ***4981.45*** *p132*
Lairney, John 24; St. Johns, N.F., 1811 ***1053.20*** *p21*
Lairsey, John 24; St. Johns, N.F., 1811 ***1053.20*** *p21*
Laisch, Auguste 10; Louisiana, 1848 ***778.6*** *p199*
Laisch, Emilie 6; Louisiana, 1848 ***778.6*** *p199*
Laisch, Goudebout 18; Louisiana, 1848 ***778.6*** *p199*
Laisch, Joseph 14; Louisiana, 1848 ***778.6*** *p199*
Laisch, Joseph 36; Louisiana, 1848 ***778.6*** *p199*
Laisch, Louise 15; Louisiana, 1848 ***778.6*** *p199*
Laisch, Louise 48; Louisiana, 1848 ***778.6*** *p199*
Laisne, Alfred; America, 1840 ***9228.50*** *p317*
Laisne, Alfred; Utah, 1830-1930 ***9228.50*** *p317*
Laisne, Julia Hamelin; Ogden, UT, 1891 ***9228.50*** *p383*
Laisne, Marie; Memphis, TN, 1830-1930 ***9228.50*** *p318*
Laisne, William John; Memphis, TN, n.d. ***9228.50*** *p317*
Laissle, Ferdinand; Valdivia, Chile, 1852 ***1192.4*** *p53*
With wife
Laitor, Benjamin; Annapolis, MD, 1725 ***1220.12*** *p480*
Lajae, Laurent 38; New Orleans, 1843 ***778.6*** *p199*
Lajeunesse, Francois 30; Quebec, 1660 ***9221.17*** *p439*
Lajeunesse, Jean; Quebec, 1652 ***9221.17*** *p257*
Lajeunesse, Pierre; Quebec, 1645 ***9221.17*** *p156*
Lajeunesse, Pierre 15; Quebec, 1642 ***9221.17*** *p118*
Lajeunesse, Pierre 23; Quebec, 1647 ***9221.17*** *p178*
Lajoie, Michel; Quebec, 1658 ***9221.17*** *p383*
LaJonas, Ely 38; America, 1848 ***778.6*** *p199*
Lakanen, Arvo 18; Minnesota, 1925 ***2769.54*** *p1378*
Lakanen, Toivo 19; Minnesota, 1925 ***2769.54*** *p1378*
Lakas, Nikolaus; America, 1870 ***5475.1*** *p304*
Lake, Barnabas; Ogden, UT, 1893 ***3687.1*** *p38*
Lake, Elizabeth 32; Ontario, 1871 ***1823.21*** *p194*
Lake, Henry 35; Ontario, 1871 ***1823.21*** *p194*
Lake, John; America, 1752 ***1220.12*** *p480*
Lake, John; America, 1755 ***1220.12*** *p480*
Lake, Jos.; Louisiana, 1874 ***4981.45*** *p296*
Lake, Lucy; America, 1749 ***1220.12*** *p480*
Lake, Matthew; America, 1774 ***1220.12*** *p480*
Lake, William; America, 1743 ***1220.12*** *p480*
Lake, William; Virginia, 1768 ***1220.12*** *p480*
Lakeland, John; Virginia, 1773 ***1220.12*** *p480*
Laken, Thomas 52; Ontario, 1871 ***1823.21*** *p194*
Lakes, Arthur; Colorado, 1862-1894 ***1029.59*** *p52*
Lakey, Hannah; America, 1775 ***1220.12*** *p480*
Lakey, Robert; Barbados, 1671 ***1220.12*** *p480*
Lakey, Robert; Maryland, 1671 ***1236.25*** *p46*
Lakey, William; America, 1743 ***1220.12*** *p480*
Lakie, Andrew 71; Ontario, 1871 ***1823.21*** *p194*
Lakie, Margaret U. 33; Ontario, 1871 ***1823.21*** *p194*
Lakin, Francis; America, 1774 ***1220.12*** *p480*
Lakin, Isabella; America, 1771 ***1220.12*** *p480*
Lakin, Robert; America, 1774 ***1220.12*** *p480*
Lakin, Samuel; America, 1694 ***1220.12*** *p480*
Lakomy, Rudolf; Wisconsin, 1895 ***2853.20*** *p235*
Laks...har, Stephan 28; New York, NY, 1893 ***1883.7*** *p37*
Lakus, Alexander; Ohio, 1809-1852 ***4511.35*** *p29*
Lala, Vaclav; Chicago, 1868 ***2853.20*** *p393*
Lalamon, Pierre Piete 25; New Orleans, 1840 ***778.6*** *p199*
Lalampree, Noel; Quebec, 1651 ***9221.17*** *p245*
Lalande, Mr. 53; Port uncertain, 1844 ***778.6*** *p199*
Lalande, Jean de; Quebec, 1638 ***9221.17*** *p78*
Lalande, Michel; New Orleans, 1840 ***778.6*** *p199*

Lalande, Rene; Quebec, 1649 ***9221.17*** *p211*
Lalanne, G. 35; America, 1843 ***778.6*** *p199*
Lalanne, Henri 36; America, 1843 ***778.6*** *p199*
Lalanne, J. 17; New Orleans, 1848 ***778.6*** *p199*
Lalanne, J. J. 40; America, 1843 ***778.6*** *p199*
Lalanne, Paul; Louisiana, 1836-1840 ***4981.45*** *p213*
Lalaune, B. 17; America, 1848 ***778.6*** *p199*
Lalaune, P. 23; America, 1848 ***778.6*** *p199*
Lalemant, Charles; Quebec, 1625 ***9221.17*** *p32*
Lalemant, Gabriel 36; Quebec, 1646 ***9221.17*** *p160*
Lalemant, Isaac 16; Quebec, 1658 ***9221.17*** *p383*
Lalemant, Jerome 45; Quebec, 1638 ***9221.17*** *p74*
Lalime, Antoine 44; Montreal, 1644 ***9221.17*** *p147*
*Son:*Louis 12
Lalime, Louis 12 *SEE* Lalime, Antoine
Lalla, Antonio; Louisiana, 1874 ***4981.45*** *p132*
Lalla, Franceso; Louisiana, 1874-1875 ***4981.45*** *p29*
Lallande, J. 22; America, 1847 ***778.6*** *p199*
Lallemand, Celestine 26; Port uncertain, 1843 ***778.6*** *p199*
Lallemand, George 26; America, 1746 ***778.6*** *p199*
Lallement, Catherina 32; Port uncertain, 1842 ***778.6*** *p199*
Lallement, Joseph 37; Port uncertain, 1842 ***778.6*** *p199*
Lallement, Michel 23; Port uncertain, 1842 ***778.6*** *p199*
Laller, Patrick; New England, 1745 ***1642*** *p27*
Lally, John; America, 1764 ***1220.12*** *p480*
Lally, Michael 40; Ontario, 1871 ***1823.21*** *p194*
Lalochetiere, Etienne; Montreal, 1652 ***9221.17*** *p268*
Lalochetiere, Jean 21; Montreal, 1653 ***9221.17*** *p301*
Laloire, Mathurin 24; Montreal, 1653 ***9221.17*** *p294*
Lalone, Charles 31; Ohio, 1880 ***4879.40*** *p259*
*Wife:*Lydia J. Zedaker 40
Lalone, Emily D. 49 *SEE* Lalone, Peter
Lalone, Lydia J. Zedaker 40 *SEE* Lalone, Charles
Lalone, Maggie 17 *SEE* Lalone, Peter
Lalone, Peter 21 *SEE* Lalone, Peter
Lalone, Peter 52; Ohio, 1880 ***4879.40*** *p258*
*Wife:*Emily D. 49
*Daughter:*Maggie 17
*Son:*Peter 21
Lalter, Peter 23; America, 1848 ***778.6*** *p200*
Laluree, Antoni 26; New Orleans, 1843 ***778.6*** *p200*
Laluzerne, Adolphe *SEE* Laluzerne, Jean Joseph, Jr.
Laluzerne, August Joseph *SEE* Laluzerne, John Joseph
Laluzerne, Augustine Denis *SEE* Laluzerne, Jean Joseph, Jr.
Laluzerne, Florence Delsipee *SEE* Laluzerne, John Joseph
Laluzerne, Guillaume *SEE* Laluzerne, John Joseph
Laluzerne, Hector Joseph *SEE* Laluzerne, Jean Joseph, Jr.
Laluzerne, Hubert Joseph *SEE* Laluzerne, John Joseph
Laluzerne, Jean Joseph, Jr.; Wisconsin, 1869 ***1495.20*** *p8*
*Wife:*Augustine Denis
*Child:*Adolphe
*Child:*Hector Joseph
*Child:*Marie Therese
*Child:*Jules Joseph
*Child:*Marie Francoise
*Child:*Marie Josephe
Laluzerne, John Joseph; Wisconsin, 1855 ***1495.20*** *p8*
*Wife:*Florence Delsipee
*Child:*Hubert Joseph
*Child:*August Joseph
*Child:*Philomene
*Child:*Marie Josephine
*Child:*Leopold
*Child:*Marie Joseph
*Child:*Guillaume
Laluzerne, Jules Joseph *SEE* Laluzerne, Jean Joseph, Jr.
Laluzerne, Leopold *SEE* Laluzerne, John Joseph
Laluzerne, Marie Francoise *SEE* Laluzerne, Jean Joseph, Jr.
Laluzerne, Marie Joseph *SEE* Laluzerne, John Joseph
Laluzerne, Marie Josephe *SEE* Laluzerne, Jean Joseph, Jr.
Laluzerne, Marie Josephine *SEE* Laluzerne, John Joseph
Laluzerne, Marie Therese *SEE* Laluzerne, Jean Joseph, Jr.
Laluzerne, Philomene *SEE* Laluzerne, John Joseph
Lam, Alexandre 28; Louisiana, 1848 ***778.6*** *p200*
Lam, Charles 16; Louisiana, 1848 ***778.6*** *p200*
Lam, Emile 8; Louisiana, 1848 ***778.6*** *p200*
Lamaigne, P. 24; America, 1848 ***778.6*** *p200*
Lamain, Marguerite; Quebec, 1670 ***4514.3*** *p330*
Laman, William; America, 1732 ***1220.12*** *p495*
Lamanna, V.; Louisiana, 1874-1875 ***4981.45*** *p29*
Lamanne, Francois; Quebec, 1648 ***9221.17*** *p200*
Lamar, J. B. 34; Port uncertain, 1842 ***778.6*** *p200*
Lamarche, Charles; Montreal, 1659 ***9221.17*** *p420*
Lamarche, Charlotte; Quebec, 1669 ***4514.3*** *p331*
Lamarche, Pierre 35; Quebec, 1658 ***9221.17*** *p380*
Lamarche, Urbain 30; Quebec, 1645 ***9221.17*** *p151*
Lamare, Genevieve 16 *SEE* Lamare, Nicolas
Lamare, Jacques 25; Quebec, 1652 ***9221.17*** *p259*
Lamare, Jacques 26 *SEE* Lamare, Nicolas
Lamare, Nicolas *SEE* Lamare, Nicolas
Lamare, Nicolas; Quebec, 1652 ***9221.17*** *p258*
*Son:*Jacques
*Daughter:*Genevieve
*Son:*Nicolas
Lamarque, Miss 4; New Orleans, 1841 ***778.6*** *p200*
Lamarque, Miss 6; New Orleans, 1841 ***778.6*** *p200*
Lamarque, Miss 8; New Orleans, 1841 ***778.6*** *p200*
Lamarque, Mrs. 32; New Orleans, 1841 ***778.6*** *p200*
Lamarque, Ms. 12; New Orleans, 1841 ***778.6*** *p200*
Lamarque, Anne; Canada, 1662 ***1142.10*** *p128*
With family
Lamarque, Anne de 14; Quebec, 1662 ***9221.17*** *p488*
*Brother:*Jacques de 19
Lamarque, Barthelemy 19; New Orleans, 1848 ***778.6*** *p200*
Lamarque, Jacques de 19 *SEE* Lamarque, Anne de
Lamarre, Anne; Quebec, 1665 ***4514.3*** *p331*
Lamazon, M.; Louisiana, 1874-1875 ***4981.45*** *p29*
Lamb, Miss; California, 1868 ***1131.61*** *p89*
Lamb, Addam 60; Ontario, 1871 ***1823.17*** *p88*
Lamb, Ann; America, 1766 ***1220.12*** *p480*
Lamb, Ann 73; Ontario, 1871 ***1823.17*** *p88*
Lamb, Anthony; Annapolis, MD, 1725 ***1220.12*** *p480*
Lamb, Charles; America, 1760 ***1220.12*** *p480*
Lamb, David 70; Ontario, 1871 ***1823.21*** *p194*
Lamb, Frederick; Ohio, 1809-1852 ***4511.35*** *p29*
Lamb, George; North Carolina, 1855 ***1088.45*** *p18*
Lamb, Henry 50; Ontario, 1871 ***1823.21*** *p194*
Lamb, Hewitt; Annapolis, MD, 1720 ***1220.12*** *p480*
Lamb, Hugh; America, 1755 ***1220.12*** *p480*
Lamb, Jacob; Ohio, 1809-1852 ***4511.35*** *p29*
Lamb, James; America, 1736 ***1220.12*** *p480*
Lamb, James; America, 1739 ***1220.12*** *p480*
Lamb, James; America, 1770 ***1220.12*** *p480*
Lamb, James 43; Ontario, 1871 ***1823.17*** *p88*
Lamb, James 61; Ontario, 1871 ***1823.21*** *p195*
Lamb, John; America, 1738 ***1220.12*** *p480*
Lamb, John; America, 1741 ***1220.12*** *p481*
Lamb, John; America, 1747 ***1220.12*** *p481*
Lamb, John; America, 1748 ***1220.12*** *p481*
Lamb, John; America, 1772 ***1220.12*** *p481*
Lamb, John 62; Ontario, 1871 ***1823.21*** *p195*
Lamb, John 69; Ontario, 1871 ***1823.17*** *p88*
Lamb, Joseph 50; Ontario, 1871 ***1823.21*** *p195*
Lamb, Joseph; Virginia, 1770 ***1220.12*** *p481*
Lamb, Kennet; America, 1719 ***1220.12*** *p481*
Lamb, Luke; Virginia, 1759 ***1220.12*** *p481*
Lamb, Peter; New Orleans, 1851 ***7242.30*** *p148*
Lamb, Peter 50; Ontario, 1871 ***1823.17*** *p88*
Lamb, Richard; Virginia, 1749 ***3675.1*** *p*
Lamb, Richard; Westfield, MA, 1700-1739 ***9228.50*** *p212*
Lamb, Robert 40; Ontario, 1871 ***1823.17*** *p88*
Lamb, Sarah; America, 1762 ***1220.12*** *p481*
Lamb, Thomas 79; Ontario, 1871 ***1823.17*** *p88*
Lamb, Thomas; Virginia, 1729 ***1220.12*** *p481*
Lamball, John; America, 1766 ***1220.12*** *p481*
Lambard, Guillaume 48; America, 1843 ***778.6*** *p200*
Lambart, Alphonse 35; Louisiana, 1848 ***778.6*** *p200*
Lambart, Eugene 12; Louisiana, 1848 ***778.6*** *p200*
Lambart, Fois. 58; Louisiana, 1848 ***778.6*** *p200*
Lambart, Jon Pierre 36; Louisiana, 1848 ***778.6*** *p200*
Lambden, John; America, 1769 ***1220.12*** *p481*
Lambe, Ann; Barbados, 1683 ***1220.12*** *p480*
Lambe, Walter; Barbados, 1667 ***1220.12*** *p481*
Lambe, William; Virginia, 1618 ***1220.12*** *p481*
Lambeaux, Aime 1; America, 1843 ***778.6*** *p200*
Lambeaux, Charles 36; America, 1843 ***778.6*** *p200*
Lambeaux, Denyse 38; America, 1843 ***778.6*** *p200*
Lambeaux, Julie 4; America, 1843 ***778.6*** *p200*
Lambeaux, Louis 8; America, 1843 ***778.6*** *p200*
Lambeaux, Zachary 10; America, 1843 ***778.6*** *p200*
Lambelin, Catha. 16; America, 1840 ***778.6*** *p200*
Lambelin, Catha. 36; America, 1840 ***778.6*** *p200*
Lambelin, Edouard 12; America, 1840 ***778.6*** *p200*
Lambelin, Eugene 6; America, 1840 ***778.6*** *p200*
Lambelin, Georg. 5; America, 1840 ***778.6*** *p200*
Lambelin, Jac...s 3; America, 1840 ***778.6*** *p200*
Lambelin, Pierre 42; America, 1840 ***778.6*** *p200*
Lambelin, Theod. 16; America, 1840 ***778.6*** *p200*
Lambere, Bernard 24; New Orleans, 1844 ***778.6*** *p201*
Lambert, Mr. 26; New Orleans, 1843 ***778.6*** *p201*
Lambert, A. 72; Port uncertain, 1845 ***778.6*** *p201*
Lambert, Adam; America, 1867 ***5475.1*** *p508*
Lambert, Alexandre 43; New Orleans, 1848 ***778.6*** *p201*
Lambert, Anna Maria 32; South America, 1857 ***5475.1*** *p543*
Lambert, Anne; America, 1700 ***1220.12*** *p481*
Lambert, Anne; America, 1730 ***1220.12*** *p481*
Lambert, Arsene 25; Port uncertain, 1840 ***778.6*** *p201*
Lambert, Auguste 29; Port uncertain, 1843 ***778.6*** *p201*
Lambert, Catherine; New Orleans, 1850 ***7242.30*** *p148*
Lambert, Charles 16; America, 1841 ***778.6*** *p201*
Lambert, Charles; New Orleans, 1850 ***7242.30*** *p148*
Lambert, Charles 1; Port uncertain, 1843 ***778.6*** *p201*
Lambert, Daniel; America, 1772 ***1220.12*** *p481*
Lambert, Elizabeth; America, 1755 ***1220.12*** *p481*
Lambert, Elizabeth; West Indies, 1686 ***1220.12*** *p481*
Lambert, Esther; New Orleans, 1850 ***7242.30*** *p148*
Lambert, Eustache 28; Quebec, 1645 ***9221.17*** *p154*
Lambert, Florentin 27; America, 1841 ***778.6*** *p201*
Lambert, James; America, 1774 ***1220.12*** *p481*
Lambert, James 43; Ontario, 1871 ***1823.17*** *p88*
Lambert, Jane; Potomac, 1729 ***1220.12*** *p481*
Lambert, Jean; Quebec, 1641 ***9221.17*** *p105*
Lambert, Jean Baptiste; Wisconsin, 1846-1856 ***1495.20*** *p29*
Lambert, Jean-Baptiste 30; New Orleans, 1848 ***778.6*** *p201*
Lambert, Jeanne; Quebec, 1669 ***4514.3*** *p331*
Lambert, Jeremiah; America, 1754 ***1220.12*** *p481*
Lambert, Johann 27; South America, 1857 ***5475.1*** *p543*
Lambert, John; America, 1742 ***1220.12*** *p481*
Lambert, John; America, 1754 ***1220.12*** *p481*
Lambert, John; New Jersey, 1715-1800 ***9228.50*** *p318*
Lambert, John; New Orleans, 1850 ***7242.30*** *p148*
Lambert, John; North Carolina, 1825 ***1088.45*** *p18*
Lambert, Joseph 16; America, 1843 ***778.6*** *p201*
Lambert, Lucien 6; Port uncertain, 1843 ***778.6*** *p201*
Lambert, Maria; America, 1886 ***5475.1*** *p485*
Lambert, Marie; Quebec, 1656 ***9221.17*** *p154*
Lambert, Marie 24; Quebec, 1656 ***9221.17*** *p339*
Lambert, Mary; New Orleans, 1850 ***7242.30*** *p148*
Lambert, Peter; America, 1876 ***5475.1*** *p292*
Lambert, Philip; America, 1754 ***1220.12*** *p481*
Lambert, Rachel 62; Ontario, 1871 ***1823.21*** *p195*
Lambert, Richard; Illinois, 1852 ***6079.1*** *p8*
Lambert, Richard 62; Ontario, 1871 ***1823.21*** *p195*
Lambert, Robert; America, 1735 ***1220.12*** *p481*
Lambert, Robert; Virginia, 1620 ***1220.12*** *p481*
Lambert, Rosilla 30; Ohio, 1880 ***4879.40*** *p259*
Lambert, Samuel; America, 1770 ***1220.12*** *p481*
Lambert, Seraphine 31; Port uncertain, 1843 ***778.6*** *p201*
Lambert, Thomas; America, 1730 ***1220.12*** *p481*
Lambert, Thomas; America, 1758 ***1220.12*** *p481*
Lambert, Thomas; America, 1775 ***1220.12*** *p481*
Lambert, Thomas; Barbados, 1669 ***1220.12*** *p481*
Lambert, Thomas; Barbados, 1679 ***1220.12*** *p481*
Lambert, William; America, 1749 ***1220.12*** *p481*
Lambert, William; America, 1754 ***1220.12*** *p481*
Lambert, William 28; Ontario, 1871 ***1823.17*** *p88*
Lambert Dumont, Eustache; Quebec, 1733 ***2314.30*** *p172*
Lambertson, Christian; Colorado, 1880 ***1029.59*** *p52*
Lambertus, Appelania 17; Port uncertain, 1843 ***778.6*** *p201*
Lambertus, Eva 10; Port uncertain, 1843 ***778.6*** *p201*
Lambertus, Thomas 14; Port uncertain, 1843 ***778.6*** *p201*
Lambeth, Ann; America, 1750 ***1220.12*** *p481*
Lambeth, Elizabeth; America, 1697 ***1220.12*** *p481*
Lambeth, Elizabeth; Annapolis, MD, 1731 ***1220.12*** *p481*
Lambeth, Ephraim; America, 1772 ***1220.12*** *p481*
Lambeth, John; Died enroute, 1725 ***1220.12*** *p481*
Lambeth, Joseph; America, 1756 ***1220.12*** *p481*
Lambeth, Joseph; America, 1766 ***1220.12*** *p481*
Lambeth, Thomas; America, 1774 ***1220.12*** *p481*
Lambichi, D. E.; Louisiana, 1874 ***4981.45*** *p296*
Lambin, Mr. 22; America, 1847 ***778.6*** *p201*
Lambkin, Henry; Ohio, 1840-1897 ***8365.35*** *p17*
Lamblin, Catherine 39; America, 1846 ***778.6*** *p201*
Lamblot, Francoise; Wisconsin, 1855 ***1495.20*** *p40*
Lambotte, Patricia; Toronto, n.d. ***9228.50*** *p21A*
Lamboulin, Jacob 25; St. Louis, 1844 ***778.6*** *p201*
Lambourn, Job 40; Ontario, 1871 ***1823.21*** *p195*
Lambourn, John; America, 1720 ***1220.12*** *p481*
Lambourn, Thomas; Marston's Wharf, 1782 ***8529.30*** *p13*
Lambourne, Matthew; America, 1730 ***1220.12*** *p481*
Lambourne, Robert; America, 1688 ***1220.12*** *p481*
Lambrecht, Carl Heinrich; America, 1871 ***7420.1*** *p291*
Lambrecht, Elise; America, 1881 ***7420.1*** *p322*
Lambrecht, Emilie; Wisconsin, 1897 ***6795.8*** *p106*
Lambrecht, Johann Hermann; America, 1867 ***7420.1*** *p259*
Lambrecht, W.; New York, 1860 ***358.56*** *p149*
Lambrecht, Wilhelm; America, 1880 ***7420.1*** *p317*
Lamdale, Walter; America, 1764 ***1220.12*** *p481*
Lame, E. H.; California, 1868 ***1131.61*** *p89*
La Measure, Joseph Tallman *SEE* La Measure, Pierre
La Measure, Pierre; Detroit, 1871-1891 ***9228.50*** *p363*
*Son:*Joseph Tallman

Lameslee, Christophe 27; Quebec, 1639 9221.17 p86
*Wife:*Jeanne Enart 16
*Daughter:*Jeanne 2
Lameslee, Jeanne 2 *SEE* Lameslee, Christophe
Lameslee, Jeanne Enart 16 *SEE* Lameslee, Christophe
Lamesnerye, Annet; Quebec, 1650 9221.17 p230
Lamesterie, Jacques 25; Quebec, 1661 9221.17 p460
L'Amie, Robina Mainland; Oregon, 1941 9157.47 p3
Lamine, Jean Baptiste; Wisconsin, 1854-1858 1495.20 p66
*Wife:*Josephine Barette
Lamine, Josephine Barette *SEE* Lamine, Jean Baptiste
Lamirault, J. 30; America, 1843 778.6 p201
Lamirault, Marguerite; Quebec, 1668 4514.3 p331
Lamkin, Russell 49; Ontario, 1871 1823.21 p195
Lamler, Isaac; North Carolina, 1854 1088.45 p18
Lamley, Francis; Virginia, 1732 1220.12 p482
Lamley, William 69; Ontario, 1871 1823.21 p195
Lamm, Leon; North Carolina, 1849 1088.45 p18
Lamm, Samuel; North Carolina, 1848 1088.45 p18
Lammacraft, Richard; Virginia, 1766 1220.12 p482
Lammadee, Robert; Ohio, 1809-1852 4511.35 p29
Lammader, Barnhart; Ohio, 1809-1852 4511.35 p29
Lammeda, Robert; Ohio, 1809-1852 4511.35 p29
Lammeder, Barnhart; Ohio, 1809-1852 4511.35 p29
Lammeder, Robert; Ohio, 1809-1852 4511.35 p29
Lammerhirt, Anna Barbara 13 *SEE* Lammerhirt, Philipp Karl
Lammerhirt, Catharine Elisabeth; America, 1867 7919.3 p529
Lammerhirt, Christiane Margarethe; America, 1868 7919.3 p531
Lammerhirt, Elisabetha 41 *SEE* Lammerhirt, Philipp Karl
Lammerhirt, Eva Margaretha 9 *SEE* Lammerhirt, Philipp Karl
Lammerhirt, Georg 15 *SEE* Lammerhirt, Philipp Karl
Lammerhirt, Juliane 3 *SEE* Lammerhirt, Philipp Karl
Lammerhirt, Philipp Karl 37; America, 1882 2526.43 p152
*Wife:*Elisabetha 41
*Son:*Georg 15
*Daughter:*Eva Margaretha 9
*Daughter:*Juliane 3
*Daughter:*Anna Barbara 13
Lammers, Bernard; Ohio, 1840-1897 8365.35 p17
Lammneck, Elisabeth *SEE* Lammneck, Peter
Lammneck, Elisabeth Knapp *SEE* Lammneck, Peter
Lammneck, Jakob *SEE* Lammneck, Peter
Lammneck, Katharina *SEE* Lammneck, Peter
Lammneck, Peter; America, 1856 5475.1 p562
*Wife:*Elisabeth Knapp
*Daughter:*Elisabeth
*Son:*Philipp
*Son:*Jakob
*Daughter:*Katharina
Lammneck, Philipp *SEE* Lammneck, Peter
Lamni, Herman 36; Minnesota, 1926 2769.54 p1383
Lamon, George; America, 1739 1220.12 p495
Lamon, Isabelle 33; Port uncertain, 1845 778.6 p201
Lamon, J. Marie 45; New Orleans, 1848 778.6 p201
Lamon, Jean-Marie 33; Port uncertain, 1845 778.6 p201
Lamon, Prosper 11; Port uncertain, 1845 778.6 p201
Lamon, Thesorine 4; Port uncertain, 1845 778.6 p201
Lamond, Alexander 38; Ontario, 1871 1823.17 p88
Lamond, Allen 25; Ontario, 1871 1823.21 p195
Lamond, Peter 32; Ontario, 1871 1823.21 p195
Lamont, Ann 33; Ontario, 1871 1823.21 p195
Lamont, Archibald 63; Ontario, 1871 1823.21 p195
Lamont, Catherine 36; Ontario, 1871 1823.21 p195
Lamont, David 55; Ontario, 1871 1823.21 p195
Lamont, Donald 35; Ontario, 1871 1823.21 p195
Lamont, Elizabeth 44; Ontario, 1871 1823.21 p195
Lamont, Isabella 72; Ontario, 1871 1823.21 p195
Lamont, James 40; Ontario, 1871 1823.21 p195
Lamont, James 42; Ontario, 1871 1823.17 p88
Lamont, Jessie 20; Ontario, 1871 1823.21 p195
Lamont, John; North Carolina, 1848 1088.45 p18
Lamont, John 35; Ontario, 1871 1823.21 p195
Lamont, John 56; Ontario, 1871 1823.21 p195
Lamont, John 60; Ontario, 1871 1823.17 p88
Lamont, Mary 64; Ontario, 1871 1823.21 p195
Lamont, Neil 57; Ontario, 1871 1823.21 p195
Lamont, Norman 77; Ontario, 1871 1823.21 p195
Lamont, Peter 56; Ontario, 1871 1823.21 p195
Lamont, Sandy 38; Ontario, 1871 1823.21 p195
Lamontagne, . . .; Quebec, 1652 9221.17 p257
Lamontagne, Francois; Quebec, 1649 9221.17 p220
Lamontagne, Noel 26; Quebec, 1654 9221.17 p310
Lamontagne, Olivier 19; Montreal, 1653 9221.17 p297
Lamontagne, Yves 20; Quebec, 1658 9221.17 p386
Lamonthe, P. L.; Louisiana, 1836-1840 4981.45 p213
Lamorandiere, Nicolas; Quebec, 1647 9221.17 p183
Lamorille, Antoine 28; Quebec, 1659 9221.17 p405
Lamorille, Francois 20; Quebec, 1651 9221.17 p246
Lamoth, Mr. 30; Louisiana, 1848 778.6 p201
Lamothe, Mr. 31; America, 1848 778.6 p201
Lamothe, Francois 39; Quebec, 1660 9221.17 p431
Lamothe, Jacques de; Quebec, 1657 9221.17 p360
Lamothe, Jean; Quebec, 1657 9221.17 p360
Lamothe, N.; Quebec, 1657 9221.17 p361
Lamothe, Pierre 43; Quebec, 1658 9221.17 p383
Lamothe Cadillac, Antoine; Quebec, 1687 2314.30 p171
Lamotte, Isaac; America, 1770 1220.12 p482
Lamotte, Jacques 1; Quebec, 1636 9221.17 p55
Lamotte, Marie; Quebec, 1649-1664 4514.3 p377
Lamotte, Marie-Sainte; Quebec, 1664 4514.3 p377
La Motte deLuciere, Dominique; Quebec, 1678 2314.30 p166
La Motte deLuciere, Dominique; Quebec, 1678 2314.30 p187
Lamount, Mary 54; Ontario, 1871 1823.21 p195
Lamoureaux, Andrew L.; Utah, 1855 9228.50 p318
Lamoureux, Antoinette; Quebec, 1667 4514.3 p331
Lamoureux, Antoinette 14; Quebec, 1662 9221.17 p488
Lamozet, Marc 25; America, 1841 778.6 p201
Lamp, F. 48; New Orleans, 1842 778.6 p201
Lampa, M.L.J.C.; New York, NY, 1845 6412.40 p149
Lampard, Elijah 32; Ontario, 1871 1823.21 p195
Lampard, Thomas; America, 1756 1220.12 p482
Lampater, Margaret; Philadelphia, 1857 8513.31 p300
Lampe, Carl; America, 1852 7420.1 p92
With son
Lampe, Engel Marie Louise; America, 1867 7420.1 p266
Lampe, Johann Heinrich Wilhelm; Port uncertain, 1835 7420.1 p9
Lampe, Therese; Philadelphia, 1880 7420.1 p317
Lamper, F. 40; America, 1847 778.6 p201
Lamper, F. 44; America, 1848 778.6 p201
Lampert, Heinrich; America, 1867 7919.3 p530
Lamperti, Fr. Karl; Brazil, 1862 5475.1 p550
Lampin, Charlotte 10; Quebec, 1870 8364.32 p24
Lampke, Wilhelm; Wisconsin, 1875 6795.8 p90
Lampoon, Daniel 18; Michigan, 1880 4491.42 p16
Lamporne, Edward; Virginia, 1735 1220.12 p481
Lampp, Albert; Philadelphia, 1867 8513.31 p321
*Wife:*Elizabeth Grieb
*Son:*Henry
*Daughter:*Margaretta
*Daughter:*Anna Maria
Lampp, Anna Maria *SEE* Lampp, Albert
Lampp, Elizabeth Grieb *SEE* Lampp, Albert
Lampp, Henry *SEE* Lampp, Albert
Lampp, Margaretta *SEE* Lampp, Albert
Lampper, Sophia; Chicago, 1856 8513.31 p416
Lampre, F. 33; New Orleans, 1840 778.6 p201
Lamprecht, Andrew; Philadelphia, 1778 8529.30 p4A
Lamprecht, Frederick Herman; Wisconsin, 1900 6795.8 p90
Lamprey, John; America, 1760 1220.12 p482
Lamprey, Sarah; America, 1756 1220.12 p482
Lamprey, Thomas; America, 1766 1220.12 p482
Lamprey, Thomas; Barbados, 1695 1220.12 p482
Lampriere, James; Quebec, 1801 9228.50 p423
Lampright, Andrew; Philadelphia, 1778 8529.30 p4A
Lampring, Bartholomew; America, 1722 1220.12 p482
Lamsdall, Adam; America, 1751 1220.12 p482
Lamuloniere, Mr. 24; America, 1844 778.6 p202
Lamuloniere, Ms. 52; America, 1844 778.6 p202
La Munyon, Edward *SEE* La Munyon, Joseph
La Munyon, Joseph; Salem, MA, 1717 9228.50 p366
*Relative:*Edward
Lamy, Isaac 21; Quebec, 1661 9221.17 p460
Lamy, Marie; Quebec, 1671 4514.3 p331
Lamy, Patrick, Jr.; Burlington, VT, 1837 3274.56 p97
Lana, Morice 19; Port uncertain, 1846 778.6 p202
Lanagan, Michael; Newfoundland, 1814 3476.10 p54
Lanaghan, John; Ohio, 1841 2763.1 p20
Lanakin, George 30; Ontario, 1871 1823.17 p88
Lanasa, Joseph; Louisiana, 1836-1840 4981.45 p213
Lancashire, William; America, 1751 1220.12 p482
Lancastell, William; Barbados, 1668 1220.12 p482
Lancaster, Miss 5; Quebec, 1870 8364.32 p24
Lancaster, Mrs. 31; Quebec, 1870 8364.32 p24
Lancaster, Ms. 13; Quebec, 1870 8364.32 p24
Lancaster, Emma 45; Ontario, 1871 1823.17 p88
Lancaster, George 34; Ontario, 1871 1823.21 p195
Lancaster, James; Virginia, 1758 1220.12 p482
Lancaster, John; Maryland, 1739 1220.12 p482
Lancaster, John 54; Ontario, 1871 1823.17 p88
Lancaster, John 15; Quebec, 1870 8364.32 p24
Lancaster, Mary; America, 1771 1220.12 p482
Lancaster, Nathaniel; America, 1742 1220.12 p482
Lancaster, Richard; Barbados, 1673 1220.12 p482
Lancaster, William; Annapolis, MD, 1731 1220.12 p482
Lancey, Henry W. 45; Ontario, 1871 1823.17 p88
Lanchart, John; Ohio, 1809-1852 4511.35 p29
Lancon, Mr. 40; Mexico, 1846 778.6 p202
Lancon, Mrs. 38; Mexico, 1846 778.6 p202
Lancon, Justin 17; Mexico, 1846 778.6 p202
Lancon, Victor 18; Mexico, 1846 778.6 p202
Land, Edmond 37; Ontario, 1871 1823.21 p195
Land, Edmund 45; Ontario, 1871 1823.21 p195
Land, Ole O.; Washington, 1886 2770.40 p195
Landa, Frantisek; Chicago, 1868 2853.20 p393
Landance, Christian; Louisiana, 1836-1840 4981.45 p213
Landbeck, . . .; Chile, 1852 1192.4 p54
With wife & child
With child 8
With child 5
Landbii, P.O.; Cleveland, OH, 1902-1903 9722.10 p122
Lande, Pierre; Quebec, 1647 9221.17 p183
Landeau, Noelle 22; Quebec, 1659 9221.17 p404
Landecker, Alexander; North Carolina, 1860 1088.45 p18
Landegren, Olof; New York, NY, 1844 6412.40 p148
Landekin, Thomas; America, 1770 1220.12 p482
Landenberger, John; New York, NY, 1890 3366.30 p70
Lander, A. Margarethe *SEE* Lander, Joh. Christ.
Lander, A. Margarethe *SEE* Lander, Johannes
Lander, Antoine 8; Missouri, 1845 778.6 p202
Lander, Denis 11; Missouri, 1845 778.6 p202
Lander, Eleanor; America, 1760 1220.12 p482
Lander, George; Maryland, 1742 1220.12 p482
Lander, George 15; Missouri, 1845 778.6 p202
Lander, Joh. Christ.; America, 1836 5475.1 p457
*Wife:*Maria Magdalena Koch
*Son:*Johann
*Son:*Peter
*Daughter:*M. Katharina
*Daughter:*A. Margarethe
*Son:*Joh. Jakob
*Son:*Joh. Christian
*Son:*Joh. Friedrich
Lander, Joh. Christian *SEE* Lander, Joh. Christ.
Lander, Joh. Friedrich *SEE* Lander, Joh. Christ.
Lander, Joh. Jakob *SEE* Lander, Joh. Christ.
Lander, Johann *SEE* Lander, Joh. Christ.
Lander, Johannes; America, 1854 5475.1 p459
*Sister:*A. Margarethe
*Sister:*Katharina
Lander, John; America, 1765 1220.12 p482
Lander, John; Marston's Wharf, 1782 8529.30 p13
Lander, Katharina *SEE* Lander, Johannes
Lander, M. Katharina *SEE* Lander, Joh. Christ.
Lander, Magdalena 21; Missouri, 1845 778.6 p202
Lander, Maria Magdalena Koch *SEE* Lander, Joh. Christ.
Lander, Marian.e 49; Missouri, 1845 778.6 p202
Lander, Marie R. 17; Missouri, 1845 778.6 p202
Lander, Mary; America, 1759 1220.12 p482
Lander, Michel 18; Missouri, 1845 778.6 p202
Lander, Michel 52; Missouri, 1845 778.6 p202
Lander, Peter *SEE* Lander, Joh. Christ.
Lander, Samuel; North Carolina, 1824 1088.45 p18
Lander, Thomas; America, 1719 1220.12 p482
Landerman, Jacob; Ohio, 1809-1852 4511.35 p29
Landers, Francis; North Carolina, 1836 1088.45 p18
Landers, Garret 25; New York, NY, 1826 6178.50 p150
Landers, James; Colorado, 1862-1894 1029.59 p52
Landers, James P.; Colorado, 1870 1029.59 p52
Landers, Nicolas 24; New York, NY, 1856 1766.1 p45
Landfriel, C.; North Carolina, 1858 1088.45 p18
Landholm, Gus; Colorado, 1893 1029.59 p52
Landholm, Gus; Colorado, 1893 1029.59 p53
Landman, James; Nevis or Jamaica, 1722 1220.12 p482
Landman, Runigiel 28; New York, NY, 1847 9176.15 p49
Landmann, Antoine 29; New Orleans, 1848 778.6 p202
Landmann, Caroline Christine Charlotte; America, 1867 7420.1 p259
Landmann, Friederike Christine Kallmeier *SEE* Landmann, Wilhelm
Landmann, Heinrich Ferdinand; America, 1867 7420.1 p259
Landmann, Wilhelm; America, 1883 7420.1 p337
*Mother:*Friederike Christine Kallmeier
Landois, Pierre; Quebec, 1648 9221.17 p200
Landoll, Christian; New York, NY, 1892 6212.1 p14
Landon, Isaac; America, 1772 1220.12 p482
Landon, John; Illinois, 1864 6079.1 p8
Landor, Henry 56; Ontario, 1871 1823.21 p195
Landoyer, Jh. 34; New Orleans, 1841 778.6 p202
Landquist, John Oskar; Cleveland, OH, 1893 9722.10 p122
Landrau, Geronomo; Puerto Rico, 1815-1915 3476.25 p113
Landreau, Marguerite 29; Montreal, 1654 9221.17 p317
Landrer, Louis 28; America, 1848 778.6 p202
Landrie, Charles 29; Ohio, 1880 4879.40 p260

Landrieux, Catherine 47; New Orleans, 1848 ***778.6*** *p202*
Landrieux, Celina 13; New Orleans, 1848 ***778.6*** *p202*
Landrieux, Eleonore 6; New Orleans, 1848 ***778.6*** *p202*
Landrieux, Emile 4; New Orleans, 1848 ***778.6*** *p202*
Landrieux, Geoffani Stan. 49; New Orleans, 1848 ***778.6*** *p202*
Landrieux, Harmonia 8; New Orleans, 1848 ***778.6*** *p202*
Landrieux, Henri 2; New Orleans, 1848 ***778.6*** *p202*
Landrieux, Melanie 27; New Orleans, 1848 ***778.6*** *p202*
Landrieux, Victor 2 months; New Orleans, 1848 ***778.6*** *p202*
Landrigan, Alice; Newbury, MA, 1756 ***1642*** *p75*
Landrin, Ozite; Nova Scotia, 1753 ***3051*** *p112*
Landrock, Charles; Ohio, 1809-1852 ***4511.35*** *p29*
Landry, Alfred A.; Colorado, 1903 ***1029.59*** *p53*
Landry, Fred; Colorado, 1904 ***1029.59*** *p53*
Landry, Gastave 5; America, 1847 ***778.6*** *p202*
Landry, Guillaume 32; Quebec, 1655 ***9221.17*** *p325*
Landry, Louis 40; America, 1847 ***778.6*** *p202*
Landry, Louise 37; America, 1847 ***778.6*** *p202*
Landry, Louise; Quebec, 1667 ***4514.3*** *p331*
Landry, Mathurin; Quebec, 1642 ***9221.17*** *p119*
Landschelten, Hans; Miami, 1935 ***4984.12*** *p39*
Landsetzer, Elise; America, 1862 ***7420.1*** *p213*
Landsetzer, Louise; America, 1870 ***7420.1*** *p395*
Landsmann, Ernst Fredrick; Iowa, 1929 ***1211.15*** *p16*
Landstrom, Bernard I.; Iowa, 1904 ***1211.15*** *p16*
Landstrom, R.; Valparaiso, Chile, 1850 ***1192.4*** *p50*
Landu, Richard; North Carolina, 1890 ***1088.45*** *p18*
Landusky, Esther 18; Quebec, 1870 ***8364.32*** *p24*
Landwick, William; America, 1752 ***1220.12*** *p482*
Landwirth, Jacob L.; Louisiana, 1888-1893 ***7710.1*** *p161*
Landwirth, Max; Louisiana, 1888-1892 ***7710.1*** *p161*
Landyszkowski, Martin; Detroit, 1890 ***9980.23*** *p97*
Lane, Aaron 12 *SEE* Lane, August
Lane, Alexander; Toronto, 1844 ***2910.35*** *p112*
Lane, Amos 35; Michigan, 1880 ***4491.36*** *p13*
Lane, Ann; Maryland, 1727 ***1220.12*** *p482*
Lane, Ann 39; Ontario, 1871 ***1823.21*** *p195*
Lane, Anna Jansdotter 36 *SEE* Lane, August
Lane, August 36; Kansas, 1880 ***777.40*** *p4*
*Wife:*Anna Jansdotter 36
*Son:*Aaron 12
*Son:*Oscar 7
*Son:*Ephram 11
Lane, Benjamin; Annapolis, MD, 1725 ***1220.12*** *p482*
Lane, Catherine 21; Ontario, 1871 ***1823.17*** *p88*
Lane, Charles; Barbados, 1679 ***1220.12*** *p482*
Lane, Edward; America, 1746 ***1220.12*** *p482*
Lane, Edward; Maryland, 1741 ***1220.12*** *p482*
Lane, Edward; Virginia, 1731 ***1220.12*** *p482*
Lane, Elisha; America, 1764 ***1220.12*** *p482*
Lane, Ellen 17; Quebec, 1870 ***8364.32*** *p24*
Lane, Ephram 11 *SEE* Lane, August
Lane, Frank 7; Santa Clara Co., CA, 1870 ***8704.1*** *p25*
Lane, Hannah; Maryland, 1742 ***1220.12*** *p482*
Lane, Hannah; Virginia, 1726 ***1220.12*** *p482*
Lane, Henry 28; Ontario, 1871 ***1823.17*** *p88*
Lane, Humfry; Virginia, 1732 ***1220.12*** *p482*
Lane, James; America, 1750 ***1220.12*** *p482*
Lane, James 45; Ontario, 1871 ***1823.21*** *p195*
Lane, James 56; Ontario, 1871 ***1823.21*** *p195*
Lane, James B. 47; Ontario, 1871 ***1823.21*** *p195*
Lane, Jane; Potomac, 1731 ***1220.12*** *p482*
Lane, Jane; Virginia, 1730 ***1220.12*** *p482*
Lane, John; America, 1741 ***1220.12*** *p482*
Lane, John; America, 1742 ***1220.12*** *p482*
Lane, John; America, 1757 ***1220.12*** *p482*
Lane, John; Barbados, 1679 ***1220.12*** *p482*
Lane, Johnathan; Ontario, 1787 ***1276.15*** *p231*
With 3 children & 3 relatives
Lane, Jos.; Ontario, 1787 ***1276.15*** *p232*
With child & relative
Lane, Joseph; America, 1738 ***1220.12*** *p482*
Lane, Joseph; America, 1743 ***1220.12*** *p482*
Lane, Joseph; America, 1765 ***1220.12*** *p482*
Lane, Levi 54; Ontario, 1871 ***1823.21*** *p196*
Lane, Margery; Barbados, 1669 ***1220.12*** *p482*
Lane, Mary; Barbados, 1681 ***1220.12*** *p483*
Lane, Mary; Ontario, 1835 ***3160.1*** *p150*
Lane, Micheal 40; Ontario, 1871 ***1823.17*** *p88*
Lane, Moses 76; Ontario, 1871 ***1823.21*** *p196*
Lane, Oscar 7 *SEE* Lane, August
Lane, Patrick 36; Ontario, 1871 ***1823.21*** *p196*
Lane, Patt; New Orleans, 1851 ***7242.30*** *p148*
Lane, Reuben 35; Ontario, 1871 ***1823.21*** *p196*
Lane, Richard; Barbados, 1698 ***1220.12*** *p483*
Lane, Robert; America, 1730 ***1220.12*** *p483*
Lane, Robert; America, 1734 ***1220.12*** *p483*
Lane, Robert; America, 1753 ***1220.12*** *p483*
Lane, Robert; Virginia, 1719 ***1220.12*** *p483*
Lane, Sarah; America, 1759 ***1220.12*** *p483*
Lane, Sarah; America, 1761 ***1220.12*** *p483*
Lane, Sarah; America, 1769 ***1220.12*** *p483*
Lane, Thomas; America, 1722 ***1220.12*** *p483*
Lane, Thomas; America, 1741 ***1220.12*** *p483*
Lane, Thomas; America, 1749 ***1220.12*** *p483*
Lane, Thomas; America, 1754 ***1220.12*** *p483*
Lane, Thomas; America, 1771 ***1220.12*** *p483*
Lane, Thomas; Virginia, 1736 ***1220.12*** *p483*
Lane, William; America, 1685 ***1220.12*** *p483*
Lane, William; America, 1759 ***1220.12*** *p483*
Lane, William; America, 1763 ***1220.12*** *p483*
Lane, William; America, 1766 ***1220.12*** *p483*
Lane, William; America, 1774 ***1220.12*** *p483*
Lane, William; Charles Town, SC, 1718 ***1220.12*** *p483*
Lane, William; Virginia, 1723 ***1220.12*** *p483*
Lanehart, John; Ohio, 1809-1852 ***4511.35*** *p29*
Lanehart, Peter; Ohio, 1809-1852 ***4511.35*** *p29*
Laneigerie, Gilles; Quebec, 1639 ***9221.17*** *p87*
Lanel, Claude 29; Port uncertain, 1841 ***778.6*** *p202*
Laner, Alex 20; Ontario, 1871 ***1823.21*** *p196*
Lanes, Elizabeth; America, 1746 ***1220.12*** *p483*
Laney, Henry 44; Ontario, 1871 ***1823.17*** *p88*
Lanfille, Marie; Quebec, 1665 ***4514.3*** *p331*
Lanford, John 25; Ontario, 1871 ***1823.21*** *p196*
Lang, Agatha; Venezuela, 1843 ***3899.5*** *p542*
Lang, Andreas; America, 1831 ***2526.42*** *p124*
With wife & 3 children
Lang, Anna Elisabetha; America, 1864 ***2526.43*** *p147*
Lang, Anna Elisabetha 38; America, 1864 ***2526.43*** *p147*
Lang, Anna Margaretha; America, 1855 ***2526.42*** *p178*
Lang, Anna Maria; America, 1866 ***2526.43*** *p174*
Lang, Anna Maria; Venezuela, 1843 ***3899.5*** *p544*
Lang, August Ludwig Oswald; America, 1864 ***7420.1*** *p225*
Lang, Augustin; Chicago, 1863-1866 ***2853.20*** *p423*
Lang, Augustin; Wisconsin, 1865-1881 ***2853.20*** *p346*
Lang, Baptist; America, 1865 ***5475.1*** *p69*
Lang, Barbara 36; America, 1856 ***5475.1*** *p287*
Lang, Bettina; America, 1868 ***7919.3*** *p529*
Lang, Caspar 35; Mississippi, 1845 ***778.6*** *p202*
Lang, Caspar; Ohio, 1809-1852 ***4511.35*** *p29*
Lang, Charles 62; Ontario, 1871 ***1823.21*** *p196*
Lang, Christoph 33; Mississippi, 1847 ***778.6*** *p203*
Lang, Christopher; America, 1751 ***1220.12*** *p483*
Lang, Elisabeth 28; Mississippi, 1845-1846 ***778.6*** *p203*
Lang, Elisabeth 55; Mississippi, 1845-1846 ***778.6*** *p203*
Lang, Emil; America, 1880 ***5475.1*** *p32*
Lang, Etienne 18; Louisiana, 1848 ***778.6*** *p203*
Lang, Euphrosine; Venezuela, 1843 ***3899.5*** *p543*
Lang, Friedrich 13 *SEE* Lang, Mrs. Friedrich
Lang, Friedrich 16; America, 1857 ***2526.42*** *p143*
Lang, Mrs. Friedrich 53; America, 1883 ***2526.42*** *p154*
*Child:*Peter Ruhl 27
*Child:*Friedrich 13
Lang, Friedrich Ludwig; America, 1848 ***7420.1*** *p60*
Lang, Gavin 28; Ontario, 1871 ***1823.17*** *p88*
Lang, Georg 14; America, 1857 ***2526.42*** *p143*
Lang, Georg, II 52; America, 1867 ***2526.42*** *p143*
With daughter 9
Lang, Georg Ludwig; America, 1853 ***2526.43*** *p206*
Lang, Georg. 24; America, 1840 ***778.6*** *p203*
Lang, George; America, 1739 ***1220.12*** *p483*
Lang, Harry; Colorado, 1897 ***1029.59*** *p53*
Lang, Helene; America, 1856 ***8115.12*** *p320*
*Child:*Katharine
*Child:*Karl
Lang, Hieronymus; America, 1852 ***2526.42*** *p136*
Lang, Ignatius; New York, 1859 ***358.56*** *p99*
Lang, Irmgard; America, 1885 ***7420.1*** *p347*
Lang, Jacob 18; Missouri, 1845 ***778.6*** *p203*
Lang, Jacob; Ohio, 1809-1852 ***4511.35*** *p29*
Lang, James; America, 1734 ***1220.12*** *p483*
Lang, James 56; Ontario, 1871 ***1823.17*** *p88*
Lang, Johann; America, 1872 ***5475.1*** *p47*
Lang, Johann 25; Missouri, 1845 ***778.6*** *p203*
Lang, Johann Adam; America, 1753 ***2526.43*** *p161*
With wife & child
Lang, Johann Adam; America, 1881 ***2526.43*** *p219*
Lang, Johann Baptist; Venezuela, 1843 ***3899.5*** *p542*
Lang, Johann Christoph; America, 1766 ***2526.43*** *p186*
Lang, Johann Eberhard; America, 1866 ***2526.43*** *p174*
Lang, John; America, 1735 ***1220.12*** *p483*
Lang, John; America, 1744 ***1220.12*** *p483*
Lang, John; Ohio, 1809-1852 ***4511.35*** *p29*
Lang, John 16; Ontario, 1871 ***1823.21*** *p196*
Lang, John 47; Ontario, 1871 ***1823.17*** *p89*
Lang, John; Texas, 1905 ***3435.45*** *p36*
Lang, Josef; Chicago, 1871 ***2853.20*** *p405*
Lang, Karl; America, 1855 ***2526.43*** *p174*
Lang, Karl *SEE* Lang, Helene
Lang, Karolina; Dakota, 1866-1918 ***554.30*** *p25*
Lang, Katharina; America, 1867 ***2526.42*** *p144*
Lang, Katharine *SEE* Lang, Helene
Lang, Konrad; Venezuela, 1843 ***3899.5*** *p543*
Lang, Konrad; Venezuela, 1843 ***3899.5*** *p543*
Lang, Konrad; Venezuela, 1843 ***3899.5*** *p544*
Lang, Leonhard; America, 1836 ***2526.42*** *p109*
With wife & children
Lang, Leonhard; Philadelphia, 1852 ***2526.42*** *p182*
Lang, Louise 2; Mississippi, 1845 ***778.6*** *p203*
Lang, Ludwig; America, 1847 ***5475.1*** *p28*
Lang, Madelaine 5; Mississippi, 1845-1846 ***778.6*** *p203*
Lang, Margarthe 19; Halifax, N.S., 1902 ***1860.4*** *p42*
Lang, Michael; America, 1820-1865 ***2526.42*** *p167*
Lang, Peter; America, 1868 ***2526.43*** *p142*
Lang, Peter; America, 1872 ***5475.1*** *p47*
Lang, Peter Ruhl 27 *SEE* Lang, Mrs. Friedrich
Lang, Philip; Ohio, 1809-1852 ***4511.35*** *p29*
Lang, Regina Magdalene; America, 1867 ***2526.43*** *p174*
Lang, Richard; New York, NY, 1882 ***5475.1*** *p34*
Lang, Robert 47; Ontario, 1871 ***1823.21*** *p196*
Lang, Rudolf; Denver, CO, 1880 ***5475.1*** *p32*
Lang, Samuel 64; Ontario, 1871 ***1823.17*** *p89*
Lang, William; New York, 1859 ***358.56*** *p55*
Lang, William 39; Ontario, 1871 ***1823.21*** *p196*
Lang, William; Virginia, 1736 ***1220.12*** *p483*
Langais, Jean; Quebec, 1643 ***9221.17*** *p131*
Langan, John 50; Ontario, 1871 ***1823.17*** *p89*
Langane, John; Ohio, 1857 ***3580.20*** *p32*
Langane, John; Ohio, 1857 ***6020.12*** *p12*
Langbein, Ernst; America, 1867 ***7919.3*** *p531*
Langcake, Anthony; America, 1735 ***1220.12*** *p483*
Langcake, Mary; America, 1761 ***1220.12*** *p483*
Langdale, John; Ohio, 1832 ***2763.1*** *p20*
Langdale, Robert; Barbados, 1669 ***1220.12*** *p483*
Langdell, Robert; Barbados, 1671 ***1220.12*** *p483*
Langdon, Mary; Ontario, 1835 ***3160.1*** *p150*
Langdon, Robert; Barbados, 1669 ***1220.12*** *p483*
Langdon, William; Ontario, 1835 ***3160.1*** *p150*
Langdon, William; Ontario, 1835 ***3160.1*** *p150*
Langdon, William; Prescott, Ont., 1835 ***3289.1*** *p61*
Lange, Alexius; North America, 1850 ***6410.15*** *p104*
Lange, Alwine 26; Portland, ME, 1911 ***970.38*** *p79*
Lange, Andrew; Louisiana, 1841-1844 ***4981.45*** *p210*
Lange, August; America, 1856 ***7420.1*** *p149*
With family
Lange, August Friedrich; America, 1868 ***7919.3*** *p531*
Lange, Bertha; America, 1883 ***7420.1*** *p339*
Lange, Bertha; Wisconsin, 1896 ***6795.8*** *p125*
Lange, C.G. Chr.; New York, NY, 1851 ***6412.40*** *p152*
Lange, Emil 21; Portland, ME, 1911 ***970.38*** *p79*
Lange, Emilie 19; Halifax, N.S., 1902 ***1860.4*** *p42*
Lange, Emma Emilie; Wisconsin, 1897 ***6795.8*** *p107*
Lange, Ferdinand 20; Halifax, N.S., 1902 ***1860.4*** *p41*
Lange, Francoise; Quebec, 1673 ***4514.3*** *p332*
Lange, Friedr.; Valdivia, Chile, 1852 ***1192.4*** *p55*
Lange, Friedrich 29; Halifax, N.S., 1902 ***1860.4*** *p42*
Lange, Friedrich Wilhelm; Port uncertain, 1856 ***7420.1*** *p150*
Lange, Friedrich Wilhelm; Wisconsin, 1913 ***6795.8*** *p168*
Lange, Gustav Herman; Wisconsin, 1886 ***6795.8*** *p175*
Lange, H. F.; Valdivia, Chile, 1850 ***1192.4*** *p48*
Lange, Johan 32; New York, NY, 1893 ***1883.7*** *p39*
Lange, Johanne; America, 1868 ***7919.3*** *p534*
Lange, Louise 27; New Orleans, 1848 ***778.6*** *p203*
Lange, Ottilie Wilhelmine; Wisconsin, 1896 ***6795.8*** *p178*
Lange, Sophie Wilhelmine Charlotte; America, 1858 ***7420.1*** *p181*
Langebrake, William; Ohio, 1840-1897 ***8365.35*** *p17*
Langel, Maxel I. 50; Ontario, 1871 ***1823.17*** *p89*
Langelier, Sebastien 36; Quebec, 1653 ***9221.17*** *p275*
Langenberg, Frdr.; America, 1889 ***7420.1*** *p400*
Langenfilden, John; America, 1752 ***1220.12*** *p483*
Langensoherdt, Edward; Illinois, 1853 ***6079.1*** *p8*
Langer, August Ernest; New York, NY, 1886 ***6212.1*** *p14*
Langerle, Katharina 29; America, 1871 ***5475.1*** *p446*
Langers, Nicholas; Ohio, 1809-1852 ***4511.35*** *p29*
Langevin, Charles; Colorado, 1880 ***1029.59*** *p53*
Langevin, Jacques; Montreal, 1652 ***9221.17*** *p268*
Langevin, Julien 26; Montreal, 1659 ***9221.17*** *p416*
Langevin, Mathurin 21; Montreal, 1653 ***9221.17*** *p294*
Langevin, Rene 21; Montreal, 1662 ***9221.17*** *p498*
Langfitt, Anthony; Barbados, 1662 ***1220.12*** *p483*
Langford, Alexander 56; Ontario, 1871 ***1823.21*** *p196*
Langford, Charles 53; Ontario, 1871 ***1823.21*** *p196*
Langford, Edward; Virginia, 1735 ***1220.12*** *p483*
Langford, Eleanor; America, 1770 ***1220.12*** *p483*
Langford, Elijah 50; Ontario, 1871 ***1823.21*** *p196*
Langford, George; Barbados, 1664 ***1220.12*** *p483*
Langford, George 35; Ontario, 1871 ***1823.21*** *p196*
Langford, Gregory 48; Ontario, 1871 ***1823.17*** *p89*
Langford, Henry 20; Ontario, 1871 ***1823.17*** *p89*
Langford, Isaac 39; Ontario, 1871 ***1823.21*** *p196*
Langford, Isaac 45; Ontario, 1871 ***1823.21*** *p196*
Langford, Isaac 53; Ontario, 1871 ***1823.21*** *p196*
Langford, Jacob; Newfoundland, 1749 ***1220.12*** *p483*
Langford, Jane; America, 1766 ***1220.12*** *p483*

Langford, Jane; Barbados, 1662 ***1220.12*** *p483*
Langford, John; America, 1685 ***1220.12*** *p483*
Langford, John; America, 1731 ***1220.12*** *p483*
Langford, John; Marston's Wharf, 1782 ***8529.30*** *p13*
Langford, John; St. Johns, N.F., 1825 ***1053.15*** *p6*
Langford, Joseph 46; Ontario, 1871 ***1823.21*** *p196*
Langford, Joseph 60; Ontario, 1871 ***1823.21*** *p196*
Langford, Martha 75; Ontario, 1871 ***1823.21*** *p196*
Langford, Samuel 27; Ontario, 1871 ***1823.21*** *p196*
Langford, Samuel 33; Ontario, 1871 ***1823.17*** *p89*
Langford, Samuel 45; Ontario, 1871 ***1823.21*** *p196*
Langford, Sanders W. 37; Ontario, 1871 ***1823.21*** *p196*
Langford, Sarah 73; Ontario, 1871 ***1823.17*** *p89*
Langford, Sophia 60; Ontario, 1871 ***1823.17*** *p89*
Langford, Thomas; America, 1741 ***1220.12*** *p483*
Langford, Thomas; Boston, 1775 ***8529.30*** *p2*
Langford, Thomas; Illinois, 1864 ***6079.1*** *p8*
Langford, Thomas A. 40; Ontario, 1871 ***1823.21*** *p196*
Langford, William 46; Ontario, 1871 ***1823.21*** *p196*
Langguth, Anton; America, 1867 ***7919.3*** *p525*
Langguth, Emilie; America, 1867 ***7919.3*** *p528*
Langguth, Ernst Ludwig; America, 1867 ***7919.3*** *p526*
Langham, John; America, 1740 ***1220.12*** *p484*
Langham, Joseph; America, 1765 ***1220.12*** *p484*
Langham, Randolph; America, 1678 ***1220.12*** *p484*
Langham, William; America, 1763 ***1220.12*** *p484*
Langham, William; New York, 1776 ***8529.30*** *p13*
Langhans, John C.; Ohio, 1809-1852 ***4511.35*** *p29*
Langhaus, John C.; Ohio, 1809-1852 ***4511.35*** *p29*
Langhorn, John; Louisiana, 1874-1875 ***4981.45*** *p29*
Langhorn, John 63; Ontario, 1871 ***1823.21*** *p196*
Langhorne, Betsy 46; Santa Clara Co., CA, 1860 ***8704.1*** *p23*
Langhorst, Anna Sophie Marie; America, 1893 ***7420.1*** *p369*
Langhorst, Heinrich; America, 1857 ***7420.1*** *p166*
Langhorst, Heinrich Christoph; Iowa, 1888 ***7420.1*** *p357*
Langhorst, Johann Friedrich; Iowa, 1883 ***7420.1*** *p337*
Langhorst, Johann Friedrich Wilhelm; America, 1859 ***7420.1*** *p187*
Langhorst, Johann Otto; America, 1869 ***7420.1*** *p280*
Langlands, Elizabeth 11; Quebec, 1870 ***8364.32*** *p24*
Langlands, Frank 13; Quebec, 1870 ***8364.32*** *p24*
Langlands, Thompson 17; Quebec, 1870 ***8364.32*** *p24*
Langlat, Mr. 22; New Orleans, 1848 ***778.6*** *p203*
Langley, Albert Wm.; California, 1894-1979 ***9228.50*** *p320*
Langley, Diana Baker Hall *SEE* Langley, Thomas Tolton
Langley, Edward; America, 1744 ***1220.12*** *p484*
Langley, Elizabeth; America, 1734 ***1220.12*** *p484*
Langley, Elizabeth; America, 1749 ***1220.12*** *p484*
Langley, George; America, 1757 ***1220.12*** *p484*
Langley, Gilbert; America, 1741 ***1220.12*** *p484*
Langley, John; America, 1738 ***1220.12*** *p484*
Langley, John; America, 1743 ***1220.12*** *p484*
Langley, John; America, 1748 ***1220.12*** *p484*
Langley, John; America, 1752 ***1220.12*** *p484*
Langley, John; America, 1775 ***1220.12*** *p484*
Langley, John; Hingham, MA, 1685 ***1642*** *p15*
Langley, Lydia; America, 1744 ***1220.12*** *p484*
Langley, Mary; America, 1764 ***1220.12*** *p484*
Langley, Muriel Gwendolyn; California, 1909-1983 ***9228.50*** *p320*
Langley, Peter; Ohio, 1821 ***9228.50*** *p318*
Langley, Rachel; Detroit, 1834-1900 ***9228.50*** *p319*
Langley, Rachel Rose *SEE* Langley, Thomas
Langley, Thomas; Quebec, 1829-1834 ***9228.50*** *p319*
*Wife:*Rachel Rose
Langley, Thomas Tolton; California, 1867-1937 ***9228.50*** *p320*
*Wife:*Diana Baker Hall
Langley, Titus; America, 1762 ***1220.12*** *p484*
Langley, William; America, 1750 ***1220.12*** *p484*
Langley, William; America, 1763 ***1220.12*** *p484*
Langley, William; America, 1765 ***1220.12*** *p484*
Langley, William; Annapolis, MD, 1722 ***1220.12*** *p484*
Langley, William; Barbados or Jamaica, 1710 ***1220.12*** *p484*
Langlois, . . .; Boston, 1879 ***9228.50*** *p533*
Langlois, Albert Wm.; California, 1894-1979 ***9228.50*** *p320*
Langlois, Anna; America, 1861-1869 ***9228.50*** *p319*
Langlois, Anne; Quebec, 1670 ***4514.3*** *p332*
Langlois, Antoinette; Quebec, 1662 ***9221.17*** *p489*
Langlois, Clement; Salem, MA, 1600-1699 ***9228.50*** *p208*
Langlois, Daniel; Boston, 1689 ***9228.50*** *p321*
Langlois, Diana Baker Hall *SEE* Langlois, Thomas Tolton
Langlois, Elizabeth M.; America, 1861-1869 ***9228.50*** *p319*
Langlois, Francoise; Quebec, 1619 ***9221.17*** *p23*
Langlois, George *SEE* Langlois, Sophia Simon
Langlois, Henry Charles; America, 1861-1869 ***9228.50*** *p319*
Langlois, Honore 19; Quebec, 1651 ***9221.17*** *p245*
Langlois, Jacqueline; Quebec, 1668 ***4514.3*** *p332*
Langlois, James; Richmond, VA, 1832 ***9228.50*** *p321*
Langlois, James M.; America, 1861-1869 ***9228.50*** *p319*
Langlois, James Mowbray; Rochester, NY, 1869-1872 ***9228.50*** *p318*
Langlois, Jane; Nova Scotia, 1731-1800 ***9228.50*** *p321*
Langlois, Jane; Salem, MA, 1720 ***9228.50*** *p321*
Langlois, Jean; Quebec, 1652 ***9221.17*** *p260*
Langlois, Jerome 52; Quebec, 1654 ***9221.17*** *p311*
*Son:*Rolin 14
Langlois, John; Hingham, MA, 1666 ***9228.50*** *p321*
Langlois, John 11; Richmond, VA, 1826-1827 ***9228.50*** *p321*
Langlois, John, Jr. *SEE* Langlois, Sophia Simon
Langlois, Margaret 23; Ontario, 1859 ***9228.50*** *p382*
Langlois, Marguerite; Quebec, 1619 ***9221.17*** *p24*
Langlois, Marguerite; Quebec, 1619 ***9221.17*** *p24*
Langlois, Maria Ann; Utah, 1810-1900 ***9228.50*** *p359*
Langlois, Marie; Quebec, 1634 ***9221.17*** *p37*
Langlois, Marie; Quebec, 1665 ***4514.3*** *p332*
Langlois, Marie; Quebec, 1667 ***4514.3*** *p332*
Langlois, Marie; Quebec, 1670 ***4514.3*** *p332*
Langlois, Martha; America, 1800-1899 ***9228.50*** *p322*
Langlois, Martha M.; America, 1861-1869 ***9228.50*** *p319*
Langlois, Mary 26; Ontario, 1863 ***9228.50*** *p321*
Langlois, Michel; Quebec, 1642 ***9221.17*** *p119*
Langlois, Muriel Gwendolyn; California, 1909-1983 ***9228.50*** *p320*
Langlois, Nicholas; Wisconsin, 1843 ***9228.50*** *p322*
Langlois, Noel 31; Quebec, 1634 ***9221.17*** *p38*
Langlois, Paul; Quebec, 1651 ***9221.17*** *p245*
Langlois, Peter; Ohio, 1807 ***9228.50*** *p57*
Langlois, Peter; Ohio, 1821 ***9228.50*** *p318*
Langlois, Peter; Quebec, 1700-1880 ***9228.50*** *p322*
Langlois, Philip; America, 1800-1899 ***9228.50*** *p322*
Langlois, Philip; America, 1861-1869 ***9228.50*** *p319*
Langlois, Philip; Massachusetts, n.d. ***9228.50*** *p207*
Langlois, Philip; Salem, MA, 1670 ***9228.50*** *p322*
L'Anglois, Philippe; Massachusetts, 1651-1734 ***9228.50*** *p207*
Langlois, Philippe; Salem, MA, 1670 ***9228.50*** *p4*
Langlois, Philippe; Salem, MA, 1670 ***9228.50*** *p24*
Langlois, Rachel; Detroit, 1834-1900 ***9228.50*** *p319*
Langlois, Rachel; Ohio, 1764-1846 ***9228.50*** *p209*
Langlois, Rachel Rose *SEE* Langlois, Thomas
Langlois, Rachel; Wisconsin, 1850 ***9228.50*** *p322*
Langlois, Rolin 14 *SEE* Langlois, Jerome
Langlois, Samuel; Ogden, UT, 1833-1875 ***9228.50*** *p322*
With children
Langlois, Sophia; Wisconsin, 1856-1889 ***9228.50*** *p321*
*Child:*George
*Child:*John, Jr.
*Child:*George
Langlois, Thomas; Quebec, 1661 ***9221.17*** *p460*
Langlois, Thomas; Quebec, 1829-1834 ***9228.50*** *p319*
*Wife:*Rachel Rose
Langlois, Thomas Tolton; California, 1867-1937 ***9228.50*** *p320*
*Wife:*Diana Baker Hall
Langmann, Wm.; Louisiana, 1874-1875 ***4981.45*** *p29*
Langmayer, Josef; St. Louis, 1866 ***2853.20*** *p414*
Langmore, John; Plymouth, MA, 1620 ***1920.45*** *p5*
Langner, Friedrich; New York, NY, 1887 ***5475.1*** *p17*
Langner, Robert; New York, NY, 1883 ***5475.1*** *p17*
Langner, Wilhelm 60; Connecticut, 1888 ***5475.1*** *p18*
Langoumois, . . .; Quebec, 1652 ***9221.17*** *p260*
Langren, Augusta; Michigan, 1888 ***1865.50*** *p39*
Langridge, James; Quebec, 1870 ***8364.32*** *p24*
Langsden, Mary; America, 1752 ***1220.12*** *p484*
Langsdorf, Anton; Wisconsin, 1873 ***6795.8*** *p98*
Langshall, Thomas; Barbados, 1664 ***1220.12*** *p484*
Langstaff, Thomas; America, 1739 ***1220.12*** *p484*
Langston, Henry; Potomac, 1729 ***1220.12*** *p484*
Langston, Jacob; America, 1754 ***1220.12*** *p484*
Langston, Robert; America, 1762 ***1220.12*** *p484*
Langston, Trott 26; Ontario, 1871 ***1823.21*** *p196*
Langton, Elizabeth; Virginia, 1721 ***1220.12*** *p484*
Langton, George, Jr.; Barbados, 1688 ***1220.12*** *p484*
Langton, William; America, 1688 ***1220.12*** *p484*
Langtry, Lillie; San Francisco, 1853-1929 ***9228.50*** *p26*
Langueseau, Francois; Quebec, 1652 ***9221.17*** *p260*
Languille, Jeanne; Quebec, 1671 ***4514.3*** *p332*
Languille, Marie-Madeleine 23; Quebec, 1659 ***9221.17*** *p404*
Languille, Prosper 36; New Orleans, 1847 ***778.6*** *p203*
Langworth, Francis 25; Virginia, 1635 ***1183.3*** *p31*
Lanham, Henry; Annapolis, MD, 1758 ***1220.12*** *p484*
Lanham, John; Annapolis, MD, 1731 ***1220.12*** *p484*
Lanham, Sarah; America, 1753 ***1220.12*** *p484*
Lanib, George; North Carolina, 1792-1862 ***1088.45*** *p18*
Laniel, Etienne 32; Quebec, 1656 ***9221.17*** *p339*
Lanier, Adam 45; New Orleans, 1847 ***778.6*** *p203*
Lanier, John 24; America, 1848 ***778.6*** *p203*
Lanier, Noe; Washington, 1889 ***2770.40*** *p79*
Lanigan, Edward; Illinois, 1834-1900 ***6020.5*** *p132*
Lanik, Frantisek; Minnesota, 1857 ***2853.20*** *p259*
Lank, John; America, 1771 ***1220.12*** *p484*
Lankhorne, William; North Carolina, 1854 ***1088.45*** *p18*
Lankin, James; North Carolina, 1855 ***1088.45*** *p18*
Lankston, William; America, 1759 ***1220.12*** *p484*
Lanman, Philippa; Virginia, 1738 ***1220.12*** *p484*
Lanmy, Samuel 55; Ontario, 1871 ***1823.17*** *p89*
Lanne, Nicolas 43; Missouri, 1847 ***778.6*** *p203*
Lannert, Elisabeth Margaretha; Illinois, 1846 ***2526.43*** *p132*
Lannert, Eva Elisabetha; America, 1857 ***2526.43*** *p123*
Lanney, Laughlin; Illinois, 1834-1900 ***6020.5*** *p132*
Lanoe, Marguerite; Quebec, 1651 ***9221.17*** *p245*
Lanos, Adelaide 22; New Orleans, 1848 ***778.6*** *p203*
Lanos, Melassie 35; New Orleans, 1848 ***778.6*** *p203*
Lanphir, Anthony 50; Ontario, 1871 ***1823.21*** *p196*
Lanqueteau, Jean 29; Quebec, 1649 ***9221.17*** *p215*
Lansden, William; America, 1774 ***1220.12*** *p484*
Lansdown, Abraham; America, 1769 ***1220.12*** *p484*
Lanski, Andrew; Detroit, 1930 ***1640.60*** *p83*
Lanson, Catherine; America, 1756 ***1220.12*** *p484*
Lanssen, John; Miami, 1935 ***4984.12*** *p39*
Lansten, Frederick; Washington, 1882 ***2770.40*** *p135*
Lanstrot, Marie Philipp 16; New York, NY, 1864 ***8425.62*** *p198*
Lanton, John; America, 1766 ***1220.12*** *p484*
Lanton, Joseph; North Carolina, 1792-1862 ***1088.45*** *p18*
Lantschek, M.; Galveston, TX, 1855 ***571.7*** *p18*
Lantwell, Bernard; America, 1767 ***1220.12*** *p484*
Lantz, Henry; Ohio, 1809-1852 ***4511.35*** *p29*
Lantz Family ; West Virginia, 1787 ***1132.30*** *p146*
Lany, Ceaser 31; America, 1843 ***778.6*** *p203*
Lanyi, Ludvik; New York, NY, 1884 ***2853.20*** *p460*
Lanyon, Mary; America, 1749 ***1220.12*** *p484*
Lanyon, William; America, 1749 ***1220.12*** *p484*
Lanz, Alexander; Ohio, 1809-1852 ***4511.35*** *p29*
Lanz, Anna; St. Paul, MN, 1887 ***1865.50*** *p35*
Lanz, Barbara 40; Missouri, 1847 ***778.6*** *p203*
Lapaille, Jean 20; Quebec, 1652 ***9221.17*** *p256*
Lapalme, . . .; Quebec, 1652 ***9221.17*** *p260*
Lapan, L. 26; America, 1841 ***778.6*** *p203*
Lape, Lazarus; Ohio, 1809-1852 ***4511.35*** *p29*
Lapein, Mr. 20; America, 1846 ***778.6*** *p203*
Lapensee, Philippe 24; Quebec, 1653 ***9221.17*** *p273*
Laperle, Aime; Quebec, 1636 ***9221.17*** *p58*
Laperle, Pierre 13; Quebec, 1648 ***9221.17*** *p202*
Laperto, Ambroise 33; Port uncertain, 1844 ***778.6*** *p203*
Lapeyre, Michel 14; New Orleans, 1846 ***778.6*** *p203*
Lapeyrolerie, Jean 19; Port uncertain, 1846 ***778.6*** *p203*
Lapeyrollerie, Jean 26; New Orleans, 1846 ***778.6*** *p203*
Lapham, Af. 47; Ontario, 1871 ***1823.17*** *p89*
Lapham, Dolph 40; Ontario, 1871 ***1823.17*** *p89*
Laphan, James; America, 1754 ***1220.12*** *p484*
Lapic, Jan; Minnesota, 1863 ***2853.20*** *p267*
Lapic, Matej; Wisconsin, 1856 ***2853.20*** *p345*
Lapierre, Bernard; Quebec, 1645 ***9221.17*** *p156*
Lapierre, Perrine; Quebec, 1665 ***4514.3*** *p332*
Lapierre, Pierre; Montreal, 1660 ***9221.17*** *p441*
Lapierre, Pierre 18; Montreal, 1653 ***9221.17*** *p295*
Lapierre, Pierre; Quebec, 1645 ***9221.17*** *p153*
Lapile, Jean; Montreal, 1659 ***9221.17*** *p425*
Lapinski, Anton 25; New York, NY, 1890 ***1883.7*** *p48*
Lapish, Thomas 60; Ontario, 1871 ***1823.17*** *p89*
Laplace, . . .; Montreal, 1650 ***9221.17*** *p232*
Laplace, B. 17; America, 1848 ***778.6*** *p203*
Laplace, Mathurin; Quebec, 1655 ***9221.17*** *p321*
Laplace, de, . . .; Montreal, 1659 ***9221.17*** *p422*
Lapland, John 45; Ontario, 1871 ***1823.21*** *p196*
Laplante, . . .; Quebec, 1654 ***9221.17*** *p311*
Laplante, Antoine 20; Quebec, 1662 ***9221.17*** *p481*
Laplante, Daniel-Joseph 26; Montreal, 1659 ***9221.17*** *p425*
Laplante, Edward 22; New Orleans, 1840 ***778.6*** *p203*
Lapointe, Celenie 40; New Orleans, 1843 ***778.6*** *p203*
Lapointe, Charles 18; Quebec, 1654 ***9221.17*** *p315*
Lapointe, Hubert 19; Quebec, 1657 ***9221.17*** *p369*
Lapointe, Pierre 20; Montreal, 1653 ***9221.17*** *p288*
Lapomier, Louis 30; New Orleans, 1848 ***778.6*** *p203*
Lapoque, J. 18; New Orleans, 1848 ***778.6*** *p203*
Laporte, Mr. 35; Mexico, 1846 ***778.6*** *p203*
Laporte, August 26; New Orleans, 1848 ***778.6*** *p203*
Laporte, J. 30; America, 1843 ***778.6*** *p204*
Laporte, J. L. 28; America, 1843 ***778.6*** *p204*
Laporte, Matthew 23; New Orleans, 1844 ***778.6*** *p204*
Laporte, Phillip 35; New Orleans, 1846 ***778.6*** *p204*
Laporte deLouvigny, Louis de; Quebec, 1683-1688 ***2314.30*** *p168*

Laporte deLouvigny, Louis de; Quebec, 1683 2314.30 p187
Laposley, John 44; New Orleans, 1841 778.6 p204
Lapoussiere, Pierre 25; Quebec, 1656 9221.17 p337
Lapouthier, . . .; Quebec, 1641 9221.17 p105
Lapp, Elisabeth; America, 1840 8115.12 p321
Lapp, Elisabeth; America, 1840 8115.12 p328
Lapp, Jakob; America, 1860 8115.12 p321
Lapp, Johann Georg; America, n.d. 8115.12 p321
Lapp, Ludwig; America, n.d. 8115.12 p321
Lappassate, John; Louisiana, 1874 4981.45 p132
Lappington, Elizabeth; America, 1770 1220.12 p485
Laprade, Michel 18; Quebec, 1649 9221.17 p218
Lapree, Nicolas 20; Quebec, 1649 9221.17 p219
Lapriestre, Nicholas; Georgia, 1795 1451.56 p118
Lapthorne, John 41; Ontario, 1871 1823.21 p196
Lapuce, Jacques; Quebec, 1639 9221.17 p84
Lapworth, Alice 42; Michigan, 1880 4491.39 p17
Lapworth, William 42; Michigan, 1880 4491.39 p17
Laquerine, Mr. 35; Port uncertain, 1843 778.6 p204
Laquette, Maline 26; America, 1847 778.6 p204
Laquintry, Lude; Louisiana, 1874 4981.45 p296
Laraway, Frank; Vermont, 1855 9228.50 p323
Laraway, John; Vermont, 1845-1921 9228.50 p323
Laraway, Peter Byron; Ohio, 1849 9228.50 p323
*Wife:*Susannah Starting
Laraway, Philip; Massachusetts, 1784 9228.50 p323
Laraway, Philip; New York, n.d. 9228.50 p395
Laraway, Susannah Starting *SEE* Laraway, Peter Byron
L'Arbalestier, Joseph; Massachusetts, 1788-1816 9228.50 p328
Larch, Joseph; Louisiana, 1874-1875 4981.45 p29
Larcher, Claude; Quebec, 1660 9221.17 p437
Larcher, Francois; Montreal, 1653 9221.17 p294
Larcher, Joseph; America, 1771 1220.12 p485
Larcher, Madeleine; Quebec, 1668-1679 1142.10 p128
Larcher, Madeleine; Quebec, 1668 4514.3 p333
Larcheveque, Claude; Quebec, 1639 9221.17 p89
Larcheveque, Francoise; Quebec, 1667 4514.3 p333
Larcom, Elizabeth Clarke *SEE* Larcom, Mordicai
Larcom, Mordicai; Ipswich, MA, 1629-1651 9228.50 p324
*Wife:*Elizabeth Clarke
Larcume, John; Virginia, 1663-1679 9228.50 p324
Lardereau, Bernard; Montreal, 1644 9221.17 p147
Lardereau, Francois; Montreal, 1644 9221.17 p147
Lardinois, Amelie Gelinne *SEE* Lardinois, Jean Pierre
Lardinois, Desiree *SEE* Lardinois, Jean Pierre
Lardinois, Jean Baptiste *SEE* Lardinois, Jean Pierre
Lardinois, Jean Pierre; Wisconsin, 1854-1858 1495.20 p50
*Wife:*Amelie Gelinne
*Child:*Desiree
*Child:*Pierre
*Child:*Jean Baptiste
Lardinois, Pierre *SEE* Lardinois, Jean Pierre
Lardner, John; America, 1774 1220.12 p485
Lardner, Roger; Charles Town, SC, 1718 1220.12 p485
Lardner, Thomas; Annapolis, MD, 1725 1220.12 p485
Larecompense, . . .; Montreal, 1651 9221.17 p252
Lareine, Jeanne 27; Quebec, 1651 9221.17 p251
Larell, Peter 35; Michigan, 1880 4491.30 p19
Lareman, Elizabeth; America, 1744 1220.12 p485
Laremon, Michael; America, 1746 1220.12 p485
Laremore, Daniel; America, 1774 1220.12 p485
Larey, Mr.; Boston, 1768 1642 p39
Larey, Arthur 65; Ontario, 1871 1823.21 p196
Larey, Jeremiah; America, 1772 1220.12 p490
Larey, John; Boston, 1765 1642 p35
Larey, Peter; Boston, 1766 1642 p36
Large, Edward 31; Ontario, 1871 1823.21 p196
Large, Eliza 33; Ontario, 1871 1823.17 p89
Large, Henry 30; Ontario, 1871 1823.21 p196
Large, James 35; Ontario, 1871 1823.21 p196
Large, John 52; Ontario, 1871 1823.21 p197
Large, Philip; Annapolis, MD, 1725 1220.12 p485
Large, Thomas; America, 1756 1220.12 p485
Large, William 41; Ontario, 1871 1823.21 p197
Largille, Pierre de; Quebec, 1647 9221.17 p183
Largin, John; Massachusetts, 1675-1676 1642 p128
Largin, John; Massachusetts, 1675-1676 1642 p129
Lariviere, Antoine 33; Quebec, 1649 9221.17 p219
Lariviere, Cardeau; Quebec, 1653 9221.17 p277
Lariviere, Francois 27; Quebec, 1639 9221.17 p85
Lariviere, Jean; Quebec, 1659 9221.17 p407
Lariviere, Laurent 23; Quebec, 1655 9221.17 p325
Lariviere, Pierre; Quebec, 1634 9221.17 p38
Lark, James; America, 1742 1220.12 p485
Larke, James; America, 1697 1220.12 p485
Larken, Thomas; Boston, 1764 1642 p33
Larken, William; Boston, 1764 1642 p33
Larken, William; New England, 1745 1642 p28
Larkham, John; America, 1685 1220.12 p485
Larkham, Robert; America, 1755 1220.12 p485
Larkin, Ann; America, 1757 1220.12 p485
Larkin, Benjamin; America, 1742 1220.12 p485
Larkin, Benjamin; Annapolis, MD, 1720 1220.12 p485
Larkin, Catherine 37; Ontario, 1871 1823.21 p197
Larkin, Eleanor; America, 1754 1220.12 p485
Larkin, Felix; Louisiana, 1836-1840 4981.45 p213
Larkin, Henry 17; Quebec, 1870 8364.32 p24
Larkin, John; Annapolis, MD, 1725 1220.12 p485
Larkin, John; Boston, 1769 1642 p40
Larkin, John; Maryland, 1723 1220.12 p485
Larkin, John 41; Ontario, 1871 1823.21 p197
Larkin, Joseph 34; Ontario, 1871 1823.21 p197
Larkin, Rich 45; St. Johns, N.F., 1811 1053.20 p20
Larkin, Richard; America, 1704 1220.12 p485
Larkin, Richard; Barbados or Jamaica, 1699 1220.12 p485
Larkin, Tim; St. John, N.B., 1847 2978.15 p36
Larkin, W.; Boston, 1728 1642 p23
Larkin, William; America, 1665 1220.12 p485
Larkman, Edward; America, 1749 1220.12 p485
Larkman, Edward; America, 1753 1220.12 p485
Larkworthy, James; America, 1770 1220.12 p485
Larmer, George; America, 1754 1220.12 p485
Larnard, Redmond; Boston, 1766 1642 p37
Larner, Ann; America, 1774 1220.12 p485
Larner, Elizabeth; America, 1759 1220.12 p485
Laroach, Ann; America, 1700 1220.12 p485
Larobardierre, Louisa 62; Michigan, 1880 4491.42 p16
Larobardierre, Sarah A. 30; Michigan, 1880 4491.42 p16
La Roche, Mr. 37; America, 1840 778.6 p204
Laroche, Constantine; America, 1769 1220.12 p485
Laroche, Geraud de 25; Quebec, 1655 9221.17 p326
Laroche, Jean 25; Montreal, 1653 9221.17 p295
Laroche, Louis 24; Quebec, 1653 9221.17 p276
Laroche, Mathurin; Quebec, 1646 9221.17 p166
Laroche, Pierre; Quebec, 1642 9221.17 p114
Larochelle, Pierre; Montreal, 1661 9221.17 p471
Laroche Vernay, Charles-Rene de; Quebec, 1750 2314.30 p170
Laroche Vernay, Charles-Rene de; Quebec, 1750 2314.30 p187
Larocque, John; Boston, 1734-1766 9228.50 p325
La Roke, . . . 15; Salem, MA, 1677 9228.50 p184
Laroke, John 27; Massachusetts, n.d. 9228.50 p324
Larolandiere, Guillaume 23; Montreal, 1653 9221.17 p291
Larose, . . .; Montreal, 1661 9221.17 p474
Larose, . . .; Quebec, 1652 9221.17 p260
Larose, . . .; Quebec, 1662 9221.17 p489
Larose, Antoine; Quebec, 1654 9221.17 p305
Larose, Barthelemy; Wisconsin, 1856 1495.20 p56
*Wife:*Marie Jos. Williquet
*Child:*Marie Therese Denise
*Child:*Fulvie Josephe Desiree
*Child:*Ferdinand
Larose, Denis; Quebec, 1652 9221.17 p253
Larose, Ferdinand *SEE* Larose, Barthelemy
Larose, Fulvie Josephe Desiree *SEE* Larose, Barthelemy
Larose, Jacques 16; Quebec, 1649 9221.17 p215
Larose, Jacques 40; Quebec, 1657 9221.17 p370
*Wife:*Marie Blondel 45
Larose, Jacques; Wisconsin, 1856 1495.20 p56
Larose, Jean 19; Quebec, 1656 9221.17 p332
Larose, Marie Blondel 45 *SEE* Larose, Jacques
Larose, Marie Jos. Williquet *SEE* Larose, Barthelemy
Larose, Marie Therese Denise *SEE* Larose, Barthelemy
Larose, Mathieu; Quebec, 1661 9221.17 p466
Larose, Pasquier 23; Quebec, 1656 9221.17 p343
Larose, Richard; Quebec, 1656 9221.17 p338
La Ross, John; America, 1772 1220.12 p485
Larramore, John; America, 1723 1220.12 p485
Larras, James 59; Ontario, 1871 1823.21 p197
Larret, James 61; Ontario, 1871 1823.17 p89
Larret, Robert; Maryland, 1674-1675 1236.25 p51
Larrett, Edmund; America, 1743 1220.12 p485
Larrett, Joseph 50; Ontario, 1871 1823.17 p89
Larrett, Robert; Barbados, 1674 1220.12 p485
Larsdotter, Christina; North America, 1858 6410.15 p105
Larsen, C.; Cleveland, OH, 1888-1897 9722.10 p122
Larsen, Emil; Iowa, 1915 1211.15 p16
Larsen, Lars Andres; Iowa, 1887 1211.15 p16
Larsen, Lars Peter; Washington, 1886 2770.40 p195
Larsen, Lauritz Peter; Iowa, 1919 1211.15 p16
Larsen, Severt Odin; Iowa, 1912 1211.15 p16
Larson, Adolph; Cleveland, OH, 1880-1892 9722.10 p122
Larson, Adolph O.; Illinois, 1854-1861 4487.25 p63
Larson, Alfred; Cleveland, OH, 1887-1894 9722.10 p122
Larson, Anders; Iowa, 1880 1211.15 p16
Larson, Andrew L.; Cleveland, OH, 1877-1899 9722.10 p122
Larson, Anna Sjostrom 26 *SEE* Larson, William
Larson, Anna; St. Paul, MN, 1887 1865.50 p93
Larson, August; Cleveland, OH, 1893-1902 9722.10 p122
Larson, August; Cleveland, OH, 1902-1903 9722.10 p122
Larson, August 1 *SEE* Larson, William
Larson, Augusta; St. Paul, MN, 1894 1865.50 p94
Larson, Betty; St. Paul, MN, 1890 1865.50 p36
Larson, Carl; Iowa, 1903 1211.15 p16
Larson, Carl Leonard; Cleveland, OH, 1893-1894 9722.10 p122
Larson, Carl Wilhelm; Cleveland, OH, 1901-1903 9722.10 p122
Larson, Charles E.; Illinois, 1854-1861 4487.25 p63
Larson, Charles J.; America, 1857 4487.25 p63
With family
Larson, Christina; St. Paul, MN, 1874-1905 1865.50 p94
Larson, Christina; St. Paul, MN, 1884 1865.50 p94
Larson, Cris; Iowa, 1885 1211.15 p16
Larson, Elise A. 14; New York, NY, 1894 6512.1 p184
Larson, Engebrit; Colorado, 1891 1029.59 p53
Larson, Erlan; Cleveland, OH, 1903 9722.10 p123
Larson, Fred; Minnesota, 1882-1886 1865.50 p94
Larson, Gustaf; St. Paul, MN, 1883 1865.50 p94
Larson, Gustaff; Iowa, 1887 1211.15 p16
Larson, Hans; Iowa, 1891 1211.15 p16
Larson, Hans M.; Iowa, 1896 1211.15 p16
Larson, Ivar; Washington, 1889 2770.40 p79
Larson, Johan S.; Colorado, 1892 1029.59 p53
Larson, John; Cleveland, OH, 1880-1898 9722.10 p123
Larson, John; Cleveland, OH, 1900-1906 9722.10 p123
Larson, John; Colorado, 1883 1029.59 p53
Larson, John; Illinois, 1861 4487.25 p63
Larson, John; Iowa, 1908 1211.15 p16
Larson, John; Springfield, IL, 1864 4487.25 p64
Larson, John; Washington, 1889 2770.40 p79
Larson, John Amandus; St. Paul, MN, 1901 1865.50 p94
Larson, John L.; Colorado, 1882 1029.59 p53
Larson, John P.; Cleveland, OH, 1886-1889 9722.10 p123
Larson, Josephine 22; New York, NY, 1894 6512.1 p184
Larson, Lars Emil; Boston, 1902 1766.20 p16
Larson, Laurits; Iowa, 1890 1211.15 p16
Larson, Lewis; Iowa, 1886 1211.15 p16
Larson, Louis; Washington, 1882 2770.40 p135
Larson, Maria M.; St. Paul, MN, 1881 1865.50 p36
Larson, Mars; Iowa, 1896 1211.15 p16
Larson, Nels; Illinois, 1861 4487.25 p64
Larson, Ove Peter; Washington, 1889 2770.40 p79
Larson, Peter; Iowa, 1893 1211.15 p16
Larson, Peter; Iowa, 1900 1211.15 p16
Larson, Robert; Iowa, 1914 1211.15 p16
Larson, Thurston; Idaho, 1907 1211.45 p133
Larson, Ulrika; St. Paul, MN, 1902 1865.50 p94
Larson, William 26; New York, 1856 6529.11 p22
*Wife:*Anna Sjostrom 26
*Son:*August 1
Larsson, Anna Sjostrom 26 *SEE* Larsson, Olof
Larsson, August 1 *SEE* Larsson, Olof
Larsson, Carl Eric; Illinois, 1854-1861 4487.25 p63
Larsson, Erik 27; New York, 1856 6529.11 p21
Larsson, Jens; Valdivia, Chile, 1850 1192.4 p49
Larsson, Lars; Kansas, 1870 777.40 p14
Larsson, Lars Fredrik; North America, 1888 6410.15 p106
Larsson, Lorents; Philadelphia, 1842 6412.40 p146
Larsson, M.; New York, NY, 1844 6412.40 p147
Larsson, Olof 26; New York, 1856 6529.11 p22
*Wife:*Anna Sjostrom 26
*Son:*August 1
Larteau, Marie; Quebec, 1667 4514.3 p333
La Rue, . . .; America, 1635 9228.50 p325
La Rue, Jane; Nova Scotia, 1843-1845 9228.50 p357
La Rue, John; Ohio, n.d. 9228.50 p326
Larvey, Alice 44; Ontario, 1871 1823.21 p197
Larwill, Robert; America, 1726 1220.12 p485
Lary, John; Boston, 1753 1642 p47
Lary, Jonathan; Massachusetts, 1774 1642 p63
Lary, Mary; America, 1769 1220.12 p490
Lary, Patrick; Boston, 1752 1642 p46
Lary, Thomas; New England, 1745 1642 p28
Lasar, H. S.; Ohio, 1860 3580.20 p32
Lasar, H. S.; Ohio, 1860 6020.12 p12
Laschner, Gustav Emil; Wisconsin, 1892 6795.8 p204
Laseke, Hans Heinrich; Port uncertain, 1834 7420.1 p7
Laseke, Ilse Marie Justine Laeseke *SEE* Laseke, Johann Heinrich
Laseke, Johann Heinrich *SEE* Laseke, Johann Heinrich

Laseke, Johann Heinrich; America, 1859 *7420.1 p186*
   *Wife:*Ilse Marie Justine Laeseke
   *Son:*Johann Heinrich
La Serre, Charles; Philadelphia, 1800-1899 *9228.50 p326*
La Serre, Octave; Ohio, 1801-1849 *9228.50 p326*
Lash, George 34; Ontario, 1871 *1823.21 p197*
Lash, Joseph; America, 1764 *1220.12 p485*
Lashbrook, Abel; America, 1720 *1220.12 p485*
Lashbrook, Richard 33; Ontario, 1871 *1823.21 p197*
Lashbrook, William; Maryland or Virginia, 1738
   1220.12 p485
Lasher, Francois; New York, 1600-1699 *9228.50 p326*
Lashford, Thomas; America, 1764 *1220.12 p485*
Lashley, Joseph; America, 1771 *1220.12 p485*
Lashure, George N.; Massachusetts, 1863-1955 *9228.50*
   p326
Lashure, Philip; Massachusetts, 1712 *9228.50 p399*
Lashure, William; Ohio, 1800-1840 *9228.50 p326*
Lashure Family ; Nova Scotia, 1800-1863 *9228.50 p326*
Lasker, Susan; America, 1741 *1220.12 p485*
Laski, Adam; Texas, 1886 *6015.15 p27*
Lasne, Guillaume; Quebec, 1645 *9221.17 p154*
Lasnon, Marie; Quebec, 1667 *4514.3 p333*
Lass, Joachim; New York, 1859 *358.56 p100*
Lassam, Ann; America, 1771 *1220.12 p485*
Lassan, L. 26; America, 1841 *778.6 p203*
Lassarade, . . .; Quebec, 1654 *9221.17 p311*
Lassen, Andrias; Colorado, 1873 *1029.59 p53*
Lassen, O.; California, 1868 *1131.61 p89*
l'Assomption, Mere de; Quebec, 1648 *9221.17 p194*
Lassurance, Paul; Quebec, 1651 *9221.17 p245*
Last, Danual 29; Ontario, 1871 *1823.21 p197*
Last, Ernest Leslie; Miami, 1935 *4984.12 p39*
Last, William; Iowa, 1888 *1211.15 p16*
Laster, Benjamin; America, 1724 *1220.12 p485*
Lastovica, Josef; Texas, 1856 *2853.20 p64*
Lasuisse, Pierre 24; Quebec, 1661 *9221.17 p460*
Lataille, Jean; Quebec, 1657 *9221.17 p353*
Lataille, Jean 2 *SEE* Lataille, Nicolas
Lataille, Nicolas 29; Quebec, 1644 *9221.17 p141*
   *Wife:*Vivienne Godeur 24
   *Son:*Jean 2
   *Son:*Pierre
Lataille, Pierre *SEE* Lataille, Nicolas
Lataille, Pierre; Quebec, 1653 *9221.17 p275*
Lataille, Vivienne Godeur 24 *SEE* Lataille, Nicolas
Latanas, C.; Louisiana, 1874-1875 *4981.45 p29*
Lataste, John; North Carolina, 1813 *1088.45 p18*
Late, Honor 28; Annapolis, MD, 1721 *1220.12 p486*
Laterner, Johann; America, 1857 *5475.1 p541*
Latham, Elizabeth; Barbados or Jamaica, 1689 *1220.12*
   p486
Latham, Henry 23; Ontario, 1871 *1823.21 p197*
Latham, Priscilla; Annapolis, MD, 1725 *1220.12 p486*
Latham, Richard; Barbados, 1690 *1220.12 p486*
Latham, Thomas; America, 1750 *1220.12 p486*
Latham, William; Plymouth, MA, 1620 *1920.45 p5*
Lathbury, Daniel; Barbados, 1680 *1220.12 p486*
Lathom, Margaret; America, 1745 *1220.12 p486*
Lathom, Thomas 45; Ontario, 1871 *1823.21 p197*
Latier, Francoise; Quebec, 1669 *4514.3 p333*
Latimer, Andrew; America, 1774 *1220.12 p486*
Latimer, John; America, 1723 *1220.12 p486*
Latola, Antti 37; Minnesota, 1926 *2769.54 p1381*
Latola, Signi 35; Minnesota, 1926 *2769.54 p1381*
LaTouche, David de; Montreal, 1643 *9221.17 p137*
Latouche, Marguerite; Quebec, 1673 *4514.3 p333*
Latour, Antoinette *SEE* Latour, Melchior
Latour, Catherine 21; Quebec, 1659 *9221.17 p404*
Latour, Charles *SEE* Latour, Melchior
Latour, Edmond *SEE* Latour, Melchior
Latour, Felicee *SEE* Latour, Melchior
Latour, Ferdinande *SEE* Latour, Melchior
Latour, Jacques 23; Quebec, 1646 *9221.17 p167*
Latour, Jean 20; Quebec, 1658 *9221.17 p383*
Latour, Louis *SEE* Latour, Melchior
Latour, Marie Joseph Sarton *SEE* Latour, Melchior
Latour, Melchior; Wisconsin, 1871 *1495.20 p28*
   *Wife:*Marie Joseph Sarton
   *Child:*Louis
   *Child:*Antoinette
   *Child:*Ferdinande
   *Child:*Seraphine
   *Grandchild:*Edmond
   *Child:*Felicee
   *Child:*Charles
Latour, Melchoir Jos.; America, 1871 *1494.20 p12*
Latour, Pierre; Quebec, 1639 *9221.17 p90*
Latour, Seraphine *SEE* Latour, Melchior
Latoush, Mary; America, 1701 *1220.12 p486*
Latra, Vincent; Detroit, 1929 *1640.55 p114*
Latreille, . . .; Montreal, 1654 *9221.17 p317*
Latreille, . . .; Quebec, 1636 *9221.17 p58*

Latreille, Jean 23; Quebec, 1661 *9221.17 p460*
Latreyte, E.; Louisiana, 1874 *4981.45 p296*
Latta, James; North Carolina, 1812 *1088.45 p18*
Lattamore, Richard; Marston's Wharf, 1782 *8529.30 p13*
Latter, John; Annapolis, MD, 1758 *1220.12 p486*
Lattermore, Richard; Marston's Wharf, 1782 *8529.30*
   p13
Lattersal, James; Philadelphia, 1830 *3274.55 p69*
Lattimer, David; America, 1719 *1220.12 p486*
Lattimore, Martha; America, 1775 *1220.12 p486*
Lattimore, Richard; Marston's Wharf, 1782 *8529.30 p13*
Lattimore, Stephen; America, 1762 *1220.12 p486*
Lattin, John; America, 1739 *1220.12 p486*
Latwesen, Anne Sophie Marie; America, 1853 *7420.1*
   p108
Latwesen, Engel Marie Sophie Dorothee; America, 1872
   7420.1 p204
Latwesen, Johann Heinrich; America, 1853 *7420.1 p108*
   *Wife:*Katharine Engel Rohrsen
Latwesen, Katharine Engel Rohrsen *SEE* Latwesen,
   Johann Heinrich
Latwesen, Sophie Louise; America, 1865 *7420.1 p238*
Latwoski, Martinus; Wisconsin, 1893 *6795.8 p59*
Latz, Barbara *SEE* Latz, Sebastian
Latz, Helena Engel *SEE* Latz, Nikolaus
Latz, Jakob *SEE* Latz, Nikolaus
Latz, Johann 23; America, 1875 *5475.1 p494*
Latz, Josef *SEE* Latz, Sebastian
Latz, Ludwig; America, 1882 *5475.1 p34*
Latz, Nikolaus; America, 1872 *5475.1 p304*
   *Wife:*Helena Engel
   *Son:*Jakob
Latz, Nikolaus *SEE* Latz, Sebastian
Latz, Peter *SEE* Latz, Sebastian
Latz, Sebastian *SEE* Latz, Sebastian
Latz, Sebastian; America, 1883 *5475.1 p316*
   *Wife:*Susanna Klein
   *Son:*Peter
   *Son:*Nikolaus
   *Daughter:*Barbara
   *Daughter:*Susanna
   *Son:*Josef
   *Son:*Sebastian
Latz, Susanna *SEE* Latz, Sebastian
Latz, Susanna Klein *SEE* Latz, Sebastian
Lau, Carl; Valdivia, Chile, 1852 *1192.4 p53*
Lau, Carl Ludwig; Wisconsin, 1859 *6795.8 p139*
Lau, Johann Gottfried; Wisconsin, 1859 *6795.8 p139*
Laub, Christina 25; New York, NY, 1898 *7951.13 p41*
Laub, Frederick; Ohio, 1809-1852 *4511.35 p29*
Laub, Jacob 25; New York, NY, 1898 *7951.13 p41*
Laub, Jakob; America, 1883 *2526.43 p152*
Laub, Johannes; America, 1883 *2526.43 p128*
Laub, Philipp; America, 1854 *2526.43 p222*
Laube, Johann Carl Heinrich; Baltimore, 1898 *6212.1*
   p14
Laubender, Michael M.; Ohio, 1809-1852 *4511.35 p29*
Lauber, Catharina; New Castle, DE, 1817-1818 *90.20*
   p152
Lauber, Christian; New Castle, DE, 1817-1818 *90.20*
   p152
Lauber, Johann Karl Heinvich; Baltimore, 1898 *6212.1*
   p13
Lauber, Joseph; New Castle, DE, 1817-1818 *90.20 p152*
Laubersheimer, Adam 23; America, 1864 *5475.1 p504*
Laubi, Xaveri 46; New Castle, DE, 1817-1818 *90.20*
   p152
Laubscher, Jacob; Ohio, 1809-1852 *4511.35 p29*
Lauch, Johannes, Jr.; America, 1892 *170.15 p34*
Lauck, Elisabeth 31; America, 1872 *5475.1 p389*
Lauck, Margarethe Thome *SEE* Lauck, Peter
Lauck, Maria *SEE* Lauck, Peter
Lauck, Mathias 27; Illinois, 1872 *5475.1 p389*
Lauck, Michel; Brazil, 1878 *5475.1 p389*
Lauck, Michel *SEE* Lauck, Peter
Lauck, Peter *SEE* Lauck, Peter
Lauck, Peter; Brazil, 1879 *5475.1 p390*
   *Wife:*Margarethe Thome
   *Daughter:*Maria
   *Son:*Michel
   *Son:*Peter
Laud, John; America, 1765 *1220.12 p486*
Laud, William; America, 1770 *1220.12 p486*
Laudenberger, Elisabetha; America, 1754 *2526.43 p214*
Lauder, David D.; North Carolina, 1837 *1088.45 p18*
Laudner, John; Nova Scotia, 1784 *7105 p24*
Laue, Mr.; America, 1863 *7420.1 p219*
Laue, Eduard Gustav Louis; America, 1890 *7420.1 p361*
Laue, Heinrich; America, 1840 *7420.1 p219*
Laue, Louis; America, 1893 *7420.1 p368*
Lauer, . . .; America, 1851 *7420.1 p81*
Lauer, A. Maria Muller *SEE* Lauer, Mathias

Lauer, Adam 44; America, 1855 *5475.1 p359*
   *Wife:*Kath. Steuer 44
   *Son:*Johann 10
   *Son:*Nikolaus
   *Daughter:*Susanna 12
Lauer, Anna Maria *SEE* Lauer, Mathias
Lauer, Barbara; America, 1853 *5475.1 p481*
Lauer, Barbara 36; America, 1860 *5475.1 p482*
Lauer, Barbara Scheid *SEE* Lauer, Johann
Lauer, Carl Wilhelm; America, 1883 *7420.1 p337*
Lauer, Elisabeth *SEE* Lauer, Mathias
Lauer, Elisabeth Schneider 43 *SEE* Lauer, Georg
Lauer, Emmerich; Chicago, 1892 *5475.1 p425*
Lauer, Eva Elisabeth; Virginia, 1831 *152.20 p61*
Lauer, Georg; America, 1837 *5475.1 p391*
   With 2 sons
Lauer, Georg; America, 1847 *5475.1 p473*
Lauer, Georg 26 *SEE* Lauer, Georg
Lauer, Georg 48; America, 1840 *5475.1 p392*
   *Wife:*Elisabeth Schneider 43
   *Son:*Heinrich 24
   *Daughter:*Luise 16
   *Son:*Georg 26
Lauer, Heinrich 24 *SEE* Lauer, Georg
Lauer, Jakob *SEE* Lauer, Mathias
Lauer, Jakob *SEE* Lauer, Johann
Lauer, Jakob; Brazil, 1881 *5475.1 p182*
Lauer, Joh. Peter *SEE* Lauer, Georg
Lauer, Johann; America, 1843 *5475.1 p305*
Lauer, Johann; America, 1853 *5475.1 p52*
   With wife & 2 children
Lauer, Johann *SEE* Lauer, Mathias
Lauer, Johann 10 *SEE* Lauer, Adam
Lauer, Johann *SEE* Lauer, Johann
Lauer, Johann; Brazil, 1879 *5475.1 p431*
   *Wife:*Barbara Scheid
   *Son:*Johann
   *Son:*Jakob
Lauer, Johann; Brazil, 1881 *5475.1 p182*
Lauer, Johann Jakob; South America, 1846 *5475.1 p531*
Lauer, Karl Johann; America, 1843 *5475.1 p505*
Lauer, Kath. Steuer 44 *SEE* Lauer, Adam
Lauer, Katharina Bluch *SEE* Lauer, Wendel
Lauer, Katharina *SEE* Lauer, Mathias
Lauer, Ludwig; Indiana, 1885 *5475.1 p381*
Lauer, Luise 16 *SEE* Lauer, Georg
Lauer, M.; New York, 1860 *358.56 p3*
Lauer, Margarethe *SEE* Lauer, Mathias
Lauer, Margarethe 14 *SEE* Lauer, Margarethe
Lauer, Margarethe 42; Pittsburgh, 1872 *5475.1 p353*
   *Daughter:*Margarethe 14
Lauer, Maria; America, 1870 *5475.1 p272*
Lauer, Maria 64; America, 1872 *5475.1 p354*
Lauer, Maria; Brazil, 1846 *5475.1 p438*
Lauer, Mathias *SEE* Lauer, Mathias
Lauer, Mathias; America, 1881 *5475.1 p357*
   *Wife:*A. Maria Muller
   *Son:*Michel
   *Daughter:*Katharina
   *Son:*Jakob
   *Son:*Joh. Peter
   *Daughter:*Margarethe
   *Son:*Johann
   *Son:*Peter
   *Daughter:*Elisabeth
   *Son:*Mathias
   *Daughter:*Anna Maria
Lauer, Mathias; America, 1884 *5475.1 p287*
Lauer, Mathias 29; America, 1846 *5475.1 p259*
Lauer, Mathias 25; Chicago, 1880 *5475.1 p306*
Lauer, Michel *SEE* Lauer, Mathias
Lauer, Nikolaus *SEE* Lauer, Mathias
Lauer, Nikolaus; America, 1873 *5475.1 p312*
Lauer, Peter *SEE* Lauer, Mathias
Lauer, Peter 22; America, 1846 *5475.1 p258*
Lauer, Peter Josef; America, 1871 *5475.1 p353*
Lauer, Philip 18; America, 1838 *5475.1 p392*
Lauer, Philipp; America, 1837 *5475.1 p391*
Lauer, Susanna 12 *SEE* Lauer, Adam
Lauer, Wendel; America, 1840 *5475.1 p437*
   *Wife:*Katharina Bluch
   With 5 children
Lauerman, Antonin *SEE* Lauerman, Josef
Lauerman, Josef; Wisconsin, 1857-1861 *2853.20 p334*
   *Brother:*Antonin
Lauermann, Elisabeth *SEE* Lauermann, Nikolaus
Lauermann, Johann 54; America, 1843 *5475.1 p270*
Lauermann, Karolina *SEE* Lauermann, Nikolaus
Lauermann, Katharina Grahser *SEE* Lauermann,
   Nikolaus
Lauermann, Maria *SEE* Lauermann, Nikolaus
Lauermann, Nikolaus *SEE* Lauermann, Nikolaus

Lauermann, Nikolaus; Ohio, 1884 ***5475.1*** *p316*
*Wife:*Katharina Grahser
*Daughter:*Elisabeth
*Daughter:*Karolina
*Son:*Nikolaus
*Daughter:*Maria
Laufaix, Jean R.; Illinois, 1852 ***6079.1*** *p8*
Laugham, Francis; Barbados, 1664 ***1220.12*** *p486*
Laughans, John C.; Ohio, 1809-1852 ***4511.35*** *p29*
Laughaus, John C.; Ohio, 1809-1852 ***4511.35*** *p29*
Laughen, John 31; Ontario, 1871 ***1823.21*** *p197*
Laughlan, Nicholas; America, 1765 ***1220.12*** *p486*
Laughland, Joseph; America, 1727 ***1220.12*** *p486*
Laughlin, Ellen 87; Ontario, 1871 ***1823.21*** *p197*
Laughlin, Samuel 30; Ontario, 1871 ***1823.17*** *p89*
Laughlin, Thomas 50; Ontario, 1871 ***1823.21*** *p197*
Laughran, Anna; Philadelphia, 1860 ***8513.31*** *p321*
Laughty, John; America, 1663 ***1220.12*** *p486*
Lauglin, Barnard 38; Ontario, 1871 ***1823.21*** *p197*
Laugtten, Edwd 22; St. Johns, N.F., 1811 ***1053.20*** *p22*
Lauinger, Damien 18; New York, NY, 1893 ***1883.7*** *p41*
Lauinger, Eva 17; New York, NY, 1898 ***7951.13*** *p43*
Lauinger, Josef 26; New York, NY, 1893 ***1883.7*** *p41*
Lauinger, Ottilia 22; New York, NY, 1893 ***1883.7*** *p41*
Lauinger, Stephania 2 months; New York, NY, 1893 ***1883.7*** *p41*
Laulunen, Isaac 41; Minnesota, 1926 ***2769.54*** *p1381*
Laulunen, Selma 38; Minnesota, 1926 ***2769.54*** *p1382*
Laulunen, Victor 40; Minnesota, 1925 ***2769.54*** *p1378*
Laulunen, Mrs. Victor 38; Minnesota, 1925 ***2769.54*** *p1378*
Laumer, Emma Auguste; Wisconsin, 1899 ***6795.8*** *p122*
Laumer, Martha Anna; Wisconsin, 1898 ***6795.8*** *p122*
Laumonnier, Barbe; Quebec, 1673 ***4514.3*** *p362*
Laun, Jakob; America, 1884 ***179.55*** *p19*
Launay, Noel; Quebec, 1651 ***9221.17*** *p245*
Launder, John; America, 1773 ***1220.12*** *p486*
Launder, Philip; America, 1745 ***1220.12*** *p486*
Launder, Robert; America, 1691 ***1220.12*** *p486*
Launders, John; Toronto, 1844 ***2910.35*** *p113*
Laundress, Sarah; America, 1737 ***1220.12*** *p486*
Laundy, Thomas 38; Ontario, 1871 ***1823.17*** *p89*
Laupscher, Nicholas; Ohio, 1809-1852 ***4511.35*** *p29*
Laupystrasser, Joseph 39; Ontario, 1871 ***1823.21*** *p197*
Laur, Josef; America, 1882 ***5475.1*** *p129*
Lauranc, John; Maine, n.d. ***9228.50*** *p327*
*Relative:*Nicolas
Lauranc, Nicolas *SEE* Lauranc, John
Laurant, C.; Louisiana, 1874-1875 ***4981.45*** *p29*
Laurant DuPortal, Louis; Quebec, 1661 ***9221.17*** *p460*
Laurence, . . .; Newfoundland, 1676 ***9228.50*** *p327*
Laurence, Genevieve; Quebec, 1664 ***4514.3*** *p333*
Laurence, Geo; Ontario, 1787 ***1276.15*** *p230*
With child & 2 relatives
Laurence, Marie; Quebec, 1656 ***9221.17*** *p154*
Laurence, Marie 24; Quebec, 1656 ***9221.17*** *p339*
Laurence, R. George 48; Ontario, 1871 ***1823.21*** *p197*
Laurence, Sidney 17; Quebec, 1870 ***8364.32*** *p24*
Laurence, William 28; Ontario, 1871 ***1823.21*** *p197*
Laurendeau, Pierre; Washington, 1884 ***6015.10*** *p16*
Laurens, . . .; Newfoundland, 1676 ***9228.50*** *p327*
Laurens, Henry; Charleston, SC, 1769 ***9228.50*** *p327*
Laurent, Alexander; Louisiana, 1874 ***4981.45*** *p132*
Laurent, Catherine; Quebec, 1667 ***4514.3*** *p334*
Laurent, Jean 21; Quebec, 1656 ***9221.17*** *p339*
Laurent, Pierre 24; Quebec, 1657 ***9221.17*** *p361*
Lauret, Pierre; Virginia, 1700 ***9230.15*** *p80*
Lauridseu, Peter C.N.; Iowa, 1899 ***1211.15*** *p16*
Lauritsen, Peter C.; Iowa, 1896 ***1211.15*** *p16*
Lausch, Hugo 19; New York, NY, 1883 ***8427.14*** *p45*
Lauson, Charles de 23; Quebec, 1652 ***9221.17*** *p261*
Lauson, Gilles 23; Montreal, 1653 ***9221.17*** *p294*
Lauson, Jean de; Quebec, 1651 ***2314.30*** *p166*
Lauson, Jean de; Quebec, 1651 ***2314.30*** *p187*
Lauson, Jean de *SEE* Lauson, Jean de
Lauson, Jean de 67; Quebec, 1651 ***9221.17*** *p234*
*Son:*Jean de
*Son:*Louis 22
Lauson, Louis 22 *SEE* Lauson, Jean de
Lauson-Charny, Charles 23; Quebec, 1652 ***9221.17*** *p261*
Lauson deCharny, Charles de; Quebec, 1652 ***2314.30*** *p166*
Lauson deCharny, Charles de; Quebec, 1652 ***2314.30*** *p187*
Lauson DeLaCitiere, Louis 22; Quebec, 1651 ***9221.17*** *p235*
Lauson deLa Citiere, Louis de; Quebec, 1651 ***2314.30*** *p166*
Lauson deLa Citiere, Louis de; Quebec, 1651 ***2314.30*** *p187*
Lautenberger, Georg; America, 1853 ***2526.43*** *p211*
Lautenberger, Heinrich; America, 1853 ***2526.42*** *p162*
Lautenberger, Johannes 40; America, 1831 ***2526.42*** *p125*
Lautenberger, Michel; America, 1854 ***2526.43*** *p128*
Lautenberger, Wilhelm; America, 1855 ***2526.42*** *p162*
Lautenschlager, Adam; America, 1885 ***2526.42*** *p109*
Lautenschlager, Johannes; America, 1852 ***2526.43*** *p222*
Lauterbach, Katharina; New York, 1884 ***5475.1*** *p430*
Lauterborn, Nikolaus; America, 1840 ***5475.1*** *p546*
Lautz, Henry; Ohio, 1809-1852 ***4511.35*** *p30*
Lauvergnat, Jacqueline; Quebec, 1663 ***4514.3*** *p334*
Lauvergnat, Jean; Quebec, 1654 ***9221.17*** *p311*
Lauvergnat, Pierre; Montreal, 1642 ***9221.17*** *p123*
Laux, Barbara *SEE* Laux, Mathias
Laux, Barbara Clemens *SEE* Laux, Mathias
Laux, Helena *SEE* Laux, Mathias
Laux, Jakob *SEE* Laux, Mathias
Laux, Johann *SEE* Laux, Mathias
Laux, Katharina *SEE* Laux, Mathias
Laux, Margarethe *SEE* Laux, Mathias
Laux, Maria *SEE* Laux, Mathias
Laux, Mathias *SEE* Laux, Mathias
Laux, Mathias; America, 1880 ***5475.1*** *p358*
*Wife:*Barbara Clemens
*Son:*Johann
*Daughter:*Susanna
*Daughter:*Katharina
*Daughter:*Barbara
*Son:*Jakob
*Daughter:*Maria
*Daughter:*Margarethe
*Son:*Mathias
*Daughter:*Helena
Laux, Mathias 42; America, 1843 ***5475.1*** *p358*
Laux, Susanna *SEE* Laux, Mathias
Lavaigne, Jacques de; Quebec, 1639 ***9221.17*** *p90*
Laval, Claude; Quebec, 1671 ***4514.3*** *p334*
Laval, Girard; Quebec, 1650 ***9221.17*** *p227*
Laval, Jacques; Montreal, 1659 ***9221.17*** *p422*
Laval, Jacques 24; Montreal, 1653 ***9221.17*** *p297*
Laval DeMontigny, Francois de 36; Quebec, 1659 ***9221.17*** *p392*
Lavalette, Marc; Illinois, 1852 ***6079.1*** *p8*
La Vallee, Mr.; Ontario, 1800-1899 ***9228.50*** *p327*
With wife
*Child:*Henry
*Child:*Thomas
Lavallee, Claude 26; Quebec, 1654 ***9221.17*** *p310*
Lavallee, Francois; Montreal, 1653 ***9221.17*** *p299*
Lavallee, Geoffroy; Quebec, 1649 ***9221.17*** *p214*
Lavallee, Guilaume 10; Montreal, 1648 ***9221.17*** *p206*
La Vallee, Henry *SEE* La Vallee, Mr.
Lavallee, Jean; Quebec, 1637 ***9221.17*** *p70*
Lavallee, Jean 17; Quebec, 1659 ***9221.17*** *p404*
*Brother:*Pierre 21
Lavallee, Pierre 21 *SEE* Lavallee, Jean
Lavallee, Pierre 26; Quebec, 1650 ***9221.17*** *p225*
La Vallee, Thomas *SEE* La Vallee, Mr.
La Valley, . . .; Georgia, 1740 ***9228.50*** *p327*
La Valley, . . .; Wisconsin, n.d. ***9228.50*** *p327*
La Valley, John; Maryland, 1657 ***9228.50*** *p327*
*Relative:*Nicholas
La Valley, Nicholas *SEE* La Valley, John
La Valley Family ; Marblehead, MA, 1700-1799 ***9228.50*** *p327*
Lavan, Hannah; America, 1756 ***1220.12*** *p486*
Lavander, William 24; Ontario, 1871 ***1823.21*** *p197*
Lavant, Mary; Potomac, 1729 ***1220.12*** *p486*
Lave, Kiohael; Wisconsin, 1878 ***6795.8*** *p189*
Lavelle, Anthony 40; Ontario, 1871 ***1823.17*** *p89*
Lavender, William; Marston's Wharf, 1782 ***8529.30*** *p13*
Lavenstine, Jacob; Ohio, 1809-1852 ***4511.35*** *p30*
Laver, James 25; Ontario, 1871 ***1823.21*** *p197*
Laver, John; America, 1685 ***1220.12*** *p486*
Laver, Richard; America, 1754 ***1220.12*** *p486*
Laver, Thomas; America, 1685 ***1220.12*** *p486*
Laverack, Robert; America, 1733 ***1220.12*** *p486*
Laverdure, . . .; Quebec, 1652 ***9221.17*** *p261*
Laverdure, Hilaire; Quebec, 1651 ***9221.17*** *p242*
Laverdure, Jacques 15; Quebec, 1643 ***9221.17*** *p130*
Laverdure, Jean 21; Montreal, 1653 ***9221.17*** *p302*
Laverdure, Marguerite; Quebec, 1665 ***4514.3*** *p334*
Laverdure, Pierre 13; Montreal, 1659 ***9221.17*** *p425*
Laverdure, Pierre 25; Quebec, 1655 ***9221.17*** *p323*
Laverick, Ralph; America, 1744 ***1220.12*** *p486*
Laverick, Walter; America, 1758 ***1220.12*** *p486*
Lavers, William; America, 1775 ***1220.12*** *p486*
Laverstick, Alice; Maryland or Virginia, 1733 ***1220.12*** *p486*
Laverty, James 50; Ontario, 1871 ***1823.21*** *p197*
Laverty, John; New York, NY, 1829 ***3274.55*** *p26*
Laveruffe, Edward 50; Ontario, 1871 ***1823.17*** *p89*
Lavery, Edward 22; Ontario, 1871 ***1823.21*** *p197*
Lavery, Edward B.; Ohio, 1836 ***3580.20*** *p32*
Lavery, Edward B.; Ohio, 1836 ***6020.12*** *p12*
Lavery, Edward B.; Ohio, 1838 ***3580.20*** *p32*
Lavery, Edward B.; Ohio, 1838 ***6020.12*** *p12*
Lavery, John 40; Ontario, 1871 ***1823.21*** *p197*
Lavess, Samuel; America, 1764 ***1220.12*** *p486*
Lavett, Thomas 36; Ontario, 1871 ***1823.17*** *p89*
La Vieville, Anne; Quebec, 1671 ***4514.3*** *p357*
Lavigne, Jean 18; Quebec, 1640 ***9221.17*** *p97*
Lavigne, Jean-Baptiste; Montreal, 1659 ***9221.17*** *p422*
Lavigne, Laurent 3 *SEE* Lavigne, Marguerite Richard
Lavigne, Louis 2 *SEE* Lavigne, Marguerite Richard
Lavigne, Marguerite; Quebec, 1651 ***9221.17*** *p97*
Lavigne, Marguerite 22; Quebec, 1651 ***9221.17*** *p247*
*Son:*Laurent 3
*Son:*Louis 2
Lavigne, Nicolas 31; Quebec, 1648 ***9221.17*** *p204*
Lavigne, Ozanie-Joseph 24; Quebec, 1661 ***9221.17*** *p463*
Lavigne, Urbain 23; Montreal, 1648 ***9221.17*** *p206*
Laville, Antoine 35; Quebec, 1657 ***9221.17*** *p362*
Laville, Francois; Quebec, 1651 ***9221.17*** *p237*
Laville, Joseph; Ohio, 1809-1852 ***4511.35*** *p30*
Lavin, John 45; Ontario, 1871 ***1823.17*** *p89*
Lavinder, Elizabeth; America, 1758 ***1220.12*** *p486*
Lavine, John; America, 1774 ***1220.12*** *p486*
Laviolette, . . .; Montreal, 1651 ***9221.17*** *p252*
Laviolette, Lieutenant; Quebec, 1634 ***9221.17*** *p32*
Laviolette, Adrien; Quebec, 1653 ***9221.17*** *p280*
With wife
Laviolette, Jacques 21; Montreal, 1653 ***9221.17*** *p298*
Laviolette, Jacques 22; Quebec, 1658 ***9221.17*** *p382*
Laviolette, Jacques 25; Quebec, 1650 ***9221.17*** *p226*
Laviolette, Jean; Montreal, 1653 ***9221.17*** *p299*
Laviolette, Jean 33; Quebec, 1659 ***9221.17*** *p396*
Laviolette, Louis 22; Quebec, 1642 ***9221.17*** *p119*
Laviolette, Mathurin 26; Quebec, 1648 ***9221.17*** *p199*
Laviolette, Pierre; Quebec, 1655 ***9221.17*** *p321*
Lavique, Mrs.; Toronto, 1844 ***2910.35*** *p112*
Lavique, Paul; Toronto, 1844 ***2910.35*** *p112*
La Vires, . . .; Ohio, n.d. ***9228.50*** *p327*
Lavires, John; Ohio, 1811 ***9228.50*** *p358*
Lavis, Henry 32; Ontario, 1871 ***1823.21*** *p197*
Lavory, Richard; Marston's Wharf, 1782 ***8529.30*** *p13*
Lavzow, Jospeh; Wisconsin, 1877 ***6795.8*** *p175*
Law, Elizabeth; Michigan, 1888-1906 ***9228.50*** *p235*
Law, Elizabeth; Philadelphia, 1851 ***8513.31*** *p305*
Law, James 21; Ontario, 1871 ***1823.17*** *p89*
Law, James; South Carolina, 1808 ***6155.4*** *p18*
Law, John; America, 1769 ***1220.12*** *p486*
Law, John; Annapolis, MD, 1720 ***1220.12*** *p486*
Law, John 27; Ontario, 1871 ***1823.21*** *p197*
Law, John 42; Ontario, 1871 ***1823.21*** *p197*
Law, John 45; Ontario, 1871 ***1823.21*** *p197*
Law, John 58; Ontario, 1871 ***1823.21*** *p197*
Law, Joseph 40; Ontario, 1871 ***1823.21*** *p197*
Law, Joseph 45; Ontario, 1871 ***1823.21*** *p197*
Law, Margaret; America, 1767 ***1220.12*** *p486*
Law, Samuel; America, 1760 ***1220.12*** *p486*
Law, Samuel; South Carolina, 1810 ***6155.4*** *p18*
Law, Thomas; America, 1769 ***1220.12*** *p486*
Law, Thomas; Marston's Wharf, 1782 ***8529.30*** *p13*
Law, William; America, 1770 ***1220.12*** *p486*
Law, William; America, 1775 ***1220.12*** *p486*
Law, William; South Carolina, 1808 ***6155.4*** *p18*
Lawder, John; Barbados, 1679 ***1220.12*** *p486*
Lawe, William; America, 1772 ***1220.12*** *p486*
Lawes, Elizabeth; Virginia, 1734 ***1220.12*** *p487*
Lawes, John; America, 1739 ***1220.12*** *p487*
Lawes, Wm. 39; Quebec, 1910 ***2897.7*** *p8*
Lawford, Adam; Virginia, 1773 ***1220.12*** *p487*
Lawford, Sarah; Virginia, 1775 ***1220.12*** *p487*
Lawin, John; America, 1747 ***1220.12*** *p487*
Lawlas, Michael 31; New York, NY, 1825 ***6178.50*** *p148*
Lawler, Catherine; America, 1748 ***1220.12*** *p487*
Lawler, Darby; Boston, 1766 ***1642*** *p37*
Lawler, Elizabeth; Died enroute, 1718 ***1220.12*** *p487*
Lawler, James; Boston, 1826 ***3274.55*** *p66*
Lawler, John; America, 1753 ***1220.12*** *p487*
Lawler, Margaret; America, 1741 ***1220.12*** *p487*
Lawless, Catherine; New Orleans, 1850 ***7242.30*** *p148*
Lawless, James; St. John, N.B., 1848 ***2978.15*** *p40*
Lawless, James; Virginia, 1739 ***1220.12*** *p487*
Lawless, James, Jr.; St. John, N.B., 1848 ***2978.15*** *p40*
Lawless, John; New Orleans, 1850 ***7242.30*** *p148*
Lawless, John; Ohio, 1809-1852 ***4511.35*** *p30*
Lawless, Lawrence 54; Ontario, 1871 ***1823.21*** *p197*
Lawless, Mary; America, 1767 ***1220.12*** *p487*
Lawless, Mary Ann; America, 1748 ***1220.12*** *p487*
Lawless, Thomas 33; Ontario, 1871 ***1823.21*** *p197*
Lawless, William; Louisiana, 1847-1850 ***7710.1*** *p151*
Lawley, Francis; America, 1753 ***1220.12*** *p487*
Lawley, Mary; America, 1769 ***1220.12*** *p487*
Lawley, William; America, 1770 ***1220.12*** *p487*
Lawlin, John; America, 1747 ***1220.12*** *p487*

262 *FOR A COMPLETE EXPLANATION OF ENTRY, SEE "HOW TO READ A CITATION" SECTION*

Lawlor, Finton; Ohio, 1838 ***3580.20*** *p32*
Lawlor, Finton; Ohio, 1838 ***6020.12*** *p12*
Lawlor, Margaret; Boston, 1742 ***1642*** *p45*
Lawlor, Thomas 35; Ontario, 1871 ***1823.21*** *p197*
Lawlore, John; America, 1740 ***1220.12*** *p487*
Lawman, Peter; Barbados or Jamaica, 1697 ***1220.12*** *p487*
Lawn, Dorothy; America, 1743 ***1220.12*** *p487*
Lawndey, Lewis; America, 1665 ***1220.12*** *p486*
Lawrance, Bartholameu 12; Ontario, 1871 ***1823.21*** *p197*
Lawrance, Benjamin 45; Ontario, 1871 ***1823.21*** *p197*
Lawrance, Clara 9; Ontario, 1871 ***1823.21*** *p197*
Lawrance, Isac 42; Ontario, 1871 ***1823.17*** *p89*
Lawrance, Thomas 33; Ontario, 1871 ***1823.17*** *p89*
Lawrane, Domingo; America, 1764 ***1220.12*** *p487*
Lawrence, . . .; Newfoundland, 1676 ***9228.50*** *p327*
Lawrence, A.; California, 1868 ***1131.61*** *p89*
With wife
Lawrence, Alfred; Marston's Wharf, 1782 ***8529.30*** *p13*
Lawrence, Anthony; America, 1721 ***1220.12*** *p487*
Lawrence, Benjamin; Annapolis, MD, 1723 ***1220.12*** *p487*
Lawrence, Charles; Barbados, 1667 ***1220.12*** *p487*
Lawrence, Daniel 60; Ontario, 1871 ***1823.21*** *p197*
Lawrence, Diana; Barbados or Jamaica, 1694 ***1220.12*** *p487*
Lawrence, Edward; Barbados, 1699 ***1220.12*** *p487*
Lawrence, Eliza J. 28; Santa Clara Co., CA, 1870 ***8704.1*** *p25*
Lawrence, Elizabeth; America, 1730 ***1220.12*** *p487*
Lawrence, Elizabeth; America, 1745 ***1220.12*** *p487*
Lawrence, Elizabeth; America, 1758 ***1220.12*** *p487*
Lawrence, Elizabeth; America, 1774 ***1220.12*** *p487*
Lawrence, George; America, 1719 ***1220.12*** *p487*
Lawrence, George; America, 1746 ***1220.12*** *p487*
Lawrence, George; North Carolina, 1815 ***1088.45*** *p18*
Lawrence, Giles; America, 1732 ***1220.12*** *p487*
Lawrence, Hannah; Maryland, 1736 ***1220.12*** *p487*
Lawrence, Henry; America, 1753 ***1220.12*** *p487*
Lawrence, Henry; America, 1756 ***1220.12*** *p487*
Lawrence, Henry; America, 1765 ***1220.12*** *p488*
Lawrence, Jacob; America, 1766 ***1220.12*** *p488*
Lawrence, James; America, 1769 ***1220.12*** *p488*
Lawrence, Jane; America, 1767 ***1220.12*** *p488*
Lawrence, Job 65; Ontario, 1871 ***1823.21*** *p198*
Lawrence, John; America, 1685 ***1220.12*** *p488*
Lawrence, John; America, 1698 ***1220.12*** *p488*
Lawrence, John; America, 1724 ***1220.12*** *p488*
Lawrence, John; America, 1743 ***1220.12*** *p488*
Lawrence, John; America, 1748 ***1220.12*** *p488*
Lawrence, John; America, 1750 ***1220.12*** *p488*
Lawrence, John; America, 1769 ***1220.12*** *p488*
Lawrence, John; America, 1773 ***1220.12*** *p488*
Lawrence, John; America, 1773 ***1220.12*** *p488*
Lawrence, John; Barbados, 1678 ***1220.12*** *p488*
Lawrence, John; Barbados, 1699 ***1220.12*** *p488*
Lawrence, John; Boston, 1713 ***9228.50*** *p327*
Lawrence, John; Charles Town, SC, 1718 ***1220.12*** *p488*
Lawrence, John; Maine, n.d. ***9228.50*** *p327*
*Relative:*Nicolas
Lawrence, John; Virginia, 1734 ***1220.12*** *p488*
Lawrence, John; Virginia, 1766 ***1220.12*** *p488*
Lawrence, Joseph 22; Ontario, 1871 ***1823.21*** *p198*
Lawrence, Martha; America, 1751 ***1220.12*** *p488*
Lawrence, Mary; America, 1757 ***1220.12*** *p488*
Lawrence, Mary; America, 1770 ***1220.12*** *p488*
Lawrence, Nathaniel; America, 1747 ***1220.12*** *p488*
Lawrence, Nicolas *SEE* Lawrence, John
Lawrence, Philip; Potomac, 1729 ***1220.12*** *p488*
Lawrence, Rebecca; America, 1746 ***1220.12*** *p488*
Lawrence, Richard; America, 1747 ***1220.12*** *p488*
Lawrence, Robert; Barbados, 1667 ***1220.12*** *p488*
Lawrence, Samuel; America, 1683 ***1220.12*** *p488*
Lawrence, Samuel; America, 1685 ***1220.12*** *p488*
Lawrence, Sarah; Potomac, 1731 ***1220.12*** *p488*
Lawrence, Thomas; America, 1685 ***1220.12*** *p488*
Lawrence, Thomas; America, 1767 ***1220.12*** *p488*
Lawrence, Thomas; Barbados, 1672 ***1220.12*** *p488*
Lawrence, Thomas 15; Michigan, 1880 ***4491.33*** *p13*
Lawrence, Walter 63; Ontario, 1871 ***1823.21*** *p198*
Lawrence, William; America, 1730 ***1220.12*** *p488*
Lawrence, William; America, 1737 ***1220.12*** *p488*
Lawrence, William; America, 1745 ***1220.12*** *p488*
Lawrence, William; America, 1750 ***1220.12*** *p488*
Lawrence, William; America, 1765 ***1220.12*** *p488*
Lawrence, William; America, 1768 ***1220.12*** *p488*
Lawrence, William; America, 1769 ***1220.12*** *p488*
Lawrence, William; America, 1774 ***1220.12*** *p489*
Lawrence, William; Annapolis, MD, 1726 ***1220.12*** *p488*
Lawrence, William; New York, NY, 1776 ***8529.30*** *p2*
Lawrence, William; Virginia, 1771 ***1220.12*** *p488*
Lawrence, William; West Indies, 1686 ***1220.12*** *p488*
Lawrenceson, John; America, 1738 ***1220.12*** *p489*
Lawrett, Mary; America, 1745 ***1220.12*** *p489*
Lawrie, Charles 4; Ontario, 1871 ***1823.21*** *p198*
Lawrie, James T. 26; Ontario, 1871 ***1823.21*** *p198*
Lawrie, Minnie 32; Ontario, 1871 ***1823.21*** *p198*
Laws, Ann; America, 1760 ***1220.12*** *p486*
Laws, Elen B. 24; Ontario, 1871 ***1823.21*** *p198*
Laws, Elizabeth; Rappahannock, VA, 1729 ***1220.12*** *p487*
Laws, George; America, 1773 ***1220.12*** *p487*
Laws, James; North America, 1750 ***1640.8*** *p233*
Laws, John; America, 1745 ***1220.12*** *p487*
Laws, John; America, 1752 ***1220.12*** *p487*
Laws, Mary; America, 1759 ***1220.12*** *p487*
Laws, Mathew; Washington, 1887 ***2770.40*** *p24*
Laws, Samuel; America, 1767 ***1220.12*** *p487*
Laws, Samuel; Annapolis, MD, 1722 ***1220.12*** *p487*
Laws, Sarah; America, 1737 ***1220.12*** *p487*
Laws, William; America, 1775 ***1220.12*** *p487*
Laws, William B. 59; Ontario, 1871 ***1823.17*** *p89*
Lawsen, John; Barbados, 1675 ***1220.12*** *p489*
Lawsen, Sarah 64; Ontario, 1871 ***1823.21*** *p198*
Lawson, Ann; America, 1736 ***1220.12*** *p489*
Lawson, Ann; Virginia, 1758 ***1220.12*** *p489*
Lawson, Charles; Colorado, 1885 ***1029.59*** *p53*
Lawson, David 38; Ontario, 1871 ***1823.21*** *p198*
Lawson, Eliza 49; Ontario, 1871 ***1823.21*** *p198*
Lawson, Elizabeth; America, 1751 ***1220.12*** *p489*
Lawson, Elizabeth; America, 1768 ***1220.12*** *p489*
Lawson, Elizabeth 70; Ontario, 1871 ***1823.17*** *p89*
Lawson, George; America, 1756 ***1220.12*** *p489*
Lawson, Isabella; America, 1773 ***1220.12*** *p489*
Lawson, Isabella; Ohio, 1801-1835 ***5024.1*** *p139*
Lawson, James; America, 1753 ***1220.12*** *p489*
Lawson, James; Long Island, 1781 ***8529.30*** *p9A*
Lawson, James 45; Ontario, 1871 ***1823.21*** *p198*
Lawson, James 58; Ontario, 1871 ***1823.17*** *p90*
Lawson, John; America, 1683 ***1220.12*** *p489*
Lawson, John; America, 1750 ***1220.12*** *p489*
Lawson, John; America, 1762 ***1220.12*** *p489*
Lawson, John 40; New York, NY, 1826 ***6178.50*** *p150*
Lawson, John 34; Ontario, 1871 ***1823.17*** *p90*
Lawson, John 34; Ontario, 1871 ***1823.21*** *p198*
Lawson, Katherine; Jamaica, 1716 ***1220.12*** *p489*
Lawson, Mannor D.; Ohio, 1844 ***2763.1*** *p20*
Lawson, Mary; America, 1700 ***1220.12*** *p489*
Lawson, Mary; America, 1731 ***1220.12*** *p489*
Lawson, Matthew; America, 1753 ***1220.12*** *p489*
Lawson, N. G.; Iowa, 1893 ***1211.15*** *p16*
Lawson, Ralph; America, 1773 ***1220.12*** *p489*
Lawson, Robert; Ohio, 1844 ***2763.1*** *p20*
Lawson, Samuel; America, 1770 ***1220.12*** *p489*
Lawson, Sara; America, 1726 ***1220.12*** *p489*
Lawson, Thomas 56; Ontario, 1871 ***1823.21*** *p198*
Lawson, Thomas 16; Quebec, 1870 ***8364.32*** *p24*
Lawson, William; America, 1767 ***1220.12*** *p489*
Lawson, William; Ohio, 1843 ***2763.1*** *p20*
Lawson, William 58; Ontario, 1871 ***1823.17*** *p90*
Lawton, Chas 42; Ontario, 1871 ***1823.21*** *p198*
Lawton, Edward 24; Ontario, 1871 ***1823.17*** *p90*
Lawton, Edwd 22; St. Johns, N.F., 1811 ***1053.20*** *p22*
Lawton, George; America, 1743 ***1220.12*** *p489*
Lawton, Moses; America, 1765 ***1220.12*** *p489*
Lawton, Samuel 39; Ontario, 1871 ***1823.21*** *p198*
Lawton, Thomas; Carolina, 1724 ***1220.12*** *p489*
Lawton, William 70; Ontario, 1871 ***1823.21*** *p198*
Lawyer, Romeyn 33; Ontario, 1871 ***1823.17*** *p90*
Lax, Ann; Virginia, 1732 ***1220.12*** *p489*
Lax, George; America, 1744 ***1220.12*** *p489*
Lax, Kjerstin; New York, 1856 ***6529.11*** *p20*
Lax, Lars 22; New York, 1856 ***6529.11*** *p20*
Lax, Martha 34; New York, 1856 ***6529.11*** *p19*
Laxon, Edmond 22; Annapolis, MD, 1721 ***1220.12*** *p489*
Laxton, Sarah; America, 1740 ***1220.12*** *p489*
Laycock, . . .; Pennsylvania, 1690 ***9228.50*** *p160*
Laycock, John; Missouri, 1899 ***3276.1*** *p2*
Laycock, Margaret; Maryland, 1674-1675 ***1236.25*** *p51*
Laycock, Martha; America, 1739 ***1220.12*** *p489*
Laycock, Matthew; Virginia, 1723 ***1220.12*** *p489*
Laycock, Richard; America, 1741 ***1220.12*** *p489*
Laydall, James; America, 1677 ***1220.12*** *p489*
Laye, George; Barbados or Jamaica, 1697 ***1220.12*** *p489*
Layer, John; Washington, 1887 ***2770.40*** *p24*
Layer, Wendel; America, 1854 ***5475.1*** *p57*
Layfield, John; America, 1721 ***1220.12*** *p489*
Layfield, William; America, 1741 ***1220.12*** *p489*
Layforton, Anthony; America, 1764 ***1220.12*** *p489*
Laykovich, Frank; Colorado, 1906 ***1029.59*** *p53*
Laykovich, Frank 26; Colorado, 1906 ***1029.59*** *p53*
Layman, Christian; Ohio, 1809-1852 ***4511.35*** *p30*
Layman, Michael; Ohio, 1809-1852 ***4511.35*** *p30*
Lays, George 41; Ontario, 1871 ***1823.17*** *p90*
Layston, Elizabeth; Virginia, 1732 ***1220.12*** *p489*
Layt, John; America, 1767 ***1220.12*** *p489*
Layton, Abraham; America, 1744 ***1220.12*** *p489*
Layton, Christopher; Utah, 1898 ***1211.45*** *p133*
Layton, Paul; Maryland, 1724 ***1220.12*** *p489*
Layton, Paul; Virginia, 1727 ***1220.12*** *p489*
Layton, Sarah; Barbados, 1679 ***1220.12*** *p489*
Layton, Thomas; Barbados or Jamaica, 1694 ***1220.12*** *p490*
Lazar, Moises; America, 1868 ***5475.1*** *p125*
Lazarchuck, Modest; New York, 1926 ***1173.1*** *p2*
Lazard, Leopold; London, Eng., 1867 ***5475.1*** *p124*
Lazarus, Isaac; America, 1773 ***1220.12*** *p490*
Lazell, John; America, 1773 ***1220.12*** *p490*
Lazenby, George 28; Ontario, 1871 ***1823.21*** *p198*
Lazenby, Thomas; Virginia, 1724 ***1220.12*** *p490*
Lazenby, William; America, 1772 ***1220.12*** *p490*
Lea, Edward; America, 1747 ***1220.12*** *p491*
Lea, Henry Heathcote 58; Ontario, 1871 ***1823.21*** *p198*
Lea, John; America, 1766 ***1220.12*** *p492*
Lea, Louis 21; New Orleans, 1848 ***778.6*** *p204*
Lea, Thomas; America, 1742 ***1220.12*** *p493*
Lea, William 35; Ontario, 1871 ***1823.21*** *p198*
Leach, Andrew 33; Michigan, 1880 ***4491.36*** *p13*
Leach, Edmund; America, 1755 ***1220.12*** *p493*
Leach, Elizabeth 44; Ontario, 1871 ***1823.21*** *p198*
Leach, George 26; Ontario, 1871 ***1823.21*** *p198*
Leach, George 40; Ontario, 1871 ***1823.17*** *p90*
Leach, George 20; Quebec, 1870 ***8364.32*** *p24*
Leach, James; America, 1755 ***1220.12*** *p493*
Leach, John; America, 1732 ***1220.12*** *p493*
Leach, John; Barbados or Jamaica, 1698 ***1220.12*** *p493*
Leach, John; Jamaica, 1661 ***1220.12*** *p493*
Leach, John 53; Ontario, 1871 ***1823.17*** *p90*
Leach, Joseph; Maryland, 1744 ***1220.12*** *p493*
Leach, Lawrence; America, 1743 ***1220.12*** *p493*
Leach, Paul; Massachusetts, 1751 ***1642*** *p72*
Leach, Richard; America, 1767 ***1220.12*** *p493*
Leach, Robert; Barbados, 1667 ***1220.12*** *p493*
Leach, Roger; America, 1755 ***1220.12*** *p493*
Leach, Simon; America, 1725 ***1220.12*** *p493*
Leach, Solomon; America, 1771 ***1220.12*** *p493*
Leach, Thomas 18; Quebec, 1870 ***8364.32*** *p24*
Leach, William; Marston's Wharf, 1782 ***8529.30*** *p13*
Leachford, John; America, 1765 ***1220.12*** *p490*
Leacock, David; America, 1771 ***1220.12*** *p490*
Leacock, John 57; Ontario, 1871 ***1823.17*** *p90*
Leacock, Thomas 36; Ontario, 1871 ***1823.17*** *p90*
Leacock, William 29; Ontario, 1871 ***1823.17*** *p90*
Leadbeater, Ann; Annapolis, MD, 1725 ***1220.12*** *p490*
Leadbeater, Edward; America, 1740 ***1220.12*** *p490*
Leadbeater, Henry 39; Ontario, 1871 ***1823.21*** *p198*
Leadbeater, William; America, 1739 ***1220.12*** *p490*
Leadbeter, John; America, 1769 ***1220.12*** *p490*
Leadbeter, Ralph; America, 1690 ***1220.12*** *p490*
Leader, Alice; Potomac, 1731 ***1220.12*** *p490*
Leader, James 40; Ontario, 1871 ***1823.17*** *p90*
Leader, William; America, 1677 ***1220.12*** *p490*
Leadley, George 56; Michigan, 1880 ***4491.39*** *p17*
Leadley, Matilda 50; Michigan, 1880 ***4491.39*** *p17*
Leadly, Mary 74; Michigan, 1880 ***4491.39*** *p17*
Leaeickum, T.; Louisiana, 1874 ***4981.45*** *p132*
Leahane, Abigail; New Orleans, 1851 ***7242.30*** *p148*
Leahane, John; New Orleans, 1851 ***7242.30*** *p148*
Leahey, Edward; Boston, 1834 ***3274.56*** *p72*
Leahy, Daniel 16; Quebec, 1870 ***8364.32*** *p24*
Leake, Edward 32; Ontario, 1871 ***1823.21*** *p198*
Leake, James; Annapolis, MD, 1726 ***1220.12*** *p490*
Leake, John; America, 1773 ***1220.12*** *p490*
Leaken, Thomas 30; Ontario, 1871 ***1823.21*** *p198*
Leaker, John; America, 1685 ***1220.12*** *p490*
Leaker, William 54; Ontario, 1871 ***1823.21*** *p198*
Leakey, John; Barbados, 1701 ***1220.12*** *p490*
Leaky, John; America, 1739 ***1220.12*** *p490*
Leaky, Robert; Maryland, 1671 ***1236.25*** *p46*
Lealan, James M. 40; Ontario, 1871 ***1823.17*** *p90*
Leale, Captain; San Francisco, 1800-1899 ***9228.50*** *p327*
Leaman, Robert; Virginia, 1761 ***1220.12*** *p490*
Leaman, William; Virginia, 1768 ***1220.12*** *p490*
Leamber, J.; Louisiana, 1874 ***4981.45*** *p132*
Leamon, Mary; Boston, 1749 ***1642*** *p46*
Leamon, Sarah; Boston, 1773 ***1642*** *p49*
Lean, Mary 53; Michigan, 1880 ***4491.36*** *p13*
Lean, Richard; America, 1733 ***1220.12*** *p490*
Lean, Richard L. 48; Ontario, 1871 ***1823.17*** *p90*
Lean, Thomas 49; Michigan, 1880 ***4491.36*** *p13*
Leane, Robert; Virginia, 1718 ***1220.12*** *p490*
Leanhart, Peter; Ohio, 1809-1852 ***4511.35*** *p30*
Leaper, Courtland 88; Ontario, 1871 ***1823.17*** *p90*
Leaper, Rachel 75; Ontario, 1871 ***1823.17*** *p90*
Lear, Edward 57; Ontario, 1871 ***1823.21*** *p198*
Lear, Joseph; America, 1737 ***1220.12*** *p490*
Lear, Mary; Philadelphia, 1858 ***8513.31*** *p304*
Lear, William; America, 1729 ***1220.12*** *p490*
Leard, Alden Warren; Iowa, 1921 ***1211.15*** *p16*
Leardon, Elizer; New England, 1745 ***1642*** *p28*

Leare, Elisabeth 19; America, 1844 ***778.6*** *p204*
Leare, Jacob 28; America, 1844 ***778.6*** *p204*
Learman, Isabella; Boston, 1766 ***1642*** *p37*
Learmouth, Alex. James; Buffalo, NY, 1883-1884 ***9228.50*** *p365*
*Wife:*Louisa Jane Nile
Learmouth, Louisa Jane Nile *SEE* Learmouth, Alex. James
Learock, John; Boston, 1734-1766 ***9228.50*** *p325*
Learst, Rebecca 74; Ontario, 1871 ***1823.17*** *p90*
Leary, Cornelius; America, 1774 ***1220.12*** *p490*
Leary, Dennis 21; St. Johns, N.F., 1811 ***1053.20*** *p21*
Leary, Jas 23; St. Johns, N.F., 1811 ***1053.20*** *p21*
Leary, Jeremy; New England, 1745 ***1642*** *p28*
Leary, Jerimiah 25; Ontario, 1871 ***1823.21*** *p198*
Leary, John; America, 1772 ***1220.12*** *p490*
Leary, John; Boston, 1772 ***1642*** *p49*
Leary, John; New Orleans, 1850 ***7242.30*** *p148*
Leary, John; Newfoundland, 1814 ***3476.10*** *p54*
Leary, Margaret; America, 1762 ***1220.12*** *p490*
Leary, Michael; New Orleans, 1851 ***7242.30*** *p148*
Leary, Patrick; Toronto, 1844 ***2910.35*** *p114*
Leary, Philip; Toronto, 1844 ***2910.35*** *p112*
Leary, Tim 22; St. Johns, N.F., 1811 ***1053.20*** *p21*
Leary, Timothy 65; Ontario, 1871 ***1823.21*** *p198*
Leasa, Anna; Wisconsin, 1899 ***6795.8*** *p74*
Lease, John; America, 1685 ***1220.12*** *p494*
Lease, John 55; Ontario, 1871 ***1823.21*** *p198*
Leash, James 47; Ontario, 1871 ***1823.17*** *p90*
Leaston, Mary 20; Ontario, 1871 ***1823.21*** *p198*
Leath, John; America, 1724 ***1220.12*** *p490*
Leather, John; Potomac, 1731 ***1220.12*** *p490*
Leatherby, Richard; America, 1764 ***1220.12*** *p490*
Leatherman, Melchior; Ohio, 1809-1852 ***4511.35*** *p30*
Leatherstone, Hannah; America, 1756 ***1220.12*** *p490*
Leathorn, James; America, 1733 ***1220.12*** *p490*
Leathorn, Robert 42; Ontario, 1871 ***1823.21*** *p198*
Leatro, Bertie 17; Quebec, 1870 ***8364.32*** *p24*
Leaver, Benjamin; America, 1755 ***1220.12*** *p496*
Leavers, Patience; America, 1750 ***1220.12*** *p490*
Leavitt, Darius *SEE* Leavitt, Seth
Leavitt, Joanna Kimball *SEE* Leavitt, Seth
Leavitt, John True Lougee *SEE* Leavitt, Seth
Leavitt, Joseph; Quebec, 1791-1878 ***9228.50*** *p407*
*Wife:*Mary Greeley Smith
*Child:*Noah Smith
Leavitt, Julia Ann *SEE* Leavitt, Seth
Leavitt, Lucinda *SEE* Leavitt, Seth
Leavitt, Mary Greeley Smith *SEE* Leavitt, Joseph
Leavitt, Noah Smith *SEE* Leavitt, Joseph
Leavitt, Samuel *SEE* Leavitt, Seth
Leavitt, Seth; Quebec, 1823-1841 ***9228.50*** *p407*
*Wife:*Joanna Kimball
*Child:*Lucinda
*Child:*Julia Ann
*Child:*John True Lougee
*Child:*Samuel
*Child:*Darius
Leavy, Michael; Boston, 1840 ***3274.55*** *p44*
Leay, Joseph; America, 1769 ***1220.12*** *p492*
Leay, Robert W. 36; Ontario, 1871 ***1823.17*** *p90*
LeBaillif, . . .; Quebec, 1632 ***9221.17*** *p20*
Le Ballister, Joseph; Massachusetts, 1788-1816 ***9228.50*** *p328*
Le Bannister, Joseph; Massachusetts, 1788-1816 ***9228.50*** *p328*
Lebarbier, Germain; Quebec, 1639 ***9221.17*** *p90*
Lebarbier, Marie 18; Quebec, 1637 ***9221.17*** *p71*
Lebarge, Joseph 45; Port uncertain, 1845 ***778.6*** *p204*
Le Baron, Francis; Plymouth, MA, 1694 ***1642*** *p55*
Lebaron, Jean 33; Montreal, 1653 ***9221.17*** *p281*
Lebaron, Louis 9 *SEE* Lebaron, Louise Grisard
Lebaron, Louise 27; Montreal, 1660 ***9221.17*** *p440*
*Son:*Louis 9
Lebart, Valery 19; New Orleans, 1846 ***778.6*** *p204*
Lebart, Walter 16; Ontario, 1871 ***1823.21*** *p198*
Le Bas, Anne; Utah, 1830-1870 ***9228.50*** *p328*
*Sister:*Elizabeth
Le Bas, Elizabeth *SEE* Le Bas, Anne
Le Bas, James; South Carolina, 1683 ***9228.50*** *p328*
Lebas, Vincent; Quebec, 1650 ***9221.17*** *p227*
Lebasque, Jean 21; Quebec, 1656 ***9221.17*** *p339*
Lebatz, Valery 19; New Orleans, 1846 ***778.6*** *p204*
Lebeau, Guillaume; Montreal, 1643 ***9221.17*** *p137*
Lebeau, Michael; Ohio, 1809-1852 ***4511.35*** *p30*
Lebeauceron, Nicolas 21; Montreal, 1653 ***9221.17*** *p297*
Lebecheur, Louis 24; Quebec, 1653 ***9221.17*** *p276*
Lebeck, Anthony; New Jersey, 1777 ***8529.30*** *p6*
Lebedelle, Hubert; Detroit, 1870 ***1494.20*** *p12*
Lebel, Charles 29; Port uncertain, 1847 ***778.6*** *p204*
Lebel, Nicolas 24; Quebec, 1656 ***9221.17*** *p339*
Lebenbruck, Nikolaus; America, 1843 ***5475.1*** *p358*
Leber, Anne 4 *SEE* Leber, Francois
Leber, Francois 34; Montreal, 1660 ***9221.17*** *p441*
*Daughter:*Anne 4
*Sister:*Marie 17
Leber, Fredericka Reitz *SEE* Leber, Friedrich
Leber, Friedrich; Philadelphia, 1852 ***8513.31*** *p322*
*Wife:*Fredericka Reitz
*Son:*Karl Friedrich
Leber, Jacques; Quebec, 1657 ***2314.30*** *p167*
Leber, Jacques; Quebec, 1696 ***2314.30*** *p187*
Leber, Jacques 16; Quebec, 1649 ***9221.17*** *p215*
Leber, Karl Friedrich *SEE* Leber, Friedrich
Leber, Marie 17 *SEE* Leber, Francois
Lebera, Laurent 21; America, 1847 ***778.6*** *p204*
Lebey, Jean; Quebec, 1655 ***9221.17*** *p320*
Lebicheux, Louis 24; Quebec, 1653 ***9221.17*** *p276*
Le Blam, Philip; Boston, 1715 ***9228.50*** *p329*
Le Blanc, Abraham *SEE* Le Blanc, Philip
Leblanc, Agnaise 30; America, 1848 ***778.6*** *p204*
Leblanc, Anne; Quebec, 1672 ***4514.3*** *p334*
Leblanc, Elisabeth; Nova Scotia, 1753 ***3051*** *p113*
Leblanc, Euseb 22; Louisiana, 1847 ***778.6*** *p204*
Leblanc, Jean 15; Montreal, 1659 ***9221.17*** *p423*
Leblanc, Jean 30; Quebec, 1643 ***9221.17*** *p131*
Leblanc, Jeanne; Quebec, 1669 ***4514.3*** *p371*
Le Blanc, John *SEE* Le Blanc, Philip
Le Blanc, John *SEE* Le Blanc, Philip
Leblanc, Joseph; Nova Scotia, 1753 ***3051*** *p112*
LeBlanc, Jules 25; America, 1843 ***778.6*** *p204*
Leblanc, Leonard 24; Quebec, 1650 ***9221.17*** *p227*
Leblanc, Nicolas 24; Quebec, 1661 ***9221.17*** *p460*
Le Blanc, Peter; Maine, n.d. ***9228.50*** *p329*
Le Blanc, Philip; Boston, 1715 ***9228.50*** *p329*
Le Blanc, Philip; Massachusetts, 1700 ***9228.50*** *p653*
*Relative:*Zachariah
*Relative:*Abraham
*Relative:*John
Le Blanc, Philip; Salem, MA, 1678 ***9228.50*** *p329*
*Relative:*Zachariah
*Relative:*John
Le Blanc, Philip; Salem, MA, 1720 ***9228.50*** *p653*
Leblanc, Regis 19; Ohio, 1880 ***4879.40*** *p258*
Leblanc, Whilheim 25; America, 1848 ***778.6*** *p204*
Le Blanc, Zachariah *SEE* Le Blanc, Philip
Le Blanc, Zachariah *SEE* Le Blanc, Philip
Le Blancq, . . .; Nova Scotia, n.d. ***9228.50*** *p329*
Le Blant, Claude; Nova Scotia, 1753 ***3051*** *p112*
*Wife:*Dorothee Richard
Le Blant, Dorothee Richard *SEE* Le Blant, Claude
Le Blond, . . .; Massachusetts, 1600-1699 ***9228.50*** *p329*
Le Blond, . . .; Pennsylvania, 1700-1799 ***9228.50*** *p329*
LeBlond, Francis 40; Ohio, 1880 ***4879.40*** *p257*
Leblond, Nicolas 17; Quebec, 1654 ***9221.17*** *p311*
Leblonde, Clotilda 5; Texas, 1843 ***778.6*** *p204*
Leblonde, Clotilda 38; Texas, 1843 ***778.6*** *p204*
Leblonde, Henrietta 11; Texas, 1843 ***778.6*** *p204*
Leblonde, Louis 35; Texas, 1843 ***778.6*** *p204*
LeBlousart DuPlessis, Francois 28; Quebec, 1649 ***9221.17*** *p215*
Leboeuf, Marguerite; Canada, 1658 ***1142.10*** *p128*
Leboeuf, Marguerite 19; Quebec, 1658 ***9221.17*** *p383*
Leboheme, Antoine 44; Montreal, 1644 ***9221.17*** *p147*
*Son:*Louis 12
Leboheme, Jean; Quebec, 1656 ***9221.17*** *p340*
*Sister:*Jeanne
Leboheme, Jeanne *SEE* Leboheme, Jean
Leboheme, Louis 12 *SEE* Leboheme, Antoine
Lebolt, Jean 26; Port uncertain, 1841 ***778.6*** *p204*
Lebon, Robert; Quebec, 1633 ***9221.17*** *p29*
Lebon De Champfleury, Marie; Quebec, 1665 ***4514.3*** *p334*
Lebondidier, Leon 36; America, 1843 ***778.6*** *p204*
Leborgne, Francoise 24; Quebec, 1661 ***9221.17*** *p457*
Le Bosquet, Nicholas 49; North Carolina, 1702 ***9228.50*** *p257*
Leboucher, Denis; Quebec, 1638 ***9221.17*** *p78*
Leboucher, Victor 16; Louisiana, 1848 ***778.6*** *p204*
Leboue, Anne 24; Quebec, 1644 ***9221.17*** *p138*
Leboulanger, Pierre 19; Montreal, 1662 ***9221.17*** *p498*
Leboulanger, Pierre 20; Quebec, 1654 ***9221.17*** *p311*
Leboule, Angelique 3; America, 1843 ***778.6*** *p204*
Leboule, Flumbert 7; America, 1843 ***778.6*** *p204*
Leboule, Jean 11; America, 1843 ***778.6*** *p204*
Leboule, Jean 43; America, 1843 ***778.6*** *p204*
Leboule, Marie 12; America, 1843 ***778.6*** *p205*
Leboule, Marie 43; America, 1843 ***778.6*** *p204*
Leboule, Pierre 1; America, 1843 ***778.6*** *p205*
Lebourdellay, Jean 23; Quebec, 1657 ***9221.17*** *p353*
Le Bourdon, . . .; Boston, 1769 ***9228.50*** *p5*
Le Bourdon, Charles; Boston, 1769 ***9228.50*** *p48*
Le Bourdon, Charles *SEE* Le Bourdon, Wm.
LeBourdon, Edward; Nantucket, MA, 1782-1807 ***9228.50*** *p123*
Le Bourdon, William; Boston, 1769 ***9228.50*** *p48*
Le Bourdon, William; Salem, MA, 1783 ***9228.50*** *p122*
Le Bourdon, Wm.; Boston, 1769 ***9228.50*** *p329*
*Relative:*Charles
Le Bourdon, Wm.; New England, 1775-1807 ***9228.50*** *p122*
Le Bourdon Family ; Massachusetts, n.d. ***9228.50*** *p126*
Lebourguignon, Jean 22; Montreal, 1652 ***9221.17*** *p268*
Le Bourveau, Colonel; America, 1776 ***9228.50*** *p329*
Lebouteleux, Jean 22; Quebec, 1660 ***9221.17*** *p437*
*Wife:*Marie Blanquet 29
Lebouteleux, Marie Blanquet 29 *SEE* Lebouteleux, Jean
Le Boutillier, Mrs.; New York, NY, 1847 ***9228.50*** *p334*
Le Boutillier, Alfred *SEE* Le Boutillier, Hugh
Le Boutillier, Ann; Cincinnati, 1850 ***9228.50*** *p333*
Le Boutillier, Ann Jane *SEE* Le Boutillier, Hugh
Le Boutillier, Anne Le Sueur *SEE* Le Boutillier, Charles
Le Boutillier, Charles; Cincinnati, 1850 ***9228.50*** *p333*
Le Boutillier, Charles *SEE* Le Boutillier, Charles
Le Boutillier, Charles; Iowa, 1851 ***9228.50*** *p330*
*Wife:*Anne Le Sueur
*Child:*Charles
*Child:*Mary
*Child:*Elizabeth
*Child:*Philip
*Child:*Rachel
*Child:*John
*Child:*Esther
Le Boutillier, Charles; Montreal, 1913 ***9228.50*** *p334*
*Wife:*Florence Renouf
*Child:*Florence
Le Boutillier, Charles C.; Philadelphia, 1844 ***9228.50*** *p334*
Le Boutillier, Edward *SEE* Le Boutillier, Philip Henry
Le Boutillier, Elias *SEE* Le Boutillier, Heloise Jane
Le Boutillier, Elizabeth 42; Cincinnati, 1850 ***9228.50*** *p333*
Le Boutillier, Elizabeth *SEE* Le Boutillier, Charles
Le Boutillier, Elizabeth; Iowa, 1854 ***9228.50*** *p92*
Le Boutillier, Emma-Jan; Texas, 1844-1878 ***9228.50*** *p334*
Le Boutillier, Ernest; Minnesota, 1880-1950 ***9228.50*** *p334*
Le Boutillier, Esther *SEE* Le Boutillier, Charles
LeBoutillier, Florence; Maine, 1931 ***9228.50*** *p334*
Le Boutillier, Florence *SEE* Le Boutillier, Charles
Le Boutillier, Florence Renouf *SEE* Le Boutillier, Charles
Le Boutillier, George; Cincinnati, 1783-1838 ***9228.50*** *p332*
Le Boutillier, Georgina *SEE* Le Boutillier, Hugh
Le Boutillier, Heloise Jane; Iowa, 1897 ***9228.50*** *p330*
*Son:*Elias
Le Boutillier, Hugh; Virginia, 1911-1920 ***9228.50*** *p330*
*Child:*Georgina
*Wife:*Margaret Boyle Beattie
*Child:*Ann Jane
*Child:*Alfred
Le Boutillier, James; Cincinnati, 1827 ***9228.50*** *p333*
*Wife:*Mary Gallier
Le Boutillier, James; Cincinnati, 1850 ***9228.50*** *p333*
Le Boutillier, Jane; Texas, 1860-1869 ***9228.50*** *p334*
LeBoutillier, Jane Elizabeth; Iowa, 1870 ***9228.50*** *p330*
*Son:*Elias, Jr.
Le Boutillier, Jane Elizabeth Le Boutillier Le Sueur *SEE* Le Boutillier, Jean
Le Boutillier, Jean; Iowa, 1870 ***9228.50*** *p330*
*Wife:*Jane Elizabeth Le Boutillier Le Sueur
With stepchild
Le Boutillier, John *SEE* Le Boutillier, Charles
Le Boutillier, John; South Carolina, 1678 ***9228.50*** *p125*
Le Boutillier, Margaret; Cincinnati, 1850 ***9228.50*** *p333*
Le Boutillier, Margaret Boyle Beattie *SEE* Le Boutillier, Hugh
Le Boutillier, Mary Gallier *SEE* Le Boutillier, James
Le Boutillier, Mary; Cincinnati, 1850 ***9228.50*** *p333*
Le Boutillier, Mary *SEE* Le Boutillier, Charles
Le Boutillier, Mary; Salem, MA, 1675 ***9228.50*** *p149*
Le Boutillier, Philip; Honolulu, 1840-1870 ***9228.50*** *p332*
Le Boutillier, Philip *SEE* Le Boutillier, Charles
Le Boutillier, Philip Henry; Minneapolis, 1891-1903 ***9228.50*** *p333*
*Child:*Edward
*Child:*Thomas Henry
Le Boutillier, Philip Henry; Quebec, 1891-1903 ***9228.50*** *p333*
Le Boutillier, Rachel 7 *SEE* Le Boutillier, Charles
Le Boutillier, Thomas; Maine, 1731 ***9228.50*** *p491*
Le Boutillier, Thomas C.; Montreal, 1880-1950 ***9228.50*** *p334*
Le Boutillier, Thomas Henry *SEE* Le Boutillier, Philip Henry
Le Boutillier Family ; Iowa, 1860 ***9228.50*** *p399*
Le Boutillier Family ; New Jersey, n.d. ***9228.50*** *p334*

264 *FOR A COMPLETE EXPLANATION OF ENTRY, SEE "HOW TO READ A CITATION" SECTION*

Le Boutillier Family ; Pennsylvania, 1800-1899 ***9228.50*** *p334*
Lebret, Elisabeth; Quebec, 1654 ***9221.17*** *p314*
Lebret, Mathurin; Quebec, 1644 ***9221.17*** *p143*
Le Breton, . . .; Louisiana, 1820 ***9228.50*** *p335*
Le Breton, . . .; Mississippi, 1820 ***9228.50*** *p335*
Le Breton, . . .; Quebec, 1534 ***9228.50*** *p3*
Le Breton, Mr.; New England, 1675-1676 ***9228.50*** *p268*
Le Breton, Aime; New York, 1820 ***9228.50*** *p335*
Le Breton, Aime; Philadelphia, 1798 ***9228.50*** *p335*
Le Breton, Aime; Rhode Island, 1686 ***9228.50*** *p335*
Le Breton, Charles William; Pittsburgh, 1903 ***9228.50*** *p334*
Le Breton, Clement; Brazil, 1800-1899 ***9228.50*** *p335*
Lebreton, Georges 20; Quebec, 1651 ***9221.17*** *p238*
Le Breton, James P.; New York, 1803 ***9228.50*** *p335*
Lebreton, Jean 23; Quebec, 1657 ***9221.17*** *p353*
Le Breton, John; Virginia, 1664 ***9228.50*** *p335*
Lebreton, Louis; Quebec, 1643 ***9221.17*** *p134*
Lebreton, Mathieu; Quebec, 1657 ***9221.17*** *p361*
Le Breton, Peter; Salem, MA, 1677 ***9228.50*** *p135*
Le Breton, Philip; FalmoutH ME, 1700-1740 ***9228.50*** *p335*
Le Breton, Thomas; Washington, D.C., 1900 ***9228.50*** *p335*
Le Breton Family ; Massachusetts, 1790 ***9228.50*** *p334*
Le Breton Family ; Ontario, n.d. ***9228.50*** *p131*
Le Bretton Family ; Massachusetts, 1790 ***9228.50*** *p334*
Lebreuil, Louise-Marie-Therese 23; Montreal, 1659 ***9221.17*** *p423*
Le Brocq, George; Boston, 1727 ***9228.50*** *p335*
Le Brocq, John; New York, 1783-1805 ***9228.50*** *p137*
Le Brocq, Marie; New England, 1698 ***9228.50*** *p335*
Le Brocq, Martha; Beverly, MA, 1698 ***9228.50*** *p159*
Le Brocq, Martha; Beverly, MA, 1698 ***9228.50*** *p159*
Le Brocq, Martha; Beverly, MA, 1698 ***9228.50*** *p159*
Le Brocq, Martha; Beverly, MA, 1698 ***9228.50*** *p159*
Le Brocq, Martha; Beverly, MA, 1698 ***9228.50*** *p159*
Le Brocq, Martha; Beverly, MA, 1698 ***9228.50*** *p159*
Le Brocq, Martha; Beverly, MA, 1698 ***9228.50*** *p159*
Le Brocq, Martha; Beverly, MA, 1698 ***9228.50*** *p335*
Le Brocq, Martha; Massachusetts, 1743 ***9228.50*** *p23*
LeBrocq, Martha; Massachusetts, 1743 ***9228.50*** *p23*
Le Brocq, Pierre; Newport, RI, 1711 ***9228.50*** *p335*
Lebrok, John; Boston, 1760-1769 ***9228.50*** *p335*
Lebroth, Ferdinand 25; Mississippi, 1845-1846 ***778.6*** *p205*
Lebroth, Gertrude 28; Mississippi, 1845-1846 ***778.6*** *p205*
Le Brun, . . .; California, 1890 ***9228.50*** *p473*
Le Brun, Child; Quebec, 1826-1900 ***9228.50*** *p336*
With 2 siblings
Le Brun, Mr.; Minnesota, 1857 ***9228.50*** *p336*
With wife
Lebrun, Alfred 7; Mississippi, 1846 ***778.6*** *p205*
Le Brun, Daniel *SEE* Le Brun, John
Lebrun, Daniel; Quebec, 1641 ***9221.17*** *p105*
Le Brun, Edouard J.; Wisconsin, 1854-1858 ***1495.20*** *p50*
Le Brun, Elizabeth; Minnesota, 1880 ***9228.50*** *p139*
Lebrun, Gilbert 25; Port uncertain, 1843 ***778.6*** *p205*
Le Brun, Isabella B. *SEE* Le Brun, John
Le Brun, Jenny; St. Louis, 1854 ***9228.50*** *p421*
*Child:*Mary Elizabeth
*Child:*Jane
Le Brun, John; Minnesota, 1821-1900 ***9228.50*** *p336*
*Wife:*Susan Sohier
Le Brun, John; Minnesota, 1847-1900 ***9228.50*** *p139*
*Wife:*Susan Sohier
*Child:*Isabella B.
Le Brun, John; Minnesota, 1862 ***9228.50*** *p336*
*Brother:*Peter
Le Brun, John; Portsmouth, NH, 1698 ***9228.50*** *p17A*
*Brother:*Daniel
Le Brun, John; Salem, MA, 1660 ***9228.50*** *p138*
Lebrun, Joseph 28; New Orleans, 1845 ***778.6*** *p205*
Lebrun, Marie; Quebec, 1667 ***4514.3*** *p334*
Le Brun, Marie Laure Catherine; Wisconsin, 1854-1858 ***1495.20*** *p49*
Le Brun, Moses; New England, 1686 ***9228.50*** *p336*
Le Brun, Peter; Minnesota, 1830-1862 ***9228.50*** *p139*
Le Brun, Peter *SEE* Le Brun, John
Lebrun, Pierre 28; Mississippi, 1846 ***778.6*** *p205*
Lebrun, Remy 30; New Orleans, 1845 ***778.6*** *p205*
Le Brun, Susan; Minnesota, 1819-1900 ***9228.50*** *p336*
Le Brun, Susan Sohier *SEE* Le Brun, John
Le Brun, Susan Sohier *SEE* Le Brun, John
Le Brun, Susan 61; Minnesota, 1880 ***9228.50*** *p336*
Lebugeux, Louis; Quebec, 1651 ***9221.17*** *p245*
Lebugle, Anne 35; Quebec, 1640 ***9221.17*** *p94*
Lebzelter, Franz; Venezuela, 1529 ***3899.5*** *p538*
Le Cain, . . .; New England, n.d. ***9228.50*** *p151*
Lecamus, Elisabeth 14; Montreal, 1659 ***9221.17*** *p423*
Lecapitaine, Constant; Wisconsin, 1856 ***1494.20*** *p13*
Le Cappelain, Elizabeth Irene *SEE* Le Cappelain, Richard Samuel
Le Cappelain, George; Ontario, 1880 ***9228.50*** *p337*
Le Cappelain, Linda Rose *SEE* Le Cappelain, Richard Samuel
Le Cappelain, Mary Jean Quinn *SEE* Le Cappelain, Richard Samuel
Le Cappelain, Richard Samuel; New York, 1929-1957 ***9228.50*** *p337*
*Wife:*Mary Jean Quinn
*Child:*Elizabeth Irene
*Child:*Linda Rose
Lecarme, Rene; Montreal, 1660 ***9221.17*** *p443*
Le Caudey, Martha Le Brocq *SEE* Le Caudey, Philip
Le Caudey, Martha Le Brocq *SEE* Le Caudey, Philippe
Le Caudey, Martha LeBrocq *SEE* Le Caudey, Philip
Le Caudey, Philip; Beverly, MA, 1698 ***9228.50*** *p159*
*Wife:*Martha Le Brocq
Le Caudey, Philip; Beverly, MA, 1698 ***9228.50*** *p335*
*Wife:*Martha LeBrocq
Le Caudey, Philip, Family; America, 1600-1699 ***9228.50*** *p337*
Le Caudey, Philippe; Massachusetts, 1743 ***9228.50*** *p23*
*Wife:*Martha Le Brocq
LeCaux, Eliz; Boston, 1716 ***9228.50*** *p273*
Le Caux, John; Boston, 1700-1799 ***9228.50*** *p337*
Le Caux, Peter; Portsmouth, NH, 1735 ***9228.50*** *p170*
Lecelier, Robert; Quebec, 1659 ***9221.17*** *p414*
Lech, Antoni; New York, NY, 1912 ***8355.1*** *p16*
Lech, Philip; Ohio, 1840-1897 ***8365.35*** *p17*
Lechelt, Samuel; Wisconsin, 1886 ***6795.8*** *p92*
Le Cheminant, Agnes *SEE* Le Cheminant, Sara Farr
Le Cheminant, Edmond *SEE* Le Cheminant, Sara Farr
Le Cheminant, Elizabeth *SEE* Le Cheminant, Sara Farr
Le Cheminant, John; Massachusetts, 1900-1983 ***9228.50*** *p338*
Le Cheminant, Osmond *SEE* Le Cheminant, Sara Farr
Le Cheminant, Peter *SEE* Le Cheminant, Sara Farr
Le Cheminant, Robert; Utah, 1850-1859 ***9228.50*** *p338*
Le Cheminant, Sara; New Orleans, 1853-1855 ***9228.50*** *p337*
*Child:*Elizabeth
*Child:*Peter
*Child:*Osmond
*Child:*Edmond
*Child:*Agnes
Lechevalier, Anne; Quebec, 1659 ***9221.17*** *p404*
Lechevalier, Catherine 15; Quebec, 1639 ***9221.17*** *p90*
Lechevalier, Pierre 19; Montreal, 1660 ***9221.17*** *p442*
Leck, Thomas; America, 1752 ***1220.12*** *p491*
Leckeblen, Francois 29; America, 1847 ***778.6*** *p205*
Leckeblen, Maria 39; America, 1847 ***778.6*** *p205*
Leckie, John 58; Ontario, 1871 ***1823.17*** *p90*
Leckie, John 92; Ontario, 1871 ***1823.17*** *p90*
Leckie, Stewart; Washington, 1882 ***2770.40*** *p135*
Leclair, Francois 30; New Orleans, 1847 ***778.6*** *p205*
Leclaire, L. Charles 31; Mississippi, 1846 ***778.6*** *p205*
LeClaire, Madalaine 53; Mississippi, 1846 ***778.6*** *p205*
Leclare, Jacob 55; Ontario, 1871 ***1823.21*** *p198*
Le Clerc, . . .; Boston, 1970-1979 ***9228.50*** *p338*
Leclerc, Mr. 18; America, 1841 ***778.6*** *p205*
Leclerc, Adriane 13; Quebec, 1661 ***9221.17*** *p461*
Leclerc, Andre; Quebec, 1647 ***9221.17*** *p183*
Leclerc, Anne; Quebec, 1668 ***4514.3*** *p334*
Leclerc, Baroche 30; Texas, 1848 ***778.6*** *p205*
Leclerc, Denise; Quebec, 1669 ***4514.3*** *p335*
Leclerc, Florent 38; Quebec, 1657 ***9221.17*** *p361*
Leclerc, Francoise; Quebec, 1668 ***4514.3*** *p335*
Leclerc, Genevieve; Quebec, 1671 ***4514.3*** *p335*
Leclerc, Jean 22; Quebec, 1660 ***9221.17*** *p437*
*Wife:*Marie Blanquet 29
Leclerc, Marguerite; Quebec, 1600-1668 ***4514.3*** *p335*
Leclerc, Marguerite; Quebec, 1665 ***4514.3*** *p335*
Leclerc, Marguerite 21; Quebec, 1661 ***9221.17*** *p461*
Leclerc, Marie 23; Quebec, 1661 ***9221.17*** *p461*
Leclerc, Marie Blanquet 29 *SEE* Leclerc, Jean
Leclerc, Pettro 50; America, 1843 ***778.6*** *p205*
Leclerc DeLaVigne, Pierre; Quebec, 1644 ***9221.17*** *p143*
Leclerc DeNarbonne, Leonard; Quebec, 1645 ***9221.17*** *p154*
Le Clercq, George; Utah, 1863 ***9228.50*** *p338*
Le Clercq, Henrietta; Utah, 1862 ***9228.50*** *p338*
*Relative:*Jane
Le Clercq, Jane *SEE* Le Clercq, Mary
Le Clercq, Jane *SEE* Le Clercq, Henrietta
Le Clercq, Mary; Utah, 1854 ***9228.50*** *p338*
*Relative:*Jane
Leclere, Joseph; Illinois, 1863 ***6079.1*** *p8*
Leclere, Nicholas; Illinois, 1852 ***6079.1*** *p8*
Le Cocq, Mr.; New Hampshire, 1697 ***9228.50*** *p338*
Lecocq, Anne-Joseph; Wisconsin, 1856 ***1495.20*** *p12*
Lecocq, Jean Baptiste; Wisconsin, 1854-1858 ***1495.20*** *p66*
Le Cocq, Thomas; Boston, 1740 ***9228.50*** *p159*
Le Cocq, Wm.; New England, 1688 ***9228.50*** *p338*
Le Cocque, Philip; Prince Edward Island, 1770-1799 ***9228.50*** *p338*
Le Cody, Martha Le Brocq *SEE* Le Cody, Philip
Le Cody, Philip; Beverly, MA, 1698 ***9228.50*** *p159*
*Wife:*Martha Le Brocq
Lecointe, Jeanne; Quebec, 1671 ***4514.3*** *p362*
LeCointre, Anne 28; Quebec, 1639 ***9221.17*** *p84*
Le Coke, Mr.; New Hampshire, 1697 ***9228.50*** *p338*
Lecol, Jean-Baptiste 29; New Orleans, 1843 ***778.6*** *p205*
Lecombe, Miotte; Quebec, 1644 ***9221.17*** *p141*
Lecombe, Miotte; Quebec, 1644 ***9221.17*** *p141*
Lecombe, Miotte; Quebec, 1644 ***9221.17*** *p141*
Lecomte, Isaac; Quebec, 1634 ***9221.17*** *p38*
Lecomte, Jean 21; Montreal, 1653 ***9221.17*** *p295*
Lecomte, Jean 27; Montreal, 1658 ***9221.17*** *p390*
Lecomte, Jeanne; Quebec, 1670 ***4514.3*** *p371*
Lecomte, Jeanne; Quebec, 1671 ***4514.3*** *p335*
Lecomte, Louis; Quebec, 1652 ***9221.17*** *p261*
Lecomte, Marguerite; Quebec, 1673 ***4514.3*** *p335*
Lecomte, Marie; Quebec, 1672 ***4514.3*** *p335*
Lecomte, Michel; Montreal, 1653 ***9221.17*** *p295*
Lecomte, Suzanne; Quebec, 1665 ***4514.3*** *p335*
Le Comte de Lusy, Auguste; Galveston, TX, 1844 ***3967.10*** *p375*
Lecondreors, Franz; Valdivia, Chile, 1851 ***1192.4*** *p50*
Le Conte, Clara Elizabeth; Virginia, 1910-1930 ***9228.50*** *p338*
Leconte, Elisabeth; Quebec, 1666 ***4514.3*** *p336*
Le Conte, Harold Benj.; America, 1876-1910 ***9228.50*** *p338*
Lecoq, Charles 23; Missouri, 1848 ***778.6*** *p205*
Lecoq, Jeanne; Quebec, 1670 ***4514.3*** *p336*
Lecoq, Robert; Quebec, 1633 ***9221.17*** *p29*
Lecordier, Michel; Quebec, 1653 ***9221.17*** *p276*
Lecordier, Pierre; Quebec, 1659 ***9221.17*** *p405*
Le Cornee Family ; Port uncertain, 1700-1789 ***9228.50*** *p339*
Le Cornu, Francis; Quebec, 1881 ***9228.50*** *p340*
Le Cornu, John; Iowa, 1835-1865 ***9228.50*** *p339*
Le Cornu, John; Utah, 1823-1893 ***9228.50*** *p339*
*Wife:*Mary Renouf
*Daughter:*Mary
Le Cornu, John Alexander; Kentucky, 1824-1845 ***9228.50*** *p339*
Le Cornu, Mary; America, 1850 ***9228.50*** *p311*
Le Cornu, Mary *SEE* Le Cornu, John
Le Cornu, Mary Renouf *SEE* Le Cornu, John
Le Cornu, Mary Ann; Michigan, n.d. ***9228.50*** *p289*
Le Cornu, Mary Ann; Quebec, n.d. ***9228.50*** *p289*
Le Cornu, Philip 33; Kansas, 1870-1871 ***9228.50*** *p339*
Le Cornue, Ann *SEE* Le Cornue, Peter
Le Cornue, Frank *SEE* Le Cornue, Peter
Le Cornue, Mary Ann Hoyles *SEE* Le Cornue, Peter
Le Cornue, Peter; Michigan, 1860 ***9228.50*** *p339*
*Wife:*Mary Ann Hoyles
*Child:*Ann
*Child:*Frank
L'Ecossais, Abraham; Quebec, 1619 ***9221.17*** *p24*
*Wife:*Marguerite Langlois
L'Ecossais, Marguerite Langlois *SEE* L'Ecossais, Abraham
Le Count, David; Annapolis, MD, 1725 ***1220.12*** *p491*
Lecourt, Jean 30; Quebec, 1643 ***9221.17*** *p131*
Lecourt, Michel 16; Quebec, 1655 ***9221.17*** *p326*
Lecoustre, Catherine 31; Quebec, 1657 ***9221.17*** *p350*
Lecoustre, Claude; Quebec, 1638 ***9221.17*** *p78*
Lecousturier, Hugues 23; Quebec, 1653 ***9221.17*** *p276*
Le Couteur, . . .; Massachusetts, 1790 ***9228.50*** *p171*
Le Couteur, Edward; Salem, MA, 1668 ***9228.50*** *p169*
Le Couteur, Edward; Salem, MA, 1668 ***9228.50*** *p340*
LeCouteur, George; New York, NY, 1897 ***9228.50*** *p446*
With father
Le Couteur, John; Boston, 1700-1713 ***9228.50*** *p340*
Le Couteur, John; Boston, 1707 ***9228.50*** *p424*
Lecoutiux, Felix Clement; Illinois, 1856 ***6079.1*** *p8*
Lecoutre, Louise; Quebec, 1665 ***4514.3*** *p336*
Le Cras, John; Boston, 1716 ***9228.50*** *p342*
Le Cras, John; Boston, 1760-1769 ***9228.50*** *p342*
Le Cras, Philip; Massachusetts, 1700-1766 ***9228.50*** *p342*
Le Cras, Wm.; Marblehead, MA, 1728 ***9228.50*** *p340*
Le Cras, Wm.; Marblehead, MA, 1819 ***9228.50*** *p171*
Le Craw, Peter B.; Brazil, 1750-1822 ***9228.50*** *p342*
Le Craw, Peter B.; New York, NY, 1822 ***9228.50*** *p342*
Le Craw, Susan; North America, 1711 ***9228.50*** *p366*
Le Craw, Wm.; Marblehead, MA, 1728 ***9228.50*** *p340*
Le Craw, Wm.; Marblehead, MA, 1819 ***9228.50*** *p171*
Le Croix, Abraham; Marblehead, MA, 1700 ***9228.50*** *p170*
Le Croix, Wm.; Marblehead, MA, 1819 ***9228.50*** *p171*
Le Cross, John; Marblehead, MA, 1700-1741 ***9228.50*** *p170*

Le Curnah, Catherine; Maine, 1680 ***9228.50*** *p339*
Ledafleur, Mr. 21; New Orleans, 1841 ***778.6*** *p205*
Ledbetter, Eliza 43; Ontario, 1871 ***1823.21*** *p198*
Ledell, Charles Alfred 41; Ontario, 1871 ***1823.21*** *p198*
Ledenicq, Jean; Quebec, 1644 ***9221.17*** *p143*
Ledepensier, Nicolas; Quebec, 1647 ***9221.17*** *p183*
Leder, Bertha; New York, 1859 ***358.56*** *p100*
Leder, John; Illinois, 1855 ***6079.1*** *p8*
Lederle, Anthony; North Carolina, 1855 ***1088.45*** *p18*
Ledger, Ann O'Shade *SEE* Ledger, Charles
Ledger, Charles; Philadelphia, 1853 ***8513.31*** *p322*
*Wife:*Ann O'Shade
Ledger, Frank; Washington, 1885 ***2770.40*** *p194*
Ledger, John; America, 1757 ***1220.12*** *p491*
Ledger, John; America, 1758 ***1220.12*** *p491*
Ledger, Joseph P.; Washington, 1882 ***2770.40*** *p135*
Ledger, Newberry; America, 1739 ***1220.12*** *p491*
Ledger, Thomas; America, 1745 ***1220.12*** *p491*
Ledgett, Joseph; Carolina, 1724 ***1220.12*** *p491*
Ledgeworth, John 28; Ontario, 1871 ***1823.21*** *p198*
Lediard, Ann; America, 1754 ***1220.12*** *p500*
Ledig, Catharina 67; America, 1846 ***778.6*** *p205*
Ledig, Charles 18; America, 1846 ***778.6*** *p205*
Ledig, Marianne 21; America, 1846 ***778.6*** *p205*
Ledley, John; America, 1755 ***1220.12*** *p491*
Ledman, Mary; America, 1739 ***1220.12*** *p491*
Ledoux, Jacquette; Quebec, 1664 ***4514.3*** *p336*
Ledra, Euphrasie 19; Louisiana, 1848 ***778.6*** *p205*
Ledran, Toussaint 23; Quebec, 1659 ***9221.17*** *p405*
Le Drew, Brigus *SEE* Le Drew, Robert
Le Drew, Robert; Newfoundland, 1871 ***9228.50*** *p343*
*Wife:*Brigus
Ledro, Euphrasie 19; Louisiana, 1848 ***778.6*** *p205*
Leduc, Antoine; Quebec, 1656 ***9221.17*** *p340*
Leduc, Antoinette 8; Port uncertain, 1846 ***778.6*** *p205*
Leduc, Eugene 5; Port uncertain, 1846 ***778.6*** *p205*
Leduc, Jean 20; Montreal, 1644 ***9221.17*** *p148*
Leduc, Jeanne 34; Port uncertain, 1846 ***778.6*** *p205*
Leduc, Jeanne; Quebec, 1666 ***4514.3*** *p309*
Ledue, Jean; Louisiana, 1874-1875 ***4981.45*** *p29*
Ledwell, Walter 35; St. Johns, N.F., 1811 ***1053.20*** *p22*
Lee, Abraham; New Hampshire, 1680 ***9228.50*** *p344*
Lee, Alexander; North Carolina, 1837 ***1088.45*** *p18*
Lee, Andrew 55; Ontario, 1871 ***1823.21*** *p198*
Lee, Ann; America, 1742 ***1220.12*** *p491*
Lee, Ann; America, 1770 ***1220.12*** *p491*
Lee, Ann; America, 1775 ***1220.12*** *p491*
Lee, Anne; America, 1743 ***1220.12*** *p491*
Lee, Benjamin; America, 1753 ***1220.12*** *p491*
Lee, Benjamin; Barbados, 1692 ***1220.12*** *p491*
Lee, Charles; America, 1765 ***1220.12*** *p491*
Lee, Charles 70; Ontario, 1871 ***1823.17*** *p90*
Lee, Daniel; America, 1757 ***1220.12*** *p491*
Lee, David; Ohio, 1831 ***3580.20*** *p32*
Lee, David; Ohio, 1831 ***6020.12*** *p12*
Lee, David E. 26; Ontario, 1871 ***1823.17*** *p90*
Lee, Downs; America, 1730 ***1220.12*** *p491*
Lee, Edmond; America, 1738 ***1220.12*** *p491*
Lee, Edward; America, 1750 ***1220.12*** *p491*
Lee, Edward; America, 1764 ***1220.12*** *p491*
Lee, Elizabeth; America, 1733 ***1220.12*** *p491*
Lee, Elizabeth 23; Annapolis, MD, 1721 ***1220.12*** *p491*
Lee, Elizabeth; Barbados, 1693 ***1220.12*** *p491*
Lee, Ellen Gilmore *SEE* Lee, Robert
Lee, Ellen; Philadelphia Co., PA, 1853 ***8513.31*** *p429*
Lee, Ferdinando; America, 1742 ***1220.12*** *p491*
Lee, Francis; America, 1700 ***1220.12*** *p491*
Lee, George; America, 1685 ***1220.12*** *p491*
Lee, George; Barbados or Jamaica, 1697 ***1220.12*** *p491*
Lee, George 21; Ontario, 1871 ***1823.21*** *p198*
Lee, George 42; Ontario, 1871 ***1823.17*** *p90*
Lee, George 55; Ontario, 1871 ***1823.21*** *p198*
Lee, Gertrude; Virginia, 1740 ***1220.12*** *p491*
Lee, Hannah; America, 1758 ***1220.12*** *p491*
Lee, Harriett 39; Ontario, 1871 ***1823.21*** *p198*
Lee, Henry 30; Ontario, 1871 ***1823.21*** *p198*
Lee, Henry 47; Ontario, 1871 ***1823.21*** *p198*
Lee, Hugh; Virginia, 1652 ***6254.4*** *p243*
Lee, James; America, 1754 ***1220.12*** *p491*
Lee, James; America, 1766 ***1220.12*** *p491*
Lee, James; America, 1770 ***1220.12*** *p491*
Lee, James; Barbados, 1668 ***1220.12*** *p491*
Lee, James; North Carolina, 1855 ***1088.45*** *p18*
Lee, James 30; Ontario, 1871 ***1823.21*** *p199*
Lee, James 35; Ontario, 1871 ***1823.17*** *p90*
Lee, James 37; Ontario, 1871 ***1823.21*** *p199*
Lee, James; Virginia, 1766 ***1220.12*** *p491*
Lee, John; America, 1700 ***1220.12*** *p491*
Lee, John; America, 1700 ***1220.12*** *p492*
Lee, John; America, 1721 ***1220.12*** *p492*
Lee, John; America, 1746 ***1220.12*** *p492*
Lee, John; America, 1749 ***1220.12*** *p492*
Lee, John; America, 1751 ***1220.12*** *p492*
Lee, John; America, 1754 ***1220.12*** *p492*
Lee, John; America, 1759 ***1220.12*** *p492*
Lee, John; America, 1764 ***1220.12*** *p492*
Lee, John; America, 1764 ***1220.12*** *p492*
Lee, John; America, 1767 ***1220.12*** *p492*
Lee, John; America, 1770 ***1220.12*** *p492*
Lee, John; America, 1774 ***1220.12*** *p492*
Lee, John; Barbados, 1671 ***1220.12*** *p491*
Lee, John; Barbados, 1692 ***1220.12*** *p491*
Lee, John; Barbados or Jamaica, 1683 ***1220.12*** *p491*
Lee, John; Boston, 1766 ***1642*** *p37*
Lee, John; Died enroute, 1722 ***1220.12*** *p492*
Lee, John 35; Ontario, 1871 ***1823.21*** *p199*
Lee, John 45; Ontario, 1871 ***1823.21*** *p199*
Lee, John; Toronto, 1825-1865 ***9228.50*** *p343*
Lee, John; Toronto, 1844 ***2910.35*** *p114*
Lee, Joseph; America, 1744 ***1220.12*** *p492*
Lee, Joseph; America, 1769 ***1220.12*** *p492*
Lee, Joseph; America, 1770 ***1220.12*** *p492*
Lee, Joseph; Annapolis, MD, 1725 ***1220.12*** *p492*
Lee, Langley; America, 1700 ***1220.12*** *p492*
Lee, Lewis; Annapolis, MD, 1731 ***1220.12*** *p492*
Lee, Lewis; North Carolina, 1822 ***1088.45*** *p18*
Lee, Lucy M. 20; Michigan, 1880 ***4491.36*** *p13*
Lee, Margaret; America, 1755 ***1220.12*** *p492*
Lee, Margaret 11; Quebec, 1870 ***8364.32*** *p24*
Lee, Martha; America, 1756 ***1220.12*** *p492*
Lee, Mary; America, 1735 ***1220.12*** *p492*
Lee, Mary; America, 1746 ***1220.12*** *p492*
Lee, Mary; America, 1765 ***1220.12*** *p492*
Lee, Mary; Annapolis, MD, 1729 ***1220.12*** *p492*
Lee, Mary; Barbados, 1676 ***1220.12*** *p492*
Lee, Matthew; America, 1765 ***1220.12*** *p492*
Lee, Ole Nielson; Washington, 1887 ***2770.40*** *p24*
Lee, Patrick; Colorado, 1888 ***1029.59*** *p53*
Lee, Patrick; Colorado, 1888 ***1029.59*** *p54*
Lee, Patrick; Colorado, 1890 ***1029.59*** *p53*
Lee, Paul; America, 1727 ***1220.12*** *p492*
Lee, Paul; America, 1736 ***1220.12*** *p492*
Lee, Peter; America, 1684 ***1220.12*** *p492*
Lee, Peter; America, 1745 ***1220.12*** *p492*
Lee, Philip; Virginia, 1734 ***1220.12*** *p492*
Lee, Rebecca; America, 1758 ***1220.12*** *p492*
Lee, Rebecca; America, 1769 ***1220.12*** *p492*
Lee, Richard; America, 1728 ***1220.12*** *p492*
Lee, Richard; America, 1738 ***1220.12*** *p492*
Lee, Richard 30; Ontario, 1871 ***1823.21*** *p199*
Lee, Richard 65; Ontario, 1871 ***1823.21*** *p199*
Lee, Richard; Virginia, 1751 ***1220.12*** *p492*
Lee, Robert; Ohio, 1843 ***2763.1*** *p20*
Lee, Robert; Ohio, 1853 ***8513.31*** *p322*
*Wife:*Ellen Gilmore
Lee, Robert 28; Ontario, 1871 ***1823.21*** *p199*
Lee, Samuel; Barbados, 1692 ***1220.12*** *p492*
Lee, Samuel; New York, 1776 ***8529.30*** *p4A*
Lee, Sarah; America, 1756 ***1220.12*** *p492*
Lee, Sarah; America, 1767 ***1220.12*** *p492*
Lee, Simon; Barbados, 1681 ***1220.12*** *p493*
Lee, Stephen 34; Ontario, 1871 ***1823.21*** *p199*
Lee, Susanna; Annapolis, MD, 1725 ***1220.12*** *p493*
Lee, Susannah; America, 1775 ***1220.12*** *p493*
Lee, Tho.; Jamestown, VA, 1633 ***1658.20*** *p211*
Lee, Thomas; America, 1728 ***1220.12*** *p493*
Lee, Thomas; America, 1732 ***1220.12*** *p493*
Lee, Thomas; America, 1737 ***1220.12*** *p493*
Lee, Thomas; America, 1757 ***1220.12*** *p493*
Lee, Thomas; America, 1757 ***1220.12*** *p493*
Lee, Thomas; America, 1762 ***1220.12*** *p493*
Lee, Thomas; America, 1765 ***1220.12*** *p493*
Lee, Thomas; America, 1774 ***1220.12*** *p493*
Lee, Thomas; Barbados or Jamaica, 1689 ***1220.12*** *p493*
Lee, Thomas 35; Ontario, 1871 ***1823.17*** *p90*
Lee, Thomas 42; Ontario, 1871 ***1823.21*** *p199*
Lee, William; America, 1700 ***1220.12*** *p493*
Lee, William; America, 1739 ***1220.12*** *p493*
Lee, William; America, 1748 ***1220.12*** *p493*
Lee, William; America, 1749 ***1220.12*** *p493*
Lee, William; America, 1751 ***1220.12*** *p493*
Lee, William; America, 1758 ***1220.12*** *p493*
Lee, William; America, 1774 ***1220.12*** *p493*
Lee, William; America, 1775 ***1220.12*** *p493*
Lee, William 37; Ontario, 1871 ***1823.21*** *p199*
Lee, William 46; Ontario, 1871 ***1823.21*** *p199*
Lee, William; Rappahannock, VA, 1728 ***1220.12*** *p493*
Lee, William; St. John, N.B., 1847 ***2978.15*** *p35*
Lee, William; Virginia, 1741 ***1220.12*** *p493*
Lee, William H. 24; Michigan, 1880 ***4491.36*** *p13*
Lee, William W. 49; Ontario, 1871 ***1823.21*** *p199*
Lee, Wm.; Ohio, 1840-1897 ***8365.35*** *p17*
Leebeck, Anthony; New Jersey, 1777 ***8529.30*** *p6*
Leech, Andrew; America, 1772 ***1220.12*** *p493*
Leech, Anne; Virginia, 1723 ***1220.12*** *p493*
Leech, Benjamin 27; Ontario, 1871 ***1823.21*** *p199*
Leech, George; Barbados or Jamaica, 1697 ***1220.12*** *p493*
Leech, John; America, 1739 ***1220.12*** *p493*
Leech, John; America, 1752 ***1220.12*** *p493*
Leech, John; America, 1769 ***1220.12*** *p493*
Leech, John; America, 1774 ***1220.12*** *p493*
Leech, John, Jr.; Barbados or Jamaica, 1691 ***1220.12*** *p493*
Leech, Thomas; Barbados, 1673 ***1220.12*** *p494*
Leech, Thomas; Maryland, 1674 ***1236.25*** *p50*
Leech, Thomas; New Orleans, 1850 ***7242.30*** *p148*
Leedam, Jonathan; America, 1735 ***1220.12*** *p494*
Leeder, Charles; America, 1752 ***1220.12*** *p490*
Leeds, Ann; Maryland, 1725 ***1220.12*** *p494*
Leeds, John; Marston's Wharf, 1782 ***8529.30*** *p13*
Leeke, Thomas; America, 1676 ***1220.12*** *p490*
Leeke, William; America, 1764 ***1220.12*** *p490*
Leely, Robert; America, 1731 ***1220.12*** *p494*
Leeman, Diedrick; New York, 1778 ***8529.30*** *p6*
Leeman, John; America, 1750 ***1220.12*** *p490*
Leer, Abraham; America, 1774 ***1220.12*** *p490*
Leer, Ann; America, 1763 ***1220.12*** *p490*
Lees, Andrew 45; St. John, N.B., 1834 ***6469.7*** *p4*
Lees, Ann; Philadelphia, 1855 ***8513.31*** *p299*
Lees, Annie 40; Ontario, 1871 ***1823.21*** *p199*
Lees, Biddy 35; St. John, N.B., 1834 ***6469.7*** *p4*
Lees, David; Colorado, 1891 ***1029.59*** *p54*
Lees, Elvy 11; St. John, N.B., 1834 ***6469.7*** *p4*
Lees, Florina 3; St. John, N.B., 1834 ***6469.7*** *p4*
Lees, George; America, 1759 ***1220.12*** *p494*
Lees, George; America, 1767 ***1220.12*** *p494*
Lees, George; America, 1773 ***1220.12*** *p494*
Lees, George 79; Ontario, 1871 ***1823.17*** *p90*
Lees, Hariet 19; Ontario, 1871 ***1823.21*** *p199*
Lees, Isabella 8; St. John, N.B., 1834 ***6469.7*** *p4*
Lees, James; America, 1756 ***1220.12*** *p494*
Lees, James 44; Indiana, 1866-1870 ***9076.20*** *p67*
Lees, Jane; America, 1747 ***1220.12*** *p494*
Lees, John; America, 1721 ***1220.12*** *p494*
Lees, John; America, 1756 ***1220.12*** *p494*
Lees, John; Died enroute, 1722 ***1220.12*** *p494*
Lees, John; Maryland, 1723 ***1220.12*** *p494*
Lees, John; Ohio, 1842 ***2763.1*** *p20*
Lees, John 47; Ontario, 1871 ***1823.21*** *p199*
Lees, Joseph; Boston, 1822 ***3274.55*** *p73*
Lees, Margt 13; St. John, N.B., 1834 ***6469.7*** *p4*
Lees, Mary; America, 1766 ***1220.12*** *p494*
Lees, Mary; Maryland, 1724 ***1220.12*** *p494*
Lees, Thomas; America, 1701 ***1220.12*** *p494*
Lees, Thomas; America, 1741 ***1220.12*** *p494*
Lees, William; America, 1735 ***1220.12*** *p494*
Leese, Daniel 57; Indiana, 1869-1870 ***9076.20*** *p67*
Leese, William 35; Indiana, 1869-1870 ***9076.20*** *p67*
Leeson, Elizabeth; America, 1749 ***1220.12*** *p494*
Leeson, Esther; America, 1773 ***1220.12*** *p494*
Leeson, John; America, 1769 ***1220.12*** *p494*
Leesor, John 48; Ontario, 1871 ***1823.21*** *p199*
Leet, William; America, 1756 ***1220.12*** *p494*
Leete, Margaret; Nova Scotia, 1800-1831 ***9228.50*** *p195*
Leetham, Jonathan; America, 1735 ***1220.12*** *p494*
Leeves, Samuel; America, 1775 ***1220.12*** *p494*
Leeworthy, William; America, 1758 ***1220.12*** *p494*
Lefarge, Joseph 45; Port uncertain, 1845 ***778.6*** *p204*
Lefauconnier, Nicolas; Quebec, 1638 ***9221.17*** *p78*
Le Favor, Anna; Massachusetts, 1750-1769 ***9228.50*** *p345*
Le Favour, Anna; Massachusetts, 1750-1769 ***9228.50*** *p345*
Le Favour, John; Marblehead, MA, 1743 ***9228.50*** *p345*
Le Favour, Maybelle; Canada, 1877-1950 ***9228.50*** *p347*
Lefebre, Mr. 38; New Orleans, 1846 ***778.6*** *p205*
Lefebre, A. 23; Port uncertain, 1845 ***778.6*** *p205*
Lefebure, Joshua; America, 1739 ***1220.12*** *p494*
Lefebvre, . . .; Quebec, 1635 ***9221.17*** *p47*
Lefebvre, Adrian; Quebec, 1659 ***9221.17*** *p414*
Lefebvre, Angelique *SEE* Lefebvre, Louis
Lefebvre, Antoinette; Quebec, 1671 ***4514.3*** *p336*
Lefebvre, Barbe; Quebec, 1668 ***4514.3*** *p337*
Lefebvre, Claude; Quebec, 1653 ***9221.17*** *p276*
Le Febvre, Elinor M.; New York, 1831-1900 ***9228.50*** *p348*
Lefebvre, Elisabeth-Agnes; Quebec, 1670 ***4514.3*** *p336*
Lefebvre, Francois 17; Quebec, 1653 ***9221.17*** *p276*
Le Febvre, Helen Ellnora; New York, 1843-1871 ***9228.50*** *p213*
Lefebvre, Hyppolite 43; America, 1846 ***778.6*** *p205*
Lefebvre, J. B. 22; Port uncertain, 1843 ***778.6*** *p206*
Lefebvre, Jacques 23; America, 1846 ***778.6*** *p206*
Lefebvre, Jacques 38; Louisiana, 1848 ***778.6*** *p206*
Lefebvre, Jacques A.; Illinois, 1852 ***6079.1*** *p8*
Lefebvre, Jean; Quebec, 1659 ***9221.17*** *p414*
Lefebvre, Joseph 21; America, 1846 ***778.6*** *p206*
Lefebvre, Julie Gohir; Wisconsin, 1855 ***1495.20*** *p8*
Lefebvre, Laurent 28; Quebec, 1656 ***9221.17*** *p340*

Lefebvre, Louis 26; America, 1843 ***778.6*** *p206*
Lefebvre, Louis; Quebec, 1665 ***4514.3*** *p298*
*Wife:*Suzanne Debure
With sister
*Daughter:*Angelique
Lefebvre, Louis 17; Quebec, 1645 ***9221.17*** *p154*
Le Febvre, Marie; Newport, RI, 1696-1698 ***9228.50*** *p348*
Lefebvre, Marie; Quebec, 1669 ***4514.3*** *p336*
Lefebvre, Marie; Quebec, 1670 ***4514.3*** *p337*
Lefebvre, Marie; Quebec, 1671 ***4514.3*** *p337*
Lefebvre, Marie Therese; Wisconsin, 1855 ***1495.20*** *p8*
Lefebvre, Marin; Quebec, 1640 ***9221.17*** *p97*
Lefebvre, Pasquiere 35; Quebec, 1662 ***9221.17*** *p494*
Lefebvre, Pierre 18; Montreal, 1653 ***9221.17*** *p295*
Lefebvre, Pierre 24; Quebec, 1655 ***9221.17*** *p326*
Lefebvre, Pierre 27; Quebec, 1644 ***9221.17*** *p143*
Lefebvre, Pierre 33; Quebec, 1655 ***9221.17*** *p326*
Lefebvre, Renaud; Quebec, 1659 ***9221.17*** *p414*
Lefebvre, Solomon 32; America, 1845 ***778.6*** *p206*
Lefebvre, Suzanne Debure *SEE* Lefebvre, Louis
Lefebvre, Thomas 16; Quebec, 1658 ***9221.17*** *p383*
Lefebvre Duplessis, Francois; Quebec, 1683-1688 ***2314.30*** *p168*
Lefebvre Duplessis, Francois; Quebec, 1687 ***2314.30*** *p188*
Lefere, L. 18; Quebec, 1870 ***8364.32*** *p24*
Lefet, Achille; Illinois, 1852 ***6079.1*** *p8*
LeFeurre, Susanna; Maine, 1640-1688 ***9228.50*** *p172*
Le Feuvre, Clement; Wisconsin, n.d. ***9228.50*** *p348*
Le Feuvre, Daniel; New Hampshire, 1770 ***9228.50*** *p348*
Le Feuvre, George Francis; Quebec, 1869-1940 ***9228.50*** *p348*
With family
Le Feuvre, Gilbert; Texas, 1870-1899 ***9228.50*** *p477*
Le Feuvre, Susanna; Maine, 1688 ***9228.50*** *p600*
Lefever, Mary; Annapolis, MD, 1733 ***1220.12*** *p494*
Lefevre, Adolphus 23; Port uncertain, 1843 ***778.6*** *p206*
Lefevre, Batist 34; New Orleans, 1847 ***778.6*** *p206*
Lefevre, Charlemagne 18; New Orleans, 1848 ***778.6*** *p206*
Le Fevre, Clement Fall; New York, NY, 1817 ***9228.50*** *p349*
Le Fevre, Clement Fall; Ontario, 1817-1821 ***9228.50*** *p349*
Lefevre, Henri; New York, NY, 1871 ***1494.20*** *p13*
Lefevre, Jacob 21; Port uncertain, 1847 ***778.6*** *p206*
Lefevre, Louis; Maryland, 1736 ***1220.12*** *p494*
Lefevre, P. J.; New York, NY, 1866 ***1494.21*** *p31*
Lefevre, Prosper 25; North America, 1841 ***778.6*** *p206*
Le Filliatre, Abraham; Maine, n.d. ***9228.50*** *p349*
Lefinds, Marie Louise 55; Ontario, 1871 ***1823.21*** *p199*
Leflot, Christophe; Montreal, 1644 ***9221.17*** *p148*
Leflot, Michelle 11; Quebec, 1652 ***9221.17*** *p261*
Lefoe, Daniel; Virginia, 1732 ***1220.12*** *p494*
Leforestier, Pierre; Quebec, 1658 ***9221.17*** *p380*
Leforme, Arnold 30; Boston, 1835 ***6424.55*** *p30*
Lefort, Francois 19; New Orleans, 1847 ***778.6*** *p206*
Lefort, Jean Pierre 58; New Orleans, 1847 ***778.6*** *p206*
Lefoulon, Mr. 45; America, 1845 ***778.6*** *p206*
Lefoulon, Mrs. 40; America, 1845 ***778.6*** *p206*
Lefoulon, A. 10; America, 1845 ***778.6*** *p206*
Lefoulon, E. 3; America, 1845 ***778.6*** *p206*
Le Fournier duVivier, Henry-Jules; Quebec, 1683-1688 ***2314.30*** *p168*
Le Fournier duVivier, Henry-Jules; Quebec, 1687 ***2314.30*** *p188*
Lefran, Alexis 30; Missouri, 1848 ***778.6*** *p206*
Lefranc, Francois 16; Quebec, 1655 ***9221.17*** *p326*
Le Franceys, Thomas 9; America, n.d. ***9228.50*** *p228*
With parents brothers & sisters
Lefrancois, Charles 31; Quebec, 1657 ***9221.17*** *p361*
Lefrancois, Francoise; Quebec, 1671 ***4514.3*** *p337*
Lefrancois, Marie-Madeleine 19; Quebec, 1654 ***9221.17*** *p312*
Lefrancois, Pierre; Quebec, 1655 ***9221.17*** *p326*
Lefrane, Jacquette 4 *SEE* Lefrane, Marguerite Corrivault
Lefrane, Marguerite Corrivault 22; Quebec, 1648 ***9221.17*** *p201*
*Son:*Jacquette 4
Leg, Catherine; America, 1772 ***1220.12*** *p494*
Legall, Noel 21; Montreal, 1659 ***9221.17*** *p423*
Le Gallais, . . .; America, 1492-1817 ***9228.50*** *p28*
Le Gallais, Mr.; New Hampshire, 1700-1799 ***9228.50*** *p349*
Le Gallais, Mr.; New Hampshire, 1700-1799 ***9228.50*** *p652*
Le Gallais, David; Boston, 1745 ***9228.50*** *p652*
Le Gallais, David; Marblehead, MA, 1727 ***9228.50*** *p349*
Le Gallais, James; Massachusetts, 1775-1820 ***9228.50*** *p122*
Le Gallais, John 78; Massachusetts, 1683 ***9228.50*** *p234*
Le Gallais, John; Salem, MA, 1635 ***9228.50*** *p18A*
Le Gallais, Mary; Quebec, 1871 ***9228.50*** *p349*
Le Gallais, Philip 72; Quebec, 1861 ***9228.50*** *p349*
Le Gallais, Reuben; New Hampshire, n.d. ***9228.50*** *p19A*
Le Gallais, Thomas; Salem, MA, 1790 ***9228.50*** *p350*
Le Gallee, Reuben; New Hampshire, n.d. ***9228.50*** *p19A*
Le Gallez, . . .; Detroit, 1970-1979 ***9228.50*** *p350*
Le Gallienne, Eva; Connecticut, 1899-1983 ***9228.50*** *p350*
Le Gallienne, Eva; New York, 1900-1983 ***9228.50*** *p236*
LeGallienne, Richard; America, 1866-1947 ***9228.50*** *p350*
Legallion, Alexandre; Quebec, 1650 ***9221.17*** *p227*
Legan, Robert; Boston, 1743 ***1642*** *p45*
Legantier deLa Vallee Rane, Francois; Quebec, 1683-1688 ***2314.30*** *p168*
Legantier deLa Vallee Rane, Francois; Quebec, 1687 ***2314.30*** *p188*
Legardeur, Catherine *SEE* Legardeur, Catherine Corde
Legardeur, Catherine; Quebec, 1636 ***9221.17*** *p58*
*Son:*Pierre
*Grandson:*Jean-Baptiste
*Granddaughter:*Catherine
*Granddaughter:*Marie-Madeleine
*Daughter-In-Law:*Marie Favery
*Son:*Charles
Legardeur, Charles 21 *SEE* Legardeur, Catherine Corde
Legardeur, Jean-Baptiste 4 *SEE* Legardeur, Catherine Corde
Legardeur, Marie Favery 20 *SEE* Legardeur, Catherine Corde
Legardeur, Marie-Madeleine *SEE* Legardeur, Catherine Corde
Legardeur, Pierre *SEE* Legardeur, Catherine Corde
Legardeur DeRepentigny, Jean-Baptiste 4; Quebec, 1636 ***9221.17*** *p59*
Legardeur deRepentigny, Pierre; Quebec, 1636 ***2314.30*** *p166*
Legardeur deRepentigny, Pierre; Quebec, 1636 ***2314.30*** *p188*
Legardeur DeRepentigny, Pierre; Quebec, 1636 ***9221.17*** *p58*
Legardeur DeTilly, Catherine; Quebec, 1636 ***9221.17*** *p58*
Legardeur deTilly, Charles; Quebec, 1636 ***2314.30*** *p166*
Legardeur deTilly, Charles; Quebec, 1636 ***2314.30*** *p188*
Legardeur DeTilly, Charles 21; Quebec, 1636 ***9221.17*** *p59*
Legardeur De Tilly, Marguerite-Marie 28; Quebec, 1636 ***9221.17*** *p59*
Legardeur DeTilly, Marguerite-Marie 28; Quebec, 1636 ***9221.17*** *p60*
Legascon, Antoine; Quebec, 1658 ***9221.17*** *p386*
Legascon, Pierre 19; Quebec, 1662 ***9221.17*** *p489*
Legassie, Isaac 35; New Orleans, 1843 ***778.6*** *p206*
Legassie, Jean 15; New Orleans, 1843 ***778.6*** *p206*
Legat, Charles 30; Louisiana, 1840 ***778.6*** *p206*
Legate, Henry; America, 1773 ***1220.12*** *p494*
Legate, John; America, 1739 ***1220.12*** *p494*
Le Gate, Peter 38; Boston, 1667 ***9228.50*** *p350*
Legay, Antonin-Hyacinthe; Quebec, 1644 ***9221.17*** *p143*
Legay, Aug..te 30; Port uncertain, 1841 ***778.6*** *p206*
Legay, Louis; America, 1774 ***1220.12*** *p494*
Legendre, Jeanne; Quebec, 1669 ***4514.3*** *p337*
Legendre, Simon; Quebec, 1655 ***9221.17*** *p326*
Leger, Mr. 25; Mexico, 1846 ***778.6*** *p206*
Leger, Mrs. 50; Mexico, 1846 ***778.6*** *p206*
Leger, Adrien 14; Quebec, 1645 ***9221.17*** *p154*
Leger, Cesar; Montreal, 1642 ***9221.17*** *p123*
Leger, Jean; Quebec, 1639 ***9221.17*** *p90*
Leger, Jean 20; Quebec, 1658 ***9221.17*** *p383*
Leger, Jean Justin 30; America, 1840 ***778.6*** *p206*
Leger, Maurice 21; Montreal, 1653 ***9221.17*** *p281*
Leger, Ovesina; Iowa, 1892 ***1211.15*** *p16*
Legerken, Lewis; North Carolina, 1857 ***1088.45*** *p18*
LeGerme, Ms. 36; Port uncertain, 1840 ***778.6*** *p206*
Legeron, Pierre 18; Quebec, 1657 ***9221.17*** *p361*
Leget, Robt.; Ontario, 1871 ***1823.17*** *p90*
Legett, George D.; Louisiana, 1836-1841 ***4981.45*** *p209*
Le Gette, . . .; California, 1900 ***9228.50*** *p350*
Le Geyt, . . .; California, 1900 ***9228.50*** *p350*
Le Geyt, Daniel; Omaha, NE, 1844-1873 ***9228.50*** *p350*
Le Geyt, John; Hartford, CT, n.d. ***9228.50*** *p350*
Le Geyt, Peter 38; Boston, 1667 ***9228.50*** *p350*
Le Geyt, Sarah Judith; Hartford, CT, 1819-1845 ***9228.50*** *p518*
Legford, John; New York, 1778 ***8529.30*** *p6*
Legg, Grace; Virginia, 1732 ***1220.12*** *p494*
Legg, Henry 60; Ontario, 1871 ***1823.21*** *p199*
Legg, James; America, 1726 ***1220.12*** *p494*
Legg, James; America, 1732 ***1220.12*** *p494*
Legg, James 40; Ontario, 1871 ***1823.21*** *p199*
Legg, Jane; Virginia, 1736 ***1220.12*** *p494*
Legg, John; America, 1740 ***1220.12*** *p494*
Legg, John 52; Ontario, 1871 ***1823.21*** *p199*
Legg, John 65; Ontario, 1871 ***1823.21*** *p199*
Legg, Margaret; America, 1721 ***1220.12*** *p494*
Legg, Richard; America, 1728 ***1220.12*** *p494*
Legg, Solomon; America, 1769 ***1220.12*** *p494*
Legg, Thomas; America, 1724 ***1220.12*** *p494*
Legg, William; Virginia, 1718 ***1220.12*** *p494*
Leggatt, Alexander 25; Ontario, 1871 ***1823.17*** *p90*
Leggatt, Benjamin; America, 1757 ***1220.12*** *p494*
Leggatt, Richard; Barbados or Jamaica, 1682 ***1220.12*** *p495*
Leggatt, Richard 27; Ontario, 1871 ***1823.17*** *p91*
Leggatt, Thomas; America, 1745 ***1220.12*** *p495*
Leggatt, Thomas 50; Ontario, 1871 ***1823.17*** *p91*
Leggatt, William; America, 1743 ***1220.12*** *p495*
Legget, John; America, 1739 ***1220.12*** *p495*
Leggett, John; Died enroute, 1725 ***1220.12*** *p494*
Leggett, Peter 38; Boston, 1667 ***9228.50*** *p350*
Leggett, Wm. B.; Washington, 1889 ***2770.40*** *p79*
Leggot, Charles 57; Ontario, 1871 ***1823.17*** *p91*
Leggott, Mathias 25; Ontario, 1871 ***1823.17*** *p91*
Legier, Gabriel John; Virginia, 1760 ***1220.12*** *p495*
Legill, Magdalena; America, 1890 ***5475.1*** *p257*
Leglebat, Bertrand de; Quebec, 1648 ***9221.17*** *p200*
L'Eglise, Jean Marie 28; America, 1845 ***778.6*** *p206*
Legmuller, Jacob 4; Halifax, N.S., 1902 ***1860.4*** *p42*
Legmuller, Josef 3; Halifax, N.S., 1902 ***1860.4*** *p42*
Legmuller, Margt. 35; Halifax, N.S., 1902 ***1860.4*** *p42*
Legmuller, Stefan 36; Halifax, N.S., 1902 ***1860.4*** *p42*
Legnay, August P. H.; Illinois, 1856 ***6079.1*** *p8*
Legnay, Henry F. A.; Illinois, 1856 ***6079.1*** *p8*
Lego, Charles; America, 1752 ***1220.12*** *p495*
Legobloteur, Guillaume; Quebec, 1641 ***9221.17*** *p106*
*Wife:*Michelle Morille
*Son:*Jean
*Daughter:*Marie
Legobloteur, Jean 14 *SEE* Legobloteur, Guillaume
Legobloteur, Marie *SEE* Legobloteur, Guillaume
Legobloteur, Michelle Morille 49 *SEE* Legobloteur, Guillaume
Le Goues deGrais, Louis-Joseph; Quebec, 1683-1688 ***2314.30*** *p168*
Le Goues deGrais, Louis-Joseph; Quebec, 1686 ***2314.30*** *p188*
LeGrand, . . .; America, 1847 ***778.6*** *p206*
Le Grand, . . .; Boston, 1769 ***9228.50*** *p5*
Legrand, Antoinette; Quebec, 1669 ***4514.3*** *p337*
Legrand, Catherine; America, 1846 ***778.6*** *p206*
Legrand, Charles 16; America, 1846 ***778.6*** *p206*
Legrand, Etienne 80; America, 1846 ***778.6*** *p206*
Legrand, Jacques; Wisconsin, 1886 ***1495.20*** *p56*
*Wife:*Marie-Louise Duchene
Legrand, Jean 23; New Orleans, 1848 ***778.6*** *p206*
Le Grand, John; Boston, 1769 ***9228.50*** *p48*
Le Grand, John; Boston, 1769 ***9228.50*** *p350*
Legrand, John Rodolph; America, 1770 ***1220.12*** *p495*
Legrand, Joseph 9; America, 1846 ***778.6*** *p207*
Le Grand, Louis; America, 1763 ***1220.12*** *p495*
Legrand, M. 42; America, 1846 ***778.6*** *p207*
Legrand, Margueritte 76; America, 1846 ***778.6*** *p207*
Legrand, Marie 47; America, 1846 ***778.6*** *p207*
Legrand, Marie-Louise Duchene *SEE* Legrand, Jacques
Legrand, N. 50; New York, NY, 1856 ***1766.1*** *p45*
Legrand, N. P. M. 24; New Orleans, 1844 ***778.6*** *p207*
Legrand, Nicole; Quebec, 1669 ***4514.3*** *p338*
Legrand, P. 35; Mexico, 1846 ***778.6*** *p207*
Le Grand, Philip 22; Toronto, 1864 ***9228.50*** *p350*
Legrand, Prosper 36; New Orleans, 1846 ***778.6*** *p207*
Legrand, Sebastien 18; America, 1846 ***778.6*** *p207*
Legrand, Sebastien 44; Quebec, 1644 ***9221.17*** *p143*
LeGrand Beauchamp, Jacques 1 *SEE* LeGrand Beauchamp, Jacques
LeGrand Beauchamp, Jacques 24; Montreal, 1659 ***9221.17*** *p416*
*Wife:*Marie Dardenne 22
*Son:*Jacques 1
LeGrand Beauchamp, Marie Dardenne 22 *SEE* LeGrand Beauchamp, Jacques
LeGrand Pierre, Pierre; Montreal, 1660 ***9221.17*** *p440*
LeGrand Pierre, Pierre 18; Montreal, 1653 ***9221.17*** *p285*
Legrapt, Martin 25; Quebec, 1658 ***9221.17*** *p382*
Le Gresley, . . .; California, 1900-1940 ***9228.50*** *p353*
Le Gresley, . . .; Quebec, 1840 ***9228.50*** *p351*
Le Gresley, Andrew; Massachusetts, 1638-1669 ***9228.50*** *p255*
Le Gresley, Arthur; Canada, 1890-1983 ***9228.50*** *p353*
Le Gresley, Betsy *SEE* Le Gresley, Philip
Le Gresley, Caroline; Philadelphia, 1813-1855 ***9228.50*** *p396*
Le Gresley, Caroline *SEE* Le Gresley, Philip
Le Gresley, Edward *SEE* Le Gresley, Philip
Le Gresley, Elizabeth *SEE* Le Gresley, John
Le Gresley, Emelie; Massachusetts, 1873 ***9228.50*** *p359*
Le Gresley, Emilie; Massachusetts, 1870 ***9228.50*** *p353*

LeGresley, Francis John; Quebec, 1890-1940 *9228.50 p352*
Le Gresley, Frank; Quebec, n.d. *9228.50 p351*
   With brother
   *Brother:*Philip
   *Brother:*John
Le Gresley, John *SEE* Le Gresley, Frank
Le Gresley, John *SEE* Le Gresley, Philip
Le Gresley, John; Utah, 1855 *9228.50 p353*
   *Relative:*Elizabeth
Le Gresley, John Walter; America, 1868-1947 *9228.50 p352*
   *Wife:*Lilian Elsie Brown
   With family
Le Gresley, Judith; Ohio, 1805-1860 *9228.50 p429*
Le Gresley, Judith Marquand *SEE* Le Gresley, Philip
Le Gresley, Lilian Elsie Brown *SEE* Le Gresley, John Walter
Le Gresley, Mary; Utah, 1819-1872 *9228.50 p423*
Le Gresley, Mary *SEE* Le Gresley, Philip
Le Gresley, Mary; Utah, 1851 *9228.50 p198*
   *Child:*John
   *Child:*Julia
   *Child:*Leah
   *Relative:*John
   *Child:*Mary
Le Gresley, Philip *SEE* Le Gresley, Frank
Le Gresley, Philip *SEE* Le Gresley, Philip
Le Gresley, Philip; Utah, 1823-1860 *9228.50 p352*
   *Wife:*Judith Marquand
   *Child:*Rachel
   *Child:*Edward
   *Child:*Betsy
   *Child:*John
   *Child:*Mary
   *Child:*Caroline
   *Child:*Philip
Le Gresley, Rachel *SEE* Le Gresley, Philip
Le Gresley, Thomas; Portsmouth, NH, 1723 *9228.50 p255*
Le Grew, Jane; Virginia, 1732 *1220.12 p495*
Legris, Auguste 28; Port uncertain, 1843 *778.6 p207*
Legris, Eugene 24; Port uncertain, 1846 *778.6 p207*
Legris, Francois; Quebec, 1659 *9221.17 p414*
Legris, Louis; Quebec, 1648 *9221.17 p200*
Le Gro, Christian; Salem, MA, 1695 *9228.50 p354*
Le Groe, John; Salem, MA, 1674 *9228.50 p354*
Le Gro Family ; Marblehead, MA, 1684 *9228.50 p255*
Le Groo, Philip; Salem, MA, 1671-1679 *9228.50 p354*
Legros, Charles T.; Illinois, 1852 *6079.1 p8*
Le Gros, Christian; Salem, MA, 1695 *9228.50 p354*
Le Gros, Emanuel; Chicago, 1850-1896 *2853.20 p405*
LeGros, Francois 25; America, 1845 *778.6 p207*
Le Gros, James; Los Angeles, 1960 *9228.50 p354*
Le Gros, John; Marblehead, MA, 1700-1736 *9228.50 p256*
Legros, Jos. 38; America, 1840 *778.6 p207*
Legros, Pierre; Quebec, 1645 *9221.17 p155*
Le Gros Family ; Chicago, n.d. *9228.50 p354*
Le Gros Family ; Marblehead, MA, 1684 *9228.50 p255*
Le Gross, Francis; Massachusetts, 1764-1781 *9228.50 p353*
Le Gross, Francis; Massachusetts, 1790 *9228.50 p354*
Legross, John; America, 1749 *1220.12 p495*
Le Groves, William; America, 1771 *1220.12 p495*
Legrow, Philip; Massachusetts, 1756-1763 *1642 p64*
Le Grow, Rebecca; Marblehead, MA, 1768 *9228.50 p82*
Le Grow Family ; Marblehead, MA, 1684 *9228.50 p256*
Le Gruche, John; Marblehead, MA, 1700-1729 *9228.50 p258*
Leguay, Jean le vieux 38; Quebec, 1647 *9221.17 p186*
Leguay, Lienarde; Quebec, 1652 *9221.17 p261*
Leguay, Madeleine; Quebec, 1668 *4514.3 p338*
Le Guedard, John, Sr. 16; Quebec, 1907 *9228.50 p354*
Leguee, Thomas 21; Ontario, 1871 *1823.17 p91*
Le Guernsieis, Guillaume; Canada, 1534 *9228.50 p260*
Leguet, Frederic 32; Louisiana, 1847 *778.6 p207*
Leguille, . . .; Quebec, 1662 *9221.17 p489*
Leguillon, Fred. 21; Port uncertain, 1840 *778.6 p207*
Leguin, Mrs. 36; New Orleans, 1841 *778.6 p207*
Leguin, Ms. 15; New Orleans, 1841 *778.6 p207*
Leguin, Ms. 16; New Orleans, 1841 *778.6 p207*
Lehavel, Joseph 22; Mississippi, 1845-1846 *778.6 p207*
Lehberger, Nikolaus 26; America, 1883 *5475.1 p421*
   With wife & 2 children
Lehe, Elisa 27; Port uncertain, 1840 *778.6 p207*
Lehe, Jacob 3; America, 1847 *778.6 p207*
Lehe, Jacques 36; America, 1847 *778.6 p207*
Lehe, Louis 6 months; America, 1847 *778.6 p207*
Lehe, Maria 26; America, 1847 *778.6 p207*
Leher, Victor Josephe; Louisiana, 1836-1840 *4981.45 p213*
Lehman, Adam A. 1; Michigan, 1880 *4491.30 p20*

Lehman, Elizabeth 50; Michigan, 1880 *4491.30 p19*
Lehman, Gustave; Ohio, 1840-1897 *8365.35 p17*
Lehman, Joseph; Ohio, 1809-1852 *4511.35 p30*
Lehman, Louis; Louisiana, 1874 *4981.45 p132*
Lehman, Nicholas; Ohio, 1809-1852 *4511.35 p30*
Lehman, Peter; Ohio, 1809-1852 *4511.35 p30*
Lehman, Sarah 21; Michigan, 1880 *4491.30 p20*
Lehman, Mr. 20; America, 1847 *778.6 p207*
Lehmann, Abraham 30; Mississippi, 1846 *778.6 p207*
Lehmann, Aron 9 months; Mississippi, 1846 *778.6 p207*
Lehmann, Aron 65; New Orleans, 1848 *778.6 p207*
Lehmann, Carl; Galveston, TX, 1855 *571.7 p17*
Lehmann, Diedrick; New York, 1778 *8529.30 p6*
Lehmann, Elisa 26; New Orleans, 1848 *778.6 p207*
Lehmann, Frederike Albertine; Wisconsin, 1882 *6795.8 p41*
Lehmann, Friedrich 15; America, 1866 *5475.1 p59*
Lehmann, Gertrude 1; Mississippi, 1846 *778.6 p207*
Lehmann, H.; New York, 1860 *358.56 p148*
Lehmann, Henry 29; Mississippi, 1846 *778.6 p207*
Lehmann, Hermann; America, 1882 *5475.1 p421*
Lehmann, Karl Ernst August Mathias; Milwaukee, 1865 *5475.1 p12*
Lehmann, Lenhard Robert; Kansas, 1917-1918 *2094.25 p50*
Lehmann, Marie 30; Mississippi, 1846 *778.6 p207*
Lehmann, Marie 30; Mississippi, 1846 *778.6 p208*
Lehmann, Moritz; Galveston, TX, 1855 *571.7 p17*
Lehmann, Moses 3; Mississippi, 1846 *778.6 p208*
Lehmann, Rudolph; Valdivia, Chile, 1852 *1192.4 p53*
Lehmann, Samuel 30; Port uncertain, 1847 *778.6 p208*
Lehmann, Theodor; Valdivia, Chile, 1851 *1192.4 p51*
Lehmensiek, Mr.; America, 1835 *7420.1 p9*
Lehmensiek, Dorothea Sophie; America, 1872 *7420.1 p397*
Lehmensiek, Hermann Gustav Adolf; America, 1892 *7420.1 p366*
Lehmkuhl, John Henry; Ohio, 1840-1897 *8365.35 p17*
Lehn, Franz 33; America, 1746 *778.6 p208*
Lehner, Christian; Ohio, 1809-1852 *4511.35 p30*
Lehner, Dorothea; New York, 1852 *5475.1 p70*
Lehnert, Andreas *SEE* Lehnert, Jakob
Lehnert, Barbara *SEE* Lehnert, Jakob
Lehnert, Heinrich; America, 1852 *7420.1 p92*
Lehnert, Jakob *SEE* Lehnert, Jakob
Lehnert, Jakob; America, 1883 *5475.1 p198*
   *Wife:*Margarethe Weyand
   *Son:*Jakob
   *Son:*Andreas
   *Son:*Johann
   *Daughter:*Barbara
   *Son:*Peter
Lehnert, Johann *SEE* Lehnert, Jakob
Lehnert, Margarethe Weyand 37 *SEE* Lehnert, Jakob
Lehnert, Mathias; America, 1872 *5475.1 p346*
Lehnert, Peter *SEE* Lehnert, Jakob
Lehnhof, Anna Maria; America, 1868 *5475.1 p139*
Lehnhoff, Katharina 44; America, 1872 *5475.1 p271*
Lehning, Philipp 48; Pennsylvania, 1850 *170.15 p34*
   With child
Lehook, Mary; America, 1758 *1220.12 p495*
Lehoux, Francoise 23 *SEE* Lehoux, Jacques
Lehoux, Jacques 75; Quebec, 1651 *9221.17 p245*
   *Daughter:*Francoise 23
   *Son:*Jean 18
   *Wife:*Jeanne Hamel 49
Lehoux, Jean 22; Montreal, 1643 *9221.17 p136*
Lehoux, Jean 18 *SEE* Lehoux, Jacques
Lehoux, Jeanne Hamel 49 *SEE* Lehoux, Jacques
Lehr, Alexander 2; New York, NY, 1893 *1883.7 p43*
Lehr, Andreas 24; New York, NY, 1885 *1883.7 p46*
Lehr, Anna Maria; America, 1866 *2526.43 p174*
Lehr, Anna Maria 65; America, 1800-1899 *5475.1 p453*
   With 2 daughters
Lehr, Barba. 22; New York, NY, 1885 *1883.7 p46*
Lehr, Catha. 23; New York, NY, 1893 *1883.7 p43*
Lehr, Charlotte *SEE* Lehr, Wilhelm
Lehr, Christe. 16; New York, NY, 1885 *1883.7 p46*
Lehr, Christe. 45; New York, NY, 1885 *1883.7 p46*
Lehr, Emma 18; New York, NY, 1885 *1883.7 p46*
Lehr, Georg; America, 1882 *2526.43 p152*
Lehr, Georg; America, 1890 *2526.43 p152*
Lehr, Georg Nikolaus; America, 1866 *2526.43 p174*
Lehr, Heinr. 35; New York, NY, 1893 *1883.7 p43*
Lehr, Helena 7; New York, NY, 1885 *1883.7 p46*
Lehr, Johann; America, 1890 *2526.43 p152*
Lehr, Johann 14; New York, NY, 1885 *1883.7 p46*
Lehr, Johann 49; New York, NY, 1885 *1883.7 p46*
Lehr, Madge. 4; New York, NY, 1885 *1883.7 p46*
Lehr, Margaretha *SEE* Lehr, Philipp
Lehr, Margaretha 38; America, 1853 *2526.43 p174*
Lehr, Maria 4; New York, NY, 1893 *1883.7 p43*
Lehr, Marie 26; America, 1853 *2526.43 p174*

Lehr, Philipp *SEE* Lehr, Philipp
Lehr, Philipp; America, 1853 *2526.43 p152*
   *Wife:*Margaretha
   *Son:*Philipp
   *Daughter:*Regina
Lehr, Regina *SEE* Lehr, Philipp
Lehr, Simon; America, 1882 *2526.43 p198*
Lehr, Sophie; America, 1867 *2526.43 p174*
Lehr, Valentin 2; New York, NY, 1885 *1883.7 p46*
Lehr, Wilhelm; America, 1892 *2526.43 p152*
   *Sister:*Charlotte
Lehr, Wladimer 3 months; New York, NY, 1893 *1883.7 p43*
Lehsel, Peter; Illinois, 1855 *5475.1 p348*
Lehst, Joachim; Ohio, 1840-1897 *8365.35 p17*
Lehto, Elli 24; Minnesota, 1926 *2769.54 p1383*
Lehu, Victor Joseph; Louisiana, 1836-1841 *4981.45 p209*
Le Huquet, Claude; Boston, 1800 *9228.50 p299*
Le Huquet, Elizabeth Susan Hamon *SEE* Le Huquet, Francis
Le Huquet, Elizabeth Susan Hamon *SEE* Le Huquet, Francis
Le Huquet, Francis; Iowa, 1833-1905 *9228.50 p355*
   *Wife:*Elizabeth Susan Hamon
   *Son:*Wm John
Le Huquet, Francis; Quebec, 1833 *9228.50 p355*
   *Wife:*Elizabeth Susan Hamon
Le Huquet, Freda *SEE* Le Huquet, Naomi
Le Huquet, Naomi; Massachusetts, 1900-1973 *9228.50 p355*
   *Sibling:*Freda
Le Huquet, Ruth Huish *SEE* Le Huquet, William
Le Huquet, Thomas; San Francisco, 1820-1900 *9228.50 p355*
Le Huquet, Wiliam; Iowa, 1800-1899 *9228.50 p355*
Le Huquet, William; Canada, 1968 *9228.50 p355*
   *Wife:*Ruth Huish
Le Huquet, Wm John *SEE* Le Huquet, Francis
Le Huray, Herbert St. John; San Francisco, 1853-1885 *9228.50 p355*
Le Huray, John *SEE* Le Huray, John
Le Huray, John; Ontario, 1800-1868 *9228.50 p355*
   *Wife:*Mary Roberge
   *Son:*John
Le Huray, Mary Roberge *SEE* Le Huray, John
LeHuray, Stephen; New York, 1918-1983 *9228.50 p355*
Le Huray, Wm. Fowler; British Columbia, 1894-1983 *9228.50 p355*
Le Huray Family ; Newfoundland, 1750 *9228.50 p233*
Leib, Anna Margarethe; America, 1847 *8115.12 p319*
   *Child:*Ludwig
Leib, Friedrich; America, 1867 *7919.3 p528*
Leib, Ludwig *SEE* Leib, Anna Margarethe
Leibenguth, Kath.; America, 1836 *5475.1 p458*
Leibenguth, M. Katharina; America, 1830 *5475.1 p458*
Leibford, Jacob; Ohio, 1809-1852 *4511.35 p30*
Leibfried, Nikolaus; Brazil, 1879 *5475.1 p382*
Leibold, Lewis; Ohio, 1809-1852 *4511.35 p30*
Leibove, Mr. 25; America, 1844 *778.6 p208*
Leicester, John; Virginia, 1732 *1220.12 p495*
Leicester, William; Barbados or Jamaica, 1699 *1220.12 p495*
Leich, Lazarus; Ohio, 1840-1897 *8365.35 p17*
Leicher, Auguste; Louisiana, 1874 *4981.45 p132*
Leicher, Maria Anna; Venezuela, 1843 *3899.5 p540*
Leichnitz, Robert; Colorado, 1894 *1029.59 p54*
Leichnitz, Robert; Kansas, 1888 *1029.59 p54*
Leichtenberger, Hubert 20; Port uncertain, 1840 *778.6 p208*
Leichtweiss, Anna; America, 1881 *5475.1 p221*
Leichtweiss, Anna; Scranton, PA, 1884 *5475.1 p221*
Leick, Elisabeth Baller *SEE* Leick, Michel
Leick, Johann 3 *SEE* Leick, Michel
Leick, Juliana 1 *SEE* Leick, Michel
Leick, Margarethe; America, 1855 *5475.1 p375*
Leick, Michel; America, 1864 *5475.1 p264*
   *Wife:*Elisabeth Baller
   *Son:*Johann
   *Daughter:*Juliana
Leid, James 65; Ontario, 1871 *1823.21 p199*
Leiden, Henry; Havana, 1782 *8529.30 p9A*
Leidenburgh, Aaron; America, 1742 *1220.12 p495*
Leidermann, Elisabetha *SEE* Leidermann, Georg Peter
Leidermann, Eva Katharina Gerbig *SEE* Leidermann, Georg Peter
Leidermann, Georg Peter; New York, 1886 *2526.43 p206*
   *Wife:*Eva Katharina Gerbig
   With 2 stepchildren
   *Daughter:*Elisabetha
   *Son:*Johann
   *Daughter:*Maria
Leidermann, Johann *SEE* Leidermann, Georg Peter

Leidermann, Maria *SEE* Leidermann, Georg Peter
Leidgen, Johann; America, 1843 ***5475.1*** *p366*
Leidig, Jakob; America, 1860-1886 ***179.55*** *p19*
Leidig, Matthaus; America, 1872 ***179.55*** *p19*
Leidinger, Johann; America, 1876 ***5475.1*** *p134*
Leidinger, Johann; Scranton, PA, 1884 ***5475.1*** *p293*
Leidinger, Peter; America, 1872 ***5475.1*** *p292*
Leidle, Francisca 11; New York, NY, 1847 ***9176.15*** *p50*
Leidle, Jacob 50; New York, NY, 1847 ***9176.15*** *p50*
Leidle, Johannes 7; New York, NY, 1847 ***9176.15*** *p50*
Leidle, Sophia 17; New York, NY, 1847 ***9176.15*** *p50*
Leidle, Veronica 8; New York, NY, 1847 ***9176.15*** *p50*
Leidle, Victoria 14; New York, NY, 1847 ***9176.15*** *p50*
Leidle, Walbrugo 45; New York, NY, 1847 ***9176.15*** *p50*
Leidler, John; New York, 1859 ***358.56*** *p100*
Leidner, Charlotte; Galveston, TX, 1855 ***571.7*** *p17*
Leidner, Fried.; Galveston, TX, 1855 ***571.7*** *p17*
Leidner, Hulda E.; Wisconsin, 1904 ***6795.8*** *p162*
Leidorf, Barbara 35 *SEE* Leidorf, Philipp
Leidorf, Karl *SEE* Leidorf, Philipp
Leidorf, Karoline 4 *SEE* Leidorf, Philipp
Leidorf, Luise 10 *SEE* Leidorf, Philipp
Leidorf, Philipp 35; Rio Grande do Sul, Brazil, 1854 ***5475.1*** *p532*
*Wife:*Barbara 35
*Son:*Karl
*Daughter:*Luise 10
*Daughter:*Karoline 4
Leidster, Mary A. 35; Ontario, 1871 ***1823.17*** *p91*
Leier, Barbara 2; New York, NY, 1893 ***1883.7*** *p38*
Leier, Ignac 4; New York, NY, 1893 ***1883.7*** *p38*
Leier, Jacob 30; New York, NY, 1893 ***1883.7*** *p38*
Leier, Petronella 27; New York, NY, 1893 ***1883.7*** *p38*
Leier, Stefan 1 months; New York, NY, 1893 ***1883.7*** *p38*
Leier, Theresia 3; New York, NY, 1893 ***1883.7*** *p38*
Leifer, August; America, 1867 ***7919.3*** *p534*
Leifer, Gustav Adolph; America, 1867 ***7919.3*** *p534*
Leifert, John; Ohio, 1809-1852 ***4511.35*** *p30*
Leigh, Edward; Annapolis, MD, 1726 ***1220.12*** *p491*
Leigh, John; America, 1664 ***1220.12*** *p491*
Leigh, John; America, 1743 ***1220.12*** *p492*
Leigh, Mathew; America, 1741 ***1220.12*** *p492*
Leigh, Richard; America, 1728 ***1220.12*** *p492*
Leigh, Richard; Barbados or Jamaica, 1712 ***1220.12*** *p492*
Leigh, William; America, 1685 ***1220.12*** *p493*
Leigh, William; America, 1749 ***1220.12*** *p493*
Leighe, Mary; Barbados, 1678 ***1220.12*** *p492*
Leighton, Agnes; Annapolis, MD, 1726 ***1220.12*** *p489*
Leighton, Albert 28; New York, NY, 1894 ***6512.1*** *p183*
Leighton, James; America, 1775 ***1220.12*** *p489*
Leighton, John; Barbados, 1688 ***1220.12*** *p489*
Leighton, Richard; Annapolis, MD, 1726 ***1220.12*** *p489*
Leillet, Claude 29; America, 1846 ***778.6*** *p208*
Leimbach, Zachariah; Ohio, 1845 ***2763.1*** *p20*
Leimer, Anton *SEE* Leimer, Jakob
Leimer, Heinrich *SEE* Leimer, Jakob
Leimer, Jakob 29; America, 1897 ***5475.1*** *p19*
*Wife:*Juliane Sold
*Son:*Heinrich
*Son:*Anton
Leimer, Juliane Sold *SEE* Leimer, Jakob
Leinberger, Nicholas; New Jersey, 1739-1774 ***927.31*** *p3*
Leind, Severin; North Carolina, 1848 ***1088.45*** *p18*
Leinen, Bernhard 38; America, 1859 ***5475.1*** *p278*
*Wife:*Maria Johannes
*Son:*Nikolaus
*Son:*Jakob
*Daughter:*Margarethe
Leinen, Gertrud 45; America, 1863 ***5475.1*** *p314*
Leinen, Jakob *SEE* Leinen, Bernhard
Leinen, Johann 27; America, 1867 ***5475.1*** *p361*
Leinen, Margarethe *SEE* Leinen, Bernhard
Leinen, Margarethe *SEE* Leinen, Mathias
Leinen, Maria Johannes *SEE* Leinen, Bernhard
Leinen, Maria; America, 1873 ***5475.1*** *p22*
Leinen, Mathias; America, 1872 ***5475.1*** *p329*
*Sister:*Margarethe
Leinen, Nikolaus *SEE* Leinen, Bernhard
Leinen, Nikolaus; America, 1882 ***5475.1*** *p339*
Leinenbach, Johannetta 3 *SEE* Leinenbach, Nikolaus
Leinenbach, Katharina Scheier 27 *SEE* Leinenbach, Nikolaus
Leinenbach, Margarethe; America, 1882 ***5475.1*** *p141*
Leinenbach, Margarethe 2 *SEE* Leinenbach, Nikolaus
Leinenbach, Nikolaus 30; America, 1846 ***5475.1*** *p451*
*Wife:*Katharina Scheier 27
*Daughter:*Margarethe 2
*Daughter:*Johannetta 3
Leinenweber, Margarethe *SEE* Leinenweber, Mathias
Leinenweber, Mathias 49; America, 1864 ***5475.1*** *p284*
*Daughter:*Margarethe
Leineweber, Mathias 58; America, 1843 ***5475.1*** *p261*
Leining, Peter; Illinois, 1856 ***6079.1*** *p8*
Leininger, Charles 23; America, 1843 ***778.6*** *p208*
Leininger, Gabriel 21; America, 1747 ***778.6*** *p208*
Leino, Frank 44; Minnesota, 1925 ***2769.54*** *p1378*
Leintinger, Nicolas 39; America, 1847 ***778.6*** *p208*
Leinz, Valentin; New York, 1860 ***358.56*** *p148*
Leion, Abr. 28; New York, NY, 1884 ***8427.14*** *p45*
Leion, Darey 2; New York, NY, 1884 ***8427.14*** *p45*
Leion, Ester 24; New York, NY, 1884 ***8427.14*** *p45*
Leion, Milley; New York, NY, 1884 ***8427.14*** *p45*
Leipheimer, Clara; Philadelphia, 1856 ***8513.31*** *p293*
Leipman, Levi; America, 1763 ***1220.12*** *p495*
Leipold, Carl Ferdinand; America, 1867 ***7919.3*** *p526*
With wife & daughter
Leipold, Elisabeth; America, 1867 ***7919.3*** *p532*
Leis, Carl August; Port uncertain, 1854 ***7420.1*** *p124*
Leisaschneider, Godfried 39; Mississippi, 1845 ***778.6*** *p208*
Leis-Bock, David; Port uncertain, 1898 ***170.15*** *p35*
Leischen, Katharina 24; America, 1861 ***5475.1*** *p492*
Leiseberg, Carl Friedrich Christian; America, 1852 ***7420.1*** *p92*
With wife 2 sons & 2 daughters
Leiseberg, Carl Friedrich Ferdinand; Illinois, 1878 ***7420.1*** *p311*
Leiseberg, Hanne Wilhelmine Caroline; America, 1867 ***7420.1*** *p260*
Leiseberg, Heinrich; America, 1852 ***7420.1*** *p92*
Leiseberg, Ludwig; America, 1854 ***7420.1*** *p124*
With wife & daughter
Leiseberg, Sophie; America, 1854 ***7420.1*** *p124*
Leiss, Adolf Eugen; America, 1887 ***2526.43*** *p222*
Leiss, Adolf Eugen *SEE* Leiss, Katharina Elisabetha Muller
Leiss, Alphon Guillaume *SEE* Leiss, Katharina Elisabetha Muller
Leiss, Anna Eva; America, 1847 ***2526.42*** *p175*
Leiss, Anna Katharina 18 *SEE* Leiss, Gottlieb
Leiss, Anna Margaretha; America, 1853 ***2526.43*** *p128*
Leiss, Anna Maria; America, 1854 ***2526.43*** *p134*
Leiss, August; America, 1855 ***7420.1*** *p138*
Leiss, Barbara; America, 1854 ***2526.43*** *p211*
Leiss, Barbara 8 *SEE* Leiss, Michael, III
Leiss, Barbara 21; America, 1842 ***2526.43*** *p134*
Leiss, Elisabetha 14 *SEE* Leiss, Michael, III
Leiss, Elisabetha 29 *SEE* Leiss, Mrs. Michael
Leiss, Fred. Hermann *SEE* Leiss, Katharina Elisabetha Muller
Leiss, Friedrich; America, 1853 ***2526.43*** *p134*
Leiss, Georg Adam; America, 1868 ***2526.43*** *p211*
Leiss, Gottlieb 50; America, 1866 ***2526.42*** *p169*
With wife
*Daughter:*Anna Katharina 18
*Daughter:*Margaretha 9
*Son:*Leonhard 7
*Son:*Johannes 15
*Daughter:*Maria Elisabetha 26
*Son:*Johann Nikolaus 22
Leiss, Heinrich 26 *SEE* Leiss, Mrs. Michael
Leiss, Johann *SEE* Leiss, Michael
Leiss, Johann Nikolaus 22 *SEE* Leiss, Gottlieb
Leiss, Johannes 15 *SEE* Leiss, Gottlieb
Leiss, Julius Emil *SEE* Leiss, Katharina Elisabetha Muller
Leiss, Katharina 4 *SEE* Leiss, Michael, III
Leiss, Katharina 32 *SEE* Leiss, Mrs. Michael
Leiss, Katharina Saul 34 *SEE* Leiss, Michael, III
Leiss, Katharina Elisabetha; America, 1854 ***2526.43*** *p211*
Leiss, Katharina Elisabetha; America, 1891 ***2526.43*** *p222*
*Son:*Julius Emil
*Son:*Alphon Guillaume
*Son:*Peter Alphon
*Son:*Fred. Hermann
*Son:*Adolf Eugen
Leiss, Leonhard 7 *SEE* Leiss, Gottlieb
Leiss, Margaretha 9 *SEE* Leiss, Gottlieb
Leiss, Margaretha 17; America, 1844 ***2526.43*** *p211*
Leiss, Maria 20 *SEE* Leiss, Mrs. Michael
Leiss, Maria Elisabetha 26 *SEE* Leiss, Gottlieb
Leiss, Michael 19; America, 1831 ***2526.43*** *p211*
With wife
*Son:*Johann
Leiss, Michael 22 *SEE* Leiss, Mrs. Michael
Leiss, Michael, III 40; America, 1855 ***2526.42*** *p96*
*Wife:*Katharina Saul 34
*Child:*Katharina 4
*Child:*Elisabetha 14
*Child:*Barbara 8
Leiss, Mrs. Michael 62; America, 1854 ***2526.43*** *p134*
*Daughter:*Katharina 32
*Daughter:*Elisabetha 29
*Son:*Michael 22
*Daughter:*Maria 20
*Son:*Heinrich 26
Leiss, Peter; America, 1832 ***2526.43*** *p211*
With wife & 5 children
Leiss, Peter Alphon *SEE* Leiss, Katharina Elisabetha Muller
Leist, Fried. Wilh.; Galveston, TX, 1855 ***571.7*** *p17*
Leist, Jakob 8 *SEE* Leist, Margarethe Fuchs
Leist, Johann; America, 1847 ***5475.1*** *p547*
Leist, Joseph; Ohio, 1809-1852 ***4511.35*** *p30*
Leist, Margarethe 38; America, 1854 ***5475.1*** *p539*
*Son:*Jakob 8
Leistekow, Fred Wm.; Wisconsin, 1887 ***6795.8*** *p88*
Leister, Edward; Plymouth, MA, 1620 ***1920.45*** *p5*
Leister, James; New York, 1783 ***8529.30*** *p13*
Leister, John; America, 1751 ***1220.12*** *p495*
Leistikow, Fred August; Wisconsin, 1884 ***6795.8*** *p88*
Leitch, Alexander 86; Ontario, 1871 ***1823.21*** *p199*
Leitch, Arch 26; Ontario, 1871 ***1823.21*** *p199*
Leitch, Archibald 32; Ontario, 1871 ***1823.17*** *p91*
Leitch, Archibald 35; Ontario, 1871 ***1823.17*** *p91*
Leitch, Archibald 36; Ontario, 1871 ***1823.17*** *p91*
Leitch, Archibald 46; Ontario, 1871 ***1823.21*** *p199*
Leitch, Arthur; North Carolina, 1837 ***1088.45*** *p18*
Leitch, Catherine 74; Ontario, 1871 ***1823.17*** *p91*
Leitch, Donald 68; Ontario, 1871 ***1823.17*** *p91*
Leitch, Dugald 46; Ontario, 1871 ***1823.21*** *p199*
Leitch, Edward 67; Ontario, 1871 ***1823.21*** *p199*
Leitch, H. J. 60; Ontario, 1871 ***1823.21*** *p199*
Leitch, Hugh 31; Ontario, 1871 ***1823.17*** *p91*
Leitch, John 58; Ontario, 1871 ***1823.21*** *p199*
Leitch, John 85; Ontario, 1871 ***1823.21*** *p199*
Leitch, Malcolm 35; Ontario, 1871 ***1823.21*** *p200*
Leitch, Malcolm 45; Ontario, 1871 ***1823.21*** *p200*
Leitch, Margaret 54; Ontario, 1871 ***1823.17*** *p91*
Leitch, Neil 53; Ontario, 1871 ***1823.21*** *p200*
Leitch, Neil 63; Ontario, 1871 ***1823.17*** *p91*
Leitch, Neil 70; Ontario, 1871 ***1823.21*** *p200*
Leitch, Neill 71; Ontario, 1871 ***1823.17*** *p91*
Leitch, William; North Carolina, 1837 ***1088.45*** *p18*
Leitch, William 43; Ontario, 1871 ***1823.21*** *p200*
Leitch, William 55; Ontario, 1871 ***1823.21*** *p200*
Leitermann, Elisabetha Katharina Blatz Seeger *SEE* Leitermann, Johann Philipp
Leitermann, Georg *SEE* Leitermann, Johann Philipp
Leitermann, Jakob; New York, 1884 ***2526.43*** *p206*
Leitermann, Johann Philipp; New York, 1883 ***2526.43*** *p126*
*Wife:*Elisabetha Katharina Blatz Seeger
*Son:*Leonhard
*Son:*Georg
*Son:*Philipp
Leitermann, Leonhard *SEE* Leitermann, Johann Philipp
Leitermann, Philipp *SEE* Leitermann, Johann Philipp
Leitermann, Wilhelm; America, 1880 ***2526.43*** *p152*
Leith, George 49; Ontario, 1871 ***1823.21*** *p200*
Leith, John; America, 1767 ***1220.12*** *p490*
Leith, William 30; Ontario, 1871 ***1823.17*** *p91*
Leithauser, M.; Nova Scotia, 1784 ***7105*** *p24*
Leitheuser, Karl Wilhelm August; America, 1886 ***7420.1*** *p351*
Leitheusser, Friedrich Wilhelm Carl Heinrich; America, 1886 ***7420.1*** *p351*
Leitner, August *SEE* Leitner, Georg
Leitner, Christian Ruff *SEE* Leitner, Georg
Leitner, Christina Fahndrich *SEE* Leitner, Georg
Leitner, Ferdinand Ruff *SEE* Leitner, Georg
Leitner, Friedrich *SEE* Leitner, Georg
Leitner, Georg *SEE* Leitner, Georg
Leitner, Georg; Dakota, 1875-1918 ***554.30*** *p25*
*Wife:*Christina Fahndrich
*Child:*Johann
*Child:*August
*Child:*Friedrich
*Child:*Georg
*Child:*Christian Ruff
*Child:*Ferdinand Ruff
*Child:*Jacob Ruff
Leitner, Jacob Ruff *SEE* Leitner, Georg
Leitner, Johann *SEE* Leitner, Georg
Leitner, Katharina; Dakota, 1888 ***554.30*** *p25*
Leitner, Maria; Dakota, 1888 ***554.30*** *p25*
Leitner, Mariane; Dakota, 1886 ***554.30*** *p25*
Leitz, Hermann; Colorado, 1895 ***1029.59*** *p22*
Leitzing, Jos.; Louisiana, 1874-1875 ***4981.45*** *p29*
Leizinsky, Petter Alexander; North America, 1847 ***6410.15*** *p104*
Le Jeune, . . .; Maryland, 1763 ***9228.50*** *p356*
Lejeune, Antoine 9; America, 1846 ***778.6*** *p208*
Lejeune, Augustine 49; Port uncertain, 1840 ***778.6*** *p208*
Le Jeune, Eliz.; Quebec, 1862 ***9228.50*** *p466*
Lejeune, Felix 5; America, 1846 ***778.6*** *p208*
Le Jeune, Gregoire; Virginia, 1621 ***9228.50*** *p356*
With wife & 4 children
Lejeune, Jean 6; America, 1846 ***778.6*** *p208*

Lejeune, Jean 48; America, 1846 *778.6 p208*
Le Jeune, John; Salem, MA, 1713 *9228.50 p656*
Lejeune, Jules 24; Port uncertain, 1840 *778.6 p208*
Lejeune, Louis 3; America, 1846 *778.6 p208*
LeJeune, Louis 31; America, 1844 *778.6 p208*
Le Jeune, Lucq; Nevis, 1684 *9228.50 p356*
Le Jeune, Lucq; St. Kitts, n.d. *9228.50 p656*
LeJeune, M. 30; America, 1844 *778.6 p208*
Lejeune, Marie 45; America, 1846 *778.6 p208*
Lejeune, Marie Therese; Wisconsin, 1855 *1495.20 p8*
LeJeune, Paul 41; Quebec, 1632 *9221.17 p23*
Le Jeune, Rachel; Utah, 1851 *9228.50 p309*
Le Jeune, William; Boston, 1880-1889 *9228.50 p356*
Lejonc, Anne 58; Quebec, 1655 *9221.17 p326*
Lejonhjort, John; St. Paul, MN, 1892 *1865.50 p94*
Lejuste, Francis 26; America, 1848 *778.6 p208*
Lejuste, Leontine 28; America, 1848 *778.6 p208*
Lelabloureur, Anne 26; Quebec, 1656 *9221.17 p340*
Le Lacheur, Caroline SEE Le Lacheur, Peter
Le Lacheur, Charlotte; Providence, RI, 1849-1900
   9228.50 p276
Le Lacheur, Elisha M.; New York, NY, 1849-1900
   9228.50 p276
Le Lacheur, Eliza M.; Providence, RI, 1849-1900
   9228.50 p276
Le Lacheur, Francois; New York, 1600-1699 *9228.50*
   p326
Le Lacheur, George N.; Massachusetts, 1863-1955
   9228.50 p326
Le Lacheur, George Nicholas; Salem, MA, 1890 *9228.50*
   p357
Le Lacheur, Gustavus; New York, 1892 *9228.50 p356*
Le Lacheur, Henry J. SEE Le Lacheur, Peter
Le Lacheur, James SEE Le Lacheur, Peter
Le Lacheur, Jane La Rue SEE Le Lacheur, Peter
Le Lacheur, Jane; Prince Edward Island, 1806 *9228.50*
   p356
   *Father:*John
Le Lacheur, John SEE Le Lacheur, Jane
Lelacheur, Mary 45; Ontario, 1871 *1823.21 p200*
Le Lacheur, Peter SEE Le Lacheur, Peter
Le Lacheur, Peter; Nova Scotia, 1843-1845 *9228.50*
   p357
   *Wife:*Jane La Rue
   *Child:*William
   *Child:*James
   *Child:*Henry J.
   *Child:*Caroline
   *Child:*Peter
Le Lacheur, William SEE Le Lacheur, Peter
Le Lacheur Family ; Nova Scotia, 1800-1863 *9228.50*
   p326
LeLacheur Family ; Prince Edward Island, 1806 *9228.50*
   p128
Leland, Isaac C.; Louisiana, 1874 *4981.45 p132*
Leland, Thomas; Havana, 1782 *8529.30 p9A*
Lelat, Pierre 20; Quebec, 1656 *9221.17 p340*
Lelauvre, J. 34; America, 1843 *778.6 p208*
Lelect, Miss 27; New Orleans, 1845 *778.6 p208*
Leleu, Angelique Desiree 24; New Orleans, 1842 *778.6*
   p208
Lelevrier, Jacques; Quebec, 1637 *9221.17 p70*
Le Lievre, . . .; Ohio, n.d. *9228.50 p327*
Lelievre, Mr. 15; America, 1841 *778.6 p208*
Lelievre, Antoine; Quebec, 1659 *9221.17 p414*
Le Lievre, Daniel; Quebec, 1766-1790 *9228.50 p358*
Lelievre, Francoise 17; Quebec, 1652 *9221.17 p261*
Lelievre, Guillaume; Quebec, 1600-1663 *4514.3 p339*
Lelievre, Guillaume 48; Quebec, 1659 *9221.17 p405*
Lelievre, Jeanne; Quebec, 1663 *4514.3 p339*
Lelievre, Mathurin 21; Montreal, 1662 *9221.17 p498*
Lellemhaga, Ja. 20; Halifax, N.S., 1902 *1860.4 p43*
Lelleongreen, Frederick; America, 1774 *1220.12 p495*
Lellig, Elisabeth 23; America, 1857 *5475.1 p282*
Lellig, Johann; America, 1867 *5475.1 p225*
Lellig, Johann; New York, 1868 *5475.1 p225*
Lellig, Mathias; America, 1854 *5475.1 p277*
Lellman, Peter; Illinois, 1859 *6079.1 p8*
Lellmann, Bernhard Paul Julius SEE Lellmann, Hermann
Lellmann, Carl August Adolf SEE Lellmann, Hermann
Lellmann, Ernst August Hubert SEE Lellmann, Hermann
Lellmann, Heinrich; America, 1904 *7420.1 p380*
Lellmann, Hermann; Rio Grande do Sul, Brazil, 1897
   7420.1 p374
   With wife
   *Son:*Bernhard Paul Julius
   *Son:*Paul Albert Carl
   *Son:*Johannes Ernst Hermann
   *Son:*Carl August Adolf
   *Son:*Ernst August Hubert
Lellmann, Johannes Ernst Hermann SEE Lellmann,
  Hermann

Lellmann, Maximilian Ludwig; Port uncertain, 1888
   7420.1 p357
Lellmann, Paul Albert Carl SEE Lellmann, Hermann
Lelong, Louis 22; Quebec, 1642 *9221.17 p119*
Lelong, Marie; Quebec, 1671 *4514.3 p338*
Lelong, Marie-Anne; Quebec, 1670 *4514.3 p338*
Leloup, Catherine; Quebec, 1668 *4514.3 p338*
Leloup, Edward; Louisiana, 1836-1841 *4981.45 p209*
Leloutre, Andre 16; Quebec, 1656 *9221.17 p331*
Leloutre, Francois; Quebec, 1648 *9221.17 p200*
Leloux, Fulvie; Wisconsin, 1880 *1495.20 p55*
Leloyal, Jacques 25; Quebec, 1642 *9221.17 p111*
Lelyonnais, Etienne 40; Quebec, 1660 *9221.17 p439*
Lem, John; America, 1764 *1220.12 p495*
Lemaignan, Jean 25; Montreal, 1661 *9221.17 p474*
Lemaine, Joseph 22; Louisiana, 1840 *778.6 p208*
Lemaire, Mr. 30; Texas, 1840 *778.6 p208*
Lemaire, Anne; Quebec, 1673 *4514.3 p338*
Lemaire, Jean 20; America, 1840 *778.6 p208*
Lemaire, Marie; Quebec, 1669 *4514.3 p339*
Le Maistre, . . .; Winnipeg, Man., n.d. *9228.50 p359*
Le Maistre, Miss; Ontario, n.d. *9228.50 p18A*
Lemaistre, Antoine 28; Quebec, 1659 *9221.17 p405*
Lemaistre, Barthelemy 26; Montreal, 1660 *9221.17 p442*
Lemaistre, Catherine 39; Quebec, 1662 *9221.17 p487*
Lemaistre, Denise 23; Montreal, 1659 *9221.17 p423*
Le Maistre, Edward; America, 1700-1793 *9228.50 p359*
   *Wife:*Rachel Durell
Le Maistre, Francis; New Jersey, 1667 *9228.50 p358*
Lemaistre, Francois 20; Quebec, 1651 *9221.17 p246*
Le Maistre, Frederick; Philadelphia, 1860 *9228.50 p359*
   *Relative:*John
   *Relative:*Peter
   *Relative:*Thomas
   *Relative:*Henry
Le Maistre, Frederick John; Pennsylvania, 1900-1983
   9228.50 p358
Le Maistre, Henry SEE Le Maistre, Frederick
Lemaistre, Jacques 42; Montreal, 1659 *9221.17 p414*
Le Maistre, John SEE Le Maistre, Frederick
Lemaistre, Noel; Quebec, 1659 *9221.17 p414*
Lemaistre, Pascal 32; Quebec, 1651 *9221.17 p246*
Le Maistre, Peter SEE Le Maistre, Frederick
Le Maistre, Peter; San Francisco, 1851 *9228.50 p192*
Le Maistre, Peter; San Francisco, 1851 *9228.50 p359*
Le Maistre, Rachel Durell SEE Le Maistre, Edward
Le Maistre, Rachel; New York, 1900-1983 *9228.50 p358*
Lemaistre, Robert; Quebec, 1659 *9221.17 p414*
Le Maistre, Thomas; Marblehead, MA, 1754-1799
   9228.50 p358
Le Maistre, Thomas SEE Le Maistre, Frederick
Le Maistre Family ; Canada, 1870-1879 *9228.50 p358*
Le Maistre Family ; Canada, n.d. *9228.50 p359*
Le Maitre, . . .; Canada, n.d. *9228.50 p18A*
Le Maitre, Abraham; Maryland, 1662 *9228.50 p358*
Lemaitre, Anne; Quebec, 1663 *4514.3 p339*
   *Daughter-In-Law:*Jeanne Lelievre
   *Grandchild:*Nicolas
   *Grandchild:*Louis
Lemaitre, Gabrielle; Quebec, 1667 *4514.3 p339*
Le Maitre, Philip; Quebec, 1889 *9228.50 p359*
Le Maitre, Rachel Mary Steen; Toronto, 1829-1908
   9228.50 p359
Lemajor, Louis 22; Quebec, 1661 *9221.17 p456*
Leman, Francis J.; North Carolina, 1825 *1088.45 p19*
Leman, Henry; Virginia, 1736 *1220.12 p495*
Lemane, Vincent 36; New Orleans, 1843 *778.6 p208*
Lemange, Peter; America, 1767 *1220.12 p495*
Lemann, Elisabeth 50; Port uncertain, 1842 *778.6 p208*
Lemann, Martin 30; Port uncertain, 1842 *778.6 p209*
Lemanne, Mr. 24; America, 1847 *778.6 p209*
Lemarchand, Jacques 18; Quebec, 1656 *9221.17 p341*
Lemarchand, Marguerite-Jeanne; Quebec, 1636 *9221.17*
   p59
   *Son:*Jacques
   *Granddaughter:*Anne
   *Son:*Michel
   *Daughter:*Marie
   *Granddaughter:*Marie-Anne
   *Daughter-In-Law:*Marguerite-Marie Legardeur De Tilly
Lemarchand, Marguerite-Jeanne; Quebec, 1636 *9221.17*
   p59
Le Marchand, Nicholas; Montreal, 1795-1867 *9228.50*
   p359
Le Marchand deLignery, Constant; Quebec, 1683-1688
   2314.30 p168
Le Marchand deLignery, Constant; Quebec, 1687
   2314.30 p188
Le Marchant, Johanna; New York, 1842-1900 *9228.50*
   p359
Lemarcom, Jane; Salem, MA, 1653-1674 *9228.50 p425*
Le Marcom, Jane; Salem, MA, 1676 *9228.50 p359*
Le Marcom, Jane 6; Salem, MA, 1659 *9228.50 p360*

Le Marcum, Jane 6; Salem, MA, 1659 *9228.50 p360*
Le Marguard, Maria Ann; Utah, 1810-1900 *9228.50*
   p359
Lemarie, Jacques 33; Quebec, 1660 *9221.17 p437*
   *Wife:*Marie Morin 31
   *Son:*Michel 7
Lemarie, Marie Morin 31 SEE Lemarie, Jacques
Lemarie, Michel 7 SEE Lemarie, Jacques
Lemarie, P. 22; America, 1840 *778.6 p209*
Lemarie, V. 16; America, 1840 *778.6 p209*
Le Marinel, . . .; New England, n.d. *9228.50 p127*
Le Marinel, Andre; Maine, n.d. *9228.50 p20A*
Le Marinel, Emelie Le Gresley SEE Le Marinel, John,
  Sr.
Le Marinel, Emilie Le Gresley SEE Le Marinel, John
Le Marinel, John; Massachusetts, 1870 *9228.50 p353*
   *Wife:*Emilie Le Gresley
Le Marinel, John, Jr. SEE Le Marinel, John, Sr.
Le Marinel, John, Sr.; Massachusetts, 1873 *9228.50*
   p359
   *Wife:*Emelie Le Gresley
   *Child:*John, Jr.
   *Child:*Theodore
Le Marinel, Theodore SEE Le Marinel, John, Sr.
Le Marinel, Thomas; Salem, MA, 1650 *9228.50 p424*
Le Marquand, Charles P.; Quebec, 1882-1926 *9228.50*
   p362
Le Marquand, Edward; Michigan, 1890 *9228.50 p362*
Le Marquand, Elias John SEE Le Marquand, Ernest
  Philip
LeMarquand, Elizabeth; Minnesota, 1857-1891 *9228.50*
   p361
Le Marquand, Ernest Philip; America, 1800-1899
   9228.50 p431
   *Brother:*Elias John
   *Brother:*Samuel James
Le Marquand, Jane 6; Salem, MA, 1659 *9228.50 p360*
Le Marquand, John; Newfoundland, 1818-1846 *9228.50*
   p361
Le Marquand, Samuel James SEE Le Marquand, Ernest
  Philip
Lemarquis, Francois; Quebec, 1643 *9221.17 p132*
le Masservier, . . .; Boston, 1769 *9228.50 p5*
Le Masservier, Charles; Boston, 1769 *9228.50 p48*
Le Masservier, Charles; Boston, 1769 *9228.50 p363*
Le Master, Abraham; Maryland, 1662 *9228.50 p358*
Le Masurier, . . .; Massachusetts, 1969 *9228.50 p50*
Le Masurier, . . .; Massachusetts, n.d. *9228.50 p19A*
Le Masurier, Amedee Ernes Pierre Lionel 3 SEE Le
  Masurier, Josue Elie
Le Masurier, Ann Jane Louise Buesnel SEE Le
  Masurier, John Philip
Le Masurier, Charles Garnet; Massachusetts, 1900-1940
   9228.50 p363
Le Masurier, George; Massachusetts, 1883-1949 *9228.50*
   p363
Le Masurier, John Philip; Canada, n.d. *9228.50 p19A*
   *Wife:*Ann Jane Louise Buesnel
Le Masurier, John T. 75; Quebec, 1901 *9228.50 p363*
Le Masurier, Josue Elie; Richmond, VA, 1847 *9228.50*
   p363
   *Son:*Amedee Ernes Pierre Lionel
Le Masurier, Thomas; Massachusetts, 1907 *9228.50*
   p362
Le Matre, Rachel Mary Steen; Toronto, 1829-1908
   9228.50 p359
Lemay, Michel 25; Quebec, 1654 *9221.17 p312*
Lemb, Mag.; New York, 1859 *358.56 p55*
Lembach, M.; New York, 1860 *358.56 p150*
Le Mee, Francis; Philadelphia, 1807 *9228.50 p363*
Lemee, Fs. Gilles 26; Missouri, 1848 *778.6 p209*
Lemeilleur, Jacques 28; Quebec, 1661 *9221.17 p461*
Lemeilleur, Pierre 19; Quebec, 1661 *9221.17 p461*
Lemelin, Jean 26; Quebec, 1657 *9221.17 p361*
Lemelle, Jean 30; America, 1840 *778.6 p209*
Lemenager, Camille SEE Lemenager, Jean Joseph
Lemenager, Celinie SEE Lemenager, Jean Joseph
Lemenager, Dieudonne SEE Lemenager, Jean Joseph
Lemenager, Eugene SEE Lemenager, Jean Joseph
Lemenager, Francois Xavier; Wisconsin, 1856 *1495.20*
   p41
Lemenager, Jean Joseph; Illinois, 1857 *1495.20 p41*
   *Child:*Dieudonne
   *Child:*Celinie
   *Child:*Eugene
   *Child:*Camille
LeMeneye, . . .; Quebec, 1657 *9221.17 p366*
Lemense, Alphonse Julien SEE Lemense, Louis Joseph
Lemense, Ferdinand SEE Lemense, Ferdinand
Lemense, Ferdinand; Wisconsin, 1855-1870 *1495.20 p8*
   *Wife:*Marie Josephe Justine Fortemps
   *Child:*Josephine

              FOR A COMPLETE EXPLANATION OF ENTRY, SEE "HOW TO READ A CITATION" SECTION

*Child:*Ferdinand
*Child:*Marie Joseph
*Child:*Jean
Lemense, Jean *SEE* Lemense, Ferdinand
Lemense, Josephine *SEE* Lemense, Ferdinand
Lemense, Louis Joseph; Wisconsin, 1855 *1495.20 p8*
  *Wife:*Marie Anastasie Fortemps
  *Child:*Marie Joseph
  *Child:*Alphonse Julien
Lemense, Marie Anastasie Fortemps *SEE* Lemense, Louis
  Joseph
Lemense, Marie Joseph *SEE* Lemense, Ferdinand
Lemense, Marie Joseph *SEE* Lemense, Louis Joseph
Lemense, Marie Josephe Justine Fortemps *SEE* Lemense,
  Ferdinand
Lemense, Marie Therese; Wisconsin, 1855 *1495.20 p8*
Lemer, Mathieu 35; Quebec, 1642 *9221.17 p119*
Lemer, Nicole; Quebec, 1635 *9221.17 p43*
Lemercher, Jean 25; Montreal, 1653 *9221.17 p295*
Le Mercier, Francois; Quebec, 1740 *2314.30 p170*
Le Mercier, Francois; Quebec, 1740 *2314.30 p189*
Lemercier, Francois-Joseph 31; Quebec, 1635 *9221.17
  p42*
Lemercier, Jean; Quebec, 1645 *9221.17 p155*
Lemercier, Marguerite; Montreal, 1653 *9221.17 p295*
Lemerle De Hautpre, Marguerite; Quebec, 1671 *4514.3
  p339*
Le Mesarier, Harriet; Utah, 1863 *9228.50 p365*
Lemesle, Catherine; Quebec, 1671 *4514.3 p339*
Lemesnager, Claude; Quebec, 1639 *9221.17 p90*
Le Messurier, Benj.; Salem, MA, 1677 *9228.50 p412*
Le Messurier, Benjamin; Salem, MA, 1650-1675
  9228.50 p440
Le Messurier, Charles; Boston, 1769 *9228.50 p363*
Le Messurier, Eliz. Allez *SEE* Le Messurier, John
Le Messurier, George; Massachusetts, n.d. *9228.50 p439*
Le Messurier, George; Newbury, MA, 1672 *9228.50
  p420*
Le Messurier, Jane; Died enroute, 1677 *9228.50 p440*
Le Messurier, John; Wisconsin, 1846 *9228.50 p19A*
  *Wife:*Eliz. Allez
  With 3 children
Le Messurier, Joseph; Salem, MA, 1655-1680 *9228.50
  p440*
Le Messurier, Joseph Tallman *SEE* Le Messurier, Pierre
Le Messurier, Laurence; Salem, MA, 1646-1670 *9228.50
  p439*
Le Messurier, Margaret *SEE* Le Messurier, Mary Le
  Prevost
Le Messurier, Martin; Massachusetts, 1652-1709 *9228.50
  p440*
Le Messurier, Mary; Wisconsin, 1847 *9228.50 p364*
  *Child:*Margaret
  *Child:*Mary Ann
  *Child:*Matilda
Le Messurier, Mary Ann *SEE* Le Messurier, Mary Le
  Prevost
Le Messurier, Mary Anne; Wisconsin, 1832-1916
  9228.50 p486
Le Messurier, Matilda *SEE* Le Messurier, Mary Le
  Prevost
Le Messurier, Matilda; Wisconsin, 1856 *9228.50 p253*
Le Messurier, Peter; Detroit, 1834-1900 *9228.50 p319*
  *Wife:*Rachel Langlois
Le Messurier, Pierre; Detroit, 1871-1891 *9228.50 p363*
  *Son:*Joseph Tallman
Le Messurier, Rachel; Baltimore, 1799-1806 *9228.50
  p228*
Le Messurier, Rachel Langlois *SEE* Le Messurier, Peter
Le Messurier, Thomas; Detroit, 1827 *9228.50 p363*
Le Messurier Family ; Wisconsin, 1840 *9228.50 p64*
Le Mesurier, Desmond; America, 1902-1983 *9228.50
  p364*
Le Mesurier, Dorothy; America, 1964-1983 *9228.50
  p365*
Le Mesurier, Elizabeth; Edmonton, Alberta, 1908
  9228.50 p508
Le Mesurier, Elizabeth; Edmonton, Alberta, 1908
  9228.50 p508
Le Mesurier, Harriet; Utah, 1863 *9228.50 p365*
Le Mesurier, Henriette; New York, 1870 *9228.50 p435*
Lemet, J. 26; Louisiana, 1847 *778.6 p209*
Lemeusnier, Perrine 32; Montreal, 1653 *9221.17 p287*
Lemieux, Gabriel 21; Quebec, 1647 *9221.17 p183*
Lemieux, Pierre 22; Quebec, 1638 *9221.17 p78*
Lemiller, John; Ohio, 1809-1852 *4511.35 p30*
Lemin, John 17; Ontario, 1871 *1823.21 p200*
Leming, Robert; Canada, 1774 *3036.5 p41*
Leming, Robert, Jr.; Canada, 1774 *3036.5 p41*
Lemire, Francois; Quebec, 1651 *9221.17 p247*
Lemire, Jean 25; Quebec, 1650 *9221.17 p247*
Lemke, Carl Wilhelm Fredrik; America, 1890 *6410.15
  p106*

Lemke, Charles Frederick; Wisconsin, 1914 *6795.8 p173*
Lemke, Ernestine; Wisconsin, 1887 *6795.8 p71*
Lemmer, Anna Marie; America, 1880 *8115.12 p325*
  *Child:*Marie
Lemmer, Marie *SEE* Lemmer, Anna Marie
Lemmermann, Charles; Louisiana, 1841-1844 *4981.45
  p210*
Lemmle, Jacob 8; New York, NY, 1893 *1883.7 p39*
Lemmle, Jacob 8; New York, NY, 1893 *1883.7 p47*
Lemmle, Johann 6; New York, NY, 1893 *1883.7 p39*
Lemmle, Johann 6; New York, NY, 1893 *1883.7 p47*
Lemmle, Johann 39; New York, NY, 1893 *1883.7 p39*
Lemmle, Johann 39; New York, NY, 1893 *1883.7 p47*
Lemmle, Katha. 10; New York, NY, 1893 *1883.7 p47*
Lemmle, Katha. 33; New York, NY, 1893 *1883.7 p47*
Lemmle, Kathe. 10; New York, NY, 1893 *1883.7 p39*
Lemmle, Kathe. 33; New York, NY, 1893 *1883.7 p39*
Lemmle, Margar. 4; New York, NY, 1893 *1883.7 p47*
Lemmle, Margare. 4; New York, NY, 1893 *1883.7 p39*
Lemmle, Philipp 8 months; New York, NY, 1893 *1883.7
  p39*
Lemmle, Philipp 9 months; New York, NY, 1893 *1883.7
  p47*
Lemmon, John; North America, 1711 *9228.50 p366*
Lemmon, Nicholas; America, 1678 *1220.12 p495*
Lemmon, Peter *SEE* Lemmon, Robert
Lemmon, Robert; Salem, MA, 1637 *9228.50 p366*
  *Relative:*Peter
Lemoal, Marie Perrine 23; America, 1846 *778.6 p209*
Lemocks, Elizabeth; Virginia, 1739 *1220.12 p495*
Lemoine, Mr. 32; America, 1842 *778.6 p209*
Lemoine, Barthelemy; Quebec, 1636 *9221.17 p59*
Lemoine, Claude 35; Quebec, 1643 *9221.17 p132*
Lemoine, Franc. 17; America, 1840 *778.6 p209*
Lemoine, Francois; Illinois, 1852 *6079.1 p8*
Lemoine, Francoise; Quebec, 1665 *4514.3 p339*
Lemoine, Jean 27; New Orleans, 1848 *778.6 p209*
Le Moine, John Charles; Newfoundland, 1816-1835
  9228.50 p366
Lemoine, Marie; Quebec, 1665 *4514.3 p339*
Le Moine, Peter *SEE* Le Moine, Robert
Lemoine, Pierre 25; New Orleans, 1848 *778.6 p209*
Le Moine, Robert; Salem, MA, 1637 *9228.50 p366*
  *Relative:*Peter
Lemoisson, Francois 23; America, 1844 *778.6 p209*
Lemon, David; America, 1770 *1220.12 p495*
Lemon, Elizabeth; America, 1736 *1220.12 p495*
Lemon, Elizabeth; Jamaica, 1661 *1220.12 p495*
Lemon, Elizabeth 40; Ontario, 1871 *1823.21 p200*
Lemon, Ignatius A.; Colorado, 1903 *1029.59 p54*
Lemon, John; Annapolis, MD, 1725 *1220.12 p495*
Lemon, John; North America, 1711 *9228.50 p366*
Lemon, Thomas; America, 1747 *1220.12 p495*
Lemon, William; America, 1741 *1220.12 p495*
Lemonee, John; North America, 1711 *9228.50 p366*
Lemonnier, Mathurin 25; Montreal, 1644 *9221.17 p148*
Le Montais, Jane; Maine, 1707 *9228.50 p367*
Le Montais, Jane; Maine, 1707 *9228.50 p367*
Le Montais, John; Boston, 1729 *9228.50 p189*
Le Montais, John; New York, 1686 *9228.50 p367*
Le Montais, Philip Joseph; Newfoundland, 1705 *9228.50
  p467*
Le Montais, Walter; Honolulu, 1875 *9228.50 p247*
Le Montes, John; Boston, 1729 *9228.50 p189*
Le Montes, John; New York, 1686 *9228.50 p367*
Le Montes, Philip Joseph; Newfoundland, 1705 *9228.50
  p467*
LeMore, A. 23; America, 1842 *778.6 p209*
Le Mote, George; Boston, 1725 *9228.50 p367*
Le Mote, Matthew; Plymouth, MA, 1728 *9228.50 p367*
Le Mottee, Clement; Maine, n.d. *9228.50 p467*
Le Mottee, Clement; New Hampshire, 1692 *9228.50
  p468*
Le Mottee, John; Massachusetts, 1800-1830 *9228.50
  p470*
Le Mottee, Matthew; Plymouth, MA, 1728 *9228.50 p367*
Lemousnier, Mathurin 25; Montreal, 1644 *9221.17 p148*
Lemoyne, . . .; Quebec, 1662 *9221.17 p489*
Lemoyne, Anne 19; Montreal, 1657 *9221.17 p372*
  *Brother:*Jacques 35
  *Sister:*Jeanne 27
Lemoyne, Charles 15; Quebec, 1641 *9221.17 p105*
Lemoyne, David 19; Montreal, 1653 *9221.17 p295*
Lemoyne, Jacques 35 *SEE* Lemoyne, Anne
Lemoyne, Jean 21; Quebec, 1656 *9221.17 p340*
Lemoyne, Jeanne 27 *SEE* Lemoyne, Anne
LeMoyne, Simon 34; Quebec, 1638 *9221.17 p75*
Lemoyne deLongueuil, Charles; Quebec, 1641 *2314.30
  p167*
Lemoyne deLongueuil, Charles; Quebec, 1668 *2314.30
  p189*
L'Empereur, Aurelie *SEE* L'Empereur, Jean Joseph
L'Empereur, Constant *SEE* L'Empereur, Jean Joseph

Lempereur, Eugene; Detroit, 1856 *1494.20 p11*
L'Empereur, Eugene *SEE* L'Empereur, Jean Joseph
L'Empereur, Ferdinande *SEE* L'Empereur, Jean Joseph
L'Empereur, Jean Joseph; Wisconsin, 1856 *1495.20 p45*
  *Wife:*Seraphine Delligne
  *Child:*Marie Catherine
  *Child:*Nestor
  *Child:*Aurelie
  *Child:*Eugene
  *Child:*Ferdinande
  *Child:*Constant
  *Child:*Octavie
L'Empereur, Marie Catherine *SEE* L'Empereur, Jean
  Joseph
L'Empereur, Nestor *SEE* L'Empereur, Jean Joseph
L'Empereur, Octavie *SEE* L'Empereur, Jean Joseph
L'Empereur, Seraphine Delligne *SEE* L'Empereur, Jean
  Joseph
Lempert, Friederike; America, 1868 *7919.3 p525*
Lempert, Georgine; America, 1868 *7919.3 p525*
  With 2 children
Lempks, David 25; Halifax, N.S., 1902 *1860.4 p44*
Lempks, Emilia; Halifax, N.S., 1902 *1860.4 p44*
Lempks, Godbina 20; Halifax, N.S., 1902 *1860.4 p44*
Lempks, Lydia 2; Halifax, N.S., 1902 *1860.4 p44*
Lempriere, . . .; Newfoundland, 1717 *9228.50 p367*
Lempriere, Arthur Reid; British Columbia, 1859 *9228.50
  p368*
Lempriere, Eva Hubert *SEE* Lempriere, John Philip
Lempriere, Geo.; Wisconsin, n.d. *9228.50 p19A*
Lempriere, George; Wisconsin, 1860-1869 *9228.50 p631*
Lempriere, John Philip; Edmonton, Alberta, 1888-1919
  9228.50 p368
  With wife
Lempriere, John Philip; Edmonton, Alberta, 1888-1964
  9228.50 p214
  *Wife:*Eva Hubert
Lempriere, Thomas; Virginia, 1671 *9228.50 p367*
Lempriere Family ; Wisconsin, n.d. *9228.50 p368*
Lena, Martin 22; America, 1847 *778.6 p209*
Lenabery, Casper; New Jersey, 1739-1774 *927.31 p3*
Lenabery, Conrad; New Jersey, 1739-1774 *927.31 p3*
Lenabery, Nicholas; New Jersey, 1739-1774 *927.31 p3*
Lenahan, Owen; St. John, N.B., 1847 *2978.15 p36*
Lenan, Thomas; Marston's Wharf, 1782 *8529.30 p13*
Lenander, C.E.; New York, NY, 1845 *6412.40 p149*
Lenard, John; America, 1773 *1220.12 p496*
Lenard, Roger; Philadelphia, 1778 *8529.30 p7A*
Lenard, Walter Joseph; Detroit, 1929 *1640.55 p116*
Lenart, Wawrzyniec 29; New York, NY, 1911 *6533.11
  p9*
Lench, Patrick; Boston, 1748 *1642 p46*
Lenderhan, James; Newfoundland, 1814 *3476.10 p54*
Lendermann, Philip Frantz; Ohio, 1809-1852 *4511.35
  p30*
Lendigren, Nathaniel; Havana, 1782 *8529.30 p9A*
Lendon, John; Virginia, 1768 *1220.12 p495*
Lendon, Joseph 39; Ontario, 1871 *1823.17 p91*
Lendrum, James 27; Ontario, 1871 *1823.21 p200*
Leneuf, Anne 4 *SEE* Leneuf, Marguerite-Jeanne
  Lemarchand
Leneuf, Jacques 30 *SEE* Leneuf, Marguerite-Jeanne
  Lemarchand
Leneuf, Marguerite-Jeanne; Quebec, 1636 *9221.17 p59*
  *Son:*Jacques
  *Granddaughter:*Anne
  *Son:*Michel
  *Daughter:*Marie
  *Granddaughter:*Marie-Anne
  *Daughter-In-Law:*Marguerite-Marie Legardeur De Tilly
Leneuf, Marguerite-Marie Legardeur De Tilly 28 *SEE*
  Leneuf, Marguerite-Jeanne Lemarchand
Leneuf, Marie 25 *SEE* Leneuf, Marguerite-Jeanne
  Lemarchand
Leneuf, Marie-Anne 4 *SEE* Leneuf, Marguerite-Jeanne
  Lemarchand
Leneuf, Michel 35 *SEE* Leneuf, Marguerite-Jeanne
  Lemarchand
Leneuf deLa Poterie, Jacques; Quebec, 1636 *2314.30
  p166*
Leneuf deLa Poterie, Jacques; Quebec, 1636 *2314.30
  p189*
Leneuf DeLaPoterie, Jacques 30; Quebec, 1636 *9221.17
  p60*
  *Wife:*Marguerite-Marie Legardeur DeTilly 28
  *Daughter:*Marie-Anne 4
Leneuf DeLaPoterie, Marguerite-Marie Legardeur
  DeTilly 28 *SEE* Leneuf DeLaPoterie, Jacques
Leneuf DeLaPoterie, Marie-Anne 4 *SEE* Leneuf
  DeLaPoterie, Jacques
Leneuf DuHerisson, Marguerite-Jeanne; Quebec, 1636
  9221.17 p59

Leneuf DuHerisson, Marie 25; Quebec, 1636 *9221.17 p60*
Leneuf duHerisson, Michel; Quebec, 1636 *2314.30 p166*
Leneuf duHerisson, Michel; Quebec, 1636 *2314.30 p189*
LeNeuf DuHerisson, Michel 35; Quebec, 1636 *9221.17 p61*
Le Neveu, David; California, 1851 *9228.50 p368*
Le Neveu, David; Victoria, B.C., 1851-1900 *9228.50 p368*
Le Neveu, Elizabeth; Canada, 1849 *9228.50 p100*
Lenfestey, Harriet; Ohio, 1826 *9228.50 p376*
Lenfestey, James; Vancouver, B.C., 1860-1869 *9228.50 p376*
Lenfestey, John; Ohio, 1860 *9228.50 p376*
Lenfestey, John; Toledo, OH, 1876-1937 *9228.50 p375*
Lenfestey, John, Sr. 62; Ontario, 1871 *1823.21 p200*
Lenfestey, Nacy; Ohio, 1815 *9228.50 p376*
Lenfestey, Peter; America, 1870 *9228.50 p376*
Lenfestey, Thomas; Norfolk, VA, 1806 *9228.50 p56*
  With wife & children
Lenfestey, Thomas; Ohio, 1806 *9228.50 p376*
Lenfestey, Thomas 56; Ontario, 1871 *1823.21 p200*
Lenfesty, Anna Young *SEE* Lenfesty, William
Lenfesty, Carterette; Ohio, 1788-1878 *9228.50 p376*
Lenfesty, Charles *SEE* Lenfesty, William
Lenfesty, Henry *SEE* Lenfesty, William
Lenfesty, James; Quebec, 1786-1814 *9228.50 p369*
Lenfesty, John; Michigan, 1868-1950 *9228.50 p376*
Lenfesty, John; Ohio, 1800-1849 *9228.50 p15*
Lenfesty, John; Pittsburgh, 1750-1837 *9228.50 p376*
Lenfesty, Mark Arthur *SEE* Lenfesty, William
Lenfesty, Peter; Maine, 1739-1775 *9228.50 p370*
Lenfesty, Robert; Philadelphia, 1770 *9228.50 p374*
Lenfesty, Sterrie Hunt; Ontario, 1885-1894 *9228.50 p369*
Lenfesty, William; Detroit, 1885 *9228.50 p369*
  *Wife:*Anna Young
  *Child:*Henry
  *Child:*Mark Arthur
  *Child:*Charles
L'Enfete, John; Ontario, 1846 *9228.50 p376*
Lenfit, John; Ontario, 1846 *9228.50 p376*
Leng, Auguste; America, 1868 *7919.3 p534*
Lengacker, Christian; Ohio, 1809-1852 *4511.35 p30*
Lenganiad, Edwin 26; Ontario, 1871 *1823.21 p200*
Lenger, Jan; South Dakota, 1869-1871 *2853.20 p246*
Lengesick, Wm.; Ohio, 1840-1897 *8365.35 p17*
Lenhart, Christian; Ohio, 1809-1852 *4511.35 p30*
Lenhart, Jacob; Ohio, 1809-1852 *4511.35 p30*
Lenhier, Pier.e 17; New Orleans, 1845 *778.6 p209*
Lenhof, Barbara; America, 1872 *5475.1 p139*
Lenhof, Barbara *SEE* Lenhof, Karl
Lenhof, Johann 68 *SEE* Lenhof, Nikolaus
Lenhof, Karl; America, 1874 *5475.1 p140*
  *Wife:*Margarethe Cannivet
  *Daughter:*Barbara
Lenhof, Katharina; America, 1873 *5475.1 p140*
Lenhof, Margarethe *SEE* Lenhof, Nikolaus
Lenhof, Margarethe Hermann *SEE* Lenhof, Nikolaus
Lenhof, Margarethe Cannivet *SEE* Lenhof, Karl
Lenhof, Nik. Math. 4 *SEE* Lenhof, Nikolaus
Lenhof, Nikolaus; America, 1870 *5475.1 p134*
  *Wife:*Margarethe Hermann
  *Father:*Johann
  *Daughter:*Susanna
  *Son:*Peter
  *Daughter:*Margarethe
  *Son:*Nik. Math.
Lenhof, Peter *SEE* Lenhof, Nikolaus
Lenhof, Peter; America, 1873 *5475.1 p140*
Lenhof, Susanna *SEE* Lenhof, Nikolaus
Lenig, C. 30; New Orleans, 1834 *1002.51 p112*
Lenior, Charles Duffy; North Carolina, 1835 *1088.45 p19*
Lennan, Mic; St. John, N.B., 1848 *2978.15 p36*
Lennard, James; America, 1757 *1220.12 p496*
Lennard, Margaret; America, 1752 *1220.12 p496*
Lenneberg, Hermann *SEE* Lenneberg, Isak
Lenneberg, Isak; America, 1938 *8023.44 p376*
  *Son:*Julius
  *Son:*Hermann
Lenneberg, Julius *SEE* Lenneberg, Isak
Lennep, C.; Louisiana, 1874-1875 *4981.45 p29*
Lennerman, Emil; Illinois, 1873-1875 *6020.5 p132*
Lennigan, John; Virginia, 1763 *1220.12 p495*
Lennon, Ignatius; Colorado, 1903 *1029.59 p54*
Lennon, John; America, 1772 *1220.12 p495*
Lennon, Michael 48; Ontario, 1871 *1823.17 p91*
Lennon, Patrick; Washington, 1884 *2770.40 p192*
Lennon, Thomas; Marston's Wharf, 1782 *8529.30 p13*
Lennon, William 31; Ontario, 1871 *1823.21 p200*
Lennox, Agnes 17; Ontario, 1871 *1823.21 p200*
Lennox, James 62; Ontario, 1871 *1823.21 p200*
Lennox, Mary Ann 80; Ontario, 1871 *1823.17 p91*

Lennox, Thomas 43; Ontario, 1871 *1823.17 p91*
Lennox, William; America, 1672 *1220.12 p495*
Lennqvist, G.L.; New York, NY, 1851 *6412.40 p153*
Lenoble, Jean; Quebec, 1651 *9221.17 p247*
Lenoch, Vaclav; Chicago, 1869-1901 *2853.20 p422*
Lenoch, Vaclav; Chicago, 1869-1910 *2853.20 p404*
Lenocher, David; Ohio, 1809-1852 *4511.35 p30*
Lenoet, Jean-Baptiste; Quebec, 1659 *9221.17 p414*
Lenoir, Antoinette; Quebec, 1669 *4514.3 p339*
Lenon, Thomas; Marston's Wharf, 1782 *8529.30 p13*
Lenorchan, Ann; America, 1763 *1220.12 p495*
Lenord, Ida 17; Michigan, 1880 *4491.30 p20*
Lenord, Ida 47; Michigan, 1880 *4491.30 p20*
Lenord, Iseral 14; Michigan, 1880 *4491.30 p20*
Lenord, Maggy 12; Michigan, 1880 *4491.30 p20*
Lenord, Mary 15; Michigan, 1880 *4491.30 p20*
Lenord, Moses 47; Michigan, 1880 *4491.30 p20*
Lenord, Peter 19; Michigan, 1880 *4491.30 p20*
Lenord, William; Jamaica, 1779 *8529.30 p13A*
Lenormand, Edouarde Joineau *SEE* Lenormand, Gervais
Lenormand, Gervais; Quebec, 1647 *9221.17 p185*
  *Wife:*Edouarde Jouineau
  *Son:*Jean
Lenormand, Jacques 27; Montreal, 1661 *9221.17 p472*
Lenormand, Jean 11 *SEE* Lenormand, Gervais
Lenormand, Jean le vieux 38; Quebec, 1647 *9221.17 p186*
Le Noury, . . .; California, 1920-1929 *9228.50 p377*
Lenox, Mary; America, 1724 *1220.12 p495*
Lent, Thomas; America, 1760 *1220.12 p495*
Lentall, Thomas 51; Ontario, 1871 *1823.21 p200*
Lentes, Bergmann August; America, 1893 *5475.1 p42*
Lentes, Nikolaus 27; New York, 1887 *5475.1 p75*
Lenthal, Samuel; America, 1749 *1220.12 p495*
Lenthall, Thomas; America, 1766 *1220.12 p495*
Lenton, Martha; America, 1763 *1220.12 p495*
Lentritz, Henry; Ohio, 1809-1852 *4511.35 p30*
Lentriz, Henry; Ohio, 1809-1852 *4511.35 p30*
Lentz, Child; Pennsylvania, 1865 *170.15 p35*
  With sibling
Lentz, Anna Katharina 22; Pennsylvania, 1848 *170.15 p35*
  With brother
Lentz, Daniel; Ohio, 1809-1852 *4511.35 p30*
Lentz, George; Ohio, 1809-1852 *4511.35 p30*
Lentz, Gertraud; Pennsylvania, 1865 *170.15 p35*
Lentz, Gertraud; Pennsylvania, 1865 *170.15 p35*
  With family
Lentz, Joshua; Ohio, 1809-1852 *4511.35 p30*
Lentz, Leopold; America, 1882 *5475.1 p130*
Lentzich, C.H.; Missouri, 1888 *3276.1 p2*
Lenz, Child; Pennsylvania, 1865 *170.15 p35*
  With 4 siblings
Lenz, August Hermann; Wisconsin, 1896 *6795.8 p74*
Lenz, Barbara Kuhn *SEE* Lenz, Peter
Lenz, Charlotte *SEE* Lenz, Nikolaus
Lenz, Eugen; America, 1867 *7919.3 p534*
  With wife & 2 children
Lenz, Gertraud; Pennsylvania, 1865 *170.15 p35*
  With family
Lenz, Heinrich Johann Jakob; Pennsylvania, 1892 *5475.1 p39*
Lenz, Johann; Brazil, 1881 *5475.1 p373*
  *Wife:*Margarethe Barbian
  *Daughter:*Margarethe
Lenz, Margarethe *SEE* Lenz, Peter
Lenz, Margarethe *SEE* Lenz, Johann
Lenz, Margarethe Barbian *SEE* Lenz, Johann
Lenz, Matern *SEE* Lenz, Nikolaus
Lenz, Nikolaus; America, 1869 *5475.1 p50*
  *Sibling:*Matern
  *Sister:*Charlotte
Lenz, Peter; Brazil, 1874 *5475.1 p372*
  *Wife:*Barbara Kuhn
  *Daughter:*Margarethe
Lenz, Wilhelmine Ernestine; Wisconsin, 1897 *6795.8 p74*
Lenz, Wilhelmine Friedericke; Wisconsin, 1884 *6795.8 p90*
Lenzi, Caspar; New Castle, DE, 1817-1818 *90.20 p152*
Lenzi, J. Martin; New Castle, DE, 1817-1818 *90.20 p152*
Lenzi, Johann; New Castle, DE, 1817-1818 *90.20 p152*
Lenzi, Wendel; New Castle, DE, 1817-1818 *90.20 p152*
Leo, James; Toronto, 1844 *2910.35 p113*
Leo, John William; America, 1772 *1220.12 p495*
Leodet, Anne 21; Quebec, 1652 *9221.17 p261*
Leogerny, Daniel 25; New York, NY, 1847 *9176.15 p50*
Leoh, William 18; Ontario, 1871 *1823.21 p200*
Leolune, John D.; America, 1867 *9076.20 p69*
Leon, J. 36; America, 1848 *778.6 p209*
Leon, Jean 16; Port uncertain, 1841 *778.6 p209*
Leon, Jean H.; Louisiana, 1836-1841 *4981.45 p209*
Leon, Leon 37; Port uncertain, 1841 *778.6 p209*

Leon, Louis 22; New Orleans, 1848 *778.6 p209*
Leon, Morris; North Carolina, 1856 *1088.45 p19*
Leon, N. 10; New Orleans, 1846 *778.6 p209*
Leonard, Catharine 57; Ontario, 1871 *1823.21 p200*
Leonard, Christian; Ohio, 1809-1852 *4511.35 p30*
Leonard, Daniel; Toronto, 1844 *2910.35 p115*
Leonard, Ed; St. John, N.B., 1847 *2978.15 p36*
Leonard, Edward 30; Ontario, 1871 *1823.21 p200*
Leonard, Elijah 56; Ontario, 1871 *1823.21 p200*
Leonard, Elizabeth; America, 1749 *1220.12 p495*
Leonard, Hugh 22; Ontario, 1871 *1823.21 p200*
Leonard, Hugh 30; Ontario, 1871 *1823.21 p200*
Leonard, Jacques; Quebec, 1661 *9221.17 p461*
Leonard, James; Ohio, 1809-1852 *4511.35 p30*
Leonard, Johann Josef; America, 1872 *5475.1 p154*
Leonard, John 35; Michigan, 1880 *4491.33 p14*
Leonard, John 50; Ontario, 1871 *1823.21 p200*
Leonard, L. C. 57; Ontario, 1871 *1823.21 p200*
Leonard, Marie; Quebec, 1666 *4514.3 p340*
Leonard, Mary 16; Michigan, 1880 *4491.39 p17*
Leonard, Mary 78; Ontario, 1871 *1823.21 p200*
Leonard, Mary; Toronto, 1844 *2910.35 p113*
Leonard, Michael 38; Ontario, 1871 *1823.21 p200*
Leonard, Michel; America, 1843 *5475.1 p428*
  With wife
  With son
  With daughter
Leonard, Patrick; Illinois, 1834-1900 *6020.5 p132*
Leonard, Patrick 50; Ontario, 1871 *1823.21 p200*
Leonard, Patrick; Toronto, 1844 *2910.35 p113*
Leonard, Sarah; Massachusetts, 1660-1669 *9228.50 p377*
Leonard, Simeon; Ohio, 1809-1852 *4511.35 p30*
Leonard, Thomas; Ohio, 1809-1852 *4511.35 p30*
Leonard, Thomas 60; Ontario, 1871 *1823.21 p200*
Leonard, William; America, 1753 *1220.12 p496*
Leonard, William; America, 1774 *1220.12 p496*
Leonard, William; Illinois, 1857 *6079.1 p8*
Leonard, William; Jamaica, 1779 *8529.30 p13A*
Leonard, William 40; Ontario, 1871 *1823.17 p91*
Leonhard, Johan 19; America, 1840 *778.6 p209*
Leonhard, Philipp; America, 1843 *5475.1 p540*
Leonhard, Philipp Peter; America, 1843 *5475.1 p540*
Leonhardt, Ernst 40; Missouri, 1848 *778.6 p209*
Leonharebz, Reinh. 2; America, 1846 *778.6 p209*
Leonhart, John; St. Paul, MN, 1892 *1865.50 p94*
Leopold, Christopher; Nova Scotia, 1784 *7105 p24*
Leopold, Her.; Louisiana, 1874-1875 *4981.45 p29*
Leopold, Hirsch 17; America, 1882 *2526.42 p125*
Leorge, Jakob; North Carolina, 1710 *3629.40 p8*
Lep, Elenore 25; Halifax, N.S., 1902 *1860.4 p41*
Lep, Emil 1; Halifax, N.S., 1902 *1860.4 p41*
Lep, Erdmann 24; Halifax, N.S., 1902 *1860.4 p41*
Le Page, Mr.; New York, 1871 *9228.50 p379*
Le Page, Elisha; Charlottetown, P.E.I., 1764-1813 *9228.50 p378*
Lepage, Germain; Quebec, 1600-1673 *4514.3 p340*
  *Brother:*Louis
  *Relative:*Reine Lory
  *Child:*Rene
Le Page, John *SEE* Le Page, Thomas
Lepage, Louis *SEE* Lepage, Germain
Lepage, Marie-Rogere; Quebec, 1667 *4514.3 p340*
Le Page, Martha; America, 1821 *9228.50 p659*
Le Page, Martha 7 *SEE* Le Page, Thomas
Le Page, Nicholas; America, 1800-1899 *9228.50 p382*
Le Page, Norman *SEE* Le Page, Thomas
Le Page, Peter 26; Ontario, 1859 *9228.50 p382*
Lepage, Prosper 26; America, 1844 *778.6 p209*
Lepage, Reine Lory *SEE* Lepage, Germain
Lepage, Rene *SEE* Lepage, Germain
Le Page, Samuel; New York, NY, 1769 *9228.50 p379*
Le Page, Thomas; America, 1800-1899 *9228.50 p382*
  *Brother:*John
  *Brother:*Norman
Le Page, Thomas; America, 1820-1900 *9228.50 p573*
Le Page, Thomas; Ohio, 1813-1869 *9228.50 p382*
Le Page, Thomas; Ohio, 1817-1889 *9228.50 p382*
Le Page, Thomas 10; Ohio, 1818 *9228.50 p377*
  With aunt
  *Sister:*Martha 7
Le Page, William N.; Massachusetts, 1848-1919 *9228.50 p26*
Le Page Family ; Kentucky, 1836 *9228.50 p165*
Le Page Family ; Prince Edward Island, 1807 *9228.50 p26*
Le Page Guille, Arthur *SEE* Le Page Guille, James Philippe
Le Page Guille, James Philippe; Virginia, 1900-1940 *9228.50 p266*
  *Son:*Arthur
Lepallier, Joachim; Montreal, 1653 *9221.17 p295*
Le Patomal, Elias James 24; Ontario, 1859 *9228.50 p382*

Le Patourel, Alfred; Pennsylvania, 1886 ***9228.50*** *p382*
*Wife:*Emily Gaudion
Le Patourel, Anthony; Pennsylvania, 1900-1983 ***9228.50*** *p382*
Le Patourel, Anthony; Pennsylvania, 1900-1983 ***9228.50*** *p419*
Le Patourel, Arthur James; Alberta, 1881-1962 ***9228.50*** *p382*
Le Patourel, Emily Gaudion *SEE* Le Patourel, Alfred
LePatourel, Francis; New Hampshire, 1909-1910 ***9228.50*** *p382*
*Wife:*Miriam Flere Bisson Ogier
Le Patourel, Frank; Pennsylvania, 1921-1983 ***9228.50*** *p484*
*Wife:*Miriam Ogier
Le Patourel, J. Lewis; Alberta, 1881-1962 ***9228.50*** *p382*
Le Patourel, Miriam Ogier *SEE* Le Patourel, Frank
LePatourel, Miriam Flere Bisson Ogier *SEE* LePatourel, Francis
Lepatron, Jamen; Quebec, 1636 ***9221.17*** *p52*
Lepatte, Laurent 16; America, 1846 ***778.6*** *p209*
Lepele, Jean 13; Quebec, 1659 ***9221.17*** *p405*
Lepele, Pierre 25; Quebec, 1652 ***9221.17*** *p262*
Le Pelley, Alfred; America, 1883-1910 ***9228.50*** *p383*
Le Pelley, Edward; America, n.d. ***9228.50*** *p383*
Le Pelley, Edward; Chicago, 1870-1899 ***9228.50*** *p383*
Le Pelley, Gladys; Boston, 1929 ***9228.50*** *p383*
Le Pelley, Gordelia; America, n.d. ***9228.50*** *p419*
Le Pelley, Harold 21; Massachusetts, 1925 ***9228.50*** *p383*
Le Pelley, Henry; Ogden, UT, 1891 ***9228.50*** *p383*
Le Pelley, John; Boston, 1927 ***9228.50*** *p383*
Le Pelley, John; Boston, 1934 ***9228.50*** *p383*
Le Pelley, John 30; Charleston, SC, 1806 ***9228.50*** *p383*
Le Pelley, John F. 33; Massachusetts, 1964 ***9228.50*** *p383*
Le Pelley, Margaret; Massachusetts, 1975 ***9228.50*** *p383*
Le Pelley, Richard; Maryland, 1664 ***9228.50*** *p383*
Le Pelley, Wilfred; Los Angeles, 1879-1979 ***9228.50*** *p383*
Le Pelley, Wm. C.; Massachusetts, 1925 ***9228.50*** *p383*
Le Penn, . . .; Newfoundland, 1700-1799 ***9228.50*** *p504*
Leper, Anne; Quebec, 1673 ***4514.3*** *p340*
Leper, Matthew; America, 1736 ***1220.12*** *p490*
LePere Veron, Jean 29; Quebec, 1659 ***9221.17*** *p406*
LePetit, Claude; Quebec, 1647 ***9221.17*** *p178*
Lepetit, Pierre 27; Quebec, 1658 ***9221.17*** *p385*
LePetit Breton, Jean; Montreal, 1653 ***9221.17*** *p298*
LePetit Claude, Claude 26; Quebec, 1650 ***9221.17*** *p223*
LePetit Homme, Francois; Quebec, 1637 ***9221.17*** *p68*
With wife
LePetit Lacroix, Mathurin 21; Montreal, 1653 ***9221.17*** *p294*
LePetit Louis, Louis 37; Montreal, 1653 ***9221.17*** *p289*
Lepgen, Wilh.; Valdivia, Chile, 1852 ***1192.4*** *p54*
LePhenlenac, S. 29; New Orleans, 1840 ***778.6*** *p209*
Lepicard, Antoine; Quebec, 1637 ***9221.17*** *p71*
With wife
Lepicard, Florence 10 *SEE* Lepicard, Pierre
Lepicard, Francois 20; Quebec, 1651 ***9221.17*** *p246*
Lepicard, Jacques; Quebec, 1656 ***9221.17*** *p345*
Lepicard, Jean 10 *SEE* Lepicard, Pierre
Lepicard, Madeleine Charlot *SEE* Lepicard, Pierre
Lepicard, Nicole-Madeleine 9 *SEE* Lepicard, Pierre
Lepicard, Pierre; Quebec, 1639 ***9221.17*** *p88*
*Wife:*Madeleine Charlot
*Daughter:*Florence
*Daughter:*Nicole-Madeleine
Lepicard, Pierre 34; Quebec, 1645 ***9221.17*** *p156*
*Wife:*Renee Suronne 29
*Son:*Jean 10
Lepicard, Renee Suronne 29 *SEE* Lepicard, Pierre
Lepidor, Laurent 27; Quebec, 1661 ***9221.17*** *p459*
Lepine, Andree; Quebec, 1666 ***4514.3*** *p340*
Lepine, Anne; Quebec, 1663 ***4514.3*** *p340*
Lepine, Jacques; Montreal, 1650 ***9221.17*** *p232*
Lepine, Julien 26; Quebec, 1647 ***9221.17*** *p185*
Lepine, Marie *SEE* Lepine, Pierre
Lepine, Marie; Quebec, 1667 ***4514.3*** *p341*
Lepine, Pierre 15; Montreal, 1650 ***9221.17*** *p231*
*Wife:*Marie
Lepine, Pierre; Quebec, 1648 ***9221.17*** *p200*
Le Poidevin, Alfred; Long Island, n.d. ***9228.50*** *p390*
Le Poidevin, Daniel; New York, NY, 1852 ***9228.50*** *p386*
Le Poidevin, Ezekiel; New Jersey, 1884 ***9228.50*** *p391*
Le Poidevin, J.; Wisconsin, 1809-1872 ***9228.50*** *p391*
Le Poidevin, Jean; Wisconsin, 1819-1842 ***9228.50*** *p384*
*Brother:*Thomas
Le Poidevin, Jean; Wisconsin, n.d. ***9228.50*** *p34*
Le Poidevin, John; Boston, 1721 ***9228.50*** *p519*
Le Poidevin, John; Nebraska, 1827-1902 ***9228.50*** *p390*
Le Poidevin, John *SEE* Le Poidevin, Thomas J.
Le Poidevin, Joseph; New York, NY, 1840-1899 ***9228.50*** *p390*
Le Poidevin, Louisa; British Columbia, 1854-1928 ***9228.50*** *p390*
Le Poidevin, Michael Goudion; Pensacola, FL, 1849-1878 ***9228.50*** *p384*
Le Poidevin, Nicholas; Nebraska, 1823-1891 ***9228.50*** *p390*
Le Poidevin, Nicholas; Ohio, 1798-1846 ***9228.50*** *p392*
Le Poidevin, Nicholas; Ohio, 1807 ***9228.50*** *p516*
Le Poidevin, Thomas *SEE* Le Poidevin, Jean
Le Poidevin, Thomas J.; Wisconsin, 1863 ***9228.50*** *p390*
*Brother:*John
Le Poidevin, Willis Thomas; Wisconsin, 1850-1885 ***9228.50*** *p391*
Lepoigneux, Leonarde; Quebec, 1658 ***9221.17*** *p382*
Le Poitevin, John; Boston, 1721 ***9228.50*** *p519*
Lepoitevin, Rene 25; Quebec, 1656 ***9221.17*** *p334*
LePoulard, Miss 16; Port uncertain, 1841 ***778.6*** *p209*
Lepoulard, Mrs. P.er.e 34; Port uncertain, 1841 ***778.6*** *p209*
Leppard, James; America, 1745 ***1220.12*** *p496*
Leppart, John 24; Ontario, 1871 ***1823.21*** *p200*
Lepper, Andrew 52; Ontario, 1871 ***1823.21*** *p200*
Lepper, Margarethe; America, 1880 ***8115.12*** *p324*
*Child:*Theodor
Lepper, Theodor *SEE* Lepper, Margarethe
Leppinen, Arvi; Oregon, 1941 ***9157.47*** *p2*
Leppingwell, James; America, 1771 ***1220.12*** *p496*
Lepple, Anton; North Dakota, 1892 ***554.30*** *p26*
*Wife:*Elizabeth
Lepple, Elizabeth *SEE* Lepple, Anton
Leprestre, Jacques 29; Montreal, 1659 ***9221.17*** *p423*
Le Prevost, Capt.; Wisconsin, 1818-1879 ***9228.50*** *p36*
Le Prevost, Deborah; Wisconsin, 1847 ***9228.50*** *p392*
Le Prevost, Louisa; Wisconsin, 1847 ***9228.50*** *p392*
*Sister:*Mary
Le Prevost, Mansell; Wisconsin, 1800-1899 ***9228.50*** *p392*
Le Prevost, Martha; Philadelphia, 1825-1856 ***9228.50*** *p630*
Le Prevost, Mary; Wisconsin, 1847 ***9228.50*** *p364*
*Child:*Margaret
*Child:*Mary Ann
*Child:*Matilda
Le Prevost, Mary *SEE* Le Prevost, Louisa
Le Prevost, N.; Wisconsin, 1818-1879 ***9228.50*** *p36*
With family
Le Prevost deBasserode, Jean-Bte-Guillaume; Quebec, 1755-1757 ***2314.30*** *p170*
Le Prevost deBasserode, Jean-Bte-Guillaume; Quebec, 1755-1757 ***2314.30*** *p189*
Leprieur, Christophe 21; Montreal, 1653 ***9221.17*** *p290*
Leprieur, Marie; Nova Scotia, 1753 ***3051*** *p113*
LePrieur, Rene; Quebec, 1642-1643 ***9221.17*** *p128*
Leprinasse, Mr. 48; America, 1842 ***778.6*** *p209*
Leprince, Jean 18; Quebec, 1639 ***9221.17*** *p90*
Leprince, Michel 30; Quebec, 1658 ***9221.17*** *p376*
Le Provost, Mary; New Jersey, 1869-1961 ***9228.50*** *p526*
Lepsa, Frantisek; Wisconsin, 1866 ***2853.20*** *p183*
Le Quelenec, Philip; Boston, n.d. ***9228.50*** *p392*
Le Quesne, . . .; New England, n.d. ***9228.50*** *p151*
Le Quesne, Richard; Marblehead, MA, 1740 ***9228.50*** *p392*
Lequien, Charles; Quebec, 1649 ***9221.17*** *p215*
Lequin, Elisabeth; Quebec, 1667 ***4514.3*** *p341*
Lequint, Lewis; America, 1774 ***1220.12*** *p496*
Lera, James; New England, 1745 ***1642*** *p28*
Lerat, Elisabeth 50; Quebec, 1654 ***9221.17*** *p304*
Lerat, Gustave; New York, NY, 1856 ***1494.21*** *p31*
Leraude, N...as 42; Louisiana, 1848 ***778.6*** *p209*
Le Ray, Margaret Tostevin *SEE* Le Ray, Peter
Le Ray, Peter; Wisconsin, 1850-1859 ***9228.50*** *p392*
Le Ray, Peter; Wisconsin, 1860 ***9228.50*** *p631*
*Wife:*Margaret Tostevin
Lerch, Philipp Josef; St. Paul, MN, 1866 ***5475.1*** *p379*
Lerdelet, Ms. 24; America, 1847 ***778.6*** *p210*
Lerdelet, C. 31; America, 1847 ***778.6*** *p210*
Lerdelet, Marie 6 months; America, 1847 ***778.6*** *p210*
Lerderich, Caroline 6; America, 1847 ***778.6*** *p210*
Lerderich, M. 55; America, 1847 ***778.6*** *p210*
Lerderich, Madeline 4; America, 1847 ***778.6*** *p210*
Lerderich, Michel 9; Port uncertain, 1847 ***778.6*** *p210*
Lereau, Marie; Quebec, 1652 ***9221.17*** *p255*
*Son:*Gervais
*Son:*Antoine
Lereau, Simon 31; Quebec, 1655 ***9221.17*** *p327*
Le Regle, John; Boston, 1752-1800 ***9228.50*** *p392*
Le Reigle, John; Boston, 1752-1800 ***9228.50*** *p392*
Leret, Mr. 20; Port uncertain, 1844 ***778.6*** *p210*
Leret, Alexandre 18; America, 1843 ***778.6*** *p210*
Leret, Jean; Louisiana, 1836-1840 ***4981.45*** *p213*
Leret, Jean Michel 29; New Orleans, 1848 ***778.6*** *p210*
Le Retilley, James, Sr.; Ohio, 1806-1850 ***9228.50*** *p540*
Le Retilley, James, Sr.; Ohio, 1825 ***9228.50*** *p392*
Le Reverend, . . .; Cuba, 1800-1830 ***9228.50*** *p393*
Lerez, Thomas; Ohio, 1840-1897 ***8365.35*** *p17*
Lerhalle, B. H.; Ohio, 1840-1897 ***8365.35*** *p17*
Le Rich, Thomas; Salem, MA, 1702 ***9228.50*** *p541*
Le Riche, . . .; Carolina, 1679 ***9228.50*** *p393*
Leriche, Anne; Quebec, 1648 ***9221.17*** *p194*
Le Riche, Thomas; Salem, MA, 1702 ***9228.50*** *p393*
Lerigal, John; Boston, 1752-1800 ***9228.50*** *p392*
Lerige Laplante, Clement; Quebec, 1685 ***2314.30*** *p172*
Le Riverend, . . .; America, 1950-1983 ***9228.50*** *p393*
Lermen, Barbara Holz *SEE* Lermen, Johann
Lermen, Elisabeth; America, 1834 ***5475.1*** *p436*
Lermen, Franz *SEE* Lermen, Johann
Lermen, Jakob; Brazil, 1862 ***5475.1*** *p441*
With wife 4 children & sister-in-law
Lermen, Jakob; Brazil, 1878 ***5475.1*** *p443*
Lermen, Johann; Brazil, 1883 ***5475.1*** *p445*
*Wife:*Barbara Holz
*Son:*Michel
*Son:*Franz
Lermen, Johann 24; Brazil, 1874 ***5475.1*** *p443*
Lermen, Josef 28; Brazil, 1872 ***5475.1*** *p442*
Lermen, Maria; America, 1800-1899 ***5475.1*** *p436*
Lermen, Maria Peter *SEE* Lermen, Michel
Lermen, Maria; America, 1852 ***5475.1*** *p439*
Lermen, Maria; Brazil, 1854 ***5475.1*** *p440*
Lermen, Mathias 37; Brazil, 1876 ***5475.1*** *p443*
Lermen, Michel; America, 1833 ***5475.1*** *p436*
*Wife:*Maria Peter
With 4 children
Lermen, Michel *SEE* Lermen, Johann
Lermen, Nikolaus; Brazil, 1846 ***5475.1*** *p438*
Lermen, Nikolaus; Brazil, 1862 ***5475.1*** *p441*
Lermen, Peter 24; Brazil, 1872 ***5475.1*** *p443*
Lermont, John; America, 1754 ***1220.12*** *p496*
Lermount, John; America, 1766 ***1220.12*** *p496*
Lerner, George; Louisiana, 1874 ***4981.45*** *p132*
Lero, Frank; Texas, 1884-1908 ***6015.15*** *p27*
Lero, Jacob; Texas, 1914 ***6015.15*** *p27*
Lero, Mike; Texas, 1920 ***6015.15*** *p27*
Lero, Paul; Texas, 1896 ***6015.15*** *p27*
Leroche, Ls. 22; New Orleans, 1848 ***778.6*** *p210*
Leronee, Julien 55; New Orleans, 1848 ***778.6*** *p210*
Lerosse, Ludovic; Barbados or Jamaica, 1694 ***1220.12*** *p496*
Le Rossignol, Annie Elizabeth; New York, 1903 ***9228.50*** *p394*
Le Rossignol, Benj.; Braintree, MA, 1689 ***9228.50*** *p478*
Le Rossignol, Edward; Canada, 1817-1900 ***9228.50*** *p394*
Le Rossignol, James Edward; Denver, CO, 1898-1902 ***9228.50*** *p393*
*Wife:*Jessie Catherine Ross
Le Rossignol, Jessie Catherine Ross *SEE* Le Rossignol, James Edward
Le Rossignol, Mary Ann; America, n.d. ***9228.50*** *p94*
Le Rossignol, Mary Anne; America, 1814-1900 ***9228.50*** *p394*
Le Rossignol, Peter; Quebec, 1826-1874 ***9228.50*** *p393*
Le Rossignol, Peter; Quebec, n.d. ***9228.50*** *p393*
Lerou, Paule 30; New Orleans, 1845 ***778.6*** *p210*
Lerouge, Francois; Quebec, 1659 ***9221.17*** *p414*
LeRouge, J. A. 19; America, 1845 ***778.6*** *p210*
Lerouge, Jean 23; Quebec, 1662 ***9221.17*** *p489*
Lerouge, Jeanne 26; Quebec, 1653 ***9221.17*** *p276*
Leroux, Andre 24; Quebec, 1661 ***9221.17*** *p461*
Leroux, Catherine; Quebec, 1670 ***4514.3*** *p341*
Leroux, Francois 25; Quebec, 1658 ***9221.17*** *p384*
Leroux, Jean; Quebec, 1659 ***9221.17*** *p414*
Leroux, Marguerite Lemercier *SEE* Leroux, Sebastien
Leroux, Marguerite; Quebec, 1665 ***4514.3*** *p341*
Leroux, Marie; Quebec, 1668 ***4514.3*** *p341*
Leroux, Mathurine 17; Quebec, 1652 ***9221.17*** *p262*
Leroux, Nicolas 29; Quebec, 1660 ***9221.17*** *p437*
Leroux, Pierre; Quebec, 1637 ***9221.17*** *p71*
Leroux, Sebastien; Montreal, 1653 ***9221.17*** *p295*
*Wife:*Marguerite Lemercier
With son 7
With daughter 5
Le Roy, . . .; Boston, 1769 ***9228.50*** *p5*
Le Roy, . . .; Philadelphia, 1769 ***9228.50*** *p394*
LeRoy, Mr. 34; New Orleans, 1834 ***1002.51*** *p113*
Leroy, Adam 20; America, 1846 ***778.6*** *p210*
Leroy, Charles 25; America, 1843 ***778.6*** *p210*
Le Roy, Francis *SEE* Le Roy, Judith
Le Roy, Francis; Boston, 1769 ***9228.50*** *p48*
Leroy, Gustave 16; Missouri, 1848 ***778.6*** *p210*
Leroy, Hippolyte 29; New York, NY, 1894 ***6512.1*** *p181*
Le Roy, James *SEE* Le Roy, Judith
Le Roy, James; Boston, 1769 ***9228.50*** *p48*
Leroy, Jeanne 27; Quebec, 1651 ***9221.17*** *p251*
Leroy, John 28; Louisiana, 1848 ***778.6*** *p210*
Leroy, Joseph 57; America, 1846 ***778.6*** *p210*

Le Roy, Judith; America, 1769 *9228.50 p394*
  *Relative:*Wm.
  *Relative:*Francis
  *Relative:*James
Le Roy, Judith; Boston, 1769 *9228.50 p48*
Leroy, Louis 25; America, 1840 *778.6 p210*
Leroy, Louis SEE Leroy, Maximilien
Leroy, Lucie SEE Leroy, Maximilien
Leroy, M. A. 24; New Orleans, 1841 *778.6 p210*
Leroy, Marie 53; America, 1846 *778.6 p210*
Leroy, Marie Alexandrine SEE Leroy, Maximilien
Leroy, Marie Joseph Motte SEE Leroy, Maximilien
Leroy, Mathurin 36; Quebec, 1646 *9221.17 p168*
Leroy, Maximilien; Wisconsin, 1878 *1495.20 p12*
  *Grandchild:*Marie Alexandrine
  *Grandchild:*Louis
  *Grandchild:*Lucie
  *Son:*Nicolas
  *Daughter-In-Law:*Marie Joseph Motte
Leroy, Michel 30; Port uncertain, 1846 *778.6 p210*
Leroy, Nicolas 30; Mississippi, 1847 *778.6 p210*
Leroy, Nicolas; Montreal, 1644 *9221.17 p148*
Leroy, Nicolas SEE Leroy, Maximilien
Leroy, Pierre 36; New Orleans, 1848 *778.6 p210*
Leroy, Robert; Quebec, 1649 *9221.17 p220*
Leroy, Simon; Montreal, 1653 *9221.17 p296*
Le Roy, William; America, 1800-1899 *9228.50 p394*
Le Roy, William; Boston, 1769 *9228.50 p48*
Le Roy, Wm. SEE Le Roy, Judith
Le Roy deLa Potherie, Claude-Charles; Quebec, 1700 *2314.30 p171*
Lerpiniere, Jean; Quebec, 1642 *9221.17 p118*
Lerraux, Francois 29; America, 1843 *778.6 p210*
Lerroy, Philipp; America, 1836 *5475.1 p549*
Lert, Etienne 27; Montreal, 1653 *9221.17 p296*
Lert, Geo. L.; California, 1868 *1131.61 p89*
Le Ruez, Philip; Massachusetts, 1784 *9228.50 p323*
Le Ruez, Philip; New York, n.d. *9228.50 p395*
Le Ruez, Thomas; America, 1705-1805 *9228.50 p98*
Lervin, William; America, 1764 *1220.12 p496*
Le Ryche Family ; Massachusetts, 1630-1639 *9228.50 p541*
Lesabotier, Louis 20; Montreal, 1653 *9221.17 p291*
Lesabre, Guillaume 31; Montreal, 1656 *9221.17 p348*
Lesage, Charles; Texas, 1851 *3435.45 p36*
Le Sage, Claude; Boston, 1760-1769 *9228.50 p395*
Lesage, Louis 35; Quebec, 1653 *9221.17 p276*
Lesage, Marguerite; Quebec, 1653 *9221.17 p25*
Lesaint, Marie; Quebec, 1671 *4514.3 p341*
Lesan, Michel 18; Quebec, 1657 *9221.17 p362*
Lesaulenier deSaint-Michel, Philippe; Quebec, 1683-1688 *2314.30 p168*
Lesaulenier deSaint-Michel, Philippe; Quebec, 1687 *2314.30 p189*
Lesbirel, John; Salem, MA, n.d. *9228.50 p578*
Lesbirel, Thomas; Salem, MA, 1718 *9228.50 p395*
Lesborough, Richard; America, 1741 *1220.12 p496*
Lesbrill, Daniel; Marblehead, MA, 1700-1749 *9228.50 p395*
Lesbros, Joseph 19; America, 1846 *778.6 p210*
Lescall, William; America, 1771 *1220.12 p496*
Lescallie, William; America, 1775 *1220.12 p496*
Lescallott, William; America, 1771 *1220.12 p496*
Lescalopier, Suzanne; Quebec, 1651 *9221.17 p247*
Lescaner, Pierre 27; America, 1846 *778.6 p210*
Lesch, George; Illinois, 1855 *6079.1 p8*
Lesch, Johannes; Nova Scotia, 1784 *7105 p24*
Leschinsky, Waclaw; Detroit, 1929-1930 *6214.5 p69*
Lescinsky, Frantisek; New York, NY, 1893 *2853.20 p469*
Lescour Wirini, Th. 18; America, 1844 *778.6 p210*
Lescow, Charles Wm.; Wisconsin, 1891 *6795.8 p103*
Lesdiller, Michelle; Quebec, 1668 *4514.3 p341*
Le Sebirel, Thomas; Salem, MA, 1718 *9228.50 p395*
Le Seelleur, Charles Josue; Quebec, 1847-1876 *9228.50 p395*
Le Seelleur, Robert; New Jersey, 1665 *9228.50 p578*
Leseke, Ilse Marie Justine Laeseke SEE Leseke, Johann Heinrich
Leseke, Johann Heinrich SEE Leseke, Johann Heinrich
Leseke, Johann Heinrich; America, 1859 *7420.1 p186*
  *Wife:*Ilse Marie Justine Laeseke
  *Son:*Johann Heinrich
Lesellier, Mathieu; Quebec, 1659 *9221.17 p414*
Leser, Leopold 22; Louisiana, 1848 *778.6 p210*
Lesh, Andrew; Ohio, 1809-1852 *4511.35 p30*
Lesh, John; Nova Scotia, 1784 *7105 p24*
Le Sheminaw, Robert; Utah, 1850-1859 *9228.50 p338*
Le Siberrel, Elias SEE Le Siberrel, Thomas
Le Siberrel, Thomas; Boston, 1766 *9228.50 p395*
  *Relative:*Elias
Le Sieur, P.; Quebec, 1849-1949 *9228.50 p396*
Lesikar, Josef; Texas, 1852 *2853.20 p59*
Lesikar, Josef K.; Galveston, TX, 1853 *2853.20 p59*

Lesikar, Vincenc; Texas, 1853 *2853.20 p60*
Lesirre, Mrs. 18; New Orleans, 1848 *778.6 p211*
Lesirre, Louis 33; New Orleans, 1848 *778.6 p210*
Leski, Mary 10; Ontario, 1871 *1823.17 p91*
Lesky, Edward 23; New York, NY, 1893 *1883.7 p43*
Lesky, Mathilde 19; New York, NY, 1893 *1883.7 p43*
Lesley, Charles; America, 1728 *1220.12 p496*
Leslie, Adam J.; Ohio, 1833 *3580.20 p32*
Leslie, Adam J.; Ohio, 1833 *6020.12 p12*
Leslie, Alexander 44; Ontario, 1871 *1823.21 p200*
Leslie, Andrew 66; Ontario, 1871 *1823.21 p200*
Leslie, Ellis 35; Ontario, 1871 *1823.21 p201*
Leslie, George 20; Ontario, 1871 *1823.21 p201*
Leslie, James 45; Ontario, 1871 *1823.21 p201*
Leslie, John; Ohio, 1824 *3580.20 p32*
Leslie, John; Ohio, 1824 *6020.12 p13*
Leslie, Mary 44; Ontario, 1871 *1823.21 p201*
Leslie, Mary 95; Ontario, 1871 *1823.21 p201*
Leslie, Robert; Ohio, 1856 *3580.20 p32*
Leslie, Robert; Ohio, 1856 *6020.12 p13*
Leslie, Robert A. 30; Ontario, 1871 *1823.21 p201*
Lesnard, Jean; Virginia, 1700 *9230.15 p80*
Lesner, Hermann; Ohio, 1840-1897 *8365.35 p17*
Lesniak, Edward 28; New York, NY, 1920 *930.50 p49*
Lesoldat, Jacques; Montreal, 1656 *9221.17 p471*
Lesont, Anne 58; Quebec, 1655 *9221.17 p326*
Lesot, Jacques-Francois 18; Quebec, 1654 *9221.17 p312*
Lespaisse, Jean; Quebec, 1654 *9221.17 p312*
Lespasse, Lucie de 26; America, 1847 *778.6 p211*
Lespasse, M. Louise de 19; America, 1847 *778.6 p211*
Lespasse, Mrs. de 55; America, 1847 *778.6 p211*
Lesperance, Jean 14; Montreal, 1648 *9221.17 p205*
Lesperance, Marie; Quebec, 1665 *4514.3 p341*
Lesperance, Pierre 27; Quebec, 1654 *9221.17 p312*
Lespinasse, Jean de; Quebec, 1636 *9221.17 p61*
Lespinasse, Jean de 32; Quebec, 1661 *9221.17 p462*
Lespinat, Leon 40; New Orleans, 1846 *778.6 p211*
Lespine, Francois; Quebec, 1658 *9221.17 p385*
Lespine, Jacques; Quebec, 1637 *9221.17 p73*
Lespine, Jacques; Quebec, 1653 *9221.17 p277*
Lespine, Jacques 28; Quebec, 1659 *9221.17 p406*
Lespine, Nicolas; Quebec, 1651 *9221.17 p244*
Lespinette, Antoine 15; Montreal, 1653 *9221.17 p282*
Lespommiers, Auguste 26; New Orleans, 1848 *778.6 p211*
Lespommiers, Justine 24; New Orleans, 1848 *778.6 p211*
Lesputre, Nicholas; Georgia, 1795 *1451.56 p118*
Lesquille, Jacques; Quebec, 1656 *9221.17 p339*
Lesquillon, Francois; Quebec, 1641 *9221.17 p105*
Lesseau, Marie; Quebec, 1657 *9221.17 p362*
Lessel, Jakob; America, 1864 *5475.1 p303*
Lessieur, Francois; New York, 1600-1699 *9228.50 p326*
Lessinger, Anna Lichtenthal SEE Lessinger, Johann
Lessinger, Joh. August SEE Lessinger, Johann
Lessinger, Johann; Rio de Janeiro, Brazil, 1879 *5475.1 p258*
  *Wife:*Anna Lichtenthal
  *Son:*Joh. August
  *Son:*Michel
Lessinger, Michel SEE Lessinger, Johann
Lesslie, David 40; Ontario, 1871 *1823.21 p201*
Lesslie, Ephraem 48; Ontario, 1871 *1823.21 p201*
Lesslie, William 32; Ontario, 1871 *1823.21 p201*
Lessman, August; North Carolina, 1854 *1088.45 p19*
Lestadau, John; America, 1764 *1220.12 p496*
Lestang, Charles; Quebec, 1661 *9221.17 p447*
Lestang, Etienne de; Quebec, 1647 *9221.17 p184*
Lestang, Michel; Quebec, 1661 *9221.17 p462*
Lestang, Michel-Mathieu 20; Quebec, 1657 *9221.17 p353*
Lestart, Marie 60; Quebec, 1655 *9221.17 p327*
Lester, Albert 55; Ontario, 1871 *1823.17 p91*
Lester, David 52; Ontario, 1871 *1823.21 p201*
Lester, Elizabeth; America, 1750 *1220.12 p495*
Lester, James; New York, 1683 *8529.30 p13*
Lester, John; Virginia, 1757 *1220.12 p495*
Lester, John B. 51; Ontario, 1871 *1823.21 p201*
Lester, John William 40; Ontario, 1871 *1823.21 p201*
Lester, Mark 24; Indiana, 1879-1880 *9076.20 p69*
Lester, Robert; New York, 1778 *8529.30 p13*
Lester, Thomas; America, 1773 *1220.12 p495*
Lester, Thomas 35; Ontario, 1871 *1823.21 p201*
Lester, Thomas 39; Ontario, 1871 *1823.21 p201*
Lester, William 63; Ontario, 1871 *1823.17 p91*
Lestina, Jan; St. Paul, MN, 1867 *2853.20 p277*
Lestoupin, Michel; Quebec, 1652 *9221.17 p262*
Lestrade, P. 23; New Orleans, 1848 *778.6 p211*
L'Estrange, Antony; New Orleans, 1840 *778.6 p211*
LeStrange, Emma 18; Quebec, 1870 *8364.32 p24*
Lestrange, Thomas; Annapolis, MD, 1726 *1220.12 p496*
Lestringuant deSt-Martin, Alexandre-Joseph de; Quebec, 1683-1688 *2314.30 p168*

Lestringuant deSt-Martin, Alexandre-Joseph de; Quebec, 1684 *2314.30 p189*
Lestroda, A. 25; New Orleans, 1841 *778.6 p211*
Le Suer, Cassandra; Maryland, 1791 *9228.50 p399*
Le Suer, . . .; North America, 1800-1870 *9228.50 p399*
LeSueur, Mr. 35; America, 1745 *778.6 p211*
LeSueur, Mr. 44; America, 1844 *778.6 p211*
Le Sueur, Anne; Iowa, 1851 *9228.50 p330*
Le Sueur, Anne; Iowa, 1851 *9228.50 p330*
Le Sueur, Arthur; Minnesota, n.d. *9228.50 p399*
Le Sueur, Caroline; Minnesota, 1872 *9228.50 p399*
Le Sueur, Caroline; Minnesota, 1872 *9228.50 p401*
Le Sueur, Caroline Le Gresley SEE Le Sueur, John
Le Sueur, Caroline Mary Turner SEE Le Sueur, John
Le Sueur, Cassandra; Maryland, 1791 *9228.50 p399*
Le Sueur, Charles; Pennsylvania, 1905-1946 *9228.50 p399*
  *Wife:*Winifred Knightly
  *Child:*Hardress Norman
Lesueur, Elias, Jr. SEE Lesueur, Jane Elizabeth LeBoutillier
Le Sueur, Francois; New York, 1600-1699 *9228.50 p326*
Le Sueur, Gilbert 19; Iowa, 1860 *9228.50 p399*
Le Sueur, Hardress Norman SEE Le Sueur, Charles
Le Sueur, Harriet Ellen SEE Le Sueur, John
Le Sueur, Hubert; New England, 1633 *9228.50 p399*
Le Sueur, Jane Caroline SEE Le Sueur, John
Lesueur, Jane Elizabeth; Iowa, 1870 *9228.50 p330*
  *Son:*Elias, Jr.
Le Sueur, John; Philadelphia, 1813-1855 *9228.50 p396*
  *Wife:*Caroline Le Gresley
  *Child:*Jane Caroline
  *Child:*Harriet Ellen
  *Child:*John Taylor
  *Child:*Caroline Mary Turner
  *Child:*Mary Ann
Le Sueur, John Taylor SEE Le Sueur, John
Le Sueur, Mary Ann SEE Le Sueur, John
Le Sueur, Mary Ann Falle SEE Le Sueur, Philippe
Le Sueur, Muriel Hunter-Watters SEE Le Sueur, Peter
Le Sueur, Nicholas; Louisiana, 1756 *9228.50 p399*
Le Sueur, Percival; Pennsylvania, 1882-1960 *9228.50 p399*
Le Sueur, Peter; Pennsylvania, 1905 *9228.50 p398*
  *Wife:*Muriel Hunter-Watters
Le Sueur, Peter; St. Johns, N.F., 1892-1905 *9228.50 p398*
Le Sueur, Philip; Massachusetts, 1712 *9228.50 p399*
Le Sueur, Philip; New York, 1828-1866 *9228.50 p399*
Le Sueur, Philip SEE Le Sueur, Philippe
Le Sueur, Philippe; Port uncertain, n.d. *9228.50 p213*
  *Wife:*Mary Ann Falle
  *Son:*Philip
Lesueur, Phillip 60; Ontario, 1871 *1823.17 p91*
Lesueur, Pierre 30; New Orleans, 1840 *778.6 p211*
Le Sueur, Susan; America, 1805-1900 *9228.50 p399*
Le Sueur, Susan Jane; New York, 1843-1871 *9228.50 p213*
  *Grandson:*Thomas
  *Granddaughter:*Elinora R.M.
  *Daughter-In-Law:*Helen Ellnora Le Febvre
  *Son:*Thomas
  *Daughter:*Mary Ann
  *Son:*Elias
  *Grandson:*Elias Thomas Marche
  *Daughter:*Annie H.
  *Daughter-In-Law:*Mary Ann Champion
Le Sueur, Winifred Knightly SEE Le Sueur, Charles
LeSueur DeSaint-Sauveur, Jean 36; Quebec, 1634 *9221.17 p32*
Lesuisse, Charlotte Mauger 42 SEE Lesuisse, Pierre
Lesuisse, Felicien; America, 1872 *1494.20 p12*
Lesuisse, Felix Joseph; Wisconsin, 1871 *1495.20 p28*
Lesuisse, Francois 15 SEE Lesuisse, Pierre
Lesuisse, Jacques 10 SEE Lesuisse, Pierre
Lesuisse, Jean; Quebec, 1662 *9221.17 p493*
Lesuisse, Marie 17 SEE Lesuisse, Pierre
Lesuisse, Marie-Madeleine 13 SEE Lesuisse, Pierre
Lesuisse, Martine-Aimee 14 SEE Lesuisse, Pierre
Lesuisse, Pierre 47; Quebec, 1649 *9221.17 p216*
  *Wife:*Charlotte Mauger 42
  *Daughter:*Martine-Aimee 14
  *Daughter:*Marie-Madeleine 13
  *Son:*Jacques 10
  *Daughter:*Suzanne 9
  *Son:*Francois 15
  *Daughter:*Marie 17
Lesuisse, Suzanne 9 SEE Lesuisse, Pierre
Lesure, Philip; Massachusetts, 1712 *9228.50 p399*
Letaillandier, Pierre 29; Quebec, 1646 *9221.17 p168*
Letailleur, Pierre; Quebec, 1660 *9221.17 p437*
Letardif, Barbe Esmard Michel; Quebec, 1648 *9221.17 p200*

Letardif, Guillaume; Quebec, 1648 *9221.17 p200*
Letardif, Olivier; Quebec, 1621 *9221.17 p24*
Letartre, . . .; Quebec, 1639 *9221.17 p90*
Letartre, Rene 34; Quebec, 1661 *9221.17 p462*
Letcher, Adam 18; New Orleans, 1840 *778.6 p211*
Letellier, Etienne 18; Quebec, 1654 *9221.17 p312*
Le Tellier, Henri; Montreal, 1905-1979 *9228.50 p400*
Letellier, Pierre; Quebec, 1635 *9221.17 p42*
Letembre, Isaac; Quebec, 1652 *9221.17 p262*
Letemple, Mr. 43; Louisiana, 1848 *778.6 p211*
Letemple, Comtesse 37; Louisiana, 1848 *778.6 p211*
Letemple, Dumarret 35; Louisiana, 1848 *778.6 p211*
Le Terrier, Jacques; Nova Scotia, 1753 *3051 p112*
Le Terrier, Jean-Baptiste; Nova Scotia, 1753 *3051 p112*
Lethbridge, Ann 38; Ontario, 1871 *1823.21 p201*
Lethbridge, Garland 41; Ontario, 1871 *1823.21 p201*
Lethbridge, George 42; Ontario, 1871 *1823.21 p201*
Lethbridge, John 46; Ontario, 1871 *1823.21 p201*
Lethbridge, John 52; Ontario, 1871 *1823.21 p201*
Lethbridge, Thomas 38; Ontario, 1871 *1823.21 p201*
Lethbridge, William; America, 1739 *1220.12 p496*
Letherby, Ann; America, 1767 *1220.12 p490*
Letherington, Elizabeth; Virginia, 1735 *1220.12 p496*
Letherland, George; America, 1741 *1220.12 p496*
Letherland, Thomas; America, 1682 *1220.12 p496*
Letkemann, Franz 9; New York, NY, 1893 *1883.7 p44*
Letkemann, Heinr. 5; New York, NY, 1893 *1883.7 p44*
Letkemann, Johann 11; New York, NY, 1893 *1883.7 p44*
Letkemann, Johann 43; New York, NY, 1893 *1883.7 p44*
Letkemann, Maria 2; New York, NY, 1893 *1883.7 p44*
Letkemann, Maria 32; New York, NY, 1893 *1883.7 p44*
Letkiewicz, Jozef 30; New York, NY, 1920 *930.50 p49*
Letondalle, Jules Alex. 25; Louisiana, 1848 *778.6 p211*
Letourangeau, Andre 20; Quebec, 1657 *9221.17 p366*
Letourangeau, Honore 26; Montreal, 1653 *9221.17 p286*
Letourangeau, Jean 26; Quebec, 1657 *9221.17 p361*
Letourneur, Bernard 13 SEE Letourneur, Louis
Letourneur, Francoise 14 SEE Letourneur, Louis
Letourneur, Francoise Dechaux 39 SEE Letourneur, Louis
Letourneur, Louis 42; Quebec, 1660 *9221.17 p432*
   Wife:Francoise Dechaux 39
   Daughter:Francoise 14
   Son:Bernard 13
Letourneur, Pierre; Quebec, 1639 *9221.17 p90*
Letouset, Hyacinthe 20; America, 1846 *778.6 p211*
Le Touzel, George; Port uncertain, 1875-1975 *9228.50 p400*
Letovsky, Jan Barta; Boston, 1854 *2853.20 p212*
Letovsky, Jan Barta; Wisconsin, 1860 *2853.20 p291*
Letovsky, Viktor Barta; Wisconsin, 1854 *2853.20 p217*
Letres, J.P. 20; New Orleans, 1846 *778.6 p309*
Letruns, Joseph 15; Ohio, 1880 *4879.40 p257*
Lett, John 77; Ontario, 1871 *1823.17 p91*
Letter, Elizabeth; America, 1758 *1220.12 p496*
Letteridge, Samuel; America, 1767 *1220.12 p496*
Letters, Christine 36; Louisiana, 1848 *778.6 p211*
Letters, Fred. 28; Louisiana, 1848 *778.6 p211*
Letts, Charles 31; Ontario, 1871 *1823.17 p91*
Letts, Eliza.; Jamestown, VA, 1633 *1658.20 p211*
Letts, Elizabeth; Virginia, 1739 *1220.12 p496*
Leu, Abram; North Carolina, 1792-1862 *1088.45 p19*
Leubschir, John; Ohio, 1809-1852 *4511.35 p30*
Leuck, Franz SEE Leuck, Peter
Leuck, Franz 25; America, 1867 *5475.1 p349*
Leuck, J. Peter SEE Leuck, Peter
Leuck, Johann SEE Leuck, Peter
Leuck, Johann; Wisconsin, 1862 *5475.1 p260*
Leuck, Katharina SEE Leuck, Peter
Leuck, Katharina Hensgen SEE Leuck, Peter
Leuck, Katharina 33; America, 1857 *5475.1 p244*
Leuck, Magdalena SEE Leuck, Peter
Leuck, Margarethe SEE Leuck, Peter
Leuck, Maria Pinten SEE Leuck, Michel
Leuck, Mathias SEE Leuck, Peter
Leuck, Mathias 9 SEE Leuck, Michel
Leuck, Michel; America, 1867 *5475.1 p349*
Leuck, Michel 2 SEE Leuck, Michel
Leuck, Michel 40; Tennessee, 1880 *5475.1 p265*
   Wife:Maria Pinten
   Son:Mathias 9
   Son:Michel 2
Leuck, Peter; America, 1872 *5475.1 p256*
Leuck, Peter; America, 1873 *5475.1 p350*
Leuck, Peter; America, 1882 *5475.1 p261*
   Wife:Katharina Hensgen
   Daughter:Katharina
   Son:Johann
   Son:Mathias
   Daughter:Margarethe

   Son:Franz
   Daughter:Magdalena
   Son:J. Peter
Leucke, Carl Wilhelm Friedrich; Wisconsin, 1866 *6795.8 p104*
Leuck-Fuss, Anna Fuss 27 SEE Leuck-Fuss, Nikolaus
Leuck-Fuss, Johann 5 SEE Leuck-Fuss, Nikolaus
Leuck-Fuss, Katharina 3 SEE Leuck-Fuss, Nikolaus
Leuck-Fuss, Nikolaus 29; America, 1867 *5475.1 p349*
   Wife:Anna Fuss 27
   Son:Johann 5
   Daughter:Susanna 3 months
   Daughter:Katharina 3
Leuck-Fuss, Susanna 3 SEE Leuck-Fuss, Nikolaus
Leuk, Katharina 48; America, 1855 *5475.1 p317*
Leupar, Henry 22; Louisiana, 1848 *778.6 p211*
Leuter, William; Washington, 1889 *2770.40 p79*
Leuthauser, Johann Michael; Nova Scotia, 1784 *7105 p24*
Leuthauser, Louis; America, 1867 *7919.3 p530*
Leutweiler, Rudolph 48; New Castle, DE, 1817-1818 *90.20 p152*
Leuty, Thomas; America, 1773 *1220.12 p500*
Leuty, William; America, 1774 *1220.12 p500*
Leutz, . . .; New Orleans, 1840 *778.6 p211*
Leutz, Pierre; New Orleans, 1840 *778.6 p211*
Levaigneur, Marguerite; Quebec, 1667 *4514.3 p342*
LeVaillant, Georges; Quebec, 1658 *9221.17 p375*
Le Vallee, Anne; Quebec, 1826 *9228.50 p631*
Le Vallee, Pierre; Marblehead, MA, 1700 *9228.50 p400*
Le Valley, John; America, 1748 *1220.12 p496*
Le Valley, Pierre; Marblehead, MA, 1700 *9228.50 p185*
Levalley, Thomas 40; Michigan, 1880 *4491.39 p17*
Levallon, Thierry 28; Quebec, 1652 *9221.17 p257*
Levander, Johannes Nicolaus August SEE Levander, Maria Christina
Levander, Margareta Johanna SEE Levander, Maria Christina
Levander, Maria Christina; North America, 1857 *6410.15 p105*
   Child:Margareta Johanna
   Child:Johannes Nicolaus August
Levasseur, Eugene 31; New Orleans, 1848 *778.6 p211*
Levasseur, Jean 18; Quebec, 1640 *9221.17 p97*
Levasseur, Jeanne; Quebec, 1654 *9221.17 p307*
Levasseur, Jeanne; Quebec, 1667 *4514.3 p342*
Levasseur, Joseph Marie 48; New Orleans, 1848 *778.6 p211*
Levasseur, Julie 31; New Orleans, 1848 *778.6 p211*
Levasseur, Laurent 3 SEE Levasseur, Marguerite Richard
Levasseur, Louis 2 SEE Levasseur, Marguerite Richard
Levasseur, Marguerite; Quebec, 1651 *9221.17 p97*
Levasseur, Marguerite 22; Quebec, 1651 *9221.17 p247*
   Son:Laurent 3
   Son:Louis 2
Levasseur, Pierre 27; Quebec, 1654 *9221.17 p312*
Levavasseur, Hardin 25; Missouri, 1845 *778.6 p212*
Le Vavasseur, Peter Jeune; Boston, 1740 *9228.50 p5*
Le Vavasseur, Thomas; Boston, 1700-1730 *9228.50 p647*
Leve, Daniel; America, 1756 *1220.12 p496*
Leveau, Mr. 16; America, 1841 *778.6 p212*
Leveau, J.P.; New York, NY, 1844 *6412.40 p148*
Leveau, Jacques; Quebec, 1648 *9221.17 p201*
Leveau, Sylvain 21; Quebec, 1660 *9221.17 p440*
Levein, Joseph 29; Ontario, 1871 *1823.17 p91*
Level, Francois 30; New Orleans, 1847 *778.6 p212*
Level, Jean 26; America, 1840 *778.6 p212*
Level, Louis 26; New Orleans, 1847 *778.6 p212*
Level, Marie 23; America, 1840 *778.6 p212*
Leven, Edward; America, 1743 *1220.12 p496*
Levenston, Jacob; Ohio, 1809-1852 *4511.35 p30*
Leventhorpe, Collet; North Carolina, 1849 *1088.45 p19*
Leveque, Marie 16; Missouri, 1845 *778.6 p212*
Leveque, Pierre 22; Missouri, 1845 *778.6 p212*
Lever, James; America, 1772 *1220.12 p496*
Lever, James; America, 1773 *1220.12 p496*
Lever, John; America, 1756 *1220.12 p496*
Lever, John; America, 1758 *1220.12 p496*
Lever, John; America, 1759 *1220.12 p496*
Lever, John; Boston, 1812 *3274.55 p25*
Lever, Samuel; America, 1758 *1220.12 p496*
Lever, Thomas; America, 1771 *1220.12 p496*
Leverett, James; America, 1773 *1220.12 p496*
Leverett, John; America, 1686 *1220.12 p496*
Levergood, George; Ohio, 1809-1852 *4511.35 p30*
Leveridge, John; America, 1771 *1220.12 p496*
Leveridge, Mary; America, 1759 *1220.12 p496*
Leverit, James; America, 1757 *1220.12 p496*
Leverit, Somon; Portsmouth, NH, 1700-1799 *9228.50 p400*
Leveritt, John; Maryland, 1741 *1220.12 p496*
Leverrier, P. 45; New Orleans, 1848 *778.6 p212*

Le Verrier deRousson, Francois; Quebec, 1683-1688 *2314.30 p168*
Le Verrier deRousson, Francois; Quebec, 1687 *2314.30 p189*
Leversedge, Allegan; America, 1685 *1220.12 p497*
Levert, Jean 26; Quebec, 1659 *9221.17 p405*
Levertsson, Oscar; Cleveland, OH, 1900-1902 *9722.10 p123*
Leves, Angele 21; New Orleans, 1848 *778.6 p212*
Leves, Rosalie 34; New Orleans, 1848 *778.6 p212*
Le Vesconte, Alfred SEE Le Vesconte, Charles
Le Vesconte, Caroline Le Sueur SEE Le Vesconte, Charles
Le Vesconte, Carrie SEE Le Vesconte, Charles
Le Vesconte, Charles SEE Le Vesconte, Charles
Le Vesconte, Charles; Minnesota, 1872 *9228.50 p401*
   Wife:Caroline Le Sueur
   Child:Ernest
   Child:Emile
   Child:John
   Child:Carrie
   Child:George
   Child:Alfred
   Child:Henry
   Child:Margaret
   Child:Charles
Le Vesconte, Emile SEE Le Vesconte, Charles
Le Vesconte, Ernest SEE Le Vesconte, Charles
Le Vesconte, George SEE Le Vesconte, Charles
Le Vesconte, Henry SEE Le Vesconte, Charles
Le Vesconte, John SEE Le Vesconte, Charles
Le Vesconte, Margaret SEE Le Vesconte, Charles
Levesque, Mr. 20; America, 1846 *778.6 p212*
Levesque, Andre; Quebec, 1649 *9221.17 p216*
Levesque, Jacques; Quebec, 1644 *9221.17 p144*
Levesque, Jacques 23; Quebec, 1656 *9221.17 p341*
Levesque, Louis 24; America, 1841 *778.6 p212*
Levesque, Marie; Virginia, 1700 *9230.15 p81*
Levesque, Noel; Quebec, 1654 *9221.17 p313*
Leveston, John; America, 1732 *1220.12 p497*
Leveston, William; America, 1710 *1220.12 p497*
Levet, Mrs. 22; New Orleans, 1848 *778.6 p212*
Levet, Mrs. 54; New Orleans, 1848 *778.6 p212*
Levet, Madelaine Rosalie 30; America, 1844 *778.6 p212*
Levet, Marie 30; America, 1845 *778.6 p212*
Levett, Agnes 65; Ontario, 1871 *1823.21 p201*
Levett, John; Barbados, 1662 *1220.12 p497*
Levett, William; America, 1735 *1220.12 p497*
Levi, Alex. 30; New Orleans, 1845 *778.6 p212*
Levi, Amelie 36; New Orleans, 1847 *778.6 p212*
Levi, August; Indiana, 1883 *5475.1 p36*
Levi, Caroline 24; Cincinnati, 1846 *778.6 p212*
Levi, David; America, 1756 *1220.12 p497*
Levi, David 6; New Orleans, 1847 *778.6 p212*
Levi, Emanuel; America, 1769 *1220.12 p497*
Levi, Emanuel Michel 26; America, 1852 *5475.1 p403*
Levi, Henri 19; New Orleans, 1847 *778.6 p212*
Levi, Hyam; America, 1756 *1220.12 p497*
Levi, Israel; America, 1756 *1220.12 p497*
Levi, Jacob; America, 1764 *1220.12 p497*
Levi, Jacob 8; New Orleans, 1847 *778.6 p212*
Levi, Jeanett 53; Cincinnati, 1846 *778.6 p212*
Levi, Jeremiah; America, 1748 *1220.12 p497*
Levi, John; America, 1759 *1220.12 p497*
Levi, Leon 22; Cincinnati, 1846 *778.6 p212*
Levi, Marthe 26; New Orleans, 1847 *778.6 p212*
Levi, Max 45; Ontario, 1871 *1823.21 p201*
Levi, Meyer 15; Cincinnati, 1846 *778.6 p212*
Levi, Michael 35; America, 1845 *778.6 p212*
Levi, Michel 73; Cincinnati, 1846 *778.6 p212*
Levi, Nanette 9; New Orleans, 1847 *778.6 p212*
Levi, Nephtalie 19; New Orleans, 1848 *778.6 p212*
Levi, Prosper 17; Cincinnati, 1846 *778.6 p212*
Levi, Rose 10; Cincinnati, 1846 *778.6 p213*
Levi, Salomon 4; New Orleans, 1847 *778.6 p213*
Levi, Samuel 20; Cincinnati, 1846 *778.6 p213*
Levi, Samuel 18; Port uncertain, 1841 *778.6 p213*
Levi, Solomon; America, 1771 *1220.12 p497*
Levicomte, Jean; Quebec, 1659 *9221.17 p405*
Levie, Aberham 24; America, 1846 *778.6 p213*
Levie, John 38; Ontario, 1871 *1823.21 p201*
Levie, Joseph 71; America, 1846 *778.6 p213*
Levieux, Claire; Quebec, 1670 *4514.3 p342*
LeVieux DeHauteville, Nicolas; Quebec, 1651 *9221.17 p247*
Le Vieux deHauteville, Nicolas; Quebec, 1654 *2314.30 p171*
Levin, Carrie; St. Paul, MN, 1885 *1865.50 p48*
Levin, Carrie; St. Paul, MN, 1894 *1865.50 p94*
Levin, John; Washington, 1889 *2770.40 p79*
Levin, Ludwicka Jelonek SEE Levin, Siegmund
Levin, Patrick; Louisiana, 1874-1875 *4981.45 p29*

Levin, Siegmund; Philadelphia, 1850 ***8513.31*** *p323*
*Wife:*Ludwicka Jelonek
Levine, John 52; Michigan, 1880 ***4491.30*** *p20*
Levine, Mary 47; Michigan, 1880 ***4491.30*** *p20*
Levings, Edward; America, 1759 ***1220.12*** *p497*
Levingston, Anna Maria; America, 1746 ***1220.12*** *p504*
Levingstone, Elizabeth; America, 1724 ***1220.12*** *p504*
Levins, Henry; Philadelphia, 1855 ***5720.10*** *p378*
Levins, Isaac; America, 1764 ***1220.12*** *p497*
Levis, Florent.C.A.; Louisiana, 1836-1841 ***4981.45*** *p209*
Levis, Joseph; Louisiana, 1836-1841 ***4981.45*** *p209*
Leviston, Ann; America, 1763 ***1220.12*** *p497*
Levit, William; America, 1768 ***1220.12*** *p497*
Leviton, Mendel 42; New York, NY, 1894 ***6512.1*** *p230*
Leviton, Merkel 18; New York, NY, 1894 ***6512.1*** *p230*
Levitt, John 42; Ontario, 1871 ***1823.21*** *p201*
Levitt, William 50; Ontario, 1871 ***1823.21*** *p201*
Levois, Mrs. 27; America, 1844 ***778.6*** *p213*
Levois, J. 29; America, 1844 ***778.6*** *p213*
Levois, Jules 32; America, 1843 ***778.6*** *p213*
Levoyer, Daniel; America, 1752 ***1220.12*** *p497*
Levraud deLangis, Leon; Quebec, 1683-1688 ***2314.30*** *p168*
Levraud deLangis, Leon; Quebec, 1687 ***2314.30*** *p190*
Levy, Abraham; America, 1772 ***1220.12*** *p497*
Levy, Abraham 12; America, 1841 ***778.6*** *p213*
Levy, Abraham 23; Missouri, 1847 ***778.6*** *p213*
Levy, Abraham 24; Ohio, 1847 ***778.6*** *p213*
Levy, Abraham; Potomac, 1731 ***1220.12*** *p497*
Levy, Agathe 9; New Orleans, 1848 ***778.6*** *p213*
Levy, Ann; America, 1775 ***1220.12*** *p497*
Levy, Archer; North Carolina, 1856 ***1088.45*** *p19*
Levy, Brina; America, 1762 ***1220.12*** *p497*
Levy, Carl; Port uncertain, 1856 ***7420.1*** *p150*
Levy, Cloyenne 49; New Orleans, 1848 ***778.6*** *p213*
Levy, Daniel; America, 1867 ***5475.1*** *p208*
Levy, Daniel *SEE* Levy, Simon
Levy, David 36; New York, NY, 1878 ***9253.2*** *p44*
Levy, Elias; America, 1771 ***1220.12*** *p497*
Levy, Elias; America, 1867 ***5475.1*** *p225*
Levy, Emelie 4; America, 1841 ***778.6*** *p213*
Levy, Felix; America, 1873 ***5475.1*** *p226*
Levy, Garret; America, 1753 ***1220.12*** *p497*
Levy, Hendrick; Louisiana, 1836-1841 ***4981.45*** *p209*
Levy, Henri 37; Texas, 1848 ***778.6*** *p213*
Levy, Henry; America, 1766 ***1220.12*** *p497*
Levy, Henry; America, 1768 ***1220.12*** *p497*
Levy, Henry; America, 1771 ***1220.12*** *p497*
Levy, Henry 24; Port uncertain, 1842 ***778.6*** *p213*
Levy, Herman; New York, NY, 1873 ***5720.10*** *p378*
Levy, Isaac 24; America, 1840 ***778.6*** *p213*
Levy, Isaac 25; New Orleans, 1847 ***778.6*** *p213*
Levy, J. M. 19; New Orleans, 1848 ***778.6*** *p213*
Levy, Jacob; America, 1773 ***1220.12*** *p497*
Levy, Jakob; America, 1852 ***5475.1*** *p403*
Levy, Joseph 25; America, 1840 ***778.6*** *p213*
Levy, Joseph 30; America, 1841 ***778.6*** *p213*
Levy, Joseph 19; New Orleans, 1848 ***778.6*** *p213*
Levy, Judah; America, 1771 ***1220.12*** *p497*
Levy, Julius; Indiana, 1877 ***5475.1*** *p32*
Levy, Lazarus; America, 1770 ***1220.12*** *p497*
Levy, Leopold; Cleveland, OH, 1845-1849 ***2853.20*** *p475*
Levy, Louis; New York, NY, 1845 ***7710.1*** *p151*
Levy, Manfred; South America, 1893 ***5475.1*** *p210*
Levy, Marcus; America, 1886 ***5475.1*** *p423*
Levy, Max 30; New Orleans, 1847 ***778.6*** *p213*
Levy, Michael; America, 1764 ***1220.12*** *p497*
Levy, Mordecai; America, 1774 ***1220.12*** *p497*
Levy, Moses Simon; America, 1771 ***1220.12*** *p497*
Levy, S.; Louisiana, 1874 ***4981.45*** *p132*
Levy, Samuel; America, 1769 ***1220.12*** *p497*
Levy, Saul; North Carolina, 1848 ***1088.45*** *p19*
Levy, Simon; America, 1891 ***5475.1*** *p38*
*Brother:*Daniel
Levy, Solomon; America, 1766 ***1220.12*** *p497*
Levy, Solomon; America, 1772 ***1220.12*** *p497*
Levy, Zacharias; America, 1858 ***5475.1*** *p283*
LeWallon, Thierry 28; Quebec, 1652 ***9221.17*** *p257*
Lewander, Charles; New York, NY, 1852 ***6410.15*** *p104*
Lewander, Jon Oscar Emanuel; North America, 1854 ***6410.15*** *p104*
Lewandowski, Anthony 41; New York, NY, 1920 ***930.50*** *p48*
Lewandowski, John; Detroit, 1929-1930 ***6214.5*** *p65*
Lewandowski, John; Texas, 1892-1900 ***6015.15*** *p10*
Lewandowski, Stanislas 30; New York, NY, 1920 ***930.50*** *p49*
Lewandowsky, John Frank; Detroit, 1929 ***1640.55*** *p114*
Leweck, Karoline 42; America, 1852 ***5475.1*** *p495*
*Daughter:*Karoline 20
*Son:*Theobald 14
*Son:*Jakob 10
*Son:*Konrad 7
*Son:*Nikolaus 11
*Daughter:*Katharina 16
Lewelleon, William 65; Ontario, 1871 ***1823.21*** *p201*
Lewellin, Elizabeth; America, 1773 ***1220.12*** *p504*
Lewen, Abraham; Virginia, 1726 ***1220.12*** *p497*
Lewen, John; Potomac, 1731 ***1220.12*** *p497*
Lewen, Joseph; America, 1740 ***1220.12*** *p497*
Lewen, William; America, 1746 ***1220.12*** *p498*
Lewendowski, John; Texas, 1892-1900 ***6015.15*** *p10*
Lewenski, Mary; Detroit, 1929 ***1640.55*** *p113*
Lewent, Mary; Maryland or Virginia, 1728 ***1220.12*** *p497*
Lewer, Catherine; Potomac, 1731 ***1220.12*** *p497*
Lewers, Joachim Johann Conrad; North Carolina, 1792-1862 ***1088.45*** *p19*
Lewes, Abraham; America, 1773 ***1220.12*** *p498*
Lewes, John; Barbados, 1670 ***1220.12*** *p499*
Lewiek, Alphonse 37; New York, NY, 1920 ***930.50*** *p48*
Lewik, Godlip; Pennsylvania, 1837 ***471.10*** *p86*
Lewin, Edward; Washington, 1889 ***2770.40*** *p79*
Lewin, Mary; Maryland, 1733 ***1220.12*** *p497*
Lewin, Peter; America, 1775 ***1220.12*** *p497*
Lewin, Ralph; America, 1772 ***1220.12*** *p497*
Lewin, Susanna; America, 1745 ***1220.12*** *p498*
Lewin, William; America, 1761 ***1220.12*** *p498*
Lewis, Abbott 60; Ontario, 1871 ***1823.21*** *p201*
Lewis, Alfred 18; Quebec, 1870 ***8364.32*** *p24*
Lewis, Ann; America, 1753 ***1220.12*** *p498*
Lewis, Ann; America, 1759 ***1220.12*** *p498*
Lewis, Ann; America, 1761 ***1220.12*** *p498*
Lewis, Ann; Maryland, 1744 ***1220.12*** *p498*
Lewis, Ann *SEE* Lewis, John R.
Lewis, Ann; Ohio, 1850 ***4022.20*** *p284*
Lewis, Anne; Annapolis, MD, 1726 ***1220.12*** *p498*
Lewis, Anne; Rappahannock, VA, 1728 ***1220.12*** *p498*
Lewis, Annie; Ontario, 1871 ***1823.21*** *p201*
Lewis, Bartholomew; America, 1763 ***1220.12*** *p498*
Lewis, Benjamin 33; Ontario, 1871 ***1823.21*** *p201*
Lewis, Bridget 70; Ontario, 1871 ***1823.17*** *p91*
Lewis, Catherine; America, 1750 ***1220.12*** *p498*
Lewis, Charles; America, 1722 ***1220.12*** *p498*
Lewis, Charles; Barbados, 1675 ***1220.12*** *p498*
Lewis, Charles Hiram; Oregon, 1941 ***9157.47*** *p3*
Lewis, Christon 48; Ontario, 1871 ***1823.21*** *p201*
Lewis, Christopher; America, 1725 ***1220.12*** *p498*
Lewis, Christopher; America, 1741 ***1220.12*** *p498*
Lewis, Christopher; America, 1759 ***1220.12*** *p498*
Lewis, Christopher; America, 1763 ***1220.12*** *p498*
Lewis, Christopher; America, 1769 ***1220.12*** *p498*
Lewis, Christopher 50; Ontario, 1871 ***1823.21*** *p201*
Lewis, Clara 20; Quebec, 1870 ***8364.32*** *p24*
Lewis, Daniel; America, 1751 ***1220.12*** *p498*
Lewis, Daniel; America, 1772 ***1220.12*** *p498*
Lewis, Daniel; Colorado, 1883 ***1029.59*** *p54*
Lewis, David; America, 1742 ***1220.12*** *p498*
Lewis, David; America, 1743 ***1220.12*** *p498*
Lewis, David; Boston, 1819 ***3274.55*** *p71*
Lewis, David; Ohio, n.d. ***4022.20*** *p286*
Lewis, David M. *SEE* Lewis, Morgan
Lewis, Devlin 31; Ontario, 1871 ***1823.21*** *p201*
Lewis, Edward; Annapolis, MD, 1723 ***1220.12*** *p498*
Lewis, Edward; Colorado, 1891 ***1029.59*** *p54*
Lewis, Edwin 40; Ontario, 1871 ***1823.21*** *p201*
Lewis, Elizabeth; America, 1751 ***1220.12*** *p498*
Lewis, Elizabeth; America, 1756 ***1220.12*** *p498*
Lewis, Elizabeth; America, 1757 ***1220.12*** *p498*
Lewis, Elizabeth; America, 1773 ***1220.12*** *p498*
Lewis, Elizabeth; America, 1774 ***1220.12*** *p498*
Lewis, Elizabeth Hughes *SEE* Lewis, Morgan
Lewis, Elizabeth 52; Ontario, 1871 ***1823.21*** *p201*
Lewis, Elizabeth; Potomac, 1729 ***1220.12*** *p498*
Lewis, Fabius; America, 1774 ***1220.12*** *p498*
Lewis, Francis; America, 1772 ***1220.12*** *p498*
Lewis, Francis; Died enroute, 1731 ***1220.12*** *p498*
Lewis, Francis 81; Ontario, 1871 ***1823.21*** *p201*
Lewis, Frank; America, 1773 ***1220.12*** *p498*
Lewis, Frank; Maine, 1869-1919 ***9228.50*** *p412*
Lewis, George 26; Ontario, 1871 ***1823.21*** *p201*
Lewis, George 48; Ontario, 1871 ***1823.21*** *p201*
Lewis, Grace; America, 1710 ***1220.12*** *p498*
Lewis, Henry; America, 1774 ***1220.12*** *p498*
Lewis, Hugh; America, 1767 ***1220.12*** *p498*
Lewis, Irenaus 32; Ontario, 1871 ***1823.21*** *p201*
Lewis, Isaac; America, 1748 ***1220.12*** *p498*
Lewis, James; America, 1736 ***1220.12*** *p498*
Lewis, James; America, 1749 ***1220.12*** *p498*
Lewis, James; America, 1751 ***1220.12*** *p498*
Lewis, James; America, 1773 ***1220.12*** *p498*
Lewis, James 38; Ontario, 1871 ***1823.21*** *p201*
Lewis, James 75; Ontario, 1871 ***1823.21*** *p202*
Lewis, Jane; America, 1719 ***1220.12*** *p499*
Lewis, Jane; America, 1746 ***1220.12*** *p499*
Lewis, Jane; America, 1765 ***1220.12*** *p499*
Lewis, Jeremiah 36; Ontario, 1871 ***1823.21*** *p202*
Lewis, Joan; America, 1758 ***1220.12*** *p499*
Lewis, John; America, 1658 ***1220.12*** *p499*
Lewis, John; America, 1685 ***1220.12*** *p499*
Lewis, John; America, 1730 ***1220.12*** *p499*
Lewis, John; America, 1741 ***1220.12*** *p499*
Lewis, John; America, 1747 ***1220.12*** *p499*
Lewis, John; America, 1752 ***1220.12*** *p499*
Lewis, John; America, 1762 ***1220.12*** *p499*
Lewis, John; America, 1763 ***1220.12*** *p499*
Lewis, John; America, 1764 ***1220.12*** *p499*
Lewis, John; America, 1768 ***1220.12*** *p499*
Lewis, John; America, 1769 ***1220.12*** *p499*
Lewis, John; America, 1772 ***1220.12*** *p499*
Lewis, John; America, 1773 ***1220.12*** *p499*
Lewis, John; America, 1774 ***1220.12*** *p499*
Lewis, John; America, 1775 ***1220.12*** *p499*
Lewis, John; Annapolis, MD, 1722 ***1220.12*** *p499*
Lewis, John; Annapolis, MD, 1725 ***1220.12*** *p499*
Lewis, John; Barbados or Jamaica, 1686 ***1220.12*** *p499*
Lewis, John *SEE* Lewis, Thomas
Lewis, John 26; Ontario, 1871 ***1823.17*** *p92*
Lewis, John 41; Ontario, 1871 ***1823.21*** *p202*
Lewis, John 50; Ontario, 1871 ***1823.21*** *p202*
Lewis, John 60; Ontario, 1871 ***1823.21*** *p202*
Lewis, John 25; Santa Clara Co., CA, 1852 ***8704.1*** *p22*
Lewis, John; Virginia, 1758 ***1220.12*** *p499*
Lewis, John; Wisconsin, 1920-1924 ***9228.50*** *p412*
Lewis, John James; America, 1763 ***1220.12*** *p499*
Lewis, John R.; Ohio, 1829 ***4022.20*** *p286*
*Wife:*Ann
With 3 children
*Child:*Zillah
Lewis, Joseph; America, 1748 ***1220.12*** *p499*
Lewis, Joseph; America, 1772 ***1220.12*** *p499*
Lewis, Josiah; America, 1744 ***1220.12*** *p499*
Lewis, Katherine; Maryland, 1719 ***1220.12*** *p498*
Lewis, Lewis; America, 1752 ***1220.12*** *p499*
Lewis, Lewis; Colorado, 1889 ***1029.59*** *p54*
Lewis, Lewis; Colorado, 1897 ***1029.59*** *p54*
Lewis, Luther 40; Ontario, 1871 ***1823.21*** *p202*
Lewis, M. 25; Ontario, 1871 ***1823.21*** *p202*
Lewis, Margaret; America, 1767 ***1220.12*** *p499*
Lewis, Margaret; Annapolis, MD, 1731 ***1220.12*** *p499*
Lewis, Margaret *SEE* Lewis, Thomas
Lewis, Margaret D. *SEE* Lewis, William
Lewis, Marie Genevieve; Bangor, ME, 1865-1920 ***9228.50*** *p412*
Lewis, Martha; America, 1719 ***1220.12*** *p499*
Lewis, Mary; America, 1755 ***1220.12*** *p499*
Lewis, Mary; America, 1774 ***1220.12*** *p499*
Lewis, Mary; Charles Town, SC, 1718 ***1220.12*** *p499*
Lewis, Mary; Died enroute, 1731 ***1220.12*** *p499*
Lewis, Mary; Ohio, 1838 ***4022.20*** *p276*
Lewis, Mary; Potomac, 1729 ***1220.12*** *p499*
Lewis, Morgan; Ohio, n.d. ***4022.20*** *p286*
*Wife:*Elizabeth Hughes
With children
*Child:*David M.
Lewis, Nathaniel; America, 1751 ***1220.12*** *p499*
Lewis, Nelson; Washington, 1889 ***2770.40*** *p79*
Lewis, Peter; America, 1722 ***1220.12*** *p499*
Lewis, Peter; America, 1742 ***1220.12*** *p499*
Lewis, Philip; America, 1766 ***1220.12*** *p499*
Lewis, Philip; Quebec, 1845 ***9228.50*** *p411*
Lewis, Phyllis; Oregon, 1941 ***9157.47*** *p2*
Lewis, Richard; America, 1704 ***1220.12*** *p499*
Lewis, Richard; America, 1750 ***1220.12*** *p500*
Lewis, Richard; America, 1764 ***1220.12*** *p500*
Lewis, Richard; America, 1773 ***1220.12*** *p500*
Lewis, Richard; Potomac, 1731 ***1220.12*** *p499*
Lewis, Robert; America, 1680 ***1220.12*** *p500*
Lewis, Robert; America, 1745 ***1220.12*** *p500*
Lewis, Robert; America, 1775 ***1220.12*** *p500*
Lewis, Robert 20; Ontario, 1871 ***1823.21*** *p202*
Lewis, Samuel; America, 1665 ***1220.12*** *p500*
Lewis, Samuel; Annapolis, MD, 1729 ***1220.12*** *p500*
Lewis, Samuel 38; Ontario, 1871 ***1823.21*** *p202*
Lewis, Sarah; America, 1758 ***1220.12*** *p500*
Lewis, Sarah *SEE* Lewis, William
Lewis, Sarah 62; Ontario, 1871 ***1823.21*** *p202*
Lewis, Sevan; Washington, 1889 ***2770.40*** *p79*
Lewis, Sibill; America, 1722 ***1220.12*** *p500*
Lewis, Simon; Louisiana, 1843-1847 ***7710.1*** *p149*
Lewis, Simon; Louisiana, 1847 ***7710.1*** *p150*
Lewis, Soloman; Louisiana, 1874-1875 ***4981.45*** *p29*
Lewis, Susan; America, 1704 ***1220.12*** *p500*
Lewis, Susanna; America, 1719 ***1220.12*** *p500*
Lewis, Thomas; America, 1753 ***1220.12*** *p500*
Lewis, Thomas; America, 1755 ***1220.12*** *p500*
Lewis, Thomas; America, 1758 ***1220.12*** *p500*
Lewis, Thomas; America, 1759 ***1220.12*** *p500*
Lewis, Thomas; America, 1767 ***1220.12*** *p500*
Lewis, Thomas; America, 1769 ***1220.12*** *p500*

276 *FOR A COMPLETE EXPLANATION OF ENTRY, SEE "HOW TO READ A CITATION" SECTION*

Lewis, Thomas; Maryland, 1744 *1220.12 p500*
Lewis, Thomas; New York, 1778 *8529.30 p4A*
Lewis, Thomas; Ohio, 1834-1837 *4022.20 p286*
 *Wife:*Margaret
 *Child:*John
Lewis, Thomas 55; Ontario, 1871 *1823.21 p202*
Lewis, Thomas 56; Ontario, 1871 *1823.17 p92*
Lewis, Thomas 60; Ontario, 1871 *1823.21 p202*
Lewis, Thomas 61; Ontario, 1871 *1823.21 p202*
Lewis, Thomas J.; Washington, 1889 *2770.40 p79*
Lewis, Walter; America, 1758 *1220.12 p500*
Lewis, William; America, 1687 *1220.12 p500*
Lewis, William; America, 1729 *1220.12 p500*
Lewis, William; America, 1730 *1220.12 p500*
Lewis, William; America, 1740 *1220.12 p500*
Lewis, William; America, 1751 *1220.12 p500*
Lewis, William; America, 1759 *1220.12 p500*
Lewis, William; America, 1765 *1220.12 p500*
Lewis, William; America, 1768 *1220.12 p500*
Lewis, William; America, 1773 *1220.12 p500*
Lewis, William; Annapolis, MD, 1725 *1220.12 p500*
Lewis, William; Ohio, 1835 *4022.20 p287*
 *Wife:*Sarah
 *Child:*Margaret D.
Lewis, William 25; Ontario, 1871 *1823.21 p202*
Lewis, Zillah SEE Lewis, John R.
Lewis Children, . . .; Quebec, 1845-1880 *9228.50 p412*
Lewitt, B.; Louisiana, 1836-1840 *4981.45 p213*
Lewitt, Thomas; Virginia, 1751 *1220.12 p500*
Lewreau, Moyse; Virginia, 1700 *9230.15 p81*
Lews, Joseph; America, 1713 *1220.12 p500*
Lewton, Thomas; America, 1772 *1220.12 p500*
Lewty, Thomas; America, 1773 *1220.12 p500*
Lex, Christian; Galveston, TX, 1855 *571.7 p17*
Lex, Conrad; Galveston, TX, 1855 *571.7 p17*
Ley, Caroline Morgan SEE Ley, William T.
Ley, Charles; Ohio, 1809-1852 *4511.35 p30*
Ley, Cuirad; Louisiana, 1874 *4981.45 p296*
Ley, John D. 38; Ontario, 1871 *1823.21 p202*
Ley, John H.; Ohio, 1809-1852 *4511.35 p30*
Ley, Mary D. 52; Ontario, 1871 *1823.21 p202*
Ley, Robert; America, 1772 *1220.12 p492*
Ley, Thomas 41; Ontario, 1871 *1823.21 p202*
Ley, William T.; Philadelphia, 1852 *8513.31 p323*
 *Wife:*Caroline Morgan
Leydecker, Jean; Illinois, 1852 *6079.1 p8*
Leyer, Elisabeth; America, 1868 *7919.3 p527*
Leygh, Francis 50; Ontario, 1871 *1823.21 p202*
Leyh, Anna; America, 1868 *7919.3 p524*
Leyh, Johann Heinrich; America, 1868 *7919.3 p524*
Leyh, Valtin; America, 1867 *7919.3 p527*
Leyhe, John; Illinois, 1851 *6079.1 p8*
Leyland, Samuel; America, 1775 *1220.12 p500*
Leyland, William; America, 1768 *1220.12 p500*
Leyman, Christian; Ohio, 1809-1852 *4511.35 p30*
Leys, Alexander 60; Ontario, 1871 *1823.17 p92*
Leysons, Richard; America, 1752 *1220.12 p500*
Lezeau, Catherine 28; Montreal, 1641 *9221.17 p108*
Lezenets, Anne 38; Quebec, 1643 *9221.17 p128*
Lezuch, Jacob; Detroit, 1929 *1640.55 p117*
L'Fabuere, Rachael 40; North Carolina, 1774 *1422.10 p56*
L'Herault, Eveline Machon SEE L'Herault, Octave
L'Herault, Octave; Massachusetts, 1903 *9228.50 p402*
 *Wife:*Eveline Machon
L'Hermite, Antoine; Quebec, 1649 *9221.17 p216*
L'Homme, Michel 21; Quebec, 1653 *9221.17 p276*
L'Honneur, Gilles; Quebec, 1654 *9221.17 p313*
L'Hoste, Michael; America, 1837 *5475.1 p468*
L'Hoste, Peter 22; America, 1865 *5475.1 p558*
Lhotka, Vaclav; Chicago, 1854 *2853.20 p387*
Lhotka, Vaclav; Quebec, 1854 *2853.20 p387*
 With family
Liana, Frank; Detroit, 1929-1930 *6214.5 p65*
Liancourt, Auguste 16; America, 1843 *778.6 p213*
Liardin, Marie; Quebec, 1668 *4514.3 p342*
Liazzo, Fillipo; Louisiana, 1874 *4981.45 p132*
Libbermann, Dominique 43; Port uncertain, 1847 *778.6 p213*
Libbey, Minnie M.; Quebec, 1915-1916 *9228.50 p408*
Libenstene, Lewis Henry; North Carolina, 1849 *1088.45 p19*
Liberge, Marie Justine 32; America, 1844 *778.6 p213*
Libert, Isidore; Detroit, 1873 *1494.20 p12*
Libert, Joseph 32; Wisconsin, 1854-1858 *1495.20 p66*
Libert, Nicolas; Milwaukee, 1871 *1494.20 p13*
Liberty, Samuel; Maryland or Virginia, 1738 *1220.12 p500*
Libetz, Chaie 25 SEE Libetz, Moses
Libetz, Moses 23; New York, NY, 1878 *9253.2 p44*
 *Wife:*Chaie 25
Libl, Jan; Iowa, 1854 *2853.20 p230*
Libo, John; Washington, 1889 *2770.40 p79*

Liborne, Jean 21; Quebec, 1659 *9221.17 p400*
Lichners, Sebastian; Louisiana, 1836-1841 *4981.45 p209*
Lichtenberger, Adam; Ohio, 1809-1852 *4511.35 p30*
Lichtenberger, George; Ohio, 1809-1852 *4511.35 p30*
Lichtenstein, Caroline; America, 1867 *7919.3 p534*
Lichtenthal, Anna; Rio de Janeiro, Brazil, 1879 *5475.1 p258*
Lichtey, John; Ohio, 1809-1852 *4511.35 p30*
Lichthardt, Engel Marie Sophie; America, 1852 *7420.1 p94*
Lichtman, Andor 27; America, 1845 *778.6 p213*
Lichtman, Georges 19; America, 1845 *778.6 p213*
Lichtman, Jacob 25; America, 1845 *778.6 p213*
Lichtman, Marie 23; America, 1845 *778.6 p213*
Lichze, Michel 23; New York, NY, 1847 *9176.15 p50*
Liciter, William; America, 1757 *1220.12 p500*
Lick, Anna Margarethe SEE Lick, Johann Jakob
Lick, Eva Giessman SEE Lick, Johann Jakob
Lick, Johann Adam SEE Lick, Johann Jakob
Lick, Johann Jakob; Virginia, 1831 *152.20 p65*
 *Wife:*Eva Giessman
 *Child:*Anna Margarethe
 *Child:*Johann Adam
Liddall, Mary; Annapolis, MD, 1730 *1220.12 p500*
Liddell, Elizabeth; America, 1758 *1220.12 p500*
Liddey, Thomas 23; Ontario, 1871 *1823.21 p202*
Liddiard, Sarah; Maryland, 1740 *1220.12 p500*
Liddie, George; Illinois, 1863 *6079.1 p8*
Liddle, Isabella; America, 1773 *1220.12 p500*
Liddle, Jessie 14; Quebec, 1870 *8364.32 p24*
Liddle, John; America, 1764 *1220.12 p500*
Liddle, Nanny 7; Quebec, 1870 *8364.32 p24*
Liddle, Robert 60; Ontario, 1871 *1823.21 p202*
Liddle, Thomas; New York, 1782 *8529.30 p13*
Liddy, Edith; Ontario, 1871 *1823.17 p92*
Lidget, Charles 46; Ontario, 1871 *1823.21 p202*
Lidget, Peter 38; Boston, 1667 *9228.50 p350*
Lidgett, Smith 48; Ontario, 1871 *1823.17 p92*
Lidgley, John; America, 1758 *1220.12 p501*
Lidley, Richard; Barbados or Jamaica, 1700 *1220.12 p501*
Lidman, Adam Persson; St. Paul, MN, 1877 *1865.50 p94*
Lidman, Carl Gust; Iowa, 1904 *1211.15 p16*
Lidman, John; Iowa, 1898 *1211.15 p16*
Lieb, Elisabeth; America, 1847 *5475.1 p474*
Lieb, Elisabeth SEE LieB, Peter
Lieb, Franz 34; New Orleans, 1848 *778.6 p214*
LieB, Friedrich SEE LieB, Peter
LieB, Heinrich SEE LieB, Peter
Lieb, J. 22; America, 1846 *778.6 p214*
Lieb, Johannetta; America, 1837 *5475.1 p468*
LieB, Karolina SEE LieB, Peter
Lieb, Katharina SEE LieB, Peter
Lieb, Maria 39; New Orleans, 1848 *778.6 p214*
LieB, P. Josef SEE LieB, Peter
LieB, Peter 56; America, 1880 *5475.1 p484*
 *Daughter:*Karolina
 *Daughter:*Elisabeth
 *Son:*Friedrich
 *Daughter:*Katharina
 *Son:*P. Josef
 *Son:*Heinrich
Lieb, Waldburga 30; New Orleans, 1848 *778.6 p214*
Liebeling, Johannes; Mexico, 1903 *7420.1 p379*
Liebermann, Johann Georg; America, 1867 *7919.3 p533*
Lieblang, Georg; Pittsburgh, 1871 *5475.1 p418*
Liebmann, Friedrich; America, 1867 *7919.3 p527*
Lied, John; New York, 1859 *358.56 p99*
Liegenbuhl, Dorothea; America, 1867 *2526.43 p206*
Liegeois, Clemence; Wisconsin, 1854-1858 *1495.20 p50*
Liegeois, Florent; Wisconsin, 1858 *1495.20 p56*
Liegeois, Jean 33; Quebec, 1634 *9221.17 p32*
Liegeois, Jean Baptiste SEE Liegeois, Jean Baptiste
Liegeois, Jean Baptiste; Wisconsin, 1854-1858 *1495.20 p50*
 *Wife:*Marie Antoinette Veckman
 *Son:*Sylvan
 *Son:*Jean Baptiste
Liegeois, Jean Joseph; Wisconsin, 1854-1858 *1495.20 p50*
Liegeois, Marie Antoinette Veckman SEE Liegeois, Jean Baptiste
Liegeois, Sylvan SEE Liegeois, Jean Baptiste
Liell, Friedrich; America, 1852 *5475.1 p481*
Liemenery, Michel 30; New Orleans, 1845 *778.6 p214*
Lienard, Sebastien 27; Quebec, 1654 *9221.17 p313*
Lienard deBeaujeu, Louis; Quebec, 1697 *2314.30 p169*
Lienard deBeaujeu, Louis; Quebec, 1697 *2314.30 p190*
Lier, B. 31; America, 1843 *778.6 p214*
Lierer, Peter; America, 1849 *5475.1 p477*
Liermann, Ferdinand; Ohio, 1840-1897 *8365.35 p17*
Lies, Edouard 32; Texas, 1848 *778.6 p214*
Liese, Anna; Wisconsin, 1899 *6795.8 p74*

Liesenfelder, Margarethe 19; New York, 1899 *5475.1 p40*
Lieser, Johann; America, 1847 *5475.1 p475*
Lieser, Peter; America, 1849 *5475.1 p477*
Liesinger, Oscar; Washington, 1889 *2770.40 p79*
Lieske, Fred William; Wisconsin, 1911 *6795.8 p172*
Lieske, Friedrich; Wisconsin, 1875 *6795.8 p125*
Lieske, Robert Amiel; Wisconsin, 1913 *6795.8 p170*
Liesner, Franz; Wisconsin, 1879 *6795.8 p226*
Liesner, Wm.; Wisconsin, 1891 *6795.8 p107*
Liesse, Marie Catherine; Wisconsin, 1854-1858 *1495.20 p50*
Liestz, Christian; Ohio, 1840-1897 *8365.35 p17*
Liette, Pierre-Charles de; Quebec, 1683-1688 *2314.30 p168*
Liette, Pierre-Charles de; Quebec, 1685 *2314.30 p190*
Lietz, Hermann; Colorado, 1895 *1029.59 p54*
Liewaldt, G. A.; Valdivia, Chile, 1852 *1192.4 p54*
Liewaldt, Herm.; Valdivia, Chile, 1852 *1192.4 p54*
Life, Robert; America, 1763 *1220.12 p501*
Lifiski, Samuel 48; Indiana, 1892 *9076.20 p73*
Lifrihin, John 43; Ontario, 1871 *1823.21 p202*
Lift, Henry; Barbados or Jamaica, 1685 *1220.12 p501*
Ligday, Josef Libor; Minnesota, 1872-1882 *2853.20 p268*
Ligday, Libor; Minnesota, 1888 *2853.20 p270*
Ligden, Harriet 14; Quebec, 1870 *8364.32 p24*
Ligeret, Miss 20; New Orleans, 1848 *778.6 p214*
Ligeret, Mr. 55; New Orleans, 1848 *778.6 p214*
Ligeret, Mrs. 50; New Orleans, 1848 *778.6 p214*
Liggett, William; America, 1736 *1220.12 p501*
Light, Esther; America, 1769 *1220.12 p501*
Light, Hester; America, 1771 *1220.12 p501*
Light, John Lemon; North Carolina, 1809 *1088.45 p19*
Light, Peter; Waldoboro, ME, 1741-1800 *9228.50 p402*
Light, Thomas; America, 1765 *1220.12 p501*
Light, William; America, 1728 *1220.12 p501*
Light, William; America, 1737 *1220.12 p501*
Lightbourn, Joseph; America, 1739 *1220.12 p501*
Lightbourne, Richard; America, 1751 *1220.12 p501*
Lightfoot, Daniel; Virginia, 1732 *1220.12 p501*
Lightfoot, George; America, 1743 *1220.12 p501*
Lightfoot, George 32; Ontario, 1871 *1823.21 p202*
Lightfoot, John; America, 1740 *1220.12 p501*
Lightfoot, John; Marblehead, MA, 1692 *9228.50 p402*
Lightfoot, John 45; Ontario, 1871 *1823.17 p92*
Lightfoot, John; Salem, MA, 1678 *9228.50 p653*
Lightfoot, Joseph 30; Ontario, 1871 *1823.21 p202*
Lightfoot, Richard; America, 1753 *1220.12 p501*
Lightfoot, Robert; Boston, 1745 *9228.50 p652*
Lightfoot, Thomas; America, 1749 *1220.12 p501*
Lightfoot, Thomas 42; Ontario, 1871 *1823.21 p202*
Lightfoot, Thomas 53; Ontario, 1871 *1823.21 p202*
Lightfoot, William; America, 1755 *1220.12 p501*
Lightfoot, William 40; Ontario, 1871 *1823.21 p202*
Lightiser, John; Nova Scotia, 1784 *7105 p24*
Lightwood, Elizabeth; America, 1756 *1220.12 p501*
Lightwood, Mary; America, 1756 *1220.12 p501*
Ligi, Edouard 26; Louisiana, 1848 *778.6 p214*
Ligler, Jan; Wisconsin, 1854 *2853.20 p290*
Lignove, Mr. 24; America, 1842 *778.6 p214*
Lihou, Adele SEE Lihou, James
Lihou, James; Detroit, 1913 *9228.50 p403*
 *Relative:*Adele
 *Relative:*Louise
Lihou, Louise SEE Lihou, James
Lile, Edward; Barbados, 1667 *1220.12 p503*
Lile, Jane; America, 1742 *1220.12 p503*
Lile, Lewis 30; Ontario, 1871 *1823.17 p92*
Liliencamp, Fritz; Ohio, 1840-1897 *8365.35 p17*
Lilienfeld, Carl SEE Lilienfeld, Salomon
Lilienfeld, Elise SEE Lilienfeld, Salomon
Lilienfeld, F.; New York, 1859 *358.56 p100*
Lilienfeld, Johanne Segelbaum SEE Lilienfeld, Salomon
Lilienfeld, Paula SEE Lilienfeld, Salomon
Lilienfeld, Salomon; America, 1881 *7420.1 p322*
 *Wife:*Johanne Segelbaum
 *Daughter:*Paula
 *Son:*Carl
 *Daughter:*Elise
Liljedahl, Carl Johan; St. Paul, MN, 1882 *1865.50 p94*
Liljengren, John P.; Illinois, 1860-1861 *4487.25 p64*
Lill, Silvester; America, 1707 *1220.12 p501*
Lilleston, John; America, 1742 *1220.12 p501*
Lilley, Charles 37; Ontario, 1871 *1823.21 p202*
Lilley, Charles 59; Ontario, 1871 *1823.17 p92*
Lilley, David 5; New Orleans, 1840 *778.6 p214*
Lilley, David 32; New Orleans, 1840 *778.6 p214*
Lilley, Edward 41; Ontario, 1871 *1823.21 p202*
Lilley, Elisa 25; New Orleans, 1840 *778.6 p214*
Lilley, Francis 17; New Orleans, 1840 *778.6 p214*
Lilley, George; America, 1773 *1220.12 p501*
Lilley, George A. 39; Ontario, 1871 *1823.17 p92*
Lilley, James 60; Ontario, 1871 *1823.21 p202*

Lilley, Jeremiah; Virginia, 1730 ***1220.12*** *p501*
Lilley, John; America, 1697 ***1220.12*** *p501*
Lilley, John; Barbados, 1665 ***1220.12*** *p501*
Lilley, Joseph 31; New Orleans, 1840 ***778.6*** *p214*
Lilley, Maria 12; New Orleans, 1840 ***778.6*** *p214*
Lilley, Maria 27; New Orleans, 1840 ***778.6*** *p214*
Lilley, Richard; America, 1656 ***1220.12*** *p501*
Lilley, Samuel; Died enroute, 1726 ***1220.12*** *p501*
Lilley, Theobald; Ohio, 1809-1852 ***4511.35*** *p30*
Lilley, William; America, 1766 ***1220.12*** *p501*
Lillig, A. Maria *SEE* Lillig, Johann
Lillig, Anna *SEE* Lillig, Peter
Lillig, Anna *SEE* Lillig, Johann
Lillig, Helena *SEE* Lillig, Peter
Lillig, Johann *SEE* Lillig, Peter
Lillig, Johann; Iowa, 1880 ***5475.1*** *p350*
*Wife:*Maria Borhofen
*Son:*Peter
*Daughter:*A. Maria
*Daughter:*Anna
*Daughter:*Katharina
Lillig, Katharina *SEE* Lillig, Peter
Lillig, Katharina *SEE* Lillig, Johann
Lillig, Maria Borhofen *SEE* Lillig, Johann
Lillig, Mathias *SEE* Lillig, Peter
Lillig, Nikolaus *SEE* Lillig, Peter
Lillig, Peter; America, 1881 ***5475.1*** *p334*
Lillig, Peter; America, 1881 ***5475.1*** *p334*
*Wife:*Regina Michels
*Daughter:*Anna
*Son:*Johann
*Son:*Mathias
*Daughter:*Regina
*Son:*Nikolaus
With son
*Daughter:*Katharina
*Daughter:*Helena
Lillig, Peter *SEE* Lillig, Johann
Lillig, Regina *SEE* Lillig, Peter
Lillig, Regina Michels *SEE* Lillig, Peter
Lillington, Elizabeth; Barbados, 1669 ***1220.12*** *p501*
Lillington, Robert; America, 1767 ***1220.12*** *p501*
Lilliston, John; America, 1735 ***1220.12*** *p501*
Lilliwood, Ann 20; St. John, N.B., 1834 ***6469.7*** *p4*
Lilljedahl, Sv.; New York, NY, 1843 ***6412.40*** *p147*
Lilly, Ann; America, 1765 ***1220.12*** *p501*
Lilly, James; Louisiana, 1836-1840 ***4981.45*** *p213*
Lilly, James 26; Ontario, 1871 ***1823.17*** *p92*
Lilly, John; America, 1750 ***1220.12*** *p501*
Lilly, John; America, 1762 ***1220.12*** *p501*
Lilly, John; America, 1766 ***1220.12*** *p501*
Lilly, John Patterson; America, 1752 ***1220.12*** *p501*
Lilly, Margaret; America, 1754 ***1220.12*** *p501*
Lilly, Robert; America, 1761 ***1220.12*** *p501*
Lilly, Sarah; America, 1722 ***1220.12*** *p501*
Lilly, Thomas; America, 1754 ***1220.12*** *p501*
Lilly, Timothy; America, 1750 ***1220.12*** *p501*
Lilly, William; Virginia, 1732 ***1220.12*** *p501*
Lily, John 48; Ontario, 1871 ***1823.17*** *p92*
Limarez, John; America, 1764 ***1220.12*** *p501*
Limbach, Andreas *SEE* Limbach, Christian
Limbach, Christian *SEE* Limbach, Christian
Limbach, Christian; New York, 1884 ***5475.1*** *p430*
*Wife:*Katharina Lauterbach
*Son:*Andreas
*Daughter:*Katharina
*Son:*Johann
*Son:*Christian
Limbach, Johann *SEE* Limbach, Christian
Limbach, Katharina *SEE* Limbach, Christian
Limbach, Katharina Lauterbach *SEE* Limbach, Christian
Limberg, Abraham 7 *SEE* Limberg, Judes
Limberg, Judes 40; New York, NY, 1878 ***9253.2*** *p45*
*Son:*Abraham 7
Limberger, John; Ohio, 1856 ***3580.20*** *p32*
Limberger, John; Ohio, 1856 ***6020.12*** *p13*
Limbrish, Thomas; America, 1728 ***1220.12*** *p501*
Limburgh, Paul; Ohio, 1844 ***2763.1*** *p20*
Limburner, Arthur 28; Michigan, 1880 ***4491.36*** *p14*
Limburner, Sarah M. 18; Michigan, 1880 ***4491.36*** *p14*
Limes, Margaret; America, 1748 ***1220.12*** *p502*
Limo, Abraham; Louisiana, 1874 ***4981.45*** *p132*
Limousin, Jacques; Quebec, 1657 ***9221.17*** *p362*
Lin, Thomas 61; Ontario, 1871 ***1823.21*** *p203*
Linakin, John; America, 1768 ***1220.12*** *p502*
Linakin, Mary; America, 1764 ***1220.12*** *p502*
Linard, Roger; Philadelphia, 1778 ***8529.30*** *p7A*
Linberger, Charles; Illinois, 1861 ***6079.1*** *p8*
Linc, Frantisek; Iowa, 1855-1856 ***2853.20*** *p237*
Linch, . . .; New Orleans, 1851 ***7242.30*** *p148*
Linch, Abigail; Boston, 1760 ***1642*** *p48*
Linch, Bartholomew; Boston, 1744 ***1642*** *p45*
Linch, Betsey; New Orleans, 1851 ***7242.30*** *p148*
Linch, Bridget; New Orleans, 1851 ***7242.30*** *p148*
Linch, Christopher; Boston, 1750 ***1642*** *p46*
Linch, Christopher; Boston, 1754 ***1642*** *p47*
Linch, Christopher; Boston, 1756 ***1642*** *p47*
Linch, Cornelius; Boston, 1738 ***1642*** *p44*
Linch, Daniel; Virginia, 1770 ***1220.12*** *p515*
Linch, David; Boston, 1771 ***1642*** *p49*
Linch, Denis; Toronto, 1844 ***2910.35*** *p113*
Linch, Edward; Boston, 1768 ***1642*** *p39*
Linch, Elizabeth; Boston, 1753 ***1642*** *p47*
Linch, Elizabeth; Boston, 1754 ***1642*** *p47*
Linch, Elizabeth; Boston, 1755 ***1642*** *p47*
Linch, James; Boston, 1750 ***1642*** *p46*
Linch, John; America, 1765 ***1220.12*** *p515*
Linch, Katharine; Boston, 1766 ***1642*** *p48*
Linch, Mary; New Orleans, 1851 ***7242.30*** *p148*
Linch, Michael; America, 1758 ***1220.12*** *p515*
Linch, North; Boston, 1766 ***1642*** *p37*
Linch, Richard; New England, 1745 ***1642*** *p27*
Linch, Richard; New England, 1745 ***1642*** *p28*
Linch, Thomas; Boston, 1765 ***1642*** *p35*
Linch, Thomas 40; Ontario, 1871 ***1823.17*** *p92*
Linch, William; Boston, 1725 ***1642*** *p25*
Linchlop, Jacob; Nova Scotia, 1784 ***7105*** *p25*
Linck, Joseph 18; America, 1846 ***778.6*** *p312*
Linck, Nicholus; Ohio, 1809-1852 ***4511.35*** *p30*
Linck, Xaver; Valdivia, Chile, 1850 ***1192.4*** *p48*
Lincke, Carl Gottlob; Valdivia, Chile, 1850 ***1192.4*** *p49*
Lincke, Gottl.; Valdivia, Chile, 1852 ***1192.4*** *p54*
With wife
With child 18
With child 8
Lincke, Joh. Friedrich; Valdivia, Chile, 1850 ***1192.4*** *p49*
Lincoln, Isaiah 25; Ontario, 1871 ***1823.17*** *p92*
Lincoln, James; America, 1752 ***1220.12*** *p502*
Lincoln, John; America, 1765 ***1220.12*** *p502*
Lincoln, Joseph 49; Ontario, 1871 ***1823.17*** *p92*
Lincoln, Rose; America, 1745 ***1220.12*** *p502*
Lincoln, Thomas; America, 1775 ***1220.12*** *p502*
Lincolne, Edward; America, 1700 ***1220.12*** *p502*
Lind, Adam 45; Ontario, 1871 ***1823.21*** *p203*
Lind, Andrew *SEE* Lind, Hans
Lind, Axel Frederick; Boston, 1899 ***1766.20*** *p3*
Lind, Betze Erickson *SEE* Lind, Hans
Lind, Catherine; Kansas, 1879 ***777.40*** *p15*
Lind, Charles F.; St. Paul, MN, 1881 ***1865.50*** *p95*
Lind, Hans; Kansas, 1876 ***777.40*** *p14*
*Wife:*Betze Erickson
With father-in-law & mother-in-law
*Son:*Andrew
Lind, Heinrich, Jr.; America, 1867 ***7919.3*** *p534*
Lind, Heinrich, Sr.; America, 1867 ***7919.3*** *p534*
With 4 children
Lind, John A.; Washington, 1887 ***2770.40*** *p24*
Lind, Nels; Colorado, 1893 ***1029.59*** *p54*
Lind, Richard; New York, NY, 1852 ***6412.40*** *p153*
Lind, Sofia; St. Paul, MN, 1894 ***1865.50*** *p95*
Lind, Thomas; America, 1728 ***1220.12*** *p502*
Lindahl, Carl G.E. *SEE* Lindahl, Daniel August
Lindahl, Daniel August; Kansas, 1870 ***777.40*** *p10*
*Wife:*Mary
*Son:*John A.
*Son:*Carl G.E.
Lindahl, G.; New York, NY, 1850 ***6412.40*** *p152*
Lindahl, John A. *SEE* Lindahl, Daniel August
Lindahl, Malcolm; Cleveland, OH, 1895-1900 ***9722.10*** *p123*
Lindahl, Mary *SEE* Lindahl, Daniel August
Lindauer, Christian; Louisiana, 1836-1840 ***4981.45*** *p213*
Lindback, Cajsa; America, 1849 ***6529.11*** *p25*
Lindberg, Alfred; Cleveland, OH, 1889-1895 ***9722.10*** *p123*
Lindberg, Andrew S.; St. Paul, MN, 1880 ***1865.50*** *p95*
Lindberg, Carl Fred.; New York, NY, 1850 ***6412.40*** *p152*
Lindberg, G.L.; Baltimore, 1846 ***6412.40*** *p149*
Lindberg, John; Washington, 1886 ***2770.40*** *p195*
Lindberg, L.; Savannah, GA, 1849 ***6412.40*** *p152*
Lindberg, Swan; Colorado, 1890 ***1029.59*** *p54*
Lindberg, Swan Gust; Colorado, 1892 ***1029.59*** *p54*
Lindblad, Jennie *SEE* Lindblad, John W.
Lindblad, John W.; St. Paul, MN, 1884 ***1865.50*** *p95*
*Wife:*Jennie
Lindblom, Olif; Washington, 1884 ***2770.40*** *p192*
Linde, Erick; Illinois, 1842-1879 ***777.40*** *p18*
Lindeblad, N. Christiansson; New York, NY, 1851 ***6412.40*** *p153*
Lindekugel, Gottlieb Johann; Wisconsin, 1889 ***6795.8*** *p229*
Lindekugel, Johann; Wisconsin, 1881 ***6795.8*** *p230*
Lindekugel, John Gottlieb; Wisconsin, 1891 ***6795.8*** *p229*
Lindel, Charles; Washington, 1885 ***2770.40*** *p194*
Lindell, J.P.; St. Paul, MN, 1871-1874 ***1865.50*** *p95*
Lindell, John; Illinois, 1861 ***4487.25*** *p64*
Lindell, Mary; St. Paul, MN, 1890 ***1865.50*** *p95*
Lindell, Nels; Illinois, 1861 ***4487.25*** *p64*
Lindeman, Dirk; North Carolina, 1824 ***1088.45*** *p19*
Lindemann, . . .; America, 1846 ***7420.1*** *p45*
With family
Lindemann, August 24; New York, NY, 1864 ***8425.62*** *p195*
Lindemann, Bertha; Wisconsin, 1892 ***6795.8*** *p79*
Lindemann, Carl; America, 1877 ***7420.1*** *p309*
Lindemann, Johann Adam; America, 1859 ***2526.43*** *p152*
Lindemann, Johann Heinrich Christian; America, 1868 ***7420.1*** *p274*
With family
Lindemann, Johannes; America, 1873 ***2526.43*** *p152*
Lindemann, Karl; Port uncertain, 1908 ***7420.1*** *p384*
Lindemann, Minna 15; New York, NY, 1864 ***8425.62*** *p196*
Lindemann, Wilhelmine Christine Charlotte; America, 1864 ***7420.1*** *p227*
*Daughter:*Wilhelmine Auguste
*Son:*Heinrich Ferdinand August
*Daughter:*Wilhelmine Sophie Charlotte
Lindemeier, Carl Friedrich August; America, 1846 ***7420.1*** *p45*
Lindemeyer, Carl Heinrich Albrecht; America, 1883 ***7420.1*** *p337*
Linden, Anna; New York, NY, 1878 ***7420.1*** *p311*
Linden, Carl August; New York, 1870 ***1766.20*** *p14*
Linden, Francois 21; America, 1847 ***778.6*** *p214*
Linden, Joseph 25; Ontario, 1871 ***1823.21*** *p203*
Linden, Per Martin; Cleveland, OH, 1892-1893 ***9722.10*** *p123*
Linden, Samual 31; Ontario, 1871 ***1823.21*** *p203*
Linder, Charles; Cleveland, OH, 1873-1888 ***9722.10*** *p123*
Linder, Godfrey Linus; New York, 1903 ***1766.20*** *p36*
Linder, Juliane 52; America, 1866 ***5475.1*** *p490*
Linder, Wm.; Illinois, 1834-1900 ***6020.5*** *p132*
Linderyon, John 30; Ontario, 1871 ***1823.21*** *p203*
Lindfast, John; Ontario, 1846 ***9228.50*** *p376*
Lindgren, Albert; Cleveland, OH, 1895 ***9722.10*** *p123*
Lindgren, Andrew; St. Paul, MN, 1887 ***1865.50*** *p95*
*Wife:*Elisabeth
*Daughter:*Anna Carolina
Lindgren, Anna Carolina *SEE* Lindgren, Andrew
Lindgren, Carl Lorens; New York, NY, 1850 ***6410.15*** *p104*
Lindgren, Christina; St. Paul, MN, 1894 ***1865.50*** *p95*
Lindgren, Einar; Cleveland, OH, 1902-1906 ***9722.10*** *p123*
Lindgren, Elisabeth *SEE* Lindgren, Andrew
Lindgren, Frank 50; Minnesota, 1925 ***2769.54*** *p1379*
Lindgren, Johanna M.; St. Paul, MN, 1904 ***1865.50*** *p96*
Lindgren, John; St. Paul, MN, 1894 ***1865.50*** *p95*
Lindgren, John Elis; Boston, 1902 ***1766.20*** *p36*
Lindgren, L.; North Carolina, 1855 ***1088.45*** *p19*
Lindgren, Olof; New York, NY, 1843 ***6412.40*** *p147*
Lindholme, Charles; Cleveland, OH, 1902-1903 ***9722.10*** *p123*
Lindhorst, Bernard; Nebraska, 1905 ***3004.30*** *p46*
Lindhorst, Henry; Nebraska, 1905 ***3004.30*** *p46*
Lindhorst, Hy; Nebraska, 1905 ***3004.30*** *p46*
Lindin, Anna Elisabetha 18; Pennsylvania, 1850 ***170.15*** *p35*
Lindinger, Egbert Hermann; Baltimore, 1878 ***7420.1*** *p311*
Lindinger, Johann Heinrich August; Baltimore, 1876 ***7420.1*** *p307*
Lindlaub, Jakob; Nova Scotia, 1784 ***7105*** *p25*
Lindley, George 51; Ontario, 1871 ***1823.21*** *p203*
Lindley, John; America, 1753 ***1220.12*** *p502*
Lindley, William; America, 1758 ***1220.12*** *p502*
Lindley, William; America, 1760 ***1220.12*** *p502*
Lindley, William; America, 1761 ***1220.12*** *p502*
Lindman, Hjalmer 37; Minnesota, 1923 ***2769.54*** *p1378*
Lindman, William 19; Minnesota, 1925 ***2769.54*** *p1378*
Lindner, George; New York, 1859 ***358.56*** *p55*
Lindner, Hedwig 17; New York, NY, 1885 ***1883.7*** *p45*
Lindoll Swenson, August; Kansas, 1870 ***777.40*** *p10*
*Wife:*Mary
*Son:*Carl G.E.
*Son:*John A.
Lindoll Swenson, Carl G.E. *SEE* Lindoll Swenson, August
Lindoll Swenson, John A. *SEE* Lindoll Swenson, August
Lindoll Swenson, Mary *SEE* Lindoll Swenson, August
Lindon, Catherine; America, 1757 ***1220.12*** *p502*
Lindquist, Hilda K.; St. Paul, MN, 1894 ***1865.50*** *p95*
Lindquist, John; Colorado, 1878 ***1029.59*** *p55*
Lindquist, Victor; Washington, 1889 ***2770.40*** *p79*
Lindqvist, Alvin; Cleveland, OH, 1901-1902 ***9722.10*** *p123*

278 *FOR A COMPLETE EXPLANATION OF ENTRY, SEE "HOW TO READ A CITATION" SECTION*

Lindqvist, Carl; Philadelphia, 1848 ***6412.40*** *p150*
Lindqvist, Hilda K.; St. Paul, MN, 1894 ***1865.50*** *p95*
Lindqvist, Mathilda; Minneapolis, 1884-1890 ***1865.50*** *p41*
Lindqvist, Wilhelm Petrus; Cleveland, OH, 1901-1903 ***9722.10*** *p123*
Lindsay, David; America, 1706 ***1220.12*** *p502*
Lindsay, George 51; Ontario, 1871 ***1823.21*** *p203*
Lindsay, Isabella 11; Quebec, 1870 ***8364.32*** *p24*
Lindsay, John; Boston, 1767 ***1642*** *p38*
Lindsay, John; North Carolina, 1825 ***1088.45*** *p19*
Lindsay, John 36; Ontario, 1871 ***1823.17*** *p92*
Lindsay, Martha 40; Ontario, 1871 ***1823.21*** *p203*
Lindsay, Neil 30; Ontario, 1871 ***1823.21*** *p203*
Lindsay, Robert; North Carolina, 1845 ***1088.45*** *p19*
Lindsay, Thomas; Washington, 1889 ***2770.40*** *p79*
Lindsay, William 80; Ontario, 1871 ***1823.21*** *p203*
Lindsay, William 16; Quebec, 1870 ***8364.32*** *p24*
Lindset, Anton; Colorado, 1880 ***1029.59*** *p55*
Lindsey, Anthony; Annapolis, MD, 1735 ***1220.12*** *p502*
Lindsey, Archibald 42; Ontario, 1871 ***1823.17*** *p92*
Lindsey, Archibald C.; North Carolina, 1809 ***1088.45*** *p19*
Lindsey, Catherine; America, 1760 ***1220.12*** *p502*
Lindsey, Hugh; America, 1732 ***1220.12*** *p502*
Lindsey, John; America, 1739 ***1220.12*** *p502*
Lindsey, Mary; America, 1758 ***1220.12*** *p502*
Lindsey, Richard; Virginia, 1721 ***1220.12*** *p502*
Lindsey, Thomas; Virginia, 1735 ***1220.12*** *p502*
Lindsey, William 36; Ontario, 1871 ***1823.21*** *p203*
Lindstahl, Ferd.; Philadelphia, 1847 ***6412.40*** *p150*
Lindstrom, Carl Simon; New York, 1902 ***1766.20*** *p14*
Lindstrom, G.; New York, NY, 1843 ***6412.40*** *p147*
Lindstrom, John; St. Paul, MN, 1874 ***1865.50*** *p95*
*Wife:*Maria
Lindstrom, Karl Fredrik; Cleveland, OH, 1892 ***9722.10*** *p123*
Lindstrom, Maria *SEE* Lindstrom, John
Lindstrom, Nicholas; Michigan, 1897-1898 ***1865.50*** *p95*
Lindstrom, O.; New York, NY, 1843 ***6412.40*** *p146*
Linduff, Benjamin A.; Ohio, 1873 ***3580.20*** *p32*
Linduff, Benjamin A.; Ohio, 1873 ***6020.12*** *p13*
Line, Thomas; America, 1755 ***1220.12*** *p502*
Line, Thomas; Boston, 1776 ***8529.30*** *p6*
Lineaux, Joseph 41; New Orleans, 1841 ***778.6*** *p214*
Lineback, Frederick; North Carolina, 1811 ***1088.45*** *p19*
Linek, Frantisek; Cleveland, OH, 1868-1910 ***2853.20*** *p498*
Lines, Ann 45; Ontario, 1871 ***1823.21*** *p203*
Lines, Mary; America, 1767 ***1220.12*** *p502*
Lines, Patrick; Toronto, 1844 ***2910.35*** *p115*
Linetzchy, Pink; Galveston, TX, 1913 ***3331.4*** *p11*
Linetzchy, Sonnia; Galveston, TX, 1913 ***3331.4*** *p11*
Linfield, William 28; Ontario, 1871 ***1823.21*** *p203*
Linfoot, George 46; Ontario, 1871 ***1823.21*** *p203*
Linfoot, John; Ontario, 1846 ***9228.50*** *p376*
Linford, Samuel; America, 1774 ***1220.12*** *p502*
Ling, Edgar Alfred; America, 1906 ***9228.50*** *p403*
*Child:*Esther
*Child:*Edgar Frederick
Ling, Edgar Frederick *SEE* Ling, Edgar Alfred
Ling, Emma Alice; America, 1857-1949 ***9228.50*** *p403*
Ling, Esther *SEE* Ling, Edgar Alfred
Ling, George; Boston, 1774 ***8529.30*** *p3*
Ling, Joseph 55; Ontario, 1871 ***1823.21*** *p203*
Ling, Maurice; America, 1729 ***1220.12*** *p502*
Ling, William 64; Ontario, 1871 ***1823.21*** *p203*
Lingard, Robert; America, 1753 ***1220.12*** *p502*
Lingham, John; America, 1749 ***1220.12*** *p502*
Lingley, Elizabeth; America, 1771 ***1220.12*** *p502*
Lingley, James; America, 1738 ***1220.12*** *p502*
Lingnowski, Barbara 42; New York, NY, 1879 ***6954.7*** *p40*
Lingnowski, Friedrich 11 months; New York, NY, 1879 ***6954.7*** *p40*
Lingnowski, Johannes 17; New York, NY, 1879 ***6954.7*** *p40*
Lingnowski, Leonore 15; New York, NY, 1879 ***6954.7*** *p40*
Linguard, Isaac; America, 1741 ***1220.12*** *p502*
Linhard, Josef; Iowa, 1854 ***2853.20*** *p230*
Linhart, John Adam; Wisconsin, 1855 ***6795.8*** *p99*
Liniere, Jeanne-Marie-Anne; Quebec, 1671 ***4514.3*** *p342*
Lininger, George; Ohio, 1809-1852 ***4511.35*** *p30*
Lininger, John; Ohio, 1809-1852 ***4511.35*** *p30*
Lininger, Philip; Ohio, 1809-1852 ***4511.35*** *p30*
Linington, Mary; Maryland, 1672 ***1236.25*** *p47*
Link, Adam; America, 1892 ***2526.43*** *p211*
*Brother:*Peter
Link, Charles William; Wisconsin, 1899 ***6795.8*** *p94*
Link, Franz; America, 1836 ***2526.42*** *p105*
Link, Franz; America, 1836 ***2526.42*** *p193*
With wife
With child 6
With child 1
With child 4
Link, Franz Michael; America, 1883 ***2526.43*** *p211*
Link, George; Colorado, 1862-1894 ***1029.59*** *p55*
Link, George; Colorado, 1873 ***1029.59*** *p55*
Link, Heinrich; America, 1885 ***2526.42*** *p163*
Link, Jakob Gottlieb; Baltimore, 1893 ***3366.30*** *p70*
Link, Mrs. Johannes; America, 1837 ***2526.42*** *p193*
With daughter & son-in-law
Link, John; Ohio, 1809-1852 ***4511.35*** *p30*
Link, Julien 19; Ohio, 1847 ***778.6*** *p214*
Link, Matthaus; America, 1836 ***2526.42*** *p105*
Link, Matthias; America, 1836 ***2526.42*** *p193*
Link, Nicholas; Ohio, 1809-1852 ***4511.35*** *p31*
Link, Nikolaus 2 *SEE* Link, Peter Paul
Link, Peter *SEE* Link, Adam
Link, Peter Paul; America, 1846 ***2526.42*** *p143*
With wife
*Child:*Nikolaus
*Child:*Philipp
Link, Philipp 4 *SEE* Link, Peter Paul
Link, Wilhelmine Maria; Wisconsin, 1897 ***6795.8*** *p63*
Link, William Fred; Wisconsin, 1892 ***6795.8*** *p90*
Linka, Jan; South Dakota, 1892 ***2853.20*** *p250*
Linka, Jan; South Dakota, 1900 ***2853.20*** *p248*
Linke, Antonie; America, 1867 ***7919.3*** *p531*
Linke, Emilie; Wisconsin, 1888 ***6795.8*** *p44*
Linke, Johann; Wisconsin, 1869 ***6795.8*** *p25*
Linke, Johanne Therese; America, 1867 ***7919.3*** *p534*
Linkenhelt, Franz 42; Port uncertain, 1843 ***778.6*** *p214*
Linker, John; Ohio, 1840-1897 ***8365.35*** *p17*
Linkherd, Thomas; America, 1749 ***1220.12*** *p503*
Linkhoner, William; North Carolina, 1854 ***1088.45*** *p19*
Linkiewicz, Antonina 20; New York, NY, 1911 ***6533.11*** *p10*
Linkowski, Ignacy 24; New York, NY, 1920 ***930.50*** *p48*
Linlowe, Elizabeth; Barbados, 1672 ***1220.12*** *p503*
Linn, A. Maria Meyer 50 *SEE* Linn, Christoph
Linn, Augusta Sofia *SEE* Linn, N. Peter
Linn, Christoph 52; Wisconsin, 1857 ***5475.1*** *p255*
*Wife:*A. Maria Meyer 50
*Son:*Johann 17
*Son:*Mathias 13
*Son:*Franz 15
Linn, Franz 15 *SEE* Linn, Christoph
Linn, Hulda Maria Augusta *SEE* Linn, N. Peter
Linn, Johann 17 *SEE* Linn, Christoph
Linn, Joseph; Toronto, 1844 ***2910.35*** *p115*
Linn, Mathias 13 *SEE* Linn, Christoph
Linn, N. Peter; St. Paul, MN, 1882 ***1865.50*** *p96*
*Wife:*Augusta Sofia
*Daughter:*Hulda Maria Augusta
Linnard, Richard; America, 1769 ***1220.12*** *p503*
Linneberger, Child; Pennsylvania, 1866 ***170.15*** *p35*
With sibling
Linneberger, Katharina; Pennsylvania, 1866 ***170.15*** *p35*
With family
Linneke, Anne Mary; Annapolis, MD, 1725 ***1220.12*** *p503*
Linnemann, Anne Sophie Marie Hattendorf *SEE* Linnemann, Heinrich Konrad
Linnemann, Engel Marie Charlotte; America, 1846 ***7420.1*** *p46*
*Sister:*Sophie Dorothee
Linnemann, Heinrich Friedr. Wilh.; America, 1846 ***7420.1*** *p46*
Linnemann, Heinrich Konrad; America, 1850 ***7420.1*** *p73*
*Wife:*Anne Sophie Marie Hattendorf
*Son:*Johann Otto
*Son:*Johann Heinrich
Linnemann, Heinrich Wilhelm August *SEE* Linnemann, Sophie Marie Dorothee
Linnemann, Heinrich Wilhelm Christian *SEE* Linnemann, Sophie Marie Dorothee
Linnemann, Johann Heinrich *SEE* Linnemann, Heinrich Konrad
Linnemann, Johann Otto *SEE* Linnemann, Heinrich Konrad
Linnemann, Sophie Dorothee *SEE* Linnemann, Engel Marie Charlotte
Linnemann, Sophie Marie Dorothee; America, 1860 ***7420.1*** *p195*
*Brother:*Heinrich Wilhelm Christian
*Brother:*Heinrich Wilhelm August
Linnerpon, George; America, 1772 ***1220.12*** *p503*
Linnett, Benjamin; America, 1730 ***1220.12*** *p503*
Linnett, Francis; America, 1772 ***1220.12*** *p503*
Linnett, Francis 30; Maryland, 1724 ***1220.12*** *p503*
Linney, Charles; America, 1765 ***1220.12*** *p503*
Linney, James; America, 1745 ***1220.12*** *p503*
Linney, John; America, 1770 ***1220.12*** *p503*
Linney, William; America, 1767 ***1220.12*** *p503*
Linnick, Robert; America, 1772 ***1220.12*** *p503*
Linnig, Anna; America, 1882 ***5475.1*** *p512*
Linnigin, John; America, 1766 ***1220.12*** *p503*
Linnington, Robert; America, 1767 ***1220.12*** *p503*
Linny, Sarah; Maryland, 1727 ***1220.12*** *p503*
Linot, Jacques; Montreal, 1653 ***9221.17*** *p296*
Linquist, Carl H.; Washington, 1885 ***2770.40*** *p194*
Linsay, Lucretia; America, 1741 ***1220.12*** *p502*
Linser, Barbara Auguste; America, 1867 ***7919.3*** *p529*
Linser, Ernst Christian; America, 1868 ***7919.3*** *p532*
With 5 children
Linsey, Jane; America, 1745 ***1220.12*** *p502*
Linsey, Mary; America, 1742 ***1220.12*** *p502*
Linsey, Thomas; America, 1770 ***1220.12*** *p502*
Linsey, Thos.; Maryland, 1673 ***1236.25*** *p48*
Linsey, William; America, 1766 ***1220.12*** *p502*
Linsey, William; America, 1773 ***1220.12*** *p502*
Linsie, Dond; Cape Fear, NC,, 1754 ***1422.10*** *p61*
Linsler, Charles 38; Missouri, 1845 ***778.6*** *p214*
Linsler, Josephine 30; Missouri, 1845 ***778.6*** *p214*
Linsley, John; America, 1722 ***1220.12*** *p503*
Linss, Dorothea; America, 1868 ***7919.3*** *p528*
*Son:*Louis
Linss, Louis *SEE* Linss, Dorothea
Linsted, Thomas; America, 1748 ***1220.12*** *p503*
Linstrom, Charley; Iowa, 1896 ***1211.15*** *p16*
Linstrom, G. A.; Iowa, 1891 ***1211.15*** *p16*
Linstruth, Chatar. 19; New York, NY, 1864 ***8425.62*** *p197*
Lintern, Edward; Maryland, 1745 ***1220.12*** *p503*
Lintern, Henry; Boston, 1831 ***3274.55*** *p73*
Lintlop, Jacob; Nova Scotia, 1784 ***7105*** *p25*
Linto, Theodor; America, n.d. ***8023.44*** *p376*
Linton, Henry; America, 1775 ***1220.12*** *p503*
Linton, Isaac 38; Ontario, 1871 ***1823.21*** *p203*
Linton, Samuel; America, 1767 ***1220.12*** *p503*
Lintott, Geo 63; Ontario, 1871 ***1823.21*** *p203*
Lintz, Ap.line 22; America, 1848 ***778.6*** *p214*
Lintz, Daniel; Ohio, 1809-1852 ***4511.35*** *p31*
Linvill, John; America, 1700 ***1220.12*** *p503*
Lioddi, Henri 16; Tennessee, 1848 ***778.6*** *p214*
Lioewski, Kasimir 33; New York, NY, 1894 ***6512.1*** *p183*
Lion, Albert; America, 1892 ***5475.1*** *p448*
Lion, Emanuel; America, 1882 ***5475.1*** *p447*
Lion, Isidor; New York, 1890 ***5475.1*** *p448*
Lion, Jakob; New York, 1888 ***5475.1*** *p448*
Lion, Joseph; North America, 1847-1848 ***5475.1*** *p402*
Lion, Karl; America, 1880 ***5475.1*** *p447*
Lion, Leon; America, 1893 ***5475.1*** *p25*
Lion, Salomon; North America, 1847 ***5475.1*** *p402*
Lion, Simon; America, 1883 ***5475.1*** *p434*
Lion, Theophile 21; America, 1845 ***778.6*** *p214*
Lion, Thomas; America, 1758 ***1220.12*** *p515*
Lion, Thomas; America, 1759 ***1220.12*** *p515*
Lion, Thomas 32; Ontario, 1871 ***1823.21*** *p203*
Lions, Barnaby; America, 1769 ***1220.12*** *p515*
Lions, Francis 42; Ontario, 1871 ***1823.21*** *p203*
Lipcraft, John; America, 1751 ***1220.12*** *p503*
Lipfert, Johanna Catharina; America, 1867 ***7919.3*** *p525*
Lipinski, Eva; Wisconsin, 1899 ***6795.8*** *p63*
Lipok, Simon; Texas, 1855-1886 ***9980.22*** *p16*
Lipovsky, Jindrich; St. Louis, 1850 ***2853.20*** *p23*
Lipp, Adam 8; New York, NY, 1898 ***7951.13*** *p43*
Lipp, Andrew; South Carolina, 1852 ***6155.4*** *p18*
Lipp, Anna 4 months; New York, NY, 1898 ***7951.13*** *p43*
Lipp, Barbara 9; New York, NY, 1898 ***7951.13*** *p43*
Lipp, Christine 35; New York, NY, 1898 ***7951.13*** *p43*
Lipp, Eva 20; New York, NY, 1898 ***7951.13*** *p43*
Lipp, Helen 52; New York, NY, 1898 ***7951.13*** *p43*
Lipp, Johann 11; New York, NY, 1898 ***7951.13*** *p43*
Lipp, Joseph 4; New York, NY, 1898 ***7951.13*** *p43*
Lipp, Joseph 13; New York, NY, 1898 ***7951.13*** *p43*
Lipp, Katherine 2; New York, NY, 1898 ***7951.13*** *p43*
Lipp, Lorentz 13; New York, NY, 1898 ***7951.13*** *p43*
Lipp, Martin 39; New York, NY, 1898 ***7951.13*** *p43*
Lipp, Mathais 11; New York, NY, 1898 ***7951.13*** *p43*
Lipp, Michael 17; New York, NY, 1898 ***7951.13*** *p43*
Lipp, Peter 10; New York, NY, 1898 ***7951.13*** *p43*
Lipp, Stephan 23; New York, NY, 1898 ***7951.13*** *p43*
Lipp, Wilhelm 4; New York, NY, 1898 ***7951.13*** *p43*
Lippe, Christine; New York, 1860 ***358.56*** *p3*
Lippelt, Fred T.; Louisiana, 1874-1875 ***4981.45*** *p29*
Lippert, Wilhelm; Wisconsin, 1874 ***6795.8*** *p154*
Lippey, William; America, 1685 ***1220.12*** *p503*
Lippitt, William; America, 1721 ***1220.12*** *p503*
Lippmann, Johann Heinrich; America, 1865 ***7420.1*** *p233*
Lippmann, Moses; Port uncertain, 1849 ***7420.1*** *p66*
Lippmann, Noah 22; Louisiana, 1848 ***778.6*** *p214*
Lippold, Gottlieb Christian; America, 1867 ***7919.3*** *p532*
Lippoth, Jacob; Ohio, 1840-1897 ***8365.35*** *p17*
Lipps, Andre 16; Missouri, 1845 ***778.6*** *p214*
Lipps, Arbroqurt 11; Missouri, 1845 ***778.6*** *p214*
Lipps, George 4; Missouri, 1845 ***778.6*** *p214*
Lipps, Gertrude 13; Missouri, 1845 ***778.6*** *p215*

Lipps, Gertrude 39; Missouri, 1845 778.6 p215
Lipps, Johann 18; Missouri, 1845 778.6 p215
Lipps, Lorenz 6; Missouri, 1845 778.6 p215
Lipps, Lorenz 48; Missouri, 1845 778.6 p215
Lipps, Louise 1; Missouri, 1845 778.6 p215
Lipps, Marie 8; Missouri, 1845 778.6 p215
Lipscomb, William; America, 1747 1220.12 p503
Lipscomb, William; West Virginia, 1787 1132.30 p146
Lipscombe, Stephen; Annapolis, MD, 1725 1220.12 p503
Lipsett, William 72; Ontario, 1871 1823.21 p203
Lipszyc, Bessie; Detroit, 1929-1930 6214.5 p69
Liptrap, Isaac; America, 1772 1220.12 p503
Liquet Bayron, Luciano; Puerto Rico, 1851 3476.25 p113
Liroux, Maximillienne; Wisconsin, 1856 1495.20 p41
Lis, Thomas; Wisconsin, 1891 6795.8 p59
Lisbona, Francisco Lalinde; Missouri, 1889 3276.1 p3
Lisbony, Joseph; Louisiana, 1841-1844 4981.45 p210
Liscot, James; America, 1751 1220.12 p503
Lisence, Ruth; Annapolis, MD, 1720 1220.12 p503
Liser, Nicolas 30; Mississippi, 1847 778.6 p215
Lisert, Mr. 30; New Orleans, 1845 778.6 p215
Lish, Thomas; America, 1772 1220.12 p503
Lishlar, George; Nova Scotia, 1784 7105 p24
Lishman, Jane; America, 1774 1220.12 p503
Lisk, Emma 22; Ontario, 1871 1823.17 p92
Liske, Julius Christoph; Wisconsin, 1872 6795.8 p37
Liskow, Joachim; New York, 1859 358.56 p101
Lisle, Captain; San Francisco, 1800-1899 9228.50 p327
Lisle, Edward; Barbados, 1667 1220.12 p503
Lismann, Franz 23; America, 1862 5475.1 p500
Lisnewsky, Rosalie 20; New York, NY, 1894 6512.1 p230
Lisot, Guillaume 19; Quebec, 1662 9221.17 p489
Lissant, Richard; America, 1685 1220.12 p503
Lissiman, Henry; America, 1755 1220.12 p503
Lissner, Marcus; North Carolina, 1860 1088.45 p19
Lisson, Daniel; Virginia, 1652 6254.4 p243
List, Adam; Ohio, 1809-1852 4511.35 p31
List, Apollonie; America, 1785 2526.43 p180
List, Christina Elisabetha; America, 1858 2526.43 p211
List, Elisabeth 18; America, 1853 2526.43 p174
List, Eva Margaretha; America, 1858 2526.43 p211
List, Georg; America, 1843 2526.42 p193
With wife & stepfather
With child 6
With child 3
With child 14
With child 9
List, Heinrich; America, 1859 2526.43 p211
List, Johannes 16; America, 1852 2526.43 p211
List, Johannes 18; America, 1850 2526.43 p211
List, John H.; Colorado, 1873 1029.59 p55
List, Leonhard; America, 1853 2526.43 p174
With wife
With child 1
With child 3
List, Philipp 16; America, 1854 2526.43 p212
List, Sophie 35; America, 1853 2526.43 p174
Listare, A. 32; Port uncertain, 1842 778.6 p215
Lister, Benjamin; Ohio, 1836 3580.20 p32
Lister, Benjamin; Ohio, 1836 6020.12 p13
Lister, Benjamin; Ohio, 1838 3580.20 p32
Lister, Benjamin; Ohio, 1838 6020.12 p13
Lister, John; America, 1729 1220.12 p503
Lister, John; America, 1753 1220.12 p503
Lister, John; America, 1770 1220.12 p503
Lister, John; America, 1772 1220.12 p503
Lister, Mary; America, 1738 1220.12 p503
Lister, William; Ohio, 1836 3580.20 p32
Lister, William; Ohio, 1836 6020.12 p13
Lister, William; Ohio, 1838 3580.20 p32
Lister, William; Ohio, 1838 6020.12 p13
Listner, Bernard; Ohio, 1840-1897 8365.35 p17
Listril, John; Salem, MA, n.d. 9228.50 p578
Lisy, . . .; Pennsylvania, 1750-1799 2853.20 p17
Litchborne, William 39; Ontario, 1871 1823.17 p92
Litchfield, Charles 47; Ontario, 1871 1823.17 p92
Litchfield, John; America, 1774 1220.12 p504
Litford, Mathew; America, 1752 1220.12 p504
Lithgoe, Henry; Barbados, 1683 1220.12 p504
Lithgow, Robert 42; Ontario, 1871 1823.17 p92
Litman, Yankel; Detroit, 1929 1640.55 p113
Litners, Thomas; America, 1772 1220.12 p504
Litt, Johannes; America, 1855 2526.43 p225
Littig, Eduard Gottfried; America, 1868 7919.3 p532
Littilton, John 42; Ontario, 1871 1823.17 p92
Littilton, William 46; Ontario, 1871 1823.17 p92
Little, Andrew; America, 1753 1220.12 p504
Little, Ann *SEE* Little, Thomas
Little, Archibald; America, 1722 1220.12 p504
Little, Charles 22; Ontario, 1871 1823.21 p203
Little, Daniel; America, 1756 1220.12 p504
Little, Edward; Barbados or Jamaica, 1685 1220.12 p504
Little, Elizabeth; America, 1732 1220.12 p504
Little, Elizabeth; America, 1752 1220.12 p504
Little, Hannah 75; Ontario, 1871 1823.17 p92
Little, Henry 47; Ontario, 1871 1823.21 p203
Little, James 38; Ontario, 1871 1823.21 p203
Little, James 52; Ontario, 1871 1823.21 p203
Little, John; America, 1754 1220.12 p504
Little, John; Boston, 1737 1642 p26
Little, John; North Carolina, 1832 1088.45 p19
Little, John 25; Ontario, 1871 1823.21 p203
Little, John 35; Ontario, 1871 1823.21 p203
Little, John 46; Ontario, 1871 1823.17 p92
Little, John 48; Ontario, 1871 1823.17 p92
Little, John 55; Ontario, 1871 1823.21 p203
Little, John 56; Ontario, 1871 1823.21 p203
Little, John 75; Ontario, 1871 1823.21 p203
Little, John; Virginia, 1732 1220.12 p504
Little, John H. 56; Ontario, 1871 1823.21 p203
Little, Joseph 59; Ontario, 1871 1823.17 p92
Little, Keziah; America, 1757 1220.12 p504
Little, Martha 56; Ontario, 1871 1823.21 p203
Little, Mary 40; Ontario, 1871 1823.21 p203
Little, Matthias; Virginia, 1760 1220.12 p504
Little, Peter; Illinois, 1856 6079.1 p8
Little, Rachael 26; Ontario, 1871 1823.21 p204
Little, Ralph; Barbados, 1665 1220.12 p504
Little, Robert 48; Ontario, 1871 1823.21 p204
Little, Thomas; America, 1750 1220.12 p504
Little, Thomas; America, 1766 1220.12 p504
Little, Thomas; Canada, 1774 3036.5 p42
*Wife:*Ann
Little, Thomas 35; Ontario, 1871 1823.17 p92
Little, Thomas 40; Ontario, 1871 1823.17 p92
Little, William; America, 1750 1220.12 p504
Little, William; Died enroute, 1729 1220.12 p504
Little, William 22; New York, NY, 1835 5024.1 p136
Little, William 32; Ontario, 1871 1823.21 p204
Little, William 35; Ontario, 1871 1823.17 p93
Little, William 52; Ontario, 1871 1823.17 p93
Little, William; Virginia, 1774 1220.12 p504
Little, William M. 67; Ontario, 1871 1823.21 p204
Littleboy, John; America, 1774 1220.12 p504
Littleford, John; America, 1751 1220.12 p504
Littlejohn, Elizabeth; America, 1771 1220.12 p504
Littlejohn, Michael; America, 1750 1220.12 p504
Littlejohn, Wilmot; Virginia, 1745 1220.12 p504
Littlejohns, Philip 37; Ontario, 1871 1823.21 p204
Littlejohns, William; America, 1745 1220.12 p504
Littler, Abigail; America, 1760 1220.12 p504
Littleton, Joseph; America, 1765 1220.12 p504
Littlewood, Edward; America, 1655 1220.12 p504
Littlewood, John 96; Ontario, 1871 1823.21 p204
Littlewood, Thomas; New York, 1778 8529.30 p13
Littleworth, James 93; Ontario, 1871 1823.17 p93
Littmann, Johann Martin; America, 1870 2526.43 p186
Litton, Thomas; Virginia, 1731 1220.12 p504
Litwinczuk, Eleanore; Detroit, 1929-1930 6214.5 p61
Litwora, Peter; Texas, 1887 6015.15 p27
Litzen, John; North Carolina, 1855 1088.45 p19
Litzler, Antoine; Louisiana, 1874 4981.45 p132
Liukonen, Hugo 40; Minnesota, 1926 2769.54 p1383
Liukonen, Ida 26; Minnesota, 1926 2769.54 p1383
Live, Joseph 17; Ontario, 1871 1823.21 p204
Lively, Elizabeth 47; Ontario, 1871 1823.21 p204
Lively, John; Barbados, 1668 1220.12 p504
Lively, John 48; Ontario, 1871 1823.21 p204
Lively, Matthew; Virginia, 1735 1220.12 p504
Livermoore, Thomas; Virginia, 1744 1220.12 p504
Livermore, Mary; America, 1750 1220.12 p504
Livermore, Thomas 28; Ontario, 1871 1823.21 p204
Livernois, Paul 27; Montreal, 1653 9221.17 p282
Liversidge, Elizabeth; America, 1755 1220.12 p504
Livesey, Thomas; Virginia, 1731 1220.12 p504
Livesly, Nathaniel; America, 1677 1220.12 p504
Livesson, John; America, 1771 1220.12 p504
Liveston, William; America, 1710 1220.12 p504
Livie, Mr. 28; America, 1847 778.6 p215
Livings, Thomas; America, 1740 1220.12 p504
Livingston, Alexr 65; Ontario, 1871 1823.21 p204
Livingston, Angus 52; Ontario, 1871 1823.17 p93
Livingston, Ann Jane 23; Ontario, 1871 1823.21 p204
Livingston, Annie 26; Ontario, 1871 1823.17 p93
Livingston, Charles 50; Michigan, 1880 4491.39 p18
Livingston, Christian 84; Ontario, 1871 1823.21 p204
Livingston, Daniel 34; Ontario, 1871 1823.17 p93
Livingston, David 68; Ontario, 1871 1823.21 p204
Livingston, Dougald 59; Ontario, 1871 1823.21 p204
Livingston, Dugald 34; Ontario, 1871 1823.17 p93
Livingston, Duncan 26; Ontario, 1871 1823.17 p93
Livingston, Duncan 41; Ontario, 1871 1823.17 p93
Livingston, John 40; Ontario, 1871 1823.21 p204
Livingston, John 67; Ontario, 1871 1823.17 p93
Livingston, Levi Henry; North Carolina, 1849 1088.45 p19
Livingston, Mitchell; Philadelphia, 1880 5720.10 p378
Livingston, Pierce 30; Ontario, 1871 1823.17 p93
Livingston, Robert 54; Ontario, 1871 1823.21 p204
Livingstone, William 67; Ontario, 1871 1823.21 p204
Livisley, Robert 41; Ontario, 1871 1823.17 p93
Livolsi, G.; Louisiana, 1874 4981.45 p296
Ljung, John Nilsson; New Orleans, 1851 6412.40 p153
Ljungberg, Johan Niclas; North America, 1858 6410.15 p105
Ljungholm, Eric Jacob; North America, 1885 6410.15 p106
Ljunglof, Carl Fredrik; New York, NY, 1842 6410.15 p103
Ljungman-Holmberg, Gustaf Otto; Cleveland, OH, 1880-1884 9722.10 p123
Ljungquist, John; Colorado, 1892 1029.59 p55
Ljungqvist, N.; New York, NY, 1843 6412.40 p147
Ljungvall, Axel; Colorado, 1883 1029.59 p55
Ljungvall, Axel; Colorado, 1896 1029.59 p55
Ljungvall, Claes; Colorado, 1884 1029.59 p55
Ljungvall, Hedvik M.; Colorado, 1894 1029.59 p55
Ljungvall, Johan Albt.; Colorado, 1882 1029.59 p55
Ljungvall, Johan Albt.; Colorado, 1894 1029.59 p55
Ljungvall, John A.; Colorado, 1882 1029.59 p55
Ljungvoll, Hedrik M.; Colorado, 1894 1029.59 p55
Ljungwall, Hedvik; Colorado, 1894 1029.59 p55
Llado, Joseph; Louisiana, 1836-1840 4981.45 p213
Llewellen, Thomas W. J.; North Carolina, 1857 1088.45 p19
Llewellin, Samuel; America, 1756 1220.12 p504
Llewellin, Thomas; America, 1742 1220.12 p505
Llewellin, William; America, 1760 1220.12 p505
Llewellyn, Evan; Washington, 1889 2770.40 p79
Llewellyn, William; Colorado, 1884 1029.59 p56
Llewellyn, William; New York, 1859 1029.59 p56
Lloyd, ; Ohio, 1840 4022.20 p287
With husband
*Child:*John
With siblings
Lloyd, Ann; Annapolis, MD, 1719 1220.12 p505
Lloyd, Anne; America, 1720 1220.12 p505
Lloyd, Daniel; Ohio, 1847 4022.20 p287
*Wife:*Mary
*Child:*Margaret D.
With children
Lloyd, David; America, 1696 1220.12 p505
Lloyd, David; Maryland, 1674-1675 1236.25 p51
Lloyd, David A. *SEE* Lloyd, John A.
Lloyd, David L.; Colorado, 1886 1029.59 p56
Lloyd, Deborah; America, 1746 1220.12 p505
Lloyd, Dorothy; America, 1759 1220.12 p505
Lloyd, Edward; America, 1685 1220.12 p505
Lloyd, Edward; America, 1720 1220.12 p505
Lloyd, Edward; America, 1769 1220.12 p505
Lloyd, Edward S. 20; New York, NY, 1894 6512.1 p183
Lloyd, Einion; Ohio, 1845-1850 4022.20 p287
Lloyd, Eleanor; America, 1761 1220.12 p505
Lloyd, Elice 44; Ontario, 1871 1823.17 p93
Lloyd, Elizabeth; America, 1675 1220.12 p505
Lloyd, Elizabeth; Rappahannock, VA, 1728 1220.12 p505
Lloyd, Elizabeth H. *SEE* Lloyd, James H.
Lloyd, Elizabeth Vance; Portland, ME, 1863-1889 9228.50 p404
Lloyd, Ellen Louisa; New Bedford, MA, 1880-1968 9228.50 p404
Lloyd, Ellis; Virginia, 1736 1220.12 p505
Lloyd, Esther *SEE* Lloyd, James H.
Lloyd, Francis 22; Ontario, 1871 1823.17 p93
Lloyd, George; America, 1753 1220.12 p505
Lloyd, Griffith; America, 1768 1220.12 p505
Lloyd, Hannah; America, 1745 1220.12 p505
Lloyd, Isabella Jane; Portland, ME, 1878-1899 9228.50 p404
Lloyd, James; Barbados, 1677 1220.12 p505
Lloyd, James H.; Ohio, 1841 4022.20 p287
*Wife:*Esther
With children
*Child:*Elizabeth H.
Lloyd, Jane *SEE* Lloyd, Lewis
Lloyd, Jane; Ohio, 1847 4022.20 p287
Lloyd, Jessie Alecta; Portland, ME, 1870-1888 9228.50 p404
Lloyd, John; America, 1694 1220.12 p505
Lloyd, John; America, 1738 1220.12 p505
Lloyd, John; America, 1744 1220.12 p505
Lloyd, John; America, 1748 1220.12 p505
Lloyd, John; America, 1750 1220.12 p505
Lloyd, John; Barbados or Jamaica, 1686 1220.12 p505
Lloyd, John *SEE* Lloyd, John A.
Lloyd, John *SEE* Lloyd, Mrs. Richards
Lloyd, John; Rappahannock, VA, 1726 1220.12 p505

280 *FOR A COMPLETE EXPLANATION OF ENTRY, SEE "HOW TO READ A CITATION" SECTION*

Lloyd, John A.; Ohio, 1840 ***4022.20*** *p287*
*Wife:*Mary Evans
*Child:*John
*Child:*Mary
*Child:*David A.
Lloyd, Joseph; America, 1750 ***1220.12*** *p505*
Lloyd, Joseph; America, 1772 ***1220.12*** *p505*
Lloyd, Joseph; America, 1775 ***1220.12*** *p505*
Lloyd, Kenneth Harry; California, 1972 ***9228.50*** *p130*
Lloyd, Lewis; Ohio, 1847 ***4022.20*** *p287*
*Wife:*Jane
With child
Lloyd, Lewis; Virginia, 1736 ***1220.12*** *p505*
Lloyd, Margaret; America, 1721 ***1220.12*** *p505*
Lloyd, Margaret; Portland, ME, 1865-1885 ***9228.50*** *p404*
Lloyd, Margaret D. *SEE* Lloyd, Daniel
Lloyd, Mary; America, 1766 ***1220.12*** *p505*
Lloyd, Mary; Barbados, 1675 ***1220.12*** *p505*
Lloyd, Mary; Barbados or Jamaica, 1702 ***1220.12*** *p505*
Lloyd, Mary *SEE* Lloyd, John A.
Lloyd, Mary Evans *SEE* Lloyd, John A.
Lloyd, Mary *SEE* Lloyd, Daniel
Lloyd, Mary; Ohio, 1849 ***4022.20*** *p287*
With husband
Lloyd, Mary; Virginia, 1736 ***1220.12*** *p505*
Lloyd, Matthew; America, 1772 ***1220.12*** *p505*
Lloyd, Nicholas; America, 1761 ***1220.12*** *p506*
Lloyd, Peter; America, 1751 ***1220.12*** *p506*
Lloyd, Philip; New Brunswick, 1831-1852 ***9228.50*** *p403*
Lloyd, Phyllis Alvina; Maine, 1884-1922 ***9228.50*** *p404*
Lloyd, Richard; America, 1767 ***1220.12*** *p506*
Lloyd, Richard; America, 1770 ***1220.12*** *p506*
Lloyd, Richard; America, 1773 ***1220.12*** *p506*
Lloyd, Richard; Virginia, 1735 ***1220.12*** *p506*
Lloyd, Robert; Annapolis, MD, 1733 ***1220.12*** *p506*
Lloyd, Robert 60; Ontario, 1871 ***1823.21*** *p204*
Lloyd, Samuel; America, 1768 ***1220.12*** *p506*
Lloyd, Sarah; America, 1773 ***1220.12*** *p506*
Lloyd, Sarah 68; Ontario, 1871 ***1823.21*** *p204*
Lloyd, Stephen; America, 1772 ***1220.12*** *p506*
Lloyd, Susanna; America, 1720 ***1220.12*** *p506*
Lloyd, Thomas; America, 1683 ***1220.12*** *p506*
Lloyd, Thomas; America, 1767 ***1220.12*** *p506*
Lloyd, Thomas; Ohio, 1809-1852 ***4511.35*** *p31*
Lloyd, Thomas 34; Ontario, 1871 ***1823.21*** *p204*
Lloyd, Thomas 17; Quebec, 1870 ***8364.32*** *p24*
Lloyd, William; America, 1759 ***1220.12*** *p506*
Lloyd, William; Maryland, 1673 ***1236.25*** *p48*
Lloyd, William 34; New York, NY, 1894 ***6512.1*** *p186*
Lloyd, William; Virginia, 1739 ***1220.12*** *p506*
Lloyd, William Lawlor; Portland, ME, 1862-1890 ***9228.50*** *p403*
Lluellin, David; America, 1743 ***1220.12*** *p504*
Lluellin, John; America, 1771 ***1220.12*** *p504*
Llullia, Jose; Louisiana, 1836-1840 ***4981.45*** *p213*
Loach, Henry; America, 1735 ***1220.12*** *p506*
Loach, Joseph 18; Quebec, 1870 ***8364.32*** *p24*
Load, John; Died enroute, 1726 ***1220.12*** *p506*
Loader, William; Barbados, 1672 ***1220.12*** *p506*
Loadley, Robert; America, 1748 ***1220.12*** *p506*
Lob, Abraham 2; New Orleans, 1848 ***778.6*** *p215*
Lob, Adam; America, 1884 ***2526.43*** *p198*
Lob, Benjamin; America, 1857 ***2526.42*** *p125*
Lob, Carolina 5; New Orleans, 1848 ***778.6*** *p215*
Lob, Catherine 22; America, 1847 ***778.6*** *p215*
Lob, Georg 38; New Orleans, 1848 ***778.6*** *p215*
Lob, Gutchen; America, 1866 ***2526.42*** *p125*
Lob, Jakob 11 *SEE* Lob, Marie Elisabetha Lust
Lob, Johann; America, 1882 ***2526.43*** *p198*
Lob, Katharine 1 *SEE* Lob, Marie Elisabetha Lust
Lob, Marie Elisabetha 41; America, 1884 ***2526.43*** *p187*
*Son:*Jakob 11
*Daughter:*Katharine 1
*Son:*Philipp 5
Lob, Moses 24; America, 1847 ***778.6*** *p215*
Lob, Philipp 5 *SEE* Lob, Marie Elisabetha Lust
Lob, Philippine; America, 1857 ***2526.43*** *p174*
Lob, Rebecca 39; New Orleans, 1848 ***778.6*** *p215*
Lob, Regina 6; New Orleans, 1848 ***778.6*** *p215*
Lob, Simon 8; New Orleans, 1848 ***778.6*** *p215*
Lob, Theodor 9; New Orleans, 1848 ***778.6*** *p215*
Lobb, Robert; Virginia, 1737 ***1220.12*** *p506*
Lobb, William F.; Colorado, 1894 ***1029.59*** *p56*
Lobban, George 30; Ontario, 1871 ***1823.21*** *p204*
Lobban, George 60; Ontario, 1871 ***1823.21*** *p204*
Lobdin, George 27; America, 1845 ***778.6*** *p215*
Lobe, Balth.; New York, 1860 ***358.56*** *p3*
Lobert, Anton 38; America, 1846 ***778.6*** *p215*
Lobinois deTourneuve, Louis-Jean de; Quebec, 1718 ***2314.30*** *p169*
Lobinois deTourneuve, Louis-Jean de; Quebec, 1718 ***2314.30*** *p190*
Lobly, Joshua; America, 1763 ***1220.12*** *p506*
Lobun, Cecil 76; New Orleans, 1845 ***778.6*** *p215*
Loca, Jacob 11; New Orleans, 1848 ***778.6*** *p215*
Loch, Anna Maria; America, 1865 ***5475.1*** *p511*
*Son:*Nikolaus
Loch, Jakob; America, 1862 ***5475.1*** *p500*
Lochard, William; North Carolina, 1790 ***1088.45*** *p19*
Lochead, William 31; Ontario, 1871 ***1823.17*** *p93*
Lochemes, Heinrich Peter *SEE* Lochemes, Peter
Lochemes, Katharina Josephine *SEE* Lochemes, Peter
Lochemes, Magdalena Barbara *SEE* Lochemes, Peter
Lochemes, Maria Katharina *SEE* Lochemes, Peter
Lochemes, Nikolaus Karl *SEE* Lochemes, Peter
Lochemes, Peter; America, 1868 ***5475.1*** *p31*
*Daughter:*Katharina Josephine
*Son:*Nikolaus Karl
*Daughter:*Magdalena Barbara
*Daughter:*Maria Katharina
*Son:*Heinrich Peter
Locher, George; Ohio, 1809-1852 ***4511.35*** *p31*
Locher, Joseph; Valdivia, Chile, 1850 ***1192.4*** *p49*
Lochert, Pierre 19; America, 1847 ***778.6*** *p215*
Lochet, Francois; Montreal, 1653 ***9221.17*** *p296*
Lochrie, Andreew; Washington, 1887 ***2770.40*** *p24*
Lochrie, Andrew; Washington, 1884 ***2770.40*** *p192*
Lock, Alfred 19; Quebec, 1870 ***8364.32*** *p24*
Lock, Benjamin; America, 1728 ***1220.12*** *p506*
Lock, Charles; America, 1773 ***1220.12*** *p506*
Lock, Elizabeth; America, 1763 ***1220.12*** *p506*
Lock, George; America, 1758 ***1220.12*** *p506*
Lock, Henry; America, 1759 ***1220.12*** *p506*
Lock, John; America, 1685 ***1220.12*** *p506*
Lock, John; America, 1758 ***1220.12*** *p506*
Lock, John; America, 1773 ***1220.12*** *p506*
Lock, John; Annapolis, MD, 1725 ***1220.12*** *p506*
Lock, Richard, Jr.; America, 1774 ***1220.12*** *p506*
Lock, Robert; America, 1756 ***1220.12*** *p506*
Lock, Thomas; America, 1730 ***1220.12*** *p506*
Lock, William; Annapolis, MD, 1725 ***1220.12*** *p506*
Lock, William; Marston's Wharf, 1782 ***8529.30*** *p13*
Lockbeare, Elias; America, 1685 ***1220.12*** *p506*
Locke, Elizabeth; America, 1754 ***1220.12*** *p506*
Locke, Isaac; America, 1769 ***1220.12*** *p506*
Locke, William; America, 1685 ***1220.12*** *p506*
Locke, William; Marston's Wharf, 1782 ***8529.30*** *p13*
Lockemaier, Johann; Chile, 1852 ***1192.4*** *p52*
Locken, Levi; Kansas, 1892 ***1447.20*** *p64*
Locker, Elizabeth; America, 1754 ***1220.12*** *p506*
Locker, Elizabeth; Barbados or Jamaica, 1689 ***1220.12*** *p506*
Locker, George; Ohio, 1809-1852 ***4511.35*** *p31*
Locker, Jacob; Ohio, 1809-1852 ***4511.35*** *p31*
Lockerby, Thomas; America, 1763 ***1220.12*** *p506*
Lockert, Therese 24; Missouri, 1845 ***778.6*** *p215*
Lockeskegg, Thomas; America, 1766 ***1220.12*** *p506*
Lockett, Benjamin; America, 1769 ***1220.12*** *p506*
Lockett, Charles; America, 1774 ***1220.12*** *p506*
Lockett, John; America, 1726 ***1220.12*** *p506*
Lockett, Jonathan; America, 1752 ***1220.12*** *p506*
Lockey, Henry; America, 1744 ***1220.12*** *p507*
Lockhart, Benjamin; America, 1767 ***1220.12*** *p507*
Lockhart, James 66; Ontario, 1871 ***1823.17*** *p93*
Lockhart, Jane; America, 1758 ***1220.12*** *p507*
Lockhart, John; America, 1768 ***1220.12*** *p507*
Lockhart, Thomas; America, 1765 ***1220.12*** *p507*
Lockhart, Thomas; America, 1767 ***1220.12*** *p507*
Lockhart, William; Illinois, 1855 ***6079.1*** *p8*
Lockhart, William 36; Ontario, 1871 ***1823.21*** *p204*
Lockie, John 31; Ontario, 1871 ***1823.17*** *p93*
Lockin, Richard; America, 1758 ***1220.12*** *p507*
Lockington, Charles; America, 1774 ***1220.12*** *p507*
Lockington, Joshuah 60; Ontario, 1871 ***1823.17*** *p93*
Lockitt, Mary; America, 1771 ***1220.12*** *p506*
Lockley, John; America, 1772 ***1220.12*** *p507*
Locks, Mary; Annapolis, MD, 1725 ***1220.12*** *p507*
Locks, William 72; Ontario, 1871 ***1823.21*** *p204*
Lockwood, Hester 60; Ontario, 1871 ***1823.21*** *p204*
Lockwood, John; America, 1737 ***1220.12*** *p507*
Lockwood, John; America, 1746 ***1220.12*** *p507*
Lockwood, Martha; America, 1746 ***1220.12*** *p507*
Lockwood, Martha; Virginia, 1748 ***1220.12*** *p507*
Lockwood, Mary; America, 1771 ***1220.12*** *p507*
Lockwood, William; America, 1703 ***1220.12*** *p507*
Lockyer, John; Virginia, 1719 ***1220.12*** *p507*
Lockyer, Joseph; America, 1738 ***1220.12*** *p507*
Lockyer, Roger; America, 1756 ***1220.12*** *p507*
Lockyer, Thomas; America, 1685 ***1220.12*** *p507*
Lockyn, Johnson John 25; Ontario, 1871 ***1823.21*** *p204*
Locock, Thomas; America, 1741 ***1220.12*** *p507*
Locup, Mary; America, 1772 ***1220.12*** *p507*
Loddy, James; Marston's Wharf, 1782 ***8529.30*** *p13*
Lodemann, Adolf 36; New York, NY, 1893 ***1883.7*** *p43*
Lodemann, Cath. 30; New York, NY, 1893 ***1883.7*** *p43*
Lodemann, Daniel 2; New York, NY, 1893 ***1883.7*** *p43*
Lodemann, Rosalie 11; New York, NY, 1893 ***1883.7*** *p43*
Lodge, Job; America, 1775 ***1220.12*** *p507*
Lodge, Mathew; Canada, 1775 ***3036.5*** *p67*
Lodge, Patrick; Louisiana, 1836-1841 ***4981.45*** *p209*
Lodge, Thomas; America, 1766 ***1220.12*** *p507*
Lodowick, William; America, 1752 ***1220.12*** *p507*
Lodr, Petr; Iowa, 1856-1858 ***2853.20*** *p211*
Lodwick, William; America, 1768 ***1220.12*** *p507*
Loe, Ann; Maryland, 1674 ***1236.25*** *p50*
Loeb, Elias; London, Eng., 1881 ***5475.1*** *p94*
Loeb, Emanuel; America, 1870 ***5475.1*** *p405*
Loeb, Jacob; North Carolina, 1855 ***1088.45*** *p19*
Loeb, Kath.; New York, 1897 ***5475.1*** *p40*
Loeb, Leopold; America, 1870 ***5475.1*** *p405*
Loeb, Mar.a 24; Port uncertain, 1842 ***778.6*** *p215*
Loeb, Nikolaus; America, 1843 ***5475.1*** *p305*
Loeb, Samuel E.; Louisiana, 1874-1875 ***4981.45*** *p29*
Loeb, Simon 52; Louisiana, 1848 ***778.6*** *p215*
Loeb, Sophie; Philadelphia, 1870 ***8513.31*** *p319*
Loeber, Christian *SEE* Loeber, Regina Katharine
Loeber, Katharine Marga. *SEE* Loeber, Regina Katharine
Loeber, Regina Katharine; America, 1840 ***8115.12*** *p320*
*Child:*Christian
*Child:*Katharine Marga.
Loeffler, Bertha; New York, 1860 ***358.56*** *p4*
Loeffler, Christian 8 months; New York, NY, 1893 ***1883.7*** *p38*
Loeffler, Joseph 22; Michigan, 1847 ***778.6*** *p215*
Loeffler, Julius; Wisconsin, 1885 ***6795.8*** *p69*
Loeffler, Maria 35; New York, NY, 1893 ***1883.7*** *p38*
Loeffler, Peter 8 months; New York, NY, 1893 ***1883.7*** *p38*
Loeffler, Vilem; Chicago, 1873 ***2853.20*** *p397*
Loegler, Columbia 27; Mississippi, 1847 ***778.6*** *p215*
Loehle, Justine Louise; America, 1884 ***7420.1*** *p343*
Loehr, Jacob, Jr.; Ohio, 1809-1852 ***4511.35*** *p31*
Loek, Hermann August Theodor; Wisconsin, 1871 ***6795.8*** *p83*
Loenrot, Joseph 18; America, 1840 ***778.6*** *p215*
Loeple, Mrs. 42; America, 1844 ***778.6*** *p215*
Loes, Richard; America, 1716 ***1220.12*** *p507*
Loesch, Barbara 11 *SEE* Loesch, Johann
Loesch, Jakob 4 *SEE* Loesch, Johann
Loesch, Johann 9 *SEE* Loesch, Johann
Loesch, Johann 43; America, 1846 ***5475.1*** *p451*
*Wife:*Katharina Fuchs 44
*Daughter:*Barbara 11
*Son:*Jakob 4
*Daughter:*Maria 6 months
*Son:*Johann 9
*Son:*Peter 15
*Daughter:*Katharina 13
Loesch, Katharina 13 *SEE* Loesch, Johann
Loesch, Katharina Fuchs 44 *SEE* Loesch, Johann
Loesch, Maria 6 *SEE* Loesch, Johann
Loesch, Nicholas; Illinois, 1859 ***6079.1*** *p8*
Loesch, Peter 15 *SEE* Loesch, Johann
Loesch, Vendel 26; Missouri, 1845 ***778.6*** *p216*
Loeser, Ignatz; America, 1825-1875 ***8023.44*** *p376*
Loesinger, Burkhard; Kansas, 1917-1918 ***1826.15*** *p81*
Loew, Franz; America, 1898 ***5475.1*** *p40*
Loewengren, Gustavus; Illinois, 1852 ***6079.1*** *p8*
Loewenstein, Adolph; North Carolina, 1852 ***1088.45*** *p19*
Loffen, Thomas; Barbados, 1664 ***1220.12*** *p507*
Loffler, Christ.; Valdivia, Chile, 1852 ***1192.4*** *p56*
Loffler, Johann Nicolaus; America, 1867 ***7919.3*** *p525*
Loffler, Wilhelm; America, 1883 ***2526.43*** *p152*
Lofgren, Eva Lovisa; St. Paul, MN, 1869 ***1865.50*** *p96*
Lofgren, Frida Matilda Olivia; Oregon, 1941 ***9157.47*** *p3*
Lofgren, Gust; Cleveland, OH, 1901-1903 ***9722.10*** *p123*
Lofgren, John; St. Paul, MN, 1868 ***1865.50*** *p96*
Lofgren, Jon Ersson 21; New York, 1856 ***6529.11*** *p22*
Lofstedt, G.S.; New York, NY, 1843 ***6412.40*** *p147*
Loft, Fishwick 46; Ontario, 1871 ***1823.21*** *p204*
Loft, Ralph; Ohio, 1840 ***3580.20*** *p32*
Loft, Ralph; Ohio, 1840 ***6020.12*** *p13*
Loft, Timothy 56; Ontario, 1871 ***1823.21*** *p204*
Loftus, Patt; New Orleans, 1851 ***7242.30*** *p148*
Loftus, Susan 54; Ontario, 1871 ***1823.21*** *p204*
Log, Samuel 45; Ontario, 1871 ***1823.21*** *p205*
Loga, Jean; Louisiana, 1874-1875 ***4981.45*** *p29*
Logan, Alexander 42; Ontario, 1871 ***1823.21*** *p205*
Logan, Andrew; New England, 1745 ***1642*** *p28*
Logan, Caroline 60; Ontario, 1871 ***1823.21*** *p205*
Logan, David; Cambridge, MA, 1745 ***1642*** *p100*
*Wife:*Susanna
Logan, Elizabeth 24; Ontario, 1871 ***1823.21*** *p205*
Logan, Mrs. F.; Toronto, 1844 ***2910.35*** *p114*
Logan, Geo 76; Ontario, 1871 ***1823.21*** *p205*
Logan, George 50; Ontario, 1871 ***1823.21*** *p205*
Logan, Gilbert; Boston, 1759 ***1642*** *p47*
Logan, Gilbert; Massachusetts, 1756 ***1642*** *p66*

Logan, Henry 53; Ontario, 1871 ***1823.21*** *p205*
Logan, Hill; Ohio, 1809-1852 ***4511.35*** *p31*
Logan, James; North Carolina, 1810 ***1088.45*** *p19*
Logan, James 49; Ontario, 1871 ***1823.21*** *p205*
Logan, James 60; Ontario, 1871 ***1823.21*** *p205*
Logan, Jane; Marblehead, MA, 1764 ***1642*** *p73*
Logan, John; Boston, 1717 ***1642*** *p24*
Logan, John; Jamaica, 1783 ***8529.30*** *p13A*
Logan, John 30; Ontario, 1871 ***1823.17*** *p93*
Logan, John 43; Ontario, 1871 ***1823.17*** *p93*
Logan, John C. 44; Michigan, 1880 ***4491.36*** *p14*
Logan, John M.; North Carolina, 1825 ***1088.45*** *p19*
Logan, Lydia; Boston, 1696 ***1642*** *p17*
Logan, Mary 45; Michigan, 1880 ***4491.39*** *p18*
Logan, Mery; Boston, 1749 ***1642*** *p46*
Logan, Nancy 33; Michigan, 1880 ***4491.36*** *p14*
Logan, Patrick 31; Ontario, 1871 ***1823.21*** *p205*
Logan, Richard; Ohio, 1840 ***3580.20*** *p32*
Logan, Richard; Ohio, 1840 ***6020.12*** *p13*
Logan, Richard 27; Ontario, 1871 ***1823.21*** *p205*
Logan, Richard 62; Ontario, 1871 ***1823.21*** *p205*
Logan, Robert; America, 1743 ***1220.12*** *p507*
Logan, Stephen; New England, 1745 ***1642*** *p28*
Logan, Susanna *SEE* Logan, David
Logan, Walter; Boston, 1761 ***1642*** *p48*
Logan, William; Boston, 1764 ***1642*** *p33*
Logan, William; Illinois, 1834-1900 ***6020.5*** *p132*
Logan, William 35; Ontario, 1871 ***1823.21*** *p205*
Logan, William D. 52; Ontario, 1871 ***1823.21*** *p205*
Logback, Andrew J.; Kansas, 1868 ***777.40*** *p17*
Logback, August 19; Kansas, 1880 ***777.40*** *p17*
Logback, Peter; Kansas, 1880 ***777.40*** *p17*
*Wife:*Sarah M. Johansdotter
Logback, Sarah M. Johansdotter *SEE* Logback, Peter
Loge, James 30; New York, NY, 1825 ***6178.50*** *p76*
Logea, Martin 31; Montreal, 1848 ***778.6*** *p216*
Logel, Adolph 3 months; America, 1847 ***778.6*** *p216*
Logel, Adolph 35; America, 1847 ***778.6*** *p216*
Logel, Barbara 9; America, 1847 ***778.6*** *p216*
Logel, Catherine 12; America, 1847 ***778.6*** *p216*
Logel, Catherine 37; America, 1847 ***778.6*** *p216*
Logel, Elisabethe 3; America, 1847 ***778.6*** *p216*
Logel, Louisa 21; America, 1847 ***778.6*** *p216*
Logel, Magdelena 7; America, 1847 ***778.6*** *p216*
Logen, John; Boston, 1765 ***1642*** *p34*
With wife & 2 children
Logen, Mary; Boston, 1731 ***1642*** *p44*
Loggin, John; New England, 1745 ***1642*** *p28*
Loggin, John; New England, 1745 ***1642*** *p28*
Loggin, V.J.; Philadelphia, 1848 ***6412.40*** *p151*
Loggins, Joseph; America, 1742 ***1220.12*** *p507*
Loggs, Henry; America, 1750 ***1220.12*** *p507*
Loghlin, Hugh L.; North Carolina, 1855 ***1088.45*** *p19*
Login, William; America, 1756 ***1220.12*** *p507*
Logis, Barbe; Wisconsin, 1854-1858 ***1495.20*** *p66*
Logliacona, Guisseppe; Louisiana, 1874 ***4981.45*** *p132*
Logue, James 30; New York, NY, 1825 ***6178.50*** *p76*
Logue, Patrick 7; New York, NY, 1821-1849 ***6178.50*** *p76*
Loh, Johann Georg; America, n.d. ***8115.12*** *p327*
Loher, Nicholas; Ohio, 1809-1852 ***4511.35*** *p31*
Lohfing, Maria Friederike; America, 1867 ***7919.3*** *p533*
Lohm, August Karl; Wisconsin, 1893 ***6795.8*** *p216*
Lohmann, Mr.; America, 1854 ***7420.1*** *p124*
With wife 2 sons & daughter
Lohmann, Anne Marie Eleonore; America, 1854 ***7420.1*** *p130*
Lohmann, Engel Marie Sophie Charlotte; America, 1853 ***7420.1*** *p106*
Lohmann, Engel Philippine; Port uncertain, 1851 ***7420.1*** *p82*
Lohmann, Friedrich Wilhelm Ludwig; America, 1867 ***7420.1*** *p260*
With family
*Daughter:*Sophie Wilhelmine Charlotte
Lohmann, Heinrich; America, 1853 ***7420.1*** *p108*
Lohmann, Heinrich Friedrich Ferdinand; America, 1853 ***7420.1*** *p108*
Lohmann, Johann 43; New Castle, DE, 1817-1818 ***90.20*** *p152*
Lohmann, Johann; Port uncertain, 1853 ***7420.1*** *p108*
Lohmann, Johann Christian Ludwig; Philadelphia, 1876 ***7420.1*** *p307*
Lohmann, Justine Sophie Wihelmine; America, 1859 ***7420.1*** *p187*
Lohmann, Louise Caroline Friederike; Philadelphia, 1876 ***7420.1*** *p307*
Lohmann, Sophie Wilhelmine Charlotte *SEE* Lohmann, Friedrich Wilhelm Ludwig
Lohme, John; Illinois, 1857 ***6079.1*** *p9*
Lohmeier, Ernst Heinrich Wilhelm; America, 1894 ***7420.1*** *p370*
Lohmeyer Sisters, . . .; America, 1883 ***7420.1*** *p337*
Lohn, Louis; Louisiana, 1874 ***4981.45*** *p132*
Lohnes, Adam; America, 1869 ***2526.43*** *p142*
Lohnes, Anna Barbara Kahl *SEE* Lohnes, Johannes
Lohnes, Anna Margaretha *SEE* Lohnes, Johannes
Lohnes, Elisabeth; America, 1870 ***2526.43*** *p193*
Lohnes, Friederike 33; America, 1882 ***2526.43*** *p226*
*Son:*Leonhard 9
*Son:*Philipp 4
*Son:*Johann 3
Lohnes, Georg; America, 1867 ***2526.43*** *p142*
Lohnes, Jakob; America, 1869 ***2526.43*** *p142*
Lohnes, Johann 3 *SEE* Lohnes, Friederike
Lohnes, Johann Christoph *SEE* Lohnes, Johannes
Lohnes, Johann Georg; America, 1752 ***2526.42*** *p167*
*Wife:*Katharina Elisabeth Kahl
*Child:*Johann Peter
Lohnes, Johann Georg; America, 1866 ***2526.43*** *p132*
Lohnes, Johann Georg *SEE* Lohnes, Johannes
Lohnes, Johann Michael *SEE* Lohnes, Johannes
Lohnes, Johann Peter *SEE* Lohnes, Johann Georg
Lohnes, Johannes *SEE* Lohnes, Johannes
Lohnes, Johannes; Nova Scotia, 1750 ***2526.42*** *p167*
*Wife:*Anna Barbara Kahl
*Child:*Anna Margaretha
*Child:*Johannes
*Child:*Johann Georg
*Child:*Johann Christoph
*Child:*Johann Michael
Lohnes, Katharina Elisabeth Kahl *SEE* Lohnes, Johann Georg
Lohnes, Katharina Elisabetha; America, 1859 ***2526.43*** *p142*
Lohnes, Katharine; America, 1870 ***2526.43*** *p193*
Lohnes, Leonhard 9 *SEE* Lohnes, Friederike
Lohnes, Philipp 4 *SEE* Lohnes, Friederike
Lohning, Emilie; Wisconsin, 1890 ***6795.8*** *p33*
Lohof, Fred Herman; Iowa, 1911 ***1211.15*** *p16*
Lohr, Jane Hilgers *SEE* Lohr, William
Lohr, Julius; Wisconsin, 1882 ***6795.8*** *p204*
Lohr, Lina; America, 1861 ***7420.1*** *p207*
Lohr, Michael; Louisiana, 1841-1844 ***4981.45*** *p210*
Lohr, Nicholas; Ohio, 1809-1852 ***4511.35*** *p31*
Lohr, Peter; Illinois, 1856 ***6079.1*** *p9*
Lohr, Theodore; Illinois, 1856 ***6079.1*** *p9*
Lohr, William; North Carolina, 1844 ***1088.45*** *p19*
Lohr, William; Philadelphia, 1861 ***8513.31*** *p323*
*Wife:*Jane Hilgers
Lohra, Konrad; Pennsylvania, 1854 ***170.15*** *p35*
With wife & 2 children
Lohrman, Adolph; Iowa, 1890 ***1211.15*** *p16*
Lohrman, Matthias; Ohio, 1809-1852 ***4511.35*** *p31*
Lohrman, Wilhelm; Iowa, 1890 ***1211.15*** *p16*
Lohrmann, Engel So. Car.; Minnesota, 1882 ***7420.1*** *p331*
Lohrmann, Friederike Regine Bartz *SEE* Lohrmann, Friedrich
Lohrmann, Friedrich; America, 1836 ***7420.1*** *p11*
*Wife:*Friederike Regine Bartz
Lohrmann, Heinrich Friedr. Wilh.; Port uncertain, 1882 ***7420.1*** *p331*
Lohse, Henry; North Carolina, 1853 ***1088.45*** *p19*
Lohse, Henry; Washington, 1886 ***2770.40*** *p195*
Loignon, Pierre 27; Quebec, 1647 ***9221.17*** *p184*
Lointo, Francis; North Carolina, 1792-1862 ***1088.45*** *p19*
Loire, Philibert A.; Illinois, 1852 ***6079.1*** *p9*
Loiseau, Anne; Quebec, 1664 ***4514.3*** *p342*
Loiseau, Francoise; Quebec, 1669 ***4514.3*** *p342*
Loiseau, Louis 35; Louisiana, 1848 ***778.6*** *p216*
Loison, F. F.; Louisiana, 1836-1841 ***4981.45*** *p209*
Loisone, Henry 30; Port uncertain, 1848 ***778.6*** *p216*
Loj, Frank; Detroit, 1929-1930 ***6214.5*** *p67*
Lokatch, Hyman; Detroit, 1929 ***1640.55*** *p116*
Loland, Hugh A.; North Carolina, 1852 ***1088.45*** *p19*
Loman, Robert; America, 1758 ***1220.12*** *p512*
Lomas, George; America, 1756 ***1220.12*** *p507*
Lomas, Richard 26; Indiana, 1903-1906 ***9076.20*** *p75*
Lomas, Samuel; America, 1772 ***1220.12*** *p507*
Lomas, Thomas; America, 1688 ***1220.12*** *p507*
Lomax, George; America, 1754 ***1220.12*** *p507*
Lomax, James 43; Ontario, 1871 ***1823.17*** *p93*
Lomax, John; America, 1775 ***1220.12*** *p507*
Lomax, John; New York, 1782 ***8529.30*** *p13*
Lomax, John 45; Ontario, 1871 ***1823.17*** *p93*
Lomax, Marsn; Marston's Wharf, 1782 ***8529.30*** *p13*
Lombar, Richard; America, 1741 ***1220.12*** *p507*
Lombard, Bernard *SEE* Lombard, Thomas
Lombard, Elisha; America, 1742 ***1220.12*** *p507*
Lombard, Joshua *SEE* Lombard, Thomas
Lombard, L.; Louisiana, 1836-1841 ***4981.45*** *p209*
Lombard, Margaret *SEE* Lombard, Thomas
Lombard, Thomas *SEE* Lombard, Thomas
Lombard, Thomas; Massachusetts, 1630 ***117.5*** *p154*
With wife
*Son:*Joshua
*Daughter:*Margaret
*Son:*Thomas
*Son:*Bernard
Lombart, John; Died enroute, 1725 ***1220.12*** *p507*
Lombeau, Rosalie; Wisconsin, 1880 ***1495.20*** *p55*
Lombrette, Noel 17 *SEE* Lombrette, Pierre
Lombrette, Pierre 52; Quebec, 1654 ***9221.17*** *p316*
*Son:*Noel 17
Lomera, Edwin 34; Ontario, 1871 ***1823.17*** *p93*
Lommer, Adulf 1; Halifax, N.S., 1902 ***1860.4*** *p39*
Lommer, Friedrich 42; Halifax, N.S., 1902 ***1860.4*** *p39*
Lommer, Ida 39; Halifax, N.S., 1902 ***1860.4*** *p39*
Lommer, Thersa 2; Halifax, N.S., 1902 ***1860.4*** *p39*
Lompon, Pierre; Quebec, 1661 ***9221.17*** *p465*
Lon, Elizabeth; America, 1699 ***1220.12*** *p507*
Londergan, John; Newfoundland, 1814 ***3476.10*** *p54*
Londigan, John; Newfoundland, 1814 ***3476.10*** *p54*
Londman, Nicolas 25; America, 1841 ***778.6*** *p216*
London, Alfred 21; New York, NY, 1878 ***9253.2*** *p45*
London, Alice; Barbados, 1665 ***1220.12*** *p507*
London, Charles; Ohio, 1809-1852 ***4511.35*** *p31*
London, Charlotte; America, 1772 ***1220.12*** *p507*
London, Eleanor; America, 1752 ***1220.12*** *p507*
London, Elener; America, 1730 ***1220.12*** *p507*
London, John; America, 1775 ***1220.12*** *p507*
London, Martha; America, 1739 ***1220.12*** *p507*
London, Mary; America, 1748 ***1220.12*** *p507*
Lone, Elizabeth; America, 1745 ***1220.12*** *p508*
Lone, John; America, 1773 ***1220.12*** *p508*
Lonegan, Patrick; North Carolina, 1844 ***1088.45*** *p19*
Lonergan, Edward; North Carolina, 1858 ***1088.45*** *p19*
Lonergan, James; North Carolina, 1842 ***1088.45*** *p19*
Lonergan, Michael 71; Ontario, 1871 ***1823.17*** *p93*
Loney, Abraham 23; Ontario, 1871 ***1823.17*** *p93*
Loney, Abraham 24; Ontario, 1871 ***1823.17*** *p93*
Loney, John, Jr. *SEE* Loney, John, Sr.
Loney, John, Sr.; New York, 1815 ***9228.50*** *p405*
*Wife:*Susan Cohu
*Child:*John, Jr.
Loney, Susan Cohu *SEE* Loney, John, Sr.
Loney, Thos 45; Ontario, 1871 ***1823.21*** *p205*
Long, Abraham 26; Ontario, 1871 ***1823.21*** *p205*
Long, Adam; Ohio, 1809-1852 ***4511.35*** *p31*
Long, Ann; America, 1748 ***1220.12*** *p508*
Long, Ann 42; Ontario, 1871 ***1823.17*** *p93*
Long, Anthony; America, 1724 ***1220.12*** *p508*
Long, Bonaparte; Toronto, 1844 ***2910.35*** *p112*
Long, Caspar; Ohio, 1809-1852 ***4511.35*** *p31*
Long, Catherine; America, 1738 ***1220.12*** *p508*
Long, Edmund 18; Ontario, 1871 ***1823.21*** *p205*
Long, Edward 40; Ontario, 1871 ***1823.21*** *p205*
Long, Elizabeth; America, 1741 ***1220.12*** *p508*
Long, Elizabeth; Jamaica, 1665 ***1220.12*** *p508*
Long, Fieldham 42; Ontario, 1871 ***1823.21*** *p205*
Long, George; Ohio, 1809-1852 ***4511.35*** *p31*
Long, Grace; Barbados, 1672 ***1220.12*** *p508*
Long, Grace; Maryland, 1734 ***1220.12*** *p508*
Long, Hannah; Annapolis, MD, 1721 ***1220.12*** *p508*
Long, Henry; America, 1772 ***1220.12*** *p508*
Long, Henry 51; Ontario, 1871 ***1823.21*** *p205*
Long, Henry D. 43; Ontario, 1871 ***1823.21*** *p205*
Long, Isaac; America, 1767 ***1220.12*** *p508*
Long, Jacob; Ohio, 1809-1852 ***4511.35*** *p31*
Long, James; America, 1721 ***1220.12*** *p508*
Long, James 37; Ontario, 1871 ***1823.21*** *p205*
Long, Jno.; Louisiana, 1874 ***4981.45*** *p296*
Long, John; America, 1685 ***1220.12*** *p508*
Long, John; America, 1744 ***1220.12*** *p508*
Long, John; America, 1751 ***1220.12*** *p508*
Long, John; America, 1753 ***1220.12*** *p508*
Long, John; America, 1761 ***1220.12*** *p508*
Long, John; America, 1764 ***1220.12*** *p508*
Long, John; Charles Town, SC, 1719 ***1220.12*** *p508*
Long, John; Illinois, 1834-1900 ***6020.5*** *p132*
Long, John; Illinois, 1851 ***6079.1*** *p9*
Long, John; Ohio, 1809-1852 ***4511.35*** *p31*
Long, John 48; Ontario, 1871 ***1823.21*** *p205*
Long, John L. 54; Ontario, 1871 ***1823.17*** *p93*
Long, Joseph; America, 1735 ***1220.12*** *p508*
Long, Lewis; America, 1740 ***1220.12*** *p508*
Long, Martha 16; Minnesota, 1923 ***2769.54*** *p1381*
Long, Mary; America, 1743 ***1220.12*** *p508*
Long, Mary; America, 1761 ***1220.12*** *p508*
Long, Mary; Charlestown, MA, 1664 ***1642*** *p100*
Long, Mary 13; Ontario, 1871 ***1823.17*** *p93*
Long, Mary 50; Ontario, 1871 ***1823.21*** *p206*
Long, Mary 18; St. John, N.B., 1834 ***6469.7*** *p5*
Long, Mary Jane; Potomac, 1731 ***1220.12*** *p508*
Long, Mikel 50; Ontario, 1871 ***1823.21*** *p206*
Long, Patrick; America, 1740 ***1220.12*** *p508*

Long, Peter; Ohio, 1809-1852 ***4511.35*** *p31*
Long, Richard; America, 1685 ***1220.12*** *p508*
Long, Robert; Virginia, 1773 ***1220.12*** *p508*
Long, Ruth 17; St. John, N.B., 1834 ***6469.7*** *p5*
Long, Sarah; America, 1760 ***1220.12*** *p508*
Long, Saul; North Carolina, 1842-1849 ***1088.45*** *p20*
Long, Thomas; America, 1765 ***1220.12*** *p508*
Long, William; America, 1736 ***1220.12*** *p508*
Long, William; America, 1745 ***1220.12*** *p508*
Long, William; New York, 1783 ***8529.30*** *p13*
Long, William 30; Ontario, 1871 ***1823.17*** *p93*
Long, William 42; Ontario, 1871 ***1823.21*** *p206*
Long, William; Toronto, 1844 ***2910.35*** *p115*
Longabaugh, Albinus; Ohio, 1809-1852 ***4511.35*** *p31*
Longabaugh, Jacob F.; Ohio, 1809-1852 ***4511.35*** *p31*
Longabuagh, Frederick F.; Ohio, 1809-1852 ***4511.35*** *p31*
Longanacre, Adam; Ohio, 1809-1852 ***4511.35*** *p31*
Longarre, Tobie; Louisiana, 1874 ***4981.45*** *p132*
Longbotham, Eli; America, 1763 ***1220.12*** *p508*
Longbottom, Elizabeth; America, 1754 ***1220.12*** *p508*
Longbridge, Francis; America, 1685 ***1220.12*** *p508*
Longden, John; America, 1756 ***1220.12*** *p508*
Longden, Joseph; America, 1747 ***1220.12*** *p508*
Longden, Mary; America, 1736 ***1220.12*** *p508*
Longel, Catherine 20; America, 1845 ***778.6*** *p216*
Longel, Sebastien 17; America, 1845 ***778.6*** *p216*
Longenbaugh, Albinus; Ohio, 1809-1852 ***4511.35*** *p31*
Longeran, William; Newfoundland, 1814 ***3476.10*** *p54*
Longerwood, John; America, 1755 ***1220.12*** *p508*
Longes, Mr. 24; America, 1841 ***778.6*** *p216*
Longfellow, John 31; Ontario, 1871 ***1823.21*** *p206*
Longfield, George 49; Ontario, 1871 ***1823.21*** *p206*
Longford, Elizabeth; America, 1771 ***1220.12*** *p508*
Longford, John; America, 1772 ***1220.12*** *p508*
Longford, Michael; Barbados, 1692 ***1220.12*** *p508*
Longford, Robert; Maryland, 1725 ***1220.12*** *p508*
Longgon, James; North Carolina, 1792-1862 ***1088.45*** *p20*
Longham, Christian; America, 1752 ***1220.12*** *p508*
Longhans, John C.; Ohio, 1809-1852 ***4511.35*** *p31*
Longhaus, John C.; Ohio, 1809-1852 ***4511.35*** *p31*
Longhurst, Elizabeth 55; Ontario, 1871 ***1823.21*** *p206*
Longis, Pierre; Louisiana, 1836-1840 ***4981.45*** *p213*
Longley, Elizabeth; America, 1734 ***1220.12*** *p508*
Longley, Thos 32; Ontario, 1871 ***1823.21*** *p206*
Longley, William 60; Ontario, 1871 ***1823.17*** *p93*
Longman, Eliza.; Maryland, 1674 ***1236.25*** *p50*
Longman, Elizab.; Maryland, 1673 ***1236.25*** *p49*
Longman, Elizabeth; Barbados, 1672 ***1220.12*** *p508*
Longman, Elizabeth; Barbados, 1673 ***1220.12*** *p509*
Longman, William; America, 1661 ***1220.12*** *p509*
Longman, William; Barbados, 1675 ***1220.12*** *p509*
Longmire, Mary E. 55; Ontario, 1871 ***1823.21*** *p206*
Longmire, William; Rappahannock, VA, 1726 ***1220.12*** *p509*
Longmore, Ann; Virginia, 1739 ***1220.12*** *p509*
Longo, Pietro; Louisiana, 1874 ***4981.45*** *p132*
Longood, Jan 20; Ontario, 1871 ***1823.17*** *p93*
Longpont, Adrien de; Quebec, 1643 ***9221.17*** *p132*
Longschamps, Genevieve 16; Quebec, 1654 ***9221.17*** *p313*
Longstaff, Henry; America, 1749 ***1220.12*** *p509*
Longstaff, J. C. 57; Ontario, 1871 ***1823.21*** *p206*
Longstaff, William; America, 1765 ***1220.12*** *p509*
Longstreet, Clarra 5; Michigan, 1880 ***4491.30*** *p20*
Longstreet, Lilliam 6; Michigan, 1880 ***4491.30*** *p20*
Longstreet, Robert 28; Michigan, 1880 ***4491.30*** *p20*
Longstreet, Sarah A. 25; Michigan, 1880 ***4491.30*** *p20*
Longsworth, Peter; Maryland, 1734 ***1220.12*** *p509*
Longua, R. 40; America, 1841 ***778.6*** *p216*
Longuemare, L. 33; America, 1841 ***778.6*** *p216*
Longuespee, Jean; Quebec, 1660 ***9221.17*** *p438*
Longueuil, Francois-Nicolas de; Quebec, 1652 ***9221.17*** *p262*
Longweaver, William; America, 1768 ***1220.12*** *p509*
Longworth, James; Ohio, 1843 ***2763.1*** *p20*
Lonnix, Levenia 20; Ontario, 1871 ***1823.21*** *p206*
Lonnvall, C.F.; New York, NY, 1846 ***6412.40*** *p149*
L'Onquetin, Elie; Quebec, 1656 ***9221.17*** *p331*
Lonquist, Carl; Colorado, 1883 ***1029.59*** *p56*
Lonrigan, Patrick; Ohio, 1809-1852 ***4511.35*** *p31*
Lonsbury, Walter 23; Michigan, 1880 ***4491.39*** *p18*
Lonsdale, Alfred G.; Colorado, 1895 ***1029.59*** *p56*
Lonsdale, Frank; Colorado, 1895 ***1029.59*** *p56*
Lonsdale, Frank; Missouri, 1890 ***1029.59*** *p56*
Lonsdale, William; America, 1770 ***1220.12*** *p509*
Lonsdale, William 36; Ontario, 1871 ***1823.21*** *p206*
Lonsdorfer, Anna; America, 1890 ***5475.1*** *p76*
Lonyaga, Salvatore; Louisiana, 1874 ***4981.45*** *p132*
Lonzo, J. 35; America, 1846 ***778.6*** *p216*
Looby, William; Toronto, 1844 ***2910.35*** *p115*
Loohor, John; America, 1700 ***1220.12*** *p509*
Look, James; New Orleans, 1850 ***7242.30*** *p148*
Looker, Ann 9; Quebec, 1870 ***8364.32*** *p24*
Looker, Caroline 13; Quebec, 1870 ***8364.32*** *p24*
Looker, John; America, 1750 ***1220.12*** *p509*
Looker, Richard; America, 1750 ***1220.12*** *p509*
Loome, John; America, 1769 ***1220.12*** *p509*
Looms, Michael; America, 1750 ***1220.12*** *p509*
Loory, Thomas; Illinois, 1834-1900 ***6020.5*** *p132*
Loose, Huldah Alwine; Wisconsin, 1891 ***6795.8*** *p95*
Loosemore, Henry; America, 1721 ***1220.12*** *p509*
Looson, N. 37; America, 1848 ***778.6*** *p216*
Looze, Antoine Joseph; New York, NY, 1856 ***1494.21*** *p31*
Looze, Elisa *SEE* Looze, Pierre Joseph
Looze, Marie Therese *SEE* Looze, Pierre Joseph
Looze, Marie Therese Massuy *SEE* Looze, Pierre Joseph
Looze, Pierre Joseph; Wisconsin, 1856 ***1495.20*** *p46*
*Wife:*Marie Therese Massuy
*Child:*Marie Therese
*Child:*Victoire
*Child:*Elisa
Looze, Victoire *SEE* Looze, Pierre Joseph
Lopeynolesey, Vital 18; America, 1848 ***778.6*** *p216*
Lopez, Mateo; Louisiana, 1836-1841 ***4981.45*** *p209*
Lopez, Pedro 50; Port uncertain, 1844 ***778.6*** *p216*
Loppe, Renee 14; Montreal, 1658 ***9221.17*** *p390*
Loquet, Antoine 18; Montreal, 1662 ***9221.17*** *p498*
Loquintrer, Adolphe 41; New Orleans, 1848 ***778.6*** *p216*
Lorance, William; New York, NY, 1776 ***8529.30*** *p2*
L'Orange, Leonard 21; Quebec, 1655 ***9221.17*** *p321*
Loranger, Jacques; Quebec, 1661 ***9221.17*** *p462*
Loranger, L. G.; Louisiana, 1874-1875 ***4981.45*** *p29*
Loranger, Robert 24; Quebec, 1662 ***9221.17*** *p492*
Lorcade, Mr. 23; Port uncertain, 1840 ***778.6*** *p216*
Lorch, Bernard; North Carolina, 1860 ***1088.45*** *p20*
Lorch, Jakob; America, 1846 ***5475.1*** *p547*
Lord, Anne; Maryland, 1728 ***1220.12*** *p509*
Lord, Benjamin; America, 1765 ***1220.12*** *p509*
Lord, John; America, 1682 ***1220.12*** *p509*
Lord, John; America, 1724 ***1220.12*** *p509*
Lord, John; America, 1741 ***1220.12*** *p509*
Lord, John; America, 1767 ***1220.12*** *p509*
Lord, Joseph; Philadelphia, 1865 ***5720.10*** *p382*
Lord, Mary; America, 1764 ***1220.12*** *p509*
Lord, Richard; America, 1759 ***1220.12*** *p509*
Lord, Robert 63; Ontario, 1871 ***1823.21*** *p206*
Lord, William; America, 1770 ***1220.12*** *p509*
Lore, Margarethe Pennerau *SEE* Lore, Michel
Lore, Michel; America, 1839 ***5475.1*** *p56*
*Wife:*Margarethe Pennerau
Lorea, Celestine; California, 1906-1909 ***3276.8*** *p20*
Loree, Moses; Washington, 1889 ***2770.40*** *p79*
Loreith, J. F. 21; America, 1847 ***778.6*** *p216*
Loreithe, Jacques E.; Louisiana, 1836-1840 ***4981.45*** *p213*
Lorenc, Frantisek; Iowa, 1859 ***2853.20*** *p228*
Lorenc, Matej; Wisconsin, 1866 ***2853.20*** *p251*
With parents
Lorent, Anne 31; New Orleans, 1848 ***778.6*** *p216*
Lorent, Louis 42; New Orleans, 1848 ***778.6*** *p216*
Lorente, Martinez Angot; Louisiana, 1836-1840 ***4981.45*** *p213*
Lorentz, Axel Theodor; New York, NY, 1850 ***6412.40*** *p151*
Lorentz, Eva 63; America, 1841 ***778.6*** *p216*
Lorentz, John; Ohio, 1809-1852 ***4511.35*** *p31*
Lorentz, Philip; Ohio, 1809-1852 ***4511.35*** *p31*
Lorenz, Anton 20; New York, NY, 1893 ***1883.7*** *p39*
Lorenz, Anton 20; New York, NY, 1893 ***1883.7*** *p47*
Lorenz, August; America, 1867 ***7919.3*** *p529*
Lorenz, Carl; Valdivia, Chile, 1850 ***1192.4*** *p49*
With wife
With daughter 1
Lorenz, Caroline 21; New York, NY, 1893 ***1883.7*** *p39*
Lorenz, Caroline 21; New York, NY, 1893 ***1883.7*** *p47*
Lorenz, Charles 46; Indiana, 1880-1894 ***9076.20*** *p73*
Lorenz, Christian 29; Halifax, N.S., 1902 ***1860.4*** *p40*
Lorenz, Elisabeth 25; America, 1864 ***5475.1*** *p45*
Lorenz, Ernst Gotth.; Valdivia, Chile, 1850 ***1192.4*** *p49*
With son 5
Lorenz, Eva 50; Port uncertain, 1847 ***778.6*** *p216*
Lorenz, Franciska; Halifax, N.S., 1902 ***1860.4*** *p40*
Lorenz, Franz 4; Halifax, N.S., 1902 ***1860.4*** *p40*
Lorenz, Franz 20; New Orleans, 1848 ***778.6*** *p216*
Lorenz, Georg 10; Port uncertain, 1847 ***778.6*** *p217*
Lorenz, Jacob 48; Port uncertain, 1847 ***778.6*** *p217*
Lorenz, Johann 36; Halifax, N.S., 1902 ***1860.4*** *p40*
Lorenz, Johanna 26; Halifax, N.S., 1902 ***1860.4*** *p40*
Lorenz, Malie 16; Port uncertain, 1847 ***778.6*** *p217*
Lorenz, Marianna; Halifax, N.S., 1902 ***1860.4*** *p40*
Lorenz, Marie 15; Port uncertain, 1847 ***778.6*** *p217*
Lorenz, Marie 40; Port uncertain, 1847 ***778.6*** *p217*
Lorenz, Mary 18; Louisiana, 1848 ***778.6*** *p217*
Lorenz, Michael; Halifax, N.S., 1902 ***1860.4*** *p40*
Lorenz, Michel 6; Port uncertain, 1847 ***778.6*** *p217*
Lorenz, Michel 40; Port uncertain, 1847 ***778.6*** *p217*
Lorenz, Nikolaus; America, 1871 ***5475.1*** *p329*
Lorenz, Nikolaus; America, 1882 ***5475.1*** *p329*
Lorenz, Walpurga 26; Halifax, N.S., 1902 ***1860.4*** *p40*
Lorenzen, Lous 40; Ontario, 1871 ***1823.17*** *p93*
Lorenzier, Fr. 23; Port uncertain, 1846 ***778.6*** *p217*
Lorenzo, Christian A.; Ohio, 1857 ***3580.20*** *p32*
Lorenzo, Christian A.; Ohio, 1857 ***6020.12*** *p13*
Lores, Inglehart 39; Michigan, 1880 ***4491.39*** *p18*
Loret, . . .; America, 1842 ***778.6*** *p217*
Loret, Mrs. 27; America, 1842 ***778.6*** *p217*
Loret, Etiennette; Quebec, 1671 ***4514.3*** *p343*
Loret, Francois; Quebec, 1651 ***9221.17*** *p248*
Lorette, Antoine 65; New Orleans, 1848 ***778.6*** *p217*
Lorg, Jakob; America, 1846 ***5475.1*** *p547*
Lorge, Euphrasie *SEE* Lorge, Jean Joseph, Jr.
Lorge, Jean Joseph; Wisconsin, 1856 ***1495.20*** *p8*
*Wife:*Marie Francoise Delwiche
*Child:*Marie Adolphine
*Child:*Jean Joseph, Jr.
*Child:*Jeanne
Lorge, Jean Joseph, Jr.; Wisconsin, 1855 ***1495.20*** *p8*
*Wife:*Marie Therese Lemense
*Daughter:*Euphrasie
Lorge, Jean Joseph, Jr. *SEE* Lorge, Jean Joseph
Lorge, Jeanne *SEE* Lorge, Jean Joseph
Lorge, Marie Adolphine *SEE* Lorge, Jean Joseph
Lorge, Marie Francoise Delwiche *SEE* Lorge, Jean Joseph
Lorge, Marie Therese Lemense *SEE* Lorge, Jean Joseph, Jr.
Lorgueil, Marie 16; Montreal, 1654 ***9221.17*** *p317*
Lorieul, Marie Adrienne 31; New Orleans, 1848 ***778.6*** *p217*
Lorig, Anna Linnig *SEE* Lorig, Peter
Lorig, Barbara 51; America, 1857 ***5475.1*** *p266*
*Son:*Johann
*Daughter:*Margarethe
Lorig, Elisabeth Derwing *SEE* Lorig, Mathias
Lorig, Johann *SEE* Lorig, Barbara Friedrich
Lorig, Johann *SEE* Lorig, Peter
Lorig, Katharina; America, 1875 ***5475.1*** *p285*
Lorig, Katharina 33; America, 1857 ***5475.1*** *p362*
Lorig, Margarethe *SEE* Lorig, Barbara Friedrich
Lorig, Mathias *SEE* Lorig, Mathias
Lorig, Mathias; America, 1873 ***5475.1*** *p362*
*Wife:*Elisabeth Derwing
*Son:*Peter
*Son:*Michel
*Son:*Mathias
*Son:*Nikolaus
Lorig, Mathias *SEE* Lorig, Peter
Lorig, Michel *SEE* Lorig, Mathias
Lorig, Nikolaus *SEE* Lorig, Mathias
Lorig, Peter *SEE* Lorig, Mathias
Lorig, Peter 51; America, 1882 ***5475.1*** *p512*
*Wife:*Anna Linnig
*Son:*Johann
*Son:*Mathias
Lorimer, Robert 48; Ontario, 1871 ***1823.21*** *p206*
Lorimier, Guillaume de; Quebec, 1683-1688 ***2314.30*** *p168*
Lorimier, Guillaume de; Quebec, 1685 ***2314.30*** *p190*
Loring, Andreas 33; Halifax, N.S., 1902 ***1860.4*** *p40*
Loring, Emmanuel; Halifax, N.S., 1902 ***1860.4*** *p40*
Loring, Johan 9; Halifax, N.S., 1902 ***1860.4*** *p40*
Loring, Katherina 8; Halifax, N.S., 1902 ***1860.4*** *p40*
Loring, Louise 3; Halifax, N.S., 1902 ***1860.4*** *p40*
Loring, Louise 32; Halifax, N.S., 1902 ***1860.4*** *p40*
Lorion, Catherine 16; Montreal, 1654 ***9221.17*** *p317*
Lorion, Jeanne 11 *SEE* Lorion, Mathurin
Lorion, Jeanne Bizette 37 *SEE* Lorion, Mathurin
Lorion, Marie 15 *SEE* Lorion, Mathurin
Lorion, Mathurin 57; Montreal, 1658 ***9221.17*** *p390*
*Daughter:*Marie 15
*Wife:*Jeanne Bizette 37
*Daughter:*Jeanne 11
*Daughter:*Renee 1
Lorion, Renee 1 *SEE* Lorion, Mathurin
Lorion, Toussaint; Quebec, 1659 ***9221.17*** *p406*
Loriot, Martin; Montreal, 1653 ***9221.17*** *p296*
Loriot, Perrette; Quebec, 1671 ***4514.3*** *p343*
Loris, George 36; Ontario, 1871 ***1823.17*** *p93*
Lorman, M. 30; New Orleans, 1845 ***778.6*** *p217*
Lornier, Francois Joseph 41; America, 1847 ***778.6*** *p217*
Lornier, Marie Magdalena 40; America, 1847 ***778.6*** *p217*
Lornier, Roselie 7 months; America, 1847 ***778.6*** *p217*
Lorniter, Celestine 4; America, 1847 ***778.6*** *p217*
Lorniter, Dominique 20; America, 1847 ***778.6*** *p217*
Lorniter, Etienne 10; America, 1847 ***778.6*** *p217*
Lorniter, Jn. Batiste 12; America, 1847 ***778.6*** *p217*
Lorniter, Marie 8; America, 1847 ***778.6*** *p217*
Lorniter, Marie 30; America, 1847 ***778.6*** *p217*

Lorniter, Nicolas 12; America, 1847 ***778.6*** *p217*
Lorrain, Francoise Haulin *SEE* Lorrain, Pierre
Lorrain, Pierre 28; Quebec, 1656 ***9221.17*** *p341*
*Wife:*Francoise Haulin
Lorrell, Mathew; Virginia, 1742 ***1220.12*** *p509*
Lorriman, Michael; America, 1746 ***1220.12*** *p485*
Lorriman, Richard; Barbados or Jamaica, 1694 ***1220.12*** *p509*
Lorrimer, Richard Francis; America, 1770 ***1220.12*** *p509*
Lorron, August; Cleveland, OH, 1885-1891 ***9722.10*** *p123*
Lorscheider, Katharina; America, 1855-1899 ***6442.17*** *p65*
Lorson, Anna *SEE* Lorson, Johann
Lorson, Barbara Ort *SEE* Lorson, Johann
Lorson, Elisabeth 3 *SEE* Lorson, Peter
Lorson, Elisabeth Huwer 22 *SEE* Lorson, Peter
Lorson, Elisabeth Reinstadler 23 *SEE* Lorson, Peter
Lorson, Franz *SEE* Lorson, Peter
Lorson, Georg 1 *SEE* Lorson, Peter
Lorson, Jakob *SEE* Lorson, Johann
Lorson, Johann; America, 1869 ***5475.1*** *p164*
Lorson, Johann; America, 1876 ***5475.1*** *p231*
Lorson, Johann *SEE* Lorson, Johann
Lorson, Johann; America, 1881 ***5475.1*** *p220*
*Wife:*Barbara Ort
*Son:*Mathias
*Son:*Michel
*Son:*Ludwig
*Son:*Jakob
*Son:*Simon
*Son:*Anna
*Son:*Johann
Lorson, Johanna; America, 1880 ***5475.1*** *p220*
Lorson, Johanna; America, 1881 ***5475.1*** *p164*
Lorson, Ludwig *SEE* Lorson, Johann
Lorson, Mathias *SEE* Lorson, Johann
Lorson, Michel *SEE* Lorson, Johann
Lorson, Nikolaus; America, 1869 ***5475.1*** *p163*
Lorson, Nikolaus; America, 1883 ***5475.1*** *p231*
Lorson, Peter; America, 1869 ***5475.1*** *p164*
*Wife:*Elisabeth Reinstadler
*Son:*Georg
*Daughter:*Elisabeth
Lorson, Peter; America, 1872 ***5475.1*** *p231*
*Wife:*Elisabeth Huwer
*Son:*Franz
*Daughter:*Therese
Lorson, Peter; America, 1873 ***5475.1*** *p164*
Lorson, Simon *SEE* Lorson, Johann
Lorson, Therese *SEE* Lorson, Peter
Lorsong, Anna; America, 1846 ***5475.1*** *p61*
Lorsong, Anna Maria Bach *SEE* Lorsong, Jakob
Lorsong, Barbara 42; America, 1846 ***5475.1*** *p61*
Lorsong, Jakob; America, 1846 ***5475.1*** *p61*
*Wife:*Anna Maria Bach
Lorsong, Johanetta; America, 1852 ***5475.1*** *p62*
Lorsong, Johanette Remark *SEE* Lorsong, Peter
Lorsong, Johann; America, 1846 ***5475.1*** *p61*
Lorsong, Magdalena; America, 1846 ***5475.1*** *p61*
Lorsong, Margarethe; America, 1852 ***5475.1*** *p62*
Lorsong, Peter; America, 1841 ***5475.1*** *p61*
*Wife:*Johanette Remark
With 4 children
Lorthotz, Mrs. Michel 28; Port uncertain, 1842 ***778.6*** *p217*
Lortorins, Henry; Louisiana, 1841-1844 ***4981.45*** *p210*
Lorus, Francis 24; Ontario, 1871 ***1823.17*** *p93*
Lorway, Ab'm; Ontario, 1787 ***1276.15*** *p230*
Lory, Johann; America, 1838 ***5475.1*** *p67*
With wife 2 stepchildren & daughter
Lory, Reine; Quebec, 1600-1673 ***4514.3*** *p340*
Losa, Vaclav; New York, NY, 1867-1894 ***2853.20*** *p182*
Losch, Caroline; America, 1868 ***7919.3*** *p534*
Losch, Catharina Margarethe; America, 1867 ***7919.3*** *p535*
Losch, Georg Adam; America, 1867 ***7919.3*** *p535*
With wife & 4 children
Losch, Heinrich; America, 1867 ***7919.3*** *p532*
Losch, Valentin; Nova Scotia, 1784 ***7105*** *p24*
Lose, Mrs. 30; America, 1848 ***778.6*** *p217*
Loseby, Peter; America, 1752 ***1220.12*** *p509*
Loseby, Richard; America, 1673 ***1220.12*** *p509*
Loseby, Thomas; America, 1764 ***1220.12*** *p509*
Losinska, Apolonia; Wisconsin, 1886 ***6795.8*** *p34*
Losinski, Apolonia; Wisconsin, 1886 ***6795.8*** *p34*
Lossmann, Franz; America, 1883 ***5475.1*** *p422*
With wife & 2 children
Lotan, Francis; America, 1768 ***1220.12*** *p509*
Lotan, Joseph 39; Ontario, 1871 ***1823.21*** *p206*
Lotan, Robert 44; Ontario, 1871 ***1823.21*** *p206*
Lothammer, Andrew; Ohio, 1809-1852 ***4511.35*** *p31*
Lothammer, Peter; Ohio, 1809-1852 ***4511.35*** *p31*
Lothian, George 53; Ontario, 1871 ***1823.21*** *p206*
Lothner, Andreas; North America, 1854 ***6410.15*** *p104*
Lotier, Catherine 17; Montreal, 1659 ***9221.17*** *p423*
Loton, Ann; America, 1774 ***1220.12*** *p509*
Loton, Richard; America, 1762 ***1220.12*** *p509*
Loton, Sophia; Virginia, 1741 ***1220.12*** *p509*
Lotouche MacCarthy, Charles; Quebec, 1737 ***2314.30*** *p171*
Lots, Peter; North Carolina, 1710 ***3629.40*** *p5*
Lott, Elizabeth; Barbados or Jamaica, 1697 ***1220.12*** *p509*
Lott, Kezia 65; Ontario, 1871 ***1823.21*** *p206*
Lotta, Stephen; America, 1767 ***1220.12*** *p509*
Lotter, Etienne 21; America, 1840 ***778.6*** *p217*
Lottiman, Michael; America, 1746 ***1220.12*** *p509*
Lotz, Joseph 26; America, 1846 ***778.6*** *p217*
Lotz, Nicolas 31; Missouri, 1845 ***778.6*** *p217*
Lotz, Philip; Ohio, 1809-1852 ***4511.35*** *p31*
Lotz, Wilhelm; Nova Scotia, 1852 ***170.15*** *p35*
With wife & 5 children
Louard, Florence Marie; Wisconsin, 1856 ***1495.20*** *p12*
Loub, Joseph; Ohio, 1854 ***3580.20*** *p32*
Loub, Joseph; Ohio, 1854 ***6020.12*** *p13*
Loubrere, Mr. 23; America, 1841 ***778.6*** *p217*
Louch, George 42; Ontario, 1871 ***1823.21*** *p206*
Loudeming, Bd. 43; New Orleans, 1848 ***778.6*** *p217*
Louder, Jonathan; America, 1758 ***1220.12*** *p511*
Loudon, Robert; Illinois, 1834-1900 ***6020.5*** *p132*
Loue, Martin; Quebec, 1643 ***9221.17*** *p132*
Loue, Martin; Quebec, 1643 ***9221.17*** *p132*
Louge, Aug. 37; New Orleans, 1844 ***778.6*** *p218*
Louge, Pierre 25; New Orleans, 1848 ***778.6*** *p218*
Louge, Richard; Massachusetts, 1630 ***117.5*** *p154*
Lougee, John; New Hampshire, 1702-1718 ***9228.50*** *p406*
Lougee, John; New Hampshire, 1710 ***9228.50*** *p47*
Louges, Mr. 24; America, 1841 ***778.6*** *p216*
Loughary, William 21; New York, NY, 1849 ***6178.50*** *p152*
Loughead, Emeline 30; Michigan, 1880 ***4491.42*** *p17*
Loughead, Lavinia 9; Michigan, 1880 ***4491.42*** *p17*
Loughead, Samuel 40; Michigan, 1880 ***4491.42*** *p17*
Lougheed, Robert 70; Ontario, 1871 ***1823.21*** *p206*
Lougheed, William 56; Ontario, 1871 ***1823.21*** *p206*
Loughin, Henery 73; Ontario, 1871 ***1823.21*** *p206*
Loughlin, Joseph; New England, 1747 ***1642*** *p29*
Loughlin, Thomas 55; Ontario, 1871 ***1823.21*** *p206*
Loughnan, John; Halifax, N.S., 1827 ***7009.9*** *p61*
Loughnane, Hugh 60; Ontario, 1871 ***1823.21*** *p206*
Loughnane, Patrick 30; Ontario, 1871 ***1823.21*** *p206*
Loughrey, Archibald 65; Ontario, 1871 ***1823.21*** *p206*
Loughrey, William 29; Ontario, 1871 ***1823.21*** *p206*
Louis, Mr. 25; America, 1843 ***778.6*** *p218*
Louis, Antoine Joseph; Wisconsin, 1856 ***1495.20*** *p46*
*Child:*Felicien
*Child:*Wivine
*Child:*Charles Alexandre
Louis, Antoinette 10; America, 1848 ***778.6*** *p218*
Louis, Anton; America, 1881 ***5475.1*** *p227*
Louis, Augustina 18; America, 1848 ***778.6*** *p218*
Louis, Augustus 21; St. Louis, 1843 ***778.6*** *p218*
Louis, Baptiste 6; America, 1846 ***778.6*** *p218*
Louis, Bernard 30; Port uncertain, 1840 ***778.6*** *p218*
Louis, Catherine 32; America, 1846 ***778.6*** *p218*
Louis, Charles Alexandre *SEE* Louis, Antoine Joseph
Louis, Claude 48; America, 1847 ***778.6*** *p218*
Louis, Etienna 50; America, 1847 ***778.6*** *p218*
Louis, Etienne 18; America, 1847 ***778.6*** *p218*
Louis, Felicien *SEE* Louis, Antoine Joseph
Louis, Ferdinand 10; America, 1848 ***778.6*** *p218*
Louis, Firmin 23; America, 1848 ***778.6*** *p218*
Louis, Francis; America, 1764 ***1220.12*** *p498*
Louis, Francis 8; America, 1848 ***778.6*** *p218*
Louis, Francois 21; America, 1847 ***778.6*** *p218*
Louis, Friedrich; America, 1847 ***2526.43*** *p222*
Louis, Friedrich *SEE* Louis, Konrad
Louis, Georg *SEE* Louis, Konrad
Louis, Geremi 4; America, 1845 ***778.6*** *p218*
Louis, Hyppolite 16; America, 1847 ***778.6*** *p218*
Louis, J. B. 36; New Orleans, 1840 ***778.6*** *p218*
Louis, Jacob 30; America, 1748 ***778.6*** *p218*
Louis, Jacques 12; America, 1848 ***778.6*** *p218*
Louis, Jean 8; America, 1845 ***778.6*** *p218*
Louis, Jean 14; America, 1848 ***778.6*** *p218*
Louis, Jean 20; America, 1847 ***778.6*** *p218*
Louis, Jeanne 12; America, 1847 ***778.6*** *p218*
Louis, Johann *SEE* Louis, Konrad
Louis, John 51; America, 1848 ***778.6*** *p218*
Louis, Joseph 16; America, 1848 ***778.6*** *p218*
Louis, Joseph 33; America, 1846 ***778.6*** *p218*
Louis, Julie 9; America, 1845 ***778.6*** *p218*
Louis, Konrad *SEE* Louis, Konrad
Louis, Konrad; America, 1880 ***5475.1*** *p172*
*Wife:*Maria Abel
*Son:*Nikolaus
*Son:*Michel
*Son:*Peter
*Son:*Johann
*Daughter:*Maria
*Daughter:*Magdalena
*Son:*Friedrich
*Son:*Wilhelm
*Son:*Georg
*Son:*Mathias
*Son:*Konrad
Louis, Louis 10; America, 1845 ***778.6*** *p218*
Louis, Magdalena *SEE* Louis, Konrad
Louis, Magnus 29; America, 1846 ***778.6*** *p218*
Louis, Maria *SEE* Louis, Konrad
Louis, Maria Abel *SEE* Louis, Konrad
Louis, Marie 6; America, 1847 ***778.6*** *p218*
Louis, Marie Natalie; Wisconsin, 1854-1858 ***1495.20*** *p66*
Louis, Mathias *SEE* Louis, Konrad
Louis, Michel *SEE* Louis, Konrad
Louis, Nicolas 30; New Orleans, 1848 ***778.6*** *p219*
Louis, Nikolaus *SEE* Louis, Konrad
Louis, Paul Andre 30; Port uncertain, 1846 ***778.6*** *p219*
Louis, Pauline; Wisconsin, 1880 ***1495.20*** *p46*
Louis, Peter *SEE* Louis, Konrad
Louis, Pierre 17; America, 1845 ***778.6*** *p219*
Louis, Salome 27; America, 1846 ***778.6*** *p219*
Louis, Sophie 9; America, 1847 ***778.6*** *p219*
Louis, Susanne 2; America, 1845 ***778.6*** *p219*
Louis, Thos. H. 30; Ontario, 1871 ***1823.17*** *p93*
Louis, Wilhelm *SEE* Louis, Konrad
Louis, William 58; Ontario, 1871 ***1823.17*** *p94*
Louis, Wivine *SEE* Louis, Antoine Joseph
Louisse, Nicolas 29; America, 1843 ***778.6*** *p219*
Louiza, Elizabeth; America, 1769 ***1220.12*** *p509*
Louman, Joseph; Virginia, 1741 ***1220.12*** *p512*
Lound, Mary; America, 1731 ***1220.12*** *p512*
Loune, Jacques; Quebec, 1659 ***9221.17*** *p414*
Loupy, Alexr. 48; America, 1845 ***778.6*** *p219*
Lourcelie, Mr. 32; America, 1842 ***778.6*** *p219*
Lourde, Mr. 19; America, 1841 ***778.6*** *p219*
Lourey, Mary A. 40; Ontario, 1871 ***1823.21*** *p206*
Lousche, Louise 45; Quebec, 1634 ***9221.17*** *p39*
Lousley, Alta M. 37; Michigan, 1880 ***4491.39*** *p18*
Lousley, Charles 4; Michigan, 1880 ***4491.39*** *p18*
Lousley, Cora B. 7; Michigan, 1880 ***4491.39*** *p18*
Lousley, Edway 12; Michigan, 1880 ***4491.39*** *p18*
Lousser, Joseph 22; Louisiana, 1840 ***778.6*** *p219*
Loustalot, Jean 18; America, 1845 ***778.6*** *p219*
Loustalot, Jean; Louisiana, 1874 ***4981.45*** *p132*
Loustaplad, P. 22; New Orleans, 1842 ***778.6*** *p219*
Loustean, Peter; Iowa, 1888 ***1211.15*** *p16*
Louvart, Jacques; Quebec, 1660 ***9221.17*** *p438*
Louvart, Michel; Montreal, 1653 ***9221.17*** *p296*
Louvet, Catherine; Quebec, 1668 ***4514.3*** *p343*
Louvier, Jean Claude; Illinois, 1852 ***6079.1*** *p9*
Lovatt, Lovat; Marston's Wharf, 1782 ***8529.30*** *p13*
Lovatt, William; America, 1751 ***1220.12*** *p510*
Love, Agnus 45; Ontario, 1871 ***1823.17*** *p94*
Love, Andrew; South Carolina, 1813 ***3208.30*** *p18*
Love, Andrew; South Carolina, 1813 ***3208.30*** *p31*
Love, Bernard; Toronto, 1844 ***2910.35*** *p114*
Love, Edward; Barbados, 1668 ***1220.12*** *p509*
Love, Eliza 12; Quebec, 1870 ***8364.32*** *p24*
Love, James; America, 1767 ***1220.12*** *p509*
Love, James 40; Ontario, 1871 ***1823.17*** *p94*
Love, John; America, 1742 ***1220.12*** *p509*
Love, John; Barbados, 1668 ***1220.12*** *p509*
Love, John 56; Ontario, 1871 ***1823.21*** *p206*
Love, John 67; Ontario, 1871 ***1823.21*** *p206*
Love, John 45; South Carolina, 1812 ***3476.30*** *p12*
Love, Mary 70; Ontario, 1871 ***1823.21*** *p206*
Love, Nicholas 20; Ontario, 1871 ***1823.17*** *p94*
Love, Peter; America, 1751 ***1220.12*** *p509*
Love, Robert; South Carolina, 1813 ***3208.30*** *p19*
Love, Robert; South Carolina, 1813 ***3208.30*** *p31*
Love, Robert 36; South Carolina, 1812 ***3476.30*** *p12*
Love, Thomas; America, 1718 ***1220.12*** *p509*
Love, Thomas; America, 1770 ***1220.12*** *p510*
Love, Thomas; Annapolis, MD, 1726 ***1220.12*** *p509*
Love, Thomas 15; Quebec, 1870 ***8364.32*** *p24*
Love, William; America, 1756 ***1220.12*** *p510*
Love, William 48; Ontario, 1871 ***1823.21*** *p206*
Love, William; South Carolina, 1813 ***3208.30*** *p18*
Love, William; South Carolina, 1813 ***3208.30*** *p31*
Love, William, Jr.; South Carolina, 1813 ***3208.30*** *p19*
Love, William, Jr.; South Carolina, 1813 ***3208.30*** *p32*
Love, Wm. 42; South Carolina, 1812 ***3476.30*** *p12*
Loveday, Joseph; America, 1771 ***1220.12*** *p510*
Loveday, Mary; Annapolis, MD, 1726 ***1220.12*** *p510*
Loveday, Thomas; America, 1769 ***1220.12*** *p510*
Loveday, Thomas 27; Ontario, 1871 ***1823.21*** *p206*
Lovegrove, James; America, 1768 ***1220.12*** *p510*
Lovegrove, John; Maryland, 1725 ***1220.12*** *p510*

Lovegrove, Mary; America, 1749 ***1220.12*** *p510*
Lovegrove, Rebecca; America, 1754 ***1220.12*** *p510*
Lovegrove, William; America, 1774 ***1220.12*** *p510*
Lovejoy, Roger; Virginia, 1749 ***1220.12*** *p510*
Lovejoy, William; Rappahannock, VA, 1729 ***1220.12*** *p510*
Lovelace, Edward; America, 1764 ***1220.12*** *p510*
Loveland, Daniel; America, 1769 ***1220.12*** *p510*
Loveless, James 63; Ontario, 1871 ***1823.21*** *p206*
Loveless, John 53; Ontario, 1871 ***1823.21*** *p206*
Loveless, Robert 71; Ontario, 1871 ***1823.21*** *p206*
Loveless, William 50; Ontario, 1871 ***1823.21*** *p206*
Lovell, Catherine; America, 1765 ***1220.12*** *p510*
Lovell, Frederick; America, 1770 ***1220.12*** *p510*
Lovell, James; America, 1769 ***1220.12*** *p510*
Lovell, James 37; Ontario, 1871 ***1823.17*** *p94*
Lovell, John; America, 1693 ***1220.12*** *p510*
Lovell, John; America, 1763 ***1220.12*** *p510*
Lovell, John; America, 1764 ***1220.12*** *p510*
Lovell, John; Boston, 1760-1769 ***9228.50*** *p411*
Lovell, John; Maine, 1711 ***9228.50*** *p411*
Lovell, John 29; Ontario, 1871 ***1823.17*** *p94*
Lovell, John 31; Ontario, 1871 ***1823.17*** *p94*
Lovell, John 52; Ontario, 1871 ***1823.17*** *p94*
Lovell, Joseph; America, 1755 ***1220.12*** *p510*
Lovell, Richard; America, 1765 ***1220.12*** *p510*
Lovell, Robert; America, 1737 ***1220.12*** *p510*
Lovell, Robert 54; Ontario, 1871 ***1823.21*** *p206*
Lovell, Thomas; America, 1740 ***1220.12*** *p510*
Lovell, William; America, 1750 ***1220.12*** *p510*
Lovell, William; Virginia, 1750 ***1220.12*** *p510*
Lovelock, Abraham; Virginia, 1748 ***1220.12*** *p510*
Lovelock, John; America, 1758 ***1220.12*** *p510*
Lovelock, Nathaniel; America, 1742 ***1220.12*** *p510*
Lovely, Martha; America, 1769 ***1220.12*** *p510*
Loven, Sven Victor; Charleston, SC, 1851 ***6412.40*** *p153*
Loverich, Richard; North Carolina, 1792-1862 ***1088.45*** *p20*
Loveridge, Bernard; America, 1685 ***1220.12*** *p510*
Loveridge, Henry; Quebec, 1885 ***1937.10*** *p52*
Loveridge, John; America, 1685 ***1220.12*** *p510*
Loveridge, John; Barbados or Jamaica, 1690 ***1220.12*** *p510*
Loveridge, William; America, 1685 ***1220.12*** *p510*
Lovering, John; America, 1752 ***1220.12*** *p510*
Lovering, Mary; Virginia, 1740 ***1220.12*** *p510*
Loveringham, Richard; Annapolis, MD, 1726 ***1220.12*** *p510*
Loveritt, William; America, 1731 ***1220.12*** *p510*
Lovett, Henry; America, 1747 ***1220.12*** *p510*
Lovett, John; Maryland or Virginia, 1738 ***1220.12*** *p510*
Lovett, Mary; America, 1759 ***1220.12*** *p510*
Lovett, Rachel; Washington, D.C., 1796-1836 ***9228.50*** *p425*
Lovett, Thomas 15; Quebec, 1870 ***8364.32*** *p24*
Lovett, Whipple H. 38; Ontario, 1871 ***1823.21*** *p207*
Lovett, William; America, 1760 ***1220.12*** *p510*
Lovett, William; Annapolis, MD, 1733 ***1220.12*** *p510*
Lovey, John; Virginia, 1730 ***1220.12*** *p510*
Lovgren, Eva Lovisa; St. Paul, MN, 1869 ***1865.50*** *p96*
Lovgren, John; St. Paul, MN, 1868 ***1865.50*** *p96*
Loving, Richard; Virginia, 1756 ***1220.12*** *p510*
Lovinguth, Joseph; Illinois, 1834-1900 ***6020.5*** *p132*
Lovis, Rachel; Washington, D.C., 1796-1836 ***9228.50*** *p425*
Lovlel, John; Boston, 1760-1769 ***9228.50*** *p411*
Lovless, George 38; Ontario, 1871 ***1823.21*** *p207*
Lovless, George 74; Ontario, 1871 ***1823.21*** *p207*
Lovyer, Daniel; America, 1752 ***1220.12*** *p510*
Low, Addison; Baton Rouge, LA, 1781 ***8529.30*** *p9A*
Low, Anne; Annapolis, MD, 1723 ***1220.12*** *p511*
Low, Benjamin; Maryland, 1742 ***1220.12*** *p511*
Low, Edmund; America, 1747 ***1220.12*** *p511*
Low, Elizabeth; America, 1698 ***1220.12*** *p511*
Low, Francis; America, 1687 ***1220.12*** *p511*
Low, Jane; Virginia, 1739 ***1220.12*** *p511*
Low, Johann Adam; America, 1771 ***2526.42*** *p183*
With wife & 3 children
Low, Johann Leonhard; America, 1886 ***2526.43*** *p219*
Low, John; America, 1743 ***1220.12*** *p511*
Low, John; America, 1749 ***1220.12*** *p511*
Low, John; America, 1758 ***1220.12*** *p511*
Low, John; Maryland, 1742 ***1220.12*** *p511*
Low, Mary; America, 1729 ***1220.12*** *p511*
Low, Mary; America, 1743 ***1220.12*** *p511*
Low, Mary; America, 1749 ***1220.12*** *p511*
Low, Mary; America, 1754 ***1220.12*** *p511*
Low, Mary; America, 1766 ***1220.12*** *p511*
Low, Samuel; America, 1752 ***1220.12*** *p511*
Low, Thomas; America, 1748 ***1220.12*** *p511*
Low, Thomas; America, 1763 ***1220.12*** *p511*
Low, Thomas; Massachusetts, 1650 ***9228.50*** *p411*
Low, William; Marston's Wharf, 1782 ***8529.30*** *p13*
Low, Zachariah; New York, 1775 ***8529.30*** *p13*
Lowack, Adolph; Valdivia, Chile, 1850 ***1192.4*** *p49*
Lowback, Christian; North Carolina, 1809 ***1088.45*** *p20*
Lowberg, Charles; North Carolina, 1849 ***1088.45*** *p20*
Lowbridge, John; America, 1758 ***1220.12*** *p511*
Low Brothers, . . .; Ontario, 1800-1899 ***9228.50*** *p411*
Lowcross, Martha; Annapolis, MD, 1733 ***1220.12*** *p511*
Lowden, Michael; America, 1771 ***1220.12*** *p511*
Lowdensledge, Frederick; North Carolina, 1841 ***1088.45*** *p20*
Lowder, Elizabeth; Virginia, 1739 ***1220.12*** *p511*
Lowder, James 20; Virginia, 1635 ***1183.3*** *p30*
Lowder, Richard; America, 1748 ***1220.12*** *p511*
Lowe, Ann; Maryland, 1674 ***1236.25*** *p50*
Lowe, Anna Catharine *SEE* Lowe, James
Lowe, Anne; Barbados, 1673 ***1220.12*** *p511*
Lowe, Barbara; Maryland, 1674-1675 ***1236.25*** *p51*
Lowe, David; Washington, 1889 ***2770.40*** *p79*
Lowe, Elizabeth; Annapolis, MD, 1721 ***1220.12*** *p511*
Lowe, Francis; Barbados or Jamaica, 1688 ***1220.12*** *p511*
Lowe, Fredrika; Colorado, 1897 ***1029.59*** *p56*
Lowe, George; Maryland, 1751 ***1220.12*** *p511*
Lowe, Henry *SEE* Lowe, James
Lowe, James; America, 1741 ***1220.12*** *p511*
Lowe, James; Philadelphia, 1867 ***8513.31*** *p324*
*Wife:*Mary Fawcett
*Daughter:*Anna Catharine
*Daughter:*Mary Josephine
*Son:*Patrick James
*Son:*Henry
Lowe, John; America, 1721 ***1220.12*** *p511*
Lowe, John; America, 1764 ***1220.12*** *p511*
Lowe, John; America, 1767 ***1220.12*** *p511*
Lowe, John; Annapolis, MD, 1720 ***1220.12*** *p511*
Lowe, John; Barbados or Jamaica, 1690 ***1220.12*** *p511*
Lowe, John; Ohio, 1809-1852 ***4511.35*** *p31*
Lowe, John 17; Ontario, 1871 ***1823.21*** *p207*
Lowe, Joseph; America, 1773 ***1220.12*** *p511*
Lowe, Mary Fawcett *SEE* Lowe, James
Lowe, Mary Josephine *SEE* Lowe, James
Lowe, Patrick James *SEE* Lowe, James
Lowe, Richard 40; Ontario, 1871 ***1823.21*** *p207*
Lowe, Robert; America, 1732 ***1220.12*** *p511*
Lowe, Rosanna; America, 1767 ***1220.12*** *p511*
Lowe, Samuel; America, 1773 ***1220.12*** *p511*
Lowe, Samuel; New York, 1775 ***8529.30*** *p3*
Lowe, Sarah; America, 1775 ***1220.12*** *p511*
Lowe, Theo; Colorado, 1862-1920 ***1029.59*** *p56*
Lowe, Theodore; Denver, CO, 1891 ***1029.59*** *p56*
Lowe, Thomas; America, 1722 ***1220.12*** *p511*
Lowe, Thomas 27; Indiana, 1870-1876 ***9076.20*** *p69*
Lowe, Thomas George 35; Ontario, 1871 ***1823.21*** *p207*
Lowe, William; America, 1771 ***1220.12*** *p511*
Lowe, William; America, 1773 ***1220.12*** *p511*
Lowe, William H.; Ohio, 1868 ***3580.20*** *p32*
Lowe, William H.; Ohio, 1868 ***6020.12*** *p13*
Lowell, Edward 15; Quebec, 1870 ***8364.32*** *p24*
Lowell, John; America, 1766 ***1220.12*** *p511*
Lowenberg, Benedix; North Carolina, 1854 ***1088.45*** *p20*
Lowenberg, Esther 36; New York, NY, 1894 ***6512.1*** *p232*
Lowenberg, Lipmann 40; New York, NY, 1894 ***6512.1*** *p232*
Lowenberg, Sarah 16; New York, NY, 1894 ***6512.1*** *p232*
Lowenberg, Solomon 13; New York, NY, 1894 ***6512.1*** *p232*
Lowenborg, Oscar; Colorado, 1883 ***1029.59*** *p56*
Lowenhaupt, Carl; America, 1854 ***7420.1*** *p124*
Lowenstein, L.; North Carolina, 1850 ***1088.45*** *p20*
Lower, Conrad Wilhelm; America, 1882 ***7420.1*** *p330*
Lower, Jacob; Ohio, 1809-1852 ***4511.35*** *p31*
Lower, John; Philadelphia, 1839 ***5720.10*** *p378*
Lower, Justus Heinrich Conrad; Chicago, 1892 ***7420.1*** *p366*
Lowers, Hans; New York, 1860 ***358.56*** *p150*
Lowerson, Mr.; Canada, 1775 ***3036.5*** *p67*
Lowerson, Mary; Canada, 1775 ***3036.5*** *p67*
Lowerson, Richard; Canada, 1774 ***3036.5*** *p41*
Lowery, Horatio; North Carolina, 1848 ***1088.45*** *p20*
Lowery, James 48; Ontario, 1871 ***1823.17*** *p94*
Lowery, William 35; Ontario, 1871 ***1823.17*** *p94*
Lowes, John; America, 1732 ***1220.12*** *p511*
Lowin, Thomas; Maryland, 1741 ***1220.12*** *p511*
Lowman, Bernard; America, 1685 ***1220.12*** *p512*
Lowman, Michael; America, 1755 ***1220.12*** *p512*
Lown, Fredrick 74; Ontario, 1871 ***1823.21*** *p207*
Lownde, John; America, 1756 ***1220.12*** *p512*
Lowndes, Elizabeth; America, 1687 ***1220.12*** *p512*
Lowrey, Catherine Myers *SEE* Lowrey, Michael
Lowrey, John *SEE* Lowrey, Michael
Lowrey, Michael; Halifax, N.S., 1827 ***7009.9*** *p61*
*Father:*John
*Mother:*Catherine Myers
Lowrey, William 38; Ontario, 1871 ***1823.17*** *p94*
Lowrie, Alexander 32; Ontario, 1871 ***1823.17*** *p94*
Lowrie, Alexander 60; Ontario, 1871 ***1823.21*** *p207*
Lowrie, Alexr 38; Ontario, 1871 ***1823.17*** *p94*
Lowrie, Eliza 44; Ontario, 1871 ***1823.21*** *p207*
Lowrie, Jane 40; Ontario, 1871 ***1823.17*** *p94*
Lowrie, John 25; Ontario, 1871 ***1823.21*** *p207*
Lowrie, John 39; Ontario, 1871 ***1823.17*** *p94*
Lowrie, John 62; Ontario, 1871 ***1823.21*** *p207*
Lowrie, Joseph 41; Ontario, 1871 ***1823.17*** *p94*
Lowry, Mr.; Canada, 1775 ***3036.5*** *p67*
Lowry, Ann; America, 1769 ***1220.12*** *p512*
Lowry, Catherine; America, 1746 ***1220.12*** *p512*
Lowry, Edward; America, 1746 ***1220.12*** *p512*
Lowry, Edward; America, 1750 ***1220.12*** *p512*
Lowry, George; America, 1749 ***1220.12*** *p512*
Lowry, Malcolm; Ohio, 1853 ***3580.20*** *p32*
Lowry, Malcolm; Ohio, 1853 ***6020.12*** *p13*
Lowry, Mary; Canada, 1775 ***3036.5*** *p67*
Lowry, Roger; America, 1736 ***1220.12*** *p512*
Lowry, William; North Carolina, 1827 ***1088.45*** *p20*
Lowson, John; America, 1762 ***1220.12*** *p512*
Lowth, James; America, 1748 ***1220.12*** *p512*
Lowther, Gawil; Ohio, 1840 ***3580.20*** *p32*
Lowther, Gawil; Ohio, 1840 ***6020.12*** *p13*
Lowther, John; Barbados, 1699 ***1220.12*** *p512*
Lowther, Richard 47; Ontario, 1871 ***1823.21*** *p207*
Lowther, Robert; America, 1724 ***1220.12*** *p512*
Lowther, Robert; Jamaica, 1777 ***8529.30*** *p13A*
Lowther, Sarah; America, 1747 ***1220.12*** *p512*
Lowther, William; America, 1765 ***1220.12*** *p512*
Lowthier, Mary; Canada, 1774 ***3036.5*** *p42*
Loxet, Amb. 38; America, 1842 ***778.6*** *p219*
Loxham, Elizabeth; America, 1767 ***1220.12*** *p512*
Loxley, Charles 61; Ontario, 1871 ***1823.21*** *p207*
Loy, Matthias; Ohio, 1840-1897 ***8365.35*** *p17*
Loyacano, Michele; Louisiana, 1874-1875 ***4981.45*** *p29*
Loyal, George 40; Ontario, 1871 ***1823.21*** *p207*
Loyce, Nicho.; Maryland, 1674-1675 ***1236.25*** *p51*
Loyd, Cath; New Orleans, 1851 ***7242.30*** *p148*
Loyd, David; Maryland, 1742 ***1220.12*** *p505*
Loyd, Elizabeth; Virginia, 1767 ***1220.12*** *p505*
Loyd, H. C. 31; Ontario, 1871 ***1823.21*** *p207*
Loyd, Jane; America, 1727 ***1220.12*** *p505*
Loyd, John; America, 1727 ***1220.12*** *p505*
Loyd, John; America, 1767 ***1220.12*** *p505*
Loyd, Joseph; Virginia, 1766 ***1220.12*** *p505*
Loyd, Owen 46; Ontario, 1871 ***1823.21*** *p207*
Loyd, Theophilus; America, 1742 ***1220.12*** *p506*
Loyd, Thomas 41; Ontario, 1871 ***1823.21*** *p207*
Loyd, William 50; Ontario, 1871 ***1823.21*** *p207*
Loyer, Guillaume; Quebec, 1648 ***9221.17*** *p201*
Loyer, Guillaume 26; Quebec, 1659 ***9221.17*** *p406*
Loyer, Jacques 23; Quebec, 1646 ***9221.17*** *p167*
Loynel, Mr. 21; America, 1745 ***778.6*** *p219*
Loynes, John J. 42; Ontario, 1871 ***1823.21*** *p207*
Loynes, Samuel 49; Ontario, 1871 ***1823.21*** *p207*
Loyseau, Andre 24; Quebec, 1654 ***9221.17*** *p313*
Loyseau, Catherine 43; Quebec, 1646 ***9221.17*** *p169*
Loyseau, Jacques 28; Quebec, 1647 ***9221.17*** *p184*
Loysel, Louis 29; Montreal, 1647 ***9221.17*** *p192*
Loze, Mr. 35; America, 1846 ***778.6*** *p219*
Lozier, Guillaume; Quebec, 1640 ***9221.17*** *p98*
Lozier, Jacques 20; Quebec, 1653 ***9221.17*** *p277*
Lozowski, Mr.; Detroit, 1929-1930 ***6214.5*** *p69*
Luan, Nai; Missouri, 1900 ***3276.1*** *p2*
Luan, Nai; Missouri, 1900 ***3276.1*** *p4*
Luard, Alfred 39; Ontario, 1871 ***1823.21*** *p207*
Lubbe, Friedrich; America, 1844 ***7420.1*** *p32*
Lubbe, Heinrich Friedrich Conrad; America, 1870 ***7420.1*** *p284*
Lubcke, Johann Heinrich Ernst; Port uncertain, 1855 ***7420.1*** *p138*
Luben, Ernest.n 3; America, 1846 ***778.6*** *p219*
Luben, J. 30; New Orleans, 1846 ***778.6*** *p219*
Lubert, Madelaine 26; Louisiana, 1848 ***778.6*** *p219*
Lubert, Marie 6 months; Louisiana, 1848 ***778.6*** *p219*
Lubert, Victor 29; Louisiana, 1848 ***778.6*** *p219*
Lubin, Ernest.n 3; America, 1846 ***778.6*** *p219*
Lubin, J. 30; New Orleans, 1846 ***778.6*** *p219*
Lubinsky, J.; Galveston, TX, 1855 ***571.7*** *p18*
Lubitz, Henriette; Wisconsin, 1907 ***6795.8*** *p177*
Lubke, Catharine Engel Dorothee Charl.; America, 1866 ***7420.1*** *p246*
Lubke, Engel Marie; Port uncertain, 1840 ***7420.1*** *p20*
Lubke, Johann; America, 1860 ***7420.1*** *p195*
Lubke, Johann; America, 1872 ***7420.1*** *p296*
Lubke, Johann Heinrich; America, 1860 ***7420.1*** *p195*
Lubke, Johann Heinrich Conrad; America, 1860 ***7420.1*** *p195*

Lubke, Johann Heinrich Ernst; America, 1855 ***7420.1*** *p138*
Lubke, Johann Otto Christoph; America, 1857 ***7420.1*** *p166*
Lubking, . . .; America, 1845 ***7420.1*** *p38*
Lubking, Carl Heinrich; America, 1850 ***7420.1*** *p73*
Lubow, H.; New York, 1859 ***358.56*** *p100*
Luby, Dennis; Illinois, 1834-1900 ***6020.5*** *p132*
Luc, Helene; California, 1906 ***3276.8*** *p20*
Lucadou, Jean; Virginia, 1700 ***9230.15*** *p81*
With wife
Lucas, . . .; Quebec, 1642 ***9221.17*** *p119*
Lucas, Ann; America, 1757 ***1220.12*** *p512*
Lucas, Anne; Quebec, 1665 ***4514.3*** *p277*
Lucas, Catherine; Virginia, 1735 ***1220.12*** *p512*
Lucas, Charles; America, 1685 ***1220.12*** *p512*
Lucas, Charles 27; New Orleans, 1748 ***778.6*** *p219*
Lucas, Edouard 28; Port uncertain, 1840 ***778.6*** *p219*
Lucas, Elie 27; Texas, 1848 ***778.6*** *p219*
Lucas, Elizabeth; Rappahannock, VA, 1728 ***1220.12*** *p512*
Lucas, Francisco 36; New Orleans, 1841 ***778.6*** *p219*
Lucas, G. M.; Louisiana, 1836-1841 ***4981.45*** *p209*
Lucas, George; America, 1769 ***1220.12*** *p512*
Lucas, H. G. 49; Ontario, 1871 ***1823.21*** *p207*
Lucas, Jacqueline 30; Quebec, 1647 ***9221.17*** *p174*
Lucas, Jacques; Quebec, 1653 ***9221.17*** *p277*
Lucas, James; America, 1772 ***1220.12*** *p512*
Lucas, James 30; Ontario, 1871 ***1823.21*** *p207*
Lucas, James 41; Ontario, 1871 ***1823.17*** *p94*
Lucas, James 67; Ontario, 1871 ***1823.17*** *p94*
Lucas, Jasper; Barbados or Jamaica, 1702 ***1220.12*** *p512*
Lucas, Jean 24; Louisiana, 1848 ***778.6*** *p219*
Lucas, John; America, 1755 ***1220.12*** *p512*
Lucas, John; California, 1800-1899 ***9228.50*** *p411*
Lucas, Jonas 29; Ontario, 1871 ***1823.17*** *p94*
Lucas, Jonathan; Ohio, 1836 ***2763.1*** *p20*
Lucas, Joseph; America, 1735 ***1220.12*** *p512*
Lucas, Joseph; America, 1749 ***1220.12*** *p512*
Lucas, Leland; Tucson, AZ, n.d. ***9228.50*** *p411*
Lucas, Louis 23; Louisiana, 1848 ***778.6*** *p219*
Lucas, Marie; Newport, RI, 1696-1698 ***9228.50*** *p348*
Lucas, Mary; America, 1759 ***1220.12*** *p512*
Lucas, Nicholas; America, 1665 ***1220.12*** *p512*
Lucas, Peter; Detroit, 1930 ***1640.60*** *p77*
Lucas, Peter; Potomac, 1729 ***1220.12*** *p512*
Lucas, Rachael; America, 1754 ***1220.12*** *p512*
Lucas, Richard; America, 1775 ***1220.12*** *p512*
Lucas, Robert; America, 1740 ***1220.12*** *p512*
Lucas, Sarah; America, 1733 ***1220.12*** *p512*
Lucas, Stephen; America, 1775 ***1220.12*** *p512*
Lucas, Susan; Barbados, 1694 ***1220.12*** *p512*
Lucas, Tho; Jamestown, VA, 1633 ***1658.20*** *p211*
Lucas, Thomas; America, 1761 ***1220.12*** *p513*
Lucas, Thomas; America, 1771 ***1220.12*** *p513*
Lucas, Thomas; Charles Town, SC, 1719 ***1220.12*** *p512*
Lucas, Thomas; Maryland, 1719 ***1220.12*** *p512*
Lucas, Thomas; Toronto, 1844 ***2910.35*** *p115*
Lucas, Thomas; Virginia, 1740 ***1220.12*** *p512*
Lucas, William; America, 1769 ***1220.12*** *p513*
Lucas, William; Died enroute, 1734 ***1220.12*** *p513*
Lucas, William; New York, 1782 ***8529.30*** *p13*
Lucas, William; Ohio, 1809-1852 ***4511.35*** *p31*
Lucas, William; Potomac, 1729 ***1220.12*** *p513*
Lucas, William; Virginia, 1764 ***1220.12*** *p513*
Lucas, William James 42; Ontario, 1871 ***1823.21*** *p207*
Lucaut, Leonard; Montreal, 1642 ***9221.17*** *p124*
Lucci, Sam; Minnesota, 1923 ***2769.54*** *p1383*
Lucci, Mrs. Sam; Minnesota, 1923 ***2769.54*** *p1383*
Luce, . . .; Boston, 1769 ***9228.50*** *p5*
Luce, Mr. 31; Port uncertain, 1840 ***778.6*** *p219*
Luce, Alexander; Portsmouth, NH, 1700-1740 ***9228.50*** *p412*
Luce, Donald; British Columbia, 1955 ***9228.50*** *p412*
Luce, Edward; Boston, 1715 ***9228.50*** *p412*
Luce, Frank; Maine, 1869-1919 ***9228.50*** *p412*
Luce, John; Wisconsin, 1920-1924 ***9228.50*** *p412*
Luce, Joseph; Boston, 1769 ***9228.50*** *p48*
Luce, Joseph; Boston, 1769 ***9228.50*** *p412*
Luce, Marie Genevieve; Bangor, ME, 1865-1920 ***9228.50*** *p412*
Luce, Philippe; Quebec, 1845 ***9228.50*** *p411*
Luce, Seth 63; Ontario, 1871 ***1823.21*** *p207*
Luce Children, . . .; Quebec, 1845-1880 ***9228.50*** *p412*
Lucey, James; America, 1752 ***1220.12*** *p513*
Luch, Luke 36; New Orleans, 1845 ***778.6*** *p219*
Luch, Martin 36; New Orleans, 1845 ***778.6*** *p219*
Luchi, Guisseppe 28; New York, NY, 1894 ***6512.1*** *p230*
Lucius, Peter; Ohio, 1809-1852 ***4511.35*** *p31*
Luck, Adolph 4; Halifax, N.S., 1902 ***1860.4*** *p39*
Luck, August 6; Halifax, N.S., 1902 ***1860.4*** *p39*
Luck, Augusta 39; Halifax, N.S., 1902 ***1860.4*** *p39*
Luck, Bertha Mene L.; Wisconsin, 1897 ***6795.8*** *p85*
Luck, Catherine; Virginia, 1727 ***1220.12*** *p513*
Luck, Georg Otto; Pittsburgh, 1880 ***5475.1*** *p64*
Luck, George; America, 1738 ***1220.12*** *p513*
Luck, Henrietta 1; Halifax, N.S., 1902 ***1860.4*** *p39*
Luck, Julian 15; Halifax, N.S., 1902 ***1860.4*** *p39*
Luck, Mary; Virginia, 1727 ***1220.12*** *p513*
Luck, Peter; America, 1752 ***1220.12*** *p513*
Lucke, Dorothea Louise Friederike; America, 1857 ***7420.1*** *p166*
Lucke, Giles; Barbados, 1702 ***1220.12*** *p513*
Lucke, Herman; North Carolina, 1856 ***1088.45*** *p20*
Lucke, Louise Charlotte Henriette; America, 1860 ***7420.1*** *p195*
Luckes, Thomas; America, 1761 ***1220.12*** *p513*
Luckey, Isabella; Virginia, 1726 ***1220.12*** *p513*
Luckhardt, Adam; Illinois, 1858 ***6079.1*** *p9*
Luckhurst, William; America, 1750 ***1220.12*** *p513*
Lucki, Michael; Detroit, 1929-1930 ***6214.5*** *p61*
Luckis, John; Barbados, 1681 ***1220.12*** *p512*
Luckis, Richard; Barbados, 1679 ***1220.12*** *p512*
Luckmann, . . .; Valdivia, Chile, 1852 ***1192.4*** *p56*
Luckston, Fred 25; Ontario, 1871 ***1823.21*** *p207*
Lucocke, Adam; America, 1681 ***1220.12*** *p513*
Lucon, Walter 19; Quebec, 1870 ***8364.32*** *p24*
Lucos, Catherine; Quebec, 1671 ***4514.3*** *p343*
Lucy, Daniel 58; Ontario, 1871 ***1823.21*** *p207*
Lucy, Franz Nicolas 29; Port uncertain, 1847 ***778.6*** *p220*
Lucy, Georg 3; Port uncertain, 1847 ***778.6*** *p220*
Lucy, Jean 1; Port uncertain, 1847 ***778.6*** *p220*
Lucy, Margaretha 33; Port uncertain, 1847 ***778.6*** *p220*
Lucy, Peter 33; Port uncertain, 1847 ***778.6*** *p220*
Lucy, William; America, 1766 ***1220.12*** *p513*
Ludbrooke, Sarah; America, 1772 ***1220.12*** *p513*
Ludde, Daniel; Illinois, 1853 ***6079.1*** *p9*
Luddington, Thomas; America, 1754 ***1220.12*** *p513*
Ludeke, Johann Heinrich; America, 1860 ***7420.1*** *p196*
Ludeking, . . .; America, 1883 ***7420.1*** *p337*
*Wife:*Sophie Caroline Ernestine Preul
*Grandson:*Friedrich Simon
*Daughter:*Caroline Friederike Charlotte
*Son:*Hermann Friedrich Wilhelm
Ludeking, Carl August *SEE* Ludeking, Hermann Heinrich
Ludeking, Caroline Friederike Charlotte *SEE* Ludeking, . . .
Ludeking, Friedrich Simon *SEE* Ludeking, . . .
Ludeking, Heinrich Friedrich *SEE* Ludeking, Hermann Heinrich
Ludeking, Hermann Friedrich Wilhelm *SEE* Ludeking, . . .
Ludeking, Hermann Heinrich; America, 1883 ***7420.1*** *p338*
*Wife:*Wilhelmine Charlotte Christoph
*Son:*Carl August
*Son:*Heinrich Friedrich
Ludeking, Sophie Caroline Ernestine Preul *SEE* Ludeking, . . .
Ludeking, Wilhelmine Charlotte Christoph *SEE* Ludeking, Hermann Heinrich
Luderin, Bart. 28; America, 1847 ***778.6*** *p220*
Luderin, Catherine 22; America, 1847 ***778.6*** *p220*
Luders, Frederick; Philadelphia, 1859 ***8513.31*** *p324*
*Wife:*Lisette Brunnett
Luders, Karl; America, 1848 ***7420.1*** *p60*
Luders, Lisette Brunnett *SEE* Luders, Frederick
Ludewing, Engel Justine Charlotte *SEE* Ludewing, Friedrich Wilhelm
Ludewing, Engel Marie Eleonore Oltrogge *SEE* Ludewing, Friedrich Wilhelm
Ludewing, Friedrich Wilhelm; America, 1869 ***7420.1*** *p280*
*Wife:*Engel Marie Eleonore Oltrogge
*Daughter:*Engel Justine Charlotte
Ludewing, Heinrich Ludwig; America, 1865 ***7420.1*** *p233*
Ludewing, Johann Heinrich Wilhelm; America, 1861 ***7420.1*** *p207*
Ludford, Francis; America, 1743 ***1220.12*** *p513*
Ludgater, Mary; America, 1700 ***1220.12*** *p513*
Luding, Barbara 18; Missouri, 1845 ***778.6*** *p220*
Luding, Eve 15; Missouri, 1845 ***778.6*** *p220*
Luding, Jacob 48; Missouri, 1845 ***778.6*** *p220*
Luding, Louis 6; Missouri, 1845 ***778.6*** *p220*
Luding, Marguerite 30; Missouri, 1845 ***778.6*** *p220*
Luding, Michel 10; Missouri, 1845 ***778.6*** *p220*
Luding, Michel 50; Missouri, 1845 ***778.6*** *p220*
Luding, Theobald 2; Missouri, 1845 ***778.6*** *p220*
Ludkins, John; America, 1759 ***1220.12*** *p513*
Ludlam, Thomas; America, 1759 ***1220.12*** *p513*
Ludloff, John; Illinois, 1852 ***6079.1*** *p9*
Ludlow, George; Massachusetts, 1630 ***117.5*** *p152*
Ludlow, Henry; America, 1768 ***1220.12*** *p513*
Ludlow, Jonathan *SEE* Ludlow, Roger
Ludlow, Mary *SEE* Ludlow, Roger
Ludlow, Richard; America, 1771 ***1220.12*** *p513*
Ludlow, Roger; Massachusetts, 1630 ***117.5*** *p152*
*Wife:*Mary
*Son:*Jonathan
Ludlowe, John; Barbados, 1669 ***1220.12*** *p513*
Ludly, William; America, 1774 ***1220.12*** *p513*
Ludveg, Catherine 8; Mississippi, 1845-1846 ***778.6*** *p220*
Ludveg, Francisca 18; Mississippi, 1845-1846 ***778.6*** *p220*
Ludveg, Francois 40; Mississippi, 1845-1846 ***778.6*** *p220*
Ludveg, Marie 22; Mississippi, 1845-1846 ***778.6*** *p220*
Ludveg, Resine 6; Mississippi, 1845-1846 ***778.6*** *p220*
Ludveg, Therese 44; Mississippi, 1845-1846 ***778.6*** *p220*
Ludvik, Boh.; New York, NY, 1893 ***2853.20*** *p469*
Ludvik, Frantisek; New York, NY, 1893 ***2853.20*** *p469*
Ludvikova, Bohumila; New York, NY, 1893 ***2853.20*** *p469*
Ludwiczewska, Mary; Detroit, 1890 ***9980.23*** *p97*
Ludwig, A. Maria 48; Rio Grande do Sul, Brazil, 1872 ***5475.1*** *p249*
Ludwig, Anna Lux *SEE* Ludwig, Nik.
Ludwig, Barbara Hargarten 49 *SEE* Ludwig, Nikolaus
Ludwig, Carl Otto; Wisconsin, 1898 ***6795.8*** *p107*
Ludwig, Elisabeth; America, 1881 ***5475.1*** *p302*
Ludwig, Elisabeth 25; America, 1864 ***5475.1*** *p248*
Ludwig, Elisabetha 47; America, 1854 ***2526.43*** *p152*
Ludwig, Felix 5; Galveston, TX, 1844 ***3967.10*** *p372*
Ludwig, Franz 38; Galveston, TX, 1846 ***3967.10*** *p378*
Ludwig, Jacob; Ohio, 1840-1897 ***8365.35*** *p17*
Ludwig, Joh. Jakob; Chicago, 1882 ***5475.1*** *p406*
Ludwig, Joh. Peter 63; America, 1843 ***5475.1*** *p258*
Ludwig, Johann; America, 1843 ***5475.1*** *p312*
Ludwig, Johann 39; Chicago, 1880 ***5475.1*** *p240*
Ludwig, Mrs. Johann; America, 1846 ***5475.1*** *p234*
Ludwig, Johann Hermann; America, 1885 ***5475.1*** *p407*
Ludwig, John; Ohio, 1809-1852 ***4511.35*** *p31*
Ludwig, Josef *SEE* Ludwig, Nik.
Ludwig, Joseph 14; Galveston, TX, 1846 ***3967.10*** *p378*
Ludwig, Josephine 1; Galveston, TX, 1844 ***3967.10*** *p372*
Ludwig, Josephine 11 months; Galveston, TX, 1846 ***3967.10*** *p378*
Ludwig, Kath.; Brazil, 1874 ***5475.1*** *p371*
Ludwig, Magdalene; America, 1883 ***5475.1*** *p303*
*Son:*Michel
*Son:*Johann
*Son:*Nikolaus
*Son:*Peter
Ludwig, Marianne 47; Galveston, TX, 1846 ***3967.10*** *p378*
Ludwig, Mathias; America, 1865-1870 ***5475.1*** *p404*
Ludwig, Mathias; America, 1881 ***5475.1*** *p302*
Ludwig, Michel 35; America, 1847 ***5475.1*** *p234*
With wife
With 3 children
Ludwig, Nik.; America, 1881 ***5475.1*** *p285*
*Wife:*Anna Lux
*Son:*Josef
Ludwig, Nikolaus; America, 1854 ***5475.1*** *p235*
Ludwig, Nikolaus 52; America, 1873 ***5475.1*** *p307*
*Wife:*Barbara Hargarten 49
*Son:*Peter 5
Ludwig, Peter; America, 1881 ***5475.1*** *p250*
Ludwig, Peter 5 *SEE* Ludwig, Nikolaus
Ludwig, Pierre 35; America, 1746 ***778.6*** *p220*
Ludwig, Rosine 28; Galveston, TX, 1844 ***3967.10*** *p372*
Ludwig, Zacharias 30; Galveston, TX, 1844 ***3967.10*** *p372*
Luebeck, Anthony; New Jersey, 1777 ***8529.30*** *p6*
Luebke, August; Wisconsin, 1883 ***6795.8*** *p83*
Luebke, Eduart Hermann Ernst; Wisconsin, 1888 ***6795.8*** *p227*
Luebkert, William H.; Colorado, 1894 ***1029.59*** *p56*
Luebkert, William H.; Colorado, 1899 ***1029.59*** *p56*
Luebkert, Wm. H.; Colorado, 1894 ***1029.59*** *p56*
Luebking, W. F.; Ohio, 1840-1897 ***8365.35*** *p17*
Luechon, Charles; Louisiana, 1874 ***4981.45*** *p132*
Lueck, Gottlieb; Wisconsin, 1858 ***6795.8*** *p25*
Lueck, Hermann August Theodor; Wisconsin, 1871 ***6795.8*** *p83*
Lueders, Heinrich Hanz George; Wisconsin, 1888 ***6795.8*** *p96*
Luedtke, August; Iowa, 1902 ***1211.15*** *p16*
Luedtke, Friedrich; Wisconsin, 1893 ***6795.8*** *p128*
Luedtke, Johann; Wisconsin, 1883 ***6795.8*** *p30*
Luehrs, Johannes Klaus; Iowa, 1930 ***1211.15*** *p16*
Luelling, Samuel; Annapolis, MD, 1735 ***1220.12*** *p504*
Luem, Katharina; Venezuela, 1843 ***3899.5*** *p545*
Luendgren, Nathaniel; Havana, 1782 ***8529.30*** *p9A*
Lueptow, Franz; Wisconsin, 1892 ***6795.8*** *p86*
Luer, Jque. Fois. 31; Missouri, 1848 ***778.6*** *p220*
Luers, Joachim Joham Conrad; North Carolina, 1855 ***1088.45*** *p20*
Luesdorf, Philip; Ohio, 1809-1852 ***4511.35*** *p31*

286 *FOR A COMPLETE EXPLANATION OF ENTRY, SEE "HOW TO READ A CITATION" SECTION*

Luetkens, H. D.; Valdivia, Chile, 1851 *1192.4 p51*
Luff, John; Rappahannock, VA, 1728 *1220.12 p513*
Luff, Robert; America, 1752 *1220.12 p513*
Luffe, John; America, 1772 *1220.12 p513*
Luffe, Richard; Barbados, 1672 *1220.12 p513*
Luft, Adam 17 *SEE* Luft, Leonhard
Luft, Adam; Illinois, 1856 *6079.1 p9*
Luft, Agathe 15 *SEE* Luft, Balthasar
Luft, Anna Maria 13 *SEE* Luft, Leonhard
Luft, Anna Marie 16 *SEE* Luft, Balthasar
Luft, Augusta; Kansas, 1917-1918 *2094.25 p50*
Luft, Balthasar; America, 1854 *2526.42 p200*
  With wife
  *Daughter:*Agathe
  *Daughter:*Margaretha
  *Daughter:*Gertrude
  *Son:*Johannes
  *Daughter:*Anna Marie
  *Son:*Balthasar
Luft, Balthasar 21 *SEE* Luft, Balthasar
Luft, Balthasar 24 *SEE* Luft, Leonhard
Luft, Friedrich 22 *SEE* Luft, Leonhard
Luft, Georg Philipp; America, 1868 *2526.43 p130*
Luft, Gertraud 17 *SEE* Luft, Leonhard
Luft, Gertrude 6 *SEE* Luft, Balthasar
Luft, Jacob; Illinois, 1856 *6079.1 p9*
Luft, Jakob; America, 1840 *2526.42 p125*
  With wife & 6 children
Luft, Jakob; America, 1868 *2526.43 p130*
Luft, Johann Leonhard; America, 1868 *2526.43 p130*
Luft, Johannes; America, 1883 *2526.43 p130*
Luft, Johannes 1 *SEE* Luft, Balthasar
Luft, John; Kansas, 1917-1918 *2094.25 p50*
Luft, Katharina Ruck 54 *SEE* Luft, Leonhard
Luft, Leonard; Illinois, 1858 *6079.1 p9*
Luft, Leonhard; America, 1854 *2526.42 p200*
  With wife
  *Daughter:*Gertraud
  *Daughter:*Anna Maria
  *Son:*Martin
  *Son:*Balthasar
Luft, Leonhard; America, 1857 *2526.43 p204*
Luft, Leonhard 15 *SEE* Luft, Leonhard
Luft, Leonhard 53; America, 1857 *2526.43 p198*
  *Wife:*Katharina Ruck 54
  *Son:*Leonhard 15
  *Daughter:*Luise 24
  *Son:*Adam 17
  *Son:*Friedrich 22
Luft, Luise 24 *SEE* Luft, Leonhard
Luft, Margaretha 8 *SEE* Luft, Balthasar
Luft, Martin 15 *SEE* Luft, Leonhard
Lugas, Francois 37; New Orleans, 1848 *778.6 p220*
Lugenbuehl, Gotleib; Ohio, 1809-1852 *4511.35 p31*
Lugenbuhl, Caleb; Ohio, 1809-1852 *4511.35 p31*
Lugenbuhl, Christian; Ohio, 1809-1852 *4511.35 p31*
Lugerat, Antoine 14 *SEE* Lugerat, Pierre
Lugerat, Jean; Montreal, 1649 *9221.17 p221*
Lugerat, Jeanne Crespeau Regnault 43 *SEE* Lugerat, Pierre
Lugerat, Pierre 49; Montreal, 1659 *9221.17 p424*
  *Wife:*Jeanne Crespeau Regnault 43
  *Son:*Antoine 14
Lugert, Johannes 21; New York, NY, 1893 *1883.7 p37*
Lugert, Veronika 20; New York, NY, 1893 *1883.7 p37*
Lugg, Edward; America, 1685 *1220.12 p513*
Lugg, Henry; Colorado, 1903 *1029.59 p57*
Lugg, Henry 26; Colorado, 1873 *1029.59 p57*
Luggervan, Thomas; America, 1729 *1220.12 p513*
Lugil, John; Ohio, 1809-1852 *4511.35 p31*
Luhmann, Friederike Wilhelmine; Kansas, 1882 *7420.1 p330*
Luhmann, Friedrich Wilhelm; America, 1896 *7420.1 p372*
Luhmann, Friedrich Wilhelm; Kansas, 1883 *7420.1 p338*
Luhmann, Johann Friedrich Gottlieb; Port uncertain, 1857 *7420.1 p166*
Luhta, Mrs. Oscar 39; Minnesota, 1923 *2769.54 p1378*
Luin, Ann; St. John, N.B., 1842 *2978.20 p7*
Luin, Margaret; St. John, N.B., 1842 *2978.20 p7*
Luin, Mary; St. John, N.B., 1842 *2978.20 p7*
Luin, Mary, Jr.; St. John, N.B., 1842 *2978.20 p7*
Luin, Patrick; St. John, N.B., 1842 *2978.20 p7*
Luing, Susannah; Died enroute, 1720 *1220.12 p498*
Lukas, Immanuel *SEE* Lukas, Jacob
Lukas, Jac.; New York, 1860 *358.56 p149*
Lukas, Jacob; South Dakota, 1892 *554.30 p26*
  *Wife:*Marie
  *Child:*Immanuel
  *Child:*Salome
  *Child:*Marie
  *Child:*Ottilie
  *Child:*Jakob

Lukas, Jakob *SEE* Lukas, Jacob
Lukas, Marie *SEE* Lukas, Jacob
Lukas, Marie *SEE* Lukas, Jacob
Lukas, Ottilie *SEE* Lukas, Jacob
Lukas, Salome *SEE* Lukas, Jacob
Lukasiuk, Mateusz 28; New York, NY, 1920 *930.50 p49*
Luke, E. Mary 3; Ontario, 1871 *1823.21 p207*
Luke, Fred; Iowa, 1878 *1211.15 p16*
Luke, George 21; Ontario, 1871 *1823.21 p207*
Luke, Hugh; America, 1771 *1220.12 p513*
Luke, John; America, 1752 *1220.12 p513*
Luke, Joseph; America, 1747 *1220.12 p513*
Luke, Thomas; North Carolina, 1844 *1088.45 p20*
Luke, William; America, 1734 *1220.12 p513*
Lukies, Thomas; America, 1767 *1220.12 p513*
Lukis, Mary; Virginia, 1756 *1220.12 p512*
Lukowitz, August 45; Portland, ME, 1906 *970.38 p79*
Luksik, Jan W.; Pennsylvania, 1900 *2853.20 p122*
Lulkowski, Philip; Texas, 1884 *6015.15 p28*
Lull, Andr. 63; America, 1840 *778.6 p220*
Lullams, John; America, 1770 *1220.12 p513*
Lullard, Marie 18; Quebec, 1870 *8364.32 p24*
Lulton, Mary 35; Ontario, 1871 *1823.21 p207*
Lum, Albrecht 38; Louisiana, 1848 *778.6 p220*
Lum, Barbera 34; Louisiana, 1848 *778.6 p220*
Luman, Frances I.; North Carolina, 1825 *1088.45 p20*
Lumb, Joseph; America, 1768 *1220.12 p514*
Lumbar, Moses; America, 1735 *1220.12 p513*
Lumbard, Robert; America, 1685 *1220.12 p507*
Lumbard, Sarah; Virginia, 1742 *1220.12 p507*
Lumber, James; Maryland, 1743 *1220.12 p513*
Lumbus, William 50; Ontario, 1871 *1823.17 p94*
Lumby, Benjamin 67; Ontario, 1871 *1823.21 p208*
Lumby, William 71; Ontario, 1871 *1823.21 p208*
Lumley, Abraham; America, 1753 *1220.12 p513*
Lumley, Diana *SEE* Lumley, Tom
Lumley, John *SEE* Lumley, Tom
Lumley, Margaret; America, 1742 *1220.12 p513*
Lumley, Ruth *SEE* Lumley, Tom
Lumley, Thomas; America, 1775 *1220.12 p514*
Lumley, Tom; Canada, 1774 *3036.5 p41*
  *Wife:*Ruth
  *Child:*Diana
  *Child:*John
Lumm, Joseph; America, 1772 *1220.12 p514*
Lumm, Samuel; North Carolina, 1848 *1088.45 p20*
Lumma, Eva 31; America, 1857 *5475.1 p374*
Lumpie, Anthony; Philadelphia, 1775 *8529.30 p3*
Lumsdale, Edmund; America, 1745 *1220.12 p514*
Lumsden, Hannah 45; Ontario, 1871 *1823.21 p208*
Lumy, George 41; Ontario, 1871 *1823.21 p208*
Lunak, Jaroslav; Cleveland, OH, 1881 *2853.20 p327*
Lunam, David 61; Ontario, 1871 *1823.17 p94*
Lunay, Sebastian 33; New Orleans, 1843 *778.6 p220*
Lunback, Carl; Iowa, 1892 *1211.15 p16*
Lund, Charles G.; Washington, 1887 *2770.40 p24*
Lund, Christian Fredrick; Washington, 1886 *2770.40 p195*
Lund, John; America, 1772 *1220.12 p514*
Lund, Mikal; Washington, 1887 *2770.40 p24*
Lund, N. H.; Louisiana, 1836-1840 *4981.45 p213*
Lund, Wm. Julius Rudolf; Washington, 1887 *2770.40 p24*
Lundahl, Anna C.; St. Paul, MN, 1882 *1865.50 p96*
  *Daughter:*Emma
  *Daughter:*Hilda
Lundahl, C.P.; Charleston, SC, 1850 *6412.40 p152*
Lundahl, Emma *SEE* Lundahl, Anna C.
Lundahl, Hilda *SEE* Lundahl, Anna C.
Lunday, Edwd 56; Ontario, 1871 *1823.17 p95*
Lundbeck, Frank; Iowa, 1900 *1211.15 p16*
Lundbeck, J.; New York, NY, 1845 *6412.40 p148*
Lundberg, August K.A.; Cleveland, OH, 1895-1903 *9722.10 p123*
Lundberg, Carl; Colorado, 1893 *1029.59 p57*
Lundberg, Charles L.; Colorado, 1874 *1029.59 p57*
Lundberg, J.; New York, NY, 1844 *6412.40 p147*
Lundberg, John A.; Colorado, 1891 *1029.59 p57*
Lundberg, John A.; Kansas, 1870 *1029.59 p57*
Lundberg, L.P.; New York, NY, 1848 *6412.40 p151*
Lundberg, Nils Amil; Iowa, 1908 *1211.15 p16*
Lundberg, Oscar Leonard; Iowa, 1909 *1211.15 p16*
Lundberg, Sven; America, 1753 *1220.12 p514*
Lundblad, Charlotte 27 *SEE* Lundblad, Henry W.
Lundblad, Emelia 5 *SEE* Lundblad, Henry W.
Lundblad, Henry W. 29; New York, NY, 1846 *6410.15 p103*
  *Wife:*Charlotte 27
  *Child:*Emelia 5
  With child 2
Lunde, John; Ohio, 1809-1852 *4511.35 p31*

Lundeen, Anders 36; New York, 1856 *6529.11 p19*
  *Wife:*Carin Persdotter 34
  *Son:*Per August 4 months
  *Daughter:*Carin 10
  *Son:*Eric 5
Lundeen, Carin 10 *SEE* Lundeen, Anders
Lundeen, Carin Persdotter 34 *SEE* Lundeen, Anders
Lundeen, Elsie; Kansas, 1888-1902 *1865.50 p98*
Lundeen, Eric 5 *SEE* Lundeen, Anders
Lundeen, John E.; Missouri, 1880-1881 *1865.50 p96*
Lundeen, Per August 4 *SEE* Lundeen, Anders
Lundergin, William; North Carolina, 1833 *1088.45 p20*
Lundgren, Agnes Johanna Maria; North America, 1856 *6410.15 p105*
Lundgren, C.; New York, NY, 1843 *6412.40 p148*
Lundgren, Edward; Cleveland, OH, 1893-1894 *9722.10 p123*
Lundgren, Frans L. 18; New York, NY, 1894 *6512.1 p184*
Lundgren, Hilma Viktoria *SEE* Lundgren, Lars
Lundgren, J.P.; New York, NY, 1850 *6412.40 p152*
Lundgren, John Alfred; Colorado, 1888 *1029.59 p57*
Lundgren, Lars; Wisconsin, 1881-1882 *1865.50 p96*
  *Wife:*Mathilda C. Kilsten
  *Child:*Hilma Viktoria
Lundgren, Mathilda C. Kilsten *SEE* Lundgren, Lars
Lundie, Elisabeth 30; Ontario, 1871 *1823.21 p208*
Lundie, William 38; Ontario, 1871 *1823.21 p208*
Lundin, Anders 36; New York, 1856 *6529.11 p19*
  *Wife:*Carin Persdotter 34
  *Son:*Eric 5
  *Son:*Per August 4 months
  *Daughter:*Carin 10
Lundin, Carin 10 *SEE* Lundin, Anders
Lundin, Carin Persdotter 34 *SEE* Lundin, Anders
Lundin, Edvard Julius; North America, 1882 *6410.15 p106*
Lundin, Eric 5 *SEE* Lundin, Anders
Lundin, John E.; Missouri, 1880-1881 *1865.50 p96*
Lundin, Olof; New York, NY, 1851 *6412.40 p153*
Lundin, Per August 4 *SEE* Lundin, Anders
Lundquist, Christina; St. Paul, MN, 1887 *1865.50 p96*
Lundquist, John; Illinois, 1861 *4487.25 p65*
Lundquist, Oscar; Cleveland, OH, 1880-1882 *9722.10 p123*
Lundqvist, Christina; St. Paul, MN, 1887 *1865.50 p96*
Lundstedt, Alfred L.; Cleveland, OH, 1896-1902 *9722.10 p123*
Lundstrom, Axel; Cleveland, OH, 1887-1890 *9722.10 p123*
Lundstrom, Ossian; Cleveland, OH, 1901-1904 *9722.10 p123*
Lundstrom, P.G.; New York, NY, 1844 *6412.40 p147*
Lunen, John 43; Ontario, 1871 *1823.17 p95*
Luney, James 23; Ontario, 1871 *1823.21 p208*
Lungans, Andrew 13; St. John, N.B., 1834 *6469.7 p5*
Lungans, Cathn 40; St. John, N.B., 1834 *6469.7 p5*
Lungans, Dan'l 20; St. John, N.B., 1834 *6469.7 p5*
Lungans, Dan'l 45; St. John, N.B., 1834 *6469.7 p5*
Lungans, John 24; St. John, N.B., 1834 *6469.7 p5*
Lungans, Mary 11; St. John, N.B., 1834 *6469.7 p5*
Lungans, Michael 9; St. John, N.B., 1834 *6469.7 p5*
Lungans, Thos 6; St. John, N.B., 1834 *6469.7 p5*
Lungans, William 17; St. John, N.B., 1834 *6469.7 p5*
Lungenbeck, Julius; Valdivia, Chile, 1850 *1192.4 p50*
Lungershausen, Carl Ludwig Arnold; America, 1885 *7420.1 p348*
Lungershausen, Theodor Wilhelm Moritz; America, 1844 *7420.1 p32*
Lungreen, Anders Hendrick; America, 1770 *1220.12 p514*
Lungreen, Jurgen Lawrence; America, 1766 *1220.12 p514*
Lungstrom, Anna Augusta; North America, 1887 *6410.15 p106*
Luniak, Anna Barbara *SEE* Luniak, Johannes
Luniak, Anna Christine *SEE* Luniak, Johannes
Luniak, Anna Margarethe *SEE* Luniak, Johannes
Luniak, Anna Margarethe Karch *SEE* Luniak, Johannes
Luniak, Johann Philipp *SEE* Luniak, Johannes
Luniak, Johannes; Virginia, 1831 *152.20 p65*
  *Wife:*Anna Margarethe Karch
  *Child:*Johann Philipp
  *Child:*Anna Margarethe
  *Child:*Anna Barbara
  *Child:*Anna Christine
Lunki, Elin Johanna; Oregon, 1941 *9157.47 p2*
Lunking, Amelia Louise; Wisconsin, 1899 *6795.8 p179*
Lunn, Andrew; Washington, 1879 *2770.40 p134*
Lunn, Ann; Rappahannock, VA, 1741 *1220.12 p514*
Lunn, John; Cleveland, OH, 1869-1882 *9722.10 p123*
Lunn, Margaret; America, 1710 *1220.12 p514*
Lunn, Nehemiah; America, 1769 *1220.12 p514*

Lunn, Thomas; America, 1763 ***1220.12*** *p514*
Lunn, Thomas 42; Ontario, 1871 ***1823.17*** *p95*
Lunncliff, Martha 20; Quebec, 1870 ***8364.32*** *p24*
Lunns, Anthony; America, 1683 ***1220.12*** *p514*
Lunt, Bridget; America, 1756 ***1220.12*** *p514*
Luom, Katharina; Venezuela, 1843 ***3899.5*** *p545*
Luoma, John 42; Minnesota, 1923 ***2769.54*** *p1378*
Luoma, Matt 33; Minnesota, 1926 ***2769.54*** *p1382*
Lupton, George; America, 1773 ***1220.12*** *p514*
Lupystrasser, Mary 38; Ontario, 1871 ***1823.21*** *p208*
Lurch, Isaac; North Carolina, 1854 ***1088.45*** *p20*
Luret, Rene; Quebec, 1643 ***9221.17*** *p132*
Luroy, Aime 26; America, 1843 ***778.6*** *p220*
Lurssen, Karl Ludwig; America, 1886 ***7420.1*** *p351*
Lus, Jacob 33; New Orleans, 1848 ***778.6*** *p220*
Lusby, James; America, 1770 ***1220.12*** *p514*
Luscher, Jacob 35; New Castle, DE, 1817-1818 ***90.20*** *p152*
Luscom, Thomas 28; Ontario, 1871 ***1823.21*** *p208*
Luscombe, Elizabeth 40; Ontario, 1871 ***1823.17*** *p95*
Luscombe, John; Virginia, 1771 ***1220.12*** *p514*
Luscombe, William 28; Ontario, 1871 ***1823.17*** *p95*
Lush, Arthur; America, 1685 ***1220.12*** *p514*
Lush, Henry; America, 1673 ***1220.12*** *p514*
Lush, John; America, 1685 ***1220.12*** *p514*
Lush, Mary; America, 1686 ***1220.12*** *p514*
Lush, William; America, 1685 ***1220.12*** *p514*
Lush, William; America, 1772 ***1220.12*** *p514*
Lush, William; America, 1773 ***1220.12*** *p514*
Lushby, William; America, 1773 ***1220.12*** *p514*
Lusich, P.; Louisiana, 1874 ***4981.45*** *p296*
Lusin, Jacob 20; New Orleans, 1848 ***778.6*** *p220*
Lusk, George 20; Michigan, 1880 ***4491.30*** *p21*
Lusk, John 40; Ontario, 1871 ***1823.17*** *p95*
Lusk, Vilem; Baltimore, 1852 ***2853.20*** *p125*
With family
Luska Family ; Chicago, 1862 ***2853.20*** *p390*
*Son:*Karel
Luska Family, Karel *SEE*
Lust, Adam; America, 1883 ***2526.42*** *p154*
Lust, Georg, II; America, 1841 ***2526.42*** *p125*
With child 6
With child 4
Lust, Georg Ludwig; America, 1847 ***2526.42*** *p125*
With wife
Lust, Jakob 43; America, 1856 ***2526.43*** *p152*
Lust, Johann Adam 20; America, 1854 ***2526.43*** *p152*
Lust, Johannes; America, 1859 ***2526.43*** *p187*
Lust, Johannes; America, 1882 ***2526.43*** *p187*
Lust, Julie; America, 1885 ***2526.43*** *p150*
Lust, Marie Elisabetha 41; America, 1884 ***2526.43*** *p187*
*Son:*Jakob 11
*Daughter:*Katharine 1
*Son:*Philipp 5
Lust, Michael; America, 1846 ***2526.43*** *p153*
Lust, Philipp; America, 1887 ***2526.43*** *p153*
Lusted, Frances; Barbados, 1671 ***1220.12*** *p514*
Luster, Charles; New York, 1859 ***358.56*** *p53*
Luster, Richard; New York, 1859 ***358.56*** *p53*
Luszczka, Aniela Piekos *SEE* Luszczka, Jozef
Luszczka, Jozef; Detroit, 1929-1930 ***6214.5*** *p60*
*Wife:*Aniela Piekos
Lute, Adam 37; New York, NY, 1893 ***1883.7*** *p42*
Lutgen, John; North Carolina, 1792-1862 ***1088.45*** *p20*
Luth, Joh.; Venezuela, 1843 ***3899.5*** *p547*
Luther, Carl; America, 1868 ***7919.3*** *p533*
With family
Luther, Edward; America, 1685 ***1220.12*** *p514*
Luther, Friedrich; America, 1857 ***7420.1*** *p166*
Luther, Johann August; Wisconsin, 1868 ***6795.8*** *p122*
Luther, John; Ohio, 1809-1852 ***4511.35*** *p32*
Luther, Karl; America, 1867 ***7919.3*** *p527*
Luther, Paul 48; Ontario, 1871 ***1823.21*** *p208*
Luther, Wilhelmine Leonore; America, 1860 ***7420.1*** *p196*
Luthmann, Nicolas 29; Mississippi, 1846 ***778.6*** *p220*
Luthy, Alexander 32; New York, NY, 1894 ***6512.1*** *p182*
Lutke, Gottlieb; Wisconsin, 1866 ***6795.8*** *p45*
Lutovsky, Matej; St. Paul, MN, 1863 ***2853.20*** *p277*
Lutringer, Joseph 25; Galveston, TX, 1844 ***3967.10*** *p372*
Lutsky, Aaron; Detroit, 1923 ***6214.5*** *p71*
Lutsky, Lena; Detroit, 1929-1930 ***6214.5*** *p71*
Lutt, Andr. 63; America, 1840 ***778.6*** *p220*
Lutt, Cath. 34; America, 1840 ***778.6*** *p221*
Lutte, Peter; Illinois, 1856 ***6079.1*** *p9*
Lutter, Mr.; America, 1899 ***7420.1*** *p375*
Lutter, Carl Friedrich Wilhelm *SEE* Lutter, Johann Heinrich Wilhelm
Lutter, Carl Heinrich Friedrich; America, 1853 ***7420.1*** *p108*
Lutter, Caroline Wilhelmine *SEE* Lutter, Johann Heinrich Wilhelm
Lutter, Christ.; America, 1852 ***7420.1*** *p93*
Lutter, Christian Friedrich Wilhelm *SEE* Lutter, Friedrich Christian
Lutter, Christian Ludwig; America, 1852 ***7420.1*** *p93*
*Wife:*Wilhelmine Sophia Baule
With son
*Son:*Heinrich Christian Ludwig
Lutter, Friedrich; Philadelphia, 1876 ***7420.1*** *p307*
Lutter, Friedrich Christian; America, 1881 ***7420.1*** *p322*
*Wife:*Sophie Wilhelmine Friederike Becher
*Son:*Christian Friedrich Wilhelm
Lutter, Heinrich; America, 1902 ***7420.1*** *p401*
With family
Lutter, Heinrich Christian Ludwig *SEE* Lutter, Christian Ludwig
Lutter, Heinrich Friedrich Ludwig; America, 1881 ***7420.1*** *p323*
Lutter, Johann Heinrich Wilhelm; America, 1859 ***7420.1*** *p187*
*Wife:*Sophia Justina Louisa Rohrkasten
*Daughter:*Justine Sophie
With stepchild
*Daughter:*Caroline Wilhelmine
*Son:*Carl Friedrich Wilhelm
Lutter, Justine Sophie *SEE* Lutter, Johann Heinrich Wilhelm
Lutter, Sophia Justina Louisa Rohrkasten *SEE* Lutter, Johann Heinrich Wilhelm
Lutter, Sophie Wilhelmine Friederike Becher *SEE* Lutter, Friedrich Christian
Lutter, Wilhelmine Kathrinhagen; America, 1852 ***7420.1*** *p93*
Lutter, Wilhelmine Louise Caroline; America, 1868 ***7420.1*** *p274*
Lutter, Wilhelmine Sophia Baule *SEE* Lutter, Christian Ludwig
Lutterel, Elizabeth; America, 1759 ***1220.12*** *p514*
Lutterell, James; America, 1759 ***1220.12*** *p514*
Lutticke, A. Paula Aloysia; America, 1928 ***8023.44*** *p376*
Lutticken, Robert; America, 1892 ***5475.1*** *p77*
*Wife:*Sophie Wahlster
*Son:*Robert Jakob
Lutticken, Robert Jakob *SEE* Lutticken, Robert
Lutticken, Sophie Wahlster *SEE* Lutticken, Robert
Luttle, John; Ipswich, MA, 1656 ***1642*** *p68*
Lutton, Paul; Annapolis, MD, 1725 ***1220.12*** *p514*
Lutts, Peter; North Carolina, 1710 ***3629.40*** *p5*
Lutwich, William; America, 1763 ***1220.12*** *p514*
Lutz, Andr. 22; New York, NY, 1893 ***1883.7*** *p44*
Lutz, Christian; New York, 1860 ***358.56*** *p3*
Lutz, Christine; America, 1859 ***5475.1*** *p522*
Lutz, Christine; Dakota, 1885 ***554.30*** *p25*
Lutz, Dorothea Albus *SEE* Lutz, Jakob
Lutz, Egide 28; New Orleans, 1847 ***778.6*** *p221*
Lutz, Ellen E. 33; Ontario, 1871 ***1823.17*** *p95*
Lutz, Henry; Ohio, 1844 ***2763.1*** *p20*
Lutz, Jacob; Ohio, 1809-1852 ***4511.35*** *p32*
Lutz, Jakob; Dakota, 1883 ***554.30*** *p25*
*Wife:*Dorothea Albus
*Child:*Magdalene
Lutz, Julius; America, 1884 ***2526.42*** *p162*
Lutz, Leonhard; Valdivia, Chile, 1852 ***1192.4*** *p53*
Lutz, Ludwig; America, 1867 ***7919.3*** *p529*
Lutz, Magdalene *SEE* Lutz, Jakob
Lutz, R. 35; America, 1847 ***778.6*** *p221*
Lutz, Thomas; North Dakota, 1892 ***554.30*** *p26*
Luvendam, Henry 18; Missouri, 1845 ***778.6*** *p221*
Luvignan, Antoin 20; America, 1848 ***778.6*** *p221*
Luvone, P. 28; New Orleans, 1840 ***778.6*** *p221*
Lux, Anna; America, 1881 ***5475.1*** *p285*
Lux, Anton; Iowa, 1892 ***1211.15*** *p16*
Lux, Antone, Jr.; Iowa, 1892 ***1211.15*** *p16*
Lux, John; America, 1721 ***1220.12*** *p514*
Lux, Nikolaus; Pennsylvania, 1888 ***5475.1*** *p47*
Lux, Susanna; America, 1881 ***5475.1*** *p285*
Luxenburger, Anna 8 *SEE* Luxenburger, Jakob
Luxenburger, Barbara 5 *SEE* Luxenburger, Peter
Luxenburger, Elisabeth; America, 1872 ***5475.1*** *p172*
Luxenburger, Elisabeth 3 *SEE* Luxenburger, Peter
Luxenburger, Georg 4 *SEE* Luxenburger, Jakob
Luxenburger, Jakob 40; America, 1866 ***5475.1*** *p170*
*Wife:*Margarethe 29
*Son:*Nikolaus 1
*Son:*Georg 4
*Daughter:*Margarethe 10
*Daughter:*Anna 8
Luxenburger, Margarethe 10 *SEE* Luxenburger, Jakob
Luxenburger, Margarethe 29 *SEE* Luxenburger, Jakob
Luxenburger, Maria 1 *SEE* Luxenburger, Peter
Luxenburger, Maria Stutz 26 *SEE* Luxenburger, Peter
Luxenburger, Nikolaus 1 *SEE* Luxenburger, Jakob
Luxenburger, Peter; America, 1873 ***5475.1*** *p219*
Luxenburger, Peter 30; America, 1866 ***5475.1*** *p170*
*Wife:*Maria Stutz 26
*Daughter:*Maria 1
*Daughter:*Elisabeth 3
*Daughter:*Barbara 5
Luxon, Henry; America, 1729 ***1220.12*** *p514*
Luxton, John 41; Ontario, 1871 ***1823.21*** *p208*
Luxton, Richard; Barbados, 1691 ***1220.12*** *p514*
Luxton, Richard 31; Ontario, 1871 ***1823.21*** *p208*
Luxton, Richard 64; Ontario, 1871 ***1823.21*** *p208*
Luy, Johann Hubert 25; Galveston, TX, 1844 ***3967.10*** *p375*
Luy, Winand 1; Galveston, TX, 1844 ***3967.10*** *p375*
Luyan, Atori 12; New Orleans, 1843 ***778.6*** *p221*
Lyall, James; America, 1697 ***1220.12*** *p514*
Lyanna, Louis E.; Illinois, 1852 ***6079.1*** *p9*
Lyberg, J.F.; New York, NY, 1842 ***6412.40*** *p146*
Lycence, Richard; America, 1719 ***1220.12*** *p514*
Lyddy, Catherine 60; Ontario, 1871 ***1823.21*** *p208*
Lyde, Edward; America, 1685 ***1220.12*** *p514*
Lyde, Elizabeth; America, 1723 ***1220.12*** *p514*
Lyde, Hannah Rutter; America, 1751 ***1220.12*** *p514*
Lyde, John; America, 1685 ***1220.12*** *p514*
Lyde, Sylvester; America, 1685 ***1220.12*** *p514*
Lydeat, James; Annapolis, MD, 1733 ***1220.12*** *p514*
Lyden, Marton; Colorado, 1866 ***1029.59*** *p57*
Lydiatt, Jane; America, 1758 ***1220.12*** *p514*
Lydrikson, Gustaf S.; Cleveland, OH, 1892-1896 ***9722.10*** *p123*
Lydy, Michael; Ohio, 1840-1897 ***8365.35*** *p17*
Lye, Edward; Toronto, 1829-1908 ***9228.50*** *p359*
*Wife:*Rachel Mary Steen Le Maitre
Lye, Elianor; Barbados or Jamaica, 1674 ***1220.12*** *p514*
Lye, Rachel Mary Steen Le Maitre *SEE* Lye, Edward
Lyes, Samuel; America, 1767 ***1220.12*** *p514*
Lyfe, Joseph; America, 1748 ***1220.12*** *p501*
Lyfolly, Richard; America, 1760 ***1220.12*** *p514*
Lyford, John; America, 1759 ***1220.12*** *p514*
Lyford, John; Plymouth, MA, 1623 ***1642*** *p1*
*Wife:*Sarah
With child
Lyford, Sarah *SEE* Lyford, John
Lyford, Thomas; Barbados or Jamaica, 1707 ***1220.12*** *p515*
Lyford, William; Virginia, 1739 ***1220.12*** *p515*
Lyger, James; America, 1755 ***1220.12*** *p515*
Lyle, Mary Ann 55; Ontario, 1871 ***1823.21*** *p208*
Lyle, Thomas 56; Ontario, 1871 ***1823.21*** *p208*
Lylie, William 40; Ontario, 1871 ***1823.21*** *p208*
Lyllyman, Robert; America, 1731 ***1220.12*** *p501*
Lymann, Carolina 50; Mississippi, 1847 ***778.6*** *p221*
Lymann, Frederic 16; Mississippi, 1847 ***778.6*** *p221*
Lymann, Henry 45; Mississippi, 1847 ***778.6*** *p221*
Lymann, Saloma 29; Mississippi, 1847 ***778.6*** *p221*
Lymes, Herman; America, 1773 ***1220.12*** *p501*
Lynch, Agness 40; Ontario, 1871 ***1823.17*** *p95*
Lynch, Andrew; Boston, 1761 ***1642*** *p48*
Lynch, Ann 18; Ontario, 1871 ***1823.21*** *p208*
Lynch, Catherine; Boston, 1764 ***1642*** *p34*
Lynch, Catherine 17; Quebec, 1870 ***8364.32*** *p24*
Lynch, Charles; Annapolis, MD, 1733 ***1220.12*** *p515*
Lynch, Charles; Died enroute, 1723 ***1220.12*** *p515*
Lynch, Disney; America, 1751 ***1220.12*** *p515*
Lynch, Edward 50; Ontario, 1871 ***1823.17*** *p95*
Lynch, Eleanor; America, 1764 ***1220.12*** *p515*
Lynch, Elizabeth; America, 1745 ***1220.12*** *p515*
Lynch, Elizabeth; Beverly, MA, 1740 ***1642*** *p64*
Lynch, Elizabeth 12; Ontario, 1871 ***1823.21*** *p208*
Lynch, Esther 50; Ontario, 1871 ***1823.21*** *p208*
Lynch, Fanny 47; Ontario, 1871 ***1823.17*** *p95*
Lynch, James; Newfoundland, 1814 ***3476.10*** *p54*
Lynch, James; Ohio, 1840-1897 ***8365.35*** *p17*
Lynch, James 25; Ontario, 1871 ***1823.17*** *p95*
Lynch, James 15; Quebec, 1870 ***8364.32*** *p24*
Lynch, Jeremiah; Ohio, 1840-1897 ***8365.35*** *p17*
Lynch, Jeremiah 55; Ontario, 1871 ***1823.21*** *p208*
Lynch, John; America, 1775 ***1220.12*** *p515*
Lynch, John; Colorado, 1873 ***1029.59*** *p57*
Lynch, John 71; Ontario, 1871 ***1823.21*** *p208*
Lynch, John W.; Washington, 1884 ***2770.40*** *p192*
Lynch, Joseph 49; Ontario, 1871 ***1823.21*** *p208*
Lynch, Mary; America, 1749 ***1220.12*** *p515*
Lynch, Mary; New Orleans, 1851 ***7242.30*** *p148*
Lynch, Michael 50; Ontario, 1871 ***1823.17*** *p95*
Lynch, Michael; Toronto, 1844 ***2910.35*** *p115*
Lynch, Pat 19; St. Johns, N.F., 1811 ***1053.20*** *p21*
Lynch, Patrick; Boston, 1747 ***1642*** *p46*
Lynch, Patrick 45; St. Johns, N.F., 1811 ***1053.20*** *p20*
Lynch, Richard B.; North Carolina, 1851 ***1088.45*** *p20*
Lynch, Robert 41; Ontario, 1871 ***1823.17*** *p95*
Lynch, S. J.; California, 1868 ***1131.61*** *p89*
Lynch, Terrence; Toronto, 1844 ***2910.35*** *p115*
Lynch, Thomas 45; Ontario, 1871 ***1823.17*** *p95*

Lynch, Thomas J.; New Orleans, 1850 *7242.30 p148*
Lynch, Tom; St. John, N.B., 1848 *2978.15 p40*
Lynch, William; Boston, 1737 *1642 p44*
Lynch, William; New Orleans, 1851 *7242.30 p148*
Lynch, Wm 21; St. Johns, N.F., 1811 *1053.20 p22*
Lyndsey, Jane; Virginia, 1726 *1220.12 p502*
Lyne, Benedictus; America, 1772 *1220.12 p502*
Lyne, Charles 49; Ontario, 1871 *1823.17 p95*
Lyne, Richard; America, 1685 *1220.12 p502*
Lyneing, William; America, 1685 *1220.12 p503*
Lyner, James; Barbados or Jamaica, 1715 *1220.12 p515*
Lynes, Elizabeth 13; Quebec, 1870 *8364.32 p24*
Lynes, John 50; Ontario, 1871 *1823.21 p208*
Lynes, Richard; America, 1722 *1220.12 p502*
Lynes, Thomas; America, 1722 *1220.12 p502*
Lynes, Thomas; America, 1757 *1220.12 p502*
Lyng, John; America, 1775 *1220.12 p502*
Lynham, Jane 46; Ontario, 1871 *1823.21 p208*
Lynley, Henry; America, 1740 *1220.12 p503*
Lynn, Ann 56; Ontario, 1871 *1823.21 p208*
Lynn, Elizabeth; America, 1722 *1220.12 p515*
Lynn, Hester; America, 1749 *1220.12 p515*
Lynn, John; America, 1718 *1220.12 p515*
Lynn, Nathaniel; America, 1719 *1220.12 p515*
Lynn, Mrs. S. G.; Toronto, 1844 *2910.35 p114*
Lynn, Samuel; America, 1715 *1220.12 p515*
Lynn, Thomas; America, 1700 *1220.12 p515*
Lynsey, Thomas; Barbados, 1672 *1220.12 p502*
Lyon, Ann; America, 1763 *1220.12 p515*
Lyon, Benjamin; Annapolis, MD, 1723 *1220.12 p515*

Lyon, Charles; America, 1772 *1220.12 p515*
Lyon, Elizabeth; America, 1763 *1220.12 p515*
Lyon, George; Massachusetts, 1675-1676 *1642 p129*
Lyon, Jacob; America, 1771 *1220.12 p515*
Lyon, John; Barbados, 1672 *1220.12 p515*
Lyon, John; Boston, 1764 *1642 p33*
Lyon, John; Massachusetts, 1620-1775 *1642 p139*
Lyon, Joseph; Massachusetts, 1675-1676 *1642 p128*
Lyon, Joseph; Massachusetts, 1675-1676 *1642 p128*
Lyon, Mary; America, 1756 *1220.12 p515*
Lyon, Mary; Barbados, 1671 *1220.12 p515*
Lyon, Mary; Maryland, 1672 *1236.25 p47*
Lyon, Moses; America, 1770 *1220.12 p515*
Lyon, Moses; America, 1774 *1220.12 p515*
Lyon, Nathaniel; Massachusetts, 1675-1676 *1642 p129*
Lyon, Thomas; Massachusetts, 1675-1676 *1642 p128*
Lyon, Thomas; Massachusetts, 1675-1676 *1642 p128*
Lyon, William; America, 1687 *1220.12 p515*
Lyon, William; America, 1758 *1220.12 p515*
Lyonne, Martin de 29; Quebec, 1643 *9221.17 p127*
Lyons, Mrs.; Toronto, 1844 *2910.35 p114*
Lyons, Abraham; America, 1772 *1220.12 p515*
Lyons, Alexander 37; Michigan, 1880 *4491.36 p14*
Lyons, Alexander 60; Ontario, 1871 *1823.21 p208*
Lyons, Annie 5; Quebec, 1870 *8364.32 p24*
Lyons, Bridget 51; Michigan, 1880 *4491.30 p21*
Lyons, Cath. 26; America, 1841 *778.6 p221*
Lyons, Catherine; America, 1772 *1220.12 p515*
Lyons, Elizabeth; America, 1742 *1220.12 p515*
Lyons, Elizabeth; Maryland, 1742 *1220.12 p515*

Lyons, Ellen 35; Michigan, 1880 *4491.36 p14*
Lyons, Honora 50; Ontario, 1871 *1823.17 p95*
Lyons, Hugh; Annapolis, MD, 1722 *1220.12 p515*
Lyons, Isaac; America, 1753 *1220.12 p515*
Lyons, John; America, 1772 *1220.12 p515*
Lyons, John; Colorado, 1869 *1029.59 p57*
Lyons, John; Toronto, 1844 *2910.35 p112*
Lyons, Joseph; America, 1771 *1220.12 p516*
Lyons, Joseph; Louisiana, 1874 *4981.45 p132*
Lyons, Lisabeth 26; America, 1841 *778.6 p221*
Lyons, Mary 41; Ontario, 1871 *1823.21 p208*
Lyons, Pauline 2; America, 1841 *778.6 p221*
Lyons, Samuel; Washington, 1888 *2770.40 p26*
Lyons, Timothy 30; New York, NY, 1844 *6178.50 p151*
Lyons, Timothy C.; North Carolina, 1859 *1088.45 p20*
Lyons, William 23; Michigan, 1880 *4491.36 p14*
Lyons, William 25; Ontario, 1871 *1823.21 p208*
Lyons, Williams 27; Ontario, 1871 *1823.17 p95*
Lypiatt, George; America, 1766 *1220.12 p503*
Lyre, Frederick; Ohio, 1809-1852 *4511.35 p32*
Lysaght, John; Toronto, 1844 *2910.35 p112*
Lysagth, Martin 43; Ontario, 1871 *1823.17 p95*
Lyseior, Anthony; North Carolina, 1848 *1088.45 p20*
Lystef, Kristian Andersen; Oregon, 1941 *9157.47 p3*
Lyster, L.G.; Iowa, 1898 *1211.15 p16*
Lyston, Robert; America, 1743 *1220.12 p503*
Lytch, John Peter; New York, NY, 1778 *8529.30 p3*
Lytgen, John; North Carolina, 1792-1862 *1088.45 p20*
Lyth, Robert; Annapolis, MD, 1732 *1220.12 p516*
Lyttle, Charlotte 18; Quebec, 1870 *8364.32 p24*

M

Maas, Anna; America, 1882 *5475.1 p229*
Maas, Anna 9 *SEE* Maas, Peter
Maas, Anna Drusch 47 *SEE* Maas, Peter
Maas, Anna *SEE* Maas, Peter
Maas, August; Wisconsin, 1887 *6795.8 p86*
Maas, Bernhard; Colorado, 1880 *1029.59 p57*
Maas, Charley; Wisconsin, 1880 *6795.8 p92*
Maas, Elise *SEE* Maas, Peter
Maas, Eva *SEE* Maas, Peter
Maas, Felix 22; Port uncertain, 1847 *778.6 p221*
Maas, Johann 19 *SEE* Maas, Peter
Maas, Johann *SEE* Maas, Peter
Maas, Katharina *SEE* Maas, Peter
Maas, Maria 17 *SEE* Maas, Peter
Maas, Maria *SEE* Maas, Peter
Maas, Maria Mai *SEE* Maas, Peter
Maas, Michel 14 *SEE* Maas, Peter
Maas, Nikolaus *SEE* Maas, Peter
Maas, Peter 46; America, 1857 *5475.1 p374*
  *Wife:*Anna Drusch 47
  *Son:*Michel 14
  *Daughter:*Anna 9
  *Son:*Johann 19
  *Daughter:*Maria 17
Maas, Peter *SEE* Maas, Peter
Maas, Peter; Wisconsin, 1891 *5475.1 p325*
  *Wife:*Maria Mai
  *Daughter:*Elise
  *Son:*Johann
  *Daughter:*Maria
  *Daughter:*Katharina
  *Daughter:*Anna
  *Daughter:*Eva
  *Son:*Nikolaus
  *Son:*Peter
Maasz, Emilie; Dakota, 1887 *554.30 p25*
Mabberly, Joseph; New York, NY, 1778 *8529.30 p3*
Mabbett, Anthony; America, 1775 *1220.12 p523*
Mabe, William; America, 1720 *1220.12 p523*
Mabeley, Everard; America, 1738 *1220.12 p523*
Mabell, John; Barbados, 1699 *1220.12 p523*
Mabille, Anne; Quebec, 1666 *4514.3 p343*
Mabille, Francois 27; Quebec, 1646 *9221.17 p167*
Mabille, Michelle 49; Quebec, 1641 *9221.17 p106*
Mablum, Moretz; South Carolina, 1843 *6155.4 p19*
Mably, Francis; Boston, 1830 *3274.55 p73*
Mably, John; Boston, 1830 *3274.55 p73*
Mabson, John 61; Ontario, 1871 *1823.21 p208*
Maby, Samuel; America, 1741 *1220.12 p523*
Macarde, Jacques; Quebec, 1654 *9221.17 p313*
Macare, Johann; America, 1846-1847 *5475.1 p67*
Macari, Anna Kleer 45 *SEE* Macari, Peter
Macari, Peter 2 *SEE* Macari, Peter
Macari, Peter 30; America, 1846 *5475.1 p401*
  *Wife:*Anna Kleer 45
  *Son:*Peter 2
Macarta, Florence; Boston, 1690-1699 *1642 p17*
Macarta, Jo; Salem, MA, 1694 *1642 p77*
Macartee, Jeremiah; Salem, MA, 1701 *1642 p78*
Macarthur, Archibald 36; Ontario, 1871 *1823.17 p95*
Macarthur, Thomas 41; Ontario, 1871 *1823.21 p209*
Macarti, Florence; Boston, 1697 *1642 p17*
Macarty, Elizabeth; Boston, 1740 *1642 p45*
Macarty, Florence; Salem, MA, 1713 *1642 p79*
  *Relative:*John
Macarty, John *SEE* Macarty, Florence

Macary, Mr., II; America, 1881 *5475.1 p44*
  *Wife:*Margarethe Weber
  *Daughter:*Elisabeth
  *Son:*Heinrich
  *Daughter:*Margarethe
  *Son:*Peter
  *Son:*Johann
Macary, Elisabeth *SEE* Macary, Mr., II
Macary, Heinrich *SEE* Macary, Mr., II
Macary, Johann *SEE* Macary, Mr., II
Macary, Margarethe *SEE* Macary, Mr., II
Macary, Margarethe Weber *SEE* Macary, Mr., II
Macary, Peter *SEE* Macary, Mr., II
Macauley, John 35; Ontario, 1871 *1823.21 p209*
Macbean, James 32; Ontario, 1871 *1823.17 p95*
Macbeath, George 26; Ontario, 1871 *1823.21 p209*
MacCallum, Neill; Prince Edward Island, 1771 *3799.30 p41*
Maccarter, Rebecca; Boston, 1714 *1642 p24*
Maccartey, Michael; Ipswich, MA, 1733 *1642 p71*
  *Wife:*Priscilla
Maccartey, Priscilla *SEE* Maccartey, Michael
Maccarthy, Rebeccah; Boston, 1716 *1642 p24*
Maccarty, Anne; Boston, 1734 *1642 p44*
Maccarty, Charles; Quebec, 1690 *1642 p15*
Maccarty, Christian; Boston, 1714 *1642 p24*
Maccarty, Eleanor; Boston, 1735 *1642 p44*
Maccarty, Elisabeth; Boston, 1736 *1642 p44*
Maccarty, Elisabeth; Boston, 1736 *1642 p44*
Maccarty, Eliza; Boston, 1710 *1642 p21*
Maccarty, Elizabeth; Boston, 1707 *1642 p24*
Maccarty, Elizabeth; Boston, 1738 *1642 p44*
Maccarty, Florence; Boston, 1686 *1642 p15*
Maccarty, Florence; Boston, 1706 *1642 p24*
Maccarty, Florence; Massachusetts, 1700-1799 *1642 p138*
Maccarty, Jeremiah; Boston, 1738 *1642 p44*
Maccarty, Luke; Boston, 1773 *1642 p49*
Maccarty, Margaret; Boston, 1708 *1642 p24*
Maccarty, Margaret; Boston, 1736 *1642 p44*
Maccarty, Margaret; Boston, 1743 *1642 p45*
Maccarty, Margaret; Boston, 1746 *1642 p46*
Maccarty, Mary; Boston, 1708 *1642 p24*
Maccarty, Mary; Boston, 1712 *1642 p24*
Maccarty, Mary; Boston, 1718 *1642 p24*
Maccarty, Mary; Boston, 1728 *1642 p25*
Maccarty, Mary; Boston, 1738 *1642 p44*
Maccarty, Mary; Boston, 1746 *1642 p46*
Maccarty, Mary; Massachusetts, 1744 *1642 p87*
Maccarty, Mary *SEE* Maccarty, Thaddeus
Maccarty, Prudence; Salem, MA, 1715 *1642 p78*
Maccarty, Ruth; Boston, 1721 *1642 p25*
Maccarty, Sarah; Boston, 1715 *1642 p24*
Maccarty, T.; Boston, 1728 *1642 p23*
Maccarty, Thaddeus; Boston, 1620-1775 *1642 p138*
Maccarty, Thaddeus; Boston, 1686 *1642 p15*
Maccarty, Thaddeus; Boston, 1743 *1642 p27*
Maccarty, Thaddeus; Boston, 1743 *1642 p45*
Maccarty, Thaddeus; Massachusetts, 1620-1775 *1642 p139*
Maccarty, Thaddeus; Worcester, MA, 1747 *1642 p114*
  *Wife:*Mary
Maccarty, Thadeus; Boston, 1716 *1642 p24*
Maccarty, Thomas; Massachusetts, 1620-1775 *1642 p138*
Maccarty, Timothy; Boston, 1740 *1642 p45*
Maccarty, William; Boston, 1714 *1642 p24*
Maccarty, William; Salem, MA, 1661 *1642 p78*
Macchone, John; Cambridge, MA, 1659 *9228.50 p418*

Macclesfield, Thomas; Annapolis, MD, 1725 *1220.12 p523*
Maccurdins, Abraham; Massachusetts, 1727 *1642 p100*
MacDaniel, Patrick; Boston, 1750 *1642 p46*
MacDiamod, Owen; Maryland, 1726 *1220.12 p518*
MacDonagh, Charles; Virginia, 1735 *1220.12 p518*
Macdonald, Dr.; Quebec, 1885 *1937.10 p52*
Macdonald, Donald 50; Ontario, 1871 *1823.21 p209*
MacDonald, Edith Maria Aletta *SEE* MacDonald, George Frederick
MacDonald, George Frederick; Toronto, 1863-1884 *9228.50 p576*
  *Wife:*Penrose Ann Savage
  *Daughter:*Edith Maria Aletta
MacDonald, James; America, 1772 *1220.12 p519*
Macdonald, James 32; Ontario, 1871 *1823.17 p95*
Macdonald, John 66; Ontario, 1871 *1823.21 p209*
MacDonald, Patrick; America, 1747 *1220.12 p519*
MacDonald, Penrose Ann Savage *SEE* MacDonald, George Frederick
MacDonell, Alexander; Quebec, 1786 *1416.15 p5*
MacDonell, Angus; Quebec, 1786 *1416.15 p5*
Macdonell, Angus Ban; Quebec, 1786 *1416.15 p5*
Macdougall, Donald 50; Ontario, 1871 *1823.17 p95*
MacDougall, Peter; Prince Edward Island, 1771 *3799.30 p41*
Macdowell, Richard; New York, NY, 1776 *8529.30 p7A*
Mace, Child; America, 1844 *778.6 p221*
Mace, Mrs. 30; America, 1844 *778.6 p221*
Mace, Agnes; Maine, 1733 *9228.50 p413*
Mace, Catherine 41; Montreal, 1659 *9221.17 p415*
Mace, Clarissa; Minnesota, 1925 *2769.54 p1382*
Mace, Edward; Barbados, 1669 *1220.12 p523*
Mace, Eug. 34; America, 1843 *778.6 p221*
Mace, Florence Isabelle; Minnesota, 1925 *2769.54 p1382*
Mace, J. 42; America, 1844 *778.6 p221*
Mace, James; Virginia, n.d. *9228.50 p413*
Mace, John; America, 1753 *1220.12 p523*
Mace, John; America, 1763 *1220.12 p523*
Mace, Julien; Montreal, 1653 *9221.17 p297*
Mace, Samuel; Carolina or Virginia, 1600-1699 *9228.50 p413*
Mace, Thomas; Barbados, 1681 *1220.12 p523*
Mace, William; America, 1752 *1220.12 p523*
MacEachine, Hector; Prince Edward Island, 1771 *3799.30 p41*
Macey, George; America, 1685 *1220.12 p523*
Macey, Jane; America, 1755 *1220.12 p523*
Macfadden, John 40; Ontario, 1871 *1823.17 p95*
Macfie, Daniel 52; Ontario, 1871 *1823.21 p209*
Macgee, Mary; America, 1765 *1220.12 p520*
Macgilvery, Duncan 45; Michigan, 1880 *4491.36 p14*
Macgladary, Thomas 30; Ontario, 1871 *1823.21 p209*
Macgraw, James 70; Ontario, 1871 *1823.21 p209*
Macgreggor, James; Virginia, 1652 *6254.4 p243*
Macgregor, Ann 36; Ontario, 1871 *1823.21 p209*
Macgregor, Archy 60; Ontario, 1871 *1823.21 p209*
MacGregor, James; Boston, 1718 *1642 p22*
MacGregor, James; Massachusetts, 1620-1775 *1642 p139*
MacGugan, Jno.; Prince Edward Island, 1771 *3799.30 p41*
MacGwin, Daniel; Virginia, 1736 *1220.12 p520*
Mach, Friedrich Ferdinand; Wisconsin, 1892 *6795.8 p43*
Mach, Jan; Nebraska, 1869 *2853.20 p161*
Mach, Jan, Sr.; Wisconsin, 1855 *2853.20 p330*
Mach, Vaclav; New York, NY, 1893 *2853.20 p469*
Macha, Josef; Cleveland, OH, 1854 *2853.20 p475*

Macha, Josef; New York, NY, 1870-1910 *2853.20 p110*
Macha, Josef Karel; Maryland, 1896 *2853.20 p210*
Machajski, Jozef 42; New York, NY, 1912 *8355.1 p16*
Machan, Fr. S.; Texas, 1895 *2853.20 p87*
Machart, Vojtech; North Dakota, 1879-1881 *2853.20 p252*
Macharty, Sarah; Salem, MA, 1746 *1642 p78*
Macharty, Thaddeus; Roxbury, MA, 1678 *1642 p107*
Machat, Josef; Nebraska, 1882 *2853.20 p136*
Machattie, Alex 29; Ontario, 1871 *1823.21 p209*
Machek, Vaclav; Chicago, 1810-1910 *2853.20 p466*
Machenhauer, Friedrich Ludwig Wilhelm; New York, 1879 *2526.42 p170*
Macher, Frederich Wilhelm 22; New York, NY, 1864 *8425.62 p195*
Macher, Josephine Rosalie 30; America, 1856 *5475.1 p560*
Machmar, Justus; Valdivia, Chile, 1852 *1192.4 p56*
Machnauer, Emilya 23; Portland, ME, 1911 *970.38 p79*
Machol, Josephus; Wisconsin, 1902 *6795.8 p193*
Machol, Paulina; Wisconsin, 1885 *6795.8 p59*
Machol, Theela; Wisconsin, 1896 *6795.8 p60*
Machold, Christiane; America, 1868 *7919.3 p525*
  With daughter
Machon, Albert Francis SEE Machon, Charles Henry
Machon, Ann; Massachusetts, 1900-1940 *9228.50 p418*
Machon, Anne; Massachusetts, 1907 *9228.50 p418*
  *Child:*Philippe
  *Child:*Christine
  *Child:*Ophelia
  *Child:*Philip
  *Child:*Theophilus
  *Child:*Eveline
  *Child:*Lydia
  *Child:*Joshua, Jr.
Machon, Charles Henry; Alberta, 1904-1908 *9228.50 p415*
  *Brother:*Albert Francis
  *Brother:*William Edward
Machon, Charles Vere SEE Machon, John Thomas
Machon, Christine; Massachusetts, 1907 *9228.50 p362*
Machon, Christine SEE Machon, Anne Queree
Machon, Daniel SEE Machon, Daniel
Machon, Daniel; Prince Edward Island, 1806 *9228.50 p413*
  *Wife:*Frances Pullem
  *Child:*Henry
  *Child:*William
  *Child:*Elizabeth
  *Child:*Daniel
Machon, Daniel; Providence, RI, 1833-1872 *9228.50 p413*
Machon, Daniel; Providence, RI, 1872-1965 *9228.50 p416*
Machon, Daniel Walter; Connecticut, 1871-1936 *9228.50 p414*
Machon, Elizabeth SEE Machon, Daniel
Machon, Emma Jane; Massachusetts, 1852-1905 *9228.50 p417*
Machon, Euphemia; Victoria, B.C., 1911 *9228.50 p413*
Machon, Eveline; Massachusetts, 1903 *9228.50 p402*
Machon, Eveline SEE Machon, Anne Queree
Machon, Frances Pullem SEE Machon, Daniel
Machon, Fred Seymour; Hartford, CT, 1874-1974 *9228.50 p414*
Machon, Freeman David; Illinois, 1902-1930 *9228.50 p416*
Machon, Gower; Los Angeles, 1874-1974 *9228.50 p414*
Machon, Henry SEE Machon, Daniel
Machon, Henry Alexander; Boston, 1898 *9228.50 p415*
Machon, Herbert J. SEE Machon, John Thomas
Machon, James; Mobile, AL, 1864 *9228.50 p418*
Machon, James; Philadelphia, 1839-1939 *9228.50 p415*
Machon, Jane B.; Lynn, MA, 1848-1889 *9228.50 p417*
Machon, John; Cambridge, MA, 1659 *9228.50 p418*
Machon, John; North Dakota, 1847-1947 *9228.50 p418*
Machon, John; Ontario, 1847-1947 *9228.50 p418*
Machon, John Thomas; Providence, RI, 1875-1911 *9228.50 p413*
  *Wife:*Mary Ann Darby Beck
  *Son:*Herbert J.
  *Son:*Charles Vere
  *Daughter:*Maude Mary
Machon, Joseph; Providence, RI, 1872-1965 *9228.50 p416*
Machon, Joshua, Jr. SEE Machon, Anne Queree
Machon, Lydia SEE Machon, Anne Queree
Machon, Mary A.; Boston, 1841-1929 *9228.50 p417*
Machon, Mary Ann Darby Beck SEE Machon, John Thomas
Machon, Mary Ellen; Providence, RI, 1872-1965 *9228.50 p416*
Machon, Maude Mary SEE Machon, John Thomas

Machon, Nancy Ann; Prince Edward Island, 1804-1850 *9228.50 p276*
Machon, Ophelia SEE Machon, Anne Queree
Machon, Peter J.; Providence, RI, 1872-1965 *9228.50 p416*
Machon, Philip SEE Machon, Anne Queree
Machon, Philippe SEE Machon, Anne Queree
Machon, Rebecca; Providence, RI, 1872-1965 *9228.50 p416*
Machon, Samuel; Providence, RI, n.d. *9228.50 p417*
Machon, Sarah; Providence, RI, 1872-1965 *9228.50 p416*
Machon, Theophilus SEE Machon, Anne Queree
Machon, Thomas; Providence, RI, 1872-1965 *9228.50 p416*
Machon, William SEE Machon, Daniel
Machon, William; Providence, RI, 1841-1941 *9228.50 p417*
Machon, William Edward SEE Machon, Charles Henry
Machone, John; Cambridge, MA, 1659 *9228.50 p418*
Machon Family ; Prince Edward Island, 1806 *9228.50 p128*
Machos, Jas.; Texas, 1890 *6015.15 p28*
Machos, Joseph; Texas, 1884-1890 *6015.15 p28*
Machos, Voytech; Texas, 1887-1890 *6015.15 p28*
Machta, Bernard; New York, NY, 1895 *3665.20 p112*
Maciborski, Mikolaj; Detroit, 1929 *1640.55 p115*
Maciejewska, Joseph; Wisconsin, 1898 *6795.8 p60*
Maciejewski, Joseph; Wisconsin, 1898 *6795.8 p60*
Macilhargy, Patrick 50; Ontario, 1871 *1823.21 p209*
Macinnes, Donald 47; Ontario, 1871 *1823.21 p209*
Macinnes, Donald 50; Ontario, 1871 *1823.21 p209*
Macinnes, Tom 34; Ontario, 1871 *1823.21 p209*
MacIntire, Donald 54; North Carolina, 1775 *1422.10 p59*
MacIntire, Duncan 5; North Carolina, 1775 *1422.10 p59*
MacIntire, John 6; North Carolina, 1775 *1422.10 p59*
MacIntire, Katherine 41; North Carolina, 1775 *1422.10 p59*
MacIntire, Margaret 9; North Carolina, 1775 *1422.10 p59*
MacIntire, Mary 12; North Carolina, 1775 *1422.10 p59*
Macintosh, Alexander 33; Ontario, 1871 *1823.21 p209*
Macintosh, Charles 28; Ontario, 1871 *1823.21 p209*
Macintyre, Mary 50; Ontario, 1871 *1823.21 p209*
Macintyre, Neil 50; Ontario, 1871 *1823.21 p209*
Macisaac, Neil 60; Ontario, 1871 *1823.21 p209*
Maciura, Kathrine; Detroit, 1929-1930 *6214.5 p61*
Maciver, James 37; Ontario, 1871 *1823.21 p209*
Mack, Adam 44; Halifax, N.S., 1902 *1860.4 p41*
Mack, Ann Elisa; New York, 1860 *358.56 p150*
Mack, Charles 40; Ontario, 1871 *1823.21 p209*
Mack, Edward 12; Ontario, 1871 *1823.21 p209*
Mack, H.; New York, 1860 *358.56 p148*
Mack, Jacob 17; Halifax, N.S., 1902 *1860.4 p41*
Mack, James; America, 1770 *1220.12 p523*
Mack, John; Ohio, 1809-1852 *4511.35 p32*
Mack, John 34; Ontario, 1871 *1823.21 p209*
Mack, Juley 79; Ontario, 1871 *1823.21 p209*
Mack, Katharine 9; Halifax, N.S., 1902 *1860.4 p41*
Mack, Leonhardt 7; Halifax, N.S., 1902 *1860.4 p41*
Mack, Magdalena 20; Halifax, N.S., 1902 *1860.4 p41*
Mack, Margarethe 3; Halifax, N.S., 1902 *1860.4 p41*
Mack, Marianne 15; Halifax, N.S., 1902 *1860.4 p41*
Mack, Mary 35; Ontario, 1871 *1823.21 p209*
Mack, Michael 11; Halifax, N.S., 1902 *1860.4 p41*
Mack, Rosa 4; Halifax, N.S., 1902 *1860.4 p41*
Mack, Rosina 42; Halifax, N.S., 1902 *1860.4 p41*
Mackallester, John; Massachusetts, 1715 *1642 p64*
Mackarell, Elizabeth; Maryland, 1674-1675 *1236.25 p52*
Mackarta, Elizabeth; Boston, 1696 *1642 p17*
Mackase, Bartholomew; America, 1749 *1220.12 p521*
Mackay, Aeneas 20; North Carolina, 1774 *1422.10 p59*
MacKay, Alex; Prince Edward Island, 1771 *3799.30 p41*
MacKay, Andrew F.; Portland, ME, 1850 *7710.1 p153*
MacKay, Archd.; Prince Edward Island, 1771 *3799.30 p41*
Mackay, Euphemia; Victoria, B.C., 1911 *9228.50 p413*
Mackay, George 29; Ontario, 1871 *1823.17 p95*
Mackay, Henry 49; Ontario, 1871 *1823.21 p209*
Mackay, Isabella Louisa; New Jersey, 1802-1808 *3845.2 p129*
Mackay, Ivar; Cape Fear, NC,, 1754 *1422.10 p62*
MacKay, Jno., Sr.; Prince Edward Island, 1771 *3799.30 p41*
Mackay, John 80; Ontario, 1871 *1823.17 p95*
MacKay, John; Prince Edward Island, 1771 *3799.30 p41*
MacKay, More; Prince Edward Island, 1771 *3799.30 p41*
MacKay, Neil; Prince Edward Island, 1771 *3799.30 p41*
Mackay, Richard; Illinois, 1834-1900 *6020.5 p132*
Mackay, William 43; Ontario, 1871 *1823.17 p95*
Mackcafee, Daniel; Massachusetts, 1741 *1642 p67*
  *Relative:*Heugh
Mackcafee, Heugh SEE Mackcafee, Daniel
Mackdonall, John; America, 1749 *1220.12 p519*

Mackdonall, Sarah; Annapolis, MD, 1733 *1220.12 p519*
Mackelson, John; Massachusetts, 1736 *1642 p89*
Macken, Wm 2; St. Johns, N.F., 1811 *1053.20 p20*
Mackenny, Alexander; Massachusetts, 1675-1676 *1642 p129*
Mackenzie, Alexander 28; Ontario, 1871 *1823.21 p209*
Mackenzie, Alexander 49; Ontario, 1871 *1823.17 p95*
Mackenzie, Alexander 60; Ontario, 1871 *1823.17 p95*
MacKenzie, Archd.; Prince Edward Island, 1771 *3799.30 p41*
Mackenzie, Catherine 58; Michigan, 1880 *4491.36 p14*
Mackenzie, Charles 36; Ontario, 1871 *1823.17 p95*
Mackenzie, Daniel 43; Ontario, 1871 *1823.17 p95*
Mackenzie, George 51; Michigan, 1880 *4491.36 p15*
Mackenzie, James; America, 1775 *1220.12 p521*
Mackenzie, James 39; Ontario, 1871 *1823.17 p96*
Mackenzie, John 66; Michigan, 1880 *4491.36 p14*
Mackenzie, John 16; North Carolina, 1774 *1422.10 p56*
Mackenzie, John 38; Ontario, 1871 *1823.21 p209*
Mackenzie, John 40; Ontario, 1871 *1823.17 p96*
Mackenzie, Mary 32; Ontario, 1871 *1823.17 p96*
Mackenzie, Mary 60; Ontario, 1871 *1823.21 p209*
Mackenzie, Naoma 35; Michigan, 1880 *4491.36 p15*
Mackenzie, Robert 51; Ontario, 1871 *1823.17 p96*
Mackenzie, Sarah 37; Michigan, 1880 *4491.36 p14*
MacKenzie, Sarah; Providence, RI, 1884-1914 *9228.50 p413*
Mackenzie, William O. 38; Ontario, 1871 *1823.17 p96*
Mackerell, John; Maryland, 1674-1675 *1236.25 p51*
Mackey, Alan; Ottawa, 1958 *9228.50 p418*
Mackey, George; America, 1749 *1220.12 p523*
Mackey, George; America, 1767 *1220.12 p523*
Mackey, Patrick; America, 1755 *1220.12 p523*
Mackey, Thomas 39; Ontario, 1871 *1823.21 p209*
Mackfarlin, Moly; Massachusetts, 1768 *1642 p90*
Mackguire, John; Boston, 1738 *1642 p44*
Mackichnia, Lilly 61; Ontario, 1871 *1823.17 p96*
Mackie, George 34; New York, NY, 1835 *5024.1 p137*
Mackie, John 20; Ontario, 1871 *1823.17 p96*
Mackie, Robert; Illinois, 1855 *6079.1 p9*
Mackies, Ellen 24; Ontario, 1871 *1823.21 p210*
Mackiewicz, Antonina Bajda SEE Mackiewicz, Wasil
Mackiewicz, Wasil; Detroit, 1930 *1640.60 p77*
  *Wife:*Antonina Bajda
Mackin, Daniel 50; Ontario, 1871 *1823.21 p210*
Mackin, Patrick; Washington, 1887 *2770.40 p24*
Mackin, R. G.; California, 1868 *1131.61 p89*
Mackintosh, Hester 34; Ontario, 1871 *1823.17 p96*
Macklin, Abram 17; Ontario, 1871 *1823.21 p210*
Macklin, Henry 37; Ontario, 1871 *1823.21 p210*
Macklin, John; America, 1754 *1220.12 p522*
Macklin, John 24; North Carolina, 1774 *1422.10 p54*
Macklin, Mary 23; North Carolina, 1774 *1422.10 p54*
Macklonghline, Olive; Boston, 1703 *1642 p24*
Mackmelin, John; America, 1765 *1220.12 p522*
Mackness, John A. 54; Ontario, 1871 *1823.17 p96*
Mackness, Thomas 41; Ontario, 1871 *1823.17 p96*
Macknob, Hector; Massachusetts, 1715 *1642 p64*
Mackowski, Joseph M.; Wisconsin, 1900 *6795.8 p50*
Mackreall, Jno; Jamestown, VA, 1633 *1658.20 p211*
Mackrell, Edward; America, 1766 *1220.12 p523*
Mackrell, John; America, 1730 *1220.12 p523*
Mackrell, John; Barbados, 1674 *1220.12 p523*
Mackrell, Sarah; America, 1762 *1220.12 p523*
Mackwalder, H.; New York, 1859 *358.56 p100*
Maclachlan, John; Colorado, 1883 *1029.59 p57*
MacLaren, Jessie G.; Warren, RI, 1902 *9228.50 p526*
MaClarty, Jno.; Prince Edward Island, 1771 *3799.30 p41*
Maclaughlin, Angus 50; Ontario, 1871 *1823.17 p96*
MacLaughlin, Mary; America, 1745 *1220.12 p522*
Maclean, George 31; Ontario, 1871 *1823.17 p96*
MacLean, Joseph; Prince Edward Island, 1771 *3799.30 p41*
Maclean, Rachal 71; Ontario, 1871 *1823.17 p96*
Macleod, Donald 33; Ontario, 1871 *1823.21 p210*
Macleod, J. M. 50; Ontario, 1871 *1823.21 p210*
MacLeonan, Neill; Prince Edward Island, 1771 *3799.30 p41*
Maclin, Marguerite 14; Montreal, 1662 *9221.17 p498*
MacMillan, George; Washington, 1886 *6015.10 p16*
Macnamara, . . .; Salem, MA, 1771 *1642 p78*
Macnamara, Mary; Boston, 1773 *1642 p49*
Macnamara, Patrick; Toronto, 1844 *2910.35 p113*
Macnaughton, James 59; Ontario, 1871 *1823.17 p96*
Macnemara, Martha SEE Macnemara, Timothy
Macnemara, Silence SEE Macnemara, Timothy
Macnemara, Timothy; Massachusetts, 1743 *1642 p111*
  *Wife:*Martha
Macnemara, Timothy; Massachusetts, 1746 *1642 p111*
  *Wife:*Silence
MacNichol, Archibald 2; North Carolina, 1775 *1422.10 p59*

MacNichol, Donald 40; North Carolina, 1775 ***1422.10*** *p59*
MacNichol, John 6; North Carolina, 1775 ***1422.10*** *p59*
MacNichol, Katherine 33; North Carolina, 1775 ***1422.10*** *p59*
MacNichol, Mary; North Carolina, 1775 ***1422.10*** *p59*
MacNichol, Nicol 4; North Carolina, 1775 ***1422.10*** *p59*
Maconely, Jenny; Massachusetts, 1774 ***1642*** *p91*
Macoppy, Jane; Nevis or Jamaica, 1722 ***1220.12*** *p518*
Macourek, Frantisek; Cleveland, OH, 1840-1910 ***2853.20*** *p476*
Macourek, Josef; Omaha, NE, 1892 ***2853.20*** *p188*
Macourek, Josef; Omaha, NE, 1892 ***2853.20*** *p191*
Macoy, James; Massachusetts, 1732 ***1642*** *p66*
Macquart, Michelle-Madeleine 17; Quebec, 1654 ***9221.17*** *p305*
Macquart, Nicolas; Quebec, 1638 ***9221.17*** *p79*
Macquire, Lewis; Georgia, 1795 ***1451.56*** *p118*
Macrae, Donald 53; Ontario, 1871 ***1823.21*** *p210*
Macray, William 21; Ontario, 1871 ***1823.17*** *p96*
Macre, Genevieve 31; Quebec, 1662 ***9221.17*** *p489*
Macreall, Jno; Jamestown, VA, 1633 ***1658.20*** *p211*
Macri, Dominick; New York, 1926 ***1173.1*** *p2*
Macrin, Mary; America, 1764 ***1220.12*** *p523*
MacShannon, Mary; Prince Edward Island, 1771 ***3799.30*** *p41*
MacShenaig, Hector; Prince Edward Island, 1771 ***3799.30*** *p41*
Mactavish, Duncan 65; Ontario, 1871 ***1823.17*** *p96*
Macumber, Francis 38; America, 1842 ***778.6*** *p221*
MacVicar, John; Prince Edward Island, 1771 ***3799.30*** *p41*
Macvicar, Stuart A. 39; Ontario, 1871 ***1823.17*** *p96*
Macwhinney, Lucy 42; Ontario, 1871 ***1823.17*** *p96*
MacWilliam, Dun; Prince Edward Island, 1771 ***3799.30*** *p41*
Macy, John 49; Ontario, 1871 ***1823.21*** *p210*
Macy, P. Henry 22; Ontario, 1871 ***1823.21*** *p210*
Maczolek, Albert; Wisconsin, 1895 ***6795.8*** *p26*
Maday, Richard 67; Ontario, 1871 ***1823.17*** *p96*
Madberry, Thomas; Barbados, 1664 ***1220.12*** *p523*
Maddelein, Henri; New York, 1902 ***1766.20*** *p25*
Maddelien, Rene; New York, 1903 ***1766.20*** *p34*
Maddell, William; America, 1744 ***1220.12*** *p523*
Madden, Edward; America, 1773 ***1220.12*** *p523*
Madden, Edward 29; Ontario, 1871 ***1823.17*** *p96*
Madden, Elizabeth *SEE* Madden, Timothy
Madden, James; Louisiana, 1874 ***4981.45*** *p296*
Madden, James; Toronto, 1844 ***2910.35*** *p113*
Madden, Jane 38; Ontario, 1871 ***1823.21*** *p210*
Madden, John; Colorado, 1891 ***1029.59*** *p57*
Madden, John; Colorado, 1903 ***1029.59*** *p57*
Madden, John 27; Ontario, 1871 ***1823.21*** *p210*
Madden, Mary; Boston, 1773 ***1642*** *p49*
Madden, Mary; Massachusetts, 1747 ***1642*** *p91*
Madden, Mary *SEE* Madden, Michael
Madden, Michael; Massachusetts, 1763 ***1642*** *p104*
*Wife:*Mary
Madden, Pat; St. John, N.B., 1847 ***2978.15*** *p40*
Madden, Stephen; Ohio, 1809-1852 ***4511.35*** *p32*
Madden, Thomas; Boston, 1774 ***1642*** *p50*
Madden, Timothy; Massachusetts, 1740 ***1642*** *p111*
*Wife:*Elizabeth
Madden, Timothy; Massachusetts, 1768 ***1642*** *p106*
Maddens, David *SEE* Maddens, Michael
Maddens, Leve *SEE* Maddens, Michael
Maddens, Mary *SEE* Maddens, Michael
Maddens, Michael; Milford, MA, 1772 ***1642*** *p106*
*Wife:*Mary
*Child:*Leve
*Child:*David
Maddens, Samuel; America, 1771 ***1220.12*** *p523*
Madder, Edward; America, 1741 ***1220.12*** *p523*
Maddern, John; America, 1755 ***1220.12*** *p523*
Madders, John; America, 1685 ***1220.12*** *p523*
Madders, William; Virginia, 1741 ***1220.12*** *p523*
Maddigan, David; Toronto, 1844 ***2910.35*** *p112*
Maddigan, Dennis; Toronto, 1844 ***2910.35*** *p115*
Maddigan, James 45; Ontario, 1871 ***1823.21*** *p210*
Maddigan, Patrick 32; Ontario, 1871 ***1823.21*** *p210*
Maddin, John; Boston, 1747 ***1642*** *p29*
Maddin, John; Dedham, MA, 1765 ***1642*** *p102*
Maddin, Susanna *SEE* Maddin, Walter
Maddin, Thomas; Boston, 1727 ***1642*** *p25*
Maddin, Walter; Newbury, MA, 1763 ***1642*** *p75*
Maddin, Walter; Newburyport, MA, 1764 ***1642*** *p76*
*Wife:*Susanna
Madding, Hannah; America, 1767 ***1220.12*** *p523*
Maddison, Anthony; Washington, 1889 ***2770.40*** *p79*
Maddison, Sarah; America, 1757 ***1220.12*** *p523*
Maddiver, Charles 49; Ontario, 1871 ***1823.21*** *p210*
Maddock, Patrick; Illinois, 1858-1861 ***6020.5*** *p132*
Maddock, Samuel 44; Ontario, 1871 ***1823.17*** *p96*
Maddock, William 54; Ontario, 1871 ***1823.17*** *p96*
Maddocks, Martha; America, 1758 ***1220.12*** *p524*
Maddocks, Martha; America, 1769 ***1220.12*** *p524*
Maddocks, Mary; America, 1773 ***1220.12*** *p524*
Maddon, Michael 48; Ontario, 1871 ***1823.17*** *p96*
Maddow, Thomas 18; Quebec, 1870 ***8364.32*** *p24*
Maddox, Ann; America, 1749 ***1220.12*** *p523*
Maddox, Elizabeth; America, 1773 ***1220.12*** *p523*
Maddox, John; America, 1767 ***1220.12*** *p523*
Maddox, Mary; America, 1775 ***1220.12*** *p524*
Maddox, Richard; America, 1766 ***1220.12*** *p524*
Maddox, Samuel; America, 1765 ***1220.12*** *p524*
Maddringham, Jane; America, 1745 ***1220.12*** *p524*
Maddy, William; America, 1738 ***1220.12*** *p524*
Madean, Alexander 69; Ontario, 1871 ***1823.21*** *p210*
Madel, Georg Ludwig; New York, NY, 1894 ***7420.1*** *p370*
Madel, Joseph W.; America, 1854 ***7420.1*** *p124*
With family
Madel, Louis; America, 1897 ***7420.1*** *p374*
Madelaine, Jacques 55; New Orleans, 1848 ***778.6*** *p221*
Maden, Adam; Ohio, 1809-1852 ***4511.35*** *p32*
Maden, Albigail *SEE* Maden, Timothy
Maden, John; Boston, 1745 ***1642*** *p45*
Maden, Richard; America, 1744 ***1220.12*** *p523*
Maden, Timothy; Massachusetts, 1769 ***1642*** *p111*
*Wife:*Albigail
Mader, Adam; Ohio, 1809-1852 ***4511.35*** *p32*
Madera, Joshua; America, 1746 ***1220.12*** *p524*
Maderak, Karol 39; New York, NY, 1904 ***8355.1*** *p15*
Madern, Ana 32; America, 1847 ***778.6*** *p221*
Madern, Jean 34; America, 1847 ***778.6*** *p221*
Madern, Maria 6 months; America, 1847 ***778.6*** *p221*
Madern, Michel 9 months; America, 1847 ***778.6*** *p221*
Maderson, Rachel; America, 1730 ***1220.12*** *p523*
Madge, William; America, 1730 ***1220.12*** *p524*
Madie, David D. 55; Ontario, 1871 ***1823.17*** *p96*
Madiford, Ann 40; Ontario, 1871 ***1823.21*** *p210*
Madigan, Dennis; North Carolina, 1856 ***1088.45*** *p20*
Madigan, James 60; Ontario, 1871 ***1823.21*** *p210*
Madigan, James 63; Ontario, 1871 ***1823.21*** *p210*
Madigan, James 64; Ontario, 1871 ***1823.21*** *p210*
Madigan, John; South Carolina, 1808 ***6155.4*** *p19*
Madigan, Timothy 55; Ontario, 1871 ***1823.21*** *p210*
Madill, John 18; Ontario, 1871 ***1823.17*** *p96*
Madill, Samuel 46; Ontario, 1871 ***1823.17*** *p96*
Madill, William; Ohio, 1809-1852 ***4511.35*** *p32*
Madis, Nicolas 30; Missouri, 1845 ***778.6*** *p221*
Madison, Lewis S.; Iowa, 1875 ***1211.15*** *p16*
Madison, Lorenze Henning; North Carolina, 1855 ***1088.45*** *p20*
Madison, Mary C.; Iowa, 1876 ***1211.15*** *p16*
Madland, Louisa 29; Ontario, 1871 ***1823.21*** *p210*
Madle, Joseph; America, 1775 ***1220.12*** *p524*
Madole, Hugh 75; Ontario, 1871 ***1823.21*** *p210*
Madosh, J. Joseph; New York, NY, 1856 ***1494.21*** *p31*
Madoule, Mr. 33; America, 1745 ***778.6*** *p221*
Madoule, F. 29; America, 1745 ***778.6*** *p221*
Madren, Mary; Annapolis, MD, 1725 ***1220.12*** *p524*
Madron, Alexander 45; New Orleans, 1847 ***778.6*** *p221*
Madruck, Miguel; Louisiana, 1874 ***4981.45*** *p133*
Madry, Jean 28; Quebec, 1654 ***9221.17*** *p313*
Madsen, John; Colorado, 1894 ***1029.59*** *p57*
Madsen, John; Colorado, 1894 ***1029.59*** *p58*
Madsen, Olaf Jermus; Iowa, 1926 ***1211.15*** *p17*
Madsen, Otto Julius Lauritz; Iowa, 1922 ***1211.15*** *p17*
Madsen, Soren Hans; Iowa, 1926 ***1211.15*** *p17*
Madson, Clemmen; Iowa, 1890 ***1211.15*** *p16*
Madson, Jens; Iowa, 1883 ***1211.15*** *p16*
Madson, Ole; Iowa, 1896 ***1211.15*** *p17*
Madwell, James; America, 1741 ***1220.12*** *p524*
Madzia, Paul; Detroit, 1930 ***1640.60*** *p77*
Maeks, Phoebe; America, 1774 ***1220.12*** *p524*
Maendlen, W. Carl F. 47; Ontario, 1871 ***1823.21*** *p210*
Maenel, Jacques 8; Port uncertain, 1843 ***778.6*** *p221*
Maenel, Jacques 33; Port uncertain, 1843 ***778.6*** *p221*
Maenel, Jean 5; Port uncertain, 1843 ***778.6*** *p222*
Maenel, Michel 3; Port uncertain, 1843 ***778.6*** *p222*
Maenel, Salomea 33; Port uncertain, 1843 ***778.6*** *p222*
Maenz, Elisab.; Valdivia, Chile, 1852 ***1192.4*** *p55*
Maer, Alexander; America, 1764 ***1220.12*** *p574*
Maerer, Christine; Dakota, 1885 ***554.30*** *p25*
Maes, Desire; New York, NY, 1881 ***1494.20*** *p13*
Maes, Katharina 22; America, 1872 ***5475.1*** *p41*
Maes, P. F. 40; America, 1846 ***778.6*** *p222*
Maettig, J. F.; Valdivia, Chile, 1850 ***1192.4*** *p49*
With wife
With child 5
With child 2
Maffey, Laudin 30; America, 1841 ***778.6*** *p222*
Magar, Jacog; Boston, 1766 ***1642*** *p36*
Magar, Robert; Boston, 1766 ***1642*** *p36*
Magard, Peter 28; America, 1867 ***5475.1*** *p166*
Magd D.K.Boehm, Anna Barbara; America, 1892 ***170.15*** *p35*
Magdelain, Jeanne; Quebec, 1669 ***4514.3*** *p343*
Magden, Joseph 18; Ontario, 1871 ***1823.21*** *p210*
Magee, Edward; Louisiana, 1841-1844 ***4981.45*** *p210*
Magee, Eleanor; Boston, 1763 ***1642*** *p48*
Magee, George; Boston, 1774 ***8529.30*** *p6*
Magee, James; Boston, 1768 ***1642*** *p39*
Magee, James 25; Ontario, 1871 ***1823.21*** *p210*
Magee, Jean; Massachusetts, 1749 ***1642*** *p85*
Magee, Luke; New Orleans, 1850 ***7242.30*** *p148*
Magee, Mary Ann 21; Ontario, 1871 ***1823.21*** *p210*
Magenas, Mary; Boston, 1737 ***1642*** *p44*
Magenis, Daniel; Massachusetts, 1675-1676 ***1642*** *p127*
Magennis, Daniel; Massachusetts, 1675-1676 ***1642*** *p128*
Mager, George; Newbury, MA, 1672 ***9228.50*** *p420*
Mager, Jacob; Ohio, 1809-1852 ***4511.35*** *p32*
Mager, John; America, 1772 ***1220.12*** *p525*
Mager, Thomas; Louisiana, 1836-1841 ***4981.45*** *p209*
Magerall, John 60; Ontario, 1871 ***1823.17*** *p96*
Magerom, Prosper 21; America, 1844 ***778.6*** *p222*
Mages, J. P. 23; America, 1848 ***778.6*** *p222*
Magetanz, Albert H.; Wisconsin, 1877 ***6795.8*** *p227*
Magg, G.; Louisiana, 1874 ***4981.45*** *p296*
Magginnis, William 54; Ontario, 1871 ***1823.21*** *p210*
Maggins, Charles; Quebec, 1870 ***8364.32*** *p24*
Maggs, Thomas 64; Ontario, 1871 ***1823.21*** *p210*
Magher, Edward; Toronto, 1844 ***2910.35*** *p113*
Magie, Jean 37; Port uncertain, 1848 ***778.6*** *p222*
Magier, Andras 25; New York, NY, 1904 ***8355.1*** *p15*
Magill, Henry; Colorado, 1880 ***1029.59*** *p58*
Magill, James 30; Ontario, 1871 ***1823.21*** *p210*
Magill, John 47; Ontario, 1871 ***1823.21*** *p210*
Magill, Peter; Toronto, 1844 ***2910.35*** *p113*
Magilvery, John 60; Ontario, 1871 ***1823.21*** *p211*
Magin, Charles; America, 1765 ***1220.12*** *p524*
Maginis, Daniel; Massachusetts, 1675-1676 ***1642*** *p128*
Maginnis, Daniel; Massachusetts, 1675-1676 ***1642*** *p127*
Magioti, Aspano; Louisiana, 1874-1875 ***4981.45*** *p30*
Magle, Mary 42; Michigan, 1880 ***4491.30*** *p21*
Magle, Nicholas 46; Michigan, 1880 ***4491.30*** *p21*
Magmard, Annette 3; New Orleans, 1848 ***778.6*** *p222*
Magmard, Benoite 32; New Orleans, 1848 ***778.6*** *p222*
Magmard, Jean-Baptiste 10; New Orleans, 1848 ***778.6*** *p222*
Magmard, Joseph 33; New Orleans, 1848 ***778.6*** *p222*
Magmard, Marie 7; New Orleans, 1848 ***778.6*** *p222*
Magnan, Anne; Quebec, 1665 ***4514.3*** *p343*
Magnan, Antoine 35; Quebec, 1657 ***9221.17*** *p362*
Magnan, Pierre 19; Montreal, 1662 ***9221.17*** *p498*
Magne, . . .; Montreal, 1659 ***9221.17*** *p424*
Magne, Mr. 28; America, 1843 ***778.6*** *p222*
Magne, Jean; Louisiana, 1836-1841 ***4981.45*** *p209*
Magne, Jean 35; Port uncertain, 1843 ***778.6*** *p222*
Magnell, August; Cleveland, OH, 1888-1891 ***9722.10*** *p123*
Magnenot, Charles Lewis; North Carolina, 1854 ***1088.45*** *p20*
Magner, James; Louisiana, 1874-1875 ***4981.45*** *p30*
Magner, James; Toronto, 1844 ***2910.35*** *p113*
Magner, Philip; Barbados or Jamaica, 1690 ***1220.12*** *p524*
Magner, S.; Louisiana, 1836-1841 ***4981.45*** *p209*
Magner, Thomas; Toronto, 1844 ***2910.35*** *p113*
Magnidotter, Anna; North America, 1854 ***6410.15*** *p104*
Magnidotter, Anna; North America, 1855 ***6410.15*** *p104*
Magnier, Mr. 36; Louisiana, 1840 ***778.6*** *p222*
Magnier, Aimable 28; America, 1848 ***778.6*** *p222*
Magnier, Marie; Quebec, 1665 ***4514.3*** *p343*
Magnifico, Isidore; Louisiana, 1874 ***4981.45*** *p132*
Magnin, August 24; New Orleans, 1848 ***778.6*** *p222*
Magnin, Jean 22; New Orleans, 1848 ***778.6*** *p222*
Magnin, Jn. Bte. 25; Louisiana, 1848 ***778.6*** *p222*
Magnin, Sylvestre 30; Louisiana, 1848 ***778.6*** *p222*
Magnin, Therese 25; New Orleans, 1848 ***778.6*** *p222*
Magnus, August; Galveston, TX, 1855 ***571.7*** *p17*
Magnus, Johann Ph.; Galveston, TX, 1855 ***571.7*** *p17*
Magnuson, Eva; St. Paul, MN, 1869-1878 ***1865.50*** *p96*
Magnuson, Eva; St. Paul, MN, 1899 ***1865.50*** *p96*
Magnusson, Aaron 12 *SEE* Magnusson, August
Magnusson, Anna Jansdotter 36 *SEE* Magnusson, August
Magnusson, August; Kansas, 1880 ***777.40*** *p4*
*Wife:*Anna Jansdotter
*Son:*Aaron
*Son:*Oscar
*Son:*Ephram
Magnusson, Bengt 48; New York, NY, 1894 ***6512.1*** *p184*
Magnusson, Carl August; Baltimore, 1849 ***6412.40*** *p155*
Magnusson, Charles; Cleveland, OH, 1872-1888 ***9722.10*** *p123*
Magnusson, Charles; Cleveland, OH, 1901-1904 ***9722.10*** *p123*

Magnusson, Emil; Iowa, 1906 *1211.15 p17*
Magnusson, Ephram 11 SEE Magnusson, August
Magnusson, Fredr.; New Orleans, 1856 *6412.40 p154*
Magnusson, Gustaf; Cleveland, OH, 1901-1903 *9722.10 p123*
Magnusson, J.; Valparaiso, Chile, 1850 *1192.4 p50*
Magnusson, Oscar 7 SEE Magnusson, August
Magolsin, Gottlieb 32; America, 1846 *778.6 p222*
Magon, Miss 25; America, 1845 *778.6 p222*
Magon, Aristide 9; America, 1845 *778.6 p222*
Magore, Mr. 35; Louisiana, 1848 *778.6 p222*
Magore, Mrs. 25; Louisiana, 1848 *778.6 p222*
Magoy, Hugh; America, 1738 *1220.12 p524*
Magrath, Edmond; Boston, 1753 *1642 p31*
MaGrath, Matthew; Toronto, 1844 *2910.35 p115*
Magrath, Roger 20; St. Johns, N.F., 1811 *1053.20 p21*
Magraugh, Timothy; Boston, 1724 *1642 p25*
Magrave, Ralph; America, 1774 *1220.12 p524*
Magrigor, Daniel 48; Ontario, 1871 *1823.21 p211*
Maguer, Dennis; Louisiana, 1874 *4981.45 p133*
Maguerey, Catherine 14; Mississippi, 1845-1846 *778.6 p222*
Maguerey, Catherine 43; Mississippi, 1845-1846 *778.6 p222*
Maguerey, Charles 8 months; Mississippi, 1845-1846 *778.6 p222*
Maguerey, Elisabeth 13; Mississippi, 1845-1846 *778.6 p222*
Maguerey, Jacques 15; Mississippi, 1845-1846 *778.6 p222*
Maguerey, Jean 39; Mississippi, 1845-1846 *778.6 p223*
Maguerey, Justine 5; Mississippi, 1845-1846 *778.6 p223*
Maguerey, Marguerite 10; Mississippi, 1845-1846 *778.6 p223*
Maguerey, Pierre 6; Mississippi, 1845-1846 *778.6 p223*
Maguet, Francoise; Quebec, 1670 *4514.3 p319*
  Son:Pierre
Maguet, Pierre SEE Maguet, Francoise Goubilleau
Maguire, Mrs.; Quebec, 1885 *1937.10 p52*
Maguire, Charles 72; Ontario, 1871 *1823.21 p211*
Maguire, J.; Toronto, 1844 *2910.35 p116*
Maguire, J.A.; Quebec, 1885 *1937.10 p52*
Maguire, James; Barbados or St. Christopher, 1780 *8529.30 p7A*
Maguire, James; Toronto, 1844 *2910.35 p115*
Maguire, Jane 34; Ontario, 1871 *1823.21 p211*
MaGuire, John; Toronto, 1844 *2910.35 p116*
Maguire, Michael; New York, NY, 1842 *3274.56 p99*
Maguire, Nancy 65; Ontario, 1871 *1823.17 p96*
Maguire, Patrick; Toronto, 1844 *2910.35 p113*
Maguire, Stewart; New York, NY, 1848 *7710.1 p153*
Maguire, William; Virginia, 1852 *7710.1 p152*
Magwood, Richard 27; Ontario, 1871 *1823.17 p96*
Magwood, William 35; Ontario, 1871 *1823.17 p96*
Mahaaner, Cornelius; Boston, 1747 *1642 p29*
Maham, John G.; North Carolina, 1792-1862 *1088.45 p20*
Mahan, John; Boston, 1766 *1642 p37*
Mahan, John 29; Ontario, 1871 *1823.17 p96*
Mahan, Joseph; America, 1769 *1220.12 p524*
Mahan, Joseph 45; Ontario, 1871 *1823.21 p211*
Mahan, Lawrence 40; Ontario, 1871 *1823.21 p211*
Mahan, Mary SEE Mahan, William
Mahan, Michael; Boston, 1826 *3274.55 p43*
Mahan, William 36; Ontario, 1871 *1823.21 p211*
Mahan, William; Worcester, MA, 1756 *1642 p114*
  Wife:Mary
Mahany, Thomas; New England, 1745 *1642 p27*
Mahar, John; St. John, N.B., 1847 *2978.15 p37*
Mahar, Patrick; Boston, 1747 *1642 p46*
Mahat, Aru; Louisiana, 1874 *4981.45 p296*
Mahau, Catherine 65; Ontario, 1871 *1823.21 p211*
Mahe, Louis Y. F.; Illinois, 1852 *6079.1 p9*
Mahedy, James; New York, NY, 1836 *3274.55 p75*
Mahen, Torrence; Colorado, 1871 *1029.59 p58*
Maher, Cath; New Orleans, 1851 *7242.30 p148*
Maher, David 50; Ontario, 1871 *1823.17 p96*
Maher, Edward; New York, NY, 1839 *3274.56 p72*
Maher, Edward 50; Ontario, 1871 *1823.21 p211*
Maher, John; Newfoundland, 1814 *3476.10 p54*
Maher, John C.; Ontario, 1871 *1823.21 p211*
Maher, John William; Louisiana, 1874 *4981.45 p296*
Maher, Thomas; Louisiana, 1874 *4981.45 p133*
Maher, Thomas; Ohio, 1809-1852 *4511.35 p32*
Mahern, John; California, 1868 *1131.61 p90*
Maheue, John; America, 1776 *9228.50 p418*
  Relative:Steven
Maheue, Steven SEE Maheue, John
Maheust, Charles; Quebec, 1639 *9221.17 p91*
Maheust, Jacques 36; Quebec, 1637 *9221.17 p71*
Maheust, Jean-Paul Corrivault 1 SEE Maheust, Marguerite Corrivault Lefranc
Maheust, Leonarde Fouquet SEE Maheust, Zacharie

Maheust, Louis; Quebec, 1644 *9221.17 p144*
Maheust, Marguerite 22; Quebec, 1648 *9221.17 p201*
  Son:Jean-Paul Corrivault 1
Maheust, Pierre 21; Quebec, 1651 *9221.17 p248*
Maheust, Pierre; Quebec, 1651 *9221.17 p8*
Maheust, Rene; Quebec, 1637 *9221.17 p71*
Maheust, Rene 21 SEE Maheust, Zacharie
Maheust, Zacharie 51; Quebec, 1653 *9221.17 p277*
  Wife:Leonarde Fouquet
  Son:Rene 21
Mahey, Pierre 27; New Orleans, 1848 *778.6 p223*
Maheyer, G. 17; America, 1843 *778.6 p223*
Mahfouz, Roomanas; Texas, 1906 *3435.45 p36*
Mahhon, Philip; Massachusetts, 1764 *1642 p109*
Mahier, Mary; Boston, 1700-1730 *9228.50 p576*
Mahier, Richard; Virginia, 1720 *9228.50 p418*
Mahill, Elizabeth 65; Ontario, 1871 *1823.21 p211*
Mahl, George; Louisiana, 1874 *4981.45 p133*
Mahler, Antoine 17; America, 1847 *778.6 p223*
Mahler, G. H.; North Carolina, 1860 *1088.45 p20*
Mahler, George 36; Ontario, 1871 *1823.21 p211*
Mahler, Johannes; Washington, 1882 *2770.40 p135*
Mahnberg, Jacob; Valdivia, Chile, 1852 *1192.4 p56*
  With wife
Mahon, Charles 36; Ontario, 1871 *1823.21 p211*
Mahon, Ellen 17; New York, NY, 1835 *5024.1 p137*
Mahon, Esther 37; New York, NY, 1835 *5024.1 p137*
Mahon, James 44; Ontario, 1871 *1823.21 p211*
Mahon, James 75; Ontario, 1871 *1823.21 p211*
Mahon, John; America, 1762 *1220.12 p524*
Mahon, John; New York, NY, 1834 *3274.56 p70*
Mahon, John 37; New York, NY, 1835 *5024.1 p137*
Mahon, John 65; Ontario, 1871 *1823.21 p211*
Mahon, Julia 45; Ontario, 1871 *1823.21 p211*
Mahon, Patrick; Boston, 1766 *1642 p35*
Mahon, Patrick; Toronto, 1844 *2910.35 p114*
Mahon, William 40; Ontario, 1871 *1823.21 p211*
Mahone, Rose; Rappahannock, VA, 1741 *1220.12 p524*
Mahone, Thomas; Boston, 1725 *1642 p25*
Mahoney, Catharine T. O'Halloran SEE Mahoney, Richard
Mahoney, D.; California, 1868 *1131.61 p89*
Mahoney, Dennis; Boston, 1766 *1642 p37*
Mahoney, Florence; America, 1770 *1220.12 p524*
Mahoney, George 61; Ontario, 1871 *1823.21 p211*
Mahoney, James; Shrewsbury, MA, 1766 *1642 p108*
Mahoney, James; Toronto, 1844 *2910.35 p114*
Mahoney, John; Illinois, 1834-1900 *6020.5 p132*
Mahoney, John; Toronto, 1844 *2910.35 p113*
Mahoney, John; Washington, 1884 *2770.40 p192*
Mahoney, Mary; Boston, 1766 *1642 p37*
Mahoney, Mary 9; Quebec, 1870 *8364.32 p24*
Mahoney, Patrick; Illinois, 1858-1861 *6020.5 p132*
Mahoney, Phillip; Boston, 1753 *1642 p47*
Mahoney, Richard; Philadelphia, 1861 *8513.31 p410*
  Wife:Catharine T. O'Halloran
Mahoney, Thomas; America, 1771 *1220.12 p524*
Mahoney, Thomas; New England, 1745 *1642 p28*
Mahony, Cornelius; Boston, 1731 *1642 p44*
Mahony, Elizabeth; Beverly, MA, 1723 *1642 p64*
Mahony, Elizabeth 22; Ontario, 1871 *1823.21 p211*
Mahony, Florence; Boston, 1743 *1642 p45*
Mahony, George; Boston, 1770 *1642 p49*
Mahony, John 32; Ontario, 1871 *1823.17 p96*
Mahony, Michael; America, 1767 *1220.12 p524*
Mahony, Nicholas 55; Ontario, 1871 *1823.17 p96*
Mahony, Timothy 41; Ontario, 1871 *1823.21 p211*
Mahoone, Sarah; Barbados or Jamaica, 1697 *1220.12 p524*
Mahou, . . .; New Orleans, 1848 *778.6 p223*
Mahou, Mrs. 33; New Orleans, 1848 *778.6 p223*
Mahou, L. Jean 41; New Orleans, 1848 *778.6 p223*
Mahr, Albrecht SEE Mahr, Antonie
Mahr, Antonie; America, 1868 *7919.3 p534*
  Son:Albrecht
Mahr, Carl; America, 1868 *7919.3 p534*
  With family
Mahr, Charlotte 16 SEE Mahr, Johannes
Mahr, Christiana; America, 1867 *7919.3 p528*
Mahr, Elisabetha 6 SEE Mahr, Johannes
Mahr, Georg 13 SEE Mahr, Johannes
Mahr, Johann Martin 19 SEE Mahr, Johannes
Mahr, Johann Nicolaus; America, 1867 *7919.3 p524*
Mahr, Johannes; America, 1846 *2526.42 p96*
  With wife
  Child:Magdalena
  Child:Elisabetha
  Child:Martin
  Child:Wilhelm
  Child:Johann Martin
  Child:Charlotte
  Child:Georg
  Child:Katharina

Mahr, John; Ohio, 1809-1852 *4511.35 p32*
Mahr, Katharina 20 SEE Mahr, Johannes
Mahr, Magdalena 7 SEE Mahr, Johannes
Mahr, Martin 4 SEE Mahr, Johannes
Mahr, Mathilde; America, 1867 *7919.3 p528*
Mahr, Wilhelm 11 SEE Mahr, Johannes
Mahrer, Joseph; Died enroute, 1817-1818 *90.20 p152*
Mahsem, Nikolaus; Illinois, 1855 *5475.1 p374*
Mahsing, Mrs.; America, 1847 *5475.1 p475*
Mahsing, Anna Schirra SEE Mahsing, Peter
Mahsing, Johann 2 SEE Mahsing, Peter
Mahsing, Johannetta 4 weeks months SEE Mahsing, Peter
Mahsing, Karl Franz; America, 1848 *5475.1 p475*
Mahsing, Katharina 4 SEE Mahsing, Peter
Mahsing, Peter; America, 1871 *5475.1 p441*
  Wife:Anna Schirra
  Son:Johann
  Daughter:Johannetta
  Daughter:Katharina
Mahsing, Peter 30; Brazil, 1872 *5475.1 p443*
Mahsion, Johann; America, 1867 *5475.1 p238*
Mahsion, Mathias; New York, 1854 *5475.1 p236*
Mahy, Amanda; Oregon, 1900-1923 *9228.50 p653*
Mahy, Anthony; Pennsylvania, 1900-1983 *9228.50 p419*
Mahy, Cecil Robert SEE Mahy, Robert C.
Mahy, Gordelia; America, n.d. *9228.50 p419*
Mahy, John; Marblehead, MA, 1700-1799 *9228.50 p451*
Mahy, John; Marblehead, MA, 1750-1800 *9228.50 p419*
  Wife:Margaret
Mahy, Joseph; Newfoundland, 1855 *9228.50 p419*
Mahy, Lydia Moriah Queripel SEE Mahy, Robert C.
Mahy, Margaret SEE Mahy, John
Mahy, Martin; Illinois, 1852 *6079.1 p9*
Mahy, Nicolas; New Brunswick, 1850-1925 *9228.50 p419*
Mahy, Rachel; Wisconsin, 1847 *9228.50 p317*
Mahy, Rachel; Wisconsin, 1847 *9228.50 p317*
Mahy, Robert C.; New Jersey, 1927-1928 *9228.50 p527*
  Wife:Lydia Moriah Queripel
  Child:Cecil Robert
Mai, Anna Maria; America, 1855 *2526.42 p116*
Mai, Daniel; New York, 1859 *358.56 p100*
Mai, Franz; America, 1855 *2526.42 p116*
Mai, Hermann; America, 1889 *2526.42 p126*
Mai, Isaak; America, 1890 *2526.42 p126*
Mai, Johann; America, 1881 *5475.1 p325*
  Wife:Maria Labuwe
Mai, Maria Labuwe SEE Mai, Johann
Mai, Maria; Wisconsin, 1891 *5475.1 p325*
Mai, Robert; America, 1868 *7919.3 p534*
  With wife & child
Mai, Stephan; New York, 1860 *358.56 p149*
Maid, James; America, 1775 *1220.12 p524*
Maid, Jane; America, 1774 *1220.12 p524*
Maiden, Ann; Maryland or Virginia, 1731 *1220.12 p524*
Maiden, Richard; Barbados or Jamaica, 1685 *1220.12 p524*
Maidenought, Michael; America, 1750 *1220.12 p524*
Maidh, Ellen Augusta SEE Maidh, Karl Arvid
Maidh, Karl Arvid; St. Paul, MN, 1901 *1865.50 p96*
  Wife:Ellen Augusta
Maidman, James; America, 1732 *1220.12 p524*
Maidment, Charles; Washington, 1889 *2770.40 p79*
Maidment, Henry 61; Ontario, 1871 *1823.17 p96*
Maidment, William 39; Ontario, 1871 *1823.17 p97*
Maier, Alexander; Missouri, 1876 *5475.1 p406*
Maier, Amalia 31; Texas, 1913 *8425.16 p31*
Maier, Emilie 5; Texas, 1913 *8425.16 p31*
Maier, Jakob 7; Texas, 1913 *8425.16 p31*
Maier, Johann 2; New York, NY, 1898 *7951.13 p41*
Maier, Johann 34; New York, NY, 1898 *7951.13 p41*
Maier, Johann 18; Texas, 1913 *8425.16 p31*
Maier, Katharina 16; Halifax, N.S., 1902 *1860.4 p40*
Maier, Lidia 1; Texas, 1913 *8425.16 p31*
Maier, Magdalena 32; New York, NY, 1898 *7951.13 p41*
Maier, Margaretha; America, 1844-1899 *6442.17 p65*
Maier, Margaretha; America, 1846 *6442.17 p65*
Maier, Maria 3; Texas, 1913 *8425.16 p31*
Maier, Martin; Illinois, 1858-1861 *6020.5 p132*
Maier, Matth; Valdivia, Chile, 1852 *1192.4 p53*
  With son 11
Maier, Moritz; America, 1872 *5475.1 p419*
Maier, Pauline 11; Halifax, N.S., 1902 *1860.4 p40*
Maier, Salomon; Missouri, 1870 *5475.1 p405*
Maifield, William 44; Ontario, 1871 *1823.17 p97*
Maignaut, J...ph Ed. 22; America, 1841 *778.6 p223*
Maignein, Simon 20; Montreal, 1662 *9221.17 p499*
Mail, Edmund; America, 1756 *1220.12 p525*
Mail, George 44; New Orleans, 1846 *778.6 p223*
Mailand, Pedro. 22; New Orleans, 1847 *778.6 p223*
Mailander, George; Illinois, 1864 *6079.1 p9*
Maile, Ernst; America, 1889 *179.55 p19*

Maile, John; America, 1755 ***1220.12*** *p525*
Maile, William; America, 1755 ***1220.12*** *p525*
Mailhes, Henry; Louisiana, 1874 ***4981.45*** *p133*
Mailhes, J. M. 19; New Orleans, 1848 ***778.6*** *p223*
Mailhes, Jean; Louisiana, 1874 ***4981.45*** *p132*
Mailhes, Laurent 30; New Orleans, 1844 ***778.6*** *p223*
Mailho, Jean 25; America, 1846 ***778.6*** *p223*
Maillard, Paul 30; America, 1841 ***778.6*** *p223*
Maillard, Peter; Ohio, 1809-1852 ***4511.35*** *p32*
Maillart, Louis; Quebec, 1656 ***9221.17*** *p341*
Maille, Jos.; Louisiana, 1874-1875 ***4981.45*** *p30*
Mailles, Andre 26; America, 1845 ***778.6*** *p223*
Maillet, Jean; Quebec, 1645 ***9221.17*** *p155*
Maillet, Marguerite; Quebec, 1659 ***9221.17*** *p395*
Maillet, Marguerite; Quebec, 1659 ***9221.17*** *p395*
Maillet, Marie 49; Montreal, 1659 ***9221.17*** *p415*
Maillet, Pierre 28; Montreal, 1659 ***9221.17*** *p424*
Maillette, Pierre Louis 38; America, 1848 ***778.6*** *p223*
Maillevin, J. P.; Louisiana, 1874 ***4981.45*** *p296*
Maillies, Mr. 22; New Orleans, 1840 ***778.6*** *p223*
Mailliet, Jacques; Quebec, 1655 ***9221.17*** *p324*
Maillon, Jules H.; Illinois, 1852 ***6079.1*** *p9*
Maillou, Pierre 26; Quebec, 1657 ***9221.17*** *p362*
Mailly, Mr. 20; Louisiana, 1848 ***778.6*** *p223*
Main, Alex 1; New York, NY, 1835 ***5024.1*** *p137*
Main, Alex 27; New York, NY, 1835 ***5024.1*** *p137*
Main, Alexandeer; Ohio, 1854 ***6020.12*** *p13*
Main, Alexander; Ohio, 1854 ***3580.20*** *p32*
Main, Betsey 7; New York, NY, 1835 ***5024.1*** *p137*
Main, Betsey 25; New York, NY, 1835 ***5024.1*** *p137*
Main, Elizabeth 48; Ontario, 1871 ***1823.21*** *p211*
Main, Henry; America, 1774 ***1220.12*** *p524*
Main, James 5; New York, NY, 1835 ***5024.1*** *p137*
Main, John; Illinois, 1918 ***6007.60*** *p9*
Main, John 44; Toronto, 1872 ***9228.50*** *p419*
Main, Mary 3; New York, NY, 1835 ***5024.1*** *p137*
Main, Robert; Boston, 1766 ***1642*** *p36*
Main, Robert; Ohio, 1854 ***3580.20*** *p32*
Main, Robert; Ohio, 1854 ***6020.12*** *p13*
Main, Thomas; America, 1759 ***1220.12*** *p525*
Main, William 44; Ontario, 1871 ***1823.17*** *p97*
Mainard, John 60; Ontario, 1871 ***1823.21*** *p211*
Maindet, Joseph; Montreal, 1651 ***9221.17*** *p251*
Maindonald, Albert James; Ontario, 1907 ***9228.50*** *p419*
Maindonald, Mary E.; Philadelphia, 1817 ***9228.50*** *p480*
Maine, . . .; Portsmouth, NH, n.d. ***9228.50*** *p419*
Maine, Charles; America, 1743 ***1220.12*** *p524*
Maine, John; America, 1728 ***1220.12*** *p524*
Maine, John 13; Quebec, 1870 ***8364.32*** *p24*
Maine, Mary; Annapolis, MD, 1758 ***1220.12*** *p524*
Mainer, John 29; Ontario, 1871 ***1823.21*** *p211*
Maines, Thomas; Burlington, VT, 1827 ***3274.55*** *p22*
Mainolly, Charlotte 40; Ontario, 1871 ***1823.17*** *p97*
Mainolly, Parnell 36; Ontario, 1871 ***1823.17*** *p97*
Mains, Henry 55; Ontario, 1871 ***1823.17*** *p97*
Mainwairing, Charles; America, 1767 ***1220.12*** *p525*
Mainwaring, Eliza; Utah, 1866 ***3687.1*** *p35*
Mainwaring, J. 17; Quebec, 1870 ***8364.32*** *p24*
Mainwaring, James; America, 1765 ***1220.12*** *p525*
Mainwaring, Winchester; Jamaica, 1732-1747 ***9228.50*** *p132*
Mainy, Lawrence; America, 1736 ***1220.12*** *p525*
Mair, William; Annapolis, MD, 1725 ***1220.12*** *p528*
Mair, William 43; Ontario, 1871 ***1823.21*** *p211*
Mairat, Donald 40; America, 1840 ***778.6*** *p223*
Mairat, Seraphine 19; America, 1840 ***778.6*** *p223*
Maire, Adolphe 18; America, 1843 ***778.6*** *p223*
Maire, Augustine 16; America, 1843 ***778.6*** *p223*
Maire, Ba.bara; Mississippi, 1846 ***778.6*** *p223*
Maire, Claude 18; America, 1843 ***778.6*** *p223*
Maire, Jeanne 56; America, 1843 ***778.6*** *p223*
Maire, Joseph 22; America, 1843 ***778.6*** *p223*
Maire, Jules 24; America, 1843 ***778.6*** *p223*
Maire, Leopold 56; America, 1843 ***778.6*** *p223*
Maire, Marie 9; America, 1843 ***778.6*** *p224*
Maire, Rosalie 27; Mississippi, 1846 ***778.6*** *p224*
Mairi, Claude Fois. 33; Louisiana, 1848 ***778.6*** *p224*
Mairs, Alexander; Ohio, 1854 ***3580.20*** *p32*
Mairs, Alexander; Ohio, 1854 ***6020.12*** *p13*
Mairs, Archibald; Illinois, 1855 ***6079.1*** *p9*
Mairs, Lewis 21; Michigan, 1880 ***4491.39*** *p18*
Maisey, John 83; Michigan, 1880 ***4491.30*** *p21*
Maisey, Katherine 68; Michigan, 1880 ***4491.30*** *p21*
Maisey, Richard 79; Michigan, 1880 ***4491.30*** *p21*
Maitland, Andrew 50; Ontario, 1871 ***1823.17*** *p97*
Maitland, David 44; Ontario, 1871 ***1823.17*** *p97*
Maitland, David J. 46; Ontario, 1871 ***1823.17*** *p97*
Maitland, Henry 39; Ontario, 1871 ***1823.21*** *p211*
Maitland, Jane 74; Ontario, 1871 ***1823.17*** *p97*
Maitland, John 71; Ontario, 1871 ***1823.21*** *p211*
Maitland, Patrick 42; Ontario, 1871 ***1823.17*** *p97*
Maitland, Stewart 23; Quebec, 1910 ***2897.7*** *p9*
Maitland, Thomas 52; Ontario, 1871 ***1823.17*** *p97*
Maiworm, Anna *SEE* Maiworm, Peter
Maiworm, Anton *SEE* Maiworm, Peter
Maiworm, Franz *SEE* Maiworm, Peter
Maiworm, Jodokus *SEE* Maiworm, Peter
Maiworm, Katharina *SEE* Maiworm, Peter
Maiworm, Paula; America, 1928 ***8023.44*** *p377*
Maiworm, Peter; Brazil, 1845 ***8023.44*** *p376*
*Son:*Jodokus
*Daughter:*Anna
*Daughter:*Katharina
*Son:*Franz
*Son:*Anton
Maiwurm, August; New York, 1859 ***358.56*** *p54*
Maixner, Frantisek; Nebraska, 1871-1872 ***2853.20*** *p176*
Maixner, Frantisek; Nebraska, 1875 ***2853.20*** *p172*
Maj, Josef; Detroit, 1929 ***1640.55*** *p116*
Majeire, George; Newbury, MA, 1672 ***9228.50*** *p420*
Majer, Jan; St. Louis, 1848 ***2853.20*** *p21*
Majer, Matej; Illinois, 1853-1910 ***2853.20*** *p471*
Majewicz, Alexander; Detroit, 1930 ***1640.60*** *p78*
Majewski, Josef; Detroit, 1929-1930 ***6214.5*** *p63*
Majewski, Walter; Detroit, 1929 ***1640.55*** *p116*
Majiry, Benjamin; Salem, MA, 1650-1675 ***9228.50*** *p440*
Majiry, George; Massachusetts, n.d. ***9228.50*** *p439*
Majiry, Jane; Died enroute, 1677 ***9228.50*** *p440*
Majiry, Joseph; Salem, MA, 1655-1680 ***9228.50*** *p440*
Majiry, Laurence; Salem, MA, 1646-1670 ***9228.50*** *p439*
Majiry, Martin; Massachusetts, 1652-1709 ***9228.50*** *p440*
Majka, Julius John; Detroit, 1929-1930 ***6214.5*** *p67*
Majkrzak, Josef 40; New York, NY, 1920 ***930.50*** *p49*
Majoie, Joseph *SEE* Majoie, Martin
Majoie, Marie Louise *SEE* Majoie, Martin
Majoie, Marie Therese *SEE* Majoie, Martin
Majoie, Martin; Wisconsin, 1856 ***1495.20*** *p46*
*Child:*Joseph
*Child:*Marie Therese
*Child:*Marie Louise
Major, Barbara 15 months; New York, NY, 1898 ***7951.13*** *p42*
Major, Elisabeth 32; New York, NY, 1898 ***7951.13*** *p42*
Major, Eliz.; Newport, RI, 1717 ***9228.50*** *p20A*
*Sister:*Mary
Major, George *SEE* Major, Richard
Major, George; New England, n.d. ***9228.50*** *p469*
Major, George; Newbury, MA, 1672 ***9228.50*** *p420*
Major, George; Virginia, 1729 ***1220.12*** *p525*
Major, Hannah; Virginia, 1770 ***1220.12*** *p525*
Major, Jacob 9; New York, NY, 1898 ***7951.13*** *p42*
Major, James; America, 1768 ***1220.12*** *p525*
Major, James; America, 1772 ***1220.12*** *p525*
Major, James 48; Ontario, 1871 ***1823.17*** *p97*
Major, Jean; New Hampshire, 1683 ***9228.50*** *p20A*
Major, John; America, 1767 ***1220.12*** *p525*
Major, John; Virginia, 1766 ***1220.12*** *p525*
Major, Katharina; America, 1884 ***5475.1*** *p229*
Major, Katherina 11; New York, NY, 1898 ***7951.13*** *p42*
Major, Marie; Quebec, 1668 ***4514.3*** *p344*
Major, Mary *SEE* Major, Eliz.
Major, Peter 7; New York, NY, 1898 ***7951.13*** *p42*
Major, Peter 32; New York, NY, 1898 ***7951.13*** *p42*
Major, Phillip 4; New York, NY, 1898 ***7951.13*** *p42*
Major, Richard; Maryland, 1634 ***9228.50*** *p420*
With wife
*Son:*George
*Son:*Robert
Major, Richard; Quebec, 1765-1801 ***9228.50*** *p447*
Major, Robert *SEE* Major, Richard
Major, Sarah; Maryland, 1727 ***1220.12*** *p525*
Major, Thomas; Barbados, 1664 ***1220.12*** *p525*
Major, Walter; America, 1774 ***1220.12*** *p525*
Majory, George; Newbury, MA, 1672 ***9228.50*** *p420*
Majory, John; Salem, MA, 1690-1693 ***9228.50*** *p440*
Majunke, Adolph; North Carolina, 1856 ***1088.45*** *p20*
Makela, Matt 37; Minnesota, 1926 ***2769.54*** *p1382*
Makenzie, Phillip 35; Ontario, 1871 ***1823.21*** *p211*
Makepeace, Anne; Annapolis, MD, 1733 ***1220.12*** *p525*
Makepeace, Elizabeth; America, 1770 ***1220.12*** *p525*
Maker, Charles 36; Ontario, 1871 ***1823.21*** *p211*
Maki, Alno Elvira; Illinois, 1930 ***121.35*** *p100*
Maki, Arthur 33; Minnesota, 1925 ***2769.54*** *p1384*
Maki, Charles 32; Minnesota, 1923 ***2769.54*** *p1383*
Maki, Frank 44; Minnesota, 1923 ***2769.54*** *p1381*
Maki, Henry 40; Minnesota, 1923 ***2769.54*** *p1381*
Maki, Ida 36; Minnesota, 1925 ***2769.54*** *p1384*
Maki, John 40; Minnesota, 1923 ***2769.54*** *p1378*
Maki, Mary 44; Minnesota, 1925 ***2769.54*** *p1381*
Maki, Oscar 47; Minnesota, 1925 ***2769.54*** *p1381*
Maki, William 30; Minnesota, 1925 ***2769.54*** *p1384*
Makin, Ellis; America, 1747 ***1220.12*** *p525*
Makin, John; America, 1752 ***1220.12*** *p525*
Makinen, August 36; Minnesota, 1925 ***2769.54*** *p1384*
Makinerney, Mary; Boston, 1740 ***1642*** *p45*
Makinon, Antoinette 25; Quebec, 1657 ***9221.17*** *p362*
Makinson, James; Ohio, 1840 ***3580.20*** *p32*
Makinson, James; Ohio, 1840 ***6020.12*** *p13*
Makmelin, John; America, 1765 ***1220.12*** *p522*
Makning, Phillip; Boston, 1742 ***1642*** *p45*
Makovsky, Jan; New York, NY, 1855 ***2853.20*** *p270*
With family
Makovsky, Jan; Wisconsin, 1855 ***2853.20*** *p304*
Makovsky, Josef; New York, NY, 1854 ***2853.20*** *p270*
With family
Makovsky Family ; New York, NY, 1855 ***2853.20*** *p270*
Makowski, Victor; Detroit, 1929-1930 ***6214.5*** *p69*
Makyn, Richard; America, 1749 ***1220.12*** *p525*
Malaise, Euphrasine *SEE* Malaise, Jean Baptiste
Malaise, Jean Baptiste; Wisconsin, 1855-1870 ***1495.20*** *p8*
*Wife:*Marie
*Daughter:*Euphrasine
Malaise, Marie *SEE* Malaise, Jean Baptiste
Malaise, Therese; Wisconsin, 1856 ***1495.20*** *p41*
Maland, Kjetel Svemungson; Iowa, 1912 ***1211.15*** *p17*
Malapart, Andre de; Quebec, 1634 ***9221.17*** *p38*
Malaplade, Mr. 20; Port uncertain, 1844 ***778.6*** *p224*
Malas, Samuel; Wisconsin, 1908 ***1822.55*** *p10*
Malat, Frantisek; Wisconsin, 1861 ***2853.20*** *p334*
Malateste, Giovanni; Washington, 1889 ***2770.40*** *p79*
Malaussina, Etienne 25; New York, NY, 1894 ***6512.1*** *p182*
Malbin, Florence *SEE* Malbin, Harry
Malbin, Gertrude *SEE* Malbin, Harry
Malbin, Gladys *SEE* Malbin, Harry
Malbin, Harry; Colorado, 1920 ***1029.59*** *p58*
*Wife:*Tillie
*Child:*Gertrude
*Child:*Florence
*Child:*Gladys
Malbin, Harry; New York, NY, 1903 ***1029.59*** *p58*
Malbin, Tillie *SEE* Malbin, Harry
Malbly, William; Ohio, 1826 ***3580.20*** *p32*
Malbly, William; Ohio, 1826 ***6020.12*** *p13*
Malburne, Elizabeth; America, 1734 ***1220.12*** *p525*
Malcah, Abraham; America, 1770 ***1220.12*** *p525*
Malchow, Christian F.W.; Wisconsin, 1871 ***6795.8*** *p224*
Malcolm, Alexander 40; Ontario, 1871 ***1823.21*** *p211*
Malcolm, Henry 36; Ontario, 1871 ***1823.21*** *p211*
Malcolm, James 36; Ontario, 1871 ***1823.21*** *p211*
Malcolm, John Ernest; Illinois, 1918 ***6007.60*** *p9*
Malcolm, Lidia; Annapolis, MD, 1736 ***1220.12*** *p525*
Malcomb, Robert; America, 1765 ***1220.12*** *p525*
Malcona, Robert; Barbados, 1668 ***1220.12*** *p525*
Maldaner, Magdalena; Saskatchewan, 1912 ***9228.50*** *p567*
Male, Catharine 15; New Orleans, 1846 ***778.6*** *p224*
Male, George 7; New Orleans, 1846 ***778.6*** *p224*
Male, George 44; New Orleans, 1846 ***778.6*** *p223*
Male, Magdaline 3; New Orleans, 1846 ***778.6*** *p224*
Male, Margaret 18; New Orleans, 1846 ***778.6*** *p224*
Male, Mary 20; New Orleans, 1846 ***778.6*** *p224*
Male, Mary 41; New Orleans, 1846 ***778.6*** *p224*
Male, Philip 9; New Orleans, 1846 ***778.6*** *p224*
Male, Robert; America, 1766 ***1220.12*** *p525*
Male, Samuel; America, 1775 ***1220.12*** *p525*
Maleasey, Cath; New Orleans, 1851 ***7242.30*** *p148*
Malebrier, Jean; Quebec, 1649 ***9221.17*** *p216*
Malec, Anna; Detroit, 1929 ***1640.55*** *p113*
Malecek, Josef; St. Louis, 1852 ***2853.20*** *p21*
Malecha, Jan; Cleveland, OH, 1886 ***2853.20*** *p493*
Malecki, Albert; Detroit, 1930 ***1640.60*** *p82*
Maledy, Martan 40; Ontario, 1871 ***1823.17*** *p97*
Maleistre, Alex. 38; America, 1842 ***778.6*** *p224*
Malekki, Michael; Wisconsin, 1875 ***6795.8*** *p50*
Malenfant, Jean; Quebec, 1647 ***9221.17*** *p184*
Malenfant, Michel; Quebec, 1661 ***9221.17*** *p462*
Maleray deLa Mollerie, Jacques; Quebec, 1683-1688 ***2314.30*** *p168*
Maleray deLa Mollerie, Jacques; Quebec, 1685 ***2314.30*** *p190*
Males, Cornelius; America, 1731 ***1220.12*** *p525*
Malespert, Marie-Anne; Quebec, 1661 ***9221.17*** *p462*
Malet, Alexandre 23; New Orleans, 1848 ***778.6*** *p224*
Malet, Leon; Colorado, 1870 ***1029.59*** *p58*
Maley, John 50; Ontario, 1871 ***1823.17*** *p97*
Maley, Patrick; America, 1767 ***1220.12*** *p525*
Malfal-lastre, Reni de; Georgia, 1795 ***1451.56*** *p118*
Malherbe, Edward, Family; America, 1900-1930 ***9228.50*** *p421*
Malherbe, Francois 18; Quebec, 1645 ***9221.17*** *p155*
Malie, Jeanne Nicolle 36; New Orleans, 1848 ***778.6*** *p224*
Malikowska, Maria 20; New York, NY, 1904 ***8355.1*** *p15*
Malikowski, Joseph; Detroit, 1890 ***9980.23*** *p97*
Malingren, Olaf F.; Halifax, N.S., 1893 ***1766.20*** *p14*
Malings, Thomas; America, 1770 ***1220.12*** *p525*
Malinofsky, Anastasia *SEE* Malinofsky, Frank

Malinofsky, Frank; Galveston, TX, 1897 *6015.15 p10*
  *Wife:*Anastasia
Malinovsky, Ivan; America, 1863 *2853.20 p293*
Malinowski, Ella *SEE* Malinowski, Richard
Malinowski, Frank; Galveston, TX, 1898 *6015.15 p13*
Malinowski, Piotr 35; New York, NY, 1920 *930.50 p49*
Malinowski, Richard; Galveston, TX, 1898 *6015.15 p13*
  *Wife:*Ella
Malinowsky, Anastasia *SEE* Malinowsky, Frank
Malinowsky, Frank; Galveston, TX, 1897 *6015.15 p10*
  *Wife:*Anastasia
Malinquist, Gustav Emil; New York, NY, 1900-1914
  6212.1 p15
Mallabar, John; Virginia, 1736 *1220.12 p525*
Mallach, Albert; Wisconsin, 1896 *6795.8 p134*
Mallach, Albert August; Wisconsin, 1894 *6795.8 p170*
Mallalieu, John; New York, NY, 1826 *3274.55 p25*
Mallan, Pierre 23; Missouri, 1846 *778.6 p224*
Mallard, Alphonse; New Orleans, 1848 *778.6 p224*
Mallard, Benjamin; America, 1731 *1220.12 p525*
Mallard, Elizabeth; America, 1688 *1220.12 p525*
Mallard, George; America, 1741 *1220.12 p525*
Mallard, Joseph; America, 1738 *1220.12 p525*
Mallard, Peter; America, 1721 *1220.12 p525*
Mallard, Richard; America, 1738 *1220.12 p525*
Mallard, Stephen; Potomac, 1731 *1220.12 p525*
Malle, Jean 26; Louisiana, 1848 *778.6 p224*
Mallean, Adolphe 29; Tennessee, 1847 *778.6 p224*
Mallefant, Claude; Virginia, 1700 *9230.15 p80*
  *Brother:*Jean
  With mother
Mallefant, Jean *SEE* Mallefant, Claude
Maller, Andre 37; America, 1845 *778.6 p224*
Maller, Jean 35; America, 1845 *778.6 p224*
Maller, Nicolas 18; America, 1845 *778.6 p224*
Mallery, Mathew; America, 1743 *1220.12 p526*
Mallet, Ms. 45; Mobile, AL, 1840 *778.6 p75*
Mallet, Augustin 22; America, 1845 *778.6 p224*
Mallet, Catherine 21; Ohio, 1840 *778.6 p224*
Mallet, Daniel; Marblehead, MA, 1720 *9228.50 p287*
Mallet, Elvina; Utah, 1856-1931 *9228.50 p422*
Mallet, Jane *SEE* Mallet, Jenny Le Brun
Mallet, Jenny; St. Louis, 1854 *9228.50 p421*
  *Child:*Mary Elizabeth
  *Child:*Jane
Mallet, Joseph 19; Ohio, 1840 *778.6 p224*
Mallet, Leonie 19; America, 1845 *778.6 p224*
Mallet, Mary 37; Ontario, 1871 *1823.21 p211*
Mallet, Mary Eliz.; Utah, 1870 *9228.50 p518*
Mallet, Mary Elizabeth *SEE* Mallet, Jenny Le Brun
Mallet, Michel; Quebec, 1639 *9221.17 p91*
Mallet, P...re 29; New Orleans, 1840 *778.6 p224*
Mallet, Perrine; Quebec, 1635 *9221.17 p33*
Mallet, Perrine 30; Quebec, 1635 *9221.17 p44*
  *Son:*Louis-Marin 5
  *Son:*Jean-Galleran 1
Mallet, Pierre; Virginia, 1700 *9230.15 p80*
Malletrat, Edward; America, 1664 *1220.12 p525*
Mallett, Hosea; Maine, 1664 *9228.50 p421*
Mallett, John; America, 1765 *1220.12 p526*
Mallett, Joseph; America, 1734 *1220.12 p526*
Mallett, William; America, 1767 *1220.12 p526*
Malley, Daniel; Marblehead, MA, 1720 *9228.50 p287*
Mallick, John; America, 1773 *1220.12 p526*
Mallien, Dieudonne; Detroit, 1871 *1494.20 p12*
Mallien, Pierre J.; Detroit, 1871 *1494.20 p12*
Malline, Baltzer; Ohio, 1809-1852 *4511.35 p32*
Malling, Edward; North Carolina, 1855 *1088.45 p20*
Mallinger, Eva 12 *SEE* Mallinger, Johann
Mallinger, Franz 10 *SEE* Mallinger, Johann
Mallinger, Johann; America, 1872 *5475.1 p275*
  *Wife:*Katharina Reiter
  *Son:*Franz
  *Son:*Johann
  *Daughter:*Margarethe
  *Daughter:*Katharina
  *Daughter:*Eva
Mallinger, Johann 5 *SEE* Mallinger, Johann
Mallinger, Katharina 15 *SEE* Mallinger, Johann
Mallinger, Katharina Reiter 35 *SEE* Mallinger, Johann
Mallinger, Margarethe 7 *SEE* Mallinger, Johann
Mallison, Thomas; America, 1758 *1220.12 p526*
Mallmann, Henry; Ohio, 1840-1897 *8365.35 p17*
Mallmann, Josef; Brazil, 1879 *5475.1 p484*
Malloch, Robert 50; Ontario, 1871 *1823.17 p97*
Mallock, John 50; Ontario, 1871 *1823.21 p211*
Mallock, Mary 15; Quebec, 1870 *8364.32 p24*
Malloes, Robert; America, 1769 *1220.12 p526*
Mallon, John; America, 1765 *1220.12 p526*
Mallon, John 30; Ontario, 1871 *1823.21 p211*
Mallon, John; Toronto, 1844 *2910.35 p114*
Mallon, Joseph 40; Ontario, 1871 *1823.17 p97*
Mallon, Robert J. 50; Ontario, 1871 *1823.21 p211*

Mallone, John; Boston, 1768 *1642 p39*
Malloney, John; Toronto, 1844 *2910.35 p114*
Malloney, Patrick; Boston, 1747 *1642 p46*
Malloney, Thomas; Jamaica, 1783 *8529.30 p13A*
Mallony, Charles; Washington, 1885 *2770.40 p194*
Malloone, John; Massachusetts, 1675-1676 *1642 p129*
Mallory, Mr.; Massachusetts, 1900 *9228.50 p422*
Mallory, Diana; America, 1766 *1220.12 p526*
Mallott, Elizabeth; America, 1765 *1220.12 p525*
Mallowney, John; Toronto, 1844 *2910.35 p114*
Mallows, Sarah; America, 1762 *1220.12 p526*
Malloy, James 68; Michigan, 1880 *4491.39 p18*
Malloy, James 46; Ontario, 1871 *1823.17 p97*
Mallyon, William; Barbados or Jamaica, 1674 *1220.12 p526*
Malm, Agathon; Cleveland, OH, 1891-1892 *9722.10 p123*
Malm, Charles; St. Paul, MN, 1883 *1865.50 p96*
Malm, Marin; St. Paul, MN, 1882 *1865.50 p96*
Malmberg, Swen P.; Illinois, 1861 *4487.25 p65*
Malmgren, J.P.; New York, NY, 1849 *6412.40 p151*
Malmon, Jean Baptiste 31; New Orleans, 1848 *778.6 p224*
Malmquist, Gottfried E.; Cleveland, OH, 1890-1897 *9722.10 p123*
Malmstedt, Adolph M.; Michigan, 1890-1893 *1865.50 p97*
Malneritch, Matt; Washington, 1886 *2770.40 p195*
Malney, Thomas; New England, 1745 *1642 p28*
Malo, Marie; Quebec, 1670 *4514.3 p344*
Malobody, Wojciech; Detroit, 1930 *1640.60 p82*
Malomey, Jean 18; Missouri, 1846 *778.6 p224*
Malon, Alois; Virginia, 1888 *2853.20 p136*
Malone, Abraham; America, 1773 *1220.12 p526*
Malone, Catharine; Baltimore, 1860 *8513.31 p300*
Malone, Cornelius; Massachusetts, 1755 *1642 p105*
  *Wife:*Elizabeth
Malone, Elizabeth *SEE* Malone, Cornelius
Malone, George 68; Ontario, 1871 *1823.17 p97*
Malone, Honora 60; Ontario, 1871 *1823.17 p97*
Malone, James 35; Ontario, 1871 *1823.17 p97*
Malone, John; America, 1752 *1220.12 p526*
Malone, John; Toronto, 1844 *2910.35 p112*
Malone, Nickolas 76; Ontario, 1871 *1823.17 p97*
Malone, Owen; Toronto, 1844 *2910.35 p113*
Malone, Patrick; Toronto, 1844 *2910.35 p113*
Malone, Rachael; New Hampshire, 1753 *1642 p31*
Malone, Samuel James; Philadelphia, 1859 *8513.31 p410*
Malone, William; America, 1765 *1220.12 p526*
Maloney, Ann; Boston, 1740 *1642 p45*
Maloney, Cornelius; Massachusetts, 1755 *1642 p105*
  *Wife:*Elizabeth
Maloney, Eleanor; Boston, 1767 *1642 p38*
Maloney, Elizabeth *SEE* Maloney, Cornelius
Maloney, James; Boston, 1832 *3274.55 p42*
Maloney, Jean 18; Missouri, 1846 *778.6 p224*
Maloney, John; Boston, 1752 *1642 p47*
Maloney, John 18; Quebec, 1870 *8364.32 p24*
Maloney, Kate 18; Ontario, 1871 *1823.21 p212*
Maloney, Mary 62; Michigan, 1880 *4491.39 p18*
Maloney, Patrick; Illinois, 1860 *6079.1 p9*
Maloney, Patrick; Louisiana, 1874 *4981.45 p133*
Maloney, Richard; Boston, 1833 *3274.55 p43*
Maloney, Thomas; America, 1766 *1220.12 p526*
Maloney, Thomas 50; Ontario, 1871 *1823.17 p97*
Malonia, Cornelius; Massachusetts, 1756 *1642 p110*
Malony, Cornelius; Massachusetts, 1755 *1642 p105*
  *Wife:*Elizabeth
Malony, Cornelius 70; Ontario, 1871 *1823.21 p212*
Malony, Daniel; America, 1754 *1220.12 p526*
Malony, Daniel; New England, 1745 *1642 p28*
Malony, Elenor; Boston, 1739 *1642 p45*
Malony, Elizabeth *SEE* Malony, Cornelius
Malony, John; Boston, 1765 *1642 p34*
Malony, John; Illinois, 1858-1861 *6020.5 p132*
Malony, Margaret; Boston, 1773 *1642 p43*
Malony, Margaret; New Orleans, 1851 *7242.30 p148*
Malony, Richard; Boston, 1767 *1642 p39*
Maloone, John; Massachusetts, 1675-1676 *1642 p129*
Malorand, August 16; New Orleans, 1848 *778.6 p224*
Malorey, Mr.; Massachusetts, 1900 *9228.50 p422*
Malow, Frederick; Wisconsin, 1864 *6795.8 p204*
Maloy, Arthur; Boston, 1747 *1642 p29*
Maloy, Nancy 60; Ontario, 1871 *1823.21 p212*
Maloy, Patrick; Ohio, 1809-1852 *4511.35 p32*
Maloye, Lawrence; America, 1766 *1220.12 p557*
Malquin, Auguste 24; Missouri, 1846 *778.6 p224*
Malsac, Georg; Pennsylvania, 1884 *5475.1 p131*
Malsack, Angela *SEE* Malsack, Johann
Malsack, Anna Grohn *SEE* Malsack, Johann
Malsack, Elisabeth *SEE* Malsack, Johann

Malsack, Johann; America, 1882 *5475.1 p276*
  *Wife:*Maria Friedrich
  *Mother:*Anna Grohn
  *Daughter:*Margarethe
  *Daughter:*Elisabeth
  *Daughter:*Katharina
  *Daughter:*Angela
  *Daughter:*Maria
Malsack, Katharina *SEE* Malsack, Johann
Malsack, Margarethe *SEE* Malsack, Johann
Malsack, Maria *SEE* Malsack, Johann
Malsack, Maria Friedrich *SEE* Malsack, Johann
Malsch, August Christian; America, 1868 *7919.3 p533*
Malsch, Johann Friedrich; America, 1867 *7919.3 p532*
  With child
Malsche, Margarethe; America, 1867 *7919.3 p529*
Malsheir, Elizabeth; America, 1700 *1220.12 p526*
Maltby, John; America, 1765 *1220.12 p526*
Maltiger, Louis 36; Louisiana, 1848 *778.6 p225*
Maltman, Thomas; Philadelphia, 1777 *8529.30 p7A*
Malton, Elizabeth 53; Ontario, 1871 *1823.21 p212*
Malton, Emily 10; Quebec, 1870 *8364.32 p24*
Malton, George 68; Ontario, 1871 *1823.21 p212*
Malumby, Michael 40; Ontario, 1871 *1823.17 p97*
Malvey, Thomas; Toronto, 1844 *2910.35 p113*
Malvill, George 35; Ontario, 1871 *1823.21 p212*
Malvin, Alexander; America, 1758 *1220.12 p526*
Malvin, Mary *SEE* Malvin, Patrick
Malvin, Patrick; Newbury, MA, 1750 *1642 p75*
  *Wife:*Mary
Maly, Antonin; Nebraska, 1874 *2853.20 p172*
Maly, Frantisek Jan; Nebraska, 1871 *2853.20 p194*
Maly, Josef; New York, 1854 *2853.20 p313*
Maly, Petr; Nebraska, 1876 *2853.20 p172*
Maly, Petr; New York, 1859 *2853.20 p261*
Maly, Simon; Nebraska, 1874 *2853.20 p172*
Maly, Vaclav; Wisconsin, 1852 *2853.20 p312*
Maly, Vojtech; Iowa, 1855 *2853.20 p217*
Maly Family ; Minnesota, 1854-1865 *2853.20 p271*
Mamiel dePontois; Jean-Louis; Quebec, 1744 *2314.30 p171*
Maminot, Auguste 17; America, 1847 *778.6 p225*
Maminot, Elisabeth 13; America, 1847 *778.6 p225*
Maminot, Joseph 24; America, 1847 *778.6 p225*
Maminot, Marie 23; America, 1847 *778.6 p225*
Maminot, Melanie 20; America, 1847 *778.6 p225*
Maminot, Pierre 50; America, 1847 *778.6 p225*
Mamnuel, Christopher F.; North Carolina, 1857 *1088.45 p20*
Mamous, Jean 23; America, 1846 *778.6 p225*
Man, Deborah; Barbados, 1667 *1220.12 p526*
Man, Henry; Annapolis, MD, 1725 *1220.12 p526*
Man, John 60; Ontario, 1871 *1823.21 p212*
Man, Mark 51; Ontario, 1871 *1823.21 p212*
Man, Mary; America, 1752 *1220.12 p527*
Man, Samuel; Barbados, 1684 *1220.12 p527*
Man, Sarah; America, 1764 *1220.12 p527*
Man, Thomas; Barbados, 1673 *1220.12 p527*
Man, Thomas 58; Ontario, 1871 *1823.21 p212*
Man, William 59; Ontario, 1871 *1823.17 p97*
Man, Zachary; Maryland, 1728 *1220.12 p527*
Manahay, William; America, 1768 *1220.12 p527*
Manale, Nieulo; Louisiana, 1874 *4981.45 p133*
Manassus, M.; Louisiana, 1874-1875 *4981.45 p30*
Mance, Jeanne 35; Montreal, 1641 *9221.17 p108*
Mancer, James; America, 1761 *1220.12 p528*
Manchon, Louis; Quebec, 1653 *9221.17 p277*
Mancill, Edward; America, 1757 *1220.12 p528*
Mancour, Mathurin; Quebec, 1657 *9221.17 p363*
Mancroft, John; Barbados or Jamaica, 1686 *1220.12 p526*
Mancy, Henry 21; Port uncertain, 1846 *778.6 p225*
Manda, Vincenzio; Louisiana, 1874 *4981.45 p133*
Mandall, Charles; North Carolina, 1854 *1088.45 p20*
Mandart, Adolphe 37; Port uncertain, 1843 *778.6 p225*
Mandel, Heinrich; Valdivia, Chile, 1851 *1192.4 p51*
  With wife
  With child 3
Mander, William; America, 1768 *1220.12 p526*
Manders, Annie 11; Quebec, 1870 *8364.32 p24*
Manders, Edward 9; Quebec, 1870 *8364.32 p24*
Manders, William 28; Ontario, 1871 *1823.17 p97*
Mandery, Auguste 7; America, 1846 *778.6 p225*
Mandery, Cecile 9; America, 1846 *778.6 p225*
Mandery, Constant 5; America, 1846 *778.6 p225*
Mandery, Marianne 36; America, 1846 *778.6 p225*
Mandery, Nicolas 38; Port uncertain, 1846 *778.6 p225*
Mandet, Mr. 12; Tennessee, 1848 *778.6 p225*
Mandet, Mrs. 40; Tennessee, 1848 *778.6 p225*
Mandet, Pierre J. 32; Tennessee, 1848 *778.6 p225*
Mandevil, Mary; America, 1738 *1220.12 p526*
Mandeville, Penelope; America, 1762 *1220.12 p526*

Mandler, Georg Caspar *SEE* Mandler, Katharine Margarethe
Mandler, Jakob *SEE* Mandler, Katharine Margarethe
Mandler, Johanne Louise Witte *SEE* Mandler, John Charles Frederick
Mandler, John Charles Frederick; Philadelphia, 1855 ***8513.31*** *p410*
*Wife:*Johanne Louise Witte
Mandler, Katharine Margarethe; Baltimore, 1850 ***8115.12*** *p321*
*Child:*Georg Caspar
*Child:*Jakob
*Child:*Ludwig
Mandler, Ludwig *SEE* Mandler, Katharine Margarethe
Mandreux, Francois 30; America, 1842 ***778.6*** *p225*
Mandural, William 35; Ontario, 1871 ***1823.17*** *p97*
Mandville, W. W. 29; Ontario, 1871 ***1823.21*** *p212*
Manecka, John Henry; Ohio, 1809-1852 ***4511.35*** *p32*
Manent, Miss 20; Texas, 1848 ***778.6*** *p225*
Manent, Bernard 40; Texas, 1848 ***778.6*** *p225*
Maneold, Mr. 25; America, 1842 ***778.6*** *p225*
Manera, Phillip 24; America, 1848 ***778.6*** *p225*
Manery, James 30; Ontario, 1871 ***1823.21*** *p212*
Manes, J.; Louisiana, 1874 ***4981.45*** *p296*
Maney, Stephen; Louisiana, 1874-1875 ***4981.45*** *p29*
Maney, William; Philadelphia, 1778 ***8529.30*** *p3*
Manfield, John; America, 1765 ***1220.12*** *p526*
Manfield, Stephen; America, 1767 ***1220.12*** *p526*
Mang, Jakob; America, 1870 ***5475.1*** *p211*
Mang, Jakob 32; America, 1880 ***5475.1*** *p213*
Mang, Konrad; America, 1880 ***5475.1*** *p173*
Mang, Margarethe; America, 1872 ***5475.1*** *p212*
Mang, Margarethe 34; America, 1854 ***5475.1*** *p53*
Mang, Maria 40; America, 1873 ***5475.1*** *p231*
Manga, M.; Louisiana, 1874-1875 ***4981.45*** *p29*
Mangat, Peter; North Carolina, 1825 ***1088.45*** *p20*
Mange, Margareth 24; Ohio, 1847 ***778.6*** *p225*
Mange, Pierre 30; Ohio, 1847 ***778.6*** *p225*
Mangea, August 22; Mississippi, 1847 ***778.6*** *p225*
Mangel, E. 23; Louisiana, 1847 ***778.6*** *p225*
Manger, Paul; Louisiana, 1874-1875 ***4981.45*** *p29*
Manger, Thomas; Toronto, 1844 ***2910.35*** *p114*
Manget, E. 23; Louisiana, 1847 ***778.6*** *p225*
Mangin, Charles 29; America, 1746 ***778.6*** *p225*
Mangin, Jean 83; America, 1846 ***778.6*** *p225*
Mangin, John; Ohio, 1809-1852 ***4511.35*** *p32*
Mangin, Justine 32; America, 1746 ***778.6*** *p225*
Mangin, Pierre; Louisiana, 1841-1844 ***4981.45*** *p211*
Mangoaga, Juan 43; Port uncertain, 1846 ***778.6*** *p225*
Mangold, Georg; Valdivia, Chile, 1852 ***1192.4*** *p53*
With wife
Mangold, Gustav; Chile, 1852 ***1192.4*** *p52*
Mangon, Master 2; America, 1848 ***778.6*** *p225*
Mangon, Miss 5; America, 1848 ***778.6*** *p226*
Mangon, Mr. 45; America, 1848 ***778.6*** *p226*
Mangon, Mrs. 35; America, 1848 ***778.6*** *p226*
Mangon, Pat 26; St. Johns, N.F., 1811 ***1053.20*** *p22*
Manhall, Elizabeth; America, 1775 ***1220.12*** *p526*
Manidoka, George; Ontario, 1871 ***1823.17*** *p97*
Manidoka, Goorof; Ontario, 1871 ***1823.17*** *p97*
Maniere, Nicolas; Quebec, 1657 ***9221.17*** *p363*
Manikowsky, Gottlieb Gustav Wilhelm; America, 1848 ***7420.1*** *p60*
Maning, David 51; Ontario, 1871 ***1823.21*** *p212*
Maning, John 50; Ontario, 1871 ***1823.17*** *p97*
Maning, William 21; Ontario, 1871 ***1823.21*** *p212*
Maninger, Valentine; Illinois, 1858-1861 ***6020.5*** *p132*
Maniotte, Eugene 30; Port uncertain, 1843 ***778.6*** *p226*
Mankowski, Stanley; Washington, 1889 ***2770.40*** *p79*
Manley, Ann Maria; Salt Lake City, 1854-1939 ***9228.50*** *p422*
Manley, Ann Maria; Salt Lake City, 1939 ***9228.50*** *p127*
Manley, Elijah 40; Ontario, 1871 ***1823.21*** *p212*
Manley, Elizabeth; America, 1751 ***1220.12*** *p526*
Manley, Hugh; America, 1758 ***1220.12*** *p526*
Manley, James; Annapolis, MD, 1730 ***1220.12*** *p526*
Manley, Margaret; Virginia, 1751 ***1220.12*** *p526*
Manley, Margrett 19; Ontario, 1871 ***1823.21*** *p212*
Manley, Michael; New York, NY, 1839 ***3274.56*** *p98*
Manley, Percy Frank; Miami, 1935 ***4984.12*** *p39*
Manley, Richard; America, 1765 ***1220.12*** *p526*
Manley, Robert 40; Ontario, 1871 ***1823.21*** *p212*
Manley, William; Virginia, 1740 ***1220.12*** *p526*
Manly, Mary 10; Ontario, 1871 ***1823.21*** *p212*
Manly, William; America, 1772 ***1220.12*** *p526*
Mann, Agnes 18; Ontario, 1871 ***1823.21*** *p212*
Mann, Ambrose 43; Ontario, 1871 ***1823.21*** *p212*
Mann, Andrew 42; Ontario, 1871 ***1823.17*** *p97*
Mann, Charles 15; Michigan, 1880 ***4491.39*** *p19*
Mann, Daniel 55; Ontario, 1871 ***1823.21*** *p212*
Mann, David; Maryland or Virginia, 1738 ***1220.12*** *p526*
Mann, David 48; Ontario, 1871 ***1823.21*** *p212*
Mann, Edward; America, 1754 ***1220.12*** *p526*
Mann, Elizabeth; America, 1771 ***1220.12*** *p526*
Mann, Elizabeth; St. John, N.B., 1842 ***2978.20*** *p7*
Mann, Emanuel; New York, 1860 ***358.56*** *p5*
Mann, Francis; Maryland or Virginia, 1738 ***1220.12*** *p526*
Mann, Frank M. 28; Michigan, 1880 ***4491.39*** *p19*
Mann, Geo.; Ohio, 1840-1897 ***8365.35*** *p17*
Mann, George 37; Ontario, 1871 ***1823.17*** *p97*
Mann, George 62; Ontario, 1871 ***1823.21*** *p212*
Mann, George; Virginia, 1774 ***1220.12*** *p526*
Mann, George A. 24; Ontario, 1871 ***1823.21*** *p212*
Mann, Helene; America, 1899 ***7420.1*** *p375*
Mann, Henry; Virginia, 1754 ***1220.12*** *p526*
Mann, Hiram 59; Ontario, 1871 ***1823.21*** *p212*
Mann, Jakob *SEE* Mann, Philippine
Mann, Jakob; America, 1857 ***5475.1*** *p314*
*Brother:*Peter
Mann, James; America, 1767 ***1220.12*** *p526*
Mann, James 44; Ontario, 1871 ***1823.21*** *p212*
Mann, Joanna; St. John, N.B., 1842 ***2978.20*** *p7*
Mann, John 35; Ontario, 1871 ***1823.17*** *p97*
Mann, John 46; Ontario, 1871 ***1823.21*** *p212*
Mann, John; Rappahannock, VA, 1726 ***1220.12*** *p526*
Mann, John M. 54; Ontario, 1871 ***1823.21*** *p212*
Mann, Karl 22; America, 1865 ***5475.1*** *p521*
Mann, Leonard 71; Ontario, 1871 ***1823.21*** *p212*
Mann, Mary; America, 1774 ***1220.12*** *p527*
Mann, Michael; North Carolina, 1792-1862 ***1088.45*** *p20*
Mann, Mitchel; Louisiana, 1874-1875 ***4981.45*** *p30*
Mann, Peter *SEE* Mann, Jakob
Mann, Philippine; America, 1856 ***5475.1*** *p520*
*Brother:*Jakob
Mann, Richard; America, 1738 ***1220.12*** *p527*
Mann, Tillie 23; Michigan, 1880 ***4491.30*** *p21*
Mann, William; America, 1754 ***1220.12*** *p527*
Mann, William; Maryland, 1725 ***1220.12*** *p527*
Mannass, Mr. 23; New Orleans, 1840 ***778.6*** *p226*
Mannebach, A. Maria *SEE* Mannebach, Mathias
Mannebach, Barbara *SEE* Mannebach, Mathias
Mannebach, Katharina Friedrich 32 *SEE* Mannebach, Mathias
Mannebach, Margarethe *SEE* Mannebach, Mathias
Mannebach, Maria *SEE* Mannebach, Mathias
Mannebach, Mathias *SEE* Mannebach, Mathias
Mannebach, Mathias 36; America, 1857 ***5475.1*** *p328*
*Wife:*Katharina Friedrich 32
*Daughter:*Margarethe
*Daughter:*Maria
*Son:*Mathias
*Daughter:*Barbara
*Daughter:*A. Maria
Manneck, Julius; Washington, 1889 ***2770.40*** *p79*
Mannen, James; America, 1764 ***1220.12*** *p527*
Manners, Andrew; America, 1750 ***1220.12*** *p527*
Manners, Charles 23; Ontario, 1871 ***1823.21*** *p212*
Manners, Joseph; America, 1681 ***1220.12*** *p527*
Manners, Robert C. 68; Ontario, 1871 ***1823.21*** *p212*
Manners, William; America, 1772 ***1220.12*** *p527*
Manners, William 25; Ontario, 1871 ***1823.21*** *p212*
Manneshagen, Anne Margarete; America, 1868 ***7919.3*** *p534*
Mannett, James; America, 1729 ***1220.12*** *p527*
Mannfeld, Auguste; America, 1868 ***7919.3*** *p528*
Mannheimer, Jakob; America, 1884 ***2526.43*** *p153*
Mannila, John 35; Minnesota, 1923 ***2769.54*** *p1381*
Manning, Abner; Illinois, 1870-1899 ***9228.50*** *p422*
Manning, Casper; Iowa, 1882 ***1211.15*** *p16*
Manning, Charles; Virginia, 1730 ***1220.12*** *p527*
Manning, Cornelius 51; Ontario, 1871 ***1823.21*** *p212*
Manning, David 27; Ontario, 1871 ***1823.17*** *p98*
Manning, Dorothy; America, 1740 ***1220.12*** *p527*
Manning, Edward; America, 1772 ***1220.12*** *p527*
Manning, Elizabeth; America, 1767 ***1220.12*** *p527*
Manning, Elizabeth; America, 1773 ***1220.12*** *p527*
Manning, G.W.; Iowa, 1892 ***1211.15*** *p16*
Manning, Hannah; America, 1765 ***1220.12*** *p527*
Manning, Henry; Virginia, 1768 ***1220.12*** *p527*
Manning, Humphrey; America, 1719 ***1220.12*** *p527*
Manning, James; America, 1764 ***1220.12*** *p527*
Manning, James; America, 1768 ***1220.12*** *p527*
Manning, Jane M. 22; Ontario, 1871 ***1823.17*** *p98*
Manning, Joan; America, 1759 ***1220.12*** *p527*
Manning, John; America, 1685 ***1220.12*** *p527*
Manning, John; America, 1761 ***1220.12*** *p527*
Manning, John; Barbados or Jamaica, 1697 ***1220.12*** *p527*
Manning, John 44; Ontario, 1871 ***1823.21*** *p213*
Manning, Margaret; Virginia, 1727 ***1220.12*** *p527*
Manning, Mary; America, 1735 ***1220.12*** *p527*
Manning, Mary; America, 1767 ***1220.12*** *p527*
Manning, Patrick; Ohio, 1857 ***3580.20*** *p32*
Manning, Patrick; Ohio, 1857 ***6020.12*** *p13*
Manning, Peter; Boston, 1766 ***1642*** *p37*
Manning, Peter 33; Ontario, 1871 ***1823.21*** *p213*
Manning, Rebecca; Annapolis, MD, 1730 ***1220.12*** *p527*
Manning, Richard; America, 1752 ***1220.12*** *p527*
Manning, Richard M. 27; Ontario, 1871 ***1823.17*** *p98*
Manning, Samuel; America, 1734 ***1220.12*** *p527*
Manning, Samuel; America, 1741 ***1220.12*** *p527*
Manning, Samuel; America, 1766 ***1220.12*** *p527*
Manning, Samuel; Annapolis, MD, 1725 ***1220.12*** *p527*
Manning, Sarah; Boston, 1732 ***1642*** *p44*
Manning, Thomas; Barbados or Jamaica, 1696 ***1220.12*** *p527*
Manning, Thomas 52; Ontario, 1871 ***1823.17*** *p98*
Manning, Thomas M. 23; Ontario, 1871 ***1823.17*** *p98*
Manning, William; America, 1764 ***1220.12*** *p527*
Manning, William; Maryland, 1738 ***1220.12*** *p527*
Mannings, John; America, 1765 ***1220.12*** *p527*
Mannings, Mathew; America, 1732 ***1220.12*** *p527*
Manniwell, Joseph; America, 1754 ***1220.12*** *p527*
Mannon, Mary; America, 1771 ***1220.12*** *p528*
Manns, Carl; Valdivia, Chile, 1852 ***1192.4*** *p56*
With wife & child
With child 20
With child 8
Manns, Eduard 19; Valdivia, Chile, 1852 ***1192.4*** *p56*
Manns, Ferdinand 13; Valdivia, Chile, 1852 ***1192.4*** *p56*
Manns, Gustav 14; Valdivia, Chile, 1852 ***1192.4*** *p56*
Manns, Johann Christian Wilhelm; America, 1886 ***7420.1*** *p351*
Manns, Julius 16; Valdivia, Chile, 1852 ***1192.4*** *p56*
Manns, Wilhelm; Valdivia, Chile, 1851 ***1192.4*** *p51*
Manntle, James; Marston's Wharf, 1780 ***8529.30*** *p13*
Manouelly DeReville, Marie-Genevieve 18; Quebec, 1661 ***9221.17*** *p462*
Manquet, Celestin 7; America, 1846 ***778.6*** *p226*
Manquet, Celestin 36; America, 1846 ***778.6*** *p226*
Manquet, Florentin 9; America, 1846 ***778.6*** *p226*
Manquet, Marianne 33; America, 1846 ***778.6*** *p226*
Manrenard, Alexander J.; Detroit, 1856 ***1494.21*** *p31*
Mans, Edward; Wisconsin, 1899 ***6795.8*** *p162*
Mans, Jourdan 25; America, 1843 ***778.6*** *p226*
Mans, Jul.; New York, 1860 ***358.56*** *p149*
Mansard, John B.; North Carolina, 1792-1862 ***1088.45*** *p20*
Mansby, William; America, 1772 ***1220.12*** *p528*
Mansel, Arndt 20; New York, NY, 1890 ***1883.7*** *p47*
Mansel, Friedke 21; New York, NY, 1890 ***1883.7*** *p47*
Mansell, James; Cleveland, OH, 1840 ***9228.50*** *p422*
Mansell, John; America, 1752 ***1220.12*** *p528*
Mansell, Samuel; America, 1772 ***1220.12*** *p528*
Mansell, Thomas; America, 1768 ***1220.12*** *p528*
Mansell, William; Maryland, 1731 ***1220.12*** *p528*
Mansell Family ; Cleveland, OH, n.d. ***9228.50*** *p36*
Mansen, Thomas; America, 1772 ***1220.12*** *p528*
Manser, Allen; America, 1745 ***1220.12*** *p528*
Mansfield, Charles 55; Ontario, 1871 ***1823.21*** *p213*
Mansfield, David; Potomac, 1729 ***1220.12*** *p528*
Mansfield, Elizabeth; America, 1761 ***1220.12*** *p528*
Mansfield, Elizabeth; Carolina, 1724 ***1220.12*** *p528*
Mansfield, George 40; Ontario, 1871 ***1823.21*** *p213*
Mansfield, Henry 34; Ontario, 1871 ***1823.17*** *p98*
Mansfield, John; Quebec, 1870 ***8364.32*** *p24*
Mansfield, John; Toronto, 1844 ***2910.35*** *p114*
Mansfield, John A.; Ohio, 1879 ***3580.20*** *p33*
Mansfield, John A.; Ohio, 1879 ***6020.12*** *p21*
Mansfield, Joseph; Barbados, 1694 ***1220.12*** *p528*
Mansfield, Peter; America, 1773 ***1220.12*** *p528*
Mansfield, Robert; Marston's Wharf, 1782 ***8529.30*** *p13*
Mansfield, Robert; Ontario, 1835 ***3160.1*** *p150*
Mansfield, Sarah; America, 1757 ***1220.12*** *p528*
Mansfield, Sarah; Annapolis, MD, 1719 ***1220.12*** *p528*
Mansfield, Thomas; Maryland, 1742 ***1220.12*** *p528*
Mansford, Samuel; Washington, 1887 ***2770.40*** *p24*
Mansill, William; America, 1757 ***1220.12*** *p528*
Mansion, Jeanne; Quebec, 1669 ***4514.3*** *p344*
Manson, Mr. 24; New Orleans, 1847 ***778.6*** *p226*
Manson, Anne 28; America, 1846 ***778.6*** *p226*
Manson, Anthony 28; Ontario, 1871 ***1823.21*** *p213*
Manson, Edward; America, 1772 ***1220.12*** *p528*
Manson, James 33; Ontario, 1871 ***1823.21*** *p213*
Manson, John 36; Ontario, 1871 ***1823.21*** *p213*
Manson, Moses 38; Ontario, 1871 ***1823.21*** *p213*
Mansson, C.A.; New Orleans, 1847 ***6412.40*** *p149*
Mansson, Johan; New York, NY, 1851 ***6412.40*** *p152*
Mansson, Wilhelm; St. Paul, MN, 1888 ***1865.50*** *p97*
Manssuy, A. 25; America, 1845 ***778.6*** *p236*
Mantaie, Joseph; Wisconsin, 1856 ***6795.8*** *p26*
Mantei, Ernst Gotthilf; Wisconsin, 1858 ***6795.8*** *p139*
Mantel, Antonia 32; America, 1840 ***778.6*** *p226*
Mantel, Gilbert 28; America, 1840 ***778.6*** *p226*
Manteo, Jean 26; America, 1841 ***778.6*** *p226*
Manteufel, Carl Friedrich August; Wisconsin, 1866 ***6795.8*** *p82*
Mantha, Daniel 23; America, 1845 ***778.6*** *p226*
Mantha, David 23; America, 1845 ***778.6*** *p226*

Manthei, Friedrich August; Wisconsin, 1874 ***6795.8*** *p82*
Manthei, Julius; Wisconsin, 1887 ***6795.8*** *p162*
Manthey, Friedrich; Wisconsin, 1875 ***6795.8*** *p139*
Manthey, Joseph; Wisconsin, 1856 ***6795.8*** *p26*
Manthey, Julius; Wisconsin, 1884 ***6795.8*** *p175*
Manthey, Julius Johann; Wisconsin, 1906 ***6795.8*** *p163*
Manthey, Otto George; Wisconsin, 1904 ***6795.8*** *p236*
Manthey, Pauline Josephina; Wisconsin, 1886 ***6795.8*** *p26*
Manthie, Friedrich; Wisconsin, 1875 ***6795.8*** *p139*
Mantik, Mike; Wisconsin, 1908 ***1822.55*** *p10*
Mantle, David; America, 1772 ***1220.12*** *p528*
Mantle, Edward; America, 1766 ***1220.12*** *p528*
Mantle, John; America, 1769 ***1220.12*** *p528*
Mantle, Joseph 50; Ontario, 1871 ***1823.21*** *p213*
Manton, Joseph; America, 1744 ***1220.12*** *p528*
Manton, Luke; America, 1766 ***1220.12*** *p528*
Manton, Mary; America, 1757 ***1220.12*** *p528*
Manton, Samuel; America, 1761 ***1220.12*** *p528*
Manton, Samuel; America, 1771 ***1220.12*** *p528*
Manton, Sarah; America, 1769 ***1220.12*** *p528*
Manton, Thomas; America, 1761 ***1220.12*** *p528*
Mantzel, Frederick; Wisconsin, 1892 ***6795.8*** *p171*
Manual, Constant 46; New Orleans, 1848 ***778.6*** *p226*
Manuel, David 29; America, 1745 ***778.6*** *p226*
Manuel, Honoree 22; Port uncertain, 1842 ***778.6*** *p226*
Manuell, James; Marston's Wharf, 1779 ***8529.30*** *p14*
Manvre, Geuesppe; Louisiana, 1874-1875 ***4981.45*** *p30*
Manzbendel, Jean 35; America, 1848 ***778.6*** *p226*
Maplesden, Mary; America, 1750 ***1220.12*** *p528*
Mapleton, John; America, 1749 ***1220.12*** *p528*
Mapolon, James; North Carolina, 1852 ***1088.45*** *p20*
Mapp, John; Annapolis, MD, 1723 ***1220.12*** *p528*
Mapp, William; America, 1751 ***1220.12*** *p528*
Mappett, Charles; America, 1746 ***1220.12*** *p528*
Mapps, Abraham; America, 1749 ***1220.12*** *p528*
Mapstone, William 59; Ontario, 1871 ***1823.21*** *p213*
Maquelieb, Jean Francois 29; America, 1847 ***778.6*** *p226*
Mar, Alphonse Stan. Ant. 22; Mississippi, 1848 ***778.6*** *p226*
Mara, James 18; Ontario, 1871 ***1823.21*** *p213*
Mara, James 66; Ontario, 1871 ***1823.17*** *p98*
Mara, John 60; Ontario, 1871 ***1823.21*** *p213*
Marah, John 59; Ontario, 1871 ***1823.21*** *p213*
Marah, Michael; Ohio, 1809-1852 ***4511.35*** *p32*
Maraim, Mary; Barbados, 1664 ***1220.12*** *p528*
Marais, Mr. 49; America, 1846 ***778.6*** *p226*
Marak, Frantisek; Galveston, TX, 1856 ***2853.20*** *p63*
Marak, Petr; Arkansas, 1892 ***2853.20*** *p376*
Maranten, Herman; New York, NY, 1870 ***1494.20*** *p12*
Marat, Martin 18; St. Johns, N.F., 1811 ***1053.20*** *p22*
Maraude, Madeleine 38; Quebec, 1650 ***9221.17*** *p229*
Marault, Pierre 23; Quebec, 1657 ***9221.17*** *p364*
Maraux, Mathering; America, 1767 ***1220.12*** *p528*
Maray deLa Chauvignerie, Louis; Quebec, 1697 ***2314.30*** *p169*
Maray deLa Chauvignerie, Louis; Quebec, 1697 ***2314.30*** *p190*
Marbach, Aloisur 1; New York, NY, 1906 ***8425.16*** *p34*
Marbach, Anton 23; Mississippi, 1847 ***778.6*** *p226*
Marbach, Anton 56; Mississippi, 1847 ***778.6*** *p226*
Marbach, Bonapurtura 11; New York, NY, 1906 ***8425.16*** *p34*
Marbach, Eva 9; New York, NY, 1906 ***8425.16*** *p34*
Marbach, Francisca 46; Mississippi, 1847 ***778.6*** *p226*
Marbach, Frank 33; New York, NY, 1905 ***8425.16*** *p34*
Marbach, Gabriel 30; New York, NY, 1898 ***7951.13*** *p42*
Marbach, Joseph 20; Mississippi, 1847 ***778.6*** *p226*
Marbach, Marie 11; Mississippi, 1847 ***778.6*** *p226*
Marbach, Regina 33; New York, NY, 1906 ***8425.16*** *p34*
Marbach, Theresia 25; New York, NY, 1898 ***7951.13*** *p42*
Marbach, Valentine 35; New York, NY, 1905 ***8425.16*** *p34*
Marbach, Wendelin 32; New Orleans, 1848 ***778.6*** *p226*
Marbaugh, John; Ohio, 1809-1852 ***4511.35*** *p32*
Marc, Anton 27; Galveston, TX, 1844 ***3967.10*** *p375*
Marcadet, Francois; Wisconsin, 1852 ***1495.20*** *p12*
  *Child:*Jean Joseph
  *Child:*Marie Barbe
  *Child:*Julie
Marcadet, Jean Joseph *SEE* Marcadet, Francois
Marcadet, Julie *SEE* Marcadet, Francois
Marcadet, Marie Barbe *SEE* Marcadet, Francois
Marcarti, Florence; Roxbury, MA, 1712 ***1642*** *p108*
Marcaut, Claude 19; Montreal, 1660 ***9221.17*** *p442*
Marcel, Alex. 43; New Orleans, 1842 ***778.6*** *p226*
Marcel, James; North Carolina, 1817 ***1088.45*** *p21*
Marcel, L.; Louisiana, 1874 ***4981.45*** *p296*
Marceline, Rene 34; New Orleans, 1845 ***778.6*** *p226*
Marcelle, Euphrasie Goffinet *SEE* Marcelle, Joseph
Marcelle, Felicien *SEE* Marcelle, Joseph
Marcelle, Francois Xavier *SEE* Marcelle, Joseph
Marcelle, Joseph; New York, NY, 1855 ***1494.21*** *p31*
Marcelle, Joseph *SEE* Marcelle, Joseph
Marcelle, Joseph; Wisconsin, 1855 ***1495.20*** *p45*
  *Wife:*Euphrasie Goffinet
  *Child:*Pauline
  *Child:*Felicien
  *Child:*Francois Xavier
  *Child:*Joseph
Marcelle, Pauline *SEE* Marcelle, Joseph
Marceloff, Francois 21; New Orleans, 1847 ***778.6*** *p227*
Marcent, F. E.; Louisiana, 1836-1840 ***4981.45*** *p213*
March, George; America, 1771 ***1220.12*** *p528*
March, James; America, 1748 ***1220.12*** *p528*
March, Jean; Virginia, 1700 ***9230.15*** *p81*
March, John; Virginia, 1734 ***1220.12*** *p528*
March, Robert 23; Ontario, 1871 ***1823.21*** *p213*
March, Thomas 17; Quebec, 1870 ***8364.32*** *p24*
Marchadie, Mr. 52; America, 1848 ***778.6*** *p227*
Marchadie, S. 24; America, 1848 ***778.6*** *p227*
Marchadre, S. 22; America, 1846 ***778.6*** *p227*
Marchal, Mr. 26; Louisiana, 1848 ***778.6*** *p227*
Marchal, Andre 59; Mississippi, 1846 ***778.6*** *p227*
Marchal, Aug. 31; Louisiana, 1840 ***778.6*** *p227*
Marchal, Charles; Illinois, 1852 ***6079.1*** *p9*
Marchal, Eugene 24; Mississippi, 1846 ***778.6*** *p227*
Marchal, Francois 19; Louisiana, 1847 ***778.6*** *p227*
Marchal, Joseph; Louisiana, 1841-1844 ***4981.45*** *p211*
Marchal, Madalaine 15; Mississippi, 1846 ***778.6*** *p227*
Marchal, Pierre Noel; Wisconsin, 1854-1858 ***1495.20*** *p49*
  *Wife:*Rosalie Moureau
Marchal, Remi 50; Louisiana, 1847 ***778.6*** *p227*
Marchal, Rosalie Moureau *SEE* Marchal, Pierre Noel
Marchal, Rosina 23; Mississippi, 1847 ***778.6*** *p227*
Marchand, Mrs. 29; America, 1846 ***778.6*** *p227*
Marchand, Mrs. 30; America, 1840 ***778.6*** *p227*
Marchand, Antoine 45; America, 1847 ***778.6*** *p227*
Marchand, Armel Alexis; Illinois, 1852 ***6079.1*** *p9*
Marchand, Arnal 34; Texas, 1848 ***778.6*** *p227*
Marchand, Baptiste 36; America, 1847 ***778.6*** *p227*
Marchand, Baptiste 32; New Orleans, 1844 ***778.6*** *p227*
Marchand, Catherine 18; Montreal, 1659 ***9221.17*** *p424*
Marchand, Catherine; Quebec, 1667 ***4514.3*** *p344*
Marchand, Charles 3; America, 1847 ***778.6*** *p227*
Marchand, David; Quebec, 1647 ***9221.17*** *p184*
Marchand, Delphine 7; America, 1847 ***778.6*** *p227*
Marchand, Elisabeth 54; Louisiana, 1848 ***778.6*** *p227*
Marchand, Jacques 18; Quebec, 1656 ***9221.17*** *p341*
Marchand, Jakob; Chicago, 1856 ***5475.1*** *p236*
Marchand, Jean 45; New Orleans, 1848 ***778.6*** *p227*
Marchand, Jean Louis 44; Texas, 1848 ***778.6*** *p227*
Marchand, Joseph 52; Louisiana, 1848 ***778.6*** *p227*
Marchand, Marie-Elisabeth; Quebec, 1670 ***4514.3*** *p344*
Marchand, Marie-Madeleine; Quebec, 1648 ***9221.17*** *p201*
Marchand, Michael 22; Louisiana, 1840 ***778.6*** *p227*
Marchand, Paris 35; America, 1847 ***778.6*** *p227*
Marchand, Pauchard 34; America, 1847 ***778.6*** *p227*
Marchand, Pierre 23; America, 1846 ***778.6*** *p227*
Marchand, Simon 42; New Orleans, 1844 ***778.6*** *p227*
Marchand, Thomas; Quebec, 1658 ***9221.17*** *p384*
Marchand, Virginie 9; America, 1847 ***778.6*** *p227*
Marchant, Charles; Virginia, 1766 ***1220.12*** *p545*
Marchant, Fred; New York, n.d. ***9228.50*** *p422*
Marchant, Henry 32; Ontario, 1871 ***1823.21*** *p213*
Marchant, Joseph; America, 1771 ***1220.12*** *p545*
Marchant, Joseph F. 45; Ontario, 1871 ***1823.21*** *p213*
Marchant, Mary; America, 1774 ***1220.12*** *p545*
Marchant, Rachel; Connecticut, 1730 ***9228.50*** *p260*
Marchant, Thomas; America, 1735 ***1220.12*** *p545*
Marchant, William; New York, 1775 ***8529.30*** *p14*
Marchard, George Emanuel; Ohio, 1809-1852 ***4511.35*** *p32*
Marchaw, George Emanuel; Ohio, 1809-1852 ***4511.35*** *p32*
Marchel, Catherine; Wisconsin, 1900 ***6795.8*** *p147*
Marcher, Miss 40; America, 1844 ***778.6*** *p227*
Marchesi, Alphonse 32; Port uncertain, 1841 ***778.6*** *p227*
Marchessault, Marie; Quebec, 1669 ***4514.3*** *p344*
Marchesseau, C.; Louisiana, 1874 ***4981.45*** *p296*
Marcheteau, Pierre; Quebec, 1645 ***9221.17*** *p155*
Marchinton, Matthew; America, 1771 ***1220.12*** *p528*
Marchling, Jean Joseph 36; America, 1847 ***778.6*** *p228*
Marchner, John F.; Ohio, 1809-1852 ***4511.35*** *p32*
Marcial, Louis 34; America, 1840 ***778.6*** *p228*
Marcilly, Pierre 46; America, 1843 ***778.6*** *p228*
Marciniak, William Andrew; Detroit, 1929-1930 ***6214.5*** *p67*
Marcinkowski, Romanus; Wisconsin, 1893 ***6795.8*** *p60*
Marck, Francois 39; New Orleans, 1848 ***778.6*** *p228*
Marcker, Karl Friedr. Jos.; America, 1867 ***5475.1*** *p505*
Marckle, Christopher; America, 1770 ***1220.12*** *p528*
Marconnier, Adri 28; America, 1843 ***778.6*** *p228*
Marconnot, Alexandre 18; Mississippi, 1847 ***778.6*** *p228*
Marconnot, Loiuise 22; Mississippi, 1847 ***778.6*** *p228*
Marconnot, Vincenz 25; Mississippi, 1847 ***778.6*** *p228*
Marconnot, Xavier 9; Mississippi, 1847 ***778.6*** *p228*
Marcot, Madeleine 28; Quebec, 1662 ***9221.17*** *p490*
Marcotte, Jean Desire 14; New Orleans, 1848 ***778.6*** *p228*
Marcotte, Louis Isidor 49; New Orleans, 1848 ***778.6*** *p228*
Marcou, Pierre 24; Quebec, 1655 ***9221.17*** *p327*
Marcs, Bernard 29; Missouri, 1845 ***778.6*** *p228*
Marcus, Mrs. 31; America, 1846 ***778.6*** *p228*
Marcus, Anna Carolina 7; America, 1846 ***778.6*** *p228*
Marcus, David; America, 1840 ***5475.1*** *p385*
Marcus, David; Louisiana, 1860 ***7710.1*** *p156*
Marcus, Josef; America, 1881 ***5475.1*** *p33*
Marcush, Miss; Halifax, N.S., 1902 ***1860.4*** *p44*
Marcush, Mr.; Halifax, N.S., 1902 ***1860.4*** *p44*
Marcush, Martin; Halifax, N.S., 1902 ***1860.4*** *p44*
Marcust, Miss; Halifax, N.S., 1902 ***1860.4*** *p44*
Marcust, Mr.; Halifax, N.S., 1902 ***1860.4*** *p44*
Marcust, Martin; Halifax, N.S., 1902 ***1860.4*** *p44*
Marcy, John; Roxbury, MA, 1662-1685 ***1642*** *p15*
Marcy, John; Roxbury, MA, 1685 ***1642*** *p107*
Marder, John; Ohio, 1809-1852 ***4511.35*** *p32*
Mardin, Humphrey; Virginia, 1763 ***1220.12*** *p528*
Mardon, Thomas; Philadelphia, 1778 ***8529.30*** *p4A*
Mardorf, B.; Valdivia, Chile, 1852 ***1192.4*** *p56*
  With wife & child
  With child 1
  With child 8
Mare, Thomas; Virginia, 1759 ***1220.12*** *p528*
Marecek, M.; New York, NY, 1843 ***2853.20*** *p98*
Marechal, Anne 36; New Orleans, 1847 ***778.6*** *p228*
Marechal, Anna 34; New Orleans, 1847 ***778.6*** *p228*
Marechal, Bertrand; Louisiana, 1836-1840 ***4981.45*** *p213*
Marechal, Joseph 7; New Orleans, 1847 ***778.6*** *p228*
Marechal, Joseph 16; New Orleans, 1848 ***778.6*** *p228*
Marechal, Josephine 17; Port uncertain, 1843 ***778.6*** *p228*
Marechal, Madeleine; Montreal, 1669-1684 ***1142.10*** *p128*
Marechal, Madeleine; Quebec, 1669 ***4514.3*** *p344*
Marechal, Marguerite; Quebec, 1669 ***4514.3*** *p345*
Marechal, Marie 6; New Orleans, 1847 ***778.6*** *p228*
Marechal, Nicolas 44; Port uncertain, 1847 ***778.6*** *p228*
Marei, Nicholas; Ohio, 1809-1852 ***4511.35*** *p32*
Marein, Catherine 28; New Orleans, 1848 ***778.6*** *p228*
Marein, Jean 3; New Orleans, 1848 ***778.6*** *p228*
Marein, Jean 32; New Orleans, 1848 ***778.6*** *p228*
Marein, Louise 28; New Orleans, 1848 ***778.6*** *p228*
Marein, Nicolas 5; New Orleans, 1848 ***778.6*** *p228*
Marein, Peter 6; New Orleans, 1848 ***778.6*** *p228*
Marek, Frank; Detroit, 1929-1930 ***6214.5*** *p65*
Mareng, Gottfried; Colorado, 1898 ***1029.59*** *p58*
Marentier, P. 40; New Orleans, 1840 ***778.6*** *p228*
Mares, Child; New Orleans, 1846 ***778.6*** *p228*
Mares, Child; New Orleans, 1846 ***778.6*** *p228*
Mares, Mrs. 24; New Orleans, 1846 ***778.6*** *p229*
Mares, Emile; New Orleans, 1846 ***778.6*** *p228*
Mares, Francois 22; Quebec, 1655 ***9221.17*** *p327*
Mares, J. 30; America, 1841 ***778.6*** *p229*
Mares, Jean 34; New Orleans, 1846 ***778.6*** *p228*
Mares, Josef; Texas, 1852 ***2853.20*** *p59*
Mares, Tomas; St. Paul, MN, 1858 ***2853.20*** *p277*
Marescot, Guillaume; Quebec, 1653 ***9221.17*** *p277*
Maret, Peter; Ohio, 1809-1852 ***4511.35*** *p32*
Maret, Richard; America, 1776 ***9228.50*** *p423*
Marett, James; Quebec, 1801 ***9228.50*** *p423*
Marett, John; Quebec, 1766-1843 ***9228.50*** *p20A*
Marett, John; Utah, 1855 ***9228.50*** *p423*
Marett, John; Utah, 1863 ***9228.50*** *p423*
Marett, Nicholas; Salem, MA, 1613-1635 ***9228.50*** *p423*
Marett, Philip; Utah, 1851 ***9228.50*** *p423*
Marette, . . .; Quebec, 1858 ***9228.50*** *p423*
Marette, Antoine; Quebec, 1659 ***9221.17*** *p406*
Marette, Jacques 28; Quebec, 1659 ***9221.17*** *p406*
Margane deLavaltrie, Seraphin; Quebec, 1665 ***2314.30*** *p167*
Margane deLavaltrie, Seraphin; Quebec, 1665 ***2314.30*** *p190*
Margat, George 19; Mississippi, 1847 ***778.6*** *p229*
Margat, Jean; Quebec, 1647 ***9221.17*** *p185*
Margeson, Edmond; Plymouth, MA, 1620 ***1920.45*** *p5*
Marget, George 19; Mississippi, 1847 ***778.6*** *p229*
Margetroide, Michael; America, 1729 ***1220.12*** *p572*
Margetts, Thomas; America, 1757 ***1220.12*** *p528*
Margin, Adrien 11; America, 1847 ***778.6*** *p229*
Margin, Claude 15; America, 1847 ***778.6*** *p229*
Margin, Claudine 16; America, 1847 ***778.6*** *p229*
Margin, Clementine 10; America, 1847 ***778.6*** *p229*
Margin, Emile 4; America, 1847 ***778.6*** *p229*
Margin, Emilie 1; America, 1847 ***778.6*** *p229*
Margin, Florian 8; America, 1847 ***778.6*** *p229*

Margin, Francoise 43; America, 1847 *778.6* p229
Margin, Jean Franc. Victor 45; America, 1847 *778.6* p229
Margin, John; Ohio, 1809-1852 *4511.35* p32
Margin, Joseph 13; America, 1847 *778.6* p229
Margin, Lucien 7; America, 1847 *778.6* p229
Margin, Marie 18; America, 1847 *778.6* p229
Margioti, H.; Louisiana, 1874-1875 *4981.45* p30
Margo, Alexander; Ohio, 1809-1852 *4511.35* p32
Margolewska, Wiktoria 17; New York, NY, 1911 *6533.11* p10
Margolis, Goldie Tribuch SEE Margolis, Harry
Margolis, Harry; Detroit, 1929-1930 *6214.5* p71
  Wife: Goldie Tribuch
Margoth, E. 18; New Orleans, 1843 *778.6* p229
Margraff, Jean 23; Port uncertain, 1846 *778.6* p229
Margraff, Louisa 25; Port uncertain, 1846 *778.6* p229
Margraff, Rosina 2; Port uncertain, 1846 *778.6* p229
Margrave, John; America, 1758 *1220.12* p529
Margue, S. L. 28; Port uncertain, 1848 *778.6* p229
Marguerie, Francois 20; Quebec, 1632 *9221.17* p20
Marguerie, Marie 21; Quebec, 1641 *9221.17* p105
Marguson, Michael 50; Ontario, 1871 *1823.21* p213
Mari, Michael; America, 1840 *5475.1* p470
Mari, Philipp; America, 1840 *5475.1* p471
Mari, Mrs. Philipp; America, 1847 *5475.1* p474
Maria, James; America, 1750 *1220.12* p529
Maria, Jean 25; America, 1847 *778.6* p229
Mariacher, George; Colorado, 1888 *1029.59* p58
Mariacher, George 25; Colorado, 1888 *1029.59* p58
Mariaha, Sabastian; Colorado, 1895 *1029.59* p58
Marian, Nicholas; America, 1773 *1220.12* p530
Marian, Welder 18; America, 1847 *778.6* p229
Mariau, U. J. 27; America, 1848 *778.6* p229
Mariauchau d'Esgly, Francois; Quebec, 1683-1688 *2314.30* p168
Mariauchau d'Esgly, Francois; Quebec, 1689 *2314.30* p191
Marichal, Eugene 28; America, 1847 *778.6* p229
Mariche, Louis; Quebec, 1648 *9221.17* p204
Marie, Albert 3; America, 1847 *778.6* p229
Marie, Denise; Quebec, 1673 *4514.3* p345
Marie, Henri 30; Port uncertain, 1845 *778.6* p229
Marie, Jean; Quebec, 1639 *9221.17* p91
Marie, Jeanne; Quebec, 1670 *4514.3* p345
Marie, Ludovick; Philadelphia, 1777 *8529.30* p4A
Marie, M. 32; New Orleans, 1841 *778.6* p229
Marie, Nicholas; Ohio, 1809-1852 *4511.35* p32
Marie, Nicolas 32; Port uncertain, 1845 *778.6* p229
Marie, Pierre 33; America, 1847 *778.6* p229
Marie, Rene; Quebec, 1652 *9221.17* p262
Marie, Virgile 4 months; America, 1847 *778.6* p230
Marie, Virginie 27; America, 1847 *778.6* p230
Mariegauld, Ann 49; Ontario, 1871 *1823.21* p213
Mariegauld, Charlotte 13; Ontario, 1871 *1823.21* p213
Mariegauld, Edward 24; Ontario, 1871 *1823.21* p213
Mariegauld, Elisa 23; Ontario, 1871 *1823.21* p213
Mariegauld, Gabriel 61; Ontario, 1871 *1823.21* p213
Mariegauld, Mary 14; Ontario, 1871 *1823.21* p213
Mariegauld, William 20; Ontario, 1871 *1823.21* p213
Mariel, Josephine 29; America, 1840 *778.6* p230
Marier, V. 69; America, 1846 *778.6* p230
Maries, Abraham 7 SEE Maries, Abraham
Maries, Abraham 30; Ohio, 1880 *4879.40* p259
  Wife: Marian 30
  Daughter: Cluffy 5
  Son: Louis 3
  Son: Abraham 7
  Daughter: Mary 9
Maries, Cluffy 5 SEE Maries, Abraham
Maries, Louis 3 SEE Maries, Abraham
Maries, Marian 30 SEE Maries, Abraham
Maries, Mary 9 SEE Maries, Abraham
Marietti, Jacob; Louisiana, 1874 *4981.45* p133
Marillac, Charles de; Quebec, 1755-1757 *2314.30* p170
Marillac, Charles de; Quebec, 1755 *2314.30* p191
Marin deLa Malgue, Charles; Quebec, 1683-1688 *2314.30* p168
Marin deLa Malgue, Charles; Quebec, 1684 *2314.30* p191
Marine, Alex. 19; America, 1848 *778.6* p230
Marine, Andre; Maine, n.d. *9228.50* p20A
Marinel, James; Maine, 1686 *9228.50* p424
Marinel, John Le, Sr.; Massachusetts, 1870 *9228.50* p50
  With wife
  With son 8
Marinelli, Loiuise 8; New Orleans, 1848 *778.6* p230
Marinelli, Marie 29; New Orleans, 1848 *778.6* p230
Mariner, Andrew; Portsmouth, NH, 1678 *9228.50* p424
Mariner, James; Maine, 1686 *9228.50* p424
Mariner, Joshua; Boston, 1789 *9228.50* p424
Mariner, Thomas; Salem, MA, 1650 *9228.50* p424
Mariner, Thomas; Salem, MA, 1650 *9228.50* p424

Maring, Gottfried; Colorado, 1895 *1029.59* p58
Maring, Susanna; America, 1843 *5475.1* p351
Maringer, Barbara; America, 1882 *5475.1* p228
Maringer, Johann; America, 1863 *5475.1* p282
Marino, Child; New Orleans, 1848 *778.6* p230
Marino, Mrs. A. 33; New Orleans, 1848 *778.6* p230
Marion, Mr. 19; New Orleans, 1848 *778.6* p230
Marion, Pedro 28; New Orleans, 1846 *778.6* p230
Mariot, John 26; Ontario, 1871 *1823.17* p98
Mariot, Ruth 55; Ontario, 1871 *1823.17* p98
Marir, Nicholas; Ohio, 1809-1852 *4511.35* p32
Marison, Charles; America, 1691 *1220.12* p529
Maritime, Mary; Virginia, 1736 *1220.12* p529
Maritt, Thomas; Cambridge, MA, 1638 *9228.50* p423
Maritz, . . .; North Carolina, 1710 *3629.40* p5
Maritz, Andre 64; Mississippi, 1846 *778.6* p230
Marius, Jean 31; America, 1844 *778.6* p230
Mariz, Bernard 21; America, 1847 *778.6* p230
Mariz, Jean 25; America, 1847 *778.6* p229
Marizinsk, Paul 29; New York, NY, 1894 *6512.1* p232
Marjery, Benjamin; Salem, MA, 1650-1675 *9228.50* p440
Marjery, George; Massachusetts, n.d. *9228.50* p439
Marjery, Jane; Died enroute, 1677 *9228.50* p440
Marjery, Joseph; Salem, MA, 1655-1680 *9228.50* p440
Marjery, Laurence; Salem, MA, 1646-1670 *9228.50* p439
Marjery, Martin; Massachusetts, 1652-1709 *9228.50* p440
Marjoram, William; Rappahannock, VA, 1728 *1220.12* p529
Marjot, Anne 24; America, 1846 *778.6* p230
Marjot, Baptiste 24; America, 1846 *778.6* p230
Marjot, Louise 9 months; America, 1846 *778.6* p230
Mark, Adam 2 SEE Mark, Philipp
Mark, Anna Eva 41; America, 1854 *2526.42* p200
Mark, Edward 26; Ontario, 1871 *1823.21* p213
Mark, Elisabetha; America, 1854 *2526.42* p200
Mark, Elisabetha 3 SEE Mark, Philipp
Mark, Eva Katharina Scholl SEE Mark, Johann Philipp
Mark, Fred 19; New York, NY, 1894 *6512.1* p228
Mark, Heinrich 14; America, 1865 *2526.42* p200
Mark, Henry 35; Ontario, 1871 *1823.21* p213
Mark, Henry 70; Ontario, 1871 *1823.21* p213
Mark, Israel; Marblehead, MA, 1750 *9228.50* p425
Mark, James 20; Ontario, 1871 *1823.21* p213
Mark, James 62; Ontario, 1871 *1823.21* p213
Mark, Johann Philipp; America, 1785 *2526.42* p126
  Wife: Eva Katharina Scholl
  With 3 children
Mark, Johannes; America, 1889 *2526.42* p109
Mark, John; America, 1754 *1220.12* p529
Mark, John; America, 1775 *1220.12* p529
Mark, Joseph 30; Ontario, 1871 *1823.21* p213
Mark, Konrad 15; America, 1854 *2526.42* p201
Mark, Peter; America, 1859 *2526.42* p201
Mark, Philipp; America, 1847 *2526.42* p126
  With wife
  Child: Elisabetha
  Child: Adam
  Child: Philipp
Mark, Philipp 5 SEE Mark, Philipp
Mark, Philipp 18; America, 1853 *2526.42* p109
Mark, Rachael 40; Ontario, 1871 *1823.21* p213
Mark, Richard 34; Ontario, 1871 *1823.21* p214
Mark, Thomas 40; Ontario, 1871 *1823.21* p214
Markahan, Pastrich; Ohio, 1857 *3580.20* p33
Markahan, Patrick; Ohio, 1857 *6020.12* p21
Marker, Philip, Jr.; Ohio, 1809-1852 *4511.35* p32
Markerson, John; Virginia, 1766 *1220.12* p529
Markerson, Walter; America, 1774 *1220.12* p529
Markert, Gustus J.; Wisconsin, 1877 *6795.8* p41
Markes, Anne; America, 1734 *1220.12* p529
Markes, Frances; Virginia, 1732 *1220.12* p529
Markes, John; America, 1685 *1220.12* p529
Markes, Mary 79; Ontario, 1871 *1823.21* p214
Markes, Thomas; America, 1685 *1220.12* p529
Markes, William; Barbados, 1669 *1220.12* p529
Market, Frederick; North Carolina, 1710 *3629.40* p5
Markey, Hugh; Illinois, 1858 *6079.1* p9
Markey, James; America, 1773 *1220.12* p529
Markey, Thomas 58; Ontario, 1871 *1823.21* p214
Markey, William; America, 1774 *1220.12* p529
Markgraf, Karoline Wilhelmine SEE Markgraf, Rich.
Markgraf, Katharina Klein SEE Markgraf, Rich.
Markgraf, Luise Katharina SEE Markgraf, Rich.
Markgraf, Rich.; Illinois, 1887 *5475.1* p75
  Wife: Katharina Klein
  Daughter: Luise Katharina
  Daughter: Karoline Wilhelmine
  Daughter: Sophie Karoline
Markgraf, Sophie Karoline SEE Markgraf, Rich.
Markham, Edward; New York, 1778 *8529.30* p4A

Markham, James; America, 1754 *1220.12* p529
Markham, Joseph; America, 1743 *1220.12* p529
Markham, Joseph 40; Ontario, 1871 *1823.21* p214
Markham, Margaret; Rappahannock, VA, 1729 *1220.12* p529
Marki, Jaques; New Castle, DE, 1817-1818 *90.20* p152
Marki, S. Ulrich 60; New Castle, DE, 1817-1818 *90.20* p152
Markin, Thomas 76; Ontario, 1871 *1823.21* p214
Markins, Samuel; America, 1756 *1220.12* p529
Markland, Joshua; America, 1767 *1220.12* p529
Markle, Barbara 30; Galveston, TX, 1844 *3967.10* p370
Markle, Conrad; Ohio, 1809-1852 *4511.35* p32
Markle, Emilie 5; Galveston, TX, 1844 *3967.10* p370
Markle, Jakob 7; Galveston, TX, 1844 *3967.10* p370
Markle, Karl 1; Galveston, TX, 1844 *3967.10* p370
Markle, Peter 32; Galveston, TX, 1844 *3967.10* p370
Markle, Peter; Ohio, 1809-1852 *4511.35* p32
Marklin, Daniel; America, 1733 *1220.12* p529
Markling, Adam; Ohio, 1809-1852 *4511.35* p32
Markovich, B.; Louisiana, 1874-1875 *4981.45* p29
Markowski, Jozef; Wisconsin, 1876 *6795.8* p69
Markowsky, Stany; New York, NY, 1885 *6015.15* p28
Markram, Thomas; America, 1757 *1220.12* p529
Marks, Elizabeth SEE Marks, Fred
Marks, Elizabeth; Virginia, 1758 *1220.12* p529
Marks, Emma 24; Michigan, 1880 *4491.30* p21
Marks, Esther; America, 1768 *1220.12* p529
Marks, Fred; Boston, 1800-1899 *9228.50* p425
  Brother: George
  Mother: Elizabeth
Marks, George SEE Marks, Fred
Marks, Hatty 16; Michigan, 1880 *4491.30* p21
Marks, Henry; New York, 1848 *471.10* p88
Marks, Henry; New York, NY, 1844 *7710.1* p150
Marks, Henry Marks 50; Ontario, 1871 *1823.17* p98
Marks, J. 17; Quebec, 1870 *8364.32* p24
Marks, Jane; Salem, MA, 1653-1674 *9228.50* p425
Marks, Jane 6; Salem, MA, 1659 *9228.50* p360
Marks, John 43; Ontario, 1871 *1823.21* p214
Marks, Martha 30; Ontario, 1871 *1823.17* p98
Marks, Nicholas; America, 1734 *1220.12* p529
Marks, Thomas; America, 1731 *1220.12* p529
Marks, Valentine; Ohio, 1809-1852 *4511.35* p32
Marks, William; Virginia, 1730 *1220.12* p529
Marks, William P. 46; Ontario, 1871 *1823.21* p214
Markson, Sharlotte; America, 1739 *1220.12* p529
Markus, Sarah L. 22; New York, NY, 1894 *6512.1* p186
Markwood, George; Ohio, 1809-1852 *4511.35* p32
Markworth, Frederick; Washington, 1889 *2770.40* p79
Marland, Henry; America, 1760 *1220.12* p529
Marlborough, Francis; Virginia, 1738 *1220.12* p529
Marler, Aloise 22; Louisiana, 1848 *778.6* p230
Marlette, Eliza C. 43; Michigan, 1880 *4491.36* p14
Marlette, Louis 50; Michigan, 1880 *4491.36* p14
Marley, Edward SEE Marley, Thomas
Marley, Henry SEE Marley, Thomas
Marley, Thomas; British Columbia, 1911-1912 *9228.50* p425
  Brother: Henry
  Brother: Edward
Marlier, Virginie; Wisconsin, 1870 *1495.20* p8
Marling, Mary; Virginia, 1735 *1220.12* p529
Marlis, Antoine 51; America, 1847 *778.6* p230
Marlock, John; America, 1765 *1220.12* p529
Marlow, Elizabeth; Maryland, 1725 *1220.12* p529
Marlow, James; America, 1737 *1220.12* p529
Marlow, John; America, 1748 *1220.12* p529
Marlow, Mary; America, 1742 *1220.12* p529
Marlow, Patrick; Boston, 1775 *8529.30* p4A
Marlow, Samuel; New York, NY, 1778 *8529.30* p3
Marlow, William; America, 1746 *1220.12* p529
Marlow, William; America, 1770 *1220.12* p529
Marlow, William 26; Michigan, 1880 *4491.33* p14
Marman, John; America, 1734 *1220.12* p529
Marman, Margaret; Virginia, 1732 *1220.12* p529
Marman, Mary; America, 1742 *1220.12* p529
Marman, Timothy; America, 1757 *1220.12* p529
Marman, William; America, 1734 *1220.12* p530
Marmon, John; America, 1751 *1220.12* p529
Marmontre, Charles 30; Port uncertain, 1841 *778.6* p230
Marmun, John; Barbados, 1669 *1220.12* p529
Marn, Thomas 13; Quebec, 1870 *8364.32* p24
Marnan, . . .; Toronto, 1844 *2910.35* p114
Marne, J. J. 23; Port uncertain, 1842 *778.6* p230
Marnes, Therese 38; Louisiana, 1848 *778.6* p230
Maroc, Voytech; Texas, 1887-1890 *6015.15* p28
Maron, Eva; Dakota, 1866-1918 *554.30* p26
Maron, Johann; Port uncertain. 1881 *5475.1* p329
Maron, Peter; America, 1860 *5475.1* p387
Marond, P. 28; America, 1845 *778.6* p230
Marouiche, Emile 61; America, 1840 *778.6* p230
Marpin, Antoine 30; Port uncertain, 1843 *778.6* p230

Marples, James; New York, 1775 ***8529.30*** *p14*
Marpurt, John; South Carolina, 1807 ***6155.4*** *p19*
Marq, Martin 21; America, 1846 ***778.6*** *p230*
Marquand, Charles *SEE* Marquand, John
Marquand, Charles; Washington, D.C., 1796-1836 ***9228.50*** *p425*
*Wife:*Rachel Lovis
*Child:*Solomon
*Child:*Sophia
*Child:*Charles E.
*Child:*John
*Child:*Peter
*Child:*Rachel
Marquand, Charles E. *SEE* Marquand, Charles
Marquand, Daniel; Massachusetts, 1732 ***9228.50*** *p430*
Marquand, David; Newburyport, MA, 1729 ***9228.50*** *p431*
Marquand, Elias John *SEE* Marquand, Ernest Philip
Marquand, Ernest Philip; America, 1800-1899 ***9228.50*** *p431*
*Brother:*Elias John
*Brother:*Samuel James
Marquand, Francis; Rhode Island, 1861-1915 ***9228.50*** *p431*
Marquand, Henry; Fairfield, CT, 1761 ***9228.50*** *p430*
Marquand, John; Boston, 1806 ***9228.50*** *p427*
*Child:*John M.
*Child:*Charles
Marquand, John; Norfolk, VA, 1806 ***9228.50*** *p56*
With family
Marquand, John; Ohio, 1760-1825 ***9228.50*** *p429*
Marquand, John *SEE* Marquand, Charles
Marquand, John M. *SEE* Marquand, John
Marquand, Judith; Ohio, 1805-1860 ***9228.50*** *p429*
Marquand, Judith; Utah, 1823-1860 ***9228.50*** *p352*
Marquand, Mary; Ohio, 1747-1846 ***9228.50*** *p545*
Marquand, Peter *SEE* Marquand, Charles
Marquand, Rachel *SEE* Marquand, Charles
Marquand, Rachel Lovis *SEE* Marquand, Charles
Marquand, Samuel James *SEE* Marquand, Ernest Philip
Marquand, Solomon *SEE* Marquand, Charles
Marquand, Sophia *SEE* Marquand, Charles
Marquand Family ; Fairfield, CT, 1700-1799 ***9228.50*** *p509*
Marquand Family ; Prince Edward Island, 1806 ***9228.50*** *p128*
Marquard, Adam; America, 1853 ***2526.42*** *p183*
Marquard, Adam; America, 1866 ***2526.42*** *p183*
Marquard, Anna Maria; America, 1850 ***2526.42*** *p183*
Marquard, Balthasar 6 *SEE* Marquard, Balthasar
Marquard, Balthasar 32; America, 1853 ***2526.43*** *p142*
*Wife:*Eva Elisabetha Schmauss 41
*Son:*Balthasar 6
*Brother:*Johann Peter 14
*Sister:*Maria Magdalena 30
*Son:*Georg Peter 4
*Son:*Johann Peter 9
Marquard, Barbara; America, 1854 ***2526.42*** *p183*
Marquard, Barbara; America, 1854 ***2526.43*** *p134*
Marquard, Eva Elisabetha Schmauss 41 *SEE* Marquard, Balthasar
Marquard, Georg 16; America, 1854 ***2526.42*** *p183*
Marquard, Georg Adam; America, 1859 ***2526.42*** *p183*
Marquard, Georg Peter 4 *SEE* Marquard, Balthasar
Marquard, Johann Peter 9 *SEE* Marquard, Balthasar
Marquard, Johann Peter 14 *SEE* Marquard, Balthasar
Marquard, Maria Magdalena 30 *SEE* Marquard, Balthasar
Marquard, Nikolaus 38; America, 1861 ***2526.42*** *p183*
With wife 39
With son 8
With daughter 10
Marquard, Philipp; America, 1864 ***2526.42*** *p183*
Marquardt, Anna Eva Kaffenberger *SEE* Marquardt, Johann Jakob
Marquardt, Anna Margaretha 18 *SEE* Marquardt, Georg
Marquardt, Elisabeth Katharina *SEE* Marquardt, Johann Jakob
Marquardt, Eva Katharina 11 *SEE* Marquardt, Georg
Marquardt, Eva Margaretha 26 *SEE* Marquardt, Georg
Marquardt, Eva Maria 9 *SEE* Marquardt, Georg
Marquardt, Friedr. Wilh; Wisconsin, 1900 ***6795.8*** *p193*
Marquardt, Georg 32; America, 1851 ***2526.43*** *p134*
*Wife:*Juliane Sauer 53
*Daughter:*Eva Katharina 11
*Daughter:*Juliane Elisabeth 14
*Son:*Johann Georg 6
*Daughter:*Eva Maria 9
*Daughter:*Eva Margaretha 26
*Son:*Johann Konrad 24
*Daughter:*Regina 22
*Daughter:*Anna Margaretha 18
Marquardt, Gustav; Wisconsin, 1878 ***6795.8*** *p26*
Marquardt, Johann Georg 6 *SEE* Marquardt, Georg
Marquardt, Johann Jakob; Virginia, 1831 ***152.20*** *p65*
*Wife:*Anna Eva Kaffenberger
*Child:*Elisabeth Katharina
Marquardt, Johann Konrad 24 *SEE* Marquardt, Georg
Marquardt, Johannes; America, 1851 ***2526.43*** *p134*
Marquardt, Juliane Sauer 53 *SEE* Marquardt, Georg
Marquardt, Juliane Elisabeth 14 *SEE* Marquardt, Georg
Marquardt, Leonhard; America, 1853 ***2526.42*** *p97*
Marquardt, Louis Fred; Wisconsin, 1889 ***6795.8*** *p107*
Marquardt, Regina 22 *SEE* Marquardt, Georg
Marquerre, Jean 23; New Orleans, 1848 ***778.6*** *p230*
Marques, Francisco; Louisiana, 1836-1840 ***4981.45*** *p213*
Marques, Henrietta 39; America, 1847 ***778.6*** *p230*
Marquis, Mr. 28; America, 1846 ***778.6*** *p230*
Marquis, Alexis 17 *SEE* Marquis, Jean Joseph
Marquis, Giles; Ontario, 1905 ***9228.50*** *p432*
Marquis, Giles; Pennsylvania, 1921 ***9228.50*** *p432*
*Wife:*Lucia Martel
*Daughter-In-Law:*Leonne-Louise Glorel
*Son:*Sidney
Marquis, Henri 8; Galveston, TX, 1844 ***3967.10*** *p375*
Marquis, Jean Joseph 60; Galveston, TX, 1844 ***3967.10*** *p375*
*Son:*Alexis 17
Marquis, Leonne-Louise Glorel *SEE* Marquis, Giles
Marquis, Leonore 22; Galveston, TX, 1844 ***3967.10*** *p375*
Marquis, Lucia Martel *SEE* Marquis, Giles
Marquis, Marie Anne 49; Galveston, TX, 1844 ***3967.10*** *p375*
Marquis, Seraphine 11; Galveston, TX, 1844 ***3967.10*** *p375*
Marquis, Sidney *SEE* Marquis, Giles
Marquiseau, Michel; Quebec, 1657 ***9221.17*** *p363*
Marr, . . .; New England, 1700-1799 ***9228.50*** *p432*
Marr, Alexander 35; Ontario, 1871 ***1823.21*** *p214*
Marr, Ann; America, 1772 ***1220.12*** *p530*
Marr, Nicholas Arthur; Boston, 1715 ***9228.50*** *p306*
Marr, Robert; America, 1756 ***1220.12*** *p530*
Marrain, Pierre 28; Missouri, 1847 ***778.6*** *p230*
Marrat, Charles; America, 1676 ***1220.12*** *p530*
Marratt, John; Barbados, 1679 ***1220.12*** *p530*
Marre, Jacques 29; America, 1846 ***778.6*** *p234*
Marret, Mary *SEE* Marret, Philip
Marret, Philip; Boston, 1650-1750 ***9228.50*** *p423*
*Wife:*Mary
Marrett, James; America, 1729 ***1220.12*** *p530*
Marrett, Nicholas; Salem, MA, 1613-1635 ***9228.50*** *p423*
Marrett, Philip; Boston, 1742-1760 ***9228.50*** *p423*
Marrett, Philip; Boston, 1792 ***9228.50*** *p423*
Marrett, Thomas; Cambridge, MA, 1638 ***9228.50*** *p423*
Marrian, Walter; America, 1775 ***1220.12*** *p530*
Marrick, John; Marston's Wharf, 1782 ***8529.30*** *p14*
Marricks, John; Marston's Wharf, 1782 ***8529.30*** *p14*
Marriette, Alice Ann; Massachusetts, 1913 ***9228.50*** *p532*
Marriette, Daniel; Ohio, 1810 ***9228.50*** *p432*
With children & grandchildren
Marriette, Elizabeth; Ohio, 1795-1813 ***9228.50*** *p432*
Marriette, Thomas; Ohio, 1791-1813 ***9228.50*** *p432*
Marriman, Thomas, Jr.; America, 1750 ***1220.12*** *p546*
Marrin, Wm O. 27; Ontario, 1871 ***1823.21*** *p214*
Marrion, Peter; St. John, N.B., 1848 ***2978.15*** *p40*
Marriot, Henry 53; Ontario, 1871 ***1823.17*** *p98*
Marriot, John; Marblehead, MA, 1674 ***9228.50*** *p423*
Marriot, Joseph; America, 1754 ***1220.12*** *p530*
Marriot, Thomas; Cambridge, MA, 1638 ***9228.50*** *p423*
Marriott, Clara 17; Ontario, 1871 ***1823.21*** *p214*
Marriott, Edward; America, 1775 ***1220.12*** *p530*
Marriott, Edward; Annapolis, MD, 1758 ***1220.12*** *p530*
Marriott, James; America, 1736 ***1220.12*** *p530*
Marriott, Joseph 45; Ontario, 1871 ***1823.21*** *p214*
Marriott, Nicholas; Salem, MA, 1613-1635 ***9228.50*** *p423*
Marriott, Richard; America, 1741 ***1220.12*** *p530*
Marriott, Samuel; America, 1773 ***1220.12*** *p530*
Marriott, Samuel; America, 1775 ***1220.12*** *p530*
Marriott, Samuel; Virginia, 1731 ***1220.12*** *p530*
Marriott, William; America, 1765 ***1220.12*** *p530*
Marritt, A. 47; Ontario, 1871 ***1823.21*** *p214*
Marritt, Thomas; Cambridge, MA, 1638 ***9228.50*** *p423*
Marromme, Claude; Quebec, 1643 ***9221.17*** *p132*
Marrow, James; Ontario, 1871 ***1823.17*** *p98*
Marrowe, William; America, 1691 ***1220.12*** *p530*
Marrs, David 58; Ontario, 1871 ***1823.21*** *p214*
Marrva, Philip; Louisiana, 1874-1875 ***4981.45*** *p30*
Marryatt, William 45; Ontario, 1871 ***1823.17*** *p98*
Mars, Child 4; New Orleans, 1840 ***778.6*** *p231*
Mars, Child 5; New Orleans, 1840 ***778.6*** *p230*
Mars, Child 7; New Orleans, 1840 ***778.6*** *p230*
Mars, Mrs. 25; New Orleans, 1840 ***778.6*** *p231*
Mars, Christian 29; America, 1846 ***778.6*** *p231*
Mars, James 32; Ontario, 1871 ***1823.21*** *p214*
Mars, Margaret 30; Ontario, 1871 ***1823.17*** *p98*
Mars, Micky 24; Ontario, 1871 ***1823.21*** *p214*
Marsa, Mathias 29; Ontario, 1871 ***1823.17*** *p98*
Marsalek, Jan; Iowa, 1910 ***2853.20*** *p235*
Marsalek, Simon; St. Louis, 1852 ***2853.20*** *p21*
Marsan, Jean 24; New Orleans, 1848 ***778.6*** *p231*
Marscey, Nathaniel; Virginia, 1728 ***1220.12*** *p530*
Marschall, Anna Elisabeth; Nova Scotia, 1751 ***2526.42*** *p179*
Marschall, Jakob 19; America, 1850 ***5475.1*** *p479*
Marschall, Louis 19; New Orleans, 1848 ***778.6*** *p231*
Marschall, Nikolaus; America, 1849 ***5475.1*** *p476*
Marschand, Abraham; Ohio, 1809-1852 ***4511.35*** *p32*
Marschand, David L.; Ohio, 1809-1852 ***4511.35*** *p32*
Marschand, Julius; Ohio, 1809-1852 ***4511.35*** *p32*
Marsden, David; Philadelphia, 1778 ***8529.30*** *p4A*
Marsden, Duane 30; Ontario, 1871 ***1823.17*** *p98*
Marsden, Ellen 51; Ontario, 1871 ***1823.21*** *p214*
Marsden, Esther 35; Ontario, 1871 ***1823.21*** *p214*
Marsden, Frederick 23; Ontario, 1871 ***1823.21*** *p214*
Marsden, James; America, 1743 ***1220.12*** *p530*
Marsden, Jonathan; America, 1773 ***1220.12*** *p530*
Marsden, Maria 61; Ontario, 1871 ***1823.21*** *p214*
Marsden, Mary; Washington, 1887 ***6015.10*** *p16*
Marseer, Laurant 32; America, 1845 ***778.6*** *p231*
Marselle, Xavier; Detroit, 1854 ***1494.21*** *p31*
Marsetteau, Jacques; Montreal, 1659 ***9221.17*** *p424*
Marsetteau, Mathurin 15; Montreal, 1659 ***9221.17*** *p424*
Marsey, Timothy; America, 1755 ***1220.12*** *p530*
Marsh, Daniel; America, 1749 ***1220.12*** *p530*
Marsh, Edward; America, 1685 ***1220.12*** *p530*
Marsh, Elizabeth; Virginia, 1745 ***1220.12*** *p530*
Marsh, Francis; Barbados, 1668 ***1220.12*** *p530*
Marsh, George; America, 1763 ***1220.12*** *p530*
Marsh, George; America, 1771 ***1220.12*** *p530*
Marsh, Henry 17; Ontario, 1871 ***1823.21*** *p214*
Marsh, Henry 20; Ontario, 1871 ***1823.21*** *p214*
Marsh, Isabel; Barbados, 1681 ***1220.12*** *p530*
Marsh, James; North Carolina, 1868 ***1088.45*** *p21*
Marsh, James 50; Ontario, 1871 ***1823.21*** *p214*
Marsh, James; Philadelphia, 1778 ***8529.30*** *p3*
Marsh, John; America, 1726 ***1220.12*** *p530*
Marsh, John; America, 1753 ***1220.12*** *p530*
Marsh, John; America, 1755 ***1220.12*** *p530*
Marsh, John; America, 1763 ***1220.12*** *p530*
Marsh, John; Barbados, 1683 ***1220.12*** *p530*
Marsh, John 34; Ontario, 1871 ***1823.17*** *p98*
Marsh, John R.; New Jersey, 1851-1917 ***9228.50*** *p434*
Marsh, John W. 53; Ontario, 1871 ***1823.21*** *p214*
Marsh, Lewis R. 53; Ontario, 1871 ***1823.21*** *p214*
Marsh, Mary; America, 1739 ***1220.12*** *p530*
Marsh, Mary; Barbados or Jamaica, 1705 ***1220.12*** *p530*
Marsh, Moses; Ohio, 1806 ***9228.50*** *p433*
Marsh, Nathaniel; America, 1758 ***1220.12*** *p530*
Marsh, Original; America, 1746 ***1220.12*** *p530*
Marsh, Phillis; Annapolis, MD, 1719 ***1220.12*** *p530*
Marsh, Richard; America, 1773 ***1220.12*** *p530*
Marsh, Richard 35; Ontario, 1871 ***1823.21*** *p214*
Marsh, Richard 46; Ontario, 1871 ***1823.21*** *p214*
Marsh, Susan; America, 1730 ***1220.12*** *p530*
Marsh, Thomas; America, 1726 ***1220.12*** *p530*
Marsh, Thomas; America, 1737 ***1220.12*** *p531*
Marsh, Thomas; America, 1738 ***1220.12*** *p531*
Marsh, Thomas; America, 1774 ***1220.12*** *p531*
Marsh, Thomas; Annapolis, MD, 1729 ***1220.12*** *p530*
Marsh, Thomas; Virginia, 1741 ***1220.12*** *p531*
Marsh, Walter; America, 1760 ***1220.12*** *p531*
Marsh, William; America, 1748 ***1220.12*** *p531*
Marsh, William 48; Ontario, 1871 ***1823.21*** *p214*
Marsh, William; Virginia, 1772 ***1220.12*** *p531*
Marshal, David 24; North Carolina, 1774 ***1422.10*** *p54*
Marshal, Edwin 20; Ontario, 1871 ***1823.17*** *p98*
Marshal, George 30; Ontario, 1871 ***1823.21*** *p214*
Marshal, Henry 22; Ontario, 1871 ***1823.21*** *p214*
Marshal, James 21; Ontario, 1871 ***1823.17*** *p98*
Marshal, James 34; Ontario, 1871 ***1823.21*** *p214*
Marshal, James 37; Ontario, 1871 ***1823.21*** *p214*
Marshal, John; America, 1752 ***1220.12*** *p531*
Marshal, John 52; Ontario, 1871 ***1823.21*** *p214*
Marshal, Joseph; Illinois, 1852 ***6079.1*** *p9*
Marshal, Joseph; Virginia, 1768 ***1220.12*** *p531*
Marshal, Simeon; America, 1771 ***1220.12*** *p532*
Marshale, George; Ohio, 1809-1852 ***4511.35*** *p32*
Marshall, Aaron; America, 1663 ***1220.12*** *p531*
Marshall, Abraham; America, 1757 ***1220.12*** *p531*
Marshall, Ann; Maryland, 1672 ***1236.25*** *p47*
Marshall, Anna 31; Michigan, 1880 ***4491.30*** *p21*
Marshall, Anne; America, 1746 ***1220.12*** *p531*
Marshall, Antonio 22; America, 1842 ***778.6*** *p231*
Marshall, Arthur 46; Ontario, 1871 ***1823.21*** *p214*
Marshall, Diggory; America, 1664 ***1220.12*** *p531*
Marshall, Edward; Annapolis, MD, 1725 ***1220.12*** *p531*
Marshall, Edward; Maryland, 1744 ***1220.12*** *p531*

Marshall, Edward; Maryland, 1772 ***1220.12*** *p531*
Marshall, Edward 16; Quebec, 1870 ***8364.32*** *p24*
Marshall, Elizabeth; America, 1763 ***1220.12*** *p531*
Marshall, Elizabeth; America, 1771 ***1220.12*** *p531*
Marshall, Elizabeth; America, 1773 ***1220.12*** *p531*
Marshall, Elizabeth Montgomery *SEE* Marshall, Harvey
Marshall, Ethel Tostevin; California, 1917 ***9228.50*** *p631*
Marshall, Felicite 21; America, 1846 ***778.6*** *p231*
Marshall, Frances; Barbados, 1683 ***1220.12*** *p531*
Marshall, Francois 27; America, 1846 ***778.6*** *p231*
Marshall, Fred 30; Ontario, 1871 ***1823.21*** *p214*
Marshall, George; America, 1722 ***1220.12*** *p531*
Marshall, George; Barbados or Jamaica, 1688 ***1220.12*** *p531*
Marshall, George 54; Ontario, 1871 ***1823.21*** *p214*
Marshall, George; South Carolina, 1808 ***6155.4*** *p19*
Marshall, Harry 20; Ontario, 1871 ***1823.21*** *p214*
Marshall, Harvey; Philadelphia, 1851 ***8513.31*** *p410*
*Wife:*Elizabeth Montgomery
Marshall, Henry; America, 1665 ***1220.12*** *p531*
Marshall, Henry; America, 1775 ***1220.12*** *p531*
Marshall, Henry 32; Barbados, 1664 ***1220.12*** *p531*
Marshall, Hugh 45; Ontario, 1871 ***1823.21*** *p214*
Marshall, Isaac; America, 1727 ***1220.12*** *p531*
Marshall, Isabella 55; New York, NY, 1835 ***5024.1*** *p136*
Marshall, Isaiah; Annapolis, MD, 1731 ***1220.12*** *p531*
Marshall, Israel; Canada, 1774 ***3036.5*** *p41*
Marshall, James; America, 1751 ***1220.12*** *p531*
Marshall, James; America, 1752 ***1220.12*** *p531*
Marshall, James 30; Ontario, 1871 ***1823.21*** *p215*
Marshall, James 37; Ontario, 1871 ***1823.17*** *p98*
Marshall, James 40; Ontario, 1871 ***1823.21*** *p215*
Marshall, James 52; Ontario, 1871 ***1823.21*** *p215*
Marshall, James; South Carolina, 1808 ***6155.4*** *p19*
Marshall, James T. C.; Illinois, 1858 ***6079.1*** *p9*
Marshall, Janet 76; Ontario, 1871 ***1823.21*** *p215*
Marshall, Jean 30; America, 1846 ***778.6*** *p231*
Marshall, John; America, 1697 ***1220.12*** *p531*
Marshall, John; America, 1726 ***1220.12*** *p531*
Marshall, John; America, 1767 ***1220.12*** *p531*
Marshall, John; America, 1774 ***1220.12*** *p531*
Marshall, John; Barbados or Jamaica, 1697 ***1220.12*** *p531*
Marshall, John; Charles Town, SC, 1719 ***1220.12*** *p531*
Marshall, John; Louisiana, 1841-1844 ***4981.45*** *p211*
Marshall, John; North Carolina, 1775 ***1422.10*** *p56*
Marshall, John 39; Ontario, 1871 ***1823.21*** *p215*
Marshall, John 45; Ontario, 1871 ***1823.21*** *p215*
Marshall, John 65; Ontario, 1871 ***1823.21*** *p215*
Marshall, John; Virginia, 1734 ***1220.12*** *p531*
Marshall, Joseph; America, 1766 ***1220.12*** *p531*
Marshall, Joseph; Boston, 1720 ***1642*** *p25*
Marshall, Joseph 45; Ontario, 1871 ***1823.21*** *p215*
Marshall, Joseph 85; Ontario, 1871 ***1823.21*** *p215*
Marshall, Joseph; South Carolina, 1808 ***6155.4*** *p19*
Marshall, Lydia; America, 1763 ***1220.12*** *p531*
Marshall, Martha; America, 1752 ***1220.12*** *p531*
Marshall, Mary; America, 1682 ***1220.12*** *p531*
Marshall, Mary; Barbados, 1683 ***1220.12*** *p531*
Marshall, Nehemiah; Annapolis, MD, 1731 ***1220.12*** *p532*
Marshall, Nicholas; Barbados, 1698 ***1220.12*** *p532*
Marshall, Phebe; Philadelphia, 1858 ***8513.31*** *p433*
Marshall, Rachael; America, 1756 ***1220.12*** *p532*
Marshall, Richard; America, 1726 ***1220.12*** *p532*
Marshall, Robert; Annapolis, MD, 1726 ***1220.12*** *p532*
Marshall, Robert F. 40; Ontario, 1871 ***1823.17*** *p98*
Marshall, Sarah; America, 1741 ***1220.12*** *p532*
Marshall, Scoter; America, 1771 ***1220.12*** *p532*
Marshall, Thomas; America, 1685 ***1220.12*** *p532*
Marshall, Thomas; America, 1732 ***1220.12*** *p532*
Marshall, Thomas; America, 1734 ***1220.12*** *p532*
Marshall, Thomas; Annapolis, MD, 1726 ***1220.12*** *p532*
Marshall, Thomas; Died enroute, 1736 ***1220.12*** *p532*
Marshall, Thomas; Ohio, 1809-1852 ***4511.35*** *p32*
Marshall, Thomas 42; Ontario, 1871 ***1823.21*** *p215*
Marshall, William; America, 1680 ***1220.12*** *p532*
Marshall, William; America, 1742 ***1220.12*** *p532*
Marshall, William; America, 1767 ***1220.12*** *p532*
Marshall, William; America, 1772 ***1220.12*** *p532*
Marshall, William; America, 1773 ***1220.12*** *p532*
Marshall, William; Illinois, 1858 ***6079.1*** *p9*
Marshall, William 43; Ontario, 1871 ***1823.21*** *p215*
Marshall, Wm J. 55; Ontario, 1871 ***1823.17*** *p98*
Marshel, L. F. 18; America, 1848 ***778.6*** *p231*
Marshell, Charles 37; Ontario, 1871 ***1823.21*** *p215*
Marshfielder, Jacob 25; Ontario, 1871 ***1823.21*** *p215*
Marshill, Edward 47; Ontario, 1871 ***1823.21*** *p215*
Marshman, Ben 52; Ontario, 1871 ***1823.21*** *p215*
Marshman, George 40; Ontario, 1871 ***1823.21*** *p215*
Marshman, James; America, 1771 ***1220.12*** *p532*
Marshman, James 70; Ontario, 1871 ***1823.21*** *p215*
Marshman, Jeremiah; Philadelphia, 1777 ***8529.30*** *p6*
Marshman, Job 38; Ontario, 1871 ***1823.21*** *p215*
Marshman, Simeon 49; Ontario, 1871 ***1823.21*** *p215*
Marshman, William; Virginia, 1751 ***1220.12*** *p532*
Marshmant, James; America, 1760 ***1220.12*** *p532*
Marsinder, Ann; Virginia, 1741 ***1220.12*** *p532*
Marsland, John 30; Ontario, 1871 ***1823.17*** *p98*
Marsolang, Mr. 24; New Orleans, 1847 ***778.6*** *p231*
Marsolang, Mrs. 19; New Orleans, 1847 ***778.6*** *p231*
Marsolet, Marie 18; Quebec, 1637 ***9221.17*** *p71*
Marsolet, Nicolas; Quebec, 1613 ***9221.17*** *p20*
Marson, John; America, 1765 ***1220.12*** *p532*
Marsot, Alexis 21; New Orleans, 1845 ***778.6*** *p231*
Marsot, Auguste 6; New Orleans, 1845 ***778.6*** *p231*
Marsot, Cecile 27; New Orleans, 1845 ***778.6*** *p231*
Marsot, Celestin 3 months; America, 1847 ***778.6*** *p231*
Marsot, Chris. Chs. 57; New Orleans, 1845 ***778.6*** *p231*
Marsot, Francois 18; New Orleans, 1845 ***778.6*** *p231*
Marsot, Jacques 16; New Orleans, 1845 ***778.6*** *p231*
Marsot, Joseph 41; America, 1847 ***778.6*** *p231*
Marsot, Julie 10; New Orleans, 1845 ***778.6*** *p231*
Marsot, Louis 12; New Orleans, 1845 ***778.6*** *p231*
Marsot, Marie 42; America, 1847 ***778.6*** *p231*
Marsot, Marie 40; New Orleans, 1845 ***778.6*** *p231*
Marsot, Pierre 7; New Orleans, 1845 ***778.6*** *p231*
Marsot, Vincent 14; New Orleans, 1845 ***778.6*** *p231*
Marsot, Xavier 5; America, 1847 ***778.6*** *p231*
Marst, Michael; Ohio, 1809-1852 ***4511.35*** *p32*
Marston, Phillip; Virginia, 1768 ***1220.12*** *p532*
Marston, William; America, 1768 ***1220.12*** *p532*
Martain, John; America, 1750 ***1220.12*** *p532*
Martain, William; Philadelphia, 1778 ***8529.30*** *p4A*
Martan, Thomas 66; Ontario, 1871 ***1823.17*** *p98*
Martayne, John; Barbados, 1668 ***1220.12*** *p533*
Martel, Mr.; Cuba, n.d. ***9228.50*** *p434*
Martel, Alice Le Mesurier *SEE* Martel, Nicholas
Martel, Henriette Le Mesurier *SEE* Martel, Nicholas
Martel, Henriette Eliza *SEE* Martel, Nicholas
Martel, Jane; Baltimore, 1830-1861 ***9228.50*** *p435*
Martel, John B.; Illinois, 1828-1863 ***9228.50*** *p436*
Martel, Judith; Ohio, 1815-1869 ***9228.50*** *p435*
Martel, Lucia; Pennsylvania, 1921 ***9228.50*** *p432*
Martel, Margaret Charlotte; Ohio, 1830 ***9228.50*** *p435*
Martel, Nicholas; New York, 1870 ***9228.50*** *p435*
*Wife:*Henriette Le Mesurier
*Daughter:*Henriette Eliza
*Daughter:*Alice Le Mesurier
Martel, Nicholas; Ohio, 1800-1823 ***9228.50*** *p434*
Martel, Peyret 27; America, 1843 ***778.6*** *p231*
Martel deBrouague, Francois; Quebec, 1726 ***2314.30*** *p172*
Martell, Carl Johan; North America, 1883 ***6410.15*** *p106*
Martell, Ellen 11; Quebec, 1870 ***8364.32*** *p24*
Martell, Jacob; New York, NY, 1849 ***6412.40*** *p152*
Marten, Carl; Wisconsin, 1877 ***6795.8*** *p204*
Marten, Carl Julius; Wisconsin, 1880 ***6795.8*** *p26*
Marten, Carl Julius; Wisconsin, 1882 ***6795.8*** *p50*
Marten, Florentine Johanna Louise; Wisconsin, 1890 ***6795.8*** *p74*
Marten, James 21; Ontario, 1871 ***1823.17*** *p98*
Marten, John; America, 1744 ***1220.12*** *p533*
Martens, Gust; Baltimore, 1893 ***1766.20*** *p25*
Martens, Gustav von; Valdivia, Chile, 1852 ***1192.4*** *p53*
Martens, Marcelin; New York, 1859 ***358.56*** *p54*
Martens, Ottilie Pauline Amalia; Wisconsin, 1888 ***6795.8*** *p74*
Martensen, Marten; Iowa, 1893 ***1211.15*** *p16*
Martensen, Mathias; Iowa, 1894 ***1211.15*** *p17*
Martenson, Andrew; Iowa, 1901 ***1211.15*** *p17*
Martenson, John W.; Cleveland, OH, 1880-1897 ***9722.10*** *p123*
Martenson, Lars Nils; Quebec, 1868 ***6212.1*** *p14*
Martenson, Martin; Iowa, 1892 ***1211.15*** *p17*
Martensson, Andrew; St. Paul, MN, 1887 ***1865.50*** *p97*
Martensson, Anna Alfrida *SEE* Martensson, Christina Hidinge
Martensson, Christina; St. Paul, MN, 1888 ***1865.50*** *p98*
*Daughter:*Anna Alfrida
*Son:*Fritz Gerhard
*Daughter:*Frida Elisabeth
Martensson, Frida Elisabeth *SEE* Martensson, Christina Hidinge
Martensson, Fritz Gerhard *SEE* Martensson, Christina Hidinge
Martensson, J.E.; New York, NY, 1845 ***6412.40*** *p149*
Marterstock, John; Ohio, 1809-1852 ***4511.35*** *p32*
Martez, Hortence 9; Missouri, 1845 ***778.6*** *p231*
Marthe, Francois 32; Mississippi, 1847 ***778.6*** *p231*
Marthe, Hipolite; Louisiana, 1874-1875 ***4981.45*** *p30*
Marthellot, Louis 21; Quebec, 1657 ***9221.17*** *p363*
Marthes, Armand 11; America, 1846 ***778.6*** *p232*
Marthes, Ja.ques 35; America, 1846 ***778.6*** *p232*
Marthez, Adolphe 6; Missouri, 1845 ***778.6*** *p231*
Marthez, Baptiste 62; Missouri, 1845 ***778.6*** *p232*
Marthez, Celine 10; Missouri, 1845 ***778.6*** *p232*
Marthez, Constance 3 months; Missouri, 1845 ***778.6*** *p232*
Marthez, Delphine 52; Missouri, 1845 ***778.6*** *p232*
Marthez, Felicie 4; Missouri, 1845 ***778.6*** *p232*
Marthez, Gustave 8; Missouri, 1845 ***778.6*** *p232*
Marthez, Melchior 2; Missouri, 1845 ***778.6*** *p232*
Marti, Jacob 47; New Castle, DE, 1817-1818 ***90.20*** *p153*
Marti, John; Missouri, 1888 ***3276.1*** *p2*
Marti, John; Missouri, 1894 ***3276.1*** *p2*
Marti, M. 23; New Orleans, 1834 ***1002.51*** *p112*
Marti, Miguel; Louisiana, 1836-1840 ***4981.45*** *p213*
Martial, Mr. 20; Louisiana, 1848 ***778.6*** *p232*
Martie, Jacob 47; New Castle, DE, 1817-1818 ***90.20*** *p153*
Martin, . . .; Montreal, 1642 ***9221.17*** *p124*
Martin, Mr. 25; America, 1846 ***778.6*** *p232*
Martin, Mr. 30; America, 1841 ***778.6*** *p232*
Martin, Mr. 34; America, 1847 ***778.6*** *p232*
Martin, Mr. 48; Louisiana, 1848 ***778.6*** *p232*
Martin, Mr. 19; New Orleans, 1848 ***778.6*** *p232*
Martin, Mr.; Newfoundland, 1450 ***9228.50*** *p3*
Martin, Abraham; Quebec, 1619 ***9221.17*** *p24*
*Wife:*Marguerite Langlois
Martin, Adam; America, 1888 ***2526.42*** *p194*
Martin, Adam; Valdivia, Chile, 1851 ***1192.4*** *p51*
Martin, Adolf; America, 1892 ***5475.1*** *p425*
Martin, Agnes 43; Ontario, 1871 ***1823.17*** *p98*
Martin, Albert 26; Ontario, 1871 ***1823.21*** *p215*
Martin, Alex 10; New York, NY, 1835 ***5024.1*** *p136*
Martin, Alex. 22; America, 1840 ***778.6*** *p232*
Martin, Alexander 45; Ontario, 1871 ***1823.21*** *p215*
Martin, Alexander; South Carolina, 1807 ***6155.4*** *p19*
Martin, Alphonse 18; New Orleans, 1843 ***778.6*** *p232*
Martin, Andrew; America, 1760 ***1220.12*** *p532*
Martin, Andrew; America, 1767 ***1220.12*** *p532*
Martin, Andrew; Portsmouth, NH, 1835 ***3274.55*** *p22*
Martin, Ann 53; Ontario, 1871 ***1823.17*** *p98*
Martin, Anna 3 months; New York, NY, 1893 ***1883.7*** *p39*
Martin, Anna 3 months; New York, NY, 1893 ***1883.7*** *p47*
Martin, Anne 32 *SEE* Martin, Galleran
Martin, Anne-Francoise; Quebec, 1669 ***4514.3*** *p364*
Martin, Anthony; America, 1676 ***1220.12*** *p532*
Martin, Anthony; Ohio, 1809-1852 ***4511.35*** *p32*
Martin, Antoine; Quebec, 1644 ***9221.17*** *p144*
Martin, Appelina 32; New Orleans, 1844 ***778.6*** *p232*
Martin, August Ludwig; America, 1864 ***5475.1*** *p72*
Martin, Augustus; Louisiana, 1836-1840 ***4981.45*** *p213*
Martin, Barbe 1; Louisiana, 1848 ***778.6*** *p232*
Martin, Bartholomew; America, 1769 ***1220.12*** *p532*
Martin, Benjamin; America, 1758 ***1220.12*** *p532*
Martin, Benjamin; America, 1774 ***1220.12*** *p532*
Martin, Benjamin; North Carolina, 1856 ***1088.45*** *p21*
Martin, Benjamin; Wisconsin, 1926 ***1822.55*** *p10*
Martin, Bryan; America, 1748 ***1220.12*** *p532*
Martin, Carl; Galveston, TX, 1855 ***571.7*** *p17*
Martin, Charles; America, 1756 ***1220.12*** *p532*
Martin, Charles 35; Ontario, 1871 ***1823.21*** *p215*
Martin, Christian 20; New York, NY, 1899 ***6406.6*** *p47*
Martin, Christina 36; New York, NY, 1899 ***6406.6*** *p47*
Martin, Christophe 4; Louisiana, 1848 ***778.6*** *p232*
Martin, Christophe 33; Louisiana, 1848 ***778.6*** *p232*
Martin, Christopher; Plymouth, MA, 1606 ***1642*** *p55*
Martin, Christopher; Plymouth, MA, 1620 ***1920.45*** *p5*
With wife
Martin, Conrad 39; Louisiana, 1848 ***778.6*** *p232*
Martin, David; Barbados, 1674 ***1220.12*** *p532*
Martin, David 4; New York, NY, 1899 ***6406.6*** *p47*
Martin, David; North Carolina, 1848 ***1088.45*** *p21*
Martin, Edward; America, 1752 ***1220.12*** *p532*
Martin, Edward 26; Ontario, 1871 ***1823.17*** *p98*
Martin, Edward; Salt Lake City, 1882 ***1211.45*** *p130*
Martin, Edward; Virginia, 1732 ***1220.12*** *p532*
Martin, Elie; Quebec, 1658 ***9221.17*** *p384*
Martin, Elisabeth 40; Port uncertain, 1843 ***778.6*** *p232*
Martin, Elisee 57; Texas, 1845 ***778.6*** *p232*
Martin, Elisha 54; Port uncertain, 1843 ***778.6*** *p232*
Martin, Elizabeth; America, 1738 ***1220.12*** *p532*
Martin, Elizabeth; America, 1740 ***1220.12*** *p532*
Martin, Elizabeth; America, 1740 ***1220.12*** *p533*
Martin, Elizabeth; Annapolis, MD, 1725 ***1220.12*** *p532*
Martin, Elizabeth; Barbados, 1665 ***1220.12*** *p532*
Martin, Elizabeth; Barbados, 1679 ***1220.12*** *p532*
Martin, Elizabeth 54; Ontario, 1871 ***1823.17*** *p98*
Martin, Elizabeth 60; Ontario, 1871 ***1823.17*** *p98*
Martin, Elizabeth 74; Ontario, 1871 ***1823.21*** *p215*
Martin, Ellen 70; Michigan, 1880 ***4491.42*** *p17*
Martin, Erhard; Philadelphia Co., PA, 1870 ***5720.10*** *p378*
Martin, Eugene 36; America, 1843 ***778.6*** *p232*
Martin, Eugene; North Carolina, 1854 ***1088.45*** *p21*

Martin, Eva 24; New York, NY, 1893 1883.7 p39
Martin, Eva 24; New York, NY, 1893 1883.7 p47
Martin, Fanny L.; Ontario, 1871 1823.21 p215
Martin, Ferdinand 13; New York, NY, 1899 6406.6 p47
Martin, Ferdinand 39; New York, NY, 1899 6406.6 p47
Martin, Frances; Annapolis, MD, 1730 1220.12 p533
Martin, Francis K.; North Carolina, 1798 1088.45 p21
Martin, Francois Marie; Illinois, 1852 6079.1 p9
Martin, Galleran 56; Quebec, 1635 9221.17 p47
*Daughter:*Anne 32
Martin, Geo 71; Ontario, 1871 1823.21 p215
Martin, George; Iowa, 1892 1211.15 p16
Martin, George 18; Ontario, 1871 1823.21 p215
Martin, George 16; Quebec, 1870 8364.32 p24
Martin, Gott 10; New York, NY, 1899 6406.6 p47
Martin, Hans 2 months; New York, NY, 1899 6406.6 p47
Martin, Heinrich; Valdivia, Chile, 1851 1192.4 p51
With wife
With child 1
With child 2
Martin, Henry; America, 1729 1220.12 p533
Martin, Henry; America, 1769 1220.12 p533
Martin, Henry; North Carolina, 1848 1088.45 p21
Martin, Henry; North Carolina, 1857 1088.45 p21
Martin, Henry; Virginia, 1773 1220.12 p533
Martin, Henry J. Chamberlain 37; Ontario, 1871 1823.17 p99
Martin, Hortense; Wisconsin, 1856 1495.20 p41
Martin, Hosea; America, 1750 1220.12 p533
Martin, Mrs. J. H.; Montreal, 1922 4514.4 p32
Martin, J. P. 24; America, 1841 778.6 p232
Martin, James; America, 1744 1220.12 p533
Martin, James; America, 1756 1220.12 p533
Martin, James; America, 1763 1220.12 p533
Martin, James; America, 1773 1220.12 p533
Martin, James; Barbados, 1683 1220.12 p533
Martin, James; Louisiana, 1836-1840 4981.45 p213
Martin, James; Maryland, 1719 1220.12 p533
Martin, James 59; New York, NY, 1835 5024.1 p136
Martin, James 25; Ontario, 1871 1823.21 p215
Martin, James 49; Ontario, 1871 1823.17 p99
Martin, James 77; Ontario, 1871 1823.17 p99
Martin, Jane; America, 1724 1220.12 p533
Martin, Jane 10; Quebec, 1870 8364.32 p24
Martin, Janet 57; New York, NY, 1835 5024.1 p136
Martin, Jean; Quebec, 1657 9221.17 p363
Martin, Jean N. 32; New Orleans, 1845 778.6 p232
Martin, Jesse 14; Quebec, 1870 8364.32 p24
Martin, Joachim; Quebec, 1649-1665 4514.3 p345
Martin, Joachim 20; Quebec, 1656 9221.17 p342
Martin, Joan; Barbados or Jamaica, 1698 1220.12 p533
Martin, Johann 10 *SEE* Martin, Johann
Martin, Johann 52; America, 1855 5475.1 p317
*Daughter:*Katharina 15
With stepchild 21
With stepchild 24
*Wife:*Katharina Leuk 48
*Son:*Michel 13
*Son:*Johann 10
Martin, Johann 4; New York, NY, 1893 1883.7 p39
Martin, Johann 4; New York, NY, 1893 1883.7 p47
Martin, Johann Georg; America, 1883 2526.42 p194
Martin, John; America, 1680 1220.12 p533
Martin, John; America, 1724 1220.12 p533
Martin, John; America, 1739 1220.12 p533
Martin, John; America, 1741 1220.12 p533
Martin, John; America, 1744 1220.12 p533
Martin, John; America, 1744 1220.12 p533
Martin, John; America, 1745 1220.12 p533
Martin, John; America, 1750 1220.12 p533
Martin, John; America, 1751 1220.12 p533
Martin, John; America, 1752 1220.12 p533
Martin, John; America, 1757 1220.12 p533
Martin, John; America, 1766 1220.12 p533
Martin, John; America, 1768 1220.12 p533
Martin, John; America, 1770 1220.12 p533
Martin, John; America, 1773 1220.12 p533
Martin, John; America, 1774 1220.12 p533
Martin, John; Annapolis, MD, 1725 1220.12 p533
Martin, John; Barbados, 1668 1220.12 p533
Martin, John; Barbados, 1684 1220.12 p533
Martin, John 8; New York, NY, 1835 5024.1 p136
Martin, John 21; Ontario, 1871 1823.17 p99
Martin, John 33; Ontario, 1871 1823.17 p99
Martin, John 34; Ontario, 1871 1823.21 p215
Martin, John 63; Ontario, 1871 1823.21 p215
Martin, John 66; Ontario, 1871 1823.17 p99
Martin, John 16; Quebec, 1870 8364.32 p25
Martin, John 18; Quebec, 1870 8364.32 p24
Martin, John 22; Quebec, 1870 8364.32 p24
Martin, John; South Carolina, 1807 6155.4 p19
Martin, John; Virginia, 1724 1220.12 p533
Martin, John; Virginia, 1731 1220.12 p533
Martin, John; Washington, 1885 2770.40 p194
Martin, John; West Indies, 1686 1220.12 p533
Martin, Jonathan; America, 1764 1220.12 p533
Martin, Joseph; America, 1727 1220.12 p533
Martin, Joseph; Illinois, 1852 6079.1 p9
Martin, Joseph 70; Ontario, 1871 1823.17 p99
Martin, Jules 30; New Orleans, 1848 778.6 p232
Martin, Julia 47; Ontario, 1871 1823.21 p215
Martin, Julien; Quebec, 1654 9221.17 p314
Martin, Justine; Wisconsin, 1856 1495.20 p41
Martin, Jutis 62; New York, NY, 1899 6406.6 p47
Martin, Katharina; America, 1882 5475.1 p330
Martin, Katharina 15 *SEE* Martin, Johann
Martin, Katharina Leuk 48 *SEE* Martin, Johann
Martin, L. 30; America, 1745 778.6 p232
Martin, L. 45; America, 1843 778.6 p232
Martin, Louis 20; Montreal, 1659 9221.17 p425
Martin, Louis; Quebec, 1656 9221.17 p342
Martin, Louise 19; New York, NY, 1899 6406.6 p47
Martin, Lydia 3; New York, NY, 1893 1883.7 p39
Martin, Lydia 3; New York, NY, 1893 1883.7 p47
Martin, Madalaine 30; Louisiana, 1848 778.6 p232
Martin, Margaret; America, 1694 1220.12 p533
Martin, Margaret; Jamaica, 1661 1220.12 p533
Martin, Margarethe; New York, NY, 1883 5475.1 p26
Martin, Margart 12; New York, NY, 1835 5024.1 p136
Martin, Marguerite; Montreal, 1659 9221.17 p425
Martin, Marguerite Langlois *SEE* Martin, Abraham
Martin, Maria 1; New York, NY, 1899 6406.6 p47
Martin, Marie 45; America, 1843 778.6 p233
Martin, Marie 26; Louisiana, 1848 778.6 p233
Martin, Marie; Quebec, 1665 4514.3 p345
Martin, Marie; Quebec, 1671 4514.3 p345
Martin, Marie 40; Quebec, 1639 9221.17 p84
Martin, Marie 41; Quebec, 1656 9221.17 p346
*Daughter:*Jeanne 14
*Daughter:*Barbe 12
*Son:*Jacques 11
Martin, Martha; America, 1758 1220.12 p534
Martin, Martin; Valdivia, Chile, 1852 1192.4 p53
With wife & child
With child 4
With child 8
Martin, Martin; Virginia, 1770 1220.12 p534
Martin, Mary; America, 1727 1220.12 p534
Martin, Mary; America, 1754 1220.12 p534
Martin, Mary; America, 1757 1220.12 p534
Martin, Mary; America, 1764 1220.12 p534
Martin, Mary; Annapolis, MD, 1730 1220.12 p534
Martin, Mary; Barbados or Jamaica, 1698 1220.12 p534
Martin, Mary; Maryland, 1734 1220.12 p534
Martin, Mary 16; Quebec, 1870 8364.32 p25
Martin, Matthew; America, 1770 1220.12 p534
Martin, Michael; Illinois, 1930 121.35 p100
Martin, Michel 13 *SEE* Martin, Johann
Martin, Michel 32; Missouri, 1845 778.6 p233
Martin, Michel 40; Ontario, 1871 1823.21 p215
Martin, Miles; North Carolina, 1850 1088.45 p21
Martin, Nathanial 35; New York, NY, 1893 1883.7 p39
Martin, Nathanial 35; New York, NY, 1893 1883.7 p47
Martin, Nicolas Lorentz 20; New Orleans, 1840 778.6 p233
Martin, Oliver; America, 1773 1220.12 p534
Martin, Olivier 19; Montreal, 1653 9221.17 p297
Martin, Patrick; New Orleans, 1850 7242.30 p148
Martin, Patrick; South Carolina, 1807 6155.4 p19
Martin, Paul 36; America, 1843 778.6 p233
Martin, Petchy; America, 1774 1220.12 p534
Martin, Peter; America, 1749 1220.12 p534
Martin, Peter; Illinois, 1858-1861 6020.5 p132
Martin, Peter; Portsmouth, NH, 1835 3274.56 p71
Martin, Philip J.; Ohio, 1809-1852 4511.35 p32
Martin, Pierre; Quebec, 1634 9221.17 p38
Martin, Pierre Paul; Louisiana, 1841-1844 4981.45 p211
Martin, Reine; Quebec, 1667 4514.3 p345
Martin, Renee; Quebec, 1668 4514.3 p329
Martin, Richard 54; Ontario, 1871 1823.17 p99
Martin, Richard; Rappahannock, VA, 1728 1220.12 p534
Martin, Richard; Virginia, 1772 1220.12 p534
Martin, Robert; America, 1751 1220.12 p534
Martin, Robert; Annapolis, MD, 1725 1220.12 p534
Martin, Robert 70; Ontario, 1871 1823.17 p99
Martin, Robert 70; Ontario, 1871 1823.21 p215
Martin, Robert; Virginia, 1757 1220.12 p534
Martin, Rowland 24; Ontario, 1871 1823.21 p215
Martin, Sampson; Maryland, 1720 1220.12 p534
Martin, Samuel 36; Ontario, 1871 1823.17 p99
Martin, Samuel 39; Ontario, 1871 1823.17 p99
Martin, Samuel 56; Ontario, 1871 1823.17 p99
Martin, Sarah; America, 1749 1220.12 p534
Martin, Sarah; America, 1770 1220.12 p534
Martin, Sarah; Maryland, 1719 1220.12 p534
Martin, Sarah; Virginia, 1741 1220.12 p534
Martin, Shadrick 37; Ontario, 1871 1823.21 p215
Martin, Sofia 7; New York, NY, 1899 6406.6 p47
Martin, Susan; America, 1695 1220.12 p534
Martin, Susanna; Annapolis, MD, 1721 1220.12 p534
Martin, Susanna; Barbados, 1694 1220.12 p534
Martin, Thomas; America, 1739 1220.12 p534
Martin, Thomas; America, 1744 1220.12 p534
Martin, Thomas; America, 1755 1220.12 p534
Martin, Thomas; America, 1767 1220.12 p534
Martin, Thomas; America, 1773 1220.12 p534
Martin, Thomas; America, 1774 1220.12 p534
Martin, Thomas; New York, 1859 358.56 p100
Martin, Thomas; Ohio, 1838 3580.20 p33
Martin, Thomas; Ohio, 1838 6020.12 p21
Martin, Thomas 37; Ontario, 1871 1823.21 p215
Martin, Thomas 41; Ontario, 1871 1823.17 p99
Martin, Thomas 60; Ontario, 1871 1823.17 p99
Martin, Thomas 66; Ontario, 1871 1823.21 p215
Martin, Thomas; Virginia, 1736 1220.12 p534
Martin, Thomas; Virginia, 1773 1220.12 p534
Martin, Wilhe. 2; New York, NY, 1893 1883.7 p39
Martin, Wilhe. 2; New York, NY, 1893 1883.7 p47
Martin, Wilhelmine; America, 1852 7420.1 p93
Martin, Wilkinson 60; Ontario, 1871 1823.21 p215
Martin, William; America, 1685 1220.12 p534
Martin, William; America, 1730 1220.12 p535
Martin, William; America, 1741 1220.12 p535
Martin, William; America, 1743 1220.12 p535
Martin, William; America, 1749 1220.12 p535
Martin, William; America, 1769 1220.12 p535
Martin, William; America, 1772 1220.12 p535
Martin, William; Annapolis, MD, 1724 1220.12 p534
Martin, William; Barbados, 1668 1220.12 p534
Martin, William; Barbados, 1676 1220.12 p534
Martin, William; Barbados, 1699 1220.12 p534
Martin, William; Died enroute, 1725 1220.12 p534
Martin, William 18; New York, NY, 1835 5024.1 p136
Martin, William; North Carolina, 1854 1088.45 p21
Martin, William; Ohio, 1809-1852 4511.35 p32
Martin, William 23; Ontario, 1871 1823.21 p216
Martin, William 55; Ontario, 1871 1823.21 p216
Martin, William 55; Ontario, 1871 1823.21 p216
Martin, Zephaniah; America, 1721 1220.12 p535
Martinac, Theodore 29; Port uncertain, 1844 778.6 p233
Martincourt, Miss 27; New Orleans, 1845 778.6 p233
Martindale, John; America, 1758 1220.12 p535
Martindale, Joseph 47; Ontario, 1871 1823.21 p216
Martineau, Jean; Montreal, 1659 9221.17 p425
Martineau, Louis 27; Quebec, 1656 9221.17 p342
Martinek, Vaclav; St. Louis, 1865-1867 2853.20 p27
Martines, Antonio; North Carolina, 1849 1088.45 p21
Martinet, Louis Joseph; Illinois, 1852 6079.1 p9
Martinet, Louise Joseph 49; New Orleans, 1848 778.6 p233
Martinet, Margaretha 49; New Orleans, 1848 778.6 p233
Martinez, B.; Louisiana, 1874 4981.45 p133
Martinez, D. V.; Louisiana, 1836-1840 4981.45 p213
Martinez, Henry; Louisiana, 1874 4981.45 p133
Marting, Hiram 76; Ontario, 1871 1823.21 p216
Martinieres, Jean 32; Port uncertain, 1842 778.6 p233
Martinshrider, David; Barbados or Jamaica, 1698 1220.12 p535
Martinson, John W.; Cleveland, OH, 1880-1897 9722.10 p123
Martinson, Thomas C.; Iowa, 1894 1211.15 p17
Martinson, William 43; Ontario, 1871 1823.21 p216
Martinstein, Anselm Wilhelm; America, 1848 5475.1 p476
Martinussen, Fredrik Kristian; Iowa, 1914 1211.15 p17
Martiny, C.; Venezuela, 1843 3899.5 p546
Martley, Richard; Virginia, 1767 1220.12 p535
Martney, Carrie; America, 1750 1220.12 p535
Marton, Frederick W. 32; Kansas, 1892 1447.20 p62
Marton, James; America, 1768 1220.12 p535
Martow, Jacob; America, 1742 1220.12 p535
Martray, Guillaume de; Quebec, 1644 9221.17 p144
Marts, Child; America, 1845 778.6 p233
Marts, Catharine 40; America, 1845 778.6 p233
Marttila, Matt 42; Minnesota, 1923 2769.54 p1381
Martwich, Ludwig Friedrich; Wisconsin, 1868 6795.8 p43
Marty, John; Ohio, 1809-1852 4511.35 p32
Marty, Jort 44; Louisiana, 1848 778.6 p233
Martyn, Benjamin; America, 1741 1220.12 p532
Martyn, John; America, 1737 1220.12 p533
Martyn, John 34; Ontario, 1871 1823.21 p216
Martyn, Joseph J. 56; Ontario, 1871 1823.21 p216
Martyn, Thomas 23; Ontario, 1871 1823.21 p216
Martyn, William; America, 1744 1220.12 p535
Martyn, William; America, 1755 1220.12 p535
Martyn, William; Barbados, 1671 1220.12 p534
Martyn, William 37; Ontario, 1871 1823.17 p99

Martyn, William; Virginia, 1729 ***1220.12*** *p535*
Martzell, John; Ohio, 1809-1852 ***4511.35*** *p33*
Marumin, Katharina 22; Halifax, N.S., 1902 ***1860.4*** *p42*
Maruszewski, Anna; Detroit, 1929-1930 ***6214.5*** *p69*
Maruszewski, Thomas; Detroit, 1924 ***6214.5*** *p69*
Marvel, Mary; Virginia, 1726 ***1220.12*** *p535*
Marvell, William; America, 1719 ***1220.12*** *p535*
Marvill, John; Toronto, 1844 ***2910.35*** *p114*
Marvill, Richard; America, 1727 ***1220.12*** *p535*
Marvin, John R. 19; Michigan, 1880 ***4491.30*** *p21*
Marwan, Ferdinand; Wisconsin, 1888 ***6795.8*** *p67*
Marwan, Wilhelm Eduard; Wisconsin, 1890 ***6795.8*** *p63*
Marwick, John; America, 1766 ***1220.12*** *p535*
Marwick, Robert 21; Ontario, 1871 ***1823.17*** *p99*
Marwood, John; America, 1685 ***1220.12*** *p535*
Marwood, John 41; Ontario, 1871 ***1823.21*** *p216*
Marwood, Jonas; Maryland, 1727 ***1220.12*** *p535*
Marx, Anna 20 *SEE* Marx, Nikolaus
Marx, Annie; Wisconsin, 1907 ***6795.8*** *p179*
Marx, Barbara; America, 1880 ***5475.1*** *p484*
Marx, Blimgen 22; America, 1874 ***2526.42*** *p194*
Marx, Camilla; America, 1898 ***2526.42*** *p163*
Marx, Catherine 18; America, 1847 ***778.6*** *p233*
Marx, Eduard; America, 1867 ***7919.3*** *p529*
Marx, Emanuel; America, 1895 ***2526.42*** *p194*
Marx, Ferdinand 15; America, 1846 ***778.6*** *p233*
Marx, Georg Peter; America, 1867 ***5475.1*** *p124*
Marx, Hermann 32; Mississippi, 1845 ***778.6*** *p233*
Marx, Ida; America, 1902 ***2526.42*** *p163*
Marx, Isaac 17; Louisiana, 1848 ***778.6*** *p233*
Marx, Johann *SEE* Marx, Nikolaus
Marx, John 33; Ontario, 1871 ***1823.21*** *p216*
Marx, Joseph; Ohio, 1809-1852 ***4511.35*** *p33*
Marx, Julius; America, 1892 ***2526.43*** *p153*
Marx, Karl; America, 1845 ***5475.1*** *p233*
Marx, Loser; America, 1879 ***2526.42*** *p194*
Marx, Margarethe Weyand 32 *SEE* Marx, Nikolaus
Marx, Martin 34; America, 1847 ***778.6*** *p233*
Marx, Mathias 26; America, 1897 ***5475.1*** *p25*
Marx, Mathias; Rochester, NY, 1870 ***5475.1*** *p143*
Marx, Minette 30; America, 1847 ***778.6*** *p233*
Marx, Morris; Louisiana, 1874-1875 ***4981.45*** *p30*
Marx, Nathan; America, 1867 ***5475.1*** *p264*
Marx, Nikolaus; America, 1868 ***5475.1*** *p239*
Marx, Nikolaus; America, 1869 ***5475.1*** *p279*
*Wife:*Margarethe Weyand
*Son:*Johann
Marx, Nikolaus 24; America, 1847 ***5475.1*** *p254*
*Sister:*Anna 20
Marx, Peter; America, 1865 ***5475.1*** *p238*
Marx, Peter; America, 1867 ***5475.1*** *p255*
Marx, R.; Louisiana, 1874 ***4981.45*** *p133*
Marx, Samuel 35; America, 1847 ***778.6*** *p233*
Marxgolf, Catharine 24; America, 1847 ***778.6*** *p233*
Mary, Johann; Ohio, 1888 ***5475.1*** *p230*
Mary, Joseph 46; America, 1848 ***778.6*** *p233*
Mary, Katharina; America, 1882 ***5475.1*** *p229*
*Son:*Nikolaus
*Daughter:*Maria
Mary, Louis 30; Port uncertain, 1841 ***778.6*** *p233*
Mary, Thomas; Rappahannock, VA, 1728 ***1220.12*** *p535*
Maryott, Thomas; Cambridge, MA, 1638 ***9228.50*** *p423*
Maryska, Frantisek; Minnesota, 1858-1860 ***2853.20*** *p259*
Marz, Catherine; New York, 1859 ***358.56*** *p54*
Marz, Jakob; America, 1870 ***5475.1*** *p274*
Marz, Johann; Connecticut, 1886 ***5475.1*** *p146*
Marz, Peter; America, 1869 ***5475.1*** *p274*
Marzec, John; Detroit, 1929-1930 ***6214.5*** *p65*
Marzec, John; Detroit, 1930 ***1640.60*** *p81*
Marzejon, August; Wisconsin, 1878 ***6795.8*** *p50*
Marzejon, Frank; Wisconsin, 1881 ***6795.8*** *p60*
Marzen, Josef; America, 1847 ***5475.1*** *p474*
Marzen, Philipp; America, 1849 ***5475.1*** *p478*
Marzolf, Anna 2; Portland, ME, 1911 ***970.38*** *p79*
Marzolf, Catha. 4 months; America, 1840 ***778.6*** *p233*
Marzolf, Freidrich 38; Portland, ME, 1911 ***970.38*** *p79*
Marzolf, George 7; America, 1840 ***778.6*** *p233*
Marzolf, Jacob 23; America, 1840 ***778.6*** *p233*
Marzolf, Johannes 4; America, 1840 ***778.6*** *p233*
Marzolf, Katarina 26; Portland, ME, 1911 ***970.38*** *p79*
Marzolf, Luisa 4; Portland, ME, 1911 ***970.38*** *p79*
Marzolf, Maria 64; America, 1840 ***778.6*** *p233*
Marzolf, Marie 10; America, 1840 ***778.6*** *p233*
Marzolf, Marie 38; America, 1840 ***778.6*** *p233*
Marzolf, Pierre 40; America, 1840 ***778.6*** *p233*
Masaryk, Tomas G.; America, 1810-1910 ***2853.20*** *p513*
Mascada, Francis; America, 1772 ***1220.12*** *p535*
Mascall, Ann; America, 1759 ***1220.12*** *p535*
Mascall, Israell; America, 1774 ***1220.12*** *p535*
Mascall, John; America, 1723 ***1220.12*** *p535*
Mascall, John; America, 1750 ***1220.12*** *p535*
Mascall, Mary; America, 1750 ***1220.12*** *p535*
Mascall, Richard; America, 1741 ***1220.12*** *p535*
Mascall, Richard; America, 1754 ***1220.12*** *p535*
Mascall, Thomas; America, 1739 ***1220.12*** *p535*
Mascare, Jean 46; America, 1846 ***778.6*** *p233*
Masch, Carl Friedrich; Wisconsin, 1877 ***6795.8*** *p96*
Maschner, John F.; Ohio, 1809-1852 ***4511.35*** *p33*
Mase, Levi 20; America, 1847 ***778.6*** *p327*
Masek, Matej; Chicago, 1857-1910 ***2853.20*** *p415*
Masek, Matej; Chicago, 1895 ***2853.20*** *p524*
Masek, Vojta; Wisconsin, 1860-1865 ***2853.20*** *p324*
Masek, Vojtech; America, 1863 ***2853.20*** *p293*
Maser, Johannes; America, 1854 ***2526.42*** *p201*
Maser, Johannes 31; America, 1857 ***2526.42*** *p201*
Masey, Thomas; America, 1772 ***1220.12*** *p523*
Mash, John; America, 1773 ***1220.12*** *p535*
Mash, Phillis; Maryland, 1719 ***1220.12*** *p535*
Mash, Richard; America, 1772 ***1220.12*** *p535*
Masham, Ann; America, 1743 ***1220.12*** *p535*
Mashman, James; America, 1769 ***1220.12*** *p535*
Masier, Nicolas; Quebec, 1647 ***9221.17*** *p185*
Masik, Josef *SEE* Masik, Josef
Masik, Josef; Houston, 1855 ***2853.20*** *p62*
With wife
*Child:*Josef
*Child:*Terezie
*Child:*Vincenc
Masik, Terezie *SEE* Masik, Josef
Masik, Vincenc *SEE* Masik, Josef
Masin, Ms. 16; America, 1841 ***778.6*** *p234*
Masin, Jnas. 26; America, 1846 ***778.6*** *p234*
Masion, Margarethe 19; Chicago, 1880 ***5475.1*** *p241*
Maskal, Henry 19; North Carolina, 1774 ***1422.10*** *p54*
Maskew, Elizabeth; America, 1750 ***1220.12*** *p535*
Maskew, Esther; America, 1758 ***1220.12*** *p535*
Maskew, Sarah; America, 1759 ***1220.12*** *p535*
Masland, Robert; Carolina, 1724 ***1220.12*** *p535*
Maslier, Jeanne 31; Quebec, 1652 ***9221.17*** *p266*
Maslin, Robert; Philadelphia, 1778 ***8529.30*** *p6*
Maslowas, Piotr 20; New York, NY, 1911 ***6533.11*** *p9*
Maslowski, Joseph; Detroit, 1929-1930 ***6214.5*** *p65*
Mason, Alexander; America, 1766 ***1220.12*** *p535*
Mason, Allen; America, 1746 ***1220.12*** *p535*
Mason, Amey; America, 1773 ***1220.12*** *p535*
Mason, Ann; Annapolis, MD, 1721 ***1220.12*** *p535*
Mason, Ann; Jamaica, 1661 ***1220.12*** *p535*
Mason, Auguste; Louisiana, 1874-1875 ***4981.45*** *p30*
Mason, Benjamin; America, 1765 ***1220.12*** *p535*
Mason, Charles; America, 1685 ***1220.12*** *p536*
Mason, Charles; America, 1773 ***1220.12*** *p536*
Mason, Charles; Virginia, 1767 ***1220.12*** *p536*
Mason, Dennis 25; Ontario, 1871 ***1823.21*** *p216*
Mason, Donald 34; Ontario, 1871 ***1823.21*** *p216*
Mason, Edward; America, 1750 ***1220.12*** *p536*
Mason, Edward; America, 1770 ***1220.12*** *p536*
Mason, Edward; America, 1772 ***1220.12*** *p536*
Mason, Edward; Annapolis, MD, 1722 ***1220.12*** *p536*
Mason, Elizabeth; America, 1766 ***1220.12*** *p536*
Mason, Elizabeth; America, 1768 ***1220.12*** *p536*
Mason, Elizabeth; America, 1775 ***1220.12*** *p536*
Mason, Elizabeth; Rappahannock, VA, 1741 ***1220.12*** *p536*
Mason, Eugene 23; Ontario, 1871 ***1823.17*** *p99*
Mason, Francis; America, 1752 ***1220.12*** *p536*
Mason, Francis Knill; America, 1757 ***1220.12*** *p536*
Mason, George; America, 1735 ***1220.12*** *p536*
Mason, Henry; Maryland, 1725 ***1220.12*** *p536*
Mason, Henry; North Carolina, 1841 ***1088.45*** *p21*
Mason, Isaac 21; Ontario, 1871 ***1823.17*** *p99*
Mason, Jabez 30; Ontario, 1871 ***1823.21*** *p216*
Mason, James; America, 1656 ***1220.12*** *p536*
Mason, James; Boston, 1830 ***3274.55*** *p24*
Mason, James 45; Ontario, 1871 ***1823.21*** *p216*
Mason, Jane 50; Ontario, 1871 ***1823.21*** *p216*
Mason, Jessie 50; Ontario, 1871 ***1823.17*** *p99*
Mason, John; America, 1683 ***1220.12*** *p536*
Mason, John; America, 1700 ***1220.12*** *p536*
Mason, John; America, 1734 ***1220.12*** *p536*
Mason, John; America, 1745 ***1220.12*** *p536*
Mason, John; America, 1747 ***1220.12*** *p536*
Mason, John; America, 1749 ***1220.12*** *p536*
Mason, John; America, 1768 ***1220.12*** *p536*
Mason, John; America, 1772 ***1220.12*** *p536*
Mason, John; America, 1773 ***1220.12*** *p536*
Mason, John; Annapolis, MD, 1722 ***1220.12*** *p536*
Mason, John; Barbados or Jamaica, 1699 ***1220.12*** *p536*
Mason, John; Charles Town, SC, 1719 ***1220.12*** *p536*
Mason, John 60; Michigan, 1880 ***4491.30*** *p21*
Mason, John 30; Ontario, 1871 ***1823.21*** *p216*
Mason, John 50; Ontario, 1871 ***1823.17*** *p99*
Mason, John 55; Ontario, 1871 ***1823.21*** *p216*
Mason, John 56; Ontario, 1871 ***1823.21*** *p216*
Mason, John 57; Ontario, 1871 ***1823.17*** *p99*
Mason, John 70; Ontario, 1871 ***1823.17*** *p99*
Mason, John C.; Louisiana, 1836-1840 ***4981.45*** *p213*
Mason, John S. 44; Ontario, 1871 ***1823.21*** *p216*
Mason, Jonathan; America, 1760 ***1220.12*** *p536*
Mason, Joseph; America, 1746 ***1220.12*** *p536*
Mason, Joseph 32; America, 1846 ***778.6*** *p234*
Mason, Katherine; America, 1737 ***1220.12*** *p536*
Mason, Margaret; Barbados or Jamaica, 1696 ***1220.12*** *p536*
Mason, Mary; America, 1745 ***1220.12*** *p536*
Mason, Mary; Nevis or Jamaica, 1722 ***1220.12*** *p536*
Mason, Mary; Virginia, 1741 ***1220.12*** *p536*
Mason, Patrick; Maryland, 1727 ***1220.12*** *p536*
Mason, Peter; America, 1759 ***1220.12*** *p536*
Mason, Peter; Maryland, 1741 ***1220.12*** *p536*
Mason, Richard; America, 1768 ***1220.12*** *p536*
Mason, Robert; America, 1724 ***1220.12*** *p536*
Mason, Robert; America, 1755 ***1220.12*** *p536*
Mason, Robert; Maryland, 1725 ***1220.12*** *p536*
Mason, Robert 34; Ontario, 1871 ***1823.21*** *p216*
Mason, Robert 44; Ontario, 1871 ***1823.21*** *p216*
Mason, Robert; Potomac, 1742 ***1220.12*** *p536*
Mason, Sarah; Barbados, 1680 ***1220.12*** *p536*
Mason, Thomas; America, 1723 ***1220.12*** *p536*
Mason, Thomas; America, 1728 ***1220.12*** *p536*
Mason, Thomas; America, 1735 ***1220.12*** *p537*
Mason, Thomas; America, 1756 ***1220.12*** *p537*
Mason, Thomas; America, 1758 ***1220.12*** *p537*
Mason, Thomas; North Carolina, 1841 ***1088.45*** *p21*
Mason, Thomas 39; Ontario, 1871 ***1823.21*** *p216*
Mason, Thos 46; Ontario, 1871 ***1823.17*** *p99*
Mason, William; America, 1675 ***1220.12*** *p537*
Mason, William; America, 1683 ***1220.12*** *p537*
Mason, William; America, 1761 ***1220.12*** *p537*
Mason, William; America, 1764 ***1220.12*** *p537*
Mason, William; America, 1767 ***1220.12*** *p537*
Mason, William 38; Ontario, 1871 ***1823.21*** *p216*
Mass, Catharine 18; New York, NY, 1874 ***6954.7*** *p39*
Mass, Catharine 50; New York, NY, 1874 ***6954.7*** *p39*
Mass, Catherina 20; New York, NY, 1885 ***1883.7*** *p45*
Mass, Christian 15; New York, NY, 1874 ***6954.7*** *p39*
Mass, Christoph 5; New York, NY, 1874 ***6954.7*** *p39*
Mass, Elisabeth 6 months; New York, NY, 1874 ***6954.7*** *p39*
Mass, Friedrich 20; New York, NY, 1885 ***1883.7*** *p45*
Mass, Johann 10; New York, NY, 1874 ***6954.7*** *p39*
Mass, Joseph 44; New Orleans, 1847 ***778.6*** *p234*
Mass, Ludwig 51; New York, NY, 1874 ***6954.7*** *p39*
Mass, Rosina 23; New York, NY, 1874 ***6954.7*** *p39*
Mass, Wilhelm 25; New York, NY, 1874 ***6954.7*** *p39*
Massader, Richard; America, 1764 ***1220.12*** *p537*
Massard, Nicolas 23; Quebec, 1658 ***9221.17*** *p384*
Massavet, Conrad; America, 1764 ***1220.12*** *p537*
Masse, Ennemond; Acadia, 1611 ***9221.17*** *p28*
Masse, Jacques 29; America, 1846 ***778.6*** *p234*
Masse, Jacques; Quebec, 1657 ***9221.17*** *p363*
Masse, Jean; Montreal, 1642 ***9221.17*** *p124*
Masse, Pierre 26; Quebec, 1643 ***9221.17*** *p132*
Masseau, Adolphus 28; Tennessee, 1848 ***778.6*** *p234*
Masseau, Emilie 20; Tennessee, 1848 ***778.6*** *p234*
Masseau, Henry 3; Tennessee, 1848 ***778.6*** *p234*
Massender, George 49; Ontario, 1871 ***1823.17*** *p99*
Masser, John P.; Ohio, 1809-1852 ***4511.35*** *p33*
Masseron, Marie; Quebec, 1672 ***4514.3*** *p346*
Masset, Antoine 23; Port uncertain, 1842 ***778.6*** *p234*
Masset, Anton 28; New York, NY, 1898 ***7951.13*** *p43*
Masset, Clara 28; New York, NY, 1898 ***7951.13*** *p43*
Masset, Eugene; Wisconsin, 1854-1858 ***1495.20*** *p50*
Masset, Katherine 4; New York, NY, 1898 ***7951.13*** *p43*
Masset, Marie Henriette; Wisconsin, 1857 ***1495.20*** *p46*
Masset, Marie Therese; Wisconsin, 1857 ***1495.20*** *p46*
Masset, Peter 24; New York, NY, 1898 ***7951.13*** *p43*
Masset, Rosina 2; New York, NY, 1898 ***7951.13*** *p43*
Masset, Stanislaus 18; New York, NY, 1898 ***7951.13*** *p43*
Massett, Anders 7; Halifax, N.S., 1902 ***1860.4*** *p44*
Massett, Eva 17; Halifax, N.S., 1902 ***1860.4*** *p44*
Massett, Joseph; Halifax, N.S., 1902 ***1860.4*** *p44*
Massett, Josephina 27; Halifax, N.S., 1902 ***1860.4*** *p44*
Massett, Katha 11; Halifax, N.S., 1902 ***1860.4*** *p44*
Massett, Marian; Halifax, N.S., 1902 ***1860.4*** *p44*
Massett, Martin 8; Halifax, N.S., 1902 ***1860.4*** *p44*
Massett, Michael 34; Halifax, N.S., 1902 ***1860.4*** *p44*
Massey, Agnes; Maine, 1733 ***9228.50*** *p413*
Massey, Ann; America, 1754 ***1220.12*** *p537*
Massey, George; America, 1747 ***1220.12*** *p537*
Massey, J.; Louisiana, 1874 ***4981.45*** *p296*
Massey, James; America, 1756 ***1220.12*** *p537*
Massey, James; Maryland, 1644 ***9228.50*** *p436*
Massey, James; Port uncertain, 1720 ***1220.12*** *p537*
Massey, James; Virginia, n.d. ***9228.50*** *p413*
Massey, Joseph 40; Ontario, 1871 ***1823.21*** *p216*
Massey, Joyce; America, 1764 ***1220.12*** *p537*
Massey, Margaret; Maryland, 1742 ***1220.12*** *p537*
Massey, Nathaniel; Rappahannock, VA, 1729 ***1220.12*** *p537*

Massey, Rachel; New York, NY, 1847 ***9228.50*** *p317*
Massey, Samuel; Boston, 1684 ***9228.50*** *p436*
Massey, Sarah; America, 1743 ***1220.12*** *p537*
Massey, Sarah; America, 1754 ***1220.12*** *p537*
Massey, Thomas; America, 1738 ***1220.12*** *p537*
Massey, Thomas; Barbados, 1668 ***1220.12*** *p537*
Massey, William; America, 1753 ***1220.12*** *p537*
Massicot, Jacques; Quebec, 1667 ***4514.3*** *p331*
Massie, Agnes; Maine, 1733 ***9228.50*** *p413*
Massier, Ludwige; Dakota, 1892-1918 ***554.30*** *p26*
Massing, Peter; Brazil, 1880 ***5475.1*** *p444*
With family
Massingham, Charles; America, 1744 ***1220.12*** *p537*
Massoe, William 39; Ontario, 1871 ***1823.21*** *p216*
Massois, Mrs. 32; America, 1844 ***778.6*** *p234*
Masson, Anne; Quebec, 1670 ***4514.3*** *p346*
Masson, Catherine 66; Missouri, 1845 ***778.6*** *p234*
Masson, Ernest 2; America, 1842 ***778.6*** *p234*
Masson, Honore 33; Missouri, 1848 ***778.6*** *p234*
Masson, Jeanne 23; America, 1842 ***778.6*** *p234*
Masson, Joseph 32; New Orleans, 1848 ***778.6*** *p234*
Masson, Pierre 31; America, 1842 ***778.6*** *p234*
Masson, Pierre 37; Quebec, 1646 ***9221.17*** *p160*
Massone, Adolf *SEE* Massone, Johann
Massone, Anna; America, 1872 ***5475.1*** *p205*
Massone, Barbara *SEE* Massone, Johann
Massone, Georg *SEE* Massone, Johann
Massone, Gertrud Schudes *SEE* Massone, Johann
Massone, Johann *SEE* Massone, Johann
Massone, Johann; America, 1873 ***5475.1*** *p205*
*Wife:*Gertrud Schudes
*Son:*Adolf
*Son:*Johann
*Son:*Georg
*Son:*Nikolaus
*Daughter:*Barbara
Massone, Nikolaus *SEE* Massone, Johann
Massoneau, Rene; Virginia, 1700 ***9230.15*** *p81*
Massony, Eulalie 33; New Orleans, 1848 ***778.6*** *p234*
Massony, Jumeline 26; New Orleans, 1848 ***778.6*** *p234*
Massuy, Marie Joseph Duccroc *SEE* Massuy, Paul
Massuy, Marie Therese; Wisconsin, 1856 ***1495.20*** *p46*
Massuy, Paul; Wisconsin, 1856 ***1495.20*** *p46*
*Wife:*Marie Joseph Duccroc
With 5 children
Massy, Agnes; Maine, 1733 ***9228.50*** *p413*
Massy, William; Louisiana, 1836-1840 ***4981.45*** *p213*
Mast, Christian; Illinois, 1857 ***6079.1*** *p9*
Mast, Daniel; Louisiana, 1874 ***4981.45*** *p133*
Masterman, John; America, 1743 ***1220.12*** *p537*
Masterman, John; Virginia, 1734 ***1220.12*** *p537*
Masters, . . .; Canada, n.d. ***9228.50*** *p18A*
Masters, Alice; America, 1715 ***1220.12*** *p537*
Masters, Alice; Barbados, 1675 ***1220.12*** *p537*
Masters, Andrew; America, 1775 ***1220.12*** *p537*
Masters, Barney; Ohio, 1855 ***3580.20*** *p33*
Masters, Barney; Ohio, 1855 ***6020.12*** *p21*
Masters, Charles 60; Ontario, 1871 ***1823.17*** *p99*
Masters, Christopher; America, 1685 ***1220.12*** *p537*
Masters, Edward; Boston, 1713 ***9228.50*** *p424*
Masters, Edward; Massachusetts, 1713 ***9228.50*** *p439*
Masters, Francis; New Jersey, 1667 ***9228.50*** *p358*
Masters, James; Annapolis, MD, 1729 ***1220.12*** *p537*
Masters, John; Died enroute, 1718 ***1220.12*** *p537*
Masters, Nicholas; Connecticut, 1688-1717 ***9228.50*** *p591*
Masters, Nicholas; Connecticut, 1720 ***9228.50*** *p436*
Masters, Richard; Virginia, 1719 ***1220.12*** *p537*
Masters, Thomas; America, 1772 ***1220.12*** *p537*
Masters, Thomas; Marblehead, MA, 1754-1799 ***9228.50*** *p358*
Masterson, James 66; Michigan, 1880 ***4491.33*** *p14*
Masterson, Margaret 60; Michigan, 1880 ***4491.33*** *p14*
Masterson, Patrick; Colorado, 1880 ***1029.59*** *p58*
Masterson, Patrick; Colorado, 1903 ***1029.59*** *p58*
Masterson, Thomas; America, 1749 ***1220.12*** *p537*
Masterson, Thomas; Ohio, 1856 ***3580.20*** *p33*
Masterson, Thomas; Ohio, 1856 ***6020.12*** *p21*
Masterton, John; America, 1751 ***1220.12*** *p537*
Mastin, Louis 28; New Orleans, 1840 ***778.6*** *p234*
Mastio, Jacque 38; America, 1842 ***778.6*** *p234*
Masurett, Frank 18; Ontario, 1871 ***1823.17*** *p99*
Masury, . . .; America, 1492-1820 ***9228.50*** *p27*
Masury, Benjamin; America, 1700 ***9228.50*** *p446*
*Sister:*Jane
Masury, Benjamin; Salem, MA, 1650-1675 ***9228.50*** *p440*
Masury, George; Massachusetts, n.d. ***9228.50*** *p439*
Masury, Jane *SEE* Masury, Benjamin
Masury, Jane; Died enroute, 1677 ***9228.50*** *p440*
Masury, Jean; New Hampshire, 1683 ***9228.50*** *p20A*
Masury, John; Salem, MA, 1690-1693 ***9228.50*** *p441*
Masury, Joseph; Salem, MA, 1655-1680 ***9228.50*** *p440*
Masury, Joseph; Salem, MA, 1679 ***9228.50*** *p445*
Masury, Laurence; Salem, MA, 1646-1670 ***9228.50*** *p439*
Masury, Martin; Massachusetts, 1652-1709 ***9228.50*** *p440*
Masury, William; Salem, MA, 1682 ***9228.50*** *p440*
Matagne, Marie Victorine; Wisconsin, 1880 ***1495.20*** *p55*
Matayer, Josephine 35; Missouri, 1845 ***778.6*** *p234*
Matcham, Henry; America, 1764 ***1220.12*** *p537*
Matches, James 36; Ontario, 1871 ***1823.21*** *p216*
Matchet, William; America, 1772 ***1220.12*** *p537*
Matchett, Christopher 60; Ontario, 1871 ***1823.17*** *p99*
Matchett, Isabel; America, 1734 ***1220.12*** *p537*
Matchett, John; America, 1675 ***1220.12*** *p537*
Matchett, Thomas; America, 1752 ***1220.12*** *p537*
Matchett, Thomas; Barbados, 1672 ***1220.12*** *p537*
Mate, Jeremiah; America, 1755 ***1220.12*** *p537*
Matecki, John; Texas, 1884-1890 ***6015.15*** *p28*
Matejcek, . . .; Pennsylvania, 1750-1799 ***2853.20*** *p17*
Matejka, Josef; Chicago, 1873-1882 ***2853.20*** *p405*
Matejka, Josef; New York, NY, 1873 ***2853.20*** *p398*
Matejovsky, Vaclav; Chicago, 1867 ***2853.20*** *p391*
Matejovsky, Vaclav; Chicago, 1872 ***2853.20*** *p424*
Matejovsky, Vaclav; Texas, 1850 ***2853.20*** *p59*
Mateju, Bohumil; New York, NY, 1904 ***2853.20*** *p109*
Matejunas, Hilary 28; New York, NY, 1920 ***930.50*** *p49*
Mater, John 24; Ontario, 1871 ***1823.17*** *p99*
Matere, Charles 45; Ontario, 1871 ***1823.21*** *p216*
Mates, Cornelius; Virginia, 1732 ***1220.12*** *p537*
Mates, Joseph; America, 1763 ***1220.12*** *p537*
Mateski, John; Texas, 1884-1890 ***6015.15*** *p28*
Mathais, Antoine; Louisiana, 1874-1875 ***4981.45*** *p29*
Mathau, Victoire 63; New Orleans, 1848 ***778.6*** *p234*
Mather, H. 19; America, 1840 ***778.6*** *p234*
Mather, Increase; Boston, 1676 ***1642*** *p130*
Mather, Margaret; America, 1751 ***1220.12*** *p537*
Mather, Matilda 71; Ontario, 1871 ***1823.21*** *p216*
Mather, Thomas; America, 1767 ***1220.12*** *p537*
Mather, Thomas; Barbados, 1673 ***1220.12*** *p537*
Matherall, John 69; Ontario, 1871 ***1823.21*** *p216*
Mathers, Alfred; Miami, 1935 ***4984.12*** *p39*
Mathers, Henry 60; Ontario, 1871 ***1823.21*** *p216*
Mathers, Wesley 48; Ontario, 1871 ***1823.21*** *p216*
Mathers, William 33; Ontario, 1871 ***1823.21*** *p216*
Mathers, Wm.; Ohio, 1840-1897 ***8365.35*** *p17*
Mathes, Christian; Louisiana, 1841-1844 ***4981.45*** *p211*
Mathes, Emma Pauline; Wisconsin, 1892 ***6795.8*** *p134*
Matheson, Ann 29; Ontario, 1871 ***1823.17*** *p99*
Matheson, Hugh 32; North Carolina, 1774 ***1422.10*** *p58*
Matheson, Jean 27; North Carolina, 1775 ***1422.10*** *p57*
Matheson, Jno. 38; North Carolina, 1775 ***1422.10*** *p57*
Matheson, Kathrine 16; North Carolina, 1774 ***1422.10*** *p58*
Matheson, Margt. 4; North Carolina, 1775 ***1422.10*** *p57*
Matheson, William 31; Ontario, 1871 ***1823.21*** *p216*
Matheson, William 60; Ontario, 1871 ***1823.21*** *p216*
Mathesson, Christina 14; Quebec, 1870 ***8364.32*** *p25*
Mathew, Andrew 4; St. John, N.B., 1834 ***6469.7*** *p5*
Mathew, Louis E.; Illinois, 1856 ***6079.1*** *p9*
Mathew, Pierre 17; America, 1748 ***778.6*** *p234*
Mathewes, Edward; Barbados, 1664 ***1220.12*** *p538*
Mathewes, Elizabeth; Barbados, 1679 ***1220.12*** *p538*
Mathews, Abraham; America, 1751 ***1220.12*** *p538*
Mathews, Albert Wilhelm; Wisconsin, 1896 ***6795.8*** *p213*
Mathews, Ann; Maryland, 1727 ***1220.12*** *p538*
Mathews, Benjamin 59; Ontario, 1871 ***1823.21*** *p216*
Mathews, Catherine; Died enroute, 1721 ***1220.12*** *p538*
Mathews, Charles 40; Ontario, 1871 ***1823.21*** *p216*
Mathews, Christopher; Charles Town, SC, 1719 ***1220.12*** *p538*
Mathews, Christopher; Maryland, 1720 ***1220.12*** *p538*
Mathews, Dorothy; Barbados, 1681 ***1220.12*** *p538*
Mathews, Edw 25; St. Johns, N.F., 1811 ***1053.20*** *p20*
Mathews, Edward; America, 1740 ***1220.12*** *p538*
Mathews, Edward; Ohio, 1844 ***2763.1*** *p20*
Mathews, Edwin; New Jersey, 1807 ***3845.2*** *p129*
Mathews, Elizabeth; America, 1772 ***1220.12*** *p538*
Mathews, George; America, 1731 ***1220.12*** *p538*
Mathews, George 45; Ontario, 1871 ***1823.21*** *p216*
Mathews, George; Potomac, 1729 ***1220.12*** *p538*
Mathews, Harriot; America, 1770 ***1220.12*** *p538*
Mathews, Henry 37; Ontario, 1871 ***1823.21*** *p216*
Mathews, James; America, 1737 ***1220.12*** *p538*
Mathews, James; Barbados, 1673 ***1220.12*** *p538*
Mathews, James; Barbados, 1677 ***1220.12*** *p538*
Mathews, James; Boston, 1715 ***1642*** *p24*
Mathews, James; Maryland, 1674 ***1236.25*** *p50*
Mathews, James 60; Ontario, 1871 ***1823.17*** *p99*
Mathews, Jane; Wisconsin, 1852 ***9228.50*** *p446*
Mathews, John; America, 1729 ***1220.12*** *p538*
Mathews, John; America, 1741 ***1220.12*** *p538*
Mathews, John; America, 1752 ***1220.12*** *p538*
Mathews, John; America, 1763 ***1220.12*** *p538*
Mathews, John; America, 1766 ***1220.12*** *p539*
Mathews, John 63; Ontario, 1871 ***1823.21*** *p216*
Mathews, Margaret Blampied Newman; Ohio, 1834 ***9228.50*** *p119*
Mathews, Mary; Maryland, 1725 ***1220.12*** *p539*
Mathews, Mathias; Long Island, 1778 ***8529.30*** *p9A*
Mathews, Pater; America, 1770 ***1220.12*** *p539*
Mathews, Paul; America, 1768 ***1220.12*** *p539*
Mathews, Paul; America, 1770 ***1220.12*** *p539*
Mathews, Perminas 71; Ontario, 1871 ***1823.17*** *p99*
Mathews, Philip 51; Ontario, 1871 ***1823.21*** *p217*
Mathews, Rebeccah; Virginia, 1741 ***1220.12*** *p539*
Mathews, Richard; America, 1737 ***1220.12*** *p539*
Mathews, Samuel; America, 1741 ***1220.12*** *p539*
Mathews, Samuel; Barbados, 1683 ***1220.12*** *p539*
Mathews, Samuel 22; Ontario, 1871 ***1823.17*** *p99*
Mathews, Samuel H. 29; Ontario, 1871 ***1823.21*** *p217*
Mathews, Thomas; America, 1693 ***1220.12*** *p539*
Mathews, Thomas; America, 1751 ***1220.12*** *p539*
Mathews, Thomas; America, 1761 ***1220.12*** *p539*
Mathews, Thomas; Maryland, 1674 ***1236.25*** *p49*
Mathews, Thomas 39; Ontario, 1871 ***1823.17*** *p99*
Mathews, William; America, 1685 ***1220.12*** *p539*
Mathews, William; America, 1729 ***1220.12*** *p539*
Mathews, William; America, 1731 ***1220.12*** *p539*
Mathews, William; America, 1775 ***1220.12*** *p540*
Mathews, William; Marston's Wharf, 1782 ***8529.30*** *p14*
Mathews, William 30; Ontario, 1871 ***1823.17*** *p99*
Mathews, William C.; Colorado, 1880 ***1029.59*** *p58*
Mathewson, Hugh 47; Ontario, 1871 ***1823.17*** *p99*
Mathewson, Rob't 37; Ontario, 1871 ***1823.21*** *p217*
Mathey, Mr. 40; New Orleans, 1848 ***778.6*** *p234*
Mathey, Ms. 30; New Orleans, 1848 ***778.6*** *p234*
Mathez, Jules 31; Missouri, 1845 ***778.6*** *p234*
Mathian, Rudolph; New York, 1860 ***358.56*** *p3*
Mathias, B. 25; America, 1847 ***778.6*** *p234*
Mathias, Catherine 29; America, 1847 ***778.6*** *p234*
Mathias, Christian; America, 1868 ***7420.1*** *p274*
Mathias, Christian Heinrich; Brazil, 1889 ***5475.1*** *p38*
Mathias, Engel Marie; America, 1855 ***7420.1*** *p138*
*Sister:*Thrine Sophia
Mathias, Francois 29; America, 1846 ***778.6*** *p234*
Mathias, Friedrich; America, 1880 ***7420.1*** *p317*
Mathias, Heinrich; America, 1866 ***7420.1*** *p245*
Mathias, Henry; Louisiana, 1874-1875 ***4981.45*** *p30*
Mathias, Johann Heinrich Conrad; America, 1864 ***7420.1*** *p225*
With family
Mathias, Pierre 18; America, 1846 ***778.6*** *p234*
Mathias, Sophie Marie; America, 1857 ***7420.1*** *p166*
Mathias, Therese 63; Missouri, 1846 ***778.6*** *p234*
Mathias, Thrine Sophia *SEE* Mathias, Engel Marie
Mathier, Julie 23; New Orleans, 1846 ***778.6*** *p235*
Mathiesan, David; Colorado, 1868 ***1029.59*** *p59*
Mathieu, . . .; America, 1846 ***778.6*** *p235*
Mathieu, Mr. 27; America, 1841 ***778.6*** *p235*
Mathieu, Catherine 26; Quebec, 1658 ***9221.17*** *p384*
Mathieu, Francois 19; Port uncertain, 1843 ***778.6*** *p235*
Mathieu, G. 22; America, 1848 ***778.6*** *p235*
Mathieu, Henry 40; America, 1848 ***778.6*** *p235*
Mathieu, Itienne; Illinois, 1852 ***6079.1*** *p9*
Mathieu, Jean 23; Quebec, 1659 ***9221.17*** *p406*
Mathieu, Julien Joseph; Wisconsin, 1854-1858 ***1495.20*** *p66*
Mathieu, Katharina; America, 1833 ***5475.1*** *p20*
Mathieu, Louisa 42; New Orleans, 1844 ***778.6*** *p235*
Mathieu, Sophie; America, 1881 ***5475.1*** *p55*
Mathis, Mr. 38; America, 1843 ***778.6*** *p235*
Mathis, Adam 5; America, 1846 ***778.6*** *p235*
Mathis, Anton *SEE* Mathis, Johann
Mathis, Barbara Hirtz 29 *SEE* Mathis, Johann
Mathis, Catherine 15; America, 1846 ***778.6*** *p235*
Mathis, Catherine 49; America, 1846 ***778.6*** *p235*
Mathis, Charles 26; America, 1846 ***778.6*** *p235*
Mathis, Charlotte 8; America, 1846 ***778.6*** *p235*
Mathis, Henri 6; America, 1846 ***778.6*** *p235*
Mathis, Jacob 13; America, 1846 ***778.6*** *p235*
Mathis, Jacob 52; America, 1846 ***778.6*** *p235*
Mathis, Johann *SEE* Mathis, Johann
Mathis, Johann 31; America, 1880 ***5475.1*** *p227*
*Wife:*Barbara Hirtz 29
*Son:*Anton
*Son:*Michel
*Son:*Johann
Mathis, Michel *SEE* Mathis, Johann
Mathis, Michel 26; America, 1880 ***5475.1*** *p226*
Mathis, Sophie 20; America, 1846 ***778.6*** *p235*
Mathisen, Nicolas 18; New Orleans, 1848 ***778.6*** *p235*
Mathison, Andrew; Iowa, 1904 ***1211.15*** *p17*
Mathison, Martin; New York, 1900 ***1766.20*** *p25*
Mathison, Peter; Iowa, 1899 ***1211.15*** *p17*
Mathizen, Jacob; Wisconsin, 1874 ***6795.8*** *p104*
Mathon, Fd. 23; America, 1843 ***778.6*** *p235*
Mathou, Philippe 29; Quebec, 1662 ***9221.17*** *p490*
Mathson, Andrew; Washington, 1889 ***2770.40*** *p79*
Mathu, Pierre Joseph; Detroit, 1871 ***1494.21*** *p31*
Mathurin, . . .; Montreal, 1642 ***9221.17*** *p124*

Mathurin, . . .; Quebec, 1636 ***9221.17*** *p61*
Mathurin, Alphonse 8; Jacksonville, FL, 1840 ***778.6*** *p235*
Mathurin, Catha. 15; Jacksonville, FL, 1840 ***778.6*** *p235*
Mathurin, Franc. 39; Jacksonville, FL, 1840 ***778.6*** *p235*
Mathurin, Leonore 10; Jacksonville, FL, 1840 ***778.6*** *p235*
Mathurin, Marg. 38; Jacksonville, FL, 1840 ***778.6*** *p235*
Mathurin, Marie 13; Jacksonville, FL, 1840 ***778.6*** *p235*
Mathurin, Nidovine 9; Jacksonville, FL, 1840 ***778.6*** *p235*
Mathy, Antoinette *SEE* Mathy, Pierre Joseph
Mathy, Augustin Joseph *SEE* Mathy, Pierre Joseph
Mathy, Charles; Philadelphia, 1880 ***1494.20*** *p13*
Mathy, Henri *SEE* Mathy, Pierre Joseph
Mathy, Louis; Philadelphia, 1879 ***1494.20*** *p13*
Mathy, Louise *SEE* Mathy, Pierre Joseph
Mathy, Marie Therese Evrard *SEE* Mathy, Pierre Joseph
Mathy, Pierre Joseph; Wisconsin, 1856 ***1495.20*** *p41*
*Wife:*Marie Therese Evrard
*Child:*Henri
*Child:*Augustin Joseph
*Child:*Rosalie
*Child:*Louise
With brother-in-law
*Child:*Antoinette
Mathy, Rosalie *SEE* Mathy, Pierre Joseph
Mathys, Frederick; Philadelphia, 1860 ***8513.31*** *p411*
Matifa, Antoine; Quebec, 1637 ***9221.17*** *p71*
With wife
Matith, Elise 21; New York, NY, 1894 ***6512.1*** *p231*
Matkins, Elizabeth; Virginia, 1735 ***1220.12*** *p537*
Matler, Martin 62; Missouri, 1845 ***778.6*** *p235*
Maton, Ann; Virginia, 1772 ***1220.12*** *p537*
Matoret, Francoise Richard; Quebec, 1671 ***4514.3*** *p374*
Matoret, Francoise Trochet; Quebec, 1671 ***4514.3*** *p374*
Matousek, Jan; St. Louis, 1896 ***2853.20*** *p54*
Matousek, Rudolf; Missouri, 1888 ***2853.20*** *p54*
Matousek, Rudolf; Missouri, 1888 ***2853.20*** *p284*
Matrat, Antoine; Illinois, 1863 ***6079.1*** *p9*
Matschnig, Johan; Colorado, 1886 ***1029.59*** *p59*
Matsenkis, Joseph 28; New York, NY, 1893 ***1883.7*** *p41*
Matson, Andrew; Cleveland, OH, 1889-1894 ***9722.10*** *p123*
Matson, August; Cleveland, OH, 1901-1905 ***9722.10*** *p123*
Matson, Gabriela 58; New Orleans, 1848 ***778.6*** *p235*
Matson, Jack; Colorado, 1904 ***1029.59*** *p59*
Matson, Jack 29; Colorado, 1904 ***1029.59*** *p59*
Matson, John; Colorado, 1892 ***1029.59*** *p59*
Matson, John; Colorado, 1904 ***1029.59*** *p59*
Matson, John 26; Colorado, 1904 ***1029.59*** *p59*
Matson, Maria 6; New Orleans, 1848 ***778.6*** *p235*
Matson, Maria 15; New Orleans, 1848 ***778.6*** *p235*
Matson, Mats; Colorado, 1885 ***1029.59*** *p59*
Matson, Michel 48; New Orleans, 1848 ***778.6*** *p235*
Matson, Susanah; Philadelphia, 1854 ***8513.31*** *p307*
Matson, William; America, 1730 ***1220.12*** *p537*
Matsson, Joh.; New York, NY, 1843 ***6412.40*** *p146*
Mattemasse, Jean; Montreal, 1642 ***9221.17*** *p124*
Mattens, Edw 25; St. Johns, N.F., 1811 ***1053.20*** *p20*
Matter, John; America, 1834-1856 ***9228.50*** *p77*
Matter, Mary, Jr.; America, 1752 ***1220.12*** *p537*
Mattern, Jakob; America, 1880 ***8115.12*** *p327*
Mattern, Konrad; America, n.d. ***8115.12*** *p325*
Mattern, Ludwig; America, n.d. ***8115.12*** *p327*
Mattes, Maria 60; America, 1882 ***5475.1*** *p555*
*Daughter:*Katharina
*Son:*Johann
Matteson, John; Ohio, 1809-1852 ***4511.35*** *p33*
Mattews, Thomas; America, 1737 ***1220.12*** *p539*
Mattews, William 61; Ontario, 1871 ***1823.21*** *p217*
Mattewson, James 43; Ontario, 1871 ***1823.21*** *p217*
Matthaei, Heinrich Philipp Eduard August; South America, 1881 ***7420.1*** *p323*
Matthas, Fr. C.; Valdivia, Chile, 1852 ***1192.4*** *p54*
Matthei, Conrad Wilhelm Bernhard Maximilian; America, 1852 ***7420.1*** *p93*
Matthei, Eduard; America, 1855 ***7420.1*** *p138*
With 2 sons
Matthei, Ernst Friedrich; America, 1859 ***7420.1*** *p187*
Matthei, Georg Christian; Port uncertain, 1853 ***7420.1*** *p108*
*Brother:*Heinrich Philipp
Matthei, Heinrich; America, 1853 ***7420.1*** *p108*
Matthei, Heinrich Philipp *SEE* Matthei, Georg Christian
Matthei, Johann Heinrich; America, 1856 ***7420.1*** *p150*
Matthei, Johanne; America, 1857 ***7420.1*** *p166*
Matthei, Louise; America, 1856 ***7420.1*** *p150*
Matthei, Philipp; America, 1853 ***7420.1*** *p108*
Matthei, Theodor; America, 1854 ***7420.1*** *p124*
Matthei, Wilhelm; America, 1852 ***7420.1*** *p93*
Matthes, Adolph; America, 1867 ***7919.3*** *p531*
Matthes, Karl Philipp; America, 1881 ***2526.42*** *p126*
Matthes, Magdalena; America, 1865 ***5475.1*** *p544*
Matthew, Louis 30; Port uncertain, 1840 ***778.6*** *p235*
Matthew, May 26; Port uncertain, 1840 ***778.6*** *p236*
Matthews, Andrew; America, 1764 ***1220.12*** *p538*
Matthews, Ann; America, 1758 ***1220.12*** *p538*
Matthews, Anne; America, 1729 ***1220.12*** *p538*
Matthews, Anthony 26; Ontario, 1871 ***1823.21*** *p217*
Matthews, Catherine Rebecca; America, 1762 ***1220.12*** *p538*
Matthews, Clement; America, 1756 ***1220.12*** *p538*
Matthews, Daniel; America, 1769 ***1220.12*** *p538*
Matthews, Darby; America, 1766 ***1220.12*** *p538*
Matthews, David; Colorado, 1883 ***1029.59*** *p59*
Matthews, Eleanor; America, 1771 ***1220.12*** *p538*
Matthews, Eliz.; Maine, 1627-1669 ***9228.50*** *p197*
Matthews, Eliz.; Maine, 1627-1669 ***9228.50*** *p197*
Matthews, Elizabeth; America, 1736 ***1220.12*** *p538*
Matthews, Elizabeth; America, 1740 ***1220.12*** *p538*
Matthews, Henry; Barbados or Jamaica, 1702 ***1220.12*** *p538*
Matthews, Hugh; America, 1749 ***1220.12*** *p538*
Matthews, James; America, 1736 ***1220.12*** *p538*
Matthews, James; America, 1740 ***1220.12*** *p538*
Matthews, James; America, 1744 ***1220.12*** *p538*
Matthews, James; America, 1761 ***1220.12*** *p538*
Matthews, James; New York, NY, 1778 ***8529.30*** *p3*
Matthews, James; Virginia, 1771 ***1220.12*** *p538*
Matthews, Jane; Wisconsin, 1853 ***9228.50*** *p131*
Matthews, John; America, 1731 ***1220.12*** *p538*
Matthews, John; America, 1733 ***1220.12*** *p538*
Matthews, John; America, 1738 ***1220.12*** *p538*
Matthews, John; America, 1764 ***1220.12*** *p539*
Matthews, John; America, 1765 ***1220.12*** *p539*
Matthews, John; America, 1770 ***1220.12*** *p539*
Matthews, John; Maryland, 1740 ***1220.12*** *p538*
Matthews, John; Potomac, 1729 ***1220.12*** *p538*
Matthews, John; Virginia, 1739 ***1220.12*** *p538*
Matthews, John; Virginia, 1740 ***1220.12*** *p538*
Matthews, Joseph; Ohio, 1809-1852 ***4511.35*** *p33*
Matthews, Joseph; Virginia, 1767 ***1220.12*** *p539*
Matthews, Joseph H.; Ohio, 1809-1852 ***4511.35*** *p33*
Matthews, Luke; Barbados or Jamaica, 1702 ***1220.12*** *p539*
Matthews, Margaret; America, 1747 ***1220.12*** *p539*
Matthews, Margaret; America, 1768 ***1220.12*** *p539*
Matthews, Margaret; Ohio, 1835 ***9228.50*** *p147*
Matthews, Maria; America, 1758 ***1220.12*** *p539*
Matthews, Mary; America, 1735 ***1220.12*** *p539*
Matthews, Mary; America, 1736 ***1220.12*** *p539*
Matthews, Mary; Annapolis, MD, 1726 ***1220.12*** *p539*
Matthews, Mary 59; Ontario, 1871 ***1823.21*** *p217*
Matthews, Mary; Virginia, 1735 ***1220.12*** *p539*
Matthews, Moses; America, 1772 ***1220.12*** *p539*
Matthews, Richard; America, 1736 ***1220.12*** *p539*
Matthews, Richard; America, 1757 ***1220.12*** *p539*
Matthews, Richard F. 39; Ontario, 1871 ***1823.21*** *p217*
Matthews, Robert; America, 1737 ***1220.12*** *p539*
Matthews, Sarah; America, 1767 ***1220.12*** *p539*
Matthews, Sarah; America, 1775 ***1220.12*** *p539*
Matthews, Sarah; America, 1904 ***6410.15*** *p108*
*Daughter:*Wendla Maria
*Daughter:*Mia Hermanna
*Daughter:*Emilie Dorothea
Matthews, Sarah; Carolina, 1724 ***1220.12*** *p539*
Matthews, Sarah; Rappahannock, VA, 1729 ***1220.12*** *p539*
Matthews, Thomas; America, 1685 ***1220.12*** *p539*
Matthews, Thomas; America, 1729 ***1220.12*** *p539*
Matthews, Thomas; America, 1751 ***1220.12*** *p539*
Matthews, Thomas; America, 1763 ***1220.12*** *p539*
Matthews, Thomas; America, 1764 ***1220.12*** *p539*
Matthews, Thomas; Charles Town, SC, 1718 ***1220.12*** *p539*
Matthews, Thomas 61; Ontario, 1871 ***1823.21*** *p217*
Matthews, William; America, 1664 ***1220.12*** *p539*
Matthews, William; America, 1744 ***1220.12*** *p539*
Matthews, William; America, 1748 ***1220.12*** *p540*
Matthews, William; America, 1752 ***1220.12*** *p540*
Matthews, William; America, 1773 ***1220.12*** *p540*
Matthews, William; Marston's Wharf, 1782 ***8529.30*** *p14*
Matthews, William C.; Colorado, 1889 ***1029.59*** *p59*
Matthewson, Alexander; North Carolina, 1838-1839 ***1088.45*** *p21*
Matthewson, Donald 54; Ontario, 1871 ***1823.21*** *p217*
Matthewson, Henry 52; Ontario, 1871 ***1823.21*** *p217*
Matthey, J. H.; Louisiana, 1836-1841 ***4981.45*** *p209*
Matthey, Minna; Wisconsin, 1888 ***6795.8*** *p26*
Matthias, Widow; America, 1861 ***7420.1*** *p207*
With family
Matthias, Anne Sophie Dorothee; America, 1855 ***7420.1*** *p138*
*Sister:*Engel Dorothee Sophie
Matthias, Catharine Engel Sophie *SEE* Matthias, Engel Dorothe
Matthias, Catherine Engel Sophie *SEE* Matthias, Johann Heinrich Christoph
Matthias, Engel Dorothe; America, 1881 ***7420.1*** *p323*
*Son:*Johann Conrad
*Daughter:*Engel Dorothea
*Son:*Heinrich Christoph
*Daughter:*Catharine Engel Sophie
Matthias, Engel Dorothea *SEE* Matthias, Engel Dorothe
Matthias, Engel Dorothee Sophie *SEE* Matthias, Anne Sophie Dorothee
Matthias, Engel Maria Dorothea; America, 1854 ***7420.1*** *p124*
Matthias, Engel Marie Sophie; America, 1857 ***7420.1*** *p166*
Matthias, H.; Port uncertain, 1853 ***7420.1*** *p108*
Matthias, Heinrich Christoph *SEE* Matthias, Engel Dorothe
Matthias, Johann Conrad; America, 1857 ***7420.1*** *p166*
Matthias, Johann Conrad *SEE* Matthias, Engel Dorothe
Matthias, Johann Heinr. Otto *SEE* Matthias, Johann Heinrich Christoph
Matthias, Johann Heinrich; America, 1860 ***7420.1*** *p196*
Matthias, Johann Heinrich Christoph; America, 1850 ***7420.1*** *p73*
*Wife:*Marie Sophie Bock
*Son:*Johann Heinrich Conrad
*Daughter:*Sophie Dorothea
*Son:*Johann Heinr. Otto
*Daughter:*Catherine Engel Sophie
Matthias, Johann Heinrich Conrad *SEE* Matthias, Johann Heinrich Christoph
Matthias, Johann Otto; America, 1857 ***7420.1*** *p166*
Matthias, Johann Wilhelm; America, 1850 ***7420.1*** *p73*
Matthias, Louise Ernestine Amalia; America, 1855 ***7420.1*** *p141*
Matthias, Marie Sophie Bock *SEE* Matthias, Johann Heinrich Christoph
Matthias, Sophie Dorothea *SEE* Matthias, Johann Heinrich Christoph
Matthias, Thrine Maria; America, 1854 ***7420.1*** *p124*
Matti, Louis; Philadelphia, 1879 ***1494.20*** *p13*
Mattil, Jacob; Ohio, 1809-1852 ***4511.35*** *p33*
Mattila, Erland 40; Minnesota, 1923 ***2769.54*** *p1379*
Mattila, Hilda 31; Minnesota, 1923 ***2769.54*** *p1379*
Mattis, Anna 19; New York, NY, 1877 ***6954.7*** *p40*
Mattis, Barbara 28; New York, NY, 1886 ***6954.7*** *p41*
Mattis, Carolina 56; New York, NY, 1887 ***6954.7*** *p41*
Mattis, Catherina 22; New York, NY, 1885 ***6954.7*** *p40*
Mattis, David 2 months; New York, NY, 1877 ***6954.7*** *p40*
Mattis, Emanuel 8; New York, NY, 1886 ***6954.7*** *p41*
Mattis, Emelia 4; New York, NY, 1886 ***6954.7*** *p41*
Mattis, Johann 23; Died enroute, 1885 ***6954.7*** *p40*
Mattis, Johann 33; New York, NY, 1886 ***6954.7*** *p41*
Mattis, Katherina 9; New York, NY, 1886 ***6954.7*** *p41*
Mattis, Paulina 3; New York, NY, 1886 ***6954.7*** *p41*
Mattis, Wilhelm 6 months; New York, NY, 1886 ***6954.7*** *p41*
Mattis, Wilhelm 23; New York, NY, 1877 ***6954.7*** *p40*
Mattison, Hugh; Annapolis, MD, 1723 ***1220.12*** *p540*
Mattlemore, Thady; Toronto, 1844 ***2910.35*** *p116*
Mattocks, John; America, 1774 ***1220.12*** *p540*
Matton, Anthonie; Virginia, 1700 ***9230.15*** *p81*
With wife
Mattot, Antoine; Wisconsin, 1855 ***1495.20*** *p45*
Matts, Roger; Annapolis, MD, 1758 ***1220.12*** *p540*
Matts, Sarah; Virginia, 1736 ***1220.12*** *p540*
Mattson, Andrew; St. Paul, MN, 1881 ***1865.50*** *p97*
Mattson, Evert 18; Minnesota, 1923 ***2769.54*** *p1381*
Mattson, Herman; New York, NY, 1873-1919 ***1029.59*** *p59*
Mattson, Johan Manfred; Cleveland, OH, 1905 ***9722.10*** *p124*
Mattson, Leonard 32; Minnesota, 1925 ***2769.54*** *p1384*
Mattson, Ludwig; Cleveland, OH, 1890-1892 ***9722.10*** *p124*
Mattson, Matt 19; Minnesota, 1925 ***2769.54*** *p1378*
Mattson, William 23; Minnesota, 1925 ***2769.54*** *p1378*
Mattsson, A.G.; Cleveland, OH, 1880-1884 ***9722.10*** *p124*
Mattsson, Dan. Johan; Philadelphia, 1847 ***6412.40*** *p150*
Mattsson, Jons 30; New York, 1856 ***6529.11*** *p22*
Mattsson, Oskar; Cleveland, OH, 1891-1892 ***9722.10*** *p124*
Mattwig, Auguste; Wisconsin, 1896 ***6795.8*** *p37*
Matty, Henry; America, 1740 ***1220.12*** *p540*
Matula, Ondrej; Texas, 1860 ***2853.20*** *p74*
Matulas, Frantisek; Texas, 1860-1865 ***2853.20*** *p67*
Matulas, Vaclav; Texas, 1860-1865 ***2853.20*** *p67*
Matusek, Jan; Texas, 1860 ***2853.20*** *p74*

Matusiak, Stanislaw 28; New York, NY, 1920 930.50 p49
Matuska, Antonin; Chicago, 1858 2853.20 p389
Matuszewski, Andrew Frank; Chicago, 1930 121.35 p100
Matuszkowicz, Jan 25; New York, NY, 1911 6533.11 p10
Matuszyk, Michael; Detroit, 1930 1640.60 p81
Matya, Frank; Wisconsin, 1899 6795.8 p60
Matya, Joseph; Wisconsin, 1897 6795.8 p60
Matysko, John; Detroit, 1930 1640.60 p78
Matz, Frederick Wilhelm; Wisconsin, 1901 6795.8 p177
Matz, Jacob; Washington, 1882 2770.40 p135
Matz, Jacques 20; America, 1846 778.6 p236
Matz, John Julius; Wisconsin, 1869 6795.8 p154
Matz, Rosine 23; America, 1846 778.6 p236
Matzinger, Catha. 28; America, 1840 778.6 p236
Matzinger, Eva 1; America, 1840 778.6 p236
Matzinger, Eva 23; America, 1840 778.6 p236
Matzinger, Georg. 6; America, 1840 778.6 p236
Matzinger, Georg. 31; America, 1840 778.6 p236
Matzinger, Marg. 27; America, 1840 778.6 p236
Matzinger, Marie 4; America, 1840 778.6 p236
Maubach, J. Mathias; Chicago, 1883 5475.1 p385
Mauch, Adam 7; Baltimore, 1906 8425.16 p31
Mauch, Adolf 2; New York, NY, 1893 1883.7 p39
Mauch, Adolf 7; New York, NY, 1893 1883.7 p47
Mauch, Anna 38; Baltimore, 1906 8425.16 p31
Mauch, Christina 54; New York, NY, 1900 8425.16 p31
Mauch, Daniel 15; New York, NY, 1893 1883.7 p39
Mauch, Daniel 15; New York, NY, 1893 1883.7 p47
Mauch, Elisabetha 20; Baltimore, 1906 8425.16 p31
Mauch, Emelia 10; Baltimore, 1906 8425.16 p31
Mauch, Ferdinand 9; New York, NY, 1893 1883.7 p39
Mauch, Ferninand 9; New York, NY, 1893 1883.7 p47
Mauch, Georg 17; Baltimore, 1906 8425.16 p31
Mauch, Gottlieb 14; New York, NY, 1893 1883.7 p39
Mauch, Gottlieb 14; New York, NY, 1893 1883.7 p47
Mauch, Gustav 1; New York, NY, 1893 1883.7 p39
Mauch, Gustav 1; New York, NY, 1893 1883.7 p47
Mauch, Johann 52; New York, NY, 1900 8425.16 p31
Mauch, Karl 19; Baltimore, 1906 8425.16 p31
Mauch, Karl 40; Baltimore, 1906 8425.16 p31
Mauch, Karl 38; New York, NY, 1893 1883.7 p39
Mauch, Karl 38; New York, NY, 1893 1883.7 p47
Mauch, Karoline 13; Baltimore, 1906 8425.16 p31
Mauch, Katharina 14; Baltimore, 1906 8425.16 p31
Mauch, Louise 38; New York, NY, 1893 1883.7 p39
Mauch, Louise 38; New York, NY, 1893 1883.7 p47
Mauch, Lydia 4; Baltimore, 1906 8425.16 p31
Mauch, Maria 11; New York, NY, 1893 1883.7 p39
Mauch, Maria 11; New York, NY, 1893 1883.7 p47
Mauch, Maria 18; New York, NY, 1900 8425.16 p31
Maucher, Amelia Henlean SEE Maucher, Charles
Maucher, Charles; Philadelphia, 1863 8513.31 p411
Wife:Amelia Henlean
Mauchey, Celestine 36; America, 1843 778.6 p236
Mauclair, Ferdinand 35; America, 1843 778.6 p236
Maud, Grace; America, 1747 1220.12 p540
Maud, Henry L. 29; Ontario, 1871 1823.21 p217
Maudet, Francois 20; Quebec, 1657 9221.17 p363
Maudin, Thomas; Annapolis, MD, 1722 1220.12 p540
Mauer, Anna Rempel SEE Mauer, Nikolaus
Mauer, Heinrich; Valdivia, Chile, 1851 1192.4 p51
With wife & 4 children
Mauer, Katharina Eckert SEE Mauer, Nikolaus
Mauer, Nikolaus; Brazil, 1886 5475.1 p432
Wife:Katharina Eckert
Mother:Anna Rempel
Son:Peter
Mauer, Peter SEE Mauer, Nikolaus
Maufay, Pierre 23; Quebec, 1652 9221.17 p262
Maufils, Pierre 21; Quebec, 1652 9221.17 p262
Maufre, Salvatore; Louisiana, 1874 4981.45 p133
Mauger, Miss; Wilmington, DE, 1800-1899 9228.50 p450
Mauger, Alfred James; Wisconsin, 1970-1979 9228.50 p449
With wife
Mauger, Charlotte 42; Quebec, 1649 9221.17 p216
Mauger, Charlotte 42; Quebec, 1649 9221.17 p216
Mauger, Charlotte 42; Quebec, 1649 9221.17 p216
Mauger, Daniel; New York, NY, 1800-1830 9228.50 p449
Mauger, Frederick; Quebec, 1903 9228.50 p447
Mauger, George; New England, n.d. 9228.50 p469
Mauger, J.W.G.; New York, NY, 1897 9228.50 p37
Mauger, John Wallace Goodenough; New York, NY, 1897 9228.50 p446
Mauger, Louise 36; Quebec, 1636 9221.17 p55
Mauger, Nicholas; Connecticut, 1659 9228.50 p472
Mauger, Richard; Quebec, 1765-1801 9228.50 p447
Mauger, Thomas; Marblehead, MA, 1674-1724 9228.50 p447
Mauger, Thomas James; New York, 1861 9228.50 p450
Maugham, Jane; America, 1764 1220.12 p540
Maugham, Mary; Annapolis, MD, 1725 1220.12 p540
Maughan, John; Barbados, 1705 1220.12 p540
Maughan, Joseph; America, 1743 1220.12 p540
Maughan, Joseph; Colorado, 1881 1029.59 p59
Maughan, Joseph; Colorado, 1903 1029.59 p59
Maugher, Edmund; Boston, 1768 1642 p39
Maugin, Edouard 33; America, 1842 778.6 p236
Maugin, John; Ohio, 1809-1852 4511.35 p33
Maugot, Daniel; Quebec, 1643 9221.17 p132
Maujean, Pierre; Quebec, 1655 9221.17 p327
Maul, Friedrich; America, 1879 5475.1 p44
Maul, John Batzer; Ohio, 1809-1852 4511.35 p33
Maul, Margarethe 33; Pennsylvania, 1898 5475.1 p46
Maul, Robert; America, 1848 2526.43 p175
Maulam, Matthew; America, 1768 1220.12 p540
Maule, Charles; North Carolina, 1842 1088.45 p21
Mauley, William; America, 1775 1220.12 p566
Maulin, J. 28; America, 1846 778.6 p236
Maulkin, John, Jr.; America, 1749 1220.12 p540
Maumert, Jean 21; America, 1840 778.6 p236
Maund, John; America, 1765 1220.12 p540
Maund, Nicholas; America, 1761 1220.12 p540
Maund, Rebecca; America, 1700 1220.12 p540
Maund, Rebecca; America, 1701 1220.12 p540
Maunder, Henry; America, 1774 1220.12 p540
Maunder, Mary; America, 1738 1220.12 p540
Maunder, Samuel; America, 1754 1220.12 p540
Maunders, Thomas; Barbados, 1690 1220.12 p540
Maundrell, Francis; America, 1754 1220.12 p540
Maundry, Humphrey; America, 1685 1220.12 p540
Maundry, William; Barbados, 1715 1220.12 p540
Maune, Gustav Adolf; Kansas, 1917-1918 2054.10 p48
Maunoury, Cardeau; Quebec, 1653 9221.17 p277
Maunoury, Jean; Quebec, 1639 9221.17 p91
Maupertuis, . . .; Quebec, 1635 9221.17 p47
Maurant, Fidel; Ohio, 1809-1852 4511.35 p33
Maurat, Fidel; Ohio, 1809-1852 4511.35 p33
Maurel deSte-Helene, Paul; Quebec, 1665 2314.30 p167
Maurel deSte-Helene, Paul; Quebec, 1665 2314.30 p191
Maurer, Anna Pistorius SEE Maurer, Johann
Maurer, Anna 3 SEE Maurer, Johann Adam
Maurer, Anna Pistorius 30 SEE Maurer, Johann Adam
Maurer, Anna Mag. 32; New York, NY, 1864 8425.62 p196
Maurer, Benedict 48; New Castle, DE, 1817-1818 90.20 p153
Maurer, Conrad; Illinois, 1851 6079.1 p9
Maurer, Elisabeth Klein 37 SEE Maurer, Peter
Maurer, Frederick; Ohio, 1809-1852 4511.35 p33
Maurer, Friedrich; America, 1851 5475.1 p30
Maurer, Georg 16; Port uncertain, 1847 778.6 p236
Maurer, Johann; America, 1836 5475.1 p65
Wife:Anna Pistorius
With child 5
With child 1
Maurer, Johann 7 SEE Maurer, Johann Adam
Maurer, Johann; Brazil, 1856 5475.1 p510
Maurer, Johann Adam; America, 1838 5475.1 p387
Wife:Anna Pistorius
Daughter:Anna
Son:Johann
Maurer, Johann Friedrich Carl; America, 1847 179.55 p19
Maurer, Johann Philipp; Brazil, 1856 5475.1 p510
Maurer, Johanne; America, 1868 7919.3 p534
Maurer, John J.; Illinois, 1834-1900 6020.5 p132
Maurer, Karl Ludwig; America, 1848 5475.1 p28
Maurer, Katharina; America, 1883 5475.1 p413
Maurer, Nikolaus; America, 1846 5475.1 p408
Maurer, Peter 50; America, 1846 5475.1 p408
Wife:Elisabeth Klein 37
With 9 children
Maurer, Peter; Illinois, 1852 6079.1 p9
Maurer, Ph. Ludwig; America, 1889 5475.1 p60
Maurer, Philippine; America, 1862 5475.1 p523
Maurer, Pierre 24; New Orleans, 1848 778.6 p236
Maurer, Sophie Katharina; America, 1880 5475.1 p55
With son
Maurice, Charles 21; Ontario, 1871 1823.21 p217
Maurice, Germain 22; Galveston, TX, 1844 3967.10 p374
Maurin, Mrs. 60; America, 1844 778.6 p236
Maurin, August 31; America, 1843 778.6 p236
Maurizi, Giulio; Illinois, 1930 121.35 p101
Maury, Louis; Louisiana, 1874 4981.45 p133
Maus, Christoph 5 SEE Maus, Georg
Maus, Friedrich 24 SEE Maus, Georg
Maus, Georg 17 SEE Maus, Georg
Maus, Georg 53; America, 1831 2526.43 p175
With wife 44
Son:Kilian 9
Son:Christoph 5
Son:Karl 6
Son:Jakob 14
With stepchild 28
Son:Friedrich 24
Son:Georg 17
Maus, Jakob 14 SEE Maus, Georg
Maus, Jean 16; New Orleans, 1846 778.6 p236
Maus, Johann; America, 1857 5475.1 p321
Maus, Karl 6 SEE Maus, Georg
Maus, Kilian 9 SEE Maus, Georg
Maus, Maria; America, 1854 2526.43 p175
Maus, Peter; America, 1857 5475.1 p308
Maus, Peter; America, 1869 5475.1 p321
Maus, Theodor; America, 1871 5475.1 p321
Mausden, David; Philadelphia, 1778 8529.30 p4A
Mausdon, David; Philadelphia, 1778 8529.30 p4A
Mausier, Francois 45; Texas, 1848 778.6 p236
Mausser, John; Illinois, 1858-1861 6020.5 p132
Mausset, J. L. 28; America, 1841 778.6 p236
Maussler, Georg Ernst 19; New York, 1883 2526.43 p175
Maussler, Karl Heinrich; New York, 1888 2526.43 p175
Maussuy, A. 25; America, 1845 778.6 p236
Mautes, Johann 48; Brazil, 1828 5475.1 p233
M'Autiff, Elizabeth; Toronto, 1844 2910.35 p114
Mautz, Christiane 20; Chile, 1852 1192.4 p52
Mautz, G. A.; Chile, 1852 1192.4 p52
Mautz, Maria 23; Chile, 1852 1192.4 p52
Mauvitzsow, Solomon F.; Louisiana, 1836-1840 4981.45 p213
Mavec, Gust 16; Minnesota, 1925 2769.54 p1382
Mavec, Joe 17; Minnesota, 1925 2769.54 p1382
Mavec, John 19; Minnesota, 1925 2769.54 p1382
Mavec, Tony 22; Minnesota, 1925 2769.54 p1382
Maverick, Abigail SEE Maverick, John
Maverick, Antipas SEE Maverick, John
Maverick, Elias SEE Maverick, John
Maverick, John SEE Maverick, John
Maverick, John; Massachusetts, 1630 117.5 p152
Wife:Mary
Daughter:Abigail
Son:Elias
Son:Moses
Son:Antipas
Daughter:Mary
Son:John
Maverick, Mary SEE Maverick, John
Maverick, Mary SEE Maverick, John
Maverick, Moses SEE Maverick, John
Mavity, John 38; Ontario, 1871 1823.17 p99
Maw, John 38; Ontario, 1871 1823.17 p99
Mawheny, Samuel; Boston, 1775 8529.30 p4A
Mawhiney, William 70; Ontario, 1871 1823.21 p217
Mawhinney, Robert 35; Ontario, 1871 1823.21 p217
Mawhiny, John 40; Ontario, 1871 1823.21 p217
Mawl, Robert; America, 1751 1220.12 p540
Mawlam, Henry 58; Ontario, 1871 1823.17 p99
Mawson, Thomas; America, 1682 1220.12 p540
Max, Johann; America, 1800-1899 5475.1 p288
Max, Sulivan; Louisiana, 1874 4981.45 p133
Maxem, Maria 43; America, 1856 5475.1 p278
Maxey, Benjamin; America, 1736 1220.12 p540
Maxey, John; Virginia, 1734 1220.12 p540
Maxey, Joseph; Illinois, 1858-1861 6020.5 p132
Maxfield, Freelove SEE Maxfield, Patrick
Maxfield, James E. 44; Ontario, 1871 1823.21 p217
Maxfield, John; America, 1749 1220.12 p540
Maxfield, Mary; America, 1754 1220.12 p540
Maxfield, Patience SEE Maxfield, Timothy, Jr.
Maxfield, Patrick; Massachusetts, 1772 1642 p85
Wife:Freelove
Maxfield, Timothy, Jr.; Massachusetts, 1736 1642 p85
Wife:Patience
Maxwell, Alexander; Ohio, 1825 3580.20 p33
Maxwell, Alexander; Ohio, 1825 6020.12 p21
Maxwell, Emily 22; Quebec, 1870 8364.32 p25
Maxwell, Ethel; America, 1890-1965 9228.50 p450
Maxwell, Hugh; Massachusetts, 1732 1642 p63
Maxwell, Hugh; Massachusetts, 1733 1642 p117
Son:Hugh, Jr.
Maxwell, Hugh; Philadelphia, 1855-1860 7074.20 p133
Maxwell, Hugh, Jr. SEE Maxwell, Hugh
Maxwell, James 28; New York, NY, 1825 6178.50 p77
Maxwell, James; Ohio, 1838 3580.20 p33
Maxwell, James; Ohio, 1838 6020.12 p21
Maxwell, Janet 23; New York, NY, 1835 5024.1 p137
Maxwell, John; America, 1756 1220.12 p540
Maxwell, John 23; New York, NY, 1835 5024.1 p137
Maxwell, John 22; Ontario, 1871 1823.17 p99

306 FOR A COMPLETE EXPLANATION OF ENTRY, SEE "HOW TO READ A CITATION" SECTION

Maxwell, John 45; Ontario, 1871 ***1823.21*** *p217*
Maxwell, Mary 28; Ontario, 1871 ***1823.21*** *p217*
Maxwell, Michael 42; Ontario, 1871 ***1823.17*** *p99*
Maxwell, Robt. 18; North Carolina, 1774 ***1422.10*** *p56*
Maxwell, Thomas; America, 1771 ***1220.12*** *p540*
Maxwell, Thomas 45; Ontario, 1871 ***1823.21*** *p217*
Maxwell, William 61; Ontario, 1871 ***1823.17*** *p99*
May, Alexander; North Carolina, 1792-1862 ***1088.45*** *p21*
May, Ann; America, 1765 ***1220.12*** *p540*
May, Anna Eva; America, 1844 ***2526.42*** *p109*
With child
May, Anne Rebecca; New York, 1853 ***8513.31*** *p421*
May, Calvin L.; Ohio, 1878 ***3580.20*** *p33*
May, Calvin L.; Ohio, 1878 ***6020.12*** *p21*
May, Catherine; America, 1733 ***1220.12*** *p540*
May, Celius; America, 1766 ***1220.12*** *p540*
May, Charles; America, 1739 ***1220.12*** *p540*
May, Eleanor; America, 1764 ***1220.12*** *p540*
May, Elizabeth; America, 1742 ***1220.12*** *p540*
May, George; Virginia, 1768 ***1220.12*** *p540*
May, Henry; America, 1770 ***1220.12*** *p540*
May, Henry; Annapolis, MD, 1719 ***1220.12*** *p540*
May, James; America, 1754 ***1220.12*** *p540*
May, James; America, 1771 ***1220.12*** *p541*
May, James 31; Ontario, 1871 ***1823.21*** *p217*
May, James 40; Ontario, 1871 ***1823.21*** *p217*
May, James 50; Ontario, 1871 ***1823.17*** *p100*
May, James 78; Ontario, 1871 ***1823.21*** *p217*
May, Jane; Died enroute, 1734 ***1220.12*** *p541*
May, Jean 30; Quebec, 1657 ***9221.17*** *p363*
May, Johannes; Carolina, 1841 ***170.15*** *p36*
With wife & 3 children
May, John; America, 1740 ***1220.12*** *p541*
May, John; America, 1747 ***1220.12*** *p541*
May, John; America, 1753 ***1220.12*** *p541*
May, John; America, 1758 ***1220.12*** *p541*
May, John; America, 1764 ***1220.12*** *p541*
May, John; America, 1768 ***1220.12*** *p541*
May, John; America, 1772 ***1220.12*** *p541*
May, John; Barbados, 1679 ***1220.12*** *p541*
May, John; Maryland, 1722 ***1220.12*** *p541*
May, John; Nova Scotia, 1784 ***7105*** *p25*
May, John 48; Ontario, 1871 ***1823.21*** *p217*
May, Joseph; Detroit, 1929 ***1640.55*** *p116*
May, Karl; America, 1845 ***2526.43*** *p175*
*Wife:*Luise Dauth
May, L. 24; America, 1848 ***778.6*** *p236*
May, Luise Dauth *SEE* May, Karl
May, Maria; America, 1882 ***5475.1*** *p228*
May, Mary; America, 1748 ***1220.12*** *p541*
May, Peter; America, 1700 ***1220.12*** *p541*
May, Peter; America, 1772 ***1220.12*** *p541*
May, Richard; America, 1725 ***1220.12*** *p541*
May, Richard; America, 1749 ***1220.12*** *p541*
May, Richard; America, 1750 ***1220.12*** *p541*
May, Richard; America, 1767 ***1220.12*** *p541*
May, Richard 66; Ontario, 1871 ***1823.17*** *p100*
May, Robert; Barbados, 1692 ***1220.12*** *p541*
May, Samuel; America, 1727 ***1220.12*** *p541*
May, Samuel; America, 1764 ***1220.12*** *p541*
May, Samuel Richard 45; Ontario, 1871 ***1823.21*** *p217*
May, Sarah; Virginia, 1721 ***1220.12*** *p541*
May, Sarah; Virginia, 1758 ***1220.12*** *p541*
May, Sarah; Virginia, 1767 ***1220.12*** *p541*
May, Stephen; Ohio, 1809-1852 ***4511.35*** *p33*
May, Susan 24; Ontario, 1871 ***1823.21*** *p217*
May, Susannah; America, 1771 ***1220.12*** *p541*
May, Thomas; America, 1727 ***1220.12*** *p541*
May, Thomas; America, 1774 ***1220.12*** *p541*
May, Thomas; Barbados, 1669 ***1220.12*** *p541*
May, Thomas; Louisiana, 1874 ***4981.45*** *p133*
May, Thos.; Louisiana, 1836-1840 ***4981.45*** *p213*
May, William; America, 1700 ***1220.12*** *p541*
May, William; America, 1724 ***1220.12*** *p541*
May, William; America, 1734 ***1220.12*** *p541*
May, William; America, 1737 ***1220.12*** *p541*
May, William; America, 1763 ***1220.12*** *p541*
May, William; Barbados, 1694 ***1220.12*** *p541*
May, William; Newfoundland, 1818 ***9228.50*** *p450*
May, William 40; Ontario, 1871 ***1823.21*** *p217*
May, William; Virginia, 1767 ***1220.12*** *p541*
May, William; Virginia, 1772 ***1220.12*** *p541*
Mayam, Robert 21; Annapolis, MD, 1721 ***1220.12*** *p541*
Mayance, Jorde; Louisiana, 1874-1875 ***4981.45*** *p30*
Mayaul, Casimir 35; New Orleans, 1848 ***778.6*** *p236*
Maybank, Elizabeth; America, 1748 ***1220.12*** *p541*
Maybrick, Charles; America, 1775 ***1220.12*** *p541*
Mayby, Ambrose; America, 1745 ***1220.12*** *p523*
Maychin, Ann; America, 1739 ***1220.12*** *p523*
Maycock, Thomas; Marston's Wharf, 1782 ***8529.30*** *p14*
Maycock, William; America, 1773 ***1220.12*** *p541*
Mayd, Ann; Barbados, 1665 ***1220.12*** *p524*
Mayel, Jean 44; Texas, 1848 ***778.6*** *p236*
Mayer, Ms. 30; America, 1844 ***778.6*** *p236*
Mayer, Abe; Texas, 1881 ***3435.45*** *p36*
Mayer, Abram R.; North Carolina, 1792-1862 ***1088.45*** *p21*
Mayer, Alphred 19; New Orleans, 1848 ***778.6*** *p236*
Mayer, Anna 18; New Orleans, 1848 ***778.6*** *p236*
Mayer, Augusta 32; New York, NY, 1894 ***6512.1*** *p181*
Mayer, Caroline 40; America, 1847 ***778.6*** *p236*
Mayer, Dorothee Louise; America, 1868 ***7420.1*** *p272*
Mayer, Elisabeth 14; New York, NY, 1898 ***7951.13*** *p44*
Mayer, Estelle 17; Missouri, 1848 ***778.6*** *p236*
Mayer, Eugene 26; New Orleans, 1848 ***778.6*** *p236*
Mayer, Ferdinand; America, 1877-1899 ***5475.1*** *p435*
Mayer, Franz 11; New York, NY, 1898 ***7951.13*** *p44*
Mayer, Franziska; America, 1872 ***5475.1*** *p160*
Mayer, Georg; Wisconsin, 1886 ***6795.8*** *p100*
Mayer, Gertrude Weber *SEE* Mayer, John
Mayer, Gottlieb; America, 1873 ***179.55*** *p19*
Mayer, Helena 4 *SEE* Mayer, Johann
Mayer, Helena *SEE* Mayer, Judith Aron
Mayer, Ignaz Joseph; Venezuela, 1843 ***3899.5*** *p544*
Mayer, Isaac, Jr.; North Carolina, 1852 ***1088.45*** *p21*
Mayer, Jacob 23; Mississippi, 1845 ***778.6*** *p237*
Mayer, Jarolim S.; Chicago, 1867-1910 ***2853.20*** *p406*
Mayer, Jean G.; Louisiana, 1836-1841 ***4981.45*** *p209*
Mayer, Johann 31; America, 1872 ***5475.1*** *p41*
*Wife:*Katharina Best 30
*Daughter:*Helena 4
*Son:*Ludwig 8
Mayer, Johann 35; New York, NY, 1898 ***7951.13*** *p44*
Mayer, Johanna 33; New York, NY, 1898 ***7951.13*** *p44*
Mayer, John; America, 1767 ***1220.12*** *p574*
Mayer, John 28; America, 1840 ***778.6*** *p237*
Mayer, John; Philadelphia, 1862 ***8513.31*** *p411*
*Wife:*Gertrude Weber
Mayer, John Phillip; Ohio, 1809-1852 ***4511.35*** *p33*
Mayer, Joseph 2; New York, NY, 1898 ***7951.13*** *p44*
Mayer, Joseph; North Carolina, 1852 ***1088.45*** *p21*
Mayer, Joseph; Venezuela, 1843 ***3899.5*** *p544*
Mayer, Josephine 57; New Orleans, 1848 ***778.6*** *p237*
Mayer, Judith 37; America, 1843 ***778.6*** *p237*
Mayer, Judith; Ohio, 1894 ***5475.1*** *p162*
*Child:*Helena
*Child:*Leopold
*Child:*Simon
Mayer, Katharina; America, 1852 ***5475.1*** *p56*
Mayer, Katharina; America, 1887 ***5475.1*** *p25*
Mayer, Katharina Best 30 *SEE* Mayer, Johann
Mayer, Laverture 32; New Orleans, 1848 ***778.6*** *p237*
Mayer, Leonhard; America, 1888 ***179.55*** *p19*
Mayer, Leonhard Karl; America, 1887 ***179.55*** *p19*
Mayer, Leopold *SEE* Mayer, Judith Aron
Mayer, Ludwig 8 *SEE* Mayer, Johann
Mayer, M. R. 35; America, 1846 ***778.6*** *p237*
Mayer, Magdalena 3; New York, NY, 1898 ***7951.13*** *p44*
Mayer, Marcus; Kansas, 1917-1918 ***2054.10*** *p48*
Mayer, Maria Emilie; New York, NY, 1884 ***7420.1*** *p344*
Mayer, Marie 40; Missouri, 1848 ***778.6*** *p237*
Mayer, Max; Texas, 1892 ***3435.45*** *p36*
Mayer, Michael 10; New York, NY, 1898 ***7951.13*** *p44*
Mayer, Petrine 3 months; New York, NY, 1898 ***7951.13*** *p44*
Mayer, Simon *SEE* Mayer, Judith Aron
Mayer, Theodor; America, 1868 ***5475.1*** *p543*
Mayer, Walburga; Venezuela, 1843 ***3899.5*** *p544*
Mayer, William; Virginia, 1772 ***1220.12*** *p574*
Mayer, William Karl Christian; Iowa, 1914 ***1211.15*** *p17*
Mayerhoeffer, Joseph; Kansas, 1917-1918 ***1826.15*** *p81*
Mayers, John; Marston's Wharf, 1782 ***8529.30*** *p14*
Mayes, George; America, 1742 ***1220.12*** *p542*
Mayes, James; America, 1766 ***1220.12*** *p542*
Mayes, Philip; America, 1733 ***1220.12*** *p542*
Mayes, Robert; Virginia, 1723 ***1220.12*** *p542*
Mayfield, Jane; Barbados or Jamaica, 1697 ***1220.12*** *p541*
Mayfield, William; America, 1774 ***1220.12*** *p541*
Mayham, James; America, 1747 ***1220.12*** *p541*
Mayham, Thomas; Maryland or Virginia, 1738 ***1220.12*** *p542*
Mayham, William; America, 1702 ***1220.12*** *p542*
Mayhan, James; America, 1739 ***1220.12*** *p541*
Mayhen, Ellen 16; Ontario, 1871 ***1823.17*** *p100*
Mayhew, Edmund; America, 1773 ***1220.12*** *p542*
Mayhew, John; America, 1727 ***1220.12*** *p542*
Mayhew, John; America, 1773 ***1220.12*** *p542*
Mayhew, Nathaniel; Maryland or Virginia, 1731 ***1220.12*** *p542*
Mayhew, Philip; America, 1741 ***1220.12*** *p542*
Mayhew, Susan; America, 1749 ***1220.12*** *p542*
Mayhood, George 65; Ontario, 1871 ***1823.21*** *p217*
Mayhoone, Margaret; Boston, 1661 ***1642*** *p9*
Maylard, Phillip 38; Ontario, 1871 ***1823.21*** *p217*
Mayle, William; America, 1716 ***1220.12*** *p525*
Maylin, Daniel; America, 1773 ***1220.12*** *p542*
Maylin, Dominique 23; New Orleans, 1845 ***778.6*** *p237*
Maylin, M. 20; America, 1843 ***778.6*** *p237*
Maynard, Anne; Maryland, 1725 ***1220.12*** *p542*
Maynard, Charles Gregory; America, 1774 ***1220.12*** *p542*
Maynard, James; America, 1685 ***1220.12*** *p542*
Maynard, Jane; America, 1743 ***1220.12*** *p542*
Maynard, John 9; New Hampshire, 1825 ***9228.50*** *p450*
Maynard, Samuel; America, 1753 ***1220.12*** *p542*
Maynard, Thomas; America, 1720 ***1220.12*** *p542*
Mayne, Henry; America, 1761 ***1220.12*** *p524*
Mayne, James; America, 1770 ***1220.12*** *p524*
Mayne, John; America, 1740 ***1220.12*** *p524*
Mayne, John; America, 1753 ***1220.12*** *p524*
Mayne, Matthew 42; Ontario, 1871 ***1823.21*** *p217*
Mayne, Richard 45; Ontario, 1871 ***1823.21*** *p217*
Mayne, Samll.; Jamestown, VA, 1633 ***1658.20*** *p211*
Mayne, Stephen; America, 1753 ***1220.12*** *p524*
Mayne, Thomas; Virginia, 1738 ***1220.12*** *p525*
Mayne, William; Maryland, 1740 ***1220.12*** *p525*
Maynes, James; Boston, 1737 ***1642*** *p26*
Maynes, John 38; Ontario, 1871 ***1823.21*** *p217*
Maynes, Margaret 20; Ontario, 1871 ***1823.21*** *p217*
Mayo, Robert; Maryland, 1720 ***1220.12*** *p542*
Mayo, Rosamund; Maryland or Virginia, 1731 ***1220.12*** *p542*
Mayo, Thomas; America, 1762 ***1220.12*** *p542*
Mayo, Thomas; America, 1764 ***1220.12*** *p542*
Mayo, William 40; Ontario, 1871 ***1823.21*** *p218*
Mayo, William 42; Ontario, 1871 ***1823.21*** *p218*
Mayoh, Edward; South Carolina, 1678 ***9228.50*** *p450*
*Relative:*Robert
Mayoh, Robert *SEE* Mayoh, Edward
Mayol, Jean-Baptiste 3; New Orleans, 1848 ***778.6*** *p237*
Mayol, Joseph Felix 12; New Orleans, 1848 ***778.6*** *p237*
Mayol, Mathieu 37; New Orleans, 1848 ***778.6*** *p237*
Mayor, John; Illinois, 1856 ***6079.1*** *p9*
Mayor, Michel 20; Ontario, 1871 ***1823.21*** *p218*
Mayoris, William; America, 1755 ***1220.12*** *p542*
Mayot, Mrs. 35; America, 1840 ***778.6*** *p237*
Mayot, L. 37; America, 1840 ***778.6*** *p237*
Maypowder, Anthony; Maryland, 1673 ***1236.25*** *p48*
Mays, Elizabeth; America, 1745 ***1220.12*** *p542*
Mays, Minvielle 17; New Orleans, 1848 ***778.6*** *p237*
Mayse, Richard; America, 1754 ***1220.12*** *p542*
Mayson, Hannah; America, 1768 ***1220.12*** *p536*
Mazac, Karel J.; Chicago, 1892 ***2853.20*** *p309*
Mazanec, Matej; St. Paul, MN, 1862 ***2853.20*** *p277*
Mazanek, Vaclav; Wisconsin, 1851 ***2853.20*** *p303*
Mazanka, Stanislaw; Detroit, 1930 ***1640.60*** *p83*
Maze, Benjamin; America, 1757 ***1220.12*** *p542*
Mazet, Francois; Illinois, 1852 ***6079.1*** *p9*
Mazey, Thomas; America, 1766 ***1220.12*** *p542*
Maziarz, Szczepan 18; New York, NY, 1912 ***8355.1*** *p15*
Mazie, John; Marston's Wharf, 1782 ***8529.30*** *p14*
Mazlech, John; Detroit, 1929-1930 ***6214.5*** *p67*
Mazoire, Raimond 55; Texas, 1848 ***778.6*** *p237*
Mazotta, Frank; Louisiana, 1874-1875 ***4981.45*** *p30*
Mazur, Felix 38; New York, NY, 1920 ***930.50*** *p49*
Mazur, Jadwiga; Detroit, 1929 ***1640.55*** *p115*
Mazur, John; Detroit, 1929-1930 ***6214.5*** *p67*
Mazur, Stanley; Detroit, 1930 ***1640.60*** *p83*
Mazure, Benjamin; Salem, MA, 1650-1675 ***9228.50*** *p440*
Mazure, George; Massachusetts, n.d. ***9228.50*** *p439*
Mazure, Jane; Died enroute, 1677 ***9228.50*** *p440*
Mazure, Joseph; Salem, MA, 1655-1680 ***9228.50*** *p440*
Mazure, Laurence; Salem, MA, 1646-1670 ***9228.50*** *p439*
Mazure, Martin; Massachusetts, 1652-1709 ***9228.50*** *p440*
Mazurie, Jean Jacques; Philadelphia, 1764-1864 ***9228.50*** *p445*
With family
Mazury, Benjamin; Salem, MA, 1650-1675 ***9228.50*** *p440*
Mazury, George; Massachusetts, n.d. ***9228.50*** *p439*
Mazury, Jane; Died enroute, 1677 ***9228.50*** *p440*
Mazury, Joseph; Salem, MA, 1655-1680 ***9228.50*** *p440*
Mazury, Laurence; Salem, MA, 1646-1670 ***9228.50*** *p439*
Mazury, Martin; Massachusetts, 1652-1709 ***9228.50*** *p440*
Mazurye, Joseph; Salem, MA, 1679 ***9228.50*** *p445*
Mazzarinni, Riccardo; Miami, 1935 ***4984.12*** *p39*
Mazzel, Johann 29; Galveston, TX, 1846 ***3967.10*** *p378*
M'Cabe, Bernard; Toronto, 1844 ***2910.35*** *p115*
McAchin, Angus 36; Ontario, 1871 ***1823.21*** *p218*
McAdam, John 34; Ontario, 1871 ***1823.21*** *p218*
McAdams, David 70; Ontario, 1871 ***1823.21*** *p218*
McAdams, Robert 28; Ontario, 1871 ***1823.17*** *p100*
McAfee, Robert; Ohio, 1809-1852 ***4511.35*** *p33*
McAffee, Samuel; North Carolina, 1819 ***1088.45*** *p21*
McAffrey, John; St. John, N.B., 1847 ***2978.15*** *p41*
McAinsh, John 38; Ontario, 1871 ***1823.21*** *p218*
McAlan, James; Jamaica, 1778 ***8529.30*** *p13A*
McAlaster, Mary 64; North Carolina, 1774 ***1422.10*** *p62*
McAleer, Margaret 32; St. John, N.B., 1834 ***6469.7*** *p6*
McAleer, Patt; Jamaica, 1778 ***8529.30*** *p13A*

McAlester, Cathn 30; North Carolina, 1774 ***1422.10 p62***
McAlester, Cathn. 30; North Carolina, 1774 ***1422.10 p58***
McAlester, Coll 24; North Carolina, 1774 ***1422.10 p61***
McAlester, Coll 24; North Carolina, 1774 ***1422.10 p63***
McAlester, Mary 31; North Carolina, 1774 ***1422.10 p61***
McAlester, Mary 31; North Carolina, 1774 ***1422.10 p63***
McAlester, Mary 64; North Carolina, 1774 ***1422.10 p58***
McAlgar, John; St. John, N.B., 1842 ***2978.20 p7***
McAlgar, Nancy; St. John, N.B., 1842 ***2978.20 p7***
McAlier, James; Jamaica, 1778 ***8529.30 p13A***
McAlier, Patt; Jamaica, 1778 ***8529.30 p13A***
McAlister, Alexander 64; Ontario, 1871 ***1823.21 p218***
McAlister, Archibald 72; Ontario, 1871 ***1823.21 p218***
McAlister, Donald 68; Ontario, 1871 ***1823.21 p218***
McAllan, A. E.; Montreal, 1922 ***4514.4 p32***
McAllister, Angus; Maine, 1763 ***9228.50 p609***
McAllister, Catharine McInnish *SEE* McAllister, Charles
McAllister, Charles; New York, 1739 ***8277.31 p115***
*Wife:*Catharine McInnish
*Son:*John
*Daughter:*Margaret
McAllister, Duncan; New York, 1739 ***8277.31 p116***
*Wife:*Effie Keith
McAllister, Effie Keith *SEE* McAllister, Duncan
McAllister, Florence; New York, 1738 ***8277.31 p115***
McAllister, John; New Hampshire, 1739-1783 ***9228.50 p607***
McAllister, John *SEE* McAllister, Charles
McAllister, Malcolm 55; Ontario, 1871 ***1823.17 p100***
McAllister, Margaret *SEE* McAllister, Charles
McAllum, Cathn 30; North Carolina, 1774 ***1422.10 p62***
McAllum, Cathn. 30; North Carolina, 1774 ***1422.10 p58***
McAllum, Duncan 22; North Carolina, 1774 ***1422.10 p58***
McAllum, Duncan 22; North Carolina, 1774 ***1422.10 p62***
McAlmoyl, Robert; Illinois, 1865 ***6079.1 p9***
McAlpin, Alexander 55; Ontario, 1871 ***1823.17 p100***
McAlpin, Barbaria 47; Ontario, 1871 ***1823.17 p100***
McAlpin, Daniel 45; Ontario, 1871 ***1823.17 p100***
McAlpin, Donald 56; Ontario, 1871 ***1823.21 p218***
McAlpin, Donald 61; Ontario, 1871 ***1823.21 p218***
McAlpin, Donald 61; Ontario, 1871 ***1823.21 p218***
McAlpin, Duncan 32; Ontario, 1871 ***1823.21 p218***
McAlpin, Duncan 64; Ontario, 1871 ***1823.21 p218***
McAlpin, Hugh 79; Ontario, 1871 ***1823.21 p218***
McAlpin, Isabella 48; Ontario, 1871 ***1823.21 p218***
McAlpin, James 35; Ontario, 1871 ***1823.21 p218***
McAlpin, James 75; Ontario, 1871 ***1823.21 p218***
McAlpin, John 29; Ontario, 1871 ***1823.21 p218***
McAlpin, John 39; Ontario, 1871 ***1823.21 p218***
McAlpin, Jonas 20; Ontario, 1871 ***1823.21 p218***
McAlpin, Macolm 68; Ontario, 1871 ***1823.21 p218***
McAlpin, Malcolm 42; Ontario, 1871 ***1823.21 p218***
McAlpin, Peter; North Carolina, 1835-1837 ***1088.45 p21***
McAlpine, Archd 68; Ontario, 1871 ***1823.21 p218***
McAlpine, Archibald 30; Ontario, 1871 ***1823.21 p218***
McAlpine, Donald 63; Ontario, 1871 ***1823.21 p218***
McAlpine, Dugald; New York, 1738 ***8277.31 p116***
*Wife:*Mary McPhaden
McAlpine, Dugald 35; Ontario, 1871 ***1823.21 p218***
McAlpine, John 68; Ontario, 1871 ***1823.21 p218***
McAlpine, Mary McPhaden *SEE* McAlpine, Dugald
McAlpine, Robert; New York, 1740 ***8277.31 p116***
McAlpine, Robert 58; Ontario, 1871 ***1823.21 p218***
McAlpine, William 61; Ontario, 1871 ***1823.17 p100***
McAnara, Anna 20; Ontario, 1871 ***1823.21 p218***
McAnartney, Michl; St. John, N.B., 1848 ***2978.15 p40***
McAnartney, Scott; St. John, N.B., 1848 ***2978.15 p40***
McAnartney, Wm.; St. John, N.B., 1848 ***2978.15 p40***
McAndless, James 45; Ontario, 1871 ***1823.21 p218***
McAndless, William 56; Ontario, 1871 ***1823.21 p218***
McAndrew, John 54; Ontario, 1871 ***1823.21 p218***
McAndrew, Peter 40; Ontario, 1871 ***1823.17 p100***
McAndrews, Martin; Washington, 1881 ***2770.40 p135***
McAneeley, John; New Orleans, 1851 ***7242.30 p148***
McAngels, William; Washington, 1884 ***2770.40 p192***
McAngus, Donald 36; Ontario, 1871 ***1823.21 p218***
McAran, P.; California, 1868 ***1131.61 p90***
McArdel, John; Washington, 1881 ***2770.40 p135***
McArdell, Catherine 100; Ontario, 1871 ***1823.21 p218***
McArdell, Henry; America, 1750 ***1220.12 p517***
McArdle, Bernard; Toronto, 1844 ***2910.35 p113***
McArdle, P.; California, 1868 ***1131.61 p89***
M'Caree, Patrick; New Orleans, 1851 ***7242.30 p148***
McArnnely, Thomas 46; Ontario, 1871 ***1823.17 p100***
McArter, Alexander John; America, 1756 ***1220.12 p517***
McArter, Janet 35; Ontario, 1871 ***1823.17 p100***
McArter, Peter 61; Ontario, 1871 ***1823.21 p219***
McArthur, Alexander *SEE* McArthur, Neil
McArthur, Alexander; New York, 1738 ***8277.31 p116***
*Wife:*Catherine
*Child:*Duncan
*Child:*Catharine
*Child:*Florence
*Child:*Donald
*Child:*John
McArthur, Alexander; New York, 1739 ***8277.31 p116***
*Wife:*Catharine Gillies
*Child:*Flora
*Child:*Duncan
McArthur, Alexander 55; Ontario, 1871 ***1823.21 p219***
McArthur, Alise 32; Ontario, 1871 ***1823.21 p219***
McArthur, Andrew 47; South Carolina, 1812 ***3476.30 p12***
McArthur, Angus 40; Ontario, 1871 ***1823.21 p219***
McArthur, Ann; North Carolina, 1774 ***1422.10 p62***
McArthur, Ann 38; North Carolina, 1774 ***1422.10 p58***
McArthur, Anna *SEE* McArthur, Duncan
McArthur, Anna McQuin *SEE* McArthur, Duncan
McArthur, Archibald 52; Ontario, 1871 ***1823.17 p100***
McArthur, Catharine *SEE* McArthur, Alexander
McArthur, Catharine Gillies *SEE* McArthur, Alexander
McArthur, Catherine *SEE* McArthur, Alexander
McArthur, Cathn 58; North Carolina, 1774 ***1422.10 p62***
McArthur, Cathn.; North Carolina, 1774 ***1422.10 p58***
McArthur, Charles *SEE* McArthur, Patrick
McArthur, Chas 28; Ontario, 1871 ***1823.21 p219***
McArthur, Chirst 52; North Carolina, 1774 ***1422.10 p62***
McArthur, Chirst. 52; North Carolina, 1774 ***1422.10 p57***
McArthur, Christian *SEE* McArthur, Neil
McArthur, Christian *SEE* McArthur, John
McArthur, Colin *SEE* McArthur, Patrick
McArthur, Colin 67; Ontario, 1871 ***1823.21 p219***
McArthur, Donald *SEE* McArthur, Alexander
McArthur, Donald 30; Ontario, 1871 ***1823.21 p219***
McArthur, Donald 68; Ontario, 1871 ***1823.21 p219***
McArthur, Donald 69; Ontario, 1871 ***1823.21 p219***
McArthur, Duncan; Cape Fear, NC,, 1754 ***1422.10 p62***
McArthur, Duncan *SEE* McArthur, Alexander
McArthur, Duncan; New York, 1738 ***8277.31 p116***
*Wife:*Anna McQuin
*Child:*Margaret
*Child:*John
*Child:*Anna
*Child:*Mary
McArthur, Duncan *SEE* McArthur, Alexander
McArthur, Duncan 51; Ontario, 1871 ***1823.21 p219***
McArthur, Elizabeth 60; Ontario, 1871 ***1823.21 p219***
McArthur, Flora *SEE* McArthur, Alexander
McArthur, Florence *SEE* McArthur, Alexander
McArthur, Isabel; New York, 1740 ***8277.31 p115***
McArthur, James 40; Ontario, 1871 ***1823.21 p219***
McArthur, James 42; Ontario, 1871 ***1823.21 p219***
McArthur, James 50; Ontario, 1871 ***1823.21 p219***
McArthur, Janet *SEE* McArthur, Patrick
McArthur, Jean; North Carolina, 1774 ***1422.10 p62***
McArthur, Jean 20; North Carolina, 1774 ***1422.10 p58***
McArthur, Jenet 40; Ontario, 1871 ***1823.21 p219***
McArthur, John *SEE* McArthur, Alexander
McArthur, John *SEE* McArthur, Duncan
McArthur, John *SEE* McArthur, Neil
McArthur, John; New York, 1740 ***8277.31 p116***
*Son:*Neil
*Daughter:*Christian
McArthur, John; North Carolina, 1774 ***1422.10 p62***
McArthur, John 16; North Carolina, 1774 ***1422.10 p58***
McArthur, John 28; North Carolina, 1774 ***1422.10 p58***
McArthur, John 45; Ontario, 1871 ***1823.21 p219***
McArthur, John 45; Ontario, 1871 ***1823.21 p219***
McArthur, John 56; Ontario, 1871 ***1823.17 p100***
McArthur, Lachlin 33; Ontario, 1871 ***1823.21 p219***
McArthur, Margaret *SEE* McArthur, Duncan
McArthur, Mary *SEE* McArthur, Duncan
McArthur, Mary Campbell *SEE* McArthur, Neil
McArthur, Mary McDougall *SEE* McArthur, Patrick
McArthur, Neil; New York, 1738 ***8277.31 p116***
*Wife:*Mary Campbell
*Child:*Christian
*Child:*John
*Child:*Alexander
McArthur, Neil *SEE* McArthur, John
McArthur, Patrick; New York, 1738 ***8277.31 p116***
*Wife:*Mary McDougall
*Child:*Charles
*Child:*Janet
*Child:*Colin
McArthur, Peter 58; North Carolina, 1774 ***1422.10 p57***
McArthur, Peter 58; North Carolina, 1774 ***1422.10 p62***
McArthur, Robert 31; Ontario, 1871 ***1823.17 p100***
McArthur, Sarah 40; Ontario, 1871 ***1823.21 p219***
McArty, Dennis; St. John, N.B., 1848 ***2978.15 p39***
McArty, Mic; St. John, N.B., 1847 ***2978.15 p40***
McArty, Tim; St. John, N.B., 1848 ***2978.15 p39***
McArty, Tim; St. John, N.B., 1848 ***2978.15 p39***
McArty, Tim; St. John, N.B., 1848 ***2978.15 p40***
McArty, Wm.; St. John, N.B., 1847 ***2978.15 p35***
McAsh, Janet 80; Ontario, 1871 ***1823.17 p100***
McAtire, Jane 55; Ontario, 1871 ***1823.17 p100***
McAulay, Catherine 25; Ontario, 1871 ***1823.21 p219***
McAulay, Ewen 37; Ontario, 1871 ***1823.17 p100***
McAulay, Samuel; Louisiana, 1833 ***7710.1 p151***
McAuley, Alexander 22; Ontario, 1871 ***1823.21 p219***
McAuley, Finley 27; Ontario, 1871 ***1823.21 p219***
McAuley, James 56; Ontario, 1871 ***1823.17 p100***
McAuley, Neil 60; Ontario, 1871 ***1823.21 p219***
M'Cauley, William; Boston, 1770 ***1642 p43***
McAuliff, Jeremiah 45; Ontario, 1871 ***1823.21 p219***
McAuliff, Mickel 38; Ontario, 1871 ***1823.21 p219***
McAuliffe, Jane 46; Ontario, 1871 ***1823.21 p219***
McAuslan, Andrew 62; Ontario, 1871 ***1823.17 p100***
McAusland, Andrew 73; Ontario, 1871 ***1823.21 p219***
McAuslin, Robert 65; Ontario, 1871 ***1823.17 p100***
McAuslin, William 41; Ontario, 1871 ***1823.17 p100***
McAvey, Martin 57; Ontario, 1871 ***1823.21 p219***
McAvoy, Ellen; Philadelphia, 1851 ***8513.31 p319***
McAvoy, John 45; Ontario, 1871 ***1823.17 p100***
McAvoy, Mary 87; Ontario, 1871 ***1823.21 p219***
McAvoy, Wm; Toronto, 1844 ***2910.35 p114***
McAway, Stephen; America, 1769 ***1220.12 p517***
McAway, William; America, 1767 ***1220.12 p517***
McBain, Alexandre; Illinois, 1857 ***6079.1 p9***
McBain, Peter 55; Ontario, 1871 ***1823.21 p219***
McBain, Sarah 32; Ontario, 1871 ***1823.21 p219***
McBain, William 57; Ontario, 1871 ***1823.21 p219***
McBane, Robert 41; Ontario, 1871 ***1823.21 p220***
McBean, Alexander 50; Ontario, 1871 ***1823.21 p220***
McBean, Alexander; Philadelphia, 1856 ***7074.20 p133***
McBean, Angus 45; Ontario, 1871 ***1823.17 p100***
McBean, Angus 54; Ontario, 1871 ***1823.21 p220***
McBean, Duncan 36; Ontario, 1871 ***1823.17 p101***
McBean, Duncan 78; Ontario, 1871 ***1823.21 p220***
McBean, Jannet 34; Ontario, 1871 ***1823.21 p220***
McBean, John 52; Ontario, 1871 ***1823.17 p101***
McBean, John 63; Ontario, 1871 ***1823.17 p101***
McBean, Lewis 49; Ontario, 1871 ***1823.17 p101***
McBean, Peter 47; Ontario, 1871 ***1823.17 p101***
McBean, William 63; Ontario, 1871 ***1823.21 p220***
McBeath, John 37; North Carolina, 1774 ***1422.10 p58***
McBee, William; America, 1732 ***1220.12 p517***
McBeth, Anne G. 44; Ontario, 1871 ***1823.21 p220***
McBeth, David 30; Ontario, 1871 ***1823.17 p101***
McBeth, James 27; Ontario, 1871 ***1823.17 p101***
McBeth, Jannet 62; Ontario, 1871 ***1823.21 p220***
McBeth, Roderich 43; Ontario, 1871 ***1823.17 p101***
McBey, William 61; St. John, N.B., 1834 ***6469.7 p6***
McBlair, John; America, 1739 ***1220.12 p517***
McBrid, Robert 50; Ontario, 1871 ***1823.21 p220***
McBride, Alexr. 22; North Carolina, 1775 ***1422.10 p57***
McBride, Archd. 7; North Carolina, 1775 ***1422.10 p57***
McBride, Christine 76; Ontario, 1871 ***1823.21 p220***
McBride, Duncan 34; Ontario, 1871 ***1823.21 p220***
McBride, Eliz 5; North Carolina, 1775 ***1422.10 p57***
McBride, James 48; Ontario, 1871 ***1823.21 p220***
McBride, James 29; St. John, N.B., 1834 ***6469.7 p6***
McBride, Jane 17; Quebec, 1870 ***8364.32 p25***
McBride, Jane 30; St. John, N.B., 1834 ***6469.7 p6***
McBride, Janet 39; North Carolina, 1775 ***1422.10 p57***
McBride, Jas. 38; North Carolina, 1775 ***1422.10 p57***
McBride, Jenny 4; North Carolina, 1775 ***1422.10 p57***
McBride, John 49; Ontario, 1871 ***1823.21 p220***
McBride, Malcolm 68; Ontario, 1871 ***1823.21 p220***
McBride, Moses; Ohio, 1809-1852 ***4511.35 p33***
McBride, Neil 77; Ontario, 1871 ***1823.21 p220***
McBride, Patrick 50; Ontario, 1871 ***1823.21 p220***
McBride, Robert 59; Ontario, 1871 ***1823.17 p101***
McBride, Samuel 52; Ontario, 1871 ***1823.21 p220***
McBride, Thomas; Toronto, 1844 ***2910.35 p115***
McBride, William 53; Ontario, 1871 ***1823.21 p220***
McBride, William 76; Ontario, 1871 ***1823.17 p101***
McBrine, Robert 49; Ontario, 1871 ***1823.17 p101***
McBrine, Sarah 48; Ontario, 1871 ***1823.17 p101***
McBroom, Thos 46; Ontario, 1871 ***1823.21 p220***
McBryan, John; Jamaica, 1778 ***8529.30 p13A***
McCabe, Brigget 80; Ontario, 1871 ***1823.17 p101***
McCabe, Charles 40; Ontario, 1871 ***1823.17 p101***
McCabe, Edward; Newport, RI, 1831 ***3274.55 p26***
McCabe, Francis; Toronto, 1844 ***2910.35 p113***
McCabe, George 45; Ontario, 1871 ***1823.17 p101***
McCabe, James 43; Ontario, 1871 ***1823.17 p101***
McCabe, John; Louisiana, 1874-1875 ***4981.45 p30***
McCabe, John 35; Ontario, 1871 ***1823.17 p101***
McCabe, John R. 32; Ohio, 1880 ***4879.40 p257***
McCabe, Lawrence; Toronto, 1844 ***2910.35 p113***
McCabe, Mary 12; Quebec, 1870 ***8364.32 p25***
McCabe, Miles 41; Ontario, 1871 ***1823.21 p220***
McCabe, Sarah; America, 1764 ***1220.12 p517***
McCabe, William; America, 1764 ***1220.12 p517***
McCabe, William 45; Ontario, 1871 ***1823.17 p101***
McCadden, Gosford P.; Ohio, 1809-1852 ***4511.35 p33***
McCadden, John; Ohio, 1809-1852 ***4511.35 p33***

McCafferty, Robert; North Carolina, 1855 ***1088.45*** *p21*
McCaffery, Hugh 66; Ontario, 1871 ***1823.21*** *p220*
McCaffrey, Elizabeth 50; Ontario, 1871 ***1823.21*** *p220*
McCaffrey, Jane A. 18; Ontario, 1871 ***1823.21*** *p220*
McCaherin, John 25; South Carolina, 1812 ***3476.30*** *p12*
McCahil, Owen; America, 1746 ***1220.12*** *p517*
McCaib, John; America, 1768 ***1220.12*** *p517*
McCain, Charles 17; Ontario, 1871 ***1823.21*** *p220*
McCall, David 42; Ontario, 1871 ***1823.17*** *p101*
McCall, Duncan 58; Ontario, 1871 ***1823.21*** *p220*
McCall, Duncan 70; Ontario, 1871 ***1823.21*** *p220*
McCall, Duncan 88; Ontario, 1871 ***1823.21*** *p220*
McCall, Elizabeth; America, 1760 ***1220.12*** *p517*
McCall, Ellen 53; Ontario, 1871 ***1823.21*** *p220*
McCall, Hugh 52; Ontario, 1871 ***1823.17*** *p101*
McCall, James; America, 1765 ***1220.12*** *p517*
McCall, John 24; Ontario, 1871 ***1823.21*** *p220*
McCall, Ronald 44; Ontario, 1871 ***1823.17*** *p101*
McCall, Samuel 74; Ontario, 1871 ***1823.21*** *p220*
McCalla, Ann; South Carolina, 1824 ***6155.4*** *p18*
McCalla, Robert; South Carolina, 1824 ***6155.4*** *p18*
McCalla, Samuel; South Carolina, 1808 ***6155.4*** *p18*
McCallam, Duncan 58; Ontario, 1871 ***1823.21*** *p220*
McCalley, Richard; Jamaica, 1776 ***8529.30*** *p13A*
McCallister, John; Illinois, 1855 ***6079.1*** *p9*
McCallor, Archibald; New York, 1738 ***8277.31*** *p118*
*Wife:*Janet Reed
McCallor, Janet Reed *SEE* McCallor, Archibald
McCallum, Alex 29; Ontario, 1871 ***1823.21*** *p220*
McCallum, Alexander 60; Ontario, 1871 ***1823.21*** *p220*
McCallum, Arch 70; Ontario, 1871 ***1823.21*** *p220*
McCallum, Archd 54; Ontario, 1871 ***1823.21*** *p220*
McCallum, Archy 48; Ontario, 1871 ***1823.21*** *p220*
McCallum, Arthur 85; Ontario, 1871 ***1823.21*** *p220*
McCallum, Barbara 64; Ontario, 1871 ***1823.21*** *p220*
McCallum, Barney 18; Ontario, 1871 ***1823.21*** *p221*
McCallum, Catherine 30; Ontario, 1871 ***1823.21*** *p221*
McCallum, Collin 46; Ontario, 1871 ***1823.17*** *p101*
McCallum, Donald 20; Ontario, 1871 ***1823.21*** *p221*
McCallum, Donald 77; Ontario, 1871 ***1823.21*** *p221*
McCallum, Duncan 30; North Carolina, 1775 ***1422.10*** *p60*
McCallum, Duncan 48; Ontario, 1871 ***1823.21*** *p221*
McCallum, Duncan 50; Ontario, 1871 ***1823.17*** *p101*
McCallum, Duncan Wilfred; Iowa, 1923 ***1211.15*** *p17*
McCallum, Edward 45; Ontario, 1871 ***1823.21*** *p221*
McCallum, Edward 61; Ontario, 1871 ***1823.21*** *p221*
McCallum, Florence 72; Ontario, 1871 ***1823.21*** *p221*
McCallum, Hugh 53; Ontario, 1871 ***1823.21*** *p221*
McCallum, James 29; Ontario, 1871 ***1823.17*** *p101*
McCallum, James 54; Ontario, 1871 ***1823.21*** *p221*
McCallum, John; Ontario, 1871 ***1823.21*** *p221*
McCallum, John 48; Ontario, 1871 ***1823.21*** *p221*
McCallum, John 70; Ontario, 1871 ***1823.21*** *p221*
McCallum, John 77; Ontario, 1871 ***1823.21*** *p221*
McCallum, John; Philadelphia, 1777 ***8529.30*** *p7A*
McCallum, Metta 6; Ontario, 1871 ***1823.21*** *p221*
McCallum, Neal 45; Ontario, 1871 ***1823.21*** *p221*
McCallum, Neale 46; Ontario, 1871 ***1823.21*** *p221*
McCallum, Patrick 22; New York, NY, 1835 ***5024.1*** *p137*
McCallum, Peter 45; Ontario, 1871 ***1823.21*** *p221*
McCallum, Peter 51; Ontario, 1871 ***1823.21*** *p221*
McCallum, Peter 59; Ontario, 1871 ***1823.17*** *p101*
McCalum, Peter 58; Ontario, 1871 ***1823.17*** *p101*
McCalumn, John 63; Ontario, 1871 ***1823.21*** *p221*
McCalvey, Mary; Pennsylvania, 1856 ***8513.31*** *p417*
McCalvy, Robert 37; Ontario, 1871 ***1823.21*** *p221*
McCan, Sarah; America, 1763 ***1220.12*** *p517*
McCandra, Patrick 50; Ontario, 1871 ***1823.17*** *p101*
McCann, Annie 9; Quebec, 1870 ***8364.32*** *p25*
McCann, Elen 19; Ontario, 1871 ***1823.21*** *p221*
McCann, Frank; Detroit, 1929 ***1640.55*** *p114*
McCann, James 30; Ontario, 1871 ***1823.21*** *p221*
McCann, James; South Carolina, 1833 ***6155.4*** *p18*
McCann, John 15; Ontario, 1871 ***1823.21*** *p221*
McCann, John 33; Ontario, 1871 ***1823.17*** *p101*
McCann, Pat; St. John, N.B., 1847 ***2978.15*** *p37*
McCann, Pat; St. John, N.B., 1847 ***2978.15*** *p41*
McCann, Patt; New Orleans, 1850 ***7242.30*** *p148*
McCann, Peter 49; Ontario, 1871 ***1823.21*** *p221*
McCann, Phillip 45; Ontario, 1871 ***1823.21*** *p221*
McCann, Wm. J.; Ohio, 1878 ***3580.20*** *p32*
McCann, Wm. J.; Ohio, 1878 ***6020.12*** *p13*
McCannon, Frederick; America, 1770 ***1220.12*** *p517*
McCannon, James; New Orleans, 1851 ***7242.30*** *p148*
McCanny, Biddy 20; St. John, N.B., 1834 ***6469.7*** *p5*
McCape, John; America, 1763 ***1220.12*** *p517*
McCardle, John; Washington, 1884 ***2770.40*** *p192*
McCarley, Charles; America, 1733 ***1220.12*** *p517*
McCarroll, Thomas; North Carolina, 1858 ***1088.45*** *p21*
McCarroll, William; North Carolina, 1835 ***1088.45*** *p21*
McCarrou, Owen; St. John, N.B., 1848 ***2978.15*** *p38*
McCart, Daniel 36; Ontario, 1871 ***1823.17*** *p101*
McCart, Daniel 62; Ontario, 1871 ***1823.17*** *p101*
McCarter, Mary; America, 1751 ***1220.12*** *p517*
McCarter, Mary; America, 1772 ***1220.12*** *p517*
McCarter, Robert 25; Ontario, 1871 ***1823.17*** *p101*
McCarter, Sarah; South Carolina, 1813 ***3208.30*** *p19*
McCarter, Sarah; South Carolina, 1813 ***3208.30*** *p32*
McCartey, William; Boston, 1768 ***1642*** *p39*
McCarthelme, William; Massachusetts, 1736 ***1642*** *p74*
McCartheo, E. 30; Ontario, 1871 ***1823.21*** *p221*
McCarthey, Eliza; Boston, 1741 ***1642*** *p45*
McCarthey, William 60; Ontario, 1871 ***1823.21*** *p221*
McCarthy, C. 60; Ontario, 1871 ***1823.21*** *p221*
McCarthy, Catherine 16; Ontario, 1871 ***1823.21*** *p221*
McCarthy, Charles; Philadelphia, 1836 ***5720.10*** *p379*
McCarthy, Cornelius; Kansas, 1889 ***1447.20*** *p63*
McCarthy, Daniel; Boston, 1759 ***1642*** *p47*
McCarthy, Daniel; Boston, 1765 ***1642*** *p34*
McCarthy, Daniel; Massachusetts, 1747 ***1642*** *p105*
*Wife:*Mary
McCarthy, Edward 60; Ontario, 1871 ***1823.21*** *p221*
McCarthy, Ellen 22; Ontario, 1871 ***1823.21*** *p221*
McCarthy, James 35; Ontario, 1871 ***1823.21*** *p221*
McCarthy, Jeremiah; Toronto, 1844 ***2910.35*** *p113*
McCarthy, John 35; Ontario, 1871 ***1823.17*** *p101*
McCarthy, John; Toronto, 1844 ***2910.35*** *p112*
McCarthy, John; Toronto, 1844 ***2910.35*** *p112*
McCarthy, John; Toronto, 1844 ***2910.35*** *p112*
McCarthy, Mrs. John; Toronto, 1844 ***2910.35*** *p112*
McCarthy, Julia D. 53; Michigan, 1880 ***4491.39*** *p19*
McCarthy, Katharine; Boston, 1740 ***1642*** *p45*
McCarthy, Maggie 20; Ontario, 1871 ***1823.21*** *p221*
McCarthy, Mary *SEE* McCarthy, Daniel
McCarthy, Michael 48; Ontario, 1871 ***1823.21*** *p221*
McCarthy, Michael; Toronto, 1844 ***2910.35*** *p113*
McCarthy, Michael; Toronto, 1844 ***2910.35*** *p116*
McCarthy, Owen; Toronto, 1844 ***2910.35*** *p116*
McCarthy, Patrick 36; New York, NY, 1894 ***6512.1*** *p228*
McCarthy, Patrick 44; Ontario, 1871 ***1823.21*** *p221*
McCarthy, Thomas; Boston, 1747 ***1642*** *p29*
McCarthy, Tim 26; St. Johns, N.F., 1811 ***1053.20*** *p20*
McCarthy, Timothy; Toronto, 1844 ***2910.35*** *p112*
McCarthy, William; Newbury, MA, 1729 ***1642*** *p75*
McCarthy, William; Newbury, MA, 1729 ***1642*** *p75*
McCartie, Sallie; Boston, 1768 ***1642*** *p39*
McCartney, Arthur; Virginia, 1736 ***1220.12*** *p517*
McCartney, George; America, 1771 ***1220.12*** *p517*
McCartney, George; Toronto, 1844 ***2910.35*** *p116*
McCartney, James; America, 1740 ***1220.12*** *p517*
McCartney, Patrick; America, 1760 ***1220.12*** *p517*
McCartney, Patrick; America, 1765 ***1220.12*** *p517*
McCartney, William; Miami, 1935 ***4984.12*** *p39*
McCarty, Mr.; Boston, 1765 ***1642*** *p34*
McCarty, Ann 45; Ontario, 1871 ***1823.21*** *p222*
McCarty, Austin; Boston, 1766 ***1642*** *p37*
McCarty, Brigget 24; Ontario, 1871 ***1823.21*** *p222*
McCarty, Catherine; New Brunswick, 1842 ***2978.20*** *p8*
McCarty, Charles; Illinois, 1864 ***6079.1*** *p9*
McCarty, Charles; Philadelphia, 1836 ***5720.10*** *p379*
McCarty, Corneilius 37; Ontario, 1871 ***1823.21*** *p222*
McCarty, Daniel; Boston, 1742 ***1642*** *p45*
McCarty, Daniel; Boston, 1743 ***1642*** *p45*
McCarty, Darby; America, 1764 ***1220.12*** *p517*
McCarty, David; America, 1755 ***1220.12*** *p517*
McCarty, Dennis; Boston, 1766 ***1642*** *p37*
McCarty, Dennis; Illinois, 1858-1861 ***6020.5*** *p132*
McCarty, Dennis; Massachusetts, 1757 ***1642*** *p66*
McCarty, Dennis 61; Ontario, 1871 ***1823.21*** *p222*
McCarty, Edward; Boston, 1768 ***1642*** *p39*
McCarty, Esther; Massachusetts, 1720 ***1642*** *p66*
McCarty, Florence; Boston, 1760 ***1642*** *p48*
McCarty, Frank; Ohio, 1840-1897 ***8365.35*** *p17*
McCarty, James; America, 1773 ***1220.12*** *p517*
McCarty, James; Boston, 1749 ***1642*** *p46*
McCarty, James; North Carolina, 1792-1862 ***1088.45*** *p21*
McCarty, James 40; Ontario, 1871 ***1823.21*** *p222*
McCarty, James 42; Ontario, 1871 ***1823.21*** *p222*
McCarty, James A.; Philadelphia, 1868 ***7074.20*** *p133*
McCarty, Jeramiah 30; Ontario, 1871 ***1823.21*** *p222*
McCarty, Jeremiah 33; Ontario, 1871 ***1823.17*** *p102*
McCarty, John; Boston, 1738 ***1642*** *p44*
McCarty, John; Boston, 1833 ***3274.56*** *p98*
McCarty, John; Louisiana, 1836-1841 ***4981.45*** *p209*
McCarty, John; New Brunswick, 1842 ***2978.20*** *p8*
McCarty, John; Ohio, 1809-1852 ***4511.35*** *p33*
McCarty, John 40; Ontario, 1871 ***1823.21*** *p222*
McCarty, John 41; Ontario, 1871 ***1823.17*** *p102*
McCarty, Margaret; Massachusetts, 1708 ***1642*** *p86*
McCarty, Mary; Annapolis, MD, 1731 ***1220.12*** *p517*
McCarty, Mary 22; Ontario, 1871 ***1823.21*** *p222*
McCarty, Mary; Rappahannock, VA, 1741 ***1220.12*** *p517*
McCarty, Michael; America, 1771 ***1220.12*** *p517*
McCarty, Michael; Boston, 1738 ***1642*** *p44*
McCarty, Michael 42; Ontario, 1871 ***1823.21*** *p222*
McCarty, Pat 40; Ontario, 1871 ***1823.21*** *p222*
McCarty, Rebecca; Salem, MA, 1716 ***1642*** *p78*
McCarty, Robert 33; Ontario, 1871 ***1823.21*** *p222*
McCarty, Terence; Boston, 1768 ***1642*** *p39*
McCarty, Thomas; Boston, 1766 ***1642*** *p37*
McCarty, Timothy; Ohio, 1836 ***3580.20*** *p32*
McCarty, Timothy; Ohio, 1836 ***6020.12*** *p13*
McCasey, William; America, 1767 ***1220.12*** *p517*
McCash, Adam; Philadelphia, 1778 ***8529.30*** *p4A*
McCathany, Mary 26; Ohio, 1880 ***4879.40*** *p260*
McCaughen, Hugh; North Carolina, 1841 ***1088.45*** *p21*
McCaul, Daniel; Toronto, 1844 ***2910.35*** *p113*
McCaulay, Alex 72; Ontario, 1871 ***1823.21*** *p222*
McCaulay, James; Toronto, 1844 ***2910.35*** *p113*
McCaulem, James 43; Ontario, 1871 ***1823.21*** *p222*
McCauley, Bridget; Pennsylvania, 1858 ***8513.31*** *p307*
McCauley, Catherine 45; Ontario, 1871 ***1823.21*** *p222*
McCauley, Eliza 50; Michigan, 1880 ***4491.33*** *p15*
McCauley, James 61; Michigan, 1880 ***4491.33*** *p15*
McCauley, James; Oregon, 1941 ***9157.47*** *p3*
McCauley, M.; Washington, 1886 ***2770.40*** *p195*
McCaullum, Daniel 54; Ontario, 1871 ***1823.21*** *p222*
McCaullum, Hugh 60; Ontario, 1871 ***1823.21*** *p222*
McCaullum, Neil 52; Ontario, 1871 ***1823.21*** *p222*
McCauly, Hugh 10; Ontario, 1871 ***1823.21*** *p222*
McCauly, Mary 19; Ontario, 1871 ***1823.21*** *p222*
McCavner, William; Philadelphia, 1856 ***5720.10*** *p379*
McCaw, John 30; Ontario, 1871 ***1823.21*** *p222*
McCaw, Margaret 54; Ontario, 1871 ***1823.21*** *p222*
McCaw, William 65; Ontario, 1871 ***1823.21*** *p222*
McCawley, Richard; Jamaica, 1776 ***8529.30*** *p13A*
McCay, William; Louisiana, 1855 ***7710.1*** *p156*
McCay, William; St. John, N.B., 1848 ***7710.1*** *p155*
McCennis, Christina 60; Ontario, 1871 ***1823.21*** *p222*
McChasney, Hamilton 41; Ontario, 1871 ***1823.21*** *p222*
McCherry, Edward; America, 1763 ***1220.12*** *p517*
McChesney, Alexr 62; Ontario, 1871 ***1823.17*** *p102*
McChesney, Elen 24; Ontario, 1871 ***1823.21*** *p222*
McChesney, Hugh 56; Ontario, 1871 ***1823.21*** *p222*
McChesney, William 62; Ontario, 1871 ***1823.21*** *p222*
McClah, Robert 20; Ontario, 1871 ***1823.21*** *p222*
McClain, Jane; Annapolis, MD, 1726 ***1220.12*** *p522*
McClain, Margrit 79; Ontario, 1871 ***1823.21*** *p222*
McClain, Peter 58; Ontario, 1871 ***1823.21*** *p222*
McClanan, Hugh; New England, 1745 ***1642*** *p28*
McClare, Maximillian; Ohio, 1809-1852 ***4511.35*** *p33*
McClaren, Lewis 17; Ontario, 1871 ***1823.17*** *p102*
McClarty, Sarah 21; Ontario, 1871 ***1823.21*** *p222*
McClary, James 21; Ontario, 1871 ***1823.21*** *p222*
McClary, Oliver 53; Ontario, 1871 ***1823.21*** *p222*
McClary, William 39; Ontario, 1871 ***1823.21*** *p222*
McClaughlan, Thomas; North Carolina, 1855 ***1088.45*** *p21*
McClean, Arch 40; Ontario, 1871 ***1823.17*** *p102*
McClean, James 27; New York, NY, 1894 ***6512.1*** *p186*
McClean, James 40; Ontario, 1871 ***1823.21*** *p222*
McClear, Hugh 79; Ontario, 1871 ***1823.17*** *p102*
McCleary, Daniel; Massachusetts, 1739 ***1642*** *p74*
McClelan, Elizabeth; Boston, 1773 ***1642*** *p49*
McClellan, Catherine 53; Ontario, 1871 ***1823.21*** *p222*
McClellan, Hugh 62; Ontario, 1871 ***1823.21*** *p222*
McClellan, Jane 20; Ontario, 1871 ***1823.21*** *p223*
McClellan, Mary 37; Ontario, 1871 ***1823.17*** *p102*
McClellan, Mary 47; Ontario, 1871 ***1823.17*** *p102*
McClellan, Susan 61; Ontario, 1871 ***1823.17*** *p102*
McClelland, John; America, 1764 ***1220.12*** *p518*
McClelland, Nathaniel; Ohio, 1825 ***3580.20*** *p32*
McClelland, Nathaniel; Ohio, 1825 ***6020.12*** *p13*
McClelland, Robert; Ohio, 1825 ***3580.20*** *p32*
McClelland, Robert; Ohio, 1825 ***6020.12*** *p13*
McClemens, Richard 32; Ontario, 1871 ***1823.17*** *p102*
McClena, Ann; Ontario, 1871 ***1823.21*** *p223*
McClenen, George 27; Ontario, 1871 ***1823.21*** *p223*
McClennan, Sadie B.; Manitoba, 1909 ***9228.50*** *p18A*
McCline, James 56; Ontario, 1871 ***1823.17*** *p102*
McClintock, James; Philadelphia, 1846 ***5720.10*** *p379*
McClocklin, Annie 22; Ontario, 1871 ***1823.21*** *p223*
McClocklin, Louisa 18; Ontario, 1858 ***9228.50*** *p450*
McClonnie, Mr.; British Columbia, 1910 ***2897.7*** *p9*
McClonnie, C. 3; Quebec, 1910 ***2897.7*** *p9*
McClonnie, Catherine 2; Quebec, 1910 ***2897.7*** *p9*
McClonnie, Cathrine 40; Quebec, 1910 ***2897.7*** *p9*
McClonnie, John 12; Quebec, 1910 ***2897.7*** *p9*
McClonnie, M. 11; Quebec, 1910 ***2897.7*** *p9*
McClonnie, R. 6; Quebec, 1910 ***2897.7*** *p9*
McCloskey, Edward 58; Ontario, 1871 ***1823.21*** *p223*
McCloud, Alexander; Marston's Wharf, 1782 ***8529.30*** *p14*
McCloud, Anna 7; Quebec, 1870 ***8364.32*** *p25*
McCloud, Catharine Graham *SEE* McCloud, Donald

McCloud, Donald; New York, 1738 ***8277.31*** *p116*
*Wife:*Catharine Graham
*Son:*Duncan
*Son:*John
McCloud, Duncan *SEE* McCloud, Donald
McCloud, Elizabeth; America, 1764 ***1220.12*** *p518*
McCloud, Isabella 59; Ontario, 1871 ***1823.21*** *p223*
McCloud, James; America, 1770 ***1220.12*** *p518*
McCloud, John; America, 1727 ***1220.12*** *p518*
McCloud, John *SEE* William 49; McCloud, Donald
McCloud, John 28; Ontario, 1871 ***1823.17*** *p102*
McCloud, Thos 37; Ontario, 1871 ***1823.21*** *p223*
McCloud, William; America, 1772 ***1220.12*** *p518*
McClough, Daniel; America, 1775 ***1220.12*** *p518*
McClow, Daniel; America, 1739 ***1220.12*** *p518*
McClure, Andrew 41; Ontario, 1871 ***1823.17*** *p102*
McClure, Donald 45; Ontario, 1871 ***1823.17*** *p102*
McClurg, John 45; Ontario, 1871 ***1823.21*** *p223*
McClury, John 40; Ontario, 1871 ***1823.21*** *p223*
McClymont, Alex 21; Ontario, 1871 ***1823.21*** *p223*
McCody, Martha Le Brocq *SEE* McCody, Philip
McCody, Philip; Beverly, MA, 1698 ***9228.50*** *p159*
*Wife:*Martha Le Brocq
McCody, Philip, Family; America, 1600-1699 ***9228.50*** *p337*
McCole, Alexander 4; North Carolina, 1775 ***1422.10*** *p60*
McCole, Ann 3; North Carolina, 1775 ***1422.10*** *p60*
McCole, Ann 38; North Carolina, 1775 ***1422.10*** *p60*
McCole, Christian 2; North Carolina, 1775 ***1422.10*** *p60*
McCole, Christian 10; North Carolina, 1775 ***1422.10*** *p60*
McCole, Christian 35; North Carolina, 1775 ***1422.10*** *p60*
McCole, Christian 40; North Carolina, 1775 ***1422.10*** *p60*
McCole, David 30; North Carolina, 1775 ***1422.10*** *p60*
McCole, Donald 12; North Carolina, 1775 ***1422.10*** *p60*
McCole, Donald 34; North Carolina, 1775 ***1422.10*** *p60*
McCole, Dougald 8; North Carolina, 1775 ***1422.10*** *p60*
McCole, Dugal 38; North Carolina, 1775 ***1422.10*** *p59*
McCole, Dugald 20; North Carolina, 1775 ***1422.10*** *p60*
McCole, Duncan 21; North Carolina, 1775 ***1422.10*** *p60*
McCole, Duncan 35; North Carolina, 1775 ***1422.10*** *p60*
McCole, Duncan 45; North Carolina, 1775 ***1422.10*** *p60*
McCole, Evan 6; North Carolina, 1775 ***1422.10*** *p60*
McCole, Johan; Philadelphia, 1861 ***8513.31*** *p296*
McCole, John 16; North Carolina, 1775 ***1422.10*** *p60*
McCole, John 49; North Carolina, 1775 ***1422.10*** *p60*
McCole, Katherine 2; North Carolina, 1775 ***1422.10*** *p60*
McCole, Katherine 3; North Carolina, 1775 ***1422.10*** *p60*
McCole, Katherine 40; North Carolina, 1775 ***1422.10*** *p60*
McCole, Marget 10; North Carolina, 1775 ***1422.10*** *p59*
McCole, Mary 8; North Carolina, 1775 ***1422.10*** *p59*
McCole, Mary 18; North Carolina, 1775 ***1422.10*** *p60*
McCole, Mildred 6; North Carolina, 1775 ***1422.10*** *p60*
McCole, Mildred 40; North Carolina, 1775 ***1422.10*** *p60*
McCole, Samuel 15; North Carolina, 1775 ***1422.10*** *p60*
McCole, Sarah 2; North Carolina, 1775 ***1422.10*** *p59*
McCole, Sarah 15; North Carolina, 1775 ***1422.10*** *p60*
McColl, Alexander 54; Ontario, 1871 ***1823.21*** *p223*
McColl, Angus B. 36; Ontario, 1871 ***1823.21*** *p223*
McColl, Catharin 49; Ontario, 1871 ***1823.21*** *p223*
McColl, Catherine 48; Ontario, 1871 ***1823.21*** *p223*
McColl, Donald 77; Ontario, 1871 ***1823.21*** *p223*
McColl, Duncan 35; Ontario, 1871 ***1823.21*** *p223*
McColl, Duncan 78; Ontario, 1871 ***1823.21*** *p223*
McColl, Hugh; North Carolina, 1792-1862 ***1088.45*** *p21*
McColl, John; North Carolina, 1808 ***1088.45*** *p21*
McColl, John; Ontario, 1871 ***1823.17*** *p102*
McColl, John 32; Ontario, 1871 ***1823.21*** *p223*
McColl, Nancy 74; Ontario, 1871 ***1823.17*** *p102*
McColl, Neil 31; Ontario, 1871 ***1823.17*** *p102*
McColl, Neil 85; Ontario, 1871 ***1823.21*** *p223*
McColl, Patrick Henry 28; Ontario, 1871 ***1823.17*** *p102*
McColl, Samuel 71; Ontario, 1871 ***1823.21*** *p223*
McCollam, Catherine 65; Ontario, 1871 ***1823.21*** *p223*
McColley, Andrew; Potomac, 1731 ***1220.12*** *p517*
McColley, Ann 2; St. John, N.B., 1834 ***6469.7*** *p4*
McColley, James 30; St. John, N.B., 1834 ***6469.7*** *p4*
McColley, Jane 3; St. John, N.B., 1834 ***6469.7*** *p4*
McColley, Mary 30; St. John, N.B., 1834 ***6469.7*** *p4*
McCollie, John; America, 1753 ***1220.12*** *p517*
McCollum, Alexander 37; Ontario, 1871 ***1823.17*** *p102*
McCollum, Alexander 46; Ontario, 1871 ***1823.17*** *p102*
McCollum, Angus 45; Ontario, 1871 ***1823.21*** *p223*
McCollum, Angus 59; Ontario, 1871 ***1823.21*** *p223*
McCollum, Ann 50; Ontario, 1871 ***1823.21*** *p223*
McCollum, Charles 49; Ontario, 1871 ***1823.21*** *p223*
McCollum, Donald 58; Ontario, 1871 ***1823.21*** *p223*
McCollum, Dugald 40; Ontario, 1871 ***1823.21*** *p223*
McCollum, Florry; New York, 1740 ***8277.31*** *p118*
McCollum, John; Boston, 1774 ***8529.30*** *p6*
McCollum, John 45; Ontario, 1871 ***1823.21*** *p223*
McCollum, John 53; Ontario, 1871 ***1823.21*** *p223*
McCollum, John 78; Ontario, 1871 ***1823.17*** *p102*
McCollum, Malcom; North Carolina, 1808 ***1088.45*** *p21*
McCollum, Marian; New York, 1740 ***8277.31*** *p118*
McCollum, Mary; New York, 1740 ***8277.31*** *p115*
McCollum, Sarah 60; Ontario, 1871 ***1823.21*** *p223*
McCollum, William 51; Ontario, 1871 ***1823.21*** *p223*
McCollum, Zachriah 68; Ontario, 1871 ***1823.21*** *p223*
McCollumn, Gilbert 57; Ontario, 1871 ***1823.21*** *p223*
McColough, Thomas 50; Ontario, 1871 ***1823.17*** *p102*
McComb, Mary; America, 1760 ***1220.12*** *p518*
McComb, William 49; Ontario, 1871 ***1823.21*** *p223*
McConachy, James 26; Ontario, 1871 ***1823.21*** *p224*
McConal, John 37; Ontario, 1871 ***1823.17*** *p102*
McConbrey, Elizabeth McMullin *SEE* McConbrey, John
McConbrey, John; Philadelphia, 1855 ***8513.31*** *p412*
*Wife:*Elizabeth McMullin
McConddra, Ann 72; Ontario, 1871 ***1823.17*** *p102*
McCone, James; Illinois, 1834-1900 ***6020.5*** *p132*
McConkey, John; Boston, 1776 ***8529.30*** *p4A*
McConlin, John; Toronto, 1844 ***2910.35*** *p115*
McConnal, Andrew 36; Ontario, 1871 ***1823.21*** *p224*
McConnel, Mr.; Boston, 1767 ***1642*** *p38*
McConnel, Samuel; Ohio, 1832 ***3580.20*** *p32*
McConnel, Samuel; Ohio, 1832 ***6020.12*** *p13*
McConnel, Thomas; Ohio, 1840 ***6020.12*** *p13*
McConnel, William 24; Ontario, 1871 ***1823.21*** *p224*
McConnell, Alexander 61; Ontario, 1871 ***1823.21*** *p224*
McConnell, Allan 16; Ontario, 1871 ***1823.21*** *p224*
McConnell, James P.; Washington, 1887 ***2770.40*** *p24*
McConnell, John; Ohio, 1809-1852 ***4511.35*** *p33*
McConnell, John 40; Ontario, 1871 ***1823.17*** *p102*
McConnell, John 45; Ontario, 1871 ***1823.21*** *p224*
McConnell, Margaret; New Jersey, 1864 ***8513.31*** *p433*
McConnell, Mary 17; Ontario, 1871 ***1823.21*** *p224*
McConnell, Mary; Potomac, 1731 ***1220.12*** *p518*
McConnell, Thomas; Ohio, 1840 ***3580.20*** *p32*
McConnell, William 37; Ontario, 1871 ***1823.17*** *p102*
McConoughey, David; Massachusetts, 1731 ***1642*** *p111*
With wife
McConvill, Edward 70; Ontario, 1871 ***1823.21*** *p224*
McConvill, John; Toronto, 1844 ***2910.35*** *p115*
McConville, Henrietta 40; Ontario, 1871 ***1823.21*** *p224*
McCook, Anson G.; Ohio, 1863 ***3580.20*** *p32*
McCook, Anson G.; Ohio, 1863 ***6020.12*** *p13*
McCool, Nels P.; Illinois, 1857-1861 ***4487.25*** *p65*
McCoomb, Thomas 50; Ontario, 1871 ***1823.21*** *p224*
McCoot, Edwd 21; St. John, N.B., 1834 ***6469.7*** *p5*
McCoppy, Jane; Nevis or Jamaica, 1722 ***1220.12*** *p518*
McCore, Archibald; New York, 1739 ***8277.31*** *p116*
McCorie, Elizabeth; Potomac, 1729 ***1220.12*** *p518*
McCorkdale, Hugh 47; Ontario, 1871 ***1823.17*** *p103*
McCorkindale, Agnes 60; Ontario, 1871 ***1823.21*** *p224*
McCorkindale, Archebald 28; Ontario, 1871 ***1823.21*** *p224*
McCorkindale, John 43; Ontario, 1871 ***1823.17*** *p103*
McCorkindle, Eliza 36; Ontario, 1871 ***1823.21*** *p224*
McCormack, A. 62; Ontario, 1871 ***1823.21*** *p224*
McCormack, Ann Bennett *SEE* McCormack, Michael
McCormack, Charles 38; Ontario, 1871 ***1823.17*** *p103*
McCormack, Elizabeth 9; Quebec, 1870 ***8364.32*** *p25*
McCormack, James 30; Ontario, 1871 ***1823.21*** *p224*
McCormack, James; Philadelphia, 1841-1844 ***7074.20*** *p133*
McCormack, John 36; Ontario, 1871 ***1823.21*** *p224*
McCormack, Mary 27; Ontario, 1871 ***1823.21*** *p224*
McCormack, Mary 30; Ontario, 1871 ***1823.21*** *p224*
McCormack, Michael; Philadelphia, 1856 ***8513.31*** *p412*
*Wife:*Ann Bennett
McCormack, Thomas; Philadelphia, 1858 ***7074.20*** *p133*
McCormack, William; North America, 1750 ***1640.8*** *p234*
McCormak, Robert 31; Ontario, 1871 ***1823.21*** *p224*
McCormic, James 39; Ontario, 1871 ***1823.17*** *p103*
McCormic, William 58; Ontario, 1871 ***1823.17*** *p103*
McCormick, Adam; America, 1746 ***1220.12*** *p518*
McCormick, Alexan 60; Ontario, 1871 ***1823.21*** *p224*
McCormick, Ann; America, 1754 ***1220.12*** *p518*
McCormick, Archibald 52; Ontario, 1871 ***1823.21*** *p224*
McCormick, Barbery 21; Ontario, 1871 ***1823.21*** *p224*
McCormick, Daniel 28; Ontario, 1871 ***1823.21*** *p224*
McCormick, Donald 48; Ontario, 1871 ***1823.21*** *p224*
McCormick, Donald 60; Ontario, 1871 ***1823.21*** *p224*
McCormick, Donald 80; Ontario, 1871 ***1823.21*** *p224*
McCormick, Edward; Ipswich, MA, 1736 ***1642*** *p70*
McCormick, Fanny 14; Ontario, 1871 ***1823.17*** *p103*
McCormick, Francis; America, 1753 ***1220.12*** *p518*
McCormick, George 77; Ontario, 1871 ***1823.21*** *p224*
McCormick, James A. 25; Michigan, 1880 ***4491.33*** *p15*
McCormick, John; Colorado, 1879 ***1029.59*** *p59*
McCormick, John; Louisiana, 1836-1841 ***4981.45*** *p209*
McCormick, John 27; Ontario, 1871 ***1823.21*** *p224*
McCormick, Joseph 53; Ontario, 1871 ***1823.17*** *p103*
McCormick, Martin; Colorado, 1882 ***1029.59*** *p59*
McCormick, Patrick; Ohio, 1809-1852 ***4511.35*** *p33*
McCormick, Peter 55; Ontario, 1871 ***1823.21*** *p224*
McCormick, Robert 26; Ontario, 1871 ***1823.17*** *p103*
McCormick, Robert 65; Ontario, 1871 ***1823.21*** *p224*
McCormick, Samuel 26; Ontario, 1871 ***1823.17*** *p103*
McCormick, Samuel 53; Ontario, 1871 ***1823.17*** *p103*
McCormick, Sarah 60; Ontario, 1871 ***1823.21*** *p224*
McCormick, Stephen 35; Ontario, 1871 ***1823.21*** *p224*
McCormick, Thomas; Ohio, 1809-1852 ***4511.35*** *p33*
McCormick, Thomas 40; Ontario, 1871 ***1823.21*** *p224*
McCormick, Thomas; Toronto, 1844 ***2910.35*** *p113*
McCormick, William; North Carolina, 1844 ***1088.45*** *p21*
McCormick, William 42; Ontario, 1871 ***1823.21*** *p224*
McCormuck, Mary 55; Ontario, 1871 ***1823.17*** *p103*
McCorry, Hugh; Ohio, 1809-1852 ***4511.35*** *p33*
McCorry, Patrick; Ohio, 1809-1852 ***4511.35*** *p33*
McCosh, Margret 22; Ontario, 1871 ***1823.21*** *p224*
McCotton, John; North Carolina, 1810 ***1088.45*** *p21*
McCoubrey, Eliza 35; Ontario, 1871 ***1823.21*** *p224*
McCoubrey, Elizabeth Le Marquand *SEE* McCoubrey, Stanley
McCoubrey, Stanley; Minnesota, 1857-1891 ***9228.50*** *p361*
*Wife:*Elizabeth Le Marquand
McCough, Timothy; Toronto, 1844 ***2910.35*** *p112*
McCoughel, Patrick; Portland, ME, 1832 ***3274.55*** *p42*
McCoulrey, John 37; Ontario, 1871 ***1823.17*** *p103*
McCowen, Alexander 53; Ontario, 1871 ***1823.21*** *p224*
McCoy, Abraham; New York, 1750 ***1640.8*** *p234*
McCoy, Angus; Washington, 1882 ***2770.40*** *p135*
McCoy, Ann; Boston, 1757 ***1642*** *p47*
McCoy, Benjamin; Maryland, 1744 ***1220.12*** *p518*
McCoy, Duncan; New York, 1740 ***8277.31*** *p118*
McCoy, Duncan 19; Ontario, 1871 ***1823.21*** *p224*
McCoy, Edwin; Ohio, 1878 ***3580.20*** *p32*
McCoy, Edwin; Ohio, 1878 ***6020.12*** *p13*
McCoy, James; America, 1742 ***1220.12*** *p518*
McCoy, John; America, 1752 ***1220.12*** *p518*
McCoy, John; Annapolis, MD, 1732 ***1220.12*** *p518*
McCoy, Martha; America, 1719 ***1220.12*** *p518*
McCoy, Mary; Potomac, 1729 ***1220.12*** *p518*
McCoy, Mary A. 42; Ontario, 1871 ***1823.21*** *p224*
McCoy, Michael 40; Ontario, 1871 ***1823.17*** *p103*
McCoy, Sandy 63; Ontario, 1871 ***1823.21*** *p224*
McCoy, Sarah; America, 1774 ***1220.12*** *p518*
McCoy, William; America, 1746 ***1220.12*** *p518*
McCracken, Alexander 36; Indiana, 1881-1896 ***9076.20*** *p74*
McCracken, Francis 27; Ontario, 1871 ***1823.21*** *p224*
McCracken, John 71; Ontario, 1871 ***1823.21*** *p224*
McCracken, Mary Jane; Philadelphia, 1847 ***8513.31*** *p424*
McCracken, Samuel 40; Ontario, 1871 ***1823.21*** *p225*
McCracken, William 45; Ontario, 1871 ***1823.21*** *p225*
McCracken, William 46; Ontario, 1871 ***1823.21*** *p225*
McCrackin, Francis; Boston, 1818 ***3274.55*** *p73*
McCrackin, John 54; Ontario, 1871 ***1823.21*** *p225*
McCrae, Wm.; Delaware, 1710 ***9228.50*** *p450*
McCrainie, Arch.; Cape Fear, NC,, 1754 ***1422.10*** *p61*
McCrainkein, John; Cape Fear, NC,, 1754 ***1422.10*** *p61*
McCraw, Thomas 40; Ontario, 1871 ***1823.21*** *p225*
McCrea, Alexander 40; Ontario, 1871 ***1823.17*** *p103*
McCrea, Donald 44; Ontario, 1871 ***1823.17*** *p103*
McCrea, John; Boston, 1775 ***8529.30*** *p4A*
McCready, Andrew 2; St. John, N.B., 1834 ***6469.7*** *p4*
McCready, Ann 3 months; St. John, N.B., 1834 ***6469.7*** *p4*
McCready, James 47; Ontario, 1871 ***1823.17*** *p103*
McCready, John 6; St. John, N.B., 1834 ***6469.7*** *p4*
McCready, Mary 5; St. John, N.B., 1834 ***6469.7*** *p4*
McCready, Mary 30; St. John, N.B., 1834 ***6469.7*** *p4*
McCreery, Anna M. 12; Michigan, 1880 ***4491.42*** *p18*
McCreery, Emily M. 41; Michigan, 1880 ***4491.42*** *p18*
McCreery, John 44; Michigan, 1880 ***4491.42*** *p18*
McCreery, Lucy 6; Michigan, 1880 ***4491.42*** *p18*
McCreery, Miles 21; Michigan, 1880 ***4491.42*** *p18*
McCreery, Olive 4; Michigan, 1880 ***4491.42*** *p18*
McCreight, Ellen; Victoria, B.C., 1892-1917 ***9228.50*** *p646*
McCreight, James 75; Ontario, 1871 ***1823.21*** *p225*
McCrew, John; America, 1767 ***1220.12*** *p518*
McCrohon, Owen; North Carolina, 1806 ***1088.45*** *p21*
McCroult, John 18; Ontario, 1871 ***1823.21*** *p225*
McCuarg, Anna; New York, 1739 ***8277.31*** *p117*
McCubbin, Daniel 58; Ontario, 1871 ***1823.21*** *p225*
McCubbin, John 40; Ontario, 1871 ***1823.21*** *p225*
McCue, Henry; Washington, 1870 ***2770.40*** *p134*
McCue, Henry; Washington, 1882 ***2770.40*** *p135*
McCue, John; Maryland or Virginia, 1738 ***1220.12*** *p521*
McCue, John G. 54; Ontario, 1871 ***1823.21*** *p225*
McCue, Margaret; New Orleans, 1851 ***7242.30*** *p148*
McCue, William; Illinois, 1834-1900 ***6020.5*** *p132*
McCuin, James 45; Ontario, 1871 ***1823.21*** *p225*
McCuish, Mary 15; Ontario, 1871 ***1823.21*** *p225*

McCuish, Neil 37; Ontario, 1871 ***1823.21*** *p225*
McCuish, Neil 45; Ontario, 1871 ***1823.21*** *p225*
McCullah, Thomas 47; Ontario, 1871 ***1823.21*** *p225*
McCullin, James; Louisiana, 1874 ***4981.45*** *p133*
McCulloch, Edwin 85; Ontario, 1871 ***1823.21*** *p225*
McCulloch, John 40; Ontario, 1871 ***1823.21*** *p225*
McCulloch, Mary 40; Ontario, 1871 ***1823.21*** *p225*
McCulloch, Robert; South Carolina, 1813 ***3208.30*** *p18*
McCulloch, Robert; South Carolina, 1813 ***3208.30*** *p31*
McCulloch, William; Washington, D.C., 1819 ***6020.12*** *p13*
McCullock, John; America, 1743 ***1220.12*** *p518*
McCullock, Robert 45; South Carolina, 1812 ***3476.30*** *p12*
McCullock, William; America, 1766 ***1220.12*** *p518*
McCullogh, Hugh; North Carolina, 1809-1814 ***1088.45*** *p21*
McCullogh, Margaret; America, 1774 ***1220.12*** *p518*
McCullogh, William; America, 1739 ***1220.12*** *p518*
McCullough, Andrew; New Jersey, 1802-1808 ***3845.2*** *p129*
McCullough, Catherine 34; Ontario, 1871 ***1823.21*** *p225*
McCullough, Ellen 49; Michigan, 1880 ***4491.39*** *p19*
McCullough, Hugh 21; Ontario, 1871 ***1823.21*** *p225*
McCullough, John 66; Michigan, 1880 ***4491.42*** *p18*
McCullough, Michael 45; Michigan, 1880 ***4491.39*** *p19*
McCullough, Robert 35; Ontario, 1871 ***1823.21*** *p225*
McCullough, Samuel 24; South Carolina, 1812 ***3476.30*** *p12*
McCullough, Thomas H. 76; Michigan, 1880 ***4491.39*** *p19*
McCullough, William; Ohio, 1826 ***3580.20*** *p32*
McCullough, Wm. 25; South Carolina, 1812 ***3476.30*** *p12*
McCullum, Peter 52; Ontario, 1871 ***1823.21*** *p225*
McCully, Irving 36; Ontario, 1871 ***1823.21*** *p225*
McCully, James 32; Ontario, 1871 ***1823.17*** *p103*
McCully, John 60; Ontario, 1871 ***1823.21*** *p225*
McCully, Joseph 73; Ontario, 1871 ***1823.21*** *p225*
McCully, Margaret 71; Ontario, 1871 ***1823.21*** *p225*
McCully, Robert 68; Ontario, 1871 ***1823.21*** *p225*
McCully, Samuel 61; Ontario, 1871 ***1823.21*** *p225*
McCumsky, Bridget 39; Ontario, 1871 ***1823.21*** *p225*
McCurdy, Archibald; Philadelphia, 1857 ***5720.10*** *p379*
McCurdy, James; Washington, 1884 ***2770.40*** *p192*
McCurdy, James A.; Ohio, 1862 ***3580.20*** *p32*
McCurdy, James A.; Ohio, 1862 ***6020.12*** *p13*
McCurdy, Margt 34; Ontario, 1871 ***1823.21*** *p225*
McCusear, John 52; Ontario, 1871 ***1823.17*** *p103*
McCush, Murdok 30; Ontario, 1871 ***1823.21*** *p225*
McCutchen, John 36; Ontario, 1871 ***1823.21*** *p225*
McCutcheon, Alex 35; Ontario, 1871 ***1823.21*** *p225*
McCutcheon, Robert 32; Ontario, 1871 ***1823.17*** *p103*
McCutcheon, Robert 60; Ontario, 1871 ***1823.21*** *p225*
McCutcheon, William 25; Ontario, 1871 ***1823.21*** *p225*
McCutchon, James 55; Ontario, 1871 ***1823.21*** *p225*
McDade, Jane; Philadelphia, 1852 ***8513.31*** *p296*
McDaniel, Ann; America, 1770 ***1220.12*** *p518*
McDaniel, Daniel; America, 1767 ***1220.12*** *p518*
McDaniel, Elizabeth; America, 1773 ***1220.12*** *p518*
McDaniel, Hugh; America, 1764 ***1220.12*** *p518*
McDaniel, James; America, 1774 ***1220.12*** *p518*
McDaniel, James; St. Johns, N.F., 1825 ***1053.15*** *p6*
McDaniel, John; Annapolis, MD, 1730 ***1220.12*** *p518*
McDaniel, Margaret; Boston, 1734 ***1642*** *p44*
McDaniel, Mary; America, 1750 ***1220.12*** *p518*
McDaniel, Mary; Virginia, 1723 ***1220.12*** *p518*
McDaniel, Neal; Virginia, 1750 ***1220.12*** *p518*
McDaniel, Robert; America, 1761 ***1220.12*** *p518*
McDaniel, Thomas; St. Johns, N.F., 1825 ***1053.15*** *p6*
McDaniel, Timothy; Boston, 1732 ***1642*** *p76*
McDaniel, William; America, 1751 ***1220.12*** *p518*
McDaniell, H. D. 40; Ontario, 1871 ***1823.21*** *p225*
McDannel, James; America, 1757 ***1220.12*** *p518*
McDannell, Mary; America, 1753 ***1220.12*** *p518*
McDavid, Robert 30; Louisiana, 1831-1847 ***7710.1*** *p149*
McDavid, Robert 32; Louisiana, 1831-1849 ***7710.1*** *p150*
McDead, Peter 28; Ontario, 1871 ***1823.21*** *p225*
McDearmid, Mary; New York, 1739 ***8277.31*** *p119*
McDermaid, Patrick 40; Ontario, 1871 ***1823.21*** *p225*
McDerment, James 70; Ontario, 1871 ***1823.21*** *p226*
McDermot, Charles 30; Ontario, 1871 ***1823.21*** *p226*
McDermot, Malcolm 39; Ontario, 1871 ***1823.17*** *p103*
McDermot, Thomas; Ohio, 1809-1852 ***4511.35*** *p33*
McDermot, Timothy; America, 1765 ***1220.12*** *p518*
McDermoth, Charles; Washington, 1882 ***2770.40*** *p135*
McDermott, Edward; Toronto, 1844 ***2910.35*** *p113*
McDermott, Hugh 13; Quebec, 1870 ***8364.32*** *p25*
McDermott, Hy; Louisiana, 1874 ***4981.45*** *p296*
McDermott, John; Louisiana, 1874 ***4981.45*** *p133*
McDermott, Julia; Philadelphia, 1867 ***8513.31*** *p317*
McDermott, Nelly; Ontario, 1835 ***3160.1*** *p150*
McDermott, Nelly; Prescott, Ont., 1835 ***3289.1*** *p61*
McDermott, P. H.; Louisiana, 1874 ***4981.45*** *p133*
McDevit, Donald 40; Ontario, 1871 ***1823.21*** *p226*
McDevitt, Fannie Garner *SEE* McDevitt, William
McDevitt, William; Philadelphia, 1846 ***8513.31*** *p412*
*Wife:*Fannie Garner
McDiamod, Owen; Maryland, 1726 ***1220.12*** *p518*
McDiarmid, Donald 25; Ontario, 1871 ***1823.21*** *p226*
McDiarmid, John 60; Ontario, 1871 ***1823.21*** *p226*
McDonaell, Francis; Toronto, 1844 ***2910.35*** *p114*
McDonagh, Charles; Virginia, 1735 ***1220.12*** *p518*
McDonagh, Mathew; Toronto, 1844 ***2910.35*** *p112*
McDonal, John 26; Ontario, 1871 ***1823.21*** *p226*
McDonald, A. 82; Ontario, 1871 ***1823.21*** *p226*
McDonald, Mrs. A.; Toronto, 1844 ***2910.35*** *p114*
McDonald, Adam 48; Ontario, 1871 ***1823.17*** *p103*
McDonald, Alec 22; Michigan, 1880 ***4491.39*** *p19*
McDonald, Alex; Cape Fear, NC,, 1754 ***1422.10*** *p61*
McDonald, Alex 29; Ontario, 1871 ***1823.21*** *p226*
McDonald, Alex 41; Ontario, 1871 ***1823.21*** *p226*
McDonald, Alex 64; Ontario, 1871 ***1823.21*** *p226*
McDonald, Alex 72; Ontario, 1871 ***1823.21*** *p226*
McDonald, Alexander; America, 1753 ***1220.12*** *p518*
McDonald, Alexander; Boston, 1775 ***8529.30*** *p4A*
McDonald, Alexander; New York, 1738 ***8277.31*** *p115*
With mother
McDonald, Alexander; North Carolina, 1774 ***1422.10*** *p58*
McDonald, Alexander; North Carolina, 1837 ***1088.45*** *p21*
McDonald, Alexander 35; Ohio, 1880 ***4879.40*** *p260*
McDonald, Alexander 37; Ontario, 1871 ***1823.17*** *p103*
McDonald, Alexander 43; Ontario, 1871 ***1823.17*** *p103*
McDonald, Alexander 54; Ontario, 1871 ***1823.21*** *p226*
McDonald, Alexander 60; Ontario, 1871 ***1823.21*** *p226*
McDonald, Alexander 62; Ontario, 1871 ***1823.21*** *p226*
McDonald, Alexander 73; Ontario, 1871 ***1823.21*** *p226*
McDonald, Alexander 75; Ontario, 1871 ***1823.21*** *p226*
McDonald, Alexander; Pictou, N.S., 1816 ***7085.8*** *p89*
With wife & 2 sons
McDonald, Alexr 21; Ontario, 1871 ***1823.21*** *p226*
McDonald, Alexr 101; Ontario, 1871 ***1823.21*** *p226*
McDonald, Allan; Ontario, 1787 ***1276.15*** *p230*
With 2 children & relative
McDonald, Allan 49; Ontario, 1871 ***1823.21*** *p226*
McDonald, Andrew; America, 1769 ***1220.12*** *p518*
McDonald, Andrew; Ohio, 1856 ***3580.20*** *p32*
McDonald, Andrew; Ohio, 1856 ***6020.12*** *p13*
McDonald, Angus; America, 1753 ***1220.12*** *p518*
McDonald, Angus; North Carolina, 1856 ***1088.45*** *p21*
McDonald, Angus; Ohio, 1809-1852 ***4511.35*** *p33*
McDonald, Angus 28; Ontario, 1871 ***1823.21*** *p226*
McDonald, Angus 29; Ontario, 1871 ***1823.21*** *p226*
McDonald, Angus 40; Ontario, 1871 ***1823.21*** *p226*
McDonald, Angus 46; Ontario, 1871 ***1823.21*** *p226*
McDonald, Angus 52; Ontario, 1871 ***1823.17*** *p104*
McDonald, Angus 55; Ontario, 1871 ***1823.21*** *p226*
McDonald, Angus 55; Ontario, 1871 ***1823.21*** *p226*
McDonald, Angus 60; Ontario, 1871 ***1823.21*** *p226*
McDonald, Angus 83; Ontario, 1871 ***1823.21*** *p226*
McDonald, Angus; Philadelphia, 1778 ***8529.30*** *p3*
McDonald, Ann; America, 1748 ***1220.12*** *p519*
McDonald, Ann; America, 1762 ***1220.12*** *p519*
McDonald, Ann; Maryland, 1742 ***1220.12*** *p519*
McDonald, Ann 21; Ontario, 1871 ***1823.21*** *p226*
McDonald, Ann 30; Ontario, 1871 ***1823.21*** *p226*
McDonald, Ann 51; Ontario, 1871 ***1823.21*** *p226*
McDonald, Anna McDuffie *SEE* McDonald, Neil
McDonald, Anna; New York, 1738 ***8277.31*** *p117*
McDonald, Arch 41; Ontario, 1871 ***1823.17*** *p104*
McDonald, Archb 49; Ontario, 1871 ***1823.21*** *p226*
McDonald, Archd 60; Ontario, 1871 ***1823.21*** *p226*
McDonald, Archebald 36; Ontario, 1871 ***1823.21*** *p226*
McDonald, Archibald; America, 1751 ***1220.12*** *p519*
McDonald, Archibald *SEE* McDonald, Neil
McDonald, Archibald; North Carolina, 1846 ***1088.45*** *p22*
McDonald, Archibald 34; Ontario, 1871 ***1823.17*** *p104*
McDonald, Archibald 57; Ontario, 1871 ***1823.17*** *p104*
McDonald, Archie; Missouri, 1890 ***3276.1*** *p3*
McDonald, Archy 44; Ontario, 1871 ***1823.21*** *p226*
McDonald, Betsey 40; Ontario, 1871 ***1823.21*** *p226*
McDonald, Catharin 74; Ontario, 1871 ***1823.21*** *p226*
McDonald, Catharine *SEE* McDonald, Neil
McDonald, Catharine; New York, 1740 ***8277.31*** *p117*
McDonald, Catharine; New York, 1740 ***8277.31*** *p117*
McDonald, Catharine; New York, 1740 ***8277.31*** *p117*
McDonald, Catherine 38; Ontario, 1871 ***1823.21*** *p227*
McDonald, Catherine 40; Ontario, 1871 ***1823.21*** *p227*
McDonald, Catherine 50; Ontario, 1871 ***1823.21*** *p227*
McDonald, Catherine 60; Ontario, 1871 ***1823.21*** *p227*
McDonald, Catherine 65; Ontario, 1871 ***1823.21*** *p226*
McDonald, Catherine 70; Ontario, 1871 ***1823.21*** *p227*
McDonald, Charles; America, 1769 ***1220.12*** *p519*
McDonald, Charles; North Carolina, 1844 ***1088.45*** *p22*
McDonald, Charles 26; Ontario, 1871 ***1823.17*** *p104*
McDonald, Christena 8 *SEE* McDonald, Martin
McDonald, Christopher; America, 1765 ***1220.12*** *p519*
McDonald, Christy 25; North Carolina, 1775 ***1422.10*** *p60*
McDonald, Coll 40; Ontario, 1871 ***1823.17*** *p104*
McDonald, Dan 32; Ontario, 1871 ***1823.21*** *p227*
McDonald, Daniel; Kansas, 1887 ***1447.20*** *p63*
McDonald, Daniel 26; Ontario, 1871 ***1823.21*** *p227*
McDonald, David 51; Ontario, 1871 ***1823.21*** *p227*
McDonald, David; Philadelphia, 1778 ***8529.30*** *p4A*
McDonald, Donald; Marston's Wharf, 1782 ***8529.30*** *p14*
McDonald, Donald *SEE* McDonald, Neil
McDonald, Donald; North America, 1750 ***1640.8*** *p234*
McDonald, Donald 29; North Carolina, 1774 ***1422.10*** *p58*
McDonald, Donald 18; Ontario, 1871 ***1823.21*** *p227*
McDonald, Donald 20; Ontario, 1871 ***1823.21*** *p227*
McDonald, Donald 28; Ontario, 1871 ***1823.21*** *p227*
McDonald, Donald 32; Ontario, 1871 ***1823.21*** *p227*
McDonald, Donald 33; Ontario, 1871 ***1823.21*** *p227*
McDonald, Donald 36; Ontario, 1871 ***1823.21*** *p227*
McDonald, Donald 38; Ontario, 1871 ***1823.21*** *p227*
McDonald, Donald 39; Ontario, 1871 ***1823.21*** *p227*
McDonald, Donald 40; Ontario, 1871 ***1823.21*** *p227*
McDonald, Donald 40; Ontario, 1871 ***1823.21*** *p227*
McDonald, Donald 45; Ontario, 1871 ***1823.17*** *p104*
McDonald, Donald 45; Ontario, 1871 ***1823.21*** *p227*
McDonald, Donald 46; Ontario, 1871 ***1823.21*** *p227*
McDonald, Donald 58; Ontario, 1871 ***1823.17*** *p104*
McDonald, Donald 60; Ontario, 1871 ***1823.21*** *p227*
McDonald, Donald 60; Ontario, 1871 ***1823.21*** *p227*
McDonald, Donald 60; Ontario, 1871 ***1823.21*** *p227*
McDonald, Donald 63; Ontario, 1871 ***1823.21*** *p227*
McDonald, Donald 71; Ontario, 1871 ***1823.17*** *p104*
McDonald, Donald; Pictou, N.S., 1816 ***7085.8*** *p89*
With wife 2 sons & 3 daughters
McDonald, Duncan 14; Ontario, 1871 ***1823.21*** *p227*
McDonald, Duncan 35; Ontario, 1871 ***1823.21*** *p227*
McDonald, Duncan 39; Ontario, 1871 ***1823.21*** *p227*
McDonald, Duncan 61; Ontario, 1871 ***1823.21*** *p227*
McDonald, Duncan 73; Ontario, 1871 ***1823.21*** *p227*
McDonald, Duncan 79; Ontario, 1871 ***1823.17*** *p104*
McDonald, Duncan J.; Washington, 1885 ***2770.40*** *p194*
McDonald, Edward 34; Ontario, 1871 ***1823.17*** *p104*
McDonald, Edward 35; Ontario, 1871 ***1823.21*** *p227*
McDonald, Edwin 42; Ontario, 1871 ***1823.21*** *p227*
McDonald, Eliz 29; North Carolina, 1774 ***1422.10*** *p58*
McDonald, Elizabeth; America, 1745 ***1220.12*** *p519*
McDonald, Elizabeth; Annapolis, MD, 1719 ***1220.12*** *p519*
McDonald, Ellen 11; Quebec, 1870 ***8364.32*** *p25*
McDonald, Farquhar 68; Ontario, 1871 ***1823.21*** *p227*
McDonald, George; North Carolina, 1774 ***1422.10*** *p58*
McDonald, Grace 27; Ontario, 1871 ***1823.21*** *p227*
McDonald, Grace 64; Ontario, 1871 ***1823.21*** *p227*
McDonald, Hector 75; North Carolina, 1774 ***1422.10*** *p58*
McDonald, Hector 25; Ontario, 1871 ***1823.21*** *p227*
McDonald, Hector 50; Ontario, 1871 ***1823.21*** *p227*
McDonald, Helen 14; Quebec, 1870 ***8364.32*** *p25*
McDonald, Henry 23; Ontario, 1871 ***1823.21*** *p227*
McDonald, Hugh; New Orleans, 1850 ***7242.30*** *p148*
McDonald, Isabella 44; Ontario, 1871 ***1823.21*** *p228*
McDonald, Isobel 36; North Carolina, 1774 ***1422.10*** *p60*
McDonald, Isobel 36; North Carolina, 1774 ***1422.10*** *p62*
McDonald, James; America, 1768 ***1220.12*** *p519*
McDonald, James; America, 1770 ***1220.12*** *p519*
McDonald, James; America, 1772 ***1220.12*** *p519*
McDonald, James; Boston, 1834 ***3274.55*** *p22*
McDonald, James; Marston's Wharf, 1782 ***8529.30*** *p14*
McDonald, James; North Carolina, 1858 ***1088.45*** *p22*
McDonald, James 49; Ohio, 1880 ***4879.40*** *p259*
McDonald, James 36; Ontario, 1871 ***1823.21*** *p228*
McDonald, James 41; Ontario, 1871 ***1823.17*** *p104*
McDonald, James 42; Ontario, 1871 ***1823.17*** *p104*
McDonald, James 43; Ontario, 1871 ***1823.21*** *p228*
McDonald, James 45; Ontario, 1871 ***1823.21*** *p228*
McDonald, James 50; Ontario, 1871 ***1823.21*** *p228*
McDonald, James 50; Ontario, 1871 ***1823.21*** *p228*
McDonald, James 50; Ontario, 1871 ***1823.21*** *p228*
McDonald, James 53; Ontario, 1871 ***1823.17*** *p104*
McDonald, James 60; Ontario, 1871 ***1823.21*** *p228*
McDonald, James; Virginia, 1738 ***1220.12*** *p519*
McDonald, James E.; Washington, 1889 ***2770.40*** *p79*
McDonald, James R.; Washington, 1885 ***2770.40*** *p194*
McDonald, Jane 30; Ontario, 1871 ***1823.21*** *p228*
McDonald, Jane 32; Ontario, 1871 ***1823.21*** *p228*
McDonald, Jannet 66; Ontario, 1871 ***1823.21*** *p228*
McDonald, Jas 40; Ontario, 1871 ***1823.21*** *p228*
McDonald, Jennet 30; Ontario, 1871 ***1823.21*** *p228*
McDonald, Jessy 2; North Carolina, 1774 ***1422.10*** *p60*
McDonald, Jessy 2; North Carolina, 1774 ***1422.10*** *p62*
McDonald, John; America, 1761 ***1220.12*** *p519*

McDonald, John; America, 1771 ***1220.12*** *p519*
McDonald, John; Annapolis, MD, 1719 ***1220.12*** *p519*
McDonald, John; California, 1868 ***1131.61*** *p90*
McDonald, John; Colorado, 1873 ***1029.59*** *p60*
McDonald, John; New York, 1739 ***8277.31*** *p116*
McDonald, John; North Carolina, 1774 ***1422.10*** *p58*
McDonald, John 49; Ohio, 1880 ***4879.40*** *p259*
McDonald, John 25; Ontario, 1871 ***1823.21*** *p228*
McDonald, John 25; Ontario, 1871 ***1823.21*** *p228*
McDonald, John 28; Ontario, 1871 ***1823.21*** *p228*
McDonald, John 32; Ontario, 1871 ***1823.21*** *p228*
McDonald, John 32; Ontario, 1871 ***1823.21*** *p228*
McDonald, John 35; Ontario, 1871 ***1823.17*** *p104*
McDonald, John 35; Ontario, 1871 ***1823.21*** *p228*
McDonald, John 38; Ontario, 1871 ***1823.21*** *p228*
McDonald, John 41; Ontario, 1871 ***1823.21*** *p228*
McDonald, John 43; Ontario, 1871 ***1823.21*** *p228*
McDonald, John 45; Ontario, 1871 ***1823.21*** *p228*
McDonald, John 45; Ontario, 1871 ***1823.21*** *p228*
McDonald, John 48; Ontario, 1871 ***1823.21*** *p228*
McDonald, John 51; Ontario, 1871 ***1823.17*** *p104*
McDonald, John 60; Ontario, 1871 ***1823.17*** *p104*
McDonald, John 63; Ontario, 1871 ***1823.17*** *p104*
McDonald, John 65; Ontario, 1871 ***1823.21*** *p228*
McDonald, John 65; Ontario, 1871 ***1823.21*** *p228*
McDonald, John 67; Ontario, 1871 ***1823.21*** *p228*
McDonald, Joseph; Iowa, 1877 ***1211.15*** *p16*
McDonald, Keneth 65; Ontario, 1871 ***1823.17*** *p104*
McDonald, Kenneth 50; Ontario, 1871 ***1823.21*** *p228*
McDonald, Kenneth; Washington, 1879 ***2770.40*** *p134*
McDonald, Lachlan 70; Ontario, 1871 ***1823.21*** *p228*
McDonald, Loavitia 63; Ontario, 1871 ***1823.21*** *p229*
McDonald, Loughlin 30; Ontario, 1871 ***1823.21*** *p229*
McDonald, Loughly 30; Ontario, 1871 ***1823.21*** *p229*
McDonald, Margaret; America, 1756 ***1220.12*** *p519*
McDonald, Margaret Nolan *SEE* McDonald, Robert
McDonald, Margret 56; Ontario, 1871 ***1823.21*** *p229*
McDonald, Marion 45; Ontario, 1871 ***1823.21*** *p229*
McDonald, Martin 33; Ohio, 1880 ***4879.40*** *p259*
*Wife:*Mary A. 32
*Daughter:*Christena 8
McDonald, Mary; America, 1740 ***1220.12*** *p519*
McDonald, Mary; Halifax, N.S., 1827 ***7009.9*** *p60*
McDonald, Mary; New York, 1738 ***8277.31*** *p118*
McDonald, Mary; New York, 1738 ***8277.31*** *p118*
McDonald, Mary; New York, 1738 ***8277.31*** *p118*
McDonald, Mary 4; North Carolina, 1774 ***1422.10*** *p60*
McDonald, Mary 4; North Carolina, 1774 ***1422.10*** *p62*
McDonald, Mary 27; Ontario, 1871 ***1823.21*** *p229*
McDonald, Mary 42; Ontario, 1871 ***1823.21*** *p229*
McDonald, Mary 48; Ontario, 1871 ***1823.21*** *p229*
McDonald, Mary 48; Ontario, 1871 ***1823.21*** *p229*
McDonald, Mary 50; Ontario, 1871 ***1823.21*** *p229*
McDonald, Mary 51; Ontario, 1871 ***1823.17*** *p104*
McDonald, Mary 60; Ontario, 1871 ***1823.17*** *p104*
McDonald, Mary 64; Ontario, 1871 ***1823.21*** *p229*
McDonald, Mary 65; Ontario, 1871 ***1823.21*** *p229*
McDonald, Mary 65; Ontario, 1871 ***1823.21*** *p229*
McDonald, Mary A. 32 *SEE* McDonald, Martin
McDonald, Mary E.; Philadelphia, 1817 ***9228.50*** *p480*
McDonald, Matthew; Maryland, 1719 ***1220.12*** *p519*
McDonald, Murdoch 50; Ontario, 1871 ***1823.17*** *p104*
McDonald, Murray 80; Ontario, 1871 ***1823.17*** *p104*
McDonald, Nancy 24; Ontario, 1871 ***1823.21*** *p229*
McDonald, Neal; America, 1753 ***1220.12*** *p519*
McDonald, Neil; New York, 1738 ***8277.31*** *p116*
*Wife:*Anna McDuffie
*Child:*Catharine
*Child:*Donald
*Child:*Archibald
McDonald, Owen 58; Ontario, 1871 ***1823.17*** *p104*
McDonald, P. A.; Colorado, 1893 ***1029.59*** *p60*
McDonald, Patrick; America, 1747 ***1220.12*** *p519*
McDonald, Patrick; Ohio, 1809-1852 ***4511.35*** *p33*
McDonald, Patrick; Salem, MA, 1749 ***1642*** *p78*
McDonald, Peter; America, 1754 ***1220.12*** *p519*
McDonald, Peter 36; Ontario, 1871 ***1823.21*** *p229*
McDonald, Peter 42; Ontario, 1871 ***1823.17*** *p104*
McDonald, Peter 48; Ontario, 1871 ***1823.21*** *p229*
McDonald, Peter 70; Ontario, 1871 ***1823.21*** *p229*
McDonald, Rachael; America, 1771 ***1220.12*** *p519*
McDonald, Ranald 40; Ontario, 1871 ***1823.21*** *p229*
McDonald, Rand'l.; Ontario, 1787 ***1276.15*** *p230*
With 2 relatives
McDonald, Randal 54; Ontario, 1871 ***1823.17*** *p105*
McDonald, Robert; Jamaica, 1777 ***8529.30*** *p13A*
McDonald, Robert; New York, NY, 1858 ***8513.31*** *p412*
*Wife:*Margaret Nolan
McDonald, Robert 42; Ohio, 1880 ***4879.40*** *p260*
McDonald, Robert 30; Ontario, 1871 ***1823.21*** *p229*
McDonald, Robert 60; Ontario, 1871 ***1823.21*** *p229*
McDonald, Robert; Virginia, 1732 ***1220.12*** *p519*
McDonald, Robert C.; Iowa, 1885 ***1211.15*** *p16*
McDonald, Roderick 40; Ontario, 1871 ***1823.21*** *p229*
McDonald, Rodk 45; Ontario, 1871 ***1823.21*** *p229*
McDonald, Rodrick 40; Ontario, 1871 ***1823.21*** *p229*
McDonald, Rodrick 45; Ontario, 1871 ***1823.21*** *p229*
McDonald, Roger; America, 1769 ***1220.12*** *p519*
McDonald, Ronald; North Carolina, 1826 ***1088.45*** *p22*
McDonald, Ronald 28; Ontario, 1871 ***1823.21*** *p229*
McDonald, Ronald 44; Ontario, 1871 ***1823.21*** *p229*
McDonald, Ronald 50; Ontario, 1871 ***1823.21*** *p229*
McDonald, Sarah; America, 1724 ***1220.12*** *p519*
McDonald, Sarah 21; Ontario, 1871 ***1823.21*** *p229*
McDonald, Sarah 25; Ontario, 1871 ***1823.21*** *p229*
McDonald, Sarah 26; Ontario, 1871 ***1823.21*** *p229*
McDonald, Sarah 60; Ontario, 1871 ***1823.21*** *p229*
McDonald, Thomas 56; Ontario, 1871 ***1823.21*** *p229*
McDonald, William; America, 1751 ***1220.12*** *p518*
McDonald, William; Iowa, 1879 ***1211.15*** *p16*
McDonald, William 40; North Carolina, 1774 ***1422.10*** *p60*
McDonald, William 40; North Carolina, 1774 ***1422.10*** *p62*
McDonald, William 71; North Carolina, 1774 ***1422.10*** *p58*
McDonald, William 25; Ontario, 1871 ***1823.21*** *p229*
McDonald, William 26; Ontario, 1871 ***1823.21*** *p229*
McDonald, William 37; Ontario, 1871 ***1823.17*** *p105*
McDonald, William 44; Ontario, 1871 ***1823.17*** *p105*
McDonald, William 50; Ontario, 1871 ***1823.17*** *p105*
McDonald, William 60; Ontario, 1871 ***1823.17*** *p105*
McDonald, William; Washington, 1888 ***2770.40*** *p26*
McDonald, Wm. 46; Ontario, 1871 ***1823.17*** *p105*
McDonall, Sarah; Annapolis, MD, 1733 ***1220.12*** *p519*
McDonaugh, John; Jamaica, 1778 ***8529.30*** *p13A*
McDonaugh, John; Marston's Wharf, 1782 ***8529.30*** *p14*
McDonaugh, John 57; Michigan, 1880 ***4491.36*** *p15*
McDonaugh, Mary 43; Michigan, 1880 ***4491.36*** *p15*
McDone, Ephraim; America, 1767 ***1220.12*** *p519*
McDonell, Alexander; Quebec, 1786 ***1416.15*** *p5*
McDonell, Alexr; Quebec, 1786 ***1416.15*** *p8*
McDonell, Alexr; Quebec, 1786 ***1416.15*** *p9*
McDonell, Allan; Quebec, 1786 ***1416.15*** *p8*
McDonell, Angus; Quebec, 1786 ***1416.15*** *p5*
McDonell, Angus; Quebec, 1786 ***1416.15*** *p8*
McDonell, Archd; Quebec, 1786 ***1416.15*** *p8*
McDonell, Donald; Quebec, 1786 ***1416.15*** *p8*
McDonell, Donald; Quebec, 1786 ***1416.15*** *p9*
McDonell, Dond; Quebec, 1786 ***1416.15*** *p9*
McDonell, Dougald; Quebec, 1786 ***1416.15*** *p8*
McDonell, Dougald; Quebec, 1786 ***1416.15*** *p8*
McDonell, Duncan; Quebec, 1786 ***1416.15*** *p8*
McDonell, Ewen; Quebec, 1786 ***1416.15*** *p8*
McDonell, Finlay; Quebec, 1786 ***1416.15*** *p8*
McDonell, Gilbert; Quebec, 1786 ***1416.15*** *p8*
McDonell, James; Quebec, 1786 ***1416.15*** *p8*
McDonell, John; Quebec, 1786 ***1416.15*** *p8*
McDonell, John; Quebec, 1786 ***1416.15*** *p9*
McDonell, Peter; Quebec, 1786 ***1416.15*** *p8*
McDonell, Rand; Quebec, 1786 ***1416.15*** *p8*
McDonell, Ranold; Quebec, 1786 ***1416.15*** *p8*
McDonell, Rodk; Quebec, 1786 ***1416.15*** *p8*
McDonell, Ronald; Quebec, 1786 ***1416.15*** *p8*
McDonell, Runold; Quebec, 1786 ***1416.15*** *p8*
McDonell, Saml; Quebec, 1786 ***1416.15*** *p8*
McDonnack, Edward; America, 1758 ***1220.12*** *p519*
McDonnagh, John; Boston, 1766 ***1642*** *p37*
McDonnell, Alexander 53; Ontario, 1871 ***1823.21*** *p230*
McDonnell, Bess; New Orleans, 1850 ***7242.30*** *p148*
McDonnell, Edward; America, 1697 ***1220.12*** *p519*
McDonnell, Elizabeth; Barbados or Jamaica, 1691 ***1220.12*** *p519*
McDonnell, Henry; America, 1718 ***1220.12*** *p519*
McDonnell, James; America, 1744 ***1220.12*** *p519*
McDonnell, James; Virginia, 1741 ***1220.12*** *p519*
McDonnell, John; New Orleans, 1850 ***7242.30*** *p148*
McDonnell, John; Virginia, 1732 ***1220.12*** *p519*
McDonnell, Maria; New Orleans, 1850 ***7242.30*** *p149*
McDonnell, Mary 48; Michigan, 1880 ***4491.39*** *p19*
McDonnell, Mary; New Orleans, 1850 ***7242.30*** *p149*
McDonnell, Mathew; New Orleans, 1850 ***7242.30*** *p149*
McDonnell, Owen 51; Michigan, 1880 ***4491.39*** *p19*
McDonnell, Patt; New Orleans, 1850 ***7242.30*** *p149*
McDonnell, Philip; Barbados, 1694 ***1220.12*** *p519*
McDonnell, Philip; New Orleans, 1850 ***7242.30*** *p149*
McDonnell, Thomas; New Orleans, 1850 ***7242.30*** *p149*
McDonogh, John; Jamaica, 1778 ***8529.30*** *p13A*
McDonough, Henry; America, 1718 ***1220.12*** *p519*
McDonough, Jno.; St. John, N.B., 1848 ***2978.15*** *p38*
McDonough, John; St. John, N.B., 1847 ***2978.15*** *p38*
McDonough, John M.; Illinois, 1860 ***6079.1*** *p9*
McDonough, Michael 77; Ontario, 1871 ***1823.21*** *p230*
McDonough, Michael; Washington, 1889 ***2770.40*** *p79*
McDonough, Thomas 42; Ontario, 1871 ***1823.21*** *p230*
McDonough, Thos 52; Ontario, 1871 ***1823.21*** *p230*
McDonough, Thos; St. John, N.B., 1847 ***2978.15*** *p36*
McDonough, William 43; Ontario, 1871 ***1823.21*** *p230*
McDorell, Andrew; America, 1769 ***1220.12*** *p519*
McDormale, Patrick; America, 1726 ***1220.12*** *p519*
McDougal, Andrew 28; Ontario, 1871 ***1823.21*** *p230*
McDougal, Hugh 66; Ontario, 1871 ***1823.21*** *p230*
McDougal, James; America, 1764 ***1220.12*** *p519*
McDougal, John 50; Ontario, 1871 ***1823.17*** *p105*
McDougal, Joseph 32; Ontario, 1871 ***1823.21*** *p230*
McDougal, Mary 46; Ontario, 1871 ***1823.21*** *p230*
McDougal, Thomas 38; Ontario, 1871 ***1823.21*** *p230*
McDougald, Alexander; Brunswick, NC, 1767 ***1422.10*** *p61*
McDougald, Alexander; Brunswick, NC, 1767 ***1422.10*** *p61*
McDougald, Alexander 63; Ontario, 1871 ***1823.21*** *p230*
McDougald, Angus; Brunswick, NC, 1767 ***1422.10*** *p61*
McDougald, Angus; Brunswick, NC, 1767 ***1422.10*** *p61*
McDougald, Angus; Quebec, 1786 ***1416.15*** *p8*
McDougald, Archd; Quebec, 1786 ***1416.15*** *p8*
McDougald, Archibald 70; Ontario, 1871 ***1823.21*** *p230*
McDougald, Archibald; Pictou, N.S., 1816 ***7085.8*** *p89*
With wife & 2 daughters
McDougald, Donald; Brunswick, NC, 1767 ***1422.10*** *p61*
McDougald, Donald; Brunswick, NC, 1767 ***1422.10*** *p61*
McDougald, Donald; Pictou, N.S., 1816 ***7085.8*** *p89*
With wife
McDougald, Donald; Quebec, 1786 ***1416.15*** *p8*
McDougald, Dougal 74; Ontario, 1871 ***1823.21*** *p230*
McDougald, Dougald; Brunswick, NC, 1767 ***1422.10*** *p61*
McDougald, Dougald; Brunswick, NC, 1767 ***1422.10*** *p61*
McDougald, Dunn; Quebec, 1786 ***1416.15*** *p8*
McDougald, Hugh; Pictou, N.S., 1816 ***7085.8*** *p89*
McDougald, Jane 80; Ontario, 1871 ***1823.21*** *p230*
McDougald, Jas 27; Ontario, 1871 ***1823.21*** *p230*
McDougald, John; Brunswick, NC, 1767 ***1422.10*** *p61*
McDougald, John 52; Ontario, 1871 ***1823.21*** *p230*
McDougald, John 55; Ontario, 1871 ***1823.21*** *p230*
McDougald, John; Pictou, N.S., 1816 ***7085.8*** *p89*
With wife 2 sons & 2 daughters
McDougald, John; Quebec, 1786 ***1416.15*** *p8*
McDougald, Malcom; Quebec, 1786 ***1416.15*** *p8*
McDougald, Neil 25; Ontario, 1871 ***1823.21*** *p230*
McDougald, Peggy; Brunswick, NC, 1767 ***1422.10*** *p61*
McDougald, R. M. 35; Ontario, 1871 ***1823.17*** *p105*
McDougall, Alexander *SEE* McDougall, Archibald
McDougall, Alexander *SEE* McDougall, Ronald
McDougall, Alexander *SEE* McDougall, Duncan
McDougall, Allan; New York, 1738 ***8277.31*** *p116*
*Wife:*Elizabeth Graham
*Daughter:*Anna
*Daughter:*Hannah
*Daughter:*Margaret
McDougall, Angus; New York, 1738 ***8277.31*** *p117*
McDougall, Angus 45; Ontario, 1871 ***1823.21*** *p230*
McDougall, Angus; Quebec, 1786 ***1416.15*** *p8*
McDougall, Anna; New York, 1738 ***8277.31*** *p114*
McDougall, Anna *SEE* McDougall, Allan
McDougall, Archibald; New York, 1738 ***8277.31*** *p116*
*Wife:*Christian McIntyre
*Son:*Alexander
*Son:*John
McDougall, Bettie *SEE* McDougall, Ronald
McDougall, Catherine 19; Ontario, 1871 ***1823.21*** *p230*
McDougall, Christian McIntyre *SEE* McDougall, Archibald
McDougall, Donald 68; Ontario, 1871 ***1823.21*** *p230*
McDougall, Dugald *SEE* McDougall, Duncan
McDougall, Duncan; New York, 1739 ***8277.31*** *p117*
*Wife:*Janet Calder
*Child:*Alexander
*Child:*Ronald
*Child:*Margaret
*Child:*Dugald
*Child:*John
McDougall, Duncan 66; Ontario, 1871 ***1823.21*** *p230*
McDougall, Elizabeth Graham *SEE* McDougall, Allan
McDougall, Flora 27; Ontario, 1871 ***1823.21*** *p230*
McDougall, Hannah *SEE* McDougall, Allan
McDougall, Hugh; New York, 1738 ***8277.31*** *p117*
McDougall, Hugh; South Carolina, 1855 ***6155.4*** *p18*
McDougall, Janet Calder *SEE* McDougall, Duncan
McDougall, John *SEE* McDougall, Archibald
McDougall, John *SEE* McDougall, Ronald
McDougall, John *SEE* McDougall, Duncan
McDougall, John 22; New York, NY, 1835 ***5024.1*** *p136*
McDougall, John 36; Ohio, 1880 ***4879.40*** *p258*
McDougall, John 32; Ontario, 1871 ***1823.21*** *p230*
McDougall, John 65; Ontario, 1871 ***1823.17*** *p105*
McDougall, John 78; Ontario, 1871 ***1823.21*** *p230*
McDougall, John 85; Ontario, 1871 ***1823.21*** *p230*
McDougall, M. 19; Ontario, 1871 ***1823.21*** *p230*
McDougall, Margaret *SEE* McDougall, Allan

McDougall, Margaret *SEE* McDougall, Duncan
McDougall, Margaret; New York, 1740 ***8277.31*** *p117*
McDougall, Margret 31; Ontario, 1871 ***1823.21*** *p230*
McDougall, Mary; New York, 1738 ***8277.31*** *p116*
McDougall, Mary 30; Ontario, 1871 ***1823.21*** *p230*
McDougall, Ronald; New York, 1738 ***8277.31*** *p117*
*Wife:*Bettie
*Son:*John
*Son:*Alexander
McDougall, Ronald *SEE* McDougall, Duncan
McDougall, Samuel 48; Ontario, 1871 ***1823.21*** *p230*
McDougall, Samuel; Philadelphia, 1856 ***8513.31*** *p413*
McDougall, Sarah 57; Ontario, 1871 ***1823.21*** *p231*
McDougall, Sarah 78; Ontario, 1871 ***1823.21*** *p231*
McDougals, Malcolm; Brunswick, NC, 1767 ***1422.10*** *p61*
McDougle, Archibald 57; Ontario, 1871 ***1823.21*** *p231*
McDoule, James; Kingston, Jamaica, 1778 ***8529.30*** *p13A*
McDoull, John; Jamaica, 1793 ***8529.30*** *p13A*
McDowale, Robert 53; Ontario, 1871 ***1823.21*** *p231*
McDowell, Eliza 58; Ontario, 1871 ***1823.21*** *p231*
McDowell, James; America, 1767 ***1220.12*** *p519*
McDowell, Jas 64; Ontario, 1871 ***1823.21*** *p231*
McDowell, Samuel; Louisiana, 1874 ***4981.45*** *p133*
McDowgall, John; Died enroute, 1725 ***1220.12*** *p519*
McDuff, John; America, 1772 ***1220.12*** *p519*
McDuffie, Anna; New York, 1738 ***8277.31*** *p116*
McDuffie, Archibald; New York, 1739 ***8277.31*** *p117*
*Wife:*Catharine Campbell
*Son:*John
*Son:*Duncan
McDuffie, Catharine Campbell *SEE* McDuffie, Archibald
McDuffie, Dudley *SEE* McDuffie, Dudley
McDuffie, Dudley; New York, 1740 ***8277.31*** *p117*
*Wife:*Margaret McDougall
*Child:*Mary
*Child:*Dudley
McDuffie, Duncan *SEE* McDuffie, Archibald
McDuffie, Janet *SEE* McDuffie, Malcolm
McDuffie, John *SEE* McDuffie, Archibald
McDuffie, Malcolm; New York, 1738 ***8277.31*** *p117*
*Wife:*Rose Docharty
*Daughter:*Janet
*Daughter:*Margart
McDuffie, Margaret; New York, 1739 ***8277.31*** *p119*
McDuffie, Margaret; New York, 1739 ***8277.31*** *p119*
McDuffie, Margaret McDougall *SEE* McDuffie, Dudley
McDuffie, Margart *SEE* McDuffie, Malcolm
McDuffie, Mary *SEE* McDuffie, Dudley
McDuffie, Rose Docharty *SEE* McDuffie, Malcolm
McDuffies, Alexander; Died enroute, 1739 ***8277.31*** *p117*
McDuffy, Donald 48; Ontario, 1871 ***1823.21*** *p231*
McDugal, Donald 48; Ontario, 1871 ***1823.17*** *p105*
McDugald, Alex 59; Ontario, 1871 ***1823.21*** *p231*
McDugald, Alex.; Cape Fear, NC,, 1754 ***1422.10*** *p62*
McDugald, Allan; Cape Fear, NC,, 1754 ***1422.10*** *p62*
McDugdale, Daniel; Barbados or Jamaica, 1699 ***1220.12*** *p519*
McDugoll, John; Boston, 1728 ***1642*** *p25*
McEachan, Duncan 46; Ontario, 1871 ***1823.17*** *p105*
McEacharn, Catherine; Ontario, 1871 ***1823.21*** *p231*
McEacharn, David 54; Ontario, 1871 ***1823.21*** *p231*
McEacharn, Donald 50; Ontario, 1871 ***1823.21*** *p231*
McEacharn, Hector 36; Ontario, 1871 ***1823.21*** *p231*
McEacharn, John 75; Ontario, 1871 ***1823.21*** *p231*
McEachem, John; Colorado, 1880 ***1029.59*** *p60*
McEachern, Mr.; Died enroute, 1816 ***7085.8*** *p89*
McEachern, Angus 43; Ontario, 1871 ***1823.21*** *p231*
McEachern, Archibald; Pictou, N.S., 1816 ***7085.8*** *p89*
With wife & 3 sons
McEachern, Catherine; Pictou, N.S., 1816 ***7085.8*** *p89*
With 2 daughters
McEachern, Christy 55; Ontario, 1871 ***1823.21*** *p231*
McEachern, Duncan 38; Ontario, 1871 ***1823.21*** *p231*
McEachern, Florence; New York, 1738 ***8277.31*** *p118*
McEachern, John; Pictou, N.S., 1816 ***7085.8*** *p89*
With wife 3 sons & 5 daughters
McEachern, Mary; New York, 1738 ***8277.31*** *p118*
McEachin, Donald 52; Ontario, 1871 ***1823.21*** *p231*
McEachin, Janet 40; Ontario, 1871 ***1823.21*** *p231*
McEachin, John 31; Ontario, 1871 ***1823.21*** *p231*
McEachin, John 42; Ontario, 1871 ***1823.21*** *p231*
McEachron, Anna McDonald *SEE* McEachron, Donald
McEachron, Catharine *SEE* McEachron, Donald
McEachron, Donald; New York, 1738 ***8277.31*** *p117*
*Wife:*Anna McDonald
*Daughter:*Catharine
McEchan, Malcolm 75; Ontario, 1871 ***1823.21*** *p231*
McElderry, Edward; Toronto, 1844 ***2910.35*** *p113*
McElderry, Margaret; South Carolina, 1813 ***3208.30*** *p19*
McElderry, Margaret; South Carolina, 1813 ***3208.30*** *p32*
McElery, Bridget *SEE* McElery, John
McElery, Catharine McDonald *SEE* McElery, John
McElery, Donald *SEE* McElery, John
McElery, Hugh *SEE* McElery, John
McElery, John; New York, 1740 ***8277.31*** *p117*
*Wife:*Catharine McDonald
*Child:*Donald
*Child:*Mary
*Child:*Bridget
*Child:*Hugh
McElery, Mary *SEE* McElery, John
McElhern, George 26; Ontario, 1871 ***1823.21*** *p231*
McElhern, Jane 58; Ontario, 1871 ***1823.21*** *p231*
McElheron, Marg I. 30; Ontario, 1871 ***1823.17*** *p105*
McElheron, Patrick 32; Ontario, 1871 ***1823.17*** *p105*
McElheron, William J. 47; Ontario, 1871 ***1823.17*** *p105*
McElhinney, Audrey 4; St. John, N.B., 1834 ***6469.7*** *p5*
McElhinney, Cathn 6; St. John, N.B., 1834 ***6469.7*** *p5*
McElhinney, James 1; St. John, N.B., 1834 ***6469.7*** *p5*
McElhinney, John 12; St. John, N.B., 1834 ***6469.7*** *p5*
McElhinney, Lady 9; St. John, N.B., 1834 ***6469.7*** *p5*
McElmoyle, James 68; Ontario, 1871 ***1823.17*** *p105*
McElmoyle, Jas, Jr. 39; Ontario, 1871 ***1823.17*** *p105*
McElmurry, James 33; Ontario, 1871 ***1823.21*** *p231*
McElree, Auguste; Wisconsin, 1905 ***6795.8*** *p224*
McElroy, Elizabeth; Boston, 1760 ***1642*** *p48*
McElroy, James 36; Ontario, 1871 ***1823.17*** *p105*
McEnnery, Patrick; Toronto, 1844 ***2910.35*** *p113*
McEnnis, Frederick; America, 1742 ***1220.12*** *p519*
McEnny, Andrew; America, 1738 ***1220.12*** *p520*
McEreth, Elizabeth; America, 1732 ***1220.12*** *p520*
McEther, Timothy; America, 1729 ***1220.12*** *p520*
McEuen, Alexander *SEE* McEuen, Anne McNeil
McEuen, Anna Johnston *SEE* McEuen, John
McEuen, Anne; New York, 1740 ***8277.31*** *p117*
*Child:*Alexander
*Child:*Hannah
*Child:*Mary
McEuen, Catherine; New York, 1739 ***8277.31*** *p115*
McEuen, Hannah *SEE* McEuen, Anne McNeil
McEuen, John; New York, 1739 ***8277.31*** *p117*
*Wife:*Anna Johnston
*Son:*Malcolm
McEuen, Malcolm *SEE* McEuen, John
McEuen, Mary; New York, 1738 ***8277.31*** *p117*
McEuen, Mary *SEE* McEuen, Anne McNeil
McEuin, George; New Jersey, 1777 ***8529.30*** *p4A*
McEury, Owen 75; Ontario, 1871 ***1823.17*** *p105*
McEver, Henry; St. John, N.B., 1847 ***2978.15*** *p36*
McEver, Michael 42; Ontario, 1871 ***1823.17*** *p105*
McEvoy, Andrew M. 34; Ontario, 1871 ***1823.21*** *p231*
McEwan, Ann 55; Ontario, 1871 ***1823.21*** *p231*
McEwan, Charles 51; Ontario, 1871 ***1823.17*** *p105*
McEwan, Duncan 53; Ontario, 1871 ***1823.17*** *p105*
McEwan, Duncan 56; Ontario, 1871 ***1823.21*** *p231*
McEwan, James 53; Ontario, 1871 ***1823.21*** *p231*
McEwan, Peter 59; Ontario, 1871 ***1823.21*** *p231*
McEwan, Robert 46; Ontario, 1871 ***1823.21*** *p231*
McEwen, Catherine 55; Ontario, 1871 ***1823.17*** *p105*
McEwen, Colin 50; Ontario, 1871 ***1823.21*** *p231*
McEwen, David 65; Ontario, 1871 ***1823.21*** *p231*
McEwen, Duncan 60; Ontario, 1871 ***1823.21*** *p231*
McEwen, Ewen 76; Ontario, 1871 ***1823.21*** *p231*
McEwen, George 39; Ontario, 1871 ***1823.21*** *p231*
McEwen, Hessie 65; Ontario, 1871 ***1823.21*** *p231*
McEwen, Robert 45; Ontario, 1871 ***1823.21*** *p232*
McEwer, Andrew 14; Ontario, 1871 ***1823.21*** *p232*
McEwer, Jane 12; Ontario, 1871 ***1823.21*** *p232*
McEwing, Agnes 65; Ontario, 1871 ***1823.21*** *p232*
McEwing, William 41; Ontario, 1871 ***1823.21*** *p232*
McFadden, David 26; Ontario, 1871 ***1823.21*** *p232*
McFadden, George 38; Ontario, 1871 ***1823.21*** *p232*
McFadden, John; Ohio, 1809-1852 ***4511.35*** *p33*
McFadden, John 28; Ontario, 1871 ***1823.21*** *p232*
McFadden, John 39; Ontario, 1871 ***1823.21*** *p232*
McFadden, John 66; Ontario, 1871 ***1823.21*** *p232*
McFadden, Joseph 54; Ontario, 1871 ***1823.21*** *p232*
McFadden, Lachlin 50; Ontario, 1871 ***1823.17*** *p105*
McFadden, Mary 46; Ontario, 1871 ***1823.21*** *p232*
McFadden, Prudence; Boston, 1760 ***1642*** *p48*
McFadden, Thomas 39; Ontario, 1871 ***1823.21*** *p232*
McFail, Christy Clark *SEE* McFail, John
McFail, John *SEE* McFail, John
McFail, John; New York, 1739 ***8277.31*** *p119*
*Wife:*Christy Clark
*Son:*John
McFall, Daniel; Boston, 1737 ***1642*** *p26*
McFall, Patrick 43; Ontario, 1871 ***1823.21*** *p232*
McFalls, Alexander 38; Ontario, 1871 ***1823.21*** *p232*
McFalls, Alexander 73; Ontario, 1871 ***1823.21*** *p232*
McFalls, John 45; Ontario, 1871 ***1823.21*** *p232*
McFalls, Steward 37; Ontario, 1871 ***1823.21*** *p232*
McFalls, Stewart 40; Ontario, 1871 ***1823.21*** *p232*
McFarlan, Daniel 35; Ontario, 1871 ***1823.17*** *p106*
McFarlan, Duncan 55; Ontario, 1871 ***1823.21*** *p232*
McFarlan, Edward 42; Michigan, 1880 ***4491.39*** *p20*
McFarlan, John 53; Ontario, 1871 ***1823.21*** *p232*
McFarland, Alex 63; Ontario, 1871 ***1823.21*** *p232*
McFarland, Andrew 58; Ontario, 1871 ***1823.21*** *p232*
McFarland, Catharine Feeney *SEE* McFarland, Hugh
McFarland, Eliza J. 35; Michigan, 1880 ***4491.36*** *p15*
McFarland, Henry 45; Michigan, 1880 ***4491.36*** *p15*
McFarland, Hugh; Pittsburgh, 1854 ***8513.31*** *p413*
*Wife:*Catharine Feeney
McFarland, J. P.; California, 1868 ***1131.61*** *p89*
McFarland, James 35; Michigan, 1880 ***4491.36*** *p15*
McFarland, James; North Carolina, 1848 ***1088.45*** *p22*
McFarland, John 34; New York, NY, 1825 ***6178.50*** *p77*
McFarland, Mary Anne 17; Ontario, 1871 ***1823.21*** *p232*
McFarland, Steward 9; New York, NY, 1821-1849 ***6178.50*** *p77*
Mc Farland, Thomas; Ohio, 1844 ***2763.1*** *p20*
McFarland, Thomas; Washington, 1885 ***2770.40*** *p194*
McFarlane, Donald 39; Ontario, 1871 ***1823.21*** *p232*
McFarlane, Donald 58; Ontario, 1871 ***1823.21*** *p232*
McFarlane, Dond. 6; North Carolina, 1774 ***1422.10*** *p57*
McFarlane, Dond. 26; North Carolina, 1774 ***1422.10*** *p57*
McFarlane, James 67; Ontario, 1871 ***1823.17*** *p106*
McFarlane, John; Nova Scotia, 1839 ***7078*** *p80*
McFarlane, John 34; Ontario, 1871 ***1823.17*** *p106*
McFarlane, John 68; Ontario, 1871 ***1823.21*** *p232*
McFarlane, Malcolm 53; Ontario, 1871 ***1823.21*** *p232*
McFarlane, Peter 35; Ontario, 1871 ***1823.17*** *p106*
McFarlane, Thomas 57; Ontario, 1871 ***1823.21*** *p232*
McFarlane, Walter 20; North Carolina, 1775 ***1422.10*** *p57*
McFarlane, Wm 37; Ontario, 1871 ***1823.21*** *p232*
McFarlin, Arch. 65; Ontario, 1871 ***1823.17*** *p106*
McFarlin, John 55; Ontario, 1871 ***1823.21*** *p232*
McFarlin, Patk 35; Ontario, 1871 ***1823.21*** *p232*
McFarling, Catherine; America, 1765 ***1220.12*** *p520*
McFarling, Daniel; Massachusetts, 1747 ***1642*** *p111*
McFarling, Mary; Virginia, 1718 ***1220.12*** *p520*
McFarling, William 43; Ontario, 1871 ***1823.17*** *p106*
McFarndall, Mark; America, 1718 ***1220.12*** *p520*
McFaston, John; America, 1722 ***1220.12*** *p520*
McFeast, Mary; America, 1771 ***1220.12*** *p520*
McFeden, John; Massachusetts, 1740 ***1642*** *p100*
McFee, Alexander 32; Ontario, 1871 ***1823.21*** *p232*
McFee, Alexander 53; Ontario, 1871 ***1823.21*** *p232*
McFee, Hector 45; Ontario, 1871 ***1823.17*** *p106*
McFee, Hector 45; Ontario, 1871 ***1823.21*** *p232*
McFee, John 70; Ontario, 1871 ***1823.21*** *p233*
McFee, Mary 49; Ontario, 1871 ***1823.21*** *p233*
McFee, Neal 32; Ohio, 1880 ***4879.40*** *p260*
McFee, Norman 41; Ontario, 1871 ***1823.21*** *p233*
McFee, Roderick 20; Ontario, 1871 ***1823.21*** *p233*
McFeet, John; America, 1766 ***1220.12*** *p520*
McFerson, Alexander 60; Ontario, 1871 ***1823.17*** *p106*
McFerston, John; America, 1722 ***1220.12*** *p520*
McFetrick, John 45; St. John, N.B., 1834 ***6469.7*** *p4*
McFetrick, Martha 45; St. John, N.B., 1834 ***6469.7*** *p4*
McFetrick, Thomas 11; St. John, N.B., 1834 ***6469.7*** *p4*
McFetrick, William 10; St. John, N.B., 1834 ***6469.7*** *p4*
McFie, Charles 58; Ontario, 1871 ***1823.21*** *p233*
McFie, Donald 50; Ontario, 1871 ***1823.21*** *p233*
McFie, John 32; Ontario, 1871 ***1823.21*** *p233*
McFie, Joseph 30; Ontario, 1871 ***1823.21*** *p233*
McFie, Malcolm 78; Ontario, 1871 ***1823.21*** *p233*
McFie, Mary 36; Ontario, 1871 ***1823.21*** *p233*
McGae, John; Boston, 1765 ***1642*** *p35*
McGaim, Mary 45; Ontario, 1871 ***1823.21*** *p233*
McGamm, Patrick 40; Ontario, 1871 ***1823.21*** *p233*
McGanley, James; America, 1774 ***1220.12*** *p520*
McGann, Mary 35; Ontario, 1871 ***1823.21*** *p233*
McGannon, James; Ohio, 1840-1897 ***8365.35*** *p17*
McGarhn, James 32; Ontario, 1871 ***1823.17*** *p106*
McGarl, James; Ohio, 1850 ***3580.20*** *p32*
McGarl, James; Ohio, 1850 ***6020.12*** *p13*
McGarrah, Edwd 50; Ontario, 1871 ***1823.21*** *p233*
Mc Garrigle, John; Louisiana, 1841-1844 ***4981.45*** *p211*
McGarvey, Edward 51; Ontario, 1871 ***1823.17*** *p106*
McGarvey, John 39; Ontario, 1871 ***1823.21*** *p233*
McGarvey, Patrick; Ohio, 1838 ***3580.20*** *p32*
McGarvey, Patrick; Ohio, 1838 ***6020.12*** *p13*
McGary, Catharine 53; Ontario, 1871 ***1823.17*** *p106*
McGary, Cathrine 53; Ontario, 1871 ***1823.21*** *p233*
McGaughlin, James 30; New York, NY, 1825 ***6178.50*** *p77*
McGavah, Andrew 56; Ontario, 1871 ***1823.21*** *p233*
McGavin, Michael; Ontario, 1871 ***1823.17*** *p106*
McGavock, William; Colorado, 1886 ***1029.59*** *p60*
McGaw, Alexander; Philadelphia, 1778 ***8529.30*** *p4A*
McGea, Andrew; America, 1738 ***1220.12*** *p520*
McGeachy, Malcolm 46; Ontario, 1871 ***1823.21*** *p233*
McGeary, George 40; Ontario, 1871 ***1823.21*** *p233*
McGeary, James 35; Ontario, 1871 ***1823.21*** *p233*
McGee, Bernard; Toronto, 1844 ***2910.35*** *p116*
McGee, Bridget 48; Ontario, 1871 ***1823.21*** *p233*

McGee, Catherine; America, 1765 *1220.12 p520*
McGee, Charles 60; Ontario, 1871 *1823.17 p106*
McGee, Charles; Philadelphia, 1777 *8529.30 p4A*
McGee, Christopher; America, 1773 *1220.12 p520*
McGee, Daniel 39; Ontario, 1871 *1823.17 p106*
McGee, George G. 56; Ontario, 1871 *1823.21 p233*
McGee, James; Philadelphia, 1777 *8529.30 p3*
McGee, James; Toronto, 1844 *2910.35 p114*
McGee, John; America, 1765 *1220.12 p520*
McGee, John; Annapolis, MD, 1726 *1220.12 p520*
McGee, John; North America, 1750 *1640.8 p234*
McGee, John 71; Ontario, 1871 *1823.21 p233*
McGee, John; Toronto, 1844 *2910.35 p114*
McGee, Margt 25; St. John, N.B., 1834 *6469.7 p4*
McGee, Martin 30; Ontario, 1871 *1823.21 p233*
McGee, Mary; America, 1765 *1220.12 p520*
McGee, Mary; America, 1771 *1220.12 p520*
McGee, Michael 34; Ontario, 1871 *1823.21 p233*
McGee, Molly 26; St. John, N.B., 1834 *6469.7 p4*
McGee, Patrick 47; Ontario, 1871 *1823.21 p233*
McGee, Robert 55; Ontario, 1871 *1823.17 p106*
McGee, Thomas; America, 1734 *1220.12 p520*
McGee, Thomas; Massachusetts, 1741 *1642 p101*
McGee, Thomas; Massachusetts, 1747 *1642 p117*
McGee, William 11; Ontario, 1871 *1823.17 p106*
McGee, William 42; Ontario, 1871 *1823.21 p233*
McGee, William 46; Ontario, 1871 *1823.21 p233*
McGee, Wm.; Toronto, 1844 *2910.35 p116*
McGehan, John; Pennsylvania, 1859 *8513.31 p413*
*Wife:*Margaret Moore
McGehan, Margaret Moore *SEE* McGehan, John
McGen, James; Ohio, 1809-1852 *4511.35 p33*
McGennes, William; America, 1764 *1220.12 p520*
McGennis, Thomas; America, 1770 *1220.12 p520*
McGettrick, John; Toronto, 1844 *2910.35 p116*
McGey, Thomas; Annapolis, MD, 1725 *1220.12 p520*
McGhee, Margaret 14; Quebec, 1870 *8364.32 p25*
McGibbon, Donald 41; Ontario, 1871 *1823.17 p106*
McGibbon, William 38; Quebec, 1910 *2897.7 p7*
McGie, Margret 33; Ontario, 1871 *1823.21 p233*
McGigar, Thomas 45; Ontario, 1871 *1823.17 p106*
McGilfry, Robert 19; Michigan, 1880 *4491.39 p20*
McGill, David 56; Ontario, 1871 *1823.21 p233*
McGill, Duncan 45; Ontario, 1871 *1823.21 p233*
McGill, Henry; Havana, 1782 *8529.30 p9A*
McGill, James 28; Ontario, 1871 *1823.17 p106*
McGill, James 38; Ontario, 1871 *1823.17 p106*
McGill, Jane 50; Ontario, 1871 *1823.21 p233*
McGill, John 43; Ontario, 1871 *1823.17 p106*
McGill, Owen 66; Ontario, 1871 *1823.17 p106*
McGill, Patrick 60; Ontario, 1871 *1823.21 p233*
McGill, Peter J.; Louisiana, 1874-1875 *4981.45 p30*
McGill, Quinten 57; Ontario, 1871 *1823.21 p233*
McGill, William 64; Ontario, 1871 *1823.17 p106*
McGilles, John; Quebec, 1786 *1416.15 p8*
McGilles, John; Washington, 1884 *2770.40 p192*
McGillicuddy, Eusebuis 37; Ontario, 1871 *1823.17 p106*
McGilligan, John 35; Ontario, 1871 *1823.21 p233*
McGillycuddy, Pamis 28; Ontario, 1871 *1823.17 p106*
McGilreach, Hugh; Cape Fear, NC,, 1754 *1422.10 p61*
McGilriach, John; Cape Fear, NC,, 1754 *1422.10 p61*
McGilveray, Finlay 30; Ontario, 1871 *1823.21 p233*
McGilvery, Bridget *SEE* McGilvery, John
McGilvery, Catharine McDonald *SEE* McGilvery, John
McGilvery, Donald *SEE* McGilvery, John
McGilvery, Duncan 45; Michigan, 1880 *4491.36 p14*
McGilvery, Hugh *SEE* McGilvery, John
McGilvery, John; New York, 1740 *8277.31 p117*
*Wife:*Catharine McDonald
*Child:*Bridget
*Child:*Mary
*Child:*Hugh
*Child:*Donald
McGilvery, John 68; Ontario, 1871 *1823.21 p233*
McGilvery, Mary *SEE* McGilvery, John
McGilvra, Martin; Quebec, 1786 *1416.15 p8*
McGiness, Calvin 40; Ontario, 1871 *1823.21 p233*
McGinis, James 45; Ontario, 1871 *1823.17 p106*
McGinn, James; St. John, N.B., 1847 *2978.15 p38*
McGinn, James; St. John, N.B., 1847 *2978.15 p39*
McGinnes, Angus 30; Ontario, 1871 *1823.21 p233*
McGinnes, Edward; North Carolina, 1834 *1088.45 p22*
McGinnis, Alexr 29; Ontario, 1871 *1823.21 p233*
McGinnis, Bridget 46; Michigan, 1880 *4491.39 p20*
McGinnis, Charles; America, 1775 *1220.12 p520*
McGinnis, Fred 6; Michigan, 1880 *4491.39 p20*
McGinnis, J. J.; Louisiana, 1874 *4981.45 p133*
McGinnis, John; America, 1764 *1220.12 p520*
McGinnis, John 28; Ontario, 1871 *1823.21 p234*
McGinnis, John 36; Ontario, 1871 *1823.17 p106*
McGinnis, John 40; Ontario, 1871 *1823.21 p234*
McGinnis, John; Quebec, 1786 *1416.15 p5*
McGinnis, Judith; America, 1769 *1220.12 p520*
McGinnis, Maggie 3; Michigan, 1880 *4491.39 p20*
McGinnis, Margeret 16; Ontario, 1871 *1823.21 p234*
McGinnis, Martin 48; Michigan, 1880 *4491.39 p20*
McGinnis, Mary 45; Michigan, 1880 *4491.39 p20*
McGinnis, Patrick; North America, 1750 *1640.8 p233*
McGinnis, Peter; Ohio, 1809-1852 *4511.35 p33*
McGinnis, Richard 43; Michigan, 1880 *4491.39 p20*
McGinnis, Thomas 45; Ontario, 1871 *1823.17 p106*
McGinnis, William 11; Michigan, 1880 *4491.39 p20*
McGinty, Ann; Philadelphia, 1857 *8513.31 p299*
McGinty, Brian 23; Michigan, 1880 *4491.30 p22*
McGinty, John A.; Ohio, 1824 *3580.20 p32*
McGinty, John A.; Ohio, 1824 *6020.12 p13*
McGinty, John A.; Ohio, 1827 *3580.20 p32*
McGinty, John A.; Ohio, 1827 *6020.12 p13*
McGirdy, Jane 75; Ontario, 1871 *1823.21 p234*
McGirdy, Robert 40; Ontario, 1871 *1823.21 p234*
McGirk, James; America, 1768 *1220.12 p520*
McGirwin, Nancy; Ontario, 1835 *3160.1 p150*
McGiven, Francis 35; Ontario, 1871 *1823.21 p234*
McGivern, Nancy; Prescott, Ont., 1835 *3289.1 p61*
McGlachan, Alex 7; New York, NY, 1835 *5024.1 p136*
McGlachan, Isabella 9; New York, NY, 1835 *5024.1 p136*
McGlachan, John 4; New York, NY, 1835 *5024.1 p136*
McGlachan, Margaret 11; New York, NY, 1835 *5024.1 p136*
McGlachan, Margaret 37; New York, NY, 1835 *5024.1 p136*
McGlachan, Neil 40; New York, NY, 1835 *5024.1 p136*
McGlade, James 18; New York, NY, 1894 *6512.1 p229*
McGlade, Neil 21; New York, NY, 1894 *6512.1 p229*
McGlashan, Peter 60; Ontario, 1871 *1823.17 p106*
McGlauchlan, Colin 55; Ontario, 1871 *1823.17 p106*
McGlaughlin, James 30; New York, NY, 1825 *6178.50 p77*
McGlaughlin, Thomas 52; Ontario, 1871 *1823.17 p106*
McGlennan, John; St. Johns, N.F., 1825 *1053.15 p6*
McGlennan, Margt; St. Johns, N.F., 1825 *1053.15 p6*
McGlew, Patrick; America, 1755 *1220.12 p520*
McGlinch, John 22; Ontario, 1871 *1823.21 p234*
McGlochlin, Mary; America, 1770 *1220.12 p520*
McGlockin, James 14; Ontario, 1871 *1823.21 p234*
McGloghlan, W. D. 31; Ontario, 1871 *1823.21 p234*
McGlouclin, William 20; Ontario, 1871 *1823.21 p234*
McGolderick, Frs; St. John, N.B., 1847 *2978.15 p37*
McGonigal, George; Colorado, 1884 *1029.59 p60*
McGorman, Margaret; Philadelphia, 1854 *8513.31 p313*
McGorman, William 24; Ontario, 1871 *1823.17 p106*
McGory, John 55; Ontario, 1871 *1823.21 p234*
McGough, Arthur 60; Ontario, 1871 *1823.17 p107*
McGouigal, George; Colorado, 1890 *1029.59 p60*
McGovern, Edward 55; Ontario, 1871 *1823.21 p234*
McGovern, Frances; Colorado, 1872 *1029.59 p60*
McGovern, Tho.; Colorado, 1873 *1029.59 p60*
McGowan, Grace Ann; Oregon, 1941 *9157.47 p2*
McGowan, James; North Carolina, 1844 *1088.45 p22*
McGowan, James; St. John, N.B., 1842 *2978.20 p9*
McGowan, John 40; Ontario, 1871 *1823.17 p107*
McGowan, Mic; St. John, N.B., 1847 *2978.15 p38*
McGowan, Mic; St. John, N.B., 1847 *2978.15 p39*
McGowan, Robert 45; Ontario, 1871 *1823.21 p234*
McGowan, Rodger; North Carolina, 1839 *1088.45 p22*
McGowen, David; Ohio, 1826 *3580.20 p32*
McGowen, David; Ohio, 1826 *6020.12 p13*
McGowing, John; America, 1769 *1220.12 p520*
McGown, Angus *SEE* McGown, John
McGown, Anna McCuarg *SEE* McGown, John
McGown, Archibald; New York, 1739 *8277.31 p117*
*Child:*Duncan
*Child:*John
*Child:*Margaret
McGown, Duncan *SEE* McGown, Archibald
McGown, John *SEE* McGown, Archibald
McGown, John; New York, 1739 *8277.31 p117*
*Wife:*Anna McCuarg
*Son:*Malcolm
*Son:*Angus
McGown, Malcolm *SEE* McGown, John
McGown, Margaret *SEE* McGown, Archibald
McGrady, James 36; Ontario, 1871 *1823.21 p234*
McGragh, James; Boston, 1826 *3274.55 p27*
McGrath, . . . 23; St. Johns, N.F., 1811 *1053.20 p21*
McGrath, Catherine 60; Ontario, 1871 *1823.21 p234*
McGrath, David 26; Ontario, 1871 *1823.17 p107*
McGrath, Edward; New York, NY, 1839 *3274.55 p44*
McGrath, Elizabeth; America, 1767 *1220.12 p520*
McGrath, Elizabeth Connelly *SEE* McGrath, Thomas
McGrath, Gilbert; Philadelphia, 1778 *8529.30 p4A*
McGrath, James; Philadelphia, 1778 *8529.30 p4A*
McGrath, John 59; Ontario, 1871 *1823.21 p234*
McGrath, Margaret; America, 1759 *1220.12 p520*
McGrath, Margaret 10; Quebec, 1870 *8364.32 p25*
McGrath, Matthew 60; Ontario, 1871 *1823.21 p234*
McGrath, Michael; Newfoundland, 1814 *3476.10 p54*
McGrath, Michael; Ohio, 1809-1852 *4511.35 p33*
McGrath, P. H.; Louisiana, 1874 *4981.45 p296*
McGrath, Patrick; Burlington, VT, 1832 *3274.55 p44*
McGrath, Patrick; New York, NY, 1836 *3274.55 p44*
McGrath, Phil J.; Louisiana, 1874-1875 *4981.45 p30*
McGrath, Thomas 34; Ontario, 1871 *1823.17 p107*
McGrath, Thomas; Philadelphia, 1854 *8513.31 p413*
*Wife:*Elizabeth Connelly
McGrath, William 50; Ontario, 1871 *1823.21 p234*
McGraw, James 40; Ontario, 1871 *1823.17 p107*
McGraw, Thomas 45; Ontario, 1871 *1823.21 p234*
McGreedy, Rosan 30; Ontario, 1871 *1823.21 p234*
McGregor, Alex 51; Ontario, 1871 *1823.17 p107*
McGregor, Alex 56; Ontario, 1871 *1823.21 p234*
McGregor, Alexander 50; Ontario, 1871 *1823.17 p107*
McGregor, Alexander 55; Ontario, 1871 *1823.17 p107*
McGregor, Alexr 37; Ontario, 1871 *1823.17 p107*
McGregor, Angus 49; Ontario, 1871 *1823.17 p107*
McGregor, Arch 39; Ontario, 1871 *1823.17 p107*
McGregor, Archibald 73; Ontario, 1871 *1823.17 p107*
McGregor, Christy A. 20; Ontario, 1871 *1823.21 p234*
McGregor, Donald 54; Ontario, 1871 *1823.21 p234*
McGregor, Duncan 28; Ontario, 1871 *1823.21 p234*
McGregor, Duncan 50; Ontario, 1871 *1823.21 p234*
McGregor, Duncan 53; Ontario, 1871 *1823.21 p234*
McGregor, Duncan 60; Ontario, 1871 *1823.17 p107*
McGregor, Gregor 38; Ontario, 1871 *1823.21 p234*
McGregor, James 26; Ontario, 1871 *1823.21 p234*
McGregor, James 36; Ontario, 1871 *1823.21 p234*
McGregor, James 37; Ontario, 1871 *1823.17 p107*
McGregor, James 40; Ontario, 1871 *1823.21 p234*
McGregor, James 43; Ontario, 1871 *1823.17 p107*
McGregor, James; Washington, 1889 *2770.40 p79*
McGregor, John 19; Ontario, 1871 *1823.21 p234*
McGregor, John 35; Ontario, 1871 *1823.21 p234*
McGregor, John 42; Ontario, 1871 *1823.21 p234*
McGregor, John 43; Ontario, 1871 *1823.21 p234*
McGregor, John 58; Ontario, 1871 *1823.21 p234*
McGregor, John 60; Ontario, 1871 *1823.17 p107*
McGregor, John 60; Ontario, 1871 *1823.21 p234*
McGregor, John 64; Ontario, 1871 *1823.17 p107*
McGregor, Margaret 73; Ontario, 1871 *1823.17 p107*
McGregor, Margaret 89; Ontario, 1871 *1823.17 p107*
McGregor, Neil 30; Ontario, 1871 *1823.17 p107*
McGregor, Peter 35; Ontario, 1871 *1823.17 p107*
McGregor, Peter 56; Ontario, 1871 *1823.17 p107*
McGregor, Peter 72; Ontario, 1871 *1823.17 p107*
McGregor, Peter R. 22; Ontario, 1871 *1823.17 p107*
McGregor, Robert; America, 1726 *1220.12 p520*
McGregor, Samuel 52; Ontario, 1871 *1823.21 p234*
McGregor, William 40; Ontario, 1871 *1823.17 p107*
McGrerdy, John 47; Ontario, 1871 *1823.21 p234*
McGrew, James; America, 1743 *1220.12 p520*
McGrew, Thomas F.; Ohio, 1842 *3580.20 p32*
McGrew, Thomas F.; Ohio, 1842 *6020.12 p13*
McGrogan, Margaret; Philadelphia, 1854 *8513.31 p313*
McGrory, Mary 24; Ontario, 1871 *1823.21 p235*
McGroty, Thomas; Illinois, 1834-1900 *6020.5 p132*
McGueire, Margaret; America, 1760 *1220.12 p520*
McGuerk, John 60; Ontario, 1871 *1823.21 p235*
McGuey, Timothy 50; Ontario, 1871 *1823.21 p235*
McGuffin, Alex 32; Ontario, 1871 *1823.21 p235*
McGuffin, Alexander; America, 1763 *1220.12 p520*
McGuffin, Alexander 84; Ontario, 1871 *1823.21 p235*
McGuffin, Joseph 60; Ontario, 1871 *1823.21 p235*
McGuffy, Alice 12; Quebec, 1870 *8364.32 p25*
McGuffy, Margaret 11; Quebec, 1870 *8364.32 p25*
McGugan, Angus 52; Ontario, 1871 *1823.17 p107*
McGugan, Archibald 41; Ontario, 1871 *1823.17 p107*
McGugan, Archy 60; Ontario, 1871 *1823.21 p235*
McGugan, Donald 38; Ontario, 1871 *1823.17 p107*
McGugan, Donald 48; Ontario, 1871 *1823.17 p107*
McGugan, Donald 54; Ontario, 1871 *1823.21 p235*
McGugan, Donald 72; Ontario, 1871 *1823.21 p235*
McGugan, John 70; Ontario, 1871 *1823.21 p235*
McGuggan, Mary 70; Ontario, 1871 *1823.21 p235*
McGuines, Bernard; Virginia, 1766 *1220.12 p520*
McGuiness, Daniel 18; Quebec, 1870 *8364.32 p25*
McGuiness, Duncan 17; Quebec, 1870 *8364.32 p25*
McGuiness, Edward; Colorado, 1873 *1029.59 p60*
McGuiness, John; America, 1771 *1220.12 p520*
McGuinis, William; Virginia, 1723 *1220.12 p520*
McGuire, Andrew 47; Ontario, 1871 *1823.17 p107*
McGuire, Ann; Boston, 1759 *1642 p47*
McGuire, Bernard 67; Ontario, 1871 *1823.21 p235*
McGuire, Catherine; America, 1749 *1220.12 p520*
McGuire, Catherine; America, 1774 *1220.12 p520*
McGuire, Christian *SEE* McGuire, Duncan
McGuire, Daniel; Potomac, 1729 *1220.12 p520*
McGuire, Daniel; Washington, 1889 *2770.40 p79*
McGuire, Dennis; America, 1771 *1220.12 p520*

314 FOR A COMPLETE EXPLANATION OF ENTRY, SEE "HOW TO READ A CITATION" SECTION

McGuire, Donald *SEE* McGuire, Duncan
McGuire, Duncan; New York, 1739 ***8277.31*** *p119*
*Wife:*Mary McIlepheder
*Child:*John
*Child:*Christian
*Child:*Gilbert
*Child:*Donald
McGuire, Elisabeth 68; Ontario, 1871 ***1823.21*** *p235*
McGuire, Eliza 60; Ontario, 1871 ***1823.21*** *p235*
McGuire, Francis; Louisiana, 1872 ***7710.1*** *p161*
McGuire, George 41; Ontario, 1871 ***1823.17*** *p107*
McGuire, Gilbert *SEE* McGuire, Duncan
McGuire, Hugh Peter 19; New York, NY, 1869 ***7710.1*** *p158*
McGuire, James; Louisiana, 1874-1875 ***4981.45*** *p30*
McGuire, James; Ohio, 1838 ***3580.20*** *p32*
McGuire, James; Ohio, 1838 ***6020.12*** *p13*
McGuire, James 59; Ontario, 1871 ***1823.21*** *p235*
McGuire, Jane; Boston, 1747 ***1642*** *p46*
McGuire, John *SEE* McGuire, Duncan
McGuire, John 32; Ontario, 1871 ***1823.17*** *p107*
McGuire, John 50; Ontario, 1871 ***1823.17*** *p107*
McGuire, John S. 18; New York, NY, 1874 ***7710.1*** *p158*
McGuire, Lockland; America, 1747 ***1220.12*** *p520*
McGuire, Martin; America, 1771 ***1220.12*** *p520*
McGuire, Mary McIlepheder *SEE* McGuire, Duncan
McGuire, Matthew; America, 1765 ***1220.12*** *p520*
McGuire, Owen 35; Ontario, 1871 ***1823.21*** *p235*
McGuire, Peter 36; Ontario, 1871 ***1823.17*** *p107*
McGuire, Philip; Long Island, 1781 ***8529.30*** *p9A*
McGuire, Philip; Louisiana, 1916 ***7710.1*** *p161*
McGuire, Rosanna 49; Ontario, 1871 ***1823.17*** *p107*
McGuire, William 25; Ontario, 1871 ***1823.21*** *p235*
McGuire, William 51; Ontario, 1871 ***1823.21*** *p235*
McGum, Patrick 50; Ontario, 1871 ***1823.21*** *p235*
McGunn, John; Colorado, 1868 ***1029.59*** *p60*
McGurdy, Thomas 36; Ontario, 1871 ***1823.21*** *p235*
McGurk, Henry 42; Ontario, 1871 ***1823.17*** *p107*
McGurk, Martha 54; Ontario, 1871 ***1823.17*** *p108*
McGurn, Ellen 20; Ontario, 1871 ***1823.21*** *p235*
McGutre, Dennis; Boston, 1734 ***1642*** *p44*
McGuy, Jane; Virginia, 1730 ***1220.12*** *p520*
McGwen, John; Louisiana, 1874 ***4981.45*** *p133*
McGwin, Daniel; Virginia, 1736 ***1220.12*** *p520*
McGwin, Michael 66; Ontario, 1871 ***1823.17*** *p108*
McHaen, Donald 33; Ontario, 1871 ***1823.21*** *p235*
McHalfpen, James; America, 1756 ***1220.12*** *p520*
McHam, Margaret; Annapolis, MD, 1725 ***1220.12*** *p521*
McHardie, Robert 29; New York, NY, 1835 ***5024.1*** *p136*
McHardy, William 54; Ontario, 1871 ***1823.21*** *p235*
McHarry, James; New York, NY, 1776 ***8529.30*** *p3*
McHarty, Daniel; America, 1680 ***1220.12*** *p517*
McHattie, George 52; Ontario, 1871 ***1823.17*** *p108*
McHaughton, James 32; Ontario, 1871 ***1823.17*** *p108*
McHiver, Lacky; Marston's Wharf, 1782 ***8529.30*** *p14*
McHobin, Ufane; America, 1719 ***1220.12*** *p521*
McHoon, Mary; Boston, 1767 ***1642*** *p38*
McHugh, Charles; Ohio, 1838 ***3580.20*** *p32*
McHugh, Charles; Ohio, 1838 ***6020.12*** *p13*
McHugh, Henry; Colorado, 1873 ***1029.59*** *p60*
McHugh, John F. 27; Michigan, 1880 ***4491.30*** *p22*
McHugh, Peter 52; Indiana, 1838-1888 ***9076.20*** *p72*
McIlepheder, Archibald; New York, 1739 ***8277.31*** *p117*
McIlepheder, Mary; New York, 1739 ***8277.31*** *p115*
McIlepheder, Mary; New York, 1739 ***8277.31*** *p119*
McIlepheder, Mary; New York, 1739 ***8277.31*** *p119*
McIlepheder, Mary; New York, 1739 ***8277.31*** *p119*
McIlepheder, Mary; New York, 1739 ***8277.31*** *p119*
McIlhargey, John 55; Ontario, 1871 ***1823.21*** *p235*
McIlhargy, Mary Ann 30; Ontario, 1871 ***1823.21*** *p235*
McIllmurry, Joseph 31; Ontario, 1871 ***1823.21*** *p235*
McIlmrry, James 61; Ontario, 1871 ***1823.17*** *p108*
McIlmurry, Samuel 66; Ontario, 1871 ***1823.17*** *p108*
McIlriach, Angus; Cape Fear, NC,, 1754 ***1422.10*** *p62*
McIlriach, Arch.; Cape Fear, NC,, 1754 ***1422.10*** *p61*
McIlriach, Arch.; Cape Fear, NC,, 1754 ***1422.10*** *p62*
McIlriach, Gilbert; Cape Fear, NC,, 1754 ***1422.10*** *p61*
McIlroy, John 49; Ontario, 1871 ***1823.17*** *p108*
McIlroy, John 52; Ontario, 1871 ***1823.17*** *p108*
McIlroy, Thos 32; Ontario, 1871 ***1823.21*** *p235*
McIlvray, Bridget *SEE* McIlvray, John
McIlvray, Catharine McDonald *SEE* McIlvray, John
McIlvray, Donald *SEE* McIlvray, John
McIlvray, Hugh *SEE* McIlvray, John
McIlvray, John; New York, 1740 ***8277.31*** *p117*
*Wife:*Catharine McDonald
*Child:*Mary
*Child:*Hugh
*Child:*Bridget
*Child:*Donald
McIlvray, Mary *SEE* McIlvray, John
McIlwain, George 45; Ontario, 1871 ***1823.17*** *p108*
McIlwain, James 53; Ontario, 1871 ***1823.17*** *p108*
McIlwain, William 52; Ontario, 1871 ***1823.17*** *p108*
McIlwayne, Margaret 13; Ontario, 1871 ***1823.21*** *p235*
McInerny, Micheal 40; Ontario, 1871 ***1823.17*** *p108*
McInish, Ann 15; North Carolina, 1775 ***1422.10*** *p60*
McInish, Archibald 4; North Carolina, 1775 ***1422.10*** *p60*
McInish, Catherine 11; North Carolina, 1775 ***1422.10*** *p60*
McInish, Donald 8; North Carolina, 1775 ***1422.10*** *p60*
McInish, Jannet 36; North Carolina, 1775 ***1422.10*** *p60*
McInish, John 20; North Carolina, 1775 ***1422.10*** *p60*
McInish, Malcolm 40; North Carolina, 1775 ***1422.10*** *p60*
McInnes, Donald 60; Ontario, 1871 ***1823.21*** *p235*
McInnes, Dugald 35; Ontario, 1871 ***1823.17*** *p108*
McInnes, John; America, 1766 ***1220.12*** *p521*
McInnes, John; Quebec, 1786 ***1416.15*** *p8*
McInnes, Peter 69; Ontario, 1871 ***1823.21*** *p236*
McInnes, Robert 47; Ontario, 1871 ***1823.17*** *p108*
McInnis, Archd 41; Ontario, 1871 ***1823.17*** *p108*
McInnis, Catherine 38; Ontario, 1871 ***1823.21*** *p236*
McInnis, Catherine 68; Ontario, 1871 ***1823.21*** *p236*
McInnis, Donald 55; Ontario, 1871 ***1823.21*** *p236*
McInnis, Dougald 32; Ontario, 1871 ***1823.21*** *p236*
McInnis, Finley 27; Ontario, 1871 ***1823.21*** *p236*
McInnis, James 49; Ontario, 1871 ***1823.21*** *p236*
McInnis, James 70; Ontario, 1871 ***1823.21*** *p236*
McInnis, John 60; Ontario, 1871 ***1823.21*** *p236*
McInnis, Kinneth 25; Ontario, 1871 ***1823.21*** *p236*
McInnis, Lachlan 63; Ontario, 1871 ***1823.21*** *p236*
McInnis, Murdoch 35; Ontario, 1871 ***1823.21*** *p236*
McInnis, Murdock 31; Ontario, 1871 ***1823.21*** *p236*
McInnish, Catharine; New York, 1739 ***8277.31*** *p115*
McInnon, Hugh 68; Ontario, 1871 ***1823.17*** *p108*
McIntire, Alex 20; Ontario, 1871 ***1823.21*** *p236*
McIntire, Ann 32; North Carolina, 1775 ***1422.10*** *p59*
McIntire, Ann 36; North Carolina, 1775 ***1422.10*** *p60*
McIntire, Ann 60; North Carolina, 1775 ***1422.10*** *p59*
McIntire, Archibald 4; North Carolina, 1775 ***1422.10*** *p59*
McIntire, Charles 11; North Carolina, 1775 ***1422.10*** *p60*
McIntire, Donald 3; North Carolina, 1775 ***1422.10*** *p60*
McIntire, Duncan 55; North Carolina, 1775 ***1422.10*** *p60*
McIntire, Elizabeth 14; North Carolina, 1775 ***1422.10*** *p60*
McIntire, Evan 5; North Carolina, 1775 ***1422.10*** *p60*
McIntire, Gilbert 34; North Carolina, 1775 ***1422.10*** *p60*
McIntire, John; North Carolina, 1775 ***1422.10*** *p59*
McIntire, John 1; North Carolina, 1775 ***1422.10*** *p60*
McIntire, John 32; North Carolina, 1775 ***1422.10*** *p60*
McIntire, John 35; North Carolina, 1775 ***1422.10*** *p59*
McIntire, John 25; Ontario, 1871 ***1823.21*** *p236*
McIntire, Katherine 17; North Carolina, 1775 ***1422.10*** *p60*
McIntire, Katherine 30; North Carolina, 1775 ***1422.10*** *p60*
McIntire, Katherine 55; North Carolina, 1775 ***1422.10*** *p60*
McIntire, Malcolm 1; North Carolina, 1775 ***1422.10*** *p60*
McIntire, Margaret 6; North Carolina, 1775 ***1422.10*** *p59*
McIntire, Margaret 9; North Carolina, 1775 ***1422.10*** *p60*
McIntire, May 24; North Carolina, 1775 ***1422.10*** *p60*
McIntire, Neil; Boston, 1743 ***1642*** *p26*
McIntire, Patrick; Ohio, 1809-1852 ***4511.35*** *p33*
McIntire, Peggy 20; St. John, N.B., 1834 ***6469.7*** *p4*
McIntosh, Alex 45; Ontario, 1871 ***1823.21*** *p236*
McIntosh, Alex 55; Ontario, 1871 ***1823.17*** *p108*
McIntosh, Alexander 29; Ontario, 1871 ***1823.21*** *p236*
McIntosh, Alexander 44; Ontario, 1871 ***1823.17*** *p108*
McIntosh, Alexander 57; Ontario, 1871 ***1823.21*** *p236*
McIntosh, Angus 37; Ontario, 1871 ***1823.21*** *p236*
McIntosh, Angus 43; Ontario, 1871 ***1823.21*** *p236*
McIntosh, Angus 46; Ontario, 1871 ***1823.21*** *p236*
McIntosh, Angus 55; Ontario, 1871 ***1823.21*** *p236*
McIntosh, Angus 61; Ontario, 1871 ***1823.21*** *p236*
McIntosh, Angus 65; Ontario, 1871 ***1823.21*** *p236*
McIntosh, Angus 94; Ontario, 1871 ***1823.21*** *p236*
McIntosh, Ann 72; Ontario, 1871 ***1823.17*** *p108*
McIntosh, Anne; Jamaica, 1716 ***1220.12*** *p521*
McIntosh, Catherine 22; Ontario, 1871 ***1823.21*** *p236*
McIntosh, Catherine 33; Ontario, 1871 ***1823.21*** *p236*
McIntosh, Charles 49; Ontario, 1871 ***1823.17*** *p108*
McIntosh, Daniel; America, 1741 ***1220.12*** *p521*
McIntosh, Daniel; America, 1754 ***1220.12*** *p521*
McIntosh, Daniel 35; Ontario, 1871 ***1823.17*** *p108*
McIntosh, David 51; Ontario, 1871 ***1823.21*** *p236*
McIntosh, David 51; Ontario, 1871 ***1823.21*** *p236*
McIntosh, Donald 29; New York, NY, 1835 ***5024.1*** *p136*
McIntosh, Donald 30; Ontario, 1871 ***1823.17*** *p108*
McIntosh, Donald 35; Ontario, 1871 ***1823.21*** *p236*
McIntosh, Donald 40; Ontario, 1871 ***1823.21*** *p236*
McIntosh, Donald 54; Ontario, 1871 ***1823.21*** *p236*
McIntosh, Dougal 30; Ontario, 1871 ***1823.21*** *p236*
McIntosh, Dougald 38; Ontario, 1871 ***1823.21*** *p236*
McIntosh, George 22; Ontario, 1871 ***1823.17*** *p108*
McIntosh, George 36; Ontario, 1871 ***1823.21*** *p236*
McIntosh, Gilbert 33; Ontario, 1871 ***1823.21*** *p236*
McIntosh, Gilbert 65; Ontario, 1871 ***1823.21*** *p236*
McIntosh, James; Ontario, 1871 ***1823.17*** *p108*
McIntosh, James 67; Ontario, 1871 ***1823.21*** *p236*
McIntosh, Jane 60; Ontario, 1871 ***1823.21*** *p236*
McIntosh, Jane L. 76; Ontario, 1871 ***1823.17*** *p108*
McIntosh, Jenet 66; Ontario, 1871 ***1823.21*** *p236*
McIntosh, John; America, 1741 ***1220.12*** *p521*
McIntosh, John; Kansas, 1885 ***1447.20*** *p63*
McIntosh, John 38; Ontario, 1871 ***1823.21*** *p237*
McIntosh, John 40; Ontario, 1871 ***1823.21*** *p236*
McIntosh, John 44; Ontario, 1871 ***1823.21*** *p236*
McIntosh, John 65; Ontario, 1871 ***1823.21*** *p236*
McIntosh, John G. 53; Ontario, 1871 ***1823.21*** *p237*
McIntosh, Julia 62; Ontario, 1871 ***1823.21*** *p237*
McIntosh, Malcolm 56; Ontario, 1871 ***1823.21*** *p237*
McIntosh, Mary 46; Ontario, 1871 ***1823.21*** *p237*
McIntosh, Mary 60; Ontario, 1871 ***1823.21*** *p237*
McIntosh, Niel 35; Ontario, 1871 ***1823.21*** *p237*
McIntosh, Peter; America, 1753 ***1220.12*** *p521*
McIntosh, Robert 53; New York, NY, 1894 ***6512.1*** *p228*
McIntosh, William; America, 1766 ***1220.12*** *p521*
McIntosh, William; America, 1779 ***8529.30*** *p14*
McIntosh, William 34; Michigan, 1880 ***4491.30*** *p22*
McIntosh, William 40; Ontario, 1871 ***1823.17*** *p108*
McIntosh, William 61; Ontario, 1871 ***1823.21*** *p237*
McIntosh, William 70; Ontario, 1871 ***1823.21*** *p237*
McIntosh, William; Pictou, N.S., 1815 ***7100*** *p20*
With family of 11
McIntye, Bridget 42; Ontario, 1871 ***1823.21*** *p237*
McIntyre, Alexander 36; Ontario, 1871 ***1823.21*** *p237*
McIntyre, Alexander 42; Ontario, 1871 ***1823.21*** *p237*
McIntyre, Alexander 60; Ontario, 1871 ***1823.17*** *p108*
McIntyre, Alexander 64; Ontario, 1871 ***1823.21*** *p237*
McIntyre, Amelia 44; Ontario, 1871 ***1823.21*** *p237*
McIntyre, Angus 40; Ontario, 1871 ***1823.21*** *p237*
McIntyre, Angus 50; Ontario, 1871 ***1823.21*** *p237*
McIntyre, Arch 32; Ontario, 1871 ***1823.21*** *p237*
McIntyre, Archd 40; Ontario, 1871 ***1823.21*** *p237*
McIntyre, Archd 50; Ontario, 1871 ***1823.21*** *p237*
McIntyre, Archy 50; Ontario, 1871 ***1823.21*** *p237*
McIntyre, C. 21; Ontario, 1871 ***1823.21*** *p237*
McIntyre, Catherine 72; Ontario, 1871 ***1823.21*** *p237*
McIntyre, Charles 29; Ontario, 1871 ***1823.17*** *p108*
McIntyre, Charles 35; Ontario, 1871 ***1823.21*** *p237*
McIntyre, Christian; New York, 1738 ***8277.31*** *p116*
McIntyre, Christy 5; North Carolina, 1774 ***1422.10*** *p57*
McIntyre, Colin 38; Ontario, 1871 ***1823.21*** *p237*
McIntyre, Dan 18; Ontario, 1871 ***1823.21*** *p237*
McIntyre, David 50; Ontario, 1871 ***1823.21*** *p237*
McIntyre, Donald; New York, 1738 ***8277.31*** *p118*
McIntyre, Donald 28; North Carolina, 1774 ***1422.10*** *p57*
McIntyre, Donald 19; Ontario, 1871 ***1823.21*** *p237*
McIntyre, Donald 38; Ontario, 1871 ***1823.21*** *p237*
McIntyre, Donald 42; Ontario, 1871 ***1823.17*** *p108*
McIntyre, Donald 48; Ontario, 1871 ***1823.17*** *p108*
McIntyre, Donald 48; Ontario, 1871 ***1823.21*** *p237*
McIntyre, Donald 52; Ontario, 1871 ***1823.21*** *p237*
McIntyre, Donald 56; Ontario, 1871 ***1823.21*** *p237*
McIntyre, Donald 61; Ontario, 1871 ***1823.21*** *p237*
McIntyre, Donald 67; Ontario, 1871 ***1823.17*** *p108*
McIntyre, Donald 80; Ontario, 1871 ***1823.21*** *p237*
McIntyre, Dond 8; North Carolina, 1774 ***1422.10*** *p57*
McIntyre, Dougald 78; Ontario, 1871 ***1823.21*** *p237*
McIntyre, Dugald 62; Ontario, 1871 ***1823.17*** *p108*
McIntyre, Dugald 63; Ontario, 1871 ***1823.17*** *p108*
McIntyre, Duncan; Colorado, 1863 ***1029.59*** *p60*
McIntyre, Duncan 40; North Carolina, 1774 ***1422.10*** *p57*
McIntyre, Duncan 39; Ontario, 1871 ***1823.17*** *p108*
McIntyre, Duncan 45; Ontario, 1871 ***1823.21*** *p237*
McIntyre, Duncan 67; Ontario, 1871 ***1823.21*** *p238*
McIntyre, Elizabeth 42; Ontario, 1871 ***1823.17*** *p108*
McIntyre, Elizabeth 72; Ontario, 1871 ***1823.21*** *p238*
McIntyre, Evina 41; Ontario, 1871 ***1823.17*** *p108*
McIntyre, Finlay 42; Ontario, 1871 ***1823.21*** *p238*
McIntyre, George 45; Ontario, 1871 ***1823.21*** *p238*
McIntyre, Hector 53; Ontario, 1871 ***1823.21*** *p238*
McIntyre, Hugh 36; Ontario, 1871 ***1823.21*** *p238*
McIntyre, Hugh 40; Ontario, 1871 ***1823.21*** *p238*
McIntyre, Isabella 18; Michigan, 1880 ***4491.39*** *p20*
McIntyre, Isobel 24; North Carolina, 1774 ***1422.10*** *p57*
McIntyre, Issabella 34; Ontario, 1871 ***1823.21*** *p238*
McIntyre, J. B. 32; Ontario, 1871 ***1823.21*** *p238*
McIntyre, James 32; Ontario, 1871 ***1823.21*** *p238*
McIntyre, James 46; Ontario, 1871 ***1823.21*** *p238*
McIntyre, John; New York, 1740 ***8277.31*** *p118*
McIntyre, John 4; North Carolina, 1774 ***1422.10*** *p57*
McIntyre, John 35; North Carolina, 1774 ***1422.10*** *p57*
McIntyre, John 45; North Carolina, 1774 ***1422.10*** *p57*
McIntyre, John; Ohio, 1840-1897 ***8365.35*** *p17*
McIntyre, John 19; Ontario, 1871 ***1823.21*** *p238*

McIntyre, John 30; Ontario, 1871 *1823.21 p238*
McIntyre, John 35; Ontario, 1871 *1823.17 p109*
McIntyre, John 35; Ontario, 1871 *1823.21 p238*
McIntyre, John 43; Ontario, 1871 *1823.17 p109*
McIntyre, John 44; Ontario, 1871 *1823.21 p238*
McIntyre, John 48; Ontario, 1871 *1823.21 p238*
McIntyre, John 50; Ontario, 1871 *1823.21 p238*
McIntyre, John 56; Ontario, 1871 *1823.21 p238*
McIntyre, John 57; Ontario, 1871 *1823.21 p238*
McIntyre, John 69; Ontario, 1871 *1823.21 p238*
McIntyre, John 69; Ontario, 1871 *1823.21 p238*
McIntyre, John 70; Ontario, 1871 *1823.21 p238*
McIntyre, John 73; Ontario, 1871 *1823.21 p238*
McIntyre, John 90; Ontario, 1871 *1823.21 p238*
McIntyre, Joseph 35; Ontario, 1871 *1823.17 p109*
McIntyre, Joseph 67; Ontario, 1871 *1823.17 p109*
McIntyre, Kathrine 40; North Carolina, 1774 *1422.10 p57*
McIntyre, Katie; Iowa, 1873 *1211.15 p16*
McIntyre, Katrine 28; North Carolina, 1774 *1422.10 p57*
McIntyre, L. C. 41; Ontario, 1871 *1823.21 p238*
McIntyre, Malcolm 38; Ontario, 1871 *1823.21 p238*
McIntyre, Malcolm 46; Ontario, 1871 *1823.21 p238*
McIntyre, Malcolm 66; Ontario, 1871 *1823.21 p238*
McIntyre, Malcolm 88; Ontario, 1871 *1823.21 p238*
McIntyre, Margt. 30; North Carolina, 1774 *1422.10 p57*
McIntyre, Mary 25; North Carolina, 1774 *1422.10 p57*
McIntyre, Mary 35; North Carolina, 1774 *1422.10 p57*
McIntyre, Mary 70; Ontario, 1871 *1823.21 p238*
McIntyre, Mary 71; Ontario, 1871 *1823.17 p109*
McIntyre, Matthew 44; Indiana, 1887-1896 *9076.20 p74*
McIntyre, Michael; Colorado, 1889 *1029.59 p60*
McIntyre, Michael 34; Michigan, 1880 *4491.39 p20*
McIntyre, Michael; Pennsylvania, 1867 *1029.59 p60*
McIntyre, Nancy 11; North Carolina, 1774 *1422.10 p57*
McIntyre, Neil 45; Ontario, 1871 *1823.21 p238*
McIntyre, Neil 50; Ontario, 1871 *1823.21 p239*
McIntyre, Neil 58; Ontario, 1871 *1823.21 p238*
McIntyre, Neil 80; Ontario, 1871 *1823.21 p238*
McIntyre, Nichol 45; Ontario, 1871 *1823.17 p109*
McIntyre, Nicol 60; Ontario, 1871 *1823.21 p239*
McIntyre, Niel 55; Ontario, 1871 *1823.21 p239*
McIntyre, Norman 49; Ontario, 1871 *1823.17 p109*
McIntyre, Patt 46; Ontario, 1871 *1823.21 p239*
McIntyre, Peter 53; Ontario, 1871 *1823.21 p239*
McIntyre, Peter 55; Ontario, 1871 *1823.21 p239*
McIntyre, Peter 56; Ontario, 1871 *1823.21 p239*
McIntyre, Robert 52; Ontario, 1871 *1823.21 p239*
McIntyre, Roderick 60; Ontario, 1871 *1823.21 p239*
McIntyre, Ronald 38; Ontario, 1871 *1823.21 p239*
McIntyre, Sterling; Ohio, 1833 *3580.20 p32*
McIntyre, Sterling; Ohio, 1833 *6020.12 p13*
McInyre, Ann 59; Ontario, 1871 *1823.17 p109*
McIsaac, Archy 53; Ontario, 1871 *1823.21 p239*
McIsaac, Donald 38; Ontario, 1871 *1823.21 p239*
McIsaac, Donald 60; Ontario, 1871 *1823.21 p239*
McIsaac, Donald 85; Ontario, 1871 *1823.21 p239*
McIsaac, John 35; Ontario, 1871 *1823.21 p239*
McIsaac, John 40; Ontario, 1871 *1823.21 p239*
McIsaac, Mary 50; Ontario, 1871 *1823.21 p239*
McIsaac, Mary 68; Ontario, 1871 *1823.21 p239*
McIsaac, Sarah 45; Ontario, 1871 *1823.21 p239*
McIvor, Esther 67; Ontario, 1871 *1823.21 p239*
McIvor, William 34; Ontario, 1871 *1823.21 p239*
McIvor, William 75; Ontario, 1871 *1823.21 p239*
McKa, Duncan; Quebec, 1786 *1416.15 p8*
McKaa, William 60; Ontario, 1871 *1823.21 p239*
McKaffrey, Henry 55; Ontario, 1871 *1823.21 p239*
McKan, John; America, 1774 *1220.12 p517*
McKane, John 61; Ontario, 1871 *1823.21 p239*
McKarty, Lawrence; America, 1749 *1220.12 p517*
McKase, Bartholomew; America, 1749 *1220.12 p521*
McKaw, Alexander; America, 1750 *1220.12 p521*
McKay, Miss; Toronto, 1844 *2910.35 p114*
McKay, Widow; Pictou, N.S., 1815 *7100 p20*
  With family of 4
McKay, Alexander; Colorado, 1873 *1029.59 p61*
McKay, Alexander; North Carolina, 1845 *1088.45 p22*
McKay, Alexander 61; Ontario, 1871 *1823.21 p239*
McKay, Angus 32; Ontario, 1871 *1823.17 p109*
McKay, Ann 45; Ontario, 1871 *1823.17 p109*
McKay, Betsy 45; Ontario, 1871 *1823.21 p239*
McKay, Bridget; Toronto, 1844 *2910.35 p114*
McKay, Catherine 10; Ontario, 1871 *1823.21 p239*
McKay, Colin 57; Ontario, 1871 *1823.21 p239*
McKay, Daniel; St. John, N.B., 1842 *2978.20 p7*
McKay, David 61; Ontario, 1871 *1823.21 p239*
McKay, Donald; Illinois, 1857 *6079.1 p9*
McKay, Donald 20; North Carolina, 1774 *1422.10 p62*
McKay, Donald 40; Ontario, 1871 *1823.21 p239*
McKay, Donald 54; Ontario, 1871 *1823.21 p239*
McKay, Donald, Jr.; Pictou, N.S., 1815 *7100 p20*
  With family of 2

McKay, Donald, Sr.; Pictou, N.S., 1815 *7100 p20*
  With family of 5
McKay, Dond. 20; North Carolina, 1774 *1422.10 p58*
McKay, Duncan; New York, 1740 *8277.31 p118*
McKay, Elizabeth; Utah, 1855 *9228.50 p635*
McKay, Florence; New York, 1739 *8277.31 p120*
McKay, George 34; New York, NY, 1835 *5024.1 p137*
McKay, George 40; North Carolina, 1774 *1422.10 p59*
McKay, George 54; Ontario, 1871 *1823.21 p239*
McKay, George 56; Ontario, 1871 *1823.21 p240*
McKay, Hugh; Pictou, N.S., 1815 *7100 p20*
  With family of 2
McKay, Hugh; Pictou, N.S., 1815 *7100 p20*
  With family of 5
McKay, Isabella 27; Ontario, 1871 *1823.21 p240*
McKay, Isabella 45; Ontario, 1871 *1823.17 p109*
McKay, J. A.; Louisiana, 1836-1840 *4981.45 p213*
McKay, James 35; Michigan, 1880 *4491.36 p15*
McKay, James; North Carolina, 1835 *1088.45 p22*
McKay, James 60; North Carolina, 1774 *1422.10 p59*
McKay, James 20; Ontario, 1871 *1823.21 p240*
McKay, James 23; Ontario, 1871 *1823.21 p240*
McKay, James 28; Ontario, 1871 *1823.17 p109*
McKay, James; Pictou, N.S., 1815 *7100 p20*
  With family of 2
McKay, James; Quebec, 1786 *1416.15 p8*
McKay, Janet 40; Ontario, 1871 *1823.21 p240*
McKay, Jannet 81; Ontario, 1871 *1823.21 p240*
McKay, Jeannet 45; Ontario, 1871 *1823.21 p240*
McKay, Jessie 12; Ontario, 1871 *1823.21 p240*
McKay, John; America, 1758 *1220.12 p521*
McKay, John 19; Ontario, 1871 *1823.17 p109*
McKay, John 43; Ontario, 1871 *1823.17 p109*
McKay, John 49; Ontario, 1871 *1823.21 p240*
McKay, John 54; Ontario, 1871 *1823.21 p240*
McKay, John 70; Ontario, 1871 *1823.17 p109*
McKay, John 81; Ontario, 1871 *1823.21 p240*
McKay, John; Pictou, N.S., 1815 *7100 p20*
  With family of 7
McKay, John; Pictou, N.S., 1815 *7100 p20*
  With family of 8
McKay, John; Pictou, N.S., 1815 *7100 p20*
  With family of 9
McKay, John; Potomac, 1743 *1220.12 p521*
McKay, Joseph 23; Ontario, 1871 *1823.21 p240*
McKay, Keneth 55; Ontario, 1871 *1823.21 p240*
McKay, Kenneth; Illinois, 1857 *6079.1 p9*
McKay, Lizzie 19; Ontario, 1871 *1823.17 p109*
McKay, Margaret; Ontario, 1835 *3160.1 p150*
McKay, Margaret 65; Ontario, 1871 *1823.21 p240*
McKay, Margaret 68; Ontario, 1871 *1823.21 p240*
McKay, Margrit 86; Ontario, 1871 *1823.21 p240*
McKay, Mary; New York, 1738 *8277.31 p114*
McKay, Mary 16; Ontario, 1871 *1823.21 p240*
McKay, Mary 56; Ontario, 1871 *1823.21 p240*
McKay, Melashus 22; Virginia, 1635 *1183.3 p31*
McKay, Murdoch 45; Ontario, 1871 *1823.17 p109*
McKay, Robert; Pictou, N.S., 1815 *7100 p20*
  With family of 3
McKay, Roderick 50; Ontario, 1871 *1823.21 p240*
McKay, Rosa 30; Michigan, 1880 *4491.36 p15*
McKay, Thomas 60; Ontario, 1871 *1823.21 p240*
McKay, William 19; Michigan, 1880 *4491.36 p15*
McKay, William 30; North Carolina, 1774 *1422.10 p58*
McKay, William 22; Ontario, 1871 *1823.21 p240*
McKay, William 60; Ontario, 1871 *1823.21 p240*
McKay, William 67; Ontario, 1871 *1823.21 p240*
McKay, William; Pictou, N.S., 1815 *7100 p20*
  With family of 4
McKay, Willm. 26; North Carolina, 1774 *1422.10 p58*
McKean, George 62; Ontario, 1871 *1823.21 p240*
McKean, John; Ohio, 1809-1852 *4511.35 p33*
McKean, Sarah 63; Ontario, 1871 *1823.21 p240*
McKean, William 26; Ontario, 1871 *1823.21 p240*
McKean, William John; Philadelphia, 1852 *5720.10 p379*
McKearne, Niel; Prescott, Ont., 1835 *3289.1 p62*
McKeath, Sarah 37; Ontario, 1871 *1823.21 p240*
McKechan, John 25; Ontario, 1871 *1823.21 p240*
McKechan, John 66; Ontario, 1871 *1823.21 p240*
McKecky, Joseph; Rappahannock, VA, 1726 *1220.12 p521*
McKee, David 58; Ontario, 1871 *1823.21 p240*
McKee, George 45; Ontario, 1871 *1823.17 p109*
McKee, George P.; North Carolina, 1841 *1088.45 p22*
McKee, John; North Carolina, 1841 *1088.45 p22*
McKee, Patrick; Barbados, 1670 *1220.12 p521*
McKee, Robert; South Carolina, 1800-1899 *6155.4 p18*
McKee, Sarah 31; Ontario, 1871 *1823.21 p240*
McKee, William; Ontario, 1871 *1823.21 p240*
McKee, William 43; Ontario, 1871 *1823.21 p240*
McKeehee, John; North Carolina, 1792-1862 *1088.45 p22*
McKeen, James M.; Colorado, 1873 *1029.59 p61*

McKeen, James M.; Colorado, 1884 *1029.59 p61*
McKeever, John; California, 1868 *1131.61 p89*
McKegan, Alexandria 38; Ontario, 1871 *1823.21 p240*
McKegnay, James; Toronto, 1844 *2910.35 p113*
McKehan, Peter 63; Ontario, 1871 *1823.21 p240*
McKehon, John 50; Ontario, 1871 *1823.21 p240*
McKeith, John 48; Ontario, 1871 *1823.21 p240*
McKeithley, Christopher; America, 1733 *1220.12 p521*
McKeiver, John 38; Ontario, 1871 *1823.21 p240*
McKellar, Adelaide 39; Ontario, 1871 *1823.21 p240*
McKellar, Alexander 50; Ontario, 1871 *1823.21 p241*
McKellar, Alexander 57; Ontario, 1871 *1823.21 p241*
McKellar, Archd 74; Ontario, 1871 *1823.21 p241*
McKellar, Archibald; New York, 1738 *8277.31 p118*
  *Wife:*Janet Reed
McKellar, Archibald 52; Ontario, 1871 *1823.21 p241*
McKellar, Catharine *SEE* McKellar, Charles
McKellar, Charles; New York, 1738 *8277.31 p118*
  *Wife:*Florence McEachern
  *Daughter:*Mary
  *Daughter:*Margaret
  *Daughter:*Catharine
McKellar, Charles 71; Ontario, 1871 *1823.21 p241*
McKellar, Christy 40; Ontario, 1871 *1823.21 p241*
McKellar, Colin 65; Ontario, 1871 *1823.21 p241*
McKellar, Donald 39; Ontario, 1871 *1823.21 p241*
McKellar, Donald 44; Ontario, 1871 *1823.21 p241*
McKellar, Donald 46; Ontario, 1871 *1823.17 p109*
McKellar, Donald 75; Ontario, 1871 *1823.17 p109*
McKellar, Dugald 47; Ontario, 1871 *1823.17 p109*
McKellar, Duncan 58; Ontario, 1871 *1823.21 p241*
McKellar, Duncan 74; Ontario, 1871 *1823.21 p241*
McKellar, Duncan 76; Ontario, 1871 *1823.21 p241*
McKellar, Emily 42; Ontario, 1871 *1823.17 p109*
McKellar, Florence McEachern *SEE* McKellar, Charles
McKellar, Isabella 84; Ontario, 1871 *1823.21 p241*
McKellar, Janet Reed *SEE* McKellar, Archibald
McKellar, Janet 80; Ontario, 1871 *1823.21 p241*
McKellar, Malcolm 46; Ontario, 1871 *1823.21 p241*
McKellar, Malcolm 78; Ontario, 1871 *1823.21 p241*
McKellar, Margaret *SEE* McKellar, Charles
McKellar, Mary *SEE* McKellar, Charles
McKellar, Neil 60; Ontario, 1871 *1823.17 p109*
McKellar, Peter 64; Ontario, 1871 *1823.17 p109*
McKellar, Peter 68; Ontario, 1871 *1823.21 p241*
McKeller, Christina 27; Ontario, 1871 *1823.17 p109*
McKeller, Dougal; New York, 1776 *8529.30 p3*
McKeller, Dugald 52; Ontario, 1871 *1823.21 p241*
McKeller, James 58; Ontario, 1871 *1823.17 p109*
McKeller, Ougald 10; Ontario, 1871 *1823.17 p109*
McKelvie, William 40; Ontario, 1871 *1823.17 p109*
McKen, Luke 65; Ontario, 1871 *1823.17 p109*
McKena, Thomas 35; Ontario, 1871 *1823.17 p110*
McKenarch, Thomas; Louisiana, 1874 *4981.45 p133*
McKendra, John; St. John, N.B., 1847 *2978.15 p37*
McKendrick, Janet 24; North Carolina, 1774 *1422.10 p58*
McKendrick, Janet 24; North Carolina, 1774 *1422.10 p62*
McKenly, Anthony 31; Ontario, 1871 *1823.17 p110*
McKenna, Andrew 57; Ontario, 1871 *1823.21 p241*
Mc Kenna, Hugh; Ohio, 1843 *2763.1 p20*
McKenna, James; Louisiana, 1874 *4981.45 p133*
McKenna, James 33; Ontario, 1871 *1823.21 p241*
McKenna, John; Washington, 1887 *2770.40 p24*
McKenna, Margaret; Ontario, 1835 *3160.1 p150*
McKenna, Mary 40; Michigan, 1880 *4491.39 p20*
McKenna, Michael; Boston, 1825 *3274.55 p27*
McKenna, Michael 54; Michigan, 1880 *4491.39 p20*
McKenna, Niel; Ontario, 1835 *3160.1 p150*
McKenna, Owen; Washington, 1885 *2770.40 p194*
McKenna, Patrick; Boston, 1830 *3274.55 p67*
McKenna, William 66; Ontario, 1871 *1823.21 p241*
McKennedy, Mary 25; Ontario, 1871 *1823.21 p241*
McKenneth, Kenzie 42; Ontario, 1871 *1823.21 p241*
McKenney, Alexander; Massachusetts, 1675-1676 *1642 p128*
McKenney, Angus 53; Ontario, 1871 *1823.21 p241*
McKennon, Rodrick 33; Ontario, 1871 *1823.21 p241*
McKenny, Chas; Louisiana, 1874-1875 *4981.45 p30*
McKenny, John 16; St. John, N.B., 1834 *6469.7 p5*
McKenny, Rose 17; St. John, N.B., 1834 *6469.7 p5*
McKenny, William; Maryland, 1736 *1220.12 p521*
McKenny, William 54; Ontario, 1871 *1823.21 p241*
McKensie, Andrew; America, 1766 *1220.12 p521*
McKensie, Susanna; America, 1766 *1220.12 p521*
McKeny, Daniel; Maryland, 1741 *1220.12 p521*
McKenzie, Alexander; America, 1765 *1220.12 p521*
McKenzie, Alexander 33; Ontario, 1871 *1823.17 p110*
McKenzie, Alexander 43; Ontario, 1871 *1823.21 p241*
McKenzie, Alexander 47; Ontario, 1871 *1823.21 p241*
McKenzie, Alexander 56; Ontario, 1871 *1823.21 p241*
McKenzie, Alexander 74; Ontario, 1871 *1823.17 p110*

McKenzie, Alexander 79; Ontario, 1871 ***1823.21*** *p241*
McKenzie, Alexr 23; Ontario, 1871 ***1823.17*** *p110*
McKenzie, Angus 43; Ontario, 1871 ***1823.21*** *p242*
McKenzie, Ann 44; Ontario, 1871 ***1823.17*** *p110*
McKenzie, Ann 45; Ontario, 1871 ***1823.21*** *p242*
McKenzie, Archibald *SEE* McKenzie, John
McKenzie, Catharine McNiven *SEE* McKenzie, George
McKenzie, Catherine 58; Michigan, 1880 ***4491.36*** *p14*
McKenzie, Catherine 75; Ontario, 1871 ***1823.21*** *p242*
McKenzie, Christena 60; Ontario, 1871 ***1823.21*** *p242*
McKenzie, Christian; America, 1743 ***1220.12*** *p521*
McKenzie, Colin *SEE* McKenzie, George
McKenzie, Colin 68; Ontario, 1871 ***1823.21*** *p242*
McKenzie, Dan 17; Ontario, 1871 ***1823.21*** *p242*
McKenzie, Daniel, Jr.; Philadelphia, 1777 ***8529.30*** *p4A*
McKenzie, Daniel, Sr.; Philadelphia, 1778 ***8529.30*** *p4A*
McKenzie, Donald *SEE* McKenzie, George
McKenzie, Donald 22; Ontario, 1871 ***1823.21*** *p242*
McKenzie, Donald 35; Ontario, 1871 ***1823.21*** *p242*
McKenzie, Donald 38; Ontario, 1871 ***1823.21*** *p242*
McKenzie, Donald 43; Ontario, 1871 ***1823.21*** *p242*
McKenzie, Donald 43; Ontario, 1871 ***1823.21*** *p242*
McKenzie, Donald 45; Ontario, 1871 ***1823.21*** *p242*
McKenzie, Dougall 78; Ontario, 1871 ***1823.17*** *p110*
McKenzie, Duncan 32; Ontario, 1871 ***1823.21*** *p242*
McKenzie, Duncan 84; Ontario, 1871 ***1823.21*** *p242*
McKenzie, Eleanor; America, 1772 ***1220.12*** *p521*
McKenzie, Elizabeth 45; Ontario, 1871 ***1823.21*** *p242*
McKenzie, Finlay 55; Ontario, 1871 ***1823.17*** *p110*
McKenzie, Florence *SEE* McKenzie, John
McKenzie, Francis 50; Ontario, 1871 ***1823.17*** *p110*
McKenzie, George 51; Michigan, 1880 ***4491.36*** *p15*
McKenzie, George; New York, 1738 ***8277.31*** *p118*
*Wife:*Catharine McNiven
*Son:*Colin
*Son:*Donald
McKenzie, George 49; Ontario, 1871 ***1823.21*** *p242*
McKenzie, Gilbert 34; North Carolina, 1774 ***1422.10*** *p60*
McKenzie, Gilbert 34; North Carolina, 1774 ***1422.10*** *p63*
McKenzie, Gordon 40; Ontario, 1871 ***1823.21*** *p242*
McKenzie, Hector 41; Ontario, 1871 ***1823.17*** *p110*
Mc Kenzie, Hugh; Ohio, 1840 ***2763.1*** *p20*
McKenzie, Hugh 31; Ontario, 1871 ***1823.17*** *p110*
McKenzie, Hugh 71; Ontario, 1871 ***1823.21*** *p242*
McKenzie, Hugh 82; Ontario, 1871 ***1823.17*** *p110*
McKenzie, James; America, 1773 ***1220.12*** *p521*
McKenzie, James; America, 1775 ***1220.12*** *p521*
McKenzie, James 66; Ontario, 1871 ***1823.21*** *p242*
McKenzie, James; Philadelphia, 1778 ***8529.30*** *p6*
McKenzie, John; America, 1765 ***1220.12*** *p521*
McKenzie, John; America, 1771 ***1220.12*** *p521*
McKenzie, John 66; Michigan, 1880 ***4491.36*** *p14*
McKenzie, John; New York, 1738 ***8277.31*** *p118*
*Wife:*Mary McVurrish
*Child:*Archibald
*Child:*Florence
McKenzie, John 20; Ontario, 1871 ***1823.17*** *p110*
McKenzie, John 23; Ontario, 1871 ***1823.21*** *p242*
McKenzie, John 30; Ontario, 1871 ***1823.21*** *p242*
McKenzie, John 31; Ontario, 1871 ***1823.17*** *p110*
McKenzie, John 53; Ontario, 1871 ***1823.17*** *p110*
McKenzie, John 54; Ontario, 1871 ***1823.21*** *p242*
McKenzie, John 54; Ontario, 1871 ***1823.21*** *p242*
McKenzie, John 64; Ontario, 1871 ***1823.21*** *p242*
McKenzie, John 73; Ontario, 1871 ***1823.21*** *p242*
McKenzie, Kenneth 55; Ontario, 1871 ***1823.17*** *p110*
McKenzie, Lawrence; North America, 1750 ***1640.8*** *p234*
McKenzie, Martha 45; North Carolina, 1775 ***1422.10*** *p57*
McKenzie, Mary; Maryland or Virginia, 1738 ***1220.12*** *p521*
McKenzie, Mary McVurrish *SEE* McKenzie, John
McKenzie, Mary 27; North Carolina, 1774 ***1422.10*** *p60*
McKenzie, Mary 27; North Carolina, 1774 ***1422.10*** *p63*
McKenzie, Mary 75; Ontario, 1871 ***1823.21*** *p242*
McKenzie, Mary 77; Ontario, 1871 ***1823.21*** *p242*
McKenzie, Murdo 20; Halifax, N.S., 1906 ***1833.5*** *p7*
McKenzie, Murdoc 52; Ontario, 1871 ***1823.21*** *p242*
McKenzie, Murdoch 72; Ontario, 1871 ***1823.21*** *p242*
McKenzie, Naoma 35; Michigan, 1880 ***4491.36*** *p15*
McKenzie, Neil C.; Ohio, 1809-1852 ***4511.35*** *p33*
McKenzie, Neill 20; Ontario, 1871 ***1823.21*** *p242*
McKenzie, Norman 77; Ontario, 1871 ***1823.21*** *p242*
McKenzie, Penelope; America, 1748 ***1220.12*** *p521*
McKenzie, Peter 64; Ontario, 1871 ***1823.17*** *p110*
McKenzie, Robert; Pictou, N.S., 1815 ***7100*** *p20*
With family of 10
McKenzie, Roderich 40; Ontario, 1871 ***1823.21*** *p242*
McKenzie, Sarah; America, 1754 ***1220.12*** *p521*
McKenzie, Sarah 37; Michigan, 1880 ***4491.36*** *p14*
McKenzie, William; America, 1773 ***1220.12*** *p521*
McKenzie, William 25; Ontario, 1871 ***1823.21*** *p242*
McKenzie, William 40; Ontario, 1871 ***1823.17*** *p110*
McKenzie, William 45; Ontario, 1871 ***1823.21*** *p242*
McKenzie, William 63; Ontario, 1871 ***1823.17*** *p110*
McKenzie, William; Philadelphia, 1778 ***8529.30*** *p4A*
McKeon, James 50; Ontario, 1871 ***1823.21*** *p242*
McKeon, Maggie 25; Ontario, 1871 ***1823.21*** *p242*
McKeon, Patrick; Boston, 1830 ***3274.55*** *p27*
McKeown, Edw's; Toronto, 1844 ***2910.35*** *p115*
McKeown, James; North Carolina, 1833 ***1088.45*** *p22*
McKeown, James 35; Ontario, 1871 ***1823.17*** *p110*
McKeown, Joseph 60; Ontario, 1871 ***1823.17*** *p110*
McKercher, Charles 35; Ontario, 1871 ***1823.21*** *p243*
McKernan, Catharine; Philadelphia, 1851 ***8513.31*** *p314*
McKeugh, Cornelius 36; Ontario, 1871 ***1823.17*** *p110*
McKeune, James 51; Ontario, 1871 ***1823.17*** *p110*
McKeune, John 55; Ontario, 1871 ***1823.17*** *p110*
McKevin, Roger 40; Ontario, 1871 ***1823.21*** *p243*
McKew, Henry; America, 1770 ***1220.12*** *p521*
McKewn, John 80; Ontario, 1871 ***1823.17*** *p110*
McKibben, Robert; Ohio, 1855 ***3580.20*** *p32*
McKibben, Robert; Ohio, 1855 ***6020.12*** *p13*
McKichan, Janet 24; North Carolina, 1774 ***1422.10*** *p58*
McKichan, Janet 24; North Carolina, 1774 ***1422.10*** *p62*
McKichan, Neil; North Carolina, 1774 ***1422.10*** *p62*
McKichan, Neil 5; North Carolina, 1774 ***1422.10*** *p58*
McKichan, Rob 32; North Carolina, 1774 ***1422.10*** *p58*
McKichan, Rob 32; North Carolina, 1774 ***1422.10*** *p62*
McKie, Mary 20; Ontario, 1871 ***1823.17*** *p110*
McKiernan, Tony; North Carolina, 1855 ***1088.45*** *p22*
McKiesuck, Sarrah 30; Ontario, 1871 ***1823.21*** *p243*
McKiggan, Angus 45; Ontario, 1871 ***1823.21*** *p243*
McKilliam, John 75; Ontario, 1871 ***1823.21*** *p243*
McKillop, A. 18; Quebec, 1910 ***2897.7*** *p7*
McKillop, Archibald 40; Ontario, 1871 ***1823.17*** *p110*
McKillop, Donald 36; Ontario, 1871 ***1823.21*** *p243*
McKillop, Henry 26; Ontario, 1871 ***1823.21*** *p243*
McKillop, Neil 40; Ontario, 1871 ***1823.21*** *p243*
McKim, Daniel 24; Ontario, 1871 ***1823.21*** *p243*
McKim, George; Ohio, 1809-1852 ***4511.35*** *p33*
McKim, William; Ohio, 1809-1852 ***4511.35*** *p33*
McKimm, George; Ohio, 1809-1852 ***4511.35*** *p33*
McKimm, Robert; Ohio, 1809-1852 ***4511.35*** *p33*
McKimmon, James; North Carolina, 1831 ***1088.45*** *p22*
McKinely, Angus 41; Ontario, 1871 ***1823.17*** *p110*
McKinely, Donald 38; Ontario, 1871 ***1823.17*** *p110*
McKinely, Donald 70; Ontario, 1871 ***1823.17*** *p110*
McKinely, Duncan 60; Ontario, 1871 ***1823.17*** *p110*
McKinily, Duncan 36; Ontario, 1871 ***1823.17*** *p110*
McKinistry, John; Massachusetts, 1620-1775 ***1642*** *p139*
McKinlay, Alex.; Toronto, 1844 ***2910.35*** *p116*
McKinlay, Angus 60; Ontario, 1871 ***1823.21*** *p243*
McKinlay, Donald 70; Ontario, 1871 ***1823.17*** *p110*
McKinlay, Duncan 37; Ontario, 1871 ***1823.17*** *p110*
McKinlay, George 17 *SEE* McKinlay, Thomas
McKinlay, James 36; Ontario, 1871 ***1823.21*** *p243*
McKinlay, James 38; Ontario, 1871 ***1823.17*** *p110*
McKinlay, John 42; Ontario, 1871 ***1823.17*** *p110*
McKinlay, Thomas 25; Halifax, N.S., n.d. ***1833.5*** *p7*
McKinlay, Thomas 25; Halifax, N.S., n.d. ***8445.10*** *p7*
*Relative:*George 17
McKinley, A.; Louisiana, 1874-1875 ***4981.45*** *p30*
McKinley, Catherine 61; Ontario, 1871 ***1823.21*** *p243*
McKinley, James; North Carolina, 1792-1862 ***1088.45*** *p22*
McKinly, Donald 60; Ontario, 1871 ***1823.21*** *p243*
McKinnae, Nicholas; North Carolina, 1823 ***1088.45*** *p22*
McKinney, Barney; Illinois, 1858-1861 ***6020.5*** *p132*
McKinney, Thomas; America, 1773 ***1220.12*** *p521*
McKinnon, Ann 57; Ontario, 1871 ***1823.21*** *p243*
McKinnon, Ann 80; Ontario, 1871 ***1823.21*** *p243*
McKinnon, Arabella 49; Ontario, 1871 ***1823.21*** *p243*
McKinnon, Charles 60; Ontario, 1871 ***1823.21*** *p243*
McKinnon, Donald 30; Ontario, 1871 ***1823.21*** *p243*
McKinnon, Donald 38; Ontario, 1871 ***1823.21*** *p243*
McKinnon, Donald 80; Ontario, 1871 ***1823.21*** *p243*
McKinnon, Eliza 70; Ontario, 1871 ***1823.21*** *p243*
McKinnon, Flora 40; Ontario, 1871 ***1823.21*** *p243*
McKinnon, Gregor 52; Ontario, 1871 ***1823.21*** *p243*
McKinnon, James 20; Ontario, 1871 ***1823.21*** *p243*
McKinnon, John 32; Ontario, 1871 ***1823.21*** *p243*
McKinnon, John 35; Ontario, 1871 ***1823.21*** *p243*
McKinnon, John 38; Ontario, 1871 ***1823.21*** *p243*
McKinnon, John 39; Ontario, 1871 ***1823.21*** *p243*
McKinnon, John 41; Ontario, 1871 ***1823.21*** *p243*
McKinnon, John 50; Ontario, 1871 ***1823.17*** *p111*
McKinnon, John 55; Ontario, 1871 ***1823.21*** *p243*
McKinnon, Margret 82; Ontario, 1871 ***1823.21*** *p243*
McKinnon, Margrett 21; Ontario, 1871 ***1823.21*** *p243*
McKinnon, Neil 26; Ontario, 1871 ***1823.21*** *p243*
McKinnon, Neil 40; Ontario, 1871 ***1823.21*** *p244*
McKinnon, Neil 44; Ontario, 1871 ***1823.21*** *p243*
McKinny, Wm 60; Ontario, 1871 ***1823.21*** *p244*
McKinsey, . . .; Iowa, 1800-1899 ***9228.50*** *p451*
McKinstry, Captain; Boston, 1740 ***1642*** *p26*
*Wife:*Jane Dickie Belknap
McKinstry, Jane Dickie Belknap *SEE* McKinstry, Captain
McKinstry, John; Boston, 1718 ***1642*** *p22*
McKinstry, John; Massachusetts, 1620-1775 ***1642*** *p138*
McKinstry, William; Boston, 1740-1741 ***1642*** *p108*
McKinvan, Donald *SEE* McKinvan, Duncan
McKinvan, Duncan; New York, 1740 ***8277.31*** *p118*
*Wife:*Marian McCollum
*Child:*Mary
*Child:*Donald
McKinvan, Marian McCollum *SEE* McKinvan, Duncan
McKinvan, Mary *SEE* McKinvan, Duncan
McKinzi, John 23; Ontario, 1871 ***1823.21*** *p244*
McKinzie, Catharine McNiven *SEE* McKinzie, George
McKinzie, Colin *SEE* McKinzie, George
McKinzie, Donald *SEE* McKinzie, George
McKinzie, George; New York, 1738 ***8277.31*** *p118*
*Wife:*Catharine McNiven
*Son:*Colin
*Son:*Donald
McKinzie, John 54; Ontario, 1871 ***1823.21*** *p244*
McKinzie, Valentine; New York, 1776 ***8529.30*** *p3*
McKirgon, Patrick; Boston, 1750 ***1642*** *p46*
McKitnick, Jonah 52; Ontario, 1871 ***1823.21*** *p244*
McKitrick, John; Illinois, 1852 ***6079.1*** *p9*
McKittrick, George; South Carolina, 1808 ***6155.4*** *p18*
McKittrick, Robert; South Carolina, 1808 ***6155.4*** *p18*
McKiver, Lacky; Marston's Wharf, 1782 ***8529.30*** *p14*
McKlauglan, Mark; Boston, 1747 ***1642*** *p46*
McKley, William; Died enroute, 1725 ***1220.12*** *p521*
McKmillman, Wm H. 25; Ontario, 1871 ***1823.21*** *p244*
McKnight, James; Philadelphia, 1850 ***8513.31*** *p414*
McKnight, John 62; Ontario, 1871 ***1823.21*** *p244*
McKnight, John; Philadelphia, 1856 ***8513.31*** *p414*
*Wife:*Mary Swann
McKnight, Mary Swann *SEE* McKnight, John
McKnight, William 55; Ontario, 1871 ***1823.21*** *p244*
McKny, William; Died enroute, 1725 ***1220.12*** *p521*
McKoan, James; America, 1767 ***1220.12*** *p521*
McKone, John 40; Ontario, 1871 ***1823.21*** *p244*
McKonnelly, Michael; America, 1764 ***1220.12*** *p518*
McKool, Elizabeth; Maryland or Virginia, 1728 ***1220.12*** *p517*
McKoone, Edward; America, 1739 ***1220.12*** *p521*
McKoskie, Katie; Wisconsin, 1891 ***6795.8*** *p60*
McKown, James 61; Ontario, 1871 ***1823.17*** *p111*
McKown, Joseph; South Carolina, 1800-1899 ***6155.4*** *p18*
McKown, Michael; Maine, 1833 ***3274.55*** *p72*
McKown, Michael; Ohio, 1836 ***3580.20*** *p32*
McKown, Michael; Ohio, 1836 ***6020.12*** *p13*
McKoy, Katherine; Boston, 1740-1749 ***1642*** *p29*
McKoy, Mary; Boston, 1740-1749 ***1642*** *p29*
McKriach, Malcom; Cape Fear, NC,, 1754 ***1422.10*** *p62*
McLachlan, Alex 45; Ontario, 1871 ***1823.21*** *p244*
McLachlan, Alex 61; Ontario, 1871 ***1823.21*** *p244*
McLachlan, Alexander 87; Ontario, 1871 ***1823.21*** *p244*
McLachlan, Allan 35; Ontario, 1871 ***1823.21*** *p244*
McLachlan, Ann 57; Ontario, 1871 ***1823.21*** *p244*
McLachlan, Archd 27; Ontario, 1871 ***1823.17*** *p111*
McLachlan, Archibald; Illinois, 1872 ***1029.59*** *p61*
McLachlan, Archibald 49; Ontario, 1871 ***1823.21*** *p244*
McLachlan, Catherine 60; Ontario, 1871 ***1823.21*** *p244*
McLachlan, Donald 70; Ontario, 1871 ***1823.21*** *p244*
McLachlan, Duncan 61; Ontario, 1871 ***1823.17*** *p111*
McLachlan, Duncan 62; Ontario, 1871 ***1823.21*** *p244*
McLachlan, Duncan 62; Ontario, 1871 ***1823.21*** *p244*
McLachlan, Euphemia 84; Ontario, 1871 ***1823.21*** *p244*
McLachlan, Hugh 30; Ontario, 1871 ***1823.21*** *p244*
McLachlan, Hugh 52; Ontario, 1871 ***1823.21*** *p244*
McLachlan, Hugh 55; Ontario, 1871 ***1823.21*** *p244*
McLachlan, James 28; New York, NY, 1835 ***5024.1*** *p136*
McLachlan, John 23; Ontario, 1871 ***1823.21*** *p244*
McLachlan, John 24; Ontario, 1871 ***1823.21*** *p244*
McLachlan, John 34; Ontario, 1871 ***1823.17*** *p111*
McLachlan, John 62; Ontario, 1871 ***1823.21*** *p244*
McLachlin, Archd 60; Ontario, 1871 ***1823.21*** *p244*
McLachlin, Donald 63; Ontario, 1871 ***1823.21*** *p244*
McLachlin, Jane 82; Ontario, 1871 ***1823.21*** *p244*
McLachlin, John 42; Ontario, 1871 ***1823.21*** *p244*
McLachlin, John 64; Ontario, 1871 ***1823.17*** *p111*
McLachlin, John 65; Ontario, 1871 ***1823.21*** *p245*
McLachlin, Lachlin 75; Ontario, 1871 ***1823.21*** *p245*
McLachlin, Lamont A.; Kansas, 1898 ***1447.20*** *p65*
McLachlin, William 47; Ontario, 1871 ***1823.21*** *p245*
McLachlon, Euphamia 80; Ontario, 1871 ***1823.21*** *p245*
McLacklan, Alexander; North Carolina, 1859 ***1088.45*** *p22*
McLacklan, Archibald; Colorado, 1888 ***1029.59*** *p61*
McLagan, Alexander 71; Ontario, 1871 ***1823.17*** *p111*
McLagan, Charles 25; Ontario, 1871 ***1823.17*** *p111*
McLagan, John 30; Ontario, 1871 ***1823.17*** *p111*
McLaghlin, Henry; America, 1744 ***1220.12*** *p522*

McLahone, Rose 28; Ontario, 1871 ***1823.21*** *p245*
McLain, James H. 29; Michigan, 1880 ***4491.42*** *p18*
McLane, Ann; Maryland, 1726 ***1220.12*** *p522*
McLane, David; America, 1771 ***1220.12*** *p522*
McLane, Jane; America, 1749 ***1220.12*** *p522*
McLane, John; Boston, 1769 ***1642*** *p49*
McLane, John; South Carolina, 1815 ***6155.4*** *p18*
McLane, Paul; America, 1746 ***1220.12*** *p522*
McLaran, Isabella 45; Ontario, 1871 ***1823.21*** *p245*
McLaren, D. 38; Ontario, 1871 ***1823.17*** *p111*
McLaren, Daniel 49; Ontario, 1871 ***1823.21*** *p245*
McLaren, Donald 12; North Carolina, 1775 ***1422.10*** *p60*
McLaren, Duncan 30; North Carolina, 1775 ***1422.10*** *p60*
McLaren, Euphremia 24; Michigan, 1880 ***4491.33*** *p15*
McLaren, Felix; North Carolina, 1824 ***1088.45*** *p22*
McLaren, James 45; Ontario, 1871 ***1823.21*** *p245*
McLaren, James; Washington, 1887 ***6015.10*** *p16*
McLaren, Lachlan 25; North Carolina, 1775 ***1422.10*** *p60*
McLaren, Marion 40; Ontario, 1871 ***1823.21*** *p245*
McLaren, Mary 28; Michigan, 1880 ***4491.33*** *p15*
McLaren, Peter 37; Ontario, 1871 ***1823.21*** *p245*
McLaren, Peter 53; Ontario, 1871 ***1823.17*** *p111*
McLaren, Peter 53; Ontario, 1871 ***1823.21*** *p245*
McLaren, Robert 45; Ontario, 1871 ***1823.21*** *p245*
McLaren, Ronald 40; Ontario, 1871 ***1823.17*** *p111*
McLaren, Wm 55; Ontario, 1871 ***1823.21*** *p245*
McLarine, Lawrine 20; North Carolina, 1775 ***1422.10*** *p60*
McLaron, Hugh 42; Ontario, 1871 ***1823.17*** *p111*
McLarty, Alexander 28; Ontario, 1871 ***1823.21*** *p245*
McLarty, Donald 66; Ontario, 1871 ***1823.21*** *p245*
McLarty, Duncan 50; Ontario, 1871 ***1823.21*** *p245*
McLarty, Hector 48; Ontario, 1871 ***1823.21*** *p245*
McLarty, John J. 47; Ontario, 1871 ***1823.21*** *p245*
McLarty, Neil 67; Ontario, 1871 ***1823.21*** *p245*
McLarty, Peter 55; Ontario, 1871 ***1823.17*** *p111*
McLarty, William 46; Ontario, 1871 ***1823.17*** *p111*
McLary, Alexander 10; Ontario, 1871 ***1823.21*** *p245*
McLary, John 81; Ontario, 1871 ***1823.17*** *p111*
McLary, Thomas 79; Ontario, 1871 ***1823.21*** *p245*
McLashan, Charles 66; Ontario, 1871 ***1823.17*** *p111*
McLashan, Margaret 40; Ontario, 1871 ***1823.17*** *p111*
McLaslin, Florence; New York, 1739 ***8277.31*** *p119*
McLaughlan, Duncan 26; Ontario, 1871 ***1823.21*** *p245*
McLaughlan, Milas 63; Ontario, 1871 ***1823.21*** *p245*
McLaughland, Hannah; America, 1762 ***1220.12*** *p522*
McLaughlin, Alex 20; St. John, N.B., 1834 ***6469.7*** *p5*
McLaughlin, Angus 30; Ontario, 1871 ***1823.17*** *p111*
McLaughlin, Archibald 52; Ontario, 1871 ***1823.17*** *p111*
McLaughlin, Archibald 63; Ontario, 1871 ***1823.21*** *p245*
McLaughlin, Archie 38; Ontario, 1871 ***1823.17*** *p111*
McLaughlin, Barnay; America, 1765 ***1220.12*** *p521*
McLaughlin, Barny 21; St. John, N.B., 1834 ***6469.7*** *p6*
McLaughlin, Bridget 50; Ontario, 1871 ***1823.21*** *p245*
McLaughlin, Burnet; North Carolina, 1843 ***1088.45*** *p22*
McLaughlin, Catharine 23; St. John, N.B., 1834 ***6469.7*** *p4*
McLaughlin, Catherine 21; St. John, N.B., 1834 ***6469.7*** *p5*
McLaughlin, Charles; Toronto, 1844 ***2910.35*** *p115*
McLaughlin, Christy 17; Ontario, 1871 ***1823.17*** *p111*
McLaughlin, D.; Toronto, 1844 ***2910.35*** *p115*
McLaughlin, Duncan 28; Ontario, 1871 ***1823.17*** *p111*
McLaughlin, Esther 56; St. John, N.B., 1834 ***6469.7*** *p4*
Mc'Laughlin, F.; Toronto, 1844 ***2910.35*** *p115*
McLaughlin, George; Hingham, MA, 1755 ***1642*** *p87*
McLaughlin, James; Boston, 1742 ***1642*** *p45*
McLaughlin, James 48; Ontario, 1871 ***1823.17*** *p111*
McLaughlin, James; Washington, 1885 ***2770.40*** *p194*
McLaughlin, Jane 30; Ontario, 1871 ***1823.21*** *p245*
McLaughlin, Jeremiah; America, 1749 ***1220.12*** *p522*
McLaughlin, Jno.; Louisiana, 1874-1875 ***4981.45*** *p30*
McLaughlin, John 34; Ontario, 1871 ***1823.21*** *p245*
McLaughlin, John 35; Ontario, 1871 ***1823.17*** *p111*
McLaughlin, John 51; Ontario, 1871 ***1823.21*** *p245*
McLaughlin, John 56; Ontario, 1871 ***1823.17*** *p111*
McLaughlin, John 58; Ontario, 1871 ***1823.21*** *p245*
McLaughlin, John 6; St. John, N.B., 1834 ***6469.7*** *p4*
McLaughlin, John 21; St. John, N.B., 1834 ***6469.7*** *p5*
McLaughlin, John 58; St. John, N.B., 1834 ***6469.7*** *p4*
McLaughlin, Margt 10; St. John, N.B., 1834 ***6469.7*** *p4*
McLaughlin, Martha 20; St. John, N.B., 1834 ***6469.7*** *p4*
McLaughlin, Martin 32; Ontario, 1871 ***1823.21*** *p245*
McLaughlin, Mary; America, 1745 ***1220.12*** *p522*
McLaughlin, Mary; Philadelphia, 1857 ***8513.31*** *p302*
McLaughlin, Mary 8; St. John, N.B., 1834 ***6469.7*** *p4*
McLaughlin, Mary 30; St. John, N.B., 1834 ***6469.7*** *p4*
McLaughlin, Melinda 59; Ontario, 1871 ***1823.21*** *p245*
McLaughlin, Michael; America, 1766 ***1220.12*** *p521*
McLaughlin, Michael; Nova Scotia, 1839 ***7078*** *p80*
McLaughlin, Michael 27; Ontario, 1871 ***1823.17*** *p111*
McLaughlin, Murdock 70; Ontario, 1871 ***1823.17*** *p111*
McLaughlin, P.; Louisiana, 1874-1875 ***4981.45*** *p30*
McLaughlin, Pat; St. John, N.B., 1847 ***2978.15*** *p36*
McLaughlin, Patrick 26; New York, NY, 1826 ***6178.50*** *p150*
McLaughlin, Patrick 33; Ontario, 1871 ***1823.17*** *p111*
McLaughlin, Patrick 38; Ontario, 1871 ***1823.21*** *p245*
McLaughlin, Patrick 63; Ontario, 1871 ***1823.17*** *p111*
McLaughlin, Peter 25; Ontario, 1871 ***1823.21*** *p245*
McLaughlin, Peter 45; Ontario, 1871 ***1823.21*** *p245*
McLaughlin, Richard; Nova Scotia, 1839 ***7078*** *p80*
McLaughlin, Robert 34; New York, NY, 1825 ***6178.50*** *p149*
McLaughlin, Samuel; North Carolina, 1853 ***1088.45*** *p22*
McLaughlin, Sarah 71; Ontario, 1871 ***1823.21*** *p245*
McLaughlin, Thomas 68; Ontario, 1871 ***1823.21*** *p245*
McLaughlin, Will 22; St. John, N.B., 1834 ***6469.7*** *p5*
McLaughlin, William 28; Ontario, 1871 ***1823.21*** *p245*
McLaughton, Grifsey; America, 1749 ***1220.12*** *p522*
McLauglin, Neil 29; Ontario, 1871 ***1823.21*** *p245*
McLay, Archibald 27; Ontario, 1871 ***1823.21*** *p245*
McLean, Agnes 7; Quebec, 1870 ***8364.32*** *p25*
McLean, Alex 40; Ontario, 1871 ***1823.21*** *p246*
McLean, Alex; Toronto, 1844 ***2910.35*** *p115*
McLean, Alexander; Colorado, 1905 ***1029.59*** *p61*
McLean, Alexander 62; Ontario, 1871 ***1823.17*** *p111*
McLean, Alexander 67; Ontario, 1871 ***1823.21*** *p246*
McLean, Alexander 69; Ontario, 1871 ***1823.21*** *p246*
McLean, Alexander; Washington, 1888 ***2770.40*** *p26*
McLean, Allen 31; Ontario, 1871 ***1823.21*** *p246*
McLean, Allen 55; Ontario, 1871 ***1823.21*** *p246*
McLean, Andrew; North Carolina, 1844 ***1088.45*** *p22*
McLean, Angus 21; Ontario, 1871 ***1823.21*** *p246*
McLean, Angus 40; Ontario, 1871 ***1823.21*** *p246*
McLean, Angus 42; Ontario, 1871 ***1823.17*** *p111*
McLean, Angus 45; Ontario, 1871 ***1823.21*** *p246*
McLean, Angus 60; Ontario, 1871 ***1823.17*** *p111*
McLean, Archibald 48; Ontario, 1871 ***1823.21*** *p246*
McLean, Archibald 51; Ontario, 1871 ***1823.17*** *p111*
McLean, Archibald 54; Ontario, 1871 ***1823.21*** *p246*
McLean, Catherine 20; Ontario, 1871 ***1823.21*** *p246*
McLean, Catherine 50; Ontario, 1871 ***1823.21*** *p246*
McLean, Catherine 55; Ontario, 1871 ***1823.21*** *p246*
McLean, Charles 59; Ontario, 1871 ***1823.21*** *p246*
McLean, Charles 63; Ontario, 1871 ***1823.17*** *p111*
McLean, Chrispin; Cape Fear, NC,, 1754 ***1422.10*** *p62*
McLean, Christina 80; Ontario, 1871 ***1823.17*** *p111*
McLean, Colin 35; Ontario, 1871 ***1823.17*** *p111*
McLean, Donald; Brunswick, NC, 1767 ***1422.10*** *p61*
McLean, Donald 38; Ontario, 1871 ***1823.17*** *p112*
McLean, Donald 42; Ontario, 1871 ***1823.17*** *p111*
McLean, Donald 60; Ontario, 1871 ***1823.17*** *p112*
McLean, Donald 60; Ontario, 1871 ***1823.21*** *p246*
McLean, Donald 62; Ontario, 1871 ***1823.21*** *p246*
McLean, Donald 64; Ontario, 1871 ***1823.21*** *p246*
McLean, Donald 69; Ontario, 1871 ***1823.17*** *p112*
McLean, Donald 72; Ontario, 1871 ***1823.21*** *p246*
McLean, Dugal 25; Ontario, 1871 ***1823.21*** *p246*
McLean, Duncan; Brunswick, NC, 1767 ***1422.10*** *p61*
McLean, Duncan 36; Ontario, 1871 ***1823.17*** *p112*
McLean, Duncan 62; Ontario, 1871 ***1823.21*** *p246*
McLean, Duncan 65; Ontario, 1871 ***1823.21*** *p246*
McLean, Eleanor; America, 1752 ***1220.12*** *p522*
McLean, Elizabeth 60; Ontario, 1871 ***1823.21*** *p246*
McLean, Euphemia 32; Ontario, 1871 ***1823.21*** *p246*
McLean, Ewen 40; Ontario, 1871 ***1823.17*** *p112*
McLean, Florence 21; Ontario, 1871 ***1823.21*** *p246*
McLean, Francis 29; Ontario, 1871 ***1823.17*** *p112*
McLean, George 21; Ontario, 1871 ***1823.21*** *p246*
McLean, Gillane 76; Ontario, 1871 ***1823.21*** *p246*
McLean, Hector 44; Ontario, 1871 ***1823.21*** *p246*
McLean, Hector 74; Ontario, 1871 ***1823.21*** *p246*
McLean, Henry 30; Ontario, 1871 ***1823.21*** *p246*
McLean, Hugh; Boston, 1750 ***1642*** *p29*
McLean, Hugh; Cape Fear, NC,, 1754 ***1422.10*** *p61*
McLean, Hugh; North Carolina, 1806 ***1088.45*** *p22*
McLean, Isabella 25; Ontario, 1871 ***1823.21*** *p246*
McLean, Isabella 40; Ontario, 1871 ***1823.21*** *p246*
McLean, Isabella 60; Ontario, 1871 ***1823.21*** *p246*
McLean, James 33; Ontario, 1871 ***1823.21*** *p246*
McLean, James 41; Ontario, 1871 ***1823.21*** *p246*
McLean, James 44; Ontario, 1871 ***1823.21*** *p246*
McLean, Jane 58; Ontario, 1871 ***1823.21*** *p246*
McLean, Janet 65; Ontario, 1871 ***1823.21*** *p247*
McLean, John; America, 1743 ***1220.12*** *p522*
McLean, John; Brunswick, NC, 1767 ***1422.10*** *p61*
McLean, John; Brunswick, NC, 1767 ***1422.10*** *p61*
McLean, John 28; Ontario, 1871 ***1823.17*** *p112*
McLean, John 29; Ontario, 1871 ***1823.21*** *p247*
McLean, John 34; Ontario, 1871 ***1823.17*** *p112*
McLean, John 37; Ontario, 1871 ***1823.21*** *p247*
McLean, John 43; Ontario, 1871 ***1823.17*** *p112*
McLean, John 53; Ontario, 1871 ***1823.21*** *p247*
McLean, John 63; Ontario, 1871 ***1823.21*** *p247*
McLean, John 68; Ontario, 1871 ***1823.21*** *p247*
McLean, John 83; Ontario, 1871 ***1823.21*** *p247*
McLean, Kate 29; Ontario, 1871 ***1823.21*** *p247*
McLean, Katherain; Cape Fear, NC,, 1754 ***1422.10*** *p61*
McLean, Lauchlin; New York, 1740 ***8277.31*** *p118*
McLean, Laughlin 48; Ontario, 1871 ***1823.21*** *p247*
McLean, Malcolm 30; Ontario, 1871 ***1823.21*** *p247*
McLean, Margaret 38; Ontario, 1871 ***1823.21*** *p247*
McLean, Martha 62; Ontario, 1871 ***1823.21*** *p247*
McLean, Mary; New York, 1739 ***8277.31*** *p115*
McLean, Mary 36; Ontario, 1871 ***1823.21*** *p247*
McLean, Mary 55; Ontario, 1871 ***1823.21*** *p247*
McLean, Mary 64; Ontario, 1871 ***1823.21*** *p247*
McLean, Nanny; Brunswick, NC, 1767 ***1422.10*** *p61*
McLean, Neal; Louisiana, 1874-1875 ***4981.45*** *p30*
McLean, Neil 32; Ontario, 1871 ***1823.21*** *p247*
McLean, Neil 38; Ontario, 1871 ***1823.21*** *p247*
McLean, Neil 50; Ontario, 1871 ***1823.21*** *p247*
McLean, Neill; Brunswick, NC, 1767 ***1422.10*** *p61*
McLean, Oliver 45; South Carolina, 1812 ***3476.30*** *p12*
McLean, Peter; Brunswick, NC, 1767 ***1422.10*** *p61*
McLean, Robert 36; Ontario, 1871 ***1823.21*** *p247*
McLean, Robert 44; Ontario, 1871 ***1823.21*** *p247*
McLean, Robert 53; Ontario, 1871 ***1823.21*** *p247*
McLean, Robert 60; Ontario, 1871 ***1823.21*** *p247*
McLean, Robert 65; Ontario, 1871 ***1823.21*** *p247*
McLean, Robert L.; North Carolina, 1845 ***1088.45*** *p22*
McLean, Thomas; America, 1772 ***1220.12*** *p522*
McLean, William; America, 1738 ***1220.12*** *p522*
McLean, William 25; Ontario, 1871 ***1823.21*** *p247*
McLeane, Frances; Virginia, 1731-1733 ***1220.12*** *p522*
McLearon, John; America, 1743 ***1220.12*** *p522*
McLeary, Ludovic 30; Ontario, 1871 ***1823.21*** *p247*
McLeary, Patrick 36; Ontario, 1871 ***1823.21*** *p247*
McLeay, Donald 60; Ontario, 1871 ***1823.17*** *p112*
McLeay, Murdo 39; Ontario, 1871 ***1823.17*** *p112*
McLeelan, John 43; Ontario, 1871 ***1823.21*** *p247*
McLeeland, William 29; Ontario, 1871 ***1823.21*** *p247*
McLeggan, Archibald 60; Ontario, 1871 ***1823.21*** *p247*
McLeish, Alex 53; Ontario, 1871 ***1823.21*** *p247*
McLeish, Archibald 40; Ontario, 1871 ***1823.21*** *p247*
McLeish, Donald 58; Ontario, 1871 ***1823.21*** *p247*
McLeish, Jean; Ontario, 1871 ***1823.21*** *p247*
McLeish, John 48; Ontario, 1871 ***1823.21*** *p247*
McLeish, John 49; Ontario, 1871 ***1823.21*** *p247*
McLeland, James 41; Ontario, 1871 ***1823.17*** *p112*
McLellah, Margaret 45; Ontario, 1871 ***1823.21*** *p247*
McLellan, Allan; Colorado, 1873 ***1029.59*** *p61*
McLellan, Angus 57; Ontario, 1871 ***1823.21*** *p247*
McLellan, Ann 52; Ontario, 1871 ***1823.21*** *p247*
McLellan, Archd 50; Ontario, 1871 ***1823.21*** *p247*
McLellan, Archibald 38; Ontario, 1871 ***1823.21*** *p247*
McLellan, Archibald 43; Ontario, 1871 ***1823.21*** *p248*
McLellan, Archibald 70; Ontario, 1871 ***1823.21*** *p248*
McLellan, Daniel 11; Ontario, 1871 ***1823.17*** *p112*
McLellan, David 52; Ontario, 1871 ***1823.21*** *p248*
McLellan, Donald 51; Ontario, 1871 ***1823.21*** *p248*
McLellan, Donald 55; Ontario, 1871 ***1823.21*** *p248*
McLellan, Donald 84; Ontario, 1871 ***1823.21*** *p248*
McLellan, Finlay 40; Ontario, 1871 ***1823.21*** *p248*
McLellan, Flora 78; Ontario, 1871 ***1823.21*** *p248*
McLellan, James 24; Ontario, 1871 ***1823.21*** *p248*
McLellan, James 54; Ontario, 1871 ***1823.21*** *p248*
McLellan, Jemima 53; Ontario, 1871 ***1823.21*** *p248*
McLellan, John 21; Ontario, 1871 ***1823.21*** *p248*
McLellan, John 30; Ontario, 1871 ***1823.21*** *p248*
McLellan, John 43; Ontario, 1871 ***1823.21*** *p248*
McLellan, John 45; Ontario, 1871 ***1823.17*** *p112*
McLellan, John 56; Ontario, 1871 ***1823.21*** *p248*
McLellan, Lisu 21; Ontario, 1871 ***1823.17*** *p112*
McLellan, Mary 49; Ontario, 1871 ***1823.17*** *p112*
McLellan, Neil 35; Ontario, 1871 ***1823.21*** *p248*
McLellan, Neil 48; Ontario, 1871 ***1823.21*** *p248*
McLellan, Ranald 50; Ontario, 1871 ***1823.21*** *p248*
McLellan, Robert 38; Ontario, 1871 ***1823.21*** *p248*
McLelland, Alexander 40; Ontario, 1871 ***1823.17*** *p112*
McLellen, George 49; Ontario, 1871 ***1823.21*** *p248*
McLellen, John 60; Ontario, 1871 ***1823.21*** *p248*
McLennan, James 40; Ontario, 1871 ***1823.21*** *p248*
McLennan, John 64; Ontario, 1871 ***1823.21*** *p248*
McLennan, Niel 55; Ontario, 1871 ***1823.17*** *p112*
McLennan, William; North Carolina, 1792-1862 ***1088.45*** *p22*
McLennan, William 41; Ontario, 1871 ***1823.21*** *p248*
McLennin, Donald 39; Ontario, 1871 ***1823.17*** *p112*
McLennon, Simon 58; Ontario, 1871 ***1823.17*** *p112*
McLenons, Mary 30; Ontario, 1871 ***1823.21*** *p248*
McLeod, Aeneas 60; North Carolina, 1774 ***1422.10*** *p59*
McLeod, Alexander; Marston's Wharf, 1782 ***8529.30*** *p14*
McLeod, Alexander 25; Ontario, 1871 ***1823.17*** *p112*
McLeod, Alexander 40; Ontario, 1871 ***1823.21*** *p248*
McLeod, Alexander; Washington, 1882 ***2770.40*** *p135*
McLeod, Angus 19; Ontario, 1871 ***1823.21*** *p248*
McLeod, Angus 73; Ontario, 1871 ***1823.21*** *p248*

McLeod, Ann 57; Ontario, 1871 ***1823.17*** *p112*
McLeod, Archibald 43; Ontario, 1871 ***1823.21*** *p248*
McLeod, Archibald 43; Ontario, 1871 ***1823.21*** *p248*
McLeod, Barbara 57; Ontario, 1871 ***1823.21*** *p248*
McLeod, Bella 18; Ontario, 1871 ***1823.21*** *p248*
McLeod, Donald; New York, 1782 ***8529.30*** *p14*
McLeod, Donald 21; Ontario, 1871 ***1823.17*** *p112*
McLeod, Donald 38; Ontario, 1871 ***1823.21*** *p248*
McLeod, Donald 50; Ontario, 1871 ***1823.21*** *p249*
McLeod, Donald 60; Ontario, 1871 ***1823.21*** *p249*
McLeod, Donald 80; Ontario, 1871 ***1823.21*** *p249*
McLeod, Duncan 39; Ontario, 1871 ***1823.21*** *p249*
McLeod, Duncan 46; Ontario, 1871 ***1823.21*** *p249*
McLeod, Finley 42; Ontario, 1871 ***1823.21*** *p249*
McLeod, George 50; Ontario, 1871 ***1823.21*** *p249*
McLeod, Hector 42; Ontario, 1871 ***1823.21*** *p249*
McLeod, Hugh 40; Ontario, 1871 ***1823.21*** *p249*
McLeod, Janet 60; Ontario, 1871 ***1823.21*** *p249*
McLeod, Jannet 21; Ontario, 1871 ***1823.21*** *p249*
McLeod, John 27; Ontario, 1871 ***1823.21*** *p249*
McLeod, John 45; Ontario, 1871 ***1823.17*** *p112*
McLeod, John 48; Ontario, 1871 ***1823.21*** *p249*
McLeod, John 52; Ontario, 1871 ***1823.21*** *p249*
McLeod, John 57; Ontario, 1871 ***1823.21*** *p249*
McLeod, John 78; Ontario, 1871 ***1823.21*** *p249*
McLeod, Kenneth 30; Ontario, 1871 ***1823.21*** *p249*
McLeod, Kitty 22; Ontario, 1871 ***1823.17*** *p112*
McLeod, Malcolm 60; Ontario, 1871 ***1823.21*** *p249*
McLeod, Margaret 20; Ontario, 1871 ***1823.17*** *p112*
McLeod, Margret 50; Ontario, 1871 ***1823.21*** *p249*
McLeod, Mungo; Philadelphia, 1778 ***8529.30*** *p4A*
McLeod, Murdoch 50; Ontario, 1871 ***1823.21*** *p249*
McLeod, Murdok 43; Ontario, 1871 ***1823.21*** *p249*
McLeod, Neil 32; Ontario, 1871 ***1823.21*** *p249*
McLeod, Roderick; Quebec, 1786 ***1416.15*** *p8*
McLeod, Ronald 35; Ontario, 1871 ***1823.21*** *p249*
McLeod, Sarah 18; Ontario, 1871 ***1823.17*** *p112*
McLeod, Simon 44; Ontario, 1871 ***1823.21*** *p249*
McLeod, Thomas 72; Ontario, 1871 ***1823.21*** *p249*
McLeod, William 20; Ontario, 1871 ***1823.21*** *p249*
McLeod, William 34; Ontario, 1871 ***1823.21*** *p249*
McLeod, Willm. 26; North Carolina, 1774 ***1422.10*** *p59*
McLeoud, Ceser 75; Ontario, 1871 ***1823.21*** *p249*
McLeoud, William 40; Ontario, 1871 ***1823.21*** *p249*
McLeran, James; North Carolina, 1835 ***1088.45*** *p22*
McLeran, Neil; North Carolina, 1812 ***1088.45*** *p22*
McLevey, John 34; Ontario, 1871 ***1823.17*** *p112*
McLillan, John 19; Ontario, 1871 ***1823.21*** *p249*
McLin, Ann; Maryland or Virginia, 1731 ***1220.12*** *p522*
McLin, Thomas; America, 1748 ***1220.12*** *p522*
McLinden, Daniel 63; Ontario, 1871 ***1823.21*** *p249*
McLinglin, Michael; America, 1766 ***1220.12*** *p521*
McLoach, James; New Hampshire, 1820 ***3274.55*** *p66*
McLochlen, Cornelius; America, 1774 ***1220.12*** *p522*
McLocklin, Edward; America, 1730 ***1220.12*** *p522*
McLocklin, Edward; America, 1739 ***1220.12*** *p522*
McLocklin, Lamont A.; Kansas, 1898 ***1447.20*** *p62*
McLoicer, Louse; North Carolina, 1859 ***1088.45*** *p22*
McLorley, John; North Carolina, 1860 ***1088.45*** *p22*
McLoud, Daniel 36; Ontario, 1871 ***1823.17*** *p113*
McLoud, Roderick; Washington, 1883 ***2770.40*** *p137*
McLoughlin, Edward; Barbados or St. Christopher, 1780 ***8529.30*** *p7A*
McLoughlin, William 31; Ontario, 1871 ***1823.21*** *p249*
McLowe, Charles 32; Ontario, 1871 ***1823.17*** *p113*
McLung, Alexander 39; Ontario, 1871 ***1823.17*** *p113*
McLure, George 72; Ontario, 1871 ***1823.17*** *p113*
McLure, John 74; Ontario, 1871 ***1823.17*** *p113*
McLurg, Robert 51; Ontario, 1871 ***1823.21*** *p249*
McLyn, John; Barbados, 1683 ***1220.12*** *p522*
McMahan, . . .; Boston, 1774 ***8529.30*** *p6*
McMahan, James 58; Ontario, 1871 ***1823.17*** *p113*
McMahan, John 49; Ontario, 1871 ***1823.17*** *p113*
McMahon, Benjamin; America, 1750 ***1220.12*** *p522*
McMahon, Bernard; Ontario, 1835 ***3160.1*** *p150*
McMahon, Bernard 37; Ontario, 1871 ***1823.21*** *p249*
McMahon, Bernard; Prescott, Ont., 1835 ***3289.1*** *p61*
McMahon, Bridget 23; Ontario, 1871 ***1823.17*** *p113*
McMahon, Dennis; Ohio, 1809-1852 ***4511.35*** *p33*
McMahon, E.; Louisiana, 1874 ***4981.45*** *p296*
McMahon, Edward; Ontario, 1835 ***3160.1*** *p150*
McMahon, James 32; Ontario, 1871 ***1823.17*** *p113*
McMahon, Jas.; Toronto, 1844 ***2910.35*** *p116*
McMahon, John; Louisiana, 1836-1840 ***4981.45*** *p213*
McMahon, John 36; Ontario, 1871 ***1823.21*** *p249*
McMahon, John 60; Ontario, 1871 ***1823.17*** *p113*
McMahon, Mary; America, 1757 ***1220.12*** *p522*
McMahon, Mary 24; Ontario, 1871 ***1823.17*** *p113*
McMahon, Michael 25; Ontario, 1871 ***1823.17*** *p113*
McMahon, Patt; New Orleans, 1851 ***7242.30*** *p149*
McMahon, Ross; New Orleans, 1851 ***7242.30*** *p149*
McMahon, Thimothy; Ohio, 1840-1897 ***8365.35*** *p17*
McManinan, Alexander; Boston, 1836 ***3274.55*** *p44*
McMann, Blanche 32; Minnesota, 1923 ***2769.54*** *p1378*
McMann, Jane 37; Michigan, 1880 ***4491.36*** *p15*
McMann, Margaret 14; Michigan, 1880 ***4491.36*** *p15*
McMann, Mary G. 16; Michigan, 1880 ***4491.36*** *p15*
Mc Mann, Michael; Ohio, 1844 ***2763.1*** *p20*
McMann, Sarah J. 18; Michigan, 1880 ***4491.36*** *p15*
McMann, Thomas 33; Michigan, 1880 ***4491.36*** *p15*
McMannas, Thomas 46; Ontario, 1871 ***1823.21*** *p250*
McMannis, Eliza 63; Ontario, 1871 ***1823.21*** *p250*
McMannus, Mary 84; Ontario, 1871 ***1823.21*** *p250*
McManus, Mrs. J.; Toronto, 1844 ***2910.35*** *p111*
McManus, James 52; Ontario, 1871 ***1823.17*** *p113*
McManus, John 45; Ontario, 1871 ***1823.17*** *p113*
McManus, John 68; Ontario, 1871 ***1823.21*** *p250*
McManus, John; Philadelphia, 1852 ***8513.31*** *p414*
*Wife:*Susan McNamee
McManus, John; Toronto, 1844 ***2910.35*** *p111*
McManus, Patrick 45; Ontario, 1871 ***1823.17*** *p113*
McManus, Patrick; Toronto, 1844 ***2910.35*** *p111*
McManus, Rodger; Toronto, 1844 ***2910.35*** *p111*
McManus, Susan McNamee *SEE* McManus, John
McManus, Terrence; Ohio, 1854 ***3580.20*** *p32*
McManus, Terrence; Ohio, 1854 ***6020.12*** *p13*
McManus, Thomas; New Orleans, 1850 ***7242.30*** *p149*
McManus, Thos.; California, 1868 ***1131.61*** *p89*
McMarcos, Margaret; Palmer, MA, 1717 ***1642*** *p119*
McMarshall, Thomas 30; Ontario, 1871 ***1823.21*** *p250*
McMartin, William 77; Ontario, 1871 ***1823.21*** *p250*
McMaster, Alexander 67; Ontario, 1871 ***1823.21*** *p250*
McMaster, Annie 12; Quebec, 1870 ***8364.32*** *p25*
McMaster, Catherine 73; Ontario, 1871 ***1823.21*** *p250*
McMaster, David 38; Ontario, 1871 ***1823.17*** *p113*
McMaster, George 8; Quebec, 1870 ***8364.32*** *p25*
McMaster, James 28; Ontario, 1871 ***1823.17*** *p113*
McMasters, John; North Carolina, 1821 ***1088.45*** *p22*
McMath, Jesse H.; Ohio, 1853 ***3580.20*** *p32*
McMath, Jesse H.; Ohio, 1853 ***6020.12*** *p13*
McMechan, Benjamin 43; Ontario, 1871 ***1823.17*** *p113*
McMechan, John; Ohio, 1838 ***3580.20*** *p32*
McMechan, John; Ohio, 1838 ***6020.12*** *p13*
McMechan, John 49; Ontario, 1871 ***1823.21*** *p250*
McMechan, Samuel 74; Ontario, 1871 ***1823.17*** *p113*
McMecken, Samuel 36; Ontario, 1871 ***1823.17*** *p113*
McMecredy, Robert 15; Ontario, 1871 ***1823.21*** *p250*
McMennin, Mary; Boston, 1738 ***1642*** *p44*
McMichael, John 25; New York, NY, 1825 ***6178.50*** *p149*
McMichael, Thomas 8; Michigan, 1880 ***4491.42*** *p18*
McMicking, Mary; Ontario, 1835 ***3160.1*** *p150*
McMiken, Janet 39; North Carolina, 1775 ***1422.10*** *p57*
McMillan, Alex 36; Ontario, 1871 ***1823.21*** *p250*
McMillan, Alexander *SEE* McMillan, Donald
McMillan, Alexander 60; Ontario, 1871 ***1823.21*** *p250*
McMillan, Angus 46; Ontario, 1871 ***1823.21*** *p250*
McMillan, Angus 54; Ontario, 1871 ***1823.21*** *p250*
McMillan, Arcd. 58; North Carolina, 1774 ***1422.10*** *p57*
McMillan, Archd; North Carolina, 1774 ***1422.10*** *p63*
McMillan, Archd.; North Carolina, 1774 ***1422.10*** *p61*
McMillan, Archibald 60; Ontario, 1871 ***1823.21*** *p250*
McMillan, Barbra 20; North Carolina, 1774 ***1422.10*** *p57*
McMillan, Benjamin 33; Ontario, 1871 ***1823.21*** *p250*
McMillan, Catharine 53; Ontario, 1871 ***1823.21*** *p250*
McMillan, Donald; New York, 1738 ***8277.31*** *p118*
*Wife:*Mary McEachern
McMillan, Donald; New York, 1739 ***8277.31*** *p118*
*Wife:*Janet Gillies
*Son:*Alexander
McMillan, Donald 25; Ontario, 1871 ***1823.21*** *p250*
McMillan, Donald 30; Ontario, 1871 ***1823.21*** *p250*
McMillan, Donald 31; Ontario, 1871 ***1823.21*** *p250*
McMillan, Donald 38; Ontario, 1871 ***1823.17*** *p113*
McMillan, Donald 57; Ontario, 1871 ***1823.21*** *p250*
McMillan, Donald 60; Ontario, 1871 ***1823.21*** *p250*
McMillan, Donald 66; Ontario, 1871 ***1823.21*** *p250*
McMillan, Donald; Quebec, 1786 ***1416.15*** *p8*
McMillan, Duncan 34; Ontario, 1871 ***1823.21*** *p250*
McMillan, Duncan 47; Ontario, 1871 ***1823.21*** *p250*
McMillan, Duncan 66; Ontario, 1871 ***1823.21*** *p250*
McMillan, Encas 35; Ontario, 1871 ***1823.21*** *p250*
McMillan, Flora 50; Ontario, 1871 ***1823.21*** *p250*
McMillan, Hugh; Washington, 1883 ***2770.40*** *p137*
McMillan, Iver 26; North Carolina, 1774 ***1422.10*** *p58*
McMillan, Iver 26; North Carolina, 1774 ***1422.10*** *p62*
McMillan, James 49; Ontario, 1871 ***1823.21*** *p250*
McMillan, Janet Gillies *SEE* McMillan, Donald
McMillan, Jean 23; North Carolina, 1774 ***1422.10*** *p58*
McMillan, Jean 23; North Carolina, 1774 ***1422.10*** *p62*
McMillan, John 39; Ontario, 1871 ***1823.21*** *p250*
McMillan, John 46; Ontario, 1871 ***1823.17*** *p113*
McMillan, John 52; Ontario, 1871 ***1823.21*** *p250*
McMillan, John 56; Ontario, 1871 ***1823.21*** *p250*
McMillan, John G. 27; Ontario, 1871 ***1823.21*** *p250*
McMillan, Lachlan 28; Ontario, 1871 ***1823.21*** *p250*
McMillan, Malcolm 56; Ontario, 1871 ***1823.21*** *p250*
McMillan, Mary McEachern *SEE* McMillan, Donald
McMillan, Mary 40; North Carolina, 1774 ***1422.10*** *p57*
McMillan, Mary 19; Ontario, 1871 ***1823.21*** *p250*
McMillan, Neal 39; Ontario, 1871 ***1823.21*** *p251*
McMillan, Neal 65; Ontario, 1871 ***1823.21*** *p250*
McMillan, Neil 50; Ontario, 1871 ***1823.21*** *p251*
McMillan, William 50; Ontario, 1871 ***1823.21*** *p251*
McMillen, Archibald 50; Ontario, 1871 ***1823.21*** *p251*
McMillen, Daniel 28; Ontario, 1871 ***1823.21*** *p251*
McMillen, James 25; Ontario, 1871 ***1823.21*** *p251*
McMillen, Thomas 35; Ontario, 1871 ***1823.21*** *p251*
McMillen, William; Virginia, 1727 ***1220.12*** *p522*
McMillin, James 66; Ontario, 1871 ***1823.17*** *p113*
McMillion, Philip; Rappahannock, VA, 1729 ***1220.12*** *p522*
McMorphee, Peter; Massachusetts, 1761 ***1642*** *p109*
McMullan, Archd; North Carolina, 1774 ***1422.10*** *p62*
McMullan, Archd. 16; North Carolina, 1774 ***1422.10*** *p58*
McMullan, Cathn 58; North Carolina, 1774 ***1422.10*** *p62*
McMullan, Cathn.; North Carolina, 1774 ***1422.10*** *p58*
McMullan, Daniel; North Carolina, 1774 ***1422.10*** *p62*
McMullan, Daniel 24; North Carolina, 1774 ***1422.10*** *p58*
McMullan, Gelbt.; North Carolina, 1774 ***1422.10*** *p62*
McMullan, Gelbt. 8; North Carolina, 1774 ***1422.10*** *p58*
McMullan, James; Jamaica, 1783 ***8529.30*** *p13A*
McMullan, Malm 58; North Carolina, 1774 ***1422.10*** *p62*
McMullan, Malm. 58; North Carolina, 1774 ***1422.10*** *p58*
McMullan, Robert 53; Ontario, 1871 ***1823.21*** *p251*
McMullan, Thomas; Jamaica, 1783 ***8529.30*** *p13A*
McMullen, Alexander *SEE* McMullen, Donald
McMullen, Alexander 21; New York, NY, 1825 ***6178.50*** *p149*
McMullen, Barbara 40; Ontario, 1871 ***1823.21*** *p251*
McMullen, Catharine; New York, NY, 1856 ***8513.31*** *p423*
McMullen, Donald; New York, 1739 ***8277.31*** *p118*
*Wife:*Janet Gillies
*Son:*Alexander
McMullen, James; Jamaica, 1778 ***8529.30*** *p13A*
McMullen, James; Kingston, Jamaica, 1780 ***8529.30*** *p13A*
Mc Mullen, James; Ohio, 1843 ***2763.1*** *p20*
McMullen, Janet Gillies *SEE* McMullen, Donald
McMullen, Neil 46; Ontario, 1871 ***1823.21*** *p251*
McMullen, Robert C. 54; Ontario, 1871 ***1823.17*** *p113*
McMullen, Thomas 38; Ontario, 1871 ***1823.21*** *p251*
McMullen, Thomas 61; Ontario, 1871 ***1823.21*** *p251*
McMullen, Thomas F. 60; Ontario, 1871 ***1823.21*** *p251*
McMullen, William 35; New York, NY, 1825 ***6178.50*** *p148*
McMullen, William 61; Ontario, 1871 ***1823.21*** *p251*
McMullin, Denis 39; Ontario, 1871 ***1823.21*** *p251*
McMullin, Elizabeth; Philadelphia, 1855 ***8513.31*** *p412*
McMulling, Mary; Virginia, 1736 ***1220.12*** *p522*
McMullins, Susanna; Boston, 1767 ***1642*** *p48*
McMurchie, Archd. 21; North Carolina, 1774 ***1422.10*** *p61*
McMurchie, Elizabeth 14; North Carolina, 1774 ***1422.10*** *p61*
McMurchie, Hugh 46; North Carolina, 1774 ***1422.10*** *p61*
McMurchie, Mary 17; North Carolina, 1774 ***1422.10*** *p61*
McMurchie, Patrick 17; North Carolina, 1774 ***1422.10*** *p61*
McMurchie, Robert 9; North Carolina, 1774 ***1422.10*** *p61*
McMurchy, Archd 21; North Carolina, 1774 ***1422.10*** *p63*
McMurchy, Elizabeth 8; North Carolina, 1774 ***1422.10*** *p63*
McMurchy, Elizabeth 14; North Carolina, 1774 ***1422.10*** *p63*
McMurchy, Hugh 46; North Carolina, 1774 ***1422.10*** *p63*
McMurchy, Mary 17; North Carolina, 1774 ***1422.10*** *p63*
McMurchy, Patrick 17; North Carolina, 1774 ***1422.10*** *p63*
McMurchy, Robert 9; North Carolina, 1774 ***1422.10*** *p63*
McMurfy, John; Boston, 1741 ***1642*** *p45*
McMurfy, Mary *SEE* McMurfy, Peter
McMurfy, Peter; Massachusetts, 1739 ***1642*** *p99*
*Wife:*Mary
McMurphy, Christina 62; Ontario, 1871 ***1823.21*** *p251*
McMurphy, Dugald 46; Ontario, 1871 ***1823.17*** *p113*
McMurphy, Dugald 63; Ontario, 1871 ***1823.21*** *p251*
McMurphy, Dugald 72; Ontario, 1871 ***1823.21*** *p251*
McMurphy, Duncan 34; Ontario, 1871 ***1823.21*** *p251*
McMurphy, John 41; Ontario, 1871 ***1823.21*** *p251*
McMurphy, Susanna; Boston, 1762 ***1642*** *p48*
McMurphy, Susanna; Boston, 1769 ***1642*** *p49*
McMurray, David 32; Ontario, 1871 ***1823.21*** *p251*
McMurray, James 84; Ontario, 1871 ***1823.21*** *p251*
McMurrien, Samuel; North Carolina, 1835-1837 ***1088.45*** *p22*
McMurry, Frank; Colorado, 1873 ***1029.59*** *p61*

McMurry, Michael 62; Ontario, 1871 ***1823.21*** *p251*
McMurtry, John 60; Ontario, 1871 ***1823.21*** *p251*
McNab, Alexander 32; Ontario, 1871 ***1823.21*** *p251*
McNab, Andrew 60; Ontario, 1871 ***1823.21*** *p251*
McNab, Archibald 33; Ontario, 1871 ***1823.21*** *p251*
McNab, Ms. S.A. 13; Quebec, 1870 ***8364.32*** *p25*
McNabb, Angus 55; Ontario, 1871 ***1823.17*** *p113*
McNabb, David 49; Ontario, 1871 ***1823.21*** *p251*
McNabb, Hugh 35; Ontario, 1871 ***1823.17*** *p113*
McNabb, John 46; Ontario, 1871 ***1823.21*** *p252*
McNabb, John 50; Ontario, 1871 ***1823.17*** *p113*
McNabb, John 60; Ontario, 1871 ***1823.17*** *p113*
McNachten, Alexander; New York, 1738 ***8277.31*** *p118*
*Wife:*Mary McDonald
*Child:*Janet
*Child:*Eleanor
*Child:*Moses
*Child:*John
McNachten, Eleanor *SEE* McNachten, Alexander
McNachten, Janet *SEE* McNachten, Alexander
McNachten, John *SEE* McNachten, Alexander
McNachten, Mary McDonald *SEE* McNachten, Alexander
McNachten, Moses *SEE* McNachten, Alexander
McNair, David 40; Ontario, 1871 ***1823.21*** *p252*
McNalas, William; Ohio, 1809-1852 ***4511.35*** *p33*
McNally, Jesa 61; Michigan, 1880 ***4491.36*** *p15*
McNally, Luke; Boston, 1747 ***1642*** *p29*
McNally, Mary 70; Ontario, 1871 ***1823.21*** *p252*
McNally, Mary S. 73; Michigan, 1880 ***4491.36*** *p15*
McNally, Thomas 47; Michigan, 1880 ***4491.36*** *p15*
McNally, Thomas 73; Michigan, 1880 ***4491.36*** *p15*
McNally, William 45; Ontario, 1871 ***1823.21*** *p252*
McNamail, Douglad; Cape Fear, NC,, 1754 ***1422.10*** *p62*
McNamaile, Dugald; Cape Fear, NC,, 1754 ***1422.10*** *p62*
McNamam, James 47; Ontario, 1871 ***1823.17*** *p114*
McNamara, Augustus; Ohio, 1856 ***3580.20*** *p32*
McNamara, Augustus; Ohio, 1856 ***6020.12*** *p13*
McNamara, James; Colorado, 1882 ***1029.59*** *p61*
McNamara, James; Salem, MA, 1771 ***1642*** *p78*
McNamara, Jeremiah; Virginia, 1762 ***1220.12*** *p522*
McNamara, Jno.; Louisiana, 1874 ***4981.45*** *p296*
McNamara, John; St. John, N.B., 1847 ***2978.15*** *p38*
McNamara, M. 50; Ontario, 1871 ***1823.21*** *p252*
McNamara, Margret 40; Ontario, 1871 ***1823.17*** *p114*
McNamara, Margt 76; Ontario, 1871 ***1823.21*** *p252*
McNamara, Martha; Massachusetts, 1769 ***1642*** *p106*
McNamara, Mary; America, 1757 ***1220.12*** *p522*
McNamara, Mathew; Boston, 1764 ***1642*** *p34*
McNamara, Michael; Colorado, 1870 ***1029.59*** *p61*
McNamara, Michael; Colorado, 1884 ***1029.59*** *p61*
McNamara, Mick; Boston, 1765 ***1642*** *p35*
McNamara, Patrick; Toronto, 1844 ***2910.35*** *p115*
McNamara, Peter; Boston, 1766 ***1642*** *p37*
McNamara, Timothy; America, 1767 ***1220.12*** *p522*
McNamee, James 62; Ontario, 1871 ***1823.21*** *p252*
McNamee, John 33; New York, NY, 1826 ***6178.50*** *p149*
McNamee, Michael 8; New York, NY, 1821-1849 ***6178.50*** *p149*
McNamee, Patrick; Jamaica, 1783 ***8529.30*** *p13A*
McNamee, Robert 30; Ontario, 1871 ***1823.21*** *p252*
McNamee, Susan; Philadelphia, 1852 ***8513.31*** *p414*
McNamee, William 35; Ontario, 1871 ***1823.21*** *p252*
McNamer, Joseph; America, 1753 ***1220.12*** *p522*
McNamera, Robert; North Carolina, 1823 ***1088.45*** *p22*
McNara, Simon; America, 1750 ***1220.12*** *p522*
McNarys, Patrick; South Carolina, 1800-1899 ***6155.4*** *p18*
McNaughton, Alexander; New York, 1738 ***8277.31*** *p118*
*Wife:*Mary McDonald
*Child:*Moses
*Child:*Janet
*Child:*Eleanor
*Child:*John
McNaughton, Catherine 31; Ontario, 1871 ***1823.21*** *p252*
McNaughton, D. 26; Ontario, 1871 ***1823.21*** *p252*
McNaughton, D.S.; Iowa, 1896 ***1211.15*** *p17*
McNaughton, Donald 59; Ontario, 1871 ***1823.21*** *p252*
McNaughton, Donald 64; Ontario, 1871 ***1823.21*** *p252*
McNaughton, Donald 66; Ontario, 1871 ***1823.21*** *p252*
McNaughton, Duncan 28; Ontario, 1871 ***1823.21*** *p252*
McNaughton, Duncan 64; Ontario, 1871 ***1823.17*** *p114*
McNaughton, Eleanor *SEE* McNaughton, Alexander
McNaughton, Henrietta 62; Ontario, 1871 ***1823.17*** *p114*
McNaughton, Janet *SEE* McNaughton, Alexander
McNaughton, John *SEE* McNaughton, Alexander
McNaughton, John 36; Ontario, 1871 ***1823.17*** *p114*
McNaughton, John 40; Ontario, 1871 ***1823.21*** *p252*
McNaughton, John 46; Ontario, 1871 ***1823.21*** *p252*
McNaughton, John 48; Ontario, 1871 ***1823.21*** *p252*
McNaughton, John 65; Ontario, 1871 ***1823.21*** *p252*
McNaughton, John; Washington, 1889 ***2770.40*** *p79*
McNaughton, Mary McDonald *SEE* McNaughton, Alexander
McNaughton, Mary 65; Ontario, 1871 ***1823.17*** *p114*
McNaughton, Moses *SEE* McNaughton, Alexander
McNaughton, Robert 55; Ontario, 1871 ***1823.21*** *p252*
McNeal, Alexander; Burlington, VT, 1839 ***3274.56*** *p99*
McNeal, Duncan 50; Ontario, 1871 ***1823.21*** *p252*
McNeal, John 42; Ontario, 1871 ***1823.21*** *p252*
McNeal, John 51; Ontario, 1871 ***1823.21*** *p252*
McNeal, Mary 60; Ontario, 1871 ***1823.21*** *p252*
McNeeson, Michael; Toronto, 1844 ***2910.35*** *p112*
McNeice, James 52; Ontario, 1871 ***1823.21*** *p252*
McNeice, Thomas 50; Ontario, 1871 ***1823.21*** *p252*
McNeil, Alex 36; Ontario, 1871 ***1823.21*** *p252*
McNeil, Alexander 42; Ontario, 1871 ***1823.17*** *p114*
McNeil, Alexander 45; Ontario, 1871 ***1823.21*** *p252*
McNeil, Alexander 49; Ontario, 1871 ***1823.21*** *p252*
McNeil, Alexander 52; Ontario, 1871 ***1823.21*** *p252*
McNeil, Alexander 58; Ontario, 1871 ***1823.21*** *p252*
McNeil, Andrew; North America, 1750 ***1640.8*** *p234*
McNeil, Angus 76; Ontario, 1871 ***1823.21*** *p252*
McNeil, Ann 80; Ontario, 1871 ***1823.21*** *p252*
McNeil, Anne; New York, 1740 ***8277.31*** *p117*
*Child:*Alexander
*Child:*Hannah
*Child:*Mary
McNeil, Archibald; New York, 1739 ***8277.31*** *p117*
McNeil, Archibald 32; Ontario, 1871 ***1823.21*** *p252*
McNeil, Barbara *SEE* McNeil, John
McNeil, Barbara 70; Ontario, 1871 ***1823.21*** *p252*
McNeil, Betty *SEE* McNeil, John
McNeil, C. 50; Ontario, 1871 ***1823.21*** *p252*
McNeil, Catharine *SEE* McNeil, John
McNeil, Catherine 50; Ontario, 1871 ***1823.21*** *p252*
McNeil, Catherine 60; Ontario, 1871 ***1823.21*** *p252*
McNeil, Daniel 55; Ontario, 1871 ***1823.21*** *p252*
McNeil, Danl; North Carolina, 1774 ***1422.10*** *p62*
McNeil, Danl. 28; North Carolina, 1774 ***1422.10*** *p58*
McNeil, Donald 50; Ontario, 1871 ***1823.21*** *p252*
McNeil, Donald 62; Ontario, 1871 ***1823.21*** *p252*
McNeil, Donald 75; Ontario, 1871 ***1823.21*** *p252*
McNeil, Elizabeth Campbell *SEE* McNeil, John
McNeil, Elizabeth 19; Ontario, 1871 ***1823.21*** *p252*
McNeil, Finlay 31; Ontario, 1871 ***1823.21*** *p253*
McNeil, Flora 23; Ontario, 1871 ***1823.21*** *p253*
McNeil, Hector; North Carolina, 1774 ***1422.10*** *p62*
McNeil, Hector 24; North Carolina, 1774 ***1422.10*** *p58*
McNeil, Hector 32; Ontario, 1871 ***1823.21*** *p253*
McNeil, Hector 42; Ontario, 1871 ***1823.21*** *p253*
McNeil, Hector 60; Ontario, 1871 ***1823.21*** *p253*
McNeil, Henry; America, 1766 ***1220.12*** *p522*
McNeil, Hugh 46; Ontario, 1871 ***1823.17*** *p114*
McNeil, Isobel 64; North Carolina, 1774 ***1422.10*** *p58*
McNeil, Isobel 64; North Carolina, 1774 ***1422.10*** *p62*
McNeil, James 54; Ontario, 1871 ***1823.21*** *p253*
McNeil, James; South Carolina, 1800-1899 ***6155.4*** *p18*
McNeil, Jean 32; North Carolina, 1774 ***1422.10*** *p60*
McNeil, Jean 32; North Carolina, 1774 ***1422.10*** *p62*
McNeil, John; New York, 1738 ***8277.31*** *p118*
*Wife:*Elizabeth Campbell
*Child:*Neil
*Child:*Peggy
*Child:*Catharine
*Child:*Betty
*Child:*Barbara
McNeil, John 28; Ontario, 1871 ***1823.21*** *p253*
McNeil, John 39; Ontario, 1871 ***1823.21*** *p253*
McNeil, John 40; Ontario, 1871 ***1823.21*** *p253*
McNeil, John 42; Ontario, 1871 ***1823.21*** *p253*
McNeil, John 46; Ontario, 1871 ***1823.21*** *p253*
McNeil, John 49; Ontario, 1871 ***1823.21*** *p253*
McNeil, John 60; Ontario, 1871 ***1823.21*** *p253*
McNeil, John 69; Ontario, 1871 ***1823.17*** *p114*
McNeil, Malcolm 39; Ontario, 1871 ***1823.21*** *p253*
McNeil, Malcolm 52; Ontario, 1871 ***1823.21*** *p253*
McNeil, Malcolm 75; Ontario, 1871 ***1823.21*** *p253*
McNeil, Margaret; New York, 1738 ***8277.31*** *p118*
McNeil, Margt 18; Ontario, 1871 ***1823.21*** *p253*
McNeil, Mary; New York, 1739 ***8277.31*** *p119*
McNeil, Mary; North Carolina, 1774 ***1422.10*** *p62*
McNeil, Mary 9; North Carolina, 1774 ***1422.10*** *p58*
McNeil, Mary 27; Ontario, 1871 ***1823.21*** *p253*
McNeil, Mary 75; Ontario, 1871 ***1823.21*** *p253*
McNeil, Nail 65; Ontario, 1871 ***1823.21*** *p253*
McNeil, Neil *SEE* McNeil, John
McNeil, Neil; North Carolina, 1774 ***1422.10*** *p62*
McNeil, Neil 18; North Carolina, 1774 ***1422.10*** *p58*
McNeil, Neil 64; North Carolina, 1774 ***1422.10*** *p58*
McNeil, Neil 64; North Carolina, 1774 ***1422.10*** *p62*
McNeil, Neil 47; Ontario, 1871 ***1823.17*** *p114*
McNeil, Neil 48; Ontario, 1871 ***1823.17*** *p114*
McNeil, Patrick; Colorado, 1869 ***1029.59*** *p61*
McNeil, Peggy *SEE* McNeil, John
McNeil, Peter; North Carolina, 1774 ***1422.10*** *p62*
McNeil, Peter 22; North Carolina, 1774 ***1422.10*** *p58*
McNeil, Peter 70; Ontario, 1871 ***1823.21*** *p253*
McNeil, Richard 26; Ontario, 1871 ***1823.21*** *p253*
McNeil, Robert 29; Ontario, 1871 ***1823.21*** *p253*
McNeil, Roger; New York, 1740 ***8277.31*** *p118*
McNeil, Ronald 48; Ontario, 1871 ***1823.21*** *p253*
McNeil, Samuel 60; Ontario, 1871 ***1823.21*** *p253*
McNeil, William 25; Ontario, 1871 ***1823.21*** *p253*
McNeil, Willm; North Carolina, 1774 ***1422.10*** *p62*
McNeil, Willm. 15; North Carolina, 1774 ***1422.10*** *p58*
McNeill, Alexander 50; Ontario, 1871 ***1823.17*** *p114*
McNeill, John 50; Ontario, 1871 ***1823.17*** *p114*
McNeill, Mary 25; Ontario, 1871 ***1823.21*** *p253*
McNeill, Mary 60; Ontario, 1871 ***1823.17*** *p114*
McNelly, James 30; Ontario, 1871 ***1823.21*** *p253*
Mc Nelly, Lawrence; Louisiana, 1841-1844 ***4981.45*** *p211*
McNelty, Patrick; North Carolina, 1839 ***1088.45*** *p22*
McNelus, John; South Carolina, 1860 ***6155.4*** *p18*
McNemaro, Michael; Boston, 1765 ***1642*** *p34*
McNemarrow, John; Massachusetts, 1755 ***1642*** *p111*
*Wife:*Ruth
McNemarrow, Ruth *SEE* McNemarrow, John
McNerney, Mary 55; Ontario, 1871 ***1823.21*** *p253*
McNerny, Micheal 22; Ontario, 1871 ***1823.17*** *p114*
McNertny, Nancy 55; Ontario, 1871 ***1823.17*** *p114*
McNeven, Angus 52; Ontario, 1871 ***1823.21*** *p253*
McNeven, Robert 49; Ontario, 1871 ***1823.21*** *p253*
McNevin, Daniel 43; Ontario, 1871 ***1823.21*** *p253*
McNevin, Flora 45; Ontario, 1871 ***1823.21*** *p253*
McNichel, John 56; Ontario, 1871 ***1823.17*** *p114*
McNichol, Donald 69; Ontario, 1871 ***1823.21*** *p253*
McNickle, James 68; Ontario, 1871 ***1823.17*** *p114*
McNicol, Angus 30; North Carolina, 1775 ***1422.10*** *p59*
McNicol, Ann 20; North Carolina, 1775 ***1422.10*** *p59*
McNicol, Annapel 8; North Carolina, 1774 ***1422.10*** *p57*
McNicol, Jean 24; North Carolina, 1774 ***1422.10*** *p57*
McNicol, John 24; North Carolina, 1774 ***1422.10*** *p57*
McNicol, Neil 26; Ontario, 1871 ***1823.21*** *p253*
McNicol, Robet 30; North Carolina, 1774 ***1422.10*** *p57*
McNiece, John 53; Ontario, 1871 ***1823.17*** *p114*
McNierney, Cornelius 40; Ontario, 1871 ***1823.17*** *p114*
McNitt, Alexander; Palmer, MA, 1744 ***1642*** *p119*
*Wife:*Sarah
McNitt, Sarah *SEE* McNitt, Alexander
McNiven, Catharine; New York, 1738 ***8277.31*** *p118*
McNiven, Catharine; New York, 1738 ***8277.31*** *p118*
McNiver, Donald 39; Ontario, 1871 ***1823.21*** *p253*
McNorton, Duncan 56; Ontario, 1871 ***1823.21*** *p253*
McNulty, Bartholomew 61; Ontario, 1871 ***1823.21*** *p253*
McNulty, James 35; Ontario, 1871 ***1823.17*** *p114*
McNulty, Michael 23; Ontario, 1871 ***1823.17*** *p114*
McNulty, Patrick 50; Ontario, 1871 ***1823.21*** *p253*
McOllester, John; America, 1756 ***1220.12*** *p517*
McOnaughy, Isabella 33; Ohio, 1880 ***4879.40*** *p259*
M'Cormick, Dr.; Toronto, 1844 ***2910.35*** *p115*
McOrmie, Math 51; Ontario, 1871 ***1823.17*** *p114*
McOsker, Hugh; Ohio, 1809-1852 ***4511.35*** *p33*
MCoy, Anna; Massachusetts, 1757 ***1642*** *p111*
McParland, Michael 47; Ontario, 1871 ***1823.17*** *p114*
McPeake, James D.; North Carolina, 1853 ***1088.45*** *p22*
McPhaden, Divorgill *SEE* McPhaden, Neil
McPhaden, Duncan *SEE* McPhaden, Duncan
McPhaden, Duncan; New York, 1740 ***8277.31*** *p118*
*Wife:*Florry McCollum
*Son:*John
*Son:*Duncan
McPhaden, Florry McCollum *SEE* McPhaden, Duncan
McPhaden, John *SEE* McPhaden, Duncan
McPhaden, Margaret *SEE* McPhaden, Neil
McPhaden, Mary; New York, 1738 ***8277.31*** *p116*
McPhaden, Mary McDearmid *SEE* McPhaden, Neil
McPhaden, Neil; New York, 1739 ***8277.31*** *p119*
*Wife:*Mary McDearmid
*Daughter:*Margaret
*Daughter:*Divorgill
McPhaden, Ruth 6; Ontario, 1871 ***1823.17*** *p114*
McPhadin, John 61; Ontario, 1871 ***1823.17*** *p114*
McPhail, . . .; Ontario, 1871 ***1823.21*** *p254*
McPhail, Archibald 39; Ontario, 1871 ***1823.21*** *p254*
McPhail, Archie 29; Ontario, 1871 ***1823.17*** *p114*
McPhail, Charles 33; Ontario, 1871 ***1823.17*** *p114*
McPhail, Christy Clark *SEE* McPhail, John
McPhail, Donald 25; Ontario, 1871 ***1823.21*** *p254*
McPhail, Donald 29; Ontario, 1871 ***1823.17*** *p114*
McPhail, Donald 61; Ontario, 1871 ***1823.17*** *p114*
McPhail, Dougal 27; Ontario, 1871 ***1823.17*** *p114*
McPhail, Dugald 45; Ontario, 1871 ***1823.17*** *p114*
McPhail, Duncan 35; Ontario, 1871 ***1823.21*** *p254*
McPhail, Duncan 38; Ontario, 1871 ***1823.21*** *p254*
McPhail, Duncan 55; Ontario, 1871 ***1823.17*** *p114*
McPhail, Duncan 58; Ontario, 1871 ***1823.17*** *p114*
McPhail, Duncan 68; Ontario, 1871 ***1823.17*** *p114*
McPhail, Hector 24; Ontario, 1871 ***1823.17*** *p114*
McPhail, James 45; Ontario, 1871 ***1823.21*** *p254*

McPhail, James 48; Ontario, 1871 ***1823.21*** *p254*
McPhail, James 50; Ontario, 1871 ***1823.17*** *p114*
McPhail, John *SEE* McPhail, John
McPhail, John; New York, 1739 ***8277.31*** *p119*
*Wife:*Christy Clark
*Son:*John
McPhail, Sarah 23; Ontario, 1871 ***1823.21*** *p254*
McPharlen, Cathrine 37; Ontario, 1871 ***1823.17*** *p114*
McPharson, James; Jamaica, 1778 ***8529.30*** *p13A*
McPhearson, Ann; America, 1749 ***1220.12*** *p522*
McPhederen, Peter 62; Ontario, 1871 ***1823.17*** *p114*
McPhee, Angus 44; Ontario, 1871 ***1823.21*** *p254*
McPhee, Archibald 40; Ontario, 1871 ***1823.21*** *p254*
McPhee, Archibald 52; Ontario, 1871 ***1823.21*** *p254*
McPhee, Archibald 60; Ontario, 1871 ***1823.21*** *p254*
McPhee, Archibald 62; Ontario, 1871 ***1823.21*** *p254*
McPhee, Christie 52; Ontario, 1871 ***1823.21*** *p254*
McPhee, Donald 33; Ontario, 1871 ***1823.21*** *p254*
McPhee, Donald 44; Ontario, 1871 ***1823.21*** *p254*
McPhee, Donald 50; Ontario, 1871 ***1823.21*** *p254*
McPhee, Donald 60; Ontario, 1871 ***1823.21*** *p254*
McPhee, Hannah 50; Ontario, 1871 ***1823.21*** *p254*
McPhee, Hector 40; Ontario, 1871 ***1823.17*** *p114*
McPhee, Hector 45; Ontario, 1871 ***1823.21*** *p254*
McPhee, Hugh 55; Ontario, 1871 ***1823.21*** *p254*
McPhee, John 21; Ontario, 1871 ***1823.21*** *p254*
McPhee, John 35; Ontario, 1871 ***1823.21*** *p254*
McPhee, John 56; Ontario, 1871 ***1823.21*** *p254*
McPhee, John 58; Ontario, 1871 ***1823.21*** *p254*
McPhee, John 65; Ontario, 1871 ***1823.21*** *p254*
McPhee, John 69; Ontario, 1871 ***1823.21*** *p254*
McPhee, Margert 63; Ontario, 1871 ***1823.17*** *p114*
McPhee, Mary 48; Ontario, 1871 ***1823.21*** *p254*
McPhee, Michael 35; Ontario, 1871 ***1823.21*** *p254*
McPhee, Neil 50; Ontario, 1871 ***1823.21*** *p254*
McPhee, William; Washington, 1889 ***2770.40*** *p79*
McPheely, Edward; Toronto, 1844 ***2910.35*** *p112*
McPherson, Alex 45; Ontario, 1871 ***1823.21*** *p254*
McPherson, Alexander; Charles Town, SC, 1718 ***1220.12*** *p522*
McPherson, Alexander 50; Ontario, 1871 ***1823.21*** *p254*
McPherson, Allen 33; Ontario, 1871 ***1823.17*** *p114*
McPherson, Allen 60; Ontario, 1871 ***1823.17*** *p115*
McPherson, Angus 31; Ontario, 1871 ***1823.17*** *p115*
McPherson, Angus 35; Ontario, 1871 ***1823.21*** *p254*
McPherson, Archibald 38; Ontario, 1871 ***1823.21*** *p254*
McPherson, Christn. 30; North Carolina, 1774 ***1422.10*** *p57*
McPherson, Donald 32; Ontario, 1871 ***1823.21*** *p254*
McPherson, Donald 40; Ontario, 1871 ***1823.21*** *p254*
McPherson, Donald 60; Ontario, 1871 ***1823.21*** *p254*
McPherson, Dugal 36; Ontario, 1871 ***1823.17*** *p115*
McPherson, Dugald 43; Ontario, 1871 ***1823.21*** *p254*
McPherson, Duncan 60; Ontario, 1871 ***1823.17*** *p115*
McPherson, Eliza 30; Ontario, 1871 ***1823.21*** *p254*
McPherson, George 47; Ontario, 1871 ***1823.17*** *p115*
McPherson, Gilbert 32; Ontario, 1871 ***1823.21*** *p254*
McPherson, Hugh 23; Ontario, 1871 ***1823.21*** *p254*
McPherson, Hugh 38; Ontario, 1871 ***1823.21*** *p254*
McPherson, Hugh 52; Ontario, 1871 ***1823.21*** *p254*
McPherson, Isabella 27; Ontario, 1871 ***1823.21*** *p255*
McPherson, James; Jamaica, 1778 ***8529.30*** *p13A*
McPherson, James 90; Ontario, 1871 ***1823.21*** *p255*
McPherson, Janet 10; North Carolina, 1774 ***1422.10*** *p57*
McPherson, Jessie 37; Ontario, 1871 ***1823.21*** *p255*
McPherson, Job; Colorado, 1901 ***1029.59*** *p61*
McPherson, John; New York, 1778 ***8529.30*** *p4A*
McPherson, John; North Carolina, 1816 ***1088.45*** *p22*
McPherson, John 32; Ontario, 1871 ***1823.21*** *p255*
McPherson, John 38; Ontario, 1871 ***1823.21*** *p255*
McPherson, John 42; Ontario, 1871 ***1823.17*** *p115*
McPherson, John 43; Ontario, 1871 ***1823.17*** *p115*
McPherson, John 50; Ontario, 1871 ***1823.21*** *p255*
McPherson, John 60; Ontario, 1871 ***1823.21*** *p255*
McPherson, John 70; Ontario, 1871 ***1823.17*** *p115*
McPherson, John P.; Colorado, 1901 ***1029.59*** *p61*
McPherson, Joseph 40; Ontario, 1871 ***1823.17*** *p115*
McPherson, Lachlin 58; Ontario, 1871 ***1823.21*** *p255*
McPherson, Malcolm 40; North Carolina, 1774 ***1422.10*** *p57*
McPherson, Malcolm 40; Ontario, 1871 ***1823.21*** *p255*
McPherson, Malcolm 76; Ontario, 1871 ***1823.21*** *p255*
McPherson, Margaret 26; Ontario, 1871 ***1823.21*** *p255*
McPherson, Martin 55; Ontario, 1871 ***1823.21*** *p255*
McPherson, Murdoch 75; Ontario, 1871 ***1823.17*** *p115*
McPherson, Neil 40; Ontario, 1871 ***1823.21*** *p255*
McPherson, Thomas; Iowa, 1887 ***1211.15*** *p16*
McPherson, Walter 60; Ontario, 1871 ***1823.21*** *p255*
McPherson, William 45; Ontario, 1871 ***1823.17*** *p115*
McPherson, Willm. 9; North Carolina, 1774 ***1422.10*** *p57*
McPhilomy, John; Philadelphia, 1851 ***5720.10*** *p379*
McPhissan, John 65; Ontario, 1871 ***1823.21*** *p255*
McPhisson, Archibald 61; Ontario, 1871 ***1823.21*** *p255*
McQuade, John; Ontario, 1871 ***1823.17*** *p115*
McQuade, John; Ontario, 1871 ***1823.17*** *p115*
McQuaid, Patrick; Toronto, 1844 ***2910.35*** *p113*
McQuarrie, Catherine 73; Ontario, 1871 ***1823.21*** *p255*
McQuarrie, Christian *SEE* McQuarrie, Duncan
McQuarrie, Donald *SEE* McQuarrie, Duncan
McQuarrie, Duncan; New York, 1739 ***8277.31*** *p119*
*Wife:*Mary McIlepheder
*Child:*John
*Child:*Gilbert
*Child:*Christian
*Child:*Donald
McQuarrie, Frank; Washington, 1886 ***6015.10*** *p16*
McQuarrie, Gilbert *SEE* McQuarrie, Duncan
McQuarrie, John *SEE* McQuarrie, Duncan
McQuarrie, Malcolm 48; Ontario, 1871 ***1823.21*** *p255*
McQuarrie, Mary McIlepheder *SEE* McQuarrie, Duncan
McQuarry, John 34; Ontario, 1871 ***1823.21*** *p255*
McQuary, Angus 50; Ontario, 1871 ***1823.21*** *p255*
McQueen, Daniel F.; Ohio, 1878 ***3580.20*** *p32*
McQueen, Daniel F.; Ohio, 1878 ***6020.12*** *p13*
McQueen, Donald 60; Ontario, 1871 ***1823.21*** *p255*
McQueen, Ewen 39; Ontario, 1871 ***1823.17*** *p115*
McQueen, John; America, 1764 ***1220.12*** *p522*
McQueen, John 67; Ontario, 1871 ***1823.21*** *p255*
McQueen, John 77; Ontario, 1871 ***1823.21*** *p255*
McQueen, Sarah; America, 1726 ***1220.12*** *p522*
McQueen, William; Quebec, 1786 ***1416.15*** *p8*
McQueeny, Thomas 58; Ontario, 1871 ***1823.21*** *p255*
McQuern, James; South Carolina, 1812 ***6155.4*** *p18*
McQuern, Samuel; South Carolina, 1810 ***6155.4*** *p18*
McQuern, Samuel, Jr.; South Carolina, 1812 ***6155.4*** *p19*
McQuigley, Catherine 9; Quebec, 1870 ***8364.32*** *p25*
McQuilkan, John; Ontario, 1871 ***1823.21*** *p255*
McQuillan, Edward 50; Ontario, 1871 ***1823.17*** *p115*
McQuillen, Ann 47; Ontario, 1871 ***1823.21*** *p255*
McQuillen, John; Illinois, 1864 ***6079.1*** *p9*
McQuin, Anna; New York, 1738 ***8277.31*** *p116*
McQuin, Daniel; America, 1749 ***1220.12*** *p522*
McQuin, Daniel 35; Ontario, 1871 ***1823.17*** *p115*
McQuin, John; America, 1736 ***1220.12*** *p522*
McQuin, John; America, 1764 ***1220.12*** *p522*
McQuines, Alexander 28; Ontario, 1871 ***1823.21*** *p255*
McQuinn, Michael; New Orleans, 1851 ***7242.30*** *p149*
McQuire, Barbara; America, 1736 ***1220.12*** *p520*
McQuire, Henry; America, 1765 ***1220.12*** *p520*
McQuire, John; North Carolina, 1792-1862 ***1088.45*** *p23*
McQuirk, Biddy; New Orleans, 1850 ***7242.30*** *p149*
McQuirk, Thomas; New York, NY, 1841 ***3274.56*** *p72*
McQuiston, Cathr. 46; North Carolina, 1775 ***1422.10*** *p57*
McQuiston, Jean 27; North Carolina, 1775 ***1422.10*** *p57*
McQuiston, Jno. 46; North Carolina, 1775 ***1422.10*** *p57*
McQulien, Edward; Toronto, 1844 ***2910.35*** *p112*
McQuore, Christian *SEE* McQuore, Duncan
McQuore, Donald *SEE* McQuore, Duncan
McQuore, Duncan; New York, 1739 ***8277.31*** *p119*
*Wife:*Mary McIlepheder
*Child:*John
*Child:*Christian
*Child:*Gilbert
*Child:*Donald
McQuore, Gilbert *SEE* McQuore, Duncan
McQuore, John *SEE* McQuore, Duncan
McQuore, Mary McIlepheder *SEE* McQuore, Duncan
McQurda, George 60; Ontario, 1871 ***1823.21*** *p255*
McRae, Alexander 45; Ontario, 1871 ***1823.21*** *p255*
McRae, Catherine 54; Ontario, 1871 ***1823.17*** *p115*
McRae, Colin 70; Ontario, 1871 ***1823.17*** *p115*
McRae, Donald 40; Ontario, 1871 ***1823.21*** *p255*
McRae, Donald 49; Ontario, 1871 ***1823.21*** *p255*
McRae, Donald 55; Ontario, 1871 ***1823.21*** *p255*
McRae, Donald D. 26; Ontario, 1871 ***1823.21*** *p255*
McRae, Duncan 40; Ontario, 1871 ***1823.21*** *p256*
McRae, Farquhar; Quebec, 1786 ***1416.15*** *p8*
McRae, Finlay 72; Ontario, 1871 ***1823.21*** *p256*
McRae, Hugh 50; Ontario, 1871 ***1823.21*** *p256*
McRae, Hugh 56; Ontario, 1871 ***1823.21*** *p256*
McRae, James 70; Ontario, 1871 ***1823.21*** *p256*
McRae, Jeannette 60; Ontario, 1871 ***1823.21*** *p256*
McRae, John 47; Ontario, 1871 ***1823.17*** *p115*
McRae, John; Quebec, 1786 ***1416.15*** *p8*
McRae, Kenneth 60; Ontario, 1871 ***1823.21*** *p256*
McRae, Malcolm 60; Ontario, 1871 ***1823.21*** *p256*
McRae, Norman 50; Ontario, 1871 ***1823.17*** *p115*
McRahn, James 45; Ontario, 1871 ***1823.21*** *p256*
McRay, Wm. 37; North Carolina, 1774 ***1422.10*** *p59*
McRea, Patrick 27; Ontario, 1871 ***1823.21*** *p256*
McRea, Philip 65; Ontario, 1871 ***1823.21*** *p256*
McRie, William 67; Ontario, 1871 ***1823.17*** *p115*
McRob, Duncan 26; North Carolina, 1774 ***1422.10*** *p60*
McRob, Duncan 26; North Carolina, 1774 ***1422.10*** *p63*
McRoberts, Andrew 78; Ontario, 1871 ***1823.21*** *p256*
McRoberts, Charles 45; Ontario, 1871 ***1823.21*** *p256*
McRoberts, David 48; Ontario, 1871 ***1823.21*** *p256*
McRoberts, James 50; Ontario, 1871 ***1823.21*** *p256*
McRoberts, James 72; Ontario, 1871 ***1823.21*** *p256*
McRoberts, James H. 65; Ontario, 1871 ***1823.21*** *p256*
McRoberts, Jessie 43; Ontario, 1871 ***1823.21*** *p256*
McRoberts, John; New York, NY, 1838 ***3274.55*** *p44*
McRoberts, John 56; Ontario, 1871 ***1823.21*** *p256*
McRoberts, John 81; Ontario, 1871 ***1823.21*** *p256*
McRoberts, Mary 46; Ontario, 1871 ***1823.21*** *p256*
McRoberts, William 49; Ontario, 1871 ***1823.21*** *p256*
McRoberts, William 50; Ontario, 1871 ***1823.21*** *p256*
McRoberts, William 61; Ontario, 1871 ***1823.21*** *p256*
McRoria, Petre 28; Ontario, 1871 ***1823.17*** *p115*
McRow, Daniel; America, 1685 ***1220.12*** *p522*
McRury, Angus 38; Ontario, 1871 ***1823.21*** *p256*
M'Crystal, Patrick; Toronto, 1844 ***2910.35*** *p113*
McShane, James; Ohio, 1809-1852 ***4511.35*** *p33*
McSherry, E.H.; Toronto, 1844 ***2910.35*** *p111*
McSkinning, Ewen; America, 1756 ***1220.12*** *p522*
McSlipheder, John; Cape Fear, NC,, 1754 ***1422.10*** *p62*
McSorley, James; Toronto, 1844 ***2910.35*** *p115*
McSpron, Robert 60; Ontario, 1871 ***1823.21*** *p256*
McStay, James 61; Ontario, 1871 ***1823.21*** *p256*
McStay, John 35; New York, NY, 1844 ***6178.50*** *p151*
McSweney, Dinish; Boston, 1767 ***1642*** *p38*
McSweney, Eleanor; Boston, 1767 ***1642*** *p38*
McSwiggin, Ann; Philadelphia, 1851 ***8513.31*** *p415*
McTagart, Angus 44; Ontario, 1871 ***1823.21*** *p256*
McTagart, Lachlin 63; Ontario, 1871 ***1823.21*** *p256*
McTagert, Hugh 50; Ontario, 1871 ***1823.21*** *p256*
McTaggart, Alexander 32; Ontario, 1871 ***1823.21*** *p257*
McTaggart, Archie 28; Ontario, 1871 ***1823.21*** *p257*
McTaggart, Dougald 41; Ontario, 1871 ***1823.17*** *p115*
McTaggart, Duncan 32; Ontario, 1871 ***1823.17*** *p115*
McTaggart, George 53; Ontario, 1871 ***1823.21*** *p257*
McTaggart, John 40; Ontario, 1871 ***1823.17*** *p115*
McTaggart, Lachlan 55; Ontario, 1871 ***1823.21*** *p257*
McTaggart, Neil 40; Ontario, 1871 ***1823.21*** *p257*
McTague, Patrick 20; St. John, N.B., 1834 ***6469.7*** *p5*
McTavish, Alexander 56; Ontario, 1871 ***1823.21*** *p257*
McTavish, Angus 68; Ontario, 1871 ***1823.21*** *p257*
McTie, Kate 35; Ontario, 1871 ***1823.21*** *p257*
McUllister, Edward; America, 1750 ***1220.12*** *p517*
McVane, Katherine 30; North Carolina, 1775 ***1422.10*** *p59*
McVane, William 42; Ontario, 1871 ***1823.21*** *p257*
McVannel, Duncan 30; Ontario, 1871 ***1823.21*** *p257*
McVarich, Florence; New York, 1739 ***8277.31*** *p119*
McVeagh, Edward; Philadelphia, 1778 ***8529.30*** *p3*
McVean, Peter 60; Ontario, 1871 ***1823.21*** *p257*
McVeigh, Francis 70; Ontario, 1871 ***1823.21*** *p257*
McVey, James 40; Ontario, 1871 ***1823.21*** *p257*
McVicar, Alexander 44; Ontario, 1871 ***1823.21*** *p257*
McVicar, Archibald 50; Ontario, 1871 ***1823.21*** *p257*
McVicar, Archibald 71; Ontario, 1871 ***1823.21*** *p257*
McVicar, Catherine 90; Ontario, 1871 ***1823.21*** *p257*
McVicar, David 39; Ontario, 1871 ***1823.21*** *p257*
McVicar, Donald 37; Ontario, 1871 ***1823.21*** *p257*
McVicar, Donald 50; Ontario, 1871 ***1823.21*** *p257*
McVicar, Dugal 45; Ontario, 1871 ***1823.21*** *p257*
McVicar, Duncan 35; Ontario, 1871 ***1823.21*** *p257*
McVicar, Duncan 55; Ontario, 1871 ***1823.17*** *p115*
McVicar, James 62; Ontario, 1871 ***1823.21*** *p257*
McVicar, Janet 58; Ontario, 1871 ***1823.21*** *p257*
McVicar, John 36; North Carolina, 1774 ***1422.10*** *p61*
McVicar, John 36; North Carolina, 1774 ***1422.10*** *p63*
McVicar, Nevin 34; Ontario, 1871 ***1823.17*** *p115*
McVicar, Niven 25; Ontario, 1871 ***1823.21*** *p257*
McVicar, Peter 52; Ontario, 1871 ***1823.21*** *p257*
McVicer, David 56; Ontario, 1871 ***1823.21*** *p257*
McVicken, James; North Carolina, 1835-1837 ***1088.45*** *p23*
McVicker, Archibald 50; Ontario, 1871 ***1823.21*** *p257*
McVicker, Daniel; New York, 1782 ***8529.30*** *p14*
McVickers, Daniel; New York, 1782 ***8529.30*** *p14*
McVoy, Charles 49; Ontario, 1871 ***1823.21*** *p257*
McVoy, Margaret 74; Ontario, 1871 ***1823.21*** *p257*
McVurich, Florence; New York, 1739 ***8277.31*** *p119*
McVurrish, Mary; New York, 1738 ***8277.31*** *p118*
McWherter, John 58; Ontario, 1871 ***1823.17*** *p116*
McWherter, Robert 34; Ontario, 1871 ***1823.17*** *p116*
McWhiney, John; Ohio, 1809-1852 ***4511.35*** *p33*
McWhinie, Barbara 50; New York, NY, 1835 ***5024.1*** *p136*
McWhinie, Elizabeth 22; New York, NY, 1835 ***5024.1*** *p136*
McWhinie, Joseph 25; New York, NY, 1835 ***5024.1*** *p136*
McWhinie, Mary 20; New York, NY, 1835 ***5024.1*** *p136*
McWhinney, Eliz.; Montreal, n.d. ***9228.50*** *p289*
McWhinney, George 45; St. John, N.B., 1834 ***6469.7*** *p5*
McWhinney, James 32; Ontario, 1871 ***1823.21*** *p257*
McWhinney, James 40; Ontario, 1871 ***1823.21*** *p257*

McWhinney, John; Ohio, 1809-1852 ***4511.35*** *p33*
McWhinney, Mary 45; St. John, N.B., 1834 ***6469.7*** *p5*
McWhorter, A. 29; South Carolina, 1812 ***3476.30*** *p12*
McWhorter, Andrew; South Carolina, 1813 ***3208.30*** *p19*
McWhorter, Andrew; South Carolina, 1813 ***3208.30*** *p31*
McWhorter, John; South Carolina, 1813 ***3208.30*** *p19*
McWhorter, John; South Carolina, 1813 ***3208.30*** *p32*
McWhorter, John 24; South Carolina, 1812 ***3476.30*** *p12*
McWhorter, Thomas; South Carolina, 1813 ***3208.30*** *p19*
McWhorter, Thomas; South Carolina, 1813 ***3208.30*** *p32*
McWhorter, Thos. 22; South Carolina, 1812 ***3476.30*** *p12*
McWiling, John 38; Ontario, 1871 ***1823.21*** *p257*
McWilliam, James 44; Ontario, 1871 ***1823.21*** *p257*
McWilliam, John 48; Ontario, 1871 ***1823.21*** *p257*
McWilliam, Norman 56; Ontario, 1871 ***1823.21*** *p257*
McWilliams, Andrew 40; Ontario, 1871 ***1823.21*** *p257*
McWilliams, John; Long Island, 1778 ***8529.30*** *p9A*
M'Donald, Ensign; Quebec, 1786 ***1416.15*** *p5*
M'Donald, Lieut.; Quebec, 1786 ***1416.15*** *p5*
M'Donald, Mrs.; Quebec, 1786 ***1416.15*** *p5*
M'Donald, Alexander; Quebec, 1786 ***1416.15*** *p5*
M'Donald, Ann; Quebec, 1786 ***1416.15*** *p5*
M'Donald, Isabella; Quebec, 1786 ***1416.15*** *p5*
M'Donald, Mary; Quebec, 1786 ***1416.15*** *p5*
M'Donald, Rod.; Quebec, 1786 ***1416.15*** *p5*
M'Donald, Ronald; Quebec, 1786 ***1416.15*** *p5*
M'Donell, Allen; Toronto, 1844 ***2910.35*** *p113*
Mea, Mary; Ontario, 1835 ***3160.1*** *p150*
Meaburne, Gerard; Barbados, 1698 ***1220.12*** *p542*
Meacham, Edward; Annapolis, MD, 1731 ***1220.12*** *p542*
Meacher, James; Colorado, 1902 ***1029.59*** *p61*
Meacher, Lucy E.; Colorado, 1902 ***1029.59*** *p61*
Meachum, Mary; Barbados or Jamaica, 1696 ***1220.12*** *p542*
Meachum, Mary; Died enroute, 1734 ***1220.12*** *p542*
Mead, Ambrose; Barbados or Jamaica, 1698 ***1220.12*** *p542*
Mead, B.F.; Buffalo, NY, 1870-1880 ***9228.50*** *p582*
Mead, Charles; Annapolis, MD, 1758 ***1220.12*** *p542*
Mead, Charles; Barbados or Jamaica, 1710 ***1220.12*** *p542*
Mead, Edward; America, 1723 ***1220.12*** *p542*
Mead, Edward; America, 1752 ***1220.12*** *p542*
Mead, George; America, 1757 ***1220.12*** *p542*
Mead, George; Barbados, 1698 ***1220.12*** *p542*
Mead, John; America, 1685 ***1220.12*** *p543*
Mead, John; America, 1698 ***1220.12*** *p543*
Mead, John; America, 1756 ***1220.12*** *p543*
Mead, John; America, 1757 ***1220.12*** *p543*
Mead, John; Annapolis, MD, 1725 ***1220.12*** *p543*
Mead, Joseph; Barbados, 1693 ***1220.12*** *p543*
Mead, Margaret; Virginia, 1727 ***1220.12*** *p543*
Mead, Martha; Annapolis, MD, 1725 ***1220.12*** *p543*
Mead, Methuselah; America, 1733 ***1220.12*** *p543*
Mead, Nicholas; America, 1745 ***1220.12*** *p543*
Mead, Nightingale; America, 1750 ***1220.12*** *p543*
Mead, Nightingale; Virginia, 1736 ***1220.12*** *p543*
Mead, Peter; Louisiana, 1874-1875 ***4981.45*** *p30*
Mead, Robert; America, 1685 ***1220.12*** *p543*
Mead, Roger; Nevis or Jamaica, 1722 ***1220.12*** *p543*
Mead, Thomas; America, 1741 ***1220.12*** *p543*
Mead, Thomas; America, 1760 ***1220.12*** *p543*
Mead, Thomas; Annapolis, MD, 1722 ***1220.12*** *p543*
Mead, Thomas, Jr.; America, 1760 ***1220.12*** *p543*
Mead, William; America, 1685 ***1220.12*** *p543*
Mead, William; America, 1756 ***1220.12*** *p543*
Meadall, William; America, 1750 ***1220.12*** *p543*
Meade, George 45; Ontario, 1871 ***1823.21*** *p257*
Meade, James 60; Ontario, 1871 ***1823.17*** *p116*
Meade, Thomas; America, 1685 ***1220.12*** *p543*
Meade, Thomas; America, 1766 ***1220.12*** *p543*
Meadford, Henry 32; Ontario, 1871 ***1823.21*** *p258*
Meadle, James; America, 1746 ***1220.12*** *p543*
Meadowcroft, Mathew; America, 1758 ***1220.12*** *p543*
Meadowcroft, Richard; New York, NY, 1837 ***3274.55*** *p75*
Meadows, Andrew 78; Ontario, 1871 ***1823.21*** *p258*
Meadows, Charles 40; Ontario, 1871 ***1823.21*** *p258*
Meadows, Eleanor; America, 1770 ***1220.12*** *p543*
Meadows, Elizabeth; Annapolis, MD, 1758 ***1220.12*** *p543*
Meadows, Thomas; America, 1750 ***1220.12*** *p543*
Meafee, Daniel; Boston, 1745 ***1642*** *p28*
Meagher, Mrs.; Ottawa, 1889-1983 ***9228.50*** *p514*
Meagher, James; Boston, 1766 ***1642*** *p36*
With wife
Meagher, James 42; Ontario, 1871 ***1823.21*** *p258*
Meagher, Patric 40; Michigan, 1880 ***4491.42*** *p18*
Meagher, Thomas; Newfoundland, 1814 ***3476.10*** *p54*
Meake, George; Jamaica, 1661 ***1220.12*** *p544*
Meakham, Samuel; America, 1773 ***1220.12*** *p543*
Meakin, Ellis; America, 1747 ***1220.12*** *p543*
Meakin, Thomas; America, 1770 ***1220.12*** *p543*
Meakings, John; America, 1730 ***1220.12*** *p543*
Meakins, John; Virginia, 1721 ***1220.12*** *p543*
Meakins, William; Nevis or Jamaica, 1722 ***1220.12*** *p543*
Meal, Abraham; America, 1770 ***1220.12*** *p543*
Meal, Henry; America, 1733 ***1220.12*** *p543*
Meal, John; America, 1741 ***1220.12*** *p543*
Meal, John; America, 1750 ***1220.12*** *p543*
Meal, John; America, 1770 ***1220.12*** *p543*
Meal, Mary; America, 1750 ***1220.12*** *p543*
Mealing, John; New York, 1783 ***8529.30*** *p14*
Mealing, Richard; Marston's Wharf, 1782 ***8529.30*** *p14*
Mealon, John; Boston, 1766 ***1642*** *p36*
Meals, Casander; America, 1763 ***1220.12*** *p543*
Meams, Charles 57; Ontario, 1871 ***1823.21*** *p258*
Mean, Thomas; Virginia, 1738 ***1220.12*** *p543*
Meaney, John; Halifax, N.S., 1827 ***7009.9*** *p61*
*Son:*Richard
Meaney, Richard *SEE* Meaney, John
Means, John; Marston's Wharf, 1782 ***8529.30*** *p14*
Meares, Thomas 32; Ontario, 1871 ***1823.17*** *p116*
Mearitte, Daniel; Ohio, 1810 ***9228.50*** *p432*
With children & grandchildren
Mearns, John 28; Ontario, 1871 ***1823.17*** *p116*
Mears, Catherine 55; Michigan, 1880 ***4491.39*** *p20*
Mears, John; Marston's Wharf, 1782 ***8529.30*** *p14*
Mears, John Philip; Washington, 1883 ***2770.40*** *p137*
Mears, Richard; America, 1765 ***1220.12*** *p544*
Mearz, Fredric; Ohio, 1840-1897 ***8365.35*** *p17*
Mease, Edward; America, 1678 ***1220.12*** *p544*
Measey, John; Marston's Wharf, 1782 ***8529.30*** *p14*
Mebert, Ferdinand; Louisiana, 1836-1840 ***4981.45*** *p213*
Mebert, Ferdinand; Louisiana, 1836-1841 ***4981.45*** *p209*
Mecabe, Bridget; Boston, 1739 ***1642*** *p45*
Mecan, William; America, 1743 ***1220.12*** *p544*
Mecanny, Alexander; Massachusetts, 1675-1676 ***1642*** *p128*
Mecaral, James; New England, 1745 ***1642*** *p27*
Mecco, Giacomo; Illinois, 1918 ***6007.60*** *p9*
Mecham, J. H. 30; Ontario, 1871 ***1823.21*** *p258*
Mechan, Edward 39; Ontario, 1871 ***1823.21*** *p258*
Mechan, J. J.; Louisiana, 1874 ***4981.45*** *p133*
Mechin, Jeanne 12; Quebec, 1642 ***9221.17*** *p119*
Mechsner, Aug.; Valdivia, Chile, 1852 ***1192.4*** *p56*
With wife & 4 children
With child 17
With child 8
Mecke, Fritz; Louisiana, 1874 ***4981.45*** *p133*
Meckison, Andrew 35; Ontario, 1871 ***1823.21*** *p258*
Mecum, John; America, 1774 ***1220.12*** *p543*
Meczynski, Fan 18; New York, NY, 1878 ***9253.2*** *p45*
Medates, Armenell; North Carolina, 1845 ***1088.45*** *p23*
Medates, Monwell; North Carolina, 1845 ***1088.45*** *p23*
Medberry, Thomas; Barbados, 1664 ***1220.12*** *p544*
Medcaf, William 39; Ontario, 1871 ***1823.21*** *p258*
Medcaff, John 46; Ontario, 1871 ***1823.17*** *p116*
Medcalf, George; America, 1741 ***1220.12*** *p547*
Medcalf, Joseph; America, 1774 ***1220.12*** *p547*
Medcalfe, Adam; America, 1758 ***1220.12*** *p547*
Medcalfe, William; America, 1702 ***1220.12*** *p547*
Medcalfe, William; America, 1775 ***1220.12*** *p547*
Medcalfe, Wm; Virginia, 1652 ***6254.4*** *p244*
Medcof, Thomas 64; Ontario, 1871 ***1823.21*** *p258*
Medcroft, George; America, 1738 ***1220.12*** *p544*
Meddison, Job; Barbados or Jamaica, 1689 ***1220.12*** *p523*
Meddocks, William; America, 1739 ***1220.12*** *p524*
Meder, Carolina 5; Port uncertain, 1840 ***778.6*** *p237*
Meder, Carolina 30; Port uncertain, 1840 ***778.6*** *p237*
Meder, Catha. 1; Port uncertain, 1840 ***778.6*** *p237*
Meder, Ch. 35; Port uncertain, 1840 ***778.6*** *p237*
Medeye, Francoise 30; America, 1847 ***778.6*** *p237*
Medhurst, George 40; Ontario, 1871 ***1823.21*** *p258*
Medhurst, William; Maryland, 1725 ***1220.12*** *p544*
Mediamole, Mr. 23; America, 1841 ***778.6*** *p237*
Medilton, Mattha 24; Ontario, 1871 ***1823.21*** *p258*
Medinger, J. M.; Chile, 1852 ***1192.4*** *p52*
With wife & 4 children
With child 1
With child 8
Medlam, William; New York, 1776 ***8529.30*** *p14*
Medlewski, Catharina; Wisconsin, 1885 ***6795.8*** *p60*
Medley, Francis 49; Ontario, 1871 ***1823.17*** *p116*
Medley, Peter; America, 1769 ***1220.12*** *p544*
Medley, Roger; Barbados, 1671 ***1220.12*** *p544*
Medley, Roger; Maryland, 1672 ***1236.25*** *p47*
Medlicot, William; America, 1764 ***1220.12*** *p544*
Medlin, Thomas; America, 1741 ***1220.12*** *p544*
Medoux, Pierre 35; Port uncertain, 1846 ***778.6*** *p237*
Medrianot, A. 19; New Orleans, 1847 ***778.6*** *p237*
Meduna, Matt; Detroit, 1929-1930 ***6214.5*** *p65*
Medve, John; New York, 1926 ***1173.1*** *p2*
Medve, Louis; New York, 1926 ***1173.1*** *p2*
Mee, Benjamin; New York, 1775 ***8529.30*** *p14*
Mee, John; Washington, 1884 ***2770.40*** *p193*
Mee, Joseph; America, 1775 ***1220.12*** *p544*
Mee, Patrick 64; Ontario, 1871 ***1823.21*** *p258*
Meech, Ann; America, 1739 ***1220.12*** *p544*
Meecham, Benjamin; Barbados or Jamaica, 1694 ***1220.12*** *p542*
Meechem, George 22; Ontario, 1871 ***1823.21*** *p258*
Meechert, John F.; Washington, 1884 ***2770.40*** *p193*
Meechin, Mary; Barbados or Jamaica, 1698 ***1220.12*** *p544*
Meed, John; America, 1775 ***1220.12*** *p543*
Meedy, Joseph; America, 1728 ***1220.12*** *p544*
Meehan, Andrew T.; Tennessee, 1893 ***3665.20*** *p112*
Meehan, Michael 46; Ontario, 1871 ***1823.21*** *p258*
Meek, John; America, 1754 ***1220.12*** *p544*
Meek, John; New York, 1860 ***358.56*** *p150*
Meek, John 63; Ontario, 1871 ***1823.21*** *p258*
Meek, Mary 60; Ontario, 1871 ***1823.21*** *p258*
Meek, Robert; America, 1765 ***1220.12*** *p544*
Meek, Thomas; America, 1774 ***1220.12*** *p544*
Meek, Thomas 65; Ontario, 1871 ***1823.21*** *p258*
Meek, Thomas; Toronto, 1844 ***2910.35*** *p116*
Meek, William; America, 1757 ***1220.12*** *p544*
Meek, William; America, 1774 ***1220.12*** *p544*
Meek, William 40; Ontario, 1871 ***1823.21*** *p258*
Meek, William 53; Ontario, 1871 ***1823.21*** *p258*
Meeke, Margaret; America, 1688 ***1220.12*** *p544*
Meekison, George 33; Ontario, 1871 ***1823.21*** *p258*
Meenan, Daniel; North Carolina, 1830 ***1088.45*** *p23*
Meenan, Hugh; North Carolina, 1825 ***1088.45*** *p23*
Meeney, John; St. John, N.B., 1848 ***2978.15*** *p40*
Meeney, John; St. John, N.B., 1848 ***2978.15*** *p40*
Meeney, John, Jr.; St. John, N.B., 1848 ***2978.15*** *p40*
Meer, Guy; Annapolis, MD, 1733 ***1220.12*** *p544*
Meer, Jacob 23; Louisiana, 1848 ***778.6*** *p237*
Meerbach, Christian; America, 1868 ***7919.3*** *p532*
With wife & 4 children
Meere, Joseph; America, 1749 ***1220.12*** *p544*
Meeres, John; America, 1655 ***1220.12*** *p544*
Meerfeld, Henriette Hauck 40 *SEE* Meerfeld, Mathias
Meerfeld, Mathias; America, 1854 ***5475.1*** *p78*
*Wife:*Henriette Hauck
With 5 children
With daughter 24
Meerholz, Nathan; North Carolina, 1852 ***1088.45*** *p23*
Meers, John; Died enroute, 1731 ***1220.12*** *p544*
Meers, Margaret; America, 1745 ***1220.12*** *p544*
Meers, Peter 61; Ontario, 1871 ***1823.21*** *p258*
Meers, William 30; Ontario, 1871 ***1823.21*** *p258*
Mees, August; Wisconsin, 1873 ***6795.8*** *p230*
Mees, Elisabeth 26; Brazil, 1862 ***5475.1*** *p496*
Mees, Margarethe 33; Brazil, 1862 ***5475.1*** *p496*
Meesburger, Catherine 15; Louisiana, 1848 ***778.6*** *p237*
Meesburger, Jn. Bte. 10; Louisiana, 1848 ***778.6*** *p237*
Meesburger, Leonard 54; Louisiana, 1848 ***778.6*** *p237*
Meesburger, Marie A. 17; Louisiana, 1848 ***778.6*** *p237*
Meesburger, Marie A. 46; Louisiana, 1848 ***778.6*** *p237*
Meesburger, Therese 6; Louisiana, 1848 ***778.6*** *p237*
Meese, Caroline Dorothee Charlotte; America, 1853 ***7420.1*** *p108*
Meese, Christoph Ludwig; America, 1843 ***7420.1*** *p29*
With family
*Son:*Heinrich Christian Ludwig
Meese, Heinrich Christian Ludwig *SEE* Meese, Christoph Ludwig
Meese, Johann Friedrich Christian; America, 1854 ***7420.1*** *p124*
Meese, Thomas; America, 1665 ***1220.12*** *p544*
Meetkerke, William; America, 1773 ***1220.12*** *p544*
Meffert, Aegidius; Pennsylvania, 1848 ***170.15*** *p36*
With 2 children
Meffert, Aegidius 47; Pennsylvania, 1848 ***170.15*** *p36*
With child 17
With child 20
Meffert, Andreas 42; America, 1849 ***170.15*** *p36*
With 3 children
Meffert, Christian; America, 1868 ***7919.3*** *p524*
With wife & 7 children
Meffert, Engel Marie Sophie; America, 1857 ***7420.1*** *p166*
Meffert, Heinrich Conrad; New York, NY, 1856 ***7420.1*** *p150*
Meffert, Johann Philipp; America, 1857 ***7420.1*** *p166*
Megary, Arthur 58; Ontario, 1871 ***1823.21*** *p258*
Megee, John; Massachusetts, 1759 ***1642*** *p89*
Megee, Mary; Massachusetts, 1774 ***1642*** *p91*
Megee, Reliance; Massachusetts, 1754 ***1642*** *p91*
Megee, Thomas; Massachusetts, 1700-1799 ***1642*** *p85*
Megel, Gottfried 25; Portland, ME, 1911 ***970.38*** *p79*
Megel, Maria Sofia 25; Portland, ME, 1911 ***970.38*** *p79*
Megenburre, Alexandre 6; Missouri, 1846 ***778.6*** *p237*
Megenburre, Auguste 8; Missouri, 1846 ***778.6*** *p238*
Megenburre, Marguerite 31; Missouri, 1846 ***778.6*** *p238*
Megenburre, Marie 29; Missouri, 1846 ***778.6*** *p238*
Megenburre, Pierre 36; Missouri, 1846 ***778.6*** *p238*

Megenburre, Pierre 40; Missouri, 1846 *778.6 p238*
Megenburre, Rosalie 2; Missouri, 1846 *778.6 p238*
Meggs, Charles 35; Ontario, 1871 *1823.21 p258*
Meggs, William; Virginia, 1745 *1220.12 p544*
Meggs, William; Virginia, 1762 *1220.12 p544*
Megher, Bierly 23; Ontario, 1871 *1823.21 p258*
Megher, David 28; Ontario, 1871 *1823.21 p258*
Megher, James Robert Richard Sledin 27; Ontario, 1866 *9228.50 p451*
Meginny, Daniel; Massachusetts, 1675-1676 *1642 p129*
Mehan, Edward; Ohio, 1836 *3580.20 p33*
Mehan, Edward; Ohio, 1836 *6020.12 p21*
Mehan, Edward; Ohio, 1838 *3580.20 p33*
Mehan, Edward; Ohio, 1838 *6020.12 p21*
Mehan, Patrick 40; Ontario, 1871 *1823.21 p258*
Mehen, John; Colorado, 1869 *1029.59 p62*
Meher, Thomas 60; Ontario, 1871 *1823.21 p258*
Mehl, Elisabeth; Rio Grande do Sul, Brazil, 1861 *5475.1 p489*
Mehlburger, Conrad; America, 1868 *7420.1 p274*
Mehlburger, Ludwig Philipp; America, 1866 *7420.1 p245*
Mehleman, Matthias; Ohio, 1809-1852 *4511.35 p33*
Mehlharn, August; Washington, 1882 *2770.40 p135*
Mehlhose, F. E.; Valdivia, Chile, 1852 *1192.4 p54*
Mehling, M. And.; New York, 1859 *358.56 p101*
Mehlman, George S.; Philadelphia, 1865-1867 *7074.20 p133*
Mehmert, Catharine Georgine; America, 1867 *7919.3 p529*
Mehoney, Mary; Marblehead, MA, 1743 *1642 p73*
Mehr, Andrew; Washington, 1884 *2770.40 p193*
Mehr, Christina; Dakota, 1877-1918 *554.30 p25*
Mehsner, Gustav; Chicago, 1882 *5475.1 p130*
Mehuy, John; Marblehead, MA, 1700-1799 *9228.50 p451*
Mehy, John; Marblehead, MA, 1700-1799 *9228.50 p451*
Mehyi, John; Marblehead, MA, 1700-1799 *9228.50 p451*
Meichel, Anna 15; Halifax, N.S., 1902 *1860.4 p43*
Meichel, Anton 43; Halifax, N.S., 1902 *1860.4 p43*
Meichel, Elizabeth 32; Halifax, N.S., 1902 *1860.4 p43*
Meichel, Franz 4; Halifax, N.S., 1902 *1860.4 p43*
Meichel, Gertrude 20; Halifax, N.S., 1902 *1860.4 p43*
Meichel, Jacob 8; Halifax, N.S., 1902 *1860.4 p43*
Meichel, Lombard 9; Halifax, N.S., 1902 *1860.4 p43*
Meichel, Peter 3; Halifax, N.S., 1902 *1860.4 p43*
Meichel, Segmund 1; Halifax, N.S., 1902 *1860.4 p43*
Meicher, Angela Wehr *SEE* Meicher, Johann
Meicher, Franz *SEE* Meicher, Johann
Meicher, Johann *SEE* Meicher, Johann
Meicher, Johann; America, 1872 *5475.1 p328*
  *Wife:*Angela Wehr
  *Son:*Johann
  *Son:*Franz
  *Daughter:*Susanna
Meicher, Susanna *SEE* Meicher, Johann
Meidhardt, Georg; America, 1868 *7919.3 p533*
  With wife & 2 children
Meidinger, Adolf 3; New York, NY, 1885 *1883.7 p46*
Meidinger, Catha. 6; New York, NY, 1885 *1883.7 p46*
Meidinger, Christa. 7; New York, NY, 1885 *1883.7 p46*
Meidinger, Christn. 18; New York, NY, 1885 *1883.7 p46*
Meidinger, Friedr. 15; New York, NY, 1885 *1883.7 p46*
Meidinger, Jacob 5; New York, NY, 1885 *1883.7 p46*
Meidinger, Johann 11 months; New York, NY, 1885 *1883.7 p46*
Meidinger, Johann 40; New York, NY, 1885 *1883.7 p46*
Meidinger, Magde. 40; New York, NY, 1885 *1883.7 p46*
Meier, . . .; America, 1849 *7420.1 p66*
Meier, Miss; America, 1886 *7420.1 p351*
Meier, Mr.; America, 1857 *7420.1 p167*
Meier, Mr.; America, 1870 *7420.1 p395*
  With wife
Meier, Mr.; America, 1886 *7420.1 p351*
Meier, Anna Maria; Pennsylvania, 1852 *8513.31 p306*
Meier, Anna Sophie Marie *SEE* Meier, Johann Heinrich Christoph
Meier, August; America, 1852 *7420.1 p93*
Meier, August; America, 1861 *7420.1 p207*
  With family
Meier, August Ferdinand; America, 1867 *7420.1 p260*
  With children
Meier, Barbara; New York, 1860 *358.56 p4*
Meier, Carl; America, 1870 *7420.1 p287*
  *Son:*Carl Heinrich Fr. Conrad
  *Son:*Carl August Wilh. Otto
  With family
Meier, Carl; America, 1892 *7420.1 p366*
Meier, Carl; Port uncertain, 1866 *7420.1 p245*
  *Sister:*Line
Meier, Carl August Wilh. Otto *SEE* Meier, Carl
Meier, Carl Friedrich Ludwig; America, 1860 *7420.1 p196*

Meier, Carl Friedrich Wilhelm; Nebraska, 1879 *7420.1 p314*
Meier, Carl Heinrich; America, 1854 *7420.1 p124*
Meier, Carl Heinrich August; America, 1868 *7420.1 p274*
  With family
Meier, Carl Heinrich August; America, 1870 *7420.1 p288*
Meier, Carl Heinrich Fr. Conrad *SEE* Meier, Carl
Meier, Carl Justus; America, 1847 *7420.1 p54*
  With wife
  With daughter 6 months
  With son 3
  With son 5
  With son 9
Meier, Caroline Sophie Ernestine; America, 1871 *7420.1 p290*
Meier, Catharina; America, 1847 *7420.1 p52*
Meier, Charlotte; America, 1860 *7420.1 p196*
Meier, Christian; America, 1853 *7420.1 p108*
  With wife son & 4 daughters
Meier, Christian; America, 1882 *7420.1 p330*
Meier, Christiane; America, 1857 *7420.1 p167*
Meier, Engel Marie; America, 1860 *7420.1 p196*
Meier, Engel Marie Sophie *SEE* Meier, Ilse Marie Charlotte
Meier, Engel Marie Sophie *SEE* Meier, Johann Heinrich Christoph
Meier, Engel Marie Sophie Dorothee *SEE* Meier, Ilse Marie Charlotte
Meier, Ernst; Wisconsin, 1888 *6795.8 p149*
Meier, Eva 20; New York, NY, 1898 *7951.13 p43*
Meier, Friederike; America, 1885 *7420.1 p348*
Meier, Friederike Konradine Amalie Stockmann *SEE* Meier, Hermann Heinrich
Meier, Friederike Sophie Karoline *SEE* Meier, Hermann Heinrich
Meier, Friedrich Carl; America, 1866 *7420.1 p245*
Meier, Friedrich Wilhelm; America, 1867 *7420.1 p260*
  With family
Meier, Georg 18; New York, NY, 1893 *1883.7 p41*
Meier, Hans Heinrich; America, 1850 *7420.1 p73*
  *Sister:*Thrine Maria Sophia
Meier, Hans Heinrich Christoph; America, 1867 *7420.1 p260*
  With family
Meier, Heinrich; America, 1846 *7420.1 p46*
Meier, Heinrich; America, 1852 *7420.1 p93*
  With wife 3 sons & 2 daughters
Meier, Heinrich Christoph *SEE* Meier, Johann Heinrich Christoph
Meier, Heinrich Conrad *SEE* Meier, Ilse Marie Charlotte
Meier, Heinrich Wilhelm; America, 1865 *7420.1 p233*
Meier, Hermann Heinrich; America, 1887 *7420.1 p354*
  *Wife:*Friederike Konradine Amalie Stockmann
  *Daughter:*Wilhelmine Friederike Amalie
  *Son:*Karl Heinrich Hermann
  *Daughter:*Friederike Sophie Karoline
Meier, Ilse Marie Charlotte; America, 1856 *7420.1 p150*
  *Daughter:*Engel Marie Sophie
  *Daughter:*Engel Marie Sophie Dorothee
  *Son:*Heinrich Conrad
Meier, Jacob J.; Nebraska, 1905 *3004.30 p46*
Meier, Jean Batist 14; America, 1848 *778.6 p238*
Meier, Johann; America, 1851 *5475.1 p68*
  With family
Meier, Johann Carl; America, 1852 *7420.1 p93*
Meier, Johann Christian; America, 1874 *7420.1 p303*
Meier, Johann Conrad; America, 1854 *7420.1 p124*
Meier, Johann Ernst *SEE* Meier, Johann Philipp
Meier, Johann Friedrich Gottlieb; America, 1848 *7420.1 p61*
Meier, Johann Heinrich; America, 1850 *7420.1 p74*
  *Wife:*Sophia Dorothea Wilhelmine Seegers
Meier, Johann Heinrich Christoph; America, 1871 *7420.1 p291*
  *Son:*Heinrich Christoph
  *Daughter:*Anna Sophie Marie
  *Daughter:*Engel Marie Sophie
  With wife
Meier, Johann Heinrich Wilhelm; America, 1860 *7420.1 p196*
Meier, Johann Heinrich Wilhelm; Port uncertain, 1854 *7420.1 p124*
Meier, Johann Otto; America, 1857 *7420.1 p167*
Meier, Johann Philipp; America, 1840 *7420.1 p19*
  *Brother:*Johann Ernst
Meier, Johann Philipp; America, 1857 *7420.1 p167*
Meier, Johannes; America, 1892 *170.15 p36*
  With wife & child
Meier, Johannes; Illinois, 1854 *6079.1 p9*
Meier, John; America, 1764 *1220.12 p574*
Meier, John; Colorado, 1870 *1029.59 p62*

Meier, Joseph; North Carolina, 1855 *1088.45 p23*
Meier, Justine; America, 1867 *7420.1 p260*
Meier, Karl Heinrich Hermann *SEE* Meier, Hermann Heinrich
Meier, Karl Ludwig Friedrich; Chicago, 1873 *7420.1 p300*
Meier, Lazarus; America, 1867 *7919.3 p525*
  With daughter
Meier, Line *SEE* Meier, Carl
Meier, Longius 24; New York, NY, 1898 *7951.13 p43*
Meier, Ludwig; America, 1867 *7420.1 p260*
  With family
Meier, Mrs. Ludwig; America, 1867 *7420.1 p260*
Meier, Maria; America, 1879 *5475.1 p372*
Meier, Maria 31; Brazil, 1857 *5475.1 p356*
Meier, Marie; New York, 1860 *358.56 p149*
Meier, Mathias; America, 1881 *5475.1 p313*
Meier, Michel; America, 1881 *5475.1 p313*
Meier, Minna; America, 1885 *7420.1 p348*
Meier, Oliver 20; Ontario, 1871 *1823.17 p116*
Meier, P. T.; Louisiana, 1836-1841 *4981.45 p209*
Meier, Sophia Dorothea Wilhelmine Seegers *SEE* Meier, Johann Heinrich
Meier, Sophie Cathar. Friederike Charl.; America, 1883 *7420.1 p340*
Meier, Sophie Marie Caroline; America, 1883 *7420.1 p339*
Meier, Thrine Maria Sophia *SEE* Meier, Hans Heinrich
Meier, Wilhelm; America, 1854 *7420.1 p125*
  With brother & sister
Meier, Wilhelm; America, 1882 *7420.1 p330*
Meier, Wilhelmine Christ.; Fort Wayne, IN, 1845 *7420.1 p37*
Meier, Wilhelmine Friederike Amalie *SEE* Meier, Hermann Heinrich
Meierhof, Engel Marie Charlotte; America, 1864 *7420.1 p222*
Meierhof, Engel Marie Charlotte; America, 1864 *7420.1 p222*
Meierhoff, Mr.; America, 1860 *7420.1 p196*
Meierhoff, Wilhelm; America, 1870 *7420.1 p207*
  With wife & 2 sons & 2 daughters
Meiers, A. Maria; America, 1881 *5475.1 p299*
Meiers, A. Maria *SEE* Meiers, Nikolaus
Meiers, Angela 59; Brazil, 1857 *5475.1 p368*
Meiers, Helena; Brazil, 1880 *5475.1 p373*
Meiers, Johann *SEE* Meiers, Nikolaus
Meiers, Katharina; America, 1857 *5475.1 p254*
Meiers, Katharina 28 *SEE* Meiers, Katharina Schmitt
Meiers, Katharina 63; America, 1857 *5475.1 p335*
  *Son:*Mathias 33
  *Daughter:*Maria 25
  *Daughter:*Katharina 28
Meiers, Katharina *SEE* Meiers, Nikolaus
Meiers, Ludwig 54; America, 1843 *5475.1 p294*
Meiers, Margarethe; America, 1860 *5475.1 p296*
Meiers, Margarethe 51; America, 1863 *5475.1 p261*
Meiers, Maria 25 *SEE* Meiers, Katharina Schmitt
Meiers, Maria 31; America, 1860 *5475.1 p360*
  *Son:*Nikolaus
  *Son:*Johann
Meiers, Mathias 33 *SEE* Meiers, Katharina Schmitt
Meiers, Mathias *SEE* Meiers, Nikolaus
Meiers, Nikolaus; Arkansas, 1880 *5475.1 p299*
  *Wife:*Susanna Becker
  *Son:*Mathias
  *Daughter:*Katharina
  *Daughter:*A. Maria
  *Son:*Johann
Meiers, Susanna; America, 1881 *5475.1 p299*
Meiers, Susanna; America, 1881 *5475.1 p300*
Meiers, Susanna Becker *SEE* Meiers, Nikolaus
Meiersick, William; Illinois, 1859 *6079.1 p9*
Meigher, Ellen 23; Ontario, 1871 *1823.17 p116*
Meijer, Fr. Bernhard; New York, NY, 1849 *6412.40 p151*
Meilchen, Anna; America, 1883 *5475.1 p164*
Meilchen, Barbara *SEE* Meilchen, Georg
Meilchen, Georg; America, 1883 *5475.1 p164*
  *Daughter:*Barbara
  *Daughter:*Maria
Meilchen, Maria *SEE* Meilchen, Georg
Meindre, Jean; Illinois, 1852 *6079.1 p9*
Meineke, Caroline Frieder. Justine; America, 1855 *7420.1 p139*
Meininger, Johannes 35; New Jersey, 1748-1774 *927.31 p2*
Meininger, Leonhard; America, 1883 *2526.43 p198*
Meinke, Ferdinand; Wisconsin, 1890 *6795.8 p26*
Meinninger, Marie Anne; Pennsylvania, 1877 *8513.31 p430*
Meinradt, Andrew 54; Port uncertain, 1845 *778.6 p238*
Meinradt, Antoine 20; Port uncertain, 1845 *778.6 p238*

Meinradt, John 24; Port uncertain, 1845 ***778.6*** *p238*
Meinradt, Joseph 21; Port uncertain, 1845 ***778.6*** *p238*
Meinradt, Magd. 14; Port uncertain, 1845 ***778.6*** *p238*
Meinradt, Marianna 15; Port uncertain, 1845 ***778.6*** *p238*
Meinradt, Morant 16; Port uncertain, 1845 ***778.6*** *p238*
Meinradt, Theresa 54; Port uncertain, 1845 ***778.6*** *p238*
Meinsola, Jean Baptiste 25; New Orleans, 1847 ***778.6*** *p238*
Meirenger, Elisabeth 39; America, 1846 ***778.6*** *p238*
Meirick, Mary; America, 1764 ***1220.12*** *p546*
Meirutt, Wm 40; St. Johns, N.F., 1811 ***1053.20*** *p20*
Meiser, A. Barbara 9 *SEE* Meiser, Johann
Meiser, Adolf Johann Jakob; America, 1871 ***5475.1*** *p154*
Meiser, Anna 49; America, 1856 ***5475.1*** *p563*
Meiser, Anna Maria 25; America, 1846 ***5475.1*** *p402*
Meiser, Barbara 16 *SEE* Meiser, Johann
Meiser, Gertrud; America, 1842 ***5475.1*** *p397*
Meiser, Gertrud 21 *SEE* Meiser, Johann
Meiser, Jakob; America, 1855 ***5475.1*** *p455*
Meiser, Jakob; America, 1882 ***5475.1*** *p464*
Meiser, Jakob; New York, 1846 ***5475.1*** *p450*
Meiser, Johann 46; America, 1846 ***5475.1*** *p386*
*Wife:*Katharina Woll 46
*Daughter:*Barbara 16
*Daughter:*A. Barbara 9
*Daughter:*Margarethe 5
*Daughter:*Katharina 13
*Daughter:*Gertrud 21
*Son:*Peter 18
Meiser, Katharina *SEE* Meiser, Michel
Meiser, Katharina 13 *SEE* Meiser, Johann
Meiser, Katharina Woll 46 *SEE* Meiser, Johann
Meiser, Katharina 46; America, 1846 ***5475.1*** *p408*
Meiser, Katharina 47; America, 1846 ***5475.1*** *p401*
Meiser, Margarethe; America, 1854 ***5475.1*** *p465*
Meiser, Margarethe 5 *SEE* Meiser, Johann
Meiser, Mathias; New York, 1884 ***5475.1*** *p59*
Meiser, Michel; America, 1833 ***5475.1*** *p461*
*Sister:*Katharina
Meiser, Nikolaus 28; America, 1872 ***5475.1*** *p418*
Meiser, Peter 18 *SEE* Meiser, Johann
Meiser, Peter 27; America, 1836 ***5475.1*** *p407*
Meisinger, Anna; America, 1895 ***2526.42*** *p110*
Meisinger, Anna Eva 5 *SEE* Meisinger, Michael
Meisinger, Anna Eva 14 *SEE* Meisinger, Philipp
Meisinger, Anna Eva 16 *SEE* Meisinger, Anton
Meisinger, Anna Katharina Kumpf *SEE* Meisinger, Balthasar
Meisinger, Anna Katharina Keil *SEE* Meisinger, Anton
Meisinger, Anna Katharina 19 *SEE* Meisinger, Anton
Meisinger, Anna Margaretha Hallstein *SEE* Meisinger, Philipp
Meisinger, Anna Maria Friedrich *SEE* Meisinger, Philipp
Meisinger, Anton; Illinois, 1846 ***2526.43*** *p132*
*Wife:*Anna Katharina Keil
*Daughter:*Anna Katharina
*Daughter:*Anna Eva
*Son:*Balthasar
*Daughter:*Eva
Meisinger, Balthasar; Illinois, 1846 ***2526.43*** *p124*
*Wife:*Anna Katharina Kumpf
*Daughter:*Katharina
*Daughter:*Maria Elisabetha
*Daughter:*Margaretha
*Son:*Johann Georg
Meisinger, Balthasar 8 *SEE* Meisinger, Anton
Meisinger, Balthasar 10 *SEE* Meisinger, Georg, II
Meisinger, Elisabeth 2 *SEE* Meisinger, Philipp
Meisinger, Elisabeth Margaretha Lannert *SEE* Meisinger, Georg, II
Meisinger, Eva 11 *SEE* Meisinger, Anton
Meisinger, Georg; America, 1831 ***2526.43*** *p187*
Meisinger, Georg 4 *SEE* Meisinger, Philipp
Meisinger, Georg, II; Illinois, 1846 ***2526.43*** *p132*
*Wife:*Elisabeth Margaretha Lannert
*Son:*Heinrich
*Son:*Balthasar
*Son:*Michael
*Son:*Konrad
Meisinger, Heinrich 3 days *SEE* Meisinger, Michael
Meisinger, Heinrich 1 *SEE* Meisinger, Georg, II
Meisinger, Johann Georg 5 *SEE* Meisinger, Balthasar
Meisinger, Johann Georg 8 *SEE* Meisinger, Philipp
Meisinger, Johannes; America, 1852 ***2526.43*** *p212*
Meisinger, Johannes 10 *SEE* Meisinger, Philipp
Meisinger, Julius Wilhelm; America, 1891 ***2526.43*** *p175*
Meisinger, Karl; America, 1867 ***2526.43*** *p142*
Meisinger, Katharina 9 *SEE* Meisinger, Balthasar
Meisinger, Katharina 12 *SEE* Meisinger, Philipp
Meisinger, Konrad 5 *SEE* Meisinger, Georg, II
Meisinger, Ludwig; America, 1881 ***2526.43*** *p142*
Meisinger, Magdalena 7 *SEE* Meisinger, Michael
Meisinger, Margaretha 2 *SEE* Meisinger, Philipp
Meisinger, Margaretha 8 *SEE* Meisinger, Balthasar
Meisinger, Maria Elisabetha 3 *SEE* Meisinger, Balthasar
Meisinger, Michael; America, 1841 ***2526.42*** *p201*
Meisinger, Michael; America, 1846 ***2526.43*** *p128*
With wife
*Son:*Heinrich
*Daughter:*Magdalena
*Daughter:*Anna Eva
Meisinger, Michael 7 *SEE* Meisinger, Georg, II
Meisinger, Peter; America, 1894 ***2526.43*** *p124*
Meisinger, Peter 6 *SEE* Meisinger, Philipp
Meisinger, Peter 6 *SEE* Meisinger, Philipp
Meisinger, Philipp; America, 1867 ***2526.43*** *p191*
*Wife:*Anna Maria Friedrich
*Son:*Peter
*Daughter:*Margaretha
Meisinger, Philipp; Illinois, 1853 ***2526.43*** *p124*
*Wife:*Anna Margaretha Hallstein
*Daughter:*Anna Eva
*Son:*Johannes
*Son:*Peter
*Daughter:*Elisabeth
*Son:*Georg
*Son:*Johann Georg
*Daughter:*Katharina
Meiss, Caroline Johanne Louise; America, 1869 ***7919.3*** *p533*
Meissel, Lazice; Louisiana, 1874 ***4981.45*** *p133*
Meissner, C.W.; Galveston, TX, 1855 ***571.7*** *p17*
Meissner, Carl; Detroit, 1890 ***9980.23*** *p97*
Meissner, Emil Henrich; America, 1867 ***7919.3*** *p530*
Meissner, Johann Georg *SEE* Meissner, Marie Katharine
Meissner, Johann Konrad *SEE* Meissner, Marie Katharine
Meissner, Marie Katharine; America, 1840 ***8115.12*** *p321*
*Child:*Johann Konrad
*Child:*Johann Georg
Meister, Alois 23; America, 1846 ***778.6*** *p238*
Meister, Conrad; Ohio, 1844 ***2763.1*** *p20*
Meistrel, Nikolaus; America, 1839 ***5475.1*** *p469*
Meistrell, Franz *SEE* Meistrell, Jakob
Meistrell, Jakob; Kansas, 1894 ***5475.1*** *p381*
*Child:*Franz
*Child:*Johann
Meistrell, Johann 18; America, 1852 ***5475.1*** *p480*
Meistrell, Johann *SEE* Meistrell, Jakob
Meitchler, Godfrey; Ohio, 1809-1852 ***4511.35*** *p33*
Meitot, Fredrick; New York, 1860 ***358.56*** *p148*
Mejory, John; Boston, 1763 ***1642*** *p32*
Mekel, John 76; Ontario, 1871 ***1823.21*** *p258*
Melady, Brian 50; Ontario, 1871 ***1823.17*** *p116*
Melander, Anna L.; St. Paul, MN, 1885 ***1865.50*** *p97*
Melander, Sven J.; St. Paul, MN, 1868 ***1865.50*** *p97*
Melarned, Abearro 4; New York, NY, 1894 ***6512.1*** *p231*
Melarned, Leje 35; New York, NY, 1894 ***6512.1*** *p231*
Melarned, Lore 1; New York, NY, 1894 ***6512.1*** *p231*
Melarned, Markel 7; New York, NY, 1894 ***6512.1*** *p231*
Melarned, Meier 15; New York, NY, 1894 ***6512.1*** *p231*
Melarned, Meilach 10; New York, NY, 1894 ***6512.1*** *p231*
Melber, Johann Georg; America, 1889 ***179.55*** *p19*
Melber, Rosine; America, 1889 ***179.55*** *p19*
Melborne, Thomas; America, 1685 ***1220.12*** *p544*
Melburne, Charles 29; Ontario, 1871 ***1823.21*** *p258*
Melcher, C.; Louisiana, 1874 ***4981.45*** *p133*
Melchers, Adolf R.; Baltimore, 1872 ***2853.20*** *p125*
Melchior, Angela *SEE* Melchior, Nikolaus
Melchior, Anna *SEE* Melchior, Nikolaus
Melchior, Anna Felz *SEE* Melchior, Nikolaus
Melchior, Heinrich 46; America, 1882 ***5475.1*** *p16*
Melchior, Johann *SEE* Melchior, Nikolaus
Melchior, Margarethe *SEE* Melchior, Nikolaus
Melchior, Maria *SEE* Melchior, Nikolaus
Melchior, Nikolaus; America, 1882 ***5475.1*** *p339*
*Wife:*Anna Felz
*Daughter:*Maria
*Daughter:*Angela
*Daughter:*Anna
*Son:*Johann
*Daughter:*Margarethe
Melchman, George; America, 1665 ***1220.12*** *p544*
Meldrum, John 15; New York, NY, 1835 ***5024.1*** *p137*
Mele, Antoine 21; New Orleans, 1848 ***778.6*** *p238*
Meler, Anna; Detroit, 1890 ***9980.23*** *p96*
Melhuish, Agnes; Virginia, 1719 ***1220.12*** *p544*
Melhuish, William; America, 1740 ***1220.12*** *p544*
Melichar, Vaclav; New York, NY, 1904 ***2853.20*** *p109*
Melichar, Vaclav; New York, NY, 1904 ***2853.20*** *p131*
Melin, Alma Carolina *SEE* Melin, Marcus
Melin, John; St. Paul, MN, 1874-1905 ***1865.50*** *p97*
Melin, Marcus; St. Paul, MN, 1891 ***1865.50*** *p97*
*Wife:*Alma Carolina
Meliot, Catherine 28; Quebec, 1662 ***9221.17*** *p490*
Mellade, Jean 20; New Orleans, 1840 ***778.6*** *p238*
Mellander, Anna L.; St. Paul, MN, 1885 ***1865.50*** *p97*
Mellander, Sven J.; St. Paul, MN, 1868 ***1865.50*** *p97*
Mellange, Mr. 34; Louisiana, 1840 ***778.6*** *p238*
Mellard, Elizabeth; Barbados or Jamaica, 1688 ***1220.12*** *p544*
Mellberg, A.; New York, NY, 1844 ***6412.40*** *p148*
Melleory, Thomas; America, 1768 ***1220.12*** *p526*
Meller, Henry; America, 1734 ***1220.12*** *p550*
Meller, Hy.; Louisiana, 1874 ***4981.45*** *p296*
Meller, John; America, 1766 ***1220.12*** *p550*
Meller, Sarah; Annapolis, MD, 1721 ***1220.12*** *p551*
Melleret, J. J. A. 29; Baton Rouge, LA, 1847 ***778.6*** *p238*
Melley, John; Died enroute, 1851 ***9228.50*** *p192*
Mellin, Alma Carolina *SEE* Mellin, Marcus
Mellin, Carl 26; Minnesota, 1925 ***2769.54*** *p1379*
Mellin, Gustaf; Cleveland, OH, 1901-1903 ***9722.10*** *p124*
Mellin, Marcus; St. Paul, MN, 1891 ***1865.50*** *p97*
*Wife:*Alma Carolina
Melline, John; Ohio, 1809-1852 ***4511.35*** *p33*
Mellis, Antoine de; Quebec, 1752 ***2314.30*** *p170*
Mellis, Antoine de; Quebec, 1752 ***2314.30*** *p191*
Mellis, George 49; Ontario, 1871 ***1823.17*** *p116*
Mellis, James 53; Ontario, 1871 ***1823.21*** *p258*
Mellon, Charles 48; Ontario, 1871 ***1823.17*** *p116*
Mellon, Christina 35; Michigan, 1880 ***4491.39*** *p20*
Mellon, Edward; America, 1769 ***1220.12*** *p544*
Mellon, Hans 37; Michigan, 1880 ***4491.39*** *p20*
Mellon, James; New York, NY, 1839 ***3274.56*** *p71*
Mellon, M. 24; America, 1846 ***778.6*** *p238*
Mellon, Patrick; Ohio, 1809-1852 ***4511.35*** *p33*
Mellon, Patrick 73; Ontario, 1871 ***1823.17*** *p116*
Mellon, Robert; Quebec, 1633 ***9221.17*** *p29*
With brother
Mellon, Thomas; New York, 1776 ***8529.30*** *p4A*
Mellon, William 41; Ontario, 1871 ***1823.21*** *p258*
Mellor, James 46; Ontario, 1871 ***1823.21*** *p258*
Mellor, Richard; America, 1775 ***1220.12*** *p544*
Mellor, William; America, 1760 ***1220.12*** *p544*
Mellors, Frances; America, 1759 ***1220.12*** *p545*
Mells, Robert; America, 1759 ***1220.12*** *p553*
Mellstedt, Wilhelm; Valdivia, Chile, 1850 ***1192.4*** *p49*
Melnick, Mike; New York, 1926 ***1173.1*** *p2*
Meloany, Mary 10; Quebec, 1870 ***8364.32*** *p25*
Melon, Rose; Wisconsin, 1856 ***1495.20*** *p41*
Melone, John; America, 1749 ***1220.12*** *p544*
Meloon, Rachael; New Hampshire, 1753 ***1642*** *p31*
Meloque, Diane; Quebec, 1656 ***9221.17*** *p331*
Meloy, John; St. John, N.B., 1847 ***2978.15*** *p37*
Melrose, F. Matthews 5; New York, NY, 1839 ***7710.1*** *p157*
Melrose, Thomas 63; Ontario, 1871 ***1823.17*** *p116*
Melshaw, Mary; Annapolis, MD, 1731 ***1220.12*** *p545*
Melsheim, Rene 21; Louisiana, 1848 ***778.6*** *p238*
Melsop, Jos; St. John, N.B., 1848 ***2978.15*** *p39*
Melsop, Thos; St. John, N.B., 1848 ***2978.15*** *p39*
Melsop, William; St. John, N.B., 1848 ***2978.15*** *p39*
Melter, Frederick; Ohio, 1809-1852 ***4511.35*** *p34*
Melton, Joseph; Barbados, 1677 ***1220.12*** *p554*
Melton, Philip; America, 1678 ***1220.12*** *p554*
Melton, Thomas; America, 1761 ***1220.12*** *p554*
Meltshaw, Sarah; America, 1739 ***1220.12*** *p545*
Melville, Margaret 23; Ontario, 1871 ***1823.21*** *p258*
Melville, Peter 72; Ontario, 1871 ***1823.21*** *p258*
Melvin, David; North Carolina, 1804 ***1088.45*** *p23*
Melvin, Elliot; America, 1773 ***1220.12*** *p545*
Melvin, Richard; America, 1760 ***1220.12*** *p545*
Melz, Anton; Colorado, 1888 ***1029.59*** *p62*
Melzer, John; Texas, 1919-1922 ***6015.15*** *p28*
Memahone, Roger; New England, 1745 ***1642*** *p28*
Meminot, Aristile 9; America, 1847 ***778.6*** *p238*
Memory, George; America, 1770 ***1220.12*** *p545*
Menacier, Louise; Quebec, 1663 ***4514.3*** *p346*
Menadier, Jules; Valdivia, Chile, 1852 ***1192.4*** *p55*
Menager, Jean; Virginia, 1700 ***9230.15*** *p80*
Menager deCourbuisson, Charles-Antoine; Quebec, 1730 ***2314.30*** *p171*
Menah, Robert 60; Ontario, 1871 ***1823.17*** *p116*
Menam, Patrick; California, 1868 ***1131.61*** *p89*
Menard, Barbe; Quebec, 1669 ***4514.3*** *p346*
Menard, Gabriel 38; New Orleans, 1847 ***778.6*** *p238*
Menard, Gabriel 40; New Orleans, 1748 ***778.6*** *p238*
Menard, Jacques 15; Quebec, 1643 ***9221.17*** *p133*
Menard, Jean; Nova Scotia, 1753 ***3051*** *p112*
Menard, M. 27; America, 1843 ***778.6*** *p238*
Menard, Pierre 22; Quebec, 1656 ***9221.17*** *p342*
Menard, Rene 35; Quebec, 1640 ***9221.17*** *p93*
Menaur, Mr. 30; Mississippi, 1847 ***778.6*** *p238*
Menchan, Mr. 30; New Orleans, 1848 ***778.6*** *p238*
Menche, Justine; America, 1868 ***7420.1*** *p274*
Mencik, Jan; St. Paul, MN, 1863 ***2853.20*** *p277*
Mendlebaum, John; North Carolina, 1843 ***1088.45*** *p23*
Mendlik, Jan; Wisconsin, 1852 ***2853.20*** *p312*
Mendlik, Ludvik; Oklahoma, 1889 ***2853.20*** *p372*

324
FOR A COMPLETE EXPLANATION OF ENTRY, SEE "HOW TO READ A CITATION" SECTION

Mendousse, Jean 20; New Orleans, 1746 778.6 p238
Menegay, Claude F. 59; New Orleans, 1848 778.6 p239
Menegay, Emelie 36; New Orleans, 1848 778.6 p239
Menegay, Joseph; Ohio, 1809-1852 4511.35 p34
Menegay, Josephine 21; New Orleans, 1848 778.6 p239
Menegay, Louis 19; New Orleans, 1848 778.6 p239
Menegay, Marie 1; New Orleans, 1848 778.6 p239
Menegay, Marie 60; New Orleans, 1848 778.6 p239
Menegay, Sedevini 26; New Orleans, 1848 778.6 p239
Menegay, Virginia 33; New Orleans, 1848 778.6 p239
Menegot, John Baptist; Ohio, 1809-1852 4511.35 p34
Meneguin, Augustin 13; Port uncertain, 1843 778.6 p239
Meneguin, Emelie 2; Port uncertain, 1843 778.6 p239
Meneguin, Etienne 37; Port uncertain, 1843 778.6 p239
Meneguin, Eugenie 4; Port uncertain, 1843 778.6 p239
Meneguin, Francoise 40; Port uncertain, 1843 778.6 p239
Meneguin, Sephirain 9; Port uncertain, 1843 778.6 p239
Menery, James 48; Ontario, 1871 1823.17 p116
Menetier, Felix 30; Port uncertain, 1843 778.6 p239
Menetier, Jeremiah 42; Port uncertain, 1843 778.6 p239
Menetre, Antoine 31; America, 1843 778.6 p239
Menetre, Emile 2; America, 1843 778.6 p239
Menetre, Francois 5; America, 1843 778.6 p239
Menetre, Jean 27; America, 1840 778.6 p238
Menetre, Magdalena 31; America, 1843 778.6 p239
Menetre, Marie 17; America, 1843 778.6 p239
Meneux, Jacques 23; Quebec, 1662 9221.17 p490
Meng, Friedrich Nikolaus; America, 1864 5475.1 p488
Menge, Anna; Wisconsin, 1895 6795.8 p130
Menge, Antoine; Louisiana, 1836-1841 4981.45 p209
Menge, Friedrich; Wisconsin, 1898 6795.8 p149
Menge, Ludwig Heinrich; America, 1860 7420.1 p196
With parents
Mengel, G.; Louisiana, 1874-1875 4981.45 p29
Menger, Benedict; Ohio, 1809-1852 4511.35 p34
Menges, Katharina 43; America, 1854 5475.1 p74
Menhenick, William 50; Ontario, 1871 1823.17 p116
Menhennick, Joseph 38; Ontario, 1871 1823.21 p258
Menhinick, Denzil 50; Ontario, 1871 1823.17 p116
Menhinick, Francis 43; Ontario, 1871 1823.17 p116
Menick, Suzanna; America, 1663 1220.12 p545
Menielle, Louis; Louisiana, 1836-1840 4981.45 p213
Meninges, Mr. 19; America, 1846 778.6 p239
Menke, Heinrich; Port uncertain, 1840 7420.1 p19
Menke, Joseph; Brazil, 1921 8023.44 p377
Menkhoff, Heinrich August; New York, NY, 1884 7420.1 p344
*Wife:*Maria Emilie Mayer
With 4 children
Menkhoff, Maria Emilie Mayer *SEE* Menkhoff, Heinrich August
Menking, Mr.; America, 1853 7420.1 p108
With family
Menking, Carl Heinrich; America, 1886 7420.1 p351
Menking, Friedrich; America, 1836 7420.1 p11
Menking, Friedrich; America, 1849 7420.1 p66
Menking, Friedrich Gottlieb; America, 1838 7420.1 p15
Menking, Johann Heinrich; America, 1854 7420.1 p125
Menlein, Carl 35; America, 1840 778.6 p239
Menlein, Johann 10; America, 1840 778.6 p239
Menlein, Maria 38; America, 1840 778.6 p239
Mennel, Crispin; Ohio, 1835 2763.1 p20
Mennel, George 61; Ontario, 1871 1823.21 p259
Menney, William; Louisiana, 1841-1844 4981.45 p211
Mennin, John Claude; Ohio, 1809-1852 4511.35 p34
Menochiz, Cecile 26; Port uncertain, 1843 778.6 p239
Menot, Abraham; Virginia, 1700 9230.15 p81
Menot, P. 28; America, 1848 778.6 p239
Menouel, Francois; Quebec, 1650 9221.17 p228
*Wife:*Louise Tiolet
Menouel, Louise Tiolet *SEE* Menouel, Francois
Menouvel, Perrine 25; America, 1840 778.6 p239
Mens, Martin; Ohio, 1809-1852 4511.35 p34
Mensching, Mr.; America, 1873 7420.1 p300
With sister
Mensching, Anna Sophie Eleonore Stockmann *SEE* Mensching, Hans Heinrich
Mensching, Anna Sophie Marie *SEE* Mensching, Hans Heinrich
Mensching, Carl; America, 1882 7420.1 p330
With 5 children
Mensching, Carl August; America, 1860 7420.1 p196
Mensching, Carl Christoph; America, 1881 7420.1 p323
Mensching, Carl Ludwig; America, 1850 7420.1 p74
Mensching, Catharine Marie; America, 1850 7420.1 p71
Mensching, Catharine Marie Charlotte; America, 1850 7420.1 p74
Mensching, Christian; America, 1857 7420.1 p167
With family
Mensching, Engel Maria; America, 1860 7420.1 p196
Mensching, Engel Marie Charlotte; America, 1847 7420.1 p57
Mensching, Engel Marie Charlotte; America, 1847 7420.1 p57
Mensching, Engel Marie Charlotte; America, 1847 7420.1 p57
Mensching, Engel Marie Dorothee Flentge *SEE* Mensching, Johann Heinrich Christoph
Mensching, Engel Sophie Dorothee; America, 1860 7420.1 p196
Mensching, Ernst; America, 1854 7420.1 p125
Mensching, Ernst; America, 1867 7420.1 p260
With daughter 5 weeks
With son 8
With wife
Mensching, Ernst Heinrich Wilhelm; America, 1876 7420.1 p307
Mensching, Friedrich *SEE* Mensching, Johann Friedrich
Mensching, Friedrich; America, 1852 7420.1 p93
With 2 sons
Mensching, Friedrich; America, 1868 7420.1 p274
With family
Mensching, Hans Heinrich; America, 1847 7420.1 p54
With wife & 2 sons & daughter
Mensching, Hans Heinrich; America, 1847 7420.1 p54
*Wife:*Anna Sophie Eleonore Stockmann
*Daughter:*Anna Sophie Marie
*Son:*Johann Friedrich
*Son:*Joh. Heinr. Christoph
Mensching, Heinrich; America, 1868 7420.1 p274
Mensching, Heinrich Christoph *SEE* Mensching, Johann Heinrich Christoph
Mensching, Heinrich Christoph; America, 1860 7420.1 p197
Mensching, Heinrich Friedrich Wilhelm; America, 1904 7420.1 p380
Mensching, Joh. Heinr. Christoph *SEE* Mensching, Hans Heinrich
Mensching, Johann August Ludwig *SEE* Mensching, Johann Friedrich
Mensching, Mrs. Johann Christoph; America, 1857 7420.1 p167
*Son:*Johann Heinrich Christ.
Mensching, Johann Friedrich *SEE* Mensching, Hans Heinrich
Mensching, Johann Friedrich; America, 1851 7420.1 p81
*Son:*Johann August Ludwig
With wife
Mensching, Johann Friedrich; America, 1852 7420.1 p93
With wife & children
*Son:*Friedrich
Mensching, Johann Heinrich; America, 1857 7420.1 p167
Mensching, Johann Heinrich Christ. *SEE* Mensching, Mrs. Johann Christoph
Mensching, Johann Heinrich Christoph; America, 1845 7420.1 p38
*Wife:*Engel Marie Dorothee Flentge
*Son:*Heinrich Christoph
Mensching, Johann Heinrich Christoph; America, 1860 7420.1 p197
Mensching, Wilhelm; America, 1855 7420.1 p139
Mensching, Wilhelm; America, 1886 7420.1 p399
Mensing, Carl; America, 1854 7420.1 p125
Menville, J. J. 19; America, 1845 778.6 p239
Menze, Ernst Heinrich Wilhelm; America, 1870 7420.1 p284
Menzel, Hermann; Valdivia, Chile, 1850 1192.4 p48
Menzel, Michael; Galveston, TX, 1855 571.7 p17
Menzele, J. F. H. 25; New Orleans, 1848 778.6 p239
Menzen, Joseph 32; America, 1840 778.6 p239
Menzer, Eva Katharina 13 *SEE* Menzer, Johannes
Menzer, Georg Peter 33; America, 1857 2526.43 p134
Menzer, Jakob; America, 1878 2526.43 p175
Menzer, Johannes; America, 1844 2526.43 p212
With wife
*Daughter:*Eva Katharina
Menzer, Konrad 28; America, 1868 2526.43 p212
With wife 28
With child 3
With child 1
Menzer, Peter 40; America, 1832 2526.42 p97
With wife
Menzies, Mary 25; North Carolina, 1775 1422.10 p57
Menzies, Robert 77; Ontario, 1871 1823.17 p116
Menzies, William 42; Ontario, 1871 1823.21 p259
Menzus, John 24; Ontario, 1871 1823.21 p259
Meon, Guillaume 21; Quebec, 1657 9221.17 p364
Meoser, Johan; Illinois, 1855 6079.1 p9
Mepham, Joseph; America, 1742 1220.12 p545
Merandino, A.; Louisiana, 1874-1875 4981.45 p30
Merar, William; Marston's Wharf, 1782 8529.30 p14
Merauld, Pierre 23; Quebec, 1657 9221.17 p364
Merbach, F. 44; America, 1846 778.6 p239
Merbite, Frederick Oswald; Illinois, 1854 6079.1 p9
Mercenier, Therese; Wisconsin, 1855-1858 1495.20 p67
Mercer, Ann Elizabeth 76; Ontario, 1880 9228.50 p451
Mercer, Elizabeth; America, 1747 1220.12 p545
Mercer, James; America, 1750 1220.12 p545
Mercer, John 64; Ontario, 1871 1823.21 p259
Mercer, Jonas; America, 1750 1220.12 p545
Mercer, Joseph; America, 1727 1220.12 p545
Mercer, Joseph; Annapolis, MD, 1725 1220.12 p545
Mercer, Peter; Virginia, 1770 1220.12 p545
Mercer, Richard; Maryland, 1733 1220.12 p545
Mercer, Samuel; America, 1773 1220.12 p545
Mercer, Sarah; America, 1766 1220.12 p545
Mercer, William; America, 1763 1220.12 p545
Mercer, William; Marston's Wharf, 1782 8529.30 p14
Mercey, Thomas; Barbados or Jamaica, 1692 1220.12 p545
Merchant, Elizabeth; America, 1767 1220.12 p545
Merchant, Emanuel; America, 1685 1220.12 p545
Merchant, George; Barbados, 1674 1220.12 p545
Merchant, George; Maryland, 1674-1675 1236.25 p52
Merchant, John; America, 1766 1220.12 p545
Merchant, John; Barbados or Jamaica, 1687 1220.12 p545
Merchant, Joseph 30; America, 1773 1220.12 p545
Merchant, Robert; America, 1768 1220.12 p545
Merchant, Stephen, Jr.; America, 1773 1220.12 p545
Merchant, Stephen, Sr.; America, 1773 1220.12 p545
Merchant, Thomas; America, 1742 1220.12 p545
Merchant, William; America, 1685 1220.12 p545
Merchant, William; America, 1750 1220.12 p545
Mercier, Catherine; Montreal, 1649 9221.17 p221
Mercier, Catherine; Montreal, 1649 9221.17 p221
Mercier, Denise; Quebec, 1641 9221.17 p101
Mercier, Francis; America, 1773 1220.12 p545
Mercier, Francis; Georgia, 1795 1451.56 p118
Mercier, G. F.; Louisiana, 1841-1844 4981.45 p211
Mercier, Isaac 36; Ontario, 1871 1823.17 p116
Mercier, Jean; Quebec, 1645 9221.17 p155
Mercier, Jean Etienne 43; Texas, 1843 778.6 p240
Mercier, Jeanne 13; Quebec, 1639 9221.17 p91
Mercier, Julien 26; Quebec, 1647 9221.17 p185
Mercier, Marie; Quebec, 1671 4514.3 p346
Mercier, Theophile 34; Texas, 1843 778.6 p240
Mercilary, Thomas; Virginia, 1759 1220.12 p545
Merckle, Daniel 29; Louisiana, 1848 778.6 p240
Mercy, Alexander 37; Indiana, 1887-1896 9076.20 p74
Mercy, James; Port uncertain, 1720 1220.12 p545
Merdell, . . .; Ontario, 1871 1823.21 p259
Merdian, Anna 2 months; New York, NY, 1893 1883.7 p37
Merdian, Helena 33; New York, NY, 1893 1883.7 p37
Merdian, Kaspar 7; New York, NY, 1893 1883.7 p37
Merdian, Mathaus 4; New York, NY, 1893 1883.7 p37
Merdian, Michael 32; New York, NY, 1893 1883.7 p37
Merdian, Monika 8; New York, NY, 1893 1883.7 p37
Merdyth, James; Philadelphia, 1777 8529.30 p4A
Mere, Jeanne 19; Montreal, 1654 9221.17 p317
Mere, John; Iowa, 1884 1211.15 p16
Merebeth, John 38; Ontario, 1871 1823.17 p116
Mereden, Joseph; America, 1773 1220.12 p546
Meredith, David; New Jersey, 1777 8529.30 p6
Meredith, Edward; America, 1751 1220.12 p545
Meredith, Edward; America, 1763 1220.12 p545
Meredith, Elizabeth; America, 1728 1220.12 p545
Meredith, Elizabeth; America, 1731 1220.12 p545
Meredith, Jane; America, 1765 1220.12 p546
Meredith, John; America, 1694 1220.12 p546
Meredith, John; America, 1743 1220.12 p546
Meredith, John Cook 61; Ontario, 1871 1823.21 p259
Meredith, John R.; Ohio, 1849 3580.20 p33
Meredith, John R.; Ohio, 1849 6020.12 p21
Meredith, Mary; America, 1734 1220.12 p546
Meredith, Mary; America, 1761 1220.12 p546
Meredith, Richard; America, 1753 1220.12 p546
Meredith, Richard; America, 1756 1220.12 p546
Meredy, Mary; Maryland, 1723 1220.12 p546
Merewether, Edward; Colorado, 1902 1029.59 p62
Merewether, Edward 21; Colorado, 1902 1029.59 p62
Merfeld, Anna Maria Wein *SEE* Merfeld, Nikolaus
Merfeld, Barbara *SEE* Merfeld, Mathias
Merfeld, Barbara *SEE* Merfeld, Peter
Merfeld, Barbara Lenhof *SEE* Merfeld, Peter
Merfeld, Gertrud *SEE* Merfeld, Mathias
Merfeld, Johann *SEE* Merfeld, Mathias
Merfeld, Johann *SEE* Merfeld, Johann
Merfeld, Johann; America, 1871 5475.1 p139
*Wife:*Margarethe Dezes
*Son:*Peter
*Son:*Josef
*Son:*Johann
Merfeld, Johann *SEE* Merfeld, Peter
Merfeld, Johann; America, 1889 5475.1 p52
Merfeld, Josef *SEE* Merfeld, Nikolaus

Merfeld, Josef *SEE* Merfeld, Mathias
Merfeld, Josef *SEE* Merfeld, Johann
Merfeld, Katharina *SEE* Merfeld, Mathias
Merfeld, Margarethe Dezes *SEE* Merfeld, Johann
Merfeld, Maria *SEE* Merfeld, Peter
Merfeld, Maria; America, 1874 ***5475.1*** *p140*
Merfeld, Mathias; America, 1869 ***5475.1*** *p139*
*Wife:*Susanna Heinz
*Daughter:*Barbara
*Son:*Nikolaus
*Son:*Johann
*Daughter:*Gertrud
*Daughter:*Susanna
*Daughter:*Katharina
*Father:*Josef
Merfeld, Mathias *SEE* Merfeld, Peter
Merfeld, Nikolaus; America, 1800-1899 ***5475.1*** *p300*
*Wife:*Anna Maria Wein
*Son:*Josef
*Son:*Peter
*Daughter:*Susanna
Merfeld, Nikolaus *SEE* Merfeld, Mathias
Merfeld, Peter *SEE* Merfeld, Nikolaus
Merfeld, Peter *SEE* Merfeld, Johann
Merfeld, Peter *SEE* Merfeld, Peter
Merfeld, Peter; America, 1872 ***5475.1*** *p139*
*Wife:*Barbara Lenhof
*Daughter:*Barbara
*Son:*Mathias
*Daughter:*Maria
*Son:*Johann
*Son:*Peter
Merfeld, Susanna *SEE* Merfeld, Nikolaus
Merfeld, Susanna *SEE* Merfeld, Mathias
Merfeld, Susanna Heinz *SEE* Merfeld, Mathias
Merfeld, Wilhelm; America, 1868 ***5475.1*** *p297*
Merfie, Margaret; Massachusetts, 1732 ***1642*** *p91*
Mergen, Anna Maria; Brazil, 1874 ***5475.1*** *p372*
Merger, W. F.; Chile, 1852 ***1192.4*** *p52*
With wife
Merges, Johann; Ohio, 1885 ***5475.1*** *p317*
Mergl, Alois; Wisconsin, 1901 ***2853.20*** *p449*
Mergle, Barbara 30; Galveston, TX, 1844 ***3967.10*** *p370*
Mergle, Emilie 5; Galveston, TX, 1844 ***3967.10*** *p370*
Mergle, Jakob 7; Galveston, TX, 1844 ***3967.10*** *p370*
Mergle, Karl 1; Galveston, TX, 1844 ***3967.10*** *p370*
Mergle, Peter 32; Galveston, TX, 1844 ***3967.10*** *p370*
Merherper, H.; Galveston, TX, 1855 ***571.7*** *p18*
Meric, Miss 15; New Orleans, 1848 ***778.6*** *p240*
Merick, Thomas; America, 1681 ***1220.12*** *p546*
Merideth, E. 36; Ontario, 1871 ***1823.21*** *p259*
Meridieth, John; Boston, 1775 ***8529.30*** *p4A*
Meridith, Mary; Annapolis, MD, 1723 ***1220.12*** *p546*
Merion, Amel 40; America, 1847 ***778.6*** *p240*
Meriot, Eleonore 27; Port uncertain, 1841 ***778.6*** *p240*
Meriot, Miss S. 25; America, 1845 ***778.6*** *p240*
Merit, Francis; Portsmouth, NH, 1733 ***9228.50*** *p452*
Merit, Joseph; America, 1659 ***9228.50*** *p452*
Merit, Mary; America, 1743-1744 ***9228.50*** *p452*
Merit, Nicholas; America, n.d. ***9228.50*** *p452*
Merit, Nicholas; Marblehead, MA, 1724 ***9228.50*** *p452*
Merit, Nicholas; Salem, MA, 1613-1635 ***9228.50*** *p423*
Merit, Nicholas, Jr.; Marblehead, MA, 1700-1701 ***9228.50*** *p452*
Merit, Philip; Boston, 1731 ***9228.50*** *p452*
Merit, Samuel; America, 1733-1737 ***9228.50*** *p452*
Merit, Stephen 38; Ontario, 1871 ***1823.21*** *p259*
Meriton, Henry; Philadelphia, 1842 ***471.10*** *p87*
Meriton, Henry; Philadelphia, 1842 ***471.10*** *p88*
Meriweather, William 23; Ontario, 1871 ***1823.17*** *p116*
Merkel, Adam 68 *SEE* Merkel, Johannes
Merkel, Elisabetha Margaretha 7 *SEE* Merkel, Johannes
Merkel, George P.; North Carolina, 1839 ***1088.45*** *p23*
Merkel, Jakob; America, 1854 ***2526.42*** *p183*
Merkel, Johann Michael; America, 1856 ***2526.43*** *p153*
Merkel, Johannes 11 *SEE* Merkel, Johannes
Merkel, Johannes 37; America, 1847 ***2526.42*** *p127*
With wife 35
*Child:*Peter 2
*Father:*Adam 68
*Child:*Johannes 11
*Child:*Elisabetha Margaretha 7
Merkel, John; Ohio, 1809-1852 ***4511.35*** *p34*
Merkel, Leonhard 25; America, 1842 ***2526.42*** *p183*
Merkel, Ludwig; America, 1889 ***2526.43*** *p153*
Merkel, Peter 2 *SEE* Merkel, Johannes
Merker, Chrisitan Frederick; Ohio, 1809-1852 ***4511.35*** *p34*
Merker, Johann Adam; America, 1904 ***2526.43*** *p175*
Merkert, Alexander 26; New York, NY, 1893 ***1883.7*** *p43*
Merkert, Friedr. 29; New York, NY, 1893 ***1883.7*** *p43*
Merkert, Julius 59; New York, NY, 1893 ***1883.7*** *p43*
Merkle, John *SEE* Merkle, Theodore
Merkle, Theodore; Colorado, 1872-1903 ***1029.59*** *p62*
*Father:*John
Merkle, Theodore; Colorado, 1903 ***1029.59*** *p62*
Merkling, Fredk. 29; America, 1847 ***778.6*** *p240*
Merla, James; Virginia, 1719 ***1220.12*** *p546*
Merle, J. 50; America, 1847 ***778.6*** *p240*
Merle, Joseph 37; America, 1843 ***778.6*** *p240*
Merlet, Baptiste 32; America, 1846 ***778.6*** *p240*
Merlet, Rose 28; America, 1846 ***778.6*** *p240*
Merlin, Agathe; Quebec, 1670 ***4514.3*** *p346*
Merlin, Josep 38; Port uncertain, 1845 ***778.6*** *p240*
Merlin, Pierre 24; Quebec, 1662 ***9221.17*** *p490*
Merling, Gaspard 24; America, 1847 ***778.6*** *p240*
Merlot, Joseph 35; America, 1844 ***778.6*** *p240*
Merni, Adele 8; Missouri, 1846 ***778.6*** *p240*
Merni, Agathe 40; Missouri, 1846 ***778.6*** *p240*
Merni, Jerome 38; Missouri, 1846 ***778.6*** *p240*
Merni, Josephine 18; Missouri, 1846 ***778.6*** *p240*
Merni, Julie 9; Missouri, 1846 ***778.6*** *p240*
Merrell, John; Barbados, 1678 ***1220.12*** *p546*
Merrem, Theodore; Galveston, TX, 1855 ***571.7*** *p17*
Merrett, Israel; America, 1726 ***1220.12*** *p546*
Merrick, Griffith; America, 1743 ***1220.12*** *p546*
Merrick, John; Marston's Wharf, 1782 ***8529.30*** *p14*
Merrick, Levi 70; Ontario, 1871 ***1823.21*** *p259*
Merrick, William; America, 1685 ***1220.12*** *p546*
Merricks, John K.; St. Paul, MN, 1874 ***1865.50*** *p97*
Merriday, Mary; America, 1756 ***1220.12*** *p546*
Merriden, John; Barbados, 1682 ***1220.12*** *p546*
Merrifield, William K. 27; Ontario, 1871 ***1823.21*** *p259*
Merrill, Mary Sarah 52; Ontario, 1871 ***1823.17*** *p116*
Merrills, Dudley 83; Ontario, 1871 ***1823.21*** *p259*
Merrils, John 87; Ontario, 1871 ***1823.21*** *p259*
Merriman, Thomas; America, 1750 ***1220.12*** *p546*
Merring, Richard; America, 1740 ***1220.12*** *p546*
Merrio, Charles A.; North Carolina, 1843 ***1088.45*** *p23*
Merriot, E. 25; America, 1844 ***778.6*** *p240*
Merrison, William; America, 1771 ***1220.12*** *p546*
Merrit, Daniel; Ohio, 1810 ***9228.50*** *p432*
With children & grandchildren
Merrit, Francis; Portsmouth, NH, 1733 ***9228.50*** *p452*
Merrit, James, Jr.; America, 1768 ***1220.12*** *p546*
Merrit, John; America, 1758 ***1220.12*** *p546*
Merrit, John C. 47; Ontario, 1871 ***1823.21*** *p259*
Merrit, Richard; America, 1731 ***1220.12*** *p546*
Merritt, Ann; America, 1758 ***1220.12*** *p546*
Merritt, Anne; Annapolis, MD, 1722 ***1220.12*** *p546*
Merritt, Charles; America, 1767 ***1220.12*** *p546*
Merritt, Daniel; Ohio, 1810 ***9228.50*** *p432*
With children & grandchildren
Merritt, Gilbert 35; Ontario, 1871 ***1823.17*** *p116*
Merritt, Isaac; New York, 1776 ***8529.30*** *p4A*
Merritt, Joseph; America, 1659 ***9228.50*** *p452*
Merritt, Leticia 54; Ontario, 1871 ***1823.21*** *p259*
Merritt, Martha 50; Ontario, 1871 ***1823.17*** *p116*
Merritt, Mary; America, 1743-1744 ***9228.50*** *p452*
Merritt, Mary Ann 39; Ontario, 1871 ***1823.21*** *p259*
Merritt, Nicholas; America, n.d. ***9228.50*** *p452*
Merritt, Nicholas; Marblehead, MA, 1724 ***9228.50*** *p452*
Merritt, Nicholas, Jr.; Marblehead, MA, 1700-1701 ***9228.50*** *p452*
Merritt, Philip; Boston, 1731 ***9228.50*** *p452*
Merritt, Rozamirah 59; Ontario, 1871 ***1823.17*** *p117*
Merritt, Samuel; America, 1733-1737 ***9228.50*** *p452*
Merritt, Thomas; Ohio, 1791-1813 ***9228.50*** *p432*
Merritt, William; America, 1760 ***1220.12*** *p546*
Merrotte, Samuel 21; Ontario, 1871 ***1823.17*** *p117*
Merry, Daniel; Marblehead, MA, 1722 ***9228.50*** *p452*
Merry, Henry; America, 1741 ***1220.12*** *p546*
Merry, James; America, 1753 ***1220.12*** *p546*
Merry, James 60; Ontario, 1871 ***1823.17*** *p117*
Merry, John 45; Ontario, 1871 ***1823.21*** *p259*
Merry, Joseph; America, 1659 ***9228.50*** *p452*
Merry, Mary; America, 1743-1744 ***9228.50*** *p452*
Merry, Nicholas; America, n.d. ***9228.50*** *p452*
Merry, Nicholas; Marblehead, MA, 1724 ***9228.50*** *p452*
Merry, Nicholas, Jr.; Marblehead, MA, 1700-1701 ***9228.50*** *p452*
Merry, Philip; Boston, 1731 ***9228.50*** *p452*
Merry, Richard; America, 1752 ***1220.12*** *p546*
Merry, Samuel; America, 1733-1737 ***9228.50*** *p452*
Merryfield, Samuel; America, 1738 ***1220.12*** *p546*
Merryman, John; America, 1743 ***1220.12*** *p546*
Merryman, John; Barbados, 1695 ***1220.12*** *p546*
Merryman, Nicholas; America, 1679 ***1220.12*** *p546*
Mersa, Antoine 26; Louisiana, 1848 ***778.6*** *p240*
Mersaro, Peter; Port uncertain, 1842 ***778.6*** *p240*
Mersch, Angela; America, 1875 ***5475.1*** *p257*
Mersch, Peter; Iowa, 1857 ***5475.1*** *p340*
Merser, Robert; Rappahannock, VA, 1728 ***1220.12*** *p545*
Mersey, William; America, 1769 ***1220.12*** *p546*
Merson, George; Virginia, 1740 ***1220.12*** *p546*
Merten, Katharina *SEE* Merten, Nikolaus
Merten, Mathias *SEE* Merten, Nikolaus
Merten, Mathias; America, 1881 ***5475.1*** *p273*
Merten, Nikolaus *SEE* Merten, Nikolaus
Merten, Nikolaus; America, 1800-1899 ***5475.1*** *p135*
*Wife:*Susanna Hermann
*Son:*Mathias
*Son:*Peter
*Daughter:*Katharina
*Son:*Nikolaus
*Daughter:*Susanna
Merten, Peter *SEE* Merten, Nikolaus
Merten, Susanna *SEE* Merten, Nikolaus
Merten, Susanna Hermann *SEE* Merten, Nikolaus
Mertens, Engel *SEE* Mertens, Sophie Buthe
Mertens, Hans Heinrich Conrad; America, 1865 ***7420.1*** *p233*
Mertens, Johann 37; America, 1843 ***5475.1*** *p305*
Mertens, Sophie; America, 1884 ***7420.1*** *p344*
*Daughter:*Engel
Mertes, A. Maria *SEE* Mertes, Johann
Mertes, Anna Gottfrois *SEE* Mertes, Johann
Mertes, Johann *SEE* Mertes, Johann
Mertes, Johann; America, 1881 ***5475.1*** *p300*
*Wife:*Anna Gottfrois
*Son:*Nikolaus
*Daughter:*A. Maria
*Son:*Johann
Mertes, Mathias; America, 1872 ***5475.1*** *p298*
Mertes, Nikolaus; America, 1870 ***5475.1*** *p353*
Mertes, Nikolaus *SEE* Mertes, Johann
Mertes, Wilhelm; America, 1879 ***5475.1*** *p299*
Mertle, Magdalaine; Virginia, 1700 ***9230.15*** *p80*
Mertz, Adolf 23; America, 1899 ***5475.1*** *p40*
Mertz, Frde 49; New York, NY, 1893 ***1883.7*** *p43*
Mertz, Lische 18; New York, NY, 1893 ***1883.7*** *p43*
Mertz, Philipp Heinrich; America, 1850 ***5475.1*** *p29*
Mertzweiller, A.; Louisiana, 1874-1875 ***4981.45*** *p29*
Mervaux, Mrs. 23; America, 1840 ***778.6*** *p240*
Merveillean, Peter; Barbados, 1682 ***1220.12*** *p546*
Mery, Anne; Quebec, 1669 ***4514.3*** *p346*
Mery, Francoise 19; Quebec, 1636 ***9221.17*** *p61*
Merz, John; Colorado, 1897 ***1029.59*** *p62*
Merziger, Michel; America, 1871 ***5475.1*** *p298*
Merzweiler, Ch...ian 5; Port uncertain, 1840 ***778.6*** *p240*
Merzweiler, Marg. 36; Port uncertain, 1840 ***778.6*** *p240*
Merzweiler, Michel 56; Port uncertain, 1840 ***778.6*** *p240*
Merzweiler, Salome 1; Port uncertain, 1840 ***778.6*** *p240*
Mesange, Marie 18; Quebec, 1661 ***9221.17*** *p462*
Mesch, Miss; America, 1882 ***7420.1*** *p328*
Mesch, Schakel; America, 1882 ***7420.1*** *p328*
Meschin, Jean; Quebec, 1645 ***9221.17*** *p155*
Mesener, M.; New York, 1860 ***358.56*** *p150*
Meserve, Clement; Portsmouth, NH, 1670 ***9228.50*** *p453*
Meserve, George; Boston, 1765 ***9228.50*** *p463*
Meservey, Clement; Portsmouth, NH, 1670 ***9228.50*** *p453*
Mesharvy, Clement; New Hampshire, n.d. ***9228.50*** *p273*
Mesiner, Gaston J.; Illinois, 1856 ***6079.1*** *p9*
Mesinger, William 48; Ontario, 1871 ***1823.17*** *p117*
Mesland, Simon; Quebec, 1655 ***9221.17*** *p327*
Mesley, Frances; Missouri, 1923 ***6212.1*** *p16*
Meslier, Dieudonne 21; Texas, 1848 ***778.6*** *p240*
Meslier, Franklin 22; Mobile, AL, 1844 ***778.6*** *p240*
Meslier, Jean 30; Quebec, 1657 ***9221.17*** *p363*
Mesnard, Louis; Quebec, 1642 ***9221.17*** *p119*
Mesner, Peter; Ohio, 1809-1852 ***4511.35*** *p34*
Mesney, Peter; New York, 1900-1930 ***9228.50*** *p452*
Mesnier, Charles Antoine; Illinois, 1852 ***6079.1*** *p9*
Mesnier, Charles Jean; Illinois, 1852 ***6079.1*** *p10*
Mesnier, Gaston Julien; Illinois, 1852 ***6079.1*** *p10*
Mesnier, Leonard 35; Quebec, 1656 ***9221.17*** *p342*
Mesple, Julian; Louisiana, 1874 ***4981.45*** *p132*
Mesquitta, Jacob Henriques; America, 1753 ***1220.12*** *p546*
Mesritz, V. H.; Louisiana, 1836-1840 ***4981.45*** *p213*
Messeb..., Marc; Quebec, 1646 ***9221.17*** *p167*
Messecont, Robert 25; New Orleans, 1840 ***778.6*** *p240*
Messenger, Elizabeth; America, 1763 ***1220.12*** *p546*
Messenger, James; America, 1775 ***1220.12*** *p546*
Messenger, John; Annapolis, MD, 1729 ***1220.12*** *p547*
Messenger, William; America, 1731 ***1220.12*** *p547*
Messer, Christopher; Illinois, 1858 ***6079.1*** *p10*
Messeray, Jean 29; America, 1745 ***778.6*** *p240*
Messeray, Marianne 24; America, 1745 ***778.6*** *p241*
Messerve, Harriet *SEE* Messerve, Josue
Messerve, Jacob; Utah, 1843 ***9228.50*** *p463*
Messerve, Jeanne Robert *SEE* Messerve, Josue
Messerve, John *SEE* Messerve, Josue
Messerve, Josephus *SEE* Messerve, Josue
Messerve, Joshua *SEE* Messerve, Josue
Messerve, Josue; Utah, 1843 ***9228.50*** *p462*
*Wife:*Jeanne Robert
*Child:*Harriet

*Child:*John
*Child:*Josephus
*Child:*Joshua
Messerve, Thomas; Massachusetts, 1714-1731 ***9228.50*** *p462*
Messerve, William C.; North America, 1972 ***9228.50*** *p38*
Messervy, Charles; West Indies, 1849-1925 ***9228.50*** *p463*
Messervy, Clement; America, 1492-1745 ***9228.50*** *p27*
Messervy, Clement; Maine, n.d. ***9228.50*** *p467*
Messervy, Clement; New Hampshire, n.d. ***9228.50*** *p273*
Messervy, Clement; Portsmouth, NH, 1670 ***9228.50*** *p453*
Messervy, George; Boston, 1760-1776 ***9228.50*** *p463*
Messervy, Harriet *SEE* Messervy, Josue
Messervy, Jacob; Utah, 1843 ***9228.50*** *p463*
Messervy, Jean Clement; Maine, 1615-1715 ***9228.50*** *p453*
Messervy, Jeanne Robert *SEE* Messervy, Josue
Messervy, John *SEE* Messervy, Josue
Messervy, Josephus *SEE* Messervy, Josue
Messervy, Joshua *SEE* Messervy, Josue
Messervy, Josue; Utah, 1843 ***9228.50*** *p462*
*Wife:*Jeanne Robert
*Child:*Josephus
*Child:*John
*Child:*Joshua
*Child:*Harriet
Messervy, Nathaniel; Nova Scotia, 1745 ***9228.50*** *p201*
Messervy, Philip; Marblehead, MA, 1727 ***9228.50*** *p464*
Messervy, William C.; North America, 1972 ***9228.50*** *p38*
Messes, Juan Simon; Puerto Rico, 1811 ***3476.25*** *p113*
Messie, Mr. 50; Texas, 1843 ***778.6*** *p241*
Messier, Jacques 11; Montreal, 1660 ***9221.17*** *p442*
Messier, Jacques 44; Montreal, 1650 ***9221.17*** *p232*
*Nephew:*Michel 9
Messier, Martine 34; Montreal, 1641 ***9221.17*** *p108*
Messier, Michel 9 *SEE* Messier, Jacques
Messing, Georg; Wisconsin, 1884 ***6795.8*** *p100*
Messing, Lorenz; New York, 1860 ***358.56*** *p4*
Messinger, Christian Ludwig; America, 1849 ***5475.1*** *p29*
Messmann, Konrad; New York, 1860 ***358.56*** *p6*
Messmer, Christian; Ohio, 1809-1852 ***4511.35*** *p34*
Messner, Canrad 40; Ontario, 1871 ***1823.17*** *p117*
Messner, Catharina 25; New Orleans, 1847 ***778.6*** *p241*
Messner, Francis; Ohio, 1809-1852 ***4511.35*** *p34*
Messner, Georg 27; New Orleans, 1847 ***778.6*** *p241*
Messner, Maria 49; New Orleans, 1847 ***778.6*** *p241*
Messner, Mathias; America, 1875 ***5475.1*** *p127*
Messner, Stephan 54; New Orleans, 1847 ***778.6*** *p241*
Messner, Theresia 29; New Orleans, 1847 ***778.6*** *p241*
Mestayer, Denis; Quebec, 1649 ***9221.17*** *p216*
*Sister:*Marie
Mestayer, Marie 24 *SEE* Mestayer, Denis
Mestee, John; Charles Town, SC, 1719 ***1220.12*** *p547*
Mestle, J. 37; Port uncertain, 1840 ***778.6*** *p241*
Mestlebrock, Joseph 57; Ontario, 1871 ***1823.17*** *p117*
Mestz, Elisa 3; America, 1745 ***778.6*** *p241*
Mestz, Elisabeth 33; America, 1745 ***778.6*** *p241*
Mestz, Philipp 32; America, 1745 ***778.6*** *p241*
Mestz, Phillip 5; America, 1745 ***778.6*** *p241*
Mesure, Marie; Quebec, 1665 ***4514.3*** *p346*
Metaggart, Allen 62; Michigan, 1880 ***4491.33*** *p15*
Metayer, Mr. 17; America, 1843 ***778.6*** *p241*
Metcalf, Anthony 47; Ontario, 1871 ***1823.21*** *p259*
Metcalf, Chri. 19; Virginia, 1635 ***1183.3*** *p30*
Metcalf, Elizabeth; America, 1753 ***1220.12*** *p547*
Metcalf, Henry 60; Ontario, 1871 ***1823.21*** *p259*
Metcalf, James; America, 1771 ***1220.12*** *p547*
Metcalf, James 33; Ontario, 1871 ***1823.21*** *p259*
Metcalf, Joseph 53; Ontario, 1871 ***1823.21*** *p259*
Metcalf, William; America, 1771 ***1220.12*** *p547*
Metcalfe, George; America, 1737 ***1220.12*** *p547*
Metcalfe, Jabez 47; Ontario, 1871 ***1823.21*** *p259*
Metcalfe, John; America, 1735 ***1220.12*** *p547*
Metcalfe, Michael; America, 1733 ***1220.12*** *p547*
Metcalfe, Simon; America, 1735 ***1220.12*** *p547*
Metcalfe, Thomas; America, 1755 ***1220.12*** *p547*
Metcalfe, Thomas; America, 1769 ***1220.12*** *p547*
Metcalfe, William; America, 1727 ***1220.12*** *p547*
Metcalfe, William 50; Ontario, 1871 ***1823.21*** *p259*
Metch, John; Ohio, 1809-1852 ***4511.35*** *p34*
Meteyi, Etienne; Louisiana, 1836-1841 ***4981.45*** *p209*
Meteyi, J. B. A.; Louisiana, 1836-1841 ***4981.45*** *p209*
Metge, Jean; Louisiana, 1836-1841 ***4981.45*** *p209*
Metgzer, Jacob 28; Ontario, 1871 ***1823.21*** *p259*
Meth, Christine *SEE* Meth, Heinrich
Meth, Heinrich *SEE* Meth, Heinrich
Meth, Heinrich; North Dakota, 1894 ***554.30*** *p26*
*Wife:*Rosiene
*Child:*Heinrich
*Child:*Katharine
*Child:*Pauline
*Child:*Johann
*Child:*Christine
Meth, Johann *SEE* Meth, Heinrich
Meth, Katharine *SEE* Meth, Heinrich
Meth, Luise; North Dakota, 1908 ***554.30*** *p26*
Meth, Pauline *SEE* Meth, Heinrich
Meth, Rosiene *SEE* Meth, Heinrich
Metham, Margaret; America, 1723 ***1220.12*** *p547*
Methe, Guillamin 28; New Orleans, 1848 ***778.6*** *p241*
Metherall, William 33; Ontario, 1871 ***1823.21*** *p259*
Metherill, John 41; Ontario, 1871 ***1823.21*** *p259*
Methier, William; Ohio, 1809-1852 ***4511.35*** *p34*
Meting, Matthew; America, 1720 ***1220.12*** *p544*
Metivier, Jacques; Montreal, 1659 ***9221.17*** *p425*
Metkins, William; America, 1713 ***1220.12*** *p547*
Metkirk, William; America, 1767 ***1220.12*** *p547*
Metru, Marie-Anne; Quebec, 1671 ***4514.3*** *p346*
Metruk, John; New York, 1926 ***1173.1*** *p2*
Metsler, Joseph; Ohio, 1809-1852 ***4511.35*** *p34*
Mett, Frank; Iowa, 1888 ***1211.15*** *p17*
Mettag, Daniel; North Carolina, 1858 ***1088.45*** *p23*
Mette, Frederick; Ohio, 1809-1852 ***4511.35*** *p34*
Mettenheimer, Elisabeth; America, 1869 ***2526.42*** *p154*
Mettenheimer, Peter; America, 1853 ***2526.42*** *p154*
Mettenheimer, Peter; America, 1869 ***2526.42*** *p155*
Metter, Thomasin; Virginia, 1745 ***1220.12*** *p547*
Metter, William; Ohio, 1809-1852 ***4511.35*** *p34*
Metters, John 59; Ontario, 1871 ***1823.21*** *p259*
Metters, Richard; Virginia, 1731 ***1220.12*** *p547*
Metthe, Wilhelmine 29; Valdivia, Chile, 1852 ***1192.4*** *p54*
Metto, Frederick; Ohio, 1809-1852 ***4511.35*** *p34*
Metton, George; America, 1750 ***1220.12*** *p547*
Metton, Jean 22; America, 1846 ***778.6*** *p241*
Metudy, B. 21; America, 1841 ***778.6*** *p241*
Metyard, John; America, 1685 ***1220.12*** *p547*
Metye, P. A. 36; America, 1848 ***778.6*** *p241*
Metz, Anna 1; New York, NY, 1898 ***7951.13*** *p44*
Metz, Anna 7; New York, NY, 1898 ***7951.13*** *p44*
Metz, Anton 5; New York, NY, 1898 ***7951.13*** *p44*
Metz, Aron 3; New York, NY, 1898 ***7951.13*** *p44*
Metz, August; America, 1867 ***7919.3*** *p534*
Metz, Carl Friedrich; America, 1867 ***7919.3*** *p534*
Metz, Carl Heinrich; New York, NY, 1853 ***7420.1*** *p109*
Metz, Elisabeth 37; New York, NY, 1898 ***7951.13*** *p44*
Metz, Elisabeth Christiane; America, 1868 ***7919.3*** *p534*
With 3 children
Metz, Eva Catharina; America, 1867 ***7919.3*** *p534*
Metz, Fritz; Canada, 1853 ***7420.1*** *p109*
Metz, Georg Christian; America, 1868 ***7919.3*** *p534*
Metz, Heidi; New York, 1964-1965 ***9228.50*** *p460*
Metz, Jacob 48; New York, NY, 1898 ***7951.13*** *p44*
Metz, Jacob; Ohio, 1809-1852 ***4511.35*** *p34*
Metz, Johann 12; New York, NY, 1898 ***7951.13*** *p44*
Metz, Katherina 48; New York, NY, 1898 ***7951.13*** *p44*
Metz, Ludwig 7; New York, NY, 1898 ***7951.13*** *p44*
Metz, Ludwig 14; New York, NY, 1898 ***7951.13*** *p44*
Metz, Margaret 17; New York, NY, 1898 ***7951.13*** *p44*
Metz, Matthew 5; New York, NY, 1898 ***7951.13*** *p44*
Metz, Pauline 9; New York, NY, 1898 ***7951.13*** *p44*
Metz, Peter 38; New York, NY, 1898 ***7951.13*** *p44*
Metz, Philip Adam; Ohio, 1809-1852 ***4511.35*** *p34*
Metz, Roselia 3; New York, NY, 1898 ***7951.13*** *p44*
Metz, Roselia 12; New York, NY, 1898 ***7951.13*** *p44*
Metz, Stephan 18; New York, NY, 1898 ***7951.13*** *p44*
Metz, Valentin 23; Port uncertain, 1846 ***778.6*** *p241*
Metzdorf, H. L.; Valdivia, Chile, 1850 ***1192.4*** *p48*
Metzdorf, Pauline; Valdivia, Chile, 1850 ***1192.4*** *p48*
Metze, Friedrich; America, 1866 ***7420.1*** *p245*
Metzer, John G. 32; Ontario, 1871 ***1823.21*** *p259*
Metzgar, Andrew; Ohio, 1809-1852 ***4511.35*** *p34*
Metzgar, Conrad; Ohio, 1809-1852 ***4511.35*** *p34*
Metzgar, John; Ohio, 1809-1852 ***4511.35*** *p34*
Metzgar, Sebastian; Ohio, 1809-1852 ***4511.35*** *p34*
Metzger, Abraham *SEE* Metzger, Johann
Metzger, Anthony 37; Michigan, 1880 ***4491.30*** *p22*
Metzger, Charlotte *SEE* Metzger, Johann
Metzger, Dorothea *SEE* Metzger, Johann
Metzger, Dorothea Kampf *SEE* Metzger, Johann
Metzger, Georg *SEE* Metzger, Johann
Metzger, Jacob; New York, 1859 ***358.56*** *p100*
Metzger, Jacques 28; Mississippi, 1847 ***778.6*** *p241*
Metzger, Jakob *SEE* Metzger, Johann
Metzger, Johann; America, 1861 ***5475.1*** *p542*
*Wife:*Dorothea Kampf
*Daughter:*Charlotte
*Daughter:*Dorothea
*Daughter:*Karoline
*Son:*Jakob
*Son:*Abraham
*Son:*Georg
*Daughter:*Katharina
Metzger, John; Ohio, 1809-1852 ***4511.35*** *p34*
Metzger, Karoline *SEE* Metzger, Johann
Metzger, Katharina *SEE* Metzger, Johann
Metzger, Nicholas; Iowa, 1888 ***1211.15*** *p16*
Metzger, Sebastian; Ohio, 1809-1852 ***4511.35*** *p34*
Metzinger, Francois 6; America, 1846 ***778.6*** *p241*
Metzinger, Veronica 31; America, 1846 ***778.6*** *p241*
Metzler, Jak. Julius; Chicago, 1889 ***5475.1*** *p190*
Metzler, Joseph; Ohio, 1809-1852 ***4511.35*** *p34*
Metzmaer, William; Louisiana, 1874 ***4981.45*** *p133*
Metzner, M.; New York, 1860 ***358.56*** *p150*
Metzo, Richard 49; Ontario, 1871 ***1823.17*** *p117*
Meuchel, Albert 22; Michigan, 1880 ***4491.30*** *p22*
Meuchel, Frank 69; Michigan, 1880 ***4491.30*** *p22*
Meuchel, Gusta 33; Michigan, 1880 ***4491.30*** *p22*
Meuchel, Lewis 31; Michigan, 1880 ***4491.30*** *p22*
Meuchel, Mary 66; Michigan, 1880 ***4491.30*** *p22*
Meudes, Robert 28; America, 1841 ***778.6*** *p241*
Meundlein, George; Ohio, 1809-1852 ***4511.35*** *p34*
Meunier, Antoinette; Quebec, 1665 ***4514.3*** *p347*
Meunier, Estere 22; Missouri, 1847 ***778.6*** *p241*
Meunier, Francoise 24; Quebec, 1658 ***9221.17*** *p384*
Meunier, Joseph 32; Missouri, 1847 ***778.6*** *p241*
Meunier, Marie; Quebec, 1665 ***4514.3*** *p347*
Meunier, Marie; Quebec, 1666 ***4514.3*** *p347*
Meunier, Michel 32; Mississippi, 1847 ***778.6*** *p241*
Meura, Julienne; Wisconsin, 1855 ***1495.20*** *p56*
Meurdefaim, Prosper 36; Missouri, 1846 ***778.6*** *p241*
Meuron, Desiree; Wisconsin, 1854-1858 ***1495.20*** *p66*
Meuron, Desiree; Wisconsin, 1854-1858 ***1495.20*** *p66*
Meuron, Hortense; Wisconsin, 1854-1858 ***1495.20*** *p66*
Meusel, Carl Hen. Christian; America, 1870 ***7420.1*** *p287*
With wife & daughter
Meuser, Peter; Illinois, 1851 ***6079.1*** *p10*
Meusnier-Preville, Jacques; Quebec, 1643 ***9221.17*** *p133*
Meuter, Carl Friedrich Eduard; America, 1849 ***7420.1*** *p66*
Mevert, Widow; America, 1865 ***7420.1*** *p233*
With 3 children
Mevert, Ernst Friedrich Christian; Paraguay, 1885 ***7420.1*** *p348*
Mevert Sisters, . . .; America, 1862 ***7420.1*** *p213*
Mewres, Samuel; America, 1747 ***1220.12*** *p547*
Mey, John; Louisiana, 1841-1844 ***4981.45*** *p211*
Mey, Louis 26; America, 1846 ***778.6*** *p241*
Meyer, . . .; America, 1846 ***7420.1*** *p46*
With family
Meyer, Mr.; America, 1858 ***7420.1*** *p180*
Meyer, Mr.; America, 1871 ***7420.1*** *p291*
Meyer, Mrs.; America, 1856 ***7420.1*** *p150*
With son & 2 daughters
Meyer, Mrs.; America, 1871 ***7420.1*** *p289*
Meyer, Widow; America, 1868 ***7420.1*** *p274*
Meyer, A. 22; America, 1848 ***778.6*** *p241*
Meyer, A. Maria 50; Wisconsin, 1857 ***5475.1*** *p255*
Meyer, Acher. 19; America, 1840 ***778.6*** *p241*
Meyer, Adolf; Port uncertain, 1846 ***7420.1*** *p46*
Meyer, Albert 22; America, 1899 ***5475.1*** *p19*
Meyer, Alexander 11 months; New York, NY, 1893 ***1883.7*** *p44*
Meyer, Amalie 3; New York, NY, 1893 ***1883.7*** *p44*
Meyer, Andreas 19; Port uncertain, 1841 ***778.6*** *p241*
Meyer, Andreas 45; Port uncertain, 1841 ***778.6*** *p241*
Meyer, Andres 4; Halifax, N.S., 1902 ***1860.4*** *p44*
Meyer, Anna 68; America, 1844 ***778.6*** *p241*
Meyer, Anna; Wisconsin, 1899 ***6795.8*** *p74*
Meyer, Anna Maria 23; America, 1875 ***5475.1*** *p331*
Meyer, Anna Marie 55; America, 1888 ***2526.42*** *p116*
Meyer, Anne Sophie Catharine; America, 1857 ***7420.1*** *p167*
Meyer, Anne Sophie Marie; America, 1858 ***7420.1*** *p182*
Meyer, Anthony; Ohio, 1809-1852 ***4511.35*** *p34*
Meyer, Anton Ludwig; Indianapolis, 1865 ***7420.1*** *p233*
With wife 3 sons & 6 daughters
Meyer, Antonio 9; America, 1843 ***778.6*** *p242*
Meyer, Apolenarias; Ohio, 1809-1852 ***4511.35*** *p34*
Meyer, Apolenarius; Ohio, 1809-1852 ***4511.35*** *p34*
Meyer, August; America, 1878 ***5475.1*** *p309*
Meyer, August; America, 1887 ***7420.1*** *p399*
Meyer, August; Wisconsin, 1914 ***6795.8*** *p167*
Meyer, Barbara; Chicago, 1880 ***5475.1*** *p347*
Meyer, Bartholomaus 45; Galveston, TX, 1846 ***3967.10*** *p378*
Meyer, Bernard; Ohio, 1809-1852 ***4511.35*** *p34*
Meyer, Blasius 13; Galveston, TX, 1844 ***3967.10*** *p375*
Meyer, C.; Louisiana, 1874-1875 ***4981.45*** *p30*
Meyer, Carl; America, 1854 ***7420.1*** *p125*
Meyer, Carl; America, 1855 ***7420.1*** *p136*
Meyer, Carl; America, 1857 ***7420.1*** *p167*
With wife son & 2 daughters
Meyer, Carl; America, 1857 ***7420.1*** *p167*
With wife & 2 stepchildren
With son 15
With son 10

Meyer, Carl; Port uncertain, 1854 *7420.1 p125*
Meyer, Carl; Wisconsin, 1891 *6795.8 p79*
Meyer, Carl August; America, 1860 *7420.1 p197*
Meyer, Carl Christian Gottlieb *SEE* Meyer, Johann Christian Carl
Meyer, Carl Ferdinand; America, 1867 *7420.1 p260*
Meyer, Carl Friedrich Wilhelm; America, 1872 *7420.1 p296*
Meyer, Carl Heinrich Conrad; America, 1866 *7420.1 p245*
Meyer, Carl Heinrich Conrad; America, 1866 *7420.1 p251*
Meyer, Carole 35; New York, NY, 1886 *8425.16 p33*
Meyer, Caroline Frieder. Justine Meineke *SEE* Meyer, Johann Heinrich Christian
Meyer, Caroline Henriette *SEE* Meyer, Hermann Conrad Heinrich
Meyer, Caroline Louise Henriette; America, 1868 *7420.1 p274*
Meyer, Caroline Philippine Mohme *SEE* Meyer, Georg Wilhelm August
Meyer, Caroline Sophie Dorothee *SEE* Meyer, Sophie Wilhelmine Friederike
Meyer, Caroline Sophie Louise; America, 1866 *7420.1 p245*
Meyer, Caroline Wilhelmine Henriette; America, 1866 *7420.1 p245*
Meyer, Catha. 11 months; New York, NY, 1893 *1883.7 p44*
Meyer, Catha. 28; New York, NY, 1893 *1883.7 p43*
Meyer, Charles; Louisiana, 1836-1840 *4981.45 p213*
Meyer, Charles; Louisiana, 1874 *4981.45 p133*
Meyer, Charles 22; Louisiana, 1848 *778.6 p242*
Meyer, Charlotte; America, 1857 *7420.1 p197*
Meyer, Christ; Nebraska, 1905 *3004.30 p46*
Meyer, Christ 35; New York, NY, 1886 *8425.16 p33*
Meyer, Christ.; Valdivia, Chile, 1852 *1192.4 p53*
Meyer, Christa 8 months; New York, NY, 1886 *8425.16 p33*
Meyer, Christian; America, 1865 *7420.1 p234*
  With wife son & daughter
Meyer, Christian; Louisiana, 1841-1844 *4981.45 p211*
Meyer, Christian 23; New York, NY, 1886 *8425.16 p33*
Meyer, Christian; Ohio, 1809-1852 *4511.35 p34*
Meyer, Christian; Valdivia, Chile, 1850 *1192.4 p50*
Meyer, Christian August; America, 1868 *7420.1 p274*
  With family
Meyer, Christian Friedrich; Port uncertain, 1854 *7420.1 p125*
Meyer, Christian Friedrich Wilhelm *SEE* Meyer, Georg Wilhelm August
Meyer, Christian Ludwig; America, 1852 *7420.1 p93*
  *Wife:*Sophie Charlotte Mohling
  With son
  *Daughter:*Wilhelmine Charlotte
  *Son:*Johann Friedrich Christian
Meyer, Christian Ludwig; America, 1868 *7420.1 p274*
  With family
Meyer, Christine 25; New York, NY, 1893 *1883.7 p44*
Meyer, Christine Sophie Charlotte *SEE* Meyer, Johann Christian Carl
Meyer, Christoph; America, 1859 *7420.1 p187*
  With wife son & daughter
Meyer, Christopher; America, 1759 *1220.12 p574*
Meyer, Claus; New York, NY, 1875 *6212.1 p16*
Meyer, Conrad; Ohio, 1809-1852 *4511.35 p34*
Meyer, Cord Heinrich; America, 1855 *7420.1 p139*
  With wife & 2 daughters
Meyer, Daniel; Ohio, 1855 *3580.20 p33*
Meyer, Daniel; Ohio, 1855 *6020.12 p21*
Meyer, David 39; America, 1843 *778.6 p242*
Meyer, Diedrich; America, 1866 *7420.1 p246*
Meyer, Dorothea *SEE* Meyer, Lina Pauly
Meyer, Dorothea Charlotte Christine; America, 1867 *7420.1 p260*
Meyer, Dorothee Sophie Cathar. *SEE* Meyer, Johann Heinrich Christian
Meyer, Edouard 29; Port uncertain, 1847 *778.6 p242*
Meyer, Eleonore; America, 1857 *7420.1 p167*
Meyer, Elisabeth Ditten *SEE* Meyer, Ludwig
Meyer, Elisabeth 23; America, 1888 *2526.42 p117*
Meyer, Elisabeth 29; America, 1840 *778.6 p242*
Meyer, Elisabeth 26; New York, NY, 1893 *1883.7 p44*
Meyer, Eliza 15; Port uncertain, 1841 *778.6 p242*
Meyer, Eliza 45; Port uncertain, 1841 *778.6 p242*
Meyer, Emilie Toelke *SEE* Meyer, Friedrich
Meyer, Emilie 6 months; New York, NY, 1886 *8425.16 p33*
Meyer, Engel Dorothee; America, 1856 *7420.1 p150*
  With daughter
Meyer, Engel Maria Eleonore; New York, NY, 1856 *7420.1 p150*
Meyer, Engel Marie; America, 1845 *7420.1 p34*

Meyer, Engel Marie Charlotte; America, 1846 *7420.1 p50*
  *Daughter:*Engel Marie Dorothee
Meyer, Engel Marie Charlotte; America, 1847 *7420.1 p57*
Meyer, Engel Marie Charlotte Mensching; America, 1847 *7420.1 p57*
Meyer, Engel Marie Sophie; America, 1846 *7420.1 p42*
Meyer, Engel Marie Sophie Lichthardt *SEE* Meyer, Johann Heinrich Christian
Meyer, Engel Marie Sophie; America, 1871 *7420.1 p293*
Meyer, Ernst; America, 1865 *7420.1 p234*
  With wife
  With daughter 14
Meyer, Mrs. Ernst; America, 1856 *7420.1 p150*
  With 2 children
Meyer, Ernst Gottlieb; Port uncertain, 1869 *7420.1 p279*
Meyer, Eva Margaretha *SEE* Meyer, Philipp
Meyer, Ferdinand; America, 1877-1899 *5475.1 p435*
Meyer, Franz; America, 1837 *2526.42 p143*
  With child 12
  With child 1
  With child 4
  With child 5
Meyer, Franz 32; Galveston, TX, 1844 *3967.10 p371*
Meyer, Franz 18; Halifax, N.S., 1902 *1860.4 p44*
Meyer, Fred; Nebraska, 1905 *3004.30 p46*
Meyer, Frederich; Louisiana, 1841-1844 *4981.45 p210*
Meyer, Frieda Friederike Sophie *SEE* Meyer, Hermann Conrad Heinrich
Meyer, Friedr. 3; New York, NY, 1886 *8425.16 p33*
Meyer, Friedrich; America, 1859 *7420.1 p187*
Meyer, Friedrich; Dakota, 1859-1918 *554.30 p26*
  *Wife:*Emilie Toelke
Meyer, Friedrich August Sigismund; America, 1883 *7420.1 p338*
Meyer, Friedrich Christian Ludw.; Iowa, 1859 *7420.1 p187*
  *Wife:*Sophie Dorothee Louise Werhahne
Meyer, Friedrich Conrad; America, 1866 *7420.1 p246*
Meyer, Friedrich Ludwig Daniel; America, 1855 *7420.1 p139*
Meyer, Friedrich Wilhelm; America, 1855 *7420.1 p139*
Meyer, Friedrich Wilhelm; America, 1864 *7420.1 p225*
Meyer, Friedrich Wilhelm; America, 1867 *7420.1 p260*
Meyer, Friedrich Wilhelm August; America, 1865 *7420.1 p234*
  With family
Meyer, Georg 3; New York, NY, 1893 *1883.7 p43*
Meyer, Georg 3; New York, NY, 1893 *1883.7 p44*
Meyer, Georg 28; New York, NY, 1893 *1883.7 p44*
Meyer, Georg; Valdivia, Chile, 1851 *1192.4 p51*
Meyer, Georg Wilhelm August; America, 1857 *7420.1 p167*
  *Wife:*Caroline Philippine Mohme
  *Son:*Christian Friedrich Wilhelm
  With 2 children
  *Daughter:*Sophie Caroline Friederike
Meyer, George; Ohio, 1809-1852 *4511.35 p34*
Meyer, Gustav A.; Kansas, 1917-1918 *2094.25 p50*
Meyer, Hans Heinrich Philipp; America, 1871 *7420.1 p291*
Meyer, Hans Heinrich Philipp; Port uncertain, 1854 *7420.1 p125*
Meyer, Heinr. 4; New York, NY, 1893 *1883.7 p44*
Meyer, Heinr. 7; New York, NY, 1893 *1883.7 p44*
Meyer, Heinr. 7; New York, NY, 1893 *1883.7 p44*
Meyer, Heinr. 35; New York, NY, 1893 *1883.7 p43*
Meyer, Heinrich; America, 1854 *7420.1 p125*
Meyer, Heinrich; America, 1857 *7420.1 p168*
Meyer, Heinrich; America, 1860 *7420.1 p197*
Meyer, Heinrich; America, 1874 *7420.1 p274*
Meyer, Heinrich; America, 1883 *5475.1 p49*
Meyer, Heinrich 23; New York, NY, 1864 *8425.62 p196*
Meyer, Heinrich 24; New York, NY, 1893 *1883.7 p44*
Meyer, Heinrich 26; New York, NY, 1882 *5475.1 p16*
Meyer, Heinrich; Valdivia, Chile, 1852 *1192.4 p53*
Meyer, Heinrich; Wisconsin, 1861 *6795.8 p158*
Meyer, Heinrich Christoph; America, 1867 *7420.1 p261*
Meyer, Heinrich Christoph Conrad; America, 1857 *7420.1 p168*
Meyer, Heinrich Conrad Christian; America, 1854 *7420.1 p125*
Meyer, Heinrich Wilhelm; America, 1857 *7420.1 p168*
Meyer, Heinrich Wilhelm; Port uncertain, 1860 *7420.1 p197*
Meyer, Helena 24; Port uncertain, 1847 *778.6 p242*
Meyer, Henry; America, 1685 *1220.12 p574*
Meyer, Henry; Louisiana, 1874 *4981.45 p133*
Meyer, Henry; North Carolina, 1853 *1088.45 p23*
Meyer, Hermann; Ohio, 1840-1897 *8365.35 p17*
Meyer, Hermann Conrad Heinrich *SEE* Meyer, Hermann Conrad Heinrich

Meyer, Hermann Conrad Heinrich; America, 1893 *7420.1 p368*
  *Wife:*Wilhelmine Sophie Louise Kromer
  *Daughter:*Frieda Friederike Sophie
  *Daughter:*Ida Friederike
  *Son:*Hermann Conrad Heinrich
  *Daughter:*Wilhelmine Sophie
  *Daughter:*Caroline Henriette
Meyer, Hermann Louis August; America, 1866 *7420.1 p246*
Meyer, Ida Friederike *SEE* Meyer, Hermann Conrad Heinrich
Meyer, Ignatz; Louisiana, 1874 *4981.45 p133*
Meyer, Ilse Dorothee Charlotte; America, 1846 *7420.1 p46*
Meyer, Isaac 52; Halifax, N.S., 1902 *1860.4 p44*
Meyer, Isador 23; America, 1847 *778.6 p242*
Meyer, J. E. Paul; Colorado, 1886 *1029.59 p62*
Meyer, J. E. Paul; Colorado, 1886 *1029.59 p62*
Meyer, J. E. Paul; Colorado, 1903 *1029.59 p62*
Meyer, J. Jaques 49; New Castle, DE, 1817-1818 *90.20 p153*
Meyer, Ja.ques 32; America, 1846 *778.6 p242*
Meyer, Jacob; Ohio, 1809-1852 *4511.35 p34*
Meyer, Jakob; America, 1840 *5475.1 p51*
  With child 7
Meyer, Jakob 27; Pennsylvania, 1888 *5475.1 p55*
  *Wife:*Sophie Jungfleisch
Meyer, Janet 3; Halifax, N.S., 1902 *1860.4 p44*
Meyer, Jean 26; America, 1846 *778.6 p242*
Meyer, Johan 17; New York, NY, 1847 *9176.15 p50*
Meyer, Johann *SEE* Meyer, Sophie Bresser
Meyer, Johann 23 *SEE* Meyer, Sebastian
Meyer, Johann Christian Carl; America, 1873 *7420.1 p300*
  *Son:*Carl Christian Gottlieb
  *Daughter:*Sophie Dorothea Charlotte
  *Daughter:*Christine Sophie Charlotte
  With wife
Meyer, Johann Conrad; America, 1867 *7420.1 p261*
Meyer, Johann Diether; America, 1753 *2526.42 p143*
  *Child:*Johann Leonhard
  *Wife:*Maria Elisabetha Schnellbacher
Meyer, Johann Friedrich; America, 1845 *7420.1 p38*
Meyer, Johann Friedrich; America, 1852 *7420.1 p94*
Meyer, Johann Friedrich; Port uncertain, 1853 *7420.1 p109*
Meyer, Johann Friedrich Christian *SEE* Meyer, Christian Ludwig
Meyer, Johann Georg 35; Galveston, TX, 1844 *3967.10 p373*
Meyer, Johann Heinrich Christian; America, 1852 *7420.1 p94*
  *Wife:*Engel Marie Sophie Lichthardt
  *Son:*Johann Heinrich Ludwig
Meyer, Johann Heinrich Christian; America, 1855 *7420.1 p139*
Meyer, Johann Heinrich Christian; America, 1855 *7420.1 p139*
  *Wife:*Caroline Frieder. Justine Meineke
  *Daughter:*Wilhelmine Charlotte
  *Daughter:*Dorothee Sophie Cathar.
Meyer, Johann Heinrich Ludwig *SEE* Meyer, Johann Heinrich Christian
Meyer, Johann Heinrich Wilhelm; America, 1862 *7420.1 p213*
Meyer, Johann Leonhard *SEE* Meyer, Johann Diether
Meyer, Johann Philipp; America, 1857 *7420.1 p168*
Meyer, Johann Wilhelm; America, 1847 *7420.1 p55*
  With wife
  With son 6
  With son 3
  With son 17
  With son 12
Meyer, Johanna 44; Halifax, N.S., 1902 *1860.4 p44*
Meyer, Johanne; America, 1864 *7420.1 p225*
Meyer, John 50; America, 1841 *778.6 p242*
Meyer, John; Baltimore, 1886 *6212.1 p15*
Meyer, John; Colorado, 1870 *1029.59 p62*
Meyer, John; Colorado, 1892 *1029.59 p62*
Meyer, John; Louisiana, 1874 *4981.45 p133*
Meyer, John; Nebraska, 1905 *3004.30 p46*
Meyer, John; Ohio, 1840-1897 *8365.35 p17*
Meyer, Johs. 18; New York, NY, 1893 *1883.7 p44*
Meyer, Johs. 33; New York, NY, 1893 *1883.7 p44*
Meyer, Josef; New York, 1882 *5475.1 p35*
Meyer, Joseph 23; America, 1846 *778.6 p242*
Meyer, Joseph 10; Galveston, TX, 1844 *3967.10 p375*
Meyer, Joseph 11; Halifax, N.S., 1902 *1860.4 p44*
Meyer, Joseph 52; New Castle, DE, 1817-1818 *90.20 p153*
Meyer, Karl; Philadelphia, 1858 *5475.1 p403*
Meyer, Katharina 27; America, 1851 *5475.1 p68*

Meyer, Katharina Altmeyer 49 *SEE* Meyer, Sebastian
Meyer, Katharina Elisabeth; America, 1866 ***2526.43*** *p176*
Meyer, Kolon; America, 1848 ***7420.1*** *p61*
With wife 5 sons & 4 daughters
Meyer, Ladd 62; Ontario, 1871 ***1823.17*** *p117*
Meyer, Lewis; Ohio, 1809-1852 ***4511.35*** *p34*
Meyer, Lina; Baltimore, 1899 ***5475.1*** *p20*
*Daughter:*Dorothea
Meyer, Louis 17; Port uncertain, 1841 ***778.6*** *p242*
Meyer, Louisa 6; Port uncertain, 1841 ***778.6*** *p242*
Meyer, Ludwig; America, 1857 ***7420.1*** *p168*
Meyer, Ludwig; America, 1881 ***5475.1*** *p15*
*Wife:*Elisabeth Ditten
Meyer, Ludwig; Valdivia, Chile, 1850 ***1192.4*** *p49*
Meyer, Luise; America, 1872 ***5475.1*** *p14*
Meyer, Manfred 20; New York, NY, 1872 ***7710.1*** *p158*
Meyer, Marg. 40; America, 1841 ***778.6*** *p242*
Meyer, Maria; America, 1880 ***5475.1*** *p54*
Meyer, Maria; Chicago, 1880 ***5475.1*** *p347*
Meyer, Maria 33; New York, NY, 1893 ***1883.7*** *p44*
Meyer, Maria Anna 9; Galveston, TX, 1844 ***3967.10*** *p375*
Meyer, Maria Elisabetha Schnellbacher *SEE* Meyer, Johann Diether
Meyer, Marie 13; Port uncertain, 1841 ***778.6*** *p242*
Meyer, Marie Dorothea; America, 1845 ***7420.1*** *p35*
Meyer, Mary 20; Halifax, N.S., 1902 ***1860.4*** *p44*
Meyer, Mathias; America, 1881 ***5475.1*** *p313*
Meyer, Mathias; America, 1881 ***5475.1*** *p351*
Meyer, Mauri 8; Halifax, N.S., 1902 ***1860.4*** *p44*
Meyer, Meier; Texas, 1894 ***5475.1*** *p425*
Meyer, Meyer 28; America, 1844 ***778.6*** *p242*
Meyer, Michel 19; America, 1846 ***778.6*** *p242*
Meyer, Michel 10; Port uncertain, 1841 ***778.6*** *p242*
Meyer, Minnie; Wisconsin, 1895 ***6795.8*** *p74*
Meyer, Moise 22; Port uncertain, 1847 ***778.6*** *p242*
Meyer, Moritz; America, 1888 ***5475.1*** *p424*
Meyer, Nikolaus; America, 1850 ***2526.42*** *p127*
Meyer, Otto; Iowa, 1931 ***1211.15*** *p17*
Meyer, Patrick; North Carolina, 1839 ***1088.45*** *p23*
Meyer, Pene 20; New York, NY, 1886 ***8425.16*** *p33*
Meyer, Peter 67; America, 1844 ***778.6*** *p242*
Meyer, Philipp; America, 1753 ***2526.42*** *p143*
*Wife:*Susanna Margaretha Old
*Child:*Eva Margaretha
Meyer, Rosina Louise; America, 1868 ***7919.3*** *p527*
Meyer, Rudolph; Louisiana, 1841-1844 ***4981.45*** *p210*
Meyer, Sebastian 25 *SEE* Meyer, Sebastian
Meyer, Sebastian 59; America, 1851 ***5475.1*** *p68*
*Wife:*Katharina Altmeyer 49
*Son:*Johann 23
*Son:*Sebastian 25
Meyer, Siegfried; England, 1883 ***7420.1*** *p338*
Meyer, Sophie; America, 1865 ***2526.43*** *p176*
Meyer, Sophie; America, 1869 ***5475.1*** *p13*
*Son:*Johann
Meyer, Sophie Jungfleisch *SEE* Meyer, Jakob
Meyer, Sophie; Port uncertain, 1853 ***7420.1*** *p109*
Meyer, Sophie Caroline Friederike *SEE* Meyer, Georg Wilhelm August
Meyer, Sophie Charlotte Mohling *SEE* Meyer, Christian Ludwig
Meyer, Sophie Dorothea Charlotte *SEE* Meyer, Johann Christian Carl
Meyer, Sophie Dorothee Louise Werhahne *SEE* Meyer, Friedrich Christian Ludw.
Meyer, Sophie Louise; America, 1871 ***7420.1*** *p291*
Meyer, Sophie Wilhelmine Friederike; America, 1855 ***7420.1*** *p139*
*Daughter:*Caroline Sophie Dorothee
Meyer, Susanna Margaretha Old *SEE* Meyer, Philipp
Meyer, Valatin 31; America, 1844 ***778.6*** *p242*
Meyer, Wilhelm; America, 1856 ***7420.1*** *p150*
Meyer, Wilhelm; America, 1868 ***7420.1*** *p274*
With family
Meyer, Wilhelm; Port uncertain, 1859 ***7420.1*** *p187*
Meyer, Wilhelmine Charlotte *SEE* Meyer, Christian Ludwig
Meyer, Wilhelmine Charlotte *SEE* Meyer, Johann Heinrich Christian
Meyer, Wilhelmine Sophie *SEE* Meyer, Hermann Conrad Heinrich
Meyer, Wilhelmine Sophie Louise Kromer *SEE* Meyer, Hermann Conrad Heinrich
Meyer, Wm.; Nebraska, 1905 ***3004.30*** *p46*
Meyer, Wolfgang 13; Missouri, 1852 ***5475.1*** *p403*
Meyers, Barbara; Philadelphia, 1858 ***8513.31*** *p311*
Meyers, Edward; Louisiana, 1836-1841 ***4981.45*** *p209*
Meyers, Felix 20; Michigan, 1880 ***4491.33*** *p15*
Meyers, Fredrick 48; Ontario, 1871 ***1823.17*** *p117*
Meyers, George; Illinois, 1860 ***6079.1*** *p10*
Meyers, Johann Nichol.; Colorado, 1862-1894 ***1029.59*** *p62*
Meyers, John J.; Louisiana, 1874 ***4981.45*** *p296*
Meyers, Michel; Arkansas, 1880 ***5475.1*** *p310*
Meyers, Moses 25; Ontario, 1871 ***1823.21*** *p259*
Meyersick, William; Illinois, 1859 ***6079.1*** *p10*
Meylin, Francois 30; America, 1843 ***778.6*** *p242*
Meynell, Christopher; America, 1678 ***1220.12*** *p547*
Meynick, Johannes Phillippus; Oregon, 1941 ***9157.47*** *p2*
Meynink, Johannes Phillippus; Oregon, 1941 ***9157.47*** *p2*
Meyrick, John; Marston's Wharf, 1782 ***8529.30*** *p14*
Meyrick, Thomas; America, 1769 ***1220.12*** *p546*
Meysen, Jean 10; New Orleans, 1847 ***778.6*** *p242*
Meysen, Jean 40; New Orleans, 1847 ***778.6*** *p242*
Meysen, Lisa 5; New Orleans, 1847 ***778.6*** *p242*
Meysen, Margarethe 1; New Orleans, 1847 ***778.6*** *p242*
Meysen, Margarethe 36; New Orleans, 1847 ***778.6*** *p242*
Mezere, Francois-Rene; Quebec, 1638 ***9221.17*** *p79*
*Brother:*Rene
Mezere, Rene 24 *SEE* Mezere, Francois-Rene
Mezger, Friedrich; America, 1875 ***179.55*** *p19*
Mezger, Friedrich F.; America, 1875 ***179.55*** *p19*
Mezger, Johann; America, 1875 ***179.55*** *p19*
Mezger, Karoline Regine; America, 1875 ***179.55*** *p19*
Mezger, Wilhelm Gotthilf; America, 1875 ***179.55*** *p19*
Mezieres deLepervanche, Charles-Francois; Quebec, 1715 ***2314.30*** *p169*
Mezieres deLepervanche, Charles-Francois; Quebec, 1715 ***2314.30*** *p191*
Mezieres deMaisonselle, Armand-Francois; Quebec, 1738 ***2314.30*** *p170*
Mezieres deMaisonselle, Armand-Francois; Quebec, 1738 ***2314.30*** *p191*
Mezlor, Jean Baptiste 39; America, 1845 ***778.6*** *p242*
Mezlor, Marg. 17; America, 1845 ***778.6*** *p242*
Mezlor, Pierr 38; America, 1845 ***778.6*** *p242*
Mezlor, Victoria 7; America, 1845 ***778.6*** *p243*
M'Gann, Charles; Toronto, 1844 ***2910.35*** *p114*
M'Gloyne, John; Toronto, 1844 ***2910.35*** *p114*
M'Guile, Duncan; Cape Fear, NC,, 1754 ***1422.10*** *p62*
Mhunial, Angus Ban A.; Quebec, 1786 ***1416.15*** *p5*
Mianeri, Antonio; Louisiana, 1874 ***4981.45*** *p133*
Miars, Edward; California, 1868 ***1131.61*** *p89*
Micaitch, Dominico; Louisiana, 1874 ***4981.45*** *p132*
Miceleau, Jean; Quebec, 1644 ***9221.17*** *p144*
Michael, August; Chile, 1852 ***1192.4*** *p54*
With wife & 3 children
With child 7
With child 21
Michael, Galbes; Texas, 1906 ***3435.45*** *p36*
Michael, Roger 19; America, 1843 ***778.6*** *p243*
Michael, Sarah; America, 1769 ***1220.12*** *p547*
Michaeli, Johann; America, 1870 ***5475.1*** *p272*
*Wife:*Maria Lauer
Michaeli, Katharina; Brazil, 1854 ***5475.1*** *p440*
Michaeli, Maria Lauer *SEE* Michaeli, Johann
Michaelis, Barba. 9 months; New York, NY, 1893 ***1883.7*** *p43*
Michaelis, Barba. 21; New York, NY, 1893 ***1883.7*** *p43*
Michaelis, Catha. 18; New York, NY, 1893 ***1883.7*** *p43*
Michaelis, Catha. 47; New York, NY, 1893 ***1883.7*** *p43*
Michaelis, Georg 7; New York, NY, 1893 ***1883.7*** *p43*
Michaelis, Georg 50; New York, NY, 1893 ***1883.7*** *p43*
Michaelis, Jacob 4; New York, NY, 1893 ***1883.7*** *p43*
Michaelis, Jacob 30; New York, NY, 1893 ***1883.7*** *p43*
Michaelis, Markus; America, 1866 ***7420.1*** *p246*
Michaell, John; Annapolis, MD, 1723 ***1220.12*** *p547*
Michaelsen, J. D.; Valparaiso, Chile, 1850 ***1192.4*** *p50*
Michaely, Barbara *SEE* Michaely, Mathias
Michaely, Barbara Knobe *SEE* Michaely, Mathias
Michaely, Johann; America, 1882 ***5475.1*** *p148*
Michaely, Mathias *SEE* Michaely, Mathias
Michaely, Mathias; America, 1879 ***5475.1*** *p175*
*Wife:*Barbara Knobe
*Daughter:*Barbara
*Son:*Mathias
Michaely, Peter; America, 1800-1899 ***5475.1*** *p148*
Michalek, Stanislaw; Detroit, 1929 ***1640.55*** *p113*
Michall, Joseph; Maine, 1745 ***9228.50*** *p465*
Michaloczy, Geza; Chicago, 1848 ***2853.20*** *p401*
Michals, James 45; Ontario, 1871 ***1823.21*** *p259*
Michalski, John 26; Texas, 1872 ***9980.22*** *p17*
Michalski, Joseph; Texas, 1855-1888 ***9980.22*** *p16*
Michalski, Joseph 72; Texas, 1888 ***9980.22*** *p17*
Michalski, Joseph; Wisconsin, 1926 ***1822.55*** *p10*
Michaud, F. F.; Louisiana, 1836-1841 ***4981.45*** *p209*
Michaud, Madeleine; Quebec, 1660 ***9221.17*** *p436*
Michaud, Marie-Louise; Quebec, 1670 ***4514.3*** *p347*
Micheau, Pierre 38; Quebec, 1656 ***9221.17*** *p342*
Michel, . . .; Quebec, 1638 ***9221.17*** *p79*
Michel, Miss 5; Havana, 1848 ***778.6*** *p243*
Michel, Miss 7; Havana, 1848 ***778.6*** *p243*
Michel, Mr. 23; America, 1843 ***778.6*** *p243*
Michel, Mr. 50; Havana, 1848 ***778.6*** *p243*
Michel, Mrs. 48; Havana, 1848 ***778.6*** *p243*
Michel, Ms. 32; America, 1745 ***778.6*** *p243*
Michel, A. 26; America, 1841 ***778.6*** *p243*
Michel, Abraham; Rio de Janeiro, Brazil, 1891 ***5475.1*** *p216*
Michel, Ada; Lexington, MA, 1926 ***9228.50*** *p465*
Michel, Anna 1 *SEE* Michel, Johann
Michel, Anna 15; America, 1847 ***778.6*** *p243*
Michel, Anna Margarethe; America, 1853 ***8115.12*** *p320*
*Child:*Johann Georg
*Child:*Magdalene
*Child:*Katharine
Michel, Anne; Quebec, 1668 ***4514.3*** *p347*
Michel, Barbara 22; America, 1847 ***778.6*** *p243*
Michel, Barbe Esmard; Quebec, 1648 ***9221.17*** *p200*
*Son:*Etienne
Michel, Bartholemy 19; New Orleans, 1848 ***778.6*** *p243*
Michel, Catherine 5; America, 1846 ***778.6*** *p243*
Michel, Catherine 20; America, 1847 ***778.6*** *p243*
Michel, Christian 12; New Orleans, 1848 ***778.6*** *p243*
Michel, Christine 23; America, 1847 ***778.6*** *p243*
Michel, Etienne 2 *SEE* Michel, Barbe Esmard
Michel, F. 45; America, 1843 ***778.6*** *p243*
Michel, Francois; Quebec, 1831-1857 ***9228.50*** *p465*
Michel, Francoise; Quebec, 1670 ***4514.3*** *p347*
Michel, Frederique 1; America, 1846 ***778.6*** *p243*
Michel, Georg; South Dakota, 1887-1900 ***3366.30*** *p70*
Michel, Georg Andreas; America, n.d. ***8115.12*** *p321*
Michel, Georg Christian; America, n.d. ***8115.12*** *p321*
Michel, Georg Pierre 28; America, 1847 ***778.6*** *p243*
Michel, Georges 2; America, 1846 ***778.6*** *p243*
Michel, Godefroi 38; America, 1846 ***778.6*** *p243*
Michel, Isaak; Brazil, 1878 ***5475.1*** *p216*
Michel, Jacob 47; New Orleans, 1848 ***778.6*** *p243*
Michel, Jacques 28; America, 1843 ***778.6*** *p243*
Michel, Jacques 43; New Orleans, 1843 ***778.6*** *p243*
Michel, Jacquette; Quebec, 1668 ***4514.3*** *p348*
Michel, James 40; Ontario, 1871 ***1823.21*** *p259*
Michel, Jean 17; America, 1847 ***778.6*** *p243*
Michel, Jean; Quebec, 1643 ***9221.17*** *p133*
Michel, Jean Pierre 2; America, 1847 ***778.6*** *p243*
Michel, Johann 11 *SEE* Michel, Johann
Michel, Johann 49; America, 1873 ***5475.1*** *p307*
*Wife:*Susanna Pignon 38
*Son:*Mathias 7
*Daughter:*Anna 1
*Daughter:*Maria 4
*Daughter:*Magdalena 12
*Son:*Johann 11
Michel, Johann Georg *SEE* Michel, Anna Margarethe
Michel, John 25; New Orleans, 1846 ***778.6*** *p243*
Michel, Joseph A.; Texas, 1851 ***3435.45*** *p36*
Michel, Julien; Nova Scotia, 1753 ***3051*** *p112*
Michel, Katharine *SEE* Michel, Anna Margarethe
Michel, Lena 3; America, 1846 ***778.6*** *p243*
Michel, Madeleine 32; America, 1846 ***778.6*** *p243*
Michel, Magdalena 12 *SEE* Michel, Johann
Michel, Magdalene *SEE* Michel, Anna Margarethe
Michel, Maria 4 *SEE* Michel, Johann
Michel, Marie; Quebec, 1667 ***4514.3*** *p348*
Michel, Marie 22; Quebec, 1644 ***9221.17*** *p142*
Michel, Marie 22; Quebec, 1644 ***9221.17*** *p142*
Michel, Mary 28; Ontario, 1871 ***1823.21*** *p259*
Michel, Mathias 7 *SEE* Michel, Johann
Michel, Mathias; Wisconsin, 1880 ***5475.1*** *p344*
Michel, Nicola 17; America, 1847 ***778.6*** *p243*
Michel, Nikolaus 22; America, 1858 ***5475.1*** *p501*
Michel, Philipp 16; New Orleans, 1848 ***778.6*** *p243*
Michel, Pierre 36; New Orleans, 1842 ***778.6*** *p243*
Michel, Pierre; Quebec, 1659 ***9221.17*** *p414*
Michel, Susanna Pignon 38 *SEE* Michel, Johann
Michel, Thomas; Quebec, 1658 ***9221.17*** *p384*
Michel, Wilhelm Salomon; Chicago, 1892 ***5475.1*** *p217*
Michel deVillebois deLa Rouvilliere, Honore; Quebec, 1737 ***2314.30*** *p171*
Micheles, Casper; Indiana, 1866-1868 ***9076.20*** *p66*
Michelet, Marie; Quebec, 1647 ***9221.17*** *p176*
Michelet, Pierre; Quebec, 1649 ***9221.17*** *p216*
Michel Family ; Salem, MA, 1693 ***9228.50*** *p465*
Michelfelder, Just; America, 1867 ***7919.3*** *p529*
Michell, Albin 30; America, 1843 ***778.6*** *p244*
Michell, Bernard; Louisiana, 1874-1875 ***4981.45*** *p29*
Michell, Hannah; Massachusetts, 1772 ***1642*** *p87*
Michell, Richard; New Jersey, 1665 ***9228.50*** *p465*
Michell, Richard; Virginia, 1665 ***9228.50*** *p53*
Michell, Scipio; America, 1773 ***1220.12*** *p556*
Michell, William; Barbados, 1668 ***1220.12*** *p556*
Michels, Anton 29; America, 1872 ***5475.1*** *p308*
Michels, Elisabeth 29; America, 1854 ***5475.1*** *p236*
Michels, Helena; America, 1872 ***6442.17*** *p65*
Michels, Jakob; America, 1872 ***6442.17*** *p65*
Michels, Johann Nikolaus 26; New York, 1854 ***5475.1*** *p236*
Michels, Josef; America, 1876 ***5475.1*** *p309*

Michels, Julius; America, 1883 ***5475.1*** *p381*
Michels, Mathias; America, 1857 ***5475.1*** *p305*
Michels, Peter *SEE* Michels, Peter
Michels, Peter 62; America, 1867 ***5475.1*** *p297*
*Son:*Peter
Michels, Regina; America, 1881 ***5475.1*** *p334*
Michelsen, Michel; Iowa, 1916 ***1211.15*** *p17*
Michelsohn, Andr. 58; New York, NY, 1885 ***1883.7*** *p46*
Michelsohn, Emanuel 16; New York, NY, 1885 ***1883.7*** *p46*
Michelsohn, Friedrich 19; New York, NY, 1876 ***6954.7*** *p39*
Michelsohn, Marie 56; New York, NY, 1885 ***1883.7*** *p46*
Michelsohn, Pauline 15; New York, NY, 1885 ***1883.7*** *p46*
Michely, A. Maria; America, 1881 ***5475.1*** *p315*
Michely, A. Maria Bernardy 27 *SEE* Michely, Michel
Michely, Katharina 2 *SEE* Michely, Michel
Michely, Margarethe 2 *SEE* Michely, Michel
Michely, Michel 30; America, 1863 ***5475.1*** *p347*
*Wife:*A. Maria Bernardy 27
*Daughter:*Katharina 2 months
*Daughter:*Margarethe 2
Michener, John; Maryland, 1722 ***1220.12*** *p547*
Michenfelder, Ant.; New York, 1860 ***358.56*** *p4*
Michie, Caroline 50; Ontario, 1871 ***1823.21*** *p259*
Michill, George; America, 1685 ***1220.12*** *p555*
Michler, Anna Margaretha; New England, 1866 ***170.15*** *p37*
With family
Michler, Charles; Missouri, 1885 ***3276.1*** *p2*
Michler, Johannes; New England, 1866 ***170.15*** *p37*
With family
Michler, Wolfgang Ludwig; New England, 1866 ***170.15*** *p37*
With family
Michlossky, Lewis; California, 1868 ***1131.61*** *p89*
Michna, Vaclav; Texas, 1860 ***2853.20*** *p74*
Michniewicz, Joseph; Detroit, 1929-1930 ***6214.5*** *p69*
Michotte, Eugene 4; New York, NY, 1856 ***1766.1*** *p45*
Michotte, Jean B. 2; New York, NY, 1856 ***1766.1*** *p45*
Michotte, Jean G. 6; New York, NY, 1856 ***1766.1*** *p45*
Micka, Ferdinand *SEE* Micka, Johann
Micka, Heinrich *SEE* Micka, Johann
Micka, Jakob; America, 1898 ***5475.1*** *p46*
Micka, Johann *SEE* Micka, Johann
Micka, Johann; America, 1881 ***5475.1*** *p46*
*Wife:*Katharina Port
*Son:*Valentin
*Son:*Johann
*Son:*Richard
*Daughter:*Katharina
*Son:*Ferdinand
*Daughter:*Maria
*Daughter:*Karoline
*Son:*Nikolaus
*Son:*Heinrich
Micka, Karoline *SEE* Micka, Johann
Micka, Katharina *SEE* Micka, Johann
Micka, Katharina Port *SEE* Micka, Johann
Micka, Maria *SEE* Micka, Johann
Micka, Nikolaus *SEE* Micka, Johann
Micka, Richard *SEE* Micka, Johann
Micka, Valentin *SEE* Micka, Johann
Mickelsohn, Georg 25; New York, NY, 1893 ***1883.7*** *p43*
Mickelson, Andrew B.; Washington, 1888 ***2770.40*** *p26*
Mickelson, Mack; Iowa, 1898 ***1211.15*** *p17*
Micker, Garrett; Massachusetts, 1660 ***1642*** *p110*
Mickey, Elizabeth; America, 1740 ***1220.12*** *p547*
Mickleborough, Thomas 36; Ontario, 1871 ***1823.21*** *p259*
Mickleburgh, Daniel; America, 1721 ***1220.12*** *p547*
Mickleburgh, John, Jr.; America, 1754 ***1220.12*** *p547*
Mickley, Adolph; Iowa, 1903 ***1211.15*** *p17*
Micolo, J. V.; Louisiana, 1874 ***4981.45*** *p296*
Middelmas, Ralph 43; Ontario, 1871 ***1823.21*** *p259*
Middlebrook, Henry; Indiana, 1893 ***9076.20*** *p73*
Middleditch, Eleanor; America, 1761 ***1220.12*** *p547*
Middlemass, William; Virginia, 1723 ***1220.12*** *p547*
Middlemis, Robert 66; Ontario, 1871 ***1823.21*** *p260*
Middlemiss, William 74; Ontario, 1871 ***1823.21*** *p260*
Middlestadt, Johan Frederick; Wisconsin, 1869 ***6795.8*** *p127*
Middleton, Albert; Illinois, 1834-1900 ***6020.5*** *p132*
Middleton, Alex 21; St. Johns, N.F., 1811 ***1053.20*** *p20*
Middleton, Alexander; America, 1772 ***1220.12*** *p547*
Middleton, Ann; America, 1764 ***1220.12*** *p547*
Middleton, Bridget; New Orleans, 1851 ***7242.30*** *p149*
Middleton, Charles; America, 1685 ***1220.12*** *p547*
Middleton, Charles; America, 1742 ***1220.12*** *p547*
Middleton, David; America, 1693 ***1220.12*** *p547*
Middleton, Edward; North Carolina, 1846 ***1088.45*** *p23*
Middleton, Elizabeth; America, 1770 ***1220.12*** *p547*
Middleton, F.; Louisiana, 1874 ***4981.45*** *p296*
Middleton, Frances; America, 1736 ***1220.12*** *p548*
Middleton, George 45; Ontario, 1871 ***1823.21*** *p260*
Middleton, Gerrard; Barbados or Jamaica, 1684 ***1220.12*** *p548*
Middleton, James 43; Ontario, 1871 ***1823.17*** *p117*
Middleton, John; America, 1724 ***1220.12*** *p548*
Middleton, John; America, 1772 ***1220.12*** *p548*
Middleton, John 48; Ontario, 1871 ***1823.21*** *p260*
Middleton, Mary; America, 1737 ***1220.12*** *p548*
Middleton, Mary; America, 1762 ***1220.12*** *p548*
Middleton, Mary; Barbados or Jamaica, 1697 ***1220.12*** *p548*
Middleton, Mary; Maryland, 1737 ***1220.12*** *p548*
Middleton, Michael; America, 1750 ***1220.12*** *p548*
Middleton, Ralph; America, 1685 ***1220.12*** *p548*
Middleton, Richard; America, 1724 ***1220.12*** *p548*
Middleton, Robert; America, 1702 ***1220.12*** *p548*
Middleton, Robert; America, 1732 ***1220.12*** *p548*
Middleton, Robert; Barbados, 1662 ***1220.12*** *p548*
Middleton, Robert; Virginia, 1741 ***1220.12*** *p548*
Middleton, Thomas; America, 1685 ***1220.12*** *p548*
Middleton, Thomas; America, 1748 ***1220.12*** *p548*
Middleton, Thomas; Annapolis, MD, 1732 ***1220.12*** *p548*
Middleton, Thomas; Virginia, 1618 ***1220.12*** *p548*
Middleton, William; America, 1680 ***1220.12*** *p548*
Middleton, William; America, 1687 ***1220.12*** *p548*
Middleton, William; America, 1753 ***1220.12*** *p548*
Middleton, William; America, 1773 ***1220.12*** *p548*
Middleton, William 47; Ontario, 1871 ***1823.21*** *p260*
Middleton, William; Virginia, 1730 ***1220.12*** *p548*
Middlewood, Mary; America, 1758 ***1220.12*** *p548*
Middlewood, Robert; Philadelphia, 1778 ***8529.30*** *p3*
Midet, Jean 27; Quebec, 1655 ***9221.17*** *p327*
Midgley, Matthew; America, 1728 ***1220.12*** *p548*
Midleton, Thomas; America, 1756 ***1220.12*** *p548*
Midwinter, John, Jr.; America, 1750 ***1220.12*** *p548*
Mieczkowski, Boleslaw; Detroit, 1929 ***1640.55*** *p113*
Miede, Sophie; Port uncertain, 1853 ***7420.1*** *p109*
Miehan, Edward; Ohio, 1836 ***3580.20*** *p33*
Miehan, Edward; Ohio, 1836 ***6020.12*** *p21*
Miekels, P.; New York, 1860 ***358.56*** *p150*
Mielcke, Adam; Chile, 1852 ***1192.4*** *p52*
Mielecki, Carl Alexander Stanislaus von; Canada, 1883 ***7420.1*** *p338*
Mielecki, Carl Alexander Stanislaus von; Port uncertain, 1883 ***7420.1*** *p338*
Mielewczyk, Augusta; Wisconsin, 1881 ***6795.8*** *p60*
Mielke, Friedrich; Wisconsin, 1904 ***6795.8*** *p209*
Mielke, Ida Hulda Adeline; Wisconsin, 1894 ***6795.8*** *p30*
Mielke, Pauline; Wisconsin, 1903 ***6795.8*** *p147*
Mienser, Laurent 26; New Orleans, 1845 ***778.6*** *p244*
Mier, Conrad; Ohio, 1809-1852 ***4511.35*** *p34*
Mier, Joseph; North Carolina, 1792-1862 ***1088.45*** *p23*
Miera, Mary; Wisconsin, 1888 ***6795.8*** *p60*
Mieroslawski, John; Detroit, 1929-1930 ***6214.5*** *p71*
Miers, Emanuel; America, 1774 ***1220.12*** *p574*
Miers, Sarah; Annapolis, MD, 1725 ***1220.12*** *p574*
Mieske, Wilhelmine; Wisconsin, 1885 ***6795.8*** *p140*
Mieszczak, Vincenty; Detroit, 1930 ***1640.60*** *p81*
Mieszkowski, Helen; Detroit, 1930 ***1640.60*** *p82*
Mieszkowski, Stanley; Detroit, 1930 ***1640.60*** *p82*
Miettinen, Elizabeth 35; Minnesota, 1923 ***2769.54*** *p1381*
Miettinen, John 38; Minnesota, 1923 ***2769.54*** *p1381*
Mietzner, Carl August; Wisconsin, 1891 ***6795.8*** *p38*
Mietzner, Wilhelmine; Wisconsin, 1896 ***6795.8*** *p134*
Mifflin, Caroline; Massachusetts, 1903 ***9228.50*** *p336*
Migeon, Henry; New York, NY, 1828 ***3274.55*** *p68*
Migeon deBranssat, Jean-Baptiste; Quebec, 1665 ***2314.30*** *p172*
Mignault, Catherine; Quebec, 1673 ***4514.3*** *p348*
Mignaux, Jean 16; Quebec, 1643 ***9221.17*** *p133*
Migneron, Jean-Baptiste 21; Quebec, 1657 ***9221.17*** *p364*
Migneron, Laurent 22; Quebec, 1661 ***9221.17*** *p463*
Mignolet, Gillette; Quebec, 1671 ***4514.3*** *p348*
Mignon, Antoinette 25; Quebec, 1657 ***9221.17*** *p362*
Mignon, Henry Victor 21; America, 1848 ***778.6*** *p244*
Mignon, Jean-Baptiste 21; Quebec, 1657 ***9221.17*** *p364*
Mignon, Jeanne 17; Quebec, 1652 ***9221.17*** *p263*
Mignonneau, Simon 40; Quebec, 1657 ***9221.17*** *p364*
Migny, George Camille 35; Colorado, 1926 ***1029.59*** *p62*
Miguot, Joseph; Illinois, 1856 ***6079.1*** *p10*
Mihan, Mark; New York, 1832 ***3274.56*** *p72*
Mihill, Edward 62; Ontario, 1871 ***1823.21*** *p260*
Mihony, John; Ohio, 1840-1897 ***8365.35*** *p17*
Mika, Frantisek; Milwaukee, 1854 ***2853.20*** *p316*
Mika, Maria 20; New York, NY, 1904 ***8355.1*** *p15*
Mikes, Vaclav; Iowa, 1854 ***2853.20*** *p230*
Mikes, Vaclav; North Dakota, 1872 ***2853.20*** *p251*
Mikeschak, Stanislaus; Wisconsin, 1884 ***6795.8*** *p169*
Mikeska, Petr; Texas, 1854 ***2853.20*** *p78*
Mikkelsen, Paul; Iowa, 1913 ***1211.15*** *p17*
Mikkonen, John 40; Minnesota, 1925 ***2769.54*** *p1384*
Mikkonen, Mary 37; Minnesota, 1925 ***2769.54*** *p1384*
Miklaszek, Tadeusz; Detroit, 1929-1930 ***6214.5*** *p61*
Mikolait, Gottlieb 20; New York, NY, 1893 ***1883.7*** *p37*
Mikolasek, Vaclav; South Dakota, 1904 ***2853.20*** *p248*
Mikota, Frantisek L.; Iowa, 1867 ***2853.20*** *p231*
Miksovsky, Josef; Kansas, 1899-1910 ***2853.20*** *p206*
Mikula, Josef; Texas, 1856 ***2853.20*** *p64*
Mikula, Karel; St. Paul, MN, 1887 ***2853.20*** *p282*
Mikulecky, Josef; Wisconsin, 1852 ***2853.20*** *p303*
Mikulecky, Josef; Wisconsin, 1855 ***2853.20*** *p304*
Mikulenka, Josef; Texas, 1850-1900 ***2853.20*** *p76*
Mikus, Joseph; Louisiana, 1836-1841 ***4981.45*** *p209*
Mikyska, Frantisek; Minnesota, 1858-1860 ***2853.20*** *p260*
Miladin, Walter George; Illinois, 1930 ***121.35*** *p100*
Milan, Edward 49; Minnesota, 1923 ***2769.54*** *p1378*
Milan, Edward 51; Minnesota, 1925 ***2769.54*** *p1378*
Milan, Patrick 51; Ontario, 1871 ***1823.21*** *p260*
Milani, G. 18; Port uncertain, 1840 ***778.6*** *p244*
Milbank, John; America, 1770 ***1220.12*** *p549*
Milbey, Agness 21; Ontario, 1871 ***1823.21*** *p260*
Milborn, Andrew 7; North Carolina, 1774 ***1422.10*** *p56*
Milborn, Christopher 2; North Carolina, 1774 ***1422.10*** *p56*
Milbourne, Catherine; Annapolis, MD, 1719 ***1220.12*** *p548*
Milbourne, John; America, 1749 ***1220.12*** *p548*
Milbourne, Thomas; America, 1750 ***1220.12*** *p548*
Milbrandt, August Ferdinand; Wisconsin, 1900 ***6795.8*** *p148*
Milbrath, Emelina Paulina; Wisconsin, 1895 ***6795.8*** *p34*
Milburn, Charles 57; Ontario, 1871 ***1823.21*** *p260*
Milburn, Elizabeth; America, 1747 ***1220.12*** *p548*
Milburn, Lenard 52; Ontario, 1871 ***1823.21*** *p260*
Milburn, Wm. 39; Ontario, 1871 ***1823.17*** *p117*
Milburne, Robert; America, 1727 ***1220.12*** *p548*
Milburne, Thomas; America, 1765 ***1220.12*** *p548*
Milcham, William; Maryland, 1720 ***1220.12*** *p548*
Milde, Anna 59; America, 1880 ***5475.1*** *p227*
*Son:*Wilhelm
With 2 grandchildren
*Daughter:*Maria
*Son:*Heinrich
Mildenberger, Johann Peter 23; America, 1857 ***5475.1*** *p540*
Mildenberger, Peter Jakob 22; America, 1857 ***5475.1*** *p551*
Mildenberger, Wilhelm 24; America, 1857 ***5475.1*** *p551*
Mildred, Hannah; America, 1749 ***1220.12*** *p548*
Mileist, Thomas; America, 1744 ***1220.12*** *p548*
Miles, Briant; America, 1774 ***1220.12*** *p548*
Miles, Charles; America, 1740 ***1220.12*** *p548*
Miles, Charles; Maryland or Virginia, 1731 ***1220.12*** *p548*
Miles, Christian; America, 1763 ***1220.12*** *p548*
Miles, Elizabeth; America, 1761 ***1220.12*** *p548*
Miles, Elizabeth; America, 1769 ***1220.12*** *p548*
Miles, George; America, 1775 ***1220.12*** *p548*
Miles, George; Maryland, 1672 ***1236.25*** *p47*
Miles, Henry 28; Ontario, 1871 ***1823.21*** *p260*
Miles, James; America, 1756 ***1220.12*** *p548*
Miles, James; America, 1763 ***1220.12*** *p549*
Miles, John; America, 1739 ***1220.12*** *p549*
Miles, John; America, 1753 ***1220.12*** *p549*
Miles, John; America, 1758 ***1220.12*** *p549*
Miles, John; America, 1772 ***1220.12*** *p549*
Miles, John; Annapolis, MD, 1725 ***1220.12*** *p549*
Miles, John; Annapolis, MD, 1726 ***1220.12*** *p549*
Miles, John; Barbados or Jamaica, 1688 ***1220.12*** *p549*
Miles, Mary; America, 1743 ***1220.12*** *p549*
Miles, Mary; America, 1751 ***1220.12*** *p549*
Miles, Mary; America, 1767 ***1220.12*** *p549*
Miles, Norah Helen; Oregon, 1941 ***9157.47*** *p2*
Miles, Peter; America, 1767 ***1220.12*** *p549*
Miles, Robert; Virginia, 1760 ***1220.12*** *p549*
Miles, Thomas; America, 1719 ***1220.12*** *p549*
Miles, Thomas; America, 1736 ***1220.12*** *p549*
Miles, Thomas; America, 1738 ***1220.12*** *p549*
Miles, Thomas; America, 1762 ***1220.12*** *p549*
Miles, Thomas; Annapolis, MD, 1720 ***1220.12*** *p549*
Miles, Thomas; Marston's Wharf, 1782 ***8529.30*** *p14*
Miles, W.E. 17; Quebec, 1870 ***8364.32*** *p25*
Miles, William; America, 1750 ***1220.12*** *p549*
Miles, William; Virginia, 1729 ***1220.12*** *p549*
Miley, Patrick; Ohio, 1856 ***3580.20*** *p33*
Mileyl, Patrick; Ohio, 1856 ***6020.12*** *p21*
Milford, David; Annapolis, MD, 1729 ***1220.12*** *p549*
Milford, John; Virginia, 1750 ***1220.12*** *p549*
Milham, William 46; Michigan, 1880 ***4491.39*** *p21*
Milhomme, Pierre 27; Quebec, 1658 ***9221.17*** *p385*
Miliet, Jean Pierre 23; New Orleans, 1845 ***778.6*** *p244*
Milinowitz, Jan 31; New York, NY, 1920 ***930.50*** *p49*
Miliom, Stephen; America, 1740 ***1220.12*** *p549*
Milius, Dorothea; America, 1856 ***7420.1*** *p151*

Milius, Johann Heinrich August; America, 1881 7420.1 p323
*Brother:*Johann Heinrich Friedrich
Milius, Johann Heinrich Christoph; America, 1886 7420.1 p351
Milius, Johann Heinrich Friedrich *SEE* Milius, Johann Heinrich August
Milkas, Jacques 24; New Orleans, 1848 778.6 p244
Milke, Christiane; America, 1868 7919.3 p533
With 4 children
Milke, George; Wisconsin, 1883 6795.8 p204
Milke, Wilhelm; Wisconsin, 1881 6795.8 p204
Milkins, William; Potomac, 1731 1220.12 p549
Milksop, Thomas; Charles Town, SC, 1719 1220.12 p549
Milkus, Maciej 21; New York, NY, 1911 6533.11 p10
Mill, Catha. 30; New York, NY, 1893 1883.7 p43
Mill, Christ 35; New York, NY, 1893 1883.7 p43
Mill, Heinr. 3; New York, NY, 1893 1883.7 p43
Mill, John A. 39; Ontario, 1871 1823.21 p260
Mill, John William 45; Ontario, 1871 1823.17 p117
Mill, Thomas; Virginia, 1740 1220.12 p549
Mill, William 54; Ontario, 1871 1823.21 p260
Millams, George; America, 1766 1220.12 p549
Millan, Mary 19; Ontario, 1871 1823.21 p260
Millan, Robert 25; Ontario, 1871 1823.21 p260
Millar, James 40; Ontario, 1871 1823.21 p260
Millar, Robert 43; Ontario, 1871 1823.21 p260
Millar, Thomas 68; Ontario, 1871 1823.21 p260
Millard, Anna 37; Michigan, 1880 4491.36 p15
Millard, Frank A. 17; Michigan, 1880 4491.36 p15
Millard, George 33; Michigan, 1880 4491.36 p15
Millard, Henry; America, 1747 1220.12 p549
Millard, John; America, 1760 1220.12 p549
Millard, John; America, 1772 1220.12 p549
Millard, John; Barbados, 1683 1220.12 p549
Millard, Joseph; America, 1764 1220.12 p549
Millard, Peter; America, 1697 1220.12 p549
Millard, Robert; America, 1685 1220.12 p549
Millard, Thomas; America, 1764 1220.12 p549
Millard, Thomas; America, 1771 1220.12 p549
Millard, Thomas; Ontario, 1787 1276.15 p230
Millard, William; America, 1752 1220.12 p549
Millard, William; America, 1770 1220.12 p549
Millard, William; Virginia, 1756 1220.12 p549
Millban, Thomas; America, 1774 1220.12 p549
Mille, Cord; America, 1867 7919.3 p528
Millea, Samuel; America, 1757 1220.12 p551
Millen, Ann McSwiggin *SEE* Millen, James
Millen, James; Philadelphia, 1851 8513.31 p415
*Wife:*Ann McSwiggin
Millen, William 55; Ontario, 1871 1823.21 p260
Miller, Mr. 27; America, 1745 778.6 p244
Miller, Mr. 36; America, 1846 778.6 p244
Miller, Abel; New York, 1828 3274.55 p70
Miller, Adam; Ohio, 1809-1852 4511.35 p34
Miller, Alexander; North Carolina, 1831 1088.45 p23
Miller, Andrew; America, 1761 1220.12 p549
Miller, Andrew 1; America, 1846 778.6 p244
Miller, Andrew; Louisiana, 1874 4981.45 p133
Miller, Andrew; Ohio, 1809-1852 4511.35 p34
Miller, Ann; America, 1757 1220.12 p549
Miller, Ann; Barbados or Jamaica, 1674 1220.12 p549
Miller, Ann; Maryland, 1721 1220.12 p549
Miller, Anna Maria; Rappahannock, VA, 1741 1220.12 p550
Miller, Anna Maria; Venezuela, 1843 3899.5 p544
Miller, Antoine; Missouri, 1891 3276.1 p2
Miller, Anton Pearson; New York, 1902 1766.20 p16
Miller, August; Pennsylvania, 1855 8513.31 p416
*Wife:*Bertha E. Buttner
Miller, August Wilhelm; New York, 1841 9722.10 p113
Miller, Axel; Iowa, 1891 1211.15 p16
Miller, Benjaman 59; Ontario, 1871 1823.21 p260
Miller, Benjamin, Jr.; America, 1767 1220.12 p550
Miller, Bertha E. Buttner *SEE* Miller, August
Miller, Bertrand 4; America, 1846 778.6 p244
Miller, Carl; Galveston, TX, 1855 571.7 p17
Miller, Casper; Ohio, 1809-1852 4511.35 p34
Miller, Cath. 72; America, 1840 778.6 p244
Miller, Catherine 5; New York, NY, 1892 8425.16 p34
Miller, Catherine 37; New York, NY, 1892 8425.16 p34
Miller, Catherine 35; Ontario, 1871 1823.21 p260
Miller, Charles; America, 1767 1220.12 p550
Miller, Charles; North Carolina, 1844 1088.45 p23
Miller, Charles; Ohio, 1809-1852 4511.35 p34
Miller, Charles 28; Ontario, 1871 1823.21 p260
Miller, Christian; Ohio, 1809-1852 4511.35 p34
Miller, Christine 11 months; New York, NY, 1892 8425.16 p34
Miller, Christopher; America, 1745 1220.12 p550
Miller, Christopher; North Carolina, 1710 3629.40 p5
Miller, Conrad; Ohio, 1809-1852 4511.35 p34
Miller, Daniel; America, 1746 1220.12 p550
Miller, Daniel; America, 1763 1220.12 p550
Miller, Daniel; America, 1771 1220.12 p550
Miller, Daniel; Ohio, 1809-1852 4511.35 p34
Miller, Daniel; Wisconsin, 1861 6795.8 p163
Miller, Danl. 10; Quebec, 1870 8364.32 p25
Miller, David; America, 1758 1220.12 p550
Miller, David; America, 1759 1220.12 p550
Miller, David; America, 1768 1220.12 p550
Miller, David 22; Ontario, 1871 1823.21 p260
Miller, David 50; Ontario, 1871 1823.17 p117
Miller, David 50; Ontario, 1871 1823.21 p260
Miller, David 55; Ontario, 1871 1823.21 p260
Miller, David 57; Ontario, 1871 1823.21 p260
Miller, Dorothy; America, 1721 1220.12 p550
Miller, Ebenezer; Colorado, 1880 1029.59 p63
Miller, Edward; America, 1772 1220.12 p550
Miller, Edward; America, 1774 1220.12 p550
Miller, Edward 52; Ontario, 1871 1823.21 p260
Miller, Edwin 35; Ontario, 1871 1823.21 p260
Miller, Elisabeth 3; New York, NY, 1892 8425.16 p34
Miller, Elizabeth; Barbados, 1700 1220.12 p550
Miller, Elizabeth; Maryland, 1744 1220.12 p550
Miller, Emil Friedrich; Wisconsin, 1892 6795.8 p169
Miller, Florentine; Ohio, 1809-1852 4511.35 p34
Miller, Forentine; Ohio, 1809-1852 4511.35 p35
Miller, Francis; Ohio, 1809-1852 4511.35 p35
Miller, Francois 21; America, 1840 778.6 p244
Miller, Frank; Illinois, 1857 6079.1 p10
Miller, Frank; Ohio, 1809-1852 4511.35 p35
Miller, Frederick 56; Ontario, 1871 1823.21 p260
Miller, Friedrich 11; New York, NY, 1892 8425.16 p34
Miller, Friedrich 20; Portland, ME, 1906 970.38 p79
Miller, Fritz J. 24; Port uncertain, 1841 778.6 p244
Miller, Ganzelius; America, 1766 1220.12 p550
Miller, George; America, 1685 1220.12 p550
Miller, George 31; Michigan, 1880 4491.36 p16
Miller, George; Ohio, 1809-1852 4511.35 p35
Miller, George 14; Quebec, 1870 8364.32 p25
Miller, George Frederick; North Carolina, 1847 1088.45 p23
Miller, H.; Louisiana, 1874-1875 4981.45 p29
Miller, Heinrich 9; New York, NY, 1892 8425.16 p34
Miller, Heinrich 39; New York, NY, 1892 8425.16 p34
Miller, Henry; California, 1868 1131.61 p89
Miller, Henry; Ohio, 1809-1852 4511.35 p35
Miller, Henry; Ohio, 1840-1897 8365.35 p17
Miller, Henry; Ohio, 1844 2763.1 p20
Miller, Henry 21; Ontario, 1871 1823.21 p260
Miller, Henry 25; Ontario, 1871 1823.21 p260
Miller, Henry 44; Ontario, 1871 1823.17 p117
Miller, Henry 50; Ontario, 1871 1823.21 p260
Miller, Henry I. 49; Ontario, 1871 1823.17 p117
Miller, Herman August; Wisconsin, 1884 6795.8 p172
Miller, Hester; America, 1741 1220.12 p550
Miller, Hiram 62; Ontario, 1871 1823.21 p260
Miller, Ignatius 50; Ontario, 1871 1823.17 p117
Miller, Jacob; Colorado, 1897 1029.59 p63
Miller, Jacob; Illinois, 1858-1861 6020.5 p132
Miller, Jacob; Louisiana, 1836-1841 4981.45 p209
Miller, Jacob 7; New York, NY, 1892 8425.16 p34
Miller, Jacob; North Carolina, 1710 3629.40 p5
Miller, Jacob; Ohio, 1809-1852 4511.35 p35
Miller, Jakob; Colorado, 1887 1029.59 p63
Miller, James; America, 1732 1220.12 p550
Miller, James; America, 1734 1220.12 p550
Miller, James; Maryland, 1719 1220.12 p550
Miller, James; North Carolina, 1826 1088.45 p23
Miller, James; Ohio, 1809-1852 4511.35 p35
Miller, James 22; Ontario, 1871 1823.17 p117
Miller, James 28; Ontario, 1871 1823.17 p117
Miller, James 45; Ontario, 1871 1823.21 p261
Miller, James 50; Ontario, 1871 1823.21 p261
Miller, James 74; Ontario, 1871 1823.17 p117
Miller, James; Philadelphia, 1778 8529.30 p6
Miller, Jane; America, 1742 1220.12 p550
Miller, Jane 16; Ontario, 1871 1823.17 p117
Miller, Jannett 36; America, 1846 778.6 p244
Miller, Jean 10; America, 1840 778.6 p244
Miller, Jean Pierre 7; America, 1840 778.6 p244
Miller, Jerome; Ohio, 1809-1852 4511.35 p35
Miller, Johannes; Venezuela, 1843 3899.5 p543
Miller, John; America, 1685 1220.12 p550
Miller, John; America, 1691 1220.12 p550
Miller, John; America, 1721 1220.12 p550
Miller, John; America, 1744 1220.12 p550
Miller, John; America, 1749 1220.12 p550
Miller, John; America, 1752 1220.12 p550
Miller, John; America, 1756 1220.12 p550
Miller, John; America, 1764 1220.12 p550
Miller, John; America, 1766 1220.12 p550
Miller, John; America, 1767 1220.12 p550
Miller, John; America, 1768 1220.12 p550
Miller, John; Annapolis, MD, 1720 1220.12 p550
Miller, John; Barbados, 1695 1220.12 p550
Miller, John; Boston, 1766 1642 p36
With son
Miller, John; Colorado, 1871 1029.59 p63
Miller, John; Died enroute, 1721 1220.12 p550
Miller, John; Illinois, 1858-1861 6020.5 p132
Miller, John; Iowa, 1893 1211.15 p16
Miller, John; New York, 1777 8529.30 p14
Miller, John; North Carolina, 1841 1088.45 p23
Miller, John; North Carolina, 1843 1088.45 p23
Miller, John; Ohio, 1809-1852 4511.35 p35
Miller, John; Ohio, 1840-1897 8365.35 p17
Miller, John 28; Ontario, 1871 1823.21 p261
Miller, John 34; Ontario, 1871 1823.17 p117
Miller, John 45; Ontario, 1871 1823.21 p261
Miller, John 48; Ontario, 1871 1823.17 p117
Miller, John 69; Ontario, 1871 1823.17 p117
Miller, John 70; Ontario, 1871 1823.17 p117
Miller, John 6; Quebec, 1870 8364.32 p25
Miller, John; South Carolina, 1813 3208.30 p18
Miller, John; South Carolina, 1813 3208.30 p31
Miller, John 29; South Carolina, 1812 3476.30 p12
Miller, John; Virginia, 1751 1220.12 p550
Miller, John C.; Ohio, 1809-1852 4511.35 p35
Miller, John Christian Elvin; North Carolina, 1839 1088.45 p23
Miller, John Jacob; Ohio, 1809-1852 4511.35 p35
Miller, John Lecher; North Carolina, 1710 3629.40 p5
Miller, John M.; Ohio, 1809-1852 4511.35 p35
Miller, John P.; Ohio, 1809-1852 4511.35 p35
Miller, Joseph; America, 1741 1220.12 p550
Miller, Joseph; America, 1760 1220.12 p550
Miller, Joseph; America, 1763 1220.12 p550
Miller, Joseph; Ohio, 1809-1852 4511.35 p35
Miller, Joseph 36; Ontario, 1871 1823.17 p117
Miller, Joseph 58; Ontario, 1871 1823.17 p117
Miller, Joseph 31; South Carolina, 1812 3476.30 p12
Miller, Joseph, Jr.; South Carolina, 1813 3208.30 p18
Miller, Joseph, Jr.; South Carolina, 1813 3208.30 p31
Miller, Julia 48; Ontario, 1871 1823.21 p261
Miller, Lawrence; America, 1745 1220.12 p551
Miller, Lawrence; America, 1763 1220.12 p551
Miller, Leopold 22; America, 1844 778.6 p244
Miller, Lewis; Ohio, 1809-1852 4511.35 p35
Miller, Louis 32; Ontario, 1871 1823.17 p117
Miller, Louis 38; Ontario, 1871 1823.21 p261
Miller, Louise; Wisconsin, 1903 6795.8 p117
Miller, Lucretia; America, 1741 1220.12 p551
Miller, Marcus; Ohio, 1809-1852 4511.35 p35
Miller, Margaret; America, 1775 1220.12 p551
Miller, Margaret; Rappahannock, VA, 1729 1220.12 p551
Miller, Maria 39; America, 1840 778.6 p244
Miller, Maria 1; Port uncertain, 1841 778.6 p244
Miller, Maria 20; Port uncertain, 1841 778.6 p244
Miller, Maria Magdalena; Venezuela, 1843 3899.5 p543
Miller, Marianne 5; America, 1846 778.6 p244
Miller, Marie 22; Portland, ME, 1906 970.38 p79
Miller, Martha Louise; Wisconsin, 1896 6795.8 p74
Miller, Mary; America, 1737 1220.12 p551
Miller, Mary; America, 1748 1220.12 p551
Miller, Mary; America, 1749 1220.12 p551
Miller, Mary; America, 1764 1220.12 p551
Miller, Mary; America, 1769 1220.12 p551
Miller, Mary; Annapolis, MD, 1725 1220.12 p551
Miller, Mary; Maryland, 1742 1220.12 p551
Miller, Mary 66; Ontario, 1871 1823.21 p261
Miller, Matthias; Ohio, 1809-1852 4511.35 p35
Miller, Maximilian; America, 1772 1220.12 p551
Miller, Melchior; Ohio, 1809-1852 4511.35 p35
Miller, Melcoir; Ohio, 1809-1852 4511.35 p35
Miller, Michael; Ohio, 1809-1852 4511.35 p35
Miller, Michael 27; Ontario, 1871 1823.17 p117
Miller, Mitchel 45; Ontario, 1871 1823.17 p118
Miller, Ness Hansen; Iowa, 1896 1211.15 p17
Miller, Nicholas; America, 1770 1220.12 p551
Miller, Nicola 38; America, 1840 778.6 p244
Miller, Nicolas 12; America, 1840 778.6 p244
Miller, Nis Hansen; Iowa, 1896 1211.15 p17
Miller, Ottwell; Barbados, 1667 1220.12 p551
Miller, Peter; Illinois, 1856 6079.1 p10
Miller, Peter; New York, NY, 1851 6412.40 p156
Miller, Peter; Ohio, 1809-1852 4511.35 p35
Miller, Philip; Ohio, 1809-1852 4511.35 p35
Miller, Philip; Ohio, 1840-1897 8365.35 p17
Miller, Pier.e 5; America, 1840 778.6 p244
Miller, Rebekah 24; Ontario, 1871 1823.17 p118
Miller, Richard; America, 1694 1220.12 p551
Miller, Richard; America, 1739 1220.12 p551
Miller, Richard; Barbados, 1663 1220.12 p551
Miller, Richard; Barbados, 1699 1220.12 p551
Miller, Robert; America, 1748 1220.12 p551
Miller, Robert; Barbados, 1669 1220.12 p551

Miller, Robert 46; Ontario, 1871 ***1823.21*** *p261*
Miller, Robert 47; Ontario, 1871 ***1823.21*** *p261*
Miller, Robert 55; Ontario, 1871 ***1823.21*** *p261*
Miller, Robert 62; Ontario, 1871 ***1823.17*** *p118*
Miller, Samuel 50; Ontario, 1871 ***1823.17*** *p118*
Miller, Sarah; Annapolis, MD, 1721 ***1220.12*** *p551*
Miller, Solomon; America, 1753 ***1220.12*** *p551*
Miller, Susanna 37; Ontario, 1871 ***1823.17*** *p118*
Miller, Susannah; Potomac, 1731 ***1220.12*** *p551*
Miller, Thomas; America, 1749 ***1220.12*** *p551*
Miller, Thomas; America, 1753 ***1220.12*** *p551*
Miller, Thomas; America, 1766 ***1220.12*** *p551*
Miller, Thomas; America, 1768 ***1220.12*** *p551*
Miller, Thomas; America, 1773 ***1220.12*** *p551*
Miller, Thomas; Boston, 1766 ***1642*** *p36*
With wife & son
Miller, Thomas 30; Ontario, 1871 ***1823.21*** *p261*
Miller, Thomas Zachariah; America, 1767 ***1220.12*** *p551*
Miller, Valentine; Ohio, 1809-1852 ***4511.35*** *p35*
Miller, Walter 37; Ontario, 1871 ***1823.17*** *p118*
Miller, Wilhelm 1; America, 1840 ***778.6*** *p244*
Miller, William; America, 1736 ***1220.12*** *p551*
Miller, William; America, 1738 ***1220.12*** *p551*
Miller, William; America, 1743 ***1220.12*** *p551*
Miller, William; America, 1749 ***1220.12*** *p551*
Miller, William; America, 1750 ***1220.12*** *p551*
Miller, William; America, 1757 ***1220.12*** *p551*
Miller, William; America, 1763 ***1220.12*** *p551*
Miller, William; America, 1764 ***1220.12*** *p551*
Miller, William; America, 1770 ***1220.12*** *p551*
Miller, William; America, 1772 ***1220.12*** *p551*
Miller, William; Ohio, 1809-1852 ***4511.35*** *p35*
Miller, William 45; Ontario, 1871 ***1823.17*** *p118*
Miller, William 56; Ontario, 1871 ***1823.21*** *p261*
Miller, William 71; Ontario, 1871 ***1823.21*** *p261*
Miller, William 14; Quebec, 1870 ***8364.32*** *p25*
Miller, William Thomas 25; Halifax, N.S., n.d. ***1833.5*** *p7*
Miller, William Thomas 25; Halifax, N.S., n.d. ***8445.10*** *p7*
Millers, James; America, 1753 ***1220.12*** *p551*
Millet, Annie 23; Ontario, 1871 ***1823.21*** *p261*
Millet, Catherine; Quebec, 1671 ***4514.3*** *p308*
Millet, Jacques; Montreal, 1659 ***9221.17*** *p425*
Millet, Jean 28; Quebec, 1656 ***9221.17*** *p342*
Millet, John C.; Ohio, 1840-1897 ***8365.35*** *p17*
Millet, Mary; Massachusetts, 1635 ***117.5*** *p157*
Millet, Nicolas 21; Montreal, 1653 ***9221.17*** *p297*
Millet, Nicolas 29; Quebec, 1656 ***9221.17*** *p343*
Millet, Pierre 48; Quebec, 1643 ***9221.17*** *p133*
Millet, Pierre 48; Quebec, 1658 ***9221.17*** *p384*
Millet, Simon; Quebec, 1651 ***9221.17*** *p248*
Millett, Ann; America, 1751 ***1220.12*** *p551*
Millett, Caleb; Barbados or Jamaica, 1698 ***1220.12*** *p551*
Millett, Mary; America, 1771 ***1220.12*** *p551*
Milley, John; America, 1769 ***1220.12*** *p552*
Millican, S. H.; Montreal, 1922 ***4514.4*** *p32*
Millichap, Richard; America, 1773 ***1220.12*** *p552*
Millickin, Robert; Annapolis, MD, 1725 ***1220.12*** *p552*
Millidge, Mary; America, 1771 ***1220.12*** *p552*
Milliford, James; America, 1758 ***1220.12*** *p552*
Milligan, George; New Jersey, 1777 ***8529.30*** *p7*
Milligan, George; Ohio, 1840 ***3580.20*** *p33*
Milligan, George; Ohio, 1840 ***6020.12*** *p21*
Milligan, Margaret 40; Ontario, 1871 ***1823.17*** *p118*
Millikan, John 79; Ontario, 1871 ***1823.17*** *p118*
Milliken, John 67; Ontario, 1871 ***1823.21*** *p261*
Milliken, Samuel 34; Ontario, 1871 ***1823.21*** *p261*
Millikin, Ann 50; Ontario, 1871 ***1823.17*** *p118*
Millikin, George; Ohio, 1825 ***3580.20*** *p33*
Millikin, George; Ohio, 1825 ***6020.12*** *p21*
Millikin, Mark; America, 1775 ***1220.12*** *p552*
Milliman, John; Ohio, 1809-1852 ***4511.35*** *p35*
Millind, John; Potomac, 1729 ***1220.12*** *p552*
Milliner, Anne; America, 1728 ***1220.12*** *p552*
Milliner, William; America, 1753 ***1220.12*** *p552*
Millington, Giles; Barbados or Jamaica, 1702 ***1220.12*** *p552*
Millington, James; America, 1745 ***1220.12*** *p552*
Millington, John; America, 1749 ***1220.12*** *p552*
Millington, Joseph; America, 1774 ***1220.12*** *p552*
Millinor, Thomas; America, 1721 ***1220.12*** *p552*
Millison, Matthew; America, 1775 ***1220.12*** *p552*
Millman, Richard 45; Ontario, 1871 ***1823.17*** *p118*
Millman, William 33; Ontario, 1871 ***1823.17*** *p118*
Milln, James 82; Ontario, 1871 ***1823.17*** *p118*
Milln, Margrat 40; Ontario, 1871 ***1823.17*** *p118*
Millner, Joseph 42; Ontario, 1871 ***1823.21*** *p261*
Millo, Herman; America, 1750 ***1220.12*** *p552*
Millon, Patrick; Ohio, 1809-1852 ***4511.35*** *p35*
Millor, Patrick; Ohio, 1809-1852 ***4511.35*** *p35*
Millor, Peter; Ontario, 1787 ***1276.15*** *p230*
With 2 relatives
Millot, Agnes 8; New Orleans, 1847 ***778.6*** *p244*
Millot, Alfred 4; Port uncertain, 1842 ***778.6*** *p244*
Millot, Edouard 2; Port uncertain, 1842 ***778.6*** *p244*
Millot, Francois 19; New Orleans, 1847 ***778.6*** *p244*
Millot, Francoise; Quebec, 1669 ***4514.3*** *p348*
Millot, Hortense 25; Port uncertain, 1842 ***778.6*** *p244*
Millot, Jean 35; Port uncertain, 1842 ***778.6*** *p244*
Millot, Jeanne 50; New Orleans, 1847 ***778.6*** *p244*
Millot, Lucie 3; Port uncertain, 1842 ***778.6*** *p245*
Millot, Nicolas 47; New Orleans, 1847 ***778.6*** *p245*
Millouer, Jean 26; Quebec, 1638 ***9221.17*** *p79*
Milloy, Archibald; North Carolina, 1835 ***1088.45*** *p23*
Mills, Abel; America, 1742 ***1220.12*** *p552*
Mills, Abraham 19; Ontario, 1871 ***1823.17*** *p118*
Mills, Adam 17; Ontario, 1871 ***1823.21*** *p261*
Mills, Alexander; America, 1769 ***1220.12*** *p552*
Mills, Alexander 32; Ontario, 1871 ***1823.17*** *p118*
Mills, Almira L. 39; Ontario, 1871 ***1823.21*** *p261*
Mills, Amelia 6; Quebec, 1870 ***8364.32*** *p25*
Mills, Ann 60; Ontario, 1871 ***1823.21*** *p261*
Mills, Anna; Iowa, 1931 ***1211.15*** *p17*
Mills, Anne; Barbados or Jamaica, 1688 ***1220.12*** *p552*
Mills, Arthur; Pennsylvania, 1856 ***8513.31*** *p416*
*Wife:*Jane A. Earnsby
Mills, Bonaventure; Barbados, 1699 ***1220.12*** *p552*
Mills, C. J.; California, 1868 ***1131.61*** *p89*
Mills, Catharine *SEE* Mills, James
Mills, Christian 21; Port uncertain, 1846 ***778.6*** *p245*
Mills, David R.; Ohio, 1825 ***6020.12*** *p21*
Mills, David R.; Ohio, 1877 ***3580.20*** *p33*
Mills, Douglass 24; Michigan, 1880 ***4491.39*** *p21*
Mills, Eleanor; America, 1723 ***1220.12*** *p552*
Mills, Eleanor; America, 1773 ***1220.12*** *p552*
Mills, Elford; America, 1749 ***1220.12*** *p552*
Mills, Elizabeth; America, 1746 ***1220.12*** *p552*
Mills, Elizabeth; America, 1754 ***1220.12*** *p552*
Mills, Elizabeth; America, 1755 ***1220.12*** *p552*
Mills, Elizabeth; America, 1763 ***1220.12*** *p552*
Mills, Elizabeth; Annapolis, MD, 1730 ***1220.12*** *p552*
Mills, Elizabeth; North Carolina, 1775 ***1422.10*** *p56*
Mills, Elizabeth Cristy *SEE* Mills, James
Mills, Emanuel; America, 1749 ***1220.12*** *p552*
Mills, Emmanuel; America, 1771 ***1220.12*** *p552*
Mills, Frances; Annapolis, MD, 1719 ***1220.12*** *p552*
Mills, Frances 52; Ontario, 1871 ***1823.21*** *p261*
Mills, George; America, 1758 ***1220.12*** *p552*
Mills, George; Barbados, 1694 ***1220.12*** *p552*
Mills, George 46; Ontario, 1871 ***1823.17*** *p118*
Mills, Gideon; Barbados, 1665 ***1220.12*** *p552*
Mills, Henry; America, 1685 ***1220.12*** *p552*
Mills, Henry; America, 1750 ***1220.12*** *p552*
Mills, Hugh 73; Ontario, 1871 ***1823.21*** *p261*
Mills, Isaac 45; Ontario, 1871 ***1823.21*** *p261*
Mills, Isabella; America, 1744 ***1220.12*** *p552*
Mills, Isabella; Maryland, 1744 ***1220.12*** *p552*
Mills, Isabella 50; Ontario, 1871 ***1823.21*** *p261*
Mills, James; America, 1750 ***1220.12*** *p552*
Mills, James 40; Ontario, 1871 ***1823.21*** *p261*
Mills, James 45; Ontario, 1871 ***1823.21*** *p261*
Mills, James; Philadelphia, 1868 ***8513.31*** *p416*
*Wife:*Elizabeth Cristy
*Child:*Catharine
Mills, Jane 60; Ontario, 1871 ***1823.21*** *p261*
Mills, Jane A. Earnsby *SEE* Mills, Arthur
Mills, John; America, 1700 ***1220.12*** *p552*
Mills, John; America, 1722 ***1220.12*** *p552*
Mills, John; America, 1736 ***1220.12*** *p552*
Mills, John; America, 1750 ***1220.12*** *p552*
Mills, John; America, 1768 ***1220.12*** *p553*
Mills, John; America, 1770 ***1220.12*** *p553*
Mills, John; America, 1773 ***1220.12*** *p553*
Mills, John; Barbados or Jamaica, 1687 ***1220.12*** *p552*
Mills, John; Boston, 1832 ***3274.55*** *p73*
Mills, John; Charles Town, SC, 1719 ***1220.12*** *p552*
Mills, John; Illinois, 1834-1900 ***6020.5*** *p132*
Mills, John; Maryland, 1726 ***1220.12*** *p552*
Mills, John; North Carolina, 1775 ***1422.10*** *p57*
Mills, John 19; Ontario, 1871 ***1823.21*** *p261*
Mills, John 21; Ontario, 1871 ***1823.21*** *p261*
Mills, John; Virginia, 1734 ***1220.12*** *p552*
Mills, Joseph; America, 1771 ***1220.12*** *p553*
Mills, Joseph 52; Ontario, 1871 ***1823.17*** *p118*
Mills, Lucy 10; Quebec, 1870 ***8364.32*** *p25*
Mills, Margaret; Annapolis, MD, 1735 ***1220.12*** *p553*
Mills, Martha; America, 1751 ***1220.12*** *p553*
Mills, Mary; America, 1749 ***1220.12*** *p553*
Mills, Mary; America, 1767 ***1220.12*** *p553*
Mills, Mary; Barbados, 1676 ***1220.12*** *p553*
Mills, Mary 47; Ontario, 1871 ***1823.21*** *p261*
Mills, Mary; Rappahannock, VA, 1741 ***1220.12*** *p553*
Mills, Michael; America, 1769 ***1220.12*** *p553*
Mills, Nathaniel; Died enroute, 1722 ***1220.12*** *p553*
Mills, Nicholas; Virginia, 1745 ***1220.12*** *p553*
Mills, Richard; Jamaica, 1716 ***1220.12*** *p553*
Mills, Richard 41; Ontario, 1871 ***1823.21*** *p261*
Mills, Richard 50; Ontario, 1871 ***1823.21*** *p261*
Mills, Robert; America, 1761 ***1220.12*** *p553*
Mills, Robert; America, 1771 ***1220.12*** *p553*
Mills, Samuel; America, 1764 ***1220.12*** *p553*
Mills, Samuel; America, 1767 ***1220.12*** *p553*
Mills, Samuel; New York, 1776 ***8529.30*** *p14*
Mills, Sarah; America, 1737 ***1220.12*** *p553*
Mills, Sarah; America, 1743 ***1220.12*** *p553*
Mills, Sarah 53; Ontario, 1871 ***1823.21*** *p262*
Mills, Sebastian; America, 1655 ***1220.12*** *p553*
Mills, Thomas; America, 1685 ***1220.12*** *p553*
Mills, Thomas; America, 1719 ***1220.12*** *p553*
Mills, Thomas; America, 1721 ***1220.12*** *p553*
Mills, Thomas; America, 1746 ***1220.12*** *p553*
Mills, Thomas; America, 1752 ***1220.12*** *p553*
Mills, Thomas; America, 1755 ***1220.12*** *p553*
Mills, Thomas; America, 1767 ***1220.12*** *p553*
Mills, Thomas; Barbados or Jamaica, 1682 ***1220.12*** *p553*
Mills, Thomas 50; Ontario, 1871 ***1823.21*** *p262*
Mills, Vincent; America, 1739 ***1220.12*** *p553*
Mills, William; America, 1721 ***1220.12*** *p553*
Mills, William; America, 1741 ***1220.12*** *p553*
Mills, William; America, 1743 ***1220.12*** *p553*
Mills, William; America, 1755 ***1220.12*** *p553*
Mills, William; America, 1760 ***1220.12*** *p553*
Mills, William; Ontario, 1871 ***1823.21*** *p262*
Mills, William 23; Ontario, 1871 ***1823.21*** *p262*
Mills, William 39; Ontario, 1871 ***1823.21*** *p262*
Mills, William; Rappahannock, VA, 1726 ***1220.12*** *p553*
Mills, William; Virginia, 1745 ***1220.12*** *p553*
Mills, William S.; Washington, 1887 ***6015.10*** *p16*
Mills, Wilson 63; Ontario, 1871 ***1823.21*** *p262*
Millson, Thomas; America, 1773 ***1220.12*** *p553*
Milluns, John 36; Ontario, 1871 ***1823.21*** *p262*
Millward, George 16; Quebec, 1870 ***8364.32*** *p25*
Millward, Harriet 19; Quebec, 1870 ***8364.32*** *p25*
Milne, Alexander 29; Ontario, 1871 ***1823.17*** *p118*
Milne, Andrew 15; Ontario, 1871 ***1823.17*** *p118*
Milne, Francis 44; Ontario, 1871 ***1823.21*** *p262*
Milne, George 55; Ontario, 1871 ***1823.21*** *p262*
Milne, James 33; Ontario, 1871 ***1823.21*** *p262*
Milne, James 34; Ontario, 1871 ***1823.21*** *p262*
Milne, James 49; Ontario, 1871 ***1823.21*** *p262*
Milne, John 73; Ontario, 1871 ***1823.21*** *p262*
Milne, William 31; Ontario, 1871 ***1823.21*** *p262*
Milner, Edward; America, 1739 ***1220.12*** *p553*
Milner, Eli; America, 1865 ***9076.20*** *p67*
Milner, Elizabeth; Barbados, 1667 ***1220.12*** *p553*
Milner, George; America, 1743 ***1220.12*** *p553*
Milner, George; America, 1754 ***1220.12*** *p553*
Milner, Jacob; America, 1746 ***1220.12*** *p553*
Milner, James; America, 1734 ***1220.12*** *p553*
Milner, James 66; Ontario, 1871 ***1823.21*** *p262*
Milner, Jane; America, 1754 ***1220.12*** *p553*
Milner, Jane 56; Ontario, 1871 ***1823.21*** *p262*
Milner, John; America, 1737 ***1220.12*** *p554*
Milner, John; America, 1758 ***1220.12*** *p554*
Milner, John 28; Ontario, 1871 ***1823.21*** *p262*
Milner, Joseph 34; Ontario, 1871 ***1823.17*** *p118*
Milner, Nathan; America, 1746 ***1220.12*** *p554*
Milner, Robert; America, 1766 ***1220.12*** *p554*
Milner, Thomas; America, 1749 ***1220.12*** *p554*
Milner, Thomas; America, 1763 ***1220.12*** *p554*
Milner, William; America, 1750 ***1220.12*** *p554*
Milner, William; America, 1754 ***1220.12*** *p554*
Milner, William 32; Ontario, 1871 ***1823.21*** *p262*
Milot, Jacques 24; Montreal, 1653 ***9221.17*** *p297*
Milot, Jean 22; Montreal, 1652 ***9221.17*** *p268*
Milsham, John; America, 1739 ***1220.12*** *p554*
Milsome, John; America, 1758 ***1220.12*** *p554*
Milson, John H. 45; Ontario, 1871 ***1823.21*** *p262*
Milstead, Edward; Barbados or Jamaica, 1674 ***1220.12*** *p554*
Milston, Thomas; America, 1770 ***1220.12*** *p554*
Milsum, Abraham; America, 1763 ***1220.12*** *p554*
Milton, Anne; Annapolis, MD, 1730 ***1220.12*** *p554*
Milton, Edward; America, 1728 ***1220.12*** *p554*
Milton, Henry; America, 1767 ***1220.12*** *p554*
Milton, J. 41; Ontario, 1871 ***1823.21*** *p262*
Milton, James; Barbados, 1714 ***1220.12*** *p554*
Milton, John; America, 1765 ***1220.12*** *p554*
Milton, John; Maryland, 1720 ***1220.12*** *p554*
Milton, Robert; Maryland, 1674-1675 ***1236.25*** *p51*
Milton, Sarah A.; Colorado, 1903 ***1029.59*** *p63*
Milton, Sarah A. 47; Colorado, 1903 ***1029.59*** *p63*
Milton, William; America, 1742 ***1220.12*** *p554*
Milusky, Peter George; Philadelphia, 1903 ***1029.59*** *p63*
Milward, Benjamin, Jr.; America, 1767 ***1220.12*** *p554*
Milward, Jane; America, 1693 ***1220.12*** *p554*
Milward, John; America, 1756 ***1220.12*** *p554*
Milward, Richard; America, 1685 ***1220.12*** *p554*
Milwood, Richard; America, 1679 ***1220.12*** *p554*

Mims, Mary; Annapolis, MD, 1720 1220.12 p554
Mina, Joseph S.; New Orleans, 1853 7710.1 p153
Minas, Barbara 40; America, 1855 5475.1 p244
Minas, Katharina 1 *SEE* Minas, Katharina
Minas, Katharina 30; America, 1885 5475.1 p246
  *Daughter:*Katharina 1
Mince, John; America, 1774 1220.12 p554
Minch, Joseph 32; New Orleans, 1848 778.6 p245
Minchan, Ferdinand 21; Portland, ME, 1912 970.38 p79
Minchell, John; Maryland, 1720 1220.12 p554
Mincher, Hannah; Barbados or Jamaica, 1712 1220.12 p554
Mincher, John; America, 1764 1220.12 p554
Mincher, John; Maryland, 1719 1220.12 p554
Minchin, Joseph; America, 1713 1220.12 p554
Minchin, William 27; Ontario, 1871 1823.21 p262
Minchinton, Harry; Toronto, 1969 9228.50 p466
Mindel, August; North Carolina, 1792-1862 1088.45 p23
Mindre, Jean 39; New Orleans, 1848 778.6 p245
Mine, Cyr. 40; Port uncertain, 1841 778.6 p245
Mine, Jean de; Quebec, 1693 2314.30 p171
Mineau, Simon 35; Quebec, 1656 9221.17 p343
Miner, Mr. 23; Mississippi, 1846 778.6 p245
Miner, Anna 3; Mississippi, 1846 778.6 p245
Miner, Ba.bara 3 months; Mississippi, 1846 778.6 p245
Miner, Ba.bara 16; Mississippi, 1846 778.6 p245
Miner, Case 28; Ontario, 1871 1823.17 p118
Miner, Cristopher 32; Mississippi, 1846 778.6 p245
Miner, Joseph 2; Mississippi, 1846 778.6 p245
Miner, Madalaine 5; Mississippi, 1846 778.6 p245
Miner, Madalaine 23; Mississippi, 1846 778.6 p245
Minerd, John 19; Ontario, 1871 1823.21 p262
Minetre, F.; Louisiana, 1874-1875 4981.45 p30
Minett, Matthew; America, 1754 1220.12 p554
Minger, Peter 24; Galveston, TX, 1844 3967.10 p374
Mingers, Adolph; North Carolina, 1856 1088.45 p23
Mingham, Benjamin; America, 1724 1220.12 p554
Mingis, Martha; America, 1754 1220.12 p554
Mingot, Elizabet; Virginia, 1700 9230.15 p81
Mingre, Andre; Montreal, 1650 9221.17 p231
Minhinnick, J. R. 33; Ontario, 1871 1823.21 p262
Minhinnick, John 45; Ontario, 1871 1823.21 p262
Miniberger, V.; Omaha, NE, 1903-1910 2853.20 p154
Miniely, Andrew 73; Ontario, 1871 1823.21 p262
Minier, Ernst Ludwig 20; America, 1854 2526.43 p176
Minier, Heinrich Friedrich; America, 1888 2526.43 p198
Minier, Maria; America, 1854 2526.43 p176
Minier, Sophie Elisabeth 51; America, 1857 2526.43 p176
Minifee, Joseph 60; Santa Clara Co., CA, 1860 8704.1 p23
Minifie, John; America, 1685 1220.12 p554
Miniger, Cristion; New Jersey, 1748-1774 927.31 p2
Miniger, Jacob; New Jersey, 1748-1774 927.31 p2
Miniger, Lowrance; New Jersey, 1748-1774 927.31 p2
Minilly, William 36; Ontario, 1871 1823.17 p118
Minime, Gilbert 20; Montreal, 1642 9221.17 p122
Mininger, John; Ohio, 1809-1852 4511.35 p35
Mink, Andrew; New Jersey, 1773-1774 927.31 p3
Minn, Juliane; America, 1856 5475.1 p560
Minn, William; Ohio, 1809-1852 4511.35 p35
Minnett, Abraham; North Carolina, 1710 3629.40 p8
Minnett, Mary; North Carolina, 1710 3629.40 p8
Minnich, Nicholas; Ohio, 1809-1852 4511.35 p35
Minnick, Michael; Ohio, 1809-1852 4511.35 p35
Minniger, Barbara 43; America, 1868 5475.1 p253
Minninger, Johann; America, 1881 5475.1 p245
Minns, Alfred; Ohio, 1844 2763.1 p20
Minns, Elizabeth; Barbados, 1676 1220.12 p554
Minns, James; America, 1774 1220.12 p554
Minns, John; Barbados, 1671 1220.12 p554
Minor, James 24; Ontario, 1871 1823.21 p262
Mins, Melin 27; New Orleans, 1840 778.6 p245
Minsall, Anne; Virginia, 1728 1220.12 p554
Minshall, Thomas; America, 1738 1220.12 p555
Minsheare, Roger; America, 1678 1220.12 p555
Minskipp, Thomas; Annapolis, MD, 1723 1220.12 p555
Minson, Richard; America, 1733 1220.12 p555
Minster, Jacob; Ohio, 1844 2763.1 p20
Minter, Desire; Plymouth, MA, 1620 1920.45 p5
Minter, John T. 29; Ontario, 1871 1823.17 p118
Minton, Thomas S. 25; Ontario, 1871 1823.21 p262
Minty, Jane 27; Michigan, 1880 4491.33 p15
Minty, John 36; Michigan, 1880 4491.33 p16
Minty, Maggie 3; Michigan, 1880 4491.33 p16
Minty, Mary; America, 1766 1220.12 p555
Minty, Mary E. 5; Michigan, 1880 4491.33 p16
Mintz, Esther *SEE* Mintz, Harry
Mintz, Harry; Detroit, 1929-1930 6214.5 p71
  *Wife:*Esther
Mintz, Simon; Texas, 1895 3435.45 p36
Minuit, Peter; New York, NY, 1626 2853.20 p97
Minville, Charlotte Mauger 42 *SEE* Minville, Pierre
Minville, Francois 15 *SEE* Minville, Pierre
Minville, Jacques 10 *SEE* Minville, Pierre
Minville, Marie 17 *SEE* Minville, Pierre
Minville, Marie-Madeleine 13 *SEE* Minville, Pierre
Minville, Martine-Aimee 14 *SEE* Minville, Pierre
Minville, Pierre 47; Quebec, 1649 9221.17 p216
  *Wife:*Charlotte Mauger 42
  *Daughter:*Martine-Aimee 14
  *Daughter:*Marie-Madeleine 13
  *Daughter:*Suzanne 9
  *Son:*Jacques 10
  *Daughter:*Marie 17
  *Son:*Francois 15
Minville, Suzanne 9 *SEE* Minville, Pierre
Minzio, Lizzo; Louisiana, 1874-1875 4981.45 p30
Minzler, Martin; North Carolina, 1860 1088.45 p23
Miol, Jean 34; New Orleans, 1848 778.6 p245
Miranda, D.; Louisiana, 1874-1875 4981.45 p29
Mirat, Gion; Louisiana, 1874 4981.45 p132
Mirault, Jean Baptiste; Illinois, 1852 6079.1 p10
Mirehouse, Joseph; America, 1744 1220.12 p555
Mires, Catherine; America, 1754 1220.12 p574
Mires, Mary; America, 1754 1220.12 p574
Mires, Thomas; America, 1772 1220.12 p574
Mirik, Pierre; Louisiana, 1874 4981.45 p296
Mirkel, Peter; Ohio, 1809-1852 4511.35 p36
Miro, Jancinto; Louisiana, 1874-1875 4981.45 p29
Miron, Mathew 50; Ontario, 1871 1823.17 p118
Mirrells, Platt 60; Ontario, 1871 1823.17 p118
Mirton, William; America, 1739 1220.12 p546
Mirus, Marcus A.; Ohio, 1809-1852 4511.35 p36
Mischaleck, V.; Galveston, TX, 1855 571.7 p18
Mischel, Adam 16; New York, NY, 1893 1883.7 p42
Mischel, Agatha 8; New York, NY, 1893 1883.7 p42
Mischel, Ferdinand 48; New York, NY, 1893 1883.7 p42
Mischel, Georg 9 months; New York, NY, 1893 1883.7 p42
Mischel, Georg 21; New York, NY, 1893 1883.7 p42
Mischel, Margaretha 4; New York, NY, 1893 1883.7 p42
Mischel, Marianna 48; New York, NY, 1893 1883.7 p42
Mischel, Rosalie 26; New York, NY, 1893 1883.7 p42
Mischel, Sebastian 26; New York, NY, 1893 1883.7 p42
Mischel, Theresa 17; New York, NY, 1893 1883.7 p42
Mischel, Veronika 3; New York, NY, 1893 1883.7 p42
Mischuk, Philip; Detroit, 1929-1930 6214.5 p69
Misener, George; Washington, 1880 2770.40 p134
Misgen, Peter 54; America, 1843 5475.1 p366
Mishelfelder, Berda; Kansas, 1917-1918 2054.10 p48
Misicka, Josef; Chicago, 1884-1899 2853.20 p460
Miskell, John 26; Ontario, 1871 1823.17 p118
Miskell, Thomas; Illinois, 1860 6079.1 p10
Misken, Isabella 21; Quebec, 1870 8364.32 p25
Miskovsky, Robert V.; New York, NY, 1881 2853.20 p145
Missae, Johann Ludwig; Wisconsin, 1858 6795.8 p159
Missall, Wilhelm; Wisconsin, 1874 6795.8 p34
Missback, Johannes; America, 1843 2526.42 p193
Misselbrook, Samuel 30; Ontario, 1871 1823.17 p118
Misselhorn, Ferdinand; America, 1859 7420.1 p187
Missiter, Richard; America, 1771 1220.12 p547
Missner, Anton 18; Port uncertain, 1847 778.6 p245
Misson, Gretian; Carolina, 1724 1220.12 p555
Mist, John; America, 1765 1220.12 p555
Mitchal, John 50; Ontario, 1871 1823.21 p263
Mitcham, William; America, 1770 1220.12 p555
Mitchel, Alexander 54; Ontario, 1871 1823.21 p263
Mitchel, Andrew 60; Ontario, 1871 1823.17 p118
Mitchel, Arthur 20; Ontario, 1871 1823.21 p263
Mitchel, Charles; North Carolina, 1824 1088.45 p23
Mitchel, Charles 30; Ontario, 1871 1823.21 p263
Mitchel, David 27; Ontario, 1871 1823.21 p263
Mitchel, Duncan 53; Ontario, 1871 1823.21 p263
Mitchel, Duncan 75; Ontario, 1871 1823.21 p263
Mitchel, Elenor *SEE* Mitchel, Lorance
Mitchel, Elisabeth *SEE* Mitchel, Lorance
Mitchel, Fancies *SEE* Mitchel, Lorance
Mitchel, George 55; Ontario, 1871 1823.21 p263
Mitchel, George 72; Ontario, 1871 1823.21 p263
Mitchel, Idacie 44; Ontario, 1871 1823.21 p263
Mitchel, James 30; Ontario, 1871 1823.21 p263
Mitchel, Jean 22; Port uncertain, 1840 778.6 p245
Mitchel, Johanna Follett *SEE* Mitchel, Sam
Mitchel, John; North Carolina, 1804 1088.45 p23
Mitchel, John 37; Ontario, 1871 1823.17 p119
Mitchel, John 39; Ontario, 1871 1823.17 p119
Mitchel, John 78; Ontario, 1871 1823.21 p263
Mitchel, John C. 58; Ontario, 1871 1823.21 p263
Mitchel, Jos.; Louisiana, 1874-1875 4981.45 p30
Mitchel, Joseph 40; Ontario, 1871 1823.21 p263
Mitchel, Joshti 26; Ontario, 1871 1823.21 p263
Mitchel, Lorance; Massachusetts, 1748 1642 p108
  *Wife:*Elisabeth
  *Child:*Elenor
  *Child:*Fancies
Mitchel, Mathew 53; Ontario, 1871 1823.21 p263
Mitchel, Patrick 34; Ontario, 1871 1823.21 p263
Mitchel, Peter 47; Ontario, 1871 1823.21 p263
Mitchel, Sam; Maine, 1762 9228.50 p226
  *Wife:*Johanna Follett
Mitchel, Samuel; America, 1769 1220.12 p556
Mitchel, William 31; Ontario, 1871 1823.21 p263
Mitchell, Adam; America, 1772 1220.12 p555
Mitchell, Agnes 55; Ontario, 1871 1823.21 p263
Mitchell, Aguilla 61; Ontario, 1871 1823.17 p119
Mitchell, Ann 19; North Carolina, 1774 1422.10 p58
Mitchell, Ann 19; North Carolina, 1774 1422.10 p62
Mitchell, Annie 34; Ontario, 1871 1823.17 p119
Mitchell, Anthony Grenfell; Washington, 1888 2770.40 p26
Mitchell, Benjamin; America, 1752 1220.12 p555
Mitchell, Charles 19; Quebec, 1870 8364.32 p25
Mitchell, Charles A.; North Carolina, 1792-1862 1088.45 p23
Mitchell, Christian; America, 1743 1220.12 p555
Mitchell, David; Burlington, VT, 1830 3274.55 p71
Mitchell, David; Iowa, 1888 1211.15 p16
Mitchell, David; Montreal, 1830 3274.55 p71
Mitchell, David; Ohio, 1840 3580.20 p33
Mitchell, David; Ohio, 1840 6020.12 p21
Mitchell, Dorothy; America, 1767 1220.12 p555
Mitchell, Edward; America, 1685 1220.12 p555
Mitchell, Edward; Barbados, 1669 1220.12 p555
Mitchell, Edward 30; Ontario, 1871 1823.17 p119
Mitchell, Elinor; Barbados or Jamaica, 1685 1220.12 p555
Mitchell, Elizabeth; America, 1747 1220.12 p555
Mitchell, Elizabeth; Barbados or Jamaica, 1695 1220.12 p555
Mitchell, Francis; New York, 1778 8529.30 p14
Mitchell, George; America, 1747 1220.12 p555
Mitchell, George; America, 1768 1220.12 p555
Mitchell, Hamilton; North Carolina, 1840 1088.45 p23
Mitchell, Henry; Philadelphia, 1777 8529.30 p4A
Mitchell, Hugh 45; Ontario, 1871 1823.21 p263
Mitchell, James; America, 1727 1220.12 p555
Mitchell, James; America, 1730 1220.12 p555
Mitchell, James; America, 1737 1220.12 p555
Mitchell, James; America, 1746 1220.12 p555
Mitchell, James; America, 1747 1220.12 p555
Mitchell, James; America, 1754 1220.12 p555
Mitchell, James; America, 1769 1220.12 p555
Mitchell, James; America, 1771 1220.12 p555
Mitchell, James; America, 1772 1220.12 p555
Mitchell, James; Annapolis, MD, 1735 1220.12 p555
Mitchell, James; Colorado, 1891 1029.59 p63
Mitchell, James 28; Colorado, 1876 1029.59 p63
Mitchell, James 50; Ontario, 1871 1823.21 p263
Mitchell, James; Toronto, 1844 2910.35 p114
Mitchell, James; Virginia, 1763 1220.12 p555
Mitchell, Jane; Barbados or Jamaica, 1710 1220.12 p555
Mitchell, John; America, 1685 1220.12 p555
Mitchell, John; America, 1730 1220.12 p555
Mitchell, John; America, 1739 1220.12 p555
Mitchell, John; America, 1740 1220.12 p555
Mitchell, John; America, 1750 1220.12 p555
Mitchell, John; America, 1767 1220.12 p555
Mitchell, John; America, 1771 1220.12 p555
Mitchell, John; America, 1771 1220.12 p556
Mitchell, John; Annapolis, MD, 1729 1220.12 p555
Mitchell, John; Maryland, 1722 1220.12 p555
Mitchell, John; Ohio, 1840 3580.20 p33
Mitchell, John; Ohio, 1840 6020.12 p21
Mitchell, John 38; Ontario, 1871 1823.17 p119
Mitchell, John 40; Ontario, 1871 1823.17 p119
Mitchell, John 40; Ontario, 1871 1823.21 p263
Mitchell, John 43; Ontario, 1871 1823.21 p263
Mitchell, John 63; Ontario, 1871 1823.21 p263
Mitchell, John S. 21; Ontario, 1871 1823.21 p263
Mitchell, Joseph; America, 1740 1220.12 p556
Mitchell, Katherine; Barbados, 1690 1220.12 p555
Mitchell, Mary; Barbados or Jamaica, 1697 1220.12 p556
Mitchell, Mary 12; Quebec, 1870 8364.32 p25
Mitchell, Mary Jane; New Jersey, 1885 9228.50 p466
Mitchell, Michael 50; Ontario, 1871 1823.21 p263
Mitchell, Patk; St. John, N.B., 1847 2978.15 p35
Mitchell, Peter; America, 1771 1220.12 p556
Mitchell, Peter 74; Ontario, 1871 1823.21 p264
Mitchell, Ralph; America, 1771 1220.12 p556
Mitchell, Richard; America, 1743 1220.12 p556
Mitchell, Richard; America, 1758 1220.12 p556
Mitchell, Richard; America, 1763 1220.12 p556
Mitchell, Richard; New Jersey, 1665 9228.50 p465
Mitchell, Richard; Virginia, 1665 9228.50 p53

Mitchell, Robert; America, 1685 *1220.12 p556*
Mitchell, Robert; America, 1765 *1220.12 p556*
Mitchell, Robert 42; Ontario, 1871 *1823.17 p119*
Mitchell, Robt 26; North Carolina, 1774 *1422.10 p62*
Mitchell, Robt. 26; North Carolina, 1774 *1422.10 p58*
Mitchell, Rossom A. 48; Ontario, 1871 *1823.21 p264*
Mitchell, Samuel; America, 1742 *1220.12 p556*
Mitchell, Sarah; America, 1741 *1220.12 p556*
Mitchell, Sarah; America, 1757 *1220.12 p556*
Mitchell, Sarah; America, 1765 *1220.12 p556*
Mitchell, Sarah; America, 1774 *1220.12 p556*
Mitchell, Thomas; America, 1685 *1220.12 p556*
Mitchell, Thomas; America, 1749 *1220.12 p556*
Mitchell, Thomas; America, 1768 *1220.12 p556*
Mitchell, Thomas; Barbados or Jamaica, 1697 *1220.12 p556*
Mitchell, Thomas; Colorado, 1882 *1029.59 p63*
Mitchell, Thomas; North Carolina, 1850 *1088.45 p23*
Mitchell, Thomas 40; Ontario, 1871 *1823.17 p119*
Mitchell, Timothy; Toronto, 1844 *2910.35 p113*
Mitchell, William; America, 1739 *1220.12 p556*
Mitchell, William; America, 1744 *1220.12 p556*
Mitchell, William; America, 1770 *1220.12 p556*
Mitchell, William; America, 1771 *1220.12 p556*
Mitchell, William; Barbados, 1674 *1220.12 p556*
Mitchell, William; North Carolina, 1775 *1422.10 p57*
Mitchell, William; North Carolina, 1829 *1088.45 p23*
Mitchell, William; North Carolina, 1856 *1088.45 p23*
Mitchell, William 38; Ontario, 1871 *1823.17 p119*
Mitchell, William 64; Ontario, 1871 *1823.21 p264*
Mitchell, William Bland; Louisiana, 1850 *7710.1 p151*
Mitchell, Willm.; Maryland, 1674-1675 *1236.25 p52*
Mitchells, Jacob; America, 1770 *1220.12 p556*
Mitchelmore, Thomas 45; Ontario, 1871 *1823.21 p264*
Mitchelson, James; America, 1765 *1220.12 p556*
Mitchelthree, Fanny 50; Ontario, 1871 *1823.21 p264*
Mitcheltree, John 38; Ontario, 1871 *1823.21 p264*
Mitchiner, Thomas; America, 1768 *1220.12 p547*
Mitchler, Nicholas; North Carolina, 1857 *1088.45 p23*
Mitermiler, Ondrej; Cleveland, OH, 1840 *2853.20 p476*
Mitnacht, Anne Marie 18; Louisiana, 1848 *778.6 p245*
Mitrenga, Stanislaus; Port uncertain, 1905 *7420.1 p380*
Mitron, Francois 31; Quebec, 1659 *9221.17 p401*
Mittan, John; New Hampshire, 1665 *9228.50 p466*
Mittans, John; Virginia, 1665 *9228.50 p53*
Mittchel, William 32; Ontario, 1871 *1823.21 p264*
Mittelbrihler, Jacob 22; New Orleans, 1848 *778.6 p245*
Mittelsdorf, Henriette; America, 1867 *7919.3 p534*
Mittelstaedt, Eduard Friede; Wisconsin, 1905 *6795.8 p123*
Mittelstaedt, Ernst Eduard; Wisconsin, 1895 *6795.8 p236*
Mittelstedt, Edward; Wisconsin, 1869 *6795.8 p186*
Mitten, John; New Hampshire, 1665 *9228.50 p466*
Mittenmeier, John; Illinois, 1858 *6079.1 p10*
Mittiga, Dom.; New York, 1926 *1173.1 p2*
Mittin, John; New Hampshire, 1665 *9228.50 p466*
Mittins, John; Virginia, 1665 *9228.50 p53*
Mittmann, Julius Alexander; Texas, 1873 *5475.1 p31*
Mitton, John; America, 1774 *1220.12 p556*
Mitton, John; New Hampshire, 1665 *9228.50 p466*
Mitton, Samuel; America, 1774 *1220.12 p556*
Mitton, William; America, 1757 *1220.12 p556*
Mitze, Gebhart; Illinois, 1863 *6079.1 p10*
Mitzel, Agatha 5 months; New York, NY, 1893 *1883.7 p41*
Mitzel, Andreas 24; New York, NY, 1893 *1883.7 p41*
Mitzel, Peter 1; New York, NY, 1893 *1883.7 p41*
Mitzel, Veronika 23; New York, NY, 1893 *1883.7 p41*
Mitzenheim, Theodor; America, 1867 *7919.3 p528*
Mitzner, Carl August; Wisconsin, 1891 *6795.8 p38*
Mitzner, Wilhelmine; Wisconsin, 1896 *6795.8 p134*
Miville, Charlotte Mauger 42 SEE Miville, Pierre
Miville, Francois 15 SEE Miville, Pierre
Miville, Jacques 10 SEE Miville, Pierre
Miville, Marie 17 SEE Miville, Pierre
Miville, Marie-Madeleine 13 SEE Miville, Pierre
Miville, Martine-Aimee 14 SEE Miville, Pierre
Miville, Pierre 47; Quebec, 1649 *9221.17 p216*
  *Wife:*Charlotte Mauger 42
  *Daughter:*Martine-Aimee 14
  *Son:*Jacques 10
  *Daughter:*Suzanne 9
  *Daughter:*Marie-Madeleine 13
  *Daughter:*Marie 17
  *Son:*Francois 15
Miville, Suzanne 9 SEE Miville, Pierre
Miville, Vincent; Quebec, 1638 *9221.17 p79*
Mixner, Frank 29; Ontario, 1871 *1823.21 p264*
Mixon, William; Virginia, 1732 *1220.12 p556*
Mizyck, Alexander 69; Ontario, 1871 *1823.21 p264*
M'Kay, Thomas; Toronto, 1844 *2910.35 p113*
M'Laughlin, P.B.; Toronto, 1844 *2910.35 p113*
Mleczko, Marya 18; New York, NY, 1911 *6533.11 p10*

Mlen, Nichol 48; Ontario, 1871 *1823.21 p264*
Mlickova, Antonie; America, 1850-1860 *2853.20 p49*
  With parents
Moaks, John 52; Ontario, 1871 *1823.21 p264*
Moar, Deborah; Boston, 1750 *1642 p46*
Moar, Elizabeth; Massachusetts, 1767 *1642 p64*
Moar, Myer 28; New York, NY, 1894 *6512.1 p229*
Moar, Solomon 25; New York, NY, 1894 *6512.1 p229*
Moate, John; America, 1751 *1220.12 p556*
Mobbs, Elizabeth; Annapolis, MD, 1722 *1220.12 p556*
Mobbs, Elizabeth; Maryland, 1737 *1220.12 p556*
Mobbs, Martha; America, 1739 *1220.12 p556*
Mobbs, Philip; America, 1732 *1220.12 p556*
Mobbs, Thomas; Annapolis, MD, 1725 *1220.12 p556*
Moberg, Anders; Cleveland, OH, 1881-1884 *9722.10 p124*
Mobson, William; America, 1699 *1220.12 p556*
Moburg, Gust Renhold; New York, 1902 *1766.20 p3*
Mock, Conrad; Ohio, 1809-1852 *4511.35 p36*
Mock, George; Ohio, 1809-1852 *4511.35 p36*
Mock, John; America, 1775 *1220.12 p556*
Mock, John; Ohio, 1809-1852 *4511.35 p36*
Mock, Philip; Ohio, 1809-1852 *4511.35 p36*
Mocklar, John 32; Ontario, 1871 *1823.21 p264*
Mockridge, Mary; America, 1743 *1220.12 p557*
Modeka, Michael; Louisiana, 1874 *4981.45 p133*
Moder, John; Ohio, 1809-1852 *4511.35 p36*
Moderecki, Isidore 39; New York, NY, 1920 *930.50 p49*
Moderson, E. H.; Louisiana, 1874-1875 *4981.45 p29*
Modeste, Sylvester; Ohio, 1809-1852 *4511.35 p36*
Modesty, Thomas; Virginia, 1727 *1220.12 p557*
Modre, Joseph; Ohio, 1809-1852 *4511.35 p36*
Modrow, Martin; Wisconsin, 1892 *6795.8 p123*
Moe, Johann; America, 1880 *7420.1 p317*
Moeand, Jean 23; America, 1840 *778.6 p245*
Moebius, August Reinhart; Kansas, 1883 *1447.20 p63*
Moede, Hermann; Wisconsin, 1858 *6795.8 p90*
Moehlenbrock, Christian Gerhard; Iowa, 1906 *1211.15 p17*
Moelders, Peter Joseph Mathias; Illinois, 1930 *121.35 p100*
Moeller, Johann Adam; America, 1895 *170.15 p37*
  With family
Moeller, Johannes; America, 1895 *170.15 p37*
  With family
Moeller, Paul; Iowa, 1889 *1211.15 p17*
Moench, Alexander; New York, NY, 1889 *3366.30 p70*
Moens, Edmond Leopold Gregoire SEE Moens, Jean Joseph
Moens, Englebert Joseph SEE Moens, Jean Joseph
Moens, Jean Francois SEE Moens, Jean Joseph
Moens, Jean Joseph; Wisconsin, 1857 *1495.20 p41*
  *Wife:*Marie Henriette Vercammen
  *Child:*Marie Emerence
  *Child:*Englebert Joseph
  *Child:*Virginie
  *Child:*Jean Francois
  *Child:*Edmond Leopold Gregoire
Moens, Marie Emerence SEE Moens, Jean Joseph
Moens, Marie Henriette Vercammen SEE Moens, Jean Joseph
Moens, Virginie SEE Moens, Jean Joseph
Moerckle, Peter; Ohio, 1809-1852 *4511.35 p36*
Moersdorf, Anna; Brazil, 1846 *5475.1 p438*
Moesch, Charles; Illinois, 1861 *6079.1 p10*
Moeser, Micholas; Illinois, 1852 *6079.1 p10*
Moestrich, John; New York, 1859 *358.56 p55*
Moffat, Andrew 71; Ontario, 1871 *1823.17 p119*
Moffat, James 48; Ontario, 1871 *1823.21 p264*
Moffat, James 70; Ontario, 1871 *1823.17 p119*
Moffat, John 35; Ontario, 1871 *1823.21 p264*
Moffat, John 41; Ontario, 1871 *1823.21 p264*
Moffat, Mary 34; Ontario, 1871 *1823.21 p264*
Moffatt, Alexander; America, 1747 *1220.12 p557*
Moffett, Samuel; America, 1771 *1220.12 p557*
Moffit, John 39; Ontario, 1871 *1823.17 p119*
Moffit, Patrick; Ohio, 1809-1852 *4511.35 p36*
Moffitt, Patrick; Ohio, 1809-1852 *4511.35 p36*
Moffitt, Richard; Ohio, 1809-1852 *4511.35 p36*
Moffitt, Thomas; Ohio, 1809-1852 *4511.35 p36*
Moge, Joseph; Maryland or Virginia, 1733 *1220.12 p557*
Moger, George; New England, n.d. *9228.50 p469*
Moggridge, Richard; America, 1728 *1220.12 p557*
Moggridge, Samuel; America, 1729 *1220.12 p557*
Moggridge, Timothy; America, 1730 *1220.12 p557*
Mogielnicki, Marcin; Detroit, 1929 *1640.55 p112*
Mognon, Jean; North Carolina, 1805 *1088.45 p24*
Mogren, Augusta; St. Paul, MN, 1892 *1865.50 p97*
Mogridge, John; America, 1685 *1220.12 p557*
Mogridge, John; Virginia, 1766 *1220.12 p557*
Mohan, Francis 55; Ontario, 1871 *1823.21 p264*
Mohany, Daniel; St. John, N.B., 1842 *2978.20 p6*
Mohany, Daniel; St. John, N.B., 1842 *2978.20 p7*

Mohany, Kitty; St. John, N.B., 1842 *2978.20 p6*
Mohany, Mary; St. John, N.B., 1842 *2978.20 p6*
Mohen, He.ry 37; America, 1846 *778.6 p245*
Mohen, Sidary 9; America, 1846 *778.6 p245*
Mohen Seronce, Miss 9; America, 1846 *778.6 p245*
Mohimont, Alphonse SEE Mohimont, Jean Francois
Mohimont, Jean Francois; Wisconsin, 1856 *1495.20 p46*
  *Wife:*Marie Therese Barras
  *Son:*Alphonse
  With sister-in-law
Mohimont, Marie Therese Barras SEE Mohimont, Jean Francois
Mohl, Charles W.; Philadelphia, 1869 *8513.31 p416*
  *Wife:*Lydia Ernestine Vogel
Mohl, Lydia Ernestine Vogel SEE Mohl, Charles W.
Mohlenpah, Adolph Georg; America, 1871 *7420.1 p291*
Mohlenpah, Fritz Ferdinand; America, 1868 *7420.1 p274*
Mohlenpah, Karl; America, 1888 *7420.1 p357*
Mohlenpah Sisters, . . .; America, 1867 *7420.1 p261*
Mohling, August; America, 1857 *7420.1 p168*
Mohling, Christian Aug. Christ. SEE Mohling, Johann Christoph
Mohling, Engel Wilh. Charl. SEE Mohling, Johann Christoph
Mohling, Friedrich; America, 1857 *7420.1 p168*
Mohling, Henrich Christ. SEE Mohling, Johann Christoph
Mohling, Johann Christ. SEE Mohling, Johann Christoph
Mohling, Johann Christoph; America, 1852 *7420.1 p94*
  *Wife:*Wilhelmine Charl. Poock
  *Son:*Johann Christ.
  *Daughter:*Engel Wilh. Charl.
  *Son:*Johann Friedr. Christ.
  *Son:*Christian Aug. Christ.
  *Son:*Henrich Christ.
Mohling, Johann Friedr. Christ. SEE Mohling, Johann Christoph
Mohling, Johann Friedrich Christoph; America, 1862 *7420.1 p213*
  With wife
Mohling, Johann Heinrich Christian; America, 1851 *7420.1 p82*
Mohling, Sophie Charlotte; America, 1852 *7420.1 p93*
Mohling, Wilhelmine Charl. Poock SEE Mohling, Johann Christoph
Mohlmann, Carl; America, 1858 *7420.1 p180*
  With son & daughter
Mohlmann, Ernst Carl Ludwig; America, 1851 *7420.1 p82*
  With wife & daughter
Mohlmann, Friedrich Wilhelm; America, 1867 *7420.1 p261*
Mohlmann, Johanne Auguste Elisabeth; America, 1865 *7420.1 p234*
Mohlmeister, Heinrich; Port uncertain, 1853 *7420.1 p109*
Mohme, Caroline Philippine; America, 1857 *7420.1 p167*
Mohme, Marie Karoline; America, 1913 *7420.1 p391*
Mohn, Barbara; Venezuela, 1843 *3899.5 p542*
Mohn, Benedikt; Venezuela, 1843 *3899.5 p542*
Mohn, George Frederick; Ohio, 1809-1852 *4511.35 p36*
Mohn, Gotfred H.; Washington, 1886 *2770.40 p195*
Mohn, Hilarius; Venezuela, 1843 *3899.5 p542*
Mohn, Jacob E.; Washington, 1889 *2770.40 p79*
Mohn, John; Ohio, 1809-1852 *4511.35 p36*
Mohn, Peter; Ohio, 1809-1852 *4511.35 p36*
Mohni, Albert; Iowa, 1910 *1211.15 p17*
Mohnn, Catherine; America, 1755 *1220.12 p557*
Mohns, Wilhelm; America, 1849 *7420.1 p66*
  With wife & 3 children
Mohr, Adam; America, 1881 *2526.42 p155*
Mohr, Angela 14; Port uncertain, 1840 *778.6 p245*
Mohr, Anna Katharina; Baltimore, 1831 *2526.43 p206*
Mohr, Anna Margaretha; Baltimore, 1831 *2526.43 p206*
Mohr, Asmus; Illinois, 1930 *121.35 p100*
Mohr, Babette; America, 1883 *2526.42 p161*
Mohr, Barbara; Illinois, 1865 *2526.42 p149*
Mohr, Carl; Wisconsin, 1860 *6795.8 p102*
Mohr, Catherine 20; Port uncertain, 1840 *778.6 p245*
Mohr, Elisabeth; America, 1881 *2526.42 p155*
Mohr, Georg Friedrich; America, 1894 *2526.43 p176*
Mohr, Georg Peter; Baltimore, 1831 *2526.43 p206*
Mohr, Jakob; America, 1865 *5475.1 p30*
  *Wife:*Maria Katharina Walter
Mohr, Jakob; America, 1881 *2526.42 p155*
Mohr, Jakob SEE Mohr, Nikolaus
Mohr, Jean 16; Port uncertain, 1840 *778.6 p245*
Mohr, Jean 24; Port uncertain, 1840 *778.6 p245*
Mohr, Johann SEE Mohr, Nikolaus
Mohr, Johann Karl; America, 1843 *5475.1 p488*
Mohr, Johann Nikolaus 20 SEE Mohr, Mrs. Michael
Mohr, Johannes; America, 1860 *2526.42 p177*
Mohr, Juliana; America, 1857 *5475.1 p512*
Mohr, Karl; America, 1847 *5475.1 p473*

Mohr, Karl; America, 1851 *5475.1 p455*
*Brother:*Peter
Mohr, Katharina; America, 1856 *5475.1 p516*
Mohr, Katharina Kuhn *SEE* Mohr, Nikolaus
Mohr, Katharina 49; America, 1880 *5475.1 p456*
Mohr, Konrad; Baltimore, 1831 *2526.43 p206*
*Wife:*Anna Katharina Mohr
*Daughter:*Marie Katharine
*Son:*Georg Peter
*Daughter:*Anna Margaretha
Mohr, Leonhard; America, 1848 *2526.43 p206*
With wife & 8 children
Mohr, Leonhard; America, 1881 *2526.42 p155*
Mohr, Leonhard; America, 1881 *2526.42 p155*
*Wife:*Margaretha Mohr
*Child:*Leonhard
*Child:*Adam
*Child:*Elisabeth
*Child:*Margaretha
Mohr, Luise; America, 1857 *5475.1 p516*
Mohr, Marg. Greiweldinger 37 *SEE* Mohr, Nik.
Mohr, Margaretha; America, 1881 *2526.42 p155*
Mohr, Margaretha; America, 1881 *2526.42 p155*
Mohr, Marguerite 9; Port uncertain, 1840 *778.6 p245*
Mohr, Maria Katharina Walter *SEE* Mohr, Jakob
Mohr, Maria Margarethe; Brazil, 1865 *5475.1 p507*
Mohr, Marie Katharine; Baltimore, 1831 *2526.43 p206*
Mohr, Martin; New Castle, DE, 1817-1818 *90.20 p153*
Mohr, Michael 15 *SEE* Mohr, Mrs. Michael
Mohr, Michael 27; America, 1857 *5475.1 p343*
Mohr, Mrs. Michael; America, 1836 *2526.43 p219*
*Son:*Johann Nikolaus
*Son:*Michael
Mohr, Nik. 33; America, 1857 *5475.1 p362*
*Wife:*Marg. Greiweldinger 37
Mohr, Nikolaus; America, 1842 *5475.1 p397*
Mohr, Nikolaus *SEE* Mohr, Nikolaus
Mohr, Nikolaus; America, 1881 *5475.1 p456*
*Wife:*Katharina Kuhn
*Son:*Nikolaus
*Son:*Peter
*Son:*Jakob
*Son:*Johann
Mohr, Nikolaus 28; America, 1843 *5475.1 p294*
Mohr, Peter; America, 1849 *5475.1 p402*
Mohr, Peter *SEE* Mohr, Karl
Mohr, Peter *SEE* Mohr, Nikolaus
Mohr, Sophie; Brazil, 1861 *5475.1 p506*
Mohr, William 41; Ontario, 1871 *1823.21 p264*
Mohranz, Conrade; Philadelphia, 1778 *8529.30 p3*
Mohrbach, Katharina 50; America, 1874 *5475.1 p463*
Mohrmann, Ch.; Galveston, TX, 1855 *571.7 p18*
Mohrmann, Friedrich Wilhelm; Port uncertain, 1835
7420.1 p9
Mohs, Nikolaus; America, 1867 *5475.1 p376*
Moidrux, Rene; Quebec, 1659 *9221.17 p406*
Moig, Joseph; North Carolina, 1852 *1088.45 p24*
Moinet, Peter; Ohio, 1809-1852 *4511.35 p36*
Moinot, John Baptist; Ohio, 1809-1852 *4511.35 p36*
Moir, Alexander 42; Ontario, 1871 *1823.21 p264*
Moir, Jas. P. 21; Quebec, 1910 *2897.7 p10*
Moir, John; North Carolina, 1846 *1088.45 p24*
Moir, John 45; Ontario, 1871 *1823.17 p119*
Moir, John 45; Ontario, 1871 *1823.21 p264*
Moir, John 51; Ontario, 1871 *1823.21 p264*
Moir, Mary; North Carolina, 1847 *1088.45 p24*
Moir, Mary 53; Ontario, 1871 *1823.21 p264*
Moir, Robert; North Carolina, 1829 *1088.45 p24*
Moisan, Francoise; Canada, 1663 *1142.10 p128*
Moisan, Francoise; Quebec, 1663 *4514.3 p348*
Moise, Joseph 25; America, 1843 *778.6 p245*
Moise, Mathias 40; New Orleans, 1848 *778.6 p245*
Moise, Simon 23; Port uncertain, 1841 *778.6 p245*
Moisey, William; America, 1734 *1220.12 p557*
Moisley, Henry 35; Michigan, 1880 *4491.39 p21*
Moisley, Nancy 50; Michigan, 1880 *4491.39 p21*
Moisne, Simon; Montreal, 1644 *9221.17 p148*
Moisnet, Simon; Montreal, 1644 *9221.17 p148*
Moisse, Willian 44; Ontario, 1871 *1823.21 p264*
Moitie, Catherine; Quebec, 1663 *4514.3 p349*
*Sister:*Marguerite
Moitie, Marguerite *SEE* Moitie, Catherine
Moitie, Marie; Quebec, 1671 *4514.3 p349*
Moitie, Noel 33; America, 1846 *778.6 p246*
Moity, Louis 26; Texas, 1848 *778.6 p246*
Moizeau, Francois 17; Quebec, 1656 *9221.17 p343*
Moje, Emil; Valdivia, Chile, 1851 *1192.4 p51*
*Wife:*Jette
Moje, Jette *SEE* Moje, Emil
Moje, Joh.; Valdivia, Chile, 1851 *1192.4 p51*
Mojzis, Karel; Iowa, 1870-1889 *2853.20 p223*
Moke, John 20; Ontario, 1871 *1823.21 p264*
Mokejewon, John 48; Ontario, 1871 *1823.21 p264*

Mol, John; Maryland, 1753 *1220.12 p557*
Molan, Daniel; New England, 1745 *1642 p28*
Molander, August; St. Paul, MN, 1887 *1865.50 p97*
Molander, Bertha; Kansas, 1868 *777.40 p9*
Molarkie, John; North Carolina, 1792-1862 *1088.45 p24*
Molberg, Sam; Colorado, 1893 *1029.59 p63*
Moldenhauer, Wilh.; Valdivia, Chile, 1852 *1192.4 p53*
Molder, Mary; America, 1741 *1220.12 p570*
Molding, William; America, 1749 *1220.12 p570*
Mole, Thomas; America, 1775 *1220.12 p557*
Molen, Thomas; Boston, 1761 *1642 p48*
Molere, Joseph; Quebec, 1640 *9221.17 p98*
Moles, George; Barbados, 1671 *1220.12 p557*
Molessant, H. 31; New Orleans, 1841 *778.6 p246*
Molesworth, Joseph; America, 1768 *1220.12 p557*
Moley, Ann; America, 1743 *1220.12 p557*
Molezun, Jean; Louisiana, 1874-1875 *4981.45 p30*
Molholm, Eli C.; Nebraska, 1899 *1029.59 p63*
Molieure, John; Virginia, 1735 *1220.12 p557*
Molin, Auguste; Louisiana, 1836-1840 *4981.45 p213*
Molin, Brita Cajsa; St. Paul, MN, 1884-1885 *1865.50 p97*
Molin, J.A.; New York, NY, 1845 *6412.40 p149*
Molinder, H.J.; Cleveland, OH, 1899-1901 *9722.10 p124*
Moline, Brita Cajsa; St. Paul, MN, 1884-1885 *1865.50 p97*
Molineaux, Jonathan; Annapolis, MD, 1726 *1220.12 p557*
Molineux, Edward; Died enroute, 1719 *1220.12 p557*
Molineux, Richard; America, 1768 *1220.12 p557*
Molineux, Robert; Barbados, 1685 *1220.12 p557*
Molineux, Sapcott; Virginia, 1618 *1220.12 p557*
Molitor, Frederick; Ohio, 1809-1852 *4511.35 p36*
Molitor, Johann; Philadelphia, 1866 *5475.1 p178*
*Wife:*Susanna Arweiler
Molitor, Josef; Chicago, 1866 *2853.20 p423*
Molitor, Katharina; Texas, 1887 *5475.1 p162*
Molitor, Nikolaus; America, 1865 *5475.1 p159*
With brother
Molitor, Peter; America, 1865 *5475.1 p159*
With 2 brothers
Molitor, Stephan; America, 1866 *5475.1 p160*
With brother
Molitor, Susanna Arweiler 24 *SEE* Molitor, Johann
Molkup, Matej; Chicago, 1870-1910 *2853.20 p415*
Moll, Francisco; America, 1762 *1220.12 p557*
Moll, Joseph; Louisiana, 1874-1875 *4981.45 p30*
Moll, Margarethe 21; America, 1866 *5475.1 p143*
Moll, Simon 35; Ontario, 1871 *1823.21 p264*
Mollan, Ernest 41; Minnesota, 1925 *2769.54 p1382*
Mollan, Gunhilda 39; Minnesota, 1925 *2769.54 p1382*
Molland, John 36; Ontario, 1871 *1823.21 p264*
Molland, Philip 65; Ontario, 1871 *1823.21 p264*
Molland, William; Maryland, 1727 *1220.12 p557*
Molland, William 45; Ontario, 1871 *1823.21 p264*
Mollenhauer, Friedrich; New York, 1882 *5475.1 p42*
Moller, Mr.; America, 1860 *7420.1 p197*
With family
Moller, Mr.; Port uncertain, 1853 *7420.1 p109*
Moller, A.; New York, NY, 1844 *6412.40 p148*
Moller, August Hermann; Iowa, 1890 *7420.1 p361*
Moller, August Wilhelm; New York, 1841 *9722.10 p113*
Moller, Carl Wilhelm Gustav; America, 1878 *7420.1 p311*
Moller, Charlotte Johanne; America, 1865 *7420.1 p234*
*Brother:*Ernst Heinrich Christian
Moller, Christian; America, 1857 *7420.1 p168*
With son wife & daughter
Moller, Christian; America, 1867 *7919.3 p530*
With wife & 9 children
Moller, Christine Luise; America, 1836 *7420.1 p11*
Moller, Christine Marie; America, 1881 *7420.1 p324*
Moller, Christine Wilhelmine Charlotte; Minnesota, 1882
7420.1 p330
*Son:*Friedrich Wilhelm Christian Ludwig
*Daughter:*Wilhelmine Sophie Luise
*Son:*Christoph Friedrich Wilhelm
With mother
*Son:*Friedrich Christian
*Daughter:*Sophie Caroline Charlotte
Moller, Christoph Friedrich Wilhelm *SEE* Moller,
Christine Wilhelmine Charlotte Kuhlmann
Moller, Engel Marie Charlotte; America, 1845 *7420.1 p38*
Moller, Engel Marie Sophie Dorothee; Iowa, 1859
7420.1 p189
Moller, Engel Marie Wilhelm Eleonore; Port uncertain, 1840 *7420.1 p17*
Moller, Ernestine Philippine; America, 1869 *7420.1 p280*
Moller, Ernst Heinrich *SEE* Moller, Karl
Moller, Ernst Heinrich Carl; America, 1871 *7420.1 p291*
Moller, Ernst Heinrich Christian *SEE* Moller, Charlotte
Johanne

Moller, Ernst Heinrich Christoph; America, 1864 *7420.1 p225*
Moller, Ernst Heinrich Wilhelm; America, 1871 *7420.1 p291*
Moller, F. A.; Louisiana, 1874-1875 *4981.45 p30*
Moller, Friedrich; America, 1867 *7420.1 p261*
With family
Moller, Friedrich; America, 1867 *7420.1 p261*
Moller, Friedrich; New York, NY, 1844 *7420.1 p33*
Moller, Friedrich Christian *SEE* Moller, Christine
Wilhelmine Charlotte Kuhlmann
Moller, Friedrich Wilhelm Christian Ludwig *SEE* Moller,
Christine Wilhelmine Charlotte Kuhlmann
Moller, Friedrich Wilhelm Heinrich; America, 1846
7420.1 p46
With wife
Moller, Georg Friedrich August; America, 1888 *7420.1 p357*
Moller, Hans Heinrich Christoph; America, 1861 *7420.1 p207*
Moller, Heinrich; America, 1855 *7420.1 p139*
Moller, Heinrich; America, 1857 *7420.1 p168*
*Son:*Johann Heinrich Wilhelm
With wife 2 sons & 2 daughters
Moller, Heinrich; Iowa, 1892 *1211.15 p16*
Moller, Heinrich August; Port uncertain, 1854 *7420.1 p125*
Moller, Heinrich Christoph; America, 1860 *7420.1 p197*
Moller, Heinrich Conrad; America, 1857 *7420.1 p168*
Moller, Heinrich Conrad Gottlieb; America, 1867 *7420.1 p261*
Moller, Heinrich Conrad Gottlieb; America, 1868 *7420.1 p275*
Moller, Heinrich Friedrich Wilhelm; Port uncertain, 1883
7420.1 p338
Moller, Heinrich Gottlieb August; America, 1865 *7420.1 p234*
Moller, Johann Chr.; America, 1855 *7420.1 p139*
Moller, Johann Ernst; America, 1866 *7420.1 p246*
With family
Moller, Johann Heinrich Philipp; America, 1857 *7420.1 p168*
Moller, Johann Heinrich Wilhelm *SEE* Moller, Heinrich
Moller, Karl; America, 1869 *7420.1 p280*
With wife & 2 daughters
*Son:*Karl Wilhelm
*Son:*Ernst Heinrich
*Son:*Karl Friedrich Wilhelm
Moller, Karl Friedrich Wilhelm *SEE* Moller, Karl
Moller, Karl Wilhelm *SEE* Moller, Karl
Moller, Louis August; America, 1865 *7420.1 p234*
Moller, Louise 19; New York, NY, 1864 *8425.62 p196*
Moller, N.P.; Philadelphia, 1847 *6412.40 p150*
Moller, Sebastian; St. Louis, 1848 *2853.20 p21*
Moller, Sophie; America, 1885 *7420.1 p349*
Moller, Sophie Caroline Charlotte *SEE* Moller, Christine
Wilhelmine Charlotte Kuhlmann
Moller, Thrine Sophia; America, 1862 *7420.1 p212*
Moller, Wilhelm; America, 1846 *7420.1 p43*
Moller, Wilhelm; Port uncertain, 1853 *7420.1 p109*
Moller, Wilhelm Carl; America, 1869 *7420.1 p280*
Moller, Wilhelm Hackshorst Einlieger; America, 1846
7420.1 p46
Moller, Wilhelmine Sophie Luise *SEE* Moller, Christine
Wilhelmine Charlotte Kuhlmann
Moller Brothers, . . .; America, 1870 *7420.1 p285*
Moller Brothers, . . .; America, 1889 *7420.1 p359*
Mollers, Frantisek; St. Louis, 1852 *2853.20 p21*
Mollers, Vaclav; St. Louis, 1852 *2853.20 p21*
Mollet, Abraham; Marblehead, MA, 1722-1723 *9228.50 p472*
Mollet, Abraham; Marblehead, MA, 1722-1723 *9228.50 p487*
Mollet, Abraham, Jr.; Marblehead, MA, 1762 *9228.50 p472*
Mollet, Eliz. Le Jeune *SEE* Mollet, John
Mollet, Esme Patricia; America, 1918-1983 *9228.50 p467*
Mollet, John; Boston, 1790 *9228.50 p467*
Mollet, John; Quebec, 1862 *9228.50 p466*
*Wife:*Margaret Carter
*Son:*Philip Carter
*Son:*John C.
*Daughter-In-Law:*Eliz. Le Jeune
Mollet, John C. *SEE* Mollet, John
Mollet, Margaret Carter *SEE* Mollet, John
Mollet, Philip Alva; Detroit, 1925-1983 *9228.50 p467*
Mollet, Philip Carter *SEE* Mollet, John
Mollett, Edward; Virginia, 1738 *1220.12 p557*
Mollett, Esme P.; Ontario, 1918-1983 *9228.50 p539*
Mollett, John 58; Ontario, 1871 *1823.21 p264*
Mollett, Mary; New York, 1864 *9228.50 p250*
Molley, Mrs. 30; North Carolina, 1774 *1422.10 p55*
Mollin, L. A.; New York, NY, 1841 *6412.40 p155*

Molloney, Michael; Boston, 1774 ***1642*** *p50*
Mollony, John; Boston, 1765 ***1642*** *p34*
Molloy, Charles; Boston, 1725 ***1642*** *p25*
Molloy, John; Boston, 1764 ***1642*** *p48*
Molloy, Mary; Virginia, 1721 ***1220.12*** *p557*
Molloy, Michael; Newfoundland, 1814 ***3476.10*** *p54*
Molloy, Patrick; Salem, MA, 1763 ***1642*** *p78*
Molloy, Roger; America, 1775 ***1220.12*** *p557*
Molloys, Marcel; Quebec, 1649 ***9221.17*** *p217*
Mollynex, John; America, 1736 ***1220.12*** *p557*
Molnar, John; New York, 1926 ***1173.1*** *p2*
Molnar, Karel V.; Chicago, 1896 ***2853.20*** *p461*
Molney, Peter; America, 1767 ***1220.12*** *p557*
Moloney, James 28; Ontario, 1871 ***1823.17*** *p119*
Moloney, Thomas 75; Ontario, 1871 ***1823.17*** *p119*
Molony, John; Boston, 1752 ***1642*** *p46*
Molotkiewicz, Anthony; Detroit, 1930 ***1640.60*** *p82*
Molson, Joseph; America, 1772 ***1220.12*** *p570*
Molter, Franz; America, 1865 ***5475.1*** *p542*
Molter, Karl; America, 1867 ***5475.1*** *p543*
Molthahn, Ernst Wilhelm; Fort Wayne, IN, 1840 ***7420.1*** *p19*
Molthan, Mr.; America, 1869 ***7420.1*** *p281*
Molthan, C. Friedrich Wilhelm; America, 1867 ***7420.1*** *p261*
Molthan, Christine Marie *SEE* Molthan, Ernst Christian Ferdinand
Molthan, Christine Philippine Spannuth *SEE* Molthan, Ernst Christian Ferdinand
Molthan, Ernestine Caroline Sophie; America, 1869 ***7420.1*** *p281*
Molthan, Ernst Carl Christian; America, 1870 ***7420.1*** *p285*
Molthan, Ernst Christian Ferdinand; America, 1872 ***7420.1*** *p296*
*Wife:*Christine Philippine Spannuth
*Daughter:*Christine Marie
*Son:*Franz Albert
Molthan, Ernst Friedrich; America, 1869 ***7420.1*** *p281*
Molthan, Franz Albert *SEE* Molthan, Ernst Christian Ferdinand
Molthan, Gottlieb; America, 1869 ***7420.1*** *p281*
With wife
Molthan, Heinrich Christian; America, 1871 ***7420.1*** *p291*
Molthan, Johann Christoph; America, 1856 ***7420.1*** *p151*
Molthan, Johann Friedrich Wilhelm *SEE* Molthan, Johann Henrich
Molthan, Johann Henrich; America, 1845 ***7420.1*** *p38*
*Brother:*Johann Friedrich Wilhelm
Molton, Anthony Theodore; Detroit, 1930 ***1640.60*** *p82*
Molton, Humphrey; America, 1685 ***1220.12*** *p570*
Molton, William; America, 1697 ***1220.12*** *p570*
Molz, Friedrich Adam; America, 1870 ***7420.1*** *p287*
Molz, Jacob 26; America, 1844 ***778.6*** *p246*
Molz, John; Chicago, 1856 ***8513.31*** *p416*
*Wife:*Sophia Lampper
Molz, Sophia Lampper *SEE* Molz, John
Momford, Thomas; America, 1745 ***1220.12*** *p572*
Mommer, Joseph; Ohio, 1809-1852 ***4511.35*** *p36*
Momsen, Lorenz Olsen; Iowa, 1924 ***1211.15*** *p17*
Monaco, John 50; Ontario, 1871 ***1823.21*** *p264*
Monaghan, Bernard; North Carolina, 1854 ***1088.45*** *p24*
Monaghan, Cormach 40; Ontario, 1871 ***1823.21*** *p264*
Monaghan, Edward 39; Michigan, 1880 ***4491.33*** *p16*
Monaghan, George 33; Ontario, 1871 ***1823.21*** *p264*
Monaghan, James; Ohio, 1809-1852 ***4511.35*** *p36*
Monaghan, John; Toronto, 1844 ***2910.35*** *p113*
Monaghan, Patrick 63; Ontario, 1871 ***1823.17*** *p119*
Monaghan, Thomas; Ohio, 1809-1852 ***4511.35*** *p36*
Monaghan, William 65; Ontario, 1871 ***1823.17*** *p119*
Monaghan, Wm.; Louisiana, 1874-1875 ***4981.45*** *p30*
Monahan, Luke 30; Michigan, 1880 ***4491.30*** *p22*
Monahan, Mary; New Orleans, 1851 ***7242.30*** *p149*
Monahan, Winafred; New Orleans, 1851 ***7242.30*** *p149*
Monard, Alexandre 15; America, 1843 ***778.6*** *p246*
Monard, Pauline 41; America, 1843 ***778.6*** *p246*
Monard, Pierre 1; America, 1843 ***778.6*** *p246*
Monassot, A. 30; America, 1843 ***778.6*** *p246*
Monballais, Eugene 34; New Orleans, 1848 ***778.6*** *p246*
Monballais, Eugenie 5; New Orleans, 1848 ***778.6*** *p246*
Monballais, Josephine 29; New Orleans, 1848 ***778.6*** *p246*
Monceau, Mrs. 35; America, 1843 ***778.6*** *p246*
Monceaux, Jean-Christophe-Marie de; Quebec, 1729 ***2314.30*** *p171*
Moncion, Marguerite; Quebec, 1670 ***4514.3*** *p320*
Monck, Mary 30; Ontario, 1871 ***1823.21*** *p264*
Moncke, Richard; America, 1683 ***1220.12*** *p558*
Moncreff, William 55; Ontario, 1871 ***1823.21*** *p264*
Moncrieff, George 26; Ontario, 1871 ***1823.17*** *p119*
Mond, Benedikt; Venezuela, 1843 ***3899.5*** *p542*
Monday, Richard; America, 1772 ***1220.12*** *p572*
Monday, William; America, 1745 ***1220.12*** *p572*
Monde, Carl A.; Galveston, TX, 1855 ***571.7*** *p17*
Mondorf, Johann Heinrich; New York, NY, 1882 ***5475.1*** *p24*
Mondry, Peter; Wisconsin, 1910 ***6795.8*** *p166*
Monela, Mrs. 28; Port uncertain, 1840 ***778.6*** *p246*
Monese, Manuel; North Carolina, 1814 ***1088.45*** *p24*
Money, Edward; America, 1690 ***1220.12*** *p557*
Money, Robert; America, 1697 ***1220.12*** *p557*
Money, Roger; Barbados, 1664 ***1220.12*** *p557*
Moneypenny, Hugh; America, 1762 ***1220.12*** *p557*
Moneypeny, Mary 43; Ontario, 1871 ***1823.17*** *p119*
Monford, Richard; America, 1758 ***1220.12*** *p557*
Monford, Thomas; America, 1727 ***1220.12*** *p557*
Monfort, P.; Louisiana, 1874 ***4981.45*** *p296*
Mong, Valentine; Ohio, 1809-1852 ***4511.35*** *p36*
Mongardain, Gabriel Armd. 26; New Orleans, 1840 ***778.6*** *p246*
Monge, F. 27; America, 1846 ***778.6*** *p246*
Mongeau, Pierre; Quebec, 1662 ***9221.17*** *p490*
Mongeon, Louis; Louisiana, 1874-1875 ***4981.45*** *p29*
Monger, Elijah 44; Ontario, 1871 ***1823.17*** *p119*
Monger, Henry 46; Ontario, 1871 ***1823.21*** *p265*
Monger, Joseph; America, 1765 ***1220.12*** *p557*
Monger, Sarah; America, 1753 ***1220.12*** *p557*
Monger, Wm F. 49; Ontario, 1871 ***1823.21*** *p265*
Mongin, L. 17; New Orleans, 1841 ***778.6*** *p249*
Monguillot, Jean; Louisiana, 1874-1875 ***4981.45*** *p30*
Monic, Joseph de; Quebec, 1691 ***2314.30*** *p171*
Monie, Jacob; Ohio, 1809-1852 ***4511.35*** *p36*
Monier, Jean Baptiste; Louisiana, 1836-1840 ***4981.45*** *p213*
Monig, A. Elisabeth; Vancouver, B.C., 1907 ***8023.44*** *p377*
Monighan, Thomas; Ohio, 1809-1852 ***4511.35*** *p36*
Monin, Charles; Ohio, 1809-1852 ***4511.35*** *p36*
Monin, J. 30; New Orleans, 1844 ***778.6*** *p246*
Monis, Nicolas 22; New Orleans, 1840 ***778.6*** *p246*
Moniso, Mr. 52; New Orleans, 1843 ***778.6*** *p246*
Monk, Ann; America, 1754 ***1220.12*** *p558*
Monk, Ann; America, 1755 ***1220.12*** *p558*
Monk, Ann; America, 1774 ***1220.12*** *p558*
Monk, Elizabeth; America, 1759 ***1220.12*** *p558*
Monk, George; America, 1740 ***1220.12*** *p558*
Monk, George; America, 1756 ***1220.12*** *p558*
Monk, George; Virginia, 1738 ***1220.12*** *p558*
Monk, John; America, 1754 ***1220.12*** *p558*
Monk, John; America, 1768 ***1220.12*** *p558*
Monk, John 76; Ontario, 1871 ***1823.21*** *p265*
Monk, Joseph; America, 1773 ***1220.12*** *p558*
Monk, Martha; America, 1744 ***1220.12*** *p558*
Monk, Mary; America, 1749 ***1220.12*** *p558*
Monk, Neil 32; Ontario, 1871 ***1823.21*** *p265*
Monk, Rinaldo; Virginia, 1742 ***1220.12*** *p558*
Monke, Elizabeth; Annapolis, MD, 1736 ***1220.12*** *p558*
Monke, Thomas; America, 1701 ***1220.12*** *p558*
Monkhouse, Jane; America, 1765 ***1220.12*** *p558*
Monkhouse, William 63; Ontario, 1871 ***1823.17*** *p119*
Monkinnick, John W. 52; Ontario, 1871 ***1823.21*** *p265*
Monks, James 50; Ontario, 1871 ***1823.21*** *p265*
Monks, William 42; Ontario, 1871 ***1823.21*** *p265*
Monlezun, P. 34; New Orleans, 1842 ***778.6*** *p246*
Monloney, John; Boston, 1763 ***1642*** *p32*
Monmerque Dubreuil, Cyr de; Quebec, 1726 ***2314.30*** *p172*
Monmouth, Charles William; America, 1698 ***1220.12*** *p558*
Monnien, Francis; Ohio, 1840-1897 ***8365.35*** *p17*
Monnier, Mr. 42; America, 1847 ***778.6*** *p246*
Monnier, Charles; Ohio, 1809-1852 ***4511.35*** *p36*
Monnier, Claudine 56; New Orleans, 1848 ***778.6*** *p246*
Monnier, F.; Louisiana, 1874 ***4981.45*** *p296*
Monnier, Louise 11; America, 1845 ***778.6*** *p246*
Monnier, Louise 46; America, 1845 ***778.6*** *p246*
Monnier, Xavier 49; New Orleans, 1848 ***778.6*** *p246*
Monnin, Ignace; Ohio, 1840-1897 ***8365.35*** *p17*
Monnin, John B.; Ohio, 1840-1897 ***8365.35*** *p17*
Monnin, Justin; Ohio, 1840-1897 ***8365.35*** *p17*
Monnot de Angle, Mr. 19; America, 1842 ***778.6*** *p246*
Monot, Francoise 17; Louisiana, 1848 ***778.6*** *p246*
Monot, Henriette 6; Louisiana, 1848 ***778.6*** *p246*
Monot, J. Bte. 9; Louisiana, 1848 ***778.6*** *p246*
Monot, Jeanne 42; Louisiana, 1848 ***778.6*** *p246*
Monot, Pauline 26; New Orleans, 1846 ***778.6*** *p246*
Monreal, Anna *SEE* Monreal, Anton
Monreal, Anton *SEE* Monreal, Anton
Monreal, Anton 41; America, 1880 ***5475.1*** *p227*
*Wife:*Magdalena Hirtz 36
*Daughter:*Anna
*Son:*Anton
Monreal, Magdalena Hirtz 36 *SEE* Monreal, Anton
Monro, Alexander 50; Ontario, 1871 ***1823.21*** *p265*
Monro, Hugh 26; North Carolina, 1774 ***1422.10*** *p59*
Monro, James; North Carolina, 1856 ***1088.45*** *p24*
Monro, Jane; Maryland or Virginia, 1738 ***1220.12*** *p558*
Monro, John; America, 1770 ***1220.12*** *p558*
Monro, Margaret; America, 1774 ***1220.12*** *p558*
Monro, Mary; America, 1750 ***1220.12*** *p558*
Monro, Willm. 34; North Carolina, 1774 ***1422.10*** *p59*
Monroe, Alexander 50; Ontario, 1871 ***1823.17*** *p119*
Monroe, Alexander 69; Ontario, 1871 ***1823.17*** *p119*
Monroe, Christina 37; Ontario, 1871 ***1823.21*** *p265*
Monroe, Christine 19; Ontario, 1871 ***1823.21*** *p265*
Monroe, E.; California, 1868 ***1131.61*** *p90*
Monroe, George 42; Michigan, 1880 ***4491.39*** *p21*
Monroe, George W.; Illinois, 1858-1861 ***6020.5*** *p132*
Monroe, Hugh 20; Ontario, 1871 ***1823.21*** *p265*
Monroe, James 13; Michigan, 1880 ***4491.39*** *p21*
Monroe, John; America, 1765 ***1220.12*** *p558*
Monroe, John, Sr. 76; Ontario, 1871 ***1823.21*** *p265*
Monroe, Joseph; America, 1750 ***1220.12*** *p558*
Monroe, Margaret; America, 1744 ***1220.12*** *p558*
Monroe, Margarett 41; Michigan, 1880 ***4491.39*** *p21*
Monroe, Robert; North Carolina, 1852 ***1088.45*** *p24*
Monroe, Robert 50; Ontario, 1871 ***1823.21*** *p265*
Monroe, William 15; Michigan, 1880 ***4491.39*** *p21*
Monroe, William; Virginia, 1749 ***3675.1*** *p*
Monrose, Mr. 16; New Orleans, 1848 ***778.6*** *p246*
Monrose, Chs. 38; New Orleans, 1842 ***778.6*** *p247*
Monrse, Manuel; North Carolina, 1842 ***1088.45*** *p24*
Monsabert, de, Baron 29; America, 1842 ***778.6*** *p247*
Monson, John E.; Iowa, 1900 ***1211.15*** *p17*
Monson, Mons; Iowa, 1892 ***1211.15*** *p16*
Monson, Peter; Iowa, 1896 ***1211.15*** *p17*
Monson, Wilhelm; St. Paul, MN, 1888 ***1865.50*** *p97*
Monsuit, Miss 32; America, 1846 ***778.6*** *p247*
Monsuit, Mathilde 19; America, 1846 ***778.6*** *p247*
Montag, Nikolaus; North America, 1834 ***5475.1*** *p52*
Montagnan, Mr. 22; New Orleans, 1840 ***778.6*** *p247*
Montagne, Martin; Quebec, 1646 ***9221.17*** *p167*
Montague, Elizabeth; Maryland, 1737 ***1220.12*** *p558*
Montague, Henry 37; Ontario, 1871 ***1823.21*** *p265*
Montague, Patrick; North Carolina, 1841 ***1088.45*** *p24*
Montague, Rhoda 47; Ontario, 1871 ***1823.21*** *p265*
Montague, Thomas; America, 1682 ***1220.12*** *p558*
Montague, Thomas; America, 1690 ***1220.12*** *p558*
Montais, Jane; Maine, 1704 ***9228.50*** *p271*
Montalant, Eugene 40; America, 1843 ***778.6*** *p247*
Montaldo, Ignacio; Illinois, 1852 ***6079.1*** *p10*
Montamat, Eugene 18; America, 1848 ***778.6*** *p247*
Montamat, Nicolas 33; America, 1845 ***778.6*** *p247*
Montana, Domnick 23; Indiana, 1892-1904 ***9076.20*** *p74*
Montandon, L. E. 34; New Orleans, 1846 ***778.6*** *p247*
Montane, Pierre 41; America, 1843 ***778.6*** *p247*
Montant, Laurens 30; America, 1842 ***778.6*** *p247*
Montanus, Ernest; North Carolina, 1856 ***1088.45*** *p24*
Montaricht, John 37; New Orleans, 1843 ***778.6*** *p247*
Montassier, Mr. 25; New Orleans, 1844 ***778.6*** *p247*
Montassier, Mr. 30; New Orleans, 1848 ***778.6*** *p247*
Montauban, Francois 29; Quebec, 1660 ***9221.17*** *p436*
Montaunt, Mr. 20; New Orleans, 1848 ***778.6*** *p247*
Montaye, Philip Joseph; Newfoundland, 1705 ***9228.50*** *p467*
Montchevreul, Pierre de; Quebec, 1647 ***9221.17*** *p185*
Montear, Martha; Annapolis, MD, 1725 ***1220.12*** *p558*
Monteaux, Mr. 30; New Orleans, 1842 ***778.6*** *p247*
Monteeth, Robert; America, 1773 ***1220.12*** *p558*
Montegut, Antoine 18; America, 1845 ***778.6*** *p247*
Montegut, Pierre 22; America, 1845 ***778.6*** *p247*
Monteil, Jean 29; New Orleans, 1840 ***778.6*** *p247*
Monteith, Henry 30; Ontario, 1871 ***1823.21*** *p265*
Monteith, John 67; Ontario, 1871 ***1823.21*** *p265*
Monteith, Robert 65; Ontario, 1871 ***1823.21*** *p265*
Monteleon, Louis de; Quebec, 1710 ***2314.30*** *p169*
Monteleon, Louis de; Quebec, 1710 ***2314.30*** *p191*
Montelius, Reinhold; New York, NY, 1844 ***6412.40*** *p148*
Monter, Sarah; America, 1766 ***1220.12*** *p558*
Montereau, A. 17; America, 1844 ***778.6*** *p247*
Montess, Jane; Maine, 1650-1750 ***9228.50*** *p467*
Montess, Jane; Maine, 1707 ***9228.50*** *p367*
Montess, Philip Joseph; Newfoundland, 1705 ***9228.50*** *p467*
Montesse, Jane; Maine, 1704 ***9228.50*** *p271*
Montesse, Jeanne; Maine, 1707 ***9228.50*** *p367*
Montet, A. 45; New Orleans, 1842 ***778.6*** *p247*
Montete, Eugen.e 6; Port uncertain, 1841 ***778.6*** *p247*
Montete, Pierre 36; Port uncertain, 1841 ***778.6*** *p247*
Montford, Robert; America, 1773 ***1220.12*** *p558*
Montfort, Emanuel; New York, NY, 1855 ***1494.21*** *p31*
Montfort, Jacques *SEE* Montfort, Jean
Montfort, Jean 52; Quebec, 1637 ***9221.17*** *p72*
*Son:*Jacques
Montfort, Pierre 38; Louisiana, 1848 ***778.6*** *p247*
Montgomary, Robert 65; Ontario, 1871 ***1823.17*** *p119*
Montgomery, Alexander; America, 1773 ***1220.12*** *p558*
Montgomery, Alexander; New York, 1738 ***8277.31*** *p119*
*Wife:*Anna Sutherland

336

FOR A COMPLETE EXPLANATION OF ENTRY, SEE "HOW TO READ A CITATION" SECTION

Montgomery, Allison 19; New York, NY, 1835 *5024.1 p137*
Montgomery, Andrew; America, 1740 *1220.12 p558*
Montgomery, Anna Sutherland SEE Montgomery, Alexander
Montgomery, Eleanor; America, 1756 *1220.12 p558*
Montgomery, Elizabeth; America, 1743 *1220.12 p558*
Montgomery, Elizabeth; Boston, 1749 *1642 p46*
Montgomery, Elizabeth; Philadelphia, 1851 *8513.31 p410*
Montgomery, Ester; Virginia, 1724 *1220.12 p558*
Montgomery, Frances; America, 1747 *1220.12 p558*
Montgomery, George 1; New York, NY, 1835 *5024.1 p137*
Montgomery, George Frederick; America, 1767 *1220.12 p558*
Montgomery, Hannah; Potomac, 1731 *1220.12 p559*
Montgomery, Hugh 15; Boston, 1730 *1642 p24*
Montgomery, Hugh; New York, 1738 *8277.31 p119*
Montgomery, Hugh; Prince Edward Island, 1771 *3799.30 p41*
Montgomery, Hugh; Prince Edward Island, 1771 *3799.30 p41*
    Wife:Mary MacShannon
    With 5 children
Montgomery, James 30; Ontario, 1871 *1823.21 p265*
Montgomery, James 35; Ontario, 1871 *1823.17 p119*
Montgomery, James 62; Ontario, 1871 *1823.17 p119*
Montgomery, Jeremiah 30; Ontario, 1871 *1823.17 p119*
Montgomery, John; America, 1766 *1220.12 p559*
Montgomery, John; Ohio, 1838 *3580.20 p33*
Montgomery, John; Ohio, 1838 *6020.12 p21*
Montgomery, John; Ontario, 1835 *3160.1 p150*
Montgomery, Margaret; America, 1770 *1220.12 p559*
Montgomery, Mary MacShannon SEE Montgomery, Hugh
Montgomery, Neill; Prince Edward Island, 1771 *3799.30 p41*
Montgomery, Peter; Boston, 1740-1749 *1642 p29*
Montgomery, Robert 22; New York, NY, 1835 *5024.1 p137*
Montgomery, Robert 32; Ontario, 1871 *1823.17 p119*
Montgomery, Thomas; Ohio, 1838 *3580.20 p33*
Montgomery, Thomas; Ohio, 1838 *6020.12 p21*
Montgomery, William 31; Ontario, 1871 *1823.17 p119*
Montgomry, Chartis 44; Ontario, 1871 *1823.17 p119*
Montgomry, John 42; Ontario, 1871 *1823.17 p119*
Montheil, Doct. 40; Port uncertain, 1845 *778.6 p247*
Montier, John 36; Ontario, 1871 *1823.21 p265*
Montier, Leon 30; America, 1845 *778.6 p247*
Montier, William 62; Ontario, 1871 *1823.21 p265*
Montieth, William 30; Ontario, 1871 *1823.21 p265*
Montigny, Pierre; Quebec, 1662 *9221.17 p479*
Montjoy, Richard 36; Ontario, 1871 *1823.21 p265*
Montminy, Barbe SEE Montminy, Charles
Montminy, Charles; Quebec, 1646-1664 *4514.3 p349*
    Child:Marie
    Child:Barbe
Montminy, Marie SEE Montminy, Charles
Montminy, Marie; Quebec, 1664 *4514.3 p349*
Montmorency, . . . 27; Quebec, 1655 *9221.17 p320*
Montois, Mr. 35; Port uncertain, 1846 *778.6 p247*
Montousee, Nic...s 38; New Orleans, 1843 *778.6 p247*
Montpellier, Antoine; Quebec, 1644 *9221.17 p144*
Montpellier, Jacques; Quebec, 1657 *9221.17 p357*
Montpere, Marie 58; Mississippi, 1846 *778.6 p247*
Montpetit, Francais 21; Ohio, 1880 *4879.40 p258*
Montplaisir, Pierre 16; Quebec, 1653 *9221.17 p272*
Montra, Lius 27 SEE Montra, Marcus
Montra, Marcus 26; Ohio, 1880 *4879.40 p257*
    Wife:Lius 27
    Daughter:Mary 1
Montra, Mary 1 SEE Montra, Marcus
Montrer, Isaac 30; America, 1846 *778.6 p247*
Montreuil, Nicolas; Quebec, 1640 *9221.17 p98*
Montross, Francis; Annapolis, MD, 1725 *1220.12 p559*
Montroy, Margarett E. 15; Ohio, 1880 *4879.40 p259*
Monvoisin, Francoise; Quebec, 1668 *4514.3 p349*
Monz, Anna Barbara 23 SEE Monz, Nikolaus
Monz, Magdalena 50; America, 1861 *5475.1 p482*
Monz, Maria 19 SEE Monz, Nikolaus
Monz, Nikolaus; America, 1836 *5475.1 p468*
    Wife:Anna Barbara
    Daughter:Maria
Mood, Philip; Ohio, 1809-1852 *4511.35 p36*
Mooden, Elizabeth; America, 1739 *1220.12 p559*
Moodie, William 54; Ontario, 1871 *1823.21 p265*
Moody, Alexander 46; Michigan, 1880 *4491.33 p16*
Moody, Andrew; Virginia, 1736 *1220.12 p559*
Moody, Charles; America, 1726 *1220.12 p559*
Moody, Clement; Maine, n.d. *9228.50 p467*
Moody, Clement; New Hampshire, 1692 *9228.50 p468*

Moody, David; Ohio, 1867 *3580.20 p33*
Moody, David; Ohio, 1867 *6020.12 p21*
Moody, Dorothy Frances Henry SEE Moody, Hunter Courtland
Moody, Earl Humphrey; Montreal, 1944 *9228.50 p455*
    Wife:Kathryn Irene Foley
    Child:John Edward
Moody, Eleanor; America, 1718 *1220.12 p559*
Moody, Eliza 36; Michigan, 1880 *4491.33 p16*
Moody, Elizabeth; America, 1739 *1220.12 p559*
Moody, Elizabeth; Charles Town, SC, 1719 *1220.12 p559*
Moody, Elizabeth; Virginia, 1767 *1220.12 p559*
Moody, Hill 80; Michigan, 1880 *4491.33 p16*
Moody, Hunter Courtland; Montreal, 1942 *9228.50 p455*
    Wife:Dorothy Frances Henry
Moody, Isaac 38; Ontario, 1871 *1823.21 p265*
Moody, Isaac 72; Ontario, 1871 *1823.21 p265*
Moody, Isaac J. 29; Michigan, 1880 *4491.33 p16*
Moody, Isabel 27; Michigan, 1880 *4491.33 p16*
Moody, Jacob 31; Michigan, 1880 *4491.33 p16*
Moody, James; America, 1685 *1220.12 p559*
Moody, James; America, 1767 *1220.12 p559*
Moody, James 61; Ontario, 1871 *1823.17 p119*
Moody, John; America, 1752 *1220.12 p559*
Moody, John; America, 1758 *1220.12 p559*
Moody, John; America, 1763 *1220.12 p559*
Moody, John; America, 1771 *1220.12 p559*
Moody, John; America, 1774 *1220.12 p559*
Moody, John 50; Ontario, 1871 *1823.21 p265*
Moody, John Edward SEE Moody, Earl Humphrey
Moody, Kathryn Irene Foley SEE Moody, Earl Humphrey
Moody, Kay Erline; Illinois, 1969 *9228.50 p455*
Moody, Nicholas; Maine, 1679 *9228.50 p468*
Moody, Philip; Maine, 1684 *9228.50 p468*
Moody, Richard; America, 1730 *1220.12 p559*
Moody, Samuel; America, 1754 *1220.12 p559*
Moody, Samuel; America, 1766 *1220.12 p559*
Moody, Solomon B. 25; Michigan, 1880 *4491.33 p16*
Moody, Thomas; America, 1733 *1220.12 p559*
Moody, William; America, 1720 *1220.12 p559*
Moody, William; America, 1735 *1220.12 p559*
Moody, William; America, 1764 *1220.12 p559*
Moog, John; Ohio, 1809-1852 *4511.35 p36*
Moohan, James; St. John, N.B., 1847 *2978.15 p36*
Moohan, Patrick 30; Ontario, 1871 *1823.21 p265*
Moole, John 64; Ontario, 1871 *1823.21 p265*
Mooley, William 42; Ontario, 1871 *1823.17 p119*
Moon, Ann; America, 1739 *1220.12 p559*
Moon, Catherine; America, 1755 *1220.12 p559*
Moon, Edward 33; Ontario, 1871 *1823.21 p265*
Moon, Elizabeth; New London, CT, 1850 *9228.50 p468*
Moon, George; America, 1742 *1220.12 p559*
Moon, Jane SEE Moon, Thomas
Moon, John Martin; Ohio, 1809-1852 *4511.35 p36*
Moon, Joseph; New York, 1829-1900 *9228.50 p468*
    Wife:Sophia Gilbert
Moon, M. W.; South Carolina, 1807 *6155.4 p19*
Moon, Samuel; Marston's Wharf, 1781 *8529.30 p14*
Moon, Sophia Gilbert SEE Moon, Joseph
Moon, Thomas; America, 1758 *1220.12 p559*
Moon, Thomas; Marblehead, MA, 1730-1760 *9228.50 p468*
    Relative:Jane
Mooney, Maryanne 6; Ontario, 1871 *1823.21 p265*
Mooney, Elizabeth 24; Ontario, 1871 *1823.17 p119*
Mooney, George 35; Ontario, 1871 *1823.21 p265*
Mooney, James 25; St. Johns, N.F., 1811 *1053.20 p19*
Mooney, John; America, 1750 *1220.12 p559*
Mooney, John; Boston, 1734 *1642 p44*
Mooney, John; Ohio, 1857 *3580.20 p33*
Mooney, John; Ohio, 1857 *6020.12 p21*
Mooney, Joseph; Boston, 1758 *1642 p47*
Mooney, Margaret; Boston, 1741 *1642 p45*
Mooney, Nicholas; America, 1768 *1220.12 p559*
Mooney, Richard; America, 1754 *1220.12 p559*
Mooney, Thomas 30; Ontario, 1871 *1823.21 p265*
Mooney, Thomas; Texas, 1872 *3435.45 p36*
Moonsinger, Charles; Ohio, 1843 *2763.1 p20*
Moony, Mary; Boston, 1761 *1642 p48*
Moony, Michael; Ohio, 1857 *6020.12 p21*
Moor, Dr.; Boston, 1763 *1642 p32*
Moor, Mr.; Boston, 1763 *1642 p32*
Moor, Mrs.; Boston, 1765 *1642 p34*
    With 2 daughters
Moor, Mrs.; North Carolina, 1763 *1642 p32*
Moor, Adam; North Carolina, 1710 *3629.40 p5*
Moor, Ann; America, 1739 *1220.12 p559*
Moor, Daniel; Boston, 1765 *1642 p34*
    With 4 children
Moor, David 21; Ontario, 1871 *1823.21 p265*
Moor, David 38; Ontario, 1871 *1823.17 p119*

Moor, Dennis; North Carolina, 1710 *3629.40 p6*
Moor, Edward; Boston, 1764 *1642 p34*
    Relative:John
Moor, Edward; Boston, 1765 *1642 p35*
Moor, Elizabeth; America, 1715 *1220.12 p560*
Moor, Elizabeth; America, 1725 *1220.12 p560*
Moor, Elizabeth; America, 1765 *1220.12 p560*
Moor, James; America, 1750 *1220.12 p560*
Moor, James; Boston, 1766 *1642 p36*
    With wife
Moor, John; America, 1723 *1220.12 p560*
Moor, John; America, 1751 *1220.12 p560*
Moor, John; Annapolis, MD, 1722 *1220.12 p560*
Moor, John; Annapolis, MD, 1729 *1220.12 p560*
Moor, John SEE Moor, Edward
Moor, John; Boston, 1765 *1642 p34*
Moor, John; Boston, 1766 *1642 p36*
Moor, John; Maryland, 1727 *1220.12 p560*
Moor, John; Massachusetts, 1733 *1642 p91*
Moor, Mary; Massachusetts, 1731 *1642 p91*
Moor, Nicholas; America, 1771 *1220.12 p561*
Moor, Rebecca; Died enroute, 1722 *1220.12 p561*
Moor, Robert; America, 1770 *1220.12 p561*
Moor, Robert; Boston, 1763 *1642 p32*
Moor, Samuel; Boston, 1737 *1642 p26*
Moor, Samuel; Marston's Wharf, 1781 *8529.30 p14*
Moor, Samuel 50; Ontario, 1871 *1823.21 p265*
Moor, Susanna; America, 1719 *1220.12 p561*
Moor, Timothy; Potomac, 1729 *1220.12 p561*
Moor, Walter 61; Ontario, 1871 *1823.21 p265*
Moor, William; America, 1770 *1220.12 p561*
Moor, William; America, 1771 *1220.12 p562*
Moor, William; Boston, 1764 *1642 p33*
Moor, William; Boston, 1766 *1642 p36*
Moor, William; Died enroute, 1725 *1220.12 p561*
Moore, Aaron; Virginia, 1744 *1220.12 p559*
Moore, Ann; America, 1755 *1220.12 p559*
Moore, Ann; America, 1759 *1220.12 p559*
Moore, Ann; Boston, 1763 *1642 p32*
Moore, Ann 45; Ontario, 1871 *1823.21 p265*
Moore, Ann; Philadelphia, 1856 *8513.31 p309*
Moore, Anthony; Died enroute, 1734 *1220.12 p559*
Moore, Archibald 44; Ontario, 1871 *1823.21 p265*
Moore, Arthur; Annapolis, MD, 1731 *1220.12 p559*
Moore, Arthur 50; Ontario, 1871 *1823.21 p265*
Moore, Augustus; New England, 1745 *1642 p28*
Moore, B. A.; California, 1868 *1131.61 p89*
    With son
Moore, Beale T. 40; Ontario, 1871 *1823.21 p265*
Moore, Benjamin; Massachusetts, 1675-1676 *1642 p127*
Moore, Benjamin 33; Ontario, 1871 *1823.17 p119*
Moore, Bridget 29; Ontario, 1871 *1823.21 p266*
Moore, Charles; America, 1749 *1220.12 p559*
Moore, Charles; Maryland, 1720 *1220.12 p559*
Moore, Charlotta 40; Ontario, 1871 *1823.21 p266*
Moore, Chas G. 52; Ontario, 1871 *1823.21 p266*
Moore, Christopher; Barbados, 1682 *1220.12 p559*
Moore, Christopher; Barbados, 1683 *1220.12 p559*
Moore, Coulter 35; Ontario, 1871 *1823.17 p119*
Moore, Daniel; America, 1763 *1220.12 p559*
Moore, Daniel 17; Quebec, 1870 *8364.32 p25*
Moore, Diana; America, 1774 *1220.12 p559*
Moore, Dorothy; Barbados, 1673 *1220.12 p559*
Moore, Dorothy; Barbados, 1677 *1220.12 p560*
Moore, Dorothy; Maryland, 1674 *1236.25 p50*
Moore, Dugald 36; Ontario, 1871 *1823.21 p266*
Moore, E. M. 28; Ontario, 1871 *1823.21 p266*
Moore, Edmond; Massachusetts, 1675-1676 *1642 p127*
Moore, Edward; Virginia, 1742 *1220.12 p560*
Moore, Edward, Jr.; America, 1735 *1220.12 p560*
Moore, Eleanor; America, 1756 *1220.12 p560*
Moore, Eliza 9; Quebec, 1870 *8364.32 p25*
Moore, Eliza H. 46; Ontario, 1871 *1823.21 p266*
Moore, Elizabeth; America, 1752 *1220.12 p560*
Moore, Elizabeth; America, 1754 *1220.12 p560*
Moore, Francis; New England, 1745 *1642 p28*
Moore, George; America, 1764 *1220.12 p560*
Moore, George; America, 1774 *1220.12 p560*
Moore, George; Barbados or Jamaica, 1680 *1220.12 p560*
Moore, George; New York, 1776 *8529.30 p7*
Moore, George 22; Ontario, 1871 *1823.21 p266*
Moore, George 40; Ontario, 1871 *1823.21 p266*
Moore, George 15; Quebec, 1870 *8364.32 p25*
Moore, George G. 42; Ontario, 1871 *1823.21 p266*
Moore, Harriet 11; Quebec, 1870 *8364.32 p25*
Moore, Henry; America, 1754 *1220.12 p560*
Moore, Henry 6; St. John, N.B., 1834 *6469.7 p6*
Moore, Hugh 42; Indiana, 1852-1865 *9076.20 p66*
Moore, Isaac; Barbados, 1695 *1220.12 p560*
Moore, Isaac; New England, 1745 *1642 p28*
Moore, Jacob 30; New Orleans, 1847 *778.6 p247*
Moore, James; America, 1685 *1220.12 p560*

Moore, James; America, 1753 ***1220.12*** *p560*
Moore, James; Boston, 1735 ***1642*** *p44*
Moore, James; Massachusetts, 1718 ***1642*** *p118*
Moore, James 26; Ontario, 1871 ***1823.17*** *p120*
Moore, James 28; Ontario, 1871 ***1823.21*** *p266*
Moore, James 61; Ontario, 1871 ***1823.17*** *p120*
Moore, James 22; St. Johns, N.F., 1811 ***1053.20*** *p20*
Moore, Jane; America, 1774 ***1220.12*** *p560*
Moore, Jane; Minnesota, 1828-1878 ***9228.50*** *p385*
Moore, Jane; Rappahannock, VA, 1741 ***1220.12*** *p560*
Moore, Jno.; Louisiana, 1874-1875 ***4981.45*** *p30*
Moore, John; America, 1621 ***1220.12*** *p560*
Moore, John; America, 1728 ***1220.12*** *p560*
Moore, John; America, 1741 ***1220.12*** *p560*
Moore, John; America, 1748 ***1220.12*** *p560*
Moore, John; America, 1750 ***1220.12*** *p560*
Moore, John; America, 1753 ***1220.12*** *p560*
Moore, John; America, 1767 ***1220.12*** *p560*
Moore, John; America, 1768 ***1220.12*** *p560*
Moore, John; America, 1769 ***1220.12*** *p560*
Moore, John; America, 1770 ***1220.12*** *p560*
Moore, John; America, 1771 ***1220.12*** *p560*
Moore, John; Barbados or Jamaica, 1689 ***1220.12*** *p560*
Moore, John; Barbados or Jamaica, 1698 ***1220.12*** *p560*
Moore, John; Jamaica, 1783 ***8529.30*** *p13A*
Moore, John; Maryland, 1674-1675 ***1236.25*** *p51*
Moore, John; Massachusetts, 1642 ***1642*** *p109*
Moore, John; Massachusetts, 1675-1676 ***1642*** *p129*
Moore, John; New England, 1745 ***1642*** *p28*
Moore, John; New York, NY, 1832 ***3274.55*** *p70*
Moore, John 29; Ontario, 1871 ***1823.17*** *p120*
Moore, John 55; Ontario, 1871 ***1823.21*** *p266*
Moore, John 56; Ontario, 1871 ***1823.21*** *p266*
Moore, John 60; Ontario, 1871 ***1823.17*** *p120*
Moore, John; Philadelphia, 1868 ***7074.20*** *p133*
Moore, John 15; Quebec, 1870 ***8364.32*** *p25*
Moore, John; St. John, N.B., 1842 ***2978.20*** *p9*
Moore, John; Virginia, 1734 ***1220.12*** *p560*
Moore, John A.; Washington, 1888 ***2770.40*** *p26*
Moore, Jonathan; Massachusetts, 1675-1676 ***1642*** *p128*
Moore, Joseph; America, 1749 ***1220.12*** *p560*
Moore, Joseph; America, 1757 ***1220.12*** *p560*
Moore, Joseph; Massachusetts, 1675-1676 ***1642*** *p127*
Moore, Joseph; Massachusetts, 1675-1676 ***1642*** *p128*
Moore, Joseph 38; Ontario, 1871 ***1823.21*** *p266*
Moore, Margaret; New Orleans, 1850 ***7242.30*** *p149*
Moore, Margaret; Pennsylvania, 1859 ***8513.31*** *p413*
Moore, Martha 59; Ontario, 1871 ***1823.21*** *p266*
Moore, Martin; St. Johns, N.F., 1825 ***1053.15*** *p6*
Moore, Mary; America, 1736 ***1220.12*** *p560*
Moore, Mary; America, 1767 ***1220.12*** *p561*
Moore, Mary; Boston, 1759 ***1642*** *p47*
Moore, Mary 47; Ontario, 1871 ***1823.21*** *p266*
Moore, Mary Jane 15; St. John, N.B., 1834 ***6469.7*** *p6*
Moore, Maryann 18; Ontario, 1871 ***1823.21*** *p266*
Moore, Matthew 47; Ontario, 1871 ***1823.21*** *p266*
Moore, Michael 35; Ontario, 1871 ***1823.21*** *p266*
Moore, Moreg 52; Ontario, 1871 ***1823.17*** *p120*
Moore, Morice; Barbados, 1693 ***1220.12*** *p561*
Moore, Moses; America, 1685 ***1220.12*** *p561*
Moore, Nathan; New England, 1745 ***1642*** *p28*
Moore, Nora 23; Michigan, 1880 ***4491.30*** *p22*
Moore, Oscar F.; Ohio, 1838 ***3580.20*** *p33*
Moore, Oscar F.; Ohio, 1838 ***6020.12*** *p21*
Moore, Peter; America, 1775 ***1220.12*** *p561*
Moore, Reuben; New England, 1745 ***1642*** *p28*
Moore, Richard; America, 1774 ***1220.12*** *p561*
Moore, Richard; Annapolis, MD, 1733 ***1220.12*** *p561*
Moore, Richard; New York, NY, 1841 ***3274.56*** *p71*
Moore, Richard 43; Ontario, 1871 ***1823.17*** *p120*
Moore, Robert; America, 1754 ***1220.12*** *p561*
Moore, Robert; America, 1766 ***1220.12*** *p561*
Moore, Robert; New England, 1745 ***1642*** *p28*
Moore, Robert; North Carolina, 1828-1840 ***1088.45*** *p24*
Moore, Robert; Philadelphia, 1778 ***8529.30*** *p4A*
Moore, Robert; South Carolina, 1800-1899 ***6155.4*** *p19*
Moore, Robert 2; St. John, N.B., 1834 ***6469.7*** *p6*
Moore, Samuel; America, 1748 ***1220.12*** *p561*
Moore, Samuel; Massachusetts, 1675-1676 ***1642*** *p127*
Moore, Samuel; Massachusetts, 1675-1676 ***1642*** *p129*
Moore, Samuel; New England, 1745 ***1642*** *p28*
Moore, Sarah; America, 1759 ***1220.12*** *p561*
Moore, Sarah; Barbados or Jamaica, 1697 ***1220.12*** *p561*
Moore, Sarah; Virginia, 1740 ***1220.12*** *p561*
Moore, Silas G. 37; Ontario, 1871 ***1823.21*** *p266*
Moore, Thomas; America, 1685 ***1220.12*** *p561*
Moore, Thomas; America, 1720 ***1220.12*** *p561*
Moore, Thomas; America, 1738 ***1220.12*** *p561*
Moore, Thomas; America, 1743 ***1220.12*** *p561*
Moore, Thomas; America, 1753 ***1220.12*** *p561*
Moore, Thomas; America, 1766 ***1220.12*** *p561*
Moore, Thomas; Barbados or Jamaica, 1699 ***1220.12*** *p561*
Moore, Thomas; Massachusetts, 1675-1676 ***1642*** *p128*
Moore, Thomas; Massachusetts, 1724 ***1642*** *p91*
Moore, Thomas; North Carolina, 1855 ***1088.45*** *p24*
Moore, Thomas 48; Ontario, 1871 ***1823.17*** *p120*
Moore, Thomas, Jr.; America, 1752 ***1220.12*** *p561*
Moore, Timothy; America, 1759 ***1220.12*** *p561*
Moore, Wildrage 60; Ontario, 1871 ***1823.17*** *p120*
Moore, William; America, 1720 ***1220.12*** *p561*
Moore, William; America, 1734 ***1220.12*** *p561*
Moore, William; America, 1739 ***1220.12*** *p561*
Moore, William; America, 1748 ***1220.12*** *p561*
Moore, William; America, 1753 ***1220.12*** *p561*
Moore, William; America, 1758 ***1220.12*** *p561*
Moore, William; America, 1767 ***1220.12*** *p561*
Moore, William; America, 1770 ***1220.12*** *p562*
Moore, William; America, 1773 ***1220.12*** *p562*
Moore, William; America, 1774 ***1220.12*** *p562*
Moore, William; Annapolis, MD, 1726 ***1220.12*** *p561*
Moore, William; Barbados, 1690 ***1220.12*** *p561*
Moore, William; Barbados, 1702 ***1220.12*** *p561*
Moore, William; Boston, 1747 ***1642*** *p46*
Moore, William; Massachusetts, 1745 ***1642*** *p28*
Moore, William; New England, 1745 ***1642*** *p28*
Moore, William; Ohio, 1809-1852 ***4511.35*** *p36*
Moore, William 27; Ontario, 1871 ***1823.21*** *p266*
Moore, William 36; Ontario, 1871 ***1823.21*** *p266*
Moore, William 49; Ontario, 1871 ***1823.21*** *p266*
Moore, William 51; Ontario, 1871 ***1823.17*** *p120*
Moore, William 51; Ontario, 1871 ***1823.21*** *p266*
Moore, William 66; Ontario, 1871 ***1823.21*** *p266*
Moore, William 69; Ontario, 1871 ***1823.21*** *p266*
Moore, William 16; Quebec, 1870 ***8364.32*** *p25*
Moore, William 4; St. John, N.B., 1834 ***6469.7*** *p6*
Moore, William; Virginia, 1734 ***1220.12*** *p561*
Moore, William, Jr.; America, 1767 ***1220.12*** *p561*
Moore, William, Sr.; America, 1767 ***1220.12*** *p561*
Moore, William C. 50; Ontario, 1871 ***1823.21*** *p266*
Moore, William H. 60; Ontario, 1871 ***1823.21*** *p266*
Moorehead, Alexander 39; Ontario, 1871 ***1823.21*** *p266*
Moorehead, Hugh; Ohio, 1809-1852 ***4511.35*** *p36*
Moorehead, James; South Carolina, 1808 ***6155.4*** *p19*
Moorehouse, Jonah 64; Ontario, 1871 ***1823.17*** *p120*
Moores, James Harvey; Washington, 1885 ***2770.40*** *p194*
Moores, John; America, 1756 ***1220.12*** *p562*
Moores, Mathew; America, 1760 ***1220.12*** *p562*
Moores, Richard; America, 1768 ***1220.12*** *p562*
Moores, Thomas; America, 1756 ***1220.12*** *p562*
Mooreton, William; Barbados, 1676 ***1220.12*** *p563*
Moorey, John; America, 1767 ***1220.12*** *p563*
Moorhead, George 36; Ontario, 1871 ***1823.21*** *p266*
Moorhead, John; Iowa, 1880 ***1211.15*** *p16*
Moorhead, Thomas 40; Ontario, 1871 ***1823.21*** *p266*
Moorhead, William 42; Ontario, 1871 ***1823.21*** *p266*
Moorhouse, Henry 50; Ontario, 1871 ***1823.17*** *p120*
Moorhouse, Joseph; New York, NY, 1835 ***3274.55*** *p43*
Moorhouse, William 30; Ontario, 1871 ***1823.21*** *p267*
Moorhouse, William 66; Ontario, 1871 ***1823.17*** *p120*
Mooring, William; America, 1757 ***1220.12*** *p562*
Mooris, Joseph A.; North Carolina, 1848 ***1088.45*** *p24*
Moorshall, Edward; America, 1773 ***1220.12*** *p531*
Moorshall, Thomas; America, 1774 ***1220.12*** *p532*
Moos, Anna Beer 44 *SEE* Moos, Mathias
Moos, Elisabeth 19; America, 1858 ***5475.1*** *p310*
Moos, Johann 11 *SEE* Moos, Mathias
Moos, Katharina 5 *SEE* Moos, Mathias
Moos, Mathias 7 *SEE* Moos, Mathias
Moos, Mathias 43; America, 1858 ***5475.1*** *p310*
*Wife:*Anna Beer 44
*Son:*Johann 11
*Son:*Mathias 7
*Daughter:*Katharina 5
*Son:*Michel 2
*Son:*Peter 9
*Son:*Nikolaus 16
Moos, Michel 2 *SEE* Moos, Mathias
Moos, Nikolaus 16 *SEE* Moos, Mathias
Moos, Peter 9 *SEE* Moos, Mathias
Mooscup, John; Ohio, 1809-1852 ***4511.35*** *p36*
Moosmann, Jakob *SEE* Moosmann, Jakob
Moosmann, Jakob; Brazil, 1861 ***5475.1*** *p503*
*Daughter:*Kath. Elisabeth
*Son:*Jakob
Moosmann, Karoline; Brazil, 1861 ***5475.1*** *p489*
Moosmann, Kath. Elisabeth *SEE* Moosmann, Jakob
Moot, John; America, 1773 ***1220.12*** *p562*
Mootz, Eva; Kansas, 1917-1918 ***1826.15*** *p81*
Mootz, George; Ohio, 1809-1852 ***4511.35*** *p36*
Mootz, Peter; Kansas, 1917-1918 ***1826.15*** *p81*
Mootz, Philip Jacob; Ohio, 1809-1852 ***4511.35*** *p36*
Mopsey, Ann; America, 1771 ***1220.12*** *p562*
Moquet, Victor Etienne; Illinois, 1854 ***6079.1*** *p10*
Mora, Julian; Texas, 1891 ***3435.45*** *p36*
Moraa, William; America, 1720 ***1220.12*** *p562*
Moraine, Patrick; Massachusetts, 1675-1676 ***1642*** *p128*
Moral, Baptiste 31; New Orleans, 1848 ***778.6*** *p247*
Moral, Jean 19; New Orleans, 1848 ***778.6*** *p248*
Moral DeSaint-Quentin, Quentin 30; Quebec, 1650 ***9221.17*** *p228*
Moran, Bridget 36; Michigan, 1880 ***4491.36*** *p16*
Moran, Catherine 31; Michigan, 1880 ***4491.36*** *p16*
Moran, Daniel; Bangor, ME, 1842 ***3274.56*** *p101*
Moran, Daniel 64; New York, NY, 1845 ***6178.50*** *p152*
Moran, Dennis; Ohio, 1840-1897 ***8365.35*** *p17*
Moran, Edward; Boston, 1752-1760 ***1642*** *p30*
Moran, Edward; New Orleans, 1851 ***7242.30*** *p149*
Moran, Francis; Ohio, 1833 ***2763.1*** *p20*
Moran, Francis 48; Ontario, 1871 ***1823.21*** *p267*
Moran, George; Washington, 1887 ***2770.40*** *p24*
Moran, J. H. 26; Ontario, 1871 ***1823.21*** *p267*
Moran, James 48; Michigan, 1880 ***4491.36*** *p16*
Moran, James 30; Ontario, 1871 ***1823.21*** *p267*
Moran, James 40; Ontario, 1871 ***1823.17*** *p120*
Moran, James N.; North Carolina, 1807 ***1088.45*** *p24*
Moran, John 30; Ontario, 1871 ***1823.17*** *p120*
Moran, John 35; Ontario, 1871 ***1823.21*** *p267*
Moran, Julia 22; Ontario, 1871 ***1823.21*** *p267*
Moran, Margaret 36; Ontario, 1871 ***1823.21*** *p267*
Moran, Marhu; Ohio, 1852 ***6020.12*** *p21*
Moran, Martin; Ohio, 1852 ***3580.20*** *p33*
Moran, Martin; Ohio, 1852 ***6020.12*** *p21*
Moran, Mary; Boston, 1736 ***1642*** *p44*
Moran, Mary 25; Ontario, 1871 ***1823.21*** *p267*
Moran, Mary 43; Ontario, 1871 ***1823.21*** *p267*
Moran, Michael; Marblehead, MA, 1763 ***1642*** *p73*
Moran, Michael; Salem, MA, 1763 ***1642*** *p78*
Moran, Nic; St. John, N.B., 1847 ***2978.15*** *p37*
Moran, Patrick 55; Ontario, 1871 ***1823.17*** *p120*
Moran, Patrick J. 33; Michigan, 1880 ***4491.36*** *p16*
Moran, Symon 38; Michigan, 1880 ***4491.36*** *p16*
Moran, Thomas; Ohio, 1834 ***2763.1*** *p20*
Moran, Thomas F.; Washington, 1889 ***2770.40*** *p79*
Moran, Winnefred; New Orleans, 1851 ***7242.30*** *p149*
Morange, Mr. 28; New Orleans, 1842 ***778.6*** *p248*
Moranowa, Anna; Detroit, 1929 ***1640.55*** *p114*
Moras, Jean; Quebec, 1661 ***9221.17*** *p463*
Morasch, Friedrich; America, 1857 ***2526.43*** *p142*
Morath, Jacob; Ohio, 1809-1852 ***4511.35*** *p36*
Morathu, Barbera 36; Louisiana, 1848 ***778.6*** *p248*
Morathu, Francois 21; Louisiana, 1848 ***778.6*** *p248*
Morathu, Henri 10; Louisiana, 1848 ***778.6*** *p248*
Morathu, Marie 40; Louisiana, 1848 ***778.6*** *p248*
Morathu, Theresia 22; Louisiana, 1848 ***778.6*** *p248*
Moratt, John; America, 1769 ***1220.12*** *p562*
Moratz, Carl; Wisconsin, 1884 ***6795.8*** *p128*
Morawski, Casimir; Detroit, 1929-1930 ***6214.5*** *p69*
Morbach, Nicolas 18; America, 1842 ***778.6*** *p248*
Morbach, Pierre 27; America, 1846 ***778.6*** *p248*
Morbacher, Johann; America, 1883 ***5475.1*** *p422*
With wife
With child 4
With child 3
Morbaugh, John, Jr.; Ohio, 1809-1852 ***4511.35*** *p36*
Morbe, Johann 27; America, 1864 ***5475.1*** *p282*
Morbrey, Boyan; Boston, 1661 ***1642*** *p9*
Morcan, Judith 41; Ontario, 1871 ***1823.21*** *p267*
Morcel, Frank; Montreal, 1900-1983 ***9228.50*** *p468*
Morcin, Hanorah 80; Ontario, 1871 ***1823.21*** *p267*
Morcin, James 35; Ontario, 1871 ***1823.21*** *p267*
Morcin, John 35; Ontario, 1871 ***1823.21*** *p267*
Morcin, Thomas 40; Ontario, 1871 ***1823.21*** *p267*
Morcomb, Nathaniel; America, 1725 ***1220.12*** *p562*
Morcombe, Josias; America, 1726 ***1220.12*** *p562*
Morcon, Thomas 35; Ontario, 1871 ***1823.21*** *p267*
Morcorn, John 61; Ontario, 1871 ***1823.21*** *p267*
Mord, Eduard Friedrich Wilhelm; America, 1864 ***7420.1*** *p225*
Mordecai, Moses; America, 1758 ***1220.12*** *p562*
Morden, Elizabeth; Carolina, 1724 ***1220.12*** *p562*
Mordicai, Samuel; America, 1769 ***1220.12*** *p562*
Mordini, Peter; Illinois, 1930 ***121.35*** *p101*
Mordock, Racheal 35; Ontario, 1871 ***1823.21*** *p267*
Mordock, Thonson 47; Ontario, 1871 ***1823.21*** *p267*
Mordoe, William; America, 1750 ***1220.12*** *p562*
Mordrum, Henry; America, 1770 ***1220.12*** *p562*
Mordus, Antonio; North Carolina, 1792-1862 ***1088.45*** *p24*
More, Ann 67; Ontario, 1871 ***1823.17*** *p161*
More, Charles 41; Ontario, 1871 ***1823.17*** *p120*
More, Colin 40; Ontario, 1871 ***1823.21*** *p267*
More, Elizabeth; Barbados, 1669 ***1220.12*** *p560*
More, Ellen; Plymouth, MA, 1606 ***1642*** *p55*
More, Ellen; Plymouth, MA, 1620 ***1920.45*** *p5*
More, George 15; Ontario, 1871 ***1823.17*** *p120*
More, Guy; America, 1733 ***1220.12*** *p560*
More, Jasper; Plymouth, MA, 1606 ***1642*** *p55*
More, Jasper; Plymouth, MA, 1620 ***1920.45*** *p5*

338 *FOR A COMPLETE EXPLANATION OF ENTRY, SEE "HOW TO READ A CITATION" SECTION*

More, John; America, 1767 ***1220.12*** *p560*
More, Joseph; America, 1738 ***1220.12*** *p560*
More, Richard; America, 1742 ***1220.12*** *p561*
More, Richard; Plymouth, MA, 1606 ***1642*** *p55*
More, Richard; Plymouth, MA, 1620 ***1920.45*** *p5*
More, Thomas; America, 1775 ***1220.12*** *p561*
More, William; Boston, 1766 ***1642*** *p36*
Moreau, Mr. 24; America, 1841 ***778.6*** *p248*
Moreau, Adele 25; New Orleans, 1844 ***778.6*** *p248*
Moreau, Barbara 34; New Orleans, 1848 ***778.6*** *p248*
Moreau, Etienne; Quebec, 1658 ***9221.17*** *p384*
Moreau, Francis; North Carolina, 1826 ***1088.45*** *p24*
Moreau, Jean 26; Quebec, 1661 ***9221.17*** *p463*
Moreau, Jean; Virginia, 1700 ***9230.15*** *p80*
Moreau, M. 33; America, 1841 ***778.6*** *p248*
Moreau, Marguerite; Quebec, 1670 ***4514.3*** *p350*
Moreau, Marguerite-Francoise; Quebec, 1670 ***4514.3*** *p350*
Moreau, Michel 27; Quebec, 1657 ***9221.17*** *p364*
Moreau, Pierre 16; Montreal, 1659 ***9221.17*** *p425*
Moreau, Pierre 24; Quebec, 1641 ***9221.17*** *p106*
Moreau, Rene 18; Montreal, 1659 ***9221.17*** *p425*
Moreau, Theodore 38; America, 1843 ***778.6*** *p248*
Moreau DeBresoles, Judith 39; Montreal, 1659 ***9221.17*** *p415*
Moreby, Richard; Virginia, 1724 ***1220.12*** *p562*
Morehane, Joseph; America, 1767 ***1220.12*** *p562*
Morehead, John; Ohio, 1809-1852 ***4511.35*** *p36*
Morehead, John 50; Ontario, 1871 ***1823.21*** *p267*
Morehouse, James 60; Ontario, 1871 ***1823.21*** *p267*
Morehouse, Jane 24; Ontario, 1871 ***1823.21*** *p267*
Morehouse, Thomas 32; Ontario, 1871 ***1823.21*** *p267*
Morehouse, William, Jr.; America, 1738 ***1220.12*** *p562*
Morein, John; Annapolis, MD, 1758 ***1220.12*** *p562*
Morekel, Lorens; Ohio, 1809-1852 ***4511.35*** *p36*
Morel, Mr. 58; America, 1841 ***778.6*** *p248*
Morel, Claude Charles 27; Texas, 1848 ***778.6*** *p248*
Morel, Etienne 21; Quebec, 1657 ***9221.17*** *p364*
Morel, Isaac; Massachusetts, n.d. ***9228.50*** *p468*
Morel, Isaac; New England, n.d. ***9228.50*** *p469*
Morel, Jean D. W.; Illinois, 1856 ***6079.1*** *p10*
Morel, Jean Sebastien 38; New Orleans, 1848 ***778.6*** *p248*
Morel, Mary; Boston, 1677 ***9228.50*** *p469*
Morel, Nick; Boston, n.d. ***9228.50*** *p468*
Morel, Nicolas; Montreal, 1661 ***9221.17*** *p474*
Morel, Peter; Georgia, 1733-1734 ***9228.50*** *p469*
With wife & 4 children
Morel, Peter; Massachusetts, n.d. ***9228.50*** *p468*
Morel, Peter; Salem, MA, 1675 ***9228.50*** *p149*
Morel, Peter; Salem, MA, 1675 ***9228.50*** *p469*
Morel, Pierre 24; Quebec, 1641 ***9221.17*** *p106*
Morel, Thomas 25; Quebec, 1661 ***9221.17*** *p446*
Moreland, John; America, 1768 ***1220.12*** *p565*
Moreland, William; Maryland or Virginia, 1738 ***1220.12*** *p565*
Morel deLa Durantaye, Olivier; Quebec, 1665 ***2314.30*** *p172*
Morell, David; Colorado, 1862-1920 ***1029.59*** *p64*
Morell, Marie 29; America, 1846 ***778.6*** *p248*
Morell, Pierre 23; America, 1846 ***778.6*** *p248*
Morelli, M. 18; New Orleans, 1844 ***778.6*** *p248*
Moreman, Mary; Barbados, 1679 ***1220.12*** *p562*
Moren, Patrick; Albany, NY, 1831 ***3274.56*** *p72*
Morenati, M.; Louisiana, 1836-1840 ***4981.45*** *p213*
Morency, . . . 27; Quebec, 1655 ***9221.17*** *p320*
Morestly, Joseph; America, 1752 ***1220.12*** *p562*
Moret, A. 23; Port uncertain, 1843 ***778.6*** *p248*
Moret, L. 40; Port uncertain, 1843 ***778.6*** *p248*
Moret, Leontine 4; Port uncertain, 1843 ***778.6*** *p248*
Moretman, Edward; Maryland, 1726 ***1220.12*** *p562*
Moreton, Benjamin; America, 1770 ***1220.12*** *p562*
Moreton, Caleb; America, 1756 ***1220.12*** *p562*
Moreton, Charles; Maryland, 1737 ***1220.12*** *p562*
Moreton, Christopher; America, 1771 ***1220.12*** *p562*
Moreton, Dyer Percy 24; Ontario, 1871 ***1823.21*** *p267*
Moreton, Henry; America, 1736 ***1220.12*** *p562*
Moreton, James; America, 1769 ***1220.12*** *p562*
Moreton, John; America, 1738 ***1220.12*** *p563*
Moreton, Mark; America, 1754 ***1220.12*** *p563*
Moreton, Rose; Virginia, 1734 ***1220.12*** *p563*
Moreton, Samuel; America, 1737 ***1220.12*** *p563*
Moreton, Sarah; America, 1775 ***1220.12*** *p563*
Moreton, William; America, 1764 ***1220.12*** *p563*
Moreton, William; Annapolis, MD, 1726 ***1220.12*** *p563*
Moreux, Etienne; Illinois, 1852 ***6079.1*** *p10*
Morey, James; America, 1769 ***1220.12*** *p563*
Morey, Joseph; America, 1738 ***1220.12*** *p563*
Morey, Stephen; America, 1741 ***1220.12*** *p563*
Morey, William; Virginia, 1750 ***1220.12*** *p563*
Morfield, William; America, 1742 ***1220.12*** *p562*
Morfitt, George; America, 1768 ***1220.12*** *p563*
Morfoot, John; America, 1754 ***1220.12*** *p563*
Morfy, William; Boston, 1739 ***1642*** *p44*
Morgan, Capt.; Nova Scotia, 1780-1880 ***9228.50*** *p574*
Morgan, Alice; America, 1679 ***1220.12*** *p563*
Morgan, Ann; Ohio, 1835 ***4022.20*** *p272*
Morgan, Caroline; Philadelphia, 1852 ***8513.31*** *p323*
Morgan, Catherine *SEE* Morgan, John D.
Morgan, Catherine; Ohio, n.d. ***4022.20*** *p287*
With mother
With father
Morgan, Chandos; America, 1751 ***1220.12*** *p563*
Morgan, Charles; America, 1763 ***1220.12*** *p563*
Morgan, Charles; America, 1768 ***1220.12*** *p563*
Morgan, Christopher; Jamaica, 1716 ***1220.12*** *p563*
Morgan, Daniel E.; Ohio, 1838 ***4022.20*** *p287*
*Wife:*Elinor
Morgan, David; America, 1760 ***1220.12*** *p563*
Morgan, David; America, 1761 ***1220.12*** *p563*
Morgan, David; Ohio, 1835 ***4022.20*** *p272*
Morgan, David *SEE* Morgan, Moses
Morgan, David; Ohio, 1841 ***4022.20*** *p287*
*Wife:*Margaret
*Child:*Elizabeth
*Child:*Margaret
*Child:*John
Morgan, David; Ohio, 1850 ***4022.20*** *p287*
*Wife:*Margaret
With children
Morgan, David 60; Ontario, 1871 ***1823.21*** *p267*
Morgan, David 72; Ontario, 1871 ***1823.21*** *p267*
Morgan, David E. *SEE* Morgan, John D.
Morgan, David J.; Ohio, 1836 ***4022.20*** *p287*
Morgan, David L.; Louisiana, 1847-1849 ***7710.1*** *p151*
Morgan, David Ll. *SEE* Morgan, Richard
Morgan, David Llywelyn; Louisiana, 1842-1847 ***7710.1*** *p149*
Morgan, David W.; Washington, 1889 ***2770.40*** *p79*
Morgan, Dennis; St. John, N.B., 1842 ***2978.20*** *p7*
Morgan, Dorcas; Barbados or Jamaica, 1685 ***1220.12*** *p563*
Morgan, Edward; America, 1723 ***1220.12*** *p563*
Morgan, Edward; America, 1736 ***1220.12*** *p563*
Morgan, Edward 61; Ontario, 1871 ***1823.21*** *p267*
Morgan, Edward L.; Illinois, 1852 ***6079.1*** *p10*
Morgan, Eleanor; America, 1754 ***1220.12*** *p563*
Morgan, Eleanor; America, 1769 ***1220.12*** *p563*
Morgan, Eleanor; Maryland, 1742 ***1220.12*** *p563*
Morgan, Eleanor *SEE* Morgan, Evan
Morgan, Eleanor *SEE* Morgan, John D.
Morgan, Elianor; America, 1764 ***1220.12*** *p563*
Morgan, Eliner; Maryland, 1723 ***1220.12*** *p563*
Morgan, Elinor *SEE* Morgan, Daniel E.
Morgan, Elizabeth; America, 1749 ***1220.12*** *p563*
Morgan, Elizabeth; America, 1767 ***1220.12*** *p563*
Morgan, Elizabeth; America, 1768 ***1220.12*** *p563*
Morgan, Elizabeth; Annapolis, MD, 1725 ***1220.12*** *p563*
Morgan, Elizabeth; Barbados, 1694 ***1220.12*** *p563*
Morgan, Elizabeth Jones *SEE* Morgan, Richard
Morgan, Elizabeth *SEE* Morgan, David
Morgan, Elizabeth 48; Ontario, 1871 ***1823.21*** *p268*
Morgan, Ellen; St. John, N.B., 1842 ***2978.20*** *p7*
Morgan, Evan; Ohio, 1837 ***4022.20*** *p288*
*Father:*George
*Mother:*Eleanor
With siblings
Morgan, Evan J. *SEE* Morgan, John D.
Morgan, George; America, 1715 ***1220.12*** *p563*
Morgan, George; America, 1763 ***1220.12*** *p563*
Morgan, George 37; North Carolina, 1774 ***1422.10*** *p59*
Morgan, George *SEE* Morgan, Evan
Morgan, George 25; Ontario, 1871 ***1823.21*** *p268*
Morgan, George 42; Ontario, 1871 ***1823.21*** *p268*
Morgan, George 55; Ontario, 1871 ***1823.17*** *p120*
Morgan, George A. 31; Ontario, 1871 ***1823.21*** *p268*
Morgan, Henry; America, 1775 ***1220.12*** *p563*
Morgan, Hugh; Ohio, n.d. ***4022.20*** *p288*
*Wife:*Mary
*Child:*Jane
Morgan, James; America, 1725 ***1220.12*** *p563*
Morgan, James; America, 1740 ***1220.12*** *p563*
Morgan, James; America, 1740 ***1220.12*** *p564*
Morgan, James; America, 1770 ***1220.12*** *p564*
Morgan, James; America, 1772 ***1220.12*** *p564*
Morgan, James; Barbados, 1673 ***1220.12*** *p563*
Morgan, James; Kingston, Jamaica, 1774 ***8529.30*** *p13A*
Morgan, James; Maryland, 1673 ***1236.25*** *p48*
Morgan, James 30; Ontario, 1871 ***1823.17*** *p120*
Morgan, James 49; Ontario, 1871 ***1823.21*** *p268*
Morgan, James 60; Ontario, 1871 ***1823.17*** *p120*
Morgan, James W.; Louisiana, 1836-1840 ***4981.45*** *p213*
Morgan, Jane; America, 1745 ***1220.12*** *p564*
Morgan, Jane; America, 1747 ***1220.12*** *p564*
Morgan, Jane *SEE* Morgan, Hugh
Morgan, Jenkin; Ohio, 1841 ***4022.20*** *p288*
Morgan, Job; America, 1734 ***1220.12*** *p564*
Morgan, John; America, 1656 ***1220.12*** *p564*
Morgan, John; America, 1698 ***1220.12*** *p564*
Morgan, John; America, 1730 ***1220.12*** *p564*
Morgan, John; America, 1732 ***1220.12*** *p564*
Morgan, John; America, 1736 ***1220.12*** *p564*
Morgan, John; America, 1738 ***1220.12*** *p564*
Morgan, John; America, 1740 ***1220.12*** *p564*
Morgan, John; America, 1750 ***1220.12*** *p564*
Morgan, John; America, 1754 ***1220.12*** *p564*
Morgan, John; America, 1759 ***1220.12*** *p564*
Morgan, John; America, 1763 ***1220.12*** *p564*
Morgan, John; America, 1764 ***1220.12*** *p564*
Morgan, John; America, 1767 ***1220.12*** *p564*
Morgan, John; America, 1770 ***1220.12*** *p564*
Morgan, John; America, 1774 ***1220.12*** *p564*
Morgan, John; Barbados or Jamaica, 1685 ***1220.12*** *p564*
Morgan, John; Illinois, 1858-1861 ***6020.5*** *p132*
Morgan, John; Maryland, 1740 ***1220.12*** *p564*
Morgan, John; North Carolina, 1852 ***1088.45*** *p24*
Morgan, John *SEE* Morgan, David
Morgan, John 49; Ontario, 1871 ***1823.21*** *p268*
Morgan, John 55; Ontario, 1871 ***1823.21*** *p268*
Morgan, John 68; Ontario, 1871 ***1823.21*** *p268*
Morgan, John; Rappahannock, VA, 1728 ***1220.12*** *p564*
Morgan, John; Washington, 1889 ***2770.40*** *p80*
Morgan, John D.; Ohio, 1847-1848 ***4022.20*** *p288*
*Wife:*Margaret
*Child:*Morgan J.
*Child:*John F.
*Child:*Evan J.
*Child:*Catherine
*Child:*David E.
*Child:*Eleanor
Morgan, John E.; Ohio, 1844 ***4022.20*** *p288*
*Wife:*Mary
Morgan, John F. *SEE* Morgan, John D.
Morgan, John William; Philadelphia, 1859-1867 ***8513.31*** *p417*
Morgan, Joseph; Jamaica, 1783 ***8529.30*** *p13A*
Morgan, Joseph 28; Ontario, 1871 ***1823.17*** *p120*
Morgan, Joseph 60; Ontario, 1871 ***1823.17*** *p120*
Morgan, Joseph; Potomac, 1729 ***1220.12*** *p564*
Morgan, L. Morgan 44; Ontario, 1871 ***1823.21*** *p268*
Morgan, Margaret *SEE* Morgan, Moses
Morgan, Margaret *SEE* Morgan, David
Morgan, Margaret *SEE* Morgan, David
Morgan, Margaret *SEE* Morgan, John D.
Morgan, Margaret *SEE* Morgan, David
Morgan, Margaret; Ohio, 1879 ***4022.20*** *p284*
Morgan, Maria 15; Ontario, 1871 ***1823.21*** *p268*
Morgan, Martha; America, 1770 ***1220.12*** *p564*
Morgan, Mary; America, 1743 ***1220.12*** *p564*
Morgan, Mary; America, 1752 ***1220.12*** *p564*
Morgan, Mary; America, 1775 ***1220.12*** *p564*
Morgan, Mary; Annapolis, MD, 1735 ***1220.12*** *p564*
Morgan, Mary Cahill *SEE* Morgan, Michael D.
Morgan, Mary; Ohio, 1834 ***4022.20*** *p272*
Morgan, Mary *SEE* Morgan, John E.
Morgan, Mary *SEE* Morgan, Hugh
Morgan, Mary; St. John, N.B., 1842 ***2978.20*** *p7*
Morgan, Mary Cahill *SEE* Morgan, Michael D.
Morgan, Mary, Jr.; St. John, N.B., 1842 ***2978.20*** *p7*
Morgan, Matthew; America, 1686 ***1220.12*** *p564*
Morgan, Michael D.; Canada, 1856-1859 ***8513.31*** *p417*
*Wife:*Mary Cahill
Morgan, Michael D.; Trenton, NJ, 1856 ***8513.31*** *p417*
*Wife:*Mary Cahill
Morgan, Morgan J. *SEE* Morgan, John D.
Morgan, Moses; Ohio, 1840-1841 ***4022.20*** *p288*
*Child:*David
*Child:*Margaret
Morgan, Moses; Virginia, 1773 ***1220.12*** *p564*
Morgan, Richard; America, 1719 ***1220.12*** *p564*
Morgan, Richard; America, 1721 ***1220.12*** *p564*
Morgan, Richard; America, 1741 ***1220.12*** *p564*
Morgan, Richard; America, 1747 ***1220.12*** *p564*
Morgan, Richard; America, 1775 ***1220.12*** *p564*
Morgan, Richard; Barbados, 1668 ***1220.12*** *p564*
Morgan, Richard; Barbados, 1670 ***1220.12*** *p564*
Morgan, Richard; Ohio, 1829-1837 ***4022.20*** *p288*
With 2 children
*Child:*David Ll.
*Wife:*Elizabeth Jones
Morgan, Richard 58; Ontario, 1871 ***1823.21*** *p268*
Morgan, Robert; Annapolis, MD, 1720 ***1220.12*** *p564*
Morgan, Robert 45; Ontario, 1871 ***1823.17*** *p120*
Morgan, Robert 48; Ontario, 1871 ***1823.17*** *p120*
Morgan, Robert; Virginia, 1726 ***1220.12*** *p564*
Morgan, Sara; Charles Town, SC, 1719 ***1220.12*** *p565*
Morgan, Sarah; America, 1756 ***1220.12*** *p565*
Morgan, Sarah; America, 1772 ***1220.12*** *p565*
Morgan, Sarah; America, 1774 ***1220.12*** *p565*
Morgan, Sarah; Died enroute, 1734 ***1220.12*** *p565*

Morgan, Sarah 95; Ontario, 1871 ***1823.21*** *p268*
Morgan, Stephen D.; Ohio, 1840 ***4022.20*** *p288*
Morgan, Susanna; Nevis or Jamaica, 1722 ***1220.12*** *p565*
Morgan, Thomas; America, 1671 ***1220.12*** *p565*
Morgan, Thomas; America, 1680 ***1220.12*** *p565*
Morgan, Thomas; America, 1742 ***1220.12*** *p565*
Morgan, Thomas; America, 1746 ***1220.12*** *p565*
Morgan, Thomas; America, 1747 ***1220.12*** *p565*
Morgan, Thomas; America, 1753 ***1220.12*** *p565*
Morgan, Thomas; America, 1764 ***1220.12*** *p565*
Morgan, Thomas; America, 1768 ***1220.12*** *p565*
Morgan, Thomas; America, 1774 ***1220.12*** *p565*
Morgan, Thomas; Long Island, 1780 ***8529.30*** *p10A*
Morgan, Thomas; Louisiana, 1874 ***4981.45*** *p133*
Morgan, Thomas 61; Ontario, 1871 ***1823.21*** *p268*
Morgan, Timothy; Washington, 1878 ***2770.40*** *p134*
Morgan, Timpthy; Washington, 1883 ***2770.40*** *p137*
Morgan, Walter; America, 1719 ***1220.12*** *p565*
Morgan, William; America, 1728 ***1220.12*** *p565*
Morgan, William; America, 1739 ***1220.12*** *p565*
Morgan, William; America, 1743 ***1220.12*** *p565*
Morgan, William; America, 1745 ***1220.12*** *p565*
Morgan, William; America, 1751 ***1220.12*** *p565*
Morgan, William; America, 1757 ***1220.12*** *p565*
Morgan, William; America, 1762 ***1220.12*** *p565*
Morgan, William; America, 1763 ***1220.12*** *p565*
Morgan, William; America, 1765 ***1220.12*** *p565*
Morgan, William; America, 1767 ***1220.12*** *p565*
Morgan, William; America, 1769 ***1220.12*** *p565*
Morgan, William; America, 1770 ***1220.12*** *p565*
Morgan, William; America, 1775 ***1220.12*** *p565*
Morgan, William; Annapolis, MD, 1725 ***1220.12*** *p565*
Morgan, William; Barbados or Jamaica, 1697 ***1220.12*** *p565*
Morgan, William 32; Ontario, 1871 ***1823.21*** *p268*
Morgan, William 33; Ontario, 1871 ***1823.17*** *p120*
Morgan, William 60; Ontario, 1871 ***1823.21*** *p268*
Morgan, William; St. John, N.B., 1842 ***2978.20*** *p7*
Morgan, William P.; Washington, 1882 ***2770.40*** *p135*
Morgan, William T.; Colorado, 1891 ***1029.59*** *p64*
Morgan, Wm H. 51; Ontario, 1871 ***1823.21*** *p268*
Morgani, Gaetano; Louisiana, 1874-1875 ***4981.45*** *p30*
Morgans, Anne *SEE* Morgans, George
Morgans, Daniel *SEE* Morgans, Morgan
Morgans, Eleanor Evans *SEE* Morgans, George
Morgans, Elizabeth Davies; Ohio, 1840 ***4022.20*** *p288*
Morgans, Evan *SEE* Morgans, George
Morgans, George; Ohio, 1837 ***4022.20*** *p288*
*Wife:*Eleanor Evans
*Child:*Anne
*Child:*Evan
With father-in-law
*Child:*Margaret
Morgans, Jane *SEE* Morgans, Morgan
Morgans, Jane Edwards *SEE* Morgans, Morgan
Morgans, John *SEE* Morgans, Morgan
Morgans, Margaret *SEE* Morgans, George
Morgans, Margaret *SEE* Morgans, Morgan
Morgans, Mary *SEE* Morgans, Morgan
Morgans, Morgan; Ohio, 1840 ***4022.20*** *p288*
*Wife:*Jane Edwards
*Child:*Margaret
*Child:*Daniel
*Child:*Jane
*Child:*John
*Child:*Mary
Morganthaler, Henry; Ohio, 1809-1852 ***4511.35*** *p37*
Morganthaler, Peter; Ohio, 1809-1852 ***4511.35*** *p37*
Morgenstern, Karl; New York, 1887 ***5475.1*** *p409*
Morgenstern, Margarethe 49; America, 1856 ***5475.1*** *p496*
Morgenthaler, Henry; Ohio, 1809-1852 ***4511.35*** *p37*
Morgenthaler, Peter; Ohio, 1809-1852 ***4511.35*** *p37*
Morgenthall, Jean 7; America, 1841 ***778.6*** *p248*
Morgenthall, Marie 51; America, 1841 ***778.6*** *p248*
Morgenweck, Matthaus; America, 1867 ***7919.3*** *p524*
Morgon, Madeline 10; America, 1843 ***778.6*** *p248*
Morhain, Nikolaus; Iowa, 1878 ***5475.1*** *p341*
Morhat, John; Illinois, 1865 ***6079.1*** *p10*
Moriarty, Johanna 42; Ontario, 1871 ***1823.21*** *p268*
Moriaux, Jean Joseph; New York, NY, 1856 ***1494.21*** *p31*
Morice, Daniel Nicholas; Philadelphia, 1804 ***9228.50*** *p469*
Morice, John; America, 1644-1663 ***9228.50*** *p469*
Morice, Marguerite; Louisiana, 1719 ***9228.50*** *p469*
Morier, Jean 29; Quebec, 1659 ***9221.17*** *p406*
Morier, Pierre 22; Quebec, 1658 ***9221.17*** *p384*
Morille, Charles; Quebec, 1639 ***9221.17*** *p91*
Morille, Michelle 49; Quebec, 1641 ***9221.17*** *p106*
Morille, Michelle 49; Quebec, 1641 ***9221.17*** *p106*
Morin, A. 23; America, 1840 ***778.6*** *p248*
Morin, Charlotte; Quebec, 1668 ***4514.3*** *p350*
Morin, Claire 21; Quebec, 1636 ***9221.17*** *p61*
Morin, Francoise 21; Quebec, 1647 ***9221.17*** *p185*
Morin, George 36; Ontario, 1871 ***1823.17*** *p120*
Morin, J.G.; New York, NY, 1848 ***6412.40*** *p151*
Morin, Jacques 26; Montreal, 1654 ***9221.17*** *p318*
Morin, Jean; Quebec, 1642 ***9221.17*** *p119*
Morin, Jean; Quebec, 1643 ***9221.17*** *p134*
Morin, John 29; Ontario, 1871 ***1823.21*** *p268*
Morin, Joseph 26; America, 1843 ***778.6*** *p248*
Morin, Margaret 32; Ontario, 1871 ***1823.17*** *p120*
Morin, Marie; Quebec, 1665 ***4514.3*** *p350*
Morin, Marie; Quebec, 1669 ***4514.3*** *p350*
Morin, Marie; Quebec, 1673 ***4514.3*** *p350*
Morin, Marie 31; Quebec, 1660 ***9221.17*** *p437*
Morin, Michel; Quebec, 1649 ***9221.17*** *p217*
Morin, Noel 24; Quebec, 1639 ***9221.17*** *p91*
Morin, Olive 35; Quebec, 1661 ***9221.17*** *p465*
*Son:*Jean 14
*Daughter:*Jacqueline 11
*Son:*Jean-Baptiste
Morin, Robert; Toronto, 1844 ***2910.35*** *p114*
Morin, Rogers; America, 1763 ***1220.12*** *p565*
Moring, Elias; America, 1765 ***1220.12*** *p565*
Moring, Thomas; America, 1741 ***1220.12*** *p565*
Moris, Etienne; Quebec, 1656 ***9221.17*** *p343*
Moris, Jan; Texas, 1860 ***2853.20*** *p74*
Morisain, James 50; Ontario, 1871 ***1823.17*** *p120*
Morisini, Mr. 2; America, 1843 ***778.6*** *p248*
Morisini, Mr. 30; America, 1843 ***778.6*** *p248*
Morisini, Mr. 36; America, 1843 ***778.6*** *p248*
Morisini, Mrs. 30; America, 1843 ***778.6*** *p248*
Morison, Alexr. 60; North Carolina, 1774 ***1422.10*** *p59*
Morison, John 52; Ontario, 1871 ***1823.21*** *p268*
Morison, John 60; Ontario, 1871 ***1823.21*** *p268*
Morison, William 60; Ontario, 1871 ***1823.21*** *p268*
Morisse, Charles; Quebec, 1639 ***9221.17*** *p91*
Morisseau, Marguerite-Madeleine 18; Quebec, 1661 ***9221.17*** *p463*
Morisset, Jean 20; Quebec, 1661 ***9221.17*** *p463*
Morisset, Mathurin; Quebec, 1645 ***9221.17*** *p155*
Morisset, Mathurin 41; Quebec, 1662 ***9221.17*** *p490*
Moriteur, Andrew 30; Port uncertain, 1846 ***778.6*** *p249*
Moritz, Barbara; America, 1847 ***5475.1*** *p474*
Moritz, Friederike Catharine; America, 1866 ***7420.1*** *p246*
Moritz, Johann 19; America, 1844 ***5475.1*** *p471*
Moritz, Josef 43; America, 1843 ***5475.1*** *p347*
Moritz, Magdalena; America, 1881 ***5475.1*** *p285*
Morkan, Michael 44; Ontario, 1871 ***1823.21*** *p268*
Morkin, Edward 35; Ontario, 1871 ***1823.21*** *p268*
Morkin, Martin 25; Ontario, 1871 ***1823.21*** *p268*
Morkin, Thomas 36; Ontario, 1871 ***1823.21*** *p268*
Morland, Edward; America, 1730 ***1220.12*** *p565*
Morland, Eleanor; America, 1774 ***1220.12*** *p565*
Morlay, John; Illinois, 1860 ***6079.1*** *p10*
Morley, Ann; America, 1766 ***1220.12*** *p565*
Morley, Charles 38; Ontario, 1871 ***1823.21*** *p268*
Morley, Edward; America, 1730 ***1220.12*** *p565*
Morley, Edward; Barbados, 1679 ***1220.12*** *p565*
Morley, Frances; America, 1665 ***1220.12*** *p565*
Morley, Giovana W.; Illinois, 1834-1900 ***6020.5*** *p132*
Morley, John; America, 1684 ***1220.12*** *p565*
Morley, John; America, 1685 ***1220.12*** *p565*
Morley, John; America, 1752 ***1220.12*** *p565*
Morley, John 43; Ontario, 1871 ***1823.17*** *p120*
Morley, John 66; Ontario, 1871 ***1823.21*** *p268*
Morley, Joseph; America, 1767 ***1220.12*** *p566*
Morley, Joseph 27; Ontario, 1871 ***1823.17*** *p120*
Morley, Joseph 29; Ontario, 1871 ***1823.21*** *p268*
Morley, Joseph 51; Ontario, 1871 ***1823.17*** *p120*
Morley, Martin 18; Quebec, 1870 ***8364.32*** *p25*
Morley, Mary; America, 1749 ***1220.12*** *p566*
Morley, Robert; Barbados, 1682 ***1220.12*** *p566*
Morley, Shadreck; America, 1685 ***1220.12*** *p566*
Morley, Thomas; America, 1754 ***1220.12*** *p566*
Morley, Thomas; America, 1771 ***1220.12*** *p566*
Morlier, E. 20; New Orleans, 1846 ***778.6*** *p249*
Morling, Gottfried; New York, 1859 ***358.56*** *p99*
Morllein, Baltzer; Ohio, 1809-1852 ***4511.35*** *p37*
Morlot, Gabriel; Illinois, 1859 ***6079.1*** *p10*
Morneau, Francois; Quebec, 1652 ***9221.17*** *p263*
Mornet, Bernard 28; New Orleans, 1840 ***778.6*** *p249*
Moroane, Patrick; Massachusetts, 1675-1676 ***1642*** *p128*
Moronie, John; America, 1775 ***1220.12*** *p566*
Morotzke, Fred; Iowa, 1892 ***1211.15*** *p16*
Morphew, John; America, 1744 ***1220.12*** *p566*
Morphy, Andrew 49; Ontario, 1871 ***1823.21*** *p269*
Morphy, Brian; Massachusetts, 1675-1676 ***1642*** *p129*
Morr, Peter; America, 1831 ***2526.43*** *p219*
Morran, Bryan; Boston, 1766 ***1642*** *p36*
Morray, Adam; America, 1774 ***1220.12*** *p573*
Morray, Roger; Virginia, 1730 ***1220.12*** *p573*
Morreance, Conrade; Philadelphia, 1778 ***8529.30*** *p3*
Morrell, Benjamin; Barbados or Jamaica, 1692 ***1220.12*** *p566*
Morrell, David; Colorado, 1882 ***1029.59*** *p64*
Morrell, Elizabeth; Potomac, 1729 ***1220.12*** *p566*
Morrell, John; Boston, 1659 ***1642*** *p9*
Morrell, John; Virginia, 1719 ***1220.12*** *p566*
Morrell, Lysbell; Boston, 1659 ***1642*** *p9*
Morrell, Mary; Barbados or Jamaica, 1694 ***1220.12*** *p566*
Morrell, Peter; Salem, MA, 1675 ***9228.50*** *p149*
Morrell, Peter; Salem, MA, 1675 ***9228.50*** *p469*
Morren, Patrick; Massachusetts, 1675-1676 ***1642*** *p127*
Morrene, Patrick; Massachusetts, 1675-1676 ***1642*** *p128*
Morres, James 25; Ontario, 1871 ***1823.21*** *p269*
Morrice, Ann; America, 1742 ***1220.12*** *p566*
Morrice, John; America, 1729 ***1220.12*** *p567*
Morrice, Richard; America, 1754 ***1220.12*** *p567*
Morrill, George 22; Ontario, 1871 ***1823.21*** *p269*
Morrill, John; Ipswich, MA, 1661 ***1642*** *p70*
Morrill, Simeon 77; Ontario, 1871 ***1823.21*** *p269*
Morris, Abraham; America, 1753 ***1220.12*** *p566*
Morris, Ang; America, 1700 ***1220.12*** *p566*
Morris, Ann; America, 1772 ***1220.12*** *p566*
Morris, Augustin; Barbados or Jamaica, 1700 ***1220.12*** *p566*
Morris, Bartholomew; Annapolis, MD, 1725 ***1220.12*** *p566*
Morris, Benjamin; America, 1765 ***1220.12*** *p566*
Morris, Catherine; America, 1767 ***1220.12*** *p566*
Morris, Charles 36; Michigan, 1880 ***4491.39*** *p21*
Morris, David; America, 1723 ***1220.12*** *p566*
Morris, David; America, 1774 ***1220.12*** *p566*
Morris, David; America, 1774 ***1220.12*** *p566*
Morris, David; Colorado, 1891 ***1029.59*** *p64*
Morris, David; Marston's Wharf, 1780 ***8529.30*** *p14*
Morris, Edward; America, 1763 ***1220.12*** *p566*
Morris, Edward; Ohio, 1837-1838 ***4022.20*** *p289*
*Wife:*Mary Morris
Morris, Eleanor; America, 1749 ***1220.12*** *p566*
Morris, Eliza; New Orleans, 1850 ***7242.30*** *p149*
Morris, Elizabeth; America, 1724 ***1220.12*** *p566*
Morris, Elizabeth; America, 1738 ***1220.12*** *p566*
Morris, Elizabeth; America, 1742 ***1220.12*** *p566*
Morris, Elizabeth; America, 1759 ***1220.12*** *p566*
Morris, Elizabeth; America, 1768 ***1220.12*** *p566*
Morris, Elizabeth; Barbados or Jamaica, 1688 ***1220.12*** *p566*
Morris, Elizabeth; Virginia, 1736 ***1220.12*** *p566*
Morris, Evan; America, 1765 ***1220.12*** *p566*
Morris, Evan; Ohio, 1849 ***4022.20*** *p289*
*Wife:*Hannah
Morris, Frances; Barbados or Jamaica, 1702 ***1220.12*** *p567*
Morris, George; America, 1764 ***1220.12*** *p567*
Morris, George; America, 1769 ***1220.12*** *p567*
Morris, George 28; Ontario, 1871 ***1823.17*** *p121*
Morris, Hanna; America, 1725 ***1220.12*** *p567*
Morris, Hannah; America, 1751 ***1220.12*** *p567*
Morris, Hannah; America, 1755 ***1220.12*** *p567*
Morris, Hannah *SEE* Morris, Evan
Morris, Hanora 70; Ontario, 1871 ***1823.21*** *p269*
Morris, Henry; America, 1717 ***1220.12*** *p567*
Morris, Henry; North Carolina, 1710 ***3629.40*** *p6*
Morris, James; America, 1758 ***1220.12*** *p567*
Morris, James; America, 1764 ***1220.12*** *p567*
Morris, James; America, 1773 ***1220.12*** *p567*
Morris, Jane; America, 1745 ***1220.12*** *p567*
Morris, Jane; Virginia, 1749 ***3675.1*** *p*
Morris, John; America, 1725 ***1220.12*** *p567*
Morris, John; America, 1736 ***1220.12*** *p567*
Morris, John; America, 1745 ***1220.12*** *p567*
Morris, John; America, 1749 ***1220.12*** *p567*
Morris, John; America, 1754 ***1220.12*** *p567*
Morris, John; America, 1761 ***1220.12*** *p567*
Morris, John; America, 1764 ***1220.12*** *p567*
Morris, John; America, 1765 ***1220.12*** *p567*
Morris, John; America, 1766 ***1220.12*** *p567*
Morris, John; America, 1769 ***1220.12*** *p567*
Morris, John; America, 1770 ***1220.12*** *p567*
Morris, John; America, 1774 ***1220.12*** *p567*
Morris, John; America, 1775 ***1220.12*** *p567*
Morris, John; Barbados, 1668 ***1220.12*** *p567*
Morris, John 21; Boston, 1747 ***1642*** *p30*
Morris, John; Charles Town, SC, 1718 ***1220.12*** *p567*
Morris, John; Colorado, 1888 ***1029.59*** *p64*
Morris, John; Dakota, 1880-1885 ***1865.50*** *p97*
Morris, John; Maryland, 1737 ***1220.12*** *p567*
Morris, John; Maryland or Virginia, 1738 ***1220.12*** *p567*
Morris, John; New York, 1783 ***8529.30*** *p14*
Morris, John; Virginia, 1742 ***1220.12*** *p567*
Morris, John; Washington, 1887 ***2770.40*** *p24*
Morris, John; Washington, 1889 ***2770.40*** *p80*
Morris, John H. 35; Ontario, 1871 ***1823.17*** *p121*
Morris, Joseph; America, 1768 ***1220.12*** *p567*

Morris, Joseph 31; Ontario, 1871 1823.21 p269
Morris, Margaret; America, 1749 1220.12 p567
Morris, Margaret; America, 1751 1220.12 p567
Morris, Mary; America, 1739 1220.12 p567
Morris, Mary; America, 1759 1220.12 p567
Morris, Mary; America, 1762 1220.12 p567
Morris, Mary; Annapolis, MD, 1719 1220.12 p567
Morris, Mary; Barbados, 1675 1220.12 p567
Morris, Mary; Ohio, 1837-1838 4022.20 p289
Morris, Matthew 26; Ontario, 1871 1823.21 p269
Morris, Morgan; America, 1770 1220.12 p567
Morris, Morris; Ohio, 1844 4022.20 p289
*Wife:*Sarah
Morris, Nicholas; Virginia, 1652 6254.4 p243
Morris, Philip; America, 1682 1220.12 p567
Morris, Richard; America, 1759 1220.12 p567
Morris, Richard; America, 1775 1220.12 p567
Morris, Richard 50; Ontario, 1871 1823.17 p121
Morris, Richard 19; Virginia, 1635 1183.3 p30
Morris, Robert; America, 1756 1220.12 p567
Morris, Robert 39; Ontario, 1871 1823.21 p269
Morris, Robert 57; Ontario, 1871 1823.21 p269
Morris, Robert 58; Ontario, 1871 1823.21 p269
Morris, Ruth; America, 1752 1220.12 p568
Morris, Sarah; America, 1757 1220.12 p568
Morris, Sarah *SEE* Morris, Morris
Morris, Silvan; America, 1685 1220.12 p568
Morris, Thomas; America, 1673 1220.12 p568
Morris, Thomas; America, 1679 1220.12 p568
Morris, Thomas; America, 1723 1220.12 p568
Morris, Thomas; America, 1736 1220.12 p568
Morris, Thomas; America, 1747 1220.12 p568
Morris, Thomas; America, 1751 1220.12 p568
Morris, Thomas; America, 1752 1220.12 p568
Morris, Thomas; America, 1765 1220.12 p568
Morris, Thomas; America, 1771 1220.12 p568
Morris, Thomas; America, 1774 1220.12 p568
Morris, Thomas; Barbados, 1670 1220.12 p568
Morris, Thomas; Barbados, 1710 1220.12 p568
Morris, Thomas; Marston's Wharf, 1780 8529.30 p14
Morris, Thomas; Maryland, 1737 1220.12 p568
Morris, Thomas 40; Ontario, 1871 1823.17 p121
Morris, Thomas 72; Ontario, 1871 1823.21 p269
Morris, Thomas; Rappahannock, VA, 1728 1220.12 p568
Morris, Thomas I.; Philadelphia, 1876-1880 7074.20 p133
Morris, Thos.; Louisiana, 1874 4981.45 p296
Morris, Thos.; Louisiana, 1874 4981.45 p296
Morris, William; America, 1738 1220.12 p568
Morris, William; America, 1743 1220.12 p568
Morris, William; America, 1769 1220.12 p568
Morris, William; America, 1771 1220.12 p568
Morris, William; Barbados, 1668 1220.12 p568
Morris, William; Barbados, 1675 1220.12 p568
Morris, William; Boston, 1743 1642 p45
Morris, William 33; Ontario, 1871 1823.21 p269
Morris, William 50; Ontario, 1871 1823.21 p269
Morris, William; Potomac, 1731 1220.12 p568
Morris, William; Washington, 1880 2770.40 p134
Morriset, Pierre; Virginia, 1700 9230.15 p80
Morrisett, Henry; North Carolina, 1710 3629.40 p6
Morrisey, Agustus 36; Ontario, 1871 1823.21 p269
Morrish, George 70; Ontario, 1871 1823.21 p269
Morrish, Jane 49; Michigan, 1880 4491.39 p21
Morrish, Louisa 17; Michigan, 1880 4491.39 p21
Morrish, Sarah; Virginia, 1763 1220.12 p568
Morrish, Thomas; Barbados, 1672 1220.12 p568
Morrish, William; America, 1772 1220.12 p568
Morrish, Wm 48; Michigan, 1880 4491.39 p21
Morrison, Mr. 30; New Orleans, 1848 778.6 p249
Morrison, Alexander 30; Ontario, 1871 1823.17 p121
Morrison, Alexander 56; Ontario, 1871 1823.17 p121
Morrison, Alexr 60; Ontario, 1871 1823.21 p269
Morrison, Andrew; North Carolina, 1839 1088.45 p24
Morrison, Andrew Jcksn; Colorado, 1890 1029.59 p64
Morrison, Angus 50; Ontario, 1871 1823.17 p121
Morrison, Angus 50; Ontario, 1871 1823.21 p269
Morrison, Angus 60; Ontario, 1871 1823.21 p269
Morrison, Archd 25; Ontario, 1871 1823.21 p269
Morrison, Archibald 27; Ontario, 1871 1823.17 p121
Morrison, Bella 22; Ontario, 1871 1823.21 p269
Morrison, Bengim 50; Ontario, 1871 1823.17 p121
Morrison, Catherine 30; Ontario, 1871 1823.21 p269
Morrison, Catherine 48; Ontario, 1871 1823.21 p269
Morrison, Cathn 20; St. John, N.B., 1834 6469.7 p6
Morrison, Charles 41; Ontario, 1871 1823.17 p121
Morrison, Daniel 26; Ontario, 1871 1823.17 p121
Morrison, David 45; Ontario, 1871 1823.17 p121
Morrison, David 57; Ontario, 1871 1823.17 p121
Morrison, Donald 34; Ontario, 1871 1823.21 p269
Morrison, Donald 45; Ontario, 1871 1823.21 p269
Morrison, Donald 60; Ontario, 1871 1823.21 p269
Morrison, Duncan 28; Ontario, 1871 1823.21 p269
Morrison, Duncan 30; Ontario, 1871 1823.21 p269
Morrison, Effa; America, 1765 1220.12 p568
Morrison, Elisabeth 42; Ontario, 1871 1823.21 p269
Morrison, Francies 36; Ontario, 1871 1823.21 p269
Morrison, George; Boston, 1776 8529.30 p4A
Morrison, George; Colorado, 1862 1029.59 p64
Morrison, George 40; Ontario, 1871 1823.17 p121
Morrison, George 60; Ontario, 1871 1823.17 p121
Morrison, Hector 23; Ontario, 1871 1823.17 p121
Morrison, Hector 23; Ontario, 1871 1823.21 p269
Morrison, Henry 60; Ontario, 1871 1823.17 p121
Morrison, Hugh 46; Ontario, 1871 1823.21 p269
Morrison, Isabella 35; Ontario, 1871 1823.21 p269
Morrison, James; Ohio, 1809-1852 4511.35 p37
Morrison, James 31; Ontario, 1871 1823.17 p121
Morrison, James 42; Ontario, 1871 1823.17 p121
Morrison, James; Washington, 1883 2770.40 p137
Morrison, Janet 67; Ontario, 1871 1823.21 p269
Morrison, John; America, 1748 1220.12 p568
Morrison, John 21; Boston, 1747 1642 p29
Morrison, John; Ohio, 1854 3580.20 p33
Morrison, John; Ohio, 1854 6020.12 p21
Morrison, John 27; Ontario, 1871 1823.21 p269
Morrison, John 32; Ontario, 1871 1823.21 p269
Morrison, John 37; Ontario, 1871 1823.17 p121
Morrison, John 48; Ontario, 1871 1823.21 p269
Morrison, John 56; Ontario, 1871 1823.17 p121
Morrison, John; St. John, N.B., 1848 2978.15 p41
Morrison, Josephine May; Detroit, 1910 9228.50 p321
Morrison, Lucy; America, 1755 1220.12 p568
Morrison, Malcolm 27; Ontario, 1871 1823.21 p269
Morrison, Malcolm 37; Ontario, 1871 1823.21 p269
Morrison, Margret 30; Ontario, 1871 1823.21 p270
Morrison, Martin 37; Ontario, 1871 1823.21 p270
Morrison, Mary 22; Ontario, 1871 1823.17 p121
Morrison, Mary 38; Ontario, 1871 1823.21 p270
Morrison, Mary Ann 44; Ontario, 1871 1823.21 p270
Morrison, Murdock 36; Ontario, 1871 1823.21 p270
Morrison, Neil; Ontario, 1871 1823.17 p121
Morrison, Neil 36; Ontario, 1871 1823.21 p270
Morrison, Neil 50; Ontario, 1871 1823.21 p270
Morrison, Norman 42; Ontario, 1871 1823.17 p121
Morrison, Peter 42; Ontario, 1871 1823.21 p270
Morrison, Robert 12; Ontario, 1871 1823.21 p270
Morrison, Robert 43; Ontario, 1871 1823.21 p270
Morrison, Robert 45; Ontario, 1871 1823.21 p270
Morrison, Robert 52; Ontario, 1871 1823.21 p270
Morrison, Samuel; America, 1743 1220.12 p568
Morrison, Sarah 41; Ontario, 1871 1823.21 p270
Morrison, William 23; Ontario, 1871 1823.17 p121
Morrison, William 59; Ontario, 1871 1823.21 p270
Morrissey, Edward; New Orleans, 1851 7242.30 p149
Morrissey, James 40; Ontario, 1871 1823.17 p121
Morrissy, John R.; Illinois, 1858-1861 6020.5 p132
Morrit, Mary; America, 1746 1220.12 p568
Morrough, John; Jamaica, 1776 8529.30 p13A
Morrous, James 56; Ontario, 1871 1823.17 p121
Morrow, Andrew 60; Ontario, 1871 1823.21 p270
Morrow, Francis 19; Ontario, 1871 1823.21 p270
Morrow, George 50; Ontario, 1871 1823.17 p121
Morrow, James 45; Ontario, 1871 1823.17 p121
Morrow, John; America, 1743 1220.12 p568
Morrow, John 14; Ontario, 1871 1823.21 p270
Morrow, John 42; Ontario, 1871 1823.21 p270
Morrow, Levi J.; New Mexico, 1914 4812.1 p87
Morrow, Nelson 57; Ontario, 1871 1823.21 p270
Morrow, Richard; Ohio, 1809-1852 4511.35 p37
Morrow, Samuel 85; Ontario, 1871 1823.21 p270
Morrow, William; Ohio, 1809-1852 4511.35 p37
Morsance, Conrade; Philadelphia, 1778 8529.30 p3
Morsch, Anna *SEE* Morsch, Johann Nik.
Morsch, Anna Maria Lambert 32 *SEE* Morsch, Johann Nik.
Morsch, Elisabeth *SEE* Morsch, Johann Nik.
Morsch, J. Nikolaus *SEE* Morsch, Johann Nik.
Morsch, Johann Nik. 47; South America, 1857 5475.1 p543
*Wife:*Anna Maria Lambert 32
*Son:*J. Nikolaus
*Daughter:*Anna
*Daughter:*Maria
*Daughter:*Elisabeth
Morsch, Maria *SEE* Morsch, Johann Nik.
Morsch, Nikolaus; America, 1846 5475.1 p547
Morsden, Walter 26; Halifax, N.S., n.d. 1833.5 p7
Morsden, Walter 26; Halifax, N.S., n.d. 8445.10 p7
Morse, Charles; America, 1751 1220.12 p568
Morse, Dinah; America, 1761 1220.12 p568
Morse, George; Ohio, 1844 2763.1 p20
Morse, John; America, 1685 1220.12 p568
Morse, John; America, 1720 1220.12 p568
Morse, John 42; Ontario, 1871 1823.21 p270
Morse, John 70; Ontario, 1871 1823.21 p270
Morse, Margaret; Philadelphia, 1863 8513.31 p296
Morse, Paul; America, 1685 1220.12 p568
Morse, Peter; Massachusetts, 1754 1642 p109
Morse, Richard; America, 1736 1220.12 p568
Morse, Samuel 45; Ontario, 1871 1823.21 p270
Morse, William; America, 1716 1220.12 p568
Morse, William; America, 1729 1220.12 p568
Morse, William; America, 1748 1220.12 p568
Morsfeldel, Katharina 53; America, 1867 5475.1 p524
Morsley, James 30; Ontario, 1871 1823.17 p121
Morsom, Henry 30; Ontario, 1871 1823.17 p121
Morson, Edward 67; Ontario, 1871 1823.21 p270
Morson, John 39; Ontario, 1871 1823.17 p122
Morson, Joseph 50; Ontario, 1871 1823.21 p270
Mort, C. J.; North Carolina, 1855 1088.45 p24
Mort, Joseph; New Jersey, 1794 3845.2 p129
Mortaigne, Francois 22; Quebec, 1637 9221.17 p69
Mortall, Charles; America, 1676 1220.12 p568
Mortar, Richard; Barbados or Jamaica, 1699 1220.12 p568
Mortebois, Robert; America, 1752 1220.12 p568
Mortell, Thomas; Washington, 1883 2770.40 p137
Morten, Mr. 42; America, 1847 778.6 p249
Morten, Mrs. 30; America, 1847 778.6 p249
Mortenson, Andrew; St. Paul, MN, 1887 1865.50 p97
Mortenson, Anna Alfrida *SEE* Mortenson, Christina Hidinge
Mortenson, Christina; St. Paul, MN, 1888 1865.50 p98
*Daughter:*Anna Alfrida
*Daughter:*Frida Elisabeth
*Son:*Fritz Gerhard
Mortenson, Frida Elisabeth *SEE* Mortenson, Christina Hidinge
Mortenson, Fritz Gerhard *SEE* Mortenson, Christina Hidinge
Mortenson, Martin C.; Washington, 1886 2770.40 p195
Mortenson, Mils C.; Iowa, 1904 1211.15 p17
Mortenson, Morten Sorensen; Iowa, 1914 1211.15 p17
Mortenson, Walter; Iowa, 1916 1211.15 p17
Morth, Pedro A. 30; America, 1844 778.6 p249
Mortilly, Victor; Louisiana, 1836-1841 4981.45 p209
Mortimer, Caroline 23; Ontario, 1871 1823.21 p270
Mortimer, Charlotte 17; Ontario, 1871 1823.21 p270
Mortimer, Edward; Maryland, 1726 1220.12 p569
Mortimer, George 27; Ontario, 1871 1823.17 p122
Mortimer, George 63; Ontario, 1871 1823.21 p270
Mortimer, John 34; Ontario, 1871 1823.21 p270
Mortimer, Philip; Boston, 1737 1642 p26
Mortimer, R.; Quebec, 1885 1937.10 p52
Mortimer, Roger; America, 1685 1220.12 p569
Mortimer, Wm 43; Ontario, 1871 1823.21 p270
Mortimor, Luke; America, 1741 1220.12 p569
Mortimore, Adeline 22; Ontario, 1871 1823.21 p270
Mortimore, George 82; Michigan, 1880 4491.42 p18
Mortimore, Henry 43; Michigan, 1880 4491.42 p18
Mortimore, John 57; Michigan, 1880 4491.42 p18
Mortimore, Mary 74; Michigan, 1880 4491.42 p18
Mortin, Miles; North Carolina, 1850 1088.45 p24
Morton, Abraham; Barbados or Jamaica, 1684 1220.12 p562
Morton, Charles 30; Ontario, 1871 1823.21 p270
Morton, Daniel; America, 1732 1220.12 p562
Morton, David; Long Island, 1781 8529.30 p10A
Morton, Edward; America, 1685 1220.12 p562
Morton, Elizabeth; America, 1769 1220.12 p562
Morton, George; America, 1766 1220.12 p562
Morton, George; America, 1767 1220.12 p562
Morton, George 13; Ontario, 1871 1823.21 p270
Morton, George 44; Ontario, 1871 1823.21 p270
Morton, Gilbert 17; Ontario, 1871 1823.17 p122
Morton, Jas 50; Ontario, 1871 1823.21 p271
Morton, John; Marston's Wharf, 1782 8529.30 p14
Morton, John 60; Ontario, 1871 1823.21 p271
Morton, Mary; America, 1772 1220.12 p563
Morton, Richard; Barbados, 1688 1220.12 p563
Morton, Ronia Goldflam; Detroit, 1929-1930 6214.5 p63
Morton, Samuel 21; Annapolis, MD, 1724 1220.12 p563
Morton, William; Marston's Wharf, 1782 8529.30 p14
Mortonson, James; Iowa, 1890 1211.15 p16
Mortrier, M. Rose 20; Missouri, 1848 778.6 p249
Mortrier, Pierre 50; Missouri, 1848 778.6 p249
Moruine, Jean 31; America, 1848 778.6 p249
Mosa, Madeline 40; Ohio, 1840 778.6 p249
Mosby, Margaret 50; Ontario, 1871 1823.21 p271
Mosel, Andreas; Ohio, 1840-1897 8365.35 p17
Moseley, Charles; America, 1749 1220.12 p569
Moseley, Hannah; America, 1762 1220.12 p569
Moseley, John; America, 1716 1220.12 p569
Moseley, John; Philadelphia, 1778 8529.30 p7
Moseley, Joseph; America, 1749 1220.12 p569
Moseley, Paul; America, 1768 1220.12 p569
Moseley, Richard; America, 1742 1220.12 p569
Moseley, Thomas; Annapolis, MD, 1730 1220.12 p569

Mosell, James 16; Quebec, 1870 *8364.32* p25
Mosely, George; Philadelphia, 1778 *8529.30* p7
Mosely, Joseph; America, 1752 *1220.12* p569
Mosely, Kate 60; Ontario, 1871 *1823.21* p271
Moser, Benedicht; Ohio, 1809-1852 *4511.35* p37
Moser, Carl Aug. Phil. Alb. *SEE* Moser, Johann
  Friedrich Gottlieb
Moser, Carl Heinr. Lud. *SEE* Moser, Johann Friedrich
  Gottlieb
Moser, Christian *SEE* Moser, John
Moser, Engel So. Car. Lohrmann *SEE* Moser, Johann
  Friedrich Gottlieb
Moser, Frances 40; Ontario, 1871 *1823.21* p271
Moser, Heinrich 21; New York, NY, 1898 *7951.13* p42
Moser, Heinrich Friedr. Wilh. *SEE* Moser, Johann
  Friedrich Gottlieb
Moser, Hermanie 1; Port uncertain, 1843 *778.6* p249
Moser, Johann Friedrich Gottlieb; Minnesota, 1882
  7420.1 p331
  *Wife:*Engel So. Car. Lohrmann
  *Son:*Carl Aug. Phil. Alb.
  *Son:*Carl Heinr. Lud.
  *Son:*Heinrich Friedr. Wilh.
Moser, John; Ohio, 1839-1877 *9228.50* p469
  *Wife:*Sarah H.
  *Child:*Christian
  *Child:*William Wesley
  *Child:*Nancy
Moser, John; Pennsylvania, 1711 *9228.50* p469
Moser, Jons 23; New York, NY, 1893 *1883.7* p41
Moser, Landelin 22; America, 1848 *778.6* p249
Moser, Ludwig; Valdivia, Chile, 1850 *1192.4* p48
Moser, Marie 23; Port uncertain, 1843 *778.6* p249
Moser, Nancy *SEE* Moser, John
Moser, Peter; America, 1868 *5475.1* p297
Moser, Peter; Ohio, 1809-1852 *4511.35* p37
Moser, R.; Valdivia, Chile, 1850 *1192.4* p48
Moser, Sarah H. *SEE* Moser, John
Moser, William Wesley *SEE* Moser, John
Moses, Abraham; North Carolina, 1811-1812 *1088.45*
  p24
Moses, Benjamin; Annapolis, MD, 1726 *1220.12* p569
Moses, Jacob; America, 1762 *1220.12* p569
Moses, Jacob; America, 1763 *1220.12* p569
Moses, Jacob; America, 1769 *1220.12* p569
Moses, Joseph; America, 1761 *1220.12* p569
Moses, Samuel; America, 1767 *1220.12* p569
Moses, Solomon; America, 1773 *1220.12* p569
Moses, Susan; America, 1727 *1220.12* p569
Moses, Susan; Virginia, 1734 *1220.12* p569
Moses, Thomas; Died enroute, 1725 *1220.12* p569
Moses, William; America, 1738 *1220.12* p569
Moses, William; America, 1775 *1220.12* p569
Mosesly, George; America, 1751 *1220.12* p569
Mosey, John; Marston's Wharf, 1782 *8529.30* p14
Mosey, Richard; Ohio, 1843 *2763.1* p20
Mosher, Samuel E.; Philadelphia, 1869 *7074.20* p133
Mosher, Thomas 53; Michigan, 1880 *4491.30* p23
Moshier, Thomas 53; Michigan, 1880 *4491.30* p23
Mosinger, Jacob; New Jersey, 1750-1774 *927.31* p3
Moskal, Albert; Detroit, 1929-1930 *6214.5* p65
Moskowitz, Dorothy; Detroit, 1929 *1640.55* p117
Moskowitz, Zeindel; Detroit, 1929-1930 *6214.5* p65
Mosley, Hen; Virginia, 1652 *6254.4* p243
Mosllein, Baltzer; Ohio, 1809-1852 *4511.35* p37
Moss, Ac 44; Ontario, 1871 *1823.17* p122
Moss, Ann; America, 1752 *1220.12* p569
Moss, Charles; America, 1771 *1220.12* p569
Moss, Christopher; America, 1727 *1220.12* p569
Moss, David; Utah, 1899 *3687.1* p38
Moss, Francis; America, 1767 *1220.12* p569
Moss, Henry 48; Ontario, 1871 *1823.21* p271
Moss, Herman Leopold; North Carolina, 1844 *1088.45*
  p24
Moss, James 40; Ontario, 1871 *1823.17* p122
Moss, Jarvis; America, 1768 *1220.12* p569
Moss, John; America, 1742 *1220.12* p569
Moss, John; America, 1759 *1220.12* p569
Moss, John 23; Ontario, 1871 *1823.21* p271
Moss, Joseph; Boston, 1775 *8529.30* p3
Moss, Laura 40; Ontario, 1871 *1823.17* p122
Moss, Peter; America, 1748 *1220.12* p569
Moss, Philip; America, 1773 *1220.12* p569
Moss, Robert; America, 1742 *1220.12* p569
Moss, Samuel Carlton; Detroit, 1929-1930 *6214.5* p65
Moss, Sarah; America, 1770 *1220.12* p569
Moss, Thomas; America, 1729 *1220.12* p569
Moss, Thomas; America, 1734 *1220.12* p569
Moss, Thomas; America, 1771 *1220.12* p569
Moss, William; America, 1730 *1220.12* p569
Moss, William; Annapolis, MD, 1732 *1220.12* p569
Moss, William 28; Ontario, 1871 *1823.21* p271
Moss, William 32; Ontario, 1871 *1823.21* p271

Moss, William 36; Ontario, 1871 *1823.21* p271
Mossberg, A. Solomon; Kansas, 1869-1872 *1865.50* p98
Mossberg, Anna M.; St. Paul, MN, 1882 *1865.50* p98
Mosse, Richard; America, 1746 *1220.12* p569
Mosser, Christian *SEE* Mosser, John
Mosser, John; Ohio, 1839-1877 *9228.50* p469
  *Wife:*Sarah H.
  *Child:*William Wesley
  *Child:*Nancy
  *Child:*Christian
Mosser, John; Pennsylvania, 1711 *9228.50* p469
Mosser, Nancy *SEE* Mosser, John
Mosser, Sarah H. *SEE* Mosser, John
Mosser, William Wesley *SEE* Mosser, John
Mosses, Joseph; Boston, 1766 *1642* p37
Mosset, Jean; Louisiana, 1874 *4981.45* p296
Mossgrove, Oliver P.; Ohio, 1854 *3580.20* p33
Mossgrove, Oliver P.; Ohio, 1854 *6020.12* p21
Mossip, John 43; Ontario, 1871 *1823.21* p271
Mossman, Flora G. 50; Quebec, 1910 *2897.7* p7
Mossman, Robert A. 54; Quebec, 1910 *2897.7* p7
Mossop, Frederick 50; Ontario, 1871 *1823.17* p122
Mossop, John 40; Ontario, 1871 *1823.21* p271
Most, Hans Heinrich; New York, NY, 1856 *7420.1* p151
  *Brother:*Johann Conrad
Most, Hans Heinrich Christoph; America, 1861 *7420.1*
  p207
Most, Johann Conrad; America, 1859 *7420.1* p188
Most, Johann Conrad *SEE* Most, Hans Heinrich
Most, Johann Heinrich; America, 1857 *7420.1* p168
Mosten, John; America, 1750 *1220.12* p569
Motais, Guy; Montreal, 1653 *9221.17* p297
Mote, Elizabeth; Annapolis, MD, 1729 *1220.12* p556
Mot...ha, Casimir 20; New York, NY, 1893 *1883.7* p37
Mothe, Bernard 19; New Orleans, 1848 *778.6* p249
Mother, Elizabeth 36; Ontario, 1871 *1823.17* p122
Motherby, Charles; Annapolis, MD, 1723 *1220.12* p569
Mothersell, William 51; Ontario, 1871 *1823.21* p271
Mothersill, Joseph 51; Ontario, 1871 *1823.21* p271
Motherway, William; Washington, 1889 *2770.40* p80
Motley, James 38; Ontario, 1871 *1823.21* p271
Motley, Mary; America, 1675 *1220.12* p569
Motley, Robert; Barbados, 1674 *1220.12* p569
Motley, Robert; Jamaica, 1665 *1220.12* p569
Motley, Robert; Maryland, 1674-1675 *1236.25* p52
Motley, William; America, 1677 *1220.12* p570
Motley, William; America, 1682 *1220.12* p570
Motley, William; Barbados, 1675 *1220.12* p570
Motloe, William; America, 1732 *1220.12* p570
Motowski, Frank; Detroit, 1929-1930 *6214.5* p67
Motquin, Desire; Wisconsin, 1871 *1494.20* p11
Motquin, J. J.; Wisconsin, 1871 *1494.20* p11
Motraigh, Jerry 20; Ohio, 1880 *4879.40* p257
Motsche, Heinrich Christoph; Port uncertain, 1885
  7420.1 p348
Mott, Elena; Detroit, 1929-1930 *6214.5* p70
Mott, John; America, 1773 *1220.12* p570
Mott, Joseph; America, 1775 *1220.12* p570
Mott, Rebecca 63; Ontario, 1871 *1823.21* p271
Mott, Richard; America, 1763 *1220.12* p570
Mott, Richard; America, 1773 *1220.12* p570
Mott, William; Barbados or Jamaica, 1676 *1220.12* p570
Mott, Wm 49; Ontario, 1871 *1823.21* p271
Mottart, Clement; Wisconsin, 1855-1858 *1495.20* p67
  *Wife:*Eleonore Vandermissen
Mottart, Eleonore Vandermissen *SEE* Mottart, Clement
Mottart, Martin; Wisconsin, 1855 *1495.20* p41
  *Wife:*Therese Fresson
  *Daughter:*Therese
Mottart, Therese *SEE* Mottart, Martin
Mottart, Therese Fresson *SEE* Mottart, Martin
Motte, Mr. 13; Port uncertain, 1844 *778.6* p249
Motte, Mrs. 35; Port uncertain, 1844 *778.6* p249
Motte, Daniel; Ohio, 1809 *9228.50* p470
Motte, Marie Joseph; Wisconsin, 1878 *1495.20* p12
Mottee, Clement; Maine, n.d. *9228.50* p467
Mottee, Jacob; Charleston, SC, 1700-1790 *9228.50* p470
Mottel, Jakub; St. Louis, 1852 *2853.20* p21
Motter, William; North Carolina, 1855 *1088.45* p24
Mottice, Peter, Sr.; Ohio, 1809-1852 *4511.35* p37
Mottie, Peter; Ohio, 1809-1852 *4511.35* p37
Mottill, Jacob; Ohio, 1809-1852 *4511.35* p37
Mottilor, Edward 33; Ontario, 1871 *1823.17* p122
Mottin, A. Marie 29; Louisiana, 1848 *778.6* p249
Mottin, Adalaide 5; Louisiana, 1848 *778.6* p249
Mottin, Nicolas 34; Louisiana, 1848 *778.6* p249
Motton, Adolf 20; New Orleans, 1848 *778.6* p249
Motton, Charles 17; New Orleans, 1848 *778.6* p249
Mottrom, John; Virginia, 1652 *6254.4* p243
Motyl, Jakob 24; New York, NY, 1912 *8355.1* p16
Motz, David; Ohio, 1809-1852 *4511.35* p37
Motz, Georg 38; New Orleans, 1848 *778.6* p249
Motz, Peter; Ohio, 1809-1852 *4511.35* p37

Motz, Philip; North Carolina, 1856 *1088.45* p24
Motz, Philip Jacob; Ohio, 1809-1852 *4511.35* p37
Moucheau, Michael; America, 1742 *1220.12* p570
Moucheur, Alexander 27; America, 1842 *778.6* p249
Mouchlin, S. 53; America, 1843 *778.6* p249
Mouet deMoras, Pierre; Quebec, 1665 *2314.30* p167
Mouet deMoras, Pierre; Quebec, 1665 *2314.30* p191
Mougeville, Gerard 21; America, 1840 *778.6* p249
Mougeville, Marg. 22; America, 1840 *778.6* p249
Mougin, Clotilde 29; Louisiana, 1848 *778.6* p249
Mougin, Desire 4; Louisiana, 1848 *778.6* p250
Mougin, Fois. Eugene 31; Louisiana, 1848 *778.6* p250
Mougin, L. 17; New Orleans, 1841 *778.6* p249
Mougon deJarimeau, Michel-Marie; Quebec, 1755-1757
  2314.30 p170
Mougon deJarimeau, Michel-Marie; Quebec, 1755-1757
  2314.30 p191
Mouillard, Eleonore; Quebec, 1671 *4514.3* p350
Moul, Timothy; Virginia, 1700 *9230.15* p81
  With wife & child
Moulard, Claude 30; Port uncertain, 1841 *778.6* p250
Mould, Daniel; America, 1748 *1220.12* p570
Mould, Jeremiah; America, 1766 *1220.12* p570
Mould, Martin; America, 1754 *1220.12* p570
Mould, William; Annapolis, MD, 1725 *1220.12* p570
Moulden, Daniel; America, 1729 *1220.12* p570
Moulden, Thomas; Maryland, 1722 *1220.12* p570
Moulder, Jacob; Ohio, 1844 *2763.1* p20
Moulder, John; Maryland or Virginia, 1733 *1220.12*
  p570
Moulder, John; Ohio, 1844 *2763.1* p20
Moulding, James; Maryland, 1737 *1220.12* p570
Moulding, William; America, 1752 *1220.12* p570
Moule, Chas; Ontario, 1871 *1823.21* p271
Moule, Edward; America, 1747 *1220.12* p570
Moule, John; America, 1740 *1220.12* p570
Moule, Robert 25; Ontario, 1871 *1823.21* p271
Moule, Thomas; America, 1686 *1220.12* p570
Mouler, Jean 22; Port uncertain, 1843 *778.6* p250
Moulieres, Pierre; Montreal, 1653 *9221.17* p297
Moulin, Abraham; Virginia, 1700 *9230.15* p81
  With wife
Moulin, Francis; Ohio, 1809-1852 *4511.35* p37
Moulin, Francois 29; Missouri, 1845 *778.6* p250
Moulin Bros, Mr. 18; New Orleans, 1840 *778.6* p250
Moulinie, V. 24; New Orleans, 1842 *778.6* p250
Moulinier, Francoise 24; Quebec, 1658 *9221.17* p384
Moulinier, Roger; Quebec, 1648 *9221.17* p202
Moulson, Robert; Annapolis, MD, 1725 *1220.12* p570
Moulson, William; America, 1730 *1220.12* p570
Moulton, Chauncy 51; Ontario, 1871 *1823.21* p271
Moulton, John 5; Quebec, 1870 *8364.32* p25
Moulton, Samuel; Maryland, 1723 *1220.12* p570
Moulton, William; America, 1765 *1220.12* p570
Moulton, William; Newburyport, MA, 1690 *1642* p76
Moulton, William; West Indies, 1686 *1220.12* p570
Mounce, Christopher; Maryland, 1700-1730 *9228.50*
  p471
  *Wife:*Martha
Mounce, Martha *SEE* Mounce, Christopher
Mounslow, John; Rappahannock, VA, 1741 *1220.12*
  p570
Mount, John; America, 1758 *1220.12* p570
Mount, John; America, 1775 *1220.12* p570
Mount, Jonas; America, 1774 *1220.12* p570
Mount, Thomas; Died enroute, 1736 *1220.12* p570
Mountague, Francis; Barbados, 1665 *1220.12* p558
Mountague, Margaret; Potomac, 1729 *1220.12* p558
Mountague, William; America, 1774 *1220.12* p558
Mountain, Mitchel 30; Ontario, 1871 *1823.21* p271
Mountain, Patrick; North Carolina, 1836 *1088.45* p24
Mountaine, Mary; Annapolis, MD, 1722 *1220.12* p570
Mountfield, Robert; America, 1739 *1220.12* p570
Mountford, James 58; Ontario, 1871 *1823.21* p271
Mountford, Robert 26; Ontario, 1871 *1823.21* p271
Mountjoy, Anscott 44; Ontario, 1871 *1823.17* p122
Mountjoy, Mary Ann 42; Ontario, 1871 *1823.21* p271
Mounts, Christopher; Maryland, 1700-1730 *9228.50* p471
  *Wife:*Martha
Mounts, Martha *SEE* Mounts, Christopher
Mountsley, Mary; Barbados or Jamaica, 1686 *1220.12*
  p570
Mountstephen, Lawrence; Barbados, 1669 *1220.12* p570
Mountstephen, Samuel; America, 1685 *1220.12* p570
Mountstephen, William; Barbados, 1665 *1220.12* p570
Mounty, William; America, 1774 *1220.12* p570
Mourant, Nita Louisa *SEE* Mourant, Philip
Mourant, Nita Louisa *SEE* Mourant, Philip
Mourant, Philip; British Columbia, 1912-1916 *9228.50*
  p183
  *Child:*Philip Waddington
  *Child:*Winifred Eva
  *Child:*Nita Louisa

Mourant, Philip; Los Angeles, 1912-1916 ***9228.50*** *p183*
*Child:*Nita Louisa
Mourant, Philip Waddington *SEE* Mourant, Philip
Mourant, Winifred Eva *SEE* Mourant, Philip
Moureau, Antoine; Wisconsin, 1854-1858 ***1495.20*** *p49*
Moureau, Auguste; Wisconsin, 1854-1858 ***1495.20*** *p49*
*Wife:*Seraphine
Moureau, Jean Baptiste; Wisconsin, 1854-1858 ***1495.20*** *p49*
Moureau, Marie Therese Desiree; Wisconsin, 1854-1858 ***1495.20*** *p49*
Moureau, Romain Martin; Wisconsin, 1854-1858 ***1495.20*** *p49*
Moureau, Rosalie; Wisconsin, 1854-1858 ***1495.20*** *p49*
Moureau, Seraphine *SEE* Moureau, Auguste
Mouren, Jean 28; America, 1846 ***778.6*** *p250*
Moures, Xavier 18; Louisiana, 1848 ***778.6*** *p250*
Mourey, Joseph 28; New Orleans, 1843 ***778.6*** *p250*
Mourier, Jean 29; Quebec, 1659 ***9221.17*** *p406*
Mourier, Pierre 22; Quebec, 1658 ***9221.17*** *p384*
Mournaz, Mr. 40; America, 1846 ***778.6*** *p250*
Mournaz, Mrs. 30; America, 1846 ***778.6*** *p250*
Mournaz, Auguste 8; America, 1846 ***778.6*** *p250*
Mournaz, Henry 6; America, 1846 ***778.6*** *p250*
Mournaz, Marie 5; America, 1846 ***778.6*** *p250*
Mourot, Sebastian L. A.; Illinois, 1852 ***6079.1*** *p10*
Mourou, Alfred 3; New Orleans, 1848 ***778.6*** *p250*
Mours, Mariane 24; New Orleans, 1846 ***778.6*** *p250*
Mouse, Catherine 32; Ontario, 1871 ***1823.21*** *p271*
Mouse, Humphrey; America, 1758 ***1220.12*** *p570*
Mouse, John 36; Ontario, 1871 ***1823.21*** *p271*
Mouser, Barb. 28; America, 1846 ***778.6*** *p250*
Moushell, Humphrey; America, 1758 ***1220.12*** *p570*
Mousnier, Jacques; Montreal, 1653 ***9221.17*** *p298*
Mousnier, Marie 44; Montreal, 1659 ***9221.17*** *p422*
*Daughter:*Urbaine 14
Mousnier, Mathurin 25; Montreal, 1644 ***9221.17*** *p148*
Mousnier, Pierre; Montreal, 1644 ***9221.17*** *p149*
Mousnier, Thomas 19; Montreal, 1660 ***9221.17*** *p442*
Moussain, Louis 21; America, 1843 ***778.6*** *p250*
Mousseaux, Jacques 21; Montreal, 1653 ***9221.17*** *p298*
Mousseron, Rerre B.; Illinois, 1856 ***6079.1*** *p10*
Mousset, Florimond; Quebec, 1649 ***9221.17*** *p218*
Moutardrin, Mr. 36; Port uncertain, 1840 ***778.6*** *p250*
Mouth, John; America, 1732 ***1220.12*** *p570*
Mouton, Miss 6 months; Texas, 1848 ***778.6*** *p250*
Mouton, Miss 25; Texas, 1848 ***778.6*** *p250*
Mouton, Jean 30; Texas, 1848 ***778.6*** *p250*
Moutrachy, Marguerite; Quebec, 1671 ***4514.3*** *p351*
Movant, A. 39; New Orleans, 1848 ***778.6*** *p250*
Mow, Rachel; America, 1727 ***1220.12*** *p571*
Mowbray, Thomas 72; Ontario, 1871 ***1823.17*** *p122*
Mowbray, William 42; Ontario, 1871 ***1823.17*** *p122*
Mowburn, George; America, 1770 ***1220.12*** *p571*
Mowls, Ann; America, 1761 ***1220.12*** *p557*
Mowser, Jo. 22; Virginia, 1635 ***1183.3*** *p30*
Mowton, Joseph 40; Ontario, 1871 ***1823.17*** *p122*
Moxley, Willis 43; Ontario, 1871 ***1823.21*** *p271*
Moy, Arthur; Louisiana, 1874-1875 ***4981.45*** *p29*
Moy, Pierre; Quebec, 1644 ***9221.17*** *p144*
Moy, Richard; America, 1770 ***1220.12*** *p571*
Moyan, O. S. 28; Ontario, 1871 ***1823.21*** *p271*
Moyen DesGranges, Elisabeth Lebret *SEE* Moyen DesGranges, Jean
Moyen DesGranges, Elisabeth 13 *SEE* Moyen DesGranges, Jean
Moyen DesGranges, Jean; Quebec, 1654 ***9221.17*** *p314*
*Wife:*Elisabeth Lebret
*Daughter:*Elisabeth
*Son:*Jean-Baptiste
*Daughter:*Marie
Moyen DesGranges, Jean-Baptiste 10 *SEE* Moyen DesGranges, Jean
Moyen DesGranges, Marie 7 *SEE* Moyen DesGranges, Jean
Moyer, Isaac; North Carolina, 1860 ***1088.45*** *p24*
Moyer, John Philip; Ohio, 1809-1852 ***4511.35*** *p37*
Moyes, David; Illinois, 1860 ***6079.1*** *p10*
Moyes, James 45; Ontario, 1871 ***1823.21*** *p271*
Moyes, John; America, 1755 ***1220.12*** *p571*
Moylan, Dennis; Illinois, 1860 ***6079.1*** *p10*
Moylan, Gregory *SEE* Moylan, Isaac
Moylan, Isaac; Philadelphia, 1867 ***8513.31*** *p417*
*Wife:*Margaret Gregory
*Child:*Mary
*Child:*Gregory
Moylan, Margaret Gregory *SEE* Moylan, Isaac
Moylan, Mary *SEE* Moylan, Isaac
Moylan, Michael 52; Ontario, 1871 ***1823.21*** *p271*
Moylau, George 29; Ontario, 1871 ***1823.21*** *p271*
Moyle, Richard 46; Ontario, 1871 ***1823.21*** *p271*
Moyle, Richard, Sr.; America, 1775 ***1220.12*** *p571*
Moyle, Thomas 53; Ontario, 1871 ***1823.21*** *p271*
Moylen, . . .; Ontario, 1871 ***1823.21*** *p271*
Moyles, Joseph 37; Ontario, 1871 ***1823.21*** *p271*
Moylin, Dennis; Philadelphia, 1778 ***8529.30*** *p7A*
Moyniau, Gilbert; Quebec, 1661 ***9221.17*** *p463*
Moynnke, Adolph; North Carolina, 1856 ***1088.45*** *p24*
Moyser, William; America, 1741 ***1220.12*** *p571*
Moyses, Samuel 34; New York, NY, 1825 ***6178.50*** *p149*
Mozzenae, Phillippe; Louisiana, 1874 ***4981.45*** *p133*
Mpherson, Duncan 67; Ontario, 1871 ***1823.17*** *p122*
Mracek, Frantisek; Pennsylvania, 1854 ***2853.20*** *p119*
Mracek, Frantisek; St. Louis, 1857-1861 ***2853.20*** *p48*
Mraz, Jan; Iowa, 1855-1910 ***2853.20*** *p237*
Mross, V.; Galveston, TX, 1855 ***571.7*** *p18*
Mrowiec, Stephen; Detroit, 1929-1930 ***6214.5*** *p61*
Mroz, Rosalia; Wisconsin, 1900 ***6795.8*** *p36*
M'Severn, Mr.; Quebec, 1786 ***1416.15*** *p5*
Mubeara, Louis 23; Mississippi, 1847 ***778.6*** *p250*
Mucek, Jan; Chicago, 1889 ***2853.20*** *p507*
Much, Hermann Johann Adam; Wisconsin, 1887 ***6795.8*** *p221*
Mucha, John; Detroit, 1929-1930 ***6214.5*** *p70*
Muckaway, Thomas; America, 1771 ***1220.12*** *p571*
Muckle, William; South Carolina, 1800-1899 ***6155.4*** *p19*
Mucklehone, James; America, 1753 ***1220.12*** *p571*
Muckleroy, Bartholomew; America, 1765 ***1220.12*** *p571*
Muckleston, Elizabeth; America, 1743 ***1220.12*** *p571*
Muckley, Adam; Ohio, 1809-1852 ***4511.35*** *p37*
Muckley, Henry; Ohio, 1809-1852 ***4511.35*** *p37*
Muckley, Humphrey; America, 1687 ***1220.12*** *p571*
Muckley, John; Ohio, 1809-1852 ***4511.35*** *p37*
Muckly, Henry; Ohio, 1809-1852 ***4511.35*** *p37*
Muczynski, Marya Pajor Nosewicz; Detroit, 1929 ***1640.55*** *p117*
Mudd, Bartholomew; Barbados or Jamaica, 1707 ***1220.12*** *p571*
Mudeford, Daniel; America, 1723 ***1220.12*** *p571*
Mudford, Robert; America, 1685 ***1220.12*** *p571*
Mudgett, Elizabeth; America, 1740 ***1220.12*** *p571*
Mudie, Thomas 60; Ontario, 1871 ***1823.17*** *p122*
Mudroch, Jan; St. Louis, 1864 ***2853.20*** *p38*
Mudry, Katherine; Detroit, 1929 ***1640.55*** *p115*
Muelich, Barbara; New York, 1859 ***358.56*** *p99*
Mueller, . . .; West Virginia, n.d. ***1132.30*** *p151*
Mueller, Albert; Wisconsin, 1899 ***6795.8*** *p34*
Mueller, Alma Emma Clara; Wisconsin, 1892 ***6795.8*** *p67*
Mueller, Arpa *SEE* Mueller, Fried. A.
Mueller, Augusta Bertha; Wisconsin, 1894 ***6795.8*** *p117*
Mueller, Caroline 46; New Orleans, 1834 ***1002.51*** *p111*
Mueller, Charles; Wisconsin, 1886 ***6795.8*** *p107*
Mueller, Christian; Philadelphia, 1852 ***8513.31*** *p417*
*Wife:*Christina Bader
Mueller, Christina Bader *SEE* Mueller, Christian
Mueller, Daniel 17; New Orleans, 1834 ***1002.51*** *p111*
Mueller, Daniel 44; New Orleans, 1834 ***1002.51*** *p111*
Mueller, Edward; Colorado, 1881 ***1029.59*** *p64*
Mueller, Edward; Wisconsin, 1884 ***6795.8*** *p204*
Mueller, Elisabeth 21; New Orleans, 1834 ***1002.51*** *p111*
Mueller, Emil Friderich; Wisconsin, 1897 ***6795.8*** *p118*
Mueller, Fredric; Wisconsin, 1899 ***6795.8*** *p26*
Mueller, Fried. A.; Dakota, 1898-1918 ***554.30*** *p26*
*Wife:*Wilhelmina Schrade
*Child:*Rosa
*Child:*Arpa
*Child:*Frieda
Mueller, Frieda *SEE* Mueller, Fried. A.
Mueller, Friedrick; Wisconsin, 1898 ***6795.8*** *p152*
Mueller, Gerhard; Missouri, 1903 ***3276.1*** *p4*
Mueller, Gustavus; Illinois, 1858-1861 ***6020.5*** *p132*
Mueller, Jacob 14; New Orleans, 1834 ***1002.51*** *p111*
Mueller, Johann Daniel 25; Pennsylvania, 1850 ***170.15*** *p37*
With wife & child
Mueller, Johann Henrich; America, 1838 ***170.15*** *p37*
Mueller, Johannes; America, 1800-1899 ***170.15*** *p37*
Mueller, Julius; Canada, 1808-1908 ***1822.55*** *p10*
Mueller, Julius; Wisconsin, 1908 ***1822.55*** *p10*
Mueller, Margaretha 19; New Orleans, 1834 ***1002.51*** *p111*
Mueller, Martin; Wisconsin, 1868 ***6795.8*** *p140*
Mueller, Rosa *SEE* Mueller, Fried. A.
Mueller, Samuel August; Wisconsin, 1869 ***6795.8*** *p43*
Mueller, Theobald 28; New Orleans, 1834 ***1002.51*** *p111*
Mueller, Ulrich; West Virginia, 1869 ***1132.30*** *p151*
Mueller, Wiiliam; Wisconsin, 1899 ***6795.8*** *p148*
Mueller, Wilhelmina Schrade *SEE* Mueller, Fried. A.
Muendlein, John; Ohio, 1809-1852 ***4511.35*** *p37*
Muendlin, George; Ohio, 1809-1852 ***4511.35*** *p37*
Muendlin, John; Ohio, 1809-1852 ***4511.35*** *p37*
Muffee, William; New England, 1745 ***1642*** *p28*
Mugan, Annie 10; Ontario, 1871 ***1823.17*** *p122*
Mugan, Anthony 56; Ontario, 1871 ***1823.17*** *p122*
Mugan, Austin 34; Ontario, 1871 ***1823.17*** *p122*
Mugan, Catherine 12; Ontario, 1871 ***1823.17*** *p122*
Mugan, James 39; Ontario, 1871 ***1823.17*** *p122*
Mugan, Michael 42; Ontario, 1871 ***1823.17*** *p*
Mugan, Thomas 47; Ontario, 1871 ***1823.17*** *p122*
Mugde, Adolphe 23; Mississippi, 1847 ***778.6*** *p250*
Mugel, Frederic 20; Louisiana, 1848 ***778.6*** *p250*
Mugel, Friedrich Wilhelm; America, 1848 ***5475.1*** *p28*
Mugel, Josephine 40; New Orleans, 1848 ***778.6*** *p250*
Mugele, Adolphe 23; Mississippi, 1847 ***778.6*** *p250*
Muget, Louis 25; Port uncertain, 1842 ***778.6*** *p250*
Mugford, Francis; America, 1755 ***1220.12*** *p571*
Muggeride, Joseph; Virginia, 1732 ***1220.12*** *p557*
Mugler, Heinrich Otto; America, 1893 ***179.55*** *p19*
Mugnier, Hippolitte Franc. 3; New Orleans, 1848 ***778.6*** *p250*
Mugnier, Jacques 27; New Orleans, 1848 ***778.6*** *p250*
Mugnier, Joseph 47; Louisiana, 1848 ***778.6*** *p250*
Mugnier, Jules 40; Louisiana, 1848 ***778.6*** *p251*
Mugnier, Marie 10; Louisiana, 1848 ***778.6*** *p251*
Mugnier, Victorine Ant. 31; New Orleans, 1848 ***778.6*** *p251*
Muhlbeyer, Catharine 8; New York, NY, 1874 ***6954.7*** *p37*
Muhlbeyer, Christina 10; New York, NY, 1874 ***6954.7*** *p37*
Muhlbeyer, Christina 38; New York, NY, 1874 ***6954.7*** *p37*
Muhlbeyer, Conrad 1 months; New York, NY, 1874 ***6954.7*** *p37*
Muhlbeyer, Conrad 38; New York, NY, 1874 ***6954.7*** *p37*
Muhlbeyer, Elizabeth 6; New York, NY, 1874 ***6954.7*** *p37*
Muhlbeyer, Friedrich 3; New York, NY, 1874 ***6954.7*** *p37*
Muhlbeyer, Jacob 9; New York, NY, 1874 ***6954.7*** *p37*
Muhlbeyer, Sophie 9 months; New York, NY, 1874 ***6954.7*** *p37*
Muhlenbacher, Charlotte Sophie Kiefer *SEE* Muhlenbacher, Philipp
Muhlenbacher, Jakob 15 *SEE* Muhlenbacher, Ludwig
Muhlenbacher, Johann 12 *SEE* Muhlenbacher, Ludwig
Muhlenbacher, Karoline 10 *SEE* Muhlenbacher, Ludwig
Muhlenbacher, Katharina 5 *SEE* Muhlenbacher, Ludwig
Muhlenbacher, Ludwig; America, 1836 ***5475.1*** *p513*
With wife
*Son:*Jakob
*Daughter:*Karoline
*Son:*Ludwig
*Daughter:*Katharina
*Son:*Johann
*Daughter:*Luise
Muhlenbacher, Ludwig 8 *SEE* Muhlenbacher, Ludwig
Muhlenbacher, Luise 16 *SEE* Muhlenbacher, Ludwig
Muhlenbacher, Philipp; America, 1881 ***5475.1*** *p14*
*Wife:*Charlotte Sophie Kiefer
Muhlenberg, . . .; America, 1832 ***7420.1*** *p6*
Muhlenen, Salome von; North Carolina, 1710 ***3629.40*** *p6*
Muhlfelder, Joseph; America, 1868 ***7919.3*** *p525*
Muhlhauser, Heinrich 20; America, 1831 ***2526.42*** *p201*
Muhlich, Marie Katharine; America, 1832 ***8115.12*** *p325*
Muhlke, Engel Marie Dorothe; America, 1857 ***7420.1*** *p168*
Muhlke, Friedrich; America, 1841 ***7420.1*** *p22*
With wife & 7 children
Muhlke, Heinrich Gottfried; Port uncertain, 1835 ***7420.1*** *p9*
Muhlmann, Minne; New York, 1859 ***358.56*** *p101*
Muhlmeister, Carl Wilhelm Christian; California, 1872 ***7420.1*** *p296*
Muhlmeister, Wilhelm Albert; England, 1867 ***7420.1*** *p261*
Muhm, Otto; Valdivia, Chile, 1852 ***1192.4*** *p56*
Muhm, Theod.; Valdivia, Chile, 1852 ***1192.4*** *p56*
Muhn, Georg Peter; America, 1867 ***2526.43*** *p120*
Muhn, Johannes; America, 1884 ***2526.43*** *p120*
Muhn, Ludwig; America, 1846 ***2526.43*** *p193*
With wife & 2 children
Muhn, Ludwig 25; America, 1846 ***2526.43*** *p204*
With wife & 2 children
Muhr, Henry; Ohio, 1809-1852 ***4511.35*** *p37*
Muhsler, Elisabeth 37; America, 1860 ***5475.1*** *p251*
Muir, Elizabeth 5; New York, NY, 1835 ***5024.1*** *p137*
Muir, Elsie 32; Ontario, 1871 ***1823.21*** *p271*
Muir, Janet 1; New York, NY, 1835 ***5024.1*** *p137*
Muir, Janet 38; New York, NY, 1835 ***5024.1*** *p137*
Muir, John 3; New York, NY, 1835 ***5024.1*** *p137*
Muir, John 40; Ontario, 1871 ***1823.21*** *p272*
Muir, Mary 7; New York, NY, 1835 ***5024.1*** *p137*
Muir, Pet.; New York, 1860 ***358.56*** *p148*
Muir, Robert; New York, 1835 ***471.10*** *p61*
Muir, Robert 35; New York, NY, 1835 ***5024.1*** *p137*

Muir, Wm. S.; Utah, 1896 ***3687.1*** *p35*
Muirhead, Margaret 40; Ontario, 1871 ***1823.17*** *p122*
Muirson, Alexander; North Carolina, 1835 ***1088.45*** *p24*
Mulanny, Josh 2; St. Johns, N.F., 1811 ***1053.20*** *p20*
Mulbens, Joseph; America, 1763 ***1220.12*** *p571*
Mulberger, Louis 36; America, 1747 ***778.6*** *p251*
Mulberger, Louisa 23; America, 1747 ***778.6*** *p251*
Mulberger, Louise 2; America, 1747 ***778.6*** *p251*
Mulberger, Margarette 4; America, 1747 ***778.6*** *p251*
Mulberger, Marie Louise 6 months; America, 1747 ***778.6*** *p251*
Mulbury, James; America, 1743 ***1220.12*** *p571*
Mulcahy, Daniel; Illinois, 1858-1861 ***6020.5*** *p132*
Mulcahy, John; Boston, 1831 ***3274.55*** *p67*
Mulcahy, Timothy; Boston, 1767 ***1642*** *p38*
Mulch, Conrad; Illinois, 1855 ***6079.1*** *p10*
Mulch, Conrad B.; Illinois, 1855 ***6079.1*** *p10*
Mulch, Gilbert; Illinois, 1858 ***6079.1*** *p10*
Mulch, Henry; Illinois, 1856 ***6079.1*** *p10*
Mulch, John; Illinois, 1857 ***6079.1*** *p10*
Mulch, John Conrad; Illinois, 1861 ***6079.1*** *p10*
Muld, Henrick; Louisiana, 1874 ***4981.45*** *p296*
Muldoney, James W.; Louisiana, 1874 ***4981.45*** *p133*
Muldoney, Laurence; Louisiana, 1874 ***4981.45*** *p133*
Muldoon, James; Pennsylvania, 1856 ***8513.31*** *p417*
*Wife:*Mary McCalvey
Muldoon, Mary McCalvey *SEE* Muldoon, James
Muldoone, Timothy; New York, NY, 1833 ***3274.55*** *p69*
Muler, Gadlibe 35; America, 1847 ***778.6*** *p251*
Mulford, David; America, 1775 ***1220.12*** *p571*
Mulgrove, James 32; Ontario, 1871 ***1823.21*** *p272*
Mulhall, Eleanor; Halifax, N.S., 1827 ***7009.9*** *p61*
Mulhall, Joseph; New Orleans, 1850 ***7242.30*** *p149*
Mulhall, Judy; New Orleans, 1850 ***7242.30*** *p149*
Mulhall, L.; New Orleans, 1850 ***7242.30*** *p149*
Mulhall, Mary; New Orleans, 1850 ***7242.30*** *p149*
Mulhall, Miles; New Orleans, 1850 ***7242.30*** *p149*
Mulhall, P.; New Orleans, 1850 ***7242.30*** *p149*
Mulhall, Thomas; Boston, 1775 ***8529.30*** *p4A*
Mulhall, William; New Orleans, 1850 ***7242.30*** *p149*
Mulheisen, Wm.; Ohio, 1840-1897 ***8365.35*** *p17*
Mulheney, Patrick; Ohio, 1809-1852 ***4511.35*** *p37*
Mulholland, Hugh 52; Ontario, 1871 ***1823.21*** *p272*
Muligan, Thomas 68; Ontario, 1871 ***1823.21*** *p272*
Mulkern, James; Washington, 1884 ***2770.40*** *p193*
Mulkern, Michael 36; Ontario, 1871 ***1823.21*** *p272*
Mull, James; America, 1767 ***1220.12*** *p571*
Mullagen, Widow; New Orleans, 1851 ***7242.30*** *p149*
Mullagen, Anne; New Orleans, 1851 ***7242.30*** *p149*
Mullagen, Edward; New Orleans, 1851 ***7242.30*** *p149*
Mullagen, John; New Orleans, 1851 ***7242.30*** *p149*
Mulland, James 28; Ontario, 1871 ***1823.21*** *p272*
Mullanny, Mrs.; Toronto, 1844 ***2910.35*** *p112*
Mullanny, Patrick; Toronto, 1844 ***2910.35*** *p112*
Mullany, Mary 47; Ontario, 1871 ***1823.21*** *p272*
Mullard, Jonah 50; Ontario, 1871 ***1823.21*** *p272*
Mullberg, Alarik; Cleveland, OH, 1902-1904 ***9722.10*** *p124*
Mulle, Marguerite 19; New York, NY, 1856 ***1766.1*** *p45*
Mullen, Alexander 47; Ontario, 1871 ***1823.21*** *p272*
Mullen, Brian; Boston, 1774 ***8529.30*** *p3*
Mullen, Darby 18; St. John, N.B., 1834 ***6469.7*** *p5*
Mullen, James 32; New York, NY, 1825 ***6178.50*** *p77*
Mullen, James 52; South Carolina, 1812 ***3476.30*** *p12*
Mullen, John; New Orleans, 1851 ***7242.30*** *p149*
Mullen, John; St. John, N.B., 1847 ***2978.15*** *p37*
Mullen, M.; Louisiana, 1874 ***4981.45*** *p296*
Mullen, Martin; New Orleans, 1850 ***7242.30*** *p149*
Mullen, Mary; New Orleans, 1851 ***7242.30*** *p149*
Mullen, Neal; North America, 1750 ***1640.8*** *p233*
Mullen, Thomas; Ohio, 1840-1897 ***8365.35*** *p17*
Mullen, Wm.; St. John, N.B., 1848 ***2978.15*** *p39*
Mullener, John; America, 1743 ***1220.12*** *p571*
Mullens, Daniel; America, 1771 ***1220.12*** *p571*
Mullens, Henry; Virginia, 1761 ***1220.12*** *p571*
Mullens, John; America, 1736 ***1220.12*** *p571*
Mullens, John; Virginia, 1761 ***1220.12*** *p571*
Mullens, Mary; America, 1763 ***1220.12*** *p571*
Mullens, Robert; America, 1685 ***1220.12*** *p571*
Mullens, Thomas; America, 1756 ***1220.12*** *p571*
Mullens, William; Plymouth, MA, 1606 ***1642*** *p55*
Muller, . . .; North Carolina, 1710 ***3629.40*** *p6*
Muller, Mr.; America, 1852 ***7420.1*** *p94*
With wife 4 sons & daughter
Muller, A. Maria; America, 1881 ***5475.1*** *p357*
Muller, A. Valeska *SEE* Muller, Georg
Muller, Adam; America, 1856 ***2526.43*** *p153*
Muller, Adam *SEE* Muller, Johann Adam
Muller, Adam; America, 1883 ***2526.43*** *p153*
Muller, Adam 21; New Orleans, 1848 ***778.6*** *p251*
Muller, Adolf *SEE* Muller, Johann
Muller, Albert; America, 1890 ***179.55*** *p19*
Muller, Amedee 6; New Orleans, 1848 ***778.6*** *p251*
Muller, And. 34; America, 1840 ***778.6*** *p251*
Muller, And..s 7; America, 1840 ***778.6*** *p251*
Muller, Anna; America, 1873 ***5475.1*** *p22*
Muller, Anna 4 *SEE* Muller, Nikolaus
Muller, Anna 40; America, 1840 ***778.6*** *p251*
Muller, Anna *SEE* Muller, Heinrich
Muller, Anna 1 *SEE* Muller, Jakob
Muller, Anna Margaretha Hofmann *SEE* Muller, Balthasar
Muller, Anna Maria Weber *SEE* Muller, Mathias
Muller, Anna Maria; Venezuela, 1843 ***3899.5*** *p544*
Muller, Anne 2; America, 1846 ***778.6*** *p251*
Muller, Anne Louise Henriette; America, 1854 ***7420.1*** *p125*
Muller, Appolonia 9 *SEE* Muller, Georg
Muller, Aug. 27; America, 1840 ***778.6*** *p251*
Muller, August; America, 1868 ***7919.3*** *p527*
Muller, August 50; New York, NY, 1886 ***8425.16*** *p32*
Muller, Auguste; America, 1867 ***7919.3*** *p530*
Muller, Auguste 4; New Orleans, 1848 ***778.6*** *p251*
Muller, Auguste Bertha; America, 1868 ***7919.3*** *p530*
Muller, Balthasar; America, 1785 ***2526.42*** *p155*
*Wife:*Anna Margaretha Hofmann
Muller, Balthasar; America, 1855 ***2526.42*** *p109*
Muller, Balthasar 39; America, 1855 ***2526.42*** *p109*
*Wife:*Magdalena Reichart 37
*Child:*Katharina Elisabetha 4
*Child:*Maria Elisabetha 9
Muller, Barbara; America, 1867 ***5475.1*** *p78*
Muller, Bernhard; America, 1849 ***5475.1*** *p477*
Muller, Bertha; Wisconsin, 1882 ***6795.8*** *p63*
Muller, C.; America, 1867 ***179.55*** *p19*
Muller, Miss C. 46; New Orleans, 1834 ***1002.51*** *p111*
Muller, Camille 8; America, 1846 ***778.6*** *p251*
Muller, Carl 16; America, 1867 ***7919.3*** *p529*
Muller, Carl Friedrich Wilhelm August; Port uncertain, 1855 ***7420.1*** *p140*
Muller, Carolina 19; Portland, ME, 1910 ***970.38*** *p79*
Muller, Caroline Melosine; Albany, NY, 1858 ***7420.1*** *p180*
With husband
Muller, Catharina; America, 1879 ***179.55*** *p19*
Muller, Catharina 14; New Orleans, 1848 ***778.6*** *p251*
Muller, Catherine 6; America, 1846 ***778.6*** *p251*
Muller, Catherine 4; Missouri, 1847 ***778.6*** *p251*
Muller, Catherine 44; Missouri, 1847 ***778.6*** *p251*
Muller, Charles H. F.; Colorado, 1896 ***1029.59*** *p64*
Muller, Charlotte; Chicago, 1891 ***7420.1*** *p363*
Muller, Christian; America, 1847 ***5475.1*** *p21*
*Wife:*Elisabeth Horr
Muller, Christian; America, 1867 ***7919.3*** *p528*
Muller, Christian *SEE* Muller, Friedrich
Muller, Christian 40; America, 1846 ***778.6*** *p251*
Muller, Christian 4; New York, NY, 1898 ***7951.13*** *p42*
Muller, Christian 29; New York, NY, 1898 ***7951.13*** *p42*
Muller, Christian Friedrich; America, 1867 ***7919.3*** *p533*
Muller, Christian Ludwig; Port uncertain, 1837 ***7420.1*** *p13*
Muller, Christiane; America, 1868 ***7919.3*** *p533*
Muller, Christiane Caroline; America, 1867 ***7919.3*** *p530*
Muller, Christina; Arkansas, 1880 ***5475.1*** *p358*
Muller, Christoph 1; America, 1846 ***778.6*** *p251*
Muller, Clement 19; America, 1841 ***778.6*** *p251*
Muller, Conrad; America, 1868 ***7919.3*** *p531*
Muller, D. 17; New Orleans, 1834 ***1002.51*** *p111*
Muller, D. 44; New Orleans, 1834 ***1002.51*** *p111*
Muller, Dominick 25; New York, NY, 1893 ***1883.7*** *p38*
Muller, Dorothea; America, 1866 ***7420.1*** *p246*
Muller, Dorothea Schlossmann *SEE* Muller, Michael, IV
Muller, Dorthe *SEE* Muller, Michael, IV
Muller, Miss E. 21; New Orleans, 1834 ***1002.51*** *p111*
Muller, Eduard; America, 1882 ***8115.12*** *p325*
Muller, Edward; New Orleans, 1851 ***7242.30*** *p149*
Muller, Elisabeth Horr *SEE* Muller, Christian
Muller, Elisabeth; America, 1857 ***5475.1*** *p518*
Muller, Elisabeth; America, 1865 ***5475.1*** *p498*
Muller, Elisabeth; America, 1866 ***2526.43*** *p151*
Muller, Elisabeth; America, 1867 ***7919.3*** *p530*
Muller, Elisabeth; America, n.d. ***8115.12*** *p325*
Muller, Elisabeth Dreystadt 22 *SEE* Muller, Peter
Muller, Elisabeth 28; America, 1857 ***5475.1*** *p494*
Muller, Elisabeth *SEE* Muller, Heinrich
Muller, Elisabeth; Brazil, 1862 ***5475.1*** *p561*
Muller, Elisabeth; Brazil, 1891 ***5475.1*** *p432*
Muller, Elisabeth 33; Brazil, 1862 ***5475.1*** *p519*
Muller, Elisabeth Brandenburger 35 *SEE* Muller, Heinrich
Muller, Elisabeth 45; Brazil, 1862 ***5475.1*** *p515*
Muller, Elisabeth *SEE* Muller, Georg
Muller, Elisabeth *SEE* Muller, Philipp
Muller, Elisabeth Bauer *SEE* Muller, Philipp
Muller, Elisabeth Forster *SEE* Muller, Johann
Muller, Elise; America, 1891 ***2526.43*** *p153*
Muller, Elizabeth 22; New Orleans, 1848 ***778.6*** *p251*
Muller, Emilie Emma Mathilde Elisabeth; America, 1867 ***7919.3*** *p526*
Muller, Engebert 34; New York, NY, 1893 ***1883.7*** *p38*
Muller, Eva; America, 1854 ***2526.43*** *p226*
With daughter
Muller, Eva Katharina 59; America, 1883 ***2526.43*** *p158*
Muller, Eva Margaretha 24 *SEE* Muller, Johannes
Muller, Ezra 11; Halifax, N.S., 1902 ***1860.4*** *p43*
Muller, F. F.; Louisiana, 1841-1844 ***4981.45*** *p211*
Muller, Ferdinand; America, 1868 ***7919.3*** *p529*
Muller, Fidel; Texas, 1851 ***3435.45*** *p36*
Muller, Florentein 38; New Castle, DE, 1817-1818 ***90.20*** *p153*
Muller, Florentine 1 months; Galveston, TX, 1844 ***3967.10*** *p375*
Muller, Frank M.; Iowa, 1877 ***1211.15*** *p16*
Muller, Franziska 28; America, 1846 ***778.6*** *p251*
Muller, Fredrick; Washington, 1887 ***2770.40*** *p24*
Muller, Friederich 26; Port uncertain, 1843 ***778.6*** *p251*
Muller, Friederich 52; Port uncertain, 1843 ***778.6*** *p251*
Muller, Friedrich *SEE* Muller, Johann
Muller, Friedrich; America, 1881 ***5475.1*** *p72*
*Wife:*Katharina Grentz
*Daughter:*Maria
*Son:*Heinr.
*Son:*Christian
*Daughter:*Katharina
Muller, Friedrich; America, 1884 ***2526.43*** *p153*
Muller, Friedrich 25; America, 1872 ***2526.43*** *p153*
Muller, Friedrich; Wisconsin, 1876 ***6795.8*** *p163*
Muller, Friedrich; Wisconsin, 1883 ***6795.8*** *p204*
Muller, Friedrich Wilhelm Ferdinand; Port uncertain, 1854 ***7420.1*** *p125*
Muller, Georg; America, 1843 ***5475.1*** *p515*
Muller, Georg; America, 1847 ***2526.42*** *p127*
With wife
*Child:*Appolonia
Muller, Georg *SEE* Muller, Johann
Muller, Georg 31; America, 1854 ***2526.43*** *p226*
Muller, Georg; Chile, 1885 ***5475.1*** *p37*
*Wife:*Valeska Birkelbach
*Daughter:*Elisabeth
*Son:*Philipp
*Daughter:*A. Valeska
*Son:*Georg Karl
Muller, Georg 37; Galveston, TX, 1844 ***3967.10*** *p371*
Muller, Georg Adam; America, 1868 ***7919.3*** *p532*
With wife & 7 children
Muller, Georg Karl *SEE* Muller, Georg
Muller, Georg. 4; America, 1840 ***778.6*** *p251*
Muller, Gertrud *SEE* Muller, Johann
Muller, Gertrude 31; America, 1846 ***778.6*** *p251*
Muller, Gottfried; America, 1894 ***179.55*** *p19*
Muller, Gottl.; Valdivia, Chile, 1852 ***1192.4*** *p54*
With wife
With child 17
With child 8
Muller, Gottlieb; Valdivia, Chile, 1851 ***1192.4*** *p51*
Muller, Gustav *SEE* Muller, Johann
Muller, Gustav Gottlob Ferdinand; Wisconsin, 1879 ***6795.8*** *p97*
Muller, Gustave 8; New Orleans, 1848 ***778.6*** *p251*
Muller, H. 27; New Orleans, 1834 ***1002.51*** *p113*
Muller, Hans Heinrich; America, 1852 ***7420.1*** *p94*
With wife & son
Muller, Hans Jacob 35; New Castle, DE, 1817-1818 ***90.20*** *p153*
Muller, Heinr. *SEE* Muller, Friedrich
Muller, Heinrich; America, 1800-1899 ***5475.1*** *p12*
Muller, Heinrich; America, 1874 ***5475.1*** *p318*
Muller, Heinrich; America, 1898 ***2526.43*** *p176*
Muller, Heinrich 24; America, 1847 ***778.6*** *p252*
Muller, Heinrich 38; Brazil, 1862 ***5475.1*** *p551*
*Wife:*Elisabeth Brandenburger 35
*Daughter:*Margarethe
*Son:*Johann
*Daughter:*Anna
*Daughter:*Elisabeth
With daughter
*Daughter:*Philippine
Muller, Heinrich 35; Galveston, TX, 1844 ***3967.10*** *p374*
Muller, Heinrich 7; New York, NY, 1898 ***7951.13*** *p42*
Muller, Heinrich August; America, 1854 ***7420.1*** *p125*
Muller, Heinrich Dietrich Wilhelm; America, 1845 ***7420.1*** *p38*
Muller, Heinrich Franz Carl Gustav; America, 1866 ***7420.1*** *p246*
Muller, Helena; America, 1865 ***5475.1*** *p49*
Muller, Helena; America, 1867 ***179.55*** *p19*
Muller, Henriette; America, 1867 ***7919.3*** *p530*
Muller, Henry; Nova Scotia, 1784 ***7105*** *p25*
Muller, Herm 33; Halifax, N.S., 1902 ***1860.4*** *p43*

Muller, Hermann; Valdivia, Chile, 1851 *1192.4 p51*
Muller, Hilda 10; Portland, ME, 1910 *970.38 p79*
Muller, Hilde; America, 1923 *8023.44 p378*
Muller, Hilde; South America, 1932 *8023.44 p377*
Muller, Ida 8; Portland, ME, 1910 *970.38 p79*
Muller, J. 14; New Orleans, 1834 *1002.51 p111*
Muller, J. 24; New Orleans, 1834 *1002.51 p111*
Muller, J. W.; Louisiana, 1836-1840 *4981.45 p213*
Muller, Jacob 40; America, 1847 *778.6 p252*
Muller, Jacob 10; New Orleans, 1848 *778.6 p252*
Muller, Jacob 21; New Orleans, 1846 *778.6 p252*
Muller, Jacob 35; New Orleans, 1848 *778.6 p252*
Muller, Jacq. 55; America, 1840 *778.6 p252*
Muller, Jacques 48; New Orleans, 1848 *778.6 p252*
Muller, Jakob; America, 1855 *2526.43 p153*
Muller, Jakob *SEE* Muller, Johann
Muller, Jakob; America, 1887 *2526.43 p153*
Muller, Jakob 10 *SEE* Muller, Jakob
Muller, Jakob 33; Chicago, 1855 *5475.1 p310*
  *Wife:*Maria Schwarz 29
  *Daughter:*Anna 1
  With mother-in-law
  *Son:*Jakob 10
  *Son:*Peter 6
Muller, Jakob 23; New York, NY, 1874 *5475.1 p26*
Muller, Jakob; Ohio, 1873 *5475.1 p167*
Muller, Jean 8; America, 1846 *778.6 p252*
Muller, Jean 37; America, 1846 *778.6 p252*
Muller, Jerome 34; America, 1846 *778.6 p252*
Muller, Joh. 2; America, 1840 *778.6 p252*
Muller, Joh. Gottlob; Valdivia, Chile, 1850 *1192.4 p49*
Muller, Joh. Josef *SEE* Muller, Johann
Muller, Johann; America, 1833 *5475.1 p436*
  *Wife:*Maria Dewes
  With 5 children
Muller, Johann; America, 1866 *5475.1 p433*
  *Wife:*Luise Ruf
  *Son:*Gustav
  *Son:*Friedrich
  *Daughter:*Magdalena
Muller, Johann; America, 1872 *5475.1 p305*
Muller, Johann *SEE* Muller, Johann
Muller, Johann; America, 1881 *5475.1 p55*
  *Wife:*Sophie Mathieu
  *Son:*Philipp
  *Son:*Jakob
  *Son:*Georg
  *Son:*Johann
  *Daughter:*Sophie
  *Son:*Adolf
Muller, Johann; America, 1881 *5475.1 p161*
  *Wife:*Maria Gartner
  *Daughter:*Gertrud
  With mother-in-law
  *Son:*Joh. Josef
Muller, Johann 1 *SEE* Muller, Nikolaus
Muller, Johann 26; America, 1867 *5475.1 p217*
Muller, Johann; Brazil, 1861 *5475.1 p276*
Muller, Johann *SEE* Muller, Johann
Muller, Johann; New Castle, DE, 1817-1818 *90.20 p153*
Muller, Johann; Pittsburgh, 1880 *5475.1 p23*
  *Wife:*Elisabeth Forster
  *Son:*Johann Nikolaus
Muller, Johann Adam; America, 1880 *2526.43 p226*
  *Wife:*Margaretha Hotz
  *Son:*Adam
  *Son:*Philipp
Muller, Johann Georg 7; America, 1831 *2526.43 p198*
Muller, Johann Georg; New Jersey, 1898 *2526.43 p176*
Muller, Johann Georg Karl; America, 1882 *2526.43 p226*
Muller, Johann Jacob; America, 1867 *7919.3 p532*
Muller, Johann Karl; New York, 1857 *2526.43 p176*
Muller, Johann Ludwig 16; America, 1853 *2526.43 p153*
Muller, Johann Max August; America, 1867 *7919.3 p529*
Muller, Johann Nikolaus *SEE* Muller, Johann
Muller, Johann Peter; America, 1867 *5475.1 p562*
Muller, Johann Peter 43; Brazil, 1862 *5475.1 p540*
  *Wife:*Katharina Krahn 39
  *Daughter:*Katharina
  *Daughter:*Margarethe
  *Son:*Peter
Muller, Johannes; America, n.d. *8115.12 p327*
Muller, Johannes 26; America, 1854 *2526.43 p219*
  *Sister:*Eva Margaretha 24
  *Sister:*Katharina 21
Muller, Johannes 49; America, 1856 *2526.43 p153*
Muller, Johannes 3; New York, NY, 1898 *7951.13 p42*
Muller, Johannes 10; New York, NY, 1893 *1883.7 p38*
Muller, Johannes; Venezuela, 1843 *3899.5 p543*
Muller, Mrs. Johannes; America, 1836 *2526.43 p187*
  With 5 children
Muller, John Martin; Illinois, 1858-1861 *6020.5 p132*
Muller, Josef Theodor; America, 1864 *5475.1 p238*

Muller, Joseph 22; America, 1847 *778.6 p252*
Muller, Julie *SEE* Muller, Michael, IV
Muller, K.H.; New York, 1860 *358.56 p3*
Muller, Karl; America, 1882 *179.55 p19*
Muller, Karl; America, 1883 *8115.12 p325*
Muller, Karl; America, 1887 *2526.43 p176*
Muller, Karl *SEE* Muller, Michael, IV
Muller, Karl Georg 18; America, 1853 *2526.43 p153*
Muller, Karl Johann 24; America, 1897 *5475.1 p19*
Muller, Karoline; America, 1883 *8115.12 p325*
Muller, Katchen *SEE* Muller, Michael, IV
Muller, Katharina *SEE* Muller, Friedrich
Muller, Katharina Grentz *SEE* Muller, Friedrich
Muller, Katharina; America, 1891 *2526.43 p153*
Muller, Katharina 21 *SEE* Muller, Johannes
Muller, Katharina 24; America, 1865 *5475.1 p544*
Muller, Katharina 30; America, 1857 *5475.1 p499*
Muller, Katharina 33; America, 1864 *5475.1 p535*
Muller, Katharina 36; America, 1856 *5475.1 p488*
Muller, Katharina 54; America, 1860 *5475.1 p269*
Muller, Katharina *SEE* Muller, Johann Peter
Muller, Katharina Krahn 39 *SEE* Muller, Johann Peter
Muller, Katharina *SEE* Muller, Philipp
Muller, Katharina Elisabetha; America, 1891 *2526.43 p222*
  *Son:*Julius Emil
  *Son:*Alphon Guillaume
  *Son:*Peter Alphon
  *Son:*Fred. Hermann
  *Son:*Adolf Eugen
Muller, Katharina Elisabetha 4 *SEE* Muller, Balthasar
Muller, Katherina 28; New York, NY, 1898 *7951.13 p42*
Muller, Konrad; America, 1881 *8115.12 p325*
Muller, Laurentius; Brazil, 1933 *8023.44 p378*
Muller, Leonhard; America, 1868 *2526.42 p110*
Muller, Lottchen *SEE* Muller, Michael, IV
Muller, Louise; America, 1867 *7919.3 p533*
Muller, Ludwig; America, 1894 *2526.43 p189*
Muller, Luise Ruf *SEE* Muller, Johann
Muller, Luise 22 *SEE* Muller, Margarethe
Muller, Miss M. 19; New Orleans, 1834 *1002.51 p111*
Muller, Mag. 27; America, 1846 *778.6 p252*
Muller, Magdalena; America, 1854 *2526.43 p198*
Muller, Magdalena; America, 1854 *2526.43 p204*
Muller, Magdalena; America, 1862 *5475.1 p523*
Muller, Magdalena *SEE* Muller, Johann
Muller, Magdalena Reichart 37 *SEE* Muller, Balthasar
Muller, Magdalena 34; New York, NY, 1893 *1883.7 p38*
Muller, Marg. 9; America, 1840 *778.6 p252*
Muller, Marg. 34; America, 1840 *778.6 p252*
Muller, Marg...te 1; America, 1840 *778.6 p252*
Muller, Margaret; New York, 1859 *358.56 p55*
Muller, Margaretha; America, 1854 *2526.43 p176*
Muller, Margaretha Hotz *SEE* Muller, Johann Adam
Muller, Margaretha 37; New Orleans, 1848 *778.6 p252*
Muller, Margaretha Elise; New York, 1870 *2526.43 p226*
Muller, Margarethe; America, 1867 *179.55 p19*
Muller, Margarethe; America, 1881 *5475.1 p214*
Muller, Margarethe 5 *SEE* Muller, Nikolaus
Muller, Margarethe Knapp 38 *SEE* Muller, Nikolaus
Muller, Margarethe 56; America, 1856 *5475.1 p488*
  *Daughter:*Luise 22
Muller, Margarethe *SEE* Muller, Johann Peter
Muller, Margarethe *SEE* Muller, Heinrich
Muller, Margarethe *SEE* Muller, Philipp
Muller, Mari.nne 29; America, 1846 *778.6 p252*
Muller, Maria Dewes *SEE* Muller, Johann
Muller, Maria; America, 1867 *179.55 p19*
Muller, Maria; America, 1868 *7919.3 p531*
Muller, Maria; America, 1872 *5475.1 p212*
Muller, Maria *SEE* Muller, Friedrich
Muller, Maria Gartner *SEE* Muller, Johann
Muller, Maria; America, 1881 *5475.1 p214*
Muller, Maria 29; America, 1843 *778.6 p252*
Muller, Maria 36; America, 1867 *5475.1 p49*
Muller, Maria Schwarz 29 *SEE* Muller, Jakob
Muller, Maria 19; New York, NY, 1885 *1883.7 p45*
Muller, Maria Elisabetha 9 *SEE* Muller, Balthasar
Muller, Maria Katharina 19 *SEE* Muller, Mrs. Peter
Muller, Maria Magdalena; Venezuela, 1843 *3899.5 p543*
Muller, Maria Ursula 30; Galveston, TX, 1844 *3967.10 p371*
Muller, Marie 5; America, 1846 *778.6 p252*
Muller, Marie 29; America, 1846 *778.6 p252*
Muller, Marie 1; Missouri, 1847 *778.6 p252*
Muller, Marie 2; Missouri, 1847 *778.6 p252*
Muller, Marie Francoise 34; New Orleans, 1848 *778.6 p252*
Muller, Martha Elisabeth; America, 1864 *7420.1 p225*
Muller, Martin 35; Galveston, TX, 1844 *3967.10 p375*
Muller, Martin P.; North Carolina, 1853 *1088.45 p24*
Muller, Mary; New York, 1859 *358.56 p100*
Muller, Math.; Missouri, 1884 *5475.1 p72*

Muller, Mathias *SEE* Muller, Mathias
Muller, Mathias; America, 1872 *5475.1 p304*
  *Wife:*Anna Maria Weber
  With sister-in-law & brother-in-law
  *Son:*Mathias
  With father-in-law 61
Muller, Mathias 8 *SEE* Muller, Nikolaus
Muller, Matthaus; America, 1860 *2526.42 p170*
Muller, Melchior 4; New York, NY, 1893 *1883.7 p38*
Muller, Michael 16; America, 1853 *2526.43 p226*
Muller, Michael 34; America, 1848 *2526.42 p163*
  With wife
  With child 2
Muller, Michael, IV; America, 1896 *2526.43 p153*
  *Wife:*Dorothea Schlossmann
  *Daughter:*Dorthe
  *Son:*Karl
  *Daughter:*Katchen
  *Daughter:*Lottchen
  *Daughter:*Julie
Muller, Michael Friedrich; America, 1885 *179.55 p19*
Muller, Michel; America, 1872 *5475.1 p212*
Muller, Michel 7 *SEE* Muller, Peter
Muller, Nikolaus; America, 1867 *5475.1 p178*
Muller, Nikolaus; America, 1872 *5475.1 p292*
Muller, Nikolaus; America, 1890 *5475.1 p168*
Muller, Nikolaus 2 *SEE* Muller, Nikolaus
Muller, Nikolaus 35; America, 1873 *5475.1 p509*
  *Wife:*Margarethe Knapp 38
  *Son:*Johann 1
  *Son:*Nikolaus 2
  *Son:*Mathias 8
  *Daughter:*Anna 4
  *Daughter:*Margarethe 5
Muller, Nikolaus; Minnesota, 1885 *5475.1 p206*
Muller, Otto; America, 1891 *7420.1 p363*
Muller, Otto; Chile, 1897 *7420.1 p374*
Muller, Pauline; America, 1883 *8115.12 p325*
Muller, Pauline; America, 1883 *8115.12 p325*
Muller, Pet.; New York, 1859 *358.56 p99*
Muller, Peter; America, 1837 *5475.1 p536*
Muller, Peter; America, 1847 *5475.1 p486*
Muller, Peter; America, 1865-1870 *5475.1 p386*
Muller, Peter; America, 1869 *5475.1 p211*
Muller, Peter 29; America, 1843 *778.6 p252*
Muller, Peter 30; America, 1856 *5475.1 p492*
Muller, Peter 36; America, 1866 *5475.1 p150*
  *Wife:*Elisabeth Dreystadt 22
  *Son:*Michel 7 months
Muller, Peter 38; America, 1877 *2526.43 p153*
Muller, Peter *SEE* Muller, Johann Peter
Muller, Peter 6 *SEE* Muller, Jakob
Muller, Peter; New York, NY, 1854 *1494.21 p31*
Muller, Mrs. Peter; America, 1832 *2526.42 p176*
  With child 16
  With child 8
  With child 6
  With child 10
Muller, Mrs. Peter 41; America, 1854 *2526.43 p226*
  *Daughter:*Maria Katharina 19
Muller, Philip 37; America, 1840 *778.6 p252*
Muller, Philipp *SEE* Muller, Johann Adam
Muller, Philipp; America, 1881 *2526.43 p153*
Muller, Philipp *SEE* Muller, Johann
Muller, Philipp; America, 1883 *8115.12 p325*
Muller, Philipp; America, 1891 *2526.43 p153*
Muller, Philipp *SEE* Muller, Georg
Muller, Philipp *SEE* Muller, Philipp
Muller, Philipp; Pittsburgh, 1863 *5475.1 p541*
  *Wife:*Elisabeth Bauer
  *Daughter:*Margarethe
  *Daughter:*Katharina
  *Daughter:*Elisabeth
  *Son:*Philipp
Muller, Philipp, I 62; America, 1836 *2526.43 p219*
  With wife & daughter
Muller, Philipp, II 24; America, 1836 *2526.43 p219*
  With wife 20
  With child 6 months
Muller, Philipp Jakob; America, 1855 *2526.43 p154*
Muller, Philippine *SEE* Muller, Heinrich
Muller, Pierre 14; New Orleans, 1748 *778.6 p252*
Muller, Regina 2; Galveston, TX, 1844 *3967.10 p371*
Muller, Regina; New York, 1860 *358.56 p3*
Muller, Regina Friederike; America, 1867 *7919.3 p530*
Muller, Rosa 21; America, 1846 *778.6 p252*
Muller, Rose Dominika 2; Galveston, TX, 1844 *3967.10 p375*
Muller, Salome 3; America, 1840 *778.6 p252*
Muller, Salome 32; America, 1840 *778.6 p252*
Muller, Sebastian; Ohio, 1840-1897 *8365.35 p17*
Muller, Sophia 8; New York, NY, 1898 *7951.13 p42*
Muller, Sophie; America, 1859 *5475.1 p522*

Muller, Sophie *SEE* Muller, Johann
Muller, Sophie Mathieu *SEE* Muller, Johann
Muller, Sophie; America, 1881 ***5475.1*** *p120*
Muller, Stephan; Chicago, 1881 ***5475.1*** *p129*
Muller, Susanna 37; America, 1873 ***5475.1*** *p179*
Muller, T. 28; New Orleans, 1834 ***1002.51*** *p111*
Muller, Theodor 31; Galveston, TX, 1844 ***3967.10*** *p370*
Muller, Ursula 3 months; Galveston, TX, 1844 ***3967.10*** *p371*
Muller, Valentin 21; America, 1855 ***2526.43*** *p226*
Muller, Valentin; New York, 1860 ***358.56*** *p148*
Muller, Valeska Birkelbach *SEE* Muller, Georg
Muller, Wendel; America, 1847 ***5475.1*** *p486*
Muller, Wendel; America, 1867 ***7919.3*** *p534*
Muller, Wilhelm; America, 1867 ***7919.3*** *p526*
Muller, Wilhelm 7; Galveston, TX, 1844 ***3967.10*** *p375*
Muller, Wilhelm Jakob; America, 1895 ***2526.43*** *p206*
Muller, Wilhelmine; America, 1854 ***5475.1*** *p459*
Muller, William 46; Ontario, 1871 ***1823.17*** *p122*
Mullet, Abraham; Marblehead, MA, 1722-1723 ***9228.50*** *p472*
Mullet, Abraham, Jr.; Marblehead, MA, 1762 ***9228.50*** *p472*
Mullet, Charles 30; Ontario, 1871 ***1823.21*** *p272*
Mullett, William; America, 1720 ***1220.12*** *p571*
Mullett, William; America, 1736 ***1220.12*** *p571*
Mulley, Abraham; Marblehead, MA, 1722-1723 ***9228.50*** *p472*
Mulley, Abraham; Marblehead, MA, 1722-1723 ***9228.50*** *p487*
Mulley, James 22; St. Johns, N.F., 1811 ***1053.20*** *p22*
Mulley, Mary; New York, 1864-1880 ***9228.50*** *p250*
Mullholand, William; Jamaica, 1778 ***8529.30*** *p13A*
Mullier, Marguerite 17; Quebec, 1646 ***9221.17*** *p165*
Mulligan, Con 70; Ontario, 1871 ***1823.21*** *p272*
Mulligan, Francis; Washington, 1889 ***2770.40*** *p80*
Mulligan, John 60; Ontario, 1871 ***1823.21*** *p272*
Mulligan, Nabby; Boston, 1773 ***1642*** *p49*
Mulligan, P.; New Orleans, 1850 ***7242.30*** *p149*
Mulligan, Patrick 40; Ontario, 1871 ***1823.21*** *p272*
Mulligan, Sophia 46; Ontario, 1871 ***1823.17*** *p122*
Mulligan, Susanna; Newburyport, MA, 1770 ***1642*** *p76*
Mulligan, Thomas 45; Ontario, 1871 ***1823.17*** *p122*
Mulligon, James; North Carolina, 1857 ***1088.45*** *p24*
Mullin, John 35; Ontario, 1871 ***1823.21*** *p272*
Mullin, John 21; St. John, N.B., 1834 ***6469.7*** *p5*
Mullin, Patrick; Toronto, 1844 ***2910.35*** *p113*
Mulliner, Thomas; America, 1773 ***1220.12*** *p571*
Mulling, Patrick; America, 1750 ***1220.12*** *p571*
Mullings, Ann; America, 1748 ***1220.12*** *p571*
Mullins, Andrew 49; Ontario, 1871 ***1823.17*** *p122*
Mullins, Charles 26; Ontario, 1871 ***1823.21*** *p272*
Mullins, Charles 56; Ontario, 1871 ***1823.21*** *p272*
Mullins, George; America, 1685 ***1220.12*** *p571*
Mullins, Henry 31; Ontario, 1871 ***1823.21*** *p272*
Mullins, James; America, 1750 ***1220.12*** *p571*
Mullins, James; America, 1755 ***1220.12*** *p571*
Mullins, John; America, 1764 ***1220.12*** *p571*
Mullins, John 75; Beverly, MA, 1755 ***1642*** *p64*
Mullins, Joseph; America, 1685 ***1220.12*** *p571*
Mullins, Joseph; Plymouth, MA, 1606 ***1642*** *p55*
With wife & 2 children
Mullins, Joseph *SEE* Mullins, Wm.
Mullins, Margaret; America, 1741 ***1220.12*** *p571*
Mullins, Matthew; America, 1756 ***1220.12*** *p571*
Mullins, Priscilla *SEE* Mullins, Wm.
Mullins, Richard; America, 1768 ***1220.12*** *p571*
Mullins, Wm.; Plymouth, MA, 1620 ***1920.45*** *p5*
With wife
*Child:*Priscilla
*Child:*Joseph
Mullis, John; America, 1766 ***1220.12*** *p571*
Mullois, Madeleine; Quebec, 1600-1665 ***4514.3*** *p351*
Mullois, Marie; Quebec, 1665 ***4514.3*** *p351*
Mulloney, Peter; New York, NY, 1841 ***3274.56*** *p96*
Mullons, Morgan; Boston, 1764 ***1642*** *p33*
Mulloy, Edward; Boston, 1769 ***1642*** *p49*
Mulloy, Mary; America, 1756 ***1220.12*** *p557*
Mulloys DeLaBorde, Madeleine 24; Montreal, 1662 ***9221.17*** *p499*
Mully, Abraham; Marblehead, MA, 1722-1723 ***9228.50*** *p472*
Mully, John; America, 1722 ***1220.12*** *p571*
Mulneed, Patrick 32; Ontario, 1871 ***1823.17*** *p122*
Mulraney, John 41; Ontario, 1871 ***1823.21*** *p272*
Mulreedy, William; New York, NY, 1822 ***3274.55*** *p27*
Mulreman, Martin; Long Island, 1778 ***8529.30*** *p10A*
Multman, Thomas; Philadelphia, 1777 ***8529.30*** *p7A*
Mulvena, Terence 34; Ontario, 1871 ***1823.21*** *p272*
Mulvey, Jeremiah; Marston's Wharf, 1779 ***8529.30*** *p14*
Mulvihill, Daniel; Ohio, 1840-1897 ***8365.35*** *p17*
Mulvihill, Maurice; Illinois, 1858-1861 ***6020.5*** *p132*
Mulvihill, Patrick; Ohio, 1840-1897 ***8365.35*** *p17*
Mulvy, Thomas; Louisiana, 1836-1841 ***4981.45*** *p209*
Mulzar, John; Barbados or Jamaica, 1692 ***1220.12*** *p571*
Muma, Michael 71; Ontario, 1871 ***1823.17*** *p122*
Mumford, Annie 22; Ontario, 1871 ***1823.21*** *p272*
Mumford, Charles; America, 1759 ***1220.12*** *p571*
Mumford, Edwin A. 30; Ontario, 1871 ***1823.21*** *p272*
Mumford, Margaret; Annapolis, MD, 1729 ***1220.12*** *p572*
Mumford, Robert; America, 1739 ***1220.12*** *p572*
Mumford, Stephen; Marston's Wharf, 1782 ***8529.30*** *p14*
Mumford, William; America, 1752 ***1220.12*** *p572*
Mummery, Stephen 64; Ontario, 1871 ***1823.21*** *p272*
Mumpman, Ann; America, 1748 ***1220.12*** *p572*
Mun, William; America, 1764 ***1220.12*** *p572*
Munat, Emanuel 34; New Orleans, 1844 ***778.6*** *p252*
Munce, John 33; Ontario, 1871 ***1823.21*** *p272*
Munch, Andre 19; Port uncertain, 1840 ***778.6*** *p253*
Munch, Andrew; New Jersey, 1773-1774 ***927.31*** *p3*
Munch, Bernhard 53; Galveston, TX, 1846 ***3967.10*** *p377*
Munch, Charles; Louisiana, 1874-1875 ***4981.45*** *p30*
Munch, Edmund; America, 1894 ***5475.1*** *p39*
Munch, Elise; America, 1854 ***2526.43*** *p176*
Munch, Erasmus 32; Galveston, TX, 1844 ***3967.10*** *p375*
Munch, George; North Carolina, 1860 ***1088.45*** *p24*
Munchen, Franz; America, 1883 ***5475.1*** *p355*
Munchen, Kath.; America, 1855 ***5475.1*** *p352*
*Daughter:*Susanna
With child 13
With child 16
*Son:*Peter
Munchen, Peter 5 *SEE* Munchen, Kath. Klauck
Munchen, Susanna 7 *SEE* Munchen, Kath. Klauck
Muncher, Katharina 27; Galveston, TX, 1845 ***3967.10*** *p376*
Munckton, Joseph; America, 1741 ***1220.12*** *p558*
Mund, Friedrich Christian Conrad; America, 1847 ***7420.1*** *p55*
With son & 2 daughters
Mund, Wilhelm 31; New York, NY, 1893 ***1883.7*** *p40*
Mund, Wilhelm 31; New York, NY, 1893 ***1883.7*** *p47*
Munday, David; America, 1727 ***1220.12*** *p572*
Munday, Edward; America, 1756 ***1220.12*** *p572*
Munday, Frances; America, 1748 ***1220.12*** *p572*
Munday, James; America, 1750 ***1220.12*** *p572*
Munday, Richard; America, 1756 ***1220.12*** *p572*
Munday, Richard; America, 1764 ***1220.12*** *p572*
Munday, Richard; Barbados or Jamaica, 1697 ***1220.12*** *p572*
Munday, Thomas; America, 1734 ***1220.12*** *p572*
Munden, James; America, 1765 ***1220.12*** *p572*
Munder, Heinrich; America, 1844 ***7420.1*** *p33*
With son 20
With son 8
With son 11
With son 18
Mundhenk, Dorothea Wilhelmine Louise; America, 1867 ***7420.1*** *p266*
Mundil, Josef M.; Nebraska, 1856-1910 ***2853.20*** *p183*
Mundinger, Jacob F.; Wisconsin, 1867 ***6795.8*** *p234*
Mundle, John; America, 1766 ***1220.12*** *p572*
Mundloch, Anton *SEE* Mundloch, Nikolaus
Mundloch, Bernhard *SEE* Mundloch, Nikolaus
Mundloch, Jakob *SEE* Mundloch, Nikolaus
Mundloch, Katharina *SEE* Mundloch, Nikolaus
Mundloch, M. Graf 40 *SEE* Mundloch, Nikolaus
Mundloch, Mathias *SEE* Mundloch, Nikolaus
Mundloch, Nikolaus *SEE* Mundloch, Nikolaus
Mundloch, Nikolaus 42; America, 1875 ***5475.1*** *p331*
*Wife:*M. Graf 40
*Son:*Anton
*Son:*Bernhard
*Son:*Mathias
*Son:*Nikolaus
*Daughter:*Katharina
*Son:*Jakob
Mundt, Friedrich Christian Conrad; America, 1847 ***7420.1*** *p55*
With son & 2 daughters
Mundt, Remus; Iowa, 1888 ***1211.15*** *p16*
Mundy, Thomas; America, 1751 ***1220.12*** *p572*
Muneck, Jose 25; Port uncertain, 1846 ***778.6*** *p253*
Munfie, John; Barbados, 1683 ***1220.12*** *p572*
Munford, Robert; America, 1685 ***1220.12*** *p572*
Mungay, Thomas; America, 1772 ***1220.12*** *p572*
Munger, Christian 28; Louisiana, 1848 ***778.6*** *p253*
Munger, Johann 19; Louisiana, 1848 ***778.6*** *p253*
Munger, Johann 28; Louisiana, 1848 ***778.6*** *p253*
Munger, Nicholas; Connecticut, 1659 ***9228.50*** *p472*
Munger, Thomas; America, 1767 ***1220.12*** *p572*
Mungerson, Samuel A.; Springfield, IL, 1864 ***4487.25*** *p65*
Mungham, Charles 43; Ontario, 1871 ***1823.17*** *p122*
Munholland, Hugh 57; Ontario, 1871 ***1823.17*** *p123*
Munier, Catherine 34; America, 1846 ***778.6*** *p253*
Munier, Pierre 31; America, 1846 ***778.6*** *p253*
Munier, Yerter 2; America, 1846 ***778.6*** *p253*
Munig, Henriette 32; America, 1864 ***5475.1*** *p41*
Munio, Pedro; Louisiana, 1874-1875 ***4981.45*** *p30*
Munk, Jane; America, 1770 ***1220.12*** *p558*
Munkes, Elisabeth Zeier *SEE* Munkes, Jakob
Munkes, H. Mathias *SEE* Munkes, Jakob
Munkes, Heinrich *SEE* Munkes, Jakob
Munkes, Jakob 40; America, 1882 ***5475.1*** *p494*
*Wife:*Elisabeth Zeier
*Son:*Pet. Josef
*Son:*H. Mathias
*Son:*Heinrich
Munkes, Pet. Josef *SEE* Munkes, Jakob
Munkhouse, John; Barbados, 1673 ***1220.12*** *p558*
Munn, Hugh 31; Ontario, 1871 ***1823.21*** *p272*
Munn, Joseph; Barbados or Jamaica, 1696 ***1220.12*** *p572*
Munn, William; Died enroute, 1726 ***1220.12*** *p572*
Munnery, John; Barbados or Jamaica, 1715 ***1220.12*** *p572*
Munnings, Fred; Washington, 1886 ***2770.40*** *p195*
Munns, James; America, 1773 ***1220.12*** *p572*
Munns, Joshua; America, 1766 ***1220.12*** *p572*
Munns, Thomas; America, 1731 ***1220.12*** *p572*
Munro, Alexander; Colorado, 1862-1894 ***1029.59*** *p64*
Munro, Alexander 78; Ontario, 1871 ***1823.21*** *p272*
Munro, Alexander; Pictou, N.S., 1815 ***7100*** *p20*
With family of 4
Munro, Archibald 47; Ontario, 1871 ***1823.21*** *p272*
Munro, Charles 37; Ontario, 1871 ***1823.21*** *p272*
Munro, Christina 61; Ontario, 1871 ***1823.21*** *p272*
Munro, Daniel 60; Ontario, 1871 ***1823.21*** *p272*
Munro, Donald 46; Ontario, 1871 ***1823.21*** *p272*
Munro, Ena Mae; Miami, 1935 ***4984.12*** *p39*
Munro, Hector 31; Ontario, 1871 ***1823.21*** *p272*
Munro, Hellen 60; Ontario, 1871 ***1823.21*** *p272*
Munro, Hugh; Colorado, 1865 ***1029.59*** *p64*
Munro, James; North Carolina, 1856 ***1088.45*** *p24*
Munro, James 28; Ontario, 1871 ***1823.21*** *p272*
Munro, James 65; Ontario, 1871 ***1823.17*** *p123*
Munro, James 66; Ontario, 1871 ***1823.17*** *p123*
Munro, John 73; Ontario, 1871 ***1823.21*** *p272*
Munro, Kenneth; Pictou, N.S., 1815 ***7100*** *p20*
With family of 5
Munro, Neil 40; Ontario, 1871 ***1823.17*** *p123*
Munro, Neil 66; Ontario, 1871 ***1823.21*** *p273*
Munro, Neil 74; Ontario, 1871 ***1823.21*** *p273*
Munro, Robert; North Carolina, 1839 ***1088.45*** *p24*
Munro, Robert; North Carolina, 1839 ***1088.45*** *p25*
Munro, Roderick 30; Ontario, 1871 ***1823.21*** *p273*
Munro, William 44; Ontario, 1871 ***1823.21*** *p273*
Munroe, Andrew; Virginia, 1652 ***6254.4*** *p243*
Munroe, Anne 70; Ontario, 1871 ***1823.17*** *p123*
Munroe, Catherine 75; Ontario, 1871 ***1823.17*** *p123*
Munroe, Donald 38; Ontario, 1871 ***1823.21*** *p273*
Munroe, Donald 52; Ontario, 1871 ***1823.21*** *p273*
Munroe, Duncan 43; Ontario, 1871 ***1823.17*** *p123*
Munroe, Frederick 38; Ohio, 1880 ***4879.40*** *p258*
*Wife:*Louisa E. 24
*Son:*Frederick J.W. 2
Munroe, Frederick J.W. 2 *SEE* Munroe, Frederick
Munroe, George 52; Ontario, 1871 ***1823.21*** *p273*
Munroe, John 45; Ontario, 1871 ***1823.21*** *p273*
Munroe, John 50; Ontario, 1871 ***1823.21*** *p273*
Munroe, John 63; Ontario, 1871 ***1823.17*** *p123*
Munroe, Louisa E. 24 *SEE* Munroe, Frederick
Munroe, Robert; America, 1751 ***1220.12*** *p558*
Muns, Samuel 76; Ontario, 1871 ***1823.21*** *p273*
Munsch, Thibault 18; Louisiana, 1848 ***778.6*** *p253*
Munseh, Mathis 26; Louisiana, 1848 ***778.6*** *p253*
Munsen, Joseph 2; America, 1845 ***778.6*** *p253*
Munsen, Maria 6; America, 1845 ***778.6*** *p253*
Munsey, Cooper *SEE* Munsey, Wm.
Munsey, Wm.; Maine, 1686 ***9228.50*** *p472*
*Relative:*Cooper
Munsinger, John; Ohio, 1844 ***2763.1*** *p20*
Munsinger, Philip; Ohio, 1844 ***2763.1*** *p20*
Munson, Charles; Washington, 1884 ***2770.40*** *p193*
Munson, Richard; Annapolis, MD, 1733 ***1220.12*** *p572*
Munsow, John; New Orleans, 1851 ***7242.30*** *p149*
Munster, Johann; America, 1881 ***5475.1*** *p308*
*Wife:*Maria Entinger
*Son:*Peter
Munster, Johann 22; America, 1836 ***5475.1*** *p468*
Munster, Johann Nikolaus; America, 1885 ***5475.1*** *p485*
Munster, Johanna Katharina 22; New York, 1885 ***5475.1*** *p485*
Munster, Maria Entinger *SEE* Munster, Johann
Munster, Peter *SEE* Munster, Johann
Munster, Raymond; Louisiana, 1874 ***4981.45*** *p133*
Munt, Elizabeth; America, 1749 ***1220.12*** *p572*
Munt, Jane; America, 1775 ***1220.12*** *p572*
Muntemann, Karl *SEE* Muntemann, Katharina

Muntemann, Katharina; America, 1881 ***2526.43*** *p143*
*Brother:*Karl
Munter, Anna 12 *SEE* Munter, Anna
Munter, Anna 55; New York, 1856 ***6529.11*** *p22*
*Daughter:*Anna 12
Muntermann, Karl; America, 1881 ***2526.43*** *p142*
Muntermann, Katharina; America, 1881 ***2526.43*** *p142*
Muntermann, Peter; England, 1862 ***2526.43*** *p189*
Muntford, Ann; Virginia, 1734 ***1220.12*** *p572*
Muntinger, Leonhard; North Carolina, 1836 ***1088.45*** *p25*
Muntz, Christian 5; New York, NY, 1890 ***1883.7*** *p47*
Muntz, Ferdinand 36; New York, NY, 1890 ***1883.7*** *p47*
Muntz, Gottlieb 7; New York, NY, 1890 ***1883.7*** *p47*
Muntz, Johanne 4; New York, NY, 1890 ***1883.7*** *p47*
Muntz, Johanne 35; New York, NY, 1890 ***1883.7*** *p47*
Muntz, Johannes 6; New York, NY, 1890 ***1883.7*** *p47*
Muntz, John; Illinois, 1834-1900 ***6020.5*** *p132*
Muntz, Pauline 6 months; New York, NY, 1890 ***1883.7*** *p47*
Munyon, Edward *SEE* Munyon, Joseph
Munyon, Joseph; Salem, MA, 1717 ***9228.50*** *p366*
*Relative:*Edward
Munz, Adolf Paul; America, 1891 ***179.55*** *p19*
Munz, Anna; America, 1891 ***179.55*** *p19*
Munz, Anna 7 *SEE* Munz, Elisabetha Brunner
Munz, Carl Friedrich; America, 1880-1890 ***179.55*** *p19*
Munz, Caroline Rosine; America, 1882-1890 ***179.55*** *p19*
Munz, Catharina; America, 1849-1890 ***179.55*** *p19*
Munz, Elisabeth; America, 1891 ***179.55*** *p19*
Munz, Elisabetha 35; America, 1857 ***2526.43*** *p154*
*Daughter:*Elise 13
*Son:*Theodor 11
*Daughter:*Jeanette 9
*Daughter:*Maria 4
*Daughter:*Anna 7
Munz, Elise 13 *SEE* Munz, Elisabetha Brunner
Munz, Friedrich; America, 1881-1890 ***179.55*** *p19*
Munz, Friedrich; America, 1891 ***179.55*** *p19*
Munz, Georg; America, 1853-1854 ***2526.43*** *p154*
Munz, Jakob; America, 1883 ***179.55*** *p19*
Munz, Jakob; America, 1891 ***179.55*** *p19*
With wife
Munz, Jeanette 9 *SEE* Munz, Elisabetha Brunner
Munz, Maria 4 *SEE* Munz, Elisabetha Brunner
Munz, Maria Rosina; America, 1877-1890 ***179.55*** *p19*
Munz, Theodor 11 *SEE* Munz, Elisabetha Brunner
Munz, Wilhelm; America, 1882 ***179.55*** *p19*
Munzenmeyer, E. G.; Valdivia, Chile, 1852 ***1192.4*** *p53*
Munzenmeyer, J. B.; Valdivia, Chile, 1852 ***1192.4*** *p53*
Mur, Ernest; New Orleans, 1851 ***7242.30*** *p150*
Murat, Antoine 23; Mississippi, 1845 ***778.6*** *p253*
Murat, Emanuel 34; New Orleans, 1844 ***778.6*** *p252*
Murault, Pierre 23; Quebec, 1657 ***9221.17*** *p364*
Murawski, Alexander; Detroit, 1929-1930 ***6214.5*** *p65*
Murch, George 25; Ontario, 1871 ***1823.21*** *p273*
Murch, Harry 37; Ontario, 1871 ***1823.21*** *p273*
Murch, James 50; Ontario, 1871 ***1823.21*** *p273*
Murchie, Archd 10; North Carolina, 1774 ***1422.10*** *p63*
Murchie, Archd. 10; North Carolina, 1774 ***1422.10*** *p60*
Murchie, Barbara 6 months; North Carolina, 1774 ***1422.10*** *p60*
Murchie, Barbara 6 months; North Carolina, 1774 ***1422.10*** *p63*
Murchie, Catherine 35; North Carolina, 1774 ***1422.10*** *p60*
Murchie, Catherine 35; North Carolina, 1774 ***1422.10*** *p62*
Murchie, Charles 5; North Carolina, 1774 ***1422.10*** *p60*
Murchie, Charles 5; North Carolina, 1774 ***1422.10*** *p63*
Murchie, Elizabeth 8; North Carolina, 1774 ***1422.10*** *p60*
Murchie, Findlay 45; North Carolina, 1774 ***1422.10*** *p62*
Murchie, Finlay 45; North Carolina, 1774 ***1422.10*** *p60*
Murchie, Neil 3; North Carolina, 1774 ***1422.10*** *p60*
Murchie, Neil 3; North Carolina, 1774 ***1422.10*** *p63*
Murchison, Andrew 45; Ontario, 1871 ***1823.21*** *p273*
Murdick, Robert; Iowa, 1894 ***1211.15*** *p17*
Murdoch, Charles 43; Ontario, 1871 ***1823.17*** *p123*
Murdoch, George; Philadelphia, 1778 ***8529.30*** *p4A*
Murdoch, James; New York, 1776 ***8529.30*** *p14*
Murdoch, Thomson; Ontario, 1871 ***1823.21*** *p273*
Murdoch, Wm 36; Ontario, 1871 ***1823.21*** *p273*
Murdock, Albert; Washington, 1883 ***2770.40*** *p137*
Murdock, Alexander; America, 1756 ***1220.12*** *p572*
Murdock, Alexander; North Carolina, 1836 ***1088.45*** *p25*
Murdock, Alexander 60; Ontario, 1871 ***1823.21*** *p273*
Murdock, George; Philadelphia, 1778 ***8529.30*** *p4A*
Murdock, Henry 46; Ontario, 1871 ***1823.17*** *p123*
Murdock, Hugh; North Carolina, 1860 ***1088.45*** *p25*
Murdock, James 40; Ontario, 1871 ***1823.21*** *p273*
Murdock, John; America, 1765 ***1220.12*** *p572*
Murdock, John 22; Ontario, 1871 ***1823.17*** *p123*
Murdock, John 36; Ontario, 1871 ***1823.17*** *p123*
Murdock, Johnston 41; Ontario, 1871 ***1823.21*** *p273*
Murdock, Margaret 53; Ontario, 1871 ***1823.17*** *p123*
Murdock, Robert 55; Ontario, 1871 ***1823.17*** *p123*
Murdock, William; North Carolina, 1839 ***1088.45*** *p25*
Murdock, Wm 86; Ontario, 1871 ***1823.21*** *p273*
Murdy, John 60; Ontario, 1871 ***1823.21*** *p273*
Murehead, David 54; Ontario, 1871 ***1823.21*** *p273*
Murei, Nicholas; Ohio, 1809-1852 ***4511.35*** *p37*
Muret, Adolph 17; St. Louis, 1847 ***778.6*** *p253*
Muret, Emile 38; St. Louis, 1847 ***778.6*** *p253*
Muret, Jacob 78; St. Louis, 1847 ***778.6*** *p253*
Muret, Louis 19; St. Louis, 1847 ***778.6*** *p253*
Murfee, Edward; Massachusetts, 1756 ***1642*** *p111*
Murfey, John; Boston, 1746 ***1642*** *p46*
Murfey, John; Boston, 1756 ***1642*** *p47*
Murfey, Peter; Boston, 1741 ***1642*** *p45*
Murfey, Timothy; America, 1755 ***1220.12*** *p573*
Murfey, William; America, 1764 ***1220.12*** *p573*
Murfle, Achille; Winnipeg, Man., 1911 ***3331.4*** *p12*
Murfy, Ann; Marblehead, MA, 1696 ***1642*** *p72*
Murfy, Ann 70; Ontario, 1871 ***1823.17*** *p123*
Murfy, John; Newburyport, MA, 1765 ***1642*** *p76*
Murgatroyd, Elizabeth; Maryland, 1725 ***1220.12*** *p572*
Murgatroyd, Joseph; America, 1757 ***1220.12*** *p572*
Murgett, Edward; America, 1681 ***1220.12*** *p572*
Murich, Jacob 30; America, 1847 ***778.6*** *p253*
Murich, Pierre 22; America, 1847 ***778.6*** *p253*
Murland, John; America, 1754 ***1220.12*** *p572*
Murna, James; New Orleans, 1850 ***7242.30*** *p150*
Murna, Mary; New Orleans, 1850 ***7242.30*** *p150*
Murna, Owen; New Orleans, 1850 ***7242.30*** *p150*
Murnin, Hugh; Illinois, 1858-1861 ***6020.5*** *p132*
Murphay, Michael; North Carolina, 1792-1862 ***1088.45*** *p25*
Murphet, Edward; America, 1721 ***1220.12*** *p566*
Murphey, Bridget; America, 1730 ***1220.12*** *p573*
Murphey, Edward; Marblehead, MA, 1753 ***1642*** *p73*
Murphey, James; North Carolina, 1835 ***1088.45*** *p25*
Murphey, Jeremiah; North Carolina, 1837 ***1088.45*** *p25*
Murphey, John; Boston, 1765 ***1642*** *p35*
Murphey, Joseph; North Carolina, 1844 ***1088.45*** *p25*
Murphey, Mary; Massachusetts, 1766 ***1642*** *p91*
Murphey, Thomas; Boston, 1763 ***1642*** *p32*
Murphey, Thomas; Boston, 1770 ***1642*** *p49*
Murphey, Thomas; Jamaica, 1783 ***8529.30*** *p13A*
Murphey, Thomas; North Carolina, 1834 ***1088.45*** *p25*
Murphey, William; Boston, 1763 ***1642*** *p32*
Murphey, William 31; Ontario, 1871 ***1823.17*** *p123*
Murphil, John Lawrence; America, 1758 ***1220.12*** *p572*
Murphy, . . .; Newburyport, MA, 1771 ***1642*** *p76*
Murphy, . . . 40; Ontario, 1871 ***1823.21*** *p273*
Murphy, Mr.; Boston, 1768 ***1642*** *p40*
Murphy, Andrew 40; Ontario, 1871 ***1823.17*** *p123*
Murphy, Andy; New Orleans, 1850 ***7242.30*** *p150*
Murphy, Ann; America, 1746 ***1220.12*** *p572*
Murphy, Ann; Boston, 1744 ***1642*** *p45*
Murphy, Ann 66; Michigan, 1880 ***4491.39*** *p21*
Murphy, Ann 10; Quebec, 1870 ***8364.32*** *p25*
Murphy, Anne; New Orleans, 1850 ***7242.30*** *p150*
Murphy, Archd 33; Ontario, 1871 ***1823.21*** *p273*
Murphy, Arthur; Newfoundland, 1814 ***3476.10*** *p54*
Murphy, Barbary; Boston, 1770 ***1642*** *p49*
Murphy, Bartho 11; Ontario, 1871 ***1823.21*** *p273*
Murphy, Betty; New Orleans, 1850 ***7242.30*** *p150*
Murphy, Biddy; New Orleans, 1850 ***7242.30*** *p150*
Murphy, Bridget; Boston, 1761 ***1642*** *p48*
Murphy, Bridget; New Orleans, 1850 ***7242.30*** *p150*
Murphy, Catherine; New Orleans, 1850 ***7242.30*** *p150*
Murphy, Damnal 81; Ontario, 1871 ***1823.17*** *p123*
Murphy, Daniel; Boston, 1754 ***1642*** *p47*
Murphy, Daniel 35; Ontario, 1871 ***1823.21*** *p273*
Murphy, Daniel 39; Ontario, 1871 ***1823.21*** *p273*
Murphy, Daniel; Toronto, 1844 ***2910.35*** *p113*
Murphy, David; Illinois, 1858-1861 ***6020.5*** *p132*
Murphy, David 40; Ontario, 1871 ***1823.17*** *p123*
Murphy, David; Salem, MA, 1769 ***1642*** *p78*
Murphy, Dennis; Massachusetts, 1754-1763 ***1642*** *p74*
Murphy, Dennis; Massachusetts, 1755 ***1642*** *p65*
Murphy, Dennis; New Orleans, 1850 ***7242.30*** *p150*
Murphy, Dennis; New Orleans, 1851 ***7242.30*** *p150*
Murphy, Edmond; New Orleans, 1850 ***7242.30*** *p150*
Murphy, Edward; America, 1764 ***1220.12*** *p573*
Murphy, Edward; America, 1772 ***1220.12*** *p573*
Murphy, Edward; Boston, 1766 ***1642*** *p37*
Murphy, Edward; New Orleans, 1850 ***7242.30*** *p150*
Murphy, Eleanor; America, 1773 ***1220.12*** *p573*
Murphy, Eleanor; Boston, 1767 ***1642*** *p38*
Murphy, Eliza 60; Ontario, 1871 ***1823.21*** *p273*
Murphy, Elizabeth; Boston, 1754 ***1642*** *p47*
Murphy, Elizabeth; Boston, 1765 ***1642*** *p34*
Murphy, Elizabeth; Maryland, 1725 ***1220.12*** *p573*
Murphy, Elizabeth 26; Ontario, 1871 ***1823.21*** *p273*
Murphy, Elizabeth *SEE* Murphy, William
Murphy, Ellen; New Orleans, 1850 ***7242.30*** *p150*
Murphy, Ellen; New Orleans, 1851 ***7242.30*** *p150*
Murphy, Ellen 60; Ontario, 1871 ***1823.21*** *p273*
Murphy, Frances; New Orleans, 1851 ***7242.30*** *p150*
Murphy, Francis; New Orleans, 1850 ***7242.30*** *p150*
Murphy, Frank; Boston, 1763 ***1642*** *p32*
Murphy, Frank; New Orleans, 1850 ***7242.30*** *p150*
Murphy, Garrett; America, 1759 ***1220.12*** *p573*
Murphy, George; New Orleans, 1850 ***7242.30*** *p150*
Murphy, George E. 35; Ontario, 1871 ***1823.17*** *p123*
Murphy, Hugh 47; Ontario, 1871 ***1823.21*** *p273*
Murphy, Hugh; St. Augustine, FL, 1777 ***8529.30*** *p10A*
Murphy, J.; California, 1868 ***1131.61*** *p89*
With family
Murphy, Mrs. J.; Toronto, 1844 ***2910.35*** *p112*
Murphy, James; America, 1753 ***1220.12*** *p573*
Murphy, James; America, 1764 ***1220.12*** *p573*
Murphy, James; America, 1766 ***1220.12*** *p573*
Murphy, James; Louisiana, 1841-1844 ***4981.45*** *p211*
Murphy, James; Louisiana, 1874-1875 ***4981.45*** *p30*
Murphy, James; Marblehead, MA, 1774 ***1642*** *p73*
Murphy, James; Massachusetts, 1755-1761 ***1642*** *p110*
Murphy, James; New York, 1783 ***8529.30*** *p14*
Murphy, James 16; Ontario, 1871 ***1823.17*** *p123*
Murphy, James 28; Ontario, 1871 ***1823.17*** *p123*
Murphy, James 57; Ontario, 1871 ***1823.17*** *p123*
Murphy, Jane; Boston, 1744 ***1642*** *p45*
Murphy, Jeffry 40; Ontario, 1871 ***1823.17*** *p123*
Murphy, Jeremiah; America, 1751 ***1220.12*** *p573*
Murphy, Jeremiah; Boston, 1766 ***1642*** *p36*
Murphy, Jerry; South Carolina, 1847 ***6155.4*** *p19*
Murphy, John; America, 1750 ***1220.12*** *p573*
Murphy, John; America, 1770 ***1220.12*** *p573*
Murphy, John; America, 1771 ***1220.12*** *p573*
Murphy, John; Annapolis, MD, 1723 ***1220.12*** *p573*
Murphy, John; Boston, 1766 ***1642*** *p37*
Murphy, John; Colorado, 1873 ***1029.59*** *p64*
Murphy, John; Hingham, MA, 1722 ***1642*** *p87*
Murphy, John; Illinois, 1834-1900 ***6020.5*** *p132*
Murphy, John; Jamaica, 1777 ***8529.30*** *p13A*
Murphy, John; Minnesota, 1842-1878 ***9228.50*** *p387*
Murphy, John; New England, 1745 ***1642*** *p28*
Murphy, John; New Orleans, 1850 ***7242.30*** *p150*
Murphy, John; New Orleans, 1851 ***7242.30*** *p150*
Murphy, John; Ohio, 1809-1852 ***4511.35*** *p37*
Murphy, John 54; Ontario, 1871 ***1823.21*** *p273*
Murphy, John 56; Ontario, 1871 ***1823.21*** *p273*
Murphy, John; Rappahannock, VA, 1741 ***1220.12*** *p573*
Murphy, John; St. John, N.B., 1847 ***2978.15*** *p39*
Murphy, John; St. John, N.B., 1848 ***2978.15*** *p38*
Murphy, John 24; St. Johns, N.F., 1811 ***1053.20*** *p21*
Murphy, John; Toronto, 1844 ***2910.35*** *p112*
Murphy, John; Toronto, 1844 ***2910.35*** *p112*
Murphy, John; Toronto, 1844 ***2910.35*** *p113*
Murphy, John; Toronto, 1844 ***2910.35*** *p113*
Murphy, John B. 35; Ontario, 1871 ***1823.21*** *p273*
Murphy, John R. 36; Michigan, 1880 ***4491.30*** *p23*
Murphy, Jonathan; New Orleans, 1850 ***7242.30*** *p150*
Murphy, Jsh; Colorado, 1873 ***1029.59*** *p64*
Murphy, Lawrence; America, 1765 ***1220.12*** *p573*
Murphy, Lawrence 46; Ontario, 1871 ***1823.17*** *p123*
Murphy, Luke M.; Illinois, 1834-1900 ***6020.5*** *p132*
Murphy, M.; New Orleans, 1850 ***7242.30*** *p150*
Murphy, Margaret; America, 1760 ***1220.12*** *p573*
Murphy, Margaret; Massachusetts, 1686 ***1642*** *p91*
Murphy, Margaret 50; Ontario, 1871 ***1823.17*** *p123*
Murphy, Martin; Colorado, 1880 ***1029.59*** *p64*
Murphy, Martin; New Orleans, 1851 ***7242.30*** *p150*
Murphy, Martin; New Orleans, 1851 ***7242.30*** *p151*
Murphy, Martin J.; Colorado, 1880 ***1029.59*** *p64*
Murphy, Mary; America, 1750 ***1220.12*** *p573*
Murphy, Mary; America, 1753 ***1220.12*** *p573*
Murphy, Mary 56; Michigan, 1880 ***4491.33*** *p16*
Murphy, Mary; Nantucket, MA, 1700-1799 ***1642*** *p89*
Murphy, Mary; New Orleans, 1850 ***7242.30*** *p151*
Murphy, Mary; New Orleans, 1851 ***7242.30*** *p151*
Murphy, Mary 36; Ontario, 1871 ***1823.17*** *p123*
Murphy, Matthew 43; Ontario, 1871 ***1823.21*** *p274*
Murphy, Michael; New Orleans, 1850 ***7242.30*** *p151*
Murphy, Michael 45; Ontario, 1871 ***1823.17*** *p123*
Murphy, Michel; Boston, 1763 ***1642*** *p48*
Murphy, Miles 22; Michigan, 1880 ***4491.39*** *p21*
Murphy, Morris; Boston, 1766 ***1642*** *p37*
Murphy, Nicholas; Boston, 1763 ***1642*** *p48*
Murphy, Nicholas; Boston, 1771 ***1642*** *p49*
Murphy, Nicholas; Boston, 1773 ***1642*** *p49*
Murphy, Nicholas 25; Michigan, 1880 ***4491.39*** *p21*
Murphy, Owen 29; Ontario, 1871 ***1823.17*** *p123*
Murphy, P.; New Orleans, 1850 ***7242.30*** *p151*
Murphy, Patk; St. John, N.B., 1847 ***2978.15*** *p35*
Murphy, Patrick; America, 1766 ***1220.12*** *p573*
Murphy, Patrick; America, 1771 ***1220.12*** *p573*
Murphy, Patrick; Boston, 1763 ***1642*** *p32*
Murphy, Patrick; California, 1868 ***1131.61*** *p89*

Murphy, Patrick 28; Michigan, 1880 4491.39 p21
Murphy, Patrick 54; Michigan, 1880 4491.33 p16
Murphy, Patrick; New Orleans, 1851 7242.30 p151
Murphy, Paul; New Orleans, 1850 7242.30 p151
Murphy, Peter; Lexington, MA, 1738 1642 p105
Murphy, Peter 45; Ontario, 1871 1823.17 p123
Murphy, Philip; Illinois, 1858-1861 6020.5 p132
Murphy, Philip 40; Ontario, 1871 1823.21 p274
Murphy, Richard; Newfoundland, 1814 3476.10 p54
Murphy, Richard 25; Ontario, 1871 1823.21 p274
Murphy, Richard; Rutland, MA, 1774 1642 p108
Murphy, Richard; Shrewsbury, MA, 1774 1642 p108
Murphy, Robert; Jamaica, 1777 8529.30 p13A
Murphy, Robert; Louisiana, 1836-1840 4981.45 p213
Murphy, Sarah; America, 1736 1220.12 p573
Murphy, Stephen; New Orleans, 1851 7242.30 p151
Murphy, Thomas; America, 1754 1220.12 p573
Murphy, Thomas; America, 1770 1220.12 p573
Murphy, Thomas; Illinois, 1858-1861 6020.5 p132
Murphy, Thomas; Massachusetts, 1770 1642 p104
Murphy, Thomas 30; Michigan, 1880 4491.39 p21
Murphy, Thomas 57; Ontario, 1871 1823.21 p274
Murphy, Timothy; Boston, 1767 1642 p38
Murphy, William; America, 1754 1220.12 p573
Murphy, William; Boston, 1766 1642 p38
Murphy, William; Boston, 1771 1642 p49
Murphy, William; Illinois, 1860 6079.1 p10
Murphy, William 30; Ontario, 1871 1823.21 p274
Murphy, William 60; Ontario, 1871 1823.21 p274
Murphy, William 70; Ontario, 1871 1823.17 p123
Murphy, William 16; Quebec, 1870 8364.32 p25
Murphy, William; Worcester, MA, 1748 1642 p114
*Wife:*Elizabeth
Murphy, Wm.; Toronto, 1844 2910.35 p111
Murrall, John; America, 1751 1220.12 p566
Murray, Adam 63; Ontario, 1871 1823.21 p274
Murray, Alexander 57; Ontario, 1871 1823.21 p274
Murray, Andrew; Louisiana, 1874 4981.45 p133
Murray, Andrew; Ohio, 1834 3580.20 p33
Murray, Andrew; Ohio, 1834 6020.12 p21
Murray, Andrew 43; Ontario, 1871 1823.21 p274
Murray, Andrew 55; Ontario, 1871 1823.17 p123
Murray, Ann 40; Ontario, 1871 1823.17 p123
Murray, Bernard 59; Ontario, 1871 1823.17 p123
Murray, Bridget 80; Ontario, 1871 1823.21 p274
Murray, Brien; America, 1770 1220.12 p573
Murray, C. 14; Quebec, 1870 8364.32 p25
Murray, Catherine 40; Michigan, 1880 4491.30 p23
Murray, Daniel 30; Ontario, 1871 1823.21 p274
Murray, David 43; Ontario, 1871 1823.21 p274
Murray, Dennis 10; Quebec, 1870 8364.32 p25
Murray, Dugald 43; Ontario, 1871 1823.21 p274
Murray, Edward; Philadelphia, 1778 8529.30 p7A
Murray, Elizabeth; America, 1747 1220.12 p573
Murray, Elizabeth; Ontario, 1835 3160.1 p150
Murray, Elizabeth; Prescott, Ont., 1835 3289.1 p61
Murray, Francis 55; Ontario, 1871 1823.21 p274
Murray, George 47; Ontario, 1871 1823.21 p274
Murray, George 49; Ontario, 1871 1823.21 p274
Murray, George 63; Ontario, 1871 1823.21 p274
Murray, Gregory; Philadelphia, 1778 8529.30 p4A
Murray, James 56; Michigan, 1880 4491.36 p16
Murray, James; North Carolina, 1858 1088.45 p25
Murray, James 18; Ontario, 1871 1823.21 p274
Murray, James 28; Ontario, 1871 1823.17 p123
Murray, James 34; Ontario, 1871 1823.17 p123
Murray, James 36; Ontario, 1871 1823.17 p123
Murray, Jane; America, 1765 1220.12 p573
Murray, Jane 61; Ontario, 1871 1823.17 p123
Murray, John; America, 1699 1220.12 p573
Murray, John; America, 1770 1220.12 p573
Murray, John; Burlington, VT, 1834 3274.55 p23
Murray, John; Massachusetts, 1620-1775 1642 p139
Murray, John 43; New York, NY, 1825 6178.50 p148
Murray, John; Newburyport, MA, 1763-1781 1642 p76
Murray, John; North America, 1750 1640.8 p234
Murray, John 30; Ontario, 1871 1823.21 p274
Murray, John 48; Ontario, 1871 1823.21 p274
Murray, John 48; Ontario, 1871 1823.21 p274
Murray, John; St. John, N.B., 1848 2978.15 p39
Murray, John D.; Colorado, 1875 1029.59 p64
Murray, John D. 46; Ontario, 1871 1823.17 p124
Murray, Judith; Virginia, 1739 1220.12 p573
Murray, Kate V.; Colorado, 1894 1029.59 p65
Murray, Larence 50; Michigan, 1880 4491.30 p23
Murray, Lawrence 35; Ontario, 1871 1823.17 p124
Murray, Malissa 20; Michigan, 1880 4491.36 p16
Murray, Margaret; Illinois, 1930 121.35 p101
Murray, Margaret 24; Michigan, 1880 4491.36 p16
Murray, Margaret 9; Quebec, 1870 8364.32 p25
Murray, Martin 33; Ontario, 1871 1823.17 p124
Murray, Mary 16; Ontario, 1871 1823.17 p124
Murray, Mary 65; Ontario, 1871 1823.21 p274
Murray, Matthew; America, 1771 1220.12 p573
Murray, Michael 60; Ontario, 1871 1823.21 p274
Murray, Owen 36; Ontario, 1871 1823.17 p124
Murray, Patrick; Ontario, 1835 3160.1 p150
Murray, Patrick 40; Ontario, 1871 1823.21 p274
Murray, Patrick; Prescott, Ont., 1835 3289.1 p61
Murray, Peter 34; Ontario, 1871 1823.21 p274
Murray, Peter 55; Ontario, 1871 1823.21 p274
Murray, Peter 55; Ontario, 1871 1823.21 p274
Murray, Rachel 55; Michigan, 1880 4491.36 p16
Murray, Re S. 45; Ontario, 1871 1823.21 p274
Murray, Richard; America, 1752 1220.12 p573
Murray, Robert; America, 1763 1220.12 p573
Murray, Robert 30; Ontario, 1871 1823.17 p124
Murray, Roger; Ohio, 1840-1897 8365.35 p17
Murray, Samuel; Ontario, 1835 3160.1 p150
Murray, Susan 10; Ontario, 1871 1823.21 p274
Murray, Susan 10; Quebec, 1870 8364.32 p25
Murray, Thomas 37; Ontario, 1871 1823.21 p274
Murray, Thomas 37; Ontario, 1871 1823.21 p274
Murray, Thomas 41; Ontario, 1871 1823.21 p274
Murray, Walter 26; Ontario, 1871 1823.17 p124
Murray, William 28; Ontario, 1871 1823.21 p274
Murray, William 54; Ontario, 1871 1823.21 p274
Murray, William 58; Ontario, 1871 1823.21 p274
Murray, William 15; Quebec, 1870 8364.32 p25
Murray, William David; Detroit, 1892 1766.20 p3
Murray, William H. 34; Ontario, 1871 1823.21 p274
Murray, William J. 22; Michigan, 1880 4491.36 p16
Murrell, Muriel; America, 1731 1220.12 p566
Murrell, Peter; Salem, MA, 1675 9228.50 p469
Murrell, Robert; America, 1772 1220.12 p566
Murrell, Sarah; America, 1741 1220.12 p566
Murrell, Sarah; America, 1765 1220.12 p566
Murrell, Sarah; America, 1773 1220.12 p566
Murrell, Susanna; America, 1722 1220.12 p566
Murrell, William 50; Ontario, 1871 1823.21 p274
Murrey, Francis; America, 1693 1220.12 p573
Murrey, Peter 44; Ontario, 1871 1823.21 p274
Murrey, Robert 40; Ontario, 1871 1823.21 p274
Murrican, John 41; Ontario, 1871 1823.21 p275
Murrick, Elizabeth; America, 1751 1220.12 p573
Murrow, Mary; America, 1746 1220.12 p573
Murry, Adam 37; Ontario, 1871 1823.17 p124
Murry, Alexander; Colorado, 1879 1029.59 p65
Murry, Donald 50; Ontario, 1871 1823.21 p275
Murry, George 45; Ontario, 1871 1823.17 p124
Murry, Henry; America, 1722 1220.12 p573
Murry, James 32; Ontario, 1871 1823.17 p124
Murry, James 42; Ontario, 1871 1823.21 p275
Murry, John; Illinois, 1858-1861 6020.5 p132
Murry, John 43; New York, NY, 1825 6178.50 p148
Murry, John 27; Ontario, 1871 1823.17 p124
Murry, Mary; Maryland or Virginia, 1733 1220.12 p573
Murry, Patrick 37; Ontario, 1871 1823.21 p275
Murry, Robert 40; Ontario, 1871 1823.21 p275
Murry, Sarah; Barbados or Jamaica, 1697 1220.12 p573
Murst, Michael; Ohio, 1809-1852 4511.35 p37
Murt, Anna *SEE* Murt, Karl
Murt, Karl; America, 1881 5475.1 p195
*Wife:*Kath. Gerardy
*Daughter:*Peter
*Daughter:*Anna
Murt, Kath. Gerardy *SEE* Murt, Karl
Murt, Peter *SEE* Murt, Karl
Murtagh, Julia 53; Ontario, 1871 1823.21 p275
Murtaugh, Patrick 44; Ontario, 1871 1823.21 p275
Murtaugh, Peter; Ohio, 1844 2763.1 p20
Murtfeld, Carl; America, 1845 7420.1 p38
With child 2
With child 1
Murtfeld, Wilhelm; America, 1832 7420.1 p6
Murthwaite, Ann; America, 1769 1220.12 p573
Murtin, James 52; Ontario, 1871 1823.17 p124
Murtogh, Bryan; America, 1739 1220.12 p573
Murton, Peter; North Carolina, 1859 1088.45 p25
Murton, William; America, 1764 1220.12 p546
Mury, Donald 44; Ontario, 1871 1823.21 p275
Musa, Antoine 26; Louisiana, 1848 778.6 p240
Musa, Lusanna 40; New York, NY, 1894 6512.1 p232
Musa, Rosa 3; New York, NY, 1894 6512.1 p232
Musch, Herman; Missouri, 1888 3276.1 p2
Musch, William; Illinois, 1834-1900 6020.5 p132
Muschgay, C. Otto v.; Valdivia, Chile, 1850 1192.4 p49
Musgrave, Andrew; America, 1771 1220.12 p574
Musgrave, Christopher; North Carolina, 1844 1088.45 p25
Musgrave, John; America, 1742 1220.12 p574
Musgrave, Maria; America, 1769 1220.12 p574
Musgrave, Nathaniel; America, 1685 1220.12 p574
Musgrove, Edward; America, 1754 1220.12 p574
Musgrove, John; America, 1742 1220.12 p574
Musgrove, John; Barbados, 1669 1220.12 p574
Musgrove, John 26; Ontario, 1871 1823.21 p275
Musgrove, Thomas; America, 1769 1220.12 p574
Musgrove, Thomas 64; Ontario, 1871 1823.21 p275
Musial, Andrew John; Detroit, 1929 1640.55 p114
Musial, Jan 36; New York, NY, 1920 930.50 p48
Musil, Jan; America, 1888 2853.20 p497
Musing, Carl Heinrich; America, 1868 7420.1 p275
Musing, Carl Wilhelm; America, 1867 7420.1 p261
Musing, Christian Friedrich *SEE* Musing, Christian Friedrich
Musing, Christian Friedrich; America, 1836 7420.1 p11
*Wife:*Christine Luise Moller
*Son:*Christian Friedrich
Musing, Christine Luise Moller *SEE* Musing, Christian Friedrich
Musing, Ludwig Wilhelm; America, 1868 7420.1 p275
With family
Musk, J.; Quebec, 1870 8364.32 p25
Muske, August; Wisconsin, 1901 6795.8 p144
Muske, Fred; Wisconsin, 1905 6795.8 p144
Muske, Ida; Wisconsin, 1898 6795.8 p144
Muske, Martha; Wisconsin, 1901 6795.8 p144
Muske, Minna; Wisconsin, 1897 6795.8 p144
Musket, James; America, 1743 1220.12 p574
Muskett, William; America, 1738 1220.12 p574
Muskman, John; America, 1614-1775 1220.12 p574
Mussedy, Thomas; America, 1710 1220.12 p574
Mussell, Ferdinand; Ohio, 1809-1852 4511.35 p37
Mussen, James; America, 1766 1220.12 p574
Musser, John; Ohio, 1809-1852 4511.35 p37
Musser, John; Pennsylvania, 1711 9228.50 p469
Musser, John P.; Ohio, 1809-1852 4511.35 p37
Musson, Thomas 33; Ontario, 1871 1823.17 p124
Mustachia, Joseph; Louisiana, 1874 4981.45 p132
Mustell, John 31; Ontario, 1871 1823.21 p275
Muster, Edwanu 19; Portland, ME, 1911 970.38 p79
Musters, Munday; America, 1764 1220.12 p574
Musto, Thomas; America, 1742 1220.12 p574
Muston, Richard Joseph; America, 1771 1220.12 p574
Mutchler, Godfrey; Ohio, 1809-1852 4511.35 p37
Mutchmore, Walter; Barbados, 1664 1220.12 p574
Mutes, Mary; Maryland, 1727 1220.12 p574
Muth, Adam; Ohio, 1809-1852 4511.35 p37
Muth, And. 18; America, 1840 778.6 p253
Muth, Charles; Ohio, 1809-1852 4511.35 p37
Muth, Elisabeth; America, 1892 170.15 p37
Mutkim, Desire; Wisconsin, 1871 1494.20 p11
Mutkin, J. J.; Wisconsin, 1871 1494.20 p11
Mutlow, Sarah; America, 1764 1220.12 p574
Mutschler, Anna Maria; Venezuela, 1843 3899.5 p544
Mutschler, Anna Maria; Venezuela, 1843 3899.5 p544
Mutschler, Barbara; Venezuela, 1843 3899.5 p543
*Child:*Joseph
*Child:*Matthaus
Mutschler, Franz Karl; Venezuela, 1843 3899.5 p543
Mutschler, Johannes; Venezuela, 1843 3899.5 p543
Mutschler, Joseph *SEE* Mutschler, Barbara
Mutschler, Leonhard; Venezuela, 1843 3899.5 p543
Mutschler, Leonhard; Venezuela, 1843 3899.5 p544
Mutschler, Magdalena; Venezuela, 1843 3899.5 p540
Mutschler, Matthaus *SEE* Mutschler, Barbara
Muttart, Lewis 62; Ontario, 1871 1823.21 p275
Mutter, Elizabeth; Wisconsin, n.d. 9228.50 p631
Mutter, Jessie P. 40; Ontario, 1871 1823.21 p275
Muttit, Elizabeth; America, 1668 1220.12 p574
Muttlebury, John; America, 1685 1220.12 p574
Mutton, Mary; America, 1767 1220.12 p574
Muttutt, Henery 84; Ontario, 1871 1823.17 p124
Mutz, Anna Marie 55; America, 1888 2526.42 p116
Mutzel, Frederick; Iowa, 1888 1211.15 p16
Mutzig, Friedrich 20; America, 1842 778.6 p253
Mutzwerller, Anton 20; America, 1746 778.6 p253
Mutzwerller, George 2; America, 1746 778.6 p253
Muvray, Hugh; North Carolina, 1848 1088.45 p25
Muysinger, Coonrod; New Jersey, 1750-1774 927.31 p3
Muzie, John; Marston's Wharf, 1782 8529.30 p14
Muzny, Hynek; Galveston, TX, 1856 2853.20 p63
Muzzaretti, Antonio; Illinois, 1930 121.35 p101
Muzzle, Joseph; America, 1748 1220.12 p574
Myalls, William; America, 1733 1220.12 p549
Myer, Abraham; America, 1770 1220.12 p574
Myer, Bernard; Ohio, 1809-1852 4511.35 p37
Myer, Charles G.; North Carolina, 1853 1088.45 p25
Myer, Christian; Ohio, 1809-1852 4511.35 p37
Myer, Christian, Jr.; Ohio, 1809-1852 4511.35 p37
Myer, Conrad; Ohio, 1809-1852 4511.35 p37
Myer, Jacob; Ohio, 1809-1852 4511.35 p37
Myer, John; Ohio, 1809-1852 4511.35 p37
Myer, Mattis 21; America, 1848 778.6 p253
Myer, Samuel; America, 1722 1220.12 p574
Myer, Ulrich; Ohio, 1809-1852 4511.35 p37
Myers, A. B.; Louisiana, 1874 4981.45 p133
Myers, Ann; America, 1767 1220.12 p574

Myers, Ann 52; Ontario, 1871 *1823.21 p275*
Myers, Catherine; Halifax, N.S., 1827 *7009.9 p61*
Myers, Daniel; America, 1720 *1220.12 p574*
Myers, Edward; America, 1720 *1220.12 p574*
Myers, Francis 23; Ontario, 1871 *1823.17 p124*
Myers, Henry; Ohio, 1809-1852 *4511.35 p37*
Myers, Henry 50; Ontario, 1871 *1823.17 p124*
Myers, Jacob; Ohio, 1809-1852 *4511.35 p38*
Myers, John; America, 1756 *1220.12 p574*
Myers, Joseph; America, 1771 *1220.12 p574*
Myers, Joseph 30; Ontario, 1871 *1823.17 p124*
Myers, Mary; America, 1719 *1220.12 p574*
Myers, Mary; America, 1748 *1220.12 p574*
Myers, Michael; Ohio, 1809-1852 *4511.35 p38*
Myers, Samuel; New Jersey, 1807 *3845.2 p129*
Myers, Seraphim; Ohio, 1809-1852 *4511.35 p38*
Myers, Ulrich; Ohio, 1809-1852 *4511.35 p38*

Myers, William; America, 1755 *1220.12 p574*
Myers, William; America, 1756 *1220.12 p574*
Myford, Elizabeth; America, 1763 *1220.12 p574*
Mygood, Nicholas; New Hampshire, 1718 *9228.50 p473*
Myles, Martha 25; Ontario, 1871 *1823.21 p275*
Mylius, August; America, 1852 *7420.1 p94*
Mylius, Engel Marie Sophia Schwiessing *SEE* Mylius, Johann Heinrich Christoph
Mylius, Hans Heinrich Christoph *SEE* Mylius, Johann Heinrich Christoph
Mylius, Johann Heinrich Carl *SEE* Mylius, Johann Heinrich Christoph
Mylius, Johann Heinrich Christoph; America, 1886 *7420.1 p351*
   *Wife:*Engel Marie Sophia Schwiessing
   *Son:*Johann Heinrich Carl

   *Son:*Hans Heinrich Christoph
   *Daughter:*Sophie Marie Wilhelmine
Mylius, Sophie Marie Wilhelmine *SEE* Mylius, Johann Heinrich Christoph
Mylls, John 22; Ontario, 1871 *1823.21 p275*
Mynott, Ebenezer; Colorado, 1873 *1029.59 p65*
Myrberg, Margareta 22; New York, 1856 *6529.11 p22*
Myre deL'Argenterie, Etienne; Quebec, 1683-1688 *2314.30 p168*
Myre deL'Argenterie, Etienne; Quebec, 1685 *2314.30 p191*
Myren, Carl Axel; Cleveland, OH, 1901-1903 *9722.10 p124*
Myres, Hannah; America, 1775 *1220.12 p574*
Myszk, August; Wisconsin, 1894 *6795.8 p60*

N

Naahyee, William 60; Ontario, 1871 *1823.17 p124*
Naas, Franz; America, 1839 *2526.42 p110*
   With wife
   With child 11
   With child 6 months
Naas, Friedrich Wilhelm Georg 25; America, 1883
   2526.43 p176
Naas, Jakob; America, 1832 *2526.43 p212*
   With wife & 4 children
   With child 20
   With child 4
Naas, Philipp Jakob; America, 1884 *2526.43 p226*
Nabb, Elizabeth; America, 1770 *1220.12 p575*
Nabbs, Elizabeth; America, 1770 *1220.12 p575*
Nabbs, Thomas; America, 1772 *1220.12 p575*
Nabersheus, Edward; Louisiana, 1874 *4981.45 p133*
Nabholz, Jacob; Valdivia, Chile, 1851 *1192.4 p51*
Nabier, T. 27; Ontario, 1871 *1823.21 p275*
Nabrick, Andrew; America, 1685 *1220.12 p575*
Nace, Pierre; Virginia, 1700 *9230.15 p80*
   With wife & 2 daughters
Nacher, Theodor; America, 1850 *5475.1 p478*
Nachten, Alexander; New York, 1738 *8277.31 p118*
   *Wife:*Mary McDonald
   *Child:*Eleanor
   *Child:*Janet
   *Child:*John
   *Child:*Moses
Nachten, Eleanor *SEE* Nachten, Alexander
Nachten, Janet *SEE* Nachten, Alexander
Nachten, John *SEE* Nachten, Alexander
Nachten, Mary McDonald *SEE* Nachten, Alexander
Nachten, Moses *SEE* Nachten, Alexander
Nacke, Catharina Marie *SEE* Nacke, Engel Marie
   Dorothea
Nacke, Catharine Marie Sophie; America, 1868 *7420.1*
   p275
Nacke, Engel Marie *SEE* Nacke, Engel Marie Dorothea
Nacke, Engel Marie Dorothea; America, 1872 *7420.1*
   p296
   *Daughter:*Engel Marie
   *Daughter:*Catharina Marie
   *Son:*Johann Heinrich
Nacke, Johann Heinrich *SEE* Nacke, Engel Marie
   Dorothea
Nackel, Louise; Port uncertain, 1843 *778.6 p253*
Nadault, Jean 23; Quebec, 1656 *9221.17 p337*
Nadault, Jean 23; Quebec, 1656 *9221.17 p343*
Nadeau, Ozanie-Joseph 24; Quebec, 1661 *9221.17 p463*
Naden, Richard; America, 1678 *1220.12 p575*
Naden, Robert; America, 1713 *1220.12 p575*
Naden, Thomas; America, 1678 *1220.12 p575*
Naden, Thomas; America, 1684 *1220.12 p575*
Naden, Thomas; America, 1764 *1220.12 p575*
Nadereau, Francoise; Canada, 1658 *1142.10 p128*
Nadereau, Francoise-Jacqueline 14; Montreal, 1658
   9221.17 p390
Nadin, Elizabeth *SEE* Nadin, John
Nadin, Jane Evans *SEE* Nadin, John
Nadin, John; Philadelphia, 1868 *8513.31 p417*
   *Wife:*Jane Evans
   *Child:*Elizabeth
Nadler, Ch..les 19; Louisiana, 1848 *778.6 p253*
Naef, L.; Louisiana, 1874 *4981.45 p296*
Naegelin, Angele 24; New Orleans, 1848 *778.6 p253*
Naegelin, Elisabeth 23; New Orleans, 1848 *778.6 p253*
Naegelin, John Ulrich; Illinois, 1856 *6079.1 p10*
Naegelin, Laurent 46; New Orleans, 1848 *778.6 p253*

Naegle, John Conrad; Mexico, 1899 *3687.1 p38*
Naested, Frederick; North Carolina, 1823 *1088.45 p25*
Nafrechoux, Isaac 22; Montreal, 1662 *9221.17 p499*
Naftal, John; America, 1818 *9228.50 p152*
Naftel, Abraham; Canada, 1814-1900 *9228.50 p166*
   *Wife:*Elizabeth Stonehouse
   With 2 sons & daughter
Naftel, Abraham; Canada, 1814-1900 *9228.50 p473*
   *Wife:*Elizabeth Stonehouse
Naftel, Caroline Slocomb *SEE* Naftel, John
Naftel, Daniel; Ohio, 1807 *9228.50 p473*
Naftel, Elizabeth Stonehouse *SEE* Naftel, Abraham
Naftel, Elizabeth Stonehouse *SEE* Naftel, Abraham
Naftel, John; Canada, 1814-1900 *9228.50 p166*
   *Wife:*Caroline Slocomb
Naftel, John; Canada, 1816-1900 *9228.50 p473*
Naftel, Thomas; Norfolk, VA, 1806 *9228.50 p56*
   With wife & children
Naftel, Thomas; Ohio, 1806 *9228.50 p473*
   With wife & children
Naftel, Thomas, Family; Ohio, 1807 *9228.50 p57*
Nagall, John 20; Quebec, 1870 *8364.32 p25*
Nagel, . . .; America, 1849 *7420.1 p66*
Nagel, Adam 17; Portland, ME, 1911 *970.38 p79*
Nagel, August Herman; Iowa, 1888 *1211.15 p17*
Nagel, August Herman; Iowa, 1888 *1211.15 p17*
Nagel, Catharina 56; America, 1843 *778.6 p253*
Nagel, Clemens 6 *SEE* Nagel, Margarethe
Nagel, Conrad; Illinois, 1859 *6079.1 p10*
Nagel, Elisabeth 30 *SEE* Nagel, Jakob
Nagel, Ella 19; New York, NY, 1886 *5475.1 p17*
Nagel, Emilie 1 *SEE* Nagel, Jakob
Nagel, Engel Christine; America, 1860 *7420.1 p197*
Nagel, Friedrich Wilhelm; America, 1882 *7420.1 p331*
Nagel, Isaac 43; Missouri, 1845 *778.6 p253*
Nagel, Jakob 33; New York, NY, 1882 *5475.1 p16*
   *Wife:*Elisabeth 30
   *Daughter:*Luise 3
   *Daughter:*Emilie 1
Nagel, Johann; Missouri, 1846 *778.6 p253*
Nagel, Johann 34; New York, 1892 *5475.1 p77*
Nagel, Johannes; Illinois, 1854 *6079.1 p10*
Nagel, John; New York, 1859-1860 *358.56 p102*
Nagel, Louise Charlotte; America, 1892 *7420.1 p367*
Nagel, Luise 3 *SEE* Nagel, Jakob
Nagel, Margarethe 27; New York, 1893 *5475.1 p77*
   *Son:*Clemens 6
   *Son:*Peter 2
Nagel, Martin Georg; Wisconsin, 1868 *6795.8 p42*
Nagel, Peter 2 *SEE* Nagel, Margarethe
Nagel, Sophie Louise; St. Louis, 1846 *7420.1 p46*
Nagel, William; Louisiana, 1874 *4981.45 p133*
Nagelheuer, Fred K. 25; New York, NY, 1847 *9176.15*
   p50
Nagelin, Jakob 13; Galveston, TX, 1844 *3967.10 p370*
Nagelin, Joseph 24; Galveston, TX, 1844 *3967.10 p370*
Nagelin, Therese 20; Galveston, TX, 1844 *3967.10 p370*
Nagels, George; Louisiana, 1874 *4981.45 p133*
Nagerle, Christian; Illinois, 1834-1900 *6020.5 p132*
Nagerle, Frederick; Illinois, 1834-1900 *6020.5 p132*
Naggington, Robert; America, 1775 *1220.12 p575*
Naggs, Charles 17; Ontario, 1871 *1823.21 p275*
Naggs, Sarah; Maryland, 1720 *1220.12 p575*
Nagle, Adam; Ohio, 1809-1852 *4511.35 p38*
Nagle, Bernard; Ohio, 1809-1852 *4511.35 p38*
Nagle, Ella 23; Ontario, 1871 *1823.21 p275*
Nagle, Frederick 15; Quebec, 1870 *8364.32 p25*
Nagle, Thomas 38; Ontario, 1871 *1823.21 p275*

Nagle, Thomas 63; Ontario, 1871 *1823.21 p275*
Nagle, Vitus; Ohio, 1809-1852 *4511.35 p38*
Nagret, Charles 41; New Orleans, 1843 *778.6 p254*
Nagues, Jean 28; America, 1842 *778.6 p254*
Nahara, Stanislaus; Wisconsin, 1879 *6795.8 p140*
Nahn, Mr. 45; America, 1846 *778.6 p254*
Nahrwold, Wilhelm; Port uncertain, 1854 *7420.1 p126*
Nahs, Amalie 9 months; New York, NY, 1893 *1883.7*
   p43
Nahs, Elisabeth 21; New York, NY, 1893 *1883.7 p43*
Nahwakodoo, John 45; Ontario, 1871 *1823.17 p124*
Nail, Jacques 28; Montreal, 1653 *9221.17 p298*
Nail, Michael 48; Ontario, 1871 *1823.17 p124*
Nailer, William; America, 1768 *1220.12 p576*
Naillest, J. 35; America, 1841 *778.6 p254*
Nailon, Mic; St. John, N.B., 1847 *2978.15 p39*
Nailor, Elizabeth; America, 1744 *1220.12 p576*
Nailor, Mary; America, 1752 *1220.12 p576*
Nairot, Michael; Ohio, 1809-1852 *4511.35 p38*
Naisby, Frances; America, 1734 *1220.12 p575*
Naish, John; Virginia, 1741 *1220.12 p575*
Naish, Susan; America, 1745 *1220.12 p575*
Naish, William; America, 1731 *1220.12 p575*
Naismith, J. J.; Montreal, 1922 *4514.4 p32*
Nakas, Dorothea Konig *SEE* Nakas, Philipp
Nakas, Philipp 44; America, 1880 *5475.1 p48*
   *Wife:*Dorothea Konig
Nakis, Christos Emmanouil; Illinois, 1930 *121.35 p100*
Nalan, Michael; Illinois, 1855 *6079.1 p10*
Nalbach, Georg; America, 1852 *5475.1 p52*
Nalbach, Sebastian; America, 1852 *5475.1 p52*
Naley, Patrick; America, 1760 *1220.12 p575*
Nalfing, Philip; Rappahannock, VA, 1728 *1220.12 p575*
Nalin, Bridget 40; Ontario, 1871 *1823.17 p124*
Nallen, James 55; Ontario, 1871 *1823.21 p275*
Nalmquist, Carl Itjalman; Canada, 1902 *1766.20 p36*
Nancy, Elizabeth; America, 1756 *1220.12 p575*
Nangle, Patrick 40; Ontario, 1871 *1823.21 p275*
Nangle, Patrick 64; Ontario, 1871 *1823.21 p275*
Nangle, Peter; Toronto, 1844 *2910.35 p112*
Nankivell, Jas; Colorado, 1880 *1029.59 p65*
Nanny, Martin; Virginia, 1732 *1220.12 p575*
Nantford, Francis; Barbados, 1672 *1220.12 p575*
Nanty, Francois 28; New Orleans, 1848 *778.6 p254*
Napen, Miss 37; America, 1844 *778.6 p254*
Napett, Samuel; America, 1768 *1220.12 p575*
Napkin, Hannah; America, 1752 *1220.12 p575*
Napoleon, Etienne 37; New Orleans, 1848 *778.6 p254*
Napoleon, J. 35; New Orleans, 1840 *778.6 p254*
Nappe, Wm 45; Ontario, 1871 *1823.21 p275*
Napper, Charles 50; Ontario, 1871 *1823.21 p275*
Napper, John; America, 1764 *1220.12 p575*
Napper, William 45; Ontario, 1871 *1823.17 p124*
Naprstek, Vojta; New York, NY, 1848 *2853.20 p100*
Naprstek, Vojta; New York, NY, 1850 *2853.20 p101*
Napton, Francis; America, 1749 *1220.12 p575*
Narder, James; America, 1753 *1220.12 p575*
Nardin, Jean-Louis 28; New Orleans, 1848 *778.6 p254*
Naren, Patrick 30; Ontario, 1871 *1823.21 p275*
Nargaud, Edouard 22; America, 1746 *778.6 p254*
Narjes, . . .; New York, NY, 1893 *7420.1 p368*
Narkiewicz, Boleslaw; Detroit, 1929 *1640.55 p117*
Narkiewicz, Michael; Detroit, 1929 *1640.55 p117*
Narp, Charles; Quebec, 1658 *9221.17 p385*
Narrot, Michel; Ohio, 1809-1852 *4511.35 p38*
Narroway, William; America, 1757 *1220.12 p575*
Nary, Andrew; America, 1774 *1220.12 p575*
Nary, Margaret; Halifax, N.S., 1827 *7009.9 p62*

Naschold, Heinrieke; America, 1845-1882 ***179.55*** *p19*
Nasey, Richard; Barbados, 1664 ***1220.12*** *p575*
Nash, Abraham; America, 1739 ***1220.12*** *p575*
Nash, Ann; America, 1763 ***1220.12*** *p575*
Nash, Benjamin 63; Ontario, 1871 ***1823.21*** *p275*
Nash, Diana; America, 1769 ***1220.12*** *p575*
Nash, Elizabeth; America, 1734 ***1220.12*** *p575*
Nash, Henry 55; Ontario, 1871 ***1823.21*** *p275*
Nash, I. H. 43; Ontario, 1871 ***1823.17*** *p124*
Nash, James 66; Michigan, 1880 ***4491.30*** *p23*
Nash, James 17; Ontario, 1871 ***1823.21*** *p275*
Nash, John; America, 1753 ***1220.12*** *p575*
Nash, John; America, 1773 ***1220.12*** *p575*
Nash, John; Annapolis, MD, 1722 ***1220.12*** *p575*
Nash, Lewis 19; Ontario, 1871 ***1823.21*** *p275*
Nash, Mary; America, 1771 ***1220.12*** *p575*
Nash, Mary; Maryland, 1741 ***1220.12*** *p575*
Nash, Mary; Virginia, 1767 ***1220.12*** *p575*
Nash, Mary A. 66; Michigan, 1880 ***4491.30*** *p23*
Nash, Mary Ann 60; Ontario, 1871 ***1823.21*** *p275*
Nash, Matthew; America, 1756 ***1220.12*** *p575*
Nash, Richard; America, 1685 ***1220.12*** *p575*
Nash, Sarah; America, 1764 ***1220.12*** *p575*
Nash, Susannah; America, 1769 ***1220.12*** *p575*
Nash, Thomas; America, 1727 ***1220.12*** *p576*
Nash, Thomas; America, 1759 ***1220.12*** *p576*
Nash, Thomas; Jamaica, 1661 ***1220.12*** *p575*
Nash, William; America, 1773 ***1220.12*** *p576*
Nash, William 33; Ontario, 1871 ***1823.21*** *p275*
Nash, William; Virginia, 1739 ***1220.12*** *p576*
Nashion, Thomas; America, 1685 ***1220.12*** *p576*
Naslund, Christina; Illinois, 1854 ***6529.11*** *p23*
With parents
Naslund, Peter; Cleveland, OH, 1892-1897 ***9722.10*** *p124*
Nasmyth, Henry 35; Ontario, 1871 ***1823.17*** *p124*
Nason, John; America, 1746 ***1220.12*** *p576*
Nass, Abraham; America, 1739 ***1220.12*** *p576*
Nassauer, Fred; North Carolina, 1859 ***1088.45*** *p25*
Nasser, Czar; Oregon, 1941 ***9157.47*** *p3*
Nastali, John; Wisconsin, 1884 ***6795.8*** *p60*
Naston, John; America, 1754 ***1220.12*** *p576*
Natash, August; Illinois, 1858-1861 ***6020.5*** *p132*
Nathan, Bernard; America, 1762 ***1220.12*** *p576*
Nathan, Peter 45; Ontario, 1871 ***1823.17*** *p124*
Nathnagel, Henry Jacob; Ohio, 1809-1852 ***4511.35*** *p38*
Nathnagle, Henry Jacob; Ohio, 1809-1852 ***4511.35*** *p38*
Nativite, Mere de la 25; Quebec, 1654 ***9221.17*** *p303*
Natt, John; America, 1771 ***1220.12*** *p576*
Natt, John; Charles Town, SC, 1718 ***1220.12*** *p576*
Nattrass, John 42; Ontario, 1871 ***1823.21*** *p276*
Nau, Anna Maria 51; America, 1837 ***5475.1*** *p399*
Nau, Barbara 13 *SEE* Nau, Jakob
Nau, Christian 27; America, 1846 ***5475.1*** *p411*
*Wife:*Katharina Jochum 27
*Mother:*Magdalena 61
*Daughter:*Katharina 1
*Daughter:*Katharina 6
Nau, Christina; America, 1846 ***5475.1*** *p411*
Nau, Christina Schuler *SEE* Nau, Peter
Nau, Franz 16 *SEE* Nau, Jakob
Nau, Jakob 20 *SEE* Nau, Jakob
Nau, Jakob 49; America, 1837 ***5475.1*** *p410*
*Daughter:*Margarethe 26
*Son:*Johann, II 8
*Son:*Jakob 20
*Son:*Franz 16
*Daughter:*Barbara 13
*Daughter:*Peter 23
Nau, Johann, II 8 *SEE* Nau, Jakob
Nau, Johann Alois; America, 1873 ***5475.1*** *p58*
Nau, Karl; America, 1887 ***2526.42*** *p163*
Nau, Karl *SEE* Nau, Nikolaus
Nau, Katharina Guldner *SEE* Nau, Nikolaus
Nau, Katharina 1 *SEE* Nau, Christian
Nau, Katharina 6 *SEE* Nau, Christian
Nau, Katharina Jochum 27 *SEE* Nau, Christian
Nau, Magdalena 61 *SEE* Nau, Christian
Nau, Margarethe Schremer *SEE* Nau, Nikolaus
Nau, Margarethe 26 *SEE* Nau, Jakob
Nau, Margarethe 29; America, 1880 ***5475.1*** *p456*
Nau, Nikolaus; America, 1854 ***5475.1*** *p57*
*Wife:*Katharina Guldner
Nau, Nikolaus; America, 1887 ***5475.1*** *p58*
*Wife:*Margarethe Schremer
*Son:*Karl
Nau, Nikolaus 65; America, 1846 ***5475.1*** *p411*
Nau, Peter; America, 1872 ***5475.1*** *p57*
*Wife:*Christina Schuler
Nau, Peter 23 *SEE* Nau, Jakob
Nau DeBeaumont, Bonaventure; Quebec, 1659 ***9221.17*** *p407*
Nau DeFossambault, Marie-Catherine 21; Quebec, 1655 ***9221.17*** *p327*
Nau DeFossambault, Michelle-Therese 18; Quebec, 1661 ***9221.17*** *p463*
Naudet, Jean Pierre 26; America, 1845 ***778.6*** *p254*
Naudier, Jean; Quebec, 1652 ***9221.17*** *p263*
Naudin, Francois; Quebec, 1649 ***9221.17*** *p218*
Naughton, Luke 30; Ontario, 1871 ***1823.21*** *p276*
Naugocks, Maria Anna; Wisconsin, 1898 ***6795.8*** *p82*
Naujocks, Maria Anna; Wisconsin, 1898 ***6795.8*** *p82*
Naumann, A. Maria Embser *SEE* Naumann, Jakob
Naumann, Balthasar; Ohio, 1809-1852 ***4511.35*** *p38*
Naumann, Barbara *SEE* Naumann, Nikolaus
Naumann, Franz Josef *SEE* Naumann, Jakob
Naumann, Friedrich *SEE* Naumann, Jakob
Naumann, Helena *SEE* Naumann, Jakob
Naumann, Helena; America, 1882 ***5475.1*** *p333*
Naumann, Jakob *SEE* Naumann, Jakob
Naumann, Jakob; America, 1854 ***5475.1*** *p459*
*Wife:*Sophie Honecker
*Son:*Friedrich
*Daughter:*Katharina
*Son:*Karl
*Daughter:*Maria
*Daughter:*Sophie
*Son:*Jakob
*Son:*Wilhelm
*Son:*Ludwig
Naumann, Jakob; America, 1881 ***5475.1*** *p334*
*Wife:*A. Maria Embser
*Son:*Franz Josef
*Daughter:*Maria
*Daughter:*Helena
Naumann, Johann; America, 1852 ***5475.1*** *p514*
Naumann, Johann *SEE* Naumann, Nikolaus
Naumann, Johann Jakob Ludwig; America, 1890 ***5475.1*** *p38*
Naumann, John Y.; Ohio, 1809-1852 ***4511.35*** *p38*
Naumann, Karl *SEE* Naumann, Jakob
Naumann, Karl Wilhelm; America, 1841 ***5475.1*** *p458*
Naumann, Katharina *SEE* Naumann, Jakob
Naumann, Katharina *SEE* Naumann, Nikolaus
Naumann, Katharina; Brazil, 1879 ***5475.1*** *p265*
Naumann, Ludwig *SEE* Naumann, Jakob
Naumann, Maria *SEE* Naumann, Jakob
Naumann, Maria *SEE* Naumann, Nikolaus
Naumann, Maria Merfeld *SEE* Naumann, Nikolaus
Naumann, Maria; America, 1880 ***5475.1*** *p272*
Naumann, Maria *SEE* Naumann, Jakob
Naumann, Maria; America, 1889 ***5475.1*** *p424*
Naumann, Mathias; America, 1881 ***5475.1*** *p276*
Naumann, Melchisadec; Ohio, 1809-1852 ***4511.35*** *p38*
Naumann, Melchisedeck; Ohio, 1809-1852 ***4511.35*** *p38*
Naumann, Nikolaus; America, 1855 ***5475.1*** *p279*
Naumann, Nikolaus *SEE* Naumann, Nikolaus
Naumann, Nikolaus; America, 1874 ***5475.1*** *p140*
*Wife:*Maria Merfeld
*Son:*Nikolaus
*Daughter:*Maria
*Daughter:*Katharina
*Daughter:*Johann
*Daughter:*Barbara
Naumann, Nikolaus; America, 1883 ***5475.1*** *p277*
Naumann, Sophie *SEE* Naumann, Jakob
Naumann, Sophie Honecker *SEE* Naumann, Jakob
Naumann, Wilhelm *SEE* Naumann, Jakob
Naundorf, Nikolaus; America, 1840 ***5475.1*** *p169*
Nausle, Jean 19; New Orleans, 1848 ***778.6*** *p254*
Navaron, Marie; Quebec, 1670 ***4514.3*** *p351*
Navarre, John 40; Ontario, 1871 ***1823.17*** *p124*
Navarre, Marguerite; Quebec, 1669 ***4514.3*** *p351*
Navell, James; America, 1685 ***1220.12*** *p576*
Navratil Family ; Minnesota, 1854-1865 ***2853.20*** *p271*
Nawnton, James; America, 1715 ***1220.12*** *p576*
Nay, John; Hampton, NH, n.d. ***9228.50*** *p473*
Nayel, Hermann; Illinois, 1858-1861 ***6020.5*** *p132*
Naylor, Ann; Potomac, 1731 ***1220.12*** *p576*
Naylor, Esther; America, 1738 ***1220.12*** *p576*
Naylor, George; Barbados or Jamaica, 1699 ***1220.12*** *p576*
Naylor, James; America, 1770 ***1220.12*** *p576*
Naylor, John; America, 1748 ***1220.12*** *p576*
Naylor, Nathaniel; America, 1767 ***1220.12*** *p576*
Naylor, Peter 63; Ontario, 1871 ***1823.17*** *p124*
Naylor, Robert; America, 1700 ***1220.12*** *p576*
Naylor, Susannah; America, 1772 ***1220.12*** *p576*
Naylor, Thomas; Washington, 1889 ***2770.40*** *p80*
Naze, Prosper; New York, NY, 1855 ***1494.21*** *p31*
NcSharry, Brian; St. John, N.B., 1847 ***2978.15*** *p38*
Neabel, Jacob; Ohio, 1809-1852 ***4511.35*** *p38*
Neable, Christian; New York, 1778 ***8529.30*** *p7*
Neaderkorn, Joseph; Ohio, 1840-1897 ***8365.35*** *p17*
Neadinn, Mary 57; Ontario, 1871 ***1823.17*** *p124*
Neagle, Jno.; St. John, N.B., 1848 ***2978.15*** *p41*
Neagle, John; St. John, N.B., 1848 ***2978.15*** *p41*
Neal, Arthur; New Orleans, 1850 ***7242.30*** *p151*
Neal, Catherine; New Orleans, 1850 ***7242.30*** *p151*
Neal, Christopher; America, 1766 ***1220.12*** *p576*
Neal, Daniel; America, 1774 ***1220.12*** *p576*
Neal, Daniel; Boston, 1737 ***1642*** *p26*
Neal, Daniel; New Orleans, 1850 ***7242.30*** *p151*
Neal, Edward; America, 1754 ***1220.12*** *p576*
Neal, Edward; Newfoundland, 1814 ***3476.10*** *p54*
Neal, Fanny; New Orleans, 1850 ***7242.30*** *p151*
Neal, Francis; New England, n.d. ***9228.50*** *p473*
Neal, George H. 40; Ontario, 1871 ***1823.21*** *p276*
Neal, Jane 48; Ontario, 1871 ***1823.21*** *p276*
Neal, John; America, 1768 ***1220.12*** *p576*
Neal, John; America, 1770 ***1220.12*** *p576*
Neal, John; New Orleans, 1851 ***7242.30*** *p151*
Neal, Laurence; New Orleans, 1850 ***7242.30*** *p151*
Neal, Lilly 13; Quebec, 1870 ***8364.32*** *p25*
Neal, Margaret; Boston, 1767 ***1642*** *p48*
Neal, Margaret; New Orleans, 1850 ***7242.30*** *p151*
Neal, Mary; Annapolis, MD, 1736 ***1220.12*** *p576*
Neal, Michael; Boston, 1766 ***1642*** *p36*
Neal, Patrick 26; Ontario, 1871 ***1823.21*** *p276*
Neal, Patrick; St. Johns, N.F., 1825 ***1053.15*** *p6*
Neal, Paul; America, 1758 ***1220.12*** *p576*
Neal, Richard 72; Ontario, 1871 ***1823.21*** *p276*
Neal, Thomas; America, 1733 ***1220.12*** *p577*
Neal, Thomas; America, 1741 ***1220.12*** *p577*
Neal, Thomas; America, 1749 ***1220.12*** *p577*
Neal, Thomas 69; Ontario, 1871 ***1823.17*** *p124*
Neal, Thomas; Virginia, 1741 ***1220.12*** *p577*
Neal, Thos 45; Ontario, 1871 ***1823.17*** *p124*
Neal, Thos; St. John, N.B., 1847 ***2978.15*** *p38*
Neal, William 62; Ontario, 1871 ***1823.21*** *p276*
Neale, Capt.; California, 1890 ***9228.50*** *p473*
Neale, Ann; Rappahannock, VA, 1741 ***1220.12*** *p576*
Neale, Anna Maria; America, 1742 ***1220.12*** *p576*
Neale, B.; New Orleans, 1850 ***7242.30*** *p151*
Neale, Charles; New Orleans, 1850 ***7242.30*** *p151*
Neale, Connell; America, 1759 ***1220.12*** *p576*
Neale, Dolly; New Orleans, 1850 ***7242.30*** *p151*
Neale, Elizabeth; Barbados, 1683 ***1220.12*** *p576*
Neale, Hannah; Barbados, 1669 ***1220.12*** *p576*
Neale, James; New Orleans, 1850 ***7242.30*** *p151*
Neale, John; America, 1743 ***1220.12*** *p576*
Neale, John; America, 1757 ***1220.12*** *p576*
Neale, John; America, 1766 ***1220.12*** *p576*
Neale, John; Barbados, 1669 ***1220.12*** *p576*
Neale, Joseph; America, 1766 ***1220.12*** *p576*
Neale, Laurence; Virginia, 1730 ***1220.12*** *p576*
Neale, Rebecca; Virginia, 1721 ***1220.12*** *p576*
Neale, Richard; America, 1769 ***1220.12*** *p576*
Neale, Richard; Virginia, 1739 ***1220.12*** *p576*
Neale, Samuel; America, 1769 ***1220.12*** *p576*
Neale, Sarah; America, 1748 ***1220.12*** *p577*
Neale, Sarah; America, 1757 ***1220.12*** *p577*
Neale, Susannah; America, 1753 ***1220.12*** *p577*
Neale, Thomas; America, 1754 ***1220.12*** *p577*
Neale, William; America, 1677 ***1220.12*** *p577*
Neale, William; America, 1739 ***1220.12*** *p577*
Neale, William; America, 1752 ***1220.12*** *p577*
Neale, William; America, 1759 ***1220.12*** *p577*
Neale, William; Virginia, 1760 ***1220.12*** *p577*
Nealer, Elizabeth; America, 1707 ***1220.12*** *p576*
Nealin, Michael; Louisiana, 1874 ***4981.45*** *p296*
Nealing, James; New York, 1776 ***8529.30*** *p3*
Nealing, Richard; Marston's Wharf, 1782 ***8529.30*** *p14*
Nealy, John; Philadelphia, 1778 ***8529.30*** *p14*
Neaman, Fritz 45; Ontario, 1871 ***1823.21*** *p276*
Near, John; Ohio, 1840-1897 ***8365.35*** *p17*
Neary, Mathew; Toronto, 1844 ***2910.35*** *p112*
Neason, Torrans; Illinois, 1861 ***6079.1*** *p10*
Neastley, John; South Carolina, 1813 ***6155.4*** *p19*
Neat, John; Ohio, 1840-1897 ***8365.35*** *p17*
Neaton, Edward; America, 1775 ***1220.12*** *p577*
Neau, Jean 13; Quebec, 1655 ***9221.17*** *p327*
Neave, John; America, 1774 ***1220.12*** *p578*
Neaves, George 60; Ontario, 1871 ***1823.21*** *p276*
Nebard, Samuel; America, 1765 ***1220.12*** *p577*
Nebauck, J.O.; New York, NY, 1844 ***6412.40*** *p148*
Nebel, Heinrich; America, 1845 ***7420.1*** *p38*
With wife & 2 children
Nebit, Frances 52; South Carolina, 1812 ***3476.30*** *p12*
Neblock, James 45; Ontario, 1871 ***1823.21*** *p276*
Neblock, John 42; Ontario, 1871 ***1823.21*** *p276*
Neblock, Joseph 58; Ontario, 1871 ***1823.21*** *p276*
Neblock, Robert 37; Ontario, 1871 ***1823.21*** *p276*
Nebors, Lewis; South Carolina, 1844 ***6155.4*** *p19*
Neborsky, John; Detroit, 1930 ***1640.60*** *p81*
Nechame, Kagan; Detroit, 1929-1930 ***6214.5*** *p61*
Nechuta, Frantisek *SEE* Nechuta, Frantisek
Nechuta, Frantisek; Wisconsin, 1853 ***2853.20*** *p303*
*Son:*Frantisek
*Son:*Karel

352 *FOR A COMPLETE EXPLANATION OF ENTRY, SEE "HOW TO READ A CITATION" SECTION*

Nechuta, Karel *SEE* Nechuta, Frantisek
Neckless, George; America, 1750 ***1220.12*** *p577*
Nedela, Frantisek; New York, NY, 1867 ***2853.20*** *p156*
Nedeli, Sebastian; Ohio, 1809-1852 ***4511.35*** *p38*
Nederhouser, Jacob; Ohio, 1809-1852 ***4511.35*** *p38*
Nedra, Louise 24; Missouri, 1845 ***778.6*** *p254*
Nedved, Frantisek; South Dakota, 1850-1910 ***2853.20*** *p246*
Nedzlnsky, Felix 24; New York, NY, 1890 ***1883.7*** *p47*
Nee, Guillaume; Quebec, 1634 ***9221.17*** *p39*
Need, William; America, 1754 ***1220.12*** *p577*
Needham, Cephas 33; Ontario, 1871 ***1823.21*** *p276*
Needham, George 52; Ontario, 1871 ***1823.17*** *p124*
Needham, James; America, 1749 ***1220.12*** *p577*
Needham, Jane 77; Ontario, 1871 ***1823.21*** *p276*
Needham, John; America, 1750 ***1220.12*** *p577*
Needham, Joseph 49; Ontario, 1871 ***1823.17*** *p124*
Needham, Richard 50; Ontario, 1871 ***1823.21*** *p276*
Needham, Thomas; America, 1749 ***1220.12*** *p577*
Needham, Thomas; Charles Town, SC, 1719 ***1220.12*** *p577*
Needham, Thomas 48; Ontario, 1871 ***1823.21*** *p276*
Needham, William; America, 1760 ***1220.12*** *p577*
Needham, William; America, 1775 ***1220.12*** *p577*
Needham, William 53; Ontario, 1871 ***1823.17*** *p125*
Needhem, Arthur; Washington, 1886 ***2770.40*** *p195*
Needs, John; America, 1685 ***1220.12*** *p577*
Needum, Mary; Barbados, 1679 ***1220.12*** *p577*
Neef, Ernst *SEE* Neef, Josef
Neef, Josef; America, 1883 ***5475.1*** *p35*
*Wife:*Katharina Beller
*Son:*Ernst
*Son:*Karl
Neef, Karl *SEE* Neef, Josef
Neef, Katharina Beller *SEE* Neef, Josef
Neel, Albert Elias; Texas, 1885 ***9228.50*** *p476*
*Wife:*Mary Hargreaves Croskell
Neel, Alfred; Montreal, 1850-1923 ***9228.50*** *p474*
Neel, Alfred; Peoria, IL, 1850-1923 ***9228.50*** *p474*
Neel, Annie Maude *SEE* Neel, Samuel Francis
Neel, Boyd Louis; Ohio, 1905-1983 ***9228.50*** *p473*
Neel, Edith Emma *SEE* Neel, Samuel Francis
Neel, Emily Sophia; Florida, 1851-1928 ***9228.50*** *p475*
Neel, Emma Jane *SEE* Neel, Samuel Francis
Neel, Florence Eliz. *SEE* Neel, Samuel Francis
Neel, Francis, Jr.; New Hampshire, 1680 ***9228.50*** *p477*
With father
Neel, Isabel Adeline *SEE* Neel, Samuel Francis
Neel, James Frederick; Texas, 1852-1916 ***9228.50*** *p475*
Neel, Lillian Gertrude *SEE* Neel, Samuel Francis
Neel, Louisa Maria; Florida, 1844-1891 ***9228.50*** *p474*
Neel, Mary Hargreaves Croskell *SEE* Neel, Albert Elias
Neel, Samuel Francis; Texas, 1873 ***9228.50*** *p473*
*Wife:*Emma Jane
*Child:*Florence Eliz.
*Child:*Lillian Gertrude
*Child:*Isabel Adeline
*Child:*Annie Maude
*Child:*Samuel Francis, Jr.
*Child:*Edith Emma
Neel, Samuel Francis, Jr. *SEE* Neel, Samuel Francis
Neeland, A. 55; South Carolina, 1812 ***3476.30*** *p12*
Neeland, Andrew; Boston, 1839 ***3274.55*** *p27*
Neeland, James 30; South Carolina, 1812 ***3476.30*** *p12*
Neelands, James; South Carolina, 1813 ***3208.30*** *p19*
Neelands, James; South Carolina, 1813 ***3208.30*** *p31*
Neeley, Mary 35; Ontario, 1871 ***1823.21*** *p276*
Neeley, Mary 71; Ontario, 1871 ***1823.21*** *p276*
Neeley, Mary; Philadelphia, 1843 ***8513.31*** *p424*
Neeley, Robert 34; Ontario, 1871 ***1823.21*** *p276*
Neeley, Samuel; South Carolina, 1813 ***3208.30*** *p18*
Neeley, Samuel; South Carolina, 1813 ***3208.30*** *p31*
Neeley, Thomas 50; Ontario, 1871 ***1823.21*** *p276*
Neelmeier, Heinrich Wilhelm; America, 1860 ***7420.1*** *p197*
Neely, John; Ohio, 1832 ***3580.20*** *p33*
Neely, John; Ohio, 1832 ***6020.12*** *p21*
Neely, Samuel 58; South Carolina, 1812 ***3476.30*** *p12*
Neely, Sarah; Philadelphia, 1853 ***8513.31*** *p304*
Nees, August 17 *SEE* Nees, Balthasar Ludwig Albrecht
Nees, Balthasar Ludwig Albrecht; America, 1833 ***2526.42*** *p127*
With wife
*Child:*Michael
*Child:*Katharina
*Child:*Friedrich
*Child:*Heinrich
*Child:*Wilhelm
*Child:*Georg
*Child:*August
Nees, Friedrich 10 *SEE* Nees, Balthasar Ludwig Albrecht
Nees, Georg 16 *SEE* Nees, Balthasar Ludwig Albrecht
Nees, Heinrich 6 *SEE* Nees, Balthasar Ludwig Albrecht
Nees, Katharina 12 *SEE* Nees, Balthasar Ludwig Albrecht
Nees, Ludwig; America, 1892 ***2526.42*** *p127*
With brother
Nees, Michael 14 *SEE* Nees, Balthasar Ludwig Albrecht
Nees, Wilhelm; America, 1834 ***2526.42*** *p127*
With wife
With child 5
Nees, Wilhelm 8 *SEE* Nees, Balthasar Ludwig Albrecht
Neesen, Joe; Nebraska, 1905 ***3004.30*** *p46*
Neeshaw, Wm. 18; Quebec, 1910 ***2897.7*** *p8*
Neff, August; America, 1881 ***2526.43*** *p176*
Neff, Chas. 30; Ontario, 1871 ***1823.17*** *p125*
Neff, Eva Margaretha 36; America, 1854 ***2526.42*** *p105*
Neff, Georg; America, 1836 ***2526.43*** *p191*
Neff, Henry; Illinois, 1858-1861 ***6020.5*** *p132*
Neff, M.E.; America, 1854 ***2526.42*** *p101*
With child
Neff, Maria; America, 1857 ***2526.43*** *p204*
Neff, Michael; America, 1881 ***2526.42*** *p97*
Neff, Philipp; America, 1853 ***2526.42*** *p101*
Negele, Carl 18; New Orleans, 1848 ***778.6*** *p254*
Negle, Thomas; America, 1747 ***1220.12*** *p577*
Negles, Jane; Boston, 1765 ***1642*** *p48*
Neglig, Valent 25; America, 1840 ***778.6*** *p254*
Negout, Jean Sebastien 16; New Orleans, 1845 ***778.6*** *p254*
Negre, Mr. 35; America, 1846 ***778.6*** *p254*
Negrier, Jean; Quebec, 1634 ***9221.17*** *p37*
Nehlig, Christi 19; America, 1847 ***778.6*** *p254*
Nehlsen, Max; Wisconsin, 1895 ***6795.8*** *p104*
Nehring, Edward 36; New York, NY, 1893 ***1883.7*** *p43*
Nehring, Ida; Wisconsin, 1901 ***6795.8*** *p229*
Nehring, Johann Sebastian; Illinois, 1852 ***6079.1*** *p10*
Nehring, John Fred; Wisconsin, 1885 ***6795.8*** *p197*
Neibel, Anna 18; Galveston, TX, 1846 ***3967.10*** *p378*
Neidemeyer, Fabian; Colorado, 1876 ***1029.59*** *p65*
Neidhardt, Gottlieb W.; Louisiana, 1841-1844 ***4981.45*** *p211*
Neidiger, Adolph; Kansas, 1887 ***1447.20*** *p63*
Neighbours, Joseph; America, 1765 ***1220.12*** *p577*
Neil, Benjamin 48; Ontario, 1871 ***1823.21*** *p276*
Neil, Benjamin 60; Ontario, 1871 ***1823.17*** *p125*
Neil, Cornelius; America, 1771 ***1220.12*** *p576*
Neil, Daniel 53; Ontario, 1871 ***1823.21*** *p276*
Neil, Daniel 60; Ontario, 1871 ***1823.21*** *p276*
Neil, Frances 45; Ontario, 1871 ***1823.21*** *p276*
Neil, Francis 68; Ontario, 1871 ***1823.21*** *p276*
Neil, Henry; New Orleans, 1850 ***7242.30*** *p151*
Neil, Henry 38; Ontario, 1871 ***1823.17*** *p125*
Neil, Isaac 37; Ontario, 1871 ***1823.21*** *p276*
Neil, James 41; Ontario, 1871 ***1823.17*** *p125*
Neil, James 58; Ontario, 1871 ***1823.21*** *p276*
Neil, John; Massachusetts, 1620-1775 ***1642*** *p138*
Neil, John; Massachusetts, 1730 ***1642*** *p91*
With wife
Neil, John; Massachusetts, 1730 ***1642*** *p91*
Neil, John 32; Ontario, 1871 ***1823.21*** *p276*
Neil, John 45; Ontario, 1871 ***1823.21*** *p276*
Neil, Margaret; New Orleans, 1850 ***7242.30*** *p151*
Neil, Pat 21; St. Johns, N.F., 1811 ***1053.20*** *p21*
Neil, Richard 50; Ontario, 1871 ***1823.21*** *p277*
Neil, Richard 65; Ontario, 1871 ***1823.21*** *p277*
Neil, Robert; Washington, 1884 ***2770.40*** *p193*
Neil, Thomas; New Orleans, 1850 ***7242.30*** *p151*
Neil, Thomas 42; Ontario, 1871 ***1823.21*** *p277*
Neil, Thomas 59; Ontario, 1871 ***1823.21*** *p277*
Neil, William 38; Ontario, 1871 ***1823.17*** *p125*
Neil, William 48; Ontario, 1871 ***1823.21*** *p277*
Neil, William 55; Ontario, 1871 ***1823.21*** *p277*
Neill, Andrew; Ohio, 1833 ***3580.20*** *p33*
Neill, Andrew; Ohio, 1833 ***6020.12*** *p21*
Neill, John; Toronto, 1844 ***2910.35*** *p112*
Neill, Philip; Louisiana, 1841-1844 ***4981.45*** *p211*
Neill, William 32; Ontario, 1871 ***1823.21*** *p277*
Neilsen, Anna Christina; St. Paul, MN, 1867 ***1865.50*** *p40*
Neilsen, Nels Borge; Oregon, 1941 ***9157.47*** *p2*
Neilson, Charles 30; New York, NY, 1835 ***5024.1*** *p136*
Neilson, David S. 31; Ontario, 1871 ***1823.21*** *p277*
Neilson, Jinnet 58; Ontario, 1871 ***1823.21*** *p277*
Neilson, Jorgen 30; Colorado, 1904 ***1029.59*** *p65*
Neilson, Neils; America, 1760 ***1220.12*** *p577*
Neilson, William 22; Ontario, 1871 ***1823.21*** *p277*
Neimi, Hannes 42; Minnesota, 1926 ***2769.54*** *p1382*
Neirengarden, Arnold; Ohio, 1809-1852 ***4511.35*** *p38*
Neirengarden, Peter; Ohio, 1809-1852 ***4511.35*** *p38*
Neis, George; Ohio, 1809-1852 ***4511.35*** *p38*
Neis, Johanna Hans *SEE* Neis, Peter
Neis, Maria Lermen *SEE* Neis, Nikolaus
Neis, Maria Lauer *SEE* Neis, Nikolaus
Neis, Nikolaus; America, 1852 ***5475.1*** *p439*
*Wife:*Maria Lermen
With 4 children
Neis, Nikolaus; Brazil, 1846 ***5475.1*** *p438*
*Wife:*Maria Lauer
With 2 children
Neis, Peter; America, 1852 ***5475.1*** *p439*
*Wife:*Johanna Hans
With 4 children
Neisius, Katharina *SEE* Neisius, Mathias
Neisius, Magdalena Deutsch *SEE* Neisius, Mathias
Neisius, Mathias *SEE* Neisius, Mathias
Neisius, Mathias; America, 1871 ***5475.1*** *p263*
*Wife:*Magdalena Deutsch
*Daughter:*Katharina
*Son:*Mathias
*Daughter:*Susanna
*Son:*Nikolaus
Neisius, Nikolaus *SEE* Neisius, Mathias
Neisius, Susanna *SEE* Neisius, Mathias
Neisznous, Christian; Ohio, 1809-1852 ***4511.35*** *p38*
Neithart, Peter; Ohio, 1809-1852 ***4511.35*** *p38*
Neitz, Friedrich Wilhelm; Port uncertain, 1858 ***7420.1*** *p180*
Neitz, Johann; America, 1893 ***7420.1*** *p369*
Neiznous, Christian; Ohio, 1809-1852 ***4511.35*** *p38*
Nekula, Jan; St. Louis, 1895 ***2853.20*** *p33*
Nell, Ann; America, 1740 ***1220.12*** *p577*
Nell, Thomas 52; Ontario, 1871 ***1823.21*** *p277*
Nelley, John; Philadelphia, 1778 ***8529.30*** *p14*
Nelligan, David; Louisiana, 1841-1844 ***4981.45*** *p211*
Nellilton, William 73; Ontario, 1871 ***1823.21*** *p277*
Nelms, Mary; America, 1772 ***1220.12*** *p577*
Nelsen, K. M.; Louisiana, 1874-1875 ***4981.45*** *p30*
Nelson, Alice *SEE* Nelson, Lena
Nelson, Alice; Maryland, 1674-1675 ***1236.25*** *p51*
Nelson, Alva Maria *SEE* Nelson, Lars E.
Nelson, Amanda; St. Paul, MN, 1894 ***1865.50*** *p98*
Nelson, Anders Peter; Iowa, 1917 ***1211.15*** *p17*
Nelson, Andrew; Iowa, 1909 ***1211.15*** *p17*
Nelson, Andrew; Washington, 1887 ***2770.40*** *p24*
Nelson, Andrew J.; Illinois, 1861 ***4487.25*** *p65*
Nelson, Andrew M.; Louisiana, 1870-1895 ***7710.1*** *p160*
Nelson, Andrew M.; New York, NY, 1870 ***7710.1*** *p160*
Nelson, Ann; America, 1753 ***1220.12*** *p577*
Nelson, Ann; America, 1763 ***1220.12*** *p577*
Nelson, Ann; Potomac, 1742 ***1220.12*** *p577*
Nelson, Anna; St. Paul, MN, 1887 ***1865.50*** *p92*
Nelson, Anna Lotta *SEE* Nelson, Lars E.
Nelson, Anna Martha; St. Paul, MN, 1902 ***1865.50*** *p98*
Nelson, Anna Mary 7; Kansas, 1880 ***777.40*** *p17*
Nelson, Aron; Colorado, 1904 ***1029.59*** *p65*
Nelson, Arvid N.; St. Paul, MN, 1900-1901 ***1865.50*** *p98*
Nelson, Asel John R.; Colorado, 1891 ***1029.59*** *p65*
Nelson, August 33; Kansas, 1879-1880 ***777.40*** *p17*
Nelson, Benjamin; Boston, 1902 ***1766.20*** *p34*
Nelson, Benjamin; Springfield, IL, 1864 ***4487.25*** *p66*
Nelson, Betty; Canada, 1863-1888 ***1865.50*** *p105*
Nelson, Betty; St. Paul, MN, 1888 ***1865.50*** *p105*
Nelson, Brigett 74; Ontario, 1871 ***1823.21*** *p277*
Nelson, Carl Erick *SEE* Nelson, Lars E.
Nelson, Carl Gustaf; Cleveland, OH, 1891-1897 ***9722.10*** *p124*
Nelson, Carl Gustaf 44; Kansas, 1869-1880 ***777.40*** *p19*
*Wife:*Mathilda Olofsdotter 33
Nelson, Carl Severin; Boston, 1905 ***1029.59*** *p65*
Nelson, Carrie; St. Paul, MN, 1874-1905 ***1865.50*** *p98*
Nelson, Catarina Anderson *SEE* Nelson, Lars E.
Nelson, Cathn 25; St. John, N.B., 1834 ***6469.7*** *p5*
Nelson, Charles; Colorado, 1891 ***1029.59*** *p65*
Nelson, Charles 30; St. John, N.B., 1834 ***6469.7*** *p5*
Nelson, Charles; Washington, 1888 ***2770.40*** *p26*
Nelson, Charles Ernst.; Colorado, 1901 ***1029.59*** *p65*
Nelson, Charles M.; Illinois, 1861 ***4487.25*** *p66*
Nelson, Charley; Cleveland, OH, 1888-1892 ***9722.10*** *p124*
Nelson, Christ; Iowa, 1896 ***1211.15*** *p17*
Nelson, Christian; Iowa, 1893 ***1211.15*** *p17*
Nelson, Christina; St. Paul, MN, 1874-1905 ***1865.50*** *p98*
Nelson, Clair 50; Ontario, 1871 ***1823.17*** *p125*
Nelson, Daniel; South Carolina, 1829 ***6155.4*** *p19*
Nelson, Edward; Cleveland, OH, 1903-1906 ***9722.10*** *p124*
Nelson, Eleanor; America, 1755 ***1220.12*** *p577*
Nelson, Elin *SEE* Nelson, Lars E.
Nelson, Ella; Minnesota, 1882-1883 ***1865.50*** *p96*
Nelson, Emma; Colorado, 1894 ***1029.59*** *p65*
Nelson, Emma; St. Paul, MN, 1874-1905 ***1865.50*** *p98*
Nelson, Erik *SEE* Nelson, Lars E.
Nelson, Erik G.; Colorado, 1884 ***1029.59*** *p65*
Nelson, Erik G.; Colorado, 1902 ***1029.59*** *p65*
Nelson, Ernest B.; Colorado, 1904 ***1029.59*** *p66*
Nelson, Everett; Miami, 1935 ***4984.12*** *p39*
Nelson, F. O.; Washington, 1884 ***2770.40*** *p193*
Nelson, Frank; St. Paul, MN, 1874-1905 ***1865.50*** *p98*
Nelson, George 51; Ontario, 1871 ***1823.21*** *p277*

Nelson, Godfrey; Philadelphia, 1902 ***6212.1*** *p13*
Nelson, Gust; Colorado, 1873 ***1029.59*** *p66*
Nelson, Gust; St. Paul, MN, 1893 ***1865.50*** *p98*
Nelson, Gustaf Emanuel *SEE* Nelson, Lars E.
Nelson, Gustaf W.; Illinois, 1861 ***4487.25*** *p66*
Nelson, Hannah Mathilda; St. Paul, MN, 1888 ***1865.50*** *p92*
Nelson, Helen *SEE* Nelson, Lena
Nelson, Henry; Annapolis, MD, 1721 ***1220.12*** *p577*
Nelson, Henry; California, 1868 ***1131.61*** *p89*
Nelson, Hezekiah 48; Ontario, 1871 ***1823.21*** *p277*
Nelson, Hilma; Minneapolis, 1881-1886 ***1865.50*** *p42*
Nelson, Hugh; America, 1739 ***1220.12*** *p577*
Nelson, Hulda Elizabeth; Cleveland, OH, 1868-1892 ***9722.10*** *p131*
Nelson, Ida; St. Paul, MN, 1892 ***1865.50*** *p110*
Nelson, Ida Fredrika; St. Paul, MN, 1889-1898 ***1865.50*** *p100*
Nelson, James; America, 1754 ***1220.12*** *p577*
Nelson, James; Iowa, 1883 ***1211.15*** *p17*
Nelson, James; New York, 1776 ***8529.30*** *p14*
Nelson, James 30; Ontario, 1871 ***1823.21*** *p277*
Nelson, James 63; Ontario, 1871 ***1823.17*** *p125*
Nelson, James S.; Washington, 1889 ***2770.40*** *p80*
Nelson, Jennie; Minnesota, 1873-1878 ***1865.50*** *p99*
Nelson, Jenny Octavia; Providence, RI, 1860-1876 ***6410.15*** *p108*
Nelson, John; America, 1689 ***1220.12*** *p577*
Nelson, John; America, 1737 ***1220.12*** *p577*
Nelson, John; America, 1761 ***1220.12*** *p577*
Nelson, John; Boston, 1775 ***8529.30*** *p4A*
Nelson, John; Cleveland, OH, 1854-1858 ***9722.10*** *p124*
Nelson, John; Cleveland, OH, 1902-1904 ***9722.10*** *p124*
Nelson, John *SEE* Nelson, Lena
Nelson, John; Jamaica, 1783 ***8529.30*** *p13A*
Nelson, John 22; Kansas, 1880 ***777.40*** *p20*
Nelson, John; New York, NY, 1902 ***1029.59*** *p1A*
Nelson, John; Ohio, 1842 ***2763.1*** *p20*
Nelson, John 31; Ontario, 1871 ***1823.17*** *p125*
Nelson, John; South Carolina, 1811 ***6155.4*** *p19*
Nelson, John *SEE* Nelson, Lars E.
Nelson, John; Washington, 1889 ***2770.40*** *p80*
Nelson, John C.; Washington, 1886 ***2770.40*** *p195*
Nelson, John Nicholas; St. Paul, MN, 1885 ***1865.50*** *p99*
Nelson, John W.; Chicago, 1864 ***4487.25*** *p66*
Nelson, Joseph; Barbados, 1665 ***1220.12*** *p577*
Nelson, Julia; St. Paul, MN, 1894 ***1865.50*** *p99*
Nelson, Julius; Colorado, 1893 ***1029.59*** *p66*
Nelson, Lars E.; St. Paul, MN, 1886 ***1865.50*** *p99*
*Wife:*Catarina Anderson
*Child:*John
*Child:*Elin
*Child:*Erik
*Child:*Gustaf Emanuel
*Child:*Alva Maria
*Child:*Carl Erick
*Child:*Anna Lotta
Nelson, Lena; Colorado, 1902-1917 ***1029.59*** *p66*
Nelson, Lena; Colorado, 1917 ***1029.59*** *p66*
*Child:*Per Gunar
*Child:*John
*Child:*Mary
*Child:*Helen
*Child:*Alice
Nelson, Lewis; Iowa, 1893 ***1211.15*** *p17*
Nelson, Louis; Illinois, 1861 ***4487.25*** *p66*
Nelson, Magnus M.; Illinois, 1861 ***4487.25*** *p66*
Nelson, Margt 3 months; St. John, N.B., 1834 ***6469.7*** *p5*
Nelson, Maria; Boston, 1881-1883 ***1865.50*** *p99*
Nelson, Mary *SEE* Nelson, Lena
Nelson, Mary; Minnesota, 1899 ***1865.50*** *p99*
Nelson, Mathilda Olofsdotter 33 *SEE* Nelson, Carl Gustaf
Nelson, Michael T.; Washington, 1889 ***2770.40*** *p80*
Nelson, N.J.; Louisiana, 1887 ***7710.1*** *p161*
Nelson, Nellie; St. Paul, MN, 1881 ***1865.50*** *p51*
Nelson, Nels; America, 1856 ***4487.25*** *p67*
With mother & siblings
Nelson, Nels; Colorado, 1892 ***1029.59*** *p66*
Nelson, Nils John; Cleveland, OH, 1890-1897 ***9722.10*** *p124*
Nelson, Olaf N.; Washington, 1887 ***2770.40*** *p25*
Nelson, Ole P.; Washington, 1886 ***2770.40*** *p195*
Nelson, Olga; St. Paul, MN, 1895 ***1865.50*** *p98*
Nelson, Olof; Iowa, 1881-1887 ***1865.50*** *p99*
Nelson, Olof; Iowa, 1886 ***1029.59*** *p66*
Nelson, Olof Christoffer; St. Paul, MN, 1896 ***1865.50*** *p99*
Nelson, Olof Gustaf; St. Paul, MN, 1902 ***1865.50*** *p99*
Nelson, Otto 15; New York, NY, 1894 ***6512.1*** *p184*
Nelson, P.O.; St. Paul, MN, 1893-1896 ***1865.50*** *p99*
Nelson, Per Gunar *SEE* Nelson, Lena
Nelson, Peter; America, 1771 ***1220.12*** *p577*
Nelson, Peter; Washington, 1889 ***2770.40*** *p80*
Nelson, Mrs. Peter A.; St. Paul, MN, 1874-1905 ***1865.50*** *p99*
Nelson, Peter Christian; Iowa, 1911 ***1211.15*** *p17*
Nelson, Peter E.; St. Paul, MN, 1867 ***1865.50*** *p99*
Nelson, Peter O.; Colorado, 1889 ***1029.59*** *p66*
Nelson, Peter O.; Colorado, 1895 ***1029.59*** *p66*
Nelson, Richard; America, 1719 ***1220.12*** *p577*
Nelson, Richard W.; Illinois, 1834-1900 ***6020.5*** *p132*
Nelson, Robert; Annapolis, MD, 1720 ***1220.12*** *p577*
Nelson, Robert; Cleveland, OH, 1897-1904 ***9722.10*** *p124*
Nelson, Robert; Iowa, 1890 ***1211.15*** *p17*
Nelson, Robert; South Carolina, 1813 ***6155.4*** *p19*
Nelson, Samuel; Kansas, 1868-1873 ***777.40*** *p16*
Nelson, Sara; St. Paul, MN, 1896 ***1865.50*** *p99*
Nelson, Severin; Cleveland, OH, 1900-1902 ***9722.10*** *p124*
Nelson, Swen A.; Illinois, 1861 ***4487.25*** *p67*
Nelson, Theodore Wilhehn; Boston, 1896 ***1766:20*** *p27*
Nelson, Theofel; Colorado, 1893 ***1029.59*** *p66*
Nelson, Theofel E.; Colorado, 1893 ***1029.59*** *p66*
Nelson, Thomas; America, 1772 ***1220.12*** *p578*
Nelson, Thomas; America, 1775 ***1220.12*** *p578*
Nelson, Thomas; Annapolis, MD, 1720 ***1220.12*** *p578*
Nelson, Victor; Illinois, 1861 ***4487.25*** *p67*
Nelson, Weste; Illinois, 1861 ***4487.25*** *p67*
Nelson, William; America, 1745 ***1220.12*** *p578*
Nelson, William; Barbados, 1665 ***1220.12*** *p578*
Nelson, William; Barbados, 1671 ***1220.12*** *p578*
Nelson, William 51; Ontario, 1871 ***1823.21*** *p277*
Nelson, Wm.; California, 1868 ***1131.61*** *p89*
Nelson-Palmer, Ann; Newfoundland, 1845-1945 ***9228.50*** *p174*
Nelson-Palmer, Eveline Wade *SEE* Nelson-Palmer, Frank Thomas
Nelson-Palmer, Frank Geoffrey *SEE* Nelson-Palmer, John Charles
Nelson-Palmer, Frank Thomas; Canada, 1923 ***9228.50*** *p174*
*Son:*Peter Robert
*Wife:*Eveline Wade
Nelson-Palmer, John Charles; Vancouver, B.C., 1910-1912 ***9228.50*** *p175*
*Wife:*Nora Marjorie Christie
*Son:*Frank Geoffrey
Nelson-Palmer, Nora Marjorie Christie *SEE* Nelson-Palmer, John Charles
Nelson-Palmer, Peter Robert *SEE* Nelson-Palmer, Frank Thomas
Nelsson, Ernst Algot; Cleveland, OH, 1902-1903 ***9722.10*** *p124*
Nemec, Frantisek; Omaha, NE, 1871 ***2853.20*** *p190*
*Wife:*Marie
Nemec, Marie *SEE* Nemec, Frantisek
Nemminger, Jn. Gges. 29; Louisiana, 1848 ***778.6*** *p254*
Nenburger, Hugo 21; America, 1840 ***778.6*** *p254*
Nepardeau, Jean 32; Quebec, 1658 ***9221.17*** *p385*
Neporte, Louis; Illinois, 1918 ***6007.60*** *p9*
Nepoty, Xavier; Illinois, 1852 ***6079.1*** *p10*
Nepper, Jacob; Ohio, 1809-1852 ***4511.35*** *p38*
Neptune, Ann; America, 1767 ***1220.12*** *p578*
Nepveu, Francois 21; Quebec, 1659 ***9221.17*** *p407*
*Brother:*Philippe 24
Nepveu, Jean; Quebec, 1645 ***9221.17*** *p156*
Nepveu, Philippe 24 *SEE* Nepveu, Francois
Nepveu, Pierre; Montreal, 1652 ***9221.17*** *p268*
Nepveu, Pierre 13; Montreal, 1659 ***9221.17*** *p425*
Nequalano, Joseph Helaire; Louisiana, 1874 ***4981.45*** *p133*
Nerbclin, C. A.; Louisiana, 1874 ***4981.45*** *p296*
Nerbert, Mr. 44; America, 1846 ***778.6*** *p254*
Neret, Pierre; Montreal, 1642 ***9221.17*** *p124*
Nerge, Mr.; Port uncertain, 1858 ***7420.1*** *p180*
Nerge, Anne Sophie Caroline *SEE* Nerge, Friedrich Christian
Nerge, Carl; America, 1855 ***7420.1*** *p140*
Nerge, Ernst Heinrich Wilhelm; America, 1889 ***7420.1*** *p359*
Nerge, Friedrich Christian; America, 1850 ***7420.1*** *p74*
*Wife:*Sophie Charlotte Thies
*Daughter:*Anne Sophie Caroline
*Son:*Johann Heinrich Wilhelm
Nerge, Hanne Sophie Charl.; America, 1851 ***7420.1*** *p81*
Nerge, Hanne Sophie Charl.; America, 1851 ***7420.1*** *p81*
Nerge, Johann Heinrich Wilhelm *SEE* Nerge, Friedrich Christian
Nerge, Sophie Charlotte Thies *SEE* Nerge, Friedrich Christian
Nering, Frank; Detroit, 1929-1930 ***6214.5*** *p70*
Nerman, Nelson 22; Ohio, 1880 ***4879.40*** *p257*
Nero, Dietrich; America, 1846 ***7420.1*** *p46*
With wife & 4 sons
Nero, Heinrich; America, 1846 ***7420.1*** *p46*
Nerring, Edward; New York, 1860 ***358.56*** *p3*
Nesbit, Frances 52; South Carolina, 1812 ***3476.30*** *p12*
Nesbit, John 56; Ontario, 1871 ***1823.21*** *p277*
Nesbit, William 65; Ontario, 1871 ***1823.21*** *p277*
Nesbitt, Elizabeth; America, 1751 ***1220.12*** *p578*
Nesbitt, James; America, 1752 ***1220.12*** *p578*
Nesbitt, James; America, 1764 ***1220.12*** *p578*
Nesbitt, William; America, 1767 ***1220.12*** *p578*
Nesbitt, William 57; Ontario, 1871 ***1823.17*** *p125*
Nescel, Michael; Illinois, 1858 ***6079.1*** *p10*
Nesel, Philip; Illinois, 1858 ***6079.1*** *p10*
Neser, Christian 18; America, 1847 ***778.6*** *p254*
Nesladek, Vaclav; Nebraska, 1867 ***2853.20*** *p168*
Nesper, Gottlieb 48; New York, NY, 1893 ***1883.7*** *p42*
Nesper, Theresia 14; New York, NY, 1893 ***1883.7*** *p42*
Ness, Christine 21; Quebec, 1870 ***8364.32*** *p25*
Ness, Knutt; Kansas, 1886 ***1447.20*** *p64*
Ness, Ole; Kansas, 1893 ***1447.20*** *p65*
Ness, Ole 26; Kansas, 1892 ***1447.20*** *p62*
Nesser, Nicolas 26; New Orleans, 1846 ***778.6*** *p254*
Nesses, Juan Simon; Puerto Rico, 1811 ***3476.25*** *p113*
Nesson, John; Maryland, 1719 ***1220.12*** *p578*
Nest, Emil Theodor; Wisconsin, 1896 ***6795.8*** *p118*
Nest, Gustav Julius; Wisconsin, 1888 ***6795.8*** *p118*
Nest, John; Maryland, 1719 ***1220.12*** *p578*
Nest, Katharina 25; America, 1871 ***5475.1*** *p72*
Nestor, Hannorah 80; Ontario, 1871 ***1823.21*** *p277*
Nestor, John 40; Ontario, 1871 ***1823.17*** *p125*
Netardus, Alois Petr; Texas, 1895 ***2853.20*** *p75*
Nethercliffe, John; America, 1733 ***1220.12*** *p578*
Nethercliffe, William; America, 1752 ***1220.12*** *p578*
Nethercote, John; America, 1737 ***1220.12*** *p578*
Nethercott, John 50; Ontario, 1871 ***1823.21*** *p277*
Netherton, John 37; Ontario, 1871 ***1823.21*** *p277*
Netherwood, Charles; North Carolina, 1852 ***1088.45*** *p25*
Netherwood, William; Maryland, 1736 ***1220.12*** *p578*
Netheway, Elizabeth; America, 1724 ***1220.12*** *p578*
Nette, Francis; New York, 1859 ***358.56*** *p54*
Netter, Abraham 24; America, 1847 ***778.6*** *p254*
Netter, Adolphe 23; New Orleans, 1748 ***778.6*** *p254*
Nettleton, John; America, 1684 ***1220.12*** *p578*
Nettmann, Charles; Illinois, 1854 ***6079.1*** *p10*
Nettway, John 21; Michigan, 1880 ***4491.33*** *p16*
Netz, Johann 19; Galveston, TX, 1846 ***3967.10*** *p378*
Netz, Joseph 49; Galveston, TX, 1846 ***3967.10*** *p378*
Netz, Walburga 40; Galveston, TX, 1846 ***3967.10*** *p378*
Netzhammer, Frank; Louisiana, 1874 ***4981.45*** *p133*
Neu, Adolf; America, 1899 ***5475.1*** *p20*
Neu, Adolph; America, 1893 ***2526.43*** *p176*
Neu, Bernhard; Ohio, 1809-1852 ***4511.35*** *p38*
Neu, Daniel 35; America, 1865 ***5475.1*** *p562*
*Wife:*M. Elisabeth Haupert 35
*Daughter:*Katharina 3
Neu, Jakob; America, 1866 ***5475.1*** *p556*
Neu, Johann Friedrich; America, 1852 ***5475.1*** *p556*
Neu, Johann Nikolaus; America, 1852 ***5475.1*** *p556*
Neu, Katharina; America, 1869 ***5475.1*** *p289*
Neu, Katharina 3 *SEE* Neu, Daniel
Neu, M. Elisabeth Haupert 35 *SEE* Neu, Daniel
Neu, Marg. Elisabeth; America, 1863 ***5475.1*** *p557*
Neu, Margarethe; America, 1877 ***5475.1*** *p452*
Neu, Marianne 52; Mississippi, 1847 ***778.6*** *p254*
Neu, Michael; Ohio, 1809-1852 ***4511.35*** *p38*
Neu, Philipp 25; America, 1836 ***5475.1*** *p65*
Neu, Valentine; Ohio, 1809-1852 ***4511.35*** *p38*
Neuahan, Michal; Colorado, 1873 ***1029.59*** *p66*
Neubal, N. 51; America, 1846 ***778.6*** *p254*
Neubaner, Joseph 60; America, 1846 ***778.6*** *p254*
Neubauer, Amelie 9 months; New York, NY, 1874 ***6954.7*** *p38*
Neubauer, Caroline 13; New York, NY, 1874 ***6954.7*** *p38*
Neubauer, Conrad 20; New York, NY, 1874 ***6954.7*** *p38*
Neubauer, Emilie Juliane; Wisconsin, 1894 ***6795.8*** *p67*
Neubauer, Ferdinand 8; New York, NY, 1874 ***6954.7*** *p38*
Neubauer, Fr.; New York, 1859 ***358.56*** *p55*
Neubauer, Francis; Ohio, 1809-1852 ***4511.35*** *p38*
Neubauer, Franz; Ohio, 1809-1852 ***4511.35*** *p38*
Neubauer, Friedrich 10; New York, NY, 1874 ***6954.7*** *p38*
Neubauer, Friedrich 33; New York, NY, 1874 ***6954.7*** *p38*
Neubauer, Karoline 32; New York, NY, 1874 ***6954.7*** *p38*
Neubauer, Nicolas 35; Mississippi, 1847 ***778.6*** *p254*
Neuberger, Martin; New York, 1860 ***358.56*** *p5*
Neubert, Bedrich; Texas, 1897 ***2853.20*** *p70*
Neubert, Eva Margarete; America, 1867 ***7919.3*** *p524*
Neubeser, Anne 17; Missouri, 1846 ***778.6*** *p254*
Neucomb, Joseph A.; Colorado, 1894 ***1029.59*** *p67*
Neudacher, Anastasie 45; Port uncertain, 1846 ***778.6*** *p254*
Neudacher, Artoise 6; Port uncertain, 1846 ***778.6*** *p255*

354 *FOR A COMPLETE EXPLANATION OF ENTRY, SEE "HOW TO READ A CITATION" SECTION*

Neudacher, Baptiste 45; Port uncertain, 1846 ***778.6*** *p255*
Neudacher, Barb..a 17; Port uncertain, 1846 ***778.6*** *p255*
Neudacher, Clara 7; Port uncertain, 1846 ***778.6*** *p255*
Neudacher, Marianne 22; Port uncertain, 1846 ***778.6*** *p255*
Neudacher, Peter 3; Port uncertain, 1846 ***778.6*** *p255*
Neudacher, Teresse 15; Port uncertain, 1846 ***778.6*** *p255*
Neudacher, Victor 5; Port uncertain, 1846 ***778.6*** *p255*
Neuendorf, August; New York, 1860 ***358.56*** *p5*
Neuer, Charles; Ohio, 1809-1852 ***4511.35*** *p38*
Neuf, Simon 38; New Orleans, 1848 ***778.6*** *p255*
Neuf, Victorine 18; New Orleans, 1848 ***778.6*** *p255*
Neufeld, Jacob 34; New York, NY, 1893 ***1883.7*** *p40*
Neufeld, Katharina 25; New York, NY, 1893 ***1883.7*** *p40*
Neugebauer, Frank; Detroit, 1930 ***1640.60*** *p76*
Neuhand, Georg 23; America, 1847 ***778.6*** *p255*
Neuhaus, Caroline; America, 1845 ***7420.1*** *p38*
Neukirsch, Conrad; Louisiana, 1836-1841 ***4981.45*** *p209*
Neukom, Conrad; Washington, 1887 ***2770.40*** *p25*
Neumann, Adelle 22; America, 1843 ***778.6*** *p255*
Neumann, Adolph 19; Portland, ME, 1912 ***970.38*** *p80*
Neumann, Andreas; America, 1867 ***7919.3*** *p534*
With sister
Neumann, August 38; Halifax, N.S., 1902 ***1860.4*** *p41*
Neumann, Bernhard 45; New York, NY, 1893 ***1883.7*** *p40*
Neumann, Bernhardt 20; New York, NY, 1893 ***1883.7*** *p40*
Neumann, C. G.; Valdivia, Chile, 1850 ***1192.4*** *p49*
With wife
With child 1
Neumann, Emma; Wisconsin, 1883 ***6795.8*** *p52*
Neumann, Helene 45; New York, NY, 1893 ***1883.7*** *p40*
Neumann, Helene Maria; America, 1867 ***7919.3*** *p534*
Neumann, Jacob; America, 1867 ***7919.3*** *p534*
Neumann, Jan N. 23; Philadelphia, 1834-1835 ***2853.20*** *p124*
Neumann, Johan 10; New York, NY, 1893 ***1883.7*** *p40*
Neumann, Julius; Valdivia, Chile, 1850 ***1192.4*** *p49*
Neumann, Karel; Chicago, 1894 ***2853.20*** *p415*
Neumann, Moise; New Orleans, 1840 ***778.6*** *p255*
Neumann, Peter 4; New York, NY, 1893 ***1883.7*** *p40*
Neumann, Philipp; Wisconsin, 1865 ***6795.8*** *p235*
Neumann, Susanne; America, 1867 ***7919.3*** *p534*
Neumeier, Robert; America, 1865 ***5475.1*** *p49*
Neumeister, Leonard; New Jersey, 1784-1786 ***927.31*** *p3*
Neumeyer, Johann; New York, 1892 ***5475.1*** *p169*
Neuner, Johann 16; America, 1871 ***5475.1*** *p418*
Neurath, Karoline; America, 1833 ***2526.42*** *p128*
With mother
Neurath, Luise; America, 1833 ***2526.42*** *p128*
With daughter
Neurohr, Catherine 10; Missouri, 1845 ***778.6*** *p255*
Neurohr, Christine 9; Missouri, 1845 ***778.6*** *p255*
Neurohr, Christine 49; Missouri, 1845 ***778.6*** *p255*
Neurohr, Gertrude 15; Missouri, 1845 ***778.6*** *p255*
Neurohr, Johann 26; America, 1871 ***5475.1*** *p50*
Neurohr, Lorenz 20; Missouri, 1845 ***778.6*** *p255*
Neurohr, Marguerite 10; Missouri, 1845 ***778.6*** *p255*
Neurohr, Paulas 48; Missouri, 1845 ***778.6*** *p255*
Neurzig, Michael; Illinois, 1834-1900 ***6020.5*** *p132*
Neuse, August; America, 1867 ***7919.3*** *p533*
Neusel, Hermann August; America, 1852 ***7420.1*** *p94*
Neusius, Jakob; America, 1874 ***5475.1*** *p324*
Neusius, Katharina; America, 1874 ***5475.1*** *p362*
Neusius, Magdalena 13 *SEE* Neusius, Nikolaus
Neusius, Margarethe; America, 1865 ***5475.1*** *p360*
Neusius, Maria Pfeifer 56 *SEE* Neusius, Nikolaus
Neusius, Nikolaus; New York, 1874 ***5475.1*** *p350*
*Wife:*Maria Pfeifer
*Daughter:*Magdalena
Neusse, Joseph 25; America, 1843 ***778.6*** *p255*
Neussel, Mr.; America, 1886 ***7420.1*** *p351*
Neussel, Ernst Ludwig Ferdinand; America, 1849 ***7420.1*** *p66*
Neussel, Hermann August; America, 1852 ***7420.1*** *p94*
Neustadt, Antonin; St. Louis, 1850-1851 ***2853.20*** *p21*
Neustel, Georg; America, 1889 ***179.55*** *p19*
Neuville, Leopold; New York, NY, 1871 ***1494.21*** *p31*
Neuwegen, Marie; New York, 1859 ***358.56*** *p99*
Neuwirth, Frantisek; Wisconsin, 1856 ***2853.20*** *p344*
Neuzil, Josef; Chicago, 1888 ***2853.20*** *p417*
Neuzil, Prokop 13; Baltimore, 1874 ***2853.20*** *p431*
With parents
Nevala, Ina 18; Minnesota, 1925 ***2769.54*** *p1380*
Nevala, Laina 16; Minnesota, 1925 ***2769.54*** *p1380*
Neve, John; America, 1753 ***1220.12*** *p578*
Neve, Samuel; Barbados, 1682 ***1220.12*** *p578*
Nevell, John; America, 1756 ***1220.12*** *p578*
Nevell, John; Rappahannock, VA, 1726 ***1220.12*** *p578*
Nevell, Mary; Maryland, 1674-1675 ***1236.25*** *p52*
Nevers, Thomas; America, 1772 ***1220.12*** *p578*
Neves, Daniel; America, 1739 ***1220.12*** *p578*
Neves, Thomas; Virginia, 1726 ***1220.12*** *p578*
Nevil, Micheal; Boston, 1753 ***1642*** *p31*
Nevile, Cavandish 35; Ontario, 1871 ***1823.17*** *p125*
Nevile, Henry; North Carolina, 1850 ***1088.45*** *p25*
Nevile, Rich 40; St. Johns, N.F., 1811 ***1053.20*** *p20*
Nevill, Eleanor; America, 1766 ***1220.12*** *p578*
Nevill, Katherine; Barbados, 1681 ***1220.12*** *p578*
Nevill, Mary; Barbados, 1674 ***1220.12*** *p578*
Nevill, Mary; Maryland, 1674-1675 ***1236.25*** *p52*
Nevill, Mayes; America, 1770 ***1220.12*** *p578*
Nevill, Thomas; Annapolis, MD, 1731 ***1220.12*** *p578*
Nevill, Thomas 75; Ontario, 1871 ***1823.17*** *p125*
Neville, Joseph; New York, NY, 1856 ***1494.20*** *p12*
Neville, Michael; Newfoundland, 1814 ***3476.10*** *p54*
Neville, Robert 44; Ontario, 1871 ***1823.21*** *p277*
Nevilles, Louis 66; Ontario, 1871 ***1823.21*** *p277*
Nevils, John 28; Ontario, 1871 ***1823.21*** *p277*
Nevin, William 45; Ontario, 1871 ***1823.21*** *p277*
Nevinson, John; Barbados, 1679 ***1220.12*** *p578*
Nevirets, Theodore 45; Port uncertain, 1846 ***778.6*** *p255*
Nevison, Margaret; Barbados, 1669 ***1220.12*** *p578*
New, Elizabeth 8; Quebec, 1870 ***8364.32*** *p25*
New, Emily 14; Quebec, 1870 ***8364.32*** *p25*
New, Richard; America, 1731 ***1220.12*** *p578*
Newall, Thomas; America, 1764 ***1220.12*** *p578*
Newbald, John; America, 1714 ***1220.12*** *p579*
Newbee, Edward; America, 1750 ***1220.12*** *p579*
Newbell, Joseph; America, 1753 ***1220.12*** *p578*
Newbergh, Aaron 29; Ontario, 1871 ***1823.21*** *p277*
Newberry, Edward; Barbados, 1682 ***1220.12*** *p578*
Newberry, Elizabeth; America, 1745 ***1220.12*** *p578*
Newberry, Elizabeth; Virginia, 1756 ***1220.12*** *p578*
Newberry, Jacob; America, 1700 ***1220.12*** *p578*
Newberry, James; America, 1740 ***1220.12*** *p578*
Newberry, Joane; America, 1720 ***1220.12*** *p578*
Newberry, John; Virginia, 1772 ***1220.12*** *p578*
Newberry, Joseph; America, 1685 ***1220.12*** *p578*
Newberry, Mary 77; Michigan, 1880 ***4491.30*** *p23*
Newberry, Robert; America, 1738 ***1220.12*** *p578*
Newberry, Robert; America, 1741 ***1220.12*** *p579*
Newberry, Robert; America, 1759 ***1220.12*** *p579*
Newberry, Thomas; America, 1734 ***1220.12*** *p579*
Newbert, Ann; America, 1759 ***1220.12*** *p579*
Newbery, Edward; Barbados or St. Christopher, 1780 ***8529.30*** *p7A*
Newbiggin, John 56; Ontario, 1871 ***1823.21*** *p277*
Newbold, Caroline 11; Quebec, 1870 ***8364.32*** *p25*
Newbold, Selina 13; Quebec, 1870 ***8364.32*** *p25*
Newbole, Henry; Virginia, 1732 ***1220.12*** *p579*
Newbolt, William; Barbados or Jamaica, 1700 ***1220.12*** *p579*
Newborn, Joseph 26; Ontario, 1871 ***1823.17*** *p125*
Newborn, Thomas; America, 1746 ***1220.12*** *p579*
Newborne, James; Annapolis, MD, 1725 ***1220.12*** *p579*
Newbound, Thomas; America, 1774 ***1220.12*** *p579*
Newbound, William; America, 1774 ***1220.12*** *p579*
Newbowl, George; America, 1751 ***1220.12*** *p579*
Newbrech, Michael; Illinois, 1852 ***6079.1*** *p10*
Newburg, Joseph; Louisiana, 1874 ***4981.45*** *p133*
Newburgh, Reka 69; Ontario, 1871 ***1823.21*** *p277*
Newby, Bever; Maryland, 1737 ***1220.12*** *p579*
Newby, Elizabeth; America, 1750 ***1220.12*** *p579*
Newby, Godfrey; America, 1770 ***1220.12*** *p579*
Newby, James; Virginia, 1736 ***1220.12*** *p579*
Newby, John; America, 1738 ***1220.12*** *p579*
Newby, Sarah; America, 1755 ***1220.12*** *p579*
Newby, Thomas; America, 1749 ***1220.12*** *p579*
Newby, William 23; Kansas, 1888 ***1447.20*** *p62*
Newcomb, Elisha; America, 1749 ***1220.12*** *p579*
Newcomb, Enoch L.; Colorado, 1894 ***1029.59*** *p67*
Newcomb, John; Cleveland, OH, 1851-1856 ***9722.10*** *p124*
Newcomb, Joseph A.; Colorado, 1880 ***1029.59*** *p67*
Newcomb, Joseph A.; Colorado, 1894 ***1029.59*** *p67*
Newcomb, Mary; Rappahannock, VA, 1741 ***1220.12*** *p579*
Newcomb, Mercy; Nova Scotia, 1743-1817 ***9228.50*** *p107*
Newcomb, Timothy; Virginia, 1740 ***1220.12*** *p579*
Newcombe, Andrew 25; Ontario, 1871 ***1823.21*** *p277*
Newcombe, Frances; America, 1769 ***1220.12*** *p579*
Newcombe, J. B. 43; Ontario, 1871 ***1823.17*** *p125*
Newcombe, John; Virginia, 1730 ***1220.12*** *p579*
Newcombe, Joseph; America, 1723 ***1220.12*** *p579*
Newcombe, Robert; America, 1766 ***1220.12*** *p579*
Newcombe, Robert; Died enroute, 1729 ***1220.12*** *p579*
Newcombe, Samuel; America, 1765 ***1220.12*** *p579*
Newcombe, William; America, 1765 ***1220.12*** *p579*
Newdale, Robert; America, 1726 ***1220.12*** *p579*
Newel, John 49; Ontario, 1871 ***1823.17*** *p125*
Newel, Robert 65; Ontario, 1871 ***1823.21*** *p278*
Newel, Robert James 40; Ontario, 1871 ***1823.21*** *p278*
Neweleky, Max 20; New York, NY, 1894 ***6512.1*** *p229*
Newell, Alexander 52; Ontario, 1871 ***1823.17*** *p125*
Newell, Ann *SEE* Newell, William
Newell, Bridget *SEE* Newell, William
Newell, Catharine Kiley *SEE* Newell, William
Newell, Elizabeth; America, 1745 ***1220.12*** *p579*
Newell, Francis; America, 1721 ***1220.12*** *p579*
Newell, Henry; Marston's Wharf, 1782 ***8529.30*** *p14*
Newell, Isabella; America, 1734 ***1220.12*** *p579*
Newell, James; America, 1773 ***1220.12*** *p579*
Newell, John; America, 1739 ***1220.12*** *p579*
Newell, John; America, 1775 ***1220.12*** *p579*
Newell, Katherine; Jamaica, 1663 ***1220.12*** *p579*
Newell, Luke; America, 1739 ***1220.12*** *p579*
Newell, Richard; America, 1750 ***1220.12*** *p579*
Newell, Sarah; Barbados or Jamaica, 1694 ***1220.12*** *p579*
Newell, Sarah; Rappahannock, VA, 1728 ***1220.12*** *p579*
Newell, Thomas *SEE* Newell, William
Newell, William; America, 1746 ***1220.12*** *p580*
Newell, William; Annapolis, MD, 1732 ***1220.12*** *p579*
Newell, William; Philadelphia, 1868 ***8513.31*** *p418*
*Wife:*Catharine Kiley
*Child:*Ann
*Child:*Thomas
*Child:*Bridget
Newell, William; Virginia, 1735 ***1220.12*** *p580*
Newerbury, I.H.; Illinois, 1858-1861 ***6020.5*** *p132*
Newett, John T.; Philadelphia, 1859 ***5720.10*** *p378*
Newey, John; America, 1678 ***1220.12*** *p580*
Newey, John; America, 1683 ***1220.12*** *p580*
Newey, John; America, 1769 ***1220.12*** *p580*
Newey, John; America, 1771 ***1220.12*** *p580*
Newey, Margaret; Barbados or Jamaica, 1677 ***1220.12*** *p580*
Newey, Thomas; Marston's Wharf, 1782 ***8529.30*** *p14*
Newey, William; America, 1679 ***1220.12*** *p580*
Newgent, Edward; Barbados or Jamaica, 1687 ***1220.12*** *p589*
Newgent, Lydia; Boston, 1752 ***1642*** *p47*
Newhahn, Frederick; Ohio, 1809-1852 ***4511.35*** *p38*
Newham, John; America, 1697 ***1220.12*** *p580*
Newholm, John F.; Ohio, 1809-1852 ***4511.35*** *p38*
Newhouse, Cornelius; America, 1752 ***1220.12*** *p580*
Newhouse, Joseph; Barbados, 1690 ***1220.12*** *p580*
Newhouse, Seth 99; Ontario, 1871 ***1823.21*** *p278*
Newill, Margaret; America, 1741 ***1220.12*** *p579*
Newington, Robert; America, 1763 ***1220.12*** *p580*
Newington, Sarah; Potomac, 1729 ***1220.12*** *p580*
Newins, Letitia; America, 1773 ***1220.12*** *p580*
Newland, Henry; America, 1774 ***1220.12*** *p580*
Newland, James; America, 1742 ***1220.12*** *p580*
Newland, James; America, 1770 ***1220.12*** *p580*
Newland, James; America, 1772 ***1220.12*** *p580*
Newland, John; America, 1719 ***1220.12*** *p580*
Newland, John; America, 1731 ***1220.12*** *p580*
Newland, John; Massachusetts, 1657 ***1642*** *p90*
Newland, William; America, 1771 ***1220.12*** *p580*
Newland, William; Massachusetts, 1657 ***1642*** *p90*
Newlands, John; Havana, 1782 ***8529.30*** *p10A*
Newlove, Sarah; America, 1740 ***1220.12*** *p580*
Newman, Agnes 56; Ontario, 1871 ***1823.21*** *p278*
Newman, Ann; America, 1737 ***1220.12*** *p580*
Newman, Ann; America, 1774 ***1220.12*** *p580*
Newman, Bridget; America, 1756 ***1220.12*** *p580*
Newman, Daniel; America, 1740 ***1220.12*** *p580*
Newman, Edward; America, 1753 ***1220.12*** *p580*
Newman, Edward; America, 1773 ***1220.12*** *p580*
Newman, Edward E. 49; Ontario, 1871 ***1823.21*** *p278*
Newman, Elias 30; Ontario, 1871 ***1823.21*** *p278*
Newman, Elizabeth; Annapolis, MD, 1723 ***1220.12*** *p580*
Newman, Henry; America, 1675 ***1220.12*** *p580*
Newman, Jacob; Detroit, 1929 ***1640.55*** *p113*
Newman, James; America, 1766 ***1220.12*** *p580*
Newman, Jane; America, 1764 ***1220.12*** *p580*
Newman, Janet 42; Ontario, 1871 ***1823.21*** *p278*
Newman, John; America, 1664 ***1220.12*** *p580*
Newman, John; America, 1753 ***1220.12*** *p580*
Newman, John; Died enroute, 1726 ***1220.12*** *p580*
Newman, John; North Carolina, 1854 ***1088.45*** *p25*
Newman, John; Virginia, 1774 ***1220.12*** *p580*
Newman, John Thomas; America, 1767 ***1220.12*** *p580*
Newman, Joseph; America, 1731 ***1220.12*** *p580*
Newman, Joseph; North Carolina, 1853 ***1088.45*** *p25*
Newman, Joseph 30; Ontario, 1871 ***1823.21*** *p278*
Newman, Joseph 73; Ontario, 1871 ***1823.21*** *p278*
Newman, Joseph; Quebec, 1870 ***8364.32*** *p25*
Newman, Margaret Blampied; Ohio, 1834 ***9228.50*** *p119*
Newman, Maria; America, 1752 ***1220.12*** *p580*
Newman, Mary; Barbados or Jamaica, 1697 ***1220.12*** *p580*
Newman, Michael; America, 1764 ***1220.12*** *p580*
Newman, Michael 37; New York, NY, 1849 ***6178.50*** *p152*
Newman, Michael; Virginia, 1736 ***1220.12*** *p580*
Newman, Nash; America, 1771 ***1220.12*** *p580*

Newman, Richard; America, 1740 ***1220.12*** *p581*
Newman, Richard; Charles Town, SC, 1718 ***1220.12*** *p580*
Newman, Rob; Virginia, 1652 ***6254.4*** *p243*
Newman, Robert; America, 1736 ***1220.12*** *p581*
Newman, Robert; Annapolis, MD, 1729 ***1220.12*** *p581*
Newman, Robert; Jamaica, 1661 ***1220.12*** *p581*
Newman, Robert; Washington, 1885 ***2770.40*** *p194*
Newman, Thomas; America, 1745 ***1220.12*** *p581*
Newman, Thomas; America, 1757 ***1220.12*** *p581*
Newman, Thomas; America, 1767 ***1220.12*** *p581*
Newman, Thomas; America, 1775 ***1220.12*** *p581*
Newman, Thomas; Annapolis, MD, 1720 ***1220.12*** *p581*
Newman, Thomas; Barbados, 1683 ***1220.12*** *p581*
Newman, Thomas; Barbados, 1699 ***1220.12*** *p581*
Newman, William; America, 1747 ***1220.12*** *p581*
Newman, William; America, 1753 ***1220.12*** *p581*
Newman, William; Maryland, 1728 ***1220.12*** *p581*
Newman, William 15; Quebec, 1870 ***8364.32*** *p25*
Newman, Willmot; Virginia, 1732 ***1220.12*** *p581*
Newman, Zachary; Barbados, 1666 ***1220.12*** *p581*
Newmarsh, Jonathan; America, 1726 ***1220.12*** *p581*
Newmaster, Leonard; New Jersey, 1784-1786 ***927.31*** *p3*
Newnham, Francis; America, 1775 ***1220.12*** *p581*
Newport, John; America, 1724 ***1220.12*** *p581*
Newport, John; America, 1761 ***1220.12*** *p581*
Newport, Richard; America, 1732 ***1220.12*** *p581*
Newport, Susanna; America, 1723 ***1220.12*** *p581*
Newport, William 22; Ontario, 1871 ***1823.21*** *p278*
Newrode, Conrad; Ohio, 1809-1852 ***4511.35*** *p38*
Newroth, Conrad; Ohio, 1809-1852 ***4511.35*** *p38*
Newson, John; America, 1770 ***1220.12*** *p581*
Newstead, Abigail; Charles Town, SC, 1719 ***1220.12*** *p581*
Newstead, Thomas; America, 1742 ***1220.12*** *p581*
Newsted, Abigail; America, 1759 ***1220.12*** *p581*
Newsted, Charlott 81; Ontario, 1871 ***1823.17*** *p125*
Newth, Sarah; America, 1747 ***1220.12*** *p581*
Newton, Ann; America, 1757 ***1220.12*** *p581*
Newton, Augustine; America, 1661 ***1220.12*** *p581*
Newton, Charles; America, 1743 ***1220.12*** *p581*
Newton, Charles 41; Ontario, 1871 ***1823.17*** *p125*
Newton, Daniel; Virginia, 1718 ***1220.12*** *p581*
Newton, Edward; America, 1679 ***1220.12*** *p581*
Newton, George; America, 1774 ***1220.12*** *p581*
Newton, George; Ohio, 1834 ***3580.20*** *p33*
Newton, George 48; Ontario, 1871 ***1823.17*** *p125*
Newton, Hugh; America, 1729 ***1220.12*** *p581*
Newton, James; America, 1677 ***1220.12*** *p581*
Newton, James; America, 1775 ***1220.12*** *p581*
Newton, James; Barbados, 1665 ***1220.12*** *p581*
Newton, James; New York, 1782 ***8529.30*** *p14*
Newton, John; America, 1733 ***1220.12*** *p581*
Newton, John; America, 1758 ***1220.12*** *p581*
Newton, John; Barbados, 1664 ***1220.12*** *p581*
Newton, John; Colorado, 1903 ***1029.59*** *p67*
Newton, John; Died enroute, 1720 ***1220.12*** *p581*
Newton, John; Dorchester, MA, 1632 ***117.5*** *p158*
Newton, John; Michigan, 1878 ***1029.59*** *p67*
Newton, John 42; Ontario, 1871 ***1823.21*** *p278*
Newton, Joseph; America, 1765 ***1220.12*** *p581*
Newton, Joseph; America, 1773 ***1220.12*** *p581*
Newton, Joseph 20; Ontario, 1871 ***1823.21*** *p278*
Newton, Mary; America, 1771 ***1220.12*** *p582*
Newton, Mary; Barbados or Jamaica, 1710 ***1220.12*** *p582*
Newton, Rachael; America, 1754 ***1220.12*** *p582*
Newton, Richard; America, 1730 ***1220.12*** *p582*
Newton, Richard; America, 1755 ***1220.12*** *p582*
Newton, Richard; Maryland, 1723 ***1220.12*** *p582*
Newton, Stephen; Virginia, 1721 ***1220.12*** *p582*
Newton, Susan; Barbados or Jamaica, 1715 ***1220.12*** *p582*
Newton, Thomas; America, 1713 ***1220.12*** *p582*
Newton, Thomas; America, 1758 ***1220.12*** *p582*
Newton, Thomas; America, 1770 ***1220.12*** *p582*
Newton, Thomas; Maryland, 1735 ***1220.12*** *p582*
Newton, William; America, 1730 ***1220.12*** *p582*
Newton, William; America, 1763 ***1220.12*** *p582*
Newton, William; America, 1769 ***1220.12*** *p582*
Newton, William; America, 1774 ***1220.12*** *p582*
Newton, William; America, 1858 ***9076.20*** *p68*
Newton, William 51; Ontario, 1871 ***1823.21*** *p278*
Newton, William; Virginia, 1765 ***1220.12*** *p582*
Newtown, George; Ohio, 1834 ***6020.12*** *p21*
Newy, Thomas; Marston's Wharf, 1782 ***8529.30*** *p14*
Ney, Jean 37; Mississippi, 1847 ***778.6*** *p255*
Ney, Margarethe 37; America, 1854 ***5475.1*** *p51*
Ney, Matthew; Iowa, 1894 ***1211.15*** *p17*
Ney, Robert J.; Iowa, 1892 ***1211.15*** *p17*
Ney, William T.; Iowa, 1892 ***1211.15*** *p17*
Neylor, Martin 48; Ontario, 1871 ***1823.21*** *p278*
Neymeyer, J.H.; Venezuela, 1843 ***3899.5*** *p546*
Niall, Allice; Ontario, 1871 ***1823.21*** *p278*
Niall, Charles 35; Ontario, 1871 ***1823.21*** *p278*
Niblett, James; America, 1699 ***1220.12*** *p582*
Niblett, Joel; Maryland, 1744 ***1220.12*** *p582*
Nibling, Michael; New York, 1860 ***358.56*** *p4*
Niblock, Stephen; Washington, 1887 ***2770.40*** *p25*
Nicaise, Gabriel; Illinois, 1856 ***6079.1*** *p10*
Nical, Charles S.; Washington, 1883 ***2770.40*** *p137*
Niccoli, William; America, 1771 ***1220.12*** *p582*
Niccolin, William; America, 1771 ***1220.12*** *p582*
Niccolls, Anne; Barbados, 1670 ***1220.12*** *p582*
Niccolls, Elizabeth; Jamaica, 1716 ***1220.12*** *p582*
Niccolls, John; Barbados, 1668 ***1220.12*** *p583*
Niccolls, Thomas; Annapolis, MD, 1724 ***1220.12*** *p583*
Niccolls, Thomas; Barbados or Jamaica, 1698 ***1220.12*** *p583*
Niccols, Paul; Barbados, 1665 ***1220.12*** *p583*
Nice, Charles; Annapolis, MD, 1736 ***1220.12*** *p582*
Nice, John; Canada, 1774 ***3036.5*** *p41*
Nichilson, Agnus 12; Ontario, 1871 ***1823.21*** *p278*
Nichleson, Samuel 35; Ontario, 1871 ***1823.17*** *p125*
Nichoel, John 20; Ontario, 1871 ***1823.21*** *p278*
Nichol, Adam 51; Ontario, 1871 ***1823.17*** *p125*
Nichol, Adam 85; Ontario, 1871 ***1823.21*** *p278*
Nichol, Charles 43; Ontario, 1871 ***1823.21*** *p278*
Nichol, Christamia 49; Ontario, 1871 ***1823.17*** *p125*
Nichol, Edward; America, 1753 ***1220.12*** *p582*
Nichol, Francis 32; Ontario, 1871 ***1823.17*** *p125*
Nichol, Francis 42; Ontario, 1871 ***1823.21*** *p278*
Nichol, George 42; Ontario, 1871 ***1823.21*** *p278*
Nichol, James 40; Ontario, 1871 ***1823.21*** *p278*
Nichol, Jane 74; Ontario, 1871 ***1823.21*** *p278*
Nichol, Jane 76; Ontario, 1871 ***1823.21*** *p278*
Nichol, Jinatus 55; Ontario, 1871 ***1823.21*** *p278*
Nichol, John 24; Ontario, 1871 ***1823.21*** *p278*
Nichol, John 26; Ontario, 1871 ***1823.17*** *p125*
Nichol, John 49; Ontario, 1871 ***1823.21*** *p278*
Nichol, John 77; Ontario, 1871 ***1823.21*** *p278*
Nichol, Peter 30; Ontario, 1871 ***1823.21*** *p278*
Nichol, Robert 15; Ontario, 1871 ***1823.21*** *p278*
Nichol, Robert 47; Ontario, 1871 ***1823.21*** *p278*
Nichol, Shubal 74; Ontario, 1871 ***1823.21*** *p278*
Nichol, Thomas 45; Ontario, 1871 ***1823.21*** *p278*
Nichol, Thomas 77; Ontario, 1871 ***1823.21*** *p278*
Nichol, Walter 44; Ontario, 1871 ***1823.21*** *p278*
Nichol, William 29; Ontario, 1871 ***1823.21*** *p278*
Nicholas, Anse 50; Ontario, 1871 ***1823.21*** *p278*
Nicholas, Antony 34; Ontario, 1871 ***1823.21*** *p279*
Nicholas, Cornelius 36; Ontario, 1871 ***1823.21*** *p279*
Nicholas, Cornelius 46; Ontario, 1871 ***1823.21*** *p279*
Nicholas, Dolly 50; Ontario, 1871 ***1823.21*** *p279*
Nicholas, George; Virginia, 1722 ***1220.12*** *p582*
Nicholas, James; America, 1688 ***1220.12*** *p582*
Nicholas, John; America, 1755 ***1220.12*** *p582*
Nicholas, John; America, 1766 ***1220.12*** *p582*
Nicholas, John 54; Ontario, 1871 ***1823.21*** *p279*
Nicholas, John; Philadelphia, 1756 ***9228.50*** *p477*
Nicholas, Joseph 48; New Orleans, 1843 ***778.6*** *p255*
Nicholas, Mathew; Barbados, 1698 ***1220.12*** *p582*
Nicholas, Robert; Illinois, 1858 ***6079.1*** *p10*
Nicholas, Robin; America, 1745 ***1220.12*** *p582*
Nicholas, Rosina 18; New York, NY, 1898 ***7951.13*** *p43*
Nicholas, Susan 70; Ontario, 1871 ***1823.21*** *p279*
Nicholas, Thomas; America, 1750 ***1220.12*** *p582*
Nicholas, William; America, 1753 ***1220.12*** *p582*
Nicholes, John; America, 1773 ***1220.12*** *p583*
Nicholes, Joseph; Ohio, 1809-1852 ***4511.35*** *p38*
Nicholet, Conrad; Ohio, 1809-1852 ***4511.35*** *p38*
Nicholet, Jacob; Ohio, 1809-1852 ***4511.35*** *p38*
Nicholeth, Jacob; Ohio, 1809-1852 ***4511.35*** *p38*
Nicholl, Thomas 40; Ontario, 1871 ***1823.21*** *p279*
Nicholl, Thomas 50; Ontario, 1871 ***1823.21*** *p279*
Nicholl, William 40; Ontario, 1871 ***1823.17*** *p125*
Nicholls, Alice 10; Quebec, 1870 ***8364.32*** *p25*
Nicholls, Allan; Barbados, 1672 ***1220.12*** *p582*
Nicholls, Ann; America, 1742 ***1220.12*** *p582*
Nicholls, Ann; America, 1745 ***1220.12*** *p582*
Nicholls, Clement; Boston, 1714 ***9228.50*** *p477*
Nicholls, Edward; America, 1774 ***1220.12*** *p582*
Nicholls, Edward 38; Ontario, 1871 ***1823.21*** *p279*
Nicholls, Elizabeth; America, 1768 ***1220.12*** *p582*
Nicholls, Emanuel; America, 1749 ***1220.12*** *p582*
Nicholls, Emanuel; America, 1762 ***1220.12*** *p582*
Nicholls, Florence 12; Quebec, 1870 ***8364.32*** *p25*
Nicholls, George; America, 1750 ***1220.12*** *p582*
Nicholls, George; America, 1752 ***1220.12*** *p582*
Nicholls, Henry; America, 1726 ***1220.12*** *p583*
Nicholls, Humphrey; America, 1735 ***1220.12*** *p583*
Nicholls, James; America, 1734 ***1220.12*** *p583*
Nicholls, James; Barbados or Jamaica, 1688 ***1220.12*** *p583*
Nicholls, Jane; America, 1756 ***1220.12*** *p583*
Nicholls, Jane 9; Quebec, 1870 ***8364.32*** *p25*
Nicholls, Joan; Barbados or Jamaica, 1684 ***1220.12*** *p583*
Nicholls, Joanna; Maryland, 1737 ***1220.12*** *p583*
Nicholls, John; America, 1724 ***1220.12*** *p583*
Nicholls, John; America, 1750 ***1220.12*** *p583*
Nicholls, John; Annapolis, MD, 1723 ***1220.12*** *p583*
Nicholls, John; Barbados, 1684 ***1220.12*** *p583*
Nicholls, Jonathan; America, 1765 ***1220.12*** *p583*
Nicholls, Joseph; America, 1766 ***1220.12*** *p583*
Nicholls, Joseph; America, 1770 ***1220.12*** *p583*
Nicholls, Mark; America, 1742 ***1220.12*** *p583*
Nicholls, Martha; Charles Town, SC, 1718 ***1220.12*** *p583*
Nicholls, Mary; America, 1746 ***1220.12*** *p583*
Nicholls, Mary; America, 1750 ***1220.12*** *p583*
Nicholls, Mathew; Barbados, 1698 ***1220.12*** *p583*
Nicholls, Matthias; America, 1750 ***1220.12*** *p583*
Nicholls, Nathaniel; America, 1742 ***1220.12*** *p583*
Nicholls, Philip; Virginia, 1749 ***1220.12*** *p583*
Nicholls, Richard; America, 1740 ***1220.12*** *p583*
Nicholls, Richard; America, 1741 ***1220.12*** *p583*
Nicholls, Richard; America, 1751 ***1220.12*** *p583*
Nicholls, Richard; America, 1763 ***1220.12*** *p583*
Nicholls, Robert; America, 1742 ***1220.12*** *p583*
Nicholls, Thomas; America, 1738 ***1220.12*** *p583*
Nicholls, Thomas; America, 1743 ***1220.12*** *p583*
Nicholls, Thomas; America, 1747 ***1220.12*** *p583*
Nicholls, Thomas 45; Ontario, 1871 ***1823.21*** *p279*
Nicholls, Walter; America, 1754 ***1220.12*** *p583*
Nicholls, Walter; America, 1769 ***1220.12*** *p583*
Nicholls, William; America, 1732 ***1220.12*** *p583*
Nicholls, William; America, 1748 ***1220.12*** *p583*
Nicholls, William; America, 1763 ***1220.12*** *p584*
Nicholls, William; America, 1769 ***1220.12*** *p584*
Nicholls, William; America, 1771 ***1220.12*** *p584*
Nicholls, William; Colorado, 1894 ***1029.59*** *p67*
Nicholls, William; Maryland, 1725 ***1220.12*** *p583*
Nicholls, Wm.; Colorado, 1880 ***1029.59*** *p67*
Nicholls, Wm. J.; Colorado, 1894 ***1029.59*** *p67*
Nichollson, Edward; America, 1741 ***1220.12*** *p584*
Nichollus, Elizabeth; America, 1765 ***1220.12*** *p582*
Nichols, Alexander *SEE* Nichols, John
Nichols, Andrew; Boston, 1730 ***9228.50*** *p509*
Nichols, Ann; Annapolis, MD, 1729 ***1220.12*** *p582*
Nichols, Anna Maria *SEE* Nichols, Lovisa
Nichols, Anne; Maryland, 1721 ***1220.12*** *p582*
Nichols, Arthur, Sr. 72; Ontario, 1871 ***1823.21*** *p279*
Nichols, Daniel; America, 1775 ***1220.12*** *p582*
Nichols, Ebenezer 77; Ontario, 1871 ***1823.21*** *p279*
Nichols, Eli; New England, 1682 ***9228.50*** *p477*
Nichols, George 45; Ontario, 1871 ***1823.21*** *p279*
Nichols, Grace May; Detroit, n.d. ***9228.50*** *p477*
Nichols, Jacob E. *SEE* Nichols, Lovisa
Nichols, James; Maryland, 1674-1675 ***1236.25*** *p51*
Nichols, James; New York, 1782 ***8529.30*** *p14*
Nichols, James 24; North Carolina, 1774 ***1422.10*** *p55*
Nichols, Johannes L. *SEE* Nichols, Lovisa
Nichols, John; America, 1751 ***1220.12*** *p583*
Nichols, John 17; Massachusetts, 1734 ***1642*** *p106*
*Brother:*William
*Brother:*Alexander
Nichols, John 74; Ontario, 1871 ***1823.21*** *p279*
Nichols, Lovisa; Minnesota, 1869-1870 ***1865.50*** *p100*
*Son:*Johannes L.
*Child:*Samuel N.
*Child:*Jacob E.
*Child:*Anna Maria
Nichols, Mary; America, 1752 ***1220.12*** *p583*
Nichols, Mary 60; Ontario, 1871 ***1823.21*** *p279*
Nichols, Nels; St. Paul, MN, 1874-1894 ***1865.50*** *p100*
Nichols, Peter 68; Ohio, 1863 ***9722.10*** *p115*
Nichols, Peter; Ontario, 1871 ***1823.21*** *p279*
Nichols, Robert; America, 1775 ***1220.12*** *p583*
Nichols, Samuel N. *SEE* Nichols, Lovisa
Nichols, Thomas 17; Quebec, 1870 ***8364.32*** *p25*
Nichols, Walter; America, 1751 ***1220.12*** *p583*
Nichols, William *SEE* Nichols, John
Nichols, William 23; Ontario, 1871 ***1823.21*** *p279*
Nichols, William 38; Ontario, 1871 ***1823.21*** *p279*
Nichols, William J.; Colorado, 1894 ***1029.59*** *p67*
Nicholson, Adam 46; Ontario, 1871 ***1823.21*** *p279*
Nicholson, Agnes 12; Quebec, 1870 ***8364.32*** *p25*
Nicholson, Alfred 26; Ontario, 1871 ***1823.21*** *p279*
Nicholson, Ann; America, 1749 ***1220.12*** *p584*
Nicholson, Anthony; Virginia, 1770 ***1220.12*** *p584*
Nicholson, Archibald 24; Ontario, 1871 ***1823.17*** *p125*
Nicholson, Bartholomew; Potomac, 1731 ***1220.12*** *p584*
Nicholson, Daniel; America, 1775 ***1220.12*** *p584*
Nicholson, Edmund; America, 1763 ***1220.12*** *p584*
Nicholson, Edward 24; Ontario, 1871 ***1823.21*** *p279*
Nicholson, Eleanor; America, 1759 ***1220.12*** *p584*
Nicholson, Elizabeth; America, 1740 ***1220.12*** *p584*
Nicholson, Emilie Allez *SEE* Nicholson, Henry Luscombe
Nicholson, George; America, 1752 ***1220.12*** *p584*
Nicholson, George; America, 1774 ***1220.12*** *p584*
Nicholson, Hannah; America, 1740 ***1220.12*** *p584*

Nicholson, Henry Luscombe; Ontario, 1880-1894 ***9228.50*** *p477*
*Wife:*Matilda Ann Cort
*Son:*William Henry Allez
*Son:*Wm. Henry Cort
*Daughter-In-Law:*Emilie Allez
Nicholson, James; America, 1720 ***1220.12*** *p584*
Nicholson, James 72; Ontario, 1871 ***1823.17*** *p125*
Nicholson, James 17; Quebec, 1870 ***8364.32*** *p25*
Nicholson, Jane; America, 1739 ***1220.12*** *p584*
Nicholson, John; America, 1766 ***1220.12*** *p584*
Nicholson, John; America, 1772 ***1220.12*** *p584*
Nicholson, John; Died enroute, 1725 ***1220.12*** *p584*
Nicholson, John; North Carolina, 1868 ***1088.45*** *p25*
Nicholson, John 74; Ontario, 1871 ***1823.17*** *p125*
Nicholson, John; Rappahannock, VA, 1729 ***1220.12*** *p584*
Nicholson, John; Virginia, 1756 ***1220.12*** *p584*
Nicholson, Kenneth; Washington, 1884 ***2770.40*** *p193*
Nicholson, Mary A. 21; Ontario, 1871 ***1823.21*** *p279*
Nicholson, Matilda Ann Cort *SEE* Nicholson, Henry Luscombe
Nicholson, Robert; Louisiana, 1869-1872 ***7710.1*** *p161*
Nicholson, Robert 43; Ontario, 1871 ***1823.21*** *p279*
Nicholson, Thomas; America, 1772 ***1220.12*** *p584*
Nicholson, William; America, 1741 ***1220.12*** *p584*
Nicholson, William; America, 1767 ***1220.12*** *p584*
Nicholson, William; America, 1772 ***1220.12*** *p584*
Nicholson, William Henry Allez *SEE* Nicholson, Henry Luscombe
Nicholson, William Henry Allez; Vancouver, B.C., 1880-1962 ***9228.50*** *p79*
Nicholson, William Henry Cort; Ontario, 1854-1925 ***9228.50*** *p79*
Nicholson, Wm. Henry Cort *SEE* Nicholson, Henry Luscombe
Nicholsson, Johan Berg; Cleveland, OH, 1888-1897 ***9722.10*** *p124*
Nichterlein, Carl; America, 1868 ***7919.3*** *p530*
With wife & 3 children
Nickander, Paul 17; Minnesota, 1925 ***2769.54*** *p1380*
Nickel, Adam; America, 1856 ***2526.43*** *p128*
Nickel, Adam 8 weeks months *SEE* Nickel, Philipp
Nickel, Anna Elisabetha; America, 1856 ***2526.43*** *p128*
Nickel, Anna Margaretha 36; America, 1856 ***2526.42*** *p181*
Nickel, Anna Maria 6 *SEE* Nickel, Georg
Nickel, Barbara *SEE* Nickel, Johann
Nickel, Edward; North Carolina, 1815 ***1088.45*** *p25*
Nickel, Eva *SEE* Nickel, Johann
Nickel, Eva Katharina; America, 1853 ***2526.42*** *p184*
Nickel, Eva Katharina 18; America, 1854 ***2526.43*** *p128*
Nickel, Eva Katharina Geidel 42 *SEE* Nickel, Georg
Nickel, Fredrick; Wisconsin, 1871 ***6795.8*** *p127*
Nickel, Friedrich August; Wisconsin, 1892 ***6795.8*** *p124*
Nickel, Georg *SEE* Nickel, Johann
Nickel, Georg 2 *SEE* Nickel, Georg
Nickel, Georg 52; America, 1855 ***2526.43*** *p128*
*Wife:*Eva Katharina Geidel 42
*Daughter:*Katharina 14
*Daughter:*Maria Magdalena 11
*Son:*Georg 2
*Daughter:*Anna Maria 6
Nickel, Jac. 21; America, 1840 ***778.6*** *p255*
Nickel, Johann; America, 1856 ***2526.43*** *p154*
*Wife:*Margaretha
*Daughter:*Barbara
*Daughter:*Eva
*Son:*Georg
*Son:*Michael
*Daughter:*Margaretha
*Son:*Johannes
Nickel, Johann Michael; America, 1871 ***2526.42*** *p97*
Nickel, Johannes; America, 1855 ***2526.43*** *p128*
Nickel, Johannes; America, 1855 ***2526.43*** *p128*
With family
Nickel, Johannes *SEE* Nickel, Johann
Nickel, Katharina 14 *SEE* Nickel, Georg
Nickel, Leonhard; America, 1856 ***2526.43*** *p128*
Nickel, Margaretha *SEE* Nickel, Johann
Nickel, Margaretha *SEE* Nickel, Johann
Nickel, Maria Elisabetha; America, 1855 ***2526.43*** *p128*
Nickel, Maria Magdalena 11 *SEE* Nickel, Georg
Nickel, Michael *SEE* Nickel, Johann
Nickel, Otto Ferdinand; Wisconsin, 1910 ***6795.8*** *p166*
Nickel, Otto Friedrich; Wisconsin, 1900 ***6795.8*** *p140*
Nickel, Paul Robert; Wisconsin, 1910 ***6795.8*** *p166*
Nickel, Peter; America, 1859 ***2526.42*** *p184*
Nickel, Peter; America, 1869 ***2526.42*** *p184*
Nickel, Philipp 15; America, 1853 ***2526.42*** *p184*
Nickel, Philipp 29; America, 1847 ***2526.42*** *p184*
With wife
*Child:*Adam 8 weeks
Nickel, Theodor; Wisconsin, 1890 ***6795.8*** *p96*
Nickel, William Albert Gotthilf; Wisconsin, 1874 ***6795.8*** *p91*
Nickels, George 44; Ontario, 1871 ***1823.21*** *p279*
Nickels, Mathias; America, 1872 ***5475.1*** *p357*
Nickelson, Robert; New Orleans, 1851 ***7242.30*** *p151*
Nickel von Furstengrund, Miss; America, 1854 ***2526.43*** *p119*
Nickerson, M. J.; California, 1868 ***1131.61*** *p89*
Nickett, John C.; Colorado, 1891 ***1029.59*** *p67*
Nickgold, John 19; Ontario, 1871 ***1823.21*** *p279*
Nicklas, Jakob; America, 1871 ***2526.43*** *p161*
Nicklas, Johannes 24; America, 1884 ***2526.43*** *p161*
Nicklas, John; Washington, 1884 ***2770.40*** *p193*
Nicklas, Marie; America, 1868 ***2526.43*** *p199*
Nicklas, Peter; America, 1869 ***2526.43*** *p161*
Nicklas, Sophie; Philadelphia, 1891 ***5475.1*** *p76*
*Son:*Johann
*Daughter:*Sophie
Nickles, Elizabeth 42; Ontario, 1871 ***1823.21*** *p279*
Nickles, Peter 60; Ontario, 1871 ***1823.21*** *p279*
Nickles, William 57; Ontario, 1871 ***1823.21*** *p279*
Nicklow, Elizabeth; America, 1763 ***1220.12*** *p584*
Nickolai, Wilhelm August; Wisconsin, 1893 ***6795.8*** *p118*
Nickolls, John; Colorado, 1873 ***1029.59*** *p67*
Nickolls, Richard; America, 1728 ***1220.12*** *p583*
Nickolls, Wm.; Colorado, 1880 ***1029.59*** *p67*
Nickols, Joseph 30; Ontario, 1871 ***1823.21*** *p279*
Nickolson, Patrick; America, 1765 ***1220.12*** *p584*
Nickolson, Robert 53; Ontario, 1871 ***1823.21*** *p279*
Nicks, John; America, 1759 ***1220.12*** *p584*
Nickson, Alice; America, 1752 ***1220.12*** *p584*
Nickson, John; Virginia, 1728 ***1220.12*** *p584*
Nickson, Thomas; Barbados, 1663 ***1220.12*** *p585*
Niclas, Jakob; America, 1863 ***5475.1*** *p519*
Nicman, David; Georgia, 1736 ***2853.20*** *p17*
Nicoble, Peter 21; Ontario, 1871 ***1823.21*** *p280*
Nicod, Abraham; Virginia, 1700 ***9230.15*** *p80*
Nicol, Miss 2; America, 1843 ***778.6*** *p255*
Nicol, Miss 6; America, 1843 ***778.6*** *p255*
Nicol, Miss 8; America, 1843 ***778.6*** *p255*
Nicol, Mr. 12; America, 1843 ***778.6*** *p255*
Nicol, Mrs. 37; America, 1843 ***778.6*** *p255*
Nicol, Holander 47; America, 1843 ***778.6*** *p255*
Nicol, James 35; Ontario, 1871 ***1823.21*** *p280*
Nicol, John; Colorado, 1868 ***1029.59*** *p67*
Nicol, John; Illinois, 1834-1900 ***6020.5*** *p132*
Nicol, Robert 52; Ontario, 1871 ***1823.21*** *p280*
Nicol, Thomas; Illinois, 1858-1861 ***6020.5*** *p132*
Nicola, Anna Maria *SEE* Nicola, Johann
Nicola, Johann; America, 1882 ***5475.1*** *p228*
*Wife:*Maria May
*Daughter:*Anna Maria
Nicola, Maria May *SEE* Nicola, Johann
Nicolai, Carl; Valdivia, Chile, 1850 ***1192.4*** *p48*
Nicolai, Ferdinand; Wisconsin, 1869 ***6795.8*** *p140*
Nicolas, Aime 30; New York, NY, 1894 ***6512.1*** *p182*
Nicolas, Charles 7; New Orleans, 1844 ***778.6*** *p255*
Nicolas, Claus 17; America, 1845 ***778.6*** *p256*
Nicolas, Francis 40; New Orleans, 1844 ***778.6*** *p256*
Nicolas, Gabriel 76; America, 1843 ***778.6*** *p256*
Nicolas, Jakob; Iowa, 1887 ***5475.1*** *p204*
Nicolas, Johann Jakob; America, 1853 ***5475.1*** *p465*
Nicolas, Justin 6; New Orleans, 1844 ***778.6*** *p256*
Nicolas, Maria 2; New Orleans, 1844 ***778.6*** *p256*
Nicolas, Melanie 9; New Orleans, 1844 ***778.6*** *p256*
Nicolas, Michel; America, 1881 ***5475.1*** *p202*
Nicolas, Nicholas 1; New Orleans, 1844 ***778.6*** *p256*
Nicolas, Philip 3; New Orleans, 1844 ***778.6*** *p256*
Nicolas, Philip 5; New Orleans, 1844 ***778.6*** *p256*
Nicolas, S. 27; America, 1844 ***778.6*** *p256*
Nicolay, Jacques; Virginia, 1700 ***9230.15*** *p80*
Nicolet, Joseph; Ohio, 1809-1852 ***4511.35*** *p38*
Nicoll, James; Nova Scotia, 1798-1820 ***9228.50*** *p314*
Nicoll, John; Ontario, 1790-1839 ***9228.50*** *p314*
Nicoll, William; Pictou, N.S., 1815 ***7100*** *p20*
With family of 7
Nicolle, Elizabeth; Boston, 1839-1930 ***9228.50*** *p478*
Nicolle, Francis; Maine, 1689 ***9228.50*** *p478*
Nicolle, John Thomas; Prince Edward Island, 1806 ***9228.50*** *p478*
Nicolle, Laura; Prince Edward Island, 1872-1939 ***9228.50*** *p478*
Nicolle, Laura Cecelia; Prince Edward Island, 1898-1978 ***9228.50*** *p478*
Nicolle, Maie W.; Prince Edward Island, 1884-1946 ***9228.50*** *p478*
Nicolle De Queteville, Julia; New York, 1862-1934 ***9228.50*** *p637*
Nicollet, Etienne; Quebec, 1640 ***9221.17*** *p98*
*Brother:*Pierre
Nicollet, Gilles; Quebec, 1643 ***9221.17*** *p128*
Nicollet, Jean; Quebec, 1619 ***9221.17*** *p20*
Nicollet, Pierre *SEE* Nicollet, Etienne
Nicolls, Elizabeth; America, 1767 ***1220.12*** *p582*
Nicolls, William 29; Ontario, 1871 ***1823.21*** *p280*
Nicols, Anna Maria *SEE* Nicols, Lovisa
Nicols, Anne 76; Ontario, 1871 ***1823.21*** *p280*
Nicols, Jacob E. *SEE* Nicols, Lovisa
Nicols, Johannes L. *SEE* Nicols, Lovisa
Nicols, John 45; Ontario, 1871 ***1823.21*** *p280*
Nicols, Lovisa; Minnesota, 1869-1870 ***1865.50*** *p100*
*Son:*Johannes L.
*Child:*Jacob E.
*Child:*Anna Maria
*Child:*Samuel N.
Nicols, Nels; St. Paul, MN, 1874-1894 ***1865.50*** *p100*
Nicols, Samuel N. *SEE* Nicols, Lovisa
Nicolson, Croft 27; Ontario, 1871 ***1823.21*** *p280*
Nicolson, John; Portland, ME, 1850 ***7710.1*** *p153*
Nicolson, Joseph 55; Ontario, 1871 ***1823.17*** *p125*
Nicolson, Robert 30; Ontario, 1871 ***1823.21*** *p280*
Nicolson, Thomas 62; Ontario, 1871 ***1823.21*** *p280*
Nicolson, William 46; Ontario, 1871 ***1823.17*** *p126*
Nicomede, Ch. 30; Port uncertain, 1846 ***778.6*** *p256*
Nicque, Jacques; Quebec, 1657 ***9221.17*** *p365*
Nideus, Jacob 24; Portland, ME, 1911 ***970.38*** *p80*
Niebel, Friedrich; America, 1868 ***179.55*** *p19*
Niebylski, Joseph Michael; Detroit, 1930 ***1640.60*** *p78*
Nied, John 50; Ontario, 1871 ***1823.21*** *p280*
Niederbracht, Wilhelm; America, 1865 ***7420.1*** *p234*
With wife daughter & mother
With sister & brother
Niedercorn, A. Maria 56; America, 1856 ***5475.1*** *p374*
Niederer, Arnold 8; St. Louis, 1847 ***778.6*** *p256*
Niederer, Barbara 35; St. Louis, 1847 ***778.6*** *p256*
Niederer, Carolina 12; St. Louis, 1847 ***778.6*** *p256*
Niederer, Edward 14; St. Louis, 1847 ***778.6*** *p256*
Niederer, Robert 6; St. Louis, 1847 ***778.6*** *p256*
Niederer, Wilhelmina 10; St. Louis, 1847 ***778.6*** *p256*
Niederkorn, A. Maria *SEE* Niederkorn, Nikolaus
Niederkorn, Barbara *SEE* Niederkorn, Nikolaus
Niederkorn, Barbara Lang 36 *SEE* Niederkorn, Nikolaus
Niederkorn, Jakob; America, 1870 ***5475.1*** *p274*
Niederkorn, Margarethe *SEE* Niederkorn, Nikolaus
Niederkorn, Mathias *SEE* Niederkorn, Nikolaus
Niederkorn, Michel *SEE* Niederkorn, Nikolaus
Niederkorn, Nikolaus 57; America, 1856 ***5475.1*** *p287*
*Wife:*Barbara Lang 36
*Daughter:*Margarethe
*Son:*Michel
*Daughter:*Barbara
*Son:*Paul
*Son:*Mathias
*Son:*Peter
*Daughter:*A. Maria
Niederkorn, Paul *SEE* Niederkorn, Nikolaus
Niederkorn, Peter *SEE* Niederkorn, Nikolaus
Niedert, Johann; Port uncertain, 1853 ***7420.1*** *p109*
With wife
Nieduzak, Joseph; Detroit, 1930 ***1640.60*** *p81*
Niedzialek, John Frank; Detroit, 1929 ***1640.55*** *p113*
Niedzwiedz, Szymon 18; New York, NY, 1912 ***8355.1*** *p16*
Nieff, Simon; Ohio, 1809-1852 ***4511.35*** *p38*
Niegert, Friedrich Wilhelm; Port uncertain, 1836 ***7420.1*** *p11*
Niel, Hugh 53; Ontario, 1871 ***1823.17*** *p126*
Niel, Madeleine; Quebec, 1667 ***4514.3*** *p351*
Niel, Pierre 26; Quebec, 1656 ***9221.17*** *p343*
Nield, George 26; Ontario, 1871 ***1823.17*** *p126*
Nielsen, Adolf; Colorado, 1862-1920 ***1029.59*** *p67*
Nielsen, Anton 19; New York, NY, 1894 ***6512.1*** *p185*
Nielsen, John; Iowa, 1930 ***1211.15*** *p17*
Nielsen, Lottie Peterson *SEE* Nielsen, Peter Johnson
Nielsen, Niels Christian; Iowa, 1914 ***1211.15*** *p17*
Nielsen, Niels Christian; Iowa, 1917 ***1211.15*** *p17*
Nielsen, Peter Johnsen; New York, NY, 1877-1898 ***1029.59*** *p68*
Nielsen, Peter Johnson 47; Colorado, 1862-1920 ***1029.59*** *p68*
*Wife:*Lottie Peterson
Nielsen, Rasmus; Iowa, 1914 ***1211.15*** *p17*
Nielsen, Rasmus 25; New York, NY, 1883 ***8427.14*** *p44*
Nielsen, Thor; Washington, 1887 ***2770.40*** *p25*
Nielson, Emanuel; Washington, 1887 ***2770.40*** *p25*
Nielson, Niels; Iowa, 1883 ***1211.15*** *p17*
Niem, Julian; Detroit, 1929-1930 ***6214.5*** *p67*
Niemann, Mr.; America, 1838 ***7420.1*** *p15*
With family
Niemann, Carl Friedrich; America, 1900 ***7420.1*** *p376*
*Brother:*Friedrich Carl Heinrich
Niemann, Carl Heinrich Daniel; America, 1882 ***7420.1*** *p331*
Niemann, Ernst Wilhelm; Illinois, 1876 ***7420.1*** *p307*
Niemann, Friedrich Carl Heinrich *SEE* Niemann, Carl Friedrich

Niemann, Friedrich Christian Christoph; America, 1882 ***7420.1*** *p331*
Niemann, H.; New York, 1859 ***358.56*** *p101*
Niemann, Sophie; America, 1857 ***7420.1*** *p169*
Niemann Brothers, . . .; America, 1881 ***7420.1*** *p323*
Niemeier, Mr.; America, 1865 ***7420.1*** *p234*
With wife & 2 children
Niemeier, Mr.; Port uncertain, 1853 ***7420.1*** *p109*
Niemeier, Christoph; Port uncertain, 1858 ***7420.1*** *p180*
With wife & 2 sons
Niemeier, Heinrich Christian *SEE* Niemeier, Johann Heinrich Christian
Niemeier, Johann Friedrich Christoph *SEE* Niemeier, Johann Heinrich Christian
Niemeier, Johann Heinrich Christian; America, 1854 ***7420.1*** *p126*
*Wife:*Maria Dorothee Russel
*Son:*Johann Heinrich Conrad
*Son:*Johann Friedrich Christoph
*Son:*Heinrich Christian
Niemeier, Johann Heinrich Christoph; America, 1867 ***7420.1*** *p261*
Niemeier, Johann Heinrich Conrad *SEE* Niemeier, Johann Heinrich Christian
Niemeier, Maria Dorothee Russel *SEE* Niemeier, Johann Heinrich Christian
Niemer, Peter G.; Wisconsin, 1900 ***6795.8*** *p52*
Niemeyer, C. H.; Chile, 1852 ***1192.4*** *p52*
With wife & child
Niemeyer, Dorette; America, 1861 ***7420.1*** *p202*
Niemeyer, Dorothee; America, 1856 ***7420.1*** *p152*
Niemeyer, Frederick; Illinois, 1851 ***6079.1*** *p10*
Niemeyer, Friedrich; America, 1855 ***7420.1*** *p140*
Niemeyer, Hans Heinrich; America, 1872 ***7420.1*** *p296*
Niemeyer, Heinrich Friedrich; America, 1867 ***7420.1*** *p261*
Niemeyer, John E.; North Carolina, 1855 ***1088.45*** *p25*
Niemi, Miss; Minnesota, 1925 ***2769.54*** *p1381*
Niemi, Henry 45; Minnesota, 1925 ***2769.54*** *p1380*
Niemi, Jalmir; Minnesota, 1923 ***2769.54*** *p1378*
Niemi, John 39; Minnesota, 1925 ***2769.54*** *p1379*
Niemi, Lembi 35; Minnesota, 1923 ***2769.54*** *p1381*
Niemi, Lyyle 36; Minnesota, 1925 ***2769.54*** *p1379*
Niemi, Mary 32; Minnesota, 1925 ***2769.54*** *p1381*
Niemi, Nester; Minnesota, 1925 ***2769.54*** *p1383*
Niepolski, Andrew; Detroit, 1929-1930 ***6214.5*** *p67*
Nies, Henri; Illinois, 1858 ***6079.1*** *p10*
Nies, Jacob; Louisiana, 1874 ***4981.45*** *p133*
Niesche, Sophia D.; Philadelphia, 1867 ***8513.31*** *p435*
Niesen, Gertrud 37; America, 1880 ***5475.1*** *p484*
*Daughter:*Maria
*Son:*Simon
*Daughter:*Helena
*Daughter:*Katharina
Niesen, Helena *SEE* Niesen, Gertrud Simon
Niesen, Katharina *SEE* Niesen, Gertrud Simon
Niesen, Maria *SEE* Niesen, Gertrud Simon
Niesen, Simon *SEE* Niesen, Gertrud Simon
Nietert, . . .; America, 1847 ***7420.1*** *p55*
*Son:*Gottlieb
With wife & 2 daughters
*Son:*Hans Heinrich
*Son:*Christian
Nietert, Mr.; Port uncertain, 1853 ***7420.1*** *p109*
Nietert, Widow; America, 1849 ***7420.1*** *p66*
Nietert, Christian *SEE* Nietert, . . .
Nietert, Engel Marie Rohrsen *SEE* Nietert, Johann Conrad
Nietert, Engel Marie Sophie *SEE* Nietert, Johann Conrad
Nietert, Friedrich; America, 1854 ***7420.1*** *p126*
*Daughter:*Sophie
With wife
Nietert, Friedrich Wilhelm *SEE* Nietert, Johann Conrad
Nietert, Gottlieb *SEE* Nietert, . . .
Nietert, Hans Heinrich *SEE* Nietert, . . .
Nietert, Heinrich Christoph *SEE* Nietert, Johann Conrad
Nietert, Johann Conrad; America, 1848 ***7420.1*** *p61*
*Wife:*Engel Marie Rohrsen
*Son:*Heinrich Christoph
*Daughter:*Engel Marie Sophie
*Son:*Friedrich Wilhelm
Nietert, Johann Friedrich; America, 1850 ***7420.1*** *p74*
Nietert, Johann Heinrich Conrad; America, 1846 ***7420.1*** *p46*
Nietert, Johann Heinrich Gottlieb; America, 1840 ***7420.1*** *p20*
Nietert, Johann Philipp *SEE* Nietert, Thrine Marie Sophie Duhlmeyer
Nietert, Sophie *SEE* Nietert, Friedrich
Nietert, Thrine Marie Sophie; America, 1852 ***7420.1*** *p94*
*Son:*Johann Philipp
Nietupski, Jacob; Detroit, 1929-1930 ***6214.5*** *p60*
Nieuswander, Peter; Ohio, 1809-1852 ***4511.35*** *p38*
Nigbor, John; Wisconsin, 1875 ***6795.8*** *p69*
Nigbur, August; Wisconsin, 1878 ***6795.8*** *p52*
Nige, James 44; Ontario, 1871 ***1823.17*** *p126*
Nigg, Georg 24; America, 1846 ***778.6*** *p256*
Night, Andrew 42; Ontario, 1871 ***1823.21*** *p280*
Night, Henry 42; Ontario, 1871 ***1823.21*** *p280*
Nightingale, Ann; America, 1754 ***1220.12*** *p584*
Nightingale, Benj.; Braintree, MA, 1689 ***9228.50*** *p478*
Nightingale, John 51; Ontario, 1871 ***1823.17*** *p126*
Nightingale, Matthew; America, 1764 ***1220.12*** *p584*
Nightingale, Peter; America, 1758 ***1220.12*** *p584*
Nightingale, William; America, 1753 ***1220.12*** *p584*
Nigle, Victoria 21; New York, NY, 1847 ***9176.15*** *p50*
Nihill, John; Illinois, 1858-1861 ***6020.5*** *p132*
Nihill, Michael; Illinois, 1858-1861 ***6020.5*** *p132*
Nihill, Simon; Illinois, 1858-1861 ***6020.5*** *p132*
Nihill, Timothy; Illinois, 1858-1861 ***6020.5*** *p132*
Nihnhelm, Louis 40; New Orleans, 1848 ***778.6*** *p256*
Nijgvist, Pener 34; New York, NY, 1894 ***6512.1*** *p229*
Niker, Barbara; Florida, 1929-1983 ***9228.50*** *p514*
Nikl, Jan; South Dakota, 1871-1910 ***2853.20*** *p247*
Niklas, Elisabeth; America, 1859 ***5475.1*** *p522*
Niklas, Jakob; America, 1831 ***2526.43*** *p142*
With wife & 2 children
Niklas, Johannes; America, 1858 ***2526.43*** *p154*
Niklas, M. Philippine; Brazil, 1859 ***5475.1*** *p522*
Niklasson, P.A.; Cleveland, OH, 1897 ***9722.10*** *p124*
Nikodem, Mrs.; Chicago, 1855 ***2853.20*** *p387*
With 4 children
Nikodem, Florian; Wisconsin, 1886 ***6795.8*** *p45*
Nikodem, Jan; Chicago, 1853 ***2853.20*** *p386*
Nikodym, Jan; Arkansas, 1895 ***2853.20*** *p376*
Nikodym, Josef; South Dakota, 1871-1910 ***2853.20*** *p247*
Nikolajsen, Cecilie 17; New York, NY, 1894 ***6512.1*** *p185*
Nikolajsen, Sven 20; New York, NY, 1894 ***6512.1*** *p185*
Nikrle, Frantisek; St. Louis, 1852 ***2853.20*** *p21*
Nile, Louisa Jane; Buffalo, NY, 1883-1884 ***9228.50*** *p365*
Niles, James 41; Michigan, 1880 ***4491.39*** *p22*
Niles, Wm 71; Ontario, 1871 ***1823.21*** *p280*
Nilles, Anna Maria; America, 1880 ***5475.1*** *p287*
Nilles, Johann; Pennsylvania, 1885 ***5475.1*** *p246*
Nilles, Katharina; America, 1860 ***5475.1*** *p375*
Nillus, Jean 9; America, 1847 ***778.6*** *p256*
Nillus, Margaretha 2; America, 1847 ***778.6*** *p256*
Nillus, Marguerite 40; America, 1847 ***778.6*** *p256*
Nillus, Mathias 4; America, 1847 ***778.6*** *p256*
Nillus, Pierre 8; America, 1847 ***778.6*** *p256*
Nillus, Wilhelm 40; America, 1847 ***778.6*** *p256*
Nilsdotter, Anna 26; New York, 1856 ***6529.11*** *p20*
Nilsdotter, Johanna; Kansas, 1873 ***777.40*** *p16*
Nilsdotter, Johanna; Kansas, 1873 ***777.40*** *p16*
Nilson, A. E.; Montreal, 1922 ***4514.4*** *p32*
Nilson, Charley; Cleveland, OH, 1902-1905 ***9722.10*** *p124*
Nilson, Mangnus; Iowa, 1879 ***1211.15*** *p17*
Nilson, Mart; Washington, 1883 ***2770.40*** *p137*
Nilson, N.; Colorado, 1862-1894 ***1029.59*** *p68*
Nilson, Nils 26; Kansas, 1880 ***777.40*** *p18*
Nilson, Ole; Iowa, 1897 ***1211.15*** *p17*
Nilsson, Anders; New York, NY, 1848 ***6412.40*** *p151*
Nilsson, Anna 23; New York, NY, 1894 ***6512.1*** *p185*
Nilsson, Anna E. 37; New York, NY, 1894 ***6512.1*** *p185*
Nilsson, Anna Emerentia; St. Paul, MN, 1895 ***1865.50*** *p100*
Nilsson, Anna Stina Berggren 30 *SEE* Nilsson, Pehr
Nilsson, August; New Mexico, 1914 ***4812.1*** *p87*
Nilsson, August Herman; Iowa, 1912 ***1211.15*** *p17*
Nilsson, B.; New York, NY, 1845 ***6412.40*** *p149*
Nilsson, Bengt; Colorado, 1882 ***1029.59*** *p68*
Nilsson, C.O.; New York, NY, 1853 ***6412.40*** *p153*
Nilsson, Carl Johan; North America, 1887 ***6410.15*** *p106*
Nilsson, Erik Gustaf; Charleston, SC, 1850 ***6412.40*** *p152*
Nilsson, Gust 44; Kansas, 1869-1880 ***777.40*** *p19*
*Wife:*Matilda Olofsdotter 33
Nilsson, Hans; Cleveland, OH, 1892-1896 ***9722.10*** *p124*
Nilsson, Hilda 34; New York, NY, 1894 ***6512.1*** *p185*
Nilsson, J.; New York, NY, 1850 ***6412.40*** *p152*
Nilsson, J.; Philadelphia, 1847 ***6412.40*** *p150*
Nilsson, J.L.; New York, NY, 1851 ***6412.40*** *p153*
Nilsson, John Ludwig; Cleveland, OH, 1902-1905 ***9722.10*** *p124*
Nilsson, John W.; Washington, 1884 ***2770.40*** *p193*
Nilsson, Jons; New Orleans, 1856 ***6412.40*** *p154*
Nilsson, Matilda Olofsdotter 33 *SEE* Nilsson, Gust
Nilsson, N.; New York, NY, 1843 ***6412.40*** *p147*
Nilsson, N.; New York, NY, 1844 ***6412.40*** *p147*
Nilsson, N.; New York, NY, 1846 ***6412.40*** *p149*
Nilsson, Nils; America, 1856 ***4487.25*** *p67*
With mother & siblings
Nilsson, Olaf G.; Cleveland, OH, 1903-1905 ***9722.10*** *p124*
Nilsson, Olof Gustaf; St. Paul, MN, 1902 ***1865.50*** *p99*
Nilsson, Pehr 22; New York, 1856 ***6529.11*** *p20*
*Wife:*Anna Stina Berggren 30
Nilsson, Pet.; New York, NY, 1846 ***6412.40*** *p149*
Nilsson, Severin; Cleveland, OH, 1900-1902 ***9722.10*** *p124*
Nilsson, Valdemar; New York, NY, 1844 ***6412.40*** *p148*
Nilsson, Victor; Cleveland, OH, 1902-1905 ***9722.10*** *p124*
Nilsson Hvenstrand, Nils Per; America, 1857 ***4487.25*** *p75*
With family
Nimke, August; Wisconsin, 1870 ***6795.8*** *p68*
Nimmo, John; America, 1773 ***1220.12*** *p584*
Nimmrich, Maria; America, 1867 ***7919.3*** *p529*
With child
Ninham, Elijah 35; Ontario, 1871 ***1823.21*** *p280*
Ninham, Henry 29; Ontario, 1871 ***1823.21*** *p280*
Ninham, Henry 69; Ontario, 1871 ***1823.21*** *p280*
Ninham, Thomas 34; Ontario, 1871 ***1823.21*** *p280*
Ninsgen, Harry 24; America, 1846 ***778.6*** *p256*
Ninsgen, P. 29; America, 1846 ***778.6*** *p256*
Niquet, Jacques; Quebec, 1657 ***9221.17*** *p365*
Nirgensinger, John; New York, 1859 ***358.56*** *p100*
Nirk, Andrew; Illinois, 1858-1861 ***6020.5*** *p132*
Nirk, William; Illinois, 1858-1861 ***6020.5*** *p132*
Nisbee, Susanna; America, 1754 ***1220.12*** *p584*
Nisbet, David 56; Ontario, 1871 ***1823.17*** *p126*
Nisbet, Francis; South Carolina, 1813 ***3208.30*** *p18*
Nisbet, Francis; South Carolina, 1813 ***3208.30*** *p31*
Nisbet, George 46; Ontario, 1871 ***1823.17*** *p126*
Nisbet, James, Sr. 67; Ontario, 1871 ***1823.17*** *p126*
Nisbett, Richard; America, 1775 ***1220.12*** *p584*
Nisbett, William; America, 1751 ***1220.12*** *p584*
Nisbitt, Nathan 32; Ontario, 1871 ***1823.17*** *p126*
Nissen, George A.; North Carolina, 1870 ***1088.45*** *p25*
Nissen, Heinrich; Iowa, 1889 ***1211.15*** *p17*
Nissen, Nicholus; Iowa, 1888 ***1211.15*** *p17*
Nissen, William; Iowa, 1897 ***1211.15*** *p17*
Nissinen, Peter; Minnesota, 1926 ***2769.54*** *p1379*
Nist, Martin; Ohio, 1809-1852 ***4511.35*** *p38*
Nistrom, Olof; Kansas, 1870-1875 ***777.40*** *p16*
Niswander, Peter; Ohio, 1809-1852 ***4511.35*** *p38*
Nithingale, Alfred 22; Port uncertain, 1840 ***778.6*** *p256*
Nitschke, John 38; Ontario, 1871 ***1823.21*** *p280*
Nittler, Anna *SEE* Nittler, Johánn
Nittler, Anna Maria 42; America, 1885 ***5475.1*** *p319*
Nittler, Elisabeth *SEE* Nittler, Johann
Nittler, Eva *SEE* Nittler, Johann
Nittler, Eva Geier *SEE* Nittler, Johann
Nittler, Hubert *SEE* Nittler, Johann
Nittler, Johann *SEE* Nittler, Johann
Nittler, Johann; America, 1881 ***5475.1*** *p342*
*Wife:*Eva Geier
*Daughter:*Elisabeth
*Son:*Michel
*Daughter:*Anna
*Son:*Nikolaus
*Daughter:*Eva
*Son:*Hubert
*Son:*Johann
Nittler, Maria 45; America, 1855 ***5475.1*** *p317*
Nittler, Michel *SEE* Nittler, Johann
Nittler, Nikolaus *SEE* Nittler, Johann
Nittler, Nikolaus 25; America, 1873 ***5475.1*** *p342*
Nittler, Susanna; Iowa, 1874 ***5475.1*** *p318*
Nitzke, Carl; Wisconsin, 1885 ***6795.8*** *p93*
Nitzke, Heinr.; Valdivia, Chile, 1852 ***1192.4*** *p55*
Niven, . . .; Ontario, 1871 ***1823.21*** *p280*
Niven, Agnew 42; Ontario, 1871 ***1823.21*** *p280*
Nivet, Mr. 28; America, 1841 ***778.6*** *p256*
Nix, Anna Amanda Alvine; Wisconsin, 1896 ***6795.8*** *p209*
Nix, Nicholas; Ohio, 1809-1852 ***4511.35*** *p38*
Nixon, Alex 40; Ontario, 1871 ***1823.21*** *p280*
Nixon, Daniel 47; Michigan, 1880 ***4491.30*** *p23*
Nixon, Dory 23; Michigan, 1880 ***4491.30*** *p23*
Nixon, Edward 22; Michigan, 1880 ***4491.30*** *p23*
Nixon, Edward 36; Ontario, 1871 ***1823.21*** *p280*
Nixon, Esther 35; Michigan, 1880 ***4491.42*** *p19*
Nixon, Francis; America, 1772 ***1220.12*** *p584*
Nixon, George 54; Ontario, 1871 ***1823.21*** *p280*
Nixon, Georgina 31; Ontario, 1871 ***1823.21*** *p280*
Nixon, James 41; Michigan, 1880 ***4491.42*** *p19*
Nixon, James 53; Ontario, 1871 ***1823.21*** *p280*
Nixon, James 81; Ontario, 1871 ***1823.21*** *p280*
Nixon, Jane; America, 1759 ***1220.12*** *p584*
Nixon, John Scott; Ontario, 1835 ***3160.1*** *p150*
Nixon, Laurence; America, 1692 ***1220.12*** *p584*
Nixon, Margaret; America, 1772 ***1220.12*** *p584*
Nixon, Nancy 46; Michigan, 1880 ***4491.30*** *p23*
Nixon, Richard; America, 1736 ***1220.12*** *p584*
Nixon, Richard; America, 1738 ***1220.12*** *p585*
Nixon, Robert; America, 1732 ***1220.12*** *p585*
Nixon, Robert; America, 1758 ***1220.12*** *p585*
Nixon, Susanna; America, 1776 ***1220.12*** *p585*

Nixon, Thomas; Barbados, 1663 *1220.12* p585
Nixon, Walter 78; Ontario, 1871 *1823.21* p280
Nixon, William; America, 1745 *1220.12* p585
Nixon, William; America, 1758 *1220.12* p585
Nixon, William 17; Michigan, 1880 *4491.30* p23
Nixon, William 46; Ontario, 1871 *1823.21* p280
Nixon, William 66; Ontario, 1871 *1823.21* p281
Niziol, John; Detroit, 1929 *1640.55* p114
Noa, Raphael; Louisiana, 1874 *4981.45* p133
Noack, Eduard; Wisconsin, 1886 *6795.8* p205
Noack, Julius; Wisconsin, 1882 *6795.8* p186
Noades, Charles E. 39; Ontario, 1871 *1823.21* p281
Noak, Carl 28; New York, NY, 1883 *8427.14* p44
Noakes, Jeremiah; America, 1766 *1220.12* p585
Noakes, Stephen, Jr.; Virginia, 1766 *1220.12* p585
Noaok, Christian; Valdivia, Chile, 1850 *1192.4* p48
Noar, William; America, 1739 *1220.12* p585
Nobbe, Friedrich Wilhelm; Port uncertain, 1853 *7420.1*
  p109
Nobbs, John; America, 1743 *1220.12* p585
Nobbs, Samuel; America, 1759 *1220.12* p585
Nobery, Philip 41; Ontario, 1871 *1823.21* p281
Nobes, Charles; Washington, 1883 *2770.40* p137
Nobis, Barbara; Valdivia, Chile, 1851 *1192.4* p51
  *Child:*Maria
Nobis, Gertrud; Valdivia, Chile, 1851 *1192.4* p51
Nobis, Maria 4 *SEE* Nobis, Barbara
Noble, Alexander 62; Ontario, 1871 *1823.21* p281
Noble, Anne; New Orleans, 1851 *7242.30* p151
Noble, Benjamin 37; Ontario, 1871 *1823.21* p281
Noble, Bess; New Orleans, 1851 *7242.30* p151
Noble, Christen; North Carolina, 1710 *3629.40* p6
Noble, Daniel; Illinois, 1858 *6079.1* p10
Noble, Elizabeth; Barbados or Jamaica, 1691 *1220.12*
  p585
Noble, Elizabeth *SEE* Noble, George
Noble, George; America, 1765 *1220.12* p585
Noble, George; New York, 1858 *8513.31* p418
  *Wife:*Jane Akens
  *Child:*Elizabeth
Noble, James 36; Ontario, 1871 *1823.21* p281
Noble, Jane Akens *SEE* Noble, George
Noble, Jarrat; New Orleans, 1851 *7242.30* p151
Noble, John; America, 1664 *1220.12* p585
Noble, John; America, 1737 *1220.12* p585
Noble, John; Boston, 1737 *1642* p26
Noble, John 35; Ontario, 1871 *1823.17* p126
Noble, John 35; Ontario, 1871 *1823.21* p281
Noble, John 35; Ontario, 1871 *1823.21* p281
Noble, John 45; Ontario, 1871 *1823.21* p281
Noble, John 58; Ontario, 1871 *1823.21* p281
Noble, John Doyl 36; Ontario, 1871 *1823.17* p126
Noble, Joseph 25; Ontario, 1871 *1823.17* p126
Noble, Margaret; Philadelphia, 1854 *8513.31* p419
Noble, Margaret 14; Quebec, 1870 *8364.32* p25
Noble, Mark; America, 1727 *1220.12* p585
Noble, Mark; America, 1754 *1220.12* p585
Noble, Matthew 47; Ontario, 1871 *1823.21* p281
Noble, Phyllis; Annapolis, MD, 1726 *1220.12* p585
Noble, Robert 28; Ontario, 1871 *1823.17* p126
Noble, Simon; Barbados, 1677 *1220.12* p585
Noble, Susannah; Maryland, 1720 *1220.12* p585
Noble, Thomas; Ohio, 1809-1852 *4511.35* p38
Noble, William 40; Ontario, 1871 *1823.21* p281
Noble, William M.C. 26; Ontario, 1871 *1823.21* p281
Noblet, Tobie 25; New Orleans, 1848 *778.6* p256
Nobody, Mary; America, 1751 *1220.12* p585
Nocenti, Giovanni; Louisiana, 1841-1844 *4981.45* p211
Nock, George; America, 1739 *1220.12* p477
Nock, William; America, 1663 *1220.12* p477
Nockliss, Mary; America, 1757 *1220.12* p585
Nockolds, Elizabeth; America, 1749 *1220.12* p585
Nocks, Catherine; America, 1724 *1220.12* p477
Nodder, John; Annapolis, MD, 1731 *1220.12* p585
Noddy, Francis; America, 1740 *1220.12* p585
Noden, John; America, 1775 *1220.12* p585
Noden, William 44; Ontario, 1871 *1823.21* p281
Noe, Joseph; New York, NY, 1907 *1029.59* p68
Noe, Katharina 28; America, 1836 *5475.1* p527
Noel, . . .; America, 1736 *9228.50* p478
Noel, A. 32; America, 1848 *778.6* p256
Noel, Albin 9; America, 1841 *778.6* p257
Noel, Asenath; New Hampshire, 1850-1950 *9228.50* p478
Noel, Claude 11; America, 1841 *778.6* p257
Noel, Claude 39; America, 1841 *778.6* p257
Noel, David; Canada, 1892-1969 *9228.50* p478
Noel, Dignory; America, 1767 *1220.12* p588
Noel, E. 39; America, 1745 *778.6* p257
Noel, Elisa 38; New Orleans, 1844 *778.6* p257
Noel, Eulalie 1; America, 1841 *778.6* p257
Noel, Gertrude 5 months; America, 1841 *778.6* p257
Noel, H. 43; Louisiana, 1848 *778.6* p257
Noel, Jacques 28; Montreal, 1653 *9221.17* p298

Noel, Jean 30; Quebec, 1637 *9221.17* p72
Noel, Jean P. 37; America, 1841 *778.6* p257
Noel, John; America, 1720 *1220.12* p588
Noel, John; Colorado, 1880 *1029.59* p68
Noel, John; Colorado, 1891 *1029.59* p68
Noel, John; Salisbury, MA, 1684 *9228.50* p479
  *Brother:*Richard
Noel, John Baptiste; Wisconsin, 1856 *1494.21* p31
Noel, John P.; Ohio, 1809-1852 *4511.35* p38
Noel, Joseph 32; Port uncertain, 1842 *778.6* p257
Noel, M. 20; Halifax, N.S., 1902 *1860.4* p43
Noel, Philip; Salem, MA, 1675 *9228.50* p478
Noel, Renouf; Canada, 1892-1983 *9228.50* p478
Noel, Richard *SEE* Noel, John
Noel, Rosina 20; Halifax, N.S., 1902 *1860.4* p43
Noell, Michael; America, 1684 *1220.12* p588
Noeten, Jules 32; Louisiana, 1848 *778.6* p257
Noffsinger, Christian; Illinois, 1858-1861 *6020.5* p132
Noffziger, August; Illinois, 1858-1861 *6020.5* p132
Nogent D'Aquin, Ange; Quebec, 1661 *9221.17* p464
Noggersalk, Anton J.; Louisiana, 1836-1841 *4981.45*
  p209
Noglebach, John; Ohio, 1809-1852 *4511.35* p38
Nohlig, Nicolas 17; America, 1841 *778.6* p257
Nohling, Andrew; Duluth, MN, 1882-1886 *1865.50* p100
Nohs, Jakob; America, 1847 *5475.1* p475
Nohs, Johann; Brazil, 1825 *5475.1* p461
  With son 21
  With daughter 9
  With daughter 3
  With daughter 6
  With son 12
  With son 18
  With son 15
Noila, Michel; Montreal, 1652 *9221.17* p268
Noilhan, Bertrand 28; Port uncertain, 1843 *778.6* p257
Noirclerc, Nicolas 48; Quebec, 1647 *9221.17* p172
Noivtt, Pierre Francis; Louisiana, 1836-1840 *4981.45*
  p213
Nojd, Joh; New York, 1856 *6529.11* p19
  *Wife:*Lisa Andersdotter
Nojd, Lisa Andersdotter *SEE* Nojd, Joh
Nokes, James; America, 1764 *1220.12* p585
Nokes, John; Virginia, 1742 *1220.12* p585
Nolais, Mrs.; America, 1830-1930 *9228.50* p479
Nolan, Andrew; New Orleans, 1850 *7242.30* p151
Nolan, Charles; Quebec, 1662 *9221.17* p490
Nolan, Eliza; New Orleans, 1850 *7242.30* p151
Nolan, James; Boston, 1711 *1642* p24
Nolan, James P.; Louisiana, 1836-1841 *4981.45* p209
Nolan, James Patrick; Louisiana, 1836-1840 *4981.45*
  p213
Nolan, Margaret; New York, NY, 1858 *8513.31* p412
Nolan, Michael; Illinois, 1866 *6079.1* p10
Nolan, Michael 50; Michigan, 1880 *4491.33* p17
Nolan, Michael; St. Johns, N.F., 1825 *1053.15* p6
Nolan, Patrick; Colorado, 1886 *1029.59* p68
Nolan, Patrick; Colorado, 1891 *1029.59* p68
Nolan, Patrick 43; Ontario, 1871 *1823.21* p281
Nolan, Pierre 19; Montreal, 1660 *9221.17* p442
Nolan, Sarah; Boston, 1754 *1642* p47
Nolan, Thomas; Illinois, 1859 *6079.1* p10
Nolan, Thomas; Roxbury, MA, 1762 *1642* p108
Noland, Andrew; Annapolis, MD, 1731 *1220.12* p585
Noland, Andrew; Detroit, 1929-1930 *6214.5* p67
Noland, Ann; Boston, 1733 *1642* p44
Noland, Bridget; Charles Town, SC, 1719 *1220.12* p585
Noland, James; Roxbury, MA, 1713 *1642* p108
Noland, John W.; North Carolina, 1838 *1088.45* p25
Noland, Patrick; Colorado, 1886 *1029.59* p68
Nolbff, Louise 22; New York, NY, 1884 *8427.14* p45
Nold, Paul; Louisiana, 1874 *4981.45* p133
Nolder, Mary; Barbados or Jamaica, 1684 *1220.12* p585
Nole, Mrs. 24; America, 1844 *778.6* p257
Nolen, James 45; Ontario, 1871 *1823.17* p126
Nolen, Mary; Boston, 1765 *1642* p48
Nolin, Charles; South Dakota, 1868-1872 *1029.59* p68
  *Wife:*Christina Nolin
Nolin, Chas.; Colorado, 1903 *1029.59* p68
Nolin, Christina; South Dakota, 1868-1872 *1029.59* p68
Nolin, Martin; Quebec, 1662 *9221.17* p490
Nolin, Pierre; Quebec, 1649 *9221.17* p218
Noll, Adolf; America, 1867 *5475.1* p178
Noll, Francis; Ohio, 1809-1852 *4511.35* p39
Noll, Jacob; Illinois, 1854 *6079.1* p10
Noll, Johann Adam; America, n.d. *8115.12* p327
Noll, Josef; South Dakota, 1871-1910 *2853.20* p247
Noll, Louis; Colorado, 1896 *1029.59* p68
Noll, Louis; Colorado, 1900 *1029.59* p68
Noller, Christian; America, 1883 *179.55* p19
Noller, David; America, 1886 *179.55* p19
Noller, Elizabeth; Annapolis, MD, 1723 *1220.12* p585
Noller, Gottlieb; America, 1892 *179.55* p19

Noller, Johann; America, 1895 *179.55* p19
Noller, Johann Georg; America, 1884 *179.55* p19
Noller, Johann Gottfried; America, 1885 *179.55* p19
Noller, Karoline; America, 1881 *179.55* p19
Noller, Michael; America, 1883 *179.55* p19
Noller, Michael; Colorado, 1873 *1029.59* p69
Noller, Michael; Colorado, 1887 *1029.59* p68
Noller, Robert Friedrich; America, 1894 *179.55* p19
Nollet, George 25; Ontario, 1871 *1823.21* p281
Nollet, William 23; Ontario, 1871 *1823.21* p281
Nolloth, William; America, 1769 *1220.12* p585
Nolot, Adele 7; Port uncertain, 1843 *778.6* p257
Nolot, Alfred 5; Port uncertain, 1843 *778.6* p257
Nolot, Claude 10; Port uncertain, 1843 *778.6* p257
Nolot, Jean 45; Port uncertain, 1843 *778.6* p257
Nolot, Jeanne 9; Port uncertain, 1843 *778.6* p257
Nolot, Marcelin 3; Port uncertain, 1843 *778.6* p257
Nolot, Marie 3 months; Port uncertain, 1843 *778.6* p257
Nolot, Therese 33; Port uncertain, 1843 *778.6* p257
Nolte, . . .; West Virginia, 1850-1860 *1132.30* p149
Nolte, Christian Heinrich; America, 1865 *7420.1* p234
Nolte, Francis; Louisiana, 1841-1844 *4981.45* p211
Nolte, George; Nova Scotia, 1784 *7105* p25
Nolte, Hans Heinrich Conrad; America, 1867 *7420.1*
  p261
Nolte, Hartman 27; Indiana, 1893-1894 *9076.20* p73
Nolte, Henry 35; Indiana, 1887-1894 *9076.20* p73
Noltemeier, Carl August; America, 1857 *7420.1* p169
Noltemeyer, Carl Friedrich Wilhelm; Port uncertain,
  1854 *7420.1* p126
Nolting, Anne Marie *SEE* Nolting, Heinrich Friedrich
  Christian
Nolting, Christian Friedrich; America, 1849 *7420.1* p66
Nolting, Engel Marie Ernest *SEE* Nolting, Heinrich
  Friedrich Christian
Nolting, Engel Sophie Wilhelmine; America, 1886
  7420.1 p350
Nolting, Gerhard; America, 1869 *7420.1* p281
Nolting, Gerhard; America, 1871 *7420.1* p291
  With family
Nolting, Heinrich; America, 1882 *7420.1* p331
  With wife & child
Nolting, Heinrich Friedrich Christian; Iowa, 1865 *7420.1*
  p235
  *Wife:*Engel Marie Ernest
  *Son:*Johann Heinr.
  *Daughter:*Sophie Ernestine
  *Daughter:*Anne Marie
  *Daughter:*Sophie Wilh.
Nolting, Heinrich Friedrich Christoph; America, 1886
  7420.1 p351
Nolting, Heinrich Tobias; America, 1870 *7420.1* p285
Nolting, Johann Heinr. *SEE* Nolting, Heinrich Friedrich
  Christian
Nolting, Otto Karl Dietrich von; Kansas, 1873 *7420.1*
  p301
Nolting, Sophie Ernestine *SEE* Nolting, Heinrich
  Friedrich Christian
Nolting, Sophie Wilh. *SEE* Nolting, Heinrich Friedrich
  Christian
Nolting, Wilhelm; America, 1857 *7420.1* p169
Nolton, James; Potomac, 1731 *1220.12* p585
Nomblalais, Eugene L.; Illinois, 1852 *6079.1* p10
Nonnengard, Adam 38; America, 1872 *5475.1* p446
  *Wife:*Katharina Theis 32
  *Daughter:*Katharina 1
  *Son:*Johann 5
Nonnengard, Johann 5 *SEE* Nonnengard, Adam
Nonnengard, Katharina 1 *SEE* Nonnengard, Adam
Nonnengard, Katharina Theis 32 *SEE* Nonnengard,
  Adam
Nonpareil, Jean; Montreal, 1649 *9221.17* p221
Nony, Pasquier 23; Quebec, 1656 *9221.17* p343
Noolan, P.; New Orleans, 1850 *7242.30* p151
Nooles, Jessy 8; Ontario, 1871 *1823.21* p281
Noon, Catherine 33; Ontario, 1871 *1823.21* p281
Noon, Henry; America, 1685 *1220.12* p586
Noon, John; America, 1754 *1220.12* p586
Noon, Mary; America, 1724 *1220.12* p586
Noon, Michl; St. John, N.B., 1848 *2978.15* p41
Noon, Thomas; America, 1713 *1220.12* p586
Noon, William; America, 1742 *1220.12* p586
Noon, William L.; Washington, 1889 *2770.40* p80
Noonan, David; Newfoundland, 1814 *3476.10* p54
Noonan, John; Philadelphia, 1778 *8529.30* p4A
Noonane, Timothy; Boston, 1768 *1642* p49
Noone, Fortunatus; America, 1675 *1220.12* p586
Noone, Joseph; Maine, 1831 *3274.55* p22
Noone, William; Burlington, VT, 1832 *3274.56* p96
Noonen, James; Illinois, 1866 *6079.1* p11
Nooney, James; America, 1764 *1220.12* p586
Noonon, John; Philadelphia, 1778 *8529.30* p4A

Noorad, Thomas; North Carolina, 1792-1862 1088.45 p25
Nopar, Louis; Illinois, 1852 6079.1 p11
Nopce, Francois-Rene; Quebec, 1638 9221.17 p79
Brother:Rene
Nopce, Rene 24 SEE Nopce, Francois-Rene
Noques, Etienne 20; New Orleans, 1746 778.6 p257
Noraway, Thomas; America, 1738 1220.12 p586
Norberg, Andra Richard; Colorado, 1894 1029.59 p69
Norberg, Andrew Rich.; Colorado, 1884 1029.59 p69
Norberg, Charles G.; Minneapolis, 1879-1883 1865.50 p100
Norberg, Dorothea; St. Paul, MN, 1886 1865.50 p100
Norberg, Sven Fredr.; San Francisco, 1855 6412.40 p153
Norbert, . . .; Quebec, 1641 9221.17 p106
Norbury, Elizabeth; America, 1774 1220.12 p586
Norbury, Hester; America, 1750 1220.12 p586
Norby, Johan Petter; New York, NY, 1845 6412.40 p149
Norby, Mattias; New York, NY, 1842 6412.40 p146
Norcott, John; America, 1698 1220.12 p586
Norcott, John; America, 1733 1220.12 p586
Nord, Barbara; America, 1785 2526.42 p130
Nord, Ernst Gustaf; Cleveland, OH, 1903-1906 9722.10 p124
Nord, Friedrich August 22; America, 1855 2526.43 p177
Nord, Jakob; America, 1865 2526.43 p177
Nord, Johannes, III; America, 1841 2526.42 p128
With wife
With child 10
With child 7
With child 4
With child 12
Nord, Karl Friedrich; America, 1866 2526.43 p177
Nord, Oskar Walter Gunnar; Illinois, 1930 121.35 p100
Nordberg, P.D.; New York, NY, 1844 6412.40 p147
Nordby, Hans H.; Washington, 1889 2770.40 p80
Nordeen, Carl 20; Minnesota, 1925 2769.54 p1382
Nordeen, Charles 45; Minnesota, 1925 2769.54 p1382
Nordeen, George 18; Minnesota, 1925 2769.54 p1382
Nordell, Charles; Washington, 1885 2770.40 p194
Nordell, J.F.; New York, NY, 1847 6412.40 p150
Norder, Axel; Cleveland, OH, 1891-1894 9722.10 p124
Nordgvist, Simon 34; New York, NY, 1894 6512.1 p229
Nordgvist, Ubrika 38; New York, NY, 1894 6512.1 p229
Nordgvist, Uisito 5; New York, NY, 1894 6512.1 p229
Nordin, Amanda 28 SEE Nordin, Frank W.
Nordin, Elof; Minnesota, 1925 2769.54 p1382
Nordin, Frank W. 44; Kansas, 1880 777.40 p5
Wife:Amanda 28
Son:Oscar 5
Nordin, Halvor; Minnesota, 1925 2769.54 p1382
Nordin, Joh.; New Orleans, 1847 6412.40 p149
Nordin, Marian; Minnesota, 1925 2769.54 p1382
Nordin, Oscar 5 SEE Nordin, Frank W.
Nordin, Signe; Minnesota, 1925 2769.54 p1382
Nordin, William; Minnesota, 1925 2769.54 p1382
Nordis, Catherine; America, 1767 1220.12 p586
Nordlund, Anna; St. Paul, MN, 1888 1865.50 p103
Nordman, Charles G.; Washington, 1889 2770.40 p80
Nordmann, Carl Heinrich Wilhelm SEE Nordmann, Christian Ludwig Wilhelm
Nordmann, Christian Friedrich Wilhelm Ludwig SEE Nordmann, Christian Ludwig Wilhelm
Nordmann, Christian Ludwig Wilhelm; America, 1881 7420.1 p325
Wife:Wilhelmine Luise Charlotte Roebbeke
Son:Christian Friedrich Wilhelm Ludwig
Daughter:Hanne Caroline Charlotte
Son:Carl Heinrich Wilhelm
Son:Johann Friedrich Ludwig
Nordmann, Hanne Caroline Charlotte SEE Nordmann, Christian Ludwig Wilhelm
Nordmann, Johann Friedrich Ludwig SEE Nordmann, Christian Ludwig Wilhelm
Nordmann, Wilhelmine Luise Charlotte Roebbeke SEE Nordmann, Christian Ludwig Wilhelm
Nordmeier, Carl Friedrich Wilhelm SEE Nordmeier, Ernst Wilhelm
Nordmeier, Caroline Friedericke SEE Nordmeier, Ernst Wilhelm
Nordmeier, Caroline Friederike SEE Nordmeier, Ernst Wilhelm
Nordmeier, Caroline Friederike Charlotte SEE Nordmeier, Ernst Wilhelm
Nordmeier, Ernst; Port uncertain, 1858 7420.1 p180
Nordmeier, Ernst Heinrich Wilhelm; New York, NY, 1890 7420.1 p361
Nordmeier, Ernst Ludwig Gerhard SEE Nordmeier, Ernst Wilhelm
Nordmeier, Ernst Wilhelm; America, 1860 7420.1 p197
With wife
Daughter:Caroline Friedericke
Daughter:Caroline Friederike
Daughter:Caroline Friederike Charlotte
Son:Heinrich Wilhelm Gerhard
Son:Carl Friedrich Wilhelm
Son:Ernst Ludwig Gerhard
Nordmeier, Friedrich Wilhelm Daniel; America, 1883 7420.1 p338
Nordmeier, Heinrich Wilhelm Gerhard SEE Nordmeier, Ernst Wilhelm
Nordmeier, Wilhelm; America, 1858 7420.1 p180
With daughter
Nordmeyer, Carl; Idaho, 1843 7420.1 p380
Nordon, Joseph; Barbados, 1699 1220.12 p586
Nordquist, Christine Pehrsdotter SEE Nordquist, Hans, Sr.
Nordquist, Hans, Jr. SEE Nordquist, Hans, Sr.
Nordquist, Hans, Sr.; Kansas, 1869 777.40 p14
Wife:Christine Pehrsdotter
Daughter:Mary
Son:Hans, Jr.
Nordquist, Mary SEE Nordquist, Hans, Sr.
Nordstrom, Albert; Cleveland, OH, 1898-1902 9722.10 p124
Nordstrom, Christina; Minnesota, 1877-1885 1865.50 p100
Nordstrom, John W.; Chicago, 1882-1884 1865.50 p100
Nordstrom, Louis P.; Iowa, 1867-1870 777.40 p10
Nordstrom, Oscar; Minnesota, 1880-1885 1865.50 p100
Nordstrom, Oskar; Cleveland, OH, 1896-1904 9722.10 p124
Nore Dumesnil, Jacques de; Quebec, 1683-1688 2314.30 p168
Nore Dumesnil, Jacques de; Quebec, 1684 2314.30 p191
Norell, Anna 29 SEE Norell, Olof
Norell, Olof 39; Kansas, 1880 777.40 p15
Wife:Anna 29
Norford, James; America, 1746 1220.12 p586
Norgaard, Hans Peter; Iowa, 1931 1211.15 p17
Norgate, Nathaniel; America, 1741 1220.12 p586
Norgate, Sarah; Barbados or Jamaica, 1674 1220.12 p586
Norgrave, Joseph; America, 1756 1220.12 p586
Norgren, John; Cleveland, OH, 1892-1902 9722.10 p124
Norha, Helen 17; Minnesota, 1925 2769.54 p1380
Norha, Martha 16; Minnesota, 1925 2769.54 p1380
Norha, Matt 55; Minnesota, 1925 2769.54 p1381
Norin, Hans 25; New York, 1856 6529.11 p21
Nork, William; America, 1728 1220.12 p586
Norlen, Andrew; Wisconsin, 1880-1881 1865.50 p100
Norlin, Andrew; Wisconsin, 1880-1881 1865.50 p100
Norlinder, Nels; Illinois, 1861 4487.25 p68
Norling, C.C.; New York, NY, 1845 6412.40 p148
Norling, Peter Johan; Cleveland, OH, 1893 9722.10 p124
Norman, Anna Maria; America, 1745 1220.12 p586
Norman, Arthur Edward; North Carolina, 1853 1088.45 p25
Norman, Carl; St. Paul, MN, 1902 1865.50 p100
Norman, Charles; America, 1695 1220.12 p586
Norman, Elizabeth; America, 1664 1220.12 p586
Norman, Elizabeth; America, 1765 1220.12 p586
Norman, Elizabeth; Virginia, 1741 1220.12 p586
Norman, George; Virginia, 1766 1220.12 p586
Norman, Hanna; Annapolis, MD, 1723 1220.12 p586
Norman, Harriet; New York, 1850-1934 9228.50 p232
Norman, Henry; America, 1746 1220.12 p586
Norman, Henry; America, 1768 1220.12 p586
Norman, Henry; America, 1769 1220.12 p586
Norman, James; America, 1766 1220.12 p586
Norman, James; New York, 1783 8529.30 p14
Norman, John; America, 1725 1220.12 p586
Norman, John; America, 1765 1220.12 p586
Norman, John; Marblehead, MA, 1660-1684 9228.50 p479
Norman, John; Maryland, 1722 1220.12 p586
Norman, John 60; Ontario, 1871 1823.21 p281
Norman, L. B. 30; America, 1843 778.6 p257
Norman, Maria 30; Ontario, 1871 1823.21 p281
Norman, Mary; America, 1736 1220.12 p586
Norman, Mary; America, 1751 1220.12 p586
Norman, Mathew 42; Ontario, 1871 1823.17 p126
Norman, Peter; America, 1739 1220.12 p586
Norman, Philip; America, 1771 1220.12 p586
Norman, Robert; Barbados, 1683 1220.12 p586
Norman, Thomas 47; Ontario, 1871 1823.21 p281
Norman, William; America, 1685 1220.12 p586
Norman, William; America, 1755 1220.12 p586
Norman, William; Maryland, 1744 1220.12 p586
Norman, William; Rappahannock, VA, 1728 1220.12 p586
Normand, Catherine; Quebec, 1665 4514.3 p351
Normand, Edouarde Jouineau SEE Normand, Gervais
Normand, Gervais; Quebec, 1647 9221.17 p185
Wife:Edouarde Jouineau
Son:Jean
Normand, Jean 11 SEE Normand, Gervais
Normand, Jean le vieux 38; Quebec, 1647 9221.17 p186
Normand, Louis 35; Mississippi, 1846 778.6 p257
Normand, Marie-Madeleine; Quebec, 1669 4514.3 p351
Normand, Pierre 20; Quebec, 1657 9221.17 p365
Normandin, J. B. 33; America, 1847 778.6 p257
Normandin, Jean 45; America, 1843 778.6 p257
Normandin, Jean; Quebec, 1600-1663 4514.3 p375
Wife:Marie Desmaisons
Son:Mathurin
Normandin, Jean; Quebec, 1650 9221.17 p228
Wife:Marie Desmaisons
Son:Mathurin
Normandin, Marie Desmaisons SEE Normandin, Jean
Normandin, Marie Desmaisons SEE Normandin, Jean
Normandin, Mathurin SEE Normandin, Jean
Normandin, Mathurin SEE Normandin, Jean
Normmill, James; Toronto, 1844 2910.35 p115
Nornevill, John; America, 1767 1220.12 p586
Norns, Lucas; Louisiana, 1874 4981.45 p133
Norquist, Niles; Colorado, 1894 1029.59 p69
Norquist, Niles; New York, NY, 1869 1029.59 p69
Norrby, J.P.; New York, NY, 1845 6412.40 p149
Norrby, Matthias; New York, NY, 1842 6412.40 p146
Norrell, Thomas Lewis; Washington, 1884 2770.40 p193
Norrie, Francis 33; Ontario, 1871 1823.21 p281
Norrington, Thomas; America, 1769 1220.12 p586
Norris, Batchellor; America, 1775 1220.12 p586
Norris, Elizabeth Wallace; Massachusetts, 1877 9228.50 p513
Norris, Frances; America, 1755 1220.12 p586
Norris, Francis; America, 1773 1220.12 p587
Norris, George; America, 1742 1220.12 p587
Norris, George 69; Ontario, 1871 1823.21 p281
Norris, James; America, 1768 1220.12 p587
Norris, John; America, 1695 1220.12 p587
Norris, John; America, 1755 1220.12 p587
Norris, John; America, 1756 1220.12 p587
Norris, John M. 33; Ontario, 1871 1823.21 p281
Norris, Joseph 60; Ontario, 1871 1823.21 p281
Norris, Letitia; America, 1759 1220.12 p587
Norris, Mary; Virginia, 1741 1220.12 p587
Norris, Michael; Barbados, 1699 1220.12 p587
Norris, Philip; America, 1755 1220.12 p587
Norris, Phillip 55; Ontario, 1871 1823.21 p281
Norris, Richard; America, 1761 1220.12 p587
Norris, Richard; America, 1765 1220.12 p587
Norris, Robert; America, 1741 1220.12 p587
Norris, Thomas; America, 1734 1220.12 p587
Norris, Thomas; America, 1750 1220.12 p587
Norris, Thomas 32; Ontario, 1871 1823.17 p126
Norris, William; America, 1725 1220.12 p587
Norris, William; America, 1742 1220.12 p587
Norris, William; America, 1770 1220.12 p587
Norris, William 50; Ontario, 1871 1823.17 p126
Norris, William 58; Ontario, 1871 1823.17 p126
Norrstrom, C.H.; Cleveland, OH, 1888-1892 9722.10 p124
Norson, Jervis; Annapolis, MD, 1720 1220.12 p587
Norstedt, Ad. Fr.; New Orleans, 1843 6412.40 p147
Norstrom, Joh.; New York, NY, 1844 6412.40 p148
Norsworthy, Chas. 39; Ontario, 1871 1823.17 p126
North, Catherine; Maryland, 1736 1220.12 p587
North, Charles 70; Ontario, 1871 1823.21 p281
North, Ebeneser 37; Ontario, 1871 1823.21 p281
North, Edward; America, 1769 1220.12 p587
North, Elizabeth; America, 1721 1220.12 p587
North, Elizabeth; America, 1736 1220.12 p587
North, George 21; Ontario, 1871 1823.21 p281
North, James; America, 1775 1220.12 p587
North, James; Maryland, 1751 1220.12 p587
North, James 63; Ontario, 1871 1823.21 p281
North, John; America, 1675 1220.12 p587
North, John; America, 1751 1220.12 p587
North, John; America, 1773 1220.12 p587
North, John; Illinois, 1858-1861 6020.5 p132
North, John Guss; Washington, 1889 2770.40 p80
North, Jonathan; America, 1775 1220.12 p587
North, Joseph; America, 1737 1220.12 p587
North, Mary; America, 1721 1220.12 p587
North, Mary; America, 1740 1220.12 p587
North, Mary; Barbados, 1680 1220.12 p587
North, Mary; Maryland, 1670 1236.25 p46
North, Mary Ann 16; Ontario, 1871 1823.21 p281
North, Richard; America, 1698 1220.12 p587
North, Thomas; America, 1745 1220.12 p587
North, Thomas; America, 1749 1220.12 p587
North, Thomas; America, 1766 1220.12 p587
North, Thomas; America, 1769 1220.12 p587
North, Thomas 39; Ontario, 1871 1823.21 p281
North, Thomas 46; Ontario, 1871 1823.21 p281
North, William; America, 1774 1220.12 p587
North, William; Barbados, 1665 1220.12 p587
North, William; Charles Town, SC, 1719 1220.12 p587

Northam, Gervas; America, 1719 ***1220.12*** *p587*
Northcote, Hazell; Virginia, 1726 ***1220.12*** *p587*
Northcote, James; America, 1771 ***1220.12*** *p587*
Northcote, Thomas 63; Ontario, 1871 ***1823.21*** *p281*
Northcott, William; Barbados, 1669 ***1220.12*** *p587*
Northey, Richard 20; Ontario, 1871 ***1823.21*** *p281*
Northmore, John 50; Ontario, 1871 ***1823.21*** *p281*
Northmore, William; Virginia, 1763 ***1220.12*** *p587*
Northom, Charles 34; Ontario, 1871 ***1823.21*** *p282*
Northover, Nicholas; Barbados, 1698 ***1220.12*** *p588*
Northrop, Agustus 40; Ontario, 1871 ***1823.21*** *p282*
Northy, Henry 28; Ontario, 1871 ***1823.21*** *p282*
Northy, Samuel; Boston, 1715 ***9228.50*** *p479*
Norton, Charles O.; America, 1849 ***4487.25*** *p68*
With parents
Norton, Eli P.; Ohio, 1844 ***3580.20*** *p33*
Norton, Eli P.; Ohio, 1844 ***6020.12*** *p21*
Norton, Elizabeth; America, 1694 ***1220.12*** *p588*
Norton, Hannah; Annapolis, MD, 1725 ***1220.12*** *p588*
Norton, Hester; America, 1736 ***1220.12*** *p588*
Norton, James; America, 1750 ***1220.12*** *p588*
Norton, John; America, 1769 ***1220.12*** *p588*
Norton, John; America, 1774 ***1220.12*** *p588*
Norton, John; Colorado, 1897 ***1029.59*** *p69*
Norton, John; Iowa, 1890 ***1029.59*** *p69*
Norton, John 54; Ontario, 1871 ***1823.21*** *p282*
Norton, Lucius 31; Ontario, 1871 ***1823.21*** *p282*
Norton, Mary; America, 1764 ***1220.12*** *p588*
Norton, Mary; America, 1765 ***1220.12*** *p588*
Norton, Mary; America, 1773 ***1220.12*** *p588*
Norton, Patrick; North Carolina, 1827 ***1088.45*** *p25*
Norton, Richard; Rappahannock, VA, 1728 ***1220.12*** *p588*
Norton, Robert; America, 1685 ***1220.12*** *p588*
Norton, Thomas; America, 1685 ***1220.12*** *p588*
Norton, Thomas; America, 1775 ***1220.12*** *p588*
Norton, William; America, 1720 ***1220.12*** *p588*
Norum, Peter Cornelius; Washington, 1889 ***2770.40*** *p80*
Norvell, Thomas Lewis; Washington, 1883 ***2770.40*** *p137*
Norvil, Robert; America, 1744 ***1220.12*** *p588*
Norwell, Thomas Lewis; Washington, 1884 ***2770.40*** *p193*
Norwidge, Robert; Annapolis, MD, 1733 ***1220.12*** *p588*
Norwood, Francis; America, 1723 ***1220.12*** *p588*
Norwood, James 29; Ontario, 1871 ***1823.17*** *p126*
Norwood, Mary Ann 23; Ontario, 1871 ***1823.17*** *p126*
Norwood, Richard; Virginia, 1727 ***1220.12*** *p588*
Norwood, Robert; America, 1775 ***1220.12*** *p588*
Norwood, William 40; Ontario, 1871 ***1823.17*** *p126*
Nosal, John H.; Detroit, 1930 ***1640.60*** *p83*
Nosarzewski, Marie; Detroit, 1929-1930 ***6214.5*** *p63*
Noseley, Thomas; Maryland, 1730 ***1220.12*** *p588*
Nosewicz, Marya; Detroit, 1929 ***1640.55*** *p116*
Noseworthy, Mary 60; Ontario, 1871 ***1823.21*** *p282*
Noss, Angela *SEE* Noss, Karl
Noss, Angela Hermann *SEE* Noss, Karl
Noss, Jno.; Louisiana, 1874 ***4981.45*** *p296*
Noss, Karl; Iowa, 1886 ***5475.1*** *p141*
*Wife:*Angela Hermann
*Daughter:*Susanna
*Daughter:*Maria
*Daughter:*Angela
*Daughter:*Margarethe
*Daughter:*Katharina
Noss, Katharina *SEE* Noss, Karl
Noss, Margarethe *SEE* Noss, Karl
Noss, Maria *SEE* Noss, Karl
Noss, Susanna *SEE* Noss, Karl
Noss, William; America, 1750 ***1220.12*** *p588*
Nossler, Querin; America, 1867 ***7919.3*** *p535*
Nostro, Eutichio; Louisiana, 1841-1844 ***4981.45*** *p211*
Nota, George; Nova Scotia, 1784 ***7105*** *p25*
Notar, Johannetta; America, 1834 ***5475.1*** *p437*
Notere, Michael; America, 1752 ***1220.12*** *p588*
Notier, Leonhard 23; Port uncertain, 1846 ***778.6*** *p257*
Notman, Mary; America, 1764 ***1220.12*** *p588*
Notre-Dame, Mere 24; Quebec, 1644 ***9221.17*** *p138*
Notson, Isabella; America, 1747 ***1220.12*** *p588*
Nott, Bridget; America, 1721 ***1220.12*** *p477*
Nott, James 40; Ontario, 1871 ***1823.21*** *p282*
Nott, Joan; America, 1746 ***1220.12*** *p477*
Nott, John; America, 1696 ***1220.12*** *p477*
Nott, Randall; America, 1770 ***1220.12*** *p477*
Nott, William, Jr.; America, 1759 ***1220.12*** *p477*
Nott, William, Sr.; America, 1759 ***1220.12*** *p477*
Nottage, John; America, 1775 ***1220.12*** *p588*
Nottger, Friedrich David; America, 1854 ***7420.1*** *p126*
With wife 2 sons & daughter
Nottger, Philipp; America, 1867 ***7420.1*** *p261*
With family
Notting, Sophie Louise Charlotte; America, 1866 ***7420.1*** *p250*
Nottingham, James; America, 1755 ***1220.12*** *p588*
Nottingham, Robert; America, 1742 ***1220.12*** *p588*
Nottingham, William; America, 1767 ***1220.12*** *p588*
Nottmeier, Carl Heinrich; America, 1854 ***7420.1*** *p126*
Nottmeier, Friedrich; America, 1888 ***7420.1*** *p357*
Nottmeier, Georg Heinrich Wilhelm; America, 1885 ***7420.1*** *p348*
Nottmeier, Sophie Wilhelmine Caroline; America, 1876 ***7420.1*** *p307*
Notton, Jakob; America, 1867 ***5475.1*** *p124*
Noulty, John 32; Ontario, 1871 ***1823.21*** *p282*
Noumann, Baltazar; Ohio, 1809-1852 ***4511.35*** *p39*
Nourice, Marin 25; Quebec, 1661 ***9221.17*** *p464*
Nourricier, Chas; Louisiana, 1874-1875 ***4981.45*** *p30*
Nourry, Jacques 13; Quebec, 1651 ***9221.17*** *p248*
Nourse, Philip; America, 1768 ***1220.12*** *p589*
Noustens, F.; Louisiana, 1874-1875 ***4981.45*** *p30*
Nouvel, Henry 38; Quebec, 1662 ***9221.17*** *p477*
Novacek, Antonin J.; Montreal, 1892 ***2853.20*** *p201*
Novacek, Antonin J.; New York, NY, 1892 ***2853.20*** *p201*
Novacek, Frantisek; Nebraska, 1871-1872 ***2853.20*** *p176*
Novacek, Frantisek, Sr.; Nebraska, 1876-1877 ***2853.20*** *p172*
Novak, Anna Sloup-Vachalova *SEE* Novak, Jan
Novak, Antonin; Milwaukee, 1866 ***2853.20*** *p309*
Novak, Antonin; New York, 1869 ***2853.20*** *p118*
Novak, Antonin; Wisconsin, 1853 ***2853.20*** *p303*
Novak, Frantisek; Chicago, 1856 ***2853.20*** *p389*
With father
Novak, Frantisek; Chicago, 1884 ***2853.20*** *p29*
Novak, Frantisek Dagobert; Chicago, 1896 ***2853.20*** *p527*
Novak, Jan; Chicago, 1868 ***2853.20*** *p393*
Novak, Jan; Wisconsin, 1853 ***2853.20*** *p303*
*Wife:*Anna Sloup-Vachalova
Novak, Josef; Cleveland, OH, 1854 ***2853.20*** *p475*
Novak, Josef J.; Chicago, 1884 ***2853.20*** *p29*
Novak, Karel; New York, NY, 1893 ***2853.20*** *p469*
Novak, Matej; Texas, 1856 ***2853.20*** *p67*
Novak, Tomas; Chicago, 1868 ***2853.20*** *p514*
Novakova, Anna; Chicago, 1868 ***2853.20*** *p393*
With parents
Novakova, Liska; New York, NY, 1893 ***2853.20*** *p469*
Noves, Marie 55; Missouri, 1846 ***778.6*** *p257*
Novinsky, Josef; Omaha, NE, 1875 ***2853.20*** *p144*
Novotny, Dr.; Chicago, 1909 ***2853.20*** *p410*
Novotny, Jan; Nebraska, 1856-1870 ***2853.20*** *p181*
Novotny, Jan Kr.; Nebraska, 1904 ***2853.20*** *p164*
Novotny, Josef; South Dakota, 1869-1871 ***2853.20*** *p246*
Novotny, Josef; Wisconsin, 1853 ***2853.20*** *p290*
Novy, Josef J.; New York, NY, 1892-1910 ***2853.20*** *p116*
Novy, Martin; Iowa, 1855-1856 ***2853.20*** *p237*
Nowak, Anna 26; New York, NY, 1912 ***8355.1*** *p16*
Nowak, Ignatius; Wisconsin, 1893 ***6795.8*** *p205*
Nowak, Jennie; Detroit, 1929 ***1640.55*** *p117*
Nowak, John; Detroit, 1929-1930 ***6214.5*** *p69*
Nowak, Wojciech; Detroit, 1930 ***1640.60*** *p82*
Nowakowski, August 42; New York, NY, 1920 ***930.50*** *p49*
Nowatny, Albert; Wisconsin, 1893 ***6795.8*** *p205*
Nowden, Ann; Virginia, 1732 ***1220.12*** *p588*
Nowel, Joan; America, 1758 ***1220.12*** *p588*
Nowell, Esther; America, 1769 ***1220.12*** *p588*
Nowell, George; America, 1685 ***1220.12*** *p588*
Nowell, James; America, 1744 ***1220.12*** *p588*
Nowell, John; Salisbury, MA, 1684 ***9228.50*** *p479*
*Brother:*Richard
Nowell, Lamprey; America, 1760 ***1220.12*** *p588*
Nowell, Philip; Salem, MA, 1675 ***9228.50*** *p478*
Nowell, Richard *SEE* Nowell, John
Nowels, Thomas; America, 1773 ***1220.12*** *p477*
Nowinska, Frances; Detroit, 1890 ***9980.23*** *p96*
Nowis, Percival; America, 1685 ***1220.12*** *p588*
Nowitsky, William John; Detroit, 1930 ***1640.60*** *p77*
Nowlan, Anne; New Orleans, 1850 ***7242.30*** *p151*
Nowlan, Catherine; New Orleans, 1850 ***7242.30*** *p151*
Nowlan, Daniel; New Orleans, 1850 ***7242.30*** *p151*
Nowlan, Darby; New Orleans, 1850 ***7242.30*** *p152*
Nowlan, Dennis; New Orleans, 1850 ***7242.30*** *p152*
Nowlan, Edward; St. Johns, N.F., 1825 ***1053.15*** *p6*
Nowlan, Eliza; New Orleans, 1850 ***7242.30*** *p152*
Nowlan, James; New Orleans, 1850 ***7242.30*** *p152*
Nowlan, James 40; St. Johns, N.F., 1811 ***1053.20*** *p22*
Nowlan, John; New Orleans, 1850 ***7242.30*** *p152*
Nowlan, John 28; Ontario, 1871 ***1823.17*** *p126*
Nowlan, Martin; New Orleans, 1850 ***7242.30*** *p152*
Nowlan, Mary; New Orleans, 1850 ***7242.30*** *p152*
Nowlan, Peter; New Orleans, 1850 ***7242.30*** *p152*
Nowlan, Sally; New Orleans, 1850 ***7242.30*** *p152*
Nowlan, Thomas; New Orleans, 1850 ***7242.30*** *p152*
Nowlan, William; Boston, 1757 ***1642*** *p47*
Nowland, Ann; America, 1731 ***1220.12*** *p585*
Nowland, James; Boston, 1768 ***1642*** *p39*
Nowland, Martha; New Orleans, 1851 ***7242.30*** *p152*
Nowland, Michael; Boston, 1754 ***1642*** *p47*
Nowland, Richard; New Orleans, 1851 ***7242.30*** *p152*
Nowland, William; New Orleans, 1851 ***7242.30*** *p152*
Nowles, John; America, 1767 ***1220.12*** *p477*
Nowlon, Eloner; Boston, 1766 ***1642*** *p36*
Nowosad, Frank; Detroit, 1929-1930 ***6214.5*** *p70*
Noxel, August 32; Ontario, 1871 ***1823.21*** *p282*
Noyelles, Nicolas-Joseph de; Quebec, 1710 ***2314.30*** *p169*
Noyelles, Nicolas-Joseph de; Quebec, 1710 ***2314.30*** *p192*
Noyes, Mary 27; America, 1846 ***778.6*** *p257*
Noyes, Richard; Barbados, 1701 ***1220.12*** *p588*
Noyes, William; America, 1774 ***1220.12*** *p588*
Noyes, William; Barbados, 1669 ***1220.12*** *p588*
Noyes, William 55; Ontario, 1871 ***1823.21*** *p282*
Noyle, Charles 28; Ontario, 1871 ***1823.21*** *p282*
Noys, James 30; Ontario, 1871 ***1823.17*** *p126*
Nubling, Albert; New Orleans, 1853 ***7710.1*** *p154*
Nucke, Richard; West Indies, 1668 ***1220.12*** *p588*
Nuechtern, Johann Friedr.; America, 1838 ***170.15*** *p38*
Nuel, John 63; Ontario, 1871 ***1823.17*** *p126*
Nuemen, Robert 23; Montreal, 1660 ***9221.17*** *p443*
Nuff, Patrick; Boston, 1765 ***1642*** *p35*
Nugent, Andrew; America, 1750 ***1220.12*** *p589*
Nugent, Cecelia 26; Ontario, 1871 ***1823.21*** *p282*
Nugent, Edward; Rappahannock, VA, 1728 ***1220.12*** *p589*
Nugent, Henry 9; St. John, N.B., 1834 ***6469.7*** *p5*
Nugent, Hugh 5; St. John, N.B., 1834 ***6469.7*** *p5*
Nugent, James; Boston, 1830 ***3274.55*** *p42*
Nugent, James 37; Ontario, 1871 ***1823.17*** *p126*
Nugent, John; America, 1768 ***1220.12*** *p589*
Nugent, Mary Kelly *SEE* Nugent, Peter
Nugent, Michael 11; St. John, N.B., 1834 ***6469.7*** *p5*
Nugent, Oliver; New Jersey, 1795 ***3845.2*** *p130*
Nugent, Patrick; America, 1753 ***1220.12*** *p589*
Nugent, Peter; Philadelphia, 1862 ***8513.31*** *p418*
*Wife:*Mary Kelly
Nugent, Philip; America, 1764 ***1220.12*** *p589*
Nugent, Thomas 30; Ontario, 1871 ***1823.17*** *p127*
Nugent, William; America, 1763 ***1220.12*** *p589*
Nugent, William 24; St. John, N.B., 1834 ***6469.7*** *p5*
Nuhan, Jeremiah; Boston, 1766 ***1642*** *p36*
Nuler, Eliz.b 23; New York, NY, 1847 ***9176.15*** *p50*
Null, Henry; Ohio, 1809-1852 ***4511.35*** *p39*
Nulle, Miss; Chicago, 1873 ***7420.1*** *p299*
Nulle, Heinrich Conrad; America, 1866 ***7420.1*** *p246*
With family
Nulty, Patrick; New York, NY, 1842 ***3274.56*** *p101*
Numa, Richard 23; Missouri, 1848 ***778.6*** *p257*
Numan, Robert 23; Montreal, 1660 ***9221.17*** *p443*
Numann, N.; New York, 1859 ***358.56*** *p100*
Nun, James; Virginia, 1721 ***1220.12*** *p589*
Nuner, Katharina 32; America, 1879 ***5475.1*** *p267*
Nunin, James; Ohio, 1809-1852 ***4511.35*** *p39*
Nunn, Elizabeth; America, 1767 ***1220.12*** *p589*
Nunn, John; America, 1695 ***1220.12*** *p589*
Nunn, William; America, 1765 ***1220.12*** *p589*
Nunny, Thomas; America, 1753 ***1220.12*** *p589*
Nurcombe, William; Barbados, 1667 ***1220.12*** *p589*
Nurmemaker, Daniel C. 25; Ontario, 1871 ***1823.21*** *p282*
Nurmi, Fannie 28; Minnesota, 1923 ***2769.54*** *p1379*
Nurmi, Gust; Minnesota, 1926 ***2769.54*** *p1379*
Nurse, Catherine; America, 1772 ***1220.12*** *p589*
Nurse, John; Barbados, 1664 ***1220.12*** *p589*
Nurse, William; America, 1750 ***1220.12*** *p589*
Nurton, William; America, 1739 ***1220.12*** *p589*
Nuss, Heinrich M.; New York, NY, 1893 ***3366.30*** *p70*
Nuss, Michael M.; New York, NY, 1893 ***3366.30*** *p70*
Nuss, Peter; Louisiana, 1841-1844 ***4981.45*** *p211*
Nussbaum, . . .; North Carolina, 1710 ***3629.40*** *p6*
Nussbaumer, Jakob 19; Galveston, TX, 1846 ***3967.10*** *p378*
Nussbaumer, Michael 21; Galveston, TX, 1846 ***3967.10*** *p378*
Nussey, William; America, 1740 ***1220.12*** *p589*
Nusz, Pierre 35; America, 1845 ***778.6*** *p257*
Nutall, Charles; North Carolina, 1855 ***1088.45*** *p25*
Nutall, Robert; Died enroute, 1729 ***1220.12*** *p589*
Nutbrown, John; America, 1751 ***1220.12*** *p589*
Nutbrown, Miles; America, 1751 ***1220.12*** *p589*
Nutcombe, George; Virginia, 1765 ***1220.12*** *p589*
Nutelet, Joseph; Wisconsin, 1856 ***1494.21*** *p31*
Nuthall, Thomas; America, 1770 ***1220.12*** *p589*
Nutkins, Thomas; America, 1749 ***1220.12*** *p589*
Nutley, Henry; Virginia, 1763 ***1220.12*** *p589*
Nutley, Hugh; America, 1718 ***1220.12*** *p589*
Nuton, William 25; Ontario, 1871 ***1823.21*** *p282*
Nuton, Wm 60; Ontario, 1871 ***1823.21*** *p282*
Nutore, William 22; Ontario, 1871 ***1823.21*** *p282*
Nutt, Elizabeth *SEE* Nutt, James
Nutt, James; New York, 1739 ***8277.31*** *p119*
*Wife:*Rebecca Creighton
*Child:*John
*Child:*Elizabeth
*Child:*Robert
Nutt, John; Charles Town, SC, 1718 ***1220.12*** *p589*
Nutt, John *SEE* Nutt, James

Nutt, John; Philadelphia, 1778 *8529.30 p4A*
Nutt, Mary; New York, 1739 *8277.31 p113*
Nutt, Rebecca Creighton *SEE* Nutt, James
Nutt, Robert *SEE* Nutt, James
Nutt, Sarah; Annapolis, MD, 1724 *1220.12 p589*
Nutt, Thomas; America, 1723 *1220.12 p589*
Nuttal, Thomas; America, 1754 *1220.12 p589*
Nuttall, George; America, 1769 *1220.12 p589*
Nuttall, Henry 33; Ontario, 1871 *1823.17 p127*
Nuttall, John; America, 1765 *1220.12 p589*
Nuttall, Mrs. M.; Montreal, 1922 *4514.4 p32*
Nuttall, Richard; America, 1662 *1220.12 p589*
Nuttall, Thomas; America, 1662 *1220.12 p589*

Nutter, Elizabeth; America, 1775 *1220.12 p589*
Nutter, Helen; West Indies, 1614 *1220.12 p589*
Nutter, Richard; America, 1752 *1220.12 p589*
Nutter, Richard 47; Ontario, 1871 *1823.17 p127*
Nutter, Sarah; America, 1768 *1220.12 p589*
Nuttier, James; Barbados, 1666 *1220.12 p589*
Nuttin, Thomas; Barbados or Jamaica, 1692 *1220.12 p589*
Nutting, Thomas; Barbados, 1662 *1220.12 p589*
Nutzel, John A.; North Carolina, 1844 *1088.45 p25*
Nyberg, Andrew L.; Indiana, 1887-1889 *1865.50 p100*
Nyberg, Erick; Illinois, 1861 *4487.25 p68*
Nyberg, Sam; Colorado, 1892 *1029.59 p69*

Nycek, Stanislaus; Detroit, 1929 *1640.55 p116*
Nydell, Peter J.; Minnesota, 1881-1886 *1865.50 p101*
Nye, Henry 35; Ontario, 1871 *1823.17 p127*
Nye, Nancy 5; Quebec, 1870 *8364.32 p25*
Nye, Valentine; Ohio, 1809-1852 *4511.35 p39*
Nyers, Henrietta 12; Quebec, 1870 *8364.32 p25*
Nygren, Peter J.A.; Cleveland, OH, 1893 *9722.10 p124*
Nyquist, Carl; Cleveland, OH, 1892-1895 *9722.10 p124*
Nyren, Fridolf Wiktor; Cleveland, OH, 1902-1906 *9722.10 p125*
Nyren, Mathilda; St. Paul, MN, 1874-1905 *1865.50 p101*
Nystrom, Olof; Kansas, 1870-1875 *777.40 p16*
Nyysella, Charles 20; Minnesota, 1923 *2769.54 p1383*

O

Oadley, Sarah; America, 1765 *1220.12 p590*
Oadway, Mary; America, 1750 *1220.12 p590*
Oag, James 34; Ontario, 1871 *1823.17 p127*
Oag, James 37; Ontario, 1871 *1823.17 p127*
Oak, William 19; Ontario, 1871 *1823.21 p284*
Oakam, James; America, 1766 *1220.12 p590*
Oakby, Phoebe 10; Quebec, 1870 *8364.32 p25*
Oakden, George; America, 1772 *1220.12 p590*
Oakeley, Thomas; Virginia, 1730 *1220.12 p590*
Oaker, Francis; America, 1663 *1220.12 p590*
Oaker, Henry; Barbados, 1715 *1220.12 p590*
Oakes, Elen Z. 15; Michigan, 1880 *4491.30 p24*
Oakes, Jeremiah; America, 1762 *1220.12 p590*
Oakes, John; America, 1746 *1220.12 p590*
Oakes, Robert 40; Ontario, 1871 *1823.17 p127*
Oakes, Samuel; America, 1766 *1220.12 p590*
Oakes, Thomas; America, 1746 *1220.12 p590*
Oakes, Thomas; Boston, 1774 *8529.30 p3*
Oakes, William; Barbados, 1664 *1220.12 p590*
Oakes, William 43; Ontario, 1871 *1823.21 p284*
Oakeson, Charles; Kansas, 1870 *777.40 p21*
Oakford, Josiah; Virginia, 1764 *1220.12 p590*
Oakley, Alice; Rappahannock, VA, 1729 *1220.12 p590*
Oakley, Benjamin; America, 1770 *1220.12 p590*
Oakley, Christopher; America, 1739 *1220.12 p590*
Oakley, Francis; Barbados, 1668 *1220.12 p590*
Oakley, George; America, 1769 *1220.12 p590*
Oakley, Hugh; Charles Town, SC, 1719 *1220.12 p590*
Oakley, James; Quebec, 1870 *8364.32 p25*
Oakley, Samuel; America, 1751 *1220.12 p590*
Oakley, Sarah; America, 1727 *1220.12 p590*
Oakley, Thomas; America, 1751 *1220.12 p590*
Oakley, Thomas; America, 1756 *1220.12 p590*
Oakley, Thomas; Annapolis, MD, 1730 *1220.12 p590*
Oakley, Thomas; Washington, 1887 *2770.40 p25*
Oakley, William; America, 1753 *1220.12 p590*
Oakley, William 68; Ontario, 1871 *1823.21 p284*
Oakly, Thomas; America, 1770 *1220.12 p590*
Oaks, George; North Carolina, 1859 *1088.45 p26*
Oaks, Hiram 54; Ontario, 1871 *1823.17 p127*
Oaks, John 33; Ontario, 1871 *1823.21 p284*
Oaks, Lawrence 51; Ontario, 1871 *1823.21 p284*
Oaks, Nancy 78; Ontario, 1871 *1823.21 p284*
Oaks, Samuel 50; Ontario, 1871 *1823.21 p284*
Oaks, Theophilus 55; Ontario, 1871 *1823.17 p128*
Oar, Thomas; America, 1772 *1220.12 p590*
Oarran, Frank; Colorado, 1873 *1029.59 p70*
Oasie, William; America, 1773 *1220.12 p590*
Oates, Elizabeth; America, 1763 *1220.12 p590*
Oates, Mary; Virginia, 1721 *1220.12 p590*
Oatley, Margaret; America, 1760 *1220.12 p590*
Oatridge, James; Virginia, 1767 *1220.12 p590*
Oats, Joseph 51; Ontario, 1871 *1823.21 p284*
Oatway, Elizabeth; America, 1765 *1220.12 p590*
Oatway, John; America, 1738 *1220.12 p590*
Obawitz, Anton 44; New York, NY, 1893 *1883.7 p40*
Obawitz, Anton 44; New York, NY, 1893 *1883.7 p47*
Obawitz, Barbara 40; New York, NY, 1893 *1883.7 p40*
Obawitz, Barbara 40; New York, NY, 1893 *1883.7 p47*
Obawitz, Peter 11; New York, NY, 1893 *1883.7 p40*
Obawitz, Peter 11; New York, NY, 1893 *1883.7 p47*
Obawitz, Veroni 16; New York, NY, 1893 *1883.7 p40*
Obawitz, Veroni 16; New York, NY, 1893 *1883.7 p47*
Obbins, Robert; America, 1743 *1220.12 p590*
Obe, Franz; America, 1878 *5475.1 p128*
Obear, Richard; Massachusetts, 1664 *9228.50 p479*
O'Beirne, Miss; Toronto, 1844 *2910.35 p112*

Oben, Catherine Jane; Nebraska, 1858-1885 *9228.50 p659*
Oben, Catherine Jane *SEE* Oben, Philip
Oben, Eliz. de Sainte Croix *SEE* Oben, Philip
Oben, John; California, 1850-1950 *9228.50 p659*
Oben, Philip *SEE* Oben, Philip
Oben, Philip; Toronto, 1860-1869 *9228.50 p659*
  *Child:*Philip
  *Wife:*Eliz. de Sainte Croix
  *Child:*Catherine Jane
Obendorff, Frederick; Louisiana, 1874 *4981.45 p296*
Obenlock, Henry; Ohio, 1809-1852 *4511.35 p39*
Ober, . . .; New England, n.d. *9228.50 p85*
Ober, Franziska; Venezuela, 1843 *3899.5 p543*
Ober, Richard; Massachusetts, 1664 *9228.50 p479*
Oberg, Carl; Cleveland, OH, 1902-1906 *9722.10 p125*
Oberg, Charles; Washington, 1883 *2770.40 p137*
Oberg, J.W.; New York, NY, 1845 *6412.40 p148*
Oberg, John; Cleveland, OH, 1895-1905 *9722.10 p125*
Oberg, John Algot; Miami, 1935 *4984.12 p39*
Oberg, Mathilda; St. Paul, MN, 1882 *1865.50 p44*
Oberkercher, Jacob; Ohio, 1809-1852 *4511.35 p39*
Oberle, Adam Karl; America, 1894 *2526.42 p195*
  *Son:*Joseph Anton
  *Daughter:*Elisabeth Caroline
Oberle, Elisabeth Caroline 4 *SEE* Oberle, Adam Karl
Oberle, Friedrich; America, 1856 *2526.42 p163*
Oberle, Joseph Anton 5 *SEE* Oberle, Adam Karl
Oberle, Matthaus; America, 1882 *2526.42 p170*
Oberleiter, Catherine; New York, 1860 *358.56 p5*
Oberlin, Franziska; Venezuela, 1843 *3899.5 p543*
Oberlin, Georg; Venezuela, 1843 *3899.5 p543*
O'Berlinger, John; North Carolina, 1849 *1088.45 p25*
Oberly, Christian; Ohio, 1809-1852 *4511.35 p39*
Obermueller, Fr. Xav.; Wisconsin, 1846-1886 *2853.20 p346*
Obernhaeuser, Johann Michael; Pennsylvania, 1850 *170.15 p38*
Oberringer, Wenda Haufs *SEE* Oberringer, Wilhelm
Oberringer, Wilhelm; Chicago, 1900 *5475.1 p427*
  *Wife:*Wenda Haufs
Oberskin, Jean 35; America, 1844 *778.6 p257*
Oberskin, Ordelle 32; America, 1844 *778.6 p258*
Oberst, Franz 45; Died enroute, 1817-1818 *90.20 p153*
Oberst, Joseph 28; New Castle, DE, 1817-1818 *90.20 p153*
Obertreis, Karl; America, 1861 *5475.1 p533*
Obland, Mary; Massachusetts, 1726 *1642 p102*
Obligschlager, Alexander 26; Galveston, TX, 1844 *3967.10 p375*
Obligschlager, Joseph 1; Galveston, TX, 1844 *3967.10 p375*
Obligschlager, Maria Anna 26; Galveston, TX, 1844 *3967.10 p375*
Obney, Robert; America, 1749 *1220.12 p590*
O'Boyle, Daniel; Toronto, 1844 *2910.35 p116*
O'Brain, James; Boston, 1735 *1642 p44*
Obrain, Thomas; Newbury, MA, 1755 *1642 p75*
O'Brian, Darby; Boston, 1753 *1642 p31*
O'Brian, James; Colorado, 1878 *1029.59 p69*
O'Brian, Joseph; North Carolina, 1825 *1088.45 p25*
Obrian, Mary; Boston, 1752 *1642 p46*
O'Brian, Mary; Massachusetts, 1769 *1642 p106*
O'Brian, Patrick; Ohio, 1854 *3580.20 p33*
O'Brian, Patrick; Ohio, 1854 *6020.12 p21*
Obrian, Thomas; Boston, 1744 *1642 p45*
Obrian, Thomas; Boston, 1752 *1642 p46*
O'Brian, Thomas 45; Ontario, 1871 *1823.21 p282*

O'Brian, William; America, 1750 *1220.12 p591*
Obriant, David; Boston, 1749 *1642 p46*
Obriant, James; Boston, 1753 *1642 p47*
O'Brien, A.; New Orleans, 1850 *7242.30 p152*
O'Brien, C.; Louisiana, 1874 *4981.45 p133*
O'Brien, Catherine; New Brunswick, 1842 *2978.20 p9*
O'Brien, Catherine 40; Ontario, 1871 *1823.17 p127*
O'Brien, Charity 80; Ontario, 1871 *1823.21 p282*
O'Brien, Dennis; America, 1768 *1220.12 p590*
O'Brien, Edward; America, 1768 *1220.12 p590*
O'Brien, Ellen 60; Ontario, 1871 *1823.21 p282*
Obrien, George; Ontario, 1871 *1823.17 p128*
O'Brien, Hannah 27; Ontario, 1871 *1823.21 p282*
O'Brien, Henry; North Carolina, 1839 *1088.45 p25*
O'Brien, James; Colorado, 1885 *1029.59 p69*
O'Brien, James; Louisiana, 1874 *4981.45 p133*
O'Brien, James; Louisiana, 1874 *4981.45 p296*
O'Brien, James 45; Ontario, 1871 *1823.17 p127*
O'Brien, James 45; Ontario, 1871 *1823.21 p282*
O'Brien, James; Toronto, 1844 *2910.35 p112*
O'Brien, Jane; America, 1764 *1220.12 p591*
O'Brien, Jeremiah 33; Ontario, 1871 *1823.21 p282*
O'Brien, John; Boston, 1746 *1642 p46*
O Brien, John; Colorado, 1887 *1029.59 p69*
O'Brien, John; Colorado, 1887 *1029.59 p69*
O'Brien, John 43; Ontario, 1871 *1823.17 p127*
O'Brien, John; Toronto, 1844 *2910.35 p114*
O'Brien, John M.; Louisiana, 1874 *4981.45 p133*
Obrien, Joseph 79; Ontario, 1871 *1823.21 p284*
O'Brien, Loramy; America, 1761 *1220.12 p591*
O'Brien, Margaret 50; Ontario, 1871 *1823.17 p127*
O'Brien, Mary; America, 1766 *1220.12 p591*
O'Brien, Mary; Boston, 1767 *1642 p39*
O'Brien, Mary Ann; New Brunswick, 1842 *2978.20 p9*
O'Brien, Patrick; Louisiana, 1874 *4981.45 p133*
O'Brien, Patrick; New York, NY, 1827 *3274.55 p69*
Obrien, Patrick 50; Ontario, 1871 *1823.17 p128*
O'Brien, Patrick; Philadelphia, 1855 *8513.31 p418*
O'Brien, Patrick C.; Colorado, 1888 *1029.59 p69*
O'Brien, Patrick C.; Illinois, 1866 *1029.59 p69*
O'Brien, Robert; Toronto, 1844 *2910.35 p113*
O'Brien, Sprier 32; Ontario, 1871 *1823.21 p283*
O'Brien, Thomas; America, 1749 *1220.12 p591*
O'Brien, Thomas 64; Ontario, 1871 *1823.21 p283*
O'Brien, Thomas 16; Quebec, 1870 *8364.32 p25*
O'Brien, Timothy 38; Ontario, 1871 *1823.21 p283*
O'Brien, Wheeney; New Brunswick, 1842 *2978.20 p9*
O'Brien, William; America, 1766 *1220.12 p591*
O'Brien, William; America, 1773 *1220.12 p591*
O'Brien, William; Ohio, 1854 *3580.20 p33*
O'Brien, William; Ohio, 1854 *6020.12 p21*
O'Brien, William 46; Ontario, 1871 *1823.21 p283*
Obrikewitz, Karl 11; Portland, ME, 1910 *970.38 p80*
Obrikewitz, Margaretha 2; Portland, ME, 1910 *970.38 p80*
Obrikewitz, Michail 30; Portland, ME, 1910 *970.38 p80*
Obrikewitz, Susanna 26; Portland, ME, 1910 *970.38 p80*
O'Bril, Timothy; Ohio, 1809-1852 *4511.35 p39*
O'Brin, Cornealus; Louisiana, 1836-1841 *4981.45 p209*
O'Brine, Henry 23; Ontario, 1871 *1823.21 p283*
O'Brine, James 48; Ontario, 1871 *1823.17 p127*
Obrine, John 40; Ontario, 1871 *1823.21 p284*
O'Brine, Mary; Dedham, MA, 1757 *1642 p102*
O'Brine, Mary 26; Ontario, 1871 *1823.21 p283*
Obringer, Balth. 20; America, 1840 *778.6 p258*
Obringer, Joh. 28; America, 1840 *778.6 p258*
Obrist, Albrecht; Ohio, 1809-1852 *4511.35 p39*
Obrist, Albright; Ohio, 1809-1852 *4511.35 p39*

Obrist PASSENGER AND IMMIGRATION LISTS INDEX: 1999 SUPPLEMENT PART 2

Obrist, Franz 45; Died enroute, 1817-1818 ***90.20*** *p153*
Obrist, Johann 45; New Castle, DE, 1817-1818 ***90.20*** *p153*
Obrist, Joseph 28; New Castle, DE, 1817-1818 ***90.20*** *p153*
Obroum, Corn; Boston, 1764 ***1642*** *p33*
O'Bryan, Eleanor; America, 1756 ***1220.12*** *p591*
O'Bryan, Hugh; Boston, 1751 ***1642*** *p46*
O'Bryan, James; America, 1765 ***1220.12*** *p591*
O'Bryan, James; Boston, 1744 ***1642*** *p45*
O'Bryan, James; Virginia, 1765 ***1220.12*** *p591*
Obryan, Joan; Boston, 1747 ***1642*** *p46*
O'Bryan, John; Boston, 1735 ***1642*** *p44*
O'Bryan, John; New England, 1745 ***1642*** *p28*
O'Bryan, John 50; Ontario, 1871 ***1823.21*** *p283*
O'Bryan, Judith; America, 1750 ***1220.12*** *p591*
O'Bryan, Mary; Boston, 1768 ***1642*** *p39*
O'Bryan, Michael 35; Ontario, 1871 ***1823.17*** *p127*
O'Bryan, Walter; America, 1738 ***1220.12*** *p591*
Obryan, William; Virginia, 1718 ***1220.12*** *p591*
Obryon, James; Boston, 1732 ***1642*** *p44*
O'Byrne, Bernard 32; Ontario, 1871 ***1823.21*** *p283*
O'Callaghan, John; Toronto, 1844 ***2910.35*** *p112*
O'Callaghan, Patrick; Toronto, 1844 ***2910.35*** *p115*
O'Callaghen, Thomas; Ohio, 1826 ***3580.20*** *p33*
O'Callaghen, Thomas; Ohio, 1826 ***6020.12*** *p21*
O'Carroll, John; Toronto, 1844 ***2910.35*** *p111*
Ochab, Teofila 20; New York, NY, 1904 ***8355.1*** *p15*
Ochler, George W.; North Carolina, 1840 ***1088.45*** *p26*
Ochler, John G.; North Carolina, 1840 ***1088.45*** *p26*
Ochler, Philip; North Carolina, 1792-1862 ***1088.45*** *p26*
Ochman, John Godfrey; North Carolina, 1830 ***1088.45*** *p26*
Ochs, Andelina 25; New York, NY, 1893 ***1883.7*** *p40*
Ochs, Joh 26; New York, NY, 1893 ***1883.7*** *p40*
Ochs, Johann; Pittsburgh, 1840 ***5475.1*** *p73*
Ochs, John; New York, 1859 ***358.56*** *p54*
Ochs, Marg 9 months; New York, NY, 1893 ***1883.7*** *p40*
Ochs, Rinteln; America, 1833 ***7420.1*** *p7*
Ochsenbecher, Henrich; New Jersey, 1764-1774 ***927.31*** *p2*
Ochsner, Jacob 71; New York, NY, 1874 ***6954.7*** *p38*
Ochszner, Amelie 1; New York, NY, 1874 ***6954.7*** *p38*
Ochszner, Andreas 20; New York, NY, 1874 ***6954.7*** *p38*
Ochszner, Anna 8; New York, NY, 1874 ***6954.7*** *p38*
Ochszner, August 2 months; New York, NY, 1874 ***6954.7*** *p38*
Ochszner, Carl 6; New York, NY, 1874 ***6954.7*** *p38*
Ochszner, Catharina 23; New York, NY, 1874 ***6954.7*** *p38*
Ochszner, Catharine 13; New York, NY, 1874 ***6954.7*** *p38*
Ochszner, Christian 1; New York, NY, 1874 ***6954.7*** *p38*
Ochszner, Christian 23; New York, NY, 1874 ***6954.7*** *p38*
Ochszner, Christina 9; New York, NY, 1874 ***6954.7*** *p38*
Ochszner, Christina 32; New York, NY, 1874 ***6954.7*** *p38*
Ochszner, Christina 37; New York, NY, 1874 ***6954.7*** *p38*
Ochszner, Christine 1 months; New York, NY, 1874 ***6954.7*** *p38*
Ochszner, Elisabeth 6; New York, NY, 1874 ***6954.7*** *p38*
Ochszner, Elisabeth 59; New York, NY, 1874 ***6954.7*** *p38*
Ochszner, Elisabethe 18; New York, NY, 1874 ***6954.7*** *p38*
Ochszner, Elisabethe 20; New York, NY, 1874 ***6954.7*** *p38*
Ochszner, Heinrich 9 months; New York, NY, 1874 ***6954.7*** *p38*
Ochszner, Jacob 10; New York, NY, 1874 ***6954.7*** *p38*
Ochszner, Jacob 25; New York, NY, 1874 ***6954.7*** *p38*
Ochszner, Jacob 37; New York, NY, 1874 ***6954.7*** *p38*
Ochszner, Johann 10; New York, NY, 1874 ***6954.7*** *p38*
Ochszner, Johann 10; New York, NY, 1874 ***6954.7*** *p38*
Ochszner, Johann 23; New York, NY, 1874 ***6954.7*** *p38*
Ochszner, Johanna 8; New York, NY, 1874 ***6954.7*** *p38*
Ochszner, Johanna 33; New York, NY, 1874 ***6954.7*** *p38*
Ochszner, Katharine 1 months; New York, NY, 1874 ***6954.7*** *p38*
Ochszner, Nicolaus 21; New York, NY, 1874 ***6954.7*** *p38*
Ochszner, Peter 7; New York, NY, 1874 ***6954.7*** *p38*
Ochszner, Peter 37; New York, NY, 1874 ***6954.7*** *p38*
Ochszner, Philipp 4; New York, NY, 1874 ***6954.7*** *p38*
Ochszner, Rosine 1 months; New York, NY, 1874 ***6954.7*** *p38*
Ochszner, Wilhelm 9; New York, NY, 1874 ***6954.7*** *p38*
Ochzet, Franziska 22; New York, NY, 1893 ***1883.7*** *p44*
Ochzet, Josef 2; New York, NY, 1893 ***1883.7*** *p44*
Ochzet, Wenzl 6 months; New York, NY, 1893 ***1883.7*** *p44*
Ocker, Charles A.; Washington, 1884 ***6015.10*** *p16*
Ockermann, Bodil 16; New York, NY, 1894 ***6512.1*** *p185*
Ockermann, Elizabeth 23; New York, NY, 1894 ***6512.1*** *p185*
Ockford, Nathaniel; America, 1734 ***1220.12*** *p591*
Ockleford, Mary; America, 1759 ***1220.12*** *p591*
Ockram, Vincent; America, 1736 ***1220.12*** *p591*
Ockynall, Tego; Boston, 1662 ***1642*** *p10*
O'Connel, Tego; Boston, 1662 ***1642*** *p10*
O'Connell, Dennis; Toronto, 1844 ***2910.35*** *p113*
O'Connell, Francis; Toronto, 1844 ***2910.35*** *p112*
O'Connell, James; Toronto, 1844 ***2910.35*** *p114*
O'Connell, John; Ohio, 1844 ***2763.1*** *p21*
O'Connell, Owen; Toronto, 1844 ***2910.35*** *p112*
O'Connell, Patrick; Toronto, 1844 ***2910.35*** *p116*
O'Connell, Phillip; Toronto, 1844 ***2910.35*** *p112*
O'Connell, Richard; Toronto, 1844 ***2910.35*** *p114*
O'Connell, Timothy; North Carolina, 1856 ***1088.45*** *p26*
O'Conner, Hugh; North Carolina, 1834 ***1088.45*** *p25*
O'Conner, James 36; Ontario, 1871 ***1823.21*** *p283*
Oconner, James 40; Ontario, 1871 ***1823.21*** *p285*
O'Conner, James; Toronto, 1844 ***2910.35*** *p113*
O'Conner, John; Toronto, 1844 ***2910.35*** *p115*
Oconner, Mary 27; Ontario, 1871 ***1823.21*** *p285*
O'Conner, Michael; Toronto, 1844 ***2910.35*** *p115*
O'Conner, Patrick; North Carolina, 1855 ***1088.45*** *p25*
O'Conner, Philip Charles; Died enroute, 1726 ***1220.12*** *p591*
O'Conner, Thomas; Toronto, 1844 ***2910.35*** *p112*
O'Conner, Timothy; America, 1772 ***1220.12*** *p591*
O'Conners, Mary 37; Ohio, 1880 ***4879.40*** *p259*
Oconnor, Bridget 53; Michigan, 1880 ***4491.39*** *p22*
Oconnor, Catherine 62; Ontario, 1871 ***1823.21*** *p285*
Oconnor, Daniel 40; Ontario, 1871 ***1823.17*** *p128*
Oconnor, Elen 28; Michigan, 1880 ***4491.39*** *p22*
Oconnor, Honora 16; Michigan, 1880 ***4491.39*** *p22*
O'Connor, James 36; Ontario, 1871 ***1823.21*** *p283*
Oconnor, James 45; Ontario, 1871 ***1823.21*** *p285*
O'Connor, John; Iowa, 1913 ***1211.15*** *p17*
O'Connor, Martin 40; Ontario, 1871 ***1823.21*** *p283*
O'Connor, Michael 40; Ontario, 1871 ***1823.21*** *p283*
Oconnor, Morris 42; Michigan, 1880 ***4491.39*** *p22*
O'Connor, Patrick; Toronto, 1844 ***2910.35*** *p113*
O'Connor, Patrick; Toronto, 1844 ***2910.35*** *p114*
O'Connor, Richard 28; Ontario, 1871 ***1823.17*** *p127*
Oconnor, Timothy 34; Michigan, 1880 ***4491.39*** *p22*
O'Connor, William 32; Ontario, 1871 ***1823.21*** *p283*
O'Connor, William 48; Ontario, 1871 ***1823.21*** *p283*
O'Connor, William; South Carolina, 1834 ***6155.4*** *p19*
Octhafer, John Jacob; Louisiana, 1874 ***4981.45*** *p133*
Octorn, John 22; America, 1848 ***778.6*** *p258*
Oczkowicz, Wladyslaw 20; New York, NY, 1911 ***6533.11*** *p9*
O'Daniel, James; Boston, 1766 ***1642*** *p37*
O'Dannell, Terence; North Carolina, 1844 ***1088.45*** *p26*
O'Davey, Conn; Colorado, 1873 ***1029.59*** *p69*
O'Day, Frances; North Carolina, 1844 ***1088.45*** *p26*
Odbert, Thomas; Ohio, 1824 ***3580.20*** *p33*
Odbert, Thomas; Ohio, 1824 ***6020.12*** *p21*
Oddershede, Anton Christ 18; New York, NY, 1894 ***6512.1*** *p185*
Odderway, James; America, 1749 ***1220.12*** *p591*
Oddon, Stephen; Ohio, 1809-1852 ***4511.35*** *p39*
Oddy, Francis; Annapolis, MD, 1726 ***1220.12*** *p591*
Oddy, Miles; Maryland, 1729 ***1220.12*** *p591*
O'Dea, Mrs. F.; Toronto, 1844 ***2910.35*** *p112*
O'Dea, Francis; Toronto, 1844 ***2910.35*** *p111*
O'Dea, Mary 37; Ontario, 1871 ***1823.21*** *p283*
Odele, Edward; America, 1764 ***1220.12*** *p591*
Odell, Cornelia 81; Ontario, 1871 ***1823.21*** *p285*
Odell, Edward; America, 1770 ***1220.12*** *p591*
Odell, Edwin 28; Ontario, 1871 ***1823.21*** *p285*
Odell, Elizabeth; America, 1769 ***1220.12*** *p591*
Odell, Fred 45; Ontario, 1871 ***1823.21*** *p285*
Odell, John; Marston's Wharf, 1782 ***8529.30*** *p14*
Odell, John; Potomac, 1729 ***1220.12*** *p591*
Odell, Lorenzo 44; Ontario, 1871 ***1823.17*** *p128*
Odell, Mary; Boston, 1734 ***1642*** *p44*
Odell, Mary 72; Ontario, 1871 ***1823.21*** *p285*
Odell, Simon; America, 1731 ***1220.12*** *p591*
Odell, William; Potomac, 1729 ***1220.12*** *p591*
Oden, J.A.; Cleveland, OH, 1893-1901 ***9722.10*** *p125*
Oden, J.P.; Philadelphia, 1848 ***6412.40*** *p150*
Odenhumer, Wm.; California, 1868 ***1131.61*** *p89*
Odetta, Henry 34; Ontario, 1871 ***1823.17*** *p128*
Odew, Hester; America, 1753 ***1220.12*** *p591*
Odford, Thomas; America, 1724 ***1220.12*** *p591*
Odger, William; America, 1773 ***1220.12*** *p591*
Odgers, John, Jr.; America, 1738 ***1220.12*** *p591*
Odi, Pierre; New York, 1860 ***358.56*** *p4*
Odile, Elie 7; Louisiana, 1848 ***778.6*** *p258*
Odlozelik, Jan; Texas, 1856 ***2853.20*** *p64*
Odon, Jean 18; Quebec, 1649 ***9221.17*** *p218*
O'Donal, Ralph; Boston, 1763 ***1642*** *p32*
O'Donald, James 34; Ontario, 1871 ***1823.17*** *p127*
Odonel, David 37; Ontario, 1871 ***1823.21*** *p285*
O'Donel, Phillip; Boston, 1767 ***1642*** *p38*
O'Donell, Charles; St. John, N.B., 1847 ***2978.15*** *p41*
O'Donell, Geo.; St. John, N.B., 1847 ***2978.15*** *p41*
O'Donell, Thomas; South Carolina, 1848 ***6155.4*** *p19*
Odonely, Catherine; Boston, 1764 ***1642*** *p33*
O'Donley, Charles 37; Ontario, 1871 ***1823.21*** *p283*
O'Donnel, Michael 74; Ontario, 1871 ***1823.21*** *p283*
O'Donnell, Jerry; Toronto, 1844 ***2910.35*** *p113*
O'Donnell, John J.; Colorado, 1882 ***1029.59*** *p70*
O'Donnell, Joseph Herbie; Illinois, 1930 ***121.35*** *p100*
O'Donnell, Mary 30; Ontario, 1871 ***1823.17*** *p127*
O'Donnell, Mathew 30; Ontario, 1871 ***1823.17*** *p127*
Odonnell, Michael 35; Ontario, 1871 ***1823.17*** *p128*
O'Donnell, Patrick; Toronto, 1844 ***2910.35*** *p113*
O'Donnell, Richard 40; Ontario, 1871 ***1823.17*** *p127*
O'Donnell, Rosanna; Philadelphia, 1858 ***8513.31*** *p30*
O'Donnell, Thos 30; Ontario, 1871 ***1823.17*** *p127*
O'Donohoe, John; Toronto, 1844 ***2910.35*** *p111*
O'Donohoe, M.; Toronto, 1844 ***2910.35*** *p111*
O'Donohue, John 42; Ontario, 1871 ***1823.21*** *p283*
O'Donoughe, John 36; Ontario, 1871 ***1823.21*** *p283*
O'Donoughue, John 41; Ontario, 1871 ***1823.21*** *p283*
O'Doud, Dominick 60; Ontario, 1871 ***1823.17*** *p127*
O'Dowd, Brainard; Ohio, 1809-1852 ***4511.35*** *p39*
Odum, James; America, 1747 ***1220.12*** *p591*
O Dwyer, Anthony 60; Ontario, 1871 ***1823.21*** *p282*
O'Dwyer, C.P.; Toronto, 1844 ***2910.35*** *p112*
O'Dwyer, Cathine 64; Ontario, 1871 ***1823.21*** *p283*
O'Dwyer, Daniel 26; Ontario, 1871 ***1823.21*** *p283*
O'Dwyer, Michael 45; Ontario, 1871 ***1823.21*** *p283*
O'Dwyer, Stephen 35; Ontario, 1871 ***1823.21*** *p283*
Odwyn, Samuel; Barbados, 1669 ***1220.12*** *p591*
Oeffner, Johanne; Wisconsin, 1884 ***6795.8*** *p89*
Oehler, Frank; Washington, 1889 ***2770.40*** *p80*
Oehlke, Albert Emil; Wisconsin, 1889 ***6795.8*** *p95*
Oehlke, Albert Gustav; Wisconsin, 1904 ***6795.8*** *p230*
Oehlke, Theodor; Wisconsin, 1901 ***6795.8*** *p232*
Oehm, Heinrich; America, 1883 ***5475.1*** *p316*
Oehst, Christian; Valdivia, Chile, 1852 ***1192.4*** *p56*
With wife
Oekenfeld, Francis; New York, 1859 ***358.56*** *p54*
Oekinger, Joseph; Valdivia, Chile, 1851 ***1192.4*** *p51*
With wife & 2 children
Oelke, Herman; Wisconsin, 1889 ***6795.8*** *p75*
Oelrich, Joseph; New York, 1859-1860 ***358.56*** *p102*
Oering, Chas. 21; America, 1841 ***778.6*** *p258*
Oertel, Casper; Ohio, 1809-1852 ***4511.35*** *p39*
Oertel, John Henry; Ohio, 1809-1852 ***4511.35*** *p39*
Oerter, Jake; Iowa, 1894 ***1211.15*** *p17*
Oeschger, Jean 46; New Castle, DE, 1817-1818 ***90.20*** *p153*
Oeser, Chr.; Venezuela, 1843 ***3899.5*** *p547*
Oesterlen, Emil; Valdivia, Chile, 1852 ***1192.4*** *p53*
Oesterreich, Wilhelm Carl Friedrich; Wisconsin, 1884 ***6795.8*** *p86*
Oetker, Ernst Heinrich; America, 1878 ***7420.1*** *p311*
Oetking, . . .; America, 1854 ***7420.1*** *p126*
With 4 daughters
Oetking, Widow; Port uncertain, 1853 ***7420.1*** *p109*
Oetking, Carl Heinrich; Port uncertain, 1891 ***7420.1*** *p363*
Oetting, Carl Heinrich Friedrich; America, 1881 ***7420.1*** *p323*
Oetting, Caroline Dorothee Marie *SEE* Oetting, Dietrich Christoph
Oetting, Christian Heinrich August; America, 1887 ***7420.1*** *p354*
Oetting, Dietrich Christoph; America, 1892 ***7420.1*** *p366*
*Wife:*Marie Louise Deiters
*Daughter:*Caroline Dorothee Marie
*Son:*Heinrich Gustav
*Son:*Friedrich Dietrich August
Oetting, Eduard Dietrich Wilhelm; America, 1872 ***7420.1*** *p297*
Oetting, Friedrich Dietrich August *SEE* Oetting, Dietrich Christoph
Oetting, Friedrich Hermann Buckeburg; Greenville, SC, 1857 ***7420.1*** *p169*
Oetting, Friedrich Wilhelm *SEE* Oetting, Louis Wilhelm
Oetting, Heinrich Gustav *SEE* Oetting, Dietrich Christoph
Oetting, Louis Wilhelm; America, 1883 ***7420.1*** *p338*
*Brother:*Friedrich Wilhelm
Oetting, Marie Louise Deiters *SEE* Oetting, Dietrich Christoph
Oettker, Heinrich; America, 1868 ***7420.1*** *p275*
With family
Oettker, Heinrich; Chicago, 1886 ***7420.1*** *p351*
O'Falvey, Edward 27; New York, NY, 1826 ***6178.50*** *p150*

364 *FOR A COMPLETE EXPLANATION OF ENTRY, SEE "HOW TO READ A CITATION" SECTION*

O'Falvy, Edward 27; New York, NY, 1826 ***6178.50*** *p150*
O'Farrell, Barnabus; North Carolina, 1795 ***1088.45*** *p26*
O'Farrell, J.; New Orleans, 1850 ***7242.30*** *p152*
Oferman, Anthony; Annapolis, MD, 1723 ***1220.12*** *p591*
O'Ferrell, John; North Carolina, 1838 ***1088.45*** *p26*
Offendale, Thomas 50; Ontario, 1871 ***1823.21*** *p285*
Offensandt, W. H.; Louisiana, 1836-1840 ***4981.45*** *p213*
Offer, John; America, 1768 ***1220.12*** *p591*
Offerton, William; Barbados, 1664 ***1220.12*** *p591*
Offery, Mathias; America, 1721 ***1220.12*** *p591*
O'Flagherty, M.; Toronto, 1844 ***2910.35*** *p112*
O'Flaharty, John; North Carolina, 1826 ***1088.45*** *p26*
O'Flaherty, Michael; Louisiana, 1845 ***7710.1*** *p154*
Ofling, Darby; Boston, 1701 ***1642*** *p24*
O'Flynn, James; Toronto, 1844 ***2910.35*** *p111*
Ogar, Charles; Detroit, 1929 ***1640.55*** *p115*
O'Gar, Michael; North Carolina, 1843 ***1088.45*** *p26*
Ogborn, Robert; America, 1775 ***1220.12*** *p591*
Ogden, Elizabeth; America, 1766 ***1220.12*** *p591*
Ogden, James; America, 1767 ***1220.12*** *p591*
Ogden, James 58; Indiana, 1869-1880 ***9076.20*** *p69*
Ogden, Joanna; Maryland, 1725 ***1220.12*** *p591*
Ogden, John; America, 1761 ***1220.12*** *p591*
Ogden, John; America, 1765 ***1220.12*** *p591*
Ogden, John; America, 1767 ***1220.12*** *p591*
Ogden, John; America, 1769 ***1220.12*** *p591*
Ogden, John 46; Ontario, 1871 ***1823.21*** *p285*
Ogden, Judith; America, 1750 ***1220.12*** *p591*
Ogden, Thomas; America, 1772 ***1220.12*** *p591*
Ogden, William; America, 1713 ***1220.12*** *p591*
Ogden, William; America, 1750 ***1220.12*** *p591*
Ogden, William; America, 1763 ***1220.12*** *p592*
Ogden, William; America, 1774 ***1220.12*** *p592*
Oger, Jean; Virginia, 1700 ***9230.15*** *p80*
With wife & 3 children
Oggers, James; America, 1731 ***1220.12*** *p591*
Oghen, Hugh; Barbados, 1667 ***1220.12*** *p592*
Ogier, . . .; California, 1920-1929 ***9228.50*** *p484*
Ogier, Catherine 16; North Carolina, 1774 ***1422.10*** *p54*
Ogier, Catherine 40; North Carolina, 1774 ***1422.10*** *p54*
Ogier, Charlotte 9; North Carolina, 1774 ***1422.10*** *p54*
Ogier, Edward *SEE* Ogier, John
Ogier, George 15; North Carolina, 1774 ***1422.10*** *p54*
Ogier, James; Ohio, 1810 ***9228.50*** *p483*
Ogier, James; Ohio, 1820 ***9228.50*** *p483*
Ogier, James; Philadelphia, 1817 ***9228.50*** *p480*
*Wife:*Mary E. Maindonald
*Son:*James, Jr.
Ogier, James, Jr. *SEE* Ogier, James
Ogier, John; Baltimore, 1809-1821 ***9228.50*** *p484*
*Son:*John, Jr.
*Wife:*Mary
Ogier, John 8; North Carolina, 1774 ***1422.10*** *p54*
Ogier, John; Ohio, 1820 ***9228.50*** *p483*
Ogier, John; Ohio, 1820 ***9228.50*** *p483*
Ogier, John; Ohio, 1848 ***9228.50*** *p483*
Ogier, John; Ohio, 1920 ***9228.50*** *p483*
*Son:*Edward
With wife daughter & 3 sons
*Daughter:*Kathleen
Ogier, John, Jr. *SEE* Ogier, John
Ogier, Joseph; Illinois, 1860 ***6079.1*** *p11*
Ogier, Kathleen *SEE* Ogier, John
Ogier, Lewis; Charleston, SC, 1783 ***9228.50*** *p484*
Ogier, Lewis 19; North Carolina, 1774 ***1422.10*** *p54*
Ogier, Lewis 47; North Carolina, 1774 ***1422.10*** *p54*
Ogier, Lucy 13; North Carolina, 1774 ***1422.10*** *p54*
Ogier, Mary *SEE* Ogier, John
Ogier, Mary 6; North Carolina, 1774 ***1422.10*** *p54*
Ogier, Mary E. Maindonald *SEE* Ogier, James
Ogier, Miriam; Pennsylvania, 1921-1983 ***9228.50*** *p484*
Ogier, Miriam Flere Bisson; New Hampshire, 1909-1910 ***9228.50*** *p382*
Ogier, Peter 5; North Carolina, 1774 ***1422.10*** *p54*
Ogier, Peter; Ohio, 1801-1876 ***9228.50*** *p484*
Ogier, Thomas 20; North Carolina, 1774 ***1422.10*** *p54*
Ogier, Thomas; Ohio, 1781-1850 ***9228.50*** *p484*
Ogier, Thomas; Ohio, 1810 ***9228.50*** *p484*
Ogier, Thomas; Ohio, 1829 ***9228.50*** *p484*
Ogier, William; Norfolk, VA, 1806 ***9228.50*** *p56*
With wife & children
Ogier, William; Ohio, 1806-1821 ***9228.50*** *p484*
Ogier, William; Ohio, 1819 ***9228.50*** *p484*
Ogier, William; Ohio, 1820 ***9228.50*** *p483*
Ogier, William, Family; Ohio, 1807 ***9228.50*** *p57*
Ogier, Wm.; America, 1807 ***9228.50*** *p484*
Ogier Family ; Canada, n.d. ***9228.50*** *p483*
Ogier Family ; Maine, n.d. ***9228.50*** *p483*
Ogilby, Catherine; Annapolis, MD, 1733 ***1220.12*** *p592*
Ogilby, George; America, 1752 ***1220.12*** *p592*
Ogilby, Thomas; America, 1771 ***1220.12*** *p592*
Ogilvie, Elsept 49; Ontario, 1871 ***1823.21*** *p285*
Ogle, Alexander; America, 1736 ***1220.12*** *p592*
Ogle, Eleanor; America, 1775 ***1220.12*** *p592*
Ogle, Katherine; America, 1675 ***1220.12*** *p592*
Ogleby, George; America, 1746 ***1220.12*** *p592*
Ogleby, George; Barbados or Jamaica, 1688 ***1220.12*** *p592*
Ogles, Mr. 24; America, 1842 ***778.6*** *p258*
Ogles, Pedro 35; America, 1846 ***778.6*** *p258*
Ogletree, Henry 57; Ontario, 1871 ***1823.17*** *p128*
Oglive, Patrick; Boston, 1712 ***1642*** *p24*
Ognier, Mrs. 28; New Orleans, 1748 ***778.6*** *p258*
Ognier, Henri 30; New Orleans, 1748 ***778.6*** *p258*
Ognier, P. Auguste 22; Mississippi, 1846 ***778.6*** *p258*
Ogonowski, John; Detroit, 1929-1930 ***6214.5*** *p65*
O'Grady, Miss; Toronto, 1844 ***2910.35*** *p114*
O'Grady, John 23; Ontario, 1871 ***1823.21*** *p283*
O'Grady, Mary 35; Ontario, 1871 ***1823.21*** *p283*
O'Grady, Peter; Colorado, 1894 ***1029.59*** *p70*
Ogrady, Peter; Colorado, 1894 ***1029.59*** *p70*
O'Grady, S. G. 41; Ontario, 1871 ***1823.17*** *p127*
Ogren, Anna Ch. Peterson *SEE* Ogren, Peter
Ogren, Peter; New York, 1881-1888 ***1865.50*** *p101*
*Wife:*Anna Ch. Peterson
O'Groats, John; Toronto, 1844 ***2910.35*** *p112*
Ogrzewalski, Joseph; Detroit, 1930 ***1640.60*** *p77*
Oha, Joseph; Illinois, 1863 ***6079.1*** *p11*
O'Hagan, Henry 28; Ontario, 1871 ***1823.17*** *p127*
O'Hagan, John 26; Ontario, 1871 ***1823.17*** *p127*
O'Hagan, Rose 20; Ontario, 1871 ***1823.17*** *p127*
Ohagan, Thomas 34; Ontario, 1871 ***1823.21*** *p285*
O'Hagen, John; North Carolina, 1858 ***1088.45*** *p26*
O'Halloran, Catharine T.; Philadelphia, 1861 ***8513.31*** p410
O'Halleron, Patrick; Toronto, 1844 ***2910.35*** *p116*
O'Hara, Ann; America, 1741 ***1220.12*** *p592*
O'Hara, John 25; Halifax, N.S., n.d. ***1833.5*** *p7*
O'Hara, John 25; Halifax, N.S., n.d. ***8445.10*** *p7*
*Relative:*Wilfred 7
O'Hara, Neel; New Orleans, 1850 ***7242.30*** *p152*
O'Hara, Wilfred 7; Halifax, N.S., n.d. ***1833.5*** *p7*
O'Hara, Wilfred 7 *SEE* O'Hara, John
O'Hare, Barbason; Boston, 1770 ***1642*** *p43*
Ohare, Bridgette 42; Michigan, 1880 ***4491.39*** *p22*
O'Hare, Francis 61; Ontario, 1871 ***1823.17*** *p127*
Oharra, John 40; Ontario, 1871 ***1823.17*** *p128*
O'Harrow, James 56; Ontario, 1871 ***1823.21*** *p283*
Ohealy, . . .; Ontario, 1871 ***1823.21*** *p285*
O'Henley, Donald 27; Ontario, 1871 ***1823.21*** *p283*
O'Henly, Donald 38; Ontario, 1871 ***1823.21*** *p283*
O'Henly, Donald 65; Ontario, 1871 ***1823.21*** *p283*
Ohenly, John 35; Ontario, 1871 ***1823.21*** *p285*
Ohenly, John 75; Ontario, 1871 ***1823.21*** *p285*
O'Herne, Daniel; Toronto, 1844 ***2910.35*** *p114*
O'Herne, Michael; Toronto, 1844 ***2910.35*** *p114*
Oheron, Daniel 53; Ontario, 1871 ***1823.21*** *p285*
O'Higgin, James 19; Ontario, 1871 ***1823.21*** *p283*
O'Higgins, Mrs. J.; Toronto, 1844 ***2910.35*** *p111*
O'Higgins, John J.; Toronto, 1844 ***2910.35*** *p111*
O'Higgins, Joseph P. 34; Ontario, 1871 ***1823.21*** *p283*
Ohl, Catharina 28; New Orleans, 1848 ***778.6*** *p258*
Ohl, Georg; New York, 1869 ***2526.42*** *p201*
Ohl, John; Ohio, 1809-1852 ***4511.35*** *p39*
Ohl, Leonhard; America, 1887 ***2526.42*** *p201*
Ohl, Philipp; America, 1867 ***2526.42*** *p201*
Ohl, Sebastian 32; New Orleans, 1848 ***778.6*** *p258*
Ohland, Anna Elizabeth; North Carolina, 1792-1862 ***1088.45*** *p26*
Ohlandh, William M.; North Carolina, 1851 ***1088.45*** *p26*
Ohlandt, Henry; North Carolina, 1859 ***1088.45*** *p26*
Ohlbach, Anna Dumat 37; New Jersey, 1734-1774 ***927.31*** *p3*
Ohlbach, Anna Eliza. 26; New Jersey, 1734-1774 ***927.31*** *p3*
Ohlbach, Anna Margret 8; New Jersey, 1734-1774 ***927.31*** *p3*
Ohlbach, Gerteruth Margreta 2; New Jersey, 1734-1774 ***927.31*** *p3*
Ohlbach, Joanis Gerard 6; New Jersey, 1734-1774 ***927.31*** *p3*
Ohlbach, Joanis Peter 2; New Jersey, 1734-1774 ***927.31*** *p3*
Ohlbach, Joanis Wilhelm 11; New Jersey, 1734-1774 ***927.31*** *p3*
Ohlbach, Johann Wilhelm 28; New Jersey, 1734-1774 ***927.31*** *p3*
Ohlbach, Zacharias 36; New Jersey, 1734-1774 ***927.31*** *p3*
Ohlendorf, Mr.; America, 1864 ***7420.1*** *p225*
Ohlendorf, Catharine Marie Charlotte; America, 1850 ***7420.1*** *p74*
Ohlendorf, Engel Sophie *SEE* Ohlendorf, Johann Heinrich Ludwig
Ohlendorf, Heinrich Christoph; New York, NY, 1856 ***7420.1*** *p151*
Ohlendorf, Johann Heinrich; America, 1852 ***7420.1*** *p94*
With wife 5 sons & 3 daughters
Ohlendorf, Johann Heinrich Ludwig; Port uncertain, 1853 ***7420.1*** *p109*
*Wife:*Sophie Wilhelmine Rust
*Daughter:*Engel Sophie
With son
Ohlendorf, Sophie Wilhelmine Rust *SEE* Ohlendorf, Johann Heinrich Ludwig
Ohlendorf, Wilhelm; America, 1868 ***7420.1*** *p275*
With family
Ohler, John; Louisiana, 1874 ***4981.45*** *p296*
Ohlert, John G.; Washington, 1886 ***2770.40*** *p195*
Ohlhorst, Miss; America, 1857 ***7420.1*** *p169*
Ohligar, Louis; Ohio, 1809-1852 ***4511.35*** *p39*
Ohliger, Ludwig; Ohio, 1809-1852 ***4511.35*** *p39*
Ohlin, J.; New York, NY, 1844 ***6412.40*** *p148*
Ohlmann, Joseph 8; Mississippi, 1845-1846 ***778.6*** *p258*
Ohlmann, Nazias 30; Mississippi, 1845-1846 ***778.6*** *p258*
Ohlsen, Johann; Washington, 1884 ***2770.40*** *p193*
Ohlsen, Maria 27; Chile, 1852 ***1192.4*** *p55*
Ohlsen, Thies; Washington, 1883 ***2770.40*** *p137*
Ohlson, James Peter; Washington, 1889 ***2770.40*** *p80*
Ohlsson, Gust; Cleveland, OH, 1888-1890 ***9722.10*** *p125*
Ohlsson, Jens; Colorado, 1887 ***1029.59*** *p70*
Ohm, Frantz Fr. W.; Wisconsin, 1893 ***6795.8*** *p163*
Ohm, Otto; Kansas, 1917-1918 ***2094.25*** *p50*
Ohman, Alexander; Cleveland, OH, 1904-1906 ***9722.10*** *p125*
Ohman, Bertha L.; Kansas, 1869 ***777.40*** *p15*
Ohman, Bertha L.; Kansas, 1869 ***777.40*** *p15*
Ohman, Brita Lorentina; Kansas, 1869 ***777.40*** *p15*
Ohmann, J. Gottfr.; Valdivia, Chile, 1852 ***1192.4*** *p54*
With wife
With child 5
Ohmann, Louis 32; Oregon, 1846 ***778.6*** *p258*
Ohmberger, Christine; Philadelphia, 1859 ***8513.31*** *p318*
Ohneberger, Jaque 27; America, 1848 ***778.6*** *p258*
Ohoohilahan, Francis 63; Ontario, 1871 ***1823.21*** *p285*
Ohrling, J.E.; New York, NY, 1844 ***6412.40*** *p147*
Ohrtmann, Friedrich Wilhelm; America, 1881 ***7420.1*** *p398*
Oie, Andrew; Washington, 1889 ***2770.40*** *p80*
Oigen, Oscar 20; Ontario, 1871 ***1823.17*** *p128*
Oinonen, Abel 29; Minnesota, 1925 ***2769.54*** *p1380*
Oja, Jaako; Oregon, 1941 ***9157.47*** *p2*
Oja, Jennie 35; Minnesota, 1925 ***2769.54*** *p1383*
Ojala, Anna 30; New York, NY, 1894 ***6512.1*** *p229*
Ojibway, David 30; Ontario, 1871 ***1823.17*** *p128*
Oke, Charles 44; Ontario, 1871 ***1823.21*** *p285*
Oke, James 36; Ontario, 1871 ***1823.17*** *p128*
Oke, James 40; Ontario, 1871 ***1823.21*** *p285*
Oke, Richard 46; Ontario, 1871 ***1823.21*** *p285*
Oke, William 37; Ontario, 1871 ***1823.17*** *p128*
O'Keaf, Mary 50; Ontario, 1871 ***1823.21*** *p283*
O'Kean, Michael; Colorado, 1873 ***1029.59*** *p70*
O'Keef, Patrick; North Carolina, 1788 ***1088.45*** *p26*
O'Keefe, Bridgett 20; Ontario, 1871 ***1823.21*** *p283*
O'Keefe, John; Illinois, 1858-1861 ***6020.5*** *p132*
O'Keefe, John; Toronto, 1844 ***2910.35*** *p112*
O'Keefe, Mary 11; Quebec, 1870 ***8364.32*** *p25*
O'Keefe, Patrick; Ohio, 1840-1897 ***8365.35*** *p17*
O'Keefe, Patrick 30; Ontario, 1871 ***1823.21*** *p283*
O Keegan, John; Toronto, 1844 ***2910.35*** *p115*
O'Keiffe, Dennis; Washington, 1876 ***2770.40*** *p134*
O'Keiffe, Dennis; Washington, 1880 ***2770.40*** *p134*
O'Kelia, David; Massachusetts, 1673 ***1642*** *p92*
O'Kelly, Jonathan; New England, 1745 ***1642*** *p28*
O'Kene, Michael; Colorado, 1873 ***1029.59*** *p70*
Okenfels, Frank W.; Ohio, 1840-1897 ***8365.35*** *p17*
Okentree, John; Barbados or Jamaica, 1700 ***1220.12*** *p592*
Okerstrom, Olof; Colorado, 1891 ***1029.59*** *p70*
Okes, Hannah; America, 1740 ***1220.12*** *p590*
Okes, Hugh 38; Ontario, 1871 ***1823.21*** *p285*
Okes, Nicholas; Ohio, 1809-1852 ***4511.35*** *p39*
Okes, Peter; Ohio, 1809-1852 ***4511.35*** *p39*
Okey, William; America, 1675 ***1220.12*** *p590*
Okie, John; Virginia, 1759 ***1220.12*** *p590*
O'Killey, Amos; Massachusetts, 1739 ***1642*** *p92*
O'Killey, Jonathan; Massachusetts, 1745 ***1642*** *p92*
Okonek, Frank; Wisconsin, 1884 ***6795.8*** *p60*
Oland, William; America, 1750 ***1220.12*** *p592*
Olander, Anna; St. Paul, MN, 1882 ***1865.50*** *p101*
Olander, Axel; Cleveland, OH, 1881-1892 ***9722.10*** *p125*
Olander, Bertha Olsdotter *SEE* Olander, Peter
Olander, Catharina; Minnesota, 1865-1900 ***1865.50*** *p101*
Olander, John; Minnesota, 1873-1900 ***1865.50*** *p101*
Olander, O.E.; Washington, 1889 ***2770.40*** *p80*
Olander, Peter; Kansas, 1869 ***777.40*** *p19*
*Wife:*Bertha Olsdotter

O'Laughlin, Daniel; Toronto, 1844 ***2910.35*** *p113*
O'Laughlin, James; Toronto, 1844 ***2910.35*** *p113*
O'Laughlin, Michael; Illinois, 1858 ***6079.1*** *p11*
Olave, John; Virginia, 1734 ***1220.12*** *p592*
Old, Adam 41; America, 1854 ***2526.42*** *p110*
*Wife:*Eva Arnold
*Child:*Elisabetha 10
*Child:*Margaretha 8
*Child:*Katharina 1
*Child:*Christian 4
*Child:*Nikolaus 13
Old, Christian 4 *SEE* Old, Adam
Old, Elisabetha 10 *SEE* Old, Adam
Old, Eva Arnold *SEE* Old, Adam
Old, Johannes; America, 1892 ***2526.42*** *p110*
Old, John; America, 1742 ***1220.12*** *p592*
Old, John; America, 1749 ***1220.12*** *p592*
Old, Katharina 1 *SEE* Old, Adam
Old, Margaretha 8 *SEE* Old, Adam
Old, Maria 46; America, 1856 ***2526.42*** *p100*
Old, Nikolaus 13 *SEE* Old, Adam
Old, Susanna Margaretha; America, 1753 ***2526.42*** *p143*
Oldard, Fanny 12; Ontario, 1871 ***1823.21*** *p285*
Oldasey, Stephen; Annapolis, MD, 1725 ***1220.12*** *p592*
Oldbury, Mark; America, 1774 ***1220.12*** *p592*
Oldbury, Samuel; Maryland, 1742 ***1220.12*** *p592*
Olden, William; America, 1675 ***1220.12*** *p592*
Oldenburg, C.; Venezuela, 1843 ***3899.5*** *p546*
Oldenburg, F.; Venezuela, 1843 ***3899.5*** *p546*
Oldendorf, Carl August Heinrich; Iowa, 1882 ***7420.1*** *p331*
Oldendorf, Carl Heinrich Wilhelm; America, 1876 ***7420.1*** *p307*
Oldendorf, Hans Chr.; America, 1856 ***7420.1*** *p151*
Oldendorf, J. Charles; Nova Scotia, 1784 ***7105*** *p25*
Oldendorfe, Charles; Nova Scotia, 1784 ***7105*** *p25*
Oldfield, Eleanor; Annapolis, MD, 1730 ***1220.12*** *p592*
Oldfield, Elizabeth 43; Michigan, 1880 ***4491.39*** *p22*
Oldfield, James 50; Michigan, 1880 ***4491.39*** *p22*
Oldfield, James G.; Louisiana, 1885 ***7710.1*** *p160*
Oldfield, James G. 23; Portland, ME, 1873 ***7710.1*** *p158*
Oldfield, John; America, 1768 ***1220.12*** *p592*
Oldfield, John; Annapolis, MD, 1719 ***1220.12*** *p592*
Oldfield, Margaret; America, 1747 ***1220.12*** *p592*
Oldham, Elizabeth *SEE* Oldham, William
Oldham, Elizabeth; America, 1754 ***1220.12*** *p592*
Oldham, Ellen; America, 1764 ***1220.12*** *p592*
Oldham, John; Barbados or Jamaica, 1694 ***1220.12*** *p592*
Oldham, William; America, 1749 ***1220.12*** *p592*
*Wife:*Elizabeth
Oldham, William 37; Ontario, 1871 ***1823.21*** *p285*
Oldin, William; America, 1754 ***1220.12*** *p592*
Olding, John; America, 1758 ***1220.12*** *p592*
Olding, Joseph; America, 1772 ***1220.12*** *p592*
Oldis, Sarah; America, 1771 ***1220.12*** *p592*
Oldman, Robert; America, 1749 ***1220.12*** *p592*
Oldreive, John 28; Ontario, 1871 ***1823.21*** *p285*
Oldswagon, Dallis 30; Michigan, 1880 ***4491.39*** *p22*
Oldt, Johann Georg; America, 1766 ***2526.42*** *p128*
O'Leary, Arthur 60; Ontario, 1871 ***1823.21*** *p283*
Oleary, Bridget 37; Michigan, 1880 ***4491.39*** *p22*
O'Leary, Catherine; New Orleans, 1851 ***7242.30*** *p152*
Oleary, Cornelius 28; Michigan, 1880 ***4491.39*** *p22*
O'Leary, Daniel; Illinois, 1858-1861 ***6020.5*** *p132*
O'Leary, Emiline 31; Ontario, 1871 ***1823.17*** *p127*
O'Leary, George; Toronto, 1844 ***2910.35*** *p116*
O'Leary, George, Jr.; Toronto, 1844 ***2910.35*** *p116*
O'Leary, James 50; Ontario, 1871 ***1823.17*** *p127*
O'Leary, James; Toronto, 1844 ***2910.35*** *p116*
O'Leary, James; Washington, 1884 ***2770.40*** *p193*
O'Leary, Jeremiah; Toronto, 1844 ***2910.35*** *p116*
O'Leary, John 45; Ontario, 1871 ***1823.17*** *p127*
O'Leary, John; Toronto, 1844 ***2910.35*** *p116*
O'Leary, Louis 68; Ontario, 1871 ***1823.21*** *p283*
O'Leary, Mark; Spokane, WA, n.d. ***9228.50*** *p80*
Oleary, Richard 42; Michigan, 1880 ***4491.39*** *p23*
O'Leary, Thomas; Toronto, 1844 ***2910.35*** *p113*
O'Leary, Thos.; Illinois, 1858-1861 ***6020.5*** *p132*
O'Leary, Timotheius; Toronto, 1844 ***2910.35*** *p112*
O'Leary, Timothy; Toronto, 1844 ***2910.35*** *p116*
O'Leary, Timothy; Washington, 1889 ***2770.40*** *p80*
O'Leary, William 55; Ontario, 1871 ***1823.17*** *p127*
Oleas, Hugo; Valdivia, Chile, 1851 ***1192.4*** *p51*
Oleksy, Ludwik; Detroit, 1929 ***1640.55*** *p114*
Oleski, Louis; Detroit, 1929 ***1640.55*** *p114*
Oleson, Anders; Iowa, 1876 ***1211.15*** *p17*
Oleson, Halver; Iowa, 1869 ***1211.15*** *p17*
Olfenbutel, August; Texas, 1891 ***3435.45*** *p36*
Olff, Jacob; Louisiana, 1836-1841 ***4981.45*** *p209*
Olford, Hugh; Charles Town, SC, 1719 ***1220.12*** *p592*
Olhmann, Antoine 15; Mississippi, 1845-1846 ***778.6*** *p258*
Oligmueller, Theo; Nebraska, 1905 ***3004.30*** *p46*
Oliiver, Edward A.; Illinois, 1918 ***6007.60*** *p9*
Olin, Jean 51; America, 1843 ***778.6*** *p4*
Oling, Beata 16; New York, NY, 1894 ***6512.1*** *p229*
Oling, Johannes 17; New York, NY, 1894 ***6512.1*** *p229*
Oliphant, James; Virginia, 1734 ***1220.12*** *p592*
Olivari, L.; Louisiana, 1874-1875 ***4981.45*** *p30*
Olive, Frances; Virginia, 1736 ***1220.12*** *p592*
Olive, James; North Carolina, 1838 ***1088.45*** *p26*
Olive, John; America, 1767 ***1220.12*** *p592*
Olive, Richard 40; Ontario, 1871 ***1823.17*** *p128*
Olive, William; Barbados, 1699 ***1220.12*** *p592*
Olive, William P. 43; Ontario, 1871 ***1823.17*** *p128*
Oliveau, Pierre; Quebec, 1648 ***9221.17*** *p202*
Olivella, Manuel; Florida, 1839 ***8481.1*** *p18*
Oliver, Andrew; North Carolina, 1812 ***1088.45*** *p26*
Oliver, Andrew 45; Ontario, 1871 ***1823.21*** *p285*
Oliver, Archibald; Carolina, 1724 ***1220.12*** *p592*
Oliver, Charles; Ohio, 1823 ***3580.20*** *p33*
Oliver, Charles; Ohio, 1823 ***6020.12*** *p21*
Oliver, Daniel; America, 1769 ***1220.12*** *p592*
Oliver, Edward 38; Ontario, 1871 ***1823.17*** *p128*
Oliver, Esther; Pennsylvania, 1817-1847 ***9228.50*** *p484*
Oliver, Evan; America, 1766 ***1220.12*** *p592*
Oliver, George 50; Ontario, 1871 ***1823.21*** *p285*
Oliver, George 60; Ontario, 1871 ***1823.21*** *p286*
Oliver, Hannah; America, 1741 ***1220.12*** *p592*
Oliver, Henry; Louisiana, 1848 ***7710.1*** *p150*
Oliver, Henry 74; Ontario, 1871 ***1823.21*** *p286*
Oliver, Isaac; Barbados, 1664 ***1220.12*** *p592*
Oliver, Isaac; Barbados, 1667 ***1220.12*** *p592*
Oliver, Jacob; America, 1769 ***1220.12*** *p592*
Oliver, James; North Carolina, 1837 ***1088.45*** *p26*
Oliver, James; Ohio, 1809-1852 ***4511.35*** *p39*
Oliver, James 63; Ontario, 1871 ***1823.21*** *p286*
Oliver, Jessie 86; Ontario, 1871 ***1823.21*** *p286*
Oliver, John; America, 1772 ***1220.12*** *p593*
Oliver, John; Annapolis, MD, 1730 ***1220.12*** *p593*
Oliver, John; Annapolis, MD, 1735 ***1220.12*** *p593*
Oliver, John; Ohio, 1843 ***2763.1*** *p21*
Oliver, Joseph; America, 1708 ***1220.12*** *p593*
Oliver, Julio 36; America, 1848 ***778.6*** *p258*
Oliver, Mary; America, 1773 ***1220.12*** *p593*
Oliver, Mary; Maryland, 1727 ***1220.12*** *p593*
Oliver, Nicholas; America, 1742 ***1220.12*** *p593*
Oliver, Nicholas; Barbados or Jamaica, 1699 ***1220.12*** *p593*
Oliver, Robert S. 40; Ontario, 1871 ***1823.17*** *p128*
Oliver, Robt. 49; Ontario, 1871 ***1823.17*** *p128*
Oliver, Samuel 70; Ontario, 1871 ***1823.21*** *p286*
Oliver, Simon; America, 1744 ***1220.12*** *p593*
Oliver, Thomas; America, 1728 ***1220.12*** *p593*
Oliver, Thomas; America, 1734 ***1220.12*** *p593*
Oliver, Thomas; America, 1754 ***1220.12*** *p593*
Oliver, Thomas; Iowa, 1806-1888 ***9228.50*** *p20A*
Oliver, Thomas; Ohio, 1809-1852 ***4511.35*** *p39*
Oliver, Walter 62; Ontario, 1871 ***1823.21*** *p286*
Oliver, Warl 39; Ontario, 1871 ***1823.21*** *p286*
Oliver, William; America, 1753 ***1220.12*** *p593*
Oliver, William; America, 1754 ***1220.12*** *p593*
Oliver, William; America, 1764 ***1220.12*** *p593*
Oliver, William; Maryland, 1720 ***1220.12*** *p593*
Oliver, William; Ohio, 1823 ***3580.20*** *p33*
Oliver, William; Ohio, 1823 ***6020.12*** *p21*
Oliver, William 29; Ontario, 1871 ***1823.21*** *p286*
Oliver, William 30; Ontario, 1871 ***1823.21*** *p286*
Oliver, William 56; Ontario, 1871 ***1823.21*** *p286*
Oliver, William 70; Ontario, 1871 ***1823.21*** *p286*
Olivera, Mrs. J.; New York, 1926 ***1173.1*** *p2*
Oliverius, Jan A.; Chicago, 1873 ***2853.20*** *p397*
Olives, P.; Louisiana, 1874 ***4981.45*** *p296*
Olivia, Dominique 3; New Orleans, 1848 ***778.6*** *p258*
Olivia, Marie 27; New Orleans, 1848 ***778.6*** *p258*
Olivia, Pierre 40; New Orleans, 1848 ***778.6*** *p258*
Olivier, . . .; Quebec, 1632 ***9221.17*** *p21*
Olivier, Le Jeune; Quebec, 1632 ***9221.17*** *p21*
Olivier, Mr. 30; New Orleans, 1840 ***778.6*** *p258*
Olivier, Agnes; Quebec, 1669 ***4514.3*** *p352*
Olivier, Felix 4; Missouri, 1846 ***778.6*** *p258*
Olivier, Jean; Montreal, 1653 ***9221.17*** *p298*
Olivier, Jeanne; Quebec, 1671 ***4514.3*** *p352*
Olivier, Louis 26; America, 1846 ***778.6*** *p258*
Olivier, Madeleine; Quebec, 1667 ***4514.3*** *p352*
Olivier, Margarethe 23; Missouri, 1846 ***778.6*** *p258*
Olivier, Marie 50; America, 1846 ***778.6*** *p258*
Olivier, Octavie 3; America, 1846 ***778.6*** *p258*
Olivier, Pierre 25; Missouri, 1846 ***778.6*** *p258*
Olivier, Virginie 22; America, 1846 ***778.6*** *p258*
Olivier deVezin, Pierre-Francois; Quebec, 1749 ***2314.30*** *p171*
Olk, Peter; New York, 1860 ***358.56*** *p149*
Olkers, Christian; Long Island, 1779 ***8529.30*** *p10A*
Ollander, Carl August Wilhelm; North America, 1888 ***6410.15*** *p106*
Ollery, Anne; Quebec, 1669 ***4514.3*** *p352*
Olley, John; America, 1768 ***1220.12*** *p593*
Olliger, Charles 8; Louisiana, 1848 ***778.6*** *p258*
Olliger, Jacques 57; Louisiana, 1848 ***778.6*** *p258*
Olliger, Jules 21; Louisiana, 1848 ***778.6*** *p259*
Olliger, Marguerite 25; Louisiana, 1848 ***778.6*** *p259*
Olliger, Marie 6; Louisiana, 1848 ***778.6*** *p259*
Olliger, Mathias; America, 1883 ***5475.1*** *p268*
Olliger, Pauline 17; Louisiana, 1848 ***778.6*** *p259*
Olliger, Reine 50; Louisiana, 1848 ***778.6*** *p259*
Olliger, Romain 16; Louisiana, 1848 ***778.6*** *p259*
Ollis, William 64; Ontario, 1871 ***1823.21*** *p286*
Olliver, . . .; Quebec, 1534 ***9228.50*** *p3*
Olliver, Edward 41; Ontario, 1871 ***1823.21*** *p286*
Olliver, Elizabeth 42; Ontario, 1871 ***1823.21*** *p286*
Olliver, Nicholas; Barbados or Jamaica, 1698 ***1220.12*** *p593*
Olliver, Thomas 42; Ontario, 1871 ***1823.21*** *p286*
Olliver, William; America, 1729 ***1220.12*** *p593*
Ollivier, Peter James 40; America, 1860 ***9228.50*** *p485*
Ollmann, John; Wisconsin, 1898 ***6795.8*** *p68*
Ollmeyer, Diederick; Louisiana, 1836-1841 ***4981.45*** *p209*
Olloway, Isiah; America, 1741 ***1220.12*** *p593*
Olmstead, William 26; Ontario, 1871 ***1823.21*** *p286*
Olofsdotter, Mathilda 33; Kansas, 1869-1880 ***777.40*** *p19*
Olofsdotter, Matilda 33; Kansas, 1869-1880 ***777.40*** *p19*
Olofsson, Brita Christina Pehrsdotter *SEE* Olofsson, Carl Fredrik
Olofsson, Carl Fredrik; Kansas, 1879 ***777.40*** *p11*
*Wife:*Brita Christina Pehrsdotter
*Son:*John Peter
*Daughter:*Jennie Cath.
Olofsson, Jennie Cath. *SEE* Olofsson, Carl Fredrik
Olofsson, John Peter *SEE* Olofsson, Carl Fredrik
Olofsson, Mathias Johan; North America, 1855 ***6410.15*** *p104*
Olofsson, Pehr 18; New York, 1856 ***6529.11*** *p21*
Olofsson, Peter; Kansas, 1865-1868 ***777.40*** *p16*
O'Lollers, Patrick; New England, 1745 ***1642*** *p28*
Olot, Louis; Ohio, 1809-1852 ***4511.35*** *p39*
Olrine, Andrew; Iowa, 1886 ***1211.15*** *p17*
Olsdotter, Anna 44; New York, 1856 ***6529.11*** *p22*
*Daughter:*Brita 16
Olsdotter, Bertha; Kansas, 1869 ***777.40*** *p19*
Olsdotter, Brita; Kansas, 1869 ***777.40*** *p19*
Olsdotter, Brita 60; Kansas, 1879-1880 ***777.40*** *p19*
Olsdotter, Brita 26; New York, 1856 ***6529.11*** *p21*
Olsdotter, Carin 46; New York, 1856 ***6529.11*** *p22*
Olsdotter, Christina; Illinois, 1869 ***777.40*** *p20*
Olsdotter, Gunilla 41; New York, 1856 ***6529.11*** *p20*
Olsen, Alfred; Colorado, 1893 ***1029.59*** *p70*
Olsen, Alfred; Colorado, 1893 ***1029.59*** *p71*
Olsen, Anders; Iowa, 1896 ***1211.15*** *p17*
Olsen, Anna; Colorado, 1895 ***1029.59*** *p70*
Olsen, Annie 20; Ontario, 1871 ***1823.17*** *p128*
Olsen, Hans; Colorado, 1892 ***1029.59*** *p70*
Olsen, Hans; Colorado, 1897 ***1029.59*** *p70*
Olsen, Herman; Iowa, 1900 ***1211.15*** *p17*
Olsen, Peter; Iowa, 1896 ***1211.15*** *p17*
Olson, A.C.; Iowa, 1887-1896 ***1865.50*** *p101*
Olson, Albert; New York, 1903 ***1766.20*** *p3*
Olson, Alfred; Colorado, 1893 ***1029.59*** *p70*
Olson, Alfred; Colorado, 1893 ***1029.59*** *p71*
Olson, Alfred; Colorado, 1896 ***1029.59*** *p70*
Olson, Andres P.; Kansas, 1873-1874 ***777.40*** *p17*
*Wife:*Carolina Pehrsdotter
*Son:*Andres W.
*Daughter:*Emilia Adolph
*Daughter:*Lydia M.A.
*Daughter:*Ida Elisabeth
*Son:*August Paer
Olson, Andres W. *SEE* Olson, Andres P.
Olson, Andrew; Colorado, 1873 ***1029.59*** *p70*
Olson, Andrew; Iowa, 1888 ***1211.15*** *p17*
Olson, Andrew; St. Paul, MN, 1893 ***1865.50*** *p101*
Olson, Andrew; St. Paul, MN, 1894 ***1865.50*** *p101*
*Wife:*Maria S.
Olson, Andrew A.; St. Paul, MN, 1882 ***1865.50*** *p101*
Olson, Anna; St. Paul, MN, 1874-1905 ***1865.50*** *p101*
Olson, Anna C. *SEE* Olson, Olof
Olson, Anna Kristina *SEE* Olson, Nels
Olson, Anton 36; Minnesota, 1926 ***2769.54*** *p1383*
Olson, August; St. Paul, MN, 1885 ***1865.50*** *p101*
Olson, August Paer *SEE* Olson, Andres P.
Olson, Barney B.; Iowa, 1892 ***1211.15*** *p17*
Olson, Ben; Colorado, 1897 ***1029.59*** *p70*
Olson, Brita Olsdotter *SEE* Olson, Peter
Olson, Cajsa; St. Paul, MN, 1883 ***1865.50*** *p44*
Olson, Carl; Cleveland, OH, 1903-1906 ***9722.10*** *p125*
Olson, Carl; New York, 1926 ***1173.1*** *p2*
Olson, Carl Emil; Iowa, 1910 ***1211.15*** *p17*
Olson, Carl Joel *SEE* Olson, John F.
Olson, Carolina Pehrsdotter *SEE* Olson, Andres P.

Olson, Carrie; St. Paul, MN, 1882 ***1865.50*** *p102*
Olson, Charles; Colorado, 1883 ***1029.59*** *p71*
Olson, Chas. E.; Colorado, 1887 ***1029.59*** *p71*
Olson, Christina; Minnesota, 1881-1882 ***1865.50*** *p102*
Olson, Christina; St. Paul, MN, 1885 ***1865.50*** *p99*
Olson, Christina; St. Paul, MN, 1894 ***1865.50*** *p102*
Olson, Christina J.; St. Paul, MN, 1881 ***1865.50*** *p44*
Olson, Christina P.; St. Paul, MN, 1894 ***1865.50*** *p102*
Olson, Eli E.; Colorado, 1898 ***1029.59*** *p71*
Olson, Elin; Colorado, 1892 ***1029.59*** *p71*
Olson, Ellen; St. Paul, MN, 1887 ***1865.50*** *p47*
Olson, Ellen; St. Paul, MN, 1887 ***1865.50*** *p47*
Olson, Ellen; St. Paul, MN, 1887 ***1865.50*** *p47*
Olson, Emanuel; St. Paul, MN, 1887 ***1865.50*** *p102*
Olson, Emil; Cleveland, OH, 1892-1893 ***9722.10*** *p125*
Olson, Emilia Adolph *SEE* Olson, Andres P.
Olson, Eva; Illinois, 1930 ***121.35*** *p101*
Olson, Frank; Washington, 1889 ***2770.40*** *p80*
Olson, Frederick; St. Paul, MN, 1889 ***1865.50*** *p102*
Olson, Gust; Cleveland, OH, 1893-1896 ***9722.10*** *p125*
Olson, Gust Albert; Colorado, 1883 ***1029.59*** *p71*
Olson, Gustaf Magnus; Louisiana, 1882-1896 ***7710.1*** *p161*
Olson, Gustaf W.; St. Paul, MN, 1882 ***1865.50*** *p102*
Olson, Gustave Adolf; Colorado, 1887 ***1029.59*** *p71*
Olson, Hannah; St. Paul, MN, 1887 ***1865.50*** *p101*
With child
Olson, Hans; Colorado, 1892 ***1029.59*** *p71*
Olson, Ida Elisabeth *SEE* Olson, Andres P.
Olson, Jennie; Minnesota, 1873-1878 ***1865.50*** *p99*
Olson, John; Cleveland, OH, 1882-1892 ***9722.10*** *p125*
Olson, John; Cleveland, OH, 1899-1903 ***9722.10*** *p125*
Olson, John; Colorado, 1892 ***1029.59*** *p71*
Olson, John; Illinois, 1869 ***777.40*** *p20*
Olson, John; Iowa, 1888 ***1211.15*** *p17*
Olson, John; New York, 1901 ***1766.20*** *p27*
Olson, John; St. Paul, MN, 1880 ***1865.50*** *p102*
*Wife:*Mathilda Gustafson
*Child:*Maria Betina
Olson, John; St. Paul, MN, 1881 ***1865.50*** *p102*
Olson, John Alfred; Cleveland, OH, 1899-1903 ***9722.10*** *p125*
Olson, John F.; St. Paul, MN, 1887 ***1865.50*** *p102*
*Wife:*Maria Svenson
*Child:*Carl Joel
Olson, John Gust; Iowa, 1904 ***1211.15*** *p17*
Olson, John O.; St. Paul, MN, 1892-1894 ***1865.50*** *p102*
Olson, Lars; Iowa, 1879 ***1211.15*** *p17*
Olson, Lawrence 42; Ontario, 1871 ***1823.17*** *p128*
Olson, Lina; St. Paul, MN, 1900 ***1865.50*** *p102*
Olson, Lydia M.A. *SEE* Olson, Andres P.
Olson, Maria Svenson *SEE* Olson, John F.
Olson, Maria Betina *SEE* Olson, John
Olson, Maria S. *SEE* Olson, Andrew
Olson, Maritn; New York, 1901 ***1766.20*** *p16*
Olson, Martha Stina; St. Paul, MN, 1882 ***1865.50*** *p103*
*Daughter:*Mary Hilma
Olson, Martin; Cleveland, OH, 1882-1895 ***9722.10*** *p125*
Olson, Mary Hilma *SEE* Olson, Martha Stina
Olson, Mathilda; Minnesota, 1879-1880 ***1865.50*** *p97*
Olson, Mathilda Gustafson *SEE* Olson, John
Olson, Mathilda C.; St. Paul, MN, 1882 ***1865.50*** *p101*
Olson, Matilda; St. Paul, MN, 1894 ***1865.50*** *p103*
Olson, Nells Peter; Cleveland, OH, 1880-1884 ***9722.10*** *p125*
Olson, Nels; Illinois, 1861 ***4487.25*** *p68*
Olson, Nels; Iowa, 1883-1904 ***1865.50*** *p103*
*Wife:*Anna Kristina
Olson, Nels; Iowa, 1898 ***1211.15*** *p17*
Olson, Ola 27; Michigan, 1880 ***4491.36*** *p16*
Olson, Olaf 45; New York, NY, 1883 ***8427.14*** *p45*
Olson, Olaf Peter; Iowa, 1911 ***1211.15*** *p17*
Olson, Olaus; Colorado, 1891 ***1029.59*** *p71*
Olson, Ole; Iowa, 1895 ***1211.15*** *p17*
Olson, Ole; Iowa, 1896 ***1211.15*** *p17*
Olson, Ole F.; Iowa, 1902 ***1211.15*** *p17*
Olson, Oliver P.; St. Paul, MN, 1879-1889 ***1865.50*** *p103*
Olson, Olof 24; Kansas, 1880 ***777.40*** *p12*
Olson, Olof; St. Paul, MN, 1894 ***1865.50*** *p103*
*Wife:*Anna C.
Olson, Olof; St. Paul, MN, 1902 ***1865.50*** *p103*
Olson, Olof; Washington, 1887 ***2770.40*** *p25*
Olson, Oscar; Iowa, 1902 ***1211.15*** *p17*
Olson, Otto; Texas, 1903 ***3435.45*** *p36*
Olson, Peder Cornelius; Iowa, 1898 ***1211.15*** *p17*
Olson, Peter; Cleveland, OH, 1889-1893 ***9722.10*** *p125*
Olson, Peter; Illinois, 1861 ***4487.25*** *p68*
Olson, Peter; Kansas, 1869 ***777.40*** *p19*
*Wife:*Brita Olsdotter
Olson, Richard; Cleveland, OH, 1903-1905 ***9722.10*** *p125*
Olson, Siver; Iowa, 1876 ***1211.15*** *p17*
Olson, Sophia; Iowa, 1882-1888 ***1865.50*** *p113*
Olson, Swen; Illinois, 1861 ***4487.25*** *p68*
Olson, Swen T.; Illinois, 1855-1861 ***4487.25*** *p69*
Olson, V. 20; New York, NY, 1894 ***6512.1*** *p184*
Olson, Valdemar; Cleveland, OH, 1904-1905 ***9722.10*** *p125*
Olson, William; Illinois, 1861 ***4487.25*** *p69*
Olsson, August; Colorado, 1883 ***1029.59*** *p71*
Olsson, C.; New York, NY, 1847 ***6412.40*** *p150*
Olsson, C.P.; New Orleans, 1856 ***6412.40*** *p154*
Olsson, Charles; Cleveland, OH, 1885-1888 ***9722.10*** *p125*
Olsson, Christian; Boston, 1847 ***6412.40*** *p150*
Olsson, D.; New York, NY, 1845 ***6412.40*** *p148*
Olsson, E.; New York, NY, 1844 ***6412.40*** *p148*
Olsson, Edv.; New York, NY, 1843 ***6412.40*** *p147*
Olsson, Elna; North Carolina, 1879 ***1088.45*** *p26*
Olsson, Emil A.; Washington, 1889 ***2770.40*** *p80*
Olsson, Eric 30; New York, 1856 ***6529.11*** *p21*
Olsson, Fredrik; New York, NY, 1849 ***6412.40*** *p151*
Olsson, Hans 17; New York, 1856 ***6529.11*** *p21*
Olsson, Joh.; New York, NY, 1844 ***6412.40*** *p148*
Olsson, Johan; San Francisco, 1849 ***6412.40*** *p151*
Olsson, Johan Emil; Cleveland, OH, 1901-1902 ***9722.10*** *p125*
Olsson, Johannes; America, 1857 ***6529.11*** *p23*
Olsson, John; Washington, 1886 ***2770.40*** *p195*
Olsson, Lars; Kansas, 1855-1858 ***777.40*** *p11*
Olsson, Nils; Colorado, 1883 ***1029.59*** *p71*
Olsson, Ol 17; New York, 1856 ***6529.11*** *p22*
Olsson, Olaf; North Carolina, 1879 ***1088.45*** *p26*
Olsson, Olof; Savannah, GA, 1849 ***6412.40*** *p152*
Olsson, P.; New York, NY, n.d. ***6412.40*** *p148*
Olsson, Pehr 18; New York, 1856 ***6529.11*** *p21*
Olstead, Johanes; Washington, 1881 ***2770.40*** *p135*
Olt, Anna Katharina; America, 1871 ***2526.42*** *p97*
Olt, Anna Margareta 7 *SEE* Olt, Konrad
Olt, Anna Margareta 35; America, 1850 ***2526.42*** *p94*
Olt, Anna Margareta 40 *SEE* Olt, Konrad
Olt, Anna Margaretha *SEE* Olt, Anna Margaretha
Olt, Anna Margaretha; America, 1849-1906 ***2526.42*** *p176*
*Daughter:*Anna Margaretha
Olt, Anna Margaretha 16; America, 1866 ***2526.42*** *p144*
Olt, Anna Margaretha 21; America, 1842 ***2526.42*** *p98*
Olt, Anna Maria; America, 1852 ***2526.42*** *p178*
Olt, Barbara 6 *SEE* Olt, Konrad
Olt, Dorothea *SEE* Olt, Johann Georg
Olt, Dorothea; America, 1857 ***2526.43*** *p154*
Olt, Elisabetha; America, 1871 ***2526.42*** *p97*
Olt, Elisabetha 17; America, 1866 ***2526.42*** *p144*
Olt, Eva Maria *SEE* Olt, Georg, II
Olt, Eva Maria *SEE* Olt, Johann Georg
Olt, Eva Maria; America, 1871 ***2526.42*** *p97*
Olt, Friedrich; America, 1856 ***2526.43*** *p189*
Olt, Georg; America, 1870 ***2526.42*** *p97*
Olt, Georg, II 68; America, 1853 ***2526.42*** *p97*
*Daughter:*Eva Maria
Olt, Georg Philipp 10 *SEE* Olt, Konrad
Olt, Heinrich; America, 1856 ***2526.42*** *p170*
Olt, Johann Adam; America, 1835-1906 ***2526.42*** *p176*
Olt, Johann Adam; America, 1869 ***2526.42*** *p97*
Olt, Johann Georg; America, 1853 ***2526.42*** *p98*
*Sister:*Eva Maria
*Sister:*Dorothea
Olt, Johann Philipp; Illinois, 1852 ***2526.42*** *p176*
Olt, Johannes; America, 1852 ***2526.42*** *p176*
Olt, Johannes; America, 1858 ***2526.42*** *p97*
Olt, Johannes; Dayton, OH, 1869 ***2526.42*** *p98*
Olt, Katharina; America, 1853 ***2526.42*** *p155*
Olt, Katharina; America, 1871 ***2526.42*** *p98*
Olt, Konrad; America, 1842 ***2526.42*** *p98*
*Wife:*Anna Margareta
*Child:*Malena
*Child:*Barbara
*Child:*Georg Philipp
*Child:*Anna Margareta
Olt, Leonhard; America, 1854 ***2526.42*** *p176*
Olt, Leonhard F.; America, 1870 ***2526.42*** *p98*
Olt, Luise; America, 1852 ***2526.43*** *p154*
Olt, M. 42; America, 1856 ***2526.42*** *p99*
*Child:*Georg
Olt, Malena 4 *SEE* Olt, Konrad
Olt, Margareta; America, 1856 ***2526.42*** *p98*
Olt, Michael; America, 1836 ***2526.42*** *p128*
With wife & 2 children
Olt, Michael; America, 1850 ***2526.42*** *p98*
Olt, Philipp; America, 1852 ***2526.43*** *p154*
Oltendorf, Ernst; America, 1852 ***7420.1*** *p94*
With wife son & 3 daughters
Oltrogge, Anna Caroline Adelheit *SEE* Oltrogge, Johann Friedrich
Oltrogge, Catharine Engel; America, 1855 ***7420.1*** *p138*
Oltrogge, Catharine Engel Dorothee Charl. Lubke *SEE* Oltrogge, Johann Philipp
Oltrogge, Charlotte Dorothee; America, 1856 ***7420.1*** *p146*
Oltrogge, Chr.; Port uncertain, 1853 ***7420.1*** *p110*
With wife & 2 children
Oltrogge, Christoph; America, 1868 ***7420.1*** *p275*
Oltrogge, Conrad; America, 1855 ***7420.1*** *p140*
Oltrogge, Engel Marie Eleonore; America, 1869 ***7420.1*** *p280*
Oltrogge, Engel Marie Sophie Caroline Wolfrath *SEE* Oltrogge, Johann Friedrich
Oltrogge, Friedrich Wilhelm; New York, NY, 1856 ***7420.1*** *p151*
Oltrogge, Heinrich Conrad; America, 1859 ***7420.1*** *p188*
Oltrogge, Johann; America, 1856 ***7420.1*** *p151*
Oltrogge, Johann Friedrich; America, 1866 ***7420.1*** *p246*
*Wife:*Engel Marie Sophie Caroline Wolfrath
*Daughter:*Sophie Wilhelmine Caroline
*Daughter:*Anna Caroline Adelheit
Oltrogge, Johann Friedrich Christian; America, 1855 ***7420.1*** *p140*
Oltrogge, Johann Heinrich; America, 1852 ***7420.1*** *p94*
Oltrogge, Johann Heinrich Christian; New York, NY, 1856 ***7420.1*** *p151*
Oltrogge, Johann Heinrich Christoph; America, 1856 ***7420.1*** *p151*
Oltrogge, Johann Heinrich Christoph; America, 1868 ***7420.1*** *p275*
Oltrogge, Johann Heinrich Friedrich; America, 1866 ***7420.1*** *p246*
Oltrogge, Johann Philipp; America, 1866 ***7420.1*** *p246*
With family
Oltrogge, Johann Philipp; America, 1866 ***7420.1*** *p246*
*Wife:*Catharine Engel Dorothee Charl. Lubke
With children
Oltrogge, Marie Dorothee Sophie; America, 1868 ***7420.1*** *p272*
Oltrogge, Sophie Wilhelmine Caroline *SEE* Oltrogge, Johann Friedrich
Oltrogge, Wilhelm; America, 1856 ***7420.1*** *p151*
Olufson, Esther *SEE* Olufson, John Gottfrie
Olufson, Eugene *SEE* Olufson, John Gottfrie
Olufson, Gladys *SEE* Olufson, John Gottfrie
Olufson, John Gottfrie; Colorado, 1921 ***1029.59*** *p71*
*Wife:*Esther
*Child:*Gladys
*Child:*Eugene
Olveque, Francois 29; Louisiana, 1848 ***778.6*** *p259*
Olver, Joseph 24; Ontario, 1871 ***1823.21*** *p286*
Omaley, Elizabeth 28; Ontario, 1871 ***1823.21*** *p286*
O'Maley, Hugh; Toronto, 1844 ***2910.35*** *p113*
Omalley, Austin 35; Ontario, 1871 ***1823.21*** *p286*
O'Malley, Martin 45; Ontario, 1871 ***1823.21*** *p283*
Omaly, John 22; Michigan, 1880 ***4491.39*** *p23*
Oman, Andrew; St. Paul, MN, 1894 ***1865.50*** *p103*
*Wife:*Betty
Oman, Betty *SEE* Oman, Andrew
Oman, Nils; New York, NY, 1844 ***6412.40*** *p147*
Oman, Philip; North Carolina, 1710 ***3629.40*** *p6*
Omann, Christopher; Detroit, 1901 ***1766.20*** *p23*
Omann, Robert; Detroit, 1901 ***1766.20*** *p23*
O'Mara, Andrew 54; Ontario, 1871 ***1823.21*** *p283*
O'Mara, Ann 37; Ontario, 1871 ***1823.17*** *p127*
O'Mara, Ellen 20; Ontario, 1871 ***1823.21*** *p284*
O'Mara, James 28; Ontario, 1871 ***1823.17*** *p127*
O'Mara, James 84; Ontario, 1871 ***1823.21*** *p284*
O'Mara, John 60; Ontario, 1871 ***1823.21*** *p284*
O'Mara, John; St. John, N.B., 1847 ***2978.15*** *p35*
Omara, Rose 59; Ontario, 1871 ***1823.17*** *p128*
O'Mara, Timothy 74; Ontario, 1871 ***1823.21*** *p284*
O'Marah, William F. 90; Ontario, 1871 ***1823.17*** *p127*
O'Marra, Richard 40; Ontario, 1871 ***1823.21*** *p284*
O'Marsh, Catherine; America, 1746 ***1220.12*** *p593*
O'Marsh, James; America, 1746 ***1220.12*** *p593*
O'Marsh, Robert; America, 1746 ***1220.12*** *p593*
O'Marsh, Thomas; America, 1746 ***1220.12*** *p593*
Ombler, Dorothy; America, 1736 ***1220.12*** *p593*
O'Meara, Bridget 18; Ontario, 1871 ***1823.21*** *p284*
O'Meara, Martin 34; Ontario, 1871 ***1823.21*** *p284*
O'Meara, Martin 44; Ontario, 1871 ***1823.21*** *p284*
O'Meara, Michl 40; Ontario, 1871 ***1823.21*** *p284*
O'Meara, Stephen 40; Ontario, 1871 ***1823.21*** *p284*
Omeiss, Katharina; Venezuela, 1843 ***3899.5*** *p542*
Omend, John; North Carolina, 1710 ***3629.40*** *p3*
Omend, Philip; North Carolina, 1710 ***3629.40*** *p6*
Omer, Dedier 25; Missouri, 1846 ***778.6*** *p259*
Omera, Margret 37; Ontario, 1871 ***1823.21*** *p286*
Omerton, John; America, 1773 ***1220.12*** *p593*
Omeyer, Louis 25; New Orleans, 1840 ***778.6*** *p259*
Omlor, Jakob; America, 1885 ***5475.1*** *p422*
O'Moro, John 45; Ontario, 1871 ***1823.21*** *p284*
Onderick, Jacob; Ohio, 1809-1852 ***4511.35*** *p39*
Ondrisek, Frantisek; Chicago, 1896 ***2853.20*** *p470*
O'Neal, Mr.; Boston, 1763 ***1642*** *p32*

O'Neal, Mr.; Boston, 1765 ***1642*** *p35*
O'Neal, Charles; America, 1763 ***1220.12*** *p593*
O'Neal, Eleanor 40; Ontario, 1871 ***1823.17*** *p127*
O'Neal, Ferdinando; Virginia, 1739 ***1220.12*** *p593*
Oneal, George 67; Ontario, 1871 ***1823.21*** *p286*
O'Neal, Henry; America, 1752 ***1220.12*** *p593*
O'Neal, James; Jamaica, 1769 ***8529.30*** *p13A*
O'Neal, James; Massachusetts, 1832 ***3274.55*** *p27*
Oneal, John 73; Ontario, 1871 ***1823.21*** *p286*
O'Neal, Joseph 45; South Carolina, 1812 ***3476.30*** *p12*
Oneal, Margrett 40; Michigan, 1880 ***4491.30*** *p24*
O'Neal, Owen; America, 1751 ***1220.12*** *p593*
O'Neal, Patrick; Illinois, 1834-1900 ***6020.5*** *p132*
Oneal, Patrick 45; Michigan, 1880 ***4491.30*** *p24*
O'Neal, Richard Patrick; Texas, 1915 ***3435.45*** *p36*
O'Neal, Roger; Jamaica, 1778 ***8529.30*** *p13A*
O'Neal, William; Illinois, 1834-1900 ***6020.5*** *p132*
Oneal, Wm 40; Ontario, 1871 ***1823.21*** *p286*
O'Neale, Honor; Barbados, 1671 ***1220.12*** *p593*
O'Neale, Margaret; Annapolis, MD, 1731 ***1220.12*** *p593*
O'Neil, Arthur 48; Ontario, 1871 ***1823.21*** *p284*
O'Neil, Arthur 50; Ontario, 1871 ***1823.21*** *p284*
Oneil, Bridget 70; Ontario, 1871 ***1823.17*** *p128*
O'Neil, Charles; Albany, NY, 1830 ***3274.56*** *p71*
O'Neil, Charles; America, 1773 ***1220.12*** *p593*
O'Neil, Cornelius; America, 1771 ***1220.12*** *p593*
O'Neil, Dennis 30; Ontario, 1871 ***1823.21*** *p284*
O'Neil, Edward; Ohio, 1809-1852 ***4511.35*** *p39*
Oneil, Ellen 25; Michigan, 1880 ***4491.39*** *p23*
O'Neil, Ellen 55; Ontario, 1871 ***1823.21*** *p284*
Oneil, Henry 55; Ontario, 1871 ***1823.21*** *p286*
Oneil, James 50; Ontario, 1871 ***1823.21*** *p286*
Oneil, James 56; Ontario, 1871 ***1823.21*** *p286*
O'Neil, John; Long Island, 1778 ***8529.30*** *p10A*
O'Neil, John; North Carolina, 1819 ***1088.45*** *p26*
O'Neil, John; Ohio, 1836 ***3580.20*** *p33*
O'Neil, John; Ohio, 1836 ***6020.12*** *p21*
O'Neil, John 40; Ontario, 1871 ***1823.21*** *p284*
O'Neil, John 60; Ontario, 1871 ***1823.21*** *p284*
Oneil, Mary A. 3; Michigan, 1880 ***4491.39*** *p23*
O'Neil, Neil 78; Ontario, 1871 ***1823.17*** *p127*
O'Neil, Owen; North Carolina, 1835 ***1088.45*** *p26*
O Neil, Patrick 38; Ontario, 1871 ***1823.21*** *p282*
Oneil, Patrick 70; Ontario, 1871 ***1823.21*** *p286*
O'Neil, Patrick; Salem, MA, 1767 ***1642*** *p78*
O'Neil, Peter J.; Toronto, 1844 ***2910.35*** *p111*
O'Neil, Rachell 68; Ontario, 1871 ***1823.21*** *p284*
O'Neil, Roger 40; Ontario, 1871 ***1823.21*** *p284*
O'Neil, T.J.; Toronto, 1844 ***2910.35*** *p111*
O'Neil, Terence J.; Toronto, 1844 ***2910.35*** *p111*
O'Neil, Thomas; Nantucket, MA, 1756 ***1642*** *p89*
O'Neil, Thomas; Washington, 1889 ***2770.40*** *p80*
O'Neill, Edward; Illinois, 1858-1861 ***6020.5*** *p132*
O'Neill, James; Jamaica, 1769 ***8529.30*** *p13A*
O'Neill, John R.; Washington, 1885 ***2770.40*** *p194*
O'Neill, Mary 17; Quebec, 1870 ***8364.32*** *p25*
O'Neill, Michael, Jr.; Toronto, 1844 ***2910.35*** *p114*
O'Neill, Michael, Sr.; Toronto, 1844 ***2910.35*** *p114*
O'Neill, Thomas; Ontario, 1871 ***1823.17*** *p127*
O'Neill, Thomas; Ottawa, 1889-1983 ***9228.50*** *p514*
With daughter
Onesby, Sara; Barbados, 1673 ***1220.12*** *p593*
Onesby, Sarah; Maryland, 1674 ***1236.25*** *p50*
Oney, John; Annapolis, MD, 1726 ***1220.12*** *p593*
Oney, Samuel; America, 1730 ***1220.12*** *p593*
Ong, James; America, 1764 ***1220.12*** *p593*
Oniel, Bridget 60; Michigan, 1880 ***4491.39*** *p23*
O'Niel, James; America, 1614-1775 ***1220.12*** *p593*
O'Niel, James 19; Quebec, 1870 ***8364.32*** *p25*
Oniel, John 60; Michigan, 1880 ***4491.39*** *p23*
O'Niel, Joseph; Ohio, 1809-1852 ***4511.35*** *p39*
O'Niel, Martin; Ohio, 1809-1852 ***4511.35*** *p39*
O'Niel, Thomas; Ohio, 1809-1852 ***4511.35*** *p39*
Onion, Edward; America, 1764 ***1220.12*** *p593*
Onion, Henry; Annapolis, MD, 1723 ***1220.12*** *p593*
Onion, Hester; America, 1753 ***1220.12*** *p593*
Onion, Thomas; America, 1753 ***1220.12*** *p593*
Onion, Thomas; America, 1763 ***1220.12*** *p594*
Onion, William; America, 1752 ***1220.12*** *p594*
Onions, Joseph; America, 1757 ***1220.12*** *p594*
Onnen, Onne Martens; Illinois, 1855 ***6079.1*** *p11*
Onrey, James 55; Ontario, 1871 ***1823.21*** *p286*
Onyon, Catherine; Virginia, 1726 ***1220.12*** *p593*
Onyon, Elizabeth; America, 1717 ***1220.12*** *p593*
Onyons, William; Barbados, 1669 ***1220.12*** *p594*
Ooler, James; America, 1764 ***1220.12*** *p594*
Opava, Vincenc; Iowa, 1884-1900 ***2853.20*** *p238*
Opel, John; Missouri, 1886 ***3276.1*** *p2*
Opel, John; Missouri, 1888 ***3276.1*** *p2*
Openheimer, Moses; Ohio, 1809-1852 ***4511.35*** *p39*
Openshaw, John; America, 1753 ***1220.12*** *p594*
Operman, Witold 18; New York, NY, 1911 ***6533.11*** *p9*
Opitz, Christian; Galveston, TX, 1855 ***571.7*** *p17*
Opitz, Karl 22; Valparaiso, Chile, 1897 ***5475.1*** *p39*
Opocensky, Josef; Texas, 1858 ***2853.20*** *p78*
Opp, Johann Philipp; New Jersey, 1768-1774 ***927.31*** *p2*
Oppelt, Benjamin; North Carolina, 1829 ***1088.45*** *p26*
Oppemheim, George 23; Ontario, 1871 ***1823.21*** *p286*
Oppen, Josef *SEE* Oppen, Mathias
Oppen, Maria *SEE* Oppen, Mathias
Oppen, Mathias *SEE* Oppen, Mathias
Oppen, Mathias 60; America, 1857 ***5475.1*** *p322*
*Son:*Mathias
*Son:*Josef
*Daughter:*Maria
*Daughter:*Susanna
Oppen, Susanna *SEE* Oppen, Mathias
Oppenheim, Mr. 30; Louisiana, 1848 ***778.6*** *p259*
Oppenheim, Louis 24; Louisiana, 1848 ***778.6*** *p259*
Oppenheimer, Clara; America, 1856 ***2526.43*** *p154*
Oppenheimer, Elias 18; America, 1852 ***2526.43*** *p177*
Oppenheimer, Goethe 27; Missouri, 1846 ***778.6*** *p259*
Oppenheimer, Hannchen 17; America, 1853 ***2526.43*** *p177*
*Sister:*Jette 15
*Brother:*Leopold 13
Oppenheimer, Hugo; America, 1897 ***2526.43*** *p154*
Oppenheimer, Jette 15 *SEE* Oppenheimer, Hannchen
Oppenheimer, Johann; America, 1857 ***5475.1*** *p489*
Oppenheimer, Joseph; New York, 1893 ***2526.42*** *p128*
Oppenheimer, Julius; America, 1891 ***2526.43*** *p154*
Oppenheimer, Koppel; America, 1867 ***2526.42*** *p128*
Oppenheimer, Leopold; America, 1889 ***2526.42*** *p128*
Oppenheimer, Leopold 13 *SEE* Oppenheimer, Hannchen
Oppenheimer, Sara 54; America, 1853 ***2526.43*** *p199*
With 2 daughters
Oppenhein, Jacob; America, 1757 ***1220.12*** *p594*
Oppenlander, Ernest; Missouri, 1896 ***3276.1*** *p2*
Oppenlander, John; Missouri, 1892 ***3276.1*** *p2*
Opperman, Emma Elizabeth; Wisconsin, 1897 ***6795.8*** *p193*
Oppermann, Ida Auguste Eleònore; America, 1851 ***7420.1*** *p78*
Oquener, Ann; Philadelphia, 1772 ***9228.50*** *p485*
Oqvist, N.G.; New York, NY, 1846 ***6412.40*** *p149*
Orage, Thomas; America, 1773 ***1220.12*** *p594*
Oram, John; America, 1685 ***1220.12*** *p594*
Oram, John; America, 1768 ***1220.12*** *p594*
Oram, Samuel; Maryland, 1737 ***1220.12*** *p594*
Orange, John 26; Ontario, 1871 ***1823.21*** *p286*
Orange, John 48; Ontario, 1871 ***1823.21*** *p286*
Orange, Louiss; Virginia, 1700 ***9230.15*** *p81*
With wife & child
Orangez, Leger; Quebec, 1642 ***9221.17*** *p119*
Orban, Anthony; Detroit, 1926 ***6214.5*** *p67*
Orban, Emilia; Detroit, 1929-1930 ***6214.5*** *p67*
Orbann, Charles; Philadelphia, 1855 ***8513.31*** *p418*
*Wife:*Pauline Buechner
Orbann, Pauline Buechner *SEE* Orbann, Charles
Orbinson, James; Jamaica, 1778 ***8529.30*** *p13A*
Orbison, James; Jamaica, 1778 ***8529.30*** *p13A*
Orchard, Abigail; America, 1736 ***1220.12*** *p594*
Orchard, Caroline Ann 35; Ontario, 1871 ***1823.21*** *p287*
Orchard, Christopher; America, 1685 ***1220.12*** *p594*
Orchard, Edmond; Ohio, 1840-1847 ***9228.50*** *p135*
*Wife:*Rachel Brochet
*Child:*James H.
*Child:*Rachel Sophia
*Child:*William E.
Orchard, George; Barbados, 1675 ***1220.12*** *p594*
Orchard, George 39; Ontario, 1871 ***1823.21*** *p287*
Orchard, James; America, 1741 ***1220.12*** *p594*
Orchard, James; Maryland or Virginia, 1731 ***1220.12*** *p594*
Orchard, James 24; Ontario, 1871 ***1823.21*** *p287*
Orchard, James H. *SEE* Orchard, Edmond
Orchard, Jane 50; Ontario, 1871 ***1823.21*** *p287*
Orchard, John; America, 1766 ***1220.12*** *p594*
Orchard, John; Annapolis, MD, 1726 ***1220.12*** *p594*
Orchard, John 30; Ontario, 1871 ***1823.17*** *p128*
Orchard, John 50; Ontario, 1871 ***1823.21*** *p287*
Orchard, Mary Ann 58; Ontario, 1871 ***1823.21*** *p287*
Orchard, Rachel Brochet *SEE* Orchard, Edmond
Orchard, Rachel Sophia *SEE* Orchard, Edmond
Orchard, Sarah; America, 1755 ***1220.12*** *p594*
Orchard, Simon 37; Ontario, 1871 ***1823.21*** *p287*
Orchard, Thomas; America, 1685 ***1220.12*** *p594*
Orchard, Thomas; America, 1725 ***1220.12*** *p594*
Orchard, Thomas; America, 1756 ***1220.12*** *p594*
Orchard, Thomas; America, 1774 ***1220.12*** *p594*
Orchard, William; America, 1765 ***1220.12*** *p594*
Orchard, William; North Carolina, 1835 ***1088.45*** *p26*
Orchard, William 50; Ontario, 1871 ***1823.21*** *p287*
Orchard, William E. *SEE* Orchard, Edmond
Ord, Cecilla 77; Ontario, 1871 ***1823.21*** *p287*
Ord, Dorothy; Potomac, 1729 ***1220.12*** *p594*
Ord, George; New York, NY, 1778 ***8529.30*** *p3*
Ord, Margaret 40; Ontario, 1871 ***1823.21*** *p287*
Ord, Richard; America, 1735 ***1220.12*** *p594*
Ord, Robert; America, 1730 ***1220.12*** *p594*
Ord, Robert; Virginia, 1773 ***1220.12*** *p594*
Orde, Elizabeth; Virginia, 1772 ***1220.12*** *p594*
Ordery, Mary; America, 1748 ***1220.12*** *p594*
Ordinere, Barbe 24; America, 1846 ***778.6*** *p259*
Ordinere, Pre. 28; America, 1846 ***778.6*** *p259*
Orditz, Joseph 42; America, 1841 ***778.6*** *p259*
Ordoquii, Antonia; California, 1872 ***3276.8*** *p19*
*Child:*Dolores
*Child:*Manuel
Ordoquii, Dolores *SEE* Ordoquii, Antonia
Ordoquii, Juan; California, 1849 ***3276.8*** *p19*
Ordoquii, Manuel *SEE* Ordoquii, Antonia
O'Rea, Hamilton 27; Ontario, 1871 ***1823.17*** *p127*
O'Reardon, William; Louisiana, 1874 ***4981.45*** *p133*
O'Reilley, James; Ohio, 1840-1897 ***8365.35*** *p17*
O'Reilly, John V.; New Jersey, 1924 ***9228.50*** *p334*
O'Reilly, Patrick T.; Ohio, 1809-1852 ***4511.35*** *p39*
O'Reilly, Terance 60; Ontario, 1871 ***1823.21*** *p284*
O'Reily, E.; Toronto, 1844 ***2910.35*** *p115*
O'Reily, Patrick; Ohio, 1809-1852 ***4511.35*** *p39*
Orel, Iwan 20; New York, NY, 1911 ***6533.11*** *p10*
Oren, Denis 27; Missouri, 1846 ***778.6*** *p259*
Oren, Victoria 22; Missouri, 1846 ***778.6*** *p259*
Oreton, Thomas; America, 1692 ***1220.12*** *p595*
Orford, Mary; America, 1744 ***1220.12*** *p594*
Organall, William; America, 1736 ***1220.12*** *p594*
Orgar, Edward; America, 1775 ***1220.12*** *p594*
Orieux, Mathurin 22; Quebec, 1661 ***9221.17*** *p464*
O'Riley, Seth; Massachusetts, 1726 ***1642*** *p90*
Orillac, Maurice 35; Port uncertain, 1841 ***778.6*** *p259*
Orin, Mathurin 22; Quebec, 1661 ***9221.17*** *p464*
Orleac, Jean; Louisiana, 1874-1875 ***4981.45*** *p30*
Orlet, Theodor Wilhelm; America, 1867 ***7919.3*** *p528*
Orman, Anna *SEE* Orman, John A.
Orman, John A.; St. Paul, MN, 1884 ***1865.50*** *p103*
*Wife:*Anna
Orman, Meredith 47; Ontario, 1871 ***1823.21*** *p287*
Ormand, David; America, 1767 ***1220.12*** *p594*
Ormand, James; Philadelphia, 1778 ***8529.30*** *p4A*
Ormand, Mary; America, 1735 ***1220.12*** *p594*
Orme, Andrew; America, 1765 ***1220.12*** *p594*
Orme, James; Antigua (Antego), 1742 ***1220.12*** *p594*
Orme, Robert; America, 1673 ***1220.12*** *p594*
Orme, Thomas 60; Ontario, 1871 ***1823.21*** *p287*
Ormeond, John; Ohio, 1840-1897 ***8365.35*** *p17*
Ormison, Young 52; Michigan, 1880 ***4491.42*** *p20*
Ormon, James; Philadelphia, 1778 ***8529.30*** *p4A*
Ormond, Catherine; New Orleans, 1850 ***7242.30*** *p152*
Ormond, Francis 34; Ontario, 1871 ***1823.21*** *p287*
Ormond, George; New York, 1753-1800 ***9228.50*** *p20A*
Ormond, James; Philadelphia, 1778 ***8529.30*** *p4A*
Ormond, Jane; America, 1762 ***1220.12*** *p594*
Ormond, Thomas; North Carolina, 1843 ***1088.45*** *p26*
Ormsbey, Edward; Virginia, 1736 ***1220.12*** *p594*
Ormsby, N. 50; Ontario, 1871 ***1823.21*** *p287*
Orne Family ; Massachusetts, 1700 ***9228.50*** *p485*
Orocke, William; Barbados, 1684 ***1220.12*** *p594*
Oromode, John 51; Ontario, 1871 ***1823.17*** *p128*
Oronos, Marie; California, 1860-1890 ***3276.8*** *p19*
Oronsko, Henry; Virginia, 1766 ***1220.12*** *p594*
O'Rorke, Charles 45; Ontario, 1871 ***1823.21*** *p284*
O'Rorke, William 45; Ontario, 1871 ***1823.21*** *p284*
Oroszi, Andrew; New York, 1926 ***1173.1*** *p2*
O'Rourk, Brian; St. John, N.B., 1847 ***2978.15*** *p37*
O'Rourk, Patrick; Maine, 1831 ***3274.55*** *p68*
Orourke, Lawrence 49; Ontario, 1871 ***1823.21*** *p287*
O'Rourke, Patrick; Boston, 1833 ***3274.56*** *p97*
Orpwood, John; America, 1766 ***1220.12*** *p594*
Orpwood, William; America, 1741 ***1220.12*** *p594*
Orr, Betty E. 21; Michigan, 1880 ***4491.42*** *p20*
Orr, Cyrus F.; Washington, 1881 ***2770.40*** *p135*
Orr, Cyrus F.; Washington, 1886 ***2770.40*** *p195*
Orr, James 42; Ontario, 1871 ***1823.21*** *p287*
Orr, James 54; Ontario, 1871 ***1823.21*** *p287*
Orr, James, Jr.; Baltimore, 1821 ***471.10*** *p86*
Orr, James, Sr.; Baltimore, 1821 ***471.10*** *p86*
Orr, James, Sr.; Indiana, 1844 ***471.10*** *p62*
Orr, John 92; Ontario, 1871 ***1823.21*** *p287*
Orr, Joseph E. 40; Michigan, 1880 ***4491.42*** *p20*
Orr, Mary 59; Ontario, 1871 ***1823.17*** *p128*
Orr, Mary A.N. 60; Ontario, 1871 ***1823.21*** *p287*
Orr, Nancy 64; Ontario, 1871 ***1823.21*** *p287*
Orr, Robert 38; Ontario, 1871 ***1823.21*** *p287*
Orr, Robert 44; Ontario, 1871 ***1823.21*** *p287*
Orr, Robinson 50; Ontario, 1871 ***1823.21*** *p287*
Orr, Samuel; Baltimore, 1821 ***471.10*** *p61*
Orr, Sarah A. 31; Michigan, 1880 ***4491.42*** *p20*
Orr, William; America, 1773 ***1220.12*** *p594*
Orr, William 70; Ontario, 1871 ***1823.21*** *p287*

Orrange, James 28; Ontario, 1871 ***1823.21*** *p287*
Orrell, John; America, 1742 ***1220.12*** *p595*
Orrell, Thomas; Barbados, 1669 ***1220.12*** *p595*
Orrett, George; America, 1766 ***1220.12*** *p595*
Orrick, Mary; Virginia, 1734 ***1220.12*** *p595*
Orris, Emily C. 30; Ontario, 1871 ***1823.17*** *p128*
Orrox, Elizabeth; America, 1764 ***1220.12*** *p595*
Orsini, Joseph; Louisiana, 1874-1875 ***4981.45*** *p30*
Orstynowicz, Stanislaw 35; New York, NY, 1920 ***930.50*** *p48*
Ort, Barbara; America, 1881 ***5475.1*** *p220*
Ort, Euft; Illinois, 1856 ***6079.1*** *p11*
Ortega, S.; California, 1868 ***1131.61*** *p89*
Ortel, Georg 36; Galveston, TX, 1844 ***3967.10*** *p375*
Orth, Adam; America, 1830 ***2526.43*** *p226*
*Wife:*Marie Gertrud
With 5 children
Orth, Adam; America, 1867 ***2526.42*** *p144*
*Wife:*Katharina Lang
*Child:*Margaretha
*Child:*Adam
Orth, Adam 6 *SEE* Orth, Adam
Orth, Mrs. Adam 56; America, 1882 ***2526.42*** *p170*
Orth, Anna Barbara; America, 1830 ***2526.43*** *p227*
Orth, Anna Elisabetha 34 *SEE* Orth, Peter, II
Orth, Balthasar; America, 1882 ***2526.42*** *p170*
*Wife:*Margaretha
*Sister:*Katharina
*Stepchild:*Elisabetha
*Daughter:*Margaretha
*Daughter:*Mina
*Sister:*Margaretha
Orth, Barbara 5 *SEE* Orth, Leonhard
Orth, Catharine 6; New Orleans, 1848 ***778.6*** *p259*
Orth, Catharine 43; New Orleans, 1848 ***778.6*** *p259*
Orth, Elisabeth 2 *SEE* Orth, Leonhard
Orth, Elisabeth Bischoff 32 *SEE* Orth, Leonhard
Orth, Elisabetha 19 *SEE* Orth, Nikolaus
Orth, Elisabetha 21 *SEE* Orth, Balthasar
Orth, Elisabetha Margaretha *SEE* Orth, Jakob Philipp
Orth, Elisabetha Margaretha; America, 1853 ***2526.43*** *p226*
Orth, Eva Margaretha *SEE* Orth, Jakob Philipp
Orth, Friedrich; America, 1885 ***2526.42*** *p176*
Orth, Georg; America, 1833 ***2526.43*** *p226*
Orth, Georg 10 *SEE* Orth, Leonhard
Orth, Georg 22; America, 1839 ***2526.42*** *p144*
Orth, Georg 12; New Orleans, 1848 ***778.6*** *p259*
Orth, Georg, II; America, 1847 ***2526.42*** *p128*
With wife
*Child:*Margaretha
Orth, Georg Adam 14 *SEE* Orth, Nikolaus
Orth, Heinrich; America, 1753 ***2526.42*** *p144*
Orth, Jacob 20; New Orleans, 1848 ***778.6*** *p259*
Orth, Jacob 47; New Orleans, 1848 ***778.6*** *p259*
Orth, Jakob Philipp; America, 1847 ***2526.43*** *p128*
*Wife:*Katharina Trockenbrod
*Daughter:*Eva Margaretha
*Daughter:*Kath. Elisabetha
*Son:*Peter
*Daughter:*Elisabetha Margaretha
Orth, Johann 3 *SEE* Orth, Peter, II
Orth, Johann Konrad 19 *SEE* Orth, Nikolaus
Orth, Johannes 9 *SEE* Orth, Leonhard
Orth, Johannes 21 *SEE* Orth, Nikolaus
Orth, Joseph S.; Ohio, 1841 ***3580.20*** *p33*
Orth, Joseph S.; Ohio, 1841 ***6020.12*** *p21*
Orth, Kath. Elisabetha *SEE* Orth, Jakob Philipp
Orth, Katharina Trockenbrod *SEE* Orth, Jakob Philipp
Orth, Katharina Lang *SEE* Orth, Adam
Orth, Katharina 15 *SEE* Orth, Balthasar
Orth, Leonhard 3 *SEE* Orth, Peter, II
Orth, Leonhard 7 *SEE* Orth, Leonhard
Orth, Leonhard 41; America, 1883 ***2526.42*** *p136*
With stepchild 13
*Child:*Johannes 9 months
*Child:*Elisabeth 2
*Child:*Philip Jakob Bischoff 13
*Child:*Leonhard 7
*Child:*Barbara 5
*Child:*Georg 10
*Wife:*Elisabeth Bischoff 32
Orth, Margaretha *SEE* Orth, Balthasar
Orth, Margaretha 1 *SEE* Orth, Georg, II
Orth, Margaretha 2 *SEE* Orth, Adam
Orth, Margaretha 12 *SEE* Orth, Balthasar
Orth, Margaretha 23 *SEE* Orth, Balthasar
Orth, Maria 7 *SEE* Orth, Peter, II
Orth, Maria Elisabetha; America, 1785 ***2526.42*** *p131*
Orth, Marie Gertrud *SEE* Orth, Adam
Orth, Mina *SEE* Orth, Balthasar
Orth, Nikolaus 51; America, 1865 ***2526.42*** *p144*
*Wife:*Sibille 43
*Child:*Johannes 21
*Child:*Elisabetha 19
*Child:*Georg Adam 14
*Child:*Philipp 7
*Child:*Sibille 5
*Child:*Wilhelm 16
*Child:*Johann Konrad 19
Orth, Peter *SEE* Orth, Jakob Philipp
Orth, Peter, II 35; America, 1853 ***2526.43*** *p128*
*Wife:*Anna Elisabetha 34
*Son:*Leonhard 3
*Son:*Johann 3 months
*Daughter:*Sophia 5
*Daughter:*Maria 7
Orth, Philip Jakob Bischoff 13 *SEE* Orth, Leonhard
Orth, Philipp; America, 1839 ***2526.42*** *p144*
With wife
With child 12
With child 13
Orth, Philipp 7 *SEE* Orth, Nikolaus
Orth, Sibille 5 *SEE* Orth, Nikolaus
Orth, Sibille 43 *SEE* Orth, Nikolaus
Orth, Sophia 5 *SEE* Orth, Peter, II
Orth, Wilhelm 16 *SEE* Orth, Nikolaus
Orthlan, Armant; Louisiana, 1874 ***4981.45*** *p296*
Orthocheid, Ant. 30; America, 1840 ***778.6*** *p259*
Orth von Zell, Adam; America, 1833 ***2526.43*** *p187*
Ortloff, Carl; America, 1867 ***7919.3*** *p525*
Orton, Johanna; Annapolis, MD, 1725 ***1220.12*** *p595*
Orton, John; America, 1751 ***1220.12*** *p595*
Orton, John; Died enroute, 1725 ***1220.12*** *p595*
Orton, Thomas; America, 1694 ***1220.12*** *p595*
Orton, Thomas; Virginia, 1773 ***1220.12*** *p595*
Orton, William; America, 1744 ***1220.12*** *p595*
Orton, William E.; Colorado, 1887 ***1029.59*** *p71*
Orts, Jacob; Ohio, 1809-1852 ***4511.35*** *p39*
Orum, Benjamin; America, 1713 ***1220.12*** *p594*
Orville, Simone; Quebec, 1635 ***9221.17*** *p45*
Orville, Simone; Quebec, 1635 ***9221.17*** *p45*
Orvis, George; Boston, 1638 ***9228.50*** *p485*
Orvis, Isaac; Toronto, 1844 ***2910.35*** *p116*
Ory, Johann; America, 1872 ***5475.1*** *p154*
Oryon, Ann; Boston, 1704 ***1642*** *p24*
Osadchuk, Fred; Detroit, 1929-1930 ***6214.5*** *p70*
Osar, Joseph; Ohio, 1809-1852 ***4511.35*** *p39*
Osbaldston, Robert; America, 1741 ***1220.12*** *p595*
Osband, James; America, 1775 ***1220.12*** *p595*
Osbeck, C. A.; Valparaiso, Chile, 1850 ***1192.4*** *p50*
Osberg, Otto; Cleveland, OH, 1902-1904 ***9722.10*** *p125*
Osbild, Magdalena 47; America, 1873 ***5475.1*** *p172*
Osborn, Alfred 42; Ontario, 1871 ***1823.21*** *p287*
Osborn, Anna Maria; Maryland or Virginia, 1738 ***1220.12*** *p595*
Osborn, Charles; America, 1730 ***1220.12*** *p595*
Osborn, George; America, 1744 ***1220.12*** *p595*
Osborn, George; America, 1775 ***1220.12*** *p595*
Osborn, Hannah; America, 1772 ***1220.12*** *p595*
Osborn, John; America, 1728 ***1220.12*** *p595*
Osborn, John; America, 1744 ***1220.12*** *p595*
Osborn, John; America, 1758 ***1220.12*** *p595*
Osborn, Joseph; America, 1773 ***1220.12*** *p595*
Osborn, Moses; America, 1685 ***1220.12*** *p595*
Osborn, Philip; America, 1774 ***1220.12*** *p595*
Osborn, Samuel; Massachusetts, 1620-1775 ***1642*** *p138*
Osborn, Samuel; Massachusetts, 1620-1775 ***1642*** *p139*
Osborn, Samuel; Massachusetts, 1718 ***1642*** *p86*
With family
Osborn, Simon; America, 1744 ***1220.12*** *p595*
Osborn, Walter; America, 1685 ***1220.12*** *p596*
Osborn, William; America, 1770 ***1220.12*** *p596*
Osborne, Amelia; Ontario, 1923-1929 ***9228.50*** *p627*
Osborne, Ann; America, 1753 ***1220.12*** *p595*
Osborne, Ann; Barbados, 1663 ***1220.12*** *p595*
Osborne, Ann; Barbados or Jamaica, 1684 ***1220.12*** *p595*
Osborne, Catherine; Ontario, 1835 ***3160.1*** *p150*
Osborne, Charles K.; Illinois, 1918 ***6007.60*** *p9*
Osborne, Elizabeth; America, 1764 ***1220.12*** *p595*
Osborne, Elizabeth; Barbados, 1681 ***1220.12*** *p595*
Osborne, Elizabeth; Barbados or Jamaica, 1697 ***1220.12*** *p595*
Osborne, Elizabeth 17; Ontario, 1871 ***1823.21*** *p287*
Osborne, G.; Quebec, 1870 ***8364.32*** *p25*
Osborne, G. P. 35; Ontario, 1871 ***1823.17*** *p128*
Osborne, George; America, 1771 ***1220.12*** *p595*
Osborne, James; New Jersey, 1770-1799 ***9228.50*** *p661*
Osborne, Jane 41; Ontario, 1871 ***1823.21*** *p287*
Osborne, John; America, 1679 ***1220.12*** *p595*
Osborne, John; America, 1730 ***1220.12*** *p595*
Osborne, John; America, 1750 ***1220.12*** *p595*
Osborne, John; America, 1772 ***1220.12*** *p595*
Osborne, John 19; Ontario, 1871 ***1823.21*** *p287*
Osborne, John, Jr.; America, 1752 ***1220.12*** *p595*
Osborne, Martha; America, 1758 ***1220.12*** *p595*
Osborne, Mary; America, 1761 ***1220.12*** *p595*
Osborne, Richard; Barbados or Jamaica, 1686 ***1220.12*** *p595*
Osborne, Richard 15; Quebec, 1870 ***8364.32*** *p25*
Osborne, Sarah; America, 1752 ***1220.12*** *p595*
Osborne, Thomas; America, 1692 ***1220.12*** *p595*
Osborne, Thomas; America, 1774 ***1220.12*** *p596*
Osborne, William; America, 1751 ***1220.12*** *p596*
Osborne, William; America, 1771 ***1220.12*** *p596*
Osborne, William; New York, 1778 ***8529.30*** *p7*
Osborne, William 73; Ontario, 1871 ***1823.21*** *p287*
Osborne, William, Jr.; America, 1773 ***1220.12*** *p596*
Osbourne, Charles 19; Quebec, 1870 ***8364.32*** *p25*
Osbourne, George; America, 1721 ***1220.12*** *p595*
Osburn, Adam 42; Ontario, 1871 ***1823.17*** *p128*
Osburn, John; America, 1726 ***1220.12*** *p595*
Osburn, Joseph 38; Ontario, 1871 ***1823.17*** *p128*
Osburn, Peter 74; Ontario, 1871 ***1823.17*** *p128*
Osburn, Thomas; America, 1764 ***1220.12*** *p596*
Oscar, Albert; Miami, 1920 ***4984.15*** *p38*
Osche, Michel 30; America, 1843 ***778.6*** *p259*
Oschger, Jean 46; New Castle, DE, 1817-1818 ***90.20*** *p153*
Oschner, John Martin; Illinois, 1854 ***6079.1*** *p11*
Osenbrugg, Louise; Valdivia, Chile, 1851 ***1192.4*** *p51*
Osene, Julien; Quebec, 1659 ***9221.17*** *p414*
Oser, Conrad; Ohio, 1809-1852 ***4511.35*** *p39*
Osetkowski, Andrew Anthony; Detroit, 1930 ***1640.60*** *p77*
Osgood, James; America, 1752 ***1220.12*** *p596*
O'Shade, Ann; Philadelphia, 1853 ***8513.31*** *p322/lv1]*
Oshagee, Joseph 35; Ontario, 1871 ***1823.17*** *p129*
O'Shaughaussey, Michael; Louisiana, 1874 ***4981.45*** *p296*
O Shea, Ellen 34; Ontario, 1871 ***1823.21*** *p282*
O'Shea, Ellin 63; Ontario, 1871 ***1823.21*** *p284*
Oshea, Michael 34; Ontario, 1871 ***1823.21*** *p287*
O'Shea, Patrick Joseph 32; Ontario, 1871 ***1823.21*** *p284*
Oshner, Michael; Illinois, 1854 ***6079.1*** *p11*
Osland, Alfred 35; Ontario, 1871 ***1823.21*** *p287*
Osler, Mary; America, 1766 ***1220.12*** *p596*
Osler, William; America, 1762 ***1220.12*** *p596*
Oslund, Anders; Iowa, 1876 ***1211.15*** *p17*
Osman, Alice; Virginia, 1746 ***1220.12*** *p596*
Osman, Elizabeth; America, 1758 ***1220.12*** *p596*
Osman, John; Barbados, 1701 ***1220.12*** *p596*
Osman, Laura; St. Paul, MN, 1894 ***1865.50*** *p103*
Osmond, Alice 14; Quebec, 1870 ***8364.32*** *p25*
Osmond, Anne; Virginia, 1743 ***1220.12*** *p596*
Osmond, Edward; America, 1747 ***1220.12*** *p596*
Osmond, Edward; Barbados, 1672 ***1220.12*** *p596*
Osmond, J.; Quebec, 1870 ***8364.32*** *p25*
Osmonds, John; America, 1755 ***1220.12*** *p596*
Osmore, Sarah; Barbados, 1679 ***1220.12*** *p596*
Osmundsen, Jens; Iowa, 1896 ***1211.15*** *p17*
Ospelt, Mathias 50; America, 1867 ***5475.1*** *p281*
Ossenkop, Mr. 29; New Orleans, 1846 ***778.6*** *p259*
Ost, Christian 6; Halifax, N.S., 1902 ***1860.4*** *p43*
Ost, Emilie 2; Halifax, N.S., 1902 ***1860.4*** *p43*
Ost, Friederike; Halifax, N.S., 1902 ***1860.4*** *p43*
Ost, Jacob; Halifax, N.S., 1902 ***1860.4*** *p43*
Ost, Johann 34; Halifax, N.S., 1902 ***1860.4*** *p43*
Ost, Katharina 3; Halifax, N.S., 1902 ***1860.4*** *p43*
Ost, Peter; Brazil, 1857 ***5475.1*** *p441*
With wife & 4 children
Ostaszewski, Ambrose; Detroit, 1929 ***1640.55*** *p117*
Ostberg, Andrew; Iowa, 1866 ***777.40*** *p10*
Ostberg, Olof; St. Paul, MN, 1880 ***1865.50*** *p103*
Ostedt, Tilda; St. Paul, MN, 1894 ***1865.50*** *p103*
Oster, Catherine 30; New Orleans, 1846 ***778.6*** *p259*
Oster, Christ..n 9; America, 1846 ***778.6*** *p259*
Oster, Christina 34; New York, NY, 1898 ***7951.13*** *p42*
Oster, Christine 8; New York, NY, 1898 ***7951.13*** *p42*
Oster, Francisca 26; America, 1846 ***778.6*** *p259*
Oster, Franz 36; New York, NY, 1898 ***7951.13*** *p42*
Oster, Henry; Ohio, 1809-1852 ***4511.35*** *p39*
Oster, Jacob 9 months; New York, NY, 1898 ***7951.13*** *p42*
Oster, Johann 3; New York, NY, 1898 ***7951.13*** *p42*
Oster, Juanita 24; America, 1846 ***778.6*** *p259*
Oster, Marie 17; America, 1846 ***778.6*** *p259*
Oster, P. 44; America, 1846 ***778.6*** *p259*
Oster, Rosina 5; New York, NY, 1898 ***7951.13*** *p42*
Oster, Veronique 27; America, 1846 ***778.6*** *p260*
Osterberg, Marten; Charleston, SC, 1850 ***6412.40*** *p152*
Osterberg, P.; Philadelphia, 1847 ***6412.40*** *p150*
Ostergren, J.U.; New York, NY, 1847 ***6412.40*** *p150*
Osterheld, Georg; America, 1904 ***2526.43*** *p193*
Ostermeier, Carl Ernst; America, 1871 ***7420.1*** *p292*

Ostermeier, Carl Friedrich Christian; America, 1841 ***7420.1*** *p23*
*Wife:*Luise Leonore Steinkamper
With 2 daughters & son
Ostermeier, Caroline; Port uncertain, 1853 ***7420.1*** *p110*
Ostermeier, Engel Marie Caroline; America, 1854 ***7420.1*** *p126*
With husband & children
Ostermeier, Heinrich Wilhelm; America, 1852 ***7420.1*** *p95*
With family
Ostermeier, Luise Leonore Steinkamper *SEE* Ostermeier, Carl Friedrich Christian
Ostermeier, Wilhelm; Chicago, 1869 ***7420.1*** *p281*
Osterwald, Carl Ferdinand; Port uncertain, 1853 ***7420.1*** *p110*
Osterwald, Georg Friedrich Rudolph; Port uncertain, 1853 ***7420.1*** *p110*
Osterwald, Wilhelm Hieronymus; Port uncertain, 1837 ***7420.1*** *p13*
Ostlee, Godfred J. 22; Colorado, 1906 ***1029.59*** *p71*
Ostler, John; America, 1758 ***1220.12*** *p596*
Ostlund, Jonas 29; New York, 1849 ***6529.11*** *p22*
Ostram, Fannie C.; Iowa, 1884 ***1211.15*** *p17*
Ostrander, And'w; Ontario, 1787 ***1276.15*** *p230*
With child
Ostreich, Ferdinant August; Wisconsin, 1877 ***6795.8*** *p86*
Ostrom, Brita Jansdotter *SEE* Ostrom, Jacob
Ostrom, Fred.; New York, NY, 1851 ***6412.40*** *p152*
Ostrom, Jacob; Iowa, 1867-1869 ***777.40*** *p9*
*Son:*John
*Son:*Peter
*Wife:*Brita Jansdotter
*Son:*Jacob, Jr.
Ostrom, Jacob, Jr. *SEE* Ostrom, Jacob
Ostrom, John *SEE* Ostrom, Jacob
Ostrom, Mattie; Kansas, 1867 ***777.40*** *p17*
Ostrom, Peter *SEE* Ostrom, Jacob
Ostrow, William; Maryland, 1741 ***1220.12*** *p596*
Ostrowska, Stella; Detroit, 1929-1930 ***6214.5*** *p70*
Ostrowski, Casimer; Detroit, 1929-1930 ***6214.5*** *p70*
O'Sullivan, Dennis 21; New York, NY, 1826 ***6178.50*** *p150*
O'Sullivan, Joanna; Newburyport, MA, 1771 ***1642*** *p76*
O'Sullivan, John; Boston, 1840 ***3274.56*** *p69*
O'Sullivan, John; New York, NY, 1833 ***3274.55*** *p42*
O'Sullivan, John 23; New York, NY, 1826 ***6178.50*** *p150*
Oswald, Andre 35; Mississippi, 1845 ***778.6*** *p260*
Oswald, Anna Maria 25; America, 1867 ***5475.1*** *p296*
Oswald, Friedrich 2; Halifax, N.S., 1902 ***1860.4*** *p43*
Oswald, Friedrich 33; Halifax, N.S., 1902 ***1860.4*** *p43*
Oswald, John; America, 1744 ***1220.12*** *p596*
Oswald, Lisa 30; Mississippi, 1845 ***778.6*** *p260*
Oswald, Margaretha; Halifax, N.S., 1902 ***1860.4*** *p43*
Oswald, Mary 23; America, 1841 ***778.6*** *p260*
Oswald, Peter; America, 1862 ***5475.1*** *p378*
Oswald, Regina 28; Halifax, N.S., 1902 ***1860.4*** *p43*
Oswald, Rosina 3; Halifax, N.S., 1902 ***1860.4*** *p43*
Oswalt, Gotleib; Ohio, 1809-1852 ***4511.35*** *p39*
Osweiler, Elisabeth; America, 1862 ***5475.1*** *p335*
Oswin, Elizabeth 13; Quebec, 1870 ***8364.32*** *p25*
Oteri, John; Louisiana, 1874-1875 ***4981.45*** *p30*
Othea, Sarah; Dedham, MA, 1664 ***1642*** *p102*
Othen, Samuel; America, 1775 ***1220.12*** *p596*
Othon, Bernard; Louisiana, 1836-1841 ***4981.45*** *p209*
Othy, Jane; America, 1764 ***1220.12*** *p596*
O'Toole, Anthony 40; Ontario, 1871 ***1823.21*** *p284*
Otradovsky, Frantisek; Nebraska, 1872 ***2853.20*** *p182*
Otridge, James; America, 1756 ***1220.12*** *p590*
Ott, Bernhard; Colorado, 1893 ***1029.59*** *p72*
Ott, Caroline 9; Halifax, N.S., 1902 ***1860.4*** *p43*
Ott, Emilie 8; Halifax, N.S., 1902 ***1860.4*** *p43*
Ott, Gottlob; Missouri, 1872 ***3276.1*** *p3*
Ott, Jacob; Halifax, N.S., 1902 ***1860.4*** *p43*
Ott, Jacob 38; Halifax, N.S., 1902 ***1860.4*** *p43*
Ott, John 60; Indiana, 1840-1876 ***9076.20*** *p69*
Ott, John 21; Kansas, 1888 ***1447.20*** *p62*
Ott, John; Missouri, 1886 ***3276.1*** *p2*
Ott, John George; Ohio, 1809-1852 ***4511.35*** *p39*
Ott, Magdalena 4; Halifax, N.S., 1902 ***1860.4*** *p43*
Ott, Magdalena 35; Halifax, N.S., 1902 ***1860.4*** *p43*
Ott, Maria 3; Halifax, N.S., 1902 ***1860.4*** *p43*
Ott, William; Illinois, 1858-1861 ***6020.5*** *p132*
Ottenhoffer, Dominick; Louisiana, 1874 ***4981.45*** *p133*
Otter, Francis; America, 1749 ***1220.12*** *p596*
Otter, John; America, 1665 ***1220.12*** *p596*
Otter, William; America, 1765 ***1220.12*** *p596*
Otterbach, Catharina; America, 1854 ***179.55*** *p19*
Otterbach, Karl; America, 1853 ***179.55*** *p19*
Otterberg, Robert; Cleveland, OH, 1900-1904 ***9722.10*** *p125*
Ottey, Abell; America, 1742 ***1220.12*** *p596*
Otting, Franz; Ohio, 1840-1897 ***8365.35*** *p17*
Ottio, Adam; Louisiana, 1874 ***4981.45*** *p133*
Ottking, Sophie Caroline; America, 1858 ***7420.1*** *p182*
Ottley, Susannah; America, 1772 ***1220.12*** *p596*
Otto, Adolphe 57; New York, NY, 1894 ***6512.1*** *p229*
Otto, August Julius; Wisconsin, 1897 ***6795.8*** *p124*
Otto, Baptiste; Chile, 1852 ***1192.4*** *p54*
Otto, Carl; Valdivia, Chile, 1852 ***1192.4*** *p53*
Otto, Carl Heinrich; Port uncertain, 1853 ***7420.1*** *p110*
Otto, Francois; Louisiana, 1836-1841 ***4981.45*** *p209*
Otto, Heinrich; America, 1866 ***7420.1*** *p246*
With family
Otto, Heinrich Conrad; America, 1866 ***7420.1*** *p246*
With family
Otto, Heinrich Heinewald; America, 1867 ***7919.3*** *p529*
Otto, Jacob; America, 1868 ***7919.3*** *p532*
With wife & 5 children
Otto, Jacque; New York, 1860 ***358.56*** *p149*
Otto, Jean Nicholas; Louisiana, 1836-1841 ***4981.45*** *p209*
Otto, Johann *SEE* Otto, Maria Meiers
Otto, Johann *SEE* Otto, Johann
Otto, Johann; America, 1879 ***5475.1*** *p22*
Otto, Johann 56; America, 1867 ***5475.1*** *p297*
*Wife:*Katharina Schmitt 52
*Daughter:*Katharina
*Son:*Michel
*Son:*Johann
*Son:*Peter
Otto, Johann Wilhelm Friedrich Bernhard; America, 1868 ***7919.3*** *p532*
With wife & 3 children
Otto, Katharina *SEE* Otto, Johann
Otto, Katharina Schmitt 52 *SEE* Otto, Johann
Otto, Maria 31; America, 1860 ***5475.1*** *p360*
*Son:*Nikolaus
*Son:*Johann
Otto, Michel *SEE* Otto, Johann
Otto, Nikolaus *SEE* Otto, Maria Meiers
Otto, Pauline; America, 1868 ***7919.3*** *p525*
Otto, Peter *SEE* Otto, Johann
Otto, Robert; Iowa, 1896 ***1211.15*** *p17*
Otto, Sophie; America, 1857 ***7420.1*** *p169*
Otto, Wilhelm F.; Wisconsin, 1904 ***6795.8*** *p149*
Otto, William; New York, 1860 ***358.56*** *p6*
Ottoson, Ellen; St. Paul, MN, 1889 ***1865.50*** *p104*
Ottoson, Hilda 19; New York, NY, 1894 ***6512.1*** *p184*
Otty, Agnes E. 55; Ontario, 1871 ***1823.21*** *p288*
Ouache, Marie-Madeleine; Quebec, 1667 ***4514.3*** *p352*
Oubelie, Jacob 42; America, 1846 ***778.6*** *p260*
Oudinet, Jn. Bte. 28; Louisiana, 1848 ***778.6*** *p260*
Ouellet, Rene 20; Quebec, 1661 ***9221.17*** *p470*
Ouimet, Jean 23; Quebec, 1659 ***9221.17*** *p407*
Ouinville, Michelle; Quebec, 1668 ***4514.3*** *p352*
Oulsden, John; Barbados, 1675 ***1220.12*** *p596*
Ourau, P. 53; America, 1842 ***778.6*** *p260*
Ourren, Mr. 35; America, 1841 ***778.6*** *p260*
Ourth, Nicholas; Ohio, 1809-1852 ***4511.35*** *p39*
Ously, Sarah; Maryland, 1674 ***1236.25*** *p50*
Outel, Casper; Ohio, 1809-1852 ***4511.35*** *p39*
Outhier, Theophilus; Illinois, 1857 ***6079.1*** *p11*
Outhwaite, Carrie 24; Kansas, 1892 ***1447.20*** *p62*
Outlas, Jean; Quebec, 1690 ***2314.30*** *p172*
Outwood, Richard; America, 1759 ***1220.12*** *p596*
Ouyn, Francoise 33; Quebec, 1653 ***9221.17*** *p278*
Ouyn, Michel; Quebec, 1654 ***9221.17*** *p314*
Ovenden, James; Ohio, 1840-1897 ***8365.35*** *p17*
Ovens, Stewart 50; Ontario, 1871 ***1823.21*** *p288*
Ovens, Thomas 30; Ontario, 1871 ***1823.21*** *p288*
Over, Henry; America, 1729 ***1220.12*** *p596*
Over, Humphry; America, 1739 ***1220.12*** *p596*
Over, John; Barbados, 1672 ***1220.12*** *p596*
Overall, John 39; Ontario, 1871 ***1823.21*** *p288*
Overan, John; America, 1773 ***1220.12*** *p596*
Overbury, Robert; America, 1746 ***1220.12*** *p596*
Overcamp, Ludwig; Colorado, 1890 ***1029.59*** *p72*
Overen, Stephen; America, 1723 ***1220.12*** *p596*
Overend, Stephen; America, 1723 ***1220.12*** *p596*
Overfrank, Anna 28; America, 1848 ***778.6*** *p260*
Overfrank, Jacob 28; America, 1848 ***778.6*** *p260*
Overfrank, N. B. 3; America, 1848 ***778.6*** *p260*
Overhill, John; Barbados or Jamaica, 1699 ***1220.12*** *p596*
Overington, Thomas; America, 1733 ***1220.12*** *p596*
Overkamp, Loudwig; Illinois, 1875 ***1029.59*** *p72*
Overs, Sarah; Virginia, 1738 ***1220.12*** *p596*
Overstedt, Charlotte Amalie; Valdivia, Chile, 1852 ***1192.4*** *p56*
With 2 children
With child 18
With child 24
Overton, Dorothy 71; Ontario, 1871 ***1823.21*** *p288*
Overton, Job; America, 1757 ***1220.12*** *p596*
Overton, John; America, 1771 ***1220.12*** *p596*
Overton, John; America, 1774 ***1220.12*** *p596*
Overton, John; Barbados, 1693 ***1220.12*** *p596*
Overton, John G. 48; Ontario, 1871 ***1823.17*** *p129*
Overton, Mathew; America, 1766 ***1220.12*** *p596*
Overton, Thomas; America, 1766 ***1220.12*** *p597*
Overton, Thomas; Maryland, 1742 ***1220.12*** *p596*
Overton, William; America, 1750 ***1220.12*** *p597*
Overy, George 18; Quebec, 1870 ***8364.32*** *p25*
Ovins, Gilbert; America, 1766 ***1220.12*** *p597*
Ovins, Mary; America, 1766 ***1220.12*** *p597*
Ovis, William; Virginia, 1741 ***1220.12*** *p597*
Owade, Wilhelm; Wisconsin, 1899 ***6795.8*** *p118*
Owell, John; Barbados or Jamaica, 1699 ***1220.12*** *p597*
Owen, Benjamin; America, 1767 ***1220.12*** *p597*
Owen, Catherine; Potomac, 1731 ***1220.12*** *p597*
Owen, Charles 25; Ontario, 1871 ***1823.21*** *p288*
Owen, David; Barbados or Jamaica, 1698 ***1220.12*** *p597*
Owen, Ebenezer; Massachusetts, 1675-1676 ***1642*** *p127*
Owen, Edward; America, 1774 ***1220.12*** *p597*
Owen, Elizabeth; America, 1748 ***1220.12*** *p597*
Owen, Elizabeth; America, 1753 ***1220.12*** *p597*
Owen, Elizabeth; America, 1764 ***1220.12*** *p597*
Owen, Elizabeth; Barbados, 1681 ***1220.12*** *p597*
Owen, Elizabeth; Barbados or Jamaica, 1674 ***1220.12*** *p597*
Owen, Elizabeth; Maryland, 1719 ***1220.12*** *p597*
Owen, Evan; Ohio, 1809-1852 ***4511.35*** *p39*
Owen, George; Maryland or Virginia, 1738 ***1220.12*** *p597*
Owen, Hanna 55; Ontario, 1871 ***1823.21*** *p288*
Owen, Henry; Annapolis, MD, 1723 ***1220.12*** *p597*
Owen, Henry; Barbados, 1664 ***1220.12*** *p597*
Owen, Hugh; America, 1763 ***1220.12*** *p597*
Owen, J.; Boston, 1728 ***1642*** *p23*
Owen, James; Annapolis, MD, 1732 ***1220.12*** *p597*
Owen, James; New England, 1745 ***1642*** *p28*
Owen, Jane; America, 1740 ***1220.12*** *p597*
Owen, Jane; America, 1767 ***1220.12*** *p597*
Owen, Jane; America, 1769 ***1220.12*** *p597*
Owen, Jenkin 23; Ontario, 1871 ***1823.21*** *p288*
Owen, John; America, 1747 ***1220.12*** *p597*
Owen, John; America, 1755 ***1220.12*** *p597*
Owen, John; America, 1767 ***1220.12*** *p597*
Owen, John; Died enroute, 1729 ***1220.12*** *p597*
Owen, John; Died enroute, 1734 ***1220.12*** *p597*
Owen, John; Marston's Wharf, 1782 ***8529.30*** *p14*
Owen, John; New England, 1745 ***1642*** *p28*
Owen, John; Virginia, 1732 ***1220.12*** *p597*
Owen, Margaret; Annapolis, MD, 1735 ***1220.12*** *p597*
Owen, Mary; America, 1745 ***1220.12*** *p597*
Owen, Mary; America, 1764 ***1220.12*** *p597*
Owen, Mary; Annapolis, MD, 1723 ***1220.12*** *p597*
Owen, Oliver 59; Ontario, 1871 ***1823.21*** *p288*
Owen, Peter; America, 1747 ***1220.12*** *p597*
Owen, Richard; America, 1743 ***1220.12*** *p597*
Owen, Richard; Maryland, 1674-1675 ***1236.25*** *p52*
Owen, Robert; America, 1774 ***1220.12*** *p597*
Owen, Robert 30; Ontario, 1871 ***1823.21*** *p288*
Owen, Samuel; America, 1745 ***1220.12*** *p597*
Owen, Stephen; Barbados or Jamaica, 1698 ***1220.12*** *p597*
Owen, Susan; America, 1729 ***1220.12*** *p597*
Owen, Thomas; America, 1739 ***1220.12*** *p597*
Owen, Thomas; America, 1755 ***1220.12*** *p597*
Owen, Thomas; America, 1762 ***1220.12*** *p597*
Owen, Thomas; Annapolis, MD, 1729 ***1220.12*** *p597*
Owen, Thomas; Barbados, 1665 ***1220.12*** *p597*
Owen, Thomas; Massachusetts, 1675-1676 ***1642*** *p129*
Owen, Thomas; Virginia, 1766 ***1220.12*** *p598*
Owen, W.; Boston, 1728 ***1642*** *p23*
Owen, Wade 50; Ontario, 1871 ***1823.21*** *p288*
Owen, William; America, 1750 ***1220.12*** *p598*
Owen, William; America, 1752 ***1220.12*** *p598*
Owen, William; America, 1770 ***1220.12*** *p598*
Owen, William; Ohio, 1809-1852 ***4511.35*** *p39*
Owens, . . . 75; Ontario, 1871 ***1823.21*** *p288*
Owens, Bartholomew 60; Ontario, 1871 ***1823.21*** *p288*
Owens, Daniel *SEE* Owens, Evan
Owens, Diana *SEE* Owens, Evan
Owens, Ellen 60; Ontario, 1871 ***1823.17*** *p129*
Owens, Evan; Ohio, 1840 ***4022.20*** *p289*
*Child:*Daniel
*Child:*Owen
*Child:*Margaret
*Child:*Diana
*Child:*Jane
Owens, Evan *SEE* Owens, Martha
Owens, Hannah; America, 1745 ***1220.12*** *p598*
Owens, Henry 28; Ontario, 1871 ***1823.21*** *p288*
Owens, James; America, 1678 ***1220.12*** *p598*
Owens, James; America, 1684 ***1220.12*** *p598*
Owens, Jane *SEE* Owens, Evan
Owens, John; Louisiana, 1874 ***4981.45*** *p133*
Owens, John 56; Ontario, 1871 ***1823.17*** *p129*
Owens, Margaret *SEE* Owens, Evan

Owens, Martha; Ohio, 1842 *4022.20 p289*
 *Father:*Evan
 With siblings
 *Mother:*Mary
Owens, Mary *SEE* Owens, Martha
Owens, Michael; America, 1737 *1220.12 p598*
Owens, Nicholas; North Carolina, 1843 *1088.45 p26*
Owens, Owen *SEE* Owens, Evan
Owens, Shelmomish 22; Michigan, 1880 *4491.30 p24*
Owens, Susanna; America, 1760 *1220.12 p598*
Owens, Thomas 79; Ontario, 1871 *1823.21 p288*
Owens, William; America, 1753 *1220.12 p598*
Owens, William; America, 1774 *1220.12 p598*
Owesney, William A.; Ohio, 1862 *3580.20 p33*
Owesney, William A.; Ohio, 1862 *6020.12 p21*
Owle, William; America, 1726 *1220.12 p598*
Owles, Joseph; America, 1768 *1220.12 p598*
Owlet, William 68; Ontario, 1871 *1823.21 p288*
Owram, James; America, 1765 *1220.12 p598*
Owsman, Moses; America, 1724 *1220.12 p598*
Ox, John; Ohio, 1809-1852 *4511.35 p39*
Ox, Paulus; Ohio, 1809-1852 *4511.35 p39*
Oxarart, Maria 25; California, 1873 *3276.8 p18*
Oxborough, Elizabeth; Barbados or Jamaica, 1716 *1220.12 p598*
Oxden, Richard; America, 1686 *1220.12 p598*
Oxen, William; America, 1766 *1220.12 p598*
Oxenbecher, Henery; New Jersey, 1764-1774 *927.31 p2*
Oxenham, Anne 23; Ontario, 1871 *1823.21 p288*

Oxenham, James 35; Ontario, 1871 *1823.17 p129*
Oxenham, James 62; Ontario, 1871 *1823.17 p129*
Oxford, John; Potomac, 1729 *1220.12 p598*
Oxland, Arthur Conrad; Calgary, Alberta, 1912 *9228.50 p485*
Oxley, Amelia 6; Quebec, 1870 *8364.32 p25*
Oxley, Anthony; America, 1766 *1220.12 p598*
Oxley, David 29; Ontario, 1871 *1823.21 p288*
Oxley, James; America, 1720 *1220.12 p598*
Oxley, Margaret; Annapolis, MD, 1731 *1220.12 p598*
Oxley, Mary 7; Quebec, 1870 *8364.32 p25*
Oxley, Michael 52; Ontario, 1871 *1823.21 p288*
Oxley, Thomas; Maryland, 1741 *1220.12 p598*
Oxrart, Maria 25; California, 1873 *3276.8 p18*
Oxtaby, John 62; Ontario, 1871 *1823.21 p288*
Oxtoby, William; America, 1775 *1220.12 p598*
Oyer, James; America, 1750 *1220.12 p598*
Oyharzabal, Domingo; California, 1863-1878 *3276.8 p20*
Oyharzabal, E.; California, 1860-1890 *3276.8 p20*
Oyley, Marik; America, 1769 *1220.12 p598*
Oyne, John; Massachusetts, 1675-1676 *1642 p128*
Oynes, John; Massachusetts, 1675-1676 *1642 p129*
Oyston, Joseph; America, 1746 *1220.12 p598*
Ozab, Josef; New York, NY, 1860-1869 *2853.20 p100*
Ozanne, Mrs. Abraham; Wisconsin, 1847 *9228.50 p487*
Ozanne, Alfred C. *SEE* Ozanne, James
Ozanne, Cornelia B.; Costa Rica, 1910-1972 *9228.50 p662*
Ozanne, Helena *SEE* Ozanne, James

Ozanne, James *SEE* Ozanne, John
Ozanne, James; Wisconsin, 1850 *9228.50 p486*
 *Child:*James, Jr.
 *Child:*John B.
 *Child:*Alfred C.
 *Child:*Helena
 *Child:*Peter
Ozanne, James, Jr. *SEE* Ozanne, James
Ozanne, John; America, 1859 *9228.50 p662*
 *Uncle:*James
Ozanne, John B. *SEE* Ozanne, James
Ozanne, John Blanche; Wisconsin, 1850-1859 *9228.50 p487*
Ozanne, Joseph; Rhode Island, 1888-1889 *9228.50 p485*
Ozanne, Peter *SEE* Ozanne, James
Ozanne, Pierre; Quebec, 1639 *9221.17 p91*
Ozanne Group, . . .; Wisconsin, 1842 *9228.50 p153*
Ozannes, Louis 38; Quebec, 1654 *9221.17 p315*
Ozard, Mr.; Wisconsin, 1848-1948 *9228.50 p487*
 With wife
Ozervedo, Charles 23; America, 1840 *778.6 p260*
Ozier, John; Ohio, 1826-1900 *9228.50 p487*
Ozog, Jozef; Detroit, 1929 *1640.55 p114*
Ozok, Ozok Zofia Chrostek *SEE* Ozok, Peter
Ozok, Peter; Detroit, 1929-1930 *6214.5 p69*
 *Wife:*Ozok Zofia Chrostek

P

Paalanen, Henry 25; Minnesota, 1925 *2769.54 p1378*
Paap, August; Wisconsin, 1879 *6795.8 p227*
Paap, Ferdinand; Wisconsin, 1881 *6795.8 p227*
Paap, Wilhelm; Wisconsin, 1883 *6795.8 p227*
Pabijan, Josef; America, 1867 *2853.20 p168*
Pabin, Joseph 31; Texas, 1843 *778.6 p260*
Pabos, Frederic; New York, 1859 *358.56 p101*
Pabron, Pierre; Illinois, 1856 *6079.1 p11*
Pabst, Adolf 16 *SEE* Pabst, Katharina
Pabst, Emilie 18 *SEE* Pabst, Katharina
Pabst, Henry Earnst; Louisiana, 1851-1855 *7710.1 p154*
Pabst, Henry Earnst; Louisiana, 1851 *7710.1 p152*
Pabst, Katharina 59; America, 1843 *5475.1 p471*
   *Daughter:*Emilie 18
   *Son:*Adolf 16
Pabutka, Aleksander; Detroit, 1930 *1640.60 p78*
Pac, Jacques 14; New Orleans, 1845 *778.6 p260*
Pacaltova, Bela; New York, NY, 1893 *2853.20 p469*
Pacaud, Jean 12; Quebec, 1652 *9221.17 p263*
Pacaud, Marie; Canada, 1664 *1142.10 p128*
   With family
Paccoiche, Nath. 22; Port uncertain, 1842 *778.6 p260*
Pace, Richard; America, 1731 *1220.12 p599*
Pace, Robert; America, 1749 *1220.12 p599*
Pacewicz, Alexander; Detroit, 1929 *1640.55 p116*
Pacey, Edward; America, 1678 *1220.12 p599*
Pacey, George 35; Ontario, 1871 *1823.21 p288*
Pacey, John; New Orleans, 1850 *7242.30 p152*
Pacey, John 63; Ontario, 1871 *1823.21 p288*
Pacey, Joseph; America, 1753 *1220.12 p599*
Pachabet, Walerian; Detroit, 1930 *1640.60 p81*
Pachabet, Walter; Detroit, 1930 *1640.60 p81*
Pachanne, Bertrand 25; Montreal, 1653 *9221.17 p288*
Pacholik, Jacob; Texas, 1898-1904 *6015.15 p29*
Pachon, Claude 25; Port uncertain, 1841 *778.6 p260*
Pachta, Jan; Iowa, 1870 *2853.20 p202*
Paciorkowski, Aron; Detroit, 1929-1930 *6214.5 p69*
Pack, Harriet; Ohio, 1821 *9228.50 p487*
Pack, John; America, 1692 *1220.12 p599*
Pack, John; America, 1767 *1220.12 p599*
Pack, John; Utah, 1852 *9228.50 p487*
Pack, Josef; America, 1849 *5475.1 p486*
Pack, Mary; Ohio, 1840-1860 *9228.50 p487*
Packenden, Robert; Barbados, 1663 *1220.12 p599*
Packer, Elizabeth; America, 1775 *1220.12 p599*
Packer, James; Virginia, 1739 *1220.12 p599*
Packer, John; America, 1764 *1220.12 p599*
Packer, Mary; Maryland, 1674-1675 *1236.25 p52*
Packer, Richard; Ohio, 1809-1852 *4511.35 p39*
Packer, William; Virginia, 1764 *1220.12 p599*
Packet, Elizabeth; America, 1760 *1220.12 p599*
Paclt, Cenek; New York, NY, 1846 *2853.20 p98*
Pacque, Jacques 14; New Orleans, 1845 *778.6 p260*
Pacquett, Louis; Georgia, 1795 *1451.56 p118*
Pacracy, Maria Rosina 21; New Castle, DE, 1817-1818
   90.20 p153
Pacreau, Marie 28; Montreal, 1658 *9221.17 p391*
Pacy, Benjamin; New York, 1843 *471.10 p62*
Pacy, Thomas; New York, 1836 *471.10 p62*
Paddee, . . .; Boston, 1752-1760 *1642 p30*
Padderson, John; America, 1737 *1220.12 p599*
Paddick, Henry 49; Ontario, 1871 *1823.17 p129*
Paddison, Thomas; America, 1740 *1220.12 p599*
Paddison, William; America, 1747 *1220.12 p599*
Paddock, Elizabeth; America, 1754 *1220.12 p599*
Paddock, Richard; America, 1739 *1220.12 p599*
Paddon, Anthony; Barbados, 1667 *1220.12 p599*
Padecky, Jakub *SEE* Padecky, Jakub

Padecky, Jakub; Chicago, 1854 *2853.20 p387*
   *Son:*Jakub
Padey, Charles 25; America, 1846 *778.6 p260*
Padge, Thomas; America, 1749 *1220.12 p851*
Padin, James; Illinois, 1834-1900 *6020.5 p132*
Padiolet, Elie; Quebec, 1642 *9221.17 p119*
Padon, Eugene 26; America, 1843 *778.6 p260*
Padovani, Noel; Louisiana, 1836-1840 *4981.45 p213*
Pady, Thomas; America, 1749 *1220.12 p599*
Paegelet, Caroline 21; New Orleans, 1848 *778.6 p260*
Paelzer, Anna Schonach 30 *SEE* Paelzer, Peter
Paelzer, Anna Maria 19 *SEE* Paelzer, Peter
Paelzer, Peter 35; America, 1861 *5475.1 p337*
   *Wife:*Anna Schonach 30
   *Daughter:*Anna Maria 19 months
Paetz, Gustaf Adolph; Denver, CO, 1921 *1029.59 p72*
Pafford, Thomas; Barbados or Jamaica, 1688 *1220.12*
   p599
Pagal, F.J.A.; Wisconsin, 1870 *6795.8 p227*
Pagans, Thomas; America, 1749 *1220.12 p599*
Page, Abraham; America, 1741 *1220.12 p599*
Page, Adam; America, 1720 *1220.12 p599*
Page, Ann; America, 1733 *1220.12 p599*
Page, Ann; America, 1747 *1220.12 p599*
Page, Ann; America, 1767 *1220.12 p599*
Page, Chas 30; Ontario, 1871 *1823.21 p288*
Page, Denise 80; Ontario, 1871 *1823.21 p288*
Page, Edward; America, 1735 *1220.12 p599*
Page, Edward; Barbados, 1672 *1220.12 p599*
Page, Elias; America, 1741 *1220.12 p599*
Page, Elizabeth; America, 1727 *1220.12 p599*
Page, Elizabeth; Barbados, 1670 *1220.12 p599*
Page, Elizabeth; Virginia, 1732 *1220.12 p599*
Page, Emma 14; Quebec, 1870 *8364.32 p25*
Page, Grace; Virginia, 1723 *1220.12 p599*
Page, Henry; America, 1662 *1220.12 p599*
Page, Henry; America, 1746 *1220.12 p599*
Page, Henry; America, 1773 *1220.12 p599*
Page, James; America, 1739 *1220.12 p599*
Page, James 54; Ontario, 1871 *1823.21 p288*
Page, Jane; America, 1756 *1220.12 p599*
Page, Jane 22; Ontario, 1871 *1823.21 p288*
Page, John; America, 1686 *1220.12 p599*
Page, John; America, 1743 *1220.12 p599*
Page, John; America, 1754 *1220.12 p600*
Page, John; America, 1756 *1220.12 p600*
Page, John; America, 1763 *1220.12 p600*
Page, John; America, 1768 *1220.12 p600*
Page, John; America, 1772 *1220.12 p600*
Page, John; America, 1774 *1220.12 p600*
Page, John; Annapolis, MD, 1722 *1220.12 p599*
Page, John; Maryland or Virginia, 1738 *1220.12 p599*
Page, John 30; Ontario, 1871 *1823.17 p129*
Page, John; Salem, MA, 1790 *9228.50 p487*
   With family of 7
Page, Jonathan; Annapolis, MD, 1725 *1220.12 p600*
Page, Joseph; America, 1767 *1220.12 p600*
Page, Joseph; Maryland, 1719 *1220.12 p600*
Page, Joshua; America, 1742 *1220.12 p600*
Page, Judith; America, 1750 *1220.12 p600*
Page, Lucas; Barbados or Jamaica, 1696 *1220.12 p600*
Page, Margaret; Rappahannock, VA, 1729 *1220.12 p600*
Page, Mark; Maryland or Virginia, 1738 *1220.12 p600*
Page, Mary; America, 1742 *1220.12 p600*
Page, Mary; America, 1762 *1220.12 p600*
Page, Matthew; America, 1767 *1220.12 p600*
Page, Richard; America, 1697 *1220.12 p600*
Page, Richard; America, 1768 *1220.12 p600*

Page, Richard; Barbados, 1663 *1220.12 p600*
Page, Richard; Barbados, 1693 *1220.12 p600*
Page, Robert; Rappahannock, VA, 1726 *1220.12 p600*
Page, Samuel; America, 1675 *1220.12 p600*
Page, Sarah; America, 1766 *1220.12 p600*
Page, Sarah; America, 1770 *1220.12 p600*
Page, Sarah; Annapolis, MD, 1731 *1220.12 p600*
Page, Sarah; Died enroute, 1723 *1220.12 p600*
Page, Sarah 16; Quebec, 1870 *8364.32 p25*
Page, Thomas; America, 1738 *1220.12 p600*
Page, Thomas; America, 1744 *1220.12 p600*
Page, Thomas; America, 1768 *1220.12 p600*
Page, Thomas; America, 1772 *1220.12 p600*
Page, William; America, 1685 *1220.12 p600*
Page, William; America, 1724 *1220.12 p600*
Page, William; America, 1773 *1220.12 p600*
Page, William; Died enroute, 1729 *1220.12 p600*
Page, William; Virginia, 1766 *1220.12 p600*
Pagel, Johann Friedrich; Wisconsin, 1873 *6795.8 p91*
Pagel, Reinhard; Wisconsin, 1879 *6795.8 p227*
Pagel, Scharlotte; Wisconsin, 1903 *6795.8 p179*
Pagelas, Elizabeth; America, 1770 *1220.12 p600*
Pagensticker, Julius; North Carolina, 1851 *1088.45 p26*
Pageot, Renny C.; Illinois, 1852 *6079.1 p11*
Pageot, Thomas 15; Quebec, 1659 *9221.17 p407*
Paget, Henry 33; Ontario, 1871 *1823.21 p288*
Paget, Henry; Virginia, 1764 *1220.12 p600*
Pagets, Etienne 2 *SEE* Pagets, Marie-Madeleine
   Bergeronne
Pagets, Marie-Madeleine 31; Quebec, 1647 *9221.17 p186*
   *Son:*Robert 5
   *Son:*Etienne 2
Pagets, Raymond 34; Quebec, 1638 *9221.17 p80*
Pagets, Robert 5 *SEE* Pagets, Marie-Madeleine
   Bergeronne
Pagett, Edward; America, 1775 *1220.12 p600*
Pagett, John; America, 1760 *1220.12 p600*
Pagett, John; America, 1769 *1220.12 p600*
Pagett, Martha; Rappahannock, VA, 1729 *1220.12 p600*
Pagitt, Elizabeth; America, 1722 *1220.12 p600*
Pagnotte, C. 43; America, 1846 *778.6 p260*
Pagnotte, Catherine 9; America, 1846 *778.6 p260*
Pagnotte, Constance 6 months; America, 1846 *778.6*
   p260
Pagnotte, Etien.e 7; America, 1846 *778.6 p260*
Pagnotte, Jea Baptiste 16; America, 1846 *778.6 p260*
Pagnotte, Josephine 9; America, 1846 *778.6 p260*
Pagnotte, Josephine 41; America, 1846 *778.6 p260*
Pagram, Mary; America, 1746 *1220.12 p600*
Pahin, Auguste 16; America, 1843 *778.6 p260*
Pahin, Claude 47; America, 1843 *778.6 p260*
Pahin, Claude-Philiberte; Quebec, 1673 *4514.3 p352*
Pahin, Josephe 19; America, 1843 *778.6 p260*
Pahl, John Samuel; Wisconsin, 1872 *6795.8 p26*
Pahlsson, Sven; New York, NY, 1851 *6412.40 p153*
Pahmeier, Ernst Dietrich; Port uncertain, 1839 *7420.1*
   p16
Paice, Ashwood; America, 1755 *1220.12 p599*
Paice, John; America, 1741 *1220.12 p599*
Paies, Robert; America, 1768 *1220.12 p611*
Paigne, Anne 32; America, 1846 *778.6 p260*
Pail, William; America, 1730 *1220.12 p600*
Paillereau, Pierre 23; Quebec, 1649 *9221.17 p218*
Pailloe, Eugene; Illinois, 1852 *6079.1 p11*
Pain, Abigail; Salem, MA, 1714 *9228.50 p487*
   *Relative:*John
   *Relative:*Jonathan
Pain, Ann 59; Ontario, 1871 *1823.17 p129*

Pain, Anne; Rappahannock, VA, 1726 ***1220.12*** *p611*
Pain, Charles; Virginia, 1758 ***1220.12*** *p612*
Pain, Hannah; Maryland, 1724 ***1220.12*** *p612*
Pain, James; America, 1739 ***1220.12*** *p612*
Pain, Joan; America, 1748 ***1220.12*** *p612*
Pain, John 48; Ontario, 1871 ***1823.21*** *p288*
Pain, John 78; Ontario, 1871 ***1823.17*** *p129*
Pain, John *SEE* Pain, Abigail
Pain, Jonathan *SEE* Pain, Abigail
Pain, Mary; America, 1744 ***1220.12*** *p612*
Pain, Stephen; America, 1765 ***1220.12*** *p612*
Pain, Susannah; Marblehead, MA, 1722-1723 ***9228.50*** *p472*
Pain, Thomas; America, 1769 ***1220.12*** *p613*
Pain, William, Sr.; New York, 1776 ***8529.30*** *p15*
Paine, Abraham; America, 1747 ***1220.12*** *p611*
Paine, Benjamin 50; Ontario, 1871 ***1823.21*** *p288*
Paine, Edward; America, 1740 ***1220.12*** *p612*
Paine, Edward; America, 1747 ***1220.12*** *p612*
Paine, Eliza 56; Ontario, 1871 ***1823.21*** *p288*
Paine, George; America, 1736 ***1220.12*** *p612*
Paine, Henry; America, 1772 ***1220.12*** *p612*
Paine, Joan; Barbados, 1666 ***1220.12*** *p612*
Paine, John; America, 1736 ***1220.12*** *p612*
Paine, John; America, 1764 ***1220.12*** *p612*
Paine, John; Maryland, 1725 ***1220.12*** *p612*
Paine, John 46; Ontario, 1871 ***1823.17*** *p129*
Paine, Joshua; Rappahannock, VA, 1729 ***1220.12*** *p612*
Paine, Matthew; America, 1738 ***1220.12*** *p612*
Paine, P. 64; Port uncertain, 1845 ***778.6*** *p260*
Paine, Peter; America, 1770 ***1220.12*** *p612*
Paine, Philip; New Hampshire, 1707-1712 ***9228.50*** *p487*
Paine, Rachel; Marblehead, MA, 1793 ***9228.50*** *p487*
Paine, Richard; America, 1714 ***1220.12*** *p612*
Paine, Richard 58; Ontario, 1871 ***1823.21*** *p288*
Paine, Samuel; Connecticut, 1663-1750 ***9228.50*** *p488*
Paine, Sarah; Rappahannock, VA, 1729 ***1220.12*** *p612*
Paine, Susanna; Marblehead, MA, 1722-1723 ***9228.50*** *p487*
Paine, Thomas; America, 1726 ***1220.12*** *p612*
Paine, Thomas; America, 1757 ***1220.12*** *p612*
Paine, Thomas; America, 1758 ***1220.12*** *p612*
Paine, W. D.; California, 1868 ***1131.61*** *p89*
Paine, William; Barbados, 1667 ***1220.12*** *p613*
Paine, William; New York, 1783 ***8529.30*** *p15*
Painter, Edward; America, 1753 ***1220.12*** *p601*
Painter, George; Maryland, 1741 ***1220.12*** *p601*
Painter, James; America, 1744 ***1220.12*** *p601*
Painter, John; America, 1764 ***1220.12*** *p601*
Painter, John; America, 1765 ***1220.12*** *p601*
Painter, John 62; Ontario, 1871 ***1823.21*** *p288*
Painter, Peter; Ohio, 1842 ***2763.1*** *p21*
Painter, Sarah; America, 1759 ***1220.12*** *p601*
Painter, Stephen; Barbados, 1684 ***1220.12*** *p601*
Painter, Thomas; America, 1759 ***1220.12*** *p601*
Painter, Thomas; America, 1774 ***1220.12*** *p601*
Painter, William; Barbados or Jamaica, 1697 ***1220.12*** *p601*
Painture, Abraham 15; Quebec, 1661 ***9221.17*** *p464*
Pairieu, Jacques; Quebec, 1645 ***9221.17*** *p156*
Pairieu, Jacques l'ermite; Quebec, 1645 ***9221.17*** *p156*
Paiseley, Thomas; Ohio, 1809-1852 ***4511.35*** *p39*
Paisley, James E.; Ohio, 1879 ***3580.20*** *p33*
Paisley, James E.; Ohio, 1879 ***6020.12*** *p21*
Paisley, Samuel 55; Ontario, 1871 ***1823.21*** *p288*
Paisory, Alfred 14; Quebec, 1870 ***8364.32*** *p25*
Pajon, Etienne 32; Quebec, 1657 ***9221.17*** *p365*
Pajor, Marya; Detroit, 1929 ***1640.55*** *p116*
Pajot, Richard; Montreal, 1659 ***9221.17*** *p425*
Pak, Gustav; Wisconsin, 1908 ***1822.55*** *p10*
Pakenham, Mr.; British Columbia, 1910 ***2897.7*** *p8*
Pakenham, Nellie 40; Quebec, 1910 ***2897.7*** *p8*
Pakes, William; America, 1737 ***1220.12*** *p601*
Pal, Marie 20; Port uncertain, 1846 ***778.6*** *p260*
Palanque, Jean 36; America, 1844 ***778.6*** *p261*
Palatin, Mr. 38; America, 1841 ***778.6*** *p261*
Palchinski, Joseph 28; Indiana, 1892-1894 ***9076.20*** *p73*
Palda, Lev J.; Chicago, 1870 ***2853.20*** *p414*
Palda, Lev J.; New York, NY, 1867 ***2853.20*** *p220*
Paldini, Ange 5; America, 1840 ***778.6*** *p261*
Paldini, Ange 34; America, 1840 ***778.6*** *p261*
Paldini, Angelique 1; America, 1840 ***778.6*** *p261*
Paldini, Honorine 26; America, 1840 ***778.6*** *p261*
Paldini, Justin 3; America, 1840 ***778.6*** *p261*
Palentin, Charles 18; Quebec, 1654 ***9221.17*** *p315*
Pales, Edward; Annapolis, MD, 1723 ***1220.12*** *p601*
Pales, P.; California, 1868 ***1131.61*** *p90*
Palfen, Clarisse 29; New Orleans, 1848 ***778.6*** *p261*
Palfery, Florence 32; Quebec, 1910 ***2897.7*** *p9*
Palfreman, Thomas; America, 1697 ***1220.12*** *p601*
Palfrey, Jonathan; Barbados, 1698 ***1220.12*** *p601*
Palfry, Robert; America, 1749 ***1220.12*** *p601*
Palister, Joseph; Canada, 1774 ***3036.5*** *p40*
Pallatt, Elizabeth; Rappahannock, VA, 1729 ***1220.12*** *p601*
Pallen, Roger; Virginia, 1652 ***6254.4*** *p243*
Pallet, Louis 30; America, 1848 ***778.6*** *p261*
Pallett, William; America, 1774 ***1220.12*** *p601*
Palley, John; America, 1726 ***1220.12*** *p601*
Pallier, Joachim; Montreal, 1653 ***9221.17*** *p295*
Pallisser, Ann; Ontario, 1835 ***3160.1*** *p150*
Pallisser, George; Ontario, 1835 ***3160.1*** *p150*
Pallisser, Mary; Ontario, 1835 ***3160.1*** *p150*
Pallister, Richard; America, 1732 ***1220.12*** *p601*
Pallister, William; America, 1757 ***1220.12*** *p601*
Pallot, Elizabeth G.; Utah, 1851 ***9228.50*** *p488*
Pallot, Francis; Portsmouth, NH, 1676 ***9228.50*** *p488*
Pallot, Jane *SEE* Pallot, Joseph
Pallot, Joseph; Hampton, NH, n.d. ***9228.50*** *p488*
*Relative:*Jane
Pallot, Joseph 25; Ontario, 1871 ***1823.21*** *p288*
Pallot, Mary A.E.; Utah, n.d. ***9228.50*** *p488*
Pallott, William 18; Ontario, 1871 ***1823.21*** *p289*
Palls, Martha; Ontario, 1835 ***3160.1*** *p150*
Palls, Martha; Prescott, Ont., 1835 ***3289.1*** *p61*
Palm, Frank Oscar; St. Paul, MN, 1892 ***1865.50*** *p104*
Palm, John; Washington, 1877 ***2770.40*** *p134*
Palm, John; Washington, 1883 ***2770.40*** *p137*
Palmer, Alice; America, 1764 ***1220.12*** *p601*
Palmer, Andrew; America, 1685 ***1220.12*** *p601*
Palmer, Ann; America, 1748 ***1220.12*** *p601*
Palmer, Ann; Annapolis, MD, 1732 ***1220.12*** *p601*
Palmer, Ann; Newfoundland, 1845-1945 ***9228.50*** *p174*
Palmer, Ann; Virginia, 1727 ***1220.12*** *p601*
Palmer, Anne Gale *SEE* Palmer, Thomas
Palmer, Anne Gale *SEE* Palmer, Thomas
Palmer, Barnabas; Boston, 1741 ***1642*** *p26*
Palmer, Benjamin; Barbados, 1666 ***1220.12*** *p601*
Palmer, Bridget; America, 1761 ***1220.12*** *p601*
Palmer, Catherine; America, 1758 ***1220.12*** *p601*
Palmer, Catherine; America, 1768 ***1220.12*** *p601*
Palmer, Ed. 15; Quebec, 1870 ***8364.32*** *p25*
Palmer, Elizabeth; America, 1748 ***1220.12*** *p601*
Palmer, Elizabeth; Maryland, 1744 ***1220.12*** *p601*
Palmer, Elizabeth 34; Michigan, 1880 ***4491.30*** *p24*
Palmer, Ethel *SEE* Palmer, Thomas
Palmer, Eveline Wade *SEE* Palmer, Frank Thomas
Palmer, Frances; America, 1769 ***1220.12*** *p601*
Palmer, Francis W. 57; Ontario, 1871 ***1823.21*** *p289*
Palmer, Frank Geoffrey *SEE* Palmer, John Charles
Palmer, Frank Thomas; Idaho, 1925 ***9228.50*** *p174*
*Wife:*Eveline Wade
*Son:*Peter Robert
Palmer, George; America, 1756 ***1220.12*** *p601*
Palmer, George 28; Ontario, 1871 ***1823.17*** *p129*
Palmer, H. S.; Louisiana, 1874 ***4981.45*** *p296*
Palmer, Hannah; Virginia, 1732 ***1220.12*** *p601*
Palmer, Henry; America, 1773 ***1220.12*** *p601*
Palmer, Hester; America, 1757 ***1220.12*** *p601*
Palmer, Isaac Charles; Colorado, 1878 ***1029.59*** *p72*
Palmer, James; America, 1763 ***1220.12*** *p601*
Palmer, James 50; Ontario, 1871 ***1823.17*** *p129*
Palmer, James; Potomac, 1742 ***1220.12*** *p601*
Palmer, Jane; America, 1742 ***1220.12*** *p601*
Palmer, Joan; Barbados, 1672 ***1220.12*** *p601*
Palmer, John; America, 1677 ***1220.12*** *p601*
Palmer, John; America, 1685 ***1220.12*** *p601*
Palmer, John; America, 1732 ***1220.12*** *p601*
Palmer, John; America, 1734 ***1220.12*** *p601*
Palmer, John; America, 1742 ***1220.12*** *p601*
Palmer, John; America, 1764 ***1220.12*** *p602*
Palmer, John; America, 1766 ***1220.12*** *p602*
Palmer, John; Barbados or Jamaica, 1688 ***1220.12*** *p601*
Palmer, John; Marblehead, MA, 1652-1734 ***9228.50*** *p488*
Palmer, John; Maryland, 1738 ***1220.12*** *p601*
Palmer, John 42; Ontario, 1871 ***1823.17*** *p129*
Palmer, John Charles; Vancouver, B.C., 1910-1912 ***9228.50*** *p175*
*Wife:*Nora Marjorie Christie
*Son:*Frank Geoffrey
Palmer, Lewis; Barbados or Jamaica, 1705 ***1220.12*** *p602*
Palmer, Louise *SEE* Palmer, Thomas
Palmer, Mary; America, 1756 ***1220.12*** *p602*
Palmer, Mary; Virginia, 1730 ***1220.12*** *p602*
Palmer, Nicholas; America, 1685 ***1220.12*** *p602*
Palmer, Nora Marjorie Christie *SEE* Palmer, John Charles
Palmer, Paul 25; Ontario, 1871 ***1823.17*** *p129*
Palmer, Peter Robert *SEE* Palmer, Frank Thomas
Palmer, Philip; America, 1742 ***1220.12*** *p602*
Palmer, Rachael; America, 1744 ***1220.12*** *p602*
Palmer, Rebecca; America, 1757 ***1220.12*** *p602*
Palmer, Richard 40; Ontario, 1871 ***1823.17*** *p129*
Palmer, Sarah; America, 1718 ***1220.12*** *p602*
Palmer, Sarah; America, 1756 ***1220.12*** *p602*
Palmer, Thomas; America, 1739 ***1220.12*** *p602*
Palmer, Thomas; America, 1749 ***1220.12*** *p602*
Palmer, Thomas; America, 1750 ***1220.12*** *p602*
Palmer, Thomas; America, 1770 ***1220.12*** *p602*
Palmer, Thomas; America, 1775 ***1220.12*** *p602*
Palmer, Thomas; Annapolis, MD, 1725 ***1220.12*** *p602*
Palmer, Thomas; Barbados or Jamaica, 1702 ***1220.12*** *p602*
Palmer, Thomas; Detroit, 1772-1884 ***9228.50*** *p488*
*Wife:*Anne Gale
*Child:*Ethel
*Child:*William
*Child:*Louise
Palmer, Thomas; Ontario, 1872-1884 ***9228.50*** *p488*
*Wife:*Anne Gale
*Child:*William
Palmer, Thomas; Virginia, 1727 ***1220.12*** *p602*
Palmer, Valentine 22; Ontario, 1871 ***1823.17*** *p129*
Palmer, Walter; North Carolina, 1858 ***1088.45*** *p26*
Palmer, William; America, 1674 ***1220.12*** *p602*
Palmer, William; America, 1720 ***1220.12*** *p602*
Palmer, William; America, 1732 ***1220.12*** *p602*
Palmer, William; America, 1753 ***1220.12*** *p602*
Palmer, William; America, 1757 ***1220.12*** *p602*
Palmer, William; America, 1774 ***1220.12*** *p602*
Palmer, William *SEE* Palmer, Thomas
Palmer, William; Ohio, 1844 ***3580.20*** *p33*
Palmer, William; Ohio, 1844 ***6020.12*** *p21*
Palmer, William *SEE* Palmer, Thomas
Palmer, William 60; Ontario, 1871 ***1823.21*** *p289*
Palmer, William; Virginia, 1734 ***1220.12*** *p602*
Palmer, Zemira; Utah, 1886 ***3687.1*** *p34*
Palmerstone, Henry; America, 1765 ***1220.12*** *p602*
Palmgren, J.; Philadelphia, 1848 ***6412.40*** *p150*
Palmisano, August; Ohio, 1840-1897 ***8365.35*** *p17*
Palmore, Wilhemina; Oregon, 1941 ***9157.47*** *p2*
Palmquist, Aaron E.; St. Paul, MN, 1890-1905 ***1865.50*** *p104*
Palmquist, John Emil; Iowa, 1896 ***1211.15*** *p18*
Palmqvist, Aaron E.; St. Paul, MN, 1890-1905 ***1865.50*** *p104*
Palo, Eileen 16; Minnesota, 1925 ***2769.54*** *p1384*
Palser, John; America, 1770 ***1220.12*** *p602*
Palser, Thomas; America, 1756 ***1220.12*** *p602*
Palso, Cecilia *SEE* Palso, John
Palso, Hilda Theresia *SEE* Palso, John
Palso, John; Cleveland, OH, 1881-1891 ***9722.10*** *p125*
*Wife:*Cecilia
*Child:*Hilda Theresia
Palson, Cecilia *SEE* Palson, John
Palson, Hilda Theresia *SEE* Palson, John
Palson, John; Cleveland, OH, 1881-1891 ***9722.10*** *p125*
*Wife:*Cecilia
*Child:*Hilda Theresia
Palson, Sarah; America, 1741 ***1220.12*** *p611*
Paltridge, Christopher 38; Ontario, 1871 ***1823.17*** *p129*
Paluga, Anna; Wisconsin, 1885 ***6795.8*** *p34*
Paly, Desire Narcisse 20; Mississippi, 1845 ***778.6*** *p261*
Palz, Barbara; Chicago, 1887 ***5475.1*** *p244*
*Son:*Mathias
Palz, Johann; America, 1876 ***5475.1*** *p346*
Palz, Peter 24; America, 1872 ***5475.1*** *p339*
Pamier, Jean 28; Quebec, 1656 ***9221.17*** *p343*
Panchol, Frederick 18; America, 1845 ***778.6*** *p261*
Panchol, Nicolas 67; America, 1845 ***778.6*** *p261*
Panckhurst, Thomas; America, 1753 ***1220.12*** *p602*
Pander, Margarett; Maryland, 1680 ***1236.25*** *p53*
Pando, Teofila 18; New York, NY, 1911 ***6533.11*** *p10*
Pane, John; Barbados, 1664 ***1220.12*** *p612*
Pane, Joseph 73; Ontario, 1871 ***1823.21*** *p289*
Panetier, Isaac; Virginia, 1700 ***9230.15*** *p80*
Paney, David 36; Ontario, 1871 ***1823.21*** *p289*
Pangriffiths, Thomas James; America, 1768 ***1220.12*** *p602*
Panie, Charles *SEE* Panie, Jacques
Panie, Isabeau *SEE* Panie, Jacques
Panie, Jacques; Quebec, 1633 ***9221.17*** *p29*
*Wife:*Marie Pousset
*Daughter:*Isabeau
*Daughter:*Marie
*Son:*Charles
Panie, Marie *SEE* Panie, Jacques
Panie, Marie Pousset *SEE* Panie, Jacques
Panier, Daniel-Joseph 26; Montreal, 1659 ***9221.17*** *p425*
Panier, Jean; Quebec, 1659 ***9221.17*** *p407*
Panis, Jean; Quebec, 1659 ***9221.17*** *p407*
Panker, Joseph; America, 1755 ***1220.12*** *p602*
Pankonin, Herman Albert; Wisconsin, 1906 ***6795.8*** *p188*
Panks, Sarah; Carolina, 1718 ***1220.12*** *p602*
Pannel, John 50; Ontario, 1871 ***1823.21*** *p289*
Pannel, William 65; Ontario, 1871 ***1823.21*** *p289*
Pannell, Thomas 33; Ontario, 1871 ***1823.21*** *p289*
Pannequin, Elie 60; New Orleans, 1848 ***778.6*** *p261*

Pannery, Honor; America, 1738 ***1220.12*** *p602*
Pannetier, Charles Alphonse; Illinois, 1852 ***6079.1*** *p11*
Pannifer, William; America, 1756 ***1220.12*** *p602*
Panoch, Ludvik Antonin; St. Augustine, FL, 1893 ***2853.20*** *p311*
Pans, Mr. 28; New Orleans, 1840 ***778.6*** *p261*
Panse, Jacques 29; Montreal, 1653 ***9221.17*** *p283*
Pant, Christopher; America, 1761 ***1220.12*** *p602*
Pantall, Thomas; America, 1749 ***1220.12*** *p602*
Panter, Emma 12; Ontario, 1871 ***1823.21*** *p289*
Pantin, Marie Louise 28; Port uncertain, 1848 ***778.6*** *p261*
Panting, Richard; America, 1772 ***1220.12*** *p602*
Panton, Edward 57; Ontario, 1871 ***1823.21*** *p289*
Pantree, John; Annapolis, MD, 1730 ***1220.12*** *p602*
Pantry, Robert; America, 1761 ***1220.12*** *p602*
Panuska, Vaclav; Cleveland, OH, 1889 ***2853.20*** *p487*
Papayanni, Panajotte 38; New York, NY, 1894 ***6512.1*** *p186*
Pape, Mr.; America, 1838 ***7420.1*** *p15*
With wife & children
Pape, Carl Friedrich August; America, 1885 ***7420.1*** *p399*
Pape, Christian; America, 1836 ***7420.1*** *p11*
Pape, Christoph; America, 1856 ***7420.1*** *p152*
With wife & 4 daughters
Pape, Conrad; America, 1854 ***7420.1*** *p126*
Pape, Engel Marie; America, 1857 ***7420.1*** *p169*
Pape, Engel Marie Sophie; America, 1866 ***7420.1*** *p247*
Pape, Heinrich Dietrich Friedrich Ernst; Port uncertain, 1880 ***7420.1*** *p317*
Pape, Johann Christoph; America, 1855 ***7420.1*** *p140*
Pape, Johann Heinrich Wilhelm; America, 1866 ***7420.1*** *p247*
Pape, Richard 40; Ontario, 1871 ***1823.21*** *p289*
Pape, Robert; America, 1767 ***1220.12*** *p602*
Papierski, Walter; Detroit, 1929-1930 ***6214.5*** *p67*
Papik, Jan; South Dakota, 1871-1910 ***2853.20*** *p247*
Papin, Madeleine; Quebec, 1672 ***4514.3*** *p353*
Papin, Pierre 24; Montreal, 1653 ***9221.17*** *p298*
Pappadackis, Demetrius Emmanuel; Iowa, 1925 ***1211.15*** *p18*
Pappenfort, Otto; Illinois, 1854 ***6079.1*** *p11*
Papper, James; America, 1753 ***1220.12*** *p602*
Papper, Sampson; America, 1738 ***1220.12*** *p602*
Papps, Gideon; America, 1754 ***1220.12*** *p603*
Papworth, William; America, 1695 ***1220.12*** *p603*
Paquet, Augustine; Wisconsin, 1856 ***1495.20*** *p28*
Paquet, Emery *SEE* Paquet, Marguerite
Paquet, Francois Alexandre 37; New Orleans, 1848 ***778.6*** *p261*
Paquet, Gabriele 7; New Orleans, 1848 ***778.6*** *p261*
Paquet, Jeanne *SEE* Paquet, Marguerite
Paquet, Jeanne Eugenie 26; New Orleans, 1848 ***778.6*** *p261*
Paquet, Marguerite; Quebec, 1667 ***4514.3*** *p353*
With sister
*Father:*Emery
*Brother:*Maurice
*Niece:*Jeanne
*Brother:*Rene
*Stepmother:*Renee Guillocheau Forget
Paquet, Maurice *SEE* Paquet, Marguerite
Paquet, Philippe 23; Quebec, 1646 ***9221.17*** *p167*
Paquet, Rene *SEE* Paquet, Marguerite
Paquet, Renee Guillocheau Forget *SEE* Paquet, Marguerite
Paqui, Nicolas 7; New Orleans, 1848 ***778.6*** *p261*
Paqui, Susanne 5; New Orleans, 1848 ***778.6*** *p261*
Paquier, Mr. 36; New Orleans, 1848 ***778.6*** *p261*
Paquol, Nicolas 58; Texas, 1848 ***778.6*** *p261*
Paquot, Joseph 22; America, 1841 ***778.6*** *p261*
Paradice, Francis, Jr.; Virginia, 1767 ***1220.12*** *p603*
Paradis, Barbe Guion 35 *SEE* Paradis, Pierre
Paradis, Guillaume 8 *SEE* Paradis, Pierre
Paradis, Jacques 11 *SEE* Paradis, Pierre
Paradis, Jean 2 *SEE* Paradis, Pierre
Paradis, Marie 10 *SEE* Paradis, Pierre
Paradis, Pierre 5 *SEE* Paradis, Pierre
Paradis, Pierre 48; Quebec, 1652 ***9221.17*** *p263*
*Wife:*Barbe Guion 35
*Son:*Jacques 11
*Daughter:*Marie 10
*Son:*Guillaume 8
*Son:*Pierre 5
*Son:*Jean 2
Paradowski, Joseph; Texas, 1920-1923 ***6015.15*** *p28*
Paralush, Frank; Detroit, 1930 ***1640.60*** *p78*
Paramour, Phoebe; America, 1751 ***1220.12*** *p603*
Paratana, A.; Louisiana, 1874 ***4981.45*** *p296*
Paratcher, Anthony; Louisiana, 1874 ***4981.45*** *p133*
Parcher, Ira 60; Ontario, 1871 ***1823.17*** *p129*
Parden, John; Potomac, 1729 ***1220.12*** *p603*
Pardo, Mary; America, 1746 ***1220.12*** *p603*
Pardoe, Elizabeth; America, 1732 ***1220.12*** *p603*
Pardon, Catherine; America, 1771 ***1220.12*** *p603*
Pardon, Sarah; America, 1760 ***1220.12*** *p603*
Pardon, Thomas; America, 1753 ***1220.12*** *p603*
Pardy, Henry 62; Ontario, 1871 ***1823.21*** *p289*
Pare, Claire-Francoise 16; Quebec, 1661 ***9221.17*** *p454*
Pare, Robert 27; Quebec, 1653 ***9221.17*** *p278*
Paremant, Perrette; Quebec, 1670 ***4514.3*** *p353*
Paren, Pierre; Louisiana, 1874-1875 ***4981.45*** *p30*
Parent, Pierre 35; Quebec, 1652 ***9221.17*** *p264*
Parenteau, Marie; Quebec, 1642-1671 ***4514.3*** *p353*
Parenteau, Marie; Quebec, 1671 ***4514.3*** *p353*
Parenteau, Marie-Madeleine 15; Quebec, 1657 ***9221.17*** *p365*
Parentelle, Marie-Madeleine 15; Quebec, 1657 ***9221.17*** *p365*
Pares, Mr. 43; New Orleans, 1845 ***778.6*** *p261*
Parett, Wm 17; Ontario, 1871 ***1823.21*** *p289*
Paretti, Paul; Louisiana, 1874-1875 ***4981.45*** *p30*
Parfect, Robert; America, 1766 ***1220.12*** *p603*
Parfen, Frank; Detroit, 1929-1930 ***6214.5*** *p63*
Parfett, Christopher; America, 1739 ***1220.12*** *p603*
Parfit, Joanna; America, 1775 ***1220.12*** *p603*
Parfitt, Albion 24; Ontario, 1871 ***1823.21*** *p289*
Parfitt, Isabella 22; Ontario, 1871 ***1823.21*** *p289*
Parfitt, Richard; America, 1732 ***1220.12*** *p603*
Parford, William; America, 1746 ***1220.12*** *p603*
Parfourru, Marcel-Louis de; Quebec, 1755-1757 ***2314.30*** *p170*
Parfourru, Marcel-Louis de; Quebec, 1755-1757 ***2314.30*** *p192*
Parfrey, Jonathan; Barbados, 1698 ***1220.12*** *p603*
Pargeter, Susanah 60; Ontario, 1871 ***1823.21*** *p289*
Pargeter, Thomas 38; Ontario, 1871 ***1823.21*** *p289*
Pargiter, William; America, 1752 ***1220.12*** *p603*
Parillo, Franceso; Louisiana, 1874 ***4981.45*** *p133*
Parin, Frank; Ohio, 1840-1897 ***8365.35*** *p17*
Parins, Celestin; New York, NY, 1869 ***1494.20*** *p11*
Parip, Rozalia 24; New York, NY, 1911 ***6533.11*** *p10*
Paris, Child 7 months; Port uncertain, 1845 ***778.6*** *p261*
Paris, Bernard; Louisiana, 1836-1840 ***4981.45*** *p213*
Paris, Daniel; America, 1755 ***1220.12*** *p603*
Paris, Eleonore Josephe; Wisconsin, 1854-1858 ***1495.20*** *p66*
Paris, Francoise; Quebec, 1673 ***4514.3*** *p353*
Paris, George 28; Ontario, 1871 ***1823.21*** *p289*
Paris, James C. 25; Port uncertain, 1845 ***778.6*** *p261*
Paris, Jane; Maryland, 1725 ***1220.12*** *p603*
Paris, John; America, 1771 ***1220.12*** *p603*
Paris, Levis 50; America, 1843 ***778.6*** *p261*
Paris, Melanie 24; Port uncertain, 1845 ***778.6*** *p261*
Paris, Richard; America, 1734 ***1220.12*** *p603*
Paris, Robert; America, 1769 ***1220.12*** *p603*
Paris, William 26; Ontario, 1871 ***1823.21*** *p289*
Parish, Alexander; Annapolis, MD, 1721 ***1220.12*** *p603*
Parish, Alice 12; Quebec, 1870 ***8364.32*** *p25*
Parish, Benjamin; America, 1756 ***1220.12*** *p603*
Parish, George; America, 1749 ***1220.12*** *p603*
Parish, George 32; Ontario, 1871 ***1823.21*** *p289*
Parish, James; America, 1774 ***1220.12*** *p603*
Parish, Jane; Annapolis, MD, 1725 ***1220.12*** *p603*
Parish, John; America, 1767 ***1220.12*** *p603*
Parish, John 24; Ontario, 1871 ***1823.21*** *p289*
Parish, Thomas; America, 1738 ***1220.12*** *p603*
Parish, Thomas; America, 1773 ***1220.12*** *p603*
Parish, William; Barbados or Jamaica, 1677 ***1220.12*** *p603*
Parisien, Michel; Quebec, 1656 ***9221.17*** *p344*
Park, Emma 23; Ontario, 1871 ***1823.21*** *p289*
Park, George; Quebec, 1870 ***8364.32*** *p25*
Park, James 35; Michigan, 1880 ***4491.36*** *p17*
Park, James 53; Ontario, 1871 ***1823.17*** *p130*
Park, James 57; Ontario, 1871 ***1823.17*** *p130*
Park, Janet 80; Ontario, 1871 ***1823.17*** *p130*
Park, John 52; Ontario, 1871 ***1823.17*** *p130*
Park, Mary 40; Michigan, 1880 ***4491.36*** *p17*
Park, Matilda 32; Michigan, 1880 ***4491.36*** *p17*
Park, Minnie 1; Ontario, 1871 ***1823.21*** *p289*
Park, Nancy 77; Michigan, 1880 ***4491.36*** *p17*
Park, Thomas 45; Ontario, 1871 ***1823.17*** *p130*
Park, Thomas 48; Ontario, 1871 ***1823.17*** *p130*
Park, William; America, 1764 ***1220.12*** *p603*
Park, William 37; Ontario, 1871 ***1823.21*** *p289*
Park, William 52; Ontario, 1871 ***1823.17*** *p130*
Parke, Edward 52; Ontario, 1871 ***1823.21*** *p289*
Parke, James 31; Ontario, 1871 ***1823.21*** *p289*
Parke, John; Barbados, 1681 ***1220.12*** *p603*
Parke, John; Philadelphia, 1778 ***8529.30*** *p4A*
Parke, Peter; Jamaica, 1663 ***1220.12*** *p603*
Parke, Richard; America, 1768 ***1220.12*** *p603*
Parke, Simpson; America, 1755 ***1220.12*** *p603*
Parke, Thomas; America, 1713 ***1220.12*** *p603*
Parker, Mr.; Canada, 1775 ***3036.5*** *p68*
Parker, Abraham; Barbados, 1673 ***1220.12*** *p603*
Parker, Alexander 53; Ontario, 1871 ***1823.21*** *p289*
Parker, Amos; Barbados, 1667 ***1220.12*** *p603*
Parker, Andrew; America, 1741 ***1220.12*** *p603*
Parker, Andrew; America, 1755 ***1220.12*** *p603*
Parker, Ann; America, 1753 ***1220.12*** *p603*
Parker, Ann; America, 1760 ***1220.12*** *p604*
Parker, Ann; America, 1775 ***1220.12*** *p604*
Parker, Annie 8; Quebec, 1870 ***8364.32*** *p25*
Parker, Arthur; Detroit, 1929-1930 ***6214.5*** *p69*
Parker, Augustine; Barbados or Jamaica, 1699 ***1220.12*** *p604*
Parker, Austin; America, 1750 ***1220.12*** *p604*
Parker, Baldwin; America, 1685 ***1220.12*** *p604*
Parker, Benjamin; America, 1736 ***1220.12*** *p604*
Parker, Benjamin; America, 1753 ***1220.12*** *p604*
Parker, Benjamin 28; Ontario, 1871 ***1823.17*** *p130*
Parker, Bridget 56; Ontario, 1871 ***1823.17*** *p130*
Parker, Catherine; America, 1766 ***1220.12*** *p604*
Parker, Catherine; Halifax, N.S., 1827 ***7009.9*** *p61*
*Husband:*Denis
Parker, Charles; America, 1677 ***1220.12*** *p604*
Parker, Charles; America, 1726 ***1220.12*** *p604*
Parker, Charles; America, 1769 ***1220.12*** *p604*
Parker, Charles; Barbados, 1665 ***1220.12*** *p604*
Parker, Charles 60; Ontario, 1871 ***1823.21*** *p289*
Parker, Chas 23; Ontario, 1871 ***1823.21*** *p289*
Parker, Edward; America, 1738 ***1220.12*** *p604*
Parker, Edward 24; Ontario, 1871 ***1823.21*** *p289*
Parker, Edward 36; Ontario, 1871 ***1823.21*** *p289*
Parker, Edward 51; Ontario, 1871 ***1823.17*** *p130*
Parker, Edward 66; Ontario, 1871 ***1823.21*** *p289*
Parker, Elen 35; Ontario, 1871 ***1823.21*** *p289*
Parker, Elizabeth; America, 1730 ***1220.12*** *p604*
Parker, Elizabeth; America, 1760 ***1220.12*** *p604*
Parker, Elizabeth; Annapolis, MD, 1722 ***1220.12*** *p604*
Parker, Elizabeth *SEE* Parker, Mary
Parker, Emma 71; Ontario, 1871 ***1823.21*** *p289*
Parker, Francis; America, 1768 ***1220.12*** *p604*
Parker, Frank 26; Ontario, 1871 ***1823.21*** *p289*
Parker, Frederick 36; Ontario, 1871 ***1823.21*** *p289*
Parker, Frederick A.; Washington, 1889 ***2770.40*** *p80*
Parker, George; America, 1740 ***1220.12*** *p604*
Parker, George 49; Ontario, 1871 ***1823.21*** *p290*
Parker, Grace; Charles Town, SC, 1719 ***1220.12*** *p604*
Parker, Hannah; America, 1766 ***1220.12*** *p604*
Parker, Henry; America, 1748 ***1220.12*** *p604*
Parker, Henry 28; Ontario, 1871 ***1823.21*** *p290*
Parker, Henry 40; Ontario, 1871 ***1823.17*** *p130*
Parker, Henry 56; Ontario, 1871 ***1823.17*** *p130*
Parker, J.C. 15; Quebec, 1870 ***8364.32*** *p25*
Parker, James; America, 1685 ***1220.12*** *p604*
Parker, James; America, 1759 ***1220.12*** *p604*
Parker, James; Barbados, 1677 ***1220.12*** *p604*
Parker, James *SEE* Parker, Mary
Parker, James 22; Ontario, 1871 ***1823.17*** *p130*
Parker, James 46; Ontario, 1871 ***1823.21*** *p290*
Parker, John; America, 1699 ***1220.12*** *p604*
Parker, John; America, 1723 ***1220.12*** *p604*
Parker, John; America, 1735 ***1220.12*** *p604*
Parker, John; America, 1749 ***1220.12*** *p604*
Parker, John; America, 1759 ***1220.12*** *p604*
Parker, John; America, 1764 ***1220.12*** *p604*
Parker, John; America, 1766 ***1220.12*** *p604*
Parker, John; America, 1769 ***1220.12*** *p604*
Parker, John; America, 1773 ***1220.12*** *p604*
Parker, John; Annapolis, MD, 1736 ***1220.12*** *p604*
Parker, John; Barbados, 1665 ***1220.12*** *p604*
Parker, John; Died enroute, 1723 ***1220.12*** *p604*
Parker, John; Died enroute, 1726 ***1220.12*** *p604*
Parker, John; Marston's Wharf, 1782 ***8529.30*** *p15*
Parker, John; Maryland or Virginia, 1728 ***1220.12*** *p604*
Parker, John; New York, NY, 1841 ***3274.56*** *p101*
Parker, John 53; Ontario, 1871 ***1823.21*** *p290*
Parker, John; Virginia, 1734 ***1220.12*** *p604*
Parker, John; Virginia, 1740 ***1220.12*** *p604*
Parker, John; Virginia, 1741 ***1220.12*** *p604*
Parker, Jonathan; America, 1766 ***1220.12*** *p604*
Parker, Jonathan 22; Michigan, 1880 ***4491.42*** *p20*
Parker, Joseph; America, 1738 ***1220.12*** *p604*
Parker, Joseph; America, 1750 ***1220.12*** *p604*
Parker, Joseph; America, 1767 ***1220.12*** *p604*
Parker, Joseph; America, 1774 ***1220.12*** *p604*
Parker, Joseph 36; Ontario, 1871 ***1823.21*** *p290*
Parker, Josiah; America, 1736 ***1220.12*** *p604*
Parker, Margaret; America, 1751 ***1220.12*** *p605*
Parker, Margaret 12; Quebec, 1870 ***8364.32*** *p25*
Parker, Martha; America, 1717 ***1220.12*** *p605*
Parker, Martha; America, 1723 ***1220.12*** *p605*
Parker, Martha; Barbados, 1673 ***1220.12*** *p605*
Parker, Mary; America, 1702 ***1220.12*** *p605*
Parker, Mary; America, 1724 ***1220.12*** *p605*
Parker, Mary; America, 1729 ***1220.12*** *p605*

Parker, Mary; America, 1750 1220.12 p605
Parker, Mary; America, 1766 1220.12 p605
Parker, Mary; America, 1772 1220.12 p605
Parker, Mary; Barbados, 1674 1220.12 p605
Parker, Mary; Canada, 1775 3036.5 p68
*Child:*Elizabeth
*Child:*James
Parker, Mary; Maryland, 1674-1675 1236.25 p52
Parker, Michael; America, 1774 1220.12 p605
Parker, Rachel A. 30; Ontario, 1871 1823.21 p290
Parker, Ralph; Barbados, 1679 1220.12 p605
Parker, Reuben 25; Ontario, 1871 1823.21 p290
Parker, Richard; America, 1685 1220.12 p605
Parker, Richard; America, 1750 1220.12 p605
Parker, Richard; America, 1754 1220.12 p605
Parker, Robert; America, 1770 1220.12 p605
Parker, Robert; America, 1771 1220.12 p605
Parker, Robert 36; Ontario, 1871 1823.17 p130
Parker, Robert 21; Virginia, 1635 1183.3 p31
Parker, Ruth; Maryland, 1736 1220.12 p605
Parker, Samuel; America, 1733 1220.12 p605
Parker, Samuel; America, 1748 1220.12 p605
Parker, Sarah; America, 1774 1220.12 p605
Parker, Stephen; America, 1694 1220.12 p605
Parker, Stephen; Maryland, 1723 1220.12 p605
Parker, Susanna; America, 1750 1220.12 p605
Parker, T. R. 20; Ontario, 1871 1823.21 p290
Parker, Thomas; America, 1736 1220.12 p605
Parker, Thomas; America, 1747 1220.12 p605
Parker, Thomas; America, 1749 1220.12 p605
Parker, Thomas; America, 1759 1220.12 p605
Parker, Thomas; America, 1769 1220.12 p605
Parker, Thomas; America, 1772 1220.12 p605
Parker, Thomas; Died enroute, 1725 1220.12 p605
Parker, Thomas; Jamaica, 1663 1220.12 p605
Parker, Thomas; New York, NY, 1854 7710.1 p156
Parker, Thomas 66; Ontario, 1871 1823.21 p290
Parker, William; America, 1685 1220.12 p605
Parker, William; America, 1694 1220.12 p605
Parker, William; America, 1721 1220.12 p605
Parker, William; America, 1756 1220.12 p605
Parker, William; America, 1758 1220.12 p605
Parker, William; America, 1766 1220.12 p605
Parker, William; America, 1769 1220.12 p605
Parker, William; America, 1772 1220.12 p605
Parker, William; America, 1773 1220.12 p605
Parker, William; America, 1774 1220.12 p605
Parker, William; Barbados, 1693 1220.12 p605
Parker, William 40; Ontario, 1871 1823.21 p290
Parker, William 74; Ontario, 1871 1823.21 p290
Parker, William; Virginia, 1670 1220.12 p605
Parker, William; Virginia, 1739 1220.12 p605
Parkers, John 45; Ontario, 1871 1823.21 p290
Parkes, Ann; America, 1756 1220.12 p606
Parkes, George; America, 1764 1220.12 p606
Parkes, Giles; America, 1774 1220.12 p606
Parkes, Isaac; America, 1753 1220.12 p606
Parkes, James; America, 1729 1220.12 p606
Parkes, John; America, 1744 1220.12 p606
Parkes, John; America, 1764 1220.12 p606
Parkes, John; Marston's Wharf, 1782 8529.30 p15
Parkes, Joseph; America, 1772 1220.12 p606
Parkes, Samuel; America, 1746 1220.12 p606
Parkes, Thomas; America, 1708 1220.12 p606
Parkes, Thomas 15; Quebec, 1870 8364.32 p25
Parkeson, Rosamiah 20; Ontario, 1871 1823.21 p290
Parkhill, Mary J. 24; Ontario, 1871 1823.17 p130
Parkhouse, Isabella; America, 1764 1220.12 p606
Parkhouse, Thomas; America, 1752 1220.12 p606
Parkhurst, James; America, 1771 1220.12 p606
Parkin, Amos; Barbados, 1667 1220.12 p606
Parkin, Edward; Barbados, 1665 1220.12 p606
Parkin, George 64; Ontario, 1871 1823.21 p290
Parkin, George 18; Quebec, 1870 8364.32 p25
Parkin, Mary Ann; Utah, 1800-1896 9228.50 p183
Parkin, Samual 26; Ontario, 1871 1823.21 p290
Parking, John 46; Ontario, 1871 1823.21 p290
Parkins, Ann 66; Ontario, 1871 1823.21 p290
Parkins, Anne; America, 1720 1220.12 p620
Parkins, John 47; Ontario, 1871 1823.21 p290
Parkins, Joseph; Philadelphia, 1854 8513.31 p419
*Wife:*Margaret Noble
Parkins, Margaret Noble *SEE* Parkins, Joseph
Parkinson, Abram 26; Ontario, 1871 1823.21 p290
Parkinson, Anne; America, 1682 1220.12 p606
Parkinson, Benjamin; America, 1770 1220.12 p606
Parkinson, David, Jr.; America, 1758 1220.12 p606
Parkinson, George 37; Ontario, 1871 1823.21 p290
Parkinson, George 72; Ontario, 1871 1823.21 p290
Parkinson, Isaac 66; Ontario, 1871 1823.21 p290
Parkinson, James; America, 1753 1220.12 p606
Parkinson, James 80; Ontario, 1871 1823.17 p130
Parkinson, John; America, 1749 1220.12 p606
Parkinson, John; Marston's Wharf, 1781 8529.30 p15
Parkinson, John 65; Ontario, 1871 1823.21 p290
Parkinson, John 65; Ontario, 1871 1823.21 p290
Parkinson, Marmaduke 36; Ontario, 1871 1823.17 p130
Parkinson, Mary; America, 1758 1220.12 p606
Parkinson, Robert 31; Ontario, 1871 1823.21 p290
Parkinson, Robert 64; Ontario, 1871 1823.21 p290
Parkinson, Samuel 55; Ontario, 1871 1823.21 p290
Parkinson, Thomas; Ohio, 1836 3580.20 p33
Parkinson, Thomas; Ohio, 1836 6020.12 p21
Parkinson, Thomas 34; Ontario, 1871 1823.21 p290
Parkinson, Thomas 38; Ontario, 1871 1823.21 p290
Parkinson, William 27; Ontario, 1871 1823.21 p290
Parks, Edward; Annapolis, MD, 1729 1220.12 p606
Parks, G. W. 41; Ontario, 1871 1823.17 p130
Parks, James; Maryland or Virginia, 1738 1220.12 p606
Parks, Joane; America, 1679 1220.12 p606
Parks, John; America, 1738 1220.12 p606
Parks, Sampson; America, 1755 1220.12 p606
Parks, Samuel; Ohio, 1809-1852 4511.35 p39
Parks, Thomas 27; Ontario, 1871 1823.17 p130
Parks, William; America, 1750 1220.12 p606
Parkway, Robert; Barbados, 1694 1220.12 p606
Parlange, Mr. 20; America, 1846 778.6 p261
Parlange, Henry 30; Port uncertain, 1845 778.6 p261
Parlby, Thomas; America, 1758 1220.12 p606
Parlebar, Henry; North Carolina, 1710 3629.40 p6
Parley, Daniel; America, 1755 1220.12 p606
Parlo, James; America, 1772 1220.12 p606
Parlour, John; America, 1750 1220.12 p606
Parlow, Edward; America, 1685 1220.12 p606
Parlow, Thomas; America, 1685 1220.12 p606
Parma, Jindrich; Texas, 1879 2853.20 p70
Parman, James 44; Ontario, 1871 1823.21 p290
Parmentier, Mr. 34; New Orleans, 1845 778.6 p262
Parmentier, Jean; Virginia, 1700 9230.15 p81
Parmentier, Jules; New York, NY, 1873 1494.20 p13
Parmer, Robert; America, 1734 1220.12 p602
Parminter, Thomas; Colorado, 1873 1029.59 p72
Parmisano, F.; Louisiana, 1874-1875 4981.45 p30
Parnaby, John; America, 1742 1220.12 p606
Parnel, Robert; America, 1742 1220.12 p606
Parnell, Alice; Ontario, 1871 1823.21 p290
Parnell, Edward 41; Ontario, 1871 1823.21 p290
Parnell, Edwin Isaac 30; Ontario, 1871 1823.17 p130
Parnell, Elizabeth; America, 1752 1220.12 p606
Parnell, John D.; Ohio, 1809-1852 4511.35 p39
Parnell, Nurse; America, 1773 1220.12 p606
Parnell, Richard; America, 1729 1220.12 p606
Parnell, Robert; America, 1763 1220.12 p606
Parnell, Stephen; America, 1741 1220.12 p606
Paroissien, Michel; Quebec, 1656 9221.17 p344
Parolewski, Paulus; Wisconsin, 1897 6795.8 p60
Parpaillon, Etienne 23; Quebec, 1659 9221.17 p408
Parquet, Charles 36; America, 1840 778.6 p262
Parquot, Frances; America, 1719 1220.12 p606
Parr, Daniel; America, 1687 1220.12 p606
Parr, Frederick 38; Ontario, 1871 1823.21 p290
Parr, John; America, 1694 1220.12 p606
Parr, John; America, 1771 1220.12 p607
Parr, Joseph 61; Ontario, 1871 1823.21 p290
Parr, Peter; America, 1767 1220.12 p607
Parr, Robert 22; Ontario, 1871 1823.21 p290
Parr, Samuel 33; Ontario, 1871 1823.21 p290
Parr, Thomas; America, 1763 1220.12 p607
Parr, Thomas; Jamaica, 1661 1220.12 p607
Parr, William; America, 1687 1220.12 p607
Parr, William; America, 1760 1220.12 p607
Parr, William; Philadelphia, 1856 5720.10 p382
Parran, Pier.e 28; Port uncertain, 1840 778.6 p262
Parransos, Jean; Virginia, 1700 9230.15 p80
Parratt, Adam; Barbados, 1667 1220.12 p607
Parrent, Paul 29; Ohio, 1880 4879.40 p259
Parrett, Alice; Barbados, 1664 1220.12 p607
Parrett, John Hugh; New York, NY, 1893 3665.20 p112
Parrett, William 27; Ontario, 1871 1823.17 p130
Parretti, Pelegro; Louisiana, 1874-1875 4981.45 p30
Parrimore, William; Maryland, 1720 1220.12 p603
Parris, Charles; America, 1680 1220.12 p603
Parris, John; America, 1762 1220.12 p603
Parris, Mary; America, 1766 1220.12 p603
Parrise, Rosa 25; America, 1848 778.6 p262
Parrot, Thomas; America, 1734 1220.12 p607
Parrot, William; North Carolina, 1857 1088.45 p26
Parrott, Ann; Maryland or Virginia, 1738 1220.12 p607
Parrott, Charles 36; Ontario, 1871 1823.17 p130
Parrott, Charles; Virginia, 1738 1220.12 p607
Parrott, Edward; Nevis or Jamaica, 1722 1220.12 p607
Parrott, Elizabeth; America, 1752 1220.12 p607
Parrott, Gawin; Barbados, 1683 1220.12 p607
Parrott, George 32; Ontario, 1871 1823.21 p291
Parrott, John; Annapolis, MD, 1736 1220.12 p607
Parrott, John, Jr.; America, 1771 1220.12 p607
Parrott, Joshua; Barbados or Jamaica, 1715 1220.12 p607
Parrott, Leonard; America, 1745 1220.12 p607
Parrott, Samuel; North Carolina, 1856 1088.45 p26
Parrott, Thomas; America, 1760 1220.12 p607
Parrott, Thomas; America, 1762 1220.12 p877
Parrott, Thomas; Died enroute, 1728 1220.12 p607
Parry, Ann; Virginia, 1727 1220.12 p607
Parry, David; Ohio, 1820 4022.20 p289
*Wife:*Mary Jones
Parry, Edward; America, 1765 1220.12 p607
Parry, Elizabeth; America, 1763 1220.12 p607
Parry, Elizabeth; Ohio, 1850 4022.20 p290
Parry, Griffith; Ohio, 1841 4022.20 p289
*Wife:*Jane Evans
Parry, H. H. 37; Ontario, 1871 1823.17 p130
Parry, Henry; America, 1724 1220.12 p607
Parry, James; America, 1775 1220.12 p607
Parry, Jane Evans *SEE* Parry, Griffith
Parry, John; America, 1727 1220.12 p607
Parry, John; America, 1729 1220.12 p607
Parry, John; America, 1767 1220.12 p607
Parry, John; America, 1774 1220.12 p607
Parry, Margaret; America, 1663 1220.12 p607
Parry, Margaret; Barbados, 1664 1220.12 p607
Parry, Mary Jones *SEE* Parry, David
Parry, Mathew; America, 1696 1220.12 p607
Parry, Rowland; America, 1751 1220.12 p607
Parry, Thomas; America, 1727 1220.12 p607
Parry, Thomas; America, 1766 1220.12 p607
Parry, Thomas; America, 1767 1220.12 p607
Parry, Thomas; America, 1770 1220.12 p607
Parry, Thomas; America, 1775 1220.12 p607
Parry, Thomas; Ohio, 1836 4022.20 p289
Parry, Thomas 13; Quebec, 1870 8364.32 p25
Parry, William; America, 1725 1220.12 p607
Parry, William; America, 1727 1220.12 p608
Parseval, Claude 35; Quebec, 1655 9221.17 p328
Parsingham, John; America, 1769 1220.12 p608
Parsley, Francis; America, 1720 1220.12 p608
Parsley, Henry; America, 1752 1220.12 p608
Parsley, John; America, 1738 1220.12 p608
Parsley, Mary; America, 1751 1220.12 p608
Parsley, Robert; North Carolina, 1807 1088.45 p26
Parslow, Edward; America, 1774 1220.12 p608
Parslow, Hannah 37; Ontario, 1871 1823.21 p291
Parson, Elisabeth; Oregon, 1941 9157.47 p3
Parson, John 40; Ontario, 1871 1823.21 p291
Parson, John B. 25; Ontario, 1871 1823.17 p130
Parsons, Angel; Virginia, 1767 1220.12 p608
Parsons, Charles 28; Ontario, 1871 1823.21 p291
Parsons, Christian; Barbados or Jamaica, 1702 1220.12 p608
Parsons, E. Bloss 26; Ontario, 1871 1823.17 p130
Parsons, Edward; America, 1758 1220.12 p608
Parsons, Elizabeth; America, 1688 1220.12 p608
Parsons, Elizabeth; America, 1742 1220.12 p608
Parsons, Elizabeth; America, 1766 1220.12 p608
Parsons, Elizabeth; Annapolis, MD, 1725 1220.12 p608
Parsons, Elizabeth; Maryland, 1744 1220.12 p608
Parsons, Elizabeth; Virginia, 1734 1220.12 p608
Parsons, Elnathen; Ontario, 1871 1823.21 p291
Parsons, George; America, 1718 1220.12 p608
Parsons, George; America, 1747 1220.12 p608
Parsons, George; America, 1770 1220.12 p608
Parsons, George 24; New York, NY, 1894 6512.1 p183
Parsons, James; America, 1739 1220.12 p608
Parsons, James; America, 1749 1220.12 p608
Parsons, James; America, 1774 1220.12 p608
Parsons, Jesse 28; Ontario, 1871 1823.21 p291
Parsons, Joan; America, 1656 1220.12 p608
Parsons, John; America, 1685 1220.12 p608
Parsons, John; America, 1729 1220.12 p608
Parsons, John; America, 1730 1220.12 p608
Parsons, John; America, 1740 1220.12 p608
Parsons, John; America, 1745 1220.12 p608
Parsons, John; America, 1769 1220.12 p608
Parsons, John; Annapolis, MD, 1731 1220.12 p608
Parsons, John; Barbados, 1676 1220.12 p608
Parsons, John; Barbados, 1695 1220.12 p608
Parsons, John 40; Ontario, 1871 1823.21 p291
Parsons, John 52; Ontario, 1871 1823.21 p291
Parsons, John; Virginia, 1743 1220.12 p608
Parsons, Jonathan; Barbados, 1683 1220.12 p608
Parsons, Joseph Dixon; Illinois, 1855 6079.1 p11
Parsons, Lott; Ohio, 1844 2763.1 p21
Parsons, Margaret; America, 1773 1220.12 p608
Parsons, Mary; America, 1762 1220.12 p608
Parsons, Mary; Annapolis, MD, 1731 1220.12 p608
Parsons, Mary; Virginia, 1739 1220.12 p608
Parsons, Nathan 22; Ontario, 1871 1823.21 p291
Parsons, Randall; Iowa, 1875 1211.15 p18
Parsons, Richard; America, 1727 1220.12 p608

Parsons, Richard; America, 1749 ***1220.12*** *p608*
Parsons, Robert; America, 1726 ***1220.12*** *p608*
Parsons, Robert; America, 1766 ***1220.12*** *p608*
Parsons, Samuel; America, 1740 ***1220.12*** *p608*
Parsons, Sarah; America, 1761 ***1220.12*** *p608*
Parsons, Thomas; America, 1685 ***1220.12*** *p608*
Parsons, Thomas; America, 1716 ***1220.12*** *p609*
Parsons, Thomas; America, 1765 ***1220.12*** *p609*
Parsons, Thomas; America, 1769 ***1220.12*** *p609*
Parsons, Thomas 43; Ontario, 1871 ***1823.21*** *p291*
Parsons, Thomas 44; Ontario, 1871 ***1823.21*** *p291*
Parsons, Thomas; Virginia, 1765 ***1220.12*** *p609*
Parsons, William; America, 1726 ***1220.12*** *p609*
Parsons, William; America, 1730 ***1220.12*** *p609*
Parsons, William; America, 1762 ***1220.12*** *p609*
Parsons, William; America, 1765 ***1220.12*** *p609*
Parsons, William; Annapolis, MD, 1723 ***1220.12*** *p609*
Parsons, William 60; Ontario, 1871 ***1823.17*** *p130*
Parsons, William; Potomac, 1729 ***1220.12*** *p609*
Parsons, William J.B. 42; Ontario, 1871 ***1823.21*** *p291*
Parsworth, Thomas; America, 1729 ***1220.12*** *p609*
Partin, Thomas; America, 1749 ***1220.12*** *p609*
Partington, Ann; America, 1763 ***1220.12*** *p609*
Partington, George; America, 1759 ***1220.12*** *p609*
Partington, John; America, 1756 ***1220.12*** *p609*
Partington, John; Barbados, 1665 ***1220.12*** *p609*
Partlow, William 26; Ontario, 1871 ***1823.21*** *p291*
Parton, John 44; New York, NY, 1826 ***6178.50*** *p151*
Parton, William; America, 1725 ***1220.12*** *p609*
Partridge, Catherine; America, 1736 ***1220.12*** *p609*
Partridge, Isabel; Barbados, 1684 ***1220.12*** *p609*
Partridge, John; America, 1685 ***1220.12*** *p609*
Partridge, Joseph; America, 1739 ***1220.12*** *p609*
Partridge, Joseph; Virginia, 1754 ***1220.12*** *p609*
Partridge, Love; America, 1733 ***1220.12*** *p609*
Partridge, Mary; America, 1730 ***1220.12*** *p609*
Partridge, Matthew; America, 1750 ***1220.12*** *p609*
Partridge, Richard; America, 1766 ***1220.12*** *p609*
Partridge, Sarah; Maryland, 1725 ***1220.12*** *p609*
Partridge, Susan; Barbados, 1668 ***1220.12*** *p609*
Partridge, Thomas; America, 1742 ***1220.12*** *p609*
Partridge, Thomas 39; Ontario, 1871 ***1823.21*** *p291*
Partridge, Thomas 60; Ontario, 1871 ***1823.21*** *p291*
Partridge, W. 69; Ontario, 1871 ***1823.21*** *p291*
Parttow, George 33; Ontario, 1871 ***1823.17*** *p130*
Partureau, Mrs. 40; America, 1848 ***778.6*** *p262*
Partureau, H. 19; America, 1848 ***778.6*** *p262*
Partureau, H. 47; America, 1848 ***778.6*** *p262*
Party, Auguste 8; America, 1843 ***778.6*** *p262*
Party, Delphine 32; America, 1843 ***778.6*** *p262*
Party, Felicien 6; America, 1843 ***778.6*** *p262*
Party, Jean 45; America, 1843 ***778.6*** *p262*
Party, Josephe 8; America, 1843 ***778.6*** *p262*
Party, Lucine 10; America, 1843 ***778.6*** *p262*
Party, Severin 14; America, 1843 ***778.6*** *p262*
Parvey, Charles; Barbados, 1669 ***1220.12*** *p609*
Parvis, Ben; New York, NY, 1776 ***8529.30*** *p3*
Pary, Jerome; Quebec, 1657 ***9221.17*** *p365*
Pascal, Jean-Baptiste 1; Galveston, TX, 1844 ***3967.10*** *p375*
Pascal, Marie Emilie 5; Galveston, TX, 1844 ***3967.10*** *p375*
Pascal, Marie-Jeanne 36; Galveston, TX, 1844 ***3967.10*** *p375*
Pascal, Richard 50; Ontario, 1871 ***1823.17*** *p130*
Pascal, Stephanie 3; Galveston, TX, 1844 ***3967.10*** *p375*
Paschen, Christ.; Valdivia, Chile, 1852 ***1192.4*** *p53*
Paschke, Ella Fanny; Miami, 1935 ***4984.12*** *p39*
Paschke, Hans Ernst Bruno; Miami, 1935 ***4984.12*** *p39*
Paschoe, Sarah; Barbados, 1688 ***1220.12*** *p609*
Paschold, Georg Heinrich; America, 1867 ***7919.3*** *p525*
With family
Paschold, Johann Georg Christoph; America, 1868 ***7919.3*** *p525*
Pascoe, George; America, 1742 ***1220.12*** *p609*
Pascoe, James; Virginia, 1719 ***1220.12*** *p609*
Pascoe, John; America, 1731 ***1220.12*** *p609*
Pascoe, Joseph; America, 1771 ***1220.12*** *p609*
Pascoe, Joseph 47; Ontario, 1871 ***1823.17*** *p130*
Pascoe, Nathaniel; America, 1771 ***1220.12*** *p609*
Pascoe, Samuel 46; Ontario, 1871 ***1823.21*** *p291*
Pascoe, Zachariah 66; Ontario, 1871 ***1823.21*** *p291*
Pasely, Jane 77; Ontario, 1871 ***1823.21*** *p291*
Pasmore, George 43; Ontario, 1871 ***1823.21*** *p291*
Pasmore, Philip 84; Ontario, 1871 ***1823.21*** *p291*
Pasmore, Rosamund; Barbados or Jamaica, 1697 ***1220.12*** *p609*
Pasmore, Thomas; Barbados or Jamaica, 1697 ***1220.12*** *p609*
Pasquereau, Pierre; Quebec, 1653 ***9221.17*** *p278*
Pasquet, Francois 45; America, 1843 ***778.6*** *p262*
Pasquet, John; Virginia, 1665 ***9228.50*** *p523*
Pasquet, M. 43; America, 1841 ***778.6*** *p262*
Pasquier, Antoine 20; Quebec, 1656 ***9221.17*** *p344*
Pasquier, Emile 1; New Orleans, 1848 ***778.6*** *p262*
Pasquier, Emile Lucas 31; New Orleans, 1848 ***778.6*** *p262*
Pasquier, Francois 23; Quebec, 1655 ***9221.17*** *p328*
Pasquier, Jean 22; Quebec, 1662 ***9221.17*** *p491*
Pasquier, Jean-Baptiste 51; Texas, 1848 ***778.6*** *p262*
Pasquier, Josephine 28; New Orleans, 1848 ***778.6*** *p262*
Pasquier, Louis Frederic 29; New Orleans, 1848 ***778.6*** *p262*
Pasquier, Louise 5; New Orleans, 1848 ***778.6*** *p262*
Pasquier, Marie; Quebec, 1667 ***4514.3*** *p353*
Pasquier, Pascal; Quebec, 1652 ***9221.17*** *p264*
Pass, Ferdinand Gustav; Wisconsin, 1875 ***6795.8*** *p227*
Pass, Joshua; America, 1763 ***1220.12*** *p609*
Pass, Samuel; America, 1734 ***1220.12*** *p609*
Pass, Wilhelm; Wisconsin, 1875 ***6795.8*** *p227*
Passalaqua, J.; Louisiana, 1874 ***4981.45*** *p296*
Passavant, Anne; Quebec, 1665 ***4514.3*** *p354*
Passe, Joseph; Colorado, 1886 ***1029.59*** *p72*
Passenger, Jonathan; America, 1744 ***1220.12*** *p609*
Passerum, Marie 10; Port uncertain, 1842 ***778.6*** *p262*
Passerum, Virginie 12; Port uncertain, 1842 ***778.6*** *p262*
Passmore, Mary; Annapolis, MD, 1733 ***1220.12*** *p609*
Passmore, Thomas 50; Ontario, 1871 ***1823.21*** *p291*
Passue, William; St. Johns, N.F., 1825 ***1053.15*** *p6*
Paste, Charles; Ohio, 1809-1852 ***4511.35*** *p39*
Paste, Charles; Ohio, 1809-1852 ***4511.35*** *p40*
Paston, James; America, 1763 ***1220.12*** *p609*
Pastor, Josef; New York, NY, 1867 ***2853.20*** *p105*
Pastureau, Juliet Ballet 28; New Orleans, 1840 ***778.6*** *p262*
Pastureau, Raymond 28; New Orleans, 1840 ***778.6*** *p262*
Patch, John; America, 1773 ***1220.12*** *p609*
Patching, James 66; Ontario, 1871 ***1823.21*** *p291*
Patching, John 33; Ontario, 1871 ***1823.21*** *p291*
Pate, Charity; America, 1742 ***1220.12*** *p609*
Pate, John; America, 1730 ***1220.12*** *p609*
Pateman, Ann; America, 1761 ***1220.12*** *p609*
Patenostre, Nicolas 27; Quebec, 1651 ***9221.17*** *p248*
Paternoster, Catherine; America, 1736 ***1220.12*** *p610*
Paternoster, Joseph; Maryland or Virginia, 1731 ***1220.12*** *p610*
Paters, Edwin 58; Ontario, 1871 ***1823.21*** *p291*
Paterson, Alexander 44; Ontario, 1871 ***1823.21*** *p291*
Paterson, Andrew 60; Ontario, 1871 ***1823.21*** *p291*
Paterson, Donald 63; Ontario, 1871 ***1823.21*** *p291*
Paterson, Duncan 52; Ontario, 1871 ***1823.21*** *p291*
Paterson, Elisabeth 86; Ontario, 1871 ***1823.21*** *p291*
Paterson, Elizabeth 40; Ontario, 1871 ***1823.21*** *p291*
Paterson, George 30; Ontario, 1871 ***1823.21*** *p291*
Paterson, Isabella; America, 1760 ***1220.12*** *p610*
Paterson, Isabella Lawson *SEE* Paterson, Robert
Paterson, Issabella 48; Ontario, 1871 ***1823.21*** *p291*
Paterson, James 36; Ontario, 1871 ***1823.17*** *p131*
Paterson, Jane; America, 1755 ***1220.12*** *p610*
Paterson, John; Cleveland, OH, 1845-1852 ***9722.10*** *p125*
Paterson, John 30; Ontario, 1871 ***1823.21*** *p291*
Paterson, John 58; Ontario, 1871 ***1823.21*** *p291*
Paterson, Margaret 60; Ontario, 1871 ***1823.21*** *p291*
Paterson, Peter; America, 1771 ***1220.12*** *p610*
Paterson, Peter 49; Ontario, 1871 ***1823.21*** *p291*
Paterson, Robert; America, 1741 ***1220.12*** *p610*
Paterson, Robert; Ohio, 1801-1835 ***5024.1*** *p139*
*Wife:*Isabella Lawson
With family
Paterson, Rodger 43; Ontario, 1871 ***1823.21*** *p291*
Paterson, Samuel 50; Ontario, 1871 ***1823.21*** *p291*
Paterson, Susanna; America, 1734 ***1220.12*** *p610*
Paterson, Thomas; America, 1726 ***1220.12*** *p610*
Paterson, Thomas 32; Ontario, 1871 ***1823.21*** *p291*
Paterson, William 37; Ontario, 1871 ***1823.17*** *p131*
Pathen, Margarethe; America, 1880 ***5475.1*** *p302*
Pathick, Thos 18; Ontario, 1871 ***1823.21*** *p291*
Patience, John; America, 1767 ***1220.12*** *p610*
Patience, John; Maryland, 1719 ***1220.12*** *p610*
Patience, William; Maryland, 1719 ***1220.12*** *p610*
Patience, William; Virginia, 1758 ***1220.12*** *p610*
Patin, Eugenia; Philadelphia, 1881 ***8513.31*** *p294*
Patin, Stanislas 28; America, 1846 ***778.6*** *p262*
Patison, Johnathan; Canada, 1774 ***3036.5*** *p40*
Patman, Edward; America, 1753 ***1220.12*** *p610*
Patman, Robert; America, 1754 ***1220.12*** *p610*
Patmore, Benjamin; America, 1769 ***1220.12*** *p610*
Patmore, Benjamin; America, 1775 ***1220.12*** *p610*
Patmore, Joseph Henry 27; Ontario, 1871 ***1823.21*** *p292*
Patmore, Lydia 24; Ontario, 1871 ***1823.21*** *p292*
Paton, Andrew 49; Ontario, 1871 ***1823.17*** *p131*
Paton, George 44; Ontario, 1871 ***1823.17*** *p131*
Paton, George 58; Ontario, 1871 ***1823.17*** *p131*
Paton, James F.; North Carolina, 1792-1862 ***1088.45*** *p26*
Patou, Catherine 21; Quebec, 1662 ***9221.17*** *p491*
Patriarche, Elizabeth Rose; Toronto, 1868 ***9228.50*** *p488*
Patriarche, Philip Charles; Ontario, n.d. ***9228.50*** *p488*
Patriarche, William Heath; Detroit, 1840-1866 ***9228.50*** *p489*
Patriarche, William Philip; Ontario, 1800-1872 ***9228.50*** *p489*
Patrick, Cary 60; Ontario, 1871 ***1823.21*** *p292*
Patrick, Christian 19; Ontario, 1871 ***1823.17*** *p131*
Patrick, George; America, 1727 ***1220.12*** *p610*
Patrick, Isabella; Boston, 1728 ***1642*** *p25*
Patrick, James; North Carolina, 1836 ***1088.45*** *p26*
Patrick, Jemimah 36; Ontario, 1871 ***1823.21*** *p292*
Patrick, Jeremiah Fitch; Boston, 1732 ***1642*** *p44*
Patrick, John 28; Ontario, 1871 ***1823.21*** *p292*
Patrick, John 60; Ontario, 1871 ***1823.21*** *p292*
Patrick, John 64; Ontario, 1871 ***1823.21*** *p292*
Patrick, John P. 37; Ontario, 1871 ***1823.21*** *p292*
Patrick, Leinus 48; Ontario, 1871 ***1823.17*** *p131*
Patrick, Robert 32; South Carolina, 1812 ***3476.30*** *p12*
Patrick, Thomas; America, 1749 ***1220.12*** *p610*
Patrick, Thomas; Boston, 1741 ***1642*** *p45*
Patrickson, Thomas; America, 1740 ***1220.12*** *p610*
Patrill, Joseph; Massachusetts, 1740-1760 ***9228.50*** *p489*
Patschewitz, Ludwig Max; New York, NY, 1900 ***6212.1*** *p13*
Patten, . . .; Newfoundland, n.d. ***9228.50*** *p490*
Patten, Catherine Body *SEE* Patten, James
Patten, James; America, 1685 ***1220.12*** *p610*
Patten, James; Ohio, 1850 ***9228.50*** *p490*
*Wife:*Catherine Body
*Son:*John
Patten, James 29; Ontario, 1871 ***1823.21*** *p292*
Patten, James 58; Ontario, 1871 ***1823.21*** *p292*
Patten, Jane; Died enroute, 1729 ***1220.12*** *p610*
Patten, John *SEE* Patten, James
Patten, Joseph 66; Michigan, 1880 ***4491.39*** *p23*
Patten, Margaret 35; St. John, N.B., 1834 ***6469.7*** *p4*
Patten, Menlagh 40; St. John, N.B., 1834 ***6469.7*** *p4*
Patten, Michael 3 months; St. John, N.B., 1834 ***6469.7*** *p4*
Patten, Thomas 56; Ontario, 1871 ***1823.21*** *p292*
Pattenaude, Jerry; Washington, 1886 ***6015.10*** *p16*
Pattenden, John; America, 1761 ***1220.12*** *p610*
Pattenger, Letitia; America, 1766 ***1220.12*** *p610*
Pattenton, Jonathan 43; Ontario, 1871 ***1823.17*** *p131*
Patterosn, Walter 55; Ontario, 1871 ***1823.17*** *p131*
Patterson, Alexander 30; Ontario, 1871 ***1823.21*** *p292*
Patterson, David 50; Ontario, 1871 ***1823.17*** *p131*
Patterson, David G.; Illinois, 1918 ***6007.60*** *p9*
Patterson, Elizabeth Colden *SEE* Patterson, James
Patterson, George 27; Ontario, 1871 ***1823.21*** *p292*
Patterson, Hanah 12; Ontario, 1871 ***1823.21*** *p292*
Patterson, Hector 70; Ontario, 1871 ***1823.17*** *p131*
Patterson, James; America, 1763 ***1220.12*** *p610*
Patterson, James 27; Ontario, 1871 ***1823.17*** *p131*
Patterson, James 41; Ontario, 1871 ***1823.21*** *p292*
Patterson, James; Philadelphia, 1849 ***8513.31*** *p420*
*Wife:*Elizabeth Colden
Patterson, James 24; Quebec, 1910 ***2897.7*** *p10*
Patterson, James; South Carolina, 1808 ***6155.4*** *p19*
Patterson, Jane; Boston, 1766 ***1642*** *p36*
Patterson, Jane 60; Ontario, 1871 ***1823.21*** *p292*
Patterson, Janet 62; Ontario, 1871 ***1823.21*** *p292*
Patterson, John; America, 1732 ***1220.12*** *p610*
Patterson, John; America, 1740 ***1220.12*** *p610*
Patterson, John; Colorado, 1873 ***1029.59*** *p72*
Patterson, John 34; New York, NY, 1826 ***6178.50*** *p150*
Patterson, John; North Carolina, 1809 ***1088.45*** *p27*
Patterson, John 40; Ontario, 1871 ***1823.21*** *p292*
Patterson, John 43; Ontario, 1871 ***1823.21*** *p292*
Patterson, John 53; Ontario, 1871 ***1823.17*** *p131*
Patterson, Joseph 28; Indiana, 1869-1872 ***9076.20*** *p67*
Patterson, Joseph H. 40; Ontario, 1871 ***1823.17*** *p131*
Patterson, Neil 64; Ontario, 1871 ***1823.17*** *p131*
Patterson, R. S. 31; Ontario, 1871 ***1823.21*** *p292*
Patterson, Robert; America, 1772 ***1220.12*** *p610*
Patterson, Robert; Ohio, 1809-1852 ***4511.35*** *p40*
Patterson, Robert 34; Ontario, 1871 ***1823.21*** *p292*
Patterson, Robert 37; Ontario, 1871 ***1823.21*** *p292*
Patterson, Robert; Philadelphia, 1777 ***8529.30*** *p4A*
Patterson, Robert; Virginia, 1772 ***1220.12*** *p610*
Patterson, Thomas 37; Ontario, 1871 ***1823.21*** *p292*
Patterson, Thomas, Sr. 64; Ontario, 1871 ***1823.21*** *p292*
Patterson, William; America, 1772 ***1220.12*** *p610*
Patterson, William; Boston, 1754 ***1642*** *p47*
Patterson, William; Ontario, 1835 ***3160.1*** *p150*
Patterson, William 45; Ontario, 1871 ***1823.21*** *p292*
Patterson, William 48; Ontario, 1871 ***1823.21*** *p292*
Patterson, William 59; Ontario, 1871 ***1823.21*** *p292*
Patterson, William 60; Ontario, 1871 ***1823.21*** *p292*
Patterson, William 65; Ontario, 1871 ***1823.21*** *p292*
Patterson, William; Washington, 1883 ***2770.40*** *p137*
Patterson, Wm 37; Ontario, 1871 ***1823.21*** *p292*
Patterson, Wm 42; Ontario, 1871 ***1823.17*** *p131*

Pattin, Anne; Barbados, 1663 ***1220.12*** *p610*
Pattin, John; America, 1751 ***1220.12*** *p610*
Pattinson, William; America, 1743 ***1220.12*** *p610*
Pattison, George; Philadelphia, 1777 ***8529.30*** *p7*
Pattison, Isaac 21; Ontario, 1871 ***1823.17*** *p131*
Pattison, Jane; Died enroute, 1725 ***1220.12*** *p610*
Pattison, John; America, 1751 ***1220.12*** *p610*
Pattison, Joseph 70; Ontario, 1871 ***1823.17*** *p131*
Pattison, Mary; America, 1760 ***1220.12*** *p610*
Pattison, Thomas 57; Ontario, 1871 ***1823.17*** *p131*
Pattison, William; America, 1739 ***1220.12*** *p610*
Pattison, William; America, 1767 ***1220.12*** *p610*
Patton, Hugh 46; Ontario, 1871 ***1823.17*** *p131*
Patton, James; North Carolina, 1838 ***1088.45*** *p27*
Patton, John 44; Ontario, 1871 ***1823.21*** *p293*
Patton, Nicholas B.; North Carolina, 1834 ***1088.45*** *p27*
Patton, Robert 41; Ontario, 1871 ***1823.21*** *p293*
Patton, William; North Carolina, 1834 ***1088.45*** *p27*
Pattorell, Joseph; Massachusetts, 1740-1760 ***9228.50*** *p489*
Pattourel, Joseph; Massachusetts, 1740-1760 ***9228.50*** *p489*
Pattrick, Richard; America, 1707 ***1220.12*** *p610*
Pattson, John; America, 1773 ***1220.12*** *p610*
Patty, Charles; Virginia, 1718 ***1220.12*** *p610*
Patty, David; America, 1737 ***1220.12*** *p610*
Patty, John; Virginia, 1771 ***1220.12*** *p610*
Patty, Mary; Boston, 1735 ***1642*** *p44*
Paty, John; America, 1753 ***1220.12*** *p610*
Patyrak, Albert; Detroit, 1930 ***1640.60*** *p76*
Patz, Carl; America, 1867 ***7420.1*** *p261*
Patz, Max Erich Adolph; America, 1871 ***7420.1*** *p292*
Pau, Paul 23; America, 1848 ***778.6*** *p262*
Pauer, Fr.; Valdivia, Chile, 1850 ***1192.4*** *p48*
Paul, Miss; Pennsylvania, 1880 ***5475.1*** *p23*
Paul, Anna Maria Sonnhalter *SEE* Paul, Josef
Paul, Anson 68; Ontario, 1871 ***1823.21*** *p293*
Paul, Benjamin; America, 1753 ***1220.12*** *p610*
Paul, Benjamin; America, 1764 ***1220.12*** *p610*
Paul, Caroline Dorothee; America, 1871 ***7420.1*** *p292*
Paul, Catherine; Quebec, 1668 ***4514.3*** *p354*
Paul, Conrad Heinrich *SEE* Paul, Johann Hermann Heinrich
Paul, Dorothy; America, 1749 ***1220.12*** *p611*
Paul, Dugald 47; Ontario, 1871 ***1823.21*** *p293*
Paul, Duncan 65; Ontario, 1871 ***1823.21*** *p293*
Paul, Ely; America, 1748 ***1220.12*** *p611*
Paul, Engel Marie Charlotte Moller *SEE* Paul, Johann Hermann Heinrich
Paul, Engel Marie Dorothea Pfingsten *SEE* Paul, Johann Heinrich
Paul, Francois 25; Texas, 1848 ***778.6*** *p262*
Paul, Fred; New York, NY, 1880 ***1029.59*** *p72*
Paul, Gabriel; America, 1748 ***1220.12*** *p611*
Paul, Gavin 24; Ontario, 1871 ***1823.17*** *p131*
Paul, Hans Heinrich *SEE* Paul, Johann Hermann Heinrich
Paul, Heinrich; America, 1860 ***7420.1*** *p198*
With wife & 4 daughters
With son 8
Paul, Heinrich; America, 1860 ***7420.1*** *p198*
Paul, Heinrich Conrad; America, 1852 ***7420.1*** *p95*
Paul, Hubert; Wisconsin, 1854-1858 ***1495.20*** *p66*
*Wife:*Marie Josephe Bacleine
*Son:*Joseph
Paul, J. M.; California, 1868 ***1131.61*** *p90*
Paul, Jacob 33; America, 1846 ***778.6*** *p262*
Paul, Jakob *SEE* Paul, Josef
Paul, James 50; Ontario, 1871 ***1823.17*** *p131*
Paul, James E. 66; Ontario, 1871 ***1823.17*** *p131*
Paul, Johann *SEE* Paul, Josef
Paul, Johann Conrad *SEE* Paul, Johann Hermann Heinrich
Paul, Johann Conrad; California, 1877 ***7420.1*** *p309*
Paul, Johann Heinrich; America, 1867 ***7420.1*** *p261*
With mother
Paul, Johann Heinrich; America, 1884 ***7420.1*** *p344*
*Wife:*Engel Marie Dorothea Pfingsten
*Son:*Johann Heinrich Conrad
Paul, Johann Heinrich Conrad; America, 1866 ***7420.1*** *p247*
Paul, Johann Heinrich Conrad *SEE* Paul, Johann Heinrich
Paul, Johann Hermann Heinrich; America, 1845 ***7420.1*** *p38*
*Wife:*Engel Marie Charlotte Moller
*Son:*Johann Conrad
*Son:*Hans Heinrich
*Son:*Conrad Heinrich
*Son:*Johann Philipp
Paul, Johann Philipp *SEE* Paul, Johann Hermann Heinrich
Paul, John; America, 1749 ***1220.12*** *p611*
Paul, John 41; Ontario, 1871 ***1823.21*** *p293*
Paul, John 47; Ontario, 1871 ***1823.17*** *p131*
Paul, John Heinrich; Illinois, 1852 ***6079.1*** *p11*
Paul, Jonathan; America, 1750 ***1220.12*** *p611*
Paul, Josef *SEE* Paul, Josef
Paul, Josef 42; America, 1874 ***5475.1*** *p78*
*Wife:*Anna Maria Sonnhalter
*Son:*Jakob
*Son:*Josef
*Son:*Johann
*Son:*Peter
Paul, Joseph; America, 1685 ***1220.12*** *p611*
Paul, Joseph 25; Ontario, 1871 ***1823.21*** *p293*
Paul, Joseph *SEE* Paul, Hubert
Paul, Malcolm 62; Ontario, 1871 ***1823.21*** *p293*
Paul, Margaret; America, 1715 ***1220.12*** *p611*
Paul, Margaret; Barbados or Jamaica, 1684 ***1220.12*** *p611*
Paul, Marie Josephe Bacleine *SEE* Paul, Hubert
Paul, Mary; America, 1759 ***1220.12*** *p611*
Paul, Mary; Annapolis, MD, 1723 ***1220.12*** *p611*
Paul, N.; America, 1852 ***7420.1*** *p95*
Paul, Peter *SEE* Paul, Josef
Paul, Philip; Ohio, 1809-1852 ***4511.35*** *p40*
Paul, Rawson; Annapolis, MD, 1725 ***1220.12*** *p611*
Paul, Richard; America, 1685 ***1220.12*** *p611*
Paul, Robert; America, 1685 ***1220.12*** *p611*
Paul, Robert 24; Ontario, 1871 ***1823.21*** *p293*
Paul, Samuel; America, 1685 ***1220.12*** *p611*
Paul, Samuel; America, 1774 ***1220.12*** *p611*
Paul, Samuel 61; Ontario, 1871 ***1823.21*** *p293*
Paul, Sophie; St. Louis, 1885 ***5475.1*** *p243*
Paul, Wilhelm; America, n.d. ***8115.12*** *p327*
Paul, William; America, 1767 ***1220.12*** *p611*
Paul, William; America, 1771 ***1220.12*** *p611*
Paul, William; Annapolis, MD, 1758 ***1220.12*** *p611*
Paul, William 58; Ontario, 1871 ***1823.21*** *p293*
Pauldock, William; America, 1764 ***1220.12*** *p611*
Pauley, John 14; Quebec, 1870 ***8364.32*** *p25*
Pauli, Daniel 47; New Castle, DE, 1817-1818 ***90.20*** *p153*
Paulin, Mr. 22; America, 1841 ***778.6*** *p262*
Paulin, Eva 48; Minnesota, 1925 ***2769.54*** *p1379*
Paulin, Jean 25; Quebec, 1658 ***9221.17*** *p385*
Pauline, Ms. 35; New Orleans, 1848 ***778.6*** *p262*
Paull, Mary; America, 1678 ***1220.12*** *p611*
Paull, Peter; Barbados or Jamaica, 1697 ***1220.12*** *p611*
Paulo, Catherine; Quebec, 1663 ***4514.3*** *p354*
Paulo, Marie; Quebec, 1600-1663 ***4514.3*** *p354*
Pauls, C. Peter; Valdivia, Chile, 1852 ***1192.4*** *p53*
Pauls, David 10; Portland, ME, 1911 ***970.38*** *p80*
Pauls, Elisabeth 36; Portland, ME, 1911 ***970.38*** *p80*
Pauls, Jakob 2; Portland, ME, 1911 ***970.38*** *p80*
Pauls, Jakob 28; Portland, ME, 1911 ***970.38*** *p80*
Pauls, Mathias 37; America, 1843 ***5475.1*** *p294*
Paulsen, Henry; Nebraska, 1905 ***3004.30*** *p46*
Paulson, Alfred; Cleveland, OH, 1903-1904 ***9722.10*** *p125*
Paulson, Anna; St. Paul, MN, 1895 ***1865.50*** *p104*
Paulson, Aron; Cleveland, OH, 1902-1904 ***9722.10*** *p125*
Paulson, Cecilia *SEE* Paulson, Johan
Paulson, Eddie; Minnesota, 1891-1893 ***1865.50*** *p104*
Paulson, Emil; Cleveland, OH, 1887 ***9722.10*** *p125*
Paulson, Francis; America, 1743 ***1220.12*** *p611*
Paulson, Gust; Cleveland, OH, 1895-1898 ***9722.10*** *p125*
Paulson, Hans Frederick; Iowa, 1888 ***1211.15*** *p18*
Paulson, Hilda Theresia *SEE* Paulson, Johan
Paulson, Johan; Cleveland, OH, 1881-1891 ***9722.10*** *p125*
*Wife:*Cecilia
*Child:*Hilda Theresia
Paulson, John; Illinois, 1861 ***4487.25*** *p69*
Paulson, John; Iowa, 1899 ***1211.15*** *p18*
Paulson, Paul Laurits; Iowa, 1896 ***1211.15*** *p18*
Paulson, Rasmus M.; Iowa, 1898 ***1211.15*** *p18*
Paulsson, Emil; Cleveland, OH, 1887 ***9722.10*** *p125*
Paulsson, Olof; New York, NY, 1844 ***6412.40*** *p148*
Paulus, Agathe 1; America, 1746 ***778.6*** *p263*
Paulus, Anna *SEE* Paulus, Mathias
Paulus, Anna Stroh 39 *SEE* Paulus, Jakob
Paulus, Anton 8; America, 1746 ***778.6*** *p263*
Paulus, Anton 52; America, 1746 ***778.6*** *p263*
Paulus, Barbara Schneider *SEE* Paulus, Mathias
Paulus, Barbara 42; America, 1746 ***778.6*** *p263*
Paulus, Jakob; America, 1880 ***5475.1*** *p554*
*Wife:*Anna Stroh
*Son:*Nikolaus
*Son:*Johann
*Son:*Peter
Paulus, Jakob *SEE* Paulus, Mathias
Paulus, Johann *SEE* Paulus, Nikolaus
Paulus, Johann *SEE* Paulus, Jakob
Paulus, Johann *SEE* Paulus, Mathias
Paulus, Joseph 14; America, 1746 ***778.6*** *p263*
Paulus, Katharina *SEE* Paulus, Nikolaus
Paulus, Margarethe *SEE* Paulus, Nikolaus
Paulus, Margarethe Straesser 29 *SEE* Paulus, Nikolaus
Paulus, Marie 7; America, 1746 ***778.6*** *p263*
Paulus, Mathias *SEE* Paulus, Mathias
Paulus, Mathias; America, 1881 ***5475.1*** *p511*
*Wife:*Barbara Schneider
*Son:*Peter
*Son:*Johann
*Son:*Mathias
*Son:*Jakob
*Daughter:*Anna
Paulus, Nikolaus; America, 1865 ***5475.1*** *p49*
*Wife:*Margarethe Straesser
*Son:*Peter
*Son:*Johann
*Daughter:*Margarethe
*Daughter:*Katharina
Paulus, Nikolaus *SEE* Paulus, Jakob
Paulus, Othellia 5; America, 1746 ***778.6*** *p263*
Paulus, Othellia 39; America, 1746 ***778.6*** *p263*
Paulus, Peter *SEE* Paulus, Nikolaus
Paulus, Peter *SEE* Paulus, Jakob
Paulus, Peter *SEE* Paulus, Mathias
Paulus Steffan, Jean 39; America, 1746 ***778.6*** *p263*
Pauly, Anna *SEE* Pauly, Johann
Pauly, Anna Lahr *SEE* Pauly, Johann
Pauly, Anna *SEE* Pauly, Johann
Pauly, Anna Lahr *SEE* Pauly, Johann
Pauly, F. Joseph; Illinois, 1858 ***6079.1*** *p11*
Pauly, Jakob *SEE* Pauly, Johann
Pauly, Jakob 24; America, 1873 ***5475.1*** *p328*
Pauly, Johann; America, 1873 ***5475.1*** *p322*
*Wife:*Anna Lahr
*Son:*Michel
*Daughter:*Anna
*Son:*Jakob
Pauly, Johann 53; America, 1873 ***5475.1*** *p328*
*Wife:*Anna Lahr
*Daughter:*Anna
Pauly, Lina; Baltimore, 1899 ***5475.1*** *p20*
*Daughter:*Dorothea
Pauly, Michel *SEE* Pauly, Johann
Pauly, Simon Joh.; Colorado, 1896 ***1029.59*** *p72*
Pauminst, Pierre Eugene 23; New Orleans, 1848 ***778.6*** *p263*
Pauntin, John; Annapolis, MD, 1725 ***1220.12*** *p611*
Pausenberger, Theodor; Valdivia, Chile, 1850 ***1192.4*** *p49*
Pauson, Mary; America, 1686 ***1220.12*** *p611*
Pauvret, Mrs. 34; Texas, 1843 ***778.6*** *p263*
Pauvret, Jean Claude 42; Texas, 1843 ***778.6*** *p263*
Pavageaut, Marie; Quebec, 1669 ***4514.3*** *p328*
Pavaillon, Antoine; Quebec, 1642 ***9221.17*** *p120*
Pavek, Jan; Minnesota, 1863 ***2853.20*** *p267*
Pavek, Josef; Wisconsin, 1856 ***2853.20*** *p345*
Pavett, Joseph; America, 1748 ***1220.12*** *p611*
Pavey, Elijah 26; Ontario, 1871 ***1823.21*** *p293*
Pavie, Marie 21; Quebec, 1657 ***9221.17*** *p365*
Pavier, John, Jr.; America, 1765 ***1220.12*** *p611*
Pavillon, Henri; Quebec, 1654 ***9221.17*** *p315*
Paviot, Marie; Quebec, 1667 ***4514.3*** *p354*
Paviour, Benjamin; America, 1734 ***1220.12*** *p611*
Paviour, John; Virginia, 1732 ***1220.12*** *p611*
Pavitt, Mary Ann 36; Ontario, 1871 ***1823.21*** *p293*
Pavlicek, Ignac; Texas, 1860 ***2853.20*** *p70*
Pavlicek, Martin; Texas, 1860 ***2853.20*** *p70*
Pavlik, Frantisek; Nebraska, 1871 ***2853.20*** *p194*
Pavlikova, Bozena; Chicago, 1898 ***2853.20*** *p418*
Pavy, Mr. 25; America, 1842 ***778.6*** *p263*
Pavy, Edwin 29; Ontario, 1871 ***1823.21*** *p293*
Pawelek, John; Detroit, 1929 ***1640.55*** *p116*
Pawlak, Josif 37; New York, NY, 1894 ***6512.1*** *p184*
Pawlet, Jane; America, 1680 ***1220.12*** *p611*
Pawlet, Munday; America, 1764 ***1220.12*** *p611*
Pawley, George; America, 1763 ***1220.12*** *p611*
Pawlowska, Martha; Wisconsin, 1899 ***6795.8*** *p61*
Pawlowski, Mary *SEE* Pawlowski, Mike
Pawlowski, Mike; Baltimore, 1886 ***6015.15*** *p13*
*Wife:*Mary
Pawlowski, Paul; Detroit, 1929-1930 ***6214.5*** *p70*
Paxford, Richard; America, 1719 ***1220.12*** *p611*
Paxman, Adam 44; Ontario, 1871 ***1823.21*** *p293*
Paxman, John; America, 1774 ***1220.12*** *p611*
Paxton, Charles; America, 1749 ***1220.12*** *p611*
Paxton, Daniel; Annapolis, MD, 1725 ***1220.12*** *p611*
Paxton, Elizabeth; America, 1751 ***1220.12*** *p611*
Paxton, Richrd; North Carolina, 1810 ***1088.45*** *p27*
Paxton, Thomas; America, 1709 ***1220.12*** *p611*
Paxton, Thomas; North Carolina, 1853 ***1088.45*** *p27*
Paxton, William; America, 1766 ***1220.12*** *p611*
Paxton, William; Charles Town, SC, 1719 ***1220.12*** *p611*
Paxton, William 66; Ontario, 1871 ***1823.21*** *p293*
Payan, Marie-Marthe; Quebec, 1670 ***4514.3*** *p354*
Paybody, John 30; Ontario, 1871 ***1823.17*** *p131*
Payce, James; America, 1752 ***1220.12*** *p599*
Payen, Hypolite 20; New Orleans, 1840 ***778.6*** *p263*

Payen deNoyan, Pierre; Quebec, 1683-1688 ***2314.30*** *p168*
Payen deNoyan, Pierre; Quebec, 1687 ***2314.30*** *p192*
Payn, Bethia *SEE* Payn, John
Payn, John; America, 1737 ***1220.12*** *p612*
Payn, John; Boston, 1712-1713 ***9228.50*** *p490*
*Wife:*Bethia
Payn, Joshua; Connecticut, 1737 ***9228.50*** *p490*
Payne, Ambrose; America, 1774 ***1220.12*** *p611*
Payne, Benjamin; America, 1771 ***1220.12*** *p611*
Payne, Burry; America, 1770 ***1220.12*** *p611*
Payne, Charles 33; Ontario, 1871 ***1823.21*** *p293*
Payne, Constabella; Annapolis, MD, 1736 ***1220.12*** *p612*
Payne, Edward; America, 1760 ***1220.12*** *p612*
Payne, Edward 44; Ontario, 1871 ***1823.21*** *p293*
Payne, Elizabeth; America, 1771 ***1220.12*** *p612*
Payne, Elizabeth; Annapolis, MD, 1722 ***1220.12*** *p612*
Payne, Elizabeth; Barbados, 1664 ***1220.12*** *p612*
Payne, George; America, 1769 ***1220.12*** *p612*
Payne, Henry; Barbados, 1662 ***1220.12*** *p612*
Payne, Jacob 54; Ontario, 1871 ***1823.21*** *p293*
Payne, James; America, 1685 ***1220.12*** *p612*
Payne, Jane; America, 1749 ***1220.12*** *p612*
Payne, John; America, 1758 ***1220.12*** *p612*
Payne, John 22; Ontario, 1871 ***1823.21*** *p293*
Payne, John; Virginia, 1732 ***1220.12*** *p612*
Payne, Joseph 34; Ontario, 1871 ***1823.17*** *p131*
Payne, Joshua 60; Ontario, 1871 ***1823.17*** *p131*
Payne, Lydia 40; Ontario, 1871 ***1823.21*** *p293*
Payne, Martha; America, 1747 ***1220.12*** *p612*
Payne, Mary; America, 1743 ***1220.12*** *p612*
Payne, Mary 63; Ontario, 1871 ***1823.21*** *p293*
Payne, Richard; America, 1767 ***1220.12*** *p612*
Payne, Robert; America, 1732 ***1220.12*** *p612*
Payne, Robert; America, 1774 ***1220.12*** *p612*
Payne, Robert 24; Ontario, 1871 ***1823.21*** *p293*
Payne, Samuel; America, 1750 ***1220.12*** *p612*
Payne, Thomas; America, 1699 ***1220.12*** *p612*
Payne, Thomas; America, 1737 ***1220.12*** *p612*
Payne, Thomas; Annapolis, MD, 1721 ***1220.12*** *p612*
Payne, Thomas 30; Ontario, 1871 ***1823.21*** *p293*
Payne, Thomas 18; Quebec, 1870 ***8364.32*** *p25*
Payne, Thos; New Orleans, 1851 ***7242.30*** *p152*
Payne, William; America, 1750 ***1220.12*** *p613*
Payne, William; America, 1765 ***1220.12*** *p613*
Payne, William; America, 1771 ***1220.12*** *p613*
Payne, William; America, 1773 ***1220.12*** *p613*
Payne, William; Virginia, 1721 ***1220.12*** *p613*
Payon, H. 55; New Orleans, 1844 ***778.6*** *p263*
Pays, Angelina 24; Port uncertain, 1843 ***778.6*** *p263*
Pays, Armand 18; Port uncertain, 1843 ***778.6*** *p263*
Pays, Jean Marie 31; New Orleans, 1842 ***778.6*** *p263*
Paysant, Louis; Nova Scotia, 1748-1749 ***9228.50*** *p490*
Paysley, Philip 68; Ontario, 1871 ***1823.21*** *p293*
Payson, John; America, 1691 ***1220.12*** *p613*
Payson, Louis; Nova Scotia, 1748-1749 ***9228.50*** *p490*
Payson, Millisa 26; Ontario, 1871 ***1823.21*** *p293*
Payton, Edward; America, 1749 ***1220.12*** *p613*
Pazdral, Vaclav; Chicago, 1892 ***2853.20*** *p66*
Pazet, C. 25; New Orleans, 1834 ***1002.51*** *p111*
Pazet, L. 18; New Orleans, 1834 ***1002.51*** *p111*
Pazour, Josef; South Dakota, 1881 ***2853.20*** *p250*
Peabody, Hannah Gallichan *SEE* Peabody, Samuel
Peabody, Samuel; New Brunswick, 1773-1822 ***9228.50*** *p234*
*Wife:*Hannah Gallichan
Peace, Charles; America, 1753 ***1220.12*** *p613*
Peace, Edward; America, 1764 ***1220.12*** *p613*
Peace, John; America, 1742 ***1220.12*** *p613*
Peace, John 56; Ontario, 1871 ***1823.21*** *p293*
Peach, Ann; America, 1745 ***1220.12*** *p613*
Peach, Henry; Colorado, 1873 ***1029.59*** *p72*
Peach, Joseph; Antigua (Antego), 1742 ***1220.12*** *p613*
Peach, Samuel; America, 1750 ***1220.12*** *p613*
Peach, William; Died enroute, 1725 ***1220.12*** *p613*
Peacham, Mary; America, 1740 ***1220.12*** *p613*
Peachey, Josiah 45; Ontario, 1871 ***1823.21*** *p293*
Peachy, Daniel; America, 1753 ***1220.12*** *p613*
Peackle, Michael; North Carolina, 1710 ***3629.40*** *p6*
Peacock, Ann J. 36; Ontario, 1871 ***1823.21*** *p293*
Peacock, Charles 39; Ontario, 1871 ***1823.21*** *p293*
Peacock, Charles 60; Ontario, 1871 ***1823.21*** *p293*
Peacock, Edward; America, 1752 ***1220.12*** *p613*
Peacock, Elizabeth; America, 1742 ***1220.12*** *p613*
Peacock, Elizabeth; America, 1757 ***1220.12*** *p613*
Peacock, Henry 31; Ontario, 1871 ***1823.21*** *p293*
Peacock, Jeffery; America, 1728 ***1220.12*** *p613*
Peacock, Jeremiah; America, 1761 ***1220.12*** *p613*
Peacock, John; America, 1765 ***1220.12*** *p613*
Peacock, John; America, 1773 ***1220.12*** *p613*
Peacock, John; Quebec, 1870 ***8364.32*** *p25*
Peacock, Mary; Annapolis, MD, 1736 ***1220.12*** *p613*
Peacock, Richard; America, 1751 ***1220.12*** *p613*
Peacock, Richard; Died enroute, 1730 ***1220.12*** *p613*
Peacock, Stephen; America, 1740 ***1220.12*** *p613*
Peacock, Thomas; America, 1754 ***1220.12*** *p613*
Peacock, Thomas; America, 1756 ***1220.12*** *p613*
Peacock, William; America, 1720 ***1220.12*** *p613*
Peacock, William; America, 1752 ***1220.12*** *p613*
Peacock, William; America, 1754 ***1220.12*** *p613*
Peacocke, Edward; America, 1673 ***1220.12*** *p613*
Peacocke, William; Jamaica, 1662 ***1220.12*** *p613*
Peacod, Richard; Virginia, 1736 ***1220.12*** *p613*
Pead, Joseph; America, 1766 ***1220.12*** *p617*
Peaden, John 31; Ontario, 1871 ***1823.21*** *p293*
Peadle, Richard; America, 1770 ***1220.12*** *p613*
Peak, Daniel; America, 1773 ***1220.12*** *p613*
Peak, Edwin 16; Quebec, 1870 ***8364.32*** *p25*
Peak, Frances; America, 1753 ***1220.12*** *p613*
Peak, Jane; America, 1722 ***1220.12*** *p613*
Peak, Samuel 14; Quebec, 1870 ***8364.32*** *p25*
Peak, Sarah; America, 1749 ***1220.12*** *p614*
Peake, Dorothy; America, 1761 ***1220.12*** *p613*
Peake, Elizabeth; Virginia, 1732 ***1220.12*** *p613*
Peake, George; America, 1759 ***1220.12*** *p613*
Peake, James; Annapolis, MD, 1733 ***1220.12*** *p613*
Peake, John; America, 1751 ***1220.12*** *p613*
Peake, Rebecca; America, 1740 ***1220.12*** *p614*
Peake, Richard; Virginia, 1736 ***1220.12*** *p614*
Peake, Samuel; America, 1767 ***1220.12*** *p614*
Peake, Thomas; America, 1745 ***1220.12*** *p614*
Peake, Thomas; America, 1767 ***1220.12*** *p614*
Peake, Thomas; Barbados, 1663 ***1220.12*** *p614*
Peake, William; America, 1740 ***1220.12*** *p614*
Peal, George; America, 1724 ***1220.12*** *p617*
Peale, Charles; Virginia, 1736 ***1220.12*** *p617*
Peale, Edward; America, 1775 ***1220.12*** *p617*
Peale, James; America, 1752 ***1220.12*** *p617*
Pean deLivaudiere, Jacques-Hugues; Quebec, 1698 ***2314.30*** *p169*
Pean deLivaudiere, Jacques-Hugues; Quebec, 1698 ***2314.30*** *p192*
Peane, Catherine 71; Ontario, 1871 ***1823.21*** *p293*
Pearce, Abram; Virginia, 1734 ***1220.12*** *p614*
Pearce, Ada; Rhode Island, 1888 ***9228.50*** *p485*
Pearce, Benjamin; America, 1773 ***1220.12*** *p614*
Pearce, Charles; America, 1755 ***1220.12*** *p614*
Pearce, Charles; America, 1764 ***1220.12*** *p614*
Pearce, Edward; America, 1771 ***1220.12*** *p614*
Pearce, Edward; Colorado, 1902 ***1029.59*** *p72*
Pearce, Edward; Michigan, 1888 ***1029.59*** *p72*
Pearce, Elizabeth; America, 1730 ***1220.12*** *p614*
Pearce, Elizabeth; America, 1733 ***1220.12*** *p614*
Pearce, Fortunatus; America, 1675 ***1220.12*** *p614*
Pearce, Frederick 26; Ontario, 1871 ***1823.17*** *p131*
Pearce, George 20; Ontario, 1871 ***1823.17*** *p131*
Pearce, George 34; Ontario, 1871 ***1823.21*** *p293*
Pearce, Gilbert; America, 1764 ***1220.12*** *p614*
Pearce, Henry; America, 1699 ***1220.12*** *p614*
Pearce, Henry; Colorado, 1894 ***1029.59*** *p72*
Pearce, Henry; Michigan, 1888 ***1029.59*** *p72*
Pearce, Henry 19; Ontario, 1871 ***1823.21*** *p293*
Pearce, Isaac; New York, 1777 ***8529.30*** *p15*
Pearce, James; America, 1760 ***1220.12*** *p614*
Pearce, James; America, 1770 ***1220.12*** *p614*
Pearce, James 25; Ontario, 1871 ***1823.21*** *p293*
Pearce, Jane; Annapolis, MD, 1722 ***1220.12*** *p614*
Pearce, Jane; Annapolis, MD, 1725 ***1220.12*** *p614*
Pearce, John; America, 1724 ***1220.12*** *p614*
Pearce, John; America, 1740 ***1220.12*** *p615*
Pearce, John; America, 1752 ***1220.12*** *p615*
Pearce, John; America, 1755 ***1220.12*** *p615*
Pearce, John; America, 1772 ***1220.12*** *p615*
Pearce, John; Antigua (Antego), 1743 ***1220.12*** *p615*
Pearce, John; North Carolina, 1847 ***1088.45*** *p27*
Pearce, Joseph; America, 1775 ***1220.12*** *p615*
Pearce, Mary; America, 1739 ***1220.12*** *p615*
Pearce, Mary; Annapolis, MD, 1725 ***1220.12*** *p615*
Pearce, Morrice; America, 1765 ***1220.12*** *p615*
Pearce, Richard; America, 1732 ***1220.12*** *p615*
Pearce, Richard; America, 1749 ***1220.12*** *p615*
Pearce, Richard; America, 1772 ***1220.12*** *p615*
Pearce, Richard; Barbados, 1671 ***1220.12*** *p615*
Pearce, Richard; Virginia, 1741 ***1220.12*** *p615*
Pearce, Robert; America, 1685 ***1220.12*** *p615*
Pearce, Robert; America, 1725 ***1220.12*** *p615*
Pearce, Robert; Annapolis, MD, 1725 ***1220.12*** *p615*
Pearce, Robert G.; Illinois, 1834-1900 ***6020.5*** *p132*
Pearce, Sarah; America, 1752 ***1220.12*** *p615*
Pearce, Thomas; America, 1733 ***1220.12*** *p615*
Pearce, Thomas; America, 1761 ***1220.12*** *p615*
Pearce, Thomas; America, 1766 ***1220.12*** *p615*
Pearce, Thomas; America, 1774 ***1220.12*** *p615*
Pearce, Thomas; Annapolis, MD, 1735 ***1220.12*** *p615*
Pearce, Thomas; Barbados or Jamaica, 1700 ***1220.12*** *p615*
Pearce, Thomas; Colorado, 1888 ***1029.59*** *p72*
Pearce, Thomas; Colorado, 1888 ***1029.59*** *p73*
Pearce, Thomas; Colorado, 1897 ***1029.59*** *p73*
Pearce, Thomas 9; Ontario, 1871 ***1823.21*** *p294*
Pearce, Thomas 24; Ontario, 1871 ***1823.21*** *p293*
Pearce, Thomas 38; Ontario, 1871 ***1823.21*** *p293*
Pearce, Thomas; Washington, 1884 ***2770.40*** *p193*
Pearce, William; America, 1725 ***1220.12*** *p615*
Pearce, William; America, 1771 ***1220.12*** *p616*
Pearce, William; Barbados or Jamaica, 1685 ***1220.12*** *p615*
Pearce, William; Charles Town, SC, 1719 ***1220.12*** *p615*
Pearce, William 32; Ontario, 1871 ***1823.21*** *p294*
Pearce, William, The Elder; America, 1767 ***1220.12*** *p616*
Pearce, William, The Younger; America, 1767 ***1220.12*** *p616*
Pearce, William T. 41; Ontario, 1871 ***1823.21*** *p294*
Pearcehouse, Thomas; Virginia, 1773 ***1220.12*** *p616*
Pearcey, Ann; America, 1735 ***1220.12*** *p616*
Pearcey, Charles; America, 1772 ***1220.12*** *p616*
Pearciball, Mary; America, 1746 ***1220.12*** *p616*
Pearkey, Mary; America, 1739 ***1220.12*** *p616*
Pearl, John; Ohio, 1809-1852 ***4511.35*** *p40*
Pearles, Uriah; America, 1754 ***1220.12*** *p616*
Pearless, Samuel; America, 1741 ***1220.12*** *p618*
Pearmain, Edward P.; Ohio, 1835 ***2763.1*** *p21*
Pears, Elizabeth; Barbados, 1702 ***1220.12*** *p614*
Pearse, Andrew; America, 1751 ***1220.12*** *p614*
Pearse, Ann; America, 1739 ***1220.12*** *p614*
Pearse, Edward; America, 1748 ***1220.12*** *p614*
Pearse, George; America, 1752 ***1220.12*** *p614*
Pearse, John; America, 1732 ***1220.12*** *p615*
Pearse, John; America, 1742 ***1220.12*** *p615*
Pearse, John; America, 1743 ***1220.12*** *p615*
Pearse, John; Barbados, 1669 ***1220.12*** *p614*
Pearse, John; Virginia, 1731 ***1220.12*** *p614*
Pearse, Mary; America, 1726 ***1220.12*** *p615*
Pearse, Peter; America, 1745 ***1220.12*** *p615*
Pearse, Philip; America, 1765 ***1220.12*** *p615*
Pearse, Richard; America, 1663 ***1220.12*** *p615*
Pearse, Robert; America, 1754 ***1220.12*** *p615*
Pearse, Sarah; America, 1735 ***1220.12*** *p615*
Pearse, William; America, 1732 ***1220.12*** *p616*
Pearse, William; America, 1737 ***1220.12*** *p616*
Pearse, William; Virginia, 1723 ***1220.12*** *p615*
Pearsey, Henry; Rappahannock, VA, 1728 ***1220.12*** *p616*
Pearslow, John; America, 1769 ***1220.12*** *p616*
Pearson, Adolph; New York, 1896 ***1766.20*** *p14*
Pearson, Adolph Fr. *SEE* Pearson, John
Pearson, Alof; Iowa, 1915 ***1211.15*** *p18*
Pearson, Ambrose; America, 1753 ***1220.12*** *p616*
Pearson, Ann; America, 1758 ***1220.12*** *p616*
Pearson, Charles; America, 1755 ***1220.12*** *p616*
Pearson, Charles John *SEE* Pearson, John
Pearson, Christina Charlotte Andersdotter *SEE* Pearson, John
Pearson, Dorah 35; Ontario, 1871 ***1823.21*** *p294*
Pearson, Edward; America, 1768 ***1220.12*** *p616*
Pearson, Francis; America, 1739 ***1220.12*** *p616*
Pearson, George; America, 1730 ***1220.12*** *p616*
Pearson, George 43; Ontario, 1871 ***1823.17*** *p131*
Pearson, Hannah; Allegheny Co., PA, 1884-1887 ***1865.50*** *p44*
Pearson, Henry; Pittsburgh, 1882-1885 ***1865.50*** *p104*
Pearson, Hugh; America, 1732 ***1220.12*** *p616*
Pearson, James; America, 1758 ***1220.12*** *p616*
Pearson, James; America, 1775 ***1220.12*** *p616*
Pearson, James; Barbados, 1688 ***1220.12*** *p616*
Pearson, James 31; Ontario, 1871 ***1823.21*** *p294*
Pearson, Johanna Maria Hansdotter *SEE* Pearson, Martin
Pearson, John; America, 1722 ***1220.12*** *p616*
Pearson, John; America, 1739 ***1220.12*** *p616*
Pearson, John; America, 1747 ***1220.12*** *p616*
Pearson, John; America, 1751 ***1220.12*** *p616*
Pearson, John; America, 1752 ***1220.12*** *p616*
Pearson, John; America, 1755 ***1220.12*** *p616*
Pearson, John; America, 1766 ***1220.12*** *p616*
Pearson, John; Kansas, 1868 ***777.40*** *p14*
*Wife:*Christina Charlotte Andersdotter
*Son:*Charles John
*Son:*Adolph Fr.
Pearson, John William; Washington, 1885 ***2770.40*** *p194*
Pearson, Joseph; America, 1766 ***1220.12*** *p616*
Pearson, Joseph; South Carolina, 1813 ***3208.30*** *p18*
Pearson, Joseph; South Carolina, 1813 ***3208.30*** *p31*
Pearson, Joseph 40; South Carolina, 1812 ***3476.30*** *p12*
Pearson, Lizzie; Minnesota, 1900-1901 ***1865.50*** *p104*
Pearson, Martin; Kansas, 1868-1869 ***777.40*** *p7*
*Wife:*Johanna Maria Hansdotter
*Daughter:*Melinda
*Daughter:*Wilhelmina
Pearson, Mary Christina; Kansas, 1857-1878 ***777.40*** *p7*
Pearson, Matilda A.; Kansas, 1853-1875 ***777.40*** *p7*

Pearson, Matthew; America, 1751 *1220.12* p616
Pearson, Melinda SEE Pearson, Martin
Pearson, Nathaniel; America, 1752 *1220.12* p617
Pearson, Nellie; Pittsburgh, 1884-1886 *1865.50* p91
Pearson, Per J.; Washington, 1889 *2770.40* p80
Pearson, Peter; Kansas, 1869-1870 *777.40* p9
Pearson, Richard John; America, 1963 *9228.50* p647
Pearson, Robert; America, 1678 *1220.12* p617
Pearson, Robert; Barbados, 1666 *1220.12* p617
Pearson, Samuel 36; Ontario, 1871 *1823.21* p294
Pearson, Sarah; Barbados, 1683 *1220.12* p617
Pearson, Sarah 50; Ontario, 1871 *1823.21* p294
Pearson, Soan; Colorado, 1891 *1029.59* p73
Pearson, Swan; Colorado, 1891 *1029.59* p73
Pearson, Temple; America, 1760 *1220.12* p617
Pearson, Thomas; America, 1740 *1220.12* p617
Pearson, Thomas; America, 1775 *1220.12* p617
Pearson, Thomas 35; Ontario, 1871 *1823.21* p294
Pearson, Thomas 51; Ontario, 1871 *1823.21* p294
Pearson, Thomas 58; Ontario, 1871 *1823.21* p294
Pearson, Wilhelmina SEE Pearson, Martin
Pearson, William; America, 1768 *1220.12* p617
Pearson, William; Louisiana, 1841-1844 *4981.45* p211
Peart, John; America, 1758 *1220.12* p617
Peart, Thomas; America, 1752 *1220.12* p617
Peasant, Dedereux; Barbados or Jamaica, 1699 *1220.12* p617
Pease, John; America, 1756 *1220.12* p617
Peasley, Robert; Ontario, 1871 *1823.21* p294
Peat, James 28; Ontario, 1871 *1823.17* p131
Peat, Richard Denton; America, 1754 *1220.12* p617
Peate, John; America, 1752 *1220.12* p617
Peate, William; Barbados, 1664 *1220.12* p617
Peate, William; Barbados or Jamaica, 1690 *1220.12* p617
Peate, William; Virginia, 1727 *1220.12* p617
Peaten, John; Annapolis, MD, 1722 *1220.12* p617
Peates, William; America, 1726 *1220.12* p617
Peattie, Robert 45; Ontario, 1871 *1823.17* p131
Peattie, William 62; Ontario, 1871 *1823.17* p131
Peaty, Thomas; America, 1742 *1220.12* p617
Peaud, Benoit 24; America, 1842 *778.6* p263
Peaverley, John; Maryland, 1732 *1220.12* p624
Peavey, Robert 37; Ontario, 1871 *1823.21* p294
Peavier Family ; Boston, 1722 *9228.50* p509
Pebbler, Dixon 33; Ontario, 1871 *1823.21* p294
Pebody, John; Virginia, 1773 *1220.12* p613
Pebus, Katharina 34; Galveston, TX, 1844 *3967.10* p370
Pebus, Wendelin 46; Galveston, TX, 1844 *3967.10* p370
Pebworth, Mary; America, 1747 *1220.12* p617
Pebworth, Matthew; America, 1720 *1220.12* p617
Pebworth, Robert; America, 1736 *1220.12* p617
Pecaudy deContrecoeur, Antoine; Quebec, 1665 *2314.30* p167
Pecaudy deContrecoeur, Antoine; Quebec, 1665 *2314.30* p192
Peccard, Henry; Washington, 1889 *2770.40* p80
Pech, Gustaw 24; Portland, ME, 1911 *970.38* p80
Pech, Harris B.; Washington, 1886 *2770.40* p195
Pech, Louisa 21; Portland, ME, 1911 *970.38* p80
Pechan, Josef; South Dakota, 1850-1910 *2853.20* p246
Pechardie, Pierre H. 21; Texas, 1848 *778.6* p263
Peche, August 38; Louisiana, 1848 *778.6* p263
Peche, M. Anne 30; Louisiana, 1848 *778.6* p263
Peche, M. Marie 7; Louisiana, 1848 *778.6* p263
Peche, Setastian 44; Louisiana, 1848 *778.6* p263
Pechina, Marie; Quebec, 1671 *4514.3* p354
Pecinovsky Family ; New York, NY, 1854 *2853.20* p230
Peck, Ann; America, 1750 *1220.12* p617
Peck, Edward; America, 1755 *1220.12* p617
Peck, Edward 40; Ontario, 1871 *1823.21* p294
Peck, Harris B.; Washington, 1887 *2770.40* p25
Peck, Helen SEE Peck, Richard
Peck, Isaac SEE Peck, Richard
Peck, James; Annapolis, MD, 1731 *1220.12* p617
Peck, Jane SEE Peck, Richard
Peck, Jane SEE Peck, Richard
Peck, Joseph SEE Peck, Richard
Peck, Mary SEE Peck, Richard
Peck, Richard SEE Peck, Richard
Peck, Richard; Canada, 1775 *3036.5* p68
  Wife:Jane
  Child:Isaac
  Child:Rose
  Child:Joseph
  Child:Richard
  Child:Robert
  Child:Helen
  Child:Mary
  Child:Jane
Peck, Robert SEE Peck, Richard
Peck, Rose SEE Peck, Richard
Peck, Samuel 49; Ontario, 1871 *1823.21* p294
Peck, Samuel C.; Washington, 1882 *2770.40* p135

Peck, Simon 84; Ontario, 1871 *1823.21* p294
Pecka, Josef Boleslav; Chicago, 1885 *2853.20* p399
Peckard, William; America, 1720 *1220.12* p627
Peckard, William; Virginia, 1737 *1220.12* p627
Pecke, David; America, 1679 *1220.12* p617
Pecke, Jane; Barbados, 1670 *1220.12* p617
Peckenten, Francois 23; America, 1843 *778.6* p263
Peckentel, Samson 32; America, 1843 *778.6* p263
Peckett, Edward; Canada, 1774 *3036.5* p40
Peckett, John; Barbados, 1668 *1220.12* p617
Peckham, Sarah; America, 1748 *1220.12* p617
Peckham, William 67; Ontario, 1871 *1823.21* p294
Pecklar, Joseph 30; America, 1845 *778.6* p263
Pecod, Thomas; America, 1760 *1220.12* p617
Pecquet, Charlotte; Quebec, 1671 *4514.3* p354
Pect, Elizabeth; Virginia, 1735 *1220.12* p617
Pedder, Charles; America, 1765 *1220.12* p617
Pedder, John; Annapolis, MD, 1729 *1220.12* p617
Peddie, Jessie 60; Ontario, 1871 *1823.21* p294
Peddington, John; America, 1771 *1220.12* p617
Peddle, Anthony; Maine, 1672 *9228.50* p491
Peddle, George; Philadelphia, 1772 *9228.50* p491
Peddoni, Juanne; Louisiana, 1874 *4981.45* p133
Pede, Heinrich 43; Portland, ME, 1911 *970.38* p80
Peden, Andrew 66; Ontario, 1871 *1823.21* p294
Pedersen, Johanne Ericha; Oregon, 1941 *9157.47* p2
Pederson, Andreas; Iowa, 1896 *1211.15* p18
Pederson, Edvart; Washington, 1889 *2770.40* p80
Pederson, Gabriel H.; Washington, 1885 *2770.40* p194
Pederson, Lars G.; Iowa, 1890 *1211.15* p18
Pederson, Peder 17; New York, NY, 1894 *6512.1* p185
Pederson, Peter Johan; Iowa, 1922 *1211.15* p18
Pediello, Pedro; Barbados or Jamaica, 1715 *1220.12* p617
Pednel, Francoise; Quebec, 1669 *4514.3* p354
Pedre, Casper; Illinois, 1854 *6079.1* p11
Pedrick, Charles; Barbados, 1688 *1220.12* p617
Pedrick, Henry 39; Ontario, 1871 *1823.17* p131
Pedvin, Daniel; New York, NY, 1852 *9228.50* p386
Pedvin, Nicholas; Nebraska, 1823-1891 *9228.50* p390
Pedweson, Loooouis; Washington, 1889 *2770.40* p80
Peeck, Caroline SEE Peeck, Sophie Heine
Peeck, Ernst Friedrich Wilhelm SEE Peeck, Sophie Heine
Peeck, Sophie; America, 1903 *7420.1* p379
  Son:Ernst Friedrich Wilhelm
  Daughter:Caroline
Peed, Nehemiah; Barbados, 1699 *1220.12* p617
Peek, Heinrich; America, 1852 *7420.1* p95
Peeke, John; America, 1760 *1220.12* p617
Peekle, Michael; North Carolina, 1710 *3629.40* p6
Peel, Jeremiah; America, 1762 *1220.12* p618
Peel, John; America, 1768 *1220.12* p618
Peel, John R. 40; Ontario, 1871 *1823.21* p294
Peel, Mary 12; Quebec, 1870 *8364.32* p25
Peel, Polyna; America, 1736 *1220.12* p618
Peel, Thomas G. 42; Ontario, 1871 *1823.21* p294
Peele, James; America, 1771 *1220.12* p618
Peele, Thomas; America, 1770 *1220.12* p618
Peele, William; America, 1764 *1220.12* p618
Peelina, Ralph; America, 1672 *1220.12* p618
Peer, Guillaume 24; America, 1840 *778.6* p263
Peerlesse, William; Barbados, 1668 *1220.12* p618
Peers, Francis; Annapolis, MD, 1719 *1220.12* p614
Peet, Henry; Ohio, 1809-1852 *4511.35* p40
Peet, John; Boston, 1774 *8529.30* p3
Peete, Petronella 13; New York, NY, 1856 *1766.1* p45
Peeter, Elisabeth 11; New York, NY, 1856 *1766.1* p45
Peeter, Guillaume 7; New York, NY, 1856 *1766.1* p45
Peeters, Jean 16; New York, NY, 1856 *1766.1* p45
Peeters, Jean B. 58; New York, NY, 1856 *1766.1* p45
Peeters, Maria 36; New York, NY, 1856 *1766.1* p45
Peeters, Pierre 18; New York, NY, 1856 *1766.1* p45
Pefferkorn, Nicolas 49; Arkansas, 1846 *778.6* p263
Pegas, John 24; New Orleans, 1840 *778.6* p263
Pegden, John; America, 1732 *1220.12* p618
Pegden, William; America, 1729 *1220.12* p618
Pegg, William; America, 1757 *1220.12* p618
Pegg, William; America, 1769 *1220.12* p618
Pegin, Jean 26; Quebec, 1659 *9221.17* p408
Peglar, Anthony 79; Ontario, 1871 *1823.21* p294
Peglar, John 56; Ontario, 1871 *1823.21* p294
Pegley, Charlotte 2; Ontario, 1871 *1823.21* p294
Pegrentz, Joseph Pierre; Louisiana, 1874 *4981.45* p133
Pehal, Jean-Baptiste 35; New Orleans, 1848 *778.6* p263
Pehrsdotter, Brita Christina; Kansas, 1879 *777.40* p11
Pehrsdotter, Carolina; Kansas, 1873-1874 *777.40* p17
Pehrsdotter, Catherine; Kansas, 1868-1870 *777.40* p15
Pehrsdotter, Christina; Kansas, 1869 *777.40* p14
Pehrsdotter, Christina; Kansas, 1870 *777.40* p14
Pehrsdotter, Christina Maria; North America, 1853 *6410.15* p104
Pehrsdotter, Christine; Kansas, 1869 *777.40* p14
Pehrsdotter, Christine; Kansas, 1870 *777.40* p14
Pehrsdotter, Christine B.; Kansas, 1879 *777.40* p11

Pehrsdotter, Christine B.; Kansas, 1879 *777.40* p11
Pehrsdotter, Fredrika; North America, 1854 *6410.15* p104
Pehrsdotter, Margta; New York, 1857 *6529.11* p25
Pehrsdotter, Maria Christina; North America, 1857 *6410.15* p105
Pehrson, Anders 5 SEE Pehrson, Jon
Pehrson, Cajsa Stina 1 SEE Pehrson, Jon
Pehrson, J.; New York, NY, 1844 *6412.40* p148
Pehrson, Jon 43; New York, 1856 *6529.11* p19
  Wife:Martha Jonsdotter 34
  Son:Anders 5
  Son:Lars 3
  Daughter:Cajsa Stina 1
  Son:Jonas 7
  Son:Pehr 9
Pehrson, Jonas 7 SEE Pehrson, Jon
Pehrson, Lars 3 SEE Pehrson, Jon
Pehrson, Martha Jonsdotter 34 SEE Pehrson, Jon
Pehrson, Pehr 9 SEE Pehrson, Jon
Pehrsson, And 30; New York, 1856 *6529.11* p22
  Wife:Great Lisa Jonsdotter 27
  Daughter:Chatar Elisabeth 1
Pehrsson, Andreas Johannes 22; Kansas, 1876-1880 *777.40* p15
Pehrsson, Chatar Elisabeth 1 SEE Pehrsson, And
Pehrsson, Gertrud 4 SEE Pehrsson, Pal
Pehrsson, Great Lisa Jonsdotter 27 SEE Pehrsson, And
Pehrsson, Gunilla Olsdotter 41 SEE Pehrsson, Pal
Pehrsson, John; Cleveland, OH, 1900-1905 *9722.10* p125
Pehrsson, Kerstin 8 SEE Pehrsson, Pal
Pehrsson, Ol 47; New York, 1856 *6529.11* p21
Pehrsson, Olof 6 SEE Pehrsson, Pal
Pehrsson, Pal 50; New York, 1856 *6529.11* p20
  Son:Olof 6
  Daughter:Kerstin 8
  Son:Pehr 10
  Wife:Gunilla Olsdotter 41
  Daughter:Gertrud 4
Pehrsson, Pehr 10 SEE Pehrsson, Pal
Pehrsson, Sven Petter; North America, 1853 *6410.15* p104
Peifer, Elisabeth; Brazil, 1873 *5475.1* p371
Peiffer, Anna; America, 1846 *6442.17* p65
Peiffer, Maria; America, 1846 *6442.17* p65
Peik, Louis; America, 1857 *7420.1* p169
Peil, Jacob 21; New Orleans, 1846 *778.6* p264
Peiras, Jean-Baptiste de; Quebec, 1665 *2314.30* p166
Peiras, Jean-Baptiste de; Quebec, 1665 *2314.30* p192
Peirce, Ann; America, 1700 *1220.12* p614
Peirce, Ann; Maryland, 1719 *1220.12* p614
Peirce, Elizabeth; Barbados, 1663 *1220.12* p614
Peirce, Henry; Barbados, 1699 *1220.12* p614
Peirce, Isaac; America, 1739 *1220.12* p614
Peirce, James; America, 1685 *1220.12* p614
Peirce, Millicent; America, 1741 *1220.12* p615
Peirce, Moses 55; Ontario, 1871 *1823.21* p294
Peirce, Richard; America, 1739 *1220.12* p615
Peirce, Thomas; America, 1666 *1220.12* p615
Peirce, Thomas; Barbados or Jamaica, 1693 *1220.12* p615
Peirce, William; Maryland, 1725 *1220.12* p615
Peircemore, Rebecca; Maryland, 1737 *1220.12* p616
Peircy, John; America, 1685 *1220.12* p616
Peircy, Richard; America, 1685 *1220.12* p616
Peircy, William; America, 1732 *1220.12* p616
Peirey, John; America, 1730 *1220.12* p616
Peirman, Thomas; America, 1742 *1220.12* p616
Peirrow, J. N.; Ohio, 1809-1852 *4511.35* p40
Peirse, Thomas; West Indies, 1614 *1220.12* p615
Peirse, William; America, 1774 *1220.12* p616
Peirson, John; America, 1745 *1220.12* p616
Peirson, John; America, 1756 *1220.12* p616
Peirson, Rachel; Annapolis, MD, 1726 *1220.12* p617
Peirson, Richard; Maryland, 1720 *1220.12* p617
Peisley, Thomas; Maryland, 1725 *1220.12* p601
Peissard, Jean; Quebec, 1642 *9221.17* p120
Peisson, Appollonia 7; America, 1840 *778.6* p264
Peisson, Catherina 3; America, 1840 *778.6* p264
Peisson, Franz 8; America, 1840 *778.6* p264
Peisson, Mary 38; America, 1840 *778.6* p264
Peisson, Nicolas 1; America, 1840 *778.6* p264
Peisson, Philippe 5; America, 1840 *778.6* p264
Pejril, Jan; Baltimore, 1854 *2853.20* p125
Pekar, Matej; Wisconsin, 1890 *2853.20* p32
Pekar, Matej; Wisconsin, 1890 *2853.20* p217
Peklo, Bedrich; Wisconsin, 1854 *2853.20* p304
Pelanne, Raymond 34; New Orleans, 1843 *778.6* p264
Pelant, K.; America, 1810-1910 *2853.20* p513
Pelaud, Jean; Quebec, 1658 *9221.17* p385
Pelaune, Mr. 28; Port uncertain, 1845 *778.6* p264
Peleau, Guillaume; Quebec, 1646 *9221.17* p168
Pelegrino, Joseph 35; New York, NY, 1894 *6512.1* p182

Pelesson, Joseph 41; Missouri, 1845 ***778.6*** *p264*
Pelesson, Pauline 23; Missouri, 1845 ***778.6*** *p264*
Pelesson, Pierre 31; Missouri, 1845 ***778.6*** *p264*
Pelesson, Pierre 41; Missouri, 1845 ***778.6*** *p264*
Pelestral, William 25; Ontario, 1871 ***1823.17*** *p132*
Pelfield, John A. 34; Ontario, 1871 ***1823.21*** *p294*
Pelfry, Nathan 25; Ontario, 1871 ***1823.17*** *p132*
Pelham, Peter; Boston, 1737 ***1642*** *p26*
Pelham, William 30; Maryland, 1721 ***1220.12*** *p618*
Pelier, Thomas; Maine, 1731 ***9228.50*** *p491*
Pelifian, Carl; New York, 1926 ***1173.1*** *p2*
Pelikan, Frantisek; Chicago, 1899 ***2853.20*** *p460*
Pelizart, Henry; Miami, 1935 ***4984.12*** *p39*
Pell, Gerrard; Charles Town, SC, 1719 ***1220.12*** *p618*
Pell, John A.; Louisiana, 1874 ***4981.45*** *p133*
Pell, Juliana; America, 1685 ***1220.12*** *p618*
Pell, Mary; Maryland, 1674-1675 ***1236.25*** *p51*
Pell, Richard; America, 1737 ***1220.12*** *p618*
Pell, William; America, 1759 ***1220.12*** *p618*
Pellegrin, Alex. 30; America, 1841 ***778.6*** *p264*
Peller, Martin; Colorado, 1898 ***1029.59*** *p73*
Pellerin, Jean; Quebec, 1651 ***9221.17*** *p248*
Pellerin, Philippe; Quebec, 1659 ***9221.17*** *p393*
Pellerin, Pierre; Quebec, 1600-1669 ***4514.3*** *p350*
Pellerin, Pierre 34; Quebec, 1653 ***9221.17*** *p278*
Pelletier, Anne; Quebec, 1665 ***4514.3*** *p354*
Pelletier, Antoine; Quebec, 1641-1646 ***9221.17*** *p106*
Pelletier, Catherine; Quebec, 1656 ***9221.17*** *p344*
Pelletier, Charles; Quebec, 1639 ***9221.17*** *p91*
Pelletier, Francois *SEE* Pelletier, Nicolas
Pelletier, Gabriel; Quebec, 1649 ***9221.17*** *p218*
Pelletier, Georges 30; Quebec, 1654 ***9221.17*** *p315*
Pelletier, Guillaume; Quebec, 1641 ***9221.17*** *p106*
*Wife:*Michelle Morille
*Son:*Jean
*Daughter:*Marie
Pelletier, Jean 3 *SEE* Pelletier, Nicolas
Pelletier, Jean 14 *SEE* Pelletier, Guillaume
Pelletier, Jeanne 21; Quebec, 1661 ***9221.17*** *p464*
Pelletier, Jeanne Deroussy 22 *SEE* Pelletier, Nicolas
Pelletier, Marie *SEE* Pelletier, Guillaume
Pelletier, Marie; Quebec, 1669 ***4514.3*** *p355*
Pelletier, Michel; Quebec, 1660 ***9221.17*** *p438*
Pelletier, Michel 18; Quebec, 1649 ***9221.17*** *p218*
Pelletier, Michelle Morille 49 *SEE* Pelletier, Guillaume
Pelletier, Nicolas 46; Quebec, 1636 ***9221.17*** *p62*
*Wife:*Jeanne Deroussy 22
*Son:*Francois
*Son:*Jean 3
Pelletier, Pierre; Quebec, 1639 ***9221.17*** *p91*
Pelletier, Pierre; Quebec, 1660 ***9221.17*** *p438*
Pellett, John; America, 1774 ***1220.12*** *p618*
Pelleuvit, Charles 21; America, 1840 ***778.6*** *p264*
Pellier, Thomas; Maine, 1731 ***9228.50*** *p491*
Pelligan, Jane; Maryland, 1672 ***1236.25*** *p47*
Pelling, John; America, 1752 ***1220.12*** *p618*
Pellingham, Jane; Barbados, 1671 ***1220.12*** *p618*
Pellingham, Jane; Maryland, 1672 ***1236.25*** *p47*
Pellington, Thomas 24; Ontario, 1871 ***1823.21*** *p294*
Pellive, Jules 26; America, 1843 ***778.6*** *p264*
Pells, John; America, 1773 ***1220.12*** *p618*
Pelluchon, Raymond; Quebec, 1660 ***9221.17*** *p438*
Pelnar, Josef; Galveston, TX, 1890 ***2853.20*** *p87*
Pelois, Marguerite; Quebec, 1665 ***4514.3*** *p355*
Pelonehaud, John; New York, 1860 ***358.56*** *p150*
Pelsome, Ellinore; Barbados or Jamaica, 1694 ***1220.12*** *p618*
Pelson, Edward; America, 1720 ***1220.12*** *p618*
Pelt, Matt 42; Minnesota, 1925 ***2769.54*** *p1378*
Pelter, James; America, 1766 ***1220.12*** *p618*
Peltz, Albert August; Wisconsin, 1882 ***6795.8*** *p229*
Peltzer, Johann Nikolaus 51; Galveston, TX, 1846 ***3967.10*** *p378*
Pelz, Joseph; Texas, 1883 ***3435.45*** *p36*
Pember, Catherine; Virginia, 1734 ***1220.12*** *p618*
Pemberton, Isaac; America, 1770 ***1220.12*** *p618*
Pemberton, James; America, 1740 ***1220.12*** *p618*
Pemberton, Jane; Virginia, 1730 ***1220.12*** *p618*
Pemberton, John; America, 1751 ***1220.12*** *p618*
Pemberton, John; Minneapolis, 1879 ***9228.50*** *p371*
Pemberton, Maria Flannelly *SEE* Pemberton, William
Pemberton, William; Maryland, 1751 ***1220.12*** *p618*
Pemberton, William; Philadelphia, 1853 ***8513.31*** *p420*
*Wife:*Maria Flannelly
Pembrooke, Arthur; Barbados, 1683 ***1220.12*** *p618*
Pemputin, John 62; Ontario, 1871 ***1823.21*** *p294*
Pen, Hannah; Annapolis, MD, 1725 ***1220.12*** *p619*
Penaluna, Richard; Colorado, 1883 ***1029.59*** *p73*
Penaluna, Richard; Indiana, 1870 ***1029.59*** *p73*
Penard DeL'Isle, Madeleine; Quebec, 1651 ***9221.17*** *p249*
Penbrook, Grace; America, 1736 ***1220.12*** *p618*
Pence, Francis Anthony; Ohio, 1809-1852 ***4511.35*** *p40*
Pendal, John; Died enroute, 1726 ***1220.12*** *p618*
Pendell, John; America, 1721 ***1220.12*** *p618*
Pendeprat, Peter; Ohio, 1809-1852 ***4511.35*** *p40*
Pender, Lawrence 58; Ontario, 1871 ***1823.21*** *p294*
Pendergast, John; Louisiana, 1874 ***4981.45*** *p133*
Pendexter, . . .; New England, n.d. ***9228.50*** *p491*
Pendexter, Edward; Portsmouth, NH, 1715 ***9228.50*** *p491*
Pendexter, Elizabeth; Maine, 1668 ***9228.50*** *p497*
Pendexter, Isaac 34; Maine, 1698 ***9228.50*** *p497*
Pendlebury, Margaret; America, 1743 ***1220.12*** *p618*
Pendrick, Jane; Virginia, 1730 ***1220.12*** *p618*
Pendrill, Charles 19; Quebec, 1870 ***8364.32*** *p25*
Pendrill, Elianor; Died enroute, 1729 ***1220.12*** *p618*
Pendrill, William 16; Quebec, 1870 ***8364.32*** *p25*
Pendroon, Jane; Virginia, 1730 ***1220.12*** *p618*
Pendry, Jane; Virginia, 1730 ***1220.12*** *p618*
Penellton, Peter 40; Ontario, 1871 ***1823.17*** *p132*
Penent, Alexandre 23; Port uncertain, 1846 ***778.6*** *p264*
Penfold, Henry 50; Ontario, 1871 ***1823.21*** *p294*
Penfold, Thomas; America, 1772 ***1220.12*** *p618*
Penfold, William; America, 1741 ***1220.12*** *p618*
Penford, Daniel; America, 1736 ***1220.12*** *p618*
Pengelly, Alexander; America, 1732 ***1220.12*** *p618*
Pengelly, Hannah; America, 1745 ***1220.12*** *p618*
Pengelly, Thomas; Virginia, 1771 ***1220.12*** *p618*
Pengilly, John; Virginia, 1738 ***1220.12*** *p618*
Penhale, George 49; Ontario, 1871 ***1823.17*** *p132*
Peniston, Doctor 24; Port uncertain, 1841 ***778.6*** *p264*
Penman, Alexander; Illinois, 1918 ***6007.60*** *p9*
Penman, John; North Carolina, 1836 ***1088.45*** *p27*
Penman, William S.; Washington, 1889 ***2770.40*** *p80*
Penn, Amy; America, 1768 ***1220.12*** *p619*
Penn, Barbara Albrecht *SEE* Penn, George
Penn, Daniel; Barbados or Jamaica, 1687 ***1220.12*** *p619*
Penn, George; Philadelphia, 1856 ***8513.31*** *p421*
*Wife:*Barbara Albrecht
Penn, James 46; Ontario, 1871 ***1823.21*** *p294*
Penn, John; America, 1749 ***1220.12*** *p619*
Penn, Mary; Annapolis, MD, 1735 ***1220.12*** *p619*
Penn, Matthew; America, 1751 ***1220.12*** *p619*
Penn, Samuel; America, 1770 ***1220.12*** *p619*
Penn, Susanna; America, 1764 ***1220.12*** *p619*
Penn, Thomas; Barbados, 1662 ***1220.12*** *p619*
Pennard, Sarah; Maryland, 1727 ***1220.12*** *p619*
Pennault, Jacques; Quebec, 1654 ***9221.17*** *p315*
Pennec, . . .; Newfoundland, 1700-1799 ***9228.50*** *p504*
Pennel, Clement; Massachusetts, 1684-1710 ***9228.50*** *p498*
*Brother:*Thomas
Pennel, Thomas *SEE* Pennel, Clement
Pennel, William 39; Ontario, 1871 ***1823.21*** *p294*
Pennel, William 16; Quebec, 1870 ***8364.32*** *p25*
Pennell, Clement; Massachusetts, 1684-1710 ***9228.50*** *p498*
*Brother:*Thomas
Pennell, Matthew; Marblehead, MA, 1743 ***9228.50*** *p504*
Pennell, Thomas; America, 1745 ***1220.12*** *p619*
Pennell, Thomas; America, 1746 ***1220.12*** *p619*
Pennell, Thomas *SEE* Pennell, Clement
Pennell, Walter; Maine, 1647 ***9228.50*** *p514*
Pennell, William Nevins; St. John, N.B., 1844-1944 ***9228.50*** *p503*
Pennerau, Margarethe; America, 1839 ***5475.1*** *p56*
Penney, . . .; Newfoundland, 1700-1799 ***9228.50*** *p504*
Penney, Edwin 38; Ontario, 1871 ***1823.17*** *p132*
Penney, Joseph; America, 1768 ***1220.12*** *p619*
Pennill, Elizabeth; America, 1745 ***1220.12*** *p619*
Pennings, Abel; America, 1766 ***1220.12*** *p619*
Pennington, Charles; America, 1695 ***1220.12*** *p619*
Pennington, Henry; America, 1767 ***1220.12*** *p619*
Pennington, John; America, 1741 ***1220.12*** *p619*
Pennington, John; America, 1775 ***1220.12*** *p619*
Pennington, Thos 60; Ontario, 1871 ***1823.21*** *p294*
Penniston, Henry 30; Maryland, 1721 ***1220.12*** *p619*
Pennithorne, Peter; America, 1760 ***1220.12*** *p619*
Pennithorne, Peter; America, 1763 ***1220.12*** *p619*
Penno, Fredrich; Wisconsin, 1908 ***1822.55*** *p10*
Pennock, William; America, 1768 ***1220.12*** *p619*
Pennon, Thomas; Jamaica, 1783 ***8529.30*** *p13A*
Pennond, Mr. 38; America, 1848 ***778.6*** *p264*
Penny, . . .; Boston, 1769 ***9228.50*** *p5*
Penny, . . .; Newfoundland, 1700-1799 ***9228.50*** *p504*
Penny, Agnes E. 17; Michigan, 1880 ***4491.42*** *p20*
Penny, Benjamin; America, 1771 ***1220.12*** *p619*
Penny, Dinah L. 8; Michigan, 1880 ***4491.42*** *p20*
Penny, Edward; America, 1734 ***1220.12*** *p619*
Penny, Edward 51; Ontario, 1871 ***1823.21*** *p294*
Penny, Eilzabeth 42; Michigan, 1880 ***4491.42*** *p20*
Penny, Elizabeth; America, 1752 ***1220.12*** *p619*
Penny, Elizabeth; America, 1764 ***1220.12*** *p619*
Penny, George; America, 1731 ***1220.12*** *p619*
Penny, Hannah; Died enroute, 1726 ***1220.12*** *p619*
Penny, Henry; Virginia, 1762 ***1220.12*** *p619*
Penny, James 15; Michigan, 1880 ***4491.42*** *p20*
Penny, John; America, 1698 ***1220.12*** *p619*
Penny, John; Barbados, 1668 ***1220.12*** *p619*
Penny, John; Barbados or Jamaica, 1682 ***1220.12*** *p619*
Penny, John 13; Michigan, 1880 ***4491.42*** *p20*
Penny, Joseph; America, 1751 ***1220.12*** *p619*
Penny, Lizabeth A. 10; Michigan, 1880 ***4491.42*** *p20*
Penny, Martha; Maryland, 1742 ***1220.12*** *p619*
Penny, P.; Boston, 1769 ***9228.50*** *p48*
Penny, P.; Boston, 1769 ***9228.50*** *p504*
Penny, Thomas; Maryland, 1744 ***1220.12*** *p619*
Penny, Thomas 46; Michigan, 1880 ***4491.42*** *p20*
Penny, William; America, 1737 ***1220.12*** *p619*
Penny, William; America, 1738 ***1220.12*** *p619*
Penny, William; America, 1766 ***1220.12*** *p619*
Pennyfather, Michael; America, 1743 ***1220.12*** *p619*
Pennylow, John; America, 1736 ***1220.12*** *p619*
Penpraise, James; America, 1752 ***1220.12*** *p619*
Penprose, Daniel; America, 1725 ***1220.12*** *p619*
Penrice, Lawrence; America, 1751 ***1220.12*** *p619*
Penrice, Robert; America, 1759 ***1220.12*** *p619*
Penrose, William; Philadelphia, 1813 ***5720.10*** *p379*
Penryn, Mary; America, 1679 ***1220.12*** *p619*
Pense, Mrs. 26; New Orleans, 1840 ***778.6*** *p264*
Pense, M. 34; New Orleans, 1840 ***778.6*** *p264*
Pensis, Gustave Joseph; Detroit, 1870 ***1494.20*** *p12*
Penson, John 36; Ontario, 1871 ***1823.21*** *p294*
Penson, William; America, 1766 ***1220.12*** *p619*
Penstone, Thomas; America, 1761 ***1220.12*** *p619*
Pentecost, James; America, 1767 ***1220.12*** *p620*
Pentecross, James; America, 1767 ***1220.12*** *p620*
Penth, Maria 26; America, 1836 ***5475.1*** *p449*
Penth, Peter; America, 1882 ***5475.1*** *p413*
Penth, Peter; America, 1882 ***5475.1*** *p456*
Penticost, Richard; America, 1741 ***1220.12*** *p620*
Pention, Ann; America, 1734 ***1220.12*** *p620*
Pentlow, Mary; America, 1763 ***1220.12*** *p620*
Pentycost, Eleanor; America, 1758 ***1220.12*** *p620*
Peosa, Lewis 22; America, 1840 ***778.6*** *p264*
Peper, Conrad; Ohio, 1809-1852 ***4511.35*** *p40*
Peper, Hanna 28; Ontario, 1871 ***1823.21*** *p294*
Pepin, Child; Texas, 1848 ***778.6*** *p264*
Pepin, Miss 15; Texas, 1848 ***778.6*** *p265*
Pepin, Miss 30; Texas, 1848 ***778.6*** *p265*
Pepin, Mr. 18; America, 1846 ***778.6*** *p264*
Pepin, Mr.; Canada, 1850-1983 ***9228.50*** *p504*
Pepin, Mr. 40; Louisiana, 1848 ***778.6*** *p264*
Pepin, Mr.; San Francisco, 1850-1983 ***9228.50*** *p504*
Pepin, Antoine 16; Quebec, 1652 ***9221.17*** *p264*
Pepin, Benjamin 35; Texas, 1848 ***778.6*** *p265*
Pepin, Etienne 55; America, 1846 ***778.6*** *p265*
Pepin, Francois; Quebec, 1658 ***9221.17*** *p385*
Pepin, Guillaume 35; Quebec, 1642 ***9221.17*** *p120*
Pepin, Helier; Ontario, 1912-1983 ***9228.50*** *p504*
Pepin, Jean; Quebec, 1642 ***9221.17*** *p120*
Pepin, Robert 19; Quebec, 1662 ***9221.17*** *p491*
Peppard, William S.; Ohio, 1853 ***3580.20*** *p33*
Peppard, William S.; Ohio, 1853 ***6020.12*** *p21*
Peppen, Walter; Barbados, 1690 ***1220.12*** *p620*
Pepper, Alexander 29; Ontario, 1871 ***1823.21*** *p294*
Pepper, Anthony; America, 1745 ***1220.12*** *p620*
Pepper, Conrad; Ohio, 1809-1852 ***4511.35*** *p40*
Pepper, Francis; America, 1767 ***1220.12*** *p620*
Pepper, Hugh 48; Ontario, 1871 ***1823.17*** *p132*
Pepper, James 33; Quebec, 1870 ***8364.32*** *p25*
Pepper, Jasper; Virginia, 1731 ***1220.12*** *p620*
Pepper, John; Maryland, 1673 ***1236.25*** *p49*
Pepper, Mary; America, 1748 ***1220.12*** *p620*
Pepper, Phillis; America, 1754 ***1220.12*** *p620*
Pepper, Richard; America, 1754 ***1220.12*** *p620*
Pepper, Thomas; Barbados or St. Christopher, 1780 ***8529.30*** *p7A*
Pepper, Thomas; Maryland, 1725 ***1220.12*** *p620*
Pepperell, Alexander; America, 1698 ***1220.12*** *p620*
Pepperell, Elizabeth; America, 1700 ***1220.12*** *p620*
Pepperell, Mary; America, 1758 ***1220.12*** *p620*
Peppers, Thos 30; Ontario, 1871 ***1823.17*** *p132*
Peppler, Anna Elisabeth; America, 1840 ***8115.12*** *p318*
Peppler, Anna Elisabeth; America, 1870 ***8115.12*** *p318*
Peppler, Johann Jakob; America, n.d. ***8115.12*** *p318*
Peppler, Johann Philipp; America, 1847 ***8115.12*** *p318*
Peppler, Konrad; America, 1870 ***8115.12*** *p318*
Pepre, Jean; Virginia, 1700 ***9230.15*** *p81*
Pequeseard, Alfred 40; Texas, 1848 ***778.6*** *p265*
Pequignot, Angelique 27; America, 1843 ***778.6*** *p265*
Pequignot, Claude 31; America, 1843 ***778.6*** *p265*
Pequignot, Jean 33; America, 1843 ***778.6*** *p265*
Pequignot, Loiuis 35; America, 1843 ***778.6*** *p265*
Pequignot, Therese 27; America, 1843 ***778.6*** *p265*
Pequignot, Xavier 29; America, 1843 ***778.6*** *p265*
Perachain, Jean 26; America, 1840 ***778.6*** *p265*
Peradona, . . .; Quebec, 1638 ***9221.17*** *p80*
Perard, Nicholas; Louisiana, 1836-1841 ***4981.45*** *p209*

Peras, Pierre 40; Montreal, 1659 9221.17 p426
Perate, Mr. 35; America, 1844 778.6 p265
Peravall, Thomas; Barbados or Jamaica, 1688 1220.12 p620
Perce, Edmund; America, 1742 1220.12 p614
Perceval, James; America, 1745 1220.12 p620
Perchard, Mary; Baltimore, 1807 9228.50 p19
Perchard, Mary; Baltimore, 1807 9228.50 p99
Percich, Victor; Louisiana, 1874-1875 4981.45 p30
Percival, Elizabeth 36; Ontario, 1871 1823.17 p132
Percival, George H. 39; Ontario, 1871 1823.17 p132
Percival, James 53; Ontario, 1871 1823.21 p294
Percival, Matilda 14; Quebec, 1870 8364.32 p25
Percival, Robert 35; Ontario, 1871 1823.21 p295
Percival, Thomas; America, 1688 1220.12 p620
Percival, Thomas; America, 1757 1220.12 p620
Percival, Thomas; Barbados, 1694 1220.12 p620
Percival, William 30; Ontario, 1871 1823.21 p295
Percival, William 47; Ontario, 1871 1823.21 p295
Percivall, Frances; America, 1782 8529.30 p15
Percivall, Joseph; America, 1727 1220.12 p620
Percy, John 32; Ontario, 1871 1823.17 p132
Percyikowsky, Abraham 29; New York, NY, 1878 9253.2 p45
Perdue, Charles; America, 1752 1220.12 p652
Perdue, Elizabeth 11; Quebec, 1870 8364.32 p25
Pere, Arnauld *SEE* Pere, Jean
Pere, B. 27; America, 1846 778.6 p265
Pere, Jean 24; Port uncertain, 1841 778.6 p265
Pere, Jean; Quebec, 1656 9221.17 p344
With wife
*Brother:*Arnauld
Perelle, Edward 12; America, 1843 778.6 p265
Peres, L. 25; America, 1848 778.6 p265
Peres, Louis 19; New Orleans, 1843 778.6 p266
Peret, P.; Louisiana, 1874-1875 4981.45 p30
Pereyeas, Francisco; Louisiana, 1874-1875 4981.45 p30
Perez, Alexander; Louisiana, 1874 4981.45 p133
Perez, Jean 28; America, 1848 778.6 p265
Pergin, James; Ohio, 1840-1897 8365.35 p17
Pergler, Antonin; Chicago, 1865 2853.20 p405
Periam, Bernard; America, 1685 1220.12 p620
Perie, Alexander 54; Ontario, 1871 1823.21 p295
Perier, Mr. 35; Louisiana, 1848 778.6 p265
Perier, Alphonse 9; Louisiana, 1848 778.6 p265
Perigau, P. 40; New Orleans, 1845 778.6 p265
Perina, Frantisek J.; America, 1888 2853.20 p415
Perineau, Bertrand; Quebec, 1656 9221.17 p345
Perira, Joseph; America, 1772 1220.12 p620
Perissain, Augustin 23; America, 1846 778.6 p265
Peritz, Wolf; New York, 1859 358.56 p100
Perius, Anna Maria; Brazil, 1879 5475.1 p436
Perkes, John; America, 1681 1220.12 p621
Perkin, James 34; Ontario, 1871 1823.21 p295
Perkin, Josiah 20; Ontario, 1871 1823.21 p295
Perkin, Lionel; Maryland, 1740 1220.12 p620
Perkin, Phillip; Colorado, 1888 1029.59 p73
Perkin, Thomas 63; Ontario, 1871 1823.21 p295
Perkin, William 42; Ontario, 1871 1823.21 p295
Perkins, . . .; Vancouver, B.C., n.d. 9228.50 p20A
Perkins, Ann; America, 1745 1220.12 p620
Perkins, Ann; America, 1756 1220.12 p620
Perkins, Ann; America, 1769 1220.12 p620
Perkins, Ann; Virginia, 1735 1220.12 p620
Perkins, Benjamin; America, 1763 1220.12 p620
Perkins, Caleb 56; Ontario, 1871 1823.21 p295
Perkins, Charles; America, 1731 1220.12 p620
Perkins, Edward; America, 1678 1220.12 p620
Perkins, Edward; Barbados or Jamaica, 1685 1220.12 p620
Perkins, Elizabeth; America, 1700 1220.12 p620
Perkins, Emma 19; Ontario, 1871 1823.21 p295
Perkins, Emma 20; Ontario, 1871 1823.21 p295
Perkins, George; Maryland, 1727 1220.12 p620
Perkins, George 35; Ontario, 1871 1823.21 p295
Perkins, Hannah; Annapolis, MD, 1722 1220.12 p620
Perkins, Harris 66; Ontario, 1871 1823.21 p295
Perkins, Henry; America, 1721 1220.12 p620
Perkins, Henry 40; Ontario, 1871 1823.21 p295
Perkins, James; America, 1678 1220.12 p620
Perkins, Jane; America, 1700 1220.12 p620
Perkins, John; America, 1727 1220.12 p620
Perkins, John; America, 1736 1220.12 p620
Perkins, John; America, 1766 1220.12 p620
Perkins, John; Colorado, 1847 1211.45 p134
Perkins, Joseph; Potomac, 1729 1220.12 p621
Perkins, Mary; America, 1740 1220.12 p621
Perkins, Mary; America, 1753 1220.12 p621
Perkins, Mary; Maryland, 1719 1220.12 p621
Perkins, Mary; Maryland, 1730 1220.12 p621
Perkins, Richard; America, 1685 1220.12 p621
Perkins, Richard; America, 1738 1220.12 p621
Perkins, Richard; America, 1753 1220.12 p621
Perkins, Robert; America, 1716 1220.12 p621
Perkins, Thomas; America, 1774 1220.12 p621
Perkins, William; America, 1747 1220.12 p621
Perkins, William; America, 1751 1220.12 p621
Perkins, William; America, 1754 1220.12 p621
Perkins, William; America, 1770 1220.12 p621
Perks, William; America, 1769 1220.12 p621
Perkyns, John; Potomac, 1731 1220.12 p620
Perleigh, Abraham; America, 1723 1220.12 p621
Perlipah, Henry; North Carolina, 1710 3629.40 p6
Perlo, Petronella 58; New York, NY, 1856 1766.1 p45
Perlot, Joseph 58; New York, NY, 1856 1766.1 p45
Perlwitz, Gustav Theodor; Wisconsin, 1871 6795.8 p66
Pernelle, Pierre; Quebec, 1638 9221.17 p80
Pernt, Josef; Nebraska, 1867 2853.20 p187
Pero, Michael; Ohio, 1809-1852 4511.35 p40
Perodeau, Marie; Quebec, 1669 4514.3 p355
Perodin, Francois 20; Port uncertain, 1843 778.6 p265
Peron, Herve 40; New Orleans, 1848 778.6 p265
Peronne, Jean; Quebec, 1660 9221.17 p438
*Son:*Michel
Peronne, Michel *SEE* Peronne, Jean
Peronne DeMaze, Louis; Quebec, 1661 9221.17 p464
Peronne DesTouches, Michel; Quebec, 1660 9221.17 p438
With father
Peronne DuMesnil, Jean; Quebec, 1660 9221.17 p438
With son
Perpignano, A.; Louisiana, 1874 4981.45 p133
Perqueme, Mr.; America, 1745 778.6 p265
Perrain, Bte. 46; America, 1846 778.6 p265
Perran, George; Colorado, 1877 1029.59 p73
Perrault, Anne; Quebec, 1669 4514.3 p355
Perree, Mr.; Canada, 1800-1899 9228.50 p509
With brother
Perree, Arthur Oswald *SEE* Perree, George Joseph
Perree, Edward *SEE* Perree, John
Perree, Elizabeth Le Mesurier *SEE* Perree, George Joseph
Perree, Ernest; Canada, 1869-1969 9228.50 p509
Perree, George Herbert *SEE* Perree, George Joseph
Perree, George Joseph; Edmonton, Alberta, 1908 9228.50 p508
*Wife:*Elizabeth Le Mesurier
*Child:*Royston Edward
*Child:*Iris Doreen Ina
*Child:*George Herbert
*Child:*Arthur Oswald
Perree, Iris Doreen Ina *SEE* Perree, George Joseph
Perree, Jack; Canada, 1869-1969 9228.50 p509
Perree, John; Quebec, 1779-1817 9228.50 p506
*Child:*Edward
*Child:*Philip
Perree, Philip *SEE* Perree, John
Perree, Royston Edward *SEE* Perree, George Joseph
Perreint, Mr. 26; Port uncertain, 1840 778.6 p265
Perrel, Elizabeth; Ohio, 1805-1875 9228.50 p505
Perrel, Nathaniel; Ohio, 1840 9228.50 p505
Perret, Claude; Quebec, 1651 9221.17 p249
Perret, John; Louisiana, 1874 4981.45 p133
Perreway, Philip; Boston, 1707 9228.50 p505
Perrey, Harman 46; Ontario, 1871 1823.17 p132
Perrey, John; Barbados, 1666 1220.12 p622
Perrey, Mary Frances; America, 1764 1220.12 p622
Perrier, . . .; Quebec, 1658 9221.17 p385
Perrier, Jean; Quebec, 1659 9221.17 p408
Perrier, P.; Quebec, 1660 9221.17 p438
Perrier, Peter; America, 1774 1220.12 p621
Perril, Enoch; Ohio, 1817 9228.50 p505
Perril, Peter; Ohio, 1848 9228.50 p505
Perriman, Betty; America, 1771 1220.12 p622
Perrin, Mr. 24; New Orleans, 1840 778.6 p265
Perrin, Anne 38; Quebec, 1647 9221.17 p182
*Son:*Jean 11
Perrin, Daniel; New Jersey, 1665-1672 9228.50 p52
Perrin, Daniel; New Jersey, 1665 9228.50 p505
Perrin, Eli; Ohio, 1844 2763.1 p21
Perrin, Eugean; Ohio, 1840-1897 8365.35 p17
Perrin, Gladys; Chicago, 1929 9228.50 p506
Perrin, Gladys; Denver, CO, 1929-1972 9228.50 p173
Perrin, Henri 26; Montreal, 1650 9221.17 p232
Perrin, Jeanne; Quebec, 1658 9221.17 p379
*Daughter:*Marie-Michelle
*Son:*Charles
*Daughter:*Madeleine
Perrin, John; America, 1747 1220.12 p621
Perrin, Judith; Utah, 1862 9228.50 p506
Perrin, Marie; Nova Scotia, 1753 3051 p112
Perrin, Sabastian; Ohio, 1840-1897 8365.35 p17
Perrin, Samuel 32; Ontario, 1871 1823.21 p295
Perrin, Samuell; Maryland, 1673 1236.25 p48
Perrin, Sarah; America, 1761 1220.12 p621
Perrin, Thomas; America, 1727 1220.12 p621
Perrine, Daniel; Virginia, 1665 9228.50 p53
Perrine, Franz 23; America, 1840 778.6 p265
Perrine, Leonard 70; Ontario, 1871 1823.21 p295
Perrine, Peter; New York, 1640-1665 9228.50 p505
Perrinett, A. Francis 32; America, 1848 778.6 p265
Perring, John; Barbados or Jamaica, 1675 1220.12 p621
Perring, Nicholas Cridge; Washington, 1884 2770.40 p193
Perring, Peter; Virginia, 1768 1220.12 p621
Perris, Hans; New York, 1859 358.56 p55
Perris, Thomas 20; New Orleans, 1840 778.6 p265
Perrit, Charles 50; Ontario, 1871 1823.21 p295
Perriy, William; Quebec, 1870 8364.32 p25
Perroche, Jacques 29; Quebec, 1646 9221.17 p167
Perrod, Joseph; Ohio, 1809-1852 4511.35 p40
Perrol, Balthasar 28; New Orleans, 1848 778.6 p265
Perron, Daniel; Quebec, 1657 9221.17 p369
Perron, Rene; Montreal, 1660 9221.17 p443
Perrot, Antoine 38; America, 1841 778.6 p266
Perrot, Charles 6; America, 1843 778.6 p266
Perrot, Francois 2; America, 1843 778.6 p266
Perrot, Jacques 25; Quebec, 1654 9221.17 p315
Perrot, Jean 36; America, 1843 778.6 p266
Perrot, John; America, 1771 1220.12 p607
Perrot, John; Virginia, 1772 1220.12 p607
Perrot, Joseph 1; America, 1843 778.6 p266
Perrot, Ludwig 23; America, 1869 5475.1 p284
Perrot, Marguerite-Cecile; Quebec, 1660 9221.17 p438
Perrot, Therese 48; America, 1843 778.6 p266
Perrot, Zephirin 4; America, 1843 778.6 p266
Perrott, Jacob; America, 1749 1220.12 p607
Perrott, Roger; America, 1767 1220.12 p607
Perrott, William; America, 1769 1220.12 p607
Perroud, Zepherin 23; New Orleans, 1848 778.6 p266
Perroys, Robert de 26; Montreal, 1659 9221.17 p426
Perrse, Anthony B.; North Carolina, 1855 1088.45 p27
Perrut, Pierre; Virginia, 1700 9230.15 p80
With wife
Perry, Mr.; Canada, 1800-1899 9228.50 p509
With brother
Perry, Alfred 41; Ohio, 1880 4879.40 p259
*Wife:*Eliza 31
Perry, Ann; America, 1746 1220.12 p621
Perry, Ann; America, 1755 1220.12 p621
Perry, Anne Rebecca May *SEE* Perry, John
Perry, Arthur Oswald *SEE* Perry, George Joseph
Perry, Barnaby; Annapolis, MD, 1731 1220.12 p621
Perry, Benjamin; America, 1727 1220.12 p621
Perry, Benjamin 13; Michigan, 1880 4491.42 p20
Perry, Benjamin; New York, 1776 8529.30 p7
Perry, Bennett; Concord, NH, 1868-1870 9228.50 p506
*Wife:*Mary Phillips
*Child:*William Harry
Perry, Catherine; Virginia, 1723 1220.12 p621
Perry, Cavalier; America, 1731 1220.12 p621
Perry, Christopher; America, 1728 1220.12 p621
Perry, Edward; America, 1743 1220.12 p621
Perry, Edward; America, 1746 1220.12 p621
Perry, Edward; America, 1752 1220.12 p621
Perry, Edward; Maryland, 1723 1220.12 p621
Perry, Edward *SEE* Perry, John
Perry, Eliza 31 *SEE* Perry, Alfred
Perry, Elizabeth; America, 1745 1220.12 p621
Perry, Elizabeth; America, 1764 1220.12 p621
Perry, Elizabeth; Barbados or Jamaica, 1697 1220.12 p621
Perry, Elizabeth Le Mesurier *SEE* Perry, George Joseph
Perry, Elizabeth; Maryland, 1733 1220.12 p621
Perry, Elsie A. 47; Ontario, 1871 1823.21 p295
Perry, Ernest; Canada, 1869-1969 9228.50 p509
Perry, Francis; Marblehead, MA, 1631 9228.50 p509
Perry, George; America, 1738 1220.12 p621
Perry, George; America, 1750 1220.12 p621
Perry, George 41; Ontario, 1871 1823.21 p295
Perry, George; Virginia, 1768 1220.12 p622
Perry, George Herbert *SEE* Perry, George Joseph
Perry, George Joseph; Edmonton, Alberta, 1908 9228.50 p508
*Wife:*Elizabeth Le Mesurier
*Child:*Iris Doreen Ina
*Child:*George Herbert
*Child:*Royston Edward
*Child:*Arthur Oswald
Perry, Hannah; America, 1762 1220.12 p622
Perry, Harry; New Hampshire, 1840-1940 9228.50 p506
Perry, Henry; Annapolis, MD, 1719 1220.12 p622
Perry, Iris Doreen Ina *SEE* Perry, George Joseph
Perry, Isabella; America, 1735 1220.12 p622
Perry, James; Virginia, 1752 1220.12 p622
Perry, James; Washington, 1888 2770.40 p26
Perry, James E.; Washington, 1887 6015.10 p16
Perry, John; America, 1716 1220.12 p622
Perry, John; America, 1731 1220.12 p622

Perry, John; Marblehead, MA, 1724 ***9228.50*** *p509*
Perry, John; Maryland, 1722 ***1220.12*** *p622*
Perry, John; New York, 1853 ***8513.31*** *p421*
*Wife:*Anne Rebecca May
Perry, John; Ohio, 1844 ***2763.1*** *p21*
Perry, John 42; Ontario, 1871 ***1823.21*** *p295*
Perry, John; Quebec, 1779-1817 ***9228.50*** *p506*
*Child:*Edward
*Child:*Philip
Perry, Joseph; America, 1770 ***1220.12*** *p622*
Perry, Martha; America, 1752 ***1220.12*** *p622*
Perry, Martha; America, 1757 ***1220.12*** *p622*
Perry, Mary; America, 1740 ***1220.12*** *p622*
Perry, Mary Phillips *SEE* Perry, Bennett
Perry, Mary; Maryland, 1742 ***1220.12*** *p622*
Perry, Mary 38; Ontario, 1871 ***1823.21*** *p295*
Perry, Mary; Salem, MA, 1677 ***9228.50*** *p509*
Perry, Mary Ann; Ontario, 1871 ***1823.21*** *p295*
Perry, Nicholas; America, 1728 ***1220.12*** *p622*
Perry, Peter; America, 1749 ***1220.12*** *p622*
Perry, Philip *SEE* Perry, John
Perry, Priscilla; America, 1757 ***1220.12*** *p622*
Perry, Rachel 44; Ontario, 1871 ***1823.21*** *p295*
Perry, Rachel 77; Ontario, 1871 ***1823.21*** *p295*
Perry, Ralph; America, 1737 ***1220.12*** *p622*
Perry, Richard; America, 1765 ***1220.12*** *p622*
Perry, Richard J.; Colorado, 1895 ***1029.59*** *p73*
Perry, Robert; Annapolis, MD, 1722 ***1220.12*** *p622*
Perry, Royston Edward *SEE* Perry, George Joseph
Perry, Samuel; America, 1753 ***1220.12*** *p622*
Perry, Simon; America, 1769 ***1220.12*** *p622*
Perry, Solomon 43; Ontario, 1871 ***1823.21*** *p295*
Perry, Strongfaith; Potomac, 1731 ***1220.12*** *p622*
Perry, Thomas; America, 1718 ***1220.12*** *p622*
Perry, Thomas; America, 1728 ***1220.12*** *p622*
Perry, Thomas; America, 1735 ***1220.12*** *p622*
Perry, Thomas; America, 1737 ***1220.12*** *p622*
Perry, Thomas; America, 1749 ***1220.12*** *p622*
Perry, Thomas; America, 1756 ***1220.12*** *p622*
Perry, Thomas; America, 1773 ***1220.12*** *p622*
Perry, Thomas; Barbados, 1715 ***1220.12*** *p622*
Perry, Thomas 40; Ontario, 1871 ***1823.21*** *p295*
Perry, Thomas 51; Ontario, 1871 ***1823.21*** *p295*
Perry, Thomas 60; Ontario, 1871 ***1823.21*** *p295*
Perry, Waino 21; Minnesota, 1925 ***2769.54*** *p1379*
Perry, William; America, 1737 ***1220.12*** *p622*
Perry, William; America, 1741 ***1220.12*** *p622*
Perry, William; America, 1769 ***1220.12*** *p622*
Perry, William; Annapolis, MD, 1720 ***1220.12*** *p622*
Perry, William 36; Ontario, 1871 ***1823.21*** *p295*
Perry, William Harry *SEE* Perry, Bennett
Perry Family ; Ohio, 1800-1830 ***9228.50*** *p509*
Perryman, John 50; Ontario, 1871 ***1823.17*** *p132*
Perryman, Robert; Charles Town, SC, 1719 ***1220.12*** *p622*
Perryman, William; New York, 1783 ***8529.30*** *p15*
Perryment, William; America, 1744 ***1220.12*** *p622*
Perryn, John; America, 1764 ***1220.12*** *p621*
Perryn, Philip; America, 1772 ***1220.12*** *p621*
Persch, Anna Bender 32 *SEE* Persch, Peter
Persch, Christ 23; New York, NY, 1886 ***8425.16*** *p33*
Persch, Karoline *SEE* Persch, Peter
Persch, Peter 36; America, 1862 ***5475.1*** *p495*
*Wife:*Anna Bender 32
*Daughter:*Karoline
Persdotter, Carin 18; New York, 1856 ***6529.11*** *p20*
Persdotter, Carin 34; New York, 1856 ***6529.11*** *p19*
Persdotter, Carin 34; New York, 1856 ***6529.11*** *p19*
Persdotter, Carin 34; New York, 1856 ***6529.11*** *p19*
Persdotter, Carin 36; New York, 1856 ***6529.11*** *p20*
Person, Adolph Fr. *SEE* Person, John
Person, Andrew; Colorado, 1890 ***1029.59*** *p73*
Person, Andrew; Colorado, 1897 ***1029.59*** *p73*
Person, Andrew; Iowa, 1895 ***1211.15*** *p18*
Person, Andro; Cleveland, OH, 1888 ***9722.10*** *p125*
Person, Anna; St. Paul, MN, 1884 ***1865.50*** *p46*
Person, Charles John *SEE* Person, John
Person, Charlotta F.; St. Paul, MN, 1888 ***1865.50*** *p99*
Person, Charlotta Frederika *SEE* Person, Olof
Person, Christina Anderson *SEE* Person, Olof
Person, Christina; Washington, 1884 ***2770.40*** *p193*
Person, Christine C. Andersdotter *SEE* Person, John
Person, Emma *SEE* Person, Henry
Person, Ester Nicolina *SEE* Person, Olof
Person, Francis; Ohio, 1809-1852 ***4511.35*** *p40*
Person, Henry; St. Paul, MN, 1894 ***1865.50*** *p104*
*Wife:*Emma
Person, Hilma; St. Paul, MN, 1888 ***1865.50*** *p49*
Person, Hulda Maria *SEE* Person, Olof
Person, John; Kansas, 1868 ***777.40*** *p14*
*Wife:*Christine C. Andersdotter
*Son:*Charles John
*Son:*Adolph Fr.
Person, Lewis; Ohio, 1809-1852 ***4511.35*** *p40*
Person, Lizzie; Minnesota, 1900-1901 ***1865.50*** *p104*
Person, Maria Cajsa; St. Paul, MN, 1899 ***1865.50*** *p104*
Person, Nels Peter *SEE* Person, Olof
Person, Nils; Colorado, 1891 ***1029.59*** *p73*
Person, Nils; Washington, 1884 ***2770.40*** *p193*
Person, Olof; St. Paul, MN, 1888 ***1865.50*** *p104*
*Wife:*Christina Anderson
*Son:*Nels Peter
*Daughter:*Ester Nicolina
*Daughter:*Charlotta Frederika
*Daughter:*Hulda Maria
Person, Peter; Washington, 1888 ***2770.40*** *p26*
Person, Soan; Colorado, 1891 ***1029.59*** *p73*
Person, Sofia 15; New York, NY, 1894 ***6512.1*** *p184*
Persson, Carin Persdotter 18 *SEE* Persson, Lars
Persson, Johan Collin; Cleveland, OH, 1889-1890 ***9722.10*** *p125*
Persson, Lars 20; New York, 1856 ***6529.11*** *p20*
*Wife:*Carin Persdotter 18
Persson, Nils; Illinois, 1857-1861 ***4487.25*** *p65*
Pertold, Seraphin 32; Port uncertain, 1843 ***778.6*** *p266*
Perton, Winifred; America, 1764 ***1220.12*** *p653*
Peru, Anna 45; America, 1840 ***778.6*** *p266*
Peru, Pierre 50; America, 1840 ***778.6*** *p266*
Peruc, Mr. 25; America, 1842 ***778.6*** *p266*
Perusseau, Pierre 24; Montreal, 1659 ***9221.17*** *p426*
Pervear Family ; Boston, 1722 ***9228.50*** *p509*
Pervier, . . .; Boston, 1769 ***9228.50*** *p5*
Pervier, John; Boston, 1769 ***9228.50*** *p48*
Pervier Family ; Boston, 1722 ***9228.50*** *p509*
Peryn, Samuel; Barbados, 1673 ***1220.12*** *p621*
Perzigan, Avedis; Illinois, 1930 ***121.35*** *p100*
Peschan, Christian G. E.; North Carolina, 1858 ***1088.45*** *p27*
Peschel, August; Wisconsin, 1882 ***6795.8*** *p175*
Peschel, Johann Karl August; Wisconsin, 1894 ***6795.8*** *p148*
Pescher, Marie; Quebec, 1671 ***4514.3*** *p355*
Pesek, Frantisek; Minnesota, 1858-1860 ***2853.20*** *p259*
Pesek, Frantisek; St. Louis, 1855 ***2853.20*** *p24*
Pesel, Louis; North Carolina, 1840 ***1088.45*** *p27*
Pesha, Francis 34; Ontario, 1871 ***1823.17*** *p132*
Pesola, Hilma 46; Minnesota, 1925 ***2769.54*** *p1380*
Pessey, David; America, 1769 ***1220.12*** *p622*
Pesson, Eli; Louisiana, 1874-1875 ***4981.45*** *p30*
Pester, Thomas; America, 1685 ***1220.12*** *p622*
Petals, William; Barbados, 1669 ***1220.12*** *p622*
Petan, Mr. 27; New Orleans, 1840 ***778.6*** *p266*
Petanaquet, Lewis 50; Ontario, 1871 ***1823.17*** *p132*
Petault, Julien; Quebec, 1646 ***9221.17*** *p167*
Petch, Francis 55; Ontario, 1871 ***1823.21*** *p295*
Petch, James 43; Ontario, 1871 ***1823.21*** *p295*
Petch, James 70; Ontario, 1871 ***1823.21*** *p295*
Petch, John 54; Ontario, 1871 ***1823.21*** *p295*
Petch, John 66; Ontario, 1871 ***1823.21*** *p296*
Petch, Robert; America, 1772 ***1220.12*** *p622*
Petcher, Nicholas; Washington, 1885 ***2770.40*** *p194*
Petchy, Elizabeth; America, 1723 ***1220.12*** *p622*
Peteau, Guillaume; Quebec, 1646 ***9221.17*** *p168*
Petel, John; Boston, 1703 ***9228.50*** *p509*
*Wife:*Rachel
Petel, Rachel *SEE* Petel, John
Petel, Rachel; Boston, 1730 ***9228.50*** *p509*
Peter, Abraham; America, 1770 ***1220.12*** *p623*
Peter, Caroline 69; Ontario, 1871 ***1823.17*** *p132*
Peter, Charles; Ohio, 1809-1852 ***4511.35*** *p40*
Peter, Charlotte 21; Mississippi, 1845 ***778.6*** *p266*
Peter, Conrad; Ohio, 1809-1852 ***4511.35*** *p40*
Peter, Dorothea 9 *SEE* Peter, Maria Schmitt
Peter, Elisabeth; America, 1856 ***5475.1*** *p440*
Peter, Elisabeth; America, 1867 ***7919.3*** *p533*
With child
Peter, Elisabeth; America, 1883 ***5475.1*** *p430*
Peter, Elisabeth 13 *SEE* Peter, Maria Schmitt
Peter, Eva 75; America, 1855 ***5475.1*** *p317*
Peter, Frederick; Ohio, 1809-1852 ***4511.35*** *p40*
Peter, Georg *SEE* Peter, Maria Schmitt
Peter, Heinrich; America, 1852 ***7420.1*** *p95*
Peter, Jacob; Illinois, 1856 ***6079.1*** *p11*
Peter, Johann; Brazil, 1878 ***5475.1*** *p431*
Peter, John; New York, 1860 ***358.56*** *p148*
Peter, Josef *SEE* Peter, Maria Schmitt
Peter, Joseph 30; Galveston, TX, 1844 ***3967.10*** *p375*
Peter, Katharina; America, 1853 ***5475.1*** *p439*
Peter, Konrad *SEE* Peter, Maria Schmitt
Peter, Maria; America, 1833 ***5475.1*** *p436*
Peter, Maria 22 *SEE* Peter, Maria Schmitt
Peter, Maria 49; America, 1833 ***5475.1*** *p58*
With relative 24
*Daughter:*Maria 22
*Son:*Georg
*Daughter:*Elisabeth 13
*Daughter:*Dorothea 9
*Son:*Josef
*Son:*Konrad
Peter, Marie 25; Mississippi, 1846 ***778.6*** *p266*
Peter, Mathias; America, 1840 ***5475.1*** *p437*
With wife & 2 children
Peter, Peter; America, 1834 ***5475.1*** *p437*
Peter, Peter; Chicago, 1857 ***5475.1*** *p318*
Peterean, Catherine 19; America, 1841 ***778.6*** *p266*
Peterean, Etienne 50; America, 1841 ***778.6*** *p266*
Peterean, Frederic 11; America, 1841 ***778.6*** *p266*
Peterean, George 5; America, 1841 ***778.6*** *p266*
Peterean, Pierre 7; America, 1841 ***778.6*** *p266*
Peterean, Sussanne 50; America, 1841 ***778.6*** *p266*
Peterhansel, Hermann; America, 1868 ***7919.3*** *p531*
Peterka, Jan; Illinois, 1853-1910 ***2853.20*** *p471*
Peterli, Maria 25; Galveston, TX, 1844 ***3967.10*** *p372*
Petermann, James 26; New Orleans, 1844 ***778.6*** *p266*
Petermann, Johann; America, 1866 ***7420.1*** *p247*
Peters, Mr. 43; Port uncertain, 1840 ***778.6*** *p266*
Peters, A. Maria *SEE* Peters, Friedrich
Peters, Anne 28; Barbados, 1664 ***1220.12*** *p623*
Peters, Anne 77; Ontario, 1871 ***1823.21*** *p296*
Peters, Charles 29; Kansas, 1880 ***777.40*** *p5*
Peters, Christine; Ohio, 1884 ***554.30*** *p25*
Peters, Claus; Valdivia, Chile, 1851 ***1192.4*** *p51*
Peters, Daniel; Virginia, 1766 ***1220.12*** *p623*
Peters, Fanny 15; Ontario, 1871 ***1823.21*** *p296*
Peters, Felix; Louisiana, 1836-1841 ***4981.45*** *p209*
Peters, Friedrich; Wisconsin, 1881 ***5475.1*** *p308*
*Wife:*Maria Griesenbeck
*Son:*Peter
*Daughter:*A. Maria
*Son:*Johann
*Daughter:*Maria
Peters, George 40; Ontario, 1871 ***1823.21*** *p296*
Peters, H. M.; Washington, 1889 ***2770.40*** *p80*
Peters, Henry 28; Boston, 1835 ***6424.55*** *p31*
Peters, J.A.; New York, 1859 ***358.56*** *p55*
Peters, Jacob 37; Port uncertain, 1842 ***778.6*** *p266*
Peters, James 36; Ontario, 1871 ***1823.21*** *p296*
Peters, Johann; America, 1874 ***5475.1*** *p357*
Peters, Johann 28; Brazil, 1857 ***5475.1*** *p320*
*Wife:*Susanna Rectenwald 23
Peters, Johann *SEE* Peters, Friedrich
Peters, John; America, 1737 ***1220.12*** *p623*
Peters, John; America, 1765 ***1220.12*** *p623*
Peters, John; North Carolina, 1848 ***1088.45*** *p27*
Peters, Josef 6 *SEE* Peters, Peter
Peters, Joseph; America, 1754 ***1220.12*** *p623*
Peters, Joseph; New York, 1783 ***8529.30*** *p15*
Peters, Karoline 3 *SEE* Peters, Peter
Peters, Karoline 33; America, 1856 ***5475.1*** *p352*
Peters, Kath. Jungblut 36 *SEE* Peters, Peter
Peters, Maria *SEE* Peters, Friedrich
Peters, Maria Griesenbeck *SEE* Peters, Friedrich
Peters, Mathew 62; Ontario, 1871 ***1823.21*** *p296*
Peters, Otto; Virginia, 1734 ***1220.12*** *p623*
Peters, Peter 36; America, 1856 ***5475.1*** *p352*
*Wife:*Kath. Jungblut 36
*Daughter:*Karoline 3 months
*Son:*Josef 6
Peters, Peter *SEE* Peters, Friedrich
Peters, Richard; America, 1756 ***1220.12*** *p623*
Peters, Robert; America, 1679 ***1220.12*** *p623*
Peters, Samuel 47; Ontario, 1871 ***1823.21*** *p296*
Peters, Solomon; America, 1759 ***1220.12*** *p623*
Peters, Susanna Rectenwald 23 *SEE* Peters, Johann
Peters, Thomas; Barbados, 1663 ***1220.12*** *p623*
Peters, Wilhelm; Iowa, 1889 ***1211.15*** *p18*
Peters, William; Annapolis, MD, 1723 ***1220.12*** *p623*
Peters, William 60; Ontario, 1871 ***1823.21*** *p296*
Petersen, Adolf; Washington, 1889 ***2770.40*** *p80*
Petersen, Carl Oscar; Cleveland, OH, 1899-1905 ***9722.10*** *p125*
Petersen, Christien; Washington, 1889 ***2770.40*** *p80*
Petersen, Jens Peter; Illinois, 1930 ***121.35*** *p100*
Petersen, Jens Peter; Iowa, 1913 ***1211.15*** *p18*
Petersen, John; Louisiana, 1874-1875 ***4981.45*** *p30*
Petersen, Niels S.; Washington, 1889 ***2770.40*** *p80*
Petersen, Peter; Iowa, 1896 ***1211.15*** *p18*
Petersen, Thomas 35; New York, NY, 1894 ***6512.1*** *p229*
Petersilia, Karl W.; North Carolina, 1849 ***1088.45*** *p27*
Peterson, Mr.; Montreal, 1922 ***4514.4*** *p32*
Peterson, Adolph; Cleveland, OH, 1887-1889 ***9722.10*** *p125*
Peterson, Alfred; Cleveland, OH, 1901-1904 ***9722.10*** *p126*
Peterson, Alfred; St. Paul, MN, 1891 ***1865.50*** *p104*
Peterson, Alma; St. Paul, MN, 1889-1890 ***1865.50*** *p104*
Peterson, Amanda C. 27; New York, NY, 1894 ***6512.1*** *p184*
Peterson, Andres; Colorado, 1900 ***1029.59*** *p73*

Peterson, Andrew; America, 1694 ***1220.12*** *p623*
Peterson, Andrew; Colorado, 1873 ***1029.59*** *p73*
Peterson, Andrew B.; St. Paul, MN, 1888 ***1865.50*** *p105*
Peterson, Andrew E.; St. Paul, MN, 1880-1889 ***1865.50*** *p105*
Peterson, Andrew F.; St. Paul, MN, 1880 ***1865.50*** *p105*
*Wife:*Johanna Gustafson
*Child:*Anna
Peterson, Andrew F.; St. Paul, MN, 1889 ***1865.50*** *p105*
*Wife:*Johanna
Peterson, Anna; St. Paul, MN, 1874 ***1865.50*** *p105*
Peterson, Anna *SEE* Peterson, Andrew F.
Peterson, Anna Ch.; New York, 1881-1888 ***1865.50*** *p101*
Peterson, Anna Ch.; New York, 1881-1888 ***1865.50*** *p101*
Peterson, Anna Sophia; St. Paul, MN, 1882 ***1865.50*** *p105*
Peterson, August; St. Paul, MN, 1902 ***1865.50*** *p105*
Peterson, Banks; Iowa, 1888 ***1211.15*** *p18*
Peterson, Carl; St. Paul, MN, 1887 ***1865.50*** *p105*
Peterson, Carl; St. Paul, MN, 1894 ***1865.50*** *p105*
Peterson, Carl Christian; Iowa, 1924 ***1211.15*** *p18*
Peterson, Carl Henrik; Oregon, 1941 ***9157.47*** *p2*
Peterson, Carl Julius; Iowa, 1920 ***1211.15*** *p18*
Peterson, Charles; Colorado, 1883 ***1029.59*** *p73*
Peterson, Charles; Colorado, 1883 ***1029.59*** *p74*
Peterson, Charles J.; St. Paul, MN, 1887 ***1865.50*** *p105*
Peterson, Charles W.; New York, NY, 1869-1870 ***777.40*** *p7*
Peterson, Charlotta; St. Paul, MN, 1869 ***1865.50*** *p115*
Peterson, Charlotta S.; St. Paul, MN, 1883-1889 ***1865.50*** *p105*
Peterson, Charly 25; Ontario, 1871 ***1823.21*** *p296*
Peterson, Chris; Iowa, 1888 ***1211.15*** *p18*
Peterson, Christian; Ohio, 1809-1852 ***4511.35*** *p40*
Peterson, Christina; Minnesota, 1876-1885 ***1865.50*** *p100*
Peterson, Christopher; America, 1743 ***1220.12*** *p623*
Peterson, Daniel; Toronto, 1844 ***2910.35*** *p112*
Peterson, E.M.; Iowa, 1883 ***1211.15*** *p18*
Peterson, Eli; Iowa, 1896 ***1211.15*** *p18*
Peterson, Elof L.; Kansas, 1879 ***777.40*** *p12*
Peterson, Emma 15; New York, NY, 1894 ***6512.1*** *p184*
Peterson, Emma; St. Paul, MN, 1874-1905 ***1865.50*** *p105*
Peterson, Emma *SEE* Peterson, Frank
Peterson, Erick 51; Kansas, 1880 ***777.40*** *p17*
Peterson, Erick Julius; Cleveland, OH, 1902-1903 ***9722.10*** *p126*
Peterson, Ernest N.; Iowa, 1902 ***1211.15*** *p18*
Peterson, Esther *SEE* Peterson, John Gott.
Peterson, Eugene *SEE* Peterson, John Gott.
Peterson, F.G.; St. Paul, MN, 1887 ***1865.50*** *p106*
Peterson, Frank; Iowa, 1888 ***1211.15*** *p18*
Peterson, Frank; St. Paul, MN, 1894 ***1865.50*** *p106*
*Wife:*Emma
Peterson, Frank L.; Chicago, 1864 ***4487.25*** *p69*
Peterson, Fred; Iowa, 1888 ***1211.15*** *p18*
Peterson, Frederick; Washington, 1886 ***2770.40*** *p195*
Peterson, Gertie 28 *SEE* Peterson, Lawrence
Peterson, Gladys *SEE* Peterson, John Gott.
Peterson, Hannah; St. Paul, MN, 1880-1892 ***1865.50*** *p106*
Peterson, Hannah; St. Paul, MN, 1885 ***1865.50*** *p106*
Peterson, Hans; Iowa, 1892 ***1211.15*** *p18*
Peterson, Hans; St. Paul, MN, 1887 ***1865.50*** *p106*
Peterson, Hans Christian; Iowa, 1922 ***1211.15*** *p18*
Peterson, Hans J.J.; Iowa, 1896 ***1211.15*** *p18*
Peterson, Hans P.; Iowa, 1876 ***1211.15*** *p18*
Peterson, Henry; Washington, 1884 ***2770.40*** *p193*
Peterson, Ida M.; St. Paul, MN, 1894 ***1865.50*** *p106*
Peterson, J. H.; Iowa, 1894 ***1211.15*** *p18*
Peterson, J.P.; Cleveland, OH, 1870-1876 ***9722.10*** *p126*
Peterson, Jacob; Iowa, 1877 ***1211.15*** *p18*
Peterson, James; Iowa, 1883 ***1211.15*** *p18*
Peterson, James; Iowa, 1894 ***1211.15*** *p18*
Peterson, Jens; Iowa, 1903 ***1211.15*** *p18*
Peterson, Joh. A. 22; Kansas, 1876-1880 ***777.40*** *p15*
Peterson, Johanna Gustafson *SEE* Peterson, Andrew F.
Peterson, Johanna *SEE* Peterson, Andrew F.
Peterson, Johanna; St. Paul, MN, 1894 ***1865.50*** *p106*
Peterson, Johanna Sophia; Minnesota, 1880-1887 ***1865.50*** *p106*
Peterson, John; America, 1755 ***1220.12*** *p623*
Peterson, John; America, 1852 ***777.40*** *p11*
Peterson, John; Illinois, 1861 ***4487.25*** *p69*
Peterson, John; Illinois, 1861 ***4487.25*** *p70*
Peterson, John 24; Kansas, 1879-1880 ***777.40*** *p11*
Peterson, John; Ohio, 1844 ***2763.1*** *p21*
Peterson, John; St. Paul, MN, 1882 ***1865.50*** *p106*
Peterson, John A.; Cleveland, OH, 1878-1893 ***9722.10*** *p126*
Peterson, John A.; St. Paul, MN, 1881-1888 ***1865.50*** *p106*
Peterson, Mrs. John A.; St. Paul, MN, 1893 ***1865.50*** *p106*
Peterson, John E.; St. Paul, MN, 1888 ***1865.50*** *p106*
Peterson, John Gott.; Colorado, 1921 ***1029.59*** *p74*
*Wife:*Esther
*Child:*Eugene
*Child:*Gladys
Peterson, John Peter; Cleveland, OH, 1893-1900 ***9722.10*** *p126*
Peterson, John V.; Cleveland, OH, 1886-1890 ***9722.10*** *p126*
Peterson, John Victor; Boston, 1880 ***1029.59*** *p74*
Peterson, Joseph; Maryland or Virginia, 1731 ***1220.12*** *p623*
Peterson, Josephine C.; Kansas, 1879 ***777.40*** *p12*
Peterson, Lawrence 30; Kansas, 1880 ***777.40*** *p4*
*Wife:*Gertie 28
Peterson, Lewis; Washington, 1884 ***2770.40*** *p193*
Peterson, Loren; Iowa, 1877 ***1211.15*** *p18*
Peterson, Lottie; Colorado, 1862-1920 ***1029.59*** *p68*
Peterson, Malkus 46; Minnesota, 1925 ***2769.54*** *p1380*
Peterson, Maria; St. Paul, MN, 1881-1894 ***1865.50*** *p107*
Peterson, Maria; St. Paul, MN, 1886 ***1865.50*** *p107*
Peterson, Martin; Iowa, 1892 ***1211.15*** *p18*
Peterson, Martin; Louisiana, 1836-1840 ***4981.45*** *p213*
Peterson, Mathilda; Minneapolis, 1888 ***1865.50*** *p107*
Peterson, Mathilda; New York, 1881-1882 ***1865.50*** *p107*
Peterson, Matilda; Washington, 1883 ***2770.40*** *p137*
Peterson, Nels; Illinois, 1861 ***4487.25*** *p70*
Peterson, Nels C.; Illinois, 1861 ***4487.25*** *p70*
Peterson, Nels N.; Illinois, 1861 ***4487.25*** *p71*
Peterson, Nicholas 32; Kansas, 1880 ***777.40*** *p7*
Peterson, Niels; Iowa, 1898 ***1211.15*** *p18*
Peterson, Niles B.; Washington, 1882 ***2770.40*** *p136*
Peterson, Ole P. D.; Washington, 1888 ***2770.40*** *p26*
Peterson, Olof; Illinois, 1861 ***4487.25*** *p71*
Peterson, Olof 68; Kansas, 1880 ***777.40*** *p12*
Peterson, Oscar Ludvig; Iowa, 1915 ***1211.15*** *p18*
Peterson, Otto 25; New York, NY, 1894 ***6512.1*** *p184*
Peterson, Otto J.; Minnesota, 1884-1885 ***1865.50*** *p107*
Peterson, P.O.; Cleveland, OH, 1870-1890 ***9722.10*** *p126*
Peterson, Perry; Iowa, 1903 ***1211.15*** *p18*
Peterson, Peter; Dakota, 1885 ***1029.59*** *p74*
Peterson, Peter; New York, 1888 ***1029.59*** *p74*
Peterson, Peter; St. Paul, MN, 1887 ***1865.50*** *p107*
Peterson, Peter; Washington, 1886 ***2770.40*** *p195*
Peterson, Peter A.; Washington, 1884 ***2770.40*** *p193*
Peterson, Peter H.; Iowa, 1896 ***1211.15*** *p18*
Peterson, Peter J.; Colorado, 1894 ***1029.59*** *p74*
Peterson, Peter Larson; Washington, 1889 ***2770.40*** *p80*
Peterson, Philip; Washington, 1889 ***2770.40*** *p80*
Peterson, Richard; Rappahannock, VA, 1741 ***1220.12*** *p623*
Peterson, Saul 75; Ontario, 1871 ***1823.21*** *p296*
Peterson, Selma; St. Paul, MN, 1902 ***1865.50*** *p109*
Peterson, Sigurd; Iowa, 1898 ***1211.15*** *p18*
Peterson, Swan; Cleveland, OH, 1890-1897 ***9722.10*** *p126*
Peterson, Swan John; Colorado, 1890 ***1029.59*** *p74*
Peterson, Swan John; Colorado, 1891 ***1029.59*** *p74*
Peterson, Swan M.; Cleveland, OH, 1893-1897 ***9722.10*** *p126*
Peterson, Swen; Illinois, 1861 ***4487.25*** *p71*
Peterson, Swen; Iowa, 1876 ***1211.15*** *p18*
Peterson, Swen M.; Illinois, 1861 ***4487.25*** *p71*
Peterson, Theodor Julius; Cleveland, OH, 1890-1892 ***9722.10*** *p126*
Peterson, Theophilus; Ohio, 1844 ***2763.1*** *p21*
Peterson, Thomas 32; Florida, 1832-1846 ***8481.1*** *p18*
Peterson, Victor; Cleveland, OH, 1903-1906 ***9722.10*** *p126*
Peterson, William; America, 1768 ***1220.12*** *p623*
Peterson, William; St. Paul, MN, 1893 ***1865.50*** *p107*
Peterson Nostrom, Louis; Iowa, 1867-1870 ***777.40*** *p10*
Petersson, Jons; Colorado, 1887 ***1029.59*** *p74*
Petgen, Nikolaus; Indiana, 1857 ***5475.1*** *p260*
Peth, Hirman 80; Ontario, 1871 ***1823.17*** *p132*
Pether, John; America, 1771 ***1220.12*** *p623*
Pether, Thomas; America, 1775 ***1220.12*** *p623*
Petherbridge, Mary A. 38; Ontario, 1871 ***1823.21*** *p296*
Petheway, Elizabeth; America, 1725 ***1220.12*** *p623*
Pethic, Charles; Ohio, 1885-1941 ***9228.50*** *p509*
Pethick, William H. 22; Ontario, 1871 ***1823.21*** *p296*
Petibeau, Gabriel 35; Havana, 1842 ***778.6*** *p266*
Petijean, John 20; New Orleans, 1840 ***778.6*** *p266*
Petincourt, Charles 29; America, 1846 ***778.6*** *p266*
Petiot DeCourbiere, Claude; Quebec, 1657 ***9221.17*** *p365*
Petissen, Mrs. 27; America, 1844 ***778.6*** *p266*
Petit, Mr. 14; America, 1848 ***778.6*** *p266*
Petit, Mr. 45; New Orleans, 1845 ***778.6*** *p266*
Petit, Barbe Laumonnier; Quebec, 1673 ***4514.3*** *p362*
Petit, Barbe Raveau; Quebec, 1673 ***4514.3*** *p362*
Petit, Catherine-Francoise; Quebec, 1647 ***9221.17*** *p186*
Petit, Charles 23; Quebec, 1662 ***9221.17*** *p491*
Petit, Charles 38; Texas, 1843 ***778.6*** *p266*
Petit, F. 37; America, 1841 ***778.6*** *p267*
Petit, Guillaume; Quebec, 1647 ***9221.17*** *p186*
Petit, Hilah 18; America, 1842 ***778.6*** *p267*
Petit, Jean Philippe Milan 30; America, 1841 ***778.6*** *p267*
Petit, Jeanne; Quebec, 1672 ***4514.3*** *p355*
Petit, Louise; Quebec, 1670 ***4514.3*** *p355*
Petit, Malvina; Massachusetts, 1854-1904 ***9228.50*** *p623*
Petit, Marie; Quebec, 1669 ***4514.3*** *p355*
Petit, Marie; Quebec, 1671 ***4514.3*** *p324*
Petit, Marie Chapelier 25; Quebec, 1649 ***9221.17*** *p210*
Petit, Marie-Rose; Quebec, 1668 ***4514.3*** *p356*
Petit, Marie-Therese; Quebec, 1669 ***4514.3*** *p356*
Petit, Nicolas 20; Quebec, 1649 ***9221.17*** *p219*
Petit, Pierre; Quebec, 1642 ***9221.17*** *p120*
Petit, Pierre; Quebec, 1645 ***9221.17*** *p156*
Petit, Pierre 27; Quebec, 1658 ***9221.17*** *p385*
Petit, Pierre 32; Texas, 1848 ***778.6*** *p267*
Petit, Thomas; America, 1752 ***1220.12*** *p623*
Petit, Victor 19; New Orleans, 1845 ***778.6*** *p267*
Petitbien, R. 41; Port uncertain, 1845 ***778.6*** *p267*
Petit deLevilliers, Charles; Quebec, 1683-1688 ***2314.30*** *p168*
Petit deLevilliers, Charles; Quebec, 1687 ***2314.30*** *p192*
Petitfils, Charles 31; America, 1840 ***778.6*** *p267*
Petitfils, Emile 12; America, 1843 ***778.6*** *p267*
Petitfils, Eugene 16; America, 1843 ***778.6*** *p267*
Petitfils, Francois 17; America, 1843 ***778.6*** *p267*
Petitfils, Joseph 44; America, 1843 ***778.6*** *p267*
Petitfils, Leonore 45; America, 1843 ***778.6*** *p267*
Petitfils, Marie 14; America, 1843 ***778.6*** *p267*
Petitfils, Marie 19; America, 1843 ***778.6*** *p267*
Petitjean, Jean; Montreal, 1644 ***9221.17*** *p146*
Petitjean, Jean 20; Montreal, 1658 ***9221.17*** *p387*
Petitjean, Jean-Baptiste 21; Quebec, 1657 ***9221.17*** *p364*
Petitory, Catherina 24; America, 1844 ***778.6*** *p267*
Petitory, Jacques 22; Port uncertain, 1844 ***778.6*** *p267*
Petitory, Suzanna 22; America, 1844 ***778.6*** *p267*
Petitpas, Marguerite; Quebec, 1636 ***9221.17*** *p63*
*Son:*Charles
*Granddaughter:*Marguerite
*Daughter-In-Law:*Marie Pichon Gaultier
*Granddaughter:*Denise
*Son:*Etienne
*Son:*Thomas
*Son:*Jacques
Petitpre, Francois; Quebec, 1633 ***9221.17*** *p30*
Petlach, Karel Z.; Nebraska, 1898-1899 ***2853.20*** *p184*
Petman, John; America, 1770 ***1220.12*** *p623*
Peto, Thomas; America, 1774 ***1220.12*** *p623*
Petr, Josef; Galveston, TX, 1856 ***2853.20*** *p63*
Petr, Josef; Galveston, TX, 1856 ***2853.20*** *p71*
Petra, Jane 26; Ontario, 1871 ***1823.21*** *p296*
Petreken, Philip; Philadelphia, 1778 ***8529.30*** *p7A*
Petrekin, Philip; Philadelphia, 1778 ***8529.30*** *p7A*
Petrell, Olga 38; Minnesota, 1925 ***2769.54*** *p1379*
Petrelli, Joe; Illinois, 1918 ***6007.60*** *p9*
Petri, Emelie 29; America, 1840 ***778.6*** *p267*
Petri, Friedrich August; America, 1883 ***7420.1*** *p338*
Petri, Heinrich Ferdinand Ludwig; America, 1882 ***7420.1*** *p331*
Petri, Minna; New York, NY, 1907 ***7420.1*** *p382*
Petricek, Frantisek; Minnesota, 1857 ***2853.20*** *p259*
Petricek, Josef; Minnesota, 1857 ***2853.20*** *p259*
Petrick, Carl; Wisconsin, 1907 ***6795.8*** *p149*
Petrick, Julius Hermann August; Wisconsin, 1889 ***6795.8*** *p75*
Petrick, Karl Fredrick; Wisconsin, 1897 ***6795.8*** *p148*
Petricka, Frantisek; Minnesota, 1857 ***2853.20*** *p259*
Petricka, Josef; Minnesota, 1857 ***2853.20*** *p259*
Petrie, James 26; Ontario, 1871 ***1823.17*** *p132*
Petrik, Martin; Wisconsin, 1873 ***6795.8*** *p34*
Petrik, Matej; South Dakota, 1871-1910 ***2853.20*** *p247*
Petrik, Vaclav; South Dakota, 1871-1910 ***2853.20*** *p247*
Petroche, J. 38; America, 1841 ***778.6*** *p267*
Petrosky, I.; Texas, 1892-1900 ***6015.15*** *p10*
Petrosky, S.; Texas, 1893 ***6015.15*** *p10*
Petrtyl, Antonin; Port uncertain, 1861-1910 ***2853.20*** *p370*
Petrtyl, Tomas; Michigan, 1868 ***2853.20*** *p370*
Petrtyl, Viktor; Chicago, 1810-1910 ***2853.20*** *p405*
Petrtyl, Viktor; Chicago, 1854 ***2853.20*** *p387*
Petrtyl, Viktor; New York, NY, 1853 ***2853.20*** *p370*
Petru, Jan; Chicago, 1875 ***2853.20*** *p429*
Petrus, Pierre 17; Montreal, 1651 ***9221.17*** *p252*
Petruschke, Richard; Wisconsin, 1896 ***6795.8*** *p82*
Petry, Anna *SEE* Petry, Nikolaus
Petry, Jacques Alexander; Illinois, 1856 ***6079.1*** *p11*
Petry, Jakob; New York, 1886 ***5475.1*** *p423*
Petry, Johann *SEE* Petry, Nikolaus
Petry, Joseph; Ontario, 1787 ***1276.15*** *p230*
With child & relative
Petry, Maria Schedler *SEE* Petry, Nikolaus

384 *FOR A COMPLETE EXPLANATION OF ENTRY, SEE "HOW TO READ A CITATION" SECTION*

Petry, Nikolaus *SEE* Petry, Nikolaus
Petry, Nikolaus; Illinois, 1887 5475.1 p391
*Wife:*Maria Schedler
*Son:*Johann
*Daughter:*Anna
*Son:*Nikolaus
Petryniak, Jozefa 18; New York, NY, 1904 8355.1 p15
Petrzelka, Vaclav J.; Nebraska, 1897 2853.20 p422
Pett, Anne; America, 1735 1220.12 p623
Pett, John; Barbados or Jamaica, 1685 1220.12 p623
Petten, . . .; Newfoundland, n.d. 9228.50 p490
Pettengill, George James; Washington, 1886 6015.10 p16
Petterson, Bernart 4; New York, NY, 1883 8427.14 p44
Petterson, Christine 11; New York, NY, 1883 8427.14 p44
Petterson, Gunder 1; New York, NY, 1883 8427.14 p44
Petterson, Hilma A. 23; New York, NY, 1894 6512.1 p184
Petterson, James 56; Ontario, 1871 1823.21 p296
Petterson, Johan A. 27; New York, NY, 1894 6512.1 p185
Petterson, Mary 39; New York, NY, 1883 8427.14 p44
Petterson, Ole 6; New York, NY, 1883 8427.14 p44
Petterson, Pauline 8; New York, NY, 1883 8427.14 p44
Pettersson, A.; New York, NY, 1845 6412.40 p148
Pettersson, And.; New York, NY, 1843 6412.40 p147
Pettersson, Bengt; New York, NY, 1850 6412.40 p152
Pettersson, Carl; New York, NY, 1849 6412.40 p151
Pettersson, Carl Fredrik Ferdinand; North America, 1887 6410.15 p106
Pettersson, Carl Henrik; Oregon, 1941 9157.47 p2
Pettersson, Erland; North America, 1858 6410.15 p105
*Wife:*Margareta Christina Johansdotter
*Child:*Jacob Edvard
Pettersson, G.W.; New York, NY, 1849 6412.40 p151
Pettersson, J.; New York, NY, 1845 6412.40 p148
Pettersson, J.; New York, NY, 1847 6412.40 p149
Pettersson, Jacob August; North America, 1887 6410.15 p106
Pettersson, Jacob Edvard *SEE* Pettersson, Erland
Pettersson, Johan; New York, NY, 1851 6412.40 p152
Pettersson, John Birger; Cleveland, OH, 1903 9722.10 p126
Pettersson, Jons; New York, NY, 1846 6412.40 p149
Pettersson, L.; New York, NY, 1845 6412.40 p149
Pettersson, Margareta Christina Johansdotter *SEE* Pettersson, Erland
Pettersson, Nils; Charleston, SC, 1851 6412.40 p153
Pettersson, Nils; New York, NY, 1845 6412.40 p149
Pettersson, Olof; Cleveland, OH, 1880-1888 9722.10 p126
Pettersson, Olof; New York, NY, 1843 6412.40 p147
Pettersson, Olof; New York, NY, 1850 6412.40 p152
Pettersson, Otto; Charleston, SC, 1851 6412.40 p153
Pettersson, P.; New York, NY, 1844 6412.40 p147
Pettersson, P.; New York, NY, 1845 6412.40 p148
Pettersson, P.; Savannah, GA, 1849 6412.40 p152
Pettersson, P.L.; Boston, 1847 6412.40 p150
Pettersson, Sven; New York, NY, 1849 6412.40 p151
Pettersson, Sven; Philadelphia, 1847 6412.40 p150
Pettersson, Sven August; New York, NY, 1850 6410.15 p104
Pettet, John; America, 1758 1220.12 p623
Pettey, Ann; America, 1740 1220.12 p623
Pettibon, Reynaud 38; America, 1843 778.6 p267
Pettifer, John; America, 1749 1220.12 p623
Pettifer, John 31; Baltimore, 1775 1220.12 p623
Pettiford, Elizabeth; Maryland, 1720 1220.12 p623
Pettin, Ann; America, 1775 1220.12 p623
Pettingale, Richard; Barbados, 1664 1220.12 p623
Pettis, Ann 26; Barbados, 1664 1220.12 p623
Pettit, Ann; America, 1758 1220.12 p623
Pettit, John; Barbados or Jamaica, 1704 1220.12 p623
Pettit, Michael; America, 1763 1220.12 p623
Pettit, Patrick 28; Ontario, 1871 1823.17 p132
Pettit, Sarah; America, 1761 1220.12 p623
Pettit, Thomas; Virginia, 1732 1220.12 p623
Pettitt, Sarah; America, 1774 1220.12 p623
Pettnich, William; Ohio, 1836 2763.1 p21
Petto, Elisabeth 49; Chicago, 1885 5475.1 p555
Petts, Elizabeth; America, 1748 1220.12 p623
Petts, Mary; America, 1748 1220.12 p623
Petts, William; Barbados, 1669 1220.12 p623
Petty, Ann; America, 1758 1220.12 p623
Petty, Francis; America, 1727 1220.12 p624
Petty, Henry; America, 1762 1220.12 p624
Petty, Isabella; America, 1755 1220.12 p624
Petty, Thomas; America, 1724 1220.12 p624
Pettyford, Charles; America, 1774 1220.12 p623
Petura, Josef *SEE* Petura, Josef
Petura, Josef; Wisconsin, 1856 2853.20 p304
*Son:*Josef
Petwageswhite, Peter 57; Ontario, 1871 1823.17 p132
Petworth, Ann 26; Barbados, 1664 1220.12 p624
Petythen, Edward 25; New Orleans, 1845 778.6 p267
Petz, Charles; Louisiana, 1874 4981.45 p133
Peuchenne, Miss 5; Port uncertain, 1844 778.6 p267
Peuchenne, Mr. 35; Port uncertain, 1844 778.6 p267
Peuchenne, Mrs. 35; Port uncertain, 1844 778.6 p267
Peudon, J. 31; America, 1846 778.6 p267
Peuplat, Andre 45; Quebec, 1656 9221.17 p345
Peusch, Pierre 34; America, 1844 778.6 p267
Peuvret, Francois; Quebec, 1651 9221.17 p249
*Brother:*Jean-Baptiste
Peuvret, Jean-Baptiste 20 *SEE* Peuvret, Francois
Peuvret DeMargontier, Francois; Quebec, 1651 9221.17 p249
Peuvret deMesnu, Jean-Baptiste; Quebec, 1651 2314.30 p172
Peuvret DeMesnu, Jean-Baptiste 20; Quebec, 1651 9221.17 p249
Peuvrier, Marguerite; Quebec, 1663 4514.3 p356
Peverett, William 40; Ontario, 1871 1823.21 p296
Peverley, Alexander; Annapolis, MD, 1732 1220.12 p624
Peverley, Rebecca; America, 1772 1220.12 p624
Pevett, Elizabeth; America, 1757 1220.12 p624
Pevier Family ; Boston, 1722 9228.50 p509
Pew, Anne; Annapolis, MD, 1725 1220.12 p651
Pew, David; America, 1749 1220.12 p651
Pew, Elizabeth 20; Virginia, 1635 1183.3 p31
Pew, Margaret; Annapolis, MD, 1726 1220.12 p651
Pew, Margaret; Ontario, 1835 3160.1 p150
Pew, Margaret; Prescott, Ont., 1835 3289.1 p61
Pew, Sarah; America, 1736 1220.12 p651
Peway, Lucy 50; Ontario, 1871 1823.17 p132
Pewe, William Peter; Iowa, 1909 1211.15 p18
Pewter, John; America, 1767 1220.12 p624
Pewter, Samuel; Maryland, 1723 1220.12 p624
Pewter, Thomas; America, 1729 1220.12 p624
Pewteres, Jane; America, 1675 1220.12 p624
Pewtinger, Richard; Virginia, 1665 9228.50 p53
Pewtriss, William; America, 1768 1220.12 p624
Peybody, John; Barbados, 1683 1220.12 p613
Peyer, Frantisek; Iowa, 1854 2853.20 p230
Peyronnet, Mrs. 36; New Orleans, 1848 778.6 p267
Peyronon, Jean 25; Quebec, 1655 9221.17 p328
Peyton, Ann; America, 1734 1220.12 p624
Peyton, Ann; America, 1760 1220.12 p624
Peyton, Edward; America, 1765 1220.12 p624
Peyton, George; America, 1749 1220.12 p624
Peyton, Honorene *SEE* Peyton, Philippe
Peyton, Luce Casgrain-Gagnon *SEE* Peyton, Philippe
Peyton, Marie Emma Sarah *SEE* Peyton, Philippe
Peyton, Philippe; New York, 1858 9228.50 p515
*Wife:*Luce Casgrain-Gagnon
*Child:*Honorene
*Child:*Marie Emma Sarah
Peyton, Philippe 32; Quebec, 1804 9228.50 p515
Peytoureau, A. Guillaume 39; New Orleans, 1848 778.6 p267
Peyuiulet, Jacq. 25; New Orleans, 1848 778.6 p267
Pez, Anna Katharina; Venezuela, 1843 3899.5 p543
Pezard DeLaTouche, Etienne 37; Quebec, 1661 9221.17 p445
Pezard deLa Touche Champlain, Etienne; Quebec, 1661 2314.30 p172
Pezbycian, John 26; Indiana, 1895-1904 9076.20 p75
Pezet, Carrie *SEE* Pezet, Walter
Pezet, Walter; Detroit, 1900-1979 9228.50 p510
*Wife:*Carrie
Pfaender, K.; New York, 1859 358.56 p99
Pfaff, Abraham; Ohio, 1809-1852 4511.35 p40
Pfaff, Mrs. Andreas; America, 1838 170.15 p38
Pfaff, Catharina 16; New Orleans, 1848 778.6 p267
Pfaff, Catharina 47; New Orleans, 1848 778.6 p267
Pfaff, Ferdinand; America, 1867 7919.3 p535
Pfaff, Friedrich Theodor; America, 1867 7919.3 p535
Pfaff, Jean-Baptiste 12; New Orleans, 1848 778.6 p267
Pfaff, Joseph 20; New Orleans, 1848 778.6 p268
Pfaff, Louisa; Wisconsin, 1895 6795.8 p237
Pfaff, Michael; America, 1868 7919.3 p535
Pfaff, Nicolas 51; New Orleans, 1848 778.6 p268
Pfaff, Peter 7; New Orleans, 1848 778.6 p268
Pfaff, Simon; New York, NY, 1889 3366.30 p70
Pfaff, Victor 9; New Orleans, 1848 778.6 p268
Pfannstiel, Charlotte; America, 1867 7919.3 p533
*Brother:*Friedrich
Pfannstiel, Friedrich *SEE* Pfannstiel, Charlotte
Pfarrer, Benedikt 26; Galveston, TX, 1846 3967.10 p378
Pfarrer, Elisabeth 21; Galveston, TX, 1846 3967.10 p378
Pfau, Christian; New York, NY, 1889 3366.30 p70
Pfau, Ida J. *SEE* Pfau, Julius
Pfau, Julius; New York, 1865-1870 9228.50 p213
*Wife:*Rachel Falle
*Daughter:*Ida J.
Pfau, Rachel Falle *SEE* Pfau, Julius
Pfeffer, Jacob 6; Portland, ME, 1906 970.38 p80
Pfeffer, Leiser 8; Portland, ME, 1906 970.38 p80
Pfeffer, Louise; America, 1868 7919.3 p526
Pfeffer, Meyer 47; Portland, ME, 1906 970.38 p80
Pfeffer, P. F.; Louisiana, 1874 4981.45 p296
Pfefferkorn, Jacob 19; Arkansas, 1846 778.6 p268
Pfeifer, Ali; America, 1868 7919.3 p525
Pfeifer, Augustine 3; New York, NY, 1898 7951.13 p43
Pfeifer, Bernhard; America, 1868 7919.3 p534
With wife & daughter
Pfeifer, Emme; New York, 1898 5475.1 p426
Pfeifer, Ferd; Wisconsin, 1899 6795.8 p95
Pfeifer, Georg; America, 1867 7919.3 p534
Pfeifer, Heinrich 27; New York, NY, 1893 1883.7 p42
Pfeifer, Johann Heinrich; Wisconsin, 1893 6795.8 p95
Pfeifer, Johann Wilhelm; America, 1868 7919.3 p528
Pfeifer, Joseph 33; New York, NY, 1898 7951.13 p43
Pfeifer, Karoline; America, 1867 5475.1 p491
Pfeifer, Katharina; Indiana, 1867 2526.43 p159
Pfeifer, Magdalena 11 months; New York, NY, 1893 1883.7 p42
Pfeifer, Magdalena 26; New York, NY, 1898 7951.13 p43
Pfeifer, Maria 56; New York, 1874 5475.1 p350
Pfeifer, Maria; Wisconsin, 1894 6795.8 p95
Pfeifer, Mathias; Ohio, 1809-1852 4511.35 p40
Pfeifer, Matthias; Ohio, 1809-1852 4511.35 p40
Pfeifer, Michel; America, 1843 5475.1 p294
With wife 2 sons & 2 daughters
Pfeifer, Philipp 28; America, 1857 5475.1 p552
Pfeifer, Roselia 18 months; New York, NY, 1898 7951.13 p43
Pfeifer, Theresia 23; New York, NY, 1893 1883.7 p42
Pfeiffer, Anna Katharina Kappes 37 *SEE* Pfeiffer, Josef
Pfeiffer, Barbara Seibert *SEE* Pfeiffer, Franz
Pfeiffer, Caspar 9; Mississippi, 1848 778.6 p268
Pfeiffer, Caspar 48; Mississippi, 1848 778.6 p268
Pfeiffer, Catherine 2; Mississippi, 1848 778.6 p268
Pfeiffer, Dorothea Rausch *SEE* Pfeiffer, Ludwig
Pfeiffer, Franz; America, 1846 6442.17 p65
*Wife:*Barbara Seibert
With 7 children
Pfeiffer, Hermann; America, 1872 7420.1 p297
Pfeiffer, Jakob; Cincinnati, 1888 5475.1 p185
Pfeiffer, Jean-Baptiste 29; New Orleans, 1848 778.6 p268
Pfeiffer, Joh.; Chile, 1879 5475.1 p282
Pfeiffer, Josef; America, 1863 5475.1 p482
*Wife:*Anna Katharina Kappes
*Son:*Oswald
Pfeiffer, Julius; America, 1866 5475.1 p404
Pfeiffer, Karl 24; New York, NY, 1900 5475.1 p26
Pfeiffer, Ludwig; America, 1881 5475.1 p34
*Wife:*Dorothea Rausch
*Son:*Michael Gustav
Pfeiffer, Marianne 7; Mississippi, 1848 778.6 p268
Pfeiffer, Michael Gustav *SEE* Pfeiffer, Ludwig
Pfeiffer, Michel; Chicago, 1888 5475.1 p185
Pfeiffer, Nikolaus; Cincinnati, 1888 5475.1 p185
Pfeiffer, Oswald *SEE* Pfeiffer, Josef
Pfeiffer, Philipp; America, 1832 5475.1 p379
With family
Pfeiffer, Therese 44; Mississippi, 1848 778.6 p268
Pfeiffer, Valentin; America, 1846 2526.43 p199
Pfeil, Conrad; Ohio, 1840-1897 8365.35 p17
Pfeil, John; Ohio, 1840-1897 8365.35 p17
Pfeiling, Peter; Marston's Wharf, 1782 8529.30 p11
Pfesterer, Lewis; Ohio, 1809-1852 4511.35 p40
Pfetzinger, Jacob; Ohio, 1840-1897 8365.35 p17
Pfeufer, Barbara Elisabeth; America, 1867 7919.3 p533
Pfeuling, Peter; Marston's Wharf, 1782 8529.30 p11
Pfingsten, Carl Heinrich Ludwig; America, 1857 7420.1 p169
Pfingsten, Caroline Louise Charlotte; America, 1866 7420.1 p247
Pfingsten, Caroline Wilhelmine Hucker *SEE* Pfingsten, Heinrich Wilhelm
Pfingsten, Caroline Wilhelmine Sophie *SEE* Pfingsten, Heinrich Wilhelm
Pfingsten, Engel Marie Dorothea; America, 1884 7420.1 p344
Pfingsten, Engel Marie Dorothea; Ohio, 1879 7420.1 p313
Pfingsten, Engel Marie Sophie; America, 1865 7420.1 p235
Pfingsten, Engel Marie Sophie Leonore Schutte *SEE* Pfingsten, Hermann Heinrich
Pfingsten, Engel Sophie Dorothea; America, 1884 7420.1 p344
Pfingsten, Friedrich Carl Ferdinand; America, 1871 7420.1 p396
With family

Pfingsten, Friedrich Wilhelm; Port uncertain, 1860 7420.1 p198
Pfingsten, Grossenheidorn; America, 1844 7420.1 p33
With wife 6 sons & daughter
Pfingsten, H. H.; Port uncertain, 1853 7420.1 p110
Pfingsten, Hans Heinrich; America, 1884 7420.1 p344
Pfingsten, Hans Heinrich; America, 1888 7420.1 p357
Pfingsten, Heinr. Friedrich Christoph *SEE* Pfingsten, Hermann Heinrich
Pfingsten, Heinrich; New York, NY, 1856 7420.1 p152
Pfingsten, Heinrich Conrad Gottlieb; America, 1868 7420.1 p275
Pfingsten, Heinrich Friedrich; America, 1886 7420.1 p352
Pfingsten, Heinrich Friedrich August; America, 1866 7420.1 p247
Pfingsten, Heinrich Friedrich Christian *SEE* Pfingsten, Heinrich Wilhelm
Pfingsten, Heinrich Wilhelm; America, 1867 7420.1 p262
*Wife:*Caroline Wilhelmine Hucker
*Daughter:*Caroline Wilhelmine Sophie
*Son:*Heinrich Friedrich Christian
Pfingsten, Hermann Heinrich; America, 1850 7420.1 p74
*Wife:*Engel Marie Sophie Leonore Schutte
With children
*Son:*Heinr. Friedrich Christoph
Pfingsten, Johann Conrad; America, 1854 7420.1 p126
Pfingsten, Johann Ernst Wilhelm; Port uncertain, 1837 7420.1 p13
Pfingsten, Sophie Louise; America, 1872 7420.1 p297
*Son:*Christian Friedrich Sch.
*Husband:*Gradierer Johann Ernst
Pfingsten, Wilhelm Christoph; Illinois, 1879 7420.1 p314
Pfinning, Godfrey; North Carolina, 1829 1088.45 p27
Pfister, Mr. 25; America, 1843 778.6 p268
Pfisterer, Andrew; Ohio, 1809-1852 4511.35 p40
Pfisterer, Philip P.; Ohio, 1809-1852 4511.35 p40
Pfitzenmyer, Wm. F.; Illinois, 1858-1861 6020.5 p132
Pflessterer, Philip P.; Ohio, 1809-1852 4511.35 p40
Pfluger, Friedrich Jakob; Port uncertain, 1837 7420.1 p13
Pflugrad, Auguste; Wisconsin, 1898 6795.8 p209
Pflugradt, Auguste; Wisconsin, 1898 6795.8 p209
Pflugradt, Julius Heinrich; Wisconsin, 1894 6795.8 p230
Pfoff, Abraham; Ohio, 1809-1852 4511.35 p40
Pfordt, Christian 28; America, 1836 5475.1 p27
Pfordt, Jakob; America, 1840 5475.1 p27
Pfost, Anna Maria; Venezuela, 1843 3899.5 p542
Pfromeier, Jacob 22; Missouri, 1845 778.6 p268
Pfund, Jean P.; Illinois, 1852 6079.1 p11
Pfund, Margaret; North Carolina, 1710 3629.40 p6
Phagin, John; Boston, 1765 1642 p34
Phair, Henry 40; Ontario, 1871 1823.21 p296
Phal, Fritz 22; New York, NY, 1864 8425.62 p197
Phalater, Abraham; Maine, 1660-1669 9228.50 p510
Phalater, Abraham; Maine, n.d. 9228.50 p349
Pharaoh, Thomas; America, 1768 1220.12 p624
Pharby, Stephen; North Carolina, 1842 1088.45 p27
Phealen, Patrick; Boston, 1753 1642 p31
Phegins, Hannah; Boston, 1718 1642 p24
Phelan, Daniel; St. Johns, N.F., 1825 1053.15 p6
Pheland, Thomas; Boston, 1744 1642 p45
Phelau, Sarah 25; Ontario, 1871 1823.21 p296
Phelen, Jacob; Colorado, 1873 1029.59 p74
Phelen, John; Boston, 1747 1642 p46
Phelippeaux, Charles; Quebec, 1653 9221.17 p278
Phelpes, William; America, 1685 1220.12 p624
Phelps, Anne *SEE* Phelps, William
Phelps, Edward; America, 1753 1220.12 p624
Phelps, Elijah; Ontario, 1787 1276.15 p230
With 2 relatives
Phelps, George T.; Colorado, 1885 1029.59 p74
Phelps, John; America, 1745 1220.12 p624
Phelps, John; America, 1756 1220.12 p624
Phelps, Joseph *SEE* Phelps, William
Phelps, Mary; America, 1748 1220.12 p624
Phelps, Nathaniel *SEE* Phelps, William
Phelps, Samuel *SEE* Phelps, William
Phelps, Thomas; America, 1752 1220.12 p624
Phelps, Thomas; America, 1775 1220.12 p624
Phelps, William; America, 1731 1220.12 p624
Phelps, William; America, 1747 1220.12 p624
Phelps, William *SEE* Phelps, William
Phelps, William; Massachusetts, 1630 117.5 p154
*Wife:*Anne
*Son:*William
*Son:*Samuel
*Son:*Joseph
*Son:*Nathaniel
Phelps, Willis 51; Ontario, 1871 1823.21 p296
Phelun, John; Boston, 1744 1642 p45
Phenix, Alice; Maryland, 1722 1220.12 p627
Phenix, Caroll; America, 1752 1220.12 p627
Phenlo, Lydia 19; Annapolis, MD, 1724 1220.12 p624
Pherson, Theophilus; Ohio, 1809-1852 4511.35 p40
Phesant, James; Maryland, 1722 1220.12 p624
Phibbs, Robert O. 40; Ontario, 1871 1823.17 p132
Phihue, Jacques; Quebec, 1646 9221.17 p164
Philbin, Bridget 60; Ontario, 1871 1823.17 p132
Philip, Joseph; Wisconsin, 1886 6795.8 p52
Philipe, Adam; Ohio, 1809-1852 4511.35 p40
Philipe, Claude; Virginia, 1700 9230.15 p81
With wife
Philipp, Anthony; Cincinnati, 1850 2853.20 p257
Philipp, Babette 25; Galveston, TX, 1844 3967.10 p371
Philipp, Eugene 18; New Orleans, 1848 778.6 p268
Philipp, Josephine 2; Galveston, TX, 1844 3967.10 p371
Philipp, Peter; Colorado, 1877 1029.59 p74
Philipp, Vinzenz 33; Galveston, TX, 1844 3967.10 p371
Philippe, Mr. 29; America, 1846 778.6 p268
Philippe, Anne; Quebec, 1671 4514.3 p356
Philippe, Felix 21; America, 1840 778.6 p268
Philippe, Jean; Montreal, 1642 9221.17 p124
Philippe, Laurent 22; Quebec, 1661 9221.17 p464
Philippe, Leonard 40; America, 1840 778.6 p268
Philippe, Maria 23; America, 1846 778.6 p268
Philippe, Marie 45; America, 1840 778.6 p268
Philippe, Marie-Madeleine; Quebec, 1668 4514.3 p356
Philippe, Prosper 29; New Orleans, 1848 778.6 p268
Philippeau, Nicole; Quebec, 1671 4514.3 p357
Philippeus, Alexander E. 45; New York, NY, 1878 9253.2 p45
Philippi, Adolf; America, 1849 5475.1 p29
Philippi, Anna; Pittsburgh, 1881 5475.1 p69
Philippi, C.; Louisiana, 1836-1840 4981.45 p213
Philippi, Georg; America, 1850 5475.1 p29
Philippi, Johann 23 *SEE* Philippi, Stephan
Philippi, Katharina; America, 1872 5475.1 p186
Philippi, Katharina 17 *SEE* Philippi, Stephan
Philippi, Ludwig; America, 1844 5475.1 p28
Philippi, Peter *SEE* Philippi, Stephan
Philippi, Stephan 57; America, 1857 5475.1 p253
*Son:*Peter
*Son:*Johann 23
*Daughter:*Katharina 17
Philippon, Guillaume; Nova Scotia, 1753 3051 p113
Philippon, Jeanne; Nova Scotia, 1753 3051 p112
Philipps, Daniel 36; Ontario, 1871 1823.21 p296
Philipps, Ellen B. 13; Ontario, 1871 1823.21 p296
Philipps, Emily 12; Ontario, 1871 1823.21 p296
Philipps, Mary 67; Ontario, 1871 1823.21 p296
Philips, Adam; Ohio, 1809-1852 4511.35 p40
Philips, Ann 45; Ontario, 1871 1823.21 p296
Philips, Franklin 34; Ontario, 1871 1823.17 p133
Philips, Frederick *SEE* Philips, Frederick
Philips, Frederick; New York, 1647-1653 2853.20 p14
*Son:*Frederick
Philips, Griffith 37; Ontario, 1871 1823.21 p296
Philips, H. 22; Ontario, 1871 1823.21 p296
Philips, James; Louisiana, 1836-1840 4981.45 p213
Philips, John 28; Ontario, 1871 1823.21 p296
Philips, John 49; Ontario, 1871 1823.21 p296
Philips, John 65; Ontario, 1871 1823.21 p296
Philips, Mary 38; Ontario, 1871 1823.21 p296
Philips, Patrick 42; Ontario, 1871 1823.21 p297
Philips, Robert 67; Ontario, 1871 1823.21 p297
Philips, Robert; Philadelphia, 1777 8529.30 p7A
Philips, William 39; Ontario, 1871 1823.21 p297
Philipse, Frederick *SEE* Philipse, Frederick
Philipse, Frederick; New York, 1647-1653 2853.20 p14
*Son:*Frederick
Phill, Frances; America, 1749 1220.12 p624
Phillicourt, F. 25; America, 1843 778.6 p268
Phillipp, Fanny; Philadelphia, 1854 8513.31 p303
Phillips, Adam; Ohio, 1809-1852 4511.35 p40
Phillips, Ann; America, 1744 1220.12 p624
Phillips, Ann; America, 1755 1220.12 p624
Phillips, Anne; Barbados, 1669 1220.12 p624
Phillips, Anne; Ohio, 1838 4022.20 p280
Phillips, Anne; Ohio, 1838 4022.20 p280
Phillips, Antone; Boston, 1826 3274.55 p73
Phillips, Benjamin; America, 1773 1220.12 p624
Phillips, Benjamin; America, 1774 1220.12 p624
Phillips, Benjamine M.; Colorado, 1891 1029.59 p74
Phillips, Charles; Virginia, 1730 1220.12 p624
Phillips, Cicely; Virginia, 1740 1220.12 p624
Phillips, Daniel; Barbados or Jamaica, 1697 1220.12 p624
Phillips, David; America, 1769 1220.12 p624
Phillips, David; Ohio, 1838 4022.20 p289
*Wife:*Margaret Williams
Phillips, David 81; Ontario, 1871 1823.21 p297
Phillips, Edward; America, 1700 1220.12 p624
Phillips, Edward; America, 1750 1220.12 p624
Phillips, Edward; America, 1751 1220.12 p624
Phillips, Edward; America, 1767 1220.12 p624
Phillips, Edward; America, 1774 1220.12 p624
Phillips, Edwin; Colorado, 1891 1029.59 p74
Phillips, Elizabeth; America, 1724 1220.12 p625
Phillips, Elizabeth; America, 1743 1220.12 p625
Phillips, Elizabeth; America, 1749 1220.12 p625
Phillips, Elizabeth; America, 1774 1220.12 p625
Phillips, Elizabeth; Ohio, 1840 4022.20 p275
Phillips, Emma; Barbados, 1666 1220.12 p625
Phillips, Emma; Barbados or Jamaica, 1677 1220.12 p625
Phillips, Evan; America, 1761 1220.12 p625
Phillips, Evan; America, 1771 1220.12 p625
Phillips, Fidelia; Barbados, 1664 1220.12 p625
Phillips, Francis 50; Ontario, 1871 1823.17 p133
Phillips, Francis 57; Ontario, 1871 1823.21 p297
Phillips, Frank 16; Quebec, 1870 8364.32 p25
Phillips, George; America, 1766 1220.12 p625
Phillips, George; Massachusetts, 1630 117.5 p157
Phillips, George 42; Ontario, 1871 1823.21 p297
Phillips, Hannah; America, 1745 1220.12 p625
Phillips, Henry 37; Ontario, 1871 1823.21 p297
Phillips, Isaac; America, 1769 1220.12 p625
Phillips, Isiah; Louisiana, 1874 4981.45 p133
Phillips, James; America, 1719 1220.12 p625
Phillips, James; America, 1769 1220.12 p625
Phillips, James; America, 1774 1220.12 p625
Phillips, James; Died enroute, 1725 1220.12 p625
Phillips, James; North Carolina, 1830 1088.45 p27
Phillips, James; Virginia, 1732 1220.12 p625
Phillips, James John; America, 1772 1220.12 p625
Phillips, Jane; America, 1756 1220.12 p625
Phillips, Jane; America, 1764 1220.12 p625
Phillips, Jane 16; Quebec, 1870 8364.32 p25
Phillips, John; America, 1697 1220.12 p625
Phillips, John; America, 1729 1220.12 p625
Phillips, John; America, 1738 1220.12 p625
Phillips, John; America, 1740 1220.12 p625
Phillips, John; America, 1745 1220.12 p625
Phillips, John; America, 1749 1220.12 p625
Phillips, John; America, 1751 1220.12 p625
Phillips, John; America, 1754 1220.12 p625
Phillips, John; America, 1760 1220.12 p625
Phillips, John; America, 1766 1220.12 p625
Phillips, John; America, 1767 1220.12 p625
Phillips, John; America, 1768 1220.12 p625
Phillips, John; America, 1771 1220.12 p625
Phillips, John; America, 1773 1220.12 p625
Phillips, John; America, 1774 1220.12 p625
Phillips, John; America, 1775 1220.12 p625
Phillips, John; Barbados, 1664 1220.12 p625
Phillips, John; Louisiana, 1874 4981.45 p133
Phillips, John; Maryland, 1672 1236.25 p47
Phillips, John; Maryland, 1737 1220.12 p625
Phillips, John; Massachusetts, 1630 117.5 p157
Phillips, John 72; Ontario, 1871 1823.21 p297
Phillips, John; Virginia, 1759 1220.12 p625
Phillips, John Maurice; Washington, 1885 2770.40 p194
Phillips, Joseph; America, 1760 1220.12 p625
Phillips, Joseph; America, 1771 1220.12 p625
Phillips, Joshua 22; Ontario, 1871 1823.17 p133
Phillips, Lewis; Ohio, 1840 4022.20 p289
Phillips, Margaret; America, 1690 1220.12 p625
Phillips, Margaret Williams *SEE* Phillips, David
Phillips, Mary; America, 1677 1220.12 p625
Phillips, Mary; America, 1753 1220.12 p625
Phillips, Mary; America, 1757 1220.12 p626
Phillips, Mary; America, 1764 1220.12 p626
Phillips, Mary; America, 1772 1220.12 p626
Phillips, Mary; Annapolis, MD, 1726 1220.12 p625
Phillips, Mary; Concord, NH, 1868-1870 9228.50 p506
Phillips, Moses; America, 1772 1220.12 p626
Phillips, Moses; America, 1774 1220.12 p626
Phillips, Paul; Maryland, 1723 1220.12 p626
Phillips, Peter; Colorado, 1877 1029.59 p75
Phillips, Philip; America, 1768 1220.12 p626
Phillips, Philip H.; Illinois, 1858-1861 6020.5 p132
Phillips, Phillip; Iowa, 1903 1211.15 p18
Phillips, Rachel; Ohio, 1849 4022.20 p278
Phillips, Ralph; America, 1728 1220.12 p626
Phillips, Richard; America, 1724 1220.12 p626
Phillips, Richard; America, 1766 1220.12 p626
Phillips, Richard 50; Ontario, 1871 1823.21 p297
Phillips, Richard; Virginia, 1754 1220.12 p626
Phillips, Richard 20; Virginia, 1635 1183.3 p31
Phillips, Robert 43; Ontario, 1871 1823.21 p297
Phillips, Robert; Philadelphia, 1777 8529.30 p7A
Phillips, Samuel; America, 1742 1220.12 p626
Phillips, Samuel; America, 1769 1220.12 p626
Phillips, Samuel; Washington, 1887 6015.10 p16
Phillips, Sarah; America, 1748 1220.12 p626
Phillips, Silas; America, 1685 1220.12 p626
Phillips, Stephen; America, 1721 1220.12 p626
Phillips, Thomas; America, 1673 1220.12 p626
Phillips, Thomas; America, 1702 1220.12 p626

Phillips, Thomas; America, 1750 ***1220.12*** *p626*
Phillips, Thomas; America, 1767 ***1220.12*** *p626*
Phillips, Thomas; America, 1771 ***1220.12*** *p626*
Phillips, Thomas; America, 1774 ***1220.12*** *p626*
Phillips, Thomas; America, 1775 ***1220.12*** *p626*
Phillips, Thomas; Barbados, 1665 ***1220.12*** *p626*
Phillips, Thomas; Colorado, 1891 ***1029.59*** *p75*
Phillips, Thomas; Maryland, 1672 ***1236.25*** *p46*
Phillips, Thos; St. John, N.B., 1847 ***2978.15*** *p39*
Phillips, Timothy; America, 1770 ***1220.12*** *p626*
Phillips, W. H. 30; Ontario, 1871 ***1823.21*** *p297*
Phillips, Walter; America, 1685 ***1220.12*** *p626*
Phillips, Walter 19; Quebec, 1870 ***8364.32*** *p25*
Phillips, William; America, 1730 ***1220.12*** *p626*
Phillips, William; America, 1737 ***1220.12*** *p626*
Phillips, William; America, 1740 ***1220.12*** *p626*
Phillips, William; America, 1754 ***1220.12*** *p626*
Phillips, William; America, 1766 ***1220.12*** *p626*
Phillips, William; Annapolis, MD, 1719 ***1220.12*** *p626*
Phillips, William; Annapolis, MD, 1725 ***1220.12*** *p626*
Phillips, William; Barbados, 1668 ***1220.12*** *p626*
Phillips, William; Barbados, 1670 ***1220.12*** *p626*
Phillips, William; Iowa, 1871 ***1211.15*** *p18*
Phillips, William; Marston's Wharf, 1782 ***8529.30*** *p15*
Phillips, William; Ontario, 1871 ***1823.17*** *p133*
Phillips, William 34; Ontario, 1871 ***1823.21*** *p297*
Phillips, William 57; Ontario, 1871 ***1823.21*** *p297*
Phillips, William 68; Ontario, 1871 ***1823.21*** *p297*
Phillips, William; Virginia, 1735 ***1220.12*** *p626*
Phillips, William; Virginia, 1740 ***1220.12*** *p626*
Phillips, Wilmot; America, 1758 ***1220.12*** *p626*
Phillipson, John; Virginia, 1739 ***1220.12*** *p626*
Phillis, Alexander; Barbados, 1665 ***1220.12*** *p626*
Phillis, Joseph; Maryland or Virginia, 1738 ***1220.12*** *p626*
Philloh, Charlotte 26; New Orleans, 1845 ***778.6*** *p268*
Philloh, Henry 4; New Orleans, 1845 ***778.6*** *p268*
Philloh, Joseph 26; New Orleans, 1845 ***778.6*** *p268*
Phillpot, E.; Louisiana, 1874 ***4981.45*** *p133*
Phillpot, William; Louisiana, 1874 ***4981.45*** *p133*
Philoe, Thomas; America, 1773 ***1220.12*** *p626*
Philomy, John; Philadelphia, 1851 ***5720.10*** *p379*
Philp, Stephen 36; Ontario, 1871 ***1823.21*** *p297*
Philpin, William; North Carolina, 1842 ***1088.45*** *p27*
Philpot, George; America, 1768 ***1220.12*** *p626*
Philpot, John; America, 1765 ***1220.12*** *p540*
Philpot, Mary; America, 1763 ***1220.12*** *p627*
Philpott, Henry; America, 1752 ***1220.12*** *p626*
Philpott, Jane; America, 1747 ***1220.12*** *p627*
Philpott, Thomas; America, 1734 ***1220.12*** *p627*
Philpotts, Edward; America, 1753 ***1220.12*** *p627*
Philps, Hugh; Barbados, 1714 ***1220.12*** *p624*
Philwood, John; Annapolis, MD, 1720 ***1220.12*** *p627*
Phineas, Joseph; America, 1767 ***1220.12*** *p627*
Phinnimore, John; America, 1685 ***1220.12*** *p627*
Phippe, John; America, 1655 ***1220.12*** *p627*
Phippen, William; America, 1685 ***1220.12*** *p627*
Phippin, Henry 37; Ontario, 1871 ***1823.21*** *p297*
Phippin, Robert 41; Ontario, 1871 ***1823.21*** *p297*
Phipps, Charles; Kansas, 1895 ***1447.20*** *p64*
Phipps, Dinah; America, 1774 ***1220.12*** *p627*
Phipps, George; America, 1751 ***1220.12*** *p627*
Phipps, James; America, 1763 ***1220.12*** *p627*
Phipps, John; America, 1655 ***1220.12*** *p627*
Phipps, John; Barbados or Jamaica, 1699 ***1220.12*** *p627*
Phipps, John; Maryland, 1727 ***1220.12*** *p627*
Phipps, Mary; America, 1612-1699 ***9228.50*** *p654*
Phipps, Mary; America, 1768 ***1220.12*** *p627*
Phipps, Paul 44; Ontario, 1871 ***1823.21*** *p297*
Phipps, Stephen; America, 1731 ***1220.12*** *p627*
Phipps, Stephen; America, 1751 ***1220.12*** *p627*
Phipps, William; America, 1680 ***1220.12*** *p627*
Phipps, William; America, 1746 ***1220.12*** *p627*
Phipps, William B.; North Carolina, 1854 ***1088.45*** *p27*
Phippy, John; America, 1661 ***1220.12*** *p627*
Phlipot, Agnes Sorin *SEE* Phlipot, Jean
Phlipot, Jean; Nova Scotia, 1753 ***3051*** *p112*
*Wife:*Agnes Sorin
Phoenix, David 37; Ontario, 1871 ***1823.21*** *p297*
Phoenix, Walter; America, 1726 ***1220.12*** *p627*
Phoinix, Matthew 49; Ontario, 1871 ***1823.21*** *p297*
Phratter, Phillis; America, 1737 ***1220.12*** *p627*
Phylis, Jacques 41; Quebec, 1662 ***9221.17*** *p484*
Pialats, Jacques 30; Port uncertain, 1841 ***778.6*** *p268*
Pian, Henry C.; Illinois, 1856 ***6079.1*** *p11*
Piasecki, Sem; Galveston, TX, 1881 ***6015.15*** *p13*
Piattoly, Mrs. J. 25; America, 1848 ***778.6*** *p268*
Piattoly, J. D. 30; America, 1848 ***778.6*** *p268*
Piau, Pierre; Quebec, 1647 ***9221.17*** *p187*
Pic, Mr. 30; America, 1841 ***778.6*** *p268*
Picard, Hugues 31; Montreal, 1653 ***9221.17*** *p298*
Picard, Jacques; Quebec, 1648 ***9221.17*** *p199*
Picard, Jacques; Quebec, 1656 ***9221.17*** *p345*
Picard, Jean 10 *SEE* Picard, Pierre
Picard, Leopold; Louisiana, 1874-1875 ***4981.45*** *p30*
Picard, Marguerite 13; Montreal, 1657 ***9221.17*** *p373*
Picard, Nicolas 15; Quebec, 1656 ***9221.17*** *p345*
Picard, Pierre 34; America, 1843 ***778.6*** *p268*
Picard, Pierre; Quebec, 1649 ***9221.17*** *p212*
Picard, Pierre 34; Quebec, 1645 ***9221.17*** *p156*
*Wife:*Renee Suronne 29
*Son:*Jean 10
Picard, Renee Suronne 29 *SEE* Picard, Pierre
Picard, Vincent; Quebec, 1659 ***9221.17*** *p408*
Picart, Adeline 6; Port uncertain, 1843 ***778.6*** *p268*
Picart, Alexandre 36; America, 1843 ***778.6*** *p268*
Picart, Augustin 22; America, 1843 ***778.6*** *p268*
Picart, Claude 61; America, 1843 ***778.6*** *p269*
Picart, Jean 30; Port uncertain, 1843 ***778.6*** *p269*
Picart, Marie 31; Port uncertain, 1843 ***778.6*** *p269*
Picart, Pierre 39; America, 1843 ***778.6*** *p269*
Picau, T. 28; New Orleans, 1845 ***778.6*** *p269*
Piceford, Robert; America, 1742 ***1220.12*** *p627*
Picha, Josef; St. Paul, MN, 1868 ***2853.20*** *p277*
Picha, Vaclav; St. Paul, MN, 1870 ***2853.20*** *p277*
Pichard, Jean 21; Montreal, 1653 ***9221.17*** *p299*
Picher, Pierre; Quebec, 1661 ***9221.17*** *p465*
Pichet, Jean 26; Quebec, 1659 ***9221.17*** *p408*
Pichler, Thomas; Colorado, 1895 ***1029.59*** *p75*
Pichon, Bernard; Quebec, 1645 ***9221.17*** *p156*
Pichon, Celestin 37; Louisiana, 1848 ***778.6*** *p269*
Pichon, Francois 20; Quebec, 1657 ***9221.17*** *p363*
Pichon, Jean 32 *SEE* Pichon, Mathurin
Pichon, Jules 10; Louisiana, 1848 ***778.6*** *p269*
Pichon, Mace 23 *SEE* Pichon, Mathurin
Pichon, Marie; Quebec, 1636 ***9221.17*** *p63*
Pichon, Mathurin; Quebec, 1659 ***9221.17*** *p408*
*Son:*Jean
*Son:*Mace
Pick, Julius; Louisiana, 1860 ***7710.1*** *p156*
Pickard, Ellen 8; Quebec, 1870 ***8364.32*** *p25*
Pickard, Frederick; New York, 1778 ***8529.30*** *p4A*
Pickard, Herbert B.; Quebec, 1885 ***1937.10*** *p52*
Pickard, Isaac 8; Ontario, 1871 ***1823.21*** *p297*
Pickard, Jane; Virginia, 1745 ***1220.12*** *p627*
Pickard, John; America, 1757 ***1220.12*** *p627*
Pickard, Thomas; America, 1774 ***1220.12*** *p627*
Pickard, William; America, 1751 ***1220.12*** *p627*
Pickel, Charles; Philadelphia, 1868 ***8513.31*** *p421*
*Wife:*Helene Balkhaus
Pickel, Contrad; Ohio, 1844 ***2763.1*** *p21*
Pickel, Friedrich; America, 1867 ***7919.3*** *p534*
With family
Pickel, Helene Balkhaus *SEE* Pickel, Charles
Pickel, Henry; Ohio, 1844 ***2763.1*** *p21*
Pickel, Michael; North Carolina, 1710 ***3629.40*** *p6*
Pickell, Henry; America, 1773 ***1220.12*** *p627*
Picken, Martha 26; North Carolina, 1774 ***1422.10*** *p57*
Picken, Willm. 32; North Carolina, 1774 ***1422.10*** *p57*
Pickens, James; West Virginia, 1856 ***1132.30*** *p149*
*Son:*James, Jr.
Pickens, James, Jr. *SEE* Pickens, James
Pickerell, William; Barbados or Jamaica, 1696 ***1220.12*** *p627*
Pickering, Benjamin; America, 1766 ***1220.12*** *p627*
Pickering, Charles; Quebec, 1870 ***8364.32*** *p25*
Pickering, Elizabeth 63; Ontario, 1871 ***1823.21*** *p297*
Pickering, George 40; Ontario, 1871 ***1823.21*** *p297*
Pickering, George; Washington, 1889 ***2770.40*** *p80*
Pickering, John; America, 1751 ***1220.12*** *p627*
Pickering, John; America, 1762 ***1220.12*** *p627*
Pickering, John; America, 1774 ***1220.12*** *p627*
Pickering, John 37; Ontario, 1871 ***1823.21*** *p297*
Pickering, John 56; Ontario, 1871 ***1823.21*** *p297*
Pickering, John; Virginia, 1729 ***1220.12*** *p627*
Pickering, John Christopher; America, 1736 ***1220.12*** *p627*
Pickernell, James; Maine, 1707 ***9228.50*** *p510*
Pickernell Family ; New England, n.d. ***9228.50*** *p510*
Pickersgill, Joe; Iowa, 1914 ***1211.15*** *p18*
Pickersgill, Thomas; America, 1760 ***1220.12*** *p627*
Picket, Edwin B. 46; Michigan, 1880 ***4491.39*** *p24*
Picket, Henry; Ohio, 1844 ***2763.1*** *p21*
Picket, John; America, 1665 ***1220.12*** *p627*
Pickett, D.J.; Quebec, 1980 ***9228.50*** *p510*
Pickett, Giles; Canada, 1774 ***3036.5*** *p41*
*Wife:*Mary
*Child:*John
*Child:*Margaret
*Child:*William
*Child:*James
Pickett, James *SEE* Pickett, Giles
Pickett, James; Potomac, 1729 ***1220.12*** *p627*
Pickett, Jane *SEE* Pickett, Nicholas
Pickett, John *SEE* Pickett, Giles
Pickett, John; Marblehead, MA, 1752 ***9228.50*** *p226*
*Wife:*Miriam
*Daughter:*Miriam
Pickett, Margaret *SEE* Pickett, Giles
Pickett, Mary *SEE* Pickett, Giles
Pickett, Miriam *SEE* Pickett, John
Pickett, Miriam *SEE* Pickett, John
Pickett, Nicholas; Marblehead, MA, 1718 ***9228.50*** *p510*
*Wife:*Jane
With children
Pickett, Nicholas; Massachusetts, 1702 ***9228.50*** *p510*
Pickett, William; Annapolis, MD, 1725 ***1220.12*** *p628*
Pickett, William *SEE* Pickett, Giles
Pickford, Joseph; America, 1725 ***1220.12*** *p628*
Pickford, Mark; America, 1737 ***1220.12*** *p628*
Pickills, Thomas; America, 1775 ***1220.12*** *p628*
Pickington, Grace; America, 1747 ***1220.12*** *p628*
Pickle, David 63; Ontario, 1871 ***1823.21*** *p297*
Pickles, John; America, 1723 ***1220.12*** *p628*
Pickles, John; America, 1759 ***1220.12*** *p628*
Pickley, Margaret 35; Ontario, 1871 ***1823.21*** *p297*
Pickmore, Thomas; America, 1722 ***1220.12*** *p628*
Picknp, Edward 42; Ontario, 1871 ***1823.17*** *p133*
Pickstock, John; America, 1757 ***1220.12*** *p628*
Pickton, John; Annapolis, MD, 1725 ***1220.12*** *p628*
Pickup, Aaron; Ohio, 1836 ***3580.20*** *p33*
Pickup, Aaron; Ohio, 1836 ***6020.12*** *p21*
Pickup, George; California, 1860 ***1211.45*** *p134*
Picone, Joseph; Louisiana, 1874 ***4981.45*** *p133*
Picot, A.; San Francisco, 1852 ***9228.50*** *p510*
Picot, A. M. 13; America, 1842 ***778.6*** *p269*
Picot, Elias; Boston, 1723 ***9228.50*** *p510*
*Wife:*Jane
Picot, Geo.; Massachusetts, 1775-1820 ***9228.50*** *p122*
Picot, Jane *SEE* Picot, Elias
Picot, John; Marblehead, MA, 1752 ***9228.50*** *p226*
*Wife:*Miriam
*Daughter:*Miriam
Picot, Miriam *SEE* Picot, John
Picot, Miriam *SEE* Picot, John
Picot, Nicholas; Massachusetts, 1702 ***9228.50*** *p510*
Picot, Robert; Quebec, 1653 ***9221.17*** *p278*
Picote DeBelestre, Perrine 15; Montreal, 1659 ***9221.17*** *p426*
*Brother:*Pierre 22
Picote DeBelestre, Pierre 22 *SEE* Picote DeBelestre, Perrine
Picote deBelestre, Pierre; Quebec, 1659 ***2314.30*** *p166*
Picote deBelestre, Pierre; Quebec, 1659 ***2314.30*** *p192*
Picton, Margaret; America, 1735 ***1220.12*** *p628*
Piddesley, Matthew; Barbados, 1673 ***1220.12*** *p628*
Piddington, Christopher 18; Virginia, 1635 ***1183.3*** *p30*
Piddington, Edward; America, 1759 ***1220.12*** *p628*
Piddington, John; America, 1764 ***1220.12*** *p628*
Piddle, James; America, 1720 ***1220.12*** *p628*
Pider, George; Ohio, 1809-1852 ***4511.35*** *p40*
Pidgeon, John; America, 1728 ***1220.12*** *p628*
Pidgeon, Mary; America, 1746 ***1220.12*** *p628*
Pidgeon, William; America, 1755 ***1220.12*** *p628*
Pidgley, James; America, 1688 ***1220.12*** *p628*
Pidhajny, Dimitrius; Detroit, 1929 ***1640.55*** *p115*
Pie, Joseph 19; America, 1845 ***778.6*** *p269*
Piece, John 51; Ontario, 1871 ***1823.21*** *p297*
Piederit, William; Illinois, 1851 ***6079.1*** *p11*
Piederluche, Wilhelmine 20; New York, NY, 1864 ***8425.62*** *p197*
Piedfort, Rosalie; Wisconsin, 1885 ***1495.20*** *p56*
Piednoel, Edouard 22; Missouri, 1848 ***778.6*** *p269*
Piednoel, Elisabeth 23; Missouri, 1848 ***778.6*** *p269*
Piedoux, Olivier; Quebec, 1649 ***9221.17*** *p219*
Piedrit, Frederick; Illinois, 1851 ***6079.1*** *p11*
Piedt, Carolina *SEE* Piedt, Johann, Jr.
Piedt, Elisabeth *SEE* Piedt, Johann, Jr.
Piedt, Friederika; Dakota, 1887 ***554.30*** *p25*
Piedt, Jakob *SEE* Piedt, Johann, Sr.
Piedt, Johann, Jr.; Dakota, 1888 ***554.30*** *p25*
*Wife:*Maria Leitner
*Child:*Carolina
*Child:*Elisabeth
Piedt, Johann, Sr.; Dakota, 1866-1918 ***554.30*** *p25*
*Child:*Jakob
*Wife:*Karolina Lang
Piedt, Karolina Lang *SEE* Piedt, Johann, Sr.
Piedt, Maria Leitner *SEE* Piedt, Johann, Jr.
Piedt, Susanna; Dakota, 1886 ***554.30*** *p25*
Piefer, H. 20; America, 1846 ***778.6*** *p269*
Piek, Louis; America, 1857 ***7420.1*** *p169*
Piekos, Aniela; Detroit, 1929-1930 ***6214.5*** *p60*
Piel, Friedrich Wilhelm; America, 1846 ***7420.1*** *p47*
*Wife:*Philippine Charlotte Regine Portge
Piel, Friedrich Wilhelm; America, 1872 ***7420.1*** *p297*
Piel, Heinrich; America, 1877 ***7420.1*** *p309*
Piel, Philippine; Illinois, 1876 ***7420.1*** *p307*

Piel, Philippine Charlotte Regine Portge *SEE* Piel, Friedrich Wilhelm
Pielaszkiewicz, Seweryn; Detroit, 1929-1930 ***6214.5*** *p65*
Pielech, Franciszek 27; New York, NY, 1904 ***8355.1*** *p15*
Pienarek, Mike; Texas, 1900 ***6015.15*** *p29*
Piep, Christ; Iowa, 1892 ***1211.15*** *p18*
Piepenbrink, Engel Marie Sophie Pfingsten *SEE* Piepenbrink, Johann Heinrich Conrad
Piepenbrink, Friedrich Conrad; America, 1864 ***7420.1*** *p226*
Piepenbrink, Friedrich Konrad *SEE* Piepenbrink, Johann Heinrich Conrad
Piepenbrink, Johann Heinrich; America, 1854 ***7420.1*** *p126*
Piepenbrink, Johann Heinrich Conrad; America, 1865 ***7420.1*** *p235*
*Wife:*Engel Marie Sophie Pfingsten
*Son:*Friedrich Konrad
Piepenbrink, Johann Otto; America, 1854 ***7420.1*** *p126*
Piepenbrink, Otto; America, 1853 ***7420.1*** *p110*
Pieper, Amalie; America, 1870 ***7420.1*** *p395*
Pieper, Engel Cathar. Margr.; America, 1855 ***7420.1*** *p140*
Pieper, Friedrich; America, 1857 ***7420.1*** *p169*
With wife & daughter-in-law
Pieper, Friedrich Conrad; America, 1853 ***7420.1*** *p110*
Pieper, Heinrich Carl August; America, 1855 ***7420.1*** *p140*
Pieper, Justine Friederike; America, 1854 ***7420.1*** *p129*
Pieper, Louise Charlotte; America, 1868 ***7420.1*** *p275*
Piepho, Mr.; America, 1854 ***7420.1*** *p126*
With wife 2 sons & daughter
Piepho, Christian; America, 1852 ***7420.1*** *p95*
Piepho, Johann Cord; America, 1857 ***7420.1*** *p169*
With wife & 2 daughters
Pier, Angela *SEE* Pier, Mathias
Pier, Anna Maria Folz *SEE* Pier, Mathias
Pier, Jakob *SEE* Pier, Mathias
Pier, Mathias; Wisconsin, 1891 ***5475.1*** *p326*
*Wife:*Anna Maria Folz
*Son:*Jakob
*Daughter:*Angela
Pier, Peter; America, 1871 ***5475.1*** *p324*
Pierard, Charles Joseph; Wisconsin, 1870 ***1495.20*** *p8*
*Wife:*Virginie Marlier
*Child:*Joachim Xavier
*Child:*Marie Josephine
Pierard, Joachim Xavier *SEE* Pierard, Charles Joseph
Pierard, Marie Josephine *SEE* Pierard, Charles Joseph
Pierard, Virginie Marlier *SEE* Pierard, Charles Joseph
Pierce, Abraham; America, 1738 ***1220.12*** *p614*
Pierce, Arthur 65; Ontario, 1871 ***1823.17*** *p133*
Pierce, David; America, 1721 ***1220.12*** *p614*
Pierce, Edward; America, 1758 ***1220.12*** *p614*
Pierce, Elizabeth; America, 1753 ***1220.12*** *p614*
Pierce, George; America, 1726 ***1220.12*** *p614*
Pierce, George; America, 1769 ***1220.12*** *p614*
Pierce, Henry 25; Ontario, 1871 ***1823.21*** *p297*
Pierce, James 23; Ontario, 1871 ***1823.17*** *p133*
Pierce, John; Barbados, 1667 ***1220.12*** *p614*
Pierce, John; Long Island, 1781 ***8529.30*** *p10A*
Pierce, John; Massachusetts, 1630 ***117.5*** *p157*
*Wife:*Parnell
Pierce, Mary; America, 1758 ***1220.12*** *p615*
Pierce, Parnell *SEE* Pierce, John
Pierce, Robert 55; Ontario, 1871 ***1823.21*** *p297*
Pierce, Thomas; America, 1743 ***1220.12*** *p615*
Pierce, Thomas; Rappahannock, VA, 1729 ***1220.12*** *p615*
Pierce, Thomas; Virginia, 1721 ***1220.12*** *p615*
Piercy, Charles; America, 1772 ***1220.12*** *p616*
Piercy, Elizabeth; America, 1738 ***1220.12*** *p616*
Piercy, John; America, 1751 ***1220.12*** *p616*
Piercy, John; America, 1755 ***1220.12*** *p616*
Pierel, Julie 2; New Orleans, 1848 ***778.6*** *p269*
Pierel, Odille 7; New Orleans, 1848 ***778.6*** *p269*
Piero, Ignatius; Ohio, 1809-1852 ***4511.35*** *p40*
Piero, Joseph; Ohio, 1809-1852 ***4511.35*** *p40*
Pieron, Desire 32; America, 1745 ***778.6*** *p269*
Pierott, Francis; Long Island, 1778 ***8529.30*** *p10A*
Pierpoint, John; Charles Town, SC, 1719 ***1220.12*** *p628*
Pierre, Adolphe 32; New Orleans, 1848 ***778.6*** *p269*
Pierre, Antoine 65; Missouri, 1845 ***778.6*** *p269*
Pierre, C. P. Girard; North Carolina, 1848 ***1088.45*** *p27*
Pierre, Charles; Quebec, 1634 ***9221.17*** *p39*
Pierre, Frederic 14; America, 1746 ***778.6*** *p269*
Pierre, James 45; Missouri, 1845 ***778.6*** *p269*
Pierre, Jean 28; Missouri, 1845 ***778.6*** *p269*
Pierre, Jean Albert 22; New Orleans, 1748 ***778.6*** *p269*
Pierre, Jean-Baptiste 24; New Orleans, 1748 ***778.6*** *p269*
Pierre, Joseph Charles; Louisiana, 1874 ***4981.45*** *p133*
Pierre, Lacalle; Louisiana, 1874-1875 ***4981.45*** *p30*
Pierre, Leon 30; America, 1746 ***778.6*** *p269*
Pierre, Louis 32; America, 1846 ***778.6*** *p269*
Pierre, Louis 34; New Orleans, 1848 ***778.6*** *p269*
Pierrecot deBailleul, Louis Audet; Quebec, 1696 ***2314.30*** *p169*
Pierrecot deBailleul, Louis Audet; Quebec, 1696 ***2314.30*** *p193*
Pierret, Francois 57; New Orleans, 1848 ***778.6*** *p269*
Pierrol, Antoine 32; New Orleans, 1848 ***778.6*** *p269*
Pierron, Mr. 30; New Orleans, 1848 ***778.6*** *p269*
Pierron, Charles 22; America, 1841 ***778.6*** *p269*
Pierron, J. N.; Ohio, 1809-1852 ***4511.35*** *p40*
Pierrot, Francois 21; Quebec, 1661 ***9221.17*** *p465*
Pierrot, Gustavus Alexander; Illinois, 1855 ***6079.1*** *p11*
Pierrow, Nicholas; Ohio, 1809-1852 ***4511.35*** *p40*
Piersey, John; America, 1741 ***1220.12*** *p616*
Pierson, Diana; America, 1757 ***1220.12*** *p616*
Pierson, Francois 28; Port uncertain, 1843 ***778.6*** *p269*
Pierson, Jeanne 23; Port uncertain, 1843 ***778.6*** *p269*
Pierson, John 24; Indiana, 1880-1881 ***9076.20*** *p70*
Pierson, John Nicholas; Ohio, 1809-1852 ***4511.35*** *p40*
Pierson, Joseph; America, 1769 ***1220.12*** *p616*
Pierson, Malta 22; Kansas, 1880 ***777.40*** *p20*
Pierson, Per Algott; New York, 1902 ***1766.20*** *p16*
Pierson, Peter; Ohio, 1809-1852 ***4511.35*** *p40*
Pierson, William; America, 1751 ***1220.12*** *p617*
Pieschke, August; Wisconsin, 1885 ***6795.8*** *p52*
Pietarila, Abram 46; Minnesota, 1923 ***2769.54*** *p1381*
Pieton, Francoise; Quebec, 1667 ***4514.3*** *p357*
Pietras, Wladyslaw; Detroit, 1930 ***1640.60*** *p81*
Pietrzak, Benjamin; Detroit, 1929 ***1640.55*** *p113*
Pietsch, Eva 20; Halifax, N.S., 1902 ***1860.4*** *p41*
Pietsch, Jacob 16; Halifax, N.S., 1902 ***1860.4*** *p41*
Pietsch, Johann 25; Halifax, N.S., 1902 ***1860.4*** *p41*
Pietsch, Nikolaus; America, 1884 ***5475.1*** *p268*
Piette, Charles *SEE* Piette, Maximilien
Piette, Flore Marie *SEE* Piette, Josephine
Piette, Josephine *SEE* Piette, Maximilien
Piette, Josephine; Wisconsin, 1880 ***1495.20*** *p45*
*Grandchild:*Marie Therese
*Grandchild:*Flore Marie
Piette, Marie Therese *SEE* Piette, Josephine
Piette, Maximilien; Wisconsin, 1857 ***1495.20*** *p45*
*Wife:*Victoire Boucher
*Child:*Josephine
*Child:*Charles
Piette, Victoire Boucher *SEE* Piette, Maximilien
Pietz, Ant. 17; America, 1840 ***778.6*** *p269*
Pietzcker, Herman; Ohio, 1809-1852 ***4511.35*** *p40*
Pietzeker, Augustus F.; Ohio, 1809-1852 ***4511.35*** *p40*
Pifarer, James; Louisiana, 1874 ***4981.45*** *p133*
Pifeteau, Pierre; Quebec, 1647 ***9221.17*** *p187*
Piffaut, Joseph 39; America, 1848 ***778.6*** *p270*
Piffeteau, Francois; Quebec, 1658 ***9221.17*** *p385*
Pifray, Jacques 22; Quebec, 1657 ***9221.17*** *p365*
Pifre, Jacques 22; Quebec, 1657 ***9221.17*** *p365*
Pifre, M. 35; Mexico, 1846 ***778.6*** *p270*
Pifre, Marie 40; Mexico, 1846 ***778.6*** *p270*
Pifret, Jacques 22; Quebec, 1657 ***9221.17*** *p365*
Pigen, John; America, 1773 ***1220.12*** *p628*
Pigeon, James; America, 1765 ***1220.12*** *p628*
Pigeon, Jeanne Josephe Sidonie; Wisconsin, 1857 ***1495.20*** *p41*
Pigeon, Mary; America, 1762 ***1220.12*** *p628*
Pigeon, Pierre 24; Montreal, 1661 ***9221.17*** *p474*
Pigeon, William; America, 1767 ***1220.12*** *p628*
Pigg, Joseph; America, 1742 ***1220.12*** *p628*
Pigget, William; America, 1737 ***1220.12*** *p628*
Piggot, John; America, 1769 ***1220.12*** *p628*
Piggot, William; America, 1742 ***1220.12*** *p628*
Piggott, Daniel; America, 1734 ***1220.12*** *p628*
Piggott, John; America, 1737 ***1220.12*** *p628*
Piggott, John; America, 1765 ***1220.12*** *p628*
Piggott, Mary; America, 1744 ***1220.12*** *p628*
Piggott, Mary; America, 1772 ***1220.12*** *p628*
Piggott, Ralph; America, 1743 ***1220.12*** *p628*
Piggott, Richard; Barbados, 1672 ***1220.12*** *p628*
Piggott, Thomas 53; Ontario, 1871 ***1823.17*** *p133*
Piggott, William; Barbados, 1670 ***1220.12*** *p628*
Pignane, Anna 18; America, 1840 ***778.6*** *p270*
Pignane, Bapt. 14; America, 1840 ***778.6*** *p270*
Pignane, Cath. 41; America, 1840 ***778.6*** *p270*
Pignane, Jean 42; America, 1840 ***778.6*** *p270*
Pignane, Joh. 18; America, 1840 ***778.6*** *p270*
Pignatel, L. 68; America, 1841 ***778.6*** *p270*
Pigneau, Rene; Montreal, 1647 ***9221.17*** *p192*
Pignon, Susanna 38; America, 1873 ***5475.1*** *p307*
Pigorsch, Alf. Aug. Evald; Wisconsin, 1897 ***6795.8*** *p197*
Pigorsch, Gustav Friedrich; Wisconsin, 1895 ***6795.8*** *p197*
Pigot, Elisa 59; Ontario, 1871 ***1823.21*** *p297*
Pigot, George; America, 1767 ***1220.12*** *p628*
Pigott, Thomas; America, 1737 ***1220.12*** *p628*
Pigott, Thomas 42; Ontario, 1871 ***1823.21*** *p298*
Pigournel Family ; New England, n.d. ***9228.50*** *p510*
Pigula, Frank; Detroit, 1930 ***1640.60*** *p83*
Pihlqvist, J.G.; New York, NY, 1845 ***6412.40*** *p148*
Pihlstrom, John Sigfrid; St. Paul, MN, 1902 ***1865.50*** *p107*
Pijart, Claude 37; Quebec, 1637 ***9221.17*** *p67*
Pijart, Pierre 27; Quebec, 1635 ***9221.17*** *p42*
Pijot, Antoine; Quebec, 1642 ***9221.17*** *p122*
Pijut, Catherine; Detroit, 1890 ***9980.23*** *p96*
Pike, David 38; Ontario, 1871 ***1823.17*** *p133*
Pike, James; Quebec, 1850-1915 ***9228.50*** *p635*
Pike, James; Quebec, 1900-1930 ***9228.50*** *p511*
Pike, John; America, 1774 ***1220.12*** *p628*
Pike, John; Marston's Wharf, 1782 ***8529.30*** *p15*
Pike, John 50; Ontario, 1871 ***1823.21*** *p298*
Pike, Joseph; America, 1739 ***1220.12*** *p628*
Pike, Mary; America, 1761 ***1220.12*** *p628*
Pike, Oliver; Barbados, 1663 ***1220.12*** *p628*
Pike, Robert; America, 1773 ***1220.12*** *p628*
Pike, Sarah; America, 1761 ***1220.12*** *p629*
Pike, Thomas 23; Ontario, 1871 ***1823.21*** *p298*
Pike, Thomas 49; Ontario, 1871 ***1823.21*** *p298*
Pikeman, Benjamin; America, 1739 ***1220.12*** *p629*
Piketz, George; Port uncertain, 1842 ***778.6*** *p270*
Pilat, Jadwiga 18; New York, NY, 1904 ***8355.1*** *p15*
Pilbean, John; America, 1775 ***1220.12*** *p629*
Pilborow, John; Barbados or Jamaica, 1685 ***1220.12*** *p629*
Pilcher, . . .; America, 1656 ***1220.12*** *p629*
Pilcher, William; America, 1757 ***1220.12*** *p629*
Pilelienne, Dominique 27; New Orleans, 1848 ***778.6*** *p270*
Pilfey, Fanny Ann 35; Ontario, 1871 ***1823.21*** *p298*
Pilger, Adam, IV; America, 1853 ***2526.42*** *p160*
Pilger, Adam, IV; America, 1853 ***2526.42*** *p163*
*Wife:*Elisabetha
With mother-in-law
*Child:*Katharina
Pilger, Mrs. Adam; America, 1836 ***2526.42*** *p163*
With child 11
With brother-in-law
With child 7
With child 9
Pilger, Elisabetha 37 *SEE* Pilger, Adam, IV
Pilger, Johann Adam; America, 1853 ***2526.42*** *p163*
Pilger, Johann Georg; America, 1836 ***2526.42*** *p163*
Pilger, Johannes; America, 1836 ***2526.42*** *p163*
With wife 2 sons & daughter
Pilger, Karl; America, 1853 ***2526.42*** *p164*
Pilger, Katharina 8 *SEE* Pilger, Adam, IV
Pilger, Michael; America, 1865 ***2526.42*** *p164*
Pilger, Sofie 17; New York, NY, 1885 ***1883.7*** *p45*
Pilgrim, Richard; America, 1742 ***1220.12*** *p629*
Pilker, Francis; America, 1734 ***1220.12*** *p629*
Pilkey, Miss; California, 1868 ***1131.61*** *p89*
Pilkie, Alexander 45; Ontario, 1871 ***1823.17*** *p133*
Pilkington, Anne; America, 1719 ***1220.12*** *p629*
Pilkington, John; Barbados, 1685 ***1220.12*** *p629*
Pilkington, Richard; America, 1765 ***1220.12*** *p629*
Pilkington, Thomas; America, 1769 ***1220.12*** *p629*
Pilkington, William; America, 1684 ***1220.12*** *p629*
Pilkington, William; America, 1734 ***1220.12*** *p629*
Pilkington, William; America, 1770 ***1220.12*** *p629*
Pill, John; Utah, 1855 ***9228.50*** *p511*
With family of 6
Pillar, Thomas; Maine, 1731 ***9228.50*** *p491*
Pillat, Catherine; Quebec, 1663 ***4514.3*** *p357*
Pillate, Mr. 25; Mobile, AL, 1840 ***778.6*** *p270*
Pille, Henry; Ohio, 1809-1852 ***4511.35*** *p40*
Pillere, H. 30; America, 1748 ***778.6*** *p270*
Pilleron, Mr. 25; New Orleans, 1841 ***778.6*** *p270*
Pilleron, Theophile 28; America, 1845 ***778.6*** *p270*
Pillet, Andre 20; Quebec, 1657 ***9221.17*** *p366*
Pillet, Antoine 18; America, 1843 ***778.6*** *p270*
Pillet, Francois 30; Quebec, 1660 ***9221.17*** *p439*
Pillet, Jean Baptiste; Wisconsin, 1854-1858 ***1495.20*** *p49*
Pilley, John; America, 1734 ***1220.12*** *p629*
Pilling, Jonathan; America, 1772 ***1220.12*** *p629*
Pilling, William; America, 1720 ***1220.12*** *p629*
Pilliod, Jacob M.; Ohio, 1809-1852 ***4511.35*** *p40*
Pillips, John; Massachusetts, 1630 ***117.5*** *p157*
Pillman, Peter; North Carolina, 1710 ***3629.40*** *p6*
Pillman, William Tindall; Washington, 1887 ***2770.40*** *p25*
Pillot, Denise 40; Quebec, 1662 ***9221.17*** *p491*
*Daughter:*Marguerite 7
*Son:*Jean 6
Pillot, Jean 6 *SEE* Pillot, Denise Gaultier
Pillot, Leonard 38; Quebec, 1657 ***9221.17*** *p366*
Pillot, Marguerite 7 *SEE* Pillot, Denise Gaultier
Pillow, Thomas 34; Ontario, 1871 ***1823.21*** *p298*
Pillsworth, John; America, 1751 ***1220.12*** *p629*
Pilman, Charles; Louisiana, 1836-1840 ***4981.45*** *p213*
Pilmer, William; America, 1764 ***1220.12*** *p629*
Pilnick, Meyer; Detroit, 1930 ***1640.60*** *p78*

Pilois, Francoise; Quebec, 1665 *4514.3 p357*
Pilois, Francoise; Quebec, 1669 *4514.3 p357*
Pilorecq, Francois; Quebec, 1644 *9221.17 p145*
Pilote, Francois 17; Montreal, 1653 *9221.17 p286*
Pilsbury, George; America, 1751 *1220.12 p629*
Pilsbury, John; America, 1753 *1220.12 p629*
Pim, Thomas; America, 1752 *1220.12 p629*
Piman, William; America, 1723 *1220.12 p629*
Pimble, Sarah; Maryland, 1725 *1220.12 p629*
Pimm, Emanuel; Virginia, 1735 *1220.12 p629*
Pimperton, Benj 48; Ontario, 1871 *1823.21 p298*
Pimperton, Joseph 49; Ontario, 1871 *1823.21 p298*
Pimssner, Karl Ludwig Hermann; Chile, 1887 *7420.1 p354*
Pin, Jacqueline 11 SEE Pin, Olive Morin
Pin, Jean 14 SEE Pin, Olive Morin
Pin, Jean-Baptiste SEE Pin, Olive Morin
Pin, Marin 42; Quebec, 1656 *9221.17 p345*
Pin, Olive 35; Quebec, 1661 *9221.17 p465*
   *Son:*Jean 14
   *Daughter:*Jacqueline 11
   *Son:*Jean-Baptiste
Pinard, Louis 13; Quebec, 1647 *9221.17 p187*
Pincard, John; Charleston, SC, 1672 *9228.50 p526*
   *Wife:*Mary
   *Son:*John, Jr.
Pincard, John, Jr. SEE Pincard, John
Pincard, Mary SEE Pincard, John
Pincemail, Mrs. 35; Port uncertain, 1844 *778.6 p270*
Pinch, Thos. 68; Ontario, 1871 *1823.21 p298*
Pinchart, Charles Antoine; New York, NY, 1856 *1494.21 p31*
Pinchart, Emile SEE Pinchart, Pierre
Pinchart, Jeanne Deprez SEE Pinchart, Pierre
Pinchart, Julienne SEE Pinchart, Pierre
Pinchart, Marie Josephine SEE Pinchart, Pierre
Pinchart, Pierre SEE Pinchart, Pierre
Pinchart, Pierre; Wisconsin, 1854-1858 *1495.20 p50*
   *Wife:*Jeanne Deprez
   *Child:*Pierre
   *Child:*Julienne
   *Child:*Marie Josephine
   *Child:*Emile
Pinchen, Francis; America, 1724 *1220.12 p629*
Pinchert, John; Charleston, SC, 1672 *9228.50 p526*
   *Wife:*Mary
   *Son:*John, Jr.
Pinchert, John, Jr. SEE Pinchert, John
Pinchert, Mary SEE Pinchert, John
Pinchest, John; America, 1768 *1220.12 p629*
Pinchin, Anne; America, 1756 *1220.12 p629*
Pinchin, James; America, 1760 *1220.12 p629*
Pinchin, John; America, 1756 *1220.12 p629*
Pinchin, John; America, 1765 *1220.12 p629*
Pinchin, Mary; America, 1756 *1220.12 p629*
Pinchin, William; Barbados, 1666 *1220.12 p629*
Pinck, Mary; Barbados or Jamaica, 1686 *1220.12 p630*
Pinckard, Richard; America, 1688 *1220.12 p629*
Pincke, Robert; Barbados, 1708 *1220.12 p630*
Pinckney, Jemima; America, 1750 *1220.12 p629*
Pinckney, William P.; North Carolina, 1857 *1088.45 p27*
Pincomb, James 55; Ontario, 1871 *1823.21 p298*
Pincombe, John 31; Ontario, 1871 *1823.21 p298*
Pincombe, John 36; Ontario, 1871 *1823.21 p298*
Pincombe, John 42; Ontario, 1871 *1823.21 p298*
Pincombe, John 64; Ontario, 1871 *1823.21 p298*
Pincombe, Richard 34; Ontario, 1871 *1823.21 p298*
Pincombe, Wm Robert 33; Ontario, 1871 *1823.21 p298*
Pincombes, Samuel 26; Ontario, 1871 *1823.21 p298*
Pindar, Elizabeth; America, 1759 *1220.12 p629*
Pindar, John; America, 1720 *1220.12 p629*
Pindar, Rachael; America, 1769 *1220.12 p630*
Pindar, William 58; Ontario, 1871 *1823.21 p298*
Pinder, Imyra 20; New York, NY, 1894 *6512.1 p183*
Pinder, William; America, 1735 *1220.12 p630*
Pinder, William T.; Miami, 1920 *4984.15 p38*
Pine, Isaac 41; Ontario, 1871 *1823.17 p133*
Pineau, Anne; Quebec, 1671 *4514.3 p357*
Pineau, Marie 35; Quebec, 1659 *9221.17 p408*
Pinegar, Humphrey; America, 1720 *1220.12 p630*
Pineigre, Anne 18; New Orleans, 1848 *778.6 p270*
Pineigre, Margaretha 36; New Orleans, 1848 *778.6 p270*
Pineigre, Renee 12; New Orleans, 1848 *778.6 p270*
Pinel, . . .; Boston, 1769 *9228.50 p5*
Pinel, Alfred; Boston, 1872 *9228.50 p512*
Pinel, Clement; Massachusetts, 1684-1710 *9228.50 p498*
   *Brother:*Thomas
Pinel, Eliza D. Killam SEE Pinel, Joseph
Pinel, Gilles 15 SEE Pinel, Nicolas
Pinel, John; Montreal, 1850-1950 *9228.50 p512*
Pinel, Joseph; Montreal, 1870-1885 *9228.50 p513*
   *Wife:*Eliza D. Killam
Pinel, Joseph; Quebec, 1870 *9228.50 p39*

Pinel, Louisa; America, 1896-1952 *9228.50 p182*
   With aunt
Pinel, Louisa; Massachusetts, 1896 *9228.50 p514*
Pinel, Madeleine Maraude 38 SEE Pinel, Nicolas
Pinel, Marie 17; Quebec, 1643 *9221.17 p134*
Pinel, Nicolas; Quebec, 1650 *9221.17 p229*
   *Wife:*Madeleine Maraude
   *Son:*Pierre
   *Son:*Gilles
Pinel, Peter; Boston, 1769 *9228.50 p48*
Pinel, Peter; Boston, 1769 *9228.50 p514*
Pinel, Philippe; Massachusetts, 1875-1921 *9228.50 p511*
Pinel, Pierre 14 SEE Pinel, Nicolas
Pinel, Thomas SEE Pinel, Clement
Pinel, Walter; Maine, 1647 *9228.50 p514*
Pinel, Walter Philip; Massachusetts, 1873 *9228.50 p513*
Pinel, William Nevins; St. John, N.B., 1844-1944
   9228.50 p503
Piner, Ann; Potomac, 1731 *1220.12 p630*
Piner, Thomas; Virginia, 1726 *1220.12 p630*
Pinet, Alphonse 52; America, 1843 *778.6 p270*
Pinet, Auguste 10; America, 1843 *778.6 p270*
Pinet, Eugene 6; America, 1843 *778.6 p270*
Pinet, Francois 2; America, 1843 *778.6 p270*
Pinet, Francoise 33; America, 1843 *778.6 p270*
Pinet, Jacque 40; America, 1843 *778.6 p270*
Pinet, Rosine 4; America, 1843 *778.6 p270*
Pinet, Xavier 8; America, 1843 *778.6 p270*
Pineteau, Etienne; Quebec, 1657 *9221.17 p366*
Pinfield, John; America, 1771 *1220.12 p630*
Pinfield, William; America, 1764 *1220.12 p630*
Pinfold, George; Barbados or Jamaica, 1682 *1220.12 p630*
Pinfold, George; Maryland, 1727 *1220.12 p630*
Pinfold, Joseph; America, 1775 *1220.12 p630*
Pinginot, Francis C.; Ohio, 1809-1852 *4511.35 p40*
Pingler, Ewald; Brazil, 1926 *8023.44 p378*
Pingrey, Francis; America, 1688 *1220.12 p630*
Pingstone, John; America, 1735 *1220.12 p630*
Pinguet, Francoise 9 SEE Pinguet, Louis-Henry
Pinguet, Guillaume 23; Quebec, 1661 *9221.17 p465*
Pinguet, Louis-Henry 43; Quebec, 1634 *9221.17 p39*
   *Wife:*Louise Lousche 45
   *Son:*Pierre 3
   *Son:*Noel-Joseph 4
   *Daughter:*Francoise 9
Pinguet, Louise Lousche 45 SEE Pinguet, Louis-Henry
Pinguet, Noel-Joseph 4 SEE Pinguet, Louis-Henry
Pinguet, Pierre 3 SEE Pinguet, Louis-Henry
Pinhart, Martin; New Jersey, 1773-1774 *927.31 p3*
Piniel, E.; New York, 1850 *9228.50 p546*
Pinion, Barbara; America, 1855 *5475.1 p266*
Pink, Georg; America, 1882 *5475.1 p146*
Pink, Johann; America, 1882 *5475.1 p146*
Pink, Richard; America, 1751 *1220.12 p630*
Pinke, Thomas; America, 1772 *1220.12 p630*
Pinkeny, Isaac; America, 1771 *1220.12 p629*
Pinkerton, George 50; Ontario, 1871 *1823.17 p133*
Pinkey, Andrew 59; Ontario, 1871 *1823.17 p133*
Pinkowitz, Anton 39; New York, NY, 1893 *1883.7 p37*
Pinkstone, Thomas; America, 1775 *1220.12 p630*
Pinn, William; America, 1749 *1220.12 p630*
Pinn, William; Annapolis, MD, 1726 *1220.12 p630*
Pinncaw, Mary; America, 1745 *1220.12 p630*
Pinnel, William Nevins; St. John, N.B., 1844-1944
   9228.50 p503
Pinner, Edward; America, 1753 *1220.12 p630*
Pinner, Elizabeth; Maryland, 1742 *1220.12 p630*
Pinner, John; Barbados, 1669 *1220.12 p630*
Pinney, Azarias; America, 1685 *1220.12 p630*
Pinney, Francis; America, 1758 *1220.12 p630*
Pinney, Humphrey; Dorchester, MA, 1633 *117.5 p158*
Pinney, John; America, 1685 *1220.12 p630*
Pinney, John; America, 1746 *1220.12 p630*
Pinnick, Ann; America, 1771 *1220.12 p630*
Pinnigar, Joseph; Virginia, 1771 *1220.12 p630*
Pinnock, Henry; America, 1758 *1220.12 p630*
Pinnock, William, Sr.; Virginia, 1749 *1220.12 p630*
Pinochet, Madeleine SEE Pinochet, Simonne
Pinochet, Simonne; Nova Scotia, 1753 *3051 p113*
   *Sister:*Madeleine
Pinone, de, Comte 30; America, 1843 *778.6 p270*
Pinot, Pierre 13; Quebec, 1648 *9221.17 p202*
Pinozek, Mike; Texas, 1900 *6015.15 p29*
Pinsart, Jean 22; Quebec, 1658 *9221.17 p386*
Pinson, Guillaume 40; Montreal, 1661 *9221.17 p474*
Pinson, Marie-Marthe 25; Montreal, 1653 *9221.17 p299*
Pinson, Roger; Jamaica, 1665 *1220.12 p630*
Pinson, Samuel; America, 1685 *1220.12 p630*
Pinson, Thomas; America, 1741 *1220.12 p630*
Pinteaux, J. 44; America, 1848 *778.6 p270*
Pinten, Angela SEE Pinten, Johann
Pinten, Angelika Hoffmann 33 SEE Pinten, Johann

Pinten, Johann 32; America, 1858 *5475.1 p328*
   *Wife:*Angelika Hoffmann 33
   *Daughter:*Katharina
   *Daughter:*Angela
Pinten, Katharina SEE Pinten, Johann
Pinten, Maria; Tennessee, 1880 *5475.1 p265*
Pinter, Elisabeth SEE Pinter, Jakob
Pinter, Jakob; Arkansas, 1880 *5475.1 p245*
   *Wife:*Maria Brill
   *Daughter:*Elisabeth
   *Son:*Johann
   *Son:*Peter
   *Son:*Nikolaus
   *Daughter:*Susanna
   *Daughter:*Katharina
Pinter, Johann SEE Pinter, Mathias
Pinter, Johann SEE Pinter, Jakob
Pinter, Kath.; Arkansas, 1880 *5475.1 p245*
Pinter, Katharina SEE Pinter, Mathias
Pinter, Katharina SEE Pinter, Jakob
Pinter, Margarethe Deutsch SEE Pinter, Mathias
Pinter, Maria Brill SEE Pinter, Jakob
Pinter, Mathias SEE Pinter, Mathias
Pinter, Mathias; America, 1856 *5475.1 p365*
   *Wife:*Margarethe Deutsch
   *Daughter:*Katharina
   *Son:*Mathias
   *Son:*Johann
Pinter, Nikolaus SEE Pinter, Jakob
Pinter, Peter SEE Pinter, Mathias
Pinter, Peter; America, 1868 *5475.1 p338*
Pinter, Peter; America, 1881 *5475.1 p299*
Pinter, Peter SEE Pinter, Jakob
Pinter, Susanna SEE Pinter, Jakob
Pinter, Wilhelm 24; America, 1868 *5475.1 p311*
Pintner, Jan; St. Louis, 1896 *2853.20 p54*
Pinto, Husto; Louisiana, 1874-1875 *4981.45 p30*
Pinton, William; America, 1773 *1220.12 p630*
Pinyard, William; America, 1756 *1220.12 p630*
Pinyon, Thomas 45; Ontario, 1871 *1823.21 p298*
Piot, Anna SEE Piot, Nik.
Piot, Barbara SEE Piot, Nik.
Piot, Elisabeth SEE Piot, Nik.
Piot, Johann SEE Piot, Nik.
Piot, Josef SEE Piot, Nik.
Piot, Margarethe SEE Piot, Nik.
Piot, Maria SEE Piot, Nik.
Piot, Maria Rupp SEE Piot, Nik.
Piot, Nik.; America, 1880 *5475.1 p173*
   *Wife:*Maria Rupp
   *Daughter:*Anna
   *Son:*Nikolaus
   *Daughter:*Elisabeth
   *Daughter:*Barbara
   *Son:*Peter
   *Daughter:*Margarethe
   *Son:*Josef
   *Son:*Johann
   *Daughter:*Maria
Piot, Nikolaus SEE Piot, Nik.
Piot, Peter SEE Piot, Nik.
Piot deLangloiserie, Charles-Gaspard; Quebec, 1683-1688 *2314.30 p168*
Piot deLangloiserie, Charles-Gaspard; Quebec, 1687 *2314.30 p193*
Piotraschke, Friedrich Richard Otto; Wisconsin, 1889 *6795.8 p91*
Piotrowski, Clemens; Detroit, 1929-1930 *6214.5 p69*
Piotrowski, Joseph; Detroit, 1929-1930 *6214.5 p67*
Piotter, Hermann Carl; Wisconsin, 1901 *6795.8 p231*
Pipal, Jan; Omaha, NE, 1892 *2853.20 p163*
Pipe, Jno.; Colorado, 1869 *1029.59 p75*
Pipe, John; Colorado, 1874 *1029.59 p75*
Pipea, William 30; Ontario, 1871 *1823.21 p298*
Piper, Conrad; Ohio, 1809-1852 *4511.35 p40*
Piper, Elizabeth; America, 1765 *1220.12 p630*
Piper, Francis; America, 1694 *1220.12 p630*
Piper, James; Virginia, 1741 *1220.12 p630*
Piper, Jane; Annapolis, MD, 1725 *1220.12 p631*
Piper, John; Barbados, 1675 *1220.12 p631*
Piper, John 43; Ontario, 1871 *1823.21 p298*
Piper, Joseph; Barbados, 1666 *1220.12 p631*
Piper, Nicholas; America, 1722 *1220.12 p631*
Piper, Richard; America, 1752 *1220.12 p631*
Piper, Richard; America, 1753 *1220.12 p631*
Piper, Richard 30; Ontario, 1871 *1823.21 p298*
Piper, Thomas 37; Ontario, 1871 *1823.21 p298*
Piper, William 56; Ontario, 1871 *1823.21 p298*
Pipes, William; Canada, 1774 *3036.5 p41*
Pipho, Christian; America, 1852 *7420.1 p95*
Pipho, Eleonore; America, 1856 *7420.1 p152*

Pipho, Heinrich; America, 1857 ***7420.1*** *p169*
With family
Piphoe, Heinrich Friedrich Wilhelm; America, 1859 ***7420.1*** *p188*
Piphoh, Sophie Caroline Louise; America, 1852 ***7420.1*** *p95*
Pipin, John Femin; Louisiana, 1836-1840 ***4981.45*** *p213*
Pipka, Frank; Wisconsin, 1879 ***6795.8*** *p61*
Pipkin, William; America, 1742 ***1220.12*** *p631*
Pipon, Mr.; Salem, MA, 1673 ***9228.50*** *p514*
Pipon, Elie; New York, 1724 ***9228.50*** *p514*
Pipp, Joseph; America, 1774 ***1220.12*** *p631*
Pippen, John; Virginia, 1718 ***1220.12*** *p631*
Pippin, Richard; America, 1721 ***1220.12*** *p631*
Pippin, Richard; America, 1754 ***1220.12*** *p631*
Pipping, Nathaniel; Annapolis, MD, 1731 ***1220.12*** *p631*
Pipson, John; America, 1768 ***1220.12*** *p631*
Pique, Ernst August; America, 1866 ***7420.1*** *p247*
Pique, Francis; Louisiana, 1874-1875 ***4981.45*** *p30*
Pique, Georg August Wilhelm; America, 1866 ***7420.1*** *p247*
Pique, J. 36; America, 1846 ***778.6*** *p270*
Piquee, Joseph 27; Texas, 1848 ***778.6*** *p270*
Piquel, Theodor 38; New Orleans, 1848 ***778.6*** *p271*
Piquer, Mr. 23; America, 1846 ***778.6*** *p271*
Piquinot, Louis; Ohio, 1840-1897 ***8365.35*** *p17*
Piquot, Jacques 21; Quebec, 1643 ***9221.17*** *p134*
Piraprez, August; Wisconsin, 1855-1880 ***1495.20*** *p46*
Piraprez, Felicien; Wisconsin, 1855-1880 ***1495.20*** *p46*
Piraube, Martial; Quebec, 1639 ***9221.17*** *p92*
Pire, Leonie; Wisconsin, 1870 ***1495.20*** *p28*
Pirlet, Anne Catherine *SEE* Pirlet, Jean Louis Desire
Pirlet, Jean Bredael *SEE* Pirlet, Jean Louis Desire
Pirlet, Jean Francois; Wisconsin, 1854-1858 ***1495.20*** *p50*
Pirlet, Jean Louis Desire; Wisconsin, 1857 ***1495.20*** *p41*
*Wife:*Jean Bredael
*Daughter:*Anne Catherine
*Daughter:*Marie Eugenie
Pirlet, Marie Eugenie *SEE* Pirlet, Jean Louis Desire
Pirlot, Antoine; New York, NY, 1856 ***1494.21*** *p31*
Pirlot, Louis; Chicago, 1857 ***1494.21*** *p31*
Pirois, Antoinette; Quebec, 1669 ***4514.3*** *p339*
Pirolles, Mr. 34; America, 1846 ***778.6*** *p271*
Pirolles, Mrs. 24; America, 1846 ***778.6*** *p271*
Pirolles, A. 9; America, 1846 ***778.6*** *p271*
Piron, Francois; Montreal, 1653 ***9221.17*** *p299*
Piron, Pierre 17; Montreal, 1653 ***9221.17*** *p299*
Pirot, Ferdinand 24; New Orleans, 1845 ***778.6*** *p271*
Pirot, Jne. Claude 24; New Orleans, 1845 ***778.6*** *p271*
Pirot, Marguerite 22; New Orleans, 1845 ***778.6*** *p271*
Pirouet, Daniel; New Brunswick, 1800-1899 ***9228.50*** *p505*
Pirouet, Philip; Boston, 1707 ***9228.50*** *p505*
Pirro, Anthony; Ohio, 1809-1852 ***4511.35*** *p41*
Pirro, Charles; Ohio, 1809-1852 ***4511.35*** *p41*
Pirrong, Anthony; Ohio, 1809-1852 ***4511.35*** *p41*
Pirrung, Elisabeth *SEE* Pirrung, Johann
Pirrung, Elisabeth Hans *SEE* Pirrung, Johann
Pirrung, Friedrich *SEE* Pirrung, Johann
Pirrung, Jakob *SEE* Pirrung, Johann
Pirrung, Johann *SEE* Pirrung, Johann
Pirrung, Johann 43; America, 1881 ***5475.1*** *p435*
*Wife:*Elisabeth Hans
*Daughter:*Elisabeth
*Daughter:*Maria
*Son:*Friedrich
*Son:*Johann
*Daughter:*Katharina
*Son:*Jakob
*Son:*Peter
Pirrung, Katharina *SEE* Pirrung, Johann
Pirrung, Maria *SEE* Pirrung, Johann
Pirrung, Peter *SEE* Pirrung, Johann
Pirtie, George 30; Ontario, 1871 ***1823.21*** *p298*
Pirvonsky, Ludwig 27; Halifax, N.S., 1902 ***1860.4*** *p42*
Pirvonsky, Peter; Halifax, N.S., 1902 ***1860.4*** *p42*
Pirvonsky, Teresia 23; Halifax, N.S., 1902 ***1860.4*** *p42*
Pisa, Josef; Iowa, 1864 ***2853.20*** *p212*
Pisano, Joseph; America, 1769 ***1220.12*** *p631*
Pisarczyk, Agnieszka 25; New York, NY, 1911 ***6533.11*** *p10*
Pisarski, Paul; Detroit, 1929 ***1640.55*** *p114*
Pischke, John Joseph; Wisconsin, 1890 ***6795.8*** *p205*
Piscopo, Giovanni; Louisiana, 1874-1875 ***4981.45*** *p30*
Pisek, Jan; South Dakota, 1850 ***2853.20*** *p246*
Pisek, Tadeas; South Dakota, 1850-1910 ***2853.20*** *p246*
Pisek, Vincenc; New York, NY, 1873 ***2853.20*** *p114*
With parents
Pisel, Antonin; Nebraska, 1870 ***2853.20*** *p194*
Pishel, Antonin; Nebraska, 1870 ***2853.20*** *p194*
Piska, Jan; South Dakota, 1850-1910 ***2853.20*** *p246*
Piska, Tadeas; South Dakota, 1850 ***2853.20*** *p246*
Piskacek, Frantisek; Texas, 1856-1906 ***2853.20*** *p64*
Pison, James; America, 1747 ***1220.12*** *p631*
Pissey, John; America, 1770 ***1220.12*** *p631*
Pisson, Edward; America, 1757 ***1220.12*** *p631*
Pistorius, Anna; America, 1836 ***5475.1*** *p65*
Pistorius, Anna 20 *SEE* Pistorius, Peter
Pistorius, Anna 30; America, 1838 ***5475.1*** *p387*
Pistorius, Katharina 15 *SEE* Pistorius, Peter
Pistorius, Maria; America, 1866 ***5475.1*** *p68*
Pistorius, Michel 12 *SEE* Pistorius, Peter
Pistorius, Peter; America, 1837 ***5475.1*** *p66*
Pistorius, Peter 48; America, 1838 ***5475.1*** *p67*
*Daughter:*Anna 20
*Son:*Michel 12
*Daughter:*Katharina 15
Pisvier, Olympe 28; America, 1843 ***778.6*** *p271*
Pita, Frank; Louisiana, 1874-1875 ***4981.45*** *p30*
Pitcher, Edward; Potomac, 1729 ***1220.12*** *p631*
Pitcher, James; America, 1774 ***1220.12*** *p631*
Pitcher, Martha; America, 1764 ***1220.12*** *p631*
Pitchers, Ritchard 36; Ontario, 1871 ***1823.21*** *p298*
Pitchey, George; America, 1758 ***1220.12*** *p631*
Pitchfield, Thomas; America, 1739 ***1220.12*** *p631*
Pitchford, William; America, 1767 ***1220.12*** *p631*
Pitchland, Richard; America, 1767 ***1220.12*** *p631*
Pitek, Stanislaw; Detroit, 1929 ***1640.55*** *p112*
Pitfield, Sarah; America, 1759 ***1220.12*** *p631*
Pitford, John; Barbados, 1694 ***1220.12*** *p631*
Pitkin, William; America, 1742 ***1220.12*** *p631*
Pitman, Henry; America, 1685 ***1220.12*** *p631*
Pitman, James; America, 1745 ***1220.12*** *p631*
Pitman, Jesse; America, 1751 ***1220.12*** *p631*
Pitman, John; America, 1767 ***1220.12*** *p631*
Pitman, Mary; America, 1766 ***1220.12*** *p631*
Pitman, Samuel; America, 1751 ***1220.12*** *p631*
Pitman, Thomas; America, 1722 ***1220.12*** *p631*
Pitman, Thomas; America, 1769 ***1220.12*** *p631*
Pitney, John; America, 1725 ***1220.12*** *p631*
Piton, Honorene *SEE* Piton, Philippe
Piton, John; Ohio, 1877 ***9228.50*** *p515*
Piton, Luce Casgrain-Gagnon *SEE* Piton, Philippe
Piton, Marie; Quebec, 1668 ***4514.3*** *p357*
Piton, Marie Emma Sarah *SEE* Piton, Philippe
Piton, Philippe; New York, 1858 ***9228.50*** *p515*
*Wife:*Luce Casgrain-Gagnon
*Child:*Marie Emma Sarah
*Child:*Honorene
Piton, Philippe 32; Quebec, 1804 ***9228.50*** *p515*
Piton, Pierre 52; Port uncertain, 1846 ***778.6*** *p271*
Pitot, Pierre; Quebec, 1648 ***9221.17*** *p202*
Pitre, Pierre; Montreal, 1660 ***9221.17*** *p443*
Pitrie, Guiseppe; Louisiana, 1874-1875 ***4981.45*** *p30*
Pitsch, Heinrich 26; Halifax, N.S., 1902 ***1860.4*** *p41*
Pitsch, Philipp; America, 1880 ***5475.1*** *p267*
Pitshi, Lucas; Ohio, 1809-1852 ***4511.35*** *p41*
Pitt, Alexander; Colorado, 1904 ***1029.59*** *p75*
Pitt, Andrew M.; Colorado, 1894 ***1029.59*** *p75*
Pitt, George; America, 1766 ***1220.12*** *p631*
Pitt, George 32; Ontario, 1871 ***1823.21*** *p298*
Pitt, John; America, 1742 ***1220.12*** *p631*
Pitt, John; America, 1766 ***1220.12*** *p631*
Pitt, John; Barbados, 1665 ***1220.12*** *p631*
Pitt, Joseph; America, 1749 ***1220.12*** *p631*
Pitt, Mary; America, 1751 ***1220.12*** *p631*
Pitt, Richard; America, 1761 ***1220.12*** *p631*
Pitt, Richard; America, 1774 ***1220.12*** *p631*
Pitt, Thomas; America, 1685 ***1220.12*** *p631*
Pitt, Thomas; America, 1754 ***1220.12*** *p632*
Pitt, William; America, 1679 ***1220.12*** *p632*
Pitt, William 46; Ontario, 1871 ***1823.17*** *p133*
Pitt, William Moss; Virginia, 1773 ***1220.12*** *p632*
Pittam, John; America, 1763 ***1220.12*** *p632*
Pittard, Mary; America, 1740 ***1220.12*** *p632*
Pittard, Thomas; America, 1685 ***1220.12*** *p632*
Pittarri, Juani; Louisiana, 1874-1875 ***4981.45*** *p30*
Pitte, Robert L.; Chicago, 1869 ***2853.20*** *p394*
Pittenger, John; Ohio, 1873 ***3580.20*** *p33*
Pittenger, John; Ohio, 1873 ***6020.12*** *p22*
Pitter, Thomas; Maryland, 1739 ***1220.12*** *p632*
Pittinger, Richard; Virginia, 1665 ***9228.50*** *p53*
Pittman, Barnhart; Ohio, 1809-1852 ***4511.35*** *p41*
Pittman, Richard; America, 1752 ***1220.12*** *p631*
Pittmann, Barnhart; Ohio, 1809-1852 ***4511.35*** *p41*
Pitts, Charles; America, 1754 ***1220.12*** *p632*
Pitts, Christian; Ohio, 1809-1852 ***4511.35*** *p41*
Pitts, Francis; America, 1738 ***1220.12*** *p632*
Pitts, Jacob; Ohio, 1809-1852 ***4511.35*** *p41*
Pitts, James; Washington, 1889 ***2770.40*** *p80*
Pitts, Jane; Virginia, 1740 ***1220.12*** *p632*
Pitts, Jeremiah; America, 1745 ***1220.12*** *p632*
Pitts, John; America, 1682 ***1220.12*** *p632*
Pitts, John; America, 1685 ***1220.12*** *p632*
Pitts, John; America, 1737 ***1220.12*** *p632*
Pitts, John; Virginia, 1721 ***1220.12*** *p632*
Pitts, Matthew; America, 1742 ***1220.12*** *p632*
Pitts, William; America, 1685 ***1220.12*** *p632*
Pittwood, Richard; Barbados, 1694 ***1220.12*** *p632*
Pitz, Chr.; New York, NY, 1893 ***1883.7*** *p39*
Pitz, Chrn. 34; New York, NY, 1893 ***1883.7*** *p47*
Pitz, Henry; Ohio, 1809-1852 ***4511.35*** *p41*
Pitz, Jacob; Ohio, 1809-1852 ***4511.35*** *p41*
Pitz, Karole 22; New York, NY, 1893 ***1883.7*** *p39*
Pitz, Karole. 22; New York, NY, 1893 ***1883.7*** *p47*
Pitz, Maria; America, 1881 ***5475.1*** *p46*
Pitz, Peter; Ohio, 1809-1852 ***4511.35*** *p41*
Piusepre, Nicolas; Quebec, 1649 ***9221.17*** *p219*
Pivaux, Marie Antoinette 27; New Orleans, 1848 ***778.6*** *p271*
Pivaux, Stanislas Jos. 24; New Orleans, 1848 ***778.6*** *p271*
Pivert, Marguerite Lesage *SEE* Pivert, Nicolas
Pivert, Nicolas; Quebec, 1623 ***9221.17*** *p25*
*Wife:*Marguerite Lesage
Pivin, Pierre; Quebec, 1646 ***9221.17*** *p168*
Pivo, Jan; Minnesota, 1890 ***2853.20*** *p274*
Pivoz, Anna; Detroit, 1929-1930 ***6214.5*** *p63*
Pixley, John; America, 1732 ***1220.12*** *p632*
Pixley, Robert; Virginia, 1734 ***1220.12*** *p632*
Pixley, Thomas; America, 1775 ***1220.12*** *p632*
Pixot, Jean 19; America, 1842 ***778.6*** *p271*
Pizasse, Jean 48; America, 1840 ***778.6*** *p271*
Pizey, Henry; America, 1750 ***1220.12*** *p632*
Pizzoni, Paul; Louisiana, 1874 ***4981.45*** *p133*
Place, Ann 75; Ontario, 1871 ***1823.21*** *p298*
Place, Anne; America, 1771 ***1220.12*** *p632*
Place, John; America, 1762 ***1220.12*** *p632*
Place, John; Maryland, 1737 ***1220.12*** *p632*
Place, William; America, 1765 ***1220.12*** *p632*
Placek, Jan; Nebraska, 1868 ***2853.20*** *p161*
Plackett, John; America, 1751 ***1220.12*** *p632*
Plagens, Heinrich; Wisconsin, 1873 ***6795.8*** *p64*
Plagens, Michael Christoph; Wisconsin, 1899 ***6795.8*** *p26*
Plagenz, Michael Christoph; Wisconsin, 1899 ***6795.8*** *p26*
Plagmann, Henry; Iowa, 1888 ***1211.15*** *p18*
Plagns, Michael Christoph; Wisconsin, 1899 ***6795.8*** *p26*
Plaim, Gerema 34; New York, NY, 1894 ***6512.1*** *p230*
Plain, Christiana 18; Ontario, 1871 ***1823.21*** *p298*
Plaisted, Mary; America, 1766 ***1220.12*** *p632*
Plaister, George; America, 1757 ***1220.12*** *p484*
Plaister, Mary; America, 1766 ***1220.12*** *p632*
Plaistow, Samuel; America, 1773 ***1220.12*** *p632*
Plaman, James 53; Ontario, 1871 ***1823.17*** *p133*
Planas, Ramon; Louisiana, 1836-1840 ***4981.45*** *p213*
Plancher, Jean 27; New Orleans, 1848 ***778.6*** *p271*
Planchet, Louise; Quebec, 1668 ***4514.3*** *p313*
Plane, George 46; Ontario, 1871 ***1823.21*** *p298*
Plane, Moses; America, 1764 ***1220.12*** *p632*
Plane, Thomas; America, 1764 ***1220.12*** *p632*
Plank, Sarah; America, 1757 ***1220.12*** *p632*
Plank, William; America, 1758 ***1220.12*** *p632*
Planque, Mrs. 24; America, 1844 ***778.6*** *p271*
Planske, Emilie 55; New York, NY, 1885 ***1883.7*** *p45*
Planske, Gottlieb 60; New York, NY, 1885 ***1883.7*** *p45*
Planson, Dieud. 56; America, 1840 ***778.6*** *p271*
Plant, Elizabeth; Maryland, 1723 ***1220.12*** *p632*
Plant, James; America, 1726 ***1220.12*** *p632*
Plant, James; America, 1775 ***1220.12*** *p632*
Plant, John; Rappahannock, VA, 1726 ***1220.12*** *p632*
Plant, Mary P. 45; Ontario, 1871 ***1823.21*** *p298*
Plante, Jean 24; Quebec, 1650 ***9221.17*** *p229*
Planteau, Isabelle; Quebec, 1671 ***4514.3*** *p357*
Plantrier, Ch. 37; New Orleans, 1843 ***778.6*** *p271*
Planz, Daniel 26; New York, 1872 ***5475.1*** *p563*
Plas, Bartolomeo; Louisiana, 1836-1840 ***4981.45*** *p213*
Plaser, Christopher; America, 1738 ***1220.12*** *p632*
Plaskett, John 33; Ontario, 1871 ***1823.21*** *p298*
Plassez, Pierre; Quebec, 1652 ***9221.17*** *p264*
Plaster, Thomas; America, 1765 ***1220.12*** *p632*
Plaszkowski, Michel 38; Missouri, 1848 ***778.6*** *p271*
Plate, Friedrich Gustav; America, 1865 ***7420.1*** *p235*
Plateau, Jean 30; America, 1843 ***778.6*** *p271*
Plateau, Jean 36; America, 1843 ***778.6*** *p271*
Plateau, Remy 29; America, 1843 ***778.6*** *p271*
Plater, Maria; Rappahannock, VA, 1741 ***1220.12*** *p632*
Platet, J. B.; Louisiana, 1836-1840 ***4981.45*** *p213*
Platt, Ammon; Ohio, 1838 ***3580.20*** *p33*
Platt, Ammon; Ohio, 1838 ***6020.12*** *p22*
Platt, Ann; Barbados, 1663 ***1220.12*** *p632*
Platt, Christian; America, n.d. ***8115.12*** *p322*
Platt, David; New York, NY, 1826 ***3274.55*** *p66*
Platt, Elizabeth; Virginia, 1727 ***1220.12*** *p632*
Platt, Georg Andreas *SEE* Platt, Marie Magdalene
Platt, Georg Andreas; America, n.d. ***8115.12*** *p321*
Platt, Jakob *SEE* Platt, Marie Magdalene
Platt, James; America, 1753 ***1220.12*** *p633*
Platt, Johann Andreas; America, 1849 ***8115.12*** *p321*
Platt, Johann Konrad; America, 1800-1844 ***8115.12*** *p321*
Platt, John; America, 1751 ***1220.12*** *p633*

Platt, John; America, 1752 ***1220.12*** *p633*
Platt, John; America, 1774 ***1220.12*** *p633*
Platt, John; Annapolis, MD, 1732 ***1220.12*** *p633*
Platt, John; Barbados or Jamaica, 1693 ***1220.12*** *p633*
Platt, John; Charles Town, SC, 1718 ***1220.12*** *p633*
Platt, John 50; Ontario, 1871 ***1823.21*** *p298*
Platt, Joseph; America, 1765 ***1220.12*** *p633*
Platt, Ludwig *SEE* Platt, Marie Magdalene
Platt, Ludwig; America, n.d. ***8115.12*** *p321*
Platt, Maria; America, 1854 ***2526.43*** *p177*
Platt, Marie Magdalene; America, 1810-1901 ***8115.12*** *p321*
Platt, Marie Magdalene; America, 1857 ***8115.12*** *p318*
*Child:*Ludwig
*Child:*Jakob
*Child:*Georg Andreas
Platt, William; America, 1748 ***1220.12*** *p633*
Platt, William; America, 1771 ***1220.12*** *p633*
Platt, William 46; Ontario, 1871 ***1823.21*** *p298*
Platte, Conrad August Gottlieb; America, 1864 ***7420.1*** *p226*
*Wife:*Dorothea Wilhelmine Struckmeier
*Son:*Heinrich Friedrich Christian
Platte, Dorothea Wilhelmine Struckmeier *SEE* Platte, Conrad August Gottlieb
Platte, Hanne Sophie Friederike; America, 1861 ***7420.1*** *p207*
Platte, Heinrich Friedrich Christian *SEE* Platte, Conrad August Gottlieb
Platte, Henriette Friederike; America, 1874 ***7420.1*** *p303*
Platte, Johann Heinrich Christoph; America, 1857 ***7420.1*** *p169*
Plattner, Johann 27; Galveston, TX, 1846 ***3967.10*** *p378*
Plattner, Katharina 21; Galveston, TX, 1846 ***3967.10*** *p378*
Platton, Samuel; America, 1765 ***1220.12*** *p633*
Platts, John; Barbados, 1682 ***1220.12*** *p633*
Platvoet, Theodore; Ohio, 1840-1897 ***8365.35*** *p17*
Platzell, Franz; Colorado, 1886 ***1029.59*** *p75*
Platzer, Franz; Colorado, 1886 ***1029.59*** *p75*
Platzer, Franz; Colorado, 1894 ***1029.59*** *p75*
Plaul, Anna 22; Valdivia, Chile, 1852 ***1192.4*** *p53*
Plaut, Elise; America, 1857 ***7420.1*** *p170*
Plaw, John; America, 1777 ***8529.30*** *p15*
Plawecki, Margaret; Detroit, 1929 ***1640.55*** *p113*
Plaxton, George 45; Ontario, 1871 ***1823.21*** *p298*
Plaxton, John 50; Ontario, 1871 ***1823.21*** *p298*
Plaxton, William 48; Ontario, 1871 ***1823.21*** *p298*
Playden, Thomas; Barbados or Jamaica, 1690 ***1220.12*** *p633*
Player, Henry; America, 1765 ***1220.12*** *p633*
Playne, James; America, 1755 ***1220.12*** *p632*
Playne, Thomas; Barbados or Jamaica, 1690 ***1220.12*** *p632*
Pleadwell, Margaret; Barbados or Jamaica, 1693 ***1220.12*** *p633*
Pleasant, Thomas 41; Ontario, 1871 ***1823.21*** *p298*
Pleasants, Charles; America, 1766 ***1220.12*** *p633*
Please, Elizabeth; Virginia, 1719 ***1220.12*** *p633*
Please, John; Virginia, 1768 ***1220.12*** *p633*
Pleciak, John; Detroit, 1929 ***1640.55*** *p112*
Pledge, William; Maryland, 1719 ***1220.12*** *p633*
Pledger, John; Barbados, 1679 ***1220.12*** *p633*
Pleimann, Henry; Ohio, 1840-1897 ***8365.35*** *p17*
Pleins, Theodor Heinrich; Dubuque Co., IA, 1862 ***5475.1*** *p237*
Plemaret, Marie-Genevieve; Quebec, 1665 ***4514.3*** *p358*
Plenge, Ernst Wilhelm; America, 1845 ***7420.1*** *p39*
With wife & 4 children
Plent, Barnard; Cleveland, OH, 1872 ***2853.20*** *p283*
With wife
Plentis, Nicholas; Detroit, 1929-1930 ***6214.5*** *p61*
Plenty, Richard; Barbados, 1662 ***1220.12*** *p633*
Plessis, Nicholas; America, 1762 ***1220.12*** *p633*
Plessmann, W.; Valdivia, Chile, 1852 ***1192.4*** *p56*
Plet, Pierre; Quebec, 1651 ***9221.17*** *p249*
Pleta, Louis; Detroit, 1930 ***1640.60*** *p81*
Pletat, Gustave; Washington, 1886 ***6015.10*** *p16*
Pletschke, Ernst; America, 1849 ***5475.1*** *p29*
Plevey, Thomas; America, 1764 ***1220.12*** *p633*
Plew, John; America, 1732 ***1220.12*** *p633*
Plewes, William 40; Ontario, 1871 ***1823.21*** *p298*
Plews, James 56; Ontario, 1871 ***1823.21*** *p298*
Plews, Robert; America, 1727 ***1220.12*** *p633*
Plichon, Bernard; Quebec, 1645 ***9221.17*** *p156*
Plisson, Peter; Barbados or Jamaica, 1674 ***1220.12*** *p633*
Plitz, Elisabeth *SEE* Plitz, Marie Katharine
Plitz, Katharine *SEE* Plitz, Marie Katharine
Plitz, Louise *SEE* Plitz, Marie Katharine
Plitz, Margarethe *SEE* Plitz, Marie Katharine
Plitz, Marie; America, 1869 ***8115.12*** *p328*
Plitz, Marie Katharine; America, 1869 ***8115.12*** *p328*
*Child:*Margarethe
*Child:*Elisabeth
*Child:*Katharine
*Child:*Louise
Plocek, Jan; Chicago, 1856 ***2853.20*** *p389*
Ploch, Caspar; Texas, 1855-1886 ***9980.22*** *p16*
Plodd, John Henry; America, 1773 ***1220.12*** *p633*
Plodvin, Nicholas; Ohio, 1807 ***9228.50*** *p57*
Plodvin, Nicholas; Ohio, 1807 ***9228.50*** *p516*
Ploeger, Adolphine; Galveston, TX, 1855 ***571.7*** *p17*
Ploetz, Aug. Friedr.; Wisconsin, 1895 ***6795.8*** *p220*
Ploetz, Franz Wilhelm; Wisconsin, 1891 ***6795.8*** *p220*
Ploetz, Wilhelm; Wisconsin, 1897 ***6795.8*** *p152*
Plomber, Samuel; America, 1722 ***1220.12*** *p634*
Plomer, Richard; America, 1685 ***1220.12*** *p634*
Plong, Christian C.; Washington, 1886 ***2770.40*** *p195*
Plonget, Ulyse 17; New Orleans, 1848 ***778.6*** *p271*
Plonka, Charles; Detroit, 1929 ***1640.55*** *p116*
Plonnies, von, Karl 22; Wyoming, 1880 ***2526.43*** *p177*
Ploom, Martin; Ohio, 1843 ***2763.1*** *p21*
Plopman, Fred; North Carolina, 1845 ***1088.45*** *p27*
Ploser, Christopher; America, 1738 ***1220.12*** *p633*
Plotnik, Morris; Detroit, 1930 ***1640.60*** *p78*
Plott, James; America, 1694 ***1220.12*** *p633*
Plouard, Marie-Madeleine; Quebec, 1667 ***4514.3*** *p358*
Ploughwright, Thomas; Barbados, 1664 ***1220.12*** *p633*
Plow, Susanna; America, 1756 ***1220.12*** *p633*
Plowman, Mary; America, 1735 ***1220.12*** *p633*
Plowman, Mary; Annapolis, MD, 1726 ***1220.12*** *p633*
Plowman, Moses; America, 1740 ***1220.12*** *p633*
Plowman, Richard; Virginia, 1750 ***1220.12*** *p633*
Plowman, Robert; America, 1752 ***1220.12*** *p633*
Plowman, Thomas; Nevis or Jamaica, 1722 ***1220.12*** *p633*
Plowman, William; America, 1726 ***1220.12*** *p633*
Plowman, William; America, 1740 ***1220.12*** *p633*
Plowright, Mary; Annapolis, MD, 1726 ***1220.12*** *p633*
Ployhard, Vaclav; South Dakota, 1863 ***2853.20*** *p249*
Pluche, Adolphe 35; America, 1842 ***778.6*** *p271*
Pluche, C.; Louisiana, 1874-1875 ***4981.45*** *p30*
Pluchon, Pierre 31; Quebec, 1648 ***9221.17*** *p202*
Plucknett, James; Illinois, 1858 ***6079.1*** *p11*
Plucknett, John; New York, 1778 ***8529.30*** *p7*
Pluckrose, John; America, 1741 ***1220.12*** *p633*
Plum, Frederick; America, 1763 ***1220.12*** *p633*
Plum, Thomas 36; Ontario, 1871 ***1823.21*** *p299*
Plumb, Albert 17; Michigan, 1880 ***4491.39*** *p24*
Plumb, Alfred 17; Michigan, 1880 ***4491.39*** *p24*
Plumb, Anna J. 15; Michigan, 1880 ***4491.39*** *p24*
Plumb, John; America, 1773 ***1220.12*** *p633*
Plumb, Sarah 55; Michigan, 1880 ***4491.39*** *p24*
Plumb, Thomas; America, 1735 ***1220.12*** *p633*
Plumb, William 52; Michigan, 1880 ***4491.39*** *p24*
Plumber, Samuel; America, 1766 ***1220.12*** *p634*
Plumbly, Matthew; America, 1727 ***1220.12*** *p634*
Plumer, Ann; America, 1775 ***1220.12*** *p634*
Plumer, Engel Marie; America, 1869 ***7420.1*** *p281*
Plumer, William; America, 1772 ***1220.12*** *p634*
Plumey, Andrew Lewis; Ohio, 1809-1852 ***4511.35*** *p41*
Plumey, Andrew Louis; Ohio, 1809-1852 ***4511.35*** *p41*
Plumley, George; America, 1685 ***1220.12*** *p634*
Plummer, . . .; Ontario, 1871 ***1823.21*** *p299*
Plummer, Charles; America, 1718 ***1220.12*** *p634*
Plummer, Daniel; America, 1738 ***1220.12*** *p634*
Plummer, Elizabeth; Barbados, 1679 ***1220.12*** *p634*
Plummer, Francis; America, 1685 ***1220.12*** *p634*
Plummer, Henry 19; Ontario, 1871 ***1823.21*** *p299*
Plummer, Isaac; Maryland, 1720 ***1220.12*** *p634*
Plummer, Jeremiah 34; Ontario, 1871 ***1823.21*** *p299*
Plummer, John 61; Ontario, 1871 ***1823.21*** *p299*
Plummer, Joseph; America, 1738 ***1220.12*** *p634*
Plummer, Lydia; America, 1769 ***1220.12*** *p634*
Plummer, Mary; America, 1755 ***1220.12*** *p634*
Plummer, Mary; America, 1756 ***1220.12*** *p634*
Plummer, Richard; America, 1738 ***1220.12*** *p634*
Plummer, Thomas; Barbados or Jamaica, 1715 ***1220.12*** *p634*
Plummer, William; Barbados, 1664 ***1220.12*** *p634*
Plummeridge, Edward; America, 1766 ***1220.12*** *p634*
Plumpe, John; Barbados or Jamaica, 1699 ***1220.12*** *p634*
Plumridge, John; America, 1741 ***1220.12*** *p634*
Plumridge, Richard; America, 1678 ***1220.12*** *p634*
Plumsey, William; America, 1737 ***1220.12*** *p634*
Plunket, James; America, 1756 ***1220.12*** *p634*
Plunket, Mary; America, 1770 ***1220.12*** *p634*
Plunkett, Abraham; Boston, 1774 ***8529.30*** *p7*
Plunkett, Ann; Virginia, 1736 ***1220.12*** *p634*
Plunkett, John; Bridgeport, CT, 1856 ***8513.31*** *p421*
*Wife:*Rosanna Eustis
Plunkett, Robert; America, 1751 ***1220.12*** *p634*
Plunkett, Rosanna Eustis *SEE* Plunkett, John
Pluschke, Anton; Valdivia, Chile, 1852 ***1192.4*** *p53*
With wife
Plusson, Pierre 31; Quebec, 1648 ***9221.17*** *p202*
Pluta, Joseph; Detroit, 1930 ***1640.60*** *p83*
Plymouth, Susanna; America, 1749 ***1220.12*** *p634*
Poanseachi, Pietro 42; New York, NY, 1894 ***6512.1*** *p230*
Pobgee, William; America, 1772 ***1220.12*** *p634*
Pochard, Louise 16; America, 1845 ***778.6*** *p271*
Pochard, Susan 34; America, 1845 ***778.6*** *p271*
Pochard, Susan 47; America, 1845 ***778.6*** *p271*
Pochel, Edward; Illinois, 1858-1861 ***6020.5*** *p132*
Pochelle, Mrs. 29; America, 1841 ***778.6*** *p271*
Pochelle, Raymond 37; America, 1841 ***778.6*** *p271*
Pochelle, Wm. 6; America, 1841 ***778.6*** *p271*
Pochmann, Coelestine; Galveston, TX, 1855 ***571.7*** *p17*
Pochmara, Stella Ostrowska *SEE* Pochmara, Walter
Pochmara, Walter; Detroit, 1929-1930 ***6214.5*** *p70*
*Wife:*Stella Ostrowska
Pock, Mr.; America, 1854 ***7420.1*** *p126*
Pock, Wilhelmine Justine Charlotte; America, 1867 ***7420.1*** *p253*
Pockett, John; Virginia, 1665 ***9228.50*** *p523*
Pockiet, Pauline; America, 1867 ***7919.3*** *p533*
Pockolik, Jacob; Texas, 1898-1904 ***6015.15*** *p29*
Pockrandt, Wilhelmine; Wisconsin, 1898 ***6795.8*** *p192*
Pocock, Charles; America, 1744 ***1220.12*** *p634*
Pocock, Frederick 30; Ontario, 1871 ***1823.21*** *p299*
Pocock, Henry 50; Ontario, 1871 ***1823.21*** *p299*
Pocock, John; America, 1750 ***1220.12*** *p634*
Pocock, John J. 51; Ontario, 1871 ***1823.21*** *p299*
Pocock, Robert; America, 1751 ***1220.12*** *p634*
Pocrnich, Tony 30; Minnesota, 1926 ***2769.54*** *p1383*
Podafka, Adolf; America, 1883 ***5475.1*** *p37*
Podany, Josef; Pennsylvania, 1858 ***2853.20*** *p119*
Podczus, Peter; Detroit, 1929-1930 ***6214.5*** *p69*
Podgorski, Mary; Detroit, 1929 ***1640.55*** *p114*
Podgurski, John; New York, 1926 ***1173.1*** *p2*
Podhola, Frantisek; Wisconsin, 1854 ***2853.20*** *p333*
Podmore, George; America, 1768 ***1220.12*** *p634*
Podney, Robert 49; Ontario, 1871 ***1823.21*** *p299*
Podoll, Ernest Otto; Wisconsin, 1899 ***6795.8*** *p118*
Podoll, Otto; Wisconsin, 1886 ***6795.8*** *p118*
Poduschnuk, Wilhelm; America, 1867 ***7919.3*** *p528*
Poe, George; America, 1741 ***1220.12*** *p634*
Poe, John; America, 1750 ***1220.12*** *p634*
Poe, Jones 56; Ontario, 1871 ***1823.21*** *p299*
Poe, Samuel; America, 1752 ***1220.12*** *p634*
Poepple, Caroline *SEE* Poepple, Georg
Poepple, Friedrich *SEE* Poepple, Johann
Poepple, Friedrich *SEE* Poepple, Michael
Poepple, Friedrich *SEE* Poepple, Georg
Poepple, Georg; Dakota, 1886 ***554.30*** *p25*
*Wife:*Maria Seibold
*Child:*Caroline
*Child:*Friedrich
*Child:*Magdalene
*Child:*Jakob
*Child:*Katharina
Poepple, Jakob *SEE* Poepple, Georg
Poepple, Johann *SEE* Poepple, Johann
Poepple, Johann; Dakota, 1884 ***554.30*** *p25*
*Wife:*Karolina Albus
*Child:*Friedrich
*Child:*Johann
Poepple, Johann *SEE* Poepple, Michael
Poepple, Karolina Albus *SEE* Poepple, Johann
Poepple, Katharina *SEE* Poepple, Georg
Poepple, Magdalene *SEE* Poepple, Michael
Poepple, Magdalene *SEE* Poepple, Georg
Poepple, Maria Seibold *SEE* Poepple, Georg
Poepple, Michael; Dakota, 1885 ***554.30*** *p25*
*Wife:*Wilhelmina Grunger
*Child:*Magdalene
*Child:*Johann
*Child:*Friedrich
Poepple, Wilhelmina Grunger *SEE* Poepple, Michael
Poet, Lillian Phoebe; San Francisco, 1910-1912 ***9228.50*** *p546*
Poete, Pauline; Quebec, 1659 ***9221.17*** *p398*
*Son:*Jean
*Daughter:*Marie
*Daughter:*Marthe
*Son:*Charles
*Daughter:*Anne
Pofahl, Anna Emilie Henriette; Wisconsin, 1897 ***6795.8*** *p231*
Poggemeier, Christian Friedrich Heinrich; New York, NY, 1882 ***6212.1*** *p13*
Pohl, Emilie; Wisconsin, 1904 ***6795.8*** *p159*
Pohl, Jacob; Illinois, 1854 ***6079.1*** *p11*

Pohl, Joh. Thomas; Valdivia, Chile, 1850 ***1192.4*** *p50*
With wife & 3 children
With child 3
With child 19
Pohl, Vaclav; New York, NY, 1836-1889 ***2853.20*** *p103*
Pohl, Vaclav; New York, NY, 1848 ***2853.20*** *p100*
Pohl, Vaclav; Wisconsin, 1857-1860 ***2853.20*** *p324*
*Brother:*Vojtech
Pohl, Vojtech; New York, NY, 1848 ***2853.20*** *p100*
Pohl, Vojtech *SEE* Pohl, Vaclav
Pohlabeln, John; Ohio, 1840-1897 ***8365.35*** *p17*
Pohler, Mr.; America, 1853 ***7420.1*** *p110*
With family
Pohler, Mr.; America, 1855 ***7420.1*** *p140*
Pohler, Carl Ernst Wilhelm; America, 1883 ***7420.1*** *p338*
Pohler, Carl Friedrich Gottlieb; America, 1864 ***7420.1*** *p226*
Pohler, Carl Heinrich; America, 1867 ***7420.1*** *p262*
With sister-in-law
Pohler, Ernst Friedrich; New York, NY, 1879 ***7420.1*** *p314*
Pohler, Ernst Friedrich Ludwig; America, 1864 ***7420.1*** *p226*
Pohler, Ernst Heinrich Wilhelm; Indiana, 1882 ***7420.1*** *p331*
Pohler, Friedrich; America, 1860 ***7420.1*** *p198*
With family
Pohler, Friedrich Gottlieb; America, 1872 ***7420.1*** *p297*
Pohler, Friedrich Gottlieb Wilhelm; America, 1891 ***7420.1*** *p363*
Pohler, Friedrich Wilhelm; America, 1883 ***7420.1*** *p338*
Pohler, Heinrich; America, 1836 ***7420.1*** *p11*
Pohler, Heinrich Gottlieb; America, 1884 ***7420.1*** *p344*
Pohler, Ludwig; America, 1851 ***7420.1*** *p82*
With wife & 2 children
Pohlig, August; America, 1868 ***7919.3*** *p533*
Pohlig, Robert; America, 1868 ***7919.3*** *p533*
Pohlke, Otto; Wisconsin, 1898 ***6795.8*** *p163*
Pohlmann, . . .; America, 1864 ***7420.1*** *p226*
Pohlmann, Heinrich; America, 1867 ***7420.1*** *p262*
Pohlmann, Johann Christoph; America, 1866 ***7420.1*** *p247*
With family
Pohlmann, Johann Conrad; America, 1865 ***7420.1*** *p235*
Pohs, Mathias; Colorado, 1899 ***1029.59*** *p75*
Pohs, Mathias; Iowa, 1886 ***1029.59*** *p75*
Pohsans, Joseph 23; Missouri, 1846 ***778.6*** *p271*
Pohsans, Julie 19; Missouri, 1846 ***778.6*** *p272*
Poidevin, Nicholas; Ohio, 1807 ***9228.50*** *p57*
Poidevin, Nicholas; Ohio, 1807 ***9228.50*** *p516*
Poier, Louis N. 46; Ohio, 1880 ***4879.40*** *p258*
Poignand, David; Boston, 1787 ***9228.50*** *p80*
*Wife:*Delicia Amiraux
Poignand, Delicia Amiraux *SEE* Poignand, David
Poignard, . . .; Lexington, KY, n.d. ***9228.50*** *p518*
Poignet, Marguerite; Quebec, 1671 ***4514.3*** *p358*
Poinceau, Marguerite 17; New Orleans, 1848 ***778.6*** *p272*
Poinctain, John; Maryland, 1724 ***1220.12*** *p634*
Poindable, Michael; New Orleans, 1851 ***7242.30*** *p152*
Poindexter, . . .; New England, n.d. ***9228.50*** *p491*
Poindexter, George; Virginia, 1600-1700 ***9228.50*** *p207*
Poindexter, George; Virginia, 1657 ***9228.50*** *p517*
Poindexter, Jacob; Salem, MA, 1600-1692 ***9228.50*** *p255*
Poingdestre, . . .; New England, n.d. ***9228.50*** *p491*
Point-Du-Jour, Leonarde Fouquet *SEE* Point-Du-Jour, Zacharie
Point-Du-Jour, Rene 21 *SEE* Point-Du-Jour, Zacharie
Point-Du-Jour, Zacharie 51; Quebec, 1653 ***9221.17*** *p277*
*Wife:*Leonarde Fouquet
*Son:*Rene 21
Pointel, Charles 28; Port uncertain, 1843 ***778.6*** *p272*
Pointel, Marthe; Quebec, 1665 ***4514.3*** *p358*
Pointel, Pierre; Quebec, 1656 ***9221.17*** *p345*
Pointer, John; America, 1755 ***1220.12*** *p634*
Pointer, John; Virginia, 1741 ***1220.12*** *p634*
Pointer, Richard; Virginia, 1738 ***1220.12*** *p634*
Pointer, Thomas; Maryland or Virginia, 1733 ***1220.12*** *p634*
Poire, Marie; Quebec, 1669 ***4514.3*** *p358*
Poireau, Jeanne; Canada, 1662 ***1142.10*** *p129*
Poireau, Jeanne 18; Quebec, 1662 ***9221.17*** *p491*
Poiret, Antoine; Wisconsin, 1869 ***1495.20*** *p56*
Poiret, Etienne 39; Missouri, 1848 ***778.6*** *p272*
Poirier, August 23; Mississippi, 1848 ***778.6*** *p272*
Poirier, Mad. 23; America, 1843 ***778.6*** *p272*
Poirier, Pierre; Quebec, 1661 ***9221.17*** *p465*
Poirier, Vincent 25; Quebec, 1652 ***9221.17*** *p264*
Poisson, Barbe 13; Quebec, 1647 ***9221.17*** *p187*
*Sister:*Mathurine 20
Poisson, Catherine; Quebec, 1673 ***4514.3*** *p358*
Poisson, Jacqueline 26; Quebec, 1648 ***9221.17*** *p202*
*Daughter:*Louise 2
*Daughter:*Jeanne-Francoise 6 months
Poisson, Jean; Quebec, 1635 ***9221.17*** *p47*
*Son:*Jean
Poisson, Jean 17 *SEE* Poisson, Jean
Poisson, Jeanne-Francoise 6 *SEE* Poisson, Jacqueline Chamboy
Poisson, Louise 2 *SEE* Poisson, Jacqueline Chamboy
Poisson, Mathurine 20 *SEE* Poisson, Barbe
Poissonnier, Nicolas; Quebec, 1642 ***9221.17*** *p120*
Poitevin, Mr. 26; America, 1845 ***778.6*** *p272*
Poitevin, A. 30; America, 1843 ***778.6*** *p272*
Poitevin, Catherine; Quebec, 1669 ***4514.3*** *p358*
Poitevin, E. 24; America, 1845 ***778.6*** *p272*
Poitiers, Anna Maria 50; America, 1872 ***5475.1*** *p354*
*Daughter:*Karoline
*Son:*Karl Alexander
*Son:*Friedrich
Poitiers, Friedrich *SEE* Poitiers, Anna Maria Becker
Poitiers, Karl Alexander *SEE* Poitiers, Anna Maria Becker
Poitiers, Karoline *SEE* Poitiers, Anna Maria Becker
Poitiers Dubuisson, Jean-Baptiste de; Quebec, 1665 ***2314.30*** *p167*
Poitiers Dubuisson, Jean-Baptiste de; Quebec, 1665 ***2314.30*** *p193*
Poitraud, Anne; Quebec, 1668 ***4514.3*** *p358*
Poitron, Anne; Quebec, 1670 ***4514.3*** *p359*
Poits, Thomas; America, 1713 ***1220.12*** *p634*
Poke, Mary; America, 1722 ***1220.12*** *p635*
Poker, John; America, 1749 ***1220.12*** *p635*
Poklinton, Arthur; Quebec, 1870 ***8364.32*** *p25*
Pokloktowska, Josephine; Wisconsin, 1886 ***6795.8*** *p30*
Pokloktowski, Josephine; Wisconsin, 1886 ***6795.8*** *p30*
Pokorny, Frantisek; Minnesota, 1891 ***2853.20*** *p273*
Pokorny, Josef; Nebraska, 1875 ***2853.20*** *p172*
Pokrywka, Joseph A.; Detroit, 1930 ***1640.60*** *p82*
Polachowska, Julianna; Detroit, 1890 ***9980.23*** *p97*
Polak, Jakub; Wisconsin, 1853 ***2853.20*** *p218*
*Cousin:*Jan
*Cousin:*Josef
Polak, Jan *SEE* Polak, Jakub
Polak, Jan; Wisconsin, 1853 ***2853.20*** *p303*
Polak, Josef *SEE* Polak, Jakub
Polak, Josef; Wisconsin, 1853 ***2853.20*** *p303*
Polak, Meyer 21; New York, NY, 1894 ***6512.1*** *p232*
Polak, Simon; New York, NY, 1837 ***2853.20*** *p21*
Polan, James 34; Ontario, 1871 ***1823.17*** *p133*
Poland, Abraham; America, 1749 ***1220.12*** *p635*
Poland, Christian; America, 1743 ***1220.12*** *p635*
Polansky, Frantisek; Nebraska, 1910 ***2853.20*** *p189*
Polasek, Robert; Minnesota, 1894 ***2853.20*** *p268*
Polatsek, J.; Louisiana, 1874 ***4981.45*** *p133*
Polaza, Aron 28; Texas, 1848 ***778.6*** *p272*
Polbentier, Alphous; New York, 1904 ***1766.20*** *p34*
Pole, James 36; Ontario, 1871 ***1823.21*** *p299*
Pole, William 26; Ontario, 1871 ***1823.17*** *p133*
Polenske, Emma Alvine; Wisconsin, 1897 ***6795.8*** *p38*
Poleyn, . . .; Carolina or Virginia, n.d. ***9228.50*** *p20A*
Polin, William; America, 1769 ***1220.12*** *p635*
Polinske, Ludwig F.; Wisconsin, 1907 ***6795.8*** *p179*
Polinske, Pauline Louise; Wisconsin, 1889 ***6795.8*** *p107*
Poliron, Louis 53; New Orleans, 1848 ***778.6*** *p272*
Polit, Tomasz 35; New York, NY, 1911 ***6533.11*** *p10*
Polkinghorne, James; America, 1772 ***1220.12*** *p635*
Polkinhorne, William; America, 1744 ***1220.12*** *p635*
Poll, Johann Carl Wilhelm; America, 1858 ***7420.1*** *p181*
Poll, Wilhelm; America, 1856 ***7420.1*** *p152*
Pollan, . . .; Tennessee, n.d. ***9228.50*** *p20A*
Pollard, Abraham; America, 1685 ***1220.12*** *p635*
Pollard, Andrew; America, 1761 ***1220.12*** *p635*
Pollard, Ann; America, 1757 ***1220.12*** *p635*
Pollard, Ann 60; Michigan, 1880 ***4491.36*** *p17*
Pollard, Catherine; Maryland, 1737 ***1220.12*** *p635*
Pollard, Elizabeth; America, 1769 ***1220.12*** *p635*
Pollard, George 65; Michigan, 1880 ***4491.36*** *p17*
Pollard, John; America, 1761 ***1220.12*** *p635*
Pollard, John; America, 1768 ***1220.12*** *p635*
Pollard, John; America, 1771 ***1220.12*** *p635*
Pollard, Jonathan; America, 1765 ***1220.12*** *p635*
Pollard, Joseph 52; Ontario, 1871 ***1823.21*** *p299*
Pollard, Margaret 37; Michigan, 1880 ***4491.36*** *p17*
Pollard, Mary; America, 1749 ***1220.12*** *p635*
Pollard, Mary; America, 1772 ***1220.12*** *p635*
Pollard, Mary; America, 1775 ***1220.12*** *p635*
Pollard, Nicholas; America, 1723 ***1220.12*** *p635*
Pollard, Samuel 39; Michigan, 1880 ***4491.36*** *p17*
Pollard, Thomas; America, 1770 ***1220.12*** *p635*
Pollard, William; America, 1750 ***1220.12*** *p635*
Pollard, William; Toronto, 1844 ***2910.35*** *p114*
Pollarth, Franz 30; America, 1840 ***778.6*** *p272*
Pollet, Elizabeth; America, 1757 ***1220.12*** *p635*
Pollet, Thomas; America, 1741 ***1220.12*** *p635*
Pollet, William; America, 1774 ***1220.12*** *p635*
Pollet deLacombe dela Pocatiere, Francois; Quebec, 1665 ***2314.30*** *p167*
Pollet deLacombe deLa Pocatiere, Francois; Quebec, 1665 ***2314.30*** *p193*
Pollett, Edward; Annapolis, MD, 1724 ***1220.12*** *p635*
Pollett, Richard; America, 1719 ***1220.12*** *p635*
Pollett, Thomas; America, 1757 ***1220.12*** *p635*
Polley, Engel Marie Sophie Charlotte Roehe *SEE* Polley, Johann Christian
Polley, Johann Christian; America, 1862 ***7420.1*** *p214*
*Wife:*Engel Marie Sophie Charlotte Roehe
Polley, John; Barbados, 1668 ***1220.12*** *p635*
Polley, Joseph; Missouri, 1863 ***3276.1*** *p3*
Polley, William 59; Ontario, 1871 ***1823.17*** *p133*
Pollock, Miss; Montreal, 1922 ***4514.4*** *p32*
Pollock, James 30; Ontario, 1871 ***1823.17*** *p133*
Pollock, John 42; Ontario, 1871 ***1823.17*** *p133*
Pollock, John 65; Ontario, 1871 ***1823.21*** *p299*
Pollock, John C. 38; Ontario, 1871 ***1823.17*** *p133*
Pollock, Thos. 60; Ontario, 1871 ***1823.17*** *p133*
Pollock, William 28; Ontario, 1871 ***1823.21*** *p299*
Pollock, William F.; North Carolina, 1852 ***1088.45*** *p27*
Polly, James 72; Ontario, 1871 ***1823.17*** *p133*
Polni, Marie 50; New Orleans, 1848 ***778.6*** *p272*
Polni, Pierre 47; New Orleans, 1848 ***778.6*** *p272*
Polo, Marie 16; Montreal, 1659 ***9221.17*** *p426*
Polock, James; America, 1771 ***1220.12*** *p635*
Polomsky, Petr; Detroit, 1909 ***2853.20*** *p364*
Poloranta, Eli 41; Minnesota, 1926 ***2769.54*** *p1382*
Polson, Christina; St. Paul, MN, 1887 ***1865.50*** *p106*
Polson, Elizabeth; America, 1718 ***1220.12*** *p639*
Polstorff, Julius Rudolf; America, 1882 ***7420.1*** *p331*
Poltee, Michael; Ohio, 1809-1852 ***4511.35*** *p41*
Polton, William; America, 1741 ***1220.12*** *p640*
Poluogt, Charles; North Carolina, 1857 ***1088.45*** *p27*
Poly, Edward 57; Ontario, 1871 ***1823.21*** *p299*
Polz, Joseph 19; America, 1844 ***778.6*** *p272*
Polzt, Caspar; America, 1867 ***7919.3*** *p530*
With wife & child
Pomelet, Charles 29; New Orleans, 1848 ***778.6*** *p272*
Pomeranke, Emma Louisa; Wisconsin, 1902 ***6795.8*** *p229*
Pomeroy, Eltweed; Dorchester, MA, 1632 ***117.5*** *p158*
Pomeroy, George; America, 1728 ***1220.12*** *p635*
Pomeroy, James; America, 1685 ***1220.12*** *p635*
Pomeroy, John; America, 1738 ***1220.12*** *p635*
Pomeroy, Samuel; America, 1685 ***1220.12*** *p635*
Pomes, J.; Louisiana, 1874 ***4981.45*** *p296*
Pomfret, Elizabeth; America, 1764 ***1220.12*** *p635*
Pomfret, Henry; America, 1768 ***1220.12*** *p635*
Pomfrett, Edward; America, 1749 ***1220.12*** *p635*
Pomfrett, Thomas; America, 1685 ***1220.12*** *p635*
Pomfrett, Thomas; Rappahannock, VA, 1741 ***1220.12*** *p635*
Pomfrey, Elizabeth; America, 1759 ***1220.12*** *p635*
Pomfrey, James; Died enroute, 1730 ***1220.12*** *p635*
Pomfrey, Susanna; America, 1724 ***1220.12*** *p635*
Pomier, J. 23; New Orleans, 1846 ***778.6*** *p272*
Pominville, Henri 24; Quebec, 1659 ***9221.17*** *p395*
Pommaud, Aimee 24; America, 1844 ***778.6*** *p272*
Pommenke, Robart; Wisconsin, 1863 ***6795.8*** *p188*
Pommenker, Julius; Wisconsin, 1866 ***6795.8*** *p205*
Pommerenke, Alexander Joseph; Wisconsin, 1899 ***6795.8*** *p197*
Pommerenke, Julius; Wisconsin, 1875 ***6795.8*** *p205*
Pommernkee, Julius; Wisconsin, 1875 ***6795.8*** *p205*
Pommerole, Marie; Quebec, 1665 ***4514.3*** *p341*
Pommes, Miss 18; New Orleans, 1848 ***778.6*** *p272*
Pommes, Miss 20; New Orleans, 1848 ***778.6*** *p272*
Pomplun, Emil Friedrich; Wisconsin, 1898 ***6795.8*** *p152*
Pomplun, Otto; Wisconsin, 1892 ***6795.8*** *p153*
Pomplun, Otto; Wisconsin, 1896 ***6795.8*** *p173*
Pomponnelle, Marie 2; Quebec, 1656 ***9221.17*** *p345*
Pomroy, John; Annapolis, MD, 1723 ***1220.12*** *p635*
Pomroy, Samuel; Virginia, 1739 ***1220.12*** *p635*
Pomy, Hermann Wilhelm Ludwig; America, 1859 ***7420.1*** *p188*
Pon, Christina 7; America, 1844 ***778.6*** *p272*
Pon, Daniel 20; America, 1844 ***778.6*** *p272*
Pon, Elizabeth 14; America, 1844 ***778.6*** *p272*
Pon, Magdeleine 28; America, 1844 ***778.6*** *p272*
Pon, Marguerita 17; America, 1844 ***778.6*** *p272*
Pon, Philip; Ohio, 1809-1852 ***4511.35*** *p41*
Ponance, . . . 50; Ontario, 1871 ***1823.17*** *p134*
Poncelet, Anna Maria Treib; America, 1882 ***5475.1*** *p137*
*Son:*Mathais
*Son:*Anton
Poncelet, Anton *SEE* Poncelet, Anna Maria Treib
Poncelet, Mathais *SEE* Poncelet, Anna Maria Treib
Poncet DeLaRiviere, Joseph-Antoine 29; Quebec, 1639 ***9221.17*** *p83*
Ponchand, Francis 36; Ontario, 1871 ***1823.21*** *p299*
Pond, Bryan; America, 1726 ***1220.12*** *p636*

Pond, Elizabeth; America, 1730 ***1220.12*** *p636*
Pond, James 55; Ontario, 1871 ***1823.21*** *p299*
Ponder, John; Maryland, 1674 ***1236.25*** *p50*
Pong, Lettice; America, 1746 ***1220.12*** *p636*
Poninou, Jean Paul 19; America, 1845 ***778.6*** *p272*
Pons, James; Louisiana, 1874 ***4981.45*** *p296*
Pons, Joseph; Louisiana, 1836-1841 ***4981.45*** *p209*
Pons, Laurent 26; Port uncertain, 1848 ***778.6*** *p272*
Pons, P.; Louisiana, 1874 ***4981.45*** *p296*
Ponsart, Benoit 21; Quebec, 1642 ***9221.17*** *p120*
Ponser, Nic. 27; America, 1840 ***778.6*** *p272*
Ponsness, Lars J.; Iowa, 1896 ***1211.15*** *p18*
Ponsness, Peder; Iowa, 1896 ***1211.15*** *p18*
Pont, Anne; Barbados, 1663 ***1220.12*** *p636*
Pont, John; America, 1743 ***1220.12*** *p636*
Pont, Margaret; Barbados, 1664 ***1220.12*** *p636*
Pontcabaret, Mr. 28; America, 1746 ***778.6*** *p272*
Pontcabaret, Mrs. 32; America, 1746 ***778.6*** *p272*
Pontey, Alexander 39; Ontario, 1871 ***1823.21*** *p299*
Pontife, Jacques 26; Quebec, 1658 ***9221.17*** *p378*
Ponting, Edward; America, 1768 ***1220.12*** *p636*
Pontoise, Jacques; Quebec, 1653 ***9221.17*** *p271*
Pontonier, Marie 13; Montreal, 1656 ***9221.17*** *p348*
Ponturini, Candido 14; New York, NY, 1894 ***6512.1*** *p182*
Ponty, Louis; Quebec, 1658 ***9221.17*** *p386*
Ponydebat, Laurent; Louisiana, 1874 ***4981.45*** *p133*
Pooch, Heinrich Wilhelm August; Wisconsin, 1895 ***6795.8*** *p91*
Pooch, Henry J.; Wisconsin, 1874 ***6795.8*** *p153*
Poock, Wilhelmine Charl.; America, 1852 ***7420.1*** *p94*
Pook, . . .; America, 1847 ***7420.1*** *p55*
Pook, Mr.; America, 1856 ***7420.1*** *p152*
*Son:*Friedrich Christian Gottlieb
*Son:*Ernst Heinrich Gottlieb
With wife & 2 sons
Pook, Widow; America, 1867 ***7420.1*** *p262*
With son 11
With son 9
With son 5
Pook, Ernst Heinrich Gottlieb *SEE* Pook, Mr.
Pook, Friedrich Christian Gottlieb *SEE* Pook, Mr.
Pook, Heinrich Aug. Christoph *SEE* Pook, Heinrich August Christoph
Pook, Heinrich August Christoph; America, 1858 ***7420.1*** *p181*
*Wife:*Sophie Wilhelmine Charlotte Lange
*Son:*Johann Heinrich Carl
*Son:*Johann Heinrich Aug.
*Daughter:*Wilhelmine Charlotte
*Son:*Heinrich Aug. Christoph
Pook, Heinrich Christoph; Port uncertain, 1858 ***7420.1*** *p181*
With family
Pook, Johann Heinrich Aug. *SEE* Pook, Heinrich August Christoph
Pook, Johann Heinrich Carl *SEE* Pook, Heinrich August Christoph
Pook, Sophie Wilhelmine Charlotte Lange *SEE* Pook, Heinrich August Christoph
Pook, Wilhelmine Charlotte *SEE* Pook, Heinrich August Christoph
Pook Family ; America, 1858 ***7420.1*** *p177*
Pool, Charles 35; Ontario, 1871 ***1823.21*** *p299*
Pool, Edward; America, 1761 ***1220.12*** *p636*
Pool, Irwin I. 40; Ontario, 1871 ***1823.21*** *p299*
Pool, James; America, 1771 ***1220.12*** *p636*
Pool, John; Illinois, 1858-1861 ***6020.5*** *p132*
Pool, John 48; Ontario, 1871 ***1823.21*** *p299*
Pool, Mary; Maryland, 1736 ***1220.12*** *p636*
Pool, Robert; America, 1724 ***1220.12*** *p636*
Poole, Abraham; America, 1762 ***1220.12*** *p636*
Poole, Anne; Barbados, 1665 ***1220.12*** *p636*
Poole, Benjamin; Barbados, 1676 ***1220.12*** *p636*
Poole, Christopher 42; Ontario, 1871 ***1823.21*** *p299*
Poole, Cyrus John; New Jersey, 1808 ***3845.2*** *p130*
Poole, Daniel 19; Barbados, 1664 ***1220.12*** *p636*
Poole, Elijah E. 33; Michigan, 1880 ***4491.39*** *p24*
Poole, George; America, 1769 ***1220.12*** *p636*
Poole, George; Annapolis, MD, 1719 ***1220.12*** *p636*
Poole, Grace; America, 1724 ***1220.12*** *p636*
Poole, James; America, 1744 ***1220.12*** *p636*
Poole, James 36; Ontario, 1871 ***1823.21*** *p299*
Poole, Jeremy; America, 1685 ***1220.12*** *p636*
Poole, John; America, 1685 ***1220.12*** *p636*
Poole, John; America, 1774 ***1220.12*** *p636*
Poole, John; Barbados, 1664 ***1220.12*** *p636*
Poole, John; Maryland or Virginia, 1733 ***1220.12*** *p636*
Poole, Joseph; America, 1769 ***1220.12*** *p636*
Poole, Josiah; Virginia, 1741 ***1220.12*** *p636*
Poole, L. J.; Montreal, 1922 ***4514.4*** *p32*
Poole, Lewis; Virginia, 1736 ***1220.12*** *p636*
Poole, Mary; Jamaica, 1717 ***1220.12*** *p636*
Poole, Rachel; America, 1740 ***1220.12*** *p636*
Poole, Richard; America, 1769 ***1220.12*** *p636*
Poole, Robert; America, 1764 ***1220.12*** *p636*
Poole, Samuel 45; Ontario, 1871 ***1823.21*** *p299*
Poole, Sarah; Potomac, 1729 ***1220.12*** *p636*
Poole, Silvester; America, 1685 ***1220.12*** *p636*
Poole, Simon; America, 1685 ***1220.12*** *p636*
Poole, Susannah; Annapolis, MD, 1723 ***1220.12*** *p636*
Poole, Thomas; America, 1769 ***1220.12*** *p636*
Poole, Thomas; Maryland, 1719 ***1220.12*** *p636*
Poole, Thomas; Virginia, 1753 ***1220.12*** *p636*
Poole, William 45; Ontario, 1871 ***1823.21*** *p299*
Pooley, John; America, 1742 ***1220.12*** *p636*
Pooley, Richard; America, 1674 ***1220.12*** *p636*
Pooley, Thomas; America, 1757 ***1220.12*** *p636*
Pooley, William; America, 1755 ***1220.12*** *p636*
Pooley, William; Barbados, 1662 ***1220.12*** *p636*
Poon, Peter; America, 1757 ***1220.12*** *p636*
Poor, Abraham; America, 1720 ***1220.12*** *p637*
Poor, Arthur; Annapolis, MD, 1758 ***1220.12*** *p637*
Poor, Charles; Ohio, 1809-1852 ***4511.35*** *p41*
Poor, Henry; Virginia, 1768 ***1220.12*** *p637*
Poor, Jane; America, 1752 ***1220.12*** *p637*
Poor, John; Boston, 1762 ***1642*** *p31*
Poor, John 50; Ontario, 1871 ***1823.21*** *p299*
Poor, Michael; Boston, 1766 ***1642*** *p36*
Poore, Abram 20; Virginia, 1635 ***1183.3*** *p31*
Poore, George; America, 1675 ***1220.12*** *p637*
Poory, David 58; Ontario, 1871 ***1823.17*** *p134*
Pop, Judith; Boston, 1767 ***1642*** *p38*
Pope, Abraham; North Carolina, 1818 ***1088.45*** *p27*
Pope, Charles A. 29; Ontario, 1871 ***1823.21*** *p299*
Pope, Dorothy; Barbados, 1684 ***1220.12*** *p637*
Pope, Edward; America, 1770 ***1220.12*** *p637*
Pope, Eliza 7; Quebec, 1870 ***8364.32*** *p25*
Pope, Elizabeth; America, 1724 ***1220.12*** *p637*
Pope, Francis; Maryland, 1736 ***1220.12*** *p637*
Pope, Garrett; America, 1729 ***1220.12*** *p637*
Pope, George; Maryland, 1742 ***1220.12*** *p637*
Pope, Humphrey; America, 1685 ***1220.12*** *p637*
Pope, Isaac; America, 1738 ***1220.12*** *p637*
Pope, James; Barbados, 1684 ***1220.12*** *p637*
Pope, John; America, 1685 ***1220.12*** *p637*
Pope, John; America, 1774 ***1220.12*** *p637*
Pope, John; Annapolis, MD, 1725 ***1220.12*** *p637*
Pope, John; Barbados, 1662 ***1220.12*** *p637*
Pope, John; Jamaica, 1717 ***1220.12*** *p637*
Pope, John 36; Ontario, 1871 ***1823.21*** *p299*
Pope, John W. 59; Ontario, 1871 ***1823.21*** *p299*
Pope, Joseph; America, 1750 ***1220.12*** *p637*
Pope, Mary; America, 1724 ***1220.12*** *p637*
Pope, Maurice; America, 1772 ***1220.12*** *p637*
Pope, Michael 32; Indiana, 1854-1868 ***9076.20*** *p66*
Pope, Robert; Barbados, 1672 ***1220.12*** *p637*
Pope, Samuel 40; Ontario, 1871 ***1823.21*** *p299*
Pope, Sarah; America, 1752 ***1220.12*** *p637*
Pope, Susan 5; Quebec, 1870 ***8364.32*** *p25*
Pope, Thomas; America, 1740 ***1220.12*** *p637*
Pope, Thomas; Barbados, 1667 ***1220.12*** *p637*
Pope, William; America, 1737 ***1220.12*** *p637*
Pope, William; America, 1749 ***1220.12*** *p637*
Pope, William; America, 1752 ***1220.12*** *p637*
Pope, William; America, 1759 ***1220.12*** *p637*
Pope, William 57; Ontario, 1871 ***1823.21*** *p299*
Popham, Henry; Barbados, 1665 ***1220.12*** *p637*
Popham, Samuel; America, 1750 ***1220.12*** *p637*
Pople, Charles; America, 1685 ***1220.12*** *p637*
Popley, William; Virginia, 1738 ***1220.12*** *p637*
Popp, Auguste; America, 1868 ***7919.3*** *p533*
Popp, Gustav John Ford; New York, 1892 ***1766.20*** *p27*
Popp, Henriette; America, 1868 ***7919.3*** *p530*
Popp, Johann Georg; America, 1867 ***7919.3*** *p527*
Popp, Maria; America, 1867 ***7919.3*** *p533*
Popp, Rosina; America, 1868 ***7919.3*** *p530*
Popp, Wilhelm; America, 1868 ***7919.3*** *p533*
Poppe, Albert; Iowa, 1898 ***1211.15*** *p18*
Poppe, Jean; Montreal, 1648 ***9221.17*** *p206*
Poppe, Jules 24; Missouri, 1848 ***778.6*** *p272*
Poppelbaum, Georg Ludwig; America, 1854 ***7420.1*** *p127*
Poppelbaum, Georg Ludwig; America, 1855 ***7420.1*** *p140*
Poppelbaum, Minna; Chicago, 1870 ***7420.1*** *p284*
With 3 children
Popper, Moritz; America, 1868 ***7919.3*** *p525*
Popper, Selma; America, 1868 ***7919.3*** *p525*
Popple, Betty; America, 1753 ***1220.12*** *p637*
Popple, Saml.; Illinois, 1834-1900 ***6020.5*** *p132*
Popplewell, John; America, 1774 ***1220.12*** *p637*
Popplewell, Mary; America, 1762 ***1220.12*** *p637*
Popplewell, Timothy; America, 1738 ***1220.12*** *p637*
Popuenville, J. B. 38; New Orleans, 1840 ***778.6*** *p272*
Populus, Mr. 70; America, 1843 ***778.6*** *p273*
Popy, J. J. 30; America, 1841 ***778.6*** *p273*
Poquet, John; Virginia, 1665 ***9228.50*** *p523*
Porat, Barbara Quirin *SEE* Porat, Karl
Porat, Georg *SEE* Porat, Karl
Porat, Johann *SEE* Porat, Karl
Porat, Josef *SEE* Porat, Karl
Porat, Karl *SEE* Porat, Karl
Porat, Karl; Pennsylvania, 1880 ***5475.1*** *p22*
*Wife:*Barbara Quirin
*Son:*Karl
*Son:*Peter
*Son:*Georg
*Son:*Josef
*Son:*Johann
Porat, Peter *SEE* Porat, Karl
Porch, George, Jr.; Barbados or Jamaica, 1688 ***1220.12*** *p637*
Porchet, Martine Duruau *SEE* Porchet, Pierre
Porchet, Pierre; Quebec, 1647 ***9221.17*** *p188*
*Wife:*Martine Duruau
With daughter
Poree, Mr. 22; America, 1846 ***778.6*** *p273*
Poree, Mrs. 48; America, 1846 ***778.6*** *p273*
Poremski, Maryanna; Detroit, 1929 ***1640.55*** *p115*
Porr, Charles; Ohio, 1809-1852 ***4511.35*** *p41*
Porr, Philip; Ohio, 1809-1852 ***4511.35*** *p41*
Porry, Alexandre E.; Louisiana, 1836-1841 ***4981.45*** *p209*
Porsail, Mr. 53; America, 1840 ***778.6*** *p273*
Porsail, Mrs. 53; America, 1840 ***778.6*** *p273*
Porsch, Wolf; New York, 1859 ***358.56*** *p102*
Porson, Sarah; America, 1771 ***1220.12*** *p611*
Port, Ann; Annapolis, MD, 1726 ***1220.12*** *p637*
Port, John; America, 1698 ***1220.12*** *p637*
Port, John 17; Quebec, 1870 ***8364.32*** *p25*
Port, Kaspar; Wisconsin, 1875 ***6795.8*** *p98*
Port, Katharina; America, 1881 ***5475.1*** *p46*
Porta, Jakob; America, 1833 ***5475.1*** *p73*
With wife
With child 10
Portail Gevront, Daniel; Quebec, 1728 ***2314.30*** *p171*
Portal, Sebastien 26; New Orleans, 1846 ***778.6*** *p273*
Porte, Ann 43; Ontario, 1871 ***1823.21*** *p299*
Porte, George 44; Ontario, 1871 ***1823.21*** *p299*
Porte, Henry; America, 1773 ***1220.12*** *p637*
Porte, Margret 56; Ontario, 1871 ***1823.21*** *p299*
Porte, Michel 16; New Orleans, 1845 ***778.6*** *p273*
Porte, Pierre 18; America, 1843 ***778.6*** *p273*
Porte, Robert 41; Ontario, 1871 ***1823.21*** *p299*
Portell, Eliza 35; Ontario, 1871 ***1823.21*** *p299*
Porter, Alexander; Ohio, 1832 ***2763.1*** *p21*
Porter, Alexander 47; Ontario, 1871 ***1823.17*** *p134*
Porter, Althea *SEE* Porter, John
Porter, Ann 30; Ontario, 1871 ***1823.21*** *p299*
Porter, Bengyman 70; Ontario, 1871 ***1823.21*** *p299*
Porter, Daniel; America, 1771 ***1220.12*** *p637*
Porter, Daniel; Maryland, 1723 ***1220.12*** *p637*
Porter, Edward; Potomac, 1742 ***1220.12*** *p637*
Porter, Eliza 11; St. John, N.B., 1834 ***6469.7*** *p5*
Porter, Elizabeth; America, 1735 ***1220.12*** *p638*
Porter, Elizabeth; America, 1747 ***1220.12*** *p638*
Porter, Elizabeth; Annapolis, MD, 1719 ***1220.12*** *p637*
Porter, Francis; America, 1768 ***1220.12*** *p638*
Porter, Frank J.; Iowa, 1837-1860 ***9228.50*** *p229*
Porter, Isabella 45; Ontario, 1871 ***1823.21*** *p299*
Porter, James; Ohio, 1832 ***2763.1*** *p21*
Porter, James 40; Ontario, 1871 ***1823.17*** *p134*
Porter, James 52; Ontario, 1871 ***1823.17*** *p134*
Porter, Jasper; America, 1725 ***1220.12*** *p638*
Porter, Jean 30; New Orleans, 1848 ***778.6*** *p273*
Porter, John; America, 1735 ***1220.12*** *p638*
Porter, John; America, 1752 ***1220.12*** *p638*
Porter, John; America, 1768 ***1220.12*** *p638*
Porter, John 46; Ontario, 1871 ***1823.21*** *p300*
Porter, John 65; Ontario, 1871 ***1823.21*** *p299*
Porter, John; Philadelphia, 1859 ***8513.31*** *p421*
*Wife:*Althea
Porter, Jonathon R.; Washington, 1886 ***2770.40*** *p195*
Porter, Joseph 54; Ontario, 1871 ***1823.21*** *p300*
Porter, Luke; America, 1685 ***1220.12*** *p638*
Porter, Margaret; America, 1766 ***1220.12*** *p638*
Porter, Margaret; America, 1771 ***1220.12*** *p638*
Porter, Martha; America, 1736 ***1220.12*** *p638*
Porter, Martha; Annapolis, MD, 1723 ***1220.12*** *p638*
Porter, Mary; America, 1734 ***1220.12*** *p638*
Porter, Mary; America, 1740 ***1220.12*** *p638*
Porter, Mary; America, 1756 ***1220.12*** *p638*
Porter, Mary; America, 1773 ***1220.12*** *p638*
Porter, Mathew; America, 1685 ***1220.12*** *p638*
Porter, Mathew 40; St. John, N.B., 1834 ***6469.7*** *p5*
Porter, Matthew; Barbados or Jamaica, 1678 ***1220.12*** *p638*
Porter, Nathan; Ohio, 1832 ***2763.1*** *p21*
Porter, Rachel 8; St. John, N.B., 1834 ***6469.7*** *p5*

Porter, Rachel 35; St. John, N.B., 1834 *6469.7 p5*
Porter, Rebecca; America, 1748 *1220.12 p638*
Porter, Richard; Annapolis, MD, 1731 *1220.12 p638*
Porter, Richard 72; Ontario, 1871 *1823.21 p300*
Porter, Robert; Barbados, 1676 *1220.12 p638*
Porter, Robert 43; Ontario, 1871 *1823.21 p300*
Porter, Robert 56; Ontario, 1871 *1823.21 p300*
Porter, Solomon; America, 1754 *1220.12 p638*
Porter, Solomon; America, 1771 *1220.12 p638*
Porter, Tabitha; America, 1688 *1220.12 p638*
Porter, Thomas; America, 1768 *1220.12 p638*
Porter, Thomas; Ohio, 1832 *2763.1 p21*
Porter, William; America, 1741 *1220.12 p638*
Porter, William; America, 1755 *1220.12 p638*
Porter, William; America, 1766 *1220.12 p638*
Porter, William; America, 1768 *1220.12 p638*
Porter, William; America, 1772 *1220.12 p638*
Porter, William 70; Ontario, 1871 *1823.17 p134*
Porter, Wm.; Maryland, 1672 *1236.25 p46*
Porterfield, Catherine 59; Ontario, 1871 *1823.21 p300*
Portes, Jean 26; New Orleans, 1846 *778.6 p273*
Portes, Margaret; America, 1733 *1220.12 p638*
Portess, William; America, 1750 *1220.12 p638*
Porte Touya, Louis 23; Port uncertain, 1841 *778.6 p273*
Portge, Philippine Charlotte Regine; America, 1846
  7420.1 p47
Porth, Frederick; Illinois, 1855 *6079.1 p11*
Portice, David 45; Ontario, 1871 *1823.21 p300*
Portice, Masden 56; Ontario, 1871 *1823.21 p300*
Portis, Ellan 60; Ontario, 1871 *1823.17 p134*
Portland, James; America, 1766 *1220.12 p638*
Portman, Richard; America, 1737 *1220.12 p638*
Portnell, John; America, 1685 *1220.12 p638*
Portobello, Elizabeth; Virginia, 1741 *1220.12 p638*
Portsmouth, Peter 39; Ontario, 1871 *1823.21 p300*
Portswood, Thomas 27; Ontario, 1871 *1823.21 p300*
Portus, John; America, 1736 *1220.12 p638*
Portwood, Christopher T. 33; Ontario, 1871 *1823.21
  p300*
Portwood, Joseph 23; Ontario, 1871 *1823.21 p300*
Portz, Mr.; America, 1842 *778.6 p273*
Portz, Johann; America, 1882 *5475.1 p336*
Portz, Nikolaus 43; America, 1843 *5475.1 p309*
Portz, Peter; America, 1881 *5475.1 p299*
Portzel, Emil Albin; America, 1867 *7919.3 p528*
Pos, Melanie; Wisconsin, 1854-1858 *1495.20 p49*
Posacin, Amalie 22; Portland, ME, 1911 *970.38 p80*
Posacin, Daniel 11; Portland, ME, 1911 *970.38 p80*
Posacin, Natalie 3; Portland, ME, 1911 *970.38 p80*
Posey, Jefferson 45; Ontario, 1871 *1823.21 p300*
Posler, Jan; Iowa, 1852 *2853.20 p217*
Posler, Jan; Wisconsin, 1850 *2853.20 p303*
Posler, Jan Josef; Missouri, 1859-1860 *2853.20 p53*
Posollo, Thomas; Washington, 1883 *2770.40 p137*
Posorski, Fred; Wisconsin, 1900 *6795.8 p229*
Pospisil, Frantisek; Detroit, 1854-1859 *2853.20 p356*
Pospisil, Jos; Nebraska, 1905 *3004.30 p46*
Possehl, John; New York, 1860 *358.56 p5*
Possey, Peggy 47; Ontario, 1871 *1823.17 p134*
Possiones, Denis 20; New Orleans, 1848 *778.6 p273*
Post, Caroline 17; Quebec, 1870 *8364.32 p25*
Post, Ernst Wilhelm; Wisconsin, 1896 *6795.8 p150*
Post, John; Barbados or Jamaica, 1710 *1220.12 p638*
Post, John Henry; Wisconsin, 1861 *6795.8 p98*
Post, John J.; Washington, 1886 *2770.40 p195*
Post, Sarah 13; Quebec, 1870 *8364.32 p25*
Postill, Edward 49; Ontario, 1871 *1823.17 p134*
Postl, Karel Antonin; Philadelphia, 1822-1836 *2853.20
  p124*
Postlethwaite, Thomas; America, 1768 *1220.12 p638*
Postlewaite, Hugh; Virginia, 1739 *1220.12 p638*
Poston, John; America, 1729 *1220.12 p638*
Postons, William; America, 1736 *1220.12 p638*
Postroin, Dennis 56; America, 1842 *778.6 p273*
Posztowica, Maryanna 25; New York, NY, 1894 *6512.1
  p231*
Potel, Jacqueline; Quebec, 1635 *9221.17 p47*
Potent, Gottfr.; Valdivia, Chile, 1852 *1192.4 p56*
Potentier, Arsene 29; America, 1846 *778.6 p273*
Potet, Sebastien; Quebec, 1660 *9221.17 p439*
Pothier, Marie; Quebec, 1670 *4514.3 p359*
Potier, Alexandre 24; Missouri, 1848 *778.6 p273*
Potier, Charles *SEE* Potier, Ferdinand Joseph
Potier, Felicienne *SEE* Potier, Ferdinand Joseph
Potier; Ferdinand Joseph; Wisconsin, 1854-1858 *1495.20
  p50*
  *Wife:*Victoire Berger
  *Child:*Victoire
  *Child:*Felicienne
  *Child:*Xavier
  *Child:*Charles
Potier, Jean; Quebec, 1651 *9221.17 p249*
Potier, Louis; Quebec, 1648 *9221.17 p203*

Potier, Victoire *SEE* Potier, Ferdinand Joseph
Potier, Victoire Berger *SEE* Potier, Ferdinand Joseph
Potier, Xavier *SEE* Potier, Ferdinand Joseph
Potley, Christopher; Virginia, 1618 *1220.12 p638*
Potschner, Charles; Ohio, 1809-1852 *4511.35 p41*
Pott, Humphrey; America, 1692 *1220.12 p638*
Pott, John; America, 1749 *1220.12 p638*
Pott, William; Barbados, 1690 *1220.12 p638*
Potten, John; America, 1732 *1220.12 p638*
Pottenger, Samuel 43; Ontario, 1871 *1823.17 p134*
Potter, Ann; Virginia, 1760 *1220.12 p638*
Potter, Bilbey 51; Ontario, 1871 *1823.21 p300*
Potter, Charles; America, 1760 *1220.12 p639*
Potter, Edward; Barbados, 1665 *1220.12 p639*
Potter, Elisha; America, 1741 *1220.12 p639*
Potter, Elizabeth; Barbados, 1681 *1220.12 p639*
Potter, George; America, 1749 *1220.12 p639*
Potter, George; America, 1757 *1220.12 p639*
Potter, George 56; Ontario, 1871 *1823.21 p300*
Potter, George 62; Ontario, 1871 *1823.21 p300*
Potter, George Mitchell 23; Ontario, 1871 *1823.21 p300*
Potter, Henry; America, 1750 *1220.12 p639*
Potter, James; America, 1744 *1220.12 p639*
Potter, James; New York, 1778 *8529.30 p4A*
Potter, Jeremiah; America, 1754 *1220.12 p639*
Potter, John; America, 1732 *1220.12 p639*
Potter, John; America, 1739 *1220.12 p639*
Potter, John; America, 1767 *1220.12 p639*
Potter, John; America, 1775 *1220.12 p639*
Potter, John; Maryland, 1740 *1220.12 p639*
Potter, John; Potomac, 1729 *1220.12 p639*
Potter, John; Virginia, 1767 *1220.12 p639*
Potter, Lawrence; America, 1721 *1220.12 p639*
Potter, Martin; America, 1767 *1220.12 p639*
Potter, Mary 85; Ontario, 1871 *1823.21 p300*
Potter, Mathew 46; Ontario, 1871 *1823.21 p300*
Potter, Rebecca; Salem, MA, 1640-1641 *1642 p78*
Potter, Richard; America, 1683 *1220.12 p639*
Potter, Richard; America, 1763 *1220.12 p639*
Potter, Robert 63; Ontario, 1871 *1823.21 p300*
Potter, Sarah; America, 1758 *1220.12 p639*
Potter, Thomas; America, 1765 *1220.12 p639*
Potter, William; America, 1723 *1220.12 p639*
Potter, William; America, 1737 *1220.12 p639*
Potter, William; America, 1739 *1220.12 p639*
Potter, William; America, 1752 *1220.12 p639*
Potter, William; America, 1770 *1220.12 p639*
Potter, William; America, 1773 *1220.12 p639*
Potter, Zachariah; Virginia, 1736 *1220.12 p639*
Potters, Rhoda 30; Ontario, 1871 *1823.21 p300*
Pottier, Adelaide 17; New Orleans, 1848 *778.6 p273*
Pottinger, Annie 21; Ontario, 1871 *1823.17 p134*
Pottinger, Henry; Barbados or Jamaica, 1690 *1220.12
  p639*
Pottinger, James 30; Ontario, 1871 *1823.17 p134*
Pottinger, Jane; Died enroute, 1729 *1220.12 p639*
Pottinger, Samuel 66; Ontario, 1871 *1823.17 p134*
Pottinger, William; America, 1738 *1220.12 p639*
Pottinger, William 25; Ontario, 1871 *1823.17 p134*
Pottle, James; America, 1756 *1220.12 p639*
Pottle, Matthew; America, 1685 *1220.12 p639*
Pottle, William; America, 1737 *1220.12 p639*
Pottman, Fred; Wisconsin, 1891 *6795.8 p104*
Potts, Abraham; America, 1716 *1220.12 p639*
Potts, Edmund; America, 1749 *1220.12 p639*
Potts, Francis; America, 1765 *1220.12 p639*
Potts, George; America, 1750 *1220.12 p639*
Potts, Henry; America, 1686 *1220.12 p639*
Potts, Joseph; North Carolina, 1819 *1088.45 p27*
Potts, Thomas; Barbados, 1683 *1220.12 p639*
Potwin, John; Boston, 1721 *9228.50 p519*
Poucard, Antoine 19; America, 1843 *778.6 p273*
Poucher, Ernest 17; America, 1848 *778.6 p273*
Pouchy, John 25; Indiana, 1840 *778.6 p273*
Poudrier, Michel 25; Quebec, 1654 *9221.17 p312*
Pouget, Francois 34; America, 1843 *778.6 p273*
Pougnon, Joseph 28; New Orleans, 1848 *778.6 p273*
Poul, Ramon; Louisiana, 1836-1840 *4981.45 p213*
Poulain, Frances; Prince Edward Island, 1806 *9228.50
  p413*
Poulain, Jules 26; New Orleans, 1843 *778.6 p273*
Poulain, Maurice 29; Quebec, 1649 *9221.17 p219*
Poulain, Susanna; New Jersey, 1665 *9228.50 p519*
Poulain, Susanna; New Jersey, 1665 *9228.50 p594*
Poulain, Susanna; Virginia, 1665 *9228.50 p53*
Poulet, Antoine 28; Quebec, 1654 *9221.17 p315*
Poulet, Joseph 46; Mexico, 1846 *778.6 p273*
Poulin, Claude 20; Quebec, 1636 *9221.17 p62*
Poulin, Jean 21; Quebec, 1661 *9221.17 p466*
Poulin, Madeleine 2 *SEE* Poulin, Pascal
Poulin, Michel; Quebec, 1656 *9221.17 p346*
Poulin, Pascal 3; Quebec, 1648 *9221.17 p203*
  *Sister:*Madeleine 2

Pouliot, Charles 21; Quebec, 1653 *9221.17 p279*
Poullain, . . .; Quebec, 1657 *9221.17 p366*
Poullard, Franc. 23; America, 1840 *778.6 p273*
Poullard, Pierre; Quebec, 1662 *9221.17 p491*
Poulleau, Charles 21; Quebec, 1653 *9221.17 p279*
Poulnois, Catherine 19; America, 1846 *778.6 p273*
Poulnois, Charles 9; America, 1846 *778.6 p273*
Poulnois, Eugene 6; America, 1846 *778.6 p273*
Poulnois, Francois 16; America, 1846 *778.6 p273*
Poulnois, J. 31; America, 1846 *778.6 p273*
Poulnois, Joseph 1; America, 1846 *778.6 p273*
Poulnois, Justin 9; America, 1846 *778.6 p274*
Poulnois, Justine 4; America, 1846 *778.6 p274*
Poulnois, Marie 44; America, 1846 *778.6 p274*
Poulnois, Nicolas 23; America, 1846 *778.6 p274*
Poulnois, Rose 22; America, 1846 *778.6 p274*
Poulson, Elizabeth; America, 1754 *1220.12 p639*
Poulsum, Mary; Virginia, 1772 *1220.12 p639*
Poulter, John; America, 1746 *1220.12 p639*
Poulter, Owen; America, 1741 *1220.12 p639*
Poulterer, Louisa; Philadelphia, 1851 *8513.31 p429*
Poultney, Thomas; America, 1740 *1220.12 p640*
Poulton, George; America, 1758 *1220.12 p640*
Poulton, Isaac; America, 1772 *1220.12 p640*
Poulton, Martha; Annapolis, MD, 1733 *1220.12 p640*
Poulton, Samuel; America, 1745 *1220.12 p640*
Pound, Daniel; America, 1756 *1220.12 p640*
Pound, Fannie J. 28; Michigan, 1880 *4491.42 p21*
Pound, John; America, 1725 *1220.12 p640*
Pound, John; America, 1773 *1220.12 p640*
Pound, John; Jamaica, 1665 *1220.12 p640*
Pound, Thomas 40; Michigan, 1880 *4491.42 p21*
Poupart, Jacques; Quebec, 1647 *9221.17 p188*
  *Wife:*Marguerite Deschamps
  *Son:*Jean
Poupart, Jean *SEE* Poupart, Jacques
Poupart, Marguerite Deschamps *SEE* Poupart, Jacques
Poupeau, Jacques; Quebec, 1647 *9221.17 p188*
  *Wife:*Marguerite Deschamps
  *Son:*Jean
Poupeau, Jean *SEE* Poupeau, Jacques
Poupeau, Marguerite Deschamps *SEE* Poupeau, Jacques
Poupegur, Jean 24; Louisiana, 1848 *778.6 p274*
Poupeney, . . .; New Orleans, 1840 *778.6 p274*
Poupeney, Mrs.; New Orleans, 1840 *778.6 p274*
Poupeney, Francois; New Orleans, 1840 *778.6 p274*
Poupin, Francois 19; Quebec, 1659 *9221.17 p409*
Poupin, Jacques 30; Quebec, 1651 *9221.17 p250*
Poupot, Francois; Quebec, 1645 *9221.17 p157*
Pouque, Amalie; America, 1847 *5475.1 p474*
Pouque, Anton; America, 1840 *5475.1 p470*
Pour, Nicholas; Ohio, 1840-1897 *8365.35 p17*
Pourbaix, Adhemar; Miami, 1935 *4984.12 p39*
Pourcher, Matthew; Barbados or Jamaica, 1678 *1220.12
  p640*
Pourda, Jacques 39; America, 1840 *778.6 p274*
Pournin, Marie 36; Montreal, 1658 *9221.17 p391*
Poushett, William; America, 1749 *1220.12 p640*
Pouson, Marie 32; Missouri, 1846 *778.6 p274*
Poussard, Adele 24; New Orleans, 1848 *778.6 p274*
Pousset, Jules Paul 4; New Orleans, 1848 *778.6 p274*
Pousset, Margueritte 42; New Orleans, 1848 *778.6 p274*
Pousset, Marie; Quebec, 1633 *9221.17 p29*
Pousset, Marie Rose 24; New Orleans, 1848 *778.6 p274*
Pousset, Paul Simon 32; New Orleans, 1848 *778.6 p274*
Poussett, Henry 32; Ontario, 1871 *1823.17 p134*
Poussett, Peter Taylor 68; Ontario, 1871 *1823.17 p134*
Poussette, Arthur 35; Ontario, 1871 *1823.17 p134*
Poussiere, Pierre 42; Port uncertain, 1846 *778.6 p274*
Poussin, Marie-Anne; Quebec, 1665 *4514.3 p359*
Pousson, Charles 28; Missouri, 1845 *778.6 p274*
Pouterel, Gaspard; Quebec, 1638 *9221.17 p145*
Pouterel, Guy 17; Quebec, 1647 *9221.17 p188*
  *Sister:*Marie-Madeleine 3
Pouterel, Marie-Madeleine 3 *SEE* Pouterel, Guy
Pouterel DuColombier, Jean-Francois 17; Quebec, 1640
  9221.17 p98
Pouterel DuColombier, Nicolas 17; Quebec, 1638
  9221.17 p80
Pouzargere, M. 21; America, 1848 *778.6 p274*
Pouztou, Pierre 19; New Orleans, 1844 *778.6 p274*
Povey, Ann; Barbados or Jamaica, 1697 *1220.12 p640*
Povey, John 4; Ontario, 1871 *1823.21 p300*
Povey, Sarah 30; Ontario, 1871 *1823.21 p300*
Povolny, Honorat; America, 1868 *2853.20 p261*
Pow, Frederick; America, 1765 *1220.12 p640*
Pow, Philip; Ohio, 1809-1852 *4511.35 p41*
Powd, Thomas; Virginia, 1760 *1220.12 p640*
Powditch, George; America, 1770 *1220.12 p640*
Powe, James 30; Ontario, 1871 *1823.21 p300*
Powe, Michael 62; Ontario, 1871 *1823.21 p300*
Powel, Andrew; Ohio, 1809-1852 *4511.35 p41*
Powel, William; Marston's Wharf, 1781 *8529.30 p15*

Powell, Aaron; Barbados, 1717 ***1220.12*** *p640*
Powell, Aaron; Boston, 1720 ***1220.12*** *p640*
Powell, Abigail 45; Michigan, 1880 ***4491.30*** *p25*
Powell, Alice; Barbados, 1675 ***1220.12*** *p640*
Powell, Ambrose 72; Ontario, 1871 ***1823.21*** *p300*
Powell, Andrew; Ohio, 1809-1852 ***4511.35*** *p41*
Powell, Anne; Annapolis, MD, 1721 ***1220.12*** *p640*
Powell, Anthony; America, 1762 ***1220.12*** *p640*
Powell, Arthur; America, 1754 ***1220.12*** *p640*
Powell, Benjamin; America, 1766 ***1220.12*** *p640*
Powell, Benjamin 23; Ontario, 1871 ***1823.21*** *p300*
Powell, Betty; America, 1740 ***1220.12*** *p640*
Powell, Catherine; America, 1720 ***1220.12*** *p640*
Powell, Charles; America, 1760 ***1220.12*** *p640*
Powell, Charles 67; Ontario, 1871 ***1823.21*** *p300*
Powell, Daniel; America, 1749 ***1220.12*** *p640*
Powell, Daniel 14; Quebec, 1870 ***8364.32*** *p25*
Powell, Edward; America, 1759 ***1220.12*** *p640*
Powell, Edward 14; Quebec, 1870 ***8364.32*** *p25*
Powell, Eleanor; America, 1733 ***1220.12*** *p640*
Powell, Eleanor; America, 1760 ***1220.12*** *p640*
Powell, Eleanor; America, 1767 ***1220.12*** *p640*
Powell, Eleanor; America, 1772 ***1220.12*** *p640*
Powell, Eliza 44; Michigan, 1880 ***4491.30*** *p25*
Powell, Elizabeth; America, 1743 ***1220.12*** *p640*
Powell, Elizabeth; America, 1774 ***1220.12*** *p640*
Powell, Elizabeth; Annapolis, MD, 1725 ***1220.12*** *p640*
Powell, Elizabeth; Maryland, 1725 ***1220.12*** *p640*
Powell, Elizabeth; Virginia, 1736 ***1220.12*** *p640*
Powell, Evan; America, 1774 ***1220.12*** *p640*
Powell, George; America, 1749 ***1220.12*** *p640*
Powell, George 25; Ontario, 1871 ***1823.21*** *p300*
Powell, George 31; Ontario, 1871 ***1823.21*** *p300*
Powell, George 54; Ontario, 1871 ***1823.21*** *p300*
Powell, George; Virginia, 1730 ***1220.12*** *p640*
Powell, Hannah; America, 1739 ***1220.12*** *p640*
Powell, Henry 24; Ontario, 1871 ***1823.21*** *p300*
Powell, Henry 40; Ontario, 1871 ***1823.21*** *p300*
Powell, Hester; Died enroute, 1730 ***1220.12*** *p640*
Powell, Humphrey; America, 1750 ***1220.12*** *p640*
Powell, Jacob; America, 1685 ***1220.12*** *p640*
Powell, James; America, 1752 ***1220.12*** *p641*
Powell, James; America, 1755 ***1220.12*** *p641*
Powell, James; America, 1768 ***1220.12*** *p641*
Powell, James; America, 1770 ***1220.12*** *p641*
Powell, James; Maryland or Virginia, 1738 ***1220.12*** *p641*
Powell, James; Ohio, 1844 ***2763.1*** *p21*
Powell, James; Virginia, 1721 ***1220.12*** *p640*
Powell, Jane; America, 1760 ***1220.12*** *p641*
Powell, Jeremiah; America, 1774 ***1220.12*** *p641*
Powell, Jo; Virginia, 1652 ***6254.4*** *p243*
Powell, John; America, 1723 ***1220.12*** *p641*
Powell, John; America, 1729 ***1220.12*** *p641*
Powell, John; America, 1758 ***1220.12*** *p641*
Powell, John; America, 1762 ***1220.12*** *p641*
Powell, John; America, 1763 ***1220.12*** *p641*
Powell, John; America, 1764 ***1220.12*** *p641*
Powell, John; America, 1766 ***1220.12*** *p641*
Powell, John; America, 1768 ***1220.12*** *p641*
Powell, John; America, 1773 ***1220.12*** *p641*
Powell, John; Annapolis, MD, 1733 ***1220.12*** *p641*
Powell, John; Barbados or Jamaica, 1688 ***1220.12*** *p641*
Powell, John; Maryland or Virginia, 1733 ***1220.12*** *p641*
Powell, John 56; Ontario, 1871 ***1823.21*** *p301*
Powell, John 59; Ontario, 1871 ***1823.21*** *p301*
Powell, John 61; Ontario, 1871 ***1823.17*** *p134*
Powell, John; Rappahannock, VA, 1741 ***1220.12*** *p641*
Powell, Joseph; America, 1755 ***1220.12*** *p641*
Powell, Joseph; America, 1764 ***1220.12*** *p641*
Powell, Luke; Virginia, 1732 ***1220.12*** *p641*
Powell, Margaret; America, 1751 ***1220.12*** *p641*
Powell, Margaret; America, 1772 ***1220.12*** *p641*
Powell, Margaret; Salt Lake City, 1868 ***9228.50*** *p287*
Powell, Mary; Barbados, 1663 ***1220.12*** *p641*
Powell, Mary; Jamaica, 1717 ***1220.12*** *p641*
Powell, Michael; America, 1685 ***1220.12*** *p641*
Powell, Michael 44; Ontario, 1871 ***1823.21*** *p301*
Powell, Rachel 26; New York, NY, 1894 ***6512.1*** *p228*
Powell, Richard; America, 1671 ***1220.12*** *p641*
Powell, Richard; America, 1739 ***1220.12*** *p641*
Powell, Richard; America, 1762 ***1220.12*** *p641*
Powell, Richard; America, 1774 ***1220.12*** *p641*
Powell, Richard; Jamaica, 1663 ***1220.12*** *p641*
Powell, Richard; Virginia, 1661 ***1220.12*** *p641*
Powell, Richard, Jr.; America, 1756 ***1220.12*** *p641*
Powell, Robert; America, 1762 ***1220.12*** *p641*
Powell, Robert; America, 1765 ***1220.12*** *p641*
Powell, Robert 43; Ontario, 1871 ***1823.21*** *p301*
Powell, Robert; South Carolina, 1808 ***6155.4*** *p19*
Powell, Roger; Virginia, 1618 ***1220.12*** *p641*
Powell, Samuel; Maryland, 1740 ***1220.12*** *p641*
Powell, Sarah; America, 1765 ***1220.12*** *p641*
Powell, Sarah; America, 1771 ***1220.12*** *p641*
Powell, Sarah; Annapolis, MD, 1735 ***1220.12*** *p641*
Powell, Sarah; Virginia, 1732 ***1220.12*** *p641*
Powell, Steven 70; Ontario, 1871 ***1823.21*** *p301*
Powell, Susan; Barbados or Jamaica, 1697 ***1220.12*** *p642*
Powell, Susannah; America, 1774 ***1220.12*** *p642*
Powell, Thomas; America, 1678 ***1220.12*** *p642*
Powell, Thomas; America, 1679 ***1220.12*** *p642*
Powell, Thomas; America, 1716 ***1220.12*** *p642*
Powell, Thomas; America, 1732 ***1220.12*** *p642*
Powell, Thomas; America, 1734 ***1220.12*** *p642*
Powell, Thomas; America, 1744 ***1220.12*** *p642*
Powell, Thomas; America, 1748 ***1220.12*** *p642*
Powell, Thomas; America, 1757 ***1220.12*** *p642*
Powell, Thomas; America, 1767 ***1220.12*** *p642*
Powell, Thomas; Annapolis, MD, 1726 ***1220.12*** *p642*
Powell, Thomas; Barbados, 1671 ***1220.12*** *p642*
Powell, Thomas; Barbados, 1677 ***1220.12*** *p642*
Powell, Thomas; Died enroute, 1728 ***1220.12*** *p642*
Powell, Thomas; Maryland, 1671-1672 ***1236.25*** *p45*
Powell, Thomas; Maryland, 1726 ***1220.12*** *p642*
Powell, Thomas 64; Ontario, 1871 ***1823.21*** *p301*
Powell, Walter 35; Ontario, 1871 ***1823.21*** *p301*
Powell, William; America, 1685 ***1220.12*** *p642*
Powell, William; America, 1730 ***1220.12*** *p642*
Powell, William; America, 1739 ***1220.12*** *p642*
Powell, William; America, 1744 ***1220.12*** *p642*
Powell, William; America, 1755 ***1220.12*** *p642*
Powell, William; America, 1762 ***1220.12*** *p642*
Powell, William; America, 1765 ***1220.12*** *p642*
Powell, William; America, 1766 ***1220.12*** *p642*
Powell, William; America, 1767 ***1220.12*** *p642*
Powell, William; Barbados or Jamaica, 1676 ***1220.12*** *p642*
Powell, William; Ohio, 1843 ***2763.1*** *p21*
Powell, William; Ohio, 1851 ***4022.20*** *p289*
Powell, William 37; Ontario, 1871 ***1823.21*** *p301*
Power, Edward; America, 1767 ***1220.12*** *p642*
Power, Edward 16; Maryland, 1722 ***1220.12*** *p642*
Power, Mrs. John; Toronto, 1844 ***2910.35*** *p114*
Power, Joseph; America, 1768 ***1220.12*** *p642*
Power, Maurice 64; Ontario, 1871 ***1823.17*** *p134*
Power, Nathaniel; America, 1725 ***1220.12*** *p642*
Power, Patrick; Boston, 1753 ***1642*** *p31*
Power, Peirce 45; Ontario, 1871 ***1823.17*** *p134*
Power, Peter; Newfoundland, 1814 ***3476.10*** *p54*
Power, Phillip; Toronto, 1844 ***2910.35*** *p116*
Power, Richard; Boston, 1753 ***1642*** *p31*
Power, Thomas; Boston, 1753 ***1642*** *p31*
Power, Thos 3; St. Johns, N.F., 1811 ***1053.20*** *p20*
Power, Walter; Newfoundland, 1814 ***3476.10*** *p54*
Power, William; New Jersey, 1776 ***8529.30*** *p7*
Power, William; Toronto, 1844 ***2910.35*** *p116*
Powers, Bridget 48; Ontario, 1871 ***1823.21*** *p301*
Powers, James 40; Ontario, 1871 ***1823.21*** *p301*
Powers, James; Washington, 1882 ***2770.40*** *p136*
Powers, John; Ohio, 1809-1852 ***4511.35*** *p41*
Powers, John 50; Ontario, 1871 ***1823.17*** *p134*
Powers, Laban 51; Ontario, 1871 ***1823.21*** *p301*
Powers, Lawrence 40; Ontario, 1871 ***1823.21*** *p301*
Powers, Patrick; Louisiana, 1874 ***4981.45*** *p133*
Powers, R.; California, 1868 ***1131.61*** *p90*
Powers, Susan 22; Ontario, 1871 ***1823.21*** *p301*
Powers, Thomas; North Carolina, 1858 ***1088.45*** *p27*
Powers, Thomas 22; Ontario, 1871 ***1823.17*** *p134*
Powers, Thomas 66; Ontario, 1871 ***1823.17*** *p134*
Powett, Mary; America, 1739 ***1220.12*** *p642*
Powis, Elizabeth; America, 1759 ***1220.12*** *p642*
Powis, Samuel; America, 1773 ***1220.12*** *p642*
Powis, Thomas; America, 1736 ***1220.12*** *p642*
Powle, James; America, 1673 ***1220.12*** *p640*
Powles, Peter 50; Ontario, 1871 ***1823.21*** *p301*
Powles, Thomas; America, 1770 ***1220.12*** *p642*
Powley, Samuel; America, 1772 ***1220.12*** *p642*
Pownall, John; America, 1730 ***1220.12*** *p642*
Pownell, Christopher; America, 1698 ***1220.12*** *p642*
Powney, Thomas; America, 1750 ***1220.12*** *p642*
Powney, William; America, 1770 ***1220.12*** *p642*
Powning, John; America, 1749 ***1220.12*** *p642*
Powrey, Thos 29; Ontario, 1871 ***1823.17*** *p134*
Powrie, David; Ontario, 1871 ***1823.17*** *p134*
Powrie, James 44; Ontario, 1871 ***1823.21*** *p301*
Pows, Thomas; America, 1713 ***1220.12*** *p642*
Poyer, James; America, 1773 ***1220.12*** *p642*
Poyhonen, Otto 38; Minnesota, 1925 ***2769.54*** *p1380*
Poyhonen, Tyyne 32; Minnesota, 1925 ***2769.54*** *p1380*
Poyner, Ann; Barbados, 1671 ***1220.12*** *p642*
Poynter, William; Barbados, 1678 ***1220.12*** *p634*
Poynting, John; America, 1751 ***1220.12*** *p634*
Poynting, Richard; Maryland, 1745 ***1220.12*** *p634*
Poynting, Stephen; America, 1756 ***1220.12*** *p634*
Poynton, William; America, 1687 ***1220.12*** *p642*
Pquaikes, Toby 27; St. Johns, N.F., 1811 ***1053.20*** *p19*
Pra, Adelaide 35; America, 1847 ***778.6*** *p122*
Prace, William; Ontario, 1871 ***1823.21*** *p301*
Pracer, Henry; Barbados, 1666 ***1220.12*** *p643*
Pracey, Thomas; America, 1763 ***1220.12*** *p643*
Prachet, Peter; Louisiana, 1836-1841 ***4981.45*** *p209*
Pracht, Fred 35; America, 1848 ***778.6*** *p274*
Pracht, Fred, Jr. 2; America, 1848 ***778.6*** *p274*
Pracht, M. 36; America, 1848 ***778.6*** *p274*
Pradeau, Guillaume; Quebec, 1642 ***9221.17*** *p121*
Praetorius, Philipp Heinrich; America, 1879 ***7420.1*** *p314*
Pragge, Thomas; America, 1699 ***1220.12*** *p643*
Prahl, Carl Albert Ludwig; Wisconsin, 1899 ***6795.8*** *p64*
Prahl, Emma Mathilde; Wisconsin, 1899 ***6795.8*** *p64*
Prahl, Frederick Augustus; Wisconsin, 1862 ***6795.8*** *p186*
Prahl, Johann Edward; Wisconsin, 1895 ***6795.8*** *p64*
Prairies, des, Sieur; New Jersey, 1655 ***9228.50*** *p647*
Prais, Frank; Detroit, 1890 ***9980.23*** *p96*
Praite, Pierre; Louisiana, 1874-1875 ***4981.45*** *p30*
Pralini, Joseph 2; America, 1848 ***778.6*** *p274*
Pralini, Julia 1; America, 1848 ***778.6*** *p274*
Pralini, Pierre 29; America, 1848 ***778.6*** *p274*
Pralini, Therese 24; America, 1848 ***778.6*** *p274*
Prambin, Hypolite 23; Mississippi, 1848 ***778.6*** *p274*
Prance, Richard 41; Ontario, 1871 ***1823.21*** *p301*
Prange, Widow; America, 1853 ***7420.1*** *p110*
*Son:*Anton Friedrich
*Daughter:*Marie Charlotte
Prange, Anton Friedrich *SEE* Prange, Widow
Prange, Anton Friedrich Gottlieb; America, 1880 ***7420.1*** *p317*
Prange, Anton Heinrich Friedrich; America, 1888 ***7420.1*** *p357*
Prange, Carl Anton; America, 1882 ***7420.1*** *p331*
Prange, Carl Friedrich; America, 1854 ***7420.1*** *p127*
Prange, Carl Friedrich; Indiana, 1880 ***7420.1*** *p317*
Prange, Carl Friedrich Heinrich; America, 1882 ***7420.1*** *p331*
Prange, Christian Friedrich Wilhelm; America, 1882 ***7420.1*** *p331*
Prange, Marie; Indianapolis, 1888 ***7420.1*** *p357*
Prange, Marie Charlotte *SEE* Prange, Widow
Prangley, Nathaniel 54; Ontario, 1871 ***1823.17*** *p134*
Prangnell, Robert, Jr.; America, 1743 ***1220.12*** *p643*
Prankitt, Robert; America, 1747 ***1220.12*** *p643*
Prasuhn, Carl Ferdinand August *SEE* Prasuhn, Friedrich Heinrich Ferdinand
Prasuhn, Caroline; America, 1881 ***7420.1*** *p323*
Prasuhn, Charlotte; America, 1868 ***7420.1*** *p275*
Prasuhn, Christoph; America, 1868 ***7420.1*** *p275*
Prasuhn, Friedrich Gottlieb; America, 1854 ***7420.1*** *p127*
Prasuhn, Friedrich Heinrich Ferdinand; America, 1884 ***7420.1*** *p344*
*Brother:*Carl Ferdinand August
Prasuhn, Heinrich; America, 1887 ***7420.1*** *p399*
Prasuhn, Heinrich Friedrich Christoph; America, 1867 ***7420.1*** *p262*
Prasuhn, Sophie Wilhelmine Charlotte; America, 1868 ***7420.1*** *p275*
Prasuhn, Sophie Wilhelmine Louise; Wisconsin, 1847 ***7420.1*** *p53*
Prasun, Carl Heinr. Ferd. *SEE* Prasun, Friedrich Wilhelm Ferdinand
Prasun, Carl Ludwig Ferd. *SEE* Prasun, Friedrich Wilhelm Ferdinand
Prasun, Caroline Wilhelmine Luise; America, 1882 ***7420.1*** *p328*
Prasun, Friedrich Wilhelm Ferdinand; America, 1847 ***7420.1*** *p55*
*Wife:*Justina Carolina Koster
*Son:*Hermann Heinr. Ferd.
*Son:*Carl Ludwig Ferd.
*Son:*Carl Heinr. Ferd.
*Daughter:*Justina Carol. Wilhelm.
Prasun, Hermann Heinr. Ferd. *SEE* Prasun, Friedrich Wilhelm Ferdinand
Prasun, Justina Carol. Wilhelm. *SEE* Prasun, Friedrich Wilhelm Ferdinand
Prasun, Justina Carolina Koster *SEE* Prasun, Friedrich Wilhelm Ferdinand
Prat, Claude; Quebec, 1665 ***4514.3*** *p359*
Prat, Vaclav; Nebraska, 1876 ***2853.20*** *p172*
Prats, J. 22; America, 1843 ***778.6*** *p274*
Prats, Pedro; Louisiana, 1841-1844 ***4981.45*** *p211*
Pratt, Alexander; America, 1775 ***1220.12*** *p643*
Pratt, Edward 47; Ontario, 1871 ***1823.21*** *p301*
Pratt, Fancy Hand *SEE* Pratt, Robert
Pratt, Fancy Hand *SEE* Pratt, Robert
Pratt, Francis; America, 1735 ***1220.12*** *p643*
Pratt, Francis; America, 1758 ***1220.12*** *p643*
Pratt, Francis; America, 1773 ***1220.12*** *p643*
Pratt, Henry; America, 1765 ***1220.12*** *p643*
Pratt, Henry 29; Ontario, 1871 ***1823.21*** *p301*
Pratt, James; America, 1741 ***1220.12*** *p643*
Pratt, James; Maryland, 1742 ***1220.12*** *p643*

Pratt, Jane *SEE* Pratt, Robert
Pratt, John; America, 1752 ***1220.12*** *p643*
Pratt, John; America, 1766 ***1220.12*** *p643*
Pratt, John 52; Ontario, 1871 ***1823.21*** *p301*
Pratt, John; Rappahannock, VA, 1728 ***1220.12*** *p643*
Pratt, Randolph; Virginia, 1736 ***1220.12*** *p643*
Pratt, Robert; Bermuda, 1851 ***8513.31*** *p421*
*Wife:*Fancy Hand
Pratt, Robert; Philadelphia, 1868 ***8513.31*** *p421*
*Wife:*Fancy Hand
*Child:*Jane
Pratt, Roger; America, 1770 ***1220.12*** *p643*
Pratt, Sarah; America, 1767 ***1220.12*** *p643*
Pratt, Sarah 58; Ontario, 1871 ***1823.21*** *p301*
Pratt, Sophia 53; Ontario, 1871 ***1823.21*** *p301*
Pratt, Thomas; America, 1772 ***1220.12*** *p643*
Pratt, Thomas 54; Ontario, 1871 ***1823.21*** *p301*
Pratt, William; America, 1770 ***1220.12*** *p643*
Pratt, William; Maryland, 1725 ***1220.12*** *p643*
Praus, Jan; Chicago, 1855 ***2853.20*** *p388*
Pravda, Frantisek; Chicago, 1868 ***2853.20*** *p514*
Prawl, Emma Mathilde; Wisconsin, 1899 ***6795.8*** *p64*
Prawl, Thomas; America, 1765 ***1220.12*** *p643*
Prawley, John; Maryland, 1742 ***1220.12*** *p643*
Pray, Quinton; Lynn, MA, 1640 ***9228.50*** *p519*
Prcan, Francis 27; St. Johns, N.F., 1811 ***1053.20*** *p20*
Pre, Nicolas; Quebec, 1655 ***9221.17*** *p328*
Prebon, Auguste 54; New Orleans, 1848 ***778.6*** *p275*
Precious, Elizabeth; Virginia, 1736 ***1220.12*** *p643*
Precious, Thos 37; Ontario, 1871 ***1823.21*** *p301*
Prediger, Anna Maria 22; America, 1872 ***5475.1*** *p150*
Prediger, L.; New York, 1859 ***358.56*** *p100*
Prediger, Susanna 46; America, 1854 ***5475.1*** *p57*
*Son:*Peter
*Daughter:*Magdalena
*Daughter:*Franziska
Preece, Edward; America, 1696 ***1220.12*** *p643*
Preece, Edward; America, 1774 ***1220.12*** *p643*
Preece, Henry; America, 1756 ***1220.12*** *p643*
Preece, Sarah; America, 1755 ***1220.12*** *p643*
Preece, Thomas; America, 1740 ***1220.12*** *p643*
Preeo, Elizee; Iowa, 1829-1865 ***9228.50*** *p521*
Preeo, John; Iowa, 1808-1863 ***9228.50*** *p519*
Preeo, Nicholas; Ohio, 1809-1863 ***9228.50*** *p521*
Preeo, Rachel; Ohio, 1821-1892 ***9228.50*** *p521*
Preeo, Thomas; California, 1826-1905 ***9228.50*** *p521*
Prees, William; America, 1768 ***1220.12*** *p643*
Preest, James; America, 1736 ***1220.12*** *p647*
Pregel, Francoise 17; Quebec, 1662 ***9221.17*** *p483*
Pregnall, Joshua; Virginia, 1741 ***1220.12*** *p643*
Preis, Karel; Texas, 1887 ***2853.20*** *p282*
Preis, Karel A.; Texas, 1887 ***2853.20*** *p83*
Preising, Daniel; Valdivia, Chile, 1851 ***1192.4*** *p51*
With wife & 3 children
Preiss, Anna Christine *SEE* Preiss, Johann Christian
Preiss, Anna Elisabeth; Virginia, 1831 ***152.20*** *p62*
Preiss, Anna Elisabeth Reimund *SEE* Preiss, Johann Nikolaus
Preiss, Anna Margarethe; Virginia, 1831 ***152.20*** *p63*
Preiss, Anna Margarethe Ripper *SEE* Preiss, Johann Christian
Preiss, Anna Susanne *SEE* Preiss, Johann Christian
Preiss, Bernhard; America, 1852 ***2526.42*** *p136*
Preiss, Christina 18; America, 1859 ***2526.43*** *p212*
*Son:*Joseph 10 weeks
Preiss, Eduard; New Mexico, 1882 ***2853.20*** *p528*
Preiss, Elisabeth Katharina *SEE* Preiss, Johann Nikolaus
Preiss, Johann Christian; Virginia, 1831 ***152.20*** *p66*
*Wife:*Anna Margarethe Ripper
*Child:*Anna Susanne
*Child:*Katharina
*Child:*Anna Christine
Preiss, Johann Georg *SEE* Preiss, Johann Nikolaus
Preiss, Johann Nikolaus; Virginia, 1831 ***152.20*** *p66*
*Wife:*Anna Elisabeth Reimund
*Child:*Johann Georg
*Child:*Elisabeth Katharina
Preiss, Joseph 10 weeks months *SEE* Preiss, Christina
Preiss, Katharina *SEE* Preiss, Johann Christian
Preiss, Michael; Brazil, 1858 ***2526.43*** *p128*
Preissel, John; New York, 1860 ***358.56*** *p150*
Preister, Miss A. 1; New Orleans, 1834 ***1002.51*** *p113*
Preister, Miss A. 25; New Orleans, 1834 ***1002.51*** *p113*
Preister, G. 6; New Orleans, 1834 ***1002.51*** *p113*
Preister, J. 32; New Orleans, 1834 ***1002.51*** *p113*
Preister, M. 4; New Orleans, 1834 ***1002.51*** *p113*
Preistley, Waddington 20; Ontario, 1871 ***1823.21*** *p301*
Prekel, Johann Friedrich Ferdinand; America, 1868 ***7420.1*** *p275*
With family
Prell, Engel Marie Sophie; America, 1872 ***7420.1*** *p397*
Prell, Engel Marie Sophie Caroline *SEE* Prell, Hans Heinrich
Prell, Hans Heinrich; Illinois, 1878 ***7420.1*** *p311*
*Wife:*Engel Marie Sophie Caroline
*Son:*Johann Heinrich
*Daughter:*Trine Marie
*Son:*Johann Friedrich
Prell, Johann Friedrich *SEE* Prell, Hans Heinrich
Prell, Johann Heinrich *SEE* Prell, Hans Heinrich
Prell, Trine Marie *SEE* Prell, Hans Heinrich
Pren, J. 32; America, 1843 ***778.6*** *p275*
Prendergast, John 35; Ontario, 1871 ***1823.21*** *p301*
Prendergast, Pat.; Toronto, 1844 ***2910.35*** *p116*
Prendergast, William; Toronto, 1844 ***2910.35*** *p114*
Prengle, Johannes; Venezuela, 1843 ***3899.5*** *p541*
Prenjtaer, Otto; Miami, 1935 ***4984.12*** *p39*
Prentice, William; America, 1759 ***1220.12*** *p643*
Prentiss, Wm. J.; Toronto, 1844 ***2910.35*** *p116*
Prentler, Franziska *SEE* Prentler, Jos.
Prentler, Jos.; America, 1923 ***8023.44*** *p378*
*Sister:*Franziska
Prenzel, Ludwig; America, 1856 ***7420.1*** *p152*
Preo, Elizee; Iowa, 1829-1865 ***9228.50*** *p521*
Preo, John; Iowa, 1808-1863 ***9228.50*** *p519*
Preo, Nicholas; Ohio, 1809-1863 ***9228.50*** *p521*
Preo, Rachel; Ohio, 1821-1892 ***9228.50*** *p521*
Preo, Thomas; California, 1826-1905 ***9228.50*** *p521*
Preoust DeFerolle, Bernard; Montreal, 1649 ***9221.17*** *p221*
Prepare, Mrs. 36; New Orleans, 1848 ***778.6*** *p275*
Prepare, M. 18; New Orleans, 1848 ***778.6*** *p275*
Prescot, Thomas 28; Ontario, 1871 ***1823.21*** *p301*
Prescott, Frederick Augustus; Philadelphia, 1777 ***8529.30*** *p7A*
Prescott, George; America, 1771 ***1220.12*** *p643*
Prescott, George 34; Ontario, 1871 ***1823.21*** *p301*
Prescott, Henry; America, 1758 ***1220.12*** *p643*
Prescott, James 51; Ontario, 1871 ***1823.17*** *p134*
Prescott, Mary; America, 1764 ***1220.12*** *p643*
Prescott, Mary; America, 1774 ***1220.12*** *p643*
Prescott, Nathan; America, 1757 ***1220.12*** *p643*
Prescott, Robert; Philadelphia, 1777 ***8529.30*** *p7A*
Prescott, Thomas 42; Ontario, 1871 ***1823.17*** *p134*
Prescott, William; America, 1745 ***1220.12*** *p643*
Prescott, William; Philadelphia, 1777 ***8529.30*** *p7A*
Presgrave, Jeremiah; Annapolis, MD, 1723 ***1220.12*** *p643*
Presgrove, Thomas; America, 1749 ***1220.12*** *p643*
Presle, . . .; Montreal, 1652 ***9221.17*** *p268*
Presle, Jacques 23; Quebec, 1655 ***9221.17*** *p328*
Presley, Willm; Virginia, 1652 ***6254.4*** *p243*
Presly, Peter; Virginia, 1652 ***6254.4*** *p243*
Press, Charles 36; Ontario, 1871 ***1823.21*** *p301*
Press, William 17; Quebec, 1870 ***8364.32*** *p25*
Pressly, John; America, 1746 ***1220.12*** *p643*
Presstand, George; America, 1774 ***1220.12*** *p643*
Prest, Thomas 50; Ontario, 1871 ***1823.21*** *p301*
Prestage, Andrew; America, 1773 ***1220.12*** *p643*
Prestidge, John; America, 1740 ***1220.12*** *p644*
Prestman, Elizabeth; America, 1757 ***1220.12*** *p647*
Prestman, James; Nevis or Jamaica, 1722 ***1220.12*** *p647*
Preston, Ann; America, 1760 ***1220.12*** *p644*
Preston, Anthony 24; Ontario, 1871 ***1823.17*** *p134*
Preston, Anthony 57; Ontario, 1871 ***1823.21*** *p301*
Preston, Charles; America, 1767 ***1220.12*** *p644*
Preston, Dorothy; America, 1742 ***1220.12*** *p644*
Preston, Edward; America, 1679 ***1220.12*** *p644*
Preston, Edward; Annapolis, MD, 1721 ***1220.12*** *p644*
Preston, James; Barbados, 1724 ***1220.12*** *p644*
Preston, Jane 80; Ontario, 1871 ***1823.21*** *p301*
Preston, Johanna; America, 1769 ***1220.12*** *p644*
Preston, John; America, 1735 ***1220.12*** *p644*
Preston, John; America, 1744 ***1220.12*** *p644*
Preston, John; America, 1768 ***1220.12*** *p644*
Preston, John; Ohio, 1809-1852 ***4511.35*** *p41*
Preston, John 70; Ontario, 1871 ***1823.17*** *p134*
Preston, Maggie; Alberta, 1904-1931 ***9228.50*** *p369*
Preston, Mary; America, 1774 ***1220.12*** *p644*
Preston, Paul; America, 1773 ***1220.12*** *p644*
Preston, Peter; Jamaica, 1663 ***1220.12*** *p644*
Preston, Richard 38; Ontario, 1871 ***1823.17*** *p135*
Preston, Robert; America, 1741 ***1220.12*** *p644*
Preston, Thomas; America, 1761 ***1220.12*** *p644*
Preston, Thomas; America, 1764 ***1220.12*** *p644*
Preston, Thomas; America, 1767 ***1220.12*** *p644*
Preston, Thomas 52; Ontario, 1871 ***1823.21*** *p301*
Preston, William James; America, 1764 ***1220.12*** *p644*
Prestrot, Jean; Montreal, 1653 ***9221.17*** *p299*
Prestwich, Sarah; America, 1752 ***1220.12*** *p644*
Prestwood, Richard; America, 1748 ***1220.12*** *p644*
Pretious, Jane; Barbados or Jamaica, 1697 ***1220.12*** *p643*
Prettig, Adam 17; America, 1853 ***2526.42*** *p129*
Pretty, Eleanor; America, 1770 ***1220.12*** *p644*
Pretty, George; America, 1764 ***1220.12*** *p644*
Pretty, Henry; Jamaica, 1661 ***1220.12*** *p644*
Pretty, Sarah; America, 1770 ***1220.12*** *p644*
Pretty, William 38; Ontario, 1871 ***1823.17*** *p135*
Pretty, William J. 40; Ontario, 1871 ***1823.17*** *p135*
Pretzlow, Caspar; Philadelphia, 1778 ***8529.30*** *p4A*
Preul, Carl Wilhelm; Port uncertain, 1885 ***7420.1*** *p399*
Preul, Sophie Caroline Ernestine; America, 1883 ***7420.1*** *p337*
Preuss, Barbara; America, 1882 ***2526.42*** *p133*
Preuss, M.; Galveston, TX, 1855 ***571.7*** *p18*
Prevear Family ; Boston, 1722 ***9228.50*** *p509*
Previrault, Jacques; Quebec, 1652 ***9221.17*** *p265*
Prevost, Adam; Virginia, 1700 ***9230.15*** *p81*
Prevost, Alexander, Sr.; Illinois, 1852 ***6079.1*** *p11*
Prevost, Claudius; Ohio, 1809-1852 ***4511.35*** *p41*
Prevost, Elisabeth; Quebec, 1671 ***4514.3*** *p359*
Prevost, Jules Alexandre; Illinois, 1852 ***6079.1*** *p11*
Prevost, Louis 55; America, 1845 ***778.6*** *p275*
Prevost, Marguerite; Quebec, 1669 ***4514.3*** *p359*
Prevost, Marie; Quebec, 1669 ***4514.3*** *p359*
*Daughter:*Marie-Madeleine
Prevost, Marie; Quebec, 1669 ***4514.3*** *p360*
Prevost, Marie; Virginia, 1700 ***9230.15*** *p81*
Prevost, N.M.; Wisconsin, 1818-1879 ***9228.50*** *p392*
Prevot, Adolphine Josephine; Wisconsin, 1880 ***1495.20*** *p55*
Prevot, Catherine Joseph; Wisconsin, 1857 ***1495.20*** *p46*
Prew, John; America, 1685 ***1220.12*** *p644*
Prew, William; America, 1742 ***1220.12*** *p644*
Prewett, John; America, 1614-1775 ***1220.12*** *p644*
Priault, Marie; Quebec, 1668 ***4514.3*** *p360*
Priaulx, Mr.; Ohio, 1830-1870 ***9228.50*** *p522*
Priaulx, Eleanor; Ohio, 1850-1854 ***9228.50*** *p521*
Priaulx, Eliza; Ohio, 1814-1837 ***9228.50*** *p521*
Priaulx, Elizabeth; Ohio, 1824-1902 ***9228.50*** *p521*
Priaulx, Elizee; Iowa, 1829-1865 ***9228.50*** *p521*
Priaulx, Ernest Blondel; Wisconsin, 1910 ***9228.50*** *p521*
Priaulx, John; Iowa, 1808-1863 ***9228.50*** *p519*
Priaulx, Mary; Ohio, 1802-1892 ***9228.50*** *p521*
Priaulx, Nicholas; Ohio, 1809-1863 ***9228.50*** *p521*
Priaulx, Rachel; Ohio, 1821-1892 ***9228.50*** *p521*
Priaulx, Rachel 15; Ohio, 1836-1837 ***9228.50*** *p521*
With 2 brothers
Priaulx, Reginald; Detroit, 1920 ***9228.50*** *p522*
Priaulx, Robert; America, 1900-1983 ***9228.50*** *p522*
Priaulx, Thomas; California, 1826-1905 ***9228.50*** *p521*
Priaulx, William Arthur; Rochester, NY, 1830-1930 ***9228.50*** *p522*
Pribramsky, Frantisek; Chicago, 1853 ***2853.20*** *p386*
Pribramsky, Frantisek; New York, NY, 1853 ***2853.20*** *p100*
Pribyl, Frantisek; Minnesota, 1883 ***2853.20*** *p266*
Pribyl, Frantisek 12; Minnesota, 1864 ***2853.20*** *p274*
With parents
Pribyl, Ignac; America, 1853 ***2853.20*** *p391*
With family
Pribyl, Josef F.; Omaha, NE, 1910 ***2853.20*** *p145*
Price, Ann; America, 1740 ***1220.12*** *p644*
Price, Ann; America, 1761 ***1220.12*** *p644*
Price, Ann; America, 1767 ***1220.12*** *p644*
Price, Anne; America, 1682 ***1220.12*** *p644*
Price, Anne; America, 1725 ***1220.12*** *p902*
Price, Anne; America, 1740 ***1220.12*** *p644*
Price, Anne 60; Ontario, 1871 ***1823.21*** *p301*
Price, Benjamin; America, 1721 ***1220.12*** *p644*
Price, Benjamin; America, 1738 ***1220.12*** *p644*
Price, Caleb; America, 1708 ***1220.12*** *p644*
Price, Catherine 30; Annapolis, MD, 1721 ***1220.12*** *p644*
Price, Catherine 71 *SEE* Price, Frederick
Price, Charles; Jamaica, 1780 ***8529.30*** *p13A*
Price, Charlotte; Ohio, 1877 ***9228.50*** *p515*
Price, Daniel; America, 1770 ***1220.12*** *p644*
Price, Daniel; America, 1774 ***1220.12*** *p644*
Price, David; America, 1738 ***1220.12*** *p644*
Price, David; America, 1769 ***1220.12*** *p644*
Price, David; America, 1774 ***1220.12*** *p644*
Price, David; America, 1775 ***1220.12*** *p644*
Price, Edward; America, 1723 ***1220.12*** *p644*
Price, Edward; America, 1726 ***1220.12*** *p645*
Price, Edward; America, 1747 ***1220.12*** *p645*
Price, Edward; America, 1753 ***1220.12*** *p645*
Price, Edward; America, 1763 ***1220.12*** *p645*
Price, Edward; America, 1771 ***1220.12*** *p645*
Price, Edward; Annapolis, MD, 1722 ***1220.12*** *p644*
Price, Edward; Illinois, 1852 ***6079.1*** *p11*
Price, Edward; Virginia, 1773 ***1220.12*** *p645*
Price, Elenor 84; Ontario, 1871 ***1823.21*** *p301*
Price, Elizabeth; America, 1704 ***1220.12*** *p645*
Price, Elizabeth; America, 1753 ***1220.12*** *p645*
Price, Elizabeth; America, 1765 ***1220.12*** *p645*
Price, Elizabeth; America, 1774 ***1220.12*** *p645*
Price, Elizabeth; Maryland, 1740 ***1220.12*** *p645*
Price, Elizabeth; Maryland, 1742 ***1220.12*** *p645*
Price, Frederick; Quebec, 1881 ***9228.50*** *p522*
*Wife:*Catherine

Price, George; North Carolina, 1844 ***1088.45*** *p27*
Price, Hannah; America, 1740 ***1220.12*** *p645*
Price, Henry; America, 1731 ***1220.12*** *p645*
Price, Henry; America, 1759 ***1220.12*** *p645*
Price, Hugh; America, 1772 ***1220.12*** *p645*
Price, James; America, 1685 ***1220.12*** *p645*
Price, James; America, 1710 ***1220.12*** *p645*
Price, James; America, 1711 ***1220.12*** *p645*
Price, James; America, 1743 ***1220.12*** *p645*
Price, James; America, 1748 ***1220.12*** *p645*
Price, James; America, 1766 ***1220.12*** *p645*
Price, James; Ohio, 1840 ***4022.20*** *p289*
With wife
*Child:*Lewis
With 2 children
Price, Jane; America, 1677 ***1220.12*** *p645*
Price, Jane; America, 1765 ***1220.12*** *p645*
Price, Jane 26; Ontario, 1871 ***1823.21*** *p302*
Price, Johanna; America, 1740 ***1220.12*** *p645*
Price, John; America, 1663 ***1220.12*** *p645*
Price, John; America, 1720 ***1220.12*** *p645*
Price, John; America, 1726 ***1220.12*** *p645*
Price, John; America, 1728 ***1220.12*** *p645*
Price, John; America, 1735 ***1220.12*** *p645*
Price, John; America, 1744 ***1220.12*** *p645*
Price, John; America, 1745 ***1220.12*** *p645*
Price, John; America, 1748 ***1220.12*** *p645*
Price, John; America, 1752 ***1220.12*** *p645*
Price, John; America, 1753 ***1220.12*** *p645*
Price, John; America, 1753 ***1220.12*** *p645*
Price, John; America, 1755 ***1220.12*** *p645*
Price, John; America, 1760 ***1220.12*** *p645*
Price, John; America, 1766 ***1220.12*** *p645*
Price, John; America, 1769 ***1220.12*** *p645*
Price, John; America, 1770 ***1220.12*** *p645*
Price, John; America, 1774 ***1220.12*** *p645*
Price, John; America, 1870 ***9076.20*** *p68*
Price, John; Annapolis, MD, 1758 ***1220.12*** *p645*
Price, John; Barbados, 1667 ***1220.12*** *p645*
Price, John; Barbados, 1668 ***1220.12*** *p645*
Price, John; New York, 1783 ***8529.30*** *p15*
Price, John; Ohio, 1839 ***4022.20*** *p289*
Price, John; Ohio, n.d. ***4022.20*** *p289*
With wife
With children
Price, John 15; Ontario, 1871 ***1823.17*** *p135*
Price, John 35; Ontario, 1871 ***1823.21*** *p302*
Price, John 35; Ontario, 1871 ***1823.21*** *p302*
Price, John; Potomac, 1729 ***1220.12*** *p645*
Price, Joseph; America, 1770 ***1220.12*** *p646*
Price, Joseph; Virginia, 1730 ***1220.12*** *p646*
Price, Lewis *SEE* Price, James
Price, Lidia; Annapolis, MD, 1736 ***1220.12*** *p646*
Price, Margaret; America, 1720 ***1220.12*** *p646*
Price, Margaret; America, 1721 ***1220.12*** *p646*
Price, Margaret; Charles Town, SC, 1719 ***1220.12*** *p646*
Price, Margaret; Ohio, 1835 ***4022.20*** *p285*
Price, Marina; America, 1739 ***1220.12*** *p646*
Price, Mary; America, 1700 ***1220.12*** *p646*
Price, Mary; America, 1740 ***1220.12*** *p646*
Price, Mary; America, 1744 ***1220.12*** *p646*
Price, Mary; America, 1762 ***1220.12*** *p646*
Price, Mary; America, 1767 ***1220.12*** *p646*
Price, Mary; America, 1772 ***1220.12*** *p646*
Price, Mary; Died enroute, 1728 ***1220.12*** *p646*
Price, Mary 39; Ontario, 1871 ***1823.21*** *p302*
Price, Mary 72; Ontario, 1871 ***1823.21*** *p302*
Price, Mary; Virginia, 1721 ***1220.12*** *p646*
Price, Maurice; Barbados, 1679 ***1220.12*** *p646*
Price, Nathaniel; America, 1737 ***1220.12*** *p646*
Price, Paul; New York, 1777 ***8529.30*** *p15*
Price, Peter; America, 1749 ***1220.12*** *p646*
Price, Peter; America, 1767 ***1220.12*** *p646*
Price, Peter; America, 1771 ***1220.12*** *p646*
Price, Peter; Maryland, 1674-1675 ***1236.25*** *p51*
Price, Philip; Annapolis, MD, 1731 ***1220.12*** *p646*
Price, Rees; America, 1733 ***1220.12*** *p646*
Price, Rees; America, 1762 ***1220.12*** *p646*
Price, Rees; America, 1775 ***1220.12*** *p646*
Price, Richard; America, 1729 ***1220.12*** *p646*
Price, Richard; America, 1751 ***1220.12*** *p646*
Price, Richard; America, 1767 ***1220.12*** *p646*
Price, Richard; America, 1768 ***1220.12*** *p646*
Price, Richard; Barbados or Jamaica, 1690 ***1220.12*** *p646*
Price, Richard; Marston's Wharf, 1782 ***8529.30*** *p15*
Price, Richard; Maryland, 1734 ***1220.12*** *p646*
Price, Richard 50; Ontario, 1871 ***1823.21*** *p302*
Price, Robert; America, 1749 ***1220.12*** *p646*
Price, Robert; America, 1769 ***1220.12*** *p646*
Price, Robert 40; Ontario, 1871 ***1823.21*** *p302*
Price, Robert 50; Ontario, 1871 ***1823.21*** *p302*
Price, Samuel; America, 1736 ***1220.12*** *p646*
Price, Samuel; America, 1759 ***1220.12*** *p646*
Price, Sarah; America, 1726 ***1220.12*** *p646*
Price, Sarah; America, 1766 ***1220.12*** *p646*
Price, Sarah; America, 1773 ***1220.12*** *p646*
Price, Simon; America, 1772 ***1220.12*** *p646*
Price, Stephen; Maryland, 1742 ***1220.12*** *p646*
Price, Thomas; America, 1715 ***1220.12*** *p646*
Price, Thomas; America, 1721 ***1220.12*** *p646*
Price, Thomas; America, 1764 ***1220.12*** *p646*
Price, Thomas; America, 1771 ***1220.12*** *p646*
Price, Thomas; America, 1772 ***1220.12*** *p646*
Price, Thomas; America, 1773 ***1220.12*** *p646*
Price, Thomas; America, 1774 ***1220.12*** *p647*
Price, Thomas; Annapolis, MD, 1722 ***1220.12*** *p646*
Price, Thomas; Maryland, 1743 ***1220.12*** *p646*
Price, Thomas 48; Ontario, 1871 ***1823.21*** *p302*
Price, Thomas 54; Ontario, 1871 ***1823.17*** *p135*
Price, William; America, 1673 ***1220.12*** *p647*
Price, William; America, 1718 ***1220.12*** *p647*
Price, William; America, 1724 ***1220.12*** *p647*
Price, William; America, 1750 ***1220.12*** *p647*
Price, William; America, 1755 ***1220.12*** *p647*
Price, William; America, 1760 ***1220.12*** *p647*
Price, William; America, 1761 ***1220.12*** *p647*
Price, William; America, 1769 ***1220.12*** *p647*
Price, William; America, 1770 ***1220.12*** *p647*
Price, William; America, 1775 ***1220.12*** *p647*
Price, William; Annapolis, MD, 1725 ***1220.12*** *p647*
Price, William 35; Ontario, 1871 ***1823.17*** *p135*
Prich, Johann Baptist 20; Galveston, TX, 1846 ***3967.10*** *p379*
Prichard, George; Boston, 1767 ***1642*** *p38*
Prichard, Sam; Boston, 1767 ***1642*** *p39*
Prichard, Thomas; Boston, 1767 ***1642*** *p39*
Prichard, Thomas; Died enroute, 1720 ***1220.12*** *p649*
Prick, Rachael; America, 1743 ***1220.12*** *p647*
Pricket, Michael; America, 1769 ***1220.12*** *p647*
Prickett, Tho; Virginia, 1652 ***6254.4*** *p243*
Prickle, Richard; Virginia, 1727 ***1220.12*** *p647*
Pricklow, John; America, 1761 ***1220.12*** *p647*
Pricou, F.; Louisiana, 1874 ***4981.45*** *p296*
Pridal, Frantisek; Texas, 1895-1910 ***2853.20*** *p89*
Priddon, Thomas; America, 1741 ***1220.12*** *p647*
Pride, Shadrake; America, 1770 ***1220.12*** *p647*
Prideaux, Grace; Marblehead, MA, 1687 ***9228.50*** *p522*
Pridham, Edward 40; Ontario, 1871 ***1823.17*** *p135*
Pridmore, Thomas; Virginia, 1735 ***1220.12*** *p647*
Priehm, Mathias 44; America, 1843 ***5475.1*** *p305*
Priepke, Bertha; Wisconsin, 1899 ***6795.8*** *p134*
Priepke, Marie; Wisconsin, 1892 ***6795.8*** *p134*
Pries, Christian W.; North Carolina, 1857 ***1088.45*** *p27*
Priest, Abraham; Maryland, 1725 ***1220.12*** *p647*
Priest, Ann; America, 1750 ***1220.12*** *p647*
Priest, Catherine; America, 1715 ***1220.12*** *p647*
Priest, Catherine; Annapolis, MD, 1723 ***1220.12*** *p647*
Priest, Daniel; Maryland, 1725 ***1220.12*** *p647*
Priest, Digerie; Plymouth, MA, 1620 ***1920.45*** *p5*
Priest, Henry; America, 1685 ***1220.12*** *p647*
Priest, Henry M.; Ohio, 1876 ***3580.20*** *p33*
Priest, Henry M.; Ohio, 1876 ***6020.12*** *p22*
Priest, James; America, 1743 ***1220.12*** *p647*
Priest, James; Barbados, 1688 ***1220.12*** *p647*
Priest, John; America, 1734 ***1220.12*** *p647*
Priest, John; America, 1770 ***1220.12*** *p647*
Priest, Joseph; Marston's Wharf, 1782 ***8529.30*** *p15*
Priest, Laurence; America, 1685 ***1220.12*** *p647*
Priest, Mary; Virginia, 1727 ***1220.12*** *p647*
Priest, Naomi; Virginia, 1729 ***1220.12*** *p647*
Priest, Nathaniel; West Indies, 1686 ***1220.12*** *p647*
Priest, Robert; New York, 1783 ***8529.30*** *p15*
Priest, Thomas; America, 1685 ***1220.12*** *p647*
Priest, Thomas; America, 1772 ***1220.12*** *p647*
Priest, William; America, 1685 ***1220.12*** *p647*
Priest, William; America, 1731 ***1220.12*** *p647*
Priest, William; America, 1747 ***1220.12*** *p647*
Priestap, Charles; Ohio, 1840-1897 ***8365.35*** *p17*
Priestland, Elizabeth; America, 1760 ***1220.12*** *p647*
Priestland, William; America, 1764 ***1220.12*** *p647*
Priestley, Thomas J. 32; Ontario, 1871 ***1823.21*** *p302*
Priestley, Waddington 18; Ontario, 1871 ***1823.21*** *p302*
Priestly, James 54; Ontario, 1871 ***1823.21*** *p302*
Priestly, John 49; Ontario, 1871 ***1823.21*** *p302*
Priestly, John H. 58; Ontario, 1871 ***1823.21*** *p302*
Priestly, John W. 36; Ontario, 1871 ***1823.21*** *p302*
Priestly, Robert; America, 1734 ***1220.12*** *p647*
Priestly, Sarah; America, 1768 ***1220.12*** *p647*
Priestman, James; Maryland or Virginia, 1731 ***1220.12*** *p647*
Priestman, William; America, 1722 ***1220.12*** *p647*
Priestt, Joseph; Marston's Wharf, 1782 ***8529.30*** *p15*
Prieur, Jean 20; Quebec, 1655 ***9221.17*** *p328*
Priewe, Ernest Henry; Wisconsin, 1889 ***6795.8*** *p68*
Prigg, Elizabeth; America, 1752 ***1220.12*** *p648*
Prigg, James; America, 1759 ***1220.12*** *p648*
Prigge, Govert; North Carolina, 1844 ***1088.45*** *p27*
Prigge, John; North Carolina, 1852 ***1088.45*** *p27*
Priller, Gerhard; Ohio, 1840-1897 ***8365.35*** *p17*
Prim, Martin; Louisiana, 1874 ***4981.45*** *p133*
Prim, Thomas; America, 1684 ***1220.12*** *p648*
Prime, James 53; Ontario, 1871 ***1823.21*** *p302*
Prime, William; America, 1775 ***1220.12*** *p648*
Primette, Jane 22; America, 1848 ***778.6*** *p275*
Primot, Antoine 35; Montreal, 1641 ***9221.17*** *p108*
*Wife:*Martine Messier 34
*Daughter:*Catherine 1
Primot, Catherine 1 *SEE* Primot, Antoine
Primot, Martine Messier 34 *SEE* Primot, Antoine
Primout, Jean 21; Quebec, 1659 ***9221.17*** *p408*
Primrose, John; North Carolina, 1830 ***1088.45*** *p27*
Primrose, Robert; America, 1708 ***1220.12*** *p648*
Primrose, Robert; North Carolina, 1819 ***1088.45*** *p27*
Primus, Thomas; America, 1721 ***1220.12*** *p648*
Prince, Andrew; America, 1764 ***1220.12*** *p648*
Prince, Anne; America, 1701 ***1220.12*** *p648*
Prince, Charles; Charleston, SC, 1763 ***9228.50*** *p522*
Prince, Charles 42; Ontario, 1871 ***1823.21*** *p302*
Prince, Charles 45; Ontario, 1871 ***1823.21*** *p302*
Prince, Elizabeth; America, 1673 ***1220.12*** *p648*
Prince, George; America, 1743 ***1220.12*** *p648*
Prince, George Harris; Wisconsin, 1909-1933 ***9228.50*** *p522*
*Wife:*Philippa Georgina De Broder
*Child:*Phyllis Maud
Prince, Hannah; America, 1740 ***1220.12*** *p648*
Prince, Henry 36; Ontario, 1871 ***1823.21*** *p302*
Prince, John; America, 1751 ***1220.12*** *p648*
Prince, John; Barbados, 1676 ***1220.12*** *p648*
Prince, John; Barbados, 1683 ***1220.12*** *p648*
Prince, John; Colorado, 1887 ***1029.59*** *p75*
Prince, John; North Carolina, 1844 ***1088.45*** *p27*
Prince, Joseph; Potomac, 1729 ***1220.12*** *p648*
Prince, Martin; America, 1722 ***1220.12*** *p648*
Prince, Mary; Barbados, 1693 ***1220.12*** *p648*
Prince, Philippa Georgina De Broder *SEE* Prince, George Harris
Prince, Phyllis Maud *SEE* Prince, George Harris
Prince, Richard; America, 1735 ***1220.12*** *p648*
Prince, William; America, 1765 ***1220.12*** *p648*
Prince, William; America, 1767 ***1220.12*** *p648*
Prineveau, Sebastien; Quebec, 1657 ***9221.17*** *p366*
Priney, Peter; Potomac, 1729 ***1220.12*** *p648*
Pring, Amos 27; Ontario, 1871 ***1823.21*** *p302*
Pring, Cyprian; Virginia, 1767 ***1220.12*** *p648*
Pringell, John; America, 1693 ***1220.12*** *p648*
Pringle, Alexander 62; Ontario, 1871 ***1823.21*** *p302*
Pringle, Jane; Ontario, 1835 ***3160.1*** *p150*
Pringle, John 32; Ontario, 1871 ***1823.21*** *p302*
Pringle, Margaret; Ontario, 1835 ***3160.1*** *p150*
Pringle, Mary; Ontario, 1835 ***3160.1*** *p150*
Pringle, P. 27; Santa Clara Co., CA, 1860 ***8704.1*** *p23*
Pringle, William 38; Ontario, 1871 ***1823.17*** *p135*
Pringle, William 60; Ontario, 1871 ***1823.21*** *p302*
Prins, Andrea 37; America, 1848 ***778.6*** *p275*
Print, Sarah; America, 1766 ***1220.12*** *p648*
Prinz, Barbara; America, 1834 ***5475.1*** *p437*
Prinz, Johann Henrich 48; Pennsylvania, 1850 ***170.15*** *p38*
With 5 children
Priollaud, Mr. 39; Mexico, 1840 ***778.6*** *p275*
Prion, Rose 30; New Orleans, 1848 ***778.6*** *p275*
Prior, Ann; America, 1752 ***1220.12*** *p648*
Prior, Elizabeth; America, 1774 ***1220.12*** *p648*
Prior, George; America, 1757 ***1220.12*** *p648*
Prior, Hannah; America, 1772 ***1220.12*** *p648*
Prior, James 48; Ontario, 1871 ***1823.17*** *p135*
Prior, John; America, 1685 ***1220.12*** *p648*
Prior, John; America, 1749 ***1220.12*** *p648*
Prior, John; America, 1750 ***1220.12*** *p648*
Prior, John; Barbados, 1668 ***1220.12*** *p648*
Prior, John 70; Ontario, 1871 ***1823.21*** *p302*
Prior, William; America, 1683 ***1220.12*** *p648*
Prior, William; America, 1741 ***1220.12*** *p648*
Prioure, Francois 17; Quebec, 1658 ***9221.17*** *p386*
Prioux, J. 32; Port uncertain, 1840 ***778.6*** *p275*
Priske, Johann; Wisconsin, 1874 ***6795.8*** *p91*
Pritchard, Ann; America, 1741 ***1220.12*** *p648*
Pritchard, Arnold; America, 1769 ***1220.12*** *p648*
Pritchard, Charles; America, 1755 ***1220.12*** *p648*
Pritchard, Charles; Iowa, 1879 ***1211.15*** *p18*
Pritchard, Edward; Virginia, 1723 ***1220.12*** *p648*
Pritchard, Elizabeth; America, 1754 ***1220.12*** *p649*
Pritchard, Ezechiel; America, 1741 ***1220.12*** *p649*
Pritchard, Henry; Barbados, 1669 ***1220.12*** *p649*
Pritchard, I. H. 26; Ontario, 1871 ***1823.21*** *p302*
Pritchard, Israel; Barbados or Jamaica, 1700 ***1220.12*** *p649*
Pritchard, Jacob; Virginia, 1765 ***1220.12*** *p649*

Pritchard, James; America, 1697 ***1220.12*** *p649*
Pritchard, James; America, 1758 ***1220.12*** *p649*
Pritchard, James; America, 1768 ***1220.12*** *p649*
Pritchard, James; America, 1770 ***1220.12*** *p649*
Pritchard, James 35; Ontario, 1871 ***1823.21*** *p302*
Pritchard, Jane; America, 1695 ***1220.12*** *p649*
Pritchard, Jane; America, 1764 ***1220.12*** *p649*
Pritchard, John; America, 1739 ***1220.12*** *p649*
Pritchard, John; America, 1747 ***1220.12*** *p649*
Pritchard, John; America, 1756 ***1220.12*** *p649*
Pritchard, John; America, 1760 ***1220.12*** *p649*
Pritchard, John; America, 1766 ***1220.12*** *p649*
Pritchard, John; America, 1773 ***1220.12*** *p649*
Pritchard, John; America, 1775 ***1220.12*** *p649*
Pritchard, John; Barbados, 1672 ***1220.12*** *p649*
Pritchard, John; Maryland, 1673 ***1236.25*** *p48*
Pritchard, Jonas; Barbados or Jamaica, 1696 ***1220.12*** *p649*
Pritchard, Joseph; Iowa, 1880 ***1211.15*** *p18*
Pritchard, Joseph 55; Michigan, 1880 ***4491.42*** *p21*
Pritchard, Margaret; America, 1715 ***1220.12*** *p649*
Pritchard, Martha; America, 1757 ***1220.12*** *p649*
Pritchard, Mary; America, 1725 ***1220.12*** *p649*
Pritchard, Philip; Barbados or Jamaica, 1696 ***1220.12*** *p649*
Pritchard, Richard; America, 1726 ***1220.12*** *p649*
Pritchard, Richard; Barbados or Jamaica, 1690 ***1220.12*** *p649*
Pritchard, Richard; Virginia, 1741 ***1220.12*** *p649*
Pritchard, Robert; America, 1748 ***1220.12*** *p649*
Pritchard, Robert 34; Ontario, 1871 ***1823.21*** *p302*
Pritchard, Samuel; Potomac, 1731 ***1220.12*** *p649*
Pritchard, Sarah; America, 1765 ***1220.12*** *p649*
Pritchard, Sarah; America, 1771 ***1220.12*** *p649*
Pritchard, Thomas; America, 1775 ***1220.12*** *p649*
Pritchard, Thos 70; Ontario, 1871 ***1823.21*** *p302*
Pritchard, William; America, 1675 ***1220.12*** *p649*
Pritchard, William; America, 1731 ***1220.12*** *p649*
Pritchard, William; America, 1749 ***1220.12*** *p649*
Pritchard, William; America, 1751 ***1220.12*** *p649*
Pritchard, William; America, 1756 ***1220.12*** *p649*
Pritchard, William; America, 1769 ***1220.12*** *p649*
Pritchard, William; America, 1772 ***1220.12*** *p649*
Pritchard, William; Maryland, 1734 ***1220.12*** *p649*
Pritchard, William 19; Quebec, 1870 ***8364.32*** *p25*
Pritchet, David; Annapolis, MD, 1724 ***1220.12*** *p649*
Pritchet, John; America, 1771 ***1220.12*** *p650*
Pritchet, Thomas 28; Ontario, 1871 ***1823.21*** *p302*
Pritchett, James; America, 1697 ***1220.12*** *p649*
Pritchett, John; Maryland, 1737 ***1220.12*** *p650*
Pritchett, Thomas 61; Ontario, 1871 ***1823.21*** *p302*
Pritchler, Caspar; Philadelphia, 1778 ***8529.30*** *p4A*
Priteman, James; Nevis or Jamaica, 1722 ***1220.12*** *p650*
Prithell, Alfred 10; Quebec, 1870 ***8364.32*** *p25*
Pritherow, Silvanus; America, 1762 ***1220.12*** *p650*
Pritzkau, Anna 50; New York, NY, 1886 ***6954.7*** *p40*
Pritzkau, Anna Maria 19; New York, NY, 1886 ***6954.7*** *p40*
Pritzkau, Elenora 21; New York, NY, 1886 ***6954.7*** *p40*
Pritzkau, Eleonora 25; New York, NY, 1886 ***6954.7*** *p40*
Pritzkau, Emelia 4; New York, NY, 1886 ***6954.7*** *p40*
Pritzkau, Heinrich 13; New York, NY, 1886 ***6954.7*** *p41*
Pritzkau, Jacob 3; New York, NY, 1886 ***6954.7*** *p41*
Pritzkau, Johann 3 months; New York, NY, 1886 ***6954.7*** *p40*
Pritzkau, Johann 9; New York, NY, 1886 ***6954.7*** *p41*
Pritzkau, Johann 27; New York, NY, 1886 ***6954.7*** *p40*
Pritzkau, Johann 38; New York, NY, 1886 ***6954.7*** *p41*
Pritzkau, Katherina 38; New York, NY, 1886 ***6954.7*** *p41*
Pritzkau, Louisa 11 months; New York, NY, 1886 ***6954.7*** *p41*
Pritzkau, Paulina 8; New York, NY, 1886 ***6954.7*** *p41*
Pritzkau, Wilhelm 4; New York, NY, 1886 ***6954.7*** *p41*
Pritzler, August; America, 1866 ***7420.1*** *p247*
Privat, Chatarine 22; Missouri, 1845 ***778.6*** *p275*
Probart, James; Ohio, 1840 ***2763.1*** *p21*
Probart, William; America, 1757 ***1220.12*** *p650*
Probeart, Thomas; America, 1774 ***1220.12*** *p650*
Probert, Alice; Annapolis, MD, 1725 ***1220.12*** *p650*
Probert, Howell; America, 1678 ***1220.12*** *p650*
Probert, Thomas; America, 1725 ***1220.12*** *p650*
Probert, Thomas; America, 1744 ***1220.12*** *p650*
Probert, Thomas; America, 1768 ***1220.12*** *p650*
Probert, William; America, 1768 ***1220.12*** *p650*
Probst, Barbara Maringer *SEE* Probst, Peter
Probst, Catherine 65; Missouri, 1846 ***778.6*** *p275*
Probst, Gertrud *SEE* Probst, Peter
Probst, Joh. Peter; Pittsburgh, 1884 ***5475.1*** *p322*
Probst, Maria; America, 1882 ***5475.1*** *p228*
Probst, Peter; America, 1882 ***5475.1*** *p228*
*Wife:*Barbara Maringer
*Daughter:*Gertrud
Probuts, William; America, 1757 ***1220.12*** *p650*
Proby, Thomas; Virginia, 1739 ***1220.12*** *p650*
Prochazka, Frantisek; Detroit, 1854-1859 ***2853.20*** *p356*
Prochnow, Karl Robert; Wisconsin, 1895 ***6795.8*** *p75*
Prockter, Thomas 23; Barbados, 1664 ***1220.12*** *p650*
Procter, Christian; America, 1743 ***1220.12*** *p650*
Procter, Christopher; America, 1740 ***1220.12*** *p650*
Procter, Elizabeth; America, 1763 ***1220.12*** *p650*
Procter, John; America, 1772 ***1220.12*** *p650*
Procter, John; America, 1773 ***1220.12*** *p650*
Procter, John 63; Ontario, 1871 ***1823.17*** *p135*
Procter, Margaret; Potomac, 1731 ***1220.12*** *p650*
Procter, Mary; America, 1743 ***1220.12*** *p650*
Procter, Thomas; America, 1773 ***1220.12*** *p650*
Procter, William; America, 1772 ***1220.12*** *p650*
Proctor, Abigail; America, 1774 ***1220.12*** *p650*
Proctor, E. M. 52; Ontario, 1871 ***1823.21*** *p302*
Proctor, James 35; Ontario, 1871 ***1823.21*** *p302*
Proctor, John 43; Ontario, 1871 ***1823.21*** *p302*
Proctor, John S.; Ohio, 1844 ***2763.1*** *p21*
Proctor, Locking 42; Ontario, 1871 ***1823.21*** *p302*
Proctor, Meiza 61; Ontario, 1871 ***1823.17*** *p135*
Proctor, Morzu 40; Ontario, 1871 ***1823.17*** *p135*
Proctor, Reuben 47; Ontario, 1871 ***1823.17*** *p135*
Proctor, Richard; America, 1756 ***1220.12*** *p650*
Proctor, Robert; Long Island, 1778 ***8529.30*** *p10A*
Proctor, Sarah; America, 1769 ***1220.12*** *p650*
Proctor, William; Ohio, 1832-1932 ***9228.50*** *p511*
Proctor, William S.; Ohio, 1844 ***2763.1*** *p21*
Prodgers, John 51; Ontario, 1871 ***1823.21*** *p302*
Proescher, Karl August; Wisconsin, 1894 ***6795.8*** *p192*
Proffit, Charlotte; Quebec, 1649 ***9221.17*** *p212*
Prokes, Jan; Nebraska, 1850-1910 ***2853.20*** *p182*
Prokop, Bridget; Detroit, 1929 ***1640.55*** *p117*
Proles, Nathaniel; Maryland, 1742 ***1220.12*** *p650*
Proll, Joseph; Colorado, 1882 ***1029.59*** *p76*
Proll, Joseph; Washington, 1888 ***2770.40*** *p26*
Prollwitz, Gustav Ewald; Wisconsin, 1908 ***1822.55*** *p10*
Prontzinski, Tony; New York, 1894 ***1766.20*** *p3*
Propfe, Charles; Illinois, 1860 ***6079.1*** *p11*
Prophett, John; America, 1734 ***1220.12*** *p650*
Propier, Mr. 35; America, 1841 ***778.6*** *p275*
Propping, Carl Heinrich Ferdinand; America, 1858 ***7420.1*** *p181*
Propping, Ernst Anton Emil; America, 1860 ***7420.1*** *p198*
Propson, Wilhelm 25; America, 1861 ***5475.1*** *p336*
Proschold, Friedrich; America, 1867 ***7919.3*** *p528*
Prosek, Jan; Port uncertain, 1870 ***2853.20*** *p265*
Prosey, William; America, 1748 ***1220.12*** *p650*
Prosiner, Mrs. 39; New Orleans, 1848 ***778.6*** *p275*
Prosiner, M. 45; New Orleans, 1848 ***778.6*** *p275*
Prosper, Pierre 35; Port uncertain, 1845 ***778.6*** *p275*
Prosser, Ann; America, 1759 ***1220.12*** *p650*
Prosser, Charles; Annapolis, MD, 1730 ***1220.12*** *p650*
Prosser, Elizabeth; America, 1719 ***1220.12*** *p650*
Prosser, James; America, 1757 ***1220.12*** *p650*
Prosser, James; America, 1766 ***1220.12*** *p650*
Prosser, John; America, 1744 ***1220.12*** *p650*
Prosser, Jonathan; America, 1764 ***1220.12*** *p650*
Prosser, Roger; America, 1721 ***1220.12*** *p650*
Prosser, Sarah; America, 1754 ***1220.12*** *p650*
Prosser, Thomas; America, 1722 ***1220.12*** *p650*
Prosser, Thomas; America, 1752 ***1220.12*** *p650*
Prosser, Thomas; America, 1753 ***1220.12*** *p650*
Prosser, William; America, 1749 ***1220.12*** *p650*
Prosser, William; America, 1760 ***1220.12*** *p650*
Protat, Antoine; Illinois, 1852 ***6079.1*** *p11*
Prothero, Evan; America, 1737 ***1220.12*** *p650*
Protherow, John; America, 1774 ***1220.12*** *p650*
Protin, A. 45; New Orleans, 1846 ***778.6*** *p275*
Protin, Angelique 33; America, 1841 ***778.6*** *p275*
Protosky, Louis 6; Louisiana, 1848 ***778.6*** *p275*
Protosky, Marie 4; Louisiana, 1848 ***778.6*** *p275*
Protosky, Marie 34; Louisiana, 1848 ***778.6*** *p275*
Protosky, Stanislas 10; Louisiana, 1848 ***778.6*** *p275*
Protosky, Stanislas 34; Louisiana, 1848 ***778.6*** *p275*
Prou, Ellen; New Jersey, 1665 ***9228.50*** *p522*
Prou, Ellen; Virginia, 1665 ***9228.50*** *p53*
Prou, Pierre; Quebec, 1644 ***9221.17*** *p145*
Proud, Jacques 39; New Orleans, 1848 ***778.6*** *p275*
Proudfoot, John J. 49; Ontario, 1871 ***1823.21*** *p302*
Proudfoot, Matthew; America, 1750 ***1220.12*** *p650*
Proudman, Daniel; Virginia, 1727 ***1220.12*** *p651*
Prouings, Henry; Maine, 1641 ***9228.50*** *p522*
Proulx, Ellen; New Jersey, 1665 ***9228.50*** *p522*
Proulz, Ellen; Virginia, 1665 ***9228.50*** *p53*
Prout, John; North Carolina, 1835 ***1088.45*** *p27*
Prout, John 52; Ontario, 1871 ***1823.17*** *p135*
Prout, John 56; Ontario, 1871 ***1823.17*** *p135*
Prout, Thomas 44; Ontario, 1871 ***1823.21*** *p302*
Prout, William 47; Ontario, 1871 ***1823.17*** *p135*
Prout, William 48; Ontario, 1871 ***1823.17*** *p135*
Proutain, Pierre 30; America, 1843 ***778.6*** *p275*
Proutost, Mathieu; Quebec, 1661 ***9221.17*** *p466*
Proutt, Lawrence *SEE* Proutt, Thomas
Proutt, Thomas; Toronto, 1844 ***2910.35*** *p112*
*Son:*Lawrence
Provencher, Sebastien 26; Quebec, 1660 ***9221.17*** *p439*
Provent, Joseph 31; America, 1846 ***778.6*** *p275*
Provent, Marguerite 29; America, 1846 ***778.6*** *p275*
Provent, Victor 2; America, 1846 ***778.6*** *p275*
Provincher, Joseph 15; Ontario, 1871 ***1823.17*** *p135*
Provizor, Jack; Detroit, 1930 ***1640.60*** *p78*
Provoe, James; Maine, 1682 ***9228.50*** *p523*
Provost, Francois; Quebec, 1665 ***2314.30*** *p167*
Provost, Francois; Quebec, 1665 ***2314.30*** *p193*
Provost, Francois 25; Quebec, 1662 ***9221.17*** *p492*
Provost, Jacques; Quebec, 1660 ***9221.17*** *p439*
Provost, Marguerite; Quebec, 1670 ***4514.3*** *p360*
Provost, Martin 28; Quebec, 1639 ***9221.17*** *p92*
Provost, Mary; America, 1741 ***1220.12*** *p651*
Provost, Mathurin; Quebec, 1646 ***9221.17*** *p168*
Provost, Pierre 21; Quebec, 1651 ***9221.17*** *p250*
Prowald, Anna Maria Gilges *SEE* Prowald, Ludwig
Prowald, Franz Ludwig *SEE* Prowald, Ludwig
Prowald, Ludwig *SEE* Prowald, Ludwig
Prowald, Ludwig; America, 1868 ***5475.1*** *p388*
*Wife:*Anna Maria Gilges
*Daughter:*Maria
*Son:*Franz Ludwig
*Son:*Ludwig
Prowald, Maria *SEE* Prowald, Ludwig
Prowce, John 71; Ontario, 1871 ***1823.21*** *p302*
Prowce, Mary 61; Ontario, 1871 ***1823.21*** *p302*
Prowelsky, G.; Galveston, TX, 1855 ***571.7*** *p18*
Prower, Salamon; Plymouth, MA, 1620 ***1920.45*** *p5*
Prowers, Brigett 70; Ontario, 1871 ***1823.21*** *p302*
Prowse, John; Virginia, 1740 ***1220.12*** *p651*
Prowse, Roger; Barbados, 1694 ***1220.12*** *p651*
Prowse, William; America, 1685 ***1220.12*** *p651*
Prowse, William; Barbados, 1683 ***1220.12*** *p651*
Prucha, Emil; Wisconsin, 1856 ***2853.20*** *p345*
Prucha, Jan; Ohio, 1891 ***2853.20*** *p496*
Prucha, Vaclav; Chicago, 1896 ***2853.20*** *p460*
Prudeau, Jean 25; Port uncertain, 1848 ***778.6*** *p275*
Pruden, Hector 26; Ontario, 1871 ***1823.21*** *p302*
Prudent, Jules T.; Illinois, 1852 ***6079.1*** *p11*
Prudent, Jules Theophile 29; New Orleans, 1848 ***778.6*** *p275*
Prudham, John 51; Ontario, 1871 ***1823.21*** *p302*
Prudhomme, Claude; Montreal, 1650 ***9221.17*** *p232*
*Wife:*Isabelle Aliomet
Prudhomme, Isabelle Aliomet *SEE* Prudhomme, Claude
Prudhomme, L. Joseph Augustin 24; Galveston, TX, 1846 ***3967.10*** *p379*
Prudhomme, Louis 38; Montreal, 1642 ***9221.17*** *p124*
Prudhomme, Marie 23; America, 1841 ***778.6*** *p275*
Prudhomme, Rene 19; America, 1841 ***778.6*** *p276*
Prudhomme, Thomas W. 30; Ontario, 1871 ***1823.21*** *p302*
Prudom, George 46; Ontario, 1871 ***1823.21*** *p302*
Prudou, Franc. 28; Port uncertain, 1840 ***778.6*** *p276*
Prudzinski, Antoni; Detroit, 1930 ***1640.60*** *p81*
Pruett, William; Rappahannock, VA, 1729 ***1220.12*** *p644*
Prumm, Johann 18; America, 1856 ***5475.1*** *p356*
Pruner, Jean 31; Port uncertain, 1842 ***778.6*** *p276*
Prunetrat, J. Martin 28; America, 1840 ***778.6*** *p276*
Prunier, Marie-Madeleine; Quebec, 1671 ***4514.3*** *p360*
Prus, William; Detroit, 1930 ***1640.60*** *p78*
Pruseau, Fabien 15; Quebec, 1661 ***9221.17*** *p466*
Pruss, R. Gregor; New York, 1859 ***358.56*** *p101*
Prusse, John 36; America, 1843 ***778.6*** *p276*
Prussing, J.; Valdivia, Chile, 1852 ***1192.4*** *p56*
Prust, Carl Henry William; Wisconsin, 1888 ***6795.8*** *p169*
Pruter, Christopher; Ohio, 1840-1897 ***8365.35*** *p17*
Pryba, Constance; Detroit, 1890 ***9980.23*** *p96*
Pryce, William; Ohio, 1809-1852 ***4511.35*** *p41*
Pryer, Mary; America, 1700 ***1220.12*** *p648*
Pryer, William; Ohio, 1809-1852 ***4511.35*** *p41*
Prygroski, Stefan; Detroit, 1930 ***1640.60*** *p81*
Pryor, Francis; America, 1665 ***1220.12*** *p648*
Pryor, Isaac; America, 1685 ***1220.12*** *p648*
Pryor, John; America, 1719 ***1220.12*** *p648*
Pryor, Matthew; America, 1685 ***1220.12*** *p648*
Pryor, Samuel; America, 1747 ***1220.12*** *p648*
Pryor, William; America, 1772 ***1220.12*** *p648*
Pryor, William; Ohio, 1809-1852 ***4511.35*** *p41*
Prystay, Roman; Detroit, 1929 ***1640.55*** *p116*
Prytherch, Silvanus; America, 1762 ***1220.12*** *p651*
Prytherow, Silvanus; America, 1762 ***1220.12*** *p650*
Przedpelski, Edward; Detroit, 1930 ***1640.60*** *p77*
Przyborowski, Stanislaus; Detroit, 1930 ***1640.60*** *p82*
Przybylko, Felix; Detroit, 1929-1930 ***6214.5*** *p67*
Przybyszcwski, Josef; Texas, 1886 ***9980.22*** *p16*
Przychodzen, Anthony; Detroit, 1930 ***1640.60*** *p82*
Psencik, Jiri; Texas, 1854 ***2853.20*** *p78*

Psenicka, Rudolf Jar.; Chicago, 1910 ***2853.20*** *p528*
Psenka, Rudolf Jar.; Chicago, 1910 ***2853.20*** *p528*
Psotta, Christian; America, 1839 ***5475.1*** *p469*
With family
Psotta, Karl; America, 1837 ***5475.1*** *p468*
Ptacek, Jan; Chicago, 1856 ***2853.20*** *p389*
Ptacnik, Josef; Nebraska, 1879 ***2853.20*** *p190*
Ptak, Boleslaw; Detroit, 1930 ***1640.60*** *p82*
Ptak, Josef; South Dakota, 1871-1910 ***2853.20*** *p247*
Ptasinsky, Josef; Texas, 1910 ***2853.20*** *p93*
Ptaszynska, Emilia; Detroit, 1929-1930 ***6214.5*** *p67*
Ptolemee, Charles 23; Montreal, 1662 ***9221.17*** *p499*
Puariea, Alfred; Washington, 1884 ***2770.40*** *p193*
Pubelskh, A.; Galveston, TX, 1855 ***571.7*** *p18*
Pucci, Lodovico; Illinois, 1930 ***121.35*** *p101*
Puchen, Louis; Louisiana, 1874-1875 ***4981.45*** *p30*
Puchovitsky, Rubin; Detroit, 1930 ***1640.60*** *p81*
Puckering, Edward; America, 1755 ***1220.12*** *p651*
Puckering, James 38; Ontario, 1871 ***1823.21*** *p303*
Puckett, Francis; America, 1685 ***1220.12*** *p651*
Puckett, John; Virginia, 1665 ***9228.50*** *p523*
Puczkowski, Wladyslaw; Detroit, 1929-1930 ***6214.5*** *p69*
Puddicomb, Abraham 56; Ontario, 1871 ***1823.21*** *p303*
Puddicomb, Fanny 18; Ontario, 1871 ***1823.21*** *p303*
Puddicomb, John 30; Ontario, 1871 ***1823.21*** *p303*
Puddicomb, Robert W. 28; Ontario, 1871 ***1823.21*** *p303*
Puddle, Hannah; America, 1770 ***1220.12*** *p651*
Puddy, William; America, 1763 ***1220.12*** *p651*
Pudeator, Jacob; Salem, MA, 1600-1692 ***9228.50*** *p255*
Pudestor, Jacob; Salem, MA, 1600-1692 ***9228.50*** *p255*
Pudil, Antonin; Virginia, 1888 ***2853.20*** *p136*
Pudiphas, Samuel; America, 1775 ***1220.12*** *p651*
Pudlo, Anna 17; New York, NY, 1911 ***6533.11*** *p10*
Pudwill, Andreas 2; New York, NY, 1886 ***6954.7*** *p40*
Pudwill, Barbara 18; New York, NY, 1886 ***6954.7*** *p40*
Pudwill, Christina 6 months; New York, NY, 1886 ***6954.7*** *p40*
Pudwill, Gottlieb 26; New York, NY, 1886 ***6954.7*** *p40*
Pudwill, Heinrich 9; New York, NY, 1886 ***6954.7*** *p40*
Pudwill, Johann 8; New York, NY, 1886 ***6954.7*** *p40*
Pudwill, Johannes 4; New York, NY, 1886 ***6954.7*** *p40*
Pudwill, Katherina 16; New York, NY, 1886 ***6954.7*** *p40*
Pudwill, Katherina 52; New York, NY, 1886 ***6954.7*** *p40*
Pudwill, Louisa 5; New York, NY, 1886 ***6954.7*** *p40*
Pudwill, Margaretha 30; New York, NY, 1886 ***6954.7*** *p40*
Pudwill, Maria 21; New York, NY, 1886 ***6954.7*** *p40*
Pudwill, Michael 32; New York, NY, 1886 ***6954.7*** *p40*
Puehta, Wolfgang; North Carolina, 1848 ***1088.45*** *p27*
Pufahl, Fritz Albert Edward; Wisconsin, 1906 ***6795.8*** *p220*
Pufahl, Leo Paul; Wisconsin, 1913 ***6795.8*** *p170*
Pufahl, Martha Renspies; Wisconsin, 1902 ***6795.8*** *p144*
Pufhal, Franz Ferd.; Valdivia, Chile, 1852 ***1192.4*** *p56*
Pugar, Joseph; North Carolina, 1710 ***3629.40*** *p6*
Pugge, Frederic; Illinois, 1852 ***6079.1*** *p11*
Puggesley, John; America, 1735 ***1220.12*** *p651*
Puggesley, William; Maryland, 1736 ***1220.12*** *p651*
Pugh, Ann; America, 1748 ***1220.12*** *p651*
Pugh, Arabella; America, 1761 ***1220.12*** *p651*
Pugh, Betty; New Orleans, 1850 ***7242.30*** *p152*
Pugh, Daniel; America, 1754 ***1220.12*** *p651*
Pugh, David; America, 1748 ***1220.12*** *p651*
Pugh, Edward 20; Ontario, 1871 ***1823.21*** *p303*
Pugh, Elizabeth; America, 1744 ***1220.12*** *p651*
Pugh, Evan; Ohio, 1854 ***4022.20*** *p290*
*Wife:*Mary Williams
Pugh, Henry; New Orleans, 1850 ***7242.30*** *p152*
Pugh, Hugh; America, 1754 ***1220.12*** *p651*
Pugh, Hugh; America, 1758 ***1220.12*** *p651*
Pugh, James; New Orleans, 1850 ***7242.30*** *p152*
Pugh, John; America, 1750 ***1220.12*** *p651*
Pugh, John; New Orleans, 1850 ***7242.30*** *p152*
Pugh, John William; America, 1774 ***1220.12*** *p651*
Pugh, Margaret; Ontario, 1835 ***3160.1*** *p150*
Pugh, Mary; America, 1754 ***1220.12*** *p651*
Pugh, Mary Williams *SEE* Pugh, Evan
Pugh, Mary; Ohio, 1855 ***4022.20*** *p273*
Pugh, Mary; Virginia, 1741 ***1220.12*** *p651*
Pugh, Philip; Annapolis, MD, 1730 ***1220.12*** *p651*
Pugh, Richard; America, 1736 ***1220.12*** *p651*
Pugh, Richard; America, 1775 ***1220.12*** *p651*
Pugh, Simon; America, 1763 ***1220.12*** *p651*
Pugh, William; America, 1729 ***1220.12*** *p651*
Pugsley, George; America, 1752 ***1220.12*** *p651*
Puhl, Anna 2 *SEE* Puhl, Johann
Puhl, Anna 12 *SEE* Puhl, Peter
Puhl, Barbara 10 *SEE* Puhl, Peter
Puhl, Barbara Sanger 37 *SEE* Puhl, Peter
Puhl, Christian *SEE* Puhl, Peter
Puhl, Friedrich *SEE* Puhl, Peter
Puhl, Gertrud 1 *SEE* Puhl, Peter
Puhl, Jakob; America, 1872 ***5475.1*** *p332*
Puhl, Jakob; Iowa, 1878 ***5475.1*** *p334*
*Wife:*Maria Jost
*Son:*Nikolaus
Puhl, Johann 40; America, 1843 ***5475.1*** *p351*
Puhl, Johann 7 *SEE* Puhl, Johann
Puhl, Johann 11 *SEE* Puhl, Peter
Puhl, Johann 36; Brazil, 1857 ***5475.1*** *p356*
*Wife:*Maria Meier 31
*Daughter:*Anna 2
*Son:*Johann 7
Puhl, Katharina 7 *SEE* Puhl, Peter
Puhl, Maria 5 *SEE* Puhl, Peter
Puhl, Maria Meier 31 *SEE* Puhl, Johann
Puhl, Maria Jost *SEE* Puhl, Jakob
Puhl, Mathias; America, 1834 ***5475.1*** *p437*
Puhl, Mathias 8 *SEE* Puhl, Peter
Puhl, Michel; America, 1884 ***5475.1*** *p333*
Puhl, Nikolaus *SEE* Puhl, Jakob
Puhl, Peter; America, 1840 ***5475.1*** *p437*
With wife & 5 children
Puhl, Peter *SEE* Puhl, Peter
Puhl, Peter; America, 1854 ***5475.1*** *p459*
*Wife:*Wilhelmine Muller
*Son:*Friedrich
*Son:*Peter
*Son:*Christian
Puhl, Peter; America, 1881 ***5475.1*** *p332*
Puhl, Peter 3 *SEE* Puhl, Peter
Puhl, Peter 39; Brazil, 1857 ***5475.1*** *p320*
*Wife:*Barbara Sanger 37
*Son:*Mathias 8
*Daughter:*Maria 5
*Daughter:*Gertrud 1
*Son:*Peter 3
*Daughter:*Katharina 7
*Daughter:*Barbara 10
*Daughter:*Anna 12
*Son:*Johann 11
Puhl, Wilhelmine Muller *SEE* Puhl, Peter
Puikes, Toby 27; St. Johns, N.F., 1811 ***1053.20*** *p19*
Puin, Richard; America, 1748 ***1220.12*** *p651*
Puiseaux DeMontrenault, Pierre 71; Quebec, 1637 ***9221.17*** *p72*
Puissant, Mr. 36; Louisiana, 1840 ***778.6*** *p276*
Pujaque, Bernard; Louisiana, 1874-1875 ***4981.45*** *p30*
Pujo, Dominique 29; Port uncertain, 1843 ***778.6*** *p276*
Pujo, Eugene 23; America, 1847 ***778.6*** *p276*
Pujol, A. 28; America, 1848 ***778.6*** *p276*
Pujol, Andre 40; America, 1846 ***778.6*** *p276*
Pujols, Guillaume 36; Louisiana, 1848 ***778.6*** *p276*
Pujols, Pierre 15; Louisiana, 1848 ***778.6*** *p276*
Pujos, P. 45; Port uncertain, 1842 ***778.6*** *p276*
Pukoff, Rubin; Detroit, 1930 ***1640.60*** *p81*
Pulfer, Lewis 37; Ontario, 1871 ***1823.17*** *p135*
Pulford, Brian; America, 1697 ***1220.12*** *p651*
Pulford, George 68; Ontario, 1871 ***1823.21*** *p303*
Pulford, Thomas; America, 1751 ***1220.12*** *p651*
Pulford, William; Barbados, 1664 ***1220.12*** *p651*
Pulham, Ann; America, 1704 ***1220.12*** *p651*
Pulham, Eliz.; Prince Edward Island, 1806 ***9228.50*** *p659*
Pulham, Elizabeth; Prince Edward Island, 1792-1823 ***9228.50*** *p128*
Pulham, Elizabeth; Prince Edward Island, 1806 ***9228.50*** *p128*
Pulham, Elizabeth; Prince Edward Island, 1806 ***9228.50*** *p129*
Pulham, Frances; Prince Edward Island, 1806 ***9228.50*** *p413*
Pulham, Robert; America, 1687 ***1220.12*** *p651*
Pulham, Thomas; America, 1738 ***1220.12*** *p651*
Pulisson, Roger; Barbados, 1674 ***1220.12*** *p651*
Puliston, Roger; Maryland, 1674-1675 ***1236.25*** *p52*
Pulla, Dominique; Virginia, 1732 ***1220.12*** *p651*
Pullam, Elizabeth; Prince Edward Island, 1792-1823 ***9228.50*** *p128*
Pullan, Richard 78; Ontario, 1871 ***1823.17*** *p135*
Pullein, John; America, 1764 ***1220.12*** *p652*
Pullem, Frances; Prince Edward Island, 1806 ***9228.50*** *p413*
Pullen, Mrs.; Boston, 1766 ***1642*** *p36*
With son
Pullen, Ambrose 55; Ontario, 1871 ***1823.21*** *p303*
Pullen, Charles; America, 1774 ***1220.12*** *p651*
Pullen, Frances; Prince Edward Island, 1806 ***9228.50*** *p413*
Pullen, George 31; Ontario, 1871 ***1823.21*** *p303*
Pullen, John; America, 1736 ***1220.12*** *p651*
Pullen, Joseph; America, 1766 ***1220.12*** *p652*
Pullen, Richard; America, 1754 ***1220.12*** *p652*
Pullen, Richard; America, 1771 ***1220.12*** *p652*
Pullen, Samuel; America, 1773 ***1220.12*** *p652*
Pullen, William; America, 1745 ***1220.12*** *p652*
Pullen, William; America, 1752 ***1220.12*** *p652*
Pullenger, William; America, 1748 ***1220.12*** *p652*
Puller, Walter; America, 1753 ***1220.12*** *p652*
Pulley, Elizabeth; America, 1745 ***1220.12*** *p652*
Pulley, Susanna; America, 1756 ***1220.12*** *p652*
Pulleyn, Robert; America, 1755 ***1220.12*** *p652*
Pullham, Sarah; America, 1770 ***1220.12*** *p651*
Pullin, John; America, 1757 ***1220.12*** *p651*
Pulling, Richard 70; Ontario, 1871 ***1823.21*** *p303*
Pulling, Thomas; Ohio, 1840 ***3580.20*** *p33*
Pulling, Thomas; Ohio, 1840 ***6020.12*** *p22*
Pulling, William 42; Ontario, 1871 ***1823.21*** *p303*
Pullison, Roger; Maryland, 1674-1675 ***1236.25*** *p52*
Pullman, Henry; Louisiana, 1874-1875 ***4981.45*** *p30*
Pullor, Joseph; America, 1750 ***1220.12*** *p652*
Pulman, Mary; America, 1730 ***1220.12*** *p652*
Pulman, William; Barbados, 1683 ***1220.12*** *p652*
Pulpitt, William; America, 1751 ***1220.12*** *p652*
Pulse, John 56; Ontario, 1871 ***1823.17*** *p135*
Pulsevir, Catherine; Virginia, 1738 ***1220.12*** *p652*
Pulson, Cicely; America, 1744 ***1220.12*** *p639*
Pulton, John; America, 1741 ***1220.12*** *p640*
Pump, Jeremiah; America, 1768 ***1220.12*** *p652*
Punchard, John; Salem, MA, 1751 ***9228.50*** *p165*
Punchard, Michel; Louisiana, n.d. ***9228.50*** *p526*
Punchard, William; Salem, MA, 1669 ***9228.50*** *p523*
Punchard, Wm.; Boston, 1715 ***9228.50*** *p523*
Punchard, Wm.; Salem, MA, 1650-1750 ***9228.50*** *p287*
Puncheon, Lawrence; America, 1773 ***1220.12*** *p652*
Punski, Frank; Detroit, 1930 ***1640.60*** *p81*
Punt, Augustine; Barbados, 1675 ***1220.12*** *p652*
Punter, John; America, 1749 ***1220.12*** *p652*
Punter, Thomas; America, 1755 ***1220.12*** *p652*
Puphal, Ernestine Alwine; Wisconsin, 1894 ***6795.8*** *p140*
Pupin, Francois 19; Quebec, 1659 ***9221.17*** *p409*
Pupret, Pierre; Quebec, 1646 ***9221.17*** *p168*
Purcell, Archibald 38; Ontario, 1871 ***1823.21*** *p303*
Purcell, Elizabeth 14; Quebec, 1870 ***8364.32*** *p25*
Purcell, Henry; Virginia, 1734 ***1220.12*** *p652*
Purcell, John; America, 1693 ***1220.12*** *p652*
Purcell, John; America, 1752 ***1220.12*** *p652*
Purcell, John; St. Johns, N.F., 1825 ***1053.15*** *p7*
Purcell, Michael; Toronto, 1844 ***2910.35*** *p112*
Purcell, Michl; St. Johns, N.F., 1825 ***1053.15*** *p7*
Purcell, Nancy; St. Johns, N.F., 1825 ***1053.15*** *p7*
Purcell, Paddy; Boston, 1735 ***1642*** *p44*
Purcell, Pat; St. Johns, N.F., 1825 ***1053.15*** *p7*
Purcell, Patrick; Illinois, 1855 ***6079.1*** *p11*
Purcell, Thomas; St. Johns, N.F., 1825 ***1053.15*** *p7*
Purcell, William; Barbados, 1664 ***1220.12*** *p652*
Purcell, Wm. E.; Louisiana, 1874 ***4981.45*** *p133*
Purcels, William 23; Ontario, 1871 ***1823.21*** *p303*
Purchase, George; Annapolis, MD, 1725 ***1220.12*** *p652*
Purchase, Richard; America, 1763 ***1220.12*** *p652*
Purchase, William; America, 1768 ***1220.12*** *p652*
Purdem, Thomas; America, 1770 ***1220.12*** *p652*
Purdom, Alexander 47; Ontario, 1871 ***1823.21*** *p303*
Purdom, Thomas 40; Ontario, 1871 ***1823.21*** *p303*
Purdon, Meriel; Died enroute, 1736 ***1220.12*** *p652*
Purdue, Charles; Charles Town, SC, 1719 ***1220.12*** *p652*
Purdue, Thomas; America, 1766 ***1220.12*** *p652*
Purdy, C.B.; Iowa, 1876 ***1211.15*** *p18*
Purdy, James 34; Ontario, 1871 ***1823.21*** *p303*
Purdy, John 39; Ontario, 1871 ***1823.17*** *p135*
Purdy, Maria 54; Ontario, 1871 ***1823.21*** *p303*
Purdy, Robert; Philadelphia, 1778 ***8529.30*** *p4A*
Purdy, Samuel 60; Ontario, 1871 ***1823.21*** *p303*
Purelle, Auguste 4; America, 1846 ***778.6*** *p276*
Purelle, Cathne. 8; America, 1846 ***778.6*** *p276*
Purelle, Eugene 8; America, 1846 ***778.6*** *p276*
Purelle, Theodre. 7; America, 1846 ***778.6*** *p276*
Purie, William; Annapolis, MD, 1725 ***1220.12*** *p652*
Purland, Margaret; America, 1749 ***1220.12*** *p652*
Purland, Mathew; America, 1749 ***1220.12*** *p652*
Purlement, Elizabeth; America, 1769 ***1220.12*** *p652*
Purnell, Ann; America, 1770 ***1220.12*** *p606*
Purnell, Samuel; Virginia, 1767 ***1220.12*** *p606*
Purney, John; America, 1769 ***1220.12*** *p652*
Purney, Mary, Jr.; America, 1737 ***1220.12*** *p652*
Purney, Mary, Sr.; Virginia, 1738 ***1220.12*** *p652*
Purney, Richard; America, 1754 ***1220.12*** *p652*
Purney, Thomas; America, 1768 ***1220.12*** *p652*
Pursall, Ann 37; Michigan, 1880 ***4491.33*** *p18*
Pursall, Catherine 62; Michigan, 1880 ***4491.33*** *p18*
Pursall, Edward 51; Michigan, 1880 ***4491.33*** *p18*
Pursall, Richard 61; Michigan, 1880 ***4491.33*** *p18*
Pursau, Xavious 18; Ohio, 1880 ***4879.40*** *p257*
Purse, Ann; Barbados, 1664 ***1220.12*** *p653*
Purse, Bernard; Maryland, 1737 ***1220.12*** *p653*
Pursely, John; Barbados or Jamaica, 1702 ***1220.12*** *p653*
Purser, Catherine; America, 1752 ***1220.12*** *p653*
Purser, Daniel 35; Ontario, 1871 ***1823.17*** *p135*
Purser, Duncan 33; Ontario, 1871 ***1823.17*** *p135*
Purser, Joseph; America, 1743 ***1220.12*** *p653*

Purser, Richard; America, 1765 *1220.12 p653*
Purslake, John; Virginia, 1718 *1220.12 p653*
Pursly, John; America, 1751 *1220.12 p653*
Purtill, Patrick; Toronto, 1844 *2910.35 p115*
Purtilo, Wiljo 19; Minnesota, 1925 *2769.54 p1378*
Purtle, Thomas; Annapolis, MD, 1731 *1220.12 p653*
Purtle, Thomas 37; Ontario, 1871 *1823.17 p135*
Purton, Henry; Barbados, 1699 *1220.12 p653*
Purvas, Ralphe; America, 1724 *1220.12 p653*
Purves, Thos 47; Ontario, 1871 *1823.17 p135*
Purvis, Ann; America, 1754 *1220.12 p653*
Purvis, David 39; Ontario, 1871 *1823.17 p135*
Purvis, James 32; Ontario, 1871 *1823.17 p135*
Purvis, James; Rappahannock, VA, 1741 *1220.12 p653*
Purvis, Robert 36; Ontario, 1871 *1823.17 p135*
Pussecune, Jacq. 27; America, 1842 *778.6 p276*
Pust, Christlieb Wilhelm Aug.; Wisconsin, 1887 *6795.8 p86*
Pustejovsky, Ignac; Galveston, TX, 1856 *2853.20 p63*
Putland, Elizabeth; America, 1741 *1220.12 p653*
Putnam, James; America, 1764 *1220.12 p653*
Putnam, Mary; America, 1771 *1220.12 p653*
Putnam, Sarah; New Hampshire, 1708-1802 *9228.50 p526*
Putnam, William; America, 1772 *1220.12 p653*
Putnam Family ; Salem, MA, 1751 *9228.50 p165*
Putt, Grace; Barbados, 1688 *1220.12 p653*
Putt, Richard; America, 1759 *1220.12 p653*
Putten, Daniel; America, 1753 *1220.12 p653*
Puttenden, John; America, 1753 *1220.12 p653*
Puttenham, William; America, 1772 *1220.12 p653*
Puttick, James; North Carolina, 1835 *1088.45 p27*
Puttman, James; America, 1685 *1220.12 p653*

Puttman, William; America, 1685 *1220.12 p653*
Puttrich, Rud.; Valdivia, Chile, 1852 *1192.4 p54*
Putts, Jacob; Texas, 1878 *6015.15 p29*
Puttyford, John; America, 1762 *1220.12 p653*
Putz, Jacob; Texas, 1878 *6015.15 p29*
Putz, Margarethe Fox 19 SEE Putz, Peter
Putz, Peter; America, 1868 *5475.1 p239*
 Wife: Margarethe Fox
Putze, Ernst Friedrich Louis; America, 1867 *7919.3 p528*
Putzkuhl, Anna C. R. Steffins SEE Putzkuhl, John Henry
Putzkuhl, Anna Maria Christina SEE Putzkuhl, John Henry
Putzkuhl, John Henry; Philadelphia, 1867 *8513.31 p421*
 Wife: Anna C. R. Steffins
 Child: Maria Elvira Theresa
 Child: Anna Maria Christina
Putzkuhl, Maria Elvira Theresa SEE Putzkuhl, John Henry
Puy, William; America, 1700 *1220.12 p653*
PuyBert, Zenon 40; Port uncertain, 1848 *778.6 p276*
Puyssegur, Jean 44; New Orleans, 1845 *778.6 p276*
Puzewicz, Felix; Detroit, 1929-1930 *6214.5 p65*
Pyall, David; America, 1772 *1220.12 p653*
Pyall, John; America, 1772 *1220.12 p653*
Pyatt, James 41; Ontario, 1871 *1823.21 p303*
Pybee, Alexander; America, 1743 *1220.12 p653*
Pybers, Thomas 26; Ontario, 1871 *1823.21 p303*
Pybus, Richard; Barbados, 1665 *1220.12 p653*
Pycroft, John; America, 1773 *1220.12 p653*
Pye, Henry 44; Ontario, 1871 *1823.17 p135*
Pye, John; America, 1730 *1220.12 p653*
Pye, John; America, 1751 *1220.12 p653*
Pye, John; America, 1772 *1220.12 p653*

Pye, John; St. John, N.B., 1847 *2978.15 p36*
Pye, Mary; Maryland, 1737 *1220.12 p653*
Pye, Richard; America, 1752 *1220.12 p653*
Pye, Thos; St. John, N.B., 1847 *2978.15 p38*
Pye, Tom; St. John, N.B., 1847 *2978.15 p38*
Pye, William; America, 1760 *1220.12 p653*
Pye, Wm.; St. John, N.B., 1847 *2978.15 p36*
Pye, Wm.; St. John, N.B., 1847 *2978.15 p38*
Pyechly, James; Virginia, 1741 *1220.12 p653*
Pyhala, Eino 20; Minnesota, 1925 *2769.54 p1380*
Pyhala, Emil 21; Minnesota, 1925 *2769.54 p1380*
Pyhala, Esther 19; Minnesota, 1925 *2769.54 p1380*
Pyhala, Hannah 17; Minnesota, 1925 *2769.54 p1380*
Pyke, Eilzsha; America, 1739 *1220.12 p628*
Pyke, Florence 11; Quebec, 1870 *8364.32 p25*
Pyke, John; Maryland, 1737 *1220.12 p628*
Pyke, John; Virginia, 1749 *1220.12 p628*
Pyke, Ruben; America, 1726 *1220.12 p629*
Pyke, Thomas; America, 1736 *1220.12 p629*
Pyke, William; America, 1754 *1220.12 p629*
Pyle, William; America, 1720 *1220.12 p629*
Pymer, Robert 65; Ontario, 1871 *1823.17 p135*
Pyne, Charles; America, 1770 *1220.12 p630*
Pyne, Richard; America, 1685 *1220.12 p630*
Pyner, John; America, 1774 *1220.12 p630*
Pyner, Thomas; America, 1751 *1220.12 p630*
Pyner, William; America, 1773 *1220.12 p630*
Pynes, Mary; Barbados or Jamaica, 1697 *1220.12 p630*
Pynn, William; Barbados, 1708 *1220.12 p630*
Pynner, John; Barbados, 1669 *1220.12 p630*
Pyper, John; America, 1764 *1220.12 p631*
Pyper, Thomas; America, 1764 *1220.12 p631*

Q

Quackinbush, Isaac 77; Ontario, 1871 *1823.21 p303*
Quade, Gustav; Wisconsin, 1884 *6795.8 p205*
Quade, Joseph; Ohio, 1809-1852 *4511.35 p41*
Quade, Wilhelm; Wisconsin, 1899 *6795.8 p118*
Quail, Jane; Philadelphia, 1853 *8513.31 p303*
Quail, Richard; Virginia, 1732 *1220.12 p654*
Quale, Edward; Annapolis, MD, 1722 *1220.12 p654*
Quales, Jany; Boston, 1766 *1642 p36*
Qualline, August 17; Galveston, TX, 1844 *3967.10 p371*
Qualline, Christine 22; Galveston, TX, 1844 *3967.10 p371*
Qualline, Clarine 23; Galveston, TX, 1844 *3967.10 p371*
Qualline, Franz 48; Galveston, TX, 1844 *3967.10 p371*
Qualline, Julie 18; Galveston, TX, 1844 *3967.10 p371*
Qualline, Therese 12; Galveston, TX, 1844 *3967.10 p371*
Quance, Henry 30; Ontario, 1871 *1823.17 p135*
Quant, Henry; America, 1685 *1220.12 p654*
Quant, William; Barbados, 1690 *1220.12 p654*
Quanteril, Robert 40; Ontario, 1871 *1823.17 p135*
Quantin, Claude 38; Quebec, 1635 *9221.17 p42*
Quantius, Anthony; Wisconsin, 1883 *6795.8 p179*
Quantrill, Prettyman; America, 1770 *1220.12 p654*
Quappe, Julius; Valdivia, Chile, 1850 *1192.4 p49*
Quard, James 1; New York, NY, 1883 *8427.14 p45*
Quard, John 11; New York, NY, 1883 *8427.14 p45*
Quard, Kate 45; New York, NY, 1883 *8427.14 p45*
Quard, Margaret 15; New York, NY, 1883 *8427.14 p45*
Quard, Mary 10; New York, NY, 1883 *8427.14 p45*
Quard, Patrick 8; New York, NY, 1883 *8427.14 p45*
Quard, William 4; New York, NY, 1883 *8427.14 p45*
Quarindon, William; America, 1745 *1220.12 p654*
Quarino, Risolino; Louisiana, 1874 *4981.45 p133*
Quarles, John; Barbados, 1679 *1220.12 p654*
Quarm, Elizabeth; Utah, 1866 *9228.50 p526*
  *Relative:*Theresa
Quarm, Theresa *SEE* Quarm, Elizabeth
Quarn, Robert; Utah, 1862 *9228.50 p526*
  *Relative:*William
Quarn, William *SEE* Quarn, Robert
Quarrington, Henry; America, 1698 *1220.12 p654*
Quarry, Henry 35; Ontario, 1871 *1823.21 p303*
Quarry, James 63; Ontario, 1871 *1823.21 p303*
Quarry, William 36; Ontario, 1871 *1823.21 p303*
Quarstman, Peter Johan; Washington, 1889 *2770.40 p80*
Quarte, Theodor; Wisconsin, 1880 *6795.8 p107*
Quartemont, A.phonse; Wisconsin, 1856 *1494.20 p11*
Quarterman, John; Maryland, 1742 *1220.12 p654*
Quartier, Helene 18; Quebec, 1657 *9221.17 p366*
Quast, Wilhelm; Wisconsin, 1868 *6795.8 p43*
Quatier, Anna 21; New York, NY, 1886 *6954.7 p40*
Quatier, Barbara 52; New York, NY, 1886 *6954.7 p40*
Quatier, Dorothea 25; New York, NY, 1876 *6954.7 p39*
Quatier, Elisabeth 68; New York, NY, 1885 *6954.7 p40*
Quatier, Friedrich 52; New York, NY, 1886 *6954.7 p40*
Quatier, Heinrich 8; New York, NY, 1886 *6954.7 p40*
Quatier, Heinrich 12; New York, NY, 1876 *6954.7 p39*
Quatier, Heinrich 24; New York, NY, 1885 *6954.7 p40*
Quatier, Johann 8 months; New York, NY, 1876 *6954.7 p39*
Quatier, Katharina 23; New York, NY, 1886 *6954.7 p40*
Quatier, Lorenz 70; New York, NY, 1885 *6954.7 p40*
Quatier, Lydia 6 months; New York, NY, 1886 *6954.7 p40*
Quatier, Michael 35; New York, NY, 1876 *6954.7 p39*
Quatier, Therisia 18; New York, NY, 1886 *6954.7 p40*
Quatier, Wilhelm 9; New York, NY, 1876 *6954.7 p40*
Quatier, Wilhelm 9; New York, NY, 1886 *6954.7 p40*
Quatrevaux, Pierre; Quebec, 1642 *9221.17 p121*

Queal, John; America, 1767 *1220.12 p654*
Quee, Ole S.; Iowa, 1897 *1211.15 p18*
Quee, Sam S.; Iowa, 1896 *1211.15 p18*
Queel, Robert; America, 1765 *1220.12 p654*
Queen, Edward 28; Ontario, 1871 *1823.17 p135*
Queen, Richard; Virginia, 1721 *1220.12 p654*
Queen, Robert 30; Ontario, 1871 *1823.21 p303*
Queenton, George 60; Ontario, 1871 *1823.21 p303*
Quelch, Moses; America, 1751 *1220.12 p654*
Quelenec, Hannah; Boston, 1719 *9228.50 p310*
Quelin, Mary 16; Ontario, 1871 *1823.17 p136*
Quell, Dorothea Lehner *SEE* Quell, Franz
Quell, Franz; New York, 1852 *5475.1 p70*
  *Wife:*Dorothea Lehner
Quelquejeu, Mrs. 50; New Orleans, 1841 *778.6 p276*
Quelsh, John; America, 1680 *1220.12 p654*
Quelsh, William; America, 1766 *1220.12 p654*
Quelve, Jeanne; Quebec, 1671 *4514.3 p360*
Quen, Charles; Quebec, 1649 *9221.17 p215*
Quenault, Elizabeth Mary Ann; Quebec, 1893 *9228.50 p116*
Quenault, Elizabeth Mary Ann; Quebec, 1893 *9228.50 p526*
Quennell, Elizabeth; America, 1683 *1220.12 p655*
Quentin, Mr. 30; America, 1848 *778.6 p276*
Quentin, Gabriel; Quebec, 1659 *9221.17 p414*
Quentin, Jean 20; Montreal, 1662 *9221.17 p499*
Quentin, Jeanne; Quebec, 1673 *4514.3 p360*
Quentin, Julien; Quebec, 1650 *9221.17 p229*
Quentin, Nicolas 27; Quebec, 1655 *9221.17 p328*
Quenzer, Adam 7; New York, NY, 1898 *7951.13 p42*
Quenzer, Elisabeth 10; New York, NY, 1898 *7951.13 p42*
Quenzer, Jacob 3; New York, NY, 1898 *7951.13 p42*
Quenzer, Johann 9; New York, NY, 1898 *7951.13 p42*
Quenzer, Johann 34; New York, NY, 1898 *7951.13 p42*
Quenzer, Karl 14; New York, NY, 1898 *7951.13 p42*
Quenzer, Karl 44; New York, NY, 1898 *7951.13 p42*
Quenzer, Katherina 1; New York, NY, 1898 *7951.13 p42*
Quenzer, Katherina 12; New York, NY, 1898 *7951.13 p42*
Quenzer, Katherina 34; New York, NY, 1898 *7951.13 p42*
Quenzer, Katherina 36; New York, NY, 1898 *7951.13 p42*
Quenzer, Magdalena 2; New York, NY, 1898 *7951.13 p42*
Quenzer, Magdalena 4 months; New York, NY, 1898 *7951.13 p42*
Quequejeu, Marie; Quebec, 1667 *4514.3 p360*
Quercy, Raymond 34; Quebec, 1638 *9221.17 p80*
Queree, Ann; Massachusetts, 1900-1940 *9228.50 p418*
Queree, Ann; Massachusetts, 1907 *9228.50 p526*
Queree, Anne; Massachusetts, 1907 *9228.50 p418*
  *Child:*Philippe
  *Child:*Christine
  *Child:*Ophelia
  *Child:*Philip
  *Child:*Theophilus
  *Child:*Eveline
  *Child:*Lydia
  *Child:*Joshua, Jr.
Queree, Marie; New Brunswick, 1800-1899 *9228.50 p505*
Queree, Simon; Canada, 1700-1789 *9228.50 p526*
Querfurth, Carl Adolph David; Wisconsin, 1868 *6795.8 p104*

Queripel, Archibald Edward; Massachusetts, 1903-1929 *9228.50 p527*
Queripel, Austin Enright; New Jersey, 1905-1927 *9228.50 p527*
Queripel, Benjamin 20; New Bedford, MA, 1882 *9228.50 p528*
Queripel, Cecile Elise Mary; New Jersey, 1900-1983 *9228.50 p527*
Queripel, Lydia Moriah; New Jersey, 1927-1928 *9228.50 p527*
Queripel, Nancy; New Jersey, 1862 *9228.50 p528*
Queripel, Sydney; Massachusetts, 1934 *9228.50 p527*
Queripel, William; San Francisco, 1880 *9228.50 p526*
Queripel, William Torrens Le Provost; Connecticut, 1920 *9228.50 p526*
Querk, John; America, 1758 *1220.12 p654*
Querk, John; Boston, 1678 *1642 p11*
Querk, Margaret; America, 1764 *1220.12 p654*
Querk, Margaret; Boston, 1769 *1642 p49*
Querri, Richard; America, 1770 *1220.12 p654*
Queruee, Simon; Canada, 1700-1789 *9228.50 p526*
Query, William; North Carolina, 1740 *9228.50 p526*
Quesnel, Pierre; Montreal, 1643 *9221.17 p137*
Quesnel, Robert; Portsmouth, NH, 1671 *9228.50 p311*
Quesnell, Magdalen; Virginia, 1726 *1220.12 p655*
Queyrouze, Leon; Louisiana, 1836-1841 *4981.45 p209*
Quick, Calvin 57; Ontario, 1871 *1823.21 p303*
Quick, Christina; St. Paul, MN, 1882 *1865.50 p107*
Quick, Elizabeth; America, 1721 *1220.12 p654*
Quick, Harriett 33; Michigan, 1880 *4491.36 p17*
Quick, Henry; America, 1685 *1220.12 p654*
Quick, Hugh; America, 1738 *1220.12 p654*
Quick, Ingrid *SEE* Quick, Solomon
Quick, Isreal 27; Ontario, 1871 *1823.21 p303*
Quick, Jacob 25; Michigan, 1880 *4491.36 p17*
Quick, James 24; Ontario, 1871 *1823.21 p303*
Quick, James 40; Ontario, 1871 *1823.21 p303*
Quick, James 49; Ontario, 1871 *1823.21 p303*
Quick, Jane 49; Ontario, 1871 *1823.21 p303*
Quick, John; America, 1685 *1220.12 p654*
Quick, John; Maryland, 1738 *1220.12 p654*
Quick, Louis W.; St. Paul, MN, 1881-1882 *1865.50 p107*
Quick, Robert; America, 1728 *1220.12 p654*
Quick, Robert; America, 1764 *1220.12 p654*
Quick, Robert 27; Ontario, 1871 *1823.21 p303*
Quick, Roger; America, 1775 *1220.12 p654*
Quick, Soloman; Ontario, 1787 *1276.15 p230*
  With child & relative
Quick, Solomon; St. Paul, MN, 1868 *1865.50 p107*
  *Wife:*Ingrid
Quick, Thomas; America, 1685 *1220.12 p654*
Quick, Thomas; America, 1685 *1220.12 p654*
Quick, William 35; Ontario, 1871 *1823.21 p304*
Quick, William 39; Ontario, 1871 *1823.21 p303*
Quick, William 71; Ontario, 1871 *1823.21 p303*
Quickley, Bartholomew; America, 1746 *1220.12 p654*
Quictet, Jean; Virginia, 1700 *9230.15 p80*
  With wife & child
Quiet, John 60; Ontario, 1871 *1823.21 p304*
Quig, James 26; New York, NY, 1825 *6178.50 p78*
Quig, John 28; New York, NY, 1825 *6178.50 p76*
Quig, Mary; Boston, 1756 *1642 p47*
Quigby, Silvester 40; Ontario, 1871 *1823.21 p304*
Quiggin, Cathrine 38; Ontario, 1871 *1823.21 p304*
Quiggin, Ellen 40; Ontario, 1871 *1823.21 p304*
Quigley, Bridget; New Orleans, 1851 *7242.30 p152*
Quigley, Dennis 29; Ontario, 1871 *1823.21 p304*
Quigley, Edward; Long Island, 1778 *8529.30 p10A*

Quigley, James; New Orleans, 1851 *7242.30 p152*
Quigley, James; Newfoundland, 1814 *3476.10 p54*
Quigley, James 40; Ontario, 1871 *1823.21 p304*
Quigley, John; Louisiana, 1874-1875 *4981.45 p30*
Quigley, John 77; Ontario, 1871 *1823.21 p304*
Quigley, Patrick; North Carolina, 1850-1853 *1088.45 p28*
Quigley, Patrick 39; Ontario, 1871 *1823.21 p304*
Quigley, Susan 10; Quebec, 1870 *8364.32 p25*
Quigley, Thomas 70; Ontario, 1871 *1823.21 p304*
Quigley, Thomas; Toronto, 1844 *2910.35 p116*
Quigley, William 56; Ontario, 1871 *1823.21 p304*
Quigly, Bridget 50; Ontario, 1871 *1823.21 p304*
Quigly, Bryan; Toronto, 1844 *2910.35 p116*
Quigly, Malachy; Toronto, 1844 *2910.35 p116*
Quilcan, John 55; Ontario, 1871 *1823.21 p304*
Quill, John; Boston, 1762 *1642 p48*
Quimby, Peter; America, 1755 *1220.12 p654*
Quin, Bryan; Ohio, 1809-1852 *4511.35 p41*
Quin, Catherine; Boston, 1768 *1642 p49*
Quin, Elizabeth; Marblehead, MA, 1771 *1642 p73*
Quin, Hugh; Massachusetts, 1700-1765 *1642 p117*
Quin, James; Ohio, 1809-1852 *4511.35 p41*
Quin, Jane 58; Ontario, 1871 *1823.21 p304*
Quin, John; America, 1753 *1220.12 p654*
Quin, Joseph; Boston, 1765 *1642 p35*
Quin, Joseph, Jr. 16; Nantucket, MA, 1772 *1642 p89*
Quin, Margaret; America, 1750 *1220.12 p654*
Quin, Margaret; America, 1762 *1220.12 p654*
Quin, Mary; America, 1749 *1220.12 p654*
Quin, Mary; America, 1758 *1220.12 p654*
Quin, Michael; Marblehead, MA, 1768 *1642 p73*
Quin, Patrick; America, 1765 *1220.12 p654*
Quin, Richard; America, 1722 *1220.12 p654*
Quin, Robert; Marblehead, MA, 1771 *1642 p73*
Quin, Thomas; America, 1762 *1220.12 p654*
Quin, Thomas; Philadelphia, 1777 *8529.30 p3*
Quin, William; America, 1765 *1220.12 p654*
Quin, Winifred; America, 1756 *1220.12 p654*
Quincey, John; America, 1761 *1220.12 p654*
Quiner, Mary; Marblehead, MA, 1758 *9228.50 p137*
Quiner, Nicholas; Marblehead, MA, 1773 *9228.50 p529*
Quinlan, Mr.; Toronto, 1844 *2910.35 p116*
Quinlan, J. 17; Quebec, 1870 *8364.32 p25*
Quinlan, John; Ohio, 1809-1852 *4511.35 p41*
Quinlan, Margart 41; Ontario, 1871 *1823.17 p136*
Quinlan, Michael; Washington, 1885 *2770.40 p194*
Quinlan, Thomas; Boston, 1766 *1642 p37*
Quinland, Jno.; Louisiana, 1874-1875 *4981.45 p30*
Quinland, John; Boston, 1728 *1642 p25*
Quinlen, James; Louisiana, 1841-1844 *4981.45 p211*
Quinlin, John 60; Ontario, 1871 *1823.17 p136*
Quinlin, Joseph; Toronto, 1844 *2910.35 p116*

Quinling, John; Ohio, 1809-1852 *4511.35 p41*
Quinlisk, Martin; Ohio, 1840-1897 *8365.35 p17*
Quinlisk, Michael; Ohio, 1840-1897 *8365.35 p17*
Quinlisk, Patrick; Ohio, 1809-1852 *4511.35 p41*
Quinlisk, Patrick; Ohio, 1840-1897 *8365.35 p17*
Quinn, Brigett 60; Ontario, 1871 *1823.21 p304*
Quinn, Charles 64; Ontario, 1871 *1823.21 p304*
Quinn, Charles 64; Ontario, 1871 *1823.21 p304*
Quinn, Charles; Toronto, 1844 *2910.35 p115*
Quinn, Daniel 40; Ontario, 1871 *1823.21 p304*
Quinn, Edward; Annapolis, MD, 1725 *1220.12 p654*
Quinn, Edward; North Carolina, 1808-1814 *1088.45 p28*
Quinn, Elizabeth *SEE* Quinn, William
Quinn, Ellen 19; Quebec, 1870 *8364.32 p25*
Quinn, George *SEE* Quinn, William
Quinn, Harriet *SEE* Quinn, William
Quinn, Isabella *SEE* Quinn, William
Quinn, James; North Carolina, 1856 *1088.45 p28*
Quinn, James 65; Ontario, 1871 *1823.17 p136*
Quinn, James; South Carolina, 1813 *3208.30 p19*
Quinn, James; South Carolina, 1813 *3208.30 p31*
Quinn, James 50; South Carolina, 1812 *3476.30 p13*
Quinn, John; Boston, 1730 *1642 p44*
Quinn, John 30; Ontario, 1871 *1823.21 p304*
Quinn, John 33; Ontario, 1871 *1823.21 p304*
Quinn, Joseph; Nantucket, MA, 1700-1799 *1642 p89*
Quinn, Joseph Hyrum *SEE* Quinn, William
Quinn, Laughlin; Toronto, 1844 *2910.35 p115*
Quinn, Louisa 16; Quebec, 1870 *8364.32 p25*
Quinn, Mary; Nantucket, MA, 1771 *1642 p89*
Quinn, Mary Ann *SEE* Quinn, William
Quinn, Mary Ann Hosking *SEE* Quinn, William
Quinn, Mary Jean; New York, 1929-1957 *9228.50 p337*
Quinn, Mic; St. John, N.B., 1848 *2978.15 p38*
Quinn, Michael; Louisiana, 1874-1875 *4981.45 p30*
Quinn, Michael; Louisiana, 1874 *4981.45 p133*
Quinn, Neal; Jamaica, 1778 *8529.30 p14A*
Quinn, Oliver; Bangor, ME, 1814 *3274.55 p27*
Quinn, Owen; Illinois, 1858-1861 *6020.5 p132*
Quinn, Pat; St. John, N.B., 1848 *2978.15 p40*
Quinn, Patrick 50; Ontario, 1871 *1823.21 p304*
Quinn, Patrick; Toronto, 1844 *2910.35 p114*
Quinn, Terence 58; Ontario, 1871 *1823.21 p304*
Quinn, Thomas; America, 1771 *1220.12 p654*
Quinn, Thomas; Louisiana, 1836-1841 *4981.45 p209*
Quinn, William 40; Ontario, 1871 *1823.21 p304*
Quinn, William; Utah, 1856 *9228.50 p530*
  *Wife:*Mary Ann Hosking
  *Child:*Joseph Hyrum
  *Child:*Isabella
  *Child:*Mary Ann
  *Child:*Harriet

  *Child:*George
  *Child:*Elizabeth
  *Child:*William R.
Quinn, William R. *SEE* Quinn, William
Quinn, Wm 35; St. Johns, N.F., 1811 *1053.20 p20*
Quinn, Wm. 24; South Carolina, 1812 *3476.30 p13*
Quinnell, Ann; America, 1741 *1220.12 p654*
Quinones, Elucterio 16; Ontario, 1871 *1823.21 p304*
Quinones, Francisco 14; Ontario, 1871 *1823.21 p304*
Quinqueneau, Marie; Canada, 1668 *1142.10 p129*
Quint, Agnes 24; Valdivia, Chile, 1852 *1192.4 p54*
Quint, Andrew; America, 1747 *1220.12 p655*
Quint, Crisset; Annapolis, MD, 1736 *1220.12 p655*
Quintal, Francois 16; Quebec, 1662 *9221.17 p492*
Quinton, Alex 21; New York, NY, 1835 *5024.1 p137*
Quinton, John; America, 1679 *1220.12 p655*
Quinton, John; Virginia, 1765 *1220.12 p655*
Quinton, Thomas; America, 1771 *1220.12 p655*
Quirim, Wm. 24; South Carolina, 1812 *3476.30 p13*
Quirin, Barbara; America, 1884 *5475.1 p69*
Quirin, Barbara; Pennsylvania, 1880 *5475.1 p22*
Quirk, David; Boston, 1766 *1642 p37*
Quirk, Margrett 25; Ontario, 1871 *1823.21 p304*
Quirk, Richard; Boston, 1766 *1642 p37*
Quirk, William; Boston, 1766 *1642 p37*
Quisse, James 50; South Carolina, 1812 *3476.30 p13*
Quisse, Francois 10; Texas, 1843 *778.6 p276*
Quisse, Jeanne Josette 14; Texas, 1843 *778.6 p276*
Quisse, Jeanne Josette 16; Texas, 1843 *778.6 p276*
Quisse, Marie Constance 7; Texas, 1843 *778.6 p276*
Quist, Bengt; Colorado, 1887 *1029.59 p76*
Quist, Charles Mikkelsen; Iowa, 1913 *1211.15 p18*
Quitafield, Abraham; Marblehead, MA, 1681 *9228.50 p312*
Quitel, Marthe; Quebec, 1665 *4514.3 p361*
Quiterfield, Clement; Connecticut, 1702 *9228.50 p530*
Quittenden, Sarah; America, 1751 *1220.12 p655*
Quitty, Daniel; Annapolis, MD, 1719 *1220.12 p655*
Qunin, Margaret 40; Ontario, 1871 *1823.21 p304*
Quynn, John; America, 1742 *1220.12 p654*
Qveck, Christina; St. Paul, MN, 1882 *1865.50 p107*
Qveck, Ingrid *SEE* Qveck, Salomon
Qveck, Lars W.; St. Paul, MN, 1881-1882 *1865.50 p107*
Qveck, Salomon; St. Paul, MN, 1868 *1865.50 p107*
  *Wife:*Ingrid
Qvick, Anna G.; St. Paul, MN, 1873 *1865.50 p110*
Qvick, Anna G.; St. Paul, MN, 1873 *1865.50 p110*
Qvick, Christina; St. Paul, MN, 1882 *1865.50 p107*
Qvick, Ingrid *SEE* Qvick, Salomon
Qvick, Lars W.; St. Paul, MN, 1881-1882 *1865.50 p107*
Qvick, Salomon; St. Paul, MN, 1868 *1865.50 p107*
  *Wife:*Ingrid

R

Raab, Adam; America, 1857 *2526.43 p191*
Raab, Adam 8 *SEE* Raab, Michael
Raab, Anna Maria 4 *SEE* Raab, Michael
Raab, Elisabetha 2 *SEE* Raab, Michael
Raab, Michael; America, 1844 *2526.43 p212*
  With wife
  *Daughter:*Elisabetha
  *Daughter:*Anna Maria
  *Son:*Michael
  *Son:*Adam
Raab, Michael 10 *SEE* Raab, Michael
Raab, William; New York, 1859 *358.56 p99*
Raase, Amalie 7; New York, NY, 1883 *5475.1 p16*
Raase, Dorothea 9; New York, NY, 1883 *5475.1 p16*
Raase, Fritz 2; New York, NY, 1883 *5475.1 p16*
Raase, Heinrich 10 months; New York, NY, 1883 *5475.1 p16*
Raase, Sophie 4; New York, NY, 1883 *5475.1 p16*
Raase, Sophie 26; New York, NY, 1883 *5475.1 p16*
Raatz, Anna Maria Louise; Wisconsin, 1891 *6795.8 p227*
Raatz, Aug. Hermann; Wisconsin, 1892 *6795.8 p217*
Raatz, Hanna Henrietta *SEE* Raatz, Wilhelm Albert
Raatz, Wilhelm Albert; Wisconsin, 1875 *6795.8 p17*
  *Wife:*Hanna Henrietta
  With children
Rab, Carl 20; America, 1845 *778.6 p276*
Rab..., Christopher; North Carolina, 1852 *1088.45 p28*
Rab, Dorothea 20; America, 1845 *778.6 p276*
Rab, Jean 58; America, 1845 *778.6 p276*
Rabady, Anne; Quebec, 1672 *4514.3 p361*
Rabay, James; Boston, 1760-1769 *9228.50 p532*
Rabbetts, Thomas; America, 1753 *1220.12 p656*
Rabe, Ann; Ohio, 1781-1866 *9228.50 p532*
Rabe, Friedrich Ferdinand; America, 1850 *7420.1 p74*
Rabe, William; Ohio, 1796-1876 *9228.50 p532*
Rabehl, Friedrich Michael; Wisconsin, 1891 *6795.8 p75*
Rabehl, Karl Ludwig; Wisconsin, 1870 *6795.8 p75*
Rabellain, Jacques; Quebec, 1645 *9221.17 p157*
Rabeneck, Dick; Louisiana, 1874-1875 *4981.45 p30*
Rabeneck, Her.; Louisiana, 1874-1875 *4981.45 p30*
Rabenschantz, Nikolaus 31; Galveston, TX, 1846 *3967.10 p378*
Rabenstein, Carl E.; Tennessee, 1904 *3665.20 p112*
Raber, Elise 21 *SEE* Raber, J. N.
Raber, J. N. 27; Rio Grande do Sul, Brazil, 1854 *5475.1 p532*
  *Wife:*Elise 21
Rabert, Jean 23; New Orleans, 1843 *778.6 p276*
Rabey, Daniel; New York, n.d. *9228.50 p532*
  *Relative:*Luther
Rabey, David; New York, 1800-1899 *9228.50 p532*
Rabey, David T.; North America, 1875-1975 *9228.50 p198*
Rabey, Elizabeth; America, n.d. *9228.50 p532*
Rabey, Henry; Ohio, 1830 *9228.50 p532*
Rabey, Kathryn; New England, 1637 *9228.50 p532*
Rabey, Luther *SEE* Rabey, Daniel
Rabey, William; Ohio, 1796-1876 *9228.50 p532*
Rabke, Carl Ludwig; America, 1853 *7420.1 p110*
  With son & 2 daughters
Rableau, Florimonde; Quebec, 1665 *4514.3 p361*
Rabnett, James; America, 1751 *1220.12 p656*
Raboteau, Mr. 50; Louisiana, 1848 *778.6 p277*
Raboteau, Mr. 40; New Orleans, 1842 *778.6 p277*
Rabouin, Jean 18; Quebec, 1656 *9221.17 p346*
Rabstejnek, Tomas L.; St. Vincent, PA, 1877 *2853.20 p247*
Rabstock, Joseph; Ohio, 1809-1852 *4511.35 p41*

Raby, Louis 30; America, 1843 *778.6 p277*
Raby, Louis 32; Galveston, TX, 1845 *3967.10 p376*
Raby, Richard; America, 1774 *1220.12 p656*
Raby, William 66; Ontario, 1871 *1823.21 p304*
Race, Charles; America, 1775 *1220.12 p656*
Race, Thomas; America, 1771 *1220.12 p656*
Racek, Bohdan; Wisconsin, 1852 *2853.20 p333*
Racek, Louisa 20; Ontario, 1871 *1823.21 p304*
Racey, Helen Matilda; Detroit, 1866 *9228.50 p489*
Rachon, Maria 19; America, 1841 *778.6 p277*
Rachow, Christian; New York, 1860 *358.56 p4*
Rachwal, Antoni 18; New York, NY, 1911 *6533.11 p9*
Racine, Claude; Quebec, 1637 *9221.17 p72*
Racine, Etienne 30; Quebec, 1637 *9221.17 p72*
Racine, Francis 26; Louisiana, 1840 *778.6 p277*
Racine, H. F. W.; Louisiana, 1836-1840 *4981.45 p213*
Rack, John; America, 1735 *1220.12 p656*
Rackett, Alice; Potomac, 1742 *1220.12 p656*
Rackley, Elizabeth; America, 1767 *1220.12 p656*
Rackley, James; America, 1768 *1220.12 p656*
Raclos, Francoise; Quebec, 1671 *4514.3 p361*
  *Father:*Godebon
  *Sister:*Madeleine
  *Sister:*Marie
Raclos, Godebon *SEE* Raclos, Francoise
Raclos, Madeleine *SEE* Raclos, Francoise
Raclos, Marie *SEE* Raclos, Francoise
Radborn, John; America, 1754 *1220.12 p656*
Radborne, Thomas; America, 1754 *1220.12 p656*
Radcliff, James; America, 1757 *1220.12 p656*
Radcliff, Joseph; America, 1752 *1220.12 p656*
Radcliff, Mary 38; Ontario, 1871 *1823.17 p136*
Radcliff, Thomas; Ohio, 1840 *2763.1 p21*
Radcliff, William 65; Ontario, 1871 *1823.21 p304*
Radcliffe, John; America, 1775 *1220.12 p656*
Radcliffe, Mary; America, 1752 *1220.12 p656*
Radcliffe, Thomas; America, 1757 *1220.12 p656*
Raddall, Charles; America, 1730 *1220.12 p656*
Radden, B.; Louisiana, 1874-1875 *4981.45 p297*
Raddigan, John 50; Ontario, 1871 *1823.17 p136*
Rade, Thomas; America, 1755 *1220.12 p656*
Radelet, Louis J.; New York, NY, 1872 *1494.21 p31*
Radely, Charles; America, 1737 *1220.12 p656*
Rademacher, Wilhelmine; Chicago, 1905-1950 *8023.44 p378*
Raden, Uslier; Boston, 1773 *1642 p49*
Raderstorff, Andrew; Ohio, 1809-1852 *4511.35 p41*
Radetzky, Friedrich; Wisconsin, 1866 *6795.8 p26*
Radford, Alice Ann Marriette *SEE* Radford, Frederick
Radford, Alice May *SEE* Radford, Frederick
Radford, Anne; Virginia, 1731 *1220.12 p656*
Radford, Cornelius; America, 1685 *1220.12 p656*
Radford, Frederick; Massachusetts, 1913 *9228.50 p532*
  *Wife:*Alice Ann Marriette
  *Daughter:*Alice May
Radford, George; Virginia, 1738 *1220.12 p656*
Radford, John; America, 1773 *1220.12 p656*
Radford, Mary; Maryland, 1730 *1220.12 p656*
Radford, Mordecai; America, 1678 *1220.12 p656*
Radford, Richard; America, 1757 *1220.12 p656*
Radford, Sarah; America, 1771 *1220.12 p656*
Radford, Thomas; America, 1736 *1220.12 p656*
Radford, Walter; America, 1738 *1220.12 p656*
Radgen, Martin; North Carolina, 1850 *1088.45 p28*
Radichel, August; Wisconsin, 1880 *6795.8 p227*
Radichel, H.J.A.; Wisconsin, 1876 *6795.8 p227*
Radichel, Heinrich; Wisconsin, 1878 *6795.8 p227*
Radichel, Herman; Wisconsin, 1879 *6795.8 p227*

Radigan, Annie 22; Ontario, 1871 *1823.17 p136*
Radisch, Edward; Philadelphia, 1856 *8513.31 p422*
  *Wife:*Huelda Boerner
Radisch, Huelda Boerner *SEE* Radisch, Edward
Radish, Alse; Died enroute, 1725 *1220.12 p656*
Radisson, Elisabeth 9; Quebec, 1646 *9221.17 p168*
Radisson, Pierre-Esprit 11; Quebec, 1651 *9221.17 p250*
Radke, Albertine; Wisconsin, 1890 *6795.8 p42*
Radke, August; Wisconsin, 1881 *6795.8 p107*
Radke, Caroline *SEE* Radke, Daniel
Radke, Daniel; North Dakota, 1890 *554.30 p26*
  *Wife:*Caroline
Radke, Edward; Wisconsin, 1875 *6795.8 p205*
Radke, Johann; Wisconsin, 1879 *6795.8 p37*
Radke, Samuel 27; New York, NY, 1893 *1883.7 p37*
Radko, Michal; Detroit, 1930 *1640.60 p81*
Radley, George; America, 1726 *1220.12 p656*
Radley, Joseph; America, 1752 *1220.12 p656*
Radley, Thomas; America, 1765 *1220.12 p656*
Radliff, Robert 47; Ontario, 1871 *1823.21 p304*
Radloff, Ludwig Andreas; America, 1867 *7919.3 p530*
Radmore, Edward; Virginia, 1749 *1220.12 p656*
Radosta, Gueiseppi; Louisiana, 1874-1875 *4981.45 p30*
Radsch, Gustav; Wisconsin, 1871 *6795.8 p118*
Radschweit, August; Wisconsin, 1896 *6795.8 p82*
Radschweit, Edward August; Wisconsin, 1897 *6795.8 p94*
Radtke, August; Wisconsin, 1878 *6795.8 p75*
Radtke, Gustavus Robert; Wisconsin, 1885 *6795.8 p188*
Radtke, Martin Ludwig; Wisconsin, 1859 *6795.8 p26*
Raduchel, Anna Bertha Wilhelmine; Wisconsin, 1896 *6795.8 p220*
Raduchel, August; Wisconsin, 1905 *6795.8 p220*
Radwell, Bernard; America, 1766 *1220.12 p656*
Radwell, Johanna; America, 1720 *1220.12 p656*
Radwell, Robert; America, 1747 *1220.12 p656*
Radwell, Thomas; America, 1731 *1220.12 p656*
Rae, Agnes 79; Ontario, 1871 *1823.17 p136*
Rae, Andrew 46; Ontario, 1871 *1823.17 p136*
Rae, Harvy 36; Ontario, 1871 *1823.17 p136*
Rae, James R. 23; Quebec, 1910 *2897.7 p10*
Rae, Janet 63; Ontario, 1871 *1823.21 p304*
Rae, John 22; Ontario, 1871 *1823.21 p304*
Rae, John; Washington, 1887 *2770.40 p25*
Rae, Robert 49; Ontario, 1871 *1823.21 p304*
Rae, Robert M. 49; Ontario, 1871 *1823.17 p136*
Rae, Thomas 16; Ontario, 1871 *1823.21 p304*
Rae, Thomas 31; Ontario, 1871 *1823.21 p304*
Rae, William 45; Ontario, 1871 *1823.21 p304*
Rae, William 57; Ontario, 1871 *1823.21 p304*
Raegen, John; Boston, 1744 *1642 p45*
Rafala, Johan 17; Halifax, N.S., 1902 *1860.4 p44*
Rafalska, Catharine; Detroit, 1890 *9980.23 p96*
Rafalski, Marion; Detroit, 1890 *9980.23 p96*
Raffael, Louis 29; America, 1845 *778.6 p277*
Rafferty, William; New Orleans, 1851 *7242.30 p152*
Rafford, William; America, 1727 *1220.12 p656*
Rafter, Ed; St. John, N.B., 1847 *2978.15 p36*
Rafter, Francis; St. John, N.B., 1847 *2978.15 p37*
Rafter, Patrick; North Carolina, 1857 *1088.45 p28*
Rafter, Thos; St. John, N.B., 1847 *2978.15 p37*
Raftopoilis, Constantinos; New York, NY, 1913 *3331.4 p12*
Ragan, James; America, 1750 *1220.12 p666*
Ragan, John 40; Ontario, 1871 *1823.21 p304*
Ragan, William; America, 1773 *1220.12 p666*
Rage, Prosper; New York, NY, 1855 *1494.21 p31*
Ragen, Margaret 71; Ontario, 1871 *1823.21 p304*

Ragen, Mary 28; Ontario, 1871 ***1823.21*** *p304*
Rageot, Etienne 40; Quebec, 1660 ***9221.17*** *p439*
Ragg, Isaac; Annapolis, MD, 1720 ***1220.12*** *p656*
Ragg, Susanna; America, 1721 ***1220.12*** *p656*
Raggio, D.; Louisiana, 1874 ***4981.45*** *p296*
Raggioni, Miss 3; Louisiana, 1848 ***778.6*** *p277*
Ragil, Joseph 22; Louisiana, 1848 ***778.6*** *p277*
Ragman, Wilmot; Barbados, 1665 ***1220.12*** *p656*
Ragne, F. A. 25; America, 1848 ***778.6*** *p277*
Ragniau, Jean; Quebec, 1648 ***9221.17*** *p203*
Ragon, Jacques; Quebec, 1643 ***9221.17*** *p134*
Ragot, Genevieve 37; America, 1844 ***778.6*** *p277*
Ragot, Jacques; Quebec, 1643 ***9221.17*** *p134*
Ragot, Louis 17; America, 1844 ***778.6*** *p277*
Ragot, Louis Victor 37; America, 1844 ***778.6*** *p277*
Ragot, Marthe; Quebec, 1663 ***4514.3*** *p361*
Ragueneau, Paul 29; Quebec, 1637 ***9221.17*** *p67*
Raguet, Francois 55; Texas, 1843 ***778.6*** *p277*
Raguette, P. E. 26; America, 1841 ***778.6*** *p277*
Raguideau, Pierre 21; Montreal, 1653 ***9221.17*** *p299*
Rahde, Miss; America, 1833 ***7420.1*** *p7*
Rahdert, Friedrich; America, 1857 ***7420.1*** *p170*
Rahkila, Hilja; Minnesota, 1925-1926 ***2769.54*** *p1382*
Rahlf, Nicolaus; Nebraska, 1905 ***3004.30*** *p46*
Rahlmeyer, August *SEE* Rahlmeyer, Henriette Ahe
Rahlmeyer, Caroline *SEE* Rahlmeyer, Henriette Ahe
Rahlmeyer, Henriette Ahe; America, 1866 ***7420.1*** *p247*
*Daughter:*Caroline
*Son:*August
Rahn, Philip 24; America, 1840 ***778.6*** *p277*
Rahncke, Otto; Washington, 1886 ***2770.40*** *p195*
Rahning, Carl; America, 1854 ***7420.1*** *p127*
With 3 sons
Rahning, Carl; Port uncertain, 1854 ***7420.1*** *p127*
With 3 sons
Rahnstrom, Brita Lorentina Ohman *SEE* Rahnstrom, John G.
Rahnstrom, John *SEE* Rahnstrom, John G.
Rahnstrom, John G.; Kansas, 1869 ***777.40*** *p15*
*Wife:*Brita Lorentina Ohman
*Son:*John
Raich, Anton 20; Minnesota, 1925 ***2769.54*** *p1384*
Raich, Barbara 40; Minnesota, 1925 ***2769.54*** *p1384*
Raidred, Charles 19; Ontario, 1871 ***1823.21*** *p304*
Raife, Mr.; Wisconsin, 1842 ***9228.50*** *p532*
With wife
Raihel, Jacob; Illinois, 1856 ***6079.1*** *p11*
Raillant, Joseph 29; America, 1845 ***778.6*** *p277*
Raillard, Cecile 13; Mexico, 1846 ***778.6*** *p277*
Raillard, Henriette 40; Mexico, 1846 ***778.6*** *p277*
Raillard, Louise 18; Mexico, 1846 ***778.6*** *p277*
Raillard, Rita 4; Mexico, 1846 ***778.6*** *p277*
Railly, Edward; Ohio, 1809-1852 ***4511.35*** *p41*
Raimbault, Jeanne; Quebec, 1668 ***4514.3*** *p361*
Raimont, Mrs. 26; America, 1841 ***778.6*** *p277*
Rainbird, Joseph; America, 1751 ***1220.12*** *p656*
Rainbow, Charles; America, 1767 ***1220.12*** *p656*
Rainbow, Robert; America, 1734 ***1220.12*** *p657*
Rainbow, Robert; Died enroute, 1726 ***1220.12*** *p657*
Raine, James; America, 1765 ***1220.12*** *p657*
Raine, Sarah; America, 1721 ***1220.12*** *p657*
Raine, Simon; Potomac, 1729 ***1220.12*** *p657*
Raines, William; Virginia, 1759 ***1220.12*** *p657*
Rainey, Samuel; North Carolina, 1847 ***1088.45*** *p28*
Rainey, Thomas; South Carolina, 1800-1899 ***6155.4*** *p19*
Rainforth, George, Jr.; America, 1749 ***1220.12*** *p657*
Rainor, John; America, 1753 ***1220.12*** *p657*
Rainsberry, Ellen 30; Ontario, 1871 ***1823.17*** *p136*
Rainsberry, John 37; Ontario, 1871 ***1823.17*** *p136*
Rainsberry, Nicholas; Ontario, 1871 ***1823.17*** *p136*
Rainsbury, Mary; Annapolis, MD, 1725 ***1220.12*** *p657*
Rainsfrow, Thomas; America, 1768 ***1220.12*** *p657*
Rairdon, Bartholomew; America, 1765 ***1220.12*** *p664*
Rairdon, Cornelius; Ohio, 1840-1897 ***8365.35*** *p17*
Rais, Herrmann; America, 1884 ***2526.43*** *p177*
Rais, Jacob; Philadelphia, 1853 ***8513.31*** *p422*
Rais, Joseph; New York, 1897 ***2526.43*** *p177*
Rais, Max; America, 1901 ***2526.43*** *p177*
Raise, William; America, 1765 ***1220.12*** *p657*
Raisin, Charles 44; Ontario, 1871 ***1823.21*** *p304*
Raisin, Marguerite; Quebec, 1670 ***4514.3*** *p362*
Raisin, Marie 23; Montreal, 1659 ***9221.17*** *p415*
Raisin, William 29; Ontario, 1871 ***1823.21*** *p305*
Raisin, Wm 48; Ontario, 1871 ***1823.21*** *p305*
Raisinski, Andrej 35; New York, NY, 1920 ***930.50*** *p49*
Raiskio, Hugo 47; Minnesota, 1926 ***2769.54*** *p1382*
Raisler, Jan; Chicago, 1857 ***2853.20*** *p389*
Raison, . . .; Quebec, 1649 ***9221.17*** *p219*
Raison, Francois; Quebec, 1646 ***9221.17*** *p168*
Raison, Marie Julienne; Wisconsin, 1854-1858 ***1495.20*** *p50*
Raison, Saml 58; Ontario, 1871 ***1823.21*** *p305*
Raivio, Elmer 16; Minnesota, 1925 ***2769.54*** *p1378*
Rajda, Louis; Detroit, 1929 ***1640.55*** *p117*
Rajman, Jar.; New York, NY, 1893 ***2853.20*** *p469*
Rajmund, Ferdinand; Oklahoma, 1889 ***2853.20*** *p372*
Rakes, Weston; America, 1752 ***1220.12*** *p657*
Rakestraw, John; Annapolis, MD, 1725 ***1220.12*** *p657*
Rakowicz, Albin 48; Texas, 1888 ***9980.22*** *p17*
Rakowicz, Joe 34; Texas, 1884 ***9980.22*** *p17*
Ralhaefner, Michael; Ohio, 1809-1852 ***4511.35*** *p41*
Rall, John; Virginia, 1718 ***1220.12*** *p657*
Rallinger, Joseph; Colorado, 1892 ***1029.59*** *p78*
Rallins, Thomas; America, 1757 ***1220.12*** *p661*
Ralph, Catherine; America, 1752 ***1220.12*** *p657*
Ralph, James 29; Ontario, 1871 ***1823.21*** *p305*
Ralph, James 17; Quebec, 1870 ***8364.32*** *p25*
Ralph, James; Virginia, 1730 ***1220.12*** *p657*
Ralph, John; America, 1725 ***1220.12*** *p657*
Ralph, John; America, 1754 ***1220.12*** *p657*
Ralph, John; America, 1763 ***1220.12*** *p657*
Ralph, John; Died enroute, 1725 ***1220.12*** *p657*
Ralph, Thomas; America, 1761 ***1220.12*** *p657*
Ralph, William; America, 1756 ***1220.12*** *p657*
Ralph, William 49; Ontario, 1871 ***1823.17*** *p136*
Ralph, Wm 46; Ontario, 1871 ***1823.21*** *p305*
Ralphs, Richard; Virginia, 1721 ***1220.12*** *p657*
Ramage, Adam; Harrisburg, PA, 1798 ***5720.10*** *p379*
Ramage, Esther-Marie 31; Quebec, 1654 ***9221.17*** *p308*
Ramage, James; America, 1755 ***1220.12*** *p657*
Ramaige, Betty; Boston, 1766 ***1642*** *p36*
Ramakers, Theo; Galveston, TX, 1855 ***571.7*** *p17*
Rambell, Lewis; America, 1768 ***1220.12*** *p657*
Rambridge, Susanna; America, 1733 ***1220.12*** *p657*
Ramel, Jacque 38; Port uncertain, 1843 ***778.6*** *p277*
Ramelot, Louis; New Mexico, 1914 ***4812.1*** *p87*
Ramesire, Nicholas; Ohio, 1809-1852 ***4511.35*** *p41*
Ramezay deLa Gesse, Claude de; Quebec, 1683-1688 ***2314.30*** *p168*
Ramezay deLa Gesse, Claude de; Quebec, 1685 ***2314.30*** *p193*
Ramfray, Louiis 32; New Orleans, 1848 ***778.6*** *p277*
Ramier, Frank 37; America, 1842 ***778.6*** *p277*
Ramier, Pierre; Quebec, 1807 ***9228.50*** *p532*
Ramier, Pierre; Wisconsin, 1841-1864 ***9228.50*** *p532*
Ramley, John; America, 1748 ***1220.12*** *p657*
Ramoisy, Amelie Joseph; Wisconsin, 1855-1858 ***1495.20*** *p67*
Ramoisy, Charles Joseph; Wisconsin, 1855-1858 ***1495.20*** *p67*
Ramoisy, Marie Francoise; Wisconsin, 1855-1858 ***1495.20*** *p67*
Ramonoher, J. 16; New Orleans, 1843 ***778.6*** *p277*
Ramow, Ernst Fredrick; Wisconsin, 1894 ***6795.8*** *p83*
Rampley, James; America, 1764 ***1220.12*** *p657*
Ramplin, James 28; Ontario, 1871 ***1823.21*** *p305*
Ramplin, Nelise 26; Ontario, 1871 ***1823.21*** *p305*
Rampon, C. 40; Port uncertain, 1843 ***778.6*** *p15*
Ramsay, Christopher; Ohio, 1809-1852 ***4511.35*** *p41*
Ramsay, E. 35; Ontario, 1871 ***1823.21*** *p305*
Ramsay, George 39; Ontario, 1871 ***1823.21*** *p305*
Ramsay, George 55; Ontario, 1871 ***1823.17*** *p136*
Ramsay, Hamilton 30; Ontario, 1871 ***1823.21*** *p305*
Ramsay, Robert; Ohio, 1809-1852 ***4511.35*** *p41*
Ramsay, Robert 45; Ontario, 1871 ***1823.21*** *p305*
Ramsay, Robert; Potomac, 1729 ***1220.12*** *p658*
Ramsay, William; Ohio, 1809-1852 ***4511.35*** *p41*
Ramsay, William 52; Ontario, 1871 ***1823.21*** *p305*
Ramsbotham, John; America, 1758 ***1220.12*** *p657*
Ramsbottam, James; America, 1768 ***1220.12*** *p657*
Ramsbottom, Nicholas; America, 1765 ***1220.12*** *p657*
Ramsbottom, Obadiah; Ohio, 1826 ***3580.20*** *p33*
Ramsbottom, Obadiah; Ohio, 1826 ***6020.12*** *p22*
Ramsbottom, Obadiah; Ohio, 1832 ***3580.20*** *p33*
Ramsbottom, Obadiah; Ohio, 1832 ***6020.12*** *p22*
Ramsbottom, Ralph; America, 1769 ***1220.12*** *p657*
Ramsdale, Annie 12; Quebec, 1870 ***8364.32*** *p25*
Ramsdale, Emily 16; Quebec, 1870 ***8364.32*** *p25*
Ramsden, Francis; America, 1741 ***1220.12*** *p657*
Ramsden, Margaret; Barbados, 1665 ***1220.12*** *p657*
Ramsden, Robert; Barbados, 1671 ***1220.12*** *p657*
Ramsden, Squire; America, 1757 ***1220.12*** *p657*
Ramsden, Thomas; America, 1741 ***1220.12*** *p657*
Ramsden, William; America, 1742 ***1220.12*** *p657*
Ramsey, Ann; America, 1751 ***1220.12*** *p657*
Ramsey, Christina 45; Ontario, 1871 ***1823.17*** *p136*
Ramsey, George; America, 1764 ***1220.12*** *p657*
Ramsey, George; Washington, 1881 ***2770.40*** *p135*
Ramsey, Hannah; America, 1724 ***1220.12*** *p657*
Ramsey, Henry; America, 1774 ***1220.12*** *p658*
Ramsey, Isabella 6 months; St. John, N.B., 1834 ***6469.7*** *p4*
Ramsey, Jane 20; St. John, N.B., 1834 ***6469.7*** *p4*
Ramsey, John; West Indies, 1740 ***9228.50*** *p533*
Ramsey, Robert 16; Ontario, 1871 ***1823.21*** *p305*
Ramsey, Robert 23; St. John, N.B., 1834 ***6469.7*** *p4*
Ramsey, Robert; Washington, 1879 ***2770.40*** *p134*
Ramsey, Thomas 35; Michigan, 1880 ***4491.36*** *p18*
Ramsey, William 1; St. John, N.B., 1834 ***6469.7*** *p4*
Ramseyer, John; Ohio, 1809-1852 ***4511.35*** *p41*
Ramseyer, Joseph; Ohio, 1809-1852 ***4511.35*** *p41*
Ramshaw, George; America, 1731 ***1220.12*** *p658*
Ramshaw, Mary; Virginia, 1734 ***1220.12*** *p658*
Ramsower, John 64; Michigan, 1880 ***4491.30*** *p25*
Ramsower, Teresa 59; Michigan, 1880 ***4491.30*** *p25*
Ramspott, George Carl; Baltimore, 1899 ***6212.1*** *p14*
Ramstedt, J.G.; New York, NY, 1851 ***6412.40*** *p151*
Ramsyre, Peter; Ohio, 1809-1852 ***4511.35*** *p41*
Ramzinski, Telesfor; Texas, 1874-1886 ***9980.22*** *p16*
Ran, Henry; America, 1748 ***1220.12*** *p659*
Ranachowska, Valentina; Detroit, 1890 ***9980.23*** *p96*
Ranahan, John 41; Ontario, 1871 ***1823.21*** *p305*
Ranault, Nicholas; Maine, 1665 ***9228.50*** *p541*
Rance, Elizabeth; America, 1741 ***1220.12*** *p658*
Rance, F. 25; America, 1840 ***778.6*** *p277*
Rance, F. G.; Louisiana, 1836-1840 ***4981.45*** *p213*
Rance, Louisa 22; America, 1840 ***778.6*** *p277*
Rance, Mary; America, 1772 ***1220.12*** *p658*
Rance, Noble; Died enroute, 1719 ***1220.12*** *p658*
Rance, Richard; America, 1765 ***1220.12*** *p658*
Ranch, Mrs. 30; Port uncertain, 1844 ***778.6*** *p277*
Rand, Benjamin; Virginia, 1730 ***1220.12*** *p658*
Rand, Clarence N. *SEE* Rand, Roy Clarence
Rand, John; America, 1691 ***1220.12*** *p658*
Rand, John; America, 1749 ***1220.12*** *p658*
Rand, Mary E. *SEE* Rand, Roy Clarence
Rand, Roy Clarence; Boston, 1899 ***1029.59*** *p76*
Rand, Roy Clarence; Colorado, 1918 ***1029.59*** *p76*
*Wife:*Mary E.
*Child:*Clarence N.
Rand, William; America, 1752 ***1220.12*** *p658*
Randa, Vaclav; Chicago, 1870 ***2853.20*** *p194*
Randa, Vaclav; Nebraska, 1869-1910 ***2853.20*** *p193*
Randal, James 74; Ontario, 1871 ***1823.21*** *p305*
Randal, Mary; America, 1764 ***1220.12*** *p658*
Randall, Abraham; Barbados, 1665 ***1220.12*** *p658*
Randall, Ann; America, 1771 ***1220.12*** *p658*
Randall, Bartholomew; America, 1685 ***1220.12*** *p658*
Randall, Charles; America, 1755 ***1220.12*** *p658*
Randall, Christopher; Barbados, 1672 ***1220.12*** *p658*
Randall, Christopher; Maryland, 1673 ***1236.25*** *p49*
Randall, Elizabeth; America, 1756 ***1220.12*** *p658*
Randall, George; America, 1741 ***1220.12*** *p658*
Randall, George 26; Ontario, 1871 ***1823.21*** *p305*
Randall, Henry; America, 1685 ***1220.12*** *p658*
Randall, Isaac 74; Ontario, 1871 ***1823.21*** *p305*
Randall, Jacob 61; Ontario, 1871 ***1823.17*** *p136*
Randall, James 41; Ontario, 1871 ***1823.21*** *p305*
Randall, James 54; Ontario, 1871 ***1823.17*** *p136*
Randall, John; America, 1740 ***1220.12*** *p658*
Randall, John; America, 1752 ***1220.12*** *p658*
Randall, John; America, 1755 ***1220.12*** *p658*
Randall, John; America, 1765 ***1220.12*** *p658*
Randall, John; America, 1770 ***1220.12*** *p658*
Randall, John; Annapolis, MD, 1725 ***1220.12*** *p658*
Randall, John; Died enroute, 1719 ***1220.12*** *p658*
Randall, John; Virginia, 1726 ***1220.12*** *p658*
Randall, John Payne; Washington, 1886 ***2770.40*** *p24*
Randall, Mary; America, 1745 ***1220.12*** *p658*
Randall, Mary; Virginia, 1728 ***1220.12*** *p658*
Randall, Nicholas; Maryland, 1725 ***1220.12*** *p658*
Randall, Richard; America, 1678 ***1220.12*** *p658*
Randall, Richard; America, 1739 ***1220.12*** *p658*
Randall, Richard; America, 1774 ***1220.12*** *p658*
Randall, Robert; America, 1752 ***1220.12*** *p658*
Randall, Samuel 50; Ontario, 1871 ***1823.21*** *p305*
Randall, Sarah; Annapolis, MD, 1733 ***1220.12*** *p658*
Randall, Shadrick 65; Ontario, 1871 ***1823.17*** *p136*
Randall, Thomas; America, 1720 ***1220.12*** *p659*
Randall, Thomas; America, 1727 ***1220.12*** *p659*
Randall, Thomas; America, 1730 ***1220.12*** *p659*
Randall, Thomas; America, 1761 ***1220.12*** *p659*
Randall, Thomas; America, 1772 ***1220.12*** *p659*
Randall, Thomas; America, 1773 ***1220.12*** *p659*
Randall, Thomas; Annapolis, MD, 1726 ***1220.12*** *p659*
Randall, Thomas; Maryland, 1720 ***1220.12*** *p659*
Randall, Thos. 45; Ontario, 1871 ***1823.17*** *p136*
Randall, William; America, 1744 ***1220.12*** *p659*
Randall, William; America, 1749 ***1220.12*** *p659*
Randall, William; America, 1750 ***1220.12*** *p659*
Randall, William; America, 1752 ***1220.12*** *p659*
Randall, William; America, 1755 ***1220.12*** *p659*
Randall, William; Barbados or Jamaica, 1694 ***1220.12*** *p659*
Randall, William 45; Ontario, 1871 ***1823.21*** *p305*
Randall, William 54; Ontario, 1871 ***1823.21*** *p305*
Randall, William 76; Ontario, 1871 ***1823.21*** *p305*
Randle, Aaron; Maryland, 1727 ***1220.12*** *p658*
Randle, John 56; Ontario, 1871 ***1823.17*** *p136*

Randle, Thomas; America, 1761 *1220.12 p659*
Randle, Thomas 64; Ontario, 1871 *1823.17 p136*
Randles, Robert; America, 1767 *1220.12 p659*
Randole, John; America, 1700 *1220.12 p658*
Randoll, Amos; Barbados, 1675 *1220.12 p658*
Randoll, Katherine; Barbados or Jamaica, 1674 *1220.12 p658*
Randoll, Sarah; America, 1742 *1220.12 p658*
Rands, Symon; America, 1680 *1220.12 p659*
Rane, Ralph; America, 1740 *1220.12 p657*
Raner, Andr 29; Halifax, N.S., 1902 *1860.4 p40*
Raner, Johann 9; Halifax, N.S., 1902 *1860.4 p40*
Raner, Pauline 29; Halifax, N.S., 1902 *1860.4 p40*
Raney, Bertrand 48; New Orleans, 1848 *778.6 p277*
Raney, David 60; Ontario, 1871 *1823.17 p136*
Raney, Patrick; Ohio, 1809-1852 *4511.35 p41*
Ranford, Edward; America, 1721 *1220.12 p659*
Ranft, George; New York, 1860 *358.56 p150*
Ranger, Job; Virginia, 1744 *1220.12 p659*
Ranger, John; America, 1758 *1220.12 p659*
Ranger, Luke; America, 1768 *1220.12 p659*
Ranger, Philip; Barbados, 1664 *1220.12 p659*
Ranger, Thomas; Virginia, 1718 *1220.12 p659*
Ranger, William 18; Quebec, 1870 *8364.32 p25*
Rangueta, Mathilde 30; Port uncertain, 1846 *778.6 p277*
Ranhol, Abraham 46; Ontario, 1871 *1823.17 p136*
Rank, Martin; America, 1767 *1220.12 p659*
Rank, Petr; Nebraska, 1850-1910 *2853.20 p182*
Ranke, Wilhelmine Caroline Eleonore; America, 1867 *7420.1 p262*
Rankey, Margaret; America, 1732 *1220.12 p659*
Rankin, Agnes 9; Quebec, 1870 *8364.32 p25*
Rankin, George 28; Ontario, 1871 *1823.17 p136*
Rankin, Hugh 67; Ontario, 1871 *1823.21 p305*
Rankin, Hugh; Philadelphia, 1813 *5720.10 p379*
Rankin, Mathew 52; Ontario, 1871 *1823.17 p136*
Rankin, Paul; America, 1747 *1220.12 p659*
Rankin, Robert; North Carolina, 1792-1862 *1088.45 p28*
Rankin, Robt.; Louisiana, 1874 *4981.45 p296*
Rann, Elizabeth; Died enroute, 1734 *1220.12 p659*
Ranney, Maurice; Louisiana, 1874 *4981.45 p134*
Rannie, John 40; Ontario, 1871 *1823.21 p305*
Rannila, Johanna 46; Minnesota, 1923 *2769.54 p1381*
Ranor, Andr 29; Halifax, N.S., 1902 *1860.4 p40*
Ranor, Johann 9; Halifax, N.S., 1902 *1860.4 p40*
Ranor, Pauline 29; Halifax, N.S., 1902 *1860.4 p40*
Ransan, R. Eugine; North Carolina, 1832 *1088.45 p28*
Ransch, Georg 9; America, 1846 *778.6 p278*
Ransey, George; Annapolis, MD, 1725 *1220.12 p659*
Ransford, David *SEE* Ransford, Edward
Ransford, Edward; Philadelphia, 1854 *8513.31 p422*
*Wife:*Julia Hartigan
*Child:*David
Ransford, John; America, 1727 *1220.12 p659*
Ransford, John; America, 1737 *1220.12 p659*
Ransford, Jonathan; America, 1720 *1220.12 p659*
Ransford, Julia Hartigan *SEE* Ransford, Edward
Ransmeier, Joseph; Illinois, 1854 *6079.1 p11*
Ransom, Elizabeth; America, 1768 *1220.12 p659*
Ransom, John 50; Ontario, 1871 *1823.21 p305*
Ransome, Margaret; America, 1675 *1220.12 p659*
Ransome, William; America, 1769 *1220.12 p659*
Ransome, William; America, 1773 *1220.12 p659*
Ranson, Edmond 31; New Orleans, 1848 *778.6 p278*
Ranson, Sarah; America, 1740 *1220.12 p659*
Ranson, William; America, 1759 *1220.12 p659*
Ranson, William H.; Colorado, 1904 *1029.59 p76*
Ranstrom, Bertha L. Ohman *SEE* Ranstrom, John G.
Ranstrom, John *SEE* Ranstrom, John G.
Ranstrom, John G.; Kansas, 1869 *777.40 p15*
*Wife:*Bertha L. Ohman
*Son:*John
Rant, James; America, 1771 *1220.12 p659*
Ranta, Johan Herman; Washington, 1889 *2770.40 p80*
Ranta, Robert 36; Minnesota, 1925 *2769.54 p1384*
Rantala, Leonard 17; Minnesota, 1923 *2769.54 p1381*
Ranton, Richard; America, 1745 *1220.12 p659*
Ranzow, Friedrich August; America, 1847 *7420.1 p55*
Ranzow, Georg; America, 1865 *7420.1 p235*
Ranzow, Hermann Christian; America, 1877 *7420.1 p309*
Ranzow, Hermann Christoph; America, 1874 *7420.1 p303*
Ranzow, Melanie; America, 1885 *7420.1 p348*
Raol, Thomas George 42; Ontario, 1871 *1823.17 p136*
Raoul, Alexandre 23; Quebec, 1659 *9221.17 p409*
Raoul, Gilles; Quebec, 1642 *9221.17 p121*
Raoul, Marie 28; Havana, 1848 *778.6 p278*
Raper, Ralph; America, 1731 *1220.12 p659*
Raper, Richard; America, 1756 *1220.12 p659*
Rapier, Mary; Barbados or Jamaica, 1685 *1220.12 p659*
Rapin, Pierre 27; America, 1843 *778.6 p278*
Rapley, Christina 25; Ontario, 1871 *1823.21 p305*
Rapley, Lorenzo 21; Ontario, 1871 *1823.21 p305*
Rapley, Thomas 45; Ontario, 1871 *1823.21 p306*
Rapley, William 56; Ontario, 1871 *1823.21 p306*
Raply, David 53; Ontario, 1871 *1823.21 p306*
Raply, Jesse 47; Ontario, 1871 *1823.21 p306*
Rapp, Anthony; Louisiana, 1874 *4981.45 p133*
Rapp, Elias; Ohio, 1809-1852 *4511.35 p41*
Rapp, Eva Dorothea; America, 1854 *2526.43 p217*
Rapp, Johannes 17; Dayton, OH, 1866 *2526.43 p135*
Rapp, Konrad 17; Dayton, OH, 1868 *2526.43 p135*
Rapp, Wilhelm Johannes; Miami, 1935 *4984.12 p39*
Rappe, M.C.F.; New York, NY, 1851 *6412.40 p153*
Rappee, Andrew; Ohio, 1809-1852 *4511.35 p41*
Rappee, Andrew; Ohio, 1809-1852 *4511.35 p42*
Rappelan, Ignatz; Louisiana, 1874 *4981.45 p134*
Rapsey, Martha 50; Ontario, 1871 *1823.21 p306*
Rapson, Andrew; America, 1685 *1220.12 p659*
Rapson, Thomas; America, 1764 *1220.12 p659*
Rarock, Coonrod; New Jersey, 1773-1774 *927.31 p3*
Rasche, Anna; America, n.d. *8023.44 p378*
Rasche, Carl Wilhelm; America, 1872 *7420.1 p297*
Rasche, Maria; America, 1923 *8023.44 p378*
Rasche, Wilhelmina; America, n.d. *8023.44 p378*
Raschel, Katharina; America, 1879 *5475.1 p141*
Rascon, Pierre 34; New Orleans, 1848 *778.6 p278*
Raset, Aine 49; Port uncertain, 1844 *778.6 p278*
Rash, Joseph; Virginia, 1736 *1220.12 p659*
Rash, Mary; Virginia, 1734 *1220.12 p660*
Rashance, J. 28; Port uncertain, 1843 *778.6 p278*
Rasher, Michael; North Carolina, 1710 *3629.40 p6*
Rashet, Anne; North Carolina, 1710 *3629.40 p8*
Rashfield, Jacob; Virginia, 1727 *1220.12 p660*
Rashfield, Joseph; America, 1727 *1220.12 p660*
Rasine, Pierre 25; Missouri, 1846 *778.6 p278*
Rasker, Christopher; Barbados, 1679 *1220.12 p660*
Rasler, Barbara 14; America, 1843 *778.6 p278*
Rasler, Barbara 34; America, 1843 *778.6 p278*
Rasler, Celestine 1; America, 1843 *778.6 p278*
Rasler, Dominik 49; America, 1843 *778.6 p278*
Rasler, Frank 18; America, 1843 *778.6 p278*
Rasler, Jean 12; America, 1843 *778.6 p278*
Rasler, Lisbeth 10; America, 1843 *778.6 p278*
Rasler, Margaretha 6; America, 1843 *778.6 p278*
Rasler, Maria 16; America, 1843 *778.6 p278*
Rasler, Susanna 10; America, 1843 *778.6 p278*
Rasler, Victor 8; America, 1843 *778.6 p278*
Rasmussen, Chris; Iowa, 1892 *1211.15 p18*
Rasmussen, Hans; Iowa, 1904 *1211.15 p18*
Rasmussen, Jacob; Colorado, 1897 *1029.59 p76*
Rasmussen, James; Iowa, 1896 *1211.15 p18*
Rasmussen, James Marcus; Iowa, 1912 *1211.15 p18*
Rasmussen, Jorgen; Washington, 1889 *2770.40 p80*
Rasmussen, Lewis; Iowa, 1891 *1211.15 p18*
Rasmussen, Peter; Iowa, 1889 *1211.15 p18*
Rasmussen, Peter; Iowa, 1889 *1211.15 p18*
Rasmussen, Rasmus; Iowa, 1896 *1211.15 p18*
Rasmussen, Rasmus; Washington, 1889 *2770.40 p80*
Rasp, Powless; Ohio, 1809-1852 *4511.35 p42*
Raspford, J. 30; Port uncertain, 1842 *778.6 p278*
Raspiller, Anna; America, 1881 *5475.1 p74*
Rassall, Thomas; America, 1739 *1220.12 p660*
Rassat, F...d; America, 1842 *778.6 p278*
Rassavouin, Yves 20; Quebec, 1658 *9221.17 p386*
Rassbach, Eva Catharine; America, 1867 *7919.3 p526*
Rassbach, Heinrich Wilhelm; America, 1867 *7919.3 p526*
With 2 children
Rassbach, Wilhelmine; America, 1867 *7919.3 p526*
Rasse, Christian; Ohio, 1809-1852 *4511.35 p42*
Rassier, Johann 31; America, 1856 *5475.1 p295*
Rassier, Josef; America, 1856 *5475.1 p295*
Rassilly, Jean Louis; Harrisburg, PA, 1799 *5720.10 p379*
Rastel deRocheblave, Pierre-Louis; Quebec, 1755 *2314.30 p170*
Rastel deRocheblave, Pierre-Louis; Quebec, 1755 *2314.30 p193*
Rasties, . . .; West Virginia, 1850-1860 *1132.30 p147*
Ratcliff, Henry; America, 1698 *1220.12 p660*
Ratcliff, Timothy; Boston, 1766 *1642 p36*
Ratcliffe, Anne; America, 1739 *1220.12 p660*
Ratcliffe, Charles; America, 1766 *1220.12 p660*
Ratcliffe, Charles; America, 1770 *1220.12 p660*
Ratcliffe, Christopher; America, 1763 *1220.12 p660*
Ratcliffe, Edward; America, 1698 *1220.12 p660*
Ratcliffe, Elizabeth; Barbados or Jamaica, 1685 *1220.12 p660*
Ratcliffe, Mary; America, 1741 *1220.12 p660*
Ratcliffe, Mary 12; Quebec, 1870 *8364.32 p25*
Ratcliffe, Robert; America, 1678 *1220.12 p660*
Ratcliffe, Thomas; America, 1656 *1220.12 p660*
Rate, Jacques 22; Quebec, 1652 *9221.17 p265*
Rate, Jean 16; Quebec, 1661 *9221.17 p466*
Ratel, Jacques; Quebec, 1636 *9221.17 p50*
Ratgen, Martin; North Carolina, 1844 *1088.45 p28*
Rath, Carl; Wisconsin, 1887 *6795.8 p235*
Rath, Jemima 64; Ontario, 1871 *1823.21 p306*
Rath, John 30; Ontario, 1871 *1823.21 p306*
Rathay, James 64; Ontario, 1871 *1823.17 p136*
Rathbone, Benjamin; New York, 1782 *8529.30 p15*
Rathe, August Christian Wilhelm; America, 1890 *7420.1 p361*
Rathe, G. J.; Louisiana, 1874 *4981.45 p296*
Rathenhofer, Oscar 18; New York, NY, 1865 *7710.1 p157*
Rathgers, Wm.; Missouri, 1888 *3276.1 p2*
Rathjen, Hans; Valdivia, Chile, 1851 *1192.4 p51*
Rathjen, Johann D.; Colorado, 1877 *1029.59 p76*
Rathjen, Johann D.; Colorado, 1888 *1029.59 p76*
Rathke, Bertha Emilie; Wisconsin, 1897 *6795.8 p27*
Rathman, Alice Ruby; Miami, 1935 *4984.12 p39*
Rathmann, Mrs. D.; Wisconsin, 1899 *6795.8 p177*
Rathmann, Herman; Colorado, 1887 *1029.59 p76*
Rathmann, Herman; Colorado, 1903 *1029.59 p76*
Rathmann, Hermann; Colorado, 1887 *1029.59 p76*
Rathmann, William; New York, NY, 1880 *6212.1 p16*
Rathray, Jane 63; Ontario, 1871 *1823.17 p136*
Rathway, Margaret 55; Ontario, 1871 *1823.17 p136*
Ratier, Pierre 40; New Orleans, 1848 *778.6 p278*
Ratifie, William; Rappahannock, VA, 1728 *1220.12 p660*
Ratigan, Michael 38; Ontario, 1871 *1823.17 p136*
Ratigan, Patrick 70; Ontario, 1871 *1823.17 p136*
Ratjen, Bernhard; North Carolina, 1844 *1088.45 p28*
Ratke, August; Wisconsin, 1878 *6795.8 p75*
Ratley, John; America, 1749 *1220.12 p660*
Rattenbury, Alice; Jamaica, 1661 *1220.12 p660*
Rattenbury, William; Virginia, 1766 *1220.12 p660*
Rattle, Daniel 62; Ontario, 1871 *1823.21 p306*
Rattlen, Sara 50; New York, NY, 1885 *1883.7 p45*
Rattray, Duncan 23; Ontario, 1871 *1823.17 p136*
Rattray, Margaret 65; Ontario, 1871 *1823.17 p137*
Rattry, John 31; Ontario, 1871 *1823.21 p306*
Ratz, Carl; Valdivia, Chile, 1850 *1192.4 p49*
Ratzburg, John Fredrick; Wisconsin, 1885 *6795.8 p229*
Ratzburg, Wilhelm; Wisconsin, 1885 *6795.8 p230*
Rau, Ernst Ludwig; Wisconsin, 1893 *6795.8 p38*
Rau, Johann Adam; America, 1867 *7919.3 p526*
Rau, Valentin; Colorado, 1894 *1029.59 p76*
Rau, Valentin; Pennsylvania, 1884 *1029.59 p76*
Rauafinoli, Vincent; North Carolina, 1831 *1088.45 p28*
Raub, Michael; Ohio, 1809-1852 *4511.35 p42*
Rauber, A. Maria 43; South America, 1857 *5475.1 p502*
Rauber, Anna Maria *SEE* Rauber, Jakob
Rauber, Elisabeth Peter *SEE* Rauber, Peter
Rauber, Elisabeth *SEE* Rauber, Johann
Rauber, Georg; Brazil, 1854 *5475.1 p440*
*Wife:*Katharina Michaeli
With 9 children
Rauber, Jakob *SEE* Rauber, Michel
Rauber, Jakob 65; Brazil, 1883 *5475.1 p517*
*Wife:*Anna Maria
Rauber, Jakob, III; Rio Grande do Sul, Brazil, 1878 *5475.1 p513*
*Daughter:*Magdalena
*Son:*Johann
Rauber, Johann 47; Brazil, 1857 *5475.1 p512*
*Wife:*Susanna Rech 28
*Daughter:*Elisabeth
Rauber, Johann *SEE* Rauber, Jakob, III
Rauber, Johann Georg; Brazil, 1846 *5475.1 p439*
With 5 children
*Wife:*Susanna Dewes
Rauber, Katharina Michaeli *SEE* Rauber, Georg
Rauber, Magdalena 27; America, 1857 *5475.1 p502*
Rauber, Magdalena *SEE* Rauber, Jakob, III
Rauber, Margarethe *SEE* Rauber, Michel
Rauber, Michel *SEE* Rauber, Michel
Rauber, Michel 37; Brazil, 1862 *5475.1 p543*
*Wife:*Susanna Scherer 37
*Son:*Michel
*Daughter:*Margarethe
*Son:*Jakob
Rauber, Nikolaus *SEE* Rauber, Peter
Rauber, Peter; America, 1843 *5475.1 p446*
Rauber, Peter; America, 1856 *5475.1 p440*
*Wife:*Elisabeth Peter
With child & mother
*Brother:*Nikolaus
Rauber, Peter; Brazil, 1853 *5475.1 p439*
Rauber, Susanna Dewes *SEE* Rauber, Johann Georg
Rauber, Susanna Rech 28 *SEE* Rauber, Johann
Rauber, Susanna Scherer 37 *SEE* Rauber, Michel
Raubin, Robert; North Carolina, 1792-1862 *1088.45 p28*
Raubly, . . .; North Carolina, 1710 *3629.40 p6*
Rauch, Agnesia Katharina Riebel; Virginia, 1831 *152.20 p67*
Rauch, Anna Barbara; Virginia, 1831 *152.20 p62*

Rauch, Anna Dorothea Christiane *SEE* Rauch, Carl August
Rauch, Auguste Friedericke Catharine *SEE* Rauch, Carl August
Rauch, Carl August; America, 1872 ***7420.1*** *p297*
With wife
*Son:*Johannes Carl
*Daughter:*Auguste Friedericke Catharine
*Daughter:*Anna Dorothea Christiane
*Daughter:*Charlotte Maria
Rauch, Carl Friedrich; America, 1886 ***7420.1*** *p352*
Rauch, Charles; Louisiana, 1836-1840 ***4981.45*** *p213*
Rauch, Charlotte Maria *SEE* Rauch, Carl August
Rauch, Eva Margaretha Neff 36 *SEE* Rauch, Sebastian
Rauch, Georg; America, 1831 ***2526.43*** *p212*
Rauch, Henrich; Port uncertain, 1864 ***170.15*** *p43*
Rauch, Johannes Carl *SEE* Rauch, Carl August
Rauch, Peter; America, 1873 ***5475.1*** *p256*
Rauch, Sebastian 46; America, 1854 ***2526.42*** *p105*
*Wife:*Eva Margaretha Neff 36
Rauch, Wilhelm 30; America, 1831 ***2526.43*** *p212*
With father 65
With 3 siblings
Rauch, Wilhelmine; America, 1880 ***7420.1*** *p317*
Raudy, Marthe; Quebec, 1670 ***4514.3*** *p362*
Rauen, Joseph; Louisiana, 1874 ***4981.45*** *p133*
Raughton, Joseph; West Indies, 1686 ***1220.12*** *p660*
Raughton, Thomas; West Indies, 1686 ***1220.12*** *p660*
Raul, Sebastian 38; Galveston, TX, 1844 ***3967.10*** *p374*
Raulph, Sarah Ann 18; Ontario, 1871 ***1823.17*** *p137*
Raupp, John; Ohio, 1809-1852 ***4511.35*** *p42*
Raupp, Michael; Ohio, 1809-1852 ***4511.35*** *p42*
Rausch, Adam; America, 1872 ***2526.43*** *p199*
*Wife:*Margaretha
Rausch, Barb. 21; America, 1846 ***778.6*** *p278*
Rausch, Barbara; America, 1860 ***2526.43*** *p120*
Rausch, Barbara; America, 1868 ***5475.1*** *p262*
Rausch, Dorothea; America, 1881 ***5475.1*** *p34*
Rausch, Elisabeth; America, 1850-1899 ***6442.17*** *p65*
Rausch, Jakob; America, 1849 ***5475.1*** *p489*
Rausch, Johann Adam; America, 1888 ***2526.43*** *p204*
Rausch, Johann Peter 18; America, 1855 ***2526.43*** *p120*
Rausch, Katharina; America, 1849 ***5475.1*** *p489*
Rausch, Margaretha; America, 1856 ***2526.43*** *p120*
Rausch, Margaretha *SEE* Rausch, Adam
Rausch, Valentin; America, 1881 ***2526.43*** *p204*
Rauscher, Francois 28; Port uncertain, 1848 ***778.6*** *p278*
Rauscher, Peter Gottlieb; America, 1868 ***7919.3*** *p530*
Rauschert, Martin; America, 1867-1868 ***7919.3*** *p525*
With wife & child
Rausen, Charlotte; America, 1881 ***5475.1*** *p24*
Rausseau, Jean Baptiste; Louisiana, 1841-1844 ***4981.45*** *p211*
Rausselon, Etienne; Louisiana, 1841-1844 ***4981.45*** *p211*
Rausser, Christian; New York, 1859 ***358.56*** *p54*
Rauth, Heinrich; America, 1835-1899 ***2526.42*** *p129*
Rauth, Heinrich 18; America, 1853 ***2526.43*** *p154*
Ravain, Jean 32; America, 1840 ***778.6*** *p278*
Ravat, Etienne; Illinois, 1852 ***6079.1*** *p11*
Rave, Christ.; Valdivia, Chile, 1852 ***1192.4*** *p56*
With wife
Raveau, Barbe; Quebec, 1673 ***4514.3*** *p362*
Raveau, F. 30; America, 1843 ***778.6*** *p278*
Ravell, Edward; America, 1775 ***1220.12*** *p660*
Raven, Anne; Annapolis, MD, 1721 ***1220.12*** *p660*
Raven, George; America, 1726 ***1220.12*** *p660*
Raven, Hannah; America, 1743 ***1220.12*** *p660*
Raven, Henry; Annapolis, MD, 1721 ***1220.12*** *p660*
Raven, Lorenzo R. 42; Ontario, 1871 ***1823.17*** *p137*
Raven, Margaret; Virginia, 1730 ***1220.12*** *p660*
Raven, Mary 42; Barbados, 1664 ***1220.12*** *p660*
Raven, Thomas; America, 1766 ***1220.12*** *p660*
Raven, William; Maryland, 1733 ***1220.12*** *p660*
Raven, William; Virginia, 1729 ***1220.12*** *p660*
Ravenhill, John; America, 1740 ***1220.12*** *p660*
Ravenscroft, Frances; Maryland or Virginia, 1733 ***1220.12*** *p660*
Ravet, Annmarie; Wisconsin, 1856 ***1495.20*** *p41*
With daughter
Ravin, Baptist 32; America, 1841 ***778.6*** *p278*
Ravins, Stephen; America, 1773 ***1220.12*** *p660*
Raw, Thomas; America, 1744 ***1220.12*** *p660*
Rawbone, Edward; America, 1685 ***1220.12*** *p660*
Rawbone, Thomas; America, 1766 ***1220.12*** *p660*
Rawden, Agar; America, 1774 ***1220.12*** *p660*
Rawianko, Antony 35; New York, NY, 1920 ***930.50*** *p49*
Rawicz, Gotzel 20; New York, NY, 1878 ***9253.2*** *p45*
Rawings, George 29; Ontario, 1871 ***1823.21*** *p306*
Rawings, Louisa M. 25; Ontario, 1871 ***1823.21*** *p306*
Rawkins, John; Virginia, 1769 ***1220.12*** *p660*
Rawle, David; America, 1746 ***1220.12*** *p660*
Rawles, Joseph; America, 1775 ***1220.12*** *p660*
Rawlett, William; America, 1750 ***1220.12*** *p660*
Rawley, Catherine; New Orleans, 1851 ***7242.30*** *p152*
Rawley, James; New Orleans, 1851 ***7242.30*** *p152*
Rawley, Johanna; New Orleans, 1851 ***7242.30*** *p152*
Rawley, Margaret; New Orleans, 1851 ***7242.30*** *p152*
Rawley, Michael; New Orleans, 1851 ***7242.30*** *p153*
Rawlings, Alb 39; Ontario, 1871 ***1823.17*** *p137*
Rawlings, Alfred 15; Quebec, 1870 ***8364.32*** *p25*
Rawlings, Charles 14; Quebec, 1870 ***8364.32*** *p25*
Rawlings, Hb 37; Ontario, 1871 ***1823.17*** *p137*
Rawlings, Henry 55; Ontario, 1871 ***1823.17*** *p137*
Rawlings, Henry 69; Ontario, 1871 ***1823.21*** *p306*
Rawlings, Hiram 41; Ontario, 1871 ***1823.17*** *p137*
Rawlings, James; Barbados, 1680 ***1220.12*** *p661*
Rawlings, John; America, 1756 ***1220.12*** *p661*
Rawlings, John 52; Ontario, 1871 ***1823.17*** *p137*
Rawlings, John 75; Ontario, 1871 ***1823.17*** *p137*
Rawlings, Thomas; America, 1746 ***1220.12*** *p661*
Rawlings, William 25; Annapolis, MD, 1721 ***1220.12*** *p661*
Rawlingson, Mary; America, 1766 ***1220.12*** *p661*
Rawlington, Elizabeth; America, 1766 ***1220.12*** *p660*
Rawlins, Charles; Virginia, 1727 ***1220.12*** *p661*
Rawlins, David; America, 1730 ***1220.12*** *p661*
Rawlins, Elizabeth; Virginia, 1730 ***1220.12*** *p661*
Rawlins, James; Annapolis, MD, 1735 ***1220.12*** *p661*
Rawlins, John; America, 1745 ***1220.12*** *p661*
Rawlins, John; Barbados, 1668 ***1220.12*** *p661*
Rawlins, Margery; Barbados, 1668 ***1220.12*** *p661*
Rawlins, Nathaniel; America, 1762 ***1220.12*** *p661*
Rawlins, Nicholas; Newbury, MA, 1678 ***1642*** *p74*
Rawlins, Richard; Philadelphia, 1778 ***8529.30*** *p4A*
Rawlins, Robert 48; Ontario, 1871 ***1823.21*** *p306*
Rawlins, Robert 65; Ontario, 1871 ***1823.21*** *p306*
Rawlins, Thomas; Annapolis, MD, 1725 ***1220.12*** *p661*
Rawlins, Thomas 39; Ontario, 1871 ***1823.21*** *p306*
Rawlinson, John; America, 1731 ***1220.12*** *p661*
Rawlinson, Margaret; America, 1745 ***1220.12*** *p661*
Rawlinson, Mary; America, 1770 ***1220.12*** *p661*
Rawlinson, William; Maryland, 1734 ***1220.12*** *p661*
Rawly, Samuel R.; Washington, 1884 ***2770.40*** *p193*
Rawnicky, Sarah Hirsch; Miami, 1935 ***4984.12*** *p39*
Rawse, John; America, 1737 ***1220.12*** *p661*
Rawson, Charles 38; Ontario, 1871 ***1823.17*** *p137*
Rawson, Daniel; Virginia, 1763 ***1220.12*** *p661*
Rawson, Elizabeth; Virginia, 1721 ***1220.12*** *p661*
Rawson, Thomas 41; Ontario, 1871 ***1823.17*** *p137*
Rawson, William; Barbados or Jamaica, 1685 ***1220.12*** *p661*
Rawsthorne, Mrs. A. P.; Montreal, 1922 ***4514.4*** *p32*
Rawsthorne, Miss N.; Montreal, 1922 ***4514.4*** *p32*
Rawston, . . .; Boston, 1879 ***9228.50*** *p533*
Rawstron, . . .; Boston, 1879 ***9228.50*** *p533*
Rawthorne, John; America, 1756 ***1220.12*** *p661*
Ray, Charles; America, 1731 ***1220.12*** *p661*
Ray, Daniel; Virginia, 1732 ***1220.12*** *p661*
Ray, Elsfret 68; Ontario, 1871 ***1823.21*** *p306*
Ray, George 31; Quebec, 1870 ***8364.32*** *p25*
Ray, Henry 66; Ontario, 1871 ***1823.21*** *p306*
Ray, James; Jamaica, 1783 ***8529.30*** *p14A*
Ray, John; America, 1730 ***1220.12*** *p661*
Ray, Peter; Toronto, 1844 ***2910.35*** *p115*
Ray, Robert 52; Ontario, 1871 ***1823.17*** *p137*
Ray, Thomas; Washington, 1879 ***2770.40*** *p134*
Ray, William; America, 1759 ***1220.12*** *p661*
Ray, William; Annapolis, MD, 1725 ***1220.12*** *p661*
Raybourn, Ann; America, 1751 ***1220.12*** *p661*
Raycraft, John 35; Ontario, 1871 ***1823.17*** *p137*
Raye, Antoine 21; America, 1841 ***778.6*** *p278*
Rayer, Andrew; Ohio, 1809-1852 ***4511.35*** *p42*
Rayer, Thomas; America, 1774 ***1220.12*** *p661*
Raymbault, Charles 35; Quebec, 1637 ***9221.17*** *p67*
Raymond, Ann; Barbados or Jamaica, 1697 ***1220.12*** *p661*
Raymond, Charles 29; New Orleans, 1844 ***778.6*** *p278*
Raymond, Edmond 63; Ontario, 1871 ***1823.21*** *p306*
Raymond, George; Kansas, 1892 ***1447.20*** *p64*
Raymond, Henry; Louisiana, 1874 ***4981.45*** *p133*
Raymond, John; America, 1772 ***1220.12*** *p661*
Raymond, John 27; Ontario, 1871 ***1823.21*** *p306*
Raymond, John 55; Ontario, 1871 ***1823.21*** *p306*
Raymond, John 19; Port uncertain, 1848 ***778.6*** *p278*
Raymond, Murfie; Louisiana, 1874 ***4981.45*** *p133*
Raymond, Owen 22; Kansas, 1888 ***1447.20*** *p62*
Raymond, Philip 25; Ontario, 1871 ***1823.17*** *p137*
Raymond, Rebecca; Virginia, 1741 ***1220.12*** *p661*
Raynard, John; America, 1737 ***1220.12*** *p667*
Raynaud deLaroche deGrandval, Philippe-Ant. de; Quebec, 1728 ***2314.30*** *p171*
Rayne, George; America, 1724 ***1220.12*** *p657*
Rayner, Barnaby; America, 1763 ***1220.12*** *p661*
Rayner, Daniel 45; Ontario, 1871 ***1823.21*** *p306*
Rayner, Edward; America, 1687 ***1220.12*** *p661*
Rayner, Elizabeth; Virginia, 1732 ***1220.12*** *p661*
Rayner, John; America, 1749 ***1220.12*** *p661*
Rayner, Joseph; America, 1749 ***1220.12*** *p661*
Rayner, Rowland; Barbados, 1662 ***1220.12*** *p662*
Rayner, Sarah; Annapolis, MD, 1725 ***1220.12*** *p662*
Rayner, Thomas; Harrisburg, PA, 1799 ***5720.10*** *p380*
Rayner, Thomas; Harrisburg, PA, 1804 ***5720.10*** *p380*
Rayner, William; America, 1762 ***1220.12*** *p662*
Raynes, John; America, 1755 ***1220.12*** *p657*
Raynor, William 39; Ontario, 1871 ***1823.17*** *p137*
Raynsdon, John; America, 1748 ***1220.12*** *p657*
Raynsford, Richard; America, 1686 ***1220.12*** *p657*
Rayton, Joseph; America, 1772 ***1220.12*** *p662*
Razerge, Joseph 19; America, 1843 ***778.6*** *p278*
Razes, Marguerite; Quebec, 1669 ***4514.3*** *p351*
Rea, Alexander 30; Ontario, 1871 ***1823.21*** *p306*
Rea, John 64; Ontario, 1871 ***1823.21*** *p306*
Rea, Johnston; Ohio, 1840 ***2763.1*** *p21*
Rea, Matthew; America, 1750 ***1220.12*** *p662*
Rea, William; America, 1673 ***1220.12*** *p662*
Reaburn, James 33; Ontario, 1871 ***1823.17*** *p137*
Reachead, Sarah; America, 1747 ***1220.12*** *p662*
Reachford, John; America, 1765 ***1220.12*** *p662*
Read, Ann; America, 1763 ***1220.12*** *p662*
Read, Ann 26; Barbados, 1664 ***1220.12*** *p662*
Read, Ann; Virginia, 1738 ***1220.12*** *p662*
Read, Benjamin; Rappahannock, VA, 1728 ***1220.12*** *p662*
Read, Call; Maryland, 1672 ***1236.25*** *p47*
Read, Calvin; Barbados, 1671 ***1220.12*** *p662*
Read, Christian; America, 1763 ***1220.12*** *p662*
Read, Christian; America, 1773 ***1220.12*** *p662*
Read, Edward; America, 1768 ***1220.12*** *p662*
Read, Elizabeth; America, 1763 ***1220.12*** *p662*
Read, Elizabeth; America, 1773 ***1220.12*** *p662*
Read, Elizabeth 45; Ontario, 1871 ***1823.17*** *p137*
Read, Ely; Virginia, 1724 ***1220.12*** *p662*
Read, Esau; America, 1744 ***1220.12*** *p662*
Read, Hannah; America, 1752 ***1220.12*** *p662*
Read, Henry; America, 1760 ***1220.12*** *p662*
Read, James; Ontario, 1835 ***3160.1*** *p150*
Read, James; Prescott, Ont., 1835 ***3289.1*** *p61*
Read, Jane; Barbados or Jamaica, 1689 ***1220.12*** *p662*
Read, John; America, 1734 ***1220.12*** *p662*
Read, John; America, 1742 ***1220.12*** *p662*
Read, John; America, 1743 ***1220.12*** *p662*
Read, John; America, 1747 ***1220.12*** *p662*
Read, John; America, 1748 ***1220.12*** *p662*
Read, John; America, 1750 ***1220.12*** *p662*
Read, John; America, 1752 ***1220.12*** *p663*
Read, John; America, 1757 ***1220.12*** *p663*
Read, John; America, 1764 ***1220.12*** *p663*
Read, John; America, 1765 ***1220.12*** *p663*
Read, John; America, 1769 ***1220.12*** *p663*
Read, John; America, 1771 ***1220.12*** *p663*
Read, John; Maryland, 1742 ***1220.12*** *p662*
Read, John; Maryland, 1744 ***1220.12*** *p662*
Read, John; Ohio, 1809-1852 ***4511.35*** *p42*
Read, Jonathan; Barbados, 1664 ***1220.12*** *p663*
Read, Joseph; America, 1767 ***1220.12*** *p663*
Read, Joseph; Virginia, 1719 ***1220.12*** *p663*
Read, Mary; America, 1771 ***1220.12*** *p663*
Read, Michael; America, 1753 ***1220.12*** *p663*
Read, Nicholas; America, 1774 ***1220.12*** *p663*
Read, Osmond; America, 1685 ***1220.12*** *p663*
Read, Rachel; America, 1757 ***1220.12*** *p663*
Read, Rebecca; Annapolis, MD, 1726 ***1220.12*** *p663*
Read, Richard; America, 1770 ***1220.12*** *p663*
Read, Robert; America, 1678 ***1220.12*** *p663*
Read, Robert; America, 1724 ***1220.12*** *p663*
Read, Robert; America, 1766 ***1220.12*** *p663*
Read, Robert; America, 1769 ***1220.12*** *p663*
Read, Robert; America, 1773 ***1220.12*** *p663*
Read, Robert; Virginia, 1734 ***1220.12*** *p663*
Read, Samuel; America, 1734 ***1220.12*** *p663*
Read, Sarah; America, 1756 ***1220.12*** *p663*
Read, Stephen; America, 1749 ***1220.12*** *p663*
Read, Stephen; Barbados, 1685 ***1220.12*** *p663*
Read, Susan; Maryland, 1719 ***1220.12*** *p663*
Read, Susanna; America, 1746 ***1220.12*** *p663*
Read, Susannah; America, 1744 ***1220.12*** *p663*
Read, Thomas; America, 1699 ***1220.12*** *p664*
Read, Thomas; America, 1755 ***1220.12*** *p664*
Read, Thomas; America, 1759 ***1220.12*** *p664*
Read, Thomas; Barbados or Jamaica, 1690 ***1220.12*** *p664*
Read, William; America, 1675 ***1220.12*** *p664*
Read, William; America, 1685 ***1220.12*** *p664*
Read, William; America, 1727 ***1220.12*** *p664*
Read, William; America, 1741 ***1220.12*** *p664*
Read, William; America, 1752 ***1220.12*** *p664*
Read, William; America, 1769 ***1220.12*** *p664*
Read, William; America, 1771 ***1220.12*** *p664*
Read, William; Boston, 1718 ***1220.12*** *p664*
Read, William 23; Ontario, 1871 ***1823.21*** *p306*
Read, William; Virginia, 1736 ***1220.12*** *p664*

406 *FOR A COMPLETE EXPLANATION OF ENTRY, SEE "HOW TO READ A CITATION" SECTION*

Readaway, James; Massachusetts, 1676 ***9228.50*** *p534*
Reade, Francis; Maryland, 1719 ***1220.12*** *p662*
Reade, George; America, 1691 ***1220.12*** *p662*
Reader, Andrew; America, 1688 ***1220.12*** *p664*
Reader, Benjamin; America, 1738 ***1220.12*** *p664*
Reader, James 33; Ontario, 1871 ***1823.17*** *p137*
Reader, Thomas; America, 1775 ***1220.12*** *p664*
Reader, Thomas 44; Ontario, 1871 ***1823.21*** *p306*
Readin, Thomas; Maine, 1834 ***3274.55*** *p43*
Reading, Edward; Washington, 1887 ***6015.10*** *p16*
Reading, Elizabeth; Barbados, 1669 ***1220.12*** *p664*
Reading, George; America, 1768 ***1220.12*** *p664*
Reading, Lambeth; America, 1769 ***1220.12*** *p664*
Reading, Richard; America, 1753 ***1220.12*** *p664*
Readon, Jeremiah; Boston, 1766 ***1642*** *p36*
Ready, Charles 48; Ontario, 1871 ***1823.21*** *p306*
Ready, Jeremiah; Ohio, 1809-1852 ***4511.35*** *p42*
Ready, Peter; America, 1756 ***1220.12*** *p664*
Ready, Thomas; America, 1771 ***1220.12*** *p664*
Reaghan, John; New England, 1745 ***1642*** *p28*
Reairdon, Dennis; Toronto, 1844 ***2910.35*** *p116*
Reakoff, John 47; Michigan, 1880 ***4491.36*** *p18*
Reamer, Herman; Iowa, 1897 ***1211.15*** *p18*
Reane, W. F.; California, 1868 ***1131.61*** *p90*
Rearden, Timothy; Boston, 1762 ***1642*** *p48*
Reardon, John; America, 1766 ***1220.12*** *p664*
Reasheat, Casper; North Carolina, 1710 ***3629.40*** *p6*
Reason, Amey; America, 1741 ***1220.12*** *p664*
Reason, Bartholomew; America, 1770 ***1220.12*** *p664*
Reason, Henry Thomas 28; Ontario, 1871 ***1823.21*** *p306*
Reason, John; America, 1685 ***1220.12*** *p664*
Reason, Philip; Boston, 1715 ***9228.50*** *p306*
Reason, Thomas; Virginia, 1740 ***1220.12*** *p664*
Reason, William; America, 1771 ***1220.12*** *p664*
Reasonover, Mathias; North Carolina, 1710 ***3629.40*** *p6*
Reasonover, Matthew; North Carolina, 1710 ***3629.40*** *p6*
Reaston, John L.; Illinois, 1858-1861 ***6020.5*** *p132*
Reaton, Etienne 34; Port uncertain, 1842 ***778.6*** *p278*
Reaudolph, Mary; America, 1767 ***1220.12*** *p692*
Reaume, Jean 20; Quebec, 1662 ***9221.17*** *p492*
Reauville, Charles; Quebec, 1654 ***9221.17*** *p315*
Reavell, Sophia; America, 1768 ***1220.12*** *p667*
Reaves, Thomas; America, 1741 ***1220.12*** *p666*
Reay, James; America, 1775 ***1220.12*** *p662*
Reay, John; America, 1734 ***1220.12*** *p664*
Rebanche, Jos. 20; America, 1840 ***778.6*** *p279*
Rebanche, Marie 6; America, 1840 ***778.6*** *p279*
Rebanche, Othan 11; America, 1840 ***778.6*** *p279*
Rebart, Antoine 38; New Orleans, 1848 ***778.6*** *p279*
Rebart, Josephine 71; New Orleans, 1848 ***778.6*** *p279*
Rebau, Mr. 30; Port uncertain, 1845 ***778.6*** *p279*
Rebaud, Capt. 45; Mexico, 1842 ***778.6*** *p279*
Rebec, Anastas; Chicago, 1891 ***2853.20*** *p438*
Rebecco, Jane; America, 1754 ***1220.12*** *p664*
Rebeck, Elisabeth Ruffing *SEE* Rebeck, Nikolaus
Rebeck, Friedrich *SEE* Rebeck, Nikolaus
Rebeck, Jakob August *SEE* Rebeck, Nikolaus
Rebeck, Johann *SEE* Rebeck, Nikolaus
Rebeck, Nikolaus *SEE* Rebeck, Nikolaus
Rebeck, Nikolaus; America, 1893 ***5475.1*** *p46*
*Wife:*Elisabeth Ruffing
*Son:*Friedrich
*Son:*Wilh. Karl
*Son:*Jakob August
*Son:*Johann
*Son:*Nikolaus
Rebeck, Wilh. Karl *SEE* Rebeck, Nikolaus
Reber, Gottlob; America, 1880 ***179.55*** *p19*
Rebet, Francois 26; New Orleans, 1845 ***778.6*** *p279*
Rebicher, Louis 35; Quebec, 1648 ***9221.17*** *p203*
Rebner, C. F.; Valdivia, Chile, 1852 ***1192.4*** *p54*
With wife
With child 8
Rebott, Jack 35; New Orleans, 1843 ***778.6*** *p279*
Rebouch, A. 35; America, 1845 ***778.6*** *p279*
Rebouch, Ant. 28; Louisiana, 1840 ***778.6*** *p279*
Rebouch, Victoire 23; Louisiana, 1840 ***778.6*** *p279*
Reboul, Miss 1; Louisiana, 1848 ***778.6*** *p279*
Reboul, Miss 4; Louisiana, 1848 ***778.6*** *p279*
Reboul, Mrs. 31; Louisiana, 1848 ***778.6*** *p279*
Reboul, Barth. 33; Louisiana, 1848 ***778.6*** *p279*
Reboulleaux, Victoire 25; New Orleans, 1846 ***778.6*** *p279*
Rebours, Jean 34; New Orleans, 1848 ***778.6*** *p279*
Rebours, Marguerite 15; Montreal, 1659 ***9221.17*** *p427*
Rebruche, Victor 19; Port uncertain, 1842 ***778.6*** *p279*
Rebscher, Jakob; America, 1852 ***2526.43*** *p204*
With wife & 2 children
Rebscher, Katharina; America, 1869 ***2526.43*** *p142*
Rebscher, Peter 15; America, 1881 ***2526.43*** *p154*
Rebu, Louis; Quebec, 1659 ***9221.17*** *p414*
Reburn, John; Harrisburg, PA, 1812 ***5720.10*** *p380*
Recaldy, J. 40; America, 1848 ***778.6*** *p279*
Rech, A. Maria Rauber 43 *SEE* Rech, Jakob
Rech, Anna Behles 51 *SEE* Rech, Josef
Rech, Elisabeth *SEE* Rech, Jakob
Rech, Eva 18; Mississippi, 1846 ***778.6*** *p279*
Rech, J. Claudius *SEE* Rech, Johann
Rech, Jakob *SEE* Rech, Jakob
Rech, Jakob 26; South America, 1857 ***5475.1*** *p512*
Rech, Jakob 48; South America, 1857 ***5475.1*** *p502*
*Wife:*A. Maria Rauber 43
*Son:*Jakob
*Daughter:*Maria
*Daughter:*Elisabeth
*Daughter:*Magdalena
*Son:*Johann
Rech, Jan; Minnesota, 1900 ***2853.20*** *p285*
Rech, Johann 25; America, 1876 ***5475.1*** *p355*
Rech, Johann 46; Brazil, 1863 ***5475.1*** *p502*
*Wife:*Maria Dewes 41
*Son:*Mathias
*Son:*J. Claudius
*Son:*Peter
With son
Rech, Johann *SEE* Rech, Jakob
Rech, Josef 48; America, 1856 ***5475.1*** *p352*
*Wife:*Anna Behles 51
*Son:*Peter 15
Rech, Magdalena *SEE* Rech, Jakob
Rech, Maria Dewes 41 *SEE* Rech, Johann
Rech, Maria *SEE* Rech, Jakob
Rech, Mathias *SEE* Rech, Johann
Rech, Peter 15 *SEE* Rech, Josef
Rech, Peter *SEE* Rech, Johann
Rech, Peter 58; Mississippi, 1846 ***778.6*** *p279*
Rech, Susanna 28; Brazil, 1857 ***5475.1*** *p512*
Rechle, Geisbroun 26; New York, NY, 1847 ***9176.15*** *p50*
Rechtenwald, Johann; Ohio, 1800-1899 ***5475.1*** *p528*
*Wife:*Luise
Rechtenwald, Luise 25 *SEE* Rechtenwald, Johann
Reckie, William 37; Ontario, 1871 ***1823.21*** *p306*
Recknagel, Max Ernst; America, 1867 ***7919.3*** *p526*
Recksiedler, Mr. 37; New York, NY, 1893 ***1883.7*** *p41*
Recksiedler, Ferdinand 6; New York, NY, 1893 ***1883.7*** *p41*
Recksiedler, Gottlieb 3; New York, NY, 1893 ***1883.7*** *p41*
Recksiedler, Henrietta 27; New York, NY, 1893 ***1883.7*** *p41*
Recksiedler, Ottilie 1; New York, NY, 1893 ***1883.7*** *p41*
Recksiedler, Wilhelmina 65; New York, NY, 1893 ***1883.7*** *p41*
Reckteenmald, John; Washington, 1889 ***2770.40*** *p80*
Recktenwald, Andreas 23; America, 1865 ***5475.1*** *p516*
Recktenwald, Anna *SEE* Recktenwald, Michel
Recktenwald, Anna Meiser 49 *SEE* Recktenwald, Michel
Recktenwald, Jakob; America, 1850 ***5475.1*** *p549*
Recktenwald, Johann; America, 1849 ***5475.1*** *p547*
Recktenwald, Katharina Schwarz 27 *SEE* Recktenwald, Lorenz
Recktenwald, Lorenz 26; America, 1867 ***5475.1*** *p558*
*Wife:*Katharina Schwarz 27
*Son:*Nikolaus
Recktenwald, Michel 59; America, 1856 ***5475.1*** *p563*
*Wife:*Anna Meiser 49
*Daughter:*Anna
*Son:*Peter
Recktenwald, Nikolaus *SEE* Recktenwald, Lorenz
Recktenwald, Nikolaus 22; America, 1867 ***5475.1*** *p558*
Recktenwald, Peter *SEE* Recktenwald, Michel
Record, Prudance 60; Ontario, 1871 ***1823.17*** *p137*
Record, William 30; Ontario, 1871 ***1823.21*** *p306*
Recordel, Rene 30; America, 1748 ***778.6*** *p279*
Rectenwald, Barbara; America, 1881 ***5475.1*** *p241*
Rectenwald, Conrad, II; America, 1846 ***5475.1*** *p546*
Rectenwald, Gertrud Reiter *SEE* Rectenwald, Johann
Rectenwald, Johann; America, 1800-1899 ***5475.1*** *p440*
*Wife:*Gertrud Reiter
With 5 children
Rectenwald, Johann; America, 1848 ***5475.1*** *p532*
Rectenwald, Josef; America, 1836 ***5475.1*** *p513*
Rectenwald, Maria; America, 1881 ***5475.1*** *p428*
Rectenwald, Susanna 23; Brazil, 1857 ***5475.1*** *p320*
Reculus, Lionel; America, 1755 ***1220.12*** *p664*
Red, James; South Carolina, 1800-1899 ***6155.4*** *p19*
Red, Robert; South Carolina, 1813 ***6155.4*** *p19*
Redasti, Stepano; Louisiana, 1874-1875 ***4981.45*** *p30*
Redaway, James; Massachusetts, 1676 ***9228.50*** *p534*
Redbeard, Thomas; America, 1685 ***1220.12*** *p664*
Redbeard, William; America, 1685 ***1220.12*** *p664*
Redbrooke, William; America, 1763 ***1220.12*** *p664*
Redburn, Thomas 8; Quebec, 1870 ***8364.32*** *p25*
Reddall, John; America, 1754 ***1220.12*** *p664*
Reddall, Mary; America, 1772 ***1220.12*** *p664*
Reddall, William; America, 1766 ***1220.12*** *p664*
Reddalls, John; America, 1757 ***1220.12*** *p664*
Reddick, John 46; Ontario, 1871 ***1823.17*** *p137*
Reddick, John G. 70; Ontario, 1871 ***1823.21*** *p306*
Reddick, Richard; North Carolina, 1835 ***1088.45*** *p28*
Reddick, Thomas 30; Ontario, 1871 ***1823.17*** *p137*
Reddiford, James; America, 1769 ***1220.12*** *p664*
Reddig, Gustav A.; North Dakota, 1900 ***554.30*** *p26*
*Wife:*Johanne
Reddig, Johanne *SEE* Reddig, Gustav A.
Reddin, James; America, 1766 ***1220.12*** *p664*
Redding, Eliza 30; Ontario, 1871 ***1823.21*** *p306*
Redding, William 22; Ontario, 1871 ***1823.21*** *p306*
Redecker, Catharine Sophie; America, 1845 ***7420.1*** *p35*
Redecker, Johann Heinrich August; America, 1869 ***7420.1*** *p281*
Redecker, Johann Otto; Port uncertain, 1841 ***7420.1*** *p23*
Redecker, Wilhelm; America, 1864 ***7420.1*** *p226*
With family
Redeker, Miss; America, 1867 ***7420.1*** *p258*
Redeker, Widow; America, 1859 ***7420.1*** *p188*
Redeker, Auguste Friederike Just. Carol. *SEE* Redeker, Henrich Christoph
Redeker, Elise Sophie Johanne; America, 1847 ***7420.1*** *p52*
Redeker, Engel Marie Stege *SEE* Redeker, Johann Christoph
Redeker, Engel Marie Dorothee; America, 1848 ***7420.1*** *p61*
Redeker, Ernestine Wilhelmine; America, 1862 ***7420.1*** *p214*
With son & 3 daughters
Redeker, Ernst Friedrich; America, 1892 ***7420.1*** *p366*
Redeker, Friedrich; America, 1855 ***7420.1*** *p140*
Redeker, Friedrich Christian Gottlieb; America, 1877 ***7420.1*** *p309*
Redeker, Heinrich; America, 1856 ***7420.1*** *p152*
Redeker, Henrich Christoph; America, 1848 ***7420.1*** *p61*
*Wife:*Justine Friederike Kathmann
With children
*Daughter:*Auguste Friederike Just. Carol.
Redeker, Johann Christoph; America, 1840 ***7420.1*** *p20*
*Wife:*Engel Marie Stege
Redeker, Johann Friedrich; America, 1854 ***7420.1*** *p127*
Redeker, Johann Philipp; America, 1865 ***7420.1*** *p235*
Redeker, Justine Friederike Kathmann *SEE* Redeker, Henrich Christoph
Redeker Brothers, . . .; America, 1865 ***7420.1*** *p235*
Redel, Anna; Wisconsin, 1888 ***6795.8*** *p34*
Redel, Herman; Wisconsin, 1898 ***6795.8*** *p27*
Redell, Johann; America, 1879 ***5475.1*** *p44*
Rederer, Andrew; Ohio, 1809-1852 ***4511.35*** *p42*
Redetzke, Friedrich; Wisconsin, 1866 ***6795.8*** *p26*
Redford, Richard; America, 1741 ***1220.12*** *p664*
Redford, Rosanna 50; Ontario, 1871 ***1823.21*** *p306*
Redford, William; America, 1766 ***1220.12*** *p664*
Redge, Emblyn; Barbados, 1679 ***1220.12*** *p665*
Redge, Thomas 48; Ontario, 1871 ***1823.21*** *p307*
Redhead, Elizabeth; America, 1736 ***1220.12*** *p665*
Redhead, Elizabeth; America, 1765 ***1220.12*** *p665*
Redhead, James; America, 1741 ***1220.12*** *p665*
Redhead, Love; America, 1753 ***1220.12*** *p665*
Redhead, Thomas; America, 1750 ***1220.12*** *p665*
Reding, John; Boston, 1764 ***1642*** *p33*
Redling, Nels; St. Paul, MN, 1882 ***1865.50*** *p107*
Redlinger, Angela 26; America, 1867 ***5475.1*** *p321*
Redlinger, Barbara 17 *SEE* Redlinger, Johann
Redlinger, Elisabeth 13 *SEE* Redlinger, Johann
Redlinger, Felix 13 *SEE* Redlinger, Johann
Redlinger, Heinrich 11 *SEE* Redlinger, Johann
Redlinger, Johann; America, 1872 ***5475.1*** *p327*
Redlinger, Johann; America, 1873 ***5475.1*** *p322*
*Wife:*Maria Dillschneider
*Son:*Peter
*Daughter:*Elisabeth
*Son:*Heinrich
*Son:*Nikolaus
*Daughter:*Magdalena
*Son:*Felix
*Son:*Michel
*Daughter:*Barbara
Redlinger, Katharina Aldenhoven *SEE* Redlinger, Michel
Redlinger, Magdalena 9 *SEE* Redlinger, Johann
Redlinger, Maria Dillschneider 42 *SEE* Redlinger, Johann
Redlinger, Michel *SEE* Redlinger, Michel
Redlinger, Michel; America, 1867 ***5475.1*** *p321*
*Wife:*Katharina Aldenhoven
*Son:*Valentin
*Son:*Peter
*Son:*Michel
Redlinger, Michel 19 *SEE* Redlinger, Johann
Redlinger, Nikolaus 7 *SEE* Redlinger, Johann
Redlinger, Peter *SEE* Redlinger, Michel

Redlinger, Peter 14 SEE Redlinger, Johann
Redlinger, Valentin SEE Redlinger, Michel
Redman, Daniel; North Carolina, 1807 *1088.45 p28*
Redman, James; Harrisburg, PA, 1816 *5720.10 p380*
Redman, James; Virginia, 1767 *1220.12 p665*
Redman, John; America, 1774 *1220.12 p665*
Redman, Letitia; America, 1727 *1220.12 p665*
Redman, Marjorie; New England, 1920-1929 *9228.50 p534*
Redman, Martha; Died enroute, 1731 *1220.12 p665*
Redman, Mary; America, 1767 *1220.12 p665*
Redman, Maurice; North Carolina, 1811 *1088.45 p28*
Redman, Samuel 61; Ontario, 1871 *1823.21 p307*
Redman, Thomas; Annapolis, MD, 1723 *1220.12 p665*
Redmann, Reinhold Fred; Wisconsin, 1905 *6795.8 p188*
Redmond, Alice; New Orleans, 1850 *7242.30 p153*
Redmond, Charles; New Orleans, 1850 *7242.30 p153*
Redmond, Edward; New Orleans, 1850 *7242.30 p153*
Redmond, Eliza; New Orleans, 1850 *7242.30 p153*
Redmond, Ellen; New Orleans, 1850 *7242.30 p153*
Redmond, Francis; America, 1766 *1220.12 p665*
Redmond, Garret; New Orleans, 1851 *7242.30 p153*
Redmond, Henry; New Orleans, 1850 *7242.30 p153*
Redmond, James; New Orleans, 1850 *7242.30 p153*
Redmond, James; New Orleans, 1850 *7242.30 p153*
Redmond, John 53; Ontario, 1871 *1823.21 p307*
Redmond, Kate; New Orleans, 1850 *7242.30 p153*
Redmond, Margaret; New Orleans, 1850 *7242.30 p153*
Redmond, Margaret 40; Ontario, 1871 *1823.21 p307*
Redmond, Martha; New Orleans, 1850 *7242.30 p153*
Redmond, Mary; New Orleans, 1850 *7242.30 p153*
Redmond, Mary; New Orleans, 1851 *7242.30 p153*
Redmond, Mathew 85; Ontario, 1871 *1823.21 p307*
Redmond, Michael 48; Ontario, 1871 *1823.21 p307*
Redmond, P.; Louisiana, 1874 *4981.45 p297*
Redmond, Patrick; New Orleans, 1850 *7242.30 p153*
Redmond, Sally; New Orleans, 1850 *7242.30 p153*
Redmond, Thomas; Louisiana, 1841-1844 *4981.45 p211*
Redmond, Thomas; New Orleans, 1851 *7242.30 p153*
Redmond, William; New Orleans, 1850 *7242.30 p153*
Redner, Andrew; Ohio, 1809-1852 *4511.35 p42*
Redner, Charles; Ohio, 1809-1852 *4511.35 p42*
Redon, Jean 23; Quebec, 1657 *9221.17 p366*
Redoute, Jean Baptiste 40; New Orleans, 1848 *778.6 p279*
Redoute, Joseph 16; New Orleans, 1848 *778.6 p279*
Redoute, Joseph Baptiste 11; New Orleans, 1848 *778.6 p279*
Redpath, Alexander 36; Ontario, 1871 *1823.21 p307*
Redriff, John; America, 1767 *1220.12 p665*
Redrup, Daniel; Maryland, 1742 *1220.12 p665*
Redshaw, Sarah; America, 1755 *1220.12 p665*
Redwood, Henry; America, 1720 *1220.12 p665*
Redwood, Thomas; America, 1685 *1220.12 p665*
Redwood, William; America, 1772 *1220.12 p665*
Redwood, William; America, 1773 *1220.12 p665*
Reeb, Louise 25; America, 1840 *778.6 p279*
Reece, Andrew; Ohio, 1809-1852 *4511.35 p42*
Reece, John; America, 1751 *1220.12 p665*
Reece, Samuel 38; Michigan, 1880 *4491.33 p19*
Reece, Thomas; America, 1739 *1220.12 p665*
Reech, James; Barbados, 1664 *1220.12 p662*
Reeck, Julius H.; Wisconsin, 1877 *6795.8 p205*
Reeck, Minna Martha; Wisconsin, 1892 *6795.8 p75*
Reed, Albert S. 34; Ohio, 1880 *4879.40 p260*
Reed, Ann SEE Reed, George
Reed, Ann; Potomac, 1731 *1220.12 p662*
Reed, Anthony; America, 1766 *1220.12 p662*
Reed, Charles 49; Indiana, 1886-1892 *9076.20 p73*
Reed, Christian; Barbados or Jamaica, 1702 *1220.12 p662*
Reed, Christopher 53; Kansas, 1888 *1447.20 p62*
Reed, Daniel 11; Ontario, 1871 *1823.17 p137*
Reed, Edward; America, 1727 *1220.12 p662*
Reed, Edward 39; Ontario, 1871 *1823.21 p307*
Reed, Eliza; Halifax, N.S., 1827 *7009.9 p62*
  *Father:*Thomas
  *Mother:*Margaret Nary
Reed, Eliza; Utah, 1862 *9228.50 p534*
Reed, Elizabeth; America, 1746 *1220.12 p662*
Reed, Francis; America, 1774 *1220.12 p662*
Reed, Francis; Harrisburg, PA, 1798 *5720.10 p380*
Reed, George SEE Reed, George
Reed, George; Canada, 1774 *3036.5 p40*
  *Wife:*Hannah
  *Child:*Ann
  *Child:*Isabella
  *Child:*George
  *Child:*John
Reed, Hannah; America, 1760 *1220.12 p662*
Reed, Hannah SEE Reed, George
Reed, Henry; Long Island, 1781 *8529.30 p10A*
Reed, Isaac; Ohio, 1809-1852 *4511.35 p42*

Reed, Isabella SEE Reed, George
Reed, James; America, 1717 *1220.12 p662*
Reed, James; Harrisburg, PA, 1798 *5720.10 p380*
Reed, James; Harrisburg, PA, 1813 *5720.10 p380*
Reed, James; Marston's Wharf, 1781 *8529.30 p15*
Reed, James; North Carolina, 1838 *1088.45 p28*
Reed, James, Jr.; America, 1727 *1220.12 p662*
Reed, Janet; New York, 1738 *8277.31 p118*
Reed, Janet; New York, 1738 *8277.31 p118*
Reed, John; America, 1723 *1220.12 p662*
Reed, John; America, 1754 *1220.12 p663*
Reed, John; America, 1769 *1220.12 p663*
Reed, John; America, 1773 *1220.12 p663*
Reed, John; America, 1774 *1220.12 p663*
Reed, John; Barbados, 1686 *1220.12 p662*
Reed, John SEE Reed, George
Reed, John; Canada, 1774 *3036.5 p40*
Reed, John; Marston's Wharf, 1781 *8529.30 p15*
Reed, John; North Carolina, 1839-1846 *1088.45 p28*
Reed, John; Ohio, 1809-1852 *4511.35 p42*
Reed, John 40; Ontario, 1871 *1823.21 p307*
Reed, John 41; Ontario, 1871 *1823.21 p307*
Reed, Joseph; America, 1756 *1220.12 p663*
Reed, Lizza 41; Michigan, 1880 *4491.30 p25*
Reed, Margaret; America, 1773 *1220.12 p663*
Reed, Margaret Nary SEE Reed, Eliza
Reed, Margret 16; Ontario, 1871 *1823.21 p307*
Reed, Martin; America, 1759 *1220.12 p663*
Reed, Martin; St. Johns, N.F., 1825 *1053.15 p7*
Reed, Mary; America, 1743 *1220.12 p663*
Reed, Mary; Annapolis, MD, 1719 *1220.12 p663*
Reed, Mary; Virginia, 1773 *1220.12 p663*
Reed, Michael; America, 1776 *1220.12 p663*
Reed, Moses; America, 1700 *1220.12 p663*
Reed, Nathaniel 54; Ontario, 1871 *1823.21 p307*
Reed, Richard; Annapolis, MD, 1723 *1220.12 p663*
Reed, Robert; America, 1723 *1220.12 p663*
Reed, Robert; Harrisburg, PA, 1813 *5720.10 p380*
Reed, Samuel 34; Ohio, 1880 *4879.40 p257*
Reed, Thomas SEE Reed, George
Reed, William; Boston, 1775 *8529.30 p3*
Reed, William; Harrisburg, PA, 1798 *5720.10 p380*
Reed, William; North Carolina, 1851 *1088.45 p28*
Reed, William; Ohio, 1809-1852 *4511.35 p42*
Reed, William 30; Ontario, 1871 *1823.21 p307*
Reeda, James; Jamaica, 1778 *8529.30 p14A*
Reeder, Conrad; Illinois, 1858-1861 *6020.5 p132*
Reeder, Henry; North Carolina, 1860 *1088.45 p28*
Reeder, John; America, 1737 *1220.12 p664*
Reeder, John; America, 1765 *1220.12 p664*
Reeder, Thomas; Long Island, 1781 *8529.30 p10A*
Reedy, John 33; Ontario, 1871 *1823.21 p307*
Reedy, John 33; Ontario, 1871 *1823.21 p307*
Reedy, Thomas 62; Ontario, 1871 *1823.21 p307*
Reef, William 36; Ontario, 1871 *1823.21 p307*
Reeg, Adam; America, 1874 *2526.43 p161*
Reeg, Adam 18; America, 1853 *2526.43 p212*
Reeg, Anna Elisabetha Steiger SEE Reeg, Jakob
Reeg, Anna Elisabetha 2 SEE Reeg, Ludwig
Reeg, Balthasar; America, 1891 *2526.43 p161*
Reeg, Balthasar; America, 1896 *2526.43 p161*
Reeg, Barbara; America, 1871 *2526.43 p212*
Reeg, Barbara 17 SEE Reeg, Peter, III
Reeg, Christina 2 SEE Reeg, Heinrich
Reeg, Christina 4 SEE Reeg, Jakob
Reeg, Elisabeth SEE Reeg, Heinrich
Reeg, Elisabeth 9 SEE Reeg, Jakob
Reeg, Georg; America, 1768-1785 *2526.43 p130*
Reeg, Georg; America, 1878 *2526.43 p213*
Reeg, Georg; America, 1884 *2526.43 p161*
Reeg, Georg Adam; America, 1860 *2526.42 p170*
Reeg, Georg Adam; America, 1887 *2526.43 p191*
Reeg, Georg Philipp; America, 1853 *2526.43 p226*
Reeg, Georg Wilhelm; America, 1882 *2526.43 p132*
Reeg, Gertraude 10 SEE Reeg, Ludwig
Reeg, Heinrich; America, 1854 *2526.43 p143*
  *Wife:*Elisabeth
  *Daughter:*Margaretha
  *Son:*Johannes
  *Daughter:*Katharina
Reeg, Heinrich 4 SEE Reeg, Heinrich
Reeg, Heinrich 30; America, 1839 *2526.43 p142*
  With wife 36
  *Daughter:*Margaretha 7
  *Daughter:*Christina 2
  *Son:*Heinrich 4
Reeg, Jakob; America, 1841 *2526.42 p176*
  *Wife:*Anna Elisabetha Steiger
  *Son:*Johannes
  *Daughter:*Elisabeth
Reeg, Jakob; America, 1883 *2526.43 p132*

Reeg, Jakob 33; America, 1838 *2526.43 p143*
  With wife 33
  *Daughter:*Katharina 6
  *Daughter:*Margaretha 2
  *Daughter:*Christina 4
Reeg, Johann; America, 1853 *2526.43 p226*
Reeg, Johann Philipp; America, 1891 *2526.43 p132*
Reeg, Johannes SEE Reeg, Jakob
Reeg, Johannes SEE Reeg, Heinrich
Reeg, Johannes; America, 1899 *2526.43 p191*
Reeg, Katharina SEE Reeg, Heinrich
Reeg, Katharina 6 SEE Reeg, Jakob
Reeg, Katharina 18 SEE Reeg, Ludwig
Reeg, Katharina Breunig 43 SEE Reeg, Ludwig
Reeg, Leonhard; America, 1853 *2526.43 p143*
Reeg, Leonhard; America, 1881 *2526.43 p131*
Reeg, Leonhard; America, 1897 *2526.43 p132*
Reeg, Leonhard 30; America, 1881 *2526.43 p191*
Reeg, Ludwig 16 SEE Reeg, Ludwig
Reeg, Ludwig 44; America, 1856 *2526.43 p132*
  *Son:*Wilhelm 13
  *Daughter:*Anna Elisabetha 2
  *Daughter:*Maria Elisabetha 6
  *Son:*Ludwig 16
  *Daughter:*Katharina 18
  *Wife:*Katharina Breunig 43
  *Son:*Nikolaus 13
  *Daughter:*Gertraude 10
  *Son:*Mathaus 8
Reeg, Ludwig Adam; America, 1866 *2526.43 p226*
Reeg, Magdalena 18; America, 1893 *2526.43 p131*
Reeg, Margaretha SEE Reeg, Heinrich
Reeg, Margaretha 2 SEE Reeg, Jakob
Reeg, Margaretha 7 SEE Reeg, Heinrich
Reeg, Maria Elisabetha 6 SEE Reeg, Ludwig
Reeg, Marie; America, 1899 *2526.43 p191*
Reeg, Mathaus 8 SEE Reeg, Ludwig
Reeg, Nikolaus 13 SEE Reeg, Ludwig
Reeg, Peter; America, 1889 *2526.43 p191*
Reeg, Peter, III 64; America, 1846 *2526.43 p161*
  With wife
  *Daughter:*Barbara 17
Reeg, Philipp; America, 1847 *2526.43 p189*
Reeg, Philipp; America, 1891 *2526.43 p132*
Reeg, Philipp; America, 1893 *2526.43 p191*
Reeg, Philipp, II 20; America, 1852 *2526.43 p226*
Reeg, Philipp Jakob; America, 1893 *2526.43 p191*
Reeg, Wilhelm; America, 1879 *2526.43 p161*
Reeg, Wilhelm; America, 1883 *2526.43 p132*
Reeg, Wilhelm 13 SEE Reeg, Ludwig
Reeh, Andreas SEE Reeh, Elisabeth Margarethe
Reeh, Andreas Gg.; America, 1859 *8115.12 p322*
Reeh, Anna Elisabeth; America, 1852 *8115.12 p317*
  *Child:*Johann Georg
  *Child:*Johann Ludwig
Reeh, Balthasar 49; America, 1831 *2526.43 p177*
  With wife
Reeh, Christian SEE Reeh, Katharina
Reeh, Elisabeth; America, 1859 *8115.12 p322*
Reeh, Elisabeth SEE Reeh, Katharina
Reeh, Elisabeth SEE Reeh, Elisabeth Margarethe
Reeh, Elisabeth Margarethe; America, n.d. *8115.12 p319*
  *Child:*Konrad
  *Child:*Elisabeth
  *Child:*Johannes
  *Child:*Margarethe
  *Child:*Andreas
  *Child:*Ludwig
Reeh, Georg Christian; America, n.d. *8115.12 p327*
Reeh, Georg Wilhelm; America, n.d. *8115.12 p327*
Reeh, Johann Georg SEE Reeh, Anna Elisabeth
Reeh, Johann Ludwig SEE Reeh, Anna Elisabeth
Reeh, Johannes SEE Reeh, Elisabeth Margarethe
Reeh, Katharina; America, n.d. *8115.12 p317*
  *Child:*Katharine
  *Child:*Konrad
  *Child:*Christian
  *Child:*Louise
  *Child:*Elisabeth
  *Child:*Ludwig
Reeh, Katharine SEE Reeh, Katharina
Reeh, Katharine Elisabeth; America, 1858 *8115.12 p328*
Reeh, Konrad SEE Reeh, Katharina
Reeh, Konrad SEE Reeh, Elisabeth Margarethe
Reeh, Louise SEE Reeh, Katharina
Reeh, Louise; America, n.d. *8115.12 p322*
Reeh, Ludwig; America, 1859 *8115.12 p322*
Reeh, Ludwig SEE Reeh, Katharina
Reeh, Ludwig SEE Reeh, Elisabeth Margarethe
Reeh, Magdalena; America, 1859 *8115.12 p322*
Reeh, Margarethe SEE Reeh, Elisabeth Margarethe
Reek, Emilie; Wisconsin, 1893 *6795.8 p75*
Reekie, Richard A.; Washington, 1889 *2770.40 p80*

Reeling, Thomas; America, 1871 *9076.20* p68
Reenor, John 45; Ontario, 1871 *1823.21* p307
Rees, Ann Richards SEE Rees, Evan
Rees, Anne; Ohio, 1840 *4022.20* p290
Rees, Charles; Ohio, 1850 *4022.20* p290
 *Wife:*Elizabeth Parry
Rees, David; Nebraska, 1905 *3004.30* p46
Rees, David M.; Colorado, 1875 *1029.59* p76
Rees, Elizabeth SEE Rees, William
Rees, Elizabeth Parry SEE Rees, Charles
Rees, Evan; America, 1724 *1220.12* p665
Rees, Evan; Ohio, 1840 *4022.20* p290
 *Wife:*Ann Richards
 With children
Rees, George; Ohio, 1809-1852 *4511.35* p42
Rees, John; America, 1756 *1220.12* p665
Rees, John; America, 1765 *1220.12* p665
Rees, John; North Carolina, 1822 *1088.45* p28
Rees, Margaret Edwards SEE Rees, William
Rees, Mary; America, 1756 *1220.12* p665
Rees, Mary SEE Rees, William
Rees, Nicholas; Ohio, 1809-1852 *4511.35* p42
Rees, Rees 50; Ontario, 1871 *1823.21* p307
Rees, Roger; West Indies, 1688 *1220.12* p665
Rees, Sarah; Ohio, 1838 *4022.20* p292
Rees, William; America, 1759 *1220.12* p665
Rees, William; America, 1775 *1220.12* p665
Rees, William; Ohio, 1838 *4022.20* p290
 *Wife:*Margaret Edwards
 *Child:*Mary
 *Child:*Elizabeth
Rees, William; Ohio, 1840-1897 *8365.35* p17
Rees, Wm.; Ohio, 1838 *4022.20* p285
Reese, Andrew; Ohio, 1809-1852 *4511.35* p42
Reese, Anne Marie; Chicago, 1857 *7420.1* p163
Reese, August Hermann; America, 1848 *7420.1* p61
Reese, Cord Heinrich; America, 1853 *7420.1* p110
 With son & daughter
Reese, Dorothee; America, 1857 *7420.1* p170
Reese, Engel Marie Sophie; America, 1847 *7420.1* p51
Reese, Engel Sophie; America, 1854 *7420.1* p123
Reese, Hans Heinrich; America, 1852 *7420.1* p95
Reese, Hans Heinrich; America, 1866 *7420.1* p247
Reese, Heinrich Christoph; America, 1866 *7420.1* p247
Reese, Heinrich Christoph August; America, 1864 *7420.1* p226
Reese, Heinrich Conrad; America, 1860 *7420.1* p198
Reese, Heinrich Hermann; America, 1866 *7420.1* p247
Reese, Johann Heinrich Wilhelm; America, 1831-1914 *7420.1* p5
Reese, John; America, 1729 *1220.12* p665
Reese, Nicholas; Harrisburg, PA, 1798 *5720.10* p380
Reese, Peter 56; Michigan, 1880 *4491.30* p25
Reese, Sophia Dorothea; America, 1847 *7420.1* p55
Reese, Wilhelm; America, 1854 *7420.1* p127
Reetz, Emil R.; Wisconsin, 1889 *6795.8* p189
Reetz, Gustav; Wisconsin, 1870 *6795.8* p127
Reeve, Ann; America, 1758 *1220.12* p665
Reeve, Dina; America, 1686 *1220.12* p665
Reeve, G. B. 28; Ontario, 1871 *1823.21* p307
Reeve, John; America, 1755 *1220.12* p665
Reeve, John; America, 1767 *1220.12* p665
Reeve, Joseph; America, 1743 *1220.12* p665
Reeve, Sarah; Potomac, 1729 *1220.12* p665
Reeve, Thomas; Virginia, 1764 *1220.12* p665
Reeve, William; America, 1770 *1220.12* p665
Reeve, William; Ohio, 1842 *2763.1* p21
Reeve, William 58; Ontario, 1871 *1823.21* p307
Reeves, Abraham; Maryland or Virginia, 1738 *1220.12* p665
Reeves, Arabella; America, 1686 *1220.12* p665
Reeves, Edmund; America, 1753 *1220.12* p665
Reeves, Elizabeth; America, 1699 *1220.12* p665
Reeves, Elizabeth; Maryland or Virginia, 1733 *1220.12* p666
Reeves, Ellen 25; Ontario, 1871 *1823.21* p307
Reeves, George; Maryland, 1741 *1220.12* p666
Reeves, George; Potomac, 1731 *1220.12* p666
Reeves, James; America, 1717 *1220.12* p666
Reeves, James; America, 1760 *1220.12* p666
Reeves, Jas W. 32; Ontario, 1871 *1823.21* p307
Reeves, John; America, 1685 *1220.12* p666
Reeves, John; America, 1765 *1220.12* p666
Reeves, John 70; Ontario, 1871 *1823.21* p307
Reeves, John 13; Quebec, 1870 *8364.32* p25
Reeves, Joseph; America, 1722 *1220.12* p666
Reeves, Joseph; America, 1765 *1220.12* p666
Reeves, Mary; America, 1765 *1220.12* p666
Reeves, Richard; America, 1773 *1220.12* p666
Reeves, Robert; America, 1685 *1220.12* p666
Reeves, Robert; America, 1770 *1220.12* p666
Reeves, Robert; Carolina, 1724 *1220.12* p666
Reeves, Thomas; Annapolis, MD, 1725 *1220.12* p666

Reeves, William; America, 1741 *1220.12* p666
Reeves, William; Jamaica, 1661 *1220.12* p666
Reeves, William; New Jersey, 1777 *8529.30* p7
Reeves, William 56; Ontario, 1871 *1823.21* p307
Reeves, William 14; Quebec, 1870 *8364.32* p25
Refetopolos, Demetres; Washington, 1882 *2770.40* p136
Refouvelat, L.; Louisiana, 1874 *4981.45* p297
Regan, Andrew; America, 1770 *1220.12* p666
Regan, Ann 11; Quebec, 1870 *8364.32* p25
Regan, Bartholomew; America, 1769 *1220.12* p666
Regan, Catherine 38; Ontario, 1871 *1823.21* p307
Regan, Cornelius 37; Ontario, 1871 *1823.21* p307
Regan, Cornelius 65; Ontario, 1871 *1823.21* p307
Regan, Cornelius 66; Ontario, 1871 *1823.21* p307
Regan, Daniel 32; Ontario, 1871 *1823.21* p307
Regan, Dennis 70; Ontario, 1871 *1823.21* p307
Regan, Ellen 33; Ontario, 1871 *1823.21* p307
Regan, James; Louisiana, 1874 *4981.45* p296
Regan, James 30; Ontario, 1871 *1823.17* p137
Regan, John; Harrisburg, PA, 1813 *5720.10* p380
Regan, John 60; Ontario, 1871 *1823.21* p307
Regan, John; St. John, N.B., 1847 *2978.15* p37
Regan, Mary; America, 1765 *1220.12* p666
Regan, Mary 13; Quebec, 1870 *8364.32* p25
Regan, Michael 74; Ontario, 1871 *1823.21* p307
Regan, Olive Myrtle; Oregon, 1941 *9157.47* p2
Regan, Patrick 38; Ontario, 1871 *1823.21* p307
Regan, Patrick 61; Ontario, 1871 *1823.21* p307
Regan, Timothy 35; Ontario, 1871 *1823.21* p308
Regaull, S. 30; New Orleans, 1834 *1002.51* p113
Regel, Franz Louis; Wisconsin, 1893 *6795.8* p209
Regert, Jakob 52; Brazil, 1857 *5475.1* p291
 *Wife:*Margarethe Knapp 44
 *Son:*Peter 6
 *Son:*Michel 23
Regert, Margarethe Knapp 44 SEE Regert, Jakob
Regert, Michel 23 SEE Regert, Jakob
Regert, Peter 6 SEE Regert, Jakob
Reggendorff, Fr.; Venezuela, 1843 *3899.5* p546
Reginas, Christian; Ohio, 1809-1852 *4511.35* p42
Reginka, Cecilia; Wisconsin, 1888 *6795.8* p61
Regitz, Jakob Peter; America, 1869 *5475.1* p71
Regitz, Ludwig Daniel; America, 1869 *5475.1* p71
Regle, John; Boston, 1752-1800 *9228.50* p392
Regnard, Louis; Quebec, 1651 *9221.17* p250
Regnard Duplessis, Georges; Quebec, 1689 *2314.30* p172
Regnault, Barbe 12 SEE Regnault, Marie Martin
Regnault, Christophe; Quebec, 1636 *9221.17* p62
Regnault, Jacques 11 SEE Regnault, Marie Martin
Regnault, Jeanne 14 SEE Regnault, Marie Martin
Regnault, Jeanne Crespeau 43; Montreal, 1659 *9221.17* p424
Regnault, Jeanne Crespeau 43; Montreal, 1659 *9221.17* p424
Regnault, Joseph-Mathurin 17; Quebec, 1661 *9221.17* p466
Regnault, Marie SEE Regnault, Vincent
Regnault, Marie 21; Quebec, 1654 *9221.17* p316
Regnault, Marie 41; Quebec, 1656 *9221.17* p346
 *Daughter:*Jeanne 14
 *Daughter:*Barbe 12
 *Son:*Jacques 11
Regnault, Vincent 39; Quebec, 1648 *9221.17* p203
 *Daughter:*Marie
Regnaut, Jacques; Quebec, 1645 *9221.17* p157
Regnier, Mr. 40; America, 1746 *778.6* p279
Regnier, F. 16; America, 1746 *778.6* p279
Regnier, Pierre; Quebec, 1642 *9221.17* p121
Regnouard, Marie 35; Quebec, 1634 *9221.17* p36
 *Daughter:*Marie 6
 *Son:*Charles 3
Regottaz, Louis; Louisiana, 1874 *4981.45* p296
Regreny, Mathurin 25; Quebec, 1659 *9221.17* p409
Regueny, Mathurin 25; Quebec, 1659 *9221.17* p409
Reguindeau, Joachim 19; Quebec, 1657 *9221.17* p367
Reh, Rosine; New York, 1859 *358.56* p100
Rehage, Henry; North Carolina, 1848 *1088.45* p28
Rehage, Henry; North Carolina, 1854 *1088.45* p28
Rehak, Jan; America, 1874 *2853.20* p168
 With wife
Rehberger, George; Washington, 1882 *2770.40* p136
Rehbock, . . .; Port uncertain, 1865 *170.15* p38
 With sibling
Rehbock, Barbara; America, 1865 *170.15* p38
 With family
Rehbock, Carol. Sophie Tebbe SEE Rehbock, Heinrich Dietrich Christian
Rehbock, Heinrich Dietrich Christian SEE Rehbock, Heinrich Friedrich Wilhelm
Rehbock, Heinrich Dietrich Christian; America, 1867 *7420.1* p262
 *Wife:*Carol. Sophie Tebbe

Rehbock, Heinrich Friedrich Wilhelm; America, 1867 *7420.1* p262
 *Uncle:*Heinrich Dietrich Christian
Rehbock, Valentin; America, 1865 *170.15* p39
 With 2 children
Rehburg, Karl Heinr. Ludwig; America, 1869 *7420.1* p281
Rehder, Johanna E.; Philadelphia, 1850 *8513.31* p423
Rehder, Margaret J.; North Carolina, 1792-1862 *1088.45* p28
Rehell, James; Toronto, 1844 *2910.35* p113
Rehell, Owen; Toronto, 1844 *2910.35* p113
Rehinam, Bridget 18; Ontario, 1871 *1823.21* p308
Rehkow, August; Colorado, 1891 *1029.59* p76
Rehkow, August; Colorado, 1891 *1029.59* p77
Rehling, Anna Sophie Dorothee; America, 1855 *7420.1* p136
Rehling, Engel Marie Stege SEE Rehling, Johann Conrad
Rehling, Engel Marie Sophie; America, 1849 *7420.1* p67
Rehling, Ernst; America, 1872 *7420.1* p297
Rehling, Friedrich; America, 1852 *7420.1* p95
Rehling, Heinrich Friedrich; America, 1872 *7420.1* p297
Rehling, Johann Conrad; America, 1846 *7420.1* p47
 *Wife:*Engel Marie Stege
 *Son:*Johann Konrad
 *Son:*Johann Hermann
Rehling, Johann Hermann SEE Rehling, Johann Conrad
Rehling, Johann Konrad SEE Rehling, Johann Conrad
Rehlinger, Angela; America, 1879 *5475.1* p376
 *Daughter:*Elisabeth
 *Son:*Peter
Rehlinger, Elisabeth SEE Rehlinger, Angela Jakobs
Rehlinger, Peter SEE Rehlinger, Angela Jakobs
Rehm, Wilhelm; Valdivia, Chile, 1851 *1192.4* p51
Rehmer, Ernst; America, 1868 *7420.1* p275
 With wife
Rehmert, Auguste Charlotte; America, 1883 *7420.1* p339
Rehmert, Caroline Wilhelmine Charl.; North America, 1884 *7420.1* p345
Rehmert, Christina Wilhelmine Charlotte Dohm SEE Rehmert, Heinrich Wilhelm
Rehmert, Christine Wilhemine Dohm SEE Rehmert, Heinrich Wilhelm
Rehmert, Friederike Wilhelmine Charlotte SEE Rehmert, Heinrich Wilhelm
Rehmert, Friedrich; America, 1846 *7420.1* p47
 With wife & 5 children
Rehmert, Hans Heinrich; America, 1853 *7420.1* p110
 With wife 3 sons & 2 daughters
Rehmert, Heinrich Friedrich August SEE Rehmert, Heinrich Wilhelm
Rehmert, Heinrich Wilhelm; America, 1847 *7420.1* p55
 *Wife:*Christina Wilhelmine Charlotte Dohm
 *Son:*Heinrich Friedrich August
 *Daughter:*Friederike Wilhelmine Charlotte
Rehmert, Heinrich Wilhelm; America, 1847 *7420.1* p55
 *Wife:*Christine Wilhemine Dohm
 *Son:*Heinrich Wilhelm Ludwig
 *Sister:*Sophie Wilhelm
Rehmert, Heinrich Wilhelm; America, 1847 *7420.1* p56
Rehmert, Heinrich Wilhelm Ludwig SEE Rehmert, Heinrich Wilhelm
Rehmert, Johann Friedrich; America, 1854 *7420.1* p127
 With wife 4 sons & 3 daughters
Rehmert, Sophie Wilhelm SEE Rehmert, Heinrich Wilhelm
Rehn, Geroge; Louisiana, 1874 *4981.45* p133
Rehn, J. B.; Louisiana, 1874-1875 *4981.45* p30
Rehn, Justice; Illinois, 1852 *6079.1* p11
Rehn, Peter; Ohio, 1809-1852 *4511.35* p42
Rehon, Stanislas 35; America, 1845 *778.6* p279
Rehovsky, Tomas; Nebraska, 1871-1872 *2853.20* p176
Reiad, George 45; Ontario, 1871 *1823.17* p137
Reib, John Michael; New York, 1860 *358.56* p148
Reiber, Gertrud; America, 1887 *5475.1* p333
Reich, Hermann Johann Martin; Port uncertain, 1881 *7420.1* p323
Reich, Jacob; Ohio, 1809-1852 *4511.35* p42
Reich, Johan 30; Portland, ME, 1911 *970.38* p80
Reich, John; Harrisburg, PA, 1806 *5720.10* p380
Reichard, Georg; America, 1867 *2526.42* p184
Reichard, Kath. 38; Brazil, 1865 *5475.1* p506
Reichard, Paul; Ohio, 1809-1852 *4511.35* p42
Reichardt, Christian Frederic; Illinois, 1856 *6079.1* p11
Reichardt, Maria Kath. 32; Brazil, 1862 *5475.1* p506
Reichart, Adam; America, 1883 *2526.42* p129
 *Mother:*Eva Katharina Hofferberth
Reichart, Caspar; Ohio, 1809-1852 *4511.35* p42
Reichart, Eva Katharina Hofferberth SEE Reichart, Adam
Reichart, Johann Simon; America, 1852 *2526.43* p222
Reichart, Magdalena 37; America, 1855 *2526.42* p109
Reiche, Carl Ludwig; America, 1865 *7420.1* p235

Reichel, Dorothea 11; Portland, ME, 1910 *970.38 p80*
Reichel, Eliza 19; Portland, ME, 1910 *970.38 p80*
Reichel, Heinrich 15; Portland, ME, 1910 *970.38 p80*
Reichel, Johann 9; Portland, ME, 1910 *970.38 p80*
Reichel, Katerina 18; Portland, ME, 1910 *970.38 p80*
Reichel, Lisbeth 50; Portland, ME, 1910 *970.38 p80*
Reichel, Michael 44; Portland, ME, 1910 *970.38 p80*
Reichenbach, Henry; Ohio, 1809-1852 *4511.35 p42*
Reichenbacher, Carl; America, 1868 *7919.3 p532*
Reichenberg, Dorothea; America, 1882 *7420.1 p331*
Reicher, Jacob 26; Halifax, N.S., 1902 *1860.4 p41*
Reicher, Sophie 20; Halifax, N.S., 1902 *1860.4 p41*
Reichert, Adam; America, 1853 *2526.43 p222*
    With wife & 3 children
Reichert, Adam 6; New York, NY, 1893 *1883.7 p42*
Reichert, Amelie 22; New York, NY, 1899 *5475.1 p19*
Reichert, Anna 26; New Orleans, 1848 *778.6 p279*
Reichert, August D.; Washington, 1883 *2770.40 p137*
Reichert, C. J.; Chile, 1852 *1192.4 p52*
Reichert, Carolinia 34; New York, NY, 1893 *1883.7 p42*
Reichert, David 3; New Orleans, 1848 *778.6 p279*
Reichert, Elisabeth 56; Brazil, 1862 *5475.1 p561*
Reichert, Elise; New York, 1860 *358.56 p5*
Reichert, Georg; America, 1850 *2526.43 p199*
    With wife
    Daughter: Katharina
Reichert, Georg 1; New Orleans, 1848 *778.6 p280*
Reichert, Georg 4; New York, NY, 1893 *1883.7 p42*
Reichert, Heinrich; Halifax, N.S., 1902 *1860.4 p41*
Reichert, Heinrich 4; Halifax, N.S., 1902 *1860.4 p41*
Reichert, Heinrich 30; Halifax, N.S., 1902 *1860.4 p41*
Reichert, Jacob 42; Halifax, N.S., 1902 *1860.4 p41*
Reichert, Jacob 34; New York, NY, 1893 *1883.7 p42*
Reichert, Jacob 24; Portland, ME, 1906 *970.38 p80*
Reichert, Jacob Edward; Louisiana, 1874 *4981.45 p134*
Reichert, Johannes 19; New York, NY, 1893 *1883.7 p42*
Reichert, Katha 29; Halifax, N.S., 1902 *1860.4 p41*
Reichert, Katha 38; Halifax, N.S., 1902 *1860.4 p41*
Reichert, Katharina SEE Reichert, Georg
Reichert, Konrad; America, 1853 *2526.43 p219*
    With wife
Reichert, Leonora 8; New York, NY, 1893 *1883.7 p42*
Reichert, Lisbet 4; Halifax, N.S., 1902 *1860.4 p41*
Reichert, Lisbeth 2; Halifax, N.S., 1902 *1860.4 p41*
Reichert, Maria 2; Halifax, N.S., 1902 *1860.4 p41*
Reichert, Mona 10; Halifax, N.S., 1902 *1860.4 p41*
Reichert, Simon 20; New Orleans, 1848 *778.6 p280*
Reichert, Wendelin 10; New York, NY, 1893 *1883.7 p42*
Reicherzer, Heinrich Theodor; America, 1849 *7420.1 p67*
Reichherzer, Friederike; Philadelphia, 1904 *7420.1 p401*
Reichimer, Andrew; Ohio, 1809-1852 *4511.35 p42*
Reichling, Karl; America, 1923 *8023.44 p378*
Reichmann, Heinrich; America, 1857 *7420.1 p170*
Reichrath, Anton; America, 1873 *5475.1 p172*
Reichwage, Ernst August Otto; America, 1900 *7420.1 p376*
Reichwein, John; Nebraska, 1871 *1029.59 p77*
Reichwein, John; New York, 1860 *358.56 p149*
Reid, Miss; Quebec, 1885 *1937.10 p52*
Reid, Alexander SEE Reid, Duncan
Reid, Alexander; North Carolina, 1792-1862 *1088.45 p28*
Reid, Angus SEE Reid, Duncan
Reid, Christian 50; Ontario, 1871 *1823.21 p308*
Reid, David; America, 1767 *1220.12 p662*
Reid, David; North Carolina, 1825 *1088.45 p28*
Reid, David; South Carolina, 1808 *6155.4 p19*
Reid, Donald SEE Reid, John
Reid, Duncan; New York, 1739 *8277.31 p119*
    Wife: Mary Semple
    Child: Angus
    Child: Jennie
    Child: Alexander
    Child: Nicholas
Reid, Duncan; Philadelphia, 1777 *8529.30 p7A*
Reid, Edmund B. 32; Ontario, 1871 *1823.21 p308*
Reid, Eliza J. 28; Michigan, 1880 *4491.42 p21*
Reid, Geo. J.; Louisiana, 1874-1875 *4981.45 p30*
Reid, George 37; Ontario, 1871 *1823.21 p308*
Reid, George 40; Ontario, 1871 *1823.17 p137*
Reid, George 46; Ontario, 1871 *1823.21 p308*
Reid, Hugh 40; Ontario, 1871 *1823.21 p308*
Reid, Hugh 71; Ontario, 1871 *1823.21 p308*
Reid, Isaiah 52; South Carolina, 1812 *3476.30 p13*
Reid, James; North Carolina, 1845 *1088.45 p28*
Reid, James 20; Ontario, 1871 *1823.21 p308*
Reid, James 35; Ontario, 1871 *1823.17 p137*
Reid, James 66; Ontario, 1871 *1823.21 p308*
Reid, James 67; Ontario, 1871 *1823.17 p137*
Reid, Jane 39; Ontario, 1871 *1823.17 p137*
Reid, Jennie SEE Reid, Duncan
Reid, Jeremiah 45; Ontario, 1871 *1823.17 p137*

Reid, John; New York, 1739 *8277.31 p119*
    Wife: Mary Hyman
    Son: Donald
Reid, John 23; Ontario, 1871 *1823.21 p308*
Reid, John 30; Ontario, 1871 *1823.17 p137*
Reid, John 32; Ontario, 1871 *1823.21 p308*
Reid, John 40; Ontario, 1871 *1823.17 p137*
Reid, John 41; Ontario, 1871 *1823.17 p137*
Reid, John 50; Ontario, 1871 *1823.21 p308*
Reid, John 59; Ontario, 1871 *1823.17 p137*
Reid, John 71; Ontario, 1871 *1823.17 p137*
Reid, John; Quebec, 1885 *1937.10 p52*
Reid, John 24; St. John, N.B., 1834 *6469.7 p5*
Reid, John H. 41; Ontario, 1871 *1823.17 p137*
Reid, John I. 37; Ontario, 1871 *1823.21 p308*
Reid, Mary Hyman SEE Reid, John
Reid, Mary Semple SEE Reid, Duncan
Reid, Nicholas SEE Reid, Duncan
Reid, Peter 40; Ontario, 1871 *1823.17 p138*
Reid, Reuben 59; Ontario, 1871 *1823.21 p308*
Reid, Richard B. 50; Ontario, 1871 *1823.17 p138*
Reid, Robert 47; Ontario, 1871 *1823.21 p308*
Reid, Roger; New York, 1739 *8277.31 p119*
Reid, Thomas 29; Ontario, 1871 *1823.21 p308*
Reid, Vincent; North Carolina, 1792-1862 *1088.45 p28*
Reid, William 45; Ontario, 1871 *1823.17 p138*
Reid, William 50; Ontario, 1871 *1823.21 p308*
Reid, William 62; Ontario, 1871 *1823.21 p308*
Reid, William 20; St. John, N.B., 1834 *6469.7 p5*
Reida, James; Jamaica, 1778 *8529.30 p14A*
Reider, Meerland 56; Ontario, 1871 *1823.21 p308*
Reidman, Thomas; Maryland, 1722 *1220.12 p666*
Reier, Lina; Wisconsin, 1907 *6795.8 p128*
Reier, Wilhelmine; Wisconsin, 1893 *6795.8 p27*
Reif, Albert 24; New York, 1854 *5475.1 p235*
Reif, Amalie Elisabeth; America, 1867 *7919.3 p534*
Reif, Anna 22; New York, 1854 *5475.1 p235*
    Sister: Maria 18
Reif, Catharine 20; Louisiana, 1848 *778.6 p280*
Reif, Christian; America, 1867 *7919.3 p531*
    With wife & child
Reif, Ernst Wilhelm; America, 1867 *7919.3 p534*
    With wife & 3 children
    Brother: Karl August
Reif, F. Fredolin 28; Louisiana, 1848 *778.6 p280*
Reif, Karl August SEE Reif, Ernst Wilhelm
Reif, Maria 18 SEE Reif, Anna
Reif, Marianne 30; Louisiana, 1848 *778.6 p280*
Reiger, Jacob; Louisiana, 1874 *4981.45 p134*
Reigh, John J.; Washington, 1889 *2770.40 p80*
Reiglen, J. L. 42; New Orleans, 1846 *778.6 p280*
Reigler, John George; Ohio, 1809-1852 *4511.35 p42*
Reignold, Samuell; Maryland, 1673 *1236.25 p49*
Reih, Jean 34; America, 1846 *778.6 p282*
Reihart, Jacob 61; America, 1845 *778.6 p280*
Reihl, Jacob; Ohio, 1809-1852 *4511.35 p42*
Reihl, John; Ohio, 1809-1852 *4511.35 p42*
Reik, Jno. M.; Louisiana, 1874-1875 *4981.45 p30*
Reik, Maria 19; America, 1846 *778.6 p280*
Reiker, J. G.; Ohio, 1840-1897 *8365.35 p17*
Reile, Goody; Rowley, MA, 1700 *1642 p77*
Reiley, Henry; Rowley, MA, 1656 *1642 p77*
Reiley, Henry; Rowley, MA, 1710 *1642 p77*
Reiley, John; St. John, N.B., 1848 *2978.15 p39*
Reiley, Sarah; Rowley, MA, 1645 *1642 p77*
Reilley, Frank 32; Ontario, 1871 *1823.21 p308*
Reilley, Jas; St. John, N.B., 1848 *2978.15 p40*
Reilley, John 41; Ontario, 1871 *1823.17 p138*
Reilly, Andrew; Ohio, 1809-1852 *4511.35 p42*
Reilly, Charles 24; New York, NY, 1825 *6178.50 p77*
Reilly, Charlotte Elizabeth SEE Reilly, Hugh
Reilly, Edward; Ohio, 1809-1852 *4511.35 p42*
Reilly, Ellen; Toronto, 1844 *2910.35 p114*
Reilly, Frances 18; Quebec, 1870 *8364.32 p25*
Reilly, Francis B. 51; Ontario, 1871 *1823.21 p308*
Reilly, Hugh 41; Ontario, 1871 *1823.17 p138*
Reilly, Hugh; Philadelphia, 1867 *8513.31 p422*
    Wife: Mary Ann Buchanan
    Child: Charlotte Elizabeth
    Child: Mary Ann
Reilly, James; Boston, 1761 *1642 p48*
Reilly, James; New Orleans, 1850 *7242.30 p153*
Reilly, James; Ohio, 1859 *3580.20 p33*
Reilly, James; Ohio, 1859 *6020.12 p22*
Reilly, John; Ohio, 1809-1852 *4511.35 p42*
Reilly, John 35; Ontario, 1871 *1823.21 p308*
Reilly, Margaret; Toronto, 1844 *2910.35 p114*
Reilly, Mary Ann SEE Reilly, Hugh
Reilly, Mary Ann Buchanan SEE Reilly, Hugh
Reilly, Patrick; New Orleans, 1850 *7242.30 p153*
Reilly, Paul; Philadelphia, 1816 *5720.10 p380*
Reilly, Philip 60; Ontario, 1871 *1823.17 p138*
Reilly, Rachael 68; Ontario, 1871 *1823.21 p308*

Reilly, Thomas; New Orleans, 1850 *7242.30 p153*
Reils, Charles W.; North Carolina, 1856 *1088.45 p28*
Reily, James; Toronto, 1844 *2910.35 p112*
Reily, Jaques; Maryland, 1720 *1220.12 p666*
Reily, Laurie 38; Ontario, 1871 *1823.17 p138*
Reily, Mary 51; Ontario, 1871 *1823.21 p308*
Reily, Patrick; Philadelphia, 1778 *8529.30 p4A*
Reily, Philip; Ohio, 1809-1852 *4511.35 p42*
Reiman, Johannes 42; New Castle, DE, 1817-1818 *90.20 p153*
Reimann, Paul Herman; Wisconsin, 1884 *6795.8 p173*
Reimann, Paul Hermann; Wisconsin, 1892 *6795.8 p153*
Reimbold, William; Illinois, 1851 *6079.1 p11*
Reimelt, Franze; Kansas, 1884 *1447.20 p63*
Reimer, Friedrich Wilhelm; America, 1856 *7420.1 p152*
Reimerdes, Otto; America, 1870 *7420.1 p287*
Reimerdes, Otto; America, 1893 *7420.1 p369*
Reimers, Charley; Nebraska, 1905 *3004.30 p46*
Reimers, Herman; Nebraska, 1905 *3004.30 p46*
Reimers, Julius; Nebraska, 1905 *3004.30 p46*
Reimey, Mary 101; Ontario, 1871 *1823.17 p138*
Reimsbach, Anna; Peru, 1877 *5475.1 p205*
Reimsbach, Peter; America, 1881 *5475.1 p193*
Reimund, Anna Elisabeth; Virginia, 1831 *152.20 p66*
Rein, Mrs. Franz; America, 1846 *2526.43 p204*
Reina, Luise 54; America, 1843 *5475.1 p528*
Reinander, D.; Galveston, TX, 1855 *571.7 p18*
Reinander, J.; Galveston, TX, 1855 *571.7 p18*
Reinbold, Emil; Colorado, 1874 *1029.59 p77*
Reine, Mr. 52; New Orleans, 1848 *778.6 p280*
Reinecke, August; Port uncertain, 1891 *7420.1 p363*
Reinecke, Carl H.; America, 1885 *7420.1 p348*
Reinecke, Carl H.; New York, NY, 1893 *7420.1 p369*
Reinecke, Carl Ludwig Hermann; America, 1885 *7420.1 p348*
Reinecke, Heinrich August Robert; America, 1893 *7420.1 p369*
    Sister: Hermine Magdalena Sophie
Reinecke, Hermine Magdalena Sophie SEE Reinecke, Heinrich August Robert
Reineking, Friedrich Carl Michael; America, 1898 *7420.1 p375*
Reineking, Georg Hermann SEE Reineking, Georg Ludwig
Reineking, Georg Ludwig; America, 1899 *7420.1 p375*
    Wife: Helene Mann
    Son: Georg Hermann
Reineking, Helene Mann SEE Reineking, Georg Ludwig
Reiner, Margret E. 3; Ontario, 1871 *1823.21 p308*
Reiner, William 31; Ontario, 1871 *1823.21 p308*
Reinert, Adam; America, 1868 *5475.1 p297*
Reinert, Barbara Josten SEE Reinert, Mathias
Reinert, Barbara; Minnesota, 1881 *5475.1 p300*
Reinert, Joh. Peter SEE Reinert, Mathias
Reinert, Johann SEE Reinert, Nikolaus
Reinert, Johann; America, 1864 *5475.1 p277*
Reinert, Johann SEE Reinert, Mathias
Reinert, Johann Peter 35; America, 1859 *5475.1 p287*
Reinert, Katharina 21 SEE Reinert, Nikolaus
Reinert, Margarethe Meiers 51 SEE Reinert, Nikolaus
Reinert, Mathias 32; America, 1868 *5475.1 p349*
Reinert, Mathias 52; America, 1887 *5475.1 p243*
    Wife: Barbara Josten
    Son: Joh. Peter
    Son: Nikolaus
    Son: Johann
    Son: Michel
Reinert, Michel SEE Reinert, Mathias
Reinert, Nikolaus SEE Reinert, Nikolaus
Reinert, Nikolaus SEE Reinert, Mathias
Reinert, Nikolaus 50; America, 1863 *5475.1 p261*
    Wife: Margarethe Meiers 51
    Son: Peter
    Son: Nikolaus
    Son: Johann
    Daughter: Katharina 21
Reinert, Peter SEE Reinert, Nikolaus
Reinert, Susanna 32; America, 1867 *5475.1 p281*
Reinhard, Elisabeth; America, 1867 *7919.3 p532*
Reinhard, Emilie; America, 1867 *7919.3 p532*
Reinhard, George; Ohio, 1809-1852 *4511.35 p42*
Reinhard, Heinrich 17; America, 1854 *2526.42 p164*
Reinhard, Johann Georg; America, 1851 *2526.42 p164*
Reinhard, Johannes; Valdivia, Chile, 1852 *1192.4 p53*
Reinhard, Nicol; America, 1867 *7919.3 p532*
    With wife & child
Reinhard, Sophie 36; America, 1871 *5475.1 p62*
Reinhard, Wilhelm; America, 1853 *2526.42 p164*
Reinhardt, Barthold; America, 1868 *7919.3 p534*
Reinhardt, Elisabeth Barbara; America, 1867 *7919.3 p532*
Reinhardt, Fritz; Port uncertain, 1912 *7420.1 p390*
Reinhardt, Georg 30; Galveston, TX, 1844 *3967.10 p373*

Reinhardt, Nicolaus; America, 1867 ***7919.3*** *p532*
With wife & 6 children
Reinhardt, Peter 32; Ontario, 1871 ***1823.21*** *p308*
Reinhart, Bertha Schwarz; Illinois, 1930 ***121.35*** *p101*
Reinhart, Jacob; Ohio, 1809-1852 ***4511.35*** *p42*
Reinheimer, Peter; Ohio, 1809-1852 ***4511.35*** *p42*
Reinig, Eva; America, 1882 ***5475.1*** *p311*
Reinig, Jakob; America, 1882 ***5475.1*** *p312*
Reinig, Johann; America, 1882 ***5475.1*** *p312*
Reinig, Leonard; Washington, 1884 ***2770.40*** *p193*
Reinig, Peter; America, 1854 ***5475.1*** *p277*
Reinig, Peter; America, 1872 ***5475.1*** *p277*
Reiniger, Lisette; Philadelphia, 1843 ***8513.31*** *p298*
Reininger, Andrew; Ohio, 1809-1852 ***4511.35*** *p43*
Reininger, Christian; Ohio, 1809-1852 ***4511.35*** *p42*
Reininger, George; Ohio, 1809-1852 ***4511.35*** *p42*
Reinke, Ernst Friedrich; Wisconsin, 1873 ***6795.8*** *p68*
Reinking, Carl Friedrich Gottlieb; America, 1864 ***7420.1*** *p226*
With parents
Reinoehl, Paul Julius; Wisconsin, 1882 ***6795.8*** *p100*
Reinolds, Chr. 24; Virginia, 1635 ***1183.3*** *p31*
Reinpel, Catha 10; Halifax, N.S., 1902 ***1860.4*** *p40*
Reinpel, Elisabeth 15; Halifax, N.S., 1902 ***1860.4*** *p40*
Reinpel, Elisbethe 49; Halifax, N.S., 1902 ***1860.4*** *p40*
Reinpel, Franz 60; Halifax, N.S., 1902 ***1860.4*** *p40*
Reinpel, Jacob 16; Halifax, N.S., 1902 ***1860.4*** *p40*
Reinpel, Johann 28; Halifax, N.S., 1902 ***1860.4*** *p40*
Reinpel, Maria 21; Halifax, N.S., 1902 ***1860.4*** *p40*
Reinschmit, Johannes 25; New Jersey, 1753-1774 ***927.31*** *p3*
Reinstadler, Elisabeth 23; America, 1869 ***5475.1*** *p164*
Reinstadler, Franz; America, 1869 ***5475.1*** *p164*
Reinstadler, Johann; America, 1871 ***5475.1*** *p212*
Reinstadler, Maria Muller *SEE* Reinstadler, Peter
Reinstadler, Peter; America, 1872 ***5475.1*** *p212*
*Wife:*Maria Muller
Reinstaedler, Katharina; America, 1876 ***5475.1*** *p151*
Reiplinger, Johann; Indiana, 1883 ***5475.1*** *p246*
*Son:*M. Josef
*Daughter:*Katharina
*Daughter:*Maria
*Daughter:*Susanna
*Wife:*Susanna Steuer
Reiplinger, Katharina *SEE* Reiplinger, Johann
Reiplinger, M. Josef; Cincinnati, 1884 ***5475.1*** *p246*
Reiplinger, M. Josef *SEE* Reiplinger, Johann
Reiplinger, Maria *SEE* Reiplinger, Johann
Reiplinger, Susanna *SEE* Reiplinger, Johann
Reiplinger, Susanna Steuer *SEE* Reiplinger, Johann
Reis, Chrostophe; Missouri, 1846 ***778.6*** *p280*
Reis, Elisa 9; America, 1745 ***778.6*** *p280*
Reis, Emil; America, 1867 ***7919.3*** *p534*
Reis, Ferdinand, Jr.; America, 1867 ***7919.3*** *p534*
Reis, Johann; America, 1886 ***5475.1*** *p197*
Reis, John James 22; Port uncertain, 1844 ***778.6*** *p280*
Reis, Louis; America, 1867 ***7919.3*** *p534*
Reis, Max; North Carolina, 1812 ***1088.45*** *p28*
Reis, Philippine; Brazil, 1859 ***5475.1*** *p523*
Reisacher, Anna Pauline 25; Galveston, TX, 1844 ***3967.10*** *p371*
Reisacher, Heinrich Eduard 25; Galveston, TX, 1844 ***3967.10*** *p371*
Reischauer, Johann Friedrich; America, 1855 ***7420.1*** *p141*
Reischauer, Wilhelm; San Francisco, 1849 ***7420.1*** *p67*
Reischmann, Anna Drum *SEE* Reischmann, Charles
Reischmann, Charles; Philadelphia, 1864 ***8513.31*** *p422*
*Wife:*Anna Drum
Reisel, Emma Auguste; Wisconsin, 1884 ***6795.8*** *p43*
Reisel, Friedrich 47; New York, NY, 1893 ***1883.7*** *p44*
Reiser, Joseph; Ohio, 1840-1897 ***8365.35*** *p17*
Reising, Christine Marie Leonore; America, 1857 ***7420.1*** *p162*
Reising, Johann Friedrich Wilhelm; America, 1883 ***7420.1*** *p339*
*Wife:*Sophie Marie Caroline Meier
*Daughter:*Sophie Marie Caroline
Reising, Sophie Marie Caroline *SEE* Reising, Johann Friedrich Wilhelm
Reising, Sophie Marie Caroline Meier *SEE* Reising, Johann Friedrich Wilhelm
Reisl, Gustav Bedrich; Omaha, NE, 1873 ***2853.20*** *p299*
Reiss, Araham 72; America, 1848 ***778.6*** *p280*
Reiss, Daniel 36; America, 1745 ***778.6*** *p280*
Reiss, Dorothea 33; America, 1745 ***778.6*** *p280*
Reiss, Engel Marie Dorothea *SEE* Reiss, Mrs. Heinrich Gottlieb
Reiss, Engel Marie Sophie *SEE* Reiss, Mrs. Heinrich Gottlieb
Reiss, Friedrich Conrad Gottlieb *SEE* Reiss, Mrs. Heinrich Gottlieb
Reiss, Georg 6; America, 1745 ***778.6*** *p280*
Reiss, Heinrich Gottlieb; America, 1866 ***7420.1*** *p248*
Reiss, Mrs. Heinrich Gottlieb; America, 1866 ***7420.1*** *p248*
*Son:*Friedrich Conrad Gottlieb
*Daughter:*Engel Marie Sophie
*Daughter:*Sophie Dorothea
*Daughter:*Engel Marie Dorothea
Reiss, Isa.c 4; New Orleans, 1848 ***778.6*** *p280*
Reiss, Jacob 6; New Orleans, 1848 ***778.6*** *p280*
Reiss, Johann Hermann; America, 1850 ***7420.1*** *p74*
Reiss, Leopold 9; New Orleans, 1848 ***778.6*** *p280*
Reiss, Louise 24; Missouri, 1845 ***778.6*** *p280*
Reiss, Pauline 40; New Orleans, 1848 ***778.6*** *p280*
Reiss, Sophie Dorothea *SEE* Reiss, Mrs. Heinrich Gottlieb
Reisse, Christian; Ohio, 1809-1852 ***4511.35*** *p42*
Reissec, Coralie 10; America, 1843 ***778.6*** *p280*
Reissec, Jeanne 37; America, 1843 ***778.6*** *p280*
Reissec, Maria 7; America, 1843 ***778.6*** *p280*
Reissinger, Jacques; Louisiana, 1841-1844 ***4981.45*** *p211*
Reister, Christian; New York, NY, 1889 ***3366.30*** *p70*
Reister, Karl; New York, NY, 1893 ***3366.30*** *p70*
Reiter, Bernhard; Philadelphia, 1870 ***8513.31*** *p422*
*Wife:*Elisabeth Kratt
*Child:*Elisa
Reiter, Elisa *SEE* Reiter, Bernhard
Reiter, Elisabeth Kratt *SEE* Reiter, Bernhard
Reiter, Gertrud; America, 1800-1899 ***5475.1*** *p440*
Reiter, Johann; America, 1883 ***5475.1*** *p197*
Reiter, Katharina; America, 1833 ***5475.1*** *p436*
Reiter, Katharina 35; America, 1872 ***5475.1*** *p275*
Reiter, Katharina Backes *SEE* Reiter, Michel
Reiter, Klaus; Chicago, 1887 ***5475.1*** *p206*
Reiter, Ludwig; Wisconsin, 1865 ***6795.8*** *p52*
Reiter, Maria; America, 1800-1899 ***5475.1*** *p440*
Reiter, Maria Both *SEE* Reiter, Michel
Reiter, Michel 27; America, 1867 ***5475.1*** *p201*
Reiter, Michel; Brazil, 1846 ***5475.1*** *p438*
*Wife:*Katharina Backes
With 2 children
Reiter, Michel; Brazil, 1846 ***5475.1*** *p438*
*Wife:*Maria Both
With child
Reiter, Nikolaus; America, 1872 ***5475.1*** *p153*
Reith, Charles; Ohio, 1809-1852 ***4511.35*** *p42*
Reith, Christine; Philadelphia, 1883 ***5475.1*** *p36*
*Child:*Rosa
*Child:*Anna
*Child:*Theodor
Reith, William H. 27; Ontario, 1871 ***1823.21*** *p308*
Reithenbach, Adelheid 19; New York, NY, 1885 ***1883.7*** *p45*
Reither, Lauretz 18; Port uncertain, 1841 ***778.6*** *p280*
Reitinger, Filip; Minnesota, 1884-1891 ***2853.20*** *p273*
Reitler, . . .; America, 1853 ***5475.1*** *p51*
Reitler, Barbara Muller *SEE* Reitler, Johann
Reitler, Franz Peter 8 *SEE* Reitler, Johann
Reitler, Johann; America, 1867 ***5475.1*** *p78*
*Wife:*Barbara Muller
*Son:*Franz Peter
Reitler, Konrad, III; America, 1846-1847 ***5475.1*** *p51*
Reitmeyer, Wilhelmine Justine Charlotte; America, 1867 ***7420.1*** *p262*
Reitonwalt, Jacob; Ohio, 1809-1852 ***4511.35*** *p42*
Reitter, Eva; New York, 1860 ***358.56*** *p3*
Reitz, Anna Margaretha 2; Pennsylvania, 1851 ***170.15*** *p39*
With family
Reitz, Anna Margaretha 22; Pennsylvania, 1848 ***170.15*** *p39*
With family
Reitz, Anna Margaretha 30; Pennsylvania, 1851 ***170.15*** *p39*
With family
Reitz, Elisabeth 5; Pennsylvania, 1851 ***170.15*** *p39*
With family
Reitz, Fredericka; Philadelphia, 1852 ***8513.31*** *p322*
Reitz, Johann Friedr. 26; Pennsylvania, 1848 ***170.15*** *p39*
With family
Reitz, Johann Henrich 1; Pennsylvania, 1848 ***170.15*** *p39*
With family
Reitz, Johann Henrich 36; Pennsylvania, 1851 ***170.15*** *p39*
With family
Reiz, Johann Friedr.; Pennsylvania, 1848 ***170.15*** *p39*
With wife & child
Reiz, Johannes 38; Portland, ME, 1906 ***970.38*** *p80*
Reiz, Katha. 36; Portland, ME, 1906 ***970.38*** *p80*
Reiz, Nikolaus; Port uncertain, 1887 ***170.15*** *p39*
Rekow, Anna; Wisconsin, 1886 ***6795.8*** *p37*
Relief, John; America, 1718 ***1220.12*** *p666*
Rellett, John; America, 1772 ***1220.12*** *p666*
Relling, Johann; Valdivia, Chile, 1852 ***1192.4*** *p56*
Rellis, Frederick 15; Quebec, 1870 ***8364.32*** *p25*
Relot, Catherine; Quebec, 1667 ***4514.3*** *p362*
Rely, John; Massachusetts, 1712 ***1642*** *p101*
Remacle, Joseph 21; Missouri, 1848 ***778.6*** *p280*
Remark, Anna; America, 1872 ***5475.1*** *p172*
Remark, Johanette; America, 1841 ***5475.1*** *p61*
Remark, Nikolaus Rudolf; Philadelphia, 1873 ***5475.1*** *p47*
Remark, Peter; America, 1867 ***5475.1*** *p163*
Remark, Peter; America, 1873 ***5475.1*** *p47*
Rembley, . . .; North Carolina, 1710 ***3629.40*** *p6*
Rembourg, Francois; Nova Scotia, 1753 ***3051*** *p113*
Rembourg, Rene; Nova Scotia, 1753 ***3051*** *p113*
Rembrandt, Francis 28; Louisiana, 1840 ***778.6*** *p280*
Remde, Christiane; America, 1868 ***7919.3*** *p532*
*Son:*Friedrich
Remde, Friedrich *SEE* Remde, Christiane
Remeike, Nikols 21; New York, NY, 1893 ***1883.7*** *p41*
Remer, John; North Carolina, 1710 ***3629.40*** *p6*
Remer, Richard; North Carolina, 1710 ***3629.40*** *p6*
Remes, Matej; Minnesota, 1858-1860 ***2853.20*** *p260*
Remes, Peter 45; Santa Clara Co., CA, 1870 ***8704.1*** *p26*
Remfry, Richard; America, 1775 ***1220.12*** *p666*
Remier, Peter 48; Ontario, 1871 ***1823.17*** *p138*
Remiger, Joseph; New York, NY, 1891 ***6212.1*** *p15*
Remilee, Thomas; Texas, 1851 ***3435.45*** *p36*
Remille, Jacob; Ohio, 1809-1852 ***4511.35*** *p42*
Remington, Thomas; Barbados, 1669 ***1220.12*** *p666*
Remm, Jon. Peter; North Carolina, 1710 ***3629.40*** *p6*
Remm, Michael; North Carolina, 1710 ***3629.40*** *p6*
Remmel, Angela 10 *SEE* Remmel, Margarethe Jakoby
Remmel, Caspar 17 *SEE* Remmel, Margarethe Jakoby
Remmel, Johann 22; America, 1856 ***5475.1*** *p323*
Remmel, Margarethe 19 *SEE* Remmel, Margarethe Jakoby
Remmel, Margarethe 41; America, 1856 ***5475.1*** *p323*
*Daughter:*Margarethe 19
*Daughter:*Angela 10
*Son:*Nikolaus 8
*Son:*Caspar 17
Remmel, Nikolaus 8 *SEE* Remmel, Margarethe Jakoby
Remmer, George 21; Ontario, 1871 ***1823.21*** *p309*
Remmett, Sarah; Virginia, 1743 ***1220.12*** *p666*
Remmington, Robert; America, 1678 ***1220.12*** *p666*
Remmle, Heinrich 28; Ontario, 1871 ***1823.21*** *p309*
Remon, Clara; Maine, 1884-1888 ***9228.50*** *p534*
Remon, Clara; Quebec, 1885 ***9228.50*** *p534*
Remon, James; Quebec, 1800-1899 ***9228.50*** *p534*
*Relative:*Thomas C.
Remon, Mary; Salt Lake City, 1854 ***9228.50*** *p198*
*Child:*Mary Ann
*Child:*Peter C.
*Child:*Jane Mary
*Child:*Elizabeth I.
*Child:*John P.
Remon, Thomas C. *SEE* Remon, James
Remondiere, Andree; Quebec, 1666 ***4514.3*** *p362*
*Mother:*Renee Riviere
Remondiere, Andree *SEE* Remondiere, Renee Riviere
Remondiere, Renee Riviere *SEE* Remondiere, Andree
Remondiere, Renee; Quebec, 1666 ***4514.3*** *p365*
*Daughter:*Andree
Remot, Pierre; Quebec, 1643 ***9221.17*** *p134*
Rempel, Anna; Brazil, 1886 ***5475.1*** *p432*
Rempel, Johann; Brazil, 1857 ***5475.1*** *p441*
With wife & 5 children
Rempel, Johann 18 *SEE* Rempel, Nikolaus
Rempel, Nikolaus 25; Brazil, 1857 ***5475.1*** *p440*
*Son:*Johann 18 months
With wife
Rempel, Mrs. Nikolaus; Brazil, 1857 ***5475.1*** *p441*
Rempis, John; Ohio, 1809-1852 ***4511.35*** *p42*
Remppes, Gottlieb; Ohio, 1809-1852 ***4511.35*** *p42*
Remser, John; Ohio, 1809-1852 ***4511.35*** *p42*
Remy, Alfred 9; America, 1840 ***778.6*** *p280*
Remy, Antoine 25; New Orleans, 1848 ***778.6*** *p280*
Remy, Barbe 37; America, 1843 ***778.6*** *p280*
Remy, Catharina 2; America, 1843 ***778.6*** *p280*
Remy, Eleonore 30; America, 1840 ***778.6*** *p280*
Remy, Jean 37; America, 1843 ***778.6*** *p281*
Remy, Jean 42; America, 1843 ***778.6*** *p281*
Remy, La.rent 4; America, 1843 ***778.6*** *p281*
Remy, Marie; Quebec, 1665 ***4514.3*** *p362*
Renaleany, Jan 39; America, 1848 ***778.6*** *p281*
Renalls, Thomas; America, 1741 ***1220.12*** *p668*
Renard, Mr. 20; America, 1841 ***778.6*** *p281*
Renard, Bernard; Louisiana, 1874 ***4981.45*** *p133*
Renard, Eugene 24; Texas, 1840 ***778.6*** *p281*
Renard, Jacques; Montreal, 1644 ***9221.17*** *p149*
Renard, Jeanne; Quebec, 1671 ***4514.3*** *p362*
Renard, Louis 24; Missouri, 1845 ***778.6*** *p281*
Renard, Marianne 22; Missouri, 1845 ***778.6*** *p281*
Renard, Marie 1; Missouri, 1845 ***778.6*** *p281*
Renard, Simon 33; Port uncertain, 1843 ***778.6*** *p281*

Renaud, Adolphe 27; America, 1845 *778.6 p281*
Renaud, Andre 24; America, 1846 *778.6 p281*
Renaud, Anne-Michelle; Quebec, 1669 *4514.3 p362*
Renaud, Denis; Illinois, 1852 *6079.1 p11*
Renaud, Elisabeth; Quebec, 1673 *4514.3 p363*
Renaud, Francois 24; Missouri, 1848 *778.6 p281*
Renaud, Francois 24; Texas, 1843 *778.6 p281*
Renaud, Isaac 13; America, 1844 *778.6 p281*
Renaud, Jean 38; New Orleans, 1848 *778.6 p281*
Renaud, Jules; Illinois, 1852 *6079.1 p11*
Renaud, Marguerite; Quebec, 1667 *4514.3 p363*
Renaud, Marie 31; America, 1844 *778.6 p281*
Renaud, Marie; Quebec, 1668 *4514.3 p363*
Renaud, Marie; Quebec, 1669-1670 *4514.3 p363*
Renaud d'Avene deDesmeloizes, Francois-Marie; Quebec, 1683-1688 *2314.30 p169*
Renaud d'Avene deDesmeloizes, Francois-Marie; Quebec, 1685 *2314.30 p194*
Renaud Dubuisson, Charles; Quebec, 1683-1688 *2314.30 p169*
Renaud Dubuisson, Charles; Quebec, 1685 *2314.30 p194*
Renaudeau, Judith 25; Quebec, 1662 *9221.17 p492*
Renaudeau, Michel 21; Quebec, 1657 *9221.17 p367*
Renaudin DeLaBlanchetiere, Marie; Quebec, 1653 *9221.17 p279*
Renault, Charles 31; New Orleans, 1848 *778.6 p281*
Renault, Jules 22; Missouri, 1848 *778.6 p281*
Renault, Nicholas; Maine, 1665 *9228.50 p541*
Renber, John; Ohio, 1809-1852 *4511.35 p42*
Rencin, Josef, Sr.; Iowa, 1850-1910 *2853.20 p218*
Rencontre, Pierre; Quebec, 1660 *9221.17 p439*
Rendall, David; America, 1728 *1220.12 p666*
Rendall, Judith; America, 1775 *1220.12 p666*
Rendall, William; America, 1755 *1220.12 p666*
Rendat, Francois 34; New Orleans, 1848 *778.6 p281*
Rendell, George 46; Ontario, 1871 *1823.21 p309*
Rendell, Samuel; America, 1773 *1220.12 p666*
Rendells, Lewis R. 35; New York, NY, 1825 *6178.50 p148*
Rendiet, Adele 24; America, 1840 *778.6 p281*
Rendiet, Adelphine 4; America, 1840 *778.6 p281*
Rendiet, Chlothilde 3; America, 1840 *778.6 p281*
Rendiet, Edward 5; America, 1840 *778.6 p281*
Rendle, James 45; Ontario, 1871 *1823.17 p138*
Rendric, Thomas 35; Quebec, 1659 *9221.17 p409*
Rene, Ms. 23; New Orleans, 1848 *778.6 p281*
Rene, Jeanne 48; New Orleans, 1848 *778.6 p281*
Reneff, Philip, Sr.; Massachusetts, 1739 *9228.50 p536*
Renelt, Frank; Iowa, 1902 *1211.15 p18*
Reneuf, Philip, Sr.; Massachusetts, 1739 *9228.50 p536*
Reney, Jean 38; New Orleans, 1844 *778.6 p281*
Renffriack, Louis; Louisiana, 1874 *4981.45 p134*
Renier, Alphonsine *SEE* Renier, Pierre Joseph
Renier, Charles Joseph *SEE* Renier, Desire
Renier, Desire; Wisconsin, 1856 *1495.20 p45*
  *Child:*Marie Ferdinande
  *Child:*Charles Joseph
Renier, Eugene *SEE* Renier, Pierre Joseph
Renier, Francois *SEE* Renier, Pierre Joseph
Renier, Marie Catherine Folon *SEE* Renier, Pierre Joseph
Renier, Marie Ferdinande *SEE* Renier, Desire
Renier, Pierre Joseph; Wisconsin, 1856 *1495.20 p45*
  *Wife:*Marie Catherine Folon
  *Child:*Francois
  *Child:*Alphonsine
  *Child:*Eugene
Reniff, Philip, Sr.; Massachusetts, 1739 *9228.50 p536*
Reninger, Andres; Ohio, 1809-1852 *4511.35 p42*
Renkel, Otto; America, 1842 *2526.43 p199*
Renker, Henry; Ohio, 1844 *2763.1 p21*
Renkert, Michael; Ohio, 1809-1852 *4511.35 p43*
Renkes, Barbara 64; America, 1869 *5475.1 p170*
Renkes, Georg; America, 1880 *5475.1 p220*
  *Wife:*Maria Stein
  *Daughter:*Maria
Renkes, Margarehte; America, 1880 *5475.1 p213*
Renkes, Maria *SEE* Renkes, Georg
Renkes, Maria Stein *SEE* Renkes, Georg
Renman, Joh.; New York, NY, 1848 *6412.40 p151*
Renn, Josef 8 *SEE* Renn, Josef
Renn, Josef 32; America, 1836 *5475.1 p449*
  *Wife:*Maria Penth 26
  *Daughter:*Maria 2
  With mother 66
  *Son:*Mathias 4
  *Son:*Josef 8
  *Son:*Peter 6
Renn, Maria 2 *SEE* Renn, Josef
Renn, Maria Penth 26 *SEE* Renn, Josef
Renn, Mathias; America, 1843 *5475.1 p450*
Renn, Mathias 4 *SEE* Renn, Josef
Renn, Peter 6 *SEE* Renn, Josef

Rennet, Joseph; America, 1739 *1220.12 p666*
Rennie, Gordon 48; Ontario, 1871 *1823.21 p309*
Rennie, John 33; Ontario, 1871 *1823.21 p309*
Rennie, John 40; Ontario, 1871 *1823.17 p138*
Renno, Sophie; Ohio, 1865 *5475.1 p21*
Rennpferd, August Fred; Wisconsin, 1889 *6795.8 p82*
Rennpferd, Wilhelmine; Wisconsin, 1883 *6795.8 p82*
Renoff Family ; America, 1840-1860 *9228.50 p535*
Renolds, Catherine 49; Ontario, 1871 *1823.17 p138*
Renolds, Samuell; Maryland, 1673 *1236.25 p49*
Renolds, Timothy; Marston's Wharf, 1782 *8529.30 p15*
Renouard, Marie-Catherine; Quebec, 1665 *4514.3 p363*
Renouard DeBellaird, Jacques 13; Quebec, 1653 *9221.17 p279*
Renouf, Mr.; Windsor, Ont., 1900 *9228.50 p539*
  With sisters & brother
Renouf, Amis; Boston, 1715 *9228.50 p537*
Renouf, Edward; Boston, 1715 *9228.50 p539*
Renouf, Edward; Marblehead, MA, 1772 *9228.50 p539*
Renouf, Edward; Massachusetts, 1772 *9228.50 p99*
Renouf, Esme P. Mollett *SEE* Renouf, John
Renouf, Florence; Montreal, 1913 *9228.50 p334*
Renouf, Harriet Ann; Massachusetts, 1857-1936 *9228.50 p539*
Renouf, Harriet Ann; Weymouth, MA, 1908 *9228.50 p209*
Renouf, Helen M.; America, 1946 *9228.50 p539*
Renouf, Jane K.; New York, 1871-1874 *9228.50 p250*
  *Child:*May Jane
  *Child:*William F.
Renouf, Jane K.; Rochester, NY, n.d. *9228.50 p537*
  *Child:*May Jane
  *Child:*William F.
Renouf, John; Ontario, 1918-1983 *9228.50 p539*
  *Wife:*Esme P. Mollett
Renouf, Kathleen; Buffalo, NY, 1850-1950 *9228.50 p539*
Renouf, Kathleen; Ontario, 1850-1950 *9228.50 p539*
Renouf, Martha *SEE* Renouf, Thomas
Renouf, Mary; Utah, 1823-1893 *9228.50 p339*
Renouf, May Jane *SEE* Renouf, Jane K. Gosselin
Renouf, May Jane *SEE* Renouf, Jane K. Gosselin
Renouf, Nicholas Bion; Pennsylvania, 1840-1874 *9228.50 p538*
Renouf, Peter; Nova Scotia, 1770-1799 *9228.50 p536*
Renouf, Ralph; New York, NY, 1912 *9228.50 p539*
Renouf, Thomas; New York, 1750-1850 *9228.50 p537*
  *Wife:*Martha
Renouf, William F. *SEE* Renouf, Jane K. Gosselin
Renouf, William F. *SEE* Renouf, Jane K. Gosselin
Renough, Philip, Sr.; Massachusetts, 1739 *9228.50 p536*
Renoul, Jean 20; Montreal, 1659 *9221.17 p427*
Rensendin, A. 43; America, 1846 *778.6 p281*
Rensendin, Jean 15; America, 1846 *778.6 p281*
Rensendin, Pierre 9; America, 1846 *778.6 p281*
Renser, John; Ohio, 1809-1852 *4511.35 p42*
Renshaw, Henry; America, 1763 *1220.12 p666*
Renshaw, Isabella; America, 1766 *1220.12 p666*
Rensing, Anna 42; Galveston, TX, 1845 *3967.10 p376*
Rensing, Anna Katharina 23; Galveston, TX, 1845 *3967.10 p376*
Rensing, Bernhard 1; Galveston, TX, 1845 *3967.10 p376*
Rensing, Heinrich 40; Galveston, TX, 1845 *3967.10 p376*
Rensing, Johann Gerhard 27; Galveston, TX, 1845 *3967.10 p376*
Rensing, Wilhelm 1; Galveston, TX, 1845 *3967.10 p376*
Rensloe, Arthur 17; Ontario, 1871 *1823.21 p309*
Rentier, Madeleine; Quebec, 1668 *4514.3 p363*
Renton, David; Washington, 1889 *2770.40 p80*
Renton, William; Nevis or Jamaica, 1722 *1220.12 p666*
Rentz, Jacob; Ohio, 1809-1852 *4511.35 p43*
Rentz, Joseph; Ohio, 1809-1852 *4511.35 p43*
Renwick, Alexander 30; Ontario, 1871 *1823.21 p309*
Renwick, Mary 60; Ontario, 1871 *1823.17 p138*
Renwick, R. G. 40; Ontario, 1871 *1823.21 p309*
Renwick, William; North Carolina, 1823 *1088.45 p28*
Renwick, Wm 45; Ontario, 1871 *1823.17 p138*
Renz, Christine 20; New York, NY, 1892 *8425.16 p34*
Renz, Friedrich 22; Halifax, N.S., 1902 *1860.4 p40*
Renz, Friedrich 22; New York, NY, 1892 *8425.16 p34*
Renz, Marie 11 months; New York, NY, 1892 *8425.16 p34*
Renz, Sebastian; Venezuela, 1529 *3899.5 p538*
Repis, Vilem J.; Cleveland, OH, 1870 *2853.20 p477*
Repkey, Gerard; New York, 1777 *8529.30 p4A*
Replat, Claude Louis 18; New Orleans, 1848 *778.6 p281*
Repoche, Francois; Quebec, 1663 *4514.3 p363*
Repoche, Jeanne; Quebec, 1663 *4514.3 p363*
  *Sister:*Marie
Repoche, Marie *SEE* Repoche, Jeanne
Repp, Nicholas; Ohio, 1809-1852 *4511.35 p43*
Repp, Peter; Ohio, 1809-1852 *4511.35 p43*
Repsow, Emilie 19; Halifax, N.S., 1902 *1860.4 p41*
Repsow, Heinrich 17; Halifax, N.S., 1902 *1860.4 p41*

Reptow, Emilie 19; Halifax, N.S., 1902 *1860.4 p41*
Reptow, Heinrich 17; Halifax, N.S., 1902 *1860.4 p41*
Requard, Jobst Heinrich; America, 1864 *7420.1 p226*
Requardt, . . .; America, 1880 *7420.1 p398*
Requardt, Friedericke Henriette; America, 1847 *7420.1 p53*
Requardt, Friedrich; America, 1870 *7420.1 p287*
Requardt, Louise Charlotte; America, 1883 *7420.1 p339*
Requath, Hans Heinrich; America, 1847 *7420.1 p56*
  With wife
  With son 14
  With son 6
  With son 11
  With son 21
Requeste, Joseph 28; New Orleans, 1840 *778.6 p281*
Rerh, Jean 34; America, 1846 *778.6 p282*
Reschke, Christopher; Ohio, 1809-1852 *4511.35 p43*
Resden, John; America, 1765 *1220.12 p666*
Resouder, Louis 27; Texas, 1843 *778.6 p282*
Ress, Abraham 53; Halifax, N.S., 1902 *1860.4 p42*
Ress, Christian; Ohio, 1809-1852 *4511.35 p43*
Ress, Jacob; Ohio, 1809-1852 *4511.35 p43*
Ress, Katha 59; Halifax, N.S., 1902 *1860.4 p42*
Ressel, Frank Edmund; Illinois, 1930 *121.35 p100*
Ressoulet, Etienne 48; New Orleans, 1846 *778.6 p282*
Ressweber, Onton 25; New Orleans, 1845 *778.6 p282*
Restall, George; America, 1770 *1220.12 p666*
Reston, Francis C.; North Carolina, 1792-1862 *1088.45 p28*
Reston, Thomas Clayton; North Carolina, 1811 *1088.45 p28*
Reston, William; North Carolina, 1792-1862 *1088.45 p28*
Restorick, Francis 34; Ontario, 1871 *1823.17 p138*
Restorick, William 37; Ontario, 1871 *1823.17 p138*
Retallack, Richard; America, 1753 *1220.12 p666*
Reth, William; America, 1729 *1220.12 p666*
Rethman, Anton; Ohio, 1840-1897 *8365.35 p17*
Retienne, Karl; America, 1888 *5475.1 p183*
Retilley, James, Sr.; Ohio, 1806-1850 *9228.50 p540*
Retilley, James, Sr.; Ohio, 1871 *9228.50 p392*
Retour, Pierre 22; Quebec, 1662 *9221.17 p492*
Retsch, Heinrich 26; Halifax, N.S., 1902 *1860.4 p41*
Rettberg, Johann Heinrich; America, 1857 *7420.1 p170*
Rettcke, Friedr.; America, 1882 *5475.1 p228*
Retti, Franz Joseph; Venezuela, 1843 *3899.5 p542*
Retti, Franziskus; Venezuela, 1843 *3899.5 p542*
Retti, Sebastian; Venezuela, 1843 *3899.5 p542*
Retti Children, . . .; Venezuela, 1843 *3899.5 p542*
Rettig, Joh.; Valdivia, Chile, 1851 *1192.4 p51*
Rettig, Michael; America, 1866 *2526.42 p164*
Rettig, Moritz; Valdivia, Chile, 1850 *1192.4 p49*
  With wife & 2 children
  With child 10
  With child 7 months
Rettin, Sophie; America, 1854 *7420.1 p127*
Rettler, Nikolaus; America, 1868 *5475.1 p376*
Retzer, Francis 51; America, 1842 *778.6 p282*
Retzius, A.W.; Philadelphia, 1847 *6412.40 p150*
Retzler, Fritz; New York, 1860 *358.56 p149*
Retzler, Maria Dorothea; America, 1867 *5475.1 p561*
  *Son:*Ludwig
  *Son:*H. Peter
Reuber, Friedrich 15 *SEE* Reuber, Georg Fr.
Reuber, Georg Fr. 43; America, 1833 *5475.1 p394*
  *Wife:*Karoline Gross
  *Daughter:*Karoline 13
  *Son:*Friedrich 15
Reuber, John; Ohio, 1809-1852 *4511.35 p43*
Reuber, Karoline Gross *SEE* Reuber, Georg Fr.
Reuber, Karoline 13 *SEE* Reuber, Georg Fr.
Reubold, Elisabeth Margarethe *SEE* Reubold, Georg, II
Reubold, Eva Maria 23; America, 1853 *2526.43 p206*
Reubold, Georg, II; America, 1885 *2526.43 p131*
  *Wife:*Elisabeth Margarethe
  *Son:*Jakob
  *Daughter:*Margarethe
Reubold, Jakob *SEE* Reubold, Georg, II
Reubold, Margarethe *SEE* Reubold, Georg, II
Reuland, Angela *SEE* Reuland, Johann
Reuland, Angela Kraus *SEE* Reuland, Johann
Reuland, Angela *SEE* Reuland, Johann
Reuland, Angela Kraus *SEE* Reuland, Johann
Reuland, Anna 60 *SEE* Reuland, Jakob
Reuland, Jakob; Wisconsin, 1872 *5475.1 p275*
  *Sister:*Anna
Reuland, Johann; America, 1867 *5475.1 p238*
  *Wife:*Angela Kraus
  *Daughter:*Angela
  *Son:*Mathias
  *Daughter:*Susanna
Reuland, Johann; America, 1867 *5475.1 p265*
  *Wife:*Angela Kraus
  *Daughter:*Susanna

*Daughter:*Angela
*Son:*Mathias
Reuland, Mathias *SEE* Reuland, Johann
Reuland, Mathias *SEE* Reuland, Johann
Reuland, Susanna *SEE* Reuland, Johann
Reuland, Susanna *SEE* Reuland, Johann
Reum, Caspar Adolph; America, 1867 *7919.3 p524*
Reum, Caspar Friedrich; America, 1868 *7919.3 p526*
  With wife & 2 children
Reum, Catharina Margarethe; America, 1868 *7919.3 p524*
  With 2 children
Reum, Catharina Rosina; America, 1867 *7919.3 p526*
Reum, Christiane Maria; America, 1867 *7919.3 p526*
Reum, Dorothea Elisabeth; America, 1867 *7919.3 p524*
Reum, Elisabeth; America, 1867 *7919.3 p524*
Reum, F.A.; New York, 1860 *358.56 p3*
Reum, Friedrich; America, 1868 *7919.3 p526*
Reum, Philip; Ohio, 1809-1852 *4511.35 p43*
Reumke, Heinrich August Ludwig; Port uncertain, 1899 *7420.1 p375*
Reunig, Jakob *SEE* Reunig, Jakob
Reunig, Jakob; America, 1873 *5475.1 p179*
  *Wife:*Susanna Muller
  *Daughter:*Magdalena
  *Daughter:*Katharina
  With daughter
  *Son:*Jakob
Reunig, Katharina *SEE* Reunig, Jakob
Reunig, Magdalena *SEE* Reunig, Jakob
Reunig, Susanna Muller 37 *SEE* Reunig, Jakob
Reusch, Francis 40; Port uncertain, 1845 *778.6 p282*
Reuss, Adelheid; America, 1857 *2526.43 p178*
Reuss, Gottl.; Valdivia, Chile, 1852 *1192.4 p53*
Reussner, Elisabeth 21 *SEE* Reussner, Leonhard
Reussner, Georg Ernst 15 *SEE* Reussner, Leonhard
Reussner, Georg Jakob 28 *SEE* Reussner, Leonhard
Reussner, Johannes 19 *SEE* Reussner, Leonhard
Reussner, Katharina Elisabetha Specht *SEE* Reussner, Leonhard
Reussner, Leonhard 54; America, 1854 *2526.43 p199*
  *Wife:*Katharina Elisabetha Specht
  *Son:*Johannes 19
  *Son:*Georg Ernst 15
  *Son:*Georg Jakob 28
  *Daughter:*Elisabeth 21
Reust, Jacob; Ohio, 1809-1852 *4511.35 p43*
Reuter, Adam 11 *SEE* Reuter, Peter
Reuter, Angela *SEE* Reuter, Gottfried
Reuter, Anna Katharina 6 *SEE* Reuter, Johannes
Reuter, Anna Maria *SEE* Reuter, Joh.
Reuter, Anton 29; America, 1856 *2526.42 p102*
Reuter, Barbara; Brazil, 1880 *5475.1 p373*
Reuter, Elisabeth 21; Valdivia, Chile, 1852 *1192.4 p56*
Reuter, Georg 32; America, 1851 *2526.42 p184*
  With wife
Reuter, Gottfried 58; Brazil, 1862 *5475.1 p369*
  *Daughter:*Angela
  *Son:*Johann
  *Son:*Nikolaus
Reuter, Heinrich 6 *SEE* Reuter, Peter
Reuter, Hermann Carl August *SEE* Reuter, Johann Christoph Ludwig
Reuter, Jacob; Valdivia, Chile, 1850 *1192.4 p48*
Reuter, Jakob *SEE* Reuter, Joh.
Reuter, Joh.; America, 1883 *5475.1 p24*
  *Wife:*Susanna Zimmermann
  *Daughter:*Margarethe
  *Son:*Nikolaus
  *Daughter:*Anna Maria
  *Son:*Julius
  *Daughter:*Maria
  *Son:*Peter
  *Son:*Johann
  *Son:*Jakob
  *Daughter:*Susanne
Reuter, Johann; America, 1857 *2526.42 p164*
Reuter, Johann *SEE* Reuter, Peter
Reuter, Johann *SEE* Reuter, Joh.
Reuter, Johann *SEE* Reuter, Gottfried
Reuter, Johann Christoph Ludwig; America, 1868 *7420.1 p275*
  With wife
  *Daughter:*Johanna Pauline Hermine
  *Son:*Hermann Carl August
Reuter, Johanna Pauline Hermine *SEE* Reuter, Johann Christoph Ludwig
Reuter, Johannes; America, 1856 *2526.42 p103*
  *Child:*Johannes
  *Child:*Anna Katharina
  *Child:*Peter
Reuter, Johannes 13 *SEE* Reuter, Peter
Reuter, Johannes 16 *SEE* Reuter, Johannes

Reuter, Julius *SEE* Reuter, Joh.
Reuter, Magdalene Hermann-Mauer *SEE* Reuter, Peter
Reuter, Margarethe *SEE* Reuter, Joh.
Reuter, Maria *SEE* Reuter, Joh.
Reuter, Marie Elisabeth 9 *SEE* Reuter, Peter
Reuter, Mathias 70; America, 1874 *5475.1 p346*
Reuter, Michel 16; America, 1880 *5475.1 p484*
Reuter, Nikolaus *SEE* Reuter, Joh.
Reuter, Nikolaus *SEE* Reuter, Gottfried
Reuter, Peter; America, 1856 *2526.42 p103*
  With wife
  *Child:*Marie Elisabeth
  *Child:*Heinrich
  *Child:*Johannes
  *Child:*Adam
Reuter, Peter *SEE* Reuter, Peter
Reuter, Peter; America, 1882 *5475.1 p141*
  *Wife:*Magdalene Hermann-Mauer
  *Son:*Peter
  *Son:*Johann
Reuter, Peter *SEE* Reuter, Joh.
Reuter, Peter 11 *SEE* Reuter, Johannes
Reuter, Sophie Wilhelmine Pauline; America, 1867 *7420.1 p263*
Reuter, Susanna Zimmermann *SEE* Reuter, Joh.
Reuter, Susanne *SEE* Reuter, Joh.
Reutermark, C.J.; New York, NY, 1848 *6412.40 p151*
Reuther, Ludwig; Iowa, 1850 *5475.1 p29*
Reutiger, Peter; North Carolina, 1710 *3629.40 p6*
Reutschler, John Michael; Illinois, 1852 *6079.1 p11*
Reutter, Charles; Illinois, 1858-1861 *6020.5 p132*
Reutter, Friede 31; Valdivia, Chile, 1852 *1192.4 p53*
  With child 3
  With child 8
Reve, Robert; America, 1741 *1220.12 p665*
Revel, James; America, 1771 *1220.12 p666*
Revel, William H. 40; Ontario, 1871 *1823.21 p309*
Revell, Hannah; America, 1738 *1220.12 p666*
Revell, John; America, 1731 *1220.12 p667*
Revell, John; Rappahannock, VA, 1726 *1220.12 p667*
Revell, Samuel; America, 1707 *1220.12 p667*
Revell, William; America, 1763 *1220.12 p667*
Reveneaud, Louis 38; New Orleans, 1848 *778.6 p282*
Revere, Apollos; Boston, 1735 *9228.50 p27*
Revere, Appollos 13; Boston, n.d. *9228.50 p541*
Revers, Anthony; Wisconsin, 1900 *6795.8 p135*
Revers, Roberts; America, 1772 *1220.12 p676*
Reves, Jane; Maryland, 1672 *1236.25 p46*
Revett, Jane; America, 1723 *1220.12 p667*
Revill, William; Antigua (Antego), 1742 *1220.12 p667*
Revington, Joseph 34; Ontario, 1871 *1823.17 p138*
Revington, Margaret 20; Ontario, 1871 *1823.21 p309*
Revis, Vilem J.; Cleveland, OH, 1870 *2853.20 p477*
Revolt, Louis 50; America, 1842 *778.6 p282*
Revord, John; America, 1751 *1220.12 p667*
Rew, Isaac; America, 1733 *1220.12 p667*
Rewald, G.; Valdivia, Chile, 1850 *1192.4 p48*
Rewell, Jane; Carolina, 1719 *1220.12 p667*
Rewit, Guy 27; Ontario, 1871 *1823.21 p309*
Rex, Charles; America, 1753 *1220.12 p667*
Rexacre, Nicholas; Ohio, 1809-1852 *4511.35 p43*
Rexer, Jacob F.; Ohio, 1840-1897 *8365.35 p17*
Rexroth, Christina; America, 1843 *2526.43 p178*
Rexroth, Elisabeth 20 *SEE* Rexroth, Kilian
Rexroth, Elisabeth Margareta; America, 1854 *2526.42 p129*
  *Child:*Philipp
  *Child:*Johann Jakob
  *Child:*Margaretha
Rexroth, Georg; America, 1860 *2526.43 p154*
Rexroth, Gustav Philipp; America, 1868 *2526.43 p178*
  *Brother:*Karl
Rexroth, Heinrich; America, 1880 *2526.43 p178*
Rexroth, Johann Jakob 1 *SEE* Rexroth, Elisabeth Margareta
Rexroth, Johann Michael Ludwig Albrecht; America, 1866 *2526.43 p178*
Rexroth, Karl *SEE* Rexroth, Gustav Philipp
Rexroth, Kilian 56; America, 1853 *2526.43 p178*
  *Daughter:*Elisabeth 20
  With son-in-law
Rexroth, Leonhard Ludwig; America, 1887 *2526.43 p179*
Rexroth, Margaretha 4 *SEE* Rexroth, Elisabeth Margareta
Rexroth, Philipp 7 *SEE* Rexroth, Elisabeth Margareta
Rey, Mr. 32; America, 1846 *778.6 p282*
Rey, Mr. 18; Louisiana, 1848 *778.6 p282*
Rey, Andre; Louisiana, 1841-1844 *4981.45 p211*
Rey, Cesarine 21; New Orleans, 1848 *778.6 p282*
Rey, Jacques 30; New Orleans, 1848 *778.6 p282*
Reybaud, Eug.; Louisiana, 1874-1875 *4981.45 p30*
Reycraft, Richard 40; Ontario, 1871 *1823.21 p309*
Reydellet, Edouard; New Orleans, 1840 *778.6 p282*
Reyer, Anna Maria; Valdivia, Chile, 1852 *1192.4 p55*

Reyers, James 24; South Carolina, 1812 *3476.30 p13*
Reyet, Peter; North Carolina, 1710 *3629.40 p6*
Reymann, Fridolin; Died enroute, 1817-1818 *90.20 p153*
Reymann, Johannes 42; New Castle, DE, 1817-1818 *90.20 p153*
Reymann, Lorenz 46; Died enroute, 1817-1818 *90.20 p153*
Reymann, Marks 44; New Castle, DE, 1817-1818 *90.20 p153*
Reymershoffer, Gustav *SEE* Reymershoffer, Jan
Reymershoffer, Jan *SEE* Reymershoffer, Jan
Reymershoffer, Jan; Galveston, TX, 1854 *2853.20 p61*
  *Wife:*Klara Holla
  *Child:*Klara
  *Child:*Zdenka
  *Child:*Jan
  *Child:*Gustav
  *Child:*Otilie
Reymershoffer, Klara *SEE* Reymershoffer, Jan
Reymershoffer, Klara Holla *SEE* Reymershoffer, Jan
Reymershoffer, Otilie *SEE* Reymershoffer, Jan
Reymershoffer, Zdenka *SEE* Reymershoffer, Jan
Reymond, Mr. 52; Port uncertain, 1843 *778.6 p282*
Reymour, Spencer 43; Ontario, 1871 *1823.21 p309*
Reynal, Nicholas; Maine, 1665 *9228.50 p541*
Reynaud, L. P. 22; America, 1841 *778.6 p282*
Reyne, Estien 28; America, 1842 *778.6 p282*
Reynells, John; America, 1685 *1220.12 p667*
Reyner, John; America, 1752 *1220.12 p661*
Reyner, Joseph; America, 1749 *1220.12 p667*
Reynier, Christine 16; Quebec, 1661 *9221.17 p466*
Reynold, Alex.; Jamestown, VA, 1633 *1658.20 p211*
Reynold, Nicholas; Maine, 1665 *9228.50 p541*
Reynold, Samuel; Barbados, 1663 *1220.12 p667*
Reynold, Thomas; Barbados or Jamaica, 1688 *1220.12 p667*
Reynolds, Miss; Toronto, 1844 *2910.35 p112*
Reynolds, Andy; New Orleans, 1851 *7242.30 p153*
Reynolds, Ann; America, 1742 *1220.12 p667*
Reynolds, Ann; America, 1771 *1220.12 p667*
Reynolds, Arnold; America, 1730 *1220.12 p667*
Reynolds, Arnold; Maryland, 1719 *1220.12 p667*
Reynolds, Arnold; Maryland, 1740 *1220.12 p667*
Reynolds, Betty; New Orleans, 1851 *7242.30 p153*
Reynolds, Bridgette 38; Michigan, 1880 *4491.39 p25*
Reynolds, Caleb; Ontario, 1787 *1276.15 p230*
Reynolds, Charles 18; Quebec, 1870 *8364.32 p25*
Reynolds, Constantine; America, 1750 *1220.12 p667*
Reynolds, Edward; America, 1770 *1220.12 p667*
Reynolds, Edward; Annapolis, MD, 1719 *1220.12 p667*
Reynolds, Edward; Barbados, 1668 *1220.12 p667*
Reynolds, Elizabeth; America, 1739 *1220.12 p667*
Reynolds, Ellen; New Orleans, 1851 *7242.30 p153*
Reynolds, Emanuel; America, 1737 *1220.12 p667*
Reynolds, Gabriel; Jamaica, 1661 *1220.12 p667*
Reynolds, George; America, 1769 *1220.12 p667*
Reynolds, George; Virginia, 1732 *1220.12 p667*
Reynolds, Hannah; America, 1768 *1220.12 p667*
Reynolds, Hannah; Died enroute, 1731 *1220.12 p667*
Reynolds, Henry; America, 1737 *1220.12 p667*
Reynolds, Henry 22; Ontario, 1871 *1823.21 p309*
Reynolds, Henry; Virginia, 1742 *1220.12 p667*
Reynolds, Isaac; America, 1758 *1220.12 p667*
Reynolds, James; America, 1745 *1220.12 p667*
Reynolds, James; Barbados or Jamaica, 1687 *1220.12 p667*
Reynolds, James; Marston's Wharf, 1782 *8529.30 p15*
Reynolds, James; Potomac, 1731 *1220.12 p667*
Reynolds, James 17; Quebec, 1870 *8364.32 p25*
Reynolds, James H.; Ohio, 1873 *3580.20 p33*
Reynolds, James H.; Ohio, 1873 *6020.12 p22*
Reynolds, Jane 41; Ontario, 1871 *1823.21 p309*
Reynolds, John; America, 1727 *1220.12 p667*
Reynolds, John; America, 1746 *1220.12 p667*
Reynolds, John; America, 1758 *1220.12 p667*
Reynolds, John; America, 1764 *1220.12 p667*
Reynolds, John; America, 1766 *1220.12 p667*
Reynolds, John; Barbados, 1664 *1220.12 p667*
Reynolds, John 54; Michigan, 1880 *4491.39 p25*
Reynolds, John 34; Ontario, 1871 *1823.21 p309*
Reynolds, Jonathan; America, 1727 *1220.12 p667*
Reynolds, Joseph; America, 1726 *1220.12 p668*
Reynolds, Josias; America, 1755 *1220.12 p668*
Reynolds, Lewis 45; Ontario, 1871 *1823.17 p138*
Reynolds, M.; Toronto, 1844 *2910.35 p112*
Reynolds, Martha; America, 1702 *1220.12 p668*
Reynolds, Mary 12; Quebec, 1870 *8364.32 p25*
Reynolds, Mary; Rappahannock, VA, 1728 *1220.12 p668*
Reynolds, Miles; America, 1767 *1220.12 p668*
Reynolds, Moses; America, 1739 *1220.12 p668*
Reynolds, Nicholas; America, 1754 *1220.12 p668*
Reynolds, Patrick; New Orleans, 1851 *7242.30 p153*
Reynolds, Peter 54; Ontario, 1871 *1823.21 p309*

Reynolds, Richard; America, 1758 ***1220.12*** *p668*
Reynolds, Richard; America, 1767 ***1220.12*** *p668*
Reynolds, Richard 29; Ontario, 1871 ***1823.21*** *p309*
Reynolds, Robert; America, 1749 ***1220.12*** *p668*
Reynolds, Robert 21; Ontario, 1871 ***1823.21*** *p309*
Reynolds, Sam'l; Ontario, 1787 ***1276.15*** *p230*
Reynolds, Samuel; America, 1731 ***1220.12*** *p668*
Reynolds, Sara 20; Ontario, 1871 ***1823.21*** *p309*
Reynolds, Stephen; America, 1723 ***1220.12*** *p668*
Reynolds, Stephen; New Orleans, 1851 ***7242.30*** *p153*
Reynolds, Thomas; America, 1713 ***1220.12*** *p668*
Reynolds, Thomas; America, 1753 ***1220.12*** *p668*
Reynolds, Thomas; America, 1774 ***1220.12*** *p668*
Reynolds, Thomas; America, 1775 ***1220.12*** *p668*
Reynolds, Thomas; Barbados, 1668 ***1220.12*** *p668*
Reynolds, Thomas; Maryland, 1720 ***1220.12*** *p668*
Reynolds, Thomas; Virginia, 1734 ***1220.12*** *p668*
Reynolds, Timothy; Marston's Wharf, 1782 ***8529.30*** *p15*
Reynolds, William; America, 1740 ***1220.12*** *p668*
Reynolds, William; America, 1751 ***1220.12*** *p668*
Reynolds, William; America, 1752 ***1220.12*** *p668*
Reynolds, William; America, 1761 ***1220.12*** *p668*
Reynolds, William; Barbados, 1668 ***1220.12*** *p668*
Reynolds, William; Barbados, 1699 ***1220.12*** *p668*
Reynolds, William 29; Michigan, 1880 ***4491.39*** *p25*
Reynolds, William; North Carolina, 1853 ***1088.45*** *p28*
Reynolds, William 24; Ontario, 1871 ***1823.17*** *p138*
Reynolds, Wm; Virginia, 1652 ***6254.4*** *p243*
Reyser, Ulrich; Missouri, 1874 ***1029.59*** *p77*
Rezenover, Jacob; North Carolina, 1710 ***3629.40*** *p6*
Rezenover, Mathias; North Carolina, 1710 ***3629.40*** *p6*
Rezenover, Matthew; North Carolina, 1710 ***3629.40*** *p6*
Reznick, Nathan; Detroit, 1929 ***1640.55*** *p116*
Rhea, Francis 70; Ontario, 1871 ***1823.21*** *p309*
Rhein, Anna 47; America, 1874 ***5475.1*** *p378*
Rhein, Franz; America, 1872 ***5475.1*** *p275*
Rhein, Jacob; Ohio, 1809-1852 ***4511.35*** *p43*
Rhein, Magdalena; Wisconsin, 1882 ***6795.8*** *p99*
Rhein, Margaretha 20; New York, NY, 1894 ***6512.1*** *p182*
Rheinberger, Heinrich; Illinois, 1854 ***6079.1*** *p11*
Rheinberger, Louis; Illinois, 1852 ***6079.1*** *p11*
Rheind, Jacob; Ohio, 1809-1852 ***4511.35*** *p43*
Rheinhard, John George; Ohio, 1809-1852 ***4511.35*** *p43*
Rheinisch, Geo.; Ohio, 1840-1897 ***8365.35*** *p17*
Rheinlander, Jakob; America, 1843 ***5475.1*** *p294*
Rheinlander, Johann; America, 1843 ***5475.1*** *p294*
Rhenitgen, Gerhard 50; Ontario, 1871 ***1823.17*** *p138*
Rhimes, Mary; America, 1753 ***1220.12*** *p675*
Rhino, Mr. 45; America, 1842 ***778.6*** *p282*
Rhoades, Alfred S.; Iowa, 1900 ***1211.15*** *p18*
Rhoades, James; America, 1772 ***1220.12*** *p668*
Rhode, John; America, 1731 ***1220.12*** *p668*
Rhode, Richard; America, 1760 ***1220.12*** *p668*
Rhode, Samuel; Ohio, 1809-1852 ***4511.35*** *p43*
Rhoden, Matthew; Virginia, 1652 ***6254.4*** *p243*
Rhodenhurst, Mary; America, 1774 ***1220.12*** *p668*
Rhodes, Ann; America, 1757 ***1220.12*** *p668*
Rhodes, Ann; America, 1768 ***1220.12*** *p668*
Rhodes, Barbara 22; Ohio, 1840 ***778.6*** *p282*
Rhodes, Barbara 55; Ohio, 1840 ***778.6*** *p282*
Rhodes, Catherine 24; Ohio, 1840 ***778.6*** *p282*
Rhodes, Christian 23; Ohio, 1840 ***778.6*** *p282*
Rhodes, Francis; West Indies, 1688 ***1220.12*** *p668*
Rhodes, Jacobine 16; Ohio, 1840 ***778.6*** *p282*
Rhodes, Jervis; Annapolis, MD, 1730 ***1220.12*** *p668*
Rhodes, John; America, 1758 ***1220.12*** *p668*
Rhodes, John; America, 1767 ***1220.12*** *p668*
Rhodes, John; America, 1775 ***1220.12*** *p668*
Rhodes, Madeline 18; Ohio, 1840 ***778.6*** *p282*
Rhodes, Mary; America, 1768 ***1220.12*** *p668*
Rhodes, Robert; America, 1687 ***1220.12*** *p668*
Rhodes, Robert; Virginia, 1721 ***1220.12*** *p668*
Rhodes, Samuel; America, 1772 ***1220.12*** *p669*
Rhodes, Thomas; America, 1772 ***1220.12*** *p669*
Rhodes, Thomas; America, 1773 ***1220.12*** *p669*
Rhohr, Henry; Ohio, 1809-1852 ***4511.35*** *p43*
Rhone, August; Iowa, 1888 ***1211.15*** *p18*
Rhuee, Thomas; America, 1705-1805 ***9228.50*** *p98*
Rhunedar, Jean 27; Port uncertain, 1841 ***778.6*** *p282*
Rhydderch, John; Ohio, 1844 ***4022.20*** *p290*
Rhymes, John 24; Ontario, 1871 ***1823.21*** *p309*
Riaggioni, Mrs. 25; Louisiana, 1848 ***778.6*** *p282*
Riaggioni, Vincent 24; Louisiana, 1848 ***778.6*** *p282*
Rial, Ruth; Massachusetts, 1688 ***1642*** *p106*
Rian, Frank; Boston, 1764 ***1642*** *p33*
Rian, Ruth; Massachusetts, 1764 ***1642*** *p109*
Ribault, Gervaise; Quebec, 1648 ***9221.17*** *p204*
Ribbeck, Auguste 27; Valdivia, Chile, 1852 ***1192.4*** *p56*
Ribbeck, Friedrich; Valdivia, Chile, 1850 ***1192.4*** *p48*
Ribbeck, Heinrich; Valdivia, Chile, 1850 ***1192.4*** *p48*
Ribbeck, Pauline 28; Valdivia, Chile, 1852 ***1192.4*** *p56*
Ribbeck, Wilhelm; Valdivia, Chile, 1850 ***1192.4*** *p48*
Ribbotta, Mr. 25; America, 1842 ***778.6*** *p282*
Ribers, Henry 44; Ontario, 1871 ***1823.17*** *p138*
Ribes, Mr. 24; America, 1841 ***778.6*** *p282*
Ribet, Mr. 23; New Orleans, 1840 ***778.6*** *p282*
Ribet, Alex; Louisiana, 1874-1875 ***4981.45*** *p30*
Ribet, Bertrand 42; New Orleans, 1848 ***778.6*** *p282*
Ribet, Jean 34; New Orleans, 1840 ***778.6*** *p282*
Ribet, Pierre Guillaume 35; New Orleans, 1845 ***778.6*** *p282*
Ribofode, Anna 57; America, 1854 ***5475.1*** *p53*
*Son:*Georg
Rican, Lewis; Louisiana, 1874-1875 ***4981.45*** *p30*
Ricard, Mr. 40; America, 1745 ***778.6*** *p283*
Ricard, Antoine 22; New Orleans, 1848 ***778.6*** *p283*
Ricard, Cornelius 71; Ontario, 1871 ***1823.21*** *p309*
Ricard, George; New Hampshire, 1670 ***9228.50*** *p541*
Ricard, Maturin; New Hampshire, 1670-1706 ***9228.50*** *p541*
Ricard, Pierre 39; America, 1844 ***778.6*** *p283*
Ricardo, Rachel B. 39; Quebec, 1910 ***2897.7*** *p9*
Ricaud, Hippolite 2; America, 1842 ***778.6*** *p283*
Ricaud, Rose 18; America, 1842 ***778.6*** *p283*
Ricaut, Jean Paul Joachim 23; New Orleans, 1840 ***778.6*** *p283*
Riccar, George; New Hampshire, 1670 ***9228.50*** *p541*
Riccar, Maturin; New Hampshire, 1670-1706 ***9228.50*** *p541*
Rice, Mrs.; California, 1868 ***1131.61*** *p89*
With child
Rice, Alexander; America, 1765 ***1220.12*** *p669*
Rice, Ann; Virginia, 1738 ***1220.12*** *p669*
Rice, Bernard; North Carolina, 1859 ***1088.45*** *p28*
Rice, David; America, 1754 ***1220.12*** *p669*
Rice, Dick; America, 1762 ***1220.12*** *p669*
Rice, Elizabeth; America, 1750 ***1220.12*** *p669*
Rice, Elizabeth; America, 1762 ***1220.12*** *p669*
Rice, Elizabeth; America, 1768 ***1220.12*** *p669*
Rice, Elizabeth; Annapolis, MD, 1758 ***1220.12*** *p669*
Rice, Elizabeth *SEE* Rice, William
Rice, George; America, 1740 ***1220.12*** *p669*
Rice, George 74; Ontario, 1871 ***1823.17*** *p138*
Rice, Ignatius; North Carolina, 1859 ***1088.45*** *p29*
Rice, James; America, 1772 ***1220.12*** *p669*
Rice, James; America, 1775 ***1220.12*** *p669*
Rice, James 27; Ontario, 1871 ***1823.21*** *p309*
Rice, James 42; Ontario, 1871 ***1823.21*** *p309*
Rice, John 41; Ontario, 1871 ***1823.21*** *p309*
Rice, Margaret Edwards *SEE* Rice, William
Rice, Mary; America, 1757 ***1220.12*** *p669*
Rice, Mary; America, 1774 ***1220.12*** *p669*
Rice, Mary; Barbados, 1669 ***1220.12*** *p669*
Rice, Mary; Maryland, 1742 ***1220.12*** *p669*
Rice, Mary *SEE* Rice, William
Rice, Mary; Virginia, 1751 ***1220.12*** *p669*
Rice, Nathaniel; America, 1750 ***1220.12*** *p669*
Rice, Patrick 45; Ontario, 1871 ***1823.17*** *p138*
Rice, Richard; Barbados, 1697 ***1220.12*** *p669*
Rice, Simon; Virginia, 1766 ***1220.12*** *p669*
Rice, Stephen; America, 1771 ***1220.12*** *p669*
Rice, Thomas; America, 1680 ***1220.12*** *p669*
Rice, Thomas; America, 1775 ***1220.12*** *p669*
Rice, Thomas; Annapolis, MD, 1723 ***1220.12*** *p669*
Rice, Thomas; Barbados or Jamaica, 1704 ***1220.12*** *p669*
Rice, Valentine; America, 1735 ***1220.12*** *p669*
Rice, Walter; America, 1758 ***1220.12*** *p669*
Rice, William; America, 1736 ***1220.12*** *p669*
Rice, William; America, 1755 ***1220.12*** *p669*
Rice, William; America, 1767 ***1220.12*** *p669*
Rice, William; America, 1770 ***1220.12*** *p669*
Rice, William; America, 1774 ***1220.12*** *p669*
Rice, William; Annapolis, MD, 1736 ***1220.12*** *p669*
Rice, William; Ohio, 1838 ***4022.20*** *p290*
*Wife:*Margaret Edwards
*Child:*Elizabeth
*Child:*Mary
Rice, William 35; Ontario, 1871 ***1823.21*** *p309*
Ricenot, Mr. 25; America, 1840 ***778.6*** *p283*
Rich, Daniel; America, 1750 ***1220.12*** *p669*
Rich, Elizabeth; America, 1729 ***1220.12*** *p669*
Rich, Elizabeth; America, 1745 ***1220.12*** *p669*
Rich, Henry; Annapolis, MD, 1725 ***1220.12*** *p669*
Rich, Henry 30; Ontario, 1871 ***1823.21*** *p309*
Rich, John; America, 1731 ***1220.12*** *p669*
Rich, John; America, 1752 ***1220.12*** *p669*
Rich, John; Annapolis, MD, 1730 ***1220.12*** *p669*
Rich, Jonathan; America, 1721 ***1220.12*** *p669*
Rich, Jonathan; Marblehead, MA, 1727 ***9228.50*** *p393*
Rich, Jonathan; Marblehead, MA, 1727 ***9228.50*** *p541*
Rich, Joseph; Barbados, 1714 ***1220.12*** *p669*
Rich, Marianna 33; New Orleans, 1848 ***778.6*** *p283*
Rich, Nicolas 13; New Orleans, 1848 ***778.6*** *p283*
Rich, Robert 43; Ontario, 1871 ***1823.21*** *p309*
Rich, Samuel; America, 1771 ***1220.12*** *p669*
Rich, Samuel; America, 1773 ***1220.12*** *p669*
Rich, Thomas; America, 1700 ***1220.12*** *p670*
Rich, Thomas; Barbados or Jamaica, 1699 ***1220.12*** *p669*
Rich, Thomas; Salem, MA, 1702 ***9228.50*** *p393*
Richacraft, Thomas 25; Annapolis, MD, 1721 ***1220.12*** *p670*
Richard, Mr. 29; America, 1844 ***778.6*** *p283*
Richard, Mr. 44; America, 1844 ***778.6*** *p283*
Richard, Mr. 45; America, 1843 ***778.6*** *p283*
Richard, Mr. 47; America, 1745 ***778.6*** *p283*
Richard, Adam 22; Louisiana, 1848 ***778.6*** *p283*
Richard, Albert 6 months; Missouri, 1848 ***778.6*** *p283*
Richard, All.in 44; Texas, 1845 ***778.6*** *p283*
Richard, Andre 49; Quebec, 1649 ***9221.17*** *p208*
Richard, Anne-Francoise; Quebec, 1669 ***4514.3*** *p364*
Richard, Babette 10; Missouri, 1848 ***778.6*** *p283*
Richard, Catherine 7; Missouri, 1848 ***778.6*** *p283*
Richard, Catherine; Quebec, 1667 ***4514.3*** *p334*
Richard, Chs. 48; Louisiana, 1848 ***778.6*** *p283*
Richard, Clement 23; Quebec, 1657 ***9221.17*** *p367*
Richard, David; Ohio, 1839 ***4022.20*** *p290*
*Wife:*Mary
Richard, Dorothee; Nova Scotia, 1753 ***3051*** *p112*
Richard, Francoise; Quebec, 1671 ***4514.3*** *p374*
Richard, George; Ohio, 1809-1852 ***4511.35*** *p43*
Richard, Jacques; Quebec, 1644 ***9221.17*** *p145*
Richard, Jaques; Virginia, 1700 ***9230.15*** *p81*
With wife
Richard, Jean 25; America, 1840 ***778.6*** *p283*
Richard, Jean 2; Missouri, 1848 ***778.6*** *p283*
Richard, Jean 46; Missouri, 1848 ***778.6*** *p283*
Richard, John; Ohio, 1809-1852 ***4511.35*** *p43*
Richard, John John; America, 1767 ***1220.12*** *p670*
Richard, Louis; Illinois, 1852 ***6079.1*** *p11*
Richard, Marguerite 46; Missouri, 1848 ***778.6*** *p283*
Richard, Marguerite; Quebec, 1651 ***9221.17*** *p97*
Richard, Marguerite; Quebec, 1651 ***9221.17*** *p97*
Richard, Marguerite 22; Quebec, 1651 ***9221.17*** *p247*
*Son:*Laurent 3
*Son:*Louis 2
Richard, Marguerite 22; Quebec, 1651 ***9221.17*** *p247*
*Son:*Laurent 3
*Son:*Louis 2
Richard, Marie 3; Missouri, 1845 ***778.6*** *p283*
Richard, Marie 16; Missouri, 1848 ***778.6*** *p283*
Richard, Marie; Quebec, 1669 ***4514.3*** *p364*
Richard, Marie 17; Quebec, 1656 ***9221.17*** *p346*
Richard, Mary *SEE* Richard, David
Richard, Mary; Virginia, 1774 ***1220.12*** *p670*
Richard, Matthew; Illinois, 1880 ***1447.20*** *p64*
Richard, Philip; Ohio, 1809-1852 ***4511.35*** *p43*
Richard, Reg. 30; America, 1745 ***778.6*** *p283*
Richard, Richard; America, 1774 ***1220.12*** *p670*
Richard, Robert; Barbados, 1688 ***1220.12*** *p670*
Richard, Rudolph; England, 1878 ***7420.1*** *p311*
Richard, Sophie 6; Missouri, 1845 ***778.6*** *p283*
Richard, William John; America, 1767 ***1220.12*** *p670*
Richarde, Jules 26; America, 1843 ***778.6*** *p283*
Richards, ; Ohio, 1840 ***4022.20*** *p287*
With husband
*Child:*John
With siblings
Richards, Mrs. 32; Quebec, 1870 ***8364.32*** *p25*
Richards, Ms.; Ohio, 1840 ***4022.20*** *p287*
Richards, Abraham; Ohio, 1809-1852 ***4511.35*** *p43*
Richards, Agnes 42; Ontario, 1871 ***1823.21*** *p309*
Richards, Alice; America, 1752 ***1220.12*** *p670*
Richards, Allen 62; Ontario, 1871 ***1823.17*** *p138*
Richards, Ann; America, 1765 ***1220.12*** *p670*
Richards, Ann; Ohio, 1840 ***4022.20*** *p290*
Richards, Ann; Ohio, 1840 ***4022.20*** *p290*
*Child:*Thomas
*Child:*Margaret
*Child:*Catherine
With 3 daughters
Richards, Anthony; America, 1767 ***1220.12*** *p670*
Richards, Catherine; Ohio, 1840 ***4022.20*** *p284*
Richards, Catherine *SEE* Richards, Ann
Richards, Charles; America, 1774 ***1220.12*** *p670*
Richards, Charles H.; Washington, 1883 ***2770.40*** *p137*
Richards, Christopher; America, 1685 ***1220.12*** *p670*
Richards, Daniel *SEE* Richards, Daniel
Richards, Daniel; Ohio, 1847 ***4022.20*** *p290*
*Wife:*Eleanor
*Child:*Daniel
*Child:*Margaret
*Child:*Gwinifred
*Child:*Hannah
*Child:*David
Richards, Daniel D. *SEE* Richards, Thomas
Richards, David *SEE* Richards, Daniel

Richards, David; Ohio, 1847 *4022.20 p290*
  *Wife:*Jane
  With child
Richards, David D.; Ohio, 1847 *4022.20 p290*
Richards, Edward; America, 1730 *1220.12 p670*
Richards, Edward; America, 1758 *1220.12 p670*
Richards, Edward; America, 1766 *1220.12 p670*
Richards, Eleanor Jones *SEE* Richards, Thomas
Richards, Eleanor *SEE* Richards, Daniel
Richards, Elizabeth; America, 1727 *1220.12 p670*
Richards, Elizabeth; America, 1736 *1220.12 p670*
Richards, Elizabeth; America, 1757 *1220.12 p670*
Richards, Elizabeth; America, 1763 *1220.12 p670*
Richards, Elizabeth; America, 1770 *1220.12 p670*
Richards, Elizabeth; America, 1772 *1220.12 p670*
Richards, Elizabeth; Virginia, 1729 *1220.12 p670*
Richards, Francis; America, 1758 *1220.12 p670*
Richards, Frederick; America, 1766 *1220.12 p670*
Richards, George C. 37; Indiana, 1879-1880 *9076.20 p69*
Richards, Gwinifred *SEE* Richards, Daniel
Richards, Hannah *SEE* Richards, Daniel
Richards, Henry; America, 1738 *1220.12 p670*
Richards, Henry 62; Ontario, 1871 *1823.21 p310*
Richards, Herbert 33; Indiana, 1867-1870 *9076.20 p67*
Richards, Humphrey; America, 1682 *1220.12 p670*
Richards, J. H. 48; Ontario, 1871 *1823.21 p310*
Richards, Jacob; Ohio, 1814-1866 *4022.20 p290*
Richards, James; America, 1749 *1220.12 p670*
Richards, James; North Carolina, 1845 *1088.45 p29*
Richards, Jane *SEE* Richards, Thomas
Richards, Jane *SEE* Richards, David
Richards, Job; America, 1774 *1220.12 p670*
Richards, John; America, 1700 *1220.12 p670*
Richards, John; America, 1737 *1220.12 p670*
Richards, John; America, 1755 *1220.12 p670*
Richards, John; America, 1767 *1220.12 p670*
Richards, John; Ohio, 1809-1852 *4511.35 p43*
Richards, John B.; Colorado, 1903 *1029.59 p77*
Richards, John B. 33; Colorado, 1888 *1029.59 p77*
Richards, Joseph; America, 1757 *1220.12 p670*
Richards, Joseph; America, 1773 *1220.12 p670*
Richards, Joseph; Long Island, 1778 *8529.30 p10A*
Richards, Joseph; New York, 1815 *3274.55 p71*
Richards, Joseph 27; Ontario, 1871 *1823.17 p138*
Richards, Katherin 19; Virginia, 1635 *1183.3 p31*
Richards, Lucy; America, 1758 *1220.12 p670*
Richards, Margaret; America, 1753 *1220.12 p670*
Richards, Margaret; America, 1760 *1220.12 p670*
Richards, Margaret; Ohio, 1840 *4022.20 p278*
Richards, Margaret *SEE* Richards, Ann
Richards, Margaret *SEE* Richards, Daniel
Richards, Mary; America, 1749 *1220.12 p670*
Richards, Mary; Annapolis, MD, 1726 *1220.12 p670*
Richards, Mary 40; Ontario, 1871 *1823.21 p310*
Richards, Mary 46; Ontario, 1871 *1823.21 p310*
Richards, Mary 11; Quebec, 1870 *8364.32 p25*
Richards, Obadiah 35; Ontario, 1871 *1823.21 p310*
Richards, Oliver; Maryland, 1674-1675 *1236.25 p51*
Richards, Paul; America, 1749 *1220.12 p670*
Richards, Peter 56; Ontario, 1871 *1823.21 p310*
Richards, Reese 40; Indiana, 1881-1888 *9076.20 p72*
Richards, Richard; America, 1766 *1220.12 p670*
Richards, Richard; America, 1772 *1220.12 p670*
Richards, Richard; Annapolis, MD, 1721 *1220.12 p670*
Richards, Richard 45; Ontario, 1871 *1823.17 p138*
Richards, Robert; America, 1685 *1220.12 p670*
Richards, Robert; Barbados, 1698 *1220.12 p670*
Richards, Robert 45; Ontario, 1871 *1823.21 p310*
Richards, Samuel; America, 1728 *1220.12 p671*
Richards, Samuel; America, 1774 *1220.12 p671*
Richards, Sarah; America, 1758 *1220.12 p671*
Richards, Sarah; America, 1759 *1220.12 p671*
Richards, Stephen; America, 1751 *1220.12 p671*
Richards, Thomas; America, 1707 *1220.12 p671*
Richards, Thomas; America, 1729 *1220.12 p671*
Richards, Thomas; America, 1750 *1220.12 p671*
Richards, Thomas; Jamaica, 1727 *1220.12 p671*
Richards, Thomas; Ohio, 1830 *4022.20 p291*
  *Wife:*Eleanor Jones
  *Child:*Daniel D.
Richards, Thomas; Ohio, 1839 *4022.20 p290*
  *Wife:*Jane
  With children
Richards, Thomas *SEE* Richards, Ann
Richards, Thomas 59; Ontario, 1871 *1823.17 p138*
Richards, William; America, 1730 *1220.12 p671*
Richards, William; America, 1738 *1220.12 p671*
Richards, William; America, 1740 *1220.12 p671*
Richards, William; America, 1748 *1220.12 p671*
Richards, William; America, 1753 *1220.12 p671*
Richards, William; America, 1768 *1220.12 p671*
Richards, William; Barbados, 1678 *1220.12 p671*
Richards, William; Colorado, 1883 *1029.59 p77*

Richards, William; Marston's Wharf, 1782 *8529.30 p15*
Richards, William; North Carolina, 1849 *1088.45 p29*
Richards, William 41; Ontario, 1871 *1823.21 p310*
Richards, William 65; Ontario, 1871 *1823.17 p138*
Richards, William H. 27; Colorado, 1880 *1029.59 p77*
Richards, William H.; North Carolina, 1861 *1088.45 p29*
Richards, Wm 50; Ontario, 1871 *1823.21 p310*
Richards, Wm.; California, 1868 *1131.61 p89*
Richards, Wm. Henry; Colorado, 1880 *1029.59 p77*
Richardson, Alexander; America, 1770 *1220.12 p671*
Richardson, Alexander; Illinois, 1834-1900 *6020.5 p133*
Richardson, Alfred 42; Ontario, 1871 *1823.21 p310*
Richardson, Anne; America, 1699 *1220.12 p671*
Richardson, Anne; Maryland, 1721 *1220.12 p671*
Richardson, Charles; America, 1757 *1220.12 p671*
Richardson, Charles; America, 1764 *1220.12 p671*
Richardson, Charles; America, 1767 *1220.12 p671*
Richardson, Daniel; America, 1750 *1220.12 p671*
Richardson, Daniel; Maryland, 1719 *1220.12 p671*
Richardson, Dawney; America, 1759 *1220.12 p671*
Richardson, Edith A. 12; Ontario, 1871 *1823.17 p138*
Richardson, Edward; America, 1743 *1220.12 p671*
Richardson, Edward; Barbados, 1680 *1220.12 p671*
Richardson, Elizabeth; America, 1751 *1220.12 p671*
Richardson, Elizabeth; Barbados, 1680 *1220.12 p671*
Richardson, Elizabeth; Potomac, 1731 *1220.12 p671*
Richardson, Elizabeth; Virginia, 1721 *1220.12 p671*
Richardson, Elizabeth; Virginia, 1735 *1220.12 p671*
Richardson, Emilee 60; Ontario, 1871 *1823.17 p138*
Richardson, Fanny 45; Ontario, 1871 *1823.21 p310*
Richardson, Francis; America, 1741 *1220.12 p671*
Richardson, Francis; Marblehead, MA, 1650-1722 *9228.50 p541*
Richardson, George; America, 1765 *1220.12 p671*
Richardson, George; Colorado, 1893 *1029.59 p77*
Richardson, George 59; Ontario, 1871 *1823.21 p310*
Richardson, Grace; America, 1730 *1220.12 p671*
Richardson, Hannah; Boston, 1725 *1642 p25*
Richardson, Henry; America, 1737 *1220.12 p671*
Richardson, Horatio N.; North Carolina, 1860 *1088.45 p29*
Richardson, James; America, 1765 *1220.12 p671*
Richardson, James 77; Ontario, 1871 *1823.21 p310*
Richardson, Jane; America, 1770 *1220.12 p671*
Richardson, Jared; Harrisburg, PA, 1799 *5720.10 p380*
Richardson, John; America, 1683 *1220.12 p671*
Richardson, John; America, 1697 *1220.12 p671*
Richardson, John; America, 1743 *1220.12 p672*
Richardson, John; America, 1749 *1220.12 p672*
Richardson, John; America, 1755 *1220.12 p672*
Richardson, John; America, 1758 *1220.12 p672*
Richardson, John; America, 1763 *1220.12 p672*
Richardson, John; America, 1766 *1220.12 p672*
Richardson, John; America, 1772 *1220.12 p672*
Richardson, John; America, 1774 *1220.12 p672*
Richardson, John; Barbados, 1685 *1220.12 p671*
Richardson, John; Barbados or Jamaica, 1677 *1220.12 p671*
Richardson, John; Barbados or Jamaica, 1698 *1220.12 p671*
Richardson, John; Maryland or Virginia, 1728 *1220.12 p671*
Richardson, John; North Carolina, 1843 *1088.45 p29*
Richardson, John 25; Ontario, 1871 *1823.21 p310*
Richardson, John 47; Ontario, 1871 *1823.17 p138*
Richardson, John 48; Ontario, 1871 *1823.21 p310*
Richardson, John 63; Ontario, 1871 *1823.17 p139*
Richardson, John; Virginia, 1736 *1220.12 p672*
Richardson, Joseph; America, 1739 *1220.12 p672*
Richardson, Joseph; America, 1756 *1220.12 p672*
Richardson, Lewis 35; Ontario, 1871 *1823.21 p310*
Richardson, Margaret; Bermuda, 1620 *1220.12 p672*
Richardson, Martha; America, 1765 *1220.12 p672*
Richardson, Mary; America, 1727 *1220.12 p672*
Richardson, Mary; America, 1741 *1220.12 p672*
Richardson, Mary; America, 1757 *1220.12 p740*
Richardson, Mary; Annapolis, MD, 1725 *1220.12 p672*
Richardson, Mary 75; Ontario, 1871 *1823.21 p310*
Richardson, Mary; Rappahannock, VA, 1728 *1220.12 p672*
Richardson, Mathew; America, 1743 *1220.12 p672*
Richardson, Nathaniel; America, 1741 *1220.12 p672*
Richardson, Nicholas; America, 1775 *1220.12 p672*
Richardson, Nightingale; America, 1754 *1220.12 p672*
Richardson, Ralph 35; North Carolina, 1774 *1422.10 p56*
Richardson, Rebecca; Ontario, 1835 *3160.1 p150*
Richardson, Richard; America, 1766 *1220.12 p672*
Richardson, Richard; America, 1768 *1220.12 p672*
Richardson, Richard; America, 1775 *1220.12 p672*
Richardson, Richard Robinson; North Carolina, 1832 *1088.45 p29*
Richardson, Robert; Barbados, 1664 *1220.12 p672*

Richardson, Robert; Maryland, 1744 *1220.12 p672*
Richardson, Robert 52; Ontario, 1871 *1823.21 p310*
Richardson, Samuel; America, 1738 *1220.12 p672*
Richardson, Samuel; America, 1755 *1220.12 p672*
Richardson, Samuel 39; Ontario, 1871 *1823.21 p310*
Richardson, Samuel 58; Ontario, 1871 *1823.21 p310*
Richardson, Sarah; America, 1736 *1220.12 p672*
Richardson, Sarah; Annapolis, MD, 1736 *1220.12 p672*
Richardson, Sarah; Virginia, 1768 *1220.12 p672*
Richardson, Sarah J. 54; Ontario, 1871 *1823.21 p310*
Richardson, Thomas; America, 1753 *1220.12 p672*
Richardson, Thomas; America, 1757 *1220.12 p672*
Richardson, Thomas; America, 1758 *1220.12 p672*
Richardson, Thomas; America, 1764 *1220.12 p672*
Richardson, Thomas; America, 1767 *1220.12 p672*
Richardson, Thomas; America, 1768 *1220.12 p672*
Richardson, Thomas; America, 1775 *1220.12 p672*
Richardson, Thomas; Died enroute, 1725 *1220.12 p672*
Richardson, Thomas; New York, 1777 *8529.30 p15*
Richardson, Thomas; North Carolina, 1842 *1088.45 p29*
Richardson, Thomas 37; Ontario, 1871 *1823.21 p310*
Richardson, Thomas 39; Ontario, 1871 *1823.21 p310*
Richardson, Thomas; Virginia, 1727 *1220.12 p672*
Richardson, William; America, 1699 *1220.12 p672*
Richardson, William; America, 1715 *1220.12 p673*
Richardson, William; America, 1756 *1220.12 p673*
Richardson, William; America, 1765 *1220.12 p673*
Richardson, William; America, 1767 *1220.12 p673*
Richardson, William; America, 1770 *1220.12 p673*
Richardson, William; America, 1771 *1220.12 p673*
Richardson, William 38; Michigan, 1880 *4491.39 p25*
Richardson, William; Ohio, 1836 *3580.20 p33*
Richardson, William; Ohio, 1836 *6020.12 p22*
Richardson, William; Ohio, 1838 *2763.1 p21*
Richardson, William 29; Ontario, 1871 *1823.17 p139*
Richardson, William 35; Ontario, 1871 *1823.17 p139*
Richardson, William 38; Ontario, 1871 *1823.17 p139*
Richardson, William 54; Ontario, 1871 *1823.21 p310*
Richardson, William 58; Ontario, 1871 *1823.17 p139*
Richardson, Wm 62; Ontario, 1871 *1823.21 p310*
Richardson, Wm 65; Ontario, 1871 *1823.17 p139*
Richardson, Wm. 72; Ontario, 1871 *1823.17 p139*
Richart, Catharina 21; America, 1845 *778.6 p283*
Richart, George; Ohio, 1809-1852 *4511.35 p43*
Richecourt, Jeanne 14; Quebec, 1659 *9221.17 p409*
Richeimer, Andrew; Ohio, 1809-1852 *4511.35 p43*
Richens, Jane; America, 1752 *1220.12 p673*
Richens, John; America, 1750 *1220.12 p673*
Richer, Cecile 30; Quebec, 1639 *9221.17 p84*
Richer, Georgette; Quebec, 1670 *4514.3 p364*
Richer, Jeanne 45; Quebec, 1646 *9221.17 p161*
Richer, Jeanne 45; Quebec, 1646 *9221.17 p161*
Richer, Marguerite; Quebec, 1672 *4514.3 p364*
Richer, Rene 20; Quebec, 1660 *9221.17 p439*
Richers, Catharina Sophia; America, 1857 *7420.1 p160*
Richers, Engel Charlotte Bleidistel *SEE* Richers, Hans Heinrich
Richers, Engel Marie *SEE* Richers, Hans Heinrich
Richers, Hans Heinrich; America, 1833 *7420.1 p7*
  *Wife:*Thrine Sophie Engelking
Richers, Hans Heinrich; America, 1846 *7420.1 p47*
  *Wife:*Engel Charlotte Bleidistel
  *Daughter:*Engel Marie
Richers, Hans Heinrich; America, 1850 *7420.1 p74*
Richers, Thrine Sophie Engelking *SEE* Richers, Hans Heinrich
Richert, Cath. 62; Died enroute, 1840 *778.6 p283*
Richert, George; Ohio, 1840-1897 *8365.35 p17*
Richert, Jacob 63; America, 1840 *778.6 p283*
Richert, Marg. 62; America, 1840 *778.6 p283*
Riches, Simeon; America, 1771 *1220.12 p673*
Richeson, Thomas; America, 1736 *1220.12 p673*
Richey, Frederick; Ohio, 1809-1852 *4511.35 p43*
Rich Family ; Massachusetts, 1630-1639 *9228.50 p541*
Richie, Agustus 20; Ontario, 1871 *1823.21 p310*
Richison, William; Philadelphia, 1778 *8529.30 p4A*
Richman, John; America, 1728 *1220.12 p673*
Richman, John; America, 1734 *1220.12 p673*
Richmann, Hans Heinrich Christian; America, 1857 *7420.1 p170*
Richmond, Ann; America, 1761 *1220.12 p673*
Richmond, Ann; America, 1763 *1220.12 p673*
Richmond, Ann; America, 1767 *1220.12 p673*
Richmond, Benjamin; Utah, 1854 *1211.45 p134*
Richmond, Edward; America, 1775 *1220.12 p673*
Richmond, Edward 32; Ontario, 1871 *1823.17 p139*
Richmond, Francis; Maryland or Virginia, 1731 *1220.12 p673*
Richmond, James; New York, 1778 *8529.30 p7*
Richmond, Jane; Annapolis, MD, 1724 *1220.12 p673*
Richmond, John; America, 1774 *1220.12 p673*
Richmond, M. A.J. 43; Ontario, 1871 *1823.21 p310*
Richmond, Mary; America, 1754 *1220.12 p673*

Richmond, Richd 54; Ontario, 1871 ***1823.21*** *p310*
Richmond, Robert 46; Ontario, 1871 ***1823.17*** *p139*
Richmond, William; America, 1718 ***1220.12*** *p673*
Richmond, William; America, 1774 ***1220.12*** *p673*
Richmond, William 34; Ontario, 1871 ***1823.17*** *p139*
Richmond, William 70; Ontario, 1871 ***1823.17*** *p139*
Richned, Grisard 30; America, 1841 ***778.6*** *p284*
Richned, Theod. 29; America, 1841 ***778.6*** *p284*
Richome, Pierre 17; Montreal, 1651 ***9221.17*** *p252*
Richome, Simon; Montreal, 1644 ***9221.17*** *p149*
Richot, Prosper; Louisiana, 1836-1841 ***4981.45*** *p209*
Richoux, F. 53; New Orleans, 1842 ***778.6*** *p284*
Richter, Adam; Ontario, 1871 ***1823.17*** *p139*
Richter, Anna; Halifax, N.S., 1902 ***1860.4*** *p39*
Richter, Anna 11 months; New York, NY, 1893 ***1883.7*** *p44*
Richter, Anton 10; New York, NY, 1893 ***1883.7*** *p44*
Richter, Anton 19; New York, NY, 1898 ***7951.13*** *p43*
Richter, Bernhd. 7; New York, NY, 1893 ***1883.7*** *p44*
Richter, Carl G.; Valdivia, Chile, 1850 ***1192.4*** *p48*
Richter, Cart Ernst; Galveston, TX, 1855 ***571.7*** *p17*
Richter, Charlotte 31; America, 1843 ***5475.1*** *p529*
Richter, Christ; Galveston, TX, 1855 ***571.7*** *p17*
Richter, Daniel 39; Halifax, N.S., 1902 ***1860.4*** *p42*
Richter, Edward 33; Halifax, N.S., 1902 ***1860.4*** *p39*
Richter, Emilie 2; Halifax, N.S., 1902 ***1860.4*** *p42*
Richter, Emilie 22; Halifax, N.S., 1902 ***1860.4*** *p42*
Richter, Emilie 32; Halifax, N.S., 1902 ***1860.4*** *p39*
Richter, Ernst; Port uncertain, 1854 ***7420.1*** *p127*
Richter, Fr.; Valdivia, Chile, 1850 ***1192.4*** *p48*
Richter, Franz; Halifax, N.S., 1902 ***1860.4*** *p39*
Richter, Franz 27; New York, NY, 1898 ***7951.13*** *p43*
Richter, Franzisca 45; New York, NY, 1893 ***1883.7*** *p44*
Richter, Gottfried; Galveston, TX, 1855 ***571.7*** *p17*
Richter, Heinrich 20; Halifax, N.S., 1902 ***1860.4*** *p42*
Richter, Heinrich Wilhelm; America, 1871 ***7420.1*** *p396*
Richter, Helene 6; Halifax, N.S., 1902 ***1860.4*** *p39*
Richter, Jan 36; Halifax, N.S., 1902 ***1860.4*** *p39*
Richter, Jan; Milwaukee, 1848-1849 ***2853.20*** *p308*
Richter, Johann 8; New York, NY, 1898 ***7951.13*** *p43*
Richter, Johann 11; New York, NY, 1893 ***1883.7*** *p44*
Richter, Johann Georg; Venezuela, 1843 ***3899.5*** *p543*
Richter, Joseph 19; New York, NY, 1898 ***7951.13*** *p43*
Richter, Karoline 4; Halifax, N.S., 1902 ***1860.4*** *p39*
Richter, Konrad; America, 1879 ***5475.1*** *p533*
Richter, Leoboldina 6 months; New York, NY, 1898 ***7951.13*** *p43*
Richter, Leon. 9; New York, NY, 1893 ***1883.7*** *p44*
Richter, Lydia 9; Halifax, N.S., 1902 ***1860.4*** *p42*
Richter, Magdalena 25; New York, NY, 1898 ***7951.13*** *p43*
Richter, Maria 23; Halifax, N.S., 1902 ***1860.4*** *p39*
Richter, Maria 5; New York, NY, 1893 ***1883.7*** *p44*
Richter, Marianna 21; New York, NY, 1898 ***7951.13*** *p43*
Richter, Martha 15; New York, NY, 1893 ***1883.7*** *p44*
Richter, Mathilde 29; New York, NY, 1899 ***5475.1*** *p19*
Richter, Micheley 4; Halifax, N.S., 1902 ***1860.4*** *p39*
Richter, Mikolnj 2; Halifax, N.S., 1902 ***1860.4*** *p39*
Richter, Pauline 18; Halifax, N.S., 1902 ***1860.4*** *p42*
Richter, Regina 33; Halifax, N.S., 1902 ***1860.4*** *p42*
Richter, Theresia 49; New York, NY, 1898 ***7951.13*** *p43*
Richter, Wendelin 3; New York, NY, 1898 ***7951.13*** *p43*
Richter, Wendelin 50; New York, NY, 1898 ***7951.13*** *p43*
Richter, Wilhelm 27; Halifax, N.S., 1902 ***1860.4*** *p42*
Richter Family ; West Virginia, 1850 ***1132.30*** *p147*
Richtor, Ralph; Illinois, 1834-1900 ***6020.5*** *p133*
Richway, Eliz.; Maryland, 1674 ***1236.25*** *p50*
Richwein, John; Colorado, 1891 ***1029.59*** *p77*
Richy, James 41; Ontario, 1871 ***1823.21*** *p310*
Rick, Christian; Wisconsin, 1860 ***6795.8*** *p140*
Rick, Frederick; North Carolina, 1865 ***1088.45*** *p29*
Rick, William; America, 1767 ***1220.12*** *p673*
Rickard, Lawrence; America, 1729 ***1220.12*** *p673*
Rickard, Martin; Ohio, 1809-1852 ***4511.35*** *p43*
Rickard, Thos 29; Ontario, 1871 ***1823.21*** *p310*
Rickards, Emilia 28; Ontario, 1871 ***1823.21*** *p310*
Rickart, Christian; Ohio, 1840-1897 ***8365.35*** *p17*
Rickart, Martin; Ohio, 1809-1852 ***4511.35*** *p43*
Rickeman, Jno.; Ontario, 1787 ***1276.15*** *p230*
Ricker, George; New Hampshire, 1670 ***9228.50*** *p541*
Ricker, John Peter 30; America, 1776 ***9228.50*** *p542*
Ricker, Maturin; New Hampshire, 1670-1706 ***9228.50*** *p541*
Ricker, Noah; Quebec, 1706-1750 ***9228.50*** *p542*
Rickerby, John 38; Ontario, 1871 ***1823.21*** *p311*
Rickerby, Thomas; America, 1742 ***1220.12*** *p673*
Rickerd, George; New Hampshire, 1670 ***9228.50*** *p541*
Rickerd, Maturin; New Hampshire, 1670-1706 ***9228.50*** *p541*
Rickerson, John; Louisiana, 1836-1840 ***4981.45*** *p213*
Rickert, Andre 33; Mississippi, 1845 ***778.6*** *p284*
Ricket, John 42; Ontario, 1871 ***1823.21*** *p311*
Rickets, Edward; America, 1720 ***1220.12*** *p673*
Rickets, Joseph; Marston's Wharf, 1782 ***8529.30*** *p15*
Rickets, Thomas; America, 1758 ***1220.12*** *p673*
Rickets, William; America, 1758 ***1220.12*** *p673*
Rickett, William; America, 1740 ***1220.12*** *p673*
Rickett, William; America, 1750 ***1220.12*** *p673*
Ricketts, Edward; America, 1692 ***1220.12*** *p673*
Ricketts, Elizabeth; America, 1759 ***1220.12*** *p673*
Ricketts, John; America, 1750 ***1220.12*** *p673*
Ricketts, John; America, 1755 ***1220.12*** *p673*
Ricketts, John; Maryland, 1723 ***1220.12*** *p673*
Ricketts, Joseph; Marston's Wharf, 1782 ***8529.30*** *p15*
Ricketts, Thomas; America, 1737 ***1220.12*** *p673*
Ricketts, William; America, 1740 ***1220.12*** *p673*
Ricketts, William; America, 1743 ***1220.12*** *p673*
Ricketts, William; America, 1750 ***1220.12*** *p673*
Ricketts, William; Barbados or Jamaica, 1686 ***1220.12*** *p673*
Ricketts, William; Maryland, 1744 ***1220.12*** *p673*
Rickham, James 46; Ontario, 1871 ***1823.21*** *p311*
Rickitt, Thomas; America, 1773 ***1220.12*** *p673*
Rickman, Levi 29; Ontario, 1871 ***1823.17*** *p139*
Ricks, James; America, 1722 ***1220.12*** *p673*
Ricks, Sarah; Annapolis, MD, 1725 ***1220.12*** *p673*
Ricks, William; Annapolis, MD, 1725 ***1220.12*** *p674*
Ricksicker, John; Ohio, 1809-1852 ***4511.35*** *p43*
Rickson, John; Potomac, 1729 ***1220.12*** *p674*
Rickyard, Martin 63; Ontario, 1871 ***1823.21*** *p311*
Ricquiert, George; New Hampshire, 1670 ***9228.50*** *p541*
Ricquiert, Maturin; New Hampshire, 1670-1706 ***9228.50*** *p541*
Riculfi, J. N.; Louisiana, 1836-1840 ***4981.45*** *p213*
Riddall, Thomas; America, 1732 ***1220.12*** *p674*
Riddell, Charles 31; Ontario, 1871 ***1823.21*** *p311*
Riddell, William 54; Ontario, 1871 ***1823.21*** *p311*
Ridderbjelke, Adolph; Washington, 1888 ***2770.40*** *p26*
Riddett, Chas Percy Lowe; Kansas, 1890 ***1447.20*** *p65*
Riddiford, Thomas; America, 1767 ***1220.12*** *p664*
Riddle, Abraham 44; Ontario, 1871 ***1823.21*** *p311*
Riddle, Andrew 56; Ontario, 1871 ***1823.21*** *p311*
Riddle, Arch 85; Ontario, 1871 ***1823.21*** *p311*
Riddle, Bathia 75; Ontario, 1871 ***1823.21*** *p311*
Riddle, Charles 28; Ontario, 1871 ***1823.21*** *p311*
Riddle, David; Illinois, 1865 ***6079.1*** *p11*
Riddle, George 41; Ontario, 1871 ***1823.21*** *p311*
Riddle, James 40; Ontario, 1871 ***1823.21*** *p311*
Riddle, John 29; Ontario, 1871 ***1823.21*** *p311*
Riddle, John 74; Ontario, 1871 ***1823.21*** *p311*
Riddle, Richard; Rappahannock, VA, 1726 ***1220.12*** *p674*
Riddle, Samuel 82; Ontario, 1871 ***1823.21*** *p311*
Riddle, William 70; Ontario, 1871 ***1823.21*** *p311*
Riddler, Elizabeth 14; Ontario, 1871 ***1823.21*** *p311*
Riddlesden, William; Maryland, 1720 ***1220.12*** *p674*
Riddlesdon, William; America, 1715 ***1220.12*** *p674*
Riddley, Alice 41; Ontario, 1871 ***1823.17*** *p139*
Rideau, J. 36; America, 1843 ***778.6*** *p284*
Rideing, Roger; America, 1753 ***1220.12*** *p674*
Ridell, Samuel 55; Ontario, 1871 ***1823.21*** *p311*
Ridenour, Jacob; West Virginia, 1787 ***1132.30*** *p146*
Rideout, James; Massachusetts, 1676 ***9228.50*** *p534*
Rider, Ann; America, 1743 ***1220.12*** *p695*
Rider, Anthony; America, 1692 ***1220.12*** *p695*
Rider, David A.; North Carolina, 1856 ***1088.45*** *p29*
Rider, Frances; Annapolis, MD, 1736 ***1220.12*** *p695*
Rider, George 23; Ontario, 1871 ***1823.21*** *p311*
Rider, John; America, 1739 ***1220.12*** *p695*
Rider, William; America, 1760 ***1220.12*** *p695*
Rider, William; America, 1764 ***1220.12*** *p695*
Rider, William 32; Ontario, 1871 ***1823.21*** *p311*
Ridewood, Richard; Barbados, 1664 ***1220.12*** *p674*
Ridge, Andrew; America, 1757 ***1220.12*** *p674*
Ridge, Charles 30; Ontario, 1871 ***1823.21*** *p311*
Ridge, John; Colorado, 1884 ***1029.59*** *p77*
Ridge, John; Colorado, 1886 ***1029.59*** *p77*
Ridge, Mary; America, 1753 ***1220.12*** *p674*
Ridge, Sarah; America, 1747 ***1220.12*** *p674*
Ridge, William; America, 1730 ***1220.12*** *p674*
Ridgeley, Richard; Potomac, 1731 ***1220.12*** *p674*
Ridgely, William; Barbados, 1668 ***1220.12*** *p674*
Ridges, William 43; Ontario, 1871 ***1823.21*** *p311*
Ridgeway, John; America, 1759 ***1220.12*** *p674*
Ridgeway, Mary 10; Quebec, 1870 ***8364.32*** *p25*
Ridgeway, Nicholas; Barbados, 1664 ***1220.12*** *p674*
Ridgley, George; Virginia, 1773 ***1220.12*** *p674*
Ridgway, Edward 13; Barbados, 1664 ***1220.12*** *p674*
Ridgway, Elizabeth; America, 1694 ***1220.12*** *p674*
Ridgway, James; America, 1661 ***1220.12*** *p674*
Ridgway, James; America, 1769 ***1220.12*** *p674*
Ridgway, John; America, 1775 ***1220.12*** *p674*
Ridgway, Sarah; America, 1719 ***1220.12*** *p674*
Ridgway, Thomas; America, 1731 ***1220.12*** *p674*
Ridgway, William; America, 1673 ***1220.12*** *p674*
Ridgway, William; America, 1731 ***1220.12*** *p674*
Ridgway, William; America, 1768 ***1220.12*** *p674*
Ridgway, William; America, 1775 ***1220.12*** *p674*
Ridgway, William; Maryland, 1674 ***1236.25*** *p49*
Riding, Henry; America, 1766 ***1220.12*** *p674*
Riding, Thomas; America, 1751 ***1220.12*** *p674*
Ridiot, Isaac; Ohio, 1809-1852 ***4511.35*** *p43*
Ridl, Frantisek; Iowa, 1854 ***2853.20*** *p216*
Ridle, James 40; Ontario, 1871 ***1823.17*** *p139*
Ridler, William 54; Ontario, 1871 ***1823.21*** *p311*
Ridley, John; America, 1774 ***1220.12*** *p674*
Ridley, Lawrence; New Orleans, 1851 ***7242.30*** *p153*
Ridley, Thomas; America, 1719 ***1220.12*** *p674*
Ridley, Thomas; Barbados, 1671 ***1220.12*** *p674*
Ridley, Thomas; Boston, 1776 ***8529.30*** *p4A*
Ridley, William; America, 1755 ***1220.12*** *p674*
Ridouet, James; Massachusetts, 1676 ***9228.50*** *p534*
Ridout, Elizabeth; America, 1768 ***1220.12*** *p674*
Ridout, Isaac; Ohio, 1809-1852 ***4511.35*** *p43*
Ridout, James; Ohio, 1809-1852 ***4511.35*** *p43*
Ridout, John; America, 1767 ***1220.12*** *p674*
Ridout, Samuel; Toronto, 1844 ***2910.35*** *p114*
Ridout, Thomas; America, 1757 ***1220.12*** *p674*
Ridout, Thomas 45; Ontario, 1871 ***1823.21*** *p311*
Riebe, William; Illinois, 1858-1861 ***6020.5*** *p133*
Riebel, Agnesia Katharina; Virginia, 1831 ***152.20*** *p67*
Riebel, Christian; New York, 1860 ***358.56*** *p5*
Riebel, Margaretha; America, 1883 ***2526.42*** *p131*
Rieber, Johann 28; Galveston, TX, 1846 ***3967.10*** *p377*
Rieber, John S.; Ohio, 1840-1897 ***8365.35*** *p17*
Rieber, Joseph 26; Galveston, TX, 1846 ***3967.10*** *p377*
Rieber, Katharina 21; Galveston, TX, 1846 ***3967.10*** *p377*
Rieberach, Johanne Rosine; Valdivia, Chile, 1852 ***1192.4*** *p54*
With 2 children
With child 4
With child 21
Riechel, Julius; Valdivia, Chile, 1850 ***1192.4*** *p49*
Riechers, Carl Wilhelm; America, 1860 ***7420.1*** *p198*
*Sister:*Engel Marie Sophie
Riechers, Catharina Maria Sophia *SEE* Riechers, Hans Heinrich
Riechers, Engel Dorothea Wille *SEE* Riechers, Hans Heinrich
Riechers, Engel Maria Sophia *SEE* Riechers, Hans Heinrich
Riechers, Engel Maria Sophia *SEE* Riechers, Johann Conrad
Riechers, Engel Marie; America, 1867 ***7420.1*** *p263*
Riechers, Engel Marie Dorothee; America, 1860 ***7420.1*** *p198*
Riechers, Engel Marie Sophie *SEE* Riechers, Carl Wilhelm
Riechers, Engel Sophia Dorothea Dohmeier *SEE* Riechers, Johann Conrad
Riechers, Hans Heinrich; America, 1854 ***7420.1*** *p127*
*Wife:*Engel Dorothea Wille
*Daughter:*Engel Maria Sophia
*Daughter:*Catharina Maria Sophia
*Son:*Hans Heinrich Conrad
Riechers, Hans Heinrich; America, 1857 ***7420.1*** *p170*
Riechers, Hans Heinrich Conrad *SEE* Riechers, Hans Heinrich
Riechers, Hans Heinrich Conrad *SEE* Riechers, Johann Conrad
Riechers, Johann Conrad; America, 1857 ***7420.1*** *p170*
*Wife:*Engel Sophia Dorothea Dohmeier
*Son:*Hans Heinrich Conrad
*Daughter:*Engel Maria Sophia
Riechers, Philipp Johann; America, 1882 ***7420.1*** *p332*
Riechers, Wilhelm; America, 1911 ***7420.1*** *p388*
Riechert, Georg 28; Port uncertain, 1843 ***778.6*** *p284*
Riechert, Heinrich; America, 1854 ***7420.1*** *p127*
Riechmann, Isaac; North Carolina, 1792-1862 ***1088.45*** *p29*
Rieck, Ida Ottilie; Wisconsin, 1896 ***6795.8*** *p30*
Rieckel, Ad.; Venezuela, 1843 ***3899.5*** *p546*
Riedel, Eva Maria; America, 1870 ***2526.42*** *p98*
Riedel, Heinrich; America, 1854 ***179.55*** *p19*
Riedel, Johanna M.; New York, 1860 ***358.56*** *p3*
Riedel, Michael 24; America, 1846 ***2526.42*** *p201*
With wife
Riedel, Nikolaus; Buffalo, NY, 1894 ***5475.1*** *p425*
Rieder, Felix; Louisiana, 1836-1840 ***4981.45*** *p213*
Rieder, Leonhard 55; New York, NY, 1893 ***1883.7*** *p44*
Riedhammer, Heinrich; America, 1849 ***5475.1*** *p476*
Riediger, Gotlieb; Ohio, 1809-1852 ***4511.35*** *p43*
Riedl, Frantisek; Iowa, 1854 ***2853.20*** *p216*
Riedlinger, Elisabeth 51; New York, NY, 1898 ***7951.13*** *p42*
Riedlinger, Jacob 18; New York, NY, 1898 ***7951.13*** *p42*
Riedlinger, Jakob 21; New York, NY, 1900 ***8425.16*** *p31*
Riedlinger, Johann 19; New York, NY, 1898 ***7951.13*** *p42*

416
FOR A COMPLETE EXPLANATION OF ENTRY, SEE "HOW TO READ A CITATION" SECTION

Riedlinger, Martin 20; New York, NY, 1898 ***7951.13*** *p42*
Riedlinger, Martin 58; New York, NY, 1898 ***7951.13*** *p42*
Riedlinger, Rosina 17; New York, NY, 1900 ***8425.16*** *p31*
Riedlinger, Wilhelm 16; New York, NY, 1898 ***7951.13*** *p42*
Riefesell, Anna 10; New York, NY, 1864 ***8425.62*** *p198*
Riefesell, Cath. 9; New York, NY, 1864 ***8425.62*** *p199*
Riefesell, Friedrich 6; New York, NY, 1864 ***8425.62*** *p199*
Riefesell, Friedrich 47; New York, NY, 1864 ***8425.62*** *p198*
Riefesell, Lucie 35; New York, NY, 1864 ***8425.62*** *p198*
Riefesell, Margarethe 13; New York, NY, 1864 ***8425.62*** *p198*
Rieffest, John A.; Ohio, 1844 ***2763.1*** *p21*
Rieg, August 31; New York, NY, 1885 ***8425.16*** *p32*
Rieg, Auguste 8; New York, NY, 1885 ***8425.16*** *p32*
Rieg, Auguste 28; New York, NY, 1885 ***8425.16*** *p32*
Rieg, Emilie 17; New York, NY, 1885 ***8425.16*** *p32*
Rieger, Catha. 22; New York, NY, 1885 ***1883.7*** *p46*
Rieger, Frieda 26; New York, NY, 1894 ***6512.1*** *p186*
Rieger, Friedr. 24; New York, NY, 1885 ***1883.7*** *p46*
Rieger, Mathew 6 months; New York, NY, 1885 ***1883.7*** *p46*
Riego, Pedro; Louisiana, 1874 ***4981.45*** *p134*
Riehel, Michel 21; Port uncertain, 1843 ***778.6*** *p284*
Riehl, Adolf 7; New York, NY, 1893 ***1883.7*** *p44*
Riehl, Adolf 11; New York, NY, 1893 ***1883.7*** *p44*
Riehl, August 5; New York, NY, 1893 ***1883.7*** *p44*
Riehl, Eva 37; Port uncertain, 1843 ***778.6*** *p284*
Riehl, Florentine 2; New York, NY, 1893 ***1883.7*** *p44*
Riehl, Gottlieb 3; New York, NY, 1893 ***1883.7*** *p44*
Riehl, Gottlieb 42; New York, NY, 1893 ***1883.7*** *p44*
Riehl, Gustav 16; New York, NY, 1893 ***1883.7*** *p44*
Riehl, Jacob 36; Port uncertain, 1843 ***778.6*** *p284*
Riehl, Jacques 7; Port uncertain, 1843 ***778.6*** *p284*
Riehl, Pauline 38; New York, NY, 1893 ***1883.7*** *p44*
Riehl, Rosalie; New York, NY, 1893 ***1883.7*** *p44*
Riehm, Elisabeth Ludwig 25 *SEE* Riehm, Johann
Riehm, Johann; America, 1864 ***5475.1*** *p248*
*Wife:*Elisabeth Ludwig
*Daughter:*Susanna
*Daughter:*Margarethe
*Daughter:*Katharina
Riehm, Katharina 3 *SEE* Riehm, Johann
Riehm, Margarethe 4 *SEE* Riehm, Johann
Riehm, Susanna 1 *SEE* Riehm, Johann
Riek, Friedrich; Wisconsin, 1894 ***6795.8*** *p129*
Rieke, Simon Heinrich; Port uncertain, 1839 ***7420.1*** *p16*
Riekenberg, Marie Christiane; America, 1861 ***7420.1*** *p208*
Rielitzke, Adam 27; New York, NY, 1893 ***1883.7*** *p37*
Riell, Robert; America, 1749 ***1220.12*** *p674*
Rielly, Mr.; Massachusetts, n.d. ***1642*** *p117*
Rielsch, Magd. 28; America, 1841 ***778.6*** *p284*
Rielsch, Michel 26; America, 1841 ***778.6*** *p284*
Riely, James 54; Ontario, 1871 ***1823.21*** *p311*
Riely, John; North Carolina, 1855 ***1088.45*** *p29*
Riely, Patrick; New York, 1776 ***8529.30*** *p3*
Riely, Patrick; Philadelphia, 1778 ***8529.30*** *p4A*
Riely, Phillip 60; Ontario, 1871 ***1823.21*** *p311*
Riemann, Adolph; Louisiana, 1836-1841 ***4981.45*** *p209*
Riemann, Heinr.; Valdivia, Chile, 1852 ***1192.4*** *p56*
With wife
Riemer, Andreas 34; Port uncertain, 1846 ***778.6*** *p284*
Riemer, Gottlieb Christian; Wisconsin, 1904 ***6795.8*** *p153*
Riemer, Gustav 21; New York, NY, 1893 ***1883.7*** *p43*
Riemert, Miss A. 21; New York, NY, 1894 ***6512.1*** *p184*
Rien, Dinish; Boston, 1767 ***1642*** *p38*
Riensche, Mr.; America, 1864 ***7420.1*** *p226*
Riensche, Carl *SEE* Riensche, Christine
Riensche, Christine; America, 1865 ***7420.1*** *p236*
*Brother:*Carl
Rierdan, Tm 25; St. Johns, N.F., 1811 ***1053.20*** *p22*
Rierl, Christoph; America, 1868 ***7919.3*** *p531*
Ries, Charlotte 10 *SEE* Ries, Wilhelm
Ries, Christian; America, 1837 ***5475.1*** *p120*
*Wife:*Dorothea Becker
*Daughter:*Katharina
*Daughter:*Maria
*Daughter:*Karoline
Ries, David Jakob *SEE* Ries, Heinrich
Ries, Dorothea Becker 32 *SEE* Ries, Christian
Ries, E. Christian *SEE* Ries, Heinrich
Ries, Elisabeth; Pittsburgh, 1881 ***5475.1*** *p60*
Ries, Ernst; America, 1880 ***5475.1*** *p55*
Ries, Ernst Christian *SEE* Ries, Heinrich
Ries, Heinrich; America, 1880 ***5475.1*** *p54*
*Wife:*Maria Meyer
*Son:*Ernst Christian
*Son:*David Jakob
*Son:*E. Christian
*Son:*Wilhelm Jakob
Ries, Johann; America, 1890 ***5475.1*** *p76*
Ries, Johann *SEE* Ries, Sophie Nicklas
Ries, Johann 33; Philadelphia, 1890 ***5475.1*** *p76*
Ries, Karl; America, 1891 ***5475.1*** *p76*
Ries, Karoline 8 *SEE* Ries, Christian
Ries, Katharina 6 *SEE* Ries, Christian
Ries, Katharina 12 *SEE* Ries, Wilhelm
Ries, Konrad; Pennsylvania, 1848 ***170.15*** *p40*
With wife & child
Ries, Maria Meyer *SEE* Ries, Heinrich
Ries, Maria 2 *SEE* Ries, Christian
Ries, Maria 21; New York, NY, 1856 ***1766.1*** *p45*
Ries, Martin; America, 1846-1847 ***5475.1*** *p63*
Ries, Nikolaus 33; America, 1890 ***5475.1*** *p76*
Ries, Philipp 14 *SEE* Ries, Wilhelm
Ries, S.; Louisiana, 1836-1840 ***4981.45*** *p213*
Ries, Sophie 8 *SEE* Ries, Wilhelm
Ries, Sophie *SEE* Ries, Sophie Nicklas
Ries, Sophie; Philadelphia, 1891 ***5475.1*** *p76*
*Son:*Johann
*Daughter:*Sophie
Ries, Sophie Dorothea Bender *SEE* Ries, Wilhelm
Ries, Stephen; Colorado, 1880 ***1029.59*** *p77*
Ries, Valentine; America, 1854 ***5475.1*** *p411*
Ries, Wilhelm; America, 1833 ***5475.1*** *p63*
With wife
With 4 children
Ries, Wilhelm 39; Ohio, 1865 ***5475.1*** *p21*
*Wife:*Sophie Dorothea Bender
*Daughter:*Katharina 12
*Daughter:*Sophie 8
*Daughter:*Charlotte 10
*Son:*Philipp 14
Ries, Wilhelm Jakob *SEE* Ries, Heinrich
Riesam, August; America, 1867 ***7919.3*** *p529*
Riesch, Friedrich Ludwig; Port uncertain, 1859 ***7420.1*** *p188*
Rieschlay, Joseph; Louisiana, 1841-1844 ***4981.45*** *p211*
Riese, Anna Helen; Wisconsin, 1898 ***6795.8*** *p82*
Riesel, Bertha Lange *SEE* Riesel, Georg Heinrich Ernst
Riesel, Georg Heinrich Ernst; America, 1883 ***7420.1*** *p339*
*Wife:*Bertha Lange
Riesle, Robert; Chicago, 1892 ***7420.1*** *p366*
Riess, Anna Gertraud 16; Pennsylvania, 1848 ***170.15*** *p40*
With family
Riess, Elisabetha 6; Pennsylvania, 1848 ***170.15*** *p40*
With family
Riess, Elisabetha 41; Pennsylvania, 1848 ***170.15*** *p40*
With family
Riess, Jacque; New York, 1860 ***358.56*** *p3*
Riess, Johann Adam 13; Pennsylvania, 1848 ***170.15*** *p40*
With family
Riess, Johannes 4; Pennsylvania, 1848 ***170.15*** *p40*
With family
Riess, Konrad 42; Pennsylvania, 1848 ***170.15*** *p40*
With family
Riessinger, Wilhelm Friedrich; America, 1892 ***2526.43*** *p199*
Riessmeyer, Albrecht; America, 1849 ***7420.1*** *p67*
With son 23
With daughter 20
Riester, Christine 28; New York, NY, 1893 ***1883.7*** *p38*
Riester, M.; New York, 1860 ***358.56*** *p148*
Riester, Peter 32; New York, NY, 1893 ***1883.7*** *p38*
Riffel, Georg 45; Portland, ME, 1906 ***970.38*** *p80*
Rigal, Eugene 23; Missouri, 1845 ***778.6*** *p284*
Rigan, John; Potomac, 1729 ***1220.12*** *p666*
Rigaud, Genevieve; Quebec, 1667 ***4514.3*** *p364*
Rigaud, Jean 22; New Orleans, 1848 ***778.6*** *p284*
Rigaud, Jeanne; Quebec, 1671 ***4514.3*** *p364*
Rigaud, Marie-Judith 23; Quebec, 1653 ***9221.17*** *p279*
Rigaud deVaudreuil, Philippe de; Quebec, 1683-1688 ***2314.30*** *p169*
Rigaud deVaudreuil, Philippe de; Quebec, 1687 ***2314.30*** *p194*
Rigby, Edwin; Washington, 1888 ***2770.40*** *p26*
Rigby, Elinor; America, 1673 ***1220.12*** *p674*
Rigby, Elizabeth; America, 1720 ***1220.12*** *p674*
Rigby, Elizabeth; America, 1737 ***1220.12*** *p674*
Rigby, Emma 21; Quebec, 1870 ***8364.32*** *p25*
Rigby, George; America, 1773 ***1220.12*** *p674*
Rigby, James; America, 1773 ***1220.12*** *p675*
Rigby, John; Virginia, 1739 ***1220.12*** *p675*
Rigby, Joseph; Philadelphia, 1866 ***8513.31*** *p423*
Rigby, Nicholas; America, 1774 ***1220.12*** *p675*
Rigdale, Alice *SEE* Rigdale, John
Rigdale, John; Plymouth, MA, 1620 ***1920.45*** *p5*
*Wife:*Alice
Riger, Michael 24; New York, NY, 1893 ***1883.7*** *p42*
Riger, Rosalia 22; New York, NY, 1893 ***1883.7*** *p42*
Riges, Victory; America, 1770 ***1220.12*** *p674*
Rigg, John 36; Ontario, 1871 ***1823.17*** *p139*
Riggens, William; Nevis or Jamaica, 1722 ***1220.12*** *p675*
Rigglesworth, William; America, 1774 ***1220.12*** *p675*
Riggs, John; Jamaica, 1661 ***1220.12*** *p675*
Riggs, John 50; Ontario, 1871 ***1823.21*** *p311*
Riggs, William; Barbados, 1683 ***1220.12*** *p675*
Riggs, William; Barbados or Jamaica, 1698 ***1220.12*** *p675*
Riggs, William; Boston, 1774 ***8529.30*** *p7*
Right, David 36; Ontario, 1871 ***1823.17*** *p139*
Right, James 20; Ontario, 1871 ***1823.21*** *p311*
Right, Lizabeth 45; Ontario, 1871 ***1823.17*** *p139*
Right, Samuel; America, 1721 ***1220.12*** *p904*
Righteous, Ellen; America, 1771 ***1220.12*** *p675*
Rigler, John George; Ohio, 1809-1852 ***4511.35*** *p43*
Rigley, Richard; America, 1766 ***1220.12*** *p905*
Rigley, William; Marston's Wharf, 1781 ***8529.30*** *p15*
Rigmaiden, William; America, 1761 ***1220.12*** *p675*
Rignaux, Ernest 25; New Orleans, 1848 ***778.6*** *p284*
Rigneau, Elisabeth 29; Mississippi, 1846 ***778.6*** *p284*
Rigneau, Ignace 4; Mississippi, 1846 ***778.6*** *p284*
Rigney, Bernard 60; Ontario, 1871 ***1823.17*** *p139*
Rigney, Francis 60; Ontario, 1871 ***1823.21*** *p311*
Rigney, Thomas; Toronto, 1844 ***2910.35*** *p111*
Rigney, William 35; Ontario, 1871 ***1823.21*** *p312*
Rigot, Johann; America, 1880 ***5475.1*** *p219*
Rigot, Maria; America, 1880 ***5475.1*** *p220*
Rigot, Paul; America, 1880 ***5475.1*** *p219*
Rigsby, Jane; Maryland or Virginia, 1733 ***1220.12*** *p675*
Riguat, Mr. 29; America, 1848 ***778.6*** *p284*
Riguel, Corneille; Wisconsin, 1855-1867 ***1495.20*** *p67*
Riha, Martin; Nebraska, 1873 ***2853.20*** *p171*
Rihn, Catharina 18; America, 1846 ***778.6*** *p284*
Rihn, Christina 21; America, 1846 ***778.6*** *p284*
Rihon, Michael; Marblehead, MA, 1763 ***1642*** *p73*
Rihs, Charles; Illinois, 1858-1861 ***6020.5*** *p133*
Rikmann, Hermann 20; New York, NY, 1894 ***6512.1*** *p230*
Riland, M. N. 28; Port uncertain, 1840 ***778.6*** *p284*
Rilett, George 60; Ontario, 1871 ***1823.21*** *p312*
Riley, Ann; America, 1763 ***1220.12*** *p675*
Riley, Ann; America, 1765 ***1220.12*** *p675*
Riley, Benjamin 35; Ontario, 1871 ***1823.21*** *p312*
Riley, C. W. 32; Ontario, 1871 ***1823.21*** *p312*
Riley, Christopher; Ohio, 1844 ***2763.1*** *p21*
Riley, Cornelius 63; Ontario, 1871 ***1823.21*** *p312*
Riley, Ellen Blesson *SEE* Riley, Michael
Riley, George; America, 1775 ***1220.12*** *p675*
Riley, Grace; America, 1754 ***1220.12*** *p675*
Riley, Hannorah 48; Michigan, 1880 ***4491.42*** *p22*
Riley, James; America, 1756 ***1220.12*** *p675*
Riley, James; Antigua (Antego), 1742 ***1220.12*** *p675*
Riley, James; New York, NY, 1841 ***3274.56*** *p99*
Riley, James; Ohio, 1809-1852 ***4511.35*** *p43*
Riley, James 24; Ontario, 1871 ***1823.21*** *p312*
Riley, John; America, 1722 ***1220.12*** *p675*
Riley, John; America, 1754 ***1220.12*** *p675*
Riley, John; America, 1758 ***1220.12*** *p675*
Riley, John; America, 1764 ***1220.12*** *p675*
Riley, John; Massachusetts, 1700-1799 ***1642*** *p138*
Riley, John 40; Michigan, 1880 ***4491.42*** *p22*
Riley, John; Springfield, MA, 1664 ***1642*** *p120*
Riley, Joseph; America, 1754 ***1220.12*** *p675*
Riley, Margaret 50; Ontario, 1871 ***1823.21*** *p312*
Riley, Martin 19; Ontario, 1871 ***1823.17*** *p139*
Riley, Mary; America, 1743 ***1220.12*** *p675*
Riley, Mary; America, 1749 ***1220.12*** *p675*
Riley, Mary; America, 1752 ***1220.12*** *p675*
Riley, Mary; America, 1754 ***1220.12*** *p675*
Riley, Mary; New York, 1855 ***8513.31*** *p315*
Riley, Mary 30; Ontario, 1871 ***1823.17*** *p139*
Riley, Mary Elinor 28; Ontario, 1871 ***1823.17*** *p139*
Riley, Michael; America, 1754 ***1220.12*** *p675*
Riley, Michael; North Carolina, 1833 ***1088.45*** *p29*
Riley, Michael; Philadelphia, 1851 ***8513.31*** *p423*
*Wife:*Ellen Blesson
Riley, Owen 63; Ontario, 1871 ***1823.21*** *p312*
Riley, Patrick; Louisiana, 1858 ***7710.1*** *p156*
Riley, Patrick; New Orleans, 1851 ***7710.1*** *p155*
Riley, Patrick; Ohio, 1844 ***2763.1*** *p21*
Riley, Patrick; Philadelphia, 1778 ***8529.30*** *p4A*
Riley, Paul; Massachusetts, 1754 ***1642*** *p100*
Riley, Peter; Illinois, 1859 ***6079.1*** *p11*
Riley, Philip; America, 1753 ***1220.12*** *p675*
Riley, Philip; Annapolis, MD, 1758 ***1220.12*** *p675*
Riley, Philip; New York, NY, 1837 ***3274.56*** *p96*
Riley, Richard; America, 1765 ***1220.12*** *p675*
Riley, Robert 38; Ontario, 1871 ***1823.17*** *p139*
Riley, Robert 45; Ontario, 1871 ***1823.21*** *p312*
Riley, Sarah; America, 1736 ***1220.12*** *p675*
Riley, Thomas; America, 1757 ***1220.12*** *p675*
Riley, William; America, 1775 ***1220.12*** *p675*

Rilley, Harris 67; Ontario, 1871 1823.21 p312
Rillot, August Jean Louis; Illinois, 1852 6079.1 p11
Rilly, Bridget 21; Ontario, 1871 1823.17 p139
Riloty, L. 24; America, 1846 778.6 p284
Rily, John; Massachusetts, 1675-1676 1642 p128
Rily, Mary 18; Ontario, 1871 1823.21 p312
Rimbault, Denis 23; Quebec, 1656 9221.17 p346
Rimele, Meinrad; Ohio, 1809-1852 4511.35 p43
Rimer, John; North Carolina, 1710 3629.40 p6
Rimer, Nicholas; North Carolina, 1710 3629.40 p6
Rimer, Richard; North Carolina, 1710 3629.40 p6
Rimes, William; America, 1742 1220.12 p675
Rimes, William; America, 1749 1220.12 p676
Rimmel, Philip; Ohio, 1809-1852 4511.35 p43
Rimmer, Jane; America, 1742 1220.12 p676
Rimmer, John; America, 1742 1220.12 p676
Rimmer, Peter 46; Ontario, 1871 1823.21 p312
Rimmington, John; America, 1764 1220.12 p676
Rimpel, Johann; Galveston, TX, 1855 571.7 p17
Rinard, Magdalen 23; America, 1846 778.6 p284
Rinch, Thomas; America, 1765 1220.12 p676
Rinck, Lorenz 20; Halifax, N.S., 1902 1860.4 p40
Rinckel, Carl 19; New York, NY, 1847 9176.15 p50
Rinder, Michael; Ohio, 1809-1852 4511.35 p43
Rinehart, Martin; New Jersey, 1773-1774 927.31 p3
Rinesmith, Bernard; New Jersey, 1753-1774 927.31 p3
Riney, Catherine; Boston, 1764 1642 p33
Riney, Charles; Boston, 1764 1642 p33
Ring, Daniel; America, 1757 1220.12 p676
Ring, Daniel; New York, 1777 8529.30 p5A
Ring, David; Washington, 1889 2770.40 p80
Ring, Johann; America, 1846 5475.1 p450
Ring, John; Ipswich, MA, 1678 1642 p70
Ring, Louise; New York, 1859 358.56 p100
Ring, Margaret 65; Ontario, 1871 1823.17 p139
Ring, Peter; America, 1837 5475.1 p450
Ring, Richard; America, 1773 1220.12 p676
Ring, William; America, 1754 1220.12 p676
Ringard, Jean-Baptiste 40; New Orleans, 1848 778.6 p284
Ringe, Lewis 40; Ontario, 1871 1823.17 p139
Ringeisen, Karolina; America, 1885 5475.1 p422
Ringer, George 29; Ontario, 1871 1823.21 p312
Ringer, J. B. 34; America, 1840 778.6 p284
Ringing, John; America, 1772 1220.12 p676
Ringius, Charles; St. Paul, MN, 1890 1865.50 p107
Ringle, Jakob 4 *SEE* Ringle, Karl
Ringle, Karl 8 *SEE* Ringle, Karl
Ringle, Karl 46; America, 1800-1899 5475.1 p63
*Wife:*Maria Wagner 40
*Daughter:*Margarethe 15
*Son:*Karl 8
*Son:*Jakob 4
Ringle, Margarethe 15 *SEE* Ringle, Karl
Ringle, Maria Wagner 40 *SEE* Ringle, Karl
Ringrose, Dulcie W.; Edmonton, Alberta, 1894-1974 9228.50 p369
Ringrose, John; Ohio, 1809-1852 4511.35 p43
Ringrose, Laurence; Alberta, 1900-1920 9228.50 p370
Ringrose, Moses; Annapolis, MD, 1725 1220.12 p676
Rings, Henry; Ohio, 1809-1852 4511.35 p43
Rings, John; Ohio, 1809-1852 4511.35 p43
Ringsmuth, Frantisek; Nebraska, 1889 2853.20 p182
Ringsmuth, Frantisek K.; Nebraska, 1887 2853.20 p223
Ringus, Charles; St. Paul, MN, 1890 1865.50 p107
Ringwood, James S.; Louisiana, 1874 4981.45 p133
Rininger, Andrew; Ohio, 1809-1852 4511.35 p43
Rininger, Christian; Ohio, 1809-1852 4511.35 p43
Rink, Sophie 32; America, 1870 5475.1 p43
Rinkal, John; Illinois, 1834-1900 6020.5 p133
Rinke, Christine 11; Halifax, N.S., 1902 1860.4 p43
Rinke, Elisabeth 41; Halifax, N.S., 1902 1860.4 p43
Rinke, Emanuel 2; Halifax, N.S., 1902 1860.4 p43
Rinke, Friedrich 10; Halifax, N.S., 1902 1860.4 p43
Rinke, Johannes 7; Halifax, N.S., 1902 1860.4 p43
Rinke, Josef 43; Halifax, N.S., 1902 1860.4 p43
Rinke, Katha 20; Halifax, N.S., 1902 1860.4 p43
Rinke, Lydia 3; Halifax, N.S., 1902 1860.4 p43
Rinke, Martha 9; Halifax, N.S., 1902 1860.4 p43
Rinn, Anna Magdalene; America, 1853 8115.12 p322
Rinn, Elisabeth; America, n.d. 8115.12 p325
Rinn, Georg Adam; America, 1854 8115.12 p322
Rinn, Joh. Georg; America, 1864 8115.12 p325
Rinn, Johann Georg; America, 1864 8115.12 p322
Rinne, . . .; America, 1846 7420.1 p47
With family
Rinne, Mr.; America, 1854 7420.1 p127
*Wife:*Engel Elisabeth Engelking
With son & daughter
Rinne, Adolph Friedrich August *SEE* Rinne, Christian Hermann
Rinne, Carl; America, 1854 7420.1 p128
With brother
Rinne, Carl August *SEE* Rinne, Friedrich
Rinne, Carl Friedrich Wilhelm; America, 1867 7420.1 p263
Rinne, Carl Hermann; America, 1883 7420.1 p339
Rinne, Caroline Justine *SEE* Rinne, Heinrich Wilhelm
Rinne, Christian Adolf *SEE* Rinne, Dorothea Louise Soffker
Rinne, Christian Hermann; America, 1880 7420.1 p317
*Brother:*Adolph Friedrich August
Rinne, Dorothea Louise; America, 1888 7420.1 p357
*Son:*Friedrich Wilhelm
*Son:*Christian Adolf
Rinne, Engel Elisabeth Engelking *SEE* Rinne, Mr.
Rinne, Friederike; America, 1857 7420.1 p170
Rinne, Friedrich; America, 1853 7420.1 p110
With family
Rinne, Friedrich; America, 1857 7420.1 p170
With wife
With daughter 13
With son 17
*Son:*Carl August
Rinne, Friedrich Adolf Rudolf; America, 1883 7420.1 p339
Rinne, Friedrich Wilhelm *SEE* Rinne, Dorothea Louise Soffker
Rinne, Friedrich Wilhelm; Port uncertain, 1838 7420.1 p15
Rinne, Hans Heinrich; America, 1867 7420.1 p263
Rinne, Heinrich; America, 1852 7420.1 p95
Rinne, Heinrich August; America, 1868 7420.1 p275
Rinne, Heinrich Wilhelm; America, 1867 7420.1 p263
*Sister:*Caroline Justine
Rinne, Heinrich Wilhelm; America, 1868 7420.1 p275
With family
Rinne, Henriette; America, 1854 7420.1 p128
Rinne, Hermann Emil; America, 1872 7420.1 p297
Rinne, Louise; America, 1856 7420.1 p152
Rinne, Ludwig; America, 1852 7420.1 p96
With wife 3 sons & daughter
Rinne, Nanny Friederike Wilhelmine Ernestine; New York, NY, 1870 7420.1 p284
Rinne, Sophie; America, 1857 7420.1 p170
Rinne, Wilhelm; America, 1846 7420.1 p47
With wife & 4 children
Rinring, George; Iowa, 1890 1211.15 p18
Rinscheid, Heinrich; North America, 1838-1938 8023.44 p378
Rinshler, Agathe; New York, 1860 358.56 p148
Rintala, Emil William; Illinois, 1930 121.35 p100
Rintals, Gertrude 17; Minnesota, 1923 2769.54 p1378
Rintelmann, Carl; America, 1844 7420.1 p33
Rintelmann, Dietrich; America, 1846 7420.1 p48
With wife & child
Rintelmann, Friedrich; America, 1844 7420.1 p33
Rintelmann, Heinrich; America, 1846 7420.1 p48
With wife & 4 children
Riollet, Elie 48; Quebec, 1657 9221.17 p367
Rion, Ambrose; Boston, 1751 1642 p46
Rion, Darby; Boston, 1766 1642 p37
Riordan, John; Boston, 1754 1642 p47
Riordan, John; Boston, 1770 1642 p43
Riorteau, Mathieu 21; Quebec, 1657 9221.17 p367
Rios, S. M.; California, 1868 1131.61 p89
Riotte, Peter; America, 1851 5475.1 p480
Ripkey, Gerard; New York, 1777 8529.30 p4A
Riplett, J. 15; Quebec, 1870 8364.32 p25
Ripley, Gerard; New York, 1777 8529.30 p4A
Ripley, William; America, 1736 1220.12 p676
Ripley, William 22; North Carolina, 1774 1422.10 p56
Riplinger, Johann; America, 1858 5475.1 p283
Ripoll, Jose; Louisiana, 1836-1840 4981.45 p213
Ripool, Mr. 20; New Orleans, 1840 778.6 p284
Ripper, Adam; America, 1891 2526.43 p189
With wife
*Daughter:*Katharina
Ripper, Anna Elisabeth *SEE* Ripper, Johann Peter
Ripper, Anna Elisabeth *SEE* Ripper, Johann Georg
Ripper, Anna Margarethe; Virginia, 1831 152.20 p66
Ripper, Appolonia Goetz *SEE* Ripper, Johann Georg
Ripper, Elisabeth *SEE* Ripper, Johann Georg
Ripper, Elisabeth Katharina *SEE* Ripper, Johann Peter
Ripper, Eva Elisabeth *SEE* Ripper, Johann Georg
Ripper, Johann Georg *SEE* Ripper, Johann Georg
Ripper, Johann Georg; Virginia, 1831 152.20 p67
*Wife:*Appolonia Goetz
*Child:*Johann Nikolaus
*Child:*Eva Elisabeth
*Child:*Anna Elisabeth
*Child:*Elisabeth
*Child:*Johann Georg
Ripper, Johann Nikolaus *SEE* Ripper, Johann Georg
Ripper, Johann Peter; Virginia, 1831 152.20 p66
*Wife:*Katharina Ross
*Child:*Elisabeth Katharina
*Child:*Johanna Sophie
*Child:*Anna Elisabeth
*Child:*Elisabeth Katharina
Ripper, Johanna Sophie *SEE* Ripper, Johann Peter
Ripper, Johannes; Argentina, 1855 2526.43 p213
With family of 8
Ripper, Katharina *SEE* Ripper, Adam
Ripper, Katharina Ross *SEE* Ripper, Johann Peter
Ripper, Philipp; America, 1882 2526.43 p161
Ripping, Robert; Annapolis, MD, 1723 1220.12 p676
Ripple, Jacob; Ohio, 1809-1852 4511.35 p43
Ripple, John; Ohio, 1809-1852 4511.35 p43
Ripple, Leonard; Illinois, 1834-1900 6020.5 p133
Ripple, Ludwig; Ohio, 1809-1852 4511.35 p43
Ripplinger, Anna; America, 1882 5475.1 p268
*Son:*Mathias
*Son:*Johann
Ripplinger, Barbara Pinion *SEE* Ripplinger, Johann
Ripplinger, Elisabeth; America, 1857 5475.1 p266
Ripplinger, Franz 23; America, 1867 5475.1 p349
Ripplinger, Johann *SEE* Ripplinger, Johann
Ripplinger, Johann; America, 1855 5475.1 p266
*Wife:*Barbara Pinion
*Son:*Michel
*Son:*Nikolaus
*Son:*Peter
*Son:*Johann
Ripplinger, Johann *SEE* Ripplinger, Peter
Ripplinger, Johann *SEE* Ripplinger, Anna Seiwert
Ripplinger, Johann 29; America, 1871 5475.1 p267
Ripplinger, Johann Baptist; Pennsylvania, 1888 5475.1 p143
Ripplinger, Katharina *SEE* Ripplinger, Peter
Ripplinger, Katharina Nuner 32 *SEE* Ripplinger, Peter
Ripplinger, Maria *SEE* Ripplinger, Peter
Ripplinger, Mathias; America, 1880 5475.1 p268
Ripplinger, Mathias *SEE* Ripplinger, Anna Seiwert
Ripplinger, Michel *SEE* Ripplinger, Johann
Ripplinger, Nikolaus *SEE* Ripplinger, Johann
Ripplinger, Peter *SEE* Ripplinger, Johann
Ripplinger, Peter 22; America, 1871 5475.1 p266
Ripplinger, Peter 40; America, 1879 5475.1 p267
*Wife:*Katharina Nuner 32
*Daughter:*Maria
*Father:*Peter 70
*Daughter:*Katharina
*Son:*Johann
Ripplinger, Peter 70 *SEE* Ripplinger, Peter
Ripplinger, Peter; Iowa, 1880 5475.1 p350
Ripplinger, Philipp; America, 1872 5475.1 p167
Rippmann, Sophia; New York, NY, 1909 6212.1 p15
Rippon, George 59; Ontario, 1871 1823.21 p312
Rippon, Henry; America, 1767 1220.12 p676
Rippon, Richard; Virginia, 1732 1220.12 p676
Rippon, William; Virginia, 1721 1220.12 p676
Ripton, Robert, Jr.; America, 1743 1220.12 p676
Ririe, Robert; Marston's Wharf, 1782 8529.30 p15
Risaouin, Yves 20; Quebec, 1658 9221.17 p386
Risch, Jno.; Ohio, 1840-1897 8365.35 p17
Risch, Johann; America, 1856 5475.1 p440
Rischmuller, Christian; America, 1852 7420.1 p96
With wife & 2 sons
Rischmuller, Henriette; America, 1895 7420.1 p372
Rischmuller, Wilhelm; America, 1854 7420.1 p128
With wife & daughter
Riscombe, Benjamin; America, 1751 1220.12 p676
Risdale, William; America, 1772 1220.12 p676
Risdon, Joseph 65; Ontario, 1871 1823.21 p312
Risdon, Lawrence; America, 1758 1220.12 p676
Riseno, Silvio; Louisiana, 1874 4981.45 p133
Riser, John J.; California, 1910 1211.45 p134
Riser, Michael; North Carolina, 1710 3629.40 p6
Risheed, Anne; North Carolina, 1710 3629.40 p8
Risheed, Casper; North Carolina, 1710 3629.40 p6
Risk, Elizabeth 47; Ontario, 1871 1823.21 p312
Risk, John 57; Ontario, 1871 1823.17 p139
Risk, Louis 16; Ontario, 1871 1823.21 p312
Risk, William 65; Ontario, 1871 1823.17 p139
Riske, Robert; Wisconsin, 1908 1822.55 p10
Rislang, Anton 21; America, 1845 778.6 p284
Risley, William; America, 1760 1220.12 p676
Rismoller, Anton Heinrich Wilhelm; America, 1868 7420.1 p276
With family
Rismoller, Anton Wilhelm Conrad; America, 1867 7420.1 p263
Rison, Martha; America, 1748 1220.12 p676
Rispin, Richard 63; Ontario, 1871 1823.21 p312
Riss, Nikolaus; South America, 1872 5475.1 p119
Risse, Laurens; Illinois, 1852 6079.1 p12

418
FOR A COMPLETE EXPLANATION OF ENTRY, SEE "HOW TO READ A CITATION" SECTION

Risser, David 22; Louisiana, 1848 778.6 p284
Risser, George P.; Washington, 1889 2770.40 p80
Risser, Heinrich; Argentina, 1924 8023.44 p378
*Wife:*Maria Russmann
Risser, Maria Russmann *SEE* Risser, Heinrich
Ristau, Edward Gustav; Wisconsin, 1891 6795.8 p212
Ristau, Johann; Wisconsin, 1889 6795.8 p212
Ristler, Rudy; North Carolina, 1710 3629.40 p6
Ritch, William; America, 1730 1220.12 p670
Ritchard, Ann; America, 1761 1220.12 p670
Ritche, Andre 4; New Orleans, 1843 778.6 p284
Ritche, Anne 30; New Orleans, 1843 778.6 p284
Ritche, Joseph 40; New Orleans, 1843 778.6 p284
Ritche, Scholastique 6; New Orleans, 1843 778.6 p285
Ritche, Sophie 2; New Orleans, 1843 778.6 p285
Ritchie, John 48; Ontario, 1871 1823.21 p312
Ritchie, Mary 25; Ontario, 1871 1823.21 p312
Ritchie, Peter; America, 1765 1220.12 p676
Ritchie, Robert 40; Ontario, 1871 1823.21 p312
Ritchie, Robert 42; Ontario, 1871 1823.17 p139
Rithock, Sarah; America, 1739 1220.12 p676
Ritner, Charles; Ohio, 1809-1852 4511.35 p44
Riton, John; America, 1744 1220.12 p905
Riton, Marie 25; Quebec, 1650 9221.17 p229
Ritski, Petrina; Kansas, 1917-1918 1826.15 p81
Ritson, John; America, 1772 1220.12 p676
Ritter, Conrad; Venezuela, 1843 3899.5 p547
Ritter, David; Ohio, 1809-1852 4511.35 p44
Ritter, Friedrich Ludwig Albert; Port uncertain, 1858 7420.1 p181
Ritter, George; Illinois, 1853 6079.1 p12
Ritter, Ida; Allegheny Co., PA, 1852 8513.31 p315
Ritter, Jean 18; New Orleans, 1848 778.6 p285
Ritter, Joseph; America, 1869 2526.42 p144
Ritter, Joseph; Ohio, 1809-1852 4511.35 p44
Ritter, Josephine 30; America, 1846 778.6 p285
Ritter, Lisette 22; Louisiana, 1848 778.6 p285
Ritter, Mathew; New York, 1860 358.56 p4
Ritter, Nikolaus; America, 1837 5475.1 p462
Ritter, Remie 27; Louisiana, 1848 778.6 p285
Ritter, Rick. 22; New York, NY, 1893 1883.7 p43
Ritter, Rudolph; Wisconsin, 1876 6795.8 p100
Ritter, Wilhelm; America, 1868 7420.1 p276
Ritter, William; Ohio, 1809-1852 4511.35 p44
Ritterbusch, Ernst Wilhelm Ludwig Wolf *SEE* Ritterbusch, Julie Dorothea Gertrud
Ritterbusch, Georg Heinrich *SEE* Ritterbusch, Julie Dorothea Gertrud
Ritterbusch, Heinrich Christian August *SEE* Ritterbusch, Julie Dorothea Gertrud
Ritterbusch, Julie Dorothea Gertrud; America, 1881 7420.1 p323
*Son:*Ernst Wilhelm Ludwig Wolf
*Son:*Wilhelm Friedrich Ferdinand
*Son:*Theodor Carl Friedrich
*Son:*Heinrich Christian August
*Son:*Georg Heinrich
Ritterbusch, Theodor Carl Friedrich *SEE* Ritterbusch, Julie Dorothea Gertrud
Ritterbusch, Wilhelm Friedrich Ferdinand *SEE* Ritterbusch, Julie Dorothea Gertrud
Rittersbaugh, George; Ohio, 1809-1852 4511.35 p44
Rittmuller, Emilie; America, 1899 5475.1 p40
Ritz, H.; New York, 1860 358.56 p6
Ritzi, Fidelis; Ohio, 1840-1897 8365.35 p17
Ritzius, Frederick; Harrisburg, PA, 1867 5720.10 p380
Ritzlog, Bernhard; Galveston, TX, 1855 571.7 p17
Ritzshke, Anthony; Colorado, 1894 1029.59 p78
Ritzshke, Anthony; Michigan, 1878 1029.59 p78
Rival, Mathilde; America, 1870 5475.1 p145
Rival, Peter 29; Connecticut, 1882 5475.1 p138
Rivard, Nicolas 31; Quebec, 1648 9221.17 p204
Rivard, Robert 24; Quebec, 1662 9221.17 p492
Rivaud, John 32; Ontario, 1871 1823.17 p139
Rivault, Charles 17; Louisiana, 1848 778.6 p285
Rive, Mr.; New Jersey, 1928-1930 9228.50 p543
Rive, Mr. 16; Ontario, 1928 9228.50 p543
Riveran, Jacquette; Quebec, 1650 9221.17 p230
Riveraud, Presse 33; New Orleans, 1848 778.6 p285
Rivereau, Mr. 41; America, 1843 778.6 p285
Rivereau, Jean; Quebec, 1657 9221.17 p367
Rivers, Mrs.; California, 1868 1131.61 p89
Rivers, Benjamin; America, 1758 1220.12 p676
Rivers, Elizabeth; America, 1756 1220.12 p676
Rivers, Elizabeth; Virginia, 1726 1220.12 p676
Rivers, Frank 22; Minnesota, 1925 2769.54 p1379
Rivers, Phil; New York, 1926 1173.1 p2
Rivers, Robert; America, 1773 1220.12 p676
Rivers, Victor 24; Minnesota, 1925 2769.54 p1380
Rivers, William; America, 1738 1220.12 p676
Rives, Edward; America, 1675 1220.12 p676
Rives, James; America, 1742 1220.12 p676
Rives, Justin 28; New Orleans, 1843 778.6 p285
Rivet, Anne; Quebec, 1665 4514.3 p364
Rivet, Catherine; Quebec, 1665 4514.3 p364
Rivet, Jules Noe 36; Port uncertain, 1840 778.6 p285
Rivett, James; Boston, 1774 8529.30 p3
Rivett, Robert; America, 1702 1220.12 p676
Riviere, Anne; Quebec, 1670 4514.3 p365
Riviere, Eugenie 36; America, 1840 778.6 p285
Riviere, Jerome; Louisiana, 1874 4981.45 p296
Riviere, Louis; America, 1766 1220.12 p676
Riviere, Marguerite 54; Quebec, 1656 9221.17 p336
Riviere, Marie; Quebec, 1671 4514.3 p365
Riviere, Marie-Jeffine 45; Quebec, 1656 9221.17 p336
*Daughter:*Marie 16
Riviere, Renee; Quebec, 1666 4514.3 p362
Riviere, Renee; Quebec, 1666 4514.3 p365
*Daughter:*Andree
Rivington, Francis; America, 1686 1220.12 p676
Rivoire, Appollos 13; Boston, n.d. 9228.50 p541
Rivollet, Mr. 36; America, 1840 778.6 p285
Rivollet, Mrs. 36; America, 1840 778.6 p285
Rix, Charles; America, 1753 1220.12 p676
Rix, Henry; America, 1731 1220.12 p676
Rix, James 28; Annapolis, MD, 1724 1220.12 p676
Rixmann, Robert 48; Chicago, 1884 5475.1 p515
With son
Rixon, Jacob; America, 1743 1220.12 p674
Rixon, John 22; North Carolina, 1774 1422.10 p55
Rixton, Thomas; Miami, 1935 4984.12 p39
Rizek, Josef; Iowa, 1870 2853.20 p202
Rizo, Pedro; Louisiana, 1836-1840 4981.45 p213
Rlander, Lewis; North Carolina, 1855 1088.45 p29
Roach, Ann; Boston, 1773 1642 p49
Roach, Cornelas 35; Ontario, 1871 1823.17 p139
Roach, Elizabeth; America, 1762 1220.12 p676
Roach, Elizabeth; Potomac, 1731 1220.12 p676
Roach, James; America, 1752 1220.12 p676
Roach, James; Boston, 1759 1642 p47
Roach, James; Boston, 1760 1642 p48
Roach, James; Boston, 1763 1642 p32
Roach, James 28; Ontario, 1871 1823.21 p312
Roach, John; America, 1749 1220.12 p676
Roach, John; America, 1750 1220.12 p676
Roach, John; America, 1762 1220.12 p677
Roach, John 52; Ontario, 1871 1823.17 p139
Roach, Judith; Boston, 1769 1642 p49
Roach, Moses; Boston, 1761 1642 p48
Roach, Moses; Boston, 1765 1642 p35
Roach, Patrick; Boston, 1766 1642 p36
Roach, Patrick; Boston, 1837 3274.55 p23
Roach, Paul 27; New York, NY, 1825 6178.50 p148
Roach, Reuben 40; Ontario, 1871 1823.21 p312
Roach, Richard; America, 1773 1220.12 p677
Roach, Robert; Annapolis, MD, 1735 1220.12 p677
Roach, Samuel; America, 1744 1220.12 p677
Roach, Sarah; America, 1775 1220.12 p677
Roach, Thomas; Boston, 1765 1642 p35
Roach, Thomas; Boston, 1766 1642 p37
Roach, Thomas; Boston, 1766 1642 p48
Roach, Thomas; Boston, 1769 1642 p49
Roach, William; Barbados or Jamaica, 1686 1220.12 p677
Roach, William; Barbados or St. Christopher, 1780 8529.30 p7A
Roach, William 13; Quebec, 1870 8364.32 p25
Roach, William Henry 49; Ontario, 1871 1823.21 p312
Roache, Eleanor; America, 1774 1220.12 p676
Roache, William; New England, 1745 1642 p28
Roache, William 33; Ontario, 1871 1823.21 p312
Road, Ann; America, 1771 1220.12 p668
Road, Patrick; Massachusetts, 1761 1642 p109
Road, Thomas; America, 1697 1220.12 p668
Roades, Benjamin; Maryland, 1719 1220.12 p668
Roades, William; America, 1752 1220.12 p669
Roadley, Samuel; America, 1765 1220.12 p677
Roadnight, Thomas 61; Ontario, 1871 1823.21 p312
Roads, Albert 15; Michigan, 1880 4491.30 p26
Roads, Hannah 38; Michigan, 1880 4491.30 p26
Roaldes, Miss 4; America, 1848 778.6 p285
Roaldes, Miss 8; America, 1848 778.6 p285
Roaldes, Mrs. 30; America, 1848 778.6 p285
Roan, John; Toronto, 1844 2910.35 p115
Roan, Thomas 47; Ontario, 1871 1823.17 p139
Roanes, Samuel; America, 1768 1220.12 p677
Roats, Henry 26; Ontario, 1871 1823.21 p312
Rob, George 64; Ontario, 1871 1823.17 p139
Roback, Stanislas 27; New York, NY, 1920 930.50 p49
Robair, Eliza 16; America, 1842 778.6 p285
Robar, Joseph; Ohio, 1809-1852 4511.35 p44
Robarts, Elinor; Barbados, 1666 1220.12 p677
Robarts, Griffith; Barbados, 1676 1220.12 p677
Robarts, Peter; America, 1757 1220.12 p679
Robat, Marie Joseph; Wisconsin, 1855 1495.20 p8
Robb, Charles 18; Quebec, 1870 8364.32 p25
Robb, James 42; Ontario, 1871 1823.21 p312
Robb, James 48; Ontario, 1871 1823.17 p139
Robb, John 63; Ontario, 1871 1823.21 p312
Robb, John; Washington, 1889 2770.40 p80
Robb, John G. 45; Ontario, 1871 1823.17 p139
Robb, Margaret 45; Ontario, 1871 1823.21 p312
Robb, Peter; America, 1772 1220.12 p677
Robbe, Victor A.; Illinois, 1852 6079.1 p12
Robbecke, Carl Heinrich Hermann; America, 1859 7420.1 p188
Robbecke, Carl Hermann; America, 1866 7420.1 p248
Robbecke, Friedrich; America, 1852 7420.1 p96
Robbeke, Gottlieb; America, 1859 7420.1 p188
Robbins, Mrs.; California, 1868 1131.61 p89
With daughter
Robbins, Aaron; Virginia, 1752 1220.12 p680
Robbins, Anne; America, 1719 1220.12 p680
Robbins, George 50; Ontario, 1871 1823.21 p312
Robbins, Jephtha; Virginia, 1759 1220.12 p680
Robbins, John; America, 1770 1220.12 p680
Robbins, John; Colorado, 1886 1029.59 p78
Robbins, John; Illinois, 1860 6079.1 p12
Robbins, John; Massachusetts, 1665 9228.50 p310
Robbins, John; Wheeling, WV, 1775-1807 9228.50 p544
Robbins, Mathew; Virginia, 1747 1220.12 p680
Robbins, Nicholas; Cambridge, MA, 1635 9228.50 p543
Robbins, Orlando 50; Ontario, 1871 1823.21 p312
Robbins, Philip; America, 1767 1220.12 p680
Robbins, Thomas; America, 1730 1220.12 p680
Robbins, William; Ohio, 1844 2763.1 p21
Robbs, William 31; Ontario, 1871 1823.21 p312
Robecke, Miss; America, 1865 7420.1 p232
Robecke, Carl Friedrich Gottlieb; Port uncertain, 1857 7420.1 p170
Robelin, Francois 35; Montreal, 1641 9221.17 p109
Roben, George; Ohio, 1809-1852 4511.35 p44
Roberdon, Andre 25; Quebec, 1661 9221.17 p466
Roberds, Ann; Virginia, 1735 1220.12 p677
Roberge, Denis 30; Quebec, 1661 9221.17 p466
Roberge, Mary; Ontario, 1800-1868 9228.50 p355
Roberson, William; North Carolina, 1836 1088.45 p29
Robert, . . .; Quebec, 1642 9221.17 p121
Robert, Mr. 30; New Orleans, 1842 778.6 p285
Robert, Mrs. 30; America, 1842 778.6 p285
Robert, Mrs. 59; North America, 1841 778.6 p285
Robert, Adelaide 9; New Orleans, 1848 778.6 p285
Robert, Alfred 4; America, 1844 778.6 p285
Robert, Christian 21; America, 1847 778.6 p285
Robert, Denis; Quebec, 1636 9221.17 p63
Robert, E. Piniel *SEE* Robert, Roy
Robert, Georges 17; New Orleans, 1848 778.6 p285
Robert, Guillaume 15; Montreal, 1653 9221.17 p285
Robert, Hodgins 66; Ontario, 1871 1823.21 p312
Robert, J. 61; North America, 1841 778.6 p285
Robert, Jean 34; New Orleans, 1848 778.6 p285
Robert, Jeanne; Idaho, 1811-1894 9228.50 p545
Robert, Jeanne; Utah, 1843 9228.50 p462
Robert, Jeanne; Utah, 1843 9228.50 p462
Robert, John; Jamaica, 1663 1220.12 p677
Robert, John *SEE* Robert, Roy
Robert, Joseph *SEE* Robert, Roy
Robert, Leopold 30; New Orleans, 1848 778.6 p285
Robert, Louis 25; America, 1842 778.6 p285
Robert, Louis 45; America, 1846 778.6 p285
Robert, Louis; Chile, 1852 1192.4 p52
Robert, Louis; Quebec, 1647 9221.17 p189
Robert, Marie 33; America, 1844 778.6 p285
Robert, Marie 28; New Orleans, 1848 778.6 p285
Robert, Marie; Quebec, 1668 4514.3 p365
Robert, Nicholas; Boston, 1760-1769 9228.50 p546
Robert, Otto; Chile, 1852 1192.4 p52
Robert, Paul; Ohio, 1807 9228.50 p57
Robert, Paul; Ohio, 1807 9228.50 p545
Robert, Peter; America, 1854 5475.1 p56
Robert, Peter; New York, 1842 9228.50 p40
Robert, Peter; Wisconsin, 1842 9228.50 p545
With wife & family
Robert, Roy; New York, 1850 9228.50 p546
*Wife:*E. Piniel
*Child:*Joseph
*Child:*John
Robert, Simon 17; New Orleans, 1848 778.6 p286
Robert, Victoire 17; Louisiana, 1845 778.6 p286
Robert DuPlessis, Philippe; Quebec, 1661 9221.17 p445
Roberteau, Jean; Quebec, 1662 9221.17 p486
Roberts, Ann; Annapolis, MD, 1725 1220.12 p677
Roberts, Anne; Annapolis, MD, 1733 1220.12 p677
Roberts, Arnold; America, 1730 1220.12 p677
Roberts, B. H.; California, 1868 1131.61 p89
With wife

Roberts, Cecil Martin; San Francisco, 1910-1912 ***9228.50*** *p546*
*Wife:*Lillian Phoebe Poet
*Child:*Violet Lilian Maud
*Child:*Thomas Early
*Child:*James Cecil Thomas Henry
Roberts, Charles; America, 1747 ***1220.12*** *p677*
Roberts, Charles; America, 1764 ***1220.12*** *p677*
Roberts, Charles; America, 1771 ***1220.12*** *p677*
Roberts, Charles; Barbados, 1683 ***1220.12*** *p677*
Roberts, Charles; Wisconsin, 1860 ***9228.50*** *p548*
Roberts, David; America, 1767 ***1220.12*** *p677*
Roberts, David; Boston, 1837 ***3274.55*** *p22*
Roberts, David; Washington, 1885 ***2770.40*** *p194*
Roberts, Dorothy; America, 1743 ***1220.12*** *p677*
Roberts, Edmund Frederick; Vancouver, B.C., 1901-1926 ***9228.50*** *p321*
Roberts, Edmund Samuel 31; Ontario, 1880 ***9228.50*** *p320*
Roberts, Edward; America, 1684 ***1220.12*** *p677*
Roberts, Edward; America, 1774 ***1220.12*** *p677*
Roberts, Edward; Annapolis, MD, 1729 ***1220.12*** *p677*
Roberts, Edward; South Carolina, 1670 ***9228.50*** *p548*
Roberts, Edward; West Indies, 1686 ***1220.12*** *p677*
Roberts, Eleanor; America, 1753 ***1220.12*** *p677*
Roberts, Elizabeth; America, 1749 ***1220.12*** *p677*
Roberts, Elizabeth; America, 1752 ***1220.12*** *p677*
Roberts, Elizabeth; America, 1765 ***1220.12*** *p677*
Roberts, Elizabeth; Carolina, 1724 ***1220.12*** *p677*
Roberts, Elizabeth 6; Quebec, 1870 ***8364.32*** *p25*
Roberts, Elizabeth; Virginia, 1732 ***1220.12*** *p677*
Roberts, Evan; America, 1764 ***1220.12*** *p677*
Roberts, Francis; America, 1772 ***1220.12*** *p677*
Roberts, Francis; Maryland, 1725 ***1220.12*** *p677*
Roberts, Frederick Wm.; Detroit, 1900 ***9228.50*** *p321*
Roberts, Geo.; Marblehead, MA, 1800-1899 ***9228.50*** *p548*
*Wife:*Sally
Roberts, George; America, 1756 ***1220.12*** *p677*
Roberts, George 42; Ontario, 1871 ***1823.21*** *p312*
Roberts, George 14; Quebec, 1870 ***8364.32*** *p25*
Roberts, George C. 30; Ontario, 1871 ***1823.17*** *p140*
Roberts, Henry; America, 1768 ***1220.12*** *p677*
Roberts, Henry; America, 1772 ***1220.12*** *p677*
Roberts, Hugh; America, 1691 ***1220.12*** *p677*
Roberts, Hugh; America, 1747 ***1220.12*** *p677*
Roberts, Hugh; America, 1771 ***1220.12*** *p677*
Roberts, Hugh; Iowa, 1886 ***1211.15*** *p18*
Roberts, Isaac; America, 1771 ***1220.12*** *p677*
Roberts, James; America, 1692 ***1220.12*** *p677*
Roberts, James; America, 1726 ***1220.12*** *p678*
Roberts, James; America, 1735 ***1220.12*** *p678*
Roberts, James; America, 1759 ***1220.12*** *p678*
Roberts, James; America, 1774 ***1220.12*** *p678*
Roberts, James; Annapolis, MD, 1726 ***1220.12*** *p678*
Roberts, James 45; Ontario, 1871 ***1823.17*** *p140*
Roberts, James Adolphus; Quebec, 1833-1915 ***9228.50*** *p546*
Roberts, James Cecil Thomas Henry *SEE* Roberts, Cecil Martin
Roberts, Jane; Virginia, 1734 ***1220.12*** *p678*
Roberts, Jenkin; Colorado, 1876 ***1029.59*** *p78*
Roberts, Joan; Virginia, 1740 ***1220.12*** *p678*
Roberts, John; America, 1693 ***1220.12*** *p678*
Roberts, John; America, 1700 ***1220.12*** *p678*
Roberts, John; America, 1721 ***1220.12*** *p678*
Roberts, John; America, 1722 ***1220.12*** *p678*
Roberts, John; America, 1737 ***1220.12*** *p678*
Roberts, John; America, 1739 ***1220.12*** *p678*
Roberts, John; America, 1744 ***1220.12*** *p678*
Roberts, John; America, 1751 ***1220.12*** *p678*
Roberts, John; America, 1753 ***1220.12*** *p678*
Roberts, John; America, 1755 ***1220.12*** *p678*
Roberts, John; America, 1756 ***1220.12*** *p678*
Roberts, John; America, 1765 ***1220.12*** *p678*
Roberts, John; America, 1767 ***1220.12*** *p678*
Roberts, John; America, 1768 ***1220.12*** *p678*
Roberts, John; America, 1769 ***1220.12*** *p678*
Roberts, John; America, 1773 ***1220.12*** *p678*
Roberts, John; Boston, 1764 ***1642*** *p34*
Roberts, John; Died enroute, 1731 ***1220.12*** *p678*
Roberts, John; Maryland, 1725 ***1220.12*** *p678*
Roberts, John; Nevis or Jamaica, 1722 ***1220.12*** *p678*
Roberts, John; Ohio, 1809-1852 ***4511.35*** *p44*
Roberts, John 34; Ontario, 1871 ***1823.17*** *p140*
Roberts, John 48; Ontario, 1871 ***1823.21*** *p313*
Roberts, John 50; Ontario, 1871 ***1823.21*** *p313*
Roberts, John G.; Colorado, 1876 ***1029.59*** *p78*
Roberts, John G.; Colorado, 1880 ***1029.59*** *p78*
Roberts, Jonathan; Annapolis, MD, 1724 ***1220.12*** *p678*
Roberts, Joseph 52; Ontario, 1871 ***1823.17*** *p140*
Roberts, Joseph H.; Ohio, 1879 ***3580.20*** *p33*
Roberts, Joseph H.; Ohio, 1879 ***6020.12*** *p22*
Roberts, Lawrence; America, 1739 ***1220.12*** *p678*
Roberts, Lenard 22; Minnesota, 1925 ***2769.54*** *p1383*
Roberts, Lillian Phoebe Poet *SEE* Roberts, Cecil Martin
Roberts, Margaret; America, 1691 ***1220.12*** *p678*
Roberts, Margaret; Annapolis, MD, 1725 ***1220.12*** *p678*
Roberts, Margaret; Maryland, 1725 ***1220.12*** *p678*
Roberts, Marjory; Barbados or Jamaica, 1688 ***1220.12*** *p678*
Roberts, Mary; America, 1730 ***1220.12*** *p678*
Roberts, Mary; America, 1742 ***1220.12*** *p678*
Roberts, Mary; America, 1762 ***1220.12*** *p678*
Roberts, Mary; America, 1766 ***1220.12*** *p678*
Roberts, Mary; America, 1770 ***1220.12*** *p678*
Roberts, Mary; America, 1771 ***1220.12*** *p679*
Roberts, Morris; America, 1741 ***1220.12*** *p679*
Roberts, Nairy 9; Quebec, 1870 ***8364.32*** *p25*
Roberts, Peter; America, 1753 ***1220.12*** *p679*
Roberts, Peter; America, 1769 ***1220.12*** *p679*
Roberts, Philip; America, 1730 ***1220.12*** *p679*
Roberts, Phoebe; America, 1769 ***1220.12*** *p679*
Roberts, Richard; America, 1677 ***1220.12*** *p679*
Roberts, Richard; America, 1736 ***1220.12*** *p679*
Roberts, Richard; America, 1764 ***1220.12*** *p679*
Roberts, Richard; America, 1765 ***1220.12*** *p679*
Roberts, Richard; America, 1772 ***1220.12*** *p679*
Roberts, Richard; America, 1774 ***1220.12*** *p679*
Roberts, Richard; Barbados, 1688 ***1220.12*** *p679*
Roberts, Richard Ernest; Miami, 1935 ***4984.12*** *p39*
Roberts, Robert; America, 1741 ***1220.12*** *p679*
Roberts, Robert; America, 1763 ***1220.12*** *p679*
Roberts, Robert; Charles Town, SC, 1719 ***1220.12*** *p679*
Roberts, Robert; Iowa, 1866-1932 ***1211.15*** *p18*
Roberts, Robert; Iowa, 1887 ***1211.15*** *p18*
Roberts, Robert 24; New York, NY, 1894 ***6512.1*** *p186*
Roberts, Robert; Philadelphia, 1828 ***5720.10*** *p381*
Roberts, Robert; Washington, 1887 ***6015.10*** *p16*
Roberts, Roberts 45; Ontario, 1871 ***1823.21*** *p313*
Roberts, Sally *SEE* Roberts, Geo.
Roberts, Samuel; Virginia, 1750 ***1220.12*** *p679*
Roberts, Sarah; America, 1727 ***1220.12*** *p679*
Roberts, Sarah; America, 1751 ***1220.12*** *p679*
Roberts, Sarah; America, 1769 ***1220.12*** *p679*
Roberts, Silas Josiah; Massachusetts, 1900 ***9228.50*** *p548*
Roberts, Thomas; America, 1733 ***1220.12*** *p679*
Roberts, Thomas; America, 1747 ***1220.12*** *p679*
Roberts, Thomas; America, 1762 ***1220.12*** *p679*
Roberts, Thomas; America, 1774 ***1220.12*** *p679*
Roberts, Thomas; Annapolis, MD, 1720 ***1220.12*** *p679*
Roberts, Thomas; Jamaica, 1665 ***1220.12*** *p679*
Roberts, Thomas; New Hampshire, 1623 ***9228.50*** *p548*
Roberts, Thomas; West Indies, 1688 ***1220.12*** *p679*
Roberts, Thomas Early *SEE* Roberts, Cecil Martin
Roberts, Thomas John; San Francisco, 1856-1936 ***9228.50*** *p546*
Roberts, Violet Lilian Maud *SEE* Roberts, Cecil Martin
Roberts, William; America, 1727 ***1220.12*** *p679*
Roberts, William; America, 1733 ***1220.12*** *p679*
Roberts, William; America, 1760 ***1220.12*** *p679*
Roberts, William; America, 1762 ***1220.12*** *p679*
Roberts, William; America, 1763 ***1220.12*** *p679*
Roberts, William; America, 1768 ***1220.12*** *p679*
Roberts, William; America, 1771 ***1220.12*** *p679*
Roberts, William; America, 1772 ***1220.12*** *p679*
Roberts, William; Barbados, 1676 ***1220.12*** *p679*
Roberts, William; Maryland, 1727 ***1220.12*** *p679*
Roberts, William 62; Ontario, 1871 ***1823.17*** *p140*
Roberts, William; Virginia, 1732 ***1220.12*** *p679*
Roberts, William; Virginia, 1735 ***1220.12*** *p679*
Roberts, William; Virginia, 1736 ***1220.12*** *p679*
Roberts, William C.; Iowa, 1877 ***1211.15*** *p18*
Roberts Family ; Prince Edward Island, 1806 ***9228.50*** *p547*
Robertson, Adam 28; Ontario, 1871 ***1823.17*** *p140*
Robertson, Andrew; America, 1752 ***1220.12*** *p679*
Robertson, Ann; America, 1755 ***1220.12*** *p679*
Robertson, Ann; Barbados or Jamaica, 1689 ***1220.12*** *p679*
Robertson, Betsey 79; Ontario, 1871 ***1823.21*** *p313*
Robertson, C. 46; Ontario, 1871 ***1823.21*** *p313*
Robertson, Charles; North Carolina, 1830 ***1088.45*** *p29*
Robertson, Charles 48; Ontario, 1871 ***1823.21*** *p313*
Robertson, D. S. 42; Ontario, 1871 ***1823.17*** *p140*
Robertson, David 36; Ontario, 1871 ***1823.17*** *p140*
Robertson, David 42; Ontario, 1871 ***1823.21*** *p313*
Robertson, Donald 47; Ontario, 1871 ***1823.21*** *p313*
Robertson, Frank 50; Ontario, 1871 ***1823.21*** *p313*
Robertson, George; America, 1685 ***1220.12*** *p679*
Robertson, George 38; Ontario, 1871 ***1823.21*** *p313*
Robertson, George 50; Ontario, 1871 ***1823.17*** *p140*
Robertson, H.D.; Iowa, 1892 ***1211.15*** *p18*
Robertson, Hanna; America, 1761 ***1220.12*** *p680*
Robertson, Harriet 20; New York, NY, 1835 ***5024.1*** *p137*
Robertson, Isabella; America, 1739 ***1220.12*** *p680*
Robertson, Isabella; America, 1766 ***1220.12*** *p680*
Robertson, Isabella 21; New York, NY, 1835 ***5024.1*** *p137*
Robertson, James; America, 1738 ***1220.12*** *p680*
Robertson, James; North Carolina, 1833 ***1088.45*** *p29*
Robertson, James 40; Ontario, 1871 ***1823.17*** *p140*
Robertson, James 59; Ontario, 1871 ***1823.21*** *p313*
Robertson, James 77; Ontario, 1871 ***1823.17*** *p140*
Robertson, James 77; Ontario, 1871 ***1823.21*** *p313*
Robertson, Jean 21; New York, NY, 1835 ***5024.1*** *p137*
Robertson, John; America, 1754 ***1220.12*** *p680*
Robertson, John; America, 1772 ***1220.12*** *p680*
Robertson, John; America, 1774 ***1220.12*** *p680*
Robertson, John 32; Ontario, 1871 ***1823.17*** *p140*
Robertson, John 38; Ontario, 1871 ***1823.17*** *p140*
Robertson, John 53; Ontario, 1871 ***1823.17*** *p140*
Robertson, John C.; North Carolina, 1860 ***1088.45*** *p29*
Robertson, Joseph; Ontario, 1787 ***1276.15*** *p231*
With 3 relatives
Robertson, Mary 60; New York, NY, 1835 ***5024.1*** *p137*
Robertson, Munro Kenn 23; Halifax, N.S., 1906 ***1833.5*** *p7*
Robertson, Peter; America, 1753 ***1220.12*** *p680*
Robertson, Peter; Ohio, 1840-1897 ***8365.35*** *p17*
Robertson, Robert 36; Ontario, 1871 ***1823.21*** *p313*
Robertson, Robert 47; Ontario, 1871 ***1823.17*** *p140*
Robertson, Thomas 40; Indiana, 1881-1884 ***9076.20*** *p70*
Robertson, Thomas; Marston's Wharf, 1779 ***8529.30*** *p15*
Robertson, Thomas 34; New York, NY, 1835 ***5024.1*** *p136*
Robertson, Thomas 45; Ontario, 1871 ***1823.21*** *p313*
Robertson, Thomas 60; Ontario, 1871 ***1823.21*** *p313*
Robertson, Thomas 18; Quebec, 1870 ***8364.32*** *p25*
Robertson, William; America, 1759 ***1220.12*** *p680*
Robertson, William; Canada, 1774 ***3036.5*** *p41*
Robertson, William; Maryland, 1719 ***1220.12*** *p680*
Robertson, William; New York, NY, 1835 ***5024.1*** *p137*
Robertson, William; North Carolina, 1832 ***1088.45*** *p29*
Robertson, William 55; Ontario, 1871 ***1823.17*** *p140*
Robertson, William 55; Ontario, 1871 ***1823.21*** *p313*
Robertson, William; Virginia, 1736 ***1220.12*** *p680*
Robertton, James; Ontario, 1787 ***1276.15*** *p230*
With relative
Robey, William 33; Ontario, 1871 ***1823.21*** *p313*
Robier, Alexandre 25; New Orleans, 1848 ***778.6*** *p286*
Robighini, Charles 43; Ontario, 1871 ***1823.17*** *p140*
Robilliard, James; Wisconsin, 1865 ***9228.50*** *p548*
Robilliard, Joseph; Montreal, 1820 ***9228.50*** *p548*
*Wife:*Rose
Robilliard, Peter; Wisconsin, 1848 ***9228.50*** *p548*
Robilliard, Rose *SEE* Robilliard, Joseph
Robin, Alfred Edwin *SEE* Robin, Peter Francis
Robin, Beulah Harriet; Rochester, NY, 1915-1983 ***9228.50*** *p548*
Robin, Etienne 20; Montreal, 1653 ***9221.17*** *p300*
Robin, Eugene; New York, 1911-1914 ***9228.50*** *p548*
*Wife:*Harriet Ingrouille
*Child:*Wilson
Robin, Eugene; Ontario, 1914 ***9228.50*** *p548*
*Child:*Gladys
*Child:*Wilson
*Wife:*Harriet Ingrouille
Robin, Gladys *SEE* Robin, Eugene
Robin, Harriet Ingrouille *SEE* Robin, Eugene
Robin, Harriet Ingrouille *SEE* Robin, Eugene
Robin, Ivy Gibson *SEE* Robin, Peter Francis
Robin, Jean Firmin 30; New Orleans, 1840 ***778.6*** *p286*
Robin, Louise; Quebec, 1671 ***4514.3*** *p365*
Robin, Mathurine; Quebec, 1636 ***9221.17*** *p56*
*Son:*Simon
*Daughter:*Marie
*Son:*Claude
*Son:*Michel
*Son:*Denis
*Son:*Francois
Robin, Matilda Amy; Wisconsin, 1866-1884 ***9228.50*** *p549*
Robin, Matilda Amy; Wisconsin, 1884 ***9228.50*** *p121*
Robin, Peter Francis; Manitoba, 1908 ***9228.50*** *p549*
*Wife:*Sarah Gibson
*Child:*Robin Peter
*Child:*Alfred Edwin
*Child:*Victor Francis
Robin, Peter Francis; Mobile, AL, 1928 ***9228.50*** *p549*
*Child:*Robin Peter
*Child:*Ivy Gibson
Robin, Robin Peter *SEE* Robin, Peter Francis
Robin, Robin Peter *SEE* Robin, Peter Francis
Robin, Sarah Gibson *SEE* Robin, Peter Francis
Robin, Thomas; Quebec, 1804-1836 ***9228.50*** *p356*
With parents

420 *FOR A COMPLETE EXPLANATION OF ENTRY, SEE "HOW TO READ A CITATION" SECTION*

Robin, Thomas; Wisconsin, 1804-1836 ***9228.50*** *p356*
With parents
Robin, Victor Francis *SEE* Robin, Peter Francis
Robin, Wilson *SEE* Robin, Eugene
Robin, Wilson *SEE* Robin, Eugene
Robineau, Louis; Quebec, 1643 ***9221.17*** *p134*
Robineau, Marguerite; Quebec, 1668 ***4514.3*** *p365*
Robineau, Marie; Quebec, 1668 ***4514.3*** *p365*
Robineau deBecancour, Rene; Quebec, 1645 ***2314.30*** *p166*
Robineau deBecancour, Rene; Quebec, 1645 ***2314.30*** *p194*
Robineau DeBecancour, Rene 20; Quebec, 1645 ***9221.17*** *p157*
Robinet, Barbara 2 *SEE* Robinet, Johann
Robinet, Christoph 10 *SEE* Robinet, Johann
Robinet, Johann; America, 1854 ***5475.1*** *p465*
*Wife:*Margarethe Meiser
*Son:*Peter
*Daughter:*Katharina
*Son:*Johann
*Daughter:*Barbara
*Son:*Peter
*Son:*Christoph
*Son:*Johann
*Daughter:*Margarethe
*Daughter:*Sophie
Robinet, Johann 8 *SEE* Robinet, Johann
Robinet, Johann 18 *SEE* Robinet, Johann
Robinet, Katharina 16 *SEE* Robinet, Johann
Robinet, Margarethe Meiser *SEE* Robinet, Johann
Robinet, Margarethe 26 *SEE* Robinet, Johann
Robinet, Peter *SEE* Robinet, Johann
Robinet, Peter 5 *SEE* Robinet, Johann
Robinet, Sophie 24 *SEE* Robinet, Johann
Robinette, Esther J. 27; Ontario, 1871 ***1823.21*** *p313*
Robinius, Michel; Chicago, 1884 ***5475.1*** *p204*
Robins, Allen; Barbados, 1679 ***1220.12*** *p680*
Robins, Edwin 38; Ontario, 1871 ***1823.21*** *p313*
Robins, George; America, 1737 ***1220.12*** *p680*
Robins, James; America, 1727 ***1220.12*** *p680*
Robins, James; Barbados, 1694 ***1220.12*** *p680*
Robins, John; America, 1685 ***1220.12*** *p680*
Robins, John; Ohio, 1807 ***9228.50*** *p57*
Robins, John; Ohio, 1809-1852 ***4511.35*** *p44*
Robins, John 21; Ontario, 1871 ***1823.21*** *p313*
Robins, John 30; Ontario, 1871 ***1823.21*** *p313*
Robins, John 38; Ontario, 1871 ***1823.21*** *p313*
Robins, John; Virginia, 1732 ***1220.12*** *p680*
Robins, John; Virginia, 1745 ***1220.12*** *p680*
Robins, John; Wheeling, WV, 1775-1807 ***9228.50*** *p544*
Robins, Joseph; America, 1685 ***1220.12*** *p680*
Robins, Lewis 24; Ontario, 1871 ***1823.17*** *p140*
Robins, Louisa; Ohio, 1842 ***9228.50*** *p545*
Robins, Mary; America, 1755 ***1220.12*** *p680*
Robins, Mary; Ohio, 1747-1846 ***9228.50*** *p545*
Robins, Mary; Ohio, 1787-1845 ***9228.50*** *p545*
Robins, Richard; America, 1741 ***1220.12*** *p680*
Robins, Simon 58; Ontario, 1871 ***1823.21*** *p313*
Robins, Tho. 17; Virginia, 1635 ***1183.3*** *p31*
Robins, Thomas; America, 1725 ***1220.12*** *p680*
Robins, Tugwell 42; Ontario, 1871 ***1823.21*** *p313*
Robins, Valentine; Virginia, 1732 ***1220.12*** *p680*
Robins, William 61; Ontario, 1871 ***1823.21*** *p313*
Robins, Wm 30; Ontario, 1871 ***1823.21*** *p313*
Robinsenson, Robert 74; Ontario, 1871 ***1823.21*** *p313*
Robinson, Miss 17; New York, NY, 1894 ***6512.1*** *p186*
Robinson, Alexander; America, 1685 ***1220.12*** *p680*
Robinson, Alexander 58; Ontario, 1871 ***1823.21*** *p313*
Robinson, Andrew; America, 1745 ***1220.12*** *p680*
Robinson, Andrew 35; Ontario, 1871 ***1823.21*** *p313*
Robinson, Andrew 40; Ontario, 1871 ***1823.21*** *p313*
Robinson, Andrew 47; Ontario, 1871 ***1823.21*** *p313*
Robinson, Ann; America, 1737 ***1220.12*** *p680*
Robinson, Ann; America, 1741 ***1220.12*** *p680*
Robinson, Ann; America, 1753 ***1220.12*** *p680*
Robinson, Ann; America, 1755 ***1220.12*** *p680*
Robinson, Ann; America, 1768 ***1220.12*** *p680*
Robinson, Ann; Annapolis, MD, 1736 ***1220.12*** *p680*
Robinson, Ann; Barbados or Jamaica, 1689 ***1220.12*** *p680*
Robinson, Ann *SEE* Robinson, John
Robinson, Ann 30; New York, NY, 1835 ***5024.1*** *p136*
Robinson, Ann; Potomac, 1731 ***1220.12*** *p680*
Robinson, Annie 9; Quebec, 1870 ***8364.32*** *p25*
Robinson, Barbara; America, 1753 ***1220.12*** *p680*
Robinson, Benjamin; America, 1773 ***1220.12*** *p680*
Robinson, Blaze; America, 1764 ***1220.12*** *p680*
Robinson, Bridget; America, 1758 ***1220.12*** *p680*
Robinson, Brittain; America, 1769 ***1220.12*** *p680*
Robinson, Catherine; America, 1752 ***1220.12*** *p680*
Robinson, Catherine; Potomac, 1731 ***1220.12*** *p680*
Robinson, Catherine 13; Quebec, 1870 ***8364.32*** *p25*
Robinson, Charles; America, 1772 ***1220.12*** *p680*
Robinson, Charles 46; Ontario, 1871 ***1823.21*** *p313*
Robinson, Charles 51; Ontario, 1871 ***1823.17*** *p140*
Robinson, Charles J. 53; Ontario, 1871 ***1823.17*** *p140*
Robinson, Christopher; America, 1762 ***1220.12*** *p680*
Robinson, Christopher; Barbados, 1699 ***1220.12*** *p680*
Robinson, Cornelius; Virginia, 1652 ***6254.4*** *p243*
Robinson, David 18; Ontario, 1871 ***1823.17*** *p140*
Robinson, David 47; Ontario, 1871 ***1823.21*** *p313*
Robinson, David; Philadelphia, 1778 ***8529.30*** *p5A*
Robinson, Edward; America, 1678 ***1220.12*** *p681*
Robinson, Edward; America, 1764 ***1220.12*** *p681*
Robinson, Edward; Maryland, 1719 ***1220.12*** *p681*
Robinson, Edwd 52; Ontario, 1871 ***1823.21*** *p313*
Robinson, Elinor; Virginia, 1734 ***1220.12*** *p681*
Robinson, Elizabeth; America, 1700 ***1220.12*** *p681*
Robinson, Elizabeth; America, 1744 ***1220.12*** *p681*
Robinson, Elizabeth; America, 1760 ***1220.12*** *p681*
Robinson, Elizabeth; Annapolis, MD, 1723 ***1220.12*** *p681*
Robinson, Elizabeth *SEE* Robinson, William
Robinson, Elizabeth 11; Quebec, 1870 ***8364.32*** *p25*
Robinson, Francis *SEE* Robinson, William
Robinson, Francis 60; Ontario, 1871 ***1823.21*** *p313*
Robinson, George; America, 1709 ***1220.12*** *p681*
Robinson, George; America, 1723 ***1220.12*** *p681*
Robinson, George; America, 1731 ***1220.12*** *p681*
Robinson, George; America, 1766 ***1220.12*** *p681*
Robinson, George; America, 1773 ***1220.12*** *p681*
Robinson, George; Annapolis, MD, 1719 ***1220.12*** *p681*
Robinson, George 22; Michigan, 1880 ***4491.39*** *p25*
Robinson, George 56; Michigan, 1880 ***4491.36*** *p18*
Robinson, George 40; Ontario, 1871 ***1823.21*** *p313*
Robinson, George A. 2; New York, NY, 1835 ***5024.1*** *p136*
Robinson, Hannah; America, 1741 ***1220.12*** *p681*
Robinson, Hannah; America, 1746 ***1220.12*** *p681*
Robinson, Harriette 50; Ontario, 1871 ***1823.21*** *p314*
Robinson, Henry; America, 1746 ***1220.12*** *p681*
Robinson, Henry; America, 1762 ***1220.12*** *p681*
Robinson, Henry; America, 1771 ***1220.12*** *p681*
Robinson, Henry; Barbados, 1675 ***1220.12*** *p681*
Robinson, Henry 50; Ontario, 1871 ***1823.21*** *p314*
Robinson, Henry 60; Ontario, 1871 ***1823.21*** *p314*
Robinson, Hester; Died enroute, 1736 ***1220.12*** *p681*
Robinson, Hugh 48; Ontario, 1871 ***1823.21*** *p314*
Robinson, Isabella 8; New York, NY, 1835 ***5024.1*** *p136*
Robinson, James; America, 1753 ***1220.12*** *p681*
Robinson, James; America, 1770 ***1220.12*** *p681*
Robinson, James; America, 1774 ***1220.12*** *p681*
Robinson, James 20; Ontario, 1871 ***1823.17*** *p140*
Robinson, James 26; Ontario, 1871 ***1823.21*** *p314*
Robinson, James 41; Ontario, 1871 ***1823.21*** *p314*
Robinson, James 42; Ontario, 1871 ***1823.17*** *p140*
Robinson, James 54; Ontario, 1871 ***1823.21*** *p314*
Robinson, James 58; Ontario, 1871 ***1823.21*** *p314*
Robinson, Jane; America, 1682 ***1220.12*** *p681*
Robinson, Jane; America, 1774 ***1220.12*** *p681*
Robinson, Jane 3; New York, NY, 1835 ***5024.1*** *p136*
Robinson, Jane; Virginia, 1735 ***1220.12*** *p681*
Robinson, Jenny *SEE* Robinson, John
Robinson, Jeremiah; America, 1753 ***1220.12*** *p681*
Robinson, Jessie Ann 9 months; New York, NY, 1835 ***5024.1*** *p136*
Robinson, John; America, 1674 ***1220.12*** *p681*
Robinson, John; America, 1722 ***1220.12*** *p681*
Robinson, John; America, 1732 ***1220.12*** *p681*
Robinson, John; America, 1738 ***1220.12*** *p681*
Robinson, John; America, 1739 ***1220.12*** *p681*
Robinson, John; America, 1744 ***1220.12*** *p681*
Robinson, John; America, 1746 ***1220.12*** *p681*
Robinson, John; America, 1748 ***1220.12*** *p681*
Robinson, John; America, 1749 ***1220.12*** *p681*
Robinson, John; America, 1752 ***1220.12*** *p682*
Robinson, John; America, 1754 ***1220.12*** *p682*
Robinson, John; America, 1756 ***1220.12*** *p682*
Robinson, John; America, 1765 ***1220.12*** *p682*
Robinson, John; America, 1766 ***1220.12*** *p682*
Robinson, John; America, 1768 ***1220.12*** *p682*
Robinson, John; America, 1769 ***1220.12*** *p682*
Robinson, John; America, 1770 ***1220.12*** *p682*
Robinson, John; America, 1773 ***1220.12*** *p682*
Robinson, John; America, 1774 ***1220.12*** *p682*
Robinson, John; Annapolis, MD, 1723 ***1220.12*** *p681*
Robinson, John; Annapolis, MD, 1726 ***1220.12*** *p681*
Robinson, John; Canada, 1775 ***3036.5*** *p68*
*Daughter:*Ann
*Daughter:*Jenny
Robinson, John; Jamaica, 1661 ***1220.12*** *p681*
Robinson, John 27; Ontario, 1871 ***1823.21*** *p314*
Robinson, John 32; Ontario, 1871 ***1823.21*** *p314*
Robinson, John 35; Ontario, 1871 ***1823.21*** *p314*
Robinson, John 40; Ontario, 1871 ***1823.17*** *p140*
Robinson, John 41; Ontario, 1871 ***1823.21*** *p314*
Robinson, John 44; Ontario, 1871 ***1823.17*** *p140*
Robinson, John 44; Ontario, 1871 ***1823.21*** *p314*
Robinson, John 52; Ontario, 1871 ***1823.21*** *p314*
Robinson, John 55; Ontario, 1871 ***1823.17*** *p140*
Robinson, John 69; Ontario, 1871 ***1823.21*** *p314*
Robinson, John 70; Ontario, 1871 ***1823.21*** *p314*
Robinson, John; Potomac, 1743 ***1220.12*** *p681*
Robinson, John; Rappahannock, VA, 1741 ***1220.12*** *p681*
Robinson, John; Virginia, 1728 ***1220.12*** *p681*
Robinson, John F. 51; Ontario, 1871 ***1823.17*** *p140*
Robinson, John P.; Iowa, 1899 ***1211.15*** *p18*
Robinson, John S. 55; Ontario, 1871 ***1823.21*** *p314*
Robinson, Jonathan *SEE* Robinson, William
Robinson, Joseph; America, 1724 ***1220.12*** *p682*
Robinson, Joseph; America, 1753 ***1220.12*** *p682*
Robinson, Joseph; America, 1765 ***1220.12*** *p682*
Robinson, Joseph; America, 1775 ***1220.12*** *p682*
Robinson, Joseph; Annapolis, MD, 1725 ***1220.12*** *p682*
Robinson, Joseph; Barbados or Jamaica, 1684 ***1220.12*** *p682*
Robinson, Joseph 44; Ontario, 1871 ***1823.17*** *p140*
Robinson, Joseph 62; Ontario, 1871 ***1823.21*** *p314*
Robinson, Joseph; Potomac, 1731 ***1220.12*** *p682*
Robinson, Joseph; Virginia, 1732 ***1220.12*** *p682*
Robinson, Josias; America, 1721 ***1220.12*** *p682*
Robinson, L. S. 30; Ontario, 1871 ***1823.17*** *p140*
Robinson, Leonard; Annapolis, MD, 1730 ***1220.12*** *p682*
Robinson, Luke 40; Ontario, 1871 ***1823.17*** *p141*
Robinson, Margaret; America, 1743 ***1220.12*** *p682*
Robinson, Margaret; America, 1764 ***1220.12*** *p682*
Robinson, Margaret 25; Michigan, 1880 ***4491.36*** *p18*
Robinson, Margaret 65; Ontario, 1871 ***1823.21*** *p314*
Robinson, Margaret; Virginia, 1726 ***1220.12*** *p682*
Robinson, Margery; America, 1727 ***1220.12*** *p682*
Robinson, Margret 25; Ontario, 1871 ***1823.21*** *p314*
Robinson, Martha; Maryland, 1737 ***1220.12*** *p682*
Robinson, Mary; America, 1699 ***1220.12*** *p682*
Robinson, Mary; America, 1742 ***1220.12*** *p682*
Robinson, Mary; America, 1755 ***1220.12*** *p682*
Robinson, Mary; America, 1762 ***1220.12*** *p682*
Robinson, Mary; America, 1764 ***1220.12*** *p682*
Robinson, Mary; America, 1772 ***1220.12*** *p682*
Robinson, Mary; Barbados, 1679 ***1220.12*** *p682*
Robinson, Mary; Barbados or Jamaica, 1692 ***1220.12*** *p682*
Robinson, Mary; Died enroute, 1726 ***1220.12*** *p682*
Robinson, Mary 12; Quebec, 1870 ***8364.32*** *p25*
Robinson, Matthew; America, 1749 ***1220.12*** *p682*
Robinson, Matthew; America, 1768 ***1220.12*** *p682*
Robinson, Michael; America, 1762 ***1220.12*** *p682*
Robinson, Michael; America, 1763 ***1220.12*** *p682*
Robinson, Nathaniel; Virginia, 1760 ***1220.12*** *p683*
Robinson, Peter; Maryland, 1732 ***1220.12*** *p683*
Robinson, Raymond 22; Michigan, 1880 ***4491.36*** *p18*
Robinson, Reuben; America, 1758 ***1220.12*** *p683*
Robinson, Richard; Maryland, 1720 ***1220.12*** *p683*
Robinson, Richard 6; New York, NY, 1835 ***5024.1*** *p136*
Robinson, Richard 16; Quebec, 1870 ***8364.32*** *p25*
Robinson, Richard; Virginia, 1735 ***1220.12*** *p683*
Robinson, Robert; America, 1752 ***1220.12*** *p683*
Robinson, Robert; America, 1753 ***1220.12*** *p683*
Robinson, Robert; America, 1759 ***1220.12*** *p683*
Robinson, Robert; Barbados or Jamaica, 1686 ***1220.12*** *p683*
Robinson, Robert; Maryland, 1725 ***1220.12*** *p683*
Robinson, Robert 32; Ontario, 1871 ***1823.21*** *p314*
Robinson, Robert 50; Ontario, 1871 ***1823.21*** *p314*
Robinson, Robert 59; Ontario, 1871 ***1823.21*** *p314*
Robinson, Robert 12; Quebec, 1870 ***8364.32*** *p25*
Robinson, Rose; America, 1745 ***1220.12*** *p683*
Robinson, Samuel; America, 1740 ***1220.12*** *p683*
Robinson, Samuel 22; Ontario, 1871 ***1823.17*** *p141*
Robinson, Samuel F. 30; Ontario, 1871 ***1823.21*** *p314*
Robinson, Sarah; America, 1765 ***1220.12*** *p683*
Robinson, Sarah; America, 1768 ***1220.12*** *p683*
Robinson, Sarah; Barbados or Jamaica, 1715 ***1220.12*** *p683*
Robinson, Sarah 38; Ontario, 1871 ***1823.17*** *p141*
Robinson, Sarah 55; Ontario, 1871 ***1823.21*** *p314*
Robinson, Susan 7; Ontario, 1871 ***1823.21*** *p314*
Robinson, Susan A. 48; Ontario, 1871 ***1823.21*** *p314*
Robinson, Susanna; America, 1721 ***1220.12*** *p683*
Robinson, Thomas; America, 1687 ***1220.12*** *p683*
Robinson, Thomas; America, 1724 ***1220.12*** *p683*
Robinson, Thomas; America, 1738 ***1220.12*** *p683*
Robinson, Thomas; America, 1750 ***1220.12*** *p683*
Robinson, Thomas; America, 1752 ***1220.12*** *p683*
Robinson, Thomas; America, 1765 ***1220.12*** *p683*
Robinson, Thomas; America, 1768 ***1220.12*** *p683*
Robinson, Thomas; America, 1769 ***1220.12*** *p683*
Robinson, Thomas; America, 1774 ***1220.12*** *p683*
Robinson, Thomas; Louisiana, 1874 ***4981.45*** *p134*
Robinson, Thomas 33; Ontario, 1871 ***1823.21*** *p314*

Robinson, Thomas 35; Ontario, 1871 ***1823.21*** *p314*
Robinson, Thomas 45; Ontario, 1871 ***1823.17*** *p141*
Robinson, Thomas 48; Ontario, 1871 ***1823.21*** *p314*
Robinson, Thomas 53; Ontario, 1871 ***1823.17*** *p141*
Robinson, Thomas 56; Ontario, 1871 ***1823.21*** *p314*
Robinson, Thomas 59; Ontario, 1871 ***1823.21*** *p314*
Robinson, Timothy; Died enroute, 1730 ***1220.12*** *p683*
Robinson, Tucker 56; Ontario, 1871 ***1823.21*** *p314*
Robinson, W. H. 30; Ontario, 1871 ***1823.21*** *p314*
Robinson, William; America, 1675 ***1220.12*** *p683*
Robinson, William; America, 1719 ***1220.12*** *p683*
Robinson, William; America, 1732 ***1220.12*** *p683*
Robinson, William; America, 1733 ***1220.12*** *p683*
Robinson, William; America, 1734 ***1220.12*** *p683*
Robinson, William; America, 1744 ***1220.12*** *p683*
Robinson, William; America, 1745 ***1220.12*** *p683*
Robinson, William; America, 1752 ***1220.12*** *p683*
Robinson, William; America, 1755 ***1220.12*** *p683*
Robinson, William; America, 1763 ***1220.12*** *p683*
Robinson, William; America, 1765 ***1220.12*** *p683*
Robinson, William; America, 1768 ***1220.12*** *p683*
Robinson, William; America, 1768 ***1220.12*** *p684*
Robinson, William; America, 1772 ***1220.12*** *p684*
Robinson, William; America, 1773 ***1220.12*** *p684*
Robinson, William; Annapolis, MD, 1723 ***1220.12*** *p683*
Robinson, William *SEE* Robinson, William
Robinson, William; Canada, 1775 ***3036.5*** *p68*
*Wife:*Elizabeth
*Child:*William
*Child:*Jonathan
*Child:*Francis
Robinson, William; Colorado, 1884 ***1029.59*** *p78*
Robinson, William 25; Indiana, 1886-1892 ***9076.20*** *p73*
Robinson, William; Jamaica, 1783 ***8529.30*** *p14A*
Robinson, William; Maryland, 1721 ***1220.12*** *p683*
Robinson, William 18; Michigan, 1880 ***4491.39*** *p25*
Robinson, William; North Carolina, 1838 ***1088.45*** *p29*
Robinson, William; Ohio, 1855 ***3580.20*** *p33*
Robinson, William; Ohio, 1855 ***6020.12*** *p22*
Robinson, William 37; Ontario, 1871 ***1823.17*** *p141*
Robinson, William 39; Ontario, 1871 ***1823.21*** *p314*
Robinson, William 40; Ontario, 1871 ***1823.17*** *p141*
Robinson, William 44; Ontario, 1871 ***1823.21*** *p314*
Robinson, William 48; Ontario, 1871 ***1823.17*** *p141*
Robinson, William 50; Ontario, 1871 ***1823.17*** *p141*
Robinson, William 55; Ontario, 1871 ***1823.21*** *p314*
Robinson, William; Virginia, 1739 ***1220.12*** *p683*
Robinson, William; Virginia, 1767 ***1220.12*** *p683*
Robinson, William W. 9; New York, NY, 1835 ***5024.1*** *p136*
Robinson, Wyman 29; Ontario, 1871 ***1823.21*** *p314*
Robishaw, Mary Ann 39; Ontario, 1871 ***1823.17*** *p141*
Robison, Elizabeth 80; Ontario, 1871 ***1823.21*** *p314*
Robison, James; Ohio, 1809-1852 ***4511.35*** *p44*
Robison, John 61; Ontario, 1871 ***1823.17*** *p141*
Robke, Miss; America, 1857 ***7420.1*** *p171*
Robke, Mr.; America, 1858 ***7420.1*** *p181*
With wife & 2 daughters
With son 11
With son 15
With son 18
Robke, Eleonore; America, 1882 ***7420.1*** *p327*
Robke, Ernst; America, 1852 ***7420.1*** *p96*
With wife brother-in-law & relatives
Robke, Ernst Anton Friedrich; America, 1881 ***7420.1*** *p324*
Robke, Heinrich; America, 1846 ***7420.1*** *p47*
Robkins, James; America, 1760 ***1220.12*** *p684*
Roble, Anna 9; New York, NY, 1885 ***1883.7*** *p47*
Roble, Eva 24; New York, NY, 1885 ***1883.7*** *p47*
Robman, Christopher; North Carolina, 1854 ***1088.45*** *p29*
Robnut, Edward; America, 1772 ***1220.12*** *p684*
Robotham, Ellen 72; Ontario, 1871 ***1823.21*** *p314*
Robotham, George; America, 1762 ***1220.12*** *p684*
Robothan, William 40; Ontario, 1871 ***1823.21*** *p314*
Robouch, Miss 57; America, 1844 ***778.6*** *p286*
Robson, Alice; America, 1765 ***1220.12*** *p684*
Robson, Barbe; Wisconsin, 1854-1858 ***1495.20*** *p66*
With son
Robson, Edward; North Carolina, 1811 ***1088.45*** *p29*
Robson, George; America, 1772 ***1220.12*** *p684*
Robson, George 28; Ontario, 1871 ***1823.21*** *p315*
Robson, George 39; Ontario, 1871 ***1823.17*** *p141*
Robson, George 70; Ontario, 1871 ***1823.21*** *p315*
Robson, George 70; Ontario, 1871 ***1823.21*** *p315*
Robson, Jacob; America, 1775 ***1220.12*** *p684*
Robson, Janet 70; Ontario, 1871 ***1823.21*** *p315*
Robson, Jennet 40; Ontario, 1871 ***1823.21*** *p315*
Robson, Jeremih 62; Ontario, 1871 ***1823.21*** *p315*
Robson, John; America, 1747 ***1220.12*** *p684*
Robson, John; America, 1758 ***1220.12*** *p684*
Robson, John 74; Ontario, 1871 ***1823.17*** *p141*
Robson, John; Virginia, 1772 ***1220.12*** *p684*
Robson, Mary; America, 1760 ***1220.12*** *p684*
Robson, Mary; America, 1775 ***1220.12*** *p684*
Robson, Matthew; America, 1768 ***1220.12*** *p684*
Robson, Peter; America, 1754 ***1220.12*** *p684*
Robson, Thomas; America, 1722 ***1220.12*** *p684*
Robson, Thomas 31; Ontario, 1871 ***1823.21*** *p315*
Robson, William; America, 1741 ***1220.12*** *p684*
Robson, William; Barbados, 1665 ***1220.12*** *p684*
Robson, William; North Carolina, 1812 ***1088.45*** *p29*
Robston, George 47; Ontario, 1871 ***1823.21*** *p315*
Robuctine, Hannah; America, 1749 ***1220.12*** *p684*
Robutel deLa Noue, Zacharie; Quebec, 1689 ***2314.30*** *p172*
Robutel DeSaint-Andre, Claude 33; Montreal, 1653 ***9221.17*** *p300*
Robutel DeSaint-Andre, Suzanne de 36; Montreal, 1659 ***9221.17*** *p427*
Roby, Mr. 38; America, 1841 ***778.6*** *p286*
Roby, Elizabeth; America, 1755 ***1220.12*** *p684*
Roby, Elizabeth; America, 1769 ***1220.12*** *p684*
Roby, William; Virginia, 1751 ***1220.12*** *p684*
Rocart, William; America, 1740 ***1220.12*** *p684*
Rocbert deLa Morandiere, Etienne; Quebec, 1690 ***2314.30*** *p172*
Rocca, Antonio Giacoma; Washington, 1889 ***2770.40*** *p80*
Roch, Jan; Wisconsin, 1857-1861 ***2853.20*** *p334*
Roch, Lewis 35; America, 1843 ***778.6*** *p286*
Roch, Mary; Boston, 1774 ***1642*** *p50*
Roch, Matthias; America, 1736 ***1220.12*** *p677*
Roche, Elizabeth; Barbados, 1695 ***1220.12*** *p676*
Roche, Florence; New Orleans, 1851 ***7242.30*** *p153*
Roche, Henry 28; America, 1844 ***778.6*** *p286*
Roche, John P.; Louisiana, 1874 ***4981.45*** *p133*
Roche, Mary; Annapolis, MD, 1736 ***1220.12*** *p677*
Roche, Mary; Wisconsin, 1845-1868 ***9228.50*** *p237*
Roche, Pierre 26; New Orleans, 1848 ***778.6*** *p286*
Roche, Wm.; Canada, 1845 ***9228.50*** *p237*
Rochebrun, John B.; Louisiana, 1836-1841 ***4981.45*** *p209*
Rochel, Nicolas; New Castle, DE, 1817-1818 ***90.20*** *p153*
Rocheleau, Pierre; Quebec, 1649 ***9221.17*** *p208*
Rochelle, Adam 17; Ohio, 1880 ***4879.40*** *p257*
Rochelle, Amelia 3 *SEE* Rochelle, Eber
Rochelle, Eber 21; Ohio, 1880 ***4879.40*** *p257*
*Wife:*Elizabeth 23
*Daughter:*Amelia 3
Rochelle, Elizabeth 23 *SEE* Rochelle, Eber
Rochereau, Euge 27; New Orleans, 1840 ***778.6*** *p286*
Rochereau, Michel 24; Quebec, 1657 ***9221.17*** *p367*
Rocheron, Antoine; Quebec, 1657 ***9221.17*** *p367*
Rocheron, Gervais 23; Quebec, 1657 ***9221.17*** *p367*
*Sister:*Marie 18
*Brother:*Simon 24
Rocheron, Marie 18 *SEE* Rocheron, Gervais
Rocheron, Michel 24; Quebec, 1657 ***9221.17*** *p367*
Rocheron, Simon 24 *SEE* Rocheron, Gervais
Rochesfort, John; Havana, 1842 ***778.6*** *p286*
Rochester, Christian; Ohio, 1809-1852 ***4511.35*** *p44*
Rochester, Daniel; Ohio, 1809-1852 ***4511.35*** *p44*
Rochester, Elizabeth; America, 1754 ***1220.12*** *p684*
Rochester, Robert; America, 1735 ***1220.12*** *p684*
Rochester, Stephen; America, 1736 ***1220.12*** *p684*
Rocheteau, Suzanne 19; Quebec, 1661 ***9221.17*** *p467*
Rochford, John; Charles Town, SC, 1719 ***1220.12*** *p684*
Rochler, Simon; America, 1844 ***778.6*** *p286*
Rochmon, Olive 85; Ontario, 1871 ***1823.21*** *p315*
Rochon, Antoine; Quebec, 1657 ***9221.17*** *p367*
Rochon, Gervais 23; Quebec, 1657 ***9221.17*** *p367*
*Sister:*Marie 18
*Brother:*Simon 24
Rochon, Jean; Quebec, 1653 ***9221.17*** *p279*
Rochon, Marie 18 *SEE* Rochon, Gervais
Rochon, Simon 24 *SEE* Rochon, Gervais
Rochow, August 18; Galveston, TX, 1855 ***571.7*** *p16*
Rochow, Dorothea 54; Galveston, TX, 1855 ***571.7*** *p16*
Rochow, Johann 58; Galveston, TX, 1855 ***571.7*** *p16*
Rochow, Joseph 16; Galveston, TX, 1855 ***571.7*** *p16*
Rochow, Maria 26; Galveston, TX, 1855 ***571.7*** *p16*
Rochow, Wilhelm 20; Galveston, TX, 1855 ***571.7*** *p16*
Rochow, Wilhmine 21; Galveston, TX, 1855 ***571.7*** *p16*
Rochrige, Adam; Ohio, 1809-1852 ***4511.35*** *p44*
Rochwite, August; Wisconsin, 1896 ***6795.8*** *p82*
Rock, Ann; Boston, 1750 ***1642*** *p46*
Rock, Edward; America, 1769 ***1220.12*** *p684*
Rock, Edward; Maryland, 1720 ***1220.12*** *p684*
Rock, Frederick; Marblehead, MA, 1744 ***9228.50*** *p550*
*Wife:*Grace
Rock, Grace *SEE* Rock, Frederick
Rock, James 30; Ontario, 1871 ***1823.21*** *p315*
Rock, Johann Friedrich; America, 1866 ***5475.1*** *p308*
Rock, John; America, 1754 ***1220.12*** *p684*
Rock, John; Marblehead, MA, 1700-1799 ***9228.50*** *p550*
Rock, John; Salem, MA, 1686 ***9228.50*** *p550*
Rock, Joseph; America, 1772 ***1220.12*** *p684*
Rock, Mary; America, 1768 ***1220.12*** *p684*
Rock, Oliver 35; Ontario, 1871 ***1823.17*** *p141*
Rock, Samuel; Maryland, 1720 ***1220.12*** *p684*
Rock, Sarah; America, 1752 ***1220.12*** *p684*
Rockett, Robert; America, 1744 ***1220.12*** *p684*
Rockgaenger, Andreas; New York, 1860 ***358.56*** *p3*
Rockmann, William; New York, 1860 ***358.56*** *p5*
Rockorge, Adam; Ohio, 1809-1852 ***4511.35*** *p44*
Rocksburger, Maria 18; New York, NY, 1893 ***1883.7*** *p43*
Rockwell, Joan *SEE* Rockwell, William
Rockwell, John *SEE* Rockwell, William
Rockwell, Susan *SEE* Rockwell, William
Rockwell, William; Massachusetts, 1630 ***117.5*** *p154*
*Wife:*Susan
*Son:*John
*Daughter:*Joan
Rocour..., Richard; Quebec, 1659 ***9221.17*** *p409*
Rocourt, Catharine McMullen *SEE* Rocourt, John
Rocourt, John; New York, NY, 1856 ***8513.31*** *p423*
*Wife:*Catharine McMullen
Rocquert, William 30; Louisiana, 1840 ***778.6*** *p286*
Rocqueville, Charles; Montreal, 1660 ***9221.17*** *p443*
Rodack, Barbara 43; New York, NY, 1876 ***6954.7*** *p39*
Rodack, Catherina 14; New York, NY, 1876 ***6954.7*** *p39*
Rodack, Dorothea 8; New York, NY, 1876 ***6954.7*** *p39*
Rodack, Emelie 18; New York, NY, 1876 ***6954.7*** *p39*
Rodack, Emmanuel 7; New York, NY, 1876 ***6954.7*** *p39*
Rodack, Ephriam 28; New York, NY, 1876 ***6954.7*** *p39*
Rodack, Heinrich 9; New York, NY, 1876 ***6954.7*** *p39*
Rodack, Heinrich 21; New York, NY, 1876 ***6954.7*** *p39*
Rodack, Michael 21; New York, NY, 1876 ***6954.7*** *p39*
Rodailler, Rene; Montreal, 1653 ***9221.17*** *p300*
Rodan, Martha; America, 1729 ***1220.12*** *p684*
Rodd, Dorothy; America, 1754 ***1220.12*** *p684*
Rodd, John; America, 1757 ***1220.12*** *p684*
Rodd, Robert, Sr.; Virginia, 1732 ***1220.12*** *p684*
Rodda, James; America, 1862 ***9076.20*** *p68*
Rodda, John; America, 1773 ***1220.12*** *p684*
Roddam, Barbara; America, 1762 ***1220.12*** *p685*
Rodder, John; America, 1773 ***1220.12*** *p684*
Roddery, Jane; America, 1769 ***1220.12*** *p685*
Roddy, John 60; Ontario, 1871 ***1823.21*** *p315*
Roddy, John George 24; New York, NY, 1825 ***6178.50*** *p76*
Roddy, Mary 23; Michigan, 1880 ***4491.39*** *p25*
Roddy, Mary; Philadelphia, 1856 ***8513.31*** *p317*
Roddy, Patrick 65; Ontario, 1871 ***1823.21*** *p315*
Roddy, Thomas 32; Michigan, 1880 ***4491.39*** *p25*
Rode, Alexander 4; Texas, 1913 ***8425.16*** *p31*
Rode, Ernst Heinrich; Port uncertain, 1840 ***7420.1*** *p20*
Rode, Johannes 11; Texas, 1913 ***8425.16*** *p31*
Rode, Katharina 35; Texas, 1913 ***8425.16*** *p31*
Rode, Richard; America, 1760 ***1220.12*** *p668*
Rode, Rudolph; Wisconsin, 1908 ***1822.55*** *p10*
Rodel, Franz Eduard; America, 1848 ***5475.1*** *p476*
Rodell, Frank O. 21; Kansas, 1880 ***777.40*** *p17*
Rodelsperger, Peter; South Carolina, 1854 ***6155.4*** *p19*
Rodemacker, Carl Wilhelm; Cleveland, OH, 1896-1900 ***9722.10*** *p126*
Rodemich, Jakob; America, 1884 ***2526.43*** *p222*
Rodenbeck, August Ernst; Nebraska, 1885 ***7420.1*** *p348*
Rodenbeck, Ernst Heinrich Friedrich; America, 1881 ***7420.1*** *p324*
Rodenhausen, Friedrich 15 *SEE* Rodenhausen, Georg
Rodenhausen, Georg 38; America, 1854 ***2526.42*** *p137*
*Wife:*Maria Elisabetha Konig
*Child:*Magdalena 13
*Child:*Maria Elisabetha 6 months
*Child:*Friedrich 15
Rodenhausen, Georg Friedrich; Pennsylvania, 1753 ***2526.43*** *p126*
Rodenhausen, Leonhard; America, 1882 ***2526.43*** *p143*
Rodenhausen, Magdalena 13 *SEE* Rodenhausen, Georg
Rodenhausen, Maria Elisabetha Konig *SEE* Rodenhausen, Georg
Rodenhausen, Maria Elisabetha 6 *SEE* Rodenhausen, Georg
Rodenhauser, Lorenz 20; America, 1849 ***2526.42*** *p164*
Rodenhauser, Philipp; America, 1836 ***2526.43*** *p154*
With wife & children
Rodenwalther, Johann Georg; America, 1754 ***2526.42*** *p129*
With wife & 4 children
Roder, Anna Margarethe; America, 1867 ***7919.3*** *p529*
Roder, Christiane Elisabeth; America, 1868 ***7919.3*** *p532*
With child
Roder, Friedrich; America, 1855 ***2526.43*** *p199*
With wife & 2 children
Roder, Georg August; America, 1868 ***7919.3*** *p531*
Roder, Julius Hermann; Wisconsin, 1878 ***6795.8*** *p75*
Roder, Mathias Josef; Chicago, 1876 ***5475.1*** *p298*
Roderick, David *SEE* Roderick, Thomas

Roderick, Emanuel; North Carolina, 1849 *1088.45 p29*
Roderick, Evan *SEE* Roderick, Thomas
Roderick, Hannah *SEE* Roderick, Thomas
Roderick, James 45; Ontario, 1871 *1823.17 p141*
Roderick, Jane; Ohio, 1847 *4022.20 p282*
Roderick, John *SEE* Roderick, Thomas
Roderick, Margaret Thomas *SEE* Roderick, Thomas
Roderick, Mary *SEE* Roderick, Thomas
Roderick, Thomas *SEE* Roderick, Thomas
Roderick, Thomas; Ohio, 1837 *4022.20 p291*
  *Wife:*Margaret Thomas
  *Child:*Thomas
  *Child:*Hannah
  *Child:*Evan
  *Child:*David
  *Child:*William W.
  *Child:*Mary
  *Child:*John
Roderick, William W. *SEE* Roderick, Thomas
Roderigue, John; North Carolina, 1821 *1088.45 p29*
Roderigues, Manuel; North Carolina, 1848 *1088.45 p29*
Rodes, Francois; Louisiana, 1836-1840 *4981.45 p213*
Rodes, Mary; America, 1753 *1220.12 p668*
Rodes, Robert; America, 1764 *1220.12 p669*
Rodger, Mr.; British Columbia, 1910 *2897.7 p9*
Rodger, Alex; Quebec, 1910 *2897.7 p9*
Rodger, Ann; America, 1771 *1220.12 p685*
Rodger, Jane 23; Quebec, 1910 *2897.7 p9*
Rodgers, Abel 71; Ontario, 1871 *1823.21 p315*
Rodgers, E.; Quebec, 1870 *8364.32 p25*
Rodgers, J.; Quebec, 1870 *8364.32 p25*
Rodgers, James; Philadelphia, 1850 *8513.31 p423*
Rodgers, John; Ohio, 1836 *3580.20 p33*
Rodgers, John; Ohio, 1836 *6020.12 p22*
Rodgers, John; Ontario, 1835 *3160.1 p150*
Rodgers, John; Ontario, 1835 *3160.1 p150*
Rodgers, John 47; Ontario, 1871 *1823.21 p315*
Rodgers, John; Prescott, Ont., 1835 *3289.1 p61*
Rodgers, Joseph; America, 1722 *1220.12 p685*
Rodgers, Joseph; Ontario, 1835 *3160.1 p150*
Rodgers, Joseph; Prescott, Ont., 1835 *3289.1 p61*
Rodgers, Marg.ret 20; America, 1848 *778.6 p286*
Rodgers, Robert 45; Ontario, 1871 *1823.21 p315*
Rodgers, Thomas; America, 1769 *1220.12 p686*
Rodiger, Reinhard; America, 1867 *7919.3 p531*
Rodin, Gustaf; Charleston, SC, 1850 *6412.40 p152*
Rodin, J.; New York, NY, 1848 *6412.40 p151*
Roding, William; America, 1738 *1220.12 p685*
Rodney, Elizabeth 27; Ontario, 1871 *1823.21 p315*
Rodney, William 38; Ontario, 1871 *1823.17 p141*
Rodof, Anna Maria 2; America, 1847 *778.6 p286*
Rodof, Barbara 28; America, 1847 *778.6 p286*
Rodof, Jenny 30; America, 1847 *778.6 p286*
Rodolf, T.; Louisiana, 1836-1840 *4981.45 p213*
Rodore, Rene; Montreal, 1653 *9221.17 p300*
Rodriguez Baldamero, Mr. 20; America, 1842 *778.6 p286*
Rodriguez Vicamar, Mr. 38; America, 1842 *778.6 p286*
Rodriques, Arthur; Louisiana, 1874 *4981.45 p133*
Rodriquez, Manuel; Louisiana, 1836-1840 *4981.45 p213*
Rodstrom, Richard; Cleveland, OH, 1903-1906 *9722.10 p126*
Roduck, Robert 43; Ontario, 1871 *1823.17 p141*
Rodur, Auguste 31; America, 1842 *778.6 p286*
Rodway, Stephen; America, 1685 *1220.12 p685*
Rodway, Thomas 31; Ontario, 1871 *1823.21 p315*
Rody, Alexander 63; Ontario, 1871 *1823.17 p141*
Rody, John 38; Ontario, 1871 *1823.17 p141*
Roe, Edward 50; Ontario, 1871 *1823.21 p315*
Roe, George; North Carolina, 1858 *1088.45 p29*
Roe, Hannah; America, 1773 *1220.12 p690*
Roe, Hugh; America, 1720 *1220.12 p690*
Roe, James; America, 1710 *1220.12 p690*
Roe, James 23; Ontario, 1871 *1823.21 p315*
Roe, John; America, 1688 *1220.12 p690*
Roe, John; America, 1750 *1220.12 p690*
Roe, John; America, 1769 *1220.12 p690*
Roe, John; America, 1771 *1220.12 p690*
Roe, John 22; Maryland, 1721 *1220.12 p690*
Roe, Mary; America, 1744 *1220.12 p690*
Roe, Nicholas; America, 1747 *1220.12 p690*
Roe, Robert; America, 1740 *1220.12 p690*
Roe, Theopiles 46; Ontario, 1871 *1823.21 p315*
Roe, Tristin 53; Ontario, 1871 *1823.21 p315*
Roe, William; America, 1765 *1220.12 p690*
Roebbeke, Wilhelmine Louise Charlotte; America, 1881 *7420.1 p325*
Roebbeke, Wilhelmine Luise Charlotte; America, 1881 *7420.1 p325*
Roebel, Mr. 24; America, 1843 *778.6 p286*
Roebuck, Thomas; America, 1765 *1220.12 p685*
Roedel, David; Ohio, 1809-1852 *4511.35 p44*
Roedel, Peter; Illinois, 1853 *6079.1 p12*

Roedemeister, Heinrich Wilhelm; America, 1885 *7420.1 p348*
Roeder, Anna; America, 1882 *5475.1 p24*
Roeder, Anton 15 *SEE* Roeder, Michel
Roeder, Elisabeth 2 *SEE* Roeder, Michel
Roeder, Friedrich 8 *SEE* Roeder, Michel
Roeder, Ignatius *SEE* Roeder, Peter
Roeder, Johann 4 *SEE* Roeder, Michel
Roeder, John Jacob; Illinois, 1851 *6079.1 p12*
Roeder, Katharina *SEE* Roeder, Peter
Roeder, Katharina Weber 48 *SEE* Roeder, Michel
Roeder, Margarethe *SEE* Roeder, Peter
Roeder, Mathias *SEE* Roeder, Peter
Roeder, Mathias 19 *SEE* Roeder, Michel
Roeder, Michel 23 *SEE* Roeder, Michel
Roeder, Michel 46; America, 1855 *5475.1 p310*
  *Wife:*Katharina Weber 48
  *Daughter:*Elisabeth 2
  *Son:*Johann 4
  *Son:*Peter 22
  *Son:*Anton 15
  *Son:*Nikolaus 13
  *Son:*Friedrich 8
  *Son:*Mathias 19
  *Son:*Michel 23
Roeder, Nikolaus *SEE* Roeder, Peter
Roeder, Nikolaus 13 *SEE* Roeder, Michel
Roeder, Peter *SEE* Roeder, Peter
Roeder, Peter 22 *SEE* Roeder, Michel
Roeder, Peter 43; America, 1868 *5475.1 p253*
  *Wife:*Susanna Steuer 42
  *Daughter:*Katharina
  *Son:*Mathias
  *Son:*Ignatius
  *Daughter:*Margarethe
  *Son:*Nikolaus
  *Son:*Peter
Roeder, Susanna Steuer 42 *SEE* Roeder, Peter
Roehe, Engel Marie Sophie Charlotte; America, 1862 *7420.1 p214*
Roehl, Gustav; Wisconsin, 1882 *6795.8 p228*
Roehler, Hans Heinrich; America, 1881 *7420.1 p324*
Roehler, Johann Conrad; America, 1890 *7420.1 p361*
Roehrig, Johann 28; America, 1856 *5475.1 p288*
Roelke, Wm.; Venezuela, 1843 *3899.5 p547*
Roellinger, Joseph; Colorado, 1892 *1029.59 p78*
Roellinger, Joseph; Colorado, 1892 *1029.59 p78*
Roemmer, Emile 9; Missouri, 1846 *778.6 p286*
Roemmer, Gustave 19; Missouri, 1846 *778.6 p286*
Roemmer, Paulina 15; Missouri, 1846 *778.6 p286*
Roemmer, Rosalie 19; Missouri, 1846 *778.6 p286*
Roemmer, Sophia 17; Missouri, 1846 *778.6 p286*
Roenz, Reinhard J.; Wisconsin, 1876 *6795.8 p205*
Roeper, Johanna E. Rehder *SEE* Roeper, John J.
Roeper, John J.; Philadelphia, 1850 *8513.31 p423*
  *Wife:*Johanna E. Rehder
Roesch, Joseph; Miami, 1935 *4984.12 p39*
Roesch, Michel 21; America, 1846 *778.6 p286*
Roese, H.; New York, 1859-1860 *358.56 p102*
Roeser, A.; Galveston, TX, 1855 *571.7 p18*
Roeser, Mary; Philadelphia, 1878 *8513.31 p306*
Roesin, Sebastian; Ohio, 1809-1852 *4511.35 p44*
Roeske, Charles; Wisconsin, 1877 *6795.8 p75*
Roeske, Ernst Wilhelm; Wisconsin, 1896 *6795.8 p217*
Roesler, Johann; Wisconsin, 1856 *6795.8 p27*
Roesler, Wilhelm Heinrich; Wisconsin, 1859 *6795.8 p140*
Roessner, Barbara Fertig *SEE* Roessner, Francis
Roessner, Francis; Philadelphia, 1843 *8513.31 p423*
  *Wife:*Barbara Fertig
Roet, J. 28; America, 1847 *778.6 p286*
Roeyret, Thiebaut 34; America, 1840 *778.6 p286*
Roff, Robert; America, 1742 *1220.12 p685*
Roffe, Edward; America, 1722 *1220.12 p685*
Rogan, Catherine; New Orleans, 1850 *7242.30 p153*
Rogan, Hugh; New Orleans, 1850 *7242.30 p153*
Rogazumks, M. 52; America, 1847 *778.6 p286*
Rogazumks, Roger 21; America, 1847 *778.6 p286*
Roger, Ch...s 26; America, 1841 *778.6 p287*
Roger, Charles 19; Quebec, 1647 *9221.17 p189*
Roger, Christophe; Montreal, 1653 *9221.17 p300*
Roger, Claude; Quebec, 1652 *9221.17 p265*
Roger, Etienne 24; America, 1846 *778.6 p287*
Roger, Ferdinand; Wisconsin, 1878 *1495.20 p28*
  *Wife:*Marie Virginie Pire Docquir
Roger, Guillaume 29; Quebec, 1661 *9221.17 p467*
Roger, Heinrich Balthasar; America, 1882 *179.55 p19*
Roger, James 46; Ontario, 1871 *1823.17 p141*
Roger, Jean; Virginia, 1700 *9230.15 p80*
Roger, Johann; America, 1882 *179.55 p19*
Roger, Louis; Quebec, 1656 *9221.17 p346*
Roger, Maria Christina; America, 1882 *179.55 p19*

Roger, Marie Virginie Pire Docquir *SEE* Roger, Ferdinand
Roger, P. D. 45; Port uncertain, 1845 *778.6 p287*
Roger, Pierre 38; New Orleans, 1848 *778.6 p287*
Roger, Renee; Quebec, 1647 *9221.17 p181*
Roger, Vincent 48; America, 1843 *778.6 p287*
Rogers, Mr. 45; America, 1846 *778.6 p287*
Rogers, Abraham; America, 1755 *1220.12 p685*
Rogers, Alexander; America, 1679 *1220.12 p685*
Rogers, Andrew 29; Ontario, 1871 *1823.21 p315*
Rogers, Ann; America, 1691 *1220.12 p685*
Rogers, Ann 69; Ontario, 1871 *1823.17 p141*
Rogers, Arnold; America, 1746 *1220.12 p685*
Rogers, Benjamin; Virginia, 1734 *1220.12 p685*
Rogers, C. 41; America, 1843 *778.6 p287*
Rogers, Charles; America, 1775 *1220.12 p685*
Rogers, Charles; Boston, 1818 *3274.56 p70*
Rogers, Charles 47; Ontario, 1871 *1823.21 p315*
Rogers, Charles; Philadelphia, 1843 *8513.31 p424*
  *Wife:*Mary Neeley
Rogers, David; North Carolina, 1826 *1088.45 p29*
Rogers, Edward; America, 1753 *1220.12 p685*
Rogers, Edward 40; Ontario, 1871 *1823.21 p315*
Rogers, Elianor; America, 1756 *1220.12 p685*
Rogers, Elinor; Barbados or Jamaica, 1686 *1220.12 p685*
Rogers, Elizabeth 45; Ontario, 1871 *1823.21 p315*
Rogers, Emma M.; Philadelphia, 1851 *8513.31 p318*
Rogers, Francis; America, 1768 *1220.12 p685*
Rogers, Frederick C. 45; Ontario, 1871 *1823.21 p315*
Rogers, George 27; Ontario, 1871 *1823.21 p315*
Rogers, George 49; Ontario, 1871 *1823.21 p315*
Rogers, Grace; Maryland, 1719 *1220.12 p685*
Rogers, Hannah; Jamaica, 1716 *1220.12 p685*
Rogers, Henry; America, 1753 *1220.12 p685*
Rogers, Henry 35; Ontario, 1871 *1823.21 p315*
Rogers, James; America, 1739 *1220.12 p685*
Rogers, James; America, 1767 *1220.12 p685*
Rogers, James; America, 1775 *1220.12 p685*
Rogers, James; Annapolis, MD, 1731 *1220.12 p685*
Rogers, James; Louisiana, 1874-1875 *4981.45 p30*
Rogers, James; Ohio, 1809-1852 *4511.35 p44*
Rogers, James 33; Ontario, 1871 *1823.21 p316*
Rogers, James 35; Ontario, 1871 *1823.17 p141*
Rogers, James 63; Ontario, 1871 *1823.21 p315*
Rogers, James H.; Ohio, 1809-1852 *4511.35 p44*
Rogers, Jane; Barbados, 1668 *1220.12 p685*
Rogers, Joan; America, 1761 *1220.12 p685*
Rogers, John; America, 1685 *1220.12 p685*
Rogers, John; America, 1726 *1220.12 p685*
Rogers, John; America, 1730 *1220.12 p685*
Rogers, John; America, 1757 *1220.12 p685*
Rogers, John; America, 1763 *1220.12 p685*
Rogers, John; America, 1772 *1220.12 p685*
Rogers, John; America, 1774 *1220.12 p685*
Rogers, John; America, 1775 *1220.12 p685*
Rogers, John; Annapolis, MD, 1719 *1220.12 p685*
Rogers, John; Annapolis, MD, 1736 *1220.12 p685*
Rogers, John; Barbados, 1668 *1220.12 p685*
Rogers, John; Marston's Wharf, 1779 *8529.30 p15*
Rogers, John; Maryland, 1725 *1220.12 p685*
Rogers, John; Ohio, 1809-1852 *4511.35 p44*
Rogers, John 21; Ontario, 1871 *1823.17 p142*
Rogers, John 21; Ontario, 1871 *1823.21 p316*
Rogers, John 24; Ontario, 1871 *1823.21 p316*
Rogers, John; Virginia, 1732 *1220.12 p685*
Rogers, Jonathan; America, 1739 *1220.12 p685*
Rogers, Joseph; Annapolis, MD, 1735 *1220.12 p686*
Rogers, Joseph *SEE* Rogers, Thomas
Rogers, Miss M.; Montreal, 1922 *4514.4 p32*
Rogers, Mary; America, 1770 *1220.12 p686*
Rogers, Mary; New York, NY, 1852 *8513.31 p426*
Rogers, Mary Neeley *SEE* Rogers, Charles
Rogers, Michael; America, 1772 *1220.12 p686*
Rogers, Patrick; North Carolina, 1792-1862 *1088.45 p29*
Rogers, Peter; New York, 1782 *8529.30 p15*
Rogers, Philip; America, 1750 *1220.12 p686*
Rogers, Richard; Annapolis, MD, 1730 *1220.12 p686*
Rogers, Richard; Barbados, 1671 *1220.12 p686*
Rogers, Robert; America, 1682 *1220.12 p686*
Rogers, Robert; America, 1752 *1220.12 p686*
Rogers, Robert; Barbados or Jamaica, 1684 *1220.12 p686*
Rogers, Sarah; America, 1760 *1220.12 p686*
Rogers, Sarah E. 51; Michigan, 1880 *4491.30 p26*
Rogers, Stephen; America, 1767 *1220.12 p686*
Rogers, Stephen; Virginia, 1617 *1220.12 p686*
Rogers, Stephen Lauren; Boston, 1898 *1029.59 p78*
Rogers, Thomas; America, 1688 *1220.12 p686*
Rogers, Thomas; America, 1691 *1220.12 p686*
Rogers, Thomas; America, 1726 *1220.12 p686*
Rogers, Thomas; America, 1729 *1220.12 p686*
Rogers, Thomas; America, 1750 *1220.12 p686*
Rogers, Thomas; America, 1753 *1220.12 p686*
Rogers, Thomas; America, 1774 *1220.12 p686*

Rogers, Thomas; Annapolis, MD, 1730 *1220.12 p686*
Rogers, Thomas; Barbados, 1682 *1220.12 p686*
Rogers, Thomas; Barbados or Jamaica, 1698 *1220.12 p686*
Rogers, Thomas 19; Ontario, 1871 *1823.21 p316*
Rogers, Thomas 33; Ontario, 1871 *1823.21 p316*
Rogers, Thomas; Plymouth, MA, 1620 *1920.45 p5*
*Son:*Joseph
Rogers, Thomas W.; Washington, 1889 *2770.40 p80*
Rogers, Walter I.; Miami, 1920 *4984.15 p38*
Rogers, Walter M. 31; Ontario, 1871 *1823.17 p142*
Rogers, William; America, 1741 *1220.12 p686*
Rogers, William; America, 1752 *1220.12 p686*
Rogers, William; Annapolis, MD, 1726 *1220.12 p686*
Rogers, William; Annapolis, MD, 1735 *1220.12 p686*
Rogers, William 24; Ontario, 1871 *1823.17 p142*
Rogers, William 91; Ontario, 1871 *1823.21 p316*
Rogers, William; Virginia, 1734 *1220.12 p686*
Rogers, William S. 41; Ontario, 1871 *1823.21 p316*
Rogers, Wm 41; Ontario, 1871 *1823.17 p142*
Rogers, Wynne; Louisiana, 1841-1844 *4981.45 p211*
Rogerson, William 53; Ontario, 1871 *1823.21 p316*
Roggow, August; Wisconsin, 1879 *6795.8 p228*
Rogowski, Jozef 28; New York, NY, 1903 *8355.1 p15*
Roguffeo, A. 18; America, 1847 *778.6 p287*
Rogus, James H.; Ohio, 1809-1852 *4511.35 p44*
Rogus, John; Ohio, 1809-1852 *4511.35 p44*
Rohan, Bridget B.; Beverly, MA, 1824-1845 *9228.50 p441*
Rohde, Auguste; Valdivia, Chile, 1851 *1192.4 p51*
Rohde, Gustav; Wisconsin, 1897 *6795.8 p124*
Rohde, Hermann; Chile, 1852 *1192.4 p52*
Rohde, John; New York, 1860 *358.56 p6*
Rohde, Juliass; Washington, 1885 *2770.40 p194*
Rohde, Ottilie Mathilde; Wisconsin, 1896 *6795.8 p150*
Rohe, Widow; America, 1852 *7420.1 p96*
With son
Rohe, Heinrich Christoph; America, 1866 *7420.1 p248*
With family
Rohe, Max Heinrich; Iowa, 1866-1932 *1211.15 p18*
Rohen, Catharine; America, 1852 *7420.1 p96*
Rohick, Barnaby; Virginia, 1736 *1220.12 p686*
Rohl, Heinrich 2; Portland, ME, 1911 *970.38 p80*
Rohl, Maria 9; Portland, ME, 1911 *970.38 p80*
Rohl, Maria 25; Portland, ME, 1911 *970.38 p80*
Rohlacher, Caspar; America, 1867 *7919.3 p531*
Rohlacher, Christoph; America, 1867 *7919.3 p531*
Rohle, Carl Friedrich; America, 1866 *7420.1 p248*
*Brother:*Christian Louis
Rohle, Christian Louis *SEE* Rohle, Carl Friedrich
Rohler, Catharina Marie *SEE* Rohler, Friedrich Christian
Rohler, Friedrich Christian; America, 1867 *7420.1 p263*
*Sister:*Catharina Marie
Rohler, Friedrich Wilhelm; California, 1865 *7420.1 p236*
Rohler, Hans Heinrich; America, 1848 *7420.1 p61*
*Brother:*Johann Conrad
Rohler, Heinrich; America, 1856 *7420.1 p152*
Rohler, Johann Conrad *SEE* Rohler, Hans Heinrich
Rohler, Johann Friedrich; America, 1867 *7420.1 p263*
Rohlffs, Ernst; Chile, 1852 *1192.4 p55*
With wife
Rohlwing, Johann Heinrich Christoph; America, 1846 *7420.1 p48*
Rohlwing, Wilhelm; America, 1881 *7420.1 p324*
Rohmeier, Friedrich Wilhelm; America, 1857 *7420.1 p171*
Rohr, Adam; America, 1867 *5475.1 p201*
*Wife:*Maria Wolf
*Son:*Nikolaus
*Daughter:*Anna
*Son:*Johann
*Son:*Peter
*Son:*Michel
*Daughter:*Maria
With son
Rohr, Adam; Ohio, 1809-1852 *4511.35 p44*
Rohr, Anna *SEE* Rohr, Adam
Rohr, Celestine 7; Missouri, 1845 *778.6 p287*
Rohr, Constant 3; Missouri, 1845 *778.6 p287*
Rohr, Henry; Ohio, 1809-1852 *4511.35 p44*
Rohr, Jean 55; Missouri, 1845 *778.6 p287*
Rohr, Jean-Bapte. 13; Missouri, 1845 *778.6 p287*
Rohr, Johann *SEE* Rohr, Adam
Rohr, Louis 9; Missouri, 1845 *778.6 p287*
Rohr, Maria *SEE* Rohr, Adam
Rohr, Maria Wolf 58 *SEE* Rohr, Adam
Rohr, Marianne 16; Missouri, 1845 *778.6 p287*
Rohr, Marianne 44; Missouri, 1845 *778.6 p287*
Rohr, Michael; Ohio, 1809-1852 *4511.35 p44*
Rohr, Michel *SEE* Rohr, Adam
Rohr, Nikolaus *SEE* Rohr, Adam
Rohr, Peter *SEE* Rohr, Adam
Rohr, Rosalie 11; Missouri, 1845 *778.6 p287*

Rohrbach, Johann Reinhard 50; America, 1849 *170.15 p40*
With 2 children
Rohrberg, A.; New York, 1860 *358.56 p4*
Rohrelsh, Antony 27; Port uncertain, 1846 *778.6 p287*
Rohrer, Edmond 1; Louisiana, 1848 *778.6 p287*
Rohrer, Eve 25; Louisiana, 1848 *778.6 p287*
Rohrer, Joseph 26; Louisiana, 1848 *778.6 p287*
Rohrig, Coonrod; New Jersey, 1773-1774 *927.31 p3*
Rohring, George; Nova Scotia, 1784 *7105 p25*
Rohrkasse, Christian Gottlieb; America, 1860 *7420.1 p199*
Rohrkasse, Heinrich Wilhelm August; Port uncertain, 1887 *7420.1 p354*
Rohrkaste, Miss; America, 1859 *7420.1 p188*
Rohrkasten, Anne Sophie Eleonore; America, 1851 *7420.1 p82*
Rohrkasten, Carl; America, 1893 *7420.1 p369*
Rohrkasten, Ernst; America, 1868 *7420.1 p276*
Rohrkasten, Friedrich; America, 1846 *7420.1 p48*
With family
Rohrkasten, Friedrich; America, 1860 *7420.1 p199*
With wife
Rohrkasten, Sophia Justina Louisa; America, 1859 *7420.1 p187*
Rohrmann, Augustin; Philadelphia, 1778 *8529.30 p5A*
Rohrmann, Augustus; New York, 1778 *8529.30 p5A*
Rohrmann, Johann; America, 1882 *5475.1 p147*
Rohrsen, Widow; America, 1874 *7420.1 p304*
*Son:*Hans Heinrich Gottlieb
Rohrsen, Carl Heinrich Friedrich; America, 1873 *7420.1 p301*
Rohrsen, Christine Louise *SEE* Rohrsen, Johann Otto
Rohrsen, Engel Mar. Dorothee *SEE* Rohrsen, Johann Otto
Rohrsen, Engel Marie; America, 1848 *7420.1 p61*
Rohrsen, Engel Marie Glade *SEE* Rohrsen, Johann Otto
Rohrsen, Engel Marie Soph. *SEE* Rohrsen, Johann Otto
Rohrsen, Hans Heinr. Phil. *SEE* Rohrsen, Johann Otto
Rohrsen, Hans Heinrich Gottlieb *SEE* Rohrsen, Widow
Rohrsen, Johann Conrad; America, 1854 *7420.1 p128*
*Son:*Johann Heinrich Christoph
With family
Rohrsen, Johann Heinr. Christ. *SEE* Rohrsen, Johann Otto
Rohrsen, Johann Heinrich Christoph *SEE* Rohrsen, Johann Conrad
Rohrsen, Johann Heinrich Christoph; Port uncertain, 1854 *7420.1 p128*
Rohrsen, Johann Otto; America, 1855 *7420.1 p141*
*Wife:*Engel Marie Glade
*Daughter:*Engel Marie Soph.
*Son:*Hans Heinr. Phil.
*Son:*Johann Heinr. Christ.
*Daughter:*Christine Louise
*Daughter:*Engel Mar. Dorothee
Rohrsen, Katharine Engel; America, 1853 *7420.1 p108*
Rohxbacher, Michel 19; Port uncertain, 1840 *778.6 p287*
Roian, Dennis; Boston, 1765 *1642 p35*
Roignon, Vincent; New Jersey, 1660-1669 *9228.50 p564*
Roissier, Henry; Wisconsin, 1855 *9228.50 p550*
Roissy, Henry; Wisconsin, 1855 *9228.50 p550*
Rojan, Johann 20; New York, 1880 *5475.1 p420*
Rojek, Jacob 27; New York, NY, 1904 *8355.1 p15*
Roland, Constant; Illinois, 1857 *6079.1 p12*
Roland, John 41; Ontario, 1871 *1823.21 p316*
Roland, Nicole 16; Quebec, 1654 *9221.17 p316*
Roland, Victor Joseph; Illinois, 1857 *6079.1 p12*
Rolay, Madeleine; Quebec, 1659 *9221.17 p409*
Rolestone, Roger 61; Ontario, 1871 *1823.17 p142*
Roley, John; America, 1775 *1220.12 p691*
Rolf, John; America, 1742 *1220.12 p686*
Rolfas, William; Ohio, 1809-1852 *4511.35 p44*
Rolfe, Arthur F. N.; North Carolina, 1851 *1088.45 p29*
Rolfe, Edward; America, 1772 *1220.12 p686*
Rolfe, Henry 42; Ontario, 1871 *1823.21 p316*
Rolfe, John; America, 1767 *1220.12 p686*
Rolfe, Joseph 69; Ontario, 1871 *1823.21 p316*
Rolfe, Mary; America, 1741 *1220.12 p686*
Rolfe, Thomas; America, 1721 *1220.12 p686*
Rolfe, Thomas; America, 1734 *1220.12 p686*
Rolfe, William 47; Ontario, 1871 *1823.21 p316*
Rolinger, Peter; America, 1864 *5475.1 p365*
Roll, Jakob *SEE* Roll, Matthaus
Roll, Matthaus; Dakota, 1864-1918 *554.30 p25*
*Wife:*Rosina Wehr
*Child:*Jakob
Roll, Rosina Wehr *SEE* Roll, Matthaus
Rolland, Mrs. 30; America, 1847 *778.6 p287*
Rolland, L. 35; America, 1847 *778.6 p287*
Rolland, Michel 30; America, 1841 *778.6 p287*
Rollande, Julien 25; America, 1846 *778.6 p287*
Rolle, Barbe 8; Missouri, 1845 *778.6 p287*

Rolle, Catherine 2; Missouri, 1845 *778.6 p287*
Rolle, Catherine 27; Missouri, 1845 *778.6 p287*
Rolle, Claude 37; Missouri, 1845 *778.6 p287*
Rolle, Emile 6; Missouri, 1845 *778.6 p287*
Rolle, Jean 22; Quebec, 1657 *9221.17 p368*
Roller, Jacques 28; Louisiana, 1848 *778.6 p287*
Roller, Louise 26; Louisiana, 1848 *778.6 p287*
Rolles, William; America, 1750 *1220.12 p691*
Rollet, J. 14; New Orleans, 1848 *778.6 p288*
Rollet, J. 70; New Orleans, 1848 *778.6 p288*
Rollet, Jno. 68; America, 1844 *778.6 p288*
Rollet, Marie; Quebec, 1617 *9221.17 p18*
Rollet, Marie; Quebec, 1617 *9221.17 p19*
*Husband:*Louis
Rollhusen, Salomon 63; New York, NY, 1893 *1883.7 p44*
Rollin, Isidore; New York, NY, 1871 *1494.20 p11*
Rolling, George 40; Ontario, 1871 *1823.21 p316*
Rollinger, Peter; America, 1864 *5475.1 p249*
Rollings, Richard; New York, 1776 *8529.30 p15*
Rollins, Henry 60; Ontario, 1871 *1823.21 p316*
Rollins, Richard; New York, 1778 *8529.30 p5A*
Rollins, Robert 60; Ontario, 1871 *1823.21 p316*
Rollinson, Mary Jane McCracken *SEE* Rollinson, Robert
Rollinson, Robert; Philadelphia, 1847 *8513.31 p424*
*Wife:*Mary Jane McCracken
Rollo, Marianna 51; New Orleans, 1847 *778.6 p288*
Rolloff, C. W. F.; Louisiana, 1874-1875 *4981.45 p30*
Rolls, Francis; America, 1677 *1220.12 p691*
Rolls, Francis; America, 1753 *1220.12 p691*
Rolls, James; America, 1752 *1220.12 p691*
Rolls, John; America, 1738 *1220.12 p691*
Rolls, John; America, 1772 *1220.12 p691*
Rolls, William 55; Ontario, 1871 *1823.21 p316*
Rollton, W. 30; Ontario, 1871 *1823.21 p316*
Rolph, David 46; Ontario, 1871 *1823.21 p316*
Rolph, Elizabeth; America, 1757 *1220.12 p686*
Rolph, Elizabeth 40; Ontario, 1871 *1823.21 p316*
Rolph, James 58; Ontario, 1871 *1823.21 p316*
Rolph, Sarah A. 19; Ontario, 1871 *1823.21 p316*
Rolph, Thomas; America, 1772 *1220.12 p686*
Rolph, William; Barbados or Jamaica, 1690 *1220.12 p686*
Rolphe, Peregrine; Barbados or Jamaica, 1687 *1220.12 p686*
Rolston, Eliza 50; Ontario, 1871 *1823.17 p142*
Rolston, James 50; Ontario, 1871 *1823.17 p142*
Rolstone, William 63; Ontario, 1871 *1823.17 p142*
Rolt, John; America, 1767 *1220.12 p687*
Romaillot, Mr. 36; Louisiana, 1848 *778.6 p288*
Romain, Mr. 28; New Orleans, 1848 *778.6 p288*
Romain, Henriette 40; America, 1845 *778.6 p288*
Romainville, Jean 30; Quebec, 1661 *9221.17 p449*
Romak, Anna; Detroit, 1929 *1640.55 p113*
Roman, Augustin; Philadelphia, 1778 *8529.30 p5A*
Roman, Karol; Detroit, 1929-1930 *6214.5 p71*
Roman, M.; Louisiana, 1874 *4981.45 p296*
Roman, Michel; Louisiana, 1841-1844 *4981.45 p211*
Romana, A. B.; North Carolina, 1855 *1088.45 p29*
Romane, Elizabeth; Rappahannock, VA, 1729 *1220.12 p687*
Romaniuk, Jennie Romaniuk *SEE* Romaniuk, Kasian
Romaniuk, Kasian; Detroit, 1929-1930 *6214.5 p63*
*Wife:*Jennie Romaniuk
Romann, Rosalie 24; Port uncertain, 1847 *778.6 p288*
Romanstoe, John; America, 1686 *1220.12 p687*
Romare, P.; New York, NY, 1847 *6412.40 p149*
Rome, Catharine M. 42; Ontario, 1871 *1823.21 p316*
Rome, George 50; Ontario, 1871 *1823.21 p316*
Romelius, Pierre 23; Quebec, 1661 *9221.17 p467*
Romeo, Pasquale; New York, 1926 *1173.1 p2*
Romer, Anna Margarethe; America, 1879 *8115.12 p325*
Romer, Heinrich; Port uncertain, 1858 *7420.1 p181*
Romeril, . . .; America, 1780 *9228.50 p552*
Romeril, Charles Abraham *SEE* Romeril, Marie Ann Billot
Romeril, Charles Durell *SEE* Romeril, Pierre
Romeril, Edwin; New York, 1947 *9228.50 p174*
*Wife:*Linda Lucy De Broder
*Son:*Robert Francis Philip
With son
Romeril, Edwin; New York, 1947 *9228.50 p552*
Romeril, Fanny Mary Ann *SEE* Romeril, Marie Ann Billot
Romeril, George; Utah, 1851 *9228.50 p552*
Romeril, J. Philip; Ohio, 1795-1850 *9228.50 p551*
Romeril, Jane Nancy *SEE* Romeril, Marie Ann Billot
Romeril, John; Ohio, 1822 *9228.50 p551*
Romeril, Linda Lucy De Broder *SEE* Romeril, Edwin
Romeril, Marie Ann; Salt Lake City, 1855 *9228.50 p552*
*Child:*Jane Nancy
*Child:*Sophia Jane

*Child:*Charles Abraham
*Child:*Fanny Mary Ann
Romeril, Matthieu; New England, 1650-1685 ***9228.50*** *p552*
Romeril, Matthieu; New England, 1685 ***9228.50*** *p551*
Romeril, Pierre; Salt Lake City, 1852-1880 ***9228.50*** *p552*
*Child:*Charles Durell
Romeril, Robert Francis Philip *SEE* Romeril, Edwin
Romeril, Simon; Salem, MA, 1660-1679 ***9228.50*** *p550*
Romeril, Sophia Jane *SEE* Romeril, Marie Ann Billot
Romhild, Elise; America, 1868 ***7919.3*** *p531*
Romier, Joseph; America, 1872 ***1494.20*** *p12*
Romieux, Pierre 23; Quebec, 1661 ***9221.17*** *p467*
Romine, Marie 64; Missouri, 1846 ***778.6*** *p288*
Rominet, Pierre 23; Quebec, 1661 ***9221.17*** *p467*
Rominger, Limon 32; Port uncertain, 1845 ***778.6*** *p288*
Rominis, M..ie 25; New Orleans, 1841 ***778.6*** *p288*
Rominis, Pedro 35; New Orleans, 1841 ***778.6*** *p288*
Rommann, Frederick; Ohio, 1840-1897 ***8365.35*** *p17*
Rommel, Andreas; America, 1867 ***7919.3*** *p527*
With wife & 2 children
Rommel, Carl Friedrich; America, 1867 ***7919.3*** *p529*
Rommel, Caspar Friedrich; America, 1867 ***7919.3*** *p535*
With wife & 5 children
Rommel, Catharine; America, 1867 ***7919.3*** *p527*
Rommel, Christine Margarethe; America, 1868 ***7919.3*** *p524*
*Sister:*Maria Barbara
Rommel, Friedrich Augut Albert; America, 1867 ***7919.3*** *p526*
Rommel, George; New York, 1860 ***358.56*** *p150*
Rommel, Maria Barbara *SEE* Rommel, Christine Margarethe
Rommel, Sophie; America, 1867 ***7919.3*** *p529*
Rommelfangen, Helena Goehl *SEE* Rommelfangen, Johann Peter
Rommelfangen, Johann Peter; America, 1880 ***5475.1*** *p194*
*Wife:*Helena Goehl
*Daughter:*Margarethe
*Daughter:*Katharina
Rommelfangen, Katharina *SEE* Rommelfangen, Johann Peter
Rommelfangen, Margarethe *SEE* Rommelfangen, Johann Peter
Romney, Tho. 19; Virginia, 1635 ***1183.3*** *p30*
Rompass, Fredk 47; Ontario, 1871 ***1823.21*** *p316*
Romph, . . .; Ontario, 1871 ***1823.21*** *p316*
Romph, George 21; Ontario, 1871 ***1823.17*** *p142*
Romph, Jacob 52; Ontario, 1871 ***1823.17*** *p142*
Romquist, Jacob; North America, 1857 ***6410.15*** *p105*
Romstein, Joseph; Louisiana, 1874 ***4981.45*** *p296*
Romuald, Ferdinande *SEE* Romuald, Gaspard
Romuald, Gaspard; Wisconsin, 1855-1870 ***1495.20*** *p8*
*Wife:*Marie Therese Decamp
*Child:*Gislain
*Child:*Ferdinande
Romuald, Gislain *SEE* Romuald, Gaspard
Romuald, Marie Therese Decamp *SEE* Romuald, Gaspard
Romulus, Pierre 23; Quebec, 1661 ***9221.17*** *p467*
Ronald, Alexander 52; Ontario, 1871 ***1823.21*** *p316*
Ronan, Hugh; South Carolina, 1808 ***6155.4*** *p19*
Ronan, Mary 86; Ontario, 1871 ***1823.21*** *p316*
Ronan, Patrick 44; Ontario, 1871 ***1823.21*** *p316*
Rond, Susan; Barbados or Jamaica, 1677 ***1220.12*** *p687*
Rondez, Jean 29; America, 1846 ***778.6*** *p288*
Rondez, Michel; Louisiana, 1836-1840 ***4981.45*** *p213*
Rondin, Jean 19; Quebec, 1659 ***9221.17*** *p409*
Rone, Katty 17; Michigan, 1880 ***4491.30*** *p26*
Ronerd, Francis; New York, 1860 ***358.56*** *p4*
Roney, Alice; America, 1765 ***1220.12*** *p687*
Rong, Helena 18; New York, NY, 1912 ***8355.1*** *p16*
Rong, John; New York, 1860 ***358.56*** *p4*
Rongret, Bridgett 50; Michigan, 1880 ***4491.30*** *p27*
Rongret, Jerry 70; Michigan, 1880 ***4491.30*** *p27*
Roning, John; America, 1750 ***1220.12*** *p687*
Ronna, Joseph 19; Port uncertain, 1846 ***778.6*** *p288*
Ronna, Joseph 45; Port uncertain, 1846 ***778.6*** *p288*
Ronnalls, Joseph 27; Ontario, 1871 ***1823.21*** *p316*
Ronnberg, Alma; Cleveland, OH, 1888-1906 ***9722.10*** *p126*
Ronner, August 10 months; New York, NY, 1893 ***1883.7*** *p41*
Ronner, John H.; Illinois, 1852 ***6079.1*** *p12*
Ronner, Lene 6; New York, NY, 1893 ***1883.7*** *p41*
Ronner, Luder; Illinois, 1852 ***6079.1*** *p12*
Ronner, Ludwig 8; New York, NY, 1893 ***1883.7*** *p41*
Ronner, Michael 2; New York, NY, 1893 ***1883.7*** *p41*
Ronner, Stanislaw 34; New York, NY, 1893 ***1883.7*** *p41*
Ronner, Wilhelmina 32; New York, NY, 1893 ***1883.7*** *p41*
Ronsewell, Thomas; America, 1685 ***1220.12*** *p687*
Ronssell, John J.; Ohio, 1809-1852 ***4511.35*** *p44*
Rood, Edward; America, 1752 ***1220.12*** *p687*
Rood, Jesse; Colorado, 1883 ***1029.59*** *p78*
Roodgers, Henry; Missouri, 1886 ***3276.1*** *p2*
Roof, Adam; Ohio, 1809-1852 ***4511.35*** *p44*
Roof, Sarah; Died enroute, 1734 ***1220.12*** *p687*
Rook, Ann; Virginia, 1727 ***1220.12*** *p687*
Rook, John; America, 1774 ***1220.12*** *p687*
Rook, Thomas; America, 1763 ***1220.12*** *p687*
Rook, Thomas; America, 1772 ***1220.12*** *p687*
Rook, William; America, 1726 ***1220.12*** *p687*
Rook, William; America, 1765 ***1220.12*** *p687*
Rooke, Henry; America, 1685 ***1220.12*** *p687*
Rooke, Henry; America, 1748 ***1220.12*** *p687*
Rooke, Joseph; America, 1755 ***1220.12*** *p687*
Rooke, Ralph; Virginia, 1618 ***1220.12*** *p687*
Rooke, Richard, Jr.; America, 1772 ***1220.12*** *p687*
Rooke, Susannah; America, 1770 ***1220.12*** *p687*
Rooker, William; America, 1775 ***1220.12*** *p687*
Rookes, Elizabeth; America, 1739 ***1220.12*** *p687*
Rooklidge, Mary 45; Ontario, 1871 ***1823.21*** *p316*
Rooks, John 50; Ontario, 1871 ***1823.21*** *p316*
Rooks, William H. 38; Ontario, 1871 ***1823.21*** *p316*
Rooks, William H. 39; Ontario, 1871 ***1823.21*** *p316*
Room, John; America, 1753 ***1220.12*** *p687*
Room, Robert 35; Ontario, 1871 ***1823.21*** *p316*
Rooney, Rose 60; Ontario, 1871 ***1823.17*** *p142*
Roos, Antoine; Quebec, 1639 ***9221.17*** *p92*
Roos, Aron 21; Port uncertain, 1847 ***778.6*** *p288*
Roos, Aron 32; Port uncertain, 1847 ***778.6*** *p288*
Roos, Bo C. H-n; New York, NY, 1851 ***6412.40*** *p153*
Roos, Charles Rudolph; Louisiana, 1874 ***4981.45*** *p134*
Roos, Georg 30; America, 1847 ***778.6*** *p288*
Roos, Isidor; Texas, 1908 ***3435.45*** *p36*
Roos, Jakob; America, 1866 ***5475.1*** *p534*
Roos, Johann 25; Port uncertain, 1847 ***778.6*** *p288*
Roos, Leon 11; Port uncertain, 1847 ***778.6*** *p288*
Roos, Salomon 22; Port uncertain, 1847 ***778.6*** *p288*
Roos, W.A.; New York, NY, 1851 ***6412.40*** *p152*
Roose, A. 10; New Orleans, 1834 ***1002.51*** *p111*
Roose, Miss A. 40; New Orleans, 1834 ***1002.51*** *p111*
Roose, G. 4; New Orleans, 1834 ***1002.51*** *p111*
Roose, J. 19; New Orleans, 1834 ***1002.51*** *p111*
Roose, M. 12; New Orleans, 1834 ***1002.51*** *p111*
Roose, M. 44; New Orleans, 1834 ***1002.51*** *p111*
Roose, V. 15; New Orleans, 1834 ***1002.51*** *p111*
Roose, William; Virginia, 1719 ***1220.12*** *p689*
Roos Family ; America, 1853 ***5475.1*** *p51*
Rooston, George; America, 1765 ***1220.12*** *p687*
Root, Austin 70; Ontario, 1871 ***1823.21*** *p316*
Root, Daniel 100; Ontario, 1871 ***1823.17*** *p142*
Root, Ephraim, Jr.; Ohio, 1818 ***3580.20*** *p33*
Root, Ephraim, Jr.; Ohio, 1818 ***6020.12*** *p22*
Root, George; America, 1765 ***1220.12*** *p687*
Root, Harriet A. 35; Michigan, 1880 ***4491.39*** *p26*
Root, Nathan 38; Ontario, 1871 ***1823.21*** *p317*
Root, Sarah 84; Ontario, 1871 ***1823.17*** *p142*
Rootham, John; America, 1736 ***1220.12*** *p687*
Roots, Henry 59; Ontario, 1871 ***1823.21*** *p317*
Roots, John 54; Ontario, 1871 ***1823.21*** *p317*
Roots, Richard 64; Ontario, 1871 ***1823.21*** *p317*
Roots, William 18; Ontario, 1871 ***1823.21*** *p317*
Ropcke, Johann Friedrich; Wisconsin, 1882 ***6795.8*** *p93*
Ropenack, Friedrich; Port uncertain, 1837 ***7420.1*** *p13*
Ropenack, Heinrich; America, 1868 ***7420.1*** *p276*
Ropenack, Wilhelmine Charlotte Caroline; America, 1874 ***7420.1*** *p303*
Roper, Christins 11; Halifax, N.S., n.d. ***1833.5*** *p7*
Roper, Christins 11 *SEE* Roper, Emily
Roper, Doris 7; Halifax, N.S., n.d. ***1833.5*** *p7*
Roper, Doris 7 *SEE* Roper, Emily
Roper, Emily 32; Halifax, N.S., n.d. ***1833.5*** *p7*
Roper, Emily 32; Halifax, N.S., n.d. ***8445.10*** *p7*
*Relative:*Doris 7
*Relative:*Christins 11
Roper, Hannah 73; Ontario, 1871 ***1823.21*** *p317*
Roper, Henry; America, 1685 ***1220.12*** *p687*
Roper, James; America, 1771 ***1220.12*** *p687*
Roper, Richard; America, 1742 ***1220.12*** *p687*
Roper, Richard; Annapolis, MD, 1730 ***1220.12*** *p687*
Ropert, Francois 28; New Orleans, 1848 ***778.6*** *p288*
Ropke, Ernst; Port uncertain, 1852 ***7420.1*** *p91*
With wife
Ropke, Ludwig; America, 1867 ***7420.1*** *p263*
Ropp, Louis 39; Indiana, 1881-1888 ***9076.20*** *p72*
Roque, Pierre Jean 25; Port uncertain, 1846 ***778.6*** *p288*
Roquer, L. 25; New Orleans, 1848 ***778.6*** *p288*
Roques, Mathien; Louisiana, 1874-1875 ***4981.45*** *p30*
Roquet, Antoine 25; Port uncertain, 1848 ***778.6*** *p288*
Rorich, Franz 35; Baltimore, 1889 ***8425.16*** *p36*
Rorich, Magdel 9 months; Baltimore, 1889 ***8425.16*** *p36*
Rorich, Marie 4; Baltimore, 1889 ***8425.16*** *p36*
Rorich, Marie 35; Baltimore, 1889 ***8425.16*** *p36*
Rorich, Michal 3; Baltimore, 1889 ***8425.16*** *p36*
Rorick, Peter 30; Ontario, 1871 ***1823.21*** *p317*
Rork, Mary; Boston, 1739 ***1642*** *p45*
Rorke, John; America, 1753 ***1220.12*** *p687*
Rorke, John; North Carolina, 1828 ***1088.45*** *p29*
Ros, Ane 76; Ontario, 1871 ***1823.21*** *p317*
Rosaile, Gabriel 25; Port uncertain, 1841 ***778.6*** *p288*
Rosaker, Detlef; Iowa, 1896 ***1211.15*** *p18*
Rosamond, John; Annapolis, MD, 1725 ***1220.12*** *p687*
Rosanske, Ewald; Wisconsin, 1893 ***6795.8*** *p140*
Rosansky, August Karl; Wisconsin, 1889 ***6795.8*** *p209*
Rosberg, Nels P.; America, 1857 ***4487.25*** *p72*
With father
Rosbourgh, Robert 48; Ontario, 1871 ***1823.17*** *p142*
Rosconnel, David 56; Ontario, 1871 ***1823.21*** *p317*
Roscow, William; America, 1737 ***1220.12*** *p687*
Roscowdrick, Thomas; America, 1728 ***1220.12*** *p687*
Rose, Mr.; America, 1842 ***7420.1*** *p26*
Rose, Alexander 49; Ontario, 1871 ***1823.21*** *p317*
Rose, Betsy *SEE* Rose, John
Rose, Daniel 58; Ontario, 1871 ***1823.21*** *p317*
Rose, Edmund; Halifax, N.S., 1902 ***1860.4*** *p40*
Rose, Edward; America, 1747 ***1220.12*** *p687*
Rose, Edward; Ohio, 1809-1852 ***4511.35*** *p44*
Rose, Edwin 43; Ontario, 1871 ***1823.17*** *p142*
Rose, Elizabeth 47; Ontario, 1871 ***1823.21*** *p317*
Rose, Francis; America, 1746 ***1220.12*** *p687*
Rose, Franklin; Ohio, 1809-1852 ***4511.35*** *p44*
Rose, George; America, 1752 ***1220.12*** *p687*
Rose, George; Maryland, 1727 ***1220.12*** *p687*
Rose, George A. 32; Ontario, 1871 ***1823.21*** *p317*
Rose, George William 26; Ontario, 1871 ***1823.21*** *p317*
Rose, Gottlieb 37; Halifax, N.S., 1902 ***1860.4*** *p40*
Rose, Gustav Emil Hugo; Wisconsin, 1906 ***6795.8*** *p230*
Rose, Harriet Mary; Quebec, 1842 ***9228.50*** *p260*
Rose, Henry; America, 1767 ***1220.12*** *p687*
Rose, Hugh 54; Ontario, 1871 ***1823.21*** *p317*
Rose, Hugh 62; Ontario, 1871 ***1823.21*** *p317*
Rose, Jacob; America, 1760 ***1220.12*** *p687*
Rose, James; America, 1743 ***1220.12*** *p687*
Rose, James; America, 1766 ***1220.12*** *p687*
Rose, James; Virginia, 1741 ***1220.12*** *p687*
Rose, Jeremiah; America, 1775 ***1220.12*** *p687*
Rose, John; America, 1751 ***1220.12*** *p688*
Rose, John; Ohio, 1844 ***2763.1*** *p21*
Rose, John 68; Ohio, 1850 ***9228.50*** *p553*
*Wife:*Betsy
Rose, John; Quebec, 1750-1850 ***9228.50*** *p553*
*Sister:*Mary
Rose, John; Virginia, 1721 ***1220.12*** *p687*
Rose, John; Virginia, 1806 ***9228.50*** *p553*
With wife
*Child:*Thompson
Rose, John R.; North Carolina, 1857 ***1088.45*** *p29*
Rose, Joseph; America, 1720 ***1220.12*** *p688*
Rose, Karoline 37; Halifax, N.S., 1902 ***1860.4*** *p40*
Rose, Louis 48; Ontario, 1871 ***1823.21*** *p317*
Rose, Mary; America, 1759 ***1220.12*** *p688*
Rose, Mary; Annapolis, MD, 1736 ***1220.12*** *p688*
Rose, Mary *SEE* Rose, John
Rose, Meyer; Ohio, 1809-1852 ***4511.35*** *p44*
Rose, Noel 19; Quebec, 1661 ***9221.17*** *p467*
Rose, Olga 2; Halifax, N.S., 1902 ***1860.4*** *p40*
Rose, Peter 47; Ontario, 1871 ***1823.21*** *p317*
Rose, Peter 50; Ontario, 1871 ***1823.21*** *p317*
Rose, Rachel; Quebec, 1829-1834 ***9228.50*** *p319*
Rose, Rachel; Quebec, 1829-1834 ***9228.50*** *p319*
Rose, Rebecca; Barbados or Jamaica, 1686 ***1220.12*** *p688*
Rose, Richard; Maryland, 1720 ***1220.12*** *p688*
Rose, Richard 57; Ontario, 1871 ***1823.21*** *p317*
Rose, Richard; Virginia, 1727 ***1220.12*** *p688*
Rose, Robert; New York, 1778 ***8529.30*** *p7*
Rose, Robert 20; North Carolina, 1774 ***1422.10*** *p54*
Rose, Sarah; America, 1721 ***1220.12*** *p688*
Rose, Thomas; America, 1750 ***1220.12*** *p688*
Rose, Thomas; America, 1754 ***1220.12*** *p688*
Rose, Thomas; America, 1758 ***1220.12*** *p688*
Rose, Thomas; New York, NY, 1838 ***3274.56*** *p101*
Rose, Thomas; Virginia, 1750 ***1220.12*** *p688*
Rose, Thompson *SEE* Rose, John
Rose, W.C.; New Mexico, 1914 ***4812.1*** *p87*
Rose, Waldine 4; Halifax, N.S., 1902 ***1860.4*** *p40*
Rose, Wilhelmine 38; Ontario, 1871 ***1823.21*** *p317*
Rose, William; America, 1740 ***1220.12*** *p688*
Rose, William; America, 1749 ***1220.12*** *p688*
Rose, William; America, 1756 ***1220.12*** *p688*
Rose, William; America, 1764 ***1220.12*** *p688*
Rose, William; America, 1765 ***1220.12*** *p688*
Rose, William; America, 1768 ***1220.12*** *p688*
Rose, William; Annapolis, MD, 1724 ***1220.12*** *p688*
Rose, William; Barbados, 1695 ***1220.12*** *p688*
Rosebrooke, Richard; Barbados or Jamaica, 1704 ***1220.12*** *p688*

Roseden, Susan; Barbados, 1673 ***1220.12*** *p688*
Roselius, O.T.; New York, NY, 1848 ***6412.40*** *p151*
Rosell, Conrad; Cleveland, OH, 1889-1893 ***9722.10*** *p126*
Rosemeier, Widow; America, 1854 ***7420.1*** *p128*
*Daughter:*Christine
Rosemeier, Carl *SEE* Rosemeier, Carl
Rosemeier, Carl; America, 1856 ***7420.1*** *p152*
With wife
*Mother-In-Law:*Dorothee
*Son:*Ernst
*Son:*Friedrich
*Daughter:*Wilhelmine
*Son:*Wilhelm
*Son:*Carl
Rosemeier, Christine *SEE* Rosemeier, Widow
Rosemeier, Dorothee *SEE* Rosemeier, Carl
Rosemeier, Ernst *SEE* Rosemeier, Carl
Rosemeier, Friedrich; America, 1854 ***7420.1*** *p128*
With family
Rosemeier, Friedrich *SEE* Rosemeier, Carl
Rosemeier, Friedrich Simon; America, 1883 ***7420.1*** *p337*
Rosemeier, Heinrich Wilhelm; America, 1883 ***7420.1*** *p339*
Rosemeier, Wilhelm *SEE* Rosemeier, Carl
Rosemeier, Wilhelmine; America, 1846 ***7420.1*** *p48*
Rosemeier, Wilhelmine *SEE* Rosemeier, Carl
Rosemond, John; North Carolina, 1835 ***1088.45*** *p29*
Rosen, Axel; Cleveland, OH, 1903-1904 ***9722.10*** *p126*
Rosen, Louisa Fredrika; St. Paul, MN, 1872 ***1865.50*** *p108*
Rosenbach, Philip 23; Portland, ME, 1906 ***970.38*** *p80*
Rosenbauer, Johann Georg; America, 1850-1872 ***179.55*** *p19*
Rosenbaum, Caroline Wilhelmine; Port uncertain, 1834 ***7420.1*** *p7*
Rosenbaum, Chaie 20; New York, NY, 1878 ***9253.2*** *p45*
*Child:*Chatzkel 10 months
Rosenbaum, Chatzkel 10 *SEE* Rosenbaum, Chaie
Rosenbaum, David; Detroit, 1929 ***1640.55*** *p114*
Rosenberg, Fredrick; New York, 1860 ***358.56*** *p4*
Rosenberg, Herman; Philadelphia, 1860 ***5720.10*** *p381*
Rosenberger, Johann 22; Louisiana, 1848 ***778.6*** *p288*
Rosenberry, Phillip 34; Ontario, 1871 ***1823.17*** *p142*
Rosenburg, Henry 40; Ontario, 1871 ***1823.17*** *p142*
Rosenbusch, Hermann; America, 1868 ***7919.3*** *p532*
*Mother:*Martha
With family
Rosenbusch, Martha *SEE* Rosenbusch, Hermann
Rosener, Miss; America, 1838 ***7420.1*** *p15*
Rosener, Anton Christian Friedrich; America, 1857 ***7420.1*** *p171*
Rosener, Anton Heinrich; Port uncertain, 1834 ***7420.1*** *p8*
Rosener, Christine Luise Leonore Bredemeyer *SEE* Rosener, Wilhelm Ludwig
Rosener, Ernst; America, 1867 ***7420.1*** *p263*
Rosener, Friedrich Wilhelm; America, 1837 ***7420.1*** *p13*
Rosener, Johann Carl Wilhelm; America, 1835 ***7420.1*** *p9*
Rosener, Leonore; America, 1884 ***7420.1*** *p345*
Rosener, Sophie Leonore; America, 1850 ***7420.1*** *p69*
Rosener, Wilhelm; America, 1869 ***7420.1*** *p281*
With family
Rosener, Wilhelm Ludwig; America, 1837 ***7420.1*** *p14*
*Wife:*Christine Luise Leonore Bredemeyer
Rosenfelter, George; Ohio, 1809-1852 ***4511.35*** *p44*
Rosenfelter, George, Jr.; Ohio, 1809-1852 ***4511.35*** *p44*
Rosenfelter, Jacob; Ohio, 1809-1852 ***4511.35*** *p44*
Rosengren, Charles G.; Little Rock, AR, 1864 ***4487.25*** *p72*
Rosenkrants, Detlof Christian; North America, 1839 ***6410.15*** *p103*
Rosenkranz, Charles; North Carolina, 1842 ***1088.45*** *p29*
Rosenkrontz, Casper; North Carolina, 1848 ***1088.45*** *p29*
Rosenkrontz, John; North Carolina, 1848 ***1088.45*** *p30*
Rosenkrontz, John Conrad; North Carolina, 1848 ***1088.45*** *p30*
Rosenstiel, Martin; North Carolina, 1846 ***1088.45*** *p30*
Rosensun, Harrie 25; New York, NY, 1894 ***6512.1*** *p229*
Rosentha, A. 21; New Orleans, 1834 ***1002.51*** *p111*
Rosenthal, C. W.; Valdivia, Chile, 1850 ***1192.4*** *p48*
Rosenthal, F.; Valdivia, Chile, 1851 ***1192.4*** *p51*
Rosenthal, Fanny; America, 1867 ***7919.3*** *p525*
Rosenthal, Harris; New York, NY, 1910 ***3331.4*** *p11*
Rosenthal, Moise 18; America, 1846 ***778.6*** *p288*
Rosenthel, Gustavous; North Carolina, 1792-1862 ***1088.45*** *p30*
Rosentsweig, John; Ohio, 1809-1852 ***4511.35*** *p44*
Rosenwasser, Eduard 13; New York, NY, 1854 ***2853.20*** *p144*
With father
Roser, Carl 21; New Orleans, 1846 ***778.6*** *p288*
Roset, Marguerite 38; Quebec, 1653 ***9221.17*** *p274*
Rosewater, Eduard 13; New York, NY, 1854 ***2853.20*** *p144*
With father
Rosewell, Alex. 50; America, 1843 ***778.6*** *p288*
Rosewell, Sarah; America, 1759 ***1220.12*** *p688*
Roshans, Amalie; Halifax, N.S., 1902 ***1860.4*** *p43*
Roshans, Emelie 2; Halifax, N.S., 1902 ***1860.4*** *p43*
Roshans, Natalie 25; Halifax, N.S., 1902 ***1860.4*** *p43*
Roshans, Peter 29; Halifax, N.S., 1902 ***1860.4*** *p43*
Rosick, Paul; North Carolina, 1792-1862 ***1088.45*** *p30*
Rosicky, Mr.; Wisconsin, 1862 ***2853.20*** *p334*
Rosicky, Jan; Chicago, 1845-1910 ***2853.20*** *p405*
Rosicky, Jan; Wisconsin, 1861-1864 ***2853.20*** *p145*
Rosicky, Jan; Wisconsin, 1861 ***2853.20*** *p334*
With uncle
Rosier, Henry; Wisconsin, 1855 ***9228.50*** *p550*
Rosier, John; America, 1754 ***1220.12*** *p688*
Rosier, John; America, 1766 ***1220.12*** *p688*
Rosier, John; Virginia, 1652 ***6254.4*** *p243*
Rosier, June; Quebec, 1827 ***9228.50*** *p554*
Rosin, Catha. 9 months; New York, NY, 1885 ***1883.7*** *p46*
Rosin, Catha. 27; New York, NY, 1885 ***1883.7*** *p46*
Rosin, Christe. 2; New York, NY, 1885 ***1883.7*** *p46*
Rosin, Georg 26; New York, NY, 1885 ***1883.7*** *p46*
Rositor, John; Annapolis, MD, 1726 ***1220.12*** *p689*
Roske, Albert Reinhard; Wisconsin, 1892 ***6795.8*** *p228*
Roskens, Edo; Iowa, 1908 ***1211.15*** *p18*
Roskens, John Edo; Iowa, 1914 ***1211.15*** *p18*
Roskronge, Ann; America, 1741 ***1220.12*** *p688*
Ross, Adam; Illinois, 1855 ***6079.1*** *p12*
Ross, Alex 22; Halifax, N.S., 1906 ***1833.5*** *p7*
Ross, Alexander; America, 1763 ***1220.12*** *p688*
Ross, Alexander; America, 1769 ***1220.12*** *p688*
Ross, Alexander 40; Ontario, 1871 ***1823.21*** *p317*
Ross, Alexander 46; Ontario, 1871 ***1823.21*** *p317*
Ross, Alsey 20; Ontario, 1871 ***1823.21*** *p317*
Ross, Andrew; America, 1765 ***1220.12*** *p688*
Ross, Andrew 25; Ontario, 1871 ***1823.21*** *p317*
Ross, Andrew 29; Ontario, 1871 ***1823.17*** *p142*
Ross, Andrew 40; Ontario, 1871 ***1823.21*** *p317*
Ross, Andrew 18; Quebec, 1870 ***8364.32*** *p25*
Ross, Andrew J. 41; Ontario, 1871 ***1823.21*** *p317*
Ross, Andrew M. 40; Ontario, 1871 ***1823.21*** *p317*
Ross, Angus 68; Ontario, 1871 ***1823.21*** *p317*
Ross, Ann; America, 1766 ***1220.12*** *p688*
Ross, Ann 35; Ontario, 1871 ***1823.21*** *p317*
Ross, Ann Elizabeth 76; Ontario, 1880 ***9228.50*** *p451*
Ross, Charles; America, 1767 ***1220.12*** *p688*
Ross, Christina 42; Ontario, 1871 ***1823.21*** *p317*
Ross, Christina 43; Ontario, 1871 ***1823.21*** *p317*
Ross, Christy 14; Ontario, 1871 ***1823.21*** *p317*
Ross, Daniel; Ohio, 1809-1852 ***4511.35*** *p44*
Ross, David; New York, 1776 ***8529.30*** *p7*
Ross, David 34; Ontario, 1871 ***1823.21*** *p317*
Ross, David 38; Ontario, 1871 ***1823.17*** *p142*
Ross, David 39; Ontario, 1871 ***1823.17*** *p142*
Ross, David 50; Ontario, 1871 ***1823.21*** *p317*
Ross, David M. 24; Ontario, 1871 ***1823.17*** *p142*
Ross, David M. 57; Ontario, 1871 ***1823.21*** *p317*
Ross, Donald 33; Ontario, 1871 ***1823.21*** *p317*
Ross, Donald 39; Ontario, 1871 ***1823.17*** *p142*
Ross, Donald 50; Ontario, 1871 ***1823.21*** *p317*
Ross, Donald 51; Ontario, 1871 ***1823.21*** *p317*
Ross, Donald 70; Ontario, 1871 ***1823.17*** *p142*
Ross, E. 26; Quebec, 1910 ***2897.7*** *p7*
Ross, Edmund; Halifax, N.S., 1902 ***1860.4*** *p40*
Ross, Elizabeth; America, 1766 ***1220.12*** *p688*
Ross, Esther; America, 1764 ***1220.12*** *p688*
Ross, Frederick L.V. 48; Ontario, 1871 ***1823.21*** *p317*
Ross, George 45; Ontario, 1871 ***1823.17*** *p142*
Ross, George H. 59; Ontario, 1871 ***1823.21*** *p317*
Ross, George M. 50; Ontario, 1871 ***1823.21*** *p317*
Ross, Gottlieb 37; Halifax, N.S., 1902 ***1860.4*** *p40*
Ross, H.; California, 1868 ***1131.61*** *p90*
Ross, Heinrich; America, 1871 ***7420.1*** *p292*
Ross, Helen 69; Ontario, 1871 ***1823.21*** *p317*
Ross, Henry; America, 1738 ***1220.12*** *p688*
Ross, Hugh 37; Ontario, 1871 ***1823.17*** *p142*
Ross, Hugh 85; Ontario, 1871 ***1823.21*** *p318*
Ross, Isabella 80; Ontario, 1871 ***1823.21*** *p318*
Ross, James; Boston, 1766 ***1642*** *p37*
Ross, James; Boston, 1766 ***1642*** *p37*
Ross, James 20; Ontario, 1871 ***1823.21*** *p318*
Ross, James 30; Ontario, 1871 ***1823.21*** *p318*
Ross, James 35; Ontario, 1871 ***1823.21*** *p318*
Ross, James 39; Ontario, 1871 ***1823.21*** *p318*
Ross, James 51; Ontario, 1871 ***1823.21*** *p318*
Ross, James 52; Ontario, 1871 ***1823.21*** *p318*
Ross, James 60; Ontario, 1871 ***1823.17*** *p142*
Ross, James 60; Ontario, 1871 ***1823.21*** *p318*
Ross, James 68; Ontario, 1871 ***1823.21*** *p318*
Ross, James C. 23; Ontario, 1871 ***1823.21*** *p318*
Ross, James I. 56; Ontario, 1871 ***1823.21*** *p318*
Ross, James W. 48; Ontario, 1871 ***1823.21*** *p318*
Ross, Jane; America, 1746 ***1220.12*** *p688*
Ross, Jane 44; Ontario, 1871 ***1823.17*** *p142*
Ross, Janet 67; Ontario, 1871 ***1823.21*** *p318*
Ross, Jannet 77; Ontario, 1871 ***1823.21*** *p318*
Ross, Jesse 39; Ontario, 1871 ***1823.21*** *p318*
Ross, Jessie Catherine; Denver, CO, 1898-1902 ***9228.50*** *p393*
Ross, John; America, 1702 ***1220.12*** *p688*
Ross, John; America, 1750 ***1220.12*** *p688*
Ross, John; America, 1757 ***1220.12*** *p688*
Ross, John; Boston, 1766 ***1642*** *p37*
Ross, John; Colorado, 1885 ***1029.59*** *p78*
Ross, John; Colorado, 1897 ***1029.59*** *p78*
Ross, John 47; North Carolina, 1774 ***1422.10*** *p59*
Ross, John 18; Ontario, 1871 ***1823.21*** *p318*
Ross, John 27; Ontario, 1871 ***1823.21*** *p318*
Ross, John 50; Ontario, 1871 ***1823.21*** *p318*
Ross, John 50; Ontario, 1871 ***1823.21*** *p318*
Ross, John 53; Ontario, 1871 ***1823.21*** *p318*
Ross, John 60; Ontario, 1871 ***1823.17*** *p142*
Ross, John; Philadelphia, 1777 ***8529.30*** *p7A*
Ross, John; Virginia, 1769 ***1220.12*** *p688*
Ross, John, Jr.; Boston, 1766 ***1642*** *p37*
Ross, John C. 53; Ontario, 1871 ***1823.17*** *p142*
Ross, Karoline 37; Halifax, N.S., 1902 ***1860.4*** *p40*
Ross, Katharina; Virginia, 1831 ***152.20*** *p66*
Ross, Ludwig; Wisconsin, 1889 ***6795.8*** *p171*
Ross, Margaret; America, 1755 ***1220.12*** *p688*
Ross, Margaret; America, 1770 ***1220.12*** *p688*
Ross, Margaret; Boston, 1766 ***1642*** *p37*
Ross, Maria 29; Port uncertain, 1844 ***778.6*** *p288*
Ross, Mariah 17; Ontario, 1871 ***1823.17*** *p142*
Ross, Mary 67; Ontario, 1871 ***1823.21*** *p318*
Ross, Mary 71; Ontario, 1871 ***1823.21*** *p318*
Ross, Mary 72; Ontario, 1871 ***1823.21*** *p318*
Ross, Olga 2; Halifax, N.S., 1902 ***1860.4*** *p40*
Ross, Patrick 35; North Carolina, 1774 ***1422.10*** *p59*
Ross, Penelope; Virginia, 1732 ***1220.12*** *p688*
Ross, Peter; America, 1750 ***1220.12*** *p689*
Ross, Peter; America, 1763 ***1220.12*** *p689*
Ross, Phineas 40; Ontario, 1871 ***1823.21*** *p318*
Ross, Robert; Colorado, 1902 ***1029.59*** *p78*
Ross, Robert 32; Ontario, 1871 ***1823.17*** *p142*
Ross, Robert 45; Ontario, 1871 ***1823.21*** *p318*
Ross, Robert 60; Ontario, 1871 ***1823.17*** *p142*
Ross, Robert; Washington, 1879 ***2770.40*** *p134*
Ross, Robert; Washington, 1884 ***2770.40*** *p193*
Ross, Robt 48; Ontario, 1871 ***1823.17*** *p142*
Ross, Sarah 19; Ontario, 1871 ***1823.21*** *p318*
Ross, Thomas; America, 1743 ***1220.12*** *p689*
Ross, Thomas; Illinois, 1858-1861 ***6020.5*** *p133*
Ross, Thomas 28; Ontario, 1871 ***1823.17*** *p142*
Ross, Waldine 4; Halifax, N.S., 1902 ***1860.4*** *p40*
Ross, William; America, 1751 ***1220.12*** *p689*
Ross, William; America, 1765 ***1220.12*** *p689*
Ross, William; Jamaica, 1774 ***8529.30*** *p14A*
Ross, William 30; Ontario, 1871 ***1823.21*** *p318*
Ross, William 38; Ontario, 1871 ***1823.21*** *p318*
Ross, William 38; Ontario, 1871 ***1823.21*** *p318*
Ross, William 41; Ontario, 1871 ***1823.21*** *p318*
Ross, William 42; Ontario, 1871 ***1823.21*** *p318*
Ross, William 65; Ontario, 1871 ***1823.21*** *p318*
Ross, William; Pictou, N.S., 1815 ***7100*** *p20*
With family of 4
Ross, William Thomas; Iowa, 1906 ***1211.15*** *p18*
Rossa, Agnes; Wisconsin, 1890 ***6795.8*** *p61*
Rossak, Thomas; America, 1769 ***1220.12*** *p689*
Rossannet, Joseph 49; Michigan, 1847 ***778.6*** *p288*
Rossart, Andreas 52; Halifax, N.S., 1902 ***1860.4*** *p40*
Rossart, Beater 17; Halifax, N.S., 1902 ***1860.4*** *p40*
Rossart, Christine 20; Halifax, N.S., 1902 ***1860.4*** *p40*
Rossart, Gottfried 20; Halifax, N.S., 1902 ***1860.4*** *p40*
Rossart, Karoline 50; Halifax, N.S., 1902 ***1860.4*** *p40*
Rossart, Rudolf 11; Halifax, N.S., 1902 ***1860.4*** *p40*
Rossberg, K.; New York, 1859 ***358.56*** *p101*
Rosse, Catherine; Charles Town, SC, 1719 ***1220.12*** *p688*
Rosse, Charles; Nova Scotia, 1753 ***3051*** *p113*
*Brother:*Georges
Rosse, Charles; Washington, 1889 ***2770.40*** *p80*
Rosse, Georges *SEE* Rosse, Charles
Rosse, John; Barbados, 1664 ***1220.12*** *p688*
Rosse, John; Potomac, 1731 ***1220.12*** *p688*
Rosse, Marie-Josephe Herpin *SEE* Rosse, Noel
Rosse, Noel; Nova Scotia, 1753 ***3051*** *p113*
*Wife:*Marie-Josephe Herpin
Rosseau, Joseph 68; Port uncertain, 1844 ***778.6*** *p289*
Rossel, Jean 24; America, 1847 ***778.6*** *p289*
Rossel, Johann; America, 1853 ***7420.1*** *p110*
Rossel, Joseph 24; America, 1847 ***778.6*** *p289*
Rossen, James; America, 1728 ***1220.12*** *p689*
Rossenberg, Herman; Philadelphia, 1860 ***5720.10*** *p381*

Rosser, Aaron; America, 1714 ***1220.12*** *p689*
Rosser, David 61; Ontario, 1871 ***1823.21*** *p318*
Rosser, Elizabeth; Ohio, 1818 ***4022.20*** *p291*
With father
With mother
Rosser, John 70; Ontario, 1871 ***1823.21*** *p318*
Rosser, Mathew 58; Ontario, 1871 ***1823.21*** *p319*
Rosser, Philip 65; Ontario, 1871 ***1823.21*** *p319*
Rosser, Solomon 26; America, 1845 ***778.6*** *p289*
Rosser, Thomas 61; Ontario, 1871 ***1823.21*** *p319*
Rosser, William; America, 1730 ***1220.12*** *p689*
Rossert, Catherina 63; Mississippi, 1847 ***778.6*** *p289*
Rossert, Johann 73; Mississippi, 1847 ***778.6*** *p289*
Rossert, Louisa 11; Mississippi, 1847 ***778.6*** *p289*
Rossert, Margarete 30; Mississippi, 1847 ***778.6*** *p289*
Rossert, Pierre 9; Mississippi, 1847 ***778.6*** *p289*
Rossert, Stephen 29; Mississippi, 1847 ***778.6*** *p289*
Rosseter, Elizabeth; America, 1773 ***1220.12*** *p689*
Rosseter, John; America, 1685 ***1220.12*** *p689*
Rosseter, Samuel; America, 1763 ***1220.12*** *p689*
Rossetter, Richard; Illinois, 1858 ***6079.1*** *p12*
Rossetti, James 30; Indiana, 1887-1888 ***9076.20*** *p72*
Rossier, John 48; Ontario, 1871 ***1823.21*** *p319*
Rossignol, Francois 27; America, 1845 ***778.6*** *p289*
Rossignol, Jean 21; America, 1845 ***778.6*** *p289*
Rossignol, Jeanne; Quebec, 1670 ***4514.3*** *p365*
Rossignol, Pierre 32; New Orleans, 1844 ***778.6*** *p289*
Rossing, Johann Heinrich; America, 1868 ***7420.1*** *p276*
Rossini, Louis; Minnesota, 1923 ***2769.54*** *p1383*
Rossini, Mrs. Louis; Minnesota, 1923 ***2769.54*** *p1383*
Rossiter, Bryan *SEE* Rossiter, Edward
Rossiter, Catherine; America, 1740 ***1220.12*** *p689*
Rossiter, Edward; Port uncertain, 1630 ***117.5*** *p152*
*Son:*Nicholas
*Daughter:*Joan
With daughter-in-law grandchild & wife
*Son:*Bryan
*Son:*Hugh
*Daughter:*Jane
Rossiter, Hannah; Maryland, 1742 ***1220.12*** *p689*
Rossiter, Henry 49; Ontario, 1871 ***1823.21*** *p319*
Rossiter, Hugh *SEE* Rossiter, Edward
Rossiter, Jane *SEE* Rossiter, Edward
Rossiter, Joan *SEE* Rossiter, Edward
Rossiter, John; America, 1740 ***1220.12*** *p689*
Rossiter, John; Virginia, 1718 ***1220.12*** *p689*
Rossiter, Nicholas; America, 1735 ***1220.12*** *p689*
Rossiter, Nicholas *SEE* Rossiter, Edward
Rossler, Georg Karl; America, 1893 ***179.55*** *p19*
Rossler, Sebastian; America, 1868 ***7919.3*** *p535*
Rossort, Andreas 52; Halifax, N.S., 1902 ***1860.4*** *p40*
Rossort, Beater 17; Halifax, N.S., 1902 ***1860.4*** *p40*
Rossort, Christine 20; Halifax, N.S., 1902 ***1860.4*** *p40*
Rossort, Gottfried 20; Halifax, N.S., 1902 ***1860.4*** *p40*
Rossort, Karoline 50; Halifax, N.S., 1902 ***1860.4*** *p40*
Rossort, Rudolf 11; Halifax, N.S., 1902 ***1860.4*** *p40*
Rossousse, Elise 39; America, 1848 ***778.6*** *p289*
Rossteutscher, Elisabeth Lisette; America, 1868 ***7919.3*** *p533*
Rossum, Mary; America, 1743 ***1220.12*** *p689*
Rost, Christine Peters *SEE* Rost, Peter
Rost, Eduard *SEE* Rost, Peter
Rost, Louis; Louisiana, 1874 ***4981.45*** *p134*
Rost, Peter; Ohio, 1884 ***554.30*** *p25*
*Wife:*Christine Peters
*Child:*Eduard
Rostator, George; Ohio, 1809-1852 ***4511.35*** *p44*
Roste, Hannah; America, 1745 ***1220.12*** *p689*
Rostelberger, Adam 21; Louisiana, 1848 ***778.6*** *p289*
Rostelberger, Christ. 17; Louisiana, 1848 ***778.6*** *p289*
Rostelberger, Colard 15; Louisiana, 1848 ***778.6*** *p289*
Rostelberger, Elisab. 45; Louisiana, 1848 ***778.6*** *p289*
Rosy, Marie Antoinette; Wisconsin, 1854-1858 ***1495.20*** *p50*
Rotchford, Thomas; America, 1765 ***1220.12*** *p684*
Rotcope, Mr. 28; America, 1846 ***778.6*** *p289*
Rotcosse, Mr. 28; America, 1846 ***778.6*** *p289*
Roteau, Barbe; Quebec, 1673 ***4514.3*** *p366*
Rotermund, Dorothee Louise Wilhelmine; America, 1845 ***7420.1*** *p36*
Roth, Adam; America, 1881 ***5475.1*** *p544*
Roth, Adolph; Dakota, 1888 ***554.30*** *p26*
*Wife:*Wilhelmine Banik
*Child:*Carl
Roth, Albert; Illinois, 1865 ***6079.1*** *p12*
Roth, Andrews; Illinois, 1851 ***6079.1*** *p12*
Roth, Anna *SEE* Roth, Stephan
Roth, Anna 28; New York, NY, 1893 ***1883.7*** *p42*
Roth, Antoine 32; Missouri, 1846 ***778.6*** *p289*
Roth, C. Theod.; Chile, 1852 ***1192.4*** *p55*
Roth, Carl *SEE* Roth, Adolph
Roth, Catharina; America, 1867 ***7919.3*** *p531*
Roth, Charles; Tennessee, 1880 ***3665.20*** *p112*
Roth, Charles Friedrich; Ohio, 1840-1897 ***8365.35*** *p17*
Roth, Elisabeth 20; America, 1846 ***778.6*** *p289*
Roth, Elisabetha 27; America, 1856 ***2526.43*** *p213*
Roth, Elisabetha 35; America, 1858 ***2526.42*** *p191*
Roth, Eva 30; Missouri, 1846 ***778.6*** *p289*
Roth, Eva Magdalena; Venezuela, 1843 ***3899.5*** *p544*
Roth, Feliz 49; New Castle, DE, 1817-1818 ***90.20*** *p153*
Roth, Franz Joseph; Venezuela, 1843 ***3899.5*** *p544*
Roth, Franzyna 3; New York, NY, 1893 ***1883.7*** *p42*
Roth, Georg; America, 1868 ***2526.42*** *p129*
Roth, Heinrich; America, 1855 ***2526.43*** *p213*
Roth, Helene *SEE* Roth, S.
Roth, Henry; Illinois, 1851 ***6079.1*** *p12*
Roth, Jacob 3; Missouri, 1846 ***778.6*** *p289*
Roth, Jakob *SEE* Roth, Stephan
Roth, Jean 27; America, 1844 ***778.6*** *p289*
Roth, Jean 34; America, 1842 ***778.6*** *p289*
Roth, Johann; America, 1836 ***5475.1*** *p495*
With wife & 6 children
Roth, Johann Georg; Port uncertain, 1887 ***170.15*** *p40*
With wife & 4 children
Roth, John; Illinois, 1854 ***6079.1*** *p12*
Roth, John; Ohio, 1809-1852 ***4511.35*** *p44*
Roth, Josef *SEE* Roth, Peter
Roth, Joseph 36; New Orleans, 1847 ***778.6*** *p289*
Roth, Karel; St. Louis, 1848 ***2853.20*** *p21*
Roth, Karl; America, 1881 ***2526.43*** *p179*
Roth, Karl 27; New York, NY, 1893 ***1883.7*** *p42*
Roth, Katharina Leischen 24 *SEE* Roth, Stephan
Roth, Ludwig; America, 1852 ***5475.1*** *p30*
Roth, M. Josephine Bauer *SEE* Roth, Peter
Roth, Madeleine 6; Missouri, 1846 ***778.6*** *p289*
Roth, Magdalena 25; America, 1842 ***778.6*** *p289*
Roth, Magdalena 39; New Orleans, 1847 ***778.6*** *p289*
Roth, Margaretha; Venezuela, 1843 ***3899.5*** *p544*
Roth, Marianne 24; Louisiana, 1848 ***778.6*** *p289*
Roth, Marianne 3; New Orleans, 1847 ***778.6*** *p289*
Roth, Mathias *SEE* Roth, Peter
Roth, Mathias 4; New Orleans, 1847 ***778.6*** *p289*
Roth, Nikolaus *SEE* Roth, Peter
Roth, Peter *SEE* Roth, Peter
Roth, Peter; America, 1881 ***5475.1*** *p152*
*Wife:*M. Josephine Bauer
*Son:*Mathias
*Son:*Josef
*Son:*Peter
*Son:*Nikolaus
Roth, Peter 20; New York, NY, 1874 ***6954.7*** *p39*
Roth, Peter Anton; America, 1883 ***2526.42*** *p196*
Roth, Philip; Illinois, 1851 ***6079.1*** *p12*
Roth, S. 62; America, 1897 ***5475.1*** *p40*
*Daughter:*Helene
Roth, Stephan 28; America, 1861 ***5475.1*** *p492*
*Wife:*Katharina Leischen 24
*Son:*Jakob
*Daughter:*Anna
Roth, Wilhelmine Banik *SEE* Roth, Adolph
Roth, Xavier 36; Louisiana, 1848 ***778.6*** *p290*
Rothacker, Christian; South Dakota, 1884 ***554.30*** *p26*
*Wife:*Veronika
*Child:*Mathaus
Rothacker, Mathaus *SEE* Rothacker, Christian
Rothacker, Veronika *SEE* Rothacker, Christian
Rothaker, Adam; Dakota, 1885 ***554.30*** *p25*
Rothann, A. 29; New Orleans, 1843 ***778.6*** *p290*
Rothberger, Joh. 18; New York, NY, 1893 ***1883.7*** *p44*
Rothchild, Lewis; North Carolina, 1860 ***1088.45*** *p30*
Rothe, A.; Galveston, TX, 1855 ***571.7*** *p18*
Rothe, Ludwig; Chile, 1852 ***1192.4*** *p52*
Rothen, Robert; America, 1923 ***8023.44*** *p378*
Rothenberg, Georg 16; New York, NY, 1878 ***9253.2*** *p45*
Rothenbuhler, Jacob; West Virginia, 1868 ***1132.30*** *p149*
Rothengatter, Georg Daniel 42; New Castle, DE, 1817-1818 ***90.20*** *p153*
Rothenhauser, Christian; America, 1831 ***2526.43*** *p179*
Rotheram, Joseph; America, 1770 ***1220.12*** *p689*
Rotherford, Robert; America, 1744 ***1220.12*** *p694*
Rotherton, John; America, 1685 ***1220.12*** *p689*
Rothgel, C. 22; New Orleans, 1834 ***1002.51*** *p112*
Rothlander, Maria Eva; Chicago, 1893 ***5475.1*** *p72*
Rothschild, Eduard; America, 1867 ***5475.1*** *p543*
Rothschild, Jakob; America, 1865 ***5475.1*** *p553*
Rothschild, Leopold; Pittsburgh, 1863 ***5475.1*** *p552*
Rothschild, Moritz; America, 1883 ***2526.43*** *p179*
Rothshild, Aaron; North Carolina, 1792-1862 ***1088.45*** *p30*
Rothstein, Axel Victor; California, 1851 ***6410.15*** *p104*
Rothwell, Caroline 42; Ontario, 1871 ***1823.21*** *p319*
Rothwell, Frederick 54; Ontario, 1871 ***1823.17*** *p143*
Rothwell, Maria 45; Ontario, 1871 ***1823.21*** *p319*
Rothwell, Richard; America, 1767 ***1220.12*** *p689*
Rothwell, Robert; Ohio, 1835 ***2763.1*** *p21*
Rothwell, Thomas W. 60; Ontario, 1871 ***1823.17*** *p143*
Rotot, Francois 14; Quebec, 1651 ***9221.17*** *p251*
Rotschild, Regina 19; America, 1857 ***5475.1*** *p552*
Rott, Eva Magdalena; Venezuela, 1843 ***3899.5*** *p544*
Rott, Martin 21; Port uncertain, 1843 ***778.6*** *p290*
Rotters, John; America, 1715 ***1220.12*** *p689*
Rottiger, Ann; New York, 1860 ***358.56*** *p150*
Rottmann, Friedrich; Port uncertain, 1840 ***7420.1*** *p20*
Rottunde, Franz; Iowa, 1923 ***1211.15*** *p18*
Rou..., John; North Carolina, 1855 ***1088.45*** *p30*
Rou, Madeleine; Quebec, 1673 ***4514.3*** *p366*
Rouaud, Antoine; Quebec, 1639 ***9221.17*** *p92*
Roubet, Mr. 65; Port uncertain, 1844 ***778.6*** *p290*
Roubet, Mrs. 40; Port uncertain, 1844 ***778.6*** *p290*
Roubet, Ms. 16; Port uncertain, 1844 ***778.6*** *p290*
Roubion, Leopold; Louisiana, 1874 ***4981.45*** *p296*
Roucek, Josef M.; Omaha, NE, 1877-1903 ***2853.20*** *p147*
With parents
Rouch, John 46; Ontario, 1871 ***1823.21*** *p319*
Rouchard, Jean 56; America, 1840 ***778.6*** *p290*
Rouchard, Jean T.; Louisiana, 1836-1840 ***4981.45*** *p213*
Rouchard, Joseph 18; America, 1840 ***778.6*** *p290*
Rouche, Catherine 28; America, 1846 ***778.6*** *p290*
Rouche, Emile 1; America, 1846 ***778.6*** *p290*
Rouche, Francis R.; North Carolina, 1842 ***1088.45*** *p30*
Rouche, John; North Carolina, 1833 ***1088.45*** *p30*
Rouche, John; North Carolina, 1855 ***1088.45*** *p30*
Rouche, Pierre 28; America, 1846 ***778.6*** *p290*
Rouchier, Marie 27; Port uncertain, 1843 ***778.6*** *p290*
Rouck, Patrick; Boston, 1731 ***1642*** *p44*
Roucu, Simon 33; Port uncertain, 1842 ***778.6*** *p290*
Roueant, P. 18; America, 1841 ***778.6*** *p290*
Rouede, J. 18; New Orleans, 1848 ***778.6*** *p291*
Rouen, P.; New York, 1860 ***358.56*** *p3*
Rouer, Antoine; Wisconsin, 1855 ***1495.20*** *p41*
*Wife:*Marie Therese Baumont
*Child:*Clement Joseph
*Child:*Julienne
Rouer, Clement Joseph *SEE* Rouer, Antoine
Rouer, Julienne *SEE* Rouer, Antoine
Rouer, Marie 44; Quebec, 1659 ***9221.17*** *p399*
*Son:*Urbain 16
Rouer, Marie Therese Baumont *SEE* Rouer, Antoine
Rouer deVilleray, Louis; Quebec, 1650-1651 ***2314.30*** *p166*
Rouer deVilleray, Louis; Quebec, 1650-1651 ***2314.30*** *p195*
Rouer DeVilleray, Louis 23; Quebec, 1652 ***9221.17*** *p265*
Rouet, Mathurin; Quebec, 1657 ***9221.17*** *p368*
Rouff, Armand; America, 1881 ***5475.1*** *p129*
Rougbie, Harriett 33; Ontario, 1871 ***1823.21*** *p319*
Rougbie, Mary White 6; Ontario, 1871 ***1823.21*** *p319*
Rougbie, Napoleon Davis; Ontario, 1871 ***1823.21*** *p319*
Rougel, Barbara 8; Port uncertain, 1843 ***778.6*** *p290*
Rougel, Barbara 42; Port uncertain, 1843 ***778.6*** *p290*
Rougel, Francois 45; Port uncertain, 1843 ***778.6*** *p290*
Rougel, Franz 3; Port uncertain, 1843 ***778.6*** *p290*
Rougel, George 4; Port uncertain, 1843 ***778.6*** *p290*
Rougel, Jean 1; Port uncertain, 1843 ***778.6*** *p290*
Rougel, Margaretha 17; Port uncertain, 1843 ***778.6*** *p290*
Rougel, Maria 12; Port uncertain, 1843 ***778.6*** *p290*
Rougel, Nicolas 15; Port uncertain, 1843 ***778.6*** *p290*
Rougel, Therese 11; Port uncertain, 1843 ***778.6*** *p290*
Rouget, Mr. 34; America, 1844 ***778.6*** *p290*
Rouget, Edouard; Quebec, 1662 ***9221.17*** *p492*
Rouget, James; New York, NY, 1800-1899 ***9228.50*** *p555*
Rouget, Jean; Quebec, 1639 ***9221.17*** *p84*
Roughley, George 34; Ontario, 1871 ***1823.21*** *p319*
Roughley, Ida 1; Ontario, 1871 ***1823.21*** *p319*
Roughsedge, William; America, 1763 ***1220.12*** *p689*
Rougon, Felix 30; New Orleans, 1848 ***778.6*** *p290*
Rouhaud, Hyppolite 19; New Orleans, 1844 ***778.6*** *p290*
Rouillard, Antoine 33; Quebec, 1649 ***9221.17*** *p219*
Rouillard, Mathieu 21; Quebec, 1661 ***9221.17*** *p467*
Rouille, Em; New York, 1859 ***358.56*** *p101*
Rouiller, Mathurin 25; Montreal, 1659 ***9221.17*** *p427*
Rouillier, Florimond 38; America, 1843 ***778.6*** *p290*
Rouland, . . .; Salt Lake City, 1880 ***9228.50*** *p555*
With sons
Rouland, . . .; Salt Lake City, 1880 ***9228.50*** *p558*
With sons
Rouland, William; Ohio, 1852 ***9228.50*** *p555*
Rouleau, Gabriel 37; Quebec, 1652 ***9221.17*** *p265*
Rouleau, Jacques; Montreal, 1660 ***9221.17*** *p443*
Roulenc, Vincenc; Nebraska, 1874 ***2853.20*** *p171*
Roullier, Mrs. 26; America, 1844 ***778.6*** *p290*
Roullier, F. 40; New Orleans, 1844 ***778.6*** *p290*
Roullier, Sivia 31; New Orleans, 1844 ***778.6*** *p290*
Roulois, Jacqueline 8 *SEE* Roulois, Michel
Roulois, Jeanne 5 *SEE* Roulois, Michel
Roulois, Jeanne Maslier 31 *SEE* Roulois, Michel

Roulois, Michel 29; Quebec, 1652 ***9221.17*** *p266*
*Wife:*Jeanne Maslier 31
*Daughter:*Jacqueline 8
*Daughter:*Jeanne 5
Roumier, Eugenie 61; New Orleans, 1844 ***778.6*** *p290*
Roumier, Pelagie 21; New Orleans, 1844 ***778.6*** *p291*
Roumier, Victor 3; New Orleans, 1844 ***778.6*** *p291*
Rouncevall, John; America, 1734 ***1220.12*** *p689*
Round, . . .; New England, 1630-1670 ***9228.50*** *p555*
Round, Henriette; North Carolina, 1855 ***1088.45*** *p30*
Round, Jacob; North Carolina, 1849 ***1088.45*** *p30*
Round, John; America, 1702 ***1220.12*** *p689*
Round, Thomas; America, 1761 ***1220.12*** *p689*
Round, Thomas; America, 1766 ***1220.12*** *p689*
Rounding, Henry 33; Ontario, 1871 ***1823.21*** *p319*
Rounds, . . .; New England, 1630-1670 ***9228.50*** *p555*
Roundy, . . .; New England, 1630-1670 ***9228.50*** *p555*
Roundy, David; America, 1744 ***1220.12*** *p689*
Roundy, Philip; Salem, MA, 1656 ***9228.50*** *p555*
Rourk, Edmund; Boston, 1727 ***1642*** *p25*
Rourk, L.; New Orleans, 1850 ***7242.30*** *p153*
Rourk, Martin; St. John, N.B., 1847 ***2978.15*** *p36*
Rourke, Bartholomew 62; Ontario, 1871 ***1823.21*** *p319*
Rourke, Bridget; New Orleans, 1850 ***7242.30*** *p153*
Rourke, Catherine; New Orleans, 1850 ***7242.30*** *p154*
Rourke, Daniel; Boston, 1773 ***1642*** *p49*
Rourke, John 34; Ontario, 1871 ***1823.21*** *p319*
Rourke, John 56; Ontario, 1871 ***1823.21*** *p319*
Rourke, Martin; New Orleans, 1850 ***7242.30*** *p154*
Rourke, Patrick; Boston, 1833 ***3274.56*** *p70*
Rourke, Patrick; Newfoundland, 1814 ***3476.10*** *p54*
Rous, Robert; America, 1758 ***1220.12*** *p689*
Rous, William; America, 1772 ***1220.12*** *p689*
Rouse, Miss A.; Montreal, 1922 ***4514.4*** *p32*
Rouse, Edward 32; Ontario, 1871 ***1823.21*** *p319*
Rouse, Francis; America, 1719 ***1220.12*** *p689*
Rouse, James 30; Ontario, 1871 ***1823.21*** *p319*
Rouse, James 56; Ontario, 1871 ***1823.21*** *p319*
Rouse, John; America, 1675 ***1220.12*** *p689*
Rouse, John; America, 1731 ***1220.12*** *p689*
Rouse, John; America, 1737 ***1220.12*** *p689*
Rouse, Margaret 62; Ontario, 1871 ***1823.17*** *p143*
Rouse, Mary; Virginia, 1741 ***1220.12*** *p689*
Rouse, Nicholas; Massachusetts, 1600-1699 ***9228.50*** *p557*
Rouse, Sarah; America, 1764 ***1220.12*** *p689*
Rouse, Thomas; America, 1689 ***9228.50*** *p563*
Rouse, Thomas; Portsmouth, NH, 1689 ***9228.50*** *p557*
Rouse, Thomas; Washington, 1885 ***2770.40*** *p194*
Rouse, William; Died enroute, 1721 ***1220.12*** *p689*
Rouse, William 41; Ontario, 1871 ***1823.17*** *p143*
Rousille, V...r 28; America, 1841 ***778.6*** *p291*
Rouso, Samuel; Boston, 1712 ***9228.50*** *p557*
Roussard, Jules 7; America, 1842 ***778.6*** *p291*
Roussdeau, Edward; America, 1842 ***778.6*** *p291*
Rousse, Mr.; America, 1843 ***778.6*** *p291*
Rousse, Mrs.; America, 1843 ***778.6*** *p291*
Rousse, John 26; America, 1843 ***778.6*** *p291*
Rousse, P. 40; New Orleans, 1848 ***778.6*** *p291*
Rousseau, Anne; Quebec, 1667 ***4514.3*** *p366*
Rousseau, Celestin 45; Port uncertain, 1843 ***778.6*** *p291*
Rousseau, Denis; Quebec, 1635 ***9221.17*** *p47*
Rousseau, Henriette; Quebec, 1668 ***4514.3*** *p366*
Rousseau, Jean; Quebec, 1642 ***9221.17*** *p121*
Rousseau, Jeanne 18; Montreal, 1654 ***9221.17*** *p318*
Rousseau, Joseph 43; Port uncertain, 1843 ***778.6*** *p291*
Rousseau, Louis 38; Port uncertain, 1841 ***778.6*** *p291*
Rousseau, Nicolas 22; Port uncertain, 1840 ***778.6*** *p291*
Rousseau, Rene; Quebec, 1647 ***9221.17*** *p189*
Rousseau, Samuel; Boston, 1712 ***9228.50*** *p557*
Rousseau, Symphorien 22; Quebec, 1657 ***9221.17*** *p368*
Rousseaux, Julien 23; Missouri, 1848 ***778.6*** *p291*
Roussel, A.; New York, NY, 1897 ***9228.50*** *p446*
Roussel, A.E.; Ontario, n.d. ***9228.50*** *p557*
Roussel, Charlotte; Quebec, 1668 ***4514.3*** *p366*
Roussel, Jean Luc 39; Texas, 1848 ***778.6*** *p291*
Roussel, M.; New York, NY, 1897 ***9228.50*** *p37*
Roussel, Marguerite; Quebec, 1673 ***4514.3*** *p366*
Roussel, Philip; Massachusetts, 1600-1699 ***9228.50*** *p557*
Roussel, Pierre Constant 24; New Orleans, 1848 ***778.6*** *p291*
Roussel, Robert M.; Marblehead, MA, 1804 ***9228.50*** *p88*
Roussel, Thomas; America, 1689 ***9228.50*** *p563*
Roussel, Thomas; Portsmouth, NH, 1689 ***9228.50*** *p557*
Rousselet, Etienne 28; Port uncertain, 1843 ***778.6*** *p291*
Rousselier, Jeanne; Quebec, 1600-1663 ***4514.3*** *p312*
Rousseliere, Jeanne 18; Montreal, 1654 ***9221.17*** *p318*
Rousselin, Suzanne; Quebec, 1665 ***4514.3*** *p366*
Roussell, John 40; America, 1847 ***778.6*** *p292*
Roussell, John P.; Ohio, 1809-1852 ***4511.35*** *p44*
Rousselot, Eliza 28; Port uncertain, 1846 ***778.6*** *p291*
Rousselot, Jean; Quebec, 1656 ***9221.17*** *p347*
Rousselot, Marguerite; Quebec, 1673 ***4514.3*** *p367*
Rousselot, Mathias 25; America, 1846 ***778.6*** *p291*
Rousselot, Remond 30; America, 1846 ***778.6*** *p291*
Rousser, Lewis; America, 1756 ***1220.12*** *p689*
Rousset, Paul; Louisiana, 1874-1875 ***4981.45*** *p30*
Roussin, Francoise 19; Quebec, 1651 ***9221.17*** *p250*
*Brother:*Nicolas 16
Roussin, Jean 53; Quebec, 1650 ***9221.17*** *p229*
*Daughter:*Madeleine 26
*Daughter:*Louise 8
Roussin, Louise 8 *SEE* Roussin, Jean
Roussin, Madeleine 26 *SEE* Roussin, Jean
Roussin, Nicolas 16 *SEE* Roussin, Francoise
Roussy, Le Compte De 32; Quebec, 1654 ***9221.17*** *p310*
Roustin, G. 35; America, 1843 ***778.6*** *p291*
Route, Sherm; Ontario, 1787 ***1276.15*** *p231*
Routh, Alexander 22; Ontario, 1871 ***1823.17*** *p143*
Routh, Christopher; America, 1748 ***1220.12*** *p689*
Routhes, Georg 38; New Orleans, 1848 ***778.6*** *p291*
Routhier, Guillaume; Quebec, 1654 ***9221.17*** *p316*
Routhier, Jean 16; Quebec, 1658 ***9221.17*** *p386*
Routledge, George 67; Ontario, 1871 ***1823.21*** *p319*
Routledge, Richard; America, 1765 ***1220.12*** *p689*
Routledge, Richard; America, 1765 ***1220.12*** *p694*
Routledge, Robert 50; Ontario, 1871 ***1823.21*** *p319*
Routledge, William 68; Ontario, 1871 ***1823.21*** *p319*
Routledge, William 76; Ontario, 1871 ***1823.21*** *p319*
Routley, Richard 42; Ontario, 1871 ***1823.21*** *p319*
Routy, Marie-Madeleine; Quebec, 1668 ***4514.3*** *p367*
Rouve, Nicolas 38; Missouri, 1845 ***778.6*** *p291*
Rouvray, Julien de; Montreal, 1659 ***9221.17*** *p427*
Roux, Mr. 40; New Orleans, 1845 ***778.6*** *p291*
Roux, Aimee; Quebec, 1669 ***4514.3*** *p367*
Roux, Etienne-Joseph 37; Galveston, TX, 1844 ***3967.10*** *p374*
Roux, Gaspard; Illinois, 1852 ***6079.1*** *p12*
Roux, Jean B. 40; America, 1845 ***778.6*** *p291*
Roux, Luise; America, 1867 ***7919.3*** *p531*
With 3 children
Roux, Michael; Virginia, 1700 ***9230.15*** *p80*
Roux, R.B. 39; Port uncertain, 1841 ***778.6*** *p291*
Rouyer, Pierre 34; Louisiana, 1848 ***778.6*** *p291*
Rouzeard, Jean; Louisiana, 1836-1840 ***4981.45*** *p213*
Rover, Hans Heinrich; America, 1852 ***7420.1*** *p96*
Rover, Hans Heinrich Christoph; Port uncertain, 1851 ***7420.1*** *p82*
Rover, Hans Henrich; Port uncertain, 1825 ***7420.1*** *p2*
Row, Charles 44; Ontario, 1871 ***1823.21*** *p319*
Row, Charles 55; Ontario, 1871 ***1823.21*** *p319*
Row, Edward; America, 1772 ***1220.12*** *p690*
Row, James; Boston, 1766 ***1642*** *p37*
Row, James; Virginia, 1765 ***1220.12*** *p690*
Row, Thomas; America, 1736 ***1220.12*** *p690*
Row, William; America, 1685 ***1220.12*** *p690*
Row, William; America, 1724 ***1220.12*** *p690*
Row, William; America, 1742 ***1220.12*** *p690*
Row, William; America, 1765 ***1220.12*** *p690*
Row, William; America, 1772 ***1220.12*** *p690*
Row, William 37; Ontario, 1871 ***1823.21*** *p319*
Rowan, M.; Louisiana, 1874-1875 ***4981.45*** *p30*
Rowan, Thomas 21; Ontario, 1871 ***1823.17*** *p143*
Rowart, Adele *SEE* Rowart, Francois Joseph
Rowart, Francois Joseph; Wisconsin, 1854-1858 ***1495.20*** *p50*
*Wife:*Adele
Rowat, Joseph 62; Ontario, 1871 ***1823.21*** *p319*
Rowbotham, George; America, 1763 ***1220.12*** *p684*
Rowcliffe, John 36; Ontario, 1871 ***1823.17*** *p143*
Rowcliffe, Robert; Quebec, 1880-1980 ***9228.50*** *p547*
Rowcliffe, Robert Gay; Quebec, 1905-1983 ***9228.50*** *p558*
Rowcliffe, Walter; Montreal, n.d. ***9228.50*** *p558*
Rowcliffe, Walter Keen; Montreal, 1911-1933 ***9228.50*** *p557*
Rowden, John 36; Ontario, 1858 ***9228.50*** *p558*
Rowden, Thomas; America, 1738 ***1220.12*** *p689*
Rowden, William; America, 1741 ***1220.12*** *p689*
Rowding, John; Virginia, 1769 ***1220.12*** *p689*
Rowdon, Sarah; America, 1769 ***1220.12*** *p689*
Rowe, Ann; Maryland, 1744 ***1220.12*** *p690*
Rowe, Anne; America, 1731 ***1220.12*** *p689*
Rowe, Christopher; America, 1685 ***1220.12*** *p690*
Rowe, George; America, 1763 ***1220.12*** *p690*
Rowe, Jane 46; Ontario, 1871 ***1823.21*** *p319*
Rowe, John; America, 1734 ***1220.12*** *p690*
Rowe, John; America, 1743 ***1220.12*** *p690*
Rowe, John; North Carolina, 1842 ***1088.45*** *p30*
Rowe, Mary; Virginia, 1732 ***1220.12*** *p690*
Rowe, Peter; America, 1685 ***1220.12*** *p690*
Rowe, Robert 60; Ontario, 1871 ***1823.21*** *p319*
Rowe, Samuel; America, 1737 ***1220.12*** *p690*
Rowe, Thomas John; New York, NY, 1896 ***1029.59*** *p78*
Rowe, William; America, 1762 ***1220.12*** *p690*
Rowe, William 45; Ontario, 1871 ***1823.21*** *p319*
Rowe, William 50; Ontario, 1871 ***1823.21*** *p319*
Rowell, Edward; America, 1663 ***1220.12*** *p690*
Rowell, Edward; Potomac, 1729 ***1220.12*** *p690*
Rowell, Francis; America, 1752 ***1220.12*** *p690*
Rowell, John 50; Ontario, 1871 ***1823.21*** *p319*
Rowell, Joseph 62; Ontario, 1871 ***1823.21*** *p320*
Rowell, Nicholas; America, 1694 ***1220.12*** *p690*
Rowell, Randolph; America, 1742 ***1220.12*** *p690*
Rowen, William 31; Ontario, 1871 ***1823.21*** *p320*
Rower, Mr.; America, 1852 ***7420.1*** *p96*
With wife
*Daughter:*Engel
*Daughter:*Philippine
*Son:*Friedrich
*Son:*Wilhelm
*Son:*Ernst
*Son:*Carl Wilhelm
Rower, Carl Wilhelm *SEE* Rower, Mr.
Rower, Engel *SEE* Rower, Mr.
Rower, Ernst *SEE* Rower, Mr.
Rower, Friedrich *SEE* Rower, Mr.
Rower, Hans Heinrich; America, 1852 ***7420.1*** *p96*
Rower, Philippine *SEE* Rower, Mr.
Rower, Sophie; America, 1851 ***7420.1*** *p82*
Rower, Wilhelm *SEE* Rower, Mr.
Rowland, . . .; Salt Lake City, 1880 ***9228.50*** *p555*
With sons
Rowland, . . .; Salt Lake City, 1880 ***9228.50*** *p558*
With sons
Rowland, Dr.; New Jersey, 1665 ***9228.50*** *p558*
Rowland, Dr.; Virginia, 1665 ***9228.50*** *p53*
Rowland, Alfred 37; Ontario, 1871 ***1823.21*** *p320*
Rowland, Arthur 20; Ontario, 1871 ***1823.17*** *p143*
Rowland, Catherine; America, 1743 ***1220.12*** *p690*
Rowland, David; America, 1767 ***1220.12*** *p690*
Rowland, David 63; Ontario, 1871 ***1823.21*** *p320*
Rowland, Edward; Marston's Wharf, 1782 ***8529.30*** *p15*
Rowland, Edward 24; Ontario, 1871 ***1823.17*** *p143*
Rowland, Edward 40; Ontario, 1871 ***1823.21*** *p320*
Rowland, Edward 61; Ontario, 1871 ***1823.21*** *p320*
Rowland, Edward; Rappahannock, VA, 1728 ***1220.12*** *p690*
Rowland, Elizabeth; America, 1751 ***1220.12*** *p690*
Rowland, Elizabeth; America, 1752 ***1220.12*** *p690*
Rowland, Elizabeth; America, 1767 ***1220.12*** *p690*
Rowland, Elizabeth; Annapolis, MD, 1723 ***1220.12*** *p690*
Rowland, Frederich 54; Ontario, 1871 ***1823.21*** *p320*
Rowland, Hannah; America, 1748 ***1220.12*** *p690*
Rowland, John; America, 1719 ***1220.12*** *p690*
Rowland, John; America, 1732 ***1220.12*** *p690*
Rowland, John; America, 1752 ***1220.12*** *p691*
Rowland, John; America, 1753 ***1220.12*** *p691*
Rowland, John; America, 1764 ***1220.12*** *p691*
Rowland, John; America, 1774 ***1220.12*** *p691*
Rowland, John; Jamaica, 1717 ***1220.12*** *p690*
Rowland, John; Marston's Wharf, 1782 ***8529.30*** *p15*
Rowland, John 27; Toronto, 1859 ***9228.50*** *p558*
Rowland, Mary 62; Ontario, 1871 ***1823.21*** *p320*
Rowland, Philip; America, 1775 ***1220.12*** *p691*
Rowland, Richard; America, 1730 ***1220.12*** *p691*
Rowland, Richard 20; Virginia, 1635 ***1183.3*** *p30*
Rowland, Robert; Barbados, 1669 ***1220.12*** *p691*
Rowland, Samuel; America, 1727 ***1220.12*** *p691*
Rowland, Samuel; America, 1774 ***1220.12*** *p691*
Rowland, Sarah; America, 1775 ***1220.12*** *p691*
Rowland, Susannah; America, 1733 ***1220.12*** *p691*
Rowland, Thomas; America, 1686 ***1220.12*** *p691*
Rowland, Thomas; America, 1734 ***1220.12*** *p691*
Rowland, Thomas; America, 1752 ***1220.12*** *p691*
Rowland, Thomas; America, 1763 ***1220.12*** *p691*
Rowland, Thomas; America, 1773 ***1220.12*** *p691*
Rowland, Thomas 26; Toronto, 1862 ***9228.50*** *p558*
Rowland, Thomas; Virginia, 1771 ***1220.12*** *p691*
Rowland, William; America, 1745 ***1220.12*** *p691*
Rowland, William; Barbados, 1663 ***1220.12*** *p691*
Rowland, William; Ohio, 1852 ***9228.50*** *p555*
Rowland, William 70; Ontario, 1871 ***1823.21*** *p320*
Rowlands, John; Ohio, 1880 ***4022.20*** *p291*
*Father:*John R.
*Mother:*Magdalen
Rowlands, John R. *SEE* Rowlands, John
Rowlands, Magdalen *SEE* Rowlands, John
Rowlandson, William; Barbados, 1679 ***1220.12*** *p691*
Rowlat, Thomas; America, 1734 ***1220.12*** *p691*
Rowler, Mary; America, 1770 ***1220.12*** *p691*
Rowles, Daniel; America, 1771 ***1220.12*** *p691*
Rowles, William; Virginia, 1767 ***1220.12*** *p691*
Rowles, William H.; Ohio, 1879 ***6020.12*** *p22*
Rowlet, John; America, 1755 ***1220.12*** *p691*
Rowlett, Elijah; Missouri, 1886 ***3276.1*** *p2*
Rowlett, Jeremiah; Missouri, 1888 ***3276.1*** *p2*
Rowley, Aletia 50; Ontario, 1871 ***1823.17*** *p143*
Rowley, Ann; America, 1772 ***1220.12*** *p691*
Rowley, Edward; America, 1736 ***1220.12*** *p691*

Rowley, Henry; America, 1737 *1220.12 p691*
Rowley, James; America, 1678 *1220.12 p691*
Rowley, John; America, 1700 *1220.12 p691*
Rowley, John; New York, NY, 1819 *3274.55 p75*
Rowley, John 34; Ontario, 1871 *1823.21 p320*
Rowley, John, Jr.; New York, NY, 1819 *3274.55 p71*
Rowley, Joseph; Barbados, 1676 *1220.12 p691*
Rowley, M. H. 60; Ontario, 1871 *1823.21 p320*
Rowley, Stephen; America, 1732 *1220.12 p691*
Rowley, Thomas; America, 1751 *1220.12 p691*
Rowley, Thomas; America, 1773 *1220.12 p691*
Rowley, William; America, 1764 *1220.12 p691*
Rowlin, Hannah; America, 1748 *1220.12 p691*
Rowling, Ann; America, 1727 *1220.12 p691*
Rowling, Elizabeth; America, 1767 *1220.12 p691*
Rowling, Thomas; America, 1772 *1220.12 p691*
Rowlins, James; America, 1769 *1220.12 p691*
Rowlins, Richard; New York, 1778 *8529.30 p5A*
Rowlinson, James; America, 1774 *1220.12 p691*
Rowna, John 38; Ontario, 1871 *1823.17 p143*
Rowsall, George; America, 1685 *1220.12 p691*
Rowsall, Henry; Barbados, 1665 *1220.12 p692*
Rowsell, John; America, 1758 *1220.12 p692*
Rowsse, John; America, 1751 *1220.12 p691*
Roxby, Thomas 51; Indiana, 1869-1880 *9076.20 p69*
Roy, Mr. 35; America, 1847 *778.6 p291*
Roy, A. F.; Colorado, 1904 *1029.59 p79*
Roy, Alfred 42; Minnesota, 1925 *2769.54 p1378*
Roy, Ann *SEE* Roy, Joseph
Roy, Anne; Quebec, 1663 *4514.3 p339*
　*Daughter-In-Law:*Jeanne Lelievre
　*Grandchild:*Nicolas
　*Grandchild:*Louis
Roy, Anne; Quebec, 1670 *4514.3 p367*
Roy, Anne; Quebec, 1671 *4514.3 p367*
Roy, Baptiste 18; America, 1846 *778.6 p291*
Roy, Baptiste 24; Texas, 1848 *778.6 p291*
Roy, Catherine; Quebec, 1673 *4514.3 p367*
Roy, Daniel; Virginia, 1700 *9230.15 p81*
Roy, Elisabeth; Quebec, 1665 *4514.3 p367*
Roy, Etienne 15 *SEE* Roy, Marguerite Bire
Roy, Felix 8; America, 1846 *778.6 p292*
Roy, Ferdinand 48; America, 1846 *778.6 p292*
Roy, Francois; Montreal, 1661 *9221.17 p474*
Roy, Francoise Bouet 19 *SEE* Roy, Jean
Roy, George; Nova Scotia, 1821 *9228.50 p107*
Roy, Jacques 12; Quebec, 1647 *9221.17 p189*
Roy, Jane; America, 1774 *1220.12 p692*
Roy, Jaques; Virginia, 1700 *9230.15 p80*
　With wife
Roy, Jean; Illinois, 1852 *6079.1 p12*
Roy, Jean 27; Montreal, 1659 *9221.17 p427*
　*Wife:*Francoise Bouet 19
Roy, Jean; Quebec, 1644 *9221.17 p145*
Roy, Jeanne Lelievre *SEE* Roy, Anne Lemaitre
Roy, Jeanne; Quebec, 1669 *4514.3 p368*
Roy, Jeanne 27; Quebec, 1651 *9221.17 p251*
Roy, Jerome; Quebec, 1643 *9221.17 p135*
Roy, John *SEE* Roy, Joseph
Roy, Joseph; Boston, 1712 *9228.50 p558*
　*Wife:*Ann
　*Son:*John
Roy, Louis *SEE* Roy, Anne Lemaitre
Roy, Marguerite; Quebec, 1665 *4514.3 p296*
Roy, Marguerite; Quebec, 1665 *4514.3 p296*
Roy, Marguerite; Quebec, 1665 *4514.3 p368*
　*Daughter:*Anne
　*Daughter:*Gabrielle
　With sister-in-law & 2 grandchildren
Roy, Marguerite 40; Quebec, 1657 *9221.17 p368*
　*Son:*Etienne 15
Roy, Marie; Quebec, 1665 *4514.3 p368*
Roy, Marie; Quebec, 1667 *4514.3 p368*
Roy, Marie-Anne; Quebec, 1670 *4514.3 p368*
Roy, Mathurin 36; Quebec, 1646 *9221.17 p168*
Roy, Nicolas; Montreal, 1644 *9221.17 p148*
Roy, Nicolas; Quebec, 1600-1663 *4514.3 p339*
Roy, Nicolas *SEE* Roy, Anne Lemaitre
Roy, Nicolas 28; Quebec, 1661 *9221.17 p467*
Roy, Robert; Illinois, 1930 *121.35 p101*
Roy, Robert; Quebec, 1649 *9221.17 p220*
Roy, William 28; Ontario, 1871 *1823.17 p143*
Royal, Elizabeth; America, 1770 *1220.12 p692*
Royce, Cornelia B.; Costa Rica, 1910-1972 *9228.50 p662*
Royce, Cornelia B.; Costa Rica, 1910-1972 *9228.50 p662*
Royce, Patrick 34; Ontario, 1871 *1823.21 p320*
Royce, Robert; America, 1767 *1220.12 p692*
Roycroft, Elizabeth; Barbados or Jamaica, 1686 *1220.12 p692*
Royer, Jean 24; Quebec, 1659 *9221.17 p410*
Royer, Nicholas; Ohio, 1809-1852 *4511.35 p44*
Royer, Nicole; Quebec, 1671 *4514.3 p368*
Royer, Philip; Ohio, 1809-1852 *4511.35 p44*

Royer, Phillip; Ohio, 1809-1852 *4511.35 p44*
Royle, James; America, 1774 *1220.12 p692*
Royley, Mary; Virginia, 1734 *1220.12 p692*
Royne, Francois 22; Montreal, 1653 *9221.17 p300*
Royssigneir, L.; Louisiana, 1874-1875 *4981.45 p30*
Royston, Abraham; America, 1737 *1220.12 p692*
Royston, Elizabeth; America, 1756 *1220.12 p692*
Royston, Robert; Barbados or Jamaica, 1697 *1220.12 p692*
Royton, John; Annapolis, MD, 1722 *1220.12 p692*
Rozanski, Wladyslaw; Detroit, 1929 *1640.55 p113*
Rozek, Joseph; Wisconsin, 1886 *6795.8 p38*
Rozenske, Theodore; Wisconsin, 1906 *6795.8 p216*
Roznorewicz, Paul; Detroit, 1930 *1640.60 p81*
Rozsevac, Josef Maria; Wisconsin, 1878-1879 *2853.20 p31*
Rozy deChauvigny, Pierre-Philippe de; Quebec, 1730 *2314.30 p171*
Ruainer, Elizabeth J. 45; Ontario, 1871 *1823.21 p320*
Ruan, Henrietta Eliza; New York, 1850-1869 *9228.50 p381*
Ruan, John; Colorado, 1887 *1029.59 p79*
Rub, Elisabeth; Venezuela, 1843 *3899.5 p542*
Rub, Elisabeth; Venezuela, 1843 *3899.5 p544*
Rubad, A.; Louisiana, 1874 *4981.45 p296*
Rubbecke, Friedrich; America, 1852 *7420.1 p96*
Rubbery, John; Barbados, 1663 *1220.12 p692*
Rubens, Joseph; New York, NY, 1856 *1494.21 p31*
Rubin, Elisabeth; Venezuela, 1843 *3899.5 p542*
Rubin, Elisabeth; Venezuela, 1843 *3899.5 p544*
Rubin, J. Jurg; New Castle, DE, 1817-1818 *90.20 p153*
Rubincaw, Christopher; North Carolina, 1842 *1088.45 p30*
Ruby, Catherine 53; Ontario, 1871 *1823.21 p320*
Ruby, Thomas; Maryland, 1742 *1220.12 p692*
Ruby, Thomas 49; Ontario, 1871 *1823.21 p320*
Ruby, William 30; Ontario, 1871 *1823.21 p320*
Ruch, Adam; Ohio, 1809-1852 *4511.35 p44*
Ruch, Christian; Ohio, 1809-1852 *4511.35 p44*
Ruch, Christian; Ohio, 1809-1852 *4511.35 p45*
Ruch, Jacob; Ohio, 1809-1852 *4511.35 p45*
Ruch, Louis 47; New Orleans, 1848 *778.6 p292*
Ruch, Michael; Ohio, 1809-1852 *4511.35 p45*
Ruchert, Heinrich; Halifax, N.S., 1902 *1860.4 p41*
Ruchert, Heinrich 30; Halifax, N.S., 1902 *1860.4 p41*
Ruchert, Katha 29; Halifax, N.S., 1902 *1860.4 p41*
Ruchert, Lisbet 4; Halifax, N.S., 1902 *1860.4 p41*
Ruchert, Maria 2; Halifax, N.S., 1902 *1860.4 p41*
Rucht, Carl 18 *SEE* Rucht, Marie
Rucht, Marie 49; New York, NY, 1878 *9253.2 p45*
　*Son:*Carl 18
Rucich, Philip; Ohio, 1809-1852 *4511.35 p45*
Ruck, Georg Julius; America, 1868 *7919.3 p533*
Ruck, Georg Karl; America, 1884 *179.55 p19*
Ruck, Jean 18; Mississippi, 1847 *778.6 p292*
Ruck, Karl; America, 1884 *179.55 p19*
Ruck, Katharina 54; America, 1857 *2526.43 p198*
Ruck, Keziah; Massachusetts, 1754 *1642 p109*
Ruck, Mathias; America, 1868 *5475.1 p225*
Rucks, Friedrick; Wisconsin, 1877 *6795.8 p205*
Ruckstuhl, Georg *SEE* Ruckstuhl, Georg Wilh.
Ruckstuhl, Georg Wilh.; America, 1873 *5475.1 p127*
　*Brother:*Georg
Ruda, Franz 43; Halifax, N.S., 1902 *1860.4 p40*
Rudd, Burlingham; America, 1728 *1220.12 p692*
Rudd, Charles B. 54; Ontario, 1871 *1823.21 p320*
Rudd, James 44; Ontario, 1871 *1823.17 p143*
Rudd, John; America, 1727 *1220.12 p692*
Rudd, John; America, 1769 *1220.12 p692*
Rudd, Timothy; America, 1767 *1220.12 p692*
Rudd, William; America, 1773 *1220.12 p692*
Rudder, Thomas; America, 1774 *1220.12 p692*
Rudderford, Margaret; America, 1740 *1220.12 p692*
Ruddiford, Mary; America, 1694 *1220.12 p692*
Ruddle, Samuel; America, 1685 *1220.12 p692*
Rudel, Christe. 1 months; New York, NY, 1893 *1883.7 p47*
Rudel, Christe. 10 months; New York, NY, 1893 *1883.7 p39*
Rudel, Friedr. 23; New York, NY, 1893 *1883.7 p39*
Rudel, Friedrich 23; New York, NY, 1893 *1883.7 p47*
Rudel, Mrs. Heinrich; America, 1884 *2526.42 p129*
　With 2 children
Rudel, Rosina 21; New York, NY, 1893 *1883.7 p39*
Rudel, Rosina 21; New York, NY, 1893 *1883.7 p47*
Rudell, Heinrich Alexander 19; New York, 1887 *5475.1 p398*
Rudert, Emilie; America, 1868 *7919.3 p532*
　With child
Rudey, Hanna 30; Portland, ME, 1911 *970.38 p80*
Rudge, Eleanor; America, 1768 *1220.12 p692*
Rudge, Thomas; America, 1758 *1220.12 p692*
Rudge, William; America, 1771 *1220.12 p692*

Rudich, Dewalt; Ohio, 1809-1852 *4511.35 p45*
Rudich, Jacob; Ohio, 1809-1852 *4511.35 p45*
Rudich, Philip; Ohio, 1809-1852 *4511.35 p45*
Rudiger, Ida Amalie; America, 1867 *7919.3 p530*
　With child
Rudin, Gustof; Colorado, 1887 *1029.59 p79*
Rudin, Nils; Colorado, 1873 *1029.59 p79*
Rudin, Nils; Colorado, 1886 *1029.59 p79*
Rudine, Andrew; St. Paul, MN, 1899 *1865.50 p108*
Rudinger, Elisabeth 19; Galveston, TX, 1846 *3967.10 p378*
Rudinger, Johann 19; Galveston, TX, 1846 *3967.10 p378*
Rudinger, Joseph 17; Galveston, TX, 1846 *3967.10 p378*
Rudinger, Joseph 49; Galveston, TX, 1846 *3967.10 p378*
Rudinger, Maria 25; Galveston, TX, 1846 *3967.10 p378*
Rudinger, Maria 51; Galveston, TX, 1846 *3967.10 p378*
Rudinger, Therese 11; Galveston, TX, 1846 *3967.10 p378*
Rudis-Jicinsky, J.; Chicago, 1884 *2853.20 p529*
Rudkin, Edward; America, 1763 *1220.12 p692*
Rudman, Thomas; Barbados, 1675 *1220.12 p692*
Rudnitz, Peter 24; New York, NY, 1890 *1883.7 p48*
Rudolf, Adolf; New York, NY, 1904 *3331.4 p12*
Rudolf, Elisabeth; New York, NY, 1903 *3331.4 p12*
Rudolf, Ferdinand; New York, NY, 1909 *3331.4 p12*
Rudolph, Johannes; America, 1887 *2526.42 p106*
Rudolph, John 28; Ontario, 1871 *1823.17 p143*
Rudolph, Katharina; America, 1853 *2526.42 p98*
Rudolph, Wilh.; Valdivia, Chile, 1852 *1192.4 p56*
Rudram, Thomas; America, 1757 *1220.12 p692*
Rudy, Nikolaus; Ottawa, 1892 *5475.1 p39*
Rudy, Peter Paul; New York, 1889 *5475.1 p38*
Rudzik, Tony; Detroit, 1930 *1640.60 p78*
Rue, . . .; America, 1635 *9228.50 p325*
Rue, Henr.ette 54; America, 1842 *778.6 p292*
Rue, Hube.t 49; America, 1842 *778.6 p292*
Rue, John De La; Ohio, 1807 *9228.50 p57*
Rue, William; America, 1772 *1220.12 p692*
Rueb, Christina 11 months; New York, NY, 1893 *1883.7 p39*
Rueb, Christoph; America, 1838 *170.15 p40*
Rueb, Elisabeth 25; New York, NY, 1893 *1883.7 p39*
Rueb, Jacob 27; New York, NY, 1893 *1883.7 p39*
Rueb, Johann 4; New York, NY, 1893 *1883.7 p39*
Rueb, Katharina 2; New York, NY, 1893 *1883.7 p39*
Rueb, Stefan; Carolina, 1841 *170.15 p40*
　With wife & child
Rueckreim, Charles; Washington, 1886 *2770.40 p24*
Ruegge, Christian Ludwig; America, 1885 *7420.1 p348*
　*Daughter:*Hanne Dorothea Charlotte
Ruegge, Hanne Dorothea Charlotte *SEE* Ruegge, Christian Ludwig
Rueggen, John W.; New York, NY, 1833 *3274.55 p23*
Ruegsegger, Hans; North Carolina, 1710 *3629.40 p6*
Ruegsegger, Hans, Jr.; North Carolina, 1710 *3629.40 p6*
Ruel, Clement 13; Quebec, 1658 *9221.17 p386*
Ruelle, M. 20; Cuba, 1841 *778.6 p292*
Ruenger, Carl Wilhelm; Wisconsin, 1899 *6795.8 p75*
Ruenholt, Anna Maria 58; New York, NY, 1864 *8425.62 p197*
Ruenholt, Charlotte 17; New York, NY, 1864 *8425.62 p197*
Ruenholt, Joh. Fr. Wm. 21; New York, NY, 1864 *8425.62 p197*
Ruenholt, Louise 19; New York, NY, 1864 *8425.62 p197*
Ruepke, Gerard; New York, 1777 *8529.30 p4A*
Ruerter, Ignatz 19; America, 1847 *778.6 p292*
Ruette D'Auteuil, Claire-Francoise Clement DuVault *SEE* Ruette D'Auteuil, Denis-Joseph
Ruette d'Auteuil, Denis-Joseph; Quebec, 1648-1649 *2314.30 p166*
Ruette d'Auteuil, Denis-Joseph; Quebec, 1648-1649 *2314.30 p195*
Ruette D'Auteuil, Denis-Joseph 32; Quebec, 1649 *9221.17 p220*
　*Wife:*Claire-Francoise Clement DuVault
Ruette D'Auteuil, Francois-Madeleine-Fortune 3; Quebec, 1660 *9221.17 p468*
Ruf, Elisabeth; Venezuela, 1843 *3899.5 p540*
Ruf, Heinrich; America, 1854 *7420.1 p128*
　With wife & daughter
Ruf, Johann 23; America, 1800-1899 *5475.1 p478*
Ruf, Luise; America, 1866 *5475.1 p433*
Ruf, Philipp; America, 1831 *2526.42 p106*
Rufer, Juide 7; New Orleans, 1847 *778.6 p292*
Rufer, Wendlin 35; New Orleans, 1847 *778.6 p292*
Ruff, Mr.; America, 1837 *5475.1 p73*
Ruff, Andri 2; Halifax, N.S., 1902 *1860.4 p41*
Ruff, Carl; Valdivia, Chile, 1851 *1192.4 p61*
Ruff, Christian; North Dakota, 1890 *554.30 p26*
　*Wife:*Rosa
Ruff, David 16; Halifax, N.S., 1902 *1860.4 p41*

Ruff, David 18; Halifax, N.S., 1902 *1860.4 p41*
Ruff, David 46; Halifax, N.S., 1902 *1860.4 p41*
Ruff, Eva 17; Halifax, N.S., 1902 *1860.4 p41*
Ruff, Friedrich; Valdivia, Chile, 1851 *1192.4 p51*
Ruff, Heinrich; Halifax, N.S., 1902 *1860.4 p41*
Ruff, Jacob; Dakota, 1892-1918 *554.30 p26*
   *Wife:*Louise
Ruff, Jacob 5; Halifax, N.S., 1902 *1860.4 p41*
Ruff, Johann 3; Halifax, N.S., 1902 *1860.4 p41*
Ruff, Johann Josef; America, 1852 *5475.1 p480*
Ruff, Lisbeth 11; Halifax, N.S., 1902 *1860.4 p41*
Ruff, Louise *SEE* Ruff, Jacob
Ruff, Margarete 40; Halifax, N.S., 1902 *1860.4 p41*
Ruff, Moua; Halifax, N.S., 1902 *1860.4 p41*
Ruff, Peter 24; Port uncertain, 1840 *778.6 p292*
Ruff, Rosa *SEE* Ruff, Christian
Ruffet, Mr. 34; New Orleans, 1845 *778.6 p292*
Ruffet, Mrs.; New Orleans, 1845 *778.6 p292*
Ruffhead, Thomas; America, 1766 *1220.12 p692*
Ruffhead, William; America, 1774 *1220.12 p692*
Ruffing, Christian *SEE* Ruffing, Karl
Ruffing, Elisabeth Peter *SEE* Ruffing, Karl
Ruffing, Elisabeth; America, 1893 *5475.1 p46*
Ruffing, Johann *SEE* Ruffing, Karl
Ruffing, Karl; America, 1883 *5475.1 p430*
   *Wife:*Elisabeth Peter
   *Daughter:*Magdalena
   *Son:*Christian
   *Son:*Johann
   *Daughter:*Maria
Ruffing, Magdalena *SEE* Ruffing, Karl
Ruffing, Maria *SEE* Ruffing, Karl
Ruffler, George; America, 1747 *1220.12 p692*
Rufflin, Augustus; Ohio, 1809-1852 *4511.35 p45*
Ruffling, Anthony; Ohio, 1809-1852 *4511.35 p45*
Ruflett, James; America, 1736 *1220.12 p692*
Rufli, Blasius 29; New Castle, DE, 1817-1818 *90.20 p153*
Rufli, Francois 19; Missouri, 1848 *778.6 p292*
Rufo, Paul; Louisiana, 1874 *4981.45 p133*
Rugby, Andrew; America, 1741 *1220.12 p692*
Ruger, Martin; Illinois, 1855 *6079.1 p12*
Rugge, Caroline; America, 1884 *7420.1 p345*
Rugge, Christian August Gottlieb; America, 1884 *7420.1 p345*
Rugge, Wihelmine Justine Charlotte; America, 1890 *7420.1 p361*
Ruggles, James; America, 1745 *1220.12 p692*
Ruggles, William; America, 1755 *1220.12 p692*
Rugh, . . .; Ontario, 1871 *1823.21 p320*
Rugles, Joseph; America, 1744 *1220.12 p692*
Rugmar, Mary; Barbados, 1674 *1220.12 p692*
Rugmar, Mary; Maryland, 1674-1675 *1236.25 p52*
Rugmore, Mary; Maryland, 1674-1675 *1236.25 p52*
Ruh, Eva; New York, 1860 *358.56 p5*
Ruh, Gustav; Colorado, 1891 *1029.59 p79*
Ruh, Gustave; Colorado, 1886 *1029.59 p79*
Ruh, Josephine 23; Port uncertain, 1846 *778.6 p292*
Ruhe, Mr.; America, 1855 *7420.1 p141*
   *Son:*Ernst
   With wife
Ruhe, Engel Sophia Doroth. *SEE* Ruhe, Johann Friedrich Ferdinand
Ruhe, Ernst *SEE* Ruhe, Mr.
Ruhe, Ferdinand Aug. Ludw. *SEE* Ruhe, Johann Friedrich Ferdinand
Ruhe, Friedrich Ludw. Aug. *SEE* Ruhe, Johann Friedrich Ferdinand
Ruhe, Johann Friedr. Wilh. *SEE* Ruhe, Johann Friedrich Ferdinand
Ruhe, Johann Friedrich Ferdinand; America, 1855 *7420.1 p141*
   *Wife:*Louise Ernestine Amalia Matthias
   *Son:*Ferdinand Aug. Ludw.
   *Daughter:*Maria Soph.
   *Daughter:*Engel Sophia Doroth.
   *Son:*Friedrich Ludw. Aug.
   *Daughter:*Justine Wilhelm. Charl.
   *Son:*Johann Friedr. Wilh.
Ruhe, Justine Wilhelm. Charl. *SEE* Ruhe, Johann Friedrich Ferdinand
Ruhe, Louise Ernestine Amalia Matthias *SEE* Ruhe, Johann Friedrich Ferdinand
Ruhe, Maria Soph. *SEE* Ruhe, Johann Friedrich Ferdinand
Ruhe, Wilhelm; America, 1854 *7420.1 p128*
Ruhenkamp, Henry; Ohio, 1840-1897 *8365.35 p17*
Ruhl, Anna Margarethe *SEE* Ruhl, Katharine Elisabeth
Ruhl, Anna Marie *SEE* Ruhl, Eleonore Christine
Ruhl, Eleonore *SEE* Ruhl, Katharine Elisabeth
Ruhl, Eleonore Christine; America, 1836 *8115.12 p326*
   *Child:*Anna Marie
Ruhl, Elisabeth; America, 1889 *5475.1 p69*

Ruhl, Elisabetha *SEE* Ruhl, Philipp
Ruhl, Elisabetha Schuler *SEE* Ruhl, Philipp
Ruhl, Elisabetha Roth 27 *SEE* Ruhl, Leonhard
Ruhl, Eva Katharina; America, 1883 *2526.42 p120*
Ruhl, Franz; America, 1865 *2526.43 p179*
Ruhl, George; Ohio, 1809-1852 *4511.35 p45*
Ruhl, Heinrich 5 *SEE* Ruhl, Leonhard
Ruhl, Jakob 1 *SEE* Ruhl, Leonhard
Ruhl, Johann Andreas; America, n.d. *8115.12 p322*
Ruhl, John; Ohio, 1809-1852 *4511.35 p45*
Ruhl, Justine; America, 1836 *8115.12 p327*
Ruhl, Justine; America, n.d. *8115.12 p327*
Ruhl, Katharina *SEE* Ruhl, Philipp
Ruhl, Katharine Elisabeth; America, 1840 *8115.12 p326*
   *Child:*Eleonore
   *Child:*Anna Margarethe
Ruhl, Konrad; America, 1881 *2526.43 p213*
Ruhl, Leonhard; America, 1856 *2526.43 p213*
   *Wife:*Elisabetha Roth
   *Son:*Heinrich
   *Son:*Jakob
Ruhl, Maria Elisabetha; America, 1752 *2526.42 p172*
Ruhl, Michael, III; America, 1888 *2526.43 p154*
   With wife 27
Ruhl, Peter 27; America, 1883 *2526.42 p154*
Ruhl, Peter 27; America, 1883 *2526.42 p155*
Ruhl, Philipp; America, 1881 *2526.43 p143*
   *Wife:*Elisabetha Schuler
   With 2 stepchildren
   *Daughter:*Elisabetha
   *Daughter:*Katharina
Ruhl, Philipp; America, 1883 *2526.42 p101*
Ruhland, Adam 2 *SEE* Ruhland, Johannes
Ruhland, Adam 12 *SEE* Ruhland, Johannes
Ruhland, Elisabetha 13 *SEE* Ruhland, Johannes
Ruhland, Elisabetha 19 *SEE* Ruhland, Johannes
Ruhland, Eva 3 *SEE* Ruhland, Johannes
Ruhland, Eva 9 *SEE* Ruhland, Johannes
Ruhland, Eva 20 *SEE* Ruhland, Johannes
Ruhland, Friedrich 7 *SEE* Ruhland, Johannes
Ruhland, Friedrich 13 *SEE* Ruhland, Johannes
Ruhland, Friedrich 24 *SEE* Ruhland, Johannes
Ruhland, Johann 7 *SEE* Ruhland, Johannes
Ruhland, Johann 17 *SEE* Ruhland, Johannes
Ruhland, Johannes; America, 1847 *2526.42 p184*
   With wife
   *Son:*Friedrich
   *Son:*Peter
   *Daughter:*Eva
   *Daughter:*Elisabetha
   *Son:*Wilhelm
Ruhland, Johannes; America, 1853 *2526.42 p164*
   With wife
   *Son:*Friedrich
   *Daughter:*Eva
   *Son:*Adam
   *Son:*Johann
   *Son:*Peter
   *Son:*Wilhelm
   With grandchild 6 months
   *Daughter:*Elisabetha
Ruhland, Johannes; America, 1864 *2526.42 p184*
   *Son:*Wilhelm
   *Son:*Peter
   *Son:*Johann
   *Son:*Adam
   *Daughter:*Eva
   *Son:*Friedrich
Ruhland, Peter 4 *SEE* Ruhland, Johannes
Ruhland, Peter 11 *SEE* Ruhland, Johannes
Ruhland, Peter 22 *SEE* Ruhland, Johannes
Ruhland, Wilhelm 11 *SEE* Ruhland, Johannes
Ruhland, Wilhelm 17 *SEE* Ruhland, Johannes
Ruhland, Wilhelm 28 *SEE* Ruhland, Johannes
Ruhler, Dominique 30; Louisiana, 1848 *778.6 p292*
Ruhleter, George; Louisiana, 1841-1844 *4981.45 p211*
Ruhlmann, Joseph; Louisiana, 1874 *4981.45 p133*
Ruhman, Michael; Ohio, 1809-1852 *4511.35 p45*
Ruihenbach, Charles; New York, 1860 *358.56 p5*
Ruishe, Pankrae; Illinois, 1852 *6079.1 p12*
Ruitty, Daniel; America, 1719 *1220.12 p692*
Ruk, Josephine 23; Louisiana, 1846 *778.6 p292*
Rukszto, Peter; Detroit, 1929-1930 *6214.5 p65*
Rul, Anna 38; Portland, ME, 1906 *970.38 p80*
Rul, David 21; Portland, ME, 1906 *970.38 p80*
Rul, Dawid 11 months; Portland, ME, 1906 *970.38 p80*
Rul, Dawid 31; Portland, ME, 1906 *970.38 p80*
Rul, Emilie 13; Portland, ME, 1906 *970.38 p80*
Rul, Heinrich 39; Portland, ME, 1906 *970.38 p80*
Rul, Julianna 18; Portland, ME, 1906 *970.38 p80*
Rul, Marie 25; Portland, ME, 1906 *970.38 p80*
Rulfs, D.A.W.; Texas, 1886 *3435.45 p36*
Rulfs, William H.; Texas, 1895 *3435.45 p36*

Rulh, Mrs. 42; New Orleans, 1846 *778.6 p292*
Rulh, Chs. Emile 12; New Orleans, 1846 *778.6 p292*
Rulh, Fs. Eugene 16; New Orleans, 1846 *778.6 p292*
Rulorrub, Friedrich 25; Portland, ME, 1906 *970.38 p80*
Ruly, John; Charles Town, SC, 1719 *1220.12 p692*
Rumball, Charles; Barbados or Jamaica, 1684 *1220.12 p692*
Rumble, John 36; Ontario, 1871 *1823.21 p320*
Rumble, Thomas 66; Ontario, 1871 *1823.21 p320*
Rumbold, Thomas; America, 1768 *1220.12 p692*
Rumbow, Edward; America, 1748 *1220.12 p692*
Rumelhart, Joseph; Ohio, 1809-1852 *4511.35 p45*
Rumella, John; Ohio, 1809-1852 *4511.35 p45*
Rumery, Simon; Salem, MA, 1660-1679 *9228.50 p550*
Rumford, William 47; Ontario, 1871 *1823.17 p143*
Rummel, Anna Maria; America, 1853 *2526.43 p155*
Rummel, Elisabeth; America, 1853 *2526.43 p155*
Rummel, Elisabeth Hill *SEE* Rummel, Johann
Rummel, Jakob; America, 1846 *2526.42 p155*
   With wife
Rummel, Johann; America, 1881 *5475.1 p23*
   *Wife:*Elisabeth Hill
Rummel, Leonard; America, 1742 *1220.12 p692*
Rummelhart, Joseph; Ohio, 1809-1852 *4511.35 p45*
Rummelmann, Christian Friedrich Ludwig; America, 1861 *7420.1 p208*
Rummler, A.; Port uncertain, 1887 *7420.1 p355*
Rumney, Andrew; America, 1746 *1220.12 p692*
Rumny, Joseph; America, 1848 *778.6 p292*
Rump, Michael; Ohio, 1840-1897 *8365.35 p17*
Rumpel, Christoph Friedrich; America, 1867 *7919.3 p532*
Rumpel, Elise; America, 1868 *7919.3 p532*
   *Brother:*Hermann
Rumpel, Hermann *SEE* Rumpel, Elise
Rumpf, Karl; America, 1882 *5475.1 p421*
Rumpfert, Christe 25; New York, NY, 1890 *1883.7 p47*
Rumpfert, Gottfried 21; New York, NY, 1890 *1883.7 p47*
Rumpfert, Gottlieb 6; New York, NY, 1890 *1883.7 p47*
Rumpfert, Math. 6; New York, NY, 1890 *1883.7 p47*
Rumpfert, Mathias 24; New York, NY, 1890 *1883.7 p47*
Rumpfert, Rike 10 months; New York, NY, 1890 *1883.7 p47*
Rumpson, John; America, 1768 *1220.12 p693*
Rumreich, Frantisek; Wisconsin, 1876 *2853.20 p252*
Rumrill, Clement; New York, 1687 *9228.50 p563*
Rumrill, Matthieu; New England, 1650-1685 *9228.50 p552*
Rumrill, Simon; New England, 1654-1754 *9228.50 p559*
Rumrill, Simon; Salem, MA, 1660-1679 *9228.50 p550*
Rumry, Simon; Salem, MA, 1660-1679 *9228.50 p550*
Rumsey, Ann; Barbados or Jamaica, 1705 *1220.12 p693*
Rumsey, John; Died enroute, 1730 *1220.12 p693*
Rumsey, John; Maryland, 1722 *1220.12 p693*
Rumsey, Thomas; Barbados, 1683 *1220.12 p693*
Run, Caroline; New Orleans, 1851 *7242.30 p154*
Run, Charles; New Orleans, 1851 *7242.30 p154*
Runckel, A. 50; New Orleans, 1834 *1002.51 p113*
Runckel, Miss A. 8; New Orleans, 1834 *1002.51 p113*
Runckel, Miss A. 43; New Orleans, 1834 *1002.51 p113*
Runckel, C. 11; New Orleans, 1834 *1002.51 p113*
Runckel, Miss J. 3; New Orleans, 1834 *1002.51 p113*
Runckel, P. 19; New Orleans, 1834 *1002.51 p113*
Runckel, Miss R. 4; New Orleans, 1834 *1002.51 p113*
Rundas, Thomas 59; Ontario, 1871 *1823.21 p320*
Runde, Heinrich 17; New York, NY, 1864 *8425.62 p197*
Runde, Louise 9; New York, NY, 1864 *8425.62 p197*
Runde, Marie 50; New York, NY, 1864 *8425.62 p197*
Runde, Sophie 8; New York, NY, 1864 *8425.62 p197*
Runde, Wilhelm 53; New York, NY, 1864 *8425.62 p197*
Rundell, Arthur 15; Quebec, 1870 *8364.32 p25*
Rundell, Richd 59; Ontario, 1871 *1823.17 p143*
Rundgvist, Amanda 22; New York, NY, 1894 *6512.1 p230*
Rundgvist, Axel 20; New York, NY, 1894 *6512.1 p230*
Rundle, Charles 25; Ontario, 1871 *1823.21 p320*
Rundle, Daniel 76; Ontario, 1871 *1823.21 p320*
Rundle, Mary Ann 30; Ontario, 1871 *1823.21 p320*
Rundle, Philip 51; Ontario, 1871 *1823.21 p320*
Rundle, Richard; America, 1737 *1220.12 p693*
Rundle, William 55; Ontario, 1871 *1823.21 p320*
Rundle, William 68; Ontario, 1871 *1823.21 p320*
Rundus, Frantisek; Iowa, 1870 *2853.20 p202*
Runells, Richard 31; Ontario, 1871 *1823.21 p320*
Rung, Friedrich 50; America, 1892 *5475.1 p425*
Runge, Ernst August; America, 1869 *7420.1 p281*
   With wife & 3 children
Runge, George H. W.; North Carolina, 1857 *1088.45 p30*
Runge, Wilhelm Gustav; New York, 1873 *5475.1 p127*
Runkel, John; New York, 1860 *358.56 p149*
Runkel, Ludwig Friedrich; America, 1867 *7919.3 p531*
   With wife

Runnell, Jacob 35; Kansas, 1904 ***1447.20*** *p62*
Runnels, Elisabeth 24; Michigan, 1880 ***4491.36*** *p18*
Runnels, Hannah 21; Ontario, 1871 ***1823.21*** *p320*
Runniard, Ann; America, 1764 ***1220.12*** *p693*
Runpel, Catha 10; Halifax, N.S., 1902 ***1860.4*** *p40*
Runpel, Elisabeth 15; Halifax, N.S., 1902 ***1860.4*** *p40*
Runpel, Elisbethe 49; Halifax, N.S., 1902 ***1860.4*** *p40*
Runpel, Franz 60; Halifax, N.S., 1902 ***1860.4*** *p40*
Runpel, Jacob 16; Halifax, N.S., 1902 ***1860.4*** *p40*
Runpel, Johann 28; Halifax, N.S., 1902 ***1860.4*** *p40*
Runpel, Maria 21; Halifax, N.S., 1902 ***1860.4*** *p40*
Runsberg, John; America, 1741 ***1220.12*** *p693*
Runser, Andrew; Ohio, 1809-1852 ***4511.35*** *p45*
Runtz, Catharine 50; America, 1841 ***778.6*** *p292*
Runtz, Jacob 11; America, 1841 ***778.6*** *p292*
Runtz, Joseph 40; America, 1841 ***778.6*** *p292*
Runtz, Marx 18; America, 1841 ***778.6*** *p292*
Runtz, Pierre 22; America, 1841 ***778.6*** *p292*
Runyan, M.; California, 1868 ***1131.61*** *p89*
Runyon, Vincent; New Jersey, 1660-1669 ***9228.50*** *p564*
Ruoss, Leonhardt; Philadelphia, 1866 ***8513.31*** *p424*
*Wife:*Margaret Hirsch
Ruoss, Margaret Hirsch *SEE* Ruoss, Leonhardt
Ruote, Rocco; Colorado, 1885 ***1029.59*** *p79*
Ruoto, Rocco; Colorado, 1885 ***1029.59*** *p79*
Rupell, Mary 20; Ontario, 1871 ***1823.21*** *p320*
Rupert, George; Ohio, 1809-1852 ***4511.35*** *p45*
Rupertus, Pius; Valdivia, Chile, 1852 ***1192.4*** *p54*
Rupnow, August; Wisconsin, 1882 ***6795.8*** *p107*
Rupp, Angela *SEE* Rupp, Johann
Rupp, Anna *SEE* Rupp, Jakob
Rupp, Anna *SEE* Rupp, Johann
Rupp, Anton *SEE* Rupp, Jakob
Rupp, Barbara; America, 1881 ***5475.1*** *p214*
Rupp, Elisabeth *SEE* Rupp, Jakob
Rupp, Elisabeth *SEE* Rupp, Johann
Rupp, Elisabeth Ruhl *SEE* Rupp, Johann Peter
Rupp, Friedrich; America, 1882 ***5475.1*** *p214*
Rupp, Jakob; America, 1873 ***5475.1*** *p172*
*Wife:*Magdalena Osbild
*Daughter:*Anna
*Daughter:*Katharina
*Daughter:*Magdalena
*Daughter:*Elisabeth
*Daughter:*Margarethe
*Son:*Anton
Rupp, Johann; America, 1873 ***5475.1*** *p145*
Rupp, Johann *SEE* Rupp, Johann
Rupp, Johann; America, 1882 ***5475.1*** *p316*
*Wife:*Katharina Klein
*Daughter:*Susanna
*Son:*Nikolaus
*Daughter:*Elisabeth
*Daughter:*Margarethe
*Son:*Johann
*Daughter:*Angela
*Daughter:*Maria
*Son:*Peter
*Daughter:*Anna
*Daughter:*Katharina
Rupp, Johann Peter; America, 1889 ***5475.1*** *p69*
*Wife:*Elisabeth Ruhl
Rupp, Katharina *SEE* Rupp, Jakob
Rupp, Katharina *SEE* Rupp, Michel
Rupp, Katharina *SEE* Rupp, Johann
Rupp, Katharina Klein *SEE* Rupp, Johann
Rupp, M. Elisabeth; America, 1880 ***5475.1*** *p173*
Rupp, Magdalena *SEE* Rupp, Jakob
Rupp, Magdalena Osbild 47 *SEE* Rupp, Jakob
Rupp, Margarethe *SEE* Rupp, Jakob
Rupp, Margarethe *SEE* Rupp, Michel
Rupp, Margarethe *SEE* Rupp, Johann
Rupp, Maria; America, 1880 ***5475.1*** *p173*
Rupp, Maria *SEE* Rupp, Johann
Rupp, Michel; America, 1881 ***5475.1*** *p174*
*Son:*Philipp
*Daughter:*Margarethe
*Daughter:*Katharina
Rupp, Nikolaus *SEE* Rupp, Johann
Rupp, Peter; America, 1881 ***5475.1*** *p174*
Rupp, Peter *SEE* Rupp, Johann
Rupp, Philipp *SEE* Rupp, Michel
Rupp, Susanna *SEE* Rupp, Johann
Ruppe, Lewis 44; Ontario, 1871 ***1823.21*** *p320*
Ruppel, Carl 30; Halifax, N.S., 1902 ***1860.4*** *p44*
Ruppel, Christine 36; Halifax, N.S., 1902 ***1860.4*** *p44*
Ruppel, Elisabetha Saul *SEE* Ruppel, Georg
Ruppel, Emilie 6; Halifax, N.S., 1902 ***1860.4*** *p44*
Ruppel, Fred 7; Halifax, N.S., 1902 ***1860.4*** *p44*
Ruppel, Georg; America, 1883 ***2526.42*** *p130*
*Wife:*Elisabetha Saul
Ruppel, Haua 18; Halifax, N.S., 1902 ***1860.4*** *p44*
Ruppel, Johann 16; Halifax, N.S., 1902 ***1860.4*** *p44*
Ruppel, Marga; Halifax, N.S., 1902 ***1860.4*** *p44*
Ruppel, Maria 10; Halifax, N.S., 1902 ***1860.4*** *p44*
Ruppel, Wilhelm 4; Halifax, N.S., 1902 ***1860.4*** *p44*
Ruppenthal, Karoline; America, 1861 ***5475.1*** *p523*
Ruppert, Andreas; America, 1843 ***2526.42*** *p196*
With wife & child
Ruppert, Andreas; America, 1845 ***2526.42*** *p189*
Ruppert, Anna Magdalene; America, n.d. ***8115.12*** *p327*
Ruppert, August 25; America, 1883 ***2526.43*** *p213*
Ruppert, Elisabetha; America, 1866 ***2526.43*** *p135*
With 2 children
Ruppert, Joseph; America, 1885 ***2526.43*** *p213*
Ruppert, Peter Joseph; America, 1856 ***2526.43*** *p213*
Ruppert, Philipp; America, 1831 ***2526.43*** *p135*
Ruppert Family ; West Virginia, 1850 ***1132.30*** *p147*
Ruprecht, Frederick; Ohio, 1809-1852 ***4511.35*** *p45*
Ruquenard, Francois 60; America, 1846 ***778.6*** *p292*
Rurheach, Catharine 17; America, 1847 ***778.6*** *p292*
Rusch, Gerhardt C.C.; Wisconsin, 1882 ***6795.8*** *p228*
Rusch, Wilhelmine Loisaa; Wisconsin, 1899 ***6795.8*** *p193*
Rusche, Francis; Texas, 1851 ***3435.45*** *p36*
Rusche, Heinrich; America, 1845 ***7420.1*** *p39*
With wife
Ruschel, Peter 23; America, 1881 ***5475.1*** *p484*
Ruscher, Eduard; America, 1867 ***7919.3*** *p528*
Ruse, Oliver E. 24; Ontario, 1871 ***1823.21*** *p320*
Ruse, Samuel 47; Ontario, 1871 ***1823.21*** *p320*
Rusel, Henry; Boston, 1720 ***9228.50*** *p564*
Rusel, Noel; Boston, 1699 ***9228.50*** *p564*
Rush, Bridget; New Orleans, 1851 ***7242.30*** *p154*
Rush, Charles 35; Ontario, 1871 ***1823.21*** *p320*
Rush, Jane 65; Ontario, 1871 ***1823.21*** *p320*
Rush, John; New Orleans, 1851 ***7242.30*** *p154*
Rush, Margaret; New Orleans, 1851 ***7242.30*** *p154*
Rush, Mary; Virginia, 1735 ***1220.12*** *p693*
Rush, Peter; New Orleans, 1851 ***7242.30*** *p154*
Rushbrooke, Benjamin; America, 1734 ***1220.12*** *p693*
Rusher, John; Ohio, 1809-1852 ***4511.35*** *p45*
Rusher, Mary; Potomac, 1731 ***1220.12*** *p693*
Rushfield, Fairfax; America, 1734 ***1220.12*** *p693*
Rushing, Jane; America, 1749 ***1220.12*** *p693*
Rusikewicz, Anna; Detroit, 1929 ***1640.55*** *p115*
Ruskamp, Lorenz; Nebraska, 1905 ***3004.30*** *p46*
Ruskin, Philip; Detroit, 1930 ***1640.60*** *p82*
Ruskin, Thomas; Virginia, 1741 ***1220.12*** *p693*
Ruskton, Thomas; America, 1771 ***1220.12*** *p693*
Russ, Antone 47; New York, NY, 1894 ***6512.1*** *p182*
Russ, Mary; America, 1768 ***1220.12*** *p693*
Russarth, John; Louisiana, 1874 ***4981.45*** *p133*
Russel, Mr.; America, 1858 ***7420.1*** *p181*
Russel, Carl Heinrich Ludwig; America, 1868 ***7420.1*** *p276*
Russel, Engel Maria Dorothea *SEE* Russel, Johann Otto
Russel, Engel Maria Dorothea Kaukenmoller *SEE* Russel, Johann Otto
Russel, Engel Maria Dorothea; America, 1867 ***7420.1*** *p263*
Russel, Engel Maria Sophia *SEE* Russel, Johann Otto
Russel, Friedrich Wilhelm *SEE* Russel, Johann Otto
Russel, Heinrich Conrad *SEE* Russel, Johann Otto
Russel, J. Ph.; New York, 1860 ***358.56*** *p3*
Russel, Jessey 32; Ontario, 1871 ***1823.21*** *p320*
Russel, Johann Heinrich Christoph; America, 1850 ***7420.1*** *p74*
Russel, Johann Otto; America, 1860 ***7420.1*** *p199*
*Wife:*Engel Maria Dorothea Kaukenmoller
*Son:*Friedrich Wilhelm
*Son:*Heinrich Conrad
*Daughter:*Engel Maria Sophia
*Daughter:*Engel Maria Dorothea
Russel, John; Boston, 1713 ***9228.50*** *p564*
Russel, John 40; Ontario, 1871 ***1823.17*** *p143*
Russel, John W.; Ohio, 1809-1852 ***4511.35*** *p45*
Russel, Maria Dorothee; America, 1854 ***7420.1*** *p126*
Russel, Robert 68; Ontario, 1871 ***1823.21*** *p321*
Russel, William E.; Ohio, 1821 ***3580.20*** *p33*
Russel, William E.; Ohio, 1821 ***6020.12*** *p22*
Russell, Mr.; Salem, MA, 1674 ***9228.50*** *p564*
Russell, Alexander; Annapolis, MD, 1732 ***1220.12*** *p693*
Russell, Ann; America, 1752 ***1220.12*** *p693*
Russell, Ann; America, 1767 ***1220.12*** *p693*
Russell, Ann; Virginia, 1618 ***1220.12*** *p693*
Russell, Cath; New Orleans, 1851 ***7242.30*** *p154*
Russell, Charles; South Carolina, 1808 ***6155.4*** *p19*
Russell, Cornelius; America, 1774 ***1220.12*** *p693*
Russell, David; America, 1772 ***1220.12*** *p693*
Russell, Eleanor; America, 1722 ***1220.12*** *p693*
Russell, Elizabeth; America, 1753 ***1220.12*** *p693*
Russell, Elizabeth; Annapolis, MD, 1723 ***1220.12*** *p693*
Russell, Elizabeth; Rappahannock, VA, 1726 ***1220.12*** *p693*
Russell, Frances; Barbados, 1676 ***1220.12*** *p693*
Russell, Francis; Barbados, 1682 ***1220.12*** *p693*
Russell, George; America, 1685 ***1220.12*** *p693*
Russell, George; America, 1775 ***1220.12*** *p693*
Russell, George F. 22; Ontario, 1871 ***1823.21*** *p321*
Russell, Hannah; America, 1765 ***1220.12*** *p693*
Russell, Henry; Louisiana, 1874-1875 ***4981.45*** *p30*
Russell, Isabella 24; New York, NY, 1835 ***5024.1*** *p137*
Russell, James; Jamaica, 1716 ***1220.12*** *p693*
Russell, James 33; Michigan, 1880 ***4491.39*** *p26*
Russell, James 41; Ontario, 1871 ***1823.17*** *p143*
Russell, James; Virginia, 1741 ***1220.12*** *p693*
Russell, Jane; America, 1743 ***1220.12*** *p693*
Russell, John; America, 1751 ***1220.12*** *p693*
Russell, John; America, 1762 ***1220.12*** *p693*
Russell, John 40; America, 1847 ***778.6*** *p292*
Russell, John; Barbados or Jamaica, 1710 ***1220.12*** *p693*
Russell, John 21; New York, NY, 1835 ***5024.1*** *p137*
Russell, John 25; Ontario, 1871 ***1823.21*** *p321*
Russell, John 27; Ontario, 1871 ***1823.21*** *p321*
Russell, John 38; Ontario, 1871 ***1823.17*** *p143*
Russell, John 44; Ontario, 1871 ***1823.17*** *p143*
Russell, John 83; Ontario, 1871 ***1823.21*** *p321*
Russell, John; Philadelphia, 1812 ***5720.10*** *p381*
Russell, John, Jr.; Virginia, 1774 ***1220.12*** *p693*
Russell, John W.; Ohio, 1809-1852 ***4511.35*** *p45*
Russell, Jonathan; Annapolis, MD, 1724 ***1220.12*** *p693*
Russell, Joseph; America, 1771 ***1220.12*** *p693*
Russell, Margaret; Charles Town, SC, 1719 ***1220.12*** *p693*
Russell, Martha 17; St. John, N.B., 1834 ***6469.7*** *p5*
Russell, Mary; America, 1718 ***1220.12*** *p693*
Russell, Mary 28; Ohio, 1880 ***4879.40*** *p259*
Russell, Nicholas; America, 1771 ***1220.12*** *p693*
Russell, Noel; Boston, 1699 ***9228.50*** *p564*
Russell, Persevel 21; Ontario, 1871 ***1823.21*** *p321*
Russell, Robert; America, 1700 ***1220.12*** *p694*
Russell, Robert; America, 1774 ***1220.12*** *p694*
Russell, Robert; Ohio, 1832 ***3580.20*** *p33*
Russell, Robert; Ohio, 1832 ***6020.12*** *p22*
Russell, Robert M.; Marblehead, MA, 1804 ***9228.50*** *p88*
Russell, Robert W.; Ohio, 1845 ***3580.20*** *p33*
Russell, Robert W.; Ohio, 1845 ***6020.12*** *p22*
Russell, Robrt 23; Halifax, N.S., n.d. ***1833.5*** *p7*
Russell, Robrt 23; Halifax, N.S., n.d. ***8445.10*** *p7*
Russell, Rosa Lena; Miami, 1935 ***4984.12*** *p39*
Russell, Samuel 40; Ontario, 1871 ***1823.21*** *p321*
Russell, Sarah; America, 1753 ***1220.12*** *p694*
Russell, Stephen; America, 1736 ***1220.12*** *p694*
Russell, Susanna; Annapolis, MD, 1725 ***1220.12*** *p694*
Russell, Thomas; Barbados or Jamaica, 1664 ***1220.12*** *p694*
Russell, Thomas 35; Michigan, 1880 ***4491.39*** *p26*
Russell, Walter; West Indies, 1686 ***1220.12*** *p694*
Russell, William; America, 1680 ***1220.12*** *p694*
Russell, William; America, 1685 ***1220.12*** *p694*
Russell, William; America, 1694 ***1220.12*** *p694*
Russell, William; America, 1748 ***1220.12*** *p694*
Russell, William; America, 1757 ***1220.12*** *p694*
Russell, William; America, 1766 ***1220.12*** *p694*
Russell, William; America, 1768 ***1220.12*** *p694*
Russell, William; America, 1771 ***1220.12*** *p694*
Russell, William; America, 1774 ***1220.12*** *p694*
Russell, William 43; Ontario, 1871 ***1823.21*** *p321*
Russen, Robert; America, 1774 ***1220.12*** *p694*
Russen, Thomas; America, 1691 ***1220.12*** *p694*
Russet, James; America, 1742 ***1220.12*** *p694*
Russmann, Franz *SEE* Russmann, Heinrich
Russmann, Heinrich; Detroit, 1903-1950 ***8023.44*** *p378*
*Brother:*Franz
*Brother:*Joh.
Russmann, Joh. *SEE* Russmann, Heinrich
Russmann, Maria; Argentina, 1924 ***8023.44*** *p378*
Russo, Augustine; Louisiana, 1874-1875 ***4981.45*** *p30*
Russo, Guisseppe; Louisiana, 1874 ***4981.45*** *p133*
Rust, . . .; America, 1846 ***7420.1*** *p48*
With family
Rust, . . .; America, 1867 ***7420.1*** *p263*
Rust, Mr.; America, 1881 ***7420.1*** *p324*
Rust, Widow; America, 1853 ***7420.1*** *p111*
Rust, Argentine; America, 1685 ***1220.12*** *p694*
Rust, Christian; America, 1867 ***7420.1*** *p263*
With family
Rust, Christian; America, 1867 ***7919.3*** *p528*
With family
Rust, Ernst; America, 1867 ***7420.1*** *p263*
With wife & 3 children
Rust, Friedrich Ludwig; America, 1881 ***7420.1*** *p324*
Rust, Heinrich; America, 1845 ***7420.1*** *p39*
With wife & 3 children
Rust, Henriette; America, 1867 ***7919.3*** *p528*
With child
Rust, Sophie Wilhelmine; Port uncertain, 1853 ***7420.1*** *p109*
Rust, Wilhelm; America, 1884 ***7420.1*** *p345*
Rust, Wilhelmina; North Dakota, 1887 ***554.30*** *p26*

Rust, William; America, 1754 1220.12 p694
Rustan, Olander; Iowa, 1916 1211.15 p18
Rustead, Richard; America, 1762 1220.12 p694
Rusted, Robert; America, 1726 1220.12 p694
Rustin, Elizabeth; America, 1739 1220.12 p694
Rustin, Mary; America, 1758 1220.12 p694
Ruston, Alice; America, 1771 1220.12 p694
Ruston, Robert; America, 1773 1220.12 p694
Ruston, William; New York, 1777 8529.30 p15
Ruteberrig, Anna 32; New York, NY, 1847 9176.15 p49
Ruteberrig, Michel 2; New York, NY, 1847 9176.15 p50
Ruteberrig, Michel 31; New York, NY, 1847 9176.15 p49
Ruter, Marie 18; New York, NY, 1864 8425.62 p198
Ruth, Anton; America, 1929 8023.44 p378
Ruth, Hein. 5; America, 1846 778.6 p292
Ruth, Jacob; America, 1751 1220.12 p694
Ruth, Marg. 5; America, 1846 778.6 p292
Ruther, Jacob 19; New York, NY, 1847 9176.15 p50
Ruther, Michel 24; New York, NY, 1847 9176.15 p50
Rutherford, Alex 37; Ontario, 1871 1823.21 p321
Rutherford, Christopher 12; New York, NY, 1821-1849 6178.50 p149
Rutherford, Christopher 41; New York, NY, 1825 6178.50 p149
Rutherford, Collingwood 8; New York, NY, 1821-1849 6178.50 p149
Rutherford, Elizabeth 41; Ontario, 1871 1823.17 p143
Rutherford, James 19; New York, NY, 1821-1849 6178.50 p149
Rutherford, John; America, 1761 1220.12 p694
Rutherford, John; America, 1766 1220.12 p694
Rutherford, John 10; New York, NY, 1821-1849 6178.50 p149
Rutherford, Mary; Virginia, 1741 1220.12 p694
Rutherford, Richard; Virginia, 1741 1220.12 p694
Rutherford, Thomas 40; Ontario, 1871 1823.21 p321
Rutherford, Walter B.; North Carolina, 1827 1088.45 p30
Rutherford, William 15; New York, NY, 1821-1849 6178.50 p149
Rutherford, William 40; Ontario, 1871 1823.17 p143
Ruthven, John; Iowa, 1878 1211.15 p18
Rutiman, Oswald 33; New Castle, DE, 1817-1818 90.20 p153
Rutland, James; America, 1764 1220.12 p694
Rutland, Jonathan; America, 1700 1220.12 p694
Rutland, Joseph; America, 1757 1220.12 p694
Rutland, Richard; America, 1700 1220.12 p694
Rutland, William; America, 1751 1220.12 p694
Rutledge, James 60; Ontario, 1871 1823.17 p143
Rutledge, John 22; Ontario, 1871 1823.21 p321
Rutledge, Mark; New York, NY, 1833 3274.55 p72
Rutledge, Thomas 27; Ontario, 1871 1823.21 p321
Rutledge, William; America, 1754 1220.12 p694
Rutlege, John; America, 1739 1220.12 p694
Rutlege, Thomas; America, 1773 1220.12 p694
Rutley, Robert; America, 1760 1220.12 p694
Rutlidge, Thomas; America, 1770 1220.12 p694
Rutliss, Wharton; America, 1736 1220.12 p694
Rutschi, C. 24; New Orleans, 1834 1002.51 p112
Rutschin, C. 8; New Orleans, 1834 1002.51 p112
Rutschin, C. 34; New Orleans, 1834 1002.51 p112
Rutschin, Miss E. 38; New Orleans, 1834 1002.51 p112
Rutschin, J. 6; New Orleans, 1834 1002.51 p112
Rutson, Richard; America, 1756 1220.12 p694
Rutt, Christopher; America, 1763 1220.12 p695
Rutt, James; America, 1743 1220.12 p695
Rutt, John; America, 1734 1220.12 p695
Rutter, Amy; Maryland, 1736 1220.12 p695
Rutter, Ann; America, 1738 1220.12 p695
Rutter, George; America, 1767 1220.12 p695
Rutter, John; America, 1728 1220.12 p695
Rutter, Minah; America, 1775 1220.12 p695
Rutter, Philip; Maryland, 1736 1220.12 p695
Rutter, Richd 45; Ontario, 1871 1823.17 p143
Rutter, Samuel; America, 1685 1220.12 p695
Rutter, Thomas; America, 1767 1220.12 p695
Ruttimann, Oswald 33; New Castle, DE, 1817-1818 90.20 p153
Ruttree, Ann; America, 1707 1220.12 p695
Rutz, Dawid 7; Portland, ME, 1906 970.38 p80
Rutz, Heinrich 37; Portland, ME, 1906 970.38 p80
Rutz, Herman; Wisconsin, 1893 6795.8 p153
Rutz, Jacob 4; Portland, ME, 1906 970.38 p80
Rutz, Lydia 11 months; Portland, ME, 1906 970.38 p80
Rutz, Marie 3; Portland, ME, 1906 970.38 p80
Rutz, Marie 33; Portland, ME, 1906 970.38 p80
Ruuska, Dan 34; Minnesota, 1923 2769.54 p1381
Ruve, Friedr.; Valdivia, Chile, 1852 1192.4 p56
Ruzicka, Frantisek; Chicago, 1810-1910 2853.20 p405
Ryadon, James; Boston, 1765 1642 p35
Ryan, . . .; Ontario, 1871 1823.21 p321
Ryan, Alfred; Washington, 1889 2770.40 p80
Ryan, Ambros; Massachusetts, 1772 1642 p66
Ryan, Ambrose; Boston, 1747 1642 p29
Ryan, Ambrose; Boston, 1752 1642 p47
Ryan, Ambrose; Massachusetts, 1744 1642 p66
Ryan, Amos 43; Ontario, 1871 1823.21 p321
Ryan, Ann 37; Ontario, 1871 1823.21 p321
Ryan, Caleb 55; Ontario, 1871 1823.21 p321
Ryan, Catharine; Boston, 1771 1642 p49
Ryan, Catharine 54; Ontario, 1871 1823.21 p321
Ryan, Catherine; Boston, 1759 1642 p47
Ryan, Catherine 60; Michigan, 1880 4491.39 p26
Ryan, Charles; New York, NY, 1827 3274.55 p66
Ryan, Chloe; Massachusetts, 1771 1642 p104
Ryan, Connor; Toronto, 1844 2910.35 p113
Ryan, Daniel; America, 1764 1220.12 p695
Ryan, Daniel; Boston, 1738 1642 p44
Ryan, Daniel; Boston, 1757 1642 p47
Ryan, Daniel; Marblehead, MA, 1770 1642 p73
Ryan, Daniel; Massachusetts, 1757 1642 p111
Ryan, Denis 37; Ontario, 1871 1823.17 p143
Ryan, Dennis 23; St. Johns, N.F., 1811 1053.20 p21
Ryan, Edward; North Carolina, 1854 1088.45 p30
Ryan, Edward 26; Ontario, 1871 1823.21 p321
Ryan, Edward 40; Ontario, 1871 1823.21 p321
Ryan, Edward; Toronto, 1844 2910.35 p113
Ryan, Edward; Toronto, 1844 2910.35 p114
Ryan, Eliza; New Orleans, 1850 7242.30 p154
Ryan, George 37; Indiana, 1858-1880 9076.20 p69
Ryan, J. H. 43; Ontario, 1871 1823.21 p321
Ryan, James; Boston, 1765 1642 p34
Ryan, James; Louisiana, 1874 4981.45 p134
Ryan, James; Massachusetts, 1763 1642 p106
Ryan, James; New Orleans, 1851 7242.30 p154
Ryan, James 34; Ontario, 1871 1823.17 p143
Ryan, James 38; Ontario, 1871 1823.21 p321
Ryan, James 58; Ontario, 1871 1823.21 p321
Ryan, James; Roxbury, MA, 1771 1642 p108
Ryan, James; St. Johns, N.F., 1825 1053.15 p6
Ryan, James J.; Louisiana, 1874 4981.45 p133
Ryan, Jean SEE Ryan, Timothy
Ryan, Jeremiah; Annapolis, MD, 1730 1220.12 p695
Ryan, Johanna 54; Michigan, 1880 4491.39 p26
Ryan, John; America, 1765 1220.12 p695
Ryan, John; America, 1774 1220.12 p695
Ryan, John; Barbados or Jamaica, 1696 1220.12 p695
Ryan, John; Boston, 1742 1642 p45
Ryan, John; Boston, 1747 1642 p46
Ryan, John; Boston, 1753 1642 p31
Ryan, John; Boston, 1757 1642 p47
Ryan, John; Boston, 1765 1642 p35
Ryan, John; Illinois, 1858-1861 6020.5 p133
Ryan, John; Louisiana, 1874 4981.45 p134
Ryan, John; Massachusetts, 1772 1642 p109
*Wife:*Sarah
Ryan, John 19; Michigan, 1880 4491.39 p26
Ryan, John; New Orleans, 1850 7242.30 p154
Ryan, John; New York, 1779 8529.30 p15
Ryan, John; Newfoundland, 1814 3476.10 p54
Ryan, John; Ohio, 1840-1897 8365.35 p18
Ryan, John 24; Ontario, 1871 1823.17 p143
Ryan, John 40; Ontario, 1871 1823.21 p321
Ryan, John 45; Ontario, 1871 1823.21 p321
Ryan, John 50; Ontario, 1871 1823.17 p143
Ryan, John 55; Ontario, 1871 1823.21 p321
Ryan, Joseph P.; North Carolina, 1858 1088.45 p30
Ryan, Judith; St. Johns, N.F., 1825 1053.15 p7
Ryan, Judy; St. Johns, N.F., 1825 1053.15 p6
Ryan, Juley 50; Ontario, 1871 1823.21 p321
Ryan, Julia 43; Ontario, 1871 1823.21 p321
Ryan, Luke; Boston, 1754 1642 p47
Ryan, Lydia SEE Ryan, Mary
Ryan, Margaret 45; Ontario, 1871 1823.21 p321
Ryan, Margaret; St. Johns, N.F., 1825 1053.15 p7
Ryan, Margret 50; Ontario, 1871 1823.21 p321
Ryan, Margret 50; Ontario, 1871 1823.21 p321
Ryan, Mary; America, 1750 1220.12 p695
Ryan, Mary; America, 1765 1220.12 p695
Ryan, Mary; Boston, 1763 1642 p32
*Relative:*Lydia
Ryan, Mary; Boston, 1767 1642 p38
With child
Ryan, Mary 17; Michigan, 1880 4491.39 p26
Ryan, Mary 41; Michigan, 1880 4491.39 p26
Ryan, Mary; New Orleans, 1850 7242.30 p154
Ryan, Mary 28; Ontario, 1871 1823.17 p143
Ryan, Mary 50; Ontario, 1871 1823.21 p321
Ryan, Mary 76; Ontario, 1871 1823.21 p321
Ryan, Matthew; Massachusetts, 1750 1642 p66
Ryan, Matthew; Massachusetts, 1752 1642 p66
Ryan, Matthew; Massachusetts, 1752 1642 p66
Ryan, Matthew 50; Ontario, 1871 1823.21 p321
Ryan, Michael; Boston, 1770 1642 p49
Ryan, Michael 48; Michigan, 1880 4491.39 p27
Ryan, Michael 61; Michigan, 1880 4491.39 p27
Ryan, Michael 35; Ontario, 1871 1823.21 p322
Ryan, Michael 42; Ontario, 1871 1823.17 p143
Ryan, Michael 45; Ontario, 1871 1823.21 p322
Ryan, Michael 50; Ontario, 1871 1823.21 p322
Ryan, Michael; Toronto, 1844 2910.35 p114
Ryan, Micheal 47; Ontario, 1871 1823.17 p143
Ryan, Nathaniel 54; Ontario, 1871 1823.21 p322
Ryan, Nicholas; St. Johns, N.F., 1825 1053.15 p6
Ryan, Owen; New Orleans, 1850 7242.30 p154
Ryan, Patrick; Boston, 1766 1642 p37
Ryan, Patrick; Illinois, 1859 6079.1 p12
Ryan, Patrick; Massachusetts, 1769 1642 p66
Ryan, Patrick 32; Michigan, 1880 4491.39 p27
Ryan, Patrick 46; Michigan, 1880 4491.39 p27
Ryan, Patrick 48; Ontario, 1871 1823.21 p322
Ryan, Patrick 55; Ontario, 1871 1823.21 p322
Ryan, Patrick; Toronto, 1844 2910.35 p116
Ryan, Phillip; Boston, 1753 1642 p31
Ryan, Richard; America, 1749 1220.12 p695
Ryan, Richard; Boston, 1763 1642 p48
Ryan, Roger; Boston, 1759 1642 p47
Ryan, Roger; Boston, 1763 1642 p32
With wife
Ryan, Roger; Newbury, MA, 1758 1642 p75
Ryan, Roger; Newbury, MA, 1758 1642 p76
Ryan, Sarah; Boston, 1752-1760 1642 p30
Ryan, Sarah; Boston, 1772 1642 p49
Ryan, Sarah; Massachusetts, 1722 1642 p66
Ryan, Sarah SEE Ryan, John
Ryan, Simon; St. Johns, N.F., 1825 1053.15 p6
Ryan, Stephen; St. Johns, N.F., 1825 1053.15 p7
Ryan, Susanna; Boston, 1746 1642 p46
Ryan, Thomas; America, 1751 1220.12 p695
Ryan, Thomas; America, 1763 1220.12 p695
Ryan, Thomas; Maryland, 1736 1220.12 p695
Ryan, Thomas; New Orleans, 1850 7242.30 p154
Ryan, Thomas 45; Ontario, 1871 1823.21 p322
Ryan, Thomas 78; Ontario, 1871 1823.21 p322
Ryan, Thomas; Toronto, 1844 2910.35 p113
Ryan, Thos; St. John, N.B., 1847 2978.15 p35
Ryan, Thos; St. John, N.B., 1848 2978.15 p39
Ryan, Timothy; Boston, 1758 1642 p47
Ryan, Timothy; Boston, 1769 1642 p49
Ryan, Timothy; Marblehead, MA, 1689 1642 p72
*Wife:*Jean
Ryan, William; Boston, 1763 1642 p32
Ryan, William 35; Michigan, 1880 4491.33 p19
Ryan, William 27; New York, NY, 1826 6178.50 p150
Ryan, William 31; New York, NY, 1826 6178.50 p150
Ryan, William H. 55; Ontario, 1871 1823.21 p322
Ryan, Winnaford 35; Ontario, 1871 1823.21 p322
Ryband, Joseph; Wisconsin, 1894 6795.8 p61
Ryband, Mary; Wisconsin, 1891 6795.8 p61
Rybicki, George; Wisconsin, 1903 6795.8 p232
Rybin, Matej; St. Louis, 1853 2853.20 p21
Ryburn, Andrew; North Carolina, 1842 1088.45 p30
Ryburn, Elizabeth 15; Quebec, 1870 8364.32 p25
Ryburn, John; North Carolina, 1838 1088.45 p30
Rychlik, Vaclav; Cleveland, OH, 1810-1910 2853.20 p476
Rychlik, Vaclav; Cleveland, OH, 1867-1873 2853.20 p498
Rychlik, Vaclav; Cleveland, OH, 1868-1910 2853.20 p498
Rychlinski, Anthony; Detroit, 1929 1640.55 p113
Rychtarik, Frantisek 9 SEE Rychtarik, Josef
Rychtarik, Josef; Wisconsin, 1854 2853.20 p157
*Brother:*Frantisek
With father
Ryckman, Gilbert 33; Ontario, 1871 1823.21 p322
Rycroft, Elizabeth; America, 1681 1220.12 p695
Rycroft, Elizabeth; Barbados or Jamaica, 1686 1220.12 p695
Rycroft, John; America, 1773 1220.12 p695
Rycroft, Thomas; America, 1755 1220.12 p695
Rydberg, Emelia; St. Paul, MN, 1894 1865.50 p108
Ryde, Job; Barbados, 1663 1220.12 p695
Rydell, C.O.; Cleveland, OH, 1880-1886 9722.10 p126
Ryder, James; America, 1770 1220.12 p695
Ryder, James 38; Ontario, 1871 1823.21 p322
Ryder, James 71; Ontario, 1871 1823.21 p322
Ryder, Jane; America, 1750 1220.12 p695
Ryder, John; America, 1724 1220.12 p695
Ryder, John; America, 1748 1220.12 p695
Ryder, John; America, 1767 1220.12 p695
Ryder, Mary; America, 1748 1220.12 p695
Ryder, Patrick 35; Ontario, 1871 1823.21 p322
Ryder, Patrick 48; Ontario, 1871 1823.21 p322
Ryder, Robert; Virginia, 1727 1220.12 p695
Ryder, Thomas; Marston's Wharf, 1782 8529.30 p15
Ryder, William; America, 1766 1220.12 p695

432 FOR A COMPLETE EXPLANATION OF ENTRY, SEE "HOW TO READ A CITATION" SECTION

Rydings, John; America, 1726 *1220.12 p674*
Rydoski, John; Louisiana, 1874 *4981.45 p134*
Rydstrom, Charles P.; St. Paul, MN, 1880-1883 *1865.50 p108*
  *Wife:*Maria
Rydstrom, Maria *SEE* Rydstrom, Charles P.
Rye, George; America, 1772 *1220.12 p695*
Rye, Rudolph; Illinois, 1858 *6079.1 p12*
Ryecheck, Michael; Miami, 1935 *4984.12 p39*
Ryecroft, Henry; America, 1759 *1220.12 p695*
Ryer, James; America, 1772 *1220.12 p695*
Rygman, John; America, 1766 *1220.12 p675*
Ryland, George 50; Ontario, 1871 *1823.21 p322*
Ryland, William; Died enroute, 1731 *1220.12 p696*
Rylande, Peter J.; Colorado, 1879 *1029.59 p79*
Rylander, August Wilh.; Colorado, 1881 *1029.59 p79*
Rylander, Peter J.; Colorado, 1879 *1029.59 p79*
Rylander, Peter J.; Colorado, 1884 *1029.59 p79*
Rylatt, Robert M.; Washington, 1880 *2770.40 p134*
Ryle, Bryant; New England, 1745 *1642 p28*
Rylett, Edward; America, 1768 *1220.12 p696*
Ryley, Ann; America, 1771 *1220.12 p675*
Ryley, Francis; America, 1750 *1220.12 p675*
Ryley, George; Virginia, 1727 *1220.12 p675*
Ryley, James; America, 1772 *1220.12 p675*
Ryley, John; America, 1681 *1220.12 p675*

Ryley, John; America, 1739 *1220.12 p675*
Ryley, Margaret; America, 1748 *1220.12 p675*
Ryley, Mat.hew; Marston's Wharf, 1780 *8529.30 p15*
Ryley, Sarah; America, 1749 *1220.12 p675*
Ryley, Sarah; America, 1755 *1220.12 p675*
Ryley, William; America, 1753 *1220.12 p675*
Ryley, William; America, 1772 *1220.12 p675*
Ryly, John; Maryland or Virginia, 1718 *1220.12 p675*
Ryman, C.J.H.; New Orleans, 1851 *6412.40 p153*
Rymas, Matthias; America, 1749 *1220.12 p696*
Rymer, George; America, 1772 *1220.12 p696*
Rymer, Martha; Rappahannock, VA, 1729 *1220.12 p696*
Rymer, Roger; America, 1764 *1220.12 p696*
Rymes, William; America, 1726 *1220.12 p675*
Rynak, Frantisek; Wisconsin, 1853 *2853.20 p303*
Rynda, Jan; St. Paul, MN, 1883 *2853.20 p280*
Ryne, Mary Ann 49; Ontario, 1871 *1823.21 p322*
Ryne, Patrick 44; Ontario, 1871 *1823.21 p322*
Ryne, Philip 27; Ontario, 1871 *1823.21 p322*
Rynkiewiez, Peter; Colorado, 1880 *1029.59 p80*
Ryon, Cornelius; Boston, 1740 *1642 p45*
Ryon, James; Boston, 1764 *1642 p33*
Ryon, John; Virginia, 1732 *1220.12 p695*
Ryon, Katharine; Boston, 1767 *1642 p49*
Rypl, Karel Josef; Texas, 1854 *2853.20 p78*
Ryre, Nicholas 50; America, 1842 *778.6 p292*

Ryrie, Robert; Marston's Wharf, 1782 *8529.30 p15*
Rysaille, Edou.rd 45; New Orleans, 1840 *778.6 p293*
Ryser, Ulrich; Colorado, 1884 *1029.59 p80*
Ryssel, Catharine Engel Sophie *SEE* Ryssel, Friedrich Wilhelm
Ryssel, Engel Dorothea *SEE* Ryssel, Friedrich Wilhelm
Ryssel, Engel Marie Dorothea Hage *SEE* Ryssel, Friedrich Wilhelm
Ryssel, Friedrich Wilhelm *SEE* Ryssel, Friedrich Wilhelm
Ryssel, Friedrich Wilhelm; America, 1882 *7420.1 p332*
  *Wife:*Engel Marie Dorothea Hage
  *Son:*Friedrich Wilhelm
  *Daughter:*Engel Dorothea
  *Daughter:*Catharine Engel Sophie
Rystrom, Charles P.; St. Paul, MN, 1880-1883 *1865.50 p108*
  *Wife:*Maria
Rystrom, Maria *SEE* Rystrom, Charles P.
Ryter, Laurets C.; Iowa, 1894 *1211.15 p18*
Rytter, Mils; Iowa, 1898 *1211.15 p18*
Ryves, Mary; Barbados or Jamaica, 1685 *1220.12 p676*
Ryzop, Theophila; Wisconsin, 1893 *6795.8 p61*
Rzepecki, Wojciech; Detroit, 1929 *1640.55 p114*
Rzewnicki, Peter; Detroit, 1930 *1640.60 p83*

S

Saal, Anthony; Ohio, 1809-1852 *4511.35 p45*
Saal, Barbara Nord *SEE* Saal, Johann Georg
Saal, Johann Georg; America, 1785 *2526.42 p130*
  With 4 children
  *Wife:*Barbara Nord
Saal, Margaretha 45; America, 1858 *2526.42 p199*
Saal, Peter; Illinois, 1860 *6079.1 p12*
Saale, Ernst; America, 1854 *7420.1 p128*
Saamanen, Lizzie 38; Minnesota, 1925 *2769.54 p1384*
Saamanen, Peter 35; Minnesota, 1925 *2769.54 p1384*
Saar, Anna Maria; America, 1854 *5475.1 p458*
Saar, Maria Elisabeth Sophie; America, 1850-1899 *6442.17 p65*
Saar, Nikolaus; America, 1865 *5475.1 p509*
Saari, Elsie; Minnesota, 1925-1926 *2769.54 p1382*
Saari, Paul; Minnesota, 1925-1926 *2769.54 p1382*
Saarikoski, Emil 37; Minnesota, 1926 *2769.54 p1382*
Sabata, Frantisek; Iowa, 1854 *2853.20 p157*
Sabata, Frantisek; Nebraska, 1874 *2853.20 p171*
Sabate, Pr. 60; America, 1840 *778.6 p293*
Sabath, Adolf J.; Chicago, 1881 *2853.20 p399*
Sabatier, Francois; Montreal, 1661 *9221.17 p474*
Sabattier, Miguel 45; Port uncertain, 1846 *778.6 p293*
Sabbark, John; North Carolina, 1710 *3629.40 p7*
Sabelfeldt, Ake; Philadelphia, 1848 *6412.40 p150*
Sabelfelt, C. Ake; New York, NY, 1845 *6412.40 p149*
Sabin, Robert; America, 1758 *1220.12 p697*
Sabine, Joseph 38; Ontario, 1871 *1823.21 p322*
Sable, John; America, 1760 *1220.12 p697*
Sablet, Abraham; Virginia, 1700 *9230.15 p80*
  With 2 children
Sablon, Paul Emile Franc. 24; New Orleans, 1848 *778.6 p293*
Sabonlard, Mr. 30; America, 1841 *778.6 p293*
Sabouni, Lewis; Ohio, 1809-1852 *4511.35 p45*
Sabourie, Lewis; Ohio, 1809-1852 *4511.35 p45*
Sabrevois, Jacques-Charles de; Quebec, 1683-1688 *2314.30 p169*
Sabrevois, Jacques-Charles de; Quebec, 1685 *2314.30 p195*
Sabrouc, Mr. 22; New Orleans, 1848 *778.6 p293*
Sacerdotte, Simon 58; America, 1843 *778.6 p293*
Sach, John; America, 1773 *1220.12 p697*
Sache, Nicholas 34; Texas, 1843 *778.6 p293*
Sachell, Emma 12; Quebec, 1870 *8364.32 p25*
Sacherer, Elise 8; Galveston, TX, 1844 *3967.10 p373*
Sacherer, Emil 1; Galveston, TX, 1844 *3967.10 p373*
Sacherer, Gabriel 38; Galveston, TX, 1844 *3967.10 p373*
Sacherer, Louise 5; Galveston, TX, 1844 *3967.10 p373*
Sacherer, Maria Anna 33; Galveston, TX, 1844 *3967.10 p373*
Sacherer, Marie 4; Galveston, TX, 1844 *3967.10 p373*
Sacheverel, Thomas; America, 1744 *1220.12 p697*
Sacheverill, Thomas; America, 1697 *1220.12 p697*
Sachs, Anton; Philadelphia, 1883 *5475.1 p36*
  *Wife:*Christine Reith Biesdorf
  With 3 stepchildren
Sachs, Christine Reith Biesdorf *SEE* Sachs, Anton
Sachs, Franz Michael; America, 1890 *2526.43 p213*
Sachs, Gertrud 39; America, 1863 *5475.1 p45*
Sachs, Jacob; America, 1867 *7919.3 p527*
Sachs, Kaspar Leo 45; Galveston, TX, 1844 *3967.10 p375*
Sack, C.P.; Philadelphia, 1848 *6412.40 p151*
Sack, Carl Friedrich; Wisconsin, 1891 *6795.8 p75*
Sack, Esther; Colorado, 1888 *1029.59 p80*
Sack, Esther; New York, NY, 1871 *1029.59 p80*
Sack, Ignatz 25; Portland, ME, 1906 *970.38 p80*

Sack, Johann 30; Portland, ME, 1906 *970.38 p80*
Sack, Johanna Louisa Carolina; Wisconsin, 1888 *6795.8 p76*
Sacke, Sidrach; Barbados, 1665 *1220.12 p697*
Sacker, George; America, 1773 *1220.12 p697*
Sacker, John; America, 1754 *1220.12 p697*
Sackman, Joseph; Colorado, 1884 *1029.59 p80*
Sackmann, Joseph; Colorado, 1884 *1029.59 p80*
Sackschewski, Johann Gottlieb; Wisconsin, 1887 *6795.8 p196*
Sackstadter, Johann; America, 1836 *5475.1 p468*
  With wife
  *Son:*Nikolaus
  *Son:*Johann
  *Son:*Peter
Sackstadter, Johann 4 *SEE* Sackstadter, Johann
Sackstadter, Nikolaus 6 weeks months *SEE* Sackstadter, Johann
Sackstadter, Peter 3 *SEE* Sackstadter, Johann
Sacky, Jan; Texas, 1860 *2853.20 p74*
Sacotte, Anne-Josephe *SEE* Sacotte, Martin
Sacotte, Florence Marie Louard *SEE* Sacotte, Martin
Sacotte, Florent; New York, NY, 1856 *1494.20 p12*
Sacotte, Florent Francois *SEE* Sacotte, Martin
Sacotte, Florentine Victoire *SEE* Sacotte, Martin
Sacotte, Francois; New York, NY, 1856 *1494.20 p12*
Sacotte, Francois *SEE* Sacotte, Martin
Sacotte, Jean Joseph *SEE* Sacotte, Martin
Sacotte, Louis *SEE* Sacotte, Martin
Sacotte, Martin; Wisconsin, 1856 *1495.20 p12*
  *Wife:*Florence Marie Louard
  *Child:*Victor
  *Child:*Louis
  *Child:*Anne-Josephe
  *Child:*Florentine Victoire
  *Child:*Florent Francois
  *Child:*Francois
  *Child:*Jean Joseph
Sacotte, Victor *SEE* Sacotte, Martin
Sacquespee deVoispreux, Joachim de; Quebec, 1725 *2314.30 p170*
Sacquespee deVoispreux, Joachim de; Quebec, 1725 *2314.30 p195*
Sacresle, Pierre 28; Texas, 1848 *778.6 p293*
Sadd, Joseph; Virginia, 1752 *1220.12 p697*
Sadd, Thomas; America, 1746 *1220.12 p697*
Sadd, William; America, 1725 *1220.12 p697*
Saddler, John 50; Ontario, 1871 *1823.21 p322*
Saddler, Thomas 45; Ontario, 1871 *1823.21 p322*
Sadecki, Franciszek 30; New York, NY, 1920 *930.50 p48*
Sadilek, Frantisek; Chicago, 1851-1896 *2853.20 p158*
Sadilek, Frantisek J.; Chicago, 1851-1910 *2853.20 p405*
Sadler, Anne; Annapolis, MD, 1721 *1220.12 p697*
Sadler, Daniel; America, 1739 *1220.12 p697*
Sadler, Francis 48; Ontario, 1871 *1823.21 p322*
Sadler, Humphry; America, 1772 *1220.12 p697*
Sadler, Isabella; America, 1742 *1220.12 p697*
Sadler, Jane; America, 1680 *1220.12 p697*
Sadler, Jane; Barbados, 1679 *1220.12 p697*
Sadler, Joseph; America, 1763 *1220.12 p697*
Sadler, Mary; America, 1742 *1220.12 p697*
Sadler, Philip; America, 1736 *1220.12 p697*
Sadler, Ralph; America, 1730 *1220.12 p697*
Sadler, Ralph; America, 1758 *1220.12 p697*
Sadler, Richard; America, 1752 *1220.12 p697*
Sadler, Robert 48; Ontario, 1871 *1823.21 p322*
Sadler, Samuel; Barbados, 1683 *1220.12 p697*

Sadler, Stephen 52; Ontario, 1871 *1823.17 p143*
Sadler, Thomas; America, 1675 *1220.12 p697*
Sadler, William; Barbados, 1675 *1220.12 p697*
Sadlier, Thomas 48; Ontario, 1871 *1823.21 p322*
Sadlier, William 25; Ontario, 1871 *1823.21 p322*
Sadot DeBelleroche, Pierre; Quebec, 1656 *9221.17 p347*
Sadowski, Anton; Galveston, TX, 1905 *6015.15 p29*
Sadowski, Frank; Detroit, 1930 *1640.60 p77*
Sadowski, Vicenty 38; New York, NY, 1920 *930.50 p48*
Safarik, Petr; Dayton, OH, 1863 *2853.20 p159*
Safegar, Susanna; Maryland, 1674 *1236.25 p50*
Saffell, Samuel; America, 1732 *1220.12 p697*
Safiets, Katie 16; Michigan, 1880 *4491.33 p19*
Sagar, James; New York, 1837 *471.10 p62*
Sagaria, Sabbato; Colorado, 1885 *1029.59 p80*
Sage, Charles 32; Indiana, 1875-1886 *9076.20 p71*
Sage, Henry; Barbados, 1668 *1220.12 p697*
Sage, James; America, 1773 *1220.12 p697*
Sage, James 59; Ontario, 1871 *1823.21 p322*
Sage, John; Illinois, 1858-1861 *6020.5 p133*
Sage, Robert; America, 1774 *1220.12 p697*
Sage, Thomas; America, 1769 *1220.12 p697*
Sageman, Elizabeth 22; Ontario, 1871 *1823.21 p322*
Sagemuller, John Diederick; America, 1750 *1220.12 p697*
Sagen, Guri; Oregon, 1941 *9157.47 p2*
Sagent, Thomas; America, 1738 *1220.12 p711*
Sageot, Genevieve; Quebec, 1667 *4514.3 p369*
Sager, August; Wisconsin, 1884 *6795.8 p130*
Sager, George; New York, 1901 *1766.20 p25*
Sagesa, Rafilo; Louisiana, 1836-1840 *4981.45 p213*
Sagl, Karel; Nebraska, 1910 *2853.20 p157*
Sago, John; America, 1752 *1220.12 p697*
Sagot, Abel 23; Quebec, 1662 *9221.17 p492*
Sagrerd, Antoine; Louisiana, 1836-1840 *4981.45 p213*
Sahlberg, Bessie 33 *SEE* Sahlberg, Peter F.
Sahlberg, Peter F. 34; Kansas, 1880 *777.40 p18*
  *Wife:*Bessie 33
  With brother-in-law
Sahlin, Axel; Missouri, 1889 *3276.1 p3*
Sahn, Marguerite 40; Port uncertain, 1840 *778.6 p293*
Sahner, Susanna 28; America, 1837 *5475.1 p395*
Sahner, Wendel; America, 1852 *5475.1 p514*
Sahnque, Eugene; Louisiana, 1874 *4981.45 p134*
Sahr, Xavier 21; America, 1843 *778.6 p293*
Sahula, Jan; Chicago, 1909 *2853.20 p452*
Sahuque, Urbain; Louisiana, 1874-1875 *4981.45 p31*
Saidwell, Arthur 25; Virginia, 1635 *1183.3 p31*
Saielli, Roberto; Illinois, 1930 *121.35 p101*
Sailer, Catherine 30; Missouri, 1848 *778.6 p293*
Sailer, George 9; Missouri, 1848 *778.6 p293*
Sailer, Henriette 4; Missouri, 1848 *778.6 p293*
Sailer, Hieronymus; Venezuela, 1529 *3899.5 p538*
Sailer, Paul 6; Missouri, 1848 *778.6 p293*
Sailer, Theresia 17; Missouri, 1848 *778.6 p293*
Sailer, Xavier 35; Missouri, 1848 *778.6 p293*
Saillard, Francois; North Carolina, 1803 *1088.45 p30*
Sailleres, Mr. 36; Port uncertain, 1841 *778.6 p293*
Sailleres, Mrs. 30; Port uncertain, 1841 *778.6 p293*
Sailliot, Antoine; Quebec, 1642 *9221.17 p121*
Sailor, John; Ohio, 1840-1897 *8365.35 p18*
Sailsbury, Bessie 33 *SEE* Sailsbury, Peter F.
Sailsbury, Peter F. 34; Kansas, 1880 *777.40 p18*
  *Wife:*Bessie 33
  With brother-in-law
Sainat, Richard; Quebec, 1645 *9221.17 p157*
Sainct, Richard; Quebec, 1645 *9221.17 p157*
Sainsbury, James T. 45; Ontario, 1871 *1823.21 p322*

Saint, John Egerton; America, 1756 ***1220.12*** *p697*
Saint-Aignan, Nicolas; Quebec, 1613 ***9221.17*** *p20*
Saint-Amant, Louis 23; Montreal, 1653 ***9221.17*** *p283*
Saint-Amant, Pierre 34; Quebec, 1653 ***9221.17*** *p278*
Saint-Amour, . . .; Montreal, 1651 ***9221.17*** *p252*
Saint-Amour, Antoine; Quebec, 1637 ***9221.17*** *p73*
Saint-Andre, Mere 26; Quebec, 1657 ***9221.17*** *p350*
Saint-Andre, Bernard de; Quebec, 1660 ***9221.17*** *p468*
Saint-Ange, Andre 19; Quebec, 1651 ***9221.17*** *p238*
Saint-Antoine, Antoine; Quebec, 1649 ***9221.17*** *p209*
Saint-Arnauld, Antoine; Quebec, 1642 ***9221.17*** *p122*
Saint-Athanase, Mere 26; Quebec, 1640 ***9221.17*** *p94*
Saint-Aubin, Jean 41; Quebec, 1662 ***9221.17*** *p493*
Saint-Augustin, Mere 16; Quebec, 1648 ***9221.17*** *p194*
Saint-Bernard, Mere 28; Quebec, 1639 ***9221.17*** *p84*
Saint-Bonaventure-de-Jesus, Mere 22; Quebec, 1639 ***9221.17*** *p84*
Saint-Claude, Claude 12; Quebec, 1648 ***9221.17*** *p205*
Saint-Cosme, Florent; Quebec, 1652 ***9221.17*** *p255*
*Wife:*Jeanne Yvon
*Daughter:*Mathurine
*Son:*Michel
Saint-Cosme, Gervais 48; Quebec, 1650 ***9221.17*** *p224*
Saint-Cosme, Jeanne Yvon 32 *SEE* Saint-Cosme, Florent
Saint-Cosme, Mathurine 15 *SEE* Saint-Cosme, Florent
Saint-Cosme, Michel 13 *SEE* Saint-Cosme, Florent
Saint-Cosme, Rene; Quebec, 1658 ***9221.17*** *p377*
Saint-Crespin, Jean 13; Quebec, 1655 ***9221.17*** *p327*
Sainte Croix, Eliz. de; Toronto, 1860-1869 ***9228.50*** *p659*
Sainte Croix, Eliz. de; Toronto, 1860-1869 ***9228.50*** *p659*
Ste. Croix, Joseph; America, 1727 ***9228.50*** *p165*
Saint Cyr, Mr. 25; New Orleans, 1848 ***778.6*** *p293*
Saint Cyr, H. J. 25; America, 1843 ***778.6*** *p293*
Saint-Denis, . . .; Quebec, 1652 ***9221.17*** *p266*
Saint-Denis, Anne 11 *SEE* Saint-Denis, Vivienne Bunelle
Saint-Denis, Antoine; Quebec, 1649 ***9221.17*** *p212*
Saint-Denis, Francois; Quebec, 1650 ***9221.17*** *p225*
Saint-Denis, Jeanne 26; Quebec, 1653 ***9221.17*** *p276*
Saint Denis, Louis 22; New Orleans, 1848 ***778.6*** *p293*
Saint-Denis, Marie-Anne 14 *SEE* Saint-Denis, Vivienne Bunelle
Saint-Denis, Pierre 16 *SEE* Saint-Denis, Vivienne Bunelle
Saint-Denis, Pierre 30; Quebec, 1655 ***9221.17*** *p328*
Saint-Denis, Vivienne 38; Quebec, 1660 ***9221.17*** *p468*
*Son:*Pierre 16
*Daughter:*Marie-Anne 14
*Daughter:*Anne 11
Sainte-Agnes, Mere 26; Quebec, 1648 ***9221.17*** *p194*
Sainte-Agnes, Mere 31; Quebec, 1657 ***9221.17*** *p350*
Sainte-Cecile, Mere; Quebec, 1644 ***9221.17*** *p138*
Sainte-Claire, Mere 35; Quebec, 1640 ***9221.17*** *p94*
Sainte-Croix, Mere 30; Quebec, 1639 ***9221.17*** *p84*
Sainte-Genevieve, Mere; Quebec, 1643 ***9221.17*** *p128*
Sainte-Marie, Mere 27; Quebec, 1640 ***9221.17*** *p94*
Sainte-Marie, Soeur 23; Quebec, 1657 ***9221.17*** *p350*
Sainte-Marthe, Marie-Anne 4; Quebec, 1662 ***9221.17*** *p494*
Sainte-Suzanne, Michel; Montreal, 1644 ***9221.17*** *p146*
Saint-Etienne DeLaTour, Charles 53; Quebec, 1646 ***9221.17*** *p159*
Saint Faurens Guenaud, Mr. 39; Port uncertain, 1841 ***778.6*** *p293*
St. Filipo, Antonio; Louisiana, 1874 ***4981.45*** *p134*
Saint Gaudeins, Child; America, 1840 ***778.6*** *p293*
Saint Gaudeins, Mrs. 25; America, 1840 ***778.6*** *p293*
Saint Gaudeins, Veuve 50; America, 1840 ***778.6*** *p293*
Saint-Georges, Jacques 27; Montreal, 1653 ***9221.17*** *p287*
Saint-Germain, . . .; Quebec, 1652 ***9221.17*** *p266*
Saint-Germain, Guillaume; Quebec, 1647 ***9221.17*** *p174*
St. Germain, H.; Louisiana, 1874-1875 ***4981.45*** *p30*
Saint-Germain, Pierre 21; Montreal, 1653 ***9221.17*** *p299*
Saint-Hilaire, Jean; Quebec, 1639 ***9221.17*** *p92*
Saint Hiller, Mr. 29; New Orleans, 1840 ***778.6*** *p293*
Saint-Ignace, Mere 29; Quebec, 1639 ***9221.17*** *p84*
Saint-Jacques, Pierre; Quebec, 1648 ***9221.17*** *p198*
Saint-James, Jacques 29; Montreal, 1653 ***9221.17*** *p282*
Saint James Glendry, Mr. 36; America, 1841 ***778.6*** *p293*
Saint-Jean, . . .; Montreal, 1651 ***9221.17*** *p252*
Saint-Joachim, Mere 33; Quebec, 1643 ***9221.17*** *p128*
St. John, Oliver; Colorado, 1869 ***1029.59*** *p85*
St. Jore, Eliza *SEE* St. Jore, Francis F.
St. Jore, Elizabeth Jena *SEE* St. Jore, Francis F.
St. Jore, Francis F.; Utah, 1855 ***9228.50*** *p193*
*Wife:*Elizabeth Jena
*Child:*Francis John
*Child:*Louisa
*Child:*Eliza
St. Jore, Francis John *SEE* St. Jore, Francis F.
St. Jore, Louisa *SEE* St. Jore, Francis F.
Saint-Joseph, Mere 23; Quebec, 1639 ***9221.17*** *p84*
Saint-Julien, Sylvestre; Montreal, 1653 ***9221.17*** *p301*
Saint Laurent, Mr. 49; Port uncertain, 1840 ***778.6*** *p293*
Saint Laurent, Mrs.; Port uncertain, 1840 ***778.6*** *p293*
Saint-Laurent, Soeur 26; Quebec, 1642 ***9221.17*** *p111*
Saint-Laurent, Nicolas 30; Quebec, 1657 ***9221.17*** *p360*
St. Lawrence, Joseph; Boston, 1737 ***1642*** *p26*
St. Ledger, Peter; New Orleans, 1850 ***7242.30*** *p154*
Saint-Leger, Jean; Quebec, 1639 ***9221.17*** *p90*
Saint-Louis, Louis; Quebec, 1658 ***9221.17*** *p386*
Saint-Loup, Claude; Quebec, 1653 ***9221.17*** *p276*
St. Marc, E. C.; Louisiana, 1874-1875 ***4981.45*** *p30*
Saint-Marc, Jacques; Quebec, 1643 ***9221.17*** *p134*
Saint-Marc, Marc 21; Quebec, 1661 ***9221.17*** *p446*
Saint Martin, Mrs. 22; New Orleans, 1847 ***778.6*** *p294*
Saint Martin, J. 23; New Orleans, 1847 ***778.6*** *p294*
Saint-Martin, Jacques 30; Quebec, 1651 ***9221.17*** *p250*
Saint-Martin, Jean; Quebec, 1656 ***9221.17*** *p347*
Saint-Martin, Jean-Jacques de; Quebec, 1750 ***2314.30*** *p170*
Saint-Martin, Jean-Jacques de; Quebec, 1750 ***2314.30*** *p195*
Saint-Martin, Martin 31; Quebec, 1643 ***9221.17*** *p129*
Saint Martin, Philip 36; Port uncertain, 1842 ***778.6*** *p294*
Saint Martin, Roland Marie 27; Port uncertain, 1842 ***778.6*** *p294*
Saint-Maurice, Louis; Quebec, 1648 ***9221.17*** *p204*
Saint-Michel, Antoine 24; Quebec, 1641 ***9221.17*** *p107*
Saint-Michel, Benjamin; Quebec, 1652 ***9221.17*** *p254*
Saint-Michel, Michel 9; Montreal, 1650 ***9221.17*** *p232*
Saint-Michel, Michel 23; Montreal, 1662 ***9221.17*** *p495*
Saint-Nicolas, Soeur 31; Quebec, 1640 ***9221.17*** *p94*
Saintomer, Cecile; Louisiana, 1845 ***778.6*** *p294*
Saintonge, Denis 22; Quebec, 1654 ***9221.17*** *p310*
Saint-Ours, Pierre de; Quebec, 1665 ***2314.30*** *p167*
Saint-Ours, Pierre de; Quebec, 1665 ***2314.30*** *p196*
Saint-Ouyn, Michel; Quebec, 1654 ***9221.17*** *p314*
St. Pasteur, Henry; Louisiana, 1874 ***4981.45*** *p134*
Saint-Pere, Catherine 14; Quebec, 1648 ***9221.17*** *p204*
*Sister:*Jeanne 21
Saint-Pere, Jean de 24; Montreal, 1642 ***9221.17*** *p124*
Saint-Pere, Jeanne 21 *SEE* Saint-Pere, Catherine
Saint-Pere, Marie-Madeleine 41; Quebec, 1647 ***9221.17*** *p178*
Saint-Pierre, . . .; Montreal, 1651 ***9221.17*** *p252*
Saint-Pierre, Pierre 20; Quebec, 1654 ***9221.17*** *p311*
Saintree, John; America, 1765 ***1220.12*** *p697*
Saint-Remond, . . .; Montreal, 1651 ***9221.17*** *p252*
Saintrong, Marie Therese Josephine; Wisconsin, 1855 ***1495.20*** *p46*
Saint Sauveur, B. de 58; America, 1840 ***778.6*** *p294*
Saint-Severin, Severin 28; Quebec, 1648 ***9221.17*** *p194*
Saint-Vincent deNarcy, Pierre de; Quebec, 1714 ***2314.30*** *p169*
Saint-Vincent deNarcy, Pierre de; Quebec, 1714 ***2314.30*** *p196*
Saint-Yves, Yves; Quebec, 1660 ***9221.17*** *p432*
With son
Saire, Greta Thereaia; Oregon, 1941 ***9157.47*** *p3*
Saires, Edward; America, 1735 ***1220.12*** *p704*
Saires, Thomas; America, 1751 ***1220.12*** *p704*
Sairs, Thomas 55; Ontario, 1871 ***1823.17*** *p144*
Saisit, Pierre 24; Port uncertain, 1841 ***778.6*** *p294*
Sajkowski, Joseph; New York, NY, 1888 ***6015.15*** *p11*
Sakowski, Francois 36; New York, NY, 1920 ***930.50*** *p49*
Salaba, Egon; New York, NY, 1904 ***2853.20*** *p413*
Salaba, Jaroslav; New York, NY, 1910 ***2853.20*** *p116*
Salaba-Vojan, Jaroslav; America, 1810-1910 ***2853.20*** *p513*
Salaberry, Michel de; Quebec, 1733 ***2314.30*** *p170*
Salaberry, Michel de; Quebec, 1733 ***2314.30*** *p196*
Salagnad, Ferdinand 6; America, 1842 ***778.6*** *p294*
Salagnad, Hypolithe 9; America, 1842 ***778.6*** *p294*
Salagnad, Lami 44; America, 1842 ***778.6*** *p294*
Salamacha, Stanley; Detroit, 1930 ***1640.60*** *p78*
Salamondra, Joseph; Detroit, 1930 ***1640.60*** *p78*
Salangrin, Gabriel; Quebec, 1658 ***9221.17*** *p386*
Salardin, Antoine; Quebec, 1637 ***9221.17*** *p73*
*Wife:*Olive Chegremond
Salardin, Olive Chegremond *SEE* Salardin, Antoine
Salas Onofre, Antonio de; Puerto Rico, 1815-1915 ***3476.25*** *p113*
Salatkewicz, Anna; Detroit, 1929 ***1640.55*** *p112*
Salbrye, Nicholas 26; Port uncertain, 1840 ***778.6*** *p294*
Sale, Ms. 12; Quebec, 1870 ***8364.32*** *p25*
Sale, Edward 92; Ontario, 1871 ***1823.21*** *p322*
Sale, Isabelle; Quebec, 1670 ***4514.3*** *p369*
Sale, Joseph; Louisiana, 1874-1875 ***4981.45*** *p31*
Sale, Madeleine-Therese; Quebec, 1670 ***4514.3*** *p369*
Sale, Mary; America, 1748 ***1220.12*** *p697*
Sale, Thomas; America, 1768 ***1220.12*** *p697*
Salerin, Andre 6; America, 1846 ***778.6*** *p294*
Salerin, Dominique 5; America, 1846 ***778.6*** *p294*
Salerin, Joseph 34; America, 1846 ***778.6*** *p294*
Salerin, Nicolas 33; America, 1846 ***778.6*** *p294*
Salerin, Victorine 1; America, 1846 ***778.6*** *p294*
Sales, Geo 57; Ontario, 1871 ***1823.21*** *p323*
Sales, Robert 84; Ontario, 1871 ***1823.21*** *p323*
Sales, Thomas; America, 1739 ***1220.12*** *p697*
Salfeld, Carl David; America, 1867 ***7420.1*** *p263*
Salge, Mr.; America, 1874 ***7420.1*** *p304*
Salge, Engel M. D.; America, 1867 ***7420.1*** *p256*
Salger, Mr.; America, 1854 ***7420.1*** *p128*
With wife & child
Salger, Ernst; America, 1852 ***7420.1*** *p96*
With family
Salidina, Laurence; Louisiana, 1874-1875 ***4981.45*** *p31*
Salie, . . .; Baltimore, 1889 ***8425.16*** *p36*
Salie, . . . 39; Baltimore, 1889 ***8425.16*** *p36*
Salie, . . . 40; Baltimore, 1889 ***8425.16*** *p36*
Salie, Margaretha; Baltimore, 1889 ***8425.16*** *p36*
Salie, Stephan; Baltimore, 1889 ***8425.16*** *p36*
Salinger, Caroline 3; Missouri, 1845 ***778.6*** *p294*
Salinger, Jacob 7; Missouri, 1845 ***778.6*** *p294*
Salinger, Madalain 34; Missouri, 1845 ***778.6*** *p294*
Salisbury, Ann; America, 1766 ***1220.12*** *p697*
Salisbury, Horace 72; Ontario, 1871 ***1823.17*** *p144*
Salisbury, Joseph; Ohio, 1843 ***2763.1*** *p21*
Salisbury, Morris; America, 1750 ***1220.12*** *p697*
Salisbury, Robert; America, 1759 ***1220.12*** *p698*
Salisbury, Tho; Virginia, 1652 ***6254.4*** *p244*
Salisbury, Thomas; America, 1685 ***1220.12*** *p698*
Salisbury, William; America, 1765 ***1220.12*** *p698*
Salkeld, Thomas; America, 1727 ***1220.12*** *p698*
Sallat, J. 29; America, 1846 ***778.6*** *p294*
Sallenburg, H.; Louisiana, 1874-1875 ***4981.45*** *p31*
Saller, Georg 30; New York, 1854 ***5475.1*** *p235*
Saller, Johann Conrad; Port uncertain, 1850 ***7420.1*** *p75*
Saller, Johann Heinrich *SEE* Saller, Johann Heinrich
Saller, Johann Heinrich; America, 1860 ***7420.1*** *p199*
With wife & daughter
*Son:*Johann Heinrich
Sallet, J. 29; America, 1846 ***778.6*** *p294*
Sallet DeBoissalet, Louis; Quebec, 1660 ***9221.17*** *p469*
Sallis, Andrew; America, 1740 ***1220.12*** *p698*
Sallmon, Christopher 31; Ontario, 1871 ***1823.21*** *p323*
Sallot, Francois 35; America, 1846 ***778.6*** *p294*
Sallot, Josephine 33; America, 1846 ***778.6*** *p294*
Sallot, Marie 3; New Orleans, 1846 ***778.6*** *p294*
Salloway, John; Barbados, 1663 ***1220.12*** *p698*
Salloway, Robert; America, 1680 ***1220.12*** *p698*
Sallows, Robert; America, 1742 ***1220.12*** *p698*
Sallway, John; Virginia, 1770 ***1220.12*** *p698*
Sallway, Mary; America, 1721 ***1220.12*** *p698*
Sally, John; America, 1677 ***1220.12*** *p698*
Sally, Judith; Halifax, N.S., 1827 ***7009.9*** *p62*
Salm, Frederick; Ohio, 1840-1897 ***8365.35*** *p18*
Salm, Hans Jacob 56; New Castle, DE, 1817-1818 ***90.20*** *p153*
Salm, Johann; America, 1874 ***5475.1*** *p362*
Salm, John Jacob; Illinois, 1858 ***6079.1*** *p12*
Salman, James; Barbados, 1677 ***1220.12*** *p698*
Salmen, Samuel 28; Ontario, 1871 ***1823.17*** *p144*
Salmen, Spencer 30; Ontario, 1871 ***1823.17*** *p144*
Salmen, Spencer 60; Ontario, 1871 ***1823.17*** *p144*
Salmi, Mrs. Emil 38; Minnesota, 1923 ***2769.54*** *p1378*
Salmon, Clement; Boston, 1660 ***1642*** *p9*
Salmon, Elianor; America, 1697 ***1220.12*** *p698*
Salmon, James 58; Ontario, 1871 ***1823.21*** *p323*
Salmon, Jean Marie 35; New Orleans, 1848 ***778.6*** *p294*
Salmon, John; America, 1740 ***1220.12*** *p698*
Salmon, John; America, 1742 ***1220.12*** *p698*
Salmon, John; America, 1774 ***1220.12*** *p698*
Salmon, John 39; Ontario, 1871 ***1823.17*** *p144*
Salmon, Mary; America, 1736 ***1220.12*** *p698*
Salmon, Mary; America, 1741 ***1220.12*** *p698*
Salmon, Mary; Annapolis, MD, 1732 ***1220.12*** *p698*
Salmon, Michael; Virginia, 1739 ***1220.12*** *p698*
Salmon, Michael; Washington, 1887 ***2770.40*** *p25*
Salmon, Pierre; Montreal, 1653 ***9221.17*** *p300*
Salmon, Richard; America, 1746 ***1220.12*** *p698*
Salmon, Richard; America, 1747 ***1220.12*** *p698*
Salmon, Rowland; America, 1727 ***1220.12*** *p698*
Salmon, Samuel; Annapolis, MD, 1723 ***1220.12*** *p698*
Salmon, Samuel; Virginia, 1730 ***1220.12*** *p698*
Salmon, Thomas; America, 1713 ***1220.12*** *p698*
Salmon, Thomas 41; Ontario, 1871 ***1823.17*** *p144*
Salmon, Walter; Virginia, 1751 ***1220.12*** *p698*
Salneuve, P. 38; America, 1840 ***778.6*** *p294*
Salo, Aino 42; Minnesota, 1925 ***2769.54*** *p1379*
Salo, John 34; Minnesota, 1923 ***2769.54*** *p1378*
Salo, John 36; Minnesota, 1925 ***2769.54*** *p1379*
Salo, S. K. 50; Minnesota, 1925 ***2769.54*** *p1380*
Salo, Mrs. S. K. 47; Minnesota, 1925 ***2769.54*** *p1380*
Salo, Toivo 30; Minnesota, 1925 ***2769.54*** *p1384*
Salomon, Louis 40; America, 1846 ***778.6*** *p294*
Salomonsen, Michael; Washington, 1882 ***2770.40*** *p136*
Salomonson, Ida *SEE* Salomonson, John A.

Salomonson, John A.; St. Paul, MN, 1894 1865.50 p108
Wife:Ida
Saloy, Pierre; Louisiana, 1874-1875 4981.45 p31
Saloy, Pierre; Louisiana, 1874-1875 4981.45 p130
Salsbury, Henry 52; Ontario, 1871 1823.21 p323
Salsbury, John 50; Ontario, 1871 1823.21 p323
Salsbury, Mary; America, 1731 1220.12 p697
Salsbury, William; Annapolis, MD, 1733 1220.12 p698
Salt, Hannah; America, 1772 1220.12 p698
Salt, Henry; Virginia, 1764 1220.12 p698
Salt, Richard; America, 1700 1220.12 p698
Salt, William; America, 1771 1220.12 p698
Salter, Benjamin; America, 1760 1220.12 p698
Salter, Charles; America, 1766 1220.12 p698
Salter, Elizabeth; America, 1743 1220.12 p698
Salter, Elizabeth SEE Salter, Francis
Salter, Francis; Marblehead, MA, 1708 9228.50 p565
Wife:Elizabeth
Salter, Hannah; America, 1732 1220.12 p698
Salter, Henry; Maryland, 1725 1220.12 p698
Salter, James; America, 1685 1220.12 p698
Salter, Jemima; Annapolis, MD, 1736 1220.12 p698
Salter, John; Annapolis, MD, 1725 1220.12 p698
Salter, John 56; Ontario, 1871 1823.21 p323
Salter, John 68; Ontario, 1871 1823.21 p323
Salter, John; Potomac, 1729 1220.12 p698
Salter, John; Virginia, 1741 1220.12 p698
Salter, Martha A. 10; Ontario, 1871 1823.21 p323
Salter, Mary SEE Salter, William
Salter, Mary; Virginia, 1726 1220.12 p698
Salter, Nicholas; America, 1685 1220.12 p698
Salter, Richard; America, 1656 1220.12 p698
Salter, Richard 28; Barbados, 1664 1220.12 p698
Salter, Samuel; America, 1745 1220.12 p699
Salter, Sarah 45; Ontario, 1871 1823.21 p323
Salter, Sophia G. 15; Ontario, 1871 1823.21 p323
Salter, Thomas; America, 1720 1220.12 p699
Salter, Thomas; America, 1775 1220.12 p699
Salter, Thomas; Barbados, 1679 1220.12 p699
Salter, Thomas; Ohio, 1809-1852 4511.35 p45
Salter, Thomas; Virginia, 1730 1220.12 p699
Salter, William; Iowa, 1870-1879 9228.50 p565
Wife:Mary
Salterwaite, Charles; America, 1764 1220.12 p699
Saltmarsh, John; America, 1750 1220.12 p699
Saltmarsh, Thomas; Barbados or Jamaica, 1685 1220.12 p699
Saltoez, Joseph; Ohio, 1809-1852 4511.35 p45
Salton, John; America, 1725 1220.12 p699
Saltz, Ethel Fitterman SEE Saltz, Julius
Saltz, Julius; Detroit, 1929-1930 6214.5 p71
Wife:Ethel Fitterman
Salvaille deTremon, Antoine; Quebec, 1726 2314.30 p172
Salvidge, Thomas; America, 1758 1220.12 p703
Salwei, Barbara 3; New York, NY, 1885 8425.16 p32
Salwei, Carolina 6 months; New York, NY, 1885 8425.16 p32
Salwei, Margaretha 9; New York, NY, 1885 8425.16 p32
Salwei, Marianna 30; New York, NY, 1885 8425.16 p32
Salwei, Michael 30; New York, NY, 1885 8425.16 p32
Salwei, Michel 7; New York, NY, 1885 8425.16 p32
Salzmann, Cathrine 39; America, 1844 778.6 p294
Salzwedel, Auguste Wilhelmine; Wisconsin, 1888 6795.8 p148
Salzwedel, Dorothea Sophia; Wisconsin, 1894 6795.8 p76
Salzwedel, Emma Auguste; Wisconsin, 1894 6795.8 p140
Salzwedel, Ernst August Theodor; Wisconsin, 1893 6795.8 p76
Salzwedel, Friedrich William; Wisconsin, 1868 6795.8 p150
Salzwedel, Herman August; Wisconsin, 1900 6795.8 p76
Salzwedel, Louise; Wisconsin, 1887 6795.8 p76
Salzwedel, Mary Frederika; Wisconsin, 1894 6795.8 p93
Salzwedel, Wilhelmine Albertine; Wisconsin, 1892 6795.8 p30
Sam, James; America, 1752 1220.12 p463
Sam, John; America, 1685 1220.12 p699
Samal, Stanislaw; Detroit, 1930 1640.60 p82
Samann, John; Iowa, 1886 1211.15 p19
Samberg, Vladimir; Chicago, 1893-1910 2853.20 p469
Sambertz, Elise 32; America, 1846 778.6 p294
Sambertz, Jean 7; America, 1846 778.6 p294
Sambola, F.; Louisiana, 1836-1840 4981.45 p213
Same, George; America, 1724 1220.12 p699
Same, John; America, 1733 1220.12 p699
Samek, Jan; Nebraska, 1876 2853.20 p172
Sammarell, Henry; America, 1763 1220.12 p699
Samme, Joseph 19; Quebec, 1870 8364.32 p25
Samme, William 17; Quebec, 1870 8364.32 p25
Sammerfield, F.W.; New York, NY, 1871 3331.4 p12
Samolej, Jan; Detroit, 1929 1640.55 p115
Samour, William 40; Ontario, 1871 1823.17 p144
Sample, Margaret 23; St. John, N.B., 1834 6469.7 p5
Sample, Reinaldo P. 30; Ontario, 1871 1823.21 p323
Sample, William; Ohio, 1843 3580.20 p33
Sample, William; Ohio, 1843 6020.12 p22
Samples, James; America, 1755 1220.12 p699
Sampson, Bartholomew; America, 1754 1220.12 p699
Sampson, Henery; Plymouth, MA, 1620 1920.45 p5
Sampson, Henry; North Carolina, 1853 1088.45 p30
Sampson, Herman; North Carolina, 1852 1088.45 p30
Sampson, James; America, 1760 1220.12 p699
Sampson, John; America, 1760 1220.12 p699
Sampson, John; America, 1769 1220.12 p699
Sampson, John; North Carolina, 1858-1859 1088.45 p30
Sampson, Jonathan; America, 1771 1220.12 p699
Sampson, Mary; America, 1760 1220.12 p699
Sampson, Michael; America, 1764 1220.12 p699
Sampson, Peter; Barbados, 1670 1220.12 p699
Sampson, Richard; America, 1756 1220.12 p699
Sampson, Richard; America, 1764 1220.12 p699
Sampson, Robert 40; Ontario, 1871 1823.21 p323
Sampson, Saml 49; Ontario, 1871 1823.21 p323
Sampson, Samuel A.; Miami, 1920 4984.15 p38
Sampson, Sarah; Virginia, 1732 1220.12 p699
Sampson, Simeon 37; Ontario, 1871 1823.21 p323
Sampson, Thomas; America, 1774 1220.12 p699
Sampson, Thomas; Virginia, 1730 1220.12 p699
Sampson, William; America, 1774 1220.12 p699
Sampson, William; America, 1775 1220.12 p699
Sampson, William 67; Ontario, 1871 1823.21 p323
Sams, Alice; America, 1751 1220.12 p699
Samsen, Wilhelm Anton Karl; America, 1885 7420.1 p348
Samson, Amellie 24; America, 1841 778.6 p294
Samson, Andre; Quebec, 1641 9221.17 p107
Samson, Anne; Nova Scotia, 1771 9228.50 p322
Samson, Elizabeth SEE Samson, John
Samson, Emelie 25; America, 1841 778.6 p294
Samson, Fanny 25; America, 1841 778.6 p294
Samson, Geo 39; Ontario, 1871 1823.21 p323
Samson, John SEE Samson, John
Samson, John; Portsmouth, NH, 1728 9228.50 p565
Wife:Elizabeth
Child:Mary
Child:Rachel
Child:John
Samson, Julius; North Carolina, 1842-1849 1088.45 p30
Samson, Marguerite; Quebec, 1670 4514.3 p369
Samson, Mary SEE Samson, John
Samson, Michel 27; America, 1841 778.6 p295
Samson, Rachel SEE Samson, John
Samson, Rene; Quebec, 1652 9221.17 p266
Samuel, Elizabeth; Ohio, 1838 4022.20 p285
Samuel, George; Louisiana, 1874-1875 4981.45 p30
Samuel, Giovani 29; America, 1848 778.6 p295
Samuel, Lester 32; Ontario, 1871 1823.21 p323
Samuel, Myers; America, 1740 1220.12 p699
Samuel, Nathan; America, 1755 1220.12 p699
Samuel, Nestir; Louisiana, 1874 4981.45 p297
Samuel, Samuel; America, 1772 1220.12 p699
Samuel, Thomas; America, 1767 1220.12 p699
Samuell, Roger; Barbados, 1683 1220.12 p699
Samuels, James 26; Ontario, 1871 1823.21 p323
Samuels, Matthew 35; Ontario, 1871 1823.21 p323
Samuels, Morris; Detroit, 1929-1930 6214.5 p69
Samuelsdotter, Anna Lena 67; Kansas, 1875-1880 777.40 p19
Samuelsdotter, Annie L. 67; Kansas, 1875-1880 777.40 p19
Samuelson, Alexander; Illinois, 1858-1861 4487.25 p72
Samuelson, Amanda SEE Samuelson, Peter
Samuelson, Andrew M.; Illinois, 1861 4487.25 p72
Samuelson, Charles; America, 1857 4487.25 p72
With family
Samuelson, Charles A.; Illinois, 1864 4487.25 p73
Samuelson, Gustaf Albin; New York, 1880 1766.20 p16
Samuelson, John; Illinois, 1861 4487.25 p73
Samuelson, John; Wisconsin, 1871-1882 1865.50 p108
Samuelson, Matilda; Kansas, 1868-1871 777.40 p11
Samuelson, Peter; St. Paul, MN, 1884 1865.50 p108
Wife:Amanda
Samuelsson, Anna Magnidotter SEE Samuelsson, Johan Magnus
Samuelsson, Anna Magnidotter SEE Samuelsson, Samuel
Samuelsson, Carin Persdotter 36 SEE Samuelsson, Pher
Samuelsson, Johan Magnus; North America, 1854 6410.15 p104
Mother:Anna Magnidotter
Samuelsson, Lisa 25 SEE Samuelsson, Matts
Samuelsson, Lisa 25; New York, 1856 6529.11 p20
Samuelsson, Matts 25; New York, 1856 6529.11 p20
Sister:Lisa 25
Samuelsson, Pher 33; New York, 1856 6529.11 p20
Wife:Carin Persdotter 36
Son:Samuel August 1
Samuelsson, Samuel; North America, 1855 6410.15 p104
Wife:Anna Magnidotter
Samuelsson, Samuel August 1 SEE Samuelsson, Pher
Sanberg, Martin; Cleveland, OH, 1900-1904 9722.10 p126
Sanbern, Abraham; Illinois, 1851 777.40 p6
Sanbidge, Thomas; New York, 1777 8529.30 p15
Sanborn, Franklin 67; Ontario, 1871 1823.21 p323
Sanborn, Malte Pehrsson 22; Kansas, 1880 777.40 p20
Sanburn, Rachel 21; Michigan, 1880 4491.30 p27
Sanchet, Ulrich; Ohio, 1809-1852 4511.35 p45
Sanchez, Joseph L.; Missouri, 1900 3276.1 p3
Sanchez, Norton 25; America, 1841 778.6 p295
Sancois, Pierre; Quebec, 1651 9221.17 p251
Sandahl, C.O.; Washington, 1889 2770.40 p80
Sandaig, Angus; Quebec, 1786 1416.15 p5
Sandalls, Joyce; America, 1763 1220.12 p699
Sandberg, Abraham; Illinois, 1851 777.40 p6
Sandberg, Andrew; Colorado, 1889 1029.59 p80
Sandberg, Andrew; Illinois, 1861 4487.25 p73
Sandberg, Anna Tomson SEE Sandberg, Carl
Sandberg, Anna Maria; St. Paul, MN, 1890-1892 1865.50 p35
Sandberg, Anna Maria SEE Sandberg, Hans A.
Sandberg, Axel; Boston, 1902 1766.20 p16
Sandberg, Axel; Boston, 1902 1766.20 p25
Sandberg, Brita Stina Johnson SEE Sandberg, Hans A.
Sandberg, Bror Amos; Cleveland, OH, 1901 9722.10 p126
Sandberg, Carl; Cleveland, OH, 1903 9722.10 p126
Wife:Anna Tomson
Child:Uno Konrad Halsten
Child:Tuve Kilkane Volrat
Sandberg, Dan. Nilsson; New York, NY, 1851 6412.40 p153
Sandberg, Gottfried; Iowa, 1908 1211.15 p19
Sandberg, Gus T.; Cleveland, OH, 1902-1904 9722.10 p126
Sandberg, Gustaf; Illinois, 1861 4487.25 p73
Sandberg, Gustaf Anders; St. Paul, MN, 1886 1865.50 p108
Sandberg, Hanna Theresia; Cleveland, OH, 1903 9722.10 p129
Sandberg, Hans A.; St. Paul, MN, 1892 1865.50 p108
Wife:Brita Stina Johnson
Child:Anna Maria
Child:Victor Johan
Sandberg, Hedvig; Cleveland, OH, 1893-1894 9722.10 p132
Sandberg, Hilda; St. Paul, MN, 1890 1865.50 p108
Sandberg, J.; New York, NY, 1845 6412.40 p148
Sandberg, John 34; Kansas, 1880 777.40 p21
Sandberg, Louis M.; St. Paul, MN, 1889 1865.50 p108
Sandberg, Martha; St. Paul, MN, 1889 1865.50 p108
Sandberg, Martin; Cleveland, OH, 1900-1904 9722.10 p126
Sandberg, Thomas; Cleveland, OH, 1902-1903 9722.10 p126
Sandberg, Tuve Kilkane Volrat SEE Sandberg, Carl
Sandberg, Uno Konrad Halsten SEE Sandberg, Carl
Sandberg, Victor Johan SEE Sandberg, Hans A.
Sandblom, A.H.; New York, NY, 1844 6412.40 p147
Sandburg, Andrew; Colorado, 1889 1029.59 p80
Sandeen, J.N.; Michigan, 1887-1903 1865.50 p108
Sandelin, J.A.; Boston, 1855 6412.40 p154
Sandell, Peter; Colorado, 1889 1029.59 p80
Sandells, John; America, 1764 1220.12 p699
Sander, Widow; America, 1880 7420.1 p317
Sander, Alexander Louis Adolph S. SEE Sander, Heinrich Wilhelm Gustav
Sander, Anna 70; America, 1854 5475.1 p53
Sander, Ernst; America, 1853 7420.1 p111
Sander, Ferdinand; America, 1868 7919.3 p527
Sander, Friedrich Wilhelm; Dayton, OH, 1865 7420.1 p236
Sander, Georg Adolph Philipp; Port uncertain, 1835 7420.1 p9
Sander, Georg Otto Louis; America, 1857 7420.1 p171
Sander, Heinrich Friedrich Wilhelm; America, 1893 7420.1 p369
Sander, Heinrich Wilhelm Gustav; Dayton, OH, 1866 7420.1 p248
Brother:Alexander Louis Adolph S.
Sander, Julius; Valdivia, Chile, 1850 1192.4 p49
Sander, Karl Ludwig; America, 1883 5475.1 p37
Sander, Katerina 25; Portland, ME, 1906 970.38 p80
Sanders, Abraham; America, 1771 1220.12 p700
Sanders, Barley; America, 1775 1220.12 p701
Sanders, Benjamin; America, 1771 1220.12 p701
Sanders, Catherine; America, 1733 1220.12 p701

Sanders, Charles 44; Ontario, 1871 ***1823.21*** *p323*
Sanders, Corney 45; Ontario, 1871 ***1823.17*** *p144*
Sanders, Edward; Saskatchewan, 1921 ***9228.50*** *p565*
*Wife:*Eliza Jane Cole
*Child:*Edward John
Sanders, Edward John *SEE* Sanders, Edward
Sanders, Eliza Jane Cole *SEE* Sanders, Edward
Sanders, Ellen 5; Quebec, 1870 ***8364.32*** *p25*
Sanders, F. 62; New Orleans, 1834 ***1002.51*** *p112*
Sanders, Friedrich Heinrich; America, 1866 ***7420.1*** *p248*
Sanders, George 32; Ontario, 1871 ***1823.21*** *p323*
Sanders, Henry; America, 1748 ***1220.12*** *p701*
Sanders, Henry; America, 1762 ***1220.12*** *p701*
Sanders, J. W.; Illinois, 1859 ***6079.1*** *p12*
Sanders, James 30; Ontario, 1871 ***1823.21*** *p323*
Sanders, John; America, 1743 ***1220.12*** *p701*
Sanders, John; Colorado, 1880 ***1029.59*** *p80*
Sanders, John; Colorado, 1903 ***1029.59*** *p80*
Sanders, Joseph; North Carolina, 1834 ***1088.45*** *p30*
Sanders, Joseph; Texas, 1891 ***3435.45*** *p36*
Sanders, Josephine; Detroit, 1929 ***1640.55*** *p115*
Sanders, Mary; America, 1748 ***1220.12*** *p701*
Sanders, Mary; America, 1754 ***1220.12*** *p701*
Sanders, Mary; Virginia, 1751 ***1220.12*** *p701*
Sanders, Mathilda 15; Quebec, 1870 ***8364.32*** *p25*
Sanders, Peter; America, 1754 ***1220.12*** *p702*
Sanders, Richard; America, 1753 ***1220.12*** *p702*
Sanders, Robert 24; Ontario, 1871 ***1823.21*** *p323*
Sanders, Sarah; Virginia, 1734 ***1220.12*** *p702*
Sanders, Susan 18; Ontario, 1871 ***1823.21*** *p323*
Sanders, Thomas; Virginia, 1741 ***1220.12*** *p702*
Sanders, William; America, 1729 ***1220.12*** *p702*
Sanders, William 60; Ontario, 1871 ***1823.21*** *p323*
Sanders, William; Virginia, 1750 ***1220.12*** *p702*
Sanderson, Austin; Ohio, 1809-1852 ***4511.35*** *p45*
Sanderson, Charles 7; Ontario, 1871 ***1823.17*** *p144*
Sanderson, Elias; America, 1656 ***1220.12*** *p702*
Sanderson, George 20; Ontario, 1871 ***1823.21*** *p323*
Sanderson, John; America, 1743 ***1220.12*** *p702*
Sanderson, John; America, 1747 ***1220.12*** *p702*
Sanderson, John; Barbados or Jamaica, 1699 ***1220.12*** *p702*
Sanderson, John 45; North Carolina, 1774 ***1422.10*** *p56*
Sanderson, John; Washington, 1889 ***2770.40*** *p81*
Sanderson, Margaret; America, 1688 ***1220.12*** *p702*
Sanderson, Robert; Washington, 1889 ***2770.40*** *p81*
Sanderson, Thomas; Ohio, 1809-1852 ***4511.35*** *p45*
Sanderson, Thomas 44; Ontario, 1871 ***1823.17*** *p144*
Sanderson, William; Colorado, 1869 ***1029.59*** *p80*
Sanderson, William 48; Ontario, 1871 ***1823.21*** *p323*
Sandersson, Johan Ludvig; Cleveland, OH, 1895-1897 ***9722.10*** *p126*
Sandford, Abraham; America, 1696 ***1220.12*** *p699*
Sandford, Benjamin; Potomac, 1731 ***1220.12*** *p699*
Sandford, John; Barbados, 1688 ***1220.12*** *p699*
Sandford, William; America, 1766 ***1220.12*** *p699*
Sandgren, Per Johan; Cleveland, OH, 1897-1898 ***9722.10*** *p126*
Sandham, Jane 40; Ontario, 1871 ***1823.21*** *p323*
Sandin, Pehr G.; New York, NY, 1851 ***6412.40*** *p152*
Sandivig, Ludivig; Washington, 1883 ***2770.40*** *p137*
Sandland, Joyce; America, 1763 ***1220.12*** *p699*
Sandmeier, Andrew; Illinois, 1858 ***6079.1*** *p12*
Sandmeier, Engel Marie Charlotte; America, 1846 ***7420.1*** *p49*
*Daughter:*Engel Marie Charl.
*Son:*Johann Heinrich Christoph
Sandmeier, Engel Marie Charlotte; America, 1847 ***7420.1*** *p49*
Sandmeier, Gottlieb Karl Wilhelm *SEE* Sandmeier, Louis Adolph
Sandmeier, Heinrich August *SEE* Sandmeier, Louis Adolph
Sandmeier, John; Illinois, 1858 ***6079.1*** *p12*
Sandmeier, Louis Adolph; America, 1865 ***7420.1*** *p236*
*Brother:*Gottlieb Karl Wilhelm
*Brother:*Heinrich August
Sandmeyer, Anna; America, 1885 ***7420.1*** *p348*
Sandmeyer, Auguste Clara Henni; America, 1884 ***7420.1*** *p345*
Sandmeyer, Carl Ludwig Hermann; America, 1889 ***7420.1*** *p359*
Sandmeyer, Engel Marie Charlotte; America, 1857 ***7420.1*** *p165*
Sandmeyer, Friedrich Ludwig; Port uncertain, 1850 ***7420.1*** *p75*
Sandquist, Alfred; Kansas, 1871 ***777.40*** *p16*
Sandquist, Anna Maria; Kansas, 1870 ***777.40*** *p10*
Sandquist, Hannah; Kansas, 1868-1873 ***777.40*** *p16*
Sandquist, Louisa Chr.; Kansas, 1867 ***777.40*** *p11*
Sandquist, Peter; Kansas, 1875-1879 ***777.40*** *p12*
Sandrock, Auguste Friederike; America, 1868 ***7420.1*** *p276*
Sandrock, Jacob; Chile, 1852 ***1192.4*** *p52*
With wife & 3 children
With child 2
With child 19
Sandrock, Johann August Ferdinand; America, 1867 ***7420.1*** *p263*
Sandry, Edwin 36; Ontario, 1871 ***1823.21*** *p324*
Sands, Ann; America, 1755 ***1220.12*** *p699*
Sands, Edward; North Carolina, 1852 ***1088.45*** *p30*
Sands, Elizabeth 40; Maryland, 1721 ***1220.12*** *p699*
Sands, Frances; Virginia, 1724 ***1220.12*** *p700*
Sands, John; America, 1750 ***1220.12*** *p700*
Sands, Margaret 60; Ontario, 1871 ***1823.21*** *p324*
Sands, Richmond 38; Ontario, 1871 ***1823.21*** *p324*
Sands, Samuel; Miami, 1920 ***4984.15*** *p38*
Sandschipper, Johann Heinrich 35; Galveston, TX, 1845 ***3967.10*** *p376*
Sandschipper, Maria 30; Galveston, TX, 1845 ***3967.10*** *p376*
Sandstedt, Charlotte; Kansas, 1867-1870 ***777.40*** *p8*
Sandstrom, Charles; Colorado, 1891 ***1029.59*** *p80*
Sandstrom, Emma; Colorado, 1894 ***1029.59*** *p81*
Sandstrom, F.; Oregon, 1845 ***6412.40*** *p147*
Sandstrom, Sven; Colorado, 1887 ***1029.59*** *p81*
Sandweiss, Aaron; Detroit, 1929 ***1640.55*** *p116*
Sandy, John; America, 1754 ***1220.12*** *p700*
Sandy, Thomas; America, 1754 ***1220.12*** *p700*
Sandys, Robert; America, 1685 ***1220.12*** *p700*
Sandys, Samuel; America, 1774 ***1220.12*** *p700*
Sane, Jean; Louisiana, 1874-1875 ***4981.45*** *p31*
Sanford, Edwin 60; Ontario, 1871 ***1823.17*** *p144*
Sanford, Francis Smith; Massachusetts, 1630 ***117.5*** *p154*
Sanford, Priscilla; America, 1720 ***1220.12*** *p699*
Sangan, James 70; Ontario, 1871 ***1823.21*** *p324*
Sanger, Adam 14; New York, NY, 1893 ***1883.7*** *p41*
Sanger, Barbara 37; Brazil, 1857 ***5475.1*** *p320*
Sanger, Catharina 31; New York, NY, 1893 ***1883.7*** *p41*
Sanger, Johann 9 months; New York, NY, 1893 ***1883.7*** *p41*
Sanger, Josef 9; New York, NY, 1893 ***1883.7*** *p41*
Sanger, Juliana 18; New York, NY, 1893 ***1883.7*** *p41*
Sanger, Max; America, 1872 ***5475.1*** *p419*
Sanger, Michael 9; New York, NY, 1893 ***1883.7*** *p41*
Sanger, Sarah; America, 1773 ***1220.12*** *p700*
Sanger, Stephen; America, 1736 ***1220.12*** *p700*
Sanger, Wendelin 39; New York, NY, 1893 ***1883.7*** *p41*
Sangiman, John 44; Ontario, 1871 ***1823.21*** *p324*
Sanglade, P. M. 18; New Orleans, 1843 ***778.6*** *p295*
Sangstor, Barbra 49; Ontario, 1871 ***1823.17*** *p144*
Sanguin, Thomas; America, 1752 ***1220.12*** *p700*
Sankey, Ellen 27; Quebec, 1870 ***8364.32*** *p25*
Sanko, Frank; Minnesota, 1926 ***2769.54*** *p1379*
Sanley, Oliver; Colorado, 1889 ***1029.59*** *p81*
Sanley, Oliver N.; Colorado, 1889 ***1029.59*** *p81*
San Luis, Jean 21; America, 1844 ***778.6*** *p295*
Sannwald, Johann Michael; America, 1881 ***179.55*** *p19*
Sannwald, Johann Michael F.; America, 1885 ***179.55*** *p19*
Sannwald, Katharina; America, 1867 ***179.55*** *p19*
Sannwald, Wilhelm Karl; America, 1885 ***179.55*** *p19*
Sanocki, Francois 19; New York, NY, 1920 ***930.50*** *p49*
Sanode, Nick; Louisiana, 1874-1875 ***4981.45*** *p31*
Sansinena, Jose; California, 1872 ***3276.8*** *p19*
Sansom, Joan; Bermuda, 1614 ***1220.12*** *p700*
Sansom, William; America, 1758 ***1220.12*** *p700*
Sansom, William; America, 1765 ***1220.12*** *p700*
Sansome, George; Barbados, 1665 ***1220.12*** *p700*
Sanson, George 40; Ontario, 1871 ***1823.17*** *p144*
Sanson, William; America, 1765 ***1220.12*** *p700*
Sanssoucy, Gabriel 37; Quebec, 1652 ***9221.17*** *p265*
Sanssoucy, Jean; Quebec, 1661 ***9221.17*** *p454*
Sanssoucy, Victor; Quebec, 1653 ***9221.17*** *p279*
Santa Cruz, Ignacio; Louisiana, 1874 ***4981.45*** *p134*
Santin, Ernest Vietn; Louisiana, 1874 ***4981.45*** *p134*
Santmeier, Andrew; Illinois, 1854 ***6079.1*** *p12*
Santmeier, Martin; Illinois, 1854 ***6079.1*** *p12*
Santmeier, Mathew; Illinois, 1854 ***6079.1*** *p12*
Santo, John 42; Ontario, 1871 ***1823.21*** *p324*
Santo, Simon; Illinois, 1852 ***6079.1*** *p12*
Santon, Henry; Barbados or St. Christopher, 1780 ***8529.30*** *p7A*
Santon, Richard; America, 1737 ***1220.12*** *p700*
Santry, Arthur; Toronto, 1844 ***2910.35*** *p116*
Santry, Daniel B.; Toronto, 1844 ***2910.35*** *p116*
Sany, Thomas; America, 1772 ***1220.12*** *p700*
Saple, Philip; Long Island, 1781 ***8529.30*** *p10A*
Sapple, Philip; Long Island, 1781 ***8529.30*** *p10A*
Sara, George 63; Ontario, 1871 ***1823.21*** *p324*
Sarandais, J. 16; America, 1847 ***778.6*** *p295*
Saranpaa, Victor 30; Minnesota, 1923 ***2769.54*** *p1381*
Sarataro, Antoine 29; New Orleans, 1848 ***778.6*** *p295*
Sarazin, J. 22; America, 1846 ***778.6*** *p295*
Sarbach, George; New Jersey, 1773-1774 ***927.31*** *p3*
Sarbaugh, Abraham; Ohio, 1809-1852 ***4511.35*** *p45*
Sarchet, Adam; Ohio, n.d. ***9228.50*** *p574*
Sarchet, Algie Marquand; Saskatchewan, 1912 ***9228.50*** *p567*
*Wife:*Magdalena Maldaner
Sarchet, Anne; Ohio, 1789-1849 ***9228.50*** *p103*
Sarchet, Anne Bichard *SEE* Sarchet, Thomas
Sarchet, David *SEE* Sarchet, Thomas
Sarchet, David *SEE* Sarchet, Thomas
Sarchet, Francis; Ohio, 1823 ***9228.50*** *p205*
Sarchet, John; Norfolk, VA, 1806 ***9228.50*** *p56*
With wife
Sarchet, John; Ohio, 1806 ***9228.50*** *p572*
With children
*Wife:*Judith Falaise
Sarchet, John *SEE* Sarchet, Thomas
Sarchet, John, Children; Ontario, 1850-1900 ***9228.50*** *p572*
Sarchet, Judith; Norfolk, VA, 1806 ***9228.50*** *p56*
Sarchet, Judith; Ohio, 1806 ***9228.50*** *p215*
Sarchet, Judith Falaise *SEE* Sarchet, John
Sarchet, Magdalena Maldaner *SEE* Sarchet, Algie Marquand
Sarchet, Margaret; Ohio, 1811 ***9228.50*** *p574*
Sarchet, Mary De Lisle *SEE* Sarchet, Thomas
Sarchet, Moses *SEE* Sarchet, Thomas
Sarchet, Moses *SEE* Sarchet, Thomas
Sarchet, Nancy *SEE* Sarchet, Thomas
Sarchet, Nancy Ann *SEE* Sarchet, Thomas
Sarchet, Nicholas; Norfolk, VA, 1806 ***9228.50*** *p56*
With wife
Sarchet, Nicholas; Ohio, 1780-1864 ***9228.50*** *p573*
Sarchet, Nicholas *SEE* Sarchet, Thomas
Sarchet, Peter; Norfolk, VA, 1806 ***9228.50*** *p56*
With wife
Sarchet, Peter *SEE* Sarchet, Thomas
Sarchet, Peter *SEE* Sarchet, Thomas
Sarchet, Peter *SEE* Sarchet, Peter
Sarchet, Peter; Ohio, 1818 ***9228.50*** *p567*
*Son:*Peter
Sarchet, Peter; Ohio, 1818 ***9228.50*** *p573*
Sarchet, Peter B. *SEE* Sarchet, Thomas
Sarchet, Peter D. *SEE* Sarchet, Thomas
Sarchet, Rachel *SEE* Sarchet, Thomas
Sarchet, Rachel; Ohio, 1807 ***9228.50*** *p101*
Sarchet, Rachel *SEE* Sarchet, Thomas
Sarchet, Rachel; Ohio, 1821 ***9228.50*** *p574*
Sarchet, Thomas; Norfolk, VA, 1806 ***9228.50*** *p5*
Sarchet, Thomas *SEE* Sarchet, Thomas
Sarchet, Thomas; Norfolk, VA, 1806 ***9228.50*** *p56*
With wife
*Son:*Thomas
Sarchet, Thomas; Ohio, 1806 ***9228.50*** *p103*
*Sibling:*David
*Sibling:*Nancy
*Sibling:*Rachel
*Sibling:*Moses
*Sibling:*Peter D.
Sarchet, Thomas; Ohio, 1807 ***9228.50*** *p566*
*Brother:*Peter
*Cousin:*Peter
*Brother:*Nicholas
*Brother:*John
Sarchet, Thomas *SEE* Sarchet, Thomas
Sarchet, Thomas *SEE* Sarchet, Thomas
Sarchet, Thomas; Ohio, 1807 ***9228.50*** *p567*
*Wife:*Mary De Lisle
*Grandchild:*Peter B.
*Grandchild:*Rachel
*Grandchild:*Moses
*Grandchild:*David
*Daughter-In-Law:*Anne Bichard
*Grandchild:*Thomas
*Grandchild:*Nancy Ann
*Son:*Thomas
Sarchet Family ; Ohio, 1806 ***9228.50*** *p433*
Sarcott, Francis; Maryland, 1723 ***1220.12*** *p700*
Sardin, Mr. 26; Louisiana, 1848 ***778.6*** *p295*
Sardin, Symon; Virginia, 1700 ***9230.15*** *p80*
Sare, David 28; Ontario, 1871 ***1823.21*** *p324*
Sares, Ann; America, 1742 ***1220.12*** *p700*
Sares, Richard; Marblehead, MA, 1637 ***9228.50*** *p577*
Sargeant, Hugh; Virginia, 1729 ***1220.12*** *p711*
Sargeant, John; America, 1675 ***1220.12*** *p711*
Sargeaton, Jean; Virginia, 1700 ***9230.15*** *p81*
With wife & child
Sargent, Frances; America, 1771 ***1220.12*** *p711*
Sargent, Isaac 30; Ontario, 1871 ***1823.21*** *p324*
Sargent, John; America, 1749 ***1220.12*** *p711*
Sargeon, Daniel; North Carolina, 1792-1862 ***1088.45*** *p30*
Sargery, John; Rappahannock, VA, 1741 ***1220.12*** *p700*
Sarjant, Thomas; America, 1774 ***1220.12*** *p711*
Sarjeant, George; America, 1769 ***1220.12*** *p711*
Sarkie, Wilhelmina; Oregon, 1941 ***9157.47*** *p2*

Sarllard, Francois; North Carolina, 1803 ***1088.45*** *p30*
Sarosick, Stanislas 49; New York, NY, 1920 ***930.50*** *p49*
Sarrabeyrouse, Mr.; New Orleans, 1845 ***778.6*** *p295*
Sarrabeyrouse, Mr. 43; New Orleans, 1845 ***778.6*** *p295*
Sarrabeyrouse, Mrs.; New Orleans, 1845 ***778.6*** *p295*
Sarrabeyrouse, J. 24; New Orleans, 1848 ***778.6*** *p295*
Sarrabeyrouse, J. 31; New Orleans, 1848 ***778.6*** *p295*
Sarramen, J. M. 24; America, 1845 ***778.6*** *p295*
Sarran, Mr. 32; Louisiana, 1848 ***778.6*** *p295*
Sarrasin, A. 60; Port uncertain, 1842 ***778.6*** *p295*
Sarrasin, J. 19; Port uncertain, 1842 ***778.6*** *p295*
Sarrat, P. 13; America, 1848 ***778.6*** *p295*
Sarrazin, E. 12; Port uncertain, 1842 ***778.6*** *p295*
Sarre, Adolphus; Ontario, 1908 ***9228.50*** *p574*
Sarre, Lewis; Ohio, 1840-1860 ***9228.50*** *p575*
Sarrene, Anne 38; New Orleans, 1840 ***778.6*** *p295*
Sarres, Richard; Marblehead, MA, 1637 ***9228.50*** *p577*
Sarrison, Sarah; America, 1753 ***1220.12*** *p700*
Sarritoff, Etienne 20; Mississippi, 1847 ***778.6*** *p295*
Sartain, James; America, 1756 ***1220.12*** *p711*
Sartaro, Antoine 5; New Orleans, 1848 ***778.6*** *p295*
Sartaro, Marguerite 23; New Orleans, 1848 ***778.6*** *p295*
Sartas, Pierre Felix; Illinois, 1852 ***6079.1*** *p12*
Sarter, Christine; Brazil, 1859 ***5475.1*** *p523*
Sarton, Marie Joseph; Wisconsin, 1871 ***1495.20*** *p28*
Sartorins, Henry; Louisiana, 1841-1844 ***4981.45*** *p211*
Sartorius, Herman Joseph Hubert; Kansas, 1917-1918 ***2054.10*** *p48*
Sartorius, M. Elizabeth; Kansas, 1917-1918 ***2054.10*** *p48*
Sartorius, Marg. Anna 32; America, 1864 ***5475.1*** *p59*
Sarvold, Engel John; Iowa, 1908 ***1211.15*** *p19*
Sary, Robert Ferdinand; Boston, 1848 ***2853.20*** *p313*
Sasse, Anton; America, 1926 ***8023.44*** *p378*
Sasse, Heinrich; America, 1832 ***7420.1*** *p6*
Sassenberg, Widow; America, 1853 ***7420.1*** *p111*
Sasser, John; Died enroute, 1743 ***1220.12*** *p700*
Sassi, . . .; West Virginia, 1865-1879 ***1132.30*** *p150*
Sassier, Ann; America, 1721 ***1220.12*** *p700*
Sassin, Francoise; Virginia, 1700 ***9230.15*** *p80*
Sassmann, Doris Sophie; America, 1866 ***7420.1*** *p248*
Sassmann, Johann Conrad Wilhelm; America, 1867 ***7420.1*** *p263*
Sasson, Catherine 24; New Orleans, 1846 ***778.6*** *p295*
Satchell, George; America, 1722 ***1220.12*** *p700*
Satcher, Thomas; America, 1739 ***1220.12*** *p700*
Satcher, Thomas; Virginia, 1730 ***1220.12*** *p700*
Satchwell, James; America, 1694 ***1220.12*** *p700*
Satchwell, Matthew; America, 1769 ***1220.12*** *p700*
Satchwell, Sarah; Virginia, 1736 ***1220.12*** *p700*
Sater, Peter E.; Washington, 1888 ***2770.40*** *p26*
Satory, William; Illinois, 1855 ***6079.1*** *p12*
Satran, Josef; Milwaukee, 1856 ***2853.20*** *p308*
Satsky, Jan; Texas, 1860 ***2853.20*** *p74*
Sattenberger, Conrad 3; America, 1847 ***778.6*** *p295*
Sattenberger, Elizabeth 37; America, 1847 ***778.6*** *p295*
Sattenberger, Johann 9; America, 1847 ***778.6*** *p295*
Sattenberger, Margaret 6; America, 1847 ***778.6*** *p295*
Sattenberger, Wilhelm 13; America, 1847 ***778.6*** *p295*
Sattenberger, Wilhelm 43; America, 1847 ***778.6*** *p295*
Satterfield, Sarah; Rappahannock, VA, 1728 ***1220.12*** *p700*
Satterholm, J.N.; New York, NY, 1851 ***6412.40*** *p153*
Satterly, Solomon; America, 1736 ***1220.12*** *p700*
Sattler, Albert; Illinois, 1858-1861 ***6020.5*** *p133*
Sattler, Johann Heinrich; America, 1846 ***7420.1*** *p48*
Satton, Joseph; America, 1744 ***1220.12*** *p700*
Satturlee, James; America, 1754 ***1220.12*** *p700*
Sauberlich, Max Arthur; Baltimore, 1902 ***6212.1*** *p13*
Sauce, John; Virginia, 1734 ***1220.12*** *p700*
Sauchet, Ulrich; Ohio, 1809-1852 ***4511.35*** *p45*
Saucisse, Ant. 35; Port uncertain, 1844 ***778.6*** *p295*
Sauer, Widow; America, 1854 ***7420.1*** *p128*
With daughter
Sauer, A.; California, 1868 ***1131.61*** *p89*
Sauer, Adam; America, 1854 ***2526.43*** *p128*
Sauer, Adam 7 *SEE* Sauer, Johannes, IV
Sauer, Anna Meisinger *SEE* Sauer, Johannes, IV
Sauer, Anna 16 *SEE* Sauer, Johannes, IV
Sauer, Balthasar; America, 1831 ***2526.43*** *p135*
Sauer, Christine *SEE* Sauer, Gottlieb
Sauer, Elisabeth 10 *SEE* Sauer, Heinrich
Sauer, Elisabetha 18; America, 1866 ***2526.42*** *p144*
Sauer, Eustas; Missouri, 1892 ***3276.1*** *p4*
Sauer, Eva 18 *SEE* Sauer, Johannes, IV
Sauer, Georg 3 *SEE* Sauer, Johannes, IV
Sauer, Georg Adam; Dayton, OH, 1854 ***2526.43*** *p135*
Sauer, Gottlieb; America, 1867 ***7919.3*** *p534*
Sauer, Gottlieb; North Dakota, 1888 ***554.30*** *p26*
*Wife:*Christine
Sauer, Heinrich; America, 1846 ***2526.42*** *p144*
With wife
*Child:*Heinrich
*Child:*Michael
*Child:*Philipp
*Child:*Elisabeth
Sauer, Heinrich 2 *SEE* Sauer, Heinrich
Sauer, Heinrich 11 *SEE* Sauer, Johannes, IV
Sauer, Heinrich Friedrich; America, 1847 ***7420.1*** *p56*
Sauer, Heinrich Friedrich; America, 1847 ***7420.1*** *p57*
Sauer, Jakob *SEE* Sauer, Johann Michel
Sauer, Joh. Michel *SEE* Sauer, Johann Michel
Sauer, Johann Michel 44; America, 1865 ***5475.1*** *p511*
*Wife:*Maria Rosina Gemmel 38
*Son:*Philipp
*Son:*Jakob
*Daughter:*Maria Anna
*Son:*Joh. Michel
Sauer, Johannes; America, 1851 ***2526.43*** *p135*
With wife & 4 children
Sauer, Johannes; America, 1865 ***5475.1*** *p510*
Sauer, Johannes; America, 1892 ***2526.42*** *p110*
Sauer, Johannes 14 *SEE* Sauer, Johannes, IV
Sauer, Johannes, IV; America, 1895 ***2526.42*** *p110*
*Wife:*Anna Meisinger
*Child:*Heinrich
*Child:*Adam
*Child:*Ludwig
*Child:*Georg
*Child:*Maria
*Child:*Johannes
*Child:*Leonhard
*Child:*Anna
*Child:*Eva
Sauer, Juliane 53; America, 1851 ***2526.43*** *p134*
Sauer, Karel; St. Louis, 1848-1849 ***2853.20*** *p21*
Sauer, Leonhard 19 *SEE* Sauer, Johannes, IV
Sauer, Ludwig 1 *SEE* Sauer, Johannes, IV
Sauer, Maria; America, 1881 ***5475.1*** *p315*
Sauer, Maria 9 *SEE* Sauer, Johannes, IV
Sauer, Maria Anna *SEE* Sauer, Johann Michel
Sauer, Maria Rosina Gemmel 38 *SEE* Sauer, Johann Michel
Sauer, Michael 1 *SEE* Sauer, Heinrich
Sauer, Michael; Dayton, OH, 1888 ***2526.42*** *p145*
Sauer, Philipp; America, 1841 ***2526.42*** *p175*
Sauer, Philipp; America, 1841 ***2526.42*** *p176*
With wife 4 children & mother-in-law
Sauer, Philipp *SEE* Sauer, Johann Michel
Sauer, Philipp 17 *SEE* Sauer, Heinrich
Sauer, Theodore J.; New York, 1859 ***358.56*** *p54*
Sauer, Vaclav; Wisconsin, 1857 ***2853.20*** *p323*
Sauer, Wilhelmine; America, 1867 ***7919.3*** *p534*
Sauerbrei, Franz Friedrich; America, 1868 ***7919.3*** *p526*
Sauerbrey, Sigmund; America, 1867 ***7919.3*** *p529*
Sauermilch, Jacob August; America, 1868 ***7919.3*** *p533*
Sauermilch, Johanne Marianne; America, 1868 ***7919.3*** *p533*
Sauermilch, Matthaus; America, 1868 ***7919.3*** *p532*
Sauers, George 35; Indiana, 1880-1887 ***9076.20*** *p71*
Sauerwein, Ms. 51; America, 1877 ***5475.1*** *p179*
Sauerwein, Heinrich Jakob; America, 1882 ***5475.1*** *p51*
*Wife:*Sophia Altpeter
*Son:*Wilhelm
*Son:*Ludwig
Sauerwein, Ludwig *SEE* Sauerwein, Heinrich Jakob
Sauerwein, Magdalena; America, 1884 ***5475.1*** *p378*
Sauerwein, Sophia Altpeter *SEE* Sauerwein, Heinrich Jakob
Sauerwein, Wilhelm *SEE* Sauerwein, Heinrich Jakob
Sauge, Francois 25; Missouri, 1848 ***778.6*** *p296*
Sauge, Francois A.; Illinois, 1852 ***6079.1*** *p12*
Sauge, Jean 27; America, 1841 ***778.6*** *p296*
Sauger, Louis; Illinois, 1852 ***6079.1*** *p12*
Saul, Adam; America, 1856 ***2526.43*** *p124*
Saul, Adam; America, 1890 ***2526.43*** *p131*
Saul, Adam 11 *SEE* Saul, Mrs. Konrad
Saul, Alfred 10; Quebec, 1870 ***8364.32*** *p25*
Saul, Anna Margaretha *SEE* Saul, Johann Leonhard
Saul, Anna Margaretha; America, 1856 ***2526.43*** *p124*
Saul, Anna Margaretha 31; America, 1867 ***2526.42*** *p145*
Saul, Anna Rosina *SEE* Saul, Johannes
Saul, Charles; Ohio, 1809-1852 ***4511.35*** *p45*
Saul, Christina 26; America, 1866 ***2526.42*** *p176*
Saul, Christine 40; America, 1831 ***2526.42*** *p176*
With daughter 6
Saul, Elisabetha; America, 1856 ***2526.43*** *p124*
Saul, Elisabetha; America, 1883 ***2526.42*** *p130*
Saul, Elisabetha 7 *SEE* Saul, Mrs. Konrad
Saul, Elisabetha Margaretha 23; America, 1867 ***2526.42*** *p145*
Saul, Friedrich; America, 1856 ***2526.43*** *p124*
Saul, Friedrich 4 *SEE* Saul, Mrs. Konrad
Saul, Georg; America, 1866 ***2526.42*** *p106*
Saul, Georg Christian 16; America, 1853 ***2526.43*** *p135*
Saul, Heinrich; America, 1856 ***2526.43*** *p124*
Saul, Heinrich 9 *SEE* Saul, Mrs. Konrad
Saul, Henry; America, 1772 ***1220.12*** *p700*
Saul, Henry; Louisiana, 1836-1840 ***4981.45*** *p213*
Saul, Henry 58; Ontario, 1871 ***1823.17*** *p144*
Saul, James 44; Ontario, 1871 ***1823.21*** *p324*
Saul, Johann Adam; America, 1753 ***2526.42*** *p145*
Saul, Johann Georg; America, 1853 ***2526.42*** *p99*
Saul, Johann Georg; America, 1867 ***2526.43*** *p135*
Saul, Johann Konrad; America, 1882 ***2526.42*** *p130*
Saul, Johann Leonhard; America, 1753 ***2526.42*** *p145*
*Wife:*Maria Magdalena Hammann
*Child:*Anna Margaretha
Saul, Johannes; America, 1832 ***2526.42*** *p177*
With mother
*Daughter:*Anna Rosina
*Wife:*Maria Katharina Hirz
Saul, John; America, 1729 ***1220.12*** *p700*
Saul, John 38; Ontario, 1871 ***1823.21*** *p324*
Saul, Joseph; Salem, MA, 1775 ***9228.50*** *p575*
Saul, Katharina; America, 1883 ***2526.42*** *p130*
Saul, Katharina 34; America, 1855 ***2526.42*** *p96*
Saul, Konrad; America, 1854 ***2526.43*** *p124*
Saul, Mrs. Konrad; America, 1855 ***2526.43*** *p124*
*Son:*Adam
*Son:*Heinrich
*Son:*Friedrich
*Son:*Peter
*Daughter:*Elisabetha
Saul, Leonhard; America, 1867 ***2526.42*** *p145*
Saul, Margaretha Elisabetha; America, 1854 ***2526.42*** *p131*
*Child:*Eva
*Child:*Heinrich
*Child:*Elisabeth
Saul, Maria Elisabetha; America, 1858 ***2526.42*** *p99*
Saul, Maria Katharina Hirz *SEE* Saul, Johannes
Saul, Maria Magdalena Hammann *SEE* Saul, Johann Leonhard
Saul, Marie Elisabeth; America, 1753 ***2526.42*** *p145*
Saul, Mary 70; Ontario, 1871 ***1823.21*** *p324*
Saul, Mary 7; Quebec, 1870 ***8364.32*** *p25*
Saul, Mrs. Michael 64; America, 1883 ***2526.42*** *p120*
Saul, Nikolaus; America, 1753 ***2526.42*** *p170*
Saul, Nikolaus; Dayton, OH, 1854 ***2526.42*** *p99*
Saul, Peter; America, 1856 ***2526.43*** *p124*
Saul, Peter 9 *SEE* Saul, Mrs. Konrad
Saul, Philipp; America, 1885 ***2526.43*** *p131*
With uncle
Saul, Philipp 25; America, 1882 ***2526.42*** *p110*
Saul, Richard 70; Ontario, 1871 ***1823.21*** *p324*
Saul, Sarah; Virginia, 1732 ***1220.12*** *p700*
Saul, Thomas; Annapolis, MD, 1719 ***1220.12*** *p700*
Saulnier, Francoise 21; Montreal, 1659 ***9221.17*** *p428*
Saulnier, Nicole; Quebec, 1669 ***4514.3*** *p369*
Saulnier DeCriel, Pierre; Montreal, 1661 ***9221.17*** *p475*
Saulter, Thomas; Ohio, 1809-1852 ***4511.35*** *p45*
Saumarez, Thomas; Yorktown, VA, 1781 ***9228.50*** *p576*
Saunby, Francis 63; Ontario, 1871 ***1823.21*** *p324*
Saunders, Abraham; America, 1746 ***1220.12*** *p700*
Saunders, Alfred 25; Ontario, 1871 ***1823.21*** *p324*
Saunders, Alice; Barbados, 1664 ***1220.12*** *p700*
Saunders, Ann; America, 1756 ***1220.12*** *p700*
Saunders, Ann; America, 1759 ***1220.12*** *p700*
Saunders, Ann; America, 1768 ***1220.12*** *p700*
Saunders, Ann; America, 1773 ***1220.12*** *p700*
Saunders, Cales 50; Ontario, 1871 ***1823.21*** *p324*
Saunders, Catherine; America, 1757 ***1220.12*** *p701*
Saunders, Catherine; America, 1767 ***1220.12*** *p701*
Saunders, Charles; Virginia, 1721 ***1220.12*** *p701*
Saunders, Charles; Virginia, 1741 ***1220.12*** *p701*
Saunders, Daniel; Virginia, 1769 ***1220.12*** *p701*
Saunders, Edward; Barbados, 1677 ***1220.12*** *p701*
Saunders, Edward; South Carolina, 1858 ***6155.4*** *p19*
Saunders, Eidth G.; Ontario, 1917 ***9228.50*** *p337*
Saunders, Elizabeth; America, 1748 ***1220.12*** *p701*
Saunders, Elizabeth; America, 1765 ***1220.12*** *p701*
Saunders, Elizabeth; America, 1766 ***1220.12*** *p701*
Saunders, Elizabeth; Charles Town, SC, 1719 ***1220.12*** *p701*
Saunders, George; Potomac, 1729 ***1220.12*** *p701*
Saunders, Hannah; America, 1760 ***1220.12*** *p701*
Saunders, Hannah; America, 1768 ***1220.12*** *p701*
Saunders, Henry; America, 1767 ***1220.12*** *p701*
Saunders, Henry 31; Ontario, 1871 ***1823.21*** *p324*
Saunders, Henry 40; Ontario, 1871 ***1823.17*** *p144*
Saunders, Humphrey; America, 1685 ***1220.12*** *p701*
Saunders, Isabel; Boston, 1923-1983 ***9228.50*** *p263*
Saunders, Isaiah; Ontario, 1871 ***1823.17*** *p144*
Saunders, Jacob 41; Ontario, 1871 ***1823.21*** *p324*
Saunders, James; America, 1751 ***1220.12*** *p701*
Saunders, James; Boston, 1718 ***1220.12*** *p701*
Saunders, James 55; Ontario, 1871 ***1823.17*** *p144*
Saunders, James 60; Ontario, 1871 ***1823.17*** *p144*
Saunders, James 79; Ontario, 1871 ***1823.21*** *p324*

Saunders, James; Virginia, 1740 ***1220.12*** *p701*
Saunders, John; America, 1685 ***1220.12*** *p701*
Saunders, John; America, 1735 ***1220.12*** *p701*
Saunders, John; America, 1754 ***1220.12*** *p701*
Saunders, John; America, 1765 ***1220.12*** *p701*
Saunders, John; America, 1768 ***1220.12*** *p701*
Saunders, John; America, 1773 ***1220.12*** *p701*
Saunders, John; Barbados or Jamaica, 1674 ***1220.12*** *p701*
Saunders, John; Barbados or Jamaica, 1702 ***1220.12*** *p701*
Saunders, John; Maryland, 1725 ***1220.12*** *p701*
Saunders, John 40; Ontario, 1871 ***1823.17*** *p144*
Saunders, John 46; Ontario, 1871 ***1823.17*** *p144*
Saunders, John 50; Ontario, 1871 ***1823.21*** *p324*
Saunders, John 61; Ontario, 1871 ***1823.21*** *p324*
Saunders, John; Virginia, 1768 ***1220.12*** *p701*
Saunders, John M.; Colorado, 1884 ***1029.59*** *p81*
Saunders, Joseph; America, 1675 ***1220.12*** *p701*
Saunders, Joseph; America, 1744 ***1220.12*** *p701*
Saunders, Joseph; Virginia, 1730 ***1220.12*** *p701*
Saunders, Kay; Boston, 1923-1983 ***9228.50*** *p263*
Saunders, Lion; America, 1771 ***1220.12*** *p701*
Saunders, Lucey; America, 1761 ***1220.12*** *p701*
Saunders, Lucretia; America, 1760 ***1220.12*** *p701*
Saunders, Mary; America, 1750 ***1220.12*** *p701*
Saunders, Mary; America, 1758 ***1220.12*** *p701*
Saunders, Mary; Boston, 1923-1983 ***9228.50*** *p263*
Saunders, Matthew; Virginia, 1735 ***1220.12*** *p701*
Saunders, Richard; America, 1757 ***1220.12*** *p702*
Saunders, Richard; Maryland or Virginia, 1738 ***1220.12*** *p702*
Saunders, Robert; America, 1753 ***1220.12*** *p702*
Saunders, Robert; Virginia, 1737 ***1220.12*** *p702*
Saunders, Samuel; Boston, 1715 ***9228.50*** *p566*
Saunders, Stephen 46; Ontario, 1871 ***1823.21*** *p324*
Saunders, Stephen; Rappahannock, VA, 1741 ***1220.12*** *p702*
Saunders, Susanna; Virginia, 1741 ***1220.12*** *p702*
Saunders, Thomas; America, 1685 ***1220.12*** *p702*
Saunders, Thomas; America, 1691 ***1220.12*** *p702*
Saunders, Thomas; America, 1724 ***1220.12*** *p702*
Saunders, Thomas; America, 1727 ***1220.12*** *p702*
Saunders, Thomas; America, 1733 ***1220.12*** *p702*
Saunders, Thomas; America, 1739 ***1220.12*** *p702*
Saunders, Thomas; America, 1743 ***1220.12*** *p702*
Saunders, Thomas; America, 1774 ***1220.12*** *p702*
Saunders, Thomas; Carolina, 1719 ***1220.12*** *p702*
Saunders, Thomas 23; Ontario, 1871 ***1823.21*** *p324*
Saunders, Thomas 46; Ontario, 1871 ***1823.17*** *p144*
Saunders, Thomas 61; Ontario, 1871 ***1823.17*** *p144*
Saunders, Thomas 80; Ontario, 1871 ***1823.17*** *p144*
Saunders, Thomas; Virginia, 1730 ***1220.12*** *p702*
Saunders, William; America, 1685 ***1220.12*** *p702*
Saunders, William; America, 1731 ***1220.12*** *p702*
Saunders, William; America, 1736 ***1220.12*** *p702*
Saunders, William; America, 1750 ***1220.12*** *p702*
Saunders, William; America, 1754 ***1220.12*** *p702*
Saunders, William; America, 1760 ***1220.12*** *p702*
Saunders, William; America, 1767 ***1220.12*** *p702*
Saunders, William; Barbados or Jamaica, 1674 ***1220.12*** *p702*
Saunders, William 34; Ontario, 1871 ***1823.21*** *p324*
Saunders, William 45; Ontario, 1871 ***1823.17*** *p144*
Saunders, William 51; Ontario, 1871 ***1823.17*** *p144*
Saunders, Wilmot; Virginia, 1745 ***1220.12*** *p702*
Saunderson, Charles; America, 1764 ***1220.12*** *p702*
Saunderson, George 25; Ontario, 1871 ***1823.21*** *p324*
Saunderson, Joseph; Virginia, 1729 ***1220.12*** *p702*
Saunderson, Thomas; America, 1729 ***1220.12*** *p702*
Saunderson, Thomas; America, 1739 ***1220.12*** *p702*
Saunderson, William; America, 1750 ***1220.12*** *p702*
Saundry, Alexander; America, 1745 ***1220.12*** *p702*
Saundry, William; North Carolina, 1838 ***1088.45*** *p30*
Saunois, Therese; Quebec, 1671 ***4514.3*** *p369*
Saurel, Pierre de; Quebec, 1665 ***2314.30*** *p167*
Saurel, Pierre de; Quebec, 1665 ***2314.30*** *p196*
Sauri, J. F.; Louisiana, 1836-1840 ***4981.45*** *p213*
Sauris Baronesa, Jose 25; Puerto Rico, 1825 ***3476.25*** *p113*
Sauser, Pierre 38; America, 1847 ***778.6*** *p296*
Sauson, George 24; Ontario, 1871 ***1823.21*** *p324*
Sausovich, Michele; Louisiana, 1874 ***4981.45*** *p134*
Sausy, Franz; America, 1880 ***5475.1*** *p257*
Sausy, Johann; America, 1874 ***5475.1*** *p309*
Sauter, Charles; Colorado, 1880 ***1029.59*** *p81*
Sauter, Dionysius 60; Galveston, TX, 1844 ***3967.10*** *p370*
Sauter, Elisabeth 15; Galveston, TX, 1844 ***3967.10*** *p370*
Sauter, John; Colorado, 1887 ***1029.59*** *p81*
Sauter, John; Colorado, 1888 ***1029.59*** *p81*
Sauter, John G.; Ohio, 1809-1852 ***4511.35*** *p45*
Sauter, Therese 58; Galveston, TX, 1844 ***3967.10*** *p370*
Sautille, Pierre 49; America, 1843 ***778.6*** *p296*
Sautrine, Jean-Baptiste 35; Port uncertain, 1843 ***778.6*** *p296*
Sautrine, Marie Louise 20; Port uncertain, 1843 ***778.6*** *p296*
Sautter, Thomas; Ohio, 1809-1852 ***4511.35*** *p45*
Sauvage, Joseph 67; New Orleans, 1847 ***778.6*** *p296*
Sauvaget, Anne Dupuy Benacis 46 *SEE* Sauvaget, Jean
Sauvaget, Jean; Quebec, 1642 ***9221.17*** *p121*
*Wife:*Anne Dupuy Benacis
Sauvaget, Jeanne 31; Quebec, 1642 ***9221.17*** *p112*
Sauvary, Mary; Maryland, 1684 ***9228.50*** *p576*
Sauviot, Jean 12 *SEE* Sauviot, Louise Brodeur Arnue
Sauviot, Louise Brodeur Arnue 48; Montreal, 1658 ***9221.17*** *p391*
With daughter 26
*Daughter:*Marguerite 17
*Brother:*Jean 12
Sauviot, Marguerite 17 *SEE* Sauviot, Louise Brodeur Arnue
Saux, Jean 27; New Orleans, 1840 ***778.6*** *p296*
Savade, Mrs.; Wisconsin, 1800-1990 ***9228.50*** *p20A*
Savadge, Mathias; America, 1749 ***1220.12*** *p703*
Savadge, Patrick; America, 1749 ***1220.12*** *p703*
Savage, Ann; America, 1752 ***1220.12*** *p702*
Savage, Ann; Virginia, 1732 ***1220.12*** *p702*
Savage, Annie 25; Ontario, 1871 ***1823.17*** *p145*
Savage, Anthony *SEE* Savage, John
Savage, Bartholomew; America, 1760 ***1220.12*** *p702*
Savage, Cane; Rappahannock, VA, 1741 ***1220.12*** *p702*
Savage, Constant; America, 1764 ***1220.12*** *p702*
Savage, Daniel; Philadelphia, 1778 ***8529.30*** *p15*
Savage, Edward; America, 1726 ***1220.12*** *p703*
Savage, Edward; Barbados, 1665 ***1220.12*** *p703*
Savage, Eliabeth *SEE* Savage, John
Savage, Francis; America, 1685 ***1220.12*** *p703*
Savage, Henry; America, 1773 ***1220.12*** *p703*
Savage, James; America, 1740 ***1220.12*** *p703*
Savage, James; America, 1757 ***1220.12*** *p703*
Savage, John; America, 1720 ***1220.12*** *p703*
Savage, John; America, 1721 ***1220.12*** *p703*
Savage, John; America, 1755 ***1220.12*** *p703*
Savage, John; America, 1758 ***1220.12*** *p703*
Savage, John; Barbados, 1701 ***1220.12*** *p703*
Savage, John; Canada, 1774 ***3036.5*** *p41*
*Wife:*Eliabeth
*Son:*Anthony
Savage, John 39; Ontario, 1871 ***1823.17*** *p145*
Savage, Joseph; America, 1747 ***1220.12*** *p703*
Savage, Mary; Annapolis, MD, 1725 ***1220.12*** *p703*
Savage, Mary; Philadelphia, 1868 ***8513.31*** *p434*
Savage, Maurice; America, 1767 ***1220.12*** *p703*
Savage, Michael 40; Ontario, 1871 ***1823.21*** *p324*
Savage, Patrick; Illinois, 1858-1861 ***6020.5*** *p133*
Savage, Penrose Ann; Toronto, 1863-1884 ***9228.50*** *p576*
Savage, Richard; America, 1749 ***1220.12*** *p703*
Savage, Sarah; America, 1752 ***1220.12*** *p703*
Savage, Thomas; America, 1739 ***1220.12*** *p703*
Savage, Thomas; Louisiana, 1836-1840 ***4981.45*** *p213*
Savage, William; America, 1755 ***1220.12*** *p703*
Savage, William; America, 1767 ***1220.12*** *p703*
Savagen, Lewis; Ohio, 1809-1852 ***4511.35*** *p45*
Savard, Gillette; Quebec, 1665 ***4514.3*** *p369*
Savaree, Elizabeth; America, 1739 ***1220.12*** *p703*
Savarese, Frank; Louisiana, 1874 ***4981.45*** *p297*
Savarian, Stanilas Vierre; Illinois, 1852 ***6079.1*** *p12*
Savariau, Stanislas 28; Texas, 1848 ***778.6*** *p296*
Savarisse, Marie 18; America, 1847 ***778.6*** *p296*
Savarit, Rene; Quebec, 1649 ***9221.17*** *p220*
Savarriau, Laurent 33; New Orleans, 1843 ***778.6*** *p296*
Savarriau, Pierre 59; New Orleans, 1843 ***778.6*** *p296*
Savary, Jean 31; New Orleans, 1848 ***778.6*** *p296*
Savary, Mary; Boston, 1700-1730 ***9228.50*** *p576*
Savary, Mary; Maryland, 1684 ***9228.50*** *p576*
Savary, Rene; Quebec, 1649 ***9221.17*** *p220*
Savary, Thomas; Plymouth, MA, 1684 ***9228.50*** *p579*
Savell, Ann; America, 1765 ***1220.12*** *p703*
Savell, James; Maryland, 1737 ***1220.12*** *p703*
Saverin, John; America, 1765 ***1220.12*** *p703*
Savident, Arthur J. *SEE* Savident, James
Savident, Eliza Jane Tostevin *SEE* Savident, James
Savident, Ernest P. *SEE* Savident, James
Savident, James; California, 1912-1950 ***9228.50*** *p576*
Savident, James; California, 1924 ***9228.50*** *p576*
With wife
*Child:*Winifred
Savident, James *SEE* Savident, James
Savident, James; Victoria, B.C., 1912 ***9228.50*** *p576*
*Wife:*Eliza Jane Tostevin
*Child:*Ernest P.
*Child:*Arthur J.
*Child:*James
Savident, Winifred *SEE* Savident, James
Savidge, Thomas; America, 1767 ***1220.12*** *p703*
Savigny, N.; Quebec, 1885 ***1937.10*** *p52*
Savil, William; America, 1743 ***1220.12*** *p703*
Savile, Richard; America, 1728 ***1220.12*** *p703*
Savill, Israel; America, 1718 ***1220.12*** *p703*
Savill, Thomas; Maryland or Virginia, 1738 ***1220.12*** *p703*
Saville, Ann; America, 1749 ***1220.12*** *p703*
Saville, Edward; America, 1721 ***1220.12*** *p703*
Saville, John; America, 1771 ***1220.12*** *p703*
Saville, Thomas; America, 1767 ***1220.12*** *p703*
Savin, Jean; Virginia, 1700 ***9230.15*** *p81*
With wife & child
Savinski, Mr.; New York, 1926 ***1173.1*** *p2*
Savinski, Mrs.; New York, 1926 ***1173.1*** *p2*
Savo, Francis; Ohio, 1809-1852 ***4511.35*** *p45*
Savon, Pierre 25; Louisiana, 1847 ***778.6*** *p296*
Savonnet, Jeanne; Quebec, 1670 ***4514.3*** *p369*
Savonnieres DeLaTroche, Marie 23; Quebec, 1639 ***9221.17*** *p84*
Savory, Ann; America, 1759 ***1220.12*** *p703*
Savory, John 98; Massachusetts, 1742 ***9228.50*** *p580*
Savory, Mary; Maryland, 1684 ***9228.50*** *p576*
Savory, Mary Ann; Havana, 1817-1900 ***9228.50*** *p581*
Savory, Richard; Marston's Wharf, 1782 ***8529.30*** *p15*
Savory, Thomas; Plymouth, MA, 1684 ***9228.50*** *p579*
Savory, William; Massachusetts, 1630-1639 ***9228.50*** *p579*
Savory, Wm.; Massachusetts, 1600-1699 ***9228.50*** *p576*
Savoy, Widow 47; America, 1845 ***778.6*** *p296*
Savoy, Charles 18; America, 1845 ***778.6*** *p296*
Savoy, Gabriel; America, 1758 ***1220.12*** *p703*
Savoyan, Louis 29; Ohio, 1847 ***778.6*** *p296*
Sawcer, William; Virginia, 1771 ***1220.12*** *p703*
Sawert, August; Iowa, 1901 ***1211.15*** *p19*
Sawford, Francis; West Indies, 1688 ***1220.12*** *p703*
Sawicki, Adolf 34; New York, NY, 1920 ***930.50*** *p49*
Sawinski, Aleksander 22; New York, NY, 1911 ***6533.11*** *p10*
Sawyer, Charles; America, 1757 ***1220.12*** *p703*
Sawyer, Charles; America, 1771 ***1220.12*** *p703*
Sawyer, Edmund; America, 1773 ***1220.12*** *p703*
Sawyer, Edward; Miami, 1920 ***4984.15*** *p38*
Sawyer, Frances; America, 1774 ***1220.12*** *p703*
Sawyer, Henry; America, 1723 ***1220.12*** *p704*
Sawyer, James; Virginia, 1747 ***1220.12*** *p704*
Sawyer, John; America, 1769 ***1220.12*** *p704*
Sawyer, Samuel; America, 1736 ***1220.12*** *p704*
Sawyer, Thomas; America, 1767 ***1220.12*** *p704*
Sawyer, W. E. 38; Ontario, 1871 ***1823.21*** *p324*
Sawyer, William; America, 1738 ***1220.12*** *p704*
Sawyer, William; Virginia, 1747 ***1220.12*** *p704*
Sax, Ann 34; New Orleans, 1845 ***778.6*** *p296*
Sax, Pinkes; Louisiana, 1887-1895 ***7710.1*** *p161*
Saxbee, Samuel; America, 1685 ***1220.12*** *p704*
Saxelby, Mary; America, 1765 ***1220.12*** *p704*
Saxon, George; America, 1758 ***1220.12*** *p704*
Saxtatter, Mary; Wisconsin, 1906 ***6795.8*** *p179*
Saxton, Margarett 51; Michigan, 1880 ***4491.39*** *p27*
Saxton, William 58; Michigan, 1880 ***4491.39*** *p27*
Say, Ephraim; Virginia, 1742 ***1220.12*** *p704*
Say, James; Virginia, 1748 ***1220.12*** *p704*
Say, John; America, 1685 ***1220.12*** *p704*
Say, Jonas; America, 1685 ***1220.12*** *p704*
Say, Richard; Virginia, 1741 ***1220.12*** *p704*
Sayce, John; America, 1675 ***1220.12*** *p704*
Saye, Jean; Virginia, 1700 ***9230.15*** *p80*
Sayer, George; America, 1754 ***1220.12*** *p704*
Sayer, John; Ohio, n.d. ***9228.50*** *p576*
Sayers, James 35; Ontario, 1871 ***1823.21*** *p324*
Sayers, William; America, 1767 ***1220.12*** *p704*
Sayers, William; Barbados or Jamaica, 1686 ***1220.12*** *p704*
Sayes, John; America, 1726 ***1220.12*** *p704*
Saynor, William 51; Ontario, 1871 ***1823.21*** *p324*
Sayre, Daniel; Salem, MA, n.d. ***9228.50*** *p576*
Sayre, John; Ohio, n.d. ***9228.50*** *p576*
Sayreter, Thiebold 5; America, 1846 ***778.6*** *p296*
Sayse, John; America, 1727 ***1220.12*** *p704*
Sayte, Jaques; Virginia, 1700 ***9230.15*** *p80*
Saythuss, James; America, 1772 ***1220.12*** *p704*
Sayward, Mary; America, 1739 ***1220.12*** *p704*
Saywell, Thomas 26; Michigan, 1880 ***4491.42*** *p23*
Saywood, Penitent; America, 1700 ***1220.12*** *p704*
Scadding, Elizabeth; Virginia, 1758 ***1220.12*** *p704*
Scadding, John; America, 1770 ***1220.12*** *p704*
Scadgell, Richard; America, 1723 ***1220.12*** *p704*
Scafe, John 45; Ontario, 1871 ***1823.21*** *p324*
Scafe, John 62; Ontario, 1871 ***1823.21*** *p324*
Scake, S. P. 41; Ontario, 1871 ***1823.21*** *p325*
Scales, Frances; Barbados or Jamaica, 1700 ***1220.12*** *p704*
Scales, Richard; America, 1736 ***1220.12*** *p704*
Scales, Richard; America, 1738 ***1220.12*** *p704*
Scales, Thomas; Washington, 1889 ***2770.40*** *p81*

Scalichi, Michele; Louisiana, 1874-1875 *4981.45 p31*
Scalichi, Michele; Louisiana, 1874-1875 *4981.45 p130*
Scaling, Hazel Heath; Oregon, 1941 *9157.47 p3*
Scallian, John; St. Johns, N.F., 1825 *1053.15 p6*
Scallian, William; St. Johns, N.F., 1825 *1053.15 p6*
Scallion, Catherine; New Orleans, 1850 *7242.30 p154*
Scallion, James; New Orleans, 1850 *7242.30 p154*
Scallion, William 70; Ontario, 1871 *1823.21 p325*
Scalthropp, John; Barbados, 1676 *1220.12 p704*
Scam, John; America, 1754 *1220.12 p704*
Scam, William; America, 1754 *1220.12 p704*
Scamell, Sarah; America, 1742 *1220.12 p704*
Scammell, Edward; Virginia, 1742 *1220.12 p704*
Scammell, John; Virginia, 1762 *1220.12 p704*
Scammell, Thomas 34; Indiana, 1881-1888 *9076.20 p71*
Scamp, Elizabeth; America, 1745 *1220.12 p704*
Scamp, James; America, 1745 *1220.12 p704*
Scamp, John; America, 1745 *1220.12 p704*
Scamp, Mary; America, 1745 *1220.12 p704*
Scamp, Mary; America, 1765 *1220.12 p704*
Scamp, Susannah; America, 1745 *1220.12 p704*
Scampey, Philip; America, 1764 *1220.12 p704*
Scampey, William; America, 1755 *1220.12 p704*
Scanado, Joseph 46; Ontario, 1871 *1823.21 p325*
Scanado, Moses 34; Ontario, 1871 *1823.21 p325*
Scanado, Thomas 33; Ontario, 1871 *1823.21 p325*
Scandon, James; America, 1766 *1220.12 p704*
Scandrell, Thomas; America, 1723 *1220.12 p705*
Scandrett, Henry; America, 1767 *1220.12 p705*
Scandrett, John 41; Ontario, 1871 *1823.21 p325*
Scandrett, Richard 52; Ontario, 1871 *1823.21 p325*
Scandrett, Thomas; America, 1723 *1220.12 p705*
Scaniin, Martin; Toronto, 1844 *2910.35 p114*
Scanlan, John 50; Ontario, 1871 *1823.21 p325*
Scanlan, John; St. John, N.B., 1848 *2978.15 p39*
Scanlan, Michael 50; Ontario, 1871 *1823.21 p325*
Scanlin, Edward 48; Ontario, 1871 *1823.17 p145*
Scanlin, John 51; Ontario, 1871 *1823.21 p325*
Scanlin, Martin 36; Ontario, 1871 *1823.21 p325*
Scanling, Simon 30; Ontario, 1871 *1823.17 p145*
Scanlon, James 34; Ontario, 1871 *1823.21 p325*
Scanlon, John; Toronto, 1844 *2910.35 p114*
Scarborough, James; America, 1755 *1220.12 p705*
Scarborough, James; America, 1773 *1220.12 p705*
Scarborough, Joseph; Virginia, 1718 *1220.12 p705*
Scarborough, Lawrence; America, 1765 *1220.12 p705*
Scarborough, Thomas; America, 1751 *1220.12 p705*
Scarcity, William; Virginia, 1736 *1220.12 p705*
Scarcliffe, William M. 57; Ontario, 1871 *1823.21 p325*
Scarenbone, John Peter; America, 1736 *1220.12 p705*
Scarfe, Jeremiah; America, 1768 *1220.12 p705*
Scarff, James 30; Quebec, 1870 *8364.32 p25*
Scarfo, Vincent; New York, 1926 *1173.1 p2*
Scarisbrick, John; America, 1755 *1220.12 p705*
Scarl, Sarah; America, 1770 *1220.12 p705*
Scarlet, Peter; America, 1768 *1220.12 p705*
Scarlett, Catherine; America, 1755 *1220.12 p705*
Scarlett, Richard; Barbados or Jamaica, 1685 *1220.12 p705*
Scarlett, Stephen; America, 1774 *1220.12 p705*
Scarlett, William; America, 1753 *1220.12 p705*
Scarr, Francis; North Carolina, 1856 *1088.45 p30*
Scarr, William; America, 1775 *1220.12 p705*
Scarratt, Mary; America, 1741 *1220.12 p705*
Scarrell, Nicholas; Maryland, 1727 *1220.12 p705*
Scarrett, George; America, 1748 *1220.12 p705*
Scarrett, Nicholas; Maryland, 1727 *1220.12 p705*
Scarritt, Anne; Carolina, 1724 *1220.12 p705*
Scatcherd, Thomas 69; Ontario, 1871 *1823.21 p325*
Scattergood, William; America, 1750 *1220.12 p705*
Scayle, John; America, 1698 *1220.12 p704*
Sceves, Charles 40; America, 1842 *778.6 p296*
Schaaf, Cath. 1; America, 1840 *778.6 p296*
Schaaf, Franz 3; America, 1840 *778.6 p296*
Schaaf, Friedrich August; America, 1881 *179.55 p19*
Schaaf, Magd. 34; America, 1840 *778.6 p296*
Schaaf, Michel 28; America, 1840 *778.6 p296*
Schaaf, Paul; Illinois, 1856 *6079.1 p12*
Schaaf, Peter 20; America, 1840 *778.6 p296*
Schaake, Heinrich Ludwig; Texas, 1845 *7420.1 p39*
  With son 9
  With son 1
Schaal, Friedrich; America, 1856 *5475.1 p491*
Schaal, Georg 18; Texas, 1913 *8425.16 p31*
Schab, Peter; Ohio, 1809-1852 *4511.35 p45*
Schad, Anton 29; America, 1857 *5475.1 p499*
  Wife: Katharina Muller 30
  Daughter: Katharina 10 months
Schad, Barbara Becker 50 SEE Schad, Jakob, II
Schad, Franz 12 SEE Schad, Jakob, II

Schad, Jakob 43; America, 1862 *5475.1 p500*
  Wife: Margarethe Grass 48
  Daughter: Margarethe 13
  Daughter: Katharina 18
Schad, Jakob, II 60; America, 1857 *5475.1 p500*
  Wife: Barbara Becker 50
  Son: Peter 17
  Son: Franz 12
Schad, Johann Georg; Pennsylvania, 1848 *170.15 p40*
Schad, Katharina 10 SEE Schad, Anton
Schad, Katharina 18 SEE Schad, Jakob
Schad, Katharina 28; America, 1857 *5475.1 p499*
  With parents & siblings
Schad, Katharina Muller 30 SEE Schad, Anton
Schad, Margarethe 13 SEE Schad, Jakob
Schad, Margarethe Grass 48 SEE Schad, Jakob
Schad, Peter 17 SEE Schad, Jakob, II
Schade, Ida Minna Helen; Wisconsin, 1898 *6795.8 p107*
Schade, John; Ohio, 1809-1852 *4511.35 p45*
Schade, Mathilde; Ohio, n.d. *8023.44 p378*
Schadeli, Miss; North Carolina, 1710 *3629.40 p7*
Schadewitz, Mrs.; Valdivia, Chile, 1850 *1192.4 p48*
  With child 10
  With child 22
  With child
Schadt, Catha. 63; New York, NY, 1893 *1883.7 p44*
Schadt, Fr. 63; New York, NY, 1893 *1883.7 p44*
Schadt, Jacob 23; New York, NY, 1893 *1883.7 p44*
Schadt, Maria 23; New York, NY, 1893 *1883.7 p44*
Schaedler, Andreas 33; New York, NY, 1886 *8425.16 p33*
Schaedler, Elisab. 8 months; New York, NY, 1886 *8425.16 p33*
Schaedler, Helene 32; New York, NY, 1886 *8425.16 p33*
Schaedler, Louise 1; New York, NY, 1886 *8425.16 p33*
Schaedler, Louise 3; New York, NY, 1886 *8425.16 p33*
Schaefer, . . .; New England, 1866 *170.15 p42*
Schaefer, . . .; New England, 1866 *170.15 p42*
  With brother & sister
Schaefer, Andrew; Ohio, 1809-1852 *4511.35 p45*
Schaefer, Anna SEE Schaefer, Jakob
Schaefer, Anna Magdalena; New England, 1866 *170.15 p42*
  With family
Schaefer, Antony 29; New Orleans, 1847 *778.6 p296*
Schaefer, Catharine Engel Sophie; America, 1870 *7420.1 p286*
Schaefer, Christian; America, 1865 *5475.1 p207*
Schaefer, Daniel SEE Schaefer, Daniel
Schaefer, Daniel 35; Brazil, 1863 *5475.1 p550*
  Son: Jakob
  Daughter: Juliana
  Son: Daniel
  Daughter: Katharina
  Daughter: Elisabeth
  Wife: Elisabeth Fickeis
  Son: Wilhelm
Schaefer, Elisabeth; America, 1847 *5475.1 p408*
Schaefer, Elisabeth SEE Schaefer, Daniel
Schaefer, Elisabeth Fickeis SEE Schaefer, Daniel
Schaefer, Engel Marie SEE Schaefer, Hans Heinrich
Schaefer, Friedrich; Ohio, 1840-1897 *8365.5 p18*
Schaefer, G. Jakob; America, 1848 *5475.1 p28*
Schaefer, Georg Heinrich; America, 1875 *7420.1 p305*
Schaefer, Hans Heinrich; Port uncertain, 1850 *7420.1 p75*
  Sister: Engel Marie
Schaefer, Heinrich; Port uncertain, 1883 *7420.1 p339*
Schaefer, Heinrich; Louisiana, 1841-1844 *4981.45 p211*
Schaefer, Jacob; New York, NY, 1888 *3366.30 p70*
Schaefer, Jak. Peter SEE Schaefer, P. Jakob
Schaefer, Jakob 29; America, 1857 *5475.1 p502*
  Wife: Magdalena Rauber 27
  Son: Peter
  Daughter: Anna
Schaefer, Jakob SEE Schaefer, Daniel
Schaefer, Johann; America, 1854 *5475.1 p463*
Schaefer, Johann Henrich; Pennsylvania, 1854 *170.15 p40*
Schaefer, Joseph 25; New Orleans, 1847 *778.6 p296*
Schaefer, Joseph; Ohio, 1809-1852 *4511.35 p45*
Schaefer, Juliana SEE Schaefer, Daniel
Schaefer, Katharina SEE Schaefer, P. Jakob
Schaefer, Katharina SEE Schaefer, Daniel
Schaefer, Luise SEE Schaefer, P. Jakob
Schaefer, Luise Kath. Schramm SEE Schaefer, P. Jakob
Schaefer, Magdalena Rauber 27 SEE Schaefer, Jakob
Schaefer, Margarethe SEE Schaefer, P. Jakob
Schaefer, Maria; America, 1871 *5475.1 p304*
Schaefer, Mary; Carolina, 1844 *170.15 p40*
Schaefer, P. Jakob; Brazil, 1863 *5475.1 p549*
  Wife: Luise Kath. Schramm
  Daughter: Margarethe

  Son: Jak. Peter
  Daughter: Luise
  Daughter: Katharina
Schaefer, Peter SEE Schaefer, Jakob
Schaefer, Sebastian; America, 1846-1847 *5475.1 p51*
Schaefer, Sophie Louise Charlotte; America, 1870 *7420.1 p282*
  Daughter: Sophie Charlotte
  Granddaughter: Engel Marie Dorothee
  Granddaughter: Catharine Marie
  Son: Johann Heinr. Conrad
  Granddaughter: Sophie Charlotte
Schaefer, Wilhelm SEE Schaefer, Daniel
Schaefer, William L.; Iowa, 1892 *1211.15 p19*
Schaefer Keinitz, Louise; Wisconsin, 1903 *6795.8 p176*
Schaeffer, Johannes; Illinois, 1851 *6079.1 p12*
Schaeffer, Julius; New York, 1860 *358.56 p5*
Schaefmann, Jean 39; New Orleans, 1848 *778.6 p296*
Schaekel, Sophie; America, 1857 *7420.1 p171*
Schaenfeld, Frederick; Wisconsin, 1900 *6795.8 p163*
Schaerf, Maria Barth 52 SEE Schaerf, Nikolaus
Schaerf, Nikolaus 52; America, 1882 *5475.1 p555*
  Wife: Maria Barth 52
Schaettgen, Joseph; Louisiana, 1841-1844 *4981.45 p211*
Schaetzke, William; Wisconsin, 1855 *6795.8 p52*
Schaezler, Maria Katharina; Venezuela, 1843 *3899.5 p541*
Schaezlin, Maria Katharina; Venezuela, 1843 *3899.5 p541*
Schafer, Adam; America, 1854 *2526.42 p201*
  With wife
  Son: Johannes
  Son: Leonhard
  Daughter: Anna Margaretha
Schafer, Adam; America, 1893 *2526.43 p155*
Schafer, Adam 10 SEE Schafer, Mrs. Michael
Schafer, Adam 54; America, 1866 *2526.43 p155*
  Wife: Katharina Helmstadter 60
  Daughter: Katharina 24
  Daughter: Kath Elisabetha 21
Schafer, Adam, VII; America, 1867 *2526.43 p155*
Schafer, Alexander 39; Ontario, 1871 *1823.21 p325*
Schafer, Amalia 22; Texas, 1913 *8425.16 p31*
Schafer, Anna; America, 1881 *5475.1 p445*
  Son: Jakob
  Daughter: Magdalena
Schafer, Anna Katharina 27 SEE Schafer, Elisabetha
Schafer, Anna Katharine; America, 1836 *8115.12 p327*
  Child: Johann Georg
Schafer, Anna Katharine; America, n.d. *8115.12 p324*
Schafer, Anna Margaretha; America, 1854 *2526.42 p106*
Schafer, Anna Margaretha; America, 1865 *2526.42 p145*
  Sibling: Maria Katharina
  Sibling: Wilhelm
Schafer, Anna Margaretha 8 SEE Schafer, Adam
Schafer, Anna Margaretha 11 SEE Schafer, Heinrich
Schafer, Anna Margaretha; Iowa, 1883 *2526.42 p121*
  With 2 sons
  Child: Philipp
Schafer, Anna Maria; America, 1853 *2526.43 p128*
Schafer, Anna Maria; America, 1868 *2526.43 p129*
Schafer, August; America, 1852 *7420.1 p96*
Schafer, Balthasar Wilhelm; America, 1884 *2526.42 p130*
Schafer, Barbara 13 SEE Schafer, Leonhard, III
Schafer, Barbara SEE Schafer, Mathias
Schafer, Carl; America, 1860 *7420.1 p199*
Schafer, Catharine Engel Sophie; America, 1863 *7420.1 p220*
Schafer, Christ.; Chile, 1852 *1192.4 p52*
  With wife
Schafer, Christian August; Port uncertain, 1835 *7420.1 p10*
Schafer, Elisabeth SEE Schafer, Johann
Schafer, Elisabeth Margaretha; America, 1868 *2526.43 p129*
Schafer, Elisabetha; America, 1853 *2526.43 p155*
  Daughter: Anna Katharina
  Son: Jakob
Schafer, Elisabetha; America, 1857 *2526.43 p155*
Schafer, Elisabetha; America, 1871 *2526.43 p126*
Schafer, Elisabetha 14 SEE Schafer, Heinrich
Schafer, Elisabetha Katharina; America, 1857 *2526.43 p155*
Schafer, Elisabetha Margaretha 17 SEE Schafer, Mrs. Michael
Schafer, Engel Maria Dorothea; America, 1859 *7420.1 p188*
Schafer, Eva Elisabetha; America, 1868 *2526.43 p129*
Schafer, Eva Katharina 60 SEE Schafer, Johannes, III

Schafer, Mrs. Franz Joseph 31; America, 1831 *2526.43 p219*
With child 8
With child 5
Schafer, Friedrich; America, 1871 *2526.42 p177*
Schafer, Friedrich; America, 1888 *2526.43 p155*
Schafer, Friedrich, II; America, 1853 *2526.42 p177*
Schafer, Friedrich Wilhelm; America, 1857 *7420.1 p171*
Schafer, Fritz; America, 1854 *7420.1 p128*
Schafer, Georg; America, 1852 *2526.43 p155*
Schafer, Georg; America, 1852 *2526.43 p155*
Schafer, Georg; America, 1853 *2526.42 p146*
Schafer, Georg *SEE* Schafer, M. Olt
Schafer, Georg; America, 1898 *2526.43 p155*
Schafer, Georg, IV; America, 1850 *2526.42 p177*
Schafer, Georg, VI; America, 1881 *2526.42 p99*
Schafer, Georg Heinrich; America, 1867 *2526.42 p103*
Schafer, Georg Philipp; America, 1884 *2526.43 p155*
Schafer, Georg Wilhelm; America, 1882 *2526.43 p155*
Schafer, Gottlieb; America, 1888 *2526.43 p155*
Schafer, Heinr. Aug.; Cleveland, OH, 1884 *5475.1 p37*
Schafer, Heinrich; America, 1844 *2526.43 p208*
Schafer, Heinrich; America, 1844 *2526.43 p213*
*Daughter:*Elisabetha
*Son:*Johann Adam
*Son:*Konrad
*Daughter:*Maria Elisabetha
*Daughter:*Katharina
*Wife:*Maria Christina
*Daughter:*Katharina Elisabetha
*Son:*Michael
*Daughter:*Margaretha Elisabetha
*Daughter:*Anna Margaretha
*Son:*Heinrich
Schafer, Heinrich; America, 1865 *2526.43 p155*
Schafer, Heinrich; America, 1869 *2526.43 p129*
Schafer, Heinrich; America, 1885 *8115.12 p322*
Schafer, Heinrich 9 *SEE* Schafer, Heinrich
Schafer, Heinrich Conrad; America, 1859 *7420.1 p188*
Schafer, Heinrich Friedrich Wilhelm; America, 1854 *7420.1 p128*
Schafer, Heinrich Friedrich Wilhelm; San Francisco, 1891 *7420.1 p363*
Schafer, Heinrich Ludwig; America, 1861 *7420.1 p208*
Schafer, Hermann; America, 1892 *179.55 p19*
Schafer, Jacob; Valdivia, Chile, 1852 *1192.4 p56*
Schafer, Jakob; America, 1866 *5475.1 p556*
*Wife:*Philippine Blind
*Daughter:*Philippine
*Daughter:*Karoline
*Son:*Karl
Schafer, Jakob *SEE* Schafer, Anna Hoffmann
Schafer, Jakob; America, n.d. *8115.12 p322*
Schafer, Jakob 3 *SEE* Schafer, Mrs. Michael
Schafer, Jakob 17 *SEE* Schafer, Philipp
Schafer, Jakob 18; America, 1854 *2526.43 p155*
Schafer, Jakob 21 *SEE* Schafer, Elisabetha
Schafer, Jakob, III 40; America, 1867 *2526.43 p155*
With wife
Schafer, Joh. Friedrich 42; Texas, 1913 *8425.16 p31*
Schafer, Johann; America, 1847-1899 *6442.17 p65*
Schafer, Johann; America, 1857 *7420.1 p171*
Schafer, Johann *SEE* Schafer, Johann
Schafer, Johann; America, 1881 *5475.1 p276*
*Wife:*Luzia Friedrich
*Son:*Peter
*Son:*Johann
*Daughter:*Elisabeth
*Son:*Nikolaus
Schafer, Johann; America, 1882 *5475.1 p445*
Schafer, Johann 19 *SEE* Schafer, Johannes, III
Schafer, Johann *SEE* Schafer, Johann
Schafer, Johann; Brazil, 1880 *5475.1 p444*
Schafer, Johann 31; Brazil, 1863 *5475.1 p502*
*Wife:*Margarethe Backes
*Son:*Peter
*Son:*Johann
Schafer, Johann; Port uncertain, 1854 *5475.1 p451*
Schafer, Johann Adam 6 *SEE* Schafer, Heinrich
Schafer, Johann Georg *SEE* Schafer, Anna Katharine
Schafer, Johann Heinrich Christian; America, 1868 *7420.1 p276*
With wife
Schafer, Mrs. Johann Nikolaus 59; America, 1882 *2526.43 p155*
Schafer, Johannes; America, 1869 *2526.42 p146*
Schafer, Johannes; America, 1871 *2526.42 p177*
Schafer, Johannes; America, 1873 *2526.42 p177*
Schafer, Johannes; America, n.d. *8115.12 p328*
Schafer, Johannes 5 *SEE* Schafer, Adam

Schafer, Johannes, III; America, 1853 *2526.43 p129*
*Wife:*Eva Katharina
*Son:*Johann
*Daughter:*Katharina
Schafer, Karl; America, 1860 *2526.43 p155*
Schafer, Karl 5 *SEE* Schafer, Jakob
Schafer, Karoline 3 *SEE* Schafer, Jakob
Schafer, Kartharina Keil *SEE* Schafer, Wilhelm, III
Schafer, Kath Elisabetha 21 *SEE* Schafer, Adam
Schafer, Katharina 6 *SEE* Schafer, Philipp
Schafer, Katharina 15 *SEE* Schafer, Heinrich
Schafer, Katharina 16 *SEE* Schafer, Johannes, III
Schafer, Katharina 24 *SEE* Schafer, Adam
Schafer, Katharina 48; America, 1872 *5475.1 p446*
Schafer, Katharina Helmstadter 60 *SEE* Schafer, Adam
Schafer, Katharina *SEE* Schafer, Mathias
Schafer, Katharina Becker *SEE* Schafer, Mathias
Schafer, Katharina Barbara 6 *SEE* Schafer, Wilhelm
Schafer, Katharina Elisabetha 1 *SEE* Schafer, Heinrich
Schafer, Katharina Elisabetha 22 *SEE* Schafer, Leonhard, III
Schafer, Katharine Margarethe; America, 1853 *8115.12 p328*
Schafer, Konrad; America, 1893 *2526.43 p155*
Schafer, Konrad 3 *SEE* Schafer, Heinrich
Schafer, Leonhard 1 *SEE* Schafer, Adam
Schafer, Leonhard 36; America, 1881 *2526.43 p155*
With wife 32
Schafer, Leonhard, III 44; America, 1846 *2526.42 p146*
With wife
*Child:*Barbara 13
*Child:*Michael 16
*Child:*Katharina Elisabetha 22
*Child:*Margaretha 18
Schafer, Ludwig; America, 1867 *2526.43 p126*
Schafer, Ludwig 18; America, 1880 *2526.43 p155*
Schafer, Luzia Friedrich *SEE* Schafer, Johann
Schafer, M. 42; America, 1856 *2526.42 p99*
*Child:*Georg
Schafer, M., II; America, 1870 *2526.43 p129*
Schafer, M. Susanna *SEE* Schafer, Mathias
Schafer, Magdalena *SEE* Schafer, Anna Hoffmann
Schafer, Magdalena; America, 1882 *5475.1 p64*
Schafer, Margaretha 18 *SEE* Schafer, Leonhard, III
Schafer, Margaretha Elisabetha 12 *SEE* Schafer, Heinrich
Schafer, Margarethe 43; America, 1881-1899 *5475.1 p74*
Schafer, Margarethe *SEE* Schafer, Mathias
Schafer, Margarethe Backes *SEE* Schafer, Johann
Schafer, Maria Christina *SEE* Schafer, Heinrich
Schafer, Maria Elisabetha 4 *SEE* Schafer, Heinrich
Schafer, Maria Katharina 24 *SEE* Schafer, Anna Margaretha
Schafer, Maria Magdalena; America, 1868 *2526.42 p184*
Schafer, Marie Elisabetha 29 *SEE* Schafer, Wilhelm
Schafer, Mathias; America, 1874 *5475.1 p348*
Schafer, Mathias; America, 1885 *5475.1 p276*
Schafer, Mathias; Arkansas, 1880 *5475.1 p299*
*Wife:*Katharina Becker
*Daughter:*Katharina
*Daughter:*Margarethe
*Daughter:*M. Susanna
*Daughter:*Susanna
*Daughter:*Barbara
Schafer, Michael; America, 1881 *2526.43 p156*
Schafer, Michael; America, 1882 *2526.43 p156*
Schafer, Michael 8 *SEE* Schafer, Heinrich
Schafer, Michael 16 *SEE* Schafer, Leonhard, III
Schafer, Michael 17; America, 1866 *2526.42 p146*
Schafer, Michael 18; America, 1853 *2526.43 p156*
Schafer, Michael 20; America, 1880 *2526.43 p156*
Schafer, Michael 24; America, 1867 *2526.42 p146*
Schafer, Mrs. Michael; America, 1857 *2526.43 p156*
With stepchild 21
*Stepchild:*Elisabetha Margaretha
*Son:*Adam
*Son:*Jakob
Schafer, Nikolaus *SEE* Schafer, Johann
Schafer, Nikolaus; Brazil, 1846 *5475.1 p438*
Schafer, Otto Konrad; America, 1883 *2526.42 p130*
Schafer, Peter; America, 1874 *5475.1 p463*
Schafer, Peter *SEE* Schafer, Johann
Schafer, Peter *SEE* Schafer, Johann
Schafer, Peter 28; Portland, ME, 1906 *970.38 p80*
Schafer, Philipp; America, 1844 *2526.43 p135*
With wife
With son 11
With son 9
Schafer, Philipp; America, 1868 *2526.42 p184*
With wife
*Son:*Wilhelm
*Daughter:*Katharina
*Son:*Jakob
Schafer, Philipp; America, 1883 *2526.43 p161*

Schafer, Philipp; Illinois, 1865 *2526.42 p177*
Schafer, Philipp Adam; America, 1882 *2526.43 p156*
Schafer, Philippine Blind *SEE* Schafer, Jakob
Schafer, Philippine 2 *SEE* Schafer, Jakob
Schafer, Simon; America, 1832 *2526.43 p135*
With wife
Schafer, Susanna *SEE* Schafer, Mathias
Schafer, Theodora A.M.; Wisconsin, 1892 *6795.8 p163*
Schafer, Wilhelm; America, 1868 *2526.42 p177*
Schafer, Wilhelm 13 *SEE* Schafer, Philipp
Schafer, Wilhelm 14 *SEE* Schafer, Anna Margaretha
Schafer, Wilhelm 32; America, 1881 *2526.43 p156*
*Wife:*Marie Elisabetha 29
*Daughter:*Katharina Barbara 6
Schafer, Wilhelm; Wisconsin, 1865 *2526.42 p146*
Schafer, Wilhelm, III; America, 1881 *2526.42 p130*
*Wife:*Kartharina Keil
Schafer, Wilhelm Jakob 23; America, 1880 *2526.43 p143*
Schafer-Hoffmann, Mrs.; Brazil, 1880 *5475.1 p444*
With 2 children
Schaff, Christian 18; Portland, ME, 1906 *970.38 p80*
Schaff, Elisabeth 52; Portland, ME, 1906 *970.38 p80*
Schaff, Peter 59; Portland, ME, 1906 *970.38 p80*
Schaff, Wm.; Missouri, 1876 *3276.1 p3*
Schaffen, Fritz; Missouri, 1892 *3276.1 p4*
Schaffer, Anna; America, 1856 *7420.1 p153*
Schaffer, Catarine 36; New York, NY, 1864 *8425.62 p197*
Schaffer, Catherine 1; Missouri, 1845 *778.6 p296*
Schaffer, Catherine 5; Missouri, 1845 *778.6 p296*
Schaffer, Elisabeth 3; Missouri, 1845 *778.6 p296*
Schaffer, Franciska; America, 1856 *7420.1 p153*
With son
Schaffer, Isidore; New York, NY, 1890 *3331.4 p11*
Schaffer, Jean Bap. 38; Missouri, 1845 *778.6 p296*
Schaffer, John; Illinois, 1834-1900 *6020.5 p133*
Schaffer, John; Nova Scotia, 1784 *7105 p25*
Schaffer, Marie 36; Missouri, 1845 *778.6 p297*
Schaffert, Johann 34; New York, NY, 1885 *1883.7 p45*
Schaffner, Caspar 48; New Castle, DE, 1817-1818 *90.20 p153*
Schaffner, Christian 22; America, 1847 *778.6 p297*
Schaffner, Rudolf 28; Louisiana, 1848 *778.6 p297*
Schaffner, Stanislas 24; Louisiana, 1847 *778.6 p297*
Schaffner, Wiegand; Ohio, 1840-1897 *8365.35 p19*
Schaffnit, Heinrich; America, 1854 *2526.43 p143*
Schafrath, George Adam; Ohio, 1809-1852 *4511.35 p45*
Schaftlein, Auguste Henriette; America, 1868 *7919.3 p527*
Schaible, Martin; Louisiana, 1874 *4981.45 p134*
Schaile, Albrecht; America, 1883 *179.55 p19*
Schaile, Christiane; America, 1883 *179.55 p19*
Schaile, Gottfried F.; America, 1883 *179.55 p19*
Schakel, Anton Carl; America, 1892 *7420.1 p366*
Schakel, Anton Heinrich; America, 1883 *7420.1 p339*
Schakel, Carl Friedrich; America, 1881 *7420.1 p324*
*Wife:*Christine Marie Moller
*Daughter:*Christine Sophie Leonore
*Daughter:*Marie Christine Louise
*Son:*Christian Carl
*Daughter:*Louise Sophie Christine
*Daughter:*Christine Louise
Schakel, Carl Heinrich Christian; America, 1881 *7420.1 p324*
Schakel, Carl Heinrich Wilhelm; America, 1880 *7420.1 p317*
Schakel, Carl Heinrich Wilhelm; America, 1884 *7420.1 p345*
Schakel, Christian Carl *SEE* Schakel, Carl Friedrich
Schakel, Christian Friedrich; America, 1870 *7420.1 p285*
Schakel, Christian Heinrich; America, 1881 *7420.1 p324*
Schakel, Christine Louise *SEE* Schakel, Carl Friedrich
Schakel, Christine Marie Moller *SEE* Schakel, Carl Friedrich
Schakel, Christine Sophie Leonore *SEE* Schakel, Carl Friedrich
Schakel, Friedrich Ernst; America, 1885 *7420.1 p348*
Schakel, Friedrich Wilhelm; Indiana, 1882 *7420.1 p332*
Schakel, Heinrich Gottlieb; America, 1890 *7420.1 p361*
Schakel, Louise Sophie Christine *SEE* Schakel, Carl Friedrich
Schakel, Marie Christine Louise *SEE* Schakel, Carl Friedrich
Schakel, Sophie; America, 1857 *7420.1 p162*
Schakow, Wilhelm; Mexico, 1908 *7420.1 p402*
With family
Schalck, Jacob Anton; Louisiana, 1841-1844 *4981.45 p211*
Schalck, Wilhelm; Louisiana, 1841-1844 *4981.45 p211*
Schaler, Aloise; America, 1747 *778.6 p297*
Schaler, Catherine 40; America, 1747 *778.6 p297*
Schaler, Georg 52; America, 1747 *778.6 p297*
Schaler, George 8; America, 1747 *778.6 p297*

FOR A COMPLETE EXPLANATION OF ENTRY, SEE "HOW TO READ A CITATION" SECTION

Schaler, Hariet 3; America, 1747 ***778.6*** *p297*
Schaler, Jacob 6; America, 1747 ***778.6*** *p297*
Schaler, Jos.phine 5; America, 1747 ***778.6*** *p297*
Schaler, Joseph 9; America, 1747 ***778.6*** *p297*
Schaler, Marie 10; America, 1747 ***778.6*** *p297*
Schaler, Roman 2; America, 1747 ***778.6*** *p297*
Schaler, Xavier 7; America, 1747 ***778.6*** *p297*
Schalk, Johanne Louise; Wisconsin, 1894 ***6795.8*** *p154*
Schaller, Anna Barbara; Virginia, 1831 ***152.20*** *p64*
Schaller, Anna Katharina; Virginia, 1831 ***152.20*** *p69*
Schaller, Anna Maria Welsch 20 *SEE* Schaller, Peter
Schaller, Lisette 22; Missouri, 1845 ***778.6*** *p297*
Schaller, Peter 28; America, 1855 ***5475.1*** *p281*
*Wife:*Anna Maria Welsch 20
Schallhammer, Anton *SEE* Schallhammer, Franz
Schallhammer, Franz; America, 1881-1899 ***5475.1*** *p74*
*Wife:*Margarethe Schafer
*Son:*Jakob
*Daughter:*Wilhelmine
*Daughter:*Magrethe
*Daughter:*Maria
*Son:*Philipp
*Son:*Anton
Schallhammer, Jakob *SEE* Schallhammer, Franz
Schallhammer, Magrethe *SEE* Schallhammer, Franz
Schallhammer, Margarethe Schafer 43 *SEE* Schallhammer, Franz
Schallhammer, Maria *SEE* Schallhammer, Franz
Schallhammer, Philipp *SEE* Schallhammer, Franz
Schallhammer, Wilhelmine *SEE* Schallhammer, Franz
Schallmo, John; Ohio, 1809-1852 ***4511.35*** *p45*
Schalmore, Jacob; Ohio, 1809-1852 ***4511.35*** *p45*
Schalmore, Jacob; Ohio, 1809-1852 ***4511.35*** *p46*
Schalow, Gottfried; Wisconsin, 1868 ***6795.8*** *p76*
Scham, Edward 7; Portland, ME, 1911 ***970.38*** *p80*
Scham, Emilie 15; Portland, ME, 1911 ***970.38*** *p80*
Scham, Emilie 35; Portland, ME, 1911 ***970.38*** *p80*
Scham, Julius 4; Portland, ME, 1911 ***970.38*** *p81*
Scham, Olga 6; Portland, ME, 1911 ***970.38*** *p81*
Scham, Regina 9; Portland, ME, 1911 ***970.38*** *p81*
Schamber, Anna 47; New York, NY, 1885 ***1883.7*** *p46*
Schamber, Peter 56; New York, NY, 1885 ***1883.7*** *p46*
Schamel, Anton 19; America, 1848 ***778.6*** *p297*
Schamon, Heinrich 40; Galveston, TX, 1844 ***3967.10*** *p375*
Schampel, Sophie; America, 1881 ***5475.1*** *p55*
Schamper, A. Margarethe Johannes *SEE* Schamper, Peter
Schamper, Anna 17 *SEE* Schamper, Johann
Schamper, Anna Adler 41 *SEE* Schamper, Johann
Schamper, Johann; Iowa, 1882 ***5475.1*** *p350*
*Wife:*Anna Adler
*Son:*Johann
*Daughter:*Anna
*Son:*Michel
*Son:*Nikolaus
*Daughter:*Maria
Schamper, Johann 19 *SEE* Schamper, Johann
Schamper, Katharina *SEE* Schamper, Peter
Schamper, Maria 22 *SEE* Schamper, Johann
Schamper, Michel 12 *SEE* Schamper, Johann
Schamper, Nikolaus 21 *SEE* Schamper, Johann
Schamper, Peter *SEE* Schamper, Peter
Schamper, Peter; America, 1858 ***5475.1*** *p283*
*Wife:*A. Margarethe Johannes
*Son:*Peter
*Daughter:*Katharina
Schande, Nicklaus; New Jersey, 1750-1774 ***927.31*** *p3*
Schandel, Christian; Ohio, 1809-1852 ***4511.35*** *p46*
Schandel, Jacob; Ohio, 1809-1852 ***4511.35*** *p46*
Schanen, Anna Bingen *SEE* Schanen, Peter
Schanen, Johann; America, 1872 ***5475.1*** *p328*
Schanen, Peter; America, 1867 ***5475.1*** *p327*
*Wife:*Anna Bingen
Schaner, Miss 6; New York, NY, 1893 ***1883.7*** *p39*
Schaner, Catha. 9; New York, NY, 1893 ***1883.7*** *p39*
Schaner, Christian 17; New York, NY, 1893 ***1883.7*** *p39*
Schaner, Christian 44; New York, NY, 1893 ***1883.7*** *p39*
Schaner, Jacob 19; New York, NY, 1893 ***1883.7*** *p39*
Schaner, Katha. 43; New York, NY, 1893 ***1883.7*** *p39*
Schaner, Ludwig 14; New York, NY, 1893 ***1883.7*** *p39*
Schaner, Margare. 7; New York, NY, 1893 ***1883.7*** *p39*
Schaner, Reinhold 14; New York, NY, 1893 ***1883.7*** *p39*
Schaner, Reinhold 14; New York, NY, 1893 ***1883.7*** *p47*
Schang, Christopher; Ohio, 1809-1852 ***4511.35*** *p46*
Schangel, Katharina; Chicago, 1880 ***5475.1*** *p335*
Schaniel, Nikolaus; America, 1846 ***5475.1*** *p301*
Schaniel, Peter; America, 1846 ***5475.1*** *p301*
Schank, Gottfried Ernst; America, 1893 ***179.55*** *p19*
Schank, Joh. Valentin; America, 1853 ***5475.1*** *p458*
*Wife:*Jul. Dorothea Kurz
*Daughter:*Luise Dorothea
*Son:*Valentin
*Daughter:*Sophie Dorothea
Schank, Jul. Dorothea Kurz *SEE* Schank, Joh. Valentin
Schank, Katharina; America, 1869-1896 ***6442.17*** *p65*
Schank, Luise Dorothea *SEE* Schank, Joh. Valentin
Schank, Sophie Dorothea *SEE* Schank, Joh. Valentin
Schank, Valentin *SEE* Schank, Joh. Valentin
Schann, Anna Maria; Brazil, 1857 ***5475.1*** *p509*
Schantz, . . . 9 months; Baltimore, 1889 ***8425.16*** *p36*
Schantz, Adam 14; America, 1853 ***2526.43*** *p191*
Schantz, Adam 23; Missouri, 1848 ***778.6*** *p297*
Schantz, Alex 7; Baltimore, 1889 ***8425.16*** *p36*
Schantz, Anna; Ohio, 1809-1852 ***4511.35*** *p46*
Schantz, Friedrich; America, 1859 ***2526.43*** *p191*
Schantz, Friedrich von Mittel-Kinzig; America, 1868 ***2526.43*** *p191*
Schantz, Gabriel 9; Baltimore, 1889 ***8425.16*** *p36*
Schantz, Georg; America, 1868 ***2526.43*** *p191*
Schantz, Georg 11; Baltimore, 1889 ***8425.16*** *p36*
Schantz, Helen 40; Baltimore, 1889 ***8425.16*** *p36*
Schantz, Johannes; America, 1865 ***2526.43*** *p191*
Schantz, Johannes; America, 1886 ***2526.43*** *p131*
Schantz, Josef 15; Baltimore, 1889 ***8425.16*** *p36*
Schantz, M. Elisabetha; America, 1871 ***2526.43*** *p191*
Schantz, Madelaine 20; Missouri, 1848 ***778.6*** *p297*
Schantz, Maria; America, 1854 ***2526.42*** *p96*
Schantz, Maria 6; Baltimore, 1889 ***8425.16*** *p36*
Schantz, Mathias 44; Baltimore, 1889 ***8425.16*** *p36*
Schantz, Michael 16; America, 1853 ***2526.43*** *p192*
Schantz, Peter; America, 1855 ***2526.43*** *p192*
Schantz, Rosa 13; Baltimore, 1889 ***8425.16*** *p36*
Schantz, Wallburga 4; Baltimore, 1889 ***8425.16*** *p36*
Schanz, Adam; Brazil, 1862 ***5475.1*** *p545*
Schanz, Eva Margaretha; America, 1806 ***2526.43*** *p189*
Schanz, Friedrich; America, 1882 ***2526.43*** *p206*
Schanz, Georg; America, 1853 ***2526.43*** *p227*
*Brother:*Johann Wilhelm
Schanz, Georg; America, 1887 ***2526.43*** *p227*
Schanz, Johann Wilhelm *SEE* Schanz, Georg
Schanz, Peter; America, 1853 ***2526.43*** *p143*
Schanz, Wilhelm; America, 1896 ***2526.43*** *p156*
Schanzenbach, Jacob 2; Baltimore, 1893 ***1883.7*** *p38*
Schanzenbach, Johann 4; Baltimore, 1893 ***1883.7*** *p38*
Schanzenbach, Johann 24; Baltimore, 1893 ***1883.7*** *p38*
Schanzenbach, Magdalena 24; Baltimore, 1893 ***1883.7*** *p38*
Schanzenbach, Rudolf 10 months; Baltimore, 1893 ***1883.7*** *p38*
Schaper, Catharine 43; New York, NY, 1864 ***8425.62*** *p195*
Schaper, Catharine 59; New York, NY, 1864 ***8425.62*** *p195*
Schaper, Engel Marie Sophie; America, 1865 ***7420.1*** *p236*
Schaper, Engel Sophie; America, 1857 ***7420.1*** *p171*
Schaper, Ernst 6; New York, NY, 1864 ***8425.62*** *p195*
Schaper, Ernst August; America, 1882 ***7420.1*** *p332*
Schaper, Heinrich; America, 1857 ***7420.1*** *p171*
Schaper, Heinrich Adolph 43; New York, NY, 1864 ***8425.62*** *p195*
Schaper, Johann Friedrich Conrad; America, 1882 ***7420.1*** *p332*
Schaper, Johann Heinrich 20; New York, NY, 1864 ***8425.62*** *p195*
Schapers, Johann Heinrich Conrad; Chicago, 1854 ***7420.1*** *p128*
Schar, Thomas; Ohio, 1809-1852 ***4511.35*** *p46*
Scharader, Andrew *SEE* Scharader, William H.
Scharader, Elizabeth *SEE* Scharader, William H.
Scharader, Mary Ellen *SEE* Scharader, William H.
Scharader, William H.; Philadelphia, 1867 ***8513.31*** *p425*
*Wife:*Elizabeth
*Child:*Andrew
*Child:*Mary Ellen
Schard, Magdalene Jakobine Augustine; Minneapolis, 1890 ***5475.1*** *p18*
Schard, Peter 25; America, 1846 ***778.6*** *p297*
Schardt, Caroline; America, 1868 ***7919.3*** *p529*
Schareo, Barney; Ohio, 1809-1852 ***4511.35*** *p46*
Schareo, Jacob; Ohio, 1809-1852 ***4511.35*** *p46*
Schareo, John; Ohio, 1809-1852 ***4511.35*** *p46*
Scharf, Elisabeth Stein *SEE* Scharf, Peter
Scharf, Elisabeth *SEE* Scharf, Nikolaus
Scharf, Jakob *SEE* Scharf, Nikolaus
Scharf, Joh. Nikolaus *SEE* Scharf, Nikolaus
Scharf, Johann *SEE* Scharf, Peter
Scharf, Karoline *SEE* Scharf, Peter
Scharf, Katharina; America, 1866 ***5475.1*** *p498*
Scharf, Katharina; Brazil, 1862 ***5475.1*** *p497*
Scharf, Katharina *SEE* Scharf, Nikolaus
Scharf, Margarethe *SEE* Scharf, Nikolaus
Scharf, Margarethe Schneider *SEE* Scharf, Nikolaus
Scharf, Maria Elisabeth; Brazil, 1862 ***5475.1*** *p497*
Scharf, Nikolaus; Brazil, 1863 ***5475.1*** *p550*
With brother-in-law
*Daughter:*Elisabeth
*Daughter:*Katharina
*Daughter:*Margarethe
*Son:*Jakob
*Wife:*Margarethe Schneider
*Son:*Joh. Nikolaus
Scharf, Peter *SEE* Scharf, Peter
Scharf, Peter; America, 1862 ***5475.1*** *p540*
*Wife:*Elisabeth Stein
*Daughter:*Karoline
*Son:*Peter
*Son:*Johann
Scharff, Cathrina 21; New Orleans, 1846 ***778.6*** *p297*
Scharrer, Donalus; Ohio, 1809-1852 ***4511.35*** *p46*
Scharrer, Jacob; Ohio, 1809-1852 ***4511.35*** *p46*
Schatsman, Peter; Ohio, 1809-1852 ***4511.35*** *p46*
Schatz, Andreas 24; New York, NY, 1885 ***8425.16*** *p32*
Schatz, Anna 37; New York, NY, 1874 ***6954.7*** *p39*
Schatz, Catharine 4; New York, NY, 1874 ***6954.7*** *p39*
Schatz, Friedrich 10; New York, NY, 1874 ***6954.7*** *p39*
Schatz, George; Illinois, 1856 ***6079.1*** *p12*
Schatz, Ignatz 5; New York, NY, 1885 ***8425.16*** *p32*
Schatz, Jacob 14; New York, NY, 1874 ***6954.7*** *p39*
Schatz, Johann 68; New York, NY, 1874 ***6954.7*** *p39*
Schatz, Johannes 46; New York, NY, 1874 ***6954.7*** *p39*
Schatz, Josef 56; New York, NY, 1885 ***8425.16*** *p32*
Schatz, Magdalena 6; New York, NY, 1874 ***6954.7*** *p39*
Schatz, Margarethe 18; New York, NY, 1885 ***8425.16*** *p32*
Schatz, Marianne 55; New York, NY, 1885 ***8425.16*** *p32*
Schatz, Marie 16; New York, NY, 1874 ***6954.7*** *p39*
Schatz, Wilhelm 18; New York, NY, 1874 ***6954.7*** *p39*
Schatzel, Georg; America, 1872 ***5475.1*** *p31*
Schatzke, Frederica; Wisconsin, 1903 ***6795.8*** *p177*
Schatzler, Maria Katharina; Venezuela, 1843 ***3899.5*** *p541*
Schau, Adam 12; America, 1747 ***778.6*** *p297*
Schau, Claus Johnson; America, 1760 ***1220.12*** *p705*
Schau, Gaspar 45; Ohio, 1847 ***778.6*** *p297*
Schau, Petre 9; America, 1747 ***778.6*** *p297*
Schaub, Jacob 40; New Castle, DE, 1817-1818 ***90.20*** *p153*
Schaubacher, J. D.; Valdivia, Chile, 1852 ***1192.4*** *p53*
Schaubacher, Nic; Valdivia, Chile, 1852 ***1192.4*** *p53*
Schauberger, Michael; Illinois, 1861 ***6079.1*** *p12*
Schauenberg, Carl Christian Frederick; Wisconsin, 1868 ***6795.8*** *p155*
Schauer, Christian; Wisconsin, 1856 ***6795.8*** *p30*
Schauerte, Alex; America, 1925 ***8023.44*** *p378*
Schauerte, Heinrich; America, 1888 ***2526.43*** *p192*
Schauerte, Joseph; America, 1882 ***2526.43*** *p192*
Schaufler, Henry Albert; Cleveland, OH, 1882 ***2853.20*** *p496*
Schaumann, Johan Ditler; Cleveland, OH, 1902-1903 ***9722.10*** *p126*
Schaun, Eduard; America, 1863 ***5475.1*** *p561*
Schauss, Heinr. Friedrich; America, 1866 ***5475.1*** *p54*
Schausten, Jacob; Illinois, 1858-1861 ***6020.5*** *p133*
Schauz, Geor 17; America, 1747 ***778.6*** *p297*
Schaver, Jacob; Ohio, 1809-1852 ***4511.35*** *p46*
Schebb, Peter 24; New York, NY, 1847 ***9176.15*** *p49*
Scheberling, Heinrich; America, 1843 ***7420.1*** *p29*
With daughter 5
With stepchild 10
With stepchild 19
With stepchild 12
With stepchild 14
Scheberra, Pierre; Louisiana, 1836-1841 ***4981.45*** *p209*
Scheck, Pauletta; Kansas, 1917-1918 ***1826.15*** *p81*
Scheder, Christophe 35; America, 1847 ***778.6*** *p297*
Schedler, Auguste Julia; Wisconsin, 1898 ***6795.8*** *p140*
Schedler, Frederick; Manitoba, 1808-1908 ***1822.55*** *p10*
Schedler, Frederick; Wisconsin, 1908 ***1822.55*** *p10*
Schedler, Herman Emil; Wisconsin, 1899 ***6795.8*** *p133*
Schedler, Margarethe Scherer *SEE* Schedler, Math.
Schedler, Maria; Illinois, 1887 ***5475.1*** *p391*
Schedler, Math.; America, 1870-1900 ***5475.1*** *p57*
*Wife:*Margarethe Scherer
*Son:*Peter
With sister-in-law
Schedler, Peter *SEE* Schedler, Math.
Scheel, August; Wisconsin, 1874 ***6795.8*** *p27*
Scheel, Lina; New York, 1860 ***358.56*** *p6*
Scheel, William; Colorado, 1884 ***1029.59*** *p81*
Scheele, August; America, 1873 ***7420.1*** *p301*
Scheele, Dietrich Friedrich Wilhelm; America, 1878 ***7420.1*** *p312*
Scheele, Heinrich Dietrich August; America, 1874 ***7420.1*** *p304*
Scheele, Wilhelm; Port uncertain, 1883 ***7420.1*** *p339*
Scheer, Christina; Pennsylvania, 1858 ***8513.31*** *p425*

Scheetz, Frederick William; Ohio, 1809-1852 *4511.35 p46*
Scheewe, Emiel; Wisconsin, 1878 *6795.8 p76*
Scheffer, Friedrich; America, 1865 *7420.1 p236*
Scheffer, Georg Carl Ernst; America, 1867 *7420.1 p263*
Scheffer, Ignace 27; America, 1840 *778.6 p297*
Scheffermann, William; New York, 1859 *358.56 p101*
Scheffler, August; Indianapolis, 1883 *7420.1 p339*
  With 3 children
Scheffler, Elisabeth 25; America, 1882 *5475.1 p241*
Scheffler, Friedrich August *SEE* Scheffler, Karoline Wilhelmine
Scheffler, Jakob; America, 1849 *5475.1 p486*
Scheffler, Jakob 19; America, 1849 *5475.1 p476*
Scheffler, Jakob 21; America, 1849 *5475.1 p476*
Scheffler, Josef; America, 1847 *5475.1 p473*
Scheffler, Karl Friedrich *SEE* Scheffler, Karoline Wilhelmine
Scheffler, Karl Friedrich August *SEE* Scheffler, Karoline Wilhelmine
Scheffler, Karoline Wilhelmine; America, 1855 *7420.1 p141*
  *Brother:*Karl Friedrich
  *Brother:*Karl Friedrich August
  *Brother:*Friedrich August
Scheffler, Katharina; America, 1847 *5475.1 p475*
Scheffler, Konrad Friedrich August; America, 1883 *7420.1 p339*
Schefner, Georg 22; America, 1847 *778.6 p297*
Scheft, Jacob 29; Louisiana, 1848 *778.6 p297*
Schegg, Ulrich; Illinois, 1860 *6079.1 p12*
Scheib, Anna *SEE* Scheib, Gertrud
Scheib, Gertrud; Brazil, 1846 *5475.1 p438*
  *Sister:*Anna
Scheib, Katharina; Brazil, 1846 *5475.1 p438*
Scheibe, . . .; America, 1852 *7420.1 p97*
  With family
Scheibe, Engel Marie Kolling *SEE* Scheibe, Johann Philipp
Scheibe, Engel Sophie Caroline; America, 1848 *7420.1 p58*
Scheibe, Hans Heinrich; America, 1860 *7420.1 p199*
Scheibe, Heinrich Christ. *SEE* Scheibe, Johann Philipp
Scheibe, Johann Friedr. Christ. *SEE* Scheibe, Johann Philipp
Scheibe, Johann Philipp; America, 1856 *7420.1 p153*
  *Wife:*Engel Marie Kolling
  With stepchild
Scheibe, Johann Philipp; America, 1869 *7420.1 p281*
  *Brother:*Johann Friedr. Christ.
  *Sister:*Thrine Sophia
  *Brother:*Heinrich Christ.
  *Sister:*Thrine Engel
Scheibe, Thrine Engel *SEE* Scheibe, Johann Philipp
Scheibe, Thrine Sophia *SEE* Scheibe, Johann Philipp
Scheibe, Wilhelmine; America, 1881 *7420.1 p324*
  With 2 daughters & 2 grandchildren
Scheibenreif, Miss 27; New York, NY, 1894 *6512.1 p181*
Scheible, Fredrik; Valparaiso, Chile, 1850 *1192.4 p50*
Scheich, Heinrich; America, 1871 *2526.42 p116*
Scheid, A. Katharina *SEE* Scheid, Johann
Scheid, Barbara; Brazil, 1879 *5475.1 p431*
Scheid, Elisabeth *SEE* Scheid, Johann
Scheid, Elisabeth Muller *SEE* Scheid, Johann
Scheid, Jakob; Brazil, 1885 *5475.1 p432*
Scheid, Jakob *SEE* Scheid, Johann
Scheid, Johann *SEE* Scheid, Mathias
Scheid, Johann *SEE* Scheid, Johann
Scheid, Johann; Brazil, 1891 *5475.1 p432*
  *Wife:*Elisabeth Muller
  *Daughter:*Elisabeth
  *Son:*Nikolaus
  *Son:*Johann
  *Son:*Peter
  *Son:*Jakob
  *Daughter:*Katharina
  *Daughter:*A. Katharina
Scheid, Kath.; Brazil, 1885 *5475.1 p432*
Scheid, Katharina *SEE* Scheid, Johann
Scheid, Katharina Theobald *SEE* Scheid, Peter
Scheid, Magdalena; Brazil, 1854 *5475.1 p440*
Scheid, Margarethe Jochum *SEE* Scheid, Mathias
Scheid, Maria; America, 1848 *5475.1 p476*
Scheid, Maria 44; South America, 1857 *5475.1 p512*
Scheid, Mathias; America, 1881 *5475.1 p50*
  *Wife:*Margarethe Jochum
  *Son:*Peter
  *Son:*Philipp
  *Son:*Johann
Scheid, Nikolaus *SEE* Scheid, Johann
Scheid, Nikolaus; Rio Grande do Sul, Brazil, 1881 *5475.1 p431*

Scheid, Peter *SEE* Scheid, Mathias
Scheid, Peter *SEE* Scheid, Johann
Scheid, Peter 71; Brazil, 1891 *5475.1 p432*
  *Wife:*Katharina Theobald
Scheid, Philipp *SEE* Scheid, Mathias
Scheider, Anna Maria 8; Portland, ME, 1910 *970.38 p81*
Scheider, Augustin 40; Portland, ME, 1910 *970.38 p81*
Scheider, Faraingha 38; Portland, ME, 1910 *970.38 p81*
Scheider, Friederike; America, 1867 *7919.3 p527*
Scheider, Johannes; Portland, ME, 1910 *970.38 p81*
Scheider, Josef 3; Portland, ME, 1910 *970.38 p81*
Scheider, Louise; America, 1868 *7919.3 p527*
Scheider, Magdalena; America, 1868 *7919.3 p527*
Scheider, Martin 6; Portland, ME, 1910 *970.38 p81*
Scheider, Michael 10; Portland, ME, 1910 *970.38 p81*
Scheider, Michel 65; America, 1847 *778.6 p297*
Scheider, Peter 15; Portland, ME, 1910 *970.38 p81*
Scheider, Philipina 11; Portland, ME, 1910 *970.38 p81*
Scheiding, Carl August; America, 1867 *7919.3 p530*
  With wife & 2 children
Scheidler, Tobias; America, 1867 *7919.3 p534*
Scheidt, Anna *SEE* Scheidt, Heinrich
Scheidt, Charlotte *SEE* Scheidt, Heinrich
Scheidt, Frederic 31; Louisiana, 1848 *778.6 p297*
Scheidt, Friedrich; America, 1867 *5475.1 p524*
Scheidt, Heinrich 59; America, 1867 *5475.1 p524*
  *Wife:*Katharina Morsfeldel 53
  *Daughter:*Charlotte
  *Daughter:*Anna
  *Son:*Ludwig
Scheidt, Heinrich; Brazil, 1863 *5475.1 p524*
Scheidt, Karoline; America, 1867 *5475.1 p524*
Scheidt, Katharina Morsfeldel 53 *SEE* Scheidt, Heinrich
Scheidt, Ludwig *SEE* Scheidt, Heinrich
Scheier, Katharina 27; America, 1846 *5475.1 p451*
Scheikel, Joseph; Louisiana, 1841-1844 *4981.45 p211*
Scheiking, Jacob; Ohio, 1809-1852 *4511.35 p46*
Scheiking, Jacob, Jr.; Ohio, 1809-1852 *4511.35 p46*
Schein, Johann August; Wisconsin, 1869 *6795.8 p118*
Scheinemann, Frederick; New York, 1777 *8529.30 p7*
Scheiner, Dr.; Chicago, 1909 *2853.20 p410*
Scheitler, Mrs. Christoph; America, 1836 *2526.42 p164*
  With 3 children
Scheive, John Jacob; North Carolina, 1710 *3629.40 p8*
Scheiwe, Johann Philipp; America, 1856 *7420.1 p153*
  With wife & son
Scheiwe, Trine Sophie Charlotte; America, 1858 *7420.1 p181*
Schejbal, Matej; Illinois, 1851-1910 *2853.20 p471*
Schejbal, Vaclav; Illinois, 1851-1910 *2853.20 p471*
Schel, Ludwig 30; New York, NY, 1885 *1883.7 p45*
Schelhorn, Engel Marie Sophie; America, 1857 *7420.1 p159*
Schelhorn, Johann Heinrich; America, 1865 *7420.1 p236*
  With wife
Schelken, Englehard; North Carolina, 1852 *1088.45 p30*
Schell, Barbara 35; New York, NY, 1893 *1883.7 p37*
Schell, Christian 1; New York, NY, 1893 *1883.7 p37*
Schell, Christine 21; New York, NY, 1893 *1883.7 p37*
Schell, Desidere 21; Michigan, 1847 *778.6 p298*
Schell, Franziska 8; New York, NY, 1893 *1883.7 p37*
Schell, Johannes 4 months; New York, NY, 1893 *1883.7 p37*
Schell, Joseph 4; New York, NY, 1893 *1883.7 p37*
Schell, Kaspar 30; New York, NY, 1893 *1883.7 p37*
Schell, Lorenz 10; New York, NY, 1893 *1883.7 p37*
Schell, Wilhelm 13; New York, NY, 1893 *1883.7 p37*
Schell, Wilhelm 37; New York, NY, 1893 *1883.7 p37*
Schellenberg, Anna Barbara; America, 1867 *7919.3 p528*
  With child
Schellenberg, Katharina Elisabeth; America, 1867 *7919.3 p528*
Schellenberger, Karl Gottl.; London, Eng., 1867 *5475.1 p84*
Scheller, Andreas Karl; America, 1868 *7919.3 p527*
Schellhaas, Barbara 19 *SEE* Schellhaas, Philipp, II
Schellhaas, Jakob 5 *SEE* Schellhaas, Philipp, II
Schellhaas, Johannes 9 *SEE* Schellhaas, Philipp, II
Schellhaas, Philipp II 40; America, 1864 *2526.42 p184*
  *Daughter:*Barbara 19
  *Son:*Jakob 5
  *Son:*Johannes 9 months
Schellhorn, Mr.; America, 1845 *7420.1 p39*
  With wife & 3 children
Schellhorn, Conrad Christoph; America, 1845 *7420.1 p39*
  With son 21
  With daughter 19
  With daughter 7
  With daughter 17
  With son 9
Schellhorn, Hans Heinrich; America, 1867 *7420.1 p264*

Schellhorn, Johann Heinr. Christoph Aug.; America, 1865 *7420.1 p236*
Schellhorn, Marie Caroline Juliane; America, 1870 *7420.1 p395*
  With daughter
Schellmann, Casper; New York, 1860 *358.56 p149*
Schelmann, William; New York, 1859 *358.56 p54*
Schemel, Catharina 28; Port uncertain, 1843 *778.6 p298*
Schemel, Jakob; America, 1881 *5475.1 p231*
Schemel, Katharina; America, 1858-1900 *5475.1 p164*
Schemel, Michel 30; Port uncertain, 1843 *778.6 p298*
Schemerber, Joseph 49; Galveston, TX, 1846 *3967.10 p377*
Schemerber, Marie 44; Galveston, TX, 1846 *3967.10 p377*
Schenger, Wilhelm 24; America, 1847 *778.6 p298*
Schenholm, G. W.; North America, 1854 *6410.15 p104*
Schenk, Godfrey Theodore; Illinois, 1851 *6079.1 p12*
Schenkel, Henry 34; America, 1847 *778.6 p298*
Schenkel, Jacob; Ohio, 1809-1852 *4511.35 p46*
Schenkle, Jacob; Ohio, 1809-1852 *4511.35 p46*
Schenkle, Peter; Ohio, 1809-1852 *4511.35 p46*
Scheperkofer, Catarine 23; New York, NY, 1864 *8425.62 p197*
Scher, Antoine 14; America, 1845 *778.6 p298*
Scher, Joseph 12; America, 1845 *778.6 p298*
Scher, Peter; Ohio, 1809-1852 *4511.35 p46*
Scher, Sophie 34; America, 1845 *778.6 p298*
Scherar, Michael; Ohio, 1840-1897 *8365.35 p18*
Scherber, Catherfina 9; New Orleans, 1848 *778.6 p298*
Scherber, Christina 38; New Orleans, 1848 *778.6 p298*
Scherber, Elisabeth 14; New Orleans, 1848 *778.6 p298*
Scherber, Jean 11; New Orleans, 1848 *778.6 p298*
Scherber, Martin; Ohio, 1809-1852 *4511.35 p46*
Scherber, Nicolas 50; New Orleans, 1848 *778.6 p298*
Scherchel, Jakob; America, 1838 *5475.1 p385*
Scheren, Paul; North Carolina, 1854 *1088.45 p30*
Scherer, Anna 3; America, 1840 *778.6 p298*
Scherer, Anna 22; Brazil, 1862 *5475.1 p289*
Scherer, Anna Katharina Breidt *SEE* Scherer, Mathias
Scherer, Anna Maria Hayo 48 *SEE* Scherer, Peter
Scherer, Anna Maria; Brazil, 1846 *5475.1 p438*
Scherer, Anna Maria *SEE* Scherer, Johann
Scherer, Barbara 35; America, 1843 *5475.1 p529*
Scherer, Barbara Bierbrauer *SEE* Scherer, Johann
Scherer, Barbara; Washington, 1886 *5475.1 p45*
Scherer, Caspar 27; New York, NY, 1885 *8425.16 p32*
Scherer, Catharine 19; New York, NY, 1885 *8425.16 p32*
Scherer, Charlotte Richter 31 *SEE* Scherer, Johann Nikolaus
Scherer, Christian *SEE* Scherer, Christian
Scherer, Christian 42; Wisconsin, 1886 *5475.1 p534*
  *Wife:*Elisabeth Werkle
  *Daughter:*Elisabeth
  *Daughter:*Katharina
  *Daughter:*Maria
  *Son:*Christian
Scherer, Claudius 58; America, 1843 *5475.1 p348*
Scherer, Conrad 40; America, 1843 *5475.1 p529*
  *Wife:*Sophia Schneider 32
  *Mother:*Katharina Zimmer 58
  *Daughter:*Sophia 9
  *Son:*Nikolaus 4
Scherer, Edward 20; Halifax, N.S., 1902 *1860.4 p42*
Scherer, Elisabeth Schneider *SEE* Scherer, Michel
Scherer, Elisabeth 6; America, 1846 *778.6 p298*
Scherer, Elisabeth 25; Brazil, 1872 *5475.1 p442*
  *Brother:*Mathias 15
Scherer, Elisabeth *SEE* Scherer, Christian
Scherer, Elisabeth Werkle *SEE* Scherer, Christian
Scherer, Eve 2; America, 1846 *778.6 p298*
Scherer, Francis Joseph; Illinois, 1864 *6079.1 p12*
Scherer, Francois 6 months; America, 1846 *778.6 p298*
Scherer, Franz 27; America, 1854 *5475.1 p57*
Scherer, Franz; Brazil, 1857 *5475.1 p368*
  *Wife:*Margarethe Barbian
  With mother-in-law 47
Scherer, Franziska 31; America, 1846 *778.6 p298*
Scherer, Franziska 14; New York, NY, 1885 *8425.16 p32*
Scherer, Jacob 9; New Orleans, 1848 *778.6 p298*
Scherer, Jakob; Pennsylvania, 1846 *170.15 p40*
Scherer, Jean 34; America, 1846 *778.6 p298*
Scherer, Jean 48; America, 1840 *778.6 p298*
Scherer, Joh. 23; America, 1840 *778.6 p298*
Scherer, Johann; America, 1843 *5475.1 p428*
  With wife
  With 3 daughters
Scherer, Johann 4 *SEE* Scherer, Johann Nikolaus
Scherer, Johann; Brazil, 1874 *5475.1 p371*
  *Wife:*Kath. Ludwig

Scherer, Johann; Brazil, 1880 *5475.1 p373*
Wife: Barbara Bierbrauer
Daughter: Maria
Daughter: Katharina
Daughter: Anna Maria
Scherer, Johann Nikolaus 33; America, 1843 *5475.1 p529*
Wife: Charlotte Richter 31
Mother: Maria Katharina Zimmer 58
Son: Johann 4
Daughter: Katharina 9
Scherer, Johanna 19; Halifax, N.S., 1902 *1860.4 p42*
Scherer, Joseph 49; Galveston, TX, 1846 *3967.10 p378*
Scherer, Joseph 11; New Orleans, 1848 *778.6 p298*
Scherer, Josephine 6 months; New Orleans, 1848 *778.6 p298*
Scherer, Karal; Ohio, 1840-1897 *8365.35 p18*
Scherer, Kath. Ludwig SEE Scherer, Johann
Scherer, Katharina SEE Scherer, Michel
Scherer, Katharina 9 SEE Scherer, Johann Nikolaus
Scherer, Katharina 35; America, 1847 *5475.1 p531*
Scherer, Katharina Zimmer 58 SEE Scherer, Conrad
Scherer, Katharina SEE Scherer, Johann
Scherer, Katharina SEE Scherer, Christian
Scherer, Katharina 49; Wisconsin, 1858 *5475.1 p260*
Scherer, Margarethe; America, 1870-1900 *5475.1 p57*
Scherer, Margarethe 23; America, 1843 *5475.1 p528*
Scherer, Margarethe Barbian 19 SEE Scherer, Franz
Scherer, Marguerite 3; America, 1846 *778.6 p298*
Scherer, Marguerite 30; America, 1846 *778.6 p298*
Scherer, Maria Hofmann SEE Scherer, Nikolaus
Scherer, Maria 14 SEE Scherer, Peter
Scherer, Maria 28; America, 1840 *778.6 p298*
Scherer, Maria SEE Scherer, Johann
Scherer, Maria SEE Scherer, Christian
Scherer, Maria Katharina Zimmer 58 SEE Scherer, Johann Nikolaus
Scherer, Marianne 8; New Orleans, 1848 *778.6 p298*
Scherer, Martin 5; America, 1846 *778.6 p298*
Scherer, Martin 32; America, 1846 *778.6 p298*
Scherer, Mathias 8; America, 1846 *778.6 p298*
Scherer, Mathias; Brazil, 1846 *5475.1 p439*
Wife: Anna Katharina Breidt
With 8 children
Scherer, Mathias 15 SEE Scherer, Elisabeth
Scherer, Michael; New York, 1859 *358.56 p53*
Scherer, Michel; America, 1865 *5475.1 p509*
Wife: Elisabeth Schneider
Daughter: Katharina
Son: Peter
Scherer, Nikolaus; America, 1836 *5475.1 p437*
Wife: Maria Hofmann
Scherer, Nikolaus 4 SEE Scherer, Conrad
Scherer, Peter; America, 1856 *2526.43 p124*
Scherer, Peter SEE Scherer, Michel
Scherer, Peter 1; America, 1840 *778.6 p298*
Scherer, Peter 54; America, 1873 *5475.1 p58*
Wife: Anna Maria Hayo 48
Daughter: Maria 14
Scherer, Peter; Brazil, 1879 *5475.1 p444*
Scherer, Philip; Ohio, 1809-1852 *4511.35 p46*
Scherer, Sophia 9 SEE Scherer, Conrad
Scherer, Sophia Schneider 32 SEE Scherer, Conrad
Scherer, Susanna; America, 1870-1900 *5475.1 p57*
Scherer, Susanna 37; Brazil, 1862 *5475.1 p543*
Scherer, Theresa 5; New Orleans, 1848 *778.6 p299*
Scherf, Anna 12 SEE Scherf, Jakob
Scherf, Helma Breit 36 SEE Scherf, Jakob
Scherf, Jakob SEE Scherf, Jakob
Scherf, Jakob; Brazil, 1837 *5475.1 p367*
Wife: Helma Breit
Daughter: Odilia
Son: Johann
Son: Jakob
Son: Mathias
Daughter: Anna
Scherf, Johann SEE Scherf, Jakob
Scherf, Mathias SEE Scherf, Jakob
Scherf, Odilia 11 SEE Scherf, Jakob
Scherhammer, Elisabeth; America, 1847 *5475.1 p474*
Scherhammer, Marianne; America, 1847 *5475.1 p474*
Scherhammer, Nikolaus; America, 1847 *5475.1 p474*
Scheriber, Anna SEE Scheriber, Carl Oscar
Scheriber, Carl Oscar; Iowa, 1908 *1029.59 p81*
Wife: Anna
Scheriber, Carl Oscar; New York, NY, 1906 *1029.59 p1A*
Schering, Mr.; America, 1874 *7420.1 p304*
With 2 sisters
Schering, Mary Hodpope; Miami, 1935 *4984.12 p39*
Scherle, Eliz. 34; New York, NY, 1847 *9176.15 p50*
Scherle, Henry 4; New York, NY, 1847 *9176.15 p50*
Scherle, Herman 36; New York, NY, 1847 *9176.15 p50*

Scherle, Horton 5; New York, NY, 1847 *9176.15 p50*
Scherle, Johanna 6 months; New York, NY, 1847 *9176.15 p50*
Scherle, Theresia 3; New York, NY, 1847 *9176.15 p50*
Scherle, Wilhelm 7; New York, NY, 1847 *9176.15 p50*
Scherlet, Peter; North Carolina, 1843 *1088.45 p30*
Schermer, Auguste Henriette; Wisconsin, 1890 *6795.8 p42*
Schermer, Catharina Engel Sophie; America, 1847 *7420.1 p57*
Schermer, Friedrich Wilhelm; America, 1871 *7420.1 p396*
Schermer, Hanne Friederike Charlotte; America, 1850 *7420.1 p77*
Schermer, Heinrich; America, 1856 *7420.1 p153*
Schermer, Michael; North Carolina, 1857 *1088.45 p30*
Schermer, Sophie Dorothee; America, 1869 *7420.1 p279*
Schermer, Wilhelmine; Wisconsin, 1882 *6795.8 p97*
Schernitzauer, Adolphe 5; America, 1843 *778.6 p299*
Schernitzauer, Andres 18; America, 1843 *778.6 p299*
Schernitzauer, Catharina 45; America, 1843 *778.6 p299*
Schernitzauer, Christina 14; America, 1843 *778.6 p299*
Schernitzauer, Elisabetha 2; America, 1843 *778.6 p299*
Schernitzauer, Joseph 16; America, 1843 *778.6 p299*
Schernitzauer, Joseph 48; America, 1843 *778.6 p299*
Schernitzauer, Louis 13; America, 1843 *778.6 p299*
Scherrer, Anna Maria 43; Galveston, TX, 1844 *3967.10 p371*
Scherrer, August 10; Galveston, TX, 1844 *3967.10 p371*
Scherrer, Frederic 35; America, 1847 *778.6 p299*
Scherrer, Jakob 15; Galveston, TX, 1844 *3967.10 p371*
Scherrer, Jakob 42; Galveston, TX, 1844 *3967.10 p371*
Scherrer, Johann Baptist 7; Galveston, TX, 1844 *3967.10 p371*
Scherrer, Joseph 13; Galveston, TX, 1844 *3967.10 p371*
Scherrer, Therese 2; Galveston, TX, 1844 *3967.10 p371*
Scherschel, Christoph; America, 1838 *5475.1 p454*
Scherschel, Elisabeth 36; America, 1836 *5475.1 p399*
Scherschel, Franz 4 SEE Scherschel, Theobald
Scherschel, Jakob 6 SEE Scherschel, Theobald
Scherschel, Jakob 11 SEE Scherschel, Theobald
Scherschel, Johann 6 SEE Scherschel, Rudolf
Scherschel, Johann 28 SEE Scherschel, Johann
Scherschel, Johann 63; America, 1836 *5475.1 p394*
Wife: Maria Woll 66
Son: Johann 28
Scherschel, Katharina 2 SEE Scherschel, Theobald
Scherschel, Ludwig 3 SEE Scherschel, Rudolf
Scherschel, Maria Weyrich 34 SEE Scherschel, Theobald
Scherschel, Maria Woll 66 SEE Scherschel, Johann
Scherschel, Nikolaus 9 SEE Scherschel, Theobald
Scherschel, Nikolaus 56; America, 1837 *5475.1 p454*
With wife 50
With daughter 9
With daughter 14
With son 22
With son 12
With daughter 19
With son 32
Scherschel, Rudolf; America, 1837 *5475.1 p395*
Wife: Susanna Sahner
Son: Ludwig
Son: Johann
Scherschel, Susanna Sahner 28 SEE Scherschel, Rudolf
Scherschel, Theobald 37; America, 1836 *5475.1 p396*
Wife: Maria Weyrich 34
Son: Franz 4
Daughter: Katharina 2
Son: Jakob 6 months
Son: Nikolaus 9
Son: Jakob 11
Scherschel, Wilhelm; America, 1838 *5475.1 p454*
Scherser, Georg 26; America, 1846 *778.6 p299*
Schertel, Peter; North Carolina, 1843 *1088.45 p31*
Schertz, Alfred 16; Galveston, TX, 1844 *3967.10 p370*
Schertz, Anna Maria 33; Galveston, TX, 1844 *3967.10 p370*
Schertz, Johann; America, 1833 *5475.1 p118*
Schertz, Johann 19; Galveston, TX, 1844 *3967.10 p371*
Schertz, Joseph 23; Galveston, TX, 1844 *3967.10 p371*
Schertz, Joseph 32; Galveston, TX, 1844 *3967.10 p370*
Schertz, Katharina 28; Galveston, TX, 1844 *3967.10 p370*
Schertz, Margaretha 12; Galveston, TX, 1844 *3967.10 p370*
Schertz, Sebastian 22; Galveston, TX, 1844 *3967.10 p370*
Schertzinger, Johann; America, 1852 *5475.1 p68*
Schertzke, Louise; Wisconsin, 1903 *6795.8 p179*
Scherver, Christian; Ohio, 1809-1852 *4511.35 p46*
Scherver, Christopher; Ohio, 1809-1852 *4511.35 p46*
Scherver, Sebastian; Ohio, 1809-1852 *4511.35 p46*
Scherver, Valentine; Ohio, 1809-1852 *4511.35 p46*

Schesler, David 34; America, 1842 *778.6 p299*
Schesler, John George; Ohio, 1809-1852 *4511.35 p46*
Schetzow, Mart.; New York, 1859 *358.56 p55*
Scheu, Christian; Ohio, 1840-1897 *8365.35 p18*
Scheub, Christian John; Missouri, 1869 *3276.1 p3*
Scheub, Gottfried; Missouri, 1893 *3276.1 p4*
Scheubly, Elisabeth; New Orleans, 1867 *5475.1 p158*
Daughter: Regina
Scheubly, Regina SEE Scheubly, Elisabeth Spitznas
Scheuer, Benjamin; Canada, 1880 *5475.1 p33*
Scheuer, Michel; New York, 1870 *5475.1 p163*
Scheuer, Wendelinus; America, 1882 *5475.1 p167*
Scheuerlein, John A.; New York, 1860 *358.56 p3*
Scheuermann, Caroline Wilhelmine Louise; America, 1888 *7420.1 p356*
Scheuermann, Maria; Philadelphia, 1860 *8513.31 p320*
Scheuermann, Peter; America, 1856 *2526.43 p200*
Scheuli, Christian 65; America, 1847 *778.6 p299*
Scheuning, G. F.; Valdivia, Chile, 1852 *1192.4 p53*
With wife
Scheup, Gottlob; Missouri, 1900 *3276.1 p4*
Scheur, Abraham; Ohio, 1809-1852 *4511.35 p46*
Scheur, August; Louisiana, 1874 *4981.45 p134*
Scheurle, Joseph; Venezuela, 1843 *3899.5 p543*
Scheurle, Matthias; Venezuela, 1843 *3899.5 p543*
Scheurle Children, . . .; Venezuela, 1843 *3899.5 p543*
Scheve, Fredrick; Wisconsin, 1871 *6795.8 p118*
Scheve, Hans Heinrich Conrad; America, 1866 *7420.1 p248*
Wife: Ilse Marie Sophie Hartmann
Scheve, Ilse Marie Sophie Hartmann SEE Scheve, Hans Heinrich Conrad
Scheve, Johann Friedrich; America, 1865 *7420.1 p236*
Scheve, Johann Otto; America, 1865 *7420.1 p236*
Schewe, Hans Heinrich Conrad; America, 1866 *7420.1 p248*
Wife: Ilse Marie Sophie Hartmann
Schewe, Ilse Marie Sophie Hartmann SEE Schewe, Hans Heinrich Conrad
Schewe, Trine Sophie Charlotte; America, 1858 *7420.1 p181*
Scheyer, Johanna; America, 1846 *5475.1 p401*
Scheyerling, George A.; Ohio, 1809-1852 *4511.35 p46*
Schezler, Maria Katharina; Venezuela, 1843 *3899.5 p541*
Schib, Maria 21; New Castle, DE, 1817-1818 *90.20 p153*
Schick, Abraham; America, 1867 *5475.1 p553*
Schickhardt, Bertha; Philadelphia, 1857 *8513.31 p304*
Schickler, Sebastion; Kansas, 1917-1918 *1826.15 p81*
Schieb, Maria 21; New Castle, DE, 1817-1818 *90.20 p153*
Schieber, Jacob; America, 1852 *179.55 p19*
Schiegal, F. Wilhelm; Colorado, 1900 *1029.59 p81*
Schiek, Heinrich; Valparaiso, Chile, 1850 *1192.4 p50*
Schiele, Franz 28; New York, NY, 1893 *1883.7 p41*
Schiele, Maria 24; New York, NY, 1893 *1883.7 p41*
Schiele, Ottilia 6 months; New York, NY, 1893 *1883.7 p41*
Schiele, Victor; Kansas, 1917-1918 *1826.15 p81*
Schiemann, Friedr. Ferd.; America, 1881 *5475.1 p33*
Schier, Anna; America, 1881 *5475.1 p45*
Schierneichen, Christine Wilhelmine; America, 1857 *7420.1 p171*
Schiesser, Geo.; Louisiana, 1874 *4981.45 p134*
Schifermeier, Johannes; Illinois, 1854 *6079.1 p12*
Schiff, August 50; Baltimore, 1889 *8425.16 p35*
Schiff, Jacob 8; Baltimore, 1889 *8425.16 p35*
Schiff, Magda 9; Baltimore, 1889 *8425.16 p35*
Schiff, Maria 41; Baltimore, 1889 *8425.16 p35*
Schiff, Valentin 7; Baltimore, 1889 *8425.16 p35*
Schiffbauer, Hermann Josef 23; New York, NY, 1882 *5475.1 p16*
Schiffer, A.; Galveston, TX, 1855 *571.7 p18*
Schiffer, Gottfried; Chicago, 1886 *5475.1 p423*
Schiffer, Jakob; America, 1847 *5475.1 p473*
Schiffgen, Coelestian; Illinois, 1851 *6079.1 p12*
Schiffler, Anna Maria SEE Schiffler, Johann Konrad
Schiffler, Anna Maria Fuchs SEE Schiffler, Johann Konrad
Schiffler, Friedrich SEE Schiffler, Johann Konrad
Schiffler, Johann Jakob; America, 1860 *5475.1 p393*
Schiffler, Johann Konrad 46; Wisconsin, 1887 *5475.1 p534*
Wife: Anna Maria Fuchs
Daughter: Sophie
Daughter: Luise
Daughter: Karolina
Daughter: Katharina
Daughter: Anna Maria
Son: Karl
Son: Friedrich
Son: Konrad
Schiffler, Karl SEE Schiffler, Johann Konrad
Schiffler, Karolina SEE Schiffler, Johann Konrad

Schiffler, Katharina; America, 1836 ***5475.1*** *p536*
Schiffler, Katharina *SEE* Schiffler, Johann Konrad
Schiffler, Konrad *SEE* Schiffler, Johann Konrad
Schiffler, Luise *SEE* Schiffler, Johann Konrad
Schiffler, Sophie *SEE* Schiffler, Johann Konrad
Schiffler, Wilhelm; America, 1883 ***5475.1*** *p452*
Schiffmacher, Anna 30; Mississippi, 1846 ***778.6*** *p299*
Schiffmacher, Ja.ques 3; Mississippi, 1846 ***778.6*** *p299*
Schiffmacher, Leonhard 50; Mississippi, 1846 ***778.6*** *p299*
Schiffman, George; Louisiana, 1841-1844 ***4981.45*** *p211*
Schiffman, Joseph; Detroit, 1929-1930 ***6214.5*** *p65*
Schiffmann, Andreas 23; America, 1857 ***5475.1*** *p282*
*Wife:*Elisabeth Lellig 23
Schiffmann, Elisabeth Lellig 23 *SEE* Schiffmann, Andreas
Schiffmann, Jakob; America, 1857 ***5475.1*** *p296*
Schiflmann, Leon 33; America, 1841 ***778.6*** *p299*
Schilb, Jemima M. 28; Ohio, 1880 ***4879.40*** *p257*
Schild, Friedrich; Ohio, 1882 ***5475.1*** *p460*
Schild, Jean 1; Mississippi, 1847 ***778.6*** *p299*
Schild, Jean 31; Mississippi, 1847 ***778.6*** *p299*
Schild, Lena 39; Mississippi, 1847 ***778.6*** *p299*
Schild, Marie 4; Mississippi, 1847 ***778.6*** *p299*
Schild, Phillipp 2; Mississippi, 1847 ***778.6*** *p299*
Schilder, Jean 8; New Orleans, 1848 ***778.6*** *p299*
Schilder, Maria 17; New Orleans, 1848 ***778.6*** *p299*
Schilder, Michel 19; New Orleans, 1848 ***778.6*** *p299*
Schilder, Thomas 6; New Orleans, 1848 ***778.6*** *p299*
Schildmeier, . . .; Port uncertain, 1836 ***7420.1*** *p11*
With family
Schildt, Jacob; Ohio, 1809-1852 ***4511.35*** *p46*
Schilf, Wilhelm; America, 1891 ***7420.1*** *p363*
Schilke, Amalia; Dakota, 1888 ***554.30*** *p25*
Schiller, Antoin 32; America, 1847 ***778.6*** *p299*
Schiller, Mich.; New York, 1860 ***358.56*** *p6*
Schillert, Julius; Wisconsin, 1889 ***6795.8*** *p118*
Schillert, Wilhelmine; Wisconsin, 1892 ***6795.8*** *p119*
Schilling, Andreas; America, 1868 ***7919.3*** *p525*
With wife & 4 children
Schilling, Barbara; Philadelphia, 1853 ***8513.31*** *p312*
Schilling, Carl; Valdivia, Chile, 1850 ***1192.4*** *p49*
Schilling, Carl; Valdivia, Chile, 1852 ***1192.4*** *p56*
Schilling, Daniel 2 *SEE* Schilling, Johann
Schilling, Friedrich; America, 1854 ***7420.1*** *p128*
Schilling, Gottlieb; America, 1868 ***7919.3*** *p525*
Schilling, Jacob; Illinois, 1852 ***6079.1*** *p12*
Schilling, Johann 26; America, 1836 ***5475.1*** *p495*
*Son:*Daniel 2
Schilling, Johann Heinrich; Port uncertain, 1850 ***7420.1*** *p75*
Schilling, John; Ohio, 1809-1852 ***4511.35*** *p46*
Schilling, Karl; Wisconsin, 1890 ***6795.8*** *p68*
Schilling, Katharina; America, 1867 ***2526.43*** *p213*
Schilling, Leonhard; America, 1881 ***2526.43*** *p213*
With mother
Schilling, Moritz; America, 1867 ***7919.3*** *p528*
Schillinger, Eugen; Colorado, 1884 ***1029.59*** *p81*
Schillinger, Leovigild; Kansas, 1917-1918 ***1826.15*** *p81*
Schillingmark, Louise; America, 1867 ***7919.3*** *p530*
With child
Schillo, Georg; America, 1855 ***5475.1*** *p248*
Schillo, Jakob; America, 1843 ***5475.1*** *p247*
Schillo, Johann Peter 49; America, 1843 ***5475.1*** *p247*
Schillo, Nikolaus; America, 1881 ***5475.1*** *p313*
Schillo, Peter; America, 1882 ***5475.1*** *p313*
Schilt, Mr. 26; Mobile, AL, 1841 ***778.6*** *p299*
Schilt, Christian; Ohio, 1809-1852 ***4511.35*** *p46*
Schilz, Henry 28; America, 1845 ***778.6*** *p299*
Schilz, Margarethe *SEE* Schilz, Peter
Schilz, Margarethe Gengler *SEE* Schilz, Peter
Schilz, Mathias 58; America, 1843 ***5475.1*** *p366*
Schilz, Peter; America, 1867 ***5475.1*** *p321*
*Wife:*Margarethe Gengler
*Daughter:*Susanna
*Daughter:*Margarethe
Schilz, Susanna *SEE* Schilz, Peter
Schimmeister, Otto Friedrich; America, 1870 ***7420.1*** *p285*
Schimmel, Augusta Louise; Wisconsin, 1886 ***6795.8*** *p76*
Schimmel, Mrs. Jakob; Pennsylvania, 1865 ***170.15*** *p41*
With 2 children
Schimmelpfennig, Barbara Rupp *SEE* Schimmelpfennig, Georg
Schimmelpfennig, Georg; America, 1881 ***5475.1*** *p214*
*Wife:*Barbara Rupp
*Son:*Michel
*Daughter:*Margarethe
Schimmelpfennig, Margarethe *SEE* Schimmelpfennig, Georg
Schimmelpfennig, Michel *SEE* Schimmelpfennig, Georg
Schimpf, Anna Katharine; America, 1887 ***8115.12*** *p323*
*Child:*Jakob
Schimpf, Friedrich; Yuma, AZ, 1882-1884 ***2526.43*** *p156*
Schimpf, Georg; America, 1841 ***2526.43*** *p126*
With wife & child
*Brother:*Nikolaus
Schimpf, Jakob *SEE* Schimpf, Anna Katharine
Schimpf, John; Philadelphia, 1839 ***5720.10*** *p381*
Schimpf, Nikolaus 12 *SEE* Schimpf, Georg
Schimpff, Martin; Ohio, 1809-1852 ***4511.35*** *p46*
Schinalofski, Emilie; Wisconsin, 1885 ***6795.8*** *p163*
Schinding, Jacob Wilhelm; America, 1868 ***7919.3*** *p533*
Schindler, Hugo Clemens; Port uncertain, 1854 ***7420.1*** *p129*
Schindler, Jacob; Illinois, 1858-1861 ***6020.5*** *p133*
Schindler, John; Illinois, 1858-1861 ***6020.5*** *p133*
Schinkhoth, Johann Christoph; Port uncertain, 1884 ***7420.1*** *p345*
Schippel, Ferdinand; America, 1867 ***7919.3*** *p531*
Schirland, Joachim; Wisconsin, 1878 ***6795.8*** *p97*
Schirlsike, Carl 36; New York, NY, 1894 ***6512.1*** *p230*
Schirlsike, Ernst 5; New York, NY, 1894 ***6512.1*** *p230*
Schirlsike, Gottfried 35; New York, NY, 1894 ***6512.1*** *p230*
Schirlsike, Martha 11 months; New York, NY, 1894 ***6512.1*** *p230*
Schirmbeck, Barbara Simon *SEE* Schirmbeck, Johann
Schirmbeck, Johann; America, 1881 ***5475.1*** *p74*
*Wife:*Barbara Simon
*Son:*Michel
*Daughter:*Magdalena
*Son:*Karl
Schirmbeck, Johann; America, 1881 ***5475.1*** *p74*
Schirmbeck, Karl *SEE* Schirmbeck, Johann
Schirmbeck, Magdalena *SEE* Schirmbeck, Johann
Schirmbeck, Michel; America, 1864 ***5475.1*** *p237*
Schirmbeck, Michel *SEE* Schirmbeck, Johann
Schirmer, Christoph; America, 1845 ***7420.1*** *p39*
Schirmer, Engel Marie Sophie; America, 1859 ***7420.1*** *p188*
Schirmer, Engel Marie Sophie; America, 1867 ***7420.1*** *p264*
Schirmer, Frederick; New York, 1859 ***358.56*** *p101*
Schirmer, Heinrich Christoph; America, 1868 ***7420.1*** *p276*
*Son:*Heinrich Friedrich Wilhelm
With family
Schirmer, Heinrich Friedrich Wilhelm *SEE* Schirmer, Heinrich Christoph
Schirmer, Johann Friedrich Conrad; America, 1856 ***7420.1*** *p153*
Schirmer, Maria Rosina; America, 1868 ***7919.3*** *p534*
Schirmer, Wilhelm; America, 1914 ***7420.1*** *p402*
Schirra, Anna; America, 1871 ***5475.1*** *p441*
Schirra, Nikolaus; Philadelphia, 1881 ***5475.1*** *p434*
Schirra, Peter; Brazil, 1855 ***5475.1*** *p440*
Schissler, John George; Ohio, 1809-1852 ***4511.35*** *p46*
Schitler, Anthony; Ohio, 1809-1852 ***4511.35*** *p46*
Schitter, Anthony; Ohio, 1809-1852 ***4511.35*** *p46*
Schitter, Christian 27; America, 1846 ***778.6*** *p299*
Schitter, Elisabeth 23; America, 1846 ***778.6*** *p299*
Schittler, Christian; Ohio, 1809-1852 ***4511.35*** *p46*
Schittli, John; Ohio, 1809-1852 ***4511.35*** *p46*
Schittly, Jacob; Ohio, 1809-1852 ***4511.35*** *p46*
Schiver, Henry; Ohio, 1809-1852 ***4511.35*** *p46*
Schlachter, Anna Zander *SEE* Schlachter, Peter
Schlachter, Friedrich 29; Minneapolis, 1890 ***5475.1*** *p18*
*Wife:*Magdalene Jakobine Augustine Schard
*Son:*Gustav Friedrich
Schlachter, Gustav Friedrich *SEE* Schlachter, Friedrich
Schlachter, Johann *SEE* Schlachter, Peter
Schlachter, Karl *SEE* Schlachter, Peter
Schlachter, Magdalene Jakobine Augustine Schard *SEE* Schlachter, Friedrich
Schlachter, Maria *SEE* Schlachter, Peter
Schlachter, Nikolaus *SEE* Schlachter, Peter
Schlachter, Peter *SEE* Schlachter, Peter
Schlachter, Peter; America, 1881 ***5475.1*** *p75*
*Wife:*Anna Zander
*Son:*Peter
*Son:*Johann
*Daughter:*Maria
*Son:*Nikolaus
*Son:*Karl
Schlachter, Simon; America, 1866 ***5475.1*** *p553*
Schlack, Mathias; New York, 1860 ***358.56*** *p5*
Schlaefle, Elisabeth 23; Mississippi, 1846 ***778.6*** *p299*
Schlaefle, Franz 40; Mississippi, 1846 ***778.6*** *p300*
Schlager, Fridolin; New Castle, DE, 1817-1818 ***90.20*** *p153*
Schlambrecht, Marie 14; America, 1846 ***778.6*** *p300*
Schlander, Anna Elisabetha 4 *SEE* Schlander, Eva Margaretha Helmstadter
Schlander, Anna Margaretha 9 *SEE* Schlander, Jakob
Schlander, Barbara 26 *SEE* Schlander, Heinrich
Schlander, Dorothea Liegenbuhl *SEE* Schlander, Heinrich
Schlander, Egidius 15 *SEE* Schlander, Eva Margaretha Helmstadter
Schlander, Elisabetha 8 *SEE* Schlander, Eva Margaretha Helmstadter
Schlander, Elisabetha Margaretha *SEE* Schlander, Jakob
Schlander, Eva Margaretha 38; America, 1857 ***2526.43*** *p192*
*Son:*Egidius 15
*Daughter:*Anna Elisabetha 4
*Daughter:*Elisabetha 8
*Son:*Johannes 5
*Son:*Philipp 6
Schlander, Eva Maria Horn *SEE* Schlander, Jakob
Schlander, Heinrich; America, 1867 ***2526.43*** *p206*
*Wife:*Dorothea Liegenbuhl
*Son:*Johann Niklaus
*Daughter:*Barbara
With grandchild 3
Schlander, Jakob; America, 1855 ***2526.43*** *p227*
*Wife:*Eva Maria Horn
*Daughter:*Elisabetha Margaretha
*Daughter:*Anna Margaretha
Schlander, Johann Niklaus 18 *SEE* Schlander, Heinrich
Schlander, Johannes 5 *SEE* Schlander, Eva Margaretha Helmstadter
Schlander, Marie; America, 1865 ***2526.43*** *p206*
Schlander, Philipp 6 *SEE* Schlander, Eva Margaretha Helmstadter
Schlander, Sophie; America, 1865 ***2526.43*** *p206*
Schlanter, John; Ohio, 1809-1852 ***4511.35*** *p46*
Schlap, J.; Galveston, TX, 1855 ***571.7*** *p18*
Schlap, S.; Galveston, TX, 1855 ***571.7*** *p18*
Schlauker, Anna Hellbruck 33 *SEE* Schlauker, Johann
Schlauker, Elisabeth 2 *SEE* Schlauker, Johann
Schlauker, Gertrud 4 *SEE* Schlauker, Johann
Schlauker, Jakob 12 *SEE* Schlauker, Johann
Schlauker, Johann 35; America, 1846 ***5475.1*** *p410*
*Wife:*Anna Hellbruck 33
*Daughter:*Elisabeth 2
*Daughter:*Gertrud 4
*Son:*Jakob 12
*Daughter:*Maria 10
Schlauker, Maria 10 *SEE* Schlauker, Johann
Schlechenmeyer, John; Ohio, 1809-1852 ***4511.35*** *p46*
Schlecht, Thibourg 21; New Orleans, 1847 ***778.6*** *p300*
Schlee, Barbara 17; America, 1747 ***778.6*** *p300*
Schlee, Catherine Xaviera 19; America, 1747 ***778.6*** *p300*
Schlee, Elizabeth 19; America, 1747 ***778.6*** *p300*
Schlee, Elizabeth 36; America, 1747 ***778.6*** *p300*
Schlee, Henry 46; America, 1747 ***778.6*** *p300*
Schleenbecker, Elisabeth; Chicago, 1881 ***8115.12*** *p327*
*Child:*Ludwig
*Child:*Heinrich
Schleenbecker, Heinrich *SEE* Schleenbecker, Elisabeth
Schleenbecker, Johannes; America, n.d. ***8115.12*** *p328*
Schleenbecker, Ludwig *SEE* Schleenbecker, Elisabeth
Schleenbecker, Ludwig; Philadelphia, n.d. ***8115.12*** *p328*
Schlegel, Carl Eduard Louis; America, 1867 ***7919.3*** *p527*
Schlegel, Christian; Ohio, 1809-1852 ***4511.35*** *p46*
Schlegel, David 32; Port uncertain, 1841 ***778.6*** *p300*
Schlegel, F. Wilhelm; New York, NY, 1887 ***1029.59*** *p81*
Schlegel, Ferdinand; Illinois, 1858-1861 ***6020.5*** *p133*
Schlegel, Herm.; Valdivia, Chile, 1850 ***1192.4*** *p49*
Schlegel, Maria *SEE* Schlegel, W. A.
Schlegel, W. A.; Valdivia, Chile, 1850 ***1192.4*** *p48*
*Wife:*Maria
Schlei, Wilhelmine Louise Albertine; Wisconsin, 1896 ***6795.8*** *p224*
Schleich, Barbara; America, 1873 ***5475.1*** *p161*
Schleiche, Madalaine 22; Arkansas, 1846 ***778.6*** *p300*
Schleichen, Peter; Philadelphia, 1777 ***8529.30*** *p3*
Schleicher, Christiane Sybille; America, 1868 ***7919.3*** *p535*
Schleicher, Furchtegott Leberecht; America, 1868 ***7919.3*** *p535*
Schleicher, Johann Georg; America, 1867 ***7919.3*** *p535*
Schleicher, Maria Sabina; America, 1867 ***7919.3*** *p535*
With 3 children
Schleicher, Wilhelm; America, 1867 ***7919.3*** *p535*
Schleier, Johann; America, 1847 ***5475.1*** *p473*
Schleimer, Peter; America, 1847 ***5475.1*** *p475*
Schleinz, Eva 40; America, 1872 ***5475.1*** *p267*
Schlemer, Cath. 36; America, 1840 ***778.6*** *p300*
Schlemer, Jacq. 4; America, 1840 ***778.6*** *p300*
Schlemer, Peter 7; America, 1840 ***778.6*** *p300*
Schlemer, Peter 41; America, 1840 ***778.6*** *p300*
Schlemnar, Charles 39; Ontario, 1871 ***1823.21*** *p325*
Schlesch, Jean 21; New Orleans, 1847 ***778.6*** *p300*
Schlesinger, Ferdinand; America, 1868 ***7919.3*** *p534*
Schlessman, Hans Christoph; New Jersey, 1752-1774 ***927.31*** *p2*

446 *FOR A COMPLETE EXPLANATION OF ENTRY, SEE "HOW TO READ A CITATION" SECTION*

Schlessman, Johann Heinrich; New Jersey, 1752-1774 ***927.31** p2*
Schlett, Adolph 28; Indiana, 1871-1874 ***9076.20** p68*
Schletzer, Joseph 33; Port uncertain, 1840 ***778.6** p300*
Schleucher, Elisabeth; America, 1860 ***2526.42** p177*
With 2 children & husband
Schleuter, Joseph; Louisiana, 1874 ***4981.45** p134*
Schlewitz, Heinrich Ernst; America, 1870 ***7420.1** p396*
Schlewitz, Philipp; America, 1854 ***7420.1** p129*
Schley, Anna Maria Saar *SEE* Schley, Johann Jakob
Schley, Christian *SEE* Schley, Johann Jakob
Schley, Jakob *SEE* Schley, Johann Jakob
Schley, Johann Jakob; America, 1854 ***5475.1** p458*
*Wife:*Anna Maria Saar
*Son:*Jakob
*Son:*Christian
*Daughter:*Sophie
*Daughter:*Maria
*Daughter:*Margarethe
Schley, Margarethe *SEE* Schley, Johann Jakob
Schley, Maria *SEE* Schley, Johann Jakob
Schley, Sophie *SEE* Schley, Johann Jakob
Schleyer, Josef; America, 1849 ***5475.1** p478*
Schlichtenmeyer, John George; Ohio, 1809-1852 ***4511.35** p46*
Schlichting, H.; Venezuela, 1843 ***3899.5** p546*
Schlick, Anton; America, 1840 ***5475.1** p549*
Schlick, Johann; America, 1847 ***5475.1** p475*
Schlick, Michael; America, 1840 ***5475.1** p470*
Schlick, Theodor; America, 1852 ***5475.1** p481*
Schlicker, Lewis; New York, 1860 ***358.56** p5*
Schlicker, Theodor; America, 1846-1847 ***5475.1** p63*
Schlie, Wilhelm Heinrich; America, 1905 ***7420.1** p401*
Schlieke, K.; New York, 1860 ***358.56** p4*
Schlieman, Andrew; North Carolina, 1840 ***1088.45** p31*
Schlientz, Peter; America, 1898 ***5475.1** p426*
Schliep, Julius; Wisconsin, 1873 ***6795.8** p86*
Schlierbach, Anna Elisabeth; America, 1864 ***8115.12** p327*
*Child:*Marie
*Child:*Christian
*Child:*Elisabeth
Schlierbach, Christian *SEE* Schlierbach, Anna Elisabeth
Schlierbach, Elisabeth *SEE* Schlierbach, Anna Elisabeth
Schlierbach, Jakob *SEE* Schlierbach, Luise
Schlierbach, Katharine Margarethe; America, n.d. ***8115.12** p322*
Schlierbach, Konrad; America, n.d. ***8115.12** p322*
Schlierbach, Konrad; Chicago, 1864 ***8115.12** p322*
Schlierbach, Ludwig; America, 1880 ***8115.12** p322*
Schlierbach, Luise; America, 1889 ***8115.12** p318*
*Child:*Jakob
*Child:*Wilhelm
Schlierbach, Marie *SEE* Schlierbach, Anna Elisabeth
Schlierbach, Wilhelm *SEE* Schlierbach, Luise
Schlimchen, Bertha; America, 1894 ***7420.1** p371*
Schling, Ch.; New York, 1859-1860 ***358.56** p102*
Schlingloff, Elisabeth; America, 1866 ***7420.1** p249*
Schlingloff, Friedrich Julius Franz; America, 1863 ***7420.1** p220*
Schlingloff, Heinrich David Theophilus; America, 1865 ***7420.1** p236*
Schlitchting, Christian; Louisiana, 1836-1841 ***4981.45** p209*
Schlitz, Joseph 9; America, 1847 ***778.6** p300*
Schloefer, Michel 18; America, 1840 ***778.6** p300*
Schloetel, Anna; America, 1883 ***7420.1** p339*
Schloetel, Ernst Christian Heinrich; America, 1885 ***7420.1** p349*
Schloetzen, Elisa 31; America, 1841 ***778.6** p300*
Schloetzen, Laurent 24; America, 1841 ***778.6** p300*
Schloetzen, Louis 31; America, 1841 ***778.6** p300*
Schloetzen, Philipp 2; America, 1841 ***778.6** p300*
Schloman, Bernard C.W.; Washington, 1887 ***2770.40** p25*
Schloss, Bertha 26; New York, NY, 1880 ***5475.1** p14*
Schloss, Hermann 24; New York, NY, 1880 ***5475.1** p14*
Schloss, Julius; North Carolina, 1860 ***1088.45** p31*
Schloss, Ludwig 34; New York, NY, 1880 ***5475.1** p14*
Schlosse, Adam 23; Louisiana, 1848 ***778.6** p300*
Schlosser, Anton 4; New York, NY, 1893 ***1883.7** p44*
Schlosser, Catherine 44; New Orleans, 1846 ***778.6** p300*
Schlosser, Frederick 9; New Orleans, 1846 ***778.6** p300*
Schlosser, Frederick 44; New Orleans, 1846 ***778.6** p300*
Schlosser, Georg 32; New Orleans, 1847 ***778.6** p300*
Schlosser, Georg August; America, 1885 ***2526.43** p200*
Schlosser, Jacob 19; New Orleans, 1846 ***778.6** p300*
Schlosser, Lorenz 20; New York, NY, 1893 ***1883.7** p44*
Schlosser, Magdalena 6 months; New York, NY, 1893 ***1883.7** p44*
Schlosser, Magdalena 13; New York, NY, 1893 ***1883.7** p44*
Schlosser, Michael 28; New York, NY, 1893 ***1883.7** p44*
Schlosser, Nicolas 28; New Orleans, 1848 ***778.6** p300*
Schlosser, Rochus 20; New York, NY, 1893 ***1883.7** p37*
Schlosser, Veronica 25; New York, NY, 1893 ***1883.7** p44*
Schlosser, Wilhelmine; America, 1857 ***5475.1** p489*
Schlossmann, Dorothea; America, 1896 ***2526.43** p153*
Schlotel, Carl August; America, 1858 ***7420.1** p181*
Schlotel, Julius August Wilhelm; America, 1882 ***7420.1** p332*
Schlothouse, Gottfried 27; Portland, ME, 1906 ***970.38** p81*
Schlothouse, Heinrich 6; Portland, ME, 1906 ***970.38** p81*
Schlothouse, Julie 2 months; Portland, ME, 1906 ***970.38** p81*
Schlothouse, Katha. 32; Portland, ME, 1906 ***970.38** p81*
Schlothouse, Marie 2; Portland, ME, 1906 ***970.38** p81*
Schlott, Ludwig Leberecht; America, 1868 ***7919.3** p535*
Schlotterbeck, G.; New York, 1859 ***358.56** p100*
Schlotz, Jacob; Ohio, 1809-1852 ***4511.35** p46*
Schlueter, Emilie Ottilie Elisabeth; Wisconsin, 1893 ***6795.8** p83*
Schlumagger, Michael; Ohio, 1809-1852 ***4511.35** p46*
Schlunegger, Michael; Ohio, 1809-1852 ***4511.35** p46*
Schlup, John; Ohio, 1809-1852 ***4511.35** p46*
Schlupp, Peter 21; America, 1746 ***778.6** p300*
Schluss, John; Ohio, 1809-1852 ***4511.35** p46*
Schluter, Charlotte; America, 1860 ***7420.1** p199*
Schluter, Henry; Colorado, 1889 ***1029.59** p81*
Schlutingt, Claus; America, 1761 ***1220.12** p705*
Schmacher, George 4; Mississippi, 1846 ***778.6** p300*
Schmacher, Joseph 25; New York, NY, 1898 ***7951.13** p43*
Schmacher, Mary 24; New York, NY, 1898 ***7951.13** p43*
Schmacher, Michael 3; New York, NY, 1898 ***7951.13** p43*
Schmacher, Theresia 18 months; New York, NY, 1898 ***7951.13** p43*
Schmadal, C.; Louisiana, 1874-1875 ***4981.45** p30*
Schmag, Franzisca 31; America, 1844 ***778.6** p300*
Schmal, Adam; America, 1843 ***5475.1** p252*
Schmal, Angela; Wisconsin, 1800-1900 ***5475.1** p326*
Schmal, Anna Biwer *SEE* Schmal, Nikolaus
Schmal, Barbara *SEE* Schmal, Nikolaus
Schmal, Jakob *SEE* Schmal, Johann
Schmal, Johann; America, 1868 ***5475.1** p253*
Schmal, Johann; Wisconsin, 1891 ***5475.1** p326*
*Wife:*Margarethe Kettenhofen
*Son:*Nikolaus
*Son:*Jakob
Schmal, Margarethe Kettenhofen *SEE* Schmal, Johann
Schmal, Maria; America, 1871 ***5475.1** p263*
Schmal, Michael; America, 1876 ***5475.1** p298*
Schmal, Nikolaus; Philadelphia, 1880 ***5475.1** p254*
*Wife:*Anna Biwer
*Daughter:*Barbara
Schmal, Nikolaus *SEE* Schmal, Johann
Schmalenberger, Miss C. 1; New Orleans, 1834 ***1002.51** p111*
Schmalenberger, Miss C. 7; New Orleans, 1834 ***1002.51** p111*
Schmalenberger, D. 4; New Orleans, 1834 ***1002.51** p111*
Schmalenberger, Miss E. 30; New Orleans, 1834 ***1002.51** p111*
Schmalenberger, J. 10; New Orleans, 1834 ***1002.51** p111*
Schmalenberger, J. 30; New Orleans, 1834 ***1002.51** p111*
Schmalenberger, J. 60; New Orleans, 1834 ***1002.51** p111*
Schmalenberger, Miss M. 65; New Orleans, 1834 ***1002.51** p111*
Schmalenberger, N. 34; New Orleans, 1834 ***1002.51** p111*
Schmall, Albert Jean 31; New Orleans, 1848 ***778.6** p301*
Schmall, Constance Angel. 31; New Orleans, 1848 ***778.6** p301*
Schmaltz, Phillip 20; New York, NY, 1898 ***7951.13** p43*
Schmalz, Maria Regine; America, 1868 ***7919.3** p532*
Schmank, Peter Franz; America, 1882 ***5475.1** p316*
Schmann, Fredk. 20; Halifax, N.S., 1902 ***1860.4** p44*
Schmauck, C. F.; Valdivia, Chile, 1852 ***1192.4** p53*
Schmauss, Adam 11 *SEE* Schmauss, Lotte
Schmauss, Eva Elisabetha 41; America, 1853 ***2526.43** p142*
Schmauss, Gottfried 9 *SEE* Schmauss, Lotte
Schmauss, Gretchen 13 *SEE* Schmauss, Lotte
Schmauss, Lotte; America, 1872 ***2526.42** p171*
*Child:*Gretchen
*Child:*Gottfried
*Child:*Theresia
*Child:*Adam
Schmauss, Theresia 6 *SEE* Schmauss, Lotte
Schmechon, William; Louisiana, 1836-1841 ***4981.45** p209*
Schmeck, August Robert; Wisconsin, 1898 ***6795.8** p76*
Schmeer, Johann Nikolaus; America, 1866 ***5475.1** p43*
Schmeer, Karoline; America, 1879 ***5475.1** p44*
Schmeer, Katharina 5 *SEE* Schmeer, Peter
Schmeer, Magdalene Karoline; America, 1866 ***5475.1** p43*
Schmeer, Peter 30; Brazil, 1872 ***5475.1** p442*
*Daughter:*Katharina 5
Schmeer, Valentin 24; America, 1833 ***5475.1** p58*
Schmel, John F.C.; Washington, 1889 ***2770.40** p81*
Schmelzer, Elisabeth 14 *SEE* Schmelzer, Valentin
Schmelzer, Georg 8 *SEE* Schmelzer, Valentin
Schmelzer, Gustav; America, 1849 ***5475.1** p28*
Schmelzer, Jakob 3 *SEE* Schmelzer, Valentin
Schmelzer, Johann Georg; America, 1846 ***5475.1** p530*
Schmelzer, Katharina 54; America, 1843 ***5475.1** p528*
*Daughter:*Charlotte 24
*Son:*Johann 23
Schmelzer, Katharina 63; America, 1843 ***5475.1** p528*
*Son:*Konrad 23
Schmelzer, Katharina 17 *SEE* Schmelzer, Valentin
Schmelzer, Konrad 23 *SEE* Schmelzer, Katharina Volz
Schmelzer, Konrad 10 *SEE* Schmelzer, Valentin
Schmelzer, Ludwig; America, 1848 ***5475.1** p28*
Schmelzer, Margarethe 7 *SEE* Schmelzer, Valentin
Schmelzer, Margarethe 43 *SEE* Schmelzer, Valentin
Schmelzer, Sophie 19 *SEE* Schmelzer, Valentin
Schmelzer, Valentin 5 *SEE* Schmelzer, Valentin
Schmelzer, Valentin 44; New York, 1854 ***5475.1** p533*
*Wife:*Margarethe 43
*Son:*Valentin 5
*Son:*Jakob 3
*Daughter:*Margarethe 7
*Daughter:*Katharina 17
*Daughter:*Elisabeth 14
*Son:*Georg 8
*Son:*Konrad 10
*Daughter:*Sophie 19
Schmerber, Morand 26; Galveston, TX, 1844 ***3967.10** p370*
Schmercel, Mr. 6; America, 1841 ***778.6** p301*
Schmercel, Ms. 25; America, 1841 ***778.6** p301*
Schmerker, Jakob, II; America, 1832 ***2526.43** p179*
With wife & child
Schmetz, Francis A.; Ohio, 1809-1852 ***4511.35** p47*
Schmid, Agathe 14; America, 1844 ***778.6** p301*
Schmid, Anne Marie 10; America, 1844 ***778.6** p301*
Schmid, Elisabeth; Venezuela, 1843 ***3899.5** p541*
Schmid, Eloise 3; America, 1844 ***778.6** p301*
Schmid, Eva Magdalena; Venezuela, 1843 ***3899.5** p541*
Schmid, Jean-Baptiste 3 months; America, 1844 ***778.6** p301*
Schmid, Johann; America, 1867 ***7919.3** p529*
With wife & 4 children
Schmid, Johann; Venezuela, 1843 ***3899.5** p541*
Schmid, Joseph 6; America, 1844 ***778.6** p301*
Schmid, Joseph; New Castle, DE, 1817-1818 ***90.20** p153*
Schmid, Joseph; Valdivia, Chile, 1850 ***1192.4** p49*
Schmid, Leon 21; America, 1844 ***778.6** p301*
Schmid, Madelaine 15; America, 1844 ***778.6** p301*
Schmid, Maria Anna; Venezuela, 1843 ***3899.5** p544*
Schmid, Nicolas 41; America, 1844 ***778.6** p301*
Schmidlin, Antoine 24; New Orleans, 1848 ***778.6** p301*
Schmidlin, Jacob 23; Mississippi, 1848 ***778.6** p301*
Schmidt, . . .; America, 1855 ***2526.43** p179*
Schmidt, . . . 55; New York, NY, 1885 ***8425.16** p32*
Schmidt, Widow; America, 1871 ***7420.1** p396*
Schmidt, Adam *SEE* Schmidt, Johann
Schmidt, Adam 39; Halifax, N.S., 1902 ***1860.4** p39*
Schmidt, Adam F.; Louisiana, 1841-1844 ***4981.45** p211*
Schmidt, Adolf 27; Halifax, N.S., 1902 ***1860.4** p43*
Schmidt, Adolph Georg Ludwig; America, 1861 ***7420.1** p208*
Schmidt, Albert; Argentina, 1920 ***8023.44** p378*
*Wife:*Pauline
Schmidt, Andrew 17; New York, NY, 1892 ***8425.16** p34*
Schmidt, Andrew P. 67; Kansas, 1935 ***1447.20** p62*
Schmidt, Anna; America, 1867 ***7420.1** p264*
Schmidt, Anna 15; America, 1881 ***5475.1** p421*
Schmidt, Anna 28; Halifax, N.S., 1902 ***1860.4** p39*
Schmidt, Anna 9; New York, NY, 1893 ***1883.7** p40*
Schmidt, Anna 16; New York, NY, 1893 ***1883.7** p44*
Schmidt, Anna Friederike Charlotte; America, 1865 ***7420.1** p236*
Schmidt, Anna Katharina *SEE* Schmidt, Johann Georg
Schmidt, Anna Maria 4; America, 1846 ***778.6** p301*
Schmidt, Anna Maria 43; America, 1846 ***778.6** p301*
Schmidt, Anna Regina; Virginia, 1831 ***152.20** p62*
Schmidt, Anna Regina *SEE* Schmidt, Johann Georg
Schmidt, Anne 25; New York, NY, 1874 ***6954.7** p39*
Schmidt, Anthony; Ohio, 1809-1852 ***4511.35** p47*
Schmidt, Antoinette; America, 1868 ***7919.3** p527*
With child

Schmidt, Anton 6; Halifax, N.S., 1902 *1860.4 p42*
Schmidt, Anton 51; Louisiana, 1848 *778.6 p301*
Schmidt, Arthur Berthold Max; America, 1868 *7919.3 p531*
Schmidt, August; America, 1864 *5475.1 p557*
Schmidt, August; America, 1867 *7919.3 p532*
  With wife & son
Schmidt, August; Wisconsin, 1873 *6795.8 p91*
Schmidt, August; Wisconsin, 1875 *6795.8 p205*
Schmidt, August Carl; America, 1868 *7919.3 p526*
Schmidt, August Georg *SEE* Schmidt, Ferdinand Gottlieb
Schmidt, B.; America, 1871 *7420.1 p289*
Schmidt, Barbara 1 *SEE* Schmidt, Nikolaus
Schmidt, Barbara 48; New York, NY, 1886 *8425.16 p32*
Schmidt, Bernh..d 25; Mississippi, 1846 *778.6 p301*
Schmidt, Bertha 19; New York, NY, 1893 *1883.7 p44*
Schmidt, C. H.; South Carolina, 1828 *6155.4 p19*
Schmidt, Carl; Galveston, TX, 1855 *571.7 p17*
Schmidt, Carl 13; New York, NY, 1893 *1883.7 p40*
Schmidt, Carl 36; New York, NY, 1893 *1883.7 p40*
Schmidt, Carl; Valdivia, Chile, 1850 *1192.4 p48*
Schmidt, Carl; Wisconsin, 1882 *6795.8 p169*
Schmidt, Carl; Wisconsin, 1903 *6795.8 p140*
Schmidt, Caroline; America, 1867 *7919.3 p530*
Schmidt, Caroline 6 *SEE* Schmidt, Philipp
Schmidt, Caroline Sophie Eleonore; America, 1857 *7420.1 p173*
Schmidt, Catharine 8; New Orleans, 1848 *778.6 p301*
Schmidt, Catharine Soph.; America, 1846 *7420.1 p49*
Schmidt, Catherine 12; New Orleans, 1848 *778.6 p301*
Schmidt, Catherine 9 months; New York, NY, 1874 *6954.7 p39*
Schmidt, Ch. 48; America, 1841 *778.6 p301*
Schmidt, Ch...na 43; America, 1841 *778.6 p301*
Schmidt, Charles 23; New Orleans, 1847 *778.6 p301*
Schmidt, Charlotte Knorzer *SEE* Schmidt, Joh. Christian
Schmidt, Charlotte; Galveston, TX, 1855 *571.7 p17*
Schmidt, Christian Johann *SEE* Schmidt, Joh. Christian
Schmidt, Christiane Elisabeth; America, 1868 *7919.3 p526*
Schmidt, Christine Sophie; America, 1893 *7420.1 p368*
Schmidt, Com; New York, 1860 *358.56 p149*
Schmidt, Conrad; America, 1857 *7420.1 p171*
Schmidt, Conrad; Washington, 1882 *2770.40 p136*
Schmidt, David; Louisiana, 1836-1841 *4981.45 p209*
Schmidt, Dorothea; America, 1836 *5475.1 p527*
Schmidt, Dorothea 2 *SEE* Schmidt, Jakob
Schmidt, E. H.; Valparaiso, Chile, 1850 *1192.4 p50*
Schmidt, Eduard 3 *SEE* Schmidt, Philipp
Schmidt, Elisabeth *SEE* Schmidt, Elisabeth Margarethe
Schmidt, Elisabeth *SEE* Schmidt, Julius
Schmidt, Elisabeth *SEE* Schmidt, Nikolaus
Schmidt, Elisabeth 10; New Orleans, 1848 *778.6 p301*
Schmidt, Elisabeth Margarethe *SEE* Schmidt, Elisabeth Margarethe
Schmidt, Elisabeth Margarethe; America, 1850 *8115.12 p321*
  Child: Elisabeth
  Child: Ernst Ludwig
  Child: Elisabeth Margarethe
  Child: Johann George
Schmidt, Elisabethe 2; America, 1847 *778.6 p301*
Schmidt, Elise 6; New Orleans, 1848 *778.6 p301*
Schmidt, Emil; Wisconsin, 1899 *6795.8 p144*
Schmidt, Emil Theodor Heinrich; America, 1874 *5475.1 p32*
Schmidt, Emilia 28; New Orleans, 1848 *778.6 p301*
Schmidt, Emma 32; New York, NY, 1893 *1883.7 p44*
Schmidt, Emmanuel 2 months; New York, NY, 1877 *6954.7 p39*
Schmidt, Ernst; America, 1867 *7919.3 p525*
Schmidt, Ernst; America, 1867 *7919.3 p531*
Schmidt, Ernst Friedrich Wilhelm; America, 1895 *7420.1 p372*
Schmidt, Ernst Ludwig *SEE* Schmidt, Elisabeth Margarethe
Schmidt, F. A.; Valdivia, Chile, 1852 *1192.4 p53*
  With wife
  With brother 26
Schmidt, F. I. H. 23; New York, NY, 1847 *9176.15 p49*
Schmidt, Ferdinand 5; Galveston, TX, 1844 *3967.10 p373*
Schmidt, Ferdinand 33; Halifax, N.S., 1902 *1860.4 p39*
Schmidt, Ferdinand; Valdivia, Chile, 1851 *1192.4 p51*
Schmidt, Ferdinand Emil; Wisconsin, 1903 *6795.8 p153*
Schmidt, Ferdinand Gottlieb; America, 1852 *7420.1 p97*
  Brother: August Georg
Schmidt, Francois 15; Louisiana, 1848 *778.6 p301*
Schmidt, Franz; America, 1865 *5475.1 p507*
Schmidt, Franz; America, 1872 *5475.1 p279*
Schmidt, Franz 4 *SEE* Schmidt, Jakob
Schmidt, Franz; Arkansas, 1880 *5475.1 p310*
Schmidt, Franz; Halifax, N.S., 1902 *1860.4 p39*

Schmidt, Frederick; New York, 1859 *358.56 p54*
Schmidt, Fredrick William; Wisconsin, 1913 *6795.8 p174*
Schmidt, Friederika 11; New York, NY, 1893 *1883.7 p40*
Schmidt, Friederika 38; New York, NY, 1893 *1883.7 p40*
Schmidt, Friedrich; America, 1868 *7919.3 p528*
Schmidt, Friedrich; America, 1872 *5475.1 p14*
Schmidt, Friedrich 7; Halifax, N.S., 1902 *1860.4 p40*
Schmidt, Friedrich 14; New Orleans, 1848 *778.6 p301*
Schmidt, Friedrich 10 *SEE* Schmidt, Philipp
Schmidt, Friedrich; Valdivia, Chile, 1852 *1192.4 p53*
Schmidt, Friedrich; Valdivia, Chile, 1852 *1192.4 p53*
Schmidt, Friedrich; Wisconsin, 1873 *6795.8 p52*
Schmidt, Friedrich Wilhelm *SEE* Schmidt, Joh. Christian
Schmidt, Friedrich Wilhelm; America, 1867 *7919.3 p530*
Schmidt, Friedrich Wilhelm; America, 1899 *7420.1 p375*
Schmidt, Friedrich Wilhelm; Wisconsin, 1892 *6795.8 p216*
Schmidt, Friedrich Wilhelm August; America, 1854 *7420.1 p129*
  Son: Heinrich Christian Friedrich
  With family
Schmidt, G. S.; Louisiana, 1874-1875 *4981.45 p31*
Schmidt, G. S.; Louisiana, 1874-1875 *4981.45 p130*
Schmidt, Georg *SEE* Schmidt, Nikolaus
Schmidt, Georg 9; America, 1846 *778.6 p301*
Schmidt, Georg 14 *SEE* Schmidt, Paul
Schmidt, Georg 45; America, 1846 *778.6 p301*
Schmidt, Georg 31; New York, NY, 1874 *6954.7 p39*
Schmidt, Georg 38; New York, NY, 1877 *6954.7 p39*
Schmidt, Georg *SEE* Schmidt, Margarethe Houy
Schmidt, Georg Ernst Julius; America, 1867 *7919.3 p532*
Schmidt, Georg Heinrich; America, 1880 *7420.1 p318*
Schmidt, Georg Wilhelm; America, 1855 *7420.1 p141*
Schmidt, George; Illinois, 1852 *6079.1 p12*
Schmidt, George; Illinois, 1854 *6079.1 p12*
Schmidt, George 18; Quebec, 1870 *8364.32 p25*
Schmidt, Gertrud Burgard *SEE* Schmidt, Julius
Schmidt, Gotleib; Ohio, 1809-1852 *4511.35 p47*
Schmidt, Gottfried; America, 1890 *179.55 p19*
Schmidt, Gustav; America, 1855 *2526.42 p164*
Schmidt, Gustav 24; New York, NY, 1893 *1883.7 p40*
Schmidt, Gustav 24; New York, NY, 1893 *1883.7 p47*
Schmidt, Gustav Theodor; Wisconsin, 1879 *6795.8 p83*
Schmidt, H.; New York, 1859 *358.56 p99*
Schmidt, Heinrich; America, 1858 *7420.1 p181*
Schmidt, Heinrich; America, 1868 *5475.1 p483*
Schmidt, Heinrich 20; New York, NY, 1893 *1883.7 p44*
Schmidt, Heinrich; Nova Scotia, 1784 *7105 p25*
Schmidt, Heinrich Christian Friedrich *SEE* Schmidt, Friedrich Wilhelm August
Schmidt, Heinrich Wilhelm August; America, 1864 *7420.1 p227*
Schmidt, Henri 21; New Orleans, 1847 *778.6 p302*
Schmidt, Henrick 3; Halifax, N.S., 1902 *1860.4 p44*
Schmidt, Henrick 38; Halifax, N.S., 1902 *1860.4 p44*
Schmidt, Henry; Washington, 1889 *2770.40 p81*
Schmidt, Henry Phillip; Texas, 1900 *3435.45 p36*
Schmidt, Herman; Halifax, N.S., 1902 *1860.4 p42*
Schmidt, Herman 7; New York, NY, 1893 *1883.7 p40*
Schmidt, Herman Johann Carl; Wisconsin, 1887 *6795.8 p224*
Schmidt, Hermann; Valdivia, Chile, 1850 *1192.4 p50*
Schmidt, Hermann Friedrich; America, 1867 *7919.3 p530*
Schmidt, Hermann Philipp; America, 1862 *7420.1 p214*
Schmidt, Ilius 23; Louisiana, 1848 *778.6 p302*
Schmidt, J. F.; Iowa, 1896 *1211.15 p19*
Schmidt, Jac.; New York, 1859 *358.56 p100*
Schmidt, Jacob 3; Halifax, N.S., 1902 *1860.4 p42*
Schmidt, Jacob F.; Texas, 1888 *3435.45 p37*
Schmidt, Jakob; America, 1836 *5475.1 p449*
Schmidt, Jakob; America, 1854 *5475.1 p465*
Schmidt, Jakob; America, 1869 *5475.1 p329*
Schmidt, Jakob 2 *SEE* Schmidt, Mathias
Schmidt, Jakob 9 *SEE* Schmidt, Johann
Schmidt, Jakob 25; America, 1846 *5475.1 p401*
  Wife: Johanna Scheyer
Schmidt, Jakob 34; America, 1846 *5475.1 p451*
  Wife: Magdalena 39
  Son: Joh. Nikolaus 6
  Son: Franz 4
  Daughter: Magdalena 1
  Son: Mathias 8
Schmidt, Jakob 37; America, 1846 *5475.1 p401*
  Wife: Wilhelmine Ansteth 35
  Daughter: Katharina 9 months
  With stepmother
  Daughter: Dorothea 2
Schmidt, Jakob; Brazil, 1879 *5475.1 p382*
Schmidt, Jakob 29; Galveston, TX, 1844 *3967.10 p375*

Schmidt, Jakob; New York, 1896 *5475.1 p426*
  Wife: Theresia Krahn
  With 3 children
Schmidt, Jakob Martin; Port uncertain, 1835 *7420.1 p10*
Schmidt, Jaspar 7; Halifax, N.S., 1902 *1860.4 p44*
Schmidt, Jean; New Castle, DE, 1817-1818 *90.20 p153*
Schmidt, Joh. Christian; America, 1833 *5475.1 p118*
  Wife: Charlotte Knorzer
  Son: Wilhelm Jakob
  Daughter: Katharina Dorothea
  Son: Friedrich Wilhelm
  Son: Christian Johann
Schmidt, Joh. Nikolaus 6 *SEE* Schmidt, Jakob
Schmidt, Johanes 25; Portland, ME, 1911 *970.38 p81*
Schmidt, Johann; America, 1854 *5475.1 p465*
  Brother: Adam
Schmidt, Johann; America, 1872 *5475.1 p272*
Schmidt, Johann *SEE* Schmidt, Nikolaus
Schmidt, Johann 3 *SEE* Schmidt, Johann
Schmidt, Johann 44; America, 1847 *5475.1 p408*
  Wife: Margarethe Fuchs 39
  Daughter: Margarethe 1
  Son: Johann 3
  Daughter: Katharina 11
  Son: Jakob 9
  Son: Peter 7
  Daughter: Maria 13
Schmidt, Johann; Halifax, N.S., 1902 *1860.4 p40*
Schmidt, Johann 2; Halifax, N.S., 1902 *1860.4 p42*
Schmidt, Johann 29; Halifax, N.S., 1902 *1860.4 p39*
Schmidt, Johann 17; New York, NY, 1886 *8425.16 p32*
Schmidt, Johann 5 *SEE* Schmidt, Philipp
Schmidt, Johann August; Wisconsin, 1874 *6795.8 p84*
Schmidt, Johann David; Nova Scotia, 1784 *7105 p25*
Schmidt, Johann Georg; Virginia, 1831 *152.20 p67*
  Wife: Johanna Elisabeth Krichbaum
  Child: Johannes
  Child: Anna Katharina
  Child: Anna Regina
Schmidt, Johann George *SEE* Schmidt, Elisabeth Margarethe
Schmidt, Johann Gottfried Julius; Wisconsin, 1879 *6795.8 p84*
Schmidt, Johann Heinrich Hermann; Wisconsin, 1874 *6795.8 p91*
Schmidt, Johann Heinrich Otto; America, 1849 *7420.1 p67*
Schmidt, Johann Nikolaus; Brazil, 1865 *5475.1 p506*
Schmidt, Johann Paul; America, 1868 *7919.3 p528*
Schmidt, Johanna Scheyer *SEE* Schmidt, Jakob
Schmidt, Johanna Elisabeth Krichbaum *SEE* Schmidt, Johann Georg
Schmidt, Johanna Emily; Wisconsin, 1892 *6795.8 p88*
Schmidt, Johannes *SEE* Schmidt, Johann Georg
Schmidt, John; Colorado, 1882 *1029.59 p85*
Schmidt, John; Illinois, 1858 *6079.1 p12*
Schmidt, John; Louisiana, 1874 *4981.45 p134*
Schmidt, John 19; New York, NY, 1892 *8425.16 p34*
Schmidt, John 45; New York, NY, 1892 *8425.16 p34*
Schmidt, John; Ohio, 1809-1852 *4511.35 p47*
Schmidt, John; Texas, 1880 *3435.45 p37*
Schmidt, Josef 22; New York, 1872 *5475.1 p483*
Schmidt, Josef *SEE* Schmidt, Margarethe Houy
Schmidt, Joseph 7; Galveston, TX, 1844 *3967.10 p373*
Schmidt, Joseph 36; Galveston, TX, 1844 *3967.10 p373*
Schmidt, Joseph; Ohio, 1809-1852 *4511.35 p47*
Schmidt, Josepha; New York, 1859 *358.56 p99*
Schmidt, Josephine 7; New Orleans, 1848 *778.6 p302*
Schmidt, Julius; America, 1881 *5475.1 p50*
  Wife: Gertrud Burgard
  Son: Reinhold
  Daughter: Elisabeth
Schmidt, Jurgen; Iowa, 1887 *1211.15 p19*
Schmidt, Karl Wilhelm Washington; New Orleans, 1882 *5475.1 p35*
Schmidt, Karoline *SEE* Schmidt, Martin
Schmidt, Katharina Buchleitner *SEE* Schmidt, Nikolaus
Schmidt, Katharina; America, 1892 *5475.1 p425*
Schmidt, Katharina 9 *SEE* Schmidt, Jakob
Schmidt, Katharina 11 *SEE* Schmidt, Johann
Schmidt, Katharina 20 *SEE* Schmidt, Paul
Schmidt, Katharina 30 *SEE* Schmidt, Nikolaus
Schmidt, Katharina Kinsinger 38 *SEE* Schmidt, Paul
Schmidt, Katharina 55; America, 1867 *5475.1 p152*
  Son: Eduard
Schmidt, Katharina 22; Galveston, TX, 1844 *3967.10 p373*
Schmidt, Katharina 12 *SEE* Schmidt, Philipp
Schmidt, Katharina Dorothea *SEE* Schmidt, Joh. Christian
Schmidt, Leipold 30; Halifax, N.S., 1902 *1860.4 p39*
Schmidt, Leonard; Ohio, 1809-1852 *4511.35 p47*
Schmidt, Lewis; Ohio, 1809-1852 *4511.35 p47*

Schmidt, Loorfa 31; Halifax, N.S., 1902 *1860.4 p39*
Schmidt, Lorenz; Chile, 1852 *1192.4 p52*
Schmidt, Louisa 4; Portland, ME, 1911 *970.38 p81*
Schmidt, Ludewig 9; New Orleans, 1848 *778.6 p302*
Schmidt, Ludwig; America, 1853 *2526.43 p200*
Schmidt, Ludwig; America, 1882 *5475.1 p15*
Schmidt, Ludwig; America, 1918 *8115.12 p322*
Schmidt, Ludwig; Halifax, N.S., 1902 *1860.4 p39*
Schmidt, Ludwig 1; Halifax, N.S., 1902 *1860.4 p39*
Schmidt, Ludwig 23; Halifax, N.S., 1902 *1860.4 p39*
Schmidt, Ludwig 1 months; New York, NY, 1886
  8425.16 p32
Schmidt, Ludwig 22; New York, NY, 1886 *8425.16 p32*
Schmidt, Ludwina 45; Halifax, N.S., 1902 *1860.4 p39*
Schmidt, Luise; America, 1883 *5475.1 p51*
Schmidt, Luise *SEE* Schmidt, Margarethe Houy
Schmidt, M. E. Christine; America, 1866 *5475.1 p550*
Schmidt, Magdalena 1 *SEE* Schmidt, Jakob
Schmidt, Magdalena 7; America, 1846 *778.6 p302*
Schmidt, Magdalena 39 *SEE* Schmidt, Jakob
Schmidt, Magdalena 41; America, 1847 *778.6 p302*
Schmidt, Margarethe Schorr *SEE* Schmidt, Nikolaus
Schmidt, Margarethe 1 *SEE* Schmidt, Johann
Schmidt, Margarethe Zimmer 28 *SEE* Schmidt, Mathias
Schmidt, Margarethe Fuchs 39 *SEE* Schmidt, Johann
Schmidt, Margarethe 65; Brazil, 1862 *5475.1 p519*
  With son-in-law
Schmidt, Margarethe 22; Halifax, N.S., 1902 *1860.4 p44*
Schmidt, Margarethe 52; Pittsburgh, 1871 *5475.1 p418*
  *Son:*Josef
  *Son:*Georg
  *Son:*Peter
  *Son:*Wilhelm
  *Daughter:*Luise
Schmidt, Margarethe Louise; America, 1867 *7919.3 p532*
Schmidt, Margarethe Luise; America, 1863 *5475.1 p12*
Schmidt, Maria 13 *SEE* Schmidt, Johann
Schmidt, Maria 14; America, 1846 *778.6 p302*
Schmidt, Maria 30; Galveston, TX, 1844 *3967.10 p373*
Schmidt, Maria 26; Halifax, N.S., 1902 *1860.4 p42*
Schmidt, Maria 5; New York, NY, 1877 *6954.7 p39*
Schmidt, Maria 36; New York, NY, 1877 *6954.7 p39*
Schmidt, Maria; Wisconsin, 1895 *6795.8 p142*
Schmidt, Maria Elisabeth Scharf *SEE* Schmidt, Martin
Schmidt, Marianna 3; Halifax, N.S., 1902 *1860.4 p39*
Schmidt, Marianna 20; New York, NY, 1893 *1883.7 p44*
Schmidt, Marianne 40; New Orleans, 1848 *778.6 p302*
Schmidt, Marie 24; America, 1847 *778.6 p302*
Schmidt, Marie 42; New York, NY, 1892 *8425.16 p34*
Schmidt, Martin; Brazil, 1862 *5475.1 p497*
Schmidt, Martin; Brazil, 1862 *5475.1 p497*
  *Wife:*Maria Elisabeth Scharf
  *Son:*Peter
  *Daughter:*Karoline
Schmidt, Mary Bertha; Wisconsin, 1907 *6795.8 p197*
Schmidt, Mathias; America, 1881 *5475.1 p193*
Schmidt, Mathias 8 *SEE* Schmidt, Jakob
Schmidt, Mathias 10; America, 1847 *778.6 p302*
Schmidt, Mathias 31; America, 1800-1899 *5475.1 p451*
  *Wife:*Margarethe Zimmer 28
  *Son:*Jakob 2
Schmidt, Mathias 4; Halifax, N.S., 1902 *1860.4 p40*
Schmidt, Menza 15; Louisiana, 1848 *778.6 p302*
Schmidt, Michael 19; New York, NY, 1893 *1883.7 p44*
Schmidt, Michael; Ohio, 1809-1852 *4511.35 p47*
Schmidt, Michel 2; New Orleans, 1848 *778.6 p302*
Schmidt, Michel 42; New Orleans, 1848 *778.6 p302*
Schmidt, Mick. 23; New York, NY, 1893 *1883.7 p43*
Schmidt, Mina Avline Helema; Wisconsin, 1890 *6795.8
p236*
Schmidt, Nicholas; Ohio, 1809-1852 *4511.35 p47*
Schmidt, Nicola 5; America, 1847 *778.6 p302*
Schmidt, Nicolaus; South Carolina, 1890 *6155.4 p19*
Schmidt, Niels Rasmussen; Iowa, 1921 *1211.15 p19*
Schmidt, Nikolaus; America, 1840 *5475.1 p56*
  *Wife:*Katharina Buchleitner
  With 4 children
Schmidt, Nikolaus; America, 1872 *5475.1 p324*
  *Wife:*Katharina
  *Daughter:*Barbara
Schmidt, Nikolaus; America, 1882 *5475.1 p161*
Schmidt, Nikolaus *SEE* Schmidt, Nikolaus
Schmidt, Nikolaus; America, 1883 *5475.1 p60*
  *Wife:*Margarethe Schorr
  *Daughter:*Elisabeth
  *Son:*Georg
  *Son:*Nikolaus
  *Son:*Johann
Schmidt, Otto 7; New York, NY, 1893 *1883.7 p40*
Schmidt, Paul 9 *SEE* Schmidt, Paul
Schmidt, Paul 53; America, 1854 *5475.1 p53*
  *Wife:*Katharina Kinsinger 38
  *Son:*Paul 9

Schmidt, Paul; New York, 1859 *358.56 p55*
Schmidt, Pauline *SEE* Schmidt, Albert
Schmidt, Pauline 19; Halifax, N.S., 1902 *1860.4 p39*
Schmidt, Peter 7 *SEE* Schmidt, Johann
Schmidt, Peter *SEE* Schmidt, Martin
Schmidt, Peter 6; New York, NY, 1886 *8425.16 p32*
Schmidt, Peter; Ohio, 1809-1852 *4511.35 p47*
Schmidt, Peter *SEE* Schmidt, Margarethe Houy
Schmidt, Phallgyt 27; Portland, ME, 1911 *970.38 p81*
Schmidt, Philipp 1 *SEE* Schmidt, Philipp
Schmidt, Philipp 42; Ohio, 1865 *5475.1 p21*
  *Son:*Friedrich 10
  *Son:*Philipp 1
  *Daughter:*Caroline 6
  *Daughter:*Katharina 12
  *Wife:*Sophie Renno
  *Son:*Johann 5
  *Son:*Eduard 3
Schmidt, Pierre 42; America, 1847 *778.6 p302*
Schmidt, Regina 25; Halifax, N.S., 1902 *1860.4 p39*
Schmidt, Reinhold *SEE* Schmidt, Julius
Schmidt, Severin 25; Galveston, TX, 1844 *3967.10 p373*
Schmidt, Sophia 17; America, 1841 *778.6 p302*
Schmidt, Sophie Renno *SEE* Schmidt, Philipp
Schmidt, Susanna 32; America, 1843 *5475.1 p252*
Schmidt, Susanna 24; Portland, ME, 1911 *970.38 p81*
Schmidt, Theobald 42; America, 1849 *170.15 p41*
  With 3 children
Schmidt, Theodor; America, 1853 *7420.1 p111*
Schmidt, Theresia Krahn *SEE* Schmidt, Jakob
Schmidt, Valentin 25; New Orleans, 1848 *778.6 p302*
Schmidt, Victor; America, 1880 *5475.1 p154*
Schmidt, Walburga 27; Galveston, TX, 1844 *3967.10
p373*
Schmidt, Wilhelm; America, 1857 *7420.1 p171*
Schmidt, Wilhelm; America, 1861 *7420.1 p208*
  With wife & son & 3 daughters
Schmidt, Wilhelm; America, 1861 *7420.1 p208*
  With family
Schmidt, Wilhelm; America, 1867 *7420.1 p264*
  With family
Schmidt, Wilhelm; America, 1867 *7919.3 p531*
Schmidt, Wilhelm *SEE* Schmidt, Margarethe Houy
Schmidt, Wilhelm; Wisconsin, 1887 *6795.8 p135*
Schmidt, Wilhelm Heinrich; America, 1872 *7420.1 p297*
  With wife
Schmidt, Wilhelm Jakob *SEE* Schmidt, Joh. Christian
Schmidt, Wilhelmine; America, 1883 *5475.1 p51*
Schmidt, Wilhelmine Ansteth 35 *SEE* Schmidt, Jakob
Schmidt, Wilhelmine 20; New York, NY, 1886 *8425.16
p32*
Schmidt, William; New York, 1889 *1766.20 p25*
Schmidt, Wm.; Venezuela, 1843 *3899.5 p546*
Schmidt, Xavier 28; Missouri, 1845 *778.6 p302*
Schmidtborn, Wilh.; Chicago, 1874 *5475.1 p419*
Schmidt Family ; West Virginia, 1850 *1132.30 p147*
Schmied, Franz 12; New Castle, DE, 1817-1818 *90.20
p153*
Schmied, Jean; New Castle, DE, 1817-1818 *90.20 p153*
Schmieding, Christian Friedrich; Port uncertain, 1838
  7420.1 p15
Schmiedle, Peter 70; Galveston, TX, 1844 *3967.10 p374*
Schmiedt, Joseph; New Castle, DE, 1817-1818 *90.20
p153*
Schmier, Adam 36; Michigan, 1880 *4491.39 p27*
Schmier, Catherine 33; Michigan, 1880 *4491.39 p27*
Schmietz, Michael; Illinois, 1856 *6079.1 p12*
Schmietz, William; Illinois, 1856 *6079.1 p12*
Schmirer, Albine 6; Portland, ME, 1906 *970.38 p81*
Schmirer, Caroline 30; Portland, ME, 1906 *970.38 p81*
Schmirer, Christian 18; Portland, ME, 1906 *970.38 p81*
Schmirer, Heinrich 20; Portland, ME, 1906 *970.38 p81*
Schmirer, Johan 14; Portland, ME, 1906 *970.38 p81*
Schmirer, Magdalena 23; Portland, ME, 1906 *970.38 p81*
Schmirer, Michael 34; Portland, ME, 1906 *970.38 p81*
Schmirer, Rosina 8; Portland, ME, 1906 *970.38 p81*
Schmit, Jost. 20; America, 1840 *778.6 p302*
Schmith, Caroline 13; Missouri, 1845 *778.6 p302*
Schmith, Dorothea 3; Missouri, 1845 *778.6 p302*
Schmith, Helene 29; America, 1845 *778.6 p302*
Schmith, John M.; Ohio, 1840-1897 *8365.35 p18*
Schmith, Joseph 42; Missouri, 1845 *778.6 p302*
Schmith, Michel 16; Missouri, 1845 *778.6 p302*
Schmith, Patrise 39; Missouri, 1845 *778.6 p302*
Schmith, Peatrix 6; Missouri, 1845 *778.6 p302*
Schmits, Henry 18; America, 1847 *778.6 p302*
Schmits, John; Louisiana, 1841-1844 *4981.45 p211*
Schmitt, A. Maria *SEE* Schmitt, Johann
Schmitt, A. Maria Goergen 71 *SEE* Schmitt, Johann
Schmitt, A. Maria *SEE* Schmitt, Gottfried

Schmitt, Adam 43; Brazil, 1864 *5475.1 p500*
  *Wife:*Margarethe Sieber 39
Schmitt, Amalia *SEE* Schmitt, Peter
Schmitt, Anna *SEE* Schmitt, Johann
Schmitt, Anna 70; America, 1854 *5475.1 p53*
Schmitt, Anna Elisabeth; America, 1840 *8115.12 p322*
Schmitt, Anna Elisabeth; America, 1840 *8115.12 p324*
  *Child:*Magdalene
  *Child:*Elisabeth
Schmitt, Anna Gertrud; America, 1800-1899 *5475.1 p140*
  *Daughter:*Katharina
  *Daughter:*Barbara
  *Grandchild:*Johann
Schmitt, Anna Katharine; America, 1849 *8115.12 p328*
  *Child:*Katharine Margarethe
  *Child:*Katharine
  *Child:*Philipp
Schmitt, Anna Margarete *SEE* Schmitt, Katharine
  Elisabeth
Schmitt, Anna Margarethe *SEE* Schmitt, Elisabeth
Schmitt, Anna Maria; America, 1876 *5475.1 p157*
Schmitt, Anna Maria Adams *SEE* Schmitt, Mathias
Schmitt, Anna Maria Perius *SEE* Schmitt, Michael
Schmitt, Barbara; America, 1855 *5475.1 p343*
  *Son:*Mathias
  *Son:*Peter
  *Son:*Johann
  *Daughter:*Magdalena
Schmitt, Barbara *SEE* Schmitt, Katharina Strasser
Schmitt, Barbara 4 *SEE* Schmitt, J. Baptist
Schmitt, Barbara 41; America, 1855 *5475.1 p309*
  *Daughter:*Magdalena 18
  *Daughter:*Elisabeth 13
  *Son:*Jakob 12
  *Son:*Peter
Schmitt, Barbara Baller 43 *SEE* Schmitt, J. Baptist
Schmitt, Barbara 59; America, 1865 *5475.1 p388*
  With children
Schmitt, Barbara; Brazil, 1879 *5475.1 p390*
Schmitt, Barbara *SEE* Schmitt, Michael
Schmitt, Bernard; America, 1881 *5475.1 p221*
Schmitt, C. 42; America, 1846 *778.6 p302*
Schmitt, Christian; America, 1800-1900 *5475.1 p65*
  *Wife:*Johanna Turck
  With 2 children
Schmitt, Christian *SEE* Schmitt, Marie
Schmitt, Christian; America, n.d. *8115.12 p324*
Schmitt, Dionysius; Pennsylvania, 1885 *5475.1 p364*
Schmitt, Elisabeth *SEE* Schmitt, Katharine Elisabeth
Schmitt, Elisabeth *SEE* Schmitt, Anna Elisabeth
Schmitt, Elisabeth; America, 1840 *8115.12 p324*
  *Child:*Helene
  *Child:*Anna Margarethe
  *Child:*Konrad
Schmitt, Elisabeth *SEE* Schmitt, Marie Katharine
Schmitt, Elisabeth *SEE* Schmitt, Peter
Schmitt, Elisabeth *SEE* Schmitt, Mathias
Schmitt, Elisabeth *SEE* Schmitt, Marie
Schmitt, Elisabeth; America, 1883 *5475.1 p232*
  *Son:*Peter
Schmitt, Elisabeth; America, n.d. *8115.12 p322*
Schmitt, Elisabeth; America, n.d. *8115.12 p322*
Schmitt, Elisabeth Wagner 28 *SEE* Schmitt, Mathias
Schmitt, Elisabeth Baltes 57 *SEE* Schmitt, Jakob
Schmitt, Elisabeth *SEE* Schmitt, Mathias
Schmitt, Elisabeth Engeldinger *SEE* Schmitt, Peter
Schmitt, Elizabeth 26; America, 1847 *778.6 p302*
Schmitt, Eva 6 *SEE* Schmitt, Mathias
Schmitt, Franz; America, 1868 *5475.1 p349*
Schmitt, Franz; America, 1870 *5475.1 p189*
Schmitt, Friedrich Heinrich Conrad; America, 1865
  7420.1 p236
  With wife & 2 children
Schmitt, Friedrich Peter; America, 1851 *8115.12 p324*
Schmitt, Georg; America, 1880 *5475.1 p231*
Schmitt, Gertrud; America, 1872 *5475.1 p319*
Schmitt, Gertrud 49; America, 1857 *5475.1 p296*
  *Son:*J. Philipp
  *Son:*Mathias
Schmitt, Gottfried 51; Brazil, 1862 *5475.1 p369*
  *Wife:*Maria Kuhn 51
  *Daughter:*A. Maria
  *Son:*Mathias
  *Daughter:*Katharina
  *Son:*Peter
  *Son:*Johann
Schmitt, Gustave; Wisconsin, 1879 *6795.8 p228*
Schmitt, Heinrich; America, n.d. *8115.12 p324*
Schmitt, Helena *SEE* Schmitt, Johann
Schmitt, Helena Naumann *SEE* Schmitt, Johann
Schmitt, Helena *SEE* Schmitt, Peter
Schmitt, Helena *SEE* Schmitt, Peter
Schmitt, Helene *SEE* Schmitt, Elisabeth

Schmitt, J. Baptist 45; America, 1863 *5475.1 p283*
  *Wife:*Barbara Baller 43
  *Son:*Mathias 15
  *Daughter:*Maria 8
  *Daughter:*Barbara 4
  *Son:*Joh. Peter 13
  *Daughter:*Magdalena 19
Schmitt, Jakob; America, 1857 *5475.1 p548*
  *Wife:*Maria Gros
  *Mother:*Elisabeth Baltes
  *Brother:*Josef
  *Daughter:*Katharina
Schmitt, Jakob; America, 1858 *8115.12 p322*
Schmitt, Jakob; America, n.d. *8115.12 p324*
Schmitt, Jakob 15 *SEE* Schmitt, Nikolaus
Schmitt, Jakob; Illinois, 1884 *5475.1 p268*
Schmitt, Jakob Nikolaus; America, 1880 *5475.1 p220*
Schmitt, Jean Pierre 30; America, 1846 *778.6 p302*
Schmitt, Joh. Peter 13 *SEE* Schmitt, J. Baptist
Schmitt, Johann; America, 1856 *5475.1 p516*
Schmitt, Johann; America, 1866 *5475.1 p431*
Schmitt, Johann *SEE* Schmitt, Johann
Schmitt, Johann; America, 1873 *5475.1 p140*
  *Wife:*Katharina Lenhof
  *Son:*Johann
  *Son:*Karl
  With father-in-law
Schmitt, Johann *SEE* Schmitt, Katharina Strasser
Schmitt, Johann *SEE* Schmitt, Johann
Schmitt, Johann; America, 1882 *5475.1 p333*
  *Wife:*Helena Naumann
  *Daughter:*Anna
  *Son:*Mathias
  *Daughter:*Helena
  *Son:*Peter
  *Daughter:*A. Maria
  *Son:*Johann
Schmitt, Johann *SEE* Schmitt, Peter
Schmitt, Johann 9 *SEE* Schmitt, Mathias
Schmitt, Johann 20 *SEE* Schmitt, Barbara Goettert
Schmitt, Johann 72; America, 1876 *5475.1 p175*
  *Wife:*A. Maria Goergen 71
Schmitt, Johann *SEE* Schmitt, Gottfried
Schmitt, Johann *SEE* Schmitt, Nikolaus
Schmitt, Johann; Brazil, 1879 *5475.1 p431*
Schmitt, Johann 1 *SEE* Schmitt, Nikolaus
Schmitt, Johann *SEE* Schmitt, Peter
Schmitt, Johann Friedrich; America, 1823-1887 *8115.12 p323*
Schmitt, Johann Friedrich; America, n.d. *8115.12 p323*
Schmitt, Johann Georg; America, 1858 *8115.12 p322*
Schmitt, Johann Georg *SEE* Schmitt, Marie
Schmitt, Johann Georg; America, n.d. *8115.12 p323*
Schmitt, Johann Jakob; America, n.d. *8115.12 p325*
Schmitt, Johann Ludwig; America, n.d. *8115.12 p322*
Schmitt, Johann Nikolaus; America, 1850 *5475.1 p532*
Schmitt, Johann Philipp; America, 1858 *8115.12 p322*
Schmitt, Johann Philipp; America, n.d. *8115.12 p323*
Schmitt, Johann Philipp; America, n.d. *8115.12 p323*
Schmitt, Johann Philipp; America, n.d. *8115.12 p323*
Schmitt, Johanna Turck *SEE* Schmitt, Christian
Schmitt, Johannes; America, n.d. *8115.12 p322*
Schmitt, Johannes; America, n.d. *8115.12 p323*
Schmitt, Johannes; America, n.d. *8115.12 p323*
Schmitt, Johannes; America, n.d. *8115.12 p328*
Schmitt, Johannetta; America, 1881 *5475.1 p364*
Schmitt, Josef *SEE* Schmitt, Jakob
Schmitt, Josef 8 *SEE* Schmitt, Nikolaus
Schmitt, Joseph 18; America, 1843 *778.6 p302*
Schmitt, Karl *SEE* Schmitt, Johann
Schmitt, Karl 6 *SEE* Schmitt, Nikolaus
Schmitt, Karl 33; Brazil, 1862 *5475.1 p496*
  *Wife:*Margarethe Mees 33
  *Son:*Peter 10 months
Schmitt, Kath Schreier 37 *SEE* Schmitt, Nikolaus
Schmitt, Katharina; America, 1843 *5475.1 p431*
Schmitt, Katharina *SEE* Schmitt, Jakob
Schmitt, Katharina *SEE* Schmitt, Peter
Schmitt, Katharina *SEE* Schmitt, Mathias
Schmitt, Katharina Lenhof *SEE* Schmitt, Johann
Schmitt, Katharina; America, 1879 *5475.1 p187*
  *Daughter:*Barbara
  *Daughter:*Maria
  With daughter
  *Son:*Johann
Schmitt, Katharina *SEE* Schmitt, Peter
Schmitt, Katharina 2 *SEE* Schmitt, Mathias
Schmitt, Katharina 22 *SEE* Schmitt, Nikolaus
Schmitt, Katharina Ginsbach 37 *SEE* Schmitt, Mathias
Schmitt, Katharina 52; America, 1867 *5475.1 p297*

Schmitt, Katharina 63; America, 1857 *5475.1 p335*
  *Son:*Mathias 33
  *Daughter:*Maria 25
  *Daughter:*Katharina 28
Schmitt, Katharina *SEE* Schmitt, Gottfried
Schmitt, Katharina *SEE* Schmitt, Michael
Schmitt, Katharina 5 *SEE* Schmitt, Nikolaus
Schmitt, Katharine *SEE* Schmitt, Anna Katharine
Schmitt, Katharine Elisabeth; America, 1840 *8115.12 p323*
  *Child:*Anna Margarete
  *Child:*Elisabeth
Schmitt, Katharine Margar.; America, 1855 *8115.12 p322*
  With siblings
Schmitt, Katharine Margarethe *SEE* Schmitt, Anna Katharine
Schmitt, Konrad *SEE* Schmitt, Elisabeth
Schmitt, Leonie 3; America, 1846 *778.6 p302*
Schmitt, Ludwig *SEE* Schmitt, Marie Katharine
Schmitt, Ludwig; America, 1870 *8115.12 p322*
Schmitt, Ludwig *SEE* Schmitt, Marie
Schmitt, Ludwig; America, n.d. *8115.12 p324*
Schmitt, Luise 11 *SEE* Schmitt, Nikolaus
Schmitt, Magdalena 19 *SEE* Schmitt, J. Baptist
Schmitt, Magdalena 23 *SEE* Schmitt, Barbara Goettert
Schmitt, Magdalene *SEE* Schmitt, Anna Elisabeth
Schmitt, Margarethe Meiers *SEE* Schmitt, Mathias
Schmitt, Margarethe; America, 1879 *5475.1 p148*
Schmitt, Margarethe *SEE* Schmitt, Marie
Schmitt, Margarethe; America, 1885 *8115.12 p322*
Schmitt, Margarethe 9 *SEE* Schmitt, Mathias
Schmitt, Margarethe *SEE* Schmitt, Mathias
Schmitt, Margarethe; Brazil, 1887 *5475.1 p42*
Schmitt, Margarethe 3 *SEE* Schmitt, Nikolaus
Schmitt, Margarethe 22; Brazil, 1864 *5475.1 p501*
Schmitt, Margarethe Mees 33 *SEE* Schmitt, Karl
Schmitt, Margarethe Sieber 39 *SEE* Schmitt, Adam
Schmitt, Margarethe *SEE* Schmitt, Peter
Schmitt, Maria Gros *SEE* Schmitt, Jakob
Schmitt, Maria *SEE* Schmitt, Peter
Schmitt, Maria *SEE* Schmitt, Mathias
Schmitt, Maria *SEE* Schmitt, Katharina Strasser
Schmitt, Maria; America, 1881 *5475.1 p220*
Schmitt, Maria *SEE* Schmitt, Peter
Schmitt, Maria 7 *SEE* Schmitt, Mathias
Schmitt, Maria 8 *SEE* Schmitt, J. Baptist
Schmitt, Maria Klein 32 *SEE* Schmitt, Peter
Schmitt, Maria 32; America, 1865 *5475.1 p388*
Schmitt, Maria 49; America, 1833 *5475.1 p58*
  With relative 24
  *Daughter:*Maria 22
  *Son:*Georg
  *Daughter:*Elisabeth 13
  *Daughter:*Dorothea 9
  *Son:*Josef
  *Son:*Konrad
Schmitt, Maria; Brazil, 1872 *5475.1 p370*
Schmitt, Maria *SEE* Schmitt, Michael
Schmitt, Maria Zorn 22 *SEE* Schmitt, Michel
Schmitt, Maria 30; Brazil, 1870 *5475.1 p370*
Schmitt, Marie; America, 1880 *8115.12 p324*
  *Child:*Margarethe
  *Child:*Christian
  *Child:*Johann Georg
  *Child:*Ludwig
  *Child:*Elisabeth
Schmitt, Marie 29; America, 1846 *778.6 p303*
Schmitt, Marie Katharine *SEE* Schmitt, Marie Katharine
Schmitt, Marie Katharine; America, 1850 *8115.12 p323*
  *Child:*Marie Katharine
  *Child:*Ludwig
  *Child:*Philipp
  *Child:*Elisabeth
Schmitt, Mathias; America, 1837 *5475.1 p52*
Schmitt, Mathias; America, 1843 *5475.1 p294*
Schmitt, Mathias; America, 1843 *5475.1 p330*
  With 2 sons
Schmitt, Mathias; America, 1860 *5475.1 p296*
  *Wife:*Margarethe Meiers
  *Son:*Mathias
  *Daughter:*Margarethe
  *Daughter:*Maria
  *Son:*Johann
Schmitt, Mathias; America, 1881 *5475.1 p332*
Schmitt, Mathias *SEE* Schmitt, Johann
Schmitt, Mathias 8 *SEE* Schmitt, Mathias
Schmitt, Mathias 15 *SEE* Schmitt, Mathias
Schmitt, Mathias 15 *SEE* Schmitt, J. Baptist
Schmitt, Mathias 26 *SEE* Schmitt, Barbara Goettert
Schmitt, Mathias 35; America, 1865 *5475.1 p389*
  *Wife:*Elisabeth Wagner 28
  *Daughter:*Katharina

  *Daughter:*Elisabeth
  *Daughter:*Maria
  *Son:*Peter
  *Son:*Nikolaus
Schmitt, Mathias 36; America, 1868 *5475.1 p323*
  *Wife:*Katharina Ginsbach 37
  *Daughter:*Katharina 2 months
  *Daughter:*Eva 6
  *Son:*Nikolaus 12
  *Son:*Mathias 8
Schmitt, Mathias 64; America, 1860 *5475.1 p42*
Schmitt, Mathias; Arkansas, 1880 *5475.1 p299*
  *Wife:*Anna Maria Adams
  *Daughter:*Susanna
  *Daughter:*Margarethe
  *Daughter:*Elisabeth
Schmitt, Mathias *SEE* Schmitt, Gottfried
Schmitt, Michael; Brazil, 1879 *5475.1 p436*
  *Wife:*Anna Maria Perius
  *Daughter:*Barbara
  *Daughter:*Maria
  *Daughter:*Katharina
Schmitt, Michel 30; Brazil, 1852 *5475.1 p500*
  *Wife:*Maria Zorn 22
Schmitt, Nikolaus; America, 1836 *5475.1 p527*
  *Daughter:*Katharina
  *Son:*Peter
Schmitt, Nikolaus *SEE* Schmitt, Peter
Schmitt, Nikolaus *SEE* Schmitt, Mathias
Schmitt, Nikolaus; America, 1866 *5475.1 p185*
Schmitt, Nikolaus; America, 1872 *5475.1 p160*
Schmitt, Nikolaus; America, 1879 *5475.1 p187*
Schmitt, Nikolaus 33; America, 1843 *5475.1 p430*
  With wife
  With 2 children
Schmitt, Nikolaus; Brazil, 1887 *5475.1 p432*
Schmitt, Nikolaus 10 *SEE* Schmitt, Nikolaus
Schmitt, Nikolaus 32; Brazil, 1857 *5475.1 p382*
  With wife
  *Son:*Johann 1
Schmitt, Nikolaus 41; Brazil, 1864 *5475.1 p502*
  *Wife:*Kath Schreier 37
  *Son:*Josef 8
  *Daughter:*Katharina 5
  *Daughter:*Luise 11 months
  *Daughter:*Margarethe 3
  *Son:*Karl 6
  *Son:*Nikolaus 10
  *Son:*Johann
  *Son:*Jakob 15
Schmitt, Nikolaus; Illinois, 1883 *5475.1 p268*
Schmitt, Peter; America, 1843 *5475.1 p366*
  With wife
  With son
Schmitt, Peter *SEE* Schmitt, Peter
Schmitt, Peter *SEE* Schmitt, Mathias
Schmitt, Peter; America, 1868 *5475.1 p376*
Schmitt, Peter; America, 1880 *5475.1 p195*
Schmitt, Peter *SEE* Schmitt, Johann
Schmitt, Peter; America, 1883 *5475.1 p364*
  *Wife:*Helena
  *Daughter:*Amalia
  *Son:*Johann
  *Daughter:*Helena
  *Daughter:*Katharina
  *Daughter:*Maria
Schmitt, Peter *SEE* Schmitt, Gottfried
Schmitt, Peter 10 *SEE* Schmitt, Karl
Schmitt, Peter; New York, 1882 *5475.1 p494*
Schmitt, Peter; Wisconsin, 1877 *5475.1 p363*
  *Wife:*Elisabeth Engeldinger
  *Daughter:*Margarethe
  *Son:*Johann
Schmitt, Philipp; America, 1840 *8115.12 p322*
Schmitt, Philipp *SEE* Schmitt, Anna Katharine
Schmitt, Philipp *SEE* Schmitt, Marie Katharine
Schmitt, Philipp; America, n.d. *8115.12 p324*
Schmitt, Stephan 16; America, 1857 *5475.1 p500*
Schmitt, Susanna *SEE* Schmitt, Mathias
Schmitt, Theobald 19; America, 1846 *778.6 p303*
Schmitt, Theobald 42; America, 1849 *170.15 p41*
  With 3 children
Schmitt, Thomas 5; America, 1846 *778.6 p303*

FOR A COMPLETE EXPLANATION OF ENTRY, SEE "HOW TO READ A CITATION" SECTION

Schmitt, Wilhelm; America, 1834 ***8115.12*** *p322*
Schmittchen, Anna 8 *SEE* Schmittchen, Nikolaus
Schmittchen, Elisabeth 9 *SEE* Schmittchen, Nikolaus
Schmittchen, Heinrich 2 *SEE* Schmittchen, Nikolaus
Schmittchen, Johanetta 4 *SEE* Schmittchen, Nikolaus
Schmittchen, Margarethe 6 *SEE* Schmittchen, Nikolaus
Schmittchen, Margarethe Mang 34 *SEE* Schmittchen, Nikolaus
Schmittchen, Nikolaus 34; America, 1854 ***5475.1*** *p53*
*Wife:*Margarethe Mang 34
*Daughter:*Johanetta 4
*Daughter:*Elisabeth 9 months
*Son:*Heinrich 2
*Daughter:*Margarethe 6
*Son:*Peter 10
*Daughter:*Anna 8
Schmittchen, Peter 10 *SEE* Schmittchen, Nikolaus
Schmitz, Adam 16; New York, NY, 1864 ***8425.62*** *p195*
Schmitz, Andr. 29; America, 1840 ***778.6*** *p303*
Schmitz, Anna Maria 43; New York, NY, 1864 ***8425.62*** *p195*
Schmitz, Anton 4; New York, NY, 1864 ***8425.62*** *p195*
Schmitz, Barbara; America, 1881 ***5475.1*** *p258*
Schmitz, Christian; Illinois, 1851 ***6079.1*** *p12*
Schmitz, Christian 8; New York, NY, 1864 ***8425.62*** *p195*
Schmitz, Gertrud Gust *SEE* Schmitz, Peter
Schmitz, Heinrich 42; New York, NY, 1864 ***8425.62*** *p195*
Schmitz, Henrich; Illinois, 1855 ***6079.1*** *p13*
Schmitz, Jacob 28; America, 1840 ***778.6*** *p303*
Schmitz, Johann *SEE* Schmitz, Peter
Schmitz, Johann 47; New York, NY, 1864 ***8425.62*** *p195*
Schmitz, Maria *SEE* Schmitz, Peter
Schmitz, Mathias 14; America, 1864 ***5475.1*** *p248*
Schmitz, Paul; Missouri, 1901 ***3276.1*** *p3*
Schmitz, Peter *SEE* Schmitz, Peter
Schmitz, Peter; America, 1872 ***5475.1*** *p153*
*Wife:*Gertrud Gust
*Son:*Johann
*Daughter:*Maria
*Son:*Peter
Schmitz, Peter; Illinois, 1851 ***6079.1*** *p13*
Schmitz, Vincent Joseph Hubert; Ohio, 1840-1897 ***8365.35*** *p18*
Schmitz, Wilhelmine 11; New York, NY, 1864 ***8425.62*** *p195*
Schmitzer, Friedrich; America, 1848 ***5475.1*** *p476*
Schmizer, Katharina; America, 1846 ***5475.1*** *p472*
Schmoe, Ernst Heinrich; America, 1889 ***7420.1*** *p359*
Schmoe, Friedrich; America, 1857 ***7420.1*** *p171*
Schmoe, Fritz; America, 1854 ***7420.1*** *p129*
Schmoe, Johann Ernst; America, 1856 ***7420.1*** *p153*
Schmoll, Carl 14; New York, NY, 1874 ***6954.7*** *p37*
Schmoll, Carl 18; New York, NY, 1874 ***6954.7*** *p37*
Schmoll, Christian 22; New York, NY, 1874 ***6954.7*** *p37*
Schmoll, Christina 8; New York, NY, 1874 ***6954.7*** *p37*
Schmoll, Daniel 10; New York, NY, 1874 ***6954.7*** *p37*
Schmoll, Elisabeth 23; New York, NY, 1874 ***6954.7*** *p37*
Schmoll, Elisabeth 35; New York, NY, 1874 ***6954.7*** *p37*
Schmoll, Heinrich 36; New York, NY, 1874 ***6954.7*** *p37*
Schmoll, Heinrich 60; New York, NY, 1874 ***6954.7*** *p37*
Schmoll, Jacob 9 months; New York, NY, 1874 ***6954.7*** *p37*
Schmoll, Jacob; Ohio, 1840-1897 ***8365.35*** *p18*
Schmoll, Johann 9 months; New York, NY, 1874 ***6954.7*** *p37*
Schmoll, Johann 27; New York, NY, 1874 ***6954.7*** *p37*
Schmoll, Margarethe; Brazil, 1862 ***5475.1*** *p540*
Schmoll, Rosina 1 months; New York, NY, 1874 ***6954.7*** *p37*
Schmonos, Henry; Louisiana, 1874-1875 ***4981.45*** *p31*
Schmonos, Henry; Louisiana, 1874-1875 ***4981.45*** *p130*
Schmuckal, Emil; Colorado, 1902 ***1029.59*** *p81*
Schmucker, Apollonie List Schonberger *SEE* Schmucker, Johann Christoph
Schmucker, Ferdinand Friedrich *SEE* Schmucker, Johann Christoph
Schmucker, Friedrich Karl; America, 1878 ***2526.43*** *p200*
Schmucker, Georg Philipp; Philadelphia, 1852 ***2526.43*** *p180*
Schmucker, Georg Wilhelm; America, 1854 ***2526.43*** *p180*
Schmucker, Gottlieb Balthasar; Philadelphia, 1887 ***2526.43*** *p180*
Schmucker, Johann Christoph; America, 1785 ***2526.43*** *p180*
*Wife:*Apollonie List Schonberger
*Son:*Johann Jakob
*Son:*Ferdinand Friedrich
*Son:*Johann Georg
Schmucker, Johann Georg *SEE* Schmucker, Johann Christoph
Schmucker, Johann Heinrich; America, 1881 ***2526.43*** *p180*
Schmucker, Johann Jakob *SEE* Schmucker, Johann Christoph
Schmucker, Kaspar; America, 1831 ***2526.43*** *p180*
With family
Schmucker, Katharina; America, 1843 ***2526.43*** *p180*
With children
Schmucker, Ludwig; America, 1840 ***2526.43*** *p180*
Schmucker, Wilhelm; America, 1854 ***2526.43*** *p227*
Schmudlach, Auguste; Wisconsin, 1898 ***6795.8*** *p135*
Schmuland, Aug. 47; Portland, ME, 1911 ***970.38*** *p81*
Schmuland, Johan 48; Portland, ME, 1911 ***970.38*** *p81*
Schmulland, Adolph 2; Portland, ME, 1910 ***970.38*** *p81*
Schmulland, Eduard 4; Portland, ME, 1910 ***970.38*** *p81*
Schmulland, Emma 17; Portland, ME, 1910 ***970.38*** *p81*
Schmulland, Gottlieb 48; Portland, ME, 1910 ***970.38*** *p81*
Schmulland, Helena 10; Portland, ME, 1910 ***970.38*** *p81*
Schmulland, Nadalia 28; Portland, ME, 1910 ***970.38*** *p81*
Schmulland, Natalia 11; Portland, ME, 1910 ***970.38*** *p81*
Schmulland, Samuel 3; Portland, ME, 1910 ***970.38*** *p81*
Schmulland, Wilhelm 18; Portland, ME, 1910 ***970.38*** *p81*
Schmutz, Christian; Ohio, 1809-1852 ***4511.35*** *p47*
Schnabel, Friedrich; America, 1884 ***2526.42*** *p185*
Schnabel, Ludwig; Iowa, 1883 ***5475.1*** *p36*
Schnackenberg, Lud.; Valdivia, Chile, 1852 ***1192.4*** *p56*
Schnadt, Friedrich; America, 1860 ***7420.1*** *p199*
Schnadt, Heinrich; America, 1860 ***7420.1*** *p199*
Schnaible, Augustine 9 months; New York, NY, 1898 ***7951.13*** *p43*
Schnaible, Helena 28; New York, NY, 1898 ***7951.13*** *p43*
Schnaible, Margaret 3; New York, NY, 1898 ***7951.13*** *p43*
Schnaible, Sigmund 2; New York, NY, 1898 ***7951.13*** *p43*
Schnaible, Sigmund 31; New York, NY, 1898 ***7951.13*** *p43*
Schnaider, Philip; Ohio, 1809-1852 ***4511.35*** *p47*
Schnauber, Anna Margaretha 10 *SEE* Schnauber, Wilhelm
Schnauber, August 26 *SEE* Schnauber, Wilhelm
Schnauber, Eva Margaretha *SEE* Schnauber, Wilhelm
Schnauber, Johann Philipp; America, 1860 ***2526.43*** *p156*
Schnauber, Ludwig 14 *SEE* Schnauber, Wilhelm
Schnauber, Maria; America, 1867 ***2526.43*** *p156*
Schnauber, Wilhelm 23 *SEE* Schnauber, Wilhelm
Schnauber, Wilhelm 50; New York, 1849 ***2526.43*** *p156*
*Son:*August 26
*Son:*Ludwig 14
*Daughter:*Anna Margaretha 10
*Daughter:*Eva Margaretha
*Son:*Wilhelm 23
Schnebele, Joseph 53; Louisiana, 1848 ***778.6*** *p303*
Schneck, Fr.; New York, 1860 ***358.56*** *p149*
Schneckenburger, Martin; New York, 1860 ***358.56*** *p150*
Schneeweis, Carl; America, 1852 ***7420.1*** *p97*
Schneeweiss, Ernst August Eduard; Port uncertain, 1850 ***7420.1*** *p75*
Schneeweiss, Hermann; America, 1849 ***7420.1*** *p67*
Schneibel, Augustine 9 months; New York, NY, 1898 ***7951.13*** *p43*
Schneibel, Helena 28; New York, NY, 1898 ***7951.13*** *p43*
Schneibel, Margaret 3; New York, NY, 1898 ***7951.13*** *p43*
Schneibel, Sigmund 2; New York, NY, 1898 ***7951.13*** *p43*
Schneibel, Sigmund 31; New York, NY, 1898 ***7951.13*** *p43*
Schneider, Mr. 25; America, 1846 ***778.6*** *p303*
Schneider, Mr. 28; America, 1841 ***778.6*** *p303*
Schneider, Miss A. 46; New Orleans, 1834 ***1002.51*** *p113*
Schneider, Miss A. 69; New Orleans, 1834 ***1002.51*** *p113*
Schneider, Abraham 47; America, 1857 ***5475.1*** *p497*
*Wife:*Elisabeth Jentes 47
*Daughter:*Katharina 7
*Son:*Karl 5
*Son:*Peter 12
*Son:*Adam 16
*Daughter:*Elisabeth 14
Schneider, Adam 16 *SEE* Schneider, Abraham
Schneider, Adam 24; Halifax, N.S., 1902 ***1860.4*** *p41*
Schneider, Adam, III 26; America, 1836 ***2526.43*** *p219*
With wife 20
With child 18 months
Schneider, Alexander 8; Halifax, N.S., 1902 ***1860.4*** *p39*
Schneider, Amalia; Baltimore, 1853 ***8513.31*** *p294*
Schneider, Amant 18; America, 1840 ***778.6*** *p303*
Schneider, Andre 20; America, 1846 ***778.6*** *p303*
Schneider, Andreas; America, n.d. ***8115.12*** *p324*
Schneider, Andreas 20 *SEE* Schneider, Georg
Schneider, Angela Backes 41 *SEE* Schneider, Michael
Schneider, Anna Peiffer *SEE* Schneider, Jakob
Schneider, Anna Wurm *SEE* Schneider, Kaspar Fried.
Schneider, Anna 47; America, 1876 ***5475.1*** *p351*
Schneider, Anna 18; Galveston, TX, 1844 ***3967.10*** *p370*
Schneider, Anna Drauz *SEE* Schneider, Francis
Schneider, Anna Gertrud 1; Galveston, TX, 1845 ***3967.10*** *p376*
Schneider, Anna Maria Franz *SEE* Schneider, Peter
Schneider, Anna Maria Scherer *SEE* Schneider, Mathias
Schneider, Ant. 38; America, 1840 ***778.6*** *p303*
Schneider, Anthony; Illinois, 1834-1900 ***6020.5*** *p133*
Schneider, Anton 2; America, 1746 ***778.6*** *p303*
Schneider, Anton 13 *SEE* Schneider, Michael
Schneider, Anton 29; America, 1746 ***778.6*** *p303*
Schneider, August; New York, 1860 ***358.56*** *p149*
Schneider, B.; Louisiana, 1874 ***4981.45*** *p297*
Schneider, Barbara; America, 1881 ***5475.1*** *p511*
Schneider, Barbara 10 *SEE* Schneider, Michael
Schneider, Barbara 23; America, 1841 ***778.6*** *p303*
Schneider, Barbara Scherer 35 *SEE* Schneider, Johann Nikolaus
Schneider, Barbara 14; New York, NY, 1898 ***7951.13*** *p44*
Schneider, Barbe 25; America, 1840 ***778.6*** *p303*
Schneider, Carl Heinrich August; America, 1892 ***7420.1*** *p367*
Schneider, Charlotte 37; America, 1840 ***778.6*** *p303*
Schneider, Charlotte 25; Missouri, 1845 ***778.6*** *p303*
Schneider, Chas. F.; Louisiana, 1874 ***4981.45*** *p134*
Schneider, Christ. 14; America, 1840 ***778.6*** *p303*
Schneider, Christian; America, 1847 ***5475.1*** *p451*
Schneider, Christian; America, 1850 ***5475.1*** *p29*
Schneider, Christian; America, 1883 ***179.55*** *p19*
Schneider, Christian; Louisiana, 1836-1841 ***4981.45*** *p209*
Schneider, Christian 1; Missouri, 1845 ***778.6*** *p303*
Schneider, Christian Wilhelm 9 *SEE* Schneider, Georg
Schneider, Christina Bousonville 34 *SEE* Schneider, Karl Ludwig
Schneider, Christina; Halifax, N.S., 1902 ***1860.4*** *p39*
Schneider, Christina Scheer *SEE* Schneider, John G.
Schneider, Christine; America, 1841 ***5475.1*** *p56*
Schneider, Christine 26; America, 1865 ***5475.1*** *p152*
Schneider, Conrad 12 *SEE* Schneider, Georg
Schneider, Dieker; America, n.d. ***8023.44*** *p379*
With family
Schneider, Eduard *SEE* Schneider, Katharina Schmidt
Schneider, Eduard 32; Galveston, TX, 1844 ***3967.10*** *p370*
Schneider, Edward 26; New York, NY, 1893 ***1883.7*** *p39*
Schneider, Elisabeth; America, 1865 ***5475.1*** *p509*
Schneider, Elisabeth 6 *SEE* Schneider, Georg
Schneider, Elisabeth 14 *SEE* Schneider, Abraham
Schneider, Elisabeth 26; America, 1746 ***778.6*** *p303*
Schneider, Elisabeth 27; America, 1846 ***778.6*** *p303*
Schneider, Elisabeth Heinrich 35 *SEE* Schneider, Ernst Karl
Schneider, Elisabeth 43; America, 1840 ***5475.1*** *p392*
Schneider, Elisabeth Jentes 47 *SEE* Schneider, Abraham
Schneider, Elisabeth Katharina; Indiana, 1882 ***5475.1*** *p191*
*Son:*Johann
*Daughter:*Maria
Schneider, Elisabeth Scholl; America, 1872 ***5475.1*** *p389*
*Daughter:*Katharina
Schneider, Elsie 20; Halifax, N.S., 1902 ***1860.4*** *p41*
Schneider, Em.; New York, 1859 ***358.56*** *p99*
Schneider, Ernst Karl 34; America, 1866 ***5475.1*** *p535*
*Wife:*Elisabeth Heinrich 35
*Daughter:*Karoline 8
Schneider, Eva 14; Halifax, N.S., 1902 ***1860.4*** *p41*
Schneider, Eva 47; Halifax, N.S., 1902 ***1860.4*** *p41*
Schneider, Eva 10; New York, NY, 1898 ***7951.13*** *p44*
Schneider, F. 51; New Orleans, 1834 ***1002.51*** *p113*
Schneider, Felix 7; Galveston, TX, 1844 ***3967.10*** *p371*
Schneider, Ferdinand 30; Halifax, N.S., 1902 ***1860.4*** *p39*
Schneider, Fidel; New Castle, DE, 1817-1818 ***90.20*** *p154*
Schneider, Francis; Philadelphia, 1854 ***8513.31*** *p425*
*Wife:*Anna Drauz
Schneider, Frank; Illinois, 1858-1861 ***6020.5*** *p133*
Schneider, Franz 2 *SEE* Schneider, Michael
Schneider, Franz 30; America, 1844 ***778.6*** *p303*
Schneider, Franz; Halifax, N.S., 1902 ***1860.4*** *p41*
Schneider, Franz 16; Missouri, 1848 ***778.6*** *p303*
Schneider, Franziska 4; Galveston, TX, 1844 ***3967.10*** *p371*
Schneider, Franziska 36; Galveston, TX, 1844 ***3967.10*** *p371*
Schneider, Frederick; Ohio, 1809-1852 ***4511.35*** *p47*
Schneider, Friedrich; America, 1883 ***5475.1*** *p61*
Schneider, Friedrich 26; America, 1866 ***5475.1*** *p521*
Schneider, Friedrich 36; New Castle, DE, 1817-1818 ***90.20*** *p153*
Schneider, Friedrich 34; Port uncertain, 1848 ***778.6*** *p303*

Schneider, Friedrich Heinrich; America, 1834 *5475.1* p516
With wife & child
Schneider, Fritz; Louisiana, 1874 *4981.45* p134
Schneider, Georg; America, 1836 *5475.1* p527
With wife
*Daughter:*Elisabeth
*Son:*Conrad
*Son:*Jakob
*Son:*Andreas
Schneider, Georg; America, 1866 *5475.1* p542
Schneider, Georg 17; America, 1887 *5475.1* p423
Schneider, Georg 25; America, 1883 *2526.43* p126
Schneider, Georg 40; America, 1864 *5475.1* p59
*Wife:*Marg. Anna Sartorius 32
*Son:*Nikolaus Wilhelm 3 months
*Son:*Konrad Christoph 3
*Son:*Christian Wilhelm 9
*Son:*Johann Heinrich 6
*Son:*Georg Martin 5
Schneider, Georg Ludwig; America, 1867 *2526.43* p126
Schneider, Georg Martin 5 *SEE* Schneider, Georg
Schneider, George 35; Kentucky, 1846 *778.6* p303
Schneider, George 1; Missouri, 1845 *778.6* p303
Schneider, Gottlieb; America, 1867 *7919.3* p533
Schneider, Gustav Adolf; America, 1892 *179.55* p19
Schneider, Heinr. Karl; America, 1847 *5475.1* p402
Schneider, Heinrich; America, 1836 *5475.1* p527
With wife
*Son:*Nikolaus
*Son:*Heinrich
*Daughter:*Katharina
Schneider, Heinrich 8 *SEE* Schneider, Heinrich
Schneider, Heinrich 8; Galveston, TX, 1845 *3967.10* p376
Schneider, Heinrich 18; Halifax, N.S., 1902 *1860.4* p39
Schneider, Heinrich 21; New York, NY, 1874 *6954.7* p39
Schneider, Helena; America, 1864 *5475.1* p264
Schneider, Henrich; North Carolina, 1852 *1088.45* p31
Schneider, Henry; Ohio, 1809-1852 *4511.35* p47
Schneider, Hermann; New York, NY, 1928 *8023.44* p379
*Brother:*K. Hugo
Schneider, Hermann; South America, 1923 *8023.44* p379
*Brother:*K. Hugo
Schneider, Ignatz 2; Halifax, N.S., 1902 *1860.4* p41
Schneider, Israel; Illinois, 1834-1900 *6020.5* p133
Schneider, Jacob 38; America, 1840 *778.6* p303
Schneider, Jacob; Colorado, 1889 *1029.59* p81
Schneider, Jacob; Colorado, 1889 *1029.59* p82
Schneider, Jakob; America, 1846 *6442.17* p65
*Wife:*Anna Peiffer
Schneider, Jakob; America, 1848 *5475.1* p532
Schneider, Jakob; America, 1866 *5475.1* p535
Schneider, Jakob 20 *SEE* Schneider, Georg
Schneider, Jakob 28; America, 1881 *5475.1* p491
Schneider, Jakob 31; America, 1849 *5475.1* p403
Schneider, Jakob 33; America, 1831 *2526.43* p219
With wife 18
With child 3 months
Schneider, Joh. Baptist *SEE* Schneider, Johann
Schneider, Johann; Akron, OH, 1882 *5475.1* p242
*Son:*Joh. Baptist
*Daughter:*Maria
Schneider, Johann; America, 1862-1899 *6442.17* p65
Schneider, Johann *SEE* Schneider, Peter
Schneider, Johann; America, 1882 *5475.1* p445
Schneider, Johann 18 *SEE* Schneider, Michael
Schneider, Johann 7; Halifax, N.S., 1902 *1860.4* p41
Schneider, Johann *SEE* Schneider, Elisabeth Katharina Hoen
Schneider, Johann Heinrich 6 *SEE* Schneider, Georg
Schneider, Johann Heinrich 44; Galveston, TX, 1845 *3967.10* p376
Schneider, Johann Jakob; America, 1852 *5475.1* p538
Schneider, Johann Jakob Peter; America, 1881 *5475.1* p460
Schneider, Johann Karl; America, 1883 *179.55* p19
Schneider, Johann Konrad; America, 1848 *5475.1* p532
Schneider, Johann Leonhard; America, 1887 *2526.43* p219
Schneider, Johann Nikolaus 41; America, 1843 *5475.1* p529
*Wife:*Barbara Scherer 35
Schneider, Johannes; America, 1853 *8115.12* p324
Schneider, Johannes 3; Halifax, N.S., 1902 *1860.4* p39
Schneider, John G.; Pennsylvania, 1858 *8513.31* p425
*Wife:*Christina Scheer
Schneider, John-Baptiste; New York, NY, 1834 *3274.55* p22
Schneider, Jonatz; Louisiana, 1874-1875 *4981.45* p31
Schneider, Jonatz; Louisiana, 1874-1875 *4981.45* p130

Schneider, Josef 5 *SEE* Schneider, Karl Ludwig
Schneider, Josef 3; Halifax, N.S., 1902 *1860.4* p41
Schneider, Joseph 29; America, 1840 *778.6* p303
Schneider, Joseph 46; New York, NY, 1898 *7951.13* p44
Schneider, Josephine; America, 1865-1900 *5475.1* p46
Schneider, Josephine 17; Galveston, TX, 1844 *3967.10* p371
Schneider, Jula 15; Halifax, N.S., 1902 *1860.4* p39
Schneider, Julia; Halifax, N.S., 1902 *1860.4* p39
Schneider, Julia 9; Halifax, N.S., 1902 *1860.4* p41
Schneider, K. Hugo *SEE* Schneider, Hermann
Schneider, K. Hugo *SEE* Schneider, Hermann
Schneider, Karl; America, 1858 *5475.1* p541
Schneider, Karl; America, 1883 *179.55* p19
Schneider, Karl 5 *SEE* Schneider, Abraham
Schneider, Karl; Scranton, PA, 1889 *5475.1* p18
Schneider, Karl Albert 17; America, 1859 *5475.1* p30
Schneider, Karl Ludwig 34; America, 1854 *5475.1* p64
*Wife:*Christina Bousonville 34
With stepchild 13
*Son:*Josef 5
*Son:*Ludwig 2
Schneider, Karoline; America, 1866 *5475.1* p542
Schneider, Karoline 8 *SEE* Schneider, Ernst Karl
Schneider, Karoline 25; America, 1857 *5475.1* p496
Schneider, Karoline 17; Halifax, N.S., 1902 *1860.4* p39
Schneider, Kaspar; America, n.d. *8023.44* p379
Schneider, Kaspar Fried.; America, 1874 *8023.44* p379
*Wife:*Anna Wurm
With child
Schneider, Kath.; America, 1881 *5475.1* p494
Schneider, Katha 11; Halifax, N.S., 1902 *1860.4* p41
Schneider, Katharina 6 *SEE* Schneider, Michael
Schneider, Katharina 7 *SEE* Schneider, Abraham
Schneider, Katharina 9 *SEE* Schneider, Heinrich
Schneider, Katharina 14 *SEE* Schneider, Elisabeth Scholl
Schneider, Katharina 55; America, 1867 *5475.1* p152
*Son:*Eduard
Schneider, Katherina 4; Halifax, N.S., 1902 *1860.4* p39
Schneider, Katherina 5; New York, NY, 1898 *7951.13* p44
Schneider, Konrad; America, 1836 *5475.1* p527
With wife & 6 children
Schneider, Konrad; America, 1849 *5475.1* p514
Schneider, Konrad Christoph 3 *SEE* Schneider, Georg
Schneider, Kristian; Halifax, N.S., 1902 *1860.4* p39
Schneider, Leonard; Ohio, 1809-1852 *4511.35* p47
Schneider, Lorence 1; New York, NY, 1898 *7951.13* p44
Schneider, Louis 6 months; America, 1746 *778.6* p303
Schneider, Louis Vincant; Washington, 1887 *2770.40* p25
Schneider, Louise 34; Galveston, TX, 1844 *3967.10* p370
Schneider, Ludwig; America, 1853 *2526.43* p129
Schneider, Ludwig 2 *SEE* Schneider, Karl Ludwig
Schneider, Ludwig 27; America, 1872 *5475.1* p72
Schneider, Ludwig; Illinois, 1891 *5475.1* p218
Schneider, Magdalena 44; New York, NY, 1898 *7951.13* p44
Schneider, Marg. Anna Sartorius 32 *SEE* Schneider, Georg
Schneider, Margaretha Maier *SEE* Schneider, Martin
Schneider, Margaretha; America, 1881 *2526.43* p126
Schneider, Margaretha 48; America, 1855 *2526.43* p166
Schneider, Margaretha; Pennsylvania, 1855 *2526.43* p200
Schneider, Margarethe; America, 1857 *5475.1* p556
Schneider, Margarethe 20; America, 1836 *5475.1* p536
Schneider, Margarethe; Brazil, 1863 *5475.1* p550
Schneider, Marguerite 2; America, 1840 *778.6* p304
Schneider, Marguerite 34; America, 1840 *778.6* p303
Schneider, Marguerite 38; Missouri, 1845 *778.6* p303
Schneider, Maria *SEE* Schneider, Johann
Schneider, Maria Peiffer *SEE* Schneider, Peter
Schneider, Maria; America, 1892 *5475.1* p79
Schneider, Maria 30; America, 1864 *5475.1* p338
Schneider, Maria 27; Halifax, N.S., 1902 *1860.4* p39
Schneider, Maria *SEE* Schneider, Elisabeth Katharina Hoen
Schneider, Maria Elizabeth 2 months; America, 1846 *778.6* p304
Schneider, Maria Katharina 5; Galveston, TX, 1845 *3967.10* p376
Schneider, Maria Katharina 42; Galveston, TX, 1845 *3967.10* p376
Schneider, Marianne 6; America, 1746 *778.6* p304
Schneider, Marianne 34; Galveston, TX, 1844 *3967.10* p371
Schneider, Martin; America, 1846 *6442.17* p65
*Wife:*Margaretha Maier
Schneider, Marton 17; Halifax, N.S., 1902 *1860.4* p41
Schneider, Marton 51; Halifax, N.S., 1902 *1860.4* p41

Schneider, Mathias; Brazil, 1846 *5475.1* p438
*Wife:*Anna Maria Scherer
With 2 children
Schneider, Matthieu 23; New Castle, DE, 1817-1818 *90.20* p153
Schneider, Michael 20 *SEE* Schneider, Michael
Schneider, Michael 43; America, 1872 *5475.1* p446
*Wife:*Angela Backes 41
*Son:*Franz 2
*Son:*Johann 18
*Son:*Anton 13
*Daughter:*Barbara 10
*Daughter:*Katharina 6
*Daughter:*Susanna 15
*Son:*Michael 20
Schneider, Michel 25; America, 1846 *778.6* p304
Schneider, Michel; Brazil, 1857 *5475.1* p441
Schneider, Nicolas 23; America, 1841 *778.6* p304
Schneider, Nicolas 24; Port uncertain, 1843 *778.6* p304
Schneider, Nikolaus; America, 1857 *5475.1* p321
Schneider, Nikolaus *SEE* Schneider, Peter
Schneider, Nikolaus 5 *SEE* Schneider, Heinrich
Schneider, Nikolaus 25; America, 1855 *5475.1* p318
Schneider, Nikolaus Wilhelm 3 *SEE* Schneider, Georg
Schneider, Peter; America, 1846 *6442.17* p65
*Wife:*Maria Peiffer
Schneider, Peter; America, 1873 *5475.1* p249
*Wife:*Anna Maria Franz
*Son:*Johann
*Son:*Nikolaus
Schneider, Peter; America, 1881 *5475.1* p511
Schneider, Peter; America, 1889 *2526.43* p219
Schneider, Peter 12 *SEE* Schneider, Abraham
Schneider, Peter 44; Brazil, 1863 *5475.1* p550
Schneider, Peter; Ohio, 1809-1852 *4511.35* p47
Schneider, Peter; Pennsylvania, 1885 *5475.1* p364
Schneider, Philip; Ohio, 1809-1852 *4511.35* p47
Schneider, Philipp 48; Galveston, TX, 1844 *3967.10* p375
Schneider, Philipp; New York, 1892 *2526.42* p130
Schneider, Pier.e 27; New York, 1846 *778.6* p304
Schneider, Pierre 2; Missouri, 1845 *778.6* p304
Schneider, Pierre 38; Missouri, 1845 *778.6* p304
Schneider, Regina 17; New York, NY, 1898 *7951.13* p44
Schneider, Rosaline 5; Galveston, TX, 1844 *3967.10* p371
Schneider, Rosina 20; Galveston, TX, 1844 *3967.10* p370
Schneider, Rosina 16; New York, NY, 1898 *7951.13* p44
Schneider, Rubart; Ohio, 1809-1852 *4511.35* p47
Schneider, Salmea 40; Kentucky, 1846 *778.6* p304
Schneider, Sophia; America, 1853 *2526.43* p129
With daughter 14
Schneider, Sophia 23; America, 1843 *5475.1* p529
Schneider, Sophia 32; America, 1843 *5475.1* p529
Schneider, Stefan 19; Halifax, N.S., 1902 *1860.4* p41
Schneider, Susanna 15 *SEE* Schneider, Michael
Schneider, Teiche 17; Galveston, TX, 1845 *3967.10* p376
Schneider, Theodore 36; Port uncertain, 1846 *778.6* p304
Schneider, Ulrich; Ohio, 1809-1852 *4511.35* p47
Schneider, V. 28; New Orleans, 1834 *1002.51* p113
Schneider, Valentin; America, 1848 *5475.1* p532
Schneider, Valentine; Ohio, 1809-1852 *4511.35* p47
Schneider, Veronica; New York, 1860 *358.56* p150
Schneider, Wendelin 25; America, 1847 *778.6* p304
Schneider, Wilhelm; America, 1867 *7420.1* p264
Schneider, Wilhelm 20; New York, 1854 *5475.1* p235
Schneider, Wilhelmine Charlotte; America, 1846 *7420.1* p48
Schneider Georg, Mr. 18; America, 1746 *778.6* p303
Schneider-Jost, Adam 15 *SEE* Schneider-Jost, Mathias
Schneider-Jost, Anna 9 *SEE* Schneider-Jost, Mathias
Schneider-Jost, Maria Klein *SEE* Schneider-Jost, Mathias
Schneider-Jost, Mathias; South America, 1856 *5475.1* p492
*Wife:*Maria Klein
*Son:*Peter
*Son:*Mathias
*Daughter:*Anna
*Son:*Adam
Schneider-Jost, Mathias 6 *SEE* Schneider-Jost, Mathias
Schneider-Jost, Peter 8 *SEE* Schneider-Jost, Mathias
Schneikart, J.; Louisiana, 1874 *4981.45* p297
Schnell, Johann; Wisconsin, 1884 *6795.8* p205
Schnellbacher, Adam; America, 1881 *2526.42* p131
Schnellbacher, Anton; America, 1881 *2526.43* p143
Schnellbacher, Elisabeth 7 *SEE* Schnellbacher, Margaretha Saul
Schnellbacher, Elisabetha Laudenberger *SEE* Schnellbacher, Johannes

Schnellbacher, Eva 9 *SEE* Schnellbacher, Margaretha Elisabetha Saul
Schnellbacher, Eva Margaretha 18; America, 1866 *2526.42 p146*
Schnellbacher, Franz; America, 1848 *2526.42 p146*
  With wife
  *Child:*Peter
  *Child:*Wilhelm
Schnellbacher, Georg; Illinois, 1880 *2526.43 p180*
Schnellbacher, Heinrich; America, 1892 *2526.43 p204*
Schnellbacher, Heinrich 1 *SEE* Schnellbacher, Margaretha Elisabetha Saul
Schnellbacher, Johann Adam; America, 1785 *2526.42 p131*
  *Wife:*Maria Elisabetha Orth
  With 5 children
Schnellbacher, Johannes; America, 1754 *2526.43 p214*
  *Wife:*Elisabetha Laudenberger
  With 5 children
Schnellbacher, Margaretha Elisabetha; America, 1854 *2526.42 p131*
  *Child:*Eva
  *Child:*Heinrich
  *Child:*Elisabeth
Schnellbacher, Maria Elisabetha; America, 1753 *2526.42 p143*
Schnellbacher, Maria Elisabetha Orth *SEE* Schnellbacher, Johann Adam
Schnellbacher, Peter 2 *SEE* Schnellbacher, Franz
Schnellbacher, Philipp, III; America, 1837 *2526.42 p106*
  With wife & 2 children
Schnellbacher, Wilhelm; America, 1887 *2526.43 p204*
Schnellbacher, Wilhelm 7 *SEE* Schnellbacher, Franz
Schnelle, Johann Conrad; Port uncertain, 1850 *7420.1 p75*
Schneller, Michael Karl; America, 1889 *2526.43 p156*
Schnerring, Sophie 27; America, 1863 *5475.1 p72*
Schnider, Adam 21; Halifax, N.S., 1902 *1860.4 p42*
Schnider, Antoin 26; New York, NY, 1847 *9176.15 p51*
Schnider, Jacob; Colorado, 1893 *1029.59 p82*
Schninder, Frederic 23; Missouri, 1845 *778.6 p304*
Schnitz, John; Ohio, 1809-1852 *4511.35 p47*
Schnobelen, Joseph; Ohio, 1809-1852 *4511.35 p47*
Schnoebalen, Joseph; Ohio, 1809-1852 *4511.35 p47*
Schnor, Friedrich 17; Portland, ME, 1911 *970.38 p81*
Schnubel, Eva; Chicago, 1887 *5475.1 p269*
Schnubel, Johann; Illinois, 1887 *5475.1 p269*
Schnur, August; America, 1889 *2526.43 p180*
Schnur, Jakob; America, 1880 *5475.1 p428*
Schnur, Johann 35; America, 1857 *5475.1 p492*
Schnur, Julius Louis; America, 1873 *7420.1 p397*
Schnur, Mathias 23; America, 1856 *5475.1 p516*
Schnur, Michel; America, 1881 *5475.1 p494*
Schnur, Peter; Arkansas, 1884 *5475.1 p494*
Schnurle, Joseph; Venezuela, 1843 *3899.5 p545*
Schnurlein, Wilhelm; America, 1842 *5475.1 p28*
Schobe, Joseph; Baltimore, 1882 *1029.59 p82*
Schober, Carl; America, 1867 *7919.3 p531*
Schober, Michael; America, 1885 *179.55 p19*
Schobitz, Gottlieb; Valdivia, Chile, 1850 *1192.4 p50*
  With wife & 3 children
  With child 22
  With child 7
Schoch, Caroline; New York, 1859 *358.56 p54*
Schoch, Julius; America, 1891 *179.55 p19*
Schock, Adam 22; New York, NY, 1893 *1883.7 p37*
Schock, Catharina 28; New York, NY, 1893 *1883.7 p40*
Schock, Elisabeth 22; New York, NY, 1893 *1883.7 p37*
Schock, George; Ohio, 1840-1897 *8365.35 p18*
Schock, Gottfried; America, 1888 *179.55 p19*
Schock, Johann 3; New York, NY, 1893 *1883.7 p40*
Schock, Johann 4 months; New York, NY, 1893 *1883.7 p37*
Schock, Josef 2; New York, NY, 1893 *1883.7 p40*
Schock, Josef 32; New York, NY, 1893 *1883.7 p40*
Schock, Ludwig 1 months; New York, NY, 1893 *1883.7 p40*
Schock, Marianna 7; New York, NY, 1893 *1883.7 p40*
Schock, Sebastian 32; America, 1847 *778.6 p304*
Schodowski, Matthew; Detroit, 1890 *9980.23 p97*
Schoech, Joseph G.; Colorado, 1897 *1029.59 p82*
Schoeck, Johann Adam 34; Pennsylvania, 1851 *170.15 p41*
  With family
Schoeck, Johannes 20; Pennsylvania, 1866 *170.15 p41*
  With family
Schoeff, Henry; Louisiana, 1836-1841 *4981.45 p209*
Schoellhammer, Theodor 40; New Orleans, 1848 *778.6 p304*
Schoenbeck, Johann Heinrich Conrad; America, 1860 *7420.1 p199*
Schoeneger, Peter; America, 1882 *5475.1 p59*
Schoeneck, Gustav; Wisconsin, 1897 *6795.8 p196*

Schoenfeld, Adolf; Wisconsin, 1898 *6795.8 p124*
Schoenfeld, Ester 20; New York, NY, 1893 *1883.7 p47*
Schoenthaler, Gotlieb 21; Louisiana, 1848 *778.6 p304*
Schoepp, Dorothea *SEE* Schoepp, Nikolaus
Schoepp, Karl *SEE* Schoepp, Nikolaus
Schoepp, Karoline *SEE* Schoepp, Nikolaus
Schoepp, Katharina *SEE* Schoepp, Nikolaus
Schoepp, Margarethe Kiefer *SEE* Schoepp, Nikolaus
Schoepp, Nikolaus *SEE* Schoepp, Nikolaus
Schoepp, Nikolaus; America, 1881 *5475.1 p48*
  *Wife:*Margarethe Kiefer
  *Daughter:*Dorothea
  *Son:*Nikolaus
  *Daughter:*Karoline
  *Daughter:*Katharina
  *Son:*Karl
Schoevaer, Joseph 18; New York, NY, 1856 *1766.1 p45*
Schoff, H.; New York, 1859 *358.56 p99*
Schoff, Nicolas 21; America, 1847 *778.6 p304*
Schofield, George 46; Michigan, 1880 *4491.39 p27*
Schofield, George 70; Michigan, 1880 *4491.39 p27*
Schofield, George H. 19; New York, NY, 1894 *6512.1 p183*
Schofield, Hannah 73; Michigan, 1880 *4491.39 p27*
Schofield, Jacob; North Carolina, 1844 *1088.45 p31*
Schofield, Martha J. 38; Michigan, 1880 *4491.39 p27*
Schoicher, Egidius; America, 1842 *2526.42 p196*
  With wife
  With child 10
  With child 6 months
  With child 12
  With child 17
  With child 15
Schoicher, Franz; America, 1844 *2526.42 p196*
  With wife
Schoicher, Michael 31; America, 1844 *2526.42 p196*
Schol, Henri 40; New Orleans, 1848 *778.6 p304*
Scholar, Michael; Ohio, 1836 *3580.20 p33*
Scholar, Michael; Ohio, 1836 *6020.12 p22*
Scholar, William; America, 1769 *1220.12 p705*
Scholcroft, James; America, 1751 *1220.12 p705*
Schold, Jacob; Washington, 1889 *2770.40 p81*
Scholder, C. H.; Ohio, 1809-1852 *4511.35 p47*
Scholder, John; Ohio, 1809-1852 *4511.35 p47*
Scholdt, Peter 35; New York, NY, 1885 *1883.7 p46*
Scholem, Markus; America, 1867 *5475.1 p561*
Scholer, Peter; America, 1888 *5475.1 p287*
Scholes, Daniel; America, 1749 *1220.12 p705*
Scholes, John; America, 1746 *1220.12 p705*
Scholfield, Thomas; America, 1750 *1220.12 p705*
Scholl, Anna 5 *SEE* Scholl, Michel
Scholl, Anna Finkler *SEE* Scholl, Michel
Scholl, Anna; Texas, 1899 *5475.1 p426*
Scholl, Anna Maria *SEE* Scholl, Michel
Scholl, Anton 25; America, 1863 *5475.1 p270*
Scholl, Barbara *SEE* Scholl, Michel
Scholl, Elisabeth 7 *SEE* Scholl, Michel
Scholl, Elisabeth Lauck 31 *SEE* Scholl, Michel
Scholl, Eva Katharina; America, 1785 *2526.42 p126*
Scholl, Friedrich 21; New York, NY, 1874 *6954.7 p38*
Scholl, Jakob; America, 1872 *5475.1 p186*
  *Wife:*Katharina Philippi
  *Daughter:*Katharina
  *Daughter:*Margarethe
  *Daughter:*Maria
  *Son:*Michel
Scholl, Jakob 10 *SEE* Scholl, Michel
Scholl, Johann; America, 1872 *5475.1 p271*
Scholl, Katharina *SEE* Scholl, Jakob
Scholl, Katharina Philippi *SEE* Scholl, Jakob
Scholl, Ludwig; America, 1882 *2526.43 p200*
Scholl, Margarethe *SEE* Scholl, Jakob
Scholl, Maria *SEE* Scholl, Jakob
Scholl, Michel *SEE* Scholl, Jakob
Scholl, Michel; America, 1872 *5475.1 p389*
  *Wife:*Elisabeth Lauck
  With sister & niece
  *Daughter:*Anna
  *Son:*Jakob
  *Daughter:*Elisabeth
Scholl, Michel *SEE* Scholl, Michel
Scholl, Michel; Brazil, 1881 *5475.1 p390*
  *Wife:*Anna Finkler
  *Son:*Michel
  *Daughter:*Anna Maria
  *Daughter:*Barbara
Scholl, Nikolaus; America, 1880 *5475.1 p390*
Scholl von Hochst, Anna Margaretha; America, 1773 *2526.42 p140*
Scholofsky, Esther; Detroit, 1930 *1640.60 p77*
Scholtz, Edward; South Carolina, 1878 *6155.4 p19*
Scholvien, L. Ernst; New York, 1859 *358.56 p99*
Scholwienski, Franz; Texas, 1892-1900 *6015.15 p11*

Scholwinski, Frank; Texas, 1892-1900 *6015.15 p11*
Scholzel, Herman 33; Indiana, 1887-1894 *9076.20 p73*
Schomacher, Marie 21; Port uncertain, 1846 *778.6 p304*
Schomaker, Johan Heinrich; Kansas, 1917-1918 *2094.25 p50*
Schommer, Anna 14 *SEE* Schommer, Nikolaus
Schommer, Anna Maria 16 *SEE* Schommer, Nikolaus
Schommer, Barbara 52; America, 1874 *5475.1 p254*
Schommer, Barbara; Chicago, 1880 *5475.1 p373*
Schommer, Barbara; Chicago, 1887 *5475.1 p244*
  *Son:*Mathias
Schommer, Elisabeth 19 *SEE* Schommer, Nikolaus
Schommer, Jakob 60; America, 1843 *5475.1 p347*
Schommer, Margarethe Herzberger 46 *SEE* Schommer, Nikolaus
Schommer, Maria 21 *SEE* Schommer, Maria Dewes
Schommer, Maria 56; America, 1856 *5475.1 p358*
  *Child:*Susanna 23
  *Child:*Maria 21
Schommer, Mathias *SEE* Schommer, Barbara Palz
Schommer, Nikolaus 49; America, 1855 *5475.1 p318*
  *Wife:*Margarethe Herzberger 46
  *Daughter:*Anna Maria 16
  *Daughter:*Anna 14
  *Daughter:*Elisabeth 19
Schommer, Susanna 23 *SEE* Schommer, Maria Dewes
Schon, Anna; America, 1840-1899 *6442.17 p65*
Schon, Gottlieb; America, 1860 *179.55 p19*
Schon, Johann; America, 1882 *179.55 p19*
Schon, Nikolaus; America, 1882 *5475.1 p228*
Schonach, Anna 30; America, 1861 *5475.1 p337*
Schonard, Georg; Louisiana, 1869 *5475.1 p460*
Schonart, Therese; Illinois, 1880 *5475.1 p373*
Schonarth, Johann; America, 1857 *5475.1 p367*
Schonarth, Margarethe 25; America, 1800-1899 *5475.1 p367*
  *Brother:*Peter 11
Schonarth, Peter 11 *SEE* Schonarth, Margarethe
Schonau, Lorentz 28; New Jersey, 1754-1774 *927.31 p2*
Schonbachler, Meinrod; Ohio, 1809-1852 *4511.35 p47*
Schonbeck, Mr.; America, 1854 *7420.1 p129*
Schonbeck, Caroline; Port uncertain, 1884 *7420.1 p345*
Schonbeck, Catharine Engel Sophie *SEE* Schonbeck, Johann Conrad
Schonbeck, Engel Marie Philippine; America, 1862 *7420.1 p211*
Schonbeck, Johann Conrad; America, 1868 *7420.1 p276*
  *Daughter:*Catharine Engel Sophie
  With wife
Schonberger, A. Ludwig *SEE* Schonberger, Nik.
Schonberger, Apollonie List; America, 1785 *2526.43 p180*
Schonberger, Elisabeth; America, 1880 *5475.1 p386*
Schonberger, Katharina Dolibois *SEE* Schonberger, Nik.
Schonberger, Maria *SEE* Schonberger, Nik.
Schonberger, Nik.; America, 1881 *5475.1 p136*
  *Wife:*Katharina Dolibois
  *Son:*A. Ludwig
  *Son:*Peter
  *Daughter:*Maria
Schonberger, Peter *SEE* Schonberger, Nik.
Schonberger, Peter; America, 1882 *5475.1 p210*
Schonberger, Peter 22; America, 1866 *5475.1 p169*
Schondel, John; Ohio, 1809-1852 *4511.35 p47*
Schondner, Martin; America, 1838 *170.15 p41*
Schone, Louise; America, 1864 *7420.1 p228*
Schonebeck, Johann Friedrich Christian; America, 1857 *7420.1 p171*
Schonebeck, Johann Heinrich Conrad; America, 1867 *7420.1 p264*
Schoneberg, Friedrich 14; New York, NY, 1864 *8425.62 p196*
Schoneberg, Johanne 50; New York, NY, 1864 *8425.62 p196*
Schoneberg, Louise 20; New York, NY, 1864 *8425.62 p196*
Schonemann, August; America, 1854 *7420.1 p129*
Schonemann, Carl Christian Friedrich; America, 1888 *7420.1 p357*
  With sister
Schonemann, Christian Wilhelm; Port uncertain, 1851 *7420.1 p82*
  *Wife:*Engel Philippine Lohmann
Schonemann, Engel Philippine Lohmann *SEE* Schonemann, Christian Wilhelm
Schonemann, Wilhelmine; America, 1852 *7420.1 p97*
Schonenberger, Mr. 19; America, 1847 *778.6 p304*
Schonenberger, Jakob; America, 1867 *5475.1 p548*
Schonenberger, Johann; America, 1846 *5475.1 p514*
Schonenberger, Johann 25; New York, 1872 *5475.1 p514*
Schonenberger, Johann 31; New York, 1872 *5475.1 p548*

Schonenberger, Wilhelm; America, 1846 *5475.1 p514*
Schonewolf, Carl Heinrich Friedrich; America, 1866 *7420.1 p249*
Schonewolf, John Bernard; North Carolina, 1710 *3629.40 p6*
Schonewolf, Marie Louise 22; Valdivia, Chile, 1852 *1192.4 p53*
Schonfeld, Mr.; America, 1854 *7420.1 p129*
Schonfeld, Abraham 44; New York, NY, 1878 *9253.2 p45*
Schonfeld, Carl; Port uncertain, 1865 *7420.1 p237*
Schonfeld, Moses; America, 1899 *7420.1 p375*
Schong, Christian; Ohio, 1809-1852 *4511.35 p47*
Schonger, Johann 30; Ohio, 1847 *778.6 p304*
Schonheit, Caroline; America, 1868 *7919.3 p531*
Schonherr, Friedrich Reinhold; America, 1867 *7919.3 p529*
Schonherr, Gotthelf Ernst; America, 1867 *7919.3 p529*
Schonherr, Gustav Adolf; America, 1868 *7919.3 p529*
Schonhofen, Johann; Brazil, 1881 *5475.1 p374*
  *Wife:*Katharina Klauck
  *Daughter:*Theres
  *Daughter:*Katharina
Schonhofen, Katharina *SEE* Schonhofen, Johann
Schonhofen, Katharina Klauck *SEE* Schonhofen, Johann
Schonhofen, Theres *SEE* Schonhofen, Johann
Schoning, Ernest; Iowa, 1897 *1211.15 p19*
Schonke, Anna Sophia; Wisconsin, 1868 *6795.8 p103*
Schonrock, John Gottlieb; Wisconsin, 1873 *6795.8 p119*
Schons, Anna; America, 1885 *5475.1 p318*
School, Jacob; Galveston, TX, 1855 *571.7 p17*
Schoor, Johann 53; America, 1858 *5475.1 p501*
  *Wife:*Katharina Hahsdenteufel 42
  *Daughter:*Katharina 17
  *Daughter:*Margarethe 15
  *Son:*Peter 21
Schoor, Katharina 17 *SEE* Schoor, Johann
Schoor, Katharina Hahsdenteufel 42 *SEE* Schoor, Johann
Schoor, Margarethe 15 *SEE* Schoor, Johann
Schoor, Peter 21 *SEE* Schoor, Johann
Schoorman, Otto; Iowa, 1914 *1211.15 p19*
Schopfer, Eduard; America, 1880 *5475.1 p380*
Schorch, Joseph G.; Colorado, 1891 *1029.59 p82*
Schorlitz, Friedrich; America, 1867 *7919.3 p534*
Schormer, Charles 35; Port uncertain, 1842 *778.6 p304*
Schormer, Charles 47; Port uncertain, 1842 *778.6 p304*
Schornack, George Fredrich; Wisconsin, 1888 *6795.8 p216*
Schornig, Friedrich Albert; America, 1868 *7919.3 p532*
Schorobien, Rudolphe 29; Missouri, 1845 *778.6 p304*
Schorp, Joseph 30; Galveston, TX, 1844 *3967.10 p372*
Schorr, Andreas 22 *SEE* Schorr, Christian
Schorr, Barbara 10 *SEE* Schorr, Mathias
Schorr, Barbara Weiland 48 *SEE* Schorr, Mathias
Schorr, Christian; America, 1834 *5475.1 p462*
  With 2 brothers
Schorr, Christian; America, 1837 *5475.1 p395*
Schorr, Christian 24; America, 1834 *5475.1 p394*
  *Brother:*Andreas 22
  *Brother:*Mathias 17
Schorr, Georg 15 *SEE* Schorr, Mathias
Schorr, J.; Brazil, 1857 *5475.1 p441*
  With wife & 4 children
Schorr, Jakob; America, 1882 *5475.1 p436*
  *Wife:*Kath. Gierend
  *Daughter:*Katharina
  *Daughter:*Maria
Schorr, Johann 12 *SEE* Schorr, Mathias
Schorr, Johann Nikolaus; America, 1846 *5475.1 p392*
Schorr, Josef 4 *SEE* Schorr, Mathias
Schorr, Kath. Gierend *SEE* Schorr, Jakob
Schorr, Katharina *SEE* Schorr, Jakob
Schorr, Katharina 8 *SEE* Schorr, Mathias
Schorr, Katharina 16 *SEE* Schorr, Mathias
Schorr, Katharina 60; America, 1800-1899 *5475.1 p558*
Schorr, Margarethe; America, 1883 *5475.1 p60*
Schorr, Margarethe 23 *SEE* Schorr, Mathias
Schorr, Maria *SEE* Schorr, Jakob
Schorr, Mathias; America, 1837 *5475.1 p395*
Schorr, Mathias 17 *SEE* Schorr, Christian
Schorr, Mathias 55; America, 1833 *5475.1 p394*
  *Wife:*Barbara Weiland 48
  *Daughter:*Barbara 10
  *Daughter:*Katharina 8
  *Son:*Josef 4
  *Daughter:*Sophie 8
  *Son:*Johann 12
  *Daughter:*Margarethe 23
  *Daughter:*Katharina 16
  *Son:*Georg 15
  With stepchild 25
Schorr, Sophie 8 *SEE* Schorr, Mathias
Schortau, Catharine Engel *SEE* Schortau, Hans Heinrich

Schortau, Engel Marie Dorothea Desenisse *SEE* Schortau, Hans Heinrich
Schortau, Engel Sophie Dorothea *SEE* Schortau, Hans Heinrich
Schortau, Hans Heinrich; America, 1882 *7420.1 p332*
  *Wife:*Engel Marie Dorothea Desenisse
  *Daughter:*Catharine Engel
  *Daughter:*Engel Sophie Dorothea
  *Son:*Hans Heinrich Wilhelm
Schortau, Hans Heinrich Wilhelm *SEE* Schortau, Hans Heinrich
Schoschneck, Luise; Wisconsin, 1883 *6795.8 p62*
Schossel, J. B. 20; Missouri, 1845 *778.6 p304*
Schott, Anton 30; Missouri, 1847 *778.6 p304*
Schott, Carl Hansen; Iowa, 1890 *1211.15 p19*
Schott, Elisabeth 8; America, 1846 *778.6 p304*
Schott, Joseph 14; America, 1846 *778.6 p304*
Schott, Louis 41; America, 1846 *778.6 p304*
Schott, Marie 1; America, 1846 *778.6 p304*
Schott, Marie 42; America, 1846 *778.6 p304*
Schott, Mathis 3; America, 1846 *778.6 p304*
Schott, Michael; America, 1885 *170.15 p41*
  With wife & 2 children
Schott, Rosina 7; America, 1846 *778.6 p305*
Schott, William; New York, 1860 *358.56 p4*
Schotte, . . .; America, 1846 *7420.1 p48*
Schotte, Mr.; America, 1853 *7420.1 p111*
  With family
Schotte, Jose 29; Port uncertain, 1841 *778.6 p305*
Schottelndreier, Widow; America, 1868 *7420.1 p276*
  With 3 children
Schottelndreyer, Mr.; America, 1845 *7420.1 p40*
Schottelndreyer, Ernestine Wilhelmine Caroline; America, 1847 *7420.1 p53*
Schottes, Johannes; America, 1925 *8023.44 p379*
Schottes, Maria; America, 1923 *8023.44 p379*
Schottmuller, Peter 30; America, 1840 *778.6 p305*
Schouller, E. 34; Port uncertain, 1846 *778.6 p305*
Schovegge, H. W. 9; New York, NY, 1864 *8425.62 p197*
Schovegge, H. W. 59; New York, NY, 1864 *8425.62 p197*
Schovell, Philip; Maryland or Virginia, 1738 *1220.12 p721*
Schrade, John; New York, 1860 *358.56 p148*
Schrade, Wilhelmina; Dakota, 1898-1918 *554.30 p26*
Schrader, Widow; America, 1856 *7420.1 p153*
  With 2 sons
Schrader, Caroline Sophia Louise; America, 1857 *7420.1 p161*
Schrader, Eduard; Port uncertain, 1845 *7420.1 p40*
Schrader, Eduard Friedrich; America, 1854 *7420.1 p129*
Schrader, Franz Wilhelm Eduard; America, 1859 *7420.1 p188*
Schrader, Friedrich Christian Sch. *SEE* Schrader, Friedrich Wilhelm
Schrader, Friedrich Wilhelm; America, 1854 *7420.1 p129*
  *Son:*Friedrich Christian Sch.
Schrader, Gustav; Galveston, TX, 1855 *571.7 p17*
Schrader, Hans Heinrich; America, 1852 *7420.1 p97*
  With family
Schrader, Heinrich; America, 1852 *7420.1 p97*
  With family
Schrader, Wilhelm; America, 1854 *7420.1 p129*
Schrader Family ; America, 1855 *7420.1 p141*
Schrage, . . .; America, 1847 *7420.1 p56*
  With wife
  With child 4
  With child 7
Schrage, Catharine Marie Charlotte; America, 1846 *7420.1 p51*
Schrage, Engel Marie Doroth. *SEE* Schrage, Johann Philipp
Schrage, Engel Marie Sophie *SEE* Schrage, Johann Philipp
Schrage, Engel Marie Sophie Wille *SEE* Schrage, Johann Philipp
Schrage, Engel Soph. *SEE* Schrage, Johann Philipp
Schrage, Hans Heinr. *SEE* Schrage, Johann Philipp
Schrage, Heinrich Wilhelm *SEE* Schrage, Wilhelm
Schrage, Johann Heinr. Phil. *SEE* Schrage, Johann Philipp
Schrage, Johann Heinrich Christoph; America, 1854 *7420.1 p129*
  *Wife:*Justine Friederike Pieper
  *Daughter:*Sophie Dorothee Friederike
Schrage, Johann Heinrich Wilhelm *SEE* Schrage, Wilhelm
Schrage, Johann Philipp; America, 1857 *7420.1 p171*
  *Wife:*Engel Marie Sophie Wille
  *Daughter:*Engel Marie Sophie
  *Daughter:*Thrine Sophie Doroth.
  *Son:*Johann Heinr. Phil.

  *Daughter:*Engel Marie Doroth.
  *Son:*Hans Heinr.
  *Daughter:*Engel Soph.
Schrage, Justine Friederike Pieper *SEE* Schrage, Johann Heinrich Christoph
Schrage, Ludwig Friedrich Wilhelm *SEE* Schrage, Wilhelm
Schrage, Sophie Dorothee Friederike *SEE* Schrage, Johann Heinrich Christoph
Schrage, Thrine Sophie Doroth. *SEE* Schrage, Johann Philipp
Schrage, Wilhelm; America, 1871 *7420.1 p292*
  *Son:*Johann Heinrich Wilhelm
  *Son:*Ludwig Friedrich Wilhelm
  *Son:*Heinrich Wilhelm
Schraid, Philipp; Pennsylvania, 1854 *170.15 p41*
  With wife & 5 children
Schram, Charity 42; Ontario, 1871 *1823.17 p145*
Schram, Margrett 67; Ontario, 1871 *1823.21 p325*
Schramm, Auguste; America, 1867 *7919.3 p532*
Schramm, Daniel 39; New York, NY, 1886 *8425.16 p33*
Schramm, Eduard Ludwig; America, 1867 *7919.3 p532*
Schramm, Elisab 39; New York, NY, 1886 *8425.16 p33*
Schramm, Elisabeth 29 *SEE* Schramm, Nikolaus
Schramm, Gustav; Wisconsin, 1888 *6795.8 p45*
Schramm, Heinrich Wilhelm; America, 1867 *7919.3 p525*
Schramm, Jacob 2 months; New York, NY, 1886 *8425.16 p33*
Schramm, Jacob Bernhard; America, 1867 *7919.3 p532*
Schramm, Jakob; New York, 1867 *5475.1 p499*
  *Wife:*Margarethe Jungbluth
Schramm, Josef 27; America, 1868 *5475.1 p254*
Schramm, Josef; Milwaukee, 1848-1849 *2853.20 p308*
Schramm, Katha 3; New York, NY, 1886 *8425.16 p33*
Schramm, Katharina; America, 1874 *5475.1 p451*
Schramm, Katharina Wiesen 65 *SEE* Schramm, Nikolaus
Schramm, Luise Kath.; Brazil, 1863 *5475.1 p549*
Schramm, Margarethe Jungbluth *SEE* Schramm, Jakob
Schramm, Nikolaus 5 *SEE* Schramm, Nikolaus
Schramm, Nikolaus 33; America, 1864 *5475.1 p348*
  *Mother:*Katharina Wiesen 65
  *Sister:*Elisabeth 29
  *Nephew:*Nikolaus 5
Schramm, Nikolaus; America, 1866 *5475.1 p177*
Schramme, Anton; America, 1855 *7420.1 p141*
Schrand, Katharina; Venezuela, 1843 *3899.5 p542*
Schrandt, Johann; Wisconsin, 1881 *6795.8 p64*
Schrang, Christopher; Ohio, 1809-1852 *4511.35 p46*
Schrebber, Wm.; Illinois, 1858-1861 *6020.5 p133*
Schreck, Heinrich; America, 1871 *2526.42 p177*
Schreck, Philipp; America, 1872 *2526.42 p177*
Schreck, Philipp; America, 1881 *2526.42 p131*
  *Wife:*Sophia
Schreck, Sophia *SEE* Schreck, Philipp
Schredder, George; Ohio, 1809-1852 *4511.35 p50*
Schreder, Karl Mathias Anton 28; America, 1882 *5475.1 p129*
Schreiber, . . .; Venezuela, 1843 *3899.5 p545*
Schreiber, Amalia 16; Portland, ME, 1911 *970.38 p81*
Schreiber, Catharine 20; Louisiana, 1848 *778.6 p305*
Schreiber, Ernst; America, 1837 *7420.1 p14*
  With family
Schreiber, Gges. 27; Louisiana, 1848 *778.6 p305*
Schreiber, Heinrich Friedrich Dietrich Wilhelm; Port uncertain, 1878 *7420.1 p312*
Schreiber, Johann; Venezuela, 1843 *3899.5 p545*
Schreiber, John F. 37; Louisiana, 1834-1846 *7710.1 p149*
Schreiber, Karl 19; Portland, ME, 1910 *970.38 p81*
Schreiber, Nicolas 36; America, 1847 *778.6 p305*
Schreiber, Theodor 31; New York, NY, 1864 *8425.62 p198*
Schreier, Barbara Rectenwald *SEE* Schreier, Christoph
Schreier, Christina; Chicago, 1880 *5475.1 p241*
Schreier, Christoph; America, 1881 *5475.1 p241*
  *Wife:*Barbara Rectenwald
  *Son:*J. Peter
  *Son:*Johann
  *Daughter:*Margarethe
  *Son:*Mathias
  *Son:*Peter
Schreier, Franz; Ohio, 1884 *5475.1 p243*
Schreier, Georg Lebrecht; Port uncertain, 1840 *7420.1 p20*
Schreier, J. Peter *SEE* Schreier, Christoph
Schreier, Jan; Nebraska, 1870 *2853.20 p193*
Schreier, Johann *SEE* Schreier, Christoph
Schreier, Kath 37; Brazil, 1864 *5475.1 p502*
Schreier, Margarethe *SEE* Schreier, Christoph
Schreier, Mathias *SEE* Schreier, Christoph
Schreier, Peter *SEE* Schreier, Christoph
Schreiner, Anna 3; America, 1893 *1883.7 p38*

Schreiner, Anna 31; America, 1893 ***1883.7*** *p38*
Schreiner, Barbara Palz Schommer; Chicago, 1887 ***5475.1*** *p244*
With son
*Son:*Johann
*Son:*Stephan
Schreiner, C.; Louisiana, 1874-1875 ***4981.45*** *p31*
Schreiner, Eva 6; America, 1893 ***1883.7*** *p38*
Schreiner, Gottfried 30; America, 1893 ***1883.7*** *p38*
Schreiner, Jacob 4 months; America, 1893 ***1883.7*** *p38*
Schreiner, Jean 30; Mississippi, 1847 ***778.6*** *p305*
Schreiner, Johann *SEE* Schreiner, Barbara Palz Schommer
Schreiner, John C.; North Carolina, 1853 ***1088.45*** *p31*
Schreiner, Konrad 55; America, 1893 ***1883.7*** *p38*
Schreiner, Stephan *SEE* Schreiner, Barbara Palz Schommer
Schreiner, Susanna 60; America, 1893 ***1883.7*** *p38*
Schremer, Margarethe; America, 1887 ***5475.1*** *p58*
Schrenck, John; Ohio, 1809-1852 ***4511.35*** *p47*
Schrenics, Anna 24; Portland, ME, 1906 ***970.38*** *p81*
Schrenics, Johannes 27; Portland, ME, 1906 ***970.38*** *p81*
Schrenk, Augustus; Ohio, 1809-1852 ***4511.35*** *p47*
Schriber, Leonard; Illinois, 1855 ***6079.1*** *p13*
Schriebel, C.; Galveston, TX, 1855 ***571.7*** *p18*
Schrieber, . . .; America, 1843 ***7420.1*** *p30*
Schrieber, Mr.; America, 1838 ***7420.1*** *p15*
With family
Schrieber, Carl Heinrich; America, 1835 ***7420.1*** *p10*
Schrieber, Friedrich; America, 1846 ***7420.1*** *p48*
With wife & 2 children
Schrieber, Kolon; Port uncertain, 1838 ***7420.1*** *p15*
With family
Schrieberger, Anna Maria 30; America, 1847 ***778.6*** *p305*
Schrieberger, Barbara 9 months; America, 1847 ***778.6*** *p305*
Schrieberger, Barbara 51; America, 1847 ***778.6*** *p305*
Schrieberger, Jacob 34; America, 1847 ***778.6*** *p305*
Schriever, Dorothea; Valdivia, Chile, 1850 ***1192.4*** *p49*
With daughter 9 months
Schriever, Joh. Wilh.; America, 1861 ***5475.1*** *p296*
Schrik, Abraham 20; America, 1847 ***778.6*** *p305*
Schriner, Herman L.; North Carolina, 1854 ***1088.45*** *p31*
Schrior, Christian 39; Ontario, 1871 ***1823.17*** *p145*
Schriver, Harman; Ohio, 1809-1852 ***4511.35*** *p47*
Schriver, Henry; Ohio, 1809-1852 ***4511.35*** *p47*
Schroder, Widow; America, 1861 ***7420.1*** *p208*
*Daughter:*Charlotte
Schroder, Widow; America, 1867 ***7420.1*** *p264*
Schroder, Anna *SEE* Schroder, Wendel
Schroder, Anna; Chicago, 1887 ***5475.1*** *p17*
*Daughter:*Emma
*Son:*Karl
*Son:*Ludwig
Schroder, Anton Heinrich; America, 1849 ***7420.1*** *p67*
Schroder, Auguste; America, 1861 ***7420.1*** *p208*
Schroder, Carl August; America, 1859 ***7420.1*** *p189*
Schroder, Carl Christian; America, 1857 ***7420.1*** *p171*
*Sister:*Engel Marie Wilhelm. Carol.
Schroder, Carl Ludwig; Wisconsin, 1872 ***6795.8*** *p37*
Schroder, Charlotte *SEE* Schroder, Widow
Schroder, Christian; Port uncertain, 1850 ***7420.1*** *p75*
Schroder, Christian Gottlieb; America, 1845 ***7420.1*** *p40*
Schroder, Christoph; America, 1855 ***7420.1*** *p141*
With son
Schroder, Elisabeth Schonberger *SEE* Schroder, Wendel
Schroder, Emma *SEE* Schroder, Anna Houy
Schroder, Engel Marie Sophie Dorothee Moller *SEE* Schroder, Johann Heinrich Ludwig
Schroder, Engel Marie Wilhelm. Carol. *SEE* Schroder, Carl Christian
Schroder, Ernst; America, 1870 ***7420.1*** *p285*
Schroder, Friedrich; America, 1867 ***7420.1*** *p262*
With family
Schroder, Hans Heinrich; New York, NY, 1856 ***7420.1*** *p153*
Schroder, Mrs. Heinrich Christoph Sch.; America, 1856 ***7420.1*** *p153*
With children
Schroder, Heinrich Ferdinand August *SEE* Schroder, Wilhelmine Christine Charlotte Lindemann
Schroder, Heinrich Wilhelm *SEE* Schroder, Johann Heinrich Ludwig
Schroder, Herman; Washington, 1883 ***2770.40*** *p137*
Schroder, J.; Venezuela, 1843 ***3899.5*** *p546*
Schroder, Jakob *SEE* Schroder, Wendel
Schroder, Johann Friedrich; America, 1852 ***7420.1*** *p97*
Schroder, Johann Heinr. Fr. *SEE* Schroder, Johann Heinrich Ludwig
Schroder, Johann Heinrich Ludwig; Iowa, 1859 ***7420.1*** *p189*
With stepmother
*Daughter:*Sophie Dorothee
*Son:*Heinrich Wilhelm
*Wife:*Engel Marie Sophie Dorothee Moller
*Son:*Johann Heinr. Fr.
Schroder, Johannes Christian; Illinois, 1852 ***6079.1*** *p13*
Schroder, Josef *SEE* Schroder, Wendel
Schroder, Josef; America, 1926 ***8023.44*** *p379*
Schroder, Joseph 21; America, 1747 ***778.6*** *p305*
Schroder, Karl *SEE* Schroder, Anna Houy
Schroder, Katharina *SEE* Schroder, Wendel
Schroder, Ludwig *SEE* Schroder, Anna Houy
Schroder, Ludwig; Wisconsin, 1880 ***6795.8*** *p96*
Schroder, Margarethe *SEE* Schroder, Wendel
Schroder, Math. Aug.; America, 1881 ***5475.1*** *p329*
Schroder, Peter *SEE* Schroder, Wendel
Schroder, Sophie; America, 1861 ***7420.1*** *p208*
With daughter
Schroder, Sophie Charlotte; Iowa, 1859 ***7420.1*** *p189*
Schroder, Sophie Dorothee *SEE* Schroder, Johann Heinrich Ludwig
Schroder, Sophie Wilhelmine Charlotte; America, 1850 ***7420.1*** *p77*
Schroder, U. F.; Valdivia, Chile, 1850 ***1192.4*** *p48*
Schroder, Wendel *SEE* Schroder, Wendel
Schroder, Wendel; America, 1880 ***5475.1*** *p386*
*Wife:*Elisabeth Schonberger
*Daughter:*Margarethe
*Daughter:*Anna
*Son:*Peter
*Son:*Jakob
*Son:*Josef
*Son:*Wendel
*Daughter:*Katharina
Schroder, Wilhelmine Auguste *SEE* Schroder, Wilhelmine Christine Charlotte Lindemann
Schroder, Wilhelmine Christine Charlotte; America, 1864 ***7420.1*** *p227*
*Daughter:*Wilhelmine Auguste
*Son:*Heinrich Ferdinand August
*Daughter:*Wilhelmine Sophie Charlotte
Schroder, Wilhelmine Sophie Charlotte *SEE* Schroder, Wilhelmine Christine Charlotte Lindemann
Schroder, William 24; Ontario, 1871 ***1823.21*** *p325*
Schroder, Wm; Louisiana, 1874-1875 ***4981.45*** *p130*
Schroder, Wm.; Louisiana, 1874-1875 ***4981.45*** *p31*
Schroeder, A. Maria 8 *SEE* Schroeder, Wilhelm
Schroeder, A. R.; Louisiana, 1874-1875 ***4981.45*** *p30*
Schroeder, Albert Carl; Wisconsin, 1875 ***6795.8*** *p216*
Schroeder, Alma 5; Portland, ME, 1911 ***970.38*** *p81*
Schroeder, August; Missouri, 1892 ***3276.1*** *p4*
Schroeder, Augusta K. 51; Portland, ME, 1911 ***970.38*** *p81*
Schroeder, Bertha 28; Portland, ME, 1911 ***970.38*** *p81*
Schroeder, Bruno Adolf Herman; Illinois, 1930 ***121.35*** *p101*
Schroeder, Carl Ludwig; Wisconsin, 1882 ***6795.8*** *p27*
Schroeder, Carl Ludwig; Wisconsin, 1899 ***6795.8*** *p27*
Schroeder, Christian; Illinois, 1858-1861 ***6020.5*** *p133*
Schroeder, Miss E. 16; New York, NY, 1894 ***6512.1*** *p181*
Schroeder, Emil; Washington, 1882 ***2770.40*** *p137*
Schroeder, Engel Marie Sophie; America, 1855 ***7420.1*** *p141*
Schroeder, Gustav; Wisconsin, 1885 ***6795.8*** *p52*
Schroeder, Hugo 3; Portland, ME, 1911 ***970.38*** *p81*
Schroeder, Jacob 26; Halifax, N.S., 1902 ***1860.4*** *p42*
Schroeder, Jacob; Ohio, 1809-1852 ***4511.35*** *p47*
Schroeder, Jakob 18 *SEE* Schroeder, Wilhelm
Schroeder, Jno; Louisiana, 1874-1875 ***4981.45*** *p130*
Schroeder, Jno.; Louisiana, 1874-1875 ***4981.45*** *p31*
Schroeder, Johann 16 *SEE* Schroeder, Wilhelm
Schroeder, Johann Conrad; America, 1860 ***7420.1*** *p200*
Schroeder, Johann Heinr. Christoph; America, 1856 ***7420.1*** *p153*
Schroeder, John Diettmer; Ohio, 1840-1897 ***8365.35*** *p18*
Schroeder, Josef 14 *SEE* Schroeder, Wilhelm
Schroeder, Joseph; Ohio, 1809-1852 ***4511.35*** *p47*
Schroeder, Karl 4 *SEE* Schroeder, Wilhelm
Schroeder, Karl 56; Portland, ME, 1911 ***970.38*** *p81*
Schroeder, Kath. 38; America, 1837 ***5475.1*** *p385*
Schroeder, Katharina 12 *SEE* Schroeder, Wilhelm
Schroeder, Katharina Meiser 47 *SEE* Schroeder, Wilhelm
Schroeder, Loring 70; Halifax, N.S., 1902 ***1860.4*** *p42*
Schroeder, Mathias; America, 1869 ***5475.1*** *p329*
Schroeder, Nicholas; Ohio, 1809-1852 ***4511.35*** *p47*
Schroeder, Rosina 64; Halifax, N.S., 1902 ***1860.4*** *p42*
Schroeder, Wilhelm 44; America, 1846 ***5475.1*** *p401*
*Wife:*Katharina Meiser 47
*Son:*Johann 16
*Daughter:*Katharina 12
*Daughter:*A. Maria 8
*Son:*Karl 4
*Son:*Josef 14
*Son:*Jakob 18
Schroer, Wm.; Ohio, 1840-1897 ***8365.35*** *p18*
Schroth, . . .; West Virginia, n.d. ***1132.30*** *p151*
Schroth, Daniel; West Virginia, 1873 ***1132.30*** *p151*
Schroth, Rudolf; Wisconsin, 1898 ***6795.8*** *p157*
Schrumpf, Elias; America, 1867 ***7919.3*** *p528*
Schrumpf, Ernestine; America, 1867 ***7919.3*** *p524*
Schu, Anna 32; America, 1846 ***5475.1*** *p401*
Schu, August; New York, NY, 1880 ***5475.1*** *p23*
Schu, Jakob; America, 1873 ***5475.1*** *p22*
Schu, Nikolaus 27; America, 1843 ***5475.1*** *p347*
Schu, Peter; Brazil, 1888 ***5475.1*** *p432*
Schu, Peter Josef; New York, NY, 1865-1900 ***5475.1*** *p24*
Schu, Stephan; America, 1855 ***5475.1*** *p507*
Schu, Stephan 34; America, 1872 ***5475.1*** *p446*
Schual, Bianca 7; America, 1846 ***778.6*** *p305*
Schual, Clara 33; America, 1846 ***778.6*** *p305*
Schual, Emile 8; America, 1846 ***778.6*** *p305*
Schual, Henri 6 months; America, 1846 ***778.6*** *p305*
Schual, Joseph 46; America, 1846 ***778.6*** *p305*
Schual, Josephine 4; America, 1846 ***778.6*** *p305*
Schual, Otto 2; America, 1846 ***778.6*** *p305*
Schubart, Oskar Carl; America, 1867 ***7919.3*** *p529*
Schubart, Wilhelm; America, 1867 ***7919.3*** *p526*
Schubert, Amial; Wisconsin, 1895 ***6795.8*** *p41*
Schubert, Emilie *SEE* Schubert, Wilhelmine Thiel
Schubert, Hugo *SEE* Schubert, Wilhelmine Thiel
Schubert, Wilhelmine *SEE* Schubert, Wilhelmine Thiel
Schubert, Wilhelmine; America, 1882 ***5475.1*** *p34*
*Daughter:*Wilhelmine
*Daughter:*Emilie
*Son:*Hugo
Schubert, William; New York, 1859 ***358.56*** *p100*
Schuberth, Anna Margarethe; America, 1867 ***7919.3*** *p526*
Schubmehl, Jakob; America, 1848 ***5475.1*** *p486*
Schubmehl, Peter 22; America, 1849 ***5475.1*** *p486*
Schuch, Charlotte; America, 1862 ***5475.1*** *p524*
Schuch, Jakob 34; America, 1865 ***5475.1*** *p504*
*Wife:*Karoline Brensecke 35
*Daughter:*Karoline 3
*Daughter:*Wilhelmine 5
*Daughter:*Pauline 4
Schuch, Johann; America, 1862 ***5475.1*** *p524*
*Wife:*Margarethe Josten
Schuch, Karoline 3 *SEE* Schuch, Jakob
Schuch, Karoline Brensecke 35 *SEE* Schuch, Jakob
Schuch, Margarethe Josten *SEE* Schuch, Johann
Schuch, Pauline 4 *SEE* Schuch, Jakob
Schuch, Peter; America, 1862 ***5475.1*** *p523*
*Wife:*Philippine Maurer
Schuch, Philippine Maurer *SEE* Schuch, Peter
Schuch, Wilhelm; America, 1862 ***5475.1*** *p524*
With relatives
Schuch, Wilhelmine 5 *SEE* Schuch, Jakob
Schuchert, Charles; Wisconsin, 1875 ***6795.8*** *p97*
Schuchert, Juliane; America, 1754 ***2526.42*** *p120*
Schucider, Elizabeth 31; Portland, ME, 1906 ***970.38*** *p81*
Schucider, Emanue 12; Portland, ME, 1906 ***970.38*** *p81*
Schucider, Emma 6; Portland, ME, 1906 ***970.38*** *p81*
Schucider, George 32; Portland, ME, 1906 ***970.38*** *p81*
Schucider, Leonard 4; Portland, ME, 1906 ***970.38*** *p81*
Schucider, Ottilie 2 months; Portland, ME, 1906 ***970.38*** *p81*
Schuck, Elisabeth; Brazil, 1859 ***5475.1*** *p523*
Schuck, Jakob 27; Brazil, 1865 ***5475.1*** *p524*
*Wife:*Karoline Wolter 34
*Daughter:*Karoline 9 months
Schuck, Karoline 9 *SEE* Schuck, Jakob
Schuck, Karoline Wolter 34 *SEE* Schuck, Jakob
Schuck, Peter; America, 1843 ***5475.1*** *p551*
Schuckart, Christina; America, 1854 ***2526.43*** *p181*
With family
Schuckhart, George; Ohio, 1809-1852 ***4511.35*** *p47*
Schuckhart, Henry; Ohio, 1809-1852 ***4511.35*** *p47*
Schudes, Gertrud; America, 1873 ***5475.1*** *p205*
Schue, Adolf; America, 1839 ***5475.1*** *p469*
Schue, Johann; America, 1837 ***5475.1*** *p468*
Schue, Karl Philipp; America, 1849 ***5475.1*** *p477*
Schue, Maria Nikolaus Engelhard; America, 1849 ***5475.1*** *p477*
Schuehagen, Herman C. E.; Iowa, 1899 ***1211.15*** *p19*
Schuel, Carl; Iowa, 1890 ***1211.15*** *p19*
Schuel, Ursule 19; Louisiana, 1848 ***778.6*** *p305*
Schueler, John; Long Island, 1781 ***8529.30*** *p10A*
Schueneman, Wilhelm; Iowa, 1888 ***1211.15*** *p19*
Schuerer, Arnost; Texas, 1854 ***2853.20*** *p78*
Schuessler, Josef Kalasansky; Chicago, 1833-1903 ***2853.20*** *p404*
Schuessler, Prokop; Milwaukee, 1858-1887 ***2853.20*** *p309*
Schuetz, Father; Kansas, 1899 ***2853.20*** *p206*
Schuetz, Gertrud; Brazil, 1846 ***5475.1*** *p439*
Schuetz, Maria *SEE* Schuetz, Mathias

Schuetz, Mathias; Brazil, 1846 *5475.1 p438*
*Sister:*Maria
Schuff, Barbara 30; New Orleans, 1834 *1002.51 p111*
Schuff, Daniel 1; New Orleans, 1834 *1002.51 p111*
Schuff, Jacob 40; New Orleans, 1834 *1002.51 p111*
Schuffenmuller, Jacques 37; Port uncertain, 1847 *778.6 p305*
Schuffer, Mr. 23; America, 1847 *778.6 p305*
Schuffler, Carl Friedrich; America, 1867 *7919.3 p525*
Schug, Elisabeth *SEE* Schug, Johann Peter
Schug, Elisabeth Geumann *SEE* Schug, Johann Peter
Schug, Elisabeth 30; America, 1857 *5475.1 p497*
Schug, Elisabeth *SEE* Schug, Peter, II
Schug, Jakob 18 *SEE* Schug, Nikolaus
Schug, Johann *SEE* Schug, Peter, II
Schug, Johann Friedrich 20; America, 1864 *5475.1 p503*
With father
Schug, Johann Peter; America, 1864 *5475.1 p503*
*Wife:*Elisabeth Geumann
*Daughter:*Katharina
*Daughter:*Elisabeth
Schug, Juliana *SEE* Schug, Peter, II
Schug, Katharina *SEE* Schug, Johann Peter
Schug, Katharina *SEE* Schug, Peter, II
Schug, Luise 41; America, 1866 *5475.1 p490*
*Daughter:*Luise 19
*Son:*Karl 15
Schug, Margarethe *SEE* Schug, Peter, II
Schug, Maria Elisabeth Henn *SEE* Schug, Peter, II
Schug, Nikolaus 51; America, 1864 *5475.1 p503*
*Son:*Jakob 18
Schug, Paul *SEE* Schug, Peter, II
Schug, Peter; Brazil, 1863 *5475.1 p498*
With father
Schug, Peter, II; Brazil, 1863 *5475.1 p498*
*Wife:*Maria Elisabeth Henn
*Son:*Johann
*Daughter:*Juliana
*Son:*Paul
With niece
*Daughter:*Katharina
*Daughter:*Margarethe
*Daughter:*Elisabeth
Schuh, A. Maria 18 *SEE* Schuh, Mathias
Schuh, Mrs. Adam; Brazil, 1862 *5475.1 p441*
Schuh, Aloise 4; America, 1846 *778.6 p305*
Schuh, Anna 9 *SEE* Schuh, Mathias
Schuh, Barbara 9 *SEE* Schuh, Mathias
Schuh, Barbara 30; America, 1846 *778.6 p305*
Schuh, Barbara Weber 42 *SEE* Schuh, Mathias
Schuh, Bernhard 2; America, 1846 *778.6 p305*
Schuh, Franz Karl Edmund; America, 1876 *5475.1 p183*
Schuh, Georg 34; Galveston, TX, 1844 *3967.10 p372*
Schuh, Helena 11 *SEE* Schuh, Mathias
Schuh, Ignaze 30; America, 1846 *778.6 p305*
Schuh, Jakob 2 *SEE* Schuh, Johann
Schuh, Johann 38; Brazil, 1857 *5475.1 p248*
*Wife:*Katharina Feltes 37
*Daughter:*Maria 16
*Son:*Jakob 2 months
*Son:*Nikolaus 10
*Son:*Peter 13
Schuh, Josephine 6; America, 1846 *778.6 p305*
Schuh, Katharina Feltes 37 *SEE* Schuh, Johann
Schuh, Magdalena 1; America, 1846 *778.6 p305*
Schuh, Maria 5 *SEE* Schuh, Mathias
Schuh, Maria 16 *SEE* Schuh, Johann
Schuh, Mathias 14 *SEE* Schuh, Mathias
Schuh, Mathias 43; America, 1864 *5475.1 p370*
*Wife:*Barbara Weber 42
*Daughter:*Barbara 9 months
*Son:*Mathias 14
*Daughter:*Anna 9
*Son:*Nikolaus 7
*Daughter:*Maria 5
*Daughter:*Helena 11
*Daughter:*A. Maria 18
Schuh, Nikolaus 7 *SEE* Schuh, Mathias
Schuh, Nikolaus 10 *SEE* Schuh, Johann
Schuh, Peter 13 *SEE* Schuh, Johann
Schuhe, Johann; America, 1881 *5475.1 p358*
Schuhmacher, Angela 30; America, 1869 *5475.1 p307*
Schuhmacher, Carl Ludwig; America, 1865 *7420.1 p237*
Schuhmacher, Friedrich Wilhelm; Port uncertain, 1899 *7420.1 p375*
Schuhmacher, Heinrich *SEE* Schuhmacher, Jakob
Schuhmacher, Jakob; America, 1857 *5475.1 p552*
Schuhmacher, Jakob; America, 1882 *5475.1 p246*
Schuhmacher, Jakob 47; America, 1860 *5475.1 p552*
*Wife:*Maria Anna Klein 48
*Son:*Heinrich
*Son:*Johann

*Daughter:*Margarethe
*Son:*Peter
Schuhmacher, Joh.; America, 1881 *5475.1 p245*
Schuhmacher, Johann *SEE* Schuhmacher, Jakob
Schuhmacher, Johann; America, 1874 *5475.1 p308*
Schuhmacher, Johann 27; America, 1852 *5475.1 p327*
Schuhmacher, Kath.; Ohio, 1886 *5475.1 p230*
Schuhmacher, Margarethe *SEE* Schuhmacher, Jakob
Schuhmacher, Maria Anna Klein 48 *SEE* Schuhmacher, Jakob
Schuhmacher, Peter *SEE* Schuhmacher, Jakob
Schuimort, Eugenie 1; Port uncertain, 1847 *778.6 p305*
Schuimort, Francoise 32; Port uncertain, 1847 *778.6 p305*
Schuimort, Mathias 32; Port uncertain, 1847 *778.6 p306*
Schuitz, Julius; Colorado, 1880 *1029.59 p82*
Schul, Angela; Pennsylvania, 1884 *5475.1 p465*
Schuldt, Hinrich; Valdivia, Chile, 1852 *1192.4 p56*
Schule, Johann Friedrich; America, 1853 *179.55 p19*
Schuler, Adam; America, 1869 *2526.43 p143*
Schuler, Adam *SEE* Schuler, Peter
Schuler, Alfred Otto; America, 1857 *7420.1 p172*
Schuler, Angela *SEE* Schuler, Elisabeth Demmer
Schuler, Anna Margaretha *SEE* Schuler, Peter
Schuler, Anna Margaretha Horn *SEE* Schuler, Peter
Schuler, Barbara; America, 1839 *5475.1 p56*
Schuler, Carl Julius; America, 1867 *7919.3 p526*
Schuler, Christina; America, 1872 *5475.1 p57*
Schuler, Christoph; America, 1867 *7919.3 p529*
With wife & 3 children
Schuler, Daniel; Valparaiso, Chile, 1850 *1192.4 p50*
Schuler, Elisabeth *SEE* Schuler, Elisabeth Demmer
Schuler, Elisabeth 32; America, 1873 *5475.1 p298*
*Daughter:*Elisabeth
*Daughter:*Gertrud
*Son:*Nikolaus
*Daughter:*Juliane
*Daughter:*Angela
Schuler, Elisabetha; America, 1881 *2526.43 p143*
Schuler, Eva 27; America, 1740-1899 *2526.42 p135*
Schuler, Eva 50; America, 1853 *2526.42 p149*
Schuler, Friedrich; America, 1867 *7919.3 p529*
With wife & daughter
Schuler, Friedrich Wilhelm; America, 1884 *2526.43 p156*
Schuler, Georg Adam; America, 1888 *2526.43 p143*
Schuler, Gertrud *SEE* Schuler, Elisabeth Demmer
Schuler, Heinrich; America, 1840 *5475.1 p56*
*Wife:*Katharina
With 5 children
Schuler, Henry 20; New York, NY, 1847 *9176.15 p51*
Schuler, Ignaz 1; New Orleans, 1847 *778.6 p306*
Schuler, Jakob; America, 1881 *5475.1 p299*
Schuler, Johan 28; New York, NY, 1847 *9176.15 p51*
Schuler, Johann *SEE* Schuler, Johann
Schuler, Johann 40; America, 1873 *5475.1 p138*
*Wife:*Margarethe Hauter 34
*Son:*Johann
Schuler, Johann Georg; America, 1882 *2526.43 p143*
Schuler, Johann Peter *SEE* Schuler, Peter
Schuler, Johannes; America, 1888 *2526.43 p143*
Schuler, John; Ohio, 1809-1852 *4511.35 p47*
Schuler, Josef; America, 1880 *5475.1 p58*
Schuler, Joseph; America, 1854 *2526.43 p143*
Schuler, Joseph 3; New Orleans, 1847 *778.6 p306*
Schuler, Joseph 35; New Orleans, 1847 *778.6 p306*
Schuler, Juliane *SEE* Schuler, Elisabeth Demmer
Schuler, Justus; Chile, 1852 *1192.4 p52*
With wife & 6 children
With child 3
With child 21
Schuler, Katharina *SEE* Schuler, Heinrich
Schuler, Katharina; America, 1881 *2526.43 p143*
Schuler, Katharina Margaretha *SEE* Schuler, Peter
Schuler, Leonhard 36; America, 1881 *2526.43 p156*
*Wife:*Charlotte Ehrhard 32
Schuler, Marcus 23; New York, NY, 1847 *9176.15 p51*
Schuler, Margaretha; America, 1867 *2526.43 p143*
Schuler, Margaretha; America, 1881 *2526.43 p143*
Schuler, Margarethe Hauter 34 *SEE* Schuler, Johann
Schuler, Maria 33; New Orleans, 1847 *778.6 p306*
Schuler, Mathias 26; America, 1843 *5475.1 p295*
Schuler, Nikolaus; America, 1867 *5475.1 p160*
Schuler, Nikolaus *SEE* Schuler, Elisabeth Demmer
Schuler, Peter; America, 1839 *5475.1 p56*
*Brother:*Wendel
Schuler, Peter; America, 1881 *2526.43 p126*
*Wife:*Anna Margaretha Horn
*Daughter:*Katharina Margaretha
*Son:*Adam
*Son:*Johann Peter
*Daughter:*Anna Margaretha
Schuler, Pierre 23; New York, NY, 1847 *9176.15 p51*

Schuler, Simpson; North Carolina, 1855 *1088.45 p31*
Schuler, Wendel *SEE* Schuler, Peter
Schuler, Wilhelm; America, 1850 *2526.43 p143*
Schulien, Helena Grunewald *SEE* Schulien, Peter
Schulien, Johann; America, 1872 *5475.1 p306*
*Wife:*Susanna Kleser
*Daughter:*Regina
*Son:*Math. Josef
Schulien, Johann *SEE* Schulien, Peter
Schulien, Math. Josef *SEE* Schulien, Johann
Schulien, Mathias; America, 1867 *5475.1 p262*
Schulien, Mathias; America, 1868 *5475.1 p305*
Schulien, Mathias *SEE* Schulien, Peter
Schulien, Michel; America, 1871 *5475.1 p262*
Schulien, Michel *SEE* Schulien, Peter
Schulien, Nikolaus; America, 1881 *5475.1 p300*
Schulien, Peter; America, 1868 *5475.1 p305*
Schulien, Peter *SEE* Schulien, Peter
Schulien, Peter; America, 1881 *5475.1 p263*
*Wife:*Helena Grunewald
*Son:*Peter
*Son:*Johann
*Son:*Mathias
*Son:*Michel
Schulien, Regina *SEE* Schulien, Johann
Schulien, Susanna Kleser *SEE* Schulien, Johann
Schulken, Engelhard; North Carolina, 1854 *1088.45 p31*
Schulken, Margaret; North Carolina, 1792-1862 *1088.45 p31*
Schulken, Martin; North Carolina, 1850 *1088.45 p31*
Schuller, Frank; Washington, 1889 *2770.40 p81*
Schuls, Emil; Wisconsin, 1902 *6795.8 p153*
Schult, George; Ohio, 1809-1852 *4511.35 p47*
Schult, John; Ohio, 1840-1897 *8365.35 p18*
Schulte, Elis. Maria *SEE* Schulte, Marg. Hacke
Schulte, Francis; New York, 1859 *358.56 p54*
Schulte, Franz 26; America, 1913 *8023.44 p379*
Schulte, Friedrich *SEE* Schulte, Marg. Hacke
Schulte, H.; Louisiana, 1874-1875 *4981.45 p31*
Schulte, Karl Maria Wilhelm; Memphis, TN, 1860 *5475.1 p12*
Schulte, Ludwig; America, 1892 *7420.1 p367*
Schulte, Marg.; America, 1886 *8023.44 p379*
*Daughter:*Elis. Maria
*Son:*Friedrich
Schultes, David 19; New York, NY, 1898 *7951.13 p42*
Schultheiss, D.; New York, 1859 *358.56 p99*
Schultheiss, Peter; Valdivia, Chile, 1852 *1192.4 p56*
Schulthies, Francis 38; Ontario, 1871 *1823.21 p325*
Schultin, John; America, 1758 *1220.12 p705*
Schults, Gotolph; America, 1773 *1220.12 p705*
Schultz, Anna 10; Halifax, N.S., 1902 *1860.4 p42*
Schultz, August; Ohio, 1840-1897 *8365.35 p18*
Schultz, Carl; Galveston, TX, 1855 *571.7 p17*
Schultz, Charles 35; America, 1844 *778.6 p306*
Schultz, Ernst Gustav; Wisconsin, 1893 *6795.8 p142*
Schultz, Frantisek; Chicago, 1854 *2853.20 p388*
Schultz, Frederick; Ohio, 1809-1852 *4511.35 p47*
Schultz, Friedrich; Valdivia, Chile, 1852 *1192.4 p53*
Schultz, Henry W.; Texas, 1904 *3435.45 p37*
Schultz, Herman Amiel; Wisconsin, 1914 *6795.8 p167*
Schultz, Joanna; North Carolina, 1792-1862 *1088.45 p31*
Schultz, Johan; Illinois, 1858-1861 *6020.5 p133*
Schultz, Johann Ludwig; Wisconsin, 1872 *6795.8 p66*
Schultz, Julia 4; Halifax, N.S., 1902 *1860.4 p42*
Schultz, Julius; Colorado, 1862-1894 *1029.59 p82*
Schultz, Lissia 3; Halifax, N.S., 1902 *1860.4 p42*
Schultz, Margarthe 30; Halifax, N.S., 1902 *1860.4 p42*
Schultz, Oscar Otto Friedrich; Wisconsin, 1888 *6795.8 p172*
Schultz, Theodore; North Carolina, 1826 *1088.45 p31*
Schultz, Theresia; Halifax, N.S., 1902 *1860.4 p42*
Schultz, Waoye 11; Halifax, N.S., 1902 *1860.4 p42*
Schultz, Wilhelmine; Valdivia, Chile, 1850 *1192.4 p48*
Schultz, Wilhelmine; Wisconsin, 1907 *6795.8 p148*
Schultz, Wilhelmine E.; Wisconsin, 1888 *6795.8 p122*
Schultze, Ernst Carl Wilhelm *SEE* Schultze, Friedrich Wilhelm August
Schultze, Friedrich Wilhelm August; America, 1872 *7420.1 p298*
With wife
*Son:*Ernst Carl Wilhelm
*Son:*Johann Friedrich Carl
Schultze, Johann Friedrich Carl *SEE* Schultze, Friedrich Wilhelm August
Schulz, Anna Wilhelmine; Wisconsin, 1897 *6795.8 p176*
Schulz, August; Valdivia, Chile, 1850 *1192.4 p50*
With wife & 2 children
With child 5
With child 19
Schulz, August Herman; Wisconsin, 1892 *6795.8 p76*

Schulz, Barbara; America, 1836 *5475.1 p495*
  *Daughter:*Maria
  *Son:*Johann
Schulz, Carl 24; Portland, ME, 1906 *970.38 p81*
Schulz, Christian; New York, 1883 *5475.1 p36*
Schulz, Christiane Caroline; America, 1867 *7919.3 p525*
Schulz, Eduard Reinhold; Port uncertain, 1904 *7420.1 p380*
Schulz, Elisabeth; America, 1881 *5475.1 p227*
Schulz, Emil; Wisconsin, 1902 *6795.8 p153*
Schulz, Erdmann 45; New York, NY, 1885 *1883.7 p46*
Schulz, Georg; America, 1843 *5475.1 p540*
Schulz, Gottfried; New York, NY, 1893 *3366.30 p70*
Schulz, Gustav 21; Portland, ME, 1911 *970.38 p81*
Schulz, Heinrich; America, 1854 *7420.1 p130*
Schulz, Heinrich; America, 1882 *5475.1 p193*
Schulz, Henrietta; Wisconsin, 1903 *6795.8 p205*
Schulz, Hermann 38; New York, NY, 1893 *1883.7 p43*
Schulz, Jakob; America, 1876-1892 *179.55 p19*
Schulz, Jean 3; America, 1846 *778.6 p306*
Schulz, Johann 12 SEE Schulz, Barbara Stoll
Schulz, Johann 27; Halifax, N.S., 1902 *1860.4 p42*
Schulz, Johann 15; New York, NY, 1885 *1883.7 p46*
Schulz, Johann Michael; America, 1845 *179.55 p19*
Schulz, John; New York, 1860 *358.56 p150*
Schulz, Joseph; America, 1881 *2526.42 p156*
Schulz, Julius Hermann; Wisconsin, 1891 *6795.8 p192*
Schulz, Karl Aug. Hermann; Wisconsin, 1892 *6795.8 p228*
Schulz, Katha. 46; New York, NY, 1885 *1883.7 p46*
Schulz, Katharina Viator SEE Schulz, Konrad
Schulz, Konrad; America, 1865 *5475.1 p482*
  *Wife:*Katharina Viator
  *Daughter:*Margarethe
  *Daughter:*Wilhelmine
  *Daughter:*Luise
Schulz, Luise 17 SEE Schulz, Konrad
Schulz, Mac. 28; America, 1840 *778.6 p306*
Schulz, Margarethe 12 SEE Schulz, Konrad
Schulz, Maria 24 SEE Schulz, Barbara Stoll
Schulz, Max; South America, 1923 *8023.44 p379*
Schulz, Michael; America, 1893 *179.55 p19*
Schulz, Ph. 6; America, 1846 *778.6 p306*
Schulz, W.; Galveston, TX, 1855 *571.7 p18*
Schulz, Wilhelmine 2 SEE Schulz, Konrad
Schulze, Carl; America, 1853 *7420.1 p111*
Schulze, Carl Friedrich Wilhelm August; America, 1871 *7420.1 p292*
Schum, Adam; America, 1854 *2526.43 p156*
Schum, Adam; America, 1868 *2526.43 p156*
Schum, Anna Maria; America, 1857 *2526.43 p156*
Schum, Eva 2 SEE Schum, Philipp
Schum, Henriette 5 SEE Schum, Philipp
Schum, Johann 1 SEE Schum, Philipp
Schum, Philipp 30; America, 1846 *2526.43 p156*
  With wife
  *Daughter:*Henriette 5
  *Son:*Johann 1
  *Daughter:*Eva 2
Schumacher, Adam 5; New York, NY, 1898 *7951.13 p44*
Schumacher, Albert H.; Louisiana, 1841-1844 *4981.45 p211*
Schumacher, Anton 31; New York, NY, 1898 *7951.13 p44*
Schumacher, Barbara Gross SEE Schumacher, Jakob
Schumacher, Christian 1 months; New York, NY, 1898 *7951.13 p44*
Schumacher, Georg SEE Schumacher, Jakob
Schumacher, H.; New York, 1859 *358.56 p100*
Schumacher, Heinrich 20; Halifax, N.S., 1902 *1860.4 p42*
Schumacher, Herman; New York, 1860 *358.56 p149*
Schumacher, Jakob; America, 1871 *5475.1 p139*
  *Wife:*Barbara Gross
  *Son:*Nikolaus
  *Son:*Georg
  *Son:*Johann
  *Son:*Karl
  *Son:*Wilhelm
  *Daughter:*Magdalena
  *Son:*P. Josef
Schumacher, Johann SEE Schumacher, Jakob
Schumacher, Karl SEE Schumacher, Jakob
Schumacher, Magdalena SEE Schumacher, Jakob
Schumacher, Magdalena 28; New York, NY, 1898 *7951.13 p44*
Schumacher, Maria 1; New York, NY, 1898 *7951.13 p44*
Schumacher, Michael 3; New York, NY, 1898 *7951.13 p44*
Schumacher, Nikolaus SEE Schumacher, Jakob
Schumacher, P. Josef SEE Schumacher, Jakob

Schumacher, Wilhelm SEE Schumacher, Jakob
Schuman, Louis; Louisiana, 1874 *4981.45 p134*
Schumann, Anna; New York, 1860 *358.56 p149*
Schumann, Dorothea; America, 1868 *7919.3 p524*
Schumann, John; Louisiana, 1874 *4981.45 p134*
Schumke, Charles 22; New York, NY, 1878 *9253.2 p45*
Schummer, Johann; America, 1881 *5475.1 p421*
Schunemann, Christian Friedrich Sch. SEE Schunemann, Sophie Louise Pfingsten
Schunemann, Georg Heinrich; America, 1865 *7420.1 p237*
Schunemann, Gradierer Johann Ernst SEE Schunemann, Sophie Louise Pfingsten
Schunemann, Heinrich August; Port uncertain, 1854 *7420.1 p129*
Schunemann, Johann Ernst; America, 1868 *7420.1 p276*
  *Daughter:*Juliane Louise
Schunemann, Johann Ernst Wilhelm; America, 1867 *7420.1 p264*
Schunemann, Johann Friedrich; America, 1867 *7420.1 p264*
Schunemann, Johann Friedrich Wilhelm; Port uncertain, 1837 *7420.1 p14*
Schunemann, Juliane Louise SEE Schunemann, Johann Ernst
Schunemann, Sophie Louise; America, 1872 *7420.1 p297*
  *Son:*Christian Friedrich Sch.
  *Husband:*Gradierer Johann Ernst
Schunk, Simon; America, 1867 *7919.3 p531*
Schuns, Frederick A.; Missouri, 1898 *3276.1 p4*
Schur, Ignas 11 months; Halifax, N.S., 1902 *1860.4 p44*
Schur, Marlinau 2; Halifax, N.S., 1902 *1860.4 p44*
Schur, Mawseha 28; Halifax, N.S., 1902 *1860.4 p44*
Schur, Peter; Illinois, 1834-1900 *6020.5 p133*
Schur, Scl.ine 26; Halifax, N.S., 1902 *1860.4 p44*
Schur, Sute; Halifax, N.S., 1902 *1860.4 p44*
Schurer, Caspar 59; New Castle, DE, 1817-1818 *90.20 p154*
Schurer, K.; New York, 1860 *358.56 p5*
Schurmann, C.; Port uncertain, 1880 *7420.1 p318*
Schurnbeck, John; Louisiana, 1836-1841 *4981.45 p209*
Schurpit, Frank; Wisconsin, 1888 *6795.8 p61*
Schurwanz, Reinhold Albert; Iowa, 1914 *1211.15 p19*
Schussler, Elisabeth Mehl SEE Schussler, Joh. Nik.
Schussler, Georg Karl SEE Schussler, Joh. Nik.
Schussler, Joh. Nik.; Rio Grande do Sul, Brazil, 1861 *5475.1 p489*
  *Wife:*Elisabeth Mehl
  *Son:*Georg Karl
  *Son:*Peter
Schussler, Maria El.; Rio Grande do Sul, Brazil, 1861 *5475.1 p489*
Schussler, Maria Katharina; Rio Grande do Sul, Brazil, 1861 *5475.1 p489*
Schussler, Peter SEE Schussler, Joh. Nik.
Schuster, . . .; New England, 1866 *170.15 p42*
Schuster, . . .; New England, 1866 *170.15 p42*
  With brother & sister
Schuster, Andreas; Pennsylvania, 1848 *170.15 p41*
Schuster, Angela 59; America, 1843 *5475.1 p253*
Schuster, Anna Magdalena; New England, 1866 *170.15 p42*
  With family
Schuster, Anna Magdalena 45; New England, 1866 *170.15 p41*
  With family
Schuster, Anna Magdalena; Port uncertain, 1866 *170.15 p41*
Schuster, Anna Regina 26; New England, 1866 *170.15 p28*
  With family
Schuster, August; Valdivia, Chile, 1850 *1192.4 p49*
Schuster, Jakob; America, 1867 *5475.1 p291*
Schuster, Johann Adam 13; New England, 1866 *170.15 p41*
  With family
Schuster, Johann Lorenz 17; New England, 1866 *170.15 p42*
  With family
Schuster, Louis 22; America, 1847 *778.6 p306*
Schuster, Luise 18; America, 1857 *5475.1 p552*
Schuster, Mrs. Melchior; Port uncertain, 1865 *170.15 p42*
  With 3 children & grandchild
Schuster, Peter; Pennsylvania, 1867 *170.15 p42*
Schut, Matt 34; New York, NY, 1847 *9176.15 p51*
Schutte, Mr.; America, 1857 *7420.1 p172*
Schutte, Mr.; America, 1868 *7420.1 p276*
  With 2 sisters
Schutte, Carl Friedrich Christian; America, 1881 *7420.1 p324*
Schutte, Carl Heinrich; America, 1854 *7420.1 p129*

Schutte, Engel Marie Sophie Leonore; America, 1850 *7420.1 p74*
Schutte, Ernst; America, 1852 *7420.1 p97*
Schutte, Friedrich; America, 1856 *7420.1 p153*
Schutte, Gustav Adolf; Chicago, 1886 *7420.1 p352*
Schutte, Heinrich Ferdinand; Chicago, 1881 *7420.1 p325*
Schutte, Heinrich Friedrich Ferdinand; Missouri, 1877 *7420.1 p309*
Schutte, Heinrich Friedrich Gottlieb; America, 1854 *7420.1 p20*
Schutte, Heinrich Rolfshagen; America, 1840 *7420.1 p20*
  With 4 daughters
Schutte, Johann Carl Friedrich; Port uncertain, 1855 *7420.1 p142*
Schutte, Johann Friedrich; America, 1856 *7420.1 p153*
  With siblings
Schutte, Johann Friedrich Wilhelm; America, 1854 *7420.1 p129*
Schutte, Johann Heinrich Gottlieb Christian; America, 1876 *7420.1 p308*
Schutte, Louise; America, 1856 *7420.1 p153*
  With son
Schutte, Ludwig; America, 1852 *7420.1 p97*
Schutte, Sophie; America, 1852 *7420.1 p97*
Schutte, Sophie Louise Charlotte; America, 1880 *7420.1 p315*
Schutte, Wilhelm; America, 1883 *7420.1 p340*
Schutters, Jacob 23; America, 1846 *778.6 p306*
Schutz, A. Margarethe Graser SEE Schutz, Johann Michael
Schutz, A. Maria SEE Schutz, Klemens
Schutz, A. Maria; Chicago, 1881 *5475.1 p246*
  *Daughter:*A. Maria
  *Son:*Peter
Schutz, Angela; America, 1843 *5475.1 p261*
Schutz, Angela Wolf SEE Schutz, Klemens
Schutz, Anna 8; America, 1848 *778.6 p306*
Schutz, Anna 10; Halifax, N.S., 1902 *1860.4 p42*
Schutz, C. 47; America, 1847 *778.6 p306*
Schutz, Christine; Port uncertain, 1850 *7420.1 p75*
Schutz, Ernst; Valparaiso, Chile, 1850 *1192.4 p50*
Schutz, Franz SEE Schutz, Klemens
Schutz, Georg 12; America, 1848 *778.6 p306*
Schutz, George 19; America, 1841 *778.6 p306*
Schutz, Gertrud 41; America, 1848 *778.6 p306*
Schutz, Herman Emil; Wisconsin, 1896 *6795.8 p122*
Schutz, Jakob SEE Schutz, Johann Michael
Schutz, Johann; America, 1853 *5475.1 p439*
Schutz, Johann; America, 1867 *5475.1 p264*
Schutz, Johann SEE Schutz, Klemens
Schutz, Johann Daniel; America, 1830 *5475.1 p458*
  *Wife:*M. Katharina Leibenguth
Schutz, Johann Michael; America, 1854 *5475.1 p459*
  *Wife:*A. Margarethe Graser
  *Son:*Peter
  *Daughter:*M. Katharina
  *Son:*Jakob
Schutz, Josef 26; America, 1843 *5475.1 p359*
Schutz, Julia 4; Halifax, N.S., 1902 *1860.4 p42*
Schutz, K.; New York, 1859 *358.56 p55*
Schutz, Karl SEE Schutz, Karl
Schutz, Karl; America, 1838 *5475.1 p458*
  *Wife:*Katharina Kurz
  *Son:*Nikolaus
  *Son:*Karl
Schutz, Katharina Kurz SEE Schutz, Karl
Schutz, Katharina SEE Schutz, Klemens
Schutz, Klemens; America, 1874 *5475.1 p258*
  *Wife:*Angela Wolf
  *Son:*Franz
  *Son:*Peter
  *Son:*Johann
  *Daughter:*Katharina
  With child
  *Daughter:*A. Maria
Schutz, Lissia 3; Halifax, N.S., 1902 *1860.4 p42*
Schutz, M. Katharina Leibenguth SEE Schutz, Johann Daniel
Schutz, M. Katharina SEE Schutz, Johann Michael
Schutz, Margaretha 18; America, 1848 *778.6 p306*
Schutz, Margarethe; America, 1841 *5475.1 p458*
Schutz, Margarethe; Brazil, 1881 *5475.1 p445*
Schutz, Margarthe 30; Halifax, N.S., 1902 *1860.4 p42*
Schutz, Maria; America, 1836 *5475.1 p457*
Schutz, Mathias; America, 1868 *5475.1 p331*
Schutz, Mathias 57; America, 1843 *5475.1 p280*
Schutz, Mathias; New York, 1887 *5475.1 p247*
Schutz, Nikolaus SEE Schutz, Karl
Schutz, Nikolaus; Chicago, 1880 *5475.1 p245*
Schutz, Nikolaus 28; New York, 1884 *5475.1 p264*
Schutz, Peter SEE Schutz, Johann Michael
Schutz, Peter SEE Schutz, Klemens
Schutz, Peter; America, 1888 *5475.1 p287*

Schutz, Theresia; Halifax, N.S., 1902 ***1860.4*** *p42*
Schutz, Waoye 11; Halifax, N.S., 1902 ***1860.4*** *p42*
Schuyler, Abraham 60; Ontario, 1871 ***1823.21*** *p325*
Schuyler, Adam; Ohio, 1809-1852 ***4511.35*** *p48*
Schuyler, Baptist 49; Ontario, 1871 ***1823.21*** *p325*
Schuyler, Betsy 80; Ontario, 1871 ***1823.21*** *p325*
Schuyler, Henry 32; Ontario, 1871 ***1823.21*** *p325*
Schuyler, James 43; Ontario, 1871 ***1823.21*** *p326*
Schuyler, Margret 70; Ontario, 1871 ***1823.21*** *p326*
Schuyler, Moses 97; Ontario, 1871 ***1823.21*** *p326*
Schuyler, Stubble 80; Ontario, 1871 ***1823.21*** *p326*
Schuyler, William 36; Ontario, 1871 ***1823.21*** *p326*
Schuyler, William 72; Ontario, 1871 ***1823.21*** *p326*
Schwaake, Heinrich Ludwig; Texas, 1845 ***7420.1*** *p40*
Schwaarke, Friedrich; America, 1866 ***7420.1*** *p249*
Schwab, Catharine 19; Portland, ME, 1911 ***970.38*** *p81*
Schwab, Catherina 25; America, 1747 ***778.6*** *p306*
Schwab, Catherine 38; Missouri, 1847 ***778.6*** *p306*
Schwab, Georg 1; America, 1747 ***778.6*** *p306*
Schwab, George; Louisiana, 1874 ***4981.45*** *p134*
Schwab, Ignaz 33; America, 1747 ***778.6*** *p306*
Schwab, Marian 2; America, 1747 ***778.6*** *p306*
Schwabauer, Anna 29; New York, NY, 1893 ***1883.7*** *p44*
Schwabauer, Charlotte 3; New York, NY, 1893 ***1883.7*** *p44*
Schwabauer, Georg 6 months; New York, NY, 1893 ***1883.7*** *p44*
Schwabe, Heinrich Friedrich Wilhelm; New York, 1857 ***7420.1*** *p172*
Schwabe, Maria; America, 1867 ***7420.1*** *p255*
Schwaberow, Christian; Ohio, 1840-1897 ***8365.35*** *p18*
Schwablein, Johann Caspar; America, 1867 ***7919.3*** *p527*
Schwake, Miss; America, 1857 ***7420.1*** *p172*
Schwake, Mr.; America, 1859 ***7420.1*** *p189*
With wife & 4 daughters
With son 9
Schwake, Caroline Wilhelmine Hartmann *SEE* Schwake, Johann Conrad
Schwake, Catharine Sophie Marie; America, 1859 ***7420.1*** *p190*
Schwake, Conrad; America, 1857 ***7420.1*** *p172*
Schwake, Engel Sophie Caroline Eleonore *SEE* Schwake, Johann Conrad
Schwake, Ernst; America, 1857 ***7420.1*** *p172*
Schwake, Ernst; America, 1867 ***7420.1*** *p264*
With family
Schwake, Friedrich August Christ. *SEE* Schwake, Johann Conrad
Schwake, Friedrich Wilhelm; America, 1866 ***7420.1*** *p249*
Schwake, Hans Heinrich *SEE* Schwake, Johann Conrad
Schwake, Heinrich; America, 1857 ***7420.1*** *p172*
With wife & son
Schwake, Heinrich Friedrich Conrad *SEE* Schwake, Johann Conrad
Schwake, Johann Conrad; America, 1857 ***7420.1*** *p172*
*Wife:*Caroline Wilhelmine Hartmann
*Son:*Friedrich August Christ.
*Daughter:*Engel Sophie Caroline Eleonore
*Son:*Heinrich Friedrich Conrad
*Son:*Hans Heinrich
Schwake, Johann Otto; America, 1871 ***7420.1*** *p396*
Schwalben, Heinr.; Valdivia, Chile, 1852 ***1192.4*** *p56*
Schwald, Catherine 23; Mississippi, 1847 ***778.6*** *p306*
Schwald, Nicolas 27; Mississippi, 1847 ***778.6*** *p306*
Schwald, Therese 1; Mississippi, 1847 ***778.6*** *p306*
Schwald, Xavier 26; Mississippi, 1847 ***778.6*** *p306*
Schwalen, David 30; Galveston, TX, 1844 ***3967.10*** *p374*
Schwalen, Franz 18; Galveston, TX, 1844 ***3967.10*** *p374*
Schwalen, Louise 25; Galveston, TX, 1844 ***3967.10*** *p374*
Schwalen, Maria Louise 6 months; Galveston, TX, 1844 ***3967.10*** *p374*
Schwalen, Nikolaus 2; Galveston, TX, 1844 ***3967.10*** *p374*
Schwalen, Nikolaus 17; Galveston, TX, 1844 ***3967.10*** *p374*
Schwalin, Martin; Ohio, 1809-1852 ***4511.35*** *p48*
Schwallen, John Peter; Ohio, 1809-1852 ***4511.35*** *p48*
Schwalm, Christian; Ohio, 1809-1852 ***4511.35*** *p48*
Schwalm, Heinr.; Valdivia, Chile, 1852 ***1192.4*** *p56*
Schwalm, Joseph; Ohio, 1809-1852 ***4511.35*** *p48*
Schwam, Nicholas; Ohio, 1809-1852 ***4511.35*** *p48*
Schwambach, Adam *SEE* Schwambach, Jakob
Schwambach, Daniel *SEE* Schwambach, Johann Philipp
Schwambach, Daniel; Brazil, 1859 ***5475.1*** *p522*
*Wife:*M. Philippine Niklas
*Son:*Jakob
*Daughter:*Philippine
Schwambach, Dorothea Hahn *SEE* Schwambach, Johann Philipp
Schwambach, Elisabeth *SEE* Schwambach, Jakob
Schwambach, Elisabeth Muller *SEE* Schwambach, Jakob
Schwambach, Elisabeth *SEE* Schwambach, Johann Adam
Schwambach, Elisabeth Killian *SEE* Schwambach, Jakob
Schwambach, Elisabeth Schuck *SEE* Schwambach, Johann Adam
Schwambach, Franziska Antoni *SEE* Schwambach, Jakob
Schwambach, Jakob *SEE* Schwambach, Jakob
Schwambach, Jakob; America, 1862 ***5475.1*** *p495*
*Wife:*Franziska Antoni
*Son:*Jakob
*Daughter:*Katharina
*Son:*Philipp
*Son:*Peter
Schwambach, Jakob; America, 1865 ***5475.1*** *p498*
*Wife:*Elisabeth Muller
*Son:*Adam
*Daughter:*Elisabeth
Schwambach, Jakob *SEE* Schwambach, Daniel
Schwambach, Jakob *SEE* Schwambach, Johann Philipp
Schwambach, Jakob *SEE* Schwambach, Johann Adam
Schwambach, Jakob; Brazil, 1859 ***5475.1*** *p523*
*Wife:*Elisabeth Killian
*Son:*Peter
Schwambach, Johann Adam; Brazil, 1859 ***5475.1*** *p523*
*Wife:*Elisabeth Schuck
*Son:*Jakob
*Daughter:*Elisabeth
Schwambach, Johann Philipp; Brazil, 1859 ***5475.1*** *p522*
*Wife:*Dorothea Hahn
*Son:*Peter
*Son:*Jakob
*Son:*Karl
*Son:*Daniel
Schwambach, Juliana; America, 1858 ***5475.1*** *p562*
Schwambach, Karl *SEE* Schwambach, Johann Philipp
Schwambach, Karoline *SEE* Schwambach, Philipp Peter
Schwambach, Karoline Kirsch *SEE* Schwambach, Philipp Peter
Schwambach, Katharina *SEE* Schwambach, Jakob
Schwambach, Katharina; Brazil, 1859 ***5475.1*** *p495*
Schwambach, M. Philippine Niklas *SEE* Schwambach, Daniel
Schwambach, Margar.; America, 1865 ***5475.1*** *p498*
Schwambach, Peter *SEE* Schwambach, Jakob
Schwambach, Peter *SEE* Schwambach, Johann Philipp
Schwambach, Peter *SEE* Schwambach, Jakob
Schwambach, Philipp *SEE* Schwambach, Jakob
Schwambach, Philipp 74; Brazil, 1859 ***5475.1*** *p522*
Schwambach, Philipp Peter; Brazil, 1859 ***5475.1*** *p523*
*Wife:*Karoline Kirsch
*Daughter:*Karoline
Schwambach, Philippine *SEE* Schwambach, Daniel
Schwambach, Regina 53; America, 1865 ***5475.1*** *p498*
Schwan, Andreas 11 months; New York, NY, 1893 ***1883.7*** *p41*
Schwan, Catharina 7; New York, NY, 1893 ***1883.7*** *p41*
Schwan, Elisabeth 10; New York, NY, 1898 ***7951.13*** *p44*
Schwan, Eva 9; New York, NY, 1893 ***1883.7*** *p41*
Schwan, Eva 9; New York, NY, 1898 ***7951.13*** *p44*
Schwan, Eva 32; New York, NY, 1893 ***1883.7*** *p41*
Schwan, Jacob 41; New York, NY, 1898 ***7951.13*** *p44*
Schwan, Joseph; Ohio, 1809-1852 ***4511.35*** *p48*
Schwan, Julianna 2; New York, NY, 1893 ***1883.7*** *p41*
Schwan, Julianna 3; New York, NY, 1898 ***7951.13*** *p44*
Schwan, Magdalena 4; New York, NY, 1893 ***1883.7*** *p41*
Schwan, Magdalena 40; New York, NY, 1898 ***7951.13*** *p44*
Schwan, Margaret 1; New York, NY, 1898 ***7951.13*** *p44*
Schwan, Paul 12; New York, NY, 1898 ***7951.13*** *p44*
Schwan, Peter 20; New York, NY, 1898 ***7951.13*** *p44*
Schwan, Peter 34; New York, NY, 1893 ***1883.7*** *p41*
Schwandt, Ferdinand; Wisconsin, 1883 ***6795.8*** *p93*
Schwandt, Herman Leopold; Wisconsin, 1897 ***6795.8*** *p84*
Schwanke, Auguste Ida; Wisconsin, 1888 ***6795.8*** *p132*
Schwanke, Edward; Wisconsin, 1883 ***6795.8*** *p208*
Schwanke, Johann J.; Wisconsin, 1874 ***6795.8*** *p129*
Schwantz, Christian; Long Island, 1779 ***8529.30*** *p10A*
Schwapps, Nicholas; Ohio, 1840-1897 ***8365.35*** *p18*
Schwarke, H. Chr.; America, 1866 ***7420.1*** *p249*
Schwarm, Nicholas; Ohio, 1809-1852 ***4511.35*** *p48*
Schwartz, Adam; Ohio, 1840-1897 ***8365.35*** *p18*
Schwartz, Anna Maria Prediger 22 *SEE* Schwartz, Josef
Schwartz, Balthasar; America, 1873 ***5475.1*** *p150*
Schwartz, Balthasar 64; America, 1869 ***5475.1*** *p149*
Schwartz, Bernard 34; New Orleans, 1841 ***778.6*** *p306*
Schwartz, Claire 19; New York, NY, 1894 ***6512.1*** *p232*
Schwartz, Eugene 9; America, 1847 ***778.6*** *p306*
Schwartz, Henry; Ohio, 1809-1852 ***4511.35*** *p48*
Schwartz, J. Peter *SEE* Schwartz, Nikolaus
Schwartz, Jakob; America, 1846 ***5475.1*** *p402*
Schwartz, Jakob *SEE* Schwartz, Josef
Schwartz, Jakob 26; America, 1869 ***5475.1*** *p149*
Schwartz, Johann *SEE* Schwartz, Nikolaus
Schwartz, Johann 24; America, 1869 ***5475.1*** *p149*
Schwartz, Johann 25; America, 1869 ***5475.1*** *p149*
Schwartz, Johann 25; Louisiana, 1848 ***778.6*** *p306*
Schwartz, Johann; New York, NY, 1890 ***3366.30*** *p70*
Schwartz, John; Ohio, 1809-1852 ***4511.35*** *p48*
Schwartz, Josef; America, 1872 ***5475.1*** *p150*
*Wife:*Anna Maria Prediger
*Son:*Jakob
With son
*Mother:*Katharina
Schwartz, Joseph 51; Louisiana, 1848 ***778.6*** *p306*
Schwartz, Joseph 29; Port uncertain, 1843 ***778.6*** *p306*
Schwartz, Kaspar *SEE* Schwartz, Nikolaus
Schwartz, Katharina 64 *SEE* Schwartz, Josef
Schwartz, Leonard; Illinois, 1852 ***6079.1*** *p13*
Schwartz, Leonard; Philadelphia, 1778 ***8529.30*** *p3*
Schwartz, Maria 26; America, 1847 ***5475.1*** *p396*
Schwartz, Nikolaus 40; America, 1872 ***5475.1*** *p149*
*Son:*Johann
*Son:*Peter
*Son:*J. Peter
*Son:*Kaspar
Schwartz, Peter *SEE* Schwartz, Nikolaus
Schwartz, Peter 28; America, 1869 ***5475.1*** *p149*
Schwartz, Peter; Ohio, 1809-1852 ***4511.35*** *p48*
Schwartz, Philip; Illinois, 1834-1900 ***6020.5*** *p133*
Schwartz, Severin; Illinois, 1858-1861 ***6020.5*** *p133*
Schwartzenbach, Maria; Detroit, 1930 ***1640.60*** *p82*
Schwartzer, Joseph; Iowa, 1922 ***1211.15*** *p19*
Schwarz, Angela 42; Brazil, 1857 ***5475.1*** *p367*
Schwarz, Anna Lonsdorfer *SEE* Schwarz, Nikolaus
Schwarz, Anna; New York, 1892 ***5475.1*** *p425*
Schwarz, Anton 22; New York, NY, 1874 ***6954.7*** *p38*
Schwarz, Barbara Bast *SEE* Schwarz, Jakob
Schwarz, Carl; America, 1866 ***7420.1*** *p249*
With son
Schwarz, Carl 45; Missouri, 1847 ***778.6*** *p306*
Schwarz, Carl 3 months; New York, NY, 1874 ***6954.7*** *p38*
Schwarz, Carl 8; New York, NY, 1874 ***6954.7*** *p38*
Schwarz, Caroline 20; New York, NY, 1874 ***6954.7*** *p38*
Schwarz, Christian 20; New York, NY, 1874 ***6954.7*** *p38*
Schwarz, Christina 9; New York, NY, 1874 ***6954.7*** *p38*
Schwarz, Christina 30; New York, NY, 1874 ***6954.7*** *p38*
Schwarz, Elisabeth; America, 1873 ***5475.1*** *p307*
Schwarz, Elisabeth 1 months; New York, NY, 1874 ***6954.7*** *p38*
Schwarz, Francois 28; New Orleans, 1845 ***778.6*** *p307*
Schwarz, Georg 1 months; New York, NY, 1874 ***6954.7*** *p38*
Schwarz, Georg 33; New York, NY, 1874 ***6954.7*** *p38*
Schwarz, Jacob 18; America, 1746 ***778.6*** *p307*
Schwarz, Jakob; America, 1830 ***5475.1*** *p410*
*Wife:*Barbara Bast
With 6 children
With child 4
With child 14
Schwarz, Jean 23; America, 1847 ***778.6*** *p307*
Schwarz, Johann; America, 1864 ***5475.1*** *p338*
Schwarz, Johann; America, 1867 ***5475.1*** *p178*
Schwarz, Johann 42; America, 1843 ***5475.1*** *p428*
With wife
With 4 children
Schwarz, Johann 23; New York, 1888 ***5475.1*** *p179*
*Brother:*Nikolaus 16
Schwarz, John; Ohio, 1842 ***2763.1*** *p21*
Schwarz, Josef; America, 1852 ***5475.1*** *p403*
Schwarz, Joseph 19; America, 1746 ***778.6*** *p307*
Schwarz, Joseph; Ohio, 1842 ***2763.1*** *p21*
Schwarz, Karoline; America, 1885 ***5475.1*** *p422*
Schwarz, Katharina; America, 1882 ***5475.1*** *p229*
*Son:*Nikolaus
*Daughter:*Maria
Schwarz, Katharina 27; America, 1867 ***5475.1*** *p558*
Schwarz, Leonard; Philadelphia, 1778 ***8529.30*** *p3*
Schwarz, Magdalena 23; New York, NY, 1874 ***6954.7*** *p38*
Schwarz, Magdalena Kiel; Chicago, 1855 ***5475.1*** *p310*
Schwarz, Margarethe *SEE* Schwarz, Margarethe
Schwarz, Margarethe; America, 1871 ***8115.12*** *p321*
*Child:*Margarethe
Schwarz, Maria *SEE* Schwarz, Katharina Mary
Schwarz, Maria 29; Chicago, 1855 ***5475.1*** *p310*
Schwarz, Mathias; America, 1871 ***5475.1*** *p534*
Schwarz, Max; America, 1867 ***7919.3*** *p534*
Schwarz, Max; Chicago, 1886 ***5475.1*** *p387*
Schwarz, Michel; America, 1878 ***5475.1*** *p163*
Schwarz, Nikolaus; America, 1873 ***5475.1*** *p133*
Schwarz, Nikolaus *SEE* Schwarz, Katharina Mary
Schwarz, Nikolaus 24; America, 1889 ***5475.1*** *p145*
Schwarz, Nikolaus 65; America, 1890 ***5475.1*** *p76*
*Wife:*Anna Lonsdorfer
Schwarz, Nikolaus 16 *SEE* Schwarz, Johann
Schwarz, Peter; America, 1872 ***5475.1*** *p388*
Schwarz, Peter; America, 1874 ***5475.1*** *p134*

Schwarz, Peter; Chicago, 1895 *5475.1 p156*
Schwarz, Peter 6; New York, NY, 1874 *6954.7 p38*
Schwarz, Peter 23; New York, NY, 1874 *6954.7 p38*
Schwarz, Philippine Friederike; America, 1836 *5475.1 p457*
Schwarz, Siegmund; America, 1867 *7919.3 p534*
Schwarz, Simon; America, 1867 *7919.3 p534*
Schwarz, Sophie 9 months; New York, NY, 1874 *6954.7 p38*
Schwarz, Sophie 13; New York, NY, 1874 *6954.7 p38*
Schwarze, Rudolph Victor Reinhard; America, 1881 *7420.1 p325*
Schwarze, Sophie; America, 1853 *7420.1 p111*
Schwarzlander, Charles; Colorado, 1900 *1029.59 p82*
Schwavy, Edward; North Carolina, 1792-1862 *1088.45 p31*
Schwaz, Katharina; America, 1881 *5475.1 p33*
Schwed, Anna SEE Schwed, Nikolaus
Schwed, Barbara SEE Schwed, Nikolaus
Schwed, Bernhard SEE Schwed, Nikolaus
Schwed, Margarethe Leinenbach SEE Schwed, Nikolaus
Schwed, Nikolaus; America, 1882 *5475.1 p141*
  *Wife:*Margarethe Leinenbach
  *Daughter:*Anna
  *Daughter:*Barbara
  *Son:*Bernhard
Schweer, . . .; America, 1845 *7420.1 p40*
Schweer, August Wilhelm; America, 1848 *7420.1 p62*
  *Wife:*Catharina Engel Sophia Homeier
Schweer, Carl Friedrich; America, 1883 *7420.1 p340*
Schweer, Catharina Engel Sophia Homeier SEE Schweer, August Wilhelm
Schweer, Catharine Marie Dorothee SEE Schweer, Engel Dorothee Louise Duhlmeyer
Schweer, Christian; America, 1854 *7420.1 p130*
Schweer, Engel Dorothee Louise; America, 1856 *7420.1 p153*
  *Daughter:*Ilse Marie Charlotte
  *Son:*Hans Heinrich Conrad
  *Son:*Johann Philipp
  *Daughter:*Catharine Marie Dorothee
Schweer, Engel Maria Sophia SEE Schweer, Johann Philipp
Schweer, Engel Marie; America, 1848 *7420.1 p59*
Schweer, Engel Marie Charlotte Hartmann SEE Schweer, Johann Christoph
Schweer, Ernst Heinrich; America, 1883 *7420.1 p340*
Schweer, Hans Heinrich Conrad SEE Schweer, Engel Dorothee Louise Duhlmeyer
Schweer, Hans Heinrich Konrad; America, 1881 *7420.1 p325*
Schweer, Hans Heinrich Otto; America, 1888 *7420.1 p357*
Schweer, Heinrich; America, 1868 *7420.1 p276*
Schweer, Heinrich Christoph; America, 1868 *7420.1 p277*
Schweer, Heinrich Friedrich Gottlieb SEE Schweer, Johann Heinrich
Schweer, Heinrich Wilhelm SEE Schweer, Johann Christoph
Schweer, Heinrich Wilhelm; America, 1881 *7420.1 p325*
Schweer, Ilse Marie Charlotte SEE Schweer, Engel Dorothee Louise Duhlmeyer
Schweer, Johann Carl Ludwig; America, 1866 *7420.1 p249*
Schweer, Johann Christoph; America, 1870 *7420.1 p287*
  *Wife:*Engel Marie Charlotte Hartmann
  *Son:*Johann Otto
  *Son:*Heinrich Wilhelm
  *Son:*Johann Friedrich Christoph
Schweer, Johann Friedrich Christoph SEE Schweer, Johann Christoph
Schweer, Johann Heinrich Conrad SEE Schweer, Johann Heinrich
Schweer, Johann Heinrich SEE Schweer, Johann Heinrich Christoph
Schweer, Johann Heinrich; America, 1854 *7420.1 p130*
  *Son:*Johann Friedrich Conrad
  *Son:*Heinrich Friedrich Gottlieb
Schweer, Johann Heinrich Christoph; America, 1849 *7420.1 p67*
  *Wife:*Kath. Sophie Borchers
  *Son:*Johann Heinrich
Schweer, Johann Heinrich Conrad; America, 1882 *7420.1 p332*
Schweer, Johann Otto SEE Schweer, Johann Christoph
Schweer, Johann Philipp; America, 1848 *7420.1 p62*
  *Sister:*Engel Maria Sophia
  *Sister:*Sophia Louise Magdalena
Schweer, Johann Philipp SEE Schweer, Engel Dorothee Louise Duhlmeyer
Schweer, Kath. Sophie Borchers SEE Schweer, Johann Heinrich Christoph

Schweer, Sophia Louise Magdalena SEE Schweer, Johann Philipp
Schwegler, Catherine 55; Ontario, 1871 *1823.17 p145*
Schweich, Ferdinand; America, 1871 *5475.1 p327*
Schweiger, Peter; America, 1836 *2526.43 p214*
  With wife
  With child 6
  With child 4
Schweighard, George 31; America, 1847 *778.6 p307*
Schweikert, Ernestine 8 SEE Schweikert, Michael
Schweikert, Georg 6 SEE Schweikert, Michael
Schweikert, Jakob 3 SEE Schweikert, Michael
Schweikert, Katharine 7 SEE Schweikert, Michael
Schweikert, Michael 41; America, 1868 *2526.43 p181*
  *Wife:*Sophie 35
  *Daughter:*Katharine 7
  *Son:*Georg 6 months
  *Son:*Jakob 3
  *Daughter:*Ernestine 8
Schweikert, Sophie 35 SEE Schweikert, Michael
Schweinsbotteher, Cath.; New York, 1859 *358.56 p55*
Schweir, Jacob; Ohio, 1809-1852 *4511.35 p48*
Schweir, Michail; Ohio, 1809-1852 *4511.35 p48*
Schweirer, George; Ohio, 1809-1852 *4511.35 p48*
Schweitzer, Anna; America, 1883 *5475.1 p176*
Schweitzer, Christian; Ohio, 1809-1852 *4511.35 p48*
Schweitzer, Christine 54; Louisiana, 1848 *778.6 p307*
Schweitzer, Claude 50; America, 1846 *778.6 p307*
Schweitzer, Elisabeth 15; Louisiana, 1848 *778.6 p307*
Schweitzer, Henry; Ohio, 1809-1852 *4511.35 p48*
Schweitzer, John Henry; Ohio, 1809-1852 *4511.35 p48*
Schweitzer, Mrs. Michel; America, 1883 *5475.1 p176*
Schweitzer, Peter; America, 1874 *2526.43 p157*
Schweizer, Joseph; New York, 1859 *358.56 p54*
Schweizer, Philipp; America, 1865 *2526.43 p157*
Schwencke, Johs.; Valdivia, Chile, 1852 *1192.4 p56*
Schwend, Katharina; Venezuela, 1843 *3899.5 p540*
Schwendler, . . .; America, 1846 *5475.1 p531*
Schwendler, Anton SEE Schwendler, Peter
Schwendler, Heinr. J.; America, 1880 *5475.1 p272*
Schwendler, Heinrich SEE Schwendler, Peter
Schwendler, Joh. Peter SEE Schwendler, Peter
Schwendler, Johann; Brazil, 1857 *5475.1 p516*
Schwendler, Katharina SEE Schwendler, Peter
Schwendler, Peter; Iowa, 1880 *5475.1 p272*
  *Wife:*Susanna Boos
  *Son:*Anton
  *Son:*Joh. Peter
  *Son:*Heinrich
  *Daughter:*Katharina
Schwendler, Susanna Boos SEE Schwendler, Peter
Schwendmann, Elisabeth; America, 1867 *7919.3 p528*
  With 3 children
Schweng, Adam 18; Halifax, N.S., 1902 *1860.4 p42*
Schwenger, Fredrich; Wisconsin, 1878 *6795.8 p188*
Schwenger, Friedrich; America, 1893 *179.55 p19*
Schwenger, Johann; America, 1869 *179.55 p19*
Schwenk, Peter; America, 1862 *5475.1 p540*
Schwer, Widow; America, 1868 *7420.1 p277*
Schwer, Dietrich; America, 1845 *7420.1 p40*
  With wife & 3 children
Schwer, Engel Dorothea; America, 1864 *7420.1 p227*
Schwer, Engel Marie Dorothea; America, 1866 *7420.1 p249*
Schwer, Heinrich Conrad Horsten; America, 1854 *7420.1 p130*
Schwerdt, Caroline; America, 1867 *7919.3 p531*
Schwerdt, Conrad Friedrich Wilhelm SEE Schwerdt, Friedrich Wilhelm
Schwerdt, Friedrich Wilhelm; Minnesota, 1873 *7420.1 p301*
  *Daughter:*Sophie Dorothea Louise
  *Son:*Conrad Friedrich Wilhelm
  With wife
Schwerdt, Sophie Dorothea Louise SEE Schwerdt, Friedrich Wilhelm
Schwerdtmann, Ludolph Philipp Eduard; Baltimore, 1873 *7420.1 p301*
  *Uncle:*Theodor
Schwerdtmann, Theodor SEE Schwerdtmann, Ludolph Philipp Eduard
Schwersinske, Emil Herman; Wisconsin, 1895 *6795.8 p42*
Schwersinske, Hulda Albertine; Wisconsin, 1896 *6795.8 p132*
Schwesinger, Johann Peter Christian; America, 1868 *7919.3 p533*
Schwesinger, Peter; America, 1868 *7919.3 p533*
  With family & grandchild
Schwidersky, Moses 17; New York, NY, 1878 *9253.2 p45*
Schwien, Alexander 2; New York, NY, 1893 *1883.7 p44*

Schwien, Amalia 9 months; New York, NY, 1893 *1883.7 p44*
Schwien, Charlotte 24; New York, NY, 1893 *1883.7 p44*
Schwier, Anton Christian Friedrich; America, 1865 *7420.1 p237*
Schwier, Anton Friedrich Wilhelm; America, 1884 *7420.1 p345*
  *Wife:*Leonore Rosener
  *Mother:*Caroline
  *Son:*Wilhelm Christian Friedrich
Schwier, Carl Friedrich; America, 1869 *7420.1 p281*
Schwier, Caroline SEE Schwier, Anton Friedrich Wilhelm
Schwier, Jacob; Ohio, 1809-1852 *4511.35 p48*
Schwier, Leonore Rosener SEE Schwier, Anton Friedrich Wilhelm
Schwier, Michael; Ohio, 1809-1852 *4511.35 p48*
Schwier, Wilhelm Christian; America, 1882 *7420.1 p332*
Schwier, Wilhelm Christian Friedrich SEE Schwier, Anton Friedrich Wilhelm
Schwiessing, Engel Marie Sophia; America, 1886 *7420.1 p351*
Schwietzer, Johann Friedrich Christoph; Port uncertain, 1853 *7420.1 p111*
Schwimmer, Margaret; New York, 1860 *358.56 p149*
Schwin, Charles; Washington, 1889 *2770.40 p81*
Schwinck, Carl; Nebraska, 1905 *3004.30 p46*
Schwind, Elisabeth 25; New England, 1866 *170.15 p42*
Schwind, Margaretha 5; New England, 1866 *170.15 p42*
Schwind, Peter 33; New England, 1866 *170.15 p42*
Schwind, Valentin 9; New England, 1866 *170.15 p42*
Schwindling, A. Maria; Chicago, 1887 *5475.1 p244*
Schwindling, Anna Kiefer SEE Schwindling, Math.
Schwindling, Math.; America, 1881 *5475.1 p325*
  *Wife:*Anna Kiefer
Schwindt, Jakob Philipp SEE Schwindt, Karl Philipp
Schwindt, Karl SEE Schwindt, Karl Philipp
Schwindt, Karl Philipp; America, 1883 *2526.42 p131*
  *Wife:*Margaretha Riebel
  *Child:*Margaretha
  *Child:*Jakob Philipp
  *Child:*Karl
Schwindt, Margaretha SEE Schwindt, Karl Philipp
Schwindt, Margaretha Riebel SEE Schwindt, Karl Philipp
Schwing, Philippe 23; New Orleans, 1845 *778.6 p307*
Schwingel, Anna Maria 13 SEE Schwingel, Konrad, III
Schwingel, Barbara 1 SEE Schwingel, Philipp
Schwingel, Christian; America, 1852 *5475.1 p495*
Schwingel, Conrad 10 SEE Schwingel, Konrad, III
Schwingel, Elisabeth 6 SEE Schwingel, Peter
Schwingel, Elisabeth Gross 31 SEE Schwingel, Peter
Schwingel, Elisabeth 38; America, 1850 *5475.1 p393*
Schwingel, Eva 119 SEE Schwingel, Konrad, III
Schwingel, Georg; America, 1837 *5475.1 p536*
Schwingel, Georg; America, 1862 *5475.1 p556*
Schwingel, Georg Jakob; America, 1836 *5475.1 p536*
  *Wife:*Katharina Schiffler
Schwingel, Georg Jakob; America, 1847 *5475.1 p537*
Schwingel, Johann 6 SEE Schwingel, Philipp
Schwingel, Johann Georg 21; New York, 1872 *5475.1 p539*
Schwingel, Katharina Schiffler SEE Schwingel, Georg Jakob
Schwingel, Katharina 5 SEE Schwingel, Philipp
Schwingel, Konrad, III; America, 1836 *5475.1 p536*
  With wife
  *Daughter:*Maria
  *Son:*Conrad
  *Son:*Nikolaus
  *Daughter:*Anna Maria
  *Daughter:*Eva
Schwingel, Luise; America, 1881 *5475.1 p539*
Schwingel, Maria 13 SEE Schwingel, Konrad, III
Schwingel, Nikolaus 6 SEE Schwingel, Konrad, III
Schwingel, Peter 50; America, 1843 *5475.1 p546*
  *Wife:*Elisabeth Gross 31
  With sister-in-law 21
  With sister-in-law 19
  *Daughter:*Elisabeth 6 months
Schwingel, Philipp; Ohio, 1843 *5475.1 p546*
  *Son:*Philipp
  *Daughter:*Barbara
  *Son:*Johann
  *Daughter:*Katharina
Schwingel, Philipp 31 SEE Schwingel, Philipp
Schwinn, . . .; America, 1882 *2526.42 p156*
  With daughter
Schwinn, Adam; America, 1853 *2526.42 p146*
Schwinn, Adam; America, 1869 *2526.42 p177*
Schwinn, Adam SEE Schwinn, Johannes
Schwinn, Adam 13 SEE Schwinn, Regina
Schwinn, Adam 56; America, 1853 *2526.42 p148*
Schwinn, Anna Margaretha 13 SEE Schwinn, Johannes, I

Schwinn, Anna Margaretha Eberhard *SEE* Schwinn, Johannes
Schwinn, Anna Maria Olt *SEE* Schwinn, Johannes, I
Schwinn, Barbara; America, 1864 ***2526.42*** *p185*
With child 2
Schwinn, Christina Thierolf *SEE* Schwinn, Johannes
Schwinn, Elisabeth 10 *SEE* Schwinn, Mrs. Friedrich, II
Schwinn, Friedrich, II; America, 1841 ***2526.43*** *p143*
Schwinn, Mrs. Friedrich, II; America, 1842 ***2526.43*** *p143*
*Daughter:*Elisabeth
*Son:*Philipp
Schwinn, Georg; America, 1827-1899 ***2526.42*** *p147*
Schwinn, Georg *SEE* Schwinn, Johannes
Schwinn, Georg Heinrich 16; America, 1853 ***2526.43*** *p124*
Schwinn, Georg Philipp; America, 1838 ***2526.42*** *p131*
With wife
With child 6 months
Schwinn, Heinrich Eberhard *SEE* Schwinn, Johannes
Schwinn, Jakob; America, 1889 ***2526.43*** *p181*
Schwinn, Jakob 21; America, 1884 ***2526.42*** *p111*
Schwinn, Jakob; Argentina, 1855 ***2526.43*** *p214*
With family of 4
Schwinn, Jakob; Pittsburgh, 1887 ***5475.1*** *p317*
Schwinn, Joh. Peter 17 *SEE* Schwinn, Johannes, I
Schwinn, Johann; America, 1892 ***2526.42*** *p111*
Schwinn, Johann Friedrich; America, 1868 ***2526.42*** *p178*
Schwinn, Johann Michael; America, 1852 ***2526.42*** *p147*
Schwinn, Johannes; America, 1884 ***2526.42*** *p131*
*Wife:*Christina Thierolf
*Child:*Adam
*Child:*Wilhelm
*Child:*Maria
*Child:*Georg
*Child:*Anna Margaretha Eberhard
*Child:*Heinrich Eberhard
Schwinn, Johannes; America, 1888 ***2526.43*** *p192*
Schwinn, Johannes 32 *SEE* Schwinn, Johannes, I
Schwinn, Johannes 43; America, 1844 ***2526.43*** *p214*
Schwinn, Johannes, I; America, 1852 ***2526.42*** *p178*
*Wife:*Anna Maria Olt
*Daughter:*Anna Margaretha
*Son:*Joh. Peter
*Son:*Johannes
Schwinn, Ludwig; America, 1867 ***2526.43*** *p189*
Schwinn, Maria *SEE* Schwinn, Johannes
Schwinn, Michael; America, 1854 ***2526.42*** *p147*
Schwinn, Nikolaus; Chicago, 1869 ***5475.1*** *p126*
Schwinn, Peter; America, 1882 ***5475.1*** *p184*
Schwinn, Philipp 7 *SEE* Schwinn, Mrs. Friedrich, II
Schwinn, Philipp 32; America, 1851 ***2526.42*** *p185*
With wife 2 children & sister
With mother 65
Schwinn, Regina; America, 1882 ***2526.42*** *p156*
*Child:*Wilhelm
*Child:*Adam
Schwinn, Wilhelm *SEE* Schwinn, Regina
Schwinn, Wilhelm *SEE* Schwinn, Johannes
Schwiser, Nikolaus 47; Galveston, TX, 1846 ***3967.10*** *p378*
Schwitzer, Conrad; America, 1853 ***7420.1*** *p111*
Schwitzer, Gerhard Conrad; America, 1849 ***7420.1*** *p68*
Schwitzer, Heinrich Friedrich Wilhelm; America, 1870 ***7420.1*** *p285*
Schwobe, Henry T.; Colorado, 1906 ***1029.59*** *p82*
Schwobe, Joseph; Wisconsin, 1884 ***1029.59*** *p82*
Schwochert, John E.; Wisconsin, 1888 ***6795.8*** *p166*
Schwochert, Joseph; Wisconsin, 1912 ***6795.8*** *p166*
Schwomeier, Mr.; America, 1855 ***7420.1*** *p142*
With wife
Schwomeier, Carl Heinrich Gottlieb; America, 1852 ***7420.1*** *p97*
Schwomeier, Christian; America, 1855 ***7420.1*** *p142*
With wife & daughter
Schwomeier, Heinrich; America, 1852 ***7420.1*** *p97*
Schwone, August; America, 1864 ***7420.1*** *p227*
Schwurm, Nicholas; Ohio, 1809-1852 ***4511.35*** *p48*
Schyall, James 65; Ontario, 1871 ***1823.21*** *p326*
Sciaeprt, Amial; Wisconsin, 1895 ***6795.8*** *p41*
Scievyer, Samuel; Virginia, 1774 ***1220.12*** *p705*
Scillia, Joseph 76; Ontario, 1871 ***1823.21*** *p326*
Scilly, Henry 38; Ontario, 1871 ***1823.21*** *p326*
Scilly, Robert 70; Ontario, 1871 ***1823.21*** *p326*
Scilly, William; Ontario, 1871 ***1823.21*** *p326*
Scior, Adam; America, 1852 ***2526.42*** *p147*
Scior, Heinrich; America, 1854 ***2526.43*** *p192*
Scior, Johann; America, 1878 ***2526.43*** *p181*
Scior, Nikolaus; America, 1883 ***2526.42*** *p131*
Scivery, Mr.; Marblehead, MA, 1629 ***9228.50*** *p579*
Sclyer, Jacob 21; America, 1847 ***778.6*** *p307*
Sclyer, Margaretta 64; America, 1847 ***778.6*** *p307*
Scobal, Ann; Boston, 1769 ***9228.50*** *p48*
Scobol, Ann; Boston, 1769 ***9228.50*** *p576*
Scoffin, George 24; Ontario, 1871 ***1823.17*** *p145*
Scofield, John; America, 1679 ***1220.12*** *p705*
Scofield, Robert; Barbados, 1693 ***1220.12*** *p705*
Scofield, William; America, 1765 ***1220.12*** *p705*
Scole, Jane; Virginia, 1735 ***1220.12*** *p705*
Scoles, John; America, 1753 ***1220.12*** *p705*
Scolfield, John; America, 1752 ***1220.12*** *p705*
Scollay, J.; Boston, 1728 ***1642*** *p23*
Scollick, Jonathan 43; Ontario, 1871 ***1823.21*** *p326*
Sconlin, James 23; Ontario, 1871 ***1823.17*** *p145*
Scoon, John; America, 1722 ***1220.12*** *p705*
Scoon, John A. 70; Ontario, 1871 ***1823.21*** *p326*
Scoon, William 39; Ontario, 1871 ***1823.21*** *p326*
Score, Joseph; America, 1766 ***1220.12*** *p705*
Scoresby, John; America, 1729 ***1220.12*** *p705*
Scorey, Anthony; Ontario, 1871 ***1823.21*** *p326*
Scot, Barrade; Annapolis, MD, 1725 ***1220.12*** *p706*
Scot, Celia; America, 1759 ***1220.12*** *p706*
Scot, Dominique 14; Quebec, 1633 ***9221.17*** *p30*
Scot, Robert 36; Ontario, 1871 ***1823.21*** *p326*
Scot, William; America, 1741 ***1220.12*** *p707*
Scother, Ann; America, 1744 ***1220.12*** *p705*
Scother, Charles 17; Quebec, 1870 ***8364.32*** *p25*
Scott, Adam 56; Ontario, 1871 ***1823.21*** *p326*
Scott, Agnes 20; Ontario, 1871 ***1823.21*** *p326*
Scott, Alexander; Ohio, 1840 ***3580.20*** *p33*
Scott, Alexander; Ohio, 1840 ***6020.12*** *p22*
Scott, Alexander 50; Ontario, 1871 ***1823.21*** *p326*
Scott, Alexander 60; Ontario, 1871 ***1823.21*** *p326*
Scott, Alexander 70; Ontario, 1871 ***1823.21*** *p326*
Scott, Andrew; Annapolis, MD, 1730 ***1220.12*** *p706*
Scott, Andrew 55; Ontario, 1871 ***1823.17*** *p145*
Scott, Ann; America, 1755 ***1220.12*** *p706*
Scott, Ann 51; Ontario, 1871 ***1823.21*** *p326*
Scott, Ann 55; Ontario, 1871 ***1823.21*** *p326*
Scott, Anna 24; Ontario, 1871 ***1823.21*** *p326*
Scott, Anna Maria; Quebec, 1790-1819 ***9228.50*** *p234*
Scott, Benjamin; America, 1758 ***1220.12*** *p706*
Scott, Benjamin 40; Ontario, 1871 ***1823.21*** *p326*
Scott, Catharine *SEE* Scott, Henry
Scott, Catherine; America, 1754 ***1220.12*** *p706*
Scott, Catherine Jane Aubin *SEE* Scott, John
Scott, Charles 44; Ontario, 1871 ***1823.21*** *p326*
Scott, Charles S. 32; Ontario, 1871 ***1823.21*** *p326*
Scott, David 12; New York, NY, 1835 ***5024.1*** *p137*
Scott, David; Ontario, 1835 ***3160.1*** *p150*
Scott, David 40; Ontario, 1871 ***1823.17*** *p145*
Scott, David 49; Ontario, 1871 ***1823.17*** *p145*
Scott, David 60; Ontario, 1871 ***1823.21*** *p326*
Scott, Edward; America, 1733 ***1220.12*** *p706*
Scott, Edward; America, 1758 ***1220.12*** *p706*
Scott, Edward; Annapolis, MD, 1725 ***1220.12*** *p706*
Scott, Edward 66; Ontario, 1871 ***1823.17*** *p145*
Scott, Eleanor; America, 1759 ***1220.12*** *p706*
Scott, Elizabeth; America, 1765 ***1220.12*** *p706*
Scott, Elizabeth; Annapolis, MD, 1725 ***1220.12*** *p706*
Scott, Elizabeth; Barbados, 1667 ***1220.12*** *p706*
Scott, Elizabeth; Barbados, 1682 ***1220.12*** *p706*
Scott, Elizabeth; Maryland, 1722 ***1220.12*** *p706*
Scott, Elizabeth 42; New York, NY, 1835 ***5024.1*** *p137*
Scott, Elizabeth 17; Ontario, 1871 ***1823.21*** *p326*
Scott, Elizabeth 32; Ontario, 1871 ***1823.17*** *p145*
Scott, Elizabeth; Potomac, 1731 ***1220.12*** *p706*
Scott, Francis W.; North Carolina, 1848 ***1088.45*** *p31*
Scott, George; America, 1719 ***1220.12*** *p706*
Scott, George; America, 1732 ***1220.12*** *p706*
Scott, George; America, 1765 ***1220.12*** *p706*
Scott, George 49; Ontario, 1871 ***1823.21*** *p326*
Scott, George 50; Ontario, 1871 ***1823.21*** *p326*
Scott, George 50; Ontario, 1871 ***1823.21*** *p326*
Scott, Hannah; America, 1774 ***1220.12*** *p706*
Scott, Harrison 50; Ontario, 1871 ***1823.21*** *p326*
Scott, Henery 72; Ontario, 1871 ***1823.21*** *p326*
Scott, Henry *SEE* Scott, Henry
Scott, Henry; Canada, 1774 ***3036.5*** *p41*
*Wife:*Mary
*Child:*Henry
*Child:*Catharine
Scott, Henry; Ohio, 1840 ***2763.1*** *p21*
Scott, Henry 50; Ontario, 1871 ***1823.17*** *p145*
Scott, Henry 64; Ontario, 1871 ***1823.21*** *p327*
Scott, Hugh, Sr. 65; Ontario, 1871 ***1823.21*** *p327*
Scott, Isabel; Virginia, 1736 ***1220.12*** *p706*
Scott, Isabele 64; Ontario, 1871 ***1823.17*** *p145*
Scott, Isabella 32; Ontario, 1871 ***1823.17*** *p145*
Scott, James; America, 1731 ***1220.12*** *p706*
Scott, James; America, 1742 ***1220.12*** *p706*
Scott, James; America, 1756 ***1220.12*** *p706*
Scott, James; Barbados, 1686 ***1220.12*** *p706*
Scott, James 36; New York, NY, 1835 ***5024.1*** *p137*
Scott, James; Ohio, 1832 ***3580.20*** *p33*
Scott, James; Ohio, 1832 ***6020.12*** *p22*
Scott, James 31; Ontario, 1871 ***1823.21*** *p327*
Scott, James 34; Ontario, 1871 ***1823.17*** *p145*
Scott, James 42; Ontario, 1871 ***1823.21*** *p327*
Scott, James 44; Ontario, 1871 ***1823.21*** *p327*
Scott, James 50; Ontario, 1871 ***1823.21*** *p327*
Scott, James 58; Ontario, 1871 ***1823.21*** *p327*
Scott, James 69; Ontario, 1871 ***1823.17*** *p145*
Scott, Jane; America, 1745 ***1220.12*** *p706*
Scott, Jane; Maryland, 1719 ***1220.12*** *p706*
Scott, Jane; Ontario, 1835 ***3160.1*** *p150*
Scott, John; America, 1719 ***1220.12*** *p706*
Scott, John; America, 1730 ***1220.12*** *p706*
Scott, John; America, 1732 ***1220.12*** *p706*
Scott, John; America, 1738 ***1220.12*** *p706*
Scott, John; America, 1742 ***1220.12*** *p706*
Scott, John; America, 1751 ***1220.12*** *p706*
Scott, John; America, 1757 ***1220.12*** *p706*
Scott, John; America, 1769 ***1220.12*** *p706*
Scott, John; Annapolis, MD, 1735 ***1220.12*** *p706*
Scott, John; Barbados or Jamaica, 1677 ***1220.12*** *p706*
Scott, John; Barbados or Jamaica, 1716 ***1220.12*** *p706*
Scott, John; Maryland, 1742 ***1220.12*** *p706*
Scott, John; Nebraska, 1858-1885 ***9228.50*** *p659*
*Wife:*Catherine Jane Aubin
Scott, John 12; New York, NY, 1835 ***5024.1*** *p137*
Scott, John; North Carolina, 1857 ***1088.45*** *p31*
Scott, John; Ohio, 1809-1852 ***4511.35*** *p48*
Scott, John; Ohio, 1840 ***2763.1*** *p21*
Scott, John 30; Ontario, 1871 ***1823.17*** *p145*
Scott, John 31; Ontario, 1871 ***1823.21*** *p327*
Scott, John 35; Ontario, 1871 ***1823.21*** *p327*
Scott, John 39; Ontario, 1871 ***1823.21*** *p327*
Scott, John 40; Ontario, 1871 ***1823.21*** *p327*
Scott, John 43; Ontario, 1871 ***1823.21*** *p327*
Scott, John 49; Ontario, 1871 ***1823.21*** *p327*
Scott, John 53; Ontario, 1871 ***1823.21*** *p327*
Scott, John 56; Ontario, 1871 ***1823.17*** *p145*
Scott, John 62; Ontario, 1871 ***1823.21*** *p327*
Scott, John 65; Ontario, 1871 ***1823.17*** *p145*
Scott, John 65; Ontario, 1871 ***1823.21*** *p327*
Scott, John; Philadelphia, 1778 ***8529.30*** *p5A*
Scott, John; Washington, 1884 ***2770.40*** *p193*
Scott, Joseph 41; Ontario, 1871 ***1823.17*** *p145*
Scott, Joseph H. 32; Ontario, 1871 ***1823.21*** *p327*
Scott, Judith; America, 1760 ***1220.12*** *p706*
Scott, Judith; Barbados, 1673 ***1220.12*** *p706*
Scott, Margaret; Barbados or Jamaica, 1677 ***1220.12*** *p706*
Scott, Margaret 16; North Carolina, 1774 ***1422.10*** *p54*
Scott, Margaret D.; Ontario, 1831-1912 ***9228.50*** *p128*
Scott, Mariah 65; Ontario, 1871 ***1823.21*** *p327*
Scott, Mary; America, 1742 ***1220.12*** *p707*
Scott, Mary; America, 1745 ***1220.12*** *p707*
Scott, Mary; America, 1758 ***1220.12*** *p707*
Scott, Mary; America, 1759 ***1220.12*** *p707*
Scott, Mary; America, 1770 ***1220.12*** *p707*
Scott, Mary; Barbados, 1663 ***1220.12*** *p707*
Scott, Mary *SEE* Scott, Henry
Scott, Mary; Charles Town, SC, 1719 ***1220.12*** *p707*
Scott, Mary; Ontario, 1835 ***3160.1*** *p150*
Scott, Mary 46; Ontario, 1871 ***1823.17*** *p145*
Scott, Mary Ann 36; Ontario, 1871 ***1823.17*** *p145*
Scott, Mathew; Ohio, 1809-1852 ***4511.35*** *p48*
Scott, Matthew; Ohio, 1809-1852 ***4511.35*** *p48*
Scott, Nathaniel; America, 1770 ***1220.12*** *p707*
Scott, Nicholas; America, 1763 ***1220.12*** *p707*
Scott, Nicholas; Barbados or Jamaica, 1697 ***1220.12*** *p707*
Scott, Pearl; Minnesota, 1926 ***2769.54*** *p1379*
Scott, Peter 39; Ontario, 1871 ***1823.17*** *p145*
Scott, Rebecca 53; Ontario, 1871 ***1823.21*** *p327*
Scott, Rebecca 56; Ontario, 1871 ***1823.21*** *p327*
Scott, Richard; Annapolis, MD, 1729 ***1220.12*** *p707*
Scott, Richard; Barbados, 1671 ***1220.12*** *p707*
Scott, Richard; Barbados or Jamaica, 1697 ***1220.12*** *p707*
Scott, Robert 22; Ontario, 1871 ***1823.17*** *p145*
Scott, Robert 41; Ontario, 1871 ***1823.21*** *p327*
Scott, Robert 43; Ontario, 1871 ***1823.21*** *p327*
Scott, Robert 43; Ontario, 1871 ***1823.21*** *p327*
Scott, Robert 47; Ontario, 1871 ***1823.21*** *p327*
Scott, Robert 48; Ontario, 1871 ***1823.17*** *p145*
Scott, Robert 58; Ontario, 1871 ***1823.21*** *p327*
Scott, Robert H. 43; Ontario, 1871 ***1823.17*** *p146*
Scott, Samuel; Illinois, 1834-1900 ***6020.5*** *p133*
Scott, Samuel 41; Ontario, 1871 ***1823.21*** *p328*
Scott, Samuel 43; Ontario, 1871 ***1823.17*** *p146*
Scott, Samuel T. 39; Ontario, 1871 ***1823.17*** *p146*
Scott, Sarah; America, 1719 ***1220.12*** *p707*
Scott, Sarah 38; Ontario, 1871 ***1823.17*** *p146*
Scott, Stephen 56; Ontario, 1871 ***1823.21*** *p328*
Scott, Steward 57; Ontario, 1871 ***1823.21*** *p328*
Scott, Thomas; America, 1719 ***1220.12*** *p707*
Scott, Thomas; America, 1748 ***1220.12*** *p707*
Scott, Thomas; America, 1755 ***1220.12*** *p707*
Scott, Thomas; America, 1770 ***1220.12*** *p707*

Scott, Thomas; America, 1771 ***1220.12*** *p707*
Scott, Thomas; America, 1774 ***1220.12*** *p707*
Scott, Thomas; Barbados, 1665 ***1220.12*** *p707*
Scott, Thomas 46; Ontario, 1871 ***1823.21*** *p328*
Scott, Thomas 55; Ontario, 1871 ***1823.17*** *p146*
Scott, Thomas 14; Quebec, 1870 ***8364.32*** *p25*
Scott, Thomas; Washington, 1884 ***2770.40*** *p193*
Scott, Thomas Rogers; Virginia, 1910 ***9228.50*** *p577*
Scott, Thomas S. W.; North Carolina, 1840 ***1088.45*** *p31*
Scott, Walter 42; Ontario, 1871 ***1823.21*** *p328*
Scott, Walter 52; Ontario, 1871 ***1823.17*** *p146*
Scott, William; America, 1732 ***1220.12*** *p707*
Scott, William; America, 1741 ***1220.12*** *p707*
Scott, William; America, 1760 ***1220.12*** *p707*
Scott, William; America, 1762 ***1220.12*** *p707*
Scott, William; America, 1773 ***1220.12*** *p707*
Scott, William; America, 1774 ***1220.12*** *p707*
Scott, William; Boston, 1766 ***1642*** *p36*
With wife
Scott, William; North Carolina, 1824 ***1088.45*** *p31*
Scott, William 21; North Carolina, 1774 ***1422.10*** *p54*
Scott, William 27; Ontario, 1871 ***1823.17*** *p146*
Scott, William 28; Ontario, 1871 ***1823.21*** *p328*
Scott, William 30; Ontario, 1871 ***1823.17*** *p146*
Scott, William 30; Ontario, 1871 ***1823.21*** *p328*
Scott, William 36; Ontario, 1871 ***1823.17*** *p146*
Scott, William 36; Ontario, 1871 ***1823.21*** *p328*
Scott, William 37; Ontario, 1871 ***1823.21*** *p328*
Scott, William 38; Ontario, 1871 ***1823.21*** *p328*
Scott, William 40; Ontario, 1871 ***1823.21*** *p328*
Scott, William 43; Ontario, 1871 ***1823.21*** *p328*
Scott, William 45; Ontario, 1871 ***1823.21*** *p328*
Scott, William 54; Ontario, 1871 ***1823.21*** *p328*
Scott, William 60; Ontario, 1871 ***1823.21*** *p328*
Scott, William 60; Ontario, 1871 ***1823.21*** *p328*
Scott, William 82; Ontario, 1871 ***1823.17*** *p146*
Scott, William; Virginia, 1767 ***1220.12*** *p707*
Scott, Wm 67; Ontario, 1871 ***1823.21*** *p328*
Scott, Wm.; Ohio, 1809-1852 ***4511.35*** *p48*
Scotus, Alexander; Quebec, 1786 ***1416.15*** *p5*
Scouler, Jasper 30; North Carolina, 1774 ***1422.10*** *p56*
Scourse, Judith; America, 1757 ***1220.12*** *p707*
Scovell, Thomas; America, 1738 ***1220.12*** *p707*
Scowfield, Jervase; America, 1773 ***1220.12*** *p705*
Scowlcroft, William; America, 1770 ***1220.12*** *p707*
Scoynes, Samuel 47; Ontario, 1871 ***1823.21*** *p328*
Scragg, I. G. 50; Ontario, 1871 ***1823.21*** *p328*
Scragg, Thomas; America, 1699 ***1220.12*** *p707*
Scratchard, Gervase; America, 1690 ***1220.12*** *p707*
Scratchley, Francis; Virginia, 1739 ***1220.12*** *p707*
Screaton, Samuel 59; Ontario, 1871 ***1823.21*** *p328*
Screen, Samuel; America, 1764 ***1220.12*** *p707*
Scriba, John; New York, NY, 1892 ***6212.1*** *p13*
Scringing, James; Maryland, 1719 ***1220.12*** *p707*
Scriven, George; Maryland, 1742 ***1220.12*** *p707*
Scriven, James; America, 1754 ***1220.12*** *p707*
Scriven, John; Barbados, 1665 ***1220.12*** *p707*
Scriven, John, Jr.; America, 1754 ***1220.12*** *p707*
Scriven, John, Sr.; America, 1754 ***1220.12*** *p707*
Scriven, Robert; America, 1760 ***1220.12*** *p707*
Scriven, Thomas; America, 1760 ***1220.12*** *p707*
Scrivener, John; America, 1752 ***1220.12*** *p708*
Scrivener, Peter; Barbados, 1665 ***1220.12*** *p708*
Scrivenor, George; America, 1762 ***1220.12*** *p707*
Scrogg, Henry 50; Ontario, 1871 ***1823.21*** *p328*
Scroggie, Robert 38; Ontario, 1871 ***1823.17*** *p146*
Scroggs, Robert; America, 1750 ***1220.12*** *p708*
Scrubiby, Christian; Colorado, 1873 ***1029.59*** *p82*
Scruce, Elizabeth; Barbados, 1669 ***1220.12*** *p708*
Scrugion, John; Barbados, 1666 ***1220.12*** *p708*
Scruton, Benjamin 32; Ontario, 1871 ***1823.17*** *p146*
Scruton, Robert; America, 1746 ***1220.12*** *p708*
Scudder, John; America, 1772 ***1220.12*** *p708*
Scuff, Miss B. 30; New Orleans, 1834 ***1002.51*** *p111*
Scuff, D. 1; New Orleans, 1834 ***1002.51*** *p111*
Scuff, J. 40; New Orleans, 1834 ***1002.51*** *p111*
Scuffam, Mary; America, 1726 ***1220.12*** *p708*
Scull, Robert; Barbados or Jamaica, 1684 ***1220.12*** *p708*
Scull, William; America, 1771 ***1220.12*** *p708*
Scullfer, William; America, 1765 ***1220.12*** *p708*
Scullin, Thomas; Louisiana, 1841-1844 ***4981.45*** *p211*
Scully, Ann; America, 1774 ***1220.12*** *p708*
Scully, Benj'n.; Illinois, 1858-1861 ***6020.5*** *p133*
Scully, Edward 21; Indiana, 1886-1888 ***9076.20*** *p72*
Scully, James 21; Indiana, 1887-1890 ***9076.20*** *p72*
Scully, James 46; Indiana, 1886-1888 ***9076.20*** *p72*
Scully, Jeremiah 56; Ontario, 1871 ***1823.17*** *p146*
Scully, Michael 23; Indiana, 1887-1896 ***9076.20*** *p74*
Scully, Patrick; Illinois, 1858-1861 ***6020.5*** *p133*
Scully, Thomas 23; Indiana, 1886-1896 ***9076.20*** *p74*
Sculovich, E.; Louisiana, 1874 ***4981.45*** *p297*
Sculthorpe, John; Rappahannock, VA, 1726 ***1220.12*** *p708*
Scupham, Thomas; America, 1738 ***1220.12*** *p708*
Scurfield, William; America, 1742 ***1220.12*** *p708*
Scurr, Alice *SEE* Scurr, Thomas
Scurr, Charles *SEE* Scurr, Thomas
Scurr, Elizabeth *SEE* Scurr, Thomas
Scurr, Elizabeth *SEE* Scurr, Thomas
Scurr, Thomas *SEE* Scurr, Thomas
Scurr, Thomas; Canada, 1774 ***3036.5*** *p40*
*Wife:*Elizabeth
*Child:*Alice
*Child:*Elizabeth
*Child:*Thomas
*Child:*William
*Child:*Charles
Scurr, William *SEE* Scurr, Thomas
Scurrier, Richard; Maryland, 1725 ***1220.12*** *p708*
Scurrier, William; America, 1685 ***1220.12*** *p708*
Scutt, John; America, 1752 ***1220.12*** *p708*
Scutt, John; Virginia, 1764 ***1220.12*** *p708*
Scutt, Mary; Virginia, 1741 ***1220.12*** *p708*
Scuyler, Abraham 37; Ontario, 1871 ***1823.21*** *p328*
Scysse, Mattis 21; America, 1848 ***778.6*** *p307*
Seablom, Charles; Cleveland, OH, 1893-1897 ***9722.10*** *p126*
Seabold, Philip; Ohio, 1809-1852 ***4511.35*** *p48*
Seaborn, William; America, 1749 ***1220.12*** *p708*
Seabright, Thomas; America, 1766 ***1220.12*** *p708*
Seabright, William; America, 1764 ***1220.12*** *p708*
Seabrook, Arthur 39; Ontario, 1871 ***1823.21*** *p328*
Seabrook, Sidney 41; Ontario, 1871 ***1823.21*** *p328*
Seabrook, William; Potomac, 1731 ***1220.12*** *p708*
Seabrooke, Thomas; America, 1749 ***1220.12*** *p708*
Seaburn, Sarah; America, 1751 ***1220.12*** *p708*
Seabury, Hannah; Boston, 1787 ***9228.50*** *p25*
Seabury, Hannah; Boston, 1787 ***9228.50*** *p306*
Seabury, Hannah; Boston, 1787 ***9228.50*** *p306*
Seaddel, Fredric 44; Ontario, 1871 ***1823.21*** *p328*
Seafort, John; Ohio, 1809-1852 ***4511.35*** *p48*
Seagar, Arthur 31; Quebec, 1870 ***8364.32*** *p25*
Seagar, Richard; Maryland, 1719 ***1220.12*** *p708*
Seager, Benjamin; America, 1774 ***1220.12*** *p708*
Seager, Charles 60; Ontario, 1871 ***1823.17*** *p146*
Seager, Thomas; America, 1774 ***1220.12*** *p708*
Seagoe, Margaret; America, 1739 ***1220.12*** *p708*
Seagrave, John; America, 1758 ***1220.12*** *p708*
Seagrove, William; America, 1744 ***1220.12*** *p708*
Seagry, Richard; America, 1754 ***1220.12*** *p708*
Seakin, Edward; America, 1722 ***1220.12*** *p708*
Seal, Ann; America, 1771 ***1220.12*** *p708*
Seal, Thomas; America, 1700 ***1220.12*** *p708*
Seal, Thomas 39; Ontario, 1871 ***1823.21*** *p328*
Seal, William; America, 1735 ***1220.12*** *p708*
Seal, William; America, 1747 ***1220.12*** *p708*
Seale, Frances; America, 1700 ***1220.12*** *p708*
Seale, Matthias; America, 1762 ***1220.12*** *p708*
Seale, Robert; New Jersey, 1665 ***9228.50*** *p578*
Seale, Robert 43; Ontario, 1871 ***1823.21*** *p328*
Seale, Robert; Virginia, 1665 ***9228.50*** *p53*
Seale, William; America, 1740 ***1220.12*** *p708*
Sealey, Joseph; Illinois, 1858-1861 ***6020.5*** *p133*
Sealey, Mary; Barbados, 1686 ***1220.12*** *p709*
Sealsfield, Charles; Philadelphia, 1822-1836 ***2853.20*** *p124*
Sealy, Hannah; America, 1733 ***1220.12*** *p709*
Sealy, Ludov'k; Ontario, 1787 ***1276.15*** *p231*
Sealy, Robert; New Jersey, 1665 ***9228.50*** *p578*
Sealy, Simon; America, 1767 ***1220.12*** *p709*
Seaman, James; America, 1767 ***1220.12*** *p709*
Seaman, Jane; America, 1773 ***1220.12*** *p709*
Seaman, Mary; America, 1722 ***1220.12*** *p709*
Seaman, Robert; America, 1685 ***1220.12*** *p709*
Seaman, Victor 38; New Orleans, 1842 ***778.6*** *p307*
Seamer, Nicholas; America, 1744 ***1220.12*** *p712*
Seamor, John; America, 1745 ***1220.12*** *p712*
Seamore, Anne; Barbados, 1672 ***1220.12*** *p712*
Seamour, Thomas; Annapolis, MD, 1733 ***1220.12*** *p712*
Seaples, Charles S.; Colorado, 1891 ***1029.59*** *p82*
Sear, Richard; America, 1738 ***1220.12*** *p709*
Sear, Thomas; America, 1770 ***1220.12*** *p709*
Seare, Stephen; America, 1680 ***1220.12*** *p709*
Seares, George; America, 1756 ***1220.12*** *p709*
Seares, William; America, 1765 ***1220.12*** *p709*
Searl, George; Ohio, 1809-1852 ***4511.35*** *p48*
Searle, Benjamin; America, 1693 ***1220.12*** *p709*
Searle, Durand Vendoline; Miami, 1935 ***4984.12*** *p39*
Searle, George; America, 1685 ***1220.12*** *p709*
Searle, George; Maryland, 1725 ***1220.12*** *p709*
Searle, James; America, 1746 ***1220.12*** *p709*
Searle, John; America, 1729 ***1220.12*** *p709*
Searle, John; Marblehead, MA, 1657-1699 ***9228.50*** *p577*
Searle, Philip; America, 1640-1660 ***9228.50*** *p577*
Searle, Samuel 40; Ontario, 1871 ***1823.17*** *p146*
Searle, Simon; Virginia, 1749 ***1220.12*** *p709*
Searle, Thomas; America, 1700 ***1220.12*** *p709*
Searle, Thomas; America, 1751 ***1220.12*** *p709*
Searle, Thomas; America, 1754 ***1220.12*** *p709*
Searle, Thomas, Jr.; America, 1773 ***1220.12*** *p709*
Searle, Thomas, Sr.; America, 1773 ***1220.12*** *p709*
Searle, William; America, 1685 ***1220.12*** *p709*
Sears, Alexander; Boston, 1752-1759 ***1642*** *p31*
Sears, George; America, 1746 ***1220.12*** *p709*
Sears, George 20; Quebec, 1870 ***8364.32*** *p26*
Sears, Giles; America, 1734 ***1220.12*** *p709*
Sears, Mary Ann; America, 1774 ***1220.12*** *p709*
Sears, Moses; America, 1755 ***1220.12*** *p709*
Sears, Richard; Marblehead, MA, 1637 ***9228.50*** *p577*
Sears, Robert; Virginia, 1736 ***1220.12*** *p709*
Searson, John 30; Ontario, 1871 ***1823.17*** *p146*
Seasdorf, Philip; Ohio, 1809-1852 ***4511.35*** *p53*
Sease, Robert; America, 1685 ***1220.12*** *p709*
Seathern, John 74; Ontario, 1871 ***1823.21*** *p328*
Seaton, Alexander 32; Ontario, 1871 ***1823.17*** *p146*
Seaton, Alexander 60; Ontario, 1871 ***1823.21*** *p329*
Seaton, Donald 54; Ontario, 1871 ***1823.21*** *p329*
Seaton, Elizabeth 58; Ontario, 1871 ***1823.21*** *p329*
Seaton, Franklin; Ohio, 1809-1852 ***4511.35*** *p48*
Seaton, Ira H.; Ohio, 1809-1852 ***4511.35*** *p48*
Seaton, Isabella 89; Ontario, 1871 ***1823.21*** *p329*
Seaton, John; Maryland, 1722 ***1220.12*** *p709*
Seaton, John 7; Ontario, 1871 ***1823.21*** *p329*
Seaton, John 50; Ontario, 1871 ***1823.21*** *p329*
Seaton, Rachel; America, 1733 ***1220.12*** *p709*
Seaton, Robert 43; Ontario, 1871 ***1823.21*** *p329*
Seaton, Samuel; Ontario, 1871 ***1823.17*** *p146*
Seaton, Samuel; Ontario, 1871 ***1823.17*** *p146*
Seaton, William 35; Ontario, 1871 ***1823.17*** *p146*
Seavell, Ann; Maryland, 1736 ***1220.12*** *p709*
Seaver, Valentine; Virginia, 1732 ***1220.12*** *p709*
Seavy, Thomas; New York, NY, 1841 ***3274.56*** *p96*
Seaward, Ann; America, 1762 ***1220.12*** *p711*
Seaward, Mathew; America, 1755 ***1220.12*** *p711*
Seawell, Mary; America, 1740 ***1220.12*** *p711*
Seba, Christian 28; Mississippi, 1847 ***778.6*** *p307*
Sebastian, Franz Josef; America, 1846 ***5475.1*** *p547*
Sebastian, Franz Josef; America, 1852 ***5475.1*** *p547*
Sebastian, Henry; Ohio, 1809-1852 ***4511.35*** *p48*
Sebastian, Johann 20; America, 1849 ***5475.1*** *p547*
Sebastian, Johann Jakob; America, 1849 ***5475.1*** *p547*
Sebastien, Reynaud 48; America, 1845 ***778.6*** *p307*
Sebeau, Michael; Ohio, 1809-1852 ***4511.35*** *p48*
Sebening, Ernst; Port uncertain, 1885 ***7420.1*** *p349*
Sebenius, John A.; Washington, 1889 ***2770.40*** *p81*
Seber, Fr.; Galveston, TX, 1855 ***571.7*** *p18*
Sebert, Henry; Boston, 1774 ***8529.30*** *p3*
Sebesta, Frantisek; Galveston, TX, 1856 ***2853.20*** *p63*
*Brother:*Pavel
Sebesta, Frantisek; Texas, 1856 ***2853.20*** *p78*
*Brother:*Parel
Sebesta, Jan; Texas, 1856 ***2853.20*** *p85*
Sebesta, Parel *SEE* Sebesta, Frantisek
Sebesta, Pavel *SEE* Sebesta, Frantisek
Sebesta, Pavel; Texas, 1856 ***2853.20*** *p78*
Sebik, Frantisek; Pennsylvania, 1901 ***2853.20*** *p122*
Sebik, Gabriel Frantisek; Texas, 1895 ***2853.20*** *p91*
Sebillon, Rene 18; Louisiana, 1848 ***778.6*** *p307*
Sebold, Lewis; Ohio, 1809-1852 ***4511.35*** *p48*
Sebold, Lewis; Ohio, 1809-1852 ***4511.35*** *p48*
Sebold, R. 41; New Orleans, 1834 ***1002.51*** *p112*
Sechre, Child; New Orleans, 1840 ***778.6*** *p307*
Sechre, Mrs. 36; New Orleans, 1840 ***778.6*** *p307*
Seckington, James; America, 1768 ***1220.12*** *p709*
Secomb, Richard 46; Ontario, 1871 ***1823.21*** *p329*
Second, R. 28; America, 1840 ***778.6*** *p307*
Secor, Matej 13; Wisconsin, 1853 ***2853.20*** *p291*
With parents
Secord, David; Ontario, 1787 ***1276.15*** *p231*
With 4 relatives
Secord, Jessey 37; Ontario, 1871 ***1823.21*** *p329*
Secord, Jno., Sr.; Ontario, 1787 ***1276.15*** *p231*
With relative
Secord, John, Jr.; Ontario, 1787 ***1276.15*** *p231*
With 2 children & relative
Secord, John S. 39; Michigan, 1880 ***4491.36*** *p18*
Secord, Julia A. 38; Michigan, 1880 ***4491.36*** *p18*
Secord, Stephen; Ontario, 1787 ***1276.15*** *p231*
With child & 2 relatives
Secretan, Christine 24; Louisiana, 1848 ***778.6*** *p307*
Secretan, Samuel 24; Louisiana, 1848 ***778.6*** *p307*
Seddon, Fanny 50; Ontario, 1871 ***1823.21*** *p329*
Seddon, Francis; America, 1740 ***1220.12*** *p709*
Seddon, George; America, 1747 ***1220.12*** *p709*
Seddon, Isaac; America, 1732 ***1220.12*** *p709*
Seddon, John; America, 1763 ***1220.12*** *p709*
Seddon, Nathan; America, 1732 ***1220.12*** *p709*

Sedel, Bridget; Canada, 1775 ***3036.5*** *p67*
*Child:*Mary
*Child:*Francis
*Child:*Sarah
Sedel, Francis *SEE* Sedel, Bridget
Sedel, Mary *SEE* Sedel, Bridget
Sedel, Sarah *SEE* Sedel, Bridget
Sederay, Jeanne; Quebec, 1669 ***4514.3*** *p370*
Sedergreen, John; Kansas, 1869 ***777.40*** *p7*
Sedgewick, John; America, 1744 ***1220.12*** *p710*
Sedgewick, Robert; Barbados or Jamaica, 1690 ***1220.12*** *p710*
Sedgeworth, John; Ontario, 1871 ***1823.21*** *p329*
Sedgware, Margaret; America, 1769 ***1220.12*** *p709*
Sedgwick, James; Nevis or Jamaica, 1722 ***1220.12*** *p710*
Sedgwick, Joseph; Ohio, 1809-1852 ***4511.35*** *p48*
Sedgwick, Marie 20; Virginia, 1635 ***1183.3*** *p31*
Sedgwick, Martha; America, 1740 ***1220.12*** *p710*
Sedgwick, Richard; America, 1739 ***1220.12*** *p710*
Sedgwick, Thomas; Ohio, 1809-1852 ***4511.35*** *p48*
Sedgwicke, John; America, 1755 ***1220.12*** *p710*
Sedgworth, Ann; America, 1743 ***1220.12*** *p710*
Sedilot, Louis 36; Quebec, 1637 ***9221.17*** *p73*
*Daughter:*Marie 10
*Wife:*Marie Grimoult 30
Sedilot, Marie 10 *SEE* Sedilot, Louis
Sedilot, Marie Grimoult 30 *SEE* Sedilot, Louis
Sedivy, Jan; Nebraska, 1870 ***2853.20*** *p193*
Sedivy, Josef; Chicago, 1865 ***2853.20*** *p193*
Sedivy, Josef; St. Paul, MN, 1863 ***2853.20*** *p277*
Sedlacek, Vaclav; New York, NY, 1850-1860 ***2853.20*** *p100*
Sedlak, Vaclav; New York, NY, 1850-1860 ***2853.20*** *p100*
Sedling, Anna Andersdotter 21 *SEE* Sedling, Jonas
Sedling, Jonas 32; New York, 1856 ***6529.11*** *p20*
*Wife:*Anna Andersdotter 21
Sedlinger, Otto; Wisconsin, 1895 ***6795.8*** *p99*
Sedlmeir, Fredrick; Kansas, 1917-1918 ***1826.15*** *p81*
See, Peter; America, 1736 ***1220.12*** *p710*
Seeba, H.; New York, 1859 ***358.56*** *p100*
Seebaum, Karl Friedrich; America, 1886 ***7420.1*** *p352*
Seebaum, Marie Dorothea Beathe; America, 1881 ***7420.1*** *p326*
Seebock, Johann; Valdivia, Chile, 1850 ***1192.4*** *p49*
Seebohm, Adolph Wilhelm; Port uncertain, 1855 ***7420.1*** *p142*
Seebohm, Carl Bernhardt Dietrich; America, 1864 ***7420.1*** *p227*
With family
Seebohm, Georg Carl; America, 1848 ***7420.1*** *p62*
Seebohm, Heinrich Ludwig Wilhelm; America, 1847 ***7420.1*** *p56*
Seebold, W. E.; Louisiana, 1874-1875 ***4981.45*** *p30*
Seebt, John; Louisiana, 1874-1875 ***4981.45*** *p30*
Seed, George 60; Ontario, 1871 ***1823.21*** *p329*
Seeds, James; Philadelphia, 1777 ***8529.30*** *p3*
Seeg, George; Ohio, 1840-1897 ***8365.35*** *p18*
Seegelbaum, Elise; America, 1861 ***7420.1*** *p209*
Seegelbaum, Liebmann; America, 1858 ***7420.1*** *p181*
Seeger, Adam; America, 1757-1903 ***2526.42*** *p165*
Seeger, Anna Barbara 44; America, 1851 ***2526.43*** *p222*
Seeger, Anna Margaretha; America, 1868 ***2526.42*** *p147*
Seeger, Elisabetha Katharina Blatz; New York, 1883 ***2526.43*** *p126*
Seeger, Georg; America, 1849 ***2526.42*** *p147*
With wife & 4 children
Seeger, Josef; Pittsburgh, 1889 ***5475.1*** *p131*
Seeger, Margaretha; America, 1868 ***2526.43*** *p189*
Seeger, Michael; America, 1869 ***2526.42*** *p147*
Seeger, Philipp 14; America, 1868 ***2526.42*** *p147*
Seegers, Anna Sophie Marie Langhorst *SEE* Seegers, Hans Heinrich Wilhelm
Seegers, Engel Marie Dorothea; America, 1867 ***7420.1*** *p264*
Seegers, Engel Marie Sophie; America, 1867 ***7420.1*** *p264*
Seegers, Hans; America, 1854 ***7420.1*** *p130*
Seegers, Hans Heinrich *SEE* Seegers, Johann Conrad
Seegers, Hans Heinrich Wilhelm; America, 1893 ***7420.1*** *p369*
*Wife:*Anna Sophie Marie Langhorst
Seegers, Heinrich Christoph *SEE* Seegers, Johann Conrad
Seegers, Johann Conrad; America, 1852 ***7420.1*** *p98*
*Brother:*Heinrich Christoph
*Brother:*Hans Heinrich
Seegers, Johann Heinrich; America, 1852 ***7420.1*** *p98*
Seegers, Johann Heinrich; America, 1852 ***7420.1*** *p98*
With wife 2 sons & 3 daughters
Seegers, Johann Heinrich Christoph; America, 1870 ***7420.1*** *p285*
Seegers, Johann Philipp; America, 1858 ***7420.1*** *p181*
Seegers, Otto Emil; America, 1849 ***7420.1*** *p68*
Seegers, Philipp; America, 1858 ***7420.1*** *p182*
Seegert, Friedrich; Port uncertain, 1866 ***7420.1*** *p249*
Seegert, Heinrich; America, 1848 ***7420.1*** *p62*
With 2 children
Seegert, Wilhelm; America, 1845 ***7420.1*** *p40*
Seehafer, Gottlieb; Wisconsin, 1894 ***6795.8*** *p145*
Seehausen, Catarine Engel; America, 1867 ***7420.1*** *p264*
*Son:*Johann Heinrich
*Daughter:*Engel Marie Sophie
*Daughter:*Engel Marie Dorothea
*Son:*Hans Heinrich Otto
*Daughter:*Engel Marie Dorothea
Seehausen, Engel Marie Dorothea *SEE* Seehausen, Catarine Engel Becker
Seehausen, Engel Marie Sophie; America, 1857 ***7420.1*** *p172*
Seehausen, Engel Marie Sophie *SEE* Seehausen, Catarine Engel Becker
Seehausen, Hans Heinrich; America, 1858 ***7420.1*** *p182*
Seehausen, Hans Heinrich Otto *SEE* Seehausen, Catarine Engel Becker
Seehausen, Heinrich; America, 1858 ***7420.1*** *p182*
Seehausen, Heinrich Conrad Dietrich; America, 1858 ***7420.1*** *p182*
Seehausen, Johann Christoph; New York, NY, 1856 ***7420.1*** *p154*
Seehausen, Johann Heinrich *SEE* Seehausen, Catarine Engel Becker
Seehausen, Marie Charlotte; America, 1853 ***7420.1*** *p111*
Seehawer, Gustav; Wisconsin, 1887 ***6795.8*** *p147*
Seeker, Mary; America, 1738 ***1220.12*** *p710*
Seeker, William 27; Ontario, 1871 ***1823.21*** *p329*
Seele, Robert; New Jersey, 1665 ***9228.50*** *p578*
Seeley, George; Barbados, 1703 ***1220.12*** *p708*
Seeley, John; America, 1675 ***1220.12*** *p709*
Seeley, Joseph; California, 1868 ***1131.61*** *p89*
Seeley, Robert; New Jersey, 1665 ***9228.50*** *p578*
Seeley, Robert; Virginia, 1665 ***9228.50*** *p53*
Seelig, Anna; America, 1885 ***7420.1*** *p399*
Seelig, Moses; New Orleans, 1849 ***7710.1*** *p153*
Seeliger, Heinrich; Wisconsin, 1883 ***6795.8*** *p87*
Seeliger, Wilhelm; Wisconsin, 1888 ***6795.8*** *p87*
Seelkopf, Caroline; America, 1867 ***7420.1*** *p264*
Seelkopf, Christoph; America, 1854 ***7420.1*** *p130*
Seelkopf, Ernst; America, 1867 ***7420.1*** *p264*
Seelleur, Thomas I. 21; Ontario, 1871 ***1823.21*** *p329*
Seelman, George; Ohio, 1809-1852 ***4511.35*** *p48*
Seels, Catherine 30; Ontario, 1871 ***1823.17*** *p146*
Seely, Francis Joseph; Illinois, 1858-1861 ***6020.5*** *p133*
Seely, Jinna P. 36; Michigan, 1880 ***4491.30*** *p28*
Seely, Robert; Barbados, 1664 ***1220.12*** *p709*
Seely, William; Maine, 1653 ***9228.50*** *p85*
Seemann, Karl Albert; Wisconsin, 1892 ***6795.8*** *p68*
Seemoneit, Adam; Argentina, 1855 ***2526.43*** *p214*
With family of 4
Seen, Peter; Washington, 1886 ***6015.10*** *p16*
Seer, Christine 14; New York, NY, 1874 ***6954.7*** *p37*
Seer, Heinrich 48; New York, NY, 1874 ***6954.7*** *p37*
Seer, James; Virginia, 1765 ***1220.12*** *p709*
Seer, Pauline 40; New York, NY, 1874 ***6954.7*** *p37*
Seers, Bernard; America, 1752 ***1220.12*** *p709*
Seesz, Henry; Ohio, 1809-1852 ***4511.35*** *p48*
Seevy, Lawrence; Portsmouth, NH, 1835 ***3274.56*** *p71*
Seferffer, Georges 18; America, 1846 ***778.6*** *p307*
Seffert, Michael; Ohio, 1809-1852 ***4511.35*** *p48*
Sefftel, Valentin; Pennsylvania, 1846 ***170.15*** *p42*
With wife & 3 children
Segar, John; Ontario, 1787 ***1276.15*** *p231*
With 3 relatives
Segar, Rolliff; Ontario, 1787 ***1276.15*** *p232*
With 2 children & 4 relatives
Segaud, Auguste; Louisiana, 1836-1841 ***4981.45*** *p209*
Segelbaum, Mrs.; America, 1881 ***7420.1*** *p325*
Segelbaum, A.; America, 1856 ***7420.1*** *p154*
Segelbaum, Adolph; America, 1868 ***7420.1*** *p277*
Segelbaum, Johanne; America, 1881 ***7420.1*** *p322*
Segelbaum, Louis; America, 1854 ***7420.1*** *p130*
Segelbaum, Meyer; America, 1866 ***7420.1*** *p249*
Segelbaum, Samuel; America, 1861 ***7420.1*** *p209*
Segelbaum, Selig; America, 1854 ***7420.1*** *p130*
Segelbaum, Seligmann; Port uncertain, 1856 ***7420.1*** *p154*
Seger, Dominick; Ohio, 1809-1852 ***4511.35*** *p48*
Segerdahl, Carl Fredrik; North America, 1868 ***6410.15*** *p105*
*Wife:*Fredrika Caroline Fogelstrom
Segerdahl, Fredrika Caroline Fogelstrom *SEE* Segerdahl, Carl Fredrik
Segerson, Ann; Boston, 1764 ***1642*** *p33*
With son
Seggebrock, Engel Marie Sophie Dorothea; America, 1861 ***7420.1*** *p209*
Seggebruch, Friederika Louisa Eleonora; America, 1859 ***7420.1*** *p189*
Seggebruch, Friedrich Adolph Heinrich; America, 1871 ***7420.1*** *p292*
Seggebruch, Friedrich Gottlieb; America, 1853 ***7420.1*** *p111*
With family
Seggin, Charles; New Jersey, 1665 ***9228.50*** *p578*
Seggin, Charles; Virginia, 1665 ***9228.50*** *p53*
Segmuller, Jacob 4; Halifax, N.S., 1902 ***1860.4*** *p42*
Segmuller, Josef 3; Halifax, N.S., 1902 ***1860.4*** *p42*
Segmuller, Margt. 35; Halifax, N.S., 1902 ***1860.4*** *p42*
Segmuller, Stefan 36; Halifax, N.S., 1902 ***1860.4*** *p42*
Segond, Drausin 29; America, 1843 ***778.6*** *p307*
Segond, Louis 31; America, 1843 ***778.6*** *p307*
Segrave, James; America, 1765 ***1220.12*** *p708*
Seguin, Charles; New Jersey, 1665 ***9228.50*** *p578*
Seguin, Francois 23; America, 1847 ***778.6*** *p307*
Seguin, Jean 22; Port uncertain, 1846 ***778.6*** *p307*
Seguine, Charles; Virginia, 1665 ***9228.50*** *p53*
Seher, Catherine 5; New York, NY, 1892 ***8425.16*** *p34*
Seher, Christian 26; New York, NY, 1892 ***8425.16*** *p34*
Seher, Christian 49; New York, NY, 1892 ***8425.16*** *p34*
Seher, Christina 21; New York, NY, 1892 ***8425.16*** *p34*
Seher, Elizabeth 19; New York, NY, 1892 ***8425.16*** *p34*
Seher, Johannes 23; New York, NY, 1892 ***8425.16*** *p34*
Seher, Mathias 17; New York, NY, 1892 ***8425.16*** *p34*
Seher, Peter 6; New York, NY, 1892 ***8425.16*** *p34*
Seher, Rosina 50; New York, NY, 1892 ***8425.16*** *p34*
Sehn, Elisabeth; America, 1837 ***5475.1*** *p410*
Sehnhang, Barb. 17; America, 1845 ***778.6*** *p307*
Sehr, Nikolaus 37; America, 1843 ***5475.1*** *p295*
Sehult, Tertulien; Virginia, 1700 ***9230.15*** *p80*
With wife & 2 children
Seib, Charles; Ontario, 1871 ***1823.17*** *p146*
Seibel, Frank; Ohio, 1840-1897 ***8365.35*** *p18*
Seibel, Gustav Adolph *SEE* Seibel, Karl Philipp
Seibel, Karl Philipp; America, 1869 ***5475.1*** *p31*
*Brother:*Gustav Adolph
Seiber, Julius; Missouri, 1902 ***3276.1*** *p3*
Seibert, Agnesia Katharina Riebel Rauch *SEE* Seibert, Johann Peter
Seibert, Anna Eva Vetter *SEE* Seibert, Johann Mkichael
Seibert, Balthasar *SEE* Seibert, Johann Mkichael
Seibert, Barbara; America, 1846 ***6442.17*** *p65*
Seibert, Charles; Illinois, 1858-1861 ***6020.5*** *p133*
Seibert, Eva Katharina; Virginia, 1831 ***152.20*** *p65*
Seibert, Eva Margaretha 9 *SEE* Seibert, Martin
Seibert, Johann Adam *SEE* Seibert, Johann Mkichael
Seibert, Johann Michael *SEE* Seibert, Johann Peter
Seibert, Johann Mkichael; Virginia, 1831 ***152.20*** *p67*
*Wife:*Anna Eva Vetter
*Child:*Johann Adam
*Child:*Johann Peter
*Child:*Balthasar
Seibert, Johann Peter; America, 1846 ***6442.17*** *p65*
*Wife:*M. Elisabeth Kubler
Seibert, Johann Peter *SEE* Seibert, Johann Mkichael
Seibert, Johann Peter; Virginia, 1831 ***152.20*** *p67*
*Wife:*Agneesia Katharina Riebel Rauch
*Child:*Johann Michael
Seibert, Johannes 17 *SEE* Seibert, Martin
Seibert, Karl; America, 1878-1899 ***6442.17*** *p65*
Seibert, M. Elisabeth Kubler *SEE* Seibert, Johann Peter
Seibert, Martin; America, 1846 ***2526.43*** *p189*
With wife
*Son:*Johannes
*Daughter:*Eva Margaretha
Seibert, Nicolas 18; New Orleans, 1840 ***778.6*** *p307*
Seibert, Nicolas 52; New Orleans, 1840 ***778.6*** *p307*
Seibold, Barbara *SEE* Seibold, Friedrich
Seibold, Friedrich *SEE* Seibold, Friedrich
Seibold, Friedrich; Dakota, 1881-1918 ***554.30*** *p25*
*Wife:*Sophia Heringer
*Child:*Katharine
*Child:*Sophie
*Child:*Marie
*Child:*Barbara
*Child:*Friedrich
Seibold, Friedrich *SEE* Seibold, Peter
Seibold, Henriette Wehr *SEE* Seibold, Johann Georg
Seibold, Jakob *SEE* Seibold, Peter
Seibold, Jakob *SEE* Seibold, Johann Georg
Seibold, Johann Georg; Dakota, 1883-1918 ***554.30*** *p25*
*Wife:*Henriette Wehr
*Child:*Thomas
*Child:*Jakob
*Child:*Magdalene
*Child:*Marie
Seibold, Johannes; New England, 1854 ***170.15*** *p42*
With wife & 2 children
Seibold, Joseph *SEE* Seibold, Peter
Seibold, Katharine *SEE* Seibold, Friedrich
Seibold, Lewis; Ohio, 1809-1852 ***4511.35*** *p48*
Seibold, Magdalene *SEE* Seibold, Johann Georg

Seibold, Maria Edinger *SEE* Seibold, Peter
Seibold, Maria; Dakota, 1886 ***554.30*** *p25*
Seibold, Marie *SEE* Seibold, Friedrich
Seibold, Marie *SEE* Seibold, Johann Georg
Seibold, Peter; Dakota, 1883-1918 ***554.30*** *p25*
*Wife:*Maria Edinger
*Child:*Joseph
*Child:*Friedrich
*Child:*Jakob
Seibold, Sophia Heringer *SEE* Seibold, Friedrich
Seibold, Sophie *SEE* Seibold, Friedrich
Seibold, Thomas *SEE* Seibold, Johann Georg
Seickel, Johannes; Port uncertain, 1887 ***170.15*** *p42*
Seide, Mrs. S.; Port uncertain, 1880 ***7420.1*** *p318*
With daughter
Seidel, Hyronimus Gerhard; America, 1867 ***7919.3*** *p525*
Seidel, Joseph 23; Louisiana, 1847 ***778.6*** *p307*
Seidel, Samuel; America, 1893 ***5475.1*** *p79*
Seidel, Samuel Friedrich; Wisconsin, 1866 ***6795.8*** *p27*
Seiden, Henry; Havana, 1782 ***8529.30*** *p9A*
Seidenfaden, Carl Friedrich Wilhelm; America, 1865 ***7420.1*** *p237*
Seidenfaden, Wilhelmine Caroline; America, 1865 ***7420.1*** *p237*
Seider, David; North Carolina, 1792-1862 ***1088.45*** *p31*
Seidler, Georgine; Valdivia, Chile, 1852 ***1192.4*** *p55*
Seidlinq, Jean 42; America, 1841 ***778.6*** *p307*
Seidlitz, Carl Friedrich; Wisconsin, 1897 ***6795.8*** *p177*
Seidlitz, Emil Herman; Wisconsin, 1896 ***6795.8*** *p142*
Seidlitz, Emil K.; Wisconsin, 1896 ***6795.8*** *p135*
Seidlitz, Emma Alvine; Wisconsin, 1893 ***6795.8*** *p142*
Seidlitz, Lina; Wisconsin, 1894 ***6795.8*** *p122*
Seiferhelde, A.; Louisiana, 1874 ***4981.45*** *p297*
Seifert, Christoph *SEE* Seifert, Ernst
Seifert, Ernst; America, 1867 ***7919.3*** *p531*
*Brother:*Christoph
Seifert, Friedrich; America, 1867 ***7919.3*** *p526*
Seifert, Friedrich; America, 1868 ***7919.3*** *p533*
With family
Seifert, Georg; America, 1893 ***2526.43*** *p200*
Seifert, Johann Georg; Dayton, OH, 1870 ***2526.43*** *p157*
Seifert, John; Ohio, 1809-1852 ***4511.35*** *p48*
Seifert, M.; New York, 1860 ***358.56*** *p5*
Seifert, Simon; Port uncertain, 1852 ***2526.43*** *p223*
Seiffert, Antonin; Georgia, 1736 ***2853.20*** *p17*
Seiffert, Wilhelmine Charlotte; America, 1846 ***7420.1*** *p48*
Seifong, William; Ohio, 1809-1852 ***4511.35*** *p48*
Seigel, Augusta 35; Michigan, 1880 ***4491.42*** *p23*
Seigel, Christ 36; Michigan, 1880 ***4491.42*** *p23*
Seiger, Barbara 8; New York, NY, 1898 ***7951.13*** *p42*
Seiger, Christine 23; New York, NY, 1898 ***7951.13*** *p42*
Seiger, David 18; New York, NY, 1898 ***7951.13*** *p42*
Seiger, Elisabeth 12; New York, NY, 1898 ***7951.13*** *p42*
Seiger, Johann 24; New York, NY, 1898 ***7951.13*** *p42*
Seiger, Katherina 19; New York, NY, 1898 ***7951.13*** *p42*
Seiger, Katherina 47; New York, NY, 1898 ***7951.13*** *p42*
Seiger, Valintine 48; New York, NY, 1898 ***7951.13*** *p42*
Seigneur, Anne; Quebec, 1668 ***4514.3*** *p370*
Seigneur, Marie; Quebec, 1670 ***4514.3*** *p370*
Seigneur, Marie-Madeleine; Quebec, 1672 ***4514.3*** *p288*
Seigneuret, Etienne 25; Quebec, 1644 ***9221.17*** *p145*
Seigrist, Rudolph; Illinois, 1864 ***6079.1*** *p13*
Seikls, William 18; Ontario, 1871 ***1823.21*** *p329*
Seil, Jean; Ohio, 1809-1852 ***4511.35*** *p48*
Seil, John; Ohio, 1809-1852 ***4511.35*** *p48*
Seil, Nicholas; Ohio, 1809-1852 ***4511.35*** *p48*
Seil, Peter; Ohio, 1809-1852 ***4511.35*** *p48*
Seilacher, Carl; America, 1854 ***179.55*** *p19*
Seilaz, Louis; Tennessee, 1891 ***3665.20*** *p112*
Seile, Barbara; New York, 1860 ***358.56*** *p3*
Seiler, Adam; North Carolina, 1823-1837 ***1088.45*** *p31*
Seiler, John; Ohio, 1809-1852 ***4511.35*** *p48*
Seilkop, Friedrich Christian Gottlieb; Cincinnati, 1870 ***7420.1*** *p285*
With daughter
*Son:*Heinrich Friedrich Gottlieb
Seilkop, Heinrich Friedrich Gottlieb *SEE* Seilkop, Friedrich Christian Gottlieb
Seily, William 38; Ontario, 1871 ***1823.21*** *p329*
Seimetz, Anna 12 *SEE* Seimetz, Nikolaus
Seimetz, Johann *SEE* Seimetz, Maria Mattes
Seimetz, Katharina *SEE* Seimetz, Maria Mattes
Seimetz, Katharina 15 *SEE* Seimetz, Nikolaus
Seimetz, Maria 60; America, 1882 ***5475.1*** *p555*
*Daughter:*Katharina
*Son:*Johann
Seimetz, Maria 42; Brazil, 1857 ***5475.1*** *p356*
Seimetz, Maria Weber 46 *SEE* Seimetz, Nikolaus
Seimetz, Mathias; America, 1873 ***5475.1*** *p554*
Seimetz, Mathias 48; Brazil, 1857 ***5475.1*** *p356*
Seimetz, Michel 23; America, 1856 ***5475.1*** *p356*
Seimetz, Michel 8 *SEE* Seimetz, Nikolaus
Seimetz, Nikolaus 6 *SEE* Seimetz, Nikolaus
Seimetz, Nikolaus 46; Brazil, 1857 ***5475.1*** *p356*
*Wife:*Maria Weber 46
*Son:*Michel 8
*Son:*Nikolaus 6
*Daughter:*Anna 12
*Daughter:*Katharina 15
Seinnenger, Catharina 18; America, 1846 ***778.6*** *p307*
Seinnenger, Henry 28; America, 1846 ***778.6*** *p308*
Seinnenger, Michel 16; America, 1846 ***778.6*** *p308*
Seip, Elisasbeth; America, 1855 ***2526.43*** *p181*
Seip, Frank; Louisiana, 1874 ***4981.45*** *p134*
Seip, Georg; America, 1888 ***2526.43*** *p181*
Seipp, Anna Elisabeth; America, 1840 ***8115.12*** *p322*
*Child:*Marie
Seipp, Friedrich; America, n.d. ***8115.12*** *p322*
Seipp, Marie *SEE* Seipp, Anna Elisabeth
Seissmann, Wilhelmine; Valdivia, Chile, 1850 ***1192.4*** *p48*
Seisz, Henry; Ohio, 1809-1852 ***4511.35*** *p48*
Seither, Frank; Louisiana, 1874-1875 ***4981.45*** *p31*
Seither, Frank; Louisiana, 1874-1875 ***4981.45*** *p130*
Seitz, Auguste 32; New Orleans, 1848 ***778.6*** *p308*
Seitz, Conrad; Ohio, 1809-1852 ***4511.35*** *p48*
Seitz, Friedrich; Valdivia, Chile, 1851 ***1192.4*** *p51*
Seitz, Georg Christian; America, 1862-1889 ***179.55*** *p19*
Seitz, Heinrich; America, 1891 ***179.55*** *p19*
Seitz, Johann; America, 1851 ***2526.43*** *p126*
Seitz, Jonas 37; Portland, ME, 1906 ***970.38*** *p81*
Seitz, Luise Charlotte; America, 1866 ***5475.1*** *p490*
Seitz, Margaretha; America, 1857 ***2526.43*** *p214*
Seitz, Wilhelm; America, 1867 ***5475.1*** *p490*
Seivers, Sophia 19; Ontario, 1871 ***1823.21*** *p329*
Seivry, Thomas; Plymouth, MA, 1684 ***9228.50*** *p579*
Seiwert, Anna; America, 1882 ***5475.1*** *p268*
*Son:*Mathias
*Son:*Johann
Seiwert, Anna Maria *SEE* Seiwert, Johann
Seiwert, Anna Maria Summa *SEE* Seiwert, Nikolaus
Seiwert, Elisabeth *SEE* Seiwert, Johann
Seiwert, Elisabeth Streit 29 *SEE* Seiwert, Johann
Seiwert, Gertrud; America, 1882 ***5475.1*** *p302*
Seiwert, Johann; America, 1868 ***5475.1*** *p335*
*Wife:*Elisabeth Streit
*Daughter:*Elisabeth
*Daughter:*Anna Maria
Seiwert, Johann 63; America, 1882 ***5475.1*** *p268*
*Wife:*Katharina Folz 63
*Son:*Mathias 29
Seiwert, Katharina Folz 63 *SEE* Seiwert, Johann
Seiwert, Maria *SEE* Seiwert, Nikolaus
Seiwert, Mathias 24; America, 1867 ***5475.1*** *p201*
Seiwert, Mathias 29 *SEE* Seiwert, Johann
Seiwert, Nikolaus; America, 1882 ***5475.1*** *p302*
*Wife:*Anna Maria Summa
*Daughter:*Maria
Seiz, Johann Georg; America, 1882 ***179.55*** *p19*
Sejk, Vaclav; Wisconsin, 1857-1860 ***2853.20*** *p324*
Sekavec, Josef; Kansas, 1866 ***2853.20*** *p201*
Sekelinberg, Frederick 23; New Orleans, 1847 ***778.6*** *p308*
Sekler, Josefa Barbara; America, 1880 ***179.55*** *p19*
Sel, Marguerite; Quebec, 1671 ***4514.3*** *p370*
Sel, Marie; Quebec, 1667 ***4514.3*** *p370*
Sel, Marie-Madeleine; Quebec, 1673 ***4514.3*** *p370*
Selberg, Emil; England, 1878 ***7420.1*** *p312*
Selberg, Georg Emil Carl; London, Eng., 1880 ***7420.1*** *p318*
Selbert, Victoria 28; New Orleans, 1848 ***778.6*** *p308*
Selby, Edward; America, 1764 ***1220.12*** *p710*
Selby, Frances; America, 1740 ***1220.12*** *p710*
Selby, George 37; Ontario, 1871 ***1823.21*** *p329*
Selby, James; America, 1752 ***1220.12*** *p710*
Selby, John; America, 1728 ***1220.12*** *p710*
Selby, Joseph; Virginia, 1768 ***1220.12*** *p710*
Selby, Mary; America, 1720 ***1220.12*** *p710*
Selby, William; America, 1739 ***1220.12*** *p710*
Selby, William 44; Ontario, 1871 ***1823.17*** *p146*
Selch, Alvarez J.; Louisiana, 1874 ***4981.45*** *p134*
Selden, Paladin 25; America, 1845 ***778.6*** *p308*
Seldon, John 38; Ontario, 1871 ***1823.21*** *p329*
Seldon, John 38; Ontario, 1871 ***1823.21*** *p329*
Selerate, John; America, 1750 ***1220.12*** *p710*
Selestman, Mary 35; New Orleans, 1845 ***778.6*** *p308*
Self, Betty; Virginia, 1738 ***1220.12*** *p710*
Self, James 35; Ontario, 1871 ***1823.21*** *p329*
Selfe, Robert; Barbados, 1680 ***1220.12*** *p710*
Selfe, William; America, 1685 ***1220.12*** *p710*
Selgardt, Mr.; America, 1837 ***5475.1*** *p468*
Selgrad, Mr.; America, 1837 ***5475.1*** *p468*
Selig, Andre 20; Missouri, 1845 ***778.6*** *p308*
Selig, Frederick; Long Island, 1778 ***8529.30*** *p10A*
Selig, George 4; Missouri, 1845 ***778.6*** *p308*
Selig, Hermann 15; Missouri, 1845 ***778.6*** *p308*
Selig, Jochim 54; Missouri, 1845 ***778.6*** *p308*
Selig, Madeleine 53; Missouri, 1845 ***778.6*** *p308*
Selig, Markus; North Carolina, 1855 ***1088.45*** *p31*
Selig, Therese 25; Missouri, 1845 ***778.6*** *p308*
Seligmann, Sigmund; America, 1884 ***5475.1*** *p422*
Selinski, Bernard 7; New York, NY, 1898 ***7951.13*** *p43*
Selinski, Johann 7; New York, NY, 1898 ***7951.13*** *p43*
Selinski, Joseph 4; New York, NY, 1898 ***7951.13*** *p43*
Selinski, Katherina 28; New York, NY, 1898 ***7951.13*** *p43*
Selinski, Maria 11 months; New York, NY, 1898 ***7951.13*** *p43*
Sell, A. G.; Louisiana, 1874-1875 ***4981.45*** *p31*
Sell, A. G.; Louisiana, 1874-1875 ***4981.45*** *p130*
Sell, Albert Charles; Wisconsin, 1899 ***6795.8*** *p76*
Sell, Charles Gottlieb Bernhard; Wisconsin, 1889 ***6795.8*** *p77*
Sell, Karl Gottlob Bernhard; Wisconsin, 1897 ***6795.8*** *p77*
Sell, William; America, 1774 ***1220.12*** *p710*
Sellars, John 64; Ontario, 1871 ***1823.21*** *p329*
Sellberg, Fr.; New York, NY, 1844 ***6412.40*** *p147*
Selle, Jacques; Quebec, 1637 ***9221.17*** *p73*
Selle, William; Colorado, 1901 ***1029.59*** *p82*
Selle, William; Colorado, 1901 ***1029.59*** *p83*
Sellen, Nikolaus; America, 1846 ***5475.1*** *p259*
Seller, John; Illinois, 1852 ***6079.1*** *p13*
Seller, Michael; Illinois, 1854 ***6079.1*** *p13*
Seller, William; America, 1775 ***1220.12*** *p710*
Sellerin, Marguerite; Quebec, 1671 ***4514.3*** *p371*
Sellers, Thomas; America, 1739 ***1220.12*** *p710*
Sellers, William; America, 1764 ***1220.12*** *p710*
Sellers, William 46; Ontario, 1871 ***1823.21*** *p329*
Sellersat, John; America, 1750 ***1220.12*** *p710*
Selley, John; America, 1761 ***1220.12*** *p710*
Selley, John; America, 1765 ***1220.12*** *p710*
Selley, Robert; New Jersey, 1665 ***9228.50*** *p578*
Selley, William 7; Ontario, 1871 ***1823.17*** *p146*
Sellick, Elizabeth; Virginia, 1746 ***1220.12*** *p710*
Sellier, Anne Julie 37; New York, NY, 1846 ***6178.50*** *p152*
Sellier, J. 48; America, 1845 ***778.6*** *p308*
Sellman, William A.; Illinois, 1834-1900 ***6020.5*** *p133*
Sellmann, Friedrich August; America, 1853 ***7420.1*** *p111*
Sells, James; America, 1772 ***1220.12*** *p710*
Sellwood, Sarah; Virginia, 1775 ***1220.12*** *p710*
Sellwood, William; America, 1685 ***1220.12*** *p710*
Selly, John; America, 1738 ***1220.12*** *p710*
Selly, Samuel; Maryland, 1742 ***1220.12*** *p710*
Selman, William 41; Ontario, 1871 ***1823.17*** *p146*
Selser, Charles 21; Louisiana, 1847 ***778.6*** *p308*
Seltitz, Fanny; America, 1868 ***7919.3*** *p527*
Seltner, Maria; America, 1868 ***7919.3*** *p531*
Selvie, George; America, 1754 ***1220.12*** *p710*
Selway, George; America, 1772 ***1220.12*** *p710*
Selwick, J. A.; Louisiana, 1874 ***4981.45*** *p134*
Selwood, Elizabeth; America, 1753 ***1220.12*** *p710*
Selwood, Richard; America, 1685 ***1220.12*** *p710*
Selwood, Sara; Virginia, 1718 ***1220.12*** *p710*
Selwood, William; Philadelphia, 1778 ***8529.30*** *p5A*
Selzer, Johann *SEE* Selzer, Johann
Selzer, Johann; America, 1881 ***5475.1*** *p359*
*Wife:*Katharina
*Son:*Stephan
*Son:*Nikolaus
*Son:*Johann
*Son:*Mathias
Selzer, Johann; Pittsburgh, 1884 ***5475.1*** *p322*
Selzer, Kath.; Arkansas, 1880 ***5475.1*** *p245*
Selzer, Katharina *SEE* Selzer, Johann
Selzer, Katharina Gaidt *SEE* Selzer, Mathias
Selzer, Mathias *SEE* Selzer, Johann
Selzer, Mathias; America, 1881 ***5475.1*** *p359*
Selzer, Mathias; America, 1884 ***5475.1*** *p333*
*Wife:*Katharina Gaidt
Selzer, Nikolaus *SEE* Selzer, Johann
Selzer, Peter; America, 1881 ***5475.1*** *p359*
Selzer, Stephan *SEE* Selzer, Johann
Seme, Eusebe 36; Mississippi, 1848 ***778.6*** *p308*
Seme, Vincent 9; Mississippi, 1848 ***778.6*** *p308*
Semes, Carolina; Miami, 1935 ***4984.12*** *p39*
Semet, Johann Georg; America, 1850-1880 ***179.55*** *p19*
Semin, Josef, Sr.; Nebraska, 1876-1877 ***2853.20*** *p172*
Sempf, Gustav; Wisconsin, 1883 ***6795.8*** *p37*
Sempf, Mrs. Heinrich; America, 1868 ***7420.1*** *p277*
Semple, Mary; New York, 1739 ***8277.31*** *p119*
Semro, August; Wisconsin, 1873 ***6795.8*** *p127*
Semro, Julius Carl; Wisconsin, 1891 ***6795.8*** *p129*
Semrow, August; Wisconsin, 1873 ***6795.8*** *p127*
Semrow, Emil E.; Wisconsin, 1890 ***6795.8*** *p216*
Semrow, Julius Carl; Wisconsin, 1891 ***6795.8*** *p129*
Sen, Jean 26; America, 1746 ***778.6*** *p308*

Sen, Johannes 47; New Castle, DE, 1817-1818 ***90.20*** *p154*
Senac, Baptiste 36; America, 1845 ***778.6*** *p308*
Senat, Bertrand 15; New Orleans, 1845 ***778.6*** *p308*
Senat, Louis; Louisiana, 1874 ***4981.45*** *p297*
Senat, Pierre 24; America, 1748 ***778.6*** *p308*
Senbey, Christopher 31; Ontario, 1871 ***1823.17*** *p146*
Sencabaugh, Sarah M.; Prince Edward Island, 1855 ***9228.50*** *p130*
Sencabaugh, Solomon; Providence, RI, 1829-1929 ***9228.50*** *p413*
Sendia, Julian V.; Louisiana, 1874 ***4981.45*** *p134*
Sendry, Thomas, Jr.; America, 1713 ***1220.12*** *p710*
Sene, Marguerite; Virginia, 1700 ***9230.15*** *p80*
With daughter
Seneca, Mary; Maryland or Virginia, 1738 ***1220.12*** *p710*
Senecal, Adrien *SEE* Senecal, Catherine
Senecal, Aimable 47; America, 1843 ***778.6*** *p308*
Senecal, Catherine; Quebec, 1670 ***4514.3*** *p371*
*Father:*Adrien
*Stepmother:*Jeanne Lecomte
*Brother:*Nicolas
Senecal, Jeanne Lecomte *SEE* Senecal, Catherine
Senecal, Louise; Quebec, 1667 ***4514.3*** *p371*
Senecal, Nicolas *SEE* Senecal, Catherine
Senfeit, George; Ohio, 1809-1852 ***4511.35*** *p48*
Senfort, George; Ohio, 1809-1852 ***4511.35*** *p48*
Senger, Alex 10; New York, NY, 1893 ***1883.7*** *p41*
Senger, Barbara 11; New York, NY, 1893 ***1883.7*** *p41*
Senger, Franc; Illinois, 1852 ***6079.1*** *p13*
Senger, Franz 2; New York, NY, 1893 ***1883.7*** *p41*
Senger, Johann 11 months; New York, NY, 1893 ***1883.7*** *p41*
Senger, Joseph 39; New York, NY, 1893 ***1883.7*** *p41*
Senger, Katharina 33; New York, NY, 1893 ***1883.7*** *p41*
Senger, Michael 4; New York, NY, 1893 ***1883.7*** *p41*
Senger, Wendelin 7; New York, NY, 1893 ***1883.7*** *p41*
Senhauser, . . .; West Virginia, n.d. ***1132.30*** *p151*
Senhauser, Gustav; West Virginia, 1873 ***1132.30*** *p151*
Senior, Jane; Rappahannock, VA, 1728 ***1220.12*** *p710*
Senior, Richard; America, 1751 ***1220.12*** *p710*
Senn, Jacob; Ohio, 1809-1852 ***4511.35*** *p49*
Senn, Johann Jakob 29; America, 1831 ***5475.1*** *p26*
With 2 children
Senn, Johannes 47; New Castle, DE, 1817-1818 ***90.20*** *p154*
Senna, Mathias 24; New Orleans, 1847 ***778.6*** *p308*
Senne, Widow; America, 1857 ***7420.1*** *p172*
*Son:*Johann Conrad
Senne, Auguste *SEE* Senne, Ernst Heinrich
Senne, Carl; America, 1885 ***7420.1*** *p349*
Senne, Caroline Wilhelmine *SEE* Senne, Ernst Heinrich
Senne, Catharine; America, 1857 ***7420.1*** *p172*
With 3 sons & 2 daughters
Senne, Engel Maria Catharina Sophia Buhr *SEE* Senne, Johann Heinrich
Senne, Engel Maria Wustenfeld *SEE* Senne, Friedrich Christoph
Senne, Engel Marie Sophie *SEE* Senne, Gottlieb
Senne, Ernestine Sophie *SEE* Senne, Ernst Heinrich
Senne, Ernst Heinrich; America, 1869 ***7420.1*** *p282*
With wife
*Daughter:*Caroline Wilhelmine
*Daughter:*Auguste
*Daughter:*Ernestine Sophie
Senne, Friedrich Christoph; Port uncertain, 1850 ***7420.1*** *p75*
*Wife:*Engel Maria Wustenfeld
Senne, Gottlieb; America, 1865 ***7420.1*** *p237*
*Daughter:*Engel Marie Sophie
Senne, Hans Heinrich; America, 1855 ***7420.1*** *p142*
Senne, Hans Heinrich Christian; America, 1873 ***7420.1*** *p301*
Senne, Johann Conrad; America, 1852 ***7420.1*** *p98*
With wife 2 sons & daughter
Senne, Johann Conrad *SEE* Senne, Widow
Senne, Johann Heinrich; Port uncertain, 1850 ***7420.1*** *p76*
*Wife:*Engel Maria Catharina Sophia Buhr
*Son:*Johann Heinrich Christoph
Senne, Johann Heinrich Christoph *SEE* Senne, Johann Heinrich
Sennebetz, T. Michel 40; Missouri, 1846 ***778.6*** *p308*
Sennet, Katharine; Boston, 1768 ***1642*** *p49*
Sennet, Patrick; Boston, 1766 ***1642*** *p48*
Sennetaire, . . .; Quebec, 1643 ***9221.17*** *p126*
Sennett, Andrew; New Orleans, 1850 ***7242.30*** *p154*
Sennett, George 27; Ontario, 1871 ***1823.21*** *p329*
Sennett, Patrick; New York, 1782 ***8529.30*** *p15*
Sennholz, Mr.; America, 1856 ***7420.1*** *p154*
With wife & 3 children
Sennholz, Mr.; America, 1869 ***7420.1*** *p282*
Sennholz, Engel Marie; America, 1858 ***7420.1*** *p182*
Sennholz, Hans Heinrich Christoph; Chicago, 1873 ***7420.1*** *p301*
Sennholz, Johann Friedrich; America, 1852 ***7420.1*** *p94*
Sennholz, Marie; America, 1856 ***7420.1*** *p154*
Sennit, John; Massachusetts, 1755 ***9228.50*** *p579*
Sennitt, Patrick; New York, 1782 ***8529.30*** *p15*
Sennot, James 37; Ontario, 1871 ***1823.21*** *p329*
Seno, William 79; Ontario, 1871 ***1823.17*** *p146*
Senoz, Alexandre 1; Texas, 1848 ***778.6*** *p308*
Senoz, Delphine 24; Texas, 1848 ***778.6*** *p308*
Senoz, Jean-Baptiste 26; Texas, 1848 ***778.6*** *p308*
Sensat, Mr. 27; America, 1841 ***778.6*** *p308*
Sente, Anne Marie; Wisconsin, 1856 ***1495.20*** *p41*
Sente, Clementin Joseph; Wisconsin, 1856 ***1495.20*** *p41*
Sentenac, Elphege 21; New Orleans, 1845 ***778.6*** *p308*
Senturelli, Joseph; America, 1750 ***1220.12*** *p710*
Sentz, Jacob 9; America, 1846 ***778.6*** *p308*
Sentz, Madeline 29; America, 1846 ***778.6*** *p308*
Sentz, N. 28; America, 1846 ***778.6*** *p308*
Sentz, Pierre 6 months; America, 1846 ***778.6*** *p309*
Senzig, Nikolaus 30; America, 1883 ***5475.1*** *p365*
Septon, Judith; America, 1744 ***1220.12*** *p710*
Septs, Mr. 22; Port uncertain, 1844 ***778.6*** *p309*
Sepure, Andre; Montreal, 1653 ***9221.17*** *p300*
Sequin, Jno; Ontario, 1787 ***1276.15*** *p231*
Serafon, Mr. 40; Port uncertain, 1844 ***778.6*** *p309*
Seramour, Jakob; America, 1857 ***5475.1*** *p253*
Seraphins, Mere des 38; Quebec, 1643 ***9221.17*** *p128*
Serb, Charles 34; Ontario, 1871 ***1823.17*** *p146*
Serbec, C.; California, 1868 ***1131.61*** *p90*
Serbel, Siegfried; New York, 1860 ***358.56*** *p5*
Serbona, Paul 27; New Orleans, 1843 ***778.6*** *p309*
Sercher, David; Ohio, 1809-1852 ***4511.35*** *p49*
Seredge, Thomas; Ohio, 1844 ***2763.1*** *p21*
Serene, Antoine; Quebec, 1658 ***9221.17*** *p386*
Seres, Jean Louis 25; New Orleans, 1845 ***778.6*** *p309*
Serf, Abraham 19; America, 1847 ***778.6*** *p309*
Serf, Ernestine 4; America, 1847 ***778.6*** *p309*
Serf, Isaac 9; America, 1847 ***778.6*** *p309*
Serf, Jeannette 32; America, 1847 ***778.6*** *p309*
Serf, Jeannette 48; America, 1847 ***778.6*** *p309*
Serf, Nathan 17; America, 1847 ***778.6*** *p309*
Serf, Salomon 14; America, 1847 ***778.6*** *p309*
Serf, Salomon 53; America, 1847 ***778.6*** *p309*
Serfous, William; Ohio, 1809-1852 ***4511.35*** *p49*
Sergeant, William; America, 1681 ***1220.12*** *p711*
Sergeant, William; New York, 1776 ***8529.30*** *p15*
Sergeason, John; America, 1748 ***1220.12*** *p775*
Serizay, Pierre; Montreal, 1653 ***9221.17*** *p301*
Serjeant, Elizabeth; America, 1767 ***1220.12*** *p711*
Serjeant, Hugh; America, 1728 ***1220.12*** *p711*
Serjeant, John; America, 1760 ***1220.12*** *p711*
Serjeant, John; America, 1769 ***1220.12*** *p711*
Serjeant, John; America, 1775 ***1220.12*** *p711*
Serjeant, John; Annapolis, MD, 1722 ***1220.12*** *p711*
Serjeant, John; Barbados or Jamaica, 1699 ***1220.12*** *p711*
Serjeant, Robert; Died enroute, 1725 ***1220.12*** *p711*
Serjeant, Susanna; Virginia, 1723 ***1220.12*** *p711*
Serjeant, Thomas; America, 1771 ***1220.12*** *p711*
Serjeant, William; America, 1726 ***1220.12*** *p711*
Serjeant, William; America, 1728 ***1220.12*** *p711*
Serjeant, William; Virginia, 1732 ***1220.12*** *p711*
Serl, John; Quebec, 1870 ***8364.32*** *p26*
Serles, Thomas; America, 1739 ***1220.12*** *p709*
Sermant, Pierre; Quebec, 1643 ***9221.17*** *p135*
Sermen, Anna Maria 40; America, 1857 ***5475.1*** *p550*
Sermentot, Marthe; Quebec, 1643 ***9221.17*** *p128*
Serne, Suzanne 19; Quebec, 1649 ***9221.17*** *p210*
Sero, Frank; Texas, 1884-1908 ***6015.15*** *p27*
Seron, Jean; Louisiana, 1874-1875 ***4981.45*** *p31*
Seron, Jean; Louisiana, 1874-1875 ***4981.45*** *p130*
Serr, Barbara 14; New York, NY, 1874 ***6954.7*** *p38*
Serr, Caroline 37; New York, NY, 1874 ***6954.7*** *p38*
Serr, Christine 14; New York, NY, 1874 ***6954.7*** *p37*
Serr, Heinrich 48; New York, NY, 1874 ***6954.7*** *p37*
Serr, Jacob 42; New York, NY, 1874 ***6954.7*** *p38*
Serr, Johann 13; New York, NY, 1874 ***6954.7*** *p38*
Serr, Pauline 40; New York, NY, 1874 ***6954.7*** *p37*
Serras, F.; Louisiana, 1874 ***4981.45*** *p297*
Serre, Antoine 18; Quebec, 1657 ***9221.17*** *p369*
Serre, Henri 21; America, 1746 ***778.6*** *p309*
Serre, John; Ohio, n.d. ***9228.50*** *p576*
Serreau, Jean 41; Quebec, 1662 ***9221.17*** *p493*
Serres, Richard; Marblehead, MA, 1637 ***9228.50*** *p577*
Serron, Mr. 28; America, 1846 ***778.6*** *p309*
Serruros, Francois-Xavier 29; Texas, 1843 ***778.6*** *p309*
Sersanou, Michel 18; New Orleans, 1848 ***778.6*** *p309*
Sertain, Thomas; Virginia, 1764 ***1220.12*** *p711*
Servant, Mary; America, 1772 ***1220.12*** *p711*
Servant, Mary 24; Michigan, 1880 ***4491.30*** *p28*
Servant, Mathias 26; America, 1747 ***778.6*** *p309*
Servent, L. 30; Port uncertain, 1842 ***778.6*** *p309*
Serverd, Master 15; America, 1847 ***778.6*** *p309*
Serverd, Mrs. 35; America, 1847 ***778.6*** *p309*
Serves, Thomas; North Carolina, 1813 ***1088.45*** *p31*
Service, Alexand 40; Ontario, 1871 ***1823.21*** *p329*
Service, Barney 62; Ontario, 1871 ***1823.21*** *p329*
Service, David 36; Ontario, 1871 ***1823.17*** *p146*
Servignan, Jeanne; Quebec, 1665 ***4514.3*** *p371*
Servigny, Julien 20; Montreal, 1659 ***9221.17*** *p417*
Serwe, Johann; Illinois, 1885 ***5475.1*** *p147*
Serwe, Nikolaus; America, 1882 ***5475.1*** *p147*
Sery, Matej; St. Louis, 1852 ***2853.20*** *p21*
*Son:*Vaclav
Sery, Vaclav *SEE* Sery, Matej
Sesnau, Patrick; Louisiana, 1874 ***4981.45*** *p134*
Sessalin, Julius; Ohio, 1809-1852 ***4511.35*** *p49*
Sessions, Alfred 42; Ontario, 1871 ***1823.21*** *p329*
Sessions, Thomas 71; Ontario, 1871 ***1823.21*** *p329*
Sessions, William; America, 1675 ***1220.12*** *p711*
Sestak, Vaclav; Nebraska, 1865 ***2853.20*** *p155*
Setall, C. 30; Port uncertain, 1845 ***778.6*** *p309*
Seth, Lewis; America, 1774 ***1220.12*** *p711*
Setres, J.P. 20; New Orleans, 1846 ***778.6*** *p309*
Sett, Jean 32; Port uncertain, 1841 ***778.6*** *p309*
Setzer, Miss 15; New York, NY, 1894 ***6512.1*** *p181*
Setzer, Miss 17; New York, NY, 1894 ***6512.1*** *p181*
Setzer, Mrs. 41; New York, NY, 1894 ***6512.1*** *p181*
Setzer, M. Ed. 44; New York, NY, 1894 ***6512.1*** *p181*
Sevanberg, Charles; Washington, 1889 ***2770.40*** *p81*
Sevengood, Benjamin 36; Ontario, 1871 ***1823.17*** *p146*
Sevens, Samuel 29; Indiana, 1881-1884 ***9076.20*** *p71*
Severa, Jiri; Iowa, 1870 ***2853.20*** *p202*
Severa, Vaclav F. 15; Wisconsin, 1868 ***2853.20*** *p218*
Severett, Philip; Portsmouth, NH, 1689 ***9228.50*** *p590*
Severight, George; America, 1753 ***1220.12*** *p711*
Severin, Frank; Iowa, 1887 ***1211.15*** *p19*
Severinsen, Rasmus Martinus; Iowa, 1917 ***1211.15*** *p19*
Severit, Johann Carl Albert; America, 1852 ***7420.1*** *p98*
Severit, Thomas; Plymouth, MA, 1684 ***9228.50*** *p579*
Severn, Caroline 27; Ontario, 1871 ***1823.21*** *p330*
Severn, Thomas; Carolina, 1724 ***1220.12*** *p711*
Severy, Mr.; Marblehead, MA, 1629 ***9228.50*** *p579*
Severy, John 98; Massachusetts, 1742 ***9228.50*** *p580*
Severy, Mary Ann; Havana, 1817-1900 ***9228.50*** *p581*
Severy, Peter; Massachusetts, 1600-1685 ***9228.50*** *p619*
Severy, Thomas; Plymouth, MA, 1684 ***9228.50*** *p579*
Sevestre, Charles 29 *SEE* Sevestre, Marguerite Petitpas
Sevestre, Denise 4 *SEE* Sevestre, Marguerite Petitpas
Sevestre, Etienne *SEE* Sevestre, Marguerite Petitpas
Sevestre, Jacques 21 *SEE* Sevestre, Marguerite Petitpas
Sevestre, Marguerite; Quebec, 1636 ***9221.17*** *p63*
*Son:*Charles
*Granddaughter:*Marguerite
*Daughter-In-Law:*Marie Pichon Gaultier
*Granddaughter:*Denise
*Son:*Etienne
*Son:*Thomas
*Son:*Jacques
Sevestre, Marguerite 1 *SEE* Sevestre, Marguerite Petitpas
Sevestre, Marie Pichon Gaultier *SEE* Sevestre, Marguerite Petitpas
Sevestre, Thomas 25 *SEE* Sevestre, Marguerite Petitpas
Sevett, John; Maryland, 1674 ***1236.25*** *p50*
Sevier, Elizabeth; America, 1733 ***1220.12*** *p711*
Seville, Mary; America, 1724 ***1220.12*** *p711*
Sevit, George E.; Louisiana, 1874 ***4981.45*** *p134*
Sevret, Thomas; Plymouth, MA, 1684 ***9228.50*** *p579*
Sevrit, Mr.; Marblehead, MA, 1629 ***9228.50*** *p579*
Sevrit, John 98; Massachusetts, 1742 ***9228.50*** *p580*
Sevrit, Mary Ann; Havana, 1817-1900 ***9228.50*** *p581*
Sevrit, Thomas; Plymouth, MA, 1684 ***9228.50*** *p579*
Sewald, Barbara Schuler *SEE* Sewald, Michel
Sewald, Christian 27; New York, 1884 ***5475.1*** *p413*
Sewald, Michel; America, 1839 ***5475.1*** *p56*
*Wife:*Barbara Schuler
With 4 children
Seward, Ebenezer; Portsmouth, NH, 1700-1799 ***9228.50*** *p591*
Seward, Geo.; Portsmouth, NH, 1729 ***9228.50*** *p495*
Seward, Henry 40; Ontario, 1871 ***1823.17*** *p146*
Seward, Henry 72; Ontario, 1871 ***1823.17*** *p146*
Seward, James; America, 1771 ***1220.12*** *p711*
Seward, John; Boston, 1716 ***9228.50*** *p591*
Seward, Lucinda 63; Ontario, 1871 ***1823.17*** *p146*
Seward, Martin; Barbados or Jamaica, 1690 ***1220.12*** *p711*
Seward, Perlina 29; Ontario, 1871 ***1823.17*** *p146*
Seward, Samuel; Maryland, 1725 ***1220.12*** *p711*
Sewell, Eliza; Quebec, 1829-1860 ***9228.50*** *p365*
Sewell, Jeremiah; Maryland, 1674 ***1236.25*** *p49*
Sewell, Jeremy; America, 1673 ***1220.12*** *p711*
Sewell, John; America, 1738 ***1220.12*** *p711*
Sewell, Margaret; America, 1741 ***1220.12*** *p711*
Sewell, Thomas; America, 1765 ***1220.12*** *p711*
Sexauer, Carl Aug.; Ohio, 1840-1897 ***8365.35*** *p18*

Sexey, George; America, 1758 1220.12 p711
Sexter, Edwzrd; New Jersey, 1777 8529.30 p5A
Sexton, Conor; St. John, N.B., 1847 2978.15 p40
Sexton, Edwzrd; New Jersey, 1777 8529.30 p5A
Sexton, George S.; Ohio, 1824 3687.1 p39
Sexton, John; America, 1748 1220.12 p711
Sexton, John; America, 1771 1220.12 p711
Sexton, Mic; St. John, N.B., 1848 2978.15 p39
Sexton, Nathaniel; America, 1742 1220.12 p711
Sexton, Pat; St. John, N.B., 1848 2978.15 p39
Sexton, Richard; America, 1675 1220.12 p712
Sexton, Stephen; Illinois, 1859 6079.1 p13
Sexton, Thomas; America, 1686 1220.12 p712
Sexton, Thomas; America, 1736 1220.12 p712
Sexton, Timothy 80; Ontario, 1871 1823.21 p330
Seyb, Mathias Karl Wilhelm; Brazil, 1874 5475.1 p420
Seyers, John; America, 1746 1220.12 p704
Seyffahrt, Fr. Philipp; America, 1878 5475.1 p69
Seyffert, E. W.; Valdivia, Chile, 1852 1192.4 p54
Seyfrard, Jean 21; Port uncertain, 1840 778.6 p309
Seymore, J. M. 39; Ontario, 1871 1823.21 p330
Seymore, John; America, 1685 1220.12 p712
Seymore, William; America, 1680 1220.12 p712
Seymore, William; South Carolina, 1808 6155.4 p19
Seymour, Ann; America, 1761 1220.12 p712
Seymour, Anne; Barbados, 1669 1220.12 p712
Seymour, Benjamin Ambrose; America, 1766 1220.12 p712
Seymour, Charles; Colorado, 1873 1029.59 p83
Seymour, Charles Stewart; America, 1739 1220.12 p712
Seymour, Elizabeth; America, 1770 1220.12 p712
Seymour, George; America, 1758 1220.12 p712
Seymour, George; Barbados, 1679 1220.12 p712
Seymour, James B. 39; Michigan, 1880 4491.33 p20
Seymour, John; America, 1751 1220.12 p712
Seymour, John; America, 1759 1220.12 p712
Seymour, John; America, 1767 1220.12 p712
Seymour, John 30; America, 1664 1220.12 p712
Seymour, John 40; America, 1664 1220.12 p712
Seymour, Mary; America, 1739 1220.12 p712
Seymour, Richard; Barbados or Jamaica, 1710 1220.12 p712
Seymour, Robert; Virginia, 1742 1220.12 p712
Seymour, William; America, 1772 1220.12 p712
Seymour, William; America, 1774 1220.12 p712
Seymour, William; Annapolis, MD, 1725 1220.12 p712
Sha, Edmund; New England, 1747 1642 p29
Sha, Patrick; New England, 1747 1642 p29
Sha..., Thomas 28; Maryland, 1721 1220.12 p712
Shaahay, Edward; Boston, 1762 1642 p31
Shackelton, Elizab 24; Ontario, 1871 1823.17 p146
Shackelton, William 15; Ontario, 1871 1823.17 p146
Shacklady, George; America, 1767 1220.12 p712
Shackleton, Edward; America, 1758 1220.12 p712
Shackleton, Margaret; America, 1751 1220.12 p712
Shackley, James; America, 1697 1220.12 p712
Shacksford, John; Barbados or Jamaica, 1698 1220.12 p712
Shadbolt, William; America, 1755 1220.12 p712
Shaddick, Thomas 37; Ontario, 1871 1823.21 p330
Shaddock, Charles; America, 1742 1220.12 p712
Shaddock, Richard 63; Ontario, 1871 1823.21 p330
Shaddows, David; America, 1745 1220.12 p712
Shadrach, Evan; Ohio, 1840 4022.20 p291
*Wife:*Jemima Thomas
With children
Shadrach, Jemima Thomas *SEE* Shadrach, Evan
Shadwell, John; America, 1765 1220.12 p712
Shae, Ann 37; Ontario, 1871 1823.21 p330
Shae, Daniel 27; Ontario, 1871 1823.21 p330
Shae, Jeremiah 70; Ontario, 1871 1823.21 p330
Shae, Michael 35; Ontario, 1871 1823.21 p330
Shaefer, Benjamin; Ohio, 1809-1852 4511.35 p49
Shaefer, Christian; Ohio, 1809-1852 4511.35 p49
Shaefer, Fautus; Illinois, 1852 6079.1 p13
Shaefer, Marquis; Illinois, 1852 6079.1 p13
Shaefer, Philip; Ohio, 1809-1852 4511.35 p49
Shaeffer, Benjamin; Ohio, 1809-1852 4511.35 p49
Shaeffer, Dewalt; Ohio, 1809-1852 4511.35 p49
Shaeffer, Henry; Ohio, 1809-1852 4511.35 p49
Shaeffer, Martin; Ohio, 1809-1852 4511.35 p49
Shaeffer, Philip; Ohio, 1809-1852 4511.35 p49
Shaen, William; America, 1760 1220.12 p712
Shafer, Adam; Baltimore, 1820 471.10 p87
Shafer, Fritz; Colorado, 1891 1029.59 p83
Shafer, John; Ohio, 1809-1852 4511.35 p49
Shaffer Family ; West Virginia, 1787 1132.30 p146
Shaffer Family ; West Virginia, 1850 1132.30 p147
Shaffner, Henry; North Carolina, 1834 1088.45 p31
Shaflbower, Christopher 39; Ontario, 1871 1823.17 p146
Shaflower, Frederick 48; Ontario, 1871 1823.17 p146
Shafrath, George A.; Ohio, 1809-1852 4511.35 p49
Shafter, J. D.; California, 1868 1131.61 p89
Shaftoe, Edward; Potomac, 1731 1220.12 p712
Shafton, Henry; America, 1738 1220.12 p712
Shailor, James; America, 1763 1220.12 p712
Shain, Kater A. 18; Ontario, 1871 1823.17 p146
Shakerly, Sampson; America, 1723 1220.12 p712
Shakespear, Samuel; America, 1779 1220.12 p712
Shakespear, William; America, 1766 1220.12 p713
Shakespeare, John; America, 1760 1220.12 p712
Shakleton, Thomas; America, 1765 1220.12 p712
Shakspeare, William; America, 1687 1220.12 p712
Shale, John; America, 1763 1220.12 p713
Shale, Robert; America, 1685 1220.12 p713
Shale, Sarah; Virginia, 1730 1220.12 p713
Shales, Daniel; America, 1764 1220.12 p713
Shales, Elizabeth; America, 1668 1220.12 p713
Shales, John; America, 1764 1220.12 p713
Shales, John; Annapolis, MD, 1726 1220.12 p713
Shall, Frederick; Ohio, 1809-1852 4511.35 p49
Shallett, Francis; America, 1685 1220.12 p713
Shallon, Thomas; Washington, 1884 2770.40 p193
Shambaw, Amelia 29 *SEE* Shambaw, Clement
Shambaw, Clement 35; Ohio, 1880 4879.40 p258
*Wife:*Amelia 29
Shamble, Elizabeth Mary; Maryland, 1742 1220.12 p713
Shambler, John; Potomac, 1742 1220.12 p713
Shanahan, Anastasia 57; Ontario, 1871 1823.21 p330
Shanahan, Anna 61; Michigan, 1880 4491.36 p19
Shanahan, Bridget; Toronto, 1844 2910.35 p114
Shanahan, James 30; Michigan, 1880 4491.36 p19
Shanahan, John; Ontario, 1871 1823.21 p330
Shanahan, Patt; New Orleans, 1851 7242.30 p154
Shanahan, Thomas 23; Michigan, 1880 4491.36 p19
Shanahan, William 68; Michigan, 1880 4491.36 p19
Shanan, Jane; Boston, 1766 1642 p36
Shand, Philip; Rappahannock, VA, 1726 1220.12 p713
Shande, Jacob; New Jersey, 1750-1774 927.31 p3
Shandel, Jacob; Ohio, 1809-1852 4511.35 p49
Shandy, Jacob; New Jersey, 1750-1774 927.31 p3
Shane, Michael 70; Ontario, 1871 1823.21 p330
Shanel, Josef; St. Louis, 1854 2853.20 p21
Shank, Mary Ann 33; Ontario, 1871 1823.21 p330
Shank, William 50; Ontario, 1871 1823.21 p330
Shanklin, Andrew; North Carolina, 1860 1088.45 p31
Shanklin, George 55; Ontario, 1871 1823.21 p330
Shanklin, William; North Carolina, 1860 1088.45 p31
Shanks, David 45; Ontario, 1871 1823.17 p147
Shanks, Elizabeth; Virginia, 1721 1220.12 p713
Shanks, John 24; Ontario, 1871 1823.21 p330
Shanks, John; Virginia, 1734 1220.12 p713
Shanks, Robert; America, 1737 1220.12 p713
Shanks, Sarah; America, 1762 1220.12 p713
Shanks, William 30; Ontario, 1871 1823.17 p147
Shanly, James 52; Ontario, 1871 1823.21 p330
Shann, William; Potomac, 1729 1220.12 p713
Shannagan, Daniel 60; Ontario, 1871 1823.21 p330
Shannagan, Denis 50; Ontario, 1871 1823.21 p330
Shannahan, John; Boston, 1765 1642 p35
Shannahan, John; Washington, 1885 2770.40 p194
Shannahan, Peter; Newfoundland, 1814 3476.10 p54
Shannan, William; Boston, 1762 1642 p31
Shannar, . . .; West Virginia, 1850-1860 1132.30 p147
Shanning, Mary; America, 1729 1220.12 p713
Shannon, Catherine 47; Ontario, 1871 1823.21 p330
Shannon, Charles 34; Ontario, 1871 1823.21 p330
Shannon, Henry 16; Quebec, 1870 8364.32 p26
Shannon, James; Boston, 1764 1642 p33
Shannon, John; Boston, 1763 1642 p32
Shannon, John 37; Ontario, 1871 1823.17 p147
Shannon, John 55; Ontario, 1871 1823.17 p147
Shannon, John D. 38; Ontario, 1871 1823.21 p330
Shannon, Michael 68; Ontario, 1871 1823.21 p330
Shannon, Michael P.; Ontario, 1871 1823.21 p330
Shannon, Robert 35; Ontario, 1871 1823.17 p147
Shannon, Robert 73; Ontario, 1871 1823.21 p330
Shannon, Sizley; Boston, 1727 1642 p25
Shannon, William 54; Ontario, 1871 1823.17 p147
Shannon, Wm. 45; Ohio, 1880 4879.40 p257
Shanohan, Edmund; Boston, 1767 1642 p38
Shapiro, Lazar; Detroit, 1929-1930 6214.5 p69
Shapiro, Leonard; Detroit, 1929-1930 6214.5 p69
Shapland, Grace; Virginia, 1740 1220.12 p713
Shapley, Andrew; America, 1722 1220.12 p713
Shaplin, William; Died enroute, 1724 1220.12 p713
Sharborn, John; America, 1765 1220.12 p718
Shard, Emanuel; America, 1727 1220.12 p713
Share, John; America, 1751 1220.12 p713
Share, John Joseph; North Carolina, 1835 1088.45 p31
Sharen, John 49; Ontario, 1871 1823.21 p330
Sharf, Andreas A.; Cleveland, OH, 1893-1900 9722.10 p118
Sharfield, Christian Fred.; North Carolina, 1710 3629.40 p8
Shargold, Robert; Barbados, 1676 1220.12 p713
Sharkey, Bernard 36; Ontario, 1871 1823.21 p330
Sharkey, Hugh 40; Ontario, 1871 1823.21 p330
Sharkey, Lewis; America, 1774 1220.12 p713
Sharland, Frank 25; Michigan, 1880 4491.42 p23
Sharlot, Henry; Boston, 1681 1642 p13
Sharlow, Elizabeth; Annapolis, MD, 1725 1220.12 p713
Sharman, Ed. 17; Quebec, 1870 8364.32 p26
Sharman, Henry; America, 1730 1220.12 p713
Sharman, James 42; Ontario, 1871 1823.21 p330
Sharman, Thomas; America, 1729 1220.12 p713
Sharnon, Richard; North Carolina, 1860 1088.45 p31
Sharon, Alexander; Ohio, 1862 3580.20 p33
Sharon, Alexander; Ohio, 1862 6020.12 p22
Sharp, Mr.; New London, CT, 1670-1699 9228.50 p591
Sharp, Archibald 28; Ontario, 1871 1823.21 p330
Sharp, Benjiman 36; Ontario, 1871 1823.17 p147
Sharp, Catherine 55; Ontario, 1871 1823.17 p147
Sharp, Dennis; Illinois, 1858-1861 6020.5 p133
Sharp, Eleanor; America, 1766 1220.12 p713
Sharp, Elizabeth; America, 1759 1220.12 p713
Sharp, Elizabeth; America, 1768 1220.12 p713
Sharp, Isiah 74; Ontario, 1871 1823.21 p330
Sharp, James; America, 1751 1220.12 p713
Sharp, James 37; Ontario, 1871 1823.21 p330
Sharp, John; America, 1737 1220.12 p713
Sharp, John; America, 1772 1220.12 p713
Sharp, John; Boston, n.d. 9228.50 p591
Sharp, John; New York, 1782 8529.30 p15
Sharp, John H. 23; Ontario, 1871 1823.21 p331
Sharp, Mary; Virginia, 1732 1220.12 p714
Sharp, Mary Ann; Philadelphia, 1847 8513.31 p296
Sharp, Michael 32; Ontario, 1871 1823.17 p147
Sharp, Nicholas; Louisiana, 1874-1875 4981.45 p31
Sharp, Rachael; America, 1773 1220.12 p714
Sharp, Robert; America, 1757 1220.12 p714
Sharp, Robert; Died enroute, 1731 1220.12 p714
Sharp, Robert 33; Ontario, 1871 1823.21 p331
Sharp, Samuel W. 21; Ontario, 1871 1823.21 p331
Sharp, Thomas; America, 1715 1220.12 p714
Sharp, Thomas; America, 1730 1220.12 p714
Sharp, Thomas; America, 1741 1220.12 p714
Sharp, Thomas; America, 1758 1220.12 p714
Sharp, Thomas; America, 1772 1220.12 p714
Sharp, Thomas; America, 1775 1220.12 p714
Sharp, Thomas 41; Ontario, 1871 1823.21 p331
Sharp, Thos 60; Ontario, 1871 1823.17 p147
Sharp, William; America, 1738 1220.12 p714
Sharp, William 30; Ontario, 1871 1823.21 p331
Sharp, William; Virginia, 1726 1220.12 p714
Sharpcliff, Thomas; Annapolis, MD, 1733 1220.12 p714
Sharpe, . . .; New London, CT, 1676 9228.50 p105
Sharpe, Allen 60; Ontario, 1871 1823.21 p331
Sharpe, Christopher; America, 1749 1220.12 p713
Sharpe, David 29; Indiana, 1854-1860 9076.20 p65
Sharpe, Elias; Rappahannock, VA, 1726 1220.12 p713
Sharpe, Elizabeth; Barbados, 1664 1220.12 p713
Sharpe, Elizabeth; Barbados or Jamaica, 1686 1220.12 p713
Sharpe, Frances; Maryland or Virginia, 1733 1220.12 p713
Sharpe, James 59; Ontario, 1871 1823.21 p331
Sharpe, John; Annapolis, MD, 1732 1220.12 p713
Sharpe, Mary; America, 1682 1220.12 p713
Sharpe, Mary; Virginia, 1766 1220.12 p714
Sharpe, Rachel; America, 1733 1220.12 p714
Sharpe, Robert; America, 1770 1220.12 p714
Sharpe, Samuel; Barbados or Jamaica, 1683 1220.12 p714
Sharpe, Sarah; America, 1701 1220.12 p714
Sharpe, Thomas; America, 1733 1220.12 p714
Sharpe, Thomas; America, 1759 1220.12 p714
Sharpe, Thomas 43; Ontario, 1871 1823.21 p331
Sharpe, William; America, 1700 1220.12 p714
Sharpe, William; America, 1719 1220.12 p714
Sharpe, William; America, 1735 1220.12 p714
Sharpells, Henry; Annapolis, MD, 1735 1220.12 p714
Sharper, William; Virginia, 1726 1220.12 p714
Sharples, John; America, 1756 1220.12 p714
Sharpless, Catherine; America, 1748 1220.12 p714
Sharpless, John; America, 1740 1220.12 p714
Sharpless, John; America, 1772 1220.12 p714
Sharpley, James; America, 1775 1220.12 p714
Sharrie, Jacob; Ohio, 1809-1852 4511.35 p49
Sharrock, Mary; Ohio, 1828 9228.50 p591
Sharrock, Timothy S.; America, 1812 9228.50 p553
With wife
Sharwell, John; America, 1767 1220.12 p714
Shathrote, Ulrich; Ohio, 1809-1852 4511.35 p49
Shattersley, John; America, 1679 1220.12 p714
Shaufmann, Jacob 21; New Orleans, 1848 778.6 p309
Shaughnashy, Michael; Boston, 1735 1642 p44
Shaughnashy, Michael; Boston, 1738 1642 p44
Shaughnessy, Michael; New York, 1778 8529.30 p7

Shaughnessy, Thos.; Toronto, 1844 ***2910.35*** *p115*
Shaughneux, Jas; St. John, N.B., 1847 ***2978.15*** *p36*
Shaul, Catherine 8; Mississippi, 1845 ***778.6*** *p309*
Shaul, George 28; Missouri, 1846 ***778.6*** *p309*
Shaul, Marie 20; Mississippi, 1845 ***778.6*** *p309*
Shaul, Martin 37; Mississippi, 1845 ***778.6*** *p310*
Shave, Henry 19; Ontario, 1871 ***1823.17*** *p147*
Shaver, Jacob 35; Ontario, 1871 ***1823.21*** *p331*
Shaver, James W.; Colorado, 1887 ***1029.59*** *p83*
Shaver, Michael; North Carolina, 1710 ***3629.40*** *p7*
Shaver, Stephen 35; Ontario, 1871 ***1823.21*** *p331*
Shaw, Alexander 51; Ontario, 1871 ***1823.17*** *p147*
Shaw, Alice; Died enroute, 1731 ***1220.12*** *p714*
Shaw, Angus 46; Ontario, 1871 ***1823.17*** *p147*
Shaw, Ann; America, 1738 ***1220.12*** *p714*
Shaw, Ann; America, 1755 ***1220.12*** *p714*
Shaw, Ann 19; Ontario, 1871 ***1823.21*** *p331*
Shaw, Ann 50; Ontario, 1871 ***1823.17*** *p147*
Shaw, Benjamin 55; Ontario, 1871 ***1823.21*** *p331*
Shaw, C. D. 62; Ontario, 1871 ***1823.21*** *p331*
Shaw, Catherine; New York, 1739 ***8277.31*** *p119*
Shaw, Charles; America, 1774 ***1220.12*** *p714*
Shaw, Charles H.; Washington, 1884 ***2770.40*** *p193*
Shaw, Chrisa 20; Ontario, 1871 ***1823.17*** *p147*
Shaw, Daniel 60; Ontario, 1871 ***1823.21*** *p331*
Shaw, David; America, 1768 ***1220.12*** *p714*
Shaw, Donald; Missouri, 1892 ***3276.1*** *p3*
Shaw, Donald *SEE* Shaw, John
Shaw, Donald 26; Ontario, 1871 ***1823.17*** *p147*
Shaw, Donald 47; Ontario, 1871 ***1823.17*** *p147*
Shaw, Dorothy; America, 1734 ***1220.12*** *p714*
Shaw, Duncan *SEE* Shaw, John
Shaw, Edward; America, 1719 ***1220.12*** *p714*
Shaw, Edward; America, 1760 ***1220.12*** *p714*
Shaw, Eliza 22; Ontario, 1871 ***1823.21*** *p331*
Shaw, Elizabeth; America, 1775 ***1220.12*** *p714*
Shaw, Elizabeth; Maryland or Virginia, 1738 ***1220.12*** *p714*
Shaw, Emanuel; America, 1769 ***1220.12*** *p714*
Shaw, Emma 12; Quebec, 1870 ***8364.32*** *p26*
Shaw, Florence McLaslin *SEE* Shaw, Neil
Shaw, George; America, 1727 ***1220.12*** *p715*
Shaw, George; Maryland, 1720 ***1220.12*** *p714*
Shaw, George; Mississippi, 1836-1838 ***7710.1*** *p150*
Shaw, George 29; Ontario, 1871 ***1823.21*** *p331*
Shaw, George 36; Ontario, 1871 ***1823.21*** *p331*
Shaw, George 40; Ontario, 1871 ***1823.21*** *p331*
Shaw, Grizziel Andrew; North Carolina, 1792-1862 ***1088.45*** *p31*
Shaw, Hugh; Iowa, 1896 ***1211.15*** *p19*
Shaw, Jackson 28; Ontario, 1871 ***1823.17*** *p147*
Shaw, James; America, 1744 ***1220.12*** *p715*
Shaw, James; New York, NY, 1827 ***3274.55*** *p71*
Shaw, James; North Carolina, 1823 ***1088.45*** *p31*
Shaw, James; Ohio, 1809-1852 ***4511.35*** *p49*
Shaw, James 45; Ontario, 1871 ***1823.21*** *p331*
Shaw, James 53; Ontario, 1871 ***1823.17*** *p147*
Shaw, James 58; Ontario, 1871 ***1823.21*** *p331*
Shaw, James 60; Ontario, 1871 ***1823.21*** *p331*
Shaw, James 64; Ontario, 1871 ***1823.17*** *p147*
Shaw, James 70; Ontario, 1871 ***1823.21*** *p331*
Shaw, James M.; Ohio, 1854 ***3580.20*** *p33*
Shaw, James M.; Ohio, 1854 ***6020.12*** *p22*
Shaw, Jane; America, 1761 ***1220.12*** *p715*
Shaw, Jane 18; Ontario, 1871 ***1823.21*** *p331*
Shaw, Jane 44; Ontario, 1871 ***1823.17*** *p147*
Shaw, John; America, 1732 ***1220.12*** *p715*
Shaw, John; America, 1751 ***1220.12*** *p715*
Shaw, John; America, 1759 ***1220.12*** *p715*
Shaw, John; America, 1771 ***1220.12*** *p715*
Shaw, John; Annapolis, MD, 1719 ***1220.12*** *p715*
Shaw, John; Barbados or Jamaica, 1697 ***1220.12*** *p715*
Shaw, John; Cape Fear, NC,, 1754 ***1422.10*** *p61*
Shaw, John; New York, 1739 ***8277.31*** *p119*
*Wife:*Mary McNeil
*Son:*Neil
*Son:*John, Sr.
*Son:*Duncan
Shaw, John; New York, 1740 ***8277.31*** *p119*
*Wife:*Merran Brown
*Child:*Margaret
*Child:*Mary
*Child:*Donald
Shaw, John; North Carolina, 1848 ***1088.45*** *p31*
Shaw, John; North Carolina, 1850 ***1088.45*** *p31*
Shaw, John 53; Ontario, 1871 ***1823.17*** *p147*
Shaw, John 70; Ontario, 1871 ***1823.17*** *p147*
Shaw, John, Jr.; Boston, 1818 ***3274.55*** *p67*
Shaw, John, Jr.; Iowa, 1896 ***1211.15*** *p19*
Shaw, John, Sr. *SEE* Shaw, John
Shaw, John B.; New York, 1856 ***8513.31*** *p426*
*Wife:*Mary A. Carlisle
Shaw, John B. 51; Ontario, 1871 ***1823.17*** *p147*
Shaw, John W. 35; Ontario, 1871 ***1823.21*** *p331*
Shaw, Jonathan; America, 1733 ***1220.12*** *p715*
Shaw, Jonathan; Barbados, 1699 ***1220.12*** *p715*
Shaw, Jonathan; Maryland, 1720 ***1220.12*** *p715*
Shaw, Joseph; America, 1741 ***1220.12*** *p715*
Shaw, Joseph; America, 1764 ***1220.12*** *p715*
Shaw, Joseph; New York, NY, 1837 ***3274.55*** *p25*
Shaw, Josephine 33; Michigan, 1880 ***4491.42*** *p24*
Shaw, Julia Harris; Iowa, 1925 ***1211.15*** *p19*
Shaw, Margaret *SEE* Shaw, John
Shaw, Mary; America, 1745 ***1220.12*** *p715*
Shaw, Mary; America, 1753 ***1220.12*** *p715*
Shaw, Mary McNeil *SEE* Shaw, John
Shaw, Mary *SEE* Shaw, John
Shaw, Mary 22; Ontario, 1871 ***1823.21*** *p331*
Shaw, Mary 9; Quebec, 1870 ***8364.32*** *p26*
Shaw, Mary A. Carlisle *SEE* Shaw, John B.
Shaw, Matthew; North Carolina, 1792-1862 ***1088.45*** *p31*
Shaw, Merran Brown *SEE* Shaw, John
Shaw, Neil *SEE* Shaw, John
Shaw, Neil; New York, 1739 ***8277.31*** *p119*
*Wife:*Florence McLaslin
Shaw, Neill; Prince Edward Island, 1771 ***3799.30*** *p41*
Shaw, Philip; America, 1730 ***1220.12*** *p715*
Shaw, Ralph; Indiana, 1843 ***471.10*** *p61*
Shaw, Richard 56; Ontario, 1871 ***1823.21*** *p331*
Shaw, Robert; Potomac, 1731 ***1220.12*** *p715*
Shaw, Samuel; America, 1682 ***1220.12*** *p715*
Shaw, Samuel; America, 1772 ***1220.12*** *p715*
Shaw, Samuel; Annapolis, MD, 1725 ***1220.12*** *p715*
Shaw, Samuel; Barbados, 1675 ***1220.12*** *p715*
Shaw, Samuel M.; Illinois, 1858-1861 ***6020.5*** *p133*
Shaw, Sarah; America, 1757 ***1220.12*** *p715*
Shaw, Sarah 47; Ontario, 1871 ***1823.21*** *p332*
Shaw, Sarah 53; Ontario, 1871 ***1823.21*** *p331*
Shaw, Sarah 77; Ontario, 1871 ***1823.21*** *p331*
Shaw, Thomas; America, 1725 ***1220.12*** *p715*
Shaw, Thomas; America, 1750 ***1220.12*** *p715*
Shaw, Thomas; America, 1751 ***1220.12*** *p715*
Shaw, Thomas; America, 1774 ***1220.12*** *p715*
Shaw, Thomas; Barbados, 1675 ***1220.12*** *p715*
Shaw, Thomas; Barbados, 1694 ***1220.12*** *p715*
Shaw, Walter; America, 1766 ***1220.12*** *p715*
Shaw, Walter; Jamaica, 1716 ***1220.12*** *p715*
Shaw, William; America, 1736 ***1220.12*** *p715*
Shaw, William; Died enroute, 1721 ***1220.12*** *p715*
Shaw, William; Died enroute, 1725 ***1220.12*** *p715*
Shaw, William; Illinois, 1858-1861 ***6020.5*** *p133*
Shaw, William; Maryland, 1740 ***1220.12*** *p715*
Shaw, William; North Carolina, 1809-1814 ***1088.45*** *p31*
Shaw, William; North Carolina, 1842-1849 ***1088.45*** *p31*
Shaw, William 17; Ontario, 1871 ***1823.17*** *p148*
Shaw, William 52; Ontario, 1871 ***1823.17*** *p148*
Shaw, William 54; Ontario, 1871 ***1823.21*** *p332*
Shaw, William 56; Ontario, 1871 ***1823.21*** *p332*
Shaw, William 67; Ontario, 1871 ***1823.17*** *p148*
Shawbridge, Robert; America, 1742 ***1220.12*** *p715*
Shawe, James; America, 1751 ***1220.12*** *p715*
Shawe, Thomas; America, 1697 ***1220.12*** *p715*
Shawe, Thomas; Antigua (Antego), 1743 ***1220.12*** *p715*
Shay, Catherine; New Brunswick, 1842 ***2978.20*** *p9*
Shay, Daniel; Massachusetts, 1772 ***1642*** *p100*
Shay, Elizabeth; New Brunswick, 1842 ***2978.20*** *p9*
Shay, Ellen; New Brunswick, 1842 ***2978.20*** *p9*
Shay, James; Massachusetts, 1768 ***1642*** *p100*
Shay, Jarvis; America, 1752 ***1220.12*** *p715*
Shay, Joanna; New Brunswick, 1842 ***2978.20*** *p9*
Shay, John; Ohio, 1840-1897 ***8365.35*** *p18*
Shay, Kate; Massachusetts, 1766 ***1642*** *p104*
Shay, Mary; Boston, 1763 ***1642*** *p48*
Shay, Patrick; Massachusetts, 1744 ***1642*** *p105*
Shay, William; New Brunswick, 1842 ***2978.20*** *p9*
Shayer, . . .; California, 1874 ***9228.50*** *p591*
Shayer, . . .; New York, 1874 ***9228.50*** *p591*
Shayhan, Patrick; Ohio, 1840-1897 ***8365.35*** *p18*
Shays, Mary; America, 1742 ***1220.12*** *p715*
She, William; Boston, 1763 ***1642*** *p32*
Shea, Christopher; Toronto, 1844 ***2910.35*** *p113*
Shea, Cornelius; South Carolina, 1835 ***6155.4*** *p19*
Shea, Daniel; Louisiana, 1874 ***4981.45*** *p297*
Shea, Daniel 59; Ontario, 1871 ***1823.17*** *p148*
Shea, Daniel; Toronto, 1844 ***2910.35*** *p115*
Shea, Frantisek; Chicago, 1866 ***2853.20*** *p68*
With parents
Shea, Honoria 40; Ontario, 1871 ***1823.21*** *p332*
Shea, James 60; Ontario, 1871 ***1823.21*** *p332*
Shea, John; Boston, 1816 ***3274.56*** *p98*
Shea, John; Toronto, 1844 ***2910.35*** *p111*
Shea, John, Jr.; Toronto, 1844 ***2910.35*** *p111*
Shea, Martin 2; St. Johns, N.F., 1811 ***1053.20*** *p22*
Shea, Patrick 47; Ontario, 1871 ***1823.17*** *p148*
Shea, Patt; New Orleans, 1850 ***7242.30*** *p154*
Shea, Thomas 70; Ontario, 1871 ***1823.21*** *p332*
Shea, Timothy; Boston, 1766 ***1642*** *p36*
Shea, Timothy 66; Ontario, 1871 ***1823.21*** *p332*
Shea, Walter; Newfoundland, 1814 ***3476.10*** *p54*
Shea, William; Newfoundland, 1814 ***3476.10*** *p54*
Sheaf, William; America, 1749 ***1220.12*** *p715*
Sheahr, Henry; Ohio, 1809-1852 ***4511.35*** *p49*
Sheal, John; America, 1736 ***1220.12*** *p715*
Shean, James; America, 1773 ***1220.12*** *p716*
Shean, John; New Orleans, 1851 ***7242.30*** *p154*
Shean, Joseph; America, 1742 ***1220.12*** *p716*
Shean, Mary; New Orleans, 1851 ***7242.30*** *p154*
Shean, Michael; New Orleans, 1851 ***7242.30*** *p154*
Sheapard, Tho; Virginia, 1652 ***6254.4*** *p243*
Shear, George R. 38; Ontario, 1871 ***1823.17*** *p148*
Shearen, John 30; Ontario, 1871 ***1823.21*** *p332*
Shearer, Henry; Ohio, 1809-1852 ***4511.35*** *p49*
Shearer, Jacob; Ohio, 1809-1852 ***4511.35*** *p49*
Shearer, Nicholas; Ohio, 1809-1852 ***4511.35*** *p49*
Shearer, Peter; Ohio, 1809-1852 ***4511.35*** *p49*
Shearing, Mary; America, 1772 ***1220.12*** *p716*
Shearing, Stephen; America, 1741 ***1220.12*** *p716*
Shearman, Elizabeth; America, 1765 ***1220.12*** *p718*
Shearman, John; America, 1750 ***1220.12*** *p718*
Shears, Christopher 31; Ontario, 1871 ***1823.21*** *p332*
Shears, Isaac; America, 1775 ***1220.12*** *p716*
Shears, Leonard; America, 1772 ***1220.12*** *p716*
Shears, Mary; America, 1761 ***1220.12*** *p716*
Shears, Mary; Maryland, 1730 ***1220.12*** *p716*
Shears, Thomas; America, 1775 ***1220.12*** *p716*
Sheat, Josias; America, 1723 ***1220.12*** *p716*
Sheave, Robert; America, 1739 ***1220.12*** *p716*
Sheaver, John 80; Ontario, 1871 ***1823.21*** *p332*
Shedduck, James 71; Ontario, 1871 ***1823.21*** *p332*
Sheean, Barbara; New Brunswick, 1842 ***2978.20*** *p8*
Sheean, Catherine, I; New Brunswick, 1842 ***2978.20*** *p8*
Sheean, Catherine, II; New Brunswick, 1842 ***2978.20*** *p8*
Sheean, Catherine, III; New Brunswick, 1842 ***2978.20*** *p8*
Sheean, Daniel, Jr.; New Brunswick, 1842 ***2978.20*** *p8*
Sheean, Daniel, Sr.; New Brunswick, 1842 ***2978.20*** *p7*
Sheean, Edward; New Brunswick, 1842 ***2978.20*** *p8*
Sheean, Edward, Sr.; New Brunswick, 1842 ***2978.20*** *p9*
Sheean, Ellen; New Brunswick, 1842 ***2978.20*** *p8*
Sheean, Jerry; New Brunswick, 1842 ***2978.20*** *p9*
Sheean, Jerry, Jr.; New Brunswick, 1842 ***2978.20*** *p8*
Sheean, Jerry, Sr.; New Brunswick, 1842 ***2978.20*** *p8*
Sheean, Joanna; New Brunswick, 1842 ***2978.20*** *p8*
Sheean, Joanna, Jr.; New Brunswick, 1842 ***2978.20*** *p8*
Sheean, John; New Brunswick, 1842 ***2978.20*** *p8*
Sheean, Judy; New Brunswick, 1842 ***2978.20*** *p8*
Sheean, Mary, I; New Brunswick, 1842 ***2978.20*** *p7*
Sheean, Mary, II; New Brunswick, 1842 ***2978.20*** *p8*
Sheean, Mary, III; New Brunswick, 1842 ***2978.20*** *p8*
Sheean, Michael; New Brunswick, 1842 ***2978.20*** *p8*
Sheean, Patrick; New Brunswick, 1842 ***2978.20*** *p8*
Sheean, Thomas; New Brunswick, 1842 ***2978.20*** *p8*
Sheeber, John; Ohio, 1809-1852 ***4511.35*** *p49*
Sheehan, Bryan; Salem, MA, 1772 ***1642*** *p78*
Sheehan, Bryan; Salem, MA, 1772 ***1642*** *p81*
Sheehan, G.B.; Washington, 1889 ***2770.40*** *p81*
Sheehan, James; Louisiana, 1874 ***4981.45*** *p134*
Sheehan, John; Colorado, 1878 ***1029.59*** *p83*
Sheeler, John; Long Island, 1781 ***8529.30*** *p10A*
Sheels, John; America, 1716 ***1220.12*** *p716*
Sheen, Mary; America, 1731 ***1220.12*** *p716*
Sheen, William; America, 1774 ***1220.12*** *p716*
Sheene, George; America, 1769 ***1220.12*** *p716*
Sheenn, Joseph; Salem, MA, 1731 ***1642*** *p78*
Sheepy, John; Charles Town, SC, 1719 ***1220.12*** *p716*
Sheereman, William; America, 1755 ***1220.12*** *p718*
Sheerer, Nicholas; Ohio, 1809-1852 ***4511.35*** *p49*
Sheeres, John; America, 1700 ***1220.12*** *p716*
Sheern, George; New York, NY, 1852 ***8513.31*** *p426*
*Wife:*Mary Rogers
Sheern, Mary Rogers *SEE* Sheern, George
Sheers, Elizabeth; America, 1757 ***1220.12*** *p716*
Sheers, John; Maryland, 1737 ***1220.12*** *p716*
Sheets, Jacob; North Carolina, 1710 ***3629.40*** *p6*
Sheffer, Mr. 26; America, 1847 ***778.6*** *p310*
Sheffield, Isaac; America, 1753 ***1220.12*** *p716*
Sheffield, John; America, 1731 ***1220.12*** *p716*
Sheffield, John; America, 1769 ***1220.12*** *p716*
Sheffield, John; Barbados, 1668 ***1220.12*** *p716*
Sheffield, Joseph; America, 1761 ***1220.12*** *p716*
Sheffield, Samuel; America, 1752 ***1220.12*** *p716*
Sheffield, Thomas; America, 1752 ***1220.12*** *p716*
Sheffield, Thomas; America, 1775 ***1220.12*** *p716*
Sheffield, William; America, 1765 ***1220.12*** *p716*
Shehan, Daniel; New York, 1824 ***3274.55*** *p71*
Shehan, Dennis; Boston, 1756 ***1642*** *p47*
Shehan, Dennis; Boston, 1758 ***1642*** *p47*
Shehane, Daniel; Salem, MA, 1767 ***1642*** *p78*
Shehr, Henry; Ohio, 1809-1852 ***4511.35*** *p49*
Sheibe, John Jacob; North Carolina, 1710 ***3629.40*** *p8*

Sheider, Xavier 24; America, 1847 778.6 p310
Sheikelane, Louis; Toronto, 1844 2910.35 p112
Sheilds, David; Illinois, 1858-1861 6020.5 p133
Sheinton, John; America, 1758 1220.12 p716
Sheldan, Andrew; America, 1742 1220.12 p716
Shelden, John; America, 1766 1220.12 p716
Sheldes, Andrew; Ohio, 1844 2763.1 p21
Sheldon, Alexr 37; Ontario, 1871 1823.17 p148
Sheldon, Andrew; Barbados, 1666 1220.12 p716
Sheldon, Benedict; Barbados, 1665 1220.12 p716
Sheldon, John; America, 1683 1220.12 p716
Sheldon, Mary; America, 1772 1220.12 p716
Sheldon, Thomas; America, 1767 1220.12 p716
Sheldon, William; America, 1683 1220.12 p716
Sheldrick, Elizabeth; America, 1732 1220.12 p716
Shelfer, Lawd.; North Carolina, 1710 3629.40 p7
Shelfer, Michael; North Carolina, 1710 3629.40 p7
Shelfer, Tobias; North Carolina, 1710 3629.40 p7
Shell, John; Louisiana, 1874 4981.45 p134
Sheller, Christopher; Ohio, 1836 3580.20 p33
Sheller, Christopher; Ohio, 1836 6020.12 p22
Shelley, Arthur 16; Quebec, 1870 8364.32 p26
Shelley, Jacob; America, 1745 1220.12 p716
Shelley, John; Barbados or Jamaica, 1710 1220.12 p716
Shelley, Philip; America, 1761 1220.12 p716
Shelley, Susannah; America, 1770 1220.12 p716
Shelly, Thomas; America, 1728 1220.12 p716
Shelock, James; America, 1756 1220.12 p716
Shelter, Stephen 43; Port uncertain, 1846 778.6 p310
Shelton, Edward; America, 1753 1220.12 p716
Shelton, Elizabeth; America, 1757 1220.12 p716
Shelton, George 31; Ontario, 1871 1823.21 p332
Shelton, Hannah; America, 1762 1220.12 p717
Shelton, Henry; Maryland or Virginia, 1731 1220.12 p717
Shelton, James; America, 1761 1220.12 p717
Shelton, John; America, 1775 1220.12 p717
Shelton, John; New York, 1778 8529.30 p15
Shelton, Jonas; America, 1758 1220.12 p717
Shelton, Mary; America, 1751 1220.12 p717
Shelton, Mary, Jr.; America, 1748 1220.12 p717
Shelton, Mary, Sr.; America, 1748 1220.12 p717
Shelton, Rachel; Massachusetts, 1814-1900 9228.50 p591
Shelton, Robert; Barbados or Jamaica, 1715 1220.12 p717
Shelton, Samuel 31; Ontario, 1871 1823.21 p332
Shelton, Thomas 30; Ontario, 1871 1823.21 p332
Shelton, Walter; Annapolis, MD, 1722 1220.12 p717
Shemmelpfenig, Stanley; Detroit, 1930 1640.60 p83
Shenburn, Peter 47; Ontario, 1871 1823.17 p148
Shendan, Andrew 17; Quebec, 1870 8364.32 p26
Shender, Julius Cereloff; Detroit, 1929-1930 6214.5 p61
Shenick, Huldah 69; Ontario, 1871 1823.21 p332
Shepard, Bernard 44; Ontario, 1871 1823.17 p148
Shepard, Charles; America, 1746 1220.12 p717
Shepard, Francis; Maryland, 1680 1236.25 p53
*Wife:*Hannah
Shepard, Hannah *SEE* Shepard, Francis
Shepard, James 54; Ontario, 1871 1823.17 p148
Shepard, William; Maryland, 1723 1220.12 p718
Shephard, David 44; Ontario, 1871 1823.17 p148
Shephard, James 60; Ontario, 1871 1823.17 p148
Shephard, James 70; Ontario, 1871 1823.21 p332
Shephard, John 50; Ontario, 1871 1823.21 p332
Shephard, John 70; Ontario, 1871 1823.21 p332
Shephard, Mary 18; Ontario, 1871 1823.21 p332
Shephard, Simpson 63; Ontario, 1871 1823.17 p148
Shephard, Thomas H.; Colorado, 1891 1029.59 p83
Shepheard, Charles; America, 1773 1220.12 p717
Shepheard, John; America, 1758 1220.12 p717
Shephens, William 40; Ontario, 1871 1823.17 p148
Shepherd, Ada Alice; Massachusetts, 1889 9228.50 p359
Shepherd, Alexander 35; Ontario, 1871 1823.21 p332
Shepherd, Ann; America, 1750 1220.12 p717
Shepherd, Ann; America, 1774 1220.12 p717
Shepherd, Benjimin 33; Ontario, 1871 1823.21 p332
Shepherd, Conrad; America, 1773 1220.12 p717
Shepherd, Dorothy; America, 1753 1220.12 p717
Shepherd, Elizabeth; Maryland, 1726 1220.12 p717
Shepherd, Elizabeth; Maryland or Virginia, 1731 1220.12 p717
Shepherd, Elizabeth; Virginia, 1730 1220.12 p717
Shepherd, Francis; Barbados, 1673 1220.12 p717
Shepherd, Geo. F.; Wisconsin, 1856-1865 9228.50 p592
*Wife:*Martha V. Fleure
Shepherd, George 58; Ontario, 1871 1823.17 p148
Shepherd, George 16; Quebec, 1870 8364.32 p26
Shepherd, J.S.; Wisconsin, 1860 9228.50 p591
Shepherd, James; America, 1766 1220.12 p717
Shepherd, James; New York, NY, 1823 3274.55 p67
Shepherd, James 30; Ontario, 1871 1823.17 p148
Shepherd, John; America, 1756 1220.12 p717
Shepherd, John; Missouri, 1894 3276.1 p4
Shepherd, John 35; Ontario, 1871 1823.21 p332
Shepherd, John 38; Ontario, 1871 1823.21 p332
Shepherd, John; Virginia, 1736 1220.12 p717
Shepherd, Laura M.; Wisconsin, 1875 9228.50 p591
Shepherd, Margaret; Annapolis, MD, 1726 1220.12 p717
Shepherd, Martha; Died enroute, 1734 1220.12 p717
Shepherd, Martha V. Fleure *SEE* Shepherd, Geo. F.
Shepherd, Mary; America, 1753 1220.12 p717
Shepherd, Richard; Virginia, 1735 1220.12 p717
Shepherd, Robert; America, 1770 1220.12 p717
Shepherd, Samuel; Annapolis, MD, 1730 1220.12 p717
Shepherd, Sara; Annapolis, MD, 1732 1220.12 p718
Shepherd, Thomas; America, 1726 1220.12 p718
Shepherd, Thomas; America, 1766 1220.12 p718
Shepherd, Thomas; Annapolis, MD, 1725 1220.12 p718
Shepherd, Thomas; Maryland, 1725 1220.12 p718
Shepherd, Thomas; Ohio, 1840 3580.20 p33
Shepherd, William; America, 1750 1220.12 p718
Shepherd, William; America, 1768 1220.12 p718
Shepherd, William; America, 1772 1220.12 p718
Shepherd, William 54; Ontario, 1871 1823.21 p332
Shepherd, Wm.; America, 1871 9076.20 p68
Shepherdl, Thomas; Ohio, 1840 6020.12 p22
Sheppach, Theodore; Illinois, 1865 6079.1 p13
Sheppard, Ambrose; Barbados, 1666 1220.12 p717
Sheppard, Charles; America, 1753 1220.12 p717
Sheppard, Charles 37; Ontario, 1871 1823.21 p332
Sheppard, David; America, 1769 1220.12 p717
Sheppard, Elizabeth; Virginia, 1750 1220.12 p717
Sheppard, George; America, 1756 1220.12 p717
Sheppard, George 36; Ontario, 1871 1823.21 p332
Sheppard, George 50; Ontario, 1871 1823.21 p332
Sheppard, Giles; America, 1748 1220.12 p717
Sheppard, Hannah; America, 1736 1220.12 p717
Sheppard, James; America, 1685 1220.12 p717
Sheppard, Mary; America, 1737 1220.12 p717
Sheppard, Mary; America, 1747 1220.12 p717
Sheppard, Mary; Barbados or Jamaica, 1694 1220.12 p717
Sheppard, Robert; America, 1774 1220.12 p717
Sheppard, Stephen; Maryland, 1674 1236.25 p49
Sheppard, Thomas; Louisiana, 1874 4981.45 p297
Sheppard, Tobias; America, 1657 1220.12 p718
Sheppard, William; America, 1685 1220.12 p718
Sheppard, William; America, 1769 1220.12 p718
Sheppard, William; America, 1774 1220.12 p718
Sheppard, William 22; Ontario, 1871 1823.21 p332
Sheppard, William 58; Ontario, 1871 1823.17 p148
Sheppard, William 17; Quebec, 1870 8364.32 p26
Sheppardson, John; America, 1773 1220.12 p718
Sheppeard, Mary; Annapolis, MD, 1722 1220.12 p717
Shepperd, John 31; Ontario, 1871 1823.21 p333
Shepperd, William 40; Ontario, 1871 1823.21 p333
Shepton, John; America, 1606 1220.12 p718
Sheran, Michael 69; Ontario, 1871 1823.21 p333
Sherborne, Sarah; America, 1721 1220.12 p718
Sherbourne, Thomas; America, 1699 1220.12 p718
Sherdin, Charles; Ohio, 1809-1852 4511.35 p49
Sherdin, Eliza 18; Quebec, 1870 8364.32 p26
Sherdin, Selena 16; Quebec, 1870 8364.32 p26
Sherdon, Paul; Virginia, 1726 1220.12 p718
Sherer, John; America, 1764 1220.12 p716
Sherer, Maria 12; America, 1840 778.6 p310
Sherer, Mary 18; America, 1840 778.6 p310
Sheridan, James; Boston, 1830 3274.55 p68
Sheridan, James; North Carolina, 1856 1088.45 p31
Sheridan, James 57; Ontario, 1871 1823.17 p148
Sheridan, John; America, 1764 1220.12 p718
Sheridan, June; North Carolina, 1856 1088.45 p31
Sheridan, Margaret; New Orleans, 1850 7242.30 p154
Sheridan, Mary 72; Ontario, 1871 1823.17 p148
Sheridan, Winifred 13; Quebec, 1870 8364.32 p26
Sheriden, John; Philadelphia, 1777 8529.30 p7
Sheriff, Matthew; America, 1737 1220.12 p718
Sheriff, Riley 45; Ontario, 1871 1823.17 p148
Sherk, Henry 46; Ontario, 1871 1823.17 p148
Sherland, John; Barbados or Jamaica, 1687 1220.12 p718
Sherland, William; America, 1729 1220.12 p718
Sherles, John; America, 1738 1220.12 p718
Sherley, Thomas; America, 1699 1220.12 p720
Sherlock, James 30; Ontario, 1871 1823.17 p148
Sherlock, John; America, 1727 1220.12 p718
Sherlock, Michael 26; Ontario, 1871 1823.21 p333
Sherlock, Patrick 29; Ontario, 1871 1823.21 p333
Sherlock, Patrick 35; Ontario, 1871 1823.21 p333
Sherlock, Ralph; America, 1750 1220.12 p718
Sherlock, Silvia; Rappahannock, VA, 1728 1220.12 p718
Sherlock, Simon; America, 1727 1220.12 p718
Sherlock, William; America, 1751 1220.12 p718
Sherman, A. 50; Ontario, 1871 1823.21 p333
Sherman, Gustave; Ohio, 1840-1897 8365.35 p18
Sherman, Henry G. 20; New York, NY, 1894 6512.1 p183
Sherman, J. L.; California, 1868 1131.61 p89
Sherman, Owen 28; Ontario, 1871 1823.17 p148
Sherman, Peter; Ohio, 1842 2763.1 p21
Sherman, Rachael; America, 1762 1220.12 p718
Sherman, Samuel; Barbados or Jamaica, 1705 1220.12 p718
Sherman, Susannah; America, 1767 1220.12 p718
Sherman, William 34; Ontario, 1871 1823.21 p333
Sherran, John P. 27; Ontario, 1871 1823.21 p333
Sherrar, William; America, 1772 1220.12 p719
Sherrard, Bernard; America, 1769 1220.12 p718
Sherrard, Francis; America, 1732 1220.12 p718
Sherrard, George; America, 1770 1220.12 p718
Sherrard, James; America, 1722 1220.12 p718
Sherrard, James; Ohio, 1789-1876 9228.50 p592
Sherrard, John; America, 1754 1220.12 p718
Sherrard, John 65; Ontario, 1871 1823.21 p333
Sherrard, Mary Bogle *SEE* Sherrard, Wm.
Sherrard, Mary Ann; Ohio, 1803-1897 9228.50 p483
Sherrard, Nathaniel; America, 1752 1220.12 p719
Sherrard, Robert; America, 1749 1220.12 p719
Sherrard, William; America, 1758 1220.12 p719
Sherrard, Wm.; Ohio, 1824 9228.50 p592
*Wife:*Mary Bogle
With children
Sherratt, John; America, 1769 1220.12 p719
Sherridan, Catherine; America, 1755 1220.12 p718
Sherridan, James 39; Ontario, 1871 1823.21 p333
Sherriff, William; Virginia, 1719 1220.12 p718
Sherriffs, George 38; Ontario, 1871 1823.21 p333
Sherriffs, Mary 82; Ontario, 1871 1823.21 p333
Sherring, George 38; Ontario, 1871 1823.21 p333
Sherring, William; America, 1751 1220.12 p719
Sherring, William; America, 1758 1220.12 p719
Sherringe, Robert; Barbados, 1669 1220.12 p719
Sherrington, William; America, 1732 1220.12 p719
Sherrord, William; America, 1758 1220.12 p719
Sherry, James 45; Ontario, 1871 1823.21 p333
Sherry, Jane; Barbados or Jamaica, 1697 1220.12 p719
Sherry, Roger; Maryland, 1672 1236.25 p46
Sherry, William; America, 1685 1220.12 p719
Sherryer, William; America, 1753 1220.12 p719
Sherston, John; America, 1743 1220.12 p719
Shervill, John; America, 1756 1220.12 p719
Sherwell, William; Barbados, 1686 1220.12 p719
Sherwin, William 34; Ontario, 1871 1823.21 p333
Sherwood, Ann Jane 29 *SEE* Sherwood, William
Sherwood, Ann Jane 29 *SEE* Sherwood, William
Sherwood, Benjamin; Maryland, 1737 1220.12 p719
Sherwood, John; America, 1694 1220.12 p719
Sherwood, John; America, 1755 1220.12 p719
Sherwood, John; America, 1759 1220.12 p719
Sherwood, Julia 55; Ontario, 1871 1823.21 p333
Sherwood, Lily 4 *SEE* Sherwood, William
Sherwood, Lily 4 *SEE* Sherwood, William
Sherwood, Minnie 7 *SEE* Sherwood, William
Sherwood, Minnie 7 *SEE* Sherwood, William
Sherwood, Peter; Quebec, 1949-1978 9228.50 p114
Sherwood, Walter 2 *SEE* Sherwood, William
Sherwood, Walter 2 *SEE* Sherwood, William
Sherwood, William; Barbados, 1668 1220.12 p719
Sherwood, William 32; Halifax, N.S., n.d. 1833.5 p7
*Wife:*Ann Jane 29
*Child:*Minnie 7
*Child:*Lily 4
*Child:*Walter 2
*Child:*Willie 10 months
Sherwood, William 32; Halifax, N.S., n.d. 8445.10 p7
*Wife:*Ann Jane 29
*Child:*Walter 2
*Child:*Willie 10 months
*Child:*Minnie 7
*Child:*Lily 4
Sherwood, Willie 10 *SEE* Sherwood, William
Sherwood, Willie 10 *SEE* Sherwood, William
Shethrote, Ulrich; Ohio, 1809-1852 4511.35 p49
Shetler, Jacob; Ohio, 1809-1852 4511.35 p49
Shetler, John; Ohio, 1809-1852 4511.35 p49
Shettle, Mahaleel; Maryland, 1724 1220.12 p719
Shettleworth, Thomas; America, 1750 1220.12 p719
Sheub, Gottfried; Missouri, 1896 3276.1 p4
Sheuds, Henri 20; America, 1841 778.6 p310
Sheufer, Anton 14; Arkansas, 1846 778.6 p310
Sheufer, Anton 45; Arkansas, 1846 778.6 p310
Sheufer, Bernhard 2; Arkansas, 1846 778.6 p310
Sheufer, Francisca 7; Arkansas, 1846 778.6 p310
Sheufer, Francisca 43; Arkansas, 1846 778.6 p310
Sheufer, Ignace 4; Arkansas, 1846 778.6 p310
Sheufer, Johann 5; Arkansas, 1846 778.6 p310
Sheufer, Joseph 14; Arkansas, 1846 778.6 p310
Sheufer, Martin 8; Arkansas, 1846 778.6 p310

Sheufer, Xavier 9; Arkansas, 1846 ***778.6*** *p310*
Shev, Motel William; Detroit, 1929-1930 ***6214.5*** *p63*
Shevent, James 61; Ontario, 1871 ***1823.21*** *p333*
Shewill, John; America, 1719 ***1220.12*** *p719*
Shewin, Sarah 43; Ontario, 1871 ***1823.21*** *p333*
Shewing, Elizabeth; America, 1770 ***1220.12*** *p719*
Shewswood, John; Potomac, 1731 ***1220.12*** *p719*
Shiblie, John; New York, NY, 1778 ***8529.30*** *p3*
Shickmon, W.E. 17; Quebec, 1870 ***8364.32*** *p26*
Shidecker, Jacob; Ohio, 1809-1852 ***4511.35*** *p49*
Shiding, Andrew; North Carolina, 1710 ***3629.40*** *p7*
Shield, Charles; Ohio, 1809-1852 ***4511.35*** *p49*
Shields, Agnes 58; Ontario, 1871 ***1823.21*** *p333*
Shields, Charles; Ohio, 1818 ***3580.20*** *p33*
Shields, Charles; Ohio, 1818 ***6020.12*** *p22*
Shields, Dennis; America, 1766 ***1220.12*** *p719*
Shields, Elizabeth; America, 1742 ***1220.12*** *p719*
Shields, Elizabeth; America, 1772 ***1220.12*** *p719*
Shields, Elizabeth; Carolina, 1724 ***1220.12*** *p719*
Shields, Francis 61; Ontario, 1871 ***1823.21*** *p333*
Shields, Henry; America, 1766 ***1220.12*** *p719*
Shields, James 40; Ontario, 1871 ***1823.21*** *p333*
Shields, James 45; Ontario, 1871 ***1823.21*** *p333*
Shields, James 50; Ontario, 1871 ***1823.21*** *p333*
Shields, John 28; Ontario, 1871 ***1823.17*** *p148*
Shields, John 40; Ontario, 1871 ***1823.21*** *p333*
Shields, John 48; Ontario, 1871 ***1823.21*** *p333*
Shields, John 53; Ontario, 1871 ***1823.21*** *p333*
Shields, Magarett 24; Ontario, 1871 ***1823.21*** *p333*
Shields, Mary; America, 1742 ***1220.12*** *p719*
Shields, Mary; America, 1773 ***1220.12*** *p719*
Shields, Michael; America, 1753 ***1220.12*** *p719*
Shields, Patrick; America, 1774 ***1220.12*** *p719*
Shields, Paul; America, 1752 ***1220.12*** *p719*
Shields, Robert; America, 1737 ***1220.12*** *p719*
Shields, Rolland 35; Ontario, 1871 ***1823.21*** *p333*
Shields, William 80; Ontario, 1871 ***1823.21*** *p333*
Shiels, Nicholas; Ohio, 1809-1852 ***4511.35*** *p49*
Shiers, Richard; America, 1773 ***1220.12*** *p716*
Shilliday, Hugh; Colorado, 1892 ***1029.59*** *p83*
Shilliday, Hugh; Colorado, 1896 ***1029.59*** *p83*
Shilling, Jacob; Ohio, 1809-1852 ***4511.35*** *p49*
Shilling, Jacob; Ohio, 1840-1897 ***8365.35*** *p18*
Shilling, John; Ohio, 1809-1852 ***4511.35*** *p49*
Shilling, John Jacob; Ohio, 1840-1897 ***8365.35*** *p18*
Shillingford, Jacob; America, 1767 ***1220.12*** *p719*
Shillingford, William; America, 1756 ***1220.12*** *p719*
Shillinglam, William 47; Ontario, 1871 ***1823.17*** *p149*
Shillington, Joseph 37; Ontario, 1871 ***1823.17*** *p149*
Shilter, Anthony; Ohio, 1809-1852 ***4511.35*** *p49*
Shilton, John; America, 1774 ***1220.12*** *p717*
Shimonek, Bedrich; Milwaukee, 1910 ***2853.20*** *p313*
Shin, Abraham; America, 1771 ***1220.12*** *p719*
Shine, Ezie; Iowa, 1916 ***1211.15*** *p19*
Shine, Harry; Iowa, 1917 ***1211.15*** *p19*
Shine, Loue; Iowa, 1910 ***1211.15*** *p19*
Shine, Sam; Iowa, 1911 ***1211.15*** *p19*
Shinfield, Martin; Barbados, 1677 ***1220.12*** *p719*
Shingfield, Mary; Barbados, 1673 ***1220.12*** *p719*
Shingfield, Mary; Maryland, 1674 ***1236.25*** *p50*
Shingle, Adam; Ohio, 1809-1852 ***4511.35*** *p49*
Shingles, Daniel 64; Ontario, 1871 ***1823.17*** *p149*
Shingloff, Nicholas; Illinois, 1858-1861 ***6020.5*** *p133*
Shinler, John; America, 1685 ***1220.12*** *p719*
Shinnehan, George; Boston, 1766 ***1642*** *p37*
Shinningfield, Hugh; Barbados, 1675 ***1220.12*** *p719*
Shino, Lawrence; New Jersey, 1754-1774 ***927.31*** *p2*
Shinwell, Samuel; America, 1727 ***1220.12*** *p719*
Shinyman, Frederick; New York, 1777 ***8529.30*** *p7*
Shipen, Nathaniel; America, 1754 ***1220.12*** *p720*
Shiples, . . .; Ontario, 1871 ***1823.21*** *p333*
Shipley, Edward 39; Ontario, 1871 ***1823.21*** *p333*
Shipley, Elizabeth *SEE* Shipley, Thomas
Shipley, Elizabeth *SEE* Shipley, Thomas
Shipley, George; America, 1763 ***1220.12*** *p719*
Shipley, Jane 65; Ontario, 1871 ***1823.21*** *p333*
Shipley, John; America, 1754 ***1220.12*** *p719*
Shipley, John; Boston, 1775 ***8529.30*** *p3*
Shipley, John 41; Ontario, 1871 ***1823.21*** *p333*
Shipley, John T. 36; Ontario, 1871 ***1823.21*** *p333*
Shipley, Joseph; Utah, 1901 ***1211.45*** *p134*
Shipley, Lionel 40; Ontario, 1871 ***1823.21*** *p333*
Shipley, Lionel 78; Ontario, 1871 ***1823.21*** *p333*
Shipley, Lionel T. 40; Ontario, 1871 ***1823.21*** *p333*
Shipley, Richard; America, 1713 ***1220.12*** *p719*
Shipley, Robert; Barbados, 1670 ***1220.12*** *p720*
Shipley, Thomas *SEE* Shipley, Thomas
Shipley, Thomas; Canada, 1774 ***3036.5*** *p41*
*Wife:*Elizabeth
*Child:*Thomas
*Child:*Elizabeth
Shipley, William 70; Ontario, 1871 ***1823.21*** *p333*
Shipman, Joseph 31; Ontario, 1871 ***1823.17*** *p149*
Shipman, Noah 37; Ontario, 1871 ***1823.17*** *p149*
Shipman, William; America, 1678 ***1220.12*** *p720*
Shipman, Wm.; California, 1868 ***1131.61*** *p89*
Shipman, Wm. 22; Virginia, 1635 ***1183.3*** *p30*
Shipmarsh, Robert; Barbados or Jamaica, 1691 ***1220.12*** *p720*
Shipper, William; America, 1745 ***1220.12*** *p720*
Shippley, George 66; Ontario, 1871 ***1823.21*** *p333*
Shippley, L. G. 43; Ontario, 1871 ***1823.21*** *p333*
Shipton, Robert; America, 1713 ***1220.12*** *p720*
Shirer, Jacob; Ohio, 1809-1852 ***4511.35*** *p49*
Shirkey, Ann; Philadelphia, 1860 ***8513.31*** *p293*
Shirley, Elizabeth; America, 1715 ***1220.12*** *p720*
Shirley, John; America, 1774 ***1220.12*** *p720*
Shirley, Mary; America, 1744 ***1220.12*** *p720*
Shirley, Thomas 57; Ontario, 1871 ***1823.17*** *p149*
Shirley, William 17; Quebec, 1870 ***8364.32*** *p26*
Shirlock, Michael 29; Ontario, 1871 ***1823.21*** *p334*
Shirving, James 37; Ontario, 1871 ***1823.17*** *p149*
Shishio, Peter 37; Minnesota, 1925 ***2769.54*** *p1382*
Shitler, Anthony; Ohio, 1809-1852 ***4511.35*** *p49*
Shitler, Christian; Ohio, 1809-1852 ***4511.35*** *p49*
Shitter, Anthony; Ohio, 1809-1852 ***4511.35*** *p49*
Shitzley, Frederick; Ohio, 1809-1852 ***4511.35*** *p49*
Shitzley, John; Ohio, 1809-1852 ***4511.35*** *p49*
Shleiche, Anton 21; Arkansas, 1846 ***778.6*** *p310*
Shleinser, Johann 26; New York, NY, 1894 ***6512.1*** *p182*
Shlygen, Peter; Philadelphia, 1777 ***8529.30*** *p3*
Shoare, Bartholomew; Jamaica, 1661 ***1220.12*** *p714*
Shobbrook, Eliza 40; Ontario, 1871 ***1823.21*** *p334*
Shobbrook, John S.; Washington, 1880 ***2770.40*** *p134*
Shobbrook, Richard 44; Ontario, 1871 ***1823.21*** *p334*
Shober, Christian; Ohio, 1809-1852 ***4511.35*** *p49*
Shober, Cyrus A.; Ohio, 1853 ***3580.20*** *p33*
Shober, Cyrus A.; Ohio, 1853 ***6020.12*** *p22*
Shodrok, Jacent; Texas, 1855-1886 ***9980.22*** *p16*
Shoebotham, John R. 55; Ontario, 1871 ***1823.21*** *p334*
Shoebotham, Mary 84; Ontario, 1871 ***1823.21*** *p334*
Shoebotham, Thomas; America, 1750 ***1220.12*** *p720*
Shoebotham, Thomas B. 57; Ontario, 1871 ***1823.21*** *p334*
Shoebotham, Thomas C. 41; Ontario, 1871 ***1823.21*** *p334*
Shoebotham, William 57; Ontario, 1871 ***1823.21*** *p334*
Shoebottom, James C. 43; Ontario, 1871 ***1823.21*** *p334*
Shoebottom, John 61; Ontario, 1871 ***1823.21*** *p334*
Shoebridge, John; Annapolis, MD, 1726 ***1220.12*** *p720*
Shoebrooks, William; America, 1773 ***1220.12*** *p720*
Shoefell, Jacob; Ohio, 1809-1852 ***4511.35*** *p50*
Shoemaker, Andrew; Ohio, 1809-1852 ***4511.35*** *p50*
Shoemaker, Francis; Ohio, 1809-1852 ***4511.35*** *p50*
Shoemaker, George; Illinois, 1854 ***6079.1*** *p13*
Shoemaker, James E.; Colorado, 1884 ***1029.59*** *p83*
Shoemaker, John; Ohio, 1809-1852 ***4511.35*** *p50*
Shoemaker, Martin; Louisiana, 1836-1841 ***4981.45*** *p209*
Shoenan, Albert; New Orleans, 1851 ***7242.30*** *p154*
Shoesmith, Robert; America, 1685 ***1220.12*** *p720*
Shoff, Andrew; Ohio, 1809-1852 ***4511.35*** *p50*
Shoffman, George 31; America, 1841 ***778.6*** *p310*
Shofiland, Joseph 28; Ontario, 1871 ***1823.21*** *p334*
Shollenberger, Jacob; Ohio, 1809-1852 ***4511.35*** *p50*
Shomarrier, Aloze 31; America, 1847 ***778.6*** *p310*
Shone, Katherine; America, 1742 ***1220.12*** *p720*
Shoning, Henrig; Iowa, 1897 ***1211.15*** *p19*
Shonk, John; America, 1760 ***1220.12*** *p720*
Shonka, Josef; Iowa, 1856-1858 ***2853.20*** *p211*
Shonnon, Miss 1; New Orleans, 1840 ***778.6*** *p310*
Shonnon, P. 35; New Orleans, 1840 ***778.6*** *p310*
Shonnon, Mrs. P. 20; New Orleans, 1840 ***778.6*** *p310*
Shony, Antony 58; Ontario, 1871 ***1823.21*** *p334*
Shooter, Charles; America, 1741 ***1220.12*** *p720*
Shooter, John; Barbados or Jamaica, 1715 ***1220.12*** *p720*
Shoppmeyer, Anton; Illinois, 1857 ***6079.1*** *p13*
Shore, Andrew; St. Johns, N.F., 1825 ***1053.15*** *p7*
Shore, Fredrick 38; Ontario, 1871 ***1823.21*** *p334*
Shore, Isaac; America, 1751 ***1220.12*** *p715*
Shore, James; America, 1737 ***1220.12*** *p715*
Shore, John; America, 1750 ***1220.12*** *p715*
Shore, John 59; Ontario, 1871 ***1823.21*** *p334*
Shore, Thomas 61; Ontario, 1871 ***1823.21*** *p334*
Shores, Edward; America, 1750 ***1220.12*** *p720*
Shores, William; America, 1738 ***1220.12*** *p720*
Shoreton, Mathew; America, 1743 ***1220.12*** *p720*
Shorey, Albright; Ohio, 1809-1852 ***4511.35*** *p50*
Shorey, Christian; Ohio, 1809-1852 ***4511.35*** *p50*
Shorey, Jacob; Ohio, 1809-1852 ***4511.35*** *p50*
Shorland, Peter; America, 1685 ***1220.12*** *p720*
Short, . . .; Canada, n.d. ***9228.50*** *p592*
Short, Adam 36; Ontario, 1871 ***1823.21*** *p334*
Short, Aron; America, 1730 ***1220.12*** *p720*
Short, Mrs. B.; Toronto, 1844 ***2910.35*** *p114*
Short, Bernard; Toronto, 1844 ***2910.35*** *p112*
Short, C.F.; California, 1900-1983 ***9228.50*** *p592*
With wife
Short, Charles 56; Ontario, 1871 ***1823.21*** *p334*
Short, Edward; America, 1699 ***1220.12*** *p720*
Short, George; America, 1768 ***1220.12*** *p720*
Short, Henry; Maryland, 1672 ***1236.25*** *p48*
Short, James 42; Ontario, 1871 ***1823.21*** *p334*
Short, Jane; Annapolis, MD, 1722 ***1220.12*** *p720*
Short, Job 36; Ontario, 1871 ***1823.21*** *p334*
Short, John; America, 1752 ***1220.12*** *p720*
Short, John; Annapolis, MD, 1725 ***1220.12*** *p720*
Short, John; Barbados, 1701 ***1220.12*** *p720*
Short, John 54; Ontario, 1871 ***1823.21*** *p334*
Short, John; Toronto, 1844 ***2910.35*** *p113*
Short, Lucas; Ohio, 1809-1852 ***4511.35*** *p50*
Short, Nicholas; Annapolis, MD, 1735 ***1220.12*** *p720*
Short, Philip; America, 1773 ***1220.12*** *p720*
Short, Reuben 36; Ontario, 1871 ***1823.21*** *p334*
Short, Reuben 55; Ontario, 1871 ***1823.17*** *p149*
Short, Reuben 64; Ontario, 1871 ***1823.21*** *p334*
Short, Richard; America, 1675 ***1220.12*** *p720*
Short, Richard; America, 1759 ***1220.12*** *p720*
Short, Richard; America, 1769 ***1220.12*** *p720*
Short, Thomas; Marston's Wharf, 1782 ***8529.30*** *p15*
Short, Thomas 26; Ontario, 1871 ***1823.21*** *p334*
Short, Thomas 29; Ontario, 1871 ***1823.21*** *p334*
Short, Thomas; Potomac, 1731 ***1220.12*** *p720*
Short, William 40; Ontario, 1871 ***1823.21*** *p334*
Short, William 62; Ontario, 1871 ***1823.21*** *p334*
Shorte, George; West Indies, 1614 ***1220.12*** *p720*
Shorter, Anne; Nevis or Jamaica, 1722 ***1220.12*** *p720*
Shorter, Henry; Barbados or Jamaica, 1690 ***1220.12*** *p720*
Shorter, John; Barbados or Jamaica, 1694 ***1220.12*** *p720*
Shorter, Martha; Barbados or Jamaica, 1694 ***1220.12*** *p720*
Shorter, Rebecca; America, 1691 ***1220.12*** *p720*
Shorthouse, Elizabeth; America, 1775 ***1220.12*** *p720*
Shorto, Thomas; Marston's Wharf, 1782 ***8529.30*** *p15*
Shortoe, George; America, 1773 ***1220.12*** *p720*
Shortoe, William; America, 1773 ***1220.12*** *p720*
Shorton, John 33; New York, NY, 1844 ***6178.50*** *p151*
Shortridge, John; North Carolina, 1846 ***1088.45*** *p32*
Shortt, Thomas 46; Ontario, 1871 ***1823.17*** *p149*
Shorttoe, Thomas; Marston's Wharf, 1782 ***8529.30*** *p15*
Shote, Augustus 36; Ontario, 1871 ***1823.21*** *p334*
Shotland, Daniel; Barbados or Jamaica, 1700 ***1220.12*** *p720*
Shott, John; Ohio, 1809-1852 ***4511.35*** *p50*
Shott, Joseph; Ohio, 1809-1852 ***4511.35*** *p50*
Shott, Wm. F.; Louisiana, 1874-1875 ***4981.45*** *p31*
Shott, Wm. F.; Louisiana, 1874-1875 ***4981.45*** *p130*
Shotton, James; America, 1772 ***1220.12*** *p720*
Shotwell, Benjamin 60; Ontario, 1871 ***1823.21*** *p335*
Shotwell, Mrs. J. M.; California, 1868 ***1131.61*** *p89*
With son
Shotwell, James 10; Ontario, 1871 ***1823.21*** *p335*
Shotwell, Keziah 71; Ontario, 1871 ***1823.21*** *p335*
Shotwell, W. G.; Montreal, 1922 ***4514.4*** *p32*
Shotwell, Zacriah 59; Ontario, 1871 ***1823.21*** *p335*
Shoug, John; America, 1739 ***1220.12*** *p721*
Shouldice, Allice 66; Ontario, 1871 ***1823.21*** *p335*
Shouldice, Joseph 74; Ontario, 1871 ***1823.21*** *p335*
Shouldice, William 22; Ontario, 1871 ***1823.21*** *p335*
Shoulter, William; Ohio, 1809-1852 ***4511.35*** *p50*
Shove, Henry; Barbados or Jamaica, 1696 ***1220.12*** *p721*
Shovel, William; Virginia, 1735 ***1220.12*** *p721*
Shovell, John; Virginia, 1721 ***1220.12*** *p721*
Shoveller, Samuel 39; Ontario, 1871 ***1823.17*** *p149*
Show, William; America, 1725 ***1220.12*** *p721*
Showell, Thomas; America, 1771 ***1220.12*** *p721*
Showerman, Irving B. 28; Ontario, 1871 ***1823.21*** *p335*
Showers, M'l.; Ontario, 1787 ***1276.15*** *p231*
With 2 children & 6 relatives
Showle, Thomas; America, 1739 ***1220.12*** *p721*
Showler, Thomas 42; Ontario, 1871 ***1823.17*** *p149*
Showlin, John G. 55; Ontario, 1871 ***1823.21*** *p335*
Showring, James; America, 1754 ***1220.12*** *p721*
Shrapnell, Elija 42; Ontario, 1871 ***1823.17*** *p149*
Shredder, George; Ohio, 1809-1852 ***4511.35*** *p50*
Shreeves, Thomas 13; Quebec, 1870 ***8364.32*** *p26*
Shreve, Robert; America, 1694 ***1220.12*** *p721*
Shrier, Jacob 60; Ontario, 1871 ***1823.21*** *p335*
Shrieve, John; America, 1747 ***1220.12*** *p721*
Shrimplin, John; America, 1749 ***1220.12*** *p721*
Shrimpton, William; Potomac, 1731 ***1220.12*** *p721*
Shrinpton, Henry N. 47; Ontario, 1871 ***1823.21*** *p335*
Shrive, Thomas; America, 1721 ***1220.12*** *p721*
Shriver, Alexander; Ohio, 1809-1852 ***4511.35*** *p50*
Shriver, Harman; Ohio, 1809-1852 ***4511.35*** *p50*
Shrobb, Edward; America, 1773 ***1220.12*** *p721*
Shroeder, George; Ohio, 1809-1852 ***4511.35*** *p50*
Shroeder, John; Texas, 1855 ***3435.45*** *p37*
Shrons, Godfrey; America, 1763 ***1220.12*** *p721*
Shropshire, John; America, 1690 ***1220.12*** *p721*
Shropshire, Mary; Virginia, 1736 ***1220.12*** *p721*

Shrouder, John; America, 1694 ***1220.12*** *p721*
Shroudy, Fanny 18; Ontario, 1871 ***1823.21*** *p335*
Shrub, Samuel; America, 1772 ***1220.12*** *p721*
Shuck, Louisa 16; Michigan, 1880 ***4491.42*** *p24*
Shuckhart, George; Ohio, 1809-1852 ***4511.35*** *p50*
Shuckley, Thomas; America, 1688 ***1220.12*** *p721*
Shudly, Peter; North Carolina, 1823 ***1088.45*** *p32*
Shudock, William; North Carolina, 1837 ***1088.45*** *p32*
Shuffle, William; Virginia, 1735 ***1220.12*** *p721*
Shufflebottom, Elizabeth; Virginia, 1738 ***1220.12*** *p721*
Shughnessy, Patrick 38; Michigan, 1880 ***4491.33*** *p20*
Shuker, Betton; America, 1768 ***1220.12*** *p721*
Shuler, John; America, 1769 ***1220.12*** *p721*
Shull, John; Ohio, 1809-1852 ***4511.35*** *p50*
Shulta, William; Ohio, 1809-1852 ***4511.35*** *p50*
Shultz, Frederick; Ohio, 1809-1852 ***4511.35*** *p50*
Shulz, Theodore; North Carolina, 1826 ***1088.45*** *p32*
Shumacker, Nick; Washington, 1888 ***2770.40*** *p26*
Shuman, Fredrick Henry; North Carolina, 1809 ***1088.45*** *p32*
Shuman, Susanna; Philadelphia, 1851 ***8513.31*** *p430*
Shun, John 48; Ontario, 1871 ***1823.21*** *p335*
Shupe, . . .; Ontario, 1871 ***1823.21*** *p335*
Shurehamer, George; Ohio, 1809-1852 ***4511.35*** *p50*
Shurman, Charles; Annapolis, MD, 1735 ***1220.12*** *p718*
Shute, Ann; America, 1741 ***1220.12*** *p721*
Shute, Hannah; America, 1759 ***1220.12*** *p721*
Shute, Henry; Virginia, 1718 ***1220.12*** *p721*
Shute, Jane; Virginia, 1759 ***1220.12*** *p721*
Shute, John Gilbert; America, 1767 ***1220.12*** *p721*
Shute, Mary; America, 1727 ***1220.12*** *p721*
Shutler, Thomas; America, 1688 ***1220.12*** *p721*
Shutt, Joseph; Ohio, 1809-1852 ***4511.35*** *p50*
Shuttlewood, John; America, 1775 ***1220.12*** *p721*
Shuttleworth, John; America, 1775 ***1220.12*** *p721*
Shutts, Jacob; Ohio, 1809-1852 ***4511.35*** *p50*
Shutts, William 70; Ontario, 1871 ***1823.21*** *p335*
Shutz, Jacob; Ohio, 1809-1852 ***4511.35*** *p50*
Siambra, A.; Louisiana, 1874-1875 ***4981.45*** *p31*
Siambra, A.; Louisiana, 1874-1875 ***4981.45*** *p130*
Sibbald, Hugh; Quebec, 1885 ***1937.10*** *p52*
Sibballs, Robert; Virginia, 1736 ***1220.12*** *p721*
Sibbons, Charles 19; Quebec, 1870 ***8364.32*** *p26*
Siberry, John; America, 1750 ***1220.12*** *p721*
Sibert, Joseph; Ohio, 1809-1852 ***4511.35*** *p50*
Sibila, George; Ohio, 1809-1852 ***4511.35*** *p50*
Sibile, Alexandre 37; Louisiana, 1848 ***778.6*** *p310*
Sibile, Auguste 5; Louisiana, 1848 ***778.6*** *p310*
Sibile, Joseph 1; Louisiana, 1848 ***778.6*** *p310*
Sibile, Marguerite 27; Louisiana, 1848 ***778.6*** *p310*
Sibille, Auguste 35; Louisiana, 1848 ***778.6*** *p310*
Sibille, Celestine 9; Louisiana, 1848 ***778.6*** *p310*
Sibille, Francois 52; Texas, 1843 ***778.6*** *p310*
Sibille, Louis 4; Louisiana, 1848 ***778.6*** *p310*
Sibille, Marie 34; Louisiana, 1848 ***778.6*** *p310*
Sibille, Marie Jos. 60; Louisiana, 1848 ***778.6*** *p311*
Sibilly, Adam; Ohio, 1809-1852 ***4511.35*** *p50*
Sibley, Henry; America, 1775 ***1220.12*** *p721*
Sibley, John; Marston's Wharf, 1782 ***8529.30*** *p15*
Sibley, Nicholas; Ohio, 1809-1852 ***4511.35*** *p50*
Sibley, Rachel 44; Ontario, 1871 ***1823.21*** *p335*
Sibley, Richard; America, 1765 ***1220.12*** *p721*
Siblie, John; Marston's Wharf, 1782 ***8529.30*** *p15*
Sibola, Nicholas; Ohio, 1809-1852 ***4511.35*** *p50*
Sibold, Dominique 35; New Orleans, 1848 ***778.6*** *p311*
Siborn, Thomas; America, 1769 ***1220.12*** *p721*
Sibre, Samuel; America, 1748 ***1220.12*** *p721*
Sibson, Peter; America, 1774 ***1220.12*** *p721*
Sibthorpe, Ann; America, 1771 ***1220.12*** *p721*
Sibthorpe, John; America, 1728 ***1220.12*** *p721*
Sibthorpe, William; America, 1756 ***1220.12*** *p721*
Siby, Dennis; Massachusetts, 1675-1676 ***1642*** *p127*
Siby, Dennis; Massachusetts, 1675-1676 ***1642*** *p128*
Sicard, Jeanne; Quebec, 1669 ***4514.3*** *p371*
Sicard, Joseph; Louisiana, 1841-1844 ***4981.45*** *p211*
Sicard deCarufel, Jean; Quebec, 1685 ***2314.30*** *p172*
Sicart, Jose 30; Martinique, 1842 ***778.6*** *p311*
Sicha, Antonin; Cleveland, OH, 1873-1877 ***2853.20*** *p498*
Sicheri, Clemente 19; New York, NY, 1894 ***6512.1*** *p182*
Sichwart, Adam 40; Portland, ME, 1911 ***970.38*** *p81*
Sicker, Edward; Ohio, 1809-1852 ***4511.35*** *p50*
Sickle, Thomas; America, 1738 ***1220.12*** *p721*
Sickles, Abraham 60; Ontario, 1871 ***1823.21*** *p335*
Sickles, Elias 30; Ontario, 1871 ***1823.21*** *p335*
Sickles, Isaac 44; Ontario, 1871 ***1823.21*** *p335*
Sickles, John 35; Ontario, 1871 ***1823.21*** *p335*
Sickles, Mary 48; Ontario, 1871 ***1823.21*** *p335*
Sicks, Nikolaus; America, 1856 ***5475.1*** *p548*
Sickwell, William; Virginia, 1734 ***1220.12*** *p721*
Sicup, Daniel 19; Ontario, 1871 ***1823.17*** *p149*
Sicut, H. 35; America, 1843 ***778.6*** *p311*
Sidaway, Samuel; America, 1753 ***1220.12*** *p722*
Sidaway, Thomas; New Jersey, 1777 ***8529.30*** *p5A*
Siday, Elizabeth; America, 1771 ***1220.12*** *p722*
Siday, John; America, 1754 ***1220.12*** *p722*
Siddah, John; America, 1724 ***1220.12*** *p722*
Siddale, Richard; Maryland, 1725 ***1220.12*** *p722*
Siddale, William 39; Ontario, 1871 ***1823.17*** *p149*
Siddall, Diana 77; Ontario, 1871 ***1823.21*** *p335*
Siddall, John; America, 1724 ***1220.12*** *p722*
Siddell, Sarah; America, 1767 ***1220.12*** *p722*
Sidden, Joseph; Maryland, 1720 ***1220.12*** *p722*
Siddons, John 44; Ontario, 1871 ***1823.21*** *p335*
Sidebottom, John; Ohio, 1831 ***3580.20*** *p33*
Sidebottom, John; Ohio, 1831 ***6020.12*** *p22*
Sidell, Ralph; Canada, 1774 ***3036.5*** *p42*
Sidle, Frederic; Illinois, 1860 ***6079.1*** *p13*
Sidler, Joseph 43; New York, NY, 1883 ***8427.14*** *p43*
Sidler, Louise 6; New York, NY, 1883 ***8427.14*** *p43*
Sidler, Madelein 36; New York, NY, 1883 ***8427.14*** *p43*
Sidler, Pauline 5; New York, NY, 1883 ***8427.14*** *p43*
Sidler, Rosa 1; New York, NY, 1883 ***8427.14*** *p43*
Sidnell, Abraham; America, 1748 ***1220.12*** *p722*
Sidnell, John; America, 1764 ***1220.12*** *p722*
Sidow, John; Annapolis, MD, 1725 ***1220.12*** *p722*
Sidwell, J. F.; California, 1868 ***1131.61*** *p89*
Sidwell, Jonathan; America, 1773 ***1220.12*** *p722*
Sidwell, William; Maryland, 1720 ***1220.12*** *p722*
Sidy, Clemintina 90; Ontario, 1871 ***1823.17*** *p149*
Siebach, Catherine 19; Louisiana, 1848 ***778.6*** *p311*
Siebach, Marie 16; Louisiana, 1848 ***778.6*** *p311*
Siebel, C.; Galveston, TX, 1855 ***571.7*** *p18*
Sieber, Anna Maria 6; Galveston, TX, 1845 ***3967.10*** *p376*
Sieber, Johann 31; Galveston, TX, 1845 ***3967.10*** *p376*
Sieber, Johann Heinrich 4; Galveston, TX, 1845 ***3967.10*** *p376*
Sieber, Johanna Maria 9 months; Galveston, TX, 1845 ***3967.10*** *p376*
Sieber, Margarethe 39; Brazil, 1864 ***5475.1*** *p500*
Sieber, Marianne 36; Galveston, TX, 1845 ***3967.10*** *p376*
Sieberns, Henry Edward; Illinois, 1858-1861 ***6020.5*** *p133*
Siebert, Andreas 27; Philadelphia, 1892 ***5475.1*** *p79*
Siebert, Fredrick William; New York, 1860 ***358.56*** *p148*
Siebert, Johannes; Chile, 1852 ***1192.4*** *p52*
Siebert, Johs.; Valdivia, Chile, 1852 ***1192.4*** *p56*
With wife
Siebert, Ludwig 25; Port uncertain, 1888 ***5475.1*** *p18*
Siebert, Rudolf Eduard; America, 1887 ***5475.1*** *p17*
Siebert, Wilhelm; Wisconsin, 1883 ***6795.8*** *p52*
Siebke, Carl; America, 1857 ***7420.1*** *p172*
Siebke, Georg Christian Ludwig; America, 1864 ***7420.1*** *p227*
Siebke, Georg Friedrich; America, 1857 ***7420.1*** *p173*
Siebke, Louise; America, 1867 ***7420.1*** *p265*
Siechli, Johann 37; New Castle, DE, 1817-1818 ***90.20*** *p154*
Sieckmann, August Dietrich Conrad; America, 1893 ***7420.1*** *p369*
Sieckmann, Carl Heinrich Wilhelm *SEE* Sieckmann, Christian Ludwig Wilhelm
Sieckmann, Christian Friedrich Wilhelm Ludwig *SEE* Sieckmann, Christian Ludwig Wilhelm
Sieckmann, Christian Ludwig Wilhelm; America, 1881 ***7420.1*** *p325*
*Wife:*Wilhelmine Louise Charlotte Roebbeke
*Son:*Johann Friedrich Ludwig
*Son:*Christian Friedrich Wilhelm Ludwig
*Daughter:*Hanne Caroline Charlotte
*Son:*Carl Heinrich Wilhelm
Sieckmann, Dietrich Wilhelm Conrad *SEE* Sieckmann, Heinrich Friedrich Christian
Sieckmann, Dorothee Sophie Marie Louise *SEE* Sieckmann, Heinrich Friedrich Christian
Sieckmann, Hanne Caroline Charlotte *SEE* Sieckmann, Christian Ludwig Wilhelm
Sieckmann, Heinrich Friedrich Christian; America, 1893 ***7420.1*** *p369*
*Daughter:*Minna Marie Christine
*Daughter:*Dorothee Sophie Marie Louise
*Wife:*Marie Dorothee Louise Behling
*Son:*Dietrich Wilhelm Conrad
Sieckmann, Johann Friedrich Ludwig *SEE* Sieckmann, Christian Ludwig Wilhelm
Sieckmann, Marie Dorothee Louise Behling *SEE* Sieckmann, Heinrich Friedrich Christian
Sieckmann, Minna Marie Christine *SEE* Sieckmann, Heinrich Friedrich Christian
Sieckmann, Wilhelmine Louise Charlotte Roebbeke *SEE* Sieckmann, Christian Ludwig Wilhelm
Siedenberg, Friedrich Wilhelm Christian; Port uncertain, 1881 ***7420.1*** *p325*
Siedenberg, Friedrich Wilhelm Ferdinand; America, 1889 ***7420.1*** *p359*
Siedlecki, Wladyslaw; Detroit, 1929 ***1640.55*** *p113*
Siefermann, Anna Marie 6 months; America, 1847 ***778.6*** *p311*
Siefermann, Anna Marie 28; America, 1847 ***778.6*** *p311*
Siefermann, Lorenz 27; America, 1847 ***778.6*** *p311*
Siefert, Friedrich; America, 1855 ***2526.43*** *p204*
Siefert, George; Ohio, 1809-1852 ***4511.35*** *p50*
Siefert, Michael; Ohio, 1809-1852 ***4511.35*** *p50*
Siefker, Joseph; Ohio, 1809-1852 ***4511.35*** *p50*
Siegel, Abe; Miami, 1920 ***4984.15*** *p38*
Siegel, Israel; America, 1883 ***2526.42*** *p132*
Siegel, Jakob; America, 1890 ***2526.42*** *p132*
Siegel, Johann; America, 1867 ***5475.1*** *p160*
*Wife:*Magdalena Balzer
*Daughter:*Katharina Adelheid
Siegel, Joseph Rachael; America, 1883 ***2526.42*** *p132*
Siegel, Katharina Adelheid 6 *SEE* Siegel, Johann
Siegel, Magdalena Balzer 25 *SEE* Siegel, Johann
Siegel, Max; Miami, 1920 ***4984.15*** *p38*
Siegel, Mendel; America, 1867 ***7919.3*** *p534*
Siegele, A. Katharina *SEE* Siegele, Heinrich
Siegele, Anna *SEE* Siegele, Heinrich
Siegele, Anna Maria *SEE* Siegele, Heinrich
Siegele, Barbara *SEE* Siegele, Heinrich
Siegele, Heinrich *SEE* Siegele, Heinrich
Siegele, Heinrich; America, 1864 ***5475.1*** *p237*
*Wife:*Kath. Juliana Fuchs
*Son:*M. August
*Daughter:*Juliana
*Son:*Barbara
*Daughter:*Anna Maria
*Daughter:*A. Katharina
*Son:*Heinrich
*Daughter:*Anna
Siegele, Juliana *SEE* Siegele, Heinrich
Siegele, Kath. Juliana Fuchs *SEE* Siegele, Heinrich
Siegele, M. August *SEE* Siegele, Heinrich
Siegfried, Caspar; New York, 1859 ***358.56*** *p55*
Siegmann, Anne Marie Eleonore; America, 1854 ***7420.1*** *p130*
Siegmann, Engel Marie Caroline; America, 1854 ***7420.1*** *p126*
With husband & children
Siegmann, Heinrich Wilhelm; America, 1844 ***7420.1*** *p33*
With family
Siegwald, Barbara 11; America, 1841 ***778.6*** *p311*
Siegwald, Eva 15; America, 1841 ***778.6*** *p311*
Siegwald, Eva 45; America, 1841 ***778.6*** *p311*
Siegwald, George 10; America, 1841 ***778.6*** *p311*
Siegwald, Jacob 5; America, 1841 ***778.6*** *p311*
Siegwald, Philipp 16; America, 1841 ***778.6*** *p311*
Siegwald, Philipp 42; America, 1841 ***778.6*** *p311*
Siekmann, Widow; America, 1857 ***7420.1*** *p173*
Siekmann, Carl Friedrich August *SEE* Siekmann, Heinrich Wilhelm Christian
Siekmann, Carl Heinrich Wilhelm *SEE* Siekmann, Wilhelm
Siekmann, Ernst Heinrich Wilhelm *SEE* Siekmann, Heinrich Wilhelm
Siekmann, Friederika Louisa Eleonora; America, 1859 ***7420.1*** *p189*
Siekmann, Friederike Louise Charl. *SEE* Siekmann, Heinrich Wilhelm
Siekmann, Friedrich Heinrich Wilhelm *SEE* Siekmann, Wilhelm
Siekmann, Heinrich Friedrich Wilhelm *SEE* Siekmann, Wilhelm
Siekmann, Heinrich Wilhelm *SEE* Siekmann, Heinrich Wilhelm
Siekmann, Heinrich Wilhelm; Port uncertain, 1850 ***7420.1*** *p76*
*Wife:*Sophie Charlotte Homeyer
*Son:*Heinrich Wilhelm
*Daughter:*Friederike Louise Charl.
*Son:*Ernst Heinrich Wilhelm
*Daughter:*Sophie Wilhelm. Carol.
Siekmann, Heinrich Wilhelm Christian; America, 1883 ***7420.1*** *p340*
*Wife:*Sophie Cathar. Friederike Charl. Meier
*Son:*Carl Friedrich August
Siekmann, Sophie Cathar. Friederike Charl. Meier *SEE* Siekmann, Heinrich Wilhelm Christian
Siekmann, Sophie Charlotte Homeyer *SEE* Siekmann, Heinrich Wilhelm
Siekmann, Sophie Wilhelm. Carol. *SEE* Siekmann, Heinrich Wilhelm
Siekmann, Wilhelm; America, 1870 ***7420.1*** *p287*
With wife & daughter
*Son:*Carl Heinrich Wilhelm
*Son:*Friedrich Heinrich Wilhelm
*Son:*Heinrich Friedrich Wilhelm
Siekmeyer, Friedrich Wilhelm; Port uncertain, 1883 ***7420.1*** *p340*
Sieler, Louis 22; America, 1845 ***778.6*** *p311*

Sielinska, Mary; Detroit, 1929-1930 ***6214.5*** *p61*
Siemkiewicz, Alexandre 26; New York, NY, 1920 ***930.50*** *p48*
Siemon, Heinrich; America, 1890 ***7420.1*** *p400*
Siemsen, H. A.; Valdivia, Chile, 1852 ***1192.4*** *p53*
With wife & 3 children
With child 8
With child 3
Sienkiewicz, Eva; Detroit, 1929 ***1640.55*** *p114*
Sieren, Peter; America, 1866 ***5475.1*** *p327*
Sieren, Peter; Wisconsin, 1891 ***5475.1*** *p326*
Sierks, Hans; Iowa, 1876 ***1211.15*** *p19*
Siers, Philippe 16; Port uncertain, 1846 ***778.6*** *p311*
Siersdorfer, Johann; America, 1872 ***5475.1*** *p167*
Siersdorfer, Maria Becker *SEE* Siersdorfer, Peter
Siersdorfer, Maria 61; America, 1883 ***5475.1*** *p203*
Siersdorfer, Peter; America, 1873 ***5475.1*** *p167*
*Wife:*Maria Becker
Sietan, Johannes; Iowa, 1889 ***1211.15*** *p19*
Sievers, John D.; North Carolina, 1840 ***1088.45*** *p32*
Siewert, Julius; Wisconsin, 1868 ***6795.8*** *p142*
Siffermann, Jacob 30; America, 1846 ***778.6*** *p311*
Sifton, Henry 44; Ontario, 1871 ***1823.17*** *p149*
Sifton, Joseph 85; Ontario, 1871 ***1823.21*** *p336*
Sifton, Joseph B. 56; Ontario, 1871 ***1823.21*** *p336*
Sigel, E. R.; Valdivia, Chile, 1852 ***1192.4*** *p53*
Siggelin, Carl Gustaf Albin; North America, 1878 ***6410.15*** *p106*
Siggins, Dudley 64; Ontario, 1871 ***1823.21*** *p336*
Siggins, Mary; Maryland, 1730 ***1220.12*** *p722*
Sigling, Johann Ernst; America, 1867 ***7919.3*** *p526*
With daughter
Siglinger, George; Ohio, 1809-1852 ***4511.35*** *p50*
Signeau, G. 28; Port uncertain, 1840 ***778.6*** *p311*
Signorth, John 27; Ontario, 1871 ***1823.21*** *p336*
Sigourney, Andre; New England, 1650-1750 ***9228.50*** *p604*
*Wife:*Mary Germain
Sigourney, Mary Germain *SEE* Sigourney, Andre
Siguet, Luciano; Puerto Rico, 1874 ***3476.25*** *p113*
Sigurquot, Loiuis 34; Port uncertain, 1842 ***778.6*** *p311*
Sihvonen, Peter; Illinois, 1930 ***121.35*** *p100*
Sikes, Edward; America, 1678 ***1220.12*** *p778*
Sikes, John; America, 1693 ***1220.12*** *p778*
Sikkard, Mary; Maryland, 1733 ***1220.12*** *p722*
Sikora, Julia; Wisconsin, 1890 ***6795.8*** *p61*
Sikorski, Ignaz; Washington Co., TX, 1900 ***6015.15*** *p29*
Sikorski, Joseph; Texas, 1887-1890 ***6015.15*** *p29*
Sikorski, Mary; New York, NY, 1891 ***6015.15*** *p29*
Sikorsky, Joseph; Texas, 1887-1890 ***6015.15*** *p29*
Silas, John 35; Ontario, 1871 ***1823.21*** *p336*
Silberhorn, George; New York, 1859 ***358.56*** *p101*
Silbernagel, George 4; New York, NY, 1898 ***7951.13*** *p43*
Silbernagel, Johann 7; New York, NY, 1898 ***7951.13*** *p43*
Silbernagel, Joseph 32; New York, NY, 1898 ***7951.13*** *p43*
Silbernagel, Leoboldina 30; New York, NY, 1898 ***7951.13*** *p43*
Silbernagel, Stephan 10 months; New York, NY, 1898 ***7951.13*** *p43*
Silberstein, Max 38; New York, NY, 1894 ***6512.1*** *p232*
Silcock, Ann; America, 1748 ***1220.12*** *p722*
Silcock, Jacob; America, 1765 ***1220.12*** *p722*
Silcox, Susan; America, 1724 ***1220.12*** *p722*
Sildon, John 40; Ontario, 1871 ***1823.21*** *p336*
Siles, Elizabeth 65; Ontario, 1871 ***1823.21*** *p336*
Silfversward, W.F.W.; New York, NY, 1843 ***6412.40*** *p146*
Silgmann, Frederick John; Wisconsin, 1893 ***6795.8*** *p104*
Silgmann, Minnie; Wisconsin, 1898 ***6795.8*** *p107*
Silk, Henery 33; Ontario, 1871 ***1823.21*** *p336*
Silk, John; America, 1765 ***1220.12*** *p722*
Silk, Mary; Annapolis, MD, 1733 ***1220.12*** *p722*
Silk, Thomas; Virginia, 1738 ***1220.12*** *p722*
Silke, John; Barbados or Jamaica, 1685 ***1220.12*** *p722*
Silkwood, Margaret; Maryland, 1725 ***1220.12*** *p722*
Sillar, Catharine 23; North Carolina, 1774 ***1422.10*** *p60*
Sillar, Catharine 62; North Carolina, 1774 ***1422.10*** *p60*
Sillar, Catherine 23; North Carolina, 1774 ***1422.10*** *p63*
Sillar, Catherine 62; North Carolina, 1774 ***1422.10*** *p63*
Sillar, Hugh 55; North Carolina, 1774 ***1422.10*** *p60*
Sillar, Hugh 55; North Carolina, 1774 ***1422.10*** *p63*
Sillar, Mary 27; North Carolina, 1774 ***1422.10*** *p60*
Sillar, Mary 27; North Carolina, 1774 ***1422.10*** *p63*
Sillen, H.E.; New York, NY, 1845 ***6412.40*** *p148*
Siller, Emilie Happel *SEE* Siller, Johann Karl Albin
Siller, Jakob; America, 1854 ***179.55*** *p19*
Siller, Jan A.; Texas, 1892 ***2853.20*** *p82*
Siller, Johann Karl Albin; America, 1868 ***7919.3*** *p535*
*Wife:*Emilie Happel
Siller, Josef; Texas, 1852 ***2853.20*** *p59*
With wife
*Son:*Josef
Siller, Josef 13 *SEE* Siller, Josef
Siller, Katha 29; Halifax, N.S., 1902 ***1860.4*** *p44*
Siller, Katherine 9 months; Halifax, N.S., 1902 ***1860.4*** *p44*
Siller, Katrina 28; Halifax, N.S., 1902 ***1860.4*** *p44*
Siller, Michael 33; Halifax, N.S., 1902 ***1860.4*** *p44*
Siller, Nicolaus 28; Halifax, N.S., 1902 ***1860.4*** *p44*
Siller, Phillippa 4 months; Halifax, N.S., 1902 ***1860.4*** *p44*
Siller, Rosalia 16; Halifax, N.S., 1902 ***1860.4*** *p44*
Siller, Rosalia 25; Halifax, N.S., 1902 ***1860.4*** *p44*
Siller, Terese 2; Halifax, N.S., 1902 ***1860.4*** *p44*
Siller, Vilem; Minnesota, 1888 ***2853.20*** *p271*
Siller, Wallenhim 31; Halifax, N.S., 1902 ***1860.4*** *p44*
Sillers, John; Washington, 1883 ***2770.40*** *p137*
Sillevan, Mary; Nantucket, MA, 1730 ***1642*** *p89*
Silley, Sarah; Maryland, 1737 ***1220.12*** *p722*
Silligh, Frederick; Long Island, 1778 ***8529.30*** *p10A*
Silliman, Christian; North Carolina, 1853 ***1088.45*** *p32*
Sillington, William 47; Ontario, 1871 ***1823.17*** *p149*
Sills, William; New York, NY, 1778 ***8529.30*** *p3*
Silly, Thomas; America, 1720 ***1220.12*** *p722*
Silman, Galbes; Texas, 1906 ***3435.45*** *p35*
Silman, Henry 46; Ontario, 1871 ***1823.17*** *p149*
Silsby, James; America, 1765 ***1220.12*** *p722*
Silva, M.; California, 1868 ***1131.61*** *p90*
Silvene, Louis; Washington, 1883 ***2770.40*** *p137*
Silver, Alexander 62; Ontario, 1871 ***1823.21*** *p336*
Silver, Ann; America, 1772 ***1220.12*** *p722*
Silver, Isaac; America, 1759 ***1220.12*** *p722*
Silver, Jacob; Detroit, 1929 ***1640.55*** *p116*
Silver, John; America, 1743 ***1220.12*** *p722*
Silver, Thomas 20; Maryland, 1724 ***1220.12*** *p722*
Silver, William; America, 1758 ***1220.12*** *p722*
Silverberg, Bernard; North Carolina, 1859 ***1088.45*** *p32*
Silverman, Abe; Detroit, 1929-1930 ***6214.5*** *p65*
Silversea, Berndt Eliasson; Cleveland, OH, 1897 ***9722.10*** *p126*
Silvester, Charles; America, 1699 ***1220.12*** *p722*
Silvester, Honore; Boston, 1760-1769 ***9228.50*** *p592*
Silvester, John; America, 1767 ***1220.12*** *p722*
Silvester, John; America, 1769 ***1220.12*** *p722*
Silvester, Richard; America, 1764 ***1220.12*** *p722*
Silvester, Richard; America, 1774 ***1220.12*** *p722*
Silvester, Thomas; America, 1773 ***1220.12*** *p722*
Silvestry, Luis; Puerto Rico, 1794 ***3476.25*** *p113*
Silvey, Aaron; America, 1772 ***1220.12*** *p722*
Silvie, Benjamin; Philadelphia, 1776 ***8529.30*** *p3*
Silvy, Thomas; America, 1775 ***1220.12*** *p722*
Silwood, William; Philadelphia, 1778 ***8529.30*** *p5A*
Silz, Fr. Wilhelm 26; America, 1846 ***5475.1*** *p401*
*Wife:*Katharina Klein 22
With child
Silz, Katharina Klein 22 *SEE* Silz, Fr. Wilhelm
Sim, Jane 24; North Carolina, 1774 ***1422.10*** *p54*
Sim, William 24; North Carolina, 1774 ***1422.10*** *p54*
Siman, Nassum; North Carolina, 1898 ***1088.45*** *p32*
Simanek, Jiri; Nebraska, 1869 ***2853.20*** *p161*
Simanek, Josef; Nebraska, 1868 ***2853.20*** *p161*
Simanek, Josef Fr.; Baltimore, 1870 ***2853.20*** *p129*
Simard, Elie; Quebec, 1648 ***9221.17*** *p204*
Simard, Noel 17 *SEE* Simard, Pierre
Simard, Pierre 52; Quebec, 1654 ***9221.17*** *p316*
*Son:*Noel 17
Simberell, Francis; America, 1773 ***1220.12*** *p722*
Simberlen, Francis; America, 1773 ***1220.12*** *p722*
Simcock, George; America, 1745 ***1220.12*** *p722*
Simcock, Theophilus; America, 1773 ***1220.12*** *p722*
Simek, Frantisek Josef; Iowa, 1856 ***2853.20*** *p212*
Simek, Josef; Wisconsin, 1857-1861 ***2853.20*** *p334*
Simek, Vaclav J.; Baltimore, 1866 ***2853.20*** *p125*
Simer, Johann 17; Portland, ME, 1906 ***970.38*** *p82*
Simeton, John 16; Ontario, 1871 ***1823.21*** *p336*
Simila, August; Oregon, 1941 ***9157.47*** *p2*
Simkin, Thomas; Virginia, 1730 ***1220.12*** *p723*
Simkins, Edward; Maryland, 1726 ***1220.12*** *p723*
Simler, Christian; Ohio, 1809-1852 ***4511.35*** *p50*
Simler, John; Ohio, 1809-1852 ***4511.35*** *p50*
Simm, John; Louisiana, 1874 ***4981.45*** *p134*
Simmerman, Jacob 22; Ohio, 1840 ***778.6*** *p311*
Simmet, Elisabeth 43; America, 1837 ***5475.1*** *p407*
Simmet, Johann Peter; America, 1882 ***5475.1*** *p406*
Simmler, Jean 20; Missouri, 1847 ***778.6*** *p311*
Simmler, Sebastian; Ohio, 1809-1852 ***4511.35*** *p50*
Simmon, Jacob; Ohio, 1809-1852 ***4511.35*** *p50*
Simmonds, Ann; Virginia, 1735 ***1220.12*** *p779*
Simmonds, Charles; Virginia, 1736 ***1220.12*** *p779*
Simmonds, Edward; America, 1769 ***1220.12*** *p779*
Simmonds, Elizabeth; America, 1774 ***1220.12*** *p779*
Simmonds, John; America, 1765 ***1220.12*** *p779*
Simmonds, John 32; Ontario, 1871 ***1823.21*** *p336*
Simmonds, John 37; Ontario, 1871 ***1823.21*** *p336*
Simmonds, Joseph 22; Ontario, 1871 ***1823.21*** *p336*
Simmonds, Margaret; America, 1756 ***1220.12*** *p780*
Simmonds, Mary A. 47; Ontario, 1871 ***1823.21*** *p336*
Simmonds, Peter; New York, 1841 ***9228.50*** *p537*
Simmonds, Sarah; America, 1744 ***1220.12*** *p780*
Simmonds, Thomas; Died enroute, 1743 ***1220.12*** *p780*
Simmonds, William; America, 1735 ***1220.12*** *p780*
Simmonds, William; America, 1738 ***1220.12*** *p780*
Simmonds, William; America, 1766 ***1220.12*** *p780*
Simmonds, William; America, 1770 ***1220.12*** *p780*
Simmonds, William; Maryland or Virginia, 1738 ***1220.12*** *p780*
Simmonds, Wm 33; Ontario, 1871 ***1823.21*** *p336*
Simmons, Amos Edward; Miami, 1935 ***4984.12*** *p39*
Simmons, Anne; America, 1745 ***1220.12*** *p779*
Simmons, Appelina 49; Michigan, 1880 ***4491.42*** *p24*
Simmons, Elizabeth; America, 1755 ***1220.12*** *p779*
Simmons, Emanuel; North Carolina, 1792-1862 ***1088.45*** *p32*
Simmons, Erod A. 60; Michigan, 1880 ***4491.42*** *p24*
Simmons, Francis 26; Ontario, 1871 ***1823.21*** *p336*
Simmons, George 34; Ontario, 1871 ***1823.17*** *p149*
Simmons, James; America, 1775 ***1220.12*** *p779*
Simmons, John; America, 1716 ***1220.12*** *p779*
Simmons, John; America, 1728 ***1220.12*** *p779*
Simmons, John; America, 1742 ***1220.12*** *p779*
Simmons, John; America, 1760 ***1220.12*** *p779*
Simmons, John; America, 1773 ***1220.12*** *p780*
Simmons, John; America, 1774 ***1220.12*** *p780*
Simmons, John; Annapolis, MD, 1730 ***1220.12*** *p779*
Simmons, John; Colorado, 1894 ***1029.59*** *p83*
Simmons, John; Illinois, 1858-1861 ***6020.5*** *p133*
Simmons, John 28; Ontario, 1871 ***1823.21*** *p336*
Simmons, Joseph; America, 1764 ***1220.12*** *p780*
Simmons, Lewis; South Carolina, 1844 ***6155.4*** *p19*
Simmons, Love; America, 1752 ***1220.12*** *p780*
Simmons, Manuel; North Carolina, 1858 ***1088.45*** *p32*
Simmons, Michael; Ohio, 1809-1852 ***4511.35*** *p50*
Simmons, Nicholas; America, 1773 ***1220.12*** *p780*
Simmons, Oliver 37; Ontario, 1871 ***1823.17*** *p149*
Simmons, R. P. 46; Ontario, 1871 ***1823.21*** *p336*
Simmons, Robert; America, 1763 ***1220.12*** *p780*
Simmons, Robert 26; Ontario, 1871 ***1823.21*** *p336*
Simmons, Samuel; America, 1769 ***1220.12*** *p780*
Simmons, Sarah; America, 1762 ***1220.12*** *p780*
Simmons, Thomas; America, 1759 ***1220.12*** *p780*
Simmons, Thomas; Virginia, 1736 ***1220.12*** *p780*
Simmons, William; America, 1751 ***1220.12*** *p780*
Simmons, William; America, 1768 ***1220.12*** *p780*
Simmons, William 21; Ontario, 1871 ***1823.17*** *p149*
Simmons, William 16; Quebec, 1870 ***8364.32*** *p26*
Simms, Ann 59; Ontario, 1871 ***1823.17*** *p149*
Simms, Elizabeth; America, 1754 ***1220.12*** *p722*
Simms, Henry; America, 1745 ***1220.12*** *p723*
Simms, James; America, 1770 ***1220.12*** *p723*
Simms, Jane; America, 1748 ***1220.12*** *p723*
Simms, John; America, 1750 ***1220.12*** *p723*
Simms, Joseph; America, 1765 ***1220.12*** *p723*
Simms, Luke 45; Ontario, 1871 ***1823.17*** *p149*
Simms, Richard; America, 1752 ***1220.12*** *p723*
Simms, Thomas 24; Ontario, 1871 ***1823.21*** *p336*
Simms, William; Illinois, 1858 ***6079.1*** *p13*
Simms, William 46; Ontario, 1871 ***1823.21*** *p336*
Simner, Mary; America, 1764 ***1220.12*** *p723*
Simola, Hjalmer; Minnesota, 1925 ***2769.54*** *p1380*
Simon, Mr. 30; New Orleans, 1848 ***778.6*** *p311*
Simon, Mr.; Quebec, n.d. ***9228.50*** *p593*
Simon, Mrs. 25; New Orleans, 1841 ***778.6*** *p312*
Simon, Adam *SEE* Simon, Jakob
Simon, Adam; America, 1867 ***7919.3*** *p526*
Simon, Adele 6; Louisiana, 1848 ***778.6*** *p311*
Simon, Alexandre 8; Louisiana, 1848 ***778.6*** *p311*
Simon, Angela; America, 1881 ***5475.1*** *p311*
Simon, Anna Margaretha; North Carolina, 1710 ***3629.40*** *p7*
Simon, Anna Margreta; North Carolina, 1710 ***3629.40*** *p7*
Simon, Anna Maria 5; Galveston, TX, 1844 ***3967.10*** *p372*
Simon, Anne Barbe 36; Louisiana, 1848 ***778.6*** *p311*
Simon, Antoine; Montreal, 1661 ***9221.17*** *p475*
Simon, Antoine; Quebec, 1642 ***9221.17*** *p122*
Simon, August; America, 1883 ***7420.1*** *p398*
Simon, Auguste; America, 1883 ***7420.1*** *p340*
Simon, Barbara; America, 1881 ***5475.1*** *p74*
Simon, Benedict; North Carolina, 1710 ***3629.40*** *p7*
With wife
Simon, Benjamin 17; Galveston, TX, 1844 ***3967.10*** *p373*
Simon, Blase 50; Port uncertain, 1841 ***778.6*** *p311*
Simon, Charles 42; Quebec, 1662 ***9221.17*** *p478*
Simon, Charlotte; America, 1868 ***7919.3*** *p530*
Simon, Conrad; Valdivia, Chile, 1852 ***1192.4*** *p55*

Simon, David; Louisiana, 1874 ***4981.45*** *p134*
Simon, Dominique 47; America, 1846 ***778.6*** *p311*
Simon, Eduard Friedrich August; America, 1867 ***7420.1*** *p265*
Simon, Eduard Samuel; Syracuse, NY, 1874 ***5475.1*** *p127*
Simon, Elie; Wisconsin, 1856 ***1494.20*** *p12*
Simon, Elisabeth; America, 1847 ***5475.1*** *p474*
Simon, Elisabeth *SEE* Simon, Peter
Simon, Elisabeth 6 weeks months *SEE* Simon, Peter
Simon, Elisabeth Michels 29 *SEE* Simon, Peter
Simon, Elisabeth *SEE* Simon, Nikolaus
Simon, Elisabeth; Brazil, 1863 ***5475.1*** *p497*
Simon, Elise; America, 1884 ***7420.1*** *p345*
Simon, Elise *SEE* Simon, Harry
Simon, Emil; Wisconsin, 1888 ***6795.8*** *p34*
Simon, Euqene; America, 1872 ***1494.20*** *p12*
Simon, Ferdinand; Buenos Aires, 1843 ***5475.1*** *p379*
Simon, Francois; America, 1872 ***1494.20*** *p13*
Simon, Francois Antoine 40; America, 1844 ***778.6*** *p311*
Simon, Francois Ralph *SEE* Simon, George
Simon, Francois Ralph *SEE* Simon, George
Simon, Friedrich *SEE* Simon, Jakob
Simon, Gaspard 45; America, 1846 ***778.6*** *p311*
Simon, Georg August; America, 1867 ***5475.1*** *p505*
Simon, George; British Columbia, 1890 ***9228.50*** *p592*
*Wife:*Louisa Bertram
*Child:*Gerald Lionel
*Child:*Julius Bertram
*Child:*Lewis Reginald
*Child:*Francois Ralph
*Child:*George Sydney
Simon, George; California, 1890 ***9228.50*** *p592*
*Wife:*Louisa Bertram
*Child:*Julius Bertram
*Child:*Francois Ralph
*Child:*Gerald Lionel
*Child:*Lewis Reginald
*Child:*George Sydney
Simon, George; Illinois, 1861 ***6079.1*** *p13*
Simon, George Sydney *SEE* Simon, George
Simon, George Sydney *SEE* Simon, George
Simon, Gerald Lionel *SEE* Simon, George
Simon, Gerald Lionel *SEE* Simon, George
Simon, Gertrud 37; America, 1880 ***5475.1*** *p484*
*Daughter:*Maria
*Son:*Simon
*Daughter:*Helena
*Daughter:*Katharina
Simon, Gregoire 18; Montreal, 1659 ***9221.17*** *p428*
Simon, Gregor 24; Galveston, TX, 1844 ***3967.10*** *p372*
Simon, Guillaume 14; Louisiana, 1848 ***778.6*** *p311*
Simon, Harry; America, 1895 ***7420.1*** *p372*
*Sister:*Elise
Simon, Heinrich *SEE* Simon, Peter
Simon, Henri 1; New Orleans, 1848 ***778.6*** *p312*
Simon, Hermann; America, 1890 ***7420.1*** *p361*
Simon, Hubert 19; Quebec, 1657 ***9221.17*** *p369*
Simon, Isaac; America, 1739 ***1220.12*** *p723*
Simon, Isaac 35; Ontario, 1871 ***1823.21*** *p336*
Simon, Jakob *SEE* Simon, Jakob
Simon, Jakob; America, 1865 ***5475.1*** *p498*
*Wife:*Kath. Jungbluth
*Daughter:*Katharina
*Son:*Adam
*Son:*Jakob
*Son:*Friedrich
Simon, Jakob 28; America, 1865 ***5475.1*** *p311*
Simon, Jakob *SEE* Simon, Nikolaus
Simon, Jean; Montreal, 1654 ***9221.17*** *p318*
Simon, Jn. Bte. 10; Louisiana, 1848 ***778.6*** *p312*
Simon, Johann; America, 1847 ***5475.1*** *p473*
Simon, Johann Adam; America, 1868 ***7919.3*** *p530*
Simon, Johann Alois *SEE* Simon, Peter
Simon, Johannes; North Carolina, 1710 ***3629.40*** *p7*
Simon, John; America, 1685 ***1220.12*** *p723*
Simon, John; America, 1753 ***1220.12*** *p723*
Simon, John; Ohio, 1840-1860 ***9228.50*** *p592*
Simon, John T.; Illinois, 1834-1900 ***6020.5*** *p133*
Simon, Josef; America, 1849 ***5475.1*** *p476*
Simon, Joseph; America, 1742 ***1220.12*** *p723*
Simon, Joseph 16; Louisiana, 1848 ***778.6*** *p312*
Simon, Julius Bertram *SEE* Simon, George
Simon, Julius Bertram *SEE* Simon, George
Simon, Karl; Brazil, 1863 ***5475.1*** *p498*
*Father:*Nikolaus
Simon, Karl Ludwig; America, 1866 ***2526.43*** *p181*
Simon, Karoline 4 *SEE* Simon, Peter
Simon, Karoline Schneider 25 *SEE* Simon, Peter
Simon, Kath. Jungbluth *SEE* Simon, Jakob
Simon, Katharina *SEE* Simon, Jakob
Simon, Katharina 2 *SEE* Simon, Peter
Simon, Katherine; Died enroute, 1710 ***3629.40*** *p7*
Simon, Lewis Reginald *SEE* Simon, George
Simon, Lewis Reginald *SEE* Simon, George
Simon, Louisa Bertram *SEE* Simon, George
Simon, Louisa Bertram *SEE* Simon, George
Simon, M. 28; New Orleans, 1841 ***778.6*** *p312*
Simon, M.; New York, 1860 ***358.56*** *p148*
Simon, Margarethe Fox *SEE* Simon, Peter
Simon, Maria; America, 1871 ***5475.1*** *p304*
Simon, Marie; Quebec, 1644 ***9221.17*** *p146*
Simon, Martin 32; America, 1846 ***778.6*** *p312*
Simon, Michael 29; Galveston, TX, 1844 ***3967.10*** *p372*
Simon, Nicholas; New York, NY, 1833 ***9228.50*** *p593*
Simon, Nicolas 48; Louisiana, 1848 ***778.6*** *p312*
Simon, Nikolaus 26; America, 1867 ***5475.1*** *p311*
Simon, Nikolaus *SEE* Simon, Karl
Simon, Nikolaus 55; Brazil, 1863 ***5475.1*** *p497*
*Daughter:*Elisabeth
*Son:*Jakob
Simon, Peter *SEE* Simon, Peter
Simon, Peter; America, 1880 ***5475.1*** *p240*
*Wife:*Margarethe Fox
*Son:*Wilhelm
*Son:*Heinrich
Simon, Peter; America, 1880 ***5475.1*** *p240*
Simon, Peter 22; America, 1864 ***5475.1*** *p502*
Simon, Peter 26; America, 1857 ***5475.1*** *p496*
*Wife:*Karoline Schneider 25
*Daughter:*Katharina 2
*Daughter:*Elisabeth 6 weeks
*Daughter:*Karoline 4
Simon, Peter 32; America, 1854 ***5475.1*** *p236*
*Wife:*Elisabeth Michels 29
*Son:*Johann Alois
*Son:*Peter
*Daughter:*Elisabeth
Simon, Philipp; America, 1857 ***5475.1*** *p504*
Simon, Rosalie 1; Galveston, TX, 1844 ***3967.10*** *p372*
Simon, Rosine 28; Galveston, TX, 1844 ***3967.10*** *p372*
Simon, Sebastian 28; Port uncertain, 1840 ***778.6*** *p312*
Simon, Silvester 28; Galveston, TX, 1844 ***3967.10*** *p372*
Simon, Simon Peter; Quebec, 1878 ***9228.50*** *p593*
Simon, Sophia; Wisconsin, 1856-1889 ***9228.50*** *p321*
*Child:*George
*Child:*John, Jr.
*Child:*George
Simon, Sophie; Wisconsin, 1856 ***9228.50*** *p593*
Simon, Wilhelm *SEE* Simon, Peter
Simon, William; Illinois, 1858-1861 ***6020.5*** *p133*
Simon DeLongpre, Catherine 16; Quebec, 1648 ***9221.17*** *p194*
Simon De Meres, Juan; Puerto Rico, 1822 ***3476.25*** *p113*
Simonds, Ann; America, 1757 ***1220.12*** *p779*
Simonds, Elizabeth; Died enroute, 1720 ***1220.12*** *p779*
Simonds, John; America, 1700 ***1220.12*** *p779*
Simonds, Margaret; America, 1726 ***1220.12*** *p780*
Simonds, Mary; Maryland, 1742 ***1220.12*** *p780*
Simoneau, Christina 16; New Orleans, 1847 ***778.6*** *p312*
Simoneau, Md. 43; New Orleans, 1847 ***778.6*** *p312*
Simonek, Jan; Chicago, 1846-1910 ***2853.20*** *p466*
Simonek, Vaclav; Wisconsin, 1854 ***2853.20*** *p313*
Simonet d'Abergemont, Jacques; Quebec, 1736 ***2314.30*** *p170*
Simonet d'Abergemont, Jacques; Quebec, 1736 ***2314.30*** *p196*
Simon Himler, Madlena; North Carolina, 1710 ***3629.40*** *p4*
Simonides, Vaclav; Nebraska, 1874 ***2853.20*** *p162*
Simonik, Frantisek; Minnesota, 1880 ***2853.20*** *p263*
Simonik, Frantisek Jul.; St. Paul, MN, 1877 ***2853.20*** *p267*
Simonils, Elizabeth 20; Ontario, 1871 ***1823.21*** *p336*
Simonin, Jn. Bapt. 26; America, 1847 ***778.6*** *p312*
Simonin, Joseph 20; America, 1840 ***778.6*** *p312*
Simonin, Pierre 28; America, 1847 ***778.6*** *p312*
Simonitz, George; America, 1742 ***1220.12*** *p723*
Simons, Abraham; America, 1772 ***1220.12*** *p779*
Simons, Catherine; Maryland, 1744 ***1220.12*** *p779*
Simons, Daniel; North Carolina, 1710 ***3629.40*** *p7*
Simons, David; America, 1774 ***1220.12*** *p779*
Simons, John; America, 1750 ***1220.12*** *p779*
Simons, John; Boston, 1718 ***1220.12*** *p779*
Simons, John; North Carolina, 1710 ***3629.40*** *p7*
Simons, John 70; Ontario, 1871 ***1823.21*** *p336*
Simons, Lewis; North Carolina, 1846 ***1088.45*** *p32*
Simons, Simon; America, 1772 ***1220.12*** *p780*
Simons, Solomon; North Carolina, 1811-1812 ***1088.45*** *p32*
Simons, William; Michigan, 1861 ***1447.20*** *p63*
Simonsen, John; Iowa, 1894 ***1211.15*** *p19*
Simonsen, Taale Berginns; Iowa, 1913 ***1211.15*** *p19*
Simonson, Axel Julius; Cleveland, OH, 1904-1906 ***9722.10*** *p126*
Simonson, David; Texas, 1888 ***3435.45*** *p37*
Simonson, Edward; Colorado, 1897 ***1029.59*** *p83*
Simonson, Soren S.; Colorado, 1884 ***1029.59*** *p83*
Simonsson, Bernhard; Cleveland, OH, 1902 ***9722.10*** *p126*
Simpcoe, Jane; America, 1685 ***1220.12*** *p723*
Simper, Sarah; Maryland, 1733 ***1220.12*** *p723*
Simpkin, Ruth; America, 1748 ***1220.12*** *p723*
Simpkins, Edward; Virginia, 1750 ***1220.12*** *p723*
Simpkins, Hannah; America, 1749 ***1220.12*** *p723*
Simpkinson, Robert; America, 1750 ***1220.12*** *p723*
Simple, James 34; Ontario, 1871 ***1823.21*** *p336*
Simpron, Robert; America, 1736 ***1220.12*** *p723*
Simpson, Adam 26; Ontario, 1871 ***1823.21*** *p336*
Simpson, Alexander; America, 1764 ***1220.12*** *p723*
Simpson, Alexander; Washington, 1889 ***2770.40*** *p81*
Simpson, Alfred 24; Ontario, 1871 ***1823.21*** *p336*
Simpson, Andrew; America, 1732 ***1220.12*** *p723*
Simpson, Ann; America, 1692 ***1220.12*** *p723*
Simpson, Ann; America, 1746 ***1220.12*** *p723*
Simpson, Ann; America, 1751 ***1220.12*** *p723*
Simpson, Ann; America, 1775 ***1220.12*** *p723*
Simpson, Anne; America, 1747 ***1220.12*** *p723*
Simpson, Anne; Virginia, 1721 ***1220.12*** *p723*
Simpson, Bella 21; Ontario, 1871 ***1823.21*** *p337*
Simpson, Catherine; America, 1739 ***1220.12*** *p723*
Simpson, Charles; America, 1749 ***1220.12*** *p723*
Simpson, Daniel; America, 1752 ***1220.12*** *p724*
Simpson, Daniel; America, 1772 ***1220.12*** *p724*
Simpson, Edward 43; Ontario, 1871 ***1823.17*** *p149*
Simpson, Elizabeth; America, 1759 ***1220.12*** *p724*
Simpson, Elizabeth 52; Ontario, 1871 ***1823.17*** *p149*
Simpson, Fred; Louisiana, 1874 ***4981.45*** *p134*
Simpson, George; America, 1754 ***1220.12*** *p724*
Simpson, George; North Carolina, 1824-1827 ***1088.45*** *p32*
Simpson, Henry; America, 1723 ***1220.12*** *p724*
Simpson, Hugh 66; Ontario, 1871 ***1823.21*** *p337*
Simpson, Hugh; South Carolina, 1813 ***3208.30*** *p18*
Simpson, Hugh; South Carolina, 1813 ***3208.30*** *p31*
Simpson, Hugh 42; South Carolina, 1812 ***3476.30*** *p13*
Simpson, Isaac 50; Ontario, 1871 ***1823.21*** *p337*
Simpson, Isobel 64; North Carolina, 1774 ***1422.10*** *p58*
Simpson, Isobel 64; North Carolina, 1774 ***1422.10*** *p62*
Simpson, Israel; America, 1736 ***1220.12*** *p724*
Simpson, James; America, 1753 ***1220.12*** *p724*
Simpson, James; America, 1760 ***1220.12*** *p724*
Simpson, James; America, 1763 ***1220.12*** *p724*
Simpson, James; America, 1767 ***1220.12*** *p724*
Simpson, James; Ohio, 1824 ***3580.20*** *p33*
Simpson, James; Ohio, 1824 ***6020.12*** *p22*
Simpson, James; Ohio, 1827 ***3580.20*** *p33*
Simpson, James; Ohio, 1827 ***6020.12*** *p22*
Simpson, James 42; Ontario, 1871 ***1823.21*** *p337*
Simpson, James 43; Ontario, 1871 ***1823.21*** *p337*
Simpson, James 45; Ontario, 1871 ***1823.17*** *p149*
Simpson, James; Rappahannock, VA, 1729 ***1220.12*** *p724*
Simpson, Jane; America, 1727 ***1220.12*** *p724*
Simpson, Jeremiah; America, 1775 ***1220.12*** *p724*
Simpson, Jessie 52; Ontario, 1871 ***1823.21*** *p337*
Simpson, John; America, 1700 ***1220.12*** *p724*
Simpson, John; America, 1723 ***1220.12*** *p724*
Simpson, John; America, 1734 ***1220.12*** *p724*
Simpson, John; America, 1753 ***1220.12*** *p724*
Simpson, John; America, 1756 ***1220.12*** *p724*
Simpson, John; America, 1757 ***1220.12*** *p724*
Simpson, John; America, 1765 ***1220.12*** *p724*
Simpson, John; Illinois, 1858-1861 ***6020.5*** *p133*
Simpson, John; Jamaica, 1716 ***1220.12*** *p724*
Simpson, John; North Carolina, 1792-1862 ***1088.45*** *p32*
Simpson, John 36; Ontario, 1871 ***1823.17*** *p149*
Simpson, John 60; Ontario, 1871 ***1823.17*** *p149*
Simpson, John 62; Ontario, 1871 ***1823.21*** *p337*
Simpson, John; Potomac, 1729 ***1220.12*** *p724*
Simpson, John D. 41; Ontario, 1871 ***1823.17*** *p150*
Simpson, John F. 54; Ontario, 1871 ***1823.21*** *p337*
Simpson, Jonathan; America, 1761 ***1220.12*** *p724*
Simpson, Joseph; America, 1773 ***1220.12*** *p724*
Simpson, Maggie 19; Ontario, 1871 ***1823.21*** *p337*
Simpson, Margaret; Barbados, 1681 ***1220.12*** *p724*
Simpson, Mary; America, 1720 ***1220.12*** *p724*
Simpson, Mary; America, 1741 ***1220.12*** *p724*
Simpson, Mary; Canada, 1774 ***3036.5*** *p40*
Simpson, Mary A.; Philadelphia, 1860 ***8513.31*** *p431*
Simpson, Mathew; Maryland, 1742 ***1220.12*** *p724*
Simpson, Nettie 5; Ontario, 1871 ***1823.17*** *p150*
Simpson, Olivia 83; Ontario, 1871 ***1823.21*** *p337*
Simpson, Ralph 52; Ontario, 1871 ***1823.21*** *p337*
Simpson, Richard; America, 1728 ***1220.12*** *p724*
Simpson, Richard; America, 1729 ***1220.12*** *p724*
Simpson, Richard; America, 1775 ***1220.12*** *p724*
Simpson, Richard 60; Ontario, 1871 ***1823.17*** *p150*
Simpson, Samuel; America, 1759 ***1220.12*** *p724*
Simpson, Stathey; Annapolis, MD, 1722 ***1220.12*** *p724*
Simpson, Thomas; America, 1701 ***1220.12*** *p724*

Simpson, Thomas; America, 1721 ***1220.12*** *p724*
Simpson, Thomas; America, 1729 ***1220.12*** *p724*
Simpson, Thomas; America, 1750 ***1220.12*** *p724*
Simpson, Thomas; America, 1763 ***1220.12*** *p724*
Simpson, Thomas; Barbados or Jamaica, 1686 ***1220.12*** *p724*
Simpson, Thomas; South Carolina, 1813 ***3208.30*** *p18*
Simpson, Thomas; South Carolina, 1813 ***3208.30*** *p31*
Simpson, Thomas 40; South Carolina, 1812 ***3476.30*** *p13*
Simpson, Walter 59; Ontario, 1871 ***1823.21*** *p337*
Simpson, William; America, 1720 ***1220.12*** *p725*
Simpson, William; America, 1743 ***1220.12*** *p725*
Simpson, William; America, 1748 ***1220.12*** *p725*
Simpson, William; America, 1750 ***1220.12*** *p725*
Simpson, William; America, 1763 ***1220.12*** *p725*
Simpson, William 43; North Carolina, 1774 ***1422.10*** *p54*
Simpson, William 31; Ontario, 1871 ***1823.17*** *p150*
Simpson, William 34; Ontario, 1871 ***1823.17*** *p150*
Simpson, William 56; Ontario, 1871 ***1823.21*** *p337*
Simpson, William 58; Ontario, 1871 ***1823.21*** *p337*
Simpson, William; Virginia, 1732 ***1220.12*** *p725*
Simpson, William B. 49; Ontario, 1871 ***1823.17*** *p150*
Simpson, William J. 47; Ontario, 1871 ***1823.21*** *p337*
Simpson, William L. 40; Ontario, 1871 ***1823.17*** *p150*
Simptree, John 30; Michigan, 1880 ***4491.39*** *p28*
Sims, George; America, 1767 ***1220.12*** *p723*
Sims, John; America, 1737 ***1220.12*** *p723*
Sims, John 60; Ontario, 1871 ***1823.21*** *p337*
Sims, Joseph 40; Ontario, 1871 ***1823.21*** *p337*
Sims, Mary; Virginia, 1749 ***1220.12*** *p723*
Sims, R.; California, 1868 ***1131.61*** *p89*
Sims, Richard; America, 1765 ***1220.12*** *p723*
Sims, Samuel 50; Ontario, 1871 ***1823.21*** *p337*
Sims, Samuel 70; Ontario, 1871 ***1823.21*** *p337*
Sims, Sarah Abigail; Massachusetts, 1845-1929 ***9228.50*** *p641*
Sims, William; Virginia, 1749 ***3675.1*** *p*
Simson, Aron 5 *SEE* Simson, Moses
Simson, Isaak; America, 1842 ***2526.43*** *p143*
With wife
With son 16
With son 13
Simson, Jakob 8 *SEE* Simson, Moses
Simson, Johannes 3 *SEE* Simson, Moses
Simson, John 57; Ontario, 1871 ***1823.21*** *p337*
Simson, Joseph 76; America, 1842 ***2526.43*** *p143*
Simson, Joseph Marx 19 *SEE* Simson, Moses
Simson, Moses; America, 1848 ***2526.43*** *p143*
With wife
*Son:*Joseph Marx
*Son:*Jakob
*Son:*Aron
*Son:*Salamon
*Son:*Johannes
Simson, Salamon 6 *SEE* Simson, Moses
Sinallon, Jeanne 22; Quebec, 1657 ***9221.17*** *p369*
Sincklowe, Jane; Barbados or Jamaica, 1685 ***1220.12*** *p725*
Sinclair, . . .; Toronto, 1844 ***2910.35*** *p114*
Sinclair, Alex. 36; North Carolina, 1774 ***1422.10*** *p58*
Sinclair, Alexander 75; Ontario, 1871 ***1823.17*** *p150*
Sinclair, Ann 65; North Carolina, 1775 ***1422.10*** *p59*
Sinclair, Annie 24; Ontario, 1871 ***1823.21*** *p337*
Sinclair, Archibald 46; Ontario, 1871 ***1823.21*** *p337*
Sinclair, Barbara 51; Ontario, 1871 ***1823.21*** *p337*
Sinclair, Christina 68; Ontario, 1871 ***1823.21*** *p337*
Sinclair, Daniel 30; Ontario, 1871 ***1823.21*** *p337*
Sinclair, David 66; Ontario, 1871 ***1823.17*** *p150*
Sinclair, Donald 75; Ontario, 1871 ***1823.21*** *p337*
Sinclair, Dougal 93; Ontario, 1871 ***1823.21*** *p337*
Sinclair, Dugald 44; Ontario, 1871 ***1823.21*** *p337*
Sinclair, Duncan 24; North Carolina, 1774 ***1422.10*** *p57*
Sinclair, Duncan 26; Ontario, 1871 ***1823.17*** *p150*
Sinclair, Duncan 27; Ontario, 1871 ***1823.17*** *p150*
Sinclair, Duncan 60; Ontario, 1871 ***1823.21*** *p338*
Sinclair, Duncan 64; Ontario, 1871 ***1823.21*** *p337*
Sinclair, Edward 30; Ontario, 1871 ***1823.21*** *p338*
Sinclair, Elizabeth 55; Ontario, 1871 ***1823.21*** *p338*
Sinclair, Euphemia 74; Ontario, 1871 ***1823.21*** *p338*
Sinclair, Isaac 53; Ontario, 1871 ***1823.17*** *p150*
Sinclair, Isobel 24; North Carolina, 1774 ***1422.10*** *p57*
Sinclair, James 21; North Carolina, 1774 ***1422.10*** *p59*
Sinclair, James; Ohio, 1854 ***3580.20*** *p33*
Sinclair, James; Ohio, 1854 ***6020.12*** *p22*
Sinclair, John 1; New York, NY, 1821-1849 ***6178.50*** *p78*
Sinclair, John 40; New York, NY, 1825 ***6178.50*** *p78*
Sinclair, John; North Carolina, 1806 ***1088.45*** *p32*
Sinclair, John 32; North Carolina, 1774 ***1422.10*** *p57*
Sinclair, John 42; Ontario, 1871 ***1823.17*** *p150*
Sinclair, John 42; Ontario, 1871 ***1823.21*** *p338*
Sinclair, John 52; Ontario, 1871 ***1823.17*** *p150*
Sinclair, John 70; Ontario, 1871 ***1823.21*** *p338*
Sinclair, John 84; Ontario, 1871 ***1823.17*** *p150*
Sinclair, John 87; Ontario, 1871 ***1823.21*** *p338*
Sinclair, Lydia 32; Ontario, 1871 ***1823.17*** *p150*
Sinclair, Margarit 25; North Carolina, 1775 ***1422.10*** *p59*
Sinclair, Mary 32; North Carolina, 1774 ***1422.10*** *p57*
Sinclair, Peggy; Brunswick, NC, 1767 ***1422.10*** *p61*
Sinclair, Peter 72; Ontario, 1871 ***1823.21*** *p338*
Sinclair, Richard 30; Ontario, 1871 ***1823.21*** *p338*
Sinclair, Robert 16; New York, NY, 1821-1849 ***6178.50*** *p78*
Sinclair, Robert 23; Ontario, 1871 ***1823.17*** *p150*
Sinclair, William; America, 1751 ***1220.12*** *p725*
Sinclair, William; Philadelphia, 1778 ***8529.30*** *p5A*
Sinclair, Wm. 3; New York, NY, 1821-1849 ***6178.50*** *p78*
Sinclar, William 36; Ontario, 1871 ***1823.21*** *p338*
Sinclare, James; America, 1688 ***1220.12*** *p725*
Sinclare, John; America, 1688 ***1220.12*** *p725*
Sinclare, Margaret 60; Ontario, 1871 ***1823.21*** *p338*
Sinclare, Nancy 60; Ontario, 1871 ***1823.21*** *p338*
Sinclear, Anthony; America, 1722 ***1220.12*** *p725*
Sinclear, Margaret; America, 1774 ***1220.12*** *p725*
Sincler, Archy 55; Ontario, 1871 ***1823.21*** *p338*
Sincler, James 16; Ontario, 1871 ***1823.21*** *p338*
Sindelar, Antonin; Iowa, 1870 ***2853.20*** *p202*
Sindelar, Josef; St. Louis, 1896 ***2853.20*** *p54*
Sindelar, Petr; Wisconsin, 1856 ***2853.20*** *p345*
Sinden, Edward; America, 1774 ***1220.12*** *p725*
Sindner, Jno.; Louisiana, 1874 ***4981.45*** *p297*
Sindt, John; Iowa, 1904 ***1211.15*** *p19*
Sinecross, Sarah; Marblehead, MA, 1732 ***9228.50*** *p316*
Sinek, Joseph 18; America, 1846 ***778.6*** *p312*
Sinek, Josephine 20; America, 1846 ***778.6*** *p312*
Sinek, Marie 25; America, 1846 ***778.6*** *p312*
Sinek, Michel 28; America, 1846 ***778.6*** *p312*
Sinek, Nicolas 26; America, 1846 ***778.6*** *p312*
Sinele, John P.; Illinois, 1860 ***6079.1*** *p13*
Sines, Jane 50; Michigan, 1880 ***4491.33*** *p21*
Sines, William 31; Michigan, 1880 ***4491.30*** *p28*
Sinewe, Peter; Indiana, 1884 ***5475.1*** *p445*
Sinewe, Peter, II; Indiana, 1884 ***5475.1*** *p445*
Siney, John; America, 1770 ***1220.12*** *p725*
Sinfield, William; America, 1721 ***1220.12*** *p725*
Sinfield, William; America, 1765 ***1220.12*** *p725*
Singcross, Joseph; America, 1727 ***9228.50*** *p165*
Singer, . . .; West Virginia, 1850-1860 ***1132.30*** *p149*
Singer, Andreas; Halifax, N.S., 1902 ***1860.4*** *p40*
Singer, Ann 35; Mississippi, 1847 ***778.6*** *p312*
Singer, Christian 33; Halifax, N.S., 1902 ***1860.4*** *p40*
Singer, Elliot; America, 1758 ***1220.12*** *p725*
Singer, Fa.ny 27; Mississippi, 1847 ***778.6*** *p312*
Singer, Heinrich 9; Halifax, N.S., 1902 ***1860.4*** *p40*
Singer, Isaac; Virginia, 1773 ***1220.12*** *p725*
Singer, Jacob; Louisiana, 1874 ***4981.45*** *p134*
Singer, Jean 6 months; Mississippi, 1847 ***778.6*** *p312*
Singer, Jean 55; Mississippi, 1847 ***778.6*** *p312*
Singer, Magdalena 7; Halifax, N.S., 1902 ***1860.4*** *p40*
Singer, Michael; America, 1774 ***1220.12*** *p725*
Singer, Pauline 2; Halifax, N.S., 1902 ***1860.4*** *p40*
Singer, Robert; America, 1769 ***1220.12*** *p725*
Singer, Rosine 32; Halifax, N.S., 1902 ***1860.4*** *p40*
Singer, Samuel C.; Colorado, 1894 ***1029.59*** *p83*
Singer, Samuel Castle 33; Colorado, 1871 ***1029.59*** *p84*
Singer, Sigmund 13; America, 1873 ***2853.20*** *p430*
Singer, Thomas; America, 1774 ***1220.12*** *p725*
Singer, Wilhelm 4; Halifax, N.S., 1902 ***1860.4*** *p40*
Singler, Mr. 10; Port uncertain, 1841 ***778.6*** *p312*
Singler, Mrs. 30; Port uncertain, 1841 ***778.6*** *p312*
Singler, Louis Charles 30; Port uncertain, 1841 ***778.6*** *p312*
Singletary, Robert; North Carolina, 1844 ***1088.45*** *p32*
Singleton, Ann; America, 1770 ***1220.12*** *p725*
Singleton, Bridget; America, 1773 ***1220.12*** *p725*
Singleton, Bridget; America, 1775 ***1220.12*** *p725*
Singleton, Edward; America, 1726 ***1220.12*** *p725*
Singleton, Edward; America, 1757 ***1220.12*** *p725*
Singleton, James; Barbados, 1662 ***1220.12*** *p725*
Singleton, Sarah; Virginia, 1736 ***1220.12*** *p725*
Singular, James 52; Ontario, 1871 ***1823.21*** *p338*
Singulon, George 29; Ontario, 1871 ***1823.21*** *p338*
Sinimin, E. Ann 60; Ontario, 1871 ***1823.21*** *p338*
Sinker, George 39; Ontario, 1871 ***1823.21*** *p338*
Sinkey, Othnile 29; Ontario, 1871 ***1823.21*** *p338*
Sinkins, George 19; Port uncertain, 1842 ***778.6*** *p312*
Sinkins, Robert 28; Port uncertain, 1842 ***778.6*** *p312*
Sinkmajer, Josef; Iowa, 1891-1892 ***2853.20*** *p118*
Sinkmajer, Josef; Wisconsin, 1891 ***2853.20*** *p216*
Sinne, Jacob 24; America, 1847 ***778.6*** *p312*
Sinne, Jean 29; America, 1847 ***778.6*** *p312*
Sinne, Peter 20; America, 1847 ***778.6*** *p312*
Sinne, Phillippe 28; America, 1847 ***778.6*** *p312*
Sinne, Wilhelm 9; America, 1847 ***778.6*** *p312*
Sinnes, Peter 54; Brazil, 1828 ***5475.1*** *p233*
Sinnett, Anne; New Orleans, 1851 ***7242.30*** *p154*
Sinnit, John; Massachusetts, 1755 ***9228.50*** *p593*
Sinnix, Emma 13; Quebec, 1870 ***8364.32*** *p26*
Sinnott, Catherine; New Orleans, 1850 ***7242.30*** *p154*
Sinnott, Richard; America, 1765 ***1220.12*** *p725*
Sinnott, Thomas; New Orleans, 1850 ***7242.30*** *p154*
Sinnou, Martin; Toronto, 1844 ***2910.35*** *p112*
Sinnvell, Johann; America, 1883 ***5475.1*** *p176*
Sinnwell, Anna Maria; Rio Grande do Sul, Brazil, 1860 ***5475.1*** *p368*
Sinot, Patrick; Boston, 1746 ***1642*** *p46*
Sins, Anthony; Louisiana, 1874-1875 ***4981.45*** *p31*
Sins, Climens; Louisiana, 1874 ***4981.45*** *p297*
Sins, George; Louisiana, 1874 ***4981.45*** *p297*
Sintas, George; North Carolina, 1792-1862 ***1088.45*** *p32*
Sinton, Robert; America, 1775 ***1220.12*** *p725*
Sinton, William; Canada, 1774 ***3036.5*** *p41*
Sintzel, Gertraud 27; Pennsylvania, 1851 ***170.15*** *p42*
With family
Sintzel, Johann Adam 4; Pennsylvania, 1851 ***170.15*** *p42*
With family
Sintzel, Johann Henrich 8; Pennsylvania, 1851 ***170.15*** *p42*
With family
Sintzel, Johann Peter 36; Pennsylvania, 1851 ***170.15*** *p42*
With family
Sinvoirat, Catharina 45; America, 1843 ***778.6*** *p313*
Sinvoirat, Pierre 45; America, 1843 ***778.6*** *p313*
Sior, Johannes; America, 1883 ***2526.42*** *p171*
Sip, Josef; Baltimore, 1872 ***2853.20*** *p125*
Sipek, Frantisek; New York, NY, 1893 ***2853.20*** *p469*
Sippel, Abraham; Iowa, 1887 ***1211.15*** *p19*
Sippel, Isaac; Iowa, 1887 ***1211.15*** *p19*
Sippi, Charles A. 27; Ontario, 1871 ***1823.21*** *p338*
Sippi, George B. 23; Ontario, 1871 ***1823.21*** *p338*
Sippola, Charles; Minnesota, 1926 ***2769.54*** *p1379*
Sipthorp, Alexander; America, 1772 ***1220.12*** *p721*
Sirbin, David; Barbados, 1668 ***1220.12*** *p725*
Sircker, Anton; America, 1847 ***5475.1*** *p474*
Sircomb, Thomas; Virginia, 1731 ***1220.12*** *p725*
Siren, Michel 18; New Orleans, 1848 ***778.6*** *p313*
Sireri, Dennis; Louisiana, 1874 ***4981.45*** *p297*
Sirre, Jean; Nova Scotia, 1753 ***3051*** *p112*
*Wife:*Marie Hebert
*Relative:*Joseph
Sirre, Joseph *SEE* Sirre, Jean
Sirre, Marie Hebert *SEE* Sirre, Jean
Sirre, Veronique; Nova Scotia, 1753 ***3051*** *p112*
Sise, Sarah; America, 1769 ***1220.12*** *p725*
Siseland, William; America, 1767 ***1220.12*** *p725*
Sisk, Wm 27; St. Johns, N.F., 1811 ***1053.20*** *p22*
Sisko, Hiram 32; Ontario, 1871 ***1823.17*** *p150*
Sisler, Sarah 46; Ontario, 1871 ***1823.21*** *p338*
Sisoz, F. 35; Mexico, 1842 ***778.6*** *p313*
Sissac, Antoine 22; Missouri, 1845 ***778.6*** *p313*
Sisse, Simon; Illinois, 1852 ***6079.1*** *p13*
Sisson, Francis; America, 1688 ***1220.12*** *p725*
Sisson, Joseph 43; Ontario, 1871 ***1823.17*** *p150*
Sissons, John; America, 1723 ***1220.12*** *p725*
Sissons, Jonathan 57; Ontario, 1871 ***1823.21*** *p338*
Sisterhenn, Peter; Ohio, 1809-1852 ***4511.35*** *p50*
Sithern, John; America, 1742 ***1220.12*** *p725*
Sittel, Julius; Ohio, 1809-1852 ***4511.35*** *p50*
Sitter, Katha 29; Halifax, N.S., 1902 ***1860.4*** *p44*
Sitter, Katherine 9 months; Halifax, N.S., 1902 ***1860.4*** *p44*
Sitter, Katrina 28; Halifax, N.S., 1902 ***1860.4*** *p44*
Sitter, Michael 33; Halifax, N.S., 1902 ***1860.4*** *p44*
Sitter, Nicholas 53; Ontario, 1871 ***1823.17*** *p150*
Sitter, Nicolaus 28; Halifax, N.S., 1902 ***1860.4*** *p44*
Sitter, Peter; Ontario, 1871 ***1823.17*** *p150*
Sitter, Phillippa 4 months; Halifax, N.S., 1902 ***1860.4*** *p44*
Sitter, Rosalia 16; Halifax, N.S., 1902 ***1860.4*** *p44*
Sitter, Rosalia 25; Halifax, N.S., 1902 ***1860.4*** *p44*
Sitter, Terese 2; Halifax, N.S., 1902 ***1860.4*** *p44*
Sitter, Wallenhim 31; Halifax, N.S., 1902 ***1860.4*** *p44*
Sitterle, Charles; Colorado, 1885 ***1029.59*** *p84*
Sitterle, Joseph; Colorado, 1880 ***1029.59*** *p84*
Sitterle, Joseph; Colorado, 1884 ***1029.59*** *p84*
Sittig, Caroline 5; America, 1846 ***778.6*** *p313*
Sittig, Jean 2; America, 1846 ***778.6*** *p313*
Sittig, Jean 40; America, 1846 ***778.6*** *p313*
Sittig, Josephine 7; America, 1846 ***778.6*** *p313*
Sittig, Marguerite 17; America, 1846 ***778.6*** *p313*
Sittig, Marie 14; America, 1846 ***778.6*** *p313*
Sittig, Marie 40; America, 1846 ***778.6*** *p313*
Sittig, Nicolas 9; America, 1846 ***778.6*** *p313*
Sittington, Henry 45; Ontario, 1871 ***1823.17*** *p150*
Sittner, Anna 23; New York, NY, 1893 ***1883.7*** *p43*
Sittner, Anna 44; New York, NY, 1893 ***1883.7*** *p43*
Sittner, Annie 19; New York, NY, 1893 ***1883.7*** *p43*
Sittner, Catha. 21; New York, NY, 1893 ***1883.7*** *p43*

Sittner, Jacob 3 months; New York, NY, 1893 *1883.7 p43*
Sittner, Jacob 43; New York, NY, 1893 *1883.7 p43*
Sittner, Magd. 6; New York, NY, 1893 *1883.7 p43*
Sittner, Marg. 7; New York, NY, 1893 *1883.7 p43*
Sittner, Rosine 10; New York, NY, 1893 *1883.7 p43*
Siverdfiger, Daniel S.; Washington, 1883 *2770.40 p137*
Siveret, Mathew; Marblehead, MA, 1745 *9228.50 p591*
Sivers, John; America, 1731 *1220.12 p725*
Sivert, Mr.; Marblehead, MA, 1629 *9228.50 p579*
Sivret, Elizabeth *SEE* Sivret, Philip
Sivret, George *SEE* Sivret, Philip
Sivret, James; Boston, 1797 *9228.50 p590*
Sivret, Philip; America, 1770-1870 *9228.50 p590*
  *Brother:*George
  *Sister:*Elizabeth
Sivyan, John 35; Ontario, 1871 *1823.17 p150*
Siweck, Wladyslaw 34; New York, NY, 1920 *930.50 p48*
Siwka, Martin; Detroit, 1890 *9980.23 p97*
Six, Gotthilf; America, 1867 *7919.3 p530*
Six, Pauline; America, 1867 *7919.3 p530*
Sixby, Chas.; California, 1868 *1131.61 p89*
Sixta, Frantisek; Wisconsin, 1867 *2853.20 p318*
Sixton, Edwzrd; New Jersey, 1777 *8529.30 p5A*
Sizler, Benjamin; Detroit, 1929-1930 *6214.5 p71*
Sjoberg, J.; New York, NY, 1845 *6412.40 p149*
Sjoberg, Nels; St. Paul, MN, 1884 *1865.50 p108*
Sjoberg, P. Edwin; St. Paul, MN, 1880 *1865.50 p109*
Sjoblad, C.G.; New York, NY, 1849 *6412.40 p152*
Sjoblom, Joh.; Philadelphia, 1848 *6412.40 p150*
Sjoblom, Karl; Cleveland, OH, 1893-1897 *9722.10 p126*
Sjoding, Axel E.; New York, NY, 1903 *6212.1 p13*
Sjogren, C.J.; New York, NY, 1844 *6412.40 p147*
Sjogren, Gustaf; Charleston, SC, 1851 *6412.40 p153*
Sjogren, N.; New York, NY, 1847 *6412.40 p150*
Sjogren, N.J.; New York, NY, 1848 *6412.40 p151*
Sjogren, O.; Philadelphia, 1848 *6412.40 p150*
Sjoholm, L.J.; New York, NY, 1846 *6412.40 p149*
Sjoholm, Peter G.; Cleveland, OH, 1894-1902 *9722.10 p126*
Sjolander, Carl; Cleveland, OH, 1902-1905 *9722.10 p126*
Sjostrand, Hannah M.; Minnesota, 1901 *1865.50 p109*
Sjostrom, Anna 26; New York, 1856 *6529.11 p22*
Sjostrom, Anna 26; New York, 1856 *6529.11 p22*
Sjostrom, Jan 29; New York, 1856 *6529.11 p22*
Skagg, Elizabeth; Died enroute, 1730 *1220.12 p725*
Skala, Vaclav; Illinois, 1853-1910 *2853.20 p471*
Skalitzky, John J.; Iowa, 1896 *1211.15 p19*
Skalmer, Emma 23 *SEE* Skalmer, Heinrich
Skalmer, Heinrich 27; New York, NY, 1878 *9253.2 p45*
  *Wife:*Emma 23
  *Child:*Marianna 11 months
Skalmer, Marianna 11 *SEE* Skalmer, Heinrich
Skaloud, Frantisek; New York, NY, 1893 *2853.20 p469*
Skalsky, Josef; New York, NY, 1893 *2853.20 p469*
Skanberg, Joh. Robert; New York, NY, 1851 *6412.40 p153*
Skane, Christian; Virginia, 1767 *1220.12 p725*
Skar, Hans P.; Washington, 1884 *2770.40 p193*
Skarda, Frantisek; New York, NY, 1868 *2853.20 p73*
Skarda, Jan *SEE* Skarda, Martin
Skarda, Martin *SEE* Skarda, Martin
Skarda, Martin; Arkansas, 1895 *2853.20 p376*
  *Son:*Martin
  *Son:*Vojtech
  *Son:*Jan
Skarda, Vojtech *SEE* Skarda, Martin
Skarnley, John; America, 1775 *1220.12 p725*
Skate, Lucy; America, 1754 *1220.12 p725*
Skatt, Timothy Featherstonehaugh; America, 1774 *1220.12 p725*
Skea, John; America, 1759 *1220.12 p725*
Skeats, John; America, 1743 *1220.12 p725*
Skeele, William; America, 1767 *1220.12 p726*
Skeem, Peter; Iowa, 1896 *1211.15 p19*
Skeet, William; America, 1771 *1220.12 p725*
Skegg, George; America, 1741 *1220.12 p726*
Skegg, William; America, 1741 *1220.12 p726*
Skeggs, James; America, 1755 *1220.12 p726*
Skelhorne, Samuel; America, 1774 *1220.12 p726*
Skelling, John 17; Quebec, 1870 *8364.32 p26*
Skellington, Catherine 30; Ontario, 1871 *1823.21 p338*
Skelly, John; Toronto, 1844 *2910.35 p115*
Skelt, John; America, 1754 *1220.12 p726*
Skelton, Ann; Canada, 1774 *3036.5 p40*
Skelton, Eleanor; America, 1749 *1220.12 p726*
Skelton, Jane; Canada, 1775 *3036.5 p67*
Skelton, John; America, 1723 *1220.12 p726*
Skelton, John; America, 1775 *1220.12 p726*
Skelton, John; Canada, 1775 *3036.5 p67*
Skelton, John; Colorado, 1866 *1029.59 p84*
Skelton, Judith; America, 1686 *1220.12 p726*

Skelton, Mary; America, 1772 *1220.12 p726*
Skelton, Ralph 70; Ontario, 1871 *1823.21 p338*
Skelton, Richard; Maryland, 1738 *1220.12 p726*
Skelton, Susannah; America, 1767 *1220.12 p726*
Skelton, William; America, 1755 *1220.12 p726*
Skene, George 40; Ontario, 1871 *1823.21 p338*
Skeoch, John 52; Ontario, 1871 *1823.17 p150*
Skerik, Jan; South Dakota, 1900 *2853.20 p251*
Skerlippens, John; Washington, 1889 *2770.40 p81*
Skernick, Samuel; North Carolina, 1854 *1088.45 p32*
Sketchley, Thomas; Virginia, 1767 *1220.12 p726*
Skett, Julius; Washington, 1887 *6015.10 p16*
Skidmore, Joseph; America, 1721 *1220.12 p726*
Skiffington, James 27; Ontario, 1871 *1823.21 p338*
Skill, John; Annapolis, MD, 1722 *1220.12 p726*
Skill, John; Barbados or Jamaica, 1698 *1220.12 p726*
Skill, Peter 37; Ontario, 1871 *1823.21 p338*
Skillam, Isaac; America, 1718 *1220.12 p726*
Skillam, Isaac; America, 1724 *1220.12 p726*
Skillard, William; Virginia, 1768 *1220.12 p726*
Skillen, Richard 44; Ontario, 1871 *1823.17 p150*
Skillett, Thomas; America, 1775 *1220.12 p726*
Skillington, William; America, 1699 *1220.12 p726*
Skinner, . . .; Virginia, 1665 *9228.50 p53*
Skinner, Ann; America, 1758 *1220.12 p726*
Skinner, Ann; America, 1762 *1220.12 p726*
Skinner, Anthony; America, 1734 *1220.12 p726*
Skinner, Charles 29; Ontario, 1871 *1823.21 p338*
Skinner, Donald 58; Ontario, 1871 *1823.17 p150*
Skinner, Edward; America, 1736 *1220.12 p726*
Skinner, Eli; Ohio, 1700-1799 *9228.50 p599*
Skinner, Eli; Ohio, 1837 *9228.50 p599*
Skinner, Elizabeth; America, 1751 *1220.12 p726*
Skinner, Isaac; America, 1769 *1220.12 p726*
Skinner, James; America, 1729 *1220.12 p726*
Skinner, John 31; Ontario, 1871 *1823.17 p150*
Skinner, Mary 26; Ontario, 1871 *1823.21 p338*
Skinner, Moses; America, 1767 *1220.12 p726*
Skinner, Richard; New Jersey, 1665 *9228.50 p594*
Skinner, Robert; America, 1729 *1220.12 p726*
Skinner, Robert; Ohio, 1841 *2763.1 p21*
Skinner, Sarah 77; Ontario, 1871 *1823.21 p338*
Skinner, Thomas; America, 1771 *1220.12 p726*
Skinner, W. H. 21; Ontario, 1871 *1823.21 p338*
Skinner, William; America, 1713 *1220.12 p726*
Skinner, William; America, 1736 *1220.12 p726*
Skinner, William 42; Ontario, 1871 *1823.21 p338*
Skinner, William 54; Ontario, 1871 *1823.21 p338*
Skip, Dennis; Newbury, MA, 1728 *1642 p75*
Skippon, Geo 37; Ontario, 1871 *1823.21 p338*
Skippon, Thomas 45; Ontario, 1871 *1823.21 p338*
Skipton, William; America, 1730 *1220.12 p726*
Skladowski, Anna 8; New York, NY, 1911 *6533.11 p9*
Skladowski, Franciszka 28; New York, NY, 1911 *6533.11 p9*
Sklenacek, Frantisek; Galveston, TX, 1856 *2853.20 p63*
Sklenar, Jan M.; America, 1881 *2853.20 p205*
  With parents
Skluzacek, Josef; Minnesota, 1858-1860 *2853.20 p259*
Skluzak, Jan; Minnesota, 1880 *2853.20 p285*
Skocek, Vilem; Texas, 1895 *2853.20 p82*
Skofield, Elizabeth; America, 1725 *1220.12 p705*
Skoglund, Fritz; St. Paul, MN, 1901-1902 *1865.50 p109*
Skoglund, Mathilda; Minnesota, 1870-1886 *1865.50 p102*
Skoglund, Olof; St. Paul, MN, 1874 *1865.50 p109*
  With wife
Skogman, Albin 32; Minnesota, 1923 *2769.54 p1379*
Skok, Frantisek; St. Paul, MN, 1866 *2853.20 p277*
Skolarzyk, Mary; Wisconsin, 1885 *6795.8 p45*
Skolbeck, Elizabeth 66; Ontario, 1871 *1823.17 p150*
Skoog, Andrew J.; St. Paul, MN, 1867 *1865.50 p109*
Skoog, Andrew L. *SEE* Skoog, Maria
Skoog, Emil *SEE* Skoog, Maria
Skoog, John; St. Paul, MN, 1868 *1865.50 p109*
Skoog, Maria; St. Paul, MN, 1868 *1865.50 p109*
  *Son:*Andrew L.
  *Son:*Emil
  *Son:*Oscar
  *Son:*Samuel
Skoog, Oscar *SEE* Skoog, Maria
Skoog, Samuel *SEE* Skoog, Maria
Skooglun, Mary; Michigan, 1884-1889 *1865.50 p109*
Skooglun, Olof A.; St. Paul, MN, 1880 *1865.50 p109*
Skooglund, Mary; Michigan, 1884-1889 *1865.50 p109*
Skooglund, Olof A.; St. Paul, MN, 1880 *1865.50 p109*
Skorch, Josef; Missouri, 1859-1860 *2853.20 p53*
Skorskowsky, William A.; Ohio, 1809-1852 *4511.35 p50*
Skov, Carl A.; Iowa, 1896 *1211.15 p19*
Skow, Emil; Wisconsin, 1885 *6795.8 p104*
Skowron, Katarzyna 20; New York, NY, 1911 *6533.11 p10*
Skowron, Walter; Detroit, 1930 *1640.60 p83*
Skragge, C.J.; New York, NY, 1843 *6412.40 p147*

Skrivanek, Josef; Texas, 1855 *2853.20 p78*
Skriven, Mark; America, 1753 *1220.12 p707*
Skrzypiec, Francois 38; New York, NY, 1920 *930.50 p48*
Skuce, Catherine; America, 1768 *1220.12 p726*
Skudamor, Jonathan; Barbados, 1670 *1220.12 p708*
Skudera, Matej; Chicago, 1867 *2853.20 p391*
Skull, Jackie; Wisconsin, 1958 *9228.50 p174*
Skull, William; America, 1771 *1220.12 p708*
Skurski, Daniel; Detroit, 1930 *1640.60 p77*
Skuse, James; Virginia, 1753 *1220.12 p726*
Skuse, John 73; Ontario, 1871 *1823.21 p339*
Skyff, John; America, 1685 *1220.12 p726*
Skylight, Margaret; Maryland, 1744 *1220.12 p726*
Skyrme, John; America, 1745 *1220.12 p726*
Skyrrell, Richard; America, 1738 *1220.12 p726*
Slabkowicz, Anna; Detroit, 1929 *1640.55 p115*
Slack, David; America, 1770 *1220.12 p726*
Slack, Elisabeth B. 75; Michigan, 1880 *4491.33 p21*
Slack, George 65; Ontario, 1871 *1823.21 p339*
Slack, John; America, 1765 *1220.12 p726*
Slack, John 58; Ontario, 1871 *1823.17 p150*
Slack, Mary; America, 1733 *1220.12 p726*
Slack, Rich 45; Ontario, 1871 *1823.21 p339*
Slack, Stephen; America, 1678 *1220.12 p726*
Slack, Thomas; America, 1755 *1220.12 p727*
Slad, William; Annapolis, MD, 1725 *1220.12 p727*
Slade, Benjamin 36; Ontario, 1871 *1823.21 p339*
Slade, Elizabeth 24; Ontario, 1871 *1823.21 p339*
Slade, Humphrey; America, 1685 *1220.12 p727*
Slade, John; America, 1685 *1220.12 p727*
Slade, John; America, 1755 *1220.12 p727*
Slade, John; Virginia, 1740 *1220.12 p727*
Slade, Mary; America, 1753 *1220.12 p727*
Slade, Moses; Virginia, 1773 *1220.12 p727*
Slade, Richard; America, 1770 *1220.12 p727*
Slade, William; America, 1755 *1220.12 p727*
Sladek, Hynek; St. Louis, 1860 *2853.20 p48*
Slader, Matthew; Barbados, 1670 *1220.12 p727*
Slake, John; America, 1772 *1220.12 p727*
Slam, James; America, 1752 *1220.12 p727*
Slamer, Elizabeth; America, 1769 *1220.12 p727*
Slaney, Mary; America, 1744 *1220.12 p727*
Slanton, Anne 17; Ontario, 1871 *1823.21 p339*
Slapak, Christian; North Carolina, 1710 *3629.40 p7*
Slape, Thomas; Maryland, 1738 *1220.12 p727*
Slark, Thomas; America, 1755 *1220.12 p727*
Slata, James 57; Ontario, 1871 *1823.21 p339*
Slate, Ann; Potomac, 1743 *1220.12 p727*
Slate, Frances; Virginia, 1724 *1220.12 p727*
Slate, George; America, 1736 *1220.12 p727*
Slate, James; America, 1749 *1220.12 p727*
Slate, John, Jr.; Barbados, 1669 *1220.12 p727*
Slater, Abraham 50; Ontario, 1871 *1823.21 p339*
Slater, Abraham 55; Ontario, 1871 *1823.21 p339*
Slater, Edward K. 37; Ontario, 1871 *1823.21 p339*
Slater, F. Sarah 61; Ontario, 1871 *1823.21 p339*
Slater, George; New York, 1783 *8529.30 p15*
Slater, George; New York, NY, 1819 *3274.55 p72*
Slater, George 65; Ontario, 1871 *1823.21 p339*
Slater, Henry 49; Ontario, 1871 *1823.17 p150*
Slater, Isaac; America, 1756 *1220.12 p727*
Slater, James; Marston's Wharf, 1782 *8529.30 p15*
Slater, James 37; Ontario, 1871 *1823.21 p339*
Slater, James 48; Ontario, 1871 *1823.17 p150*
Slater, John; America, 1745 *1220.12 p727*
Slater, John; America, 1749 *1220.12 p727*
Slater, John; Marston's Wharf, 1782 *8529.30 p15*
Slater, John; Maryland, 1674 *1236.25 p50*
Slater, Joshua; Barbados, 1675 *1220.12 p727*
Slater, Margaret; America, 1755 *1220.12 p727*
Slater, Michael; Marston's Wharf, 1782 *8529.30 p15*
Slater, Richard; Marston's Wharf, 1782 *8529.30 p15*
Slater, Robert; America, 1758 *1220.12 p727*
Slater, Samuel 47; Ontario, 1871 *1823.21 p339*
Slater, Simeon 24; Ontario, 1871 *1823.21 p339*
Slater, Thomas; Colorado, 1882 *1029.59 p84*
Slater, William; America, 1743 *1220.12 p727*
Slater, William; America, 1768 *1220.12 p727*
Slater, William 16; Quebec, 1870 *8364.32 p26*
Slates, William; Maryland, 1725 *1220.12 p727*
Slatford, Joseph; America, 1773 *1220.12 p727*
Slattery, Patrick 50; Ontario, 1871 *1823.17 p150*
Slaught, Jessie 62; Ontario, 1871 *1823.21 p339*
Slaughter, Henry; Barbados or Jamaica, 1683 *1220.12 p727*
Slaughter, James 37; Ontario, 1871 *1823.17 p150*
Slaughter, John; America, 1674 *1220.12 p727*
Slaughter, John; America, 1757 *1220.12 p727*
Slaughter, John; America, 1764 *1220.12 p727*
Slaughter, John; Maryland, 1674 *1236.25 p50*
Slaughter, Mary; America, 1732 *1220.12 p727*
Slaughter, Mary; America, 1754 *1220.12 p727*

Slaughter, Rebecca; Annapolis, MD, 1722 ***1220.12*** *p727*
Slaughter, Robert; Barbados, 1663 ***1220.12*** *p727*
Slaven, Hugh; Illinois, 1854 ***6079.1*** *p13*
Slaven, Sally; Ontario, 1835 ***3160.1*** *p150*
Slavik, Jan; New York, NY, 1852 ***2853.20*** *p386*
Slavik, Matej; Nebraska, 1875 ***2853.20*** *p172*
Slavin, Cornelius; America, 1768 ***1220.12*** *p727*
Slavin, Thomas 51; Ontario, 1871 ***1823.17*** *p150*
Slaving, Elizabeth; America, 1768 ***1220.12*** *p727*
Slawinski, John; Galveston, TX, 1894-1901 ***6015.15*** *p13*
*Wife:*Pelagia
Slawinski, Pelagia *SEE* Slawinski, John
Slayman, Cornelius; Barbados, 1694 ***1220.12*** *p727*
Slaytor, Mary; America, 1740 ***1220.12*** *p727*
Sleater, Robert; Illinois, 1856 ***6079.1*** *p13*
Sleath, Joseph; America, 1767 ***1220.12*** *p727*
Slee, Thomas; America, 1734 ***1220.12*** *p727*
Sleeman, William; Virginia, 1770 ***1220.12*** *p727*
Sleesman, Christopher; New Jersey, 1752-1774 ***927.31*** *p2*
Sleid, Giles S. 32; Ontario, 1871 ***1823.21*** *p339*
Sleightholme, Thomas; America, 1765 ***1220.12*** *p728*
Sleiter, John; Detroit, 1930 ***1640.60*** *p82*
Sleith, William 55; Ontario, 1871 ***1823.21*** *p339*
Sleno, Samuel 30; Ontario, 1871 ***1823.17*** *p150*
Slesinger, Libor Alois; Iowa, 1857 ***2853.20*** *p143*
Slesman, Christopher; New Jersey, 1752-1774 ***927.31*** *p2*
Slesser, Robert 43; Ontario, 1871 ***1823.21*** *p339*
Sletzer, George; Ohio, 1840-1897 ***8365.35*** *p18*
Slezak, Josef; Iowa, 1856-1858 ***2853.20*** *p211*
Slice, John; America, 1719 ***1220.12*** *p728*
Slider, Mary; Annapolis, MD, 1726 ***1220.12*** *p728*
Sliger, John; Illinois, 1864 ***6079.1*** *p13*
Slight, John; America, 1775 ***1220.12*** *p728*
Slight, Joseph 43; Ontario, 1871 ***1823.21*** *p339*
Slight, William 49; Ontario, 1871 ***1823.21*** *p339*
Slighthorn, William 34; Ontario, 1871 ***1823.21*** *p339*
Slim, Abraham; America, 1771 ***1220.12*** *p728*
Slim, John; Annapolis, MD, 1726 ***1220.12*** *p728*
Sliman, Galbes; Texas, 1906 ***3435.45*** *p36*
Slimmer, John 24; Ontario, 1871 ***1823.21*** *p339*
Sling, Mary; Detroit, 1930 ***1640.60*** *p78*
Slingland, Ant'y; Ontario, 1787 ***1276.15*** *p231*
With relative
Slingland, Dirk; Ontario, 1787 ***1276.15*** *p231*
With child & 2 relatives
Slingsby, Ebenezer; Massachusetts, 1717 ***1642*** *p65*
Slingsby, Thomas 40; Ontario, 1871 ***1823.21*** *p339*
Sloan, Ann; America, 1722 ***1220.12*** *p728*
Sloan, David 38; Ontario, 1871 ***1823.17*** *p151*
Sloan, James; Worcester, MA, 1733 ***1642*** *p114*
*Wife:*Mary
*Child:*John
Sloan, Jno. J. 34; South Carolina, 1812 ***3476.30*** *p13*
Sloan, John *SEE* Sloan, James
Sloan, Mary *SEE* Sloan, James
Sloan, Robert 42; Ontario, 1871 ***1823.21*** *p339*
Sloan, Samuel 32; Ontario, 1871 ***1823.21*** *p339*
Sloan, Samuel H.; Washington, 1889 ***2770.40*** *p81*
Sloan, William 65; Ontario, 1871 ***1823.17*** *p151*
Sloane, Edward 60; Ontario, 1871 ***1823.17*** *p151*
Slobbock, Christian; North Carolina, 1710 ***3629.40*** *p7*
Slobbock, Christopher, Jr.; North Carolina, 1710 ***3629.40*** *p7*
Sloboch, Christian; North Carolina, 1710 ***3629.40*** *p7*
Slocomb, Caroline; Canada, 1814-1900 ***9228.50*** *p166*
Slocomb, Sarah; America, 1757 ***1220.12*** *p728*
Slocombe, Benjamin; America, 1730 ***1220.12*** *p728*
Slocombe, George; Maryland, 1738 ***1220.12*** *p728*
Slocombe, Henry; Barbados, 1675 ***1220.12*** *p728*
Slocombe, Isaac; America, 1773 ***1220.12*** *p728*
Slocombe, John; America, 1728 ***1220.12*** *p728*
Slocum, James 44; Ontario, 1871 ***1823.17*** *p151*
Slocum, Walter 36; Ontario, 1871 ***1823.17*** *p151*
Sloffens, Henry; Illinois, 1858-1861 ***6020.5*** *p133*
Slopah, Christian; North Carolina, 1710 ***3629.40*** *p7*
Slote, John; America, 1764 ***1220.12*** *p728*
Sloup-Vachalova, Anna; Wisconsin, 1853 ***2853.20*** *p303*
Slovrn, Samuel 9; Ontario, 1871 ***1823.17*** *p151*
Slow, Edward; America, 1733 ***1220.12*** *p728*
Slow, John; America, 1688 ***1220.12*** *p728*
Sloway, Patrick; Toronto, 1844 ***2910.35*** *p112*
Slowe, Ann; Barbados, 1683 ***1220.12*** *p728*
Slowienski, Albert; Texas, 1892-1905 ***6015.15*** *p11*
Slowienski, John; Galveston, TX, 1894 ***6015.15*** *p11*
Slowly, John; America, 1753 ***1220.12*** *p728*
Slubak, Christian; North Carolina, 1710 ***3629.40*** *p7*
Slubak, John; North Carolina, 1710 ***3629.40*** *p7*
Slubbach, Christian; North Carolina, 1710 ***3629.40*** *p7*
Slubbach, Christopher, Jr.; North Carolina, 1710 ***3629.40*** *p7*
Sludescrud, S. 35; Halifax, N.S., 1902 ***1860.4*** *p44*
Slunecko, Milos; Chicago, 1892 ***2853.20*** *p446*
Sly, John; America, 1757 ***1220.12*** *p728*
Sly, William; America, 1726 ***1220.12*** *p728*
Slye, Robert; America, 1685 ***1220.12*** *p728*
Slye, Robert; America, 1772 ***1220.12*** *p728*
Slye, Thomas; Annapolis, MD, 1725 ***1220.12*** *p728*
Smaddall, Richard; America, 1766 ***1220.12*** *p728*
Smaldy, John; Maryland or Virginia, 1731 ***1220.12*** *p728*
Smale, Elizabeth; Virginia, 1736 ***1220.12*** *p728*
Smale, Elizabeth; Virginia, 1762 ***1220.12*** *p728*
Smale, John; Virginia, 1728 ***1220.12*** *p728*
Smale, Joseph; Virginia, 1737 ***1220.12*** *p728*
Smale, Mary; Virginia, 1740 ***1220.12*** *p728*
Small, Andrew 50; Ontario, 1871 ***1823.21*** *p339*
Small, David 40; Ontario, 1871 ***1823.21*** *p339*
Small, Dorrell; America, 1738 ***1220.12*** *p728*
Small, Elizabeth 32; Ontario, 1871 ***1823.21*** *p339*
Small, Francis; Barbados, 1681 ***1220.12*** *p728*
Small, Jacob 21; Ontario, 1871 ***1823.21*** *p339*
Small, James 30; Ontario, 1871 ***1823.21*** *p339*
Small, James 53; Ontario, 1871 ***1823.21*** *p339*
Small, James; Quebec, 1870 ***8364.32*** *p26*
Small, James; Virginia, 1754 ***1220.12*** *p728*
Small, John 30; Ontario, 1871 ***1823.21*** *p339*
Small, Joseph S. 30; Ontario, 1871 ***1823.21*** *p339*
Small, Mary; America, 1767 ***1220.12*** *p728*
Small, Mary; Maryland, 1736 ***1220.12*** *p728*
Small, Mary 35; Ontario, 1871 ***1823.21*** *p339*
Small, Robert; America, 1764 ***1220.12*** *p728*
Small, Robert; North Carolina, 1834 ***1088.45*** *p32*
Small, Thomas; America, 1767 ***1220.12*** *p728*
Small, Tobias; America, 1750 ***1220.12*** *p728*
Small, William; America, 1752 ***1220.12*** *p728*
Small, William 42; Ontario, 1871 ***1823.17*** *p151*
Smallacombe, Thomasin; America, 1742 ***1220.12*** *p728*
Smalldon, Richard 26; Ontario, 1871 ***1823.17*** *p151*
Smalley, George; America, 1751 ***1220.12*** *p728*
Smallman, Ann; America, 1757 ***1220.12*** *p728*
Smallman, James 66; Ontario, 1871 ***1823.21*** *p339*
Smallman, John; America, 1764 ***1220.12*** *p728*
Smallman, Martin; Illinois, 1918 ***6007.60*** *p9*
Smallman, William; America, 1774 ***1220.12*** *p728*
Smallpass, Richard; America, 1750 ***1220.12*** *p729*
Smallridge, Samuel; America, 1773 ***1220.12*** *p729*
Smallwood, Charlotte 33; Ontario, 1871 ***1823.21*** *p339*
Smallwood, Joseph; America, 1770 ***1220.12*** *p729*
Smallwood, William; Marston's Wharf, 1782 ***8529.30*** *p15*
Smalman, Martha; America, 1721 ***1220.12*** *p728*
Smalman, Mary; Barbados or Jamaica, 1677 ***1220.12*** *p728*
Smalyk, Agnes; Detroit, 1929 ***1640.55*** *p116*
Smarbeck, Christian 29; Ontario, 1871 ***1823.17*** *p151*
Smarsz, Jacob; Wisconsin, 1886 ***6795.8*** *p34*
Smart, Alfred 25; Ontario, 1871 ***1823.21*** *p340*
Smart, Ann; America, 1745 ***1220.12*** *p729*
Smart, Ann 47; Ontario, 1871 ***1823.21*** *p340*
Smart, Archibald 51; Michigan, 1880 ***4491.36*** *p19*
Smart, Charles; America, 1696 ***1220.12*** *p729*
Smart, Elizabeth 73; Ontario, 1871 ***1823.21*** *p340*
Smart, Emma Eliza; America, 1848-1948 ***9228.50*** *p650*
Smart, Francis; America, 1764 ***1220.12*** *p729*
Smart, Gabriel; America, 1685 ***1220.12*** *p729*
Smart, George 56; Ontario, 1871 ***1823.21*** *p340*
Smart, Hanna; Annapolis, MD, 1723 ***1220.12*** *p729*
Smart, James; America, 1759 ***1220.12*** *p729*
Smart, James; Iowa, 1890 ***1211.15*** *p19*
Smart, James 41; Ontario, 1871 ***1823.21*** *p340*
Smart, Jane 76; Michigan, 1880 ***4491.39*** *p28*
Smart, John; America, 1750 ***1220.12*** *p729*
Smart, John; America, 1758 ***1220.12*** *p729*
Smart, John; America, 1768 ***1220.12*** *p729*
Smart, John 44; Ontario, 1871 ***1823.21*** *p340*
Smart, John 50; Ontario, 1871 ***1823.21*** *p340*
Smart, Jonas; Maryland, 1719 ***1220.12*** *p729*
Smart, Mary; America, 1745 ***1220.12*** *p729*
Smart, Richard; Barbados, 1664 ***1220.12*** *p729*
Smart, Robert; Barbados, 1683 ***1220.12*** *p729*
Smart, Sarah; America, 1763 ***1220.12*** *p729*
Smart, Stephen; America, 1764 ***1220.12*** *p729*
Smart, Thomas; America, 1728 ***1220.12*** *p729*
Smart, Thomas 24; Ontario, 1871 ***1823.21*** *p340*
Smart, William; America, 1751 ***1220.12*** *p729*
Smat, Frantisek; Chicago, 1868 ***2853.20*** *p514*
Smathwit, John; Barbados, 1682 ***1220.12*** *p729*
Smatlan, Josef; Nebraska, 1869-1910 ***2853.20*** *p181*
Smayles, Isaac; Boston, 1830 ***3274.55*** *p25*
Smaza, Paul; Detroit, 1930 ***1640.60*** *p76*
Smeddell, Richard; America, 1766 ***1220.12*** *p729*
Smede, Johannes 19; New York, NY, 1894 ***6512.1*** *p229*
Smedley, Ralph; North Carolina, 1835 ***1088.45*** *p32*
Smee, Edward 44; Ontario, 1871 ***1823.21*** *p340*
Smee, Robert; America, 1750 ***1220.12*** *p729*
Smeeton, David; America, 1768 ***1220.12*** *p729*
Smeeton, Job; Colorado, 1874 ***1029.59*** *p84*
Smeeton, Job Samuel; Colorado, 1874 ***1029.59*** *p84*
Smeeton, John; America, 1764 ***1220.12*** *p729*
Smeeton, Robert; America, 1752 ***1220.12*** *p729*
Smeiser, George; Ohio, 1809-1852 ***4511.35*** *p50*
Smeiser, George; Ohio, 1809-1852 ***4511.35*** *p51*
Smelley, John; America, 1756 ***1220.12*** *p729*
Smellie, William 54; Ontario, 1871 ***1823.17*** *p151*
Smetana, Josef *SEE* Smetana, Josef
Smetana, Josef; Wisconsin, 1854 ***2853.20*** *p304*
*Son:*Josef
Smethurst, Elizabeth; America, 1750 ***1220.12*** *p729*
Smethurst, John; America, 1740 ***1220.12*** *p729*
Smethurst, Thomas; America, 1753 ***1220.12*** *p729*
Smethurst, William; America, 1753 ***1220.12*** *p729*
Smibert, George 36; Ontario, 1871 ***1823.21*** *p340*
Smibert, William 59; Ontario, 1871 ***1823.21*** *p340*
Smid, Jan; New York, NY, 1853 ***2853.20*** *p100*
Smidl Family ; Iowa, 1855-1856 ***2853.20*** *p237*
Smidt, Geo; Missouri, 1887 ***3276.1*** *p2*
Smidt, Sophia Augusta 16; Boston, 1835 ***6424.55*** *p31*
Smigielski, Frank; Detroit, 1929 ***1640.55*** *p113*
Smilka, Joseph; Detroit, 1924 ***6214.5*** *p61*
Smilka, Kathrine; Detroit, 1929-1930 ***6214.5*** *p61*
Smipson, Charles; Canada, 1774 ***3036.5*** *p40*
Smith, Mr.; Dedham, MA, 1640 ***1642*** *p101*
Smith, Mr.; Massachusetts, 1766 ***1642*** *p102*
Smith, Mrs.; California, 1868 ***1131.61*** *p89*
Smith, A. L. 57; Ontario, 1871 ***1823.17*** *p151*
Smith, Aaron 37; Indiana, 1851-1868 ***9076.20*** *p66*
Smith, Abel; America, 1766 ***1220.12*** *p729*
Smith, Abraham; America, 1747 ***1220.12*** *p729*
Smith, Abraham; Annapolis, MD, 1725 ***1220.12*** *p729*
Smith, Abraham 57; Ontario, 1871 ***1823.21*** *p340*
Smith, Abraham 61; Ontario, 1871 ***1823.21*** *p340*
Smith, Absalom 55; Ontario, 1871 ***1823.21*** *p340*
Smith, Adam; America, 1685 ***1220.12*** *p729*
Smith, Adam; South Carolina, 1826 ***6155.4*** *p19*
Smith, Adolphus; Illinois, 1851 ***6079.1*** *p13*
Smith, Albert; Illinois, 1834-1900 ***6020.5*** *p133*
Smith, Alex; Quebec, 1870 ***8364.32*** *p26*
Smith, Alexander; America, 1730 ***1220.12*** *p729*
Smith, Alexander; America, 1737 ***1220.12*** *p729*
Smith, Alexander; America, 1768 ***1220.12*** *p729*
Smith, Alexander 30; Ontario, 1871 ***1823.21*** *p340*
Smith, Alexander 32; Ontario, 1871 ***1823.21*** *p340*
Smith, Alexander 40; Ontario, 1871 ***1823.21*** *p340*
Smith, Alexander 56; Ontario, 1871 ***1823.21*** *p340*
Smith, Alexander Duncan; Washington, 1882 ***2770.40*** *p136*
Smith, Alexr 37; Ontario, 1871 ***1823.21*** *p340*
Smith, Alexr 50; Ontario, 1871 ***1823.21*** *p340*
Smith, Alfred 20; Ontario, 1871 ***1823.21*** *p340*
Smith, Alfred 31; Ontario, 1871 ***1823.17*** *p151*
Smith, Alfred Maurice; Colorado, 1888 ***1029.59*** *p84*
Smith, Alice; America, 1763 ***1220.12*** *p729*
Smith, Alice; America, 1768 ***1220.12*** *p729*
Smith, Alice 17; Quebec, 1870 ***8364.32*** *p26*
Smith, Alphred 44; Ontario, 1871 ***1823.17*** *p151*
Smith, Alva W. 43; Michigan, 1880 ***4491.42*** *p25*
Smith, Ambrose; America, 1618 ***1220.12*** *p729*
Smith, Ambrose; North Carolina, 1798 ***1088.45*** *p32*
Smith, Amelia 41; Ontario, 1871 ***1823.21*** *p340*
Smith, Amelia 50; Ontario, 1871 ***1823.21*** *p340*
Smith, Amy; America, 1764 ***1220.12*** *p729*
Smith, Amy 20; Ontario, 1871 ***1823.21*** *p340*
Smith, Andrew; America, 1730 ***1220.12*** *p729*
Smith, Angus 47; Ontario, 1871 ***1823.17*** *p151*
Smith, Ann; America, 1692 ***1220.12*** *p730*
Smith, Ann; America, 1695 ***1220.12*** *p730*
Smith, Ann; America, 1716 ***1220.12*** *p730*
Smith, Ann; America, 1733 ***1220.12*** *p730*
Smith, Ann; America, 1736 ***1220.12*** *p730*
Smith, Ann; America, 1738 ***1220.12*** *p730*
Smith, Ann; America, 1740 ***1220.12*** *p730*
Smith, Ann; America, 1741 ***1220.12*** *p730*
Smith, Ann; America, 1746 ***1220.12*** *p730*
Smith, Ann; America, 1749 ***1220.12*** *p730*
Smith, Ann; America, 1754 ***1220.12*** *p730*
Smith, Ann; America, 1760 ***1220.12*** *p730*
Smith, Ann; America, 1765 ***1220.12*** *p730*
Smith, Ann; America, 1766 ***1220.12*** *p730*
Smith, Ann; America, 1767 ***1220.12*** *p730*
Smith, Ann; America, 1771 ***1220.12*** *p730*
Smith, Ann; America, 1774 ***1220.12*** *p730*
Smith, Ann; Annapolis, MD, 1721 ***1220.12*** *p730*
Smith, Ann; Barbados, 1664 ***1220.12*** *p729*
Smith, Ann; Barbados or Jamaica, 1693 ***1220.12*** *p730*
Smith, Ann; Maryland, 1674 ***1236.25*** *p50*
Smith, Ann; Maryland, 1734 ***1220.12*** *p730*
Smith, Ann; Potomac, 1731 ***1220.12*** *p730*
Smith, Ann; Virginia, 1735 ***1220.12*** *p730*
Smith, Anne; America, 1722 ***1220.12*** *p730*

Smith, Anne; America, 1735 *1220.12 p730*
Smith, Anne; Barbados, 1668 *1220.12 p730*
Smith, Anne; Died enroute, 1718 *1220.12 p730*
Smith, Anne; Virginia, 1730 *1220.12 p730*
Smith, Annie 18; Ontario, 1871 *1823.21 p340*
Smith, Anthony; America, 1736 *1220.12 p730*
Smith, Anthony; America, 1751 *1220.12 p730*
Smith, Anthony; America, 1768 *1220.12 p730*
Smith, Anthony; Ohio, 1809-1852 *4511.35 p51*
Smith, Anthony 50; Ontario, 1871 *1823.21 p340*
Smith, Archibald; Ohio, 1809-1852 *4511.35 p51*
Smith, Archibald 45; Ontario, 1871 *1823.21 p340*
Smith, Arthur 36; Ontario, 1871 *1823.17 p151*
Smith, Augustia R. 41; Ontario, 1871 *1823.21 p340*
Smith, Barwell; America, 1754 *1220.12 p730*
Smith, Benjamin; America, 1687 *1220.12 p730*
Smith, Benjamin; America, 1752 *1220.12 p730*
Smith, Benjamin; America, 1756 *1220.12 p730*
Smith, Benjamin; America, 1760 *1220.12 p730*
Smith, Benjamin; America, 1765 *1220.12 p730*
Smith, Benjamin; America, 1768 *1220.12 p730*
Smith, Benjamin; America, 1770 *1220.12 p731*
Smith, Benjamin; Charles Town, SC, 1719 *1220.12 p730*
Smith, Bernard 64; Ontario, 1871 *1823.21 p340*
Smith, Bethurah 72; Ontario, 1871 *1823.21 p340*
Smith, Betsy 19; Ontario, 1871 *1823.21 p340*
Smith, Blemyre; Pennsylvania, 1863 *8513.31 p427*
Smith, Brian; America, 1708 *1220.12 p731*
Smith, Bryan; America, 1700 *1220.12 p731*
Smith, Caroline 21; Michigan, 1880 *4491.36 p20*
Smith, Catherine; America, 1741 *1220.12 p731*
Smith, Catherine; America, 1751 *1220.12 p731*
Smith, Catherine; America, 1767 *1220.12 p731*
Smith, Catherine; America, 1769 *1220.12 p731*
Smith, Catherine; America, 1773 *1220.12 p731*
Smith, Catherine; Maryland, 1722 *1220.12 p731*
Smith, Charles; America, 1744 *1220.12 p731*
Smith, Charles; America, 1750 *1220.12 p731*
Smith, Charles; America, 1761 *1220.12 p731*
Smith, Charles; America, 1764 *1220.12 p731*
Smith, Charles; America, 1767 *1220.12 p731*
Smith, Charles; Illinois, 1855 *6079.1 p13*
Smith, Charles; Illinois, 1856 *6079.1 p13*
Smith, Charles; Illinois, 1858 *6079.1 p13*
Smith, Charles; Maryland, 1674 *1236.25 p49*
Smith, Charles; North Carolina, 1866 *1088.45 p32*
Smith, Charles 19; Ontario, 1871 *1823.17 p151*
Smith, Charles 36; Ontario, 1871 *1823.17 p151*
Smith, Charles 43; Ontario, 1871 *1823.21 p340*
Smith, Charles 59; Ontario, 1871 *1823.17 p151*
Smith, Charles 81; Ontario, 1871 *1823.21 p341*
Smith, Charles A.; Colorado, 1884 *1029.59 p84*
Smith, Charles J.; North Carolina, 1854 *1088.45 p32*
Smith, Charlotte; America, 1738 *1220.12 p731*
Smith, Charlotte; America, 1768 *1220.12 p731*
Smith, Charlotte; Virginia, 1735 *1220.12 p731*
Smith, Christian; Wisconsin, 1906 *6795.8 p148*
Smith, Christopher; Maryland, 1744 *1220.12 p731*
Smith, Christopher 49; North Carolina, 1774 *1422.10 p56*
Smith, Claudius; America, 1723 *1220.12 p731*
Smith, Colin 22; Ontario, 1871 *1823.21 p341*
Smith, Conrad 20; Kentucky, 1840 *778.6 p313*
Smith, Cornesford 33; Ontario, 1871 *1823.21 p341*
Smith, Daniel; America, 1745 *1220.12 p731*
Smith, Daniel; America, 1756 *1220.12 p731*
Smith, Daniel; America, 1774 *1220.12 p731*
Smith, Daniel; Marston's Wharf, 1782 *8529.30 p15*
Smith, Daniel 70; Ontario, 1871 *1823.17 p151*
Smith, David; America, 1763 *1220.12 p731*
Smith, David; North Carolina, 1842 *1088.45 p32*
Smith, David; Nova Scotia, 1776 *9228.50 p602*
  Wife:Elizabeth Godfrey
Smith, David; Nova Scotia, 1784 *7105 p25*
Smith, David 50; Ontario, 1871 *1823.17 p151*
Smith, David 54; Ontario, 1871 *1823.21 p341*
Smith, David 70; Ontario, 1871 *1823.21 p341*
Smith, David 82; Ontario, 1871 *1823.21 p341*
Smith, Deborah; America, 1702 *1220.12 p731*
Smith, Deborah; Died enroute, 1721 *1220.12 p731*
Smith, Dewalt; Ohio, 1809-1852 *4511.35 p51*
Smith, Dickey; Barbados or Jamaica, 1694 *1220.12 p731*
Smith, Donald 50; Ontario, 1871 *1823.21 p341*
Smith, Donald 50; Ontario, 1871 *1823.21 p341*
Smith, Donald 64; Ontario, 1871 *1823.17 p151*
Smith, Dorothy; America, 1733 *1220.12 p731*
Smith, Duncan 89; Ontario, 1871 *1823.21 p341*
Smith, Edward; America, 1700 *1220.12 p731*
Smith, Edward; America, 1741 *1220.12 p731*
Smith, Edward; America, 1750 *1220.12 p731*
Smith, Edward; America, 1752 *1220.12 p731*
Smith, Edward; America, 1753 *1220.12 p731*
Smith, Edward; America, 1756 *1220.12 p731*
Smith, Edward; America, 1757 *1220.12 p731*

Smith, Edward; America, 1762 *1220.12 p731*
Smith, Edward; America, 1764 *1220.12 p731*
Smith, Edward; America, 1766 *1220.12 p731*
Smith, Edward; America, 1771 *1220.12 p731*
Smith, Edward; America, 1772 *1220.12 p731*
Smith, Edward; America, 1772 *1220.12 p732*
Smith, Edward; Barbados, 1679 *1220.12 p731*
Smith, Edward 50; Indiana, 1843-1868 *9076.20 p66*
Smith, Edward 35; Ontario, 1871 *1823.17 p151*
Smith, Edward 48; Ontario, 1871 *1823.21 p341*
Smith, Edward B. 30; Ontario, 1871 *1823.17 p151*
Smith, Edwin 3; Ontario, 1871 *1823.21 p341*
Smith, Edwin; Quebec, 1870 *8364.32 p26*
Smith, Edwin John 25; Ontario, 1871 *1823.21 p341*
Smith, Eleanor; America, 1769 *1220.12 p732*
Smith, Eleanor; Maryland, 1737 *1220.12 p732*
Smith, Elias; Barbados or Jamaica, 1687 *1220.12 p732*
Smith, Elisabeth 24; Ontario, 1871 *1823.21 p341*
Smith, Eliza 54; Michigan, 1880 *4491.42 p25*
Smith, Eliza 39; Ontario, 1871 *1823.21 p341*
Smith, Elizabeth; America, 1656 *1220.12 p732*
Smith, Elizabeth; America, 1700 *1220.12 p732*
Smith, Elizabeth; America, 1732 *1220.12 p732*
Smith, Elizabeth; America, 1736 *1220.12 p732*
Smith, Elizabeth; America, 1738 *1220.12 p732*
Smith, Elizabeth; America, 1740 *1220.12 p732*
Smith, Elizabeth; America, 1750 *1220.12 p732*
Smith, Elizabeth; America, 1753 *1220.12 p732*
Smith, Elizabeth; America, 1754 *1220.12 p732*
Smith, Elizabeth; America, 1757 *1220.12 p732*
Smith, Elizabeth; America, 1762 *1220.12 p732*
Smith, Elizabeth; America, 1763 *1220.12 p732*
Smith, Elizabeth; America, 1772 *1220.12 p732*
Smith, Elizabeth; America, 1773 *1220.12 p733*
Smith, Elizabeth; America, 1774 *1220.12 p733*
Smith, Elizabeth; America, 1775 *1220.12 p733*
Smith, Elizabeth; Annapolis, MD, 1719 *1220.12 p732*
Smith, Elizabeth; Annapolis, MD, 1723 *1220.12 p732*
Smith, Elizabeth; Annapolis, MD, 1730 *1220.12 p732*
Smith, Elizabeth; Barbados, 1694 *1220.12 p732*
Smith, Elizabeth; Barbados or Jamaica, 1677 *1220.12 p732*
Smith, Elizabeth; Barbados or Jamaica, 1680 *1220.12 p732*
Smith, Elizabeth; Barbados or Jamaica, 1700 *1220.12 p732*
Smith, Elizabeth *SEE* Smith, Nathaniel
Smith, Elizabeth *SEE* Smith, Nathaniel
Smith, Elizabeth; Died enroute, 1736 *1220.12 p732*
Smith, Elizabeth; Jamaica, 1661 *1220.12 p732*
Smith, Elizabeth; Maryland, 1735 *1220.12 p732*
Smith, Elizabeth; Maryland, 1736 *1220.12 p732*
Smith, Elizabeth; Maryland or Virginia, 1731 *1220.12 p732*
Smith, Elizabeth Godfrey *SEE* Smith, David
Smith, Elizabeth 39; Ontario, 1871 *1823.21 p341*
Smith, Elizabeth 44; Ontario, 1871 *1823.21 p341*
Smith, Elizabeth; Potomac, 1731 *1220.12 p732*
Smith, Elizabeth; Virginia, 1721 *1220.12 p732*
Smith, Elizabeth; Virginia, 1724 *1220.12 p732*
Smith, Elizabeth; Virginia, 1736 *1220.12 p732*
Smith, Elizabeth; Virginia, 1772 *1220.12 p732*
Smith, Elizabeth, Jr.; America, 1772 *1220.12 p732*
Smith, Elizabeth Jane; Ohio, 1840 *9228.50 p377*
Smith, Ella 18; Ontario, 1871 *1823.17 p151*
Smith, Elvas Clay *SEE* Smith, Richard
Smith, Emanuel; America, 1741 *1220.12 p733*
Smith, Emily 12; Quebec, 1870 *8364.32 p26*
Smith, Emma 51; Michigan, 1880 *4491.39 p28*
Smith, Esther; North Carolina, 1842 *1088.45 p32*
Smith, Esther 35; North Carolina, 1774 *1422.10 p56*
Smith, Feidor Martha; Wisconsin, 1894 *6795.8 p150*
Smith, Finlay 42; Ontario, 1871 *1823.17 p151*
Smith, Frances; America, 1745 *1220.12 p733*
Smith, Frances; Annapolis, MD, 1725 *1220.12 p733*
Smith, Frances 63; Ontario, 1871 *1823.21 p341*
Smith, Frances; Potomac, 1731 *1220.12 p733*
Smith, Francis; America, 1685 *1220.12 p733*
Smith, Francis; America, 1762 *1220.12 p733*
Smith, Francis; Maryland, 1719 *1220.12 p733*
Smith, Francis; Maryland, 1739 *1220.12 p733*
Smith, Francis; New York, NY, 1778 *8529.30 p3*
Smith, Francis; Ontario, 1835 *3160.1 p150*
Smith, Francis 24; Ontario, 1871 *1823.21 p341*
Smith, Francis 34; Ontario, 1871 *1823.17 p151*
Smith, Francis 19; St. Johns, N.F., 1811 *1053.20 p21*
Smith, Francis; Washington, 1884 *2770.40 p193*
Smith, Francis, Sr. 73; Ontario, 1871 *1823.21 p341*
Smith, Francis Abraham *SEE* Smith, James
Smith, Fred; New York, n.d. *9228.50 p602*
Smith, Fred. Cecil; America, 1912 *9228.50 p21A*
Smith, Fred. L.; America, 1905 *9228.50 p21A*
  With family

Smith, Frederick; Ohio, 1809-1852 *4511.35 p51*
Smith, Gabriel; America, 1775 *1220.12 p733*
Smith, Geo C. 44; Ontario, 1871 *1823.17 p151*
Smith, George; America, 1685 *1220.12 p733*
Smith, George; America, 1714 *1220.12 p733*
Smith, George; America, 1731 *1220.12 p733*
Smith, George; America, 1732 *1220.12 p733*
Smith, George; America, 1742 *1220.12 p733*
Smith, George; America, 1753 *1220.12 p733*
Smith, George; America, 1756 *1220.12 p733*
Smith, George; America, 1763 *1220.12 p733*
Smith, George; America, 1767 *1220.12 p733*
Smith, George; America, 1773 *1220.12 p733*
Smith, George; Annapolis, MD, 1730 *1220.12 p733*
Smith, George; Barbados, 1664 *1220.12 p733*
Smith, George; Barbados or Jamaica, 1686 *1220.12 p733*
Smith, George; Illinois, 1858 *6079.1 p13*
Smith, George; Ohio, 1809-1852 *4511.35 p51*
Smith, George 40; Ontario, 1871 *1823.21 p341*
Smith, George 42; Ontario, 1871 *1823.21 p341*
Smith, George 42; Ontario, 1871 *1823.21 p341*
Smith, George 47; Ontario, 1871 *1823.21 p341*
Smith, George 48; Ontario, 1871 *1823.21 p341*
Smith, George 50; Ontario, 1871 *1823.17 p152*
Smith, George 50; Ontario, 1871 *1823.17 p152*
Smith, George 57; Ontario, 1871 *1823.21 p341*
Smith, George 68; Ontario, 1871 *1823.21 p341*
Smith, George; Virginia, 1727 *1220.12 p733*
Smith, George; Virginia, 1735 *1220.12 p733*
Smith, George E. 27; Michigan, 1880 *4491.39 p28*
Smith, George G.; North Carolina, 1845 *1088.45 p32*
Smith, Gideon; America, 1769 *1220.12 p733*
Smith, Giles; Barbados, 1672 *1220.12 p733*
Smith, Gittos; Barbados or Jamaica, 1710 *1220.12 p733*
Smith, Hannah; America, 1756 *1220.12 p733*
Smith, Hannah; America, 1774 *1220.12 p733*
Smith, Hannah 46; Ontario, 1871 *1823.21 p341*
Smith, Hannah; Virginia, 1726 *1220.12 p733*
Smith, Harry 30; Ontario, 1871 *1823.21 p341*
Smith, Havilah 43; Michigan, 1880 *4491.36 p20*
Smith, Henry; America, 1730 *1220.12 p733*
Smith, Henry; America, 1732 *1220.12 p733*
Smith, Henry; America, 1749 *1220.12 p733*
Smith, Henry; America, 1750 *1220.12 p733*
Smith, Henry; America, 1752 *1220.12 p733*
Smith, Henry; America, 1759 *1220.12 p733*
Smith, Henry; America, 1762 *1220.12 p733*
Smith, Henry; America, 1763 *1220.12 p733*
Smith, Henry; America, 1765 *1220.12 p733*
Smith, Henry; America, 1771 *1220.12 p733*
Smith, Henry; America, 1773 *1220.12 p733*
Smith, Henry; America, 1773 *1220.12 p734*
Smith, Henry; America, 1774 *1220.12 p734*
Smith, Henry; Colorado, 1888 *1029.59 p84*
Smith, Henry; Colorado, 1893 *1029.59 p84*
Smith, Henry; Louisiana, 1874-1875 *4981.45 p30*
Smith, Henry; Massachusetts, 1630 *117.5 p154*
  With mother
Smith, Henry 32; Michigan, 1880 *4491.33 p21*
Smith, Henry; Nova Scotia, 1784 *7105 p25*
Smith, Henry 35; Ontario, 1871 *1823.17 p152*
Smith, Henry 38; Ontario, 1871 *1823.21 p342*
Smith, Henry 50; Ontario, 1871 *1823.21 p342*
Smith, Henry 57; Ontario, 1871 *1823.21 p342*
Smith, Henry 18; Quebec, 1870 *8364.32 p26*
Smith, Henry; South Carolina, 1813 *3208.30 p18*
Smith, Henry; South Carolina, 1813 *3208.30 p31*
Smith, Henry J.; Ohio, 1809-1852 *4511.35 p51*
Smith, Henry Thomas 31; Ontario, 1871 *1823.21 p342*
Smith, Herman; Wisconsin, 1882 *6795.8 p108*
Smith, Hester; America, 1740 *1220.12 p734*
Smith, Honor; America, 1763 *1220.12 p734*
Smith, Hugh; North Carolina, 1825 *1088.45 p32*
Smith, Hugh 52; Ontario, 1871 *1823.17 p152*
Smith, Hugh 55; Ontario, 1871 *1823.21 p342*
Smith, Humfrey; America, 1731 *1220.12 p734*
Smith, Humphry; America, 1756 *1220.12 p734*
Smith, Ignatius; Ohio, 1809-1852 *4511.35 p51*
Smith, Isaac; America, 1734 *1220.12 p734*
Smith, Isaac; America, 1747 *1220.12 p734*
Smith, Isaac; Annapolis, MD, 1733 *1220.12 p734*
Smith, Isaac; Barbados or Jamaica, 1686 *1220.12 p734*
Smith, Isabella 89; Ontario, 1871 *1823.21 p342*
Smith, Ivingo; America, 1742 *1220.12 p734*
Smith, J.; Quebec, 1870 *8364.32 p26*
Smith, J. B. 50; Ontario, 1871 *1823.21 p342*
Smith, J. L. 24; America, 1848 *778.6 p313*
Smith, J. S. 45; Ontario, 1871 *1823.21 p342*
Smith, Jacob 71; Ontario, 1871 *1823.21 p342*
Smith, James; America, 1685 *1220.12 p734*
Smith, James; America, 1729 *1220.12 p734*
Smith, James; America, 1730 *1220.12 p734*
Smith, James; America, 1738 *1220.12 p734*

Smith, James; America, 1743 ***1220.12*** *p734*
Smith, James; America, 1746 ***1220.12*** *p734*
Smith, James; America, 1751 ***1220.12*** *p734*
Smith, James; America, 1756 ***1220.12*** *p734*
Smith, James; America, 1762 ***1220.12*** *p734*
Smith, James; America, 1763 ***1220.12*** *p734*
Smith, James; America, 1764 ***1220.12*** *p734*
Smith, James; America, 1765 ***1220.12*** *p734*
Smith, James; America, 1766 ***1220.12*** *p734*
Smith, James; America, 1767 ***1220.12*** *p734*
Smith, James; America, 1768 ***1220.12*** *p734*
Smith, James; America, 1769 ***1220.12*** *p734*
Smith, James; America, 1770 ***1220.12*** *p735*
Smith, James; America, 1771 ***1220.12*** *p735*
Smith, James; America, 1773 ***1220.12*** *p735*
Smith, James; America, 1775 ***1220.12*** *p735*
Smith, James; Annapolis, MD, 1725 ***1220.12*** *p734*
Smith, James; Annapolis, MD, 1729 ***1220.12*** *p734*
Smith, James; Barbados, 1673 ***1220.12*** *p734*
Smith, James; Barbados or Jamaica, 1690 ***1220.12*** *p734*
Smith, James; Barbados or Jamaica, 1698 ***1220.12*** *p734*
Smith, James; Barbados or Jamaica, 1702 ***1220.12*** *p734*
Smith, James; Iowa, 1844 ***9228.50*** *p331*
*Wife:*Sarah Hill
*Son:*Francis Abraham
Smith, James; Jamaica, 1661 ***1220.12*** *p734*
Smith, James; North Carolina, 1792 ***1088.45*** *p32*
Smith, James; North Carolina, 1829 ***1088.45*** *p32*
Smith, James; North Carolina, 1833 ***1088.45*** *p32*
Smith, James 21; North Carolina, 1774 ***1422.10*** *p55*
Smith, James; Ohio, 1857 ***3580.20*** *p33*
Smith, James; Ohio, 1857 ***6020.12*** *p22*
Smith, James 23; Ontario, 1871 ***1823.21*** *p342*
Smith, James 31; Ontario, 1871 ***1823.21*** *p342*
Smith, James 36; Ontario, 1871 ***1823.21*** *p342*
Smith, James 37; Ontario, 1871 ***1823.21*** *p342*
Smith, James 40; Ontario, 1871 ***1823.21*** *p342*
Smith, James 42; Ontario, 1871 ***1823.21*** *p342*
Smith, James 47; Ontario, 1871 ***1823.21*** *p342*
Smith, James 49; Ontario, 1871 ***1823.17*** *p152*
Smith, James 52; Ontario, 1871 ***1823.21*** *p342*
Smith, James 58; Ontario, 1871 ***1823.17*** *p152*
Smith, James 59; Ontario, 1871 ***1823.21*** *p342*
Smith, James; Philadelphia, 1778 ***8529.30*** *p15*
Smith, James; Toronto, 1844 ***2910.35*** *p115*
Smith, James; West Indies, 1686 ***1220.12*** *p734*
Smith, James A. 37; Ontario, 1871 ***1823.17*** *p152*
Smith, James Arthur; Miami, 1935 ***4984.12*** *p39*
Smith, James C.; North Carolina, 1820-1823 ***1088.45*** *p32*
Smith, James M. 26; Indiana, 1868-1873 ***9076.20*** *p68*
Smith, James Robert; Washington, 1889 ***2770.40*** *p81*
Smith, James W. 35; Ontario, 1871 ***1823.21*** *p342*
Smith, Jane; America, 1739 ***1220.12*** *p735*
Smith, Jane; America, 1745 ***1220.12*** *p735*
Smith, Jane; America, 1749 ***1220.12*** *p735*
Smith, Jane; America, 1764 ***1220.12*** *p735*
Smith, Jane; America, 1771 ***1220.12*** *p735*
Smith, Jane 58; Ontario, 1871 ***1823.17*** *p152*
Smith, Jas J. 54; Ontario, 1871 ***1823.21*** *p342*
Smith, Jasper; America, 1674 ***1220.12*** *p735*
Smith, Jasper; America, 1771 ***1220.12*** *p735*
Smith, Jasper; Maryland, 1674-1675 ***1236.25*** *p52*
Smith, Jeremiah; America, 1760 ***1220.12*** *p735*
Smith, Jeremiah; Boston, 1726 ***1642*** *p23*
With wife
Smith, Jeremiah; Massachusetts, 1620-1775 ***1642*** *p138*
Smith, Jeremiah; Rappahannock, VA, 1728 ***1220.12*** *p735*
Smith, Jesse 24; Ontario, 1871 ***1823.21*** *p342*
Smith, Jessie 49; Michigan, 1880 ***4491.39*** *p28*
Smith, Jessie 24; Ontario, 1871 ***1823.21*** *p342*
Smith, Johanna; America, 1678 ***1220.12*** *p735*
Smith, John; America, 1663 ***1220.12*** *p735*
Smith, John; America, 1674 ***1220.12*** *p735*
Smith, John; America, 1678 ***1220.12*** *p735*
Smith, John; America, 1682 ***1220.12*** *p735*
Smith, John; America, 1685 ***1220.12*** *p735*
Smith, John; America, 1698 ***1220.12*** *p735*
Smith, John; America, 1701 ***1220.12*** *p735*
Smith, John; America, 1713 ***1220.12*** *p735*
Smith, John; America, 1721 ***1220.12*** *p735*
Smith, John; America, 1722 ***1220.12*** *p735*
Smith, John; America, 1723 ***1220.12*** *p735*
Smith, John; America, 1725 ***1220.12*** *p735*
Smith, John; America, 1726 ***1220.12*** *p735*
Smith, John; America, 1727 ***1220.12*** *p735*
Smith, John; America, 1730 ***1220.12*** *p736*
Smith, John; America, 1731 ***1220.12*** *p736*
Smith, John; America, 1734 ***1220.12*** *p736*
Smith, John; America, 1735 ***1220.12*** *p736*
Smith, John; America, 1737 ***1220.12*** *p736*
Smith, John; America, 1739 ***1220.12*** *p736*
Smith, John; America, 1740 ***1220.12*** *p736*
Smith, John; America, 1741 ***1220.12*** *p736*
Smith, John; America, 1742 ***1220.12*** *p736*
Smith, John; America, 1743 ***1220.12*** *p736*
Smith, John; America, 1744 ***1220.12*** *p736*
Smith, John; America, 1745 ***1220.12*** *p736*
Smith, John; America, 1746 ***1220.12*** *p736*
Smith, John; America, 1748 ***1220.12*** *p736*
Smith, John; America, 1749 ***1220.12*** *p736*
Smith, John; America, 1750 ***1220.12*** *p736*
Smith, John; America, 1751 ***1220.12*** *p736*
Smith, John; America, 1752 ***1220.12*** *p736*
Smith, John; America, 1753 ***1220.12*** *p736*
Smith, John; America, 1754 ***1220.12*** *p736*
Smith, John; America, 1755 ***1220.12*** *p736*
Smith, John; America, 1756 ***1220.12*** *p736*
Smith, John; America, 1756 ***1220.12*** *p737*
Smith, John; America, 1757 ***1220.12*** *p737*
Smith, John; America, 1758 ***1220.12*** *p737*
Smith, John; America, 1759 ***1220.12*** *p737*
Smith, John; America, 1760 ***1220.12*** *p737*
Smith, John; America, 1762 ***1220.12*** *p737*
Smith, John; America, 1763 ***1220.12*** *p737*
Smith, John; America, 1764 ***1220.12*** *p737*
Smith, John; America, 1765 ***1220.12*** *p737*
Smith, John; America, 1766 ***1220.12*** *p737*
Smith, John; America, 1767 ***1220.12*** *p737*
Smith, John; America, 1768 ***1220.12*** *p737*
Smith, John; America, 1769 ***1220.12*** *p737*
Smith, John; America, 1772 ***1220.12*** *p737*
Smith, John; America, 1773 ***1220.12*** *p737*
Smith, John; America, 1774 ***1220.12*** *p737*
Smith, John; America, 1775 ***1220.12*** *p737*
Smith, John; Annapolis, MD, 1721 ***1220.12*** *p735*
Smith, John; Annapolis, MD, 1726 ***1220.12*** *p735*
Smith, John; Annapolis, MD, 1730 ***1220.12*** *p736*
Smith, John; Barbados, 1664 ***1220.12*** *p735*
Smith, John; Barbados, 1669 ***1220.12*** *p735*
Smith, John; Barbados, 1679 ***1220.12*** *p735*
Smith, John; Barbados or Jamaica, 1683 ***1220.12*** *p735*
Smith, John; Barbados or Jamaica, 1684 ***1220.12*** *p735*
Smith, John; Barbados or Jamaica, 1686 ***1220.12*** *p735*
Smith, John; Barbados or Jamaica, 1700 ***1220.12*** *p735*
Smith, John; Boston, 1642 ***1642*** *p7*
Smith, John; Boston, 1721 ***1642*** *p25*
Smith, John; Boston, 1776 ***8529.30*** *p5A*
Smith, John *SEE* Smith, Nathaniel
Smith, John; Canada, 1774 ***3036.5*** *p41*
Smith, John; Colorado, 1882 ***1029.59*** *p85*
Smith, John; Colorado, 1889 ***1029.59*** *p84*
Smith, John; Colorado, 1892 ***1029.59*** *p84*
Smith, John; Died enroute, 1719 ***1220.12*** *p735*
Smith, John; Illinois, 1856 ***6079.1*** *p13*
Smith, John; Illinois, 1858-1861 ***6020.5*** *p133*
Smith, John 31; Indiana, 1890 ***9076.20*** *p72*
Smith, John; Iowa, 1919 ***1211.15*** *p19*
Smith, John; Louisiana, 1874-1875 ***4981.45*** *p30*
Smith, John; Maryland, 1674 ***1236.25*** *p50*
Smith, John; Maryland, 1736 ***1220.12*** *p736*
Smith, John; Maryland, 1742 ***1220.12*** *p736*
Smith, John; North Carolina, 1835 ***1088.45*** *p32*
Smith, John 22; North Carolina, 1774 ***1422.10*** *p55*
Smith, John; Ohio, 1809-1852 ***4511.35*** *p51*
Smith, John; Ohio, 1836 ***3580.20*** *p33*
Smith, John; Ohio, 1836 ***6020.12*** *p22*
Smith, John; Ohio, 1840-1897 ***8365.35*** *p18*
Smith, John; Ohio, 1840 ***2763.1*** *p22*
Smith, John 24; Ontario, 1871 ***1823.21*** *p343*
Smith, John 25; Ontario, 1871 ***1823.17*** *p152*
Smith, John 25; Ontario, 1871 ***1823.21*** *p342*
Smith, John 26; Ontario, 1871 ***1823.21*** *p343*
Smith, John 28; Ontario, 1871 ***1823.21*** *p343*
Smith, John 28; Ontario, 1871 ***1823.21*** *p343*
Smith, John 30; Ontario, 1871 ***1823.21*** *p343*
Smith, John 31; Ontario, 1871 ***1823.21*** *p343*
Smith, John 32; Ontario, 1871 ***1823.17*** *p152*
Smith, John 35; Ontario, 1871 ***1823.21*** *p342*
Smith, John 36; Ontario, 1871 ***1823.17*** *p152*
Smith, John 38; Ontario, 1871 ***1823.21*** *p342*
Smith, John 41; Ontario, 1871 ***1823.21*** *p342*
Smith, John 42; Ontario, 1871 ***1823.21*** *p342*
Smith, John 44; Ontario, 1871 ***1823.17*** *p152*
Smith, John 46; Ontario, 1871 ***1823.17*** *p152*
Smith, John 48; Ontario, 1871 ***1823.17*** *p152*
Smith, John 49; Ontario, 1871 ***1823.21*** *p343*
Smith, John 50; Ontario, 1871 ***1823.21*** *p342*
Smith, John 54; Ontario, 1871 ***1823.21*** *p342*
Smith, John 55; Ontario, 1871 ***1823.17*** *p152*
Smith, John 56; Ontario, 1871 ***1823.21*** *p342*
Smith, John 56; Ontario, 1871 ***1823.21*** *p342*
Smith, John 60; Ontario, 1871 ***1823.21*** *p343*
Smith, John 60; Ontario, 1871 ***1823.21*** *p343*
Smith, John 67; Ontario, 1871 ***1823.21*** *p343*
Smith, John 78; Ontario, 1871 ***1823.17*** *p152*
Smith, John 82; Ontario, 1871 ***1823.17*** *p152*
Smith, John; Philadelphia, 1778 ***8529.30*** *p15*
Smith, John; Virginia, 1721 ***1220.12*** *p735*
Smith, John; Virginia, 1730 ***1220.12*** *p735*
Smith, John; Virginia, 1738 ***1220.12*** *p736*
Smith, John; Virginia, 1741 ***1220.12*** *p736*
Smith, John; Virginia, 1745 ***1220.12*** *p736*
Smith, John; Virginia, 1765 ***1220.12*** *p737*
Smith, John; Washington, 1889 ***2770.40*** *p81*
Smith, John Adam; America, 1768 ***1220.12*** *p737*
Smith, John Daniel; Washington, 1886 ***2770.40*** *p24*
Smith, John L. 74; Ontario, 1871 ***1823.21*** *p343*
Smith, John U.; North Carolina, 1824 ***1088.45*** *p32*
Smith, John V.; Ohio, 1809-1852 ***4511.35*** *p51*
Smith, John W. 41; Ontario, 1871 ***1823.21*** *p343*
Smith, Jonas; America, 1737 ***1220.12*** *p737*
Smith, Jonas 22; Virginia, 1635 ***1183.3*** *p30*
Smith, Jonathan; America, 1749 ***1220.12*** *p738*
Smith, Jonathan; Maryland or Virginia, 1738 ***1220.12*** *p737*
Smith, Jophenix; Maryland, 1725 ***1220.12*** *p738*
Smith, Joseph; America, 1738 ***1220.12*** *p738*
Smith, Joseph; America, 1742 ***1220.12*** *p738*
Smith, Joseph; America, 1744 ***1220.12*** *p738*
Smith, Joseph; America, 1746 ***1220.12*** *p738*
Smith, Joseph; America, 1751 ***1220.12*** *p738*
Smith, Joseph; America, 1752 ***1220.12*** *p738*
Smith, Joseph; America, 1757 ***1220.12*** *p738*
Smith, Joseph; America, 1764 ***1220.12*** *p738*
Smith, Joseph; America, 1766 ***1220.12*** *p738*
Smith, Joseph; America, 1767 ***1220.12*** *p738*
Smith, Joseph; America, 1768 ***1220.12*** *p738*
Smith, Joseph; America, 1769 ***1220.12*** *p738*
Smith, Joseph; America, 1770 ***1220.12*** *p738*
Smith, Joseph; America, 1771 ***1220.12*** *p738*
Smith, Joseph; America, 1772 ***1220.12*** *p738*
Smith, Joseph; America, 1773 ***1220.12*** *p738*
Smith, Joseph; Annapolis, MD, 1723 ***1220.12*** *p738*
Smith, Joseph; Annapolis, MD, 1729 ***1220.12*** *p738*
Smith, Joseph; Barbados, 1668 ***1220.12*** *p738*
Smith, Joseph; Barbados or Jamaica, 1674 ***1220.12*** *p738*
Smith, Joseph; Charles Town, SC, 1719 ***1220.12*** *p738*
Smith, Joseph; Maryland, 1725 ***1220.12*** *p738*
Smith, Joseph; Ohio, 1840 ***3580.20*** *p33*
Smith, Joseph; Ohio, 1840 ***6020.12*** *p22*
Smith, Joseph 35; Ontario, 1871 ***1823.17*** *p152*
Smith, Joseph 39; Ontario, 1871 ***1823.17*** *p152*
Smith, Joseph; South Carolina, 1813 ***3208.30*** *p18*
Smith, Joseph; South Carolina, 1813 ***3208.30*** *p31*
Smith, Joseph 26; South Carolina, 1812 ***3476.30*** *p13*
Smith, Joseph; Virginia, 1769 ***1220.12*** *p738*
Smith, Joshua; America, 1766 ***1220.12*** *p738*
Smith, Josiah; Massachusetts, 1743 ***1642*** *p89*
Smith, Judith; Virginia, 1730 ***1220.12*** *p738*
Smith, Julius; Colorado, 1884 ***1029.59*** *p84*
Smith, Julius D.; Ohio, 1840-1897 ***8365.35*** *p18*
Smith, Katherine; America, 1680 ***1220.12*** *p731*
Smith, Katherine; Barbados or Jamaica, 1687 ***1220.12*** *p731*
Smith, L. 10; Quebec, 1870 ***8364.32*** *p26*
Smith, Lawrence; America, 1772 ***1220.12*** *p738*
Smith, Leonard 50; Ontario, 1871 ***1823.21*** *p343*
Smith, Leslie; South Carolina, 1840 ***6155.4*** *p19*
Smith, Levy; Virginia, 1767 ***1220.12*** *p738*
Smith, Lewis; Ohio, 1809-1852 ***4511.35*** *p51*
Smith, Lewis H. 31; Ontario, 1871 ***1823.21*** *p343*
Smith, Lonsom 60; Ontario, 1871 ***1823.21*** *p343*
Smith, Loomus; America, 1758 ***1220.12*** *p738*
Smith, Louisa; America, 1770 ***1220.12*** *p738*
Smith, Lucy C. 35; Michigan, 1880 ***4491.36*** *p19*
Smith, Luke; America, 1724 ***1220.12*** *p738*
Smith, Luke; America, 1765 ***1220.12*** *p738*
Smith, Lydia 59; Ontario, 1871 ***1823.21*** *p343*
Smith, Lyon; America, 1766 ***1220.12*** *p738*
Smith, Maire E. 58; Ontario, 1871 ***1823.21*** *p343*
Smith, Maisey; America, 1758 ***1220.12*** *p738*
Smith, Malcolm 45; Ontario, 1871 ***1823.21*** *p343*
Smith, Malm 64; North Carolina, 1774 ***1422.10*** *p62*
Smith, Malm. 64; North Carolina, 1774 ***1422.10*** *p58*
Smith, Malon 38; Ohio, 1880 ***4879.40*** *p257*
Smith, Mandana 56; Ontario, 1871 ***1823.21*** *p343*
Smith, Margaret; America, 1683 ***1220.12*** *p738*
Smith, Margaret; America, 1737 ***1220.12*** *p738*
Smith, Margaret; America, 1745 ***1220.12*** *p738*
Smith, Margaret; America, 1746 ***1220.12*** *p738*
Smith, Margaret; America, 1756 ***1220.12*** *p738*
Smith, Margaret; America, 1759 ***1220.12*** *p738*
Smith, Margaret; America, 1760 ***1220.12*** *p738*
Smith, Margaret; Annapolis, MD, 1719 ***1220.12*** *p738*
Smith, Margaret; Boston, 1752 ***1642*** *p46*
Smith, Margaret 56; Michigan, 1880 ***4491.33*** *p21*
Smith, Margaret; New Orleans, 1851 ***7242.30*** *p154*
Smith, Margaret 40; Ontario, 1871 ***1823.21*** *p343*
Smith, Margery; Barbados, 1694 ***1220.12*** *p738*

Smith, Mark; Barbados, 1671 ***1220.12*** *p738*
Smith, Martha; America, 1739 ***1220.12*** *p739*
Smith, Martha; America, 1744 ***1220.12*** *p739*
Smith, Martha; America, 1753 ***1220.12*** *p739*
Smith, Martha; America, 1772 ***1220.12*** *p739*
Smith, Martha; Virginia, 1721 ***1220.12*** *p738*
Smith, Marthe; America, 1745 ***1220.12*** *p739*
Smith, Martin 47; Ontario, 1871 ***1823.17*** *p152*
Smith, Mary; America, 1699 ***1220.12*** *p739*
Smith, Mary; America, 1715 ***1220.12*** *p739*
Smith, Mary; America, 1716 ***1220.12*** *p739*
Smith, Mary; America, 1719 ***1220.12*** *p739*
Smith, Mary; America, 1722 ***1220.12*** *p739*
Smith, Mary; America, 1724 ***1220.12*** *p739*
Smith, Mary; America, 1727 ***1220.12*** *p739*
Smith, Mary; America, 1734 ***1220.12*** *p739*
Smith, Mary; America, 1743 ***1220.12*** *p739*
Smith, Mary; America, 1744 ***1220.12*** *p739*
Smith, Mary; America, 1746 ***1220.12*** *p739*
Smith, Mary; America, 1747 ***1220.12*** *p739*
Smith, Mary; America, 1748 ***1220.12*** *p739*
Smith, Mary; America, 1750 ***1220.12*** *p739*
Smith, Mary; America, 1751 ***1220.12*** *p740*
Smith, Mary; America, 1753 ***1220.12*** *p740*
Smith, Mary; America, 1755 ***1220.12*** *p740*
Smith, Mary; America, 1756 ***1220.12*** *p740*
Smith, Mary; America, 1757 ***1220.12*** *p740*
Smith, Mary; America, 1758 ***1220.12*** *p740*
Smith, Mary; America, 1760 ***1220.12*** *p740*
Smith, Mary; America, 1761 ***1220.12*** *p740*
Smith, Mary; America, 1763 ***1220.12*** *p740*
Smith, Mary; America, 1764 ***1220.12*** *p740*
Smith, Mary; America, 1765 ***1220.12*** *p740*
Smith, Mary; America, 1766 ***1220.12*** *p740*
Smith, Mary; America, 1767 ***1220.12*** *p740*
Smith, Mary; America, 1770 ***1220.12*** *p740*
Smith, Mary; America, 1772 ***1220.12*** *p740*
Smith, Mary; America, 1773 ***1220.12*** *p740*
Smith, Mary; America, 1774 ***1220.12*** *p740*
Smith, Mary; America, 1775 ***1220.12*** *p740*
Smith, Mary; Annapolis, MD, 1722 ***1220.12*** *p739*
Smith, Mary; Annapolis, MD, 1731 ***1220.12*** *p739*
Smith, Mary; Annapolis, MD, 1736 ***1220.12*** *p739*
Smith, Mary; Barbados, 1671 ***1220.12*** *p739*
Smith, Mary; Barbados, 1681 ***1220.12*** *p739*
Smith, Mary; Barbados, 1694 ***1220.12*** *p739*
Smith, Mary; Barbados or Jamaica, 1691 ***1220.12*** *p739*
Smith, Mary; Barbados or Jamaica, 1694 ***1220.12*** *p739*
Smith, Mary; Canada, 1774 ***3036.5*** *p41*
Smith, Mary; Charles Town, SC, 1718 ***1220.12*** *p739*
Smith, Mary; Died enroute, 1734 ***1220.12*** *p739*
Smith, Mary; Jamaica, 1661 ***1220.12*** *p739*
Smith, Mary; Maryland, 1720 ***1220.12*** *p739*
Smith, Mary; Maryland, 1735 ***1220.12*** *p739*
Smith, Mary; New Orleans, 1851 ***7242.30*** *p154*
Smith, Mary; North Carolina, 1774 ***1422.10*** *p62*
Smith, Mary 19; North Carolina, 1774 ***1422.10*** *p58*
Smith, Mary 64; North Carolina, 1774 ***1422.10*** *p58*
Smith, Mary 64; North Carolina, 1774 ***1422.10*** *p62*
Smith, Mary 20; Ontario, 1871 ***1823.17*** *p152*
Smith, Mary 23; Ontario, 1871 ***1823.17*** *p152*
Smith, Mary 35; Ontario, 1871 ***1823.21*** *p343*
Smith, Mary 35; Ontario, 1871 ***1823.21*** *p343*
Smith, Mary 60; Ontario, 1871 ***1823.21*** *p343*
Smith, Mary; Potomac, 1731 ***1220.12*** *p739*
Smith, Mary; Virginia, 1728 ***1220.12*** *p739*
Smith, Mary; Virginia, 1732 ***1220.12*** *p739*
Smith, Mary; Virginia, 1735 ***1220.12*** *p739*
Smith, Mary; Virginia, 1736 ***1220.12*** *p739*
Smith, Mary; Virginia, 1738 ***1220.12*** *p739*
Smith, Mary; Virginia, 1741 ***1220.12*** *p739*
Smith, Mary E. 26; Ohio, 1880 ***4879.40*** *p259*
Smith, Mary Greeley; Quebec, 1791-1878 ***9228.50*** *p407*
Smith, Mary R. 25; Ontario, 1871 ***1823.21*** *p343*
Smith, Maryann 51; Ontario, 1871 ***1823.21*** *p343*
Smith, Mathew; America, 1768 ***1220.12*** *p740*
Smith, Matthew; America, 1720 ***1220.12*** *p740*
Smith, Matthias; Ohio, 1809-1852 ***4511.35*** *p51*
Smith, Michael; America, 1740 ***1220.12*** *p740*
Smith, Michael; Illinois, 1858-1861 ***6020.5*** *p133*
Smith, Michael; Maryland, 1720 ***1220.12*** *p740*
Smith, Michael; North Carolina, 1860 ***1088.45*** *p32*
Smith, Michael; Ohio, 1809-1852 ***4511.35*** *p51*
Smith, Michael 31; Ontario, 1871 ***1823.21*** *p343*
Smith, Michael 63; Ontario, 1871 ***1823.17*** *p152*
Smith, Middlemore; Virginia, 1739 ***1220.12*** *p740*
Smith, Mtgomery 33; Ontario, 1871 ***1823.21*** *p343*
Smith, Nathan; Boston, 1775 ***8529.30*** *p3*
Smith, Nathaniel; America, 1729 ***1220.12*** *p740*
Smith, Nathaniel *SEE* Smith, Nathaniel
Smith, Nathaniel; Canada, 1774 ***3036.5*** *p40*
*Wife:*Elizabeth
*Child:*Nathaniel
*Child:*Robert
*Child:*Elizabeth
*Child:*Rachael
*Child:*John
Smith, Neil 17; Ontario, 1871 ***1823.21*** *p343*
Smith, Nelson; Cleveland, OH, 1881-1892 ***9722.10*** *p127*
Smith, Nelson 31; Ontario, 1871 ***1823.21*** *p343*
Smith, Nichlas; North Carolina, 1876 ***1088.45*** *p33*
Smith, Nicholas; America, 1685 ***1220.12*** *p740*
Smith, Nicholas; Illinois, 1858-1861 ***6020.5*** *p133*
Smith, Nicholas; Ohio, 1809-1852 ***4511.35*** *p51*
Smith, Ophelia; America, 1720 ***1220.12*** *p740*
Smith, Oramatha 28; Ontario, 1871 ***1823.17*** *p152*
Smith, Parker; America, 1745 ***1220.12*** *p740*
Smith, Patrick; America, 1767 ***1220.12*** *p740*
Smith, Patrick; Ohio, 1809-1852 ***4511.35*** *p51*
Smith, Patrick; Toronto, 1844 ***2910.35*** *p115*
Smith, Patt; Jamaica, 1776 ***8529.30*** *p14A*
Smith, Peter; America, 1770 ***1220.12*** *p740*
Smith, Peter 26; Kentucky, 1840 ***778.6*** *p313*
Smith, Peter; North Carolina, 1774 ***1422.10*** *p62*
Smith, Peter 23; North Carolina, 1774 ***1422.10*** *p58*
Smith, Peter; Ohio, 1809-1852 ***4511.35*** *p51*
Smith, Peter 31; Ontario, 1871 ***1823.21*** *p344*
Smith, Peter 44; Ontario, 1871 ***1823.21*** *p344*
Smith, Peter 46; Ontario, 1871 ***1823.21*** *p344*
Smith, Peter 50; Ontario, 1871 ***1823.17*** *p152*
Smith, Peter 70; Ontario, 1871 ***1823.21*** *p344*
Smith, Philip; America, 1685 ***1220.12*** *p740*
Smith, Philip; Maine, 1840 ***3274.56*** *p101*
Smith, Philip; Ohio, 1809-1852 ***4511.35*** *p51*
Smith, Philo D. 35; Michigan, 1880 ***4491.36*** *p20*
Smith, R. C. 67; Ontario, 1871 ***1823.21*** *p344*
Smith, R. Fredrick 39; Ontario, 1871 ***1823.21*** *p344*
Smith, Rachael; America, 1715 ***1220.12*** *p740*
Smith, Rachael *SEE* Smith, Nathaniel
Smith, Ralph; America, 1721 ***1220.12*** *p740*
Smith, Ralph; America, 1767 ***1220.12*** *p740*
Smith, Ralph; Barbados, 1694 ***1220.12*** *p740*
Smith, Randall; America, 1754 ***1220.12*** *p740*
Smith, Rebecca; America, 1772 ***1220.12*** *p740*
Smith, Reuben G.; North Carolina, 1860 ***1088.45*** *p33*
Smith, Richard; America, 1662 ***1220.12*** *p740*
Smith, Richard; America, 1713 ***1220.12*** *p741*
Smith, Richard; America, 1721 ***1220.12*** *p741*
Smith, Richard; America, 1729 ***1220.12*** *p741*
Smith, Richard; America, 1739 ***1220.12*** *p741*
Smith, Richard; America, 1741 ***1220.12*** *p741*
Smith, Richard; America, 1743 ***1220.12*** *p741*
Smith, Richard; America, 1753 ***1220.12*** *p741*
Smith, Richard; America, 1754 ***1220.12*** *p741*
Smith, Richard; America, 1755 ***1220.12*** *p741*
Smith, Richard; America, 1756 ***1220.12*** *p741*
Smith, Richard; America, 1760 ***1220.12*** *p741*
Smith, Richard; America, 1763 ***1220.12*** *p741*
Smith, Richard; America, 1764 ***1220.12*** *p741*
Smith, Richard; America, 1765 ***1220.12*** *p741*
Smith, Richard; America, 1767 ***1220.12*** *p741*
Smith, Richard; America, 1768 ***1220.12*** *p741*
Smith, Richard; America, 1769 ***1220.12*** *p741*
Smith, Richard; America, 1770 ***1220.12*** *p741*
Smith, Richard; America, 1772 ***1220.12*** *p741*
Smith, Richard; America, 1773 ***1220.12*** *p741*
Smith, Richard; Annapolis, MD, 1730 ***1220.12*** *p741*
Smith, Richard; Barbados, 1683 ***1220.12*** *p740*
Smith, Richard; Barbados or Jamaica, 1693 ***1220.12*** *p740*
Smith, Richard; Barbados or Jamaica, 1700 ***1220.12*** *p740*
Smith, Richard; Jamestown, VA, 1633 ***1658.20*** *p211*
*Wife:*Elvas Clay
With daughter
Smith, Richard; Louisiana, 1874 ***4981.45*** *p297*
Smith, Richard; Maryland, 1672 ***1236.25*** *p47*
Smith, Richard; New York, 1775 ***8529.30*** *p16*
Smith, Richard 55; Ontario, 1871 ***1823.21*** *p344*
Smith, Richard 60; Ontario, 1871 ***1823.17*** *p152*
Smith, Richard P. 39; Ontario, 1871 ***1823.17*** *p152*
Smith, Ritchard 55; Ontario, 1871 ***1823.21*** *p344*
Smith, Robert; America, 1674 ***1220.12*** *p741*
Smith, Robert; America, 1680 ***1220.12*** *p741*
Smith, Robert; America, 1685 ***1220.12*** *p741*
Smith, Robert; America, 1725 ***1220.12*** *p741*
Smith, Robert; America, 1732 ***1220.12*** *p741*
Smith, Robert; America, 1741 ***1220.12*** *p741*
Smith, Robert; America, 1749 ***1220.12*** *p741*
Smith, Robert; America, 1760 ***1220.12*** *p741*
Smith, Robert; America, 1766 ***1220.12*** *p741*
Smith, Robert; America, 1767 ***1220.12*** *p741*
Smith, Robert; America, 1769 ***1220.12*** *p741*
Smith, Robert; America, 1774 ***1220.12*** *p741*
Smith, Robert; Barbados, 1699 ***1220.12*** *p741*
Smith, Robert; Barbados or Jamaica, 1693 ***1220.12*** *p741*
Smith, Robert *SEE* Smith, Nathaniel
Smith, Robert; Colorado, 1881 ***1029.59*** *p85*
Smith, Robert; Jamaica, 1778 ***8529.30*** *p14A*
Smith, Robert; Maryland, 1729 ***1220.12*** *p741*
Smith, Robert; Maryland or Virginia, 1731 ***1220.12*** *p741*
Smith, Robert 54; Michigan, 1880 ***4491.33*** *p21*
Smith, Robert; North Carolina, 1798 ***1088.45*** *p33*
Smith, Robert; Ohio, 1840-1897 ***8365.35*** *p18*
Smith, Robert 37; Ontario, 1871 ***1823.21*** *p344*
Smith, Robert 38; Ontario, 1871 ***1823.21*** *p344*
Smith, Robert 43; Ontario, 1871 ***1823.17*** *p153*
Smith, Robert 46; Ontario, 1871 ***1823.21*** *p344*
Smith, Robert 48; Ontario, 1871 ***1823.17*** *p153*
Smith, Robert 50; Ontario, 1871 ***1823.21*** *p344*
Smith, Robert 50; Ontario, 1871 ***1823.21*** *p344*
Smith, Robert; Philadelphia, 1778 ***8529.30*** *p5A*
Smith, Robert; Potomac, 1729 ***1220.12*** *p741*
Smith, Robert; South Carolina, 1813 ***3208.30*** *p18*
Smith, Robert; South Carolina, 1813 ***3208.30*** *p31*
Smith, Robert 29; South Carolina, 1812 ***3476.30*** *p13*
Smith, Robert; Virginia, 1652 ***6254.4*** *p243*
Smith, Robt 64; Ontario, 1871 ***1823.21*** *p344*
Smith, Roger; America, 1721 ***1220.12*** *p741*
Smith, Roger; Barbados, 1701 ***1220.12*** *p741*
Smith, Roger 65; Ontario, 1871 ***1823.21*** *p344*
Smith, Rose; Maryland or Virginia, 1740 ***1220.12*** *p742*
Smith, Russell B. 28; Ontario, 1871 ***1823.21*** *p344*
Smith, Salina 18; Ontario, 1871 ***1823.21*** *p344*
Smith, Samuel; America, 1688 ***1220.12*** *p742*
Smith, Samuel; America, 1695 ***1220.12*** *p742*
Smith, Samuel; America, 1735 ***1220.12*** *p742*
Smith, Samuel; America, 1737 ***1220.12*** *p742*
Smith, Samuel; America, 1738 ***1220.12*** *p742*
Smith, Samuel; America, 1751 ***1220.12*** *p742*
Smith, Samuel; America, 1758 ***1220.12*** *p742*
Smith, Samuel; America, 1764 ***1220.12*** *p742*
Smith, Samuel; America, 1767 ***1220.12*** *p742*
Smith, Samuel; America, 1770 ***1220.12*** *p742*
Smith, Samuel; America, 1772 ***1220.12*** *p742*
Smith, Samuel; America, 1774 ***1220.12*** *p742*
Smith, Samuel 41; Ontario, 1871 ***1823.17*** *p153*
Smith, Samuel 44; Ontario, 1871 ***1823.21*** *p344*
Smith, Samuel; Philadelphia, 1778 ***8529.30*** *p3*
Smith, Sara; Barbados, 1677 ***1220.12*** *p742*
Smith, Sarah; America, 1734 ***1220.12*** *p742*
Smith, Sarah; America, 1744 ***1220.12*** *p742*
Smith, Sarah; America, 1751 ***1220.12*** *p742*
Smith, Sarah; America, 1755 ***1220.12*** *p742*
Smith, Sarah; America, 1757 ***1220.12*** *p742*
Smith, Sarah; America, 1762 ***1220.12*** *p742*
Smith, Sarah; America, 1764 ***1220.12*** *p742*
Smith, Sarah; America, 1769 ***1220.12*** *p742*
Smith, Sarah; America, 1771 ***1220.12*** *p742*
Smith, Sarah; America, 1773 ***1220.12*** *p742*
Smith, Sarah; America, 1774 ***1220.12*** *p742*
Smith, Sarah; Annapolis, MD, 1719 ***1220.12*** *p742*
Smith, Sarah; Died enroute, 1736 ***1220.12*** *p742*
Smith, Sarah Hill *SEE* Smith, James
Smith, Sarah 48; Ontario, 1871 ***1823.17*** *p153*
Smith, Sarah; Virginia, 1735 ***1220.12*** *p742*
Smith, Sarah Ann 36; Ontario, 1871 ***1823.21*** *p344*
Smith, Sarah E. 50; Ontario, 1871 ***1823.21*** *p344*
Smith, Selena 36; Ontario, 1871 ***1823.17*** *p153*
Smith, Sharpisis; America, 1742 ***1220.12*** *p742*
Smith, Sidney 63; Ontario, 1871 ***1823.21*** *p344*
Smith, Simon; America, 1682 ***1220.12*** *p742*
Smith, Simon; America, 1753 ***1220.12*** *p742*
Smith, Smith; America, 1756 ***1220.12*** *p742*
Smith, Solomon; America, 1751 ***1220.12*** *p742*
Smith, Stephen; America, 1739 ***1220.12*** *p742*
Smith, Stephen; America, 1753 ***1220.12*** *p742*
Smith, Stephen; America, 1759 ***1220.12*** *p742*
Smith, Stephen; America, 1764 ***1220.12*** *p742*
Smith, Susan; Annapolis, MD, 1736 ***1220.12*** *p742*
Smith, Susan; Barbados, 1681 ***1220.12*** *p742*
Smith, Susanna; America, 1722 ***1220.12*** *p742*
Smith, Susanna; America, 1748 ***1220.12*** *p742*
Smith, Susanna; America, 1754 ***1220.12*** *p743*
Smith, Susanna; America, 1755 ***1220.12*** *p743*
Smith, Susanna; Maine, 1640-1688 ***9228.50*** *p172*
Smith, Susanna; Maine, 1640-1688 ***9228.50*** *p172*
Smith, Susanna; Maine, 1688 ***9228.50*** *p600*
Smith, Susannah; America, 1721 ***1220.12*** *p742*
Smith, Susannah; America, 1759 ***1220.12*** *p743*
Smith, Susannah; America, 1767 ***1220.12*** *p743*
Smith, Susannah; Virginia, 1774 ***1220.12*** *p743*
Smith, Tabitha 24; Ontario, 1871 ***1823.21*** *p344*
Smith, Terence; America, 1761 ***1220.12*** *p743*
Smith, Theobalt; Ohio, 1809-1852 ***4511.35*** *p51*
Smith, Thomas; America, 1672 ***1220.12*** *p743*
Smith, Thomas; America, 1678 ***1220.12*** *p743*
Smith, Thomas; America, 1685 ***1220.12*** *p743*
Smith, Thomas; America, 1688 ***1220.12*** *p743*
Smith, Thomas; America, 1692 ***1220.12*** *p743*
Smith, Thomas; America, 1694 ***1220.12*** *p743*

Smith, Thomas; America, 1700 ***1220.12*** *p743*
Smith, Thomas; America, 1715 ***1220.12*** *p743*
Smith, Thomas; America, 1727 ***1220.12*** *p743*
Smith, Thomas; America, 1728 ***1220.12*** *p743*
Smith, Thomas; America, 1736 ***1220.12*** *p743*
Smith, Thomas; America, 1739 ***1220.12*** *p743*
Smith, Thomas; America, 1741 ***1220.12*** *p743*
Smith, Thomas; America, 1742 ***1220.12*** *p743*
Smith, Thomas; America, 1744 ***1220.12*** *p743*
Smith, Thomas; America, 1745 ***1220.12*** *p743*
Smith, Thomas; America, 1746 ***1220.12*** *p743*
Smith, Thomas; America, 1749 ***1220.12*** *p743*
Smith, Thomas; America, 1750 ***1220.12*** *p743*
Smith, Thomas; America, 1751 ***1220.12*** *p743*
Smith, Thomas; America, 1752 ***1220.12*** *p743*
Smith, Thomas; America, 1753 ***1220.12*** *p744*
Smith, Thomas; America, 1754 ***1220.12*** *p744*
Smith, Thomas; America, 1755 ***1220.12*** *p744*
Smith, Thomas; America, 1756 ***1220.12*** *p744*
Smith, Thomas; America, 1758 ***1220.12*** *p744*
Smith, Thomas; America, 1759 ***1220.12*** *p744*
Smith, Thomas; America, 1760 ***1220.12*** *p744*
Smith, Thomas; America, 1761 ***1220.12*** *p744*
Smith, Thomas; America, 1764 ***1220.12*** *p744*
Smith, Thomas; America, 1765 ***1220.12*** *p744*
Smith, Thomas; America, 1767 ***1220.12*** *p744*
Smith, Thomas; America, 1769 ***1220.12*** *p744*
Smith, Thomas; America, 1771 ***1220.12*** *p744*
Smith, Thomas; America, 1772 ***1220.12*** *p744*
Smith, Thomas; America, 1775 ***1220.12*** *p744*
Smith, Thomas; Annapolis, MD, 1723 ***1220.12*** *p743*
Smith, Thomas 35; Annapolis, MD, 1721 ***1220.12*** *p743*
Smith, Thomas 31; Baltimore, 1775 ***1220.12*** *p744*
Smith, Thomas; Barbados, 1666 ***1220.12*** *p743*
Smith, Thomas; Barbados, 1679 ***1220.12*** *p743*
Smith, Thomas; Barbados, 1698 ***1220.12*** *p743*
Smith, Thomas; Barbados or Jamaica, 1685 ***1220.12*** *p743*
Smith, Thomas; Charles Town, SC, 1719 ***1220.12*** *p743*
Smith, Thomas; Died enroute, 1723 ***1220.12*** *p743*
Smith, Thomas; Died enroute, 1725 ***1220.12*** *p743*
Smith, Thomas; New York, 1778 ***8529.30*** *p7*
Smith, Thomas; North Carolina, 1839 ***1088.45*** *p33*
Smith, Thomas; North Carolina, 1854 ***1088.45*** *p33*
Smith, Thomas 5; Ontario, 1871 ***1823.21*** *p344*
Smith, Thomas 34; Ontario, 1871 ***1823.17*** *p153*
Smith, Thomas 45; Ontario, 1871 ***1823.21*** *p344*
Smith, Thomas 50; Ontario, 1871 ***1823.17*** *p153*
Smith, Thomas 52; Ontario, 1871 ***1823.21*** *p344*
Smith, Thomas 59; Ontario, 1871 ***1823.21*** *p344*
Smith, Thomas 80; Ontario, 1871 ***1823.21*** *p344*
Smith, Thomas; Toronto, 1844 ***2910.35*** *p115*
Smith, Thomas; Virginia, 1721 ***1220.12*** *p743*
Smith, Thomas; Virginia, 1767 ***1220.12*** *p744*
Smith, Thomas; Virginia, 1768 ***1220.12*** *p744*
Smith, Thomas, Jr.; Toronto, 1844 ***2910.35*** *p115*
Smith, Thomas Francis 26; Ontario, 1871 ***1823.21*** *p344*
Smith, Thomas L. 40; Ontario, 1871 ***1823.17*** *p153*
Smith, Thomas P.; Ohio, 1836 ***2763.1*** *p22*
Smith, Thompson S.; Colorado, 1891 ***1029.59*** *p85*
Smith, Tilden 18; Ontario, 1871 ***1823.17*** *p153*
Smith, Uryas; Jamestown, VA, 1633 ***1658.20*** *p211*
Smith, W. S. 50; Ontario, 1871 ***1823.21*** *p344*
Smith, Walter 52; Ontario, 1871 ***1823.21*** *p344*
Smith, Walter 66; Ontario, 1871 ***1823.17*** *p153*
Smith, William; America, 1656 ***1220.12*** *p744*
Smith, William; America, 1678 ***1220.12*** *p744*
Smith, William; America, 1683 ***1220.12*** *p744*
Smith, William; America, 1684 ***1220.12*** *p744*
Smith, William; America, 1685 ***1220.12*** *p744*
Smith, William; America, 1697 ***1220.12*** *p744*
Smith, William; America, 1698 ***1220.12*** *p744*
Smith, William; America, 1700 ***1220.12*** *p744*
Smith, William; America, 1701 ***1220.12*** *p745*
Smith, William; America, 1720 ***1220.12*** *p745*
Smith, William; America, 1721 ***1220.12*** *p745*
Smith, William; America, 1722 ***1220.12*** *p745*
Smith, William; America, 1724 ***1220.12*** *p745*
Smith, William; America, 1726 ***1220.12*** *p745*
Smith, William; America, 1727 ***1220.12*** *p745*
Smith, William; America, 1728 ***1220.12*** *p745*
Smith, William; America, 1731 ***1220.12*** *p745*
Smith, William; America, 1733 ***1220.12*** *p745*
Smith, William; America, 1735 ***1220.12*** *p745*
Smith, William; America, 1743 ***1220.12*** *p745*
Smith, William; America, 1744 ***1220.12*** *p745*
Smith, William; America, 1749 ***1220.12*** *p745*
Smith, William; America, 1750 ***1220.12*** *p745*
Smith, William; America, 1751 ***1220.12*** *p745*
Smith, William; America, 1753 ***1220.12*** *p745*
Smith, William; America, 1754 ***1220.12*** *p745*
Smith, William; America, 1755 ***1220.12*** *p745*
Smith, William; America, 1756 ***1220.12*** *p745*
Smith, William; America, 1757 ***1220.12*** *p745*
Smith, William; America, 1758 ***1220.12*** *p745*
Smith, William; America, 1759 ***1220.12*** *p745*
Smith, William; America, 1762 ***1220.12*** *p745*
Smith, William; America, 1763 ***1220.12*** *p745*
Smith, William; America, 1764 ***1220.12*** *p746*
Smith, William; America, 1765 ***1220.12*** *p746*
Smith, William; America, 1766 ***1220.12*** *p746*
Smith, William; America, 1767 ***1220.12*** *p746*
Smith, William; America, 1768 ***1220.12*** *p746*
Smith, William; America, 1769 ***1220.12*** *p746*
Smith, William; America, 1770 ***1220.12*** *p746*
Smith, William; America, 1771 ***1220.12*** *p746*
Smith, William; America, 1772 ***1220.12*** *p746*
Smith, William; America, 1773 ***1220.12*** *p746*
Smith, William; America, 1774 ***1220.12*** *p746*
Smith, William; Annapolis, MD, 1726 ***1220.12*** *p745*
Smith, William; Annapolis, MD, 1731 ***1220.12*** *p745*
Smith, William; Annapolis, MD, 1735 ***1220.12*** *p745*
Smith, William; Barbados, 1668 ***1220.12*** *p744*
Smith, William; Barbados, 1694 ***1220.12*** *p744*
Smith, William; Barbados or Jamaica, 1697 ***1220.12*** *p744*
Smith, William; Barbados or Jamaica, 1700 ***1220.12*** *p744*
Smith, William; Barbados or Jamaica, 1715 ***1220.12*** *p745*
Smith, William; Illinois, 1855 ***6079.1*** *p13*
Smith, William; Jamaica, 1783 ***8529.30*** *p14A*
Smith, William; Long Island, 1781 ***8529.30*** *p10A*
Smith, William; Louisiana, 1874 ***4981.45*** *p134*
Smith, William; Maryland, 1726 ***1220.12*** *p745*
Smith, William; North Carolina, 1842 ***1088.45*** *p33*
Smith, William; Ohio, 1809-1852 ***4511.35*** *p51*
Smith, William 24; Ontario, 1871 ***1823.21*** *p345*
Smith, William 25; Ontario, 1871 ***1823.17*** *p153*
Smith, William 25; Ontario, 1871 ***1823.21*** *p345*
Smith, William 27; Ontario, 1871 ***1823.17*** *p153*
Smith, William 30; Ontario, 1871 ***1823.21*** *p345*
Smith, William 31; Ontario, 1871 ***1823.21*** *p344*
Smith, William 31; Ontario, 1871 ***1823.21*** *p345*
Smith, William 32; Ontario, 1871 ***1823.21*** *p345*
Smith, William 33; Ontario, 1871 ***1823.21*** *p345*
Smith, William 34; Ontario, 1871 ***1823.21*** *p345*
Smith, William 36; Ontario, 1871 ***1823.21*** *p344*
Smith, William 36; Ontario, 1871 ***1823.21*** *p345*
Smith, William 37; Ontario, 1871 ***1823.17*** *p153*
Smith, William 37; Ontario, 1871 ***1823.21*** *p345*
Smith, William 38; Ontario, 1871 ***1823.21*** *p345*
Smith, William 39; Ontario, 1871 ***1823.21*** *p344*
Smith, William 40; Ontario, 1871 ***1823.21*** *p344*
Smith, William 42; Ontario, 1871 ***1823.21*** *p345*
Smith, William 45; Ontario, 1871 ***1823.21*** *p344*
Smith, William 49; Ontario, 1871 ***1823.21*** *p345*
Smith, William 50; Ontario, 1871 ***1823.21*** *p344*
Smith, William 52; Ontario, 1871 ***1823.17*** *p153*
Smith, William 54; Ontario, 1871 ***1823.17*** *p153*
Smith, William 56; Ontario, 1871 ***1823.17*** *p153*
Smith, William 76; Ontario, 1871 ***1823.17*** *p153*
Smith, William; Toronto, 1844 ***2910.35*** *p113*
Smith, William; Virginia, 1723 ***1220.12*** *p745*
Smith, William; Virginia, 1726 ***1220.12*** *p745*
Smith, William; Virginia, 1736 ***1220.12*** *p745*
Smith, William; Virginia, 1740 ***1220.12*** *p745*
Smith, William; Virginia, 1741 ***1220.12*** *p745*
Smith, William; Virginia, 1760 ***1220.12*** *p745*
Smith, William; Virginia, 1764 ***1220.12*** *p746*
Smith, William; Virginia, 1767 ***1220.12*** *p746*
Smith, William; Virginia, 1772 ***1220.12*** *p746*
Smith, William C. 33; Ontario, 1871 ***1823.21*** *p345*
Smith, William F. 51; Ontario, 1871 ***1823.17*** *p153*
Smith, William H. 31; Ontario, 1871 ***1823.21*** *p345*
Smith, William S. 48; Ontario, 1871 ***1823.17*** *p153*
Smith, William S. 50; Ontario, 1871 ***1823.21*** *p345*
Smith, William Watkins; America, 1763 ***1220.12*** *p746*
Smith, Winifred; America, 1720 ***1220.12*** *p746*
Smith, Wm 80; Ontario, 1871 ***1823.21*** *p345*
Smith, Wm B. 44; Ontario, 1871 ***1823.21*** *p345*
Smith, Wm.; Ohio, 1840-1897 ***8365.35*** *p18*
Smith, Wm. 50; Ontario, 1871 ***1823.17*** *p153*
Smith, Zachary; America, 1724 ***1220.12*** *p746*
Smitham, Stacey; Maryland, 1721 ***1220.12*** *p746*
Smither, John; Barbados, 1665 ***1220.12*** *p746*
Smithergill, John; America, 1694 ***1220.12*** *p746*
Smithern, John; Colorado, 1891 ***1029.59*** *p85*
Smithern, John; Colorado, 1902 ***1029.59*** *p85*
Smithern, Mary J. 20; Ontario, 1871 ***1823.21*** *p345*
Smithers, Ann; America, 1773 ***1220.12*** *p746*
Smithers, Elijah 28; Ontario, 1871 ***1823.21*** *p345*
Smithers, Elizabeth; America, 1757 ***1220.12*** *p746*
Smithers, William 58; Ontario, 1871 ***1823.21*** *p345*
Smithhurst, Sidney; North Carolina, 1858 ***1088.45*** *p33*
Smithiard, Giles 21; Barbados, 1664 ***1220.12*** *p746*
Smithiman, Thomas; America, 1750 ***1220.12*** *p746*
Smithrim, Ann 50; Ontario, 1871 ***1823.21*** *p345*
Smithrim, Richard 43; Ontario, 1871 ***1823.21*** *p345*
Smithson, John; America, 1761 ***1220.12*** *p746*
Smithson, Joseph; America, 1738 ***1220.12*** *p746*
Smithson, Mary 26; Maryland, 1721 ***1220.12*** *p746*
Smithson, William; America, 1769 ***1220.12*** *p746*
Smithson, William 46; Ontario, 1871 ***1823.21*** *p345*
Smithurst, William; Virginia, 1721 ***1220.12*** *p747*
Smittberg, P.; New York, NY, 1851 ***6412.40*** *p153*
Smola, Frank; Detroit, 1930 ***1640.60*** *p82*
Smola, Frantisek; St. Louis, 1850 ***2853.20*** *p21*
Smola, Vaclav Martin; Illinois, 1851-1910 ***2853.20*** *p471*
Smolarciff, David 30; New York, NY, 1894 ***6512.1*** *p184*
Smolik, Vaclav; South Dakota, 1869-1871 ***2853.20*** *p246*
Smolinski, Boleslaw 19; New York, NY, 1911 ***6533.11*** *p9*
Smolinski, Stefan 30; New York, NY, 1920 ***930.50*** *p49*
Smout, John; America, 1767 ***1220.12*** *p747*
Smowing, Thomas; America, 1775 ***1220.12*** *p747*
Smrcek, Pavel; Wisconsin, 1855 ***2853.20*** *p304*
Smrcka, . . .; Pennsylvania, 1750-1799 ***2853.20*** *p17*
Smuck, Sarah 22; Michigan, 1880 ***4491.36*** *p20*
Smuck, Truman J. 31; Michigan, 1880 ***4491.36*** *p20*
Smurfitt, Thomas; Barbados, 1671 ***1220.12*** *p747*
Smye, Nathan; Washington, 1886 ***6015.10*** *p16*
Smyth, Alexander 30; Ontario, 1871 ***1823.17*** *p153*
Smyth, Alfred G. 46; Ontario, 1871 ***1823.21*** *p345*
Smyth, Anne; Barbados, 1673 ***1220.12*** *p730*
Smyth, Anne; Barbados, 1681 ***1220.12*** *p730*
Smyth, Anne; Barbados, 1682 ***1220.12*** *p730*
Smyth, Anne; St. Johns, N.F., 1825 ***1053.15*** *p7*
Smyth, Charles; Barbados, 1673 ***1220.12*** *p731*
Smyth, Charles 55; Ontario, 1871 ***1823.21*** *p345*
Smyth, Christopher; Barbados, 1682 ***1220.12*** *p731*
Smyth, Elizabeth; America, 1677 ***1220.12*** *p732*
Smyth, George 29; Ontario, 1871 ***1823.21*** *p345*
Smyth, George 65; Ontario, 1871 ***1823.17*** *p153*
Smyth, Henry 30; Ontario, 1871 ***1823.21*** *p345*
Smyth, James; Canada, 1776 ***8529.30*** *p14A*
Smyth, James 5; New York, NY, 1835 ***5024.1*** *p137*
Smyth, Jane; Barbados, 1667 ***1220.12*** *p735*
Smyth, John; Barbados, 1662 ***1220.12*** *p735*
Smyth, John 3; New York, NY, 1835 ***5024.1*** *p137*
Smyth, John 30; New York, NY, 1835 ***5024.1*** *p137*
Smyth, John B. 43; Ontario, 1871 ***1823.21*** *p345*
Smyth, Maxwell 48; Ontario, 1871 ***1823.21*** *p345*
Smyth, Miles; Barbados, 1676 ***1220.12*** *p740*
Smyth, Richard; America, 1736 ***1220.12*** *p741*
Smyth, Robert; America, 1694 ***1220.12*** *p741*
Smyth, Robert; Barbados, 1676 ***1220.12*** *p741*
Smyth, Robert 1; Died enroute, 1835 ***5024.1*** *p137*
Smyth, Thomas; America, 1749 ***1220.12*** *p743*
Smyth, Thomas; Barbados, 1664 ***1220.12*** *p743*
Smyth, William; Barbados, 1673 ***1220.12*** *p744*
Smyth, William; St. Johns, N.F., 1825 ***1053.15*** *p7*
Smythe, James 44; Ontario, 1871 ***1823.21*** *p345*
Smytheman, Samuel; America, 1744 ***1220.12*** *p746*
Smyther, Sarah; America, 1735 ***1220.12*** *p746*
Smyths, Samuell; Virginia, 1652 ***6254.4*** *p243*
Smythurst, Nathaniel; Barbados, 1675 ***1220.12*** *p746*
Snaesby, James; Virginia, 1736 ***1220.12*** *p747*
Snagg, Thomas; Maryland, 1720 ***1220.12*** *p747*
Snagman, Lewis; North Carolina, 1792-1862 ***1088.45*** *p33*
Snail, William; America, 1737 ***1220.12*** *p747*
Snailam, Richard; America, 1756 ***1220.12*** *p747*
Snailes, Hannah; Annapolis, MD, 1732 ***1220.12*** *p747*
Snailhouse, Hannah; Annapolis, MD, 1732 ***1220.12*** *p747*
Snailum, Thomas; America, 1772 ***1220.12*** *p747*
Snajdr, Vaclav; Cleveland, OH, 1868-1910 ***2853.20*** *p498*
Snajdr, Vaclav; New York, NY, 1869 ***2853.20*** *p503*
Snalham, Henry; America, 1773 ***1220.12*** *p747*
Snape, Mary; America, 1767 ***1220.12*** *p747*
Snape, Nathaniel; Virginia, 1735 ***1220.12*** *p747*
Snape, William; America, 1752 ***1220.12*** *p747*
Snapp, William; America, 1749 ***1220.12*** *p747*
Snart, Elizabeth 18; Ontario, 1871 ***1823.17*** *p153*
Snart, John 20; Ontario, 1871 ***1823.17*** *p153*
Snawden, Robert; Barbados, 1673 ***1220.12*** *p747*
Snaxton, Elizabeth; Barbados or Jamaica, 1699 ***1220.12*** *p747*
Snead, Elizabeth; Barbados, 1675 ***1220.12*** *p747*
Sneechall, Sarah; America, 1765 ***1220.12*** *p747*
Sneed, Robert; America, 1742 ***1220.12*** *p747*
Sneesby, Richard; America, 1773 ***1220.12*** *p747*
Sneider, John; Nova Scotia, 1784 ***7105*** *p25*
Sneidor, George; North Carolina, 1710 ***3629.40*** *p7*
Snelgrove, John Franklin; Detroit, 1902 ***1766.20*** *p25*
Snell, Benjamin; America, 1762 ***1220.12*** *p747*
Snell, Daniel; Ohio, 1840-1897 ***8365.35*** *p18*
Snell, James; America, 1746 ***1220.12*** *p747*
Snell, James 39; Ontario, 1871 ***1823.21*** *p346*

478 *FOR A COMPLETE EXPLANATION OF ENTRY, SEE "HOW TO READ A CITATION" SECTION*

Snell, James 43; Ontario, 1871 1823.17 p153
Snell, James; Virginia, 1769 1220.12 p747
Snell, Jennie 60; Ontario, 1871 1823.21 p346
Snell, John 30; Ontario, 1871 1823.21 p346
Snell, John 55; Ontario, 1871 1823.17 p153
Snell, Mary; Barbados, 1682 1220.12 p747
Snell, Richard; Annapolis, MD, 1729 1220.12 p747
Snell, Richard; Maryland, 1725 1220.12 p747
Snell, Thomas; America, 1656 1220.12 p747
Snell, Thomas; America, 1758 1220.12 p747
Snell, Thomas 46; Ontario, 1871 1823.21 p346
Snell, Thos 24; Ontario, 1871 1823.21 p346
Snell, William 35; Ontario, 1871 1823.21 p346
Snell, William 42; Ontario, 1871 1823.21 p346
Snellgrove, Joseph 65; Ontario, 1871 1823.21 p346
Snellgrove, William 66; Ontario, 1871 1823.21 p346
Snellham, Henry; America, 1773 1220.12 p747
Snelling, James; America, 1771 1220.12 p747
Snelling, John; America, 1757 1220.12 p747
Snelling, Rebecca; Barbados, 1670 1220.12 p747
Snelling, Thomas; America, 1691 1220.12 p747
Snellock, James; America, 1751 1220.12 p747
Snellock, Thomas; Long Island, 1781 8529.30 p10A
Sneyd, John; America, 1763 1220.12 p747
Sniboden, Adolph 21; New York, NY, 1883 8427.14 p43
Snider, David; Ohio, 1809-1852 4511.35 p51
Snider, Fritz 47; Ontario, 1871 1823.17 p153
Snider, Henry 25; Boston, 1835 6424.55 p30
Snider, Jacob; Ohio, 1809-1852 4511.35 p51
Snider, John; Ohio, 1809-1852 4511.35 p51
Snider, Ulrich; Ohio, 1809-1852 4511.35 p51
Snipe, Elizabeth; Barbados, 1668 1220.12 p747
Snipe, John 30; Ontario, 1871 1823.21 p346
Snively, Isaac B.; Ohio, 1809-1852 4511.35 p51
Snodgrass, William; New York, 1776 8529.30 p16
Snooden, Richard 69; Ontario, 1871 1823.21 p346
Snook, Andrew 32; Ontario, 1871 1823.21 p346
Snook, George; America, 1770 1220.12 p747
Snook, John; Maryland, 1672 1236.25 p47
Snook, Richard; America, 1685 1220.12 p747
Snook, Samuel 49; Ontario, 1871 1823.21 p346
Snooke, Henry; America, 1685 1220.12 p747
Snooke, Thomas; America, 1685 1220.12 p747
Snooke, Thomas; Barbados, 1678 1220.12 p747
Snorter, Jacob 8 months; St. Louis, 1844 778.6 p313
Snorter, Joseph 5; St. Louis, 1844 778.6 p313
Snorter, Thomas 3; St. Louis, 1844 778.6 p313
Snoud, William; America, 1740 1220.12 p747
Snow, Bridget Hogan *SEE* Snow, James
Snow, Charles; South Carolina, 1812 6155.4 p19
Snow, Daberough; Philadelphia, 1777 8529.30 p7A
Snow, Erasmus John; America, 1759 1220.12 p747
Snow, Estelle *SEE* Snow, James
Snow, George; America, 1685 1220.12 p747
Snow, James; New York, 1862-1927 9228.50 p604
Snow, James; New York, 1909 9228.50 p603
*Wife:*Bridget Hogan
*Child:*John Alexander
*Child:*James Gerald
*Child:*Mary
*Child:*Estelle
*Child:*Loretta
Snow, James Gerald *SEE* Snow, James
Snow, John; America, 1734 1220.12 p748
Snow, John; America, 1766 1220.12 p748
Snow, John; Maryland, 1723 1220.12 p748
Snow, John Alexander; Mexico City, 1905-1983 9228.50 p604
Snow, John Alexander *SEE* Snow, James
Snow, John Brown; America, 1768 1220.12 p748
Snow, Loretta *SEE* Snow, James
Snow, Mary *SEE* Snow, James
Snow, Nicholas; America, 1623 9228.50 p603
Snow, Robert; America, 1746 1220.12 p748
Snow, William; America, 1766 1220.12 p748
Snowden, David 30; Ontario, 1871 1823.21 p346
Snowden, Edward; America, 1743 1220.12 p748
Snowden, Jessie 50; Ontario, 1871 1823.21 p346
Snowden, Matthew; America, 1740 1220.12 p748
Snowe, Henry; Barbados, 1669 1220.12 p748
Snyden, Philip 32; Ontario, 1871 1823.17 p153
Snyder, Adam; Ohio, 1809-1852 4511.35 p51
Snyder, Caspar; Illinois, 1861 6079.1 p13
Snyder, Edward; New York, NY, 1836 3274.55 p24
Snyder, Felix 8; St. Louis, 1844 778.6 p313
Snyder, Francisha 32; St. Louis, 1844 778.6 p313
Snyder, George; North Carolina, 1710 3629.40 p7
Snyder, George F.; Ohio, 1809-1852 4511.35 p51
Snyder, George Michael; Ohio, 1809-1852 4511.35 p51
Snyder, Jacob 49; Ontario, 1871 1823.21 p346
Snyder, Josephine 19; St. Louis, 1844 778.6 p313
Snyder, Louise 8; St. Louis, 1844 778.6 p313
Snyder, Mary Ann 17; St. Louis, 1844 778.6 p313
Snyder, Michel 42; St. Louis, 1844 778.6 p313
Snyder, Rosalie 7; St. Louis, 1844 778.6 p313
Soady, Isaac 25; Ontario, 1871 1823.21 p346
Soady, James 30; Ontario, 1871 1823.21 p346
Soave, Annie 16; Quebec, 1870 8364.32 p26
Sobala, Anna 17; New York, NY, 1911 6533.11 p10
Sobbe, Ernst Meinsen; America, 1852 7420.1 p98
With family
Sobcziewski, Joseph; Wisconsin, 1885 6795.8 p61
Sobczyk, Jan 25; New York, NY, 1920 930.50 p48
Sobczynski, Walter; Detroit, 1929-1930 6214.5 p67
Sobieraj, Stanislava; Wisconsin, 1886 6795.8 p39
Sobierajska, Ladislava; Wisconsin, 1885 6795.8 p27
Sobierajski, Peter; Wisconsin, 1885 6795.8 p27
Sobkowicz, Karoline; Detroit, 1929-1930 6214.5 p70
Sobkowicz, Waclaw; Detroit, 1929-1930 6214.5 p70
Sobolewski, Waclaw; Detroit, 1929-1930 6214.5 p61
Sobolik, Frantisek; Nebraska, 1873 2853.20 p171
Sobotka, Aug. Fr.; St. Paul, MN, 1884 2853.20 p448
Sobotka, Josef; Missouri, 1859-1860 2853.20 p53
Socei, Charles A.; Ohio, 1809-1852 4511.35 p51
Socie, Charles Ambrose; Ohio, 1809-1852 4511.35 p51
Socie, Paul; Ohio, 1809-1852 4511.35 p51
Sockett, Andrew; America, 1761 1220.12 p748
Sockett, Martha; America, 1773 1220.12 p748
Socquet, Marie Francoise; Wisconsin, 1855-1857 1495.20 p41
Soddi, Elizabeth; America, 1770 1220.12 p748
Soden, John; Annapolis, MD, 1720 1220.12 p748
Soder, F.; Galveston, TX, 1855 571.7 p18
Soderberg, C.; Philadelphia, 1847 6412.40 p150
Soderburg, August; Colorado, 1888 1029.59 p85
Soderling, G. E.; Valparaiso, Chile, 1850 1192.4 p50
Soderlund, Carl Gustaf; Cleveland, OH, 1892 9722.10 p127
Soderlund, J.; New York, NY, 1851 6412.40 p152
Soderman, E.; New York, NY, 1843 6412.40 p147
Soderqvist, Karl Edvard; Cleveland, OH, 1892 9722.10 p127
Soderstrom, A.F.; New York, NY, 1846 6412.40 p149
Soderstrom, Augusta; Colorado, 1897 1029.59 p85
Soderstrom, C.F.; New York, NY, 1844 6412.40 p148
Soderstrom, Chas.; Colorado, 1903 1029.59 p85
Soderstrom, Chas. G.; Colorado, 1892 1029.59 p85
Soderstrom, Jacob; North America, 1855 6410.15 p105
Soderstrom, Johan Frederick; St. Paul, MN, 1880 1865.50 p109
Sodling, C. E.; Valdivia, Chile, 1850 1192.4 p50
Sodling, C. E.; Valparaiso, Chile, 1850 1192.4 p50
Sodrok, Jacent; Texas, 1855-1886 9980.22 p16
Soduin, Samuel 51; Ontario, 1871 1823.21 p346
Soe, Elizabeth; Barbados, 1673 1220.12 p748
Soehlke, Engel Marie Sophie; America, 1854 7420.1 p130
Soehrberger, Solomon; New York, 1860 358.56 p150
Soelke, Ernst Conrad; America, 1852 7420.1 p98
Soelke, Johann Heinrich; America, 1852 7420.1 p98
Soelter, Mr.; America, 1863 7420.1 p220
Soffker, Anna; America, 1895 7420.1 p372
Soffker, Carl Friedrich Wilhelm *SEE* Soffker, Gerhard Wilhelm
Soffker, Carl Ludwig *SEE* Soffker, Heinrich
Soffker, Caroline Wilhelmine; America, 1884 7420.1 p346
Soffker, Dorothea *SEE* Soffker, Heinrich
Soffker, Dorothea Louise; America, 1888 7420.1 p357
*Son:*Friedrich Wilhelm
*Son:*Christian Adolf
Soffker, Ernst August Gerhard *SEE* Soffker, Gerhard Wilhelm
Soffker, Friedrich; America, 1853 7420.1 p111
Soffker, Gerhard Wilhelm *SEE* Soffker, Gerhard Wilhelm
Soffker, Gerhard Wilhelm; America, 1863 7420.1 p220
*Wife:*Justine Wilhelmine Charlotte Wallbaum
*Son:*Ernst August Gerhard
*Son:*Carl Friedrich Wilhelm
*Son:*Gerhard Wilhelm
Soffker, Heinrich; America, 1860 7420.1 p200
*Sister:*Dorothea
*Brother:*Carl Ludwig
Soffker, Justine Wilhelmine Charlotte Wallbaum *SEE* Soffker, Gerhard Wilhelm
Soffker, Wilhelmine; Port uncertain, 1846 7420.1 p48
Sofker, Carl Ludwig *SEE* Sofker, Wilhelm
Sofker, Ferdinand; America, 1854 7420.1 p130
Sofker, Gerhard Gottlieb; America, 1864 7420.1 p227
Sofker, Gerhard Wilhelm; America, 1857 7420.1 p173
Sofker, Ludwig; America, 1854 7420.1 p130
Sofker, Rosine; America, 1866 7420.1 p249
Sofker, Wilhelm; America, 1860 7420.1 p200
*Son:*Carl Ludwig
Sogg, Elizabeth; America, 1769 1220.12 p748
Soher, Wilhelm; Wisconsin, 1878 6795.8 p208
Sohier, Edward, III; Boston, 1750 9228.50 p604
Sohier, George; New York, 1866 9228.50 p605
Sohier, Isabella B.; Minnesota, 1847-1900 9228.50 p139
Sohier, John; Minnesota, 1847-1900 9228.50 p139
*Wife:*Susan Sohier
*Child:*Isabella B.
Sohier, Susan; Minnesota, 1821-1900 9228.50 p336
Sohier, Susan; Minnesota, 1847-1900 9228.50 p139
Sohier, Susan; Minnesota, 1847-1900 9228.50 p139
Sohl, Carl Heinrich; Port uncertain, 1835 7420.1 p10
Sohl, Henry 61; Ontario, 1871 1823.17 p154
Sohle, . . .; America, 1846 7420.1 p48
Sohle, Caroline Sophie Eleonore Schmidt *SEE* Sohle, Johann Henrich
Sohle, Johann Henrich; America, 1857 7420.1 p173
*Wife:*Caroline Sophie Eleonore Schmidt
With children
Sohlinger, Luise; Philadelphia, 1891 5475.1 p76
Sohlke, Friedrich Heinrich Ferdinand; America, 1891 7420.1 p363
Sohlke, Johann Friedrich; America, 1854 7420.1 p130
Sohm, Anton; Venezuela, 1843 3899.5 p545
Sohm, Maria Anna; Venezuela, 1843 3899.5 p545
Sohn, Agatha 25; Mississippi, 1846 778.6 p313
Sohn, Agatha 59; Mississippi, 1846 778.6 p313
Sohn, Ba.bara 8; Mississippi, 1846 778.6 p313
Sohn, Chatarine 50; Missouri, 1845 778.6 p313
Sohn, Gustav Wilh; Wisconsin, 1903 6795.8 p237
Sohn, Ignace 58; Mississippi, 1846 778.6 p313
Sohnlen, Adele 24; Galveston, TX, 1844 3967.10 p374
Sohnlen, Ludwig 23; Galveston, TX, 1844 3967.10 p374
Sohnlen, Theobald 1; Galveston, TX, 1844 3967.10 p374
Sohns, Heinrich Karl 6 *SEE* Sohns, Maria Theobald
Sohns, M. Karoline 6 *SEE* Sohns, Maria Theobald
Sohns, Maria; America, 1866 5475.1 p382
*Son:*Heinrich Karl
*Daughter:*M. Karoline
Sohoeb, Jean 67; New Orleans, 1848 778.6 p313
Soish, John 48; Ontario, 1871 1823.17 p154
Soisson, P. 32; Port uncertain, 1843 778.6 p314
Sojkowski, Joseph; New York, NY, 1888 6015.15 p11
Solace, John; America, 1758 1220.12 p748
Solace, Joseph; America, 1758 1220.12 p748
Soland, Henry; Illinois, 1855 6079.1 p13
Soland, Jacob; Illinois, 1852 6079.1 p13
Solaniet, Mr. 22; New Orleans, 1847 778.6 p314
Solbach, Elise 28; Chicago, 1900 5475.1 p20
Solbach, Heinrich 19; New York, NY, 1882 5475.1 p15
Solbach, Johann 5; Chicago, 1900 5475.1 p20
Solbach, Josef; Chile, 1950 8023.44 p378
Sold, Juliane; America, 1897 5475.1 p19
Solde, Jeanne 24; Montreal, 1653 9221.17 p301
Solding, John; America, 1766 1220.12 p748
Sole, Thomas 47; Ontario, 1871 1823.17 p154
Soleby, Thomas; America, 1764 1220.12 p748
Soleim, Edward; Iowa, 1901 1211.15 p19
Solier, Unis 11; Ontario, 1871 1823.21 p346
Solikowski, Kazimierz; Detroit, 1930 1640.60 p82
Solivan, Honora; Boston, 1769 1642 p49
Soll, Genoveva 22; America, 1881 5475.1 p421
Solle, Jeanne 32; Port uncertain, 1846 778.6 p314
Solle, Josephine 3; Port uncertain, 1846 778.6 p314
Solle, Philippe 2; Port uncertain, 1846 778.6 p314
Sollinger, John; Illinois, 1860 6079.1 p13
Sollis, Elizabeth; Virginia, 1732 1220.12 p748
Sollman, Nicholas; Ohio, 1809-1852 4511.35 p51
Sollon, James; America, 1746 1220.12 p748
Sollow, John; Ohio, 1809-1852 4511.35 p51
Sollowin, Margaret; America, 1762 1220.12 p748
Solly, Richard; America, 1724 1220.12 p748
Solme, Jacob; America, 1741 1220.12 p748
Solomon, Aaron; America, 1772 1220.12 p748
Solomon, Aaron; Ohio, 1809-1852 4511.35 p52
Solomon, Abraham; America, 1749 1220.12 p748
Solomon, Alley; America, 1770 1220.12 p748
Solomon, Barnard; America, 1764 1220.12 p748
Solomon, Barnard; America, 1773 1220.12 p748
Solomon, Benjamin; America, 1774 1220.12 p748
Solomon, David; America, 1752 1220.12 p748
Solomon, Emanuel; America, 1751 1220.12 p748
Solomon, Ezekiel; North Carolina, 1814 1088.45 p33
Solomon, Hyam; America, 1770 1220.12 p748
Solomon, Isaac; America, 1762 1220.12 p748
Solomon, Joshua; America, 1774 1220.12 p748
Solomon, Røbert; America, 1750 1220.12 p748
Solomon, Samuel; America, 1766 1220.12 p748
Solomon, Saunders; America, 1760 1220.12 p748
Solomon, Wolfe; America, 1774 1220.12 p748
Solomons, Joseph; America, 1774 1220.12 p748
Solomons, Lazarus; America, 1771 1220.12 p748
Solomons, Rachael; America, 1765 1220.12 p748
Solomons, Solomon; America, 1765 1220.12 p748
Solomons, Solomon; America, 1771 1220.12 p748

Solon, Ingersoll 36; Ontario, 1871 ***1823.17*** *p154*
Solon, Thomas 73; Ontario, 1871 ***1823.17*** *p154*
Soloven, Anne; Boston, 1764 ***1642*** *p33*
Solter, Johann Christian; America, 1855 ***7420.1*** *p142*
Solter, Johann Friedrich Christoph; Port uncertain, 1855 ***7420.1*** *p142*
Soltysiak, Wallace; Detroit, 1929 ***1640.55*** *p117*
Soltzmann, Charles; Ohio, 1840-1897 ***8365.35*** *p18*
Somarell, Benjamin; America, 1737 ***1220.12*** *p774*
Somarell, Stephen; America, 1737 ***1220.12*** *p774*
Somena, Manuel 57; New Orleans, 1840 ***778.6*** *p314*
Somenzi, Mary; Illinois, 1930 ***121.35*** *p101*
Somer, Jonas; Barbados, 1667 ***1220.12*** *p774*
Somereisen, Jean 33; Port uncertain, 1843 ***778.6*** *p314*
Somereisen, Magdalena 2; Port uncertain, 1843 ***778.6*** *p314*
Somereisen, Maria 6 months; Port uncertain, 1843 ***778.6*** *p314*
Somereisen, Maria 29; Port uncertain, 1843 ***778.6*** *p314*
Somerel, Jane; America, 1763 ***1220.12*** *p774*
Somerfeld, Friedrich Hermann; Wisconsin, 1891 ***6795.8*** *p30*
Somerfelt, Christopher; Wisconsin, 1886 ***6795.8*** *p163*
Somerhays, John; America, 1732 ***1220.12*** *p774*
Somers, Elizabeth; New Orleans, 1850 ***7242.30*** *p154*
Somers, John; America, 1732 ***1220.12*** *p774*
Somers, John; Barbados, 1690 ***1220.12*** *p774*
Somers, Joseph; America, 1721 ***1220.12*** *p774*
Somers, Timothy; New Orleans, 1850 ***7242.30*** *p154*
Somerton, John; America, 1765 ***1220.12*** *p774*
Somervell, Thomas; Virginia, 1749 ***1220.12*** *p774*
Somerville, Robert B. 58; Ontario, 1871 ***1823.17*** *p154*
Somerville, William 28; Ontario, 1871 ***1823.17*** *p154*
Somerville, Wm.; Toronto, 1844 ***2910.35*** *p116*
Somes, John; America, 1700 ***1220.12*** *p748*
Somes, Sarah; America, 1745 ***1220.12*** *p748*
Somes, Thomas; America, 1727 ***1220.12*** *p749*
Somiac, V. 28; Cuba, 1840 ***778.6*** *p314*
Sommefeldt, Auguste Alvine; Wisconsin, 1895 ***6795.8*** *p108*
Sommelmann, George; Louisiana, 1836-1841 ***4981.45*** *p209*
Sommer, Adam; New York, 1860 ***358.56*** *p148*
Sommer, Alwine 29; Galveston, TX, 1855 ***571.7*** *p16*
Sommer, Andre; Louisiana, 1836-1841 ***4981.45*** *p209*
Sommer, August 31; Galveston, TX, 1855 ***571.7*** *p16*
Sommer, Barthelemy 30; America, 1846 ***778.6*** *p314*
Sommer, Carl 20; Kentucky, 1846 ***778.6*** *p314*
Sommer, Catherine 28; America, 1846 ***778.6*** *p314*
Sommer, Charlotte Ernestine Auguste; America, 1865 ***7420.1*** *p237*
Sommer, Elisabeth 3; America, 1846 ***778.6*** *p314*
Sommer, Ferdinand Edward; Wisconsin, 1879 ***6795.8*** *p77*
Sommer, Henry 25; America, 1847 ***778.6*** *p314*
Sommer, Johann Bernhard; America, 1865 ***7420.1*** *p237*
Sommer, Joseph 28; America, 1845 ***778.6*** *p314*
Sommer, Joseph; North Carolina, 1835 ***1088.45*** *p33*
Sommer, Ludwig 7; Galveston, TX, 1855 ***571.7*** *p16*
Sommer, Marie 2; America, 1846 ***778.6*** *p314*
Sommer, Marie 32; America, 1846 ***778.6*** *p314*
Sommer, Marie; Galveston, TX, 1855 ***571.7*** *p17*
Sommer, P. 22; New Orleans, 1834 ***1002.51*** *p111*
Sommer, Rosalie 14; America, 1846 ***778.6*** *p314*
Sommer, Wilhelmine 2; Galveston, TX, 1855 ***571.7*** *p16*
Sommerfeld, Christoph Edward; Wisconsin, 1869 ***6795.8*** *p142*
Sommerfeld, Emilie; Wisconsin, 1892 ***6795.8*** *p24*
Sommerfeld, Karl; Baltimore, 1868 ***5475.1*** *p383*
Sommerfeld, Rudolf; Wisconsin, 1888 ***6795.8*** *p69*
Sommerfeldt, Auguste Alvine; Wisconsin, 1895 ***6795.8*** *p108*
Sommerfeldt, Rudolph H.; Wisconsin, 1891 ***6795.8*** *p142*
Sommers, Joseph; America, 1753 ***1220.12*** *p774*
Sommers, Joseph; Ohio, 1809-1852 ***4511.35*** *p52*
Sommers, Sarah; America, 1753 ***1220.12*** *p774*
Sommers, Sarah; Virginia, 1738 ***1220.12*** *p774*
Somner, Jonas; America, 1667 ***1220.12*** *p749*
Somner, Jonas; Barbados, 1667 ***1220.12*** *p774*
Somppi, Matt; Minnesota, 1925 ***2769.54*** *p1383*
Sompron, P. 32; America, 1848 ***778.6*** *p314*
Sonder, Rosine Frederike; America, 1881 ***179.55*** *p19*
Sonderlin, Jorgan; Miami, 1920 ***4984.15*** *p38*
Sone, Fredk.; Ohio, 1809-1852 ***4511.35*** *p52*
Sonee, Ann; Maryland, 1744 ***1220.12*** *p749*
Soneson, G.; New York, NY, 1844 ***6412.40*** *p147*
Sonet, Michel; Quebec, 1634 ***9221.17*** *p40*
Soney, Charles 35; Ontario, 1871 ***1823.17*** *p154*
Soney, Johnson 48; Ontario, 1871 ***1823.17*** *p154*
Songe, Mr. 42; America, 1848 ***778.6*** *p314*
Sonier, Francoise 21; Montreal, 1659 ***9221.17*** *p428*
Sonisborg, Jason; North Carolina, 1710 ***3629.40*** *p8*
Sonjer, George 21; Ontario, 1871 ***1823.21*** *p346*
Sonka, Josef; Iowa, 1856-1858 ***2853.20*** *p211*
Sonne, Susan; America, 1678 ***1220.12*** *p749*
Sonneberg, John; Wisconsin, 1886 ***6795.8*** *p39*
Sonnefeld, Bernhard Emil; America, 1868 ***7919.3*** *p525*
Sonnefeld, Josef Friedrich; America, 1867 ***7919.3*** *p526*
Sonnefrank, John; Virginia, 1777-1804 ***9228.50*** *p615*
Sonnenberg, Herman August; Wisconsin, 1914 ***6795.8*** *p166*
Sonnenberg, Louis B.; Louisiana, 1841-1844 ***4981.45*** *p211*
Sonnhalter, Anna Maria; America, 1874 ***5475.1*** *p78*
Sonniborn, John G.; Illinois, 1855 ***6079.1*** *p13*
Sonntag, Bernard; Louisiana, 1874-1875 ***4981.45*** *p31*
Sontea, Isaac 34; Indiana, 1887-1896 ***9076.20*** *p74*
Sooler, Bernhard 17; Port uncertain, 1846 ***778.6*** *p314*
Soon, Charles; Boston, 1774 ***8529.30*** *p5A*
Soper, Harriet E. 29; Michigan, 1880 ***4491.33*** *p21*
Soper, James; America, 1685 ***1220.12*** *p749*
Soper, Mary Ann; Utah, 1851 ***9228.50*** *p605*
Sopincoska, Franzisca 19; New York, NY, 1883 ***8427.14*** *p44*
Sopitt, William; America, 1740 ***1220.12*** *p749*
Sopko, Konstanty; Detroit, 1930 ***1640.60*** *p83*
Sorbe, Mr. 17; America, 1845 ***778.6*** *p314*
Sorbe, Mr. 21; America, 1845 ***778.6*** *p314*
Sorbe, Mrs. 51; America, 1845 ***778.6*** *p314*
Sorbe, Ms. 14; America, 1845 ***778.6*** *p314*
Sorbe, Ms. 19; America, 1845 ***778.6*** *p314*
Sorbe, Jerome Tourne 63; America, 1845 ***778.6*** *p314*
Sorbe, Victor Raymond 18; America, 1845 ***778.6*** *p314*
Sorbet, Bernard; Louisiana, 1874-1875 ***4981.45*** *p31*
Sorbet, Bernard; Louisiana, 1874-1875 ***4981.45*** *p130*
Soregheus, George; Ohio, 1809-1852 ***4511.35*** *p52*
Sorensen, Arthur Eldre; Iowa, 1913 ***1211.15*** *p19*
Sorensen, Christian; Chicago, 1930 ***121.35*** *p100*
Sorensen, Hans M. 34; New York, NY, 1894 ***6512.1*** *p185*
Sorenson, Emil; Iowa, 1899 ***1211.15*** *p19*
Sorenson, Emildus; Iowa, 1914 ***1211.15*** *p19*
Sorenson, Haakon Andrew; Iowa, 1918 ***1211.15*** *p19*
Sorenson, Hans Peter; Iowa, 1888 ***1211.15*** *p19*
Sorenson, Lars C.; Iowa, 1896 ***1211.15*** *p19*
Sorenson, Neils Peter; Iowa, 1903 ***1211.15*** *p19*
Sorenson, Nels; Iowa, 1877 ***1211.15*** *p19*
Sorenson, Sedolf M.; Iowa, 1896 ***1211.15*** *p19*
Sorenson, Soren Jensen Ivan; Iowa, 1917 ***1211.15*** *p19*
Sorg, Heinrich; America, 1860 ***5475.1*** *p463*
Sorg, Johann Wilhelm; America, 1840 ***5475.1*** *p463*
Sorg, Magdalena; America, 1837 ***2526.42*** *p143*
Sorg, Wilhelm; America, 1847 ***5475.1*** *p455*
Sorge, Christian; America, 1868 ***7919.3*** *p531*
With wife & 3 children
Sorge, Maria; America, 1868 ***7919.3*** *p531*
*Daughter:*Lina
*Granddaughter:*Maria
Sorigheus, George; Ohio, 1809-1852 ***4511.35*** *p52*
Sorigheus, Michael; Ohio, 1809-1852 ***4511.35*** *p52*
Sorin, Agnes; Nova Scotia, 1753 ***3051*** *p112*
Sorin, Elisabeth 25; Quebec, 1657 ***9221.17*** *p358*
Sorin, Elisabeth 25; Quebec, 1657 ***9221.17*** *p358*
Sorle, John 32; Ontario, 1871 ***1823.21*** *p346*
Sorrell, Daniel; America, 1737 ***1220.12*** *p749*
Sorrell, John; America, 1757 ***1220.12*** *p749*
Sorrell, Joseph; America, 1763 ***1220.12*** *p749*
Sorvari, Hilja Jemiina; Oregon, 1941 ***9157.47*** *p2*
Sorvisto, Leonard 16; Minnesota, 1925 ***2769.54*** *p1378*
Sorvisto, Richard 17; Minnesota, 1925 ***2769.54*** *p1378*
Sosel, Josef; New York, NY, 1848 ***2853.20*** *p218*
Sosin, Stanislaw 24; New York, NY, 1911 ***6533.11*** *p10*
Sosinska, Marie; Detroit, 1929-1930 ***6214.5*** *p63*
Sostmann, Sophie; America, 1865 ***7420.1*** *p237*
Sostmann, Sophie Wilhelmine Charlotte; America, 1868 ***7420.1*** *p277*
Sother, Anna *SEE* Sother, Mathias
Sother, Katharina *SEE* Sother, Mathias
Sother, Margarethe Bach 28 *SEE* Sother, Mathias
Sother, Mathias; America, 1864 ***5475.1*** *p282*
*Wife:*Margarethe Bach
*Daughter:*Katharina
*Son:*Peter
*Daughter:*Anna
Sother, Peter *SEE* Sother, Mathias
Sott, Josef; New York, NY, 1870-1910 ***2853.20*** *p110*
Souard, Marie-Madeline; Canada, 1689-1695 ***9228.50*** *p617*
Souart, Gabriel 46; Montreal, 1657 ***9221.17*** *p371*
Souba, Ignac; Minnesota, 1855-1910 ***2853.20*** *p270*
Souba, Ignac; Wisconsin, 1854 ***2853.20*** *p304*
Souba, Vaclav; Wisconsin, 1854 ***2853.20*** *p304*
Soubien, Francis 16; Louisiana, 1845 ***778.6*** *p315*
Soubira, P. 37; America, 1841 ***778.6*** *p315*
Soublanc, S. 17; America, 1846 ***778.6*** *p315*
Soubragon, . . .; Virginia, 1700 ***9230.15*** *p80*
Soucaret, Mr. 28; America, 1747 ***778.6*** *p315*
Soudamore, Thomas 41; Ontario, 1871 ***1823.17*** *p154*
Souet, Michel; Quebec, 1634 ***9221.17*** *p40*
Souhrada, Matej; South Dakota, 1869-1871 ***2853.20*** *p246*
Souillard, Nicole; Quebec, 1665 ***4514.3*** *p371*
Souillas, Pierre 21; Quebec, 1658 ***9221.17*** *p378*
Souillat, Jean 21; Port uncertain, 1846 ***778.6*** *p315*
Soukes, Rowland; America, 1766 ***1220.12*** *p749*
Soukup, Jakub; Kansas, 1869-1910 ***2853.20*** *p201*
Soukup, Tomas; Wisconsin, 1882-1898 ***2853.20*** *p349*
Soul, John; America, 1774 ***1220.12*** *p749*
Soul, Thomas; America, 1763 ***1220.12*** *p749*
Soulage, Catherine; Quebec, 1600-1664 ***4514.3*** *p283*
Soulage, Catherine; Quebec, 1650 ***9221.17*** *p223*
*Daughter:*Catherine
*Daughter:*Marie
Soulard, Mathurin; Montreal, 1659 ***9221.17*** *p428*
Soulas, Claude de; Quebec, 1657 ***9221.17*** *p369*
Soule, George; Plymouth, MA, 1620 ***1920.45*** *p5*
Soule, Luke 31; Ontario, 1871 ***1823.21*** *p346*
Soule, Robert 42; Ontario, 1871 ***1823.21*** *p346*
Souled, Catherine 53; New Orleans, 1848 ***778.6*** *p315*
Soules, Louis 18; America, 1845 ***778.6*** *p315*
Soulinie, Marie 21; Montreal, 1652 ***9221.17*** *p268*
Souls, William; New York, NY, 1830 ***3274.55*** *p69*
Soulsby, John; America, 1769 ***1220.12*** *p749*
Soulsby, Thomas; Virginia, 1772 ***1220.12*** *p749*
Soulter, John; America, 1700 ***1220.12*** *p698*
Soumandre, Pierre 29; Quebec, 1646 ***9221.17*** *p168*
Souper, Robert; Virginia, 1721 ***1220.12*** *p749*
Sousch, Catherine 22; America, 1847 ***778.6*** *p315*
Sousch, Johann 26; America, 1847 ***778.6*** *p315*
Sousch, Ludovic 1; America, 1847 ***778.6*** *p315*
Souspra, Jacques; Quebec, 1651 ***9221.17*** *p251*
Soustre, Jacques; Quebec, 1651 ***9221.17*** *p251*
South, Francis; America, 1766 ***1220.12*** *p749*
South, John; America, 1752 ***1220.12*** *p749*
South, Mary; Maryland or Virginia, 1733 ***1220.12*** *p749*
South, Phillip; Illinois, 1864 ***6079.1*** *p13*
South, Samuel; America, 1761 ***1220.12*** *p749*
South, Samuel; America, 1762 ***1220.12*** *p749*
South, Thomas; America, 1744 ***1220.12*** *p749*
South, Thos; New Orleans, 1850 ***7242.30*** *p154*
South, William; America, 1742 ***1220.12*** *p749*
Southake, Cyprian; Barbados, 1681 ***1220.12*** *p749*
Southall, Edward; America, 1719 ***1220.12*** *p749*
Southall, Elizabeth; America, 1767 ***1220.12*** *p749*
Southall, Joseph; America, 1771 ***1220.12*** *p749*
Southall, Solomon; Annapolis, MD, 1725 ***1220.12*** *p749*
Southam, Mary 45; Ontario, 1871 ***1823.21*** *p346*
Southam, Thomas; America, 1773 ***1220.12*** *p749*
Southan, William; America, 1775 ***1220.12*** *p749*
Southcott, John James 21; Ontario, 1871 ***1823.21*** *p346*
Southcott, Richard; Massachusetts, 1630 ***117.5*** *p152*
Southcott, Thomas; Massachusetts, 1630 ***117.5*** *p153*
Southen, Thomas; America, 1736 ***1220.12*** *p749*
Southeran, Elizabeth; America, 1756 ***1220.12*** *p749*
Southerby, Mary; America, 1754 ***1220.12*** *p749*
Southerland, Barnard; Died enroute, 1736 ***1220.12*** *p775*
Southerland, Jane; America, 1767 ***1220.12*** *p775*
Southern, James 27; Ontario, 1871 ***1823.21*** *p346*
Southern, Thomas 40; Ontario, 1871 ***1823.17*** *p154*
Southerne, Thomas; America, 1766 ***1220.12*** *p749*
Southernwood, Anne; Annapolis, MD, 1725 ***1220.12*** *p749*
Southerton, Richard; America, 1737 ***1220.12*** *p749*
Southier, James; America, 1706 ***1220.12*** *p749*
Southray, Samuel; America, 1752 ***1220.12*** *p749*
Southurst, Robert; America, 1766 ***1220.12*** *p749*
Southward, Eleanor; America, 1762 ***1220.12*** *p749*
Southwell, John; America, 1742 ***1220.12*** *p749*
Southwell, Thomas; America, 1766 ***1220.12*** *p750*
Southwood, John; America, 1742 ***1220.12*** *p750*
Southworth, Annie 79; Ontario, 1871 ***1823.17*** *p154*
Southworth, Eleazer 46; Ontario, 1871 ***1823.17*** *p154*
Southworth, J. Q. 43; Ontario, 1871 ***1823.17*** *p154*
Southworth, Josiah E. 37; Ontario, 1871 ***1823.17*** *p154*
Southworth, Levi 52; Ontario, 1871 ***1823.17*** *p154*
Southworth, Nelson 49; Ontario, 1871 ***1823.17*** *p154*
Soutiere, Nicola 49; America, 1847 ***778.6*** *p315*
Soutor, Samuel 35; Ontario, 1871 ***1823.17*** *p154*
Soutter, John M. 34; Michigan, 1880 ***4491.36*** *p20*
Soutter, William; America, 1720 ***1220.12*** *p750*
Souvigner, John; New York, NY, 1867 ***1494.20*** *p12*
Souyard, Charles 27; Louisiana, 1848 ***778.6*** *p315*
Souyard, Elisab. 34; Louisiana, 1848 ***778.6*** *p315*
Souyard, Eugene 6 months; Louisiana, 1848 ***778.6*** *p315*
Souyard, Jean-Baptiste 35; Louisiana, 1848 ***778.6*** *p315*
Sovaih, Sylvester 26; Ohio, 1880 ***4879.40*** *p257*
Sowa, Jozef; Detroit, 1930 ***1640.60*** *p82*
Sowa, Walenty; Detroit, 1930 ***1640.60*** *p77*
Sowbridge, Caspar; North Carolina, 1710 ***3629.40*** *p8*

Sowdell, William; Barbados, 1677 ***1220.12*** *p750*
Sowden, Benjamin; America, 1774 ***1220.12*** *p750*
Sowden, Michael; America, 1771 ***1220.12*** *p750*
Sowell, Jeremiah; Maryland, 1674 ***1236.25*** *p49*
Sowerbutts, Ellen; America, 1765 ***1220.12*** *p750*
Sowerbutts, Richard; America, 1765 ***1220.12*** *p750*
Sowerpeak, George; New Jersey, 1773-1774 ***927.31*** *p3*
Sowgate, James; Barbados or Jamaica, 1692 ***1220.12*** *p750*
Sowl, Sylvester 21; Ontario, 1871 ***1823.17*** *p154*
Sowray, Malachy; Annapolis, MD, 1731 ***1220.12*** *p750*
Sowter, Jane 50; Ontario, 1871 ***1823.21*** *p346*
Sowton, Mary; Maryland, 1737 ***1220.12*** *p750*
Soye, J. 20; America, 1847 ***778.6*** *p315*
Soyez, Albert 44; New Orleans, 1848 ***778.6*** *p315*
Soyez, Ernest 9; New Orleans, 1848 ***778.6*** *p315*
Soyez, Henri 16; New Orleans, 1848 ***778.6*** *p315*
Soyez, Joseph 15; New Orleans, 1848 ***778.6*** *p315*
Soyez, Jules 4; New Orleans, 1848 ***778.6*** *p315*
Soyez, Maria 5; New Orleans, 1848 ***778.6*** *p315*
Soyez, Marie 21; New Orleans, 1848 ***778.6*** *p315*
Soyez, Victoire 40; New Orleans, 1848 ***778.6*** *p315*
Soys, Barnhard; Ohio, 1809-1852 ***4511.35*** *p52*
Spackman, Charles; America, 1751 ***1220.12*** *p750*
Spackman, Margaret; America, 1743 ***1220.12*** *p750*
Spackman, Rebecca; America, 1768 ***1220.12*** *p750*
Spacy, John; America, 1768 ***1220.12*** *p750*
Spaeter, Karl 16; America, 1863 ***5475.1*** *p488*
Spahn, George 17; America, 1847 ***778.6*** *p315*
Spahn, Nicolas 47; America, 1847 ***778.6*** *p315*
Spahn, Osignige 50; America, 1847 ***778.6*** *p315*
Spain, Augustin; America, 1740 ***1220.12*** *p750*
Spaish, James; America, 1767 ***1220.12*** *p750*
Spalding, Elizabeth; America, 1749 ***1220.12*** *p750*
Spanel, Alex 27; New York, NY, 1835 ***5024.1*** *p136*
Spang, Franz; America, 1843 ***5475.1*** *p416*
Spang, Friedrich; America, 1856 ***5475.1*** *p327*
Spang, Philippine; America, 1843 ***5475.1*** *p416*
Spangenberg, Catharine Wilhelmine Elisabeth; America, 1853 ***7420.1*** *p102*
Spangenberg, Liese 32; Valdivia, Chile, 1852 ***1192.4*** *p53*
Spangenberger, Michael; New York, NY, 1893 ***3366.30*** *p70*
Spanger, Anna Maria Heinz 35 *SEE* Spanger, Nikolaus
Spanger, Elisabeth *SEE* Spanger, Nikolaus
Spanger, Jakob *SEE* Spanger, Nikolaus
Spanger, Margarethe *SEE* Spanger, Nikolaus
Spanger, Nikolaus *SEE* Spanger, Nikolaus
Spanger, Nikolaus 45; America, 1856 ***5475.1*** *p289*
*Wife:*Anna Maria Heinz 35
*Child:*Elisabeth
*Child:*Nikolaus
*Child:*Jakob
*Child:*Margarethe
Spanier, Johann; America, 1873 ***5475.1*** *p324*
Spanier, Johann 30; America, 1843 ***5475.1*** *p252*
Spanier, Susanna; America, 1880 ***5475.1*** *p23*
Spaniol, Barbara Knorst 30 *SEE* Spaniol, Jakob
Spaniol, Georg *SEE* Spaniol, Johann
Spaniol, Jakob *SEE* Spaniol, Johann
Spaniol, Jakob; Brazil, 1857 ***5475.1*** *p368*
*Wife:*Barbara Knorst
*Son:*Stephan
*Daughter:*Margarethe
*Son:*Peter
*Son:*Nikolaus
Spaniol, Johann *SEE* Spaniol, Johann
Spaniol, Johann; America, 1882 ***5475.1*** *p64*
*Wife:*Magdalena Schafer
*Daughter:*Maria
*Daughter:*Katharina
*Son:*Jakob
*Son:*Mathias
*Son:*Johann
*Son:*Georg
Spaniol, Katharina *SEE* Spaniol, Johann
Spaniol, Magdalena Schafer *SEE* Spaniol, Johann
Spaniol, Margarethe; America, 1847 ***5475.1*** *p393*
Spaniol, Margarethe *SEE* Spaniol, Jakob
Spaniol, Maria *SEE* Spaniol, Johann
Spaniol, Mathias *SEE* Spaniol, Johann
Spaniol, Nikolaus *SEE* Spaniol, Jakob
Spaniol, Peter *SEE* Spaniol, Jakob
Spaniol, Stephan *SEE* Spaniol, Jakob
Spanner, Friedrich August; America, 1867 ***7420.1*** *p265*
Spanner, Heinrich Christian Ludwig; America, 1867 ***7420.1*** *p265*
Spanning, A.; Louisiana, 1874 ***4981.45*** *p297*
Spannuth, Mr.; America, 1874 ***7420.1*** *p304*
Spannuth, Carl; America, 1853 ***7420.1*** *p111*
With wife
Spannuth, Christine Philippine; America, 1872 ***7420.1*** *p296*
Spannuth, Friedrich Christian; America, 1885 ***7420.1*** *p349*
*Wife:*Sophie Moller
Spannuth, Heinrich Wilhelm; Port uncertain, 1839 ***7420.1*** *p16*
Spannuth, Sophie Moller *SEE* Spannuth, Friedrich Christian
Spano, Joseph; Louisiana, 1874-1875 ***4981.45*** *p31*
Spany, Ura 17; Galveston, TX, 1844 ***3967.10*** *p374*
Sparey, John; America, 1767 ***1220.12*** *p750*
Spariner, Richard; America, 1730 ***1220.12*** *p750*
Sparke, Benjamin; America, 1685 ***1220.12*** *p750*
Sparke, Elizabeth; Barbados, 1681 ***1220.12*** *p750*
Sparke, John; Virginia, 1732 ***1220.12*** *p750*
Sparke, Samuel; America, 1751 ***1220.12*** *p750*
Sparke, Thomas; America, 1720 ***1220.12*** *p750*
Sparke, William; America, 1746 ***1220.12*** *p750*
Sparkes, Charles; America, 1770 ***1220.12*** *p750*
Sparkes, Henry; America, 1754 ***1220.12*** *p750*
Sparkes, John; Annapolis, MD, 1725 ***1220.12*** *p750*
Sparkes, John 26; Barbados, 1664 ***1220.12*** *p750*
Sparkes, Margaret; Maryland, 1734 ***1220.12*** *p750*
Sparkes, Samuel; America, 1754 ***1220.12*** *p750*
Sparkes, Samuel; America, 1763 ***1220.12*** *p750*
Sparkes, William; America, 1740 ***1220.12*** *p750*
Sparkes, William; America, 1755 ***1220.12*** *p750*
Sparkes, William; Maryland or Virginia, 1738 ***1220.12*** *p750*
Sparkman, Samuel; America, 1758 ***1220.12*** *p750*
Sparks, Alice; Maryland, 1723 ***1220.12*** *p750*
Sparks, Edward; America, 1770 ***1220.12*** *p750*
Sparks, Emiley 30; Ontario, 1871 ***1823.21*** *p346*
Sparks, George 28; Ontario, 1871 ***1823.17*** *p154*
Sparks, George; St. Johns, N.F., 1825 ***1053.15*** *p6*
Sparks, Mary; America, 1734 ***1220.12*** *p750*
Sparks, Sarah; America, 1747 ***1220.12*** *p750*
Sparks, Sarah; St. Johns, N.F., 1825 ***1053.15*** *p6*
Sparks, Thomas 37; Ontario, 1871 ***1823.21*** *p346*
Sparling, Christopher 25; Ontario, 1871 ***1823.17*** *p154*
Sparling, George 49; Ontario, 1871 ***1823.17*** *p154*
Sparling, Thomas 38; Ontario, 1871 ***1823.17*** *p154*
Sparling, William 32; Ontario, 1871 ***1823.17*** *p154*
Sparribell, Isaac; Virginia, 1768 ***1220.12*** *p750*
Sparrow, Elizabeth; Barbados, 1671 ***1220.12*** *p750*
Sparrow, James; America, 1771 ***1220.12*** *p750*
Sparrow, John; America, 1698 ***1220.12*** *p751*
Sparrow, John; America, 1765 ***1220.12*** *p751*
Sparrow, John; America, 1774 ***1220.12*** *p750*
Sparrow, Joseph; America, 1738 ***1220.12*** *p751*
Sparrow, Joseph; America, 1752 ***1220.12*** *p751*
Sparrow, Joseph; America, 1765 ***1220.12*** *p751*
Sparrow, Mary; America, 1754 ***1220.12*** *p751*
Sparrow, Robert; America, 1756 ***1220.12*** *p751*
Sparrow, William; America, 1752 ***1220.12*** *p751*
Sparrowhawk, Richard 32; Ontario, 1871 ***1823.21*** *p347*
Sparry, Ann; America, 1687 ***1220.12*** *p752*
Spatz, Eva Katharina; America, 1853 ***2526.43*** *p187*
Spatz, Eva Maria; America, 1858 ***2526.43*** *p187*
Spatz, Mrs. Jakob 54; America, 1859 ***2526.43*** *p187*
*Son:*Peter 25
*Daughter:*Katharina 19
*Son:*Konrad 22
Spatz, Katharina 19 *SEE* Spatz, Mrs. Jakob
Spatz, Konrad 22 *SEE* Spatz, Mrs. Jakob
Spatz, Leonhard; America, 1867 ***2526.42*** *p99*
Spatz, Peter 25 *SEE* Spatz, Mrs. Jakob
Spatz, Sophie; New York, NY, 1870 ***7420.1*** *p395*
Spaul, John; America, 1740 ***1220.12*** *p751*
Spaul, Thomas; Potomac, 1731 ***1220.12*** *p751*
Spaulding, Alexander 38; Ontario, 1871 ***1823.17*** *p154*
Spaulding, James 34; Ontario, 1871 ***1823.17*** *p154*
Spaulding, Jane 73; Ontario, 1871 ***1823.17*** *p154*
Spavold, John; America, 1768 ***1220.12*** *p751*
Spaw, Esther; Maryland, 1732 ***1220.12*** *p751*
Spawfoot, William; America, 1727 ***1220.12*** *p751*
Spawford, Mary; Maryland, 1727 ***1220.12*** *p751*
Spawl, John; Maryland or Virginia, 1731 ***1220.12*** *p751*
Speake, Mary; America, 1730 ***1220.12*** *p751*
Speaker, John; New York, NY, 1778 ***8529.30*** *p3*
Speakman, John; Ohio, 1809-1852 ***4511.35*** *p52*
Spear, Frederick 16; Ontario, 1871 ***1823.21*** *p347*
Spear, Joseph; Charles Town, SC, 1719 ***1220.12*** *p751*
Spear, Ruben 17; Ontario, 1871 ***1823.21*** *p347*
Spear, Samuel 21; Ontario, 1871 ***1823.21*** *p347*
Spearin, James; America, 1765 ***1220.12*** *p751*
Spearing, John; America, 1685 ***1220.12*** *p751*
Spearman, Andrew 40; Ontario, 1871 ***1823.17*** *p154*
Spearman, James 42; Ontario, 1871 ***1823.17*** *p154*
Spearman, John 48; Ontario, 1871 ***1823.17*** *p154*
Spearman, Mary; Maryland, 1721 ***1220.12*** *p751*
Spearman, Simon 50; Ontario, 1871 ***1823.17*** *p154*
Spearman, Wm 55; Ontario, 1871 ***1823.17*** *p154*
Specht, Georg; America, 1867 ***7919.3*** *p533*
Specht, Heinrich; America, 1865 ***2526.43*** *p181*
With family
Specht, Heinrich Christoph; America, 1886 ***7420.1*** *p352*
Specht, Jacob 29; America, 1845 ***778.6*** *p315*
Specht, Johann Georg; America, 1865 ***2526.43*** *p181*
Specht, Katharina Elisabetha; America, 1854 ***2526.43*** *p199*
Specht, Konrad; Port uncertain, 1842 ***170.15*** *p42*
With wife
Specht, Sebastian; America, 1903 ***2526.42*** *p156*
Specht, Victoria 21; America, 1845 ***778.6*** *p315*
Speciall, Edward; America, 1700 ***1220.12*** *p751*
Speck, Ernst; New York, 1859 ***358.56*** *p100*
Speck, John; America, 1764 ***1220.12*** *p751*
Speckhard, Barbara *SEE* Speckhard, Margaretha
Speckhard, Eva Margaretha; America, 1856 ***2526.43*** *p124*
Speckhard, Margaretha; America, 1856 ***2526.43*** *p124*
*Daughter:*Barbara
Spector, Morris A.; New York, NY, 1890 ***3331.4*** *p11*
Spedding, William; America, 1775 ***1220.12*** *p751*
Speed, Benjamin; Charles Town, SC, 1718 ***1220.12*** *p751*
Speed, Benjamin; Maryland, 1720 ***1220.12*** *p751*
Speed, Eliz. 8; Quebec, 1870 ***8364.32*** *p26*
Speed, Francis; Died enroute, 1730 ***1220.12*** *p751*
Speed, George; Iowa, 1902 ***1211.15*** *p19*
Speed, John; North Carolina, 1792-1862 ***1088.45*** *p33*
Speed, John, Jr.; America, 1725 ***1220.12*** *p751*
Speed, Mary; America, 1756 ***1220.12*** *p751*
Speed, Richard; America, 1740 ***1220.12*** *p751*
Speed, Simon; America, 1770 ***1220.12*** *p751*
Speed, Thomas; America, 1685 ***1220.12*** *p751*
Speer, Robert; Ohio, 1834 ***3580.20*** *p33*
Speer, Robert; Ohio, 1834 ***6020.12*** *p22*
Speer, William; Ohio, 1834 ***3580.20*** *p33*
Speer, William; Ohio, 1834 ***6020.12*** *p22*
Speerman, Patrick 50; Ontario, 1871 ***1823.21*** *p347*
Speers, Catherine; New Jersey, 1927 ***9228.50*** *p527*
Speicher, Anna; America, 1836 ***5475.1*** *p65*
Speicher, Georg; America, 1837 ***5475.1*** *p66*
Speicher, Jakob; Brazil, 1837 ***5475.1*** *p66*
Speicher, Johann; America, 1800-1899 ***5475.1*** *p43*
Speicher, Johann; America, 1838 ***5475.1*** *p67*
With wife & 2 children
Speicher, Louis 21; America, 1844 ***778.6*** *p315*
Speicher, Margarethe 35; America, 1837 ***5475.1*** *p66*
Speicher, Maria 26; America, 1857 ***5475.1*** *p68*
Speicher, Mathias; Brazil, 1850 ***5475.1*** *p68*
Speicher, Peter; America, 1837 ***5475.1*** *p66*
Speier, Bettchen 6 *SEE* Speier, Mrs. Moses, II
Speier, Loser 8 *SEE* Speier, Mrs. Moses, II
Speier, Mrs. Moses, II 30; America, 1853 ***2526.43*** *p144*
*Child:*Loser 8
*Daughter:*Bettchen 6
*Daughter:*Rebeckchen 2
Speier, Moses Joel 34; America, 1869 ***2526.43*** *p144*
Speier, Rebeckchen 2 *SEE* Speier, Mrs. Moses, II
Speier, Wolf; America, 1867 ***2526.43*** *p144*
Speight, Christopher; America, 1759 ***1220.12*** *p751*
Speight, Ellen 58; Ontario, 1871 ***1823.21*** *p347*
Speight, Mary; America, 1756 ***1220.12*** *p751*
Speil, Christoph 37; America, 1832 ***2526.43*** *p181*
With wife & 4 children
Speir, Alexander 19; North Carolina, 1774 ***1422.10*** *p61*
Speir, Alexander 19; North Carolina, 1774 ***1422.10*** *p63*
Speirs, Henry; Louisiana, 1874 ***4981.45*** *p134*
Speke, Tho; Virginia, 1652 ***6254.4*** *p243*
Spellicly, Michael 45; Ontario, 1871 ***1823.21*** *p347*
Spelman, Jeremiah; North Carolina, 1853 ***1088.45*** *p33*
Spelman, John; North Carolina, 1854 ***1088.45*** *p33*
Spelman, John; North Carolina, 1860 ***1088.45*** *p33*
Spelman, Martin; North Carolina, 1858 ***1088.45*** *p32*
Spelman, Martin; North Carolina, 1858 ***1088.45*** *p33*
Spelman, Thos; St. John, N.B., 1848 ***2978.15*** *p37*
Speltigue, Joseph 45; Ontario, 1871 ***1823.21*** *p347*
Spence, Alexander 22; Ontario, 1871 ***1823.17*** *p154*
Spence, Andrew; America, 1724 ***1220.12*** *p751*
Spence, David 25; Ontario, 1871 ***1823.17*** *p154*
Spence, David 40; Ontario, 1871 ***1823.21*** *p347*
Spence, Henry 50; Ontario, 1871 ***1823.21*** *p347*
Spence, James; America, 1685 ***1220.12*** *p751*
Spence, James 73; Ontario, 1871 ***1823.21*** *p347*
Spence, John; Illinois, 1855 ***6079.1*** *p13*
Spence, John; Palmer, MA, 1753 ***1642*** *p119*
Spence, Nathaniel 62; Ontario, 1871 ***1823.21*** *p347*
Spence, Samuel; South Carolina, 1808 ***6155.4*** *p19*
Spence, Smith 41; Ontario, 1871 ***1823.21*** *p347*
Spence, Thomas; America, 1730 ***1220.12*** *p751*
Spence, Thomas 42; Ontario, 1871 ***1823.21*** *p347*
Spence, William 31; Ontario, 1871 ***1823.21*** *p347*
Spenceley, George; America, 1765 ***1220.12*** *p751*

Spenceley, John; Annapolis, MD, 1735 ***1220.12*** *p751*
Spencer, Ann; America, 1767 ***1220.12*** *p751*
Spencer, Ann; Barbados or Jamaica, 1688 ***1220.12*** *p751*
Spencer, Arthur; America, 1747 ***1220.12*** *p751*
Spencer, Charles; New Orleans, 1850 ***7242.30*** *p154*
Spencer, Edward; America, 1759 ***1220.12*** *p751*
Spencer, Edward; America, 1775 ***1220.12*** *p751*
Spencer, Elianor; Barbados or Jamaica, 1710 ***1220.12*** *p752*
Spencer, Elizabeth; America, 1773 ***1220.12*** *p752*
Spencer, Gilhad A. 53; Michigan, 1880 ***4491.36*** *p20*
Spencer, Henry; America, 1678 ***1220.12*** *p752*
Spencer, J.; Louisiana, 1874 ***4981.45*** *p297*
Spencer, James; America, 1750 ***1220.12*** *p752*
Spencer, Jane; America, 1747 ***1220.12*** *p752*
Spencer, Jane; America, 1767 ***1220.12*** *p752*
Spencer, John; America, 1675 ***1220.12*** *p752*
Spencer, John; America, 1754 ***1220.12*** *p752*
Spencer, John; America, 1768 ***1220.12*** *p752*
Spencer, John; America, 1771 ***1220.12*** *p752*
Spencer, John; America, 1773 ***1220.12*** *p752*
Spencer, John; Barbados or Jamaica, 1690 ***1220.12*** *p752*
Spencer, Joseph 35; Ontario, 1871 ***1823.21*** *p347*
Spencer, Katrin; Detroit, 1929 ***1640.55*** *p117*
Spencer, Laurence; America, 1742 ***1220.12*** *p752*
Spencer, Mark 27; Ontario, 1871 ***1823.21*** *p347*
Spencer, Martha; America, 1720 ***1220.12*** *p752*
Spencer, Martin; America, 1769 ***1220.12*** *p752*
Spencer, Mary; America, 1749 ***1220.12*** *p752*
Spencer, Mary; America, 1762 ***1220.12*** *p752*
Spencer, Mary; America, 1772 ***1220.12*** *p752*
Spencer, Moses; America, 1768 ***1220.12*** *p752*
Spencer, Robert; America, 1769 ***1220.12*** *p752*
Spencer, Robert; Barbados or Jamaica, 1702 ***1220.12*** *p752*
Spencer, Rowland; America, 1753 ***1220.12*** *p752*
Spencer, Sarah 35; Ontario, 1871 ***1823.21*** *p347*
Spencer, Thomas; America, 1763 ***1220.12*** *p752*
Spencer, Thomas; Barbados or Jamaica, 1690 ***1220.12*** *p752*
Spencer, Thomas; New York, 1781 ***8529.30*** *p16*
Spencer, Thomas; Philadelphia, 1778 ***8529.30*** *p7*
Spencer, Thomas P.; Ohio, 1866 ***3580.20*** *p33*
Spencer, Thomas P.; Ohio, 1866 ***6020.12*** *p22*
Spencer, Walter; Philadelphia, 1778 ***8529.30*** *p5A*
Spencer, William; America, 1673 ***1220.12*** *p752*
Spencer, William; America, 1759 ***1220.12*** *p752*
Spencer, William; Annapolis, MD, 1730 ***1220.12*** *p752*
Spencer, William; Died enroute, 1722 ***1220.12*** *p752*
Spencer, William 51; Ontario, 1871 ***1823.21*** *p347*
Spencer, Wm. 17; Virginia, 1635 ***1183.3*** *p30*
Spender, John; America, 1735 ***1220.12*** *p752*
Spendler, Anthony; Philadelphia, 1778 ***8529.30*** *p3*
Spengler, Catherine 31; Mississippi, 1845 ***778.6*** *p315*
Spengler, Jacob 4; Mississippi, 1845 ***778.6*** *p315*
Spengler, Marguerite 15; Mississippi, 1845 ***778.6*** *p316*
Spengler, Marguerite 35; Mississippi, 1845 ***778.6*** *p316*
Spengler, Wilhelm 7; Mississippi, 1845 ***778.6*** *p316*
Spenler, Heinrich; America, 1841 ***5475.1*** *p27*
Spenner, Carl Christian Ludwig; America, 1868 ***7420.1*** *p277*
Spenner, Mrs. Chr. Ludwig; America, 1868 ***7420.1*** *p277*
*Daughter:*Sophie Wilhelmine Louise
Spenner, Sophie Wilhelmine Louise *SEE* Spenner, Mrs. Chr. Ludwig
Spenrice, Thomas 50; Ontario, 1871 ***1823.21*** *p347*
Sperandio, Giovanni 23; New York, NY, 1894 ***6512.1*** *p182*
Sperr, Jacob; Philadelphia, 1863 ***8513.31*** *p427*
*Wife:*Mary Fisher
Sperr, Mary Fisher *SEE* Sperr, Jacob
Sperrey, William; Barbados, 1670 ***1220.12*** *p752*
Sperring, John; Barbados, 1676 ***1220.12*** *p752*
Sperwood, Timothy; Marston's Wharf, 1781 ***8529.30*** *p16*
Spessert, Anna Margaretha 3; Pennsylvania, 1851 ***170.15*** *p42*
Spessert, Anna Margaretha 6; Pennsylvania, 1851 ***170.15*** *p42*
Spessert, Johann Michael 1; Pennsylvania, 1851 ***170.15*** *p42*
Spessert, Johann Peter 37; Pennsylvania, 1851 ***170.15*** *p42*
Spessert, Katharina 30; Pennsylvania, 1851 ***170.15*** *p42*
Spessert, Michael 28; Pennsylvania, 1851 ***170.15*** *p42*
Speth, Miss 20; New York, NY, 1894 ***6512.1*** *p181*
Speth, Margarethe; Texas, 1894 ***5475.1*** *p162*
Spettel, Johann Baptist 20; Galveston, TX, 1846 ***3967.10*** *p377*
Spettigue, Burchett; Virginia, 1718 ***1220.12*** *p752*
Spettigue, Richard 23; Ontario, 1871 ***1823.21*** *p347*
Spettigue, William 59; Ontario, 1871 ***1823.21*** *p347*
Speyer, Joseph; New York, 1860 ***358.56*** *p5*
Speyer, Philip; Ohio, 1809-1852 ***4511.35*** *p52*
Spice, Richard; America, 1747 ***1220.12*** *p752*
Spicei, Henry 28; Ontario, 1871 ***1823.21*** *p347*
Spicer, Elizabeth; America, 1772 ***1220.12*** *p752*
Spicer, Francis; Annapolis, MD, 1730 ***1220.12*** *p752*
Spicer, George; America, 1765 ***1220.12*** *p752*
Spicer, Jane; America, 1769 ***1220.12*** *p752*
Spicer, John 44; Ontario, 1871 ***1823.21*** *p347*
Spicer, John; Virginia, 1741 ***1220.12*** *p752*
Spicer, Jonathan; America, 1773 ***1220.12*** *p752*
Spicer, Richard; Ohio, 1842 ***2763.1*** *p22*
Spicer, Robert; America, 1769 ***1220.12*** *p752*
Spicer, Robert; Annapolis, MD, 1725 ***1220.12*** *p752*
Spicer, Samuel; America, 1768 ***1220.12*** *p752*
Spicer, Thomas; America, 1769 ***1220.12*** *p752*
Spicer, Wm; Virginia, 1652 ***6254.4*** *p243*
Spiecker, Hermann 20; New York, NY, 1864 ***8425.62*** *p195*
Spiedler, Susanna; America, 1867 ***5475.1*** *p281*
Spiegel, Adolf 16; America, 1873 ***2526.43*** *p181*
Spiegel, Anna Barbara 18 *SEE* Spiegel, Christoph
Spiegel, Anna Katharina 10 *SEE* Spiegel, Christoph
Spiegel, Christoph; America, 1853 ***2526.43*** *p181*
*Son:*Johann Jakob
*Daughter:*Elisabetha
*Daughter:*Anna Katharina
*Son:*Georg Wilhelm
*Daughter:*Anna Barbara
*Wife:*Elisabeth Thyrolf
*Daughter:*Magdalena
Spiegel, Dorothea 11 *SEE* Spiegel, Georg Ernst
Spiegel, Elisabeth Thyrolf 43 *SEE* Spiegel, Christoph
Spiegel, Elisabetha 3 *SEE* Spiegel, Georg Ernst
Spiegel, Elisabetha 9 *SEE* Spiegel, Christoph
Spiegel, Georg Ernst; America, 1847 ***2526.43*** *p182*
With wife
*Daughter:*Dorothea
*Son:*Johann Christoph
*Son:*Jakob
*Daughter:*Katharina
*Daughter:*Elisabetha
*Son:*Johann Adam
Spiegel, Georg Wilhelm 17 *SEE* Spiegel, Christoph
Spiegel, Jakob 6 *SEE* Spiegel, Georg Ernst
Spiegel, Jakob; Cincinnati, 1832 ***2526.43*** *p182*
With wife
With child 18
With child 21
With child 16
With child 5
With child 3
With child 1
With child 4
With child 15
Spiegel, Johann Adam 7 *SEE* Spiegel, Georg Ernst
Spiegel, Johann Christoph 9 *SEE* Spiegel, Georg Ernst
Spiegel, Johann Jakob; America, 1865 ***2526.43*** *p182*
With wife
Spiegel, Johann Jakob 14 *SEE* Spiegel, Christoph
Spiegel, Katharina 6 *SEE* Spiegel, Georg Ernst
Spiegel, Magdalena 9 *SEE* Spiegel, Christoph
Spiegleburg, John; Ohio, 1844 ***2763.1*** *p22*
Spielman, Conrad 10; Halifax, N.S., 1902 ***1860.4*** *p39*
Spielman, Conrad 34; Halifax, N.S., 1902 ***1860.4*** *p39*
Spielman, Consatins; Halifax, N.S., 1902 ***1860.4*** *p39*
Spielman, Ferdinand 5; Halifax, N.S., 1902 ***1860.4*** *p39*
Spielman, Johannes 3; Halifax, N.S., 1902 ***1860.4*** *p39*
Spielman, Marie 33; Halifax, N.S., 1902 ***1860.4*** *p39*
Spielmann, Elisabeth 28; America, 1867 ***5475.1*** *p508*
Spielmann, Hans Heinrich; America, 1847 ***7420.1*** *p56*
Spier, . . .; America, 1841 ***7420.1*** *p23*
Spier, Mr.; America, 1872 ***7420.1*** *p298*
Spier, August; America, 1854 ***7420.1*** *p130*
Spier, Carl; America, 1860 ***7420.1*** *p200*
Spier, Christine; America, 1868 ***7420.1*** *p277*
Spier, Dorothea Hartung *SEE* Spier, Heinrich Gottlieb
Spier, Ferdinand; America, 1869 ***7420.1*** *p282*
With wife
Spier, Friedrich Wilhelm; America, 1839 ***7420.1*** *p16*
Spier, Friedrich Wilhelm Heinrich; America, 1872 ***7420.1*** *p298*
Spier, Georg Wilhelm; America, 1871 ***7420.1*** *p292*
Spier, Heinrich Friedrich; America, 1907 ***7420.1*** *p383*
Spier, Heinrich Friedrich Wilhelm; America, 1870 ***7420.1*** *p287*
With family
*Son:*Heinrich Wilhelm
Spier, Heinrich Gottl. *SEE* Spier, Heinrich Gottlieb
Spier, Heinrich Gottlieb; America, 1835 ***7420.1*** *p10*
*Wife:*Dorothea Hartung
*Son:*Heinrich Gottl.
Spier, Heinrich Wilhelm *SEE* Spier, Heinrich Friedrich Wilhelm
Spier, Johann Otto; Quebec, 1820 ***7420.1*** *p1*
Spier, Moses, II; America, 1852 ***2526.43*** *p144*
Spier, Philippine Caroline; America, 1857 ***7420.1*** *p173*
Spier, Sophie Caroline Wilhelmine; America, 1886 ***7420.1*** *p399*
Spier, Tons Heinrich; America, 1882 ***7420.1*** *p332*
Spiers, Mary 63; Ontario, 1871 ***1823.21*** *p347*
Spiess, Gottfr.; Valdivia, Chile, 1852 ***1192.4*** *p54*
Spiesz, Katharina; Dakota, 1886 ***554.30*** *p25*
Spiet, Anna Maria 29; America, 1847 ***778.6*** *p316*
Spiet, Anna Maria 40; America, 1847 ***778.6*** *p316*
Spiet, George 37; America, 1847 ***778.6*** *p316*
Spiet, Johann 52; America, 1847 ***778.6*** *p316*
Spiet, Michael 27; America, 1847 ***778.6*** *p316*
Spiet, Philippe 22; America, 1847 ***778.6*** *p316*
Spigournel Family ; New England, n.d. ***9228.50*** *p510*
Spikeman, William; Barbados, 1695 ***1220.12*** *p752*
Spilker, Anton Louis Carl; America, 1893 ***7420.1*** *p369*
Spilker, George; Baltimore, 1839 ***471.10*** *p62*
Spiller, David; Virginia, 1652 ***6254.4*** *p243*
Spiller, Richard; America, 1685 ***1220.12*** *p752*
Spiller, Robert; Barbados, 1717 ***1220.12*** *p752*
Spiller, Thomas 30; Ontario, 1871 ***1823.17*** *p154*
Spilsbury, George; America, 1751 ***1220.12*** *p753*
Spindel, Martin; Louisiana, 1841-1844 ***4981.45*** *p211*
Spindle, John; America, 1732 ***1220.12*** *p753*
Spindler, Caspar; America, 1868 ***7919.3*** *p527*
With family
Spindler, Engel Marie Sophie Charlotte; America, 1855 ***7420.1*** *p134*
Spindler, Peter Adam; Louisiana, 1841-1844 ***4981.45*** *p211*
Spindler, Richard; America, 1767 ***1220.12*** *p753*
Spines, Thomas; America, 1767 ***1220.12*** *p753*
Spink, John; America, 1739 ***1220.12*** *p753*
Spink, John; America, 1756 ***1220.12*** *p753*
Spink, Robert; America, 1769 ***1220.12*** *p753*
Spinke, Jeffry; America, 1743 ***1220.12*** *p753*
Spinkova, Anna; Detroit, 1869 ***2853.20*** *p356*
Spinks, Daniel; America, 1751 ***1220.12*** *p753*
Spinks, James; America, 1765 ***1220.12*** *p753*
Spinks, Thomas; America, 1771 ***1220.12*** *p753*
Spinler, Jacob 22; America, 1844 ***778.6*** *p316*
Spinner, Thomas; America, 1734 ***1220.12*** *p753*
Spinnweber, Barbara 20; America, 1849 ***5475.1*** *p415*
Spire, Andrew; Barbados, 1679 ***1220.12*** *p753*
Spires, Deborah; Virginia, 1727 ***1220.12*** *p753*
Spires, William; America, 1772 ***1220.12*** *p753*
Spiring, John; America, 1738 ***1220.12*** *p753*
Spirk, Jan Fr.; Nebraska, 1910 ***2853.20*** *p157*
Spitgerber, Amalia Bertha; Wisconsin, 1884 ***6795.8*** *p45*
Spitsnagle, Conrad; Ohio, 1809-1852 ***4511.35*** *p52*
Spittal, Robert 30; Ontario, 1871 ***1823.21*** *p347*
Spittgerber, Amalia Bertha; Wisconsin, 1884 ***6795.8*** *p45*
Spittle, John; America, 1682 ***1220.12*** *p753*
Spittle, Richard; Barbados, 1681 ***1220.12*** *p753*
Spittle, Robert; America, 1751 ***1220.12*** *p753*
Spittsner, Casper; Ohio, 1809-1852 ***4511.35*** *p52*
Spitz, Ana 36; America, 1747 ***778.6*** *p316*
Spitz, Catherine 16; America, 1747 ***778.6*** *p316*
Spitz, Dagobert 4; America, 1747 ***778.6*** *p316*
Spitz, Froman 27; America, 1747 ***778.6*** *p316*
Spitz, Georg 43; America, 1747 ***778.6*** *p316*
Spitz, Ignaz 7; America, 1747 ***778.6*** *p316*
Spitz, John Henry; Illinois, 1851 ***6079.1*** *p13*
Spitzer, Laurent 34; America, 1845 ***778.6*** *p316*
Spitzer, Victoria 24; America, 1845 ***778.6*** *p316*
Spitzlein, Casper; New York, 1860 ***358.56*** *p148*
Spitzler, John; Colorado, 1888 ***1029.59*** *p85*
Spitzler, John; Michigan, 1876 ***1029.59*** *p85*
Spitznagle, Conrad; Ohio, 1809-1852 ***4511.35*** *p52*
Spitznas, Elisabeth; New Orleans, 1867 ***5475.1*** *p158*
*Daughter:*Regina
Spivey, James; America, 1751 ***1220.12*** *p753*
Splavec, Karel; Chicago, 1893-1910 ***2853.20*** *p469*
*Wife:*Otilie
Splavec, Otilie *SEE* Splavec, Karel
Splichal, Frantisek; Wisconsin, 1854 ***2853.20*** *p304*
Splichal, Josef; Iowa, 1870 ***2853.20*** *p202*
Spoarck, John; Washington, 1881 ***2770.40*** *p135*
Spock, Steve; New York, 1926 ***1173.1*** *p2*
Spoerle, Christian; Missouri, 1886 ***3276.1*** *p2*
Spoerle, Gotlobb; Missouri, 1891 ***3276.1*** *p4*
Spoerle, Gottlob; Missouri, 1886 ***3276.1*** *p2*
Spohn, Maria 36; Brazil, 1872 ***5475.1*** *p443*
Spohr, Alfred; Kansas, 1917-1918 ***2094.25*** *p50*
Spohr, Mrs. Alfred; Kansas, 1917-1918 ***2094.25*** *p50*
Spohr, Jacob 21; America, 1840 ***778.6*** *p316*
Spohr, Johann; America, 1889 ***2526.43*** *p214*
Spoke, Ann; America, 1758 ***1220.12*** *p753*
Spole, Jabob 27; Ontario, 1871 ***1823.17*** *p154*
Spole, Thomas; Ontario, 1871 ***1823.17*** *p154*
Spolly, Phillip; Boston, 1740 ***1642*** *p45*
Spong, George 48; Ontario, 1871 ***1823.21*** *p347*

Spooler, Christopher; Ohio, 1809-1852 *4511.35 p52*
Spooler, Henry; Ohio, 1809-1852 *4511.35 p52*
Spooler, Jacob; Ohio, 1809-1852 *4511.35 p52*
Spooler, John; Ohio, 1809-1852 *4511.35 p52*
Spooler, Joseph; Ohio, 1809-1852 *4511.35 p52*
Spooner, Albert 39; Ontario, 1871 *1823.21 p347*
Spooner, John; America, 1722 *1220.12 p753*
Spooner, John; America, 1775 *1220.12 p753*
Spooner, Peter; Virginia, 1734 *1220.12 p753*
Spor, Clara; America, 1892 *2526.43 p157*
Sporl, Hermann Wilhelm Franz; Brazil, 1894 *7420.1 p373*
Sporl, Wilhelm Georg August; Brazil, 1889 *7420.1 p359*
Sporleder, Engel Doroth. Just. SEE Sporleder, Johann Friedr. Wilhelm
Sporleder, Engel Maria Dorothea Tatge SEE Sporleder, Johann Friedr. Wilhelm
Sporleder, Heinr. Wilh. SEE Sporleder, Johann Friedr. Wilhelm
Sporleder, Joh. Heinr. SEE Sporleder, Johann Friedr. Wilhelm
Sporleder, Johann Friedr. Wilhelm; America, 1845 *7420.1 p40*
  Wife:Engel Maria Dorothea Tatge
  Son:Johann Heinr. Wilh.
  Son:Heinr. Wilh.
  Daughter:Engel Doroth. Just.
  Daughter:Sophie Doroth. Louise
  Son:Joh. Heinr.
Sporleder, Johann Heinr. Wilh. SEE Sporleder, Johann Friedr. Wilhelm
Sporleder, Sophie Doroth. Louise SEE Sporleder, Johann Friedr. Wilhelm
Spours, John; America, 1772 *1220.12 p753*
Sprackland, James; Virginia, 1718 *1220.12 p753*
Spragg, Abraham; America, 1750 *1220.12 p753*
Spragg, John; America, 1765 *1220.12 p753*
Spragg, Samuel, Jr.; America, 1766 *1220.12 p753*
Spraggs, Thomas; America, 1741 *1220.12 p753*
Sprague, John, Jr.; America, 1764 *1220.12 p753*
Sprague, Michael; America, 1767 *1220.12 p753*
Sprague, Richard; Boston, 1715 *9228.50 p306*
Sprake, Charles 15; Quebec, 1870 *8364.32 p26*
Sprake, John; America, 1685 *1220.12 p753*
Spraklin, Eliza 53; Ontario, 1871 *1823.21 p347*
Sprangley, John; Maryland, 1742 *1220.12 p753*
Spratley, Millicent; America, 1764 *1220.12 p753*
Spratlye, James; Maryland, 1721 *1220.12 p753*
Spratt, Francis; America, 1680 *1220.12 p753*
Spratt, John; Barbados or Jamaica, 1707 *1220.12 p753*
Spratt, Joseph; America, 1752 *1220.12 p753*
Spratt, Philemon; Maryland, 1743 *1220.12 p753*
Spratt, Richard; Barbados or Jamaica, 1680 *1220.12 p753*
Spratt, Sarah; America, 1737 *1220.12 p753*
Spratt, Sarah; Virginia, 1772 *1220.12 p753*
Spratt, Thomas; America, 1751 *1220.12 p753*
Spratt, William; America, 1754 *1220.12 p753*
Spratt Family ; Canada, n.d. *9228.50 p606*
Sprawl, John; Ohio, 1840-1897 *8365.35 p18*
Spray Family ; West Virginia, 1850 *1132.30 p147*
Spreadbarrow, John; America, 1741 *1220.12 p753*
Spreate, William; America, 1685 *1220.12 p753*
Spreschbach, Henry 31; America, 1847 *778.6 p316*
Sprick, Hermann Friedrich; America, 1854 *7420.1 p130*
  With wife 2 sons & 2 daughters
Spriggs, Frederick 50; Ontario, 1871 *1823.21 p347*
Spriggs, Stephen; America, 1758 *1220.12 p753*
Sprightley, Hannah; America, 1746 *1220.12 p753*
Sprigmore, Elizabeth; America, 1767 *1220.12 p754*
Sprimont, Camille Antoine SEE Sprimont, Ignace
Sprimont, Caroline SEE Sprimont, Ignace
Sprimont, Clemence Thunus SEE Sprimont, Ignace
Sprimont, Eugene SEE Sprimont, Ignace
Sprimont, Florence; Wisconsin, 1856 *1495.20 p45*
Sprimont, Hortense SEE Sprimont, Ignace
Sprimont, Ignace; Wisconsin, 1854-1858 *1495.20 p50*
  Wife:Clemence Thunus
  Child:Caroline
  Child:Marie Josephine
  Child:Isidore
  Child:Eugene
  Child:Camille Antoine
  Child:Hortense
Sprimont, Isidore SEE Sprimont, Ignace
Sprimont, Marie Josephine SEE Sprimont, Ignace
Spring, Gottfried; Missouri, 1894 *3276.1 p4*
Spring, Gottfried; Missouri, 1898 *3276.1 p4*
Spring, Robert; Virginia, 1741 *1220.12 p754*
Spring, Rowland 12; Ontario, 1871 *1823.21 p347*
Spring, Samuel; Missouri, 1885 *3276.1 p2*
Spring, Solomon; America, 1688 *1220.12 p754*
Springborn, Charles; Wisconsin, 1877 *6795.8 p96*

Springborn, Hermann; Valdivia, Chile, 1852 *1192.4 p53*
Springer, Eliza 49; Ontario, 1871 *1823.21 p347*
Springet, Daniel 32; Ontario, 1871 *1823.21 p347*
Springet, Robert 48; Ontario, 1871 *1823.21 p347*
Springett, Hester; America, 1753 *1220.12 p754*
Springett, William; America, 1770 *1220.12 p754*
Springinsguth, Ernst Heinr. Christoph SEE Springinsguth, Johann Heinrich
Springinsguth, Johann Heinrich; Port uncertain, 1850 *7420.1 p76*
  Brother:Ernst Heinr. Christoph
Springstead, Donald 32; Ontario, 1871 *1823.21 p347*
Springstead, Mary 29; Ontario, 1871 *1823.21 p347*
Springthorp, Ruth; Annapolis, MD, 1725 *1220.12 p754*
Sproat, Joseph; America, 1773 *1220.12 p754*
Sproat, Thomas 45; Ontario, 1871 *1823.21 p347*
Sprosly, Henry; America, 1688 *1220.12 p754*
Sproson, John; America, 1771 *1220.12 p754*
Sproul, James; Ohio, 1826 *3580.20 p33*
Sproul, James; Ohio, 1826 *6020.12 p22*
Sproul, Tamer 57; Ontario, 1871 *1823.17 p155*
Sproule, Master; Quebec, 1885 *1937.10 p52*
Sproule, Mr.; Quebec, 1885 *1937.10 p52*
Sproule, Egbert Wilson; Iowa, 1911 *1211.15 p19*
Sprowl, Robert; South Carolina, 1808 *6155.4 p19*
Spruce, Apswell; America, 1769 *1220.12 p754*
Spruce, John; America, 1700 *1220.12 p754*
Sprunt, Alexander; North Carolina, 1854 *1088.45 p33*
Sprunt, James M.; North Carolina, 1845 *1088.45 p33*
Spry, Abraham W. 44; Ontario, 1871 *1823.21 p348*
Spry, John; America, 1739 *1220.12 p754*
Spry, John 36; Ontario, 1871 *1823.17 p155*
Spry, William; Jamestown, VA, 1633 *1658.20 p211*
Spulke, Gustav 15; New York, NY, 1893 *1883.7 p43*
Spurgeon, Ann; Maryland, 1719 *1220.12 p754*
Spurgeon, James; Maryland, 1719 *1220.12 p754*
Spurgeon, John; Potomac, 1729 *1220.12 p754*
Spurgeon, William; Maryland, 1719 *1220.12 p754*
Spurham, George; America, 1743 *1220.12 p754*
Spurk, A. Maria SEE Spurk, Johann
Spurk, Barbara SEE Spurk, Johann
Spurk, Johann SEE Spurk, Johann
Spurk, Johann; America, 1881 *5475.1 p198*
  Wife:Maria Futscher
  Son:Johann
  Son:Peter
  Daughter:A. Maria
  Daughter:Barbara
  Daughter:Katharina
  Daughter:Maria
  With son
Spurk, Katharina SEE Spurk, Johann
Spurk, Maria SEE Spurk, Johann
Spurk, Maria Futscher 47 SEE Spurk, Johann
Spurk, Peter SEE Spurk, Johann
Spurling, Elizabeth; America, 1749 *1220.12 p754*
Spurling, Mary; America, 1726 *1220.12 p754*
Spurling, Nicholas; America, 1749 *1220.12 p754*
Spurr, Joseph 3; Ontario, 1871 *1823.21 p348*
Spurr, Milicant 29; Ontario, 1871 *1823.21 p348*
Spurr, Minnie 7; Ontario, 1871 *1823.21 p348*
Spurr, Moses; America, 1764 *1220.12 p754*
Spurr, Thomas; America, 1709 *1220.12 p754*
Spurr, William; America, 1764 *1220.12 p754*
Spurrier, Elizabeth; Annapolis, MD, 1725 *1220.12 p754*
Spurry, John; America, 1766 *1220.12 p754*
Spurway, Daniel; America, 1742 *1220.12 p754*
Spurway, Robert; America, 1685 *1220.12 p754*
Spycer, Francis; Marston's Wharf, 1782 *8529.30 p16*
Spyer, Francis; Marston's Wharf, 1782 *8529.30 p16*
Spynk, Robt. 20; Virginia, 1635 *1183.3 p30*
Square, John 60; Ontario, 1871 *1823.21 p348*
Squelpyn, Abraham; America, 1655 *1220.12 p754*
Squire, Anne; America, 1719 *1220.12 p754*
Squire, James W. 32; Ontario, 1871 *1823.21 p348*
Squire, John; America, 1766 *1220.12 p754*
Squire, Peter; America, 1760 *1220.12 p754*
Squire, Philip 55; Ontario, 1871 *1823.21 p348*
Squire, Robert; America, 1733 *1220.12 p754*
Squire, Robert; America, 1769 *1220.12 p754*
Squire, Thomas; America, 1722 *1220.12 p754*
Squire, William; Virginia, 1772 *1220.12 p754*
Squires, Edward H. 67; Ontario, 1871 *1823.21 p348*
Squires, Harry 39; Ontario, 1871 *1823.21 p348*
Squires, J.; Quebec, 1870 *8364.32 p26*
Squires, James; America, 1761 *1220.12 p754*
Squires, Mary; America, 1761 *1220.12 p754*
Squires, Mary Ann 51; Ontario, 1871 *1823.21 p348*
Squires, Rachel 14; Ontario, 1871 *1823.21 p348*
Squires, Rich 37; Ontario, 1871 *1823.21 p348*
Squires, Robert; America, 1743 *1220.12 p754*
Squires, Samual 36; Ontario, 1871 *1823.21 p348*
Squires, William; America, 1765 *1220.12 p754*

Squires, William 54; Ontario, 1871 *1823.21 p348*
Squirrell, Elizabeth; America, 1745 *1220.12 p754*
Srajer, Jan; Nebraska, 1870 *2853.20 p193*
Sramek, Frantisek; Illinois, 1851-1910 *2853.20 p471*
Sramek, Ignac; Galveston, TX, 1856 *2853.20 p63*
Sranahan, Tom 26; Ontario, 1871 *1823.21 p348*
Srevenson, Sane 12; Quebec, 1870 *8364.32 p26*
Staab, Eva Margaretha 31; America, 1864 *2526.43 p151*
Staab, Philipp; America, 1882 *2526.43 p157*
Staab, Regina; America, 1882 *2526.43 p157*
Staab, Wendel; America, 1882 *2526.43 p157*
Staaf, John; Illinois, 1855 *6079.1 p13*
Staakmann, Anne Marie Catharine SEE Staakmann, Johann Friedrich
Staakmann, Georg Wilhelm SEE Staakmann, Johann Friedrich
Staakmann, Johann Friedrich; America, 1857 *7420.1 p173*
  Sister:Anne Marie Catharine
  Brother:Georg Wilhelm
Staarup, Thomas Sorenson; Iowa, 1925 *1211.15 p19*
Stabbler, John 71; Ontario, 1871 *1823.17 p155*
Stabler, John; America, 1760 *1220.12 p754*
Stabs, Gotthielf; Wisconsin, 1881 *6795.8 p82*
Stace, William 42; Ontario, 1871 *1823.17 p155*
Stacey, Alice; Barbados, 1664 *1220.12 p754*
Stacey, Catherine Serna SEE Stacey, Ross
Stacey, Charles Heber SEE Stacey, Ross
Stacey, Clifford Leslie SEE Stacey, Ross
Stacey, George F. SEE Stacey, Ross
Stacey, Howard Ephraim SEE Stacey, Ross
Stacey, John; Barbados, 1683 *1220.12 p755*
Stacey, John; Barbados or Jamaica, 1696 *1220.12 p755*
Stacey, Ross; Cambridge, MA, 1880-1894 *9228.50 p314*
  Wife:Susan Alma Bagnell
  Child:Catherine Serna
  Child:Howard Ephraim
  Child:George F.
  Child:Charles Heber
  Child:Clifford Leslie
Stacey, Susan Alma Bagnell SEE Stacey, Ross
Stacey, Thomas; America, 1745 *1220.12 p755*
Stacey, William 27; Ontario, 1871 *1823.17 p155*
Stach, Kristan; Greenland, 1733 *2853.20 p18*
Stach, Matej; Greenland, 1733 *2853.20 p18*
Stach, Matej; North Carolina, 1775-1787 *2853.20 p18*
Stach, Piotr; Detroit, 1929 *1640.55 p114*
Stachelscheid, Lorenz; America, 1928 *8023.44 p379*
Stachowicz, Andrew; Detroit, 1930 *1640.60 p81*
Stacie, Wm John 28; Ontario, 1871 *1823.21 p348*
Stack, Richard; Virginia, 1766 *1220.12 p755*
Stackhouse, William 19; Ontario, 1871 *1823.21 p348*
Stackmann, Friedrich; America, 1854 *7420.1 p131*
  With son
Stackmann, Heinrich Christoph Christian; America, 1887 *7420.1 p355*
Stackpool, George; Maryland, 1742 *1220.12 p755*
Stackwell, John 25; Barbados, 1664 *1220.12 p755*
Stacy, Samuel 19; Ontario, 1871 *1823.21 p348*
Stacy, Thomas 34; Ontario, 1871 *1823.21 p348*
Stacy, William 59; Ontario, 1871 *1823.17 p155*
Stacy, William; Virginia, 1756 *1220.12 p755*
Stacz, Florin; New York, NY, 1882 *6015.15 p29*
Staddon, John; America, 1742 *1220.12 p755*
Staddon, William; America, 1764 *1220.12 p755*
Staddow, John; America, 1746 *1220.12 p755*
Stadelmann, Emil Eduard; America, 1867 *7919.3 p529*
Stadelmann, J. 33; New Orleans, 1834 *1002.51 p112*
Stadelmeyer, Jean 1; New Orleans, 1848 *778.6 p316*
Stadelmeyer, Sophia 27; New Orleans, 1848 *778.6 p316*
Stader, Robert; Potomac, 1731 *1220.12 p755*
Stader, Thomas; Potomac, 1731 *1220.12 p755*
Stades, John; America, 1721 *1220.12 p755*
Stading, Sophie; America, 1868 *7420.1 p277*
Stadlemann, John; Washington, 1886 *2770.40 p24*
Stadler, . . .; West Virginia, 1865-1895 *1132.30 p150*
Stadler, Charlotte 47; Michigan, 1880 *4491.39 p28*
Stadler, Jacob 43; Michigan, 1880 *4491.39 p29*
Stadler, Jay 34; Michigan, 1880 *4491.39 p29*
Stadler, Mary A. 45; Michigan, 1880 *4491.39 p29*
Stadler, Samuel 40; Michigan, 1880 *4491.39 p29*
Stadtler, Johann; America, 1867 *7919.3 p533*
Staehle, Fred.; Louisiana, 1874-1875 *4981.45 p30*
Staff, Henry; Illinois, 1860 *6079.1 p13*
Stafford, Ann; America, 1756 *1220.12 p755*
Stafford, Ann; America, 1767 *1220.12 p755*
Stafford, Edmund; New Orleans, 1850 *7242.30 p155*
Stafford, Elizabeth; America, 1727 *1220.12 p755*
Stafford, Hannah; America, 1772 *1220.12 p755*
Stafford, John; America, 1766 *1220.12 p755*
Stafford, John; America, 1770 *1220.12 p755*
Stafford, Matthew; Annapolis, MD, 1721 *1220.12 p755*
Stafford, May Lidgett; Oregon, 1941 *9157.47 p2*

Stafford, Nathaniel; America, 1764 ***1220.12*** *p755*
Stafford, Rachael 38; Ontario, 1871 ***1823.17*** *p155*
Stafford, Thomas, Jr.; America, 1756 ***1220.12*** *p755*
Stafford, William; America, 1695 ***1220.12*** *p755*
Stafford, William; Barbados or Jamaica, 1688 ***1220.12*** *p755*
Stage, Heinrich; America, 1866 ***7420.1*** *p249*
Stagg, Grace; Virginia, 1742 ***1220.12*** *p755*
Stagg, John; Died enroute, 1759 ***1220.12*** *p755*
Stagni, Alphonsus 22; America, 1846 ***778.6*** *p316*
Stahl, A. 50; New Orleans, 1834 ***1002.51*** *p111*
Stahl, Miss A. 27; New Orleans, 1834 ***1002.51*** *p111*
Stahl, Adele 25; Missouri, 1845 ***778.6*** *p316*
Stahl, Anna Maria 36; America, 1847 ***5475.1*** *p531*
Stahl, Miss C. 57; New Orleans, 1834 ***1002.51*** *p111*
Stahl, Catharina 36; America, 1847 ***778.6*** *p316*
Stahl, David 27; New York, NY, 1847 ***9176.15*** *p50*
Stahl, Frederick; Illinois, 1858-1861 ***6020.5*** *p133*
Stahl, Frederick; Ohio, 1809-1852 ***4511.35*** *p52*
Stahl, Henri 1; America, 1847 ***778.6*** *p316*
Stahl, Hermann; America, n.d. ***8023.44*** *p379*
Stahl, Jean 36; America, 1847 ***778.6*** *p316*
Stahl, John; Philadelphia, 1778 ***8529.30*** *p7*
Stahl, John Casper; New York, NY, 1834 ***3274.55*** *p22*
Stahl, John M.; Ohio, 1809-1852 ***4511.35*** *p52*
Stahl, Joseph 6; America, 1847 ***778.6*** *p316*
Stahl, Louis Gustav; Illinois, 1861 ***6079.1*** *p13*
Stahl, Miss M. 22; New Orleans, 1834 ***1002.51*** *p111*
Stahl, Michael 23; America, 1842 ***2526.42*** *p99*
Stahl, Nikolaus; America, 1876 ***5475.1*** *p250*
Stahl, Paul; America, 1923 ***8023.44*** *p379*
Stahl, Peter; America, n.d. ***8023.44*** *p379*
Stahl, Susanna 4; America, 1847 ***778.6*** *p316*
Stahlberg, Hermann; Wisconsin, 1896 ***6795.8*** *p208*
Stahle, Anton; Valdivia, Chile, 1850 ***1192.4*** *p49*
Stahler, John; Ohio, 1809-1852 ***4511.35*** *p52*
Stahlhammar, B.H.; Philadelphia, 1847 ***6412.40*** *p150*
Stahlhut, Mr.; America, 1880 ***7420.1*** *p318*
Stahlhut, Carl Heinrich Wilhelm *SEE* Stahlhut, Christian Gottlieb
Stahlhut, Caroline Dorothee Paul *SEE* Stahlhut, Christian Gottlieb
Stahlhut, Christian Gottlieb; America, 1871 ***7420.1*** *p292*
*Wife:*Caroline Dorothee Paul
*Daughter:*Engel Marie Sophie Carol
*Daughter:*Engel Marie Caroline
*Son:*Ernst Heinrich Gottlieb
*Son:*Carl Heinrich Wilhelm
Stahlhut, Engel Marie Caroline *SEE* Stahlhut, Christian Gottlieb
Stahlhut, Engel Marie Dorothee Dettmer *SEE* Stahlhut, Johann Heinrich
Stahlhut, Engel Marie Sophie Carol *SEE* Stahlhut, Christian Gottlieb
Stahlhut, Ernst Heinrich Gottlieb *SEE* Stahlhut, Christian Gottlieb
Stahlhut, Friedrich Wilhelm; Indianapolis, 1888 ***7420.1*** *p357*
*Wife:*Marie Prange
Stahlhut, Heinrich Wilhelm Conrad; America, 1881 ***7420.1*** *p325*
Stahlhut, Johann Heinrich; America, 1856 ***7420.1*** *p154*
*Wife:*Engel Marie Dorothee Dettmer
With 2 sons
Stahlhut, Marie Prange *SEE* Stahlhut, Friedrich Wilhelm
Stahlhuth, . . .; America, 1866 ***7420.1*** *p249*
With wife
With daughter 5
With daughter 7
With son 1
Stahlhuth, E. H.; America, 1847 ***7420.1*** *p56*
With family
Stahlhuth, Heinrich Friedrich Wilhelm; America, 1871 ***7420.1*** *p292*
Stahlmann, Wilh.; Chile, 1852 ***1192.4*** *p55*
Stahlschmitt, Adam 64; America, 1867 ***5475.1*** *p543*
*Wife:*Marianne Stuber 68
*Son:*Johann
Stahlschmitt, Johann *SEE* Stahlschmitt, Adam
Stahlschmitt, Marianne Stuber 68 *SEE* Stahlschmitt, Adam
Staible, Mathias 28; Mississippi, 1847 ***778.6*** *p316*
Staible, Valentin 23; Mississippi, 1847 ***778.6*** *p316*
Stainbank, William; Annapolis, MD, 1725 ***1220.12*** *p755*
Staines, Elizabeth; Barbados, 1679 ***1220.12*** *p755*
Staines, Elizabeth; Barbados, 1681 ***1220.12*** *p755*
Staines, Ruth; Barbados or Jamaica, 1691 ***1220.12*** *p755*
Staines, Thomas; America, 1737 ***1220.12*** *p755*
Staines, William; America, 1770 ***1220.12*** *p755*
Stainforth, Isaac; America, 1758 ***1220.12*** *p755*
Stains, Benjamin; America, 1745 ***1220.12*** *p755*
Stains, William; America, 1754 ***1220.12*** *p755*
Stainton, James 48; Ontario, 1871 ***1823.21*** *p348*
Stainton, John; Barbados, 1699 ***1220.12*** *p755*
Stainton, John 40; Ontario, 1871 ***1823.21*** *p348*
Stainton, Mary; America, 1744 ***1220.12*** *p755*
Stajewski, Wladyslaw 30; New York, NY, 1911 ***6533.11*** *p9*
Staker, Joseph 31; Ontario, 1871 ***1823.21*** *p348*
Stalder, Antoine 44; New Castle, DE, 1817-1818 ***90.20*** *p154*
Stalder, Johann Adam 38; Died enroute, 1817-1818 ***90.20*** *p154*
Stalder, Joseph 56; New Castle, DE, 1817-1818 ***90.20*** *p154*
Stale, Andrew; Ohio, 1809-1852 ***4511.35*** *p52*
Staley, Andrew; America, 1685 ***1220.12*** *p755*
Stalhammar, Baltzar Henrik; America, 1853-1902 ***6412.40*** *p156*
Stalhuth, Heinrich; America, 1852 ***7420.1*** *p98*
Stalker, William 29; Ontario, 1871 ***1823.21*** *p348*
Stall, Achd. 36; New York, NY, 1835 ***5024.1*** *p136*
Stall, Cath. 14; America, 1847 ***778.6*** *p316*
Stall, Christian 4; America, 1847 ***778.6*** *p317*
Stall, Christian 28; America, 1847 ***778.6*** *p317*
Stall, Franziska 6 months; America, 1847 ***778.6*** *p317*
Stall, Frederick; Ohio, 1809-1852 ***4511.35*** *p52*
Stall, Gaspard 16; America, 1847 ***778.6*** *p317*
Stall, Georg 8; America, 1847 ***778.6*** *p317*
Stall, John; Philadelphia, 1778 ***8529.30*** *p7*
Stall, Joseph 9; America, 1847 ***778.6*** *p317*
Stall, Joseph 42; America, 1847 ***778.6*** *p317*
Stall, Mag. 43; America, 1847 ***778.6*** *p317*
Stall, Magda. 3; America, 1847 ***778.6*** *p317*
Stall, Marga. 29; America, 1847 ***778.6*** *p317*
Stallard, Sarah; America, 1769 ***1220.12*** *p755*
Stallard, William; America, 1765 ***1220.12*** *p755*
Staller, Esther Scholofsky *SEE* Staller, William
Staller, William; Detroit, 1930 ***1640.60*** *p77*
*Wife:*Esther Scholofsky
Stallward, Charles 33; Ontario, 1871 ***1823.21*** *p348*
Stalmacher, Agnes 35; Michigan, 1880 ***4491.36*** *p21*
Stalmacher, John 47; Michigan, 1880 ***4491.36*** *p21*
Stalp, Theo; Nebraska, 1905 ***3004.30*** *p46*
Stalwood, George 35; Ontario, 1871 ***1823.21*** *p348*
St-Amand, Pierre; Quebec, 1600-1669 ***4514.3*** *p350*
Stamm, Adam; America, 1905 ***8023.44*** *p380*
Stamm, George; Illinois, 1858 ***6079.1*** *p13*
Stamm, Karl; America, 1865 ***2526.43*** *p223*
With family
Stammers, John; America, 1775 ***1220.12*** *p755*
Stamp, Roger; America, 1746 ***1220.12*** *p756*
Stamp, Thomas 28; New York, NY, 1825 ***6178.50*** *p78*
Stamp, Thomas 36; Ontario, 1871 ***1823.21*** *p348*
Stamper, George; Washington, 1880 ***2770.40*** *p134*
Stamper, Robert; America, 1752 ***1220.12*** *p756*
Stamps, William; America, 1768 ***1220.12*** *p756*
Stamton, Ellen; Ontario, 1871 ***1823.21*** *p348*
Stamton, Ellen 83; Ontario, 1871 ***1823.21*** *p348*
Stan, Anton; North Carolina, 1856 ***1088.45*** *p33*
Stanard, . . .; Potomac, 1729 ***1220.12*** *p757*
Stanborough, John; Nevis or Jamaica, 1722 ***1220.12*** *p756*
Stanburn, Robert; America, 1730 ***1220.12*** *p756*
Stanbury, Ann; America, 1746 ***1220.12*** *p756*
Stanbury, Gerthrud; America, 1724 ***1220.12*** *p756*
Stanbury, John; America, 1756 ***1220.12*** *p756*
Stanbury, Roger; Jamaica, 1661 ***1220.12*** *p756*
Stanbury, William; America, 1733 ***1220.12*** *p756*
Standeford, William; America, 1759 ***1220.12*** *p756*
Standerd, John; Louisiana, 1836-1840 ***4981.45*** *p213*
Standerwick, Nathaniel; America, 1685 ***1220.12*** *p756*
Standfad, Mary; America, 1743 ***1220.12*** *p756*
Standfast, Richard; America, 1729 ***1220.12*** *p756*
Standidge, Sarah; America, 1753 ***1220.12*** *p756*
Standish, Miles; Plymouth, MA, 1620 ***1920.45*** *p5*
*Wife:*Rose
Standish, Rose *SEE* Standish, Miles
Standitch, Mary; America, 1738 ***1220.12*** *p756*
Standke, Christian Friedrich Wm.; Wisconsin, 1896 ***6795.8*** *p177*
Standley, Humphry; Virginia, 1775 ***1220.12*** *p756*
Standworth, Henry; America, 1745 ***1220.12*** *p756*
Stanecki, Helen; Detroit, 1929-1930 ***6214.5*** *p61*
Staneford, Ephraim; Philadelphia, 1778 ***8529.30*** *p5A*
Stanek, Frances; Detroit, 1930 ***1640.60*** *p77*
Stanek, Jan; Wisconsin, 1856 ***2853.20*** *p345*
Stanek, Jerry; Nebraska, 1905 ***3004.30*** *p46*
Stanek, Vincent; Detroit, 1930 ***1640.60*** *p77*
Stanely, William; America, 1758 ***1220.12*** *p757*
Stanes, Ezekiel; America, 1741-1744 ***1220.12*** *p755*
Stanfart, John; Virginia, 1740 ***1220.12*** *p756*
Stanfield, Elizabeth; America, 1766 ***1220.12*** *p756*
Stanfield, Elizabeth; Potomac, 1743 ***1220.12*** *p756*
Stanfield, John 58; Ontario, 1871 ***1823.21*** *p348*
Stanfield, Joseph 40; Ontario, 1871 ***1823.21*** *p348*
Stanfield, Julian 28; Ontario, 1871 ***1823.21*** *p348*
Stanfield, Richard 40; Ontario, 1871 ***1823.21*** *p348*
Stanfield, Theophilus 27; Ontario, 1871 ***1823.21*** *p348*
Stanfield, William 46; Ontario, 1871 ***1823.21*** *p348*
Stanford, Augustine; Barbados, 1672 ***1220.12*** *p756*
Stanford, Elizabeth; America, 1774 ***1220.12*** *p756*
Stanford, James; America, 1662 ***1220.12*** *p756*
Stanford, Margaret; America, 1720 ***1220.12*** *p756*
Stanford, William; America, 1748 ***1220.12*** *p756*
Stanford, William; Virginia, 1739 ***1220.12*** *p756*
Stange, Died.; New York, 1860 ***358.56*** *p149*
Stanger, Henry 26; Ontario, 1871 ***1823.17*** *p155*
Stangroom, Susannah; America, 1769 ***1220.12*** *p756*
Stanhope, John; America, 1756 ***1220.12*** *p756*
Staniell, Edward; Barbados, 1675 ***1220.12*** *p756*
Staniford, Walter; America, 1770 ***1220.12*** *p756*
Stanisiere, Jean 20; New Orleans, 1846 ***778.6*** *p317*
Stanisstreet, Richard; Marston's Wharf, 1782 ***8529.30*** *p16*
Stanistreet, Richard; Marston's Wharf, 1782 ***8529.30*** *p16*
Stanke, Charles; Wisconsin, 1882 ***6795.8*** *p77*
Stanke, Ernestine 19; New York, NY, 1885 ***1883.7*** *p45*
Stanke, Ernst. 51; New York, NY, 1885 ***1883.7*** *p45*
Stanke, Johanne. 54; New York, NY, 1885 ***1883.7*** *p45*
Stanke, Louise 9; New York, NY, 1885 ***1883.7*** *p45*
Stanke, Wilhelm Friedrich; Wisconsin, 1893 ***6795.8*** *p77*
Stanke, Wilhelm Friedrich Christian; Wisconsin, 1889 ***6795.8*** *p77*
Stankie, Minnie; Wisconsin, 1898 ***6795.8*** *p142*
Stankist, Jan 24; New York, NY, 1890 ***1883.7*** *p48*
Stankovsky, Josef; St. Louis, 1848-1849 ***2853.20*** *p21*
*Brother:*Matej
Stankovsky, Matej *SEE* Stankovsky, Josef
Stanland, John; Maryland, 1736 ***1220.12*** *p756*
Stanley, Angelina 17; Quebec, 1870 ***8364.32*** *p26*
Stanley, Ann; America, 1765 ***1220.12*** *p756*
Stanley, Anne; America, 1739 ***1220.12*** *p756*
Stanley, David; Illinois, 1855 ***6079.1*** *p13*
Stanley, Edward; America, 1743 ***1220.12*** *p756*
Stanley, Edward; America, 1772 ***1220.12*** *p756*
Stanley, Edward 58; Ontario, 1871 ***1823.21*** *p348*
Stanley, Fanny 25; New York, NY, 1894 ***6512.1*** *p181*
Stanley, James; America, 1764 ***1220.12*** *p756*
Stanley, James; Maryland, 1737 ***1220.12*** *p756*
Stanley, James; Maryland, 1744 ***1220.12*** *p756*
Stanley, James 52; Ontario, 1871 ***1823.21*** *p348*
Stanley, Jane 18; Ontario, 1871 ***1823.21*** *p349*
Stanley, Jane 63; Ontario, 1871 ***1823.21*** *p349*
Stanley, Joanna; Maryland, 1674 ***1236.25*** *p50*
Stanley, Johanna; America, 1674 ***1220.12*** *p756*
Stanley, John; America, 1702 ***1220.12*** *p756*
Stanley, John; America, 1747 ***1220.12*** *p756*
Stanley, John; America, 1748 ***1220.12*** *p756*
Stanley, John; America, 1753 ***1220.12*** *p756*
Stanley, John; America, 1755 ***1220.12*** *p756*
Stanley, John; America, 1767 ***1220.12*** *p756*
Stanley, John; America, 1772 ***1220.12*** *p756*
Stanley, John 60; Ontario, 1871 ***1823.21*** *p349*
Stanley, John; Virginia, 1736 ***1220.12*** *p756*
Stanley, John; Virginia, 1773 ***1220.12*** *p756*
Stanley, Jonas 35; Ontario, 1871 ***1823.21*** *p349*
Stanley, Joseph; Long Island, 1781 ***8529.30*** *p10A*
Stanley, Laurence 64; Ontario, 1871 ***1823.17*** *p155*
Stanley, Mary; America, 1733 ***1220.12*** *p757*
Stanley, Mary; America, 1750 ***1220.12*** *p757*
Stanley, Mary; Barbados, 1668 ***1220.12*** *p756*
Stanley, Michael; Marston's Wharf, 1782 ***8529.30*** *p16*
Stanley, Nathaniel; America, 1730 ***1220.12*** *p757*
Stanley, Patrick 66; Ontario, 1871 ***1823.17*** *p155*
Stanley, Peter; America, 1764 ***1220.12*** *p757*
Stanley, Samuel; America, 1766 ***1220.12*** *p757*
Stanley, Temperance; Annapolis, MD, 1726 ***1220.12*** *p757*
Stanley, Thomas; America, 1678 ***1220.12*** *p757*
Stanley, Thomas; America, 1734 ***1220.12*** *p757*
Stanley, Thomas; America, 1751 ***1220.12*** *p757*
Stanley, Thomas; America, 1754 ***1220.12*** *p757*
Stanley, Thomas; America, 1772 ***1220.12*** *p757*
Stanley, Thomas; America, 1775 ***1220.12*** *p757*
Stanley, Thomas 22; Ontario, 1871 ***1823.21*** *p349*
Stanley, Thomas 23; Ontario, 1871 ***1823.21*** *p349*
Stanley, Thomas 50; Ontario, 1871 ***1823.17*** *p155*
Stanley, William; America, 1767 ***1220.12*** *p757*
Stanley, William; Maryland, 1719 ***1220.12*** *p757*
Stanley, William 15; Quebec, 1870 ***8364.32*** *p26*
Stanley Family ; Canada, n.d. ***9228.50*** *p21A*
Stanlins, Edward; America, 1772 ***1220.12*** *p757*
Stanly, Robert 41; Ontario, 1871 ***1823.21*** *p349*
Stanly, Thomas 62; Ontario, 1871 ***1823.21*** *p349*
Stanmore, Elizabeth; America, 1765 ***1220.12*** *p757*
Stannard, Elizabeth; America, 1767 ***1220.12*** *p757*
Stannard, James; Colorado, 1887 ***1029.59*** *p85*
Stannard, James; Colorado, 1894 ***1029.59*** *p85*

Stannard, Stephen; America, 1771 ***1220.12*** *p757*
Stanner, Anna 20; Port uncertain, 1846 ***778.6*** *p317*
Stanner, Nicolas 25; Port uncertain, 1846 ***778.6*** *p317*
Stanners, George; America, 1754-1773 ***1220.12*** *p757*
Stannesstreet, Richard; Marston's Wharf, 1782 ***8529.30*** *p16*
Stanney, William; West Indies, 1686 ***1220.12*** *p757*
Stannifer, Mary; America, 1746 ***1220.12*** *p757*
Stanning, John; Virginia, 1736 ***1220.12*** *p757*
Stanninot, William; America, 1751 ***1220.12*** *p757*
Stannton, Esther 20; Ontario, 1871 ***1823.21*** *p349*
Stannum, John; Barbados or Jamaica, 1683 ***1220.12*** *p757*
Stanour, Michael; Ohio, 1809-1852 ***4511.35*** *p52*
Stansbury, Jonathan; America, 1768 ***1220.12*** *p757*
Stansbury, Mary; America, 1744 ***1220.12*** *p757*
Stansby, Joanna; Maryland, 1674 ***1236.25*** *p50*
Stansfield, James; America, 1760 ***1220.12*** *p757*
Stansfield, James; America, 1774 ***1220.12*** *p757*
Stansfield, Samuel 66; Ontario, 1871 ***1823.21*** *p349*
Stanter, Joseph; Cleveland, OH, 1852-1854 ***9722.10*** *p127*
Stanton, Adam; America, 1739 ***1220.12*** *p757*
Stanton, Anne; America, 1727 ***1220.12*** *p757*
Stanton, Benjamin; Ohio, 1833 ***3580.20*** *p33*
Stanton, Benjamin; Ohio, 1833 ***6020.12*** *p22*
Stanton, Bridget; New Brunswick, 1842 ***2978.20*** *p9*
Stanton, Bridget; New Orleans, 1851 ***7242.30*** *p155*
Stanton, Charles; Virginia, 1752 ***1220.12*** *p757*
Stanton, Elizabeth; America, 1733 ***1220.12*** *p757*
Stanton, James; America, 1775 ***1220.12*** *p757*
Stanton, James 55; Ontario, 1871 ***1823.21*** *p349*
Stanton, James 17; Quebec, 1870 ***8364.32*** *p26*
Stanton, John; America, 1726 ***1220.12*** *p757*
Stanton, John; America, 1742 ***1220.12*** *p757*
Stanton, John; America, 1750 ***1220.12*** *p757*
Stanton, John; America, 1773 ***1220.12*** *p757*
Stanton, John; Detroit, 1929-1930 ***6214.5*** *p69*
Stanton, John 61; Ontario, 1871 ***1823.21*** *p349*
Stanton, John C.; Pennsylvania, 1866 ***8513.31*** *p428*
Stanton, Margaret; New Brunswick, 1842 ***2978.20*** *p9*
Stanton, Mary; New Brunswick, 1842 ***2978.20*** *p9*
Stanton, Patrick; Colorado, 1867 ***1029.59*** *p86*
Stanton, Patrick; New Brunswick, 1842 ***2978.20*** *p9*
Stanton, Peter; America, 1740 ***1220.12*** *p757*
Stanton, Phoebe A. 46; Michigan, 1880 ***4491.39*** *p29*
Stanton, Thomas 60; Michigan, 1880 ***4491.39*** *p29*
Stanton, Thomas; New Brunswick, 1842 ***2978.20*** *p9*
Stanton, Thomas 52; Ontario, 1871 ***1823.21*** *p349*
Stanton, William; America, 1728 ***1220.12*** *p758*
Stanton, William; Barbados or Jamaica, 1702 ***1220.12*** *p757*
Stanton, William; New Orleans, 1850 ***7242.30*** *p155*
Stanton, William 48; Ontario, 1871 ***1823.21*** *p349*
Stanyland, Thomas; America, 1729 ***1220.12*** *p758*
Stanz, J.B.; New York, 1860 ***358.56*** *p3*
Stanzell, Nicholas; America, 1700 ***1220.12*** *p758*
Stapel, Ernst Johann; Wisconsin, 1903 ***6795.8*** *p142*
Stapf, Gottfried; America, 1886 ***179.55*** *p19*
Staple, Abraham; America, 1656 ***1220.12*** *p758*
Staple, Joseph 19; Ontario, 1871 ***1823.21*** *p349*
Staple, Leonard; America, 1685 ***1220.12*** *p758*
Stapleford, John 65; Ontario, 1871 ***1823.17*** *p155*
Stapleford, Richard 22; Ontario, 1871 ***1823.21*** *p349*
Stapler, John; America, 1754 ***1220.12*** *p758*
Stapler, John 18; Quebec, 1870 ***8364.32*** *p26*
Staples, Ann; America, 1770 ***1220.12*** *p758*
Staples, Charles S.; Colorado, 1884 ***1029.59*** *p86*
Staples, Charles S.; Colorado, 1891 ***1029.59*** *p86*
Staples, Daniel; America, 1743 ***1220.12*** *p758*
Staples, Henry 15; Quebec, 1870 ***8364.32*** *p26*
Staples, James; America, 1723 ***1220.12*** *p758*
Staples, John; America, 1771 ***1220.12*** *p758*
Staples, John; Ohio, 1845 ***2763.1*** *p22*
Staples, Mary; America, 1742 ***1220.12*** *p758*
Staples, Mathew; America, 1775 ***1220.12*** *p758*
Staples, Tom 19; Quebec, 1870 ***8364.32*** *p26*
Staples, William; America, 1744 ***1220.12*** *p758*
Staples, William 32; Ontario, 1871 ***1823.17*** *p155*
Stapleton, Arthur 40; Ontario, 1871 ***1823.21*** *p349*
Stapleton, Arthur 83; Ontario, 1871 ***1823.21*** *p349*
Stapleton, Benjamin; America, 1767 ***1220.12*** *p758*
Stapleton, Charles; Maryland or Virginia, 1733 ***1220.12*** *p758*
Stapleton, James 45; Ontario, 1871 ***1823.17*** *p155*
Stapleton, John 50; Ontario, 1871 ***1823.17*** *p155*
Stapleton, Mathew 38; Ontario, 1871 ***1823.17*** *p155*
Stapleton, Sarah; Maryland or Virginia, 1733 ***1220.12*** *p758*
Stapleton, Thomas; America, 1768 ***1220.12*** *p758*
Stapleton, Timothy; Colorado, 1887 ***1029.59*** *p86*
Stapleton, William; America, 1769 ***1220.12*** *p758*
Stapleton, William 55; Ontario, 1871 ***1823.21*** *p349*
Stapling, Ambrose; Barbados or Jamaica, 1686 ***1220.12*** *p758*
Stapp, Georg; America, 1846 ***2526.42*** *p147*
Stappelton, Karl Ludwig; America, 1882 ***2526.43*** *p182*
Star, James; America, 1778 ***8529.30*** *p16*
Star, John; Colorado, 1887 ***1029.59*** *p86*
Star, John; Colorado, 1895 ***1029.59*** *p86*
Starbuck, Richard; America, 1757 ***1220.12*** *p758*
Starck, Peter; Pennsylvania, 1848 ***170.15*** *p43*
With wife
Stardin, Nicolas; Quebec, 1654 ***9221.17*** *p316*
Stare, Knut Wilhelm; Philadelphia, 1876 ***6410.15*** *p105*
Starek, . . .; Pennsylvania, 1750-1799 ***2853.20*** *p17*
Stark, Alven 16; Minnesota, 1925 ***2769.54*** *p1384*
Stark, Anna G.; St. Paul, MN, 1873 ***1865.50*** *p110*
Stark, Dominique 45; New Orleans, 1848 ***778.6*** *p317*
Stark, Eino 23; Minnesota, 1925 ***2769.54*** *p1384*
Stark, Eloy 1; America, 1840 ***778.6*** *p317*
Stark, George 2; America, 1840 ***778.6*** *p317*
Stark, Hannah Katarina; St. Paul, MN, 1879 ***1865.50*** *p110*
Stark, Madelaine 28; America, 1840 ***778.6*** *p317*
Stark, Michel 26; America, 1840 ***778.6*** *p317*
Stark, William 50; Ontario, 1871 ***1823.21*** *p349*
Starke, Franz; America, 1922 ***8023.44*** *p380*
Starkey, George; Virginia, 1727 ***1220.12*** *p758*
Starkey, John; Nevis or Jamaica, 1722 ***1220.12*** *p758*
Starkey, John; Ohio, 1809-1852 ***4511.35*** *p52*
Starkey, Richard; America, 1754 ***1220.12*** *p758*
Starkey, Sarah; America, 1721 ***1220.12*** *p758*
Starkie, William; Barbados, 1664 ***1220.12*** *p758*
Starkloff, Hugo M.; Illinois, 1861 ***4487.25*** *p73*
Starky, Hanna; Annapolis, MD, 1723 ***1220.12*** *p758*
Starlin, Thomas; America, 1750 ***1220.12*** *p758*
Starling, Edward; America, 1773 ***1220.12*** *p758*
Starling, Elizabeth; Died enroute, 1729 ***1220.12*** *p758*
Starling, George; Barbados, 1676 ***1220.12*** *p758*
Starling, Sarah; America, 1724 ***1220.12*** *p758*
Starnell, William; Barbados or Jamaica, 1678 ***1220.12*** *p758*
Starnglanz, David; North Carolina, 1860 ***1088.45*** *p33*
Starosta, Anna; Detroit, 1929 ***1640.55*** *p114*
Starr, Dennis; Washington, 1884 ***2770.40*** *p193*
Starr, Edward; Ohio, 1840-1897 ***8365.35*** *p18*
Starr, Joan; Barbados, 1663 ***1220.12*** *p758*
Starr, John; America, 1758 ***1220.12*** *p758*
Starr, John; Iowa, 1888 ***1211.15*** *p19*
Starr, Matheur 29; Ontario, 1871 ***1823.17*** *p155*
Starr, Mathias; Iowa, 1888 ***1211.15*** *p19*
Starr, Sarah; America, 1775 ***1220.12*** *p758*
Starr, Stephen; Barbados, 1663 ***1220.12*** *p758*
Starr, Stephen 46; Ontario, 1871 ***1823.21*** *p349*
Starr, William; Maryland, 1737 ***1220.12*** *p758*
Starr, William 50; Ontario, 1871 ***1823.21*** *p349*
Starre, Elizabeth; Barbados or Jamaica, 1697 ***1220.12*** *p758*
Starry, Jacob; Ohio, 1809-1852 ***4511.35*** *p52*
Stars, John; America, 1768 ***1220.12*** *p758*
Start, John; Rappahannock, VA, 1729 ***1220.12*** *p758*
Startin, Thomas; America, 1750 ***1220.12*** *p758*
Starting, Susannah; Ohio, 1849 ***9228.50*** *p323*
Startzman, David; West Virginia, 1787 ***1132.30*** *p146*
Starzman, Christian; Washington, 1887 ***6015.10*** *p16*
Stashefsky, Ben; Detroit, 1929-1930 ***6214.5*** *p61*
Stastny, Josef *SEE* Stastny, Josef
Stastny, Josef; Texas, 1856 ***2853.20*** *p75*
*Father:*Josef
State, Edward; America, 1754 ***1220.12*** *p758*
States, Francis; America, 1726 ***1220.12*** *p758*
Statham, Thomas; Barbados or Jamaica, 1697 ***1220.12*** *p758*
Stather, William; America, 1762 ***1220.12*** *p758*
Stathum, Silas; North Carolina, 1852 ***1088.45*** *p33*
Staton, Samuel 37; Ontario, 1871 ***1823.21*** *p349*
Staub, Jacob; Louisiana, 1836-1840 ***4981.45*** *p213*
Staub, Johannes; New England, 1867 ***170.15*** *p43*
With wife & 2 children
Staub, John; Louisiana, 1874 ***4981.45*** *p134*
Staubli, Anton; New Castle, DE, 1817-1818 ***90.20*** *p154*
Staubli, Conrad 50; New Castle, DE, 1817-1818 ***90.20*** *p154*
Staubli, Karl 50; New Castle, DE, 1817-1818 ***90.20*** *p154*
Staubli, Nicolas 49; New Castle, DE, 1817-1818 ***90.20*** *p154*
Stauch, Henrich; Port uncertain, 1864 ***170.15*** *p43*
Stauder, Margaretha 55; America, 1848 ***778.6*** *p317*
Staudt, Jakob 29; New York, 1881 ***5475.1*** *p196*
Staudt, Johann; America, 1877 ***5475.1*** *p134*
*Wife:*Margarethe Engstler
*Son:*Karl
*Daughter:*Margarethe
*Son:*Mathias
*Son:*Nikolaus
*Son:*Peter
Staudt, Johann; America, 1877 ***5475.1*** *p135*
Staudt, Karl *SEE* Staudt, Johann
Staudt, Katharina; America, 1876 ***5475.1*** *p141*
Staudt, Margarethe *SEE* Staudt, Johann
Staudt, Margarethe Engstler *SEE* Staudt, Johann
Staudt, Mathias *SEE* Staudt, Johann
Staudt, Nikolaus *SEE* Staudt, Johann
Staudt, Peter *SEE* Staudt, Johann
Staudt, Peter; America, 1883 ***5475.1*** *p130*
Stauffacher, Henry; Illinois, 1855 ***6079.1*** *p13*
Staunton, William; America, 1685 ***1220.12*** *p757*
Staup, John; Ohio, 1809-1852 ***4511.35*** *p52*
Staut, Michel 25; America, 1840 ***778.6*** *p317*
Stave, Sarah; America, 1746 ***1220.12*** *p758*
Staveley, Elizabeth; America, 1760 ***1220.12*** *p758*
Staveraugh, Elizabeth; America, 1745 ***1220.12*** *p759*
Stavey, William; Rappahannock, VA, 1726 ***1220.12*** *p759*
Stawarz, John; Detroit, 1929-1930 ***6214.5*** *p70*
Staydon, William; Boston, 1774 ***8529.30*** *p3*
Stayner, Richard; America, 1730 ***1220.12*** *p755*
Staynes, Daniel; America, 1700 ***1220.12*** *p755*
Stclair, John L. 23; Ontario, 1871 ***1823.21*** *p349*
St Clair, Moses 42; Ontario, 1871 ***1823.21*** *p348*
St Clair, William 55; Ontario, 1871 ***1823.17*** *p155*
Stead, Charles 64; Ontario, 1871 ***1823.21*** *p349*
Stead, James; America, 1769 ***1220.12*** *p759*
Stead, John 33; Michigan, 1880 ***4491.36*** *p21*
Stead, Joshua 47; Ontario, 1871 ***1823.21*** *p349*
Stead, Thomas 17; North Carolina, 1774 ***1422.10*** *p56*
Steadman, Ann; America, 1742 ***1220.12*** *p759*
Steadman, Catherine; Virginia, 1741 ***1220.12*** *p759*
Steadman, James; America, 1742 ***1220.12*** *p759*
Steadman, Michael 35; Ontario, 1871 ***1823.21*** *p349*
Steadman, Robert 74; Ontario, 1871 ***1823.17*** *p155*
Steadman, Thomas 60; Ontario, 1871 ***1823.21*** *p349*
Steads, Margaret 40; Ontario, 1871 ***1823.21*** *p349*
Steads, Richard; America, 1769 ***1220.12*** *p759*
Steale, Anthony; America, 1724 ***1220.12*** *p759*
Steale, Thomas; Barbados or Jamaica, 1696 ***1220.12*** *p759*
Steale, William; America, 1772 ***1220.12*** *p760*
Stearn, Joseph; America, 1768 ***1220.12*** *p759*
Stearns, J. P.; California, 1868 ***1131.61*** *p89*
Steavens, James; Virginia, 1734 ***1220.12*** *p761*
Stebbing, Aaron; America, 1773 ***1220.12*** *p759*
Stebbing, Thomas; America, 1756 ***1220.12*** *p759*
Stebbings, William; Colorado, 1885 ***1029.59*** *p86*
Stebbins, John; America, 1675 ***1220.12*** *p759*
Stebbs, John; America, 1757 ***1220.12*** *p759*
Steber, John George; New York, 1860 ***358.56*** *p149*
Stecher, Franz; Washington, 1884 ***2770.40*** *p193*
Steckel, Baron 58; New York, NY, 1878 ***9253.2*** *p45*
Steckler, Adelia 16; New York, NY, 1898 ***7951.13*** *p44*
Steckler, Ambros 14; New York, NY, 1898 ***7951.13*** *p44*
Steckler, Elisabeth 9; New York, NY, 1898 ***7951.13*** *p44*
Steckler, Ignatz 3; New York, NY, 1898 ***7951.13*** *p44*
Steckler, Ignatz 28; New York, NY, 1898 ***7951.13*** *p44*
Steckler, Jacob 12; New York, NY, 1898 ***7951.13*** *p44*
Steckler, Katherina 5; New York, NY, 1898 ***7951.13*** *p44*
Steckler, Ludwig 40; New York, NY, 1898 ***7951.13*** *p44*
Steckler, Monika 3 months; New York, NY, 1898 ***7951.13*** *p44*
Steckler, Monika 37; New York, NY, 1898 ***7951.13*** *p44*
Steckler, Nicholas 10; New York, NY, 1898 ***7951.13*** *p44*
Steckler, Rapheal 3; New York, NY, 1898 ***7951.13*** *p44*
Steckler, Rosa 2; New York, NY, 1898 ***7951.13*** *p44*
Steckler, Rosa 6 months; New York, NY, 1898 ***7951.13*** *p44*
Steckler, Theresia 2; New York, NY, 1898 ***7951.13*** *p44*
Steckler, Theresia 23; New York, NY, 1898 ***7951.13*** *p44*
Steddall, Elizabeth; America, 1742 ***1220.12*** *p759*
Stedden, Frank; Ohio, 1809-1852 ***4511.35*** *p52*
Steding, Carl; America, 1870 ***7420.1*** *p286*
Steding, Friedrich; America, 1900 ***7420.1*** *p401*
Steding, Gerhard; America, 1852 ***7420.1*** *p98*
Steding, Gustav; America, 1902 ***7420.1*** *p378*
With 3 children
Steding, Gustav; America, 1904 ***7420.1*** *p401*
Steding, Heinrich; America, 1907 ***7420.1*** *p383*
Steding, Ludwig; America, 1854 ***7420.1*** *p131*
Steding, Wilhelm; America, 1912 ***7420.1*** *p402*
Stedman, Christopher; America, 1737 ***1220.12*** *p759*
Stedman, Jane 26; Ontario, 1871 ***1823.17*** *p155*
Stedman, John, Jr.; America, 1737 ***1220.12*** *p759*
Stedman, John, Sr.; America, 1737 ***1220.12*** *p759*
Stedman, Samuel; America, 1758 ***1220.12*** *p759*
Stedman, William; America, 1773 ***1220.12*** *p759*
Stedronsky, Jan; South Dakota, 1871-1910 ***2853.20*** *p247*
Stedronsky, Josef Jan; Cleveland, OH, 1852 ***2853.20*** *p475*
Stedwell, John D. 57; Ontario, 1871 ***1823.21*** *p349*

Steebens, Wm. 22; Virginia, 1635 *1183.3 p31*
Steed, John 85; Ontario, 1871 *1823.17 p156*
Steed, Samuel; America, 1749 *1220.12 p759*
Steedman, William 43; Ontario, 1871 *1823.21 p349*
Steeds, William 54; Ontario, 1871 *1823.21 p350*
Steeg, Jacob; Louisiana, 1836-1840 *4981.45 p213*
Steege, Mr.; America, 1862 *7420.1 p215*
Steege, Anne Marie Henriette Homeier *SEE* Steege,
Johann Otto
Steege, Anne Sophie Marie *SEE* Steege, Johann Otto
Steege, Anne Sophie Marie; America, 1858 *7420.1 p182*
Steege, Catharine Soph. Schmidt *SEE* Steege, Conrad
Heinrich Philipp
Steege, Catharine Sophie; America, 1860 *7420.1 p200*
Steege, Catharine Sophie; America, 1860 *7420.1 p202*
Steege, Conrad Heinrich Philipp; America, 1846 *7420.1*
p49
  *Wife:*Catharine Soph. Schmidt
  With son 8
  With daughter 13
  With son 4
  With daughter 11
Steege, Conrad Wilhelm *SEE* Steege, Johann Heinrich
Christoph
Steege, Dorothee Charlotte; America, 1856 *7420.1 p145*
Steege, Engel Marie Bade *SEE* Steege, Johann Conrad
Steege, Engel Marie Charl. *SEE* Steege, Engel Marie
Charlotte Sandmeier
Steege, Engel Marie Charlotte; America, 1846 *7420.1*
p49
  *Daughter:*Engel Marie Charl.
  *Son:*Johann Heinrich Christoph
Steege, Engel Marie Sophie *SEE* Steege, Johann Conrad
Steege, Friedrich; America, 1854 *7420.1 p131*
Steege, Friedrich Wilhelm; America, 1866 *7420.1 p250*
Steege, Hans Heinrich *SEE* Steege, Johann Conrad
Steege, Hans Heinrich; America, 1864 *7420.1 p227*
Steege, Hans Heinrich; America, 1866 *7420.1 p250*
Steege, Hans Heinrich; Port uncertain, 1850 *7420.1 p76*
Steege, Hans Heinrich Conrad; America, 1848 *7420.1*
p62
  *Wife:*Katharine Sophie Bruns
Steege, Hans Heinrich Conrad; Port uncertain, 1856
7420.1 p154
Steege, Hans Heinrich Wilhelm; America, 1846 *7420.1*
p49
Steege, Heinrich; America, 1882 *7420.1 p332*
  With wife & 2 children
Steege, Heinrich Christian; America, 1867 *7420.1 p265*
Steege, Heinrich Conrad; America, 1871 *7420.1 p292*
Steege, Heinrich Conrad Christoph *SEE* Steege, Johann
Heinrich Christoph
Steege, Heinrich Wilhelm; America, 1867 *7420.1 p265*
Steege, Johann Christian; America, 1854 *7420.1 p131*
Steege, Johann Conrad *SEE* Steege, Johann Conrad
Steege, Johann Conrad; America, 1856 *7420.1 p154*
  *Son:*Johann Conrad
  *Wife:*Engel Marie Bade
  *Son:*Hans Heinrich
  *Son:*Johann Friedr. Conrad
  *Daughter:*Engel Marie Sophie
Steege, Johann Friedr. Conrad *SEE* Steege, Johann
Conrad
Steege, Johann Friedrich; America, 1881 *7420.1 p325*
Steege, Johann Friedrich Conrad; America, 1866 *7420.1*
p250
Steege, Johann Heinrich; America, 1852 *7420.1 p98*
Steege, Johann Heinrich; America, 1854 *7420.1 p131*
Steege, Johann Heinrich Christoph *SEE* Steege, Engel
Marie Charlotte Sandmeier
Steege, Johann Heinrich Christoph; America, 1882
7420.1 p332
  *Wife:*Sophie Dorothea Vesche
  *Son:*Heinrich Conrad Christoph
  *Son:*Conrad Wilhelm
Steege, Johann Otto; America, 1846 *7420.1 p49*
  *Wife:*Anne Marie Henriette Homeier
  With child
  *Daughter:*Anne Sophie Marie
Steege, Johann Tonnies; America, 1851 *7420.1 p83*
Steege, Katharine Sophie Bruns *SEE* Steege, Hans
Heinrich Conrad
Steege, Marie Sophie; America, 1906 *7420.1 p401*
Steege, Sophie Dorothea Vesche *SEE* Steege, Johann
Heinrich Christoph
Steege, Thrine Sophie Marie; Port uncertain, 1850 *7420.1*
p76
Steel, Alexander; North Carolina, 1710 *3629.40 p7*
Steel, Ann 28; Ontario, 1871 *1823.21 p350*
Steel, Ann 47; Ontario, 1871 *1823.21 p350*
Steel, Charles; America, 1772 *1220.12 p759*
Steel, Donald 34; Ontario, 1871 *1823.21 p350*
Steel, Donald 49; Ontario, 1871 *1823.21 p350*

Steel, Donald 50; Ontario, 1871 *1823.21 p350*
Steel, John; America, 1740 *1220.12 p759*
Steel, John; America, 1757 *1220.12 p759*
Steel, John; America, 1772 *1220.12 p759*
Steel, John; America, 1774 *1220.12 p759*
Steel, John; North Carolina, 1837 *1088.45 p33*
Steel, John; North Carolina, 1856 *1088.45 p33*
Steel, John 40; Ontario, 1871 *1823.21 p350*
Steel, John; Rappahannock, VA, 1726 *1220.12 p759*
Steel, Mary; America, 1750 *1220.12 p759*
Steel, Mary; America, 1753 *1220.12 p759*
Steel, Michael; America, 1766 *1220.12 p759*
Steel, Owen; St. John, N.B., 1847 *2978.15 p40*
Steel, Richard; America, 1751 *1220.12 p759*
Steel, Richard; America, 1753 *1220.12 p759*
Steel, Robert 27; Ontario, 1871 *1823.21 p350*
Steel, Rory 39; Ontario, 1871 *1823.21 p350*
Steel, William; America, 1768 *1220.12 p759*
Steel, William; America, 1771 *1220.12 p759*
Steel, William J. 22; Indiana, 1850-1872 *9076.20 p67*
Steel, William R. 26; Indiana, 1870-1874 *9076.20 p68*
Steele, Alice; America, 1678 *1220.12 p759*
Steele, Anthony 74; Ontario, 1871 *1823.21 p350*
Steele, E. W.; California, 1868 *1131.61 p89*
Steele, Elizabeth; America, 1765 *1220.12 p759*
Steele, F. N.; California, 1868 *1131.61 p89*
Steele, Francis; New Hampshire, 1694 *9228.50 p613*
Steele, Henry 20; New York, NY, 1835 *5024.1 p137*
Steele, James; America, 1768 *1220.12 p759*
Steele, James W. 15; Michigan, 1880 *4491.36 p21*
Steele, John; Annapolis, MD, 1720 *1220.12 p759*
Steele, John *SEE* Steele, Sarah
Steele, John 25; Ontario, 1871 *1823.21 p350*
Steele, John 49; Ontario, 1871 *1823.21 p350*
Steele, Joseph; America, 1755 *1220.12 p759*
Steele, Joseph; America, 1765 *1220.12 p759*
Steele, Joseph; Halifax, N.S., 1760 *9228.50 p606*
Steele, Joseph; Massachusetts, 1731 *9228.50 p606*
Steele, Joseph *SEE* Steele, Sarah
Steele, Joseph 37; Michigan, 1880 *4491.36 p21*
Steele, Margaret A. 13; Michigan, 1880 *4491.36 p21*
Steele, Mary; America, 1774 *1220.12 p759*
Steele, Mary A. 34; Michigan, 1880 *4491.36 p21*
Steele, Matthew 66; Ontario, 1871 *1823.21 p350*
Steele, Peter 72; Ontario, 1871 *1823.21 p350*
Steele, Ralph; America, 1733 *1220.12 p759*
Steele, Samuel; America, 1680 *1220.12 p759*
Steele, Sarah; Barbados or Jamaica, 1691 *1220.12 p759*
Steele, Sarah; Massachusetts, 1735-1739 *9228.50 p606*
  *Brother:*John
  *Brother:*Joseph
Steele, Thomas; America, 1732 *1220.12 p759*
Steele, Thomas; America, 1771 *1220.12 p759*
Steele, William; America, 1767 *1220.12 p759*
Steele, William 32; Ontario, 1871 *1823.17 p156*
Steele, William 43; Ontario, 1871 *1823.21 p350*
Steeles, John 44; Ontario, 1871 *1823.21 p350*
Steels, Duke 40; Ontario, 1871 *1823.21 p350*
Steenken, George; North Carolina, 1853 *1088.45 p33*
Steensen, Johmer; Louisiana, 1874 *4981.45 p134*
Steeper, Mathew 57; Ontario, 1871 *1823.21 p350*
Steer, Hugh; America, 1773 *1220.12 p760*
Steer, James 42; Ontario, 1871 *1823.21 p350*
Steer, John, Sr.; America, 1744 *1220.12 p760*
Steer, Stephen 44; Ontario, 1871 *1823.21 p350*
Steer, Thomas; America, 1775 *1220.12 p760*
Steere, Daniel; America, 1726 *1220.12 p760*
Steere, Elizabeth; Barbados, 1679 *1220.12 p760*
Steeres, John; Barbados or Jamaica, 1686 *1220.12 p760*
Steeres, Mary; America, 1682 *1220.12 p760*
Steers, John; America, 1769 *1220.12 p760*
Steers, William; America, 1770 *1220.12 p760*
Steffan, Adam 19; America, 1846 *778.6 p317*
Steffan, Franz 3; America, 1746 *778.6 p317*
Steffan, Jean 6; America, 1746 *778.6 p317*
Steffan, Joseph 7; America, 1746 *778.6 p317*
Steffan, Magdalena 6 months; America, 1746 *778.6 p317*
Steffan, Michel 8; America, 1746 *778.6 p317*
Steffans, William; Iowa, 1894 *1211.15 p19*
Steffansson, Jon; New York, NY, 1846 *6412.40 p149*
Steffen, Anna *SEE* Steffen, Johann
Steffen, Barbara; America, 1800-1899 *5475.1 p148*
Steffen, Charles; Illinois, 1854 *6079.1 p13*
Steffen, Christian; Ohio, 1809-1852 *4511.35 p52*
Steffen, Elisabeth *SEE* Steffen, Johann
Steffen, Gustav; Washington, 1888 *2770.40 p26*
Steffen, Helena Weyand 49 *SEE* Steffen, Johann
Steffen, Henry; Iowa, 1887 *1211.15 p19*
Steffen, Jean 23; America, 1847 *778.6 p317*
Steffen, Johann *SEE* Steffen, Johann
Steffen, Johann 57; America, 1860 *5475.1 p360*
  *Wife:*Helena Weyand 49
  *Daughter:*Maria

  *Son:*Johann
  *Daughter:*Elisabeth
  *Daughter:*Anna
  *Son:*Nikolaus
  *Daughter:*Susanna
Steffen, Johann Conrad; America, 1845 *7420.1 p40*
  With wife
  With daughter 2
  With daughter 10
  With daughter 6
Steffen, Johann Friedrich Christoph; America, 1847
7420.1 p57
  With wife
  With daughter 1
  With daughter 4
  With daughter 13
Steffen, Jophie; New York, 1859 *358.56 p100*
Steffen, Margarethe Muller *SEE* Steffen, Michel
Steffen, Maria *SEE* Steffen, Johann
Steffen, Michel; America, 1881 *5475.1 p214*
  *Wife:*Margarethe Muller
Steffen, Nikolaus *SEE* Steffen, Johann
Steffen, Susanna *SEE* Steffen, Johann
Steffens, Henry; Iowa, 1887 *1211.15 p19*
Steffens, Henry Richard; Iowa, 1922 *1211.15 p19*
Steffens, M.; New York, 1860 *358.56 p3*
Steffensky, Anna Becker *SEE* Steffensky, Johann
Steffensky, Jakob *SEE* Steffensky, Johann
Steffensky, Joh. Peter *SEE* Steffensky, Johann
Steffensky, Johann *SEE* Steffensky, Johann
Steffensky, Johann; Texas, 1881 *5475.1 p202*
  *Wife:*Anna Becker
  *Son:*Joh. Peter
  *Son:*Jakob
  *Son:*Johann
  *Daughter:*Louise
  *Son:*Mathias
  *Son:*Peter
Steffensky, Louise *SEE* Steffensky, Johann
Steffensky, Margarethe; America, 1881 *5475.1 p203*
  *Daughter:*Barbara
  *Son:*Peter
  *Daughter:*Maria
Steffensky, Maria Stein *SEE* Steffensky, Peter
Steffensky, Mathias *SEE* Steffensky, Johann
Steffensky, Peter *SEE* Steffensky, Johann
Steffensky, Peter; Texas, 1885 *5475.1 p204*
  *Wife:*Maria Stein
Steffins, Anna C. R.; Philadelphia, 1867 *8513.31 p421*
Stefl, Leopold; St. Louis, 1901 *2853.20 p32*
Ste-Foy, Marguerite; Quebec, 1667 *4514.3 p281*
Stege, Anne Sophie Dorothea *SEE* Stege, Hans Heinrich
Conrad
Stege, Catharina Sophia; America, 1845 *7420.1 p41*
Stege, Catharine Sophie Gewecke *SEE* Stege, Hans
Heinrich Conrad
Stege, Catharine Sophie Dorothee *SEE* Stege, Hans
Heinrich Conrad
Stege, Conrad; America, 1857 *7420.1 p173*
Stege, Dorothea; America, 1857 *7420.1 p173*
  With 2 daughters
Stege, Engel Marie; America, 1840 *7420.1 p20*
Stege, Engel Marie; America, 1846 *7420.1 p47*
Stege, Engel Marie Lubke; America, 1840 *7420.1 p20*
Stege, Engel Marie Sophie; America, 1855 *7420.1 p142*
Stege, Engel Sophie *SEE* Stege, Hans Heinrich Conrad
Stege, Ernst Heinrich; America, 1888 *7420.1 p358*
Stege, Hans Heinrich Conrad; New York, NY, 1856
7420.1 p154
  *Wife:*Catharine Sophie Gewecke
  *Daughter:*Catharine Sophie Dorothee
  *Daughter:*Engel Sophie
  *Daughter:*Anne Sophie Dorothea
Stege, Hans Heinrich Wilhelm; Port uncertain, 1850
7420.1 p76
Stege, Heinrich Ernst; Port uncertain, 1888 *7420.1 p358*
Stege, Johann Heinrich; America, 1857 *7420.1 p173*
Stegemann, Remo; Iowa, 1890 *1211.15 p19*
Stegemann, William; Iowa, 1890 *1211.15 p19*
Stegger, William; Louisiana, 1874 *4981.45 p134*
Stegmaier, Gottlieb; America, 1854-1882 *179.55 p19*
Stegmann, Heinrich Dietrich Wilhelm; New York, NY,
1901 *7420.1 p377*
Stegmann, Wilhelm; Port uncertain, 1901 *7420.1 p377*
Stegmayer, Adam; Chile, 1852 *1192.4 p52*
  With wife
Stegmoller, Carl; Valdivia, Chile, 1850 *1192.4 p49*
Stegner, Daniel 22; America, 1846 *778.6 p317*
Stehlik, Josef; Minnesota, 1856 *2853.20 p259*
Stehlik, Josef; Wisconsin, 1881 *2853.20 p299*
Stehlik, Vaclav; Wisconsin, 1856 *2853.20 p345*
Steiber, . . .; St. Louis, 1846 *7420.1 p49*

Steierberg, Engel Marie Sophie; America, 1870 *7420.1 p396*
Steierberg, Friedrich; America, 1852 *7420.1 p98*
Steierberg, Friedrich Christian; America, 1866 *7420.1 p250*
Steies, Nikolaus; America, 1873 *5475.1 p318*
Steiger, Adam; America, 1841 *2526.42 p178*
  *Son:*Johannes
Steiger, Adam; America, 1854 *2526.43 p214*
Steiger, Adam 14 *SEE* Steiger, Peter
Steiger, Mrs. Adam; America, 1836 *2526.42 p165*
Steiger, Anna 12 *SEE* Steiger, Peter
Steiger, Anna Elisabetha; America, 1841 *2526.42 p176*
Steiger, Christian; America, 1855 *2526.43 p214*
Steiger, Christiana Elisabetha; America, 1858 *2526.43 p214*
Steiger, Christiane Louise; America, 1855 *2526.43 p214*
Steiger, Elisabeth; America, 1854 *2526.42 p156*
Steiger, Eva Elisabetha; Cincinnati, 1854 *2526.42 p174*
Steiger, Eva Katharina 52 *SEE* Steiger, Peter
Steiger, Georg; America, 1838 *2526.42 p178*
Steiger, Georg 22 *SEE* Steiger, Peter
Steiger, George; Ohio, 1809-1852 *4511.35 p52*
Steiger, Heinrich; America, 1836 *2526.43 p121*
Steiger, Johann 40; Louisiana, 1848 *778.6 p317*
Steiger, Johann Dieter 26 *SEE* Steiger, Peter
Steiger, Johannes; America, 1832 *2526.42 p178*
  With wife & child
  *Sister:*M.E.
  *Father:*Philipp
Steiger, Johannes; America, 1838 *2526.42 p178*
  With 3 children
  *Wife:*Magdalena Beck
Steiger, Johannes *SEE* Steiger, Adam
Steiger, Katharina; America, 1879 *2526.43 p168*
Steiger, Leonhard; America, 1852 *2526.43 p144*
  With 3 daughters & son
Steiger, M.E. *SEE* Steiger, Johannes
Steiger, Magdalena Beck *SEE* Steiger, Johannes
Steiger, Margaretha 28 *SEE* Steiger, Peter
Steiger, Maria Elisabetha; America, 1858 *2526.43 p215*
Steiger, Peter; America, 1882 *2526.42 p156*
Steiger, Peter 24 *SEE* Steiger, Peter
Steiger, Peter 54; America, 1882 *2526.42 p156*
  *Wife:*Eva Katharina 52
  *Son:*Georg 22
  *Son:*Adam 14
  *Daughter:*Anna 12
  *Daughter:*Margaretha 28
  *Son:*Peter 24
  *Son:*Johann Dieter 26
Steiger, Philipp *SEE* Steiger, Johannes
Steigerman, Herman; Ohio, 1840-1897 *8365.35 p18*
Steigerwald, Anna Katharina 35; New England, 1866 *170.15 p43*
  With family
Steigerwald, Anna Margaretha 1; Pennsylvania, 1848 *170.15 p43*
  With family
Steigerwald, Anna Margaretha 37; Pennsylvania, 1848 *170.15 p43*
  With family
Steigerwald, Mrs. Fridrich; New England, 1866 *170.15 p43*
  With 3 sons
Steigerwald, Friedrich; New England, 1866 *170.15 p43*
  With family
Steigerwald, Friedrich 35; New England, 1866 *170.15 p43*
Steigerwald, Friedrich; Port uncertain, 1866 *170.15 p43*
Steigerwald, Georg; Pennsylvania, 1848 *170.15 p43*
Steigerwald, Georg 44; Pennsylvania, 1848 *170.15 p43*
  With family
Steigerwald, Johann Henrich 4; Pennsylvania, 1848 *170.15 p43*
  With family
Steigerwald, Johann Peter; New England, 1866 *170.15 p43*
  With family
Steigerwald, Johannes; New England, 1866 *170.15 p43*
  With 2 children
Steigerwald, Johannes; Pennsylvania, 1866 *170.15 p43*
  With wife & 2 children
Steigerwald, Johannes; Port uncertain, 1866 *170.15 p43*
Steigerwald, Karl Otto; New England, 1866 *170.15 p43*
  With family
Steigerwald, Maria Elisabeth 11; Pennsylvania, 1848 *170.15 p43*
  With family
Steiker, Rosalie 29; Louisiana, 1848 *778.6 p317*
Steil, Christine 19; America, 1840 *778.6 p317*
Steil, Johann; America, 1860 *5475.1 p251*
Steil, Walburga 27; Galveston, TX, 1844 *3967.10 p373*

Steilbeburger, Alfred 17; Quebec, 1870 *8364.32 p26*
Steimer, Maria; America, 1852 *5475.1 p439*
Steimkemper, Henry; Washington, 1889 *2770.40 p81*
Stein, Mr.; America, 1854 *7420.1 p131*
  With wife 4 sons & 2 daughters
Stein, A. Maria *SEE* Stein, Reinhard
Stein, Adam; America, 1855 *2526.42 p167*
  With 2 siblings
Stein, Adolf; Ohio, 1885 *5475.1 p230*
Stein, Andrew; Louisiana, 1874-1875 *4981.45 p31*
Stein, Andrew; Louisiana, 1874-1875 *4981.45 p130*
Stein, Auguste 5; New Orleans, 1845 *778.6 p317*
Stein, C.; Venezuela, 1843 *3899.5 p546*
Stein, Carl; Venezuela, 1843 *3899.5 p546*
Stein, Catherine 30; Missouri, 1848 *778.6 p318*
Stein, Charles 9; New Orleans, 1845 *778.6 p318*
Stein, Charlotte 3; New Orleans, 1845 *778.6 p318*
Stein, Charlotte 37; New Orleans, 1845 *778.6 p318*
Stein, Elisabeth; America, 1862 *5475.1 p540*
Stein, Elisabeth 3 *SEE* Stein, Jakob
Stein, Elisabeth Muller *SEE* Stein, Jakob
Stein, Francois 1; New Orleans, 1845 *778.6 p318*
Stein, Franz; America, 1881 *5475.1 p221*
Stein, Friedrich 46; Brazil, 1857 *5475.1 p510*
  *Son:*Jakob
  *Daughter:*Magdalena
  *Daughter:*Karolina
  *Son:*Heinrich
  *Daughter:*Katharina
Stein, George 40; New Orleans, 1845 *778.6 p318*
Stein, Gertrud *SEE* Stein, Reinhard
Stein, Heinrich *SEE* Stein, Friedrich
Stein, Herman; Louisiana, 1850 *7710.1 p152*
Stein, Herman; New York, NY, 1843 *7710.1 p151*
Stein, Jakob 9 *SEE* Stein, Jakob
Stein, Jakob 41; America, 1857 *5475.1 p494*
  *Wife:*Elisabeth Muller 28
  *Son:*Jakob 9 months
  *Son:*Johann 10
  *Daughter:*Elisabeth 3
Stein, Jakob *SEE* Stein, Friedrich
Stein, Johann 10 *SEE* Stein, Jakob
Stein, Johann 20; New York, NY, 1898 *7951.13 p41*
Stein, Karolina *SEE* Stein, Friedrich
Stein, Katharina *SEE* Stein, Friedrich
Stein, Levy; Louisiana, 1855 *7710.1 p154*
Stein, M. Anna *SEE* Stein, Reinhard
Stein, Magdalena Greff 59 *SEE* Stein, Sebastian
Stein, Magdalena *SEE* Stein, Friedrich
Stein, Margte. 6 months; Missouri, 1848 *778.6 p318*
Stein, Maria; America, 1880 *5475.1 p220*
Stein, Maria; America, 1881 *5475.1 p220*
Stein, Maria *SEE* Stein, Reinhard
Stein, Maria; Texas, 1885 *5475.1 p204*
Stein, Maria Anna; America, 1853 *2526.43 p145*
Stein, Marie Elisabetha 56; America, 1853 *2526.43 p127*
Stein, Melville 17; Louisiana, 1872-1883 *7710.1 p158*
Stein, Nicolas 8; Missouri, 1848 *778.6 p318*
Stein, Nicolas 40; Missouri, 1848 *778.6 p318*
Stein, Nikolaus; Iowa, 1884 *5475.1 p377*
Stein, Peter *SEE* Stein, Reinhard
Stein, Reinhard; America, 1883 *5475.1 p333*
  *Daughter:*Maria
  *Daughter:*M. Anna
  *Daughter:*Gertrud
  *Son:*Peter
  *Daughter:*A. Maria
Stein, Sebastian 69; America, 1854 *5475.1 p53*
  *Wife:*Magdalena Greff 59
Stein, Thomas 47; Ontario, 1871 *1823.17 p156*
Stein, Zikmund; Cleveland, OH, 1845-1849 *2853.20 p475*
Steinacher, Michael 45; New Castle, DE, 1817-1818 *90.20 p154*
Steinbach, Josef; America, 1839 *5475.1 p56*
  *Wife:*Katharina
  With 6 children
Steinbach, Katharina *SEE* Steinbach, Josef
Steinbauer, Jakub; America, 1855 *2853.20 p282*
  With parents
Steinbaugh, Christian; Ohio, 1809-1852 *4511.35 p52*
Steinberg, William; America, 1891 *7420.1 p364*
Steinberger, Anna Katharina; Port uncertain, 1865 *170.15 p43*
  With family
Steinberger, Johannes; Pennsylvania, 1866 *170.15 p43*
  With wife & 4 children
Steinberger, Johannes; Port uncertain, 1865 *170.15 p43*
  With family
Steinbrinck, Heinrich Ludwig Wilhelm; Texas, 1845 *7420.1 p40*
Steinbring, . . .; Kansas, 1917-1918 *2094.25 p50*
Steiner, Elisabeth *SEE* Steiner, Johann
Steiner, Famille; New Castle, DE, 1817-1818 *90.20 p154*

Steiner, Famille; New Castle, DE, 1817-1818 *90.20 p154*
Steiner, J. Friedrich *SEE* Steiner, Johann
Steiner, Jacob; Ohio, 1809-1852 *4511.35 p52*
Steiner, Johann *SEE* Steiner, Johann
Steiner, Johann; America, 1881 *5475.1 p456*
  *Wife:*Katharina Weyrich
  *Son:*Peter
  *Daughter:*Katharina
  *Son:*J. Friedrich
  *Daughter:*Elisabeth
  *Son:*Johann
Steiner, Johann Friedrich Carl; America, 1868 *7919.3 p525*
Steiner, Johannes; America, 1868 *7919.3 p525*
  With wife & 7 children
Steiner, John; Ohio, 1809-1852 *4511.35 p52*
Steiner, John M.; Ohio, 1809-1852 *4511.35 p52*
Steiner, Julius; America, 1867 *7919.3 p525*
Steiner, Katharina *SEE* Steiner, Johann
Steiner, Katharina Weyrich *SEE* Steiner, Johann
Steiner, Peter *SEE* Steiner, Johann
Steinert, Conrad 30; Texas, 1913 *8425.16 p31*
Steinert, Eva Elisabeth 24; Texas, 1913 *8425.16 p31*
Steinert, Friedrich Wilhelm; America, 1868 *7420.1 p277*
Steinert, Jakob; America, 1856 *5475.1 p412*
Steinert, Johann; America, 1856 *5475.1 p412*
Steinert, Johann 31; New York, NY, 1898 *7951.13 p42*
Steinert, Johann Heinrich; America, 1856 *7420.1 p155*
Steinert, Johann Peter; America, 1766 *2526.43 p215*
Steinert, Julianna 2; New York, NY, 1898 *7951.13 p42*
Steinert, Marie 5; Texas, 1913 *8425.16 p31*
Steinert, Michel; America, 1856 *5475.1 p412*
Steinert, Peter; America, 1856 *5475.1 p412*
Steinert, Rosina 25; New York, NY, 1898 *7951.13 p42*
Steines, Gerhard; America, 1884 *5475.1 p243*
Steinfeld, Alexander; America, 1854 *7420.1 p131*
  With wife & 3 sons
Steinfeld, Raphael; America, 1854 *7420.1 p131*
  With wife & 5 sons
Steinfeld, Simon; America, 1866 *7420.1 p250*
Steinhanses, Hubert; America, 1926 *8023.44 p380*
Steinhauer, Augustin 34; New Castle, DE, 1817-1818 *90.20 p154*
Steinhaus, Auguste Maria Magdalena; Wisconsin, 1895 *6795.8 p158*
Steinhaus, Augustin 34; New Castle, DE, 1817-1818 *90.20 p154*
Steinhaus, Fredrick Ferdinand; Wisconsin, 1913 *6795.8 p173*
Steinhauser, Katharina; America, 1867 *179.55 p19*
Steinhoff, . . .; Ontario, 1871 *1823.21 p350*
Steinholz, Lorenz 26; Mississippi, 1845 *778.6 p318*
Steiniger, John; New Jersey, 1773-1774 *927.31 p3*
Steinkamper, Luise Leonore; America, 1841 *7420.1 p23*
Steinke, Emilie; Wisconsin, 1896 *6795.8 p34*
Steinke, Fred; Wisconsin, 1903 *6795.8 p208*
Steinke, Leopold Michael; Wisconsin, 1894 *6795.8 p28*
Steinkraus, Ludwig; New York, 1859 *358.56 p55*
Steinkraus, Wilhelmine; Wisconsin, 1891 *6795.8 p91*
Steinkrauss, Freidrich; Wisconsin, 1880 *6795.8 p86*
Steinkrauss, Otto; Wisconsin, 1888 *6795.8 p91*
Steinkrauss, Wilhelmine; Wisconsin, 1891 *6795.8 p91*
Steinman, Emilie 9 months; New York, NY, 1893 *1883.7 p42*
Steinman, Louise 23; New York, NY, 1893 *1883.7 p42*
Steinman, Michael 29; New York, NY, 1893 *1883.7 p42*
Steinmann, Andrew; Long Island, 1781 *8529.30 p10A*
Steinmann, Dorothea; America, 1882 *7420.1 p333*
Steinmann, Heinrich Friedrich August; America, 1870 *7420.1 p288*
Steinmann, Johann Jakob; America, 1888 *179.55 p19*
Steinmeier, Ernst Heinrich Wilhelm; Illinois, 1869 *7420.1 p282*
  *Brother:*Friedrich Ernst
Steinmeier, Friedrich; America, 1867 *7420.1 p265*
Steinmeier, Friedrich Ernst *SEE* Steinmeier, Ernst Heinrich Wilhelm
Steinmets, Cath. 12; America, 1846 *778.6 p318*
Steinmets, Jacob 8; America, 1846 *778.6 p318*
Steinmets, Nicolas 4; America, 1846 *778.6 p318*
Steinmetz, Catharina 20; Port uncertain, 1847 *778.6 p318*
Steinmetz, Joseph 19; America, 1746 *778.6 p318*
Steinmetz, Margarethe 43; America, 1856 *5475.1 p491*
  *Daughter:*El. Margarethe 17
  *Son:*Joh. Peter 20
  *Son:*Jakob 13
  *Daughter:*Karoline 11
  *Daughter:*Luise 8
Steinmetz, Marianna 27; America, 1847 *778.6 p318*
Steinmetz, Michel 25; America, 1847 *778.6 p318*
Steinmuller, Christian *SEE* Steinmuller, Marie Magdalene

Steinmuller, Elisabeth *SEE* Steinmuller, Marie Magdalene
Steinmuller, Georg Andreas *SEE* Steinmuller, Marie Magdalene
Steinmuller, Katharine *SEE* Steinmuller, Marie Magdalene
Steinmuller, Ludwig *SEE* Steinmuller, Marie Magdalene
Steinmuller, Magdalene *SEE* Steinmuller, Marie Magdalene
Steinmuller, Marie Magdalene; America, 1847 ***8115.12*** *p321*
*Child:*Christian
*Child:*Elisabeth
*Child:*Ludwig
*Child:*Katharine
*Child:*Magdalene
*Child:*Georg Andreas
Steins, Caspar; Illinois, 1863 ***6079.1*** *p13*
Steinsiek, Hermann Georg; London, Eng., 1874 ***7420.1*** *p304*
Steinwax, John; Ontario, 1787 ***1276.15*** *p232*
Steinwentel, Minna; Nebraska, 1883 ***7420.1*** *p334*
Steir, Ernestus; Philadelphia, 1778 ***8529.30*** *p5A*
Steir, John 37; Ontario, 1871 ***1823.21*** *p350*
Steirs, George 53; Ontario, 1871 ***1823.21*** *p350*
Steiwer, Georg; America, 1866 ***5475.1*** *p54*
Stejskal, Frantisek *SEE* Stejskal, Frantisek
Stejskal, Frantisek; Chicago, 1854 ***2853.20*** *p387*
*Father:*Frantisek
Stejskal, Frantisek; Nebraska, 1874 ***2853.20*** *p171*
Stelfox, Sarah; America, 1771 ***1220.12*** *p760*
Stelgner, Johann Gustav; America, 1867 ***7919.3*** *p525*
Stellard, Daniel 25; Ontario, 1871 ***1823.21*** *p350*
Stellenberg, August 33; Portland, ME, 1911 ***970.38*** *p82*
Stelling, Friedrich Wilhelm; America, 1893 ***7420.1*** *p369*
Stelling, Johann Heinrich Christoph; America, 1883 ***7420.1*** *p340*
Stellmacher, Gustav William; Wisconsin, 1888 ***6795.8*** *p66*
Stellwagen, M.; New York, 1859 ***358.56*** *p53*
Stellyes, Diedrich; North Carolina, 1857 ***1088.45*** *p33*
Stelmach, Anna; Wisconsin, 1883 ***6795.8*** *p61*
Stelmach, William; Detroit, 1929-1930 ***6214.5*** *p70*
Stelsner, Lewis; Illinois, 1853 ***6079.1*** *p13*
Stelter, Alvine Pauline; Wisconsin, 1900 ***6795.8*** *p124*
Stelter, August; Wisconsin, 1894 ***6795.8*** *p124*
Stelter, Augusta; Wisconsin, 1902 ***6795.8*** *p119*
Stelter, Auguste Amalie; Wisconsin, 1906 ***6795.8*** *p124*
Stelter, Mrs. D.; Wisconsin, 1899 ***6795.8*** *p177*
Stelter, Friedrich Gustav; Wisconsin, 1884 ***6795.8*** *p166*
Stelter, Johann Gottlieb; Wisconsin, 1869 ***6795.8*** *p142*
Stelter, Julius; Wisconsin, 1891 ***6795.8*** *p108*
Steltmann, Heinrich; America, 1852 ***2526.42*** *p197*
Stelz, Adam 3 *SEE* Stelz, Leonhard
Stelz, Anna Eva 19 *SEE* Stelz, Philipp
Stelz, Anna Maria 5 *SEE* Stelz, Philipp
Stelz, Anna Maria Diehl 45 *SEE* Stelz, Martin
Stelz, Dorothea 11 *SEE* Stelz, Martin
Stelz, Elisabeth *SEE* Stelz, Philipp
Stelz, Georg 6 *SEE* Stelz, Leonhard
Stelz, Georg 13 *SEE* Stelz, Philipp
Stelz, Georg 15 *SEE* Stelz, Martin
Stelz, Heinrich 3 *SEE* Stelz, Leonhard
Stelz, Johannes 2 *SEE* Stelz, Philipp
Stelz, Karl 17 *SEE* Stelz, Philipp
Stelz, Leonhard 33; America, 1846 ***2526.42*** *p202*
*Daughter:*Margaretha 8
*Son:*Peter 10
With wife
*Son:*Georg 6
*Son:*Heinrich 3 months
*Son:*Adam 3
Stelz, Magdalena 15 *SEE* Stelz, Philipp
Stelz, Margaretha 8 *SEE* Stelz, Leonhard
Stelz, Margaretha 21 *SEE* Stelz, Philipp
Stelz, Martin 50; America, 1854 ***2526.42*** *p202*
*Wife:*Anna Maria Diehl 45
*Daughter:*Dorothea 11
*Son:*Georg 15
Stelz, Peter 8 *SEE* Stelz, Philipp
Stelz, Peter 10 *SEE* Stelz, Leonhard
Stelz, Philipp; America, 1857 ***2526.42*** *p202*
*Wife:*Elisabeth
*Son:*Johannes
*Daughter:*Anna Maria
*Son:*Karl
*Daughter:*Magdalena
*Son:*Georg
*Son:*Peter
*Son:*Philipp
*Daughter:*Anna Eva
*Daughter:*Margaretha
Stelz, Philipp 10 *SEE* Stelz, Philipp
Stelz, Wilhelm; America, 1856 ***2526.42*** *p202*
Stelzer, L. Katharina; America, 1871 ***5475.1*** *p384*
Stem, Joseph; North Carolina, 1850 ***1088.45*** *p33*
Stemer, Henry 27; New Orleans, 1840 ***778.6*** *p318*
Stemme, Carl; America, 1852 ***7420.1*** *p98*
With wife & 4 daughters
Stemmerman, Claus; North Carolina, 1847 ***1088.45*** *p33*
Stemmetz, Martin; Ohio, 1809-1852 ***4511.35*** *p52*
Stemple Family ; West Virginia, 1787 ***1132.30*** *p146*
Stempston, John; America, 1755 ***1220.12*** *p760*
Stenberg, Eric; America, 1855 ***6529.11*** *p26*
Stenberg, Goran Olsson; New York, NY, 1849 ***6412.40*** *p152*
Stenbom, Carl Johan Petter; North America, 1887 ***6410.15*** *p106*
Stenbom, Elisabeth; St. Paul, MN, 1899 ***1865.50*** *p109*
Stence, John 66; Ontario, 1871 ***1823.17*** *p156*
Stenholm, Jac.; New York, NY, 1848 ***6412.40*** *p151*
Stenicka, Frantisek; Wisconsin, 1865 ***2853.20*** *p299*
Stenmark, Oscar; Cleveland, OH, 1884-1896 ***9722.10*** *p127*
Stennard, Lawrence; America, 1736 ***1220.12*** *p757*
Stennett, Absolom; America, 1752 ***1220.12*** *p760*
Stennings, William; Barbados, 1664 ***1220.12*** *p760*
Stenon, Francois; Quebec, 1649 ***9221.17*** *p220*
Stenske, Gottlieb; Wisconsin, 1908 ***1822.55*** *p10*
Stenson, James; America, 1749 ***1220.12*** *p760*
Stenstrom, Anders Gustaf; St. Paul, MN, 1900 ***1865.50*** *p109*
*Wife:*Anna Lovisa
Stenstrom, Anna Lovisa *SEE* Stenstrom, Anders Gustaf
Stent, Deborah; Charles Town, SC, 1719 ***1220.12*** *p760*
Stent, Henry; America, 1665 ***1220.12*** *p760*
Stent, Thomas; America, 1742 ***1220.12*** *p760*
Stent, Thomas; America, 1775 ***1220.12*** *p760*
Stenting, Edward; America, 1734 ***1220.12*** *p760*
Stenton, George; America, 1775 ***1220.12*** *p760*
Stenton, Richard; America, 1735 ***1220.12*** *p760*
Stentzel, Julius; Wisconsin, 1873 ***6795.8*** *p37*
Stenzel, Emma; Wisconsin, 1888 ***6795.8*** *p45*
Stenzhorn, Charlotte; America, 1865 ***5475.1*** *p562*
*Son:*Wilhelm
Stenzhorn, Katharina 27; America, 1865 ***5475.1*** *p562*
Stenzhorn, Margarethe; America, 1865 ***5475.1*** *p541*
Stenzhorn, Wilhelm *SEE* Stenzhorn, Charlotte
Stepan, Blazej; Minnesota, 1862 ***2853.20*** *p267*
Stepan, Jan; Minnesota, 1863 ***2853.20*** *p267*
Stepan, Vaclav; Kansas, 1904 ***2853.20*** *p209*
Steph, Dominique 33; America, 1840 ***778.6*** *p318*
Steph, Joseph 12; America, 1840 ***778.6*** *p318*
Stephan, Agathe Arnold 25 *SEE* Stephan, Johann
Stephan, Alvena; Wisconsin, 1900 ***6795.8*** *p233*
Stephan, Christian 21; Missouri, 1845 ***778.6*** *p318*
Stephan, David; Ohio, 1840-1897 ***8365.35*** *p18*
Stephan, Engel Marie Charlotte Mensching *SEE* Stephan, Johann Friedrich Christoph
Stephan, J. B. 62; Philadelphia, 1842 ***778.6*** *p318*
Stephan, Jean 22; Port uncertain, 1846 ***778.6*** *p318*
Stephan, Johan A. W.; Ohio, 1840-1897 ***8365.35*** *p18*
Stephan, Johann 29; Baltimore, 1893 ***1883.7*** *p38*
Stephan, Johann 30; Galveston, TX, 1844 ***3967.10*** *p372*
*Wife:*Agathe Arnold 25
Stephan, Johann Friedrich Christoph; America, 1847 ***7420.1*** *p57*
*Wife:*Engel Marie Charlotte Mensching
With child
Stephan, Johannes; Pennsylvania, 1848 ***170.15*** *p43*
Stephan, Karolina 11 months; Baltimore, 1893 ***1883.7*** *p38*
Stephan, Regina 25; Baltimore, 1893 ***1883.7*** *p38*
Stephani, Elisabeth 47; America, 1859 ***5475.1*** *p332*
Stephany, Barbara *SEE* Stephany, Margarethe Klinkner
Stephany, Johann *SEE* Stephany, Margarethe Klinkner
Stephany, Margaretha *SEE* Stephany, Margarethe Klinkner
Stephany, Margarethe; America, 1872 ***5475.1*** *p289*
*Child:*Barbara
*Child:*Margaretha
*Child:*Johann
Stephany, Mathias 40; America, 1843 ***5475.1*** *p289*
Stephen, David; Ohio, 1842 ***2763.1*** *p22*
Stephen, Engel Marie Charlotte Mensching; America, 1847 ***7420.1*** *p57*
Stephen, George; Ohio, 1809-1852 ***4511.35*** *p52*
Stephen, James 33; Ontario, 1871 ***1823.21*** *p350*
Stephen, Robert 26; Ontario, 1871 ***1823.21*** *p350*
Stephens, Charles; America, 1708 ***1220.12*** *p760*
Stephens, Charles 27; Ontario, 1871 ***1823.21*** *p350*
Stephens, Daniel; Annapolis, MD, 1758 ***1220.12*** *p760*
Stephens, Edward; America, 1720 ***1220.12*** *p760*
Stephens, Eled 55; Ontario, 1871 ***1823.21*** *p350*
Stephens, Elias; America, 1685 ***1220.12*** *p760*
Stephens, Elizabeth; America, 1719 ***1220.12*** *p760*
Stephens, Esther; America, 1738 ***1220.12*** *p760*
Stephens, Evan; Colorado, 1876 ***1029.59*** *p86*
Stephens, Evan; Colorado, 1876 ***1029.59*** *p86*
Stephens, Grace; America, 1710 ***1220.12*** *p761*
Stephens, Grace; America, 1752 ***1220.12*** *p761*
Stephens, H. W. 40; Ontario, 1871 ***1823.21*** *p350*
Stephens, Hanna; Barbados or Jamaica, 1683 ***1220.12*** *p761*
Stephens, Henry; Illinois, 1858-1861 ***6020.5*** *p133*
Stephens, Isaac; America, 1757 ***1220.12*** *p761*
Stephens, Jane; Barbados, 1679 ***1220.12*** *p761*
Stephens, John; America, 1739 ***1220.12*** *p761*
Stephens, John; America, 1740 ***1220.12*** *p761*
Stephens, John; America, 1741 ***1220.12*** *p761*
Stephens, John; America, 1743 ***1220.12*** *p761*
Stephens, John; America, 1750 ***1220.12*** *p761*
Stephens, John; America, 1759 ***1220.12*** *p761*
Stephens, John; Barbados, 1700-1710 ***1220.12*** *p761*
Stephens, John; Barbados or Jamaica, 1682 ***1220.12*** *p761*
Stephens, John 80; Ontario, 1871 ***1823.21*** *p350*
Stephens, John; Rappahannock, VA, 1741 ***1220.12*** *p761*
Stephens, John; Virginia, 1742 ***1220.12*** *p761*
Stephens, Joseph; America, 1766 ***1220.12*** *p761*
Stephens, Joseph; America, 1768 ***1220.12*** *p762*
Stephens, Joseph; Barbados or Jamaica, 1693 ***1220.12*** *p761*
Stephens, Luke; America, 1773 ***1220.12*** *p762*
Stephens, Mary; America, 1767 ***1220.12*** *p762*
Stephens, Mary; Annapolis, MD, 1722 ***1220.12*** *p762*
Stephens, Mary; Annapolis, MD, 1725 ***1220.12*** *p762*
Stephens, Mary; Barbados, 1676 ***1220.12*** *p762*
Stephens, Mary; Barbados, 1679 ***1220.12*** *p762*
Stephens, Paul; America, 1749 ***1220.12*** *p762*
Stephens, Peter; America, 1752 ***1220.12*** *p762*
Stephens, Richard; America, 1685 ***1220.12*** *p762*
Stephens, Richard; America, 1767 ***1220.12*** *p762*
Stephens, Richard; Annapolis, MD, 1730 ***1220.12*** *p762*
Stephens, Richard 62; Ontario, 1871 ***1823.21*** *p350*
Stephens, Richard; Virginia, 1734 ***1220.12*** *p762*
Stephens, Robert; America, 1728 ***1220.12*** *p762*
Stephens, Robert; America, 1740 ***1220.12*** *p762*
Stephens, Robert; America, 1772 ***1220.12*** *p762*
Stephens, Roger; Annapolis, MD, 1723 ***1220.12*** *p762*
Stephens, Thomas; America, 1696 ***1220.12*** *p762*
Stephens, Thomas; America, 1700 ***1220.12*** *p762*
Stephens, Thomas; America, 1764 ***1220.12*** *p762*
Stephens, Thomas; America, 1766 ***1220.12*** *p762*
Stephens, Thomas; Virginia, 1735 ***1220.12*** *p762*
Stephens, Walter; Barbados or Jamaica, 1693 ***1220.12*** *p763*
Stephens, William; America, 1688 ***1220.12*** *p763*
Stephens, William; America, 1716 ***1220.12*** *p763*
Stephens, William; America, 1734 ***1220.12*** *p763*
Stephens, William; America, 1768 ***1220.12*** *p763*
Stephens, William; Boston, 1766 ***1642*** *p37*
Stephens, William; Died enroute, 1728 ***1220.12*** *p763*
Stephens, William 60; Ontario, 1871 ***1823.17*** *p156*
Stephenson, Ann; America, 1763 ***1220.12*** *p763*
Stephenson, Ann; America, 1774 ***1220.12*** *p763*
Stephenson, Annie 21; Ontario, 1871 ***1823.21*** *p350*
Stephenson, Catherine 65; Ontario, 1871 ***1823.21*** *p350*
Stephenson, Daniel; America, 1764 ***1220.12*** *p763*
Stephenson, Duncan 50; Ontario, 1871 ***1823.21*** *p350*
Stephenson, Elizabeth; America, 1757 ***1220.12*** *p763*
Stephenson, Henry 58; Ontario, 1871 ***1823.17*** *p156*
Stephenson, Hugh 66; Ontario, 1871 ***1823.17*** *p156*
Stephenson, John; America, 1749 ***1220.12*** *p763*
Stephenson, John 29; St. John, N.B., 1834 ***6469.7*** *p5*
Stephenson, Joseph 61; Ontario, 1871 ***1823.21*** *p351*
Stephenson, Joseph 65; Ontario, 1871 ***1823.21*** *p351*
Stephenson, Joseph 69; Ontario, 1871 ***1823.21*** *p351*
Stephenson, Margaret 64; Ontario, 1871 ***1823.21*** *p351*
Stephenson, Mary 74; Ontario, 1871 ***1823.21*** *p351*
Stephenson, Rebecca 19; St. John, N.B., 1834 ***6469.7*** *p5*
Stephenson, Richard 53; Ontario, 1871 ***1823.17*** *p156*
Stephenson, Robert 19; Ontario, 1871 ***1823.21*** *p351*
Stephenson, Sarah 15; St. John, N.B., 1834 ***6469.7*** *p5*
Stephenson, Sephin 31; Ontario, 1871 ***1823.21*** *p351*
Stephenson, Susan 12; Quebec, 1870 ***8364.32*** *p26*
Stephenson, Susanna; America, 1756 ***1220.12*** *p763*
Stephenson, Thomas; America, 1713 ***1220.12*** *p763*
Stephenson, Thomas; America, 1751 ***1220.12*** *p763*
Stephenson, Thomas; Barbados or Jamaica, 1685 ***1220.12*** *p763*
Stephenson, Thomas 35; Ontario, 1871 ***1823.21*** *p351*
Stephenson, Thomas 37; Ontario, 1871 ***1823.17*** *p156*
Stephenson, William; America, 1758 ***1220.12*** *p763*
Stephenson, William; America, 1766 ***1220.12*** *p763*
Stephenson, William 31; Ontario, 1871 ***1823.21*** *p351*
Stephenson, William 55; Ontario, 1871 ***1823.21*** *p351*
Stephson, Sarah 20; St. John, N.B., 1834 ***6469.7*** *p4*
Stepka, Matej; St. Paul, MN, 1856 ***2853.20*** *p258*
Stepler, John P. 35; Ontario, 1871 ***1823.21*** *p351*

Steps, Peter; Annapolis, MD, 1719 ***1220.12*** *p760*
Steptoe, William; America, 1760 ***1220.12*** *p760*
Sterling, David; North Carolina, 1837 ***1088.45*** *p33*
Sterling, Hugh; Ohio, 1818 ***3580.20*** *p33*
Sterling, Hugh; Ohio, 1818 ***6020.12*** *p22*
Sterling, Robert 40; Ontario, 1871 ***1823.21*** *p351*
Sterling, William 22; New York, NY, 1835 ***5024.1*** *p137*
Stern, Emile 20; Louisiana, 1848 ***778.6*** *p318*
Stern, Gabriel; Illinois, 1834-1900 ***6020.5*** *p133*
Stern, Joseph; North Carolina, 1710 ***3629.40*** *p7*
Stern, Rose; Detroit, 1929-1930 ***6214.5*** *p70*
Stern, Salomon 28; Louisiana, 1848 ***778.6*** *p318*
Sternberg, Johann Dietrich Bernhard; Port uncertain, 1836 ***7420.1*** *p12*
Sterney, Susanna; America, 1753 ***1220.12*** *p760*
Stern Himler, Johannes; North Carolina, 1710 ***3629.40*** *p4*
Stern Himler, Madlena; North Carolina, 1710 ***3629.40*** *p4*
Sterns, Auristus 70; Ontario, 1871 ***1823.21*** *p351*
Sterrett, Charles 60; Ontario, 1871 ***1823.21*** *p351*
Sterry, Richard; America, 1767 ***1220.12*** *p760*
Stersont, F. 22; America, 1848 ***778.6*** *p318*
Stetka, Frantisek; Baltimore, 1872 ***2853.20*** *p126*
Stetz, Florin; New York, NY, 1882 ***6015.15*** *p29*
Steuber, Catharine Engel; America, 1868 ***7420.1*** *p272*
Steuber, Christian; Washington, 1889 ***2770.40*** *p81*
Steuber, Johann Friedrich Christoph; America, 1848 ***7420.1*** *p62*
*Sister:*Thrine Engel
Steuber, Sophie Charlotte; America, 1857 ***7420.1*** *p164*
Steuber, Thrine Engel *SEE* Steuber, Johann Friedrich Christoph
Steuer, A. Maria *SEE* Steuer, A. Maria Schutz
Steuer, A. Maria; Chicago, 1881 ***5475.1*** *p246*
*Daughter:*A. Maria
*Son:*Peter
Steuer, Barbara Schommer 52 *SEE* Steuer, Johann
Steuer, Franz; America, 1882 ***5475.1*** *p334*
Steuer, Johann; America, 1873 ***5475.1*** *p254*
Steuer, Johann 52; America, 1874 ***5475.1*** *p254*
*Wife:*Barbara Schommer 52
*Son:*Peter
*Daughter:*Maria
*Daughter:*Katharina
Steuer, Kath. 44; America, 1855 ***5475.1*** *p359*
Steuer, Katharina *SEE* Steuer, Johann
Steuer, Maria *SEE* Steuer, Johann
Steuer, Michel; America, 1881 ***5475.1*** *p245*
Steuer, Peter *SEE* Steuer, Johann
Steuer, Peter *SEE* Steuer, A. Maria Schutz
Steuer, Susanna 42; America, 1868 ***5475.1*** *p253*
Steuer, Susanna; Indiana, 1883 ***5475.1*** *p246*
Steuerberg, Heinrich Gottlieb; America, 1846 ***7420.1*** *p49*
Steuk, Michael Ernst; Wisconsin, 1879 ***6795.8*** *p32*
Steul, Anna Katharina; Pennsylvania, 1848 ***170.15*** *p43*
Steul, Maria Katharina; Pennsylvania, 1848 ***170.15*** *p43*
Stevan, Francois; Quebec, 1649 ***9221.17*** *p220*
Stevanson, Susan 12; Ontario, 1871 ***1823.21*** *p351*
Stevely, John 29; Indiana, 1906 ***9076.20*** *p75*
Stevely, William 36; Ontario, 1871 ***1823.21*** *p351*
Steven, Chrn. 23; North Carolina, 1775 ***1422.10*** *p57*
Steven, Jas. 27; North Carolina, 1775 ***1422.10*** *p57*
Steven, John 46; Ontario, 1871 ***1823.17*** *p156*
Steven, Richard 72; Ontario, 1871 ***1823.21*** *p351*
Steven, Sarah 16; North Carolina, 1775 ***1422.10*** *p57*
Steven, Thos. 11; North Carolina, 1775 ***1422.10*** *p57*
Stevens, . . .; Winnipeg, Man., 1900-1983 ***9228.50*** *p614*
Stevens, Abraham; America, 1746 ***1220.12*** *p760*
Stevens, Alexander; Marston's Wharf, 1782 ***8529.30*** *p16*
Stevens, Ambrose 47; Ontario, 1871 ***1823.21*** *p351*
Stevens, Amelia; America, 1755 ***1220.12*** *p760*
Stevens, Ann; Potomac, 1742 ***1220.12*** *p760*
Stevens, Catharine 27; Michigan, 1880 ***4491.30*** *p29*
Stevens, Catherine; America, 1762 ***1220.12*** *p760*
Stevens, Charity; Virginia, 1719 ***1220.12*** *p760*
Stevens, Edward; America, 1760 ***1220.12*** *p760*
Stevens, Edward; Barbados, 1675 ***1220.12*** *p760*
Stevens, Edward L.; North Carolina, 1838 ***1088.45*** *p33*
Stevens, Elias; America, 1695 ***1220.12*** *p760*
Stevens, Elizabeth; Died enroute, 1736 ***1220.12*** *p760*
Stevens, Elizabeth 65; Ontario, 1871 ***1823.17*** *p156*
Stevens, Elizabeth; Virginia, 1762 ***1220.12*** *p728*
Stevens, Fanny 62; Ontario, 1871 ***1823.21*** *p351*
Stevens, Francis; America, 1771 ***1220.12*** *p760*
Stevens, George; America, 1772 ***1220.12*** *p761*
Stevens, Henry; America, 1747 ***1220.12*** *p761*
Stevens, Henry; America, 1750 ***1220.12*** *p761*
Stevens, Henry 10; Ontario, 1871 ***1823.17*** *p156*
Stevens, Israel; Washington, 1887 ***2770.40*** *p25*
Stevens, James; America, 1727 ***1220.12*** *p761*
Stevens, James; America, 1742 ***1220.12*** *p761*
Stevens, James; America, 1772 ***1220.12*** *p761*
Stevens, James 30; Ontario, 1871 ***1823.21*** *p351*
Stevens, Jane; America, 1755 ***1220.12*** *p761*
Stevens, Joan; America, 1722 ***1220.12*** *p761*
Stevens, John; America, 1738 ***1220.12*** *p761*
Stevens, John; America, 1738 ***1220.12*** *p761*
Stevens, John; America, 1739 ***1220.12*** *p761*
Stevens, John; America, 1743 ***1220.12*** *p761*
Stevens, John; America, 1750 ***1220.12*** *p761*
Stevens, John; America, 1755 ***1220.12*** *p761*
Stevens, John; America, 1758 ***1220.12*** *p761*
Stevens, John; America, 1763 ***1220.12*** *p761*
Stevens, John; America, 1765 ***1220.12*** *p761*
Stevens, John; America, 1771 ***1220.12*** *p761*
Stevens, John; America, 1775 ***1220.12*** *p761*
Stevens, John; Annapolis, MD, 1725 ***1220.12*** *p761*
Stevens, John; Annapolis, MD, 1729 ***1220.12*** *p761*
Stevens, John; Barbados, 1666 ***1220.12*** *p761*
Stevens, John; Barbados or Jamaica, 1690 ***1220.12*** *p761*
Stevens, John; Illinois, 1858-1861 ***6020.5*** *p133*
Stevens, John; Marston's Wharf, 1782 ***8529.30*** *p16*
Stevens, John; New Jersey, 1777 ***8529.30*** *p7*
Stevens, John 54; Ontario, 1871 ***1823.21*** *p351*
Stevens, Jonas; America, 1765 ***1220.12*** *p761*
Stevens, Jos.; Louisiana, 1874 ***4981.45*** *p297*
Stevens, Joseph; America, 1756 ***1220.12*** *p761*
Stevens, Joseph; America, 1767 ***1220.12*** *p761*
Stevens, Joseph; Annapolis, MD, 1735 ***1220.12*** *p761*
Stevens, Mary; America, 1753 ***1220.12*** *p762*
Stevens, Mary 24; Ontario, 1871 ***1823.21*** *p351*
Stevens, Mary; Rappahannock, VA, 1726 ***1220.12*** *p762*
Stevens, Moses; Boston, 1775 ***8529.30*** *p5A*
Stevens, Philip; America, 1742 ***1220.12*** *p762*
Stevens, Philip; Virginia, 1732 ***1220.12*** *p762*
Stevens, Richard; America, 1675 ***1220.12*** *p762*
Stevens, Richard; America, 1713 ***1220.12*** *p762*
Stevens, Richard; America, 1749 ***1220.12*** *p762*
Stevens, Richard; America, 1753 ***1220.12*** *p762*
Stevens, Richard; America, 1762 ***1220.12*** *p762*
Stevens, Richard 52; Ontario, 1871 ***1823.21*** *p351*
Stevens, Robert; America, 1727 ***1220.12*** *p762*
Stevens, Robert; America, 1738 ***1220.12*** *p762*
Stevens, Robert; Virginia, 1741 ***1220.12*** *p762*
Stevens, Sarah; America, 1774 ***1220.12*** *p762*
Stevens, Stephen; America, 1739 ***1220.12*** *p762*
Stevens, Susanna; America, 1736 ***1220.12*** *p762*
Stevens, Thomas; America, 1732 ***1220.12*** *p762*
Stevens, Thomas; America, 1742 ***1220.12*** *p762*
Stevens, Thomas; America, 1758 ***1220.12*** *p762*
Stevens, Thomas; America, 1765 ***1220.12*** *p762*
Stevens, Thomas; America, 1767 ***1220.12*** *p763*
Stevens, Thomas; America, 1774 ***1220.12*** *p763*
Stevens, Thomas; Annapolis, MD, 1719 ***1220.12*** *p762*
Stevens, Thomas; Ontario, 1871 ***1823.17*** *p156*
Stevens, Thomas 26; Ontario, 1871 ***1823.21*** *p351*
Stevens, Thomas 40; Ontario, 1871 ***1823.17*** *p156*
Stevens, Thomas 42; Ontario, 1871 ***1823.21*** *p351*
Stevens, Thomas 75; Ontario, 1871 ***1823.17*** *p156*
Stevens, Thomas; Virginia, 1736 ***1220.12*** *p762*
Stevens, William; America, 1675 ***1220.12*** *p763*
Stevens, William; America, 1750 ***1220.12*** *p763*
Stevens, William; America, 1757 ***1220.12*** *p763*
Stevens, William; America, 1770 ***1220.12*** *p763*
Stevens, William; America, 1775 ***1220.12*** *p763*
Stevens, William; Annapolis, MD, 1725 ***1220.12*** *p763*
Stevens, William; Barbados or Jamaica, 1696 ***1220.12*** *p763*
Stevens, William; North Carolina, 1848 ***1088.45*** *p33*
Stevens, William 38; Ontario, 1871 ***1823.21*** *p351*
Stevens, William; Salem, MA, 1661 ***9228.50*** *p614*
Stevens, William; Virginia, 1718 ***1220.12*** *p763*
Stevenson, Alexander 28; Ontario, 1871 ***1823.21*** *p351*
Stevenson, Allan 52; Ontario, 1871 ***1823.21*** *p351*
Stevenson, Alma 11; Quebec, 1870 ***8364.32*** *p26*
Stevenson, Arthur; America, 1774 ***1220.12*** *p763*
Stevenson, Barnabas; America, 1762 ***1220.12*** *p763*
Stevenson, Edward; Barbados, 1664 ***1220.12*** *p763*
Stevenson, Ellen; Ontario, 1871 ***1823.21*** *p351*
Stevenson, Esabella 40; Ontario, 1871 ***1823.17*** *p156*
Stevenson, Frank; Washington, 1884 ***2770.40*** *p193*
Stevenson, George; America, 1765 ***1220.12*** *p763*
Stevenson, George 25; Ontario, 1871 ***1823.21*** *p351*
Stevenson, George 58; Ontario, 1871 ***1823.17*** *p156*
Stevenson, Hector 33; Ontario, 1871 ***1823.17*** *p156*
Stevenson, Hugh 72; Ontario, 1871 ***1823.21*** *p351*
Stevenson, James; America, 1755 ***1220.12*** *p763*
Stevenson, James 50; Ontario, 1871 ***1823.21*** *p351*
Stevenson, James 67; Ontario, 1871 ***1823.21*** *p351*
Stevenson, John; Boston, 1720 ***9228.50*** *p615*
Stevenson, John; Marston's Wharf, 1782 ***8529.30*** *p16*
Stevenson, John; New Hampshire, 1764 ***9228.50*** *p614*
Stevenson, John 24; Ontario, 1871 ***1823.21*** *p351*
Stevenson, John 35; Ontario, 1871 ***1823.17*** *p156*
Stevenson, John 69; Ontario, 1871 ***1823.21*** *p351*
Stevenson, John; Portsmouth, NH, 1716 ***9228.50*** *p615*
Stevenson, Leonard 58; Ontario, 1871 ***1823.17*** *p156*
Stevenson, Mary 51; Ontario, 1871 ***1823.21*** *p352*
Stevenson, Otto 25; Minnesota, 1925 ***2769.54*** *p1383*
Stevenson, Robert 70; Ontario, 1871 ***1823.21*** *p352*
Stevenson, Sam 40; Ontario, 1871 ***1823.21*** *p352*
Stevenson, Solomon; America, 1734 ***1220.12*** *p763*
Stevenson, Susan 27; Ontario, 1871 ***1823.21*** *p352*
Stevenson, Thomas; America, 1749 ***1220.12*** *p763*
Stevenson, Thomas; Illinois, 1851 ***6079.1*** *p13*
Stevenson, Thomas; Marston's Wharf, 1782 ***8529.30*** *p16*
Stevenson, Thomas 35; Ontario, 1871 ***1823.21*** *p352*
Stevenson, Thomas B. 40; Ontario, 1871 ***1823.21*** *p352*
Stevenson, William; America, 1728 ***1220.12*** *p763*
Stevenson, William; America, 1735 ***1220.12*** *p763*
Stevenson, William; America, 1758 ***1220.12*** *p763*
Stevenson, William; America, 1761 ***1220.12*** *p763*
Stevenson, William 26; Ontario, 1871 ***1823.17*** *p156*
Stevenson, William 55; Ontario, 1871 ***1823.21*** *p352*
Stevenson, William; Philadelphia, 1864 ***8513.31*** *p428*
Stevenson, Wm 73; Ontario, 1871 ***1823.21*** *p352*
Steventon, George; America, 1768 ***1220.12*** *p763*
Steventon, Titus; America, 1741 ***1220.12*** *p763*
Steventon, William; America, 1741 ***1220.12*** *p763*
Steverding, Carmen ons de; Miami, 1935 ***4984.12*** *p39*
Stew, John; America, 1743 ***1220.12*** *p763*
Steward, Anne; America, 1678 ***1220.12*** *p763*
Steward, Charles; America, 1726 ***1220.12*** *p763*
Steward, Charles 70; Ontario, 1871 ***1823.21*** *p352*
Steward, Daniel; America, 1751 ***1220.12*** *p763*
Steward, Elizabeth; America, 1753 ***1220.12*** *p763*
Steward, Elizabeth; Annapolis, MD, 1723 ***1220.12*** *p763*
Steward, Geo.; Ontario, 1787 ***1276.15*** *p231*
With 3 children & 3 relatives
Steward, George; America, 1751 ***1220.12*** *p764*
Steward, George; America, 1774 ***1220.12*** *p764*
Steward, James; America, 1727 ***1220.12*** *p764*
Steward, James; America, 1740 ***1220.12*** *p764*
Steward, James; America, 1770 ***1220.12*** *p764*
Steward, Jane; America, 1680 ***1220.12*** *p764*
Steward, Jane; Barbados or Jamaica, 1683 ***1220.12*** *p764*
Steward, John; America, 1695 ***1220.12*** *p764*
Steward, John; America, 1758 ***1220.12*** *p764*
Steward, John; America, 1769 ***1220.12*** *p764*
Steward, John; America, 1774 ***1220.12*** *p764*
Steward, John 26; Ontario, 1871 ***1823.21*** *p352*
Steward, Margaret; America, 1730 ***1220.12*** *p764*
Steward, Mary; Rappahannock, VA, 1741 ***1220.12*** *p764*
Steward, Mathew; America, 1755 ***1220.12*** *p764*
Steward, Miriam; America, 1758 ***1220.12*** *p764*
Steward, Peter; Jamaica, 1663 ***1220.12*** *p764*
Steward, Stephen, Jr.; Died enroute, 1725 ***1220.12*** *p764*
Steward, William; America, 1768 ***1220.12*** *p764*
Stewardson, Samuel 49; Ontario, 1871 ***1823.21*** *p352*
Stewardson, Thomas 47; Ontario, 1871 ***1823.21*** *p352*
Stewart, Alex 52; Ontario, 1871 ***1823.21*** *p352*
Stewart, Alex 65; Ontario, 1871 ***1823.21*** *p352*
Stewart, Alexander; America, 1746 ***1220.12*** *p764*
Stewart, Alexander; America, 1766 ***1220.12*** *p764*
Stewart, Alexander; America, 1769 ***1220.12*** *p764*
Stewart, Alexander; Chicago, 1894 ***1766.20*** *p14*
Stewart, Alexander; Detroit, 1894 ***1766.20*** *p16*
Stewart, Alexander; Marston's Wharf, 1782 ***8529.30*** *p16*
Stewart, Alexander 4; North Carolina, 1775 ***1422.10*** *p59*
Stewart, Alexander 14; North Carolina, 1775 ***1422.10*** *p60*
Stewart, Alexander 35; North Carolina, 1775 ***1422.10*** *p60*
Stewart, Alexander; Ohio, 1827 ***3580.20*** *p33*
Stewart, Alexander; Ohio, 1827 ***6020.12*** *p22*
Stewart, Alexander 26; Ontario, 1871 ***1823.21*** *p352*
Stewart, Alexander 57; Ontario, 1871 ***1823.21*** *p352*
Stewart, Alexander B.; Washington, 1885 ***2770.40*** *p194*
Stewart, Allan 44; North Carolina, 1775 ***1422.10*** *p60*
Stewart, Allan; Ohio, 1836 ***3580.20*** *p33*
Stewart, Allan; Ohio, 1836 ***6020.12*** *p22*
Stewart, Andw 35; Ontario, 1871 ***1823.21*** *p352*
Stewart, Angus 64; Ontario, 1871 ***1823.21*** *p352*
Stewart, Angus C. 21; Ontario, 1871 ***1823.21*** *p352*
Stewart, Ann; America, 1753 ***1220.12*** *p764*
Stewart, Ann 80; Ontario, 1871 ***1823.21*** *p352*
Stewart, Annabella *SEE* Stewart, Dugald
Stewart, Archd 41; Ontario, 1871 ***1823.21*** *p352*
Stewart, Archibald 30; North Carolina, 1775 ***1422.10*** *p59*
Stewart, Archibald 50; Ontario, 1871 ***1823.21*** *p352*
Stewart, Arthur 22; Ontario, 1871 ***1823.21*** *p352*
Stewart, Banco 3; North Carolina, 1775 ***1422.10*** *p60*
Stewart, Catherine 24; Ontario, 1871 ***1823.21*** *p352*
Stewart, Catherine 41; Ontario, 1871 ***1823.21*** *p352*
Stewart, Cathrin 60; Ontario, 1871 ***1823.21*** *p352*
Stewart, Charles; America, 1766 ***1220.12*** *p764*

Stewart, Charles; Annapolis, MD, 1732 *1220.12 p764*
Stewart, Charles 15; North Carolina, 1775 *1422.10 p60*
Stewart, Charles 30; Ontario, 1871 *1823.21 p352*
Stewart, Charles 45; Ontario, 1871 *1823.21 p352*
Stewart, Charles 47; Ontario, 1871 *1823.21 p352*
Stewart, Charles 77; Ontario, 1871 *1823.17 p156*
Stewart, Charles 17; Quebec, 1870 *8364.32 p26*
Stewart, Charlotte V. 19; Ontario, 1871 *1823.17 p156*
Stewart, Christian 3; North Carolina, 1775 *1422.10 p60*
Stewart, Colin 45; Ontario, 1871 *1823.21 p352*
Stewart, David 17; Ontario, 1871 *1823.17 p157*
Stewart, David 45; Ontario, 1871 *1823.21 p352*
Stewart, Dinual 38; Ontario, 1871 *1823.21 p352*
Stewart, Donald 28; New York, NY, 1835 *5024.1 p136*
Stewart, Donald; North Carolina, 1838 *1088.45 p33*
Stewart, Donald 51; Ontario, 1871 *1823.21 p352*
Stewart, Dorothy; America, 1758 *1220.12 p764*
Stewart, Dougald 40; North Carolina, 1775 *1422.10 p59*
Stewart, Dugald; Prince Edward Island, 1770 *3799.30 p40*
　Sister: Annabella
　Brother-In-Law: Robert
Stewart, Dugald; Prince Edward Island, 1771 *3799.30 p41*
Stewart, Duncan; Maryland or Virginia, 1728 *1220.12 p764*
Stewart, Duncan 36; Ontario, 1871 *1823.21 p352*
Stewart, Duncan 60; Ontario, 1871 *1823.21 p352*
Stewart, Elizabeth 3; North Carolina, 1775 *1422.10 p59*
Stewart, Elizabeth 46; North Carolina, 1775 *1422.10 p59*
Stewart, Finley 56; Ontario, 1871 *1823.21 p352*
Stewart, Francis; Charles Town, SC, 1718 *1220.12 p764*
Stewart, Francis 14; Ontario, 1871 *1823.21 p353*
Stewart, Frederick H. 23; Ontario, 1871 *1823.17 p157*
Stewart, George; Louisiana, 1874-1875 *4981.45 p31*
Stewart, George; Louisiana, 1874-1875 *4981.45 p130*
Stewart, George 56; Ontario, 1871 *1823.17 p157*
Stewart, Hannah; Rappahannock, VA, 1741 *1220.12 p764*
Stewart, Henry; Cleveland, OH, 1857-1874 *9722.10 p127*
Stewart, Henry 45; Ontario, 1871 *1823.17 p157*
Stewart, Herman B.; Washington, 1868 *2770.40 p134*
Stewart, Herman B.; Washington, 1884 *2770.40 p193*
Stewart, Hugh; Chicago, 1901 *1766.20 p23*
Stewart, Hugh 33; Michigan, 1880 *4491.36 p21*
Stewart, Isobel 30; North Carolina, 1775 *1422.10 p60*
Stewart, James; America, 1767 *1220.12 p764*
Stewart, James; America, 1775 *1220.12 p764*
Stewart, James; Annapolis, MD, 1723 *1220.12 p764*
Stewart, James; Annapolis, MD, 1725 *1220.12 p764*
Stewart, James; Annapolis, MD, 1726 *1220.12 p764*
Stewart, James; Boston, 1764 *1642 p33*
Stewart, James; North Carolina, 1835 *1088.45 p33*
Stewart, James 10; North Carolina, 1775 *1422.10 p59*
Stewart, James 25; Ontario, 1871 *1823.17 p157*
Stewart, James 30; Ontario, 1871 *1823.21 p353*
Stewart, James 32; Ontario, 1871 *1823.21 p353*
Stewart, James 35; Ontario, 1871 *1823.17 p157*
Stewart, James 35; Ontario, 1871 *1823.21 p353*
Stewart, James 39; Ontario, 1871 *1823.21 p353*
Stewart, James 44; Ontario, 1871 *1823.17 p157*
Stewart, James 49; Ontario, 1871 *1823.21 p353*
Stewart, James 57; Ontario, 1871 *1823.21 p353*
Stewart, James 58; Ontario, 1871 *1823.21 p353*
Stewart, James 70; Ontario, 1871 *1823.21 p353*
Stewart, Jane; America, 1750 *1220.12 p764*
Stewart, Jane 70; Ontario, 1871 *1823.17 p157*
Stewart, Jane 20; Quebec, 1870 *8364.32 p26*
Stewart, Janet 12; North Carolina, 1775 *1422.10 p59*
Stewart, Jannet 23; Ontario, 1871 *1823.21 p353*
Stewart, John; America, 1754 *1220.12 p764*
Stewart, John; America, 1767 *1220.12 p765*
Stewart, John; America, 1774 *1220.12 p765*
Stewart, John; Barbados or Jamaica, 1694 *1220.12 p764*
Stewart, John; Colorado, 1884 *1029.59 p86*
Stewart, John; Died enroute, 1743 *1220.12 p764*
Stewart, John 5; North Carolina, 1775 *1422.10 p60*
Stewart, John 15; North Carolina, 1775 *1422.10 p59*
Stewart, John 16; North Carolina, 1775 *1422.10 p59*
Stewart, John 48; North Carolina, 1775 *1422.10 p59*
Stewart, John; Ohio, 1809-1852 *4511.35 p52*
Stewart, John; Ohio, 1846 *3580.20 p33*
Stewart, John; Ohio, 1846 *6020.12 p22*
Stewart, John 25; Ontario, 1871 *1823.17 p157*
Stewart, John 25; Ontario, 1871 *1823.21 p353*
Stewart, John 35; Ontario, 1871 *1823.17 p157*
Stewart, John 43; Ontario, 1871 *1823.21 p353*
Stewart, John 50; Ontario, 1871 *1823.21 p353*
Stewart, John 52; Ontario, 1871 *1823.17 p157*
Stewart, John 55; Ontario, 1871 *1823.17 p157*
Stewart, John 60; Ontario, 1871 *1823.21 p353*
Stewart, John 63; Ontario, 1871 *1823.21 p353*
Stewart, John 66; Ontario, 1871 *1823.21 p353*

Stewart, John 67; Ontario, 1871 *1823.21 p353*
Stewart, John; Potomac, 1729 *1220.12 p764*
Stewart, John A. 27; Ontario, 1871 *1823.21 p353*
Stewart, Joseph; America, 1738 *1220.12 p765*
Stewart, Josie 33; Ontario, 1871 *1823.21 p353*
Stewart, Kenneth 40; North Carolina, 1775 *1422.10 p60*
Stewart, Lilly 7; North Carolina, 1775 *1422.10 p60*
Stewart, Louis 36; Ontario, 1871 *1823.21 p353*
Stewart, Margaret 13; North Carolina, 1775 *1422.10 p59*
Stewart, Margaret 46; Ontario, 1871 *1823.17 p157*
Stewart, Margaret 66; Ontario, 1871 *1823.17 p157*
Stewart, Maria 60; Ontario, 1871 *1823.17 p157*
Stewart, Mary; America, 1757 *1220.12 p765*
Stewart, Mary 25; Michigan, 1880 *4491.36 p21*
Stewart, Mary 35; Ontario, 1871 *1823.21 p353*
Stewart, Mary 57; Ontario, 1871 *1823.21 p353*
Stewart, Mary; Virginia, 1730 *1220.12 p765*
Stewart, Mary Ann 71; Ontario, 1871 *1823.21 p353*
Stewart, Mary V. 15; Ontario, 1871 *1823.17 p157*
Stewart, Matthew; Ohio, 1809-1852 *4511.35 p52*
Stewart, Neil 40; Ontario, 1871 *1823.21 p353*
Stewart, Neil 69; Ontario, 1871 *1823.21 p353*
Stewart, Patrick 6; North Carolina, 1775 *1422.10 p59*
Stewart, Peter; America, 1747 *1220.12 p765*
Stewart, Peter 40; New York, 1827 *9228.50 p615*
Stewart, Peter; Prince Edward Island, 1771 *3799.30 p40*
Stewart, Robert; America, 1738 *1220.12 p765*
Stewart, Robert; America, 1757 *1220.12 p765*
Stewart, Robert; North Carolina, 1835 *1088.45 p33*
Stewart, Robert 40; Ontario, 1871 *1823.17 p157*
Stewart, Robert; Prince Edward Island, 1767 *3799.30 p39*
Stewart, Robert *SEE* Stewart, Dugald
Stewart, Mrs. Robert; Prince Edward Island, 1771 *3799.30 p41*
Stewart, Ronald 56; Ontario, 1871 *1823.17 p157*
Stewart, S. 27; America, 1845 *778.6 p318*
Stewart, Sarah; America, 1744 *1220.12 p765*
Stewart, Susanna; America, 1722 *1220.12 p765*
Stewart, Theresa 16; Ontario, 1871 *1823.21 p353*
Stewart, Theressa 10; Quebec, 1870 *8364.32 p26*
Stewart, Thomas; Colorado, 1869 *1029.59 p86*
Stewart, Thomas 6; North Carolina, 1775 *1422.10 p59*
Stewart, Thomas 36; Ontario, 1871 *1823.21 p353*
Stewart, Violatte; America, 1755 *1220.12 p765*
Stewart, William; Boston, 1737 *1642 p26*
Stewart, William; Maryland, 1740 *1220.12 p765*
Stewart, William; North Carolina, 1775 *1422.10 p60*
Stewart, William 34; Ontario, 1871 *1823.17 p157*
Stewart, William 39; Ontario, 1871 *1823.17 p157*
Stewart, William 42; Ontario, 1871 *1823.17 p157*
Stewart, William; Washington, 1883 *2770.40 p137*
Stewart, William F. 60; Ontario, 1871 *1823.17 p157*
Stewartson, Richard; New York, NY, 1840 *3274.56 p99*
Stewer, Frances; Virginia, 1762 *1220.12 p765*
Stewkley, Alice; Jamaica, 1661 *1220.12 p765*
Stewkly, William; America, 1686 *1220.12 p765*
Steyg, Anna Margaretha 1; Pennsylvania, 1848 *170.15 p43*
　With family
Steyg, Anna Margaretha 37; Pennsylvania, 1848 *170.15 p43*
　With family
Steyg, Georg 44; Pennsylvania, 1848 *170.15 p43*
　With family
Steyg, Johann Henrich 4; Pennsylvania, 1848 *170.15 p43*
　With family
Steyg, Maria Elisabeth 11; Pennsylvania, 1848 *170.15 p43*
　With family
Sthober, John; Ohio, 1809-1852 *4511.35 p52*
Stibb, Gottlieb; Wisconsin, 1897 *6795.8 p176*
Stibb, Gustine; Wisconsin, 1894 *6795.8 p177*
Stibbard, Thomas; America, 1759 *1220.12 p765*
Stibbs, Elizabeth; Carolina, 1724 *1220.12 p765*
Stibitz, M. Elisabeth 37; Brazil, 1862 *5475.1 p496*
Stibral, Karel; South Dakota, 1871-1910 *2853.20 p247*
　Son: Vaclav
Stibral, Vaclav *SEE* Stibral, Karel
Stich, Jan 24; New York, NY, 1893 *1883.7 p44*
Stichbury, Alexander; America, 1750 *1220.12 p765*
Stichbury, Isaac; America, 1749 *1220.12 p765*
Stichnoth, William; Illinois, 1853 *6079.1 p13*
Stick, Philipp 55; Port uncertain, 1840 *778.6 p318*
Stickel, Peter; Ohio, 1809-1852 *4511.35 p52*
Stickem, Memory 35; Boston, 1835 *6424.55 p30*
Stickland, Fred P. 25; Ontario, 1871 *1823.21 p353*
Stickland, Henry; America, 1766 *1220.12 p765*
Stickland, Josiah; America, 1742 *1220.12 p765*
Stickwood, Jonathan; America, 1769 *1220.12 p765*
Stidefor, Samuel; North Carolina, 1856 *1088.45 p33*
Stidfold, John; America, 1756 *1220.12 p765*
Stidl, John; Washington, 1881 *2770.40 p135*

Stie, Salemy; New York, NY, 1910 *3331.4 p11*
Stiebel, Eugen 29; America, 1866 *5475.1 p48*
Stieber, Andrew; Ohio, 1809-1852 *4511.35 p52*
Stiefel, Baroline 20; New Orleans, 1847 *778.6 p318*
Stiefel, Bertha 2; New Orleans, 1847 *778.6 p318*
Stiefel, Friedrich; America, 1889 *179.55 p19*
Stiefel, Julia 52; New Orleans, 1847 *778.6 p318*
Stiefel, Manuel 11; New Orleans, 1847 *778.6 p318*
Stiefel, Maria 13; New Orleans, 1847 *778.6 p319*
Stiefel, Rosalia 9; New Orleans, 1847 *778.6 p319*
Stiefel, Sarah 7; New Orleans, 1847 *778.6 p319*
Stiefelmeier, Anne Marie Cathar. Sophie; America, 1867 *7420.1 p252*
Stiegel, Hieronymus; America, 1867 *7919.3 p527*
Stiegelar, Franz; Colorado, 1895 *1029.59 p86*
Stiegeler, Franz; Philadelphia, 1887 *1029.59 p86*
Stiegeler, Simon 27; Missouri, 1848 *778.6 p319*
Stieh, Luise Karol. Elisabeth; America, 1867 *5475.1 p545*
Stielmann, August; Wisconsin, 1889 *6795.8 p193*
Stienecker, Henry; Ohio, 1840-1897 *8365.35 p18*
Stienmet, E. 31; Port uncertain, 1846 *778.6 p319*
Stienmetz, E. 31; Port uncertain, 1846 *778.6 p319*
Stiennon, Antoinette; Wisconsin, 1854-1858 *1495.20 p50*
　Son: Casimir Joseph
Stiennon, Casimir Joseph *SEE* Stiennon, Antoinette
Stiennon, Marie Therese; Wisconsin, 1856 *1495.20 p45*
Stier, Carl; America, 1868 *7919.3 p531*
Stier, John; Washington, 1889 *2770.40 p81*
Stieren, Charles; Nebraska, 1905 *3004.30 p46*
Stierhoof, Philip; Ohio, 1809-1852 *4511.35 p52*
Stife, Richard; America, 1768 *1220.12 p765*
Stifeld, Louis 27; New Orleans, 1843 *778.6 p319*
Stiff, Abraham; America, 1749 *1220.12 p765*
Stiff, John; America, 1762 *1220.12 p765*
Stiff, Robert 18; Quebec, 1870 *8364.32 p26*
Stiff, Thomas; America, 1760 *1220.12 p765*
Stiffe, Elizabeth; America, 1719 *1220.12 p765*
Stiffney, John; Annapolis, MD, 1735 *1220.12 p765*
Stiggard, Mary; America, 1755 *1220.12 p765*
Stigwood, Walter; America, 1748 *1220.12 p765*
Stika, Jan; Wisconsin, 1854 *2853.20 p323*
Stile, Betty; America, 1721 *1220.12 p773*
Stile, C. I. 66; Ontario, 1871 *1823.21 p353*
Stiles, Catherine 42; Ontario, 1871 *1823.21 p353*
Stiles, Elizabeth; Kansas, 1886 *1447.20 p64*
Stiles, Elizabeth; Virginia, 1721 *1220.12 p773*
Stiles, Felitia; America, 1756 *1220.12 p773*
Stiles, James; America, 1740 *1220.12 p773*
Stiles, James 31; Ontario, 1871 *1823.17 p157*
Stiles, Jane; America, 1739 *1220.12 p773*
Stiles, John; America, 1765 *1220.12 p773*
Stiles, John; Annapolis, MD, 1735 *1220.12 p773*
Stiles, John 40; Ontario, 1871 *1823.21 p353*
Stiles, John 72; Ontario, 1871 *1823.21 p353*
Stiles, Mary; Potomac, 1729 *1220.12 p773*
Stiles, Peter; Ohio, 1809-1852 *4511.35 p52*
Stiles, William; America, 1752 *1220.12 p773*
Stilgebauer, Jacob; Ohio, 1809-1852 *4511.35 p52*
Stilgebauer, Michael; Ohio, 1809-1852 *4511.35 p52*
Stilgebour, Nicholas; Ohio, 1809-1852 *4511.35 p52*
Stiling, John; America, 1766 *1220.12 p773*
Still, Andrew; America, 1767 *1220.12 p765*
Still, Edward; Washington, 1883 *2770.40 p137*
Still, Elizabeth; America, 1715 *1220.12 p765*
Still, James; America, 1747 *1220.12 p765*
Still, Mary; Barbados or Jamaica, 1700 *1220.12 p765*
Still, Richard; America, 1753 *1220.12 p765*
Still, Richard; Maryland, 1744 *1220.12 p765*
Still, William; America, 1741 *1220.12 p765*
Still, William; Virginia, 1726 *1220.12 p765*
Stille, Hans Heinrich; America, 1866 *7420.1 p250*
Stillebauer, Jacob; Ohio, 1809-1852 *4511.35 p52*
Stillemunkes, Karl 16; America, 1860 *5475.1 p552*
Stillenmunkes, Heinrich; America, 1865 *5475.1 p553*
Stiller, Otto; Wisconsin, 1882 *6795.8 p230*
Stillert, Gustav; Wisconsin, 1870 *6795.8 p32*
Stillert, Reinhardt; Wisconsin, 1871 *6795.8 p32*
Stillfried, Hugo; Chile, 1852 *1192.4 p55*
Stilling, Thomas; America, 1683 *1220.12 p765*
Stillita, Jane; Maryland, 1725 *1220.12 p765*
Stillwell, Johanna 12; Quebec, 1870 *8364.32 p26*
Stillwell, Mary 7; Quebec, 1870 *8364.32 p26*
Stillwell, William 17; Quebec, 1870 *8364.32 p26*
Stilson, Elizabeth 55; Ontario, 1871 *1823.21 p354*
Stilson, Luther 66; Ontario, 1871 *1823.21 p354*
Stilton, John; America, 1680 *1220.12 p765*
Stimac, Frank; Chicago, 1930 *121.35 p100*
Stimart, Adrien Joseph; Wisconsin, 1880 *1495.20 p56*
Stimart, Cecile Bayot *SEE* Stimart, Francois
Stimart, Felicien *SEE* Stimart, Francois
Stimart, Florent *SEE* Stimart, Francois
Stimart, Francois; Philadelphia, 1880 *1494.20 p13*

Stimart, Francois; Wisconsin, 1880 ***1495.20*** *p56*
*Wife:*Cecile Bayot
*Child:*Felicien
*Child:*Florent
*Child:*Louis
Stimart, Louis *SEE* Stimart, Francois
Stimart, Marie Louise; Wisconsin, 1880 ***1495.20*** *p56*
Stimpson, Edward; Barbados, 1664 ***1220.12*** *p765*
Stimpson, Thomas; America, 1713 ***1220.12*** *p766*
Stimson, Ralph; America, 1759 ***1220.12*** *p766*
Stimson, Richard; America, 1752 ***1220.12*** *p766*
Stimson, William; New York, 1778 ***8529.30*** *p5A*
Stinchcomb, Ruban 31; Ontario, 1871 ***1823.21*** *p354*
Stinchcomb, William 43; Ontario, 1871 ***1823.21*** *p354*
Stindt, Johannes; Port uncertain, 1889 ***7420.1*** *p359*
Stinele, Frank; Ohio, 1840-1897 ***8365.35*** *p18*
Stineman, Andrew; Long Island, 1781 ***8529.30*** *p10A*
Stiner, Jacob; America, 1765 ***1220.12*** *p755*
Stiner, John M.; Ohio, 1809-1852 ***4511.35*** *p52*
Stinieg, Aurelie 30; America, 1841 ***778.6*** *p319*
Stinieg, George 10; America, 1841 ***778.6*** *p319*
Stinieg, Isidore 5; America, 1841 ***778.6*** *p319*
Stinieg, Pierre 28; America, 1841 ***778.6*** *p319*
Stinn, Johann; America, n.d. ***8023.44*** *p380*
Stinnard, Joseph; America, 1723 ***1220.12*** *p766*
Stinson, Gellan 32; Ontario, 1871 ***1823.21*** *p354*
Stinson, James 44; Ontario, 1871 ***1823.21*** *p354*
Stinson, James 51; Ontario, 1871 ***1823.21*** *p354*
Stinson, James 70; Ontario, 1871 ***1823.21*** *p354*
Stinson, James; Philadelphia, 1850 ***8513.31*** *p428*
*Wife:*Margaret Gilchrist
Stinson, Margaret Gilchrist *SEE* Stinson, James
Stinson, Saml A. 29; Ontario, 1871 ***1823.21*** *p354*
Stinson, William 37; Ontario, 1871 ***1823.21*** *p354*
Stinson, Wm 48; Ontario, 1871 ***1823.21*** *p354*
Stint, Richard; America, 1772 ***1220.12*** *p766*
Stip, August; Wisconsin, 1879 ***6795.8*** *p61*
Stirh, David 36; America, 1847 ***778.6*** *p319*
Stirling, James 55; Ontario, 1871 ***1823.17*** *p157*
Stirn, Veneranda; Kansas, 1917-1918 ***1826.15*** *p81*
Stirrett, George 45; Ontario, 1871 ***1823.17*** *p157*
Stirrett, James 50; Ontario, 1871 ***1823.21*** *p354*
Stirrit, John 57; Ontario, 1871 ***1823.17*** *p157*
Stirtan, James 59; Ontario, 1871 ***1823.17*** *p157*
Stirton, John 42; Ontario, 1871 ***1823.21*** *p354*
Stis, Vaclav; Illinois, 1851-1910 ***2853.20*** *p471*
Stitchborne, Richard; Barbados or Jamaica, 1699 ***1220.12*** *p766*
Stitt, Mary 70; Ontario, 1871 ***1823.21*** *p354*
Stjernberg, C.A.; Charleston, SC, 1850 ***6412.40*** *p152*
Stluka, Josef; North Dakota, 1872 ***2853.20*** *p251*
Stoakes, Anne; Annapolis, MD, 1729 ***1220.12*** *p766*
Stoakes, Eleanor; Boston, 1767 ***1642*** *p39*
Stoakes, Isaac; Boston, 1767 ***1642*** *p38*
Stoakes, John; America, 1753 ***1220.12*** *p766*
Stoakes, John; Maryland, 1723 ***1220.12*** *p766*
Stoakes, Thomas; Barbados, 1665 ***1220.12*** *p767*
Stoakes, William; Barbados, 1664 ***1220.12*** *p767*
Stoakes, Zachary; Barbados, 1665 ***1220.12*** *p767*
Stoakley, John; America, 1715 ***1220.12*** *p766*
Stoaks, Mary; Boston, 1767 ***1642*** *p39*
Stoat, Dortha 55; Ontario, 1871 ***1823.21*** *p354*
Stoat, James 65; Ontario, 1871 ***1823.21*** *p354*
Stobbe, Alphonse; Detroit, 1929 ***1640.55*** *p113*
Stober, Georg Julius Hermann; America, 1865 ***7420.1*** *p237*
Stober, Johann Carl Heinrich August; America, 1866 ***7420.1*** *p250*
Stobia, Peter 36; Ontario, 1871 ***1823.17*** *p157*
Stock, Miss; Nevada, 1873 ***7420.1*** *p300*
Stock, Ana; America, 1772 ***1220.12*** *p766*
Stock, C.; Louisiana, 1874 ***4981.45*** *p297*
Stock, Dr. Carl; Valdivia, Chile, 1852 ***1192.4*** *p56*
Stock, Caroline Justine; Nevada, 1880 ***7420.1*** *p318*
Stock, Friedrich; Port uncertain, 1864 ***170.15*** *p43*
Stock, Friedrich Wilhelm; Port uncertain, 1881 ***7420.1*** *p325*
With wife
Stock, George; America, 1715 ***1220.12*** *p766*
Stock, Gerhard; Port uncertain, 1856 ***7420.1*** *p155*
Stock, Heinrich Eduard; New York, NY, 1873 ***7420.1*** *p301*
Stock, Heinrich Wilhelm *SEE* Stock, Louise Pauline Sophie
Stock, James; Toronto, 1844 ***2910.35*** *p114*
Stock, Johann Heinrich; America, 1866 ***7420.1*** *p250*
With family
Stock, Johann Ludwig; America, 1847 ***7420.1*** *p57*
Stock, Johann Otto; Port uncertain, 1855 ***7420.1*** *p142*
Stock, Johann Otto; Port uncertain, 1856 ***7420.1*** *p155*
Stock, Johanne Caroline Amalie; America, 1890 ***7420.1*** *p400*
Stock, John; America, 1738 ***1220.12*** *p766*
Stock, John; America, 1741 ***1220.12*** *p766*
Stock, Louise Pauline Sophie; Nevada, 1873 ***7420.1*** *p300*
Stock, Louise Pauline Sophie; Nevada, 1873 ***7420.1*** *p301*
With family
*Brother-In-Law:*Heinrich Wilhelm
Stock, Marie Dorothee Charlotte; America, 1848 ***7420.1*** *p63*
Stock, Nikolaus; Pennsylvania, 1865 ***170.15*** *p44*
With wife & 8 children
Stock, Samuel; America, 1758 ***1220.12*** *p766*
Stock, Wilhelm; America, 1854 ***7420.1*** *p131*
Stockbridge, Herbert; America, 1761 ***1220.12*** *p766*
Stockdale, Daniel; America, 1740 ***1220.12*** *p766*
Stockdale, Elianor; Virginia, 1721 ***1220.12*** *p766*
Stockdale, Elizabeth; America, 1763 ***1220.12*** *p766*
Stockdale, Jane 21; Ontario, 1871 ***1823.21*** *p354*
Stockdale, Joseph; Canada, 1774 ***3036.5*** *p41*
Stockdale, Thomas; Barbados, 1682 ***1220.12*** *p766*
Stocker, Francis; Barbados or Jamaica, 1682 ***1220.12*** *p766*
Stocker, Lydia; Barbados or Jamaica, 1690 ***1220.12*** *p766*
Stocker, William; America, 1755 ***1220.12*** *p766*
Stockert, Anna Margaretha; America, 1854 ***2526.42*** *p147*
Stockert, Eva Katharina; America, 1853 ***2526.42*** *p157*
Stockert, Georg 16; America, 1863 ***2526.42*** *p157*
Stockert, Heinrich *SEE* Stockert, Mrs. Heinrich
Stockert, Heinrich 12 *SEE* Stockert, Mrs. Heinrich
Stockert, Mrs. Heinrich; America, 1854 ***2526.42*** *p111*
*Child:*Heinrich
*Brother:*Heinrich
*Child:*Johannette
Stockert, Jakob 4 *SEE* Stockert, Jakob
Stockert, Jakob 36; America, 1854 ***2526.42*** *p111*
*Wife:*Maria Katharina
*Child:*Jakob 4
Stockert, Johann; Dayton, OH, 1871 ***2526.42*** *p157*
Stockert, Johannette 9 *SEE* Stockert, Mrs. Heinrich
Stockert, Katharina; America, 1871 ***2526.42*** *p157*
Stockert, Maria Katharina *SEE* Stockert, Jakob
Stockhaus, Aug.; Valdivia, Chile, 1852 ***1192.4*** *p54*
Stockhill, John; America, 1758 ***1220.12*** *p766*
Stockhof, William; Ohio, 1840-1897 ***8365.35*** *p18*
Stockin, Elizabeth; America, 1681 ***1220.12*** *p766*
Stockman, Daniel; Virginia, 1736 ***1220.12*** *p766*
Stockman, David; Boston, 1766 ***1642*** *p36*
Stockmann, Anna Sophie Eleonore; America, 1847 ***7420.1*** *p54*
Stockmann, Friederike Konradine Amalie; America, 1887 ***7420.1*** *p354*
Stockmeyer, Aug.; Chile, 1852 ***1192.4*** *p52*
Stocks, John; America, 1738 ***1220.12*** *p766*
Stocks, Thomas; America, 1753 ***1220.12*** *p766*
Stockton, Eliza 21; Ontario, 1871 ***1823.17*** *p157*
Stockton, William; America, 1744 ***1220.12*** *p766*
Stockum, Anna Margaretha Grunewald *SEE* Stockum, Johann Philipp
Stockum, Anna Margaretha Lang *SEE* Stockum, Johannes
Stockum, Anna Maria *SEE* Stockum, Johann Philipp
Stockum, Anna Maria 10 *SEE* Stockum, Johannes
Stockum, Eva Maria *SEE* Stockum, Johannes
Stockum, Georg 23 *SEE* Stockum, Johannes
Stockum, Heinrich 18 *SEE* Stockum, Johannes
Stockum, Jakob; America, 1852 ***2526.42*** *p178*
Stockum, Johann Philipp; America, 1832 ***2526.42*** *p178*
*Wife:*Anna Margaretha Grunewald
*Daughter:*Anna Maria
Stockum, Johannes; America, 1852 ***2526.42*** *p178*
Stockum, Johannes; America, 1855 ***2526.42*** *p178*
*Wife:*Anna Margaretha Lang
*Daughter:*Eva Maria
Stockum, Johannes 52; America, 1844 ***2526.42*** *p147*
*Child:*Georg 23
*Child:*Heinrich 18
*Child:*Anna Maria 10
Stockum, Mrs. Johannes; America, 1854 ***2526.42*** *p178*
Stockum, Maria Elisabetha; America, 1752 ***2526.42*** *p175*
Stockum, Peter; America, 1836 ***2526.42*** *p111*
With wife
With daughter 11
With daughter 3
With son 9
With son 20
With son 16
Stockum, Peter; America, 1852 ***2526.42*** *p178*
Stockwell, Banzellae 31; Ontario, 1871 ***1823.21*** *p354*
Stockwell, Caleb 54; Ontario, 1871 ***1823.21*** *p354*
Stockwell, Hosea T.; Ohio, 1846 ***3580.20*** *p33*
Stockwell, Hosea T.; Ohio, 1846 ***6020.12*** *p22*
Stockwell, James; Virginia, 1730 ***1220.12*** *p766*
Stockwell, John; America, 1731 ***1220.12*** *p766*
Stockwell, John 25; Barbados, 1664 ***1220.12*** *p766*
Stockwell, Thomas; America, 1774 ***1220.12*** *p766*
Stocum, Alonzo 66; Ontario, 1871 ***1823.21*** *p354*
Stodart, John 53; Ontario, 1871 ***1823.21*** *p354*
Stodart, Thomas 31; Ontario, 1871 ***1823.17*** *p157*
Stoddan, Thomas 61; Ontario, 1871 ***1823.21*** *p354*
Stoddard, E. L. 54; Ontario, 1871 ***1823.17*** *p157*
Stoddard, Martha; America, 1767 ***1220.12*** *p766*
Stoddart, David 18; Ontario, 1871 ***1823.21*** *p354*
Stoddart, David 51; Ontario, 1871 ***1823.21*** *p354*
Stoddart, James 25; Ontario, 1871 ***1823.21*** *p354*
Stoddart, Joseph; America, 1749 ***1220.12*** *p766*
Stoddort, George 53; Ontario, 1871 ***1823.17*** *p157*
Stodler, Frederick; Ohio, 1809-1852 ***4511.35*** *p52*
Stodler, Frederick; Ohio, 1809-1852 ***4511.35*** *p53*
Stodola, Petr; Illinois, 1853-1910 ***2853.20*** *p471*
Stoeckle, George; New York, 1860 ***358.56*** *p149*
Stoehel, Margaret 19; Mississippi, 1847 ***778.6*** *p319*
Stoehel, St. Marie 21; Mississippi, 1847 ***778.6*** *p319*
Stoehr, Jacob; Ohio, 1809-1852 ***4511.35*** *p53*
Stoehr, Maria Th. S. Trutzel *SEE* Stoehr, Max
Stoehr, Max; Philadelphia, 1852 ***8513.31*** *p428*
*Wife:*Maria Th. S. Trutzel
Stoek, Francois 30; America, 1846 ***778.6*** *p319*
Stoenzel, Gottfried; Wisconsin, 1861 ***6795.8*** *p129*
Stoesser, Jacque; New York, 1860 ***358.56*** *p3*
Stoffel, Joh. Peter; America, 1869 ***5475.1*** *p307*
*Wife:*Magdalena Biehl
*Son:*Nikolaus
*Daughter:*Magdalena
*Daughter:*Katharina
With daughter
*Son:*Johann
Stoffel, Johann *SEE* Stoffel, Joh. Peter
Stoffel, Katharina *SEE* Stoffel, Joh. Peter
Stoffel, Magdalena *SEE* Stoffel, Joh. Peter
Stoffel, Magdalena Biehl *SEE* Stoffel, Joh. Peter
Stoffel, Mathias; America, 1880 ***5475.1*** *p194*
Stoffel, Nikolaus *SEE* Stoffel, Joh. Peter
Stoffel, Peter; Wisconsin, 1855 ***5475.1*** *p259*
Stoffregen, Amalie; America, 1868 ***7420.1*** *p277*
With child
Stohlner, Mons; Cleveland, OH, 1890-1897 ***9722.10*** *p127*
Stohr, Helena; America, 1867 ***7919.3*** *p534*
With daughter
Stokes, Edward; America, 1732 ***1220.12*** *p766*
Stokes, Elizabeth; America, 1750 ***1220.12*** *p766*
Stokes, Francis; America, 1772 ***1220.12*** *p766*
Stokes, John; America, 1739 ***1220.12*** *p766*
Stokes, John; America, 1745 ***1220.12*** *p766*
Stokes, John 27; Ontario, 1871 ***1823.21*** *p354*
Stokes, John 75; Ontario, 1871 ***1823.17*** *p157*
Stokes, Joseph; America, 1734 ***1220.12*** *p766*
Stokes, Margaret; America, 1769 ***1220.12*** *p767*
Stokes, Margaret; Rappahannock, VA, 1728 ***1220.12*** *p767*
Stokes, Richard; America, 1738 ***1220.12*** *p767*
Stokes, Robert; America, 1752 ***1220.12*** *p767*
Stokes, Robert; America, 1767 ***1220.12*** *p767*
Stokes, Stephen 33; Quebec, 1870 ***8364.32*** *p26*
Stokes, Thomas S. 41; Ontario, 1871 ***1823.17*** *p157*
Stokes, William; America, 1749 ***1220.12*** *p767*
Stokes, William; America, 1772 ***1220.12*** *p767*
Stokes, William; America, 1772 ***1220.12*** *p767*
Stokes, William; Virginia, 1742 ***1220.12*** *p767*
Stolberg, Amalia; St. Paul, MN, 1874-1905 ***1865.50*** *p109*
Stolery, Brice; America, 1758 ***1220.12*** *p767*
Stolicker, Alexander 32; Ontario, 1871 ***1823.17*** *p158*
Stolkes, William 63; Ontario, 1871 ***1823.17*** *p158*
Stoll, Barbara; America, 1836 ***5475.1*** *p495*
*Daughter:*Maria
*Son:*Johann
Stoll, Catharina 20; Louisiana, 1848 ***778.6*** *p319*
Stoll, Dorothea; America, 1854 ***5475.1*** *p459*
Stoll, Franz; America, 1867 ***5475.1*** *p535*
Stoll, Georg; Valdivia, Chile, 1851 ***1192.4*** *p51*
Stoll, Katharina; America, 1848 ***5475.1*** *p476*
Stoll, Michel 19; Missouri, 1846 ***778.6*** *p319*
Stoll, Peter; Brazil, 1862 ***5475.1*** *p550*
Stollard, Robert; Philadelphia, 1777 ***8529.30*** *p3*
Stolle, Wilhelm; America, 1868 ***7420.1*** *p277*
With daughter 1
With wife
Stolley, William Claus; Iowa, 1925 ***1211.15*** *p19*
Stollt, G.; New York, 1859-1860 ***358.56*** *p102*
Stolp, Hulda Auguste; Wisconsin, 1884 ***6795.8*** *p64*
Stolpe, Esaias; St. Paul, MN, 1901 ***1865.50*** *p109*
Stolpe, Peter Gottfried Jakob; Argentina, 1896 ***5475.1*** *p19*
Stolpe, Severinna; St. Paul, MN, 1874-1905 ***1865.50*** *p110*
Stolte, Mr.; America, 1852 ***7420.1*** *p99*
With wife & 3 children

Stolte, Widow; America, 1856 ***7420.1*** *p155*
*Son:*Friedrich Wilhelm
With 2 daughters
With son 12
With son 15
Stolte, Friedrich Wilhelm 21 *SEE* Stolte, Widow
Stolte, Johann Friedrich; America, 1871 ***7420.1*** *p396*
With family
Stolte, Wilhelm; America, 1881 ***7420.1*** *p398*
Stoltenberg, Ferdinand; Iowa, 1887 ***1211.15*** *p19*
Stolter, Henry; North Carolina, 1792-1862 ***1088.45*** *p33*
Stoltz, A.; Louisiana, 1874-1875 ***4981.45*** *p30*
Stoltz, Lewis; Ohio, 1809-1852 ***4511.35*** *p53*
Stoltzing, Paul; Valdivia, Chile, 1852 ***1192.4*** *p56*
Stolz, Barbara 6 months; Missouri, 1845 ***778.6*** *p319*
Stolz, C.; Louisiana, 1874 ***4981.45*** *p297*
Stolz, Charles; Ohio, 1809-1852 ***4511.35*** *p53*
Stolz, Eva 55; America, 1864 ***5475.1*** *p266*
Stolz, F. 4; New Orleans, 1834 ***1002.51*** *p112*
Stolz, F. 32; New Orleans, 1834 ***1002.51*** *p111*
Stolz, Frederic 8; Missouri, 1845 ***778.6*** *p319*
Stolz, J. 1; New Orleans, 1834 ***1002.51*** *p112*
Stolz, Joseph; Ohio, 1809-1852 ***4511.35*** *p53*
Stolz, Miss M. 26; New Orleans, 1834 ***1002.51*** *p111*
Stolz, Marie 36; Missouri, 1845 ***778.6*** *p319*
Stolze, Simon August; America, 1881 ***7420.1*** *p325*
Stolzenbach, Jacob; Valdivia, Chile, 1852 ***1192.4*** *p56*
Stomse, J. H.; Louisiana, 1874 ***4981.45*** *p297*
Stonall, John; North Carolina, 1845 ***1088.45*** *p33*
Stone, A. C. 52; Ontario, 1871 ***1823.21*** *p354*
Stone, Ann; America, 1743 ***1220.12*** *p767*
Stone, Charles 27; Ontario, 1871 ***1823.17*** *p158*
Stone, Elizabeth; America, 1763 ***1220.12*** *p767*
Stone, Elizabeth; Virginia, 1734 ***1220.12*** *p767*
Stone, Eric; Cleveland, OH, 1902-1903 ***9722.10*** *p127*
Stone, Francis; Barbados, 1670 ***1220.12*** *p767*
Stone, George; America, 1737 ***1220.12*** *p767*
Stone, George 56; Michigan, 1880 ***4491.39*** *p29*
Stone, George 20; Ontario, 1871 ***1823.21*** *p354*
Stone, George F. 24; Ontario, 1871 ***1823.17*** *p158*
Stone, Hannah 34; Michigan, 1880 ***4491.39*** *p29*
Stone, Henry; Barbados, 1683 ***1220.12*** *p767*
Stone, Hercules; America, 1771 ***1220.12*** *p767*
Stone, James; America, 1744 ***1220.12*** *p767*
Stone, James; America, 1748 ***1220.12*** *p767*
Stone, James; America, 1750 ***1220.12*** *p767*
Stone, James; America, 1773 ***1220.12*** *p767*
Stone, James 18; Ontario, 1871 ***1823.21*** *p354*
Stone, James 70; Ontario, 1871 ***1823.21*** *p354*
Stone, James W. 60; Ontario, 1871 ***1823.17*** *p158*
Stone, Jane 18; Ontario, 1871 ***1823.17*** *p158*
Stone, John; America, 1680 ***1220.12*** *p767*
Stone, John; America, 1685 ***1220.12*** *p767*
Stone, John; America, 1749 ***1220.12*** *p767*
Stone, John; America, 1765 ***1220.12*** *p767*
Stone, John; America, 1768 ***1220.12*** *p767*
Stone, John 12; Michigan, 1880 ***4491.39*** *p29*
Stone, John; Washington, 1889 ***2770.40*** *p81*
Stone, Martha; America, 1756 ***1220.12*** *p767*
Stone, Mary; America, 1765 ***1220.12*** *p767*
Stone, Mathew; America, 1752 ***1220.12*** *p767*
Stone, Nicholas; America, 1749 ***1220.12*** *p767*
Stone, Philip; Virginia, 1742 ***1220.12*** *p767*
Stone, Richard 40; Ontario, 1871 ***1823.21*** *p354*
Stone, Samuel; America, 1770 ***1220.12*** *p767*
Stone, Susan; Jamaica, 1665 ***1220.12*** *p767*
Stone, Thomas; America, 1770 ***1220.12*** *p767*
Stone, Thomas; Barbados, 1664 ***1220.12*** *p767*
Stone, Thomas; Virginia, 1718 ***1220.12*** *p767*
Stone, Thomas; Virginia, 1740 ***1220.12*** *p767*
Stone, Thomas; Virginia, 1743 ***1220.12*** *p767*
Stone, Thomas; Virginia, 1773 ***1220.12*** *p767*
Stone, William; America, 1699 ***1220.12*** *p767*
Stone, William; America, 1726 ***1220.12*** *p767*
Stone, William; America, 1736 ***1220.12*** *p767*
Stone, William; America, 1741 ***1220.12*** *p767*
Stone, William; America, 1755 ***1220.12*** *p767*
Stone, William; America, 1766 ***1220.12*** *p767*
Stone, William; America, 1773 ***1220.12*** *p768*
Stone, William; Barbados, 1678 ***1220.12*** *p767*
Stone, William; New York, 1776 ***8529.30*** *p16*
Stone, William 56; Ontario, 1871 ***1823.17*** *p158*
Stone, William 16; Quebec, 1870 ***8364.32*** *p26*
Stonefield, Charles; Ohio, 1809-1852 ***4511.35*** *p53*
Stoneham, James; Annapolis, MD, 1719 ***1220.12*** *p768*
Stonehill, John; America, 1748 ***1220.12*** *p768*
Stonehouse, David 40; Ontario, 1871 ***1823.21*** *p355*
Stonehouse, Edward 30; Ontario, 1871 ***1823.21*** *p355*
Stonehouse, Edward C. 40; Ontario, 1871 ***1823.21*** *p355*
Stonehouse, Elizabeth; Canada, 1814-1900 ***9228.50*** *p166*
Stonehouse, Elizabeth; Canada, 1814-1900 ***9228.50*** *p473*
Stonehouse, George 70; Ontario, 1871 ***1823.21*** *p355*
Stonehouse, Henry 45; Ontario, 1871 ***1823.17*** *p158*
Stonehouse, Jame 59; Ontario, 1871 ***1823.21*** *p355*
Stonehouse, Joseph 51; Ontario, 1871 ***1823.17*** *p158*
Stonehouse, Mary 67; Ontario, 1871 ***1823.21*** *p355*
Stonehouse, Mary E. 58; Ontario, 1871 ***1823.21*** *p355*
Stonehouse, William; America, 1746 ***1220.12*** *p768*
Stonehouse, William 66; Ontario, 1871 ***1823.17*** *p158*
Stoneker, John; New Jersey, 1773-1774 ***927.31*** *p3*
Stonelake, Elizabeth; New Jersey, 1862 ***9228.50*** *p615*
Stonell, Richard; America, 1773 ***1220.12*** *p768*
Stoneman, Henry 50; Ontario, 1871 ***1823.21*** *p355*
Stoneman, William; America, 1739 ***1220.12*** *p768*
Stonemark, Oscar; Cleveland, OH, 1884-1896 ***9722.10*** *p127*
Stoner, Francis; America, 1752 ***1220.12*** *p768*
Stoner, George; Ohio, 1840-1897 ***8365.35*** *p18*
Stoner, Sarah; America, 1754 ***1220.12*** *p768*
Stones, Rebecca; America, 1773 ***1220.12*** *p768*
Stoney, Sarah 36; Ontario, 1871 ***1823.21*** *p355*
Stonicar, John; New Jersey, 1773-1774 ***927.31*** *p3*
Stonilake, Mary; America, 1752 ***1220.12*** *p768*
Stoning, Edward; America, 1752 ***1220.12*** *p768*
Stonnell, David; America, 1734 ***1220.12*** *p768*
Stoodley, James; Barbados, 1708 ***1220.12*** *p768*
Stoodley, John; America, 1685 ***1220.12*** *p768*
Stook, Richard 99; Ontario, 1871 ***1823.21*** *p355*
Stooke, Robert; America, 1745 ***1220.12*** *p768*
Stool, Mary; America, 1750 ***1220.12*** *p768*
Stoop, Samuel 38; Ontario, 1871 ***1823.17*** *p158*
Stoops, William 42; Ontario, 1871 ***1823.21*** *p355*
Stop, John; America, 1766 ***1220.12*** *p768*
Stopard, Thomas; America, 1726 ***1220.12*** *p768*
Stophert, John 30; Ontario, 1871 ***1823.17*** *p158*
Stopkolft, H. 28; America, 1841 ***778.6*** *p319*
Stoppe, Adolf 2; Portland, ME, 1906 ***970.38*** *p82*
Stoppe, Ekaterina 11 months; Portland, ME, 1906 ***970.38*** *p82*
Stoppe, Eudakia 25; Portland, ME, 1906 ***970.38*** *p82*
Stoppe, Wilhelm 25; Portland, ME, 1906 ***970.38*** *p82*
Stopper, Margaret; Barbados, 1679 ***1220.12*** *p768*
Stopps, Thomas; America, 1772 ***1220.12*** *p768*
Stor, Anna Escher *SEE* Stor, Johann
Stor, Conrad 26; New York, NY, 1883 ***8427.14*** *p43*
Stor, Georg *SEE* Stor, Johann
Stor, Johann; America, 1881 ***5475.1*** *p23*
*Wife:*Anna Escher
*Daughter:*Karoline
*Son:*Georg
Stor, Karoline *SEE* Stor, Johann
Storandt, Johann Jacob; America, 1868 ***7919.3*** *p535*
*Sister:*Margarethe Elisabeth
With child
Storandt, Margarethe Elisabeth *SEE* Storandt, Johann Jacob
Storandt, Sebastian; America, 1868 ***7919.3*** *p535*
Storandt, Susanna Margarethe; America, 1868 ***7919.3*** *p535*
Storch, William; Philadelphia, 1778 ***8529.30*** *p7*
Storck, Anna Elisabeth *SEE* Storck, Anna Margarethe
Storck, Anna Magdalene *SEE* Storck, Anna Margarethe
Storck, Anna Margarethe; America, 1817-1820 ***8115.12*** *p320*⟨/lvv1⟩
*Child:*Anna Magdalene
*Child:*Anna Elisabeth
Storck, Konrad; Port uncertain, 1866 ***170.15*** *p44*
With wife & daughter
Storck, Ludwig *SEE* Storck, Marie Katharine
Storck, Marie Katharine; America, 1846 ***8115.12*** *p323*
*Child:*Ludwig
Storen, Mathew 62; Ontario, 1871 ***1823.21*** *p355*
Storer, Henry; America, 1745 ***1220.12*** *p768*
Storer, Henry; America, 1764 ***1220.12*** *p768*
Storer, John; Maryland, 1741 ***1220.12*** *p768*
Storer, Samuel; America, 1775 ***1220.12*** *p768*
Storer, Thomas; America, 1743 ***1220.12*** *p768*
Storer, Thomas; America, 1773 ***1220.12*** *p768*
Storer, William; America, 1764 ***1220.12*** *p768*
Storey, Ann; Potomac, 1731 ***1220.12*** *p768*
Storey, Elizabeth; Barbados or Jamaica, 1694 ***1220.12*** *p768*
Storey, George 27; Ontario, 1871 ***1823.21*** *p355*
Storey, Henry; Annapolis, MD, 1735 ***1220.12*** *p768*
Storey, James; America, 1775 ***1220.12*** *p768*
Storey, John; America, 1694 ***1220.12*** *p768*
Storey, John; America, 1765 ***1220.12*** *p768*
Storey, John; Annapolis, MD, 1722 ***1220.12*** *p768*
Storey, John; Virginia, 1734 ***1220.12*** *p768*
Storey, Robert 70; Ontario, 1871 ***1823.17*** *p158*
Storey, William; America, 1774 ***1220.12*** *p768*
Storey, William 35; Ontario, 1871 ***1823.17*** *p158*
Storey, William 47; Ontario, 1871 ***1823.21*** *p355*
Storie, Richard; Bermuda, 1614 ***1220.12*** *p768*
Storing, Nelson 37; Ontario, 1871 ***1823.21*** *p355*
Storit, Donald 24; Ontario, 1871 ***1823.21*** *p355*
Stork, Josef; Wisconsin, 1854 ***2853.20*** *p333*
Stork, Thomas; America, 1729 ***1220.12*** *p768*
Storke, William; Philadelphia, 1778 ***8529.30*** *p7*
Storla, Ole Olson; Iowa, 1868 ***1211.15*** *p18*
Storm, A. 28; Port uncertain, 1840 ***778.6*** *p319*
Storm, Beata 19; New York, NY, 1894 ***6512.1*** *p229*
Storm, John; Colorado, 1873 ***1029.59*** *p86*
Storm, Michael; America, 1750 ***1220.12*** *p769*
Storm, Michael; Ohio, 1809-1852 ***4511.35*** *p53*
Storman, Samuel; America, 1725 ***1220.12*** *p769*
Stormont, Peter 32; Ontario, 1871 ***1823.21*** *p355*
Storms, John; Ohio, 1809-1852 ***4511.35*** *p53*
Storne, Marjeret 55; Ontario, 1871 ***1823.21*** *p355*
Storor, Mary Ann; Wisconsin, 1841-1844 ***9228.50*** *p299*
Storor, Mary Ann; Wisconsin, 1841-1844 ***9228.50*** *p299*
Storr, Marie 17; New York, NY, 1894 ***6512.1*** *p183*
Storr, Thomas; America, 1738 ***1220.12*** *p769*
Storrow, William; America, 1775 ***1220.12*** *p769*
Storsteen, M.; Iowa, 1895 ***1211.15*** *p19*
Story, Catherine; Annapolis, MD, 1721 ***1220.12*** *p768*
Story, Edward 40; Ontario, 1871 ***1823.21*** *p355*
Story, Elias; Plymouth, MA, 1620 ***1920.45*** *p5*
Story, Elizabeth; Charles Town, SC, 1719 ***1220.12*** *p768*
Story, John; Died enroute, 1721 ***1220.12*** *p768*
Story, Thomas; America, 1751 ***1220.12*** *p768*
Story, Thomas; Boston, 1718 ***1220.12*** *p768*
Story, Thomas 40; Ontario, 1871 ***1823.21*** *p355*
Story, William; America, 1742 ***1220.12*** *p768*
Story, William 70; Ontario, 1871 ***1823.21*** *p355*
Storz, Frans 36; America, 1846 ***778.6*** *p319*
Stossel, Frank; Washington, 1889 ***2770.40*** *p81*
Stot, Richard; America, 1775 ***1220.12*** *p769*
Stothart, James; America, 1753 ***1220.12*** *p766*
Stothers, John; America, 1775 ***1220.12*** *p769*
Stott, Elizabeth; America, 1766 ***1220.12*** *p769*
Stott, George; America, 1763 ***1220.12*** *p769*
Stott, James; America, 1761 ***1220.12*** *p769*
Stott, John; America, 1768 ***1220.12*** *p769*
Stott, John 33; Ontario, 1871 ***1823.21*** *p355*
Stoude, Francis; Louisiana, 1836-1840 ***4981.45*** *p213*
Stough, John; West Virginia, 1787 ***1132.30*** *p146*
Stoughter, John; America, 1764 ***1220.12*** *p769*
Stoughton, Katherine *SEE* Stoughton, Thomas
Stoughton, Thomas; America, 1716 ***1220.12*** *p769*
Stoughton, Thomas; Charles Town, SC, 1719 ***1220.12*** *p769*
Stoughton, Thomas *SEE* Stoughton, Thomas
Stoughton, Thomas; Massachusetts, 1630 ***117.5*** *p155*
*Son:*Thomas
*Daughter:*Katherine
Stoup, Jacque 19; America, 1847 ***778.6*** *p319*
Stourbridge, Chris'n; Ontario, 1787 ***1276.15*** *p232*
With 2 children & 6 relatives
Stourton, Robert; America, 1774 ***1220.12*** *p769*
Stout, Henry 36; Ontario, 1871 ***1823.17*** *p158*
Stoutenberg, Chester 18; Michigan, 1880 ***4491.42*** *p26*
Stoutenberg, James 61; Michigan, 1880 ***4491.42*** *p26*
Stoutenberg, Melinda 21; Michigan, 1880 ***4491.42*** *p26*
Stoutenberg, Melinda 61; Michigan, 1880 ***4491.42*** *p26*
Stoutenberg, Sarah 26; Michigan, 1880 ***4491.42*** *p26*
Stoutz, Jacob; Illinois, 1858-1861 ***6020.5*** *p133*
Stovell, Henry 18; Ontario, 1871 ***1823.21*** *p355*
Stover, William; Marston's Wharf, 1782 ***8529.30*** *p16*
Stow, Mr.; California, 1868 ***1131.61*** *p89*
Stow, Abraham; America, 1775 ***1220.12*** *p769*
Stow, Chs.; California, 1868 ***1131.61*** *p89*
Stow, Jane; America, 1750 ***1220.12*** *p769*
Stowe, Mary Anne; America, 1762 ***1220.12*** *p769*
Stowell, George; America, 1771 ***1220.12*** *p769*
Stower, John; America, 1685 ***1220.12*** *p769*
Stower, Robert; Barbados, 1708 ***1220.12*** *p769*
Stowers, James; America, 1767 ***1220.12*** *p769*
Stowman, Ann; America, 1754 ***1220.12*** *p769*
Stowman, William; America, 1742 ***1220.12*** *p769*
Stoyle, Richard; New York, NY, 1830 ***3274.55*** *p74*
Straben, Jacob 29; New York, NY, 1883 ***8427.14*** *p44*
Stracey, Ann; America, 1746 ***1220.12*** *p769*
Strachan, John; New York, 1776 ***8529.30*** *p3*
Strachan, John; Ontario, 1835 ***3160.1*** *p150*
Strachan, John; Prescott, Ont., 1835 ***3289.1*** *p61*
Strachan, Mary 60; Ontario, 1871 ***1823.21*** *p355*
Strachem, Campbell 75; Ontario, 1871 ***1823.21*** *p355*
Strachem, Malcolm 70; Ontario, 1871 ***1823.21*** *p355*
Strachezck, Fr.; Galveston, TX, 1855 ***571.7*** *p17*
Strack, Alois 33; New York, NY, 1847 ***9176.15*** *p49*
Strackbein, Anna Marie; America, 1856-1865 ***8115.12*** *p320*
*Child:*Johann Georg
*Child:*Christian
*Child:*Jakob
*Child:*Ludwig
Strackbein, Christian *SEE* Strackbein, Anna Marie
Strackbein, Jakob *SEE* Strackbein, Anna Marie

492 *FOR A COMPLETE EXPLANATION OF ENTRY, SEE "HOW TO READ A CITATION" SECTION*

Strackbein, Johann Georg *SEE* Strackbein, Anna Marie
Strackbein, Ludwig *SEE* Strackbein, Anna Marie
Strader, Henry; New Jersey, 1749-1774 ***927.31*** *p2*
Stradley, Samuel; North Carolina, 1863 ***1088.45*** *p33*
Stradling, Edward; America, 1747 ***1220.12*** *p769*
Stradter, Caspar; New Jersey, 1749-1774 ***927.31*** *p2*
Stradter, Johann Henrich; New Jersey, 1749-1774 ***927.31*** *p2*
Stradter, Johannes; New Jersey, 1749-1774 ***927.31*** *p2*
Stradter, John Henry; New Jersey, 1749-1774 ***927.31*** *p2*
Straesser, Margarethe 29; America, 1865 ***5475.1*** *p49*
Strafford, Susanna; America, 1756 ***1220.12*** *p769*
Strafser, Louis 42; America, 1846 ***778.6*** *p319*
Strahan, James; Havana, 1782 ***8529.30*** *p10A*
Strahan, Robert; America, 1773 ***1220.12*** *p769*
Strahl, Konrad; Pennsylvania, 1848 ***170.15*** *p44*
Strahle, Edmund 8; Halifax, N.S., 1902 ***1860.4*** *p40*
Strahle, Jacob 37; Halifax, N.S., 1902 ***1860.4*** *p40*
Strahle, Johanna 10; Halifax, N.S., 1902 ***1860.4*** *p40*
Strahle, Juliane 34; Halifax, N.S., 1902 ***1860.4*** *p40*
Strahle, Rosine 11; Halifax, N.S., 1902 ***1860.4*** *p40*
Straihle, William; Illinois, 1858-1861 ***6020.5*** *p133*
Strain, Barney 24; New York, NY, 1825 ***6178.50*** *p78*
Strain, Elizabeth 13; Quebec, 1870 ***8364.32*** *p26*
Strait, George; America, 1739 ***1220.12*** *p769*
Straitch, William 32; Ontario, 1871 ***1823.21*** *p355*
Straith, George 23; Ontario, 1871 ***1823.21*** *p355*
Straka, Petr; Wisconsin, 1851 ***2853.20*** *p312*
Strand, Amund; Iowa, 1877 ***1211.15*** *p19*
Strand, Carl Oscar; Cleveland, OH, 1905 ***9722.10*** *p127*
Strandberg, Gust A.; Cleveland, OH, 1865-1873 ***9722.10*** *p127*
Strandberg, N.; Boston, 1847 ***6412.40*** *p150*
Strang, Thomas; Barbados, 1698 ***1220.12*** *p769*
Strangbridge, Christopher; Maryland, 1737 ***1220.12*** *p769*
Strange, Mrs.; Toronto, 1844 ***2910.35*** *p114*
Strange, Edward; America, 1757 ***1220.12*** *p769*
Strange, John; America, 1756 ***1220.12*** *p769*
Strange, Katherine; Annapolis, MD, 1731 ***1220.12*** *p769*
Strange, Mary; America, 1752 ***1220.12*** *p769*
Strange, Robert 61; Ontario, 1871 ***1823.17*** *p158*
Strange, Thomas; America, 1771 ***1220.12*** *p769*
Strange, William 31; Ontario, 1871 ***1823.21*** *p355*
Strangeways, John; America, 1738 ***1220.12*** *p769*
Strangis, Arthur; America, 1730 ***1220.12*** *p769*
Strangway, Walter 31; Ontario, 1871 ***1823.17*** *p158*
Strangway, William 51; Ontario, 1871 ***1823.17*** *p158*
Strangwich, Anthony; Barbados or Jamaica, 1684 ***1220.12*** *p769*
Strangwish, John; America, 1738 ***1220.12*** *p769*
Stransky, A.; Iowa, 1870 ***2853.20*** *p202*
Stransky, Antonin; Wisconsin, 1854 ***2853.20*** *p304*
Stransky, Jan; Wisconsin, 1854 ***2853.20*** *p304*
Stransky, Vojtech; Wisconsin, 1854 ***2853.20*** *p323*
Strasburg, Peter; Ohio, 1809-1852 ***4511.35*** *p53*
Strass, Maria Barbara; America, 1872 ***5475.1*** *p186*
Strass, Peter; Ohio, 1809-1852 ***4511.35*** *p53*
Strassel, Joseph; Ohio, 1809-1852 ***4511.35*** *p53*
Strasser, Antone; North Carolina, 1792-1862 ***1088.45*** *p34*
Strasser, John; Wisconsin, 1880 ***6795.8*** *p99*
Strasser, Katharina; America, 1879 ***5475.1*** *p187*
*Daughter:*Barbara
*Daughter:*Maria
With daughter
*Son:*Johann
Strasser, Maria; America, 1879 ***5475.1*** *p187*
With siblings
Strasser, Nikolaus; America, 1879 ***5475.1*** *p187*
Strasser, Peter; America, 1879 ***5475.1*** *p187*
Strasz, Peter; Ohio, 1809-1852 ***4511.35*** *p53*
Stratford, Aun 16; Quebec, 1870 ***8364.32*** *p26*
Stratford, Henry 28; Ontario, 1871 ***1823.21*** *p355*
Stratford, John; America, 1741 ***1220.12*** *p769*
Stratford, John; Barbados or Jamaica, 1684 ***1220.12*** *p769*
Strathan, Thomas 35; Ontario, 1871 ***1823.21*** *p355*
Strathdee, George 48; Ontario, 1871 ***1823.21*** *p355*
Strathe, Christian Friedrich August; America, 1881 ***7420.1*** *p325*
Strathen, Martha 82; Ontario, 1871 ***1823.21*** *p355*
Strathfull, Richard 19; Ontario, 1871 ***1823.21*** *p355*
Strathman, Reinold; Ohio, 1840-1897 ***8365.35*** *p18*
Strathy, Alexander 89; Ontario, 1871 ***1823.21*** *p355*
Strathy, James B. 57; Ontario, 1871 ***1823.21*** *p355*
Stratton, Ann 22; Ontario, 1871 ***1823.21*** *p355*
Stratton, J. D.; California, 1868 ***1131.61*** *p89*
Stratton, John; America, 1683 ***1220.12*** *p769*
Stratton, John 57; Ontario, 1871 ***1823.17*** *p158*
Stratton, Lilly 35; Ontario, 1871 ***1823.21*** *p355*
Stratton, Thomas; America, 1752 ***1220.12*** *p770*
Stratton, William; America, 1758 ***1220.12*** *p770*
Stratton, William; America, 1772 ***1220.12*** *p770*
Stratton, William; America, 1775 ***1220.12*** *p770*
Stratz, Andrew; Washington, 1887 ***2770.40*** *p25*
Straub, Adam; America, 1889 ***2526.43*** *p144*
Straub, Anna *SEE* Straub, Johann Philipp
Straub, Anna Elisabetha Hofmann 33 *SEE* Straub, Ludwig
Straub, Christoph; America, 1860 ***2526.42*** *p137*
Straub, Edward; Iowa, 1894 ***1211.15*** *p19*
Straub, Elisabeth; America, 1752 ***2526.42*** *p174*
Straub, Elisabeth *SEE* Straub, Johann Philipp
Straub, Georg; America, 1831 ***2526.43*** *p121*
With wife
Straub, Georg *SEE* Straub, Johann Philipp
Straub, Georg Wilhelm; America, 1854 ***2526.43*** *p157*
Straub, Jakob; America, 1853 ***2526.43*** *p144*
Straub, Johann Kaspar; Venezuela, 1843 ***3899.5*** *p542*
Straub, Johann Philipp; America, 1883 ***2526.43*** *p215*
With wife 37
*Daughter:*Elisabeth
*Son:*Philipp
*Son:*Georg
*Son:*Leonhard
*Son:*Johannes
*Daughter:*Anna
Straub, Johannes *SEE* Straub, Johann Philipp
Straub, Leonhard *SEE* Straub, Johann Philipp
Straub, Ludwig 37; America, 1841 ***2526.43*** *p144*
*Wife:*Anna Elisabetha Hofmann 33
Straub, Michael; America, 1853 ***2526.43*** *p162*
Straub, Philipp; America, 1842 ***2526.42*** *p114*
With wife
With child 7 months
Straub, Philipp; America, 1866 ***2526.43*** *p162*
Straub, Philipp; America, 1881 ***2526.42*** *p137*
Straub, Philipp *SEE* Straub, Johann Philipp
Straubelein, Eckardt; Chile, 1852 ***1192.4*** *p52*
Strauch, Isaac 15; America, 1847 ***778.6*** *p319*
Straue, Michael; Illinois, 1859 ***6079.1*** *p13*
Straughan, Wm. 22; Virginia, 1635 ***1183.3*** *p31*
Straus, Adelheid; America, 1856 ***2526.43*** *p182*
Straus, Anna Margaretha 49; America, 1851 ***2526.43*** *p221*
*Son:*Heinrich 20
Straus, Aron; America, 1869 ***2526.43*** *p182*
Straus, Aron Raphael 48; America, 1854 ***2526.43*** *p144*
With wife 45
*Daughter:*Ester 13
*Son:*Salamon 10
*Child:*Mauche 8
*Son:*Daniel 12
*Daughter:*Gutel 16
*Son:*Joseph 19
Straus, Daniel 12 *SEE* Straus, Aron Raphael
Straus, David; America, 1892 ***2526.43*** *p182*
Straus, Ester 13 *SEE* Straus, Aron Raphael
Straus, Gutel 16 *SEE* Straus, Aron Raphael
Straus, Isaak; America, 1859 ***2526.43*** *p182*
Straus, Joseph 19 *SEE* Straus, Aron Raphael
Straus, Mauche 8 *SEE* Straus, Aron Raphael
Straus, Salamon 10 *SEE* Straus, Aron Raphael
Straus, Sara; America, 1864 ***2526.43*** *p182*
Straus, Zadock; America, 1865 ***2526.43*** *p182*
Strause, Peter; Ohio, 1809-1852 ***4511.35*** *p53*
Strauss, Elisabeth; America, 1890 ***5475.1*** *p398*
Strauss, Hans Hugo von; Canada, 1894 ***7420.1*** *p371*
Strauss, Heinrich; America, 1864 ***2526.43*** *p183*
Strauss, Jakob; America, 1864 ***2526.43*** *p157*
Strauss, Jakob; New York, 1867 ***2526.43*** *p157*
Strauss, L.; Louisiana, 1874 ***4981.45*** *p297*
Strauss, Lazarus; America, 1877 ***2526.43*** *p157*
Strauss, Magdalene; America, 1881 ***5475.1*** *p429*
Strauss, Malchen; America, 1866 ***2526.43*** *p157*
Strauss, Margarethe; America, 1881 ***5475.1*** *p429*
Strauss, Marie 24; New Orleans, 1848 ***778.6*** *p319*
Strauss, Sara 32; America, 1843 ***2526.43*** *p157*
With child 11
Strauss, Zadock; America, 1854 ***2526.43*** *p183*
Straw, Mary; America, 1753 ***1220.12*** *p770*
Strawbridge, Richard; Annapolis, MD, 1725 ***1220.12*** *p770*
Strawinsky, Joseph 29; New York, NY, 1893 ***1883.7*** *p37*
Stray, Thomas 38; Ontario, 1871 ***1823.21*** *p356*
Streader, Caspar; New Jersey, 1749-1774 ***927.31*** *p2*
Streader, Johann Henrich; New Jersey, 1749-1774 ***927.31*** *p2*
Streader, Johannes; New Jersey, 1749-1774 ***927.31*** *p2*
Streader, John Henry; New Jersey, 1749-1774 ***927.31*** *p2*
Streak, Francis; America, 1774 ***1220.12*** *p770*
Stream, John; America, 1771 ***1220.12*** *p770*
Streat, William 25; Ontario, 1871 ***1823.17*** *p158*
Streb, John; Ohio, 1809-1852 ***4511.35*** *p53*
Streb, Peter; Ohio, 1809-1852 ***4511.35*** *p53*
Streck, John; America, 1715 ***1220.12*** *p770*
Streck, Magdalena; Venezuela, 1843 ***3899.5*** *p540*
Streck, Xaver; Venezuela, 1843 ***3899.5*** *p540*
Strecker, Frederic 21; Louisiana, 1848 ***778.6*** *p319*
Strecker, Heinrich Louis Christian Jacob; America, 1866 ***7420.1*** *p250*
Streek, Thomas 26; Louisiana, 1848 ***778.6*** *p319*
Street, A. 54; New Orleans, 1848 ***778.6*** *p319*
Street, Abraham; America, 1764 ***1220.12*** *p770*
Street, Ann; America, 1772 ***1220.12*** *p770*
Street, Diana; America, 1736 ***1220.12*** *p770*
Street, Edith; Maryland, 1731 ***1220.12*** *p770*
Street, Henry; America, 1738 ***1220.12*** *p770*
Street, John; Virginia, 1749 ***1220.12*** *p770*
Street, Lawrence; Virginia, 1774 ***1220.12*** *p770*
Street, Margaret 68; Ontario, 1871 ***1823.21*** *p356*
Street, Mary 79; Ontario, 1871 ***1823.21*** *p356*
Street, Moses 37; Ontario, 1871 ***1823.21*** *p356*
Street, Peter 52; Indiana, 1892 ***9076.20*** *p73*
Street, Rebecca; Annapolis, MD, 1735 ***1220.12*** *p770*
Street, Richard; Virginia, 1750 ***1220.12*** *p770*
Street, Robert H.; Washington, 1889 ***2770.40*** *p81*
Street, S. A. 16; New Orleans, 1848 ***778.6*** *p319*
Street, Sam'l; Ontario, 1787 ***1276.15*** *p231*
Street, Saul A. 18; New Orleans, 1848 ***778.6*** *p319*
Street, William; America, 1750 ***1220.12*** *p770*
Street, William; America, 1765 ***1220.12*** *p770*
Street, William; Virginia, 1741 ***1220.12*** *p770*
Streeter, Henry 60; Ontario, 1871 ***1823.21*** *p356*
Strehle, Annette 24; Louisiana, 1848 ***778.6*** *p319*
Strehle, Batistine 5; Louisiana, 1848 ***778.6*** *p320*
Strehle, Gottlieb 19; Louisiana, 1848 ***778.6*** *p320*
Strehle, Hypolite 4; Louisiana, 1848 ***778.6*** *p320*
Strehle, Jacob 16; Louisiana, 1848 ***778.6*** *p320*
Strehte, Edmund 8; Halifax, N.S., 1902 ***1860.4*** *p40*
Strehte, Jacob 37; Halifax, N.S., 1902 ***1860.4*** *p40*
Strehte, Johanna 10; Halifax, N.S., 1902 ***1860.4*** *p40*
Strehte, Juliane 34; Halifax, N.S., 1902 ***1860.4*** *p40*
Strehte, Rosine 11; Halifax, N.S., 1902 ***1860.4*** *p40*
Streibel, Amalia Schilke *SEE* Streibel, Heinrich
Streibel, Heinrich; Dakota, 1888 ***554.30*** *p25*
*Wife:*Amalia Schilke
*Child:*Rinata
Streibel, Rinata *SEE* Streibel, Heinrich
Streicher, Anna; America, 1881 ***5475.1*** *p151*
*Son:*Johann
Streicher, Johann *SEE* Streicher, Anna Wolf
Streicher, Margarethe; America, 1893 ***5475.1*** *p152*
Streicher, Peter; America, 1870 ***5475.1*** *p150*
Streif, Marie 58; America, 1846 ***778.6*** *p320*
Streige, Johann; Wisconsin, 1899 ***6795.8*** *p231*
Streip, Joseph 27; Port uncertain, 1847 ***778.6*** *p320*
Streit, Angela; America, 1879 ***5475.1*** *p376*
Streit, Anton; America, 1857 ***5475.1*** *p375*
Streit, Elisabeth Osweiler *SEE* Streit, Peter
Streit, Elisabeth 29; America, 1868 ***5475.1*** *p335*
Streit, Eva; America, 1879 ***5475.1*** *p267*
Streit, Eva; Wisconsin, 1887 ***5475.1*** *p268*
Streit, Johann *SEE* Streit, Johann
Streit, Johann; America, 1855 ***5475.1*** *p375*
*Wife:*Margarethe Leick
*Son:*Johann
*Daughter:*Margarethe
*Daughter:*Maria
With daughter
*Daughter:*Margarethe
Streit, Joseph; Colorado, 1890 ***1029.59*** *p86*
Streit, Joseph; Colorado, 1895 ***1029.59*** *p86*
Streit, Katharina; America, 1857 ***5475.1*** *p375*
*Sister:*Maria
Streit, Margarethe *SEE* Streit, Johann
Streit, Margarethe Leick *SEE* Streit, Johann
Streit, Margarethe Neusius *SEE* Streit, Nikolaus
Streit, Margarethe 9 *SEE* Streit, Nikolaus
Streit, Maria *SEE* Streit, Johann
Streit, Maria *SEE* Streit, Katharina
Streit, Michel; America, 1876 ***5475.1*** *p267*
Streit, Nikolaus; America, 1859 ***5475.1*** *p266*
Streit, Nikolaus; America, 1865 ***5475.1*** *p360*
*Wife:*Margarethe Neusius
*Daughter:*Margarethe
Streit, Peter; America, 1858 ***5475.1*** *p283*
Streit, Peter; America, 1862 ***5475.1*** *p335*
*Wife:*Elisabeth Osweiler
Strempel, Johann Wilhelm; New Jersey, 1752-1774 ***927.31*** *p2*
Streppard, Thomas 45; New Orleans, 1848 ***778.6*** *p320*
Stretham, William; America, 1723 ***1220.12*** *p770*
Streton, Thomas; America, 1745 ***1220.12*** *p770*
Stretton, Elizabeth; Barbados, 1663 ***1220.12*** *p769*
Stretton, John; America, 1700 ***1220.12*** *p770*
Strevel, William 21; Ontario, 1871 ***1823.17*** *p158*
Strey, Fredrick; Wisconsin, 1885 ***6795.8*** *p228*

Stricker, Bernard; Ohio, 1840-1897 *8365.35 p18*
Stricker, C.; Galveston, TX, 1855 *571.7 p18*
Strickett, Arthur; America, 1743 *1220.12 p770*
Strickland, Anthony; Barbados, 1668 *1220.12 p770*
Strickland, George; America, 1771 *1220.12 p770*
Strickland, John; America, 1740 *1220.12 p770*
Strid, Anton Melcher; America, 1849 *4487.25 p74*
   With parents
Strid, Pehr 18; New York, 1856 *6529.11 p21*
Strid, Walter; America, 1849 *4487.25 p73*
   With parents
Stride, Joseph; America, 1764 *1220.12 p770*
Striger, Joseph; America, 1765 *1220.12 p770*
Strike, Arthur James; Iowa, 1901 *1211.15 p19*
Strike, Walter E.; Iowa, 1905 *1211.15 p19*
Strimple, William; New Jersey, 1752-1774 *927.31 p2*
Stringer, Ann; Maryland, 1740 *1220.12 p770*
Stringer, Elizabeth; Annapolis, MD, 1736 *1220.12 p770*
Stringer, George; America, 1731 *1220.12 p770*
Stringer, Hannah; America, 1749 *1220.12 p770*
Stringer, James; Virginia, 1618 *1220.12 p770*
Stringer, John; America, 1724 *1220.12 p770*
Stringer, John; Annapolis, MD, 1726 *1220.12 p770*
Stringer, Mary; America, 1753 *1220.12 p770*
Stringer, Mary; America, 1768 *1220.12 p770*
Stringer, Mary; Virginia, 1726 *1220.12 p770*
Stringer, Michael; America, 1731 *1220.12 p770*
Stringer, Peter; America, 1774 *1220.12 p770*
Stringer, Ralph; Maryland, 1736 *1220.12 p770*
Stringer, Robert; America, 1747 *1220.12 p770*
Stringer, Samuel 37; Ontario, 1871 *1823.21 p356*
Stringer, Samuel 72; Ontario, 1871 *1823.21 p356*
Stringer, Thomas; America, 1762 *1220.12 p771*
Stringer, Thomas; Barbados or Jamaica, 1677 *1220.12 p771*
Stringer, William; America, 1767 *1220.12 p771*
Stringer, William; North Carolina, 1835 *1088.45 p34*
Stringfellow, Thomas; Barbados, 1664 *1220.12 p771*
Strinkner, William; America, 1736 *1220.12 p771*
Strinz, Elisabeth 62; Missouri, 1845 *778.6 p320*
Stripps, Thomas 60; Ontario, 1871 *1823.21 p356*
Stritch, Walter; Barbados, 1679 *1220.12 p771*
Stritecky, Daniel; Minnesota, 1852 *2853.20 p272*
Stritesky, Daniel; Wisconsin, 1852 *2853.20 p303*
Stritesky, Jan; Wisconsin, 1852 *2853.20 p303*
Stritesky, Josef; Wisconsin, 1854 *2853.20 p304*
Stritesky, Vaclav; Wisconsin, 1854 *2853.20 p304*
Strobel, Caroline 3; New York, NY, 1885 *8425.16 p32*
Strobel, Caroline 22; New York, NY, 1885 *8425.16 p32*
Strobel, Catharina; Valdivia, Chile, 1850 *1192.4 p48*
Strobel, Cathr. 7; New York, NY, 1885 *8425.16 p32*
Strobel, Dorothea Sophie Anna; Dakota, 1885 *7420.1 p343*
Strobel, E. P. A.; Valdivia, Chile, 1850 *1192.4 p48*
   With wife & 2 children
   With child 6
   With child 19
Strobel, Frdr. 4; New York, NY, 1885 *8425.16 p32*
Strobel, Friedr. 34; New York, NY, 1885 *8425.16 p32*
Strobel, Gotfrey; Ohio, 1809-1852 *4511.35 p53*
Strobel, Gottfried; America, 1852-1883 *179.55 p19*
Strobel, Joseph 42; New Castle, DE, 1817-1818 *90.20 p154*
Strobel, Katharina; America, 1892 *179.55 p19*
Strobel, Mathias 26; Missouri, 1845 *778.6 p320*
Strobel, Minna; Chicago, 1870 *7420.1 p284*
   With 3 children
Strode, Edward; America, 1767 *1220.12 p771*
Stroder, Caspar; New Jersey, 1749-1774 *927.31 p2*
Stroder, Johann Henrich; New Jersey, 1749-1774 *927.31 p2*
Stroder, Johannes; New Jersey, 1749-1774 *927.31 p2*
Stroder, John Henry; New Jersey, 1749-1774 *927.31 p2*
Strodtbeck, Johann Ludwig; America, 1870 *179.55 p19*
Strodtbeck, Rosina Carolina; America, 1870 *179.55 p19*
Stroebel, Sophie 21; America, 1747 *778.6 p320*
Stroh, Anna 39; America, 1880 *5475.1 p554*
Stroh, Louis; Louisiana, 1874-1875 *4981.45 p31*
Stroh, Peter 36; New Orleans, 1848 *778.6 p320*
Strohl, Christian 50; America, 1843 *778.6 p320*
Strohl, Peter; Pennsylvania, 1848 *170.15 p44*
Strohl, Peter 36; Pennsylvania, 1848 *170.15 p44*
   With wife
Strohmann, Adolf Mathias; America, 1849 *5475.1 p29*
Strohmann, Pierre 20; America, 1841 *778.6 p320*
Strohmeier, Catharine Marie Dorothee Bartels *SEE* Strohmeier, Friedrich Christian Gottlieb
Strohmeier, Friedrich Christian Gottlieb; America, 1851 *7420.1 p83*
   *Wife:*Catharine Marie Dorothee Bartels
   With 3 daughters
Strohschein, Emil Hermann; Wisconsin, 1906 *6795.8 p147*

Strol, Andrus 27; Halifax, N.S., 1902 *1860.4 p44*
Strol, Anna 23; Halifax, N.S., 1902 *1860.4 p44*
Strom, Alfred; Cleveland, OH, 1901-1905 *9722.10 p127*
Strom, Brita 27; New York, 1856 *6529.11 p21*
Strom, Edna; Detroit, 1930 *1640.60 p78*
Strom, Jacob C.; Valdivia, Chile, 1851 *1192.4 p50*
Strom, Johan; New York, NY, 1843 *6412.40 p147*
Strom, Johanna; St. Paul, MN, 1892 *1865.50 p110*
Strombeck, Johan; New York, NY, 1843 *6412.40 p148*
Strombeck, Thure; San Francisco, 1849 *6412.40 p151*
Stromberg, Heinrich; America, 1852 *7420.1 p99*
   With wife 3 sons & 3 daughters
Stromberg, Johann Heinrich; America, 1845 *7420.1 p40*
Stromborg, Oscar; Cleveland, OH, 1898-1903 *9722.10 p127*
Stromeier, Miss; America, 1855 *7420.1 p136*
Stromer, Reinhold; Washington, 1889 *2770.40 p81*
Stronach, William; North Carolina, 1835 *1088.45 p34*
Stronck, Aug. W. 24; New York, NY, 1847 *9176.15 p49*
Stronck, Iecamet 26; New York, NY, 1847 *9176.15 p49*
Strong, Anna G.; St. Paul, MN, 1873 *1865.50 p110*
Strong, Charles; America, 1685 *1220.12 p771*
Strong, Charles; America, 1758 *1220.12 p771*
Strong, Elizabeth; Philadelphia, 1842 *8513.31 p294*
Strong, Hannah Katarina; St. Paul, MN, 1879 *1865.50 p110*
Strong, Henry 51; Ontario, 1871 *1823.21 p356*
Strong, James; Virginia, 1727 *1220.12 p771*
Strong, Jane; America, 1747 *1220.12 p771*
Strong, John; America, 1748 *1220.12 p771*
Strong, John; America, 1751 *1220.12 p771*
Strong, John; America, 1772 *1220.12 p771*
Strong, John; Dorchester, MA, 1635 *117.5 p158*
Strong, John 25; Ontario, 1871 *1823.21 p356*
Strong, Mary; Virginia, 1741 *1220.12 p771*
Strong, Peter; America, 1757 *1220.12 p771*
Strong, Peter Nicholas; Cleveland, OH, 1900-1904 *9722.10 p127*
Strong, Samuel 49; Ontario, 1871 *1823.21 p356*
Strong, Thomas; America, 1749 *1220.12 p771*
Strong, Thomas; America, 1754 *1220.12 p771*
Strong, Thomas; Barbados, 1698 *1220.12 p771*
Strong, William; America, 1768 *1220.12 p771*
Strongarm, William; Virginia, 1732 *1220.12 p771*
Stronghill, Thomas 65; Ontario, 1871 *1823.21 p356*
Strongman, Fred R. 11; Ontario, 1871 *1823.21 p356*
Strongman, William J. 17; Ontario, 1871 *1823.21 p356*
Strood, Richard; America, 1752 *1220.12 p771*
Strosser, Anton 20; Galveston, TX, 1846 *3967.10 p377*
Strosser, Katharina 9 months; Galveston, TX, 1846 *3967.10 p377*
Strosser, Katharina 30; Galveston, TX, 1846 *3967.10 p377*
Strosser, Paul 32; Galveston, TX, 1846 *3967.10 p377*
Strotmann, Heinrich August *SEE* Strotmann, Heinrich Friedrich Ludwig
Strotmann, Heinrich Friedrich Ludwig; America, 1862 *7420.1 p215*
   *Son:*Heinrich August
   *Son:*Heinrich Friedrich Wilhelm
   With wife
   *Son:*Heinrich Wilhelm
   *Daughter:*Justine Caroline Louise
   *Daughter:*Justine Wilhelmine Charlotte
Strotmann, Heinrich Friedrich Wilhelm *SEE* Strotmann, Heinrich Friedrich Ludwig
Strotmann, Heinrich Wilhelm *SEE* Strotmann, Heinrich Friedrich Ludwig
Strotmann, Justine Caroline Louise *SEE* Strotmann, Heinrich Friedrich Ludwig
Strotmann, Justine Wilhelmine Charlotte *SEE* Strotmann, Heinrich Friedrich Ludwig
Strotten, Thomas; America, 1773 *1220.12 p771*
Strotton, Thomas; America, 1740 *1220.12 p771*
Stroub, Elisabeth 5; Port uncertain, 1842 *778.6 p320*
Stroub, Elisabeth 40; Port uncertain, 1842 *778.6 p320*
Stroub, Eva 12; Port uncertain, 1842 *778.6 p320*
Stroub, Jacob 10; Port uncertain, 1842 *778.6 p320*
Stroub, Jean 34; Port uncertain, 1842 *778.6 p320*
Stroub, Johannes 14; Port uncertain, 1842 *778.6 p320*
Stroub, Salemie 3; Port uncertain, 1842 *778.6 p320*
Stroud, Ann; America, 1769 *1220.12 p771*
Stroud, John; Philadelphia, 1776 *8529.30 p3*
Stroud, Martha; America, 1697 *1220.12 p771*
Stroud, Richard; America, 1770 *1220.12 p771*
Stroud, Thomas; America, 1678 *1220.12 p771*
Strouhal, Josef; Chicago, 1893-1910 *2853.20 p469*
Stroup, Charles; North Carolina, 1792-1862 *1088.45 p34*
Stroup, William; North Carolina, 1857 *1088.45 p34*
Strous, Mr. 24; America, 1844 *778.6 p320*
Strous, Daberough; Philadelphia, 1777 *8529.30 p7A*
Strouse, John; North Carolina, 1853 *1088.45 p34*
Strouse, Peter; Ohio, 1809-1852 *4511.35 p53*

Strouss, John William; North Carolina, 1853 *1088.45 p34*
Strout, Jasper; America, 1759 *1220.12 p771*
Strowder, John; America, 1686 *1220.12 p771*
Strowte, John; America, 1740 *1220.12 p771*
Strozzin, William Alexander; North Carolina, 1844 *1088.45 p34*
Strub, Franz Anton; Venezuela, 1843 *3899.5 p542*
Strub, Franz Anton, Sr.; Venezuela, 1843 *3899.5 p542*
Strub, Johann Kaspar; Venezuela, 1843 *3899.5 p542*
Strub, Matthias; Venezuela, 1843 *3899.5 p542*
Strub Children, . . .; Venezuela, 1843 *3899.5 p542*
Strube, Margaretha 27; America, 1841 *778.6 p320*
Strubel, Bernard 36; Louisiana, 1848 *778.6 p320*
Strubel, Francoise 34; Louisiana, 1848 *778.6 p320*
Strubinger, Franz; Venezuela, 1843 *3899.5 p542*
Strubinger Children, . . .; Venezuela, 1843 *3899.5 p542*
Struchen, Alexander; Iowa, 1895 *1211.15 p19*
Struck, Emmy; America, 1884 *7420.1 p345*
Struck, Friedrich; Wisconsin, 1875 *6795.8 p228*
Struckmann, Carl; Port uncertain, 1874 *7420.1 p304*
Struckmann, Carl Heinrich; America, 1870 *7420.1 p288*
   *Daughter:*Sophie Juliane
   *Son:*Heinrich Wilhelm Ferdinand
   *Son:*Friedrich Wilhelm
Struckmann, Carl Wilhelm; America, 1867 *7420.1 p265*
Struckmann, Friederike; America, 1869 *7420.1 p282*
Struckmann, Friedrich; Indianapolis, 1865 *7420.1 p238*
Struckmann, Friedrich Ernst; America, 1845 *7420.1 p40*
Struckmann, Friedrich Wilhelm *SEE* Struckmann, Carl Heinrich
Struckmann, Gottlieb Lebrecht; Port uncertain, 1850 *7420.1 p76*
   *Wife:*Sophie Eleonore Krull
   With 2 sons & 2 daughters
Struckmann, Heinrich Wilhelm Ferdinand *SEE* Struckmann, Carl Heinrich
Struckmann, Ludwig; America, 1857 *7420.1 p173*
Struckmann, Sophie Eleonore Krull *SEE* Struckmann, Gottlieb Lebrecht
Struckmann, Sophie Juliane *SEE* Struckmann, Carl Heinrich
Struckmann, Wilhelm; Indianapolis, 1867 *7420.1 p265*
Struckmeier, August Gottlieb Ferdinand; America, 1870 *7420.1 p288*
   *Sister:*Louise Sophie Caroline
Struckmeier, Carl Heinrich Friedrich *SEE* Struckmeier, Caroline Wilhelmine Charlotte
Struckmeier, Caroline Wilhelmine Charlotte; America, 1871 *7420.1 p292*
   *Son:*Carl Heinrich Friedrich
   *Daughter:*Wilhelmine Caroline Charlotte
Struckmeier, Christian Ludwig *SEE* Struckmeier, Rehren
Struckmeier, Christian Wilhelm; America, 1867 *7420.1 p265*
Struckmeier, Dorothea Wilhelmine; America, 1864 *7420.1 p226*
Struckmeier, Johann Ernst Wilhelm *SEE* Struckmeier, Rehren
Struckmeier, Johann Heinrich Christian; America, 1853 *7420.1 p112*
Struckmeier, Karoline Charlotte; Chicago, 1883 *7420.1 p336*
Struckmeier, Louise; America, 1871 *7420.1 p396*
Struckmeier, Louise Sophie Caroline *SEE* Struckmeier, August Gottlieb Ferdinand
Struckmeier, Rehren; America, 1867 *7420.1 p265*
   *Son:*Christian Ludwig
   *Son:*Johann Ernst Wilhelm
Struckmeier, Wilhelmine Caroline Charlotte *SEE* Struckmeier, Caroline Wilhelmine Charlotte
Struckmeyer, Engel D.; Port uncertain, 1883 *7420.1 p340*
Struckmeyer, Engel Wilhelmine Louise; America, 1866 *7420.1 p250*
Struckmeyer, Friedrich Ludwig Wilhelm; America, 1866 *7420.1 p250*
Strude, William; America, 1764 *1220.12 p771*
Strudell, Michael; America, 1759 *1220.12 p771*
Strudwick, George; America, 1773 *1220.12 p771*
Strudwick, Thomas; America, 1771 *1220.12 p771*
Strudwick, William; America, 1738 *1220.12 p771*
Struebing, G.; Galveston, TX, 1855 *571.7 p18*
Struermann, Friedrich Ernst; America, 1848 *7420.1 p62*
Strugala, Stanley; Detroit, 1929-1930 *6214.5 p63*
Strugler, William; America, 1740 *1220.12 p771*
Strumpel, Johann Friedrich Conrad; New York, NY, 1856 *7420.1 p155*
Strunk, Anton Friedrich Wilhelm; America, 1860 *7420.1 p200*
Strupp, Peter; America, 1881 *5475.1 p257*
Struthers, James 56; Ontario, 1871 *1823.17 p158*
Struthers, Lorance; Colorado, 1873 *1029.59 p87*

Strutt, Daniel; America, 1770 ***1220.12*** *p771*
Strutt, Elizabeth; America, 1767 ***1220.12*** *p771*
Strutt, Mary; America, 1682 ***1220.12*** *p771*
Strutt, Sarah; America, 1769 ***1220.12*** *p771*
Strutton, John; Barbados or Jamaica, 1692 ***1220.12*** *p771*
Strutton, Sarah; America, 1769 ***1220.12*** *p771*
Strutton, William; America, 1751 ***1220.12*** *p771*
Strutton, William; America, 1758 ***1220.12*** *p771*
Strutz, Robert Edward Johannes; Wisconsin, 1896 ***6795.8*** *p77*
Struve, . . .; America, 1847 ***7420.1*** *p57*
With family
Struve, Heinrich Christian; America, 1847 ***7420.1*** *p57*
With wife
With daughter 9
With son 3
With son 1
With daughter 11
With daughter 14
With son 7
Struve Family ; America, 1847 ***7420.1*** *p56*
Stryce, Silver; America, 1750 ***1220.12*** *p771*
Strycharski, Martin; Texas, 1884-1904 ***6015.15*** *p29*
Strzalkowska, Eve; Detroit, 1890 ***9980.23*** *p97*
Strzalkowski, Joseph; Detroit, 1890 ***9980.23*** *p97*
Strzebielinska, Matilda; Wisconsin, 1894 ***6795.8*** *p61*
Strzebielinski, Matilda; Wisconsin, 1894 ***6795.8*** *p61*
Strzelbicki, Walter; Detroit, 1929 ***1640.55*** *p117*
Stuam, Christian 25; Halifax, N.S., 1902 ***1860.4*** *p40*
Stuam, Christine 25; Halifax, N.S., 1902 ***1860.4*** *p40*
Stuart, Alexander; Marston's Wharf, 1782 ***8529.30*** *p16*
Stuart, Alexander; New Jersey, 1777 ***8529.30*** *p7*
Stuart, Alexander; Ohio, 1840-1897 ***8365.35*** *p18*
Stuart, Alexander 40; Ontario, 1871 ***1823.21*** *p356*
Stuart, Barbara 34; Ontario, 1871 ***1823.21*** *p356*
Stuart, Charles; North Carolina, 1792-1862 ***1088.45*** *p34*
Stuart, Duncan 36; Ontario, 1871 ***1823.21*** *p356*
Stuart, Elizabeth; Virginia, 1739 ***1220.12*** *p764*
Stuart, George 45; Ontario, 1871 ***1823.17*** *p158*
Stuart, Henry Charles; North Carolina, 1844 ***1088.45*** *p34*
Stuart, Hugh; America, 1773 ***1220.12*** *p764*
Stuart, J. F.; California, 1868 ***1131.61*** *p89*
Stuart, Jane 70; Ontario, 1871 ***1823.21*** *p356*
Stuart, Jelina 18; Ontario, 1871 ***1823.17*** *p158*
Stuart, John; New York, 1776 ***8529.30*** *p16*
Stuart, John; Ohio, 1809-1852 ***4511.35*** *p53*
Stuart, Mary; America, 1746 ***1220.12*** *p765*
Stuart, Peter; America, 1769 ***1220.12*** *p765*
Stuart, Robert; North Carolina, 1792-1862 ***1088.45*** *p34*
Stubb, Andrew O.; Washington, 1888 ***2770.40*** *p26*
Stubbe, Albert; Detroit, 1929-1930 ***6214.5*** *p61*
Stubbe, Aug.; Wisconsin, 1886 ***6795.8*** *p52*
Stubbe, Gottfried; Wisconsin, 1858 ***6795.8*** *p142*
Stubbe, Wilhelmine; Wisconsin, 1904 ***6795.8*** *p176*
Stubbendorff, Joh.; Valdivia, Chile, 1852 ***1192.4*** *p56*
Stubberfield, John; Barbados, 1679 ***1220.12*** *p772*
Stubbing, John; America, 1757 ***1220.12*** *p772*
Stubbings, John; America, 1675 ***1220.12*** *p772*
Stubbings, John; Virginia, 1727 ***1220.12*** *p772*
Stubbins, Hannah; America, 1753 ***1220.12*** *p772*
Stubbins, John; America, 1740 ***1220.12*** *p772*
Stubbins, William; America, 1755 ***1220.12*** *p772*
Stubbs, Mr.; Canada, 1877-1950 ***9228.50*** *p347*
*Wife:*Maybelle Le Favour
Stubbs, Ann; America, 1756 ***1220.12*** *p772*
Stubbs, Ann; America, 1762 ***1220.12*** *p772*
Stubbs, Anne; America, 1682 ***1220.12*** *p772*
Stubbs, Arend; Louisiana, 1841-1844 ***4981.45*** *p211*
Stubbs, Charles 45; Ontario, 1871 ***1823.21*** *p356*
Stubbs, Edward 80; Ontario, 1871 ***1823.17*** *p158*
Stubbs, Frances; America, 1756 ***1220.12*** *p772*
Stubbs, James 63; Ontario, 1871 ***1823.17*** *p158*
Stubbs, John; America, 1756 ***1220.12*** *p772*
Stubbs, John; Maryland, 1737 ***1220.12*** *p772*
Stubbs, John; Virginia, 1735 ***1220.12*** *p772*
Stubbs, Mary; America, 1749 ***1220.12*** *p772*
Stubbs, Maybelle Le Favour *SEE* Stubbs, Mr.
Stubbs, Samuel; Barbados or Jamaica, 1700 ***1220.12*** *p772*
Stuber, Barbara Hoffmann 24 *SEE* Stuber, Peter
Stuber, Georg; America, 1866 ***5475.1*** *p542*
Stuber, Karl; America, 1863 ***5475.1*** *p542*
Stuber, Luise Margarethe 15 *SEE* Stuber, Peter
Stuber, Maria 30; America, 1864 ***5475.1*** *p41*
Stuber, Marianne 68; America, 1867 ***5475.1*** *p543*
Stuber, Peter; America, 1800-1899 ***5475.1*** *p41*
*Wife:*Barbara Hoffmann
*Daughter:*Luise Margarethe
Stuber, Philipp Ludwig; America, 1849 ***5475.1*** *p29*
Stubhong, Ole A.; Washington, 1885 ***2770.40*** *p194*
Stubing, Friedrich Philipp Ludwig; America, 1860 ***7420.1*** *p201*
Stuchlik, Josef; Chicago, 1854 ***2853.20*** *p388*
*Son:*Vaclav
Stuchlik, Vaclav *SEE* Stuchlik, Josef
Stucke, John; Ohio, 1809-1852 ***4511.35*** *p53*
Stuckenberg, Charlotte; America, 1880 ***7420.1*** *p318*
Stuckenberg, Friederike; America, 1884 ***7420.1*** *p345*
With 3 daughters
Stuckenberg, Marie; America, 1891 ***7420.1*** *p364*
Stuckenberg, Marie Louise Juliane; America, 1867 ***7420.1*** *p265*
Stucker, Ambrose; Ohio, 1809-1852 ***4511.35*** *p53*
Stucker, Augustus; Ohio, 1809-1852 ***4511.35*** *p53*
Stucker, Francis; Ohio, 1809-1852 ***4511.35*** *p53*
Stucker, Jacob 22; New York, NY, 1893 ***1883.7*** *p43*
Stucker, Theobald; Ohio, 1809-1852 ***4511.35*** *p53*
Stuckey, Charles; Illinois, 1858-1861 ***6020.5*** *p133*
Stuckey, John; Ohio, 1809-1852 ***4511.35*** *p53*
Stuckey, Pasche; America, 1685 ***1220.12*** *p772*
Stuckey, Robert; America, 1685 ***1220.12*** *p772*
Stuckey, Ulrich; Ohio, 1809-1852 ***4511.35*** *p53*
Stuckler, Joseph; Galveston, TX, 1855 ***571.7*** *p17*
Stuckler, Pauline; Galveston, TX, 1855 ***571.7*** *p17*
Studd, William; America, 1767 ***1220.12*** *p772*
Studder, Elizabeth; America, 1736 ***1220.12*** *p772*
Studder, Henry; Virginia, 1739 ***1220.12*** *p772*
Studder, John; America, 1747 ***1220.12*** *p772*
Studders, William 39; Ontario, 1871 ***1823.21*** *p356*
Studer, Georg 42; Galveston, TX, 1846 ***3967.10*** *p377*
Studer, Joseph 6; Galveston, TX, 1846 ***3967.10*** *p377*
Studer, Michael 10; Galveston, TX, 1846 ***3967.10*** *p377*
Studer, Therese 39; Galveston, TX, 1846 ***3967.10*** *p377*
Studham, Thomas; Barbados, 1669 ***1220.12*** *p772*
Studman, Thomas; Barbados, 1662 ***1220.12*** *p772*
Studt, Johann Peter; America, 1865 ***5475.1*** *p508*
Studzinski, Mary; Detroit, 1929-1930 ***6214.5*** *p63*
Stuebs, Herman; Wisconsin, 1875 ***6795.8*** *p228*
Stuemer, George; Colorado, 1874 ***1447.20*** *p64*
Stuermer, Clara Elise; Philadelphia, 1883 ***8513.31*** *p430*
Stueve, Andrew A.; Colorado, 1899 ***1029.59*** *p87*
Stueve, Edward A.; Colorado, 1899 ***1029.59*** *p87*
Stuf, Charles; Wisconsin, 1874 ***6795.8*** *p84*
Stuffy, John; Ohio, 1809-1852 ***4511.35*** *p53*
Stuford, Mary; America, 1730 ***1220.12*** *p772*
Stuhlfanth, Philip 24; America, 1840 ***778.6*** *p320*
Stuhlmiller, Bernhardine Walde *SEE* Stuhlmiller, Conrad
Stuhlmiller, Conrad; Philadelphia, 1875 ***8513.31*** *p428*
*Wife:*Bernhardine Walde
Stuhlsatz, Anna *SEE* Stuhlsatz, Johann
Stuhlsatz, J. Peter *SEE* Stuhlsatz, Johann
Stuhlsatz, Johann; America, 1893 ***5475.1*** *p152*
*Wife:*Margarethe Streicher
*Son:*Paul
*Daughter:*Magdalena
*Son:*J. Peter
*Son:*Peter
*Daughter:*Anna
*Son:*Nikolaus
Stuhlsatz, Magdalena *SEE* Stuhlsatz, Johann
Stuhlsatz, Margarethe Streicher *SEE* Stuhlsatz, Johann
Stuhlsatz, Nikolaus *SEE* Stuhlsatz, Johann
Stuhlsatz, Paul *SEE* Stuhlsatz, Johann
Stuhlsatz, Peter *SEE* Stuhlsatz, Johann
Stuhmann, Heinrich Dietrich Wilhelm; America, 1869 ***7420.1*** *p282*
Stukas, Wilhelm; Galveston, TX, 1855 ***571.7*** *p17*
Stuldreher, Anthony; Ohio, 1809-1852 ***4511.35*** *p53*
Stuldreher, Frank; Ohio, 1809-1852 ***4511.35*** *p53*
Stuldreher, Theodore; Ohio, 1809-1852 ***4511.35*** *p53*
Stuldreher, William; Ohio, 1809-1852 ***4511.35*** *p53*
Stulig, Anna Maria 10; America, 1747 ***778.6*** *p320*
Stulig, Johan 41; America, 1747 ***778.6*** *p320*
Stulig, Marie 7; America, 1747 ***778.6*** *p320*
Stulig, Marie 38; America, 1747 ***778.6*** *p320*
Stulig, Petre 2; America, 1747 ***778.6*** *p320*
Stulik, Karel; Chicago, 1885-1889 ***2853.20*** *p409*
Stumke, Widow; America, 1853 ***7420.1*** *p112*
*Son:*Heinrich Friedrich Wilhelm
With daughter 22
With daughter 18
Stumke, Heinrich Friedrich Wilhelm *SEE* Stumke, Widow
Stumm, Anna Maria Sermen 40 *SEE* Stumm, Heinrich
Stumm, Elisabeth 7 *SEE* Stumm, Heinrich
Stumm, Heinrich 37; America, 1857 ***5475.1*** *p550*
*Wife:*Anna Maria Sermen 40
*Daughter:*Katharina 1
*Son:*Jakob 10
*Son:*Peter 4
*Daughter:*Elisabeth 7
Stumm, Jakob 10 *SEE* Stumm, Heinrich
Stumm, Katharina 1 *SEE* Stumm, Heinrich
Stumm, Peter 4 *SEE* Stumm, Heinrich
Stummbillig, Maria; America, 1871 ***5475.1*** *p418*
Stummeier, Heinrich; Port uncertain, 1906 ***7420.1*** *p401*
Stump, John Martin; New York, 1860 ***358.56*** *p150*
Stumpf, Christian; America, 1847 ***5475.1*** *p28*
Stumpfeisen, Louise; New York, 1860 ***358.56*** *p150*
Stumpfle, Jacob; Valdivia, Chile, 1852 ***1192.4*** *p53*
Stumpke, Heinrich Wilhelm Philipp; Port uncertain, 1850 ***7420.1*** *p76*
Stumpner, Johan Georg; Wisconsin, 1899 ***6795.8*** *p234*
Stunkel, Bernhard Carl Heinrich Hermann Hugo; America, 1853 ***7420.1*** *p112*
Stunkel, Georg Friedrich; Port uncertain, 1893 ***7420.1*** *p369*
Stunkel, Henry; Missouri, 1887 ***3276.1*** *p2*
Stunkel, Henry; Missouri, 1892 ***3276.1*** *p2*
Stunkel, Johann Friedrich; New York, NY, 1856 ***7420.1*** *p155*
With family
Stunkel, Louis Carl Friedrich; America, 1855 ***7420.1*** *p142*
Stunkel, Wm.; Missouri, 1891 ***3276.1*** *p2*
Stunwax, John; Ontario, 1787 ***1276.15*** *p232*
Stupecky, Frantisek; Wisconsin, 1852 ***2853.20*** *p312*
Stupl, Antonin; Texas, 1861 ***2853.20*** *p60*
Stupp, Johann Peter; America, 1840 ***5475.1*** *p470*
Stuppi, Jakob *SEE* Stuppi, Wilhelm
Stuppi, Johann *SEE* Stuppi, Wilhelm
Stuppi, Katharina *SEE* Stuppi, Wilhelm
Stuppi, Leondina Jennewein *SEE* Stuppi, Wilhelm
Stuppi, Margarethe *SEE* Stuppi, Wilhelm
Stuppi, Wilhelm; America, 1869 ***5475.1*** *p428*
*Wife:*Leondina Jennewein
*Daughter:*Katharina
*Daughter:*Margarethe
*Son:*Johann
*Son:*Jakob
Stupple, John; America, 1758 ***1220.12*** *p772*
Stuppy, John; Ohio, 1809-1852 ***4511.35*** *p53*
Stuppy, Joseph; Ohio, 1809-1852 ***4511.35*** *p53*
Sturdivant, Emma 40; Ontario, 1871 ***1823.17*** *p158*
Sturdivant, Ira 61; Ontario, 1871 ***1823.17*** *p158*
Sturdy, Michael 35; Ontario, 1871 ***1823.17*** *p159*
Sturdy, William 25; Ontario, 1871 ***1823.17*** *p159*
Sturgeon, James 36; Ontario, 1871 ***1823.21*** *p356*
Sturgeon, James 52; Ontario, 1871 ***1823.17*** *p159*
Sturgeon, James 71; Ontario, 1871 ***1823.21*** *p356*
Sturgeon, John; America, 1739 ***1220.12*** *p772*
Sturgeon, Obediah; Maryland, 1737 ***1220.12*** *p772*
Sturgeon, Robert; Watertown, MA, 1722 ***1642*** *p112*
Sturgeon, William; America, 1745 ***1220.12*** *p772*
Sturges, William; Maryland, 1726 ***1220.12*** *p772*
Sturgis, Abram; America, 1673 ***1220.12*** *p772*
Sturgis, Jane; America, 1673 ***1220.12*** *p772*
Sturgis, John; Virginia, 1748 ***1220.12*** *p772*
Sturgis, Richard; America, 1755 ***1220.12*** *p772*
Sturm, Beate; America, 1867 ***7919.3*** *p533*
Sturm, J. George; New Castle, DE, 1817-1818 ***90.20*** *p154*
Sturm, Johann 67; America, 1846 ***778.6*** *p320*
Sturm, Julius Heinrich Conrad; Port uncertain, 1850 ***7420.1*** *p76*
Sturm, Katharina 30; Galveston, TX, 1844 ***3967.10*** *p372*
Sturm, Madeleine 22; America, 1846 ***778.6*** *p320*
Sturney, John; America, 1775 ***1220.12*** *p760*
Sturrick, John; America, 1685 ***1220.12*** *p772*
Sturt, Elizabeth; America, 1741 ***1220.12*** *p772*
Sturt, George; America, 1768 ***1220.12*** *p772*
Sturt, John; America, 1738 ***1220.12*** *p772*
Sturt, John; Virginia, 1735 ***1220.12*** *p772*
Sturt, Robert; Maryland, 1720 ***1220.12*** *p772*
Sturt, Thomas; America, 1752 ***1220.12*** *p772*
Sturt, Thomas; America, 1768 ***1220.12*** *p772*
Sturte, Thomas; America, 1655 ***1220.12*** *p772*
Sturter, Gabriel; Virginia, 1700 ***9230.15*** *p81*
Sturvohl, John Henry; Ohio, 1840-1897 ***8365.35*** *p18*
Sturwold, Bernard; Ohio, 1840-1897 ***8365.35*** *p18*
Stuter, Anne Josephe; Wisconsin, 1854-1858 ***1495.20*** *p50*
Stutherd, Thomas; America, 1734 ***1220.12*** *p766*
Stuthers, James 69; Ontario, 1871 ***1823.21*** *p356*
Stuthers, Nancy 68; Ontario, 1871 ***1823.21*** *p356*
Stuthers, Stephen 60; Ontario, 1871 ***1823.21*** *p356*
Stutt, . . . 34; Ontario, 1871 ***1823.17*** *p159*
Stuttmeister, Rud.; Chile, 1852 ***1192.4*** *p55*
Stutz, Anna 2 *SEE* Stutz, Johann
Stutz, Barbara Fischer 26 *SEE* Stutz, Johann
Stutz, Friedrich 4 *SEE* Stutz, Johann
Stutz, Johann 28; America, 1866 ***5475.1*** *p170*
*Wife:*Barbara Fischer 26
*Daughter:*Anna 2
*Son:*Friedrich 4
Stutz, Maria 26; America, 1866 ***5475.1*** *p170*
Stutz, Maria Elisabeth; Venezuela, 1843 ***3899.5*** *p544*
Stutz, Nikolaus; America, 1867 ***5475.1*** *p170*

Stutz, Peter; America, 1873 ***5475.1*** *p172*
Stutzer, Karl Heinrich; New York, NY, 1882 ***5475.1*** *p15*
Stutzman, . . .; West Virginia, n.d. ***1132.30*** *p151*
Stuver, Adolph; America, 1853 ***7420.1*** *p112*
Stuyvesant, Peter; New York, 1647 ***2853.20*** *p11*
Stuz, Johannes Christian Konrad; Venezuela, 1843 ***3899.5*** *p544*
Stuz, Maria Elisabeth; Venezuela, 1843 ***3899.5*** *p544*
Styblo, Karel; Chicago, 1810-1910 ***2853.20*** *p406*
Styck, Dorothy; America, 1768 ***1220.12*** *p765*
Styers, Thomas; America, 1758 ***1220.12*** *p772*
Stykeman, Charles A. 36; Ohio, 1880 ***4879.40*** *p259*
*Wife:*Mary O'Conners 37
Stykeman, Mary O'Conners 37 *SEE* Stykeman, Charles A.
Style, Charles; America, 1758 ***1220.12*** *p773*
Styles, Eliza; America, 1740 ***1220.12*** *p773*
Styles, James 54; Ontario, 1871 ***1823.17*** *p159*
Styles, Joane; America, 1740 ***1220.12*** *p773*
Styles, John A.; America, 1732 ***1220.12*** *p773*
Styles, Mary; America, 1740 ***1220.12*** *p773*
Styles, Robert 43; Ontario, 1871 ***1823.17*** *p159*
Styles, Thomas 30; Ontario, 1863 ***9228.50*** *p322*
Styles, William; America, 1773 ***1220.12*** *p773*
Styling, Mary; America, 1761 ***1220.12*** *p773*
Suarez, Jean; Louisiana, 1874-1875 ***4981.45*** *p31*
Suberbuc, Marie 25; America, 1843 ***778.6*** *p321*
Subtel, Mr. 37; America, 1845 ***778.6*** *p321*
Such, William; Marston's Wharf, 1782 ***8529.30*** *p16*
Suchanek, George; Washington, 1889 ***2770.40*** *p81*
Suchard, Hippolite 28; Ohio, 1847 ***778.6*** *p321*
Sucher, Charles William; Detroit, 1929 ***1640.55*** *p117*
Suchy, Leo; Wisconsin, 1873 ***2853.20*** *p310*
Sucich, F.; Louisiana, 1874-1875 ***4981.45*** *p30*
Sucklin, Balthazar; Barbados or Jamaica, 1700 ***1220.12*** *p773*
Sud, Hugh 55; Ontario, 1871 ***1823.21*** *p356*
Suda, Antonin; St. Louis, 1848 ***2853.20*** *p21*
Sudacropky, Hieman 31; New York, NY, 1894 ***6512.1*** *p229*
Sudders, Richard; America, 1766 ***1220.12*** *p773*
Suddery, John; Virginia, 1738 ***1220.12*** *p773*
Suder, Michael 36; New York, NY, 1920 ***930.50*** *p48*
Sudler, Ralph; America, 1740 ***1220.12*** *p773*
Sudman, John 54; Ontario, 1871 ***1823.17*** *p159*
Sudmeier, Ernst Heinrich Robert; America, 1883 ***7420.1*** *p340*
Sudot, Michael; Detroit, 1929 ***1640.55*** *p115*
Sudrie, Ferdinand; Louisiana, 1874 ***4981.45*** *p134*
Sudry, Mrs. 35; Port uncertain, 1844 ***778.6*** *p321*
Sudry, Elisa 18; Port uncertain, 1844 ***778.6*** *p321*
Sudry, Jacqueline 10; Port uncertain, 1844 ***778.6*** *p321*
Sudweeks, Edwin 53; Ontario, 1871 ***1823.17*** *p159*
Suebe, Jean Jos.; Louisiana, 1874-1875 ***4981.45*** *p31*
Sueezdorff, Philip; Ohio, 1809-1852 ***4511.35*** *p53*
Suele, L.; California, 1868 ***1131.61*** *p90*
Sues, Marim; North Carolina, 1857 ***1088.45*** *p34*
Suesdorf, Philip; Ohio, 1809-1852 ***4511.35*** *p53*
Suessenguth, Henry G. F.; Philadelphia, 1856 ***8513.31*** *p428*
*Wife:*Johanne Hohl
Suessenguth, Johanne Hohl *SEE* Suessenguth, Henry G. F.
Sueve, Edmond de; Quebec, 1665 ***2314.30*** *p167*
Sueve, Edmond de; Quebec, 1665 ***2314.30*** *p196*
Suey, James; Illinois, 1859 ***6079.1*** *p13*
Suffel, Heinrich *SEE* Suffel, Philipp
Suffel, Philipp *SEE* Suffel, Philipp
Suffel, Philipp 60; America, 1867 ***5475.1*** *p554*
*Son:*Philipp
*Son:*Heinrich
Suffold, William; Barbados or Jamaica, 1690 ***1220.12*** *p773*
Suffolk, George; Marston's Wharf, 1782 ***8529.30*** *p16*
Suffolk, John; America, 1768 ***1220.12*** *p773*
Suffolk, Richard; America, 1772 ***1220.12*** *p773*
Suffron, John 27; Ontario, 1871 ***1823.17*** *p159*
Sugar, Edward; America, 1771 ***1220.12*** *p773*
Sugar, John; Barbados, 1665 ***1220.12*** *p773*
Sugarek, Frantisek; Galveston, TX, 1856 ***2853.20*** *p63*
Sugden, Robert 79; Ontario, 1871 ***1823.21*** *p356*
Sugdon, David 54; Ontario, 1871 ***1823.17*** *p159*
Sugg, Elizabeth; America, 1729 ***1220.12*** *p773*
Suggs, Mary; America, 1774 ***1220.12*** *p773*
Sughrue, Humphrey; Louisiana, 1874 ***4981.45*** *p134*
Suha, Michael; Illinois, 1856 ***6079.1*** *p13*
Suhler, Alfred 37; Ontario, 1871 ***1823.17*** *p159*
Suhlfleisch, Julius Oskar; America, 1869 ***7919.3*** *p526*
Suhlfleisch, Sabine; America, 1868 ***7919.3*** *p532*
Suhr, Anna Wilhelmine Sophie *SEE* Suhr, Wilhelmine Christine Friederike Krop
Suhr, Carolina 10; New York, NY, 1874 ***6954.7*** *p37*
Suhr, Catharina 15; New York, NY, 1874 ***6954.7*** *p37*
Suhr, Christian 40; New York, NY, 1874 ***6954.7*** *p37*
Suhr, Christoph 9; New York, NY, 1874 ***6954.7*** *p37*
Suhr, Friederike Wilhelmine Charlotte *SEE* Suhr, Hermann Friedrich Wilhelm
Suhr, Georg 8 months; New York, NY, 1874 ***6954.7*** *p37*
Suhr, Hanne Christine *SEE* Suhr, Hermann Friedrich Wilhelm
Suhr, Heinrich; America, 1867 ***7420.1*** *p265*
With family
Suhr, Heinrich Friedrich Wilhelm *SEE* Suhr, Hermann Friedrich Wilhelm
Suhr, Hermann Friedrich Wilhelm; America, 1885 ***7420.1*** *p349*
*Sister:*Friederike Wilhelmine Charlotte
*Sister:*Hanne Christine
*Brother:*Heinrich Friedrich Wilhelm
Suhr, Jacob 7; New York, NY, 1874 ***6954.7*** *p37*
Suhr, Johann 4; New York, NY, 1874 ***6954.7*** *p37*
Suhr, Rosina 37; New York, NY, 1874 ***6954.7*** *p37*
Suhr, Wilhelmine Christine Friederike; America, 1894 ***7420.1*** *p371*
*Daughter:*Anna Wilhelmine Sophie
Suire, Daniel; Quebec, 1657 ***9221.17*** *p369*
Suitor, Francis 22; Ontario, 1871 ***1823.17*** *p159*
Sukowski, Anna 15; New York, NY, 1885 ***1883.7*** *p45*
Sukowski, Rosaline 12; New York, NY, 1885 ***1883.7*** *p45*
Sulak, F.X.; Minnesota, 1875 ***2853.20*** *p262*
Sulak, Frantisek; Chicago, 1865 ***2853.20*** *p423*
Sulak, Frantisek; Nebraska, 1865-1871 ***2853.20*** *p161*
Sulavan, Johannah; Boston, 1747 ***1642*** *p46*
Sulavin, Own 50; Ontario, 1871 ***1823.21*** *p356*
Sulch, John; Died enroute, 1725 ***1220.12*** *p773*
Suleavan, Margaret; Lynn, MA, 1653 ***1642*** *p71*
Suledge, Samuel; America, 1771 ***1220.12*** *p773*
Sulek, Antonin; Iowa, 1810-1910 ***2853.20*** *p217*
Sulentic, Tomo; Chicago, 1930 ***121.35*** *p100*
Sulivan, Bridget; New Orleans, 1851 ***7242.30*** *p155*
Sulivan, Daniel 41; Ontario, 1871 ***1823.21*** *p356*
Sulivan, Dennis; Ohio, 1840-1897 ***8365.35*** *p18*
Sulivan, James 23; Ontario, 1871 ***1823.17*** *p159*
Sulivan, Mary 72; Ontario, 1871 ***1823.17*** *p159*
Sulivan, Thymothy 30; Ontario, 1871 ***1823.21*** *p356*
Suliven, James 40; Ontario, 1871 ***1823.21*** *p356*
Sulkus, Francois 39; New York, NY, 1920 ***930.50*** *p49*
Sullardine, Elizabeth; Massachusetts, 1789 ***1642*** *p102*
Sulliman, Thomas; Ohio, 1809-1852 ***4511.35*** *p53*
Sullindin, John; Massachusetts, 1680 ***1642*** *p102*
Sullinge, Edward; America, 1767 ***1220.12*** *p773*
Sullinge, Richard; America, 1767 ***1220.12*** *p773*
Sullivan, . . . 18; St. Johns, N.F., 1811 ***1053.20*** *p21*
Sullivan, Mrs.; California, 1868 ***1131.61*** *p89*
Sullivan, Mrs.; California, 1868 ***1131.61*** *p89*
Sullivan, Abbey; Boston, 1762 ***1642*** *p48*
Sullivan, Ann; Boston, 1747 ***1642*** *p46*
Sullivan, Bal; Boston, 1766 ***1642*** *p37*
Sullivan, Bridget; New Brunswick, 1842 ***2978.20*** *p7*
Sullivan, Cath; New Orleans, 1851 ***7242.30*** *p155*
Sullivan, Catharine; Boston, 1766 ***1642*** *p37*
Sullivan, Catherine; America, 1754 ***1220.12*** *p773*
Sullivan, Catherine; America, 1758 ***1220.12*** *p773*
Sullivan, Cornelius; America, 1749 ***1220.12*** *p773*
Sullivan, Cornelius; Boston, 1743 ***1642*** *p45*
Sullivan, Cornelius; Boston, 1752 ***1642*** *p47*
Sullivan, Cornelius; Boston, 1766 ***1642*** *p37*
Sullivan, Cornelius; New England, 1745 ***1642*** *p28*
Sullivan, Cornelius; Ohio, 1809-1852 ***4511.35*** *p53*
Sullivan, Dan 2; St. Johns, N.F., 1811 ***1053.20*** *p22*
Sullivan, Daniel; America, 1740 ***1220.12*** *p773*
Sullivan, Daniel 33; Michigan, 1880 ***4491.33*** *p22*
Sullivan, Daniel 57; Michigan, 1880 ***4491.39*** *p29*
Sullivan, Daniel; New York, 1776 ***8529.30*** *p7*
Sullivan, Daniel 70; Ontario, 1871 ***1823.21*** *p356*
Sullivan, Daniel 15; Quebec, 1870 ***8364.32*** *p26*
Sullivan, David; Boston, 1765 ***1642*** *p35*
Sullivan, Dennis; America, 1773 ***1220.12*** *p773*
Sullivan, Dennis; New Orleans, 1851 ***7242.30*** *p155*
Sullivan, Dennis; Ohio, 1809-1852 ***4511.35*** *p53*
Sullivan, Elenor; Boston, 1739 ***1642*** *p44*
Sullivan, Elizabeth; America, 1744 ***1220.12*** *p773*
Sullivan, Francis; Toronto, 1844 ***2910.35*** *p112*
Sullivan, George H.; Boston, 1752-1760 ***1642*** *p30*
Sullivan, Hannah 18; Ontario, 1871 ***1823.21*** *p357*
Sullivan, Herbert; America, 1750 ***1220.12*** *p773*
Sullivan, Hugh 30; Ontario, 1871 ***1823.21*** *p357*
Sullivan, Humphrey; New Brunswick, 1842 ***2978.20*** *p7*
Sullivan, Isabella; America, 1773 ***1220.12*** *p773*
Sullivan, James; America, 1771 ***1220.12*** *p773*
Sullivan, James; New Orleans, 1851 ***7242.30*** *p155*
Sullivan, James 50; Ontario, 1871 ***1823.17*** *p159*
Sullivan, James; Toronto, 1844 ***2910.35*** *p113*
Sullivan, James; Toronto, 1844 ***2910.35*** *p116*
Sullivan, Jane 67; Massachusetts, 1806 ***1642*** *p88*
Sullivan, Jane 56; Michigan, 1880 ***4491.39*** *p29*
Sullivan, Jenny; Massachusetts, 1772 ***1642*** *p88*
Sullivan, Jerry 34; Ontario, 1871 ***1823.21*** *p357*
Sullivan, Jerry; St. John, N.B., 1847 ***2978.15*** *p40*
Sullivan, Jno; St. John, N.B., 1847 ***2978.15*** *p41*
Sullivan, Jno; St. John, N.B., 1847 ***2978.15*** *p41*
Sullivan, John; America, 1766 ***1220.12*** *p773*
Sullivan, John; America, 1771 ***1220.12*** *p773*
Sullivan, John; Boston, 1738 ***1642*** *p44*
Sullivan, John; Boston, 1742 ***1642*** *p45*
Sullivan, John; Boston, 1749 ***1642*** *p46*
Sullivan, John; Boston, 1756 ***1642*** *p47*
Sullivan, John; Boston, 1765 ***1642*** *p35*
Sullivan, John; Boston, 1766 ***1642*** *p48*
Sullivan, John; Marblehead, MA, 1772 ***1642*** *p73*
Sullivan, John; New Jersey, 1777 ***8529.30*** *p7*
Sullivan, John 23; New York, NY, 1826 ***6178.50*** *p150*
Sullivan, John 45; Ontario, 1871 ***1823.21*** *p357*
Sullivan, John 70; Ontario, 1871 ***1823.21*** *p357*
Sullivan, John; Plymouth, MA, 1756 ***1642*** *p90*
Sullivan, John; St. Johns, N.F., 1811 ***1053.20*** *p20*
Sullivan, John 36; St. Johns, N.F., 1811 ***1053.20*** *p21*
Sullivan, John; Toronto, 1844 ***2910.35*** *p113*
Sullivan, John; Toronto, 1844 ***2910.35*** *p113*
Sullivan, John; Washington, 1886 ***2770.40*** *p24*
Sullivan, Kate; Massachusetts, 1760 ***1642*** *p117*
Sullivan, Lawrence 58; Ontario, 1871 ***1823.21*** *p357*
Sullivan, Margaret; Boston, 1764 ***1642*** *p48*
Sullivan, Margaret; Boston, 1770 ***1642*** *p49*
Sullivan, Margaret 50; Michigan, 1880 ***4491.39*** *p29*
Sullivan, Martin; America, 1749 ***1220.12*** *p773*
Sullivan, Mary; Boston, 1754 ***1642*** *p47*
Sullivan, Mary 19; Ontario, 1871 ***1823.21*** *p357*
Sullivan, Mary 45; Ontario, 1871 ***1823.21*** *p357*
Sullivan, Mary 68; Ontario, 1871 ***1823.21*** *p357*
Sullivan, Mary; Virginia, 1732 ***1220.12*** *p773*
Sullivan, Maurice 35; Ontario, 1871 ***1823.21*** *p357*
Sullivan, Michael; Boston, 1746 ***1642*** *p46*
Sullivan, Michael 33; Ontario, 1871 ***1823.21*** *p357*
Sullivan, Michael 35; Ontario, 1871 ***1823.17*** *p159*
Sullivan, Michael; Worcester, MA, 1844 ***3274.56*** *p98*
Sullivan, Mick 23; St. Johns, N.F., 1811 ***1053.20*** *p21*
Sullivan, Morris 38; Ontario, 1871 ***1823.21*** *p357*
Sullivan, Pat; St. John, N.B., 1848 ***2978.15*** *p38*
Sullivan, Patrick; Louisiana, 1874 ***4981.45*** *p134*
Sullivan, Patrick; Ohio, 1840-1897 ***8365.35*** *p18*
Sullivan, Patrick 35; Ontario, 1871 ***1823.21*** *p357*
Sullivan, Patrick 50; Ontario, 1871 ***1823.21*** *p357*
Sullivan, Patrick 66; Ontario, 1871 ***1823.21*** *p357*
Sullivan, Patrick 20; St. Johns, N.F., 1811 ***1053.20*** *p21*
Sullivan, Patrick; Washington, 1889 ***2770.40*** *p81*
Sullivan, Patt; New Orleans, 1851 ***7242.30*** *p155*
Sullivan, Roger; America, 1773 ***1220.12*** *p773*
Sullivan, Samuel 27; Ontario, 1871 ***1823.21*** *p357*
Sullivan, Thomas 34; Ontario, 1871 ***1823.17*** *p159*
Sullivan, Thomas 40; Ontario, 1871 ***1823.21*** *p357*
Sullivan, Thomas 50; Ontario, 1871 ***1823.21*** *p357*
Sullivan, Thomas 15; Quebec, 1870 ***8364.32*** *p26*
Sullivan, Tim 22; St. Johns, N.F., 1811 ***1053.20*** *p22*
Sullivan, Timothy; America, 1749 ***1220.12*** *p774*
Sullivan, Timothy; Boston, 1759 ***1642*** *p47*
Sullivan, Timothy; Worcester, MA, 1763 ***1642*** *p114*
Sullivan, Valentine; Boston, 1763 ***1642*** *p48*
Sullivin, John 40; Ontario, 1871 ***1823.21*** *p357*
Sully, Elizabeth; America, 1752 ***1220.12*** *p774*
Sully, Joshua; America, 1685 ***1220.12*** *p774*
Sully, Richard; Barbados, 1683 ***1220.12*** *p774*
Sully, Richard 71; Ontario, 1871 ***1823.21*** *p357*
Sulowski, Frank 40; New York, NY, 1920 ***930.50*** *p49*
Sulzer, Heinrich; Chile, 1852 ***1192.4*** *p52*
Sulzer, Nicolaus; Chile, 1852 ***1192.4*** *p52*
Suman, Henery 43; Ontario, 1871 ***1823.21*** *p357*
Sumbellick, Aleck; Louisiana, 1874 ***4981.45*** *p134*
Sumeling, Adolph Heinrich Conrad; St. Louis, 1873 ***7420.1*** *p397*
Sumenara, Carl 25; New York, NY, 1893 ***1883.7*** *p44*
Sumening, Widow; America, 1861 ***7420.1*** *p209*
Sumer, Anne Marie 23; America, 1847 ***778.6*** *p321*
Sumer, Christoph 28; America, 1847 ***778.6*** *p321*
Sumer, Elisabeth 8 months; America, 1847 ***778.6*** *p321*
Sumersbye, Sarah; America, 1762 ***1220.12*** *p774*
Summa, Anna Maria; America, 1882 ***5475.1*** *p302*
Summer, Henry; Ohio, 1809-1852 ***4511.35*** *p53*
Summer, Jacob; Ohio, 1809-1852 ***4511.35*** *p53*
Summer, John; Ohio, 1809-1852 ***4511.35*** *p53*
Summer, Joseph; Ohio, 1809-1852 ***4511.35*** *p53*
Summer, Michael; Ohio, 1809-1852 ***4511.35*** *p53*
Summerbell, D. R.; Iowa, 1894 ***1211.15*** *p19*
Summerfield, Joseph; America, 1765 ***1220.12*** *p774*
Summerfield, Joseph; America, 1768 ***1220.12*** *p774*
Summerfield, Thomas; America, 1765 ***1220.12*** *p774*
Summerfield, William; Maryland, 1723 ***1220.12*** *p774*
Summerhatter, Rudolph; Illinois, 1858 ***6079.1*** *p13*

Summerhayes, Ann; America, 1771 ***1220.12*** *p774*
Summerholter, Mary 38; Kansas, 1888 ***1447.20*** *p62*
Summers, Ames 37; Ontario, 1871 ***1823.21*** *p357*
Summers, Antony 58; Ontario, 1871 ***1823.21*** *p357*
Summers, David 54; Ontario, 1871 ***1823.21*** *p357*
Summers, Elizabeth 84; Ontario, 1871 ***1823.21*** *p357*
Summers, George 47; Ontario, 1871 ***1823.21*** *p357*
Summers, Henry; Washington, 1883 ***2770.40*** *p137*
Summers, John; America, 1664 ***1220.12*** *p774*
Summers, John; America, 1749 ***1220.12*** *p774*
Summers, John; Barbados or Jamaica, 1686 ***1220.12*** *p774*
Summers, John; New Orleans, 1850 ***7242.30*** *p155*
Summers, John 50; Ontario, 1871 ***1823.21*** *p357*
Summers, Margaret 28; Ontario, 1871 ***1823.21*** *p357*
Summers, Maria 52; Ontario, 1871 ***1823.21*** *p357*
Summers, Mary; America, 1774 ***1220.12*** *p774*
Summers, Richard 46; Ontario, 1871 ***1823.21*** *p357*
Summers, Robert 60; Ontario, 1871 ***1823.21*** *p357*
Summers, Samuel; America, 1736 ***1220.12*** *p774*
Summers, Sarah; Virginia, 1756 ***1220.12*** *p774*
Summers, Thomas; America, 1768 ***1220.12*** *p774*
Summers, Thomas; Jamaica, 1759 ***8529.30*** *p14A*
Summers, Thomas 54; Ontario, 1871 ***1823.21*** *p357*
Summerton, Hester; America, 1746 ***1220.12*** *p774*
Summervill, Mary 59; Ontario, 1871 ***1823.21*** *p358*
Summerville, James; America, 1751 ***1220.12*** *p774*
Summerville, Robert 30; Ohio, 1880 ***4879.40*** *p258*
Summerville, Thos 48; Ontario, 1871 ***1823.17*** *p159*
Summor, Joseph; Ohio, 1809-1852 ***4511.35*** *p53*
Sumner, George; Colorado, 1868 ***1029.59*** *p87*
Sumner, Henry; Colorado, 1880 ***1029.59*** *p87*
Sumner, James; America, 1753 ***1220.12*** *p774*
Sumner, Jonas; America, 1667 ***1220.12*** *p749*
Sumner, Margaret; America, 1769 ***1220.12*** *p774*
Sumner, Margaret; America, 1773 ***1220.12*** *p774*
Sumner, Mary; America, 1756 ***1220.12*** *p774*
Sumner, Saml 76; Ontario, 1871 ***1823.21*** *p358*
Sumner, Stephen; Maryland, 1742 ***1220.12*** *p774*
Sumner, Syrus 70; Ontario, 1871 ***1823.21*** *p358*
Sumner, Thomas 80; Ontario, 1871 ***1823.21*** *p358*
Sumner, William; America, 1741 ***1220.12*** *p774*
Sumner, William; America, 1773 ***1220.12*** *p774*
Sumners, Thomas; America, 1773 ***1220.12*** *p774*
Sundahl, Bernhard Johan; New York, 1864 ***6410.15*** *p105*
Sundberg, Andrew; St. Paul, MN, 1878 ***1865.50*** *p110*
Sundberg, Carl; Colorado, 1893 ***1029.59*** *p87*
Sundberg, J.P.; New York, NY, 1844 ***6412.40*** *p147*
Sundberg, John G.; St. Paul, MN, 1882 ***1865.50*** *p110*
Sundberg, Peter J.; America, 1852 ***4487.25*** *p74*
With wife
Sundberg, Sven W.; Illinois, 1866 ***1865.50*** *p110*
Sundeen, Oliver; Colorado, 1891 ***1029.59*** *p87*
Sunderlan, J.; New Orleans, 1850 ***7242.30*** *p155*
Sunderland, Frances; America, 1719 ***1220.12*** *p774*
Sunderland, John; Marston's Wharf, 1782 ***8529.30*** *p16*
Sunderland, Nathaniel; Barbados, 1684 ***1220.12*** *p774*
Sunderland, William; America, 1774 ***1220.12*** *p774*
Sundermeier, Carl; America, 1854 ***7420.1*** *p131*
With wife
Sundermeier, Caroline; America, 1856 ***7420.1*** *p155*
Sundermeier, Heinrich; America, 1866 ***7420.1*** *p250*
With family
Sundgren, Hakan; New York, NY, 1848 ***6412.40*** *p151*
Sunding, Frederick; Washington, 1889 ***2770.40*** *p81*
Sundling, Thor 37; Minnesota, 1925 ***2769.54*** *p1384*
Sundmacher, . . .; America, 1836 ***7420.1*** *p12*
Sundmacher, Carl; America, 1836 ***7420.1*** *p12*
Sundmacher, Georg Friedrich Wilhelm; America, 1867 ***7420.1*** *p265*
Sundown, Thomas 50; Ontario, 1871 ***1823.21*** *p358*
Sundquist, Hjalmar; Minneapolis, 1889 ***1865.50*** *p110*
Sundqvist, Hjalmar; Minneapolis, 1889 ***1865.50*** *p110*
Sundrey, Francis; America, 1740 ***1220.12*** *p774*
Sundsten, J.O.; New York, NY, 1845 ***6412.40*** *p148*
Sundstrom, B.; Charleston, SC, 1851 ***6412.40*** *p153*
Sundstrom, C. Edv.; New York, NY, 1849 ***6412.40*** *p152*
Sundstrom, C.E.; New York, NY, 1850 ***6412.40*** *p152*
Sundstrom, Fredr. Reinh.; Charleston, SC, 1851 ***6412.40*** *p153*
Sunley, Richard; America, 1774 ***1220.12*** *p774*
Sunley, Thomas; America, 1727 ***1220.12*** *p774*
Sunnafrank, Frances; Ohio, 1789-1816 ***9228.50*** *p616*
Sunnafrank, John; Ohio, 1804-1805 ***9228.50*** *p615*
Sunnafrank, John; Virginia, 1777-1804 ***9228.50*** *p615*
Sunnafrank, Margaret; Ohio, 1774-1851 ***9228.50*** *p617*
Suomi, Urho 32; Minnesota, 1925 ***2769.54*** *p1384*
Supervielle, Mr. 46; Port uncertain, 1845 ***778.6*** *p321*
Superville, Antoine 35; America, 1843 ***778.6*** *p321*
Superville, F. 20; Port uncertain, 1842 ***778.6*** *p321*
Superville, Francois 40; America, 1843 ***778.6*** *p321*
Superville, Prosper 31; America, 1843 ***778.6*** *p321*
Supik, Vaclav; New York, NY, 1870-1910 ***2853.20*** *p110*
Supli, Jeanne 27; Quebec, 1640 ***9221.17*** *p94*
Suppey, R. 17; New Orleans, 1848 ***778.6*** *p321*
Supple, Ferdinand; America, 1867 ***179.55*** *p19*
Supple, Georg; America, 1853 ***179.55*** *p19*
Supple, Jakob; America, 1854 ***179.55*** *p19*
Supple, Kaspar; America, 1867 ***179.55*** *p19*
Supple, Richard; Toronto, 1844 ***2910.35*** *p115*
Surahan, Aarn; St. John, N.B., 1847 ***2978.15*** *p41*
Surbei, Jacob; Ohio, 1809-1852 ***4511.35*** *p53*
Surble, Guillaume M.; Illinois, 1852 ***6079.1*** *p13*
Surblet, Guil...me 22; Louisiana, 1848 ***778.6*** *p321*
Surcoat, Francis; Annapolis, MD, 1723 ***1220.12*** *p774*
Surdich, Stepano; Louisiana, 1874 ***4981.45*** *p134*
Sureau, Theodore 32; Quebec, 1659 ***9221.17*** *p410*
Suremy, Francois 7; Port uncertain, 1846 ***778.6*** *p321*
Suremy, Francois 45; Port uncertain, 1846 ***778.6*** *p321*
Suremy, Francoise 41; Port uncertain, 1846 ***778.6*** *p321*
Suremy, Madeleine 21; Port uncertain, 1846 ***778.6*** *p321*
Suremy, P. Victoire 12; Port uncertain, 1846 ***778.6*** *p321*
Suret, Catherine; Quebec, 1669 ***4514.3*** *p371*
Suret, Marie 32; New Orleans, 1848 ***778.6*** *p321*
Surfill, John; Barbados, 1682 ***1220.12*** *p775*
Surgeon, John; America, 1767 ***1220.12*** *p775*
Surget, Madeleine 22; Quebec, 1659 ***9221.17*** *p410*
Surley, John; Colorado, 1873 ***1029.59*** *p87*
Surnesburg, Christopher; North Carolina, 1845 ***1088.45*** *p34*
Surnett, Richard; Barbados, 1669 ***1220.12*** *p775*
Suronne, Renee 29; Quebec, 1645 ***9221.17*** *p156*
Suronne, Renee 29; Quebec, 1645 ***9221.17*** *p156*
Surplice, Edward 61; Ontario, 1871 ***1823.21*** *p358*
Surrey, Susanna; America, 1754 ***1220.12*** *p775*
Surridge, Richard; America, 1729 ***1220.12*** *p775*
Surry, John; America, 1766 ***1220.12*** *p775*
Surry, Ruth; Virginia, 1736 ***1220.12*** *p775*
Surtis, John; America, 1757 ***1220.12*** *p775*
Surven, John 29; America, 1845 ***778.6*** *p321*
Susan, Mathew 73; Ontario, 1871 ***1823.21*** *p358*
Susnar, George; Quebec, 1786 ***1416.15*** *p8*
Suster, Jan B.; Chicago, 1867 ***2853.20*** *p218*
Sutcliff, James 39; Ontario, 1871 ***1823.17*** *p159*
Sutcliff, Margaret; America, 1772 ***1220.12*** *p775*
Sutcliffe, James; Rappahannock, VA, 1729 ***1220.12*** *p775*
Sutcliffe, Richard; America, 1766 ***1220.12*** *p775*
Sutcliffe, Samuel; America, 1747 ***1220.12*** *p775*
Sutcliffe, William; America, 1723 ***1220.12*** *p775*
Suter, Dominicus 46; New Castle, DE, 1817-1818 ***90.20*** *p154*
Suter, John; North Carolina, 1842 ***1088.45*** *p34*
Suter, Joseph; America, 1772 ***1220.12*** *p775*
Suter, Rudolf 33; Kansas, 1896 ***1029.59*** *p87*
Suter, Rudolph 48; New Castle, DE, 1817-1818 ***90.20*** *p154*
Suter, Samuel 35; New Castle, DE, 1817-1818 ***90.20*** *p154*
Suter, Samuel; Ohio, 1809-1852 ***4511.35*** *p53*
Suter, Selma 43; Minnesota, 1925 ***2769.54*** *p1380*
Sutherby, Aaron 49; Michigan, 1880 ***4491.36*** *p22*
Sutherby, Andrew 18; Michigan, 1880 ***4491.36*** *p22*
Sutherby, George 21; Michigan, 1880 ***4491.36*** *p22*
Sutherby, Mary 42; Michigan, 1880 ***4491.36*** *p22*
Sutherland, Mrs.; California, 1868 ***1131.61*** *p89*
With family
Sutherland, Alex 25; Ontario, 1871 ***1823.21*** *p358*
Sutherland, Alex 63; Ontario, 1871 ***1823.21*** *p358*
Sutherland, Alexander 31; Ontario, 1871 ***1823.21*** *p358*
Sutherland, Alexander 32; Ontario, 1871 ***1823.17*** *p159*
Sutherland, Alexander 54; Ontario, 1871 ***1823.21*** *p358*
Sutherland, Ann; America, 1761 ***1220.12*** *p775*
Sutherland, Anna; New York, 1738 ***8277.31*** *p119*
Sutherland, Catharine 91; Ontario, 1871 ***1823.21*** *p358*
Sutherland, Daniel; New York, 1782 ***8529.30*** *p16*
Sutherland, David 28; Ontario, 1871 ***1823.21*** *p358*
Sutherland, Donald 30; Ontario, 1871 ***1823.17*** *p159*
Sutherland, Donald 52; Ontario, 1871 ***1823.21*** *p358*
Sutherland, Duncan 41; Ontario, 1871 ***1823.21*** *p358*
Sutherland, Elizabeth 62; Ontario, 1871 ***1823.21*** *p358*
Sutherland, Francis 49; Ontario, 1871 ***1823.17*** *p159*
Sutherland, George 32; Ontario, 1871 ***1823.17*** *p159*
Sutherland, George 60; Ontario, 1871 ***1823.17*** *p159*
Sutherland, George D. 40; Ontario, 1871 ***1823.21*** *p358*
Sutherland, J. G. 43; Ontario, 1871 ***1823.21*** *p358*
Sutherland, James; America, 1775 ***1220.12*** *p775*
Sutherland, James 88; Ontario, 1871 ***1823.21*** *p358*
Sutherland, James M.; Ohio, 1840-1897 ***8365.35*** *p18*
Sutherland, John; America, 1772 ***1220.12*** *p775*
Sutherland, John 61; Ontario, 1871 ***1823.21*** *p358*
Sutherland, John 66; Ontario, 1871 ***1823.21*** *p358*
Sutherland, Margaret; America, 1748 ***1220.12*** *p775*
Sutherland, Margaret; America, 1756 ***1220.12*** *p775*
Sutherland, Neil 55; Ontario, 1871 ***1823.21*** *p358*
Sutherland, Robert 28; Ontario, 1871 ***1823.21*** *p358*
Sutherland, Robert 45; Ontario, 1871 ***1823.21*** *p358*
Sutherland, Robert 60; Ontario, 1871 ***1823.21*** *p358*
Sutherland, Sarah 26; Ontario, 1871 ***1823.17*** *p159*
Sutherland, Thomas 74; Ontario, 1871 ***1823.17*** *p159*
Sutherland, William 27; Colorado, 1904 ***1029.59*** *p87*
Sutherland, William 45; Ontario, 1871 ***1823.21*** *p358*
Sutherland, William 49; Ontario, 1871 ***1823.21*** *p358*
Sutherland, William 66; Ontario, 1871 ***1823.21*** *p358*
Sutherland, Willm. 24; North Carolina, 1774 ***1422.10*** *p59*
Sutherland, Wm. 40; North Carolina, 1774 ***1422.10*** *p58*
Suthertuck, John 30; Ontario, 1871 ***1823.21*** *p358*
Suthmeier Sisters, . . .; America, 1868 ***7420.1*** *p277*
Suthmeyer, Friedrich; America, 1842 ***7420.1*** *p26*
With brother-in-law
Suthmeyer, Friedrich; Port uncertain, 1842 ***7420.1*** *p24*
Sutler, Jacob 27; Louisiana, 1848 ***778.6*** *p321*
Sutlow, Samuel; America, 1747 ***1220.12*** *p775*
Sutor, Adam 18; America, 1851 ***2526.42*** *p137*
Sutor, Rudolf; Colorado, 1862-1920 ***1029.59*** *p87*
Sutorios, Frederick; New York, 1859 ***358.56*** *p99*
Sutron, William; America, 1735 ***1220.12*** *p775*
Sutter, D. 3; New Orleans, 1834 ***1002.51*** *p111*
Sutter, Dominicus 46; New Castle, DE, 1817-1818 ***90.20*** *p154*
Sutter, J. 8; New Orleans, 1834 ***1002.51*** *p111*
Sutter, John; Illinois, 1856 ***6079.1*** *p13*
Sutter, Miss L. 6; New Orleans, 1834 ***1002.51*** *p111*
Sutter, M. 12; New Orleans, 1834 ***1002.51*** *p111*
Sutter, Maria; New York, 1881 ***5475.1*** *p434*
With son
Sutter, Miss P. 16; New Orleans, 1834 ***1002.51*** *p111*
Sutter, Miss P. 44; New Orleans, 1834 ***1002.51*** *p111*
Sutter, Rudolph 48; New Castle, DE, 1817-1818 ***90.20*** *p154*
Sutter, Samuel 35; New Castle, DE, 1817-1818 ***90.20*** *p154*
Sutter, Samuel; Washington, 1884 ***2770.40*** *p193*
Sutter, T. 53; New Orleans, 1834 ***1002.51*** *p111*
Sutterlin, George; Louisiana, 1841-1844 ***4981.45*** *p211*
Suttie, James; Illinois, 1858 ***6079.1*** *p14*
Suttinen, John 33; Minnesota, 1925 ***2769.54*** *p1384*
Sutton, Abram; Maryland, 1737 ***1220.12*** *p775*
Sutton, Anne; Barbados, 1673 ***1220.12*** *p775*
Sutton, Anne; Virginia, 1752 ***1220.12*** *p775*
Sutton, Celena 42; Ontario, 1871 ***1823.21*** *p358*
Sutton, Edward; America, 1750 ***1220.12*** *p775*
Sutton, Edward; America, 1759 ***1220.12*** *p775*
Sutton, Edward; Barbados, 1676 ***1220.12*** *p775*
Sutton, Edward; Virginia, 1732 ***1220.12*** *p775*
Sutton, Elizabeth; Maryland, 1742 ***1220.12*** *p775*
Sutton, George; America, 1754 ***1220.12*** *p775*
Sutton, George; Virginia, 1736 ***1220.12*** *p775*
Sutton, Hannah; America, 1733 ***1220.12*** *p775*
Sutton, James; America, 1765 ***1220.12*** *p775*
Sutton, James 32; Ontario, 1871 ***1823.21*** *p358*
Sutton, John; America, 1688 ***1220.12*** *p775*
Sutton, John; America, 1691 ***1220.12*** *p775*
Sutton, John; America, 1736 ***1220.12*** *p775*
Sutton, John; America, 1737 ***1220.12*** *p775*
Sutton, John; America, 1739 ***1220.12*** *p776*
Sutton, John; America, 1750 ***1220.12*** *p776*
Sutton, John; America, 1757 ***1220.12*** *p776*
Sutton, John; America, 1770 ***1220.12*** *p776*
Sutton, John; Barbados, 1676 ***1220.12*** *p775*
Sutton, John; Barbados, 1680 ***1220.12*** *p775*
Sutton, John; Maryland, 1738 ***1220.12*** *p775*
Sutton, John 63; Ontario, 1871 ***1823.17*** *p159*
Sutton, Jonathan; America, 1685 ***1220.12*** *p776*
Sutton, Joseph; America, 1775 ***1220.12*** *p776*
Sutton, Joseph; Maryland, 1723 ***1220.12*** *p776*
Sutton, Katherine; America, 1737 ***1220.12*** *p775*
Sutton, Magaret 55; Ontario, 1871 ***1823.21*** *p359*
Sutton, Mary; America, 1719 ***1220.12*** *p776*
Sutton, Richard 38; Ontario, 1871 ***1823.21*** *p359*
Sutton, Robert; Annapolis, MD, 1723 ***1220.12*** *p776*
Sutton, Samuel; America, 1752 ***1220.12*** *p776*
Sutton, Samuel 52; Ontario, 1871 ***1823.17*** *p159*
Sutton, Sarah; America, 1656 ***1220.12*** *p776*
Sutton, Sarah; America, 1716 ***1220.12*** *p776*
Sutton, Thomas; America, 1745 ***1220.12*** *p776*
Sutton, Thomas; America, 1769 ***1220.12*** *p776*
Sutton, Thomas; America, 1773 ***1220.12*** *p776*
Sutton, Thomas; America, 1774 ***1220.12*** *p776*
Sutton, Thomas 25; Indiana, 1881-1884 ***9076.20*** *p70*
Sutton, Thomas 51; Ontario, 1871 ***1823.21*** *p359*
Sutton, William; America, 1767 ***1220.12*** *p776*
Sutton, William; Barbados or Jamaica, 1686 ***1220.12*** *p776*
Sutton, William 74; Ontario, 1871 ***1823.21*** *p359*
Sutton, William; Virginia, 1766 ***1220.12*** *p776*
Sutu, Daniel; Texas, 1851 ***3435.45*** *p37*
Sutur, Thomas; America, 1752 ***1220.12*** *p775*
Suwer, Christine Sophie; America, 1849 ***7420.1*** *p68*

Svacina, Jan; Omaha, NE, 1878 ***2853.20*** *p144*
Svantner, Vaclav; Arkansas, 1892 ***2853.20*** *p376*
Svatos, Frantisek; South Dakota, 1871-1910 ***2853.20*** *p247*
Svaty, Frantisek; Wisconsin, 1853 ***2853.20*** *p312*
Svec, Stepan; New York, NY, 1852 ***2853.20*** *p386*
Svedberg, Eva Charlotta; Michigan, 1881-1888 ***1865.50*** *p110*
Svedenberg, Hannah T.; St. Paul, MN, 1884 ***1865.50*** *p110*
Svedenberg, Julia; St. Paul, MN, 1889 ***1865.50*** *p110*
Svehla, Frantisek J.; New York, NY, 1854 ***2853.20*** *p201*
With parents
Svendsen, Christian 21; New York, NY, 1894 ***6512.1*** *p185*
Svensdotter, Agnes Emilia; Cleveland, OH, 1903-1904 ***9722.10*** *p128*
Svenson, Agnes W.; St. Paul, MN, 1898 ***1865.50*** *p110*
Svenson, Alona 18; New York, NY, 1894 ***6512.1*** *p184*
Svenson, Amanda; St. Paul, MN, 1880 ***1865.50*** *p110*
Svenson, Anders; St. Paul, MN, 1888 ***1865.50*** *p110*
Svenson, Andrew; St. Paul, MN, 1889 ***1865.50*** *p111*
*Wife:*Karolina
Svenson, Anna C.; St. Paul, MN, 1894 ***1865.50*** *p111*
Svenson, Anna Cajsa; St. Paul, MN, 1872 ***1865.50*** *p111*
Svenson, Anna Ch.; Michigan, 1889-1893 ***1865.50*** *p111*
Svenson, August; Chicago, 1876-1881 ***1865.50*** *p111*
Svenson, August Alfred; Minnesota, 1875-1879 ***1865.50*** *p111*
Svenson, Brita Stina; Minnesota, 1867-1891 ***1865.50*** *p40*
Svenson, Carl A.; Cleveland, OH, 1901-1902 ***9722.10*** *p127*
Svenson, Carl Oscar; Chicago, 1891 ***1865.50*** *p111*
Svenson, Carolina; New York, NY, 1887-1888 ***1865.50*** *p51*
Svenson, Clara; St. Paul, MN, 1892 ***1865.50*** *p111*
Svenson, Edla; St. Paul, MN, 1900 ***1865.50*** *p111*
Svenson, Emil; Michigan, 1874-1879 ***1865.50*** *p111*
Svenson, Emma; Chicago, 1891-1892 ***1865.50*** *p111*
Svenson, Ernest W.; St. Paul, MN, 1886 ***1865.50*** *p111*
Svenson, Ester; St. Paul, MN, 1894 ***1865.50*** *p111*
Svenson, Ester S. *SEE* Svenson, Sven P.
Svenson, Jennie; St. Paul, MN, 1902 ***1865.50*** *p112*
Svenson, Johanna; St. Paul, MN, 1868 ***1865.50*** *p97*
Svenson, Josephina; St. Paul, MN, 1891 ***1865.50*** *p104*
Svenson, Karolina *SEE* Svenson, Andrew
Svenson, Lars J.; St. Paul, MN, 1894 ***1865.50*** *p112*
Svenson, Lena Lisa; St. Paul, MN, 1871 ***1865.50*** *p112*
Svenson, Maja Lisa; St. Paul, MN, 1891 ***1865.50*** *p112*
Svenson, Maria; St. Paul, MN, 1887 ***1865.50*** *p102*
Svenson, Mathilda; Chicago, 1868-1869 ***1865.50*** *p114*
Svenson, Svante; St. Paul, MN, 1894 ***1865.50*** *p112*
Svenson, Sven P.; St. Paul, MN, 1881 ***1865.50*** *p112*
Svenson, Sven P.; St. Paul, MN, 1887 ***1865.50*** *p112*
*Wife:*Ester S.
Svensson, Anna Lovisa *SEE* Svensson, Petter Magnus
Svensson, Aron *SEE* Svensson, Petter Magnus
Svensson, Carl; New York, NY, 1849 ***6412.40*** *p151*
Svensson, Christina Pehrsdotter *SEE* Svensson, Hans, Sr.
Svensson, Christina Johansdotter *SEE* Svensson, Petter Magnus
Svensson, Constans *SEE* Svensson, Petter Magnus
Svensson, Hans, Jr. *SEE* Svensson, Hans, Sr.
Svensson, Hans, Sr.; Kansas, 1869 ***777.40*** *p14*
*Wife:*Christina Pehrsdotter
*Son:*Hans, Jr.
*Daughter:*Mary
Svensson, Mary *SEE* Svensson, Hans, Sr.
Svensson, N.; New York, NY, 1843 ***6412.40*** *p147*
Svensson, Nils; Cleveland, OH, 1903-1904 ***9722.10*** *p132*
Svensson, Petter Magnus; North America, 1854 ***6410.15*** *p104*
*Wife:*Christina Johansdotter
*Daughter:*Anna Lovisa
*Son:*Aron
*Son:*Constans
Svensson, T.E.; New York, NY, 1852 ***6412.40*** *p153*
Svoboda, Antonin; Madison, WI, 1895 ***2853.20*** *p334*
Svoboda, Antonin; Nebraska, 1876 ***2853.20*** *p172*
Svoboda, Jan M.; Nebraska, 1866 ***2853.20*** *p155*
Svoboda, Matej; Nebraska, 1875 ***2853.20*** *p172*
Svoboda, Tomas; Minnesota, 1857 ***2853.20*** *p259*
Svrdlik, Florian; Iowa, 1899 ***2853.20*** *p225*
Swaby, Joseph James; America, 1750 ***1220.12*** *p776*
Swadder, John 65; Ontario, 1871 ***1823.21*** *p359*
Swadlowe, Margaret; America, 1675 ***1220.12*** *p776*
Swaff, Margaret; America, 1686 ***1220.12*** *p776*
Swafford, James 30; Ontario, 1871 ***1823.21*** *p359*
Swailes, John; America, 1729 ***1220.12*** *p776*
Swain, Mr. 12; Quebec, 1870 ***8364.32*** *p26*
Swain, Antonie; North Carolina, 1860 ***1088.45*** *p34*
Swain, Christian; Baltimore, 1833 ***471.10*** *p87*
Swain, Giles; America, 1753 ***1220.12*** *p776*
Swain, Martin 28; Ontario, 1871 ***1823.17*** *p159*
Swain, Robert; America, 1769 ***1220.12*** *p776*
Swain, Sarah; America, 1770 ***1220.12*** *p776*
Swain, Susan 73; Ontario, 1871 ***1823.17*** *p159*
Swaine, Edward; Barbados, 1679 ***1220.12*** *p776*
Swaine, George; America, 1775 ***1220.12*** *p776*
Swaine, James; America, 1764 ***1220.12*** *p776*
Swaine, Richard; America, 1727 ***1220.12*** *p776*
Swaine, William; America, 1736 ***1220.12*** *p776*
Swaine, William; America, 1765 ***1220.12*** *p776*
Swainman, Lawrence; America, 1726 ***1220.12*** *p776*
Swains, John; America, 1737 ***1220.12*** *p776*
Swainson, Rowland; Virginia, 1725 ***1220.12*** *p776*
Swales, Isaac 53; Ontario, 1871 ***1823.21*** *p359*
Swales, John; America, 1759 ***1220.12*** *p776*
Swales, William 26; Ontario, 1871 ***1823.21*** *p359*
Swallow, Richard; America, 1740 ***1220.12*** *p776*
Swan, Charles 27; Ontario, 1871 ***1823.17*** *p159*
Swan, Charles; Washington, 1888 ***2770.40*** *p26*
Swan, Elizabeth; America, 1740 ***1220.12*** *p776*
Swan, Elizabeth; America, 1750 ***1220.12*** *p776*
Swan, Gustaf 25; Kansas, 1880 ***777.40*** *p5*
Swan, Isabel; Maine, 1839-1858 ***9228.50*** *p496*
Swan, James 46; Ontario, 1871 ***1823.17*** *p159*
Swan, Jane; America, 1736 ***1220.12*** *p776*
Swan, John; Ohio, 1809-1852 ***4511.35*** *p53*
Swan, Mary; America, 1761 ***1220.12*** *p776*
Swan, Mary; Died enroute, 1736 ***1220.12*** *p776*
Swan, Mary; Virginia, 1734 ***1220.12*** *p776*
Swan, Peter; America, 1746 ***1220.12*** *p776*
Swan, Priscilla; America, 1747 ***1220.12*** *p776*
Swan, Ralph; America, 1757 ***1220.12*** *p776*
Swan, Robert; America, 1761 ***1220.12*** *p777*
Swan, Thomas; America, 1723 ***1220.12*** *p777*
Swan, William; America, 1718 ***1220.12*** *p673*
Swan, William 34; Ontario, 1871 ***1823.17*** *p159*
Swan, William 39; Ontario, 1871 ***1823.17*** *p159*
Swanander, John F.; Louisiana, 1836-1840 ***4981.45*** *p213*
Swanbeck, Swen Emil; Cleveland, OH, 1892-1897 ***9722.10*** *p127*
Swaney, Edmund; Boston, 1766 ***1642*** *p37*
Swaney, John; America, 1749 ***1220.12*** *p777*
Swank, George; Ohio, 1809-1852 ***4511.35*** *p53*
Swank, George; Ohio, 1809-1852 ***4511.35*** *p54*
Swanlund, Otto; Nebraska, 1887 ***1029.59*** *p87*
Swann, Christie; America, 1773 ***1220.12*** *p776*
Swann, Gus 25; Kansas, 1880 ***777.40*** *p5*
Swann, Mary; Philadelphia, 1856 ***8513.31*** *p414*
Swann, Thomas; America, 1757 ***1220.12*** *p777*
Swannock, John; America, 1750 ***1220.12*** *p777*
Swans, James; America, 1737 ***1220.12*** *p777*
Swansby, Richard; Annapolis, MD, 1723 ***1220.12*** *p777*
Swanscombe, Richard; America, 1771 ***1220.12*** *p777*
Swanskin, John; America, 1766 ***1220.12*** *p777*
Swanson, Andrew; Cleveland, OH, 1889-1894 ***9722.10*** *p127*
Swanson, August; Chicago, 1876-1881 ***1865.50*** *p111*
Swanson, C. J.; Colorado, 1873 ***1029.59*** *p87*
Swanson, Carl Henrik; Iowa, 1914 ***1211.15*** *p19*
Swanson, Elizabeth; America, 1753 ***1220.12*** *p777*
Swanson, Emelia; St. Paul, MN, 1887 ***1865.50*** *p99*
Swanson, Ernest; Minnesota, 1925 ***2769.54*** *p1382*
Swanson, Ester S. *SEE* Swanson, Swan P.
Swanson, Esther; Minnesota, 1925 ***2769.54*** *p1382*
Swanson, Gideon; Cleveland, OH, 1893-1897 ***9722.10*** *p127*
Swanson, Gust; Iowa, 1883 ***1211.15*** *p19*
Swanson, Jane; America, 1749 ***1220.12*** *p777*
Swanson, John; Cleveland, OH, 1881-1893 ***9722.10*** *p127*
Swanson, John; Cleveland, OH, 1894-1897 ***9722.10*** *p127*
Swanson, John; Colorado, 1892 ***1029.59*** *p87*
Swanson, John Nelson; Colorado, 1891 ***1029.59*** *p88*
Swanson, John S.; Iowa, 1896 ***1211.15*** *p19*
Swanson, Margaret 52; Ontario, 1871 ***1823.17*** *p159*
Swanson, Maria C.; St. Paul, MN, 1882-1885 ***1865.50*** *p112*
Swanson, Nils; Cleveland, OH, 1902 ***9722.10*** *p127*
Swanson, O.; Cleveland, OH, 1896-1901 ***9722.10*** *p127*
Swanson, Peter; Illinois, 1859 ***6079.1*** *p14*
Swanson, Peter; Iowa, 1900 ***1211.15*** *p19*
Swanson, Peter; New York, 1902 ***1766.20*** *p36*
Swanson, Sara Maria; Minnesota, 1894-1897 ***1865.50*** *p112*
Swanson, Swan Gotthard; New York, 1903 ***1766.20*** *p36*
Swanson, Swan P.; St. Paul, MN, 1881 ***1865.50*** *p112*
Swanson, Swan P.; St. Paul, MN, 1887 ***1865.50*** *p112*
*Wife:*Ester S.
Swanson, Thomas; America, 1733 ***1220.12*** *p777*
Swanton, Jasper *SEE* Swanton, Johanna Hibbard
Swanton, Johanna; Canada, 1689-1695 ***9228.50*** *p617*
*Child:*Mary
*Child:*Jasper
Swanton, John; Beverly, MA, 1674 ***9228.50*** *p617*
Swanton, Mary *SEE* Swanton, Johanna Hibbard
Swanton, Rowland; Died enroute, 1726 ***1220.12*** *p777*
Swantz, Christian; Long Island, 1779 ***8529.30*** *p10A*
Swarby, William 16; Quebec, 1870 ***8364.32*** *p26*
Swarm, Lewis; Ohio, 1809-1852 ***4511.35*** *p54*
Swart, Michael; Maryland, 1744 ***1220.12*** *p777*
Swarton, Jasper *SEE* Swarton, Johanna Hibbard
Swarton, Johanna; Canada, 1689-1695 ***9228.50*** *p617*
*Child:*Mary
*Child:*Jasper
Swarton, John; Beverly, MA, 1674 ***9228.50*** *p617*
Swarton, Mary *SEE* Swarton, Johanna Hibbard
Swarts, John L. 62; Ontario, 1871 ***1823.21*** *p359*
Swarts, Leonard; Philadelphia, 1778 ***8529.30*** *p3*
Swartz, Albert; North Carolina, 1854 ***1088.45*** *p34*
Swartz, Daniel; Ohio, 1809-1852 ***4511.35*** *p54*
Swartz, George; Ohio, 1809-1852 ***4511.35*** *p54*
Swartz, Helen E. 12; Ontario, 1871 ***1823.21*** *p359*
Swartz, Henry; Ohio, 1809-1852 ***4511.35*** *p54*
Swartz, Peter; Ohio, 1809-1852 ***4511.35*** *p54*
Swartz, Peter R. 17; Ontario, 1871 ***1823.21*** *p359*
Swartz, Thomas E. 19; Ontario, 1871 ***1823.21*** *p359*
Swarz, Louis 28; America, 1747 ***778.6*** *p321*
Swasey, John *SEE* Swasey, John
Swasey, John; Salem, MA, 1632 ***9228.50*** *p618*
*Son:*John
*Son:*Joseph
Swasey, John; Salem, MA, 1640-1660 ***9228.50*** *p618*
Swasey, Joseph *SEE* Swasey, John
Swat, Martha 60; Ontario, 1871 ***1823.17*** *p159*
Swat, Philip 24; Ontario, 1871 ***1823.17*** *p159*
Swatlo, Blanche; Detroit, 1929 ***1640.55*** *p113*
Swawbrook, Magdalen; America, 1745 ***1220.12*** *p777*
Swayne, Elizabeth; America, 1665 ***1220.12*** *p776*
Swayze, Walter J.; Colorado, 1891 ***1029.59*** *p88*
Swazman, Lewis; North Carolina, 1849 ***1088.45*** *p34*
Sweatman, Arthur 37; Ontario, 1871 ***1823.21*** *p359*
Swedberg, Charlotte; Michigan, 1881-1888 ***1865.50*** *p110*
Swedberg, Emma 11; New York, NY, 1883 ***8427.14*** *p45*
Swedberg, Maria 19; New York, NY, 1883 ***8427.14*** *p45*
Swedenborg, Hannah T.; St. Paul, MN, 1884 ***1865.50*** *p110*
Swedenborg, Julia; St. Paul, MN, 1889 ***1865.50*** *p110*
Sweemy, Hugh; North Carolina, 1855 ***1088.45*** *p34*
Sweeney, Alexander; Boston, 1768 ***1642*** *p40*
Sweeney, Biddy 30; St. John, N.B., 1834 ***6469.7*** *p5*
Sweeney, Bridget Wheeler *SEE* Sweeney, Peter
Sweeney, Catherine 20; Ontario, 1871 ***1823.21*** *p359*
Sweeney, Eliza 16; Quebec, 1870 ***8364.32*** *p26*
Sweeney, Francis 50; Ontario, 1871 ***1823.21*** *p359*
Sweeney, George 2; St. John, N.B., 1834 ***6469.7*** *p5*
Sweeney, James 25; St. John, N.B., 1834 ***6469.7*** *p5*
Sweeney, John; Louisiana, 1874 ***4981.45*** *p134*
Sweeney, John; Newfoundland, 1814 ***3476.10*** *p54*
Sweeney, John 42; Ontario, 1871 ***1823.17*** *p160*
Sweeney, John 3; St. John, N.B., 1834 ***6469.7*** *p5*
Sweeney, John S.; New London, CT, 1832 ***3274.55*** *p27*
Sweeney, Miles; Washington, 1884 ***2770.40*** *p193*
Sweeney, Patrick 34; Ontario, 1871 ***1823.17*** *p160*
Sweeney, Peter; Philadelphia, 1852 ***8513.31*** *p428*
*Wife:*Bridget Wheeler
Sweeney, Timothy 55; Ontario, 1871 ***1823.21*** *p359*
Sweeny, Hugh; North Carolina, 1855 ***1088.45*** *p34*
Sweeny, Patrick 44; Ontario, 1871 ***1823.21*** *p359*
Sweeny, Willian; Boston, 1770 ***1642*** *p49*
Sweep, John; America, 1747 ***1220.12*** *p777*
Sweet, James 60; Ontario, 1871 ***1823.21*** *p359*
Sweet, John; America, 1740 ***1220.12*** *p777*
Sweet, Noah; Massachusetts, 1670-1770 ***9228.50*** *p619*
Sweet, Robert, Jr.; America, 1685 ***1220.12*** *p777*
Sweet, William; America, 1685 ***1220.12*** *p777*
Sweething, Nathaniel; America, 1752 ***1220.12*** *p777*
Sweeting, Henry; America, 1665 ***1220.12*** *p777*
Sweeting, Manford; Miami, 1920 ***4984.15*** *p38*
Sweeting, Samuel; America, 1685 ***1220.12*** *p777*
Sweetman, Ann; Annapolis, MD, 1722 ***1220.12*** *p777*
Sweetman, Edward; America, 1750 ***1220.12*** *p777*
Sweetman, John; America, 1767 ***1220.12*** *p777*
Sweetman, Richard Matthew; America, 1762 ***1220.12*** *p777*
Sweetman, Robert; America, 1685 ***1220.12*** *p777*
Sweetman, William; Virginia, 1732 ***1220.12*** *p777*
Sweetzer, Frederich; Illinois, 1856 ***6079.1*** *p14*
Sweetzer, Frederick; Illinois, 1856 ***6079.1*** *p14*
Swegat, Christoph 23; New York, NY, 1883 ***8427.14*** *p44*
Swein, James 29; Ontario, 1871 ***1823.17*** *p160*
Sweislend, Earnest 24; Ontario, 1871 ***1823.21*** *p359*
Swendson, Ewen; Valdivia, Chile, 1850 ***1192.4*** *p49*
Sweney, William; Boston, 1767 ***1642*** *p38*
Swenson, Andrew; Iowa, 1898 ***1211.15*** *p19*
Swenson, Anna Maria Sandquist *SEE* Swenson, Daniel August
Swenson, Bengt; Illinois, 1861 ***4487.25*** *p74*

Swenson, Carl G.E. *SEE* Swenson, Daniel August
Swenson, Daniel August; Kansas, 1870 ***777.40*** *p10*
*Wife:*Anna Maria Sandquist
*Son:*Carl G.E.
*Son:*John A.
Swenson, Erick; America, 1850 ***4487.25*** *p74*
With family
Swenson, George Anton; Iowa, 1913 ***1211.15*** *p19*
Swenson, Johannes; Iowa, 1875 ***1211.15*** *p18*
Swenson, John A. *SEE* Swenson, Daniel August
Swenson, John Ben; Cleveland, OH, 1902-1906 ***9722.10*** *p127*
Swenson, John E.; Illinois, 1861 ***4487.25*** *p74*
Swenson, John P. 44; Kansas, 1880 ***777.40*** *p11*
Swenson, John W.; Cleveland, OH, 1888-1891 ***9722.10*** *p127*
Swenson, Swen; Illinois, 1861 ***4487.25*** *p75*
Swenson, Swen G.; Illinois, 1852-1861 ***4487.25*** *p75*
Swenssen, Lars Johan; Colorado, 1883 ***1029.59*** *p88*
Sweny, Francis; Boston, 1774 ***8529.30*** *p7*
Swerns, Christian; Louisiana, 1841-1844 ***4981.45*** *p211*
Swersinske, Emil Herman; Wisconsin, 1895 ***6795.8*** *p42*
Swersinske, Hulda Albertine; Wisconsin, 1896 ***6795.8*** *p132*
Swetland, Peter; America, 1739 ***1220.12*** *p777*
Swetland, Peter; America, 1751 ***1220.12*** *p777*
Swetman, George; Barbados, 1686 ***1220.12*** *p777*
Swetman, John; Died enroute, 1726 ***1220.12*** *p777*
Swetman, Thomas; America, 1745 ***1220.12*** *p777*
Swetman, William; Barbados, 1671 ***1220.12*** *p777*
Swett, Benjamin *SEE* Swett, John
Swett, John; Massachusetts, 1629-1651 ***9228.50*** *p619*
*Child:*John, Jr.
*Child:*Stephen
*Child:*Benjamin
Swett, John; Salem, MA, 1636 ***9228.50*** *p618*
Swett, John, Jr. *SEE* Swett, John
Swett, Stephen *SEE* Swett, John
Swiatek, Joseph; Detroit, 1930 ***1640.60*** *p78*
Swiatlowski, Adam; Detroit, 1929 ***1640.55*** *p117*
Swiderska, Mariann; Wisconsin, 1886 ***6795.8*** *p39*
Swiderski, Anthony; Detroit, 1929 ***1640.55*** *p112*
Swiderski, Mariann; Wisconsin, 1886 ***6795.8*** *p39*
Swiech, Henry; Detroit, 1929 ***1640.55*** *p115*
Swiecicki, Franciszek 29; New York, NY, 1911 ***6533.11*** *p9*
Swierczynski, Joseph; Detroit, 1930 ***1640.60*** *p83*
Swift, Mrs.; Toronto, 1844 ***2910.35*** *p114*
Swift, Ann; America, 1765 ***1220.12*** *p777*
Swift, Ann; Virginia, 1741 ***1220.12*** *p777*
Swift, Anne; Barbados, 1673 ***1220.12*** *p777*
Swift, Eleanor; America, 1763 ***1220.12*** *p777*
Swift, Elizabeth; America, 1727 ***1220.12*** *p777*
Swift, Elizabeth; America, 1754 ***1220.12*** *p777*
Swift, Gabriel; Died enroute, 1736 ***1220.12*** *p777*
Swift, George 37; Ontario, 1871 ***1823.21*** *p359*
Swift, Jeremiah; America, 1750 ***1220.12*** *p777*
Swift, John; America, 1763 ***1220.12*** *p777*
Swift, John; America, 1769 ***1220.12*** *p777*
Swift, John; Virginia, 1729 ***1220.12*** *p777*
Swift, Richard; America, 1764 ***1220.12*** *p778*
Swift, Samuel; America, 1755 ***1220.12*** *p778*
Swift, Thomas; America, 1735 ***1220.12*** *p778*
Swift, William; America, 1766 ***1220.12*** *p778*
Swigg, William; America, 1760 ***1220.12*** *p778*
Swigg, William; America, 1771 ***1220.12*** *p778*
Swiggleson, Robert; Illinois, 1858 ***6079.1*** *p14*
Swiles, James 36; Ontario, 1871 ***1823.21*** *p359*
Swinbank, Elizabeth; America, 1759 ***1220.12*** *p778*
Swinburn, Richard; Maryland, 1723 ***1220.12*** *p778*
Swinburn, William 46; Ontario, 1871 ***1823.21*** *p359*
Swindells, Elizabeth; America, 1775 ***1220.12*** *p778*
Swindels, Lancelot; America, 1756 ***1220.12*** *p778*
Swindles, John; America, 1772 ***1220.12*** *p778*
Swindon, White; America, 1722 ***1220.12*** *p778*
Swindon, William 16; Quebec, 1870 ***8364.32*** *p26*
Swinfeild, Mary; Maryland, 1674 ***1236.25*** *p50*
Swingfield, Thomas; Barbados, 1664 ***1220.12*** *p778*
Swingley, John; Barbados, 1679 ***1220.12*** *p778*
Swingwood, James; America, 1759 ***1220.12*** *p778*
Swiniar, Ewa 18; New York, NY, 1912 ***8355.1*** *p16*
Swinne, Rose 44; America, 1664 ***1220.12*** *p778*
Swinney, Ann; America, 1759 ***1220.12*** *p778*
Swinney, Bridget; America, 1773 ***1220.12*** *p778*
Swinney, Edmund; America, 1765 ***1220.12*** *p778*
Swinney, Edward; America, 1719 ***1220.12*** *p778*
Swinney, James Rigley; America, 1765 ***1220.12*** *p778*
Swinney, Mary; Boston, 1758 ***1642*** *p47*
Swinshead, Job; America, 1767 ***1220.12*** *p778*
Swinstead, Hambleton; Barbados, 1679 ***1220.12*** *p778*
Swinston, Francis; America, 1748 ***1220.12*** *p778*
Swint, Peter; New York, 1872 ***1132.30*** *p150*
With family
Swinton, John; America, 1745 ***1220.12*** *p778*
Swinton, John; America, 1758 ***1220.12*** *p778*
Swinyard, Edward; America, 1756 ***1220.12*** *p778*
Swiselman, Ernest; Rappahannock, VA, 1728 ***1220.12*** *p778*
Switler, Elizabeth 34; Ontario, 1871 ***1823.21*** *p359*
Switser, Catherine 30; Ontario, 1871 ***1823.21*** *p359*
Switzer, Bantlet 62; Ontario, 1871 ***1823.21*** *p359*
Switzer, Christian S. 28; Ontario, 1871 ***1823.21*** *p359*
Switzer, Jacob; Ohio, 1809-1852 ***4511.35*** *p54*
Switzer, John 26; Ontario, 1871 ***1823.21*** *p360*
Switzer, John Henry; Ohio, 1809-1852 ***4511.35*** *p54*
Switzer, Lewis; Ohio, 1809-1852 ***4511.35*** *p54*
Swope, Lewis; Ohio, 1809-1852 ***4511.35*** *p54*
Sworm, Lewis; Ohio, 1809-1852 ***4511.35*** *p54*
Swours, Mr. 16; America, 1847 ***778.6*** *p321*
Swours, Mr. 40; America, 1847 ***778.6*** *p321*
Swours, Roger 18; America, 1847 ***778.6*** *p321*
Swynny, Roger; America, 1682 ***1220.12*** *p778*
Sy, Constant 33; America, 1843 ***778.6*** *p321*
Sybilla, Adam; Ohio, 1809-1852 ***4511.35*** *p54*
Syby, Dennis; Massachusetts, 1675-1676 ***1642*** *p128*
Sydenham, John, Jr.; America, 1749 ***1220.12*** *p778*
Syder, Horace Harry; Washington, 1883 ***2770.40*** *p137*
Syer, Alfred J. 42; Ontario, 1871 ***1823.17*** *p160*
Syer, Robert; America, 1737 ***1220.12*** *p778*
Sykes, Anna 61; Ontario, 1871 ***1823.17*** *p160*
Sykes, Elizabeth; America, 1763 ***1220.12*** *p778*
Sykes, Elizabeth 63; Ontario, 1871 ***1823.17*** *p160*
Sykes, Francis; Virginia, 1736 ***1220.12*** *p778*
Sykes, George 29; Ontario, 1871 ***1823.17*** *p160*
Sykes, Henrey 28; Ontario, 1871 ***1823.17*** *p160*
Sykes, John; America, 1745 ***1220.12*** *p778*
Sykes, John 56; Ontario, 1871 ***1823.17*** *p160*
Sykes, Nathaniel; America, 1773 ***1220.12*** *p778*
Sykes, Richard; New York, NY, 1829 ***3274.55*** *p70*
Sykes, Thomas; Barbados, 1671 ***1220.12*** *p778*
Sykes, William; America, 1770 ***1220.12*** *p778*
Sykes, William; Virginia, 1741 ***1220.12*** *p778*
Sykora, Frantisek Xaver; Cleveland, OH, 1854 ***2853.20*** *p475*
Sykora, Jan Baptist; Iowa, 1856-1858 ***2853.20*** *p211*
Sykora, Vaclav J.; Cleveland, OH, 1863 ***2853.20*** *p476*
Sykowski, Joseph; New York, NY, 1888 ***6015.15*** *p11*
Syll, Joseph; Massachusetts, 1675-1676 ***1642*** *p128*
Sylvander, Ida Sophia; St. Paul, MN, 1895-1896 ***1865.50*** *p112*
Sylvestre, Claude; Quebec, 1636 ***9221.17*** *p65*
Sym, Margaret 75; Ontario, 1871 ***1823.17*** *p160*
Symcocks, William; America, 1677 ***1220.12*** *p722*
Symes, Henry; America, 1685 ***1220.12*** *p778*
Symes, James; America, 1773 ***1220.12*** *p778*
Symes, John; Barbados, 1668 ***1220.12*** *p778*
Symes, John; Virginia, 1769 ***1220.12*** *p778*
Symes, Joseph; America, 1772 ***1220.12*** *p778*
Symes, Mary; America, 1733 ***1220.12*** *p778*
Symes, Richard; America, 1685 ***1220.12*** *p779*
Symes, Thomas; America, 1744 ***1220.12*** *p779*
Symes, William; Barbados, 1666 ***1220.12*** *p779*
Symes, William 57; Ontario, 1871 ***1823.21*** *p360*
Symington, Alexander 45; Ontario, 1871 ***1823.17*** *p160*
Symington, Ellen 57; Ontario, 1871 ***1823.17*** *p160*
Symington, George 55; Ontario, 1871 ***1823.17*** *p160*
Symington, Isabella 59; Ontario, 1871 ***1823.17*** *p160*
Symington, Thomas 49; Ontario, 1871 ***1823.17*** *p160*
Symington, William 50; Ontario, 1871 ***1823.17*** *p160*
Symmes, Mary; Barbados, 1668 ***1220.12*** *p723*
Symmonds, John 42; Ontario, 1871 ***1823.21*** *p360*
Symmonds, Thomas; America, 1756 ***1220.12*** *p780*
Symmons, Frances; America, 1740 ***1220.12*** *p779*
Symonds, Ann; America, 1738 ***1220.12*** *p779*
Symonds, Ann; Barbados, 1681 ***1220.12*** *p779*
Symonds, Elizabeth; Maryland, 1720 ***1220.12*** *p779*
Symonds, Elizabeth; West Indies, 1686 ***1220.12*** *p779*
Symonds, Ephraim; Marston's Wharf, 1782 ***8529.30*** *p16*
Symonds, Francis; Barbados or Jamaica, 1686 ***1220.12*** *p779*
Symonds, Hannah; Annapolis, MD, 1725 ***1220.12*** *p779*
Symonds, Harry Chls 22; Ontario, 1871 ***1823.21*** *p360*
Symonds, Jane; America, 1675 ***1220.12*** *p779*
Symonds, John; America, 1729 ***1220.12*** *p779*
Symonds, John; America, 1735 ***1220.12*** *p779*
Symonds, John; America, 1742 ***1220.12*** *p779*
Symonds, John; America, 1753 ***1220.12*** *p779*
Symonds, John; America, 1760 ***1220.12*** *p779*
Symonds, John; America, 1770 ***1220.12*** *p779*
Symonds, John; America, 1773 ***1220.12*** *p780*
Symonds, John; Barbados or Jamaica, 1693 ***1220.12*** *p779*
Symonds, John; Died enroute, 1725 ***1220.12*** *p779*
Symonds, Peter; America, 1727 ***1220.12*** *p780*
Symonds, Peter; America, 1738 ***1220.12*** *p780*
Symonds, Robert; Barbados, 1668 ***1220.12*** *p780*
Symonds, Samuel; America, 1769 ***1220.12*** *p780*
Symonds, Thomas; America, 1763 ***1220.12*** *p780*
Symonds, Thomas; Barbados, 1675 ***1220.12*** *p780*
Symonds, Vincent; America, 1747 ***1220.12*** *p780*
Symonds, William; America, 1730 ***1220.12*** *p780*
Symonds, William; America, 1757 ***1220.12*** *p780*
Symonds, William; America, 1774 ***1220.12*** *p780*
Symonds, William; Annapolis, MD, 1720 ***1220.12*** *p780*
Symonds, William; Maryland, 1723 ***1220.12*** *p780*
Symons, Christian; America, 1752 ***1220.12*** *p779*
Symons, Elizabeth; America, 1767 ***1220.12*** *p779*
Symons, James V.; North Carolina, 1845 ***1088.45*** *p34*
Symons, John; America, 1675 ***1220.12*** *p779*
Symons, John; America, 1741 ***1220.12*** *p779*
Symons, John; Barbados, 1665 ***1220.12*** *p779*
Symons, Marie 67; Ontario, 1871 ***1823.21*** *p360*
Symons, Richard; America, 1685 ***1220.12*** *p780*
Symons, Thomas; America, 1744 ***1220.12*** *p780*
Symons, Thomas; North Carolina, 1860 ***1088.45*** *p34*
Symons, William, Jr.; North Carolina, 1845 ***1088.45*** *p34*
Symons, William, Sr.; North Carolina, 1845 ***1088.45*** *p34*
Sympson, Geo. 19; Virginia, 1635 ***1183.3*** *p31*
Sympson, Mary; Annapolis, MD, 1725 ***1220.12*** *p724*
Sympson, Thomas; Annapolis, MD, 1722 ***1220.12*** *p724*
Sympson, William; America, 1731 ***1220.12*** *p725*
Syms, Henry; America, 1685 ***1220.12*** *p723*
Syms, Isaac; Barbados or Jamaica, 1694 ***1220.12*** *p723*
Syms, Isabel; Barbados, 1683 ***1220.12*** *p723*
Syms, Isabella; America, 1738 ***1220.12*** *p723*
Syms, John; America, 1752 ***1220.12*** *p723*
Syms, Richard; Jamaica, 1661 ***1220.12*** *p723*
Syms, Thomas; America, 1736 ***1220.12*** *p723*
Syms, William; Virginia, 1750 ***1220.12*** *p723*
Synam, John 61; Ontario, 1871 ***1823.17*** *p160*
Syndergaard, Simon Hansen; Iowa, 1904 ***1211.15*** *p19*
Synnamon, Thomas; America, 1719 ***1220.12*** *p780*
Sypher, Rebecca; New Mexico, 1914 ***4812.1*** *p87*
Syren, Nikolaus 45; Galveston, TX, 1844 ***3967.10*** *p372*
Syret, Louis 32; America, 1843 ***778.6*** *p321*
Syrjanen, Matt 37; Minnesota, 1925 ***2769.54*** *p1380*
Syszkutosk, Paul 37; New York, NY, 1920 ***930.50*** *p48*
Sythe, Jane 30; Ontario, 1871 ***1823.21*** *p360*
Syverson, Carl Julius; Washington, 1889 ***2770.40*** *p81*
Syvett, John; Maryland, 1674 ***1236.25*** *p50*
Syvett, Joseph; Barbados, 1673 ***1220.12*** *p780*
Syvret, Mr.; Marblehead, MA, 1629 ***9228.50*** *p579*
Syvret, Mr.; New York, 1910 ***9228.50*** *p579*
Syvret, Amelia; Massachusetts, 1800-1899 ***9228.50*** *p620*
Syvret, John 98; Massachusetts, 1742 ***9228.50*** *p580*
Syvret, Mary; Maryland, 1684 ***9228.50*** *p576*
Syvret, Mary Ann; Havana, 1817-1900 ***9228.50*** *p581*
Syvret, Peter; Massachusetts, 1600-1685 ***9228.50*** *p619*
Syvret, Philip; Portsmouth, NH, 1671 ***9228.50*** *p619*
Syvret, Philip; Portsmouth, NH, 1689 ***9228.50*** *p590*
Syvret, Thomas; Plymouth, MA, 1684 ***9228.50*** *p579*
Szabelski, Stanislaw; Detroit, 1930 ***1640.60*** *p77*
Szafran, Stella; Detroit, 1890 ***9980.23*** *p97*
Szalankiewicz, Michal; Detroit, 1929 ***1640.55*** *p116*
Szczesniak, Martin; Detroit, 1890 ***9980.23*** *p96*
Szczuk, Julianna 18; New York, NY, 1911 ***6533.11*** *p10*
Szczyz, Jan 32; New York, NY, 1911 ***6533.11*** *p10*
Szeiner, Magdalena; Detroit, 1929 ***1640.55*** *p114*
Szelogewski, Stanislaiv; Washington, 1888 ***2770.40*** *p26*
Szewczyk, Andrew; Detroit, 1930 ***1640.60*** *p82*
Szkula, Paul; Detroit, 1929 ***1640.55*** *p116*
Sznurkowski, Henry 40; New York, NY, 1920 ***930.50*** *p49*
Szokowski, Victor; Detroit, 1929 ***1640.55*** *p115*
Szornock, August; Detroit, 1890 ***9980.23*** *p97*
Szostek, Julianus; Wisconsin, 1894 ***6795.8*** *p61*
Szpilur, Stephan; Detroit, 1930 ***1640.60*** *p78*
Szpilur, Stephan; Detroit, 1930 ***1640.60*** *p78*
Szrejber, Rosalia; Detroit, 1890 ***9980.23*** *p96*
Szuba, Antoni 18; New York, NY, 1911 ***6533.11*** *p9*
Szuba, Apolonia 20; New York, NY, 1904 ***8355.1*** *p15*
Szulc, Anna; Detroit, 1890 ***9980.23*** *p96*
Szurpit, Amial; Wisconsin, 1895 ***6795.8*** *p41*
Szurpit, Frank; Wisconsin, 1888 ***6795.8*** *p61*
Szushay, Stephen; Ohio, 1867-1920 ***9228.50*** *p620*
Szwacynberg, Wladislaw 37; New York, NY, 1920 ***930.50*** *p49*
Szydlowski, Franciszek; Detroit, 1929 ***1640.55*** *p115*
Szymanek, John; Detroit, 1929-1930 ***6214.5*** *p63*
Szymanska, Cecilia 3; New York, NY, 1904 ***8355.1*** *p15*
Szymanska, Franciszka 2; New York, NY, 1904 ***8355.1*** *p15*
Szymanska, Wiktoria 27; New York, NY, 1904 ***8355.1*** *p15*
Szymanski, Andrexej 30; New York, NY, 1894 ***6512.1*** *p231*

Szymanski, Michal 31; New York, NY, 1903 *8355.1 p15*
Szymanski, Piotr; Detroit, 1929 *1640.55 p113*

Szymeczek, Jadwiga 24; New York, NY, 1911 *6533.11 p10*

T

Taafe, Elizabeth; America, 1750 *1220.12 p781*
Tabarlet, Claude 43; America, 1843 *778.6 p321*
Tabarlet, Marie 9; America, 1843 *778.6 p322*
Tabb, Thomas 33; Ontario, 1871 *1823.21 p360*
Tabbert, Hermann; Wisconsin, 1876 *6795.8 p77*
Tabellier, Lewis; America, 1726 *1220.12 p781*
Tabellion, Nikolaus; America, 1874 *5475.1 p172*
Tabner, Benjamin 32; Ontario, 1871 *1823.21 p360*
Tabner, Emma 25; Ontario, 1871 *1823.21 p360*
Tabor, Philip; America, 1753 *1220.12 p781*
Tabor, William; Barbados, 1677 *1220.12 p781*
Tabourot, Antoine; Quebec, 1637 *9221.17 p73*
Tabuteau, Alexandre 21; Texas, 1848 *778.6 p322*
Tacha, Harry Nathan; Detroit, 1929-1930 *6214.5 p61*
Tachna, Abraham; Detroit, 1929-1930 *6214.5 p65*
Tachna, Hirsch; Detroit, 1929-1930 *6214.5 p61*
Tackabury, John 66; Ontario, 1871 *1823.21 p360*
Tackett, Edward; America, 1731 *1220.12 p781*
Tackle, Abednego; America, 1750 *1220.12 p781*
Tackle, John; America, 1750 *1220.12 p781*
Tadge, Ernst Heinrich Christian; America, 1882 *7420.1 p333*
Tadge, Heinrich Wilhelm; America, 1867 *7420.1 p265*
Tadge, Johann Heinrich Wilhelm; America, 1894 *7420.1 p371*
Tadlock, Dorothy; Annapolis, MD, 1720 *1220.12 p781*
Taffe, Henry; America, 1770 *1220.12 p781*
Taffe, Mary; America, 1679 *1220.12 p781*
Taffe, Mary; Barbados, 1677 *1220.12 p781*
Tafilowski, Franciszek; Detroit, 1929 *1640.55 p113*
Taft, Thomas; New York, 1776 *8529.30 p3*
Tagatz, Louise; Wisconsin, 1903 *6795.8 p179*
Tagg, Daniel; America, 1753 *1220.12 p781*
Tagg, Hester; America, 1748 *1220.12 p781*
Taggart, Delia 54; Ontario, 1871 *1823.21 p360*
Taggart, J.; Louisiana, 1874 *4981.45 p297*
Taggart, Michael 38; Ontario, 1871 *1823.21 p360*
Taggart, William 29; Ontario, 1871 *1823.17 p160*
Taggart, William 55; Ontario, 1871 *1823.21 p360*
Taggert, Rebecca Kyle *SEE* Taggert, Robert
Taggert, Robert; Philadelphia, 1860 *8513.31 p429*
 Wife:Rebecca Kyle
Tahlier, Desire; New York, NY, 1864 *1494.20 p13*
Tailby, John; Virginia, 1767 *1220.12 p781*
Taillandier, Clarisse 21; New Orleans, 1848 *778.6 p322*
Taillandier, Jules 41; New Orleans, 1848 *778.6 p322*
Taillandier, Marie 4; New Orleans, 1848 *778.6 p322*
Taillefer, R.; Louisiana, 1874-1875 *4981.45 p130*
Taillet, Celestine; Wisconsin, 1854-1858 *1495.20 p66*
Tailleur deSaint-Per, Hyppolyte; Quebec, 1711 *2314.30 p171*
Tailor, Robert 40; Ontario, 1871 *1823.21 p360*
Tainton, William; Died enroute, 1768 *1220.12 p781*
Tait, Francis 55; Ontario, 1871 *1823.21 p360*
Tait, George 58; Ontario, 1871 *1823.21 p360*
Tait, James 72; Ontario, 1871 *1823.17 p160*
Tait, William 33; Ontario, 1871 *1823.21 p360*
Tait, Wm. Campbell; Colorado, 1873 *1029.59 p88*
Takkonen, William; Minnesota, 1925 *2769.54 p1381*
Talamon, Mr. 30; America, 1844 *778.6 p322*
Talandier, Leon; New Orleans, 1848 *778.6 p322*
Talaru, de, Marquis 65; Port uncertain, 1846 *778.6 p322*
Talborn, Elizabeth; America, 1758 *1220.12 p781*
Talbot, Ann 94; Ontario, 1871 *1823.21 p360*
Talbot, Anne; Quebec, 1670 *4514.3 p371*
Talbot, Charles; Marston's Wharf, 1782 *8529.30 p16*
Talbot, Charles 37; Ontario, 1871 *1823.21 p360*
Talbot, Edward 69; Ontario, 1871 *1823.21 p360*

Talbot, Elizabeth; America, 1770 *1220.12 p781*
Talbot, Elizabeth 69; Ontario, 1871 *1823.21 p360*
Talbot, Ely 60; Ontario, 1871 *1823.21 p360*
Talbot, Francis; America, 1773 *1220.12 p781*
Talbot, George 16; Ontario, 1871 *1823.17 p160*
Talbot, Henry; America, 1762 *1220.12 p781*
Talbot, James; America, 1756 *1220.12 p781*
Talbot, James 67; Ontario, 1871 *1823.17 p160*
Talbot, John; America, 1766 *1220.12 p781*
Talbot, Martha; Ontario, 1871 *1823.21 p360*
Talbot, Mary; America, 1773 *1220.12 p781*
Talbot, Patrick; Newfoundland, 1814 *3476.10 p54*
Talbot, Richard; Virginia, 1762 *1220.12 p781*
Talbot, Sarah 57; Ontario, 1871 *1823.21 p360*
Talbot, Thomas; America, 1755 *1220.12 p781*
Talbot, William R. 75; Ontario, 1871 *1823.21 p361*
Talbott, Benjamin; America, 1766 *1220.12 p781*
Talbott, Charles; Marston's Wharf, 1782 *8529.30 p16*
Talbott, Henry; America, 1763 *1220.12 p781*
Talbott, Jane; Barbados, 1664 *1220.12 p781*
Talbott, Jo. 27; Virginia, 1635 *1183.3 p31*
Talbott, John; America, 1739 *1220.12 p781*
Talbott, Richard; Barbados, 1668 *1220.12 p781*
Talbott, Thomas; America, 1744-1751 *1220.12 p781*
Talcott, Carl Albin; St. Paul, MN, 1891 *1865.50 p112*
Talcut, Carl Albin; St. Paul, MN, 1891 *1865.50 p112*
Talent, Richard; Barbados or Jamaica, 1697 *1220.12 p781*
Talich, Jan; Wisconsin, 1855 *2853.20 p333*
Tall, Mary; America, 1742 *1220.12 p781*
Tallant, Patrick; America, 1751 *1220.12 p781*
Tallard, John; America, 1735 *1220.12 p781*
Tallard, Marie Elisabeth; Nova Scotia, 1753 *3051 p113*
Tallcut, Carl Albin; St. Paul, MN, 1891 *1865.50 p112*
Tallemye, Michel; Montreal, 1652 *9221.17 p268*
Talley, William; America, 1749 *1220.12 p781*
Tallia, Desire; New York, NY, 1864 *1494.20 p13*
Tallis, Thomas; Louisiana, 1874 *4981.45 p134*
Tallman, James 27; Ontario, 1871 *1823.21 p361*
Tallmarsh, William; Nevis or Jamaica, 1722 *1220.12 p781*
Tallon, Andrew 48; Ontario, 1871 *1823.21 p361*
Talloway, Elizabeth; America, 1744 *1220.12 p781*
Talloway, Samuel; America, 1771 *1220.12 p781*
Tally, Thomazine; Barbados or Jamaica, 1688 *1220.12 p781*
Talmige, John; America, 1741 *1220.12 p781*
Talmy, John; America, 1772 *1220.12 p781*
Talon, Charles; Quebec, 1660 *9221.17 p439*
Taltezon, Sophie; Washington, 1887 *2770.40 p25*
Tambaroux, Louis; Louisiana, 1874-1875 *4981.45 p130*
Tamble, Angela *SEE* Tamble, Mathias
Tamble, Anna Maria 32; Pennsylvania, 1897 *5475.1 p26*
Tamble, Elisabeth *SEE* Tamble, Mathias
Tamble, Johann *SEE* Tamble, Mathias
Tamble, Katharina *SEE* Tamble, Mathias
Tamble, Mathias; America, 1881 *5475.1 p300*
 Wife:Susanna Meiers
 Daughter:Elisabeth
 Daughter:Katharina
 Son:Johann
 Daughter:Susanna
 Son:Peter
 Daughter:Angela
Tamble, Peter *SEE* Tamble, Mathias
Tamble, Susanna *SEE* Tamble, Mathias
Tamble, Susanna Meiers *SEE* Tamble, Mathias
Tambour, Antoine; Montreal, 1662 *9221.17 p499*

Tame, John; America, 1755 *1220.12 p781*
Tame, John; America, 1766 *1220.12 p782*
Tamfrey, William; Philadelphia, 1778 *8529.30 p3*
Tamlin, Charles 57; Ontario, 1871 *1823.21 p361*
Tamlin, George 27; Ontario, 1871 *1823.21 p361*
Tamlin, Thomas 40; Ontario, 1871 *1823.21 p361*
Tamlin, William 46; Ontario, 1871 *1823.21 p361*
Tamm, Otto; Washington, 1889 *2770.40 p81*
Tampir, Josef, Sr.; Kansas, 1866-1910 *2853.20 p201*
Tamplin, Anthony; America, 1752 *1220.12 p782*
Tanasac, Mr. 47; Port uncertain, 1845 *778.6 p322*
Tancker, Joseph; Ohio, 1809-1852 *4511.35 p54*
Tancl, Jakub; New York, NY, 1852 *2853.20 p386*
Tancler, Jakub; New York, NY, 1852 *2853.20 p386*
Tancock, James 37; Ontario, 1871 *1823.21 p361*
Tancock, John 39; Ontario, 1871 *1823.17 p160*
Tancock, Thirza 37; Ontario, 1871 *1823.17 p160*
Tancock, William 32; Ontario, 1871 *1823.17 p160*
Tandy, John Merry; America, 1769 *1220.12 p782*
Tanffe, Emily B. 33; Ontario, 1871 *1823.21 p361*
Tanfield, James; America, 1775 *1220.12 p782*
Tanfield, Richard; America, 1754 *1220.12 p782*
Tangring, Algot; Cleveland, OH, 1905-1906 *9722.10 p127*
Tank, Bernhardt; Louisiana, 1874-1875 *4981.45 p130*
Tankard, Edward; Nevis or Jamaica, 1722 *1220.12 p782*
Tanklin, John; America, 1758 *1220.12 p782*
Tanner, Alphred 38; Ontario, 1871 *1823.17 p160*
Tanner, Caroline; America, 1867 *7919.3 p534*
Tanner, Charles; America, 1743 *1220.12 p782*
Tanner, Charles 48; Ontario, 1871 *1823.17 p160*
Tanner, Christopher William; America, 1765 *1220.12 p782*
Tanner, Edward; America, 1730 *1220.12 p782*
Tanner, Edward 35; Ontario, 1871 *1823.17 p160*
Tanner, Elizabeth; Barbados or Jamaica, 1696 *1220.12 p782*
Tanner, George; America, 1765 *1220.12 p782*
Tanner, George; Illinois, 1855 *6079.1 p14*
Tanner, George 37; Ontario, 1871 *1823.21 p361*
Tanner, Gilbert; Virginia, 1740 *1220.12 p782*
Tanner, James 52; Ontario, 1871 *1823.17 p160*
Tanner, Jane; America, 1684 *1220.12 p782*
Tanner, John; America, 1770 *1220.12 p782*
Tanner, John; Illinois, 1852 *6079.1 p14*
Tanner, John; Illinois, 1859 *6079.1 p14*
Tanner, John; Maryland, 1672 *1236.25 p47*
Tanner, John 32; Ontario, 1871 *1823.17 p160*
Tanner, John 57; Ontario, 1871 *1823.17 p160*
Tanner, John 65; Ontario, 1871 *1823.17 p160*
Tanner, John, Sr.; America, 1729 *1220.12 p782*
Tanner, Joseph; Ontario, 1871 *1823.17 p160*
Tanner, Joseph 40; Ontario, 1871 *1823.17 p160*
Tanner, Lucy; America, 1745 *1220.12 p782*
Tanner, Martin 44; Ontario, 1871 *1823.21 p361*
Tanner, Martin Peter; Annapolis, MD, 1730 *1220.12 p782*
Tanner, Mary; America, 1743 *1220.12 p782*
Tanner, Mary; America, 1764 *1220.12 p782*
Tanner, Mary; Virginia, 1730 *1220.12 p782*
Tanner, Maurice; America, 1663 *1220.12 p782*
Tanner, Michael; Illinois, 1856 *6079.1 p14*
Tanner, Samuel; Virginia, 1756 *1220.12 p782*
Tanner, Stephen; Virginia, 1753 *1220.12 p782*
Tanner, Thomas; America, 1741 *1220.12 p782*
Tanner, Tobias; Maryland, 1719 *1220.12 p782*
Tanner, William; America, 1680 *1220.12 p782*
Tanner, William; America, 1728 *1220.12 p782*

Tantau, Matthews; Louisiana, 1841-1844 ***4981.45*** *p211*
Tanten, . . .; Ontario, 1871 ***1823.21*** *p361*
Tanton, Henry P. 32; Ontario, 1871 ***1823.21*** *p361*
Tanton, John 41; Ontario, 1871 ***1823.21*** *p361*
Tanton, Thomas 39; Ontario, 1871 ***1823.21*** *p361*
Tanttu, Victor 37; Minnesota, 1923 ***2769.54*** *p1384*
Tap, Elizabeth; America, 1761 ***1220.12*** *p782*
Tapcas, Pierre 24; Montreal, 1659 ***9221.17*** *p426*
Tape, Geo.; St. John, N.B., 1847 ***2978.15*** *p35*
Tapeas, Pierre 24; Montreal, 1659 ***9221.17*** *p426*
Tapfield, John; Barbados, 1665 ***1220.12*** *p782*
Taplin, John; America, 1765 ***1220.12*** *p782*
Taplin, John; America, 1768 ***1220.12*** *p782*
Tapling, John; America, 1754 ***1220.12*** *p782*
Tapling, William; Maryland, 1727 ***1220.12*** *p782*
Tapp, Henry; America, 1773 ***1220.12*** *p782*
Tapp, Richard; Virginia, 1770 ***1220.12*** *p782*
Tapp, Samuel, Sr. 61; Ontario, 1871 ***1823.21*** *p361*
Tappe, Carl; America, 1857 ***7420.1*** *p173*
Tappe, Ferdinand; Port uncertain, 1878 ***7420.1*** *p312*
Tappe, Wilhelm; America, 1870 ***7420.1*** *p396*
Tapper, James; America, 1755 ***1220.12*** *p782*
Tapper, Joseph; America, 1757 ***1220.12*** *p782*
Tapper, Richard; America, 1685 ***1220.12*** *p782*
Tapper, William; America, 1755 ***1220.12*** *p782*
Tappin, James; America, 1775 ***1220.12*** *p782*
Tappin, John; America, 1750 ***1220.12*** *p782*
Tapping, John; Barbados, 1668 ***1220.12*** *p782*
Tapping, Thomas; America, 1775 ***1220.12*** *p783*
Tapscott, William; America, 1685 ***1220.12*** *p783*
Tapsell, Mary; America, 1758 ***1220.12*** *p783*
Taque, Jean Batiste 27; Port uncertain, 1845 ***778.6*** *p322*
Taraba, Filip; Chicago, 1901 ***2853.20*** *p405*
Tarabilda, Mikelas; Baltimore, 1903 ***1766.20*** *p36*
Tarafelli, Attilo; New Mexico, 1914 ***4812.1*** *p87*
Tarbock, George; America, 1751 ***1220.12*** *p783*
Tarborne, Sarah; America, 1721 ***1220.12*** *p783*
Tarbox, Eloner 70; Ontario, 1871 ***1823.17*** *p160*
Tarbuck, Charles 10; Quebec, 1870 ***8364.32*** *p26*
Tarbutt, Charlotte 15; Ontario, 1871 ***1823.21*** *p361*
Tarczydlo, Wincenty 21; New York, NY, 1911 ***6533.11*** *p10*
Tardieu, Jean; Virginia, 1700 ***9230.15*** *p80*
Tardif, Alexander; America, 1900-1983 ***9228.50*** *p620*
*Daughter:*Vera
Tardif, Robert; Maine, 1670-1679 ***9228.50*** *p620*
Tardif, Vera 6 *SEE* Tardif, Alexander
Tardif, William; New York, NY, 1832 ***9228.50*** *p621*
Tardivel, Francois 30; Montreal, 1662 ***9221.17*** *p499*
Tardivet, Francois 30; Montreal, 1662 ***9221.17*** *p499*
Tardos, Louis 19; Port uncertain, 1846 ***778.6*** *p322*
Tares, Henry; Ontario, 1871 ***1823.21*** *p361*
Targe, Elisabeth 24; Quebec, 1659 ***9221.17*** *p410*
Targer, Elisabeth; Quebec, 1642-1663 ***4514.3*** *p372*
Targer, Marie; Quebec, 1663 ***4514.3*** *p372*
Taride, Bertrand 40; America, 1844 ***778.6*** *p322*
Tarieu deLanaudiere, Thomas; Quebec, 1665 ***2314.30*** *p167*
Tarieu deLanaudiere, Thomas; Quebec, 1665 ***2314.30*** *p197*
Tarkelson, Beda; Colorado, 1894 ***1029.59*** *p88*
Tarleton, Elizabeth; Barbados, 1679 ***1220.12*** *p783*
Tarlton, Mary; Barbados or Jamaica, 1715 ***1220.12*** *p783*
Tarnaska, Michael; New York, NY, 1893 ***3366.30*** *p70*
Tarnell, Mary; Barbados, 1679 ***1220.12*** *p783*
Tarner, John; America, 1731 ***1220.12*** *p783*
Tarr, John; America, 1771 ***1220.12*** *p783*
Tarr, Thomas; America, 1744 ***1220.12*** *p783*
Tarr, William; Virginia, 1749 ***1220.12*** *p783*
Tarrant, Henry; Virginia, 1732 ***1220.12*** *p783*
Tarrant, John; America, 1754 ***1220.12*** *p783*
Tarrant, Lewis H. 33; Ontario, 1871 ***1823.21*** *p361*
Tarrant, Thomas; Virginia, 1768 ***1220.12*** *p783*
Tarrant, William; America, 1739 ***1220.12*** *p783*
Tarranto, Joseph; Louisiana, 1874-1875 ***4981.45*** *p130*
Tarride, F.; Louisiana, 1874 ***4981.45*** *p297*
Tarrs, William; America, 1680 ***1220.12*** *p783*
Tarry, Henry 33; Ontario, 1871 ***1823.21*** *p361*
Tart, Mary; America, 1750 ***1220.12*** *p783*
Tarte, Whitfield R.; Washington, 1884 ***2770.40*** *p193*
Tarte, William J.; Washington, 1887 ***2770.40*** *p25*
Tarver, John; America, 1749 ***1220.12*** *p783*
Tasch, Theodor; Valdivia, Chile, 1852 ***1192.4*** *p56*
Tasche, Clement; Quebec, 1650 ***9221.17*** *p230*
Tascher, Henry; Ohio, 1809-1852 ***4511.35*** *p54*
Tascher, Valentine; Ohio, 1809-1852 ***4511.35*** *p54*
Tascher, Volentine; Ohio, 1809-1852 ***4511.35*** *p54*
Taschereau, Thomas-Jacques; Quebec, 1726 ***2314.30*** *p170*
Taschereau, Thomas-Jacques; Quebec, 1726 ***2314.30*** *p197*
Tascheron, Jean; Quebec, 1645 ***9221.17*** *p157*
Tase, William 70; Ontario, 1871 ***1823.21*** *p361*
Tasel, Louis Marie 50; New Orleans, 1848 ***778.6*** *p322*
Tasewell, Nicholas; America, 1725 ***1220.12*** *p783*
Task, Deborah; America, 1769 ***1220.12*** *p783*
Tasker, David; America, 1735 ***1220.12*** *p783*
Tasker, George; Maryland, 1740 ***1220.12*** *p783*
Tasker, Grace; America, 1763 ***1220.12*** *p783*
Tasker, Margaret; America, 1763 ***1220.12*** *p783*
Tasker, William; America, 1686 ***1220.12*** *p783*
Tasker, William; America, 1750 ***1220.12*** *p783*
Tasse, Lazar 40; America, 1843 ***778.6*** *p322*
Tassin, Jacques; Quebec, 1642 ***9221.17*** *p122*
Taster, Ann; Barbados or Jamaica, 1680 ***1220.12*** *p783*
Taswell, William; Barbados or Jamaica, 1684 ***1220.12*** *p783*
Tatchwell, John; America, 1679 ***1220.12*** *p783*
Tate, George; Maryland, 1727 ***1220.12*** *p783*
Tate, James 48; Ontario, 1871 ***1823.17*** *p160*
Tate, James; Virginia, 1730 ***1220.12*** *p783*
Tate, John; America, 1753 ***1220.12*** *p783*
Tate, Joseph 30; Ontario, 1871 ***1823.21*** *p361*
Tate, Margaret; America, 1775 ***1220.12*** *p783*
Tate, Mary; America, 1741 ***1220.12*** *p783*
Tate, Mary; Virginia, 1734 ***1220.12*** *p783*
Tate, Michael; America, 1769 ***1220.12*** *p783*
Tate, Rosamond; America, 1765 ***1220.12*** *p783*
Tate, Thomas; America, 1736 ***1220.12*** *p783*
Tate, William; America, 1765 ***1220.12*** *p783*
Tatem, William; America, 1773 ***1220.12*** *p783*
Tatge, Carl August Arthur; America, 1858 ***7420.1*** *p182*
Tatge, Catharina Engel; America, 1857 ***7420.1*** *p173*
Tatge, Engel Maria Dorothea; America, 1845 ***7420.1*** *p40*
Tatge, Engel Marie; America, 1857 ***7420.1*** *p173*
With son
Tatge, Engel Marie Dorothea; America, 1866 ***7420.1*** *p250*
Tatge, Engel Marie Dorothee; America, 1857 ***7420.1*** *p161*
Tatge, Ernst Wilhelm; America, 1846 ***7420.1*** *p49*
With son 3
With son 3 months
With daughter 5
Tatge, Johann Conrad; America, 1872 ***7420.1*** *p298*
Tatge, Johann Heinrich; America, 1857 ***7420.1*** *p173*
Tatge, Johann Heinrich Christoph; America, 1857 ***7420.1*** *p173*
Tatham, Thomas; America, 1770 ***1220.12*** *p783*
Tatje, Engel Marie Caroline Wilhelmine; America, 1857 ***7420.1*** *p173*
*Daughter:*Ilse Marie Dorothee
*Son:*Johann Heinrich Conrad Christoph
*Son:*Heinrich Philipp
Tatje, Heinrich Philipp *SEE* Tatje, Engel Marie Caroline Wilhelmine Wille
Tatje, Ilse Marie Dorothee *SEE* Tatje, Engel Marie Caroline Wilhelmine Wille
Tatje, Johann Conrad; America, 1846 ***7420.1*** *p49*
Tatje, Johann Heinrich Christoph; America, 1849 ***7420.1*** *p68*
Tatje, Johann Heinrich Conrad Christoph *SEE* Tatje, Engel Marie Caroline Wilhelmine Wille
Tatje, Johann Heinrich Philipp; America, 1847 ***7420.1*** *p57*
Tatje, Marie; America, 1889 ***7420.1*** *p360*
*Daughter:*Sophie Dorothee Louise
Tatje, Sophie Caroline; America, 1849 ***7420.1*** *p68*
Tatje, Sophie Dorothee Louise *SEE* Tatje, Marie Hodann
Tatler, Joseph; America, 1767 ***1220.12*** *p783*
Tatlock, Jane 13; Quebec, 1870 ***8364.32*** *p26*
Taton, Miss 2; Louisiana, 1848 ***778.6*** *p322*
Tattersall, Edmund; America, 1773 ***1220.12*** *p783*
Tattershell, James; Virginia, 1727 ***1220.12*** *p783*
Tattle, Margery; Barbados, 1668 ***1220.12*** *p783*
Tatton, Ellen; America, 1769 ***1220.12*** *p783*
Tatton, Joseph; America, 1743 ***1220.12*** *p784*
Tatum, Diana; Canada, 1774 ***3036.5*** *p41*
Tatum, J. 17; Quebec, 1870 ***8364.32*** *p26*
Taube, Eduard; Valparaiso, Chile, 1850 ***1192.4*** *p50*
Tauber, Josef; Texas, 1854 ***2853.20*** *p60*
Taubler, Andreas 10 months; New York, NY, 1886 ***8425.16*** *p33*
Taubler, Gottlieb 18; New York, NY, 1886 ***8425.16*** *p33*
Taubman, Thomas; America, 1764 ***1220.12*** *p784*
Taubmann, Christian; America, 1868 ***7919.3*** *p530*
Taudvin Family ; Prince Edward Island, 1806 ***9228.50*** *p128*
Taught, John; America, 1738 ***1220.12*** *p784*
Tauk, S. G.; Texas, 1852 ***3435.45*** *p37*
Taulton, John; Rappahannock, VA, 1729 ***1220.12*** *p784*
Taumann, Lina; America, 1867 ***7919.3*** *p534*
Taunch, Robert; Carolina, 1719 ***1220.12*** *p784*
Tauner, Marie 8; New Orleans, 1848 ***778.6*** *p322*
Tauner, Victor 6; New Orleans, 1848 ***778.6*** *p322*
Taunton, Giles; Barbados, 1663 ***1220.12*** *p784*
Taunton, Samuel; Barbados, 1663 ***1220.12*** *p784*
Taupier, Marie 24; Quebec, 1660 ***9221.17*** *p469*
Taure, Daniel; Virginia, 1700 ***9230.15*** *p81*
With 2 children
Tausewell, Nicholas; America, 1725 ***1220.12*** *p784*
Tavaroz, Frank; Louisiana, 1874 ***4981.45*** *p134*
Tavarre, Mr. 35; Port uncertain, 1842 ***778.6*** *p322*
Taverly, Ann; America, 1754 ***1220.12*** *p584*
Taverner, George; America, 1753 ***1220.12*** *p784*
Taverner, George 21; North Carolina, 1774 ***1422.10*** *p55*
Taverner, George; Potomac, 1731 ***1220.12*** *p784*
Taverner, John; America, 1763 ***1220.12*** *p784*
Taverner, Joseph; Died enroute, 1730 ***1220.12*** *p784*
Taverner, Sarah; Annapolis, MD, 1729 ***1220.12*** *p784*
Taverner, Thomas; Barbados, 1694 ***1220.12*** *p784*
Tavernier, Anne; Quebec, 1665 ***4514.3*** *p372*
Tavernier, Eloi; Quebec, 1643 ***9221.17*** *p135*
*Wife:*Marguerite Gagnon
*Daughter:*Marguerite
*Daughter:*Marie
Tavernier, Gustav; Valdivia, Chile, 1850 ***1192.4*** *p49*
Tavernier, Jean 21; Montreal, 1653 ***9221.17*** *p301*
Tavernier, Marguerite 16 *SEE* Tavernier, Eloi
Tavernier, Marguerite Gagnon 45 *SEE* Tavernier, Eloi
Tavernier, Marie 12 *SEE* Tavernier, Eloi
Tavernier, Noel; Quebec, 1657 ***9221.17*** *p369*
Taverny, Jean; Quebec, 1659 ***9221.17*** *p414*
Tavis, John D.; North Carolina, 1815 ***1088.45*** *p34*
Tavrey, Martine; Quebec, 1670 ***4514.3*** *p372*
Tawbling, George 60; Ontario, 1871 ***1823.21*** *p361*
Tawner, William; Ohio, 1809-1852 ***4511.35*** *p54*
Tay, Thomas; America, 1769 ***1220.12*** *p784*
Tayler, Mr.; Canada, 1900-1983 ***9228.50*** *p621*
With 2 brothers
Tayler, Mr.; Salt Lake City, 1900-1983 ***9228.50*** *p621*
With brother
Tayler, Alice Dorey *SEE* Tayler, Cyrus
Tayler, Alice Dorey *SEE* Tayler, Cyrus
Tayler, Ann; America, 1728 ***1220.12*** *p784*
Tayler, Cyrus; Canada, 1920 ***9228.50*** *p621*
*Wife:*Alice Dorey
With 2 daughters
Tayler, Cyrus; Salt Lake City, 1920-1983 ***9228.50*** *p621*
*Wife:*Alice Dorey
With 2 daughters
Tayler, Edward; America, 1772 ***1220.12*** *p784*
Tayler, George; America, 1713 ***1220.12*** *p785*
Tayler, James; America, 1678 ***1220.12*** *p785*
Tayler, John; America, 1697 ***1220.12*** *p786*
Tayler, John; America, 1713 ***1220.12*** *p786*
Tayler, John; America, 1755 ***1220.12*** *p786*
Tayler, John; New Jersey, 1665 ***9228.50*** *p621*
Tayler, John; Virginia, 1742 ***1220.12*** *p786*
Tayler, Josias; Ontario, 1812 ***9228.50*** *p621*
Tayler, Martin; America, 1720 ***1220.12*** *p787*
Tayler, Richard; America, 1725 ***1220.12*** *p787*
Tayler, Richard; America, 1742 ***1220.12*** *p787*
Taylor, Colonel; America, 1754 ***1220.12*** *p784*
Taylor, Abraham; America, 1772 ***1220.12*** *p784*
Taylor, Agnes; America, 1762 ***1220.12*** *p784*
Taylor, Albert 49; New York, NY, 1894 ***6512.1*** *p183*
Taylor, Alexander; America, 1755 ***1220.12*** *p784*
Taylor, Alexander 36; Ontario, 1871 ***1823.17*** *p161*
Taylor, Alice; America, 1732 ***1220.12*** *p784*
Taylor, Alice; America, 1766 ***1220.12*** *p784*
Taylor, Ann; America, 1762 ***1220.12*** *p784*
Taylor, Ann; America, 1774 ***1220.12*** *p784*
Taylor, Ann; America, 1754 ***1220.12*** *p584*
Taylor, Ann; Barbados, 1700 ***1220.12*** *p784*
Taylor, Ann *SEE* Taylor, Michael
Taylor, Ann; Died enroute, 1735 ***1220.12*** *p784*
Taylor, Ann 67; Ontario, 1871 ***1823.17*** *p161*
Taylor, Ann; Virginia, 1735 ***1220.12*** *p784*
Taylor, Anne; Maryland or Virginia, 1733 ***1220.12*** *p784*
Taylor, Anne Elizabeth *SEE* Taylor, John Antony
Taylor, Annie 12; Ontario, 1871 ***1823.17*** *p161*
Taylor, Annie 11; Quebec, 1870 ***8364.32*** *p26*
Taylor, Archibald 46; Ontario, 1871 ***1823.17*** *p161*
Taylor, Aubrey Lewis; Iowa, 1916 ***1211.15*** *p19*
Taylor, Balsar 37; Ontario, 1871 ***1823.17*** *p161*
Taylor, Benjamin 46; Ontario, 1871 ***1823.21*** *p361*
Taylor, Celia; America, 1749 ***1220.12*** *p784*
Taylor, Charles; America, 1737 ***1220.12*** *p784*
Taylor, Charles; America, 1767 ***1220.12*** *p784*
Taylor, Charles; America, 1770 ***1220.12*** *p784*
Taylor, Charles; Illinois, 1858-1861 ***6020.5*** *p133*
Taylor, Charles 20; Ontario, 1871 ***1823.21*** *p361*
Taylor, Charles 24; Ontario, 1871 ***1823.21*** *p361*
Taylor, Charles 35; Ontario, 1871 ***1823.21*** *p361*
Taylor, Charles 40; Ontario, 1871 ***1823.17*** *p161*
Taylor, Charles 40; Ontario, 1871 ***1823.21*** *p361*
Taylor, Charles 59; Ontario, 1871 ***1823.17*** *p161*

Taylor, Charles Tyler; Louisville, KY, 1834 *9228.50 p621*
Taylor, Chas. John Edw; Colorado, 1872 *1029.59 p88*
Taylor, Christopher; Annapolis, MD, 1732 *1220.12 p784*
Taylor, Cordelia; Potomac, 1743 *1220.12 p784*
Taylor, Daniel 45; Ontario, 1871 *1823.17 p161*
Taylor, Daniel; Virginia, 1721 *1220.12 p784*
Taylor, David; Colorado, 1883 *1029.59 p88*
Taylor, Dimock; New York, 1776 *8529.30 p7*
Taylor, Donald; Colorado, 1882 *1029.59 p88*
Taylor, Donald 42; Ontario, 1871 *1823.17 p161*
Taylor, Duncan; New York, 1738 *8277.31 p119*
  *Wife:*Mary Gillies
  *Daughter:*Mary
Taylor, Duncan 45; Ontario, 1871 *1823.17 p161*
Taylor, Duncan 53; Ontario, 1871 *1823.21 p361*
Taylor, Edmund; America, 1755 *1220.12 p784*
Taylor, Edward; America, 1709 *1220.12 p784*
Taylor, Edward; America, 1735 *1220.12 p784*
Taylor, Edward; America, 1738 *1220.12 p784*
Taylor, Edward; America, 1741 *1220.12 p784*
Taylor, Edward; America, 1765 *1220.12 p784*
Taylor, Edward; America, 1770 *1220.12 p784*
Taylor, Edward; America, 1771 *1220.12 p784*
Taylor, Edward; America, 1773 *1220.12 p785*
Taylor, Edward; Barbados, 1664 *1220.12 p784*
Taylor, Edward; Virginia, 1734 *1220.12 p784*
Taylor, Elias; America, 1763 *1220.12 p785*
Taylor, Elias; Jamestown, VA, 1633 *1658.20 p211*
Taylor, Mrs. Elias; Jamestown, VA, 1633 *1658.20 p211*
  With daughter
Taylor, Eliza 10; Quebec, 1870 *8364.32 p26*
Taylor, Elizabeth; America, 1675 *1220.12 p785*
Taylor, Elizabeth; America, 1741 *1220.12 p785*
Taylor, Elizabeth; America, 1750 *1220.12 p785*
Taylor, Elizabeth; America, 1754 *1220.12 p785*
Taylor, Elizabeth; America, 1764 *1220.12 p785*
Taylor, Elizabeth; Died enroute, 1734 *1220.12 p785*
Taylor, Elizabeth; Maryland, 1736 *1220.12 p785*
Taylor, Elizabeth 49; Michigan, 1880 *4491.33 p22*
Taylor, Elizabeth 12; Quebec, 1870 *8364.32 p26*
Taylor, Elizabeth 16; Quebec, 1870 *8364.32 p26*
Taylor, Elizabeth; Virginia, 1732 *1220.12 p785*
Taylor, Elizabeth; Virginia, 1735 *1220.12 p785*
Taylor, Ely; America, 1748 *1220.12 p785*
Taylor, Emma 19; Ontario, 1871 *1823.21 p361*
Taylor, Emma 60; Ontario, 1871 *1823.21 p361*
Taylor, Esther; America, 1756 *1220.12 p785*
Taylor, Francis; America, 1731 *1220.12 p785*
Taylor, Francis; America, 1748 *1220.12 p785*
Taylor, Francis; America, 1753 *1220.12 p785*
Taylor, Francis 54; Ontario, 1871 *1823.21 p361*
Taylor, Garrick; America, 1741 *1220.12 p785*
Taylor, Geo. W. 11; America, 1835 *9228.50 p21A*
  With parents
Taylor, George; America, 1685 *1220.12 p785*
Taylor, George; America, 1728 *1220.12 p785*
Taylor, George; America, 1736 *1220.12 p785*
Taylor, George; America, 1759 *1220.12 p785*
Taylor, George; America, 1761 *1220.12 p785*
Taylor, George; America, 1764 *1220.12 p785*
Taylor, George; America, 1766 *1220.12 p785*
Taylor, George; America, 1771 *1220.12 p785*
Taylor, George; Canada, 1774 *3036.5 p41*
Taylor, George; Iowa, 1904 *1211.15 p19*
Taylor, George 20; Ontario, 1871 *1823.21 p362*
Taylor, George 27; Ontario, 1871 *1823.21 p362*
Taylor, George 46; Ontario, 1871 *1823.17 p161*
Taylor, George 47; Ontario, 1871 *1823.17 p161*
Taylor, George 52; Ontario, 1871 *1823.21 p362*
Taylor, George 55; Ontario, 1871 *1823.21 p361*
Taylor, George; Washington, 1885 *2770.40 p194*
Taylor, George W. 34; Ontario, 1871 *1823.21 p362*
Taylor, Hannah; America, 1686 *1220.12 p785*
Taylor, Harriet 48; New York, NY, 1894 *6512.1 p183*
Taylor, Harry; America, 1748 *1220.12 p785*
Taylor, Helen 45; Quebec, 1910 *2897.7 p10*
Taylor, Henry; America, 1754 *1220.12 p785*
Taylor, Henry; America, 1768 *1220.12 p785*
Taylor, Henry; Annapolis, MD, 1732 *1220.12 p785*
Taylor, Henry; Ohio, 1826 *3580.20 p33*
Taylor, Henry; Ohio, 1826 *6020.12 p22*
Taylor, Henry 29; Ontario, 1871 *1823.17 p161*
Taylor, Henry 29; Ontario, 1871 *1823.21 p362*
Taylor, Henry 41; Ontario, 1871 *1823.17 p161*
Taylor, Henry 87; Ontario, 1871 *1823.17 p161*
Taylor, Henry; Virginia, 1732 *1220.12 p785*
Taylor, Ishmael; Virginia, 1736 *1220.12 p785*
Taylor, J. A. 31; Ontario, 1871 *1823.17 p161*
Taylor, J. L. 30; Ontario, 1871 *1823.21 p362*
Taylor, James; America, 1745 *1220.12 p785*
Taylor, James; America, 1764 *1220.12 p785*
Taylor, James; America, 1765 *1220.12 p785*

Taylor, James; America, 1766 *1220.12 p785*
Taylor, James; America, 1767 *1220.12 p785*
Taylor, James; America, 1772 *1220.12 p785*
Taylor, James; America, 1774 *1220.12 p785*
Taylor, James; Kingston, Jamaica, 1776 *8529.30 p14A*
Taylor, James 35; Ontario, 1871 *1823.21 p362*
Taylor, James 40; Ontario, 1871 *1823.21 p362*
Taylor, James 43; Ontario, 1871 *1823.17 p161*
Taylor, James 44; Ontario, 1871 *1823.21 p362*
Taylor, James 44; Ontario, 1871 *1823.21 p362*
Taylor, James 50; Ontario, 1871 *1823.21 p362*
Taylor, James 55; Ontario, 1871 *1823.21 p362*
Taylor, James 67; Ontario, 1871 *1823.17 p161*
Taylor, James; Virginia, 1764 *1220.12 p785*
Taylor, James; Washington, 1885 *2770.40 p194*
Taylor, James V.; Washington, 1884 *2770.40 p193*
Taylor, Jane; America, 1663 *1220.12 p785*
Taylor, Jane; America, 1728 *1220.12 p785*
Taylor, Jane; America, 1773 *1220.12 p786*
Taylor, Jane; Annapolis, MD, 1731 *1220.12 p785*
Taylor, Jane; Virginia, 1734 *1220.12 p785*
Taylor, Jeremiah; America, 1765 *1220.12 p786*
Taylor, Jno. W.; Louisiana, 1874 *4981.45 p297*
Taylor, John; America, 1675 *1220.12 p786*
Taylor, John; America, 1722 *1220.12 p786*
Taylor, John; America, 1724 *1220.12 p786*
Taylor, John; America, 1737 *1220.12 p786*
Taylor, John; America, 1740 *1220.12 p786*
Taylor, John; America, 1741 *1220.12 p786*
Taylor, John; America, 1744 *1220.12 p786*
Taylor, John; America, 1745 *1220.12 p786*
Taylor, John; America, 1747 *1220.12 p786*
Taylor, John; America, 1749 *1220.12 p786*
Taylor, John; America, 1753 *1220.12 p786*
Taylor, John; America, 1754 *1220.12 p786*
Taylor, John; America, 1755 *1220.12 p786*
Taylor, John; America, 1764 *1220.12 p786*
Taylor, John; America, 1766 *1220.12 p786*
Taylor, John; America, 1767 *1220.12 p786*
Taylor, John; America, 1768 *1220.12 p786*
Taylor, John; America, 1770 *1220.12 p786*
Taylor, John; America, 1773 *1220.12 p786*
Taylor, John; America, 1774 *1220.12 p786*
Taylor, John; America, 1775 *1220.12 p786*
Taylor, John; Annapolis, MD, 1733 *1220.12 p786*
Taylor, John; Barbados, 1662 *1220.12 p786*
Taylor, John; Boston, 1718 *1220.12 p786*
Taylor, John 41; Indiana, 1865-1869 *9076.20 p66*
Taylor, John; Jamaica, 1783 *8529.30 p14A*
Taylor, John; Maryland, 1720 *1220.12 p786*
Taylor, John 35; Ontario, 1871 *1823.17 p161*
Taylor, John 35; Ontario, 1871 *1823.21 p362*
Taylor, John 36; Ontario, 1871 *1823.21 p362*
Taylor, John 37; Ontario, 1871 *1823.17 p161*
Taylor, John 38; Ontario, 1871 *1823.21 p362*
Taylor, John 46; Ontario, 1871 *1823.21 p362*
Taylor, John 52; Ontario, 1871 *1823.21 p362*
Taylor, John 54; Ontario, 1871 *1823.21 p362*
Taylor, John 65; Ontario, 1871 *1823.21 p362*
Taylor, John 69; Ontario, 1871 *1823.21 p362*
Taylor, John; Philadelphia, 1778 *8529.30 p5A*
Taylor, John; Potomac, 1731 *1220.12 p786*
Taylor, John; Virginia, 1665 *9228.50 p53*
Taylor, John; Virginia, 1724 *1220.12 p786*
Taylor, John; Virginia, 1736 *1220.12 p786*
Taylor, John Antony; Toronto, 1956 *9228.50 p621*
  *Wife:*Anne Elizabeth
Taylor, Joseph; America, 1731 *1220.12 p786*
Taylor, Joseph; America, 1751 *1220.12 p786*
Taylor, Joseph; America, 1756 *1220.12 p786*
Taylor, Joseph; America, 1764 *1220.12 p786*
Taylor, Joseph; America, 1766 *1220.12 p786*
Taylor, Joseph; America, 1771 *1220.12 p786*
Taylor, Joseph; Annapolis, MD, 1726 *1220.12 p786*
Taylor, Joseph; Barbados or Jamaica, 1690 *1220.12 p786*
Taylor, Joseph; Colorado, 1895 *1029.59 p88*
Taylor, Joseph 44; Indiana, 1886-1888 *9076.20 p72*
Taylor, Joseph 47; Michigan, 1880 *4491.33 p22*
Taylor, Joseph; Ohio, 1809-1852 *4511.35 p54*
Taylor, Joseph 29; Ontario, 1871 *1823.17 p161*
Taylor, Joseph 67; Ontario, 1871 *1823.17 p161*
Taylor, Joseph C.; Colorado, 1891 *1029.59 p88*
Taylor, Joseph C.; Colorado, 1895 *1029.59 p88*
Taylor, Judith; America, 1747 *1220.12 p786*
Taylor, Margaret; America, 1715 *1220.12 p787*
Taylor, Margaret; America, 1727 *1220.12 p787*
Taylor, Margaret; America, 1749 *1220.12 p787*
Taylor, Margaret 44; Ontario, 1871 *1823.21 p362*
Taylor, Margaret; Watertown, MA, 1690 *1642 p112*
Taylor, Margret 19; Ontario, 1871 *1823.21 p362*
Taylor, Margret 56; Ontario, 1871 *1823.21 p362*
Taylor, Marion 21; North Carolina, 1774 *1422.10 p58*
Taylor, Marion 21; North Carolina, 1774 *1422.10 p62*

Taylor, Mary; America, 1699 *1220.12 p787*
Taylor, Mary; America, 1723 *1220.12 p787*
Taylor, Mary; America, 1736 *1220.12 p787*
Taylor, Mary; America, 1744 *1220.12 p787*
Taylor, Mary; America, 1749 *1220.12 p787*
Taylor, Mary; America, 1754 *1220.12 p787*
Taylor, Mary; America, 1764 *1220.12 p787*
Taylor, Mary; America, 1768 *1220.12 p787*
Taylor, Mary *SEE* Taylor, Duncan
Taylor, Mary Gillies *SEE* Taylor, Duncan
Taylor, Mary 40; North Carolina, 1774 *1422.10 p57*
Taylor, Mary; Virginia, 1734 *1220.12 p787*
Taylor, Mary; Virginia, 1735 *1220.12 p787*
Taylor, Mary A. 56; Ontario, 1871 *1823.17 p161*
Taylor, Mary Ann 67; Ontario, 1871 *1823.21 p362*
Taylor, Matthew; America, 1765 *1220.12 p787*
Taylor, Michael; Canada, 1774 *3036.5 p40*
  *Wife:*Ann
Taylor, Michael; Canada, 1774 *3036.5 p41*
Taylor, Michael Thomas; America, 1773 *1220.12 p787*
Taylor, Minnie 37; Ontario, 1871 *1823.17 p161*
Taylor, Oscar 2; Ontario, 1871 *1823.21 p362*
Taylor, P.; California, 1868 *1131.61 p89*
Taylor, Percival Walter; Vancouver, B.C., 1920-1979 *9228.50 p621*
Taylor, Peter 35; Ontario, 1871 *1823.17 p161*
Taylor, Phebe 36; Ontario, 1871 *1823.17 p161*
Taylor, Philip; America, 1701 *1220.12 p787*
Taylor, Ralph; America, 1735 *1220.12 p787*
Taylor, Richard; America, 1671 *1220.12 p787*
Taylor, Richard; America, 1672 *1220.12 p787*
Taylor, Richard; America, 1731 *1220.12 p787*
Taylor, Richard; America, 1766 *1220.12 p787*
Taylor, Richard 44; Ontario, 1871 *1823.17 p161*
Taylor, Richard 75; Ontario, 1871 *1823.21 p362*
Taylor, Robert; America, 1684 *1220.12 p787*
Taylor, Robert; America, 1700 *1220.12 p787*
Taylor, Robert; America, 1756 *1220.12 p787*
Taylor, Robert; America, 1761 *1220.12 p787*
Taylor, Robert; America, 1768 *1220.12 p787*
Taylor, Robert; America, 1772 *1220.12 p787*
Taylor, Robert; Maryland, 1674-1675 *1236.25 p51*
Taylor, Robert; North Carolina, 1780 *1088.45 p34*
Taylor, Robert 25; Ontario, 1871 *1823.21 p362*
Taylor, Robert 52; Ontario, 1871 *1823.21 p362*
Taylor, Robert 65; Ontario, 1871 *1823.21 p362*
Taylor, Robert 71; Ontario, 1871 *1823.21 p362*
Taylor, Robert 76; Ontario, 1871 *1823.21 p362*
Taylor, Robert, Jr.; Barbados, 1683 *1220.12 p787*
Taylor, S. B.; Iowa, 1884 *1211.15 p19*
Taylor, Samuel; America, 1750 *1220.12 p787*
Taylor, Samuel; America, 1771 *1220.12 p787*
Taylor, Samuel; America, 1773 *1220.12 p787*
Taylor, Samuel; America, 1774 *1220.12 p787*
Taylor, Samuel 40; Ontario, 1871 *1823.21 p362*
Taylor, Samuel 48; Ontario, 1871 *1823.21 p362*
Taylor, Samuel; Springfield, MA, 1675 *1642 p120*
Taylor, Sarah; America, 1729 *1220.12 p787*
Taylor, Sarah; America, 1743 *1220.12 p787*
Taylor, Sarah; America, 1758 *1220.12 p787*
Taylor, Sarah; America, 1775 *1220.12 p787*
Taylor, Sarah; Barbados or Jamaica, 1690 *1220.12 p787*
Taylor, Sarah 78; Ontario, 1871 *1823.17 p161*
Taylor, Sarah; Potomac, 1743 *1220.12 p787*
Taylor, Simon; New York, 1778 *8529.30 p7*
Taylor, Solomon; America, 1757 *1220.12 p787*
Taylor, Stephen; America, 1742 *1220.12 p787*
Taylor, Stephen; Barbados, 1682 *1220.12 p787*
Taylor, Susan; America, 1675 *1220.12 p787*
Taylor, Susannah; America, 1745 *1220.12 p787*
Taylor, Thomas; America, 1691 *1220.12 p787*
Taylor, Thomas; America, 1722 *1220.12 p787*
Taylor, Thomas; America, 1730 *1220.12 p788*
Taylor, Thomas; America, 1733 *1220.12 p788*
Taylor, Thomas; America, 1738 *1220.12 p788*
Taylor, Thomas; America, 1739 *1220.12 p788*
Taylor, Thomas; America, 1750 *1220.12 p788*
Taylor, Thomas; America, 1759 *1220.12 p788*
Taylor, Thomas; America, 1760 *1220.12 p788*
Taylor, Thomas; America, 1761 *1220.12 p788*
Taylor, Thomas; America, 1770 *1220.12 p788*
Taylor, Thomas; America, 1771 *1220.12 p788*
Taylor, Thomas; America, 1772 *1220.12 p788*
Taylor, Thomas; America, 1774 *1220.12 p788*
Taylor, Thomas; America, 1775 *1220.12 p788*
Taylor, Thomas; America, 1869 *9076.20 p68*
Taylor, Thomas; Died enroute, 1725 *1220.12 p788*
Taylor, Thomas; Louisiana, 1836-1841 *4981.45 p209*
Taylor, Thomas; Maryland, 1734 *1220.12 p788*
Taylor, Thomas; Maryland, 1741 *1220.12 p788*
Taylor, Thomas; New York, 1778 *8529.30 p7*
Taylor, Thomas 31; Ontario, 1871 *1823.17 p161*
Taylor, Thomas 43; Ontario, 1871 *1823.21 p362*

Taylor, Thomas 50; Ontario, 1871 ***1823.21*** *p362*
Taylor, Thomas 50; Ontario, 1871 ***1823.21*** *p362*
Taylor, Thomas 51; Ontario, 1871 ***1823.21*** *p362*
Taylor, Thomas 53; Ontario, 1871 ***1823.21*** *p362*
Taylor, Thomas; Virginia, 1732 ***1220.12*** *p788*
Taylor, Thomas; Washington, 1886 ***2770.40*** *p24*
Taylor, Timothy; America, 1738 ***1220.12*** *p788*
Taylor, Tisdal 56; Ontario, 1871 ***1823.17*** *p161*
Taylor, Walter; Barbados, 1693 ***1220.12*** *p788*
Taylor, William; America, 1665 ***1220.12*** *p788*
Taylor, William; America, 1729 ***1220.12*** *p788*
Taylor, William; America, 1735 ***1220.12*** *p788*
Taylor, William; America, 1741 ***1220.12*** *p788*
Taylor, William; America, 1743 ***1220.12*** *p788*
Taylor, William; America, 1744 ***1220.12*** *p788*
Taylor, William; America, 1745 ***1220.12*** *p788*
Taylor, William; America, 1749 ***1220.12*** *p788*
Taylor, William; America, 1752 ***1220.12*** *p788*
Taylor, William; America, 1754 ***1220.12*** *p788*
Taylor, William; America, 1760 ***1220.12*** *p788*
Taylor, William; America, 1761 ***1220.12*** *p788*
Taylor, William; America, 1764 ***1220.12*** *p788*
Taylor, William; America, 1766 ***1220.12*** *p788*
Taylor, William; America, 1767 ***1220.12*** *p788*
Taylor, William; America, 1768 ***1220.12*** *p788*
Taylor, William; America, 1768 ***1220.12*** *p789*
Taylor, William; America, 1770 ***1220.12*** *p789*
Taylor, William; America, 1771 ***1220.12*** *p789*
Taylor, William; America, 1772 ***1220.12*** *p789*
Taylor, William; America, 1773 ***1220.12*** *p789*
Taylor, William; Barbados, 1679 ***1220.12*** *p788*
Taylor, William; Barbados or Jamaica, 1696 ***1220.12*** *p788*
Taylor, William; Died enroute, 1726 ***1220.12*** *p788*
Taylor, William; Maryland, 1737 ***1220.12*** *p788*
Taylor, William; North Carolina, 1835 ***1088.45*** *p34*
Taylor, William; Ohio, 1809-1852 ***4511.35*** *p54*
Taylor, William 30; Ontario, 1871 ***1823.17*** *p161*
Taylor, William 30; Ontario, 1871 ***1823.21*** *p362*
Taylor, William 34; Ontario, 1871 ***1823.21*** *p363*
Taylor, William 35; Ontario, 1871 ***1823.21*** *p363*
Taylor, William 39; Ontario, 1871 ***1823.17*** *p162*
Taylor, William 39; Ontario, 1871 ***1823.21*** *p363*
Taylor, William 40; Ontario, 1871 ***1823.21*** *p363*
Taylor, William 40; Ontario, 1871 ***1823.21*** *p363*
Taylor, William 48; Ontario, 1871 ***1823.21*** *p363*
Taylor, William 57; Ontario, 1871 ***1823.17*** *p162*
Taylor, William 64; Ontario, 1871 ***1823.21*** *p363*
Taylor, William; South Carolina, 1822 ***6155.4*** *p19*
Taylor, William; Virginia, 1718 ***1220.12*** *p788*
Taylor, William; Virginia, 1729 ***1220.12*** *p788*
Taylor, William; Virginia, 1730 ***1220.12*** *p788*
Taylor, William; Virginia, 1731 ***1220.12*** *p788*
Taylor, William; Virginia, 1773 ***1220.12*** *p789*
Taylor, William; Washington, 1880 ***2770.40*** *p134*
Taylor, Wm; Jamestown, VA, 1633 ***1658.20*** *p211*
Taylor, Wm. 52; Quebec, 1910 ***2897.7*** *p10*
Taylors, William 37; Ontario, 1871 ***1823.21*** *p363*
Taylour, William; America, 1752 ***1220.12*** *p788*
Tayson, Timothy; Marston's Wharf, 1782 ***8529.30*** *p16*
Tchorzelewskie, Anton 38; New York, NY, 1883 ***8427.14*** *p44*
Tchorzelewskie, Marianne 35; New York, NY, 1883 ***8427.14*** *p44*
Tea, Elizabeth; Virginia, 1736 ***1220.12*** *p789*
Teache, August; Ohio, 1809-1852 ***4511.35*** *p13*
Teachout, Peter 45; Michigan, 1880 ***4491.30*** *p30*
Teachout, William 49; Michigan, 1880 ***4491.30*** *p30*
Teage, Peter; America, 1731 ***1220.12*** *p789*
Teague, John; America, 1683 ***1220.12*** *p789*
Teague, Sarah; Quebec, 1910 ***2897.7*** *p7*
Teal, Rebeca 72; Ontario, 1871 ***1823.21*** *p363*
Teale, Christopher 52; Ontario, 1871 ***1823.21*** *p363*
Teale, John 37; Ontario, 1871 ***1823.21*** *p363*
Teape, Robert; America, 1685 ***1220.12*** *p789*
Teape, Walter; America, 1685 ***1220.12*** *p789*
Tear, Edward; Barbados or Jamaica, 1693 ***1220.12*** *p789*
Teare, Robert; North Carolina, 1812 ***1088.45*** *p34*
Teare, Thomas; Missouri, 1887 ***3276.1*** *p4*
Tearer, Robert; America, 1755 ***1220.12*** *p789*
Tearne, John; New England, 1745 ***1642*** *p28*
Tearne, Thomas; Barbados, 1675 ***1220.12*** *p789*
Tearney, John 72; Ontario, 1871 ***1823.21*** *p363*
Tearney, Lawrence 51; Ontario, 1871 ***1823.17*** *p162*
Teasdale, George; America, 1772 ***1220.12*** *p789*
Teasdle, George 47; Ontario, 1871 ***1823.21*** *p363*
Teat, William 35; Ontario, 1871 ***1823.21*** *p363*
Tebbe, Carol. Sophie; America, 1867 ***7420.1*** *p262*
Tebbe, Catharina Maria Louise Charlotte Kolling *SEE* Tebbe, Hans Heinrich
Tebbe, Hans Heinrich; America, 1840 ***7420.1*** *p20*
*Wife:*Catharina Maria Louise Charlotte Kolling
Tebbutt, William; America, 1755 ***1220.12*** *p789*
Tebby, John; America, 1753 ***1220.12*** *p789*
Tebby, Thomas; America, 1748 ***1220.12*** *p789*
Tecklenburg, Mr.; Illinois, 1857 ***7420.1*** *p174*
Tecklenburg, Anne Catherine Sophie; America, 1851 ***7420.1*** *p80*
Tecklenburg, Carl Friedrich Wilhelm; America, 1859 ***7420.1*** *p189*
With wife
With daughter 3
*Brother:*Carl Ludwig T.
With daughter 4
With daughter 6
Tecklenburg, Carl Ludwig T. *SEE* Tecklenburg, Carl Friedrich Wilhelm
Tecklenburg, Christine Witte *SEE* Tecklenburg, Friedrich Leopold
Tecklenburg, Ernst Fr. L. *SEE* Tecklenburg, Friedrich Leopold
Tecklenburg, Friederike L. *SEE* Tecklenburg, Friedrich Leopold
Tecklenburg, Friedrich Leopold; America, 1842 ***7420.1*** *p26*
*Wife:*Christine Witte
*Daughter:*Sophie A. F.
*Son:*Joh. Fr. F.
*Son:*Ernst Fr. L.
*Daughter:*Henriette J.W.
*Daughter:*Friederike L.
*Son:*Heinrich Fr. W.
Tecklenburg, Heinrich Fr. W. *SEE* Tecklenburg, Friedrich Leopold
Tecklenburg, Henriette J.W. *SEE* Tecklenburg, Friedrich Leopold
Tecklenburg, Joh. Fr. F. *SEE* Tecklenburg, Friedrich Leopold
Tecklenburg, Sophie A. F. *SEE* Tecklenburg, Friedrich Leopold
Teckoe, Richard; America, 1755 ***1220.12*** *p789*
Tecmede, Zoe 12; New Orleans, 1848 ***778.6*** *p322*
Tecton, Thomas; America, 1694 ***1220.12*** *p789*
Tedar, Joseph; America, 1760 ***1220.12*** *p789*
Tedball, Robert 59; Ontario, 1871 ***1823.17*** *p162*
Teddall, Christopher; Jamaica, 1716 ***1220.12*** *p789*
Tedder, George; America, 1729 ***1220.12*** *p789*
Tedder, John 58; Ontario, 1871 ***1823.21*** *p363*
Tedder, Mary 21; Ontario, 1871 ***1823.21*** *p363*
Tedder, Richard; Maryland, 1720 ***1220.12*** *p789*
Tedder, Thomas 1; Ontario, 1871 ***1823.21*** *p363*
Tedder, Thomas 32; Ontario, 1871 ***1823.21*** *p363*
Teddy, John; America, 1773 ***1220.12*** *p789*
Tedeman, Peter Jacobson; Iowa, 1896 ***1211.15*** *p19*
Tedford, John; New York, 1778 ***8529.30*** *p5A*
Tediman, John H.; North Carolina, 1851 ***1088.45*** *p35*
Tedstell, John; America, 1761 ***1220.12*** *p789*
Tedstill, Christopher; America, 1772 ***1220.12*** *p789*
Tee, John; America, 1755 ***1220.12*** *p789*
Tee, Joseph; America, 1754 ***1220.12*** *p789*
Teefy, Matthew; Toronto, 1844 ***2910.35*** *p113*
Teeper, Jacob; Ohio, 1809-1852 ***4511.35*** *p54*
Teeple, Edward 64; Ontario, 1871 ***1823.21*** *p363*
Teeple, Jemima 74; Ontario, 1871 ***1823.21*** *p363*
Teeple, John; Ohio, 1809-1852 ***4511.35*** *p54*
Teeple, Peter 42; Ontario, 1871 ***1823.21*** *p363*
Tees, John; North Carolina, 1792-1862 ***1088.45*** *p34*
Teesdale, Hugh; Illinois, 1852 ***6079.1*** *p14*
Teesdale, Robert; Illinois, 1852 ***6079.1*** *p14*
Teesdale, Thomas; Illinois, 1858 ***6079.1*** *p14*
Teevan, James; Toronto, 1844 ***2910.35*** *p113*
Teff, Danial 39; Ontario, 1871 ***1823.21*** *p363*
Tegg, Carl 13; Halifax, N.S., 1902 ***1860.4*** *p40*
Tegg, Carl 49; Halifax, N.S., 1902 ***1860.4*** *p40*
Tegg, Friederika 6; Halifax, N.S., 1902 ***1860.4*** *p40*
Tegg, Jacob 16; Halifax, N.S., 1902 ***1860.4*** *p40*
Tegg, Jacob 35; Halifax, N.S., 1902 ***1860.4*** *p40*
Tegg, Johannes 4; Halifax, N.S., 1902 ***1860.4*** *p40*
Tegg, Magdalene 8; Halifax, N.S., 1902 ***1860.4*** *p40*
Tegg, Margaretha 11; Halifax, N.S., 1902 ***1860.4*** *p40*
Tegg, Margaretha 41; Halifax, N.S., 1902 ***1860.4*** *p40*
Tegtmeier, Miss; America, 1871 ***7420.1*** *p288*
Tegtmeier, Anne Marie Sophie *SEE* Tegtmeier, Johann Heinrich
Tegtmeier, August; America, 1854 ***7420.1*** *p131*
Tegtmeier, Carl; America, 1857 ***7420.1*** *p174*
With wife son & daughter
Tegtmeier, Carl August *SEE* Tegtmeier, Carl Friedrich Ludwig
Tegtmeier, Carl Friedrich Ludwig; America, 1893 ***7420.1*** *p369*
*Wife:*Engel Sophie Wilhelmine Ackemann
*Son:*Wilhelm August
*Daughter:*Friederike Auguste
*Daughter:*Emilie Auguste
*Son:*Carl August
*Son:*Louis Hermann
Tegtmeier, Carl Friedrich Wilhelm; Ohio, 1884 ***7420.1*** *p345*
*Wife:*Caroline Wilhelmine Teigeler
Tegtmeier, Caroline; America, 1842 ***7420.1*** *p25*
Tegtmeier, Caroline Wilhelmine Teigeler *SEE* Tegtmeier, Carl Friedrich Wilhelm
Tegtmeier, Catharine Engel Dorothea; America, 1866 ***7420.1*** *p250*
*Daughter:*Catharine Engel Sophie
Tegtmeier, Catharine Engel Sophie *SEE* Tegtmeier, Catharine Engel Dorothea
Tegtmeier, Conrad Ludwig; America, 1839 ***7420.1*** *p17*
Tegtmeier, Dorothea Friederike Henriette; America, 1865 ***7420.1*** *p238*
*Daughter:*Wilhelmine Charlotte
Tegtmeier, Eduard; America, 1891 ***7420.1*** *p364*
Tegtmeier, Emilie Auguste *SEE* Tegtmeier, Carl Friedrich Ludwig
Tegtmeier, Engel Marie Sophie Stege *SEE* Tegtmeier, Johann Heinrich
Tegtmeier, Engel Marie Sophie; America, 1891 ***7420.1*** *p362*
Tegtmeier, Engel Sophie Wilhelmine Ackemann *SEE* Tegtmeier, Carl Friedrich Ludwig
Tegtmeier, Ferdinand; America, 1867 ***7420.1*** *p265*
Tegtmeier, Friederike Auguste *SEE* Tegtmeier, Carl Friedrich Ludwig
Tegtmeier, Friederike Charlotte; America, 1857 ***7420.1*** *p174*
Tegtmeier, Friedrich; America, 1891 ***7420.1*** *p364*
Tegtmeier, Friedrich August Wilhelm; America, 1882 ***7420.1*** *p333*
Tegtmeier, Friedrich Christian; Port uncertain, 1839 ***7420.1*** *p17*
Tegtmeier, Friedrich Heinrich Wilhelm; America, 1892 ***7420.1*** *p367*
*Brother:*Wilhelm August
Tegtmeier, Friedrich Wilhelm; America, 1855 ***7420.1*** *p142*
Tegtmeier, Friedrich Wilhelm; Port uncertain, 1840 ***7420.1*** *p21*
Tegtmeier, Hans Heinrich; America, 1850 ***7420.1*** *p77*
Tegtmeier, Hans Heinrich; America, 1855 ***7420.1*** *p142*
Tegtmeier, Heinrich; America, 1854 ***7420.1*** *p131*
Tegtmeier, Heinrich; America, 1893 ***7420.1*** *p370*
Tegtmeier, Heinrich August; America, 1884 ***7420.1*** *p345*
*Wife:*Melusine Auguste Justine Sophie Kruger
*Son:*Heinrich Friedrich August
Tegtmeier, Heinrich Christian Ludwig; America, 1870 ***7420.1*** *p288*
Tegtmeier, Heinrich Christian Wilhelm; America, 1872 ***7420.1*** *p298*
Tegtmeier, Heinrich Conrad; America, 1860 ***7420.1*** *p201*
Tegtmeier, Heinrich Conrad; America, 1870 ***7420.1*** *p288*
*Son:*Heinrich Friedrich Wilhelm
With family
Tegtmeier, Heinrich Conrad; America, 1884 ***7420.1*** *p399*
Tegtmeier, Heinrich Friedrich August *SEE* Tegtmeier, Heinrich August
Tegtmeier, Heinrich Friedrich Conrad; America, 1866 ***7420.1*** *p250*
Tegtmeier, Heinrich Friedrich Wilhelm *SEE* Tegtmeier, Heinrich Conrad
Tegtmeier, Heinrich Friedrich Wilhelm; America, 1891 ***7420.1*** *p364*
Tegtmeier, Heinrich Wilhelm Hermann; America, 1886 ***7420.1*** *p352*
Tegtmeier, Heinrich Wilhelm Leopold; America, 1881 ***7420.1*** *p326*
Tegtmeier, Hermann Gottfried Ludwig; America, 1871 ***7420.1*** *p292*
Tegtmeier, Johann Friedrich Christian; America, 1867 ***7420.1*** *p265*
Tegtmeier, Johann Friedrich Christoph; America, 1882 ***7420.1*** *p333*
Tegtmeier, Johann Heinrich; America, 1852 ***7420.1*** *p99*
Tegtmeier, Johann Heinrich; America, 1855 ***7420.1*** *p142*
*Wife:*Engel Marie Sophie Stege
*Daughter:*Anne Marie Sophie
Tegtmeier, Johann Heinrich Conrad; America, 1850 ***7420.1*** *p77*
Tegtmeier, Justine; America, 1891 ***7420.1*** *p364*
Tegtmeier, Louis Hermann *SEE* Tegtmeier, Carl Friedrich Ludwig
Tegtmeier, Ludwig; America, 1854 ***7420.1*** *p131*
Tegtmeier, Melusine Auguste Justine Sophie Kruger *SEE* Tegtmeier, Heinrich August
Tegtmeier, Philipp; America, 1854 ***7420.1*** *p131*
Tegtmeier, Sophie Dorothea Charlotte; America, 1867 ***7420.1*** *p265*

Tegtmeier, Wilhelm; America, 1854 ***7420.1*** *p131*
With wife & 2 sons
Tegtmeier, Wilhelm; America, 1871 ***7420.1*** *p396*
Tegtmeier, Wilhelm August *SEE* Tegtmeier, Friedrich Heinrich Wilhelm
Tegtmeier, Wilhelm August *SEE* Tegtmeier, Carl Friedrich Ludwig
Tegtmeier, Wilhelmine Charlotte *SEE* Tegtmeier, Dorothea Friederike Henriette
Tegtmeier, Wilhelmine Christiane Charlotte; America, 1865 ***7420.1*** *p238*
Tegtmeyer, Caroline Sophie Louise Charlotte *SEE* Tegtmeyer, Christoph Carl Christian
Tegtmeyer, Christian Ludwig Wilhelm *SEE* Tegtmeyer, Christoph Carl Christian
Tegtmeyer, Christoph Carl Christian; America, 1866 ***7420.1*** *p250*
*Wife:*Sophie Louise Charlotte Notting
*Daughter:*Marie Caroline Wilhelmine
*Daughter:*Wilhelmine Christiane Charlotte
*Son:*Christian Ludwig Wilhelm
*Daughter:*Caroline Sophie Louise Charlotte
Tegtmeyer, Conrad; America, 1845 ***7420.1*** *p41*
Tegtmeyer, Friedrich Christian; America, 1848 ***7420.1*** *p62*
Tegtmeyer, Marie Caroline Wilhelmine *SEE* Tegtmeyer, Christoph Carl Christian
Tegtmeyer, Sophie Louise Charlotte Notting *SEE* Tegtmeyer, Christoph Carl Christian
Tegtmeyer, Wilhelmine Christiane Charlotte *SEE* Tegtmeyer, Christoph Carl Christian
Tehany, James; Toronto, 1844 ***2910.35*** *p116*
Tehany, Luke, Jr.; Toronto, 1844 ***2910.35*** *p116*
Tehany, Luke, Sr.; Toronto, 1844 ***2910.35*** *p116*
Teibel, Josef; South Dakota, 1871-1910 ***2853.20*** *p247*
Teibort, Barbara 27; New York, NY, 1885 ***8425.16*** *p32*
Teibort, Jacob 4; New York, NY, 1885 ***8425.16*** *p32*
Teibort, Michael 28; New York, NY, 1885 ***8425.16*** *p32*
Teibort, Wendelin 1 months; New York, NY, 1885 ***8425.16*** *p32*
Teich, Otto 25; America, 1899 ***5475.1*** *p47*
Teichelmann, F.; Valdivia, Chile, 1850 ***1192.4*** *p50*
Teichelmann, Wilhelm; Chile, 1852 ***1192.4*** *p52*
With wife & child
With child 16
With child 24
Teigeler, . . .; America, 1846 ***7420.1*** *p50*
With family
Teigeler, Adolph; America, 1854 ***7420.1*** *p132*
Teigeler, Caroline Wilhelmine; Ohio, 1884 ***7420.1*** *p345*
Teigeler, Catharine Sophie; America, 1866 ***7420.1*** *p251*
Teigeler, Charlotte; America, 1853 ***7420.1*** *p112*
Teigeler, Christine Wilhelmine Charl.; America, 1850 ***7420.1*** *p69*
Teigeler, Heinrich Conrad; New York, NY, 1856 ***7420.1*** *p155*
Teigeler, Heinrich Wilhelm; America, 1847 ***7420.1*** *p57*
Teigeler, Johann Christoph; America, 1857 ***7420.1*** *p174*
Teigeler, Johann Friedrich; America, 1861 ***7420.1*** *p209*
Teigeler Brothers, . . .; America, 1880 ***7420.1*** *p318*
Teillard, L...s 26; Port uncertain, 1846 ***778.6*** *p322*
Teipel, Alma; Brazil, 1922 ***8023.44*** *p380*
Teipel, Julius; Brazil, 1922 ***8023.44*** *p380*
Teklenburg, Christian; America, 1852 ***7420.1*** *p99*
Telfar, Thomas; North Carolina, 1812 ***1088.45*** *p34*
Telfer, Mary 65; Ontario, 1871 ***1823.21*** *p363*
Telfer, Walter 42; Ontario, 1871 ***1823.21*** *p363*
Telisiting, Carolina 14; New Orleans, 1846 ***778.6*** *p322*
Tellak, Albert Johann August; Wisconsin, 1889 ***6795.8*** *p213*
Telley, William; America, 1742 ***1220.12*** *p789*
Tellier, Francine 23; New Orleans, 1848 ***778.6*** *p322*
Tellier, Jeanne; Quebec, 1670 ***4514.3*** *p372*
Tellier, John; America, 1686 ***1220.12*** *p789*
Tellier, Louis 25; America, 1843 ***778.6*** *p322*
Telsted, Mark; America, 1772 ***1220.12*** *p789*
Temberman, Gaspar; North Carolina, 1710 ***3629.40*** *p7*
Temer, Francoise 28; Missouri, 1846 ***778.6*** *p322*
Temer, Louis 29; Missouri, 1846 ***778.6*** *p322*
Temme, Fr. Wm. 33; New York, NY, 1864 ***8425.62*** *p197*
Tempest, Joshua; America, 1774 ***1220.12*** *p789*
Temple, George 41; Ontario, 1871 ***1823.21*** *p363*
Temple, John; America, 1726 ***1220.12*** *p789*
Temple, John; America, 1766 ***1220.12*** *p789*
Temple, Mary; Maryland, 1725 ***1220.12*** *p789*
Temple, Samuel 47; Ontario, 1871 ***1823.21*** *p363*
Temple, William; America, 1685 ***1220.12*** *p789*
Temple, William; Barbados or Jamaica, 1697 ***1220.12*** *p789*
Temple, William 37; Ontario, 1871 ***1823.21*** *p363*
Templeman, Edward; America, 1731 ***1220.12*** *p789*
Templeman, Henry; Maryland, 1723 ***1220.12*** *p789*
Templeman, William 28; North Carolina, 1774 ***1422.10*** *p55*
Templemore, J.; Toronto, 1844 ***2910.35*** *p114*
Templer, Fredrick 32; Ontario, 1871 ***1823.21*** *p363*
Templer, James; America, 1774 ***1220.12*** *p789*
Templeton, Andrew 25; Ontario, 1871 ***1823.21*** *p363*
Templeton, Frederick 64; Ontario, 1871 ***1823.21*** *p363*
Templeton, Mary 58; Ontario, 1871 ***1823.21*** *p364*
Ten, Louis; Detroit, 1929-1930 ***6214.5*** *p69*
Tenant, Thomas 53; Ontario, 1871 ***1823.21*** *p364*
Tenard, Marguerite; Quebec, 1666 ***4514.3*** *p372*
Ten Broeck, Captain; Ontario, 1787 ***1276.15*** *p231*
With child & 7 relatives
Tencza, John Joseph; Detroit, 1929 ***1640.55*** *p114*
Tennant, Elizabeth; America, 1774 ***1220.12*** *p789*
Tennant, George 56; Ontario, 1871 ***1823.17*** *p162*
Tennant, James 29; Ontario, 1871 ***1823.17*** *p162*
Tennant, John 33; Ontario, 1871 ***1823.17*** *p162*
Tennant, Judith; America, 1767 ***1220.12*** *p790*
Tennant, Susanna; America, 1752 ***1220.12*** *p790*
Tennant, William 57; Ontario, 1871 ***1823.21*** *p364*
Tennen, Charles Horton; Detroit, 1929-1930 ***6214.5*** *p69*
Tenner, Albert; America, 1867 ***7919.3*** *p534*
Tenner, Andreas; America, 1867 ***7919.3*** *p534*
Tenner, Carl; America, 1867 ***7919.3*** *p535*
Tenner, Willie; Detroit, 1929 ***1640.55*** *p113*
Tenneson, William 59; Ontario, 1871 ***1823.17*** *p162*
Tenniswood, John 37; Ontario, 1871 ***1823.21*** *p364*
Teno, Elizabeth; Virginia, 1735 ***1220.12*** *p790*
Tenpenny, Nathaniel; America, 1764 ***1220.12*** *p790*
Teori, Louis; New York, 1860 ***358.56*** *p150*
Teppell, Mary; America, 1768 ***1220.12*** *p790*
Tepper, Andrew 50; Ontario, 1871 ***1823.21*** *p364*
Tepper, Fred 32; Ontario, 1871 ***1823.21*** *p364*
Tepperwien, Heinrich Friedrich; America, 1871 ***7420.1*** *p293*
Terczak, Frank; Detroit, 1929-1930 ***6214.5*** *p63*
Tereure, Robert; Quebec, 1659 ***9221.17*** *p414*
Terillon, Genevieve; Quebec, 1672 ***4514.3*** *p372*
Terme, Jean; Quebec, 1662 ***9221.17*** *p493*
Ternan, Hugh; New York, 1783 ***8529.30*** *p16*
Ternla, Joseph 21; America, 1841 ***778.6*** *p322*
Ternon, Hugh; New York, 1783 ***8529.30*** *p16*
Terral, William; America, 1778 ***8529.30*** *p16*
Terratt, William; Barbados, 1663 ***1220.12*** *p790*
Terre, Anna *SEE* Terre, Nikolaus
Terre, Barbara *SEE* Terre, Nikolaus
Terre, Blaise; Quebec, 1660 ***9221.17*** *p469*
Terre, Josef; America, 1872 ***5475.1*** *p140*
Terre, Katharina *SEE* Terre, Nikolaus
Terre, Margarethe *SEE* Terre, Nikolaus
Terre, Maria *SEE* Terre, Nikolaus
Terre, Maria Fries *SEE* Terre, Nikolaus
Terre, Nikolaus; America, 1873 ***5475.1*** *p140*
*Wife:*Maria Fries
*Son:*Peter
*Daughter:*Maria
*Daughter:*Anna
*Daughter:*Barbara
*Daughter:*Margarethe
*Daughter:*Katharina
Terre, Peter *SEE* Terre, Nikolaus
Terrece, Frank; Washington, 1889 ***2770.40*** *p81*
Terrell, John; America, 1683 ***1220.12*** *p790*
Terreman, John 45; Ontario, 1871 ***1823.17*** *p162*
Terrett, Catherine; Maryland, 1726 ***1220.12*** *p790*
Terretta, Jaicomo; Louisiana, 1874-1875 ***4981.45*** *p130*
Terrey, Francis; America, 1664 ***1220.12*** *p790*
Terrey, John; Barbados or Jamaica, 1686 ***1220.12*** *p790*
Terrey, Richard; Barbados, 1669 ***1220.12*** *p790*
Terrey, Richard; Barbados, 1674 ***1220.12*** *p790*
Terrien, Andre 25; Quebec, 1656 ***9221.17*** *p347*
Terrien, Perrine 22; Quebec, 1662 ***9221.17*** *p493*
Terrien, Pierre 21; Quebec, 1656 ***9221.17*** *p347*
Terrier, Marin; Quebec, 1638 ***9221.17*** *p80*
Terrier deFrancheville, Marin; Quebec, 1638 ***9221.17*** *p80*
Terrier deRepentigny, Marin; Quebec, 1638 ***9221.17*** *p80*
Terrill, S.; Colorado, 1901 ***1029.59*** *p88*
Terrill, Samuel; Colorado, 1901 ***1029.59*** *p88*
Terrill, Susan; America, 1690 ***1220.12*** *p790*
Territt, William; America, 1767 ***1220.12*** *p790*
Terry, Ann; America, 1744 ***1220.12*** *p790*
Terry, Charles I. 40; Ontario, 1871 ***1823.17*** *p162*
Terry, Eliza G. 52; Ontario, 1871 ***1823.21*** *p364*
Terry, Elizabeth; America, 1727 ***1220.12*** *p790*
Terry, Elizabeth; America, 1750 ***1220.12*** *p790*
Terry, Elizabeth; America, 1754 ***1220.12*** *p790*
Terry, Elizabeth 17; Quebec, 1870 ***8364.32*** *p26*
Terry, George; America, 1769 ***1220.12*** *p790*
Terry, George; Barbados or Jamaica, 1712 ***1220.12*** *p790*
Terry, John; America, 1664 ***1220.12*** *p790*
Terry, Martha; Maryland, 1742 ***1220.12*** *p790*
Terry, Mary; America, 1775 ***1220.12*** *p790*
Terry, Richard; Maryland, 1674-1675 ***1236.25*** *p52*
Terry, Samuel; America, 1759 ***1220.12*** *p790*
Terry, Stephen; America, 1768 ***1220.12*** *p790*
Terry, Stephen; Massachusetts, 1630 ***117.5*** *p155*
Terry, Thomas; America, 1768 ***1220.12*** *p790*
Tersey, Francis; America, 1664 ***1220.12*** *p807*
Tertipes, Andrew Angelos; Iowa, 1917 ***1211.15*** *p20*
Tertrou, A. 25; America, 1847 ***778.6*** *p322*
Tertrou, A. 30; America, 1847 ***778.6*** *p322*
Terutch, Richard; Boston, 1767 ***1642*** *p38*
Tervo, Arnie 16; Minnesota, 1925 ***2769.54*** *p1378*
Tesalm, Clementine 19; America, 1847 ***778.6*** *p322*
Teschner, Agatha 11 months; New York, NY, 1893 ***1883.7*** *p40*
Teschner, Andreas 4; New York, NY, 1893 ***1883.7*** *p40*
Teschner, Anna 1; New York, NY, 1893 ***1883.7*** *p40*
Teschner, Catharina 7; New York, NY, 1893 ***1883.7*** *p40*
Teschner, Elisabeth 2; New York, NY, 1893 ***1883.7*** *p40*
Teschner, Elisabeth 29; New York, NY, 1893 ***1883.7*** *p40*
Teschner, Heinrich 35; New York, NY, 1893 ***1883.7*** *p40*
Teshew, John; Marblehead, MA, 1751-1838 ***9228.50*** *p626*
Teske, Caroline; Wisconsin, 1895 ***6795.8*** *p178*
Teske, Friedrich Ferdinand; Wisconsin, 1887 ***6795.8*** *p208*
Teske, Louis; Colorado, 1873 ***1029.59*** *p88*
Teske, Matilde; Wisconsin, 1893 ***6795.8*** *p135*
Teske, Theo. Karl; Wisconsin, 1895 ***6795.8*** *p142*
Teske, Theodor; Wisconsin, 1900 ***6795.8*** *p178*
Teskey, Edward 61; Ontario, 1871 ***1823.21*** *p364*
Tessa, Dominique; Illinois, 1852 ***6079.1*** *p14*
Tessier, Mr. 36; America, 1843 ***778.6*** *p322*
Tessier, Mathurin 18; Quebec, 1657 ***9221.17*** *p370*
Tessier, Pierre 24; Montreal, 1662 ***9221.17*** *p499*
Tessier, Urbain 23; Montreal, 1648 ***9221.17*** *p206*
Tessiman, George; America, 1719 ***1220.12*** *p790*
Tessimond, William; America, 1729 ***1220.12*** *p790*
Tessman, William; Illinois, 1834-1900 ***6020.5*** *p133*
Tessmer, Emma; Wisconsin, 1891 ***6795.8*** *p34*
Tessmer, Gusta Maria; Wisconsin, 1892 ***6795.8*** *p85*
Tesso, Bartolome 21; New Orleans, 1845 ***778.6*** *p322*
Tesson, Barthelemy 43; Quebec, 1662 ***9221.17*** *p493*
Tesson, Marguerite; Canada, 1669 ***1142.10*** *p129*
Tesson, Marguerite; Quebec, 1669 ***4514.3*** *p372*
Testard, Charles 20; Montreal, 1660 ***9221.17*** *p443*
Testard, Jean; Quebec, 1652 ***9221.17*** *p266*
Testard, Jeanne 19; Montreal, 1662 ***9221.17*** *p500*
Testard DeLaforest, Jacques 22; Quebec, 1652 ***9221.17*** *p267*
Testard deMontigny, Jacques; Quebec, 1698 ***2314.30*** *p172*
Teste, Marie 20; Quebec, 1659 ***9221.17*** *p410*
Teste-Pelee, . . .; Quebec, 1652 ***9221.17*** *p267*
Tetchey, . . .; North Carolina, 1710 ***3629.40*** *p3*
Tetchey, Daniel; North Carolina, 1710 ***3629.40*** *p7*
Tetherish, William 18; Ontario, 1871 ***1823.21*** *p364*
Tetherly, Richard; Virginia, 1740 ***1220.12*** *p790*
Tetley, William; America, 1775 ***1220.12*** *p790*
Tetloe, Nic. 35; Virginia, 1635 ***1183.3*** *p30*
Tetlow, John W.; North Carolina, 1840 ***1088.45*** *p34*
Tetrean, Alex 31; Ontario, 1871 ***1823.17*** *p162*
Tetreault, Louis 26; Quebec, 1660 ***9221.17*** *p469*
Tettenborn, Wilhelm; Wisconsin, 1883 ***6795.8*** *p93*
Tetu, Madeleine; Quebec, 1669 ***4514.3*** *p373*
Tetzlaff, Bertha Emilie; Wisconsin, 1898 ***6795.8*** *p122*
Tetzlaff, Ernst; Wisconsin, 1898 ***6795.8*** *p153*
Tetzlaff, Friedrich; Wisconsin, 1887 ***6795.8*** *p77*
Tetzlaff, Herman Martin; Wisconsin, 1885 ***6795.8*** *p122*
Tetzlaff, Hermann; Wisconsin, 1901 ***6795.8*** *p224*
Teuac, Prosper; Louisiana, 1836-1840 ***4981.45*** *p213*
Teulade, E. 36; America, 1844 ***778.6*** *p323*
Teuscher, G. B.; Valdivia, Chile, 1851 ***1192.4*** *p51*
Teuschler, Carl Ludwig; America, 1867 ***7919.3*** *p528*
Teusser, Ernst Friedrich Wilhelm; Port uncertain, 1880 ***7420.1*** *p318*
Tevhill, Anthony 55; Ontario, 1871 ***1823.21*** *p364*
Teviot, Ann 15; Ontario, 1871 ***1823.21*** *p364*
Teviot, Eliza 17; Ontario, 1871 ***1823.21*** *p364*
Tew, Michael; America, 1729 ***1220.12*** *p790*
Tew, William; America, 1775 ***1220.12*** *p790*
Teward, John; Barbados or Jamaica, 1684 ***1220.12*** *p790*
Tewey, Sarah 35; Ontario, 1871 ***1823.21*** *p364*
Tewksbury, John; Barbados, 1699 ***1220.12*** *p790*
Tewmey, William; Newburyport, MA, 1773 ***1642*** *p76*
Tews, Andreas Carl; Wisconsin, 1868 ***6795.8*** *p188*
Tews, Friedrich Christoph; Wisconsin, 1891 ***6795.8*** *p66*
Teyssier, Leon 19; Texas, 1848 ***778.6*** *p323*
Thable, Richard 19; Ontario, 1871 ***1823.21*** *p364*
Thacker, Esther; Maryland, 1732 ***1220.12*** *p790*
Thacker, George; America, 1764 ***1220.12*** *p790*

Thacker, George; America, 1773 ***1220.12*** *p790*
Thacker, Jane; America, 1747 ***1220.12*** *p790*
Thacker, William; America, 1770 ***1220.12*** *p790*
Thacker, William; North Carolina, 1835 ***1088.45*** *p34*
Thackeray, William; America, 1753 ***1220.12*** *p790*
Thackerill, Edward; America, 1759 ***1220.12*** *p790*
Thackham, William; America, 1743 ***1220.12*** *p790*
Thackston, Thomas; Barbados or Jamaica, 1696 ***1220.12*** *p791*
Thaddeus, Mr.; Massachusetts, 1744 ***1642*** *p87*
*Wife:*Mary Maccarty
Thaddeus, Mary Maccarty *SEE* Thaddeus, Mr.
Thadieck, C. F. J.; Ohio, 1840-1897 ***8365.35*** *p18*
Thaine, Robert; America, 1729 ***1220.12*** *p790*
Thaire, John; Barbados, 1669 ***1220.12*** *p790*
Thalacker, H.A.L.; Wisconsin, 1867 ***6795.8*** *p158*
Thalacker, Michael; America, 1700-1899 ***179.55*** *p19*
Thaler, Joseph 21; America, 1846 ***778.6*** *p323*
Thaller, Albert 27; America, 1844 ***778.6*** *p323*
Thaller, John; North Carolina, 1854 ***1088.45*** *p34*
Tham, Julius; Colorado, 1904 ***1029.59*** *p89*
Than, Antoine 18; America, 1847 ***778.6*** *p323*
Thane, James Wallis; America, 1774 ***1220.12*** *p790*
Thanhouser, Samuel; North Carolina, 1857 ***1088.45*** *p34*
Tharold, Theodore; Washington, 1889 ***2770.40*** *p81*
Tharp, James 26; Indiana, 1869-1872 ***9076.20*** *p67*
Tharp, William 45; Ontario, 1871 ***1823.21*** *p364*
Tharpe, Joseph; America, 1754 ***1220.12*** *p791*
Thatcher, Abraham; America, 1750 ***1220.12*** *p791*
Thatcher, Anne; America, 1722 ***1220.12*** *p791*
Thatcher, Elizabeth; America, 1758 ***1220.12*** *p791*
Thatcher, Henry; America, 1774 ***1220.12*** *p791*
Thatcher, John; America, 1774 ***1220.12*** *p791*
Thatcher, Mary; America, 1722 ***1220.12*** *p791*
Thatcher, Thomas; Annapolis, MD, 1722 ***1220.12*** *p791*
Thatchwell, John; Barbados, 1679 ***1220.12*** *p791*
Thauvernin, Ligisbertus; Ohio, 1809-1852 ***4511.35*** *p54*
Thavenet, Marguerite-Josephe de 16; Montreal, 1662 ***9221.17*** *p500*
Thaxter, Thomas; Boston, 1696 ***1642*** *p17*
Thaxton, Susannah; Virginia, 1732 ***1220.12*** *p791*
Thay, James; Kingston, Jamaica, 1774 ***8529.30*** *p13A*
Thayer, Simeon 34; Ontario, 1871 ***1823.17*** *p162*
Thayer, William; America, 1740 ***1220.12*** *p791*
Thayne, Robert; America, 1752 ***1220.12*** *p790*
Thays, Joseph; Wisconsin, 1863 ***1494.20*** *p13*
Theast, John; Virginia, 1763 ***1220.12*** *p791*
Thebant, Joseph Dennis; Ohio, 1809-1852 ***4511.35*** *p54*
Thebaut, Joseph Dennis; Ohio, 1809-1852 ***4511.35*** *p54*
Thedbout, James D.; Ohio, 1809-1852 ***4511.35*** *p54*
Thede, Charles; Wisconsin, 1891 ***6795.8*** *p108*
Thede, Ludwig Karl Theodor; Wisconsin, 1870 ***6795.8*** *p96*
Thedieck, F. H. A.; Ohio, 1840-1897 ***8365.35*** *p18*
Theed, Richard; America, 1746 ***1220.12*** *p791*
Theed, Thomas; Virginia, 1734 ***1220.12*** *p791*
Thees, Fanny; America, 1868 ***7919.3*** *p526*
Thees, Heinrich; America, 1868 ***7919.3*** *p526*
Thees, Luise; America, 1868 ***7919.3*** *p526*
Theig, Xavier 4; Port uncertain, 1847 ***778.6*** *p323*
Theil, Jacob; Philadelphia, 1777 ***8529.30*** *p5A*
Theila, Frank; Louisiana, 1874 ***4981.45*** *p134*
Thein, Abraham 44; Port uncertain, 1841 ***778.6*** *p323*
Theis, A. Maria *SEE* Theis, Adam Melchior
Theis, Adam Melchior; Chicago, 1894 ***5475.1*** *p156*
*Wife:*Anna Maria Freichel
*Son:*Peter
*Son:*Christian
*Son:*Johann
*Daughter:*A. Maria
*Daughter:*Franziska
Theis, Anna Maria Freichel *SEE* Theis, Adam Melchior
Theis, Charles; Ohio, 1809-1852 ***4511.35*** *p54*
Theis, Christian *SEE* Theis, Adam Melchior
Theis, Franziska *SEE* Theis, Adam Melchior
Theis, Jacob Adolf Heinrich; New York, 1902 ***1766.20*** *p16*
Theis, Johann *SEE* Theis, Adam Melchior
Theis, Katharina 32; America, 1872 ***5475.1*** *p446*
Theis, Peter *SEE* Theis, Adam Melchior
Theisen, Anna Germann *SEE* Theisen, Johann
Theisen, Johann *SEE* Theisen, Johann
Theisen, Johann 40; America, 1881 ***5475.1*** *p190*
*Wife:*Anna Germann
*Son:*Philipp
*Son:*Johann
Theisen, Martin; Colorado, 1885 ***1029.59*** *p89*
Theisen, Peter W.; Colorado, 1884 ***1029.59*** *p89*
Theisen, Philipp *SEE* Theisen, Johann
Theiss, P.J.; Galveston, TX, 1855 ***571.7*** *p17*
Thelander, C.J.; New York, NY, 1847 ***6412.40*** *p150*
Thelhillens, Pentz 37; America, 1847 ***778.6*** *p323*
Thelland, Alphonse; New Hampshire, 1869-1969 ***9228.50*** *p623*
Thelland, Edwidge; Massachusetts, 1873-1973 ***9228.50*** *p623*
Thelland, Francois; Quebec, 1823 ***9228.50*** *p622*
Thelland, Jean; Massachusetts, 1883 ***9228.50*** *p623*
Thelland, Joseph; Massachusetts, 1866-1922 ***9228.50*** *p623*
Thelland, Malvina; Massachusetts, 1854-1904 ***9228.50*** *p623*
Thelland, Napoleon-Paul; Massachusetts, 1882 ***9228.50*** *p623*
Thellen, Napoleon-Paul; Massachusetts, 1882 ***9228.50*** *p623*
Thely, Mr. 20; America, 1842 ***778.6*** *p323*
Them, Fredrieka; Philadelphia, 1854 ***8513.31*** *p320*
Thensted, Frederick; Louisiana, 1874 ***4981.45*** *p134*
Theobald, Anna; America, 1891 ***5475.1*** *p148*
Theobald, Anton; America, 1882 ***5475.1*** *p210*
Theobald, Hannah; America, 1731 ***1220.12*** *p791*
Theobald, Jakob; Brazil, 1879 ***5475.1*** *p431*
Theobald, Jakob; Brazil, 1887 ***5475.1*** *p432*
Theobald, Kath.; America, 1873 ***5475.1*** *p341*
Theobald, Katharina; Brazil, 1891 ***5475.1*** *p432*
Theobald, Maria; America, 1866 ***5475.1*** *p382*
*Son:*Heinrich Karl
*Daughter:*M. Karoline
Theobald, Maria; America, 1883 ***5475.1*** *p204*
*Son:*Andreas
*Son:*Joh. Peter
*Daughter:*A. Maria
*Daughter:*Anna
Theobald, Mathias; America, 1881 ***5475.1*** *p210*
Theobald, Nikolaus; Brazil, 1878 ***5475.1*** *p431*
Theobald, Nikolaus; Brazil, 1879 ***5475.1*** *p431*
Theobald, Peter; Texas, 1884 ***5475.1*** *p161*
Theobald, Robert; America, 1765 ***1220.12*** *p791*
Theobold, Johann 26; Mississippi, 1847 ***778.6*** *p323*
Theodore, Michel 19; Montreal, 1653 ***9221.17*** *p301*
Theogh, M.; New Orleans, 1850 ***7242.30*** *p155*
Theogh, P.; New Orleans, 1850 ***7242.30*** *p155*
Theray, Jean 36; America, 1843 ***778.6*** *p323*
Therean, Wm.; Louisiana, 1874 ***4981.45*** *p297*
Theriault, Andre; Montreal, 1659 ***9221.17*** *p428*
Therme, Joseph Blaise 27; Texas, 1848 ***778.6*** *p323*
Therme, Leon; Illinois, 1859 ***6079.1*** *p14*
Thermes, Constant; Illinois, 1852 ***6079.1*** *p14*
Thermes, Joseph; Illinois, 1852 ***6079.1*** *p14*
Thern, Gerhard 26; Mississippi, 1847 ***778.6*** *p323*
Theron, Isaac; America, 1746 ***1220.12*** *p791*
Therre, Katharina; Brazil, 1857 ***5475.1*** *p541*
Theru, Gerhard 26; Mississippi, 1847 ***778.6*** *p323*
Thetford, Edward; Annapolis, MD, 1725 ***1220.12*** *p791*
Thetul, John; New York, 1859 ***358.56*** *p101*
Theurer, Martin; Ohio, 1840-1897 ***8365.35*** *p18*
Thevithick, Richard; Colorado, 1887 ***1029.59*** *p89*
Thewes, Johann 2 *SEE* Thewes, Nikolaus
Thewes, Nikolaus 40; Brazil, 1857 ***5475.1*** *p383*
*Son:*Johann 2
With family
Thexton, Ann 28; Ontario, 1871 ***1823.17*** *p162*
Thexton, Robert 30; Ontario, 1871 ***1823.17*** *p162*
Thexton, Thomas 63; Ontario, 1871 ***1823.17*** *p162*
Theys, Martin; Wisconsin, 1855-1867 ***1495.20*** *p67*
Theze, Auguste 17; New Orleans, 1848 ***778.6*** *p323*
Thibault, C. 31; Port uncertain, 1843 ***778.6*** *p323*
Thibault, Etienne; Montreal, 1652 ***9221.17*** *p268*
Thibault, Guillaume 21; Quebec, 1638 ***9221.17*** *p80*
Thibault, Mathurine; Quebec, 1663 ***4514.3*** *p373*
Thibault, Pierre; Quebec, 1642 ***9221.17*** *p122*
Thibault, Therese 23; New Orleans, 1848 ***778.6*** *p323*
Thibaut, Hieronymus Renatus; Venezuela, 1843 ***3899.5*** *p542*
Thibaut, Maria Magdalena; Venezuela, 1843 ***3899.5*** *p542*
Thibeaudo, Harriet 60; Ontario, 1871 ***1823.21*** *p364*
Thibierge, Gabriel 6 *SEE* Thibierge, Hippolyte
Thibierge, Gencien 4 *SEE* Thibierge, Hippolyte
Thibierge, Hippolyte 31; Quebec, 1660 ***9221.17*** *p469*
*Wife:*Renee Herve 25
*Son:*Gabriel 6
*Son:*Gencien 4
Thibierge, Marie-Madeleine; Quebec, 1670 ***4514.3*** *p373*
Thibierge, Renee Herve 25 *SEE* Thibierge, Hippolyte
Thibodeau, Catherine Aurard 31 *SEE* Thibodeau, Mathurin
Thibodeau, Marguerite 9 *SEE* Thibodeau, Mathurin
Thibodeau, Mathurin 33; Montreal, 1659 ***9221.17*** *p428*
*Wife:*Catherine Aurard 31
*Daughter:*Marguerite 9 months
Thick, Morgan 40; Ontario, 1871 ***1823.21*** *p364*
Thickhead, William; Maryland, 1724 ***1220.12*** *p791*
Thiebaut, Appolline 10; America, 1843 ***778.6*** *p323*
Thiebaut, Auguste 3 months; America, 1843 ***778.6*** *p323*
Thiebaut, Catharina 15; America, 1843 ***778.6*** *p323*
Thiebaut, Emil 3; America, 1843 ***778.6*** *p323*
Thiebaut, Eugene 10; America, 1843 ***778.6*** *p323*
Thiebaut, Francois 46; America, 1843 ***778.6*** *p323*
Thiebaut, Genevieve 6; America, 1843 ***778.6*** *p323*
Thiebaut, Hieronymus Renatus; Venezuela, 1843 ***3899.5*** *p542*
Thiebaut, Marie 42; America, 1843 ***778.6*** *p323*
Thiebaut, Pierre 18; America, 1843 ***778.6*** *p323*
Thiebot, Marie 70; America, 1745 ***778.6*** *p323*
Thiebou, Guillaume; Quebec, 1659 ***9221.17*** *p414*
Thiede, Frank; Wisconsin, 1913 ***6795.8*** *p170*
Thiel, Anna; America, 1879 ***5475.1*** *p187*
Thiel, August; Wisconsin, 1856 ***6795.8*** *p97*
Thiel, Jakob 28; America, 1867 ***5475.1*** *p545*
Thiel, Johann 54; America, 1833 ***5475.1*** *p64*
With 5 children
Thiel, Joseph 26; America, 1848 ***778.6*** *p323*
Thiel, Katharina Peter *SEE* Thiel, Nikolaus
Thiel, Katharina; America, 1881 ***5475.1*** *p315*
Thiel, Margarethe Giering *SEE* Thiel, Michel
Thiel, Maria; America, 1856 ***5475.1*** *p440*
With 3 children
Thiel, Michel; America, 1834 ***5475.1*** *p437*
*Wife:*Margarethe Giering
With 2 children
Thiel, Nikolaus; America, 1853 ***5475.1*** *p439*
*Wife:*Katharina Peter
With 3 children
Thiel, Phillipe A. J.; North Carolina, 1851 ***1088.45*** *p34*
Thiel, Robert; America, 1887 ***5475.1*** *p42*
Thiel, Wilhelmine; America, 1882 ***5475.1*** *p34*
*Daughter:*Wilhelmine
*Daughter:*Emilie
*Son:*Hugo
Thiel, Wilhelmine A.; Wisconsin, 1892 ***6795.8*** *p108*
Thiel, William; Wisconsin, 1866 ***6795.8*** *p68*
Thielborger, Friedrich Gerhard; England, 1874 ***7420.1*** *p304*
Thiele, August; New York, NY, 1845 ***7420.1*** *p41*
*Wife:*Dorothee Kraas
Thiele, Dorothee Kraas *SEE* Thiele, August
Thiele, Gotlob; Ohio, 1809-1852 ***4511.35*** *p54*
Thiele, Gottlob; Ohio, 1809-1852 ***4511.35*** *p54*
Thiele, Gustav Heinrich Wilhelm; New York, NY, 1899 ***7420.1*** *p375*
Thiele, Heinrich; America, 1848 ***7420.1*** *p62*
With wife & 2 children
Thiele, Hermann; Denver, CO, 1894 ***7420.1*** *p373*
Thielen, Magdalena 57; America, 1856 ***5475.1*** *p270*
Thielen, Nikolaus; America, 1867 ***5475.1*** *p310*
Thielen, Mrs. Nikolaus 37; New York, 1880 ***5475.1*** *p299*
Thielen, P.; Brazil, 1857 ***5475.1*** *p441*
Thierey, Francis A.; Ohio, 1809-1852 ***4511.35*** *p54*
Thierolf, Adam; America, 1845 ***2526.43*** *p129*
With wife
*Son:*Johann Dieter
Thierolf, Adam; America, 1883 ***2526.42*** *p132*
Thierolf, Balthasar; America, 1869 ***2526.42*** *p99*
Thierolf, Christina; America, 1884 ***2526.42*** *p131*
Thierolf, Elisabeth; America, 1883 ***2526.43*** *p188*
Thierolf, Georg; America, 1831 ***2526.42*** *p197*
Thierolf, Johann Dieter 3 *SEE* Thierolf, Adam
Thierolf, Johann Leonhard; America, 1807 ***2526.42*** *p132*
Thierolf, Johannes 26; America, 1846 ***2526.42*** *p116*
Thierolf, Michael; America, 1836 ***2526.42*** *p197*
With wife
Thierolf, Philipp; America, 1883 ***2526.42*** *p132*
Thierry, Catherine 1; Montreal, 1641 ***9221.17*** *p108*
Thierry, Francis A.; Ohio, 1809-1852 ***4511.35*** *p54*
Thierry, Jean; Quebec, 1656 ***9221.17*** *p347*
Thierry, Raphael; Quebec, 1657 ***9221.17*** *p370*
Thiersant deJantis, Francois-Gabriel; Quebec, 1715 ***2314.30*** *p171*
Thiery, Alphonse; Louisiana, 1874 ***4981.45*** *p134*
Thiery, Anne 39; America, 1846 ***778.6*** *p323*
Thiery, Anton; Philadelphia, 1860 ***8513.31*** *p429*
*Wife:*Dorothea Dannenhauer
Thiery, August.n 13; America, 1846 ***778.6*** *p323*
Thiery, Charles 9; New Orleans, 1847 ***778.6*** *p323*
Thiery, Charles 37; New Orleans, 1847 ***778.6*** *p323*
Thiery, Dorothea Dannenhauer *SEE* Thiery, Anton
Thiery, Emilie 3; New Orleans, 1847 ***778.6*** *p323*
Thiery, J. B. 44; America, 1846 ***778.6*** *p324*
Thiery, Joseph 8; America, 1846 ***778.6*** *p324*
Thiery, Joseph 4; New Orleans, 1847 ***778.6*** *p324*
Thiery, Julie 36; New Orleans, 1847 ***778.6*** *p324*
Thiery, Sidonie 6; New Orleans, 1847 ***778.6*** *p324*
Thiery, Victoria 4; America, 1846 ***778.6*** *p324*
Thies, . . .; America, 1846 ***7420.1*** *p50*
With family
Thies, Adolph; America, 1854 ***7420.1*** *p132*

Thies, Adolph Siegfried; America, 1866 ***7420.1*** *p251*
*Brother:*Robert Adolph Ludolf
Thies, Charles; Ohio, 1809-1852 ***4511.35*** *p54*
Thies, Engel Dorothea Justine Eleonore Laging *SEE* Thies, Johann Heinrich Christolph
Thies, Eugen Oskar; Pennsylvania, 1873 ***7420.1*** *p301*
Thies, Friedrich Ernst Ferdinand; America, 1864 ***7420.1*** *p227*
Thies, Friedrich Wilhelm Ernst Ferdinand; America, 1856 ***7420.1*** *p155*
Thies, Hanne Friederike Charlotte Schermer *SEE* Thies, Johann Conrad
Thies, Johann Conrad; America, 1850 ***7420.1*** *p77*
*Wife:*Hanne Friederike Charlotte Schermer
With family
Thies, Johann Heinrich Christolph; America, 1850 ***7420.1*** *p77*
*Daughter:*Engel Dorothea Justine Eleonore Laging
Thies, Magdalena 45; Pittsburgh, 1872 ***5475.1*** *p354*
Thies, Mathias 32; America, 1843 ***5475.1*** *p363*
Thies, Robert Adolph Ludolf *SEE* Thies, Adolph Siegfried
Thies, Sophie Charlotte; America, 1850 ***7420.1*** *p74*
Thiesen, Joseph; Illinois, 1863 ***6079.1*** *p14*
Thieser, Barbara *SEE* Thieser, Michel
Thieser, Johann *SEE* Thieser, Michel
Thieser, Michel; America, 1880 ***5475.1*** *p336*
*Wife:*Veronika Faha
*Daughter:*Barbara
*Son:*Nikolaus
*Son:*Johann
Thieser, Nikolaus *SEE* Thieser, Michel
Thieser, Veronika Faha *SEE* Thieser, Michel
Thieson, Mrs. 37; America, 1844 ***778.6*** *p324*
Thiesselon, Pierre 25; America, 1843 ***778.6*** *p324*
Thieulin, Pierre; Illinois, 1852 ***6079.1*** *p14*
Thifries, Frederick; New York, NY, 1778 ***8529.30*** *p3*
Thilman, C. 24; America, 1847 ***778.6*** *p324*
Thilman, Pierre 19; America, 1847 ***778.6*** *p324*
Thim, Gust Olson; Iowa, 1923 ***1211.15*** *p20*
Thimbleby, Samuel; America, 1728 ***1220.12*** *p791*
Thimmer, Mathias 27; America, 1856 ***5475.1*** *p260*
Thiniert, Catharine 8; New Orleans, 1847 ***778.6*** *p324*
Thiniert, Catharine 36; New Orleans, 1847 ***778.6*** *p324*
Thiniert, Jean 6 months; New Orleans, 1847 ***778.6*** *p324*
Thiniert, Jean 32; New Orleans, 1847 ***778.6*** *p324*
Thiniert, Marie 4; New Orleans, 1847 ***778.6*** *p324*
Thinnes, Heinr.; Brazil, 1876 ***5475.1*** *p483*
Thinnes, Hubert; America, 1891 ***5475.1*** *p277*
Thinwood, John; America, 1729 ***1220.12*** *p791*
Thio, Catherina 22; New Orleans, 1848 ***778.6*** *p324*
Thirby, Mary; Maryland, 1719 ***1220.12*** *p791*
Thirchild, Edward; America, 1759 ***1220.12*** *p791*
Thirement, Anne; Quebec, 1670 ***4514.3*** *p373*
Thirion, Rosalie; Wisconsin, 1855 ***1495.20*** *p56*
Thiriot, Jakob Heinrich 28; America, 1833 ***5475.1*** *p27*
Thirske, Elizabeth; America, 1750 ***1220.12*** *p791*
Thirtehell, James 16; Quebec, 1870 ***8364.32*** *p26*
Thirtle, Bartholomew; America, 1757 ***1220.12*** *p791*
Thiry, Marie Catherine; Illinois, 1856 ***1495.20*** *p28*
This, August 4; New Orleans, 1847 ***778.6*** *p324*
This, Charles 11; New Orleans, 1847 ***778.6*** *p324*
This, Claud. 6; New Orleans, 1847 ***778.6*** *p324*
This, Dominique 1; New Orleans, 1847 ***778.6*** *p324*
This, Dominique 6; New Orleans, 1847 ***778.6*** *p324*
This, Dominique 49; New Orleans, 1847 ***778.6*** *p324*
This, Eugen 9; New Orleans, 1847 ***778.6*** *p324*
This, Felice 10; New Orleans, 1847 ***778.6*** *p324*
This, Felix 2; New Orleans, 1847 ***778.6*** *p324*
This, Francois 8; New Orleans, 1847 ***778.6*** *p324*
This, Francois 41; New Orleans, 1847 ***778.6*** *p324*
This, Jean 8; New Orleans, 1847 ***778.6*** *p324*
This, Jeanne 46; New Orleans, 1847 ***778.6*** *p324*
This, Marie 14; New Orleans, 1847 ***778.6*** *p324*
This, Marie 40; New Orleans, 1847 ***778.6*** *p324*
This, Victorie 4; New Orleans, 1847 ***778.6*** *p324*
Thison, Henry Landi; Washington, 1884 ***2770.40*** *p193*
Thistle, Eleanor Catherine; Oregon, 1941 ***9157.47*** *p2*
Thistle, Richard; America, 1715 ***1220.12*** *p791*
Thode, Henry; Washington, 1889 ***2770.40*** *p81*
Thody, Elijah 55; Ontario, 1871 ***1823.21*** *p364*
Thoews, Carl; Wisconsin, 1878 ***6795.8*** *p208*
Thoke, Heinrich; Port uncertain, 1835 ***7420.1*** *p10*
Thoke, Wilhelm; America, 1852 ***7420.1*** *p99*
Tholen, Theodore; Kansas, 1917-1918 ***1826.15*** *p81*
Tholey, Franz *SEE* Tholey, Franz
Tholey, Franz; America, 1853 ***5475.1*** *p481*
*Son:*Franz
*Son:*Josef
Tholey, Franz; America, 1867 ***5475.1*** *p417*
Tholey, Franz; America, 1880 ***5475.1*** *p484*
Tholey, Jakob; America, 1846 ***5475.1*** *p472*
Tholey, Josef *SEE* Tholey, Franz
Tholey, Philipp; America, 1847 ***5475.1*** *p475*
Thom, Carl August; Wisconsin, 1878 ***6795.8*** *p68*
Thom, James 50; Ontario, 1871 ***1823.21*** *p364*
Thom, James 50; Ontario, 1871 ***1823.21*** *p364*
Thom, Leslie; Quebec, 1870 ***8364.32*** *p26*
Thoma, Jean 19; America, 1847 ***778.6*** *p325*
Thomann, Famille; New Castle, DE, 1817-1818 ***90.20*** *p154*
Thomann, Ignace 19; America, 1846 ***778.6*** *p325*
Thomann, Joseph 18; America, 1846 ***778.6*** *p325*
Thomann, Joseph; Illinois, 1858-1861 ***6020.5*** *p133*
Thomas, . . .; Massachusetts, 1870-1880 ***9228.50*** *p623*
Thomas, Mr. 21; America, 1844 ***778.6*** *p325*
Thomas, Abraham; America, 1685 ***1220.12*** *p791*
Thomas, Abraham *SEE* Thomas, David
Thomas, Agnes 50; New York, NY, 1885 ***1883.7*** *p47*
Thomas, Alice; Annapolis, MD, 1719 ***1220.12*** *p791*
Thomas, Amos 57; Ontario, 1871 ***1823.21*** *p364*
Thomas, Amous 85; Ontario, 1871 ***1823.21*** *p364*
Thomas, Angela 47; Brazil, 1857 ***5475.1*** *p368*
Thomas, Ann; America, 1746 ***1220.12*** *p791*
Thomas, Ann; America, 1748 ***1220.12*** *p791*
Thomas, Ann; America, 1758 ***1220.12*** *p791*
Thomas, Ann; America, 1771 ***1220.12*** *p791*
Thomas, Ann; Barbados or Jamaica, 1689 ***1220.12*** *p791*
Thomas, Ann; Charles Town, SC, 1719 ***1220.12*** *p791*
Thomas, Ann *SEE* Thomas, Thomas
Thomas, Ann; Ohio, 1847 ***4022.20*** *p282*
Thomas, Ann; Virginia, 1739 ***1220.12*** *p791*
Thomas, Anna *SEE* Thomas, Nikolaus
Thomas, Anna Lara *SEE* Thomas, John
Thomas, Anne; Barbados, 1679 ***1220.12*** *p791*
Thomas, Anne; Quebec, 1665 ***4514.3*** *p373*
Thomas, Archibald; Boston, 1737 ***1642*** *p26*
Thomas, B. F.; Ohio, 1847 ***4022.20*** *p292*
With parents
Thomas, Barbara 54; America, 1847 ***778.6*** *p325*
Thomas, Blanch; Barbados, 1681 ***1220.12*** *p791*
Thomas, Catharina 36; America, 1847 ***778.6*** *p325*
Thomas, Catherine; America, 1763 ***1220.12*** *p791*
Thomas, Catherine *SEE* Thomas, William
Thomas, Charles; America, 1736 ***1220.12*** *p791*
Thomas, Charles; America, 1773 ***1220.12*** *p791*
Thomas, Charles; America, 1774 ***1220.12*** *p791*
Thomas, Charles; Ohio, 1809-1852 ***4511.35*** *p54*
Thomas, David; America, 1685 ***1220.12*** *p791*
Thomas, David; America, 1728 ***1220.12*** *p791*
Thomas, David; America, 1769 ***1220.12*** *p792*
Thomas, David; America, 1775 ***1220.12*** *p792*
Thomas, David; Barbados, 1667 ***1220.12*** *p791*
Thomas, David; Ohio, 1829 ***4022.20*** *p291*
Thomas, David; Ohio, 1837-1838 ***4022.20*** *p291*
*Wife:*Jessedinah
*Child:*Abraham
With child
*Child:*Elizabeth
Thomas, David 40; Ontario, 1871 ***1823.21*** *p364*
Thomas, David 50; Ontario, 1871 ***1823.17*** *p162*
Thomas, Diana; America, 1727 ***1220.12*** *p792*
Thomas, Dorothy; Barbados, 1679 ***1220.12*** *p792*
Thomas, Dorothy; Barbados, 1680 ***1220.12*** *p792*
Thomas, E. J. 50; Ontario, 1871 ***1823.21*** *p364*
Thomas, Edmond; America, 1768 ***1220.12*** *p792*
Thomas, Edmund; Baton Rouge, LA, 1781 ***8529.30*** *p10A*
Thomas, Edward; America, 1742 ***1220.12*** *p792*
Thomas, Edward; America, 1769 ***1220.12*** *p792*
Thomas, Edward; America, 1770 ***1220.12*** *p792*
Thomas, Edward; America, 1772 ***1220.12*** *p792*
Thomas, Edward; Annapolis, MD, 1722 ***1220.12*** *p792*
Thomas, Edward; Barbados, 1669 ***1220.12*** *p792*
Thomas, Edward; Maryland, 1725 ***1220.12*** *p792*
Thomas, Edward; Ohio, 1839 ***4022.20*** *p291*
Thomas, Edward 23; Ontario, 1871 ***1823.17*** *p162*
Thomas, Edward 32; Ontario, 1871 ***1823.21*** *p364*
Thomas, Edward 35; Ontario, 1871 ***1823.21*** *p364*
Thomas, Edward; West Indies, 1686 ***1220.12*** *p792*
Thomas, Elias; America, 1775 ***1220.12*** *p792*
Thomas, Elijah 36; Ontario, 1871 ***1823.17*** *p162*
Thomas, Elisabeth 1; America, 1847 ***778.6*** *p325*
Thomas, Elisabeth Barth 58 *SEE* Thomas, Nikolaus
Thomas, Elizabeth; America, 1767 ***1220.12*** *p792*
Thomas, Elizabeth; America, 1772 ***1220.12*** *p792*
Thomas, Elizabeth; Annapolis, MD, 1725 ***1220.12*** *p792*
Thomas, Elizabeth 9; Halifax, N.S., 1903 ***1860.4*** *p44*
Thomas, Elizabeth *SEE* Thomas, David
Thomas, Ellen; America, 1771 ***1220.12*** *p792*
Thomas, Ellen *SEE* Thomas, Evan D.
Thomas, Enoch; Ohio, 1841 ***4022.20*** *p291*
*Wife:*Margaret
Thomas, Enoch; Ohio, 1842 ***4022.20*** *p291*
*Wife:*Margaret
Thomas, Eugene 20; America, 1841 ***778.6*** *p325*
Thomas, Evan D.; Ohio, 1844 ***4022.20*** *p291*
*Mother:*Ellen
Thomas, Felix 62; Ontario, 1871 ***1823.17*** *p162*
Thomas, Frances 79; Ontario, 1871 ***1823.17*** *p162*
Thomas, Francis 29; Ontario, 1871 ***1823.17*** *p162*
Thomas, Francois 5; America, 1847 ***778.6*** *p325*
Thomas, Francois 29; America, 1846 ***778.6*** *p325*
Thomas, Francois 32; Port uncertain, 1847 ***778.6*** *p325*
Thomas, Frank; Detroit, 1930 ***1640.60*** *p78*
Thomas, G. 36; New Orleans, 1844 ***778.6*** *p325*
Thomas, G. 37; New Orleans, 1845 ***778.6*** *p325*
Thomas, Gabriel 50; New York, NY, 1885 ***1883.7*** *p47*
Thomas, George; America, 1773 ***1220.12*** *p792*
Thomas, George; Maryland or Virginia, 1731 ***1220.12*** *p792*
Thomas, George 49; Ontario, 1871 ***1823.21*** *p364*
Thomas, Grace; Virginia, 1742 ***1220.12*** *p792*
Thomas, Griffith; America, 1749 ***1220.12*** *p792*
Thomas, Griffith; America, 1769 ***1220.12*** *p792*
Thomas, Griffith; Barbados, 1699 ***1220.12*** *p792*
Thomas, Hannah; America, 1751 ***1220.12*** *p792*
Thomas, Heden 45; Ontario, 1871 ***1823.21*** *p364*
Thomas, Henry; America, 1693 ***1220.12*** *p792*
Thomas, Henry; America, 1746 ***1220.12*** *p792*
Thomas, Henry; America, 1760 ***1220.12*** *p792*
Thomas, Henry; Barbados, 1664 ***1220.12*** *p792*
Thomas, Henry 31; Ontario, 1871 ***1823.21*** *p364*
Thomas, Hester; America, 1755 ***1220.12*** *p792*
Thomas, Hopkins; Philadelphia, 1835 ***5720.10*** *p378*
Thomas, Hugh; Annapolis, MD, 1730 ***1220.12*** *p792*
Thomas, Huldah A. 25; Michigan, 1880 ***4491.39*** *p30*
Thomas, Isaac; America, 1736 ***1220.12*** *p792*
Thomas, J. 30; New Orleans, 1845 ***778.6*** *p325*
Thomas, J. A.; Valdivia, Chile, 1852 ***1192.4*** *p54*
Thomas, Jacob; America, 1766 ***1220.12*** *p792*
Thomas, Jacob 50; Halifax, N.S., 1902 ***1860.4*** *p43*
Thomas, Jacques; Quebec, 1659 ***9221.17*** *p414*
Thomas, James; America, 1771 ***1220.12*** *p792*
Thomas, James; America, 1773 ***1220.12*** *p792*
Thomas, James; Maryland, 1720 ***1220.12*** *p792*
Thomas, James; Ontario, 1871 ***1823.21*** *p364*
Thomas, James 36; Ontario, 1871 ***1823.21*** *p364*
Thomas, James 45; Ontario, 1871 ***1823.21*** *p364*
Thomas, James 58; Ontario, 1871 ***1823.21*** *p364*
Thomas, James 64; Ontario, 1871 ***1823.17*** *p162*
Thomas, James 67; Ontario, 1871 ***1823.21*** *p364*
Thomas, Jane; America, 1728 ***1220.12*** *p792*
Thomas, Jane; America, 1743 ***1220.12*** *p792*
Thomas, Jane; America, 1763 ***1220.12*** *p792*
Thomas, Jane 60; Ontario, 1871 ***1823.21*** *p365*
Thomas, Jean 52; America, 1847 ***778.6*** *p325*
Thomas, Jean Pierre 37; America, 1847 ***778.6*** *p325*
Thomas, Jeanne 26; Quebec, 1648 ***9221.17*** *p194*
Thomas, Jemima; Ohio, 1840 ***4022.20*** *p291*
Thomas, Jemima 54; Ontario, 1871 ***1823.21*** *p365*
Thomas, Jessedinah *SEE* Thomas, David
Thomas, Joan 25; Annapolis, MD, 1724 ***1220.12*** *p793*
Thomas, John; America, 1662 ***1220.12*** *p793*
Thomas, John; America, 1687 ***1220.12*** *p793*
Thomas, John; America, 1698 ***1220.12*** *p793*
Thomas, John; America, 1722 ***1220.12*** *p793*
Thomas, John; America, 1731 ***1220.12*** *p793*
Thomas, John; America, 1734 ***1220.12*** *p793*
Thomas, John; America, 1735 ***1220.12*** *p793*
Thomas, John; America, 1737 ***1220.12*** *p793*
Thomas, John; America, 1739 ***1220.12*** *p793*
Thomas, John; America, 1741 ***1220.12*** *p793*
Thomas, John; America, 1743 ***1220.12*** *p793*
Thomas, John; America, 1750 ***1220.12*** *p793*
Thomas, John; America, 1753 ***1220.12*** *p793*
Thomas, John; America, 1760 ***1220.12*** *p793*
Thomas, John; America, 1763 ***1220.12*** *p793*
Thomas, John; America, 1764 ***1220.12*** *p793*
Thomas, John; America, 1765 ***1220.12*** *p793*
Thomas, John; America, 1766 ***1220.12*** *p793*
Thomas, John; America, 1768 ***1220.12*** *p793*
Thomas, John; America, 1769 ***1220.12*** *p793*
Thomas, John; America, 1773 ***1220.12*** *p793*
Thomas, John; America, 1775 ***1220.12*** *p793*
Thomas, John; Barbados, 1699 ***1220.12*** *p793*
Thomas, John; Canada, n.d. ***9228.50*** *p526*
*Wife:*Anna Lara
Thomas, John; Carolina, 1719 ***1220.12*** *p793*
Thomas, John; Jamaica, 1661 ***1220.12*** *p793*
Thomas, John; Maryland, 1723 ***1220.12*** *p793*
Thomas, John; Maryland or Virginia, 1738 ***1220.12*** *p793*
Thomas, John; New York, 1783 ***8529.30*** *p16*
Thomas, John; Ohio, 1809-1852 ***4511.35*** *p54*
Thomas, John; Ohio, 1830-1831 ***4022.20*** *p291*
Thomas, John; Ohio, 1837 ***4022.20*** *p291*
*Wife:*Margaret Evans
Thomas, John *SEE* Thomas, Thomas
Thomas, John 30; Ontario, 1871 ***1823.21*** *p365*

Thomas, John 40; Ontario, 1871 ***1823.21*** *p365*
Thomas, John 56; Ontario, 1871 ***1823.17*** *p162*
Thomas, John 61; Ontario, 1871 ***1823.17*** *p162*
Thomas, John; Portsmouth, NH, 1718 ***9228.50*** *p623*
Thomas, John; Virginia, 1718 ***1220.12*** *p793*
Thomas, John G. 52; Michigan, 1880 ***4491.30*** *p30*
Thomas, John N.; Colorado, 1873 ***1029.59*** *p89*
Thomas, John N.; Colorado, 1894 ***1029.59*** *p89*
Thomas, Josef; America, 1881 ***5475.1*** *p202*
Thomas, Joseph; America, 1765 ***1220.12*** *p793*
Thomas, Judith; Jamaica, 1661 ***1220.12*** *p793*
Thomas, Katharina *SEE* Thomas, Nikolaus
Thomas, Lewis 30; Ontario, 1871 ***1823.17*** *p162*
Thomas, Louis 35; Ontario, 1871 ***1823.21*** *p365*
Thomas, Margaret; America, 1731 ***1220.12*** *p793*
Thomas, Margaret; America, 1770 ***1220.12*** *p793*
Thomas, Margaret; Barbados, 1671 ***1220.12*** *p793*
Thomas, Margaret Evans *SEE* Thomas, John
Thomas, Margaret; Ohio, 1837 ***4022.20*** *p291*
Thomas, Margaret *SEE* Thomas, Thomas
Thomas, Margaret *SEE* Thomas, Enoch
Thomas, Margaret *SEE* Thomas, Enoch
Thomas, Margaret; Ohio, 1857 ***4022.20*** *p291*
*Husband:*Robert
Thomas, Margaret; Ohio, 1857 ***4022.20*** *p*
Thomas, Margaret 46; Ontario, 1871 ***1823.17*** *p162*
Thomas, Margaret 56; Ontario, 1871 ***1823.17*** *p162*
Thomas, Margâret Mary; Salem, MA, 1895-1900 ***9228.50*** *p357*
Thomas, Marguerite 22; Quebec, 1655 ***9221.17*** *p329*
Thomas, Maria 7; America, 1847 ***778.6*** *p325*
Thomas, Maria 60; Ontario, 1871 ***1823.21*** *p365*
Thomas, Marianna 3; America, 1847 ***778.6*** *p325*
Thomas, Mary; America, 1745 ***1220.12*** *p793*
Thomas, Mary; America, 1751 ***1220.12*** *p793*
Thomas, Mary; America, 1754 ***1220.12*** *p793*
Thomas, Mary; America, 1762 ***1220.12*** *p793*
Thomas, Mary; Dedham, MA, 1742 ***1642*** *p102*
Thomas, Mary; Maryland or Virginia, 1733 ***1220.12*** *p793*
Thomas, Mary *SEE* Thomas, William E.
Thomas, Mary; West Indies, 1686 ***1220.12*** *p793*
Thomas, Mary S. *SEE* Thomas, Thomas
Thomas, Matthew; America, 1736 ***1220.12*** *p794*
Thomas, Matthew; Barbados, 1665 ***1220.12*** *p794*
Thomas, Matthew; Barbados or Jamaica, 1692 ***1220.12*** *p794*
Thomas, Michael; America, 1767 ***1220.12*** *p794*
Thomas, Nikolaus; Indiana, 1885 ***5475.1*** *p555*
*Wife:*Elisabeth Barth
*Daughter:*Katharina
*Son:*Peter
*Daughter:*Anna
Thomas, Peter *SEE* Thomas, Nikolaus
Thomas, Philip; Virginia, 1734 ***1220.12*** *p794*
Thomas, Phillip 42; Ontario, 1871 ***1823.21*** *p365*
Thomas, Rebecca; America, 1727 ***1220.12*** *p794*
Thomas, Rees; Colorado, 1883 ***1029.59*** *p89*
Thomas, Rees *SEE* Thomas, Thomas
Thomas, Rees 59; Ontario, 1871 ***1823.17*** *p162*
Thomas, Richard; America, 1665 ***1220.12*** *p794*
Thomas, Richard; America, 1750 ***1220.12*** *p794*
Thomas, Richard; America, 1756 ***1220.12*** *p794*
Thomas, Richard; America, 1764 ***1220.12*** *p794*
Thomas, Richard; America, 1770 ***1220.12*** *p794*
Thomas, Richard; America, 1772 ***1220.12*** *p794*
Thomas, Richard; America, 1774 ***1220.12*** *p794*
Thomas, Richard; Annapolis, MD, 1725 ***1220.12*** *p794*
Thomas, Richard 52; Ontario, 1871 ***1823.17*** *p162*
Thomas, Richard; Virginia, 1758 ***1220.12*** *p794*
Thomas, Richard 20; Virginia, 1635 ***1183.3*** *p31*
Thomas, Robert; America, 1700 ***1220.12*** *p794*
Thomas, Robert; Maryland, 1734 ***1220.12*** *p794*
Thomas, Robert 37; Ontario, 1871 ***1823.17*** *p162*
Thomas, Samuel; America, 1766 ***1220.12*** *p794*
Thomas, Samuel; America, 1767 ***1220.12*** *p794*
Thomas, Samuel; America, 1775 ***1220.12*** *p794*
Thomas, Sarah; Barbados or Jamaica, 1696 ***1220.12*** *p794*
Thomas, Sarah *SEE* Thomas, Thomas
Thomas, Sarah Rees *SEE* Thomas, Thomas
Thomas, Sarah 44; Ontario, 1871 ***1823.21*** *p365*
Thomas, Sarah 45; Ontario, 1871 ***1823.21*** *p365*
Thomas, Sebastian 20; New York, NY, 1898 ***7951.13*** *p43*
Thomas, Smalman; America, 1731 ***1220.12*** *p794*
Thomas, Sophia *SEE* Thomas, Thomas
Thomas, Stephen 31; Ontario, 1871 ***1823.21*** *p365*
Thomas, Thomas; America, 1743 ***1220.12*** *p794*
Thomas, Thomas; America, 1771 ***1220.12*** *p794*
Thomas, Thomas *SEE* Thomas, Thomas
Thomas, Thomas; Ohio, 1838 ***4022.20*** *p292*
*Wife:*Sarah Rees
*Child:*Sarah
*Child:*Margaret
*Child:*John
*Child:*Mary S.
*Child:*Rees
*Child:*Sophia
*Child:*Thomas
Thomas, Thomas; Ohio, 1841 ***4022.20*** *p292*
*Wife:*Ann
With 4 children
Thomas, Thomas; Ohio, 1843 ***4022.20*** *p292*
With family
Thomas, Thomas 24; Ontario, 1871 ***1823.21*** *p365*
Thomas, Thomas 58; Ontario, 1871 ***1823.17*** *p162*
Thomas, Thomas J. 35; Indiana, 1879-1888 ***9076.20*** *p72*
Thomas, Thomas W.; Washington, 1884 ***2770.40*** *p193*
Thomas, Walter; America, 1738 ***1220.12*** *p794*
Thomas, Walter; Barbados, 1700 ***1220.12*** *p794*
Thomas, Walter 45; New York, NY, 1894 ***6512.1*** *p186*
Thomas, Warrin 38; Ontario, 1871 ***1823.21*** *p365*
Thomas, Will; Virginia, 1652 ***6254.4*** *p243*
Thomas, William; America, 1719 ***1220.12*** *p794*
Thomas, William; America, 1722 ***1220.12*** *p794*
Thomas, William; America, 1726 ***1220.12*** *p794*
Thomas, William; America, 1736 ***1220.12*** *p794*
Thomas, William; America, 1746 ***1220.12*** *p794*
Thomas, William; America, 1749 ***1220.12*** *p794*
Thomas, William; America, 1750 ***1220.12*** *p794*
Thomas, William; America, 1754 ***1220.12*** *p794*
Thomas, William; America, 1756 ***1220.12*** *p794*
Thomas, William; America, 1759 ***1220.12*** *p794*
Thomas, William; America, 1763 ***1220.12*** *p794*
Thomas, William; America, 1770 ***1220.12*** *p794*
Thomas, William; America, 1774 ***1220.12*** *p794*
Thomas, William; America, 1775 ***1220.12*** *p794*
Thomas, William; America, 1775 ***1220.12*** *p795*
Thomas, William; Annapolis, MD, 1726 ***1220.12*** *p794*
Thomas, William; Annapolis, MD, 1733 ***1220.12*** *p794*
Thomas, William; Barbados, 1715 ***1220.12*** *p794*
Thomas, William; Barbados or Jamaica, 1685 ***1220.12*** *p794*
Thomas, William; Boston, 1749 ***1642*** *p46*
Thomas, William 28; Maryland, 1724 ***1220.12*** *p794*
Thomas, William; Ohio, 1814-1880 ***4022.20*** *p292*
Thomas, William; Ohio, 1847 ***4022.20*** *p292*
With children
*Child:*Catherine
Thomas, William 29; Ontario, 1871 ***1823.17*** *p163*
Thomas, William 33; Ontario, 1871 ***1823.21*** *p365*
Thomas, William 42; Ontario, 1871 ***1823.17*** *p162*
Thomas, William 42; Ontario, 1871 ***1823.21*** *p365*
Thomas, William 63; Ontario, 1871 ***1823.21*** *p365*
Thomas, William; Virginia, 1761 ***1220.12*** *p794*
Thomas, William E.; Ohio, 1855 ***4022.20*** *p292*
*Wife:*Mary
Thomas, William H.; Washington, 1883 ***2770.40*** *p137*
Thomas, William J.; Washington, 1887 ***2770.40*** *p25*
Thomas, William R. 42; Ontario, 1871 ***1823.21*** *p365*
Thomas, Winifred; America, 1736 ***1220.12*** *p795*
Thomasen, Jens; Washington, 1884 ***2770.40*** *p193*
Thomason, John; Washington, 1889 ***2770.40*** *p81*
Thomason, William; America, 1772 ***1220.12*** *p795*
Thomasson, Carolina; St. Paul, MN, 1896 ***1865.50*** *p48*
Thome, A. Barbara 57; America, 1878 ***5475.1*** *p447*
Thome, Adam 39; Brazil, 1876 ***5475.1*** *p383*
Thome, Anna Maria 26; Brazil, 1857 ***5475.1*** *p368*
Thome, Helena 38; Brazil, 1855 ***5475.1*** *p319*
Thome, John; Louisiana, 1836-1841 ***4981.45*** *p209*
Thome, Josef; Pennsylvania, 1884 ***5475.1*** *p271*
Thome, Margarethe; Brazil, 1879 ***5475.1*** *p390*
Thome, Maria 34; America, 1857 ***5475.1*** *p492*
Thome, Peter; Philadelphia, 1878 ***5475.1*** *p293*
Thome, Peter Josef; America, 1867 ***5475.1*** *p291*
Thomes, Est. 44; New Orleans, 1840 ***778.6*** *p325*
Thomlinson, James; Barbados, 1664 ***1220.12*** *p805*
Thomlinson, Joseph; America, 1662 ***1220.12*** *p805*
Thomlinson, Robert; Boston, 1817 ***3274.55*** *p69*
Thompson, Mrs.; Quebec, 1885 ***1937.10*** *p52*
Thompson, Ms. 27; New Orleans, 1848 ***778.6*** *p325*
Thompson, Alex 65; Ontario, 1871 ***1823.21*** *p365*
Thompson, Alexander; America, 1744 ***1220.12*** *p795*
Thompson, Alexander; America, 1760 ***1220.12*** *p795*
Thompson, Alexander 35; Ontario, 1871 ***1823.21*** *p365*
Thompson, Alice; America, 1761 ***1220.12*** *p795*
Thompson, Alice; Maryland, 1721 ***1220.12*** *p795*
Thompson, And 60; Ontario, 1871 ***1823.21*** *p365*
Thompson, Andrew; America, 1749 ***1220.12*** *p795*
Thompson, Andrew; America, 1773 ***1220.12*** *p795*
Thompson, Andrew; North Carolina, 1848 ***1088.45*** *p34*
Thompson, Andrew 30; Ontario, 1871 ***1823.21*** *p365*
Thompson, Andrew 50; Ontario, 1871 ***1823.21*** *p365*
Thompson, Ann; America, 1716 ***1220.12*** *p795*
Thompson, Ann; America, 1739 ***1220.12*** *p795*
Thompson, Ann; America, 1746 ***1220.12*** *p795*
Thompson, Ann; America, 1763 ***1220.12*** *p795*
Thompson, Ann; America, 1773 ***1220.12*** *p795*
Thompson, Ann; America, 1775 ***1220.12*** *p795*
Thompson, Ann; Annapolis, MD, 1731 ***1220.12*** *p795*
Thompson, Ann; Concord, NH, 1859-1959 ***9228.50*** *p417*
Thompson, Ann 78; Ontario, 1871 ***1823.21*** *p365*
Thompson, Ann 80; Ontario, 1871 ***1823.21*** *p365*
Thompson, Ann; Virginia, 1736 ***1220.12*** *p795*
Thompson, Annie 40; Ontario, 1871 ***1823.21*** *p365*
Thompson, Anthony; Canada, 1774 ***3036.5*** *p40*
Thompson, Anthony; Port uncertain, 1729 ***1220.12*** *p795*
Thompson, Archibald *SEE* Thompson, Dugald
Thompson, Archie 51; Ontario, 1871 ***1823.21*** *p365*
Thompson, Baptist 34; Ontario, 1871 ***1823.21*** *p365*
Thompson, Benjamin; America, 1732 ***1220.12*** *p795*
Thompson, Miss C.; Quebec, 1885 ***1937.10*** *p52*
Thompson, Carsten; Washington, 1887 ***2770.40*** *p25*
Thompson, Catherine 30; Ontario, 1871 ***1823.17*** *p163*
Thompson, Cecilia 70; Ontario, 1871 ***1823.17*** *p163*
Thompson, Charles; America, 1720 ***1220.12*** *p795*
Thompson, Charles; Virginia, 1735 ***1220.12*** *p795*
Thompson, Christ'r 47; Ontario, 1871 ***1823.17*** *p163*
Thompson, Christie *SEE* Thompson, Dugald
Thompson, Cuthbert; America, 1765 ***1220.12*** *p795*
Thompson, Daniel; America, 1764 ***1220.12*** *p795*
Thompson, David 19; Ontario, 1871 ***1823.21*** *p366*
Thompson, David 38; Ontario, 1871 ***1823.17*** *p163*
Thompson, David 52; Ontario, 1871 ***1823.21*** *p365*
Thompson, David M. 52; Ontario, 1871 ***1823.21*** *p366*
Thompson, Dorothy; America, 1724 ***1220.12*** *p795*
Thompson, Dugald; New York, 1739 ***8277.31*** *p119*
*Wife:*Margaret McDuffie
*Child:*Christie
*Child:*Archibald
*Child:*Duncan
Thompson, Duncan *SEE* Thompson, Dugald
Thompson, Edward; America, 1689 ***1220.12*** *p795*
Thompson, Edward; America, 1737 ***1220.12*** *p795*
Thompson, Edward; America, 1745 ***1220.12*** *p795*
Thompson, Edward; America, 1752 ***1220.12*** *p795*
Thompson, Edward; America, 1764 ***1220.12*** *p795*
Thompson, Edward; America, 1775 ***1220.12*** *p795*
Thompson, Edward 44; Ontario, 1871 ***1823.17*** *p163*
Thompson, Edward; Plymouth, MA, 1620 ***1920.45*** *p5*
Thompson, Eleazer 19; Michigan, 1880 ***4491.39*** *p30*
Thompson, Elianor; Barbados, 1705 ***1220.12*** *p795*
Thompson, Eliza Jane 27; Ontario, 1871 ***1823.21*** *p366*
Thompson, Elizabeth; America, 1717 ***1220.12*** *p795*
Thompson, Elizabeth; America, 1750 ***1220.12*** *p795*
Thompson, Elizabeth; America, 1753 ***1220.12*** *p795*
Thompson, Elizabeth; America, 1758 ***1220.12*** *p795*
Thompson, Elizabeth; America, 1759 ***1220.12*** *p795*
Thompson, Elizabeth; America, 1766 ***1220.12*** *p795*
Thompson, Elizabeth; America, 1774 ***1220.12*** *p795*
Thompson, Elizabeth; Virginia, 1734 ***1220.12*** *p795*
Thompson, Ellen 25; Ontario, 1871 ***1823.21*** *p366*
Thompson, Etta; Charlottesville, VA, 1909-1983 ***9228.50*** *p417*
Thompson, Francis; America, 1771 ***1220.12*** *p795*
Thompson, G. W. 29; Ontario, 1871 ***1823.21*** *p366*
Thompson, George; America, 1729 ***1220.12*** *p795*
Thompson, George; America, 1739 ***1220.12*** *p796*
Thompson, George; America, 1745 ***1220.12*** *p796*
Thompson, George; America, 1768 ***1220.12*** *p796*
Thompson, George; America, 1773 ***1220.12*** *p796*
Thompson, George; Barbados, 1683 ***1220.12*** *p795*
Thompson, George; Barbados, 1698 ***1220.12*** *p795*
Thompson, George 33; Ontario, 1871 ***1823.17*** *p163*
Thompson, George 45; Ontario, 1871 ***1823.21*** *p366*
Thompson, George 61; Ontario, 1871 ***1823.21*** *p366*
Thompson, Grace; America, 1773 ***1220.12*** *p796*
Thompson, Hannah; America, 1740 ***1220.12*** *p796*
Thompson, Harrison 66; Ontario, 1871 ***1823.21*** *p366*
Thompson, Henry; America, 1688 ***1220.12*** *p796*
Thompson, Henry; Barbados or Jamaica, 1688 ***1220.12*** *p796*
Thompson, Henry; Maryland, 1719 ***1220.12*** *p796*
Thompson, Henry 20; Ontario, 1871 ***1823.17*** *p163*
Thompson, Henry 24; Ontario, 1871 ***1823.17*** *p163*
Thompson, Henry 50; Ontario, 1871 ***1823.21*** *p366*
Thompson, Henry L. 61; Ontario, 1871 ***1823.21*** *p366*
Thompson, Hester; America, 1750 ***1220.12*** *p796*
Thompson, Hugh 34; Ontario, 1871 ***1823.21*** *p366*
Thompson, Hugh 36; Ontario, 1871 ***1823.21*** *p366*
Thompson, Ida; Minnesota, 1882-1898 ***1865.50*** *p112*
Thompson, Izabela 40; Ontario, 1871 ***1823.21*** *p366*
Thompson, J. D.; California, 1868 ***1131.61*** *p89*
Thompson, Jacob; Washington, 1883 ***2770.40*** *p137*
Thompson, James; America, 1734 ***1220.12*** *p796*
Thompson, James; America, 1738 ***1220.12*** *p796*
Thompson, James; America, 1749 ***1220.12*** *p796*
Thompson, James; America, 1753 ***1220.12*** *p796*
Thompson, James; America, 1756 ***1220.12*** *p796*

Thompson, James; America, 1758 ***1220.12*** *p796*
Thompson, James; America, 1766 ***1220.12*** *p796*
Thompson, James; America, 1767 ***1220.12*** *p796*
Thompson, James; America, 1769 ***1220.12*** *p796*
Thompson, James; America, 1770 ***1220.12*** *p796*
Thompson, James; America, 1773 ***1220.12*** *p796*
Thompson, James; Maryland, 1719 ***1220.12*** *p796*
Thompson, James 19; Ontario, 1871 ***1823.21*** *p366*
Thompson, James 27; Ontario, 1871 ***1823.21*** *p366*
Thompson, James 42; Ontario, 1871 ***1823.17*** *p163*
Thompson, James 45; Ontario, 1871 ***1823.17*** *p163*
Thompson, James 50; Ontario, 1871 ***1823.21*** *p366*
Thompson, James 62; Ontario, 1871 ***1823.21*** *p366*
Thompson, James 65; Ontario, 1871 ***1823.21*** *p366*
Thompson, James 66; Ontario, 1871 ***1823.21*** *p366*
Thompson, James 69; Ontario, 1871 ***1823.17*** *p163*
Thompson, James 69; Ontario, 1871 ***1823.21*** *p366*
Thompson, James 72; Ontario, 1871 ***1823.21*** *p366*
Thompson, James C. 61; Ontario, 1871 ***1823.21*** *p366*
Thompson, Jane; America, 1719 ***1220.12*** *p796*
Thompson, Jane; America, 1745 ***1220.12*** *p796*
Thompson, Jane; America, 1758 ***1220.12*** *p796*
Thompson, Jane; Pennsylvania, 1859 ***8513.31*** *p306*
Thompson, Jemima 56; Ontario, 1871 ***1823.21*** *p366*
Thompson, Jenkin; America, 1684 ***1220.12*** *p796*
Thompson, Jeremiah; America, 1767 ***1220.12*** *p796*
Thompson, John; America, 1700 ***1220.12*** *p796*
Thompson, John; America, 1713 ***1220.12*** *p796*
Thompson, John; America, 1730 ***1220.12*** *p796*
Thompson, John; America, 1738 ***1220.12*** *p796*
Thompson, John; America, 1740 ***1220.12*** *p796*
Thompson, John; America, 1740 ***1220.12*** *p797*
Thompson, John; America, 1748 ***1220.12*** *p797*
Thompson, John; America, 1750 ***1220.12*** *p797*
Thompson, John; America, 1751 ***1220.12*** *p797*
Thompson, John; America, 1754 ***1220.12*** *p797*
Thompson, John; America, 1756 ***1220.12*** *p797*
Thompson, John; America, 1760 ***1220.12*** *p797*
Thompson, John; America, 1763 ***1220.12*** *p797*
Thompson, John; America, 1764 ***1220.12*** *p797*
Thompson, John; America, 1766 ***1220.12*** *p797*
Thompson, John; America, 1768 ***1220.12*** *p797*
Thompson, John; America, 1773 ***1220.12*** *p797*
Thompson, John; America, 1774 ***1220.12*** *p797*
Thompson, John; Annapolis, MD, 1722 ***1220.12*** *p796*
Thompson, John; Barbados, 1669 ***1220.12*** *p796*
Thompson, John; Barbados or Jamaica, 1685 ***1220.12*** *p796*
Thompson, John; Barbados or Jamaica, 1686 ***1220.12*** *p796*
Thompson, John; Barbados or Jamaica, 1691 ***1220.12*** *p796*
Thompson, John; Barbados or Jamaica, 1697 ***1220.12*** *p796*
Thompson, John; Canada, 1774 ***3036.5*** *p41*
Thompson, John; Died enroute, 1725 ***1220.12*** *p796*
Thompson, John; Marston's Wharf, 1782 ***8529.30*** *p16*
Thompson, John; Maryland, 1736 ***1220.12*** *p796*
Thompson, John; Massachusetts, 1859-1959 ***9228.50*** *p417*
Thompson, John; North Carolina, 1838 ***1088.45*** *p34*
Thompson, John 26; Ontario, 1871 ***1823.21*** *p367*
Thompson, John 27; Ontario, 1871 ***1823.21*** *p367*
Thompson, John 34; Ontario, 1871 ***1823.17*** *p163*
Thompson, John 34; Ontario, 1871 ***1823.21*** *p366*
Thompson, John 35; Ontario, 1871 ***1823.17*** *p163*
Thompson, John 40; Ontario, 1871 ***1823.21*** *p367*
Thompson, John 41; Ontario, 1871 ***1823.17*** *p163*
Thompson, John 42; Ontario, 1871 ***1823.21*** *p366*
Thompson, John 52; Ontario, 1871 ***1823.21*** *p366*
Thompson, John 55; Ontario, 1871 ***1823.21*** *p366*
Thompson, John 60; Ontario, 1871 ***1823.17*** *p163*
Thompson, John 60; Ontario, 1871 ***1823.21*** *p366*
Thompson, John 65; Ontario, 1871 ***1823.21*** *p366*
Thompson, John; Philadelphia, 1777 ***8529.30*** *p3*
Thompson, John; Virginia, 1730 ***1220.12*** *p796*
Thompson, John; West Indies, 1688 ***1220.12*** *p796*
Thompson, Joseph; America, 1747 ***1220.12*** *p797*
Thompson, Joseph; America, 1754 ***1220.12*** *p797*
Thompson, Joseph; America, 1755 ***1220.12*** *p797*
Thompson, Joseph; America, 1770 ***1220.12*** *p797*
Thompson, Joseph; Canada, 1774 ***3036.5*** *p41*
Thompson, Joseph 53; Ontario, 1871 ***1823.21*** *p367*
Thompson, Joseph 70; Ontario, 1871 ***1823.21*** *p367*
Thompson, Judith; America, 1768 ***1220.12*** *p797*
Thompson, Judith; Maryland, 1726 ***1220.12*** *p797*
Thompson, Kate 54; Ontario, 1871 ***1823.21*** *p367*
Thompson, Krist; Washington, 1889 ***2770.40*** *p81*
Thompson, Lena Annie; Miami, 1935 ***4984.12*** *p39*
Thompson, Louisa; Philadelphia, 1851 ***8513.31*** *p429*
Thompson, Luctria 59; Ontario, 1871 ***1823.21*** *p367*
Thompson, Luke; America, 1772 ***1220.12*** *p797*
Thompson, Margaret; America, 1766 ***1220.12*** *p797*
Thompson, Margaret; America, 1767 ***1220.12*** *p797*
Thompson, Margaret McDuffie *SEE* Thompson, Dugald
Thompson, Margaret 36; Ontario, 1871 ***1823.21*** *p367*
Thompson, Margaret Dinsmore *SEE* Thompson, William
Thompson, Martha; Massachusetts, 1873-1902 ***9228.50*** *p417*
Thompson, Martin; Washington, 1889 ***2770.40*** *p81*
Thompson, Mary; America, 1751 ***1220.12*** *p797*
Thompson, Mary; America, 1754 ***1220.12*** *p797*
Thompson, Mary; America, 1760 ***1220.12*** *p797*
Thompson, Mary; America, 1761 ***1220.12*** *p797*
Thompson, Mary; America, 1762 ***1220.12*** *p797*
Thompson, Mary; America, 1764 ***1220.12*** *p797*
Thompson, Mary; Died enroute, 1728 ***1220.12*** *p797*
Thompson, Mary 16; Ontario, 1871 ***1823.21*** *p367*
Thompson, Mary 20; Ontario, 1871 ***1823.21*** *p367*
Thompson, Mary 50; Ontario, 1871 ***1823.21*** *p367*
Thompson, Mary; Potomac, 1731 ***1220.12*** *p797*
Thompson, Mathew 50; Ontario, 1871 ***1823.21*** *p367*
Thompson, Mathias 68; Ontario, 1871 ***1823.17*** *p163*
Thompson, Matthew; America, 1758 ***1220.12*** *p797*
Thompson, Nicholas; Virginia, 1741 ***1220.12*** *p797*
Thompson, Ole; Washington, 1889 ***2770.40*** *p81*
Thompson, Patrick; America, 1730 ***1220.12*** *p797*
Thompson, R. G.; North Carolina, 1860 ***1088.45*** *p35*
Thompson, Richard; America, 1673 ***1220.12*** *p797*
Thompson, Richard; America, 1754 ***1220.12*** *p797*
Thompson, Richard; America, 1757 ***1220.12*** *p797*
Thompson, Richard; America, 1760 ***1220.12*** *p797*
Thompson, Richard; America, 1775 ***1220.12*** *p797*
Thompson, Richard; Canada, 1774 ***3036.5*** *p41*
Thompson, Richard; Maryland, 1721 ***1220.12*** *p797*
Thompson, Richard 35; Ontario, 1871 ***1823.21*** *p367*
Thompson, Richard 54; Ontario, 1871 ***1823.21*** *p367*
Thompson, Richard 69; Ontario, 1871 ***1823.21*** *p367*
Thompson, Robert; America, 1729 ***1220.12*** *p797*
Thompson, Robert; America, 1740 ***1220.12*** *p797*
Thompson, Robert; America, 1752 ***1220.12*** *p797*
Thompson, Robert; America, 1756 ***1220.12*** *p797*
Thompson, Robert; America, 1761 ***1220.12*** *p798*
Thompson, Robert; Died enroute, 1719 ***1220.12*** *p797*
Thompson, Robert; Ohio, 1809-1852 ***4511.35*** *p54*
Thompson, Robert; Ohio, 1818 ***3580.20*** *p33*
Thompson, Robert; Ohio, 1818 ***6020.12*** *p22*
Thompson, Robert 26; Ontario, 1871 ***1823.21*** *p367*
Thompson, Robert 42; Ontario, 1871 ***1823.21*** *p367*
Thompson, Robert 55; Ontario, 1871 ***1823.21*** *p367*
Thompson, Robert 60; Ontario, 1871 ***1823.21*** *p367*
Thompson, Robert 64; Ontario, 1871 ***1823.21*** *p367*
Thompson, Robert 73; Ontario, 1871 ***1823.21*** *p367*
Thompson, Roger; New York, 1740 ***8277.31*** *p119*
Thompson, Sam 72; Ontario, 1871 ***1823.21*** *p367*
Thompson, Samuel; America, 1749 ***1220.12*** *p798*
Thompson, Samuel; America, 1775 ***1220.12*** *p798*
Thompson, Samuel 13; Ontario, 1871 ***1823.21*** *p367*
Thompson, Samuel 60; Ontario, 1871 ***1823.21*** *p367*
Thompson, Samuel P.; Washington, 1888 ***2770.40*** *p26*
Thompson, Sarah; America, 1768 ***1220.12*** *p798*
Thompson, Sayer 46; Ontario, 1871 ***1823.21*** *p367*
Thompson, Simpson 38; Ontario, 1871 ***1823.21*** *p367*
Thompson, Stephen; America, 1741 ***1220.12*** *p798*
Thompson, Susanna; America, 1722 ***1220.12*** *p798*
Thompson, Susanna; America, 1747 ***1220.12*** *p798*
Thompson, Thomas; America, 1747 ***1220.12*** *p798*
Thompson, Thomas; America, 1765 ***1220.12*** *p798*
Thompson, Thomas; America, 1770 ***1220.12*** *p798*
Thompson, Thomas; Ohio, 1809-1852 ***4511.35*** *p54*
Thompson, Thomas 52; Ontario, 1871 ***1823.21*** *p367*
Thompson, Thomas; Potomac, 1731 ***1220.12*** *p798*
Thompson, Thomas, Jr.; America, 1773 ***1220.12*** *p798*
Thompson, W.; Quebec, 1885 ***1937.10*** *p52*
Thompson, Walla 54; Ontario, 1871 ***1823.21*** *p367*
Thompson, William; America, 1719 ***1220.12*** *p798*
Thompson, William; America, 1728 ***1220.12*** *p798*
Thompson, William; America, 1733 ***1220.12*** *p798*
Thompson, William; America, 1736 ***1220.12*** *p798*
Thompson, William; America, 1738 ***1220.12*** *p798*
Thompson, William; America, 1742 ***1220.12*** *p798*
Thompson, William; America, 1748 ***1220.12*** *p798*
Thompson, William; America, 1749 ***1220.12*** *p798*
Thompson, William; America, 1750 ***1220.12*** *p798*
Thompson, William; America, 1753 ***1220.12*** *p798*
Thompson, William; America, 1765 ***1220.12*** *p798*
Thompson, William; America, 1766 ***1220.12*** *p798*
Thompson, William; America, 1768 ***1220.12*** *p798*
Thompson, William; Annapolis, MD, 1733 ***1220.12*** *p798*
Thompson, William; Barbados, 1671 ***1220.12*** *p798*
Thompson, William; Barbados or Jamaica, 1698 ***1220.12*** *p798*
Thompson, William; Boston, 1775 ***8529.30*** *p5A*
Thompson, William; Died enroute, 1721 ***1220.12*** *p798*
Thompson, William; Maryland, 1726 ***1220.12*** *p798*
Thompson, William; North Carolina, 1835 ***1088.45*** *p35*
Thompson, William; North Carolina, 1838 ***1088.45*** *p35*
Thompson, William; Ohio, 1838 ***3580.20*** *p33*
Thompson, William; Ohio, 1838 ***6020.12*** *p22*
Thompson, William 26; Ontario, 1871 ***1823.17*** *p163*
Thompson, William 28; Ontario, 1871 ***1823.21*** *p368*
Thompson, William 29; Ontario, 1871 ***1823.17*** *p163*
Thompson, William 30; Ontario, 1871 ***1823.21*** *p368*
Thompson, William 33; Ontario, 1871 ***1823.21*** *p368*
Thompson, William 40; Ontario, 1871 ***1823.21*** *p368*
Thompson, William 46; Ontario, 1871 ***1823.21*** *p368*
Thompson, William 49; Ontario, 1871 ***1823.21*** *p368*
Thompson, William 50; Ontario, 1871 ***1823.17*** *p163*
Thompson, William 60; Ontario, 1871 ***1823.21*** *p367*
Thompson, William 70; Ontario, 1871 ***1823.17*** *p163*
Thompson, William; Philadelphia, 1855 ***8513.31*** *p429*
*Wife:*Margaret Dinsmore
Thompson, William; Virginia, 1773 ***1220.12*** *p798*
Thompson, William; Washington, 1888 ***2770.40*** *p26*
Thompson, Wm 37; Ontario, 1871 ***1823.21*** *p368*
Thompson, Wm 42; Ontario, 1871 ***1823.21*** *p368*
Thompson, Wm 49; Ontario, 1871 ***1823.21*** *p368*
Thompson, Zachariah; America, 1743 ***1220.12*** *p798*
Thompson, Zachariah; America, 1767 ***1220.12*** *p798*
Thompson, Zacharias; Barbados or Jamaica, 1686 ***1220.12*** *p798*
Thomsen, Asmus; Mexico, 1902 ***7420.1*** *p378*
Thomsen, Carsten; Washington, 1889 ***2770.40*** *p81*
Thomsen, Hans; Washington, 1889 ***2770.40*** *p81*
Thomsen, Hans Christian K.; Iowa, 1913 ***1211.15*** *p19*
Thomson, Alec; Iowa, 1900 ***1211.15*** *p19*
Thomson, Alexander; America, 1744 ***1220.12*** *p795*
Thomson, Andrew 43; Ontario, 1871 ***1823.21*** *p368*
Thomson, Andrew 65; Ontario, 1871 ***1823.17*** *p163*
Thomson, Ann J. 44; Ontario, 1871 ***1823.21*** *p368*
Thomson, Donald 50; Ontario, 1871 ***1823.17*** *p163*
Thomson, Ebenezer 47; Ontario, 1871 ***1823.17*** *p163*
Thomson, Edward; America, 1766 ***1220.12*** *p795*
Thomson, George 68; Ontario, 1871 ***1823.21*** *p368*
Thomson, Isabella 55; Ontario, 1871 ***1823.17*** *p164*
Thomson, John 63; Ontario, 1871 ***1823.21*** *p368*
Thomson, John; Philadelphia, 1777 ***8529.30*** *p3*
Thomson, Malcolm 52; Ontario, 1871 ***1823.17*** *p164*
Thomson, Mary 32; Ontario, 1871 ***1823.17*** *p164*
Thomson, Neil 23; North Carolina, 1774 ***1422.10*** *p58*
Thomson, Neil 23; North Carolina, 1774 ***1422.10*** *p62*
Thomson, Thomas A. 33; Ontario, 1871 ***1823.17*** *p164*
Thomson, William 57; Ontario, 1871 ***1823.21*** *p368*
Thomy, Helier; Boston, 1763 ***9228.50*** *p624*
Thonant, Martin 67; New Orleans, 1847 ***778.6*** *p325*
Thone, Johannes; Venezuela, 1843 ***3899.5*** *p546*
Thonge, Richard; Annapolis, MD, 1733 ***1220.12*** *p798*
Thonitier, David; Virginia, 1700 ***9230.15*** *p81*
With wife
Thons, George 43; Ontario, 1871 ***1823.21*** *p368*
Thorburn, James; America, 1754 ***1220.12*** *p798*
Thorburn, Jessie 20; Died enroute, 1835 ***5024.1*** *p136*
Thorburn, Mary 8 months; New York, NY, 1835 ***5024.1*** *p136*
Thorburn, Murry 26; New York, NY, 1835 ***5024.1*** *p136*
Thorburn, Thomas 46; Ontario, 1871 ***1823.21*** *p368*
Thoreau, . . .; America, 1492-1817 ***9228.50*** *p28*
Thoreau, Alfred Thomas; Canada, 1850-1896 ***9228.50*** *p624*
Thoreau, Alfred Thomas; New York, NY, 1896 ***9228.50*** *p624*
Thoreau, Ann Touet *SEE* Thoreau, Philip
Thoreau, Ann Touet *SEE* Thoreau, Philip
Thoreau, Jean; Boston, 1773 ***9228.50*** *p623*
Thoreau, Philip; America, 1870 ***9228.50*** *p623*
*Wife:*Ann Touet
Thoreau, Philip; America, 1870 ***9228.50*** *p631*
*Wife:*Ann Touet
Thoreau, Philip; Iowa, n.d. ***9228.50*** *p623*
Thoreau, Philip Edward; Canada, 1770-1800 ***9228.50*** *p624*
Thorel, Jean Pierre 24; Texas, 1848 ***778.6*** *p325*
Thorel, Maria; New Jersey, 1655 ***9228.50*** *p624*
Thorel, Maria; Virginia, 1665 ***9228.50*** *p53*
Thorel, Marie; New Jersey, 1665-1672 ***9228.50*** *p52*
Thorel, Marie; New York, 1666 ***9228.50*** *p505*
Thorkil, . . .; Rhode Island, 1670-1699 ***9228.50*** *p632*
Thorley, Jane; America, 1766 ***1220.12*** *p798*
Thorley, Thomas; America, 1750 ***1220.12*** *p798*
Thorley, William 18; Quebec, 1870 ***8364.32*** *p26*
Thorm, Malcom; Washington, 1884 ***2770.40*** *p193*
Thorman, Thomas; America, 1769 ***1220.12*** *p798*
Thorn, Elen 40; Ontario, 1871 ***1823.21*** *p368*
Thorn, Isaac; America, 1746 ***1220.12*** *p799*
Thorn, Jane 60; Ontario, 1871 ***1823.17*** *p164*
Thorn, John; America, 1737 ***1220.12*** *p799*
Thorn, Ralph 19; Ontario, 1871 ***1823.21*** *p368*
Thorn, Robert; America, 1732 ***1220.12*** *p799*
Thorn, Robert; America, 1751 ***1220.12*** *p799*

Thorn, Sarah; Virginia, 1768 ***1220.12*** *p799*
Thorn, William; America, 1737 ***1220.12*** *p799*
Thorn, William; America, 1752 ***1220.12*** *p799*
Thorn, William 61; Ontario, 1871 ***1823.21*** *p368*
Thornally, Francis; America, 1770 ***1220.12*** *p798*
Thornaway, James; America, 1771 ***1220.12*** *p799*
Thornber, Henry; Illinois, 1864 ***6079.1*** *p14*
Thornberry, Daniel; Barbados or Jamaica, 1716 ***1220.12*** *p799*
Thornberry, Edward; Barbados or Jamaica, 1716 ***1220.12*** *p799*
Thornbury, Edward 28; Ontario, 1871 ***1823.17*** *p164*
Thornbury, Edward 60; Ontario, 1871 ***1823.17*** *p164*
Thornbury, James 26; Ontario, 1871 ***1823.17*** *p164*
Thornbury, Mary; America, 1773 ***1220.12*** *p799*
Thornbury, Richard; America, 1715 ***1220.12*** *p799*
Thornbury, Walter 30; Ontario, 1871 ***1823.17*** *p164*
Thorncraft, Mathew 41; Ontario, 1871 ***1823.21*** *p368*
Thorne, Ann; America, 1735 ***1220.12*** *p799*
Thorne, Charles 35; Ontario, 1871 ***1823.21*** *p368*
Thorne, Daniel; America, 1772 ***1220.12*** *p799*
Thorne, Francis; Barbados or Jamaica, 1696 ***1220.12*** *p799*
Thorne, George; Annapolis, MD, 1723 ***1220.12*** *p799*
Thorne, Jane; America, 1748 ***1220.12*** *p799*
Thorne, John; America, 1729 ***1220.12*** *p799*
Thorne, John; America, 1730 ***1220.12*** *p799*
Thorne, John; America, 1752 ***1220.12*** *p799*
Thorne, John; America, 1758 ***1220.12*** *p799*
Thorne, John; America, 1759 ***1220.12*** *p799*
Thorne, John; Barbados, 1686 ***1220.12*** *p799*
Thorne, Richard; America, 1731 ***1220.12*** *p799*
Thorne, Sarah; Potomac, 1731 ***1220.12*** *p799*
Thorne, Thomas; America, 1735 ***1220.12*** *p799*
Thorne, Thomas; Barbados, 1668 ***1220.12*** *p799*
Thorne, William; America, 1756 ***1220.12*** *p799*
Thorne, William; America, 1762 ***1220.12*** *p799*
Thorne, William; Maryland, 1731 ***1220.12*** *p799*
Thorner, James; America, 1752 ***1220.12*** *p799*
Thorneton, Blackstone; Barbados or Jamaica, 1687 ***1220.12*** *p799*
Thornham, Thomas; America, 1767 ***1220.12*** *p799*
Thornhill, Benjamin; America, 1771 ***1220.12*** *p799*
Thornhill, Hallsworth; America, 1757 ***1220.12*** *p799*
Thornhill, Peter; Marston's Wharf, 1782 ***8529.30*** *p16*
Thornhill, Robert; Maryland, 1674 ***1236.25*** *p49*
Thornhill, W. J.; Louisiana, 1874-1875 ***4981.45*** *p130*
Thornivel, Thomas; America, 1768 ***1220.12*** *p799*
Thornley, John; America, 1775 ***1220.12*** *p799*
Thornley, Peter; America, 1770 ***1220.12*** *p799*
Thornton, Almedie 9; Ontario, 1871 ***1823.21*** *p368*
Thornton, Ann; America, 1771 ***1220.12*** *p799*
Thornton, Benjamin; America, 1771 ***1220.12*** *p799*
Thornton, Christopher; America, 1764 ***1220.12*** *p799*
Thornton, Elizabeth; Virginia, 1741 ***1220.12*** *p799*
Thornton, George; America, 1725 ***1220.12*** *p799*
Thornton, George; Marston's Wharf, 1782 ***8529.30*** *p16*
Thornton, Henry 16; Quebec, 1870 ***8364.32*** *p26*
Thornton, James 58; Ontario, 1871 ***1823.17*** *p164*
Thornton, Jane; Annapolis, MD, 1723 ***1220.12*** *p799*
Thornton, Jane; Maryland, 1729 ***1220.12*** *p800*
Thornton, John; America, 1748 ***1220.12*** *p800*
Thornton, John; America, 1749 ***1220.12*** *p800*
Thornton, Joseph; America, 1765 ***1220.12*** *p800*
Thornton, Mary; America, 1769 ***1220.12*** *p800*
Thornton, Richard; America, 1675 ***1220.12*** *p800*
Thornton, Robert 40; New York, NY, 1825 ***6178.50*** *p77*
Thornton, Samuel; America, 1765 ***1220.12*** *p800*
Thornton, Samuel 50; Ontario, 1871 ***1823.21*** *p368*
Thornton, Sarah; America, 1758 ***1220.12*** *p800*
Thornton, Susanna; America, 1746 ***1220.12*** *p800*
Thornton, Thomas; America, 1757 ***1220.12*** *p800*
Thornton, Thomas; America, 1771 ***1220.12*** *p800*
Thornton, Thomas; New York, NY, 1820 ***3274.55*** *p70*
Thornton, William 37; Ontario, 1871 ***1823.21*** *p368*
Thoroughwood, Richard; America, 1713 ***1220.12*** *p800*
Thorovit, Louisa; Maryland or Virginia, 1731 ***1220.12*** *p800*
Thorowgood, George; America, 1752 ***1220.12*** *p800*
Thorowgood, Mary; America, 1767 ***1220.12*** *p800*
Thorowitz, Louisa; Maryland or Virginia, 1731 ***1220.12*** *p800*
Thorp, Emma 43; Ontario, 1871 ***1823.21*** *p368*
Thorp, Isachar; America, 1760 ***1220.12*** *p800*
Thorp, John; America, 1755 ***1220.12*** *p800*
Thorp, John; America, 1766 ***1220.12*** *p800*
Thorp, Joseph; America, 1760 ***1220.12*** *p800*
Thorp, Thomas; America, 1768 ***1220.12*** *p800*
Thorp, Thomas Jefferson; Ohio, 1809-1852 ***4511.35*** *p54*
Thorpe, Edward; America, 1765 ***1220.12*** *p800*
Thorpe, Helen; Jamaica, 1661 ***1220.12*** *p800*
Thorpe, Henry; Annapolis, MD, 1725 ***1220.12*** *p800*
Thorpe, James; America, 1763 ***1220.12*** *p800*
Thorpe, John; America, 1749 ***1220.12*** *p800*
Thorpe, John; America, 1750 ***1220.12*** *p800*
Thorpe, John; America, 1753 ***1220.12*** *p800*
Thorpe, John; Barbados, 1668 ***1220.12*** *p800*
Thorpe, Josiah; America, 1751 ***1220.12*** *p800*
Thorpe, Richard; America, 1752 ***1220.12*** *p800*
Thorpe, Richard; America, 1768 ***1220.12*** *p800*
Thorpe, Seymour 44; Ontario, 1871 ***1823.21*** *p368*
Thorpe, Thomas; America, 1737 ***1220.12*** *p800*
Thorpe, William; America, 1762 ***1220.12*** *p800*
Thorrington, John; America, 1744 ***1220.12*** *p800*
Thorrowgood, John; America, 1665 ***1220.12*** *p800*
Thorslund, Gudm.; New York, NY, 1845 ***6412.40*** *p148*
Thorsnes, Berent Andreas; Oregon, 1941 ***9157.47*** *p2*
Thorson, Hannah; St. Paul, MN, 1893 ***1865.50*** *p112*
Thorson, Mary; Colorado, 1897 ***1029.59*** *p89*
Thorson, Olof; Colorado, 1897 ***1029.59*** *p89*
Thos, Catherine 60; America, 1847 ***778.6*** *p325*
Thouard, Alphonsine 35; America, 1846 ***778.6*** *p325*
Thouchard, Felix 39; Port uncertain, 1846 ***778.6*** *p325*
Thoumine, Augustus *SEE* Thoumine, Dorcas Fannie Jessup
Thoumine, Dorcas *SEE* Thoumine, Dorcas Fannie Jessup
Thoumine, Dorcas Fannie; New York, 1886-1907 ***9228.50*** *p624*
*Child:*Augustus
*Child:*Dorcas
*Child:*Florence
Thoumine, Dorcas Jessup; New York, NY, 1907 ***9228.50*** *p249*
Thoumine, Dorcas Jessup; New York, NY, 1907 ***9228.50*** *p249*
Thoumine, Florence *SEE* Thoumine, Dorcas Fannie Jessup
Thoumine, Lucas 36; New York, 1828 ***9228.50*** *p624*
Thoury, Francois 36; America, 1846 ***778.6*** *p325*
Thouvenin, Augustus; Ohio, 1809-1852 ***4511.35*** *p54*
Thouvet, Francois 19; Missouri, 1847 ***778.6*** *p325*
Thowe, Andreas *SEE* Thowe, Andreas
Thowe, Andreas; America, 1854 ***5475.1*** *p459*
*Wife:*Dorothea Stoll
*Son:*Friedrich
*Son:*Andreas
Thowe, Dorothea Stoll *SEE* Thowe, Andreas
Thowe, Friedrich *SEE* Thowe, Andreas
Thowe, Friedrich *SEE* Thowe, Peter
Thowe, Jakob; Michigan, 1882 ***5475.1*** *p460*
Thowe, Johann Jakob; America, 1854 ***5475.1*** *p459*
*Wife:*M. Barbara Will
Thowe, Johann Peter *SEE* Thowe, Peter
Thowe, Lina *SEE* Thowe, Peter
Thowe, M. Barbara Will *SEE* Thowe, Johann Jakob
Thowe, Maria *SEE* Thowe, Peter
Thowe, Maria Hell *SEE* Thowe, Peter
Thowe, Peter *SEE* Thowe, Peter
Thowe, Peter; America, 1882 ***5475.1*** *p460*
*Wife:*Maria Hell
*Son:*Friedrich
*Father:*Johann Peter
*Daughter:*Lina
*Daughter:*Wilhelmine
*Son:*Peter
*Daughter:*Sophia
*Daughter:*Maria
Thowe, Sophia *SEE* Thowe, Peter
Thowe, Wilhelmine *SEE* Thowe, Peter
Thranum, Lars; New York, NY, 1893 ***3366.30*** *p70*
Threadwell, Joseph; America, 1738 ***1220.12*** *p800*
Threch, Xavie; Colorado, 1892 ***1029.59*** *p89*
Thredgall, John; America, 1736 ***1220.12*** *p800*
Threed, William; America, 1727 ***1220.12*** *p800*
Thresher, James; America, 1731 ***1220.12*** *p800*
Thresher, Richard; America, 1730 ***1220.12*** *p800*
Thrift, Elizabeth; America, 1749 ***1220.12*** *p800*
Thrift, Hester; Rappahannock, VA, 1741 ***1220.12*** *p800*
Thrift, James; America, 1752 ***1220.12*** *p800*
Thrift, John; America, 1772 ***1220.12*** *p800*
Thrift, Peter; America, 1767 ***1220.12*** *p800*
Thrift, William; America, 1757 ***1220.12*** *p800*
Thro, Francoise 30; America, 1842 ***778.6*** *p325*
Thro, Johannes 3; America, 1842 ***778.6*** *p325*
Throckmorton, Isaac 37; Ontario, 1871 ***1823.21*** *p368*
Throer, Isac 52; Ontario, 1871 ***1823.21*** *p368*
Throop, Ella R. 12; Michigan, 1880 ***4491.30*** *p30*
Throup, James; America, 1771 ***1220.12*** *p800*
Thrower, Charles 86; Ontario, 1871 ***1823.21*** *p368*
Thrower, Henry; America, 1761 ***1220.12*** *p801*
Thrower, Stephen 55; Ontario, 1871 ***1823.21*** *p368*
Thrustlecock, John; America, 1757 ***1220.12*** *p801*
Thubieres DeQueylus, Gabriel 45; Montreal, 1657 ***9221.17*** *p371*
Thuet, Alphons; Colorado, 1896 ***1029.59*** *p89*
Thuet, Alphons; San Francisco, 1891 ***1029.59*** *p90*
Thuet, Joseph; Colorado, 1886 ***1029.59*** *p90*
Thul, Jakob *SEE* Thul, Johann
Thul, Johann *SEE* Thul, Johann
Thul, Johann; America, 1871 ***5475.1*** *p384*
*Wife:*L. Katharina Stelzer
*Son:*Johann
*Daughter:*Maria
*Son:*Jakob
Thul, L. Katharina Stelzer *SEE* Thul, Johann
Thul, Maria *SEE* Thul, Johann
Thull, Fedinand; America, 1889 ***5475.1*** *p452*
Thull, Johann Nikolaus 25; America, 1890 ***5475.1*** *p452*
Thult, Haver; Colorado, 1887 ***1029.59*** *p90*
Thumann, John; Louisiana, 1841-1844 ***4981.45*** *p211*
Thumb, John; Boston, 1766 ***1642*** *p36*
Thumm, Jacob F.; Philadelphia, 1862 ***8513.31*** *p429*
Thunemann, Charles; Ohio, 1809-1852 ***4511.35*** *p54*
Thunqvist, P. M. Nilsson; Charleston, SC, 1850 ***6412.40*** *p152*
Thunus, Clemence; Wisconsin, 1854-1858 ***1495.20*** *p50*
Thurby, Mary; Maryland, 1719 ***1220.12*** *p801*
Thurine, T. 30; Port uncertain, 1840 ***778.6*** *p325*
Thuringer, Tobias; America, 1867 ***7919.3*** *p526*
Thurland, Mary; Jamaica, 1716 ***1220.12*** *p801*
Thurland, Thomas; America, 1715 ***1220.12*** *p801*
Thurley, Maurice 52; New Orleans, 1848 ***778.6*** *p325*
Thurloe, George; America, 1758 ***1220.12*** *p801*
Thurman, Charles; Maryland, 1735 ***1220.12*** *p801*
Thurman, Jaun 38; Ontario, 1871 ***1823.21*** *p368*
Thurnau, Anna Sophie Catharine *SEE* Thurnau, Heinrich Christoph
Thurnau, Carl; America, 1857 ***7420.1*** *p174*
Thurnau, Engel Marie Sophie; America, 1856 ***7420.1*** *p155*
Thurnau, Ferdinand; America, 1857 ***7420.1*** *p174*
Thurnau, Hans Heinrich; America, 1854 ***7420.1*** *p132*
Thurnau, Heinrich; America, 1852 ***7420.1*** *p99*
With wife son & 3 daughters
Thurnau, Heinrich Christoph; America, 1866 ***7420.1*** *p251*
*Sister:*Anna Sophie Catharine
*Brother:*Johann Heinrich
Thurnau, Johann Heinrich *SEE* Thurnau, Heinrich Christoph
Thurnau, Wilhelm; America, 1852 ***7420.1*** *p99*
Thurowgood, John; Barbados or Jamaica, 1685 ***1220.12*** *p800*
Thursby, Anthony; America, 1764 ***1220.12*** *p801*
Thursby, Sarah; Virginia, 1735 ***1220.12*** *p801*
Thursdale, Anthony; America, 1764 ***1220.12*** *p801*
Thurstan, John; America, 1759 ***1220.12*** *p801*
Thurston, Anne; Barbados or Jamaica, 1677 ***1220.12*** *p801*
Thurston, George; America, 1684 ***1220.12*** *p801*
Thurston, John; America, 1753 ***1220.12*** *p801*
Thurston, Mary; America, 1759 ***1220.12*** *p801*
Thurston, William; America, 1754 ***1220.12*** *p801*
Thurston, William; America, 1769 ***1220.12*** *p801*
Thurwell, Arthur 50; Ontario, 1871 ***1823.21*** *p368*
Thussol, James 24; Ontario, 1871 ***1823.17*** *p164*
Thwaites, William; America, 1772 ***1220.12*** *p801*
Thwaits, John; America, 1772 ***1220.12*** *p801*
Thyberg, Hans Christian; Washington, 1882 ***2770.40*** *p136*
Thygeson, Christian; Washington, 1876 ***2770.40*** *p134*
Thygeson, Christian; Washington, 1882 ***2770.40*** *p136*
Thyren, J.; Cleveland, OH, 1903-1906 ***9722.10*** *p127*
Thyrolf, Elisabeth 43; America, 1853 ***2526.43*** *p181*
Tibballs, James; Barbados, 1668 ***1220.12*** *p801*
Tibballs, Samuel; America, 1774 ***1220.12*** *p801*
Tibbet, John; America, 1740 ***1220.12*** *p801*
Tibbett, Elizabeth; America, 1745 ***1220.12*** *p801*
Tibbetts, Jane 35; Ontario, 1871 ***1823.21*** *p369*
Tibbish, Francis; Marston's Wharf, 1782 ***8529.30*** *p16*
Tibbish, Imanuel; Marston's Wharf, 1782 ***8529.30*** *p16*
Tibble, William; Barbados, 1670 ***1220.12*** *p801*
Tibbs, Abraham 25; Ontario, 1871 ***1823.21*** *p369*
Tibbs, John; America, 1759 ***1220.12*** *p801*
Tibbs, John; Annapolis, MD, 1725 ***1220.12*** *p801*
Tibbs, John 46; Ontario, 1871 ***1823.21*** *p369*
Tibbs, William; America, 1715 ***1220.12*** *p801*
Tibbs, William 25; Ontario, 1871 ***1823.21*** *p369*
Tibbs, William 54; Ontario, 1871 ***1823.21*** *p369*
Tibbworth, Susannah; America, 1767 ***1220.12*** *p801*
Tibeau, Maria Magdalena; Venezuela, 1843 ***3899.5*** *p542*
Tiberg, Peter J.; Illinois, 1861 ***4487.25*** *p75*
Tiblemont, Nicolas 22; Quebec, 1657 ***9221.17*** *p370*
Tibley, Robert; Maryland, 1736 ***1220.12*** *p801*
Tibo, Maria Magdalena; Venezuela, 1843 ***3899.5*** *p542*
Tibodo, Francis; Maine, 1826 ***3274.55*** *p25*
Tibodo, Madeleine Iquain *SEE* Tibodo, Olivier
Tibodo, Olivier; Nova Scotia, 1753 ***3051*** *p113*
*Wife:*Madeleine Iquain

Tice, Robert; America, 1726 ***1220.12*** *p801*
Ticehurst, Thomas; America, 1757 ***1220.12*** *p801*
Tichnor, H. B.; California, 1868 ***1131.61*** *p89*
With wife
Tichy, Frantisek; Milwaukee, 1873-1874 ***2853.20*** *p263*
Tichy, Jan Frantisek; St. Louis, 1898 ***2853.20*** *p32*
Ticken, Peter; America, 1685 ***1220.12*** *p801*
Tickmeir, William; Illinois, 1860 ***6079.1*** *p14*
Tickner, Peter; America, 1747 ***1220.12*** *p801*
Tickner, Peter; America, 1753 ***1220.12*** *p801*
Tickner, William; Virginia, 1732 ***1220.12*** *p801*
Ticknor, Thomas 51; Ontario, 1871 ***1823.17*** *p164*
Ticoulet, Mr. 27; Port uncertain, 1845 ***778.6*** *p325*
Tidbury, Joseph; America, 1774 ***1220.12*** *p801*
Tidcombe, William; America, 1762 ***1220.12*** *p801*
Tidd, Henry; America, 1748 ***1220.12*** *p801*
Tidder, Richard; America, 1728 ***1220.12*** *p789*
Tidemanson, H. Oliver; Iowa, 1869 ***1211.15*** *p19*
Tidey, William; America, 1768 ***1220.12*** *p801*
Tidmarsh, Grace; America, 1737 ***1220.12*** *p801*
Tidy, Robert; Maine, 1670-1679 ***9228.50*** *p620*
Tiedemann, Carl; Valdivia, Chile, 1850 ***1192.4*** *p49*
Tiefenbronner, Alfred *SEE* Tiefenbronner, Karoline Wirth
Tiefenbronner, Hedwig *SEE* Tiefenbronner, Karoline Wirth
Tiefenbronner, Karoline; America, 1892 ***5475.1*** *p39*
*Child:*Klara
*Child:*Alfred
*Child:*Hedwig
Tiefenbronner, Klara *SEE* Tiefenbronner, Karoline Wirth
Tielburg, John; Iowa, 1908 ***1211.15*** *p19*
Tieleman, Jonas; Valdivia, Chile, 1852 ***1192.4*** *p53*
Tielking, Mr.; America, 1854 ***7420.1*** *p132*
With wife & 3 daughters
Tielking, Christian Wilhelm Ludwig; America, 1868 ***7420.1*** *p277*
Tielking, Friedrich; America, 1855 ***7420.1*** *p134*
Tielking, Friedrich; America, 1855 ***7420.1*** *p142*
With family
Tiemann, Anna Marie 61; New York, NY, 1864 ***8425.62*** *p197*
Tiemann, Aug. Heinrich 20; New York, NY, 1864 ***8425.62*** *p197*
Tiemann, Bernhard 61; New York, NY, 1864 ***8425.62*** *p197*
Tiemann, Bertha; New York, 1859 ***358.56*** *p100*
Tiemann, Fr. Wilhelm 29; New York, NY, 1864 ***8425.62*** *p197*
Tiemann, J.; New York, 1859 ***358.56*** *p99*
Tiemann, John; Washington, 1889 ***2770.40*** *p81*
Tiemann, P.; New York, 1859 ***358.56*** *p100*
Tieprich, Joseph; New York, 1860 ***358.56*** *p3*
Tier, William 62; Ontario, 1871 ***1823.21*** *p369*
Tierce, Francoise; Quebec, 1671 ***4514.3*** *p373*
Tiernay, John 50; Ontario, 1871 ***1823.21*** *p369*
Tierney, James; Massachusetts, 1841 ***3274.55*** *p23*
Tierney, John 37; Ontario, 1871 ***1823.21*** *p369*
Tierney, Kate 25; Ontario, 1871 ***1823.21*** *p369*
Tierney, Patrick 55; Ontario, 1871 ***1823.21*** *p369*
Tiernon, Joseph; America, 1769 ***1220.12*** *p801*
Tiery, Julieanne 9; America, 1846 ***778.6*** *p326*
Tieste, Christine Sophie Suwer *SEE* Tieste, Georg August
Tieste, Georg August; America, 1849 ***7420.1*** *p68*
*Wife:*Christine Sophie Suwer
Tieste, Georg Ludwig; America, 1849 ***7420.1*** *p68*
With brother
Tietz, Pauline; Chile, 1852 ***1192.4*** *p55*
With 3 children
With child 2
With child 14
Tieverton, Thomas 45; Ontario, 1871 ***1823.21*** *p369*
Tiffen, Joseph; America, 1752 ***1220.12*** *p801*
Tiffin, Richard 25; Ontario, 1871 ***1823.17*** *p164*
Tifoot, Mary; America, 1749 ***1220.12*** *p801*
Tigagne, Antoin 32; New Orleans, 1845 ***778.6*** *p326*
Tigges, Amalie; America, 1867 ***7919.3*** *p532*
Tigges, Hildegard; America, 1867 ***7919.3*** *p532*
Tiggins, Thomas; America, 1759 ***1220.12*** *p801*
Tigh, Henry; America, 1770 ***1220.12*** *p818*
Tighe, John; Albany, NY, 1826 ***3274.55*** *p67*
Tighe, John; North Carolina, 1856 ***1088.45*** *p35*
Tighe, Michael; Illinois, 1858-1861 ***6020.5*** *p133*
Tignac, Elizabet; Virginia, 1700 ***9230.15*** *p80*
Tigner, William 74; Ontario, 1871 ***1823.21*** *p369*
Tigneres, Miss 20; Texas, 1848 ***778.6*** *p326*
Tigneres, Giraud 53; Texas, 1848 ***778.6*** *p326*
Tigneres, Jan 18; Texas, 1848 ***778.6*** *p326*
Tigwell, Thomas; America, 1742 ***1220.12*** *p802*
Tikalsky, Jan; Nebraska, 1870 ***2853.20*** *p193*
Tikalsky, Josef; Nebraska, 1870 ***2853.20*** *p193*
Tilborow, William, Jr.; Barbados, 1668 ***1220.12*** *p802*
Tilburn, Joseph; Illinois, 1855 ***6079.1*** *p14*
Tilbury, Anne; Died enroute, 1728 ***1220.12*** *p802*
Tildsley, William; America, 1754 ***1220.12*** *p802*
Tiler, Hannah; America, 1737 ***1220.12*** *p818*
Tiley, John; America, 1675 ***1220.12*** *p802*
Tiley, Marmaduke; America, 1736 ***1220.12*** *p802*
Tilford, Adam; New York, 1777 ***8529.30*** *p16*
Tilhn, E. D.; California, 1868 ***1131.61*** *p90*
Tilkin, Margaretha Gierend *SEE* Tilkin, Peter
Tilkin, Peter; America, 1864-1899 ***6442.17*** *p65*
*Wife:*Margaretha Gierend
With 8 children
Till, George 37; Ontario, 1871 ***1823.21*** *p369*
Till, John; America, 1763 ***1220.12*** *p802*
Till, John; America, 1775 ***1220.12*** *p802*
Till, John; Barbados, 1668 ***1220.12*** *p802*
Till, Martha; America, 1759 ***1220.12*** *p802*
Till, William; America, 1733 ***1220.12*** *p802*
Till, William; America, 1765 ***1220.12*** *p802*
Till, William 30; Ontario, 1871 ***1823.21*** *p369*
Till, Xaver; Wisconsin, 1895 ***2853.20*** *p349*
Tillaboo, John; America, 1771 ***1220.12*** *p802*
Tillard, Elizabeth; Died enroute, 1728 ***1220.12*** *p802*
Tillard, Jean; Quebec, 1659 ***9221.17*** *p410*
Tillbree, Sarah; Annapolis, MD, 1731 ***1220.12*** *p802*
Tillbry, Sarah; Annapolis, MD, 1731 ***1220.12*** *p802*
Tillett, William; America, 1767 ***1220.12*** *p802*
Tillewar, James; America, 1764 ***1220.12*** *p802*
Tilley, Abraham; America, 1768 ***1220.12*** *p802*
Tilley, Ann; America, 1755 ***1220.12*** *p802*
Tilley, Ann *SEE* Tilley, Edward
Tilley, Christopher; West Indies, 1686 ***1220.12*** *p802*
Tilley, Edward; Barbados, 1668 ***1220.12*** *p802*
Tilley, Edward; Plymouth, MA, 1620 ***1920.45*** *p5*
*Wife:*Ann
Tilley, Eelizabeth *SEE* Tilley, John
Tilley, John; America, 1685 ***1220.12*** *p802*
Tilley, John; Barbados, 1688 ***1220.12*** *p802*
Tilley, John; Plymouth, MA, 1620 ***1920.45*** *p5*
With wife
*Daughter:*Eelizabeth
Tilley, Joseph; America, 1730 ***1220.12*** *p802*
Tilley, Joseph 26; Ontario, 1871 ***1823.17*** *p164*
Tilley, Richard; Jamaica, 1664 ***1220.12*** *p802*
Tilley, Robert; Philadelphia, 1777 ***8529.30*** *p7*
Tilley, William; America, 1730 ***1220.12*** *p802*
Tilley, William; Died enroute, 1729 ***1220.12*** *p802*
Tilliard, Desire; New York, NY, 1864 ***1494.20*** *p13*
Tillie, James; America, 1754 ***1220.12*** *p802*
Tillier, Jacques; Quebec, 1659 ***9221.17*** *p414*
Tillison, William; America, 1764 ***1220.12*** *p802*
Tillman, Andrew 33; Port uncertain, 1845 ***778.6*** *p326*
Tillman, Antony 32; Ontario, 1871 ***1823.21*** *p369*
Tillman, Louisa 33; Port uncertain, 1845 ***778.6*** *p326*
Tillotson, Miles; America, 1774 ***1220.12*** *p802*
Tillott, John; America, 1775 ***1220.12*** *p802*
Tillou, Pierre; Virginia, 1700 ***9230.15*** *p81*
Tillson, Roger; Barbados, 1671 ***1220.12*** *p802*
Tilly, James; America, 1773 ***1220.12*** *p802*
Tilly, Mary; Maryland, 1735 ***1220.12*** *p802*
Tilly, Simon; America, 1750 ***1220.12*** *p802*
Tilman, Martha; America, 1758 ***1220.12*** *p802*
Tilsey, Mary; America, 1772 ***1220.12*** *p802*
Tilsley, John; America, 1758 ***1220.12*** *p802*
Tilson, Henry; America, 1734 ***1220.12*** *p802*
Tilson, John; Maryland, 1671-1672 ***1236.25*** *p45*
Timber, W.N.; Quebec, 1870 ***8364.32*** *p26*
Timberwell, George; America, 1751 ***1220.12*** *p802*
Timbrell, Thomas 35; Ontario, 1871 ***1823.21*** *p369*
Timer, Ann; America, 1747 ***1220.12*** *p802*
Times, Richard; America, 1713 ***1220.12*** *p802*
Timeus, Christian; Ohio, 1840-1897 ***8365.35*** *p18*
Timeus, Frederick; Ohio, 1840-1897 ***8365.35*** *p18*
Timeus, Wm.; Ohio, 1840-1897 ***8365.35*** *p18*
Timewell, Ann; America, 1747 ***1220.12*** *p802*
Timinson, Joseph; Philadelphia, 1778 ***8529.30*** *p3*
Timleh, Mary; America, 1775 ***1220.12*** *p802*
Timler, Hermann 20; America, 1893 ***1883.7*** *p38*
Timm, Emilie; Wisconsin, 1887 ***6795.8*** *p154*
Timm, Frederick T.; Wisconsin, 1867 ***6795.8*** *p188*
Timm, Gotleib; Wisconsin, 1888 ***6795.8*** *p224*
Timmerman, Gaspar; North Carolina, 1710 ***3629.40*** *p7*
Timmerman, Martin; Ohio, 1809-1852 ***4511.35*** *p54*
Timmes, Henry; America, 1656 ***1220.12*** *p803*
Timmings, Edward; America, 1758 ***1220.12*** *p802*
Timmins, Lawrence; America, 1773 ***1220.12*** *p802*
Timmis, John 40; Ontario, 1871 ***1823.21*** *p369*
Timmis, Thomas; New York, 1776 ***8529.30*** *p16*
Timmons, John; America, 1769 ***1220.12*** *p802*
Timmons, Mary; New Orleans, 1850 ***7242.30*** *p155*
Timms, John; America, 1750 ***1220.12*** *p803*
Timms, John; America, 1758 ***1220.12*** *p803*
Timms, Richard; America, 1713 ***1220.12*** *p803*
Timothe, Austain; Louisiana, 1874-1875 ***4981.45*** *p130*
Timothy, John; America, 1685 ***1220.12*** *p803*
Timperley, Robert; America, 1757 ***1220.12*** *p803*
Timpson, Thomas; Maryland, 1723 ***1220.12*** *p803*
Timpson, William; America, 1731 ***1220.12*** *p803*
Tims, Elizabeth; America, 1744 ***1220.12*** *p803*
Tims, Jane; America, 1742 ***1220.12*** *p803*
Tims, Philip; Barbados or Jamaica, 1698 ***1220.12*** *p803*
Timson, Moan; Annapolis, MD, 1723 ***1220.12*** *p803*
Tinbert, Celestine 26; Missouri, 1845 ***778.6*** *p326*
Tinchan, Mr. 11; New Orleans, 1843 ***778.6*** *p326*
Tinchan, Mr. 42; New Orleans, 1843 ***778.6*** *p326*
Tindale, Thomas; Ontario, 1871 ***1823.17*** *p164*
Tindall, Elizabeth 60; Ontario, 1871 ***1823.21*** *p369*
Tindall, Richd 60; Ontario, 1871 ***1823.21*** *p369*
Tindall, Thomas; America, 1740 ***1220.12*** *p803*
Tindell, Henry; America, 1769 ***1220.12*** *p803*
Tindle, Richard 44; Ontario, 1871 ***1823.21*** *p369*
Tindy, Richard; America, 1751 ***1220.12*** *p803*
Tine, Katharina Major *SEE* Tine, Peter
Tine, Peter; America, 1884 ***5475.1*** *p229*
*Wife:*Katharina Major
Tingle, James; America, 1722 ***1220.12*** *p803*
Tingle, Simon; America, 1678 ***1220.12*** *p803*
Tingley, F. C.; Washington, 1880 ***2770.40*** *p134*
Tingley, F. D.; Washington, 1883 ***2770.40*** *p137*
Tink, Garence, Jr.; America, 1755 ***1220.12*** *p803*
Tink, John, Jr.; America, 1767 ***1220.12*** *p803*
Tinker, Closs; North Carolina, 1792-1862 ***1088.45*** *p35*
Tinker, Michael; America, 1749 ***1220.12*** *p803*
Tinker, Thomas; Plymouth, MA, 1620 ***1920.45*** *p5*
With wife & son
Tinkins, Frederick; Ontario, 1871 ***1823.21*** *p369*
Tinkler, Joseph; Ohio, 1809-1852 ***4511.35*** *p54*
Tinkler, William; Marston's Wharf, 1782 ***8529.30*** *p16*
Tinkley, William; Marston's Wharf, 1782 ***8529.30*** *p16*
Tinley, John; America, 1765 ***1220.12*** *p803*
Tinley, John; America, 1768 ***1220.12*** *p803*
Tinling, Robert; America, 1765 ***1220.12*** *p803*
Tinnery, John; New York, 1782 ***8529.30*** *p16*
Tinnes, Gertrud *SEE* Tinnes, Jakob
Tinnes, Jakob; America, 1880 ***5475.1*** *p23*
*Wife:*Susanna Spanier
*Son:*Peter
*Daughter:*Gertrud
Tinnes, Peter *SEE* Tinnes, Jakob
Tinnes, Susanna Spanier *SEE* Tinnes, Jakob
Tinney, Ellen; Philadelphia Co., PA, 1853 ***8513.31*** *p429*
Tinning, H. L.; Valdivia, Chile, 1852 ***1192.4*** *p56*
Tinsey, John; America, 1768 ***1220.12*** *p803*
Tinsley, Ann; America, 1754 ***1220.12*** *p803*
Tinsley, George 36; Ontario, 1871 ***1823.21*** *p369*
Tinsley, John; America, 1765 ***1220.12*** *p803*
Tinsley, John; America, 1767 ***1220.12*** *p803*
Tinsley, John; South Carolina, 1811 ***6155.4*** *p19*
Tinsley, Peter 38; Ontario, 1871 ***1823.21*** *p369*
Tinsley, Thomas; Annapolis, MD, 1723 ***1220.12*** *p803*
Tinsley, William; America, 1754 ***1220.12*** *p803*
Tinson, Duke; America, 1731 ***1220.12*** *p803*
Tinson, John 50; Ontario, 1871 ***1823.21*** *p369*
Tintamare, Jean; Quebec, 1652 ***9221.17*** *p263*
Tintinger, Peter Joh.; Chicago, 1892 ***5475.1*** *p194*
Tintolet, Jean; Louisiana, 1836-1840 ***4981.45*** *p213*
Tintunger, Catherina 48; America, 1846 ***778.6*** *p326*
Tintunger, Catherine 10; America, 1846 ***778.6*** *p326*
Tintunger, N. 41; America, 1846 ***778.6*** *p326*
Tiolet, Louise; Quebec, 1650 ***9221.17*** *p228*
Tipits, George 73; Ontario, 1871 ***1823.21*** *p369*
Tiplee, George; North Carolina, 1792-1862 ***1088.45*** *p35*
Tipler, Ann; Annapolis, MD, 1729 ***1220.12*** *p803*
Tippe, Jacob 20; Halifax, N.S., 1902 ***1860.4*** *p42*
Tipper, James; America, 1747 ***1220.12*** *p803*
Tipper, John; America, 1742 ***1220.12*** *p803*
Tipper, Mary; America, 1757 ***1220.12*** *p803*
Tippett, Abraham; America, 1753 ***1220.12*** *p803*
Tippett, Jane; America, 1770 ***1220.12*** *p803*
Tippett, Matthew; Virginia, 1736 ***1220.12*** *p803*
Tippett, Thomas; Virginia, 1718 ***1220.12*** *p803*
Tipping, Francis; America, 1766 ***1220.12*** *p803*
Tipping, James; America, 1738 ***1220.12*** *p803*
Tipping, John; America, 1739 ***1220.12*** *p803*
Tipping, Mary; Maryland, 1725 ***1220.12*** *p803*
Tipping, Thomas; America, 1748 ***1220.12*** *p803*
Tipping, Thomas; America, 1770 ***1220.12*** *p803*
Tiptee, Bathsheba; America, 1758 ***1220.12*** *p803*
Tipton, Elizabeth; America, 1742 ***1220.12*** *p803*
Tipton, Francis; America, 1773 ***1220.12*** *p804*
Tiran, Pierre; Montreal, 1650 ***9221.17*** *p233*
Tireau, Toussaint; Quebec, 1643 ***9221.17*** *p135*
Tireman, John; America, 1771 ***1220.12*** *p804*
Tiremont, Noelle; Quebec, 1670 ***4514.3*** *p374*
Tireur, Louis Joseph; Wisconsin, 1880 ***1495.20*** *p56*
*Wife:*Marie Julie Bergilez
Tireur, Marie Julie Bergilez *SEE* Tireur, Louis Joseph

Tirey, Pierre; Louisiana, 1836-1840 ***4981.45*** *p213*
Tiron, Joseph 18; Missouri, 1845 ***778.6*** *p326*
Tisdale, Rebecca; America, 1762 ***1220.12*** *p804*
Tisdall, Charles; Potomac, 1731 ***1220.12*** *p804*
Tisdell, Elizabeth; Barbados or Jamaica, 1686 ***1220.12*** *p804*
Tisdell, William Adams; Virginia, 1759 ***1220.12*** *p804*
Tisden, Mary; Maryland, 1734 ***1220.12*** *p804*
Tisely, John; America, 1766 ***1220.12*** *p804*
Tislaige, Alphonse 25; New Orleans, 1848 ***778.6*** *p326*
Tisne, Aug.; Louisiana, 1874 ***4981.45*** *p297*
Tison, Henry; America, 1751 ***1220.12*** *p819*
Tissac, Jan 27; America, 1848 ***778.6*** *p326*
Tissant, James; Annapolis, MD, 1723 ***1220.12*** *p804*
Tisserand, Mr. 27; America, 1841 ***778.6*** *p326*
Tisserand, Edingen 19; Missouri, 1845 ***778.6*** *p326*
Tisserand, Jean; Quebec, 1642 ***9221.17*** *p122*
Tisserand, Madeleine; Quebec, 1673 ***4514.3*** *p374*
Tisserand, Remy 25; Louisiana, 1848 ***778.6*** *p326*
Tissier, Paul; Quebec, 1650 ***9221.17*** *p230*
Tisson, Pierre 31; New Orleans, 1848 ***778.6*** *p326*
Tissue, William; Pennsylvania, 1772 ***9228.50*** *p625*
Titchborn, Ann; America, 1752 ***1220.12*** *p804*
Titchborne, Elizabeth; America, 1758 ***1220.12*** *p804*
Titherington, Elizabeth; Barbados, 1697 ***1220.12*** *p804*
Titman, William; America, 1726 ***1220.12*** *p804*
Titmus, William; America, 1765 ***1220.12*** *p804*
Titsworth, Isaac; New Jersey, 1773-1774 ***927.31*** *p2*
Titten, Richard; America, 1752 ***1220.12*** *p804*
Tittle, William; Charles Town, SC, 1718 ***1220.12*** *p804*
Titz, Anastasia 6 months; New York, NY, 1883 ***8427.14*** *p44*
Titz, Francis; New York, 1859 ***358.56*** *p53*
Titz, H. Martin 31; New York, NY, 1883 ***8427.14*** *p44*
Titz, Maria 34; New York, NY, 1883 ***8427.14*** *p44*
Tiverton, Joseph; America, 1766 ***1220.12*** *p804*
Tiverton, William; America, 1685 ***1220.12*** *p804*
Tivey, James; America, 1677 ***1220.12*** *p804*
Tizard, Elizabeth; America, 1754 ***1220.12*** *p804*
Tizard, Henry; America, 1685 ***1220.12*** *p804*
Tizard, John; Potomac, 1731 ***1220.12*** *p804*
Tizzard, John; Maryland, 1740 ***1220.12*** *p804*
Tjernstrom, Wilfred; Cleveland, OH, 1895-1899 ***9722.10*** *p127*
Tjust, Olof Emil; Cleveland, OH, 1887-1894 ***9722.10*** *p127*
Toal, William 42; Ontario, 1871 ***1823.21*** *p369*
Toale, George; America, 1747 ***1220.12*** *p805*
Toamy, William; America, 1766 ***1220.12*** *p804*
Toamy, William; Boston, 1756 ***1642*** *p47*
Toane, Jane 44; Ontario, 1871 ***1823.21*** *p369*
Toane, William 60; Ontario, 1871 ***1823.21*** *p369*
Toasten, Mary; America, 1746 ***1220.12*** *p804*
Toban, Michael; Boston, 1769 ***1642*** *p40*
Tobeings, Ann; America, 1758 ***1220.12*** *p804*
Tobias, Mr.; Kansas, 1855 ***2853.20*** *p201*
Tobin, . . .; Ontario, 1871 ***1823.21*** *p369*
Tobin, Bridget; New Orleans, 1851 ***7242.30*** *p155*
Tobin, Edward; America, 1695 ***1220.12*** *p804*
Tobin, Garrett; America, 1749 ***1220.12*** *p804*
Tobin, Georg. H.; Louisiana, 1836-1841 ***4981.45*** *p209*
Tobin, James; America, 1754 ***1220.12*** *p804*
Tobin, James 47; Ontario, 1871 ***1823.21*** *p369*
Tobin, John; Louisiana, 1836-1840 ***4981.45*** *p213*
Tobin, Patrick; New Orleans, 1851 ***7242.30*** *p155*
Tobin, Patrick 25; Ontario, 1871 ***1823.17*** *p164*
Tobin, Patt; New Orleans, 1851 ***7242.30*** *p155*
Tobin, Thomas 46; Ontario, 1871 ***1823.17*** *p164*
Tobin, Walter; Virginia, 1763 ***1220.12*** *p804*
Tobolt, Wilhelm; Wisconsin, 1900 ***6795.8*** *p129*
Toburen, Frederick; Ohio, 1809-1852 ***4511.35*** *p54*
Tock, Nikolaus Victor; America, 1881 ***5475.1*** *p161*
Tocki, Joseph; Detroit, 1890 ***9980.23*** *p96*
Tocque, George; Beverly, MA, 1701 ***9228.50*** *p469*
Tod, Alexander 30; Ontario, 1871 ***1823.21*** *p369*
Todard, Joseph; Wisconsin, 1901 ***6795.8*** *p130*
Todd, Andrew 40; Ontario, 1871 ***1823.17*** *p164*
Todd, Ann; Virginia, 1732 ***1220.12*** *p804*
Todd, Charles; America, 1771 ***1220.12*** *p804*
Todd, David; Maryland, 1744 ***1220.12*** *p804*
Todd, David 31; Ontario, 1871 ***1823.21*** *p369*
Todd, Disney; America, 1726 ***1220.12*** *p804*
Todd, Edwin 44; Ontario, 1871 ***1823.21*** *p370*
Todd, Gilbert 55; Ontario, 1871 ***1823.21*** *p370*
Todd, James; America, 1772 ***1220.12*** *p804*
Todd, John; America, 1760 ***1220.12*** *p804*
Todd, John; Barbados, 1679 ***1220.12*** *p804*
Todd, John 52; Ontario, 1871 ***1823.21*** *p370*
Todd, Mary A. 38; Michigan, 1880 ***4491.42*** *p27*
Todd, Richard; America, 1738 ***1220.12*** *p804*
Todd, Robert; America, 1732 ***1220.12*** *p804*
Todd, Robert; America, 1740 ***1220.12*** *p804*
Todd, Robert; Barbados or Jamaica, 1685 ***1220.12*** *p804*
Todd, Samuel; America, 1760 ***1220.12*** *p804*
Todd, Sarah; America, 1755 ***1220.12*** *p804*
Todd, Thomas; Annapolis, MD, 1725 ***1220.12*** *p804*
Todd, William; America, 1721 ***1220.12*** *p804*
Todd, William; America, 1726 ***1220.12*** *p804*
Todd, William; America, 1743 ***1220.12*** *p804*
Todd, William; America, 1764 ***1220.12*** *p805*
Todd, William; America, 1768 ***1220.12*** *p805*
Todd, William; America, 1769 ***1220.12*** *p805*
Todd, William; America, 1772 ***1220.12*** *p805*
Todell, John; America, 1773 ***1220.12*** *p805*
Todhunter, Thomas; Barbados, 1683 ***1220.12*** *p805*
Todman, John; America, 1728 ***1220.12*** *p805*
Toelke, Emilie; Dakota, 1859-1918 ***554.30*** *p26*
Toepfer, Vaclav; Milwaukee, 1854 ***2853.20*** *p308*
Toes, William; America, 1733 ***1220.12*** *p807*
Toews, Franz Richard; Wisconsin, 1901 ***6795.8*** *p237*
Toft, James; America, 1753 ***1220.12*** *p805*
Toft, William; America, 1763 ***1220.12*** *p805*
Togerdell, John 36; Ontario, 1871 ***1823.21*** *p370*
Togni, Celestini 18; New Orleans, 1748 ***778.6*** *p326*
Tohey, Mary 20; Ontario, 1871 ***1823.21*** *p370*
Tohey, William 45; Ontario, 1871 ***1823.21*** *p370*
Toineboin, Engel Marie Sophie; America, 1856 ***7420.1*** *p144*
Toineboin, Engel Marie Sophie; America, 1856 ***7420.1*** *p144*
Toivonen, Charles 43; Minnesota, 1926 ***2769.54*** *p1383*
Toivonen, Jennie 27; Minnesota, 1926 ***2769.54*** *p1383*
Toivonen, Louise 34; Minnesota, 1923 ***2769.54*** *p1383*
Tokarsky, Malwine; Wisconsin, 1897 ***6795.8*** *p216*
Tokman, Wolf; Detroit, 1929 ***1640.55*** *p116*
Toland, John; South Carolina, 1808 ***6155.4*** *p19*
Toland, John W.; North Carolina, 1792-1862 ***1088.45*** *p35*
Tolar, Jan; Illinois, 1851-1910 ***2853.20*** *p471*
Tole, Patrick 72; Ontario, 1871 ***1823.17*** *p164*
Tole, Richard; Virginia, 1736 ***1220.12*** *p806*
Toleard, Ursula; Maryland, 1719 ***1220.12*** *p805*
Toleman, Timothy; America, 1685 ***1220.12*** *p805*
Toles, Samuel 41; Ontario, 1871 ***1823.21*** *p370*
Tolhorst, Edward 25; Ontario, 1871 ***1823.21*** *p370*
Tolhorst, John William 23; Ontario, 1871 ***1823.21*** *p370*
Tolhurst, John; America, 1742 ***1220.12*** *p805*
Tolhurst, John; America, 1766 ***1220.12*** *p805*
Tolke, Johann Heinrich Conrad; Port uncertain, 1836 ***7420.1*** *p12*
Tolkin, F.; California, 1868 ***1131.61*** *p90*
Toll, Frantisek; Wisconsin, 1853 ***2853.20*** *p303*
Toll, Peter 29; Ontario, 1871 ***1823.21*** *p370*
Toll, Thomas; Barbados or Jamaica, 1684 ***1220.12*** *p805*
Tollerfield, William; America, 1752 ***1220.12*** *p805*
Tolley, John; America, 1766 ***1220.12*** *p805*
Tollington, William; America, 1774 ***1220.12*** *p805*
Tolman, Samuel; Barbados, 1688 ***1220.12*** *p805*
Tolmy, John; America, 1772 ***1220.12*** *p805*
Tolrstad, John Mattson; New York, 1895 ***1766.20*** *p18*
Tolson, Jno; Jamestown, VA, 1633 ***1658.20*** *p211*
Tomas, John; Portsmouth, NH, 1718 ***9228.50*** *p623*
Tomasek, Karel; Wisconsin, 1856 ***2853.20*** *p344*
Tomassin, Charles; Louisiana, 1874 ***4981.45*** *p134*
Tomasz, Andrej 36; New York, NY, 1920 ***930.50*** *p49*
Tomaszewska, Clara; Wisconsin, 1897 ***6795.8*** *p61*
Tomaszewski, Anthony; Detroit, 1930 ***1640.60*** *p82*
Tomaszewski, Jan 42; New York, NY, 1920 ***930.50*** *p48*
Tomazo, Jacobina 14; Quebec, 1870 ***8364.32*** *p26*
Tombal, Josephine; Wisconsin, 1869 ***1495.20*** *p56*
Tomblinson, William; America, 1773 ***1220.12*** *p805*
Tombs, Edward; America, 1762 ***1220.12*** *p807*
Tombs, Francis; America, 1753 ***1220.12*** *p807*
Tombs, James; America, 1736 ***1220.12*** *p807*
Tomek, Vaclav; Nebraska, 1870 ***2853.20*** *p193*
Tomey, Bridget 13 *SEE* Tomey, Michael
Tomey, Margrett 15 *SEE* Tomey, Michael
Tomey, Michael 19; Ohio, 1880 ***4879.40*** *p259*
*Sister:*Margrett 15
*Sister:*Bridget 13
Tomilson, Samuel 68; Ontario, 1871 ***1823.17*** *p164*
Tomilson, Thomas 45; Ontario, 1871 ***1823.21*** *p370*
Tominson, Joseph; Philadelphia, 1778 ***8529.30*** *p3*
Tomkins, John; America, 1763 ***1220.12*** *p806*
Tomkins, Joseph; America, 1757 ***1220.12*** *p806*
Tomkins, William; America, 1694 ***1220.12*** *p806*
Tomkins, William; America, 1749 ***1220.12*** *p806*
Tomkinson, Albert; Colorado, 1900 ***1029.59*** *p90*
Tomkinson, Thomas; America, 1692 ***1220.12*** *p805*
Tomkyns, Thomas; America, 1757 ***1220.12*** *p806*
Tomkyns, Thomas; America, 1770 ***1220.12*** *p806*
Tomlin, Elizabeth; Maryland, 1735 ***1220.12*** *p805*
Tomlin, John; America, 1774 ***1220.12*** *p805*
Tomlin, John 40; Ontario, 1871 ***1823.17*** *p164*
Tomlin, John 56; Ontario, 1871 ***1823.21*** *p370*
Tomlin, Mary; America, 1732 ***1220.12*** *p805*
Tomlin, Mary; America, 1752 ***1220.12*** *p805*
Tomlin, Richard; America, 1770 ***1220.12*** *p805*
Tomlin, Thomas; Maryland, 1723 ***1220.12*** *p805*
Tomlin, William; America, 1768 ***1220.12*** *p805*
Tomlin, William; Maryland, 1723 ***1220.12*** *p805*
Tomlin, William; Maryland, 1725 ***1220.12*** *p805*
Tomlin, William 43; Ontario, 1871 ***1823.17*** *p164*
Tomlin, William 50; Ontario, 1871 ***1823.21*** *p370*
Tomlins, Frances; America, 1715 ***1220.12*** *p805*
Tomlins, George; America, 1774 ***1220.12*** *p805*
Tomlins, Martha; America, 1719 ***1220.12*** *p805*
Tomlinson, Daniel 53; Michigan, 1880 ***4491.30*** *p31*
Tomlinson, Edward; America, 1751 ***1220.12*** *p805*
Tomlinson, Harriett 48; Michigan, 1880 ***4491.30*** *p31*
Tomlinson, James; America, 1733 ***1220.12*** *p805*
Tomlinson, James 61; Ontario, 1871 ***1823.21*** *p370*
Tomlinson, John; America, 1759 ***1220.12*** *p805*
Tomlinson, John; America, 1770 ***1220.12*** *p805*
Tomlinson, John; Maryland, 1753 ***1220.12*** *p805*
Tomlinson, Joseph; Maryland, 1744 ***1220.12*** *p805*
Tomlinson, Michael; America, 1767 ***1220.12*** *p805*
Tomlinson, Richard; America, 1754 ***1220.12*** *p805*
Tomlinson, Samuel; Ontario, 1871 ***1823.17*** *p164*
Tomlinson, Thomas; America, 1738 ***1220.12*** *p805*
Tomlinson, William 50; Ontario, 1871 ***1823.21*** *p370*
Tommey, Dorothy; Jamaica, 1665 ***1220.12*** *p805*
Tommey, Patrick; Colorado, 1873 ***1029.59*** *p90*
Tompkin, Martha; Maryland, 1719 ***1220.12*** *p806*
Tompkins, Benjamin; Barbados, 1675 ***1220.12*** *p806*
Tompkins, Elizabeth; Barbados or Jamaica, 1700 ***1220.12*** *p806*
Tompkins, Henry; America, 1753 ***1220.12*** *p806*
Tompkins, Thomas; Ohio, 1840 ***2763.1*** *p22*
Tompkins, Wm. A.; Colorado, 1880 ***1029.59*** *p90*
Tompkinson, Edward 59; Michigan, 1880 ***4491.36*** *p22*
Tompor, John; Detroit, 1929-1930 ***6214.5*** *p67*
Tompson, Richard; America, 1768 ***1220.12*** *p797*
Tompson, Samuel; America, 1770 ***1220.12*** *p798*
Tompson, William; America, 1774 ***1220.12*** *p798*
Tompson, Wm.; Maryland, 1672 ***1236.25*** *p47*
Toms, Christiana; Maryland, 1726 ***1220.12*** *p806*
Toms, David; America, 1747 ***1220.12*** *p806*
Toms, Edward; America, 1772 ***1220.12*** *p806*
Toms, Elizabeth; America, 1770 ***1220.12*** *p806*
Toms, George; America, 1773 ***1220.12*** *p806*
Toms, James; America, 1759 ***1220.12*** *p806*
Toms, John; America, 1694 ***1220.12*** *p806*
Toms, John; America, 1750 ***1220.12*** *p806*
Toms, John; Maryland, 1741 ***1220.12*** *p806*
Toms, John; Massachusetts, 1870-1879 ***9228.50*** *p627*
Toms, Sarah; America, 1767 ***1220.12*** *p806*
Tomson, Anna; Cleveland, OH, 1903 ***9722.10*** *p126*
Tomson, Archibald *SEE* Tomson, Dugald
Tomson, Christie *SEE* Tomson, Dugald
Tomson, Dugald; New York, 1739 ***8277.31*** *p119*
*Wife:*Margaret McDuffie
*Child:*Duncan
*Child:*Christie
*Child:*Archibald
Tomson, Duncan *SEE* Tomson, Dugald
Tomson, Margaret McDuffie *SEE* Tomson, Dugald
Toncar, Jakub; New York, NY, 1852 ***2853.20*** *p386*
Tonebone, Johann Friedrich; America, 1855 ***7420.1*** *p142*
Tong, Miss 16; North Carolina, 1774 ***1422.10*** *p55*
Tong, William; Marston's Wharf, 1782 ***8529.30*** *p16*
Tonge, Mary; America, 1745 ***1220.12*** *p806*
Tongison, Mary; Virginia, 1726 ***1220.12*** *p806*
Tongring, Geo; Cleveland, OH, 1903-1904 ***9722.10*** *p127*
Tongue, Charles; America, 1743 ***1220.12*** *p806*
Tongue, John; Annapolis, MD, 1725 ***1220.12*** *p806*
Tongue, Mary; America, 1743 ***1220.12*** *p806*
Tongue, William; Marston's Wharf, 1782 ***8529.30*** *p16*
Tonhill, Samuel 45; Ontario, 1871 ***1823.21*** *p370*
Tonjes, Gerhard 23; New York, NY, 1864 ***8425.62*** *p196*
Tonkin, Edward 48; Ontario, 1871 ***1823.21*** *p370*
Tonkin, Elizabeth 11; Quebec, 1870 ***8364.32*** *p26*
Tonkins, James; America, 1768 ***1220.12*** *p806*
Tonks, Aaron; America, 1766 ***1220.12*** *p806*
Tonks, William; America, 1774 ***1220.12*** *p806*
Tonkyn, John; America, 1756 ***1220.12*** *p806*
Tonn, August; Wisconsin, 1894 ***6795.8*** *p127*
Tonn, Emil; Wisconsin, 1913 ***6795.8*** *p169*
Tonn, Emil Johann; Wisconsin, 1900 ***6795.8*** *p133*
Tonn, Johann Wilhelm; Wisconsin, 1871 ***6795.8*** *p34*
Tonn, Theodor Ed.; Wisconsin, 1890 ***6795.8*** *p133*
Tonn, William; Wisconsin, 1885 ***6795.8*** *p52*
Tonne, Antoine *SEE* Tonne, Pierre Joseph
Tonne, Emmanuel *SEE* Tonne, Pierre Joseph
Tonne, Jean Joseph *SEE* Tonne, Pierre Joseph
Tonne, Marie Therese *SEE* Tonne, Pierre Joseph
Tonne, Marie Therese Josephine Saintrong *SEE* Tonne, Pierre Joseph

512 *FOR A COMPLETE EXPLANATION OF ENTRY, SEE "HOW TO READ A CITATION" SECTION*

Tonne, Pierre Joseph; Wisconsin, 1855 ***1495.20*** *p46*
*Wife:*Marie Therese Josephine Saintrong
*Child:*Marie Therese
*Child:*Antoine
*Child:*Marie Therese
*Child:*Emmanuel
*Child:*Jean Joseph
Tonneslier, Anne 56; Mississippi, 1847 ***778.6*** *p326*
Tonneslier, Catherina 32; Mississippi, 1847 ***778.6*** *p326*
Tonneslier, Jacob 12; Mississippi, 1847 ***778.6*** *p326*
Tonneslier, Johan 30; Mississippi, 1847 ***778.6*** *p326*
Tonneslier, Maria 25; Mississippi, 1847 ***778.6*** *p326*
Tonneslier, Maria 25; Mississippi, 1847 ***778.6*** *p326*
Tonneslier, Pierre 19; Mississippi, 1847 ***778.6*** *p326*
Tonnoffski, George H.; North Carolina, 1837 ***1088.45*** *p35*
Tonty, Alphonse de; Quebec, 1683-1688 ***2314.30*** *p169*
Tonty, Alphonse de; Quebec, 1685 ***2314.30*** *p197*
Tonty, Henri de; Quebec, 1678 ***2314.30*** *p166*
Tonty, Henri de; Quebec, 1678 ***2314.30*** *p197*
Tony, Anthony; America, 1736 ***1220.12*** *p806*
Toogood, James; America, 1749 ***1220.12*** *p806*
Toogood, John; America, 1749 ***1220.12*** *p806*
Toogood, William 22; Ontario, 1871 ***1823.17*** *p164*
Toohey, Bridget 35; Ontario, 1871 ***1823.21*** *p370*
Toohey, Catherine 50; Ontario, 1871 ***1823.21*** *p370*
Toohey, Denis 72; Ontario, 1871 ***1823.21*** *p370*
Toohey, James 35; Ontario, 1871 ***1823.21*** *p370*
Toohey, John 30; Ontario, 1871 ***1823.21*** *p370*
Toohey, John 57; Ontario, 1871 ***1823.21*** *p370*
Toohey, Margret 34; Ontario, 1871 ***1823.21*** *p370*
Toohey, Mary 71; Ontario, 1871 ***1823.21*** *p370*
Toohey, Patrick 80; Ontario, 1871 ***1823.21*** *p370*
Toohey, Timothy 42; Ontario, 1871 ***1823.21*** *p370*
Toohey, Timothy 50; Ontario, 1871 ***1823.21*** *p370*
Toohill, Mary 90; Ontario, 1871 ***1823.21*** *p370*
Toohill, Patrick; Illinois, 1834-1900 ***6020.5*** *p133*
Toohy, Michael; Illinois, 1834-1900 ***6020.5*** *p133*
Took, S. G.; Texas, 1852 ***3435.45*** *p37*
Tool, Alice; Boston, 1743 ***1642*** *p45*
Tool, Anstis; Boston, 1744 ***1642*** *p45*
Tool, Christian; Virginia, 1726 ***1220.12*** *p806*
Tool, David; America, 1768 ***1220.12*** *p806*
Tool, James; Boston, 1766 ***1642*** *p36*
Toole, Anne; New Orleans, 1850 ***7242.30*** *p155*
Toole, Boyan; Boston, 1723 ***1642*** *p25*
Toole, Catherine; New Orleans, 1850 ***7242.30*** *p155*
Toole, Christopher; Virginia, 1734 ***1220.12*** *p806*
Toole, James; America, 1767 ***1220.12*** *p806*
Toole, James; New Orleans, 1850 ***7242.30*** *p155*
Toole, John; Boston, 1740 ***1642*** *p45*
Toole, John 46; Michigan, 1880 ***4491.39*** *p30*
Toole, John; New Orleans, 1850 ***7242.30*** *p155*
Toole, Margaret; New Orleans, 1850 ***7242.30*** *p155*
Toole, Martin 28; New York, NY, 1817-1844 ***3274.55*** *p42*
Toole, Mary; Barbados, 1677 ***1220.12*** *p806*
Toole, Mary 44; Michigan, 1880 ***4491.39*** *p30*
Toole, Mary; New Orleans, 1850 ***7242.30*** *p155*
Toole, Owen; New Orleans, 1850 ***7242.30*** *p155*
Toole, Rich'd; New Orleans, 1851 ***7242.30*** *p155*
Toole, Thomas; America, 1768 ***1220.12*** *p806*
Toole, Tobias; Boston, 1749 ***1642*** *p46*
Toole, William; New Orleans, 1850 ***7242.30*** *p155*
Tooley, Elizabeth; Maryland, 1719 ***1220.12*** *p806*
Tooley, Elizabeth; Virginia, 1736 ***1220.12*** *p806*
Tooley, Fool; America, 1746 ***1220.12*** *p806*
Tooley, John; America, 1754 ***1220.12*** *p806*
Tooley, Mary; America, 1765 ***1220.12*** *p806*
Tooley, Richard 50; Ontario, 1871 ***1823.21*** *p370*
Tooll, Mary; Massachusetts, 1663 ***1642*** *p101*
Tooly, Richard 24; Ontario, 1871 ***1823.21*** *p370*
Tooly, William 23; Ontario, 1871 ***1823.21*** *p370*
Toombes, Ann; America, 1673 ***1220.12*** *p807*
Toombes, John; America, 1767 ***1220.12*** *p807*
Toone, James; America, 1723 ***1220.12*** *p807*
Toone, William; America, 1758 ***1220.12*** *p807*
Tooney, David; Toronto, 1844 ***2910.35*** *p115*
Toop, Joseph; America, 1740 ***1220.12*** *p807*
Toop, William; America, 1752 ***1220.12*** *p807*
Toope, Francis; Boston, 1720 ***1642*** *p25*
Toope, Nicholas; Barbados, 1665 ***1220.12*** *p807*
Tootell, John; America, 1768 ***1220.12*** *p807*
Tootell, Robert; America, 1768 ***1220.12*** *p807*
Tooth, Mary; America, 1732 ***1220.12*** *p807*
Tooth, Robert 52; Ontario, 1871 ***1823.21*** *p370*
Tooth, William; Barbados or Jamaica, 1683 ***1220.12*** *p807*
Toovey, John; America, 1767 ***1220.12*** *p807*
Toovey, Thomas; America, 1752 ***1220.12*** *p807*
Tooworth, Ann; America, 1744 ***1220.12*** *p807*
Topham, John; Barbados or Jamaica, 1696 ***1220.12*** *p807*
Topham, Peter 49; Ontario, 1871 ***1823.21*** *p370*
Topham, Sarah; America, 1773 ***1220.12*** *p807*
Tophurst, Francis; America, 1765 ***1220.12*** *p807*
Topka, Tomas; Minnesota, 1858-1860 ***2853.20*** *p260*
Topliss, Joseph 35; Ontario, 1871 ***1823.21*** *p370*
Toplitz, S. Solomn; Texas, 1893 ***3435.45*** *p37*
Toponet, Francois 45; Port uncertain, 1847 ***778.6*** *p326*
Toponet, Louis 13; Port uncertain, 1847 ***778.6*** *p326*
Topp, Carl Victor; St. Paul, MN, 1889 ***1865.50*** *p113*
*Wife:*Emma A. Johnson
Topp, Emma A. Johnson *SEE* Topp, Carl Victor
Topp, William; Maryland, 1742 ***1220.12*** *p807*
Toppin, Calvin 30; Ontario, 1871 ***1823.21*** *p370*
Toppin, Henry; Virginia, 1652 ***6254.4*** *p243*
Toppin, Mary; America, 1740 ***1220.12*** *p807*
Topping, Henry; America, 1700 ***1220.12*** *p807*
Topping, Henry; America, 1758 ***1220.12*** *p807*
Topping, James; America, 1757 ***1220.12*** *p807*
Topping, John; America, 1775 ***1220.12*** *p807*
Topping, John 62; Ontario, 1871 ***1823.21*** *p371*
Topping, Joyce; America, 1762 ***1220.12*** *p807*
Topping, Mikel 77; Ontario, 1871 ***1823.21*** *p371*
Topping, William; Virginia, 1736 ***1220.12*** *p807*
Topps, Susanna; America, 1755 ***1220.12*** *p807*
Topsan, Catherine; Quebec, 1667 ***4514.3*** *p374*
Toralle, Jean Pierre 45; New Orleans, 1848 ***778.6*** *p326*
Torance, Connoly 30; Ontario, 1871 ***1823.21*** *p371*
Torance, Jane 50; Ontario, 1871 ***1823.21*** *p371*
Torance, Samuel 70; Ontario, 1871 ***1823.21*** *p371*
Torance, William 44; Ontario, 1871 ***1823.21*** *p371*
Torankuz, Antoni 39; New York, NY, 1920 ***930.50*** *p49*
Toratti, Imby 24; Minnesota, 1926 ***2769.54*** *p1382*
Torcapel, Jean; Quebec, 1659 ***9221.17*** *p393*
Tordeur, Amelie; Wisconsin, 1869 ***1495.20*** *p56*
Tordeur, Caroline; Wisconsin, 1869 ***1495.20*** *p56*
Tordeur, Etienne; Wisconsin, 1855 ***1495.20*** *p56*
*Wife:*Rosalie Bourguignon
Tordeur, Henri; Wisconsin, 1855 ***1495.20*** *p56*
*Wife:*Seraphine Bourguignon
*Son:*Joseph
Tordeur, Joseph *SEE* Tordeur, Henri
Tordeur, Joseph; Wisconsin, 1870 ***1495.20*** *p56*
Tordeur, Marie; Wisconsin, 1856 ***1495.20*** *p56*
Tordeur, Marie Therese; Wisconsin, 1856 ***1495.20*** *p56*
Tordeur, Rosalie Bourguignon *SEE* Tordeur, Etienne
Tordeur, Seraphine Bourguignon *SEE* Tordeur, Henri
Torgler, . . .; West Virginia, n.d. ***1132.30*** *p151*
Torkelson, Jul; Minnesota, 1888 ***1029.59*** *p90*
Torkelson, Jul; New York, NY, 1885 ***1029.59*** *p90*
Torkelson, Torkel; Iowa, 1866 ***1211.15*** *p19*
Tornberg, Christina; St. Paul, MN, 1880 ***1865.50*** *p113*
Tornblety, Mary; Ontario, 1835 ***3160.1*** *p150*
Tornblom, Anna; St. Paul, MN, 1887 ***1865.50*** *p45*
Torner, A.F.; New York, NY, 1845 ***6412.40*** *p149*
Torney, Hans Hugo von; Canada, 1894 ***7420.1*** *p371*
Tornow, Anna; Wisconsin, 1884 ***6795.8*** *p77*
Tornqvist, Frans Otto; St. Paul, MN, 1901 ***1865.50*** *p113*
*Wife:*Hulda M.
Tornqvist, Hulda M. *SEE* Tornqvist, Frans Otto
Torode, Alfred; Ontario, 1920-1929 ***9228.50*** *p627*
*Wife:*Mary Dorey
*Child:*Clifford
With family
Torode, Clifford *SEE* Torode, Alfred
Torode, Ella Louise; Ontario, 1900-1983 ***9228.50*** *p630*
Torode, James; Ohio, 1780-1812 ***9228.50*** *p630*
Torode, John; Ohio, 1807 ***9228.50*** *p57*
Torode, John; Ohio, 1807 ***9228.50*** *p627*
*Brother:*Peter
Torode, Mary Dorey *SEE* Torode, Alfred
Torode, Nicholas; Ohio, 1820 ***9228.50*** *p630*
With wife & 2 sons
Torode, Peter; Ohio, 1807 ***9228.50*** *p57*
Torode, Peter *SEE* Torode, John
Torode Brothers, . . .; America, 1807 ***9228.50*** *p147*
With sisters
Torode Family ; Illinois, 1840 ***9228.50*** *p64*
Torowsky, Franz 38; Baltimore, 1889 ***8425.16*** *p35*
Torquet, Paul; Canada, 1827-1864 ***9228.50*** *p630*
Torquet, Paul; San Francisco, 1864 ***9228.50*** *p630*
Torrance, John 48; Ontario, 1871 ***1823.21*** *p371*
Torrey, Samuel *SEE* Torrey, Wm.
Torrey, William *SEE* Torrey, Wm.
Torrey, Wm.; New England, 1640 ***9228.50*** *p275*
*Son:*Samuel
*Son:*William
Torrince, Abraham; America, 1764 ***1220.12*** *p807*
Torry, Catharine *SEE* Torry, James
Torry, Florence McKay *SEE* Torry, James
Torry, James; New York, 1739 ***8277.31*** *p120*
*Wife:*Florence McKay
*Child:*Mary
*Child:*Catharine
Torry, Mary *SEE* Torry, James
Torscell, John; Cleveland, OH, 1884-1892 ***9722.10*** *p127*
Tortoria, Antonnio; Louisiana, 1874 ***4981.45*** *p134*
Tory, John M. 23; Ontario, 1871 ***1823.21*** *p371*
Tose, Henry; Barbados, 1679 ***1220.12*** *p807*
Tosh, Adam; Washington, 1882 ***2770.40*** *p136*
Tosh, John; Washington, 1887 ***2770.40*** *p25*
Tossick, James; America, 1758 ***1220.12*** *p807*
Tosswick, James; America, 1758 ***1220.12*** *p807*
Tostevin, Ada; Victoria, B.C., 1886-1983 ***9228.50*** *p631*
Tostevin, Alfred *SEE* Tostevin, John
Tostevin, Arthur; New Hampshire, 1912 ***9228.50*** *p631*
Tostevin, Clifford; Victoria, B.C., 1901-1983 ***9228.50*** *p631*
Tostevin, Eliza Jane; Victoria, B.C., 1912 ***9228.50*** *p576*
Tostevin, Elizabeth; Wisconsin, n.d. ***9228.50*** *p631*
Tostevin, Ethel; Victoria, B.C., 1917 ***9228.50*** *p631*
Tostevin, George; Wisconsin, 1860-1869 ***9228.50*** *p631*
Tostevin, Harry; New Hampshire, 1889-1973 ***9228.50*** *p631*
Tostevin, Jack; New Hampshire, 1884-1974 ***9228.50*** *p631*
Tostevin, James P.; Wisconsin, 1860 ***9228.50*** *p631*
*Wife:*Julia Burgess
Tostevin, John *SEE* Tostevin, John
Tostevin, John; Philadelphia, 1825-1856 ***9228.50*** *p630*
*Wife:*Martha Le Prevost
*Child:*Alfred
*Child:*Rachel
*Child:*John
*Child:*Martha
Tostevin, John; Wisconsin, 1850 ***9228.50*** *p631*
Tostevin, Julia Burgess *SEE* Tostevin, James P.
Tostevin, Margaret; Wisconsin, 1860 ***9228.50*** *p631*
Tostevin, Martha *SEE* Tostevin, John
Tostevin, Martha Le Prevost *SEE* Tostevin, John
Tostevin, Nicholas; Quebec, 1826 ***9228.50*** *p631*
Tostevin, Rachel *SEE* Tostevin, John
Tostevin, Reta; California, 1917-1973 ***9228.50*** *p631*
Tostevin, Reta; Victoria, B.C., 1917 ***9228.50*** *p631*
Totell, Samuel; America, 1685 ***1220.12*** *p807*
Totten, Edward 24; Ontario, 1871 ***1823.21*** *p371*
Tottle, Jasper; America, 1746 ***1220.12*** *p807*
Totton, Henry 50; Ontario, 1871 ***1823.21*** *p371*
Totty, Frances; Annapolis, MD, 1723 ***1220.12*** *p807*
Totty, James; America, 1740 ***1220.12*** *p807*
Touaille, Charles; Quebec, 1659 ***9221.17*** *p414*
Touan, B. 40; Port uncertain, 1843 ***778.6*** *p327*
Touchard, H., Jr. 23; America, 1847 ***778.6*** *p327*
Touchbourne, Andrew 43; Ontario, 1871 ***1823.17*** *p164*
Toucher, Denis Riviere 22; Texas, 1848 ***778.6*** *p327*
Touchet, Nicolas; Quebec, 1649 ***9221.17*** *p221*
Touchet, Simon 5 *SEE* Touchet, Suzanne Ferrier
Touchet, Suzanne; Quebec, 1661 ***9221.17*** *p470*
*Relative:*Simon
Touchet, Thomas 26; Quebec, 1645 ***9221.17*** *p157*
Touet, Ann; America, 1870 ***9228.50*** *p623*
Touet, Ann; America, 1870 ***9228.50*** *p631*
Tough, John; Barbados, 1694 ***1220.12*** *p807*
Touk, Richard; Virginia, 1768 ***1220.12*** *p806*
Toulandou, Pierre 19; New Orleans, 1844 ***778.6*** *p327*
Toulson, Clement; America, 1673 ***1220.12*** *p807*
Toumakis, Christafis 45; New York, NY, 1894 ***6512.1*** *p186*
Toumakis, Constantin 7; New York, NY, 1894 ***6512.1*** *p186*
Toumakis, Georges 50; New York, NY, 1894 ***6512.1*** *p186*
Toumakis, Panayota 15; New York, NY, 1894 ***6512.1*** *p186*
Toumine, Lucas 36; New York, 1828 ***9228.50*** *p624*
Tounch, Robert; America, 1718 ***1220.12*** *p807*
Toupin, Michel; Quebec, 1652 ***9221.17*** *p262*
Toupin, Toussaint 23; Quebec, 1638 ***9221.17*** *p81*
Touraillon, Francois; Quebec, 1660 ***9221.17*** *p439*
Tourault, Francoise 47; Quebec, 1647 ***9221.17*** *p173*
Tourault, Jacquette 41; Quebec, 1653 ***9221.17*** *p275*
*Daughter:*Suzanne 10
Tourault, Jacquette 41; Quebec, 1653 ***9221.17*** *p275*
*Daughter:*Suzanne 10
Toure, Ma.c Antoine 54; New Orleans, 1848 ***778.6*** *p327*
Tourgee, . . .; America, 1670-1730 ***9228.50*** *p634*
Tourgee, . . .; Rhode Island, 1670-1699 ***9228.50*** *p632*
Tourgee, Peter; Rhode Island, 1686 ***9228.50*** *p632*
With brothers
Tourgee, Peter, Jr.; Rhode Island, 1722 ***9228.50*** *p632*
Tourgis, . . .; Rhode Island, 1670-1699 ***9228.50*** *p632*
Tourgis, Peter; Rhode Island, 1686 ***9228.50*** *p632*
With brothers
Tourmente, Pierre; Quebec, 1646 ***9221.17*** *p169*
Tourne, Guillaume 16; New Orleans, 1848 ***778.6*** *p327*
Tourne, J. 22; Port uncertain, 1843 ***778.6*** *p327*
Tourne, J. A. 18; New Orleans, 1843 ***778.6*** *p327*
Tourneuf, Adrien 19; America, 1842 ***778.6*** *p327*

Tourneuf, Amelie 14; America, 1842 ***778.6*** *p327*
Tourneuf, Eugenie 10; America, 1842 ***778.6*** *p327*
Tourneuf, Henriette 39; America, 1842 ***778.6*** *p327*
Tournie, Antoine 25; New Orleans, 1848 ***778.6*** *p327*
Toursey, Francis; America, 1664 ***1220.12*** *p807*
Tousing, Christofer; Maryland, 1673 ***1236.25*** *p48*
Toussaint, Eugenie Lecordier; America, 1866 ***9228.50*** *p164*
Toussaint, Jean 30; New Orleans, 1848 ***778.6*** *p327*
Toussaint, Marie-Jeanne; Quebec, 1670 ***4514.3*** *p374*
Toussaint, Pierre 33; America, 1845 ***778.6*** *p327*
Toutin, Eloi; Montreal, 1661 ***9221.17*** *p475*
Touze, Jeanne; Quebec, 1668 ***4514.3*** *p374*
Touzeau, Michel; Quebec, 1657 ***9221.17*** *p370*
Touzel, Francis; Baltimore, 1870-1879 ***9228.50*** *p21A*
Touzel, John; Massachusetts, 1700 ***9228.50*** *p635*
Tovell, Robert; America, 1760 ***1220.12*** *p807*
Tover, Elizabeth 75; Ontario, 1871 ***1823.17*** *p164*
Tover, James 75; Ontario, 1871 ***1823.17*** *p164*
Tovey, Ann; America, 1766 ***1220.12*** *p807*
Tovey, Hannah; America, 1770 ***1220.12*** *p807*
Tovey, Henry; Barbados, 1678 ***1220.12*** *p807*
Tovey, Richard; America, 1693 ***1220.12*** *p807*
Tow, Joseph 63; Ontario, 1871 ***1823.21*** *p371*
Towe, John 62; Ontario, 1871 ***1823.21*** *p371*
Towell, Anthony; America, 1738 ***1220.12*** *p808*
Towell, Thomas; America, 1769 ***1220.12*** *p808*
Tower, Jane 30; Ontario, 1871 ***1823.21*** *p371*
Towers, Charles; America, 1724 ***1220.12*** *p808*
Towers, Charles 39; Ontario, 1871 ***1823.21*** *p371*
Towers, Daniel; America, 1766 ***1220.12*** *p808*
Towers, Dennis; New York, 1783 ***8529.30*** *p16*
Towers, James; America, 1767 ***1220.12*** *p808*
Towers, Jane; America, 1723 ***1220.12*** *p808*
Towers, Jean; California, 1959 ***9228.50*** *p635*
Towers, John; America, 1751 ***1220.12*** *p808*
Towers, John; America, 1764 ***1220.12*** *p808*
Towers, John; America, 1773 ***1220.12*** *p808*
Towers, Mary; America, 1758 ***1220.12*** *p808*
Towers, Richard; America, 1726 ***1220.12*** *p808*
Towers, Thomas; America, 1673 ***1220.12*** *p808*
Towers, Thomas; Maryland, 1674 ***1236.25*** *p50*
Towgood, James; America, 1772 ***1220.12*** *p806*
Towine, Augustin; Louisiana, 1874-1875 ***4981.45*** *p130*
Towkinson, Albert; Colorado, 1900 ***1029.59*** *p90*
Towl, James; America, 1773 ***1220.12*** *p808*
Towle, Charles 27; Ontario, 1871 ***1823.21*** *p371*
Towle, George 19; Ontario, 1871 ***1823.21*** *p371*
Towle, Peter; America, 1729 ***1220.12*** *p808*
Towle, Stephen 39; Ontario, 1871 ***1823.21*** *p371*
Towler, Thomas; America, 1738 ***1220.12*** *p808*
Towler, Walter; America, 1682 ***1220.12*** *p808*
Towly, Eliza 65; Ontario, 1871 ***1823.21*** *p371*
Town, James; America, 1773 ***1220.12*** *p808*
Towndry, Robert; America, 1719 ***1220.12*** *p808*
Townes, Martha; America, 1724 ***1220.12*** *p808*
Townesend, Thomas; Barbados or Jamaica, 1677 ***1220.12*** *p808*
Towney, Thomas; Louisiana, 1836-1841 ***4981.45*** *p209*
Towning, William; Virginia, 1768 ***1220.12*** *p808*
Townley, John; America, 1751 ***1220.12*** *p808*
Townley, Mary; America, 1756 ***1220.12*** *p808*
Townley, Mary; Annapolis, MD, 1721 ***1220.12*** *p808*
Towns, William 63; Ontario, 1871 ***1823.21*** *p371*
Townsend, Al; Colorado, 1892 ***1029.59*** *p90*
Townsend, Alexander; America, 1685 ***1220.12*** *p808*
Townsend, Christofer; Maryland, 1673 ***1236.25*** *p48*
Townsend, Christopher; Barbados, 1672 ***1220.12*** *p808*
Townsend, Edward; America, 1714 ***1220.12*** *p808*
Townsend, Edward 22; Ontario, 1871 ***1823.21*** *p371*
Townsend, Elizabeth; America, 1751 ***1220.12*** *p808*
Townsend, Elizabeth; Barbados or Jamaica, 1685 ***1220.12*** *p808*
Townsend, Erasmus; Barbados or Jamaica, 1694 ***1220.12*** *p808*
Townsend, Jacob; America, 1759 ***1220.12*** *p808*
Townsend, James; America, 1775 ***1220.12*** *p808*
Townsend, Mary; America, 1737 ***1220.12*** *p808*
Townsend, Mary; Nevis or Jamaica, 1722 ***1220.12*** *p808*
Townsend, Thomas; America, 1685 ***1220.12*** *p808*
Townsend, Thomas; America, 1722 ***1220.12*** *p808*
Townsend, Thomas; America, 1742 ***1220.12*** *p808*
Townsend, Thomas; America, 1765 ***1220.12*** *p808*
Townsend, Thomas; America, 1767 ***1220.12*** *p808*
Townsend, Thomas; America, 1772 ***1220.12*** *p808*
Townsend, Thomas 26; Ontario, 1871 ***1823.17*** *p165*
Townsend, William; America, 1768 ***1220.12*** *p808*
Townshend, Isaac; Ohio, 1834 ***2763.1*** *p22*
Townshend, Joel; Ohio, 1836 ***2763.1*** *p22*
Townshend, Joel, II; Ohio, 1836 ***2763.1*** *p22*
Townshend, John; Ohio, 1836 ***2763.1*** *p22*
Townsprough, Edward 50; Ontario, 1871 ***1823.21*** *p371*
Towsend, John 60; Ontario, 1871 ***1823.21*** *p371*
Towser, George; America, 1766 ***1220.12*** *p808*
Towsey, Thomas; America, 1730 ***1220.12*** *p808*
Towzer, Henry 19; Ontario, 1871 ***1823.21*** *p371*
Towzer, Richard; America, 1751 ***1220.12*** *p808*
Toy, Frederick N. 38; Toronto, 1866 ***9228.50*** *p635*
Toy, Margaret; Maryland, 1725 ***1220.12*** *p809*
Toy, Samuel; America, 1756 ***1220.12*** *p809*
Toynton, Gervase; America, 1709 ***1220.12*** *p809*
Tozeland, Henry 36; Ontario, 1871 ***1823.21*** *p371*
Tozer, John; America, 1749 ***1220.12*** *p808*
Traber, Dagobert 3; Galveston, TX, 1844 ***3967.10*** *p371*
Traber, Joseph 9; Galveston, TX, 1844 ***3967.10*** *p371*
Traber, Joseph 40; Galveston, TX, 1844 ***3967.10*** *p371*
Traber, Marie Elisabeth 34; Galveston, TX, 1844 ***3967.10*** *p371*
Traber, Wilhelmine 4; Galveston, TX, 1844 ***3967.10*** *p371*
Trabert, Bonaventure; North Carolina, 1792-1862 ***1088.45*** *p35*
Trabold, Adam 12 *SEE* Trabold, Heinrich
Trabold, Anna Maria Gotz 42 *SEE* Trabold, Heinrich
Trabold, Barbara Barth 31 *SEE* Trabold, Georg
Trabold, Elisabeth 5 *SEE* Trabold, Heinrich
Trabold, Georg; America, 1740-1899 ***2526.42*** *p132*
Trabold, Georg 9 *SEE* Trabold, Heinrich
Trabold, Georg 29; America, 1854 ***2526.42*** *p116*
*Wife:*Barbara Barth 31
*Child:*Johannes 7
*Child:*Heinrich 2
Trabold, Heinrich; America, 1853 ***2526.42*** *p114*
*Wife:*Anna Maria Gotz
*Child:*Elisabeth
*Child:*Adam
*Child:*Georg
Trabold, Heinrich 2 *SEE* Trabold, Georg
Trabold, Johannes 7 *SEE* Trabold, Georg
Trace, George 32; Ontario, 1871 ***1823.21*** *p371*
Trace, William 45; Ontario, 1871 ***1823.21*** *p371*
Tracey, C.J.; Toronto, 1844 ***2910.35*** *p112*
Tracey, Catherine; America, 1759 ***1220.12*** *p809*
Tracey, Catherine; Annapolis, MD, 1733 ***1220.12*** *p809*
Tracey, Dorothy; America, 1749 ***1220.12*** *p809*
Tracey, George; America, 1738 ***1220.12*** *p809*
Tracey, James; New York, NY, 1778 ***8529.30*** *p3*
Tracey, John; America, 1766 ***1220.12*** *p809*
Tracey, John; Illinois, 1858-1861 ***6020.5*** *p133*
Tracey, John; Toronto, 1844 ***2910.35*** *p114*
Tracey, Mary; Virginia, 1735 ***1220.12*** *p809*
Tracey, Patrick; Newburyport, MA, 1773 ***1642*** *p76*
Tracey, Robert; America, 1721 ***1220.12*** *p809*
Tracey, Robert; Virginia, 1736 ***1220.12*** *p809*
Tracey, William; Toronto, 1844 ***2910.35*** *p113*
Trache, Christophe 26; America, 1847 ***778.6*** *p327*
Trache, Johan 29; America, 1847 ***778.6*** *p327*
Tracht, Anna Elisabetha *SEE* Tracht, Johann Adam
Tracht, Anna Elisabetha Dingeldein *SEE* Tracht, Johann Adam
Tracht, Anna Katharina Vollhard *SEE* Tracht, Johannes
Tracht, Anna Katharina Schaller *SEE* Tracht, Johann Philipp
Tracht, Anna Margaretha *SEE* Tracht, Johann Adam
Tracht, Anna Margaretha; Virginia, 1831 ***152.20*** *p69*
Tracht, Elisabeth Katharina *SEE* Tracht, Johann Adam
Tracht, Eva Elisabetha *SEE* Tracht, Johann Adam
Tracht, Eva Katharina; Virginia, 1831 ***152.20*** *p69*
Tracht, Eva Maria *SEE* Tracht, Johann Philipp
Tracht, Friederike Regina Elisa *SEE* Tracht, Johannes
Tracht, Georg Leo *SEE* Tracht, Johannes
Tracht, Gottfried Nikolaus *SEE* Tracht, Johannes
Tracht, Gustav Ludwig *SEE* Tracht, Johannes
Tracht, Johann Adam; Virginia, 1831 ***152.20*** *p68*
*Wife:*Anna Elisabetha Dingeldein
*Child:*Eva Elisabetha
*Child:*Anna Elisabetha
*Child:*Johann Peter
*Child:*Anna Margaretha
*Child:*Elisabeth Katharina
Tracht, Johann Jakob; Virginia, 1831 ***152.20*** *p69*
Tracht, Johann Peter *SEE* Tracht, Johann Adam
Tracht, Johann Peter *SEE* Tracht, Johannes
Tracht, Johann Peter; Virginia, 1831 ***152.20*** *p69*
Tracht, Johann Philipp; Virginia, 1831 ***152.20*** *p69*
*Wife:*Anna Katharina Schaller
*Child:*Peter
*Child:*Eva Maria
Tracht, Johannes; Virginia, 1831 ***152.20*** *p68*
*Wife:*Anna Katharina Vollhard
*Child:*Georg Leo
*Child:*Friederike Regina Elisa
*Child:*Marie Margarethe Katharina
*Child:*Gottfried Nikolaus
*Child:*Johann Peter
*Child:*Gustav Ludwig
Tracht, Marie Margarethe Katharina *SEE* Tracht, Johannes
Tracht, Peter; Ohio, 1836 ***3580.20*** *p33*
Tracht, Peter; Ohio, 1836 ***6020.12*** *p22*
Tracht, Peter *SEE* Tracht, Johann Philipp
Tracht, Phillip; Ohio, 1836 ***6020.12*** *p22*
Tracht, Phulip; Ohio, 1836 ***3580.20*** *p33*
Trachy, Carole May; Victoria, B.C., 1939-1983 ***9228.50*** *p635*
Trachy, Mary; Quebec, 1850-1915 ***9228.50*** *p635*
Trachy, Mary; Quebec, 1900-1930 ***9228.50*** *p511*
Tracy, Francis; America, 1688 ***1220.12*** *p809*
Tracy, John 45; Ontario, 1871 ***1823.17*** *p165*
Tracy, John 56; Ontario, 1871 ***1823.21*** *p371*
Tracy, Ralph L.; Colorado, 1903 ***1029.59*** *p90*
Tracy, Ralph L.; Port uncertain, 1894 ***1029.59*** *p90*
Tracy, William W.; Ohio, 1825 ***3580.20*** *p33*
Tracy, William W.; Ohio, 1825 ***6020.12*** *p22*
Tracz, Stanislas 27; New York, NY, 1920 ***930.50*** *p49*
Tradinick, Nicholas; North Carolina, 1834 ***1088.45*** *p35*
Traffick, Jeremiah; America, 1745 ***1220.12*** *p809*
Trafford, Charles; America, 1767 ***1220.12*** *p809*
Trafford, Robert 67; Ontario, 1871 ***1823.17*** *p165*
Trafford, Thomas 30; Ontario, 1871 ***1823.21*** *p371*
Trageser, Johann Adam; Port uncertain, 1887 ***170.15*** *p44*
With wife & 2 children
Trahan, Elisabeth Leblanc *SEE* Trahan, Jean Baptiste
Trahan, Jean Baptiste; Nova Scotia, 1753 ***3051*** *p113*
*Wife:*Elisabeth Leblanc
Traharne, John 42; Ontario, 1871 ***1823.21*** *p371*
Traher, John C. 26; Ontario, 1871 ***1823.21*** *p371*
Trahern, Mary; America, 1736 ***1220.12*** *p809*
Trahern, Thomas; America, 1761 ***1220.12*** *p809*
Traherne, Samuel; America, 1665 ***1220.12*** *p809*
Traherne, William; America, 1721 ***1220.12*** *p809*
Trail, Christian; America, 1764 ***1220.12*** *p809*
Trainer, James; Louisiana, 1874 ***4981.45*** *p297*
Trainer, James; New York, 1833 ***3274.56*** *p101*
Trainer, John; America, 1768 ***1220.12*** *p809*
Trainer, John; North Carolina, 1854 ***1088.45*** *p35*
Trainer, John H. S.; Ohio, 1848 ***3580.20*** *p33*
Trainer, John H. S.; Ohio, 1848 ***6020.12*** *p22*
Trainer, Patrick; America, 1773 ***1220.12*** *p809*
Traisch, Dorothea Maria; America, 1867 ***7919.3*** *p524*
Trajot, Andre 16; Montreal, 1662 ***9221.17*** *p500*
Traling, Rosina; Wisconsin, 1904 ***6795.8*** *p177*
Trallacke, Frances; America, 1665 ***1220.12*** *p809*
Tramer, Peter 40; Port uncertain, 1843 ***778.6*** *p327*
Tramp, Anna; Wisconsin, 1899 ***6795.8*** *p62*
Tranceys, Richard; Virginia, 1730 ***1220.12*** *p809*
Traner, Peter; Louisiana, 1852 ***7710.1*** *p153*
Tranexmoht, F. T.; Missouri, 1891 ***3276.1*** *p4*
Trangmore, Sara; Barbados, 1677 ***1220.12*** *p809*
Tranquena, Tarugo; Louisiana, 1874-1875 ***4981.45*** *p130*
Trant, Johann 28; Portland, ME, 1906 ***970.38*** *p82*
Tranter, Mary; America, 1774 ***1220.12*** *p809*
Trantom, John; America, 1745 ***1220.12*** *p809*
Trantsetter, George; North Carolina, 1710 ***3629.40*** *p8*
Trantum, Samuel; America, 1774 ***1220.12*** *p809*
Trapagnier, Jean 28; Texas, 1848 ***778.6*** *p327*
Trapnell, John; Virginia, 1750 ***1220.12*** *p809*
Trapp, Hugh 40; Ontario, 1871 ***1823.17*** *p165*
Trapp, William; Barbados or Jamaica, 1691 ***1220.12*** *p809*
Trappall, Simon; America, 1723 ***1220.12*** *p809*
Trarbach, Karoline *SEE* Trarbach, Peter
Trarbach, Katharina *SEE* Trarbach, Peter
Trarbach, M. Elisabeth Stibitz 37 *SEE* Trarbach, Peter
Trarbach, Peter *SEE* Trarbach, Peter
Trarbach, Peter 43; Brazil, 1862 ***5475.1*** *p496*
*Wife:*M. Elisabeth Stibitz 37
*Son:*Peter
*Daughter:*Karoline
*Daughter:*Katharina
Trase, Levi 20; America, 1847 ***778.6*** *p327*
Trasforest, H. Paul 38; New Orleans, 1846 ***778.6*** *p327*
Trask, Benjamin; America, 1685 ***1220.12*** *p809*
Trask, Johannes; Illinois, 1930 ***121.35*** *p100*
Trask, Susannah; Virginia, 1769 ***1220.12*** *p809*
Trast, Esther 32; America, 1843 ***778.6*** *p327*
Traube, Henry 31; New York, NY, 1893 ***1883.7*** *p44*
Traudmann, Elisabetha; America, 1853 ***2526.42*** *p157*
Traudmann, Maria; America, 1853 ***2526.42*** *p157*
Trausin, Alexis 45; America, 1847 ***778.6*** *p327*
Trausin, August 8; America, 1847 ***778.6*** *p327*
Trausin, Felix 9; America, 1847 ***778.6*** *p327*
Trausin, Francois 19; America, 1847 ***778.6*** *p327*
Trausin, Francoise 6; America, 1847 ***778.6*** *p327*
Trausin, Jean Bt. 9; America, 1847 ***778.6*** *p327*
Trausin, Jean E. 7; America, 1847 ***778.6*** *p327*
Trausin, Jean Pierre 5; America, 1847 ***778.6*** *p327*
Trausin, Jeanne 46; America, 1847 ***778.6*** *p327*
Trausin, Joseph 9; America, 1847 ***778.6*** *p327*

Trausin, Pierre 20; America, 1847 ***778.6*** *p328*
Traut, Wilhelm; America, 1867 ***7919.3*** *p528*
With wife & 2 children
Trautmann, Adam; America, 1867 ***2526.43*** *p144*
Trautmann, Adam; America, 1887 ***2526.43*** *p183*
Trautmann, Anna Margaretha; America, 1854 ***2526.43*** *p227*
*Daughter:*Elisabetha Barbara
*Granddaughter:*Eva Katharina
Trautmann, August; New York, 1859 ***358.56*** *p53*
Trautmann, Barbara; America, 1854 ***2526.43*** *p227*
Trautmann, Barbara; America, 1867 ***2526.43*** *p144*
Trautmann, Carl 9 months; New York, NY, 1874 ***6954.7*** *p38*
Trautmann, Christine 36; New York, NY, 1874 ***6954.7*** *p38*
Trautmann, Elisabeth 10; New York, NY, 1874 ***6954.7*** *p38*
Trautmann, Elisabetha Barbara *SEE* Trautmann, Anna Margaretha
Trautmann, Eva Katharina *SEE* Trautmann, Anna Margaretha
Trautmann, Friedrich 3; New York, NY, 1874 ***6954.7*** *p38*
Trautmann, Fritz; Brazil, 1895 ***7420.1*** *p372*
Trautmann, Georg 17; New York, NY, 1874 ***6954.7*** *p38*
Trautmann, Georg Adam; America, 1869 ***2526.43*** *p162*
Trautmann, Johannes; America, 1831 ***2526.43*** *p124*
With wife & 4 children
Trautmann, Johannes; America, 1852 ***2526.43*** *p162*
Trautmann, Kath. Elisabeth; America, 1836 ***5475.1*** *p457*
Trautmann, Magdalena 15; New York, NY, 1874 ***6954.7*** *p38*
Trautmann, Maria Elisabetha; America, 1833 ***2526.43*** *p227*
Trautmann, Peter 5; New York, NY, 1874 ***6954.7*** *p38*
Trautmann, Peter 40; New York, NY, 1874 ***6954.7*** *p38*
Trautmann, Philipp; America, 1885 ***2526.43*** *p157*
Trautmann, Philipp; America, 1892 ***2526.43*** *p183*
Trautvetter, Ernst; America, 1867 ***7919.3*** *p533*
Trautvetter, George; Illinois, 1855 ***6079.1*** *p14*
Trautwein, Christiane; America, 1868 ***7919.3*** *p530*
With child
Travel, Thomas; America, 1754 ***1220.12*** *p809*
Travers, Elizabeth; Maryland, 1727 ***1220.12*** *p809*
Travers, Michael 39; Ontario, 1871 ***1823.21*** *p371*
Travers, Peter; New Orleans, 1850 ***7242.30*** *p155*
Travers, Phillis; America, 1736 ***1220.12*** *p809*
Traverse, John; America, 1766 ***1220.12*** *p809*
Traverse, John; Barbados, 1695 ***1220.12*** *p809*
Traversy, Noel 31; Quebec, 1634 ***9221.17*** *p38*
Traves, Mary Ann 39; Ontario, 1871 ***1823.21*** *p371*
Travillion, Simon; America, 1736 ***1220.12*** *p809*
Travis, Barney; Louisiana, 1873-1890 ***7710.1*** *p160*
Travis, Daniel R.; Nevada, 1846-1880 ***9228.50*** *p641*
Travis, Joseph; Maryland or Virginia, 1738 ***1220.12*** *p809*
Travis, William 65; Ontario, 1871 ***1823.21*** *p371*
Traviss, John; Maryland, 1734 ***1220.12*** *p809*
Travnicek, Frantisek; Wisconsin, 1857-1861 ***2853.20*** *p334*
Travnicek, Nechuta; Wisconsin, 1853 ***2853.20*** *p303*
Trawinska, Victoria; Detroit, 1929 ***1640.55*** *p112*
Trawnski, Stanislas 32; New York, NY, 1920 ***930.50*** *p49*
Trayford, Thomas; America, 1766 ***1220.12*** *p809*
Trayner, Tristram; Barbados, 1663 ***1220.12*** *p809*
Traynor, P.; New Orleans, 1850 ***7242.30*** *p155*
Trayte, George 31; Ontario, 1871 ***1823.21*** *p371*
Treacle, George; America, 1743 ***1220.12*** *p809*
Treacle, John 55; Ontario, 1871 ***1823.21*** *p371*
Treadwell, John; America, 1758 ***1220.12*** *p810*
Treadwell, Wm 43; Ontario, 1871 ***1823.21*** *p371*
Treagher, James 63; Ontario, 1871 ***1823.21*** *p371*
Treagus, John 42; Ontario, 1871 ***1823.21*** *p372*
Treane, Thomas; Barbados, 1675 ***1220.12*** *p810*
Treapleton, . . .; Ontario, 1871 ***1823.21*** *p372*
Treaver, Jacob; North Carolina, 1710 ***3629.40*** *p8*
Trebbin, Charles; Iowa, 1889 ***1211.15*** *p19*
Trebein, Dietrich Christian; Port uncertain, 1839 ***7420.1*** *p17*
Trebein, Heinrich Wilhelm Carl Adolf; America, 1853 ***7420.1*** *p112*
Trebilcock, Charles 26; Ontario, 1871 ***1823.21*** *p372*
Trebilcock, Harriet 48; Ontario, 1871 ***1823.21*** *p372*
Trebilcock, Thos 36; Ontario, 1871 ***1823.21*** *p372*
Trebilcock, William 74; Ontario, 1871 ***1823.21*** *p372*
Treble, William; America, 1772 ***1220.12*** *p810*
Treblicock, William 45; Ontario, 1871 ***1823.21*** *p372*
Trebolet, Samuel; Ohio, 1809-1852 ***4511.35*** *p54*
Trechard, J. Ba.tist 25; New Orleans, 1846 ***778.6*** *p328*
Tredeage, Thomas; America, 1758 ***1220.12*** *p810*
Tredenick, Richard; North Carolina, 1843 ***1088.45*** *p35*
Treder, Sophia; Wisconsin, 1893 ***6795.8*** *p62*
Tredgit, William; America, 1734 ***1220.12*** *p810*
Tredway, Thomas; Barbados, 1663 ***1220.12*** *p810*
Tredwell, Richard; Annapolis, MD, 1733 ***1220.12*** *p810*
Tree, Robert; America, 1756 ***1220.12*** *p810*
Tree, Stephen B. 63; Ontario, 1871 ***1823.21*** *p372*
Tree, Thomas; America, 1744 ***1220.12*** *p810*
Treen, Joseph; America, 1726 ***1220.12*** *p810*
Treene, Nowell; America, 1685 ***1220.12*** *p810*
Treffert, Peter; Louisiana, 1874 ***4981.45*** *p134*
Treffle, Francois 14; Quebec, 1651 ***9221.17*** *p251*
Trefry, Agnes; Marblehead, MA, 1743 ***9228.50*** *p504*
Tregilgas, Edward; America, 1756 ***1220.12*** *p810*
Tregonning, Richard; America, 1743 ***1220.12*** *p810*
Tregowith, John; Port uncertain, 1760 ***1220.12*** *p810*
Trehard, Jean; Quebec, 1648 ***9221.17*** *p204*
Treharn, James; America, 1771 ***1220.12*** *p810*
Treharne, Thomas 50; Ontario, 1871 ***1823.21*** *p372*
Treharnie, David 39; Ontario, 1871 ***1823.21*** *p372*
Treharnie, Thomas 82; Ontario, 1871 ***1823.21*** *p372*
Treib, Johann Georg; America, 1882 ***5475.1*** *p137*
Treib, Maria; America, 1882 ***5475.1*** *p137*
Treib, Mathias; Pennsylvania, 1886 ***5475.1*** *p188*
Treiber, Martin 25; Port uncertain, 1845 ***778.6*** *p328*
Treinan, William; Ohio, 1809-1852 ***4511.35*** *p54*
Treinen, William; Ohio, 1809-1852 ***4511.35*** *p54*
Treiner, Michael; Ohio, 1809-1852 ***4511.35*** *p54*
Treise, John; America, 1731 ***1220.12*** *p810*
Treiss, Emilie 14; New York, NY, 1885 ***1883.7*** *p45*
Treiss, Mike 20; New York, NY, 1885 ***1883.7*** *p45*
Trelly, James; North Carolina, 1811-1812 ***1088.45*** *p35*
Treloar, William; North Carolina, 1849 ***1088.45*** *p35*
Trelure, Thomas; North Carolina, 1852 ***1088.45*** *p35*
Tremain, Eliza 43; Ontario, 1871 ***1823.17*** *p165*
Tremain, Martha; Virginia, 1734 ***1220.12*** *p810*
Tremane, Michael 45; Ontario, 1871 ***1823.17*** *p165*
Tremayne, Mary; Barbados, 1665 ***1220.12*** *p810*
Tremblay, Pierre 21; Quebec, 1647 ***9221.17*** *p189*
Tremble, George; America, 1768 ***1220.12*** *p810*
Trembley, Corney; America, 1764 ***1220.12*** *p810*
Tremeere, George 29; Ontario, 1871 ***1823.21*** *p372*
Tremell, Richard 35; Ontario, 1871 ***1823.17*** *p165*
Tremond, Daniel; Quebec, 1647 ***9221.17*** *p190*
Trempler, August; New York, 1859 ***358.56*** *p54*
Tremson, Elie; Virginia, 1700 ***9230.15*** *p80*
*Wife:*Elizabet Tignac
Tremson, Elizabet Tignac *SEE* Tremson, Elie
Trenarry, Richard; America, 1742 ***1220.12*** *p810*
Trenchard, Aaron; America, 1769 ***1220.12*** *p810*
Trend, John; Virginia, 1767 ***1220.12*** *p810*
Trendal, William 50; Ontario, 1871 ***1823.17*** *p165*
Trendelmann, Mr.; America, 1864 ***7420.1*** *p227*
*Son:*Christian Friedrich
With wife
Trendelmann, Carl Friedrich Wilhelm; America, 1882 ***7420.1*** *p333*
Trendelmann, Christian Friedrich *SEE* Trendelmann, Mr.
Trendelmann, Christine Louise Leonore; America, 1855 ***7420.1*** *p143*
Trendelmann, Ernst Heinrich; America, 1881 ***7420.1*** *p326*
Trendenburg, Rudolf; America, 1882 ***7420.1*** *p333*
Treneer, William M. 1; Ontario, 1871 ***1823.21*** *p372*
Trenham, James 22; North Carolina, 1774 ***1422.10*** *p56*
Trenor, Dr.; Toronto, 1844 ***2910.35*** *p112*
Trenor, Miss D.; Toronto, 1844 ***2910.35*** *p112*
Trenor, Daniel; Toronto, 1844 ***2910.35*** *p112*
Trenor, Peter; Toronto, 1844 ***2910.35*** *p112*
Trent, Charles 45; Michigan, 1880 ***4491.36*** *p22*
Trentham, John; America, 1722 ***1220.12*** *p810*
Trenton, Edward; America, 1752 ***1220.12*** *p810*
Trenul, Marable 20; America, 1843 ***778.6*** *p328*
Trenz, Friedrich; America, 1882 ***5475.1*** *p161*
Trep, Neils C.; Iowa, 1894 ***1211.15*** *p19*
Trepine, Judith; America, 1756 ***1220.12*** *p810*
Trepton, William; New York, 1859 ***358.56*** *p100*
Treptow, F.H.M.; Wisconsin, 1879 ***6795.8*** *p228*
Tresdale, John 59; Ontario, 1871 ***1823.21*** *p372*
Treseder, Elizabeth McKay *SEE* Treseder, Richard Doughty
Treseder, Richard Doughty; Utah, 1855 ***9228.50*** *p635*
*Wife:*Elizabeth McKay
With 8 children
Treser, Adam; America, 1757-1849 ***2526.42*** *p165*
Treser, Johannes; America, 1836 ***2526.42*** *p165*
Treser, Karl 17; America, 1854 ***2526.42*** *p185*
Tresize, Charles; America, 1766 ***1220.12*** *p810*
Tresler, John; America, 1770 ***1220.12*** *p810*
Tressen, Eugene Dominic; Detroit, 1929-1930 ***6214.5*** *p69*
Tressenberg, Eugene Dominic; Detroit, 1929-1930 ***6214.5*** *p69*
Tressler, Peter; Ohio, 1809-1852 ***4511.35*** *p55*
Trestain, George 78; Ontario, 1871 ***1823.21*** *p372*
Trestine, John 36; Ontario, 1871 ***1823.21*** *p372*
Treston, William 31; Ontario, 1871 ***1823.21*** *p372*
Trestour, P. E.; Louisiana, 1836-1840 ***4981.45*** *p213*
Trestrayle, William; Barbados, 1672 ***1220.12*** *p810*
Treswell, Loring John; America, 1764 ***1220.12*** *p810*
Trethewey, John; America, 1753 ***1220.12*** *p810*
Trethewey, Joseph; America, 1758 ***1220.12*** *p810*
Trethewey, Thomas; America, 1773 ***1220.12*** *p810*
Treton, Henry; Virginia, 1740 ***1220.12*** *p810*
Treu, Gustav Adolf Friedrich; America, 1888 ***179.55*** *p19*
Treu, Richard; America, 1892 ***179.55*** *p19*
Treusch, Adam; America, 1831 ***2526.43*** *p183*
With wife 21
With child 9 months
Trevascus, Arthur; America, 1731 ***1220.12*** *p810*
Trevealan, Ann 75; Ontario, 1871 ***1823.21*** *p372*
Trevetick, Samuel 49; Ontario, 1871 ***1823.21*** *p372*
Trevett, Charles; America, 1692 ***1220.12*** *p810*
Trevett, Noah; America, 1756 ***1220.12*** *p810*
Trevillian, Mary; Maryland or Virginia, 1733 ***1220.12*** *p810*
Trevis, John; America, 1771 ***1220.12*** *p809*
Trevis, Philip; America, 1756 ***1220.12*** *p809*
Trevis, Richard; Barbados, 1664 ***1220.12*** *p809*
Trevis, William; America, 1774 ***1220.12*** *p809*
Treviss, John; America, 1766 ***1220.12*** *p809*
Trevit, John; America, 1753 ***1220.12*** *p810*
Trevith, Mary; America, 1756 ***1220.12*** *p810*
Trevitt, Robert; Virginia, 1729 ***1220.12*** *p810*
Trevor, Thomas; America, 1713 ***1220.12*** *p810*
Trevore, . . .; Plymouth, MA, 1620 ***1920.45*** *p5*
Trevore, William; Plymouth, MA, 1606 ***1642*** *p55*
Trew, Thomas C. 20; Ontario, 1871 ***1823.21*** *p372*
Trewalla, James; North Carolina, 1843 ***1088.45*** *p35*
Trewalla, John C.; North Carolina, 1838 ***1088.45*** *p35*
Treweek, Nicholas; America, 1743 ***1220.12*** *p810*
Trewert, Hans Heinrich; America, 1840 ***7420.1*** *p21*
With son 13
With daughter 6
With son 19
With daughter 11
Trewhitt, William; America, 1726 ***1220.12*** *p810*
Trezise, Thomas; Colorado, 1892 ***1029.59*** *p90*
Trezise, Thomas 31; Colorado, 1888 ***1029.59*** *p90*
Triary, B.; Louisiana, 1874-1875 ***4981.45*** *p130*
Tribault, Joseph 28; New Orleans, 1748 ***778.6*** *p328*
Tribe, Anthony; Boston, 1718 ***1220.12*** *p810*
Tribold, Caroline Wilhelmine Soffker *SEE* Tribold, Justine Caroline Louise
Tribold, Constantin; America, 1852 ***7420.1*** *p99*
Tribold, Friedrich Wilhelm Ludwig *SEE* Tribold, Justine Caroline Louise
Tribold, Justine Caroline Louise; America, 1884 ***7420.1*** *p346*
*Father:*Friedrich Wilhelm Ludwig
*Mother:*Caroline Wilhelmine Soffker
Tribolet, Adolph G.; Ohio, 1809-1852 ***4511.35*** *p55*
Triboulet, Claude 36; Louisiana, 1848 ***778.6*** *p328*
Triboulet, Emile 3; Louisiana, 1848 ***778.6*** *p328*
Triboulet, Eugenie 8; Louisiana, 1848 ***778.6*** *p328*
Triboulet, Fois. 7; Louisiana, 1848 ***778.6*** *p328*
Triboulet, Jeanne; Quebec, 1671 ***4514.3*** *p352*
Triboulet, Jules 5; Louisiana, 1848 ***778.6*** *p328*
Triboulet, Jules 40; Louisiana, 1848 ***778.6*** *p328*
Triboulet, Pre. 9; Louisiana, 1848 ***778.6*** *p328*
Tribuch, Goldie; Detroit, 1929-1930 ***6214.5*** *p71*
Trichard, Jeanne 18; Port uncertain, 1846 ***778.6*** *p328*
Trichard, Jules 30; Port uncertain, 1846 ***778.6*** *p328*
Tricheret, Pierre 23; America, 1840 ***778.6*** *p328*
Trick, Walter 26; Ontario, 1871 ***1823.21*** *p372*
Trickens, Mary; America, 1773 ***1220.12*** *p810*
Tricket, Edward; America, 1766 ***1220.12*** *p810*
Trickett, James; Marston's Wharf, 1782 ***8529.30*** *p16*
Trickett, Joseph; Marston's Wharf, 1782 ***8529.30*** *p16*
Tricketts, Joseph; Marston's Wharf, 1782 ***8529.30*** *p16*
Tricks, Lewis; America, 1685 ***1220.12*** *p811*
Tricky, Joseph; America, 1701 ***1220.12*** *p811*
Tricon, Francois; Louisiana, 1874-1875 ***4981.45*** *p130*
Tricot, Jean Baptiste; Wisconsin, 1856 ***1495.20*** *p46*
Tricou, Mrs. 40; America, 1846 ***778.6*** *p328*
Tricou, Henry 14; America, 1846 ***778.6*** *p328*
Triddis, Charles 52; Ontario, 1871 ***1823.21*** *p372*
Triebner, Johanne Friederike; America, 1867 ***7919.3*** *p530*
With granddaughter & 4 children
Triebold, August Christian *SEE* Triebold, Friedrich Ludwig
Triebold, Caroline Wilhelmine Charlotte Wellhausen *SEE* Triebold, Friedrich Ludwig
Triebold, Franz Albert Eduard Constantin; America, 1853 ***7420.1*** *p112*
Triebold, Friedrich Heinrich Ludwig; America, 1864 ***7420.1*** *p227*

Triebold, Friedrich Ludwig; America, 1885 ***7420.1*** *p349*
*Wife:*Caroline Wilhelmine Charlotte Wellhausen
*Son:*August Christian
Triebold, Heinrich Ludwig; America, 1867 ***7420.1*** *p266*
With family
Trier, Abraham; Louisiana, 1836-1840 ***4981.45*** *p213*
Trier, Abraham; Louisiana, 1836-1841 ***4981.45*** *p209*
Trierweiler, Elisabeth 40; America, 1885 ***5475.1*** *p319*
Trierweiler, Maria 42; America, 1885 ***5475.1*** *p319*
Triest, Peter; America, 1766 ***1220.12*** *p811*
Triezer, Nicolas 28; Missouri, 1847 ***778.6*** *p328*
Trigg, Daniel; America, 1770 ***1220.12*** *p811*
Trigg, John; America, 1723 ***1220.12*** *p811*
Trigger, Mary; Died enroute, 1726 ***1220.12*** *p811*
Triggs, Elizabeth; America, 1767 ***1220.12*** *p811*
Triller, Philip; New Jersey, 1773-1774 ***927.31*** *p3*
Trim, Adam 35; America, 1845 ***778.6*** *p328*
Trimble, George 49; Ontario, 1871 ***1823.21*** *p372*
Trimble, John; America, 1769 ***1220.12*** *p810*
Trimble, William; America, 1769 ***1220.12*** *p810*
Trimby, Stephen; America, 1773 ***1220.12*** *p811*
Trimels, Robert 45; Ontario, 1871 ***1823.17*** *p165*
Trimlett, Ann; Virginia, 1734 ***1220.12*** *p811*
Trimlin, Thomas; Virginia, 1741 ***1220.12*** *p811*
Trimmer, Elizabeth 45; Ontario, 1871 ***1823.21*** *p372*
Trimnell, John; America, 1725 ***1220.12*** *p811*
Trimnell, Richard; America, 1750 ***1220.12*** *p811*
Trindall, Nathaniel; America, 1716 ***1220.12*** *p811*
Triner, Josef; Chicago, 1861-1910 ***2853.20*** *p406*
Trink, Peter; America, 1752 ***1220.12*** *p811*
Trint, Heinrich; Valdivia, Chile, 1852 ***1192.4*** *p53*
Triot, Marie-Madeleine 17; Quebec, 1658 ***9221.17*** *p387*
Trip, John; America, 1740 ***1220.12*** *p811*
Triphook, Joseph; America, 1723 ***1220.12*** *p811*
Tripier, Jean 24; Quebec, 1656 ***9221.17*** *p347*
Triponet, John Francis; Jamaica, 1665 ***1220.12*** *p811*
Tripp, Catharina 2; America, 1842 ***778.6*** *p328*
Tripp, Fran. 60; America, 1842 ***778.6*** *p328*
Tripp, John H.; Ohio, 1843 ***3580.20*** *p33*
Tripp, John H.; Ohio, 1843 ***6020.12*** *p22*
Tripp, Maria 38; America, 1842 ***778.6*** *p328*
Tripp, Thomas; America, 1743 ***1220.12*** *p811*
Tripp, William; America, 1778 ***1220.12*** *p811*
Trippett, Joseph; America, 1769 ***1220.12*** *p811*
Trippett, William; America, 1690 ***1220.12*** *p811*
Trippitt, William; America, 1768 ***1220.12*** *p811*
Trippup, John; America, 1719 ***1220.12*** *p811*
Triquett, Peter; America, 1742 ***1220.12*** *p811*
Triska, Matej; Iowa, 1855-1856 ***2853.20*** *p237*
Tristram, James; America, 1732 ***1220.12*** *p811*
Tristram, Joseph; America, 1754 ***1220.12*** *p811*
Tristram, Thomas; Barbados, 1714 ***1220.12*** *p811*
Tristrum, Joseph; America, 1754 ***1220.12*** *p811*
Tritton, Daniel; Annapolis, MD, 1725 ***1220.12*** *p811*
Trives, Robert; America, 1772 ***1220.12*** *p811*
Trivet, Mary; America, 1755 ***1220.12*** *p811*
Trivier, Edward; Washington, 1889 ***2770.40*** *p81*
Trix, Robert; America, 1719 ***1220.12*** *p811*
Trnka, Josef; St. Paul, MN, 1858-1859 ***2853.20*** *p277*
Troale, Anne; Maryland, 1725 ***1220.12*** *p811*
Troat, John; North Carolina, 1710 ***3629.40*** *p8*
Trobst, Francois 26; Port uncertain, 1843 ***778.6*** *p328*
Trochet, Francoise; Quebec, 1671 ***4514.3*** *p374*
Trocinska, Cecilia; Wisconsin, 1898 ***6795.8*** *p37*
Trockenbrod, Katharina; America, 1847 ***2526.43*** *p128*
Trodd, Barrard 23; Ontario, 1871 ***1823.21*** *p372*
Troesch, Jacob; New Mexico, 1914 ***4812.1*** *p87*
Troester, Maria 31; New Orleans, 1847 ***778.6*** *p328*
Troester, Marianna 2; New Orleans, 1847 ***778.6*** *p328*
Troester, Peter 4; New Orleans, 1847 ***778.6*** *p328*
Troester, Peter 40; New Orleans, 1847 ***778.6*** *p328*
Troike, Albert; Washington, 1882 ***2770.40*** *p136*
Troisieme, Katharina Berg *SEE* Troisieme, Peter
Troisieme, Peter *SEE* Troisieme, Peter
Troisieme, Peter; America, 1881 ***5475.1*** *p227*
*Wife:*Katharina Berg
*Son:*Peter
Trojan, Frantisek; St. Louis, 1857 ***2853.20*** *p25*
Trojan, Frantisek; Wisconsin, 1857-1861 ***2853.20*** *p334*
Trojanek, Frantisek; Wisconsin, 1856 ***2853.20*** *p345*
Trojanek, Frantisek; Wisconsin, 1857-1861 ***2853.20*** *p334*
Trojanowska, Kamila 19; New York, NY, 1911 ***6533.11*** *p10*
Trojanowski, Wolf; Detroit, 1929 ***1640.55*** *p113*
Trokur, Anton 26; Brazil, 1879 ***5475.1*** *p390*
*Wife:*Katharina Holz 26
*Daughter:*Barbara
*Daughter:*Katharina
*Daughter:*Maria
Trokur, Barbara *SEE* Trokur, Anton
Trokur, Johann 23; Brazil, 1876 ***5475.1*** *p389*
Trokur, Katharina *SEE* Trokur, Anton
Trokur, Katharina Holz 26 *SEE* Trokur, Anton
Trokur, Maria *SEE* Trokur, Anton
Troller, Philip; New Jersey, 1773-1774 ***927.31*** *p3*
Trolley, Archd 19; Ontario, 1871 ***1823.21*** *p372*
Trolley, John; America, 1688 ***1220.12*** *p811*
Troman, F. 30; Port uncertain, 1844 ***778.6*** *p328*
Trombling, G. H. A.; Louisiana, 1836-1841 ***4981.45*** *p209*
Trombly, Alexander 45; Ohio, 1880 ***4879.40*** *p258*
*Nephew:*Morris 19
Trombly, Morris 19 *SEE* Trombly, Alexander
Tromley, Arthur 21; Ohio, 1880 ***4879.40*** *p258*
Trommer, Ferdinand; North Carolina, 1850 ***1088.45*** *p35*
Tronchet, Francois 31; Missouri, 1845 ***778.6*** *p328*
Tronk, Joseph 45; America, 1845 ***778.6*** *p328*
Tronquet, Guillaume; Quebec, 1640 ***9221.17*** *p99*
Troop, Isabella; America, 1758 ***1220.12*** *p811*
Troop, William; Virginia, 1774 ***1220.12*** *p811*
Troope, Edward; Barbados or Jamaica, 1697 ***1220.12*** *p811*
Troost, Mrs.; America, 1923 ***8023.44*** *p380*
Tropf, John J.; Ohio, 1809-1852 ***4511.35*** *p55*
Trosche, Johann 1; Baltimore, 1889 ***8425.16*** *p35*
Trosche, Johannes 33; Baltimore, 1889 ***8425.16*** *p35*
Trosche, Rosina 5; Baltimore, 1889 ***8425.16*** *p35*
Trosche, Rosina 36; Baltimore, 1889 ***8425.16*** *p35*
Troscheid, Heinrich; America, 1884 ***7420.1*** *p346*
Troscheit, Friedrich Carl Gottfried; America, 1884 ***7420.1*** *p346*
Troscinski, Jan; Detroit, 1930 ***1640.60*** *p81*
Tross, Paul 9; America, 1848 ***778.6*** *p328*
Trost, Nikolaus; America, 1833 ***5475.1*** *p467*
With wife & 4 children
Trost, Nikolaus; America, 1849 ***5475.1*** *p477*
Troster, Catha. 13; New York, NY, 1885 ***1883.7*** *p45*
Troster, Friedr. 24; New York, NY, 1885 ***1883.7*** *p45*
Troster, Joh. 16; New York, NY, 1885 ***1883.7*** *p45*
Troster, Marie 4; New York, NY, 1885 ***1883.7*** *p45*
Troster, Mathe. 21; New York, NY, 1885 ***1883.7*** *p45*
Troster, Rosine 20; New York, NY, 1885 ***1883.7*** *p45*
Troster, Wilh. 9; New York, NY, 1885 ***1883.7*** *p45*
Troswell, Edw. 21; New Orleans, 1845 ***778.6*** *p329*
Trot, Samuel; America, 1755 ***1220.12*** *p811*
Trotin, Marie 17; Quebec, 1662 ***9221.17*** *p493*
Trotin, Victor; Quebec, 1653 ***9221.17*** *p279*
Trotman, George; America, 1768 ***1220.12*** *p811*
Trotman, John; America, 1774 ***1220.12*** *p811*
Trotman, Moses 42; Ontario, 1871 ***1823.21*** *p372*
Trotman, Samuel 38; Ontario, 1871 ***1823.21*** *p372*
Trotot, Joseph 32; America, 1841 ***778.6*** *p329*
Trott, John; America, 1722 ***1220.12*** *p811*
Trott, John; America, 1724 ***1220.12*** *p811*
Trott, John; Barbados or Jamaica, 1677 ***1220.12*** *p811*
Trott, John 46; Ontario, 1871 ***1823.17*** *p165*
Trott, John, Sr. 58; Ontario, 1871 ***1823.21*** *p372*
Trott, Joseph 42; Ontario, 1871 ***1823.17*** *p165*
Trott, Judith; Barbados, 1673 ***1220.12*** *p811*
Trott, Richard; America, 1770 ***1220.12*** *p811*
Trott, Thomas; America, 1685 ***1220.12*** *p811*
Trott, William 20; Ontario, 1871 ***1823.21*** *p372*
Trott, William 32; Ontario, 1871 ***1823.21*** *p372*
Trotter, Abraham; America, 1744 ***1220.12*** *p811*
Trotter, David 35; Ontario, 1871 ***1823.17*** *p165*
Trotter, Elizabeth; America, 1729 ***1220.12*** *p812*
Trotter, Jacob; America, 1740 ***1220.12*** *p812*
Trotter, James; America, 1770 ***1220.12*** *p812*
Trotter, James; America, 1772 ***1220.12*** *p812*
Trotter, James; Illinois, 1858-1861 ***6020.5*** *p133*
Trotter, James; Virginia, 1759 ***1220.12*** *p812*
Trotter, John; America, 1740 ***1220.12*** *p812*
Trotter, John; Illinois, 1858-1861 ***6020.5*** *p133*
Trotter, Richard; America, 1750 ***1220.12*** *p812*
Trottier, Antoine 5 *SEE* Trottier, Gilles
Trottier, Catherine Loyseau 43 *SEE* Trottier, Gilles
Trottier, Gilles 6 *SEE* Trottier, Gilles
Trottier, Gilles 55; Quebec, 1646 ***9221.17*** *p169*
*Wife:*Catherine Loyseau 43
*Son:*Gilles 6
*Son:*Antoine 5
*Son:*Pierre 2
*Son:*Julien 10
Trottier, Julien 10 *SEE* Trottier, Gilles
Trottier, Pierre 2 *SEE* Trottier, Gilles
Trottle, Robert; Virginia, 1718 ***1220.12*** *p812*
Trotzig, Albin; Iowa, 1896 ***1211.15*** *p19*
Trou, Gabriel; Quebec, 1647 ***9221.17*** *p190*
Trouillard, Antoine; Virginia, 1700 ***9230.15*** *p80*
Trouslot, Francois X. A.; Illinois, 1852 ***6079.1*** *p14*
Trout, Joseph; Ohio, 1809-1852 ***4511.35*** *p55*
Trouteaud, Christine Emma *SEE* Trouteaud, Eugene Elias
Trouteaud, Edward *SEE* Trouteaud, Eugene Elias
Trouteaud, Emma Eliza Hancock *SEE* Trouteaud, Eugene Elias
Trouteaud, Eugene Elias; America, 1876-1902 ***9228.50*** *p636*
*Wife:*Emma Eliza Hancock
*Child:*Edward
*Child:*Christine Emma
*Child:*Henry
Trouteaud, Henry *SEE* Trouteaud, Eugene Elias
Troutman, George; Ohio, 1809-1852 ***4511.35*** *p55*
Troutman, Peter; Ohio, 1809-1852 ***4511.35*** *p55*
Troutsetter, George; North Carolina, 1710 ***3629.40*** *p8*
Trouvand, Francois 24; Louisiana, 1847 ***778.6*** *p329*
Trow, John; America, 1729 ***1220.12*** *p812*
Trow, John; America, 1753 ***1220.12*** *p812*
Troward, Edward; America, 1757 ***1220.12*** *p812*
Trowell, Eleanor; America, 1763 ***1220.12*** *p812*
Trowell, John; Barbados, 1669 ***1220.12*** *p812*
Trowhill, Samuel 42; Ontario, 1871 ***1823.21*** *p372*
Troxell, Peter; Ohio, 1809-1852 ***4511.35*** *p55*
Troxler, Joseph; Louisiana, 1836-1841 ***4981.45*** *p209*
Troy, William; America, 1770 ***1220.12*** *p812*
Troy, William; Ohio, 1840 ***2763.1*** *p22*
Troye, Edmond 34; New Orleans, 1848 ***778.6*** *p329*
Tru, Suzanne; Quebec, 1666 ***4514.3*** *p374*
Truan, Joseph 40; Ontario, 1871 ***1823.17*** *p165*
Truar, Katharina; America, 1871 ***5475.1*** *p168*
Trubbs, George; America, 1685 ***1220.12*** *p812*
Truberiete, P. 22; America, 1848 ***778.6*** *p329*
Trubert, Jacques 34; New Orleans, 1848 ***778.6*** *p329*
Trubody, Theophilus; Virginia, 1729 ***1220.12*** *p812*
Trubshaw, Ann; America, 1758 ***1220.12*** *p812*
Trubyer, Helen; Virginia, 1700 ***9230.15*** *p81*
Trucha, Jan; Wisconsin, 1854 ***2853.20*** *p304*
Trucheteau, Pre. 40; New Orleans, 1843 ***778.6*** *p329*
Truchses, Ernst; Valdivia, Chile, 1852 ***1192.4*** *p54*
Truckenbrodt, Heinrich Martin; America, 1867 ***7919.3*** *p528*
Truckey, Joseph; Barbados or Jamaica, 1701 ***1220.12*** *p812*
Trudelle, Jean 26; Quebec, 1655 ***9221.17*** *p329*
Trudelle, Jean; Quebec, 1655 ***9221.17*** *p8*
Trudlee, Mr. 24; Louisiana, 1848 ***778.6*** *p329*
Trudlee, Mr. 26; Louisiana, 1848 ***778.6*** *p329*
True, John; America, 1769 ***1220.12*** *p812*
True, Thomas; America, 1765 ***1220.12*** *p812*
True, William 45; Ontario, 1871 ***1823.17*** *p165*
Trueas, Charles; Louisiana, 1874 ***4981.45*** *p134*
Trueboy, Richard; Maryland, 1726 ***1220.12*** *p812*
Truebridge, Mary; America, 1772 ***1220.12*** *p812*
Truelock, Giles; America, 1761 ***1220.12*** *p812*
Truelove, John; America, 1698 ***1220.12*** *p812*
Truelove, Robert; America, 1764 ***1220.12*** *p812*
Trueman, Alice; America, 1751 ***1220.12*** *p812*
Trueman, George 26; Ontario, 1871 ***1823.21*** *p372*
Trueman, Ilene 61; Ontario, 1871 ***1823.17*** *p165*
Trueman, Jane; America, 1766 ***1220.12*** *p812*
Trueman, Robert; America, 1767 ***1220.12*** *p812*
Trueman, Sarah; America, 1723 ***1220.12*** *p812*
Trueman, Thomas; America, 1743 ***1220.12*** *p812*
Trueman, Timothy; Colorado, 1862-1894 ***1029.59*** *p90*
Trueman, William; America, 1765 ***1220.12*** *p812*
Truemper, Charlote; Philadelphia, 1867 ***8513.31*** *p296*
Truesdale, Hugh 35; Ontario, 1871 ***1823.17*** *p165*
Trufard, Walter 44; Ontario, 1871 ***1823.17*** *p165*
Truffault, Rene; Montreal, 1653 ***9221.17*** *p301*
Truhitt, Roger; America, 1755 ***1220.12*** *p812*
Truillie, Jean 33; New Orleans, 1843 ***778.6*** *p329*
Trull, John; America, 1755 ***1220.12*** *p812*
Trull, John 35; Ontario, 1871 ***1823.21*** *p372*
Trull, Mary; America, 1762 ***1220.12*** *p812*
Trulock, James; Virginia, 1764 ***1220.12*** *p812*
Truman, Ann *SEE* Truman, William
Truman, John 47; Ontario, 1871 ***1823.17*** *p165*
Truman, William *SEE* Truman, William
Truman, William; Canada, 1774 ***3036.5*** *p41*
*Wife:*Ann
*Son:*William
Trumey, Frederick 50; Ontario, 1871 ***1823.21*** *p372*
Trump, Mr. 33; Port uncertain, 1843 ***778.6*** *p329*
Trump, Humphrey; America, 1685 ***1220.12*** *p812*
Trump, James; America, 1763 ***1220.12*** *p812*
Trump, Richard; America, 1741 ***1220.12*** *p812*
Trumpf, Paul; Louisiana, 1836-1840 ***4981.45*** *p213*
Trumpfheller, Adam; America, 1891 ***2526.43*** *p157*
Trumpfheller, Anna Katharina; America, 1854 ***2526.43*** *p223*
Trumpfheller, Elisabeth Katharina; America, 1854 ***2526.43*** *p119*
Trumpfheller, Friedrich; America, 1883 ***2526.43*** *p183*
Trumpfheller, Jakob; America, 1885 ***2526.43*** *p157*
Trumpfheller, Johann Adam 14; America, 1856 ***2526.43*** *p223*

516 *FOR A COMPLETE EXPLANATION OF ENTRY, SEE "HOW TO READ A CITATION" SECTION*

Trumpfheller, Leonhard; America, 1865 ***2526.43*** *p223*
With brother-in-law
Trumpfheller, Marie; America, 1867 ***2526.43*** *p183*
Trumpfheller, Michael; America, 1881 ***2526.43*** *p157*
Trumpfheller, Wilhelm; America, 1854 ***2526.43*** *p223*
Tru...nn, Jacob 56; New York, NY, 1893 ***1883.7*** *p40*
Tru...nn, Marie 56; New York, NY, 1893 ***1883.7*** *p40*
Trunzler, A. Maria *SEE* Trunzler, Mathias
Trunzler, Elisabeth *SEE* Trunzler, Mathias
Trunzler, Elisabeth Gunder *SEE* Trunzler, Mathias
Trunzler, Elisabeth; America, 1883 ***5475.1*** *p232*
*Son:*Peter
Trunzler, Johann *SEE* Trunzler, Mathias
Trunzler, Katharina *SEE* Trunzler, Mathias
Trunzler, Margarethe *SEE* Trunzler, Mathias
Trunzler, Mathias *SEE* Trunzler, Mathias
Trunzler, Mathias; America, 1881 ***5475.1*** *p151*
*Wife:*Elisabeth Gunder
*Daughter:*A. Maria
*Son:*Peter
*Daughter:*Katharina
*Son:*Johann
*Son:*Mathias
*Daughter:*Elisabeth
*Daughter:*Margarethe
Trunzler, Peter *SEE* Trunzler, Mathias
Trunzler, Peter *SEE* Trunzler, Elisabeth Schmitt
Trupe, Ernst; Illinois, 1864 ***6079.1*** *p14*
Trupe, John; Ohio, 1809-1852 ***4511.35*** *p55*
Trupp, Carl; America, 1868 ***7919.3*** *p525*
Truren, John; America, 1685 ***1220.12*** *p812*
Trusbado, L. 18; New Orleans, 1848 ***778.6*** *p329*
Trusler, Absolom 55; Ontario, 1871 ***1823.17*** *p165*
Trusler, Ester 55; Ontario, 1871 ***1823.17*** *p165*
Trusler, John 84; Ontario, 1871 ***1823.17*** *p165*
Trusler, Reuben 45; Ontario, 1871 ***1823.17*** *p165*
Truslove, Samuel; Virginia, 1768 ***1220.12*** *p812*
Truss, John; America, 1753 ***1220.12*** *p812*
Trussell, Ann; America, 1761 ***1220.12*** *p812*
Trussell, John; Virginia, 1652 ***6254.4*** *p243*
Trussin, Elizabeth; America, 1750 ***1220.12*** *p812*
Trust, Herrman; Ohio, 1840-1897 ***8365.35*** *p18*
Trusty, John; America, 1774 ***1220.12*** *p812*
Trut, Jacques 15; Quebec, 1656 ***9221.17*** *p347*
Trut, Mathurin 26; Quebec, 1647 ***9221.17*** *p190*
Trute, Carl Christian Wilhelm; England, 1885 ***7420.1*** *p349*
Trute, Heinrich; America, 1855 ***7420.1*** *p143*
With wife son & 2 daughters
Truteau, Etienne 18; Montreal, 1659 ***9221.17*** *p428*
Truthan, Bertha; America, 1867 ***7919.3*** *p530*
Truthan, Georg; America, 1867 ***7919.3*** *p530*
With wife & daughter
Trutner, Catharine Margarete Elisabeth; America, 1845 ***7420.1*** *p41*
Trutzel, Maria Th. S.; Philadelphia, 1852 ***8513.31*** *p428*
Trygoal, John; Virginia, 1765 ***1220.12*** *p812*
Trymary, Tho.; Maryland, 1672 ***1236.25*** *p47*
Tryner, Josef; Pennsylvania, 1860-1869 ***2853.20*** *p119*
Trzaskalski, Leon; Detroit, 1890 ***9980.23*** *p97*
Tschopp, Henry; Missouri, 1892 ***3276.1*** *p4*
Tubb, Jacob; Maryland, 1728 ***1220.12*** *p812*
Tubb, Thomas; America, 1751 ***1220.12*** *p812*
Tubbe, William; Texas, 1867 ***3435.45*** *p37*
Tubbins, James 33; Ontario, 1871 ***1823.17*** *p165*
Tuberville, James 30; Ontario, 1871 ***1823.21*** *p372*
Tubeuf, Nicolas; Quebec, 1643 ***9221.17*** *p136*
Tucek, Josef *SEE* Tucek, Vaclav
Tucek, Vaclav; Cleveland, OH, 1864 ***2853.20*** *p144*
*Son:*Josef
Tucheuf, Jean 31; America, 1844 ***778.6*** *p329*
Tuchmann, Franz; Valdivia, Chile, 1851 ***1192.4*** *p51*
Tuchscherer, Catharina 24; New York, NY, 1885 ***8425.16*** *p32*
Tuchscherer, Dominick 25; New York, NY, 1885 ***8425.16*** *p32*
Tuchscherer, Johanna 2; New York, NY, 1885 ***8425.16*** *p32*
Tuchscherer, Katharina 17; New York, NY, 1893 ***1883.7*** *p41*
Tuchscherer, Philippina 16; New York, NY, 1893 ***1883.7*** *p41*
Tuchscherer, Simon 21; New York, NY, 1893 ***1883.7*** *p41*
Tuchscherer, Wend 9; New York, NY, 1893 ***1883.7*** *p41*
Tuck, Charles 41; Ontario, 1871 ***1823.21*** *p372*
Tuck, Edward 40; Ontario, 1871 ***1823.21*** *p372*
Tuck, George; Beverly, MA, 1701 ***9228.50*** *p469*
Tuck, Henry 45; Ontario, 1871 ***1823.17*** *p165*
Tuck, Henry; Virginia, 1771 ***1220.12*** *p812*
Tuck, James; America, 1721 ***1220.12*** *p812*
Tuck, John; America, 1737 ***1220.12*** *p812*
Tuck, Joseph; America, 1728 ***1220.12*** *p812*
Tuck, Philip; Died enroute, 1772 ***1220.12*** *p813*
Tucker, Deborah 65; Ontario, 1871 ***1823.21*** *p373*
Tucker, Edward; America, 1749 ***1220.12*** *p813*
Tucker, Elizabeth; America, 1724 ***1220.12*** *p813*
Tucker, Elizabeth; Barbados or Jamaica, 1677 ***1220.12*** *p813*
Tucker, Emanuel; America, 1772 ***1220.12*** *p813*
Tucker, Freelove; America, 1763 ***1220.12*** *p813*
Tucker, Gabriell; America, 1697 ***1220.12*** *p813*
Tucker, George; America, 1763 ***1220.12*** *p813*
Tucker, Grace; America, 1674 ***1220.12*** *p813*
Tucker, Grace; America, 1742 ***1220.12*** *p813*
Tucker, Grace; Maryland, 1674 ***1236.25*** *p50*
Tucker, Gregory; America, 1766 ***1220.12*** *p813*
Tucker, Henry; America, 1685 ***1220.12*** *p813*
Tucker, Isaac 40; Ontario, 1871 ***1823.17*** *p165*
Tucker, James; America, 1755 ***1220.12*** *p813*
Tucker, James; America, 1775 ***1220.12*** *p813*
Tucker, John; America, 1744 ***1220.12*** *p813*
Tucker, John; America, 1749 ***1220.12*** *p813*
Tucker, John; America, 1774 ***1220.12*** *p813*
Tucker, John; Barbados, 1693 ***1220.12*** *p596*
Tucker, John 50; Ontario, 1871 ***1823.21*** *p373*
Tucker, John 53; Ontario, 1871 ***1823.21*** *p373*
Tucker, John; Virginia, 1740 ***1220.12*** *p813*
Tucker, Joseph; America, 1772 ***1220.12*** *p813*
Tucker, Lewis; America, 1729 ***1220.12*** *p813*
Tucker, Mariah 78; Ohio, 1880 ***4879.40*** *p260*
Tucker, Mary; America, 1760 ***1220.12*** *p813*
Tucker, Mary 3; Ontario, 1871 ***1823.17*** *p165*
Tucker, Mathew 25; Ontario, 1871 ***1823.21*** *p373*
Tucker, Patricia; Toronto, n.d. ***9228.50*** *p21A*
Tucker, Peter; Virginia, 1732 ***1220.12*** *p813*
Tucker, Richard; Barbados, 1672 ***1220.12*** *p813*
Tucker, Richard; Maryland, 1736 ***1220.12*** *p813*
Tucker, Robert; America, 1723 ***1220.12*** *p813*
Tucker, Robert; America, 1740 ***1220.12*** *p813*
Tucker, Robert; America, 1754 ***1220.12*** *p813*
Tucker, Roger; Barbados, 1690 ***1220.12*** *p813*
Tucker, Stephen 32; Ontario, 1871 ***1823.21*** *p373*
Tucker, Thomas; America, 1734 ***1220.12*** *p813*
Tucker, Thomas; America, 1751 ***1220.12*** *p813*
Tucker, Thomas; Marston's Wharf, 1782 ***8529.30*** *p16*
Tucker, Thomas; Washington, 1886 ***2770.40*** *p24*
Tucker, William; America, 1680 ***1220.12*** *p813*
Tucker, William; America, 1685 ***1220.12*** *p813*
Tucker, William; America, 1727 ***1220.12*** *p813*
Tucker, William; America, 1755 ***1220.12*** *p813*
Tucker, William; America, 1775 ***1220.12*** *p813*
Tucker, William 53; Ontario, 1871 ***1823.21*** *p373*
Tuckett, Thomas 53; Ontario, 1871 ***1823.21*** *p373*
Tuckey, John; America, 1773 ***1220.12*** *p813*
Tuckey, Thomas; America, 1685 ***1220.12*** *p813*
Tuckfield, Elizabeth; America, 1736 ***1220.12*** *p813*
Tuckfield, James; Barbados, 1668 ***1220.12*** *p813*
Tuckman, William; Detroit, 1929 ***1640.55*** *p116*
Tuder, Richard; Maryland, 1719 ***1220.12*** *p813*
Tudhope, Elizabeth 70; Ontario, 1871 ***1823.17*** *p165*
Tudor, Frances; America, 1771 ***1220.12*** *p813*
Tudor, George; America, 1729 ***1220.12*** *p813*
Tudor, Hervey; America, 1772 ***1220.12*** *p813*
Tudor, Nathaniel F.; Washington, 1879 ***2770.40*** *p134*
Tudor, Samuel; America, 1768 ***1220.12*** *p813*
Tudor, Sanford 35; Ontario, 1871 ***1823.21*** *p373*
Tudor, Woodward; Virginia, 1729 ***1220.12*** *p813*
Tudyk, Anton; Texas, 1855-1886 ***9980.22*** *p16*
Tudyk, Joseph; Texas, 1855-1884 ***9980.22*** *p16*
Tudyk, Joseph; Texas, 1855-1886 ***9980.22*** *p16*
Tudyk, Nicholas; Texas, 1855-1886 ***9980.22*** *p16*
Tue, Whitehill; America, 1739 ***1220.12*** *p790*
Tuedale, William 49; Ontario, 1871 ***1823.21*** *p373*
Tufay, Edouard 39; America, 1847 ***778.6*** *p329*
Tuff, Mary; Massachusetts, 1768 ***1642*** *p100*
Tuffeild, Samuel 46; Ontario, 1871 ***1823.17*** *p165*
Tuffield, William; America, 1729 ***1220.12*** *p813*
Tuffin, Samuel 40; Ontario, 1871 ***1823.21*** *p373*
Tuffnal, James; America, 1775 ***1220.12*** *p813*
Tuffnell, James; America, 1775 ***1220.12*** *p813*
Tuft, John; America, 1748 ***1220.12*** *p814*
Tuft, Thomas; America, 1761 ***1220.12*** *p814*
Tugby, John; America, 1770 ***1220.12*** *p814*
Tugman, James; America, 1755 ***1220.12*** *p814*
Tugwell, Elizabeth; America, 1773 ***1220.12*** *p814*
Tuhamel, Francois 32; Mississippi, 1847 ***778.6*** *p329*
Tuhrn, Henry 44; Indiana, 1887-1896 ***9076.20*** *p74*
Tuillier, Jacques 19; Montreal, 1661 ***9221.17*** *p475*
Tuischer, Frederick; Ohio, 1809-1852 ***4511.35*** *p55*
Tuishler, Frederick; Ohio, 1809-1852 ***4511.35*** *p55*
Tuite, Thomas; New Orleans, 1850 ***7242.30*** *p155*
Tujaque, Bernard; Louisiana, 1874-1875 ***4981.45*** *p130*
Tujaque, F. 23; New Orleans, 1848 ***778.6*** *p329*
Tujaque, Guillaume 20; New Orleans, 1848 ***778.6*** *p329*
Tujaque, Pierre 20; New Orleans, 1843 ***778.6*** *p329*
Tujaque, Silvian; Louisiana, 1874-1875 ***4981.45*** *p130*
Tuke, John W. 51; Ontario, 1871 ***1823.21*** *p373*
Tuke, William F. 35; Ontario, 1871 ***1823.21*** *p373*
Tuker, James 39; Ontario, 1871 ***1823.17*** *p166*
Tuker, Jane 64; Ontario, 1871 ***1823.17*** *p166*
Tulby, Jessie 12; Quebec, 1870 ***8364.32*** *p26*
Tulett, Thomas 38; Ontario, 1871 ***1823.21*** *p373*
Tulett, William 43; Ontario, 1871 ***1823.21*** *p373*
Tuley, John; America, 1754 ***1220.12*** *p806*
Tulick, Emma 19; Ontario, 1871 ***1823.21*** *p373*
Tull, Robert 50; Ontario, 1871 ***1823.21*** *p373*
Tulle, Samuel 44; Ontario, 1871 ***1823.21*** *p373*
Tullet, Thomas; Colorado, 1905 ***1029.59*** *p90*
Tulley, Dennis 42; Ontario, 1871 ***1823.17*** *p166*
Tulley, Edward 57; Ontario, 1871 ***1823.17*** *p166*
Tulley, Ralph; Barbados or Jamaica, 1677 ***1220.12*** *p814*
Tulloch, Ann 73; Ontario, 1871 ***1823.17*** *p166*
Tulloch, David 50; Ontario, 1871 ***1823.17*** *p166*
Tulloch, John 37; Ontario, 1871 ***1823.17*** *p166*
Tully, Andrew; New Orleans, 1851 ***7242.30*** *p155*
Tully, Ann 46; Ontario, 1871 ***1823.17*** *p166*
Tully, Catherine; New Orleans, 1851 ***7242.30*** *p155*
Tully, James; New Orleans, 1851 ***7242.30*** *p155*
Tully, James 32; Ontario, 1871 ***1823.21*** *p373*
Tully, John; New Orleans, 1851 ***7242.30*** *p155*
Tully, Mary; New Orleans, 1851 ***7242.30*** *p155*
Tully, Susanna; America, 1763 ***1220.12*** *p814*
Tuma, Karel F.; Chicago, 1875 ***2853.20*** *p504*
Tummer, John; America, 1763 ***1220.12*** *p814*
Tummon, Thomas; America, 1743 ***1220.12*** *p814*
Tummon, William 42; Ontario, 1871 ***1823.21*** *p373*
Tunbridge, Samuel; America, 1750 ***1220.12*** *p814*
Tunchel, Anna Margarethe; America, 1867 ***7919.3*** *p529*
*Daughter:*Sophia Pelz
Tunchel, Sophia Pelz *SEE* Tunchel, Anna Margarethe
Tune, Wm.; Toronto, 1844 ***2910.35*** *p114*
Tunicliff, Ann; America, 1761 ***1220.12*** *p814*
Tuniola, Margaret; America, 1761 ***1220.12*** *p814*
Tunks, James 74; Ontario, 1871 ***1823.21*** *p373*
Tunmore, David 68; Ontario, 1871 ***1823.17*** *p166*
Tunn, James 40; Ontario, 1871 ***1823.17*** *p166*
Tunnermann, Carl Friedrich Wilhelm; America, 1893 ***7420.1*** *p370*
Tunnermann, Friedrich August; America, 1883 ***7420.1*** *p340*
Tunnermann, Friedrich Wilhelm; America, 1846 ***7420.1*** *p50*
With son 9
With son 1
With daughter 4
With son 6
Tunnermann, Georg August *SEE* Tunnermann, Hans Heinrich
Tunnermann, Hans Heinrich; America, 1847 ***7420.1*** *p56*
Tunnermann, Hans Heinrich; America, 1847 ***7420.1*** *p57*
*Wife:*Sophie Catharine Dreier
*Son:*Georg August
*Daughter:*Rosine Wilhelmine Charlotte
Tunnermann, Karl; America, 1903 ***7420.1*** *p379*
Tunnermann, Rosine Wilhelmine Charlotte *SEE* Tunnermann, Hans Heinrich
Tunnermann, Sophie Catharine Dreier *SEE* Tunnermann, Hans Heinrich
Tunnermann, Sophie Wilhelmine; Wisconsin, 1855 ***7420.1*** *p143*
Tunnermann, Wilhelm; America, 1891 ***7420.1*** *p364*
Tunningley, John; America, 1770 ***1220.12*** *p814*
Tunnis, W.H. 17; Quebec, 1870 ***8364.32*** *p26*
Tunstall, John; America, 1742 ***1220.12*** *p814*
Tunstall, William; America, 1762 ***1220.12*** *p814*
Tuoe, John; New Orleans, 1851 ***7242.30*** *p155*
Tuomala, Maria 32; Minnesota, 1923 ***2769.54*** *p1383*
Tuomy, Patrick 28; New York, NY, 1825 ***6178.50*** *p77*
Tupe, Edward; Barbados, 1668 ***1220.12*** *p807*
Tupery, J. N. 35; America, 1841 ***778.6*** *p329*
Tupholme, Cordley 45; Ontario, 1871 ***1823.21*** *p373*
Tupin, Simon; Montreal, 1653 ***9221.17*** *p301*
Tupper, Ferdinand; Nova Scotia, 1816 ***9228.50*** *p636*
Tupper, Thomas; Massachusetts, 1600-1630 ***9228.50*** *p636*
Tupy, Ladislav; Chicago, 1872-1910 ***2853.20*** *p415*
Turbar, Ursule-Madeleine; Quebec, 1667 ***4514.3*** *p374*
Turbett, Hannah; America, 1736 ***1220.12*** *p814*
Turbett, Mary; America, 1751 ***1220.12*** *p814*
Turbutt, Isaac; America, 1736 ***1220.12*** *p814*
Turbutt, Samuel 25; Ontario, 1871 ***1823.21*** *p373*
Turbutt, William; America, 1745 ***1220.12*** *p814*
Turby, John; Potomac, 1731 ***1220.12*** *p814*
Turck, Johanna; America, 1800-1900 ***5475.1*** *p65*
Turcot, Abel 31; Quebec, 1662 ***9221.17*** *p493*
Turcot, Jean; Quebec, 1647 ***9221.17*** *p190*
Turczyn, Joseph; Detroit, 1929 ***1640.55*** *p115*
Ture, William 45; Ontario, 1871 ***1823.21*** *p373*

Turek, Jozefa 20; New York, NY, 1911 ***6533.11*** *p9*
Tureur, Elisa *SEE* Tureur, Olivier
Tureur, Ernest *SEE* Tureur, Olivier
Tureur, Louise Josephine *SEE* Tureur, Olivier
Tureur, Marie Eugenie *SEE* Tureur, Olivier
Tureur, Marie Louise Stimart *SEE* Tureur, Olivier
Tureur, Olivier; Wisconsin, 1880 ***1495.20*** *p56*
*Child:*Olivier, Jr.
*Wife:*Marie Louise Stimart
*Child:*Marie Eugenie
*Child:*Elisa
*Child:*Ernest
*Child:*Louise Josephine
Tureur, Olivier, Jr. *SEE* Tureur, Olivier
Turey, James 30; New York, NY, 1825 ***6178.50*** *p149*
Turgeon, Charles 41; Quebec, 1662 ***9221.17*** *p494*
*Wife:*Pasquiere Lefebvre 35
*Daughter:*Marie-Claire 11
*Son:*Jacques 9
*Daughter:*Marie-Anne 4
Turgeon, Jacques 9 *SEE* Turgeon, Charles
Turgeon, Marie-Anne 4 *SEE* Turgeon, Charles
Turgeon, Marie-Claire 11 *SEE* Turgeon, Charles
Turgeon, Pasquiere Lefebvre 35 *SEE* Turgeon, Charles
Turja, Hilda 42; Minnesota, 1926 ***2769.54*** *p1384*
Turja, Matt 44; Minnesota, 1926 ***2769.54*** *p1384*
Turk, Esau; America, 1772 ***1220.12*** *p814*
Turk, Fidel 26; America, 1846 ***778.6*** *p329*
Turker, Antoine 36; America, 1846 ***778.6*** *p329*
Turker, William; America, 1755 ***1220.12*** *p814*
Turla, Adela 18; New York, NY, 1911 ***6533.11*** *p9*
Turle, James; America, 1685 ***1220.12*** *p814*
Turle, John; America, 1685 ***1220.12*** *p814*
Turley, Andrew 53; Ontario, 1871 ***1823.21*** *p373*
Turmel, Francois 18; Quebec, 1655 ***9221.17*** *p329*
Turmidge, John; Barbados or Jamaica, 1696 ***1220.12*** *p814*
Turnam, Thomas; America, 1770 ***1220.12*** *p817*
Turnau, . . .; America, 1848 ***7420.1*** *p62*
Turnau, Mr.; America, 1845 ***7420.1*** *p41*
With wife & 5 children
Turnau, Engel Sophie Dorothee *SEE* Turnau, Heinrich Wilhelm
Turnau, Heinrich Wilhelm; America, 1848 ***7420.1*** *p63*
*Wife:*Marie Dorothee Charlotte Stock
*Son:*Joh. Heinr. Wilh. Christoph
*Daughter:*Engel Sophie Dorothee
Turnau, Joh. Heinr. Wilh. Christoph *SEE* Turnau, Heinrich Wilhelm
Turnau, Marie Dorothee Charlotte Stock *SEE* Turnau, Heinrich Wilhelm
Turnay, Daniel; North Carolina, 1850 ***1088.45*** *p35*
Turnbull, . . . 60; Ontario, 1871 ***1823.21*** *p373*
Turnbull, Elizabeth 76; Ontario, 1871 ***1823.21*** *p373*
Turnbull, Ellen; New Brunswick, 1842 ***2978.20*** *p8*
Turnbull, Francis; New Brunswick, 1842 ***2978.20*** *p8*
Turnbull, Hannah; America, 1755 ***1220.12*** *p814*
Turnbull, James; New Brunswick, 1842 ***2978.20*** *p8*
Turnbull, John; America, 1763 ***1220.12*** *p814*
Turnbull, John 39; Ontario, 1871 ***1823.21*** *p373*
Turnbull, John; Toronto, 1844 ***2910.35*** *p114*
Turnbull, Joseph; New Brunswick, 1842 ***2978.20*** *p8*
Turnbull, Luke 64; Ontario, 1871 ***1823.17*** *p166*
Turnbull, Margaret 40; Ontario, 1871 ***1823.21*** *p373*
Turnbull, Robert 39; Ontario, 1871 ***1823.21*** *p373*
Turnbull, William; America, 1748 ***1220.12*** *p814*
Turnbull, William 61; Ontario, 1871 ***1823.17*** *p166*
Turner, Abraham; America, 1754 ***1220.12*** *p814*
Turner, Abraham; Barbados or Jamaica, 1694 ***1220.12*** *p814*
Turner, Alice; Barbados, 1667 ***1220.12*** *p814*
Turner, Ann; America, 1736 ***1220.12*** *p814*
Turner, Ann; America, 1747 ***1220.12*** *p814*
Turner, Ann; America, 1749 ***1220.12*** *p814*
Turner, Ann; America, 1750 ***1220.12*** *p814*
Turner, Ann; America, 1754 ***1220.12*** *p814*
Turner, Ann; America, 1758 ***1220.12*** *p814*
Turner, Ann 62; Michigan, 1880 ***4491.33*** *p22*
Turner, Ann Harvey; America, 1768 ***1220.12*** *p814*
Turner, Anne; America, 1727 ***1220.12*** *p814*
Turner, Arthur; America, 1740 ***1220.12*** *p814*
Turner, Augustine; America, 1738 ***1220.12*** *p814*
Turner, Caroline Hale *SEE* Turner, Charles Patten
Turner, Catherine 14; Quebec, 1870 ***8364.32*** *p26*
Turner, Charles; America, 1770 ***1220.12*** *p814*
Turner, Charles 38; Ontario, 1871 ***1823.17*** *p166*
Turner, Charles Edwin *SEE* Turner, Charles Patten
Turner, Charles F. 40; Ontario, 1871 ***1823.21*** *p373*
Turner, Charles Patten; New York, 1858 ***9228.50*** *p636*
*Wife:*Caroline Hale
*Child:*Charles Edwin
With children
Turner, Daniel; America, 1767 ***1220.12*** *p814*
Turner, Duncan 53; Ontario, 1871 ***1823.17*** *p166*
Turner, Duncan; Philadelphia, 1837 ***3274.56*** *p98*
Turner, Edw'd; Ontario, 1787 ***1276.15*** *p231*
Turner, Edward; Died enroute, 1725 ***1220.12*** *p814*
Turner, Eliz. 22; Quebec, 1910 ***2897.7*** *p10*
Turner, Elizabeth; America, 1739 ***1220.12*** *p814*
Turner, Elizabeth; America, 1755 ***1220.12*** *p815*
Turner, Elizabeth; America, 1766 ***1220.12*** *p815*
Turner, Elizabeth; America, 1769 ***1220.12*** *p815*
Turner, Elizabeth; America, 1775 ***1220.12*** *p815*
Turner, Elizabeth; Annapolis, MD, 1732 ***1220.12*** *p814*
Turner, Elizabeth; Virginia, 1726 ***1220.12*** *p814*
Turner, Frances; America, 1767 ***1220.12*** *p815*
Turner, Francis; America, 1739 ***1220.12*** *p815*
Turner, Francis 52; Ontario, 1871 ***1823.21*** *p373*
Turner, George; America, 1723 ***1220.12*** *p815*
Turner, George; America, 1726 ***1220.12*** *p815*
Turner, George; America, 1760 ***1220.12*** *p815*
Turner, George; America, 1764 ***1220.12*** *p815*
Turner, George; America, 1768 ***1220.12*** *p815*
Turner, George 45; Ontario, 1871 ***1823.17*** *p166*
Turner, Henry 45; Ontario, 1871 ***1823.21*** *p373*
Turner, Hugh 42; Ontario, 1871 ***1823.21*** *p373*
Turner, Isaac; America, 1766 ***1220.12*** *p815*
Turner, Isaac; America, 1775 ***1220.12*** *p815*
Turner, James; America, 1686 ***1220.12*** *p815*
Turner, James; America, 1739 ***1220.12*** *p815*
Turner, James; America, 1765 ***1220.12*** *p815*
Turner, James; Ohio, 1809-1852 ***4511.35*** *p55*
Turner, James 30; Ontario, 1871 ***1823.21*** *p373*
Turner, James, Jr.; Boston, 1820 ***3274.55*** *p72*
Turner, Jane; America, 1679 ***1220.12*** *p815*
Turner, Jane; America, 1770 ***1220.12*** *p815*
Turner, Jane 47; Ontario, 1871 ***1823.21*** *p374*
Turner, Jas; Illinois, 1918 ***6007.60*** *p9*
Turner, Jo. 19; Virginia, 1635 ***1183.3*** *p31*
Turner, John; America, 1673 ***1220.12*** *p815*
Turner, John; America, 1708 ***1220.12*** *p815*
Turner, John; America, 1720 ***1220.12*** *p815*
Turner, John; America, 1729 ***1220.12*** *p815*
Turner, John; America, 1732 ***1220.12*** *p815*
Turner, John; America, 1736 ***1220.12*** *p815*
Turner, John; America, 1737 ***1220.12*** *p815*
Turner, John; America, 1738 ***1220.12*** *p815*
Turner, John; America, 1749 ***1220.12*** *p815*
Turner, John; America, 1750 ***1220.12*** *p815*
Turner, John; America, 1752 ***1220.12*** *p815*
Turner, John; America, 1763 ***1220.12*** *p815*
Turner, John; America, 1768 ***1220.12*** *p815*
Turner, John; America, 1769 ***1220.12*** *p815*
Turner, John; America, 1770 ***1220.12*** *p815*
Turner, John; Annapolis, MD, 1719 ***1220.12*** *p815*
Turner, John; Annapolis, MD, 1732 ***1220.12*** *p815*
Turner, John; Barbados, 1667 ***1220.12*** *p815*
Turner, John; Barbados, 1671 ***1220.12*** *p815*
Turner, John; Barbados, 1679 ***1220.12*** *p815*
Turner, John; Barbados, 1679 ***1220.12*** *p815*
Turner, John; Barbados, 1699 ***1220.12*** *p815*
Turner, John; Barbados, 1715 ***1220.12*** *p815*
Turner, John; Barbados or Jamaica, 1702 ***1220.12*** *p815*
Turner, John; Colorado, 1883 ***1029.59*** *p91*
Turner, John 42; Ontario, 1871 ***1823.21*** *p374*
Turner, John; Plymouth, MA, 1620 ***1920.45*** *p5*
With 2 sons
Turner, Joseph; America, 1730 ***1220.12*** *p815*
Turner, Joseph; America, 1764 ***1220.12*** *p816*
Turner, Joseph; America, 1765 ***1220.12*** *p816*
Turner, Joseph; America, 1766 ***1220.12*** *p816*
Turner, Joseph; America, 1769 ***1220.12*** *p816*
Turner, Joseph; Virginia, 1725 ***1220.12*** *p815*
Turner, Julia 14; Quebec, 1870 ***8364.32*** *p26*
Turner, Lewis; North Carolina, 1853 ***1088.45*** *p35*
Turner, Lissie 36; Michigan, 1880 ***4491.33*** *p22*
Turner, Mary; America, 1759 ***1220.12*** *p816*
Turner, Mary; America, 1766 ***1220.12*** *p816*
Turner, Mary; America, 1772 ***1220.12*** *p816*
Turner, Matthew; America, 1675 ***1220.12*** *p816*
Turner, Matthew; Maryland, 1733 ***1220.12*** *p816*
Turner, Peter; New York, NY, 1851 ***7710.1*** *p155*
Turner, Philip; America, 1739 ***1220.12*** *p816*
Turner, Philip; America, 1753 ***1220.12*** *p816*
Turner, Philip 36; Ontario, 1871 ***1823.17*** *p166*
Turner, Richard; America, 1685 ***1220.12*** *p816*
Turner, Richard; America, 1720 ***1220.12*** *p816*
Turner, Richard; America, 1741 ***1220.12*** *p816*
Turner, Richard; America, 1742 ***1220.12*** *p816*
Turner, Richard; Barbados, 1663 ***1220.12*** *p816*
Turner, Richard; North Carolina, 1849 ***1088.45*** *p35*
Turner, Richard 22; Ontario, 1871 ***1823.17*** *p166*
Turner, Richard 40; Ontario, 1871 ***1823.17*** *p166*
Turner, Richard, Jr.; Maryland, 1725 ***1220.12*** *p816*
Turner, Robert; Marston's Wharf, 1782 ***8529.30*** *p16*
Turner, Robert 63; Michigan, 1880 ***4491.33*** *p22*
Turner, Robert 35; Ontario, 1871 ***1823.17*** *p166*
Turner, S. M.; California, 1868 ***1131.61*** *p90*
Turner, Samuel; America, 1744 ***1220.12*** *p816*
Turner, Samuel; America, 1761 ***1220.12*** *p816*
Turner, Samuel; America, 1763 ***1220.12*** *p816*
Turner, Samuel; America, 1772 ***1220.12*** *p816*
Turner, Samuel; Virginia, 1759 ***1220.12*** *p816*
Turner, Sara; America, 1726 ***1220.12*** *p816*
Turner, Sarah; America, 1766 ***1220.12*** *p816*
Turner, Stephen; America, 1726 ***1220.12*** *p816*
Turner, Stephen; America, 1736 ***1220.12*** *p816*
Turner, Stephen; Virginia, 1765 ***1220.12*** *p816*
Turner, Susan; America, 1727 ***1220.12*** *p816*
Turner, Susan; Virginia, 1738 ***1220.12*** *p816*
Turner, Thomas; America, 1687 ***1220.12*** *p816*
Turner, Thomas; America, 1750 ***1220.12*** *p816*
Turner, Thomas; America, 1754 ***1220.12*** *p816*
Turner, Thomas; America, 1758 ***1220.12*** *p816*
Turner, Thomas; America, 1767 ***1220.12*** *p816*
Turner, Thomas; Annapolis, MD, 1725 ***1220.12*** *p816*
Turner, Thomas; Annapolis, MD, 1729 ***1220.12*** *p816*
Turner, Thomas; Barbados, 1663 ***1220.12*** *p816*
Turner, William; America, 1710 ***1220.12*** *p816*
Turner, William; America, 1721 ***1220.12*** *p816*
Turner, William; America, 1737 ***1220.12*** *p816*
Turner, William; America, 1741 ***1220.12*** *p816*
Turner, William; America, 1741 ***1220.12*** *p816*
Turner, William; America, 1749 ***1220.12*** *p816*
Turner, William; America, 1750 ***1220.12*** *p817*
Turner, William; America, 1760 ***1220.12*** *p817*
Turner, William; America, 1765 ***1220.12*** *p817*
Turner, William; America, 1768 ***1220.12*** *p817*
Turner, William; America, 1769 ***1220.12*** *p817*
Turner, William; America, 1770 ***1220.12*** *p817*
Turner, William; America, 1772 ***1220.12*** *p817*
Turner, William; America, 1774 ***1220.12*** *p817*
Turner, William; Barbados, 1664 ***1220.12*** *p816*
Turner, William 39; Ontario, 1871 ***1823.21*** *p374*
Turner, William, Jr.; Virginia, 1740 ***1220.12*** *p816*
Turner, William, Sr.; Virginia, 1740 ***1220.12*** *p816*
Turner, William P. 38; Ontario, 1871 ***1823.21*** *p374*
Turnes, Anna Forster 47 *SEE* Turnes, Nik.
Turnes, Jakob 16 *SEE* Turnes, Nik.
Turnes, Johann 22 *SEE* Turnes, Nik.
Turnes, Katharina 13 *SEE* Turnes, Nik.
Turnes, Nik. 43; America, 1846 ***5475.1*** *p401*
*Wife:*Anna Forster 47
*Daughter:*Katharina 13
*Son:*Johann 22
*Son:*Jakob 16
Turney, William; Boston, 1714 ***1642*** *p24*
Turnham, Thomas; America, 1739 ***1220.12*** *p817*
Turnhill, Peter 16; Quebec, 1870 ***8364.32*** *p26*
Turnig, Alois 31; Port uncertain, 1847 ***778.6*** *p329*
Turnow, John F.; Wisconsin, 1874 ***6795.8*** *p208*
Turnpenny, Samuel; America, 1774 ***1220.12*** *p817*
Turnquist, Frans Otto; St. Paul, MN, 1901 ***1865.50*** *p113*
*Wife:*Hulda M.
Turnquist, Hulda M. *SEE* Turnquist, Frans Otto
Turpein, Benjamin; Illinois, 1856 ***6079.1*** *p14*
Turpin, Mr.; America, 1900-1950 ***9228.50*** *p636*
With brother
Turpin, Daniel; America, 1749 ***1220.12*** *p817*
Turpin, Elizabeth; Maryland, 1719 ***1220.12*** *p817*
Turpin, Francois; Quebec, 1649 ***9221.17*** *p221*
Turpin, George 43; Ontario, 1871 ***1823.21*** *p374*
Turpin, John; America, 1750 ***1220.12*** *p817*
Turpin, John; America, 1768 ***1220.12*** *p817*
Turpin, Oliver; Barbados, 1679 ***1220.12*** *p817*
Turpin, Thomas; America, 1727 ***1220.12*** *p817*
Turpin, Tirwhite; America, 1694 ***1220.12*** *p817*
Turpitt, Mary; Virginia, 1750 ***1220.12*** *p817*
Turquaire, Alexander; America, 1723 ***1220.12*** *p817*
Turrall, Alice; Barbados, 1664 ***1220.12*** *p817*
Turreau, Henri 22; New Orleans, 1847 ***778.6*** *p329*
Turrell, John; America, 1763 ***1220.12*** *p817*
Turrell, Mary; America, 1773 ***1220.12*** *p817*
Turrill, Anne 40; Ontario, 1871 ***1823.17*** *p166*
Turtle, John 65; Ontario, 1871 ***1823.17*** *p166*
Turtle, William 15; Ontario, 1871 ***1823.17*** *p166*
Turtle, William, Sr.; America, 1772 ***1220.12*** *p817*
Turton, Elizabeth 45; Ontario, 1871 ***1823.21*** *p374*
Turton, Francis 37; Ontario, 1871 ***1823.17*** *p166*
Turton, Mary; America, 1755 ***1220.12*** *p817*
Turtsa, Theodor 34; New York, NY, 1894 ***6512.1*** *p182*
Turvel, Ann; America, 1771 ***1220.12*** *p817*
Turvey, Edward; Barbados, 1686 ***1220.12*** *p817*
Turvey, Joseph; America, 1767 ***1220.12*** *p817*
Turvey, William; America, 1771 ***1220.12*** *p817*
Turvie, James; America, 1744 ***1220.12*** *p817*
Turville, William 60; Ontario, 1871 ***1823.21*** *p374*
Tusken, Alexander 28; Ontario, 1871 ***1823.21*** *p374*
Tusky, Philip 51; Ontario, 1871 ***1823.21*** *p374*

Tuson, Richard 23; Ontario, 1871 *1823.21 p374*
Tusseau, . . .; Bermuda, 1620-1699 *9228.50 p636*
Tusseau, . . .; Jamestown, VA, 1620 *9228.50 p636*
Tusseau, . . .; Quebec, n.d. *9228.50 p636*
Tustey, Thomas; America, 1665 *1220.12 p817*
Tustin, Thomas; Virginia, 1740 *1220.12 p817*
Tutcher, Thomas; Annapolis, MD, 1726 *1220.12 p817*
Tutfold, William; Barbados, 1679 *1220.12 p817*
Tutin, Daniel; America, 1724 *1220.12 p817*
Tutorists, Anton; Illinois, 1918 *6007.60 p9*
Tutt, Jacob; America, 1733 *1220.12 p817*
Tutt, Susan; Barbados, 1675 *1220.12 p817*
Tuttell, Elizabeth 25; Virginia, 1635 *1183.3 p31*
Tuttle, Catharine 45; Ontario, 1871 *1823.21 p374*
Tuttle, Elanson; Salt Lake City, 1879 *1211.45 p135*
Tutty, James; New Orleans, 1850 *7242.30 p156*
Tutty, John 70; Ontario, 1871 *1823.21 p374*
Tuxworth, Thomas; America, 1759 *1220.12 p817*
Tuz, Nicholas; Detroit, 1929-1930 *6214.5 p69*
Tuzo, . . .; Quebec, n.d. *9228.50 p636*
Tuzo, Alice; Bermuda, 1830-1930 *9228.50 p638*
Tuzo, Joseph Stowe; Quebec, 1816-1825 *9228.50 p637*
  *Wife:*Mary Eve
Tuzo, Mary Eve *SEE* Tuzo, Joseph Stowe
Tuzo, Thomas B.; Quebec, n.d. *9228.50 p636*
Tvet, Andrew J.; Iowa, 1892 *1211.15 p19*
Tvrdy, Frantisek; New York, NY, 1848 *2853.20 p100*
Twaddle, John 70; Ontario, 1871 *1823.21 p374*
Twaite, Sampson; America, 1753 *1220.12 p817*
Twaites, William; America, 1740 *1220.12 p817*
Twanhy, Patrick; Ohio, 1809-1852 *4511.35 p55*
Twanmey, John; America, 1773 *1220.12 p817*
Twedt, Tom J.; Iowa, 1893 *1211.15 p20*
Tweedale, Thomas 56; Ontario, 1871 *1823.21 p374*
Twells, Alice; America, 1741 *1220.12 p817*
Twelves, Elizabeth; Maryland, 1721 *1220.12 p817*
Twelves, George; America, 1750 *1220.12 p817*
Twelves, George; Annapolis, MD, 1719 *1220.12 p817*
Twiddy, Mary; Annapolis, MD, 1722 *1220.12 p817*
Twiggs, Peter; America, 1744 *1220.12 p817*
Twigley, Mack 20; Ontario, 1871 *1823.21 p374*
Twine, Thomas; Virginia, 1756 *1220.12 p818*
Twiner, James; Ohio, 1809-1852 *4511.35 p55*
Twinney, William; America, 1725 *1220.12 p818*
Twisdale, Roger; Annapolis, MD, 1719 *1220.12 p818*
Twiss, Mary; America, 1771 *1220.12 p818*
Twiss, Robert 20; Ontario, 1871 *1823.21 p374*
Twissell, Wm. 28; Indiana, 1862-1870 *9076.20 p67*
Twist, Ann; Maryland, 1674 *1236.25 p50*
Twist, Benjamin; America, 1741 *1220.12 p818*
Twist, Charles; Barbados, 1686 *1220.12 p818*

Twist, Mary; America, 1771 *1220.12 p818*
Twist, Thomas; America, 1742 *1220.12 p818*
Twitt, Katherine; Annapolis, MD, 1729 *1220.12 p818*
Twogood, James 23; Ontario, 1871 *1823.17 p166*
Twohy, Catherine; Boston, 1766 *1642 p37*
Twohy, John; Boston, 1766 *1642 p37*
Twomey, Daniel; New Orleans, 1851 *7242.30 p156*
Twomey, John; Louisiana, 1874-1875 *4981.45 p130*
Twomey, John; New Orleans, 1850 *7242.30 p156*
Twonby, Patrick; Ohio, 1809-1852 *4511.35 p55*
Twongby, Patrick; Ohio, 1809-1852 *4511.35 p55*
Twonny, Michael; Boston, 1838 *3274.56 p69*
Tworek, Anthony; Detroit, 1929-1930 *6214.5 p69*
Tworney, Michael; Boston, 1837 *3274.56 p98*
Twyford, Downs; America, 1730 *1220.12 p818*
Twyford, Henry; America, 1770 *1220.12 p818*
Twyner, John; America, 1769 *1220.12 p818*
Twyner, John; Barbados, 1669 *1220.12 p818*
Tyas, Edward; America, 1744 *1220.12 p818*
Tyas, George; Ontario, 1871 *1823.21 p374*
Tyas, Jonathan; Illinois, 1858-1861 *6020.5 p133*
Tyas, Paul; Illinois, 1834-1900 *6020.5 p133*
Tyberg, Christina; St. Paul, MN, 1894 *1865.50 p113*
Tyberg, Erick; St. Paul, MN, 1887 *1865.50 p113*
Tyburski, Jozef 31; New York, NY, 1911 *6533.11 p9*
Tyce, Edward; America, 1744 *1220.12 p818*
Tycer, Benjamin; Charles Town, SC, 1719 *1220.12 p818*
Tydey, Thomas; America, 1730 *1220.12 p801*
Tydyk, Nicholas; Texas, 1855-1873 *9980.22 p16*
Tye, Mary; Barbados or Jamaica, 1690 *1220.12 p818*
Tye, Richard; America, 1770 *1220.12 p818*
Tye, Samuel 43; Ontario, 1871 *1823.21 p374*
Tyer, John; America, 1764 *1220.12 p818*
Tyeror, Anthony; North Carolina, 1844 *1088.45 p35*
Tyerrell, William 23; Ontario, 1871 *1823.17 p166*
Tyers, Ann; Virginia, 1736 *1220.12 p818*
Tyers, Richard; America, 1757 *1220.12 p818*
Tyers, Sarah; America, 1750 *1220.12 p818*
Tyler, Edward; America, 1772 *1220.12 p818*
Tyler, George 51; Ontario, 1871 *1823.17 p166*
Tyler, Hannah; Maryland, 1720 *1220.12 p818*
Tyler, James; Barbados, 1663 *1220.12 p818*
Tyler, John; America, 1730 *1220.12 p818*
Tyler, John; America, 1749 *1220.12 p818*
Tyler, John; America, 1753 *1220.12 p818*
Tyler, John; America, 1755 *1220.12 p818*
Tyler, John; New Jersey, 1665 *9228.50 p621*
Tyler, John 40; Ontario, 1871 *1823.21 p374*
Tyler, Joseph; America, 1752 *1220.12 p818*
Tyler, Joseph; Ohio, 1809-1852 *4511.35 p55*
Tyler, Margaret; America, 1683 *1220.12 p818*

Tyler, Mary; America, 1755 *1220.12 p818*
Tyler, Mary; America, 1774 *1220.12 p818*
Tyler, Mary; Annapolis, MD, 1726 *1220.12 p818*
Tyler, Thomas; Barbados, 1664 *1220.12 p818*
Tyler, William; America, 1774 *1220.12 p818*
Tyler, William; Colorado, 1904 *1029.59 p91*
Tyler, William; Maryland, 1727 *1220.12 p818*
Tyley, John; America, 1754 *1220.12 p818*
Tymperley, Thomas; America, 1768 *1220.12 p803*
Tymson, James; Barbados or Jamaica, 1705 *1220.12 p803*
Tynan, John 30; Ontario, 1871 *1823.21 p374*
Tynan, Patrick 42; Ontario, 1871 *1823.21 p374*
Tyndell, Mabel Maria; Miami, 1935 *4984.12 p39*
Tyne, Sarah; America, 1768 *1220.12 p818*
Tyner, Joseph; America, 1766 *1220.12 p818*
Tyng, Geo.; California, 1868 *1131.61 p89*
Typo, Maria Magdalena; Venezuela, 1843 *3899.5 p542*
Tyrala, Ewa 27; New York, NY, 1911 *6533.11 p10*
Tyrala, Katarzyna 6; New York, NY, 1911 *6533.11 p10*
Tyre, John; Louisiana, 1874 *4981.45 p134*
Tyrell, Elizabeth; America, 1760 *1220.12 p819*
Tyrell, John; Louisiana, 1874 *4981.45 p134*
Tyres, Samuell 21; Virginia, 1635 *1183.3 p30*
Tyroldt, Joh. M.; Chile, 1852 *1192.4 p55*
  With wife
Tyrrall, Edward 23; New York, NY, 1844 *6178.50 p151*
Tyrrell, Adam; America, 1721 *1220.12 p819*
Tyrrell, Adam 56; Ontario, 1871 *1823.17 p166*
Tyrrell, Edward 23; New York, NY, 1844 *6178.50 p151*
Tyrrell, Francis; America, 1772 *1220.12 p819*
Tyrrell, Thomas; America, 1754 *1220.12 p819*
Tysier, Ms. 54; Port uncertain, 1845 *778.6 p329*
Tysoe, James; America, 1770 *1220.12 p819*
Tysoe, Richard; America, 1765 *1220.12 p819*
Tyson, Bartlett 30; Ontario, 1871 *1823.17 p166*
Tyson, John; Missouri, 1894 *3276.1 p4*
Tyson, John 33; Ontario, 1871 *1823.21 p374*
Tyson, Joseph; America, 1771 *1220.12 p819*
Tyson, Lewis; Maryland, 1719 *1220.12 p819*
Tyson, Nicelo 24; Michigan, 1880 *4491.42 p27*
Tyson, Thomas; Missouri, 1850 *3276.1 p4*
Tyson, William; Missouri, 1894 *3276.1 p4*
Tythcott, John; Iowa, 1890 *1211.15 p19*
Tythe, Mary; America, 1751 *1220.12 p819*
Tyther, John; America, 1680 *1220.12 p819*
Tyther, John; America, 1736 *1220.12 p819*
Tytler, Alexander 36; Ontario, 1871 *1823.21 p374*
Tytler, John 40; Ontario, 1871 *1823.21 p374*
Tzschirer, Joseph; Valdivia, Chile, 1852 *1192.4 p54*

U

Ubel, Conrad; Kansas, 1917-1918 *1826.15 p81*
Ubel, John; Ohio, 1809-1852 *4511.35 p55*
Ubel, Katharina Krauter *SEE* Ubel, Valentin
Ubel, Margarethe *SEE* Ubel, Valentin
Ubel, Valentin; Pennsylvania, 1887 *5475.1 p17*
   *Wife:*Katharina Krauter
   *Daughter:*Margarethe
Udall, John; America, 1750 *1220.12 p820*
Udall, Richard; Barbados, 1673 *1220.12 p820*
Udbye, Esten; Valdivia, Chile, 1850 *1192.4 p49*
Uden, William; America, 1773 *1220.12 p820*
Uder, A. Maria *SEE* Uder, Johann
Uder, Andreas *SEE* Uder, Johann
Uder, Jakob *SEE* Uder, Johann
Uder, Johann *SEE* Uder, Johann
Uder, Johann; America, 1881 *5475.1 p273*
   *Wife:*Katharina Boss
   *Daughter:*Maria
   *Daughter:*A. Maria
   *Daughter:*Katharina
   *Son:*Nikolaus
   *Son:*Andreas
   *Son:*Peter
   *Son:*Jakob
   *Son:*Johann
Uder, Katharina *SEE* Uder, Johann
Uder, Katharina Boss *SEE* Uder, Johann
Uder, Maria *SEE* Uder, Johann
Uder, Nikolaus *SEE* Uder, Johann
Uder, Peter *SEE* Uder, Johann
Udith, James; America, 1768 *1220.12 p820*
Ueber, Jacob; Louisiana, 1841-1844 *4981.45 p211*
Uebler, Michael; New York, 1860 *358.56 p5*
Uecker, Louise; Wisconsin, 1891 *6795.8 p79*
Uelhoff, Jos. 49; America, 1913 *8023.44 p380*
Uen, Margret 30; Ontario, 1871 *1823.21 p374*
Ueo, Eliza 20; Ontario, 1871 *1823.21 p374*
Uffell, Roger; America, 1738 *1220.12 p820*
Uffleman, Peter; America, 1722 *1220.12 p820*
Ufheil, John; Ohio, 1809-1852 *4511.35 p55*
Uggles, Richard; America, 1761 *1220.12 p820*
Uglow, William 36; Ontario, 1871 *1823.21 p374*
Ugolnik, Carl; Detroit, 1929-1930 *6214.5 p61*
Uhe, Johanna Mathilde Henriette; America, 1867 *7420.1 p265*
Uhe, Wilhelmine; America, 1864 *7420.1 p227*
Uher, Alois; Chicago, 1810-1910 *2853.20 p405*
Uher, Mathias; Wisconsin, 1883 *6795.8 p234*
Uhl, August; Wisconsin, 1885 *6795.8 p208*
Uhl, George 22; Missouri, 1845 *778.6 p329*
Uhl, Johann 27; America, 1853 *2526.43 p200*
Uhl, Johann Peter; Pennsylvania, 1867 *170.15 p44*
Uhl, Johann Peter 20; Pennsylvania, 1867 *170.15 p44*
Uhl, Margaretha; New England, 1867 *170.15 p44*
Uhland, Christina 15 *SEE* Uhland, Joseph
Uhland, Franz 17 *SEE* Uhland, Joseph
Uhland, Guerard 25; Missouri, 1845 *778.6 p329*
Uhland, Joseph; America, 1844 *2526.43 p215*
   With wife
   *Daughter:*Maria
   *Son:*Ludwig
   *Daughter:*Katharina Elisabetha
   *Daughter:*Katharina
   *Son:*Franz
   *Daughter:*Christina
Uhland, Katharina 14 *SEE* Uhland, Joseph
Uhland, Katharina Elisabetha 8 *SEE* Uhland, Joseph
Uhland, Ludwig 3 *SEE* Uhland, Joseph

Uhland, Maria 10 *SEE* Uhland, Joseph
Uhle, Alfred 7 months; New York, NY, 1893 *1883.7 p39*
Uhle, Emma 22; New York, NY, 1893 *1883.7 p39*
Uhle, Herman F.; Ohio, 1809-1852 *4511.35 p55*
Uhle, Jacob 30; New York, NY, 1893 *1883.7 p39*
Uhle, Rudolf 2; New York, NY, 1893 *1883.7 p39*
Uhlman, Arnold; Louisiana, 1836-1841 *4981.45 p209*
Uhlmueller, Margaretha; Pennsylvania, 1867 *170.15 p44*
Uhmann, Peter; Nova Scotia, 1784 *7105 p25*
Uhrich, Dorothea; America, 1866 *2526.43 p183*
Uhrig, Anna Maria 24; Ohio, 1864 *2526.42 p99*
Uhrig, Barbara; Ohio, 1864 *2526.42 p96*
Uhrig, Daniel 26; America, 1846 *2526.43 p157*
Uhrig, Johannes; America, 1853 *2526.42 p148*
Uhrig, Johannes; America, 1870 *2526.42 p100*
Uhrig, Karl Albrecht; New Jersey, 1890 *2526.43 p183*
Uhrig, Magdalena; America, 1853 *2526.42 p100*
Uhrik, Paul; Chicago, 1930 *121.35 p100*
Uhrmacher, Katharina 27; New Orleans, 1860 *5475.1 p328*
Uinquist, Andrew A.; Missouri, 1876 *3276.1 p4*
Ulbrecht, John; Long Island, 1781 *8529.30 p10A*
Ulbricht, John; Long Island, 1781 *8529.30 p10A*
Ulbright, John; Long Island, 1781 *8529.30 p10A*
Ulc, Vaclav; Iowa, 1855 *2853.20 p217*
Ulerich, Franziska 27; Halifax, N.S., 1902 *1860.4 p40*
Ulerich, Margaretha 20; Halifax, N.S., 1902 *1860.4 p40*
Ulerich, Michael; Halifax, N.S., 1902 *1860.4 p40*
Ulerich, Michael 30; Halifax, N.S., 1902 *1860.4 p40*
Ulin, Eric; Washington, 1879 *2770.40 p134*
Ulinder, J.P.; Charleston, SC, 1851 *6412.40 p153*
Ullerich, Jacob; Ohio, 1809-1852 *4511.35 p55*
Ullman, Henry; Philadelphia, 1851 *8513.31 p430*
   *Wife:*Susanna Shuman
Ullman, Morris; North Carolina, 1857 *1088.45 p35*
Ullman, Susanna Shuman *SEE* Ullman, Henry
Ullmann, Barbara; America, 1857 *2526.42 p202*
Ullmann, Barbara 20 *SEE* Ullmann, Elisabetha
Ullmann, Elisabetha; America, 1854 *2526.42 p202*
   *Daughter:*Barbara
   *Daughter:*Elisabetha
   *Son:*Michael
Ullmann, Elisabetha 14 *SEE* Ullmann, Elisabetha
Ullmann, Kaspar 33; America, 1846 *2526.42 p202*
   With wife
   *Daughter:*Margaretha 2
Ullmann, Margaretha 2 *SEE* Ullmann, Kaspar
Ullmann, Mathias 21; America, 1847 *778.6 p329*
Ullmann, Michael 9 *SEE* Ullmann, Elisabetha
Ullmann, Siegmund; England, 1897 *2526.43 p144*
Ullrich, Herrmann; Valdivia, Chile, 1851 *1192.4 p51*
Ullrich, John; Louisiana, 1836-1841 *4981.45 p209*
Ullrich, Louis; America, 1867 *7919.3 p529*
Ulm, Antoine 8; New Orleans, 1848 *778.6 p329*
Ulm, Antoine 41; New Orleans, 1848 *778.6 p329*
Ulm, Catharine 11; New Orleans, 1848 *778.6 p329*
Ulm, Eva 33; America, 1847 *778.6 p329*
Ulm, Lorentz 8; America, 1847 *778.6 p329*
Ulm, Lorenz 35; America, 1847 *778.6 p330*
Ulm, Marguerite 4; America, 1847 *778.6 p330*
Ulm, Marianna 51; New Orleans, 1848 *778.6 p330*
Ulm, Michel 17; New Orleans, 1848 *778.6 p330*
Ulm, Nicolas 1; New Orleans, 1848 *778.6 p330*
Ulman, John; Ohio, 1809-1852 *4511.35 p55*
Ulmer, Andreas 18; New York, NY, 1874 *6954.7 p39*
Ulmer, Carl 1 months; New York, NY, 1874 *6954.7 p39*
Ulmer, Carl 15; New York, NY, 1874 *6954.7 p39*
Ulmer, Caroline 10; New York, NY, 1874 *6954.7 p39*

Ulmer, Catharine 15; New York, NY, 1874 *6954.7 p39*
Ulmer, Christian; Dakota, 1894-1918 *554.30 p26*
   *Wife:*Christine
Ulmer, Christian 7; New York, NY, 1874 *6954.7 p39*
Ulmer, Christina 50; New York, NY, 1874 *6954.7 p39*
Ulmer, Christine *SEE* Ulmer, Christian
Ulmer, Elizabeth 34; New York, NY, 1874 *6954.7 p39*
Ulmer, Friedricke 9 months; New York, NY, 1874 *6954.7 p39*
Ulmer, Gottlieb 14; New York, NY, 1874 *6954.7 p39*
Ulmer, Jacob 5; New York, NY, 1874 *6954.7 p39*
Ulmer, Jacob 58; New York, NY, 1874 *6954.7 p39*
Ulmer, Karl Christoph; America, 1866 *179.55 p19*
Ulmer, Louise 19; New York, NY, 1874 *6954.7 p39*
Ulmer, Ludwig; America, 1882 *2526.43 p200*
Ulmer, Marie 8; New York, NY, 1874 *6954.7 p39*
Ulmer, Mathais 39; New York, NY, 1874 *6954.7 p39*
Ulmer, Matilda; Philadelphia, 1867 *8513.31 p431*
Ulmer, Matthew; Illinois, 1834-1900 *6020.5 p133*
Ulmer, Wilhelm 9; New York, NY, 1874 *6954.7 p39*
Ulmer, Wilhelm 17; New York, NY, 1874 *6954.7 p39*
Ulph, Charles; America, 1753 *1220.12 p820*
Ulph, John; America, 1749 *1220.12 p820*
Ulph, Samuel; Annapolis, MD, 1723 *1220.12 p820*
Ulrich, Alexander 6; Portland, ME, 1906 *970.38 p82*
Ulrich, Benjamin 4; Portland, ME, 1906 *970.38 p82*
Ulrich, Bernard; Ohio, 1809-1852 *4511.35 p55*
Ulrich, Carolina; America, 1872 *5475.1 p419*
Ulrich, Christian 16; Portland, ME, 1906 *970.38 p82*
Ulrich, Dan; Louisiana, 1874-1875 *4981.45 p130*
Ulrich, Eduard Wilhelm; America, 1867 *7919.3 p526*
Ulrich, Ferd; Nebraska, 1905 *3004.30 p46*
Ulrich, Georg 42; Portland, ME, 1906 *970.38 p82*
Ulrich, Jacob 11; Portland, ME, 1906 *970.38 p82*
Ulrich, Johann 13; Portland, ME, 1906 *970.38 p82*
Ulrich, Johann Henrich; Port uncertain, 1866 *170.15 p44*
Ulrich, Johannes; America, 1867 *7919.3 p526*
Ulrich, Julius; Washington, 1885 *2770.40 p194*
Ulrich, Katarina 10; Portland, ME, 1906 *970.38 p82*
Ulrich, Katarina 40; Portland, ME, 1906 *970.38 p82*
Ulrich, Ludwig; Ohio, 1809-1852 *4511.35 p55*
Ulrich, Michael 39; Pennsylvania, 1848 *170.15 p44*
   With 3 children
Ulrich, Michael 39; Pennsylvania, 1848 *170.15 p44*
   With 2 children
Ulrich, Ottilie 5 months; Portland, ME, 1906 *970.38 p82*
Ulrich, Paul; New York, 1860 *358.56 p4*
Ulrich, Ph.; New York, 1859 *358.56 p54*
Ulrich, Samuel; Ohio, 1840-1897 *8365.35 p18*
Ulrich, Simen; Ohio, 1840-1897 *8365.35 p18*
Ulrich, Theobald; America, 1840 *5475.1 p555*
Ulrich, William; North Carolina, 1860 *1088.45 p35*
Ulvestad, Andrew O.; Washington, 1885 *2770.40 p194*
Umbach, Carl; America, 1854 *7420.1 p132*
   With wife 4 sons & daughter
Umble, Margaret; Jamaica, 1716 *1220.12 p820*
Umbreit, Traugott; Wisconsin, 1860 *6795.8 p97*
Umpelback, Mr. 28; America, 1844 *778.6 p330*
Umpisson, John; America, 1768 *1220.12 p820*
Umpris, Mary 72; Ontario, 1871 *1823.21 p374*
Umpris, William 44; Ontario, 1871 *1823.21 p374*
Uncherich, Peter; Ohio, 1809-1852 *4511.35 p55*
Uncle, Benjamin, Jr.; America, 1765 *1220.12 p820*
Uncles, Elizabeth; America, 1774 *1220.12 p820*
Uncles, Thomas; America, 1708 *1220.12 p820*
Undereiner, Jacob 18; America, 1846 *778.6 p330*
Undereiner, Pierre 17; America, 1846 *778.6 p330*
Underhill, George; America, 1745 *1220.12 p820*

Underhill, Henry; America, 1749 *1220.12* *p820*
Underhill, Henry; Marston's Wharf, 1782 *8529.30* *p16*
Underhill, Henry; New York, 1776 *8529.30* *p16*
Underhill, James; America, 1767 *1220.12* *p820*
Underhill, Joseph; America, 1756 *1220.12* *p820*
Underhill, Joseph 69; Ontario, 1871 *1823.21* *p374*
Underhill, Mary; Virginia, 1738 *1220.12* *p820*
Underhill, Robert, Jr.; Virginia, 1718 *1220.12* *p820*
Underhill, William; America, 1756 *1220.12* *p820*
Underhill, William; Virginia, 1718 *1220.12* *p820*
Underrenner, Georges 21; New Orleans, 1846 *778.6* *p330*
Underwood, Andrew; Ohio, 1832 *3580.20* *p33*
Underwood, Andrew; Ohio, 1832 *6020.12* *p23*
Underwood, Ann; America, 1770 *1220.12* *p820*
Underwood, Anthony; Maryland, 1737 *1220.12* *p820*
Underwood, Christopher; Virginia, 1768 *1220.12* *p820*
Underwood, Dorothy; America, 1768 *1220.12* *p820*
Underwood, Elizabeth; America, 1731 *1220.12* *p820*
Underwood, Humphrey; Barbados, 1664 *1220.12* *p820*
Underwood, Jacob Fosbrook; America, 1745 *1220.12* *p820*
Underwood, John; America, 1752 *1220.12* *p820*
Underwood, John; America, 1753 *1220.12* *p820*
Underwood, John; America, 1770 *1220.12* *p820*
Underwood, John; Virginia, 1744 *1220.12* *p820*
Underwood, Thomas; America, 1769 *1220.12* *p820*
Underwood, William; America, 1680 *1220.12* *p820*
Underwood, William; America, 1757 *1220.12* *p820*
Underwood, William; Virginia, 1768 *1220.12* *p820*
Underwood, Wm 52; Ontario, 1871 *1823.21* *p374*
Undurin, Catha. 29; America, 1847 *778.6* *p330*
Ungaush, A. 59; Mississippi, 1846 *778.6* *p330*
Unger, Mr. 25; America, 1847 *778.6* *p330*
Unger, Mr. 26; America, 1847 *778.6* *p330*
Unger, Christiana; America, 1867 *7919.3* *p533*
Unger, Friedr. 14; New York, NY, 1885 *1883.7* *p45*
Unger, Per O.; Colorado, 1894 *1029.59* *p91*
Unger, Petder; Colorado, 1884 *1029.59* *p91*
Unger, Peter O.; Colorado, 1884 *1029.59* *p91*
Ungern, Marc 45; Texas, 1848 *778.6* *p330*
Unit, Bertholomy 35; New Orleans, 1845 *778.6* *p330*
Unite, John, Jr.; America, 1767 *1220.12* *p820*
Unkelar, Peter W.; North Carolina, 1856 *1088.45* *p35*
Unkert, Bernhard; America, 1867 *7919.3* *p528*
Unkert, Johann Christoph; America, 1868 *7919.3* *p528*
Unkert, Matthias; America, 1868 *7919.3* *p528*
With wife & 5 children
Unkeschicht, Michael; Ohio, 1809-1852 *4511.35* *p55*
Unkeshicht, Michael; Ohio, 1809-1852 *4511.35* *p55*
Unmuth, Barbara; Venezuela, 1843 *3899.5* *p542*
Unser, Peter 17; New York, NY, 1898 *7951.13* *p43*
Unsworth, John; America, 1752 *1220.12* *p820*
Unsworth, John; America, 1763 *1220.12* *p820*
Unterimer, John; Louisiana, 1874 *4981.45* *p134*
Unterimer, Juan Baptiste; Louisiana, 1874 *4981.45* *p134*
Untersiner, Cath. 2; America, 1840 *778.6* *p330*
Untersiner, Georg 29; America, 1840 *778.6* *p330*
Untersiner, Marg. 24; America, 1840 *778.6* *p330*
Untersiner, Peter 14; America, 1840 *778.6* *p330*
Unthank, Daniel; America, 1770 *1220.12* *p821*
Unwin, Francis; America, 1770 *1220.12* *p821*
Unwin, John; Virginia, 1721 *1220.12* *p821*
Unwin, Joseph; America, 1774 *1220.12* *p821*
Up, Philip; New Jersey, 1768-1774 *927.31* *p2*
Upchurch, John; America, 1746 *1220.12* *p821*
Upcroft, John; America, 1751 *1220.12* *p821*
Updale, Elizabeth; America, 1724 *1220.12* *p821*
Upfield, George; America, 1743 *1220.12* *p821*
Upgood, John; America, 1766 *1220.12* *p821*
Upham, Comfort; America, 1754 *1220.12* *p821*
Upham, John; America, 1742 *1220.12* *p821*
Upham, Robert; America, 1775 *1220.12* *p821*
Upham, Thomas; America, 1726 *1220.12* *p821*
Upham, Thomas; America, 1772 *1220.12* *p821*
Uphill, William; America, 1742 *1220.12* *p821*
Uphus, Johann Bernhard 26; Galveston, TX, 1845 *3967.10* *p376*
Upington, William; America, 1750 *1220.12* *p821*
Uppington, Elizabeth; America, 1754 *1220.12* *p821*
Uppstrom, O.E.; Cleveland, OH, 1901-1903 *9722.10* *p127*
Upsall, Nicholas; Massachusetts, 1630 *117.5* *p155*

Upson, Mary; America, 1756 *1220.12* *p821*
Upton, Edward; America, 1763 *1220.12* *p821*
Upton, Edward 60; Ontario, 1871 *1823.21* *p374*
Upton, Elizabeth; America, 1754 *1220.12* *p821*
Upton, Elizabeth; Carolina, 1724 *1220.12* *p821*
Upton, George; America, 1752 *1220.12* *p821*
Upton, Hannah; America, 1768 *1220.12* *p821*
Upton, John; America, 1768 *1220.12* *p821*
Upton, John 40; Ontario, 1871 *1823.17* *p166*
Upton, Nicholas; America, 1691 *1220.12* *p821*
Upton, Thomas; Virginia, 1735 *1220.12* *p821*
Upton, William; America, 1742 *1220.12* *p821*
Upwin, John; America, 1742 *1220.12* *p821*
Uquet, Manuel; Louisiana, 1874 *4981.45* *p297*
Urbach, Franz 23; New York, NY, 1893 *1883.7* *p43*
Urbain, Nicolas 27; America, 1846 *778.6* *p330*
Urban, Anthony SEE Urban, John
Urban, Antonin Dominik; Iowa, 1865 *2853.20* *p231*
Urban, John; North Carolina, 1828 *1088.45* *p35*
   *Relative:*Anthony
   *Relative:*Juna
   *Relative:*Maurice
   *Relative:*Josephine
Urban, Josephine SEE Urban, John
Urban, Juna SEE Urban, John
Urban, Maurice SEE Urban, John
Urban, Michael; Detroit, 1929 *1640.55* *p116*
Urban, Nicolas 25; Port uncertain, 1843 *778.6* *p330*
Urbanek, . . .; Nebraska, 1874 *2853.20* *p172*
Urbaniak, Victoria; Detroit, 1929 *1640.55* *p112*
Urbanski, Ignacy; Texas, 1894-1905 *6015.15* *p11*
Urbanski, Walenty; Detroit, 1930 *1640.60* *p81*
Urbanus, Anna Maria SEE Urbanus, Nikolaus
Urbanus, Eva Stolz 55 SEE Urbanus, Nikolaus
Urbanus, Johann SEE Urbanus, Nikolaus
Urbanus, Katharina SEE Urbanus, Nikolaus
Urbanus, Margarethe SEE Urbanus, Nikolaus
Urbanus, Nikolaus SEE Urbanus, Nikolaus
Urbanus, Nikolaus 66; America, 1864 *5475.1* *p266*
   *Wife:*Eva Stolz 55
   *Daughter:*Katharina
   *Son:*Nikolaus
   *Daughter:*Margarethe
   *Daughter:*Anna Maria
   *Son:*Johann
Urbany, J.; Louisiana, 1874-1875 *4981.45* *p130*
Ure, John 59; Ontario, 1871 *1823.21* *p375*
Urech, Hans Ulrich 42; New Castle, DE, 1817-1818 *90.20* *p154*
Urech, Jacob 43; New Castle, DE, 1817-1818 *90.20* *p154*
Urech, Rudolph 46; New Castle, DE, 1817-1818 *90.20* *p154*
Urell, James; Quebec, 1870 *8364.32* *p26*
Uren, Andrew; Washington, 1888 *2770.40* *p26*
Uren, Elizabeth; Virginia, 1735 *1220.12* *p821*
Uren, Jane; America, 1773 *1220.12* *p821*
Urg, Hjelmen 21; Minnesota, 1923 *2769.54* *p1379*
Uri, Johannetta Notar SEE Uri, Peter
Uri, John; Ohio, 1843 *2763.1* *p22*
Uri, Peter; America, 1834 *5475.1* *p437*
   *Wife:*Johannetta Notar
   With 4 children
Uri, William; Ohio, 1844 *2763.1* *p22*
Urich, Daniel 37; America, 1868 *2526.43* *p157*
   *Wife:*Eva Katharina Hofferbert 40
   *Daughter:*Eva Katharina 18
   *Son:*Georg 13
   *Daughter:*Eva Margaretha 4
   With son I
Urich, Eva Katharina 18 SEE Urich, Daniel
Urich, Eva Katharina Hofferbert 40 SEE Urich, Daniel
Urich, Eva Margaretha 4 SEE Urich, Daniel
Urich, Georg 13 SEE Urich, Daniel
Urich, Jacob 43; New Castle, DE, 1817-1818 *90.20* *p154*
Urich, Wilhelmine; America, 1864 *2526.43* *p183*
Uridge, Ruth; America, 1742 *1220.12* *p821*
Urlau, Friedrich Gottlieb; America, 1868 *7919.3* *p532*
Urlin, Elizabeth; Barbados, 1664 *1220.12* *p821*
Urnier, Alexander; North America, 1837 *6410.15* *p103*
Urquhart, Allan 30; Ontario, 1871 *1823.17* *p167*
Urquhart, Donald 70; Ontario, 1871 *1823.21* *p375*
Urquhart, Sarah 55; Ontario, 1871 *1823.21* *p375*
Urquhart, William; Annapolis, MD, 1758 *1220.12* *p821*

Urry, James; America, 1736 *1220.12* *p821*
Urry, James; America, 1763 *1220.12* *p821*
Urschel, Daniel; Ohio, 1809-1852 *4511.35* *p55*
Urschel, John; Ohio, 1809-1852 *4511.35* *p55*
Urshehel, John; Ohio, 1809-1852 *4511.35* *p55*
Urshel, Daniel; Ohio, 1809-1852 *4511.35* *p55*
Ursin, Mary; America, 1745 *1220.12* *p821*
Ursino, Goelf 24; America, 1841 *778.6* *p330*
Ursino, Math.eu 21; America, 1841 *778.6* *p330*
Ursino, Raphae 20; America, 1841 *778.6* *p330*
Ursula, Mary 25; Ontario, 1871 *1823.21* *p375*
Urtermann, Leopold 28; America, 1840 *778.6* *p330*
Urtermann, Moretz 20; America, 1840 *778.6* *p330*
Urtermann, Saml. 24; America, 1840 *778.6* *p330*
Urton, John; Maryland or Virginia, 1773 *1220.12* *p821*
Urvoy, Toussaint Felix; America, 1762 *1220.12* *p821*
Urwin, Grifsey; America, 1749 *1220.12* *p821*
Urwin, Isabel; Barbados, 1686 *1220.12* *p821*
Urwin, Susanna; America, 1748 *1220.12* *p821*
Ury, Johann 23 SEE Ury, Margarethe
Ury, Margarethe; America, 1800-1899 *5475.1* *p439*
   *Son:*Johann
Uryga, Albert; Detroit, 1929-1930 *6214.5* *p63*
Uryga, John; Detroit, 1929-1930 *6214.5* *p61*
Usborne, Thomas; Barbados or Jamaica, 1692 *1220.12* *p821*
Useley, Barbara; Maryland or Virginia, 1733 *1220.12* *p821*
Usher, Isaac; America, 1764 *1220.12* *p821*
Usher, John; America, 1772 *1220.12* *p821*
Usher, Sarah; America, 1722 *1220.12* *p821*
Usher, William; North Carolina, 1822 *1088.45* *p35*
Usit, Bertholomy 35; New Orleans, 1845 *778.6* *p330*
Usk, Samuel; Annapolis, MD, 1723 *1220.12* *p821*
Uslar, Ferd.; Valdivia, Chile, 1852 *1192.4* *p55*
Usman, Mateo; Louisiana, 1874-1875 *4981.45* *p130*
Uss, Francis; Long Island, 1781 *8529.30* *p10A*
Uszla, Joanna; Detroit, 1890 *9980.23* *p97*
Utber, John; America, 1730 *1220.12* *p821*
Uthemann, Rud.; Valdivia, Chile, 1850 *1192.4* *p49*
Uthmeier, Friedrich Wilhelm Christian; America, 1871 *7420.1* *p293*
Uthmeyer, Marianne Friederike; America, 1903 *7420.1* *p379*
Uthmeyer, Wilhelm; America, 1904 *7420.1* *p401*
Utke, Ernst Henry; Wisconsin, 1895 *6795.8* *p86*
Utley, John; America, 1773 *1220.12* *p821*
Utsey, George; Ohio, 1809-1852 *4511.35* *p55*
Uttenveiler, Titus; Illinois, 1852 *6079.1* *p14*
Utter, Israel 34; Ontario, 1871 *1823.21* *p375*
Utting, Heinrich Ernst; America, 1868 *7919.3* *p533*
Uttrecht, Bertha 9; Halifax, N.S., 1902 *1860.4* *p40*
Uttrecht, Dorothea 33; Halifax, N.S., 1902 *1860.4* *p40*
Uttrecht, Elisabeth; Halifax, N.S., 1902 *1860.4* *p40*
Uttrecht, Emilie 14; Halifax, N.S., 1902 *1860.4* *p40*
Uttrecht, Friedrich 3; Halifax, N.S., 1902 *1860.4* *p40*
Uttrecht, Friedrich 37; Halifax, N.S., 1902 *1860.4* *p40*
Uttrecht, Gottfried 3; Halifax, N.S., 1902 *1860.4* *p40*
Uttrecht, Gottfried 4; Halifax, N.S., 1902 *1860.4* *p40*
Uttrecht, Lusa 31; Halifax, N.S., 1902 *1860.4* *p40*
Uttrecht, Magda 65; Halifax, N.S., 1902 *1860.4* *p40*
Uttrecht, Pauline 5; Halifax, N.S., 1902 *1860.4* *p40*
Uttrecht, Rosa 3; Halifax, N.S., 1902 *1860.4* *p40*
Uttrecht, Rosina 25; Halifax, N.S., 1902 *1860.4* *p40*
Uttrecht, Samuel 35; Halifax, N.S., 1902 *1860.4* *p40*
Uttrecht, Wildemer 7; Halifax, N.S., 1902 *1860.4* *p40*
Uttrscht, Dorothea 33; Halifax, N.S., 1902 *1860.4* *p40*
Uttrscht, Elisabeth; Halifax, N.S., 1902 *1860.4* *p40*
Uttrscht, Emilie 14; Halifax, N.S., 1902 *1860.4* *p40*
Uttrscht, Friedrich 37; Halifax, N.S., 1902 *1860.4* *p40*
Uttrscht, Gottfried 3; Halifax, N.S., 1902 *1860.4* *p40*
Uttrscht, Rosina 25; Halifax, N.S., 1902 *1860.4* *p40*
Utzig, Jakob; America, 1860-1899 *6442.17* *p65*
Utzig, Jakob; America, 1887-1899 *6442.17* *p69*
   *Wife:*Margaretha Hans
Utzig, Katharina Conrad SEE Utzig, Peter
Utzig, Margaretha Hans SEE Utzig, Jakob
Utzig, Peter; America, 1852-1899 *6442.17* *p69*
   *Wife:*Katharina Conrad
   With 4 children
Utzig, Peter 32; America, 1890 *5475.1* *p544*
Uzell, John 35; Ontario, 1871 *1823.21* *p375*

FOR A COMPLETE EXPLANATION OF ENTRY, SEE "HOW TO READ A CITATION" SECTION

V

Vaccaro, Joseph; Louisiana, 1874 *4981.45 p134*
Vacek, Martin; Nebraska, 1875 *2853.20 p188*
Vache, Pierre; Quebec, 1638 *9221.17 p81*
Vacher, Joseph 28; Mississippi, 1846 *778.6 p330*
Vacher, Sylvestre; Montreal, 1653 *9221.17 p301*
Vacula, Paul 23; Quebec, 1653 *9221.17 p280*
Vacula, A. Vendelin; Baltimore, 1870-1875 *2853.20 p107*
Vacula, Valentin; Baltimore, 1870 *2853.20 p128*
Vaculik, M.; San Antonio, TX, 1893 *2853.20 p83*
Vadaich, Nicolas 17; Mississippi, 1845-1846 *778.6 p331*
Vady, Patrick; Boston, 1744 *1642 p45*
Vaes, Christophe; Wisconsin, 1857 *1495.20 p41*
  *Wife:*Jeanne Josephe Sidonie Pigeon
  *Daughter:*Marie Isabelle
Vaes, Jeanne Josephe Sidonie Pigeon *SEE* Vaes, Christophe
Vaes, Marie Isabelle *SEE* Vaes, Christophe
Vager, George; America, 1727 *1220.12 p822*
Vagg, Annie *SEE* Vagg, Richard
Vagg, Edward; America, 1685 *1220.12 p822*
Vagg, Edward Langrish; America, 1890 *9228.50 p638*
  *Daughter:*Esther
Vagg, Esther *SEE* Vagg, Richard
Vagg, Esther *SEE* Vagg, Edward Langrish
Vagg, Henry *SEE* Vagg, Richard
Vagg, Margaret *SEE* Vagg, Richard
Vagg, Richard; America, 1890-1910 *9228.50 p638*
  *Relative:*Henry
  *Relative:*Annie
  *Relative:*Margaret
  *Relative:*Esther
Vagg, William; San Francisco, n.d. *9228.50 p638*
Vagner, Jean 33; Port uncertain, 1840 *778.6 p331*
Vahey, William 56; Ontario, 1871 *1823.17 p167*
Vahon, Tho.; Maryland, 1672 *1236.25 p48*
Vahrenkamp, Wilhelm 24; America, 1863 *5475.1 p30*
Vaill, George; America, 1749 *1220.12 p822*
Vaillant, Mr. 50; America, 1841 *778.6 p331*
Vaillant, Marguerite; Quebec, 1668 *4514.3 p375*
Vaillant, Perrette; Quebec, 1669 *4514.3 p375*
Vails, Zachary; Barbados or Jamaica, 1696 *1220.12 p822*
Vainwright, John; America, 1772 *1220.12 p829*
Vala, Simon; Nebraska, 1874 *2853.20 p171*
Valade, Marie; Quebec, 1600-1663 *4514.3 p375*
Valade, Marie; Quebec, 1663 *4514.3 p375*
Valade, Marie 16; Quebec, 1658 *9221.17 p387*
Valasek, Josef; Cleveland, OH, 1895 *2853.20 p146*
Valbon, Jean 46; America, 1845 *778.6 p331*
Valck, Christ. Heinr.; Valdivia, Chile, 1852 *1192.4 p56*
  With wife
Vale, Elizabeth; America, 1739 *1220.12 p822*
Vale, Harriat 75; Ontario, 1871 *1823.21 p375*
Vale, John 19; Quebec, 1870 *8364.32 p26*
Vale, Moses 75; Ontario, 1871 *1823.21 p375*
Vale, Robert; America, 1729 *1220.12 p822*
Valek, Kristian R.; Chicago, 1869 *2853.20 p394*
Valence, Thomas; America, 1756 *1220.12 p822*
Valenta, Frantisek Adolf; New York, NY, 1849 *2853.20 p386*
Valenta, Josef; Wisconsin, 1855 *2853.20 p323*
Valentien, Gottfried Emil; Wisconsin, 1897 *6795.8 p197*
Valentin, Anna Magdalene; America, n.d. *8115.12 p323*
  *Child:*Magdalene
Valentin, Anna Margarethe; America, 1840 *8115.12 p327*
Valentin, Frederic 30; New Orleans, 1848 *778.6 p331*
Valentin, Jakob; Pittsburgh, 1852 *8115.12 p324*
Valentin, Johann Philipp; America, n.d. *8115.12 p324*

Valentin, Johannes; America, 1840 *8115.12 p328*
Valentin, Johannes; America, n.d. *8115.12 p328*
Valentin, Konrad; Illinois, 1864 *8115.12 p324*
Valentin, Magdalene *SEE* Valentin, Anna Magdalene
Valentine, Esther 49; Ontario, 1871 *1823.21 p375*
Valentine, Frank; Louisiana, 1874 *4981.45 p134*
Valentine, John; Massachusetts, 1720-1763 *1642 p86*
Valentine, Mary; America, 1750 *1220.12 p822*
Valentine Family ; Boston, 1620-1775 *1642 p138*
Valentiny, Anna Hild 57 *SEE* Valentiny, Joh.
Valentiny, Elisabeth *SEE* Valentiny, Joh.
Valentiny, Helena *SEE* Valentiny, Joh.
Valentiny, Joh.; America, 1875 *5475.1 p256*
  *Wife:*Anna Hild
  *Daughter:*Maria
  *Daughter:*Margarethe
  *Daughter:*Helena
  *Daughter:*Elisabeth
Valentiny, Margarethe *SEE* Valentiny, Joh.
Valentiny, Maria *SEE* Valentiny, Joh.
Valerie, Andre 31; Louisiana, 1848 *778.6 p331*
Valerie, Marie Cath. 27; Louisiana, 1848 *778.6 p331*
Valery, Jean Louis 10; Louisiana, 1848 *778.6 p331*
Valery, Odile 7; Louisiana, 1848 *778.6 p331*
Valery, Philippe 16; Louisiana, 1848 *778.6 p331*
Valery, Philippe 42; Louisiana, 1848 *778.6 p331*
Valery, Victoire 37; Louisiana, 1848 *778.6 p331*
Valet, Mr. 35; New Orleans, 1848 *778.6 p331*
Valet, Ms. 35; New Orleans, 1848 *778.6 p331*
Valet, Barbara 26; Port uncertain, 1847 *778.6 p331*
Valet, Cecile; Quebec, 1669 *4514.3 p375*
Valet, Claude; Quebec, 1640 *9221.17 p99*
Valet, Guillaume; Nova Scotia, 1753 *3051 p113*
  *Wife:*Marie Leprieur
Valet, Louise; Quebec, 1670 *4514.3 p375*
Valet, Marie Leprieur *SEE* Valet, Guillaume
Valet, Mathurine; Quebec, 1659 *9221.17 p403*
  *Daughter:*Marie
  *Daughter:*Barbe
  *Daughter:*Elisabeth
Valet, Rene 20; Quebec, 1661 *9221.17 p470*
Valeton, Louis Leopold; Louisiana, 1841-1844 *4981.45 p211*
Valets, Jean 20; Montreal, 1653 *9221.17 p302*
Valier, Treve 48; Ohio, 1880 *4879.40 p260*
Valisier, John 23; New Orleans, 1845 *778.6 p331*
Valladon, Triolin 24; New Orleans, 1848 *778.6 p331*
Vallance, William 13; Quebec, 1870 *8364.32 p26*
Vallas, A. A.; Louisiana, 1874 *4981.45 p297*
Vallee, Madeleine-Judith; Quebec, 1669 *4514.3 p375*
Vallee, Perrette; Quebec, 1665 *4514.3 p376*
Vallee, Renee; Quebec, 1669 *3051 p112*
Vallenharst, Henry; Ohio, 1809-1852 *4511.35 p55*
Vallenhorst, Henry; Ohio, 1809-1852 *4511.35 p55*
Vallet, Emile; Illinois, 1856 *6079.1 p14*
Vallet, Jacques Piene; Illinois, 1852 *6079.1 p14*
Vallet, Justin Pierre; Illinois, 1852 *6079.1 p14*
Vallet, M. Jean 39; Louisiana, 1848 *778.6 p331*
Vallet, Madelaine 31; Missouri, 1847 *778.6 p331*
Vallett, Elizabeth; America, 1728 *1220.12 p822*
Vallett, James; America, 1774 *1220.12 p822*
Valley, Julus 28; Ontario, 1871 *1823.17 p167*
Vallier, Louisa 50; Ontario, 1871 *1823.21 p375*
Valliquet, Jean 21; Montreal, 1653 *9221.17 p302*
Vallis, John; America, 1768 *1220.12 p822*
Vallis, Stephen; America, 1768 *1220.12 p822*
Vallony, John; Barbados or Jamaica, 1684 *1220.12 p822*

Vallony, Robert; Barbados or Jamaica, 1684 *1220.12 p822*
Vallori, Bartolomio; Louisiana, 1836-1840 *4981.45 p213*
Vallot, Louis 28; Louisiana, 1848 *778.6 p331*
Vallot, Nicholas, Family; New Jersey, n.d. *9228.50 p638*
Vallot, Pierre 28; Ohio, 1847 *778.6 p331*
Vallote, Claude; New Jersey, 1665 *9228.50 p638*
Vallote, Claude; Virginia, 1665 *9228.50 p53*
Vallots, Claude; Virginia, 1665 *9228.50 p53*
Valmet, Mr. 30; Port uncertain, 1843 *778.6 p331*
Valo, Sigvald Andreas; Oregon, 1941 *9157.47 p2*
Valogner, Catherine 33; Louisiana, 1848 *778.6 p331*
Valogner, Charles 33; Louisiana, 1848 *778.6 p331*
Valogner, Henri 6 months; Louisiana, 1848 *778.6 p331*
Valorri, Jules 36; New Orleans, 1847 *778.6 p331*
Valose, Gustave 25; America, 1841 *778.6 p331*
Valpey, Richard; Salem, MA, 1777 *9228.50 p21A*
Valpy, . . .; Massachusetts, n.d. *9228.50 p639*
Valpy, Andrew; Quebec, 1800-1899 *9228.50 p639*
Valpy, Benjamin; Nova Scotia, 1700-1799 *9228.50 p639*
Valpy, Benjamin; Nova Scotia, 1773-1850 *9228.50 p643*
Valpy, Calvin; Nova Scotia, 1810 *9228.50 p640*
Valpy, Calvin; San Francisco, 1850 *9228.50 p642*
Valpy, Dupre Andrew; British Columbia, 1863-1932 *9228.50 p642*
Valpy, John; California, 1849 *9228.50 p640*
Valpy, John; Nova Scotia, 1770-1779 *9228.50 p639*
Valpy, John; Nova Scotia, 1795 *9228.50 p640*
Valpy, Richard; Salem, MA, 1777 *9228.50 p21A*
Valtaganigue, Nicolas 19; Quebec, 1658 *9221.17 p377*
Valter, A.J.; Louisiana, 1874-1875 *4981.45 p130*
Valtner, Sebastian; Ohio, 1809-1852 *4511.35 p55*
Valurans, Faster 60; Ontario, 1871 *1823.21 p375*
Valvin, Robert; America, 1770 *1220.12 p822*
Van Aalden, Harm; Iowa, 1897 *1211.15 p20*
Vanacken, Basile; New York, 1901 *1766.20 p3*
Van Aken, Barney; Detroit, 1893 *1766.20 p23*
Vanalstine, John 30; Ontario, 1871 *1823.17 p167*
Van Alstyne, H.; Ontario, 1787 *1276.15 p232*
  With 3 children & 5 relatives
Vanamburg, George 62; Ontario, 1871 *1823.17 p167*
Vanankin, Clark 33; Ontario, 1871 *1823.17 p167*
Vanasek, Frantisek, Sr.; Minnesota, 1858-1860 *2853.20 p260*
Vanau, Bernard; Ohio, 1840-1897 *8365.35 p18*
Vance, David 52; Michigan, 1880 *4491.36 p23*
Vance, Eliz 59; Ontario, 1871 *1823.17 p167*
Vance, Ellenor Armstrong *SEE* Vance, Martin
Vance, Henry 55; Ontario, 1871 *1823.17 p167*
Vance, Isabella 15; Michigan, 1880 *4491.36 p23*
Vance, John 26; Michigan, 1880 *4491.36 p23*
Vance, Margarite 48; Michigan, 1880 *4491.36 p23*
Vance, Martha 17; Michigan, 1880 *4491.36 p23*
Vance, Martin; Philadelphia, 1852 *8513.31 p430*
  *Wife:*Ellenor Armstrong
Vance, Mary 26; Michigan, 1880 *4491.36 p23*
Vance, Robert 50; Ontario, 1871 *1823.17 p167*
Vanconsant, Peter; Ohio, 1809-1852 *4511.35 p55*
Vancooler, John; America, 1764 *1220.12 p822*
Van Court, Elias; New Jersey, 1691-1750 *9228.50 p643*
Van Debergh, I.; Ontario, 1787 *1276.15 p232*
  With 5 children & 3 relatives
Van Delinder, M. 40; Ontario, 1871 *1823.21 p375*
Vandelo, Sidley; Barbados, 1683 *1220.12 p822*
Vandenack, Prosper; Wisconsin, 1855 *1495.20 p46*
Vandenbergh, Benoist 31; America, 1847 *778.6 p331*
Van Den Broucke, Jos; Louisiana, 1874-1875 *4981.45 p130*

Vandeneden, Marie Jeane 28; New Orleans, 1848 ***778.6*** *p331*
Vandenhaute, Guillaume; New York, NY, 1856 ***1494.21*** *p31*
Vanderancker, Elizabeth; Virginia, 1726 ***1220.12*** *p822*
Vanderbilt, Franc; New York, 1859 ***358.56*** *p55*
Vanderhoff, Aert; Iowa, 1884 ***1211.15*** *p20*
Vanderhoff, Arend; Iowa, 1888 ***1211.15*** *p20*
Vanderhurst, John; America, 1724 ***1220.12*** *p822*
Van der Keikooe, Marie 20; New York, NY, 1884 ***8427.14*** *p45*
van der Kooi, Maas Booken 35; Galveston, TX, 1844 ***3967.10*** *p375*
Vandermade, Leonard 22; Ontario, 1871 ***1823.21*** *p375*
Vandermeuse, Marie Therese; Wisconsin, 1856 ***1495.20*** *p46*
Vandermissen, Clemence Josephe Disteche *SEE* Vandermissen, Joseph
Vandermissen, Eleonore; Wisconsin, 1855-1858 ***1495.20*** *p67*
Vandermissen, Ernest Antoine *SEE* Vandermissen, Joseph
Vandermissen, Eugene *SEE* Vandermissen, Joseph
Vandermissen, Hortense *SEE* Vandermissen, Joseph
Vandermissen, Hortense Josephe *SEE* Vandermissen, Jean Joseph
Vandermissen, Jean Joseph *SEE* Vandermissen, Jean Joseph
Vandermissen, Jean Joseph; Wisconsin, 1854-1858 ***1495.20*** *p50*
*Wife:*Marie Therese
*Child:*Jean Joseph
*Child:*Hortense Josephe
*Child:*Marie Stephanie
Vandermissen, Joseph *SEE* Vandermissen, Joseph
Vandermissen, Joseph; Wisconsin, 1854-1858 ***1495.20*** *p50*
*Wife:*Clemence Josephe Disteche
*Child:*Joseph
*Child:*Eugene
*Child:*Ernest Antoine
*Child:*Hortense
Vandermissen, Marie Stephanie *SEE* Vandermissen, Jean Joseph
Vandermissen, Marie Therese *SEE* Vandermissen, Jean Joseph
Van der Mulen, Abr. 10; New York, NY, 1884 ***8427.14*** *p45*
Van der Mulen, Cath. 38; New York, NY, 1884 ***8427.14*** *p45*
Van der Mulen, Fran. 11; New York, NY, 1884 ***8427.14*** *p45*
Van der Mulen, Jacques; New York, NY, 1884 ***8427.14*** *p45*
Van der Mulen, Jane 9; New York, NY, 1884 ***8427.14*** *p45*
Van der Mulen, Jeanette 3; New York, NY, 1884 ***8427.14*** *p45*
Van der Mulen, Max 7; New York, NY, 1884 ***8427.14*** *p45*
Van der Mulen, Michel 4; New York, NY, 1884 ***8427.14*** *p45*
Van der Mulen, Reg. 2; New York, NY, 1884 ***8427.14*** *p45*
Vanderson, Ann; America, 1716 ***1220.12*** *p822*
Vandervenvell, Jan Jonas; America, 1762 ***1220.12*** *p822*
Vanderwinevald, Camille 35; New York, NY, 1894 ***6512.1*** *p182*
Vandevate, Peter; Rochester, NY, 1894-1896 ***9228.50*** *p537*
Van de Wiele, Victor; New Mexico, 1914 ***4812.1*** *p87*
Vandling, Adele 37; New Orleans, 1848 ***778.6*** *p331*
Vandling, Anthony 27; New Orleans, 1848 ***778.6*** *p331*
Vandling, Francois 4; New Orleans, 1848 ***778.6*** *p332*
Vandling, Marie 2 months; New Orleans, 1848 ***778.6*** *p332*
Vandokie, George 80; Ontario, 1871 ***1823.17*** *p167*
Vandorslaer, Sophie; Wisconsin, 1854 ***1495.20*** *p29*
Vandrincourt, R. A.; Louisiana, 1836-1840 ***4981.45*** *p213*
Vanduskey, James 55; Ontario, 1871 ***1823.17*** *p167*
Van Dyk, Cornelis; Iowa, 1931 ***1211.15*** *p20*
Van Dyk, Elles; Iowa, 1931 ***1211.15*** *p20*
Van Earp, John; Ohio, 1840-1897 ***8365.35*** *p18*
Vanek, Vaclav; Baltimore, 1894 ***2853.20*** *p133*
Vanek, Vaclav; Cleveland, OH, 1842-1910 ***2853.20*** *p476*
Vanek, Vaclav; Cleveland, OH, 1891 ***2853.20*** *p460*
Vanens, Anton Charles; Iowa, 1904 ***1211.15*** *p20*
Vanestone, William 47; Ontario, 1871 ***1823.21*** *p375*
Van Every, Bj'n; Ontario, 1787 ***1276.15*** *p231*
With child & relative
Van Every, S'l; Ontario, 1787 ***1276.15*** *p231*
With relative
Van Gadwey, Jacob; America, 1746 ***1220.12*** *p822*
Van Gam, Reider; New York, 1860 ***358.56*** *p5*
VanGlalin, Christopher; North Carolina, 1855 ***1088.45*** *p35*
VanGlohn, Dedrick; North Carolina, 1852 ***1088.45*** *p35*
Van Gorden, Geo.; California, 1868 ***1131.61*** *p89*
With wife
Van Hausen, John; Philadelphia, 1777 ***8529.30*** *p3*
VanHorn, Thomas; Washington, 1889 ***2770.40*** *p81*
Vanhosmal, Adolphe *SEE* Vanhosmal, Henri
Vanhosmal, Eloise *SEE* Vanhosmal, Henri
Vanhosmal, Eugene *SEE* Vanhosmal, Henri
Vanhosmal, Henri; Wisconsin, 1854-1858 ***1495.20*** *p50*
*Wife:*Hortense Jallet
*Child:*Julienne
*Child:*Eugene
*Child:*Julie
*Child:*Marie Therese
*Child:*Eloise
*Child:*Adolphe
Vanhosmal, Hortense Jallet *SEE* Vanhosmal, Henri
Vanhosmal, Julie *SEE* Vanhosmal, Henri
Vanhosmal, Julienne *SEE* Vanhosmal, Henri
Vanhosmal, Marie Therese *SEE* Vanhosmal, Henri
Vanicek, Jan; North Dakota, 1907 ***2853.20*** *p255*
Vanier, Catherine; Quebec, 1656 ***9221.17*** *p344*
VanKennel, Abraham; Ohio, 1809-1852 ***4511.35*** *p55*
VanKennel, Jacob; Ohio, 1809-1852 ***4511.35*** *p55*
Van Malderen, Jeanne; Wisconsin, 1854-1858 ***1495.20*** *p66*
Van Mierlo, J. 37; Port uncertain, 1840 ***778.6*** *p331*
Vannage, Elias; Barbados, 1668 ***1220.12*** *p822*
Vannes, Gregoire; Wisconsin, 1865 ***1495.20*** *p29*
Vannes, Jean Baptiste; Wisconsin, 1855 ***1495.20*** *p29*
Vannesson, Auguste 25; New Orleans, 1848 ***778.6*** *p332*
Vannier, Louis Victor Mathias; Illinois, 1852 ***6079.1*** *p14*
Vanous, Frantisek; Chicago, 1903 ***2853.20*** *p442*
Vanous, Frantisek; Chicago, 1903 ***2853.20*** *p453*
Vanoutch, A. 25; America, 1845 ***778.6*** *p332*
Vanstaden, William George 37; Ontario, 1871 ***1823.21*** *p375*
Vanstechelen, Ann; Maryland, 1735 ***1220.12*** *p822*
Vanstone, George G. 37; Ontario, 1871 ***1823.21*** *p375*
Vanstone, James 34; Ontario, 1871 ***1823.21*** *p375*
Vanstone, James W.; Ontario, 1871 ***1823.21*** *p375*
Vanstone, Jonas; America, 1737 ***1220.12*** *p822*
Vanstone, Joseph 59; Ontario, 1871 ***1823.21*** *p375*
van Straalen, Heinrich 26; New York, 1899 ***5475.1*** *p40*
Vanstrut Family ; West Virginia, 1850 ***1132.30*** *p147*
Vantabon, Andre; Montreal, 1644 ***9221.17*** *p147*
Vantear, John; Annapolis, MD, 1725 ***1220.12*** *p822*
Van Tifflin, Peter 84; Michigan, 1880 ***4491.33*** *p23*
Vantuyl, Benjamin 31; Ontario, 1871 ***1823.17*** *p167*
Vanwormer, John W. 65; Ontario, 1871 ***1823.21*** *p375*
Vanzegue, Anne-Marie; Canada, 1673 ***1142.10*** *p129*
Vanzegue, Anne-Marie; Quebec, 1673 ***4514.3*** *p376*
Vaquelin, Jn. Bte. 34; Louisiana, 1848 ***778.6*** *p332*
Vaquet, Marie; Quebec, 1670 ***4514.3*** *p376*
Vaqueth, Caroline 32; America, 1847 ***778.6*** *p332*
Vaqueth, Emile 6; America, 1847 ***778.6*** *p332*
Vaqueth, Gustave 7; America, 1847 ***778.6*** *p332*
Vara, Marie; Quebec, 1671 ***4514.3*** *p376*
Varace, James; Washington, 1886 ***2770.40*** *p24*
Varcoe, Jane 56; Ontario, 1871 ***1823.21*** *p375*
Vardell, Thomas; Barbados, 1674 ***1220.12*** *p822*
Vardon, Jean 25; Quebec, 1638 ***9221.17*** *p81*
Vardon, Lilly; Ontario, 1850-1950 ***9228.50*** *p645*
Vare, Augustus; America, 1840-1860 ***9228.50*** *p645*
Vareil deLa Brejoniere, Louis-Melchior de; Quebec, 1748 ***2314.30*** *p171*
Vargess, Elizabeth; America, 1747 ***1220.12*** *p822*
Varien, Fabian; North Carolina, 1792-1862 ***1088.45*** *p36*
Varin, Catherine; Quebec, 1665 ***4514.3*** *p376*
Varin, Marie; Quebec, 1667 ***4514.3*** *p376*
Varin deLa Marre, Jean-Victor; Quebec, 1733 ***2314.30*** *p171*
Varity, John; America, 1726 ***1220.12*** *p824*
Varity, William; Maryland, 1726 ***1220.12*** *p824*
Varker, James; North Carolina, 1841 ***1088.45*** *p36*
Varlat, Nicholas, Family; New Jersey, n.d. ***9228.50*** *p638*
Varley, Mary 70; Ontario, 1871 ***1823.21*** *p375*
Varley, Thos 51; Ontario, 1871 ***1823.21*** *p376*
Varley, William; America, 1766 ***1220.12*** *p822*
Varley, William; America, 1770 ***1220.12*** *p822*
Varnanan, Mary; Charles Town, SC, 1719 ***1220.12*** *p822*
Varndell, John; America, 1760 ***1220.12*** *p822*
Varnell, Arthur; America, 1663 ***1220.12*** *p822*
Varnell, Johanne; America, 1663 ***1220.12*** *p822*
Varner, Thomas; North Carolina, 1841 ***1088.45*** *p36*
Varnham, Thomas; America, 1770 ***1220.12*** *p822*
Varnial, Mary; America, 1773 ***1220.12*** *p822*
Varnom, John; America, 1737 ***1220.12*** *p823*
Varnum, Nancy 85; Ontario, 1871 ***1823.21*** *p376*
Varnum, Oliver; Annapolis, MD, 1729 ***1220.12*** *p823*
Varron, Thomas; America, 1754 ***1220.12*** *p823*
Varson, William 31; Ontario, 1871 ***1823.21*** *p376*
Vartry, Mary; Virginia, 1732 ***1220.12*** *p823*
Varty, John 48; New York, NY, 1894 ***6512.1*** *p186*
Varuelli, Justine 22; Ontario, 1871 ***1823.17*** *p167*
Varvelli, Gustave 25; Ontario, 1871 ***1823.17*** *p167*
Vasco, Valyko 33; New York, NY, 1894 ***6512.1*** *p232*
Vasel, Bernhard Karl W.; America, 1881 ***179.55*** *p19*
Vasel, Rosine Friedrich; America, 1881 ***179.55*** *p19*
Vasel, Ursula; America, 1848-1892 ***179.55*** *p19*
Vasicek, Jan; Iowa, 1870 ***2853.20*** *p202*
Vaslin, . . .; Massachusetts, 1870-1879 ***9228.50*** *p645*
Vason, Isaac; Quebec, 1662 ***9221.17*** *p494*
Vass, David 63; Ontario, 1871 ***1823.21*** *p376*
Vassal, Francoise; Quebec, 1667 ***4514.3*** *p376*
Vassal deMonviel, Germain; Quebec, 1755-1757 ***2314.30*** *p170*
Vassal deMonviel, Germain; Quebec, 1757 ***2314.30*** *p197*
Vassan, Jean-Francois de; Quebec, 1727 ***2314.30*** *p170*
Vassan, Jean-Francois de; Quebec, 1727 ***2314.30*** *p197*
Vasselin, . . .; America, n.d. ***9228.50*** *p21A*
Vasselin, . . .; Massachusetts, 1870-1879 ***9228.50*** *p645*
Vassell, Matthew; Barbados, 1669 ***1220.12*** *p823*
Vasseron, Adele 4; Mississippi, 1846 ***778.6*** *p332*
Vasseron, Elisabeth 39; Mississippi, 1846 ***778.6*** *p332*
Vasseron, Nicolas 36; Mississippi, 1846 ***778.6*** *p332*
Vasserot, C. 28; Cuba, 1841 ***778.6*** *p332*
Vasseur, Mrs. 32; America, 1843 ***778.6*** *p332*
Vasseur, Emanuel 10; America, 1843 ***778.6*** *p332*
Vasseur, L. 42; America, 1843 ***778.6*** *p332*
Vasseur, Louis 7; America, 1843 ***778.6*** *p332*
Vassey, William; America, 1762 ***1220.12*** *p823*
Vassi, Etienne 3; New Orleans, 1848 ***778.6*** *p332*
Vassine, Adele 24; Port uncertain, 1843 ***778.6*** *p332*
Vassine, Alexander 34; Port uncertain, 1843 ***778.6*** *p332*
Vasso, Cs. 30; America, 1848 ***778.6*** *p332*
Vasterlund, Carl; St. Paul, MN, 1871-1884 ***1865.50*** *p114*
Vasterlund, Martha; St. Paul, MN, 1881 ***1865.50*** *p114*
Vasthold, Martin; America, 1766 ***1220.12*** *p823*
Vate, Jean; Quebec, 1659 ***9221.17*** *p410*
Vater, Robert; America, 1685 ***1220.12*** *p823*
Vater, William; America, 1754 ***1220.12*** *p823*
Vaters, Catherine; America, 1740 ***1220.12*** *p823*
Vaters, John; America, 1740 ***1220.12*** *p823*
Vatiere, Peter; Annapolis, MD, 1735 ***1220.12*** *p823*
Vatinen, Jules 39; New Orleans, 1848 ***778.6*** *p332*
Vaublin, Marie; Quebec, 1665 ***4514.3*** *p377*
Vaucher, Louise; Quebec, 1668 ***4514.3*** *p377*
Vauchlin, Francis; Annapolis, MD, 1724 ***1220.12*** *p823*
Vauclin, Jacques 40; Quebec, 1657 ***9221.17*** *p370*
*Wife:*Marie Blondel 45
Vauclin, Marie Blondel 45 *SEE* Vauclin, Jacques
Vaudin, Doris Eileen *SEE* Vaudin, Edward Henry Osborne
Vaudin, Edward Henry Osborne; Victoria, B.C., 1892-1917 ***9228.50*** *p646*
*Wife:*Ellen McCreight
*Child:*Doris Eileen
Vaudin, Ellen McCreight *SEE* Vaudin, Edward Henry Osborne
Vaudin, John; Salem, MA, 1674 ***9228.50*** *p646*
Vaudin, Moses; Massachusetts, 1616-1716 ***9228.50*** *p646*
Vaudry, Jacques 24; Quebec, 1660 ***9221.17*** *p440*
Vaughan, Charles; New Orleans, 1851 ***7242.30*** *p156*
Vaughan, Edward; America, 1747 ***1220.12*** *p823*
Vaughan, Edward; Louisiana, 1839-1855 ***7710.1*** *p155*
Vaughan, Edward; Potomac, 1729 ***1220.12*** *p823*
Vaughan, Elizabeth; America, 1675 ***1220.12*** *p823*
Vaughan, Elizabeth 19; New York, NY, 1894 ***6512.1*** *p186*
Vaughan, Florence; Barbados or Jamaica, 1699 ***1220.12*** *p823*
Vaughan, George; America, 1767 ***1220.12*** *p823*
Vaughan, George; Maryland, 1736 ***1220.12*** *p823*
Vaughan, George; Maryland, 1740 ***1220.12*** *p823*
Vaughan, George; Virginia, 1734 ***1220.12*** *p823*
Vaughan, Henry; America, 1765 ***1220.12*** *p823*
Vaughan, Henry; Barbados, 1670 ***1220.12*** *p823*
Vaughan, Hester; America, 1729 ***1220.12*** *p823*
Vaughan, Isaac; Barbados or Jamaica, 1687 ***1220.12*** *p823*
Vaughan, James; America, 1724 ***1220.12*** *p823*
Vaughan, John; America, 1740 ***1220.12*** *p823*
Vaughan, John; America, 1746 ***1220.12*** *p823*
Vaughan, John; America, 1755 ***1220.12*** *p823*
Vaughan, John; America, 1767 ***1220.12*** *p823*
Vaughan, John; America, 1773 ***1220.12*** *p823*
Vaughan, John; Annapolis, MD, 1722 ***1220.12*** *p823*
Vaughan, John; Annapolis, MD, 1725 ***1220.12*** *p823*
Vaughan, Minnie 16; New York, NY, 1894 ***6512.1*** *p186*
Vaughan, Philip; America, 1766 ***1220.12*** *p823*
Vaughan, Richard; America, 1710 ***1220.12*** *p823*

Vaughan, Richard; America, 1731 ***1220.12*** *p823*
Vaughan, Richard; America, 1761 ***1220.12*** *p823*
Vaughan, Sarah A. 41; New York, NY, 1894 ***6512.1*** *p186*
Vaughan, Thomas; America, 1720 ***1220.12*** *p823*
Vaughan, Thomas; America, 1734 ***1220.12*** *p823*
Vaughan, Thomas; America, 1743 ***1220.12*** *p823*
Vaughan, Thomas; America, 1768 ***1220.12*** *p823*
Vaughan, William; America, 1760 ***1220.12*** *p823*
Vaughan, William; America, 1764 ***1220.12*** *p823*
Vaughan, William; America, 1769 ***1220.12*** *p823*
Vaughn, Leonard B. 36; Ontario, 1871 ***1823.17*** *p167*
Vaughne, Florents; Barbados or Jamaica, 1688 ***1220.12*** *p823*
Vaumeser, Mr. 25; America, 1846 ***778.6*** *p332*
Vaund, John 84; Ontario, 1871 ***1823.21*** *p376*
Vaupel, Ernst; Port uncertain, 1834 ***7420.1*** *p8*
Vauqier, Charles; Ohio, 1840-1897 ***8365.35*** *p18*
Vauquelin, Robert; Virginia, 1665 ***9228.50*** *p54*
Vauquellin, Anne *SEE* Vauquellin, Robert
Vauquellin, Jeanne *SEE* Vauquellin, Robert
Vauquellin, Robert; New Jersey, 1655 ***9228.50*** *p647*
*Wife:*Jeanne
*Daughter:*Anne
Vause, Thomas; Virginia, 1648 ***1658.20*** *p208*
Vaussan, Francois 52; America, 1843 ***778.6*** *p332*
Vauth, Ernst Heinrich; Indianapolis, 1879 ***7420.1*** *p314*
Vautier, Elaine; Canada, 1964 ***9228.50*** *p647*
Vautier, Emile John; Canada, 1952 ***9228.50*** *p647*
Vautier, Geoffrey; Seattle, 1925-1983 ***9228.50*** *p647*
Vautier, Jacques; Montreal, 1654 ***9221.17*** *p318*
Vauvilliers, Jeanne 20; Quebec, 1657 ***9221.17*** *p370*
Vavak, Matej; Nebraska, 1868 ***2853.20*** *p161*
Vavasour, Thomas; Boston, 1700-1730 ***9228.50*** *p647*
Vavasseur, Gerard F. P. 26; America, 1848 ***778.6*** *p332*
Vavra, Emerich Herman; Chicago, 1867 ***2853.20*** *p405*
Vavra, Jan; New York, 1819-1910 ***2853.20*** *p118*
Vavrik, Antonin; North Dakota, 1879-1881 ***2853.20*** *p252*
Vavrina, V.; Wisconsin, 1884 ***2853.20*** *p34*
With parents
Vavrovsky, Jan; St. Paul, MN, 1864 ***2853.20*** *p277*
Vaydie, Jean; Montreal, 1644 ***9221.17*** *p149*
Veacher, George 40; Ontario, 1871 ***1823.21*** *p376*
Veal, Jane; America, 1742 ***1220.12*** *p824*
Veal, John; America, 1757 ***1220.12*** *p824*
Veal, John; America, 1773 ***1220.12*** *p824*
Veale, Daniel; Annapolis, MD, 1722 ***1220.12*** *p824*
Veale, Jane; America, 1744 ***1220.12*** *p824*
Veale, Jno. 53; South Carolina, 1812 ***3476.30*** *p13*
Veale, Richard 46; Ontario, 1871 ***1823.21*** *p376*
Veale, Thomas; America, 1759 ***1220.12*** *p824*
Veares, Daniel; America, 1678 ***1220.12*** *p824*
Veares, Joseph; America, 1682 ***1220.12*** *p824*
Veauthier, Helena 24; America, 1880 ***5475.1*** *p289*
Veauthier, Margarethe; America, 1873 ***5475.1*** *p351*
Veauthier, Maria 17; America, 1880 ***5475.1*** *p289*
Veavea, Arthur; Boston, 1766 ***1642*** *p37*
Veber, . . .; Massachusetts, 1680-1689 ***9228.50*** *p648*
Veboier, Paolo 24; America, 1848 ***778.6*** *p332*
Veckel, Hannah; Canada, 1774 ***3036.5*** *p40*
Veckel, Mary; Canada, 1774 ***3036.5*** *p40*
Veckman, Marie Antoinette; Wisconsin, 1854-1858 ***1495.20*** *p50*
Vedebrand, Carl Gustaf; St. Paul, MN, 1882-1887 ***1865.50*** *p113*
Vedebrand, Hannah *SEE* Vedebrand, Marta
Vedebrand, Marta; St. Paul, MN, 1887 ***1865.50*** *p113*
*Daughter:*Hannah
Vedet, Antoine; Montreal, 1644 ***9221.17*** *p149*
*Wife:*Francoise Bugon
Vedet, Francoise Bugon 14 *SEE* Vedet, Antoine
Vedman, Andrew; Cleveland, OH, 1879-1888 ***9722.10*** *p128*
Veezey, Katherine; America, 1750 ***1220.12*** *p824*
Vehling, Mr.; America, 1866 ***7420.1*** *p251*
With wife
*Daughter:*Sophie
*Son:*Friedrich
*Son:*Heinrich
*Daughter:*Wilhelmine
Vehling, Christian; America, 1846 ***7420.1*** *p50*
Vehling, Christian Heinrich; America, 1868 ***7420.1*** *p277*
With mother & stepfather
Vehling, Ernst Heinrich Christian; America, 1846 ***7420.1*** *p50*
Vehling, Friedrich *SEE* Vehling, Mr.
Vehling, Heinrich *SEE* Vehling, Mr.
Vehling, Heinrich Conrad Wilhelm; America, 1884 ***7420.1*** *p346*
Vehling, Sophie *SEE* Vehling, Mr.
Vehling, Wilhelm August; America, 1883 ***7420.1*** *p340*
Vehling, Wilhelmine *SEE* Vehling, Mr.
Vehrmann, August; Wisconsin, 1898 ***6795.8*** *p178*
Veidlun, Fredrick; Colorado, 1884 ***1029.59*** *p91*
Veidner, Jindrich; Chicago, 1893-1910 ***2853.20*** *p469*
Veil, Ann; America, 1773 ***1220.12*** *p822*
Veillon, Sebastienne 16; Quebec, 1647 ***9221.17*** *p178*
Veit, Daniel; New Jersey, 1773-1774 ***927.31*** *p3*
Veit, Helene 34; New York, NY, 1885 ***1883.7*** *p46*
Veit, Jacob; Long Island, 1778 ***8529.30*** *p9A*
Veit, John; New Jersey, 1773-1774 ***927.31*** *p3*
Veit, Ludwig 52; New York, NY, 1885 ***1883.7*** *p46*
Veit, Mathilde 16; New York, NY, 1885 ***1883.7*** *p46*
Veit, Wilhelm 7; New York, NY, 1885 ***1883.7*** *p46*
Veit, Wilhelmine 4; New York, NY, 1885 ***1883.7*** *p46*
Veitch, John 30; Ontario, 1871 ***1823.21*** *p376*
Veitch, Robert 28; Ontario, 1871 ***1823.21*** *p376*
Veitch, William 37; Ontario, 1871 ***1823.21*** *p376*
Veitz, Cazmir 18; Baltimore, 1889 ***8425.16*** *p36*
Vejle, Mads Christenson; Iowa, 1914 ***1211.15*** *p20*
Velan, Pierre 26; Port uncertain, 1847 ***778.6*** *p332*
Velar, Pierre 26; Port uncertain, 1847 ***778.6*** *p332*
Veleba, Martin; Nebraska, 1876 ***2853.20*** *p172*
Velek, Vaclav; North Dakota, 1879-1881 ***2853.20*** *p252*
Velfl, Josef *SEE* Velfl, Vavrinec
Velfl, Vavrinec; Wisconsin, 1854 ***2853.20*** *p304*
*Son:*Josef
Velharticky, Jan; North Dakota, 1872 ***2853.20*** *p251*
Velik, Josef; Chicago, 1854 ***2853.20*** *p388*
Vellardsen, Laurets; Iowa, 1896 ***1211.15*** *p20*
Vellen, Anna 9; America, 1847 ***778.6*** *p332*
Vellen, Clare 36; America, 1847 ***778.6*** *p332*
Vellen, Jean 2; America, 1847 ***778.6*** *p333*
Vellen, Marie 8; America, 1847 ***778.6*** *p332*
Vellen, Mary 45; America, 1847 ***778.6*** *p332*
Vellen, Rosa 7; America, 1847 ***778.6*** *p332*
Vellen, Theresa 17; America, 1847 ***778.6*** *p332*
Veltgen, Peter; America, 1745 ***1220.12*** *p824*
Vemmer, Wilhelmine 23; New York, NY, 1864 ***8425.62*** *p197*
Ven, Edward; America, 1685 ***1220.12*** *p824*
Venables, George; America, 1740 ***1220.12*** *p824*
Venables, Jane; America, 1739 ***1220.12*** *p824*
Vencl, . . .; Pennsylvania, 1750-1799 ***2853.20*** *p17*
Vender, Mary; America, 1765 ***1220.12*** *p824*
Vender, Nicolas 51; America, 1846 ***778.6*** *p333*
Vender, Thomas; America, 1772 ***1220.12*** *p824*
Venderlinz, Jacob 66; America, 1846 ***778.6*** *p333*
Vendrick, John; North Carolina, 1710 ***3629.40*** *p8*
Venham, Philip; Virginia, 1726 ***1220.12*** *p824*
Venice, Thomas; America, 1750 ***1220.12*** *p824*
Venies, John; Ohio, 1809-1852 ***4511.35*** *p55*
Venill, William; Virginia, 1744 ***1220.12*** *p824*
Venn, Jane; America, 1769 ***1220.12*** *p824*
Venn, Martha; America, 1766 ***1220.12*** *p824*
Vennell, Richard; Virginia, 1767 ***1220.12*** *p824*
Vennell, William; America, 1766 ***1220.12*** *p824*
Venner, Isaac; America, 1774 ***1220.12*** *p824*
Venner, James; America, 1749 ***1220.12*** *p824*
Venner, John; America, 1736 ***1220.12*** *p824*
Venner, John; Barbados, 1668 ***1220.12*** *p824*
Venner, John 48; Ontario, 1871 ***1823.21*** *p376*
Venner, Solomon 35; Ontario, 1871 ***1823.21*** *p376*
Venner, Thomas; America, 1685 ***1220.12*** *p824*
Venner, William 58; Ontario, 1871 ***1823.21*** *p376*
Vennette, Celestine; Colorado, 1886 ***1029.59*** *p91*
Venning, Andrew 36; Ontario, 1871 ***1823.21*** *p376*
Venning, John 30; Ontario, 1871 ***1823.21*** *p376*
Venning, Richard 41; Ontario, 1871 ***1823.21*** *p376*
Venning, Richard 69; Ontario, 1871 ***1823.21*** *p376*
Venning, Thomas 33; Ontario, 1871 ***1823.21*** *p376*
Venniti, Michele; Louisiana, 1874-1875 ***4981.45*** *p130*
Vennor, Thomas 56; Ontario, 1871 ***1823.21*** *p376*
Ventham, Richard; America, 1743 ***1220.12*** *p824*
Ventham, Richard; America, 1754 ***1220.12*** *p824*
Venting, William; America, 1685 ***1220.12*** *p824*
Ventland, Elizabeth; Virginia, 1732 ***1220.12*** *p824*
Ventris, Benjamin; America, 1749 ***1220.12*** *p824*
Ventris, John; America, 1756 ***1220.12*** *p824*
Venus, Elizabeth; Maryland, 1736 ***1220.12*** *p824*
Venus, Harold 28; Ontario, 1871 ***1823.21*** *p376*
Venus, John; America, 1749 ***1220.12*** *p824*
Ver, Rosa; Venezuela, 1843 ***3899.5*** *p545*
Veravene, Antoine; Detroit, 1870 ***1494.20*** *p12*
Verbracken, Thomas; America, 1692 ***1220.12*** *p824*
Vercammen, Marie Henriette; Wisconsin, 1857 ***1495.20*** *p41*
Verde, Emma 26; America, 1848 ***778.6*** *p333*
Verdeler, Pierre 30; New Orleans, 1840 ***778.6*** *p333*
Verdinier, Mrs. 23; America, 1845 ***778.6*** *p333*
Verdinier, A. 22; America, 1845 ***778.6*** *p333*
Verdon, Francois; Quebec, 1642 ***9221.17*** *p122*
Verdon, Joseph; America, 1764 ***1220.12*** *p824*
Verdon, Vincent 15; Quebec, 1657 ***9221.17*** *p370*
Vere, Cecily; America, 1762 ***1220.12*** *p824*
Vere, Sarah; America, 1736 ***1220.12*** *p824*
Veret, Guillaume; Quebec, 1651 ***9221.17*** *p251*
Verge, Francois; Quebec, 1659 ***9221.17*** *p414*
Verge, Joseph; Boston, 1755 ***9228.50*** *p21A*
Verge, Joseph; Nova Scotia, 1755-1800 ***9228.50*** *p21A*
*Wife:*Mary Blewett
Verge, Mary Blewett *SEE* Verge, Joseph
Verge Family ; Nova Scotia, n.d. ***9228.50*** *p650*
Verger, Marie; Quebec, 1670 ***4514.3*** *p377*
Vergery, Pierre 21; America, 1845 ***778.6*** *p333*
Verges, Mr. 25; Port uncertain, 1844 ***778.6*** *p333*
Verges, P. B. 19; Port uncertain, 1840 ***778.6*** *p333*
Vergne, Mr. 30; America, 1842 ***778.6*** *p333*
Vergoe, William; America, 1721 ***1220.12*** *p826*
Vergona, John; Louisiana, 1874 ***4981.45*** *p134*
Verhaghen, Jean Baptiste *SEE* Verhaghen, Jean Joseph
Verhaghen, Jean Joseph; Wisconsin, 1855 ***1495.20*** *p56*
*Wife:*Julienne Meura
*Child:*Justine
*Child:*Marie Josephe
*Child:*Louis Joseph
*Child:*Jean Baptiste
Verhaghen, Julienne Meura *SEE* Verhaghen, Jean Joseph
Verhaghen, Justine *SEE* Verhaghen, Jean Joseph
Verhaghen, Louis Joseph *SEE* Verhaghen, Jean Joseph
Verhaghen, Marie Josephe *SEE* Verhaghen, Jean Joseph
Verhoef, Heinrich; Venezuela, 1843 ***3899.5*** *p547*
Verhoff, Frederic; New Castle, DE, 1817-1818 ***90.20*** *p154*
Veriel, Camille 2; America, 1843 ***778.6*** *p333*
Veriel, Eliza 7; America, 1843 ***778.6*** *p333*
Veriel, Justin 9; America, 1843 ***778.6*** *p333*
Veriel, Louis 5; America, 1843 ***778.6*** *p333*
Veriel, Louisa 3 months; America, 1843 ***778.6*** *p333*
Veriel, Maria 33; America, 1843 ***778.6*** *p333*
Veriel, Pierre 41; America, 1843 ***778.6*** *p333*
Verieul, Nicolas 21; Quebec, 1656 ***9221.17*** *p348*
Verieul, Thomas; Quebec, 1647 ***9221.17*** *p190*
Verignonneau, Denis 21; Quebec, 1662 ***9221.17*** *p494*
Verignonneau, Etienne 21; Quebec, 1661 ***9221.17*** *p470*
Verity, John; America, 1754 ***1220.12*** *p824*
Verity, Robert; America, 1773 ***1220.12*** *p824*
Verkin, James; Virginia, 1758 ***1220.12*** *p824*
Vermeche, Agathon 25; New Orleans, 1848 ***778.6*** *p333*
Vermin, Charles; Virginia, 1721 ***1220.12*** *p824*
Vermont, Marie 30; Louisiana, 1847 ***778.6*** *p333*
Vermont, Theophile 33; Louisiana, 1847 ***778.6*** *p333*
Vermouler, Caroline 25; Port uncertain, 1843 ***778.6*** *p333*
Vernall, Richard; America, 1755 ***1220.12*** *p825*
Vernam, Sarah; America, 1755 ***1220.12*** *p824*
Vernan, Thomas 22; North Carolina, 1774 ***1422.10*** *p54*
Verncombe, Henry; America, 1771 ***1220.12*** *p825*
Vernell, George; America, 1773 ***1220.12*** *p825*
Verner, William Henry; Iowa, 1919 ***1211.15*** *p20*
Vernet, Lady; Port uncertain, 1845 ***778.6*** *p333*
Vernet, Mr. 48; Port uncertain, 1845 ***778.6*** *p333*
Vernet, Ann Eve 29; Port uncertain, 1845 ***778.6*** *p333*
Vernet, Louis 29; Port uncertain, 1845 ***778.6*** *p333*
Vernett, Julia 40; Michigan, 1880 ***4491.39*** *p31*
Verney, William; America, 1773 ***1220.12*** *p825*
Vernham, Albert; America, 1727 ***1220.12*** *p825*
Vernier, Augustus; Ohio, 1809-1852 ***4511.35*** *p55*
Vernier, Lewis; Ohio, 1809-1852 ***4511.35*** *p55*
Vernier, Louis; Ohio, 1809-1852 ***4511.35*** *p55*
Vernis, Claire 33; America, 1845 ***778.6*** *p91*
Vernive, Xavier, I 28; St. Louis, 1847 ***778.6*** *p333*
Vernive, Xavier, II 23; St. Louis, 1847 ***778.6*** *p333*
Vernom, Ann; Virginia, 1732 ***1220.12*** *p825*
Vernon, Elizabeth; America, 1737 ***1220.12*** *p825*
Vernon, Henry; America, 1774 ***1220.12*** *p825*
Vernon, John; Barbados, 1668 ***1220.12*** *p825*
Vernon, Mary 67; Michigan, 1880 ***4491.39*** *p31*
Vernon, Patrick 63; Michigan, 1880 ***4491.39*** *p31*
Vernon, Richard 35; Ontario, 1871 ***1823.21*** *p376*
Vernon, Sarah; America, 1755 ***1220.12*** *p825*
Vernon, Thomas; Virginia, 1769 ***1220.12*** *p825*
Verodich, Andrew; Louisiana, 1874 ***4981.45*** *p134*
Veron, Mr. 24; New Orleans, 1841 ***778.6*** *p333*
Veron, Jean; Quebec, 1645 ***9221.17*** *p158*
Veroni, Joseph; America, 1775 ***1220.12*** *p825*
Verq, Eugene 29; Port uncertain, 1842 ***778.6*** *p333*
Verreau, Barthelemy 31; Montreal, 1662 ***9221.17*** *p500*
Verrier, Catherine; Quebec, 1669 ***4514.3*** *p377*
Verrier, James; America, 1769 ***1220.12*** *p825*
Verries, Francis; Ohio, 1809-1852 ***4511.35*** *p55*
Verries, John; Ohio, 1809-1852 ***4511.35*** *p55*
Verriner, James; America, 1769 ***1220.12*** *p825*
Verrowne, John; Barbados, 1668 ***1220.12*** *p825*
Verry, Isaac; Virginia, 1700 ***9230.15*** *p81*
Verryard, William; America, 1685 ***1220.12*** *p825*
Verston, Charles; Detroit, 1930 ***1640.60*** *p81*
Vert, Catherine; Annapolis, MD, 1733 ***1220.12*** *p825*
Vertee, . . .; New England, n.d. ***9228.50*** *p86*
Vertee, John; America, 1755-1781 ***9228.50*** *p648*

Vertee, John; Massachusetts, 1751-1790 ***9228.50*** *p654*
Verth, Wilhelm H.; Wisconsin, 1888 ***6795.8*** *p150*
Verty, . . .; New England, n.d. ***9228.50*** *p86*
Verzal, Rose Marie; Utah, 1953 ***9228.50*** *p304*
Vesche, Sophie Dorothea; America, 1882 ***7420.1*** *p332*
Vesely, Antonin F.; Chicago, 1896-1898 ***2853.20*** *p420*
Vesin, Mr. 30; Louisiana, 1848 ***778.6*** *p333*
Vesin, Mrs. 20; Louisiana, 1848 ***778.6*** *p333*
Vesper, Mary; Potomac, 1731 ***1220.12*** *p825*
Vesseriat, Joseph; Ohio, 1809-1852 ***4511.35*** *p55*
Vesseriot, Joseph; Ohio, 1809-1852 ***4511.35*** *p56*
Vesseriot, Peter; Ohio, 1809-1852 ***4511.35*** *p56*
Vesseron, Jean 31; America, 1843 ***778.6*** *p334*
Vesserot, C. 36; America, 1843 ***778.6*** *p334*
Vester, Frederick; Ohio, 1809-1852 ***4511.35*** *p56*
Vette, Elise Sophie Johanne; America, 1847 ***7420.1*** *p52*
Vetter, Mr. 16; America, 1840 ***778.6*** *p334*
Vetter, Adam 4; New York, NY, 1898 ***7951.13*** *p42*
Vetter, Anna Eva; Virginia, 1831 ***152.20*** *p67*
Vetter, Anna Katharina 52; America, 1853 ***2526.42*** *p120*
Vetter, Anna Maria 45; New York, NY, 1898 ***7951.13*** *p42*
Vetter, Annas 64; America, 1840 ***778.6*** *p334*
Vetter, Anton 14; New York, NY, 1898 ***7951.13*** *p42*
Vetter, Baltasar 18 months; New York, NY, 1898 ***7951.13*** *p42*
Vetter, Baltasar 41; New York, NY, 1898 ***7951.13*** *p42*
Vetter, Brigitta 38; New York, NY, 1898 ***7951.13*** *p42*
Vetter, Carl 1 months; New York, NY, 1874 ***6954.7*** *p37*
Vetter, Catharina 15; New York, NY, 1874 ***6954.7*** *p37*
Vetter, Ch...ph 72; America, 1840 ***778.6*** *p334*
Vetter, Christine 9; New York, NY, 1874 ***6954.7*** *p37*
Vetter, Elisabeth 9 months; New York, NY, 1874 ***6954.7*** *p37*
Vetter, Francisca 11; New York, NY, 1898 ***7951.13*** *p42*
Vetter, Georg Peter; America, 1867 ***2526.43*** *p192*
Vetter, Jacob 7; New York, NY, 1874 ***6954.7*** *p37*
Vetter, Jacob 38; New York, NY, 1874 ***6954.7*** *p37*
Vetter, Jacob; Ohio, 1843 ***2763.1*** *p22*
Vetter, Jacobina 35; New York, NY, 1874 ***6954.7*** *p37*
Vetter, Johann 3; New York, NY, 1898 ***7951.13*** *p42*
Vetter, Johann 23; New York, NY, 1898 ***7951.13*** *p42*
Vetter, Johann 26; New York, NY, 1898 ***7951.13*** *p42*
Vetter, Johannes; America, 1867 ***2526.43*** *p192*
Vetter, Johannes; America, 1871 ***2526.43*** *p192*
Vetter, John 59; Ontario, 1871 ***1823.17*** *p167*
Vetter, Josephine 21; New York, NY, 1898 ***7951.13*** *p42*
Vetter, Magdalena 15; New York, NY, 1898 ***7951.13*** *p42*
Vetter, Magdalena 21; New York, NY, 1898 ***7951.13*** *p42*
Vetter, Marianna 7; New York, NY, 1898 ***7951.13*** *p42*
Vetter, Marie 21; America, 1840 ***778.6*** *p334*
Vetter, Martin 48; New York, NY, 1898 ***7951.13*** *p42*
Vetter, Michael 13; New York, NY, 1898 ***7951.13*** *p42*
Vetter, Thomas 29; New York, NY, 1898 ***7951.13*** *p42*
Vetterlova, Anna; Detroit, 1869 ***2853.20*** *p356*
Veverka Family ; Nebraska, 1875 ***2853.20*** *p172*
Vevers, John; America, 1768 ***1220.12*** *p825*
Vevien, Angelina 17; America, 1842 ***778.6*** *p334*
Vevien, Napoleon 1; America, 1842 ***778.6*** *p334*
Vevieu, Angelina 17; America, 1842 ***778.6*** *p334*
Vevieu, Napoleon 1; America, 1842 ***778.6*** *p334*
Veyhl, Henriette; Port uncertain, 1880 ***7420.1*** *p318*
Veysey, Ann; Virginia, 1749 ***1220.12*** *p825*
Vezina, Selim; Colorado, 1904 ***1029.59*** *p91*
Vezina, Selin; Colorado, 1904 ***1029.59*** *p91*
Vezinat, Jacques 49; Quebec, 1659 ***9221.17*** *p411*
Viagus, Emanuel; North Carolina, 1792-1862 ***1088.45*** *p36*
Viala, Pierre 30; America, 1840 ***778.6*** *p334*
Vian, John 28; Ontario, 1871 ***1823.21*** *p376*
Vian, Joseph 33; New Orleans, 1843 ***778.6*** *p334*
Viard, Francois 19; America, 1846 ***778.6*** *p334*
Viard, Marguerite; Quebec, 1671 ***4514.3*** *p377*
Viardez, Francois 45; Texas, 1848 ***778.6*** *p334*
Viardol, Marie 47; New Orleans, 1848 ***778.6*** *p334*
Viator, Katharina; America, 1865 ***5475.1*** *p482*
Viau, Child; New Orleans, 1840 ***778.6*** *p334*
Viau, Mrs. 34; New Orleans, 1840 ***778.6*** *p334*
Viau, Joseph 33; New Orleans, 1843 ***778.6*** *p334*
Viau, M. 38; New Orleans, 1840 ***778.6*** *p334*
Viau, Sylvain 21; Quebec, 1660 ***9221.17*** *p440*
Vibault, Lancelot; Virginia, 1739 ***1220.12*** *p825*
Vibber, . . .; Massachusetts, 1680-1689 ***9228.50*** *p648*
Viber, . . .; Massachusetts, 1680-1689 ***9228.50*** *p648*
Viberg, Hilda 18; New York, NY, 1894 ***6512.1*** *p185*
Vibert, . . .; Massachusetts, 1680-1689 ***9228.50*** *p648*
Vibert, James; New Hampshire, 1724-1725 ***9228.50*** *p100*
Vibert, Julia; New York, 1862-1934 ***9228.50*** *p637*
Vibert, Sarah; New Hampshire, 1703-1788 ***9228.50*** *p148*
Vicars, Emma 64; Ontario, 1871 ***1823.21*** *p376*
Vicary, Mary; Annapolis, MD, 1725 ***1220.12*** *p825*
Vicary, Philip; America, 1764 ***1220.12*** *p825*
Viccars, Thomas; America, 1685 ***1220.12*** *p825*
Viccary, Hugh; America, 1744 ***1220.12*** *p825*
Viccary, John; America, 1740 ***1220.12*** *p825*
Viccary, Nicholas; America, 1722 ***1220.12*** *p825*
Vice, Thomas; America, 1763 ***1220.12*** *p825*
Vich, Jan; Iowa, 1870 ***2853.20*** *p202*
Vick, John; Utah, 1855 ***9228.50*** *p649*
*Relative:*Nancy
Vick, Nancy *SEE* Vick, John
Vick, Richard 28; Ontario, 1871 ***1823.21*** *p376*
Vickars, Joseph; America, 1750 ***1220.12*** *p825*
Vickars, Robert; America, 1719 ***1220.12*** *p825*
Vickars, Robert; America, 1767 ***1220.12*** *p825*
Vickers, John; America, 1773 ***1220.12*** *p825*
Vickers, John; Marston's Wharf, 1782 ***8529.30*** *p16*
Vickers, Mrs. R. G.; California, 1868 ***1131.61*** *p89*
With child
Vickers, Thomas; America, 1755 ***1220.12*** *p825*
Vickers, William; America, 1768 ***1220.12*** *p825*
Vickery, Edward 23; Quebec, 1870 ***8364.32*** *p26*
Vicklund, Anton; Cleveland, OH, 1901-1906 ***9722.10*** *p128*
Vicklund, John; Cleveland, OH, 1892-1894 ***9722.10*** *p128*
Vicory, William 40; Ontario, 1871 ***1823.21*** *p376*
Vicq, John; Utah, 1855 ***9228.50*** *p649*
*Relative:*Nancy
Vicq, Nancy *SEE* Vicq, John
Victal, William 47; Ontario, 1871 ***1823.17*** *p167*
Victor, Adolf; America, 1887 ***5475.1*** *p435*
Victor, Ant. 30; America, 1840 ***778.6*** *p334*
Victor, Felix; Missouri, 1884 ***5475.1*** *p435*
Victor, H. 33; Port uncertain, 1842 ***778.6*** *p334*
Victor, Isidor; America, 1885 ***5475.1*** *p434*
*Brother:*Maximilian
Victor, Joseph 18; America, 1840 ***778.6*** *p334*
Victor, Karl; Missouri, 1866 ***5475.1*** *p433*
Victor, Leopold; Missouri, 1878 ***5475.1*** *p433*
Victor, Maximilian *SEE* Victor, Isidor
Victor, Victor; America, 1878 ***5475.1*** *p433*
Victorin, Hannah; St. Paul, MN, 1880-1892 ***1865.50*** *p106*
Victorin, John W.; Chicago, 1880 ***1865.50*** *p113*
*Wife:*Margareta C. Erickson
Victorin, Margareta C. Erickson *SEE* Victorin, John W.
Victuals, Elizabeth; America, 1773 ***1220.12*** *p825*
Vidal, A. B. 32; New Orleans, 1841 ***778.6*** *p334*
Vidal, A. B. 30; Port uncertain, 1842 ***778.6*** *p334*
Vidal, Alexander 57; Ontario, 1871 ***1823.17*** *p167*
Vidal, Antoine; Illinois, 1852 ***6079.1*** *p14*
Vidal, B. 32; Port uncertain, 1842 ***778.6*** *p334*
Vidal, B. H. 30; Ontario, 1871 ***1823.21*** *p376*
Vidal, Baptiste 35; Ohio, 1847 ***778.6*** *p334*
Vidal, Charles; Louisiana, 1874-1875 ***4981.45*** *p130*
Vidal, Chs. 26; New Orleans, 1844 ***778.6*** *p334*
Vidal, Francisco; Washington, 1882 ***2770.40*** *p136*
Vidal, Townsend 45; Ontario, 1871 ***1823.17*** *p167*
Vidau, Jean; Virginia, 1700 ***9230.15*** *p80*
Vidault, Anne 18; Quebec, 1662 ***9221.17*** *p494*
Videau, Child; New Orleans, 1848 ***778.6*** *p334*
Videau, Mrs.; New Orleans, 1848 ***778.6*** *p335*
Videau, Jacques 50; New Orleans, 1848 ***778.6*** *p334*
Videnka, Jan; Baltimore, 1880 ***2853.20*** *p129*
Videnka, Jan; Pennsylvania, 1871 ***2853.20*** *p122*
Videnka, Jan E.; Wisconsin, 1882 ***2853.20*** *p321*
Vidgeon, Thomas; America, 1749 ***1220.12*** *p825*
Vidon, Simon 38; New Orleans, 1746 ***778.6*** *p335*
Vidou, Mr. 19; Port uncertain, 1844 ***778.6*** *p335*
Vidou, Simon 38; New Orleans, 1746 ***778.6*** *p335*
Vidre, Harry; Detroit, 1929-1930 ***6214.5*** *p61*
Vidreux, Louis H. N. 25; America, 1843 ***778.6*** *p335*
Vie, Marie; Quebec, 1649-1664 ***4514.3*** *p377*
Vie, Marie-Sainte; Quebec, 1664 ***4514.3*** *p377*
Viegener, Hedwig; New York, 1923 ***8023.44*** *p371*
Viegener, Hedwig; New York, 1923 ***8023.44*** *p371*
Viegener, Hermann; Argentina, 1919 ***8023.44*** *p380*
Vieillard, Inder 55; New Orleans, 1848 ***778.6*** *p335*
Vieillot, Catherine; Quebec, 1667 ***4514.3*** *p378*
Viel, Geo.; Quebec, 1881 ***9228.50*** *p650*
*Wife:*Sophia
*Child:*Geo. Amice
*Child:*Sophie Isabel
Viel, Geo. Amice *SEE* Viel, Geo.
Viel, Marie-Therese; Quebec, 1671 ***4514.3*** *p378*
Viel, Sophia *SEE* Viel, Geo.
Viel, Sophie Isabel *SEE* Viel, Geo.
Vielhack, K.; New York, 1860 ***358.56*** *p149*
Vielle, Mr. 46; America, 1844 ***778.6*** *p335*
Vielle, Joseph V. 30; America, 1840 ***778.6*** *p335*
Vien, Etienne; Quebec, 1647 ***9221.17*** *p190*
*Wife:*Marie DeLaMartiniere
*Daughter:*Marie
Vien, Marie 8 *SEE* Vien, Etienne
Vien, Marie DeLaMartiniere 41 *SEE* Vien, Etienne
Vien, Rene 25; Quebec, 1656 ***9221.17*** *p348*
Viennot, Benigne; Quebec, 1644 ***9221.17*** *p146*
Viennot, Denis; Quebec, 1642 ***9221.17*** *p122*
Viepont, Thomas; America, 1738 ***1220.12*** *p825*
Viergil, Carl; Iowa, 1893 ***1211.15*** *p20*
Viersac, Pierre Francois 57; America, 1847 ***778.6*** *p335*
Vierschilling, Anton 26; America, 1897 ***5475.1*** *p19*
Viery, Ja.que 46; Missouri, 1845 ***778.6*** *p335*
Viery, Margarette 40; Missouri, 1845 ***778.6*** *p335*
Viet, David; Ohio, 1809-1852 ***4511.35*** *p56*
Vietenhorn, Jacob; Ohio, 1809-1852 ***4511.35*** *p56*
Vieterhorn, Jacob; Ohio, 1809-1852 ***4511.35*** *p56*
Vieth, Friedrich Wilhelm Adolph; America, 1864 ***7420.1*** *p227*
Vieth, John; Louisiana, 1836-1841 ***4981.45*** *p209*
Vietmeyer, Carl Ludwig; America, 1833 ***7420.1*** *p7*
Vietmeyer, Conrad Ludwig; America, 1850 ***7420.1*** *p77*
Vietti, Luigi; Illinois, 1918 ***6007.60*** *p9*
Vieux, Marie 27; Port uncertain, 1843 ***778.6*** *p335*
Viez, Marie 16; Quebec, 1659 ***9221.17*** *p411*
Vigan, Robert 56; Ontario, 1871 ***1823.21*** *p376*
Vigar, Lydia 46; Ontario, 1871 ***1823.21*** *p376*
Vigen, George; Barbados, 1664 ***1220.12*** *p825*
Viger, Agnes 37; Minnesota, 1926 ***2769.54*** *p1383*
Viger, Francoise 16; Quebec, 1662 ***9221.17*** *p495*
Viger, Nicolas N. 27; America, 1845 ***778.6*** *p335*
Viger, Peter 39; Minnesota, 1926 ***2769.54*** *p1383*
Vigey, Nicholas; Louisiana, 1841-1844 ***4981.45*** *p211*
Vignal, Guillaume 33; Quebec, 1648 ***9221.17*** *p193*
Vignaud, Jeanne 21; Quebec, 1657 ***9221.17*** *p371*
Vigne, Eugenie 32; New Orleans, 1848 ***778.6*** *p335*
Vigne, Jos.; Louisiana, 1874-1875 ***4981.45*** *p130*
Vigne, Ullalie 12; New Orleans, 1848 ***778.6*** *p335*
Vigneaux, B. 40; America, 1843 ***778.6*** *p335*
Vignerie, Mr. 38; Port uncertain, 1845 ***778.6*** *p335*
Vigneron, Rene; Quebec, 1647 ***9221.17*** *p191*
Vignes, Adam; Virginia, 1700 ***9230.15*** *p80*
Vignes, Antoinette 27; Port uncertain, 1843 ***778.6*** *p335*
Vignes, Dorothee 10; Port uncertain, 1843 ***778.6*** *p335*
Vignes, Joseph 11; Port uncertain, 1843 ***778.6*** *p335*
Vignes, Louis; Louisiana, 1874 ***4981.45*** *p134*
Vigneux, Charles; Montreal, 1653 ***9221.17*** *p302*
Vignon, Michel; Montreal, 1650 ***9221.17*** *p233*
Vignos, Joseph; Ohio, 1809-1852 ***4511.35*** *p56*
Vigny, Charles 41; America, 1843 ***778.6*** *p335*
Vigny, Marie; Quebec, 1673 ***4514.3*** *p378*
Vigoreau, Emilio; Puerto Rico, 1836 ***3476.25*** *p113*
Vigue, Desiree 28; New Orleans, 1840 ***778.6*** *p335*
Viguerie, Jean 22; Port uncertain, 1846 ***778.6*** *p335*
Vigures, James; America, 1771 ***1220.12*** *p825*
Vigures, Mary; Virginia, 1767 ***1220.12*** *p825*
Viita, Eino 33; Minnesota, 1923 ***2769.54*** *p1379*
Vike, John; Washington, 1885 ***2770.40*** *p194*
Vikland, John; Cleveland, OH, 1892-1894 ***9722.10*** *p128*
Viklund, Oscar; Cleveland, OH, 1901-1906 ***9722.10*** *p128*
Viktor, Martin *SEE* Viktor, Vaclav
Viktor, Matej *SEE* Viktor, Vaclav
Viktor, Vaclav; Wisconsin, 1855 ***2853.20*** *p333*
*Brother:*Martin
*Brother:*Matej
Vilain, Jean-Baptiste; Quebec, 1600-1655 ***4514.3*** *p378*
Vilain, Jeanne; Quebec, 1670 ***4514.3*** *p378*
Vildaigre, Jacques 25; Quebec, 1654 ***9221.17*** *p315*
Vildey, Edward; America, 1685 ***1220.12*** *p825*
Vile, Christopher; America, 1754 ***1220.12*** *p825*
Vile, Edward; America, 1685 ***1220.12*** *p825*
Vile, Thomas; America, 1685 ***1220.12*** *p825*
Viles, Thomas; America, 1685 ***1220.12*** *p825*
Viles, William; Ohio, 1840 ***2763.1*** *p22*
Vilett, Nicholas; Virginia, 1744 ***1220.12*** *p825*
Vilim, Frantisek; Chicago, 1854 ***2853.20*** *p388*
Vilimek, Vaclav; Iowa, 1855 ***2853.20*** *p239*
Villa, G. 28; New Orleans, 1847 ***778.6*** *p335*
Villain, Annet; Quebec, 1650 ***9221.17*** *p230*
Villain, Pierre; Montreal, 1653 ***9221.17*** *p302*
Villan, William; Virginia, 1740 ***1220.12*** *p825*
Villar, J. 37; New Orleans, 1846 ***778.6*** *p335*
Villate, Marguerite; Quebec, 1665 ***4514.3*** *p341*
Villatte, Pierre 35; New Orleans, 1848 ***778.6*** *p335*
Villedonne, Etienne de; Quebec, 1683-1688 ***2314.30*** *p169*
Villedonne, Etienne de; Quebec, 1685 ***2314.30*** *p197*
Villemain, Francoise 34; Mississippi, 1846 ***778.6*** *p335*
Villemain, Joseph; Illinois, 1857 ***6079.1*** *p14*
Villemain, Marie 1; Mississippi, 1846 ***778.6*** *p335*
Villemain, Pierre 33; Mississippi, 1846 ***778.6*** *p335*
Villemain, T. 3; Mississippi, 1846 ***778.6*** *p335*
Villembits, J. 19; New Orleans, 1848 ***778.6*** *p335*
Villeneuse, Charles; Washington, 1885 ***2770.40*** *p194*
Villeneuve, Mr. 20; America, 1841 ***778.6*** *p335*
Villeneuve, Elie 24; Quebec, 1650 ***9221.17*** *p223*
Villeneuve, Mathieu 6; Quebec, 1636 ***9221.17*** *p51*

526 *FOR A COMPLETE EXPLANATION OF ENTRY, SEE "HOW TO READ A CITATION" SECTION*

Viller, Mrs.; Texas, 1843 ***778.6*** *p336*
Viller, Catherine 64; America, 1848 ***778.6*** *p335*
Viller, Charles 41; America, 1848 ***778.6*** *p336*
Viller, Francois Joseph 11; Texas, 1843 ***778.6*** *p336*
Viller, Georges 6; Texas, 1843 ***778.6*** *p336*
Viller, Jean-Baptiste 3; Texas, 1843 ***778.6*** *p336*
Viller, Joseph 14; Texas, 1843 ***778.6*** *p336*
Viller, Joseph Auguste 19; Texas, 1843 ***778.6*** *p336*
Viller, Marie Louise 17; Texas, 1843 ***778.6*** *p336*
Viller, Pierre Marie 38; Texas, 1843 ***778.6*** *p336*
Viller, Victor 3; Texas, 1843 ***778.6*** *p336*
Villers, Victor; Detroit, 1856 ***1494.21*** *p31*
Villersot, Jean 23; Louisiana, 1848 ***778.6*** *p336*
Villet, Leon 30; America, 1845 ***778.6*** *p336*
Villhard, Peter; America, 1854 ***2526.43*** *p124*
Villier, C. 32; New Orleans, 1846 ***778.6*** *p336*
Villiers, Marie de 26; Quebec, 1657 ***9221.17*** *p350*
Villieu, Sebastien de; Quebec, 1665 ***2314.30*** *p167*
Villieu, Sebastien de; Quebec, 1665 ***2314.30*** *p197*
Villigas, Frank; Louisiana, 1874-1875 ***4981.45*** *p130*
Villigas, Richard; Washington, 1887 ***2770.40*** *p25*
Villis, Edward; America, 1752 ***1220.12*** *p825*
Villouin, . . .; Quebec, 1662 ***9221.17*** *p495*
Villy, Balthasar 2; Missouri, 1845 ***778.6*** *p336*
Villy, Firena 1 months; Missouri, 1845 ***778.6*** *p336*
Villy, Firena 35; Missouri, 1845 ***778.6*** *p336*
Villy, Pierre 33; Missouri, 1845 ***778.6*** *p336*
Vilott, Ferrand 35; New Orleans, 1848 ***778.6*** *p336*
Vimont, Barthelemy; Acadia, 1629-1630 ***9221.17*** *p83*
Vince, Jean Baptiste; Wisconsin, 1854-1858 ***1495.20*** *p66*
Vince, John; America, 1767 ***1220.12*** *p825*
Vince, Marie Francoise; Wisconsin, 1854-1858 ***1495.20*** *p66*
Vincent, . . .; New Orleans, 1840 ***778.6*** *p336*
Vincent, Child; America, 1843 ***778.6*** *p336*
Vincent, Mr. 40; America, 1843 ***778.6*** *p336*
Vincent, Mrs.; America, 1843 ***778.6*** *p336*
Vincent, Alphonse; Detroit, 1855 ***1494.21*** *p31*
Vincent, Annette 32; Louisiana, 1848 ***778.6*** *p336*
Vincent, Aug..te; New Orleans, 1840 ***778.6*** *p336*
Vincent, Charles; America, 1754 ***1220.12*** *p825*
Vincent, Edward; America, 1702 ***1220.12*** *p825*
Vincent, Eleazer; Ohio, 1844 ***2763.1*** *p22*
Vincent, Emma Eliza Smart *SEE* Vincent, John Richard
Vincent, George 48; Ontario, 1871 ***1823.21*** *p376*
Vincent, Hezekiah; America, 1751 ***1220.12*** *p826*
Vincent, Jessie 8; Ontario, 1871 ***1823.21*** *p376*
Vincent, John; America, 1685 ***1220.12*** *p826*
Vincent, John; America, 1722 ***1220.12*** *p826*
Vincent, John; America, 1727 ***1220.12*** *p826*
Vincent, John; America, 1742 ***1220.12*** *p826*
Vincent, John; America, 1765 ***1220.12*** *p826*
Vincent, John; America, 1770 ***1220.12*** *p826*
Vincent, John 52; Ontario, 1871 ***1823.21*** *p376*
Vincent, John 71; Ontario, 1871 ***1823.21*** *p376*
Vincent, John; Philadelphia, 1778 ***8529.30*** *p16*
Vincent, John Richard; America, 1848-1948 ***9228.50*** *p650*
*Wife:*Emma Eliza Smart
Vincent, Joseph 32; America, 1846 ***778.6*** *p336*
Vincent, Joshua; America, 1686 ***1220.12*** *p826*
Vincent, Levi; Ohio, 1844 ***2763.1*** *p22*
Vincent, Margaret; America, 1752 ***1220.12*** *p826*
Vincent, Mary 35; Ontario, 1871 ***1823.21*** *p376*
Vincent, Michael 77; Ontario, 1871 ***1823.21*** *p376*
Vincent, Michel 20; Quebec, 1656 ***9221.17*** *p348*
Vincent, Nicholas; Virginia, 1738 ***1220.12*** *p826*
Vincent, Peter; America, 1741 ***1220.12*** *p826*
Vincent, Richard; America, 1729 ***1220.12*** *p826*
Vincent, Richard; America, 1737 ***1220.12*** *p826*
Vincent, Samuel; America, 1767 ***1220.12*** *p826*
Vincent, Sarah; America, 1766 ***1220.12*** *p826*
Vincent, William; Virginia, 1652 ***6254.4*** *p243*
Vincent, William King; New York, NY, 1834 ***3274.55*** *p74*
Vincent, Wm Thos 34; Ontario, 1871 ***1823.21*** *p376*
Vinchelez, Elizabeth; Marblehead, MA, 1705 ***9228.50*** *p165*
Vinckland, Elizabeth; Virginia, 1732 ***1220.12*** *p826*
Vinconneau, Jean 29; Quebec, 1659 ***9221.17*** *p411*
Vin-D'Espagne, Francois 19; Quebec, 1651 ***9221.17*** *p237*
Vine, Edward; Annapolis, MD, 1723 ***1220.12*** *p826*
Vine, Henry 20; Ontario, 1871 ***1823.21*** *p376*
Vine, James; America, 1767 ***1220.12*** *p826*
Vine, Michael; America, 1720 ***1220.12*** *p826*
Vine, Rowland; America, 1722 ***1220.12*** *p826*
Vine, Susanna; Potomac, 1729 ***1220.12*** *p826*
Vinegar, Ann; America, 1754 ***1220.12*** *p826*
Viner, Jane; Annapolis, MD, 1735 ***1220.12*** *p826*
Viner, Richard; America, 1729 ***1220.12*** *p826*
Viner, Thomas; America, 1672 ***1220.12*** *p826*
Vines, Daniel; America, 1758 ***1220.12*** *p826*
Vines, John; America, 1753 ***1220.12*** *p826*
Vines, Mary; Virginia, 1727 ***1220.12*** *p826*
Vinet, Catherine; Quebec, 1662 ***9221.17*** *p481*
*Daughter:*Marie
Vinet, Jean 17; Quebec, 1662 ***9221.17*** *p495*
Viney, Edward; America, 1749 ***1220.12*** *p826*
Viney, Thomas; America, 1749 ***1220.12*** *p826*
Ving, Susanna; America, 1876 ***5475.1*** *p271*
Vinicombe, Thomas; America, 1765 ***1220.12*** *p826*
Vinicott, Joseph; America, 1685 ***1220.12*** *p826*
Viniet, Louis 51; Port uncertain, 1846 ***778.6*** *p336*
Viniet, Marie 46; Port uncertain, 1846 ***778.6*** *p336*
Vining, Abraham; America, 1774 ***1220.12*** *p826*
Vining, Ambrose; America, 1685 ***1220.12*** *p826*
Vining, Charlotte 79; Ontario, 1871 ***1823.21*** *p376*
Vining, Salmon 73; Ontario, 1871 ***1823.21*** *p377*
Vining, Wilber R. 51; Ontario, 1871 ***1823.21*** *p377*
Vinle, Jacques; Quebec, 1651 ***9221.17*** *p251*
Vinn, Allexand 27; America, 1841 ***778.6*** *p336*
Vinn, John 27; America, 1841 ***778.6*** *p336*
Vinney, George; Ohio, 1809-1852 ***4511.35*** *p56*
Vinson, Charles T.; Kansas, 1903 ***1447.20*** *p65*
Vintner, Henry; America, 1682 ***1220.12*** *p826*
Vinyard, Abraham; America, 1753 ***1220.12*** *p826*
Vinz, Amelia Louise; Wisconsin, 1899 ***6795.8*** *p179*
Vinz, John Ernst Conrad; Wisconsin, 1883 ***6795.8*** *p97*
Vinz, Mary Catherine; Wisconsin, 1888 ***6795.8*** *p108*
Violand, Joseph; Ohio, 1809-1852 ***4511.35*** *p56*
Violant, Joseph; Ohio, 1809-1852 ***4511.35*** *p56*
Violaut, Joseph; Ohio, 1809-1852 ***4511.35*** *p56*
Violette, Adrien; Quebec, 1653 ***9221.17*** *p280*
With wife
Violette, Louis 27; Port uncertain, 1840 ***778.6*** *p336*
Viosca, Salvadore; Louisiana, 1836-1840 ***4981.45*** *p213*
Vipond, Isaac; America, 1730 ***1220.12*** *p826*
Vipont, Isaac; America, 1730 ***1220.12*** *p826*
Vippach, Lorenz; America, 1867 ***7919.3*** *p528*
Viraemer, Catharine 22; America, 1841 ***778.6*** *p336*
Viraemer, Michel 48; America, 1841 ***778.6*** *p337*
Virage, Nicholas 39; America, 1848 ***778.6*** *p337*
Viras, Jaques; Virginia, 1700 ***9230.15*** *p81*
With wife
Virgails, Charles; Illinois, 1834-1900 ***6020.5*** *p133*
Virgee, Joseph; Boston, 1755 ***9228.50*** *p21A*
Virgee, Joseph; Nova Scotia, 1755-1800 ***9228.50*** *p21A*
*Wife:*Mary Blewett
Virgee, Mary Blewett *SEE* Virgee, Joseph
Virgine, Catherine; America, 1771 ***1220.12*** *p826*
Virgl, Antonin; Nebraska, 1873 ***2853.20*** *p171*
Virgl, Petr; Nebraska, 1876 ***2853.20*** *p172*
Virgo, Thomas; America, 1756 ***1220.12*** *p826*
Virlee, Antoine; Detroit, 1870 ***1494.20*** *p11*
Vironceau, Catherine 31; Quebec, 1640 ***9221.17*** *p94*
Virtue, Robert 50; Ontario, 1871 ***1823.17*** *p167*
Virtue, Thomas; America, 1757 ***1220.12*** *p826*
Visage, George; America, 1736 ***1220.12*** *p826*
Visage, Rene; Quebec, 1647 ***9221.17*** *p191*
Vischler, Bernard 24; New Castle, DE, 1817-1818 ***90.20*** *p154*
Visemer, Jacob; North Carolina, 1710 ***3629.40*** *p7*
Visemer, Johnes; North Carolina, 1710 ***3629.40*** *p7*
Visiter, Elizabeth; America, 1767 ***1220.12*** *p826*
Vissing, Amalia 23; Halifax, N.S., 1902 ***1860.4*** *p42*
Vital, J. Pierre 31; Port uncertain, 1843 ***778.6*** *p337*
Vitard, Louise; Quebec, 1671 ***4514.3*** *p378*
Vitek, . . .; Pennsylvania, 1750-1799 ***2853.20*** *p17*
Vitek, Josef; Nebraska, 1870 ***2853.20*** *p181*
Viton, Jan; Cleveland, OH, 1852 ***2853.20*** *p475*
Vitot, G. 40; America, 1840 ***778.6*** *p337*
Vitousek, Jan; Iowa, 1854 ***2853.20*** *p218*
Vitry, Marguerite; Quebec, 1669 ***4514.3*** *p378*
Vittals, Elizabeth; America, 1773 ***1220.12*** *p826*
Vitter, Victor; Louisiana, 1874 ***4981.45*** *p297*
Vitzthurn, Oswald Paul R.; Washington, 1887 ***2770.40*** *p25*
Viverey, Jacquette; Quebec, 1650 ***9221.17*** *p230*
Vivian, Charles 44; Ontario, 1871 ***1823.17*** *p167*
Vivian, John 54; Ontario, 1871 ***1823.17*** *p167*
Vivian, Samuel; Ontario, 1871 ***1823.17*** *p167*
Vivian, Samuel 51; Ontario, 1871 ***1823.21*** *p377*
Vivian, William; Virginia, 1718 ***1220.12*** *p826*
Vivien, Marie-Rose; Quebec, 1673 ***4514.3*** *p378*
Vivier, Jacques; Quebec, 1657 ***9221.17*** *p362*
Vivier, Jacquette; Quebec, 1650 ***9221.17*** *p230*
Vivray, Jacquette; Quebec, 1650 ***9221.17*** *p230*
Vizard, John; America, 1755 ***1220.12*** *p826*
Vizard, Nathaniel; Maryland, 1737 ***1220.12*** *p827*
Vizard, Thomas; Virginia, 1749 ***1220.12*** *p827*
Vlach, Josef; Iowa, 1854 ***2853.20*** *p216*
Vlasak, Frantisek V.; New York, NY, 1836 ***2853.20*** *p98*
Vlasak, Klem.; Baltimore, 1885 ***2853.20*** *p129*
Vlasak, Klement; New York, NY, 1887 ***2853.20*** *p110*
Vlcek, Antonin; Cleveland, OH, 1884 ***2853.20*** *p487*
Vlcek, Jan; Omaha, NE, 1893 ***2853.20*** *p152*
Vlna, Frantisek; Cleveland, OH, 1865-1910 ***2853.20*** *p476*
Vock, Leonhard; America, 1853 ***2526.42*** *p157*
Vockeroth, Johann Georg; America, 1856 ***7420.1*** *p155*
Vockroth, Carl August Emil; America, 1882 ***7420.1*** *p333*
Vockroth, Georg Carl; America, 1880 ***7420.1*** *p318*
Vockroth, Louise; America, 1881 ***7420.1*** *p326*
Vodden, Thomas 22; Ontario, 1871 ***1823.21*** *p377*
Vodden, William 28; Ontario, 1871 ***1823.21*** *p377*
Vodicka, Vaclav L.; Omaha, NE, 1867 ***2853.20*** *p144*
Vodin, John; Salem, MA, 1674 ***9228.50*** *p646*
Vodin, Moses; Massachusetts, 1616-1716 ***9228.50*** *p646*
Vodrazka, Jan; New York, NY, 1854 ***2853.20*** *p250*
Voegele, Auguste 4; Mississippi, 1846 ***778.6*** *p337*
Voegele, Berdolf 6; Mississippi, 1846 ***778.6*** *p337*
Voegele, Johann 34; Mississippi, 1846 ***778.6*** *p337*
Voegele, Wilhelm 8; Mississippi, 1846 ***778.6*** *p337*
Voegelgesong, Henry Lewis; Ohio, 1809-1852 ***4511.35*** *p56*
Voegeli, August 19; New Orleans, 1847 ***778.6*** *p337*
Voegeli, Marian.a 14; New Orleans, 1847 ***778.6*** *p337*
Voegelle, Johann; New York, NY, 1889 ***3366.30*** *p70*
Voegely, August 78; New Orleans, 1847 ***778.6*** *p337*
Voegely, Fidele 25; New Orleans, 1847 ***778.6*** *p337*
Voegely, Marie Anne 19; New Orleans, 1847 ***778.6*** *p337*
Voegle, Balth. 30; America, 1840 ***778.6*** *p337*
Voegle, Joseph 28; America, 1840 ***778.6*** *p337*
Voelcker, Konrad; Port uncertain, 1810 ***170.15*** *p45*
Voelker, E. 17; Port uncertain, 1846 ***778.6*** *p337*
Voelker, John Philip; Louisiana, 1841-1844 ***4981.45*** *p211*
Voge, Johann G.; Wisconsin, 1858 ***6795.8*** *p143*
Vogel, . . .; West Virginia, 1865-1879 ***1132.30*** *p150*
Vogel, Anthony; New York, 1860 ***358.56*** *p5*
Vogel, Babet 29; Port uncertain, 1847 ***778.6*** *p337*
Vogel, Barbara Preuss *SEE* Vogel, Michael
Vogel, Charles; Colorado, 1891 ***1029.59*** *p91*
Vogel, Charles; Colorado, 1895 ***1029.59*** *p91*
Vogel, Charlotte 19; Mississippi, 1848 ***778.6*** *p337*
Vogel, Elisabetha Katharina 33; America, 1855 ***2526.43*** *p123*
*Son:*Johannes 12
*Son:*Georg 10
*Son:*Heinrich 2
*Son:*Jakob 7
Vogel, Georg; America, 1885 ***2526.42*** *p133*
Vogel, Israel; New York, 1860 ***358.56*** *p150*
Vogel, Jn. Baptiste 11; Mississippi, 1847 ***778.6*** *p337*
Vogel, Johann Baptist; America, 1849 ***5475.1*** *p478*
Vogel, Lydia Ernestine; Philadelphia, 1869 ***8513.31*** *p416*
Vogel, Michael; America, 1882 ***2526.42*** *p133*
*Wife:*Barbara Preuss
Vogel, Paul; South Dakota, 1887-1900 ***3366.30*** *p70*
Vogel, Philipp; New York, 1886 ***5475.1*** *p381*
Vogel, Vilem; Ohio, 1881-1889 ***2853.20*** *p505*
Vogel, Wilamina 3; Port uncertain, 1847 ***778.6*** *p337*
Vogel, Wolfgang; Wisconsin, 1886 ***6795.8*** *p99*
Vogel, Xavier 31; Mississippi, 1847 ***778.6*** *p337*
Vogelmann, Christine; America, 1886 ***179.55*** *p19*
Vogelmann, Gotthilf; America, 1700-1899 ***179.55*** *p19*
Vogelmann, Gottlieb; America, 1886 ***179.55*** *p19*
Vogelmann, Karoline; America, 1886 ***179.55*** *p19*
Vogelsburgh, Christopher 53; Michigan, 1880 ***4491.39*** *p31*
Vogelsburgh, Minnie 49; Michigan, 1880 ***4491.39*** *p31*
Vogely, Fredile 52; Galveston, TX, 1844 ***3967.10*** *p370*
Vogely, Marie 19; Galveston, TX, 1844 ***3967.10*** *p370*
Voges, Henri 21; Port uncertain, 1840 ***778.6*** *p337*
Voght, Francis; Ohio, 1809-1852 ***4511.35*** *p56*
Vogle, John; Illinois, 1834-1900 ***6020.5*** *p133*
Vogler, Frank; Illinois, 1858-1861 ***6020.5*** *p133*
Vogsel, Anne 24; New Orleans, 1748 ***778.6*** *p337*
Vogt, Adam 49; Texas, 1844 ***2526.43*** *p183*
With wife
*Daughter:*Anna Maria 7
*Son:*Philipp Adam 2
*Son:*Johann Heinrich 10
*Daughter:*Anna Maria Barbara 12
Vogt, Anna Maria 7 *SEE* Vogt, Adam
Vogt, Anna Maria Barbara 12 *SEE* Vogt, Adam
Vogt, Anne Marie Christine; America, 1904 ***7420.1*** *p380*
Vogt, Anthony; Ohio, 1809-1852 ***4511.35*** *p56*
Vogt, August Heinrich Friedrich Wilhelm *SEE* Vogt, Johann Heinrich Gottlieb
Vogt, August Heinrich Friedrich Wilhelm *SEE* Vogt, Johann Heinrich Gottlieb
Vogt, Auguste Sophie Marie; America, 1904 ***7420.1*** *p380*
Vogt, Carl Friedrich; America, 1868 ***7420.1*** *p277*
Vogt, Dorothea Wilhelmine Louise; America, 1867 ***7420.1*** *p266*
Vogt, Elisabeth Friederike; America, 1867 ***7919.3*** *p532*
Vogt, Elisabetha 6 *SEE* Vogt, Georg, II
Vogt, Frans Bernh.; New York, NY, 1849 ***6412.40*** *p151*

Vogt, Friedrich Gerhard; Port uncertain, 1867 ***7420.1*** *p266*
Vogt, Friedrich Wilhelm; America, 1840 ***7420.1*** *p21*
Vogt, Friedrich Wilhelm Otto; America, 1853 ***7420.1*** *p112*
Vogt, Georg; America, 1840 ***2526.42*** *p133*
With wife
With child 12
Vogt, Georg, II; America, 1846 ***2526.43*** *p158*
With wife
*Daughter:*Elisabetha
*Daughter:*Katharina
Vogt, Gottlieb; America, 1897 ***7420.1*** *p374*
With family
Vogt, Heinrich; America, 1864 ***7420.1*** *p227*
Vogt, Heinrich Christoph; America, 1904 ***7420.1*** *p380*
Vogt, Heinrich Christoph; America, 1904 ***7420.1*** *p380*
*Wife:*Sophie Justine Luise Vogt
*Daughter:*Auguste Sophie Marie
*Daughter:*Anne Marie Christine
*Daughter:*Sophie Marie
*Son:*Heinrich Christoph
*Daughter:*Lina Sophie
*Son:*Heinrich Wilhelm
*Daughter:*Sophie Ida Frieda
Vogt, Heinrich Friedrich Gottlieb *SEE* Vogt, Johann Heinrich Gottlieb
Vogt, Heinrich Friedrich Gottlieb; America, 1894 ***7420.1*** *p371*
*Brother:*Heinrich Wilhelm August
Vogt, Heinrich Tonjes; America, 1860 ***7420.1*** *p201*
With wife & daughter
Vogt, Heinrich Wilhelm; America, 1904 ***7420.1*** *p380*
Vogt, Heinrich Wilhelm August *SEE* Vogt, Johann Heinrich Gottlieb
Vogt, Heinrich Wilhelm August *SEE* Vogt, Heinrich Friedrich Gottlieb
Vogt, J.; Galveston, TX, 1855 ***571.7*** *p18*
Vogt, Johann Friedrich Wilhelm; America, 1840 ***7420.1*** *p21*
With child 11
With child 7
With child 5
With child 3
With child 8
Vogt, Johann Heinrich 10 *SEE* Vogt, Adam
Vogt, Johann Heinrich Gottlieb; America, 1882 ***7420.1*** *p333*
*Wife:*Sophie Marie Dorothea Huckemeier
*Son:*Heinrich Friedrich Gottlieb
*Son:*Heinrich Wilhelm August
*Son:*August Heinrich Friedrich Wilhelm
*Daughter:*Marie Wilhelmine Dorothea
Vogt, Johann Heinrich Gottlieb; America, 1897 ***7420.1*** *p374*
*Wife:*Sophie Marie Dorothea Huckemeier
*Son:*August Heinrich Friedrich Wilhelm
Vogt, Karl; Illinois, 1852 ***6079.1*** *p14*
Vogt, Katharina 10 *SEE* Vogt, Georg, II
Vogt, Lina Sophie; America, 1904 ***7420.1*** *p380*
Vogt, Marie Wilhelmine Dorothea *SEE* Vogt, Johann Heinrich Gottlieb
Vogt, Nicolaus Friedrich; America, 1868 ***7919.3*** *p532*
With wife & 3 children
Vogt, Philipp; America, 1870 ***2526.42*** *p133*
Vogt, Philipp Adam 2 *SEE* Vogt, Adam
Vogt, Sophie Ida Frieda; America, 1904 ***7420.1*** *p380*
Vogt, Sophie Justine Luise; America, 1904 ***7420.1*** *p380*
Vogt, Sophie Marie; America, 1904 ***7420.1*** *p380*
Vogt, Sophie Marie Dorothea Huckemeier *SEE* Vogt, Johann Heinrich Gottlieb
Vogt, Sophie Marie Dorothea Huckemeier *SEE* Vogt, Johann Heinrich Gottlieb
Vogt, Tonnies; America, 1871 ***7420.1*** *p396*
Vogt, W. G.; Nebraska, 1905 ***3004.30*** *p46*
Vogt, Wilhelmine; America, 1867 ***7420.1*** *p266*
With daughters
Voguer, Marie; Quebec, 1669 ***4514.3*** *p379*
Vogwell, George; Virginia, 1771 ***1220.12*** *p827*
Voice, George; America, 1769 ***1220.12*** *p827*
Voidie, Jeanne 18; Quebec, 1654 ***9221.17*** *p316*
Voight, Frederick; Texas, 1851 ***3435.45*** *p37*
Voight, Henry; Texas, 1854 ***3435.45*** *p37*
Voigt, Frank C.; Wisconsin, 1882 ***6795.8*** *p229*
Voigt, Ludwig; America, 1867 ***7919.3*** *p531*
Voigt, Scharlotte; Wisconsin, 1903 ***6795.8*** *p179*
Voigt, William; Texas, 1851 ***3435.45*** *p37*
Voilquin, Mr. 14; Louisiana, 1848 ***778.6*** *p337*
Voilquin, Mr. 68; Louisiana, 1848 ***778.6*** *p337*
Voilquin, Mrs. 36; Louisiana, 1848 ***778.6*** *p337*
Voinich, Joseph; Washington, 1889 ***2770.40*** *p81*
Voisin, Miss 30; New Orleans, 1845 ***778.6*** *p337*
Voisin, Mr. 26; New Orleans, 1848 ***778.6*** *p337*
Voisin, Geffin; Quebec, 1657 ***9221.17*** *p371*
Voisin, Theodore 25; America, 1841 ***778.6*** *p337*
Voisin, Theodore 33; New Orleans, 1842 ***778.6*** *p337*
Voisjean, Joseph 31; Ohio, 1847 ***778.6*** *p337*
Voit, John Peter; Illinois, 1858-1861 ***6020.5*** *p133*
Voiturier, Modeste 19; Louisiana, 1848 ***778.6*** *p338*
Voiturier, Victor; Illinois, 1852 ***6079.1*** *p14*
Voiturier, Victor; Illinois, 1856 ***6079.1*** *p14*
Vojan, Egon; New York, NY, 1904 ***2853.20*** *p413*
Vojan, Jaroslav; New York, NY, 1910 ***2853.20*** *p116*
Vojta, Frantisek *SEE* Vojta, Jan
Vojta, Jan; St. Louis, 1848 ***2853.20*** *p21*
*Brother:*Frantisek
*Brother:*Tomas
*Brother:*Vaclav
Vojta, Tomas *SEE* Vojta, Jan
Vojta, Vaclav *SEE* Vojta, Jan
Vojtech, Jan; St. Louis, 1850-1870 ***2853.20*** *p49*
Vojtisek, Josef; Galveston, TX, 1853 ***2853.20*** *p229*
With parents
Vojtisek, Vincenc; New York, NY, 1866 ***2853.20*** *p100*
Vokal, Jan; New York, NY, 1860-1869 ***2853.20*** *p100*
Vokes, James F. 45; Ontario, 1871 ***1823.21*** *p377*
Vokes, Thomas; North Carolina, 1817 ***1088.45*** *p36*
Vokner, Fr.; Nebraska, 1870 ***2853.20*** *p193*
Volant, Claude 12; Quebec, 1648 ***9221.17*** *p205*
Volger, Albert; America, 1883 ***7420.1*** *p340*
Volhert, Pierre 25; Port uncertain, 1846 ***778.6*** *p338*
Volk, Adam; America, 1869 ***2526.43*** *p192*
Volk, Adam, II; America, 1852 ***2526.42*** *p157*
Volk, Alfred 49; Galveston, TX, 1845 ***3967.10*** *p376*
Volk, Aloisia 4; New York, NY, 1893 ***1883.7*** *p37*
Volk, Angela 23; New York, NY, 1893 ***1883.7*** *p37*
Volk, Anna Eva 5 *SEE* Volk, Johannes
Volk, Balthasar 8 *SEE* Volk, Johannes
Volk, Barbara; America, 1870 ***2526.42*** *p157*
Volk, Barbara 3; New York, NY, 1898 ***7951.13*** *p44*
Volk, Christine 14; Galveston, TX, 1845 ***3967.10*** *p376*
Volk, Clemens 8; New York, NY, 1898 ***7951.13*** *p44*
Volk, Eberhard, II; America, 1831 ***2526.43*** *p183*
Volk, Elisabeth 31; New York, NY, 1893 ***1883.7*** *p37*
Volk, Elisabetha Margaretha 24 *SEE* Volk, Heinrich
Volk, Eva Margaretha 18 *SEE* Volk, Heinrich
Volk, Franz 9; New York, NY, 1893 ***1883.7*** *p37*
Volk, Friedrich 3 months; Galveston, TX, 1845 ***3967.10*** *p376*
Volk, Georg; America, 1853 ***2526.42*** *p157*
Volk, Georg 19; Galveston, TX, 1845 ***3967.10*** *p376*
Volk, Georg Adam; America, 1872 ***2526.43*** *p192*
Volk, Georg Christian; America, 1867 ***7919.3*** *p529*
Volk, Heinrich; America, 1892 ***2526.43*** *p126*
Volk, Heinrich 49; America, 1853 ***2526.42*** *p111*
With wife 52
*Child:*Eva Margaretha 18
*Child:*Philipp 14
*Child:*Elisabetha Margaretha 24
*Child:*Maria Elisabetha 23
Volk, Heinrich 38; New York, NY, 1893 ***1883.7*** *p37*
Volk, Heinrich; Toledo, OH, 1881 ***2526.42*** *p165*
Volk, Jacob 20; Halifax, N.S., 1902 ***1860.4*** *p43*
Volk, Jacob 7 months; New York, NY, 1893 ***1883.7*** *p37*
Volk, Jakob; America, 1854 ***2526.43*** *p192*
Volk, Jakob; America, 1856 ***2526.42*** *p157*
Volk, Johann Georg 17; America, 1851 ***2526.42*** *p158*
Volk, Johanna Elisabetha 21 *SEE* Volk, Johannes
Volk, Johannes; America, 1842 ***2526.42*** *p186*
With wife
*Son:*Philipp
*Son:*Balthasar
*Daughter:*Anna Eva
*Daughter:*Johanna Elisabetha
*Son:*Nikolaus
Volk, Johannes; America, 1885 ***2526.42*** *p158*
Volk, Josef 2 months; New York, NY, 1893 ***1883.7*** *p37*
Volk, Joseph 7; New York, NY, 1898 ***7951.13*** *p43*
Volk, Joseph 37; New York, NY, 1898 ***7951.13*** *p43*
Volk, Kaspar; America, 1853 ***2526.42*** *p158*
Volk, Kaspar; America, 1853 ***2526.43*** *p192*
Volk, Leonhard 25; America, 1851 ***2526.42*** *p158*
Volk, Magdalena 3; Galveston, TX, 1845 ***3967.10*** *p376*
Volk, Margaret 33; New York, NY, 1898 ***7951.13*** *p44*
Volk, Maria; America, 1868 ***2526.42*** *p158*
Volk, Maria Elisabetha 23 *SEE* Volk, Heinrich
Volk, Marie 39; Galveston, TX, 1845 ***3967.10*** *p376*
Volk, Nikolaus 24 *SEE* Volk, Johannes
Volk, Philipp; America, 1900 ***2526.43*** *p126*
Volk, Philipp 11 *SEE* Volk, Johannes
Volk, Philipp 14 *SEE* Volk, Heinrich
Volk, Ramano 30; New York, NY, 1893 ***1883.7*** *p37*
Volk, Rosina 36; New York, NY, 1898 ***7951.13*** *p43*
Volk, Rosine 17; Galveston, TX, 1845 ***3967.10*** *p376*
Volk, Salomea 8; Galveston, TX, 1845 ***3967.10*** *p376*
Volk, Vincent 34; New York, NY, 1898 ***7951.13*** *p44*
Volk, Wilhelm; America, 1890 ***2526.42*** *p100*
Volke, Clemens; Ohio, 1840-1897 ***8365.35*** *p18*
Volkening, Mr.; America, 1867 ***7420.1*** *p266*
With wife & 5 daughters
With son 9
Volkening, Carl Friedrich; America, 1853 ***7420.1*** *p112*
Volkening, Friedrich Wilhelm; America, 1862 ***7420.1*** *p215*
With wife & 2 children
Volkening, Heinrich; America, 1847 ***7420.1*** *p57*
Volker, Anna Maria Bock *SEE* Volker, Jakob
Volker, Anthony; Ohio, 1809-1852 ***4511.35*** *p56*
Volker, Jakob; America, 1880 ***5475.1*** *p241*
*Wife:*Anna Maria Bock
*Son:*Peter
*Son:*M. Johann
*Daughter:*Katharina
Volker, Johannes; America, 1868 ***2526.43*** *p187*
Volker, Katharina *SEE* Volker, Jakob
Volker, M. Johann *SEE* Volker, Jakob
Volker, Peter *SEE* Volker, Jakob
Volkmann, Ms. 26; America, 1848 ***778.6*** *p338*
Volksen, Heinrich Wilhelm; America, 1872 ***7420.1*** *p298*
Volksen, Johann Heinrich; America, 1867 ***7420.1*** *p266*
Voll, Gustav Carl; Wisconsin, 1883 ***6795.8*** *p127*
Voll, John; Louisiana, 1836-1841 ***4981.45*** *p209*
Vollard, Peter; America, 1691 ***1220.12*** *p827*
Volle, Jacques; Quebec, 1639 ***9221.17*** *p92*
Voller, Elisabeth 59; New York, NY, 1893 ***1883.7*** *p42*
Voller, Josef 19; New York, NY, 1893 ***1883.7*** *p42*
Voller, Peter 17; New York, NY, 1893 ***1883.7*** *p42*
Vollers, Carsten H.; North Carolina, 1854 ***1088.45*** *p36*
Vollers, Hankle; North Carolina, 1850 ***1088.45*** *p36*
Vollers, Ludwig; North Carolina, 1792-1862 ***1088.45*** *p36*
Vollers, Luke; North Carolina, 1854 ***1088.45*** *p36*
Vollery, Jacques; Illinois, 1852 ***6079.1*** *p14*
Volles, Jakob; America, 1861 ***5475.1*** *p504*
*Daughter:*Luise
*Son:*Karl
*Daughter:*Katharina
*Son:*Philipp
Volles, Karl *SEE* Volles, Jakob
Volles, Katharina *SEE* Volles, Jakob
Volles, Luise *SEE* Volles, Jakob
Volles, Philipp *SEE* Volles, Jakob
Vollhard, Anna Katharina; Virginia, 1831 ***152.20*** *p68*
Vollhardt, Anna Maria Kriegbaum *SEE* Vollhardt, Jakob
Vollhardt, Elisabeth *SEE* Vollhardt, Jakob
Vollhardt, Jakob; Virginia, 1831 ***152.20*** *p70*
*Wife:*Anna Maria Kriegbaum
*Child:*Elisabeth
Vollmer, Mr.; America, 1862 ***7420.1*** *p215*
Vollmer, Charles Alphons; Pennsylvania, 1877 ***8513.31*** *p430*
*Wife:*Marie Anne Meinninger
Vollmer, Dorothea 28; Chile, 1852 ***1192.4*** *p52*
Vollmer, Fredericke; Philadelphia, 1875 ***8513.31*** *p435*
Vollmer, Marie Anne Meinninger *SEE* Vollmer, Charles Alphons
Vollmerhausen, Robert; Brazil, 1925 ***8023.44*** *p380*
Vollmers, Herman; Missouri, 1894 ***3276.1*** *p4*
Vollmers, Jacob Henry; Missouri, 1844 ***3276.1*** *p3*
Vollmers, Jacob Henry; Missouri, 1893 ***3276.1*** *p4*
Vollrath, John; Louisiana, 1841-1844 ***4981.45*** *p211*
Volltmer, Henry Geo.; Missouri, 1900 ***3276.1*** *p4*
Volmers, John; Missouri, 1893 ***3276.1*** *p4*
Volte, Arnella 20; Halifax, N.S., 1902 ***1860.4*** *p43*
Volte, Catherine 11 months; Halifax, N.S., 1902 ***1860.4*** *p43*
Volte, Louise 3; Halifax, N.S., 1902 ***1860.4*** *p43*
Volte, Peter 32; Halifax, N.S., 1902 ***1860.4*** *p43*
Volte, Rocharda 24; Halifax, N.S., 1902 ***1860.4*** *p43*
Voltman, . . .; Iowa, 1870 ***2853.20*** *p202*
Voltner, Henry; Missouri, 1877 ***3276.1*** *p3*
Voltz, Christine; America, n.d. ***8115.12*** *p324*
Voltz, Conrad; Ohio, 1809-1852 ***4511.35*** *p56*
Voltz, Friedrich Konrad; America, n.d. ***8115.12*** *p324*
Voltz, Heinrich Ludwig *SEE* Voltz, Louise
Voltz, Jacob; Ohio, 1809-1852 ***4511.35*** *p56*
Voltz, Louise; America, n.d. ***8115.12*** *p322*
*Child:*Wilhelmine
*Child:*Heinrich Ludwig
Voltz, Ludwig; America, n.d. ***8115.12*** *p324*
Voltz, Ludwig Ferdinand; America, n.d. ***8115.12*** *p324*
Voltz, Margarethe; America, n.d. ***8115.12*** *p324*
Voltz, Marie Wilhelmine; America, 1859-1860 ***8115.12*** *p324*
With siblings
Voltz, Valentine; Ohio, 1809-1852 ***4511.35*** *p15*
Voltz, Wilhelmine *SEE* Voltz, Louise
Volz, Barbara 4; Halifax, N.S., 1902 ***1860.4*** *p43*
Volz, Christine 8; Halifax, N.S., 1902 ***1860.4*** *p43*
Volz, David 26; Halifax, N.S., 1902 ***1860.4*** *p44*

Volz, Elesfarina 11; Halifax, N.S., 1902 *1860.4 p43*
Volz, Elesfarina 40; Halifax, N.S., 1902 *1860.4 p43*
Volz, Friedeg 10; Halifax, N.S., 1902 *1860.4 p43*
Volz, Helena 23; Halifax, N.S., 1902 *1860.4 p44*
Volz, J. 44; Halifax, N.S., 1902 *1860.4 p43*
Volz, Jacob; Ohio, 1809-1852 *4511.35 p56*
Volz, Johann 14 *SEE* Volz, Michel
Volz, Joseph; Halifax, N.S., 1902 *1860.4 p44*
Volz, Katharina 63; America, 1843 *5475.1 p528*
  *Son:*Konrad 23
Volz, Maria; America, 1838 *5475.1 p458*
Volz, Maria 12 *SEE* Volz, Michel
Volz, Michel; America, 1836 *5475.1 p513*
  With wife
  *Daughter:*Maria
  *Son:*Nikolaus
  *Son:*Peter
  *Son:*Johann
Volz, Nikolaus 5 *SEE* Volz, Michel
Volz, Peter 1 *SEE* Volz, Michel
Volz, Wilhelm 6 months; Halifax, N.S., 1902 *1860.4 p43*
Vomberg, Marianne; America, 1868 *7919.3 p534*
Vomund, Alexius; Venezuela, 1843 *3899.5 p544*
Vomund, Benedikt; Venezuela, 1843 *3899.5 p544*
Vomund, Franz Anton; Venezuela, 1843 *3899.5 p543*
Vomund, Joseph; Venezuela, 1843 *3899.5 p543*
Vomund, Joseph; Venezuela, 1843 *3899.5 p544*
Vomund, Theresia; Venezuela, 1843 *3899.5 p545*
Vonar, Joseph 42; Louisiana, 1847 *778.6 p338*
Vonar, Marianne 38; Louisiana, 1847 *778.6 p338*
Von Arx, Joseph; Illinois, 1852 *6079.1 p14*
Von Arx, Urs; Illinois, 1852 *6079.1 p14*
Vonau, Agathe 26; New Orleans, 1848 *778.6 p338*
Vonau, Christina 1; New Orleans, 1848 *778.6 p338*
Vonau, Ignaz 46; New Orleans, 1848 *778.6 p338*
Vonbanck, Elisabeth; America, 1855 *5475.1 p327*
Vonbanck, Johann; America, 1855 *5475.1 p255*
  With family
von Buchwald, Friedrich Eduard 23; New York, NY,
  1872 *5475.1 p14*
  *Brother:*Wilhelm Rudolf 23
von Buchwald, Rudolph 33; New York, NY, 1881
  5475.1 p15
von Buchwald, Wilhelm Rudolf 23 *SEE* von Buchwald,
  Friedrich Eduard
Vonderheid, Bernard; Ohio, 1840-1897 *8365.35 p18*
von der Heide, Edward; New York, 1859 *358.56 p54*
Vonderscher, Carl 23; New Orleans, 1848 *778.6 p338*
von der Wall, Felix; New York, 1859 *358.56 p54*
von Ehr, A. Maria 28; Brazil, 1864 *5475.1 p501*
Vones, Jan; Chicago, 1894 *2853.20 p418*
Vones, Methodej; Chicago, 1901 *2853.20 p434*
von Hof, Helene; America, 1868 *7919.3 p529*
von Hutten, Philipp; Venezuela, 1529 *3899.5 p538*
Von Knobelsdorf, Julia; Galveston, TX, 1855 *571.7 p17*
Von Loeben, Clara Elise Stuermer *SEE* Von Loeben,
  Wolf Edmund Wilhelm
Von Loeben, Wolf Edmund Wilhelm; Philadelphia, 1883
  8513.31 p430
  *Wife:*Clara Elise Stuermer

Von May, Leopold; Galveston, TX, 1855 *571.7 p17*
Vonmund, Alexius; Venezuela, 1843 *3899.5 p544*
VonPressentin, Bernard M.E.; Washington, 1887
  2770.40 p25
Von Rycken, George; New Hampshire, 1670 *9228.50
  p541*
Von Rycken, Maturin; New Hampshire, 1670-1706
  9228.50 p541
von Schroder, G.A.; North America, 1819 *6410.15 p103*
von Speyer, George; Venezuela, 1529 *3899.5 p538*
Von Stein, . . .; Virginia, 1831 *152.20 p70*
Vonstewart, James 55; Ontario, 1871 *1823.21 p377*
von Vegesack, Ernst; Leeward Islands, 1850 *6410.15
  p104*
Vopalecky, Eduard; Cleveland, OH, 1845-1910 *2853.20
  p476*
Vopalecky Brothers, . . .; Cleveland, OH, 1866 *2853.20
  p499*
Vopatek, Tomas; Port uncertain, 1883-1902 *2853.20
  p434*
  With parents
Vopelius, Adolf 26; America, 1897 *5475.1 p73*
Vopicka, Karel J.; Chicago, 1880 *2853.20 p399*
Vorbach, Daniel; Port uncertain, 1800-1899 *170.15 p45*
Vordermark, Henry; Ohio, 1840-1897 *8365.35 p18*
Vorel, Vaclav; Iowa, 1857 *2853.20 p237*
Vorlicek, Jan J.; Wisconsin, 1898 *2853.20 p338*
Vormand, N. 36; America, 1748 *778.6 p338*
Vosatka, Jan F.; New York, NY, 1868 *2853.20 p101*
Vosind, Mr. 25; New Orleans, 1843 *778.6 p338*
Vosmek, Jan; Iowa, 1867 *2853.20 p218*
Vosoba, Frantisek; Iowa, 1855 *2853.20 p239*
Vosoba, M.B.; Iowa, 1855 *2853.20 p239*
Vosper, Richard; America, 1746 *1220.12 p827*
Voss, Anton 32; New York, NY, 1864 *5475.1 p21*
Voss, J. Ch.; New York, 1859 *358.56 p99*
Voss, Robert; Wisconsin, 1884 *6795.8 p79*
Vossais, Pierre 37; America, 1841 *778.6 p338*
Vosse, Jane; Barbados, 1679 *1220.12 p827*
Vosse, Mary; Barbados or Jamaica, 1685 *1220.12 p827*
Vosse, Morris; America, 1685 *1220.12 p827*
Vossick, Johann Wilhelm; Port uncertain, 1892 *7420.1
  p367*
Vostrovsky, Jaroslav; Illinois, 1863 *2853.20 p377*
Votava, Frantisek; Iowa, 1856 *2853.20 p252*
Votier, Elizabeth; America, 1727 *1220.12 p827*
Votiere, Peter; Annapolis, MD, 1735 *1220.12 p827*
Votsch, . . . 7; Baltimore, 1889 *8425.16 p35*
Votsch, Antonia 3; Baltimore, 1889 *8425.16 p35*
Votsch, Dominicus 1; Baltimore, 1889 *8425.16 p35*
Votsch, Eva 6 months; Baltimore, 1889 *8425.16 p35*
Votsch, Franz 31; Baltimore, 1889 *8425.16 p35*
Votsch, Georg 22; Baltimore, 1889 *8425.16 p35*
Votsch, Jacob 58; Baltimore, 1889 *8425.16 p35*
Votsch, Lorenz 2; Baltimore, 1889 *8425.16 p35*
Votsch, Magda 2; Baltimore, 1889 *8425.16 p35*
Votsch, Magdalena 24; Baltimore, 1889 *8425.16 p35*
Votsch, Magdalena 29; Baltimore, 1889 *8425.16 p35*
Votsch, Margaretha 17; Baltimore, 1889 *8425.16 p35*
Votsch, Margaretha 59; Baltimore, 1889 *8425.16 p35*

Votsch, Maria 31; Baltimore, 1889 *8425.16 p35*
Votsch, Melchior; Baltimore, 1889 *8425.16 p35*
Votsch, Michal 9; Baltimore, 1889 *8425.16 p35*
Votsch, Peter 35; Baltimore, 1889 *8425.16 p35*
Votypka, Cyril; Texas, 1855 *2853.20 p60*
Votypka, Jan; Texas, 1854 *2853.20 p60*
Votypka, Karel; Michigan, 1889 *2853.20 p370*
Votypka, Karel; North Dakota, 1898 *2853.20 p253*
Vouden, John; Salem, MA, 1674 *9228.50 p646*
Vouden, Moses; Massachusetts, 1616-1716 *9228.50 p646*
Vow, Thomas; Washington, 1886 *2770.40 p24*
Vowden, John; Salem, MA, 1674 *9228.50 p646*
Vowden, Moses; Massachusetts, 1616-1716 *9228.50 p646*
Vowells, John; New York, NY, 1778 *8529.30 p3*
Vowells, Mary; America, 1742 *1220.12 p827*
Vowles, Florenda; Utah, 1890 *9228.50 p288*
Vowles, Michael; America, 1749 *1220.12 p827*
Voyer, Pierre 25; Quebec, 1658 *9221.17 p387*
Voyer D'Argenson, Pierre 32; Quebec, 1658 *9221.17
  p374*
Voyes, Jaques; Virginia, 1700 *9230.15 p81*
Vozab, Frantiska; Wisconsin, 1852 *2853.20 p312*
Vozniak, Jos.; Texas, 1893 *6015.15 p29*
Vrabek, Frantisek; Minnesota, 1858-1860 *2853.20 p260*
  *Father:*Josef
  With brothers
Vrabek, Josef *SEE* Vrabek, Frantisek
Vrai, Jean 24; New Orleans, 1848 *778.6 p338*
Vrana, Julius Vitezslav; Galveston, TX, 1890 *2853.20
  p68*
Vranek, Jan; Nebraska, 1890 *2853.20 p150*
Vranek, Josef; Baltimore, 1857 *2853.20 p125*
Vranken, Olivier; New York, NY, 1856 *1494.20 p11*
Vray, Marguerite; Quebec, 1650 *9221.17 p230*
Vraz, Stanko; America, 1810-1910 *2853.20 p513*
Vrba, Frantisek; Iowa, 1889 *2853.20 p234*
Vrchota, Vaclav; Wisconsin, 1856 *2853.20 p345*
Vrignard, Auguste 32; New Orleans, 1848 *778.6 p338*
Vroege, Willem; Colorado, 1887 *1029.59 p91*
Vroege, Willem; Iowa, 1872 *1029.59 p91*
Vrtis, Tomas; Minnesota, 1857 *2853.20 p259*
Vrtis, Vojtech; St. Paul, MN, 1856 *2853.20 p258*
Vsetecka, Josef; Wisconsin, 1856 *2853.20 p345*
Vuil, Daniel; Quebec, 1659 *9221.17 p411*
Vuilliet, Joh. Nik.; America, 1866 *5475.1 p224*
Vuorela, Arri 25; Minnesota, 1925 *2769.54 p1379*
Vyborny, Josef; South Dakota, 1871-1910 *2853.20 p247*
Vychodil, Alois; Wisconsin, 1888 *2853.20 p322*
Vychopen, Jan; Galveston, TX, 1856 *2853.20 p63*
Vye, Henry; America, 1726 *1220.12 p827*
Vyhlidal, Frantisek; Nebraska, 1860-1910 *2853.20 p168*
  *Wife:*Karolina Jandova
Vyhlidal, Frantiska *SEE* Vyhlidal, Jan
Vyhlidal, Jan; Nebraska, 1825-1910 *2853.20 p168*
  *Wife:*Frantiska
Vyhlidal, Jan; Nebraska, 1866-1900 *2853.20 p161*
Vyhlidal, Karolina Jandova *SEE* Vyhlidal, Frantisek
Vyvala, Josef; Texas, 1860-1865 *2853.20 p67*

W

Waak, Geroge; Ohio, 1809-1852 *4511.35* *p56*
Waber, Adam; Illinois, 1834-1900 *6020.5* *p133*
Wachholtz, Tielka Louise; Wisconsin, 1897 *6795.8* *p153*
Wachholz, Emil Leopold; Wisconsin, 1877 *6795.8* *p163*
Wachholz, Wilhelmine Caroline Albertine; Wisconsin, 1897 *6795.8* *p87*
Wachly, John; Ohio, 1809-1852 *4511.35* *p56*
Wachnicki, Kazimierz; Detroit, 1929-1930 *6214.5* *p65*
Wacholtz, Tielea Louise; Wisconsin, 1897 *6795.8* *p224*
Wacholtz, Tielka Louise; Wisconsin, 1897 *6795.8* *p153*
Wachowska, Franciszka 22; New York, NY, 1911 *6533.11* *p9*
Wachowska, Jadwiga 2; New York, NY, 1911 *6533.11* *p9*
Wachowska, Janina 3; New York, NY, 1911 *6533.11* *p9*
Wachsmith, C.; New York, 1860 *358.56* *p149*
Wachsning, Dorothea Wilhelmine; America, 1861 *7420.1* *p209*
Wachsning, Heinrich Friedrich August; America, 1866 *7420.1* *p251*
Wachter, Carl; Valdivia, Chile, 1850 *1192.4* *p49*
Wachter, Christoph; America, 1857 *7420.1* *p174*
Wachter, Jakob; America, 1892 *5475.1* *p383*
Wachtler, Magdalena; Venezuela, 1843 *3899.5* *p542*
Wack, Friedrich Wilhelm; America, 1854 *5475.1* *p30*
Wack, Karl; America, 1850 *5475.1* *p29*
Wacker, Bernhard; America, 1889 *179.55* *p19*
Wacker, Carl Heinrich Friedrich; America, 1873 *7420.1* *p301*
Wacker, Elizabeth; Philadelphia, 1853 *8513.31* *p295*
Wacker, Magdalena Catharina; America, 1870 *179.55* *p19*
Wacker Siblings, . . .; America, 1872 *7420.1* *p298*
Wackett, Joseph; America, 1765 *1220.12* *p828*
Wackford, John; Washington, 1889 *2770.40* *p81*
Wadcase, Richard; America, 1773 *1220.12* *p828*
Waddel, George 39; Ontario, 1871 *1823.17* *p168*
Waddell, George 40; Indiana, 1880-1884 *9076.20* *p70*
Waddell, Joseph 30; Ontario, 1871 *1823.21* *p377*
Waddell, Robert 49; Ontario, 1871 *1823.21* *p377*
Waddesley, John; America, 1754 *1220.12* *p828*
Waddilove, Mary; America, 1723 *1220.12* *p828*
Waddingham, Edward; America, 1692 *1220.12* *p828*
Waddington, Alice; America, 1762 *1220.12* *p828*
Waddington, Edward 35; Ontario, 1871 *1823.17* *p168*
Waddington, Edward 36; Ontario, 1871 *1823.17* *p168*
Waddington, John; America, 1721 *1220.12* *p828*
Waddington, John; America, 1771 *1220.12* *p828*
Waddington, Ralph; America, 1758 *1220.12* *p828*
Waddington, Richard; Barbados, 1682 *1220.12* *p828*
Waddington, Robert; America, 1738 *1220.12* *p828*
Waddington, Robert; America, 1770 *1220.12* *p828*
Waddle, Agnes 21; New York, NY, 1835 *5024.1* *p137*
Waddle, James 47; Ontario, 1871 *1823.17* *p168*
Waddle, John 49; Ontario, 1871 *1823.17* *p168*
Waddy, Antho.; Jamestown, VA, 1633 *1658.20* *p211*
Waddy, John; Virginia, 1652 *6254.4* *p243*
Wade, Alexander 40; Ontario, 1871 *1823.21* *p377*
Wade, Ann; America, 1763 *1220.12* *p828*
Wade, Anne 57; Ontario, 1871 *1823.21* *p377*
Wade, Elinor; Charles Town, SC, 1719 *1220.12* *p828*
Wade, Elizabeth; America, 1768 *1220.12* *p828*
Wade, Elizabeth; Rappahannock, VA, 1728 *1220.12* *p828*
Wade, Evan Christian; Iowa, 1928 *1211.15* *p20*
Wade, Eveline; Canada, 1923 *9228.50* *p174*
Wade, Eveline; Idaho, 1925 *9228.50* *p174*
Wade, Eveline; Winnipeg, Man., 1923 *9228.50* *p174*
Wade, George; America, 1728 *1220.12* *p828*

Wade, George; America, 1744 *1220.12* *p828*
Wade, George 36; Ontario, 1871 *1823.17* *p168*
Wade, Henry; America, 1753 *1220.12* *p828*
Wade, Henry; Annapolis, MD, 1725 *1220.12* *p828*
Wade, James 38; Ontario, 1871 *1823.17* *p168*
Wade, John; America, 1663 *1220.12* *p828*
Wade, John; America, 1743 *1220.12* *p828*
Wade, John; America, 1747 *1220.12* *p828*
Wade, John; America, 1749 *1220.12* *p828*
Wade, John; America, 1762 *1220.12* *p828*
Wade, Joseph; America, 1756 *1220.12* *p828*
Wade, Joseph; America, 1768 *1220.12* *p828*
Wade, Joseph; America, 1772 *1220.12* *p828*
Wade, Joseph 4; Quebec, 1870 *8364.32* *p26*
Wade, Margaret; America, 1715 *1220.12* *p828*
Wade, Margaret; America, 1764 *1220.12* *p828*
Wade, Mary; Charles Town, SC, 1719 *1220.12* *p828*
Wade, Mary 58; Ontario, 1871 *1823.21* *p377*
Wade, Mary Ann 66; Ontario, 1871 *1823.17* *p168*
Wade, Michael; America, 1770 *1220.12* *p828*
Wade, Sarah; America, 1746 *1220.12* *p828*
Wade, Sarah; America, 1772 *1220.12* *p828*
Wade, Sarah; America, 1774 *1220.12* *p828*
Wade, Thomasin; America, 1745 *1220.12* *p828*
Wade, William; America, 1764 *1220.12* *p828*
Wade, William; Maryland, 1721 *1220.12* *p828*
Wade, William 7; Quebec, 1870 *8364.32* *p26*
Wadecki, Joseph 33; New York, NY, 1920 *930.50* *p49*
Wadford, William; America, 1685 *1220.12* *p828*
Wadge, John 39; Ontario, 1871 *1823.21* *p377*
Wadham, Elizabeth; America, 1745 *1220.12* *p829*
Wadham, Richard; America, 1685 *1220.12* *p829*
Wadhams, Richard; America, 1759 *1220.12* *p829*
Wadhams, William; Virginia, 1771 *1220.12* *p829*
Wadley, Elizabeth; America, 1774 *1220.12* *p829*
Wadling, Charles 17; Quebec, 1870 *8364.32* *p26*
Wadman, Praise; Long Island, 1781 *8529.30* *p10A*
Wadmen, Whitehill; America, 1739 *1220.12* *p829*
Wadow, Edwin 18; Quebec, 1870 *8364.32* *p26*
Wadsworth, James; America, 1751 *1220.12* *p829*
Wadsworth, Thomas; Annapolis, MD, 1733 *1220.12* *p829*
Wadsworth, William; Virginia, 1751 *1220.12* *p829*
Waechter, Philip; Ohio, 1809-1852 *4511.35* *p56*
Waee, Laura 14; Quebec, 1870 *8364.32* *p26*
Waentig, Carl Gottlob; Valdivia, Chile, 1850 *1192.4* *p49*
Waep, Frederick; Illinois, 1854 *6079.1* *p14*
Waertzner, L.; Galveston, TX, 1855 *571.7* *p18*
Waesner, George; Ohio, 1809-1852 *4511.35* *p56*
Wafer, Michael; New Orleans, 1851 *7242.30* *p156*
Wagener, Adolf Georg Hermann; America, 1882 *7420.1* *p333*
Wagener, Ernst Heinrich Friedrich Wilhelm; America, 1885 *7420.1* *p349*
Wagenfuhr, August; Illinois, 1858-1861 *6020.5* *p133*
Wagenschwanz, Gottlieb; America, 1867 *7919.3* *p532*
Wagg, Thomas; America, 1698 *1220.12* *p829*
Wagg, Thomas; Potomac, 1731 *1220.12* *p829*
Wagger, Thomas; America, 1749 *1220.12* *p829*
Waggoner, Christian; North Carolina, 1824 *1088.45* *p36*
Waggoner, Frank 36; Ontario, 1871 *1823.17* *p168*
Waggott, Thomas; America, 1765 *1220.12* *p829*
Wagner, . . .; West Virginia, 1865-1879 *1132.30* *p150*
Wagner, Albert; Wisconsin, 1885 *6795.8* *p228*
Wagner, Alfred; America, 1898 *2526.43* *p184*
Wagner, Andreas SEE Wagner, Katharine Wilhelmine
Wagner, Angela SEE Wagner, Jakob
Wagner, Anna SEE Wagner, Georg

Wagner, Anna SEE Wagner, Jakob
Wagner, Anna 6 months; Louisiana, 1847 *778.6* *p338*
Wagner, Anna 30; Louisiana, 1847 *778.6* *p338*
Wagner, Anna 33; Louisiana, 1847 *778.6* *p339*
Wagner, Anna Magdalene; America, 1850 *8115.12* *p327*
Wagner, Anna Margarethe; America, 1840 *8115.12* *p323*
  *Child:*Johann Philipp
  *Child:*Johann Ludwig
  *Child:*Konrad
Wagner, Anna Maria SEE Wagner, Johann
Wagner, Anne Maria 15; Port uncertain, 1847 *778.6* *p338*
Wagner, August; America, 1882 *5475.1* *p43*
Wagner, Mrs. Balthasar; America, 1853 *2526.43* *p184*
Wagner, Barbara 5 SEE Wagner, Franz
Wagner, Barbara Becker 41 SEE Wagner, Nikolaus
Wagner, Barbara 70; New Orleans, 1848 *778.6* *p338*
Wagner, Bernhard; Massachusetts, 1862 *5475.1* *p377*
Wagner, Bernhardine; America, 1868 *7919.3* *p531*
Wagner, C.; Died enroute, 1834 *1002.51* *p112*
Wagner, Caroline Louise; America, 1868 *7919.3* *p530*
Wagner, Caspar; America, 1867 *7919.3* *p529*
Wagner, Catharine 4; Port uncertain, 1847 *778.6* *p338*
Wagner, Chas.; California, 1868 *1131.61* *p89*
Wagner, Christine Becker SEE Wagner, Johann
Wagner, Cornelius SEE Wagner, Georg
Wagner, D. 7; New Orleans, 1834 *1002.51* *p112*
Wagner, D. 32; New Orleans, 1834 *1002.51* *p112*
Wagner, Dorothea 8 SEE Wagner, Klemens
Wagner, Dorothea 24; New York, NY, 1885 *1883.7* *p45*
Wagner, E.; Galveston, TX, 1855 *571.7* *p18*
Wagner, Miss E. 26; New Orleans, 1834 *1002.51* *p112*
Wagner, Elisabeth; America, 1819 *8115.12* *p322*
  *Child:*Magdalene
Wagner, Elisabeth SEE Wagner, Georg
Wagner, Elisabeth SEE Wagner, Jakob
Wagner, Elisabeth 28; America, 1865 *5475.1* *p389*
Wagner, Emil; America, 1882 *5475.1* *p35*
Wagner, Ernest Emil; Missouri, 1903 *3276.1* *p4*
Wagner, Ernst; America, 1849 *5475.1* *p538*
Wagner, Eva Finkler 36 SEE Wagner, Johann
Wagner, Fann 34; Halifax, N.S., 1902 *1860.4* *p42*
Wagner, Felicite 15; Port uncertain, 1847 *778.6* *p338*
Wagner, Ferdinand 39; Missouri, 1846 *778.6* *p338*
Wagner, Francis; Ohio, 1809-1852 *4511.35* *p56*
Wagner, Fransi.ca 5; Louisiana, 1847 *778.6* *p338*
Wagner, Franz 3 SEE Wagner, Franz
Wagner, Franz 39; Brazil, 1878 *5475.1* *p372*
  *Wife:*Susanna 34
  *Daughter:*Barbara 5
  *Son:*Peter 6 months
  *Son:*Franz 3
  *Son:*Jakob 8
  *Daughter:*Katharina 14
  *Son:*Mathias 9
Wagner, Franziska 23; New Orleans, 1848 *778.6* *p338*
Wagner, Fredrick 24; Indiana, 1852-1860 *9076.20* *p65*
Wagner, Friederic 23; Mississippi, 1847 *778.6* *p338*
Wagner, Friedr. 5; New York, NY, 1885 *1883.7* *p45*
Wagner, Friedr. 28; New York, NY, 1885 *1883.7* *p45*
Wagner, Friedr. 60; New York, NY, 1885 *1883.7* *p45*
Wagner, Friedrich 4 SEE Wagner, Klemens
Wagner, Georg SEE Wagner, Georg
Wagner, Georg; America, 1833 *5475.1* *p20*
  *Wife:*Katharina Mathieu
  *Daughter:*Magdalena
  *Daughter:*Elisabeth
  *Son:*Peter

*Son:*Georg
*Son:*Philipp
*Daughter:*Maria
*Daughter:*Anna
*Son:*Joh. Georg
*Son:*Cornelius
*Daughter:*Katharina
*Son:*Nikolaus
*Son:*Johann
Wagner, Georg; America, 1865 *5475.1 p223*
Wagner, George; Ohio, 1809-1852 *4511.35 p56*
Wagner, Gregoire 9; Port uncertain, 1847 *778.6 p338*
Wagner, Heinrich; America, n.d. *8115.12 p328*
Wagner, Heinrich 11 *SEE* Wagner, Klemens
Wagner, Henry 33; Louisiana, 1847 *778.6 p338*
Wagner, Henry F.; Boston, 1855 *1029.59 p91*
Wagner, Henry F.; Colorado, 1903 *1029.59 p91*
Wagner, J.; Galveston, TX, 1855 *571.7 p18*
Wagner, J. 3; New Orleans, 1834 *1002.51 p112*
Wagner, Jacob 22; America, 1847 *778.6 p338*
Wagner, Jacob; Ohio, 1809-1852 *4511.35 p56*
Wagner, Jacob; Ohio, 1840-1897 *8365.35 p18*
Wagner, Jakob; America, 1846-1847 *5475.1 p63*
Wagner, Jakob; America, 1883 *5475.1 p20*
*Wife:*Katharina Cornelius
*Daughter:*Katharina
*Daughter:*Margaretha
*Son:*Johann
*Son:*Philipp
*Daughter:*Magdalena
*Daughter:*Elisabeth
With 2 children
*Son:*Lorenz
*Daughter:*Anna
Wagner, Jakob *SEE* Wagner, Karl
Wagner, Jakob 4 *SEE* Wagner, Karl
Wagner, Jakob 8 *SEE* Wagner, Franz
Wagner, Jakob 36; Brazil, 1862 *5475.1 p369*
*Wife:*Margarethe Hoff 36
*Daughter:*Angela
*Son:*Peter
*Daughter:*Margarethe
Wagner, Jakob 37; Halifax, N.S., 1902 *1860.4 p40*
Wagner, Jan; New York, NY, 1882-1886 *2853.20 p115*
Wagner, Jean 44; Port uncertain, 1847 *778.6 p338*
Wagner, Jean Pierre 11; Port uncertain, 1847 *778.6 p338*
Wagner, Joh. Georg *SEE* Wagner, Georg
Wagner, Johann *SEE* Wagner, Georg
Wagner, Johann; America, 1843 *5475.1 p248*
Wagner, Johann; America, 1881 *5475.1 p154*
Wagner, Johann; America, 1881 *5475.1 p312*
Wagner, Johann; America, 1882 *5475.1 p59*
Wagner, Johann *SEE* Wagner, Jakob
Wagner, Johann 10 *SEE* Wagner, Johann
Wagner, Johann 26; America, 1882 *5475.1 p340*
Wagner, Johann 40; America, 1857 *5475.1 p352*
*Wife:*Eva Finkler 36
*Daughter:*Katharina 13
*Daughter:*Maria 8
*Son:*Johann 10
*Daughter:*Anna Maria
Wagner, Johann 54; America, 1874 *5475.1 p361*
*Wife:*Christine Becker
*Daughter:*Margarethe
*Daughter:*Maria
Wagner, Johann; Brazil, 1857 *5475.1 p367*
Wagner, Johann *SEE* Wagner, Karl
Wagner, Johann 2 *SEE* Wagner, Karl
Wagner, Johann 10 *SEE* Wagner, Nikolaus
Wagner, Johann 25; Brazil, 1857 *5475.1 p502*
Wagner, Johann 39; Halifax, N.S., 1902 *1860.4 p40*
Wagner, Johann; Valdivia, Chile, 1851 *1192.4 p51*
Wagner, Johann; Wisconsin, 1890 *5475.1 p325*
Wagner, Johann Georg; America, n.d. *8115.12 p324*
Wagner, Johann Jost; Ohio, 1840-1897 *8365.35 p18*
Wagner, Johann Ludwig; America, 1814-1857 *8115.12 p328*
Wagner, Johann Ludwig *SEE* Wagner, Anna Margarethe
Wagner, Johann Philipp *SEE* Wagner, Anna Margarethe
Wagner, Johann Philipp; America, n.d. *8115.12 p328*
Wagner, Johannes; America, 1852 *8115.12 p328*
Wagner, John; New York, 1859 *358.56 p101*
Wagner, John; Ohio, 1809-1852 *4511.35 p56*
Wagner, John Frank; Detroit, 1929 *1640.55 p113*
Wagner, Josephine 19; New Orleans, 1848 *778.6 p338*
Wagner, Julia 25; New York, NY, 1911 *6533.11 p10*
Wagner, K.; New York, 1859-1860 *358.56 p102*
Wagner, Karl; Brazil, 1870 *5475.1 p370*
*Wife:*Maria Schmitt
*Son:*Jakob
*Son:*Mathias
*Son:*Johann
*Son:*Karl

Wagner, Karl *SEE* Wagner, Karl
Wagner, Karl; Brazil, 1872 *5475.1 p370*
*Wife:*Maria Schmitt
*Son:*Johann
*Son:*Jakob
*Son:*Karl
Wagner, Karl 7 *SEE* Wagner, Karl
Wagner, Karl; Halifax, N.S., 1902 *1860.4 p40*
Wagner, Karl 7; Halifax, N.S., 1902 *1860.4 p40*
Wagner, Karl 10; Halifax, N.S., 1902 *1860.4 p42*
Wagner, Karoline 5 *SEE* Wagner, Klemens
Wagner, Katharina Folz *SEE* Wagner, Mathias
Wagner, Katharina *SEE* Wagner, Georg
Wagner, Katharina Mathieu *SEE* Wagner, Georg
Wagner, Katharina; America, 1846-1847 *5475.1 p51*
Wagner, Katharina Folz *SEE* Wagner, Mathias
Wagner, Katharina; America, 1857 *2526.43 p184*
Wagner, Katharina *SEE* Wagner, Jakob
Wagner, Katharina Cornelius *SEE* Wagner, Jakob
Wagner, Katharina; America, 1883 *5475.1 p342*
Wagner, Katharina 13 *SEE* Wagner, Johann
Wagner, Katharina 14 *SEE* Wagner, Franz
Wagner, Katharine; America, 1850 *8115.12 p328*
Wagner, Katharine; America, 1864 *8115.12 p328*
Wagner, Katharine Wilhelmine; America, 1853 *8115.12 p324*
*Child:*Ludwig
*Child:*Andreas
*Child:*Margarethe
Wagner, Klemens 61; America, 1854 *5475.1 p51*
*Wife:*Margarethe Ney 37
*Daughter:*Karoline 5
*Daughter:*Luise 7
*Daughter:*Konrad 3 months
*Daughter:*Maria 2
*Son:*Friedrich 4
*Daughter:*Margarethe 13
*Son:*Heinrich 11
*Daughter:*Sophie 9
*Daughter:*Dorothea 8
Wagner, Konrad *SEE* Wagner, Anna Margarethe
Wagner, Konrad; America, 1852 *5475.1 p538*
Wagner, Konrad 3 *SEE* Wagner, Klemens
Wagner, Konrad 27; America, 1856 *5475.1 p539*
Wagner, Lina; America, 1867 *7919.3 p532*
Wagner, Lorenz *SEE* Wagner, Jakob
Wagner, Lorenz 28; New Orleans, 1848 *778.6 p338*
Wagner, Louisa 13; Port uncertain, 1847 *778.6 p338*
Wagner, Ludmilha 2; Halifax, N.S., 1902 *1860.4 p40*
Wagner, Ludwig *SEE* Wagner, Katharine Wilhelmine
Wagner, Ludwig; America, n.d. *8115.12 p328*
Wagner, Luise 7 *SEE* Wagner, Klemens
Wagner, Madelaine 62; New Orleans, 1848 *778.6 p339*
Wagner, Magdalena *SEE* Wagner, Georg
Wagner, Magdalena *SEE* Wagner, Jakob
Wagner, Magdalene *SEE* Wagner, Elisabeth
Wagner, Marga. 60; New York, NY, 1885 *1883.7 p45*
Wagner, Margaretha *SEE* Wagner, Jakob
Wagner, Margarethe *SEE* Wagner, Katharine Wilhelmine
Wagner, Margarethe; America, 1867 *5475.1 p224*
Wagner, Margarethe *SEE* Wagner, Johann
Wagner, Margarethe 13 *SEE* Wagner, Klemens
Wagner, Margarethe Ney 37 *SEE* Wagner, Klemens
Wagner, Margarethe 40; America, 1864 *5475.1 p353*
Wagner, Margarethe *SEE* Wagner, Jakob
Wagner, Margarethe Hoff 36 *SEE* Wagner, Jakob
Wagner, Maria *SEE* Wagner, Georg
Wagner, Maria *SEE* Wagner, Johann
Wagner, Maria 2 *SEE* Wagner, Klemens
Wagner, Maria 8 *SEE* Wagner, Johann
Wagner, Maria 28; America, 1871 *5475.1 p62*
Wagner, Maria 40; America, 1800-1899 *5475.1 p63*
Wagner, Maria Schmitt *SEE* Wagner, Karl
Wagner, Maria Schmitt 30 *SEE* Wagner, Karl
Wagner, Maria 25; Halifax, N.S., 1902 *1860.4 p40*
Wagner, Marie 20; America, 1745 *778.6 p339*
Wagner, Marie 66; New Orleans, 1848 *778.6 p339*
Wagner, Martin 9; Halifax, N.S., 1902 *1860.4 p40*
Wagner, Mathe. 19; New York, NY, 1885 *1883.7 p45*
Wagner, Mathias; America, 1800-1899 *5475.1 p342*
*Wife:*Katharina Folz
*Son:*Peter
Wagner, Mathias; America, 1854 *5475.1 p377*
Wagner, Mathias; America, 1856 *5475.1 p342*
*Wife:*Katharina Folz
Wagner, Mathias; America, 1883 *5475.1 p342*
Wagner, Mathias 6 *SEE* Wagner, Karl
Wagner, Mathias 9 *SEE* Wagner, Franz
Wagner, Michael 51; America, 1832 *2526.43 p184*
Wagner, Michel, II; America, 1857 *5475.1 p509*
Wagner, Milton 60; Ontario, 1871 *1823.21 p377*
Wagner, Nicolas 14; Port uncertain, 1847 *778.6 p339*
Wagner, Nikolaus *SEE* Wagner, Georg

Wagner, Nikolaus; America, 1843 *5475.1 p333*
With wife
Wagner, Nikolaus; America, 1856 *5475.1 p352*
Wagner, Nikolaus; America, 1874 *5475.1 p361*
Wagner, Nikolaus 26; America, 1868 *5475.1 p176*
Wagner, Nikolaus; Brazil, 1857 *5475.1 p368*
*Wife:*Barbara Becker
*Son:*Peter
*Son:*Johann
Wagner, Nikolaus 33; New York, 1872 *5475.1 p539*
Wagner, Ottilie 4; New York, NY, 1885 *1883.7 p45*
Wagner, Otto; Halifax, N.S., 1902 *1860.4 p42*
Wagner, Peter *SEE* Wagner, Mathias
Wagner, Peter *SEE* Wagner, Georg
Wagner, Peter; America, 1867 *5475.1 p291*
Wagner, Peter 28; America, 1842 *778.6 p339*
Wagner, Peter *SEE* Wagner, Jakob
Wagner, Peter 6 *SEE* Wagner, Franz
Wagner, Peter 12 *SEE* Wagner, Nikolaus
Wagner, Philipp *SEE* Wagner, Georg
Wagner, Philipp *SEE* Wagner, Jakob
Wagner, Regina 32; Halifax, N.S., 1902 *1860.4 p40*
Wagner, Rudolf 6; Halifax, N.S., 1902 *1860.4 p42*
Wagner, Rudolph; America, 1891 *5475.1 p381*
Wagner, Salomon 11; Halifax, N.S., 1902 *1860.4 p42*
Wagner, Sol 37; Halifax, N.S., 1902 *1860.4 p42*
Wagner, Sophie; America, 1883 *5475.1 p52*
Wagner, Sophie 9 *SEE* Wagner, Klemens
Wagner, Susanna 34 *SEE* Wagner, Franz
Wagner, Ulrich 49; Galveston, TX, 1846 *3967.10 p378*
Wagner, Valentin; America, 1837 *5475.1 p549*
With wife
Wagner, Valentin; America, 1840 *5475.1 p549*
With wife
With 2 daughters
Wagner, Vojtech; South Dakota, 1869-1871 *2853.20 p246*
Wagner, Wilh.; Valdivia, Chile, 1851 *1192.4 p51*
With wife
Wagner, Wilhelm; America, 1857 *2526.43 p184*
Wagner, Wilhelm 6 months; New York, NY, 1885 *1883.7 p45*
Wagner, Mrs. Wilhelm; America, 1843 *5475.1 p416*
With 4 children
Wagner, Wimon 34; New Orleans, 1847 *778.6 p339*
Wagner, Xaver 41; Galveston, TX, 1846 *3967.10 p377*
Wagoner, Henry; Ohio, 1809-1852 *4511.35 p56*
Wagoner, Jacob; West Virginia, 1787 *1132.30 p146*
Wagoner, John; Ohio, 1809-1852 *4511.35 p56*
Wagoner, Michael; Ohio, 1809-1852 *4511.35 p56*
Wagstaff, Charles 29; Ontario, 1871 *1823.17 p168*
Wagstaff, Joseph G.; North Carolina, 1848 *1088.45 p36*
Wagstaff, Thomas; Rappahannock, VA, 1729 *1220.12 p829*
Wagstaff, William; Rappahannock, VA, 1728 *1220.12 p829*
Wagstaffe, Mary; America, 1736 *1220.12 p829*
Wagstaffe, Thomas; America, 1698 *1220.12 p829*
Wagstuff, Ludwig; Wisconsin, 1874 *6795.8 p108*
Wahenpfenning, Charles F.; Illinois, 1852 *6079.1 p14*
Wahl, Anton; Valdivia, Chile, 1850 *1192.4 p49*
Wahl, Baptiste 58; America, 1846 *778.6 p339*
Wahl, Catharina Barbara; America, 1867 *7919.3 p531*
Wahl, Christian; America, 1852 *179.55 p19*
Wahl, Elisabeth 1; America, 1846 *778.6 p339*
Wahl, George; Ohio, 1809-1852 *4511.35 p56*
Wahl, Gottfried; America, 1866 *179.55 p19*
Wahl, Johann Karl; America, 1885 *179.55 p19*
Wahl, Karl; America, 1894 *179.55 p19*
Wahl, Kaspar; America, 1837 *5475.1 p410*
Wahl, Marguerite 28; America, 1846 *778.6 p339*
Wahl, Marie; America, 1888 *179.55 p19*
Wahl, Marie 24; Port uncertain, 1847 *778.6 p339*
Wahl, Mary 25; America, 1847 *778.6 p339*
Wahl, Paul; Washington, 1885 *2770.40 p194*
Wahl, Peter; America, 1836 *5475.1 p536*
With wife
Wahlberg, August; Colorado, 1893 *1029.59 p92*
Wahlberg, J. H.; Colorado, 1887 *1029.59 p92*
Wahlberg, John; Iowa, 1881-1888 *1865.50 p113*
Wahlberg, Olof; Iowa, 1881-1882 *1865.50 p113*
Wahlblom, Carl; St. Paul, MN, 1866-1868 *1865.50 p114*
Wahlen, Johann; America, 1881 *5475.1 p359*
*Wife:*Susanna Ehlen
Wahlen, Susanna Ehlen *SEE* Wahlen, Johann
Wahlgren, Ingrid; St. Paul, MN, 1889 *1865.50 p104*
Wahlgren, Olof; Charleston, SC, 1851 *6412.40 p153*
Wahlhart, Joe; Colorado, 1883 *1029.59 p92*
Wahlin, David H.; Cleveland, OH, 1890-1894 *9722.10 p128*
Wahlmann, Carl F. W. *SEE* Wahlmann, Christian

FOR A COMPLETE EXPLANATION OF ENTRY, SEE "HOW TO READ A CITATION" SECTION

Wahlmann, Christian; America, 1852 ***7420.1*** *p99*
With wife & child
*Son:*Heinrich W.
*Son:*Friedrich C.
*Son:*Carl F. W.
Wahlmann, Engel Marie Sophie Caroline; America, 1872 ***7420.1*** *p296*
Wahlmann, Ernst; America, 1852 ***7420.1*** *p99*
Wahlmann, Ernst Wilhelm; America, 1854 ***7420.1*** *p132*
Wahlmann, Friedrich C. *SEE* Wahlmann, Christian
Wahlmann, Heinrich Gottlieb; America, 1849 ***7420.1*** *p68*
Wahlmann, Heinrich W. *SEE* Wahlmann, Christian
Wahlmann, Johann Otto; Port uncertain, 1861 ***7420.1*** *p209*
Wahlmann, Sophie Wilhelmine; America, 1852 ***7420.1*** *p99*
Wahlqvist, Emil; St. Paul, MN, 1874 ***1865.50*** *p114*
Wahlqvist, Pehr Aug.; New York, NY, 1851 ***6412.40*** *p153*
Wahls, John; Illinois, 1858-1861 ***6020.5*** *p133*
Wahlsted, David; Cleveland, OH, 1903-1904 ***9722.10*** *p128*
Wahlster, Katharina; America, 1892 ***5475.1*** *p76*
Wahlster, Sophie; America, 1892 ***5475.1*** *p77*
Wahlster, Wilhelmine; America, 1892 ***5475.1*** *p77*
Wahlstrom, C. Aug.; New York, NY, 1849 ***6412.40*** *p152*
Wahlstrom, C.A.; New York, NY, 1850 ***6412.40*** *p152*
Wahlund, Emanuel; St. Paul, MN, 1894 ***1865.50*** *p113*
Wahn, Baptiste 32; America, 1846 ***778.6*** *p339*
Wahren, Jackob; North Carolina, 1710 ***3629.40*** *p7*
With brother
Wahron, Mr. 35; Louisiana, 1848 ***778.6*** *p339*
Waid, Robert; New York, 1777 ***8529.30*** *p5A*
Waidner, Maria Magdalena; Venezuela, 1843 ***3899.5*** *p542*
Waight, Daniel; America, 1740 ***1220.12*** *p829*
Waiker, August; Colorado, 1894 ***1029.59*** *p92*
Wail, . . .; America, 1736 ***1220.12*** *p859*
Wail, Patrick; Toronto, 1844 ***2910.35*** *p115*
Wain, John; America, 1752 ***1220.12*** *p849*
Wain, Sarah; America, 1721 ***1220.12*** *p849*
Waine, George 16; Quebec, 1870 ***8364.32*** *p26*
Waine, John; America, 1749 ***1220.12*** *p849*
Waine, Richard; America, 1722 ***1220.12*** *p849*
Waines, Frances; America, 1745 ***1220.12*** *p829*
Wainewright, Elizabeth; Barbados or Jamaica, 1677 ***1220.12*** *p829*
Wainewright, George; America, 1754 ***1220.12*** *p829*
Wainewright, Hester; Barbados, 1682 ***1220.12*** *p829*
Wainman, Lawrence; America, 1726 ***1220.12*** *p829*
Wainscoate, George; America, 1743 ***1220.12*** *p829*
Wainscott, Richard; America, 1727 ***1220.12*** *p829*
Wainwick, Thomas; America, 1744 ***1220.12*** *p829*
Wainwright, Esther; America, 1753 ***1220.12*** *p829*
Wainwright, John; America, 1757 ***1220.12*** *p829*
Wainwright, Thomas; America, 1678 ***1220.12*** *p829*
Wainwright, William; America, 1766 ***1220.12*** *p829*
Waistell, Agnes 36; Ontario, 1871 ***1823.21*** *p377*
Wait, David 50; Ontario, 1871 ***1823.21*** *p377*
Wait, Solomon 22; Ontario, 1871 ***1823.17*** *p168*
Wait, William 42; Ontario, 1871 ***1823.21*** *p377*
Waite, Andrew; Barbados or Jamaica, 1700 ***1220.12*** *p829*
Waite, Charles; America, 1765 ***1220.12*** *p829*
Waite, John; America, 1736 ***1220.12*** *p829*
Waite, John; America, 1740 ***1220.12*** *p829*
Waite, John; America, 1746 ***1220.12*** *p829*
Waite, John; Annapolis, MD, 1732 ***1220.12*** *p829*
Waite, Richard; America, 1767 ***1220.12*** *p829*
Waite, Robert; America, 1681 ***1220.12*** *p829*
Waite, Thomas; America, 1759 ***1220.12*** *p829*
Waite, Thomas; America, 1768 ***1220.12*** *p829*
Waites, Samuel; America, 1756 ***1220.12*** *p830*
Waites, Thomas; America, 1767 ***1220.12*** *p830*
Waits, Edward Wallace; Missouri, 1854 ***3276.1*** *p3*
Waitz, Carl Ludwig Henri; Mexico, 1883 ***7420.1*** *p340*
Waiz, Mrs. Joh.Geor; Pennsylvania, 1854 ***170.15*** *p45*
With 5 children
Wake, James; America, 1685 ***1220.12*** *p830*
Wake, James 24; Ontario, 1871 ***1823.21*** *p377*
Wake, Walter 39; Ontario, 1871 ***1823.17*** *p168*
Wake, William; Barbados or Jamaica, 1697 ***1220.12*** *p830*
Wakefield, Benjamin 36; Ontario, 1871 ***1823.17*** *p168*
Wakefield, James; America, 1723 ***1220.12*** *p830*
Wakefield, John; America, 1752 ***1220.12*** *p830*
Wakefield, Joseph 58; Ontario, 1871 ***1823.17*** *p168*
Wakefield, Mary; America, 1727 ***1220.12*** *p830*
Wakefield, Richard; Barbados, 1663 ***1220.12*** *p830*
Wakefield, Samuel; America, 1741 ***1220.12*** *p830*
Wakefield, Sarah; America, 1761 ***1220.12*** *p830*
Wakefield, Thomas; America, 1727 ***1220.12*** *p830*
Wakefield, Thomas; America, 1773 ***1220.12*** *p830*
Wakefield, William 39; Ontario, 1871 ***1823.17*** *p168*
Wakeford, George; Barbados or Jamaica, 1684 ***1220.12*** *p830*
Wakeham, Loveday; America, 1750 ***1220.12*** *p830*
Wakeham, William; America, 1752 ***1220.12*** *p830*
Wakeley, Mary *SEE* Wakeley, William
Wakeley, William; Utah, 1863 ***9228.50*** *p651*
*Relative:*Mary
Wakelin, Elizabeth 71; Michigan, 1880 ***4491.30*** *p31*
Wakelin, John; America, 1757 ***1220.12*** *p830*
Wakelin, Thomas; Annapolis, MD, 1723 ***1220.12*** *p830*
Wakelin, Thomas 72; Michigan, 1880 ***4491.30*** *p31*
Wakeling, Elizabeth; Annapolis, MD, 1725 ***1220.12*** *p830*
Wakeling, Elizabeth 56; Ontario, 1871 ***1823.21*** *p377*
Wakeling, John; America, 1756 ***1220.12*** *p830*
Wakeling, John; America, 1770 ***1220.12*** *p830*
Wakeling, John; America, 1771 ***1220.12*** *p830*
Wakeling, William 58; Ontario, 1871 ***1823.21*** *p377*
Wakelings, Samuel; America, 1774 ***1220.12*** *p830*
Wakelinn, Robert; America, 1690 ***1220.12*** *p830*
Wakely, John; America, 1775 ***1220.12*** *p830*
Wakely, Sarah; Virginia, 1759 ***1220.12*** *p830*
Wakelyn, Daniel; America, 1740 ***1220.12*** *p830*
Waker, Edward; America, 1767 ***1220.12*** *p830*
Waklgemuth, Francois 18; America, 1843 ***778.6*** *p339*
Wal..., John; America, 1699 ***1220.12*** *p830*
Walbancke, John; America, 1685 ***1220.12*** *p830*
Walbancke, John; Barbados or Jamaica, 1682 ***1220.12*** *p830*
Walbaum, Mr.; America, 1857 ***7420.1*** *p174*
With son 28
With son 10
Walbe, Peter 36; Ontario, 1871 ***1823.21*** *p377*
Walberg, Clas; Colorado, 1890 ***1029.59*** *p92*
Walbrech, Anna Katharine; America, 1876-1877 ***8115.12*** *p326*
*Child:*Katharine
*Child:*Katharine Margarethe
*Child:*Louise
*Child:*Elisabeth
*Child:*Caroline
*Child:*Marie
Walbrech, Caroline *SEE* Walbrech, Anna Katharine
Walbrech, Elisabeth *SEE* Walbrech, Anna Katharine
Walbrech, Katharine *SEE* Walbrech, Anna Katharine
Walbrech, Katharine Margarethe *SEE* Walbrech, Anna Katharine
Walbrech, Louise *SEE* Walbrech, Anna Katharine
Walbrech, Marie *SEE* Walbrech, Anna Katharine
Walbrook, Thomas; America, 1728 ***1220.12*** *p830*
Walburg, Christ.; Valdivia, Chile, 1852 ***1192.4*** *p54*
Walby, Elizabeth; America, 1745 ***1220.12*** *p830*
Walch, Adam *SEE* Walch, Johannes
Walch, Auguste *SEE* Walch, Caroline
Walch, Caroline; America, 1867 ***7919.3*** *p534*
*Child:*Auguste
Walch, Elisabetha; America, 1867 ***7919.3*** *p531*
Walch, J. L.; Texas, 1892 ***3435.45*** *p37*
Walch, Johannes; America, 1867 ***7919.3*** *p531*
*Brother:*Adam
Walch, Michael; Boston, 1818 ***3274.55*** *p22*
Walcher, Joseph; Colorado, 1882 ***1029.59*** *p92*
Walcraft, Thomas; America, 1768 ***1220.12*** *p830*
Walczak, Walter; Detroit, 1929 ***1640.55*** *p113*
Waldaner, Abraham; North Carolina, 1850 ***1088.45*** *p36*
Waldbraun, John; New York, 1859 ***358.56*** *p99*
Walde, Bernhardine; Philadelphia, 1875 ***8513.31*** *p428*
Waldecker, Georg; America, 1851 ***5475.1*** *p480*
Walden, Anne; Annapolis, MD, 1722 ***1220.12*** *p830*
Walden, Carl 48; Minnesota, 1925 ***2769.54*** *p1380*
Walden, Francis 67; Ontario, 1871 ***1823.21*** *p377*
Walden, James; America, 1773 ***1220.12*** *p830*
Walden, James 39; Ontario, 1871 ***1823.17*** *p168*
Walden, Mandy M. 35; Minnesota, 1925 ***2769.54*** *p1380*
Walden, Susanna; America, 1767 ***1220.12*** *p830*
Walden, Thomas 63; Ontario, 1871 ***1823.21*** *p377*
Walden, William; America, 1753 ***1220.12*** *p830*
Waldin, Hannah *SEE* Waldin, John Gustaf
Waldin, John Gustaf; Minnesota, 1880-1886 ***1865.50*** *p113*
*Wife:*Hannah
Walding, John; America, 1772 ***1220.12*** *p830*
Waldmayer, Joseph 17; Louisiana, 1848 ***778.6*** *p339*
Waldmeyer, Heinrich; Died enroute, 1817-1818 ***90.20*** *p154*
Waldmeyer, Simon 46; Died enroute, 1817-1818 ***90.20*** *p154*
Waldock, Charles 45; Ontario, 1871 ***1823.21*** *p377*
Waldon, Edward; America, 1769 ***1220.12*** *p830*
Waldren, Lawrence; Virginia, 1721 ***1220.12*** *p831*
Waldron, Elizabeth; America, 1736 ***1220.12*** *p830*
Waldron, Elizabeth; America, 1753 ***1220.12*** *p830*
Waldron, Joan; America, 1748 ***1220.12*** *p830*
Waldron, Mary; Barbados, 1667 ***1220.12*** *p831*
Waldron, Roger; Newburyport, MA, 1690 ***1642*** *p76*
Waldron, Solomon 76; Ontario, 1871 ***1823.17*** *p168*
Waldrond, Grace; Virginia, 1731 ***1220.12*** *p830*
Waldschmidt, Elisabeth *SEE* Waldschmidt, Elisabeth
Waldschmidt, Elisabeth; America, 1871 ***8115.12*** *p328*
*Child:*Elisabeth
Waldschmidt, Johann Georg *SEE* Waldschmidt, Marie Katharine
Waldschmidt, Johann Jakob; America, 1834 ***8115.12*** *p324*
Waldschmidt, Johann Ludwig; America, n.d. ***8115.12*** *p324*
Waldschmidt, Konrad *SEE* Waldschmidt, Marie Katharine
Waldschmidt, Konrad; America, n.d. ***8115.12*** *p325*
Waldschmidt, Ludwig; America, n.d. ***8115.12*** *p325*
Waldschmidt, Ludwig; America, n.d. ***8115.12*** *p328*
Waldschmidt, Marie Katharine *SEE* Waldschmidt, Marie Katharine
Waldschmidt, Marie Katharine; America, 1854 ***8115.12*** *p322*
*Child:*Konrad
*Child:*Marie Katharine
*Child:*Johann Georg
*Child:*Susanne Margarethe
Waldschmidt, Peter; America, n.d. ***8115.12*** *p328*
Waldschmidt, Susanne Margarethe *SEE* Waldschmidt, Marie Katharine
Waldvogel, Lydia; Illinois, 1930 ***121.35*** *p100*
Wale, Ann; America, 1732 ***1220.12*** *p859*
Wale, Edward; America, 1685 ***1220.12*** *p859*
Wale, John; America, 1685 ***1220.12*** *p859*
Wale, John T.; Colorado, 1904 ***1029.59*** *p92*
Wale, Mary; America, 1753 ***1220.12*** *p859*
Wale, William; America, 1714 ***1220.12*** *p859*
Wale, William; America, 1773 ***1220.12*** *p859*
Walen, Thomas; Boston, 1769 ***1642*** *p40*
Walender, Josef; Wisconsin, 1855 ***2853.20*** *p323*
Wales, Cornelius 32; Ontario, 1871 ***1823.17*** *p168*
Wales, James; Annapolis, MD, 1758 ***1220.12*** *p831*
Wales, John; America, 1724 ***1220.12*** *p859*
Wales, John 47; Ontario, 1871 ***1823.21*** *p377*
Waleton, Henry 24; Port uncertain, 1840 ***778.6*** *p339*
Walford, John; Virginia, 1652 ***6254.4*** *p243*
Walford, Thomas; America, 1767 ***1220.12*** *p834*
Walford, William; Virginia, 1768 ***1220.12*** *p834*
Walheider, Christian 28; Port uncertain, 1847 ***778.6*** *p339*
Walich, John A.; Ohio, 1809-1852 ***4511.35*** *p56*
Waligora, Stanislaw; Detroit, 1929 ***1640.55*** *p115*
Walin, Nester 31; Minnesota, 1925 ***2769.54*** *p1383*
Waling, William; North Carolina, 1852 ***1088.45*** *p36*
Walk, Anna 36; Mississippi, 1846 ***778.6*** *p339*
Walk, Anton 37; Mississippi, 1846 ***778.6*** *p339*
Walk, Ba.bara 9; Mississippi, 1846 ***778.6*** *p339*
Walk, Caroline 3; Mississippi, 1846 ***778.6*** *p339*
Walk, Jacob 28; America, 1846 ***778.6*** *p339*
Walk, Louis 3 months; Mississippi, 1846 ***778.6*** *p339*
Walk, Madalaine 5; Mississippi, 1846 ***778.6*** *p339*
Walke, Thomas; Barbados, 1600-1662 ***9228.50*** *p651*
Walke, Thomas; Virginia, 1662 ***9228.50*** *p651*
Walker, . . .; England, 1847 ***7420.1*** *p57*
Walker, Alex; St. John, N.B., 1847 ***2978.15*** *p36*
Walker, Alice; America, 1772 ***1220.12*** *p831*
Walker, Alice; America, 1774 ***1220.12*** *p831*
Walker, Andrew; Died enroute, 1726 ***1220.12*** *p831*
Walker, Angus 28; Ontario, 1871 ***1823.21*** *p378*
Walker, Ann; America, 1732 ***1220.12*** *p831*
Walker, Ann; America, 1767 ***1220.12*** *p831*
Walker, Ann; America, 1772 ***1220.12*** *p831*
Walker, Ann; America, 1775 ***1220.12*** *p831*
Walker, Ann 23; Ontario, 1871 ***1823.21*** *p378*
Walker, Ann; Virginia, 1734 ***1220.12*** *p831*
Walker, Anne; Annapolis, MD, 1725 ***1220.12*** *p831*
Walker, Anton 32; Arkansas, 1846 ***778.6*** *p339*
Walker, Antony 60; Ontario, 1871 ***1823.21*** *p378*
Walker, Archibald 57; Ontario, 1871 ***1823.21*** *p378*
Walker, Atty; America, 1740 ***1220.12*** *p831*
Walker, August; Colorado, 1882 ***1029.59*** *p92*
Walker, August; Colorado, 1894 ***1029.59*** *p92*
Walker, Ba.bara 29; Arkansas, 1846 ***778.6*** *p339*
Walker, Benjamin 42; Ontario, 1871 ***1823.17*** *p168*
Walker, Burton 33; Ontario, 1871 ***1823.21*** *p378*
Walker, Caleb; America, 1742 ***1220.12*** *p831*
Walker, Catherine 26; Arkansas, 1846 ***778.6*** *p339*
Walker, Cathr. 46; North Carolina, 1775 ***1422.10*** *p57*
Walker, Charles; America, 1758 ***1220.12*** *p831*
Walker, Chrisper 75; Ontario, 1871 ***1823.21*** *p378*
Walker, Christen; North Carolina, 1710 ***3629.40*** *p7*
With wife & 8 children
Walker, Christian; North Carolina, 1710 ***3629.40*** *p7*

Walker, Christina 25; New York, NY, 1893 ***1883.7*** *p37*
Walker, Christopher; America, 1759 ***1220.12*** *p831*
Walker, David 48; Ontario, 1871 ***1823.21*** *p378*
Walker, David 58; Ontario, 1871 ***1823.21*** *p378*
Walker, Denis 2; Arkansas, 1846 ***778.6*** *p339*
Walker, Ebenezer 51; Ontario, 1871 ***1823.21*** *p378*
Walker, Edward 24; Ontario, 1871 ***1823.17*** *p168*
Walker, Edward 30; Ontario, 1871 ***1823.21*** *p378*
Walker, Edward 75; Ontario, 1871 ***1823.21*** *p378*
Walker, Edward T. 30; Ontario, 1871 ***1823.17*** *p168*
Walker, Eleanor; America, 1769 ***1220.12*** *p831*
Walker, Eleanor; Maryland or Virginia, 1733 ***1220.12*** *p831*
Walker, Eliza 45; Ontario, 1871 ***1823.21*** *p378*
Walker, Elizabeth; America, 1735 ***1220.12*** *p831*
Walker, Elizabeth; America, 1745 ***1220.12*** *p831*
Walker, Elizabeth; America, 1748 ***1220.12*** *p831*
Walker, Elizabeth; America, 1749 ***1220.12*** *p831*
Walker, Elizabeth; Annapolis, MD, 1723 ***1220.12*** *p831*
Walker, Elizabeth; Annapolis, MD, 1724 ***1220.12*** *p831*
Walker, Elizabeth; Annapolis, MD, 1725 ***1220.12*** *p831*
Walker, Elizabeth 40; Ontario, 1871 ***1823.21*** *p378*
Walker, Elizabeth 40; Ontario, 1871 ***1823.21*** *p378*
Walker, Elizabeth; St. Johns, N.F., 1825 ***1053.15*** *p6*
Walker, Esther; America, 1749 ***1220.12*** *p831*
Walker, Fansher 49; Ontario, 1871 ***1823.17*** *p168*
Walker, Fra.; Jamestown, VA, 1633 ***1658.20*** *p211*
Walker, Francis; America, 1771 ***1220.12*** *p831*
Walker, George; America, 1730 ***1220.12*** *p831*
Walker, George; America, 1768 ***1220.12*** *p831*
Walker, George; America, 1770 ***1220.12*** *p831*
Walker, George; America, 1775 ***1220.12*** *p831*
Walker, George 35; Michigan, 1880 ***4491.33*** *p23*
Walker, George; Ohio, 1809-1852 ***4511.35*** *p56*
Walker, George 25; Ontario, 1871 ***1823.17*** *p168*
Walker, George 40; Ontario, 1871 ***1823.21*** *p378*
Walker, George 45; Ontario, 1871 ***1823.21*** *p378*
Walker, George 53; Ontario, 1871 ***1823.21*** *p378*
Walker, George 18; Quebec, 1870 ***8364.32*** *p26*
Walker, Gottlieb 28; New York, NY, 1893 ***1883.7*** *p37*
Walker, Mrs. H.; Montreal, 1922 ***4514.4*** *p32*
Walker, Heinrich 22; New York, NY, 1893 ***1883.7*** *p37*
Walker, Helena 2; New York, NY, 1893 ***1883.7*** *p37*
Walker, Helena 2; New York, NY, 1893 ***1883.7*** *p37*
Walker, Henry; Barbados, 1692 ***1220.12*** *p831*
Walker, Henry; Quebec, 1870 ***8364.32*** *p26*
Walker, Henry B. 55; Ontario, 1871 ***1823.17*** *p168*
Walker, Hugh; Annapolis, MD, 1725 ***1220.12*** *p831*
Walker, Hugh 60; Ontario, 1871 ***1823.21*** *p378*
Walker, Hugh; Philadelphia, 1833 ***471.10*** *p87*
Walker, Hugh 45; South Carolina, 1812 ***3476.30*** *p13*
Walker, Humphrey; Barbados, 1683 ***1220.12*** *p831*
Walker, Isaac; America, 1752 ***1220.12*** *p831*
Walker, Isabell; America, 1731 ***1220.12*** *p831*
Walker, Isabella 42; Ontario, 1871 ***1823.21*** *p378*
Walker, Israel; America, 1758 ***1220.12*** *p831*
Walker, Jakob 1; New York, NY, 1893 ***1883.7*** *p37*
Walker, James; America, 1764 ***1220.12*** *p831*
Walker, James; America, 1765 ***1220.12*** *p831*
Walker, James; America, 1768 ***1220.12*** *p831*
Walker, James; America, 1772 ***1220.12*** *p831*
Walker, James 60; Michigan, 1880 ***4491.42*** *p28*
Walker, James 22; Ontario, 1871 ***1823.17*** *p168*
Walker, James 42; Ontario, 1871 ***1823.21*** *p378*
Walker, James 44; Ontario, 1871 ***1823.21*** *p378*
Walker, James 48; Ontario, 1871 ***1823.21*** *p378*
Walker, James 52; Ontario, 1871 ***1823.17*** *p168*
Walker, James 52; Ontario, 1871 ***1823.21*** *p378*
Walker, James 53; Ontario, 1871 ***1823.17*** *p168*
Walker, James 68; Ontario, 1871 ***1823.21*** *p378*
Walker, James L.; Washington, 1884 ***2770.40*** *p193*
Walker, Jane; Utah, 1855 ***9228.50*** *p651*
Walker, John; America, 1627 ***1220.12*** *p831*
Walker, John; America, 1655 ***1220.12*** *p831*
Walker, John; America, 1730 ***1220.12*** *p832*
Walker, John; America, 1731 ***1220.12*** *p832*
Walker, John; America, 1738 ***1220.12*** *p832*
Walker, John; America, 1739 ***1220.12*** *p832*
Walker, John; America, 1740 ***1220.12*** *p832*
Walker, John; America, 1748 ***1220.12*** *p832*
Walker, John; America, 1751 ***1220.12*** *p832*
Walker, John; America, 1753 ***1220.12*** *p832*
Walker, John; America, 1754 ***1220.12*** *p832*
Walker, John; America, 1756 ***1220.12*** *p832*
Walker, John; America, 1763 ***1220.12*** *p832*
Walker, John; America, 1764 ***1220.12*** *p832*
Walker, John; America, 1766 ***1220.12*** *p832*
Walker, John; America, 1767 ***1220.12*** *p832*
Walker, John; America, 1774 ***1220.12*** *p832*
Walker, John; Barbados or Jamaica, 1685 ***1220.12*** *p832*
Walker, John; Barbados or Jamaica, 1712 ***1220.12*** *p832*
Walker, John; Louisiana, 1874 ***4981.45*** *p297*
Walker, John; Maryland, 1737 ***1220.12*** *p832*
Walker, John 20; Ontario, 1871 ***1823.21*** *p378*
Walker, John 23; Ontario, 1871 ***1823.17*** *p168*
Walker, John 35; Ontario, 1871 ***1823.21*** *p378*
Walker, John 38; Ontario, 1871 ***1823.17*** *p168*
Walker, John 39; Ontario, 1871 ***1823.21*** *p378*
Walker, John 41; Ontario, 1871 ***1823.17*** *p168*
Walker, John 41; Ontario, 1871 ***1823.21*** *p378*
Walker, John 45; Ontario, 1871 ***1823.17*** *p168*
Walker, John 45; Ontario, 1871 ***1823.21*** *p378*
Walker, John 47; Ontario, 1871 ***1823.17*** *p168*
Walker, John 55; Ontario, 1871 ***1823.21*** *p378*
Walker, John 60; Ontario, 1871 ***1823.17*** *p168*
Walker, John 74; Ontario, 1871 ***1823.21*** *p378*
Walker, John; Virginia, 1734 ***1220.12*** *p832*
Walker, John Howard; Miami, 1920 ***4984.15*** *p38*
Walker, John S. 34; Ontario, 1871 ***1823.21*** *p378*
Walker, Johnston 44; Ontario, 1871 ***1823.21*** *p378*
Walker, Joseph; America, 1693 ***1220.12*** *p832*
Walker, Joseph; Annapolis, MD, 1726 ***1220.12*** *p832*
Walker, Joseph 59; Ontario, 1871 ***1823.21*** *p378*
Walker, Joseph 68; Ontario, 1871 ***1823.21*** *p378*
Walker, Letitia; America, 1751 ***1220.12*** *p832*
Walker, Ludwig 29; New York, NY, 1893 ***1883.7*** *p37*
Walker, Mabell; Annapolis, MD, 1736 ***1220.12*** *p832*
Walker, Madalaine 1; Arkansas, 1846 ***778.6*** *p339*
Walker, Margaret; America, 1737 ***1220.12*** *p832*
Walker, Margaret; America, 1771 ***1220.12*** *p832*
Walker, Margaret 70; Ontario, 1871 ***1823.17*** *p169*
Walker, Margaret; Potomac, 1731 ***1220.12*** *p832*
Walker, Marriah 24; Ontario, 1871 ***1823.21*** *p378*
Walker, Martha; America, 1771 ***1220.12*** *p832*
Walker, Mary; America, 1686 ***1220.12*** *p832*
Walker, Mary; America, 1721 ***1220.12*** *p832*
Walker, Mary; America, 1740 ***1220.12*** *p832*
Walker, Mary; America, 1748 ***1220.12*** *p832*
Walker, Mary; America, 1754 ***1220.12*** *p832*
Walker, Mary; America, 1759 ***1220.12*** *p832*
Walker, Mary; America, 1773 ***1220.12*** *p832*
Walker, Mary; Annapolis, MD, 1722 ***1220.12*** *p832*
Walker, Mary; Annapolis, MD, 1723 ***1220.12*** *p832*
Walker, Mary; Annapolis, MD, 1729 ***1220.12*** *p832*
Walker, Mary 58; Ontario, 1871 ***1823.17*** *p169*
Walker, Mary Jane; Utah, 1852 ***9228.50*** *p651*
Walker, Mathias; Boston, 1826 ***3274.55*** *p71*
Walker, Meredith; America, 1757 ***1220.12*** *p832*
Walker, Mitchell 44; Ontario, 1871 ***1823.21*** *p378*
Walker, Patrick; Boston, 1737 ***1642*** *p26*
Walker, Peter; America, 1752 ***1220.12*** *p832*
Walker, Philip; America, 1656 ***1220.12*** *p832*
Walker, Priscilla; Maryland, 1726 ***1220.12*** *p832*
Walker, Rich; Virginia, 1652 ***6254.4*** *p243*
Walker, Richard; America, 1707 ***1220.12*** *p832*
Walker, Richard; America, 1730 ***1220.12*** *p832*
Walker, Richard; America, 1751 ***1220.12*** *p833*
Walker, Richard; America, 1752 ***1220.12*** *p833*
Walker, Richard; America, 1756 ***1220.12*** *p833*
Walker, Richard; America, 1763 ***1220.12*** *p833*
Walker, Robert; America, 1766 ***1220.12*** *p833*
Walker, Robert; America, 1772 ***1220.12*** *p833*
Walker, Robert; America, 1773 ***1220.12*** *p833*
Walker, Robert; Barbados or Jamaica, 1674 ***1220.12*** *p833*
Walker, Robert; Barbados or Jamaica, 1694 ***1220.12*** *p833*
Walker, Robert 30; Ontario, 1871 ***1823.21*** *p379*
Walker, Robert 36; Ontario, 1871 ***1823.21*** *p379*
Walker, Robert 38; Ontario, 1871 ***1823.17*** *p169*
Walker, Robert 42; Ontario, 1871 ***1823.21*** *p379*
Walker, Robert 60; Ontario, 1871 ***1823.21*** *p379*
Walker, Robert 60; Ontario, 1871 ***1823.21*** *p379*
Walker, Ruth; Ontario, 1835 ***3160.1*** *p150*
Walker, Ruth; Prescott, Ont., 1835 ***3289.1*** *p61*
Walker, Samuel; America, 1769 ***1220.12*** *p833*
Walker, Samuel; Maryland or Virginia, 1738 ***1220.12*** *p833*
Walker, Samuel; Virginia, 1735 ***1220.12*** *p833*
Walker, Sarah; America, 1762 ***1220.12*** *p833*
Walker, Sophia 9; Ontario, 1871 ***1823.21*** *p379*
Walker, Stephen; Annapolis, MD, 1724 ***1220.12*** *p833*
Walker, Susan 9; Quebec, 1870 ***8364.32*** *p26*
Walker, Thomas; America, 1683 ***1220.12*** *p833*
Walker, Thomas; America, 1741 ***1220.12*** *p833*
Walker, Thomas; America, 1765 ***1220.12*** *p833*
Walker, Thomas; America, 1768 ***1220.12*** *p833*
Walker, Thomas; America, 1771 ***1220.12*** *p833*
Walker, Thomas; America, 1772 ***1220.12*** *p833*
Walker, Thomas; America, 1774 ***1220.12*** *p833*
Walker, Thomas; Died enroute, 1721 ***1220.12*** *p833*
Walker, Thomas 31; Ontario, 1871 ***1823.21*** *p379*
Walker, Timothy; America, 1768 ***1220.12*** *p833*
Walker, Tristram; Canada, 1774 ***3036.5*** *p41*
Walker, Walter 73; Michigan, 1880 ***4491.33*** *p23*
Walker, William; America, 1731 ***1220.12*** *p833*
Walker, William; America, 1749 ***1220.12*** *p833*
Walker, William; America, 1750 ***1220.12*** *p833*
Walker, William; America, 1753 ***1220.12*** *p833*
Walker, William; America, 1765 ***1220.12*** *p833*
Walker, William; America, 1775 ***1220.12*** *p833*
Walker, William; Annapolis, MD, 1723 ***1220.12*** *p833*
Walker, William; Colorado, 1873 ***1029.59*** *p92*
Walker, William; New York, 1783 ***8529.30*** *p16*
Walker, William 37; North Carolina, 1774 ***1422.10*** *p55*
Walker, William 49; Ontario, 1871 ***1823.17*** *p169*
Walker, William 49; Ontario, 1871 ***1823.21*** *p379*
Walker, William 65; Ontario, 1871 ***1823.21*** *p379*
Walker, William 18; Quebec, 1870 ***8364.32*** *p26*
Walker, William; St. Johns, N.F., 1825 ***1053.15*** *p6*
Walkey, Benjamin; Maryland or Virginia, 1738 ***1220.12*** *p833*
Walkky, Jack 34; Minnesota, 1925 ***2769.54*** *p1383*
Walklin, Thomas; America, 1773 ***1220.12*** *p833*
Walko, Andreas 44; New York, NY, 1894 ***6512.1*** *p183*
Walkordine, David 41; Ontario, 1871 ***1823.17*** *p169*
Wall, Ann; America, 1757 ***1220.12*** *p833*
Wall, Charles; America, 1772 ***1220.12*** *p833*
Wall, Charles; America, 1774 ***1220.12*** *p833*
Wall, Christian 44; New York, NY, 1885 ***1883.7*** *p45*
Wall, Christy; Ohio, 1809-1852 ***4511.35*** *p56*
Wall, David 60; Ontario, 1871 ***1823.17*** *p169*
Wall, Dorothea 7; New York, NY, 1885 ***1883.7*** *p45*
Wall, Edward; America, 1757 ***1220.12*** *p833*
Wall, Edwd 33; St. Johns, N.F., 1811 ***1053.20*** *p21*
Wall, Elisabeth 8; New York, NY, 1885 ***1883.7*** *p45*
Wall, Elizabeth 58; Ontario, 1871 ***1823.17*** *p169*
Wall, Francis; America, 1741 ***1220.12*** *p833*
Wall, Garrett; Toronto, 1844 ***2910.35*** *p116*
Wall, George; America, 1769 ***1220.12*** *p833*
Wall, George; America, 1774 ***1220.12*** *p833*
Wall, Henry 45; Ontario, 1871 ***1823.17*** *p169*
Wall, Jacob 9; New York, NY, 1885 ***1883.7*** *p45*
Wall, Jane; America, 1744 ***1220.12*** *p833*
Wall, Johann 66; America, 1864 ***5475.1*** *p45*
*Wife:*Wilhelmine Carl 66
*Daughter:*Maria 20
*Daughter:*Karoline 15
Wall, John; America, 1682 ***1220.12*** *p833*
Wall, John; America, 1722 ***1220.12*** *p833*
Wall, John; America, 1723 ***1220.12*** *p833*
Wall, John; America, 1741 ***1220.12*** *p833*
Wall, John 30; New York, NY, 1826 ***6178.50*** *p150*
Wall, John 66; Ontario, 1871 ***1823.21*** *p379*
Wall, John C.; New York, 1859 ***358.56*** *p55*
Wall, John T.; Colorado, 1862-1920 ***1029.59*** *p92*
Wall, Karoline 15 *SEE* Wall, Johann
Wall, Louise 43; New York, NY, 1885 ***1883.7*** *p45*
Wall, Lucia 27; America, 1864 ***5475.1*** *p45*
Wall, Luke; Maryland, 1727 ***1220.12*** *p833*
Wall, Maria 20 *SEE* Wall, Johann
Wall, Mary; America, 1744 ***1220.12*** *p834*
Wall, Mary; America, 1747 ***1220.12*** *p834*
Wall, Mary; America, 1771 ***1220.12*** *p834*
Wall, Mary; Annapolis, MD, 1725 ***1220.12*** *p833*
Wall, Mathilde 14; New York, NY, 1885 ***1883.7*** *p45*
Wall, Nicholas 49; Ontario, 1871 ***1823.17*** *p169*
Wall, Patrick; America, 1750 ***1220.12*** *p834*
Wall, Patrick; Boston, 1768 ***1642*** *p49*
Wall, Philip 40; Ontario, 1871 ***1823.21*** *p379*
Wall, Richard; America, 1735 ***1220.12*** *p834*
Wall, Richard; America, 1749 ***1220.12*** *p834*
Wall, Richard 40; Ontario, 1871 ***1823.21*** *p379*
Wall, Stephen 41; Ontario, 1871 ***1823.17*** *p169*
Wall, Thomas; America, 1737 ***1220.12*** *p834*
Wall, Thomas 40; Ontario, 1871 ***1823.21*** *p379*
Wall, Thomas 45; Ontario, 1871 ***1823.17*** *p169*
Wall, Wilhelm 1; New York, NY, 1885 ***1883.7*** *p45*
Wall, Wilhelmine Carl 66 *SEE* Wall, Johann
Wall, William; America, 1730 ***1220.12*** *p834*
Wall, William; America, 1746 ***1220.12*** *p834*
Wall, William 44; Ontario, 1871 ***1823.21*** *p379*
Wallace, Alfred 28; Ontario, 1871 ***1823.17*** *p169*
Wallace, Alice 20; Ontario, 1871 ***1823.21*** *p379*
Wallace, Andrew 19; New York, NY, 1835 ***5024.1*** *p136*
Wallace, Arthur 26; Ontario, 1871 ***1823.17*** *p169*
Wallace, Arthur 52; Ontario, 1871 ***1823.21*** *p379*
Wallace, Charles 70; Ontario, 1871 ***1823.21*** *p379*
Wallace, Elizabeth; South Carolina, 1813 ***3208.30*** *p19*
Wallace, Elizabeth; South Carolina, 1813 ***3208.30*** *p32*
Wallace, George; America, 1767 ***1220.12*** *p834*
Wallace, Hendry; America, 1762 ***1220.12*** *p834*
Wallace, Isaac 52; Ontario, 1871 ***1823.21*** *p379*
Wallace, James 39; Ontario, 1871 ***1823.17*** *p169*
Wallace, James; South Carolina, 1813 ***3208.30*** *p18*
Wallace, James; South Carolina, 1813 ***3208.30*** *p31*
Wallace, James 27; South Carolina, 1812 ***3476.30*** *p13*
Wallace, Jas. 24; South Carolina, 1812 ***3476.30*** *p13*
Wallace, John; North Carolina, 1792-1862 ***1088.45*** *p36*

Wallace, John 32; Ontario, 1871 ***1823.17*** *p169*
Wallace, John 58; Ontario, 1871 ***1823.21*** *p379*
Wallace, John 63; Ontario, 1871 ***1823.17*** *p169*
Wallace, John 35; Santa Clara Co., CA, 1860 ***8704.1*** *p24*
Wallace, Lawrence; America, 1771 ***1220.12*** *p835*
Wallace, Patrick 46; Ontario, 1871 ***1823.21*** *p379*
Wallace, Peter 50; Ontario, 1871 ***1823.21*** *p379*
Wallace, Richard 25; Ontario, 1871 ***1823.21*** *p379*
Wallace, Thomas; Louisiana, 1874 ***4981.45*** *p134*
Wallace, Walter 27; Ontario, 1871 ***1823.21*** *p379*
Wallace, William; New Brunswick, 1842 ***2978.20*** *p7*
Wallace, William; Ontario, 1871 ***1823.17*** *p169*
Wallace, William 18; Ontario, 1871 ***1823.21*** *p379*
Wallace, William 31; Ontario, 1871 ***1823.21*** *p379*
Wallace, William 52; Ontario, 1871 ***1823.21*** *p379*
Wallaner, Frederick; Philadelphia, 1860 ***8513.31*** *p431*
*Wife:*Rosa Hackett
Wallaner, Rosa Hackett *SEE* Wallaner, Frederick
Wallat, H.; New York, 1859 ***358.56*** *p99*
Wallbaum, August; America, 1852 ***7420.1*** *p99*
Wallbaum, Carl Friedr. Wilh. *SEE* Wallbaum, Friedrich August
Wallbaum, Carl Heinr. Ferd. *SEE* Wallbaum, Friedrich August
Wallbaum, Carl Heinrich Wilhelm; America, 1853 ***7420.1*** *p112*
Wallbaum, Caroline *SEE* Wallbaum, Wilhelm Carl
Wallbaum, Caroline Wilh. Just. Deiterding *SEE* Wallbaum, Friedrich August
Wallbaum, Friedrich; America, 1853 ***7420.1*** *p113*
Wallbaum, Friedrich August; America, 1883 ***7420.1*** *p341*
*Wife:*Caroline Wilh. Just. Deiterding
*Son:*Carl Friedr. Wilh.
*Son:*Wilhelm Friedr. Ludw
*Son:*Louis Eduard
*Son:*Carl Heinr. Ferd.
*Son:*Friedrich Wilh.
Wallbaum, Friedrich Carl Heinrich; America, 1884 ***7420.1*** *p346*
Wallbaum, Friedrich Wilh. *SEE* Wallbaum, Friedrich August
Wallbaum, Johann Heinrich August; America, 1852 ***7420.1*** *p99*
Wallbaum, Justine Wilhelmine Charlotte; America, 1863 ***7420.1*** *p220*
Wallbaum, Karl Heinrich August; America, 1882 ***7420.1*** *p333*
*Sister:*Philippine Friederike Justine
Wallbaum, Louis Eduard *SEE* Wallbaum, Friedrich August
Wallbaum, Philippine Friederike Justine *SEE* Wallbaum, Karl Heinrich August
Wallbaum, Wilhelm; America, 1854 ***7420.1*** *p132*
Wallbaum, Wilhelm Carl; America, 1852 ***7420.1*** *p99*
*Wife:*Caroline
With child
Wallbaum, Wilhelm Friedr. Ludw *SEE* Wallbaum, Friedrich August
Wallblom, Charles; St. Paul, MN, 1866-1868 ***1865.50*** *p114*
Wallbrandt, John; New York, 1860 ***358.56*** *p150*
Walldeck, Joseph; America, 1769 ***1220.12*** *p834*
Walle, Johann 15; New Orleans, 1848 ***778.6*** *p339*
Walleck, Kristian R.; Chicago, 1869 ***2853.20*** *p394*
Wallen, Carl Oscar; Hawaii, 1844 ***6412.40*** *p147*
Wallen, Eric 30; New York, 1856 ***6529.11*** *p21*
Wallen, John; America, 1720 ***1220.12*** *p834*
Wallen, John; New York, 1900 ***1766.20*** *p27*
Wallenbrock, Heinrich; Illinois, 1859 ***6079.1*** *p14*
Waller, Anton 27; Louisiana, 1847 ***778.6*** *p339*
Waller, Edward; America, 1756 ***1220.12*** *p834*
Waller, Elizabeth; America, 1752 ***1220.12*** *p834*
Waller, Elizabeth; America, 1770 ***1220.12*** *p834*
Waller, Francis; Barbados or Jamaica, 1700 ***1220.12*** *p834*
Waller, Jane; America, 1750 ***1220.12*** *p834*
Waller, John; America, 1750 ***1220.12*** *p834*
Waller, John; New York, 1728 ***1220.12*** *p834*
Waller, Joseph 45; Ontario, 1871 ***1823.17*** *p169*
Waller, Mary; America, 1723 ***1220.12*** *p834*
Waller, Mary; America, 1742 ***1220.12*** *p834*
Waller, Mary; America, 1761 ***1220.12*** *p834*
Waller, Peter; America, 1756 ***1220.12*** *p834*
Waller, Samuel; New York, 1728 ***1220.12*** *p834*
Waller, Samuel; South Carolina, 1813 ***3208.30*** *p19*
Waller, Samuel; South Carolina, 1813 ***3208.30*** *p31*
Waller, Thomas; Barbados or Jamaica, 1710 ***1220.12*** *p834*
Waller, William; America, 1770 ***1220.12*** *p834*
Wallerich, Anna *SEE* Wallerich, Johann
Wallerich, Barbara *SEE* Wallerich, Johann
Wallerich, Johann *SEE* Wallerich, Johann
Wallerich, Johann; America, 1856 ***5475.1*** *p278*
*Wife:*Maria Maxem
*Son:*Johann
*Daughter:*Anna
*Son:*Peter
*Daughter:*Maria
*Son:*Michel
*Son:*Peter
*Daughter:*Magdalena
*Daughter:*Barbara
Wallerich, Magdalena *SEE* Wallerich, Johann
Wallerich, Maria *SEE* Wallerich, Johann
Wallerich, Maria Maxem 43 *SEE* Wallerich, Johann
Wallerich, Michel *SEE* Wallerich, Johann
Wallerich, Peter *SEE* Wallerich, Johann
Wallerius, Katharina; America, 1880 ***5475.1*** *p240*
Wallern, Frederick J.; South Carolina, 1810 ***6155.4*** *p19*
Wallerson, George; North Carolina, 1827 ***1088.45*** *p36*
Wallerson, John; North Carolina, 1824 ***1088.45*** *p36*
Wallett, Charles; America, 1728 ***1220.12*** *p834*
Wallexelson, Thomas; Virginia, 1730 ***1220.12*** *p834*
Walley, Richard; America, 1727 ***1220.12*** *p834*
Wallford, Lucas; America, 1728 ***1220.12*** *p834*
Wallford, Mary; Rappahannock, VA, 1741 ***1220.12*** *p834*
Wallgren, August S.; St. Paul, MN, 1881 ***1865.50*** *p114*
Wallgrove, Roger; Rappahannock, VA, 1741 ***1220.12*** *p834*
Wallice, Henry 28; Ontario, 1871 ***1823.21*** *p379*
Wallin, Ann; Barbados, 1671 ***1220.12*** *p834*
Wallin, John; America, 1764 ***1220.12*** *p834*
Wallin, Lars Johan Wilhelm; North America, 1885 ***6410.15*** *p106*
Walling, Edward; North Carolina, 1855 ***1088.45*** *p36*
Walling, Peter; Barbados, 1688 ***1220.12*** *p834*
Walling, William; North Carolina, 1852 ***1088.45*** *p36*
Wallington, Ann; America, 1761 ***1220.12*** *p834*
Wallington, Cartes 53; Ontario, 1871 ***1823.21*** *p379*
Wallington, Daniel 42; Ontario, 1871 ***1823.17*** *p169*
Wallington, William; America, 1736 ***1220.12*** *p834*
Wallis, Mrs.; Toronto, 1844 ***2910.35*** *p114*
Wallis, Andrew; North Carolina, 1710 ***3629.40*** *p7*
Wallis, Ann; America, 1756 ***1220.12*** *p834*
Wallis, Christopher 40; Ontario, 1871 ***1823.21*** *p379*
Wallis, Edward; America, 1700 ***1220.12*** *p834*
Wallis, Eleanor; America, 1759 ***1220.12*** *p834*
Wallis, Francis; America, 1741 ***1220.12*** *p834*
Wallis, Geo; Toronto, 1844 ***2910.35*** *p116*
Wallis, George; America, 1765 ***1220.12*** *p834*
Wallis, Hannah; Virginia, 1732 ***1220.12*** *p834*
Wallis, Henry; America, 1763 ***1220.12*** *p835*
Wallis, Isaac 56; Ontario, 1871 ***1823.21*** *p379*
Wallis, James; America, 1769 ***1220.12*** *p835*
Wallis, James; New Jersey, 1668 ***9228.50*** *p656*
Walliss, James 26; Ontario, 1871 ***1823.21*** *p379*
Wallis, Jane; America, 1768 ***1220.12*** *p835*
Wallis, John; America, 1730 ***1220.12*** *p835*
Wallis, John; America, 1737 ***1220.12*** *p835*
Wallis, John; America, 1741 ***1220.12*** *p835*
Wallis, John; America, 1764 ***1220.12*** *p835*
Wallis, John; America, 1768 ***1220.12*** *p835*
Wallis, John; Barbados, 1664 ***1220.12*** *p835*
Wallis, John; Maryland, 1742 ***1220.12*** *p835*
Wallis, John 47; Ontario, 1871 ***1823.21*** *p379*
Wallis, Joseph 32; New Orleans, 1848 ***778.6*** *p340*
Wallis, Margaret; America, 1773 ***1220.12*** *p835*
Wallis, Peter; America, 1754 ***1220.12*** *p835*
Wallis, Richard; America, 1738 ***1220.12*** *p835*
Wallis, Robert; America, 1675 ***1220.12*** *p835*
Wallis, Robert; America, 1772 ***1220.12*** *p835*
Wallis, Robert; Barbados, 1670 ***1220.12*** *p835*
Wallis, Robert; Virginia, 1665 ***9228.50*** *p54*
Wallis, Samuel; America, 1742 ***1220.12*** *p835*
Wallis, Tho.; Maryland, 1672 ***1236.25*** *p47*
Wallis, Thomas; America, 1737 ***1220.12*** *p835*
Wallis, Thomas; America, 1750 ***1220.12*** *p835*
Wallis, Thomas; America, 1763 ***1220.12*** *p835*
Wallis, Thomas; Barbados, 1663 ***1220.12*** *p835*
Wallis, Thomas, Jr.; Barbados or Jamaica, 1710 ***1220.12*** *p835*
Wallis, William; America, 1723 ***1220.12*** *p835*
Wallis, William; America, 1774 ***1220.12*** *p835*
Wallis, William; Maryland, 1725 ***1220.12*** *p835*
Wallis, William 39; Ontario, 1871 ***1823.17*** *p169*
Wallis, William; Toronto, 1844 ***2910.35*** *p116*
Wallis, Mrs. Wm.; Toronto, 1844 ***2910.35*** *p114*
Walliss, Joseph H. 37; Ontario, 1871 ***1823.21*** *p379*
Wall-Lane, Frances 12; Quebec, 1870 ***8364.32*** *p26*
Wallne, John; Boston, 1774 ***8529.30*** *p3*
Walloni, Hella 35; Louisiana, 1848 ***778.6*** *p340*
Wallows, Hannah; America, 1742 ***1220.12*** *p835*
Wallquist, Emil; St. Paul, MN, 1874 ***1865.50*** *p114*
Wallrath, Dorothea 56; America, 1852 ***5475.1*** *p74*
Wallrot, Anders 25; New York, 1856 ***6529.11*** *p21*
Walls, Dorothy; America, 1766 ***1220.12*** *p835*
Walls, Dorothy; America, 1772 ***1220.12*** *p835*
Walls, Fritz; Illinois, 1834-1900 ***6020.5*** *p133*
Walls, Mary; America, 1765 ***1220.12*** *p835*
Walls, Samuel 36; Ontario, 1871 ***1823.21*** *p379*
Walls, Thomas 43; Ontario, 1871 ***1823.21*** *p379*
Wallstedt, An 28; New York, 1856 ***6529.11*** *p22*
Wallsten, August; St. Paul, MN, 1887 ***1865.50*** *p114*
Wallstrom, Andrew Fred; Cleveland, OH, 1881-1889 ***9722.10*** *p128*
Wally, Mary; Annapolis, MD, 1719 ***1220.12*** *p834*
Walmsley, John 45; Ontario, 1871 ***1823.21*** *p380*
Walmsley, Philip; America, 1770 ***1220.12*** *p835*
Walmsley, Sarah; America, 1733 ***1220.12*** *p835*
Walmsley, Thomas 8; Ontario, 1871 ***1823.21*** *p380*
Walmsley, William; America, 1730 ***1220.12*** *p835*
Walmsley, William 38; Ontario, 1871 ***1823.21*** *p380*
Walper, Jakob; America, 1881 ***5475.1*** *p14*
Walpole, Edward; America, 1767 ***1220.12*** *p835*
Walpole, John; America, 1739 ***1220.12*** *p835*
Walpole, John; America, 1758 ***1220.12*** *p835*
Walpole, William; America, 1767 ***1220.12*** *p835*
Walrath, Francois 27; New York, NY, 1894 ***6512.1*** *p182*
Wals, Caroline 6; New York, NY, 1886 ***8425.16*** *p33*
Wals, Eva 28; New York, NY, 1886 ***8425.16*** *p33*
Wals, Jacob 4 months; New York, NY, 1886 ***8425.16*** *p33*
Wals, Jacob 31; New York, NY, 1886 ***8425.16*** *p33*
Wals, Johannes 2; New York, NY, 1886 ***8425.16*** *p33*
Walsby, Annie 14; Quebec, 1870 ***8364.32*** *p26*
Walsby, Ms. C. 16; Quebec, 1870 ***8364.32*** *p26*
Walsby, Jane 12; Quebec, 1870 ***8364.32*** *p26*
Walsh, Ann; New Orleans, 1850 ***7242.30*** *p156*
Walsh, Ann 97; Ontario, 1871 ***1823.21*** *p380*
Walsh, Bartholomew; Newfoundland, 1814 ***3476.10*** *p54*
Walsh, Cath; New Orleans, 1851 ***7242.30*** *p156*
Walsh, Edmond; Colorado, 1873 ***1029.59*** *p92*
Walsh, Edmund; Newfoundland, 1814 ***3476.10*** *p54*
Walsh, Edward; America, 1773 ***1220.12*** *p835*
Walsh, Edward; Toronto, 1844 ***2910.35*** *p114*
Walsh, Elizabeth; Boston, 1679 ***1642*** *p13*
Walsh, Ella; Massachusetts, 1888-1929 ***9228.50*** *p527*
Walsh, Henry; North Carolina, 1852 ***1088.45*** *p36*
Walsh, Henry 36; Ontario, 1871 ***1823.21*** *p380*
Walsh, J.; New Orleans, 1850 ***7242.30*** *p156*
Walsh, J. L.; Texas, 1892 ***3435.45*** *p37*
Walsh, James 32; Ontario, 1871 ***1823.21*** *p380*
Walsh, James 33; Ontario, 1871 ***1823.17*** *p169*
Walsh, James; Toronto, 1844 ***2910.35*** *p116*
Walsh, James F.; Philadelphia, 1876 ***7074.20*** *p133*
Walsh, John 27; Ontario, 1871 ***1823.21*** *p380*
Walsh, John 41; Ontario, 1871 ***1823.21*** *p380*
Walsh, John 46; Ontario, 1871 ***1823.21*** *p380*
Walsh, John 59; Ontario, 1871 ***1823.17*** *p169*
Walsh, John 68; Ontario, 1871 ***1823.21*** *p380*
Walsh, John; Toronto, 1844 ***2910.35*** *p115*
Walsh, Joseph; St. Johns, N.F., 1825 ***1053.15*** *p6*
Walsh, Judith; St. Johns, N.F., 1825 ***1053.15*** *p7*
Walsh, Lawrence; Toronto, 1844 ***2910.35*** *p114*
Walsh, Luke; Palmer, MA, 1771 ***1642*** *p119*
Walsh, Margaret 43; Ontario, 1871 ***1823.21*** *p380*
Walsh, Mary; America, 1762 ***1220.12*** *p835*
Walsh, Mary 48; Ontario, 1871 ***1823.21*** *p380*
Walsh, Matthew; Toronto, 1844 ***2910.35*** *p116*
Walsh, Michael 37; Ontario, 1871 ***1823.21*** *p380*
Walsh, Michael 60; Ontario, 1871 ***1823.21*** *p380*
Walsh, Michael; Philadelphia, 1777 ***8529.30*** *p7A*
Walsh, Michael; Washington, 1883 ***2770.40*** *p137*
Walsh, Nathaniel; Boston, 1737 ***1642*** *p26*
Walsh, Pat 21; St. Johns, N.F., 1811 ***1053.20*** *p21*
Walsh, Pat 30; St. Johns, N.F., 1811 ***1053.20*** *p19*
Walsh, Patrick; Boston, 1760 ***1642*** *p48*
Walsh, Patrick; Halifax, N.S., 1827 ***7009.9*** *p62*
With wife & 7 children
Walsh, Patrick; Louisiana, 1874 ***4981.45*** *p134*
Walsh, Patrick 60; Ontario, 1871 ***1823.21*** *p380*
Walsh, Patrick; Toronto, 1844 ***2910.35*** *p112*
Walsh, Patrick; Toronto, 1844 ***2910.35*** *p113*
Walsh, Patrick; Toronto, 1844 ***2910.35*** *p114*
Walsh, Philip; Ipswich, MA, 1678 ***1642*** *p70*
Walsh, Philip; Massachusetts, 1675-1676 ***1642*** *p128*
Walsh, Richard; St. Johns, N.F., 1825 ***1053.15*** *p7*
Walsh, Robert; Jamaica, 1780 ***8529.30*** *p14A*
Walsh, Robert; Toronto, 1844 ***2910.35*** *p115*
Walsh, Stephen; America, 1685 ***1220.12*** *p835*
Walsh, Thomas; Colorado, 1884 ***1029.59*** *p92*
Walsh, Thomas 47; Ontario, 1871 ***1823.21*** *p380*
Walsh, Tim; Louisiana, 1874 ***4981.45*** *p297*
Walsh, William; New Jersey, 1777 ***8529.30*** *p7*
Walsh, William A.; North Carolina, 1839 ***1088.45*** *p36*
Walsh, Wm 32; St. Johns, N.F., 1811 ***1053.20*** *p20*
Walsham, Robert; America, 1742 ***1220.12*** *p835*
Walsingham, Benjamin; America, 1775 ***1220.12*** *p835*

Walsingham, John; America, 1775 ***1220.12*** *p835*
Walsom, Isaac; America, 1724 ***1220.12*** *p836*
Walsom, Thomas; America, 1774 ***1220.12*** *p836*
Walstad, Hans Jacobsen; Colorado, 1862-1894 ***1029.59*** *p92*
Walstead, Edw Jacobson; Colorado, 1873 ***1029.59*** *p92*
Walstrom, Charles; Iowa, 1893 ***1211.15*** *p20*
Walstrom, M.; Iowa, 1885 ***1211.15*** *p20*
Walte, Ernst Friedrich Wilhelm; America, 1840 ***7420.1*** *p21*
Waltemate, Mr.; America, 1858 ***7420.1*** *p182*
With wife
*Son:*Wilhelm
*Daughter:*Philippine
Waltemate, Ludwig; America, 1854 ***7420.1*** *p132*
Waltemate, Philippine *SEE* Waltemate, Mr.
Waltemate, Wilhelm *SEE* Waltemate, Mr.
Waltemathe, Carl Heinrich August; America, 1880 ***7420.1*** *p318*
Waltemathe, Christian Ludwig; America, 1843 ***7420.1*** *p30*
With son 2
With 3 daughters
With daughter 9
With daughter 18
Waltemathe, Heinrich Ferdinand; America, 1870 ***7420.1*** *p288*
Walter, Adam; Ohio, 1809-1852 ***4511.35*** *p56*
Walter, Andreas; Nova Scotia, 1751 ***2526.42*** *p179*
*Wife:*Anna Elisabeth Marschall
*Son:*Johann Georg
Walter, Ann; America, 1752 ***1220.12*** *p836*
Walter, Anna Elisabeth Marschall *SEE* Walter, Andreas
Walter, Barbara 34; Kentucky, 1846 ***778.6*** *p340*
Walter, Blakley 14; Ontario, 1871 ***1823.17*** *p169*
Walter, Catha. 9; America, 1840 ***778.6*** *p340*
Walter, Catha. 31; America, 1840 ***778.6*** *p340*
Walter, Catherina 21; New Orleans, 1848 ***778.6*** *p340*
Walter, Catherine 8; America, 1846 ***778.6*** *p340*
Walter, Catherine 28; Louisiana, 1848 ***778.6*** *p340*
Walter, Charlotte 3 months; New York, NY, 1893 ***1883.7*** *p42*
Walter, Conrad 47; New York, NY, 1893 ***1883.7*** *p42*
Walter, Elizabeth; America, 1737 ***1220.12*** *p836*
Walter, Erhard 19; New York, NY, 1893 ***1883.7*** *p40*
Walter, Erhard 19; New York, NY, 1893 ***1883.7*** *p47*
Walter, Francis; New York, 1860 ***358.56*** *p148*
Walter, Francois 12; America, 1846 ***778.6*** *p340*
Walter, Franz; America, 1882 ***5475.1*** *p329*
Walter, Frederick 6 months; Kentucky, 1846 ***778.6*** *p340*
Walter, Georges 29; Louisiana, 1848 ***778.6*** *p340*
Walter, Hannah; America, 1766 ***1220.12*** *p836*
Walter, Heinrich 18 *SEE* Walter, Susanna Geidel
Walter, Henry 3; Kentucky, 1846 ***778.6*** *p340*
Walter, Henry; Ohio, 1809-1852 ***4511.35*** *p56*
Walter, Hy. 24; America, 1840 ***778.6*** *p340*
Walter, Jacob 18; New York, NY, 1893 ***1883.7*** *p42*
Walter, Jacob Antona; Ohio, 1809-1852 ***4511.35*** *p56*
Walter, James; Barbados, 1686 ***1220.12*** *p836*
Walter, Jean 18; America, 1847 ***778.6*** *p340*
Walter, Jean 19; America, 1747 ***778.6*** *p340*
Walter, Johann 33; Louisiana, 1848 ***778.6*** *p340*
Walter, Johann 9; New York, NY, 1893 ***1883.7*** *p42*
Walter, Johann Georg *SEE* Walter, Andreas
Walter, John; America, 1685 ***1220.12*** *p836*
Walter, John; America, 1731 ***1220.12*** *p836*
Walter, John; America, 1749 ***1220.12*** *p836*
Walter, John; Illinois, 1855 ***6079.1*** *p14*
Walter, John; Ohio, 1809-1852 ***4511.35*** *p56*
Walter, John George; New York, 1860 ***358.56*** *p149*
Walter, John J.; Ohio, 1809-1852 ***4511.35*** *p56*
Walter, John Joseph; Ohio, 1809-1852 ***4511.35*** *p56*
Walter, Joseph A.; New York, 1859 ***358.56*** *p99*
Walter, Julius; Louisiana, 1874-1875 ***4981.45*** *p130*
Walter, Kath. 54; America, 1857 ***5475.1*** *p550*
Walter, Katharina 1; New York, NY, 1893 ***1883.7*** *p42*
Walter, Katharina 43; New York, NY, 1893 ***1883.7*** *p42*
Walter, Konrad; America, 1854 ***2526.42*** *p133*
Walter, Konrad; America, 1868 ***2526.43*** *p215*
Walter, Konrad 9 *SEE* Walter, Konrad
Walter, Konrad 40; America, 1837 ***5475.1*** *p70*
*Wife:*Magdalena Becker 30
*Daughter:*Wilhelmina 8
*Son:*Konrad 9 months
*Son:*Ludwig 6
Walter, Leonard; Ohio, 1809-1852 ***4511.35*** *p56*
Walter, Lorenz 22; America, 1747 ***778.6*** *p340*
Walter, Louise 5; America, 1846 ***778.6*** *p340*
Walter, Louise 35; America, 1846 ***778.6*** *p340*
Walter, Louise 30; Missouri, 1845 ***778.6*** *p340*
Walter, Ludwig 6 *SEE* Walter, Konrad
Walter, M. 19; America, 1846 ***778.6*** *p340*
Walter, Magdalena Becker 30 *SEE* Walter, Konrad
Walter, Margaretha 11; New York, NY, 1893 ***1883.7*** *p42*
Walter, Margaretha 16; New York, NY, 1893 ***1883.7*** *p42*
Walter, Maria Katharina; America, 1865 ***5475.1*** *p30*
Walter, Marie 7; America, 1846 ***778.6*** *p340*
Walter, Mariona 29; New Orleans, 1848 ***778.6*** *p340*
Walter, Mary; America, 1728 ***1220.12*** *p836*
Walter, Mary; Virginia, 1726 ***1220.12*** *p836*
Walter, Michel 41; America, 1846 ***778.6*** *p340*
Walter, Michel 36; Kentucky, 1846 ***778.6*** *p340*
Walter, Nehemiah; Boston, 1679 ***1642*** *p12*
Walter, Nehemiah; Massachusetts, 1620-1775 ***1642*** *p138*
Walter, Nehemiah; Nova Scotia, 1684-1688 ***1642*** *p12*
Walter, Peter; Philadelphia, 1875 ***5475.1*** *p263*
Walter, Richard; America, 1767 ***1220.12*** *p836*
Walter, Samuel; Annapolis, MD, 1721 ***1220.12*** *p836*
Walter, Sandolin 22; Mississippi, 1847 ***778.6*** *p340*
Walter, Steven; Detroit, 1930 ***1640.60*** *p82*
Walter, Susanna 57; America, 1882 ***2526.43*** *p158*
*Son:*Heinrich 18
Walter, Theodor 37; America, 1882 ***5475.1*** *p456*
Walter, Thomas; America, 1685 ***1220.12*** *p836*
Walter, Thomas; America, 1750 ***1220.12*** *p836*
Walter, Thomas; America, 1751 ***1220.12*** *p836*
Walter, Thomas; Boston, 1679 ***1642*** *p11*
Walter, Thomas; Massachusetts, 1620-1775 ***1642*** *p138*
Walter, Wilhelmina 8 *SEE* Walter, Konrad
Walter, William; America, 1685 ***1220.12*** *p836*
Walter, Willibald N. B.; Washington, 1887 ***2770.40*** *p25*
Walter Family ; Massachusetts, 1620-1775 ***1642*** *p139*
Waltering, Joseph; North Carolina, 1841 ***1088.45*** *p36*
Walters, Ann; Barbados or Jamaica, 1697 ***1220.12*** *p836*
Walters, Charles John; Utah, 1840-1860 ***9228.50*** *p651*
Walters, David 61; Ontario, 1871 ***1823.21*** *p380*
Walters, Edward; Virginia, 1740 ***1220.12*** *p836*
Walters, Elizabeth; America, 1754 ***1220.12*** *p836*
Walters, Elizabeth; America, 1765 ***1220.12*** *p836*
Walters, Isaac; America, 1724 ***1220.12*** *p836*
Walters, James; America, 1734 ***1220.12*** *p836*
Walters, James 44; Ontario, 1871 ***1823.21*** *p380*
Walters, John; America, 1733 ***1220.12*** *p836*
Walters, John; America, 1766 ***1220.12*** *p836*
Walters, John; America, 1771 ***1220.12*** *p836*
Walters, John; America, 1773 ***1220.12*** *p836*
Walters, John *SEE* Walters, John
Walters, John; Ohio, 1838-1839 ***4022.20*** *p292*
*Wife:*Ursula
*Child:*John
*Child:*Margaret
*Child:*Mary
Walters, Joseph; Massachusetts, 1675-1676 ***1642*** *p128*
Walters, Margaret *SEE* Walters, John
Walters, Margaret; Potomac, 1731 ***1220.12*** *p836*
Walters, Martha; Barbados or Jamaica, 1692 ***1220.12*** *p836*
Walters, Mary *SEE* Walters, John
Walters, Mary Ann 51; Ontario, 1871 ***1823.21*** *p380*
Walters, Philip; Annapolis, MD, 1730 ***1220.12*** *p836*
Walters, Redfern; America, 1765 ***1220.12*** *p836*
Walters, Richard; America, 1733 ***1220.12*** *p836*
Walters, Thomas; Barbados, 1674 ***1220.12*** *p836*
Walters, Thomas; Maryland, 1674-1675 ***1236.25*** *p52*
Walters, Thomas 25; Ontario, 1871 ***1823.21*** *p380*
Walters, Ursula *SEE* Walters, John
Walters, Walter S. 66; Ontario, 1871 ***1823.21*** *p380*
Walters, William; America, 1800-1899 ***9228.50*** *p652*
Walters, William Henry; Utah, 1862 ***9228.50*** *p652*
Walterscheid, Frederick William; Illinois, 1855 ***6079.1*** *p14*
Waltersperger, Lorenz; Venezuela, 1843 ***3899.5*** *p541*
Waltersperger, Rosina; Venezuela, 1843 ***3899.5*** *p541*
Walterton, James; Annapolis, MD, 1725 ***1220.12*** *p836*
Walthemathe, Carl Christian Friedrich; America, 1866 ***7420.1*** *p251*
Walthemathe, Heinrich Wilhelm August; America, 1880 ***7420.1*** *p318*
Walther, Anna Margareta; America, 1856 ***2526.42*** *p100*
Walther, Anna Maria 3 *SEE* Walther, Kilian
Walther, Bernard; Washington, 1885 ***2770.40*** *p194*
Walther, Eva Maria; America, 1856 ***2526.42*** *p100*
Walther, Franz Wilhelm 17 *SEE* Walther, Friedrich Theodor
Walther, Frederick; Illinois, 1866 ***6079.1*** *p14*
Walther, Friedrich Theodor 50; America, 1857 ***2526.43*** *p184*
*Daughter:*Katharina 19
*Son:*Franz Wilhelm 17
Walther, Georg; America, 1893 ***2526.43*** *p201*
Walther, Georg 27; America, 1860 ***2526.43*** *p220*
With wife
With child 14 days
With child 2
Walther, Georg Jakob 24; America, 1854 ***2526.43*** *p220*
Walther, Hannchen; America, 1867 ***7919.3*** *p533*
Walther, Johann Jakob; Dayton, OH, 1882 ***2526.43*** *p201*
Walther, Johann Jakob; Dayton, OH, 1893 ***2526.43*** *p201*
Walther, Johann Michael; America, 1883 ***2526.42*** *p197*
Walther, Johannes; America, 1856 ***2526.42*** *p100*
Walther, Johannes 19 *SEE* Walther, Kilian
Walther, Katharina; America, 1842 ***2526.43*** *p199*
Walther, Katharina; America, 1856 ***2526.42*** *p100*
Walther, Katharina 19 *SEE* Walther, Friedrich Theodor
Walther, Katharina 21 *SEE* Walther, Kilian
Walther, Katharine; America, 1853 ***2526.43*** *p201*
Walther, Kilian 11 *SEE* Walther, Kilian
Walther, Kilian 46; America, 1856 ***2526.42*** *p100*
*Wife:*Maria Old 46
*Child:*Kilian 11
*Child:*Anna Maria 3
*Child:*Johannes 19
*Child:*Katharina 21
Walther, Leonhard; America, 1853 ***2526.43*** *p223*
Walther, Magdalena; America, 1853 ***2526.42*** *p100*
Walther, Maria Old 46 *SEE* Walther, Kilian
Walther, Maria Elisabeth; America, 1853 ***2526.43*** *p201*
Walther, Marie; America, 1853 ***2526.43*** *p201*
Walther, Michael; America, 1843 ***2526.42*** *p197*
With wife
With child 2
With child 11
With child 6
Walther, Sophie; America, 1853 ***2526.43*** *p201*
Walther, Wilhelm; America, 1852 ***2526.43*** *p201*
Walthew, Jane; America, 1752 ***1220.12*** *p836*
Walton, Alice; America, 1765 ***1220.12*** *p836*
Walton, Anne; Jamaica, 1665 ***1220.12*** *p836*
Walton, Charles; America, 1727 ***1220.12*** *p836*
Walton, Edward; Potomac, 1729 ***1220.12*** *p836*
Walton, Elizabeth; Barbados or Jamaica, 1691 ***1220.12*** *p836*
Walton, Elizabeth; Virginia, 1736 ***1220.12*** *p836*
Walton, Ellen 39; Ontario, 1871 ***1823.17*** *p169*
Walton, Esther; America, 1749 ***1220.12*** *p836*
Walton, George; America, 1755 ***1220.12*** *p836*
Walton, George 25; Ontario, 1871 ***1823.21*** *p380*
Walton, Henry 24; Ontario, 1871 ***1823.21*** *p380*
Walton, Henry 84; Ontario, 1871 ***1823.17*** *p169*
Walton, John A.; Washington, 1887 ***2770.40*** *p25*
Walton, Joseph; America, 1738 ***1220.12*** *p836*
Walton, Joseph; America, 1746 ***1220.12*** *p836*
Walton, Joseph; America, 1774 ***1220.12*** *p836*
Walton, Joseph S. 35; Ontario, 1871 ***1823.17*** *p169*
Walton, Margaret; America, 1767 ***1220.12*** *p836*
Walton, Mary; America, 1735 ***1220.12*** *p836*
Walton, Mary 71; Ontario, 1871 ***1823.21*** *p380*
Walton, Matthew; America, 1700 ***1220.12*** *p837*
Walton, Nicholas; America, 1673 ***1220.12*** *p837*
Walton, Nicholas 45; Ontario, 1871 ***1823.21*** *p380*
Walton, Roger; Annapolis, MD, 1722 ***1220.12*** *p837*
Walton, Samuel; America, 1753 ***1220.12*** *p837*
Walton, Sara; America, 1718 ***1220.12*** *p837*
Walton, Susannah; Virginia, 1741 ***1220.12*** *p837*
Walton, Thomas; America, 1723 ***1220.12*** *p837*
Walton, Thomas; America, 1742 ***1220.12*** *p837*
Walton, Thomas; America, 1766 ***1220.12*** *p837*
Walton, Thomas; Barbados, 1705 ***1220.12*** *p837*
Walton, Thomas; Canada, 1775 ***3036.5*** *p68*
Walton, William; America, 1627 ***1220.12*** *p837*
Walton, William 21; Ontario, 1871 ***1823.21*** *p380*
Walton, William 26; Ontario, 1871 ***1823.21*** *p380*
Waltz, Constantine; Ohio, 1809-1852 ***4511.35*** *p56*
Waltz, George; West Virginia, 1787 ***1132.30*** *p146*
Waltz, John 52; Ontario, 1871 ***1823.21*** *p380*
Waltz, John; Washington, 1889 ***2770.40*** *p81*
Waluga, Bartlomiej 35; New York, NY, 1920 ***930.50*** *p49*
Walund, Emanuel; St. Paul, MN, 1894 ***1865.50*** *p113*
Walz, Andreas 57; New York, NY, 1874 ***6954.7*** *p38*
Walz, Caroline 10; New York, NY, 1874 ***6954.7*** *p38*
Walz, Esther 67; New York, NY, 1880 ***5475.1*** *p14*
Walz, Friedrich 9 months; New York, NY, 1874 ***6954.7*** *p38*
Walz, Gottl. 18; New York, NY, 1886 ***8425.16*** *p33*
Walz, Leopold 7; New York, NY, 1874 ***6954.7*** *p38*
Walz, Louis 18; New Orleans, 1848 ***778.6*** *p340*
Walz, Louise 1 months; New York, NY, 1874 ***6954.7*** *p38*
Walz, Margarethe 46; New York, NY, 1874 ***6954.7*** *p38*
Walz, Marie 8; New York, NY, 1874 ***6954.7*** *p38*
Walz, Matilde; Wisconsin, 1892 ***6795.8*** *p32*
Walz, Sophie 9; New York, NY, 1874 ***6954.7*** *p38*
Walz, Theodore; New York, 1859 ***358.56*** *p99*
Walzauer, Heinrich; America, 1889 ***179.55*** *p19*
Walzberg, Carl Wilhelm; America, 1854 ***7420.1*** *p132*
Walzer, Carl 3; Missouri, 1848 ***778.6*** *p340*

Walzer, Elisabeth *SEE* Walzer, Elisabeth
Walzer, Elisabeth; Philadelphia, 1896 ***5475.1*** *p39*
*Daughter:*Elisabeth
*Son:*Ludwig
*Daughter:*Maria
Walzer, Eugene; Ohio, 1840-1897 ***8365.35*** *p18*
Walzer, Francois 7; Missouri, 1848 ***778.6*** *p340*
Walzer, Ludwig *SEE* Walzer, Elisabeth
Walzer, Maria *SEE* Walzer, Elisabeth
Walzer, Marie 4; Missouri, 1848 ***778.6*** *p340*
Walzer, Marie 36; Missouri, 1848 ***778.6*** *p340*
Walzer, Peter G.; Ohio, 1840-1897 ***8365.35*** *p18*
Walzinger, Wilhelmina; Philadelphia, 1876 ***8513.31*** *p298*
Wambaugh, Ebenezer 52; Indiana, 1848-1880 ***9076.20*** *p70*
Wamser, Konrad; America, 1847 ***2526.43*** *p189*
With wife
With child 6 months
Wamsley, John; Annapolis, MD, 1723 ***1220.12*** *p835*
Wananouricz, Constantin 34; New York, NY, 1920 ***930.50*** *p48*
Wandless, Thomas; America, 1773 ***1220.12*** *p837*
Wandon, Richard; America, 1744 ***1220.12*** *p837*
Wang, Joseph 30; America, 1845 ***778.6*** *p340*
Wanger, Angela Schwarz 42 *SEE* Wanger, Peter
Wanger, Anna *SEE* Wanger, Peter
Wanger, Johann *SEE* Wanger, Peter
Wanger, Margarethe *SEE* Wanger, Peter
Wanger, Mathias *SEE* Wanger, Peter
Wanger, Peter *SEE* Wanger, Peter
Wanger, Peter; Brazil, 1857 ***5475.1*** *p367*
*Wife:*Angela Schwarz
*Son:*Mathias
*Son:*Johann
*Daughter:*Anna
*Son:*Peter
*Daughter:*Theres
*Daughter:*Margarethe
Wanger, Theres *SEE* Wanger, Peter
Wangler, Lantolin 28; New Orleans, 1848 ***778.6*** *p341*
Waning, Joseph; Ohio, 1809-1852 ***4511.35*** *p56*
Waninger, Franz; Iowa, 1873 ***5475.1*** *p328*
Wanklin, Francis; Annapolis, MD, 1724 ***1220.12*** *p837*
Wanles, James 48; Ontario, 1871 ***1823.17*** *p169*
Wanless, Elizabeth; America, 1750 ***1220.12*** *p837*
Wanless, Margaret; America, 1765 ***1220.12*** *p837*
Wanless, Robert 26; Ontario, 1871 ***1823.17*** *p169*
Wanless, William 42; Ontario, 1871 ***1823.17*** *p169*
Wann, Richard; America, 1743 ***1220.12*** *p837*
Wannacott, Emanuel 46; Ontario, 1871 ***1823.21*** *p380*
Wanne, Elizabeth; Barbados or Jamaica, 1693 ***1220.12*** *p837*
Wannenmacher, Bernhard; America, 1881 ***5475.1*** *p221*
Wanner, Catherina 30; Port uncertain, 1847 ***778.6*** *p341*
Wanner, Wilhelm; America, 1700-1899 ***179.55*** *p19*
Wannop, James; America, 1764 ***1220.12*** *p837*
Wanow, Agnete 5; Portland, ME, 1906 ***970.38*** *p82*
Wanow, Anna 3; Portland, ME, 1906 ***970.38*** *p82*
Wanow, Helene 11; Portland, ME, 1906 ***970.38*** *p82*
Wanow, Helene 41; Portland, ME, 1906 ***970.38*** *p82*
Wanow, Justine 8; Portland, ME, 1906 ***970.38*** *p82*
Wanow, Martin 33; Portland, ME, 1906 ***970.38*** *p82*
Wanrong, Francois 17; America, 1847 ***778.6*** *p341*
Wans, Alice 26; Quebec, 1870 ***8364.32*** *p26*
Wanstreet Family ; West Virginia, 1850 ***1132.30*** *p147*
Wantz, Eva 22; America, 1846 ***778.6*** *p341*
Wanzlaff, Julius; New York, NY, 1891 ***3366.30*** *p70*
Wapshot, Jane; Maryland, 1674-1675 ***1236.25*** *p52*
Wapshott, James; America, 1774 ***1220.12*** *p837*
Wapshott, Jane; Barbados, 1674 ***1220.12*** *p837*
War, Betty; America, 1753 ***1220.12*** *p841*
Warbey, Edward; America, 1758 ***1220.12*** *p837*
Warburton, Edye; America, 1718 ***1220.12*** *p837*
Warburton, John; Barbados, 1664 ***1220.12*** *p837*
Warburton, Margaret; America, 1745 ***1220.12*** *p837*
Warburton, Mary; America, 1726 ***1220.12*** *p837*
Warburton, Thomas; America, 1767 ***1220.12*** *p837*
Warburton, William; America, 1765 ***1220.12*** *p837*
Warburton, William; America, 1772 ***1220.12*** *p837*
Warby, James; America, 1773 ***1220.12*** *p837*
Ward, Ann; America, 1741 ***1220.12*** *p837*
Ward, Ann; America, 1757 ***1220.12*** *p837*
Ward, Ann; America, 1760 ***1220.12*** *p837*
Ward, Ann; America, 1771 ***1220.12*** *p837*
Ward, Ann; Annapolis, MD, 1735 ***1220.12*** *p837*
Ward, Ann; Barbados, 1665 ***1220.12*** *p837*
Ward, Anna 17; Quebec, 1870 ***8364.32*** *p26*
Ward, Annie; Quebec, 1867 ***9228.50*** *p411*
Ward, Annie 12; Quebec, 1870 ***8364.32*** *p26*
Ward, Benjamin 65; Ontario, 1871 ***1823.21*** *p380*
Ward, Bernard; Toronto, 1844 ***2910.35*** *p115*
Ward, Bridget; America, 1673 ***1220.12*** *p837*
Ward, Catherine; America, 1722 ***1220.12*** *p837*
Ward, Catherine; America, 1752 ***1220.12*** *p837*
Ward, Catherine; Annapolis, MD, 1733 ***1220.12*** *p837*
Ward, Catherine 50; Ontario, 1871 ***1823.21*** *p380*
Ward, Celia; America, 1764 ***1220.12*** *p837*
Ward, Christopher; America, 1751 ***1220.12*** *p837*
Ward, D.; New Orleans, 1850 ***7242.30*** *p156*
Ward, Dorah 40; Ontario, 1871 ***1823.21*** *p380*
Ward, Dorothy; America, 1755 ***1220.12*** *p837*
Ward, Edmund; America, 1765 ***1220.12*** *p837*
Ward, Edward; America, 1755 ***1220.12*** *p837*
Ward, Edward; America, 1763 ***1220.12*** *p837*
Ward, Edward; America, 1765 ***1220.12*** *p838*
Ward, Edward; North Carolina, 1833 ***1088.45*** *p36*
Ward, Eli; Indiana, 1865 ***9076.20*** *p66*
Ward, Eli 31; Indiana, 1887-1888 ***9076.20*** *p71*
Ward, Elizabeth; America, 1740 ***1220.12*** *p838*
Ward, Elizabeth; America, 1749 ***1220.12*** *p838*
Ward, Elizabeth; America, 1755 ***1220.12*** *p838*
Ward, Elizabeth; America, 1756 ***1220.12*** *p838*
Ward, Elizabeth; America, 1771 ***1220.12*** *p838*
Ward, Elizabeth; Virginia, 1739 ***1220.12*** *p838*
Ward, Ellen 16; Quebec, 1870 ***8364.32*** *p26*
Ward, Esther; Maryland, 1726 ***1220.12*** *p838*
Ward, Francis; America, 1756 ***1220.12*** *p838*
Ward, Francis; America, 1765 ***1220.12*** *p838*
Ward, Francis; America, 1768 ***1220.12*** *p838*
Ward, Francis 39; Ontario, 1871 ***1823.17*** *p169*
Ward, Frank; Louisiana, 1874-1875 ***4981.45*** *p130*
Ward, Frank; Louisiana, 1874 ***4981.45*** *p134*
Ward, George; America, 1728 ***1220.12*** *p838*
Ward, George; America, 1752 ***1220.12*** *p838*
Ward, George; America, 1765 ***1220.12*** *p838*
Ward, George 28; Indiana, 1887-1888 ***9076.20*** *p71*
Ward, George 40; Indiana, 1881-1884 ***9076.20*** *p71*
Ward, George 65; Michigan, 1880 ***4491.42*** *p28*
Ward, George; New York, 1782 ***8529.30*** *p16*
Ward, George 34; Ontario, 1871 ***1823.17*** *p169*
Ward, Hannah 70; Ontario, 1871 ***1823.21*** *p381*
Ward, Henry; America, 1682 ***1220.12*** *p838*
Ward, Henry H. 44; Ontario, 1871 ***1823.21*** *p381*
Ward, Hugh; St. John, N.B., 1848 ***2978.15*** *p36*
Ward, Isaac; Barbados or Jamaica, 1687 ***1220.12*** *p838*
Ward, James; America, 1750 ***1220.12*** *p838*
Ward, James; America, 1763 ***1220.12*** *p838*
Ward, James; America, 1771 ***1220.12*** *p838*
Ward, James 29; Ontario, 1871 ***1823.21*** *p381*
Ward, James 30; Ontario, 1871 ***1823.21*** *p381*
Ward, James 50; Ontario, 1871 ***1823.21*** *p381*
Ward, James Wilber 57; Ontario, 1871 ***1823.17*** *p169*
Ward, Job; America, 1738 ***1220.12*** *p838*
Ward, John; America, 1731 ***1220.12*** *p838*
Ward, John; America, 1742 ***1220.12*** *p838*
Ward, John; America, 1744 ***1220.12*** *p838*
Ward, John; America, 1747 ***1220.12*** *p838*
Ward, John; America, 1748 ***1220.12*** *p838*
Ward, John; America, 1754 ***1220.12*** *p838*
Ward, John; America, 1755 ***1220.12*** *p838*
Ward, John; America, 1758 ***1220.12*** *p838*
Ward, John; America, 1759 ***1220.12*** *p838*
Ward, John; America, 1767 ***1220.12*** *p838*
Ward, John; America, 1768 ***1220.12*** *p838*
Ward, John; America, 1769 ***1220.12*** *p838*
Ward, John; America, 1770 ***1220.12*** *p838*
Ward, John; America, 1772 ***1220.12*** *p838*
Ward, John; America, 1773 ***1220.12*** *p838*
Ward, John; America, 1774 ***1220.12*** *p838*
Ward, John; Barbados, 1667 ***1220.12*** *p838*
Ward, John 30; Barbados, 1664 ***1220.12*** *p838*
Ward, John; Jamaica, 1665 ***1220.12*** *p838*
Ward, John; Maryland, 1725 ***1220.12*** *p838*
Ward, John; Maryland, 1729 ***1220.12*** *p838*
Ward, John; Maryland, 1741 ***1220.12*** *p838*
Ward, John; New Orleans, 1850 ***7242.30*** *p156*
Ward, John; New York, 1777 ***8529.30*** *p5A*
Ward, John 44; Ontario, 1871 ***1823.21*** *p381*
Ward, John 55; Ontario, 1871 ***1823.21*** *p381*
Ward, John 63; Ontario, 1871 ***1823.21*** *p381*
Ward, John 70; Ontario, 1871 ***1823.21*** *p381*
Ward, John 72; Ontario, 1871 ***1823.21*** *p381*
Ward, John 80; Ontario, 1871 ***1823.21*** *p381*
Ward, John; St. John, N.B., 1847 ***2978.15*** *p37*
Ward, John; Virginia, 1727 ***1220.12*** *p838*
Ward, John Moor; America, 1770 ***1220.12*** *p838*
Ward, Joseph; America, 1681 ***1220.12*** *p838*
Ward, Joseph; America, 1730 ***1220.12*** *p839*
Ward, Joseph; America, 1743 ***1220.12*** *p839*
Ward, Joseph; America, 1769 ***1220.12*** *p839*
Ward, Joseph; America, 1771 ***1220.12*** *p839*
Ward, Joseph; America, 1775 ***1220.12*** *p839*
Ward, Joseph; Illinois, 1855 ***6079.1*** *p14*
Ward, Joseph P. 23; Ontario, 1871 ***1823.21*** *p381*
Ward, Katherine; America, 1662 ***1220.12*** *p837*
Ward, L.; New Orleans, 1850 ***7242.30*** *p156*
Ward, L. H.; Montreal, 1922 ***4514.4*** *p32*
Ward, Luke; America, 1747 ***1220.12*** *p839*
Ward, Margaret; America, 1773 ***1220.12*** *p839*
Ward, Mary; America, 1759 ***1220.12*** *p839*
Ward, Mary; America, 1765 ***1220.12*** *p839*
Ward, Mary; America, 1769 ***1220.12*** *p839*
Ward, Mary; America, 1770 ***1220.12*** *p839*
Ward, Mary; Annapolis, MD, 1726 ***1220.12*** *p839*
Ward, Mary; Barbados or Jamaica, 1699 ***1220.12*** *p839*
Ward, Mary; Barbados or Jamaica, 1702 ***1220.12*** *p839*
Ward, Mary 43; Ontario, 1871 ***1823.21*** *p381*
Ward, Mary; Virginia, 1738 ***1220.12*** *p839*
Ward, Mary B. 62; Michigan, 1880 ***4491.42*** *p28*
Ward, Mathew; Rappahannock, VA, 1729 ***1220.12*** *p839*
Ward, Michael 50; Ontario, 1871 ***1823.21*** *p381*
Ward, Michael; Virginia, 1730 ***1220.12*** *p839*
Ward, N.; New Orleans, 1850 ***7242.30*** *p156*
Ward, Nathan 45; Ontario, 1871 ***1823.17*** *p170*
Ward, Neil; St. John, N.B., 1847 ***2978.15*** *p37*
Ward, Pat.; Toronto, 1844 ***2910.35*** *p112*
Ward, Patrick; America, 1742 ***1220.12*** *p839*
Ward, Patrick; America, 1775 ***1220.12*** *p839*
Ward, Patrick; Toronto, 1844 ***2910.35*** *p113*
Ward, Peter 53; Ontario, 1871 ***1823.21*** *p381*
Ward, Richard; America, 1722 ***1220.12*** *p839*
Ward, Richard; America, 1760 ***1220.12*** *p839*
Ward, Richard 22; Maryland, 1724 ***1220.12*** *p839*
Ward, Robert; America, 1721 ***1220.12*** *p839*
Ward, Robert; America, 1749 ***1220.12*** *p839*
Ward, Robert; America, 1764 ***1220.12*** *p839*
Ward, Robert; New York, 1776 ***8529.30*** *p5A*
Ward, Samson 88; Ontario, 1871 ***1823.17*** *p170*
Ward, Samuel; America, 1757 ***1220.12*** *p839*
Ward, Samuel; America, 1774 ***1220.12*** *p839*
Ward, Samuel; America, 1775 ***1220.12*** *p839*
Ward, Samuel 59; Ontario, 1871 ***1823.17*** *p170*
Ward, Samuel; Virginia, 1751 ***1220.12*** *p839*
Ward, Sara; Annapolis, MD, 1720 ***1220.12*** *p839*
Ward, Sara; Charles Town, SC, 1719 ***1220.12*** *p839*
Ward, Sarah; America, 1755 ***1220.12*** *p839*
Ward, Tho; Colorado, 1871 ***1029.59*** *p93*
Ward, Thomas; America, 1739 ***1220.12*** *p839*
Ward, Thomas; America, 1767 ***1220.12*** *p839*
Ward, Thomas; America, 1770 ***1220.12*** *p839*
Ward, Thomas; America, 1771 ***1220.12*** *p839*
Ward, Thomas; America, 1772 ***1220.12*** *p840*
Ward, Thomas; America, 1775 ***1220.12*** *p840*
Ward, Thomas; Barbados, 1665 ***1220.12*** *p839*
Ward, Thomas; Barbados, 1670 ***1220.12*** *p839*
Ward, Thomas; Barbados or Jamaica, 1688 ***1220.12*** *p839*
Ward, Thomas; Colorado, 1871 ***1029.59*** *p93*
Ward, Thomas; Colorado, 1903 ***1029.59*** *p93*
Ward, Thomas; Maryland, 1720 ***1220.12*** *p839*
Ward, Thomas; Maryland or Virginia, 1731 ***1220.12*** *p839*
Ward, Thomas 36; Ontario, 1871 ***1823.21*** *p381*
Ward, Thomas 40; Ontario, 1871 ***1823.21*** *p381*
Ward, Thomas 17; Quebec, 1870 ***8364.32*** *p26*
Ward, William; America, 1747 ***1220.12*** *p840*
Ward, William; America, 1760 ***1220.12*** *p840*
Ward, William; America, 1763 ***1220.12*** *p840*
Ward, William; America, 1766 ***1220.12*** *p840*
Ward, William; America, 1768 ***1220.12*** *p840*
Ward, William; America, 1769 ***1220.12*** *p840*
Ward, William; America, 1772 ***1220.12*** *p840*
Ward, William; America, 1774 ***1220.12*** *p840*
Ward, William; Annapolis, MD, 1726 ***1220.12*** *p840*
Ward, William; Barbados, 1669 ***1220.12*** *p840*
Ward, William; Barbados, 1671 ***1220.12*** *p840*
Ward, William; Barbados, 1686 ***1220.12*** *p840*
Ward, William; Barbados or Jamaica, 1705 ***1220.12*** *p840*
Ward, William; Died enroute, 1718 ***1220.12*** *p840*
Ward, William; Illinois, 1856 ***6079.1*** *p14*
Ward, William; Maryland, 1722 ***1220.12*** *p840*
Ward, William; Ohio, 1855 ***3580.20*** *p33*
Ward, William; Ohio, 1855 ***6020.12*** *p23*
Ward, William 33; Ontario, 1871 ***1823.17*** *p170*
Ward, William 47; Ontario, 1871 ***1823.21*** *p381*
Ward, William 60; Ontario, 1871 ***1823.21*** *p381*
Ward, William 70; Ontario, 1871 ***1823.21*** *p381*
Ward, William; Potomac, 1729 ***1220.12*** *p840*
Ward, William; Rappahannock, VA, 1729 ***1220.12*** *p840*
Warde, John; Maryland, 1674-1675 ***1236.25*** *p51*
Warde, Robert; Barbados, 1672 ***1220.12*** *p839*
Wardell, Hannah; America, 1775 ***1220.12*** *p840*
Wardell, John; New York, 1782 ***8529.30*** *p16*
Wardell, Leonard; America, 1774 ***1220.12*** *p840*
Wardell, Richard, Sr.; America, 1775 ***1220.12*** *p840*
Wardell, William Wallace; Washington, 1887 ***2770.40*** *p25*
Warden, Albin; Cleveland, OH, 1901-1904 ***9722.10*** *p128*
Warden, Arthur; America, 1775 ***1220.12*** *p840*

Warden, Edwin; Cleveland, OH, 1900-1903 ***9722.10*** *p128*
Warden, Elizabeth; America, 1770 ***1220.12*** *p840*
Warden, James; America, 1769 ***1220.12*** *p840*
Warden, Jane 18; Ontario, 1871 ***1823.21*** *p381*
Warden, Richard Morse; America, 1763 ***1220.12*** *p840*
Warden, Thomas; Died enroute, 1725 ***1220.12*** *p840*
Warden, William; America, 1746 ***1220.12*** *p840*
Warden, William; America, 1763 ***1220.12*** *p840*
Wardenbaugh, Charles; Ohio, 1809-1852 ***4511.35*** *p56*
Wardenburg, Charles; Ohio, 1809-1852 ***4511.35*** *p56*
Wardenhoff, Anthony; Florida, 1845 ***8481.1*** *p18*
Wardens, James; America, 1772 ***1220.12*** *p840*
Warder, Henry; Marston's Wharf, 1782 ***8529.30*** *p16*
Warder, Mark; America, 1772 ***1220.12*** *p840*
Warder, Willoughby; America, 1741 ***1220.12*** *p840*
Warder, Wm; Virginia, 1652 ***6254.4*** *p243*
Wardibe, John 37; Ontario, 1871 ***1823.17*** *p170*
Wardin, John; America, 1769 ***1220.12*** *p840*
Wardle, Hannah; America, 1775 ***1220.12*** *p840*
Wardle, Richard, Sr.; America, 1775 ***1220.12*** *p840*
Wardle, William; America, 1684 ***1220.12*** *p840*
Wardle, William 56; Ontario, 1871 ***1823.21*** *p381*
Wardley, Francis; America, 1760 ***1220.12*** *p840*
Wardley, John; America, 1770 ***1220.12*** *p840*
Wardlow, William; Maryland, 1735 ***1220.12*** *p840*
Wardrill, Francis; America, 1764 ***1220.12*** *p840*
Wardsell, Mos; Virginia, 1652 ***6254.4*** *p243*
Ware, Agnes; Maryland, 1736 ***1220.12*** *p840*
Ware, Edward; America, 1757 ***1220.12*** *p840*
Ware, Ellen; Maryland, 1672 ***1236.25*** *p47*
Ware, James; America, 1742 ***1220.12*** *p840*
Ware, John; America, 1756 ***1220.12*** *p840*
Ware, L.; New Orleans, 1850 ***7242.30*** *p156*
Ware, Margaret; America, 1759 ***1220.12*** *p845*
Ware, P.; New Orleans, 1850 ***7242.30*** *p156*
Ware, Robert; America, 1768 ***1220.12*** *p840*
Ware, Susanna; America, 1722 ***1220.12*** *p841*
Ware, Thomas; Virginia, 1750 ***1220.12*** *p841*
Ware, William; America, 1713 ***1220.12*** *p841*
Ware, William; Annapolis, MD, 1730 ***1220.12*** *p841*
Wareham, William; America, 1764 ***1220.12*** *p841*
Wareing, John; America, 1757 ***1220.12*** *p841*
Wareing, William; America, 1703 ***1220.12*** *p841*
Warffs, Pierre 54; America, 1841 ***778.6*** *p341*
Warfield, John; Barbados, 1677 ***1220.12*** *p841*
Warg, August; Michigan, 1872 ***9722.10*** *p128*
Wargowsky, Julius Erdman; Wisconsin, 1892 ***6795.8*** *p153*
Wargula, Anthony; Wisconsin, 1903 ***6795.8*** *p208*
Wargula, Francis; Wisconsin, 1885 ***6795.8*** *p45*
Warham, John; Massachusetts, 1630 ***117.5*** *p153*
With wife
*Son:*Samuel
Warham, Samuel *SEE* Warham, John
Warhtel, Martin 55; America, 1847 ***778.6*** *p341*
Waring, Ann; America, 1742 ***1220.12*** *p841*
Waring, Ann; America, 1748 ***1220.12*** *p841*
Waring, Charles 42; Ontario, 1871 ***1823.21*** *p381*
Waring, Edward 68; Ontario, 1871 ***1823.21*** *p381*
Waring, Kingston 40; Ontario, 1871 ***1823.21*** *p381*
Wark, John 65; Ontario, 1871 ***1823.21*** *p381*
Warken, Barbara *SEE* Warken, Johann
Warken, Barbara Schmitt *SEE* Warken, Johann
Warken, Johann; Brazil, 1879 ***5475.1*** *p390*
*Wife:*Barbara Schmitt
*Son:*Josef
*Daughter:*Barbara
*Son:*Peter
Warken, Josef *SEE* Warken, Johann
Warken, Michel; Brazil, 1880 ***5475.1*** *p444*
Warken, Nikolaus; America, 1882 ***5475.1*** *p175*
Warken, Peter; America, 1882 ***5475.1*** *p445*
Warken, Peter *SEE* Warken, Johann
Warley, Francis; Ohio, 1809-1852 ***4511.35*** *p56*
Warley, Henry; Ohio, 1809-1852 ***4511.35*** *p56*
Warling, Nicholas; Ohio, 1809-1852 ***4511.35*** *p56*
Warlinger, Carl 22; New York, NY, 1885 ***8425.16*** *p33*
Warlinger, Casimir 24; New York, NY, 1885 ***8425.16*** *p33*
Warlinger, Cathr. 22; New York, NY, 1885 ***8425.16*** *p33*
Warlot, Charles 23; Ohio, 1847 ***778.6*** *p341*
Warman, Margaret; America, 1728 ***1220.12*** *p841*
Warman, Thomas; Died enroute, 1718 ***1220.12*** *p841*
Warmark, C. A.; Valparaiso, Chile, 1850 ***1192.4*** *p50*
Warmbach, Doris; New York, 1860 ***358.56*** *p150*
Warminger, James; Annapolis, MD, 1722 ***1220.12*** *p841*
Warmoll, Charles; Toronto, 1844 ***2910.35*** *p114*
Warmsley, Mathew 27; Ontario, 1871 ***1823.21*** *p381*
Warn, Richard; America, 1752 ***1220.12*** *p841*
Warncke, Marie Adelheid; Illinois, 1930 ***121.35*** *p101*
Warne, Caroline 13; Quebec, 1870 ***8364.32*** *p26*
Warne, James; America, 1750 ***1220.12*** *p841*
Warne, John; America, 1753 ***1220.12*** *p841*
Warne, Samuel; Colorado, 1894 ***1029.59*** *p93*
Warnecke, Heinrich Wilhelm; America, 1862 ***7420.1*** *p216*
Warnecke, Johann Friedrich August; America, 1862 ***7420.1*** *p216*
Warnecke, Johann Friedrich Christian; America, 1866 ***7420.1*** *p251*
Warnecke, Johann Heinrich; America, 1866 ***7420.1*** *p251*
Warnecke, Johann Heinrich Conrad; America, 1867 ***7420.1*** *p266*
Warnecke, Johann Otto; America, 1866 ***7420.1*** *p251*
Warnecke, Sophie; America, 1857 ***7420.1*** *p174*
Warnemunde, John; New York, 1860 ***358.56*** *p4*
Warner, Daniel; America, 1753 ***1220.12*** *p841*
Warner, Daniel; Rappahannock, VA, 1729 ***1220.12*** *p841*
Warner, Edmund; America, 1773 ***1220.12*** *p841*
Warner, Edward; America, 1728 ***1220.12*** *p841*
Warner, Elizabeth; America, 1682 ***1220.12*** *p841*
Warner, Elizabeth; America, 1770 ***1220.12*** *p841*
Warner, Elizabeth; Annapolis, MD, 1725 ***1220.12*** *p841*
Warner, Henry 36; Ontario, 1871 ***1823.21*** *p381*
Warner, John; America, 1752 ***1220.12*** *p841*
Warner, John; America, 1753 ***1220.12*** *p841*
Warner, John; America, 1761 ***1220.12*** *p841*
Warner, John; America, 1772 ***1220.12*** *p841*
Warner, Joseph; America, 1687 ***1220.12*** *p841*
Warner, Joseph; Barbados, 1679 ***1220.12*** *p841*
Warner, Mary; Maryland, 1672 ***1236.25*** *p46*
Warner, Michael; America, 1755 ***1220.12*** *p841*
Warner, Paul; Illinois, 1858 ***6079.1*** *p14*
Warner, Peter; Washington, 1888 ***2770.40*** *p26*
Warner, Richard; America, 1746 ***1220.12*** *p841*
Warner, Richard; Barbados, 1663 ***1220.12*** *p841*
Warner, Seraphim; Ohio, 1809-1852 ***4511.35*** *p57*
Warner, Simon; America, 1722 ***1220.12*** *p841*
Warner, Stephen; Barbados, 1663 ***1220.12*** *p841*
Warner, Stephen; Ohio, 1809-1852 ***4511.35*** *p57*
Warner, Thomas; America, 1754 ***1220.12*** *p841*
Warner, Thomas; America, 1767 ***1220.12*** *p841*
Warner, Thomas 45; Indiana, 1846-1880 ***9076.20*** *p69*
Warner, Thomas 50; Ontario, 1871 ***1823.21*** *p381*
Warner, William; America, 1737 ***1220.12*** *p841*
Warner, William; America, 1749 ***1220.12*** *p841*
Warner, William; America, 1750 ***1220.12*** *p841*
Warner, William; America, 1756 ***1220.12*** *p841*
Warner, William; America, 1768 ***1220.12*** *p841*
Warner, William 58; Ontario, 1871 ***1823.21*** *p382*
Warner, William; Virginia, 1731 ***1220.12*** *p841*
Warner, Zavier; Ohio, 1809-1852 ***4511.35*** *p57*
Warnham, Joseph 45; Ontario, 1871 ***1823.21*** *p382*
Warnholz, Elise 21; Halifax, N.S., 1902 ***1860.4*** *p41*
Warnholz, Emma 17; Halifax, N.S., 1902 ***1860.4*** *p41*
Warnholz, Hanna 9; Halifax, N.S., 1902 ***1860.4*** *p41*
Warnholz, Hermann 19; Halifax, N.S., 1902 ***1860.4*** *p41*
Warnholz, Johann 11; Halifax, N.S., 1902 ***1860.4*** *p41*
Warnholz, Julius 6; Halifax, N.S., 1902 ***1860.4*** *p41*
Warnholz, Julius 50; Halifax, N.S., 1902 ***1860.4*** *p41*
Warnholz, Marie 22; Halifax, N.S., 1902 ***1860.4*** *p41*
Warnholz, Marie 48; Halifax, N.S., 1902 ***1860.4*** *p41*
Warnholz, Markus 4; Halifax, N.S., 1902 ***1860.4*** *p41*
Warnholz, Martha 18; Halifax, N.S., 1902 ***1860.4*** *p41*
Warnicke, Frederick Cheistof; Wisconsin, 1884 ***6795.8*** *p103*
Warnke, Emil Robert; Wisconsin, 1887 ***6795.8*** *p119*
Warnke, Johann Gottlieb; Wisconsin, 1858 ***6795.8*** *p42*
Warnke, Julia; Wisconsin, 1890 ***6795.8*** *p42*
Warnke, Julia; Wisconsin, 1890 ***6795.8*** *p68*
Warnke, Maria Wilhelmine; Wisconsin, 1885 ***6795.8*** *p119*
Warnke, Wilhelm; Wisconsin, 1875 ***6795.8*** *p28*
Warnloff, Otto; Wisconsin, 1880-1886 ***1865.50*** *p114*
Warno, Rachel 27; New York, NY, 1894 ***6512.1*** *p232*
Warnock, Barbara 52; Ontario, 1871 ***1823.17*** *p170*
Warnock, John 18; St. John, N.B., 1834 ***6469.7*** *p5*
Warnock, Samuel; South Carolina, 1850 ***6155.4*** *p19*
Warns, Peter; Wisconsin, 1869 ***6795.8*** *p103*
Warnum, John; Barbados, 1669 ***1220.12*** *p841*
Warowy, Fedor 24; New York, NY, 1904 ***8355.1*** *p15*
Warowy, Maria 58; New York, NY, 1904 ***8355.1*** *p15*
Warowy, Piotr 26; New York, NY, 1904 ***8355.1*** *p15*
Warr, Ann; America, 1758 ***1220.12*** *p841*
Warr, Benjamin; Boston, 1776 ***8529.30*** *p5A*
Warr, Edith; America, 1753 ***1220.12*** *p842*
Warr, Jeremiah; America, 1752 ***1220.12*** *p842*
Warr, John; America, 1775 ***1220.12*** *p842*
Warran, William; Philadelphia, 1778 ***8529.30*** *p3*
Warrecker, William; America, 1770 ***1220.12*** *p842*
Warrel, James 35; Ontario, 1871 ***1823.21*** *p382*
Warren, Alexander 25; Ontario, 1871 ***1823.21*** *p382*
Warren, Alexander; Rappahannock, VA, 1726 ***1220.12*** *p842*
Warren, Ann; America, 1750 ***1220.12*** *p842*
Warren, Ann; America, 1767 ***1220.12*** *p842*
Warren, Anna R.; Indiana, 1867 ***9228.50*** *p652*
Warren, Anthony; America, 1738 ***1220.12*** *p842*
Warren, Birtle; America, 1773 ***1220.12*** *p842*
Warren, Catherine; Maryland or Virginia, 1733 ***1220.12*** *p842*
Warren, Charles 37; Ontario, 1871 ***1823.21*** *p382*
Warren, Charles; Virginia, 1765 ***1220.12*** *p842*
Warren, Duncan 60; Ontario, 1871 ***1823.17*** *p170*
Warren, F. E.; Iowa, 1881 ***1211.15*** *p20*
Warren, Francis; America, 1742 ***1220.12*** *p842*
Warren, Francis; Philadelphia, 1778 ***8529.30*** *p5A*
Warren, George; America, 1685 ***1220.12*** *p842*
Warren, George; America, 1741 ***1220.12*** *p842*
Warren, Jacob; America, 1763 ***1220.12*** *p842*
Warren, James; America, 1769 ***1220.12*** *p842*
Warren, James 50; Ontario, 1871 ***1823.21*** *p382*
Warren, James 17; Quebec, 1870 ***8364.32*** *p26*
Warren, Jane; America, 1734 ***1220.12*** *p842*
Warren, Jasper; Rappahannock, VA, 1741 ***1220.12*** *p842*
Warren, John; America, 1685 ***1220.12*** *p842*
Warren, John; America, 1725 ***1220.12*** *p842*
Warren, John; America, 1736 ***1220.12*** *p842*
Warren, John; America, 1739 ***1220.12*** *p842*
Warren, John; America, 1752 ***1220.12*** *p842*
Warren, John; America, 1754 ***1220.12*** *p842*
Warren, John; America, 1764 ***1220.12*** *p842*
Warren, John; America, 1774 ***1220.12*** *p842*
Warren, John 41; Ontario, 1871 ***1823.21*** *p382*
Warren, John 51; Ontario, 1871 ***1823.21*** *p382*
Warren, John; Virginia, 1774 ***1220.12*** *p842*
Warren, John R.; Ohio, 1843 ***2763.1*** *p22*
Warren, Joseph; America, 1685 ***1220.12*** *p842*
Warren, Joseph; America, 1753 ***1220.12*** *p842*
Warren, Joseph 76; Ontario, 1871 ***1823.21*** *p382*
Warren, Lawrence; Maryland, 1672 ***1236.25*** *p47*
Warren, Margaret; America, 1741 ***1220.12*** *p842*
Warren, Margaret; America, 1747 ***1220.12*** *p842*
Warren, Nicholas; America, 1685 ***1220.12*** *p842*
Warren, Peter; Maryland, 1725 ***1220.12*** *p842*
Warren, Rebea 35; Ontario, 1871 ***1823.17*** *p170*
Warren, Rebecka 34; Ontario, 1871 ***1823.17*** *p170*
Warren, Richard; North Carolina, 1837 ***1088.45*** *p36*
Warren, Richard; Plymouth, MA, 1620 ***1920.45*** *p5*
Warren, Robert; America, 1734 ***1220.12*** *p842*
Warren, Samuel; Colorado, 1883 ***1029.59*** *p93*
Warren, Samuel; Colorado, 1888 ***1029.59*** *p93*
Warren, Stephen; Ohio, 1809-1852 ***4511.35*** *p57*
Warren, Susanna; America, 1749 ***1220.12*** *p842*
Warren, Susanna; Maryland or Virginia, 1733 ***1220.12*** *p842*
Warren, Thomas; America, 1771 ***1220.12*** *p842*
Warren, Thomas; New York, 1778 ***8529.30*** *p5A*
Warren, Thomas 22; Ontario, 1871 ***1823.21*** *p382*
Warren, Thomas 23; Ontario, 1871 ***1823.21*** *p382*
Warren, Thomas; Virginia, 1743 ***1220.12*** *p842*
Warren, William; America, 1685 ***1220.12*** *p842*
Warren, William; America, 1741 ***1220.12*** *p842*
Warren, William; Colorado, 1862-1894 ***1029.59*** *p93*
Warren, William 45; Ontario, 1871 ***1823.21*** *p382*
Warren, William 50; Ontario, 1871 ***1823.17*** *p170*
Warren, William, Jr.; America, 1773 ***1220.12*** *p842*
Warret, Anthony Adrian; North Carolina, 1792-1862 ***1088.45*** *p36*
Warriker, Abraham; America, 1756 ***1220.12*** *p842*
Warrin, Catherine; Rappahannock, VA, 1741 ***1220.12*** *p842*
Warrin, Henry 70; Ontario, 1871 ***1823.21*** *p382*
Warriner, Edmund; America, 1770 ***1220.12*** *p842*
Warrington, Elizabeth; America, 1764 ***1220.12*** *p842*
Warrington, Mary; America, 1763 ***1220.12*** *p842*
Warrington, William; America, 1774 ***1220.12*** *p843*
Warrington, William; Barbados, 1693 ***1220.12*** *p843*
Warschburger, Nikolaus; America, 1881 ***5475.1*** *p456*
Warsdail, George; America, 1726 ***1220.12*** *p843*
Warsdale, Francis; America, 1772 ***1220.12*** *p843*
Warsinski, August; Wisconsin, 1901 ***6795.8*** *p197*
Warson, John; Ohio, 1809-1852 ***4511.35*** *p57*
Warsop, William; America, 1760 ***1220.12*** *p843*
Warsop, William; America, 1761 ***1220.12*** *p843*
Warsup, Samuel; America, 1753 ***1220.12*** *p843*
Wartell, Francis; America, 1753 ***1220.12*** *p843*
Warters, Thomas; Marston's Wharf, 1782 ***8529.30*** *p16*
Wartlin, Antonn 35; New Castle, DE, 1817-1818 ***90.20*** *p154*
Wartman, Michael 40; Ontario, 1871 ***1823.21*** *p382*
Warwick, Christopher; America, 1773 ***1220.12*** *p843*
Warwick, Edward; Rappahannock, VA, 1729 ***1220.12*** *p843*
Warwick, James; America, 1769 ***1220.12*** *p843*
Warwick, James 51; Ontario, 1871 ***1823.17*** *p170*
Warwick, John; Ohio, 1809-1852 ***4511.35*** *p57*
Warwick, Joseph; America, 1737 ***1220.12*** *p843*

Warwick, Richard; America, 1745 **1220.12** *p843*
Warwick, Richard; Maryland, 1744 **1220.12** *p843*
Warwick, Thomas; America, 1726 **1220.12** *p843*
Warwick, Thomas; America, 1767 **1220.12** *p843*
Warwick, William; America, 1751 **1220.12** *p843*
Wash, James; America, 1741 **1220.12** *p843*
Washfield, James; Annapolis, MD, 1723 **1220.12** *p843*
Washford, Mary; America, 1738 **1220.12** *p843*
Washing, Charles; North Carolina, 1842 **1088.45** *p36*
Washington, George 72; Ontario, 1871 **1823.21** *p382*
Washington, Henry 24; Ontario, 1871 **1823.21** *p382*
Washington, James 42; Ontario, 1871 **1823.17** *p170*
Washington, Mary 53; Ontario, 1871 **1823.21** *p382*
Washington, Philip; Barbados, 1695 **1220.12** *p843*
Washington, Richard; America, 1718 **1220.12** *p843*
Wasielewski, Edward; Detroit, 1929 **1640.55** *p114*
Wasielewski, Hermine Gindler *SEE* Wasielewski, Michael
Wasielewski, Michael; Philadelphia, 1856 **8513.31** *p431*
*Wife:*Hermine Gindler
Waskett, Ann; America, 1740 **1220.12** *p843*
Waskett, Mary, Jr.; America, 1759 **1220.12** *p843*
Waskett, William; America, 1759 **1220.12** *p843*
Wasmer, Meinrod; New York, 1872 **1132.30** *p150*
Wasmuth, Wilhelm; Colorado, 1888 **5475.1** *p174*
Wasner, . . .; West Virginia, 1865-1879 **1132.30** *p150*
Wasner, Seraphim; Ohio, 1809-1852 **4511.35** *p57*
Wasp, Jonathan 65; Ontario, 1871 **1823.21** *p382*
Wass, George; America, 1736 **1220.12** *p843*
Wass, Samuel; Ohio, 1809-1852 **4511.35** *p57*
Wassaerzieher, Edward; Illinois, 1854 **6079.1** *p14*
Wassenzieher, Otto; Illinois, 1858 **6079.1** *p14*
Wasserau, Jacob 40; America, 1843 **778.6** *p341*
Wassereau, Nicolaus 36; America, 1843 **778.6** *p341*
Wasserman, Mollie; Detroit, 1929-1930 **6214.5** *p67*
Wassermeier, Charlotte; America, 1882 **7420.1** *p333*
Wassermeier, Marie; America, 1884 **7420.1** *p346*
Wassermeyer, Charlotte; New York, NY, 1906 **7420.1** *p381*
*Sister:*Minna
Wassermeyer, Minna *SEE* Wassermeyer, Charlotte
Wassmann, Caroline; America, 1900 **7420.1** *p376*
Wassmer, Seraphim; Ohio, 1809-1852 **4511.35** *p57*
Wassmuth, Christian; America, 1872 **5475.1** *p171*
Wassnich, Anna Maria; America, 1837 **5475.1** *p468*
Wassnich, Barbara; Cincinnati, 1867 **5475.1** *p482*
Wassnich, Johann Josef; America, 1851 **5475.1** *p479*
Wassnich, Josef; America, 1840 **5475.1** *p470*
Wassnich, Nikolaus 17; America, 1849 **5475.1** *p478*
Wassnich, Wendel; America, 1847 **5475.1** *p474*
Wasson, Alexander; Ohio, 1809-1852 **4511.35** *p57*
Wasson, Robert; Ohio, 1809-1852 **4511.35** *p57*
Wassor, Marie 20; Mississippi, 1845 **778.6** *p341*
Wassum, Anna Margaretha 46 *SEE* Wassum, Leonhard
Wassum, Anton; America, 1858 **2526.42** *p100*
Wassum, Eva Elisabetha 12 *SEE* Wassum, Leonhard
Wassum, Johann Leonhard; America, 1752 **2526.43** *p135*
Wassum, Johann Michael; America, 1753 **2526.43** *p135*
Wassum, Johann Peter 22; America, 1882 **2526.43** *p135*
Wassum, Johannes; America, 1752 **2526.43** *p215*
Wassum, Johannes; America, 1858 **2526.42** *p100*
Wassum, Johannes; America, 1858 **2526.43** *p215*
Wassum, Johannes; America, 1881 **2526.43** *p215*
*Sister:*Margaretha
Wassum, Johannes; America, 1891 **2526.42** *p100*
Wassum, Konrad; America, 1752 **2526.43** *p215*
With wife & child
Wassum, Konrad; America, 1856 **2526.43** *p215*
Wassum, Leonhard 45; America, 1853 **2526.43** *p215*
*Wife:*Anna Margaretha 46
*Son:*Michael 23
*Daughter:*Eva Elisabetha 12
*Daughter:*Marie Katharina 11
Wassum, Margaretha *SEE* Wassum, Johannes
Wassum, Margaretha; America, 1881 **2526.43** *p215*
Wassum, Maria Wilhelmine; America, 1856 **2526.43** *p215*
Wassum, Marie Katharina 11 *SEE* Wassum, Leonhard
Wassum, Michael 23 *SEE* Wassum, Leonhard
Wassum, Philipp; Argentina, 1855 **2526.43** *p215*
With family of 5
Wassum, Wilhelm; America, 1881 **2526.43** *p215*
Wassuqe, Charles 45; Ontario, 1871 **1823.21** *p382*
Wast, Susannah; America, 1755 **1220.12** *p843*
Wastfield, John; Barbados, 1677 **1220.12** *p843*
Watcham, Henry; Ohio, 1809-1852 **4511.35** *p57*
Watcher, Richard 51; Ontario, 1871 **1823.17** *p170*
Watcher, William 37; Ontario, 1871 **1823.21** *p382*
Wate, Jonathan; Barbados, 1673 **1220.12** *p829*
Wateman, Edward; America, 1736 **1220.12** *p843*
Water, Thomas; America, 1675 **1220.12** *p843*
Watercombe, Thomas; Barbados or Jamaica, 1702 **1220.12** *p843*
Waterer, John, Jr.; America, 1735 **1220.12** *p843*
Waterfall, John; America, 1682 **1220.12** *p843*
Waterfall, Peter; America, 1682 **1220.12** *p843*
Waterherst, Francis; Ohio, 1809-1852 **4511.35** *p57*
Waterhorst, Francis; Ohio, 1809-1852 **4511.35** *p57*
Waterhouse, Elizabeth; America, 1773 **1220.12** *p843*
Waterhouse, Henry 46; Ontario, 1871 **1823.17** *p170*
Waterhouse, Jerry; New York, NY, 1820 **3274.55** *p68*
Waterhouse, John; America, 1739 **1220.12** *p843*
Waterhouse, Martha 28; Ontario, 1871 **1823.21** *p382*
Waterhouse, Thomas 39; Ontario, 1871 **1823.21** *p382*
Waterhouse, Thomas; Virginia, 1723 **1220.12** *p843*
Wateridge, Nathaniel; Barbados, 1665 **1220.12** *p843*
Waterland, Edward 41; Ontario, 1871 **1823.21** *p382*
Waterland, Thomas; Barbados, 1665 **1220.12** *p843*
Waterman, Alfred 21; Ontario, 1871 **1823.21** *p382*
Waterman, Emily S. 38; Michigan, 1880 **4491.33** *p23*
Waterman, John; America, 1738 **1220.12** *p843*
Waterman, Laurence; America, 1713 **1220.12** *p843*
Waterman, Michael; America, 1763 **1220.12** *p843*
Waterman, William R. 24; Ontario, 1871 **1823.21** *p382*
Watermann, Mr.; America, 1852 **7420.1** *p99*
Watermann, Anna Marie Mathilde *SEE* Watermann, Karl Heinrich Christian
Watermann, August; America, 1893 **7420.1** *p370*
With family
Watermann, August Christian Ferdinand; America, 1867 **7420.1** *p266*
Watermann, Carl Friedrich Gottlieb *SEE* Watermann, Carl Hermann
Watermann, Carl Gottlieb; America, 1867 **7420.1** *p266*
Watermann, Carl Heinrich Wilhelm *SEE* Watermann, Friedrich Wilhelm
Watermann, Carl Hermann; America, 1862 **7420.1** *p216*
*Son:*Carl Friedrich Gottlieb
With wife & 3 daughters
Watermann, Caroline Friederike Charlotte *SEE* Watermann, Friedrich Wilhelm
Watermann, Caroline Louise Charlotte; America, 1866 **7420.1** *p251*
Watermann, Christian; America, 1870 **7420.1** *p288*
With wife & 2 daughters
Watermann, Christian; Port uncertain, 1891 **7420.1** *p364*
With family
Watermann, Christine Marie Luise; America, 1891 **7420.1** *p364*
Watermann, Engel Sophie Friederike Buthe *SEE* Watermann, Karl Heinrich Christian
Watermann, Engel Sophie Karol *SEE* Watermann, Karl Heinrich Christian
Watermann, Engel Wilh. Marie *SEE* Watermann, Karl Heinrich Christian
Watermann, Ernst Wilhelm; America, 1867 **7420.1** *p266*
Watermann, Friedrich; America, 1891 **7420.1** *p364*
Watermann, Friedrich Christian Ludwig; America, 1868 **7420.1** *p277*
Watermann, Friedrich Wilhelm; America, 1892 **7420.1** *p367*
*Wife:*Louise Charlotte Nagel
*Daughter:*Caroline Friederike Charlotte
*Son:*Carl Heinrich Wilhelm
*Daughter:*Wilhelmine Caroline Charlotte
Watermann, Heinrich Carl Wilhelm; America, 1866 **7420.1** *p251*
Watermann, Heinrich Friedr. Christian *SEE* Watermann, Karl Heinrich Christian
Watermann, Heinrich Friedrich Christian; America, 1866 **7420.1** *p245*
Watermann, Heinrich Friedrich Christian; America, 1866 **7420.1** *p251*
Watermann, Heinrich Friedrich Wilhelm; America, 1891 **7420.1** *p364*
Watermann, Heinrich Ludwig; America, 1882 **7420.1** *p333*
Watermann, Heinrich Wilhelm; America, 1867 **7420.1** *p266*
Watermann, Johann Carl Ludwig; America, 1868 **7420.1** *p278*
With family
Watermann, Karl Heinrich Christian; America, 1891 **7420.1** *p364*
*Wife:*Engel Sophie Friederike Buthe
*Daughter:*Engel Sophie Karol
*Daughter:*Anna Marie Mathilde
*Daughter:*Engel Wilh. Marie
*Daughter:*Sophie Wilhelmine
*Son:*Heinrich Friedr. Christian
Watermann, Louis; Port uncertain, 1861 **7420.1** *p209*
Watermann, Louise Charlotte Nagel *SEE* Watermann, Friedrich Wilhelm
Watermann, Ludwig Ferdinand; America, 1867 **7420.1** *p266*
Watermann, Sophie; America, 1857 **7420.1** *p174*
With son
Watermann, Sophie Wilhelmine *SEE* Watermann, Karl Heinrich Christian
Watermann, Sophie Wilhelmine Caroline; America, 1864 **7420.1** *p228*
Watermann, Wilhelmine Caroline Charlotte *SEE* Watermann, Friedrich Wilhelm
Watermann, Wilhelmine Juliane; America, 1867 **7420.1** *p266*
Waters, Abel; America, 1766 **1220.12** *p843*
Waters, Catherine; America, 1773 **1220.12** *p843*
Waters, Catherine; Potomac, 1731 **1220.12** *p843*
Waters, Denis 44; Ontario, 1871 **1823.17** *p170*
Waters, Donald 69; Ontario, 1871 **1823.21** *p382*
Waters, Elizabeth; America, 1756 **1220.12** *p844*
Waters, Holden; America, 1735 **1220.12** *p844*
Waters, James; America, 1721 **1220.12** *p844*
Waters, James; America, 1738 **1220.12** *p844*
Waters, James; America, 1755 **1220.12** *p844*
Waters, James 71; Ontario, 1871 **1823.21** *p382*
Waters, John; America, 1768 **1220.12** *p844*
Waters, John; America, 1772 **1220.12** *p844*
Waters, John; Barbados or Jamaica, 1698 **1220.12** *p844*
Waters, John 25; Ontario, 1871 **1823.21** *p382*
Waters, John 30; Ontario, 1871 **1823.21** *p382*
Waters, John 41; Ontario, 1871 **1823.21** *p382*
Waters, John; Virginia, 1739 **1220.12** *p844*
Waters, John, Jr.; America, 1735 **1220.12** *p844*
Waters, John W. 20; Ontario, 1871 **1823.21** *p382*
Waters, Joseph; America, 1742 **1220.12** *p844*
Waters, Joseph; America, 1768 **1220.12** *p844*
Waters, Leonard; America, 1765 **1220.12** *p844*
Waters, Margaret; Annapolis, MD, 1729 **1220.12** *p844*
Waters, Martha; America, 1751 **1220.12** *p844*
Waters, Mary; America, 1744 **1220.12** *p844*
Waters, Mary; Barbados or Jamaica, 1697 **1220.12** *p844*
Waters, Moses; America, 1769 **1220.12** *p844*
Waters, Phillip 66; Ontario, 1871 **1823.17** *p170*
Waters, Richard; America, 1747 **1220.12** *p844*
Waters, Sarah; America, 1764 **1220.12** *p844*
Waters, T.; Louisiana, 1874-1875 **4981.45** *p130*
Waters, Thomas; America, 1754 **1220.12** *p844*
Waters, Thomas; America, 1763 **1220.12** *p844*
Waters, Thomas; America, 1774 **1220.12** *p844*
Waters, Thomas; Marston's Wharf, 1782 **8529.30** *p16*
Waters, Thomas; Maryland or Virginia, 1738 **1220.12** *p844*
Waters, William; America, 1743 **1220.12** *p844*
Waters, William; America, 1761 **1220.12** *p844*
Waters, William; America, 1773 **1220.12** *p844*
Waters, William; New York, NY, 1776 **8529.30** *p3*
Waters, William 31; Ontario, 1871 **1823.21** *p382*
Wath, Thomas; Illinois, 1858-1861 **6020.5** *p133*
Watham, Thomas; Marston's Wharf, 1782 **8529.30** *p16*
Wathan, James; Marston's Wharf, 1781 **8529.30** *p16*
Wathan, Thomas; Marston's Wharf, 1782 **8529.30** *p16*
Wathen, Thomas; Marston's Wharf, 1782 **8529.30** *p16*
Watkin, James; America, 1752 **1220.12** *p844*
Watkins, Ann; America, 1756 **1220.12** *p844*
Watkins, Benjamin; America, 1770 **1220.12** *p844*
Watkins, Christian; America, 1740 **1220.12** *p844*
Watkins, Daniel; America, 1719 **1220.12** *p844*
Watkins, Edward; Philadelphia, 1777 **8529.30** *p7A*
Watkins, Elizabeth; America, 1758 **1220.12** *p844*
Watkins, Elizabeth; Potomac, 1729 **1220.12** *p844*
Watkins, Eustace; Virginia, 1732 **1220.12** *p844*
Watkins, George; America, 1727 **1220.12** *p844*
Watkins, Griffith; Annapolis, MD, 1725 **1220.12** *p844*
Watkins, Hannah; America, 1757 **1220.12** *p844*
Watkins, James; America, 1750 **1220.12** *p844*
Watkins, James; America, 1751 **1220.12** *p844*
Watkins, James; America, 1765 **1220.12** *p844*
Watkins, James; Barbados or Jamaica, 1684 **1220.12** *p844*
Watkins, Jane; America, 1745 **1220.12** *p844*
Watkins, Jane; Annapolis, MD, 1719 **1220.12** *p844*
Watkins, John; America, 1729 **1220.12** *p845*
Watkins, John; America, 1741 **1220.12** *p845*
Watkins, John; America, 1765 **1220.12** *p845*
Watkins, John; America, 1767 **1220.12** *p845*
Watkins, John; America, 1774 **1220.12** *p845*
Watkins, John; America, 1775 **1220.12** *p845*
Watkins, John; Annapolis, MD, 1724 **1220.12** *p844*
Watkins, John; Barbados, 1681 **1220.12** *p844*
Watkins, John; Maryland, 1725 **1220.12** *p845*
Watkins, John 30; Ontario, 1871 **1823.21** *p383*
Watkins, John; Salem, MA, 1640-1643 **1642** *p78*
Watkins, Joseph; America, 1769 **1220.12** *p845*
Watkins, Margaret; America, 1759 **1220.12** *p845*
Watkins, Marmaduke; America, 1752 **1220.12** *p845*
Watkins, Martha; America, 1765 **1220.12** *p845*
Watkins, Mary; America, 1758 **1220.12** *p873*

Watkins, Mary; America, 1764 ***1220.12*** *p845*
Watkins, Mary; America, 1766 ***1220.12*** *p845*
Watkins, Philip 21; Barbados, 1664 ***1220.12*** *p845*
Watkins, Richard; America, 1762 ***1220.12*** *p845*
Watkins, Richard; America, 1764 ***1220.12*** *p845*
Watkins, Samuel; America, 1759 ***1220.12*** *p845*
Watkins, Thomas; America, 1675 ***1220.12*** *p845*
Watkins, Thomas; America, 1752 ***1220.12*** *p845*
Watkins, Thomas; America, 1753 ***1220.12*** *p845*
Watkins, Thomas; America, 1754 ***1220.12*** *p845*
Watkins, Thomas; America, 1764 ***1220.12*** *p845*
Watkins, Thomas; America, 1768 ***1220.12*** *p845*
Watkins, Thomas; America, 1773 ***1220.12*** *p845*
Watkins, Thurstus; Virginia, 1732 ***1220.12*** *p845*
Watkins, Trevor; America, 1727 ***1220.12*** *p845*
Watkins, Walter; America, 1761 ***1220.12*** *p845*
Watkins, Walter; America, 1766 ***1220.12*** *p845*
Watkins, William; America, 1688 ***1220.12*** *p845*
Watkins, William; America, 1736 ***1220.12*** *p845*
Watkins, William; America, 1752 ***1220.12*** *p845*
Watkins, William; America, 1765 ***1220.12*** *p845*
Watkins, William; America, 1767 ***1220.12*** *p845*
Watkins, William; America, 1770 ***1220.12*** *p845*
Watkins, William; America, 1774 ***1220.12*** *p845*
Watkins, William 45; Ontario, 1871 ***1823.17*** *p170*
Watkins, William 57; Ontario, 1871 ***1823.21*** *p383*
Watkinson, Alice; America, 1766 ***1220.12*** *p845*
Watkinson, Elizabeth; America, 1719 ***1220.12*** *p845*
Watkinson, James; America, 1773 ***1220.12*** *p845*
Watling, John; America, 1742 ***1220.12*** *p845*
Watling, John; America, 1753 ***1220.12*** *p845*
Watman, Margaret 35; Ontario, 1871 ***1823.17*** *p170*
Watmore, James; America, 1740 ***1220.12*** *p845*
Watmore, James; America, 1758 ***1220.12*** *p845*
Watmore, R.; Quebec, 1870 ***8364.32*** *p26*
Watnall, John; America, 1732 ***1220.12*** *p845*
Watran, George 80; Ontario, 1871 ***1823.17*** *p170*
Watry, Nicholas; Ohio, 1809-1852 ***4511.35*** *p57*
Watshaholm, Henry; North Carolina, 1839 ***1088.45*** *p36*
Watson, A. W. 56; Ontario, 1871 ***1823.17*** *p170*
Watson, Alexander 43; Ontario, 1871 ***1823.17*** *p170*
Watson, Alexander 51; Ontario, 1871 ***1823.17*** *p170*
Watson, Andrew 48; Ontario, 1871 ***1823.21*** *p383*
Watson, Ann; America, 1746 ***1220.12*** *p845*
Watson, Ann; America, 1760 ***1220.12*** *p845*
Watson, Anna 80; Ontario, 1871 ***1823.17*** *p170*
Watson, Anthony; America, 1771 ***1220.12*** *p845*
Watson, Archibald 66; Ontario, 1871 ***1823.17*** *p170*
Watson, Arthur; Annapolis, MD, 1724 ***1220.12*** *p846*
Watson, Arthur 44; Ontario, 1871 ***1823.21*** *p383*
Watson, Charles 20; America, 1841 ***778.6*** *p341*
Watson, Christopher; America, 1767 ***1220.12*** *p846*
Watson, Daniel; America, 1743 ***1220.12*** *p846*
Watson, David 24; Ontario, 1871 ***1823.17*** *p170*
Watson, David 37; Ontario, 1871 ***1823.17*** *p170*
Watson, Ebenezer 53; Ontario, 1871 ***1823.17*** *p171*
Watson, Ebenezier P. 40; Ontario, 1871 ***1823.17*** *p171*
Watson, Edward; Barbados or Jamaica, 1683 ***1220.12*** *p846*
Watson, Elizabeth; America, 1740 ***1220.12*** *p846*
Watson, Elizabeth; America, 1750 ***1220.12*** *p846*
Watson, Elizabeth; Maryland, 1742 ***1220.12*** *p846*
Watson, Elizabeth 56; Ontario, 1871 ***1823.21*** *p383*
Watson, Esther; Virginia, 1732 ***1220.12*** *p846*
Watson, F.G. 16; Quebec, 1870 ***8364.32*** *p26*
Watson, F.H.; California, 1953 ***9228.50*** *p452*
Watson, Frances; Barbados, 1676 ***1220.12*** *p846*
Watson, Francis; America, 1665 ***1220.12*** *p846*
Watson, Francis; Canada, 1775 ***3036.5*** *p68*
Watson, Francis; Maryland or Virginia, 1738 ***1220.12*** *p846*
Watson, Franklin 40; Ontario, 1871 ***1823.17*** *p171*
Watson, Fred; Iowa, 1895 ***1211.15*** *p20*
Watson, George; America, 1762 ***1220.12*** *p846*
Watson, George; America, 1763 ***1220.12*** *p846*
Watson, George; America, 1766 ***1220.12*** *p846*
Watson, George; America, 1773 ***1220.12*** *p846*
Watson, George; Nevis or Jamaica, 1722 ***1220.12*** *p846*
Watson, George 24; Ontario, 1871 ***1823.17*** *p171*
Watson, George 57; Ontario, 1871 ***1823.21*** *p383*
Watson, H. H.; Montreal, 1922 ***4514.4*** *p32*
Watson, Hannah 54; Ontario, 1871 ***1823.21*** *p383*
Watson, Henry; Barbados, 1671 ***1220.12*** *p846*
Watson, Henry 36; Ontario, 1871 ***1823.17*** *p171*
Watson, Henry Drake; America, 1774 ***1220.12*** *p846*
Watson, Isaac; Virginia, 1670 ***1220.12*** *p846*
Watson, Isabella; America, 1763 ***1220.12*** *p846*
Watson, James; America, 1774 ***1220.12*** *p846*
Watson, James; America, 1775 ***1220.12*** *p846*
Watson, James 29; Ontario, 1871 ***1823.17*** *p171*
Watson, James 36; Ontario, 1871 ***1823.21*** *p383*
Watson, James 43; Ontario, 1871 ***1823.21*** *p383*
Watson, James 45; Ontario, 1871 ***1823.17*** *p171*
Watson, James 47; Ontario, 1871 ***1823.21*** *p383*
Watson, James 48; Ontario, 1871 ***1823.17*** *p171*
Watson, James 54; Ontario, 1871 ***1823.21*** *p383*
Watson, James; Philadelphia, 1777 ***8529.30*** *p3*
Watson, James; Washington, 1885 ***2770.40*** *p194*
Watson, James John 40; Ontario, 1871 ***1823.21*** *p383*
Watson, James William; America, 1771 ***1220.12*** *p846*
Watson, Jane; America, 1743 ***1220.12*** *p846*
Watson, Jane; America, 1747 ***1220.12*** *p846*
Watson, Jane; Died enroute, 1729 ***1220.12*** *p846*
Watson, Jane 52; Ontario, 1871 ***1823.21*** *p383*
Watson, Jennett; America, 1732 ***1220.12*** *p846*
Watson, Jo. 22; Virginia, 1635 ***1183.3*** *p30*
Watson, John; America, 1736 ***1220.12*** *p846*
Watson, John; America, 1738 ***1220.12*** *p846*
Watson, John; America, 1746 ***1220.12*** *p846*
Watson, John; America, 1751 ***1220.12*** *p846*
Watson, John; America, 1753 ***1220.12*** *p846*
Watson, John; America, 1754 ***1220.12*** *p846*
Watson, John; America, 1764 ***1220.12*** *p846*
Watson, John; America, 1767 ***1220.12*** *p846*
Watson, John; America, 1770 ***1220.12*** *p846*
Watson, John; Barbados, 1694 ***1220.12*** *p846*
Watson, John; Canada, 1774 ***3036.5*** *p41*
Watson, John 22; Ontario, 1871 ***1823.21*** *p383*
Watson, John 26; Ontario, 1871 ***1823.17*** *p171*
Watson, John 38; Ontario, 1871 ***1823.21*** *p383*
Watson, John 41; Ontario, 1871 ***1823.17*** *p171*
Watson, John 41; Ontario, 1871 ***1823.21*** *p383*
Watson, John 43; Ontario, 1871 ***1823.17*** *p171*
Watson, John 45; Ontario, 1871 ***1823.21*** *p383*
Watson, John 50; Ontario, 1871 ***1823.21*** *p383*
Watson, John 62; Ontario, 1871 ***1823.17*** *p171*
Watson, John 78; Ontario, 1871 ***1823.17*** *p171*
Watson, John B. 24; Ontario, 1871 ***1823.17*** *p171*
Watson, John J.; Ohio, 1873 ***3580.20*** *p33*
Watson, John J.; Ohio, 1873 ***6020.12*** *p23*
Watson, Joseph 27; Ontario, 1871 ***1823.21*** *p383*
Watson, Joseph 58; Ontario, 1871 ***1823.17*** *p171*
Watson, Joseph; Virginia, 1724 ***1220.12*** *p846*
Watson, Joshua; America, 1746 ***1220.12*** *p846*
Watson, Kate 40; Ontario, 1871 ***1823.17*** *p171*
Watson, Kerby; Illinois, 1834-1900 ***6020.5*** *p133*
Watson, Margaret; Barbados, 1673 ***1220.12*** *p846*
Watson, Margt.; Maryland, 1674 ***1236.25*** *p50*
Watson, Mary; America, 1748 ***1220.12*** *p846*
Watson, Mary; Annapolis, MD, 1731 ***1220.12*** *p846*
Watson, Mary; Annapolis, MD, 1733 ***1220.12*** *p846*
Watson, Mary 2; Ontario, 1871 ***1823.21*** *p383*
Watson, Mary; Potomac, 1731 ***1220.12*** *p846*
Watson, Mat; Washington, 1886 ***6015.10*** *p16*
Watson, Nathaniel; America, 1702 ***1220.12*** *p846*
Watson, Nicholas; America, 1751 ***1220.12*** *p847*
Watson, Noah 50; Ontario, 1871 ***1823.21*** *p383*
Watson, Noble 30; Ontario, 1871 ***1823.17*** *p171*
Watson, Rachael; America, 1732 ***1220.12*** *p847*
Watson, Ralph; Barbados or Jamaica, 1685 ***1220.12*** *p847*
Watson, Reuben 35; Ontario, 1871 ***1823.17*** *p171*
Watson, Richard; America, 1755 ***1220.12*** *p847*
Watson, Richard; America, 1773 ***1220.12*** *p847*
Watson, Richard; America, 1774 ***1220.12*** *p847*
Watson, Richard; Maryland or Virginia, 1733 ***1220.12*** *p847*
Watson, Richard; Virginia, 1732 ***1220.12*** *p847*
Watson, Ritchard 45; Ontario, 1871 ***1823.21*** *p383*
Watson, Robert; America, 1749 ***1220.12*** *p847*
Watson, Robert; America, 1770 ***1220.12*** *p847*
Watson, Robert; Virginia, 1723 ***1220.12*** *p847*
Watson, Sarah; America, 1718 ***1220.12*** *p847*
Watson, Sarah; America, 1752 ***1220.12*** *p847*
Watson, Thomas; America, 1758 ***1220.12*** *p847*
Watson, Thomas; America, 1763 ***1220.12*** *p847*
Watson, Thomas; America, 1769 ***1220.12*** *p847*
Watson, Thomas; America, 1773 ***1220.12*** *p847*
Watson, Thomas; Barbados, 1665 ***1220.12*** *p847*
Watson, Thomas; Jamaica, 1661 ***1220.12*** *p847*
Watson, Thomas; Maryland, 1723 ***1220.12*** *p847*
Watson, Thomas 26; Ontario, 1871 ***1823.21*** *p383*
Watson, Thomas 28; Ontario, 1871 ***1823.17*** *p171*
Watson, Thomas 43; Ontario, 1871 ***1823.21*** *p383*
Watson, Thomas; Virginia, 1732 ***1220.12*** *p847*
Watson, Thos J.; North Carolina, 1853 ***1088.45*** *p36*
Watson, W. H. 32; Ontario, 1871 ***1823.17*** *p171*
Watson, William; America, 1742 ***1220.12*** *p847*
Watson, William; America, 1749 ***1220.12*** *p847*
Watson, William; America, 1753 ***1220.12*** *p847*
Watson, William; America, 1763 ***1220.12*** *p847*
Watson, William; America, 1764 ***1220.12*** *p847*
Watson, William; Iowa, 1890 ***1211.15*** *p20*
Watson, William; Maryland, 1726 ***1220.12*** *p847*
Watson, William 21; Ontario, 1871 ***1823.17*** *p171*
Watson, William 32; Ontario, 1871 ***1823.21*** *p383*
Watson, William 36; Ontario, 1871 ***1823.21*** *p383*
Watson, William 38; Ontario, 1871 ***1823.17*** *p171*
Watson, William 38; Ontario, 1871 ***1823.17*** *p171*
Watson, William 42; Ontario, 1871 ***1823.21*** *p383*
Watson, William 73; Ontario, 1871 ***1823.17*** *p171*
Watson, William 74; Ontario, 1871 ***1823.17*** *p171*
Watson, William; Philadelphia, 1778 ***8529.30*** *p17*
Watson, William; Virginia, 1723 ***1220.12*** *p847*
Watson, Wm Henry; Louisiana, 1874-1875 ***4981.45*** *p130*
Watt, Adam 34; Ontario, 1871 ***1823.21*** *p383*
Watt, Hubert 19; Ohio, 1847 ***778.6*** *p341*
Watt, James 18; Quebec, 1870 ***8364.32*** *p26*
Watt, John; North Carolina, 1835 ***1088.45*** *p36*
Watt, Robert 65; Ontario, 1871 ***1823.21*** *p383*
Watt, Mrs. Thomas 55; Ontario, 1871 ***1823.17*** *p171*
Watt, William; America, 1767 ***1220.12*** *p847*
Watt, William 66; Ontario, 1871 ***1823.17*** *p171*
Wattam, John 42; Ontario, 1871 ***1823.21*** *p383*
Wattar, John; Potomac, 1729 ***1220.12*** *p847*
Wattay, Charles John Daniel; North Carolina, 1853 ***1088.45*** *p36*
Watter, John G. G.; North Carolina, 1852 ***1088.45*** *p36*
Watterman, Heeman 37; Ontario, 1871 ***1823.21*** *p383*
Watterman, Isaac 30; Ontario, 1871 ***1823.21*** *p383*
Watters, Charles; Iowa, 1888 ***1211.15*** *p20*
Watters, Fred; Iowa, 1890 ***1211.15*** *p20*
Watters, Hayden 48; Ontario, 1871 ***1823.21*** *p383*
Watters, Lawrence Felix; New York, 1821 ***471.10*** *p86*
Watters, Sarah 81; Ontario, 1871 ***1823.21*** *p383*
Watters, Thomas; Maryland, 1674-1675 ***1236.25*** *p52*
Wattie, John 46; Ontario, 1871 ***1823.17*** *p171*
Wattiers, J.C. 26; New York, NY, 1856 ***1766.1*** *p45*
Wattison, Joseph; Maryland, 1719 ***1220.12*** *p847*
Wattkowski, Samuel; North Carolina, 1860 ***1088.45*** *p36*
Wattler, Fra.cois 49; New Orleans, 1846 ***778.6*** *p341*
Watton, . . .; Boston, 1769 ***9228.50*** *p5*
Watton, Elias; Boston, 1769 ***9228.50*** *p48*
Watton, James; America, 1754 ***1220.12*** *p847*
Watton, John; America, 1750 ***1220.12*** *p847*
Watton, Joseph; America, 1774 ***1220.12*** *p847*
Watton, Robert; Barbados, 1694 ***1220.12*** *p901*
Watts, Ann; America, 1771 ***1220.12*** *p847*
Watts, Anne; Barbados, 1665 ***1220.12*** *p847*
Watts, Barbary; Boston, 1764 ***1642*** *p33*
Watts, Charles; America, 1748 ***1220.12*** *p847*
Watts, Daniel; New Jersey, 1777 ***8529.30*** *p7*
Watts, David; America, 1741 ***1220.12*** *p847*
Watts, Edward; America, 1770 ***1220.12*** *p847*
Watts, Edward 58; Ontario, 1871 ***1823.17*** *p171*
Watts, Elizabeth; Virginia, 1750 ***1220.12*** *p847*
Watts, George; America, 1771 ***1220.12*** *p847*
Watts, Hannah; America, 1764 ***1220.12*** *p847*
Watts, Henry; America, 1728 ***1220.12*** *p847*
Watts, Henry; America, 1747 ***1220.12*** *p847*
Watts, Henry; America, 1765 ***1220.12*** *p848*
Watts, Henry 16; Quebec, 1870 ***8364.32*** *p26*
Watts, Isaac; Virginia, 1770 ***1220.12*** *p848*
Watts, Ms. J. 14; Quebec, 1870 ***8364.32*** *p26*
Watts, James 74; Ontario, 1871 ***1823.21*** *p384*
Watts, James; Virginia, 1740 ***1220.12*** *p848*
Watts, Jane; Annapolis, MD, 1725 ***1220.12*** *p848*
Watts, Jane; Barbados, 1673 ***1220.12*** *p848*
Watts, Jane; Maryland, 1674 ***1236.25*** *p50*
Watts, Joan; Virginia, 1736 ***1220.12*** *p848*
Watts, John; America, 1685 ***1220.12*** *p848*
Watts, John; America, 1764 ***1220.12*** *p848*
Watts, John; America, 1767 ***1220.12*** *p848*
Watts, John; America, 1770 ***1220.12*** *p848*
Watts, John; America, 1775 ***1220.12*** *p848*
Watts, John; Barbados or Jamaica, 1697 ***1220.12*** *p848*
Watts, Margaret; America, 1769 ***1220.12*** *p848*
Watts, Mary; America, 1770 ***1220.12*** *p848*
Watts, Mary; Died enroute, 1730 ***1220.12*** *p848*
Watts, Samuel; America, 1721 ***1220.12*** *p848*
Watts, Samuel; America, 1767 ***1220.12*** *p848*
Watts, Sarah 10; Quebec, 1870 ***8364.32*** *p26*
Watts, Thomas; America, 1741 ***1220.12*** *p848*
Watts, Thomas; America, 1741 ***1220.12*** *p848*
Watts, Thomas; America, 1755 ***1220.12*** *p848*
Watts, Thomas; America, 1761 ***1220.12*** *p848*
Watts, Thomas; America, 1771 ***1220.12*** *p833*
Watts, Thomas; America, 1775 ***1220.12*** *p848*
Watts, Thomas; Maryland, 1723 ***1220.12*** *p848*
Watts, Thomas 25; Maryland, 1724 ***1220.12*** *p848*
Watts, Will; Boston, 1764 ***1642*** *p33*
Watts, William; America, 1750 ***1220.12*** *p848*
Watts, William; America, 1756 ***1220.12*** *p848*
Watts, William; America, 1762 ***1220.12*** *p848*
Watts, William; Jamaica, 1716 ***1220.12*** *p848*
Watts, William 8; Quebec, 1870 ***8364.32*** *p26*
Watts, William; South Carolina, 1809 ***6155.4*** *p19*
Wattson, Ann; Virginia, 1735 ***1220.12*** *p845*
Wattson, Martin 48; Ontario, 1871 ***1823.17*** *p171*
Wattson, Stephen; America, 1739 ***1220.12*** *p847*

Waud, John 26; Ontario, 1871 ***1823.21*** *p384*
Waugh, Charles 55; Ontario, 1871 ***1823.21*** *p384*
Waugh, Christopher 79; Ontario, 1871 ***1823.21*** *p384*
Waugh, Robart 54; Ontario, 1871 ***1823.21*** *p384*
Waugh, Thomas; America, 1764 ***1220.12*** *p848*
Waugh, Thomas 34; Ontario, 1871 ***1823.21*** *p384*
Waugh, William 19; Ontario, 1871 ***1823.21*** *p384*
Waukle, John Christian; South Carolina, 1811 ***6155.4*** *p19*
Waul, Micl, II; St. John, N.B., 1848 ***2978.15*** *p38*
Waun, Robert 45; Ontario, 1871 ***1823.21*** *p384*
Wautelet, Joseph; Wisconsin, 1856 ***1494.21*** *p31*
Wautier, Gregoire; New York, NY, 1870 ***1494.20*** *p12*
Wautier, Joseph; New York, NY, 1869 ***1494.20*** *p11*
Wautlet, Josephine; Wisconsin, 1854-1858 ***1495.20*** *p66*
Waw, John 22; Ontario, 1871 ***1823.21*** *p384*
Wawby, Thomas; America, 1683 ***1220.12*** *p848*
Wawdby, John 56; Ontario, 1871 ***1823.21*** *p384*
Wawn, John; America, 1713 ***1220.12*** *p848*
Wawrzyniak, Anna; Wisconsin, 1897 ***6795.8*** *p62*
Wawzyniak, Karl; America, 1891 ***5475.1*** *p79*
*Wife:*Katharina Beckendorf
Wawzyniak, Katharina Beckendorf *SEE* Wawzyniak, Karl
Wax, Joseph 18; Ontario, 1871 ***1823.21*** *p384*
Waxdell, Johann; North Carolina, 1710 ***3629.40*** *p9*
Way, Aaron; Salem, MA, 1674 ***9228.50*** *p652*
Way, Edward; America, 1685 ***1220.12*** *p848*
Way, George; America, 1720 ***1220.12*** *p848*
Way, George; Barbados, 1701 ***1220.12*** *p848*
Way, George; Barbados, 1715 ***1220.12*** *p848*
Way, Henry; New England, 1631 ***117.5*** *p159*
Way, Richard; America, 1753 ***1220.12*** *p848*
Waybank, Elizabeth; Virginia, 1732 ***1220.12*** *p848*
Wayland, Ann; America, 1741 ***1220.12*** *p848*
Wayland, Elizabeth; Annapolis, MD, 1723 ***1220.12*** *p848*
Wayland, John; America, 1751 ***1220.12*** *p848*
Waylett, Samuel 33; Ontario, 1871 ***1823.17*** *p171*
Wayman, . . .; West Virginia, 1850-1860 ***1132.30*** *p149*
Wayman, Samuel; America, 1729 ***1220.12*** *p848*
Waymark, Sarah; America, 1750 ***1220.12*** *p848*
Wayne, John; America, 1739 ***1220.12*** *p849*
Wayne, William; America, 1767 ***1220.12*** *p849*
Wayte, Gerrard; Barbados, 1664 ***1220.12*** *p829*
Wayte, Jonathan; Maryland, 1674 ***1236.25*** *p50*
Wayte, Thomas; America, 1768 ***1220.12*** *p829*
Weaber, Frederick; Ohio, 1809-1852 ***4511.35*** *p57*
Wead, James; America, 1768 ***1220.12*** *p852*
Weadock, William 20; New York, NY, 1844 ***6178.50*** *p151*
Weakland, Dorothy; America, 1765 ***1220.12*** *p849*
Weal, John; Annapolis, MD, 1729 ***1220.12*** *p849*
Wealand, Joseph 59; Ontario, 1871 ***1823.17*** *p172*
Weale, John; America, 1680 ***1220.12*** *p849*
Weale, Nathaniel; America, 1685 ***1220.12*** *p849*
Weales, Mariah; Maryland, 1725 ***1220.12*** *p849*
Wear, Samuel; America, 1751 ***1220.12*** *p840*
Wear, William 38; Ontario, 1871 ***1823.21*** *p384*
Wearne, John; America, 1758 ***1220.12*** *p849*
Weatherell, James; America, 1746 ***1220.12*** *p858*
Weatherhead, James 26; Ontario, 1871 ***1823.21*** *p384*
Weatherhead, William 40; Ontario, 1871 ***1823.21*** *p384*
Weatherill, Francis; America, 1759 ***1220.12*** *p858*
Weatherill, Peter 44; Ontario, 1871 ***1823.21*** *p384*
Weatherley, John; America, 1741 ***1220.12*** *p859*
Weatherspun, Elizabeth; America, 1757 ***1220.12*** *p893*
Weatherstone, William 62; Ontario, 1871 ***1823.21*** *p384*
Weatherwick, William 63; Ontario, 1871 ***1823.21*** *p384*
Weatholder, William; Ohio, 1840-1897 ***8365.35*** *p18*
Weaver, Charles; America, 1708 ***1220.12*** *p849*
Weaver, Charles E.; Ohio, 1845 ***3580.20*** *p33*
Weaver, Charles E.; Ohio, 1845 ***6020.12*** *p23*
Weaver, Conrad 49; Ontario, 1871 ***1823.17*** *p172*
Weaver, Elizabeth; America, 1758 ***1220.12*** *p849*
Weaver, Frederick; Ohio, 1809-1852 ***4511.35*** *p57*
Weaver, George; Ohio, 1809-1852 ***4511.35*** *p57*
Weaver, Hannah; America, 1757 ***1220.12*** *p849*
Weaver, Isaac; Virginia, 1652 ***6254.4*** *p243*
Weaver, Jacob; Ohio, 1809-1852 ***4511.35*** *p57*
Weaver, John; America, 1758 ***1220.12*** *p849*
Weaver, John; America, 1759 ***1220.12*** *p849*
Weaver, John; America, 1763 ***1220.12*** *p849*
Weaver, John; Barbados or Jamaica, 1697 ***1220.12*** *p849*
Weaver, John; Barbados or Jamaica, 1715 ***1220.12*** *p849*
Weaver, John; Ohio, 1809-1852 ***4511.35*** *p57*
Weaver, John 48; Ontario, 1871 ***1823.21*** *p384*
Weaver, Mary; America, 1754 ***1220.12*** *p849*
Weaver, Mary; Barbados, 1664 ***1220.12*** *p849*
Weaver, Michael; Ohio, 1809-1852 ***4511.35*** *p57*
Weaver, Richard; America, 1757 ***1220.12*** *p849*
Weaver, Richard; America, 1766 ***1220.12*** *p849*
Weaver, Samuel; America, 1685 ***1220.12*** *p849*
Weaver, Samuel; Illinois, 1852 ***6079.1*** *p14*
Weaver, Stephen; Virginia, 1736 ***1220.12*** *p849*
Weaver, Thomas; America, 1738 ***1220.12*** *p849*
Weaver, Thomas; America, 1749 ***1220.12*** *p849*
Weaver, Thomas; America, 1753 ***1220.12*** *p849*
Weaver, William; America, 1690 ***1220.12*** *p849*
Weaver, William; America, 1769 ***1220.12*** *p849*
Weaver, William; America, 1771 ***1220.12*** *p849*
Webb, Andrew; America, 1765 ***1220.12*** *p849*
Webb, Ann; America, 1744 ***1220.12*** *p849*
Webb, Ann 24; Ontario, 1871 ***1823.21*** *p384*
Webb, Arthur 47; Ontario, 1871 ***1823.21*** *p384*
Webb, Catherine 17; Quebec, 1870 ***8364.32*** *p26*
Webb, Daniel; Virginia, 1741 ***1220.12*** *p849*
Webb, Elizabeth; Barbados or Jamaica, 1686 ***1220.12*** *p849*
Webb, Elizabeth 37; Ontario, 1871 ***1823.21*** *p384*
Webb, Henry; America, 1685 ***1220.12*** *p849*
Webb, Henry; America, 1745 ***1220.12*** *p849*
Webb, Henry; America, 1758 ***1220.12*** *p849*
Webb, Henry; North Carolina, 1855 ***1088.45*** *p36*
Webb, Henry 35; Ontario, 1871 ***1823.21*** *p384*
Webb, Henry 40; Ontario, 1871 ***1823.21*** *p384*
Webb, J.; Quebec, 1870 ***8364.32*** *p26*
Webb, James; America, 1685 ***1220.12*** *p849*
Webb, James; America, 1773 ***1220.12*** *p849*
Webb, James 87; Ontario, 1871 ***1823.21*** *p384*
Webb, Jane; America, 1738 ***1220.12*** *p849*
Webb, Jane; America, 1744 ***1220.12*** *p849*
Webb, John; America, 1685 ***1220.12*** *p849*
Webb, John; America, 1742 ***1220.12*** *p850*
Webb, John; America, 1746 ***1220.12*** *p850*
Webb, John; America, 1753 ***1220.12*** *p850*
Webb, John; America, 1754 ***1220.12*** *p850*
Webb, John; America, 1758 ***1220.12*** *p850*
Webb, John; America, 1764 ***1220.12*** *p850*
Webb, John; America, 1766 ***1220.12*** *p850*
Webb, John; America, 1770 ***1220.12*** *p850*
Webb, John; America, 1772 ***1220.12*** *p850*
Webb, John; Barbados, 1684 ***1220.12*** *p849*
Webb, John; Barbados or Jamaica, 1694 ***1220.12*** *p849*
Webb, John; Maryland or Virginia, 1731 ***1220.12*** *p850*
Webb, John; Maryland or Virginia, 1740 ***1220.12*** *p850*
Webb, John 45; Ontario, 1871 ***1823.21*** *p384*
Webb, Jonathan; America, 1765 ***1220.12*** *p850*
Webb, Joseph; America, 1768 ***1220.12*** *p850*
Webb, Joseph 55; Ontario, 1871 ***1823.21*** *p384*
Webb, Louisa 15; Ontario, 1871 ***1823.21*** *p384*
Webb, Louisa 32; Ontario, 1871 ***1823.21*** *p384*
Webb, Margaret; Virginia, 1734 ***1220.12*** *p850*
Webb, Mary; America, 1747 ***1220.12*** *p850*
Webb, Mary; America, 1768 ***1220.12*** *p850*
Webb, Mary; Maryland or Virginia, 1728 ***1220.12*** *p850*
Webb, Nathaniel; America, 1737 ***1220.12*** *p850*
Webb, Nicholas; Died enroute, 1725 ***1220.12*** *p850*
Webb, R. J. 50; Ontario, 1871 ***1823.21*** *p384*
Webb, Ri.; Maryland, 1672 ***1236.25*** *p48*
Webb, Richard; America, 1729 ***1220.12*** *p850*
Webb, Richard; America, 1732 ***1220.12*** *p850*
Webb, Richard; America, 1738 ***1220.12*** *p850*
Webb, Richard; America, 1754 ***1220.12*** *p850*
Webb, Richard; America, 1755 ***1220.12*** *p850*
Webb, Richard; Boston, 1718 ***1220.12*** *p850*
Webb, Samuel; America, 1758 ***1220.12*** *p850*
Webb, Samuel; America, 1759 ***1220.12*** *p850*
Webb, Samuel; America, 1775 ***1220.12*** *p850*
Webb, Sarah; Annapolis, MD, 1735 ***1220.12*** *p850*
Webb, Sarah; Virginia, 1742 ***1220.12*** *p850*
Webb, Stephen; America, 1740 ***1220.12*** *p850*
Webb, Thomas; America, 1734 ***1220.12*** *p850*
Webb, Thomas; America, 1743 ***1220.12*** *p850*
Webb, Thomas; America, 1767 ***1220.12*** *p850*
Webb, Thomas; America, 1771 ***1220.12*** *p850*
Webb, Thomas; America, 1772 ***1220.12*** *p850*
Webb, Thomas 55; Ontario, 1871 ***1823.21*** *p384*
Webb, Thomas 68; Ontario, 1871 ***1823.21*** *p385*
Webb, Thomas P. 39; Ontario, 1871 ***1823.21*** *p385*
Webb, Timothy; Virginia, 1719 ***1220.12*** *p850*
Webb, Walter; America, 1769 ***1220.12*** *p850*
Webb, William; America, 1736 ***1220.12*** *p850*
Webb, William; America, 1747 ***1220.12*** *p850*
Webb, William; America, 1754 ***1220.12*** *p850*
Webb, William; America, 1758 ***1220.12*** *p850*
Webb, William; America, 1768 ***1220.12*** *p850*
Webb, William; America, 1775 ***1220.12*** *p850*
Webb, William 43; Ontario, 1871 ***1823.21*** *p385*
Webb, William 44; Ontario, 1871 ***1823.21*** *p385*
Webb, William 50; Ontario, 1871 ***1823.21*** *p385*
Webb, William 54; Ontario, 1871 ***1823.21*** *p385*
Webb, William 65; Ontario, 1871 ***1823.21*** *p385*
Webber, Betty; America, 1761 ***1220.12*** *p850*
Webber, Charity; America, 1757 ***1220.12*** *p850*
Webber, Elizabeth; America, 1774 ***1220.12*** *p851*
Webber, Elizabeth; New Hampshire, 1700-1799 ***9228.50*** *p349*
Webber, Elizabeth; New Hampshire, 1700-1799 ***9228.50*** *p652*
Webber, John; America, 1767 ***1220.12*** *p851*
Webber, John; America, 1771 ***1220.12*** *p851*
Webber, John; Boston, 1745 ***9228.50*** *p652*
Webber, John; Massachusetts, 1675 ***9228.50*** *p652*
Webber, John 30; Ontario, 1871 ***1823.21*** *p385*
Webber, John 44; Ontario, 1871 ***1823.21*** *p385*
Webber, Josiah; America, 1740 ***1220.12*** *p851*
Webber, Katherine; Barbados, 1679 ***1220.12*** *p850*
Webber, Marley; Canada, 1911-1912 ***9228.50*** *p652*
Webber, Mary; America, 1751 ***1220.12*** *p851*
Webber, Nathaniel; America, 1685 ***1220.12*** *p851*
Webber, Nathaniel; America, 1767 ***1220.12*** *p851*
Webber, Richard; America, 1757 ***1220.12*** *p851*
Webber, Richard; America, 1767 ***1220.12*** *p851*
Webber, Robert; America, 1766 ***1220.12*** *p851*
Webber, Robert; America, 1768 ***1220.12*** *p851*
Webber, Ruth; America, 1677 ***1220.12*** *p851*
Webber, Sarah; America, 1766 ***1220.12*** *p851*
Webber, Sarah; America, 1772 ***1220.12*** *p851*
Webber, Susannah; Virginia, 1761 ***1220.12*** *p851*
Webber, Thomas; America, 1733 ***1220.12*** *p851*
Webber, Thomas; America, 1773 ***1220.12*** *p851*
Webber, William; America, 1749 ***1220.12*** *p851*
Webber, William; America, 1769 ***1220.12*** *p851*
Webbing, Heinrich 9; New York, NY, 1864 ***8425.62*** *p195*
Webbing, Hermann; New York, NY, 1864 ***8425.62*** *p195*
Webbing, Hermann 24; New York, NY, 1864 ***8425.62*** *p195*
Webbing, Margarethe 26; New York, NY, 1864 ***8425.62*** *p195*
Webbing, Marie 18; New York, NY, 1864 ***8425.62*** *p195*
Webbing, Marie 56; New York, NY, 1864 ***8425.62*** *p195*
Webbing, Wilhelm 4; New York, NY, 1864 ***8425.62*** *p195*
Webbing, Wilhelm 59; New York, NY, 1864 ***8425.62*** *p195*
Webdell, Thomas; America, 1753 ***1220.12*** *p851*
Webel, John; Washington, 1889 ***2770.40*** *p81*
Weber, Infant 7; Portland, ME, 1911 ***970.38*** *p82*
Weber, Abraham 56; America, 1856 ***5475.1*** *p540*
*Daughter:*Luise 28
*Grandson:*Johann 6
Weber, Adam; America, 1830 ***2526.43*** *p227*
*Wife:*Anna Barbara Orth
With child 1
With child 5
With child 4
With child 2
Weber, Adam 3 weeks months *SEE* Weber, Michael
Weber, Andrew; Ohio, 1809-1852 ***4511.35*** *p57*
Weber, Angela 9 *SEE* Weber, Michel
Weber, Anna Wein *SEE* Weber, Peter, III
Weber, Anna 27; America, 1851 ***5475.1*** *p317*
Weber, Anna Barbara Orth *SEE* Weber, Adam
Weber, Anna Elisabeth *SEE* Weber, Anna Marie
Weber, Anna Magdalena 57; America, 1860 ***2526.43*** *p119*
With child 18
With child 8
Weber, Anna Margaretha; America, 1863 ***8115.12*** *p319*
Weber, Anna Margarethe *SEE* Weber, Anna Marie
Weber, Anna Maria; America, 1872 ***5475.1*** *p304*
Weber, Anna Maria 21 *SEE* Weber, Michael
Weber, Anna Maria 24 *SEE* Weber, Georg
Weber, Anna Maria 9; Galveston, TX, 1844 ***3967.10*** *p375*
Weber, Anna Marie; America, 1850 ***8115.12*** *p326*
*Child:*Anna Elisabeth
*Child:*Katharine Margarethe
*Child:*Marie Katharine
*Child:*Anna Margarethe
*Child:*Johann Ludwig
Weber, Antoine 9 months; America, 1747 ***778.6*** *p341*
Weber, Anton; New York, 1860 ***358.56*** *p3*
Weber, Barbara 42; America, 1864 ***5475.1*** *p370*
Weber, Barbara 16 *SEE* Weber, Johann
Weber, Miss C. 3; New Orleans, 1834 ***1002.51*** *p110*
Weber, Carolina 9 months; New York, NY, 1874 ***6954.7*** *p38*
Weber, Caroline 25; America, 1846 ***778.6*** *p341*
Weber, Caroline 9 months; New York, NY, 1874 ***6954.7*** *p37*
Weber, Cath. 50; Texas, 1840 ***778.6*** *p341*
Weber, Catharina 7; New York, NY, 1874 ***6954.7*** *p38*
Weber, Catherine 36; New York, NY, 1883 ***8427.14*** *p43*
Weber, Chris; Louisiana, 1874 ***4981.45*** *p297*
Weber, Christian 1 months; New York, NY, 1874 ***6954.7*** *p38*

Weber, Christian 35; New York, NY, 1874 *6954.7 p38*
Weber, Christian Philipp Adolph; America, 1852 *7420.1 p100*
Weber, Christina 10 *SEE* Weber, Michel
Weber, Christina 15; New York, NY, 1898 *7951.13 p42*
Weber, Christine 5; New York, NY, 1874 *6954.7 p37*
Weber, Christine 14; New York, NY, 1874 *6954.7 p37*
Weber, Christoph 19; Texas, 1840 *778.6 p341*
Weber, Conrad; America, 1854 *7420.1 p132*
Weber, Elisa 25; Port uncertain, 1843 *778.6 p341*
Weber, Elisab. 27; Louisiana, 1848 *778.6 p341*
Weber, Elisabeth *SEE* Weber, Elisabeth Margarethe
Weber, Elisabeth; America, 1862 *2526.43 p119*
Weber, Elisabeth; America, 1867 *5475.1 p491*
   *Daughter:*Karoline
   *Daughter:*Amalia
   *Daughter:*Florina
   *Son:*Wilhelm
   *Daughter:*Charlotte
Weber, Elisabeth *SEE* Weber, Peter, III
Weber, Elisabeth *SEE* Weber, Elisabeth
Weber, Elisabeth; America, 1881 *8115.12 p324*
   *Child:*Elisabeth
   *Child:*Karl
   *Child:*Ludwig
Weber, Elisabeth 30 *SEE* Weber, Mrs. Friedrich
Weber, Elisabeth Kaiser 36 *SEE* Weber, Michel
Weber, Elisabeth *SEE* Weber, Peter
Weber, Elisabeth 8; New York, NY, 1874 *6954.7 p37*
Weber, Elisabeth 10; New York, NY, 1898 *7951.13 p42*
Weber, Elisabeth 35; New York, NY, 1874 *6954.7 p37*
Weber, Elisabeth 40; New York, NY, 1898 *7951.13 p42*
Weber, Elisabeth; Virginia, 1831 *152.20 p61*
Weber, Elisabeth Margarethe; America, 1847 *8115.12 p327*
   *Child:*Ludwig
   *Child:*Philipp
   *Child:*Elisabeth
Weber, Elisabethe 5 *SEE* Weber, Philipp
Weber, Emilie 25; Portland, ME, 1911 *970.38 p82*
Weber, Eva 29; America, 1853 *2526.43 p127*
Weber, Eva Elisabethe 6 *SEE* Weber, Philipp
Weber, Eva Katharina 22 *SEE* Weber, Georg
Weber, Ferdinand; America, 1848 *7420.1 p63*
   With family
   With daughter 2
   With daughter 10
   With daughter 6
   With daughter 8
Weber, Fr. Wilh.; Valdivia, Chile, 1852 *1192.4 p54*
Weber, Fr..d 50; Texas, 1840 *778.6 p341*
Weber, Francis J.; Ohio, 1809-1852 *4511.35 p57*
Weber, Francis Xavier; Ohio, 1809-1852 *4511.35 p57*
Weber, Friedrich; America, 1847 *7420.1 p57*
Weber, Friedrich; America, 1856 *2526.43 p119*
Weber, Friedrich *SEE* Weber, Sophie
Weber, Friedrich; Brazil, 1863 *5475.1 p550*
   *Wife:*Maria Luise Eifler
   *Daughter:*Luise
Weber, Friedrich 9; New York, NY, 1898 *7951.13 p42*
Weber, Mrs. Friedrich 57; America, 1860 *2526.43 p119*
   *Daughter:*Elisabeth 30
   *Son:*Philipp 8
   *Daughter:*Katharina 16
   *Daughter:*Katharina Elisabeth 22
   *Son:*Konrad 17
Weber, Georg; America, 1851 *2526.43 p184*
Weber, Georg; America, 1852-1862 *5475.1 p404*
Weber, Georg; America, 1861 *2526.43 p187*
   *Daughter:*Anna Maria
   *Son:*Georg
   *Daughter:*Eva Katharina
Weber, Georg; America, 1863 *5475.1 p49*
Weber, Georg 18 *SEE* Weber, Georg
Weber, Georg Ernst; America, 1846 *2526.43 p201*
Weber, Georg Friedrich Wilhelm; America, 1884 *7420.1 p346*
Weber, George; Ohio, 1809-1852 *4511.35 p57*
Weber, Gertrude; Philadelphia, 1862 *8513.31 p411*
Weber, Gottlieb 19; New York, NY, 1874 *6954.7 p37*
Weber, H.D.; Galveston, TX, 1855 *571.7 p17*
Weber, Heinrich *SEE* Weber, Sophie
Weber, Heinrich 7; New York, NY, 1874 *6954.7 p37*
Weber, Heinrich 70; New York, NY, 1874 *6954.7 p37*
Weber, Helena Thome 38 *SEE* Weber, Johann
Weber, Henry; Louisiana, 1874 *4981.45 p134*
Weber, Ignatz; America, 1882 *4981.45 p134*
Weber, J. 24; New Orleans, 1834 *1002.51 p110*
Weber, Miss J. 1; New Orleans, 1834 *1002.51 p110*
Weber, Jacob; Colorado, 1878 *1029.59 p93*
Weber, Jacob; Louisiana, 1874 *4981.45 p134*
Weber, Jacob; New York, 1859 *358.56 p100*
Weber, Jacob 15; New York, NY, 1898 *7951.13 p42*

Weber, Jacob 26; New York, NY, 1874 *6954.7 p37*
Weber, Jakob; America, 1843 *5475.1 p295*
Weber, Jakob; America, 1853 *2526.43 p220*
Weber, Jakob; America, 1873 *5475.1 p269*
Weber, Jakob *SEE* Weber, Mathias
Weber, Jakob *SEE* Weber, Nikolaus
Weber, Jakob; America, 1882 *5475.1 p464*
Weber, Jakob 61; America, 1872 *5475.1 p304*
   *Daughter:*Katharina
   *Son:*Josef
Weber, Jakob *SEE* Weber, Katharina Kronenberger
Weber, Jean 30; New Orleans, 1848 *778.6 p341*
Weber, Jean 39; New Orleans, 1848 *778.6 p341*
Weber, Joh. 56; New York, NY, 1883 *8427.14 p43*
Weber, Joh. Philipp; America, 1871 *5475.1 p338*
Weber, Johann; America, 1863 *5475.1 p49*
Weber, Johann *SEE* Weber, Mathias
Weber, Johann *SEE* Weber, Nikolaus
Weber, Johann 6 *SEE* Weber, Abraham
Weber, Johann; Brazil, 1850 *5475.1 p68*
Weber, Johann 4 *SEE* Weber, Johann
Weber, Johann 13 *SEE* Weber, Johann
Weber, Johann 39; Brazil, 1855 *5475.1 p319*
   *Wife:*Helena Thome 38
   *Son:*Johann 4
   *Son:*Mathias 1 months
   *Son:*Michel 2
   *Son:*Peter 6
   *Son:*Johann 13
   *Daughter:*Margarethe 11
   *Son:*Nikolaus 8
   *Daughter:*Barbara 16
Weber, Johann; Venezuela, 1843 *3899.5 p542*
Weber, Johann Friedrich; Port uncertain, 1837 *7420.1 p14*
Weber, Johann Gottlieb Fried.; Wisconsin, 1887 *6795.8 p148*
Weber, Johann Ludwig *SEE* Weber, Anna Marie
Weber, Johannes 54; Carolina, 1844 *170.15 p45*
   With 6 children
Weber, Johannes 39; New York, NY, 1874 *6954.7 p37*
Weber, Jonshua 31; Ontario, 1871 *1823.21 p385*
Weber, Josef *SEE* Weber, Jakob
Weber, Josef; Ohio, 1881-1889 *2853.20 p505*
Weber, Joseph 40; Galveston, TX, 1844 *3967.10 p375*
Weber, Josephine 38; Galveston, TX, 1844 *3967.10 p375*
Weber, Karl *SEE* Weber, Maria Alt
Weber, Karl *SEE* Weber, Elisabeth
Weber, Karl *SEE* Weber, Katharina Kronenberger
Weber, Karoline *SEE* Weber, Peter
Weber, Karoline 4; New York, NY, 1898 *7951.13 p42*
Weber, Katarina 60; Portland, ME, 1911 *970.38 p42*
Weber, Kath. Reichard 38 *SEE* Weber, Peter
Weber, Katharina *SEE* Weber, Jakob
Weber, Katharina *SEE* Weber, Nikolaus
Weber, Katharina 16 *SEE* Weber, Mrs. Friedrich
Weber, Katharina 22 *SEE* Weber, Michael
Weber, Katharina Friedrich 40 *SEE* Weber, Nikolaus
Weber, Katharina 43 *SEE* Weber, Michael
Weber, Katharina 43; America, 1883 *5475.1 p270*
Weber, Katharina 48; America, 1855 *5475.1 p310*
Weber, Katharina Mohrbach 50 *SEE* Weber, Mathias
Weber, Katharina *SEE* Weber, Peter
Weber, Katharina 6; Galveston, TX, 1844 *3967.10 p375*
Weber, Katharina; New York, 1893 *5475.1 p391*
   *Daughter:*Rosa
   *Daughter:*Margarethe
   *Son:*Nikolaus
   *Son:*Jakob
   *Son:*Karl
   *Son:*Rudolph
Weber, Katharina Elisabeth 22 *SEE* Weber, Mrs. Friedrich
Weber, Katharine Margarethe *SEE* Weber, Anna Marie
Weber, Konrad 17 *SEE* Weber, Mrs. Friedrich
Weber, Lily 33; Louisiana, 1848 *778.6 p341*
Weber, Lorenz 18; New Orleans, 1848 *778.6 p341*
Weber, Louis 24; New Orleans, 1848 *778.6 p341*
Weber, Louise 10; New York, NY, 1874 *6954.7 p37*
Weber, Ludwig *SEE* Weber, Elisabeth Margarethe
Weber, Ludwig *SEE* Weber, Elisabeth
Weber, Ludwig 3; New York, NY, 1898 *7951.13 p42*
Weber, Luise *SEE* Weber, Peter, III
Weber, Luise 28 *SEE* Weber, Abraham
Weber, Luise *SEE* Weber, Friedrich
Weber, Luise *SEE* Weber, Peter
Weber, Magdalena 19 *SEE* Weber, Michel
Weber, Magdalena 45; America, 1847 *5475.1 p254*
Weber, Magdalena 6 months; New York, NY, 1874 *6954.7 p37*
Weber, Magdalena 10; New York, NY, 1874 *6954.7 p38*
Weber, Magdalena 23; New York, NY, 1874 *6954.7 p37*

Weber, Magdalena 27; New York, NY, 1874 *6954.7 p37*
Weber, Margaret 9 months; New York, NY, 1898 *7951.13 p42*
Weber, Margarethe *SEE* Weber, Peter, III
Weber, Margarethe; America, 1881 *5475.1 p44*
Weber, Margarethe 11 *SEE* Weber, Johann
Weber, Margarethe *SEE* Weber, Katharina Kronenberger
Weber, Maria; America, 1847 *5475.1 p345*
Weber, Maria; America, 1879 *5475.1 p157*
Weber, Maria; America, 1882 *5475.1 p313*
Weber, Maria 21; America, 1747 *778.6 p341*
Weber, Maria 56; America, 1863 *5475.1 p49*
   *Son:*Karl
Weber, Maria 46; Brazil, 1857 *5475.1 p356*
Weber, Maria 31; New York, NY, 1874 *6954.7 p38*
Weber, Maria Luise Eifler *SEE* Weber, Friedrich
Weber, Marianne 32; New Orleans, 1848 *778.6 p341*
Weber, Marie Katharine *SEE* Weber, Anna Marie
Weber, Martin 25; America, 1854 *5475.1 p56*
   With sister 23
Weber, Martin 19; Missouri, 1840 *778.6 p341*
Weber, Mathias; America, 1874 *5475.1 p463*
   *Wife:*Katharina Mohrbach
   *Son:*Johann
   *Son:*Jakob
Weber, Mathias *SEE* Weber, Nikolaus
Weber, Mathias 23; America, 1843 *5475.1 p295*
Weber, Mathias 31; America, 1843 *5475.1 p367*
Weber, Mathias 1 *SEE* Weber, Johann
Weber, Mathias 30; Brazil, 1828 *5475.1 p233*
Weber, Matthias; Venezuela, 1843 *3899.5 p542*
Weber, Michael 17; America, 1833 *2526.43 p187*
   *Sister:*Anna Maria 21
   With brother-in-law
Weber, Michael 29; America, 1846 *2526.43 p187*
   *Wife:*Katharina 22
   *Son:*Adam 3 weeks
Weber, Michael 43; America, 1847 *5475.1 p254*
   *Wife:*Katharina 43
   With stepchild 24
   With stepchild 20
Weber, Michael 40; New York, NY, 1898 *7951.13 p42*
Weber, Michel 7 *SEE* Weber, Michel
Weber, Michel 49; America, 1856 *5475.1 p277*
   *Wife:*Elisabeth Kaiser 36
   *Daughter:*Christina 10
   *Son:*Michel 7
   *Daughter:*Angela 9 months
   *Daughter:*Magdalena 19
Weber, Michel 56; America, 1843 *5475.1 p295*
Weber, Michel 2 *SEE* Weber, Johann
Weber, Michel 40; Port uncertain, 1843 *778.6 p341*
Weber, Nikolaus; America, 1847 *5475.1 p345*
Weber, Nikolaus; America, 1854 *2526.43 p119*
Weber, Nikolaus *SEE* Weber, Nikolaus
Weber, Nikolaus; America, 1880 *5475.1 p362*
   *Wife:*Katharina Friedrich
   *Son:*Mathias
   *Son:*Jakob
   *Daughter:*Katharina
   *Son:*Nikolaus
   *Son:*Johann
   With son
Weber, Nikolaus; America, 1881 *5475.1 p365*
Weber, Nikolaus 8 *SEE* Weber, Johann
Weber, Nikolaus; Kansas, 1886 *5475.1 p142*
Weber, Nikolaus *SEE* Weber, Katharina Kronenberger
Weber, Otto; America, 1875 *5475.1 p346*
Weber, Peter; America, 1863 *5475.1 p524*
Weber, Peter 16; America, 1883 *2526.42 p137*
Weber, Peter 56; America, 1843 *5475.1 p309*
Weber, Peter 6 *SEE* Weber, Johann
Weber, Peter 40; Brazil, 1865 *5475.1 p506*
   *Wife:*Kath. Reichard 38
   *Daughter:*Katharina
   *Daughter:*Luise
   *Daughter:*Karoline
   *Daughter:*Elisabeth
Weber, Peter 37; Galveston, TX, 1844 *3967.10 p375*
Weber, Peter 35; New York, NY, 1874 *6954.7 p37*
Weber, Peter, III; America, 1881 *5475.1 p44*
   *Wife:*Anna Wein
   *Daughter:*Margarethe
   *Daughter:*Luise
   *Daughter:*Elisabeth
Weber, Philipp *SEE* Weber, Elisabeth Margarethe
Weber, Philipp; America, 1854 *2526.43 p119*
   With wife
   *Daughter:*Elisabethe
   *Daughter:*Eva Elisabethe
Weber, Philipp; America, 1863 *5475.1 p49*
Weber, Philipp; America, 1892 *2526.43 p201*
Weber, Philipp 8 *SEE* Weber, Mrs. Friedrich

Weber, Philipp 29; America, 1747 ***778.6*** *p341*
Weber, Philipp 6; Port uncertain, 1843 ***778.6*** *p341*
Weber, Rosa *SEE* Weber, Katharina Kronenberger
Weber, Rosina 7; New York, NY, 1898 ***7951.13*** *p42*
Weber, Rudolph 39; New Castle, DE, 1817-1818 ***90.20*** *p154*
Weber, Rudolph *SEE* Weber, Katharina Kronenberger
Weber, Samuel 30; New Castle, DE, 1817-1818 ***90.20*** *p154*
Weber, Silvester 23; Mississippi, 1846 ***778.6*** *p341*
Weber, Sophia 17; New York, NY, 1898 ***7951.13*** *p42*
Weber, Sophie; America, 1883 ***5475.1*** *p75*
*Son:*Friedrich
*Son:*Heinrich
Weber, Valentin 20; America, 1853 ***2526.43*** *p184*
Weber, Valentin; Chicago, 1886 ***5475.1*** *p340*
Weber, Valentin 12; Louisiana, 1848 ***778.6*** *p342*
Weber, Veronika 3; Galveston, TX, 1844 ***3967.10*** *p375*
Weber, William; New York, 1860 ***358.56*** *p3*
Weber-Elzen, Nikolaus; Wisconsin, 1887 ***5475.1*** *p309*
Webinetha, Walter 30; Ontario, 1871 ***1823.21*** *p385*
Webley, Ann; America, 1746 ***1220.12*** *p851*
Webley, Benjamin; America, 1738 ***1220.12*** *p851*
Webley, Henry; America, 1767 ***1220.12*** *p851*
Webley, Percifall; America, 1714 ***1220.12*** *p851*
Webley, Percival; America, 1726 ***1220.12*** *p851*
Webley, William; America, 1747 ***1220.12*** *p851*
Weblin, Samuel; America, 1743 ***1220.12*** *p851*
Weblin, William; Rappahannock, VA, 1741 ***1220.12*** *p851*
Webre, Elizabeth 19; Texas, 1843 ***778.6*** *p342*
Websoh, Catherine; New York, 1859 ***358.56*** *p54*
Webster, Alexander; North Carolina, 1792-1862 ***1088.45*** *p36*
Webster, Alison; Barbados, 1670 ***1220.12*** *p851*
Webster, David 36; Ontario, 1871 ***1823.17*** *p172*
Webster, George 44; Ontario, 1871 ***1823.21*** *p385*
Webster, George 60; Ontario, 1871 ***1823.21*** *p385*
Webster, H. F.; California, 1868 ***1131.61*** *p89*
Webster, Helen 30; New York, NY, 1835 ***5024.1*** *p137*
Webster, Hellen 28; Ontario, 1871 ***1823.21*** *p385*
Webster, Henry 45; Ontario, 1871 ***1823.17*** *p172*
Webster, Isaac 53; Ontario, 1871 ***1823.21*** *p385*
Webster, Isabella 28; Ontario, 1871 ***1823.21*** *p385*
Webster, Isabella 28; Ontario, 1871 ***1823.21*** *p385*
Webster, Isabella 29; Ontario, 1871 ***1823.21*** *p385*
Webster, James 48; Ontario, 1871 ***1823.17*** *p172*
Webster, John; America, 1740 ***1220.12*** *p851*
Webster, John; America, 1765 ***1220.12*** *p851*
Webster, John; America, 1772 ***1220.12*** *p851*
Webster, John 37; Ontario, 1871 ***1823.21*** *p385*
Webster, John 56; Ontario, 1871 ***1823.17*** *p172*
Webster, John Michael; America, 1770 ***1220.12*** *p851*
Webster, Jonathan; America, 1723 ***1220.12*** *p851*
Webster, Jonathan; Illinois, 1858-1861 ***6020.5*** *p133*
Webster, Margaret; America, 1742 ***1220.12*** *p851*
Webster, Martha; America, 1741 ***1220.12*** *p851*
Webster, Mary; America, 1763 ***1220.12*** *p851*
Webster, Mary; America, 1772 ***1220.12*** *p851*
Webster, Robert 60; Ontario, 1871 ***1823.21*** *p385*
Webster, Robert 60; Ontario, 1871 ***1823.21*** *p385*
Webster, Sarah; America, 1739 ***1220.12*** *p851*
Webster, Thomas; America, 1664 ***1220.12*** *p851*
Webster, Thomas; America, 1716 ***1220.12*** *p851*
Webster, Thomas; America, 1749 ***1220.12*** *p851*
Webster, Thomas; America, 1749 ***1220.12*** *p851*
Webster, Thomas; America, 1768 ***1220.12*** *p851*
Webster, Thomas; Annapolis, MD, 1725 ***1220.12*** *p851*
Webster, Thomas 58; Ontario, 1871 ***1823.17*** *p172*
Webster, Thomas 61; Ontario, 1871 ***1823.21*** *p385*
Webster, William; America, 1734 ***1220.12*** *p851*
Webster, William; America, 1741 ***1220.12*** *p852*
Webster, William; America, 1752 ***1220.12*** *p852*
Webster, William; America, 1773 ***1220.12*** *p852*
Webster, William; Colorado, 1873 ***1029.59*** *p93*
Webster, William 19; Ontario, 1871 ***1823.21*** *p385*
Webster, William 36; Ontario, 1871 ***1823.21*** *p385*
Webster, William 51; Ontario, 1871 ***1823.17*** *p172*
Webster, William 57; Ontario, 1871 ***1823.17*** *p172*
Webster, William 70; Ontario, 1871 ***1823.21*** *p385*
Wecera, Stanislawa; Detroit, 1929 ***1640.55*** *p115*
Wechter, George; Ohio, 1809-1852 ***4511.35*** *p57*
Wechter, Joseph; Ohio, 1809-1852 ***4511.35*** *p57*
Wechter, Mathias; America, 1846 ***5475.1*** *p234*
Wechter, Philip; Ohio, 1809-1852 ***4511.35*** *p57*
Weck, Johan Nicol; New Jersey, 1764-1774 ***927.31*** *p2*
Weck, Michl.; New Jersey, 1764-1774 ***927.31*** *p2*
Weckbach, Anna Maria 8 *SEE* Weckbach, Johannes
Weckbach, Elisabetha Daum 32 *SEE* Weckbach, Johannes
Weckbach, Georg 2 *SEE* Weckbach, Johannes
Weckbach, Johanna 6 *SEE* Weckbach, Johannes
Weckbach, Johannes 30; America, 1858 ***2526.43*** *p144*
*Wife:*Elisabetha Daum 32
*Daughter:*Johanna 6
*Son:*Georg 2
*Daughter:*Anna Maria 8
Weckedall, Martin; Ohio, 1809-1852 ***4511.35*** *p57*
Wecker, Mathias; America, 1843 ***5475.1*** *p382*
Weckerle, John; Ohio, 1809-1852 ***4511.35*** *p57*
Weckerle, Wendelin; Ohio, 1809-1852 ***4511.35*** *p57*
Weckert, Georg *SEE* Weckert, Isidor
Weckert, Isidor 28; America, 1882 ***5475.1*** *p155*
*Wife:*Theresia Wolscht 28
*Son:*Georg
*Son:*Johann
*Son:*Peter
Weckert, Johann *SEE* Weckert, Isidor
Weckert, Peter *SEE* Weckert, Isidor
Weckert, Theresia Wolscht 28 *SEE* Weckert, Isidor
Weckler, Ruppert; Wisconsin, 1881 ***5475.1*** *p434*
Weckmann, Jakob; America, 1846 ***5475.1*** *p472*
Wecks, William; Louisiana, 1874 ***4981.45*** *p134*
Wedde, Marie; Wisconsin, 1905 ***6795.8*** *p196*
Weddell, James; North Carolina, 1842 ***1088.45*** *p36*
Weddell, Mathew; North Carolina, 1844 ***1088.45*** *p36*
Wedebrand, Carl Gustaf; St. Paul, MN, 1882-1887 ***1865.50*** *p113*
Wedebrand, Hannah *SEE* Wedebrand, Marta
Wedebrand, Marta; St. Paul, MN, 1887 ***1865.50*** *p113*
*Daughter:*Hannah
Wedekind, August; Valdivia, Chile, 1850 ***1192.4*** *p49*
Wedekind, Ludwig; America, 1868 ***7420.1*** *p278*
Wedel, Ernst; America, 1867 ***7919.3*** *p524*
Wedel, Georg Adam; America, 1868 ***7919.3*** *p524*
With wife & 4 children
Wedel, Ludwig; America, 1867 ***7919.3*** *p526*
Wedemeier, Mr.; America, 1862 ***7420.1*** *p216*
Wedemeier, Heinrich Christoph; America, 1868 ***7420.1*** *p278*
Wedemeier, Heinrich Philipp Wilhelm; America, 1857 ***7420.1*** *p174*
Weder, Fried.; Valdivia, Chile, 1852 ***1192.4*** *p54*
Weder, Joh. Friedrich; Valdivia, Chile, 1850 ***1192.4*** *p49*
Wedertz, Carl; America, 1860 ***7420.1*** *p201*
Wedge, Jane; Maryland, 1674 ***1236.25*** *p50*
Wedge, John 60; Ontario, 1871 ***1823.21*** *p385*
Wedgwood, John; Annapolis, MD, 1723 ***1220.12*** *p852*
Wedin, Julia; St. Paul, MN, 1888 ***1865.50*** *p114*
Wedin, Peter Jacobsson; St. Paul, MN, 1870-1874 ***1865.50*** *p114*
Weding, Jette Pauline; Oregon, 1941 ***9157.47*** *p2*
Wedmore, Thomas 21; Ontario, 1871 ***1823.21*** *p385*
Wedrycka, Bronislawa 3; New York, NY, 1911 ***6533.11*** *p10*
Wedrycka, Jozefa 37; New York, NY, 1911 ***6533.11*** *p10*
Wedrycki, Jan 8; New York, NY, 1911 ***6533.11*** *p10*
Wedrycki, Ludwik 9; New York, NY, 1911 ***6533.11*** *p10*
Weeb, Thomas 44; Ontario, 1871 ***1823.21*** *p385*
Weech, John; America, 1685 ***1220.12*** *p852*
Weech, John; America, 1728 ***1220.12*** *p852*
Weech, Rebecca; America, 1759 ***1220.12*** *p852*
Weeden, Edward; America, 1741 ***1220.12*** *p852*
Weedon, George 29; Ontario, 1866 ***9228.50*** *p652*
Weedon, Isaac; America, 1721 ***1220.12*** *p852*
Weedon, James; America, 1755 ***1220.12*** *p852*
Weedon, Jane; Annapolis, MD, 1720 ***1220.12*** *p852*
Weedon, Lewis 17; Quebec, 1870 ***8364.32*** *p26*
Weedon, Robert; Barbados or Jamaica, 1674 ***1220.12*** *p852*
Weedon, William; America, 1727 ***1220.12*** *p852*
Weeds, Stephen; America, 1767 ***1220.12*** *p852*
Weekes, Christopher; Barbados, 1668 ***1220.12*** *p852*
Weekes, John; Jamaica, 1665 ***1220.12*** *p852*
Weekes, Richard; America, 1688 ***1220.12*** *p852*
Weekes, Thomas; Barbados, 1677 ***1220.12*** *p852*
Weekes, Thomas 52; Ontario, 1871 ***1823.21*** *p385*
Weekes, Walter; Virginia, 1652 ***6254.4*** *p243*
Weekes, William 37; Ontario, 1871 ***1823.21*** *p385*
Weekley, Roger; Barbados or Jamaica, 1684 ***1220.12*** *p852*
Weeks, Agnes; Virginia, 1736 ***1220.12*** *p852*
Weeks, Elizabeth; Virginia, 1752 ***1220.12*** *p852*
Weeks, Francis; Virginia, 1769 ***1220.12*** *p852*
Weeks, Georgbe 31; Ontario, 1871 ***1823.21*** *p385*
Weeks, James; America, 1765 ***1220.12*** *p852*
Weeks, James 25; Ontario, 1871 ***1823.21*** *p385*
Weeks, John; America, 1747 ***1220.12*** *p852*
Weeks, John; America, 1767 ***1220.12*** *p852*
Weeks, John 58; Ontario, 1871 ***1823.21*** *p385*
Weeks, Knight; America, 1752 ***1220.12*** *p852*
Weeks, Phillippa; America, 1730 ***1220.12*** *p852*
Weeks, Samuel; America, 1754 ***1220.12*** *p852*
Weeks, Samuel; Virginia, 1736 ***1220.12*** *p852*
Weeks, Susanna; America, 1759 ***1220.12*** *p852*
Weeks, Thomas; Barbados, 1715 ***1220.12*** *p852*
Weeks, William 43; Ontario, 1871 ***1823.21*** *p385*
Weeks, William 58; Ontario, 1871 ***1823.17*** *p172*
Weel, Maria 28; Port uncertain, 1844 ***778.6*** *p342*
Weene, John; Barbados, 1683 ***1220.12*** *p852*
Wefler, John; Ohio, 1809-1852 ***4511.35*** *p57*
Wefler, Maria; Ohio, 1809-1852 ***4511.35*** *p57*
Wege, Cord Heinrich Philipp; America, 1846 ***7420.1*** *p50*
Wegel, Eduard; America, 1887 ***2526.43*** *p227*
Wegel, Leopold; America, 1884 ***2526.43*** *p227*
Wegele, Emma 7; America, 1893 ***1883.7*** *p38*
Wegele, Jacob 27; America, 1893 ***1883.7*** *p38*
Wegele, Rosina 7 months; America, 1893 ***1883.7*** *p38*
Wegele, Rosina 27; America, 1893 ***1883.7*** *p38*
Wegener, Heinrich Diedrich Albrecht; America, 1846 ***7420.1*** *p50*
Wegener, K.; New York, 1860 ***358.56*** *p4*
Wegener, Martin; Galveston, TX, 1855 ***571.7*** *p17*
Weger, Albert Gottlieb; America, 1889 ***179.55*** *p19*
Wegerly, Adam; New York, 1833 ***471.10*** *p87*
Weghorst, Peter H.W. 40; Boston, 1835 ***6424.55*** *p31*
Wegman, George; Illinois, 1860 ***6079.1*** *p14*
Wegner, Christian; America, 1856 ***7420.1*** *p155*
With wife son & daughter
Wegner, Julius; Nebraska, 1905 ***3004.30*** *p46*
Wegner, Julius; Wisconsin, 1894 ***6795.8*** *p217*
Wegner, Julius; Wisconsin, 1898 ***6795.8*** *p213*
Wegst, John; Philadelphia, 1867 ***8513.31*** *p431*
*Wife:*Matilda Ulmer
*Child:*Mary
Wegst, Mary *SEE* Wegst, John
Wegst, Matilda Ulmer *SEE* Wegst, John
Weh, Jacob; Illinois, 1862 ***6079.1*** *p15*
Wehage, Wilhelmine Marie Ernestine; Nevada, 1880 ***7420.1*** *p318*
Wehka, Frank 41; Minnesota, 1925 ***2769.54*** *p1379*
Wehka, Saimi 36; Minnesota, 1925 ***2769.54*** *p1379*
Wehle, Fr. Aug.; Valdivia, Chile, 1852 ***1192.4*** *p54*
With wife child & baby
With child 8
Wehler, Christian; New York, 1860 ***358.56*** *p149*
Wehling, Mr.; America, 1860 ***7420.1*** *p201*
Wehling, Adolf Wilhelm Ludwig; Port uncertain, 1888 ***7420.1*** *p358*
Wehling, Catharine Sophie Marie Schwake *SEE* Wehling, Johann Heinrich Wilhelm
Wehling, Engel Marie Louise Lampe *SEE* Wehling, Heinrich Christoph Wilhelm
Wehling, Engel Marie Sophie; Port uncertain, 1859 ***7420.1*** *p190*
Wehling, Engel Marie Sophie Christine *SEE* Wehling, Heinrich Friedrich Wilhelm
Wehling, Friedrich Christian; America, 1849 ***7420.1*** *p68*
Wehling, Gerhard; America, 1854 ***7420.1*** *p132*
With family
Wehling, Heinrich; America, 1866 ***7420.1*** *p251*
Wehling, Heinrich; America, 1868 ***7420.1*** *p278*
Wehling, Heinrich Christoph Wilhelm; America, 1867 ***7420.1*** *p266*
*Wife:*Engel Marie Louise Lampe
*Son:*Johann Heinrich Gottlieb
With children
Wehling, Heinrich Friedrich Wilhelm; America, 1873 ***7420.1*** *p301*
*Sister:*Engel Marie Sophie Christine
Wehling, Johann Friedrich Christian; America, 1857 ***7420.1*** *p174*
Wehling, Johann Heinrich Gottlieb *SEE* Wehling, Heinrich Christoph Wilhelm
Wehling, Johann Heinrich Wilhelm; America, 1859 ***7420.1*** *p190*
*Wife:*Catharine Sophie Marie Schwake
Wehling, Wackerfeld; America, 1840 ***7420.1*** *p21*
With 6 children
Wehmeier, Simon Philipp Albert; America, 1893 ***7420.1*** *p370*
Wehmeyer, Heinrich Carl August; America, 1867 ***7420.1*** *p267*
Wehmhofer, Engel Marie *SEE* Wehmhofer, Hans Heinrich
Wehmhofer, Engel Marie Dorothea Bute *SEE* Wehmhofer, Hans Heinrich
Wehmhofer, Hans Heinrich; America, 1894 ***7420.1*** *p373*
Wehmhofer, Hans Heinrich; Iowa, 1876 ***7420.1*** *p308*
*Wife:*Engel Marie Dorothea Bute
*Daughter:*Engel Marie
Wehmhofer, Heinrich; America, 1854 ***7420.1*** *p132*
Wehmhofer, Johann *SEE* Wehmhofer, Wilhelm
Wehmhofer, Johann Friedrich Christian; Port uncertain, 1836 ***7420.1*** *p12*
Wehmhofer, Johann Karl Ludwig; America, 1850 ***7420.1*** *p77*

Wehmhofer, Wilhelm; America, 1867 *7420.1 p267*
  *Brother:*Johann
Wehner, Hugo; America, 1868 *7919.3 p528*
Wehner, Michael; Louisiana, 1841-1844 *4981.45 p211*
Wehning, Elisabeth 22; Galveston, TX, 1845 *3967.10 p376*
Wehning, Theodor 29; Galveston, TX, 1845 *3967.10 p376*
Wehr, Angela; America, 1872 *5475.1 p328*
Wehr, Angela Redlinger 26 *SEE* Wehr, Mathias
Wehr, Anna Jakob *SEE* Wehr, Johann
Wehr, Anna Hammen 39 *SEE* Wehr, Johann
Wehr, Christian *SEE* Wehr, Ferdinand
Wehr, Christine Maerer *SEE* Wehr, Ferdinand
Wehr, Emilie; America, 1899 *5475.1 p40*
Wehr, Ferdinand *SEE* Wehr, Ferdinand
Wehr, Ferdinand; Dakota, 1885 *554.30 p25*
  *Wife:*Christine Maerer
  *Child:*Magdalene
  *Child:*Christian
  *Child:*Jakob
  *Child:*Johann
  *Child:*Ferdinand
Wehr, Henriette; Dakota, 1883-1918 *554.30 p25*
Wehr, Jakob *SEE* Wehr, Ferdinand
Wehr, Johann; America, 1872 *5475.1 p321*
  *Wife:*Anna Jakob
Wehr, Johann *SEE* Wehr, Ferdinand
Wehr, Johann; Iowa, 1863 *5475.1 p340*
  *Wife:*Anna Hammen
  *Daughter:*Susanna
  *Daughter:*Margarethe
  *Son:*Nikolaus
Wehr, Magdalene *SEE* Wehr, Ferdinand
Wehr, Margarethe 16 *SEE* Wehr, Johann
Wehr, Mathias; America, 1867 *5475.1 p321*
  *Wife:*Angela Redlinger
Wehr, Nikolaus 9 *SEE* Wehr, Johann
Wehr, Rosina; Dakota, 1864-1918 *554.30 p25*
Wehr, Susanna 4 *SEE* Wehr, Johann
Wehrden, Valentin; America, 1854 *5475.1 p78*
Wehrenberg, D. E.; Valdivia, Chile, 1852 *1192.4 p54*
Wehrhahn, August Conrad; America, 1881 *7420.1 p326*
Wehrhahn, Catharine Margarete Elisabeth Trutner *SEE* Wehrhahn, Johann Heinrich
Wehrhahn, Engel Maria Sophia *SEE* Wehrhahn, Johann Heinrich
Wehrhahn, Engel Sophia Doroth. *SEE* Wehrhahn, Johann Heinrich
Wehrhahn, Ernst; America, 1854 *7420.1 p132*
Wehrhahn, Friedrich Wilhelm; Nevada, 1880 *7420.1 p319*
Wehrhahn, Friedrich Wilhelm Ludwig; America, 1861 *7420.1 p209*
Wehrhahn, Johann Heinrich; America, 1845 *7420.1 p41*
  *Wife:*Catharine Margarete Elisabeth Trutner
  *Daughter:*Engel Sophia Doroth.
  *Daughter:*Engel Maria Sophia
Wehrhan, Johann; Illinois, 1848 *7420.1 p63*
  With wife
  With son 7
  With son 26
  With son 11
Wehrheim, Konrad; Pennsylvania, 1855 *170.15 p46*
  With wife & 6 children
Wehring, Christian 21; America, 1746 *778.6 p342*
Wehrle, Anna Maria; Venezuela, 1843 *3899.5 p544*
Wehrle, Katharina; Venezuela, 1843 *3899.5 p542*
Wehrlin, Anna Maria; Venezuela, 1843 *3899.5 p544*
Wehrmacher, Charlotte; America, 1852 *7420.1 p100*
Wehrmacher, Heinrich Christoph; America, 1866 *7420.1 p251*
Wehrmacher, Johann Otto; America, 1856 *7420.1 p155*
Wehrmacher, Johann Otto; America, 1866 *7420.1 p252*
Wehrmann, Carl Friedrich Ludwig; America, 1846 *7420.1 p50*
  With wife
  With daughter 4
  With daughter 1
  With son 14
  With son 12
Wehrmann, Heinrich; Port uncertain, 1887 *7420.1 p355*
Wehrmann, Heinrich Carl Ferdinand; Port uncertain, 1890 *7420.1 p361*
Wehrmann, Heinrich Wilhelm; Port uncertain, 1840 *7420.1 p21*
Wehrmann, William; Ohio, 1840-1897 *8365.35 p18*
Wehsner, August; Wisconsin, 1894 *6795.8 p186*
Weiand, Peter; America, 1850 *5475.1 p478*
Weibel, Jakob *SEE* Weibel, Jakob
Weibel, Jakob; America, 1855 *5475.1 p544*
  *Wife:*Magdalena Matthes
  *Daughter:*Margarethe

  *Son:*Johann
  *Son:*Jakob
Weibel, Johann *SEE* Weibel, Jakob
Weibel, Magdalena Matthes *SEE* Weibel, Jakob
Weibel, Margarethe *SEE* Weibel, Jakob
Weibert, Marie 27; New York, NY, 1893 *1883.7 p43*
Weibert, Mell 2; New York, NY, 1893 *1883.7 p43*
Weibert, Peter 4; New York, NY, 1893 *1883.7 p43*
Weibrecht, Anna Elisabeth; America, 1867 *7919.3 p529*
Weichel, Abraham; America, 1856 *5475.1 p520*
  *Brother:*Johann
  *Sister:*Karoline
Weichel, Adam 15; America, 1869 *2526.42 p158*
Weichel, Christina 35; America, 1856 *5475.1 p553*
Weichel, Dorotheas 11; America, 1848 *2526.42 p124*
Weichel, Georg Friedrich; America, 1881 *2526.43 p129*
Weichel, Johann; America, 1856 *2526.43 p129*
Weichel, Johann *SEE* Weichel, Abraham
Weichel, Johann Georg 6 *SEE* Weichel, Peter
Weichel, Johann Philipp 2 *SEE* Weichel, Peter
Weichel, Johannes; America, 1785 *2526.42 p133*
  *Wife:*Maria Margaretha Eisenhauer
Weichel, Karoline *SEE* Weichel, Abraham
Weichel, Katharina Elisabeth 8 *SEE* Weichel, Peter
Weichel, Margarethe Stenzhorn *SEE* Weichel, Peter
Weichel, Maria Margaretha Eisenhauer *SEE* Weichel, Johannes
Weichel, Peter; America, 1752 *2526.42 p179*
  *Wife:*Rosina Heck
  *Son:*Johann Philipp
  *Son:*Johann Georg
  *Daughter:*Katharina Elisabeth
Weichel, Peter; America, 1865 *5475.1 p541*
  *Wife:*Margarethe Stenzhorn
Weichel, Peter; America, 1867 *5475.1 p521*
Weichel, Rosina Heck *SEE* Weichel, Peter
Weichel, Wilhelm 25; America, 1872 *2526.43 p158*
Weicht, Frederick; Ohio, 1809-1852 *4511.35 p57*
Weide, Gustav; America, 1881 *5475.1 p33*
Weidel, . . .; West Virginia, 1850-1860 *1132.30 p149*
Weideliner, Jacob; Valdivia, Chile, 1850 *1192.4 p49*
Weideman, Johanes 25; America, 1747 *778.6 p342*
Weideman, Wilhelmin; Wisconsin, 1879 *6795.8 p208*
Weidemann, Anne Marie Louise; America, 1858 *7420.1 p182*
Weidemann, Christ. 29; America, 1840 *778.6 p342*
Weidemann, Engel Marie; America, 1866 *7420.1 p252*
Weidemann, Engel Marie Charlotte; America, 1846 *7420.1 p50*
  *Daughter:*Engel Marie Dorothee
Weidemann, Engel Marie Dorothee *SEE* Weidemann, Engel Marie Charlotte Meyer
Weidemann, Johann Heinrich Ludwig; America, 1854 *7420.1 p132*
Weidemann, Johann Heinrich Ludwig; America, 1859 *7420.1 p190*
  With wife 2 sons & 5 daughters
Weidemann, Johann Heinrich Wilhelm; America, 1857 *7420.1 p174*
  With wife & 2 sons
  With mother 70
Weidemann, Johann Heinrich Wilhelm; America, 1857 *7420.1 p175*
Weidemann, Wilhelmin; Wisconsin, 1879 *6795.8 p208*
Weidemann Brothers, . . .; America, 1863 *7420.1 p221*
Weidenbach, Adam 4; New York, NY, 1874 *6954.7 p38*
Weidenbach, Andreas 1 months; New York, NY, 1874 *6954.7 p38*
Weidenbach, Catharine 10; New York, NY, 1874 *6954.7 p38*
Weidenbach, Christina 5; New York, NY, 1874 *6954.7 p38*
Weidenbach, Georg 7; New York, NY, 1874 *6954.7 p38*
Weidenbach, Heinrich 8; New York, NY, 1874 *6954.7 p38*
Weidenbach, Jacob 7 months; New York, NY, 1874 *6954.7 p38*
Weidenbach, Johann 14; New York, NY, 1874 *6954.7 p38*
Weidenbach, Johann 40; New York, NY, 1874 *6954.7 p38*
Weidenbach, Louise 36; New York, NY, 1874 *6954.7 p38*
Weidenthal, Bernard; Cleveland, OH, 1845-1849 *2853.20 p475*
Weidlich, Jiri; New York, NY, 1875 *2853.20 p106*
Weidling, Jacob; Ohio, 1809-1852 *4511.35 p57*
Weidman, Adolf; Detroit, 1930 *1640.60 p78*
Weidman, Caroline Pauline; Wisconsin, 1895 *6795.8 p95*
Weidmann, Anna Maria 44; America, 1846 *2526.43 p162*
  With son-in-law
Weidmann, Anna Marie; America, 1846 *2526.43 p159*

Weidmann, Caroline Pauline; Wisconsin, 1895 *6795.8 p95*
Weidmann, Christina Dumarin *SEE* Weidmann, Francis Xavier
Weidmann, Francis Xavier; Trenton, NJ, 1853 *8513.31 p431*
  *Wife:*Christina Dumarin
Weidner, Caroline; New York, 1859 *358.56 p99*
Weiermuller, Johann Nikolaus 40; America, 1842 *5475.1 p513*
  With wife & 6 children
Weigand, . . .; West Virginia, 1850-1860 *1132.30 p149*
Weigand, Daniel Gotthart; America, 1867 *7919.3 p532*
Weigand, Eduard *SEE* Weigand, Ernst
Weigand, Ernst; Texas, 1848 *2526.43 p184*
  *Wife:*Luise Hessig
  *Son:*Eduard
Weigand, Joseph 42; America, 1846 *778.6 p342*
Weigand, Luise Hessig *SEE* Weigand, Ernst
Weigel, A. Margarethe Hahn *SEE* Weigel, Georg Adam
Weigel, Friedrich *SEE* Weigel, Georg Adam
Weigel, Georg; America, 1885 *2526.42 p158*
Weigel, Georg Adam; Brazil, 1862 *5475.1 p519*
  *Wife:*A. Margarethe Hahn
  *Son:*Friedrich
  *Son:*Philipp
Weigel, Jean 20; America, 1847 *778.6 p342*
Weigel, Meitsel 16; America, 1847 *778.6 p342*
Weigel, Philipp *SEE* Weigel, Georg Adam
Weigele, Wilhelm; Colorado, 1884 *1029.59 p93*
Weighill, James; Virginia, 1723 *1220.12 p852*
Weight, Elizabeth; Annapolis, MD, 1725 *1220.12 p829*
Weight, Jonathan; Maryland, 1674 *1236.25 p50*
Weihe, Carl August; America, 1846 *7420.1 p50*
  With family
Weihe, Carl August; America, 1855 *7420.1 p143*
Weihe, Catharine Engel Sophie *SEE* Weihe, Johann Heinrich
Weihe, Catharine Engel Sophie Schaefer *SEE* Weihe, Johann Heinrich
Weihe, Friedrich Wilhelm; America, 1855 *7420.1 p143*
  *Wife:*Sophie Louise Beisner
  *Son:*Wilhelm August
  With children
Weihe, Johann Heinrich; America, 1870 *7420.1 p286*
  *Wife:*Catharine Engel Sophie Schaefer
  *Son:*Johann Heinrich Philipp
  *Daughter:*Catharine Engel Sophie
Weihe, Johann Heinrich Philipp *SEE* Weihe, Johann Heinrich
Weihe, Sophie Charlotte; Iowa, 1859 *7420.1 p189*
Weihe, Sophie Charlotte; Iowa, 1859 *7420.1 p189*
Weihe, Sophie Louise Beisner *SEE* Weihe, Friedrich Wilhelm
Weihe, Wilhelm August *SEE* Weihe, Friedrich Wilhelm
Weihrauch, Caspar Friedrich; America, 1867 *7919.3 p525*
Weihrauch, Johanne; America, 1868 *7919.3 p530*
Weihrauch, Michael; America, 1868 *7919.3 p530*
  With wife & 5 children
Weihrauch, Michael; America, 1869 *2526.42 p148*
Weihrauch, Sybilla; America, 1869 *2526.42 p148*
Weihrecht, Sophie; America, 1868 *7919.3 p534*
Weikum, Friedrich 1; New York, NY, 1874 *6954.7 p38*
Weikum, Philippine 9 months; New York, NY, 1874 *6954.7 p38*
Weikum, Philippine 28; New York, NY, 1874 *6954.7 p38*
Weikum, Wilhelm 33; New York, NY, 1874 *6954.7 p38*
Weil, Adam, II; America, 1846 *2526.43 p158*
  With wife
  *Son:*Georg
  *Daughter:*Anna Eva
  *Daughter:*Dorothea
  *Daughter:*Maria Elisabetha
  *Daughter:*Katharina
  *Daughter:*Eva Elisabetha
Weil, Anna Eva 20 *SEE* Weil, Adam, II
Weil, Benjamin 21; New Orleans, 1848 *778.6 p342*
Weil, Caroline 20; Mississippi, 1846 *778.6 p342*
Weil, Catherine 35; New Orleans, 1848 *778.6 p342*
Weil, Charles 9; New Orleans, 1848 *778.6 p342*
Weil, Charles 15; New Orleans, 1848 *778.6 p342*
Weil, Dorothea 15 *SEE* Weil, Adam, II
Weil, Edouard 3; New Orleans, 1848 *778.6 p342*
Weil, Eva Elisabetha 12 *SEE* Weil, Adam, II
Weil, Fanny 21; New Orleans, 1848 *778.6 p342*
Weil, Georg 6 *SEE* Weil, Adam, II
Weil, Katharina 10 *SEE* Weil, Adam, II
Weil, Leopold; North Carolina, 1859 *1088.45 p36*
Weil, Lion; America, 1870 *5475.1 p208*
Weil, Marc 22; New Orleans, 1848 *778.6 p342*
Weil, Marc 36; New Orleans, 1848 *778.6 p342*

Weil, Maria Elisabetha 12 *SEE* Weil, Adam, II
Weil, Nanette 24; New Orleans, 1847 *778.6 p342*
Weil, Nathan; North Carolina, 1855 *1088.45 p37*
Weil, Nicolas 24; America, 1747 *778.6 p342*
Weil, Philipp 7; New Orleans, 1848 *778.6 p342*
Weil, Philipp 37; New Orleans, 1848 *778.6 p342*
Weil, Regina 6; Mississippi, 1846 *778.6 p342*
Weil, Samu.l 28; Missouri, 1845 *778.6 p342*
Weil, Sarah 28; New Orleans, 1848 *778.6 p342*
Weiland, A. Maria 6 *SEE* Weiland, Georg
Weiland, Albert August Luis; Wisconsin, 1899 *6795.8 p147*
Weiland, Angelika 14 *SEE* Weiland, Georg
Weiland, Anna Maria Jenner *SEE* Weiland, Nikolaus
Weiland, Barbara 48; America, 1833 *5475.1 p394*
Weiland, Christ.; America, 1852 *7420.1 p100*
Weiland, Christoph Heinrich; Iowa, 1921 *1211.15 p20*
Weiland, Ernst Wilhelm; America, 1851 *7420.1 p83*
Weiland, Friedrich Anton; America, 1883 *7420.1 p341*
Weiland, Georg 46; America, 1837 *5475.1 p385*
 Wife: Kath. Schroeder 38
 Son: Johann 2
 Son: Paulus 4
 Daughter: Angelika 14
 Daughter: A. Maria 6
 Daughter: Margarethe 9
Weiland, Jakob 36; America, 1833 *5475.1 p461*
 With wife
 Daughter: Maria
 Daughter: Margarethe
 Daughter: Magdalena
 With 2 children
Weiland, Jakob *SEE* Weiland, Nikolaus
Weiland, Joh. Peter *SEE* Weiland, Nikolaus
Weiland, Johann 2 *SEE* Weiland, Georg
Weiland, Johann; Brazil, 1855 *5475.1 p440*
 With family of 5
Weiland, Johann *SEE* Weiland, Nikolaus
Weiland, Kath. Schroeder 38 *SEE* Weiland, Georg
Weiland, Magdalena *SEE* Weiland, Jakob
Weiland, Margarethe *SEE* Weiland, Jakob
Weiland, Margarethe 9 *SEE* Weiland, Georg
Weiland, Maria *SEE* Weiland, Jakob
Weiland, Mariana 65; America, 1747 *778.6 p342*
Weiland, Mathias *SEE* Weiland, Nikolaus
Weiland, Nikolaus 25; America, 1833 *5475.1 p394*
Weiland, Nikolaus *SEE* Weiland, Nikolaus
Weiland, Nikolaus; New York, 1884 *5475.1 p71*
 Wife: Anna Maria Jenner
 Son: Mathias
 Son: Peter
 Son: Jakob
 Son: Johann
 Son: Joh. Peter
 Son: Nikolaus
Weiland, Paulus 4 *SEE* Weiland, Georg
Weiland, Peter *SEE* Weiland, Nikolaus
Weiland, Sophie Caroline Ottking *SEE* Weiland, Wilhelm
Weiland, Wilhelm; America, 1858 *7420.1 p182*
 Wife: Sophie Caroline Ottking
 With children
Weiler, Christine 22; America, 1846 *778.6 p342*
Weiler, Emanuel; America, 1882 *5475.1 p190*
Weiler, Isidor; Philadelphia, 1891 *5475.1 p191*
Weiler, Jakob; America, 1879 *5475.1 p380*
Weiler, John; New York, 1859 *358.56 p101*
Weiler, Joseph; Ohio, 1809-1852 *4511.35 p57*
Weiler, Matthias; Ohio, 1809-1852 *4511.35 p57*
Weilerman, L.; Louisiana, 1874-1875 *4981.45 p130*
Weill, Abram; North Carolina, 1859 *1088.45 p37*
Weill, Salomon 24; Louisiana, 1848 *778.6 p342*
Weill, Seligmund 23; New Orleans, 1848 *778.6 p342*
Weiller, Adelheid *SEE* Weiller, Emanuel
Weiller, Emanuel; Ohio, 1891 *5475.1 p162*
 Wife: Maria Anna Heimann
 Daughter: Adelheid
 Son: Hermann
 Son: Leo
 Son: Max
Weiller, Hermann *SEE* Weiller, Emanuel
Weiller, Leo *SEE* Weiller, Emanuel
Weiller, Maria Anna Heimann *SEE* Weiller, Emanuel
Weiller, Max *SEE* Weiller, Emanuel
Weils, William; West Virginia, 1787 *1132.30 p146*
Weimann, Carl; America, 1858 *7420.1 p183*
Weimann, Peter; Illinois, 1855 *6079.1 p15*
Weimann, Peter; Illinois, 1858 *6079.1 p15*
Weimar, Georg Christoph; America, 1892 *2526.43 p184*
Weimar, Henry; Long Island, 1781 *8529.30 p10A*
Weimer, Frederick; Ohio, 1809-1852 *4511.35 p57*
Weimer, John; Ohio, 1809-1852 *4511.35 p57*
Weimer, Michael; Ohio, 1809-1852 *4511.35 p57*

Wein, Anna; America, 1881 *5475.1 p44*
Wein, Anna *SEE* Wein, Johann
Wein, Anna Maria; America, 1800-1899 *5475.1 p300*
Wein, Barbara Reinert *SEE* Wein, Johann
Wein, Johann; Minnesota, 1881 *5475.1 p300*
 Wife: Barbara Reinert
 Son: Mathias
 Daughter: Anna
Wein, Margarethe 34; America, 1867 *5475.1 p201*
Wein, Mathias *SEE* Wein, Johann
Weinand, Johann Jakob; America, 1846 *5475.1 p547*
Weinberg, Mr.; America, 1850 *7420.1 p77*
 With wife & children
Weinberger, Bernhard 17; New York, NY, 1878 *9253.2 p45*
Weinberger, Emil; Colorado, 1880 *1029.59 p93*
Weinberger, Georg Friedrich; America, 1867 *7919.3 p534*
Weinbertg, Samuel; Philadelphia, 1871 *5720.10 p381*
Weineck, Eduard Carl; America, 1867 *7919.3 p525*
Weinessig, George; Long Island, 1781 *8529.30 p10A*
Weinfurter, Jacob; Louisiana, 1841-1844 *4981.45 p211*
Weingardt, C. 9; New Orleans, 1834 *1002.51 p110*
Weingardt, Miss C. 11; New Orleans, 1834 *1002.51 p110*
Weingardt, Miss C. 18; New Orleans, 1834 *1002.51 p110*
Weingardt, Miss C. 24; New Orleans, 1834 *1002.51 p110*
Weingardt, Miss E. 14; New Orleans, 1834 *1002.51 p110*
Weingardt, J. 22; New Orleans, 1834 *1002.51 p110*
Weingardt, J. 46; New Orleans, 1834 *1002.51 p110*
Weingardt, Miss M. 42; New Orleans, 1834 *1002.51 p110*
Weingardt, P. 4; New Orleans, 1834 *1002.51 p110*
Weingardt, Miss P. 19; New Orleans, 1834 *1002.51 p110*
Weingartner, Andreas 9 months; New Orleans, 1847 *778.6 p342*
Weingartner, Catherina 7; New Orleans, 1847 *778.6 p342*
Weingartner, Catherine 38; New Orleans, 1847 *778.6 p342*
Weingartner, Franz 6; New Orleans, 1847 *778.6 p343*
Weingartner, Martin 9; New Orleans, 1847 *778.6 p343*
Weingartner, Martin 38; New Orleans, 1847 *778.6 p343*
Weinich, Ludwig; Ohio, 1809-1852 *4511.35 p58*
Weininger, Barbara 26; New York, NY, 1898 *7951.13 p43*
Weininger, Katherina 18 months; New York, NY, 1898 *7951.13 p43*
Weininger, Margaret 4; New York, NY, 1898 *7951.13 p43*
Weinkauf, Auguste; Wisconsin, 1893 *6795.8 p145*
Weinkauf, Christopher; Wisconsin, 1856 *6795.8 p45*
Weinknecht, J.; Galveston, TX, 1855 *571.7 p18*
Weinman, Valtin; Philadelphia, 1853 *5720.10 p382*
Weinmann, Andreas; North Carolina, 1710 *3629.40 p7*
Weinmann, Anna Margreta; North Carolina, 1710 *3629.40 p7*
Weinmister, Disapda; Halifax, N.S., 1902 *1860.4 p41*
Weinmister, Heinrich 35; Halifax, N.S., 1902 *1860.4 p41*
Weinmister, Katha 4; Halifax, N.S., 1902 *1860.4 p41*
Weinmister, Katha 30; Halifax, N.S., 1902 *1860.4 p41*
Weinmister, Ren.ick 2; Halifax, N.S., 1902 *1860.4 p41*
Weinne, Herman; Detroit, 1893 *3366.30 p70*
Weinreich, P. F.; Louisiana, 1836-1841 *4981.45 p209*
Weinschenk, Daniel; Ohio, 1840-1897 *8365.35 p18*
Weinstein, Berl 8; New York, NY, 1894 *6512.1 p230*
Weinstein, Brinah 2; New York, NY, 1894 *6512.1 p230*
Weinstein, Isaac 6; New York, NY, 1894 *6512.1 p230*
Weinstein, Leah 34; New York, NY, 1894 *6512.1 p230*
Weinstein, Levi; North Carolina, 1858 *1088.45 p37*
Weinstein, Mear; North Carolina, 1855 *1088.45 p37*
Weinstein, Solomon 11; New York, NY, 1894 *6512.1 p230*
Weinstein, William; North Carolina, 1853 *1088.45 p37*
Weintraub, Philip; Detroit, 1929-1930 *6214.5 p65*
Weinz, Anna 7; America, 1896 *5475.1 p19*
Weinzheimer, W. 45; New Orleans, 1834 *1002.51 p113*
Weir, Alexander 69; Ontario, 1871 *1823.21 p385*
Weir, Andrew 74; Ontario, 1871 *1823.21 p385*
Weir, Catherine 54; Ontario, 1871 *1823.21 p385*
Weir, James 45; Ontario, 1871 *1823.21 p385*
Weir, Jane 80; Ontario, 1871 *1823.21 p385*
Weir, John 46; Michigan, 1880 *4491.36 p24*
Weir, John 34; Ontario, 1871 *1823.21 p386*
Weir, John 46; Ontario, 1871 *1823.21 p386*
Weir, John 48; Ontario, 1871 *1823.21 p385*
Weir, John 60; Ontario, 1871 *1823.21 p386*
Weir, John 62; Ontario, 1871 *1823.21 p386*
Weir, Joseph 51; Ontario, 1871 *1823.21 p386*

Weir, Louisa 22; Ontario, 1871 *1823.21 p386*
Weir, Mary 19; Ontario, 1871 *1823.21 p386*
Weir, Mary 80; Ontario, 1871 *1823.21 p386*
Weir, Robert 62; Ontario, 1871 *1823.21 p386*
Weir, Robert B. 28; Michigan, 1880 *4491.36 p23*
Weir, Sevilla A. 26; Michigan, 1880 *4491.36 p23*
Weir, Thomas; Ohio, 1836 *3580.20 p33*
Weir, Thomas; Ohio, 1836 *6020.12 p23*
Weir, Wallace 27; Michigan, 1880 *4491.36 p23*
Weir, William 45; Ontario, 1871 *1823.21 p386*
Weir, William 57; Ontario, 1871 *1823.21 p386*
Weirauch, Leonard; Ohio, 1809-1852 *4511.35 p57*
Weirich, Anna Maria 14 *SEE* Weirich, Nikolaus
Weirich, Elisabeth 16 *SEE* Weirich, Nikolaus
Weirich, Kath. Walter 54 *SEE* Weirich, Nikolaus
Weirich, Ludwig; Ohio, 1809-1852 *4511.35 p58*
Weirich, Margarethe 8 *SEE* Weirich, Nikolaus
Weirich, Nikolaus 57; America, 1857 *5475.1 p550*
 Wife: Kath. Walter 54
 Daughter: Margarethe 8
 Daughter: Elisabeth 16
 Daughter: Anna Maria 14
Weis, Antonio 19; America, 1847 *778.6 p343*
Weis, Christian; Ohio, 1809-1852 *4511.35 p57*
Weis, Ernst Frederick; Illinois, 1858-1861 *6020.5 p133*
Weis, Josef; Illinois, 1880 *5475.1 p315*
Weis, Leopold; North Carolina, 1859 *1088.45 p37*
Weis, Martin; Ohio, 1809-1852 *4511.35 p57*
Weisbeck, Johann 20; New York, NY, 1893 *1883.7 p42*
Weisbeck, Wendelin 17; New York, NY, 1893 *1883.7 p42*
Weisberg, Abraham; Detroit, 1929 *1640.55 p117*
Weisbrod, Joseph; Illinois, 1855 *6079.1 p15*
Weisel, Anna; America, 1872 *6442.17 p69*
Weisel, Conrad; Wisconsin, 1861 *6795.8 p98*
Weisel, Conrad; Wisconsin, 1882 *6795.8 p98*
Weiserist, Benedict; Ohio, 1809-1852 *4511.35 p58*
Weisert, Michael; Ohio, 1809-1852 *4511.35 p58*
Weisgerber, Anton; America, 1846 *5475.1 p472*
Weisgerber, Franz 19; America, 1849 *5475.1 p477*
Weisgerber, Johann; America, 1881 *5475.1 p182*
Weishaar, Ch. Francois; Louisiana, 1841-1844 *4981.45 p211*
Weishaar, David F.; Kansas, 1876 *1447.20 p64*
Weishaar, Friedrich Herman; Wisconsin, 1885 *6795.8 p147*
Weiskircher, Andreas *SEE* Weiskircher, Joh.
Weiskircher, Elisabeth Strauss *SEE* Weiskircher, Joh.
Weiskircher, Joh.; America, 1890 *5475.1 p398*
 Wife: Elisabeth Strauss
 Son: Karl
 Daughter: Maria
 Son: Andreas
 Son: Nikolaus
 Son: Josef
 Son: Konrad
 Daughter: Magdalena
 Daughter: Katharina
Weiskircher, Josef *SEE* Weiskircher, Joh.
Weiskircher, Karl *SEE* Weiskircher, Joh.
Weiskircher, Katharina *SEE* Weiskircher, Joh.
Weiskircher, Konrad *SEE* Weiskircher, Joh.
Weiskircher, Magdalena *SEE* Weiskircher, Joh.
Weiskircher, Maria *SEE* Weiskircher, Joh.
Weiskircher, Nikolaus *SEE* Weiskircher, Joh.
Weislogle, George; Ohio, 1809-1852 *4511.35 p58*
Weislogle, Michael; Ohio, 1809-1852 *4511.35 p58*
Weiss, Andrew; Colorado, 1890 *1029.59 p93*
Weiss, Andrew; Colorado, 1903 *1029.59 p93*
Weiss, Anna 26; Missouri, 1845 *778.6 p343*
Weiss, Bernhard 35; New Orleans, 1847 *778.6 p343*
Weiss, Daniel; Wisconsin, 1905 *6795.8 p232*
Weiss, Dietrich Conrad; America, 1847 *7420.1 p57*
Weiss, Dorothe 15; America, 1841 *778.6 p343*
Weiss, Emilie; Wisconsin, 1901 *6795.8 p232*
Weiss, George 20; America, 1841 *778.6 p343*
Weiss, George 32; America, 1840 *778.6 p343*
Weiss, Goran 55; New Orleans, 1847 *778.6 p343*
Weiss, Henri 27; America, 1841 *778.6 p343*
Weiss, Henri 72; America, 1841 *778.6 p343*
Weiss, J. Christoph; Chile, 1852 *1192.4 p52*
 With wife
Weiss, Jacob; Ohio, 1809-1852 *4511.35 p58*
Weiss, Jacque 40; America, 1842 *778.6 p343*
Weiss, John; New York, 1859 *358.56 p55*
Weiss, Magdalena 52; America, 1841 *778.6 p343*
Weiss, Michel 19; America, 1840 *778.6 p343*
Weiss, Olgo; Wisconsin, 1905 *6795.8 p232*
Weiss, Wilhelmine; America, 1878 *7420.1 p397*
Weissbrodt, Carl; America, 1867 *7919.3 p533*
Weissdel, Regina 24; America, 1845 *778.6 p343*
Weisse, Jean 28; America, 1840 *778.6 p343*
Weissel, G. F.; Louisiana, 1836-1840 *4981.45 p213*

Weissemann, Gottlieb; America, 1833 ***5475.1*** *p73*
With wife
With child 6
With child 1
With child 8
Weissenberger, Jacob; Illinois, 1858-1861 ***6020.5*** *p133*
Weissenborn, Wilhelm August; America, 1867 ***7919.3*** *p533*
Weissenfeld, Georg *SEE* Weissenfeld, Michel
Weissenfeld, Karl *SEE* Weissenfeld, Michel
Weissenfeld, Maria *SEE* Weissenfeld, Michel
Weissenfeld, Maria Probst *SEE* Weissenfeld, Michel
Weissenfeld, Michel *SEE* Weissenfeld, Michel
Weissenfeld, Michel; America, 1882 ***5475.1*** *p228*
*Wife:*Maria Probst
*Son:*Michel
*Daughter:*Maria
*Son:*Karl
*Son:*Georg
Weissflog, Johannes; America, 1867 ***7919.3*** *p530*
Weissflog, Louise; America, 1867 ***7919.3*** *p530*
With child
Weissgerber, Christina; America, 1860 ***2526.42*** *p171*
Weissgerber, Georg; America, 1868-1906 ***2526.42*** *p179*
Weissgerber, Leonhard; America, 1859 ***2526.43*** *p144*
Weissheit, Johannes; America, 1867 ***7919.3*** *p527*
With wife & 3 children
Weissich, Moritz; America, 1861 ***7420.1*** *p209*
Weissiengar, John; Illinois, 1857 ***6079.1*** *p15*
Weisswenger, Carl; America, 1854 ***179.55*** *p19*
Weisz, Jacob; Ohio, 1809-1852 ***4511.35*** *p58*
Weiten, Anna; Kentucky, 1887 ***5475.1*** *p365*
Weiten, Johann; America, 1881 ***5475.1*** *p133*
Weiten, Johann *SEE* Weiten, Johann
Weiten, Johann; America, 1884 ***5475.1*** *p378*
*Wife:*Magdalena Sauerwein
*Son:*Johann
*Son:*Nikolaus
*Son:*Mathias
Weiten, Magdalena Sauerwein *SEE* Weiten, Johann
Weiten, Mathias *SEE* Weiten, Johann
Weiten, Nikolaus *SEE* Weiten, Johann
Weiten, Susanna; America, 1874 ***5475.1*** *p339*
Weiter, Jean 22; America, 1840 ***778.6*** *p343*
Weith, Jean 33; New Orleans, 1848 ***778.6*** *p343*
Weitz, Catherine 50; America, 1844 ***778.6*** *p343*
Weitzel, Alexander 4; Portland, ME, 1911 ***970.38*** *p82*
Weitzel, Jacob 28; Portland, ME, 1911 ***970.38*** *p82*
Weitzel, Johannes; America, 1892 ***170.15*** *p46*
With wife & 3 children
Weitzel, Otto 11; Portland, ME, 1911 ***970.38*** *p82*
Weitzel, Rosa 2; Portland, ME, 1911 ***970.38*** *p82*
Weitzel, Theresa 25; Portland, ME, 1911 ***970.38*** *p82*
Weizenkorn, Carl Ernst Friedrich; America, 1889 ***7420.1*** *p360*
Weizer, . . .; North Carolina, 1710 ***3629.40*** *p7*
Wejolowski, Charles 22; Ontario, 1871 ***1823.17*** *p172*
Welb, George 24; Ontario, 1871 ***1823.21*** *p386*
Welb, John 63; Ontario, 1871 ***1823.21*** *p386*
Welbeloved, John; America, 1765 ***1220.12*** *p852*
Welbred, Mary; America, 1774 ***1220.12*** *p852*
Welch, Abraham 52; New York, NY, 1893 ***1883.7*** *p40*
Welch, Alice; America, 1739 ***1220.12*** *p854*
Welch, Andrew; America, 1772 ***1220.12*** *p854*
Welch, Bartholomew; Boston, 1727 ***1642*** *p25*
Welch, Daniel; New England, 1745 ***1642*** *p28*
Welch, Davis; Massachusetts, 1750 ***1642*** *p100*
Welch, Dennis; Boston, 1765 ***1642*** *p35*
Welch, Edmund; America, 1736 ***1220.12*** *p854*
Welch, Edward; America, 1772 ***1220.12*** *p854*
Welch, Edward; Annapolis, MD, 1731 ***1220.12*** *p854*
Welch, Edward; Boston, 1728 ***1642*** *p25*
Welch, Edward; Ipswich, MA, 1661 ***1642*** *p69*
Welch, Edward; New England, 1745 ***1642*** *p28*
Welch, Edward 65; Ontario, 1871 ***1823.21*** *p386*
Welch, Edward; Salem, MA, 1654 ***1642*** *p78*
Welch, Elisabeth 16; New York, NY, 1893 ***1883.7*** *p40*
Welch, Elizabeth; America, 1700 ***1220.12*** *p855*
Welch, Elizabeth; America, 1771 ***1220.12*** *p855*
Welch, George 24; Ontario, 1871 ***1823.17*** *p172*
Welch, Hannah; America, 1771 ***1220.12*** *p855*
Welch, Heinrich 18; New York, NY, 1893 ***1883.7*** *p40*
Welch, Helena 14; New York, NY, 1893 ***1883.7*** *p40*
Welch, Henry; America, 1768 ***1220.12*** *p855*
Welch, Henry; America, 1774 ***1220.12*** *p855*
Welch, Jacob 5; New York, NY, 1893 ***1883.7*** *p40*
Welch, James; America, 1756 ***1220.12*** *p855*
Welch, James; America, 1762 ***1220.12*** *p855*
Welch, James; America, 1767 ***1220.12*** *p855*
Welch, James; America, 1769 ***1220.12*** *p855*
Welch, James; America, 1771 ***1220.12*** *p855*
Welch, James; America, 1774 ***1220.12*** *p855*
Welch, James; New England, 1745 ***1642*** *p28*
Welch, James; Ohio, 1840-1897 ***8365.35*** *p18*
Welch, James; Rappahannock, VA, 1728 ***1220.12*** *p855*
Welch, James; Washington, 1887 ***2770.40*** *p25*
Welch, John; America, 1741 ***1220.12*** *p855*
Welch, John; America, 1752 ***1220.12*** *p855*
Welch, John; America, 1755 ***1220.12*** *p855*
Welch, John; America, 1766 ***1220.12*** *p855*
Welch, John; America, 1771 ***1220.12*** *p855*
Welch, John; America, 1773 ***1220.12*** *p855*
Welch, John; Boston, 1763 ***1642*** *p32*
Welch, John; Colorado, 1862-1894 ***1029.59*** *p93*
Welch, John; New England, 1745 ***1642*** *p28*
Welch, John; Ohio, 1809-1852 ***4511.35*** *p58*
Welch, John 18; Quebec, 1870 ***8364.32*** *p26*
Welch, John; St. John, N.B., 1847 ***2978.15*** *p40*
Welch, Joseph; America, 1750 ***1220.12*** *p855*
Welch, Justine 51; New York, NY, 1893 ***1883.7*** *p40*
Welch, Laurence; Barbados or Jamaica, 1689 ***1220.12*** *p855*
Welch, Lawrence; America, 1749 ***1220.12*** *p855*
Welch, Luke; Boston, 1766 ***1642*** *p37*
Welch, Luke; New England, 1745 ***1642*** *p28*
Welch, Margaret 42; Ontario, 1871 ***1823.17*** *p172*
Welch, Margaretha 22; New York, NY, 1893 ***1883.7*** *p40*
Welch, Marie 20; New York, NY, 1893 ***1883.7*** *p40*
Welch, Martha; America, 1761 ***1220.12*** *p855*
Welch, Mary; America, 1756 ***1220.12*** *p855*
Welch, Mary; America, 1762 ***1220.12*** *p855*
Welch, Mary; America, 1763 ***1220.12*** *p855*
Welch, Mary; Boston, 1763 ***1642*** *p48*
Welch, Mary 42; Michigan, 1880 ***4491.39*** *p32*
Welch, Mary; Virginia, 1732 ***1220.12*** *p855*
Welch, Michael; America, 1771 ***1220.12*** *p855*
Welch, Michael 48; Michigan, 1880 ***4491.39*** *p32*
Welch, Michal 47; Ontario, 1871 ***1823.17*** *p172*
Welch, Morris; New England, 1745 ***1642*** *p28*
Welch, Nicholas; Ohio, 1809-1852 ***4511.35*** *p58*
Welch, Patrick; Boston, 1747 ***1642*** *p46*
Welch, Patrick; Boston, 1763 ***1642*** *p32*
Welch, Patrick; Illinois, 1834-1900 ***6020.5*** *p133*
Welch, Philip; America, 1772 ***1220.12*** *p855*
Welch, Philip 16; Ipswich, MA, 1654 ***1642*** *p68*
Welch, Philip; Massachusetts, 1620-1775 ***1642*** *p139*
Welch, Philip; Massachusetts, 1666 ***1642*** *p82*
Welch, Philip; Massachusetts, 1671 ***1642*** *p81*
Welch, Richard; America, 1740 ***1220.12*** *p855*
Welch, Richard; America, 1762 ***1220.12*** *p855*
Welch, Richard; Boston, 1761 ***1642*** *p48*
Welch, Robert; America, 1755 ***1220.12*** *p855*
Welch, Robert; America, 1764 ***1220.12*** *p855*
Welch, Samuel 54; Ontario, 1871 ***1823.21*** *p386*
Welch, Susannah; America, 1773 ***1220.12*** *p855*
Welch, Thomas; America, 1700 ***1220.12*** *p855*
Welch, Thomas; America, 1755 ***1220.12*** *p855*
Welch, Thomas; America, 1757 ***1220.12*** *p856*
Welch, Thomas; America, 1770 ***1220.12*** *p856*
Welch, Thomas; Illinois, 1860 ***6079.1*** *p15*
Welch, Thomas; New York, 1781 ***8529.30*** *p17*
Welch, Timothy; Ohio, 1840-1897 ***8365.35*** *p18*
Welch, William; America, 1724 ***1220.12*** *p856*
Welch, William; America, 1738 ***1220.12*** *p856*
Welch, William; America, 1740 ***1220.12*** *p856*
Welch, William 23; Boston, 1753 ***1642*** *p31*
Welch, William; Maryland, 1733 ***1220.12*** *p856*
Welch, William A.; North Carolina, 1853 ***1088.45*** *p37*
Welchborne, Thomas; America, 1760 ***1220.12*** *p852*
Welchenbach, Francis; Ohio, 1809-1852 ***4511.35*** *p58*
Welchlies, . . .; West Virginia, n.d. ***1132.30*** *p151*
Welchman, Samuel; Nevis or Jamaica, 1722 ***1220.12*** *p852*
Welck, Christina 22; New York, NY, 1893 ***1883.7*** *p38*
Welck, Ludwig 28; New York, NY, 1893 ***1883.7*** *p38*
Weld, William 46; Ontario, 1871 ***1823.21*** *p386*
Welden, Thomas, Jr. 35; Ontario, 1871 ***1823.21*** *p386*
Welding, Thomas 35; Ontario, 1871 ***1823.21*** *p386*
Weldon, Andrew *SEE* Weldon, Ann
Weldon, Andrew 40; Ontario, 1871 ***1823.21*** *p386*
Weldon, Ann *SEE* Weldon, Ann
Weldon, Ann; Canada, 1774 ***3036.5*** *p42*
*Child:*Andrew
*Child:*Thomas
*Child:*Ann
*Child:*Elizabeth
Weldon, Darby; New Orleans, 1851 ***7242.30*** *p156*
Weldon, Elizabeth *SEE* Weldon, Ann
Weldon, John; Maryland, 1723 ***1220.12*** *p852*
Weldon, Peggy; New Orleans, 1851 ***7242.30*** *p156*
Weldon, Robert Walker; America, 1772 ***1220.12*** *p852*
Weldon, Thomas *SEE* Weldon, Ann
Weldon, Thos Skelton 1; Ontario, 1871 ***1823.21*** *p386*
Weldon, William; America, 1765 ***1220.12*** *p853*
Weldron, Kate 21; Ontario, 1871 ***1823.21*** *p386*
Welfl, Frantisek; South Dakota, 1871-1910 ***2853.20*** *p247*
Welford, Gaius 48; Ontario, 1871 ***1823.21*** *p386*
Welham, James; America, 1774 ***1220.12*** *p853*
Welier, Helene; Halifax, N.S., 1902 ***1860.4*** *p41*
Welier, Jacob 25; Halifax, N.S., 1902 ***1860.4*** *p41*
Welier, Rosa 24; Halifax, N.S., 1902 ***1860.4*** *p41*
Welin, Joh. Olsson; Philadelphia, 1848 ***6412.40*** *p150*
Welintz, William Frederick Herman; Wisconsin, 1895 ***6795.8*** *p68*
Welk, Anna Maria 45; New York, NY, 1898 ***7951.13*** *p42*
Welk, Anton 2; New York, NY, 1898 ***7951.13*** *p42*
Welk, Baltasar 15; New York, NY, 1898 ***7951.13*** *p42*
Welk, Baltasar 16; New York, NY, 1898 ***7951.13*** *p42*
Welk, Francisca 11; New York, NY, 1898 ***7951.13*** *p42*
Welk, Franz 17; New York, NY, 1898 ***7951.13*** *p42*
Welk, Johann 11; New York, NY, 1898 ***7951.13*** *p42*
Welk, Johann 21; New York, NY, 1898 ***7951.13*** *p42*
Welk, Magdalena 19; New York, NY, 1898 ***7951.13*** *p42*
Welk, Magdalena 56; New York, NY, 1898 ***7951.13*** *p42*
Welk, Marcus 53; New York, NY, 1898 ***7951.13*** *p42*
Welk, Margaret 50; New York, NY, 1898 ***7951.13*** *p42*
Welk, Marianna 18; New York, NY, 1898 ***7951.13*** *p42*
Welk, Michael 49; New York, NY, 1898 ***7951.13*** *p42*
Welker, John; Illinois, 1865 ***6079.1*** *p15*
Welker, John; New Orleans, 1846 ***7710.1*** *p153*
Welker, Joseph 34; Galveston, TX, 1846 ***3967.10*** *p378*
Welker, Marianne 30; Galveston, TX, 1846 ***3967.10*** *p378*
Welker, Martin; Ohio, 1809-1852 ***4511.35*** *p58*
Welker, Wilhelm; Louisiana, 1836-1841 ***4981.45*** *p209*
Welkley, John; Ohio, 1809-1852 ***4511.35*** *p58*
Well, Richard 75; Ontario, 1871 ***1823.21*** *p386*
Well, Walter 35; St. Johns, N.F., 1811 ***1053.20*** *p22*
Wellam, Robert; America, 1750 ***1220.12*** *p853*
Welland, Nicholas; Barbados, 1715 ***1220.12*** *p853*
Welland, Richard; America, 1767 ***1220.12*** *p853*
Wellar, John; America, 1758 ***1220.12*** *p853*
Wellard, Thomas; America, 1746 ***1220.12*** *p853*
Wellbrand, Mary; America, 1774 ***1220.12*** *p853*
Welldon, George; America, 1769 ***1220.12*** *p852*
Wellenstein, Anna 20 *SEE* Wellenstein, Johann
Wellenstein, Franz 14 *SEE* Wellenstein, Johann
Wellenstein, Jakob 19 *SEE* Wellenstein, Johann
Wellenstein, Johann 55; America, 1854 ***5475.1*** *p255*
*Wife:*Johannetta Gales 55
*Son:*Jakob 19
*Son:*Franz 14
*Sister:*Margrethe 42
*Daughter:*Anna 20
*Daughter:*Johannetta 24
Wellenstein, Johann; Wisconsin, 1847 ***5475.1*** *p254*
Wellenstein, Johannetta 24 *SEE* Wellenstein, Johann
Wellenstein, Johannetta Gales 55 *SEE* Wellenstein, Johann
Wellenstein, Margrethe 42 *SEE* Wellenstein, Johann
Wellenstein, Nikolaus; America, 1872 ***5475.1*** *p256*
Wellenstein, Peter; America, 1873 ***5475.1*** *p256*
Weller, Anton 53; America, 1856 ***5475.1*** *p348*
*Wife:*Eva Berg 59
*Daughter:*Margarethe 13
Weller, Elisabeth 28; America, 1856 ***5475.1*** *p348*
Weller, Eva; America, 1881 ***179.55*** *p19*
Weller, Eva Berg 59 *SEE* Weller, Anton
Weller, George; Illinois, 1858-1861 ***6020.5*** *p133*
Weller, Helene 18; New York, NY, 1882 ***5475.1*** *p15*
Weller, Jakob; America, 1891 ***179.55*** *p19*
Weller, Jakob; America, 1891 ***179.55*** *p19*
Weller, Johann; America, 1700-1899 ***179.55*** *p19*
Weller, Johann Michael; America, 1854 ***179.55*** *p19*
Weller, John; Ohio, 1840-1897 ***8365.35*** *p18*
Weller, John; Rappahannock, VA, 1741 ***1220.12*** *p853*
Weller, Katharina; America, 1881 ***179.55*** *p19*
Weller, Lina 11 months; New York, NY, 1882 ***5475.1*** *p15*
Weller, Margarethe 13 *SEE* Weller, Anton
Weller, Melissa 42; Ontario, 1871 ***1823.21*** *p386*
Weller, Moses 49; Ontario, 1871 ***1823.21*** *p386*
Weller, Thomas; Barbados, 1663 ***1220.12*** *p853*
Weller, William; America, 1722 ***1220.12*** *p853*
Welles, Samuel 22; Ontario, 1871 ***1823.21*** *p386*
Wellf, Ant. 24; America, 1840 ***778.6*** *p343*
Wellham, Robert; America, 1768 ***1220.12*** *p853*
Wellhausen, Caroline Wilhelmine Charlotte; America, 1885 ***7420.1*** *p349*
Wellhausen, Friedrich; America, 1852 ***7420.1*** *p100*
With wife & 3 daughters
Wellhausen, Heinrich; America, 1851 ***7420.1*** *p83*
Wellhausen, Heinrich Christian Wilhelm; Port uncertain, 1860 ***7420.1*** *p201*
Welling, Elizabeth; Rappahannock, VA, 1741 ***1220.12*** *p853*
Welling, James; Barbados, 1668 ***1220.12*** *p853*
Welling, John; Barbados, 1682 ***1220.12*** *p853*

Welling, Richard; America, 1752 **1220.12** *p853*

Welling, Thomas; America, 1755 **1220.12** *p853*

Wellinger, Elnaria 49; Ohio, 1880 **4879.40** *p259*

Wellington, . . . 31; Ontario, 1871 **1823.17** *p172*

Wellington, George; America, 1758 **1220.12** *p853*

Wellington, Henry 33; Ontario, 1871 **1823.17** *p172*

Wellington, J. 28; Ontario, 1871 **1823.21** *p387*

Wellington, James; America, 1759 **1220.12** *p853*

Wellington, James 48; Ontario, 1871 **1823.17** *p172*

Wellington, Mark 38; Ontario, 1871 **1823.17** *p172*

Wellington, Mary 34; Barbados, 1664 **1220.12** *p853*

Wellington, Peter 35; Ontario, 1871 **1823.17** *p172*

Wellington, Sarah 71; Ontario, 1871 **1823.17** *p172*

Wellins, John; America, 1765 **1220.12** *p853*

Wellman, Richard; America, 1765 **1220.12** *p853*

Wellman, Simon; Louisiana, 1874 **4981.45** *p297*

Wells, Ann; America, 1740 **1220.12** *p853*

Wells, Ann; America, 1755 **1220.12** *p853*

Wells, Ann; America, 1763 **1220.12** *p853*

Wells, Ann; Virginia, 1732 **1220.12** *p853*

Wells, Anne; Virginia, 1720 **1220.12** *p853*

Wells, Benjamin T. 45; Ontario, 1871 **1823.21** *p387*

Wells, Bruce James; Miami, 1920 **4984.15** *p38*

Wells, Catherine; America, 1758 **1220.12** *p853*

Wells, Charles; America, 1686 **1220.12** *p853*

Wells, Charles; Barbados, 1672 **1220.12** *p853*

Wells, Daniel; America, 1739 **1220.12** *p853*

Wells, David; St. Johns, N.F., 1825 **1053.15** *p7*

Wells, David S.; Ohio, 1861 **3580.20** *p33*

Wells, David S.; Ohio, 1861 **6020.12** *p23*

Wells, Edmund; America, 1775 **1220.12** *p853*

Wells, Edward; America, 1773 **1220.12** *p853*

Wells, Edward; Virginia, 1739 **1220.12** *p853*

Wells, Elizabeth; Barbados or Jamaica, 1704 **1220.12** *p853*

Wells, Elizabeth 62; Ontario, 1871 **1823.17** *p172*

Wells, Elizabeth; Virginia, 1721 **1220.12** *p853*

Wells, Elizabeth Mary; Maryland, 1742 **1220.12** *p853*

Wells, George; America, 1685 **1220.12** *p853*

Wells, George; America, 1758 **1220.12** *p853*

Wells, George 59; Ontario, 1871 **1823.21** *p387*

Wells, Granby Thomas; America, 1771 **1220.12** *p853*

Wells, Hezekiah G.; Ohio, 1832 **3580.20** *p33*

Wells, Hezekiah G.; Ohio, 1832 **6020.12** *p23*

Wells, Hiram E.; Washington, 1886 **2770.40** *p24*

Wells, Isaac 32; Ontario, 1871 **1823.21** *p387*

Wells, J. 22; New Orleans, 1834 **1002.51** *p112*

Wells, Jacob; America, 1750 **1220.12** *p853*

Wells, James; America, 1742 **1220.12** *p853*

Wells, James; America, 1758 **1220.12** *p853*

Wells, James 40; Ontario, 1871 **1823.21** *p387*

Wells, James 44; Ontario, 1871 **1823.21** *p387*

Wells, Jane 35; Ontario, 1871 **1823.21** *p387*

Wells, Jane 36; Ontario, 1871 **1823.21** *p387*

Wells, Jeremiah; America, 1741 **1220.12** *p853*

Wells, Jeremiah; America, 1772 **1220.12** *p854*

Wells, John; America, 1687 **1220.12** *p854*

Wells, John; America, 1729 **1220.12** *p854*

Wells, John; America, 1748 **1220.12** *p854*

Wells, John; America, 1763 **1220.12** *p854*

Wells, John; America, 1774 **1220.12** *p854*

Wells, John; America, 1775 **1220.12** *p854*

Wells, John; Illinois, 1863 **6079.1** *p15*

Wells, John; Louisiana, 1874 **4981.45** *p297*

Wells, John 37; Ontario, 1871 **1823.21** *p387*

Wells, John 74; Ontario, 1871 **1823.21** *p387*

Wells, John 79; Ontario, 1871 **1823.21** *p387*

Wells, John; Virginia, 1739 **1220.12** *p854*

Wells, Joseph; America, 1723 **1220.12** *p854*

Wells, Joseph; America, 1727 **1220.12** *p854*

Wells, Joseph; America, 1738 **1220.12** *p854*

Wells, Joseph; America, 1740 **1220.12** *p854*

Wells, Joshua; America, 1766 **1220.12** *p854*

Wells, Katherine; America, 1721 **1220.12** *p853*

Wells, Mariah; Maryland, 1725 **1220.12** *p854*

Wells, Mary; America, 1719 **1220.12** *p854*

Wells, Mary; America, 1721 **1220.12** *p854*

Wells, Mary 45; Ontario, 1871 **1823.21** *p387*

Wells, Meketabel; Newburyport, MA, 1765 **1642** *p76*

Wells, Michael; Illinois, 1863 **6079.1** *p15*

Wells, Nathaniel; Barbados or Jamaica, 1704 **1220.12** *p854*

Wells, Paul William; America, 1768 **1220.12** *p854*

Wells, Richard; Barbados, 1671 **1220.12** *p854*

Wells, Robert; America, 1678 **1220.12** *p854*

Wells, Samuel; America, 1739 **1220.12** *p854*

Wells, Sarah; Annapolis, MD, 1723 **1220.12** *p854*

Wells, Sarah; Maryland, 1720 **1220.12** *p854*

Wells, Sarah 64; Ontario, 1871 **1823.17** *p172*

Wells, Sarah 10; Quebec, 1870 **8364.32** *p26*

Wells, Thomas; America, 1698 **1220.12** *p854*

Wells, Thomas; America, 1736 **1220.12** *p854*

Wells, Thomas; America, 1737 **1220.12** *p854*

Wells, Thomas; America, 1766 **1220.12** *p854*

Wells, Thomas; America, 1772 **1220.12** *p854*

Wells, Thomas 24; Ontario, 1871 **1823.21** *p387*

Wells, Valentine; America, 1753 **1220.12** *p854*

Wells, William; America, 1673 **1220.12** *p854*

Wells, William; America, 1742 **1220.12** *p854*

Wells, William; America, 1749 **1220.12** *p854*

Wells, William; America, 1752 **1220.12** *p854*

Wells, William; America, 1757 **1220.12** *p854*

Wells, William; America, 1758 **1220.12** *p854*

Wells, William; America, 1774 **1220.12** *p854*

Wells, William 38; Ontario, 1871 **1823.17** *p172*

Wells, William 52; Ontario, 1871 **1823.21** *p387*

Wellum, Jane; Maryland, 1723 **1220.12** *p853*

Wellwood, Joseph; Washington, 1884 **2770.40** *p193*

Welly, Peter; America, 1685 **1220.12** *p854*

Welman, Matthew; America, 1736 **1220.12** *p853*

Welmund, Joseph L. 39; Ontario, 1871 **1823.17** *p172*

Welsandt, Peter; New York, NY, 1871 **6212.1** *p14*

Welsandt, Thomas; New York, NY, 1881 **6212.1** *p13*

Welsby, Margaret; Jamaica, 1665 **1220.12** *p854*

Welsch, Angela Becker *SEE* Welsch, Peter

Welsch, Anna Maria 20; America, 1855 **5475.1** *p281*

Welsch, Elisabeth; America, 1881 **5475.1** *p213*

Welsch, Georg *SEE* Welsch, Peter

Welsch, Johann *SEE* Welsch, Michel

Welsch, Johann; America, 1881 **5475.1** *p214*

Welsch, Johann; Chicago, 1890 **5475.1** *p190*

Welsch, John; Illinois, 1866 **6079.1** *p15*

Welsch, Katharina *SEE* Welsch, Peter

Welsch, Konrad *SEE* Welsch, Peter

Welsch, Konrad *SEE* Welsch, Michel

Welsch, Maria *SEE* Welsch, Michel

Welsch, Maria Muller *SEE* Welsch, Michel

Welsch, Michel *SEE* Welsch, Michel

Welsch, Michel; America, 1881 **5475.1** *p214*
*Wife:*Maria Muller
*Son:*Konrad
*Son:*Johann
*Daughter:*Sophie
*Son:*Peter
*Son:*Michel
*Daughter:*Maria

Welsch, Peter *SEE* Welsch, Peter

Welsch, Peter; America, 1880 **5475.1** *p213*
*Wife:*Angela Becker
*Son:*Georg
*Son:*Peter
*Daughter:*Katharina
*Son:*Konrad

Welsch, Peter *SEE* Welsch, Michel

Welsch, Sophie *SEE* Welsch, Michel

Welseck, Antoine 34; Mississippi, 1846 **778.6** *p343*

Welsh, Abraham; Barbados, 1693 **1220.12** *p854*

Welsh, Ann; America, 1747 **1220.12** *p854*

Welsh, Caroline 48; Ontario, 1871 **1823.21** *p387*

Welsh, Catharine; Philadelphia, 1857 **8513.31** *p297*

Welsh, Charles 32; Ontario, 1871 **1823.21** *p387*

Welsh, Edward; Boston, 1768 **1642** *p39*

Welsh, Edward 50; Ontario, 1871 **1823.21** *p387*

Welsh, Eleanor; Virginia, 1739 **1220.12** *p855*

Welsh, Ellen; Philadelphia, 1857 **8513.31** *p301*

Welsh, George; Maryland, 1736 **1220.12** *p855*

Welsh, James 50; Michigan, 1880 **4491.30** *p32*

Welsh, James 49; Ontario, 1871 **1823.17** *p172*

Welsh, James; Washington, 1887 **2770.40** *p25*

Welsh, Jane 10; Quebec, 1870 **8364.32** *p26*

Welsh, John; America, 1728 **1220.12** *p855*

Welsh, John; America, 1738 **1220.12** *p855*

Welsh, John; America, 1747 **1220.12** *p855*

Welsh, John; Boston, 1739 **1642** *p44*

Welsh, John 36; Ontario, 1871 **1823.17** *p172*

Welsh, John 36; Ontario, 1871 **1823.21** *p387*

Welsh, John 37; Ontario, 1871 **1823.21** *p387*

Welsh, John 46; Ontario, 1871 **1823.17** *p172*

Welsh, John 54; Ontario, 1871 **1823.21** *p387*

Welsh, Joseph; America, 1741 **1220.12** *p855*

Welsh, Mary; America, 1743 **1220.12** *p855*

Welsh, Mary 14; Quebec, 1870 **8364.32** *p26*

Welsh, Michael 60; Ontario, 1871 **1823.17** *p172*

Welsh, Nancy 60; Ontario, 1871 **1823.21** *p387*

Welsh, Nicholas; Ohio, 1809-1852 **4511.35** *p58*

Welsh, Patrick; Boston, 1766 **1642** *p37*

Welsh, Patrick; Newfoundland, 1814 **3476.10** *p54*

Welsh, Patrick 27; Ontario, 1871 **1823.21** *p387*

Welsh, Philip; Ipswich, MA, 1661 **1642** *p69*

Welsh, Richard; Boston, 1763 **1642** *p32*

Welsh, Richard 55; Ontario, 1871 **1823.17** *p172*

Welsh, Robert; America, 1671 **1220.12** *p855*

Welsh, Robert; Barbados or Jamaica, 1691 **1220.12** *p855*

Welsh, Robert 38; Ontario, 1871 **1823.21** *p387*

Welsh, Samuel; America, 1768 **1220.12** *p855*

Welsh, Thomas; America, 1739 **1220.12** *p855*

Welsh, Thomas; America, 1746 **1220.12** *p855*

Welsh, Thomas; America, 1748 **1220.12** *p855*

Welsh, Thomas 32; Ontario, 1871 **1823.21** *p387*

Welsh, Thomas 37; Ontario, 1871 **1823.17** *p172*

Welsh, Thomas 64; Ontario, 1871 **1823.17** *p172*

Welsh, Walter 17; Ontario, 1871 **1823.21** *p387*

Welsh, William H.; Ohio, 1829 **3580.20** *p33*

Welsh, William H.; Ohio, 1829 **6020.12** *p23*

Welshman, John; Havana, 1782 **8529.30** *p10A*

Welter, Andreas; America, 1850 **5475.1** *p549*

Welter, August; America, 1800-1899 **5475.1** *p34*
With 2 stepchildren

Welter, August; America, 1872 **5475.1** *p239*

Welter, Johann; America, 1846 **5475.1** *p547*

Welter, Karl; America, 1881 **5475.1** *p241*

Welter, Katharina; America, 1881 **5475.1** *p33*

Welter, Nikolaus 20; America, 1850 **5475.1** *p478*

Welter, William 21; Ontario, 1871 **1823.21** *p387*

Weltham, John 38; Ontario, 1871 **1823.21** *p387*

Welthresher, Joseph; America, 1747 **1220.12** *p856*

Welton, Edward; America, 1741 **1220.12** *p856*

Welton, James; Marston's Wharf, 1780 **8529.30** *p17*

Welton, John; Marston's Wharf, 1780 **8529.30** *p17*

Welty, Andreas 70; New Orleans, 1847 **778.6** *p343*

Welty, Anna Maria 22; New Orleans, 1847 **778.6** *p343*

Welty, Dominick; Ohio, 1809-1852 **4511.35** *p58*

Welty, Franz 7; New Orleans, 1847 **778.6** *p343*

Welty, Ignaz 3 months; New Orleans, 1847 **778.6** *p343*

Welty, Jean 9; New Orleans, 1847 **778.6** *p343*

Welty, Johannis 36; New Orleans, 1847 **778.6** *p343*

Welty, John Martin; Ohio, 1809-1852 **4511.35** *p58*

Welty, Maria 33; New Orleans, 1847 **778.6** *p343*

Welty, Marianne 5; New Orleans, 1847 **778.6** *p343*

Welty, Matthias; Ohio, 1809-1852 **4511.35** *p58*

Welwood, William 34; Ontario, 1871 **1823.21** *p387*

Welz, J.G.F.; Venezuela, 1843 **3899.5** *p547*

Wemhofer, Anna Sophie; America, 1866 **7420.1** *p252*

Wemhofer, Johann Friedrich Wilhelm; America, 1850 **7420.1** *p77*

Wemmer, Anna Maria; America, 1854 **179.55** *p19*

Wemmer, Barbara; America, 1854 **179.55** *p19*

Wemmer, Friedrich; America, 1854 **179.55** *p19*

Wemmer, Jakob F.; America, 1854 **179.55** *p19*

Wemmer, Katharina; America, 1854 **179.55** *p19*

Wemmer, Maria; America, 1854 **179.55** *p19*

Wendeberg, August; America, 1882 **2526.43** *p184*

Wendel, George; Louisiana, 1874-1875 **4981.45** *p130*

Wendel, George; New York, 1859 **358.56** *p99*

Wendel, Joseph 39; Galveston, TX, 1845 **3967.10** *p377*

Wendel, Leonhard 20 *SEE* Wendel, Mrs. Nikolaus

Wendel, Mrs. Nikolaus 55; America, 1846 **2526.43** *p189*
*Son:*Leonhard 20

Wenden, James; America, 1767 **1220.12** *p856*

Wendland, Carl 7; Halifax, N.S., 1902 **1860.4** *p42*

Wendland, Ernst; Wisconsin, 1901 **6795.8** *p164*

Wendland, Jacob 3; Halifax, N.S., 1902 **1860.4** *p42*

Wendland, Johann 11; Halifax, N.S., 1902 **1860.4** *p42*

Wendland, John Edward; Wisconsin, 1880 **6795.8** *p39*

Wendland, Ludwig 4; Halifax, N.S., 1902 **1860.4** *p42*

Wendland, Ludwig 36; Halifax, N.S., 1902 **1860.4** *p42*

Wendland, Peter August; Wisconsin, 1870 **6795.8** *p39*

Wendland, Sophie 2; Halifax, N.S., 1902 **1860.4** *p42*

Wendland, Sophie 33; Halifax, N.S., 1902 **1860.4** *p42*

Wendland, Wilhelm 9; Halifax, N.S., 1902 **1860.4** *p42*

Wendland, Wilhelmine; Wisconsin, 1893 **6795.8** *p27*

Wendler, Wilhelm; California, 1853 **7420.1** *p113*

Wendling, Catherine 17; Port uncertain, 1840 **778.6** *p343*

Wendling, Jacob; Ohio, 1809-1852 **4511.35** *p58*

Wendrick, Benadictus; North Carolina, 1710 **3629.40** *p9*

Wendrick, John; North Carolina, 1710 **3629.40** *p8*

Wendt, Emil Theodor; Wisconsin, 1874 **6795.8** *p91*

Wendt, Friedrich; Wisconsin, 1877 **6795.8** *p37*

Wendt, Friedrich Christian; America, 1849 **7420.1** *p68*

Wendt, Friedrich Gerhardt Christian; America, 1868 **7420.1** *p278*

Wendt, Rudolf John Richard; Wisconsin, 1879 **6795.8** *p108*

Wendt, Rudolph Johann Richard; Wisconsin, 1870 **6795.8** *p91*

Wendta, John; Wisconsin, 1876 **6795.8** *p52*

Wendtland, Emma; Wisconsin, 1896 **6795.8** *p143*

Wengart, John; Ohio, 1809-1852 **4511.35** *p58*

Wengen, Klemens; America, 1853 **5475.1** *p51*
With wife & 9 children

Wenger, Anton 28; America, 1846 **778.6** *p343*

Wenger, Christian 34; America, 1846 **778.6** *p344*

Wenger, Elisabeth 21; America, 1846 **778.6** *p344*

Wenger, Geo.; Ohio, 1840-1897 **8365.35** *p18*

Wenger, Johannes; Illinois, 1854 **6079.1** *p15*

Wenger, Magdalena 9; America, 1846 **778.6** *p344*

Wenger, Michel 4; America, 1846 **778.6** *p344*

Wengert, Barbara; America, 1885 **179.55** *p19*

Wengert, Catharina; America, 1885 **179.55** *p19*

Wengert, Georg F.; America, 1885 *179.55 p19*
Wengert, Johannes; America, 1888 *179.55 p19*
Wengert, Maria; America, 1885 *179.55 p19*
Wengert, Rosina; America, 1885 *179.55 p19*
Wenich, Ludwig; Ohio, 1809-1852 *4511.35 p58*
Wenig, Anna Margarethe; America, 1867 *7919.3 p533*
Wenino, Elizabeth 44; Ontario, 1871 *1823.17 p173*
Wenino, Paul 37; Ontario, 1871 *1823.17 p173*
Wenioh, Simon 29; Missouri, 1848 *778.6 p344*
Wenk, Anna Maria; America, 1867 *7919.3 p533*
Wenker, Frantz; Ohio, 1840-1897 *8365.35 p18*
Wenlock, Edward; America, 1675 *1220.12 p856*
Wenn, John; America, 1710 *1220.12 p856*
Wenn, John 27; Michigan, 1880 *4491.36 p23*
Wennblad, Joh.; New Orleans, 1845 *6412.40 p148*
Wenner, Barbara Lorsong 42 *SEE* Wenner, Jakob
Wenner, Jakob 45; America, 1846 *5475.1 p61*
  *Wife:*Barbara Lorsong 42
  With 8 children
Wennerberg, S. Fr.; Charleston, SC, 1851 *6412.40 p153*
Wennerstrom, J.E.; New York, NY, 1845 *6412.40 p149*
Wensierski, Leon; Texas, 1889 *6015.15 p30*
Wensley, Thomas; America, 1731 *1220.12 p856*
Wenstrand, Nels P.; America, 1857 *4487.25 p75*
  With family
Went, Elizabeth; America, 1759 *1220.12 p856*
Went, James; America, 1740 *1220.12 p856*
Went, Joseph; Detroit, 1929-1930 *6214.5 p67*
Wenta, Michael; Wisconsin, 1878 *6795.8 p53*
Wente, Mr.; America, 1853 *7420.1 p113*
  With family
Wente, Carl; Port uncertain, 1881 *7420.1 p326*
Wente, Christoph; America, 1857 *7420.1 p175*
Wente, Christoph; America, 1857 *7420.1 p175*
Wente, Friederike; America, 1859 *7420.1 p190*
Wente, Sophie Wilhelmine Charlotte; America, 1850
  7420.1 p77
Wentel, Karl 26; America, 1881 *5475.1 p42*
Wenthe, Mr.; America, 1852 *7420.1 p100*
Wenthe, Carl Ludwig; America, 1864 *7420.1 p228*
  *Wife:*Louise Schone
Wenthe, Caroline; America, 1856 *7420.1 p156*
Wenthe, Caroline; America, 1857 *7420.1 p175*
Wenthe, Christian; America, 1852 *7420.1 p100*
Wenthe, Conrad; America, 1862 *7420.1 p216*
Wenthe, Ernst August Christian; America, 1871 *7420.1*
  p293
Wenthe, Friedrich; America, 1859 *7420.1 p190*
Wenthe, Friedrich Wilhelm; America, 1883 *7420.1 p341*
  *Wife:*Hanne Caroline Wilhelmine Fabrice
  *Son:*Heinrich Friedrich Wilhelm
  *Daughter:*Wilhelmine Caroline Charlotte
Wenthe, Friedrich Wilhelm Ferd. *SEE* Wenthe, Heinrich
  August
Wenthe, Hanna Sophie Caroline; Iowa, 1871 *7420.1*
  p289
Wenthe, Hanne Caroline Wilhelmine Fabrice *SEE*
  Wenthe, Friedrich Wilhelm
Wenthe, Heinrich; America, 1883 *7420.1 p341*
  With family
Wenthe, Heinrich August; America, 1860 *7420.1 p201*
  *Brother:*Friedrich Wilhelm Ferd.
Wenthe, Heinrich Friedrich Wilhelm *SEE* Wenthe,
  Friedrich Wilhelm
Wenthe, Heinrich Ludwig Ferdinand; America, 1866
  7420.1 p252
  *Mother:*Sophie Louise
Wenthe, Johann Christian; America, 1860 *7420.1 p190*
  With wife & daughter
Wenthe, Louise Schone *SEE* Wenthe, Carl Ludwig
Wenthe, Ludwig; America, 1863 *7420.1 p221*
  With family
Wenthe, Ludwig Kathrinhagen; America, 1856 *7420.1*
  p156
Wenthe, Sophie; America, 1856 *7420.1 p156*
Wenthe, Sophie; America, 1857 *7420.1 p175*
Wenthe, Sophie Louise *SEE* Wenthe, Heinrich Ludwig
  Ferdinand
Wenthe, Wilhelm; America, 1852 *7420.1 p100*
Wenthe, Wilhelmine Caroline Charlotte *SEE* Wenthe,
  Friedrich Wilhelm
Wentland, Ann; Virginia, 1732 *1220.12 p856*
Wentland, Fred'k Aug.; Wisconsin, 1896 *6795.8 p143*
Wentling, Adam; Ohio, 1809-1852 *4511.35 p58*
Wentworth, Ellzabeth; America, 1773 *1220.12 p856*
Wentworth, James; America, 1750 *1220.12 p856*
Wentworth, Nathaniel; Barbados, 1694 *1220.12 p856*
Wentz, John M.; Ohio, 1809-1852 *4511.35 p58*
Wentz, Joseph; Ohio, 1809-1852 *4511.35 p58*
Wentz, Philip; Ohio, 1809-1852 *4511.35 p58*
Wentzel, Lorenz 50; Pennsylvania, 1848 *170.15 p46*
  With 3 children
Wentzel, Philipp; Pennsylvania, 1848 *170.15 p46*

Wentzel, Philipp 52; Pennsylvania, 1848 *170.15 p46*
  With 3 children
Wenz, Elisabeth 4; New York, NY, 1898 *7951.13 p42*
Wenz, Jacob 10; New York, NY, 1898 *7951.13 p42*
Wenz, Jacob 32; New York, NY, 1898 *7951.13 p42*
Wenz, Jacob 56; New York, NY, 1898 *7951.13 p42*
Wenz, Johann 15 months; New York, NY, 1898 *7951.13*
  p42
Wenz, Katherina 28; New York, NY, 1898 *7951.13 p42*
Wenz, Katherine 1 months; New York, NY, 1898
  7951.13 p42
Wenz, Lorenz 21; New Orleans, 1847 *778.6 p344*
Wenz, Margaret 3; New York, NY, 1898 *7951.13 p42*
Wenz, Salomea 60; New York, NY, 1898 *7951.13 p42*
Wenzel, . . .; Pennsylvania, 1848 *170.15 p46*
  With 2 siblings
Wenzel, Anna; Wisconsin, 1889 *6795.8 p129*
Wenzel, Anton Ernst; America, 1881 *5475.1 p129*
Wenzel, Carl Heinrich Dietrich Wilhelm; America, 1873
  7420.1 p302
Wenzel, Casper; Ohio, 1809-1852 *4511.35 p58*
Wenzel, Emilie H.; Wisconsin, 1886 *6795.8 p129*
Wenzel, Emilius Gustav; America, 1868 *7919.3 p526*
Wenzel, Friedrich Wilhelm Rudolf; America, 1889
  7420.1 p360
Wenzel, Mathias; Wisconsin, 1857 *6795.8 p98*
Weosner, Delia; Wisconsin, 1900 *6795.8 p232*
Werber, Frederick; South Carolina, 1854 *6155.4 p19*
Werdein, John; New York, NY, 1883 *6212.1 p16*
Were, George; America, 1728 *1220.12 p852*
Wergengarden, Arnold; Ohio, 1809-1852 *4511.35 p58*
Werger, . . .; North Carolina, 1710 *3629.40 p7*
Wergin, Heinrich *SEE* Wergin, Karl
Wergin, Karl *SEE* Wergin, Karl
Wergin, Karl; America, 1879 *5475.1 p44*
  *Wife:*Karoline Schmeer
  *Daughter:*Katharina
  *Son:*Karl
  *Daughter:*Karoline
  *Son:*Philipp
  *Son:*Heinrich
  *Daughter:*Luise
  *Son:*Wilhelm
  *Daughter:*Maria
Wergin, Karoline *SEE* Wergin, Karl
Wergin, Karoline Schmeer *SEE* Wergin, Karl
Wergin, Katharina *SEE* Wergin, Karl
Wergin, Luise *SEE* Wergin, Karl
Wergin, Maria *SEE* Wergin, Karl
Wergin, Philipp *SEE* Wergin, Karl
Wergin, Wilhelm *SEE* Wergin, Karl
Werhahne, Sophie Dorothee Louise; Iowa, 1859 *7420.1*
  p187
Werhrle, Bernard 23; America, 1847 *778.6 p344*
Werich, Franziska 27; Halifax, N.S., 1902 *1860.4 p40*
Werich, Margaretha 20; Halifax, N.S., 1902 *1860.4 p40*
Werich, Michael; Halifax, N.S., 1902 *1860.4 p40*
Werich, Michael 30; Halifax, N.S., 1902 *1860.4 p40*
Werimo, Elizabeth 44; Ontario, 1871 *1823.17 p173*
Werimo, Paul 37; Ontario, 1871 *1823.17 p173*
Weringer, Peter; Louisiana, 1874 *4981.45 p134*
Werkle, Elisabeth; Wisconsin, 1886 *5475.1 p534*
Werkle, Heinrich 19; America, 1836 *5475.1 p513*
Werkmeister, Mr.; America, 1871 *7420.1 p293*
  *Son:*Wilhelm Carl Ernst
  *Brother:*Ernst Friedrich Wilhelm
  *Brother:*Daniel
  *Sister:*Christine Caroline Wilhelmine
  With parents
Werkmeister, Christine Caroline Wilhelmine *SEE*
  Werkmeister, Mr.
Werkmeister, Daniel *SEE* Werkmeister, Mr.
Werkmeister, Ernst Friedrich Wilhelm *SEE* Werkmeister,
  Mr.
Werkmeister, Heinrich; Chile, 1852 *1192.4 p52*
  With wife & 4 children
  With child 2
  With child 18
Werkmeister, Wilhelm Carl Ernst *SEE* Werkmeister, Mr.
Werle, Heinrich 60; New Jersey, 1737-1774 *927.31 p3*
Werlein, John; Louisiana, 1836-1841 *4981.45 p209*
Werline, Joseph 19; America, 1847 *778.6 p344*
Werlklin, Elisabeth 34; New Orleans, 1847 *778.6 p344*
Wern, J.; New Orleans, 1850 *7242.30 p156*
Wern, James; New Orleans, 1850 *7242.30 p156*
Werner, Mr. 24; America, 1843 *778.6 p344*
Werner, Adolph *SEE* Werner, Sophie Klein
Werner, Albert Louis; America, 1885 *7420.1 p349*
Werner, Andrew; Ohio, 1809-1852 *4511.35 p58*
Werner, Anna Elisabeth; America, n.d. *8115.12 p325*
Werner, Anna Stena; Wisconsin, 1911 *6795.8 p177*
Werner, August Heinrich Louis Cuno Franz; America,
  1878 *7420.1 p312*

Werner, Barbara; America, 1880 *5475.1 p70*
  *Son:*Joh. Nikolaus
  *Daughter:*Emilie
  *Son:*Ph. Konrad
  *Daughter:*Katharina
Werner, Carl Christel Otto; Chicago, 1880 *7420.1 p319*
Werner, Carl Ludwig; America, 1857 *7420.1 p162*
  With parents
Werner, Carl Ludwig; America, 1857 *7420.1 p175*
  With parents
Werner, Charlotte *SEE* Werner, Sophie Klein
Werner, Daniel; Wisconsin, 1869 *6795.8 p108*
Werner, Daniel; Wisconsin, 1898 *6795.8 p135*
Werner, Daniel; Wisconsin, 1902 *6795.8 p135*
Werner, Elisabeth 8 *SEE* Werner, Jakob
Werner, Emilie *SEE* Werner, Sophie Klein
Werner, Ernst; Wisconsin, 1858 *6795.8 p39*
Werner, Francis 40; America, 1846 *778.6 p344*
Werner, Frederick; Louisiana, 1846 *7710.1 p149*
Werner, Frederick; Ohio, 1840-1897 *8365.35 p18*
Werner, Frederick August; Wisconsin, 1870 *6795.8 p143*
Werner, Henri 28; Louisiana, 1848 *778.6 p344*
Werner, Henriette; New York, 1859 *358.56 p55*
Werner, Henriette Antoinette Ernestine; America, 1883
  7420.1 p341
Werner, Henry; Illinois, 1834-1900 *6020.5 p133*
Werner, Jakob; America, 1847 *2526.43 p184*
  With wife
  *Daughter:*Margaretha
  *Daughter:*Elisabeth
  *Daughter:*Katharina
  *Son:*Karl
Werner, Jean Pierre 32; New Orleans, 1848 *778.6 p344*
Werner, Joh. Gottl.; Valdivia, Chile, 1852 *1192.4 p54*
  With wife & baby & child
Werner, Johann Andreas; America, n.d. *8115.12 p326*
Werner, Joseph 27; America, 1844 *778.6 p344*
Werner, Julius; Detroit, 1930 *1640.60 p77*
Werner, Julus; Detroit, 1930 *1640.60 p77*
Werner, Karl 10 *SEE* Werner, Jakob
Werner, Karl *SEE* Werner, Sophie Klein
Werner, Kaspar; America, 1892 *170.15 p46*
  With wife & 4 children
Werner, Katharina 12 *SEE* Werner, Jakob
Werner, Katharina 34; Brazil, 1865 *5475.1 p521*
Werner, Louis 31; America, 1846 *778.6 p344*
Werner, Margaretha 4 *SEE* Werner, Jakob
Werner, Maria 2; America, 1846 *778.6 p344*
Werner, Martin; Ohio, 1809-1852 *4511.35 p58*
Werner, Sophie *SEE* Werner, Sophie Klein
Werner, Sophie; St. Louis, 1880 *5475.1 p33*
  *Daughter:*Sophie
  *Daughter:*Charlotte
  *Son:*Karl
  *Son:*Adolph
  *Daughter:*Emilie
Werner, Valentin; Missouri, 1846 *778.6 p344*
Werner, Valtin; America, 1868 *7919.3 p529*
Werner, Wilhelm; America, 1888 *2526.42 p197*
Wernet, Ignatius; Ohio, 1809-1852 *4511.35 p58*
Wernet, John; Ohio, 1809-1852 *4511.35 p58*
Wernet, Joseph; Ohio, 1809-1852 *4511.35 p58*
Wernich, Gottlieb Paul 19; South America, 1862 *5475.1*
  p30
Werninger, Albert 49; New York, NY, 1893 *1883.7 p42*
Werninger, Catharina 7; New York, NY, 1893 *1883.7*
  p42
Werninger, Franz 17; New York, NY, 1893 *1883.7 p42*
Werninger, Georg 9; New York, NY, 1893 *1883.7 p42*
Werninger, Magdalena 46; New York, NY, 1893 *1883.7*
  p42
Werninger, Stefen 20; New York, NY, 1893 *1883.7 p42*
Wernlof, Otto; Wisconsin, 1880-1886 *1865.50 p114*
Weron, Louis 33; Port uncertain, 1847 *778.6 p344*
Werre, Catharina 29; New York, NY, 1874 *6954.7 p37*
Werre, Joseph 25; New York, NY, 1874 *6954.7 p37*
Werre, Magdalena 9 months; New York, NY, 1874
  6954.7 p37
Werrell, Henry 37; Ontario, 1871 *1823.21 p388*
Werrengarden, Peter; Ohio, 1809-1852 *4511.35 p58*
Werth, Adam; America, 1847 *5475.1 p475*
Werth, Charles; New York, 1860 *358.56 p148*
Werthor, Josepha 19; New Orleans, 1847 *778.6 p344*
Wertz, Henry; Ohio, 1809-1852 *4511.35 p58*
Wescott, Edward 65; Michigan, 1880 *4491.33 p23*
Wescott, Rose 49; Michigan, 1880 *4491.33 p23*
Wescott, Thomas R. 57; Ontario, 1871 *1823.21 p388*
Wesenbeck, George; New York, 1859 *358.56 p100*
Weslely, John 35; Ontario, 1871 *1823.17 p173*
Wesner, Frederick August; Wisconsin, 1870 *6795.8 p143*
Wessberg, J.A.; New York, NY, 1847 *6412.40 p151*
Wessel, Jacob; North Carolina, 1844 *1088.45 p37*

Wesseling, Friedrich; America, 1858 ***7420.1*** *p183*
With family
Wessells, Francis; America, 1755 ***1220.12*** *p856*
Wesseriat, John C.; Ohio, 1809-1852 ***4511.35*** *p58*
Wessing, Edward Joseph; Wisconsin, 1901 ***6795.8*** *p179*
Wessling, Carl Heinrich Gottl; America, 1880 ***7420.1*** *p319*
*Wife:*Sophie Christine Brandt
Wessling, Heinrich Christian Gottlieb; Wisconsin, 1880 ***7420.1*** *p319*
Wessling, Sophie Christine Brandt *SEE* Wessling, Carl Heinrich Gottl
Wessman, F.W.; New York, NY, 1850 ***6412.40*** *p151*
Wessner, Jacob 17; New York, NY, 1890 ***1883.7*** *p47*
Wessner, Jacob 24; New York, NY, 1890 ***1883.7*** *p47*
Wessner, Maria 21; New York, NY, 1890 ***1883.7*** *p47*
Wessyel, Cristop.e 29; New Orleans, 1846 ***778.6*** *p344*
West, Ann; America, 1771 ***1220.12*** *p856*
West, Ann; Charles Town, SC, 1719 ***1220.12*** *p856*
West, Ann 47; Ontario, 1871 ***1823.17*** *p173*
West, Aron 67; Ontario, 1871 ***1823.17*** *p173*
West, Benjamin; America, 1733 ***1220.12*** *p856*
West, Benjamin; America, 1758 ***1220.12*** *p856*
West, Denima; America, 1758 ***1220.12*** *p856*
West, E. H.; California, 1868 ***1131.61*** *p89*
West, Edward 39; Ontario, 1871 ***1823.21*** *p388*
West, George 64; Ontario, 1871 ***1823.17*** *p173*
West, Gibbs; Colorado, 1900 ***1029.59*** *p93*
West, Gibbs; New York, NY, 1868 ***1029.59*** *p94*
West, Henry; America, 1738 ***1220.12*** *p856*
West, Henry; America, 1773 ***1220.12*** *p856*
West, Henry; Barbados, 1673 ***1220.12*** *p856*
West, Henry; Maryland, 1673 ***1236.25*** *p48*
West, James; America, 1765 ***1220.12*** *p856*
West, James; America, 1774 ***1220.12*** *p856*
West, James; America, 1775 ***1220.12*** *p856*
West, Jarvis; Annapolis, MD, 1736 ***1220.12*** *p856*
West, Jo. 30; Virginia, 1635 ***1183.3*** *p30*
West, Johan Alfred; Oregon, 1941 ***9157.47*** *p2*
West, John; America, 1726 ***1220.12*** *p856*
West, John; America, 1754 ***1220.12*** *p856*
West, John; America, 1755 ***1220.12*** *p856*
West, John; America, 1759 ***1220.12*** *p856*
West, John; America, 1761 ***1220.12*** *p856*
West, John; America, 1763 ***1220.12*** *p856*
West, John; America, 1764 ***1220.12*** *p856*
West, John; America, 1766 ***1220.12*** *p856*
West, John; America, 1768 ***1220.12*** *p857*
West, John; America, 1772 ***1220.12*** *p857*
West, John; America, 1774 ***1220.12*** *p857*
West, John; Jamaica, 1663 ***1220.12*** *p856*
West, John; Jamaica, 1777 ***8529.30*** *p14A*
West, John; Maryland, 1720 ***1220.12*** *p856*
West, John; Maryland, 1727 ***1220.12*** *p856*
West, John 28; North Carolina, 1774 ***1422.10*** *p56*
West, John 37; Ontario, 1871 ***1823.21*** *p388*
West, John 69; Ontario, 1871 ***1823.21*** *p388*
West, John 70; Ontario, 1871 ***1823.21*** *p388*
West, John; Virginia, 1742 ***1220.12*** *p856*
West, John; Washington, 1884 ***2770.40*** *p193*
West, Jonathan; New York, 1778 ***8529.30*** *p7*
West, Joseph; America, 1747 ***1220.12*** *p857*
West, Joseph; America, 1753 ***1220.12*** *p857*
West, Joseph 43; Ontario, 1871 ***1823.17*** *p173*
West, Joshua; America, 1752 ***1220.12*** *p857*
West, Luke; America, 1765 ***1220.12*** *p857*
West, Luke; America, 1772 ***1220.12*** *p857*
West, Luke 35; Ontario, 1871 ***1823.21*** *p388*
West, Mark 60; Ontario, 1871 ***1823.21*** *p388*
West, Martha; Barbados, 1699 ***1220.12*** *p857*
West, Mary; America, 1675 ***1220.12*** *p857*
West, Mary; America, 1721 ***1220.12*** *p857*
West, Mary; America, 1751 ***1220.12*** *p857*
West, Mary; Maryland or Virginia, 1738 ***1220.12*** *p857*
West, Mary A.; Philadelphia, 1860 ***8513.31*** *p431*
West, Matthew; America, 1758 ***1220.12*** *p857*
West, Richard; America, 1685 ***1220.12*** *p857*
West, Richard; America, 1754 ***1220.12*** *p857*
West, Richard; Boston, 1774 ***8529.30*** *p3*
West, Richard 60; Ontario, 1871 ***1823.21*** *p388*
West, Roger; America, 1749 ***1220.12*** *p857*
West, Samuel; America, 1717 ***1220.12*** *p857*
West, Samuel; America, 1779 ***8529.30*** *p17*
West, Samuel 52; Ontario, 1871 ***1823.21*** *p388*
West, Sarah; America, 1762 ***1220.12*** *p857*
West, Stephen 54; Ontario, 1871 ***1823.17*** *p173*
West, Thomas; America, 1768 ***1220.12*** *p857*
West, Thomas; Maryland or Virginia, 1738 ***1220.12*** *p857*
West, Thomas; Virginia, 1726 ***1220.12*** *p857*
West, William; America, 1743 ***1220.12*** *p857*
West, William; America, 1747 ***1220.12*** *p857*
West, William; America, 1766 ***1220.12*** *p857*
West, William; America, 1771 ***1220.12*** *p857*
West, William; Barbados, 1682 ***1220.12*** *p857*
West, William; Maryland, 1726 ***1220.12*** *p857*
West, William; Maryland, 1727 ***1220.12*** *p857*
West, William 49; Ontario, 1871 ***1823.21*** *p388*
West, William; Virginia, 1732 ***1220.12*** *p857*
Westaway, . . .; Prince Edward Island, 1800-1840 ***9228.50*** *p153*
Westaway, John; New York, NY, 1850-1950 ***9228.50*** *p652*
Westaway, John; South America, 1850-1950 ***9228.50*** *p652*
Westberg, Jacob; New York, NY, 1848 ***6412.40*** *p151*
Westbrook, William; America, 1771 ***1220.12*** *p857*
Westbrooke, Samuel; America, 1698 ***1220.12*** *p857*
Westby, James 43; Ontario, 1871 ***1823.17*** *p173*
Westby, Thomas 50; Ontario, 1871 ***1823.21*** *p388*
Westcar, John; America, 1737 ***1220.12*** *p857*
Westcoat, John; America, 1727 ***1220.12*** *p857*
Westcoate, Josias; Barbados, 1688 ***1220.12*** *p857*
Westcoate, Peter; America, 1771 ***1220.12*** *p857*
Westcombe, Thomas; America, 1764 ***1220.12*** *p857*
Westcombe, William; America, 1734 ***1220.12*** *p857*
Westcote, Thomas; America, 1755 ***1220.12*** *p857*
Westcott, James; America, 1729 ***1220.12*** *p857*
Westcott, James 47; Ontario, 1871 ***1823.21*** *p388*
Westcott, Stephen; America, 1729 ***1220.12*** *p857*
Westcott, Thomas; America, 1743 ***1220.12*** *p857*
Westcutt, John; Barbados or Jamaica, 1700 ***1220.12*** *p857*
Weste, Michael 28; Galveston, TX, 1844 ***3967.10*** *p375*
Westeel, Richard 46; Ontario, 1871 ***1823.21*** *p388*
Westell, John; Ohio, 1845 ***2763.1*** *p22*
Westell, Patience; Annapolis, MD, 1729 ***1220.12*** *p857*
Westen, Eduard; America, 1850 ***5475.1*** *p393*
*Wife:*Elisabeth Schwingel
*Son:*Joh. Nikolaus
*Daughter:*Katharina
*Son:*Valentin
Westen, Elisabeth Schwingel 38 *SEE* Westen, Eduard
Westen, Joh. Nikolaus 6 *SEE* Westen, Eduard
Westen, Katharina 17 *SEE* Westen, Eduard
Westen, Valentin 12 *SEE* Westen, Eduard
Westenberg, Andrew; Iowa, 1891 ***1211.15*** *p20*
Wester, Johannes; Port uncertain, 1858 ***7420.1*** *p183*
With family
Wester, K.S.; St. Paul, MN, 1905 ***1865.50*** *p114*
Wester, P. M.; Illinois, 1859 ***6079.1*** *p15*
Wester, Ursula; America, 1739 ***1220.12*** *p857*
Westerberg, C.L.; New York, NY, 1846 ***6412.40*** *p149*
Westerberg, Charles J.; Colorado, 1884 ***1029.59*** *p94*
Westerberg, Chas. John; Colorado, 1894 ***1029.59*** *p94*
Westerberg, J. Th.; Baltimore, 1846 ***6412.40*** *p149*
Westerblad, John A.; Illinois, 1861 ***4487.25*** *p76*
Westerhaus, Henry; Louisiana, 1874-1875 ***4981.45*** *p130*
Westerhoff, Jacob; Illinois, 1859 ***6079.1*** *p15*
Westerhoff, John; Illinois, 1859 ***6079.1*** *p15*
Westerhoff, William; Illinois, 1859 ***6079.1*** *p15*
Westerick, John; Ohio, 1809-1852 ***4511.35*** *p58*
Westerick, Philip; Ohio, 1809-1852 ***4511.35*** *p58*
Westerlund, Andrew; America, 1850 ***4487.25*** *p76*
With parents
Westerlund, Charles; St. Paul, MN, 1871-1884 ***1865.50*** *p114*
Westerlund, Hans; America, 1850 ***4487.25*** *p76*
With parents
Westerlund, Martha; St. Paul, MN, 1881 ***1865.50*** *p114*
Westerlund, S.F.; New York, NY, 1856 ***6412.40*** *p154*
Westerman, August; Wisconsin, 1884 ***6795.8*** *p235*
Westerman, Henry; North Carolina, 1792-1862 ***1088.45*** *p37*
Westerman, Thomas; America, 1741 ***1220.12*** *p857*
Westermann, Karl Friedr. Wilhelm; America, 1867 ***5475.1*** *p72*
Westermann, Richard Ferdinand; America, 1879 ***5475.1*** *p72*
Westermark, Ant.; New York, NY, 1844 ***6412.40*** *p148*
Western, Elicia 50; Ontario, 1871 ***1823.17*** *p173*
Western, John; America, 1764 ***1220.12*** *p857*
Westerne, John; Barbados, 1715 ***1220.12*** *p857*
Westerne, Robert; Barbados, 1687 ***1220.12*** *p858*
Westfield, Elizabeth; America, 1775 ***1220.12*** *p858*
Westfield, Grace; America, 1716 ***1220.12*** *p858*
Westfield, Richard; America, 1745 ***1220.12*** *p858*
Westgate, Alberta 24; Ontario, 1871 ***1823.21*** *p388*
Westgate, Edmund; America, 1744 ***1220.12*** *p858*
Westgate, George 46; Ontario, 1871 ***1823.17*** *p173*
Westgate, James 35; Ontario, 1871 ***1823.17*** *p173*
Westgate, Thomas 60; Ontario, 1871 ***1823.17*** *p173*
Westgood, William; America, 1775 ***1220.12*** *p858*
Westhall, Henry; America, 1775 ***1220.12*** *p858*
Westhaver, William; Washington, 1889 ***2770.40*** *p81*
Westheimer, Henry; North Carolina, 1849 ***1088.45*** *p37*
Westhin, Johannes; Nova Scotia, 1784 ***7105*** *p27*
Westin, John; Nova Scotia, 1784 ***7105*** *p27*
Westlake, Jane; America, 1751 ***1220.12*** *p858*
Westlake, John; America, 1685 ***1220.12*** *p858*
Westlake, Joseph; Virginia, 1718 ***1220.12*** *p858*
Westlake, Richard; Barbados, 1693 ***1220.12*** *p858*
Westlake, William 47; Ontario, 1871 ***1823.21*** *p388*
Westlake, William; Virginia, 1759 ***1220.12*** *p858*
Westland, Francis 73; Ontario, 1871 ***1823.21*** *p388*
Westland, G. P. 35; Ontario, 1871 ***1823.21*** *p388*
Westland, Wm 38; Ontario, 1871 ***1823.21*** *p388*
Westle, James 48; Ontario, 1871 ***1823.21*** *p388*
Westley, Samuel; America, 1763 ***1220.12*** *p858*
Westley, Thomas; America, 1737 ***1220.12*** *p858*
Westley, William; America, 1746 ***1220.12*** *p858*
Westlin, Johan Alfred; Oregon, 1941 ***9157.47*** *p2*
Westlogle, Michael; Ohio, 1809-1852 ***4511.35*** *p58*
Westman, Alfred 30; Ontario, 1871 ***1823.21*** *p388*
Westman, C.A.U.; Baltimore, 1851 ***6412.40*** *p152*
Westman, George 30; Ontario, 1871 ***1823.21*** *p388*
Westman, Henry 56; Ontario, 1871 ***1823.21*** *p388*
Westman, Isaac 38; Ontario, 1871 ***1823.21*** *p388*
Westman, James 36; Ontario, 1871 ***1823.21*** *p388*
Westman, Joh.; New York, NY, 1849 ***6412.40*** *p152*
Westman, Richard 48; Ontario, 1871 ***1823.21*** *p388*
Westmayer, Anne 23; Missouri, 1846 ***778.6*** *p344*
Westmore, Elizabeth; Annapolis, MD, 1731 ***1220.12*** *p858*
Westoby, William 40; Ontario, 1871 ***1823.21*** *p388*
Weston, Abraham; America, 1760 ***1220.12*** *p858*
Weston, Alfred L.; Colorado, 1893 ***1029.59*** *p94*
Weston, Alfred Lorenzo; New York, NY, 1888 ***1029.59*** *p1A*
Weston, Amos 47; Ontario, 1871 ***1823.21*** *p388*
Weston, Ann 30; North Carolina, 1774 ***1422.10*** *p56*
Weston, Ann; Virginia, 1758 ***1220.12*** *p858*
Weston, Charles; Barbados, 1677 ***1220.12*** *p858*
Weston, George; America, 1754 ***1220.12*** *p858*
Weston, George; America, 1758 ***1220.12*** *p858*
Weston, James; America, 1759 ***1220.12*** *p858*
Weston, James 53; Ontario, 1871 ***1823.21*** *p388*
Weston, John; America, 1748 ***1220.12*** *p858*
Weston, John; America, 1756 ***1220.12*** *p858*
Weston, John 30; Ontario, 1871 ***1823.21*** *p388*
Weston, John Christopher; Nova Scotia, 1784 ***7105*** *p27*
Weston, Joseph; America, 1755 ***1220.12*** *p858*
Weston, Kathleen; Colorado, 1862-1920 ***1029.59*** *p94*
Weston, Margaret; America, 1766 ***1220.12*** *p858*
Weston, Mary; America, 1754 ***1220.12*** *p858*
Weston, Peter 51; Ontario, 1871 ***1823.21*** *p388*
Weston, Thomas; America, 1775 ***1220.12*** *p858*
Weston, W. A.; Colorado, 1893 ***1029.59*** *p94*
Weston, Wilkinson 33; Ontario, 1871 ***1823.21*** *p389*
Weston, Wilkinson 62; Ontario, 1871 ***1823.21*** *p389*
Weston, William; America, 1775 ***1220.12*** *p858*
Weston, William; New York, 1777 ***8529.30*** *p5A*
Weston, William 70; Ontario, 1871 ***1823.21*** *p389*
Westover, Mary E. 29; Michigan, 1880 ***4491.30*** *p32*
Westphal, Christian Friedrich; Wisconsin, 1896 ***6795.8*** *p157*
Westphal, Conrad; America, 1862 ***7420.1*** *p216*
With family
Westrack, Charles Julius; Wisconsin, 1892 ***6795.8*** *p43*
Westrich, Josef 34; America, 1897 ***5475.1*** *p25*
Westrich, Mathias 44; New York, NY, 1890 ***5475.1*** *p18*
Westrick, John; Ohio, 1809-1852 ***4511.35*** *p58*
Westrick, Lewis; Ohio, 1809-1852 ***4511.35*** *p58*
Westrick, Louis; Ohio, 1809-1852 ***4511.35*** *p58*
Westrick, Philip; Ohio, 1809-1852 ***4511.35*** *p58*
Westwood, George; Colorado, 1875 ***1029.59*** *p94*
Westwood, James 29; Ontario, 1871 ***1823.17*** *p173*
Westwood, John; Jamaica, 1665 ***1220.12*** *p858*
Westwood, Richard; America, 1747 ***1220.12*** *p858*
Westwood, William; America, 1755 ***1220.12*** *p858*
Westyn, Leopold; Louisiana, 1874 ***4981.45*** *p134*
Wethager, Wilhelm; America, 1852 ***7420.1*** *p100*
With wife & son
Wetherall, Charles 39; Ontario, 1871 ***1823.17*** *p173*
Wetherall, Jane; America, 1763 ***1220.12*** *p858*
Wetherall, William; Port uncertain, 1720 ***1220.12*** *p858*
Wetherell, Francis; Annapolis, MD, 1725 ***1220.12*** *p858*
Wetherell, George; Virginia, 1723 ***1220.12*** *p858*
Wetherell, John; America, 1757 ***1220.12*** *p858*
Wetherell, Margaret; America, 1742 ***1220.12*** *p858*
Wetherford, Thomas; America, 1750 ***1220.12*** *p859*
Wetherill, John; America, 1683 ***1220.12*** *p858*
Wetherill, William; Virginia, 1721 ***1220.12*** *p859*
Wetherley, James; America, 1746 ***1220.12*** *p859*
Wetman, William; America, 1741 ***1220.12*** *p859*
Wett, Auguste 8; New York, NY, 1885 ***1883.7*** *p46*
Wett, Auguste 37; New York, NY, 1885 ***1883.7*** *p46*
Wett, Bertha 10; New York, NY, 1885 ***1883.7*** *p46*
Wett, Johanna 5; New York, NY, 1885 ***1883.7*** *p46*
Wett, Maria 6; New York, NY, 1885 ***1883.7*** *p46*
Wett, Martin 40; New York, NY, 1885 ***1883.7*** *p46*

Wett, Otto 6 months; New York, NY, 1885 ***1883.7*** *p46*
Wette, Adolphe; Louisiana, 1841-1844 ***4981.45*** *p211*
Wetterlund, J.N.; Philadelphia, 1848 ***6412.40*** *p150*
Wetthauer, Caroline Christine; America, 1866 ***7420.1*** *p245*
Wettie, Thomas; America, 1750 ***1220.12*** *p859*
Wettig, Peter; Valdivia, Chile, 1852 ***1192.4*** *p56*
With wife & 6 children
With child 3
With child 21
Wettinger, Frederick 37; Ontario, 1871 ***1823.21*** *p389*
Wettingle, Fred 42; Ontario, 1871 ***1823.21*** *p389*
Wettstein, Catharina 14; New York, NY, 1893 ***1883.7*** *p42*
Wettstein, Margaretha 11; New York, NY, 1893 ***1883.7*** *p42*
Wettstein, Margaretha 53; New York, NY, 1893 ***1883.7*** *p42*
Wettstein, Mathew 20; New York, NY, 1893 ***1883.7*** *p42*
Wettstein, Mayefa 18; New York, NY, 1893 ***1883.7*** *p42*
Wettstein, Michael 23; New York, NY, 1893 ***1883.7*** *p42*
Wettstein, Michael 58; New York, NY, 1893 ***1883.7*** *p42*
Wettstein, Theresia 16; New York, NY, 1893 ***1883.7*** *p42*
Wettwer, Jacob; Ohio, 1809-1852 ***4511.35*** *p58*
Wetwer, Jacob; Ohio, 1809-1852 ***4511.35*** *p58*
Wetwer, John; Ohio, 1809-1852 ***4511.35*** *p58*
Wetworth, Richard; Philadelphia, 1778 ***8529.30*** *p5A*
Wetzel, Mr. 23; America, 1843 ***778.6*** *p344*
Wetzel, Mr. 28; America, 1843 ***778.6*** *p344*
Wetzel, A.; Louisiana, 1874 ***4981.45*** *p297*
Wetzel, Adam; Valdivia, Chile, 1852 ***1192.4*** *p56*
Wetzel, Augustus; Ohio, 1809-1852 ***4511.35*** *p58*
Wetzel, Barbara 19; America, 1847 ***778.6*** *p344*
Wetzel, Conrad; Valdivia, Chile, 1852 ***1192.4*** *p56*
Wetzel, Jacob; Louisiana, 1836-1841 ***4981.45*** *p209*
Wetzel, Jean 24; New Orleans, 1848 ***778.6*** *p344*
Wetzele, Augustine; Ohio, 1809-1852 ***4511.35*** *p58*
Weulander, Kaisa 41; Minnesota, 1926 ***2769.54*** *p1382*
Weulander, Kate 40; Minnesota, 1923 ***2769.54*** *p1381*
Wever, Adolphus; Ohio, 1809-1852 ***4511.35*** *p58*
Wever, Ant. 35; America, 1844 ***778.6*** *p344*
Wexel, Johann; North Carolina, 1710 ***3629.40*** *p9*
Wexelberger, John; Washington, 1887 ***2770.40*** *p25*
Wexham, Margaret; Barbados, 1667 ***1220.12*** *p859*
Wey, Carl August; America, 1867 ***7919.3*** *p531*
Wey, Reuben; America, 1758 ***1220.12*** *p859*
Wey, Susanna Margarethe Storandt *SEE* Wey, Wilhelm
Wey, Wilhelm; America, 1868 ***7919.3*** *p535*
*Wife:*Susanna Margarethe Storandt
With 3 children
Weyand, Auguste; New York, NY, 1892 ***5475.1*** *p25*
Weyand, Barbara; Cincinnati, 1867 ***5475.1*** *p482*
Weyand, Helena 49; America, 1860 ***5475.1*** *p360*
Weyand, Johann; America, 1866 ***5475.1*** *p198*
Weyand, Margarethe 32; America, 1869 ***5475.1*** *p279*
Weyand, Margarethe 37; America, 1883 ***5475.1*** *p198*
Weyer, Karl; New Castle, DE, 1817-1818 ***90.20*** *p154*
Weyerbacher, Franz; America, 1858 ***5475.1*** *p507*
Weyl, Jacques 47; New Orleans, 1845 ***778.6*** *p344*
Weyland, Nikolaus; America, 1837 ***5475.1*** *p395*
Weyler, Jacob 60; Ontario, 1871 ***1823.21*** *p389*
Weyman, Michael; Annapolis, MD, 1729 ***1220.12*** *p848*
Weymar, Anna Maria 21; Pennsylvania, 1851 ***170.15*** *p47*
Weymar, Kaspar 35; Pennsylvania, 1851 ***170.15*** *p47*
Weymar, Katharina; Pennsylvania, 1899 ***170.15*** *p47*
Weymer, Henry; Long Island, 1781 ***8529.30*** *p10A*
Weynand, Anna Maria 54; America, 1857 ***5475.1*** *p548*
Weyrauch, Adam 5 *SEE* Weyrauch, Leonhard
Weyrauch, Bernhard; America, 1831 ***2526.43*** *p201*
Weyrauch, Bernhard 31; America, 1831 ***2526.43*** *p204*
Weyrauch, Heinrich; America, 1893 ***2526.43*** *p223*
Weyrauch, Heinrich Frank Gottgetreu; America, 1868 ***7919.3*** *p530*
Weyrauch, Johann Peter 9 *SEE* Weyrauch, Leonhard
Weyrauch, Leonhard; America, 1832 ***2526.43*** *p223*
With wife & child
Weyrauch, Leonhard; America, 1846 ***2526.43*** *p184*
With wife & 5 children
Weyrauch, Leonhard 36; America, 1853 ***2526.42*** *p148*
With father-in-law 56
*Child:*Adam 5
*Child:*Johann Peter 9 months
*Child:*Michael 3
*Wife:*Sybilla 32
Weyrauch, Michael 3 *SEE* Weyrauch, Leonhard
Weyrauch, Moritz; America, 1867 ***7919.3*** *p525*
Weyrauch, Sybilla 32 *SEE* Weyrauch, Leonhard
Weyrich, Adam; America, 1857 ***2526.43*** *p136*
Weyrich, Adam 46; Dayton, OH, 1855 ***2526.43*** *p135*
*Wife:*Katharina Eckert 38
*Son:*Georg Adam 3
*Daughter:*Elisabetha 6
*Son:*Konrad 17
*Daughter:*Anna Katharina 8
Weyrich, Angela; America, 1882 ***5475.1*** *p464*
Weyrich, Anna Katharina 8 *SEE* Weyrich, Adam
Weyrich, Elisabeth; America, 1837 ***5475.1*** *p395*
Weyrich, Elisabeth Baermann *SEE* Weyrich, Franz
Weyrich, Elisabetha 6 *SEE* Weyrich, Adam
Weyrich, Franz 52; America, 1842 ***5475.1*** *p397*
*Wife:*Elisabeth Baermann
*Son:*Georg
*Son:*Friedrich
*Son:*Jakob
*Daughter:*Katharina
Weyrich, Friedrich *SEE* Weyrich, Franz
Weyrich, Georg *SEE* Weyrich, Franz
Weyrich, Georg Adam 3 *SEE* Weyrich, Adam
Weyrich, Jakob; America, 1842 ***2526.42*** *p203*
Weyrich, Jakob *SEE* Weyrich, Franz
Weyrich, Johann; America, 1842 ***5475.1*** *p397*
Weyrich, Johann; Dayton, OH, 1867 ***2526.43*** *p136*
Weyrich, Johannes; America, 1884 ***2526.43*** *p216*
Weyrich, Katharina *SEE* Weyrich, Franz
Weyrich, Katharina; America, 1881 ***5475.1*** *p456*
Weyrich, Katharina Eckert 38 *SEE* Weyrich, Adam
Weyrich, Konrad 17 *SEE* Weyrich, Adam
Weyrich, M. Elisabetha; America, 1869 ***2526.43*** *p216*
Weyrich, Maria 34; America, 1836 ***5475.1*** *p396*
Weyrich, Mathias; America, 1837 ***5475.1*** *p396*
Weyrich, Michael 25; America, 1836 ***2526.43*** *p216*
Weyrich, Peter 23; America, 1740-1906 ***2526.42*** *p203*
Weyrich, Philipp; America, 1839 ***2526.42*** *p203*
Weyrich, Robert; America, 1866 ***5475.1*** *p379*
Wezel, John G.; Pittsburgh, 1850 ***8513.31*** *p432*
*Wife:*Louise Hinderer
Wezel, Louise Hinderer *SEE* Wezel, John G.
Wezmann, Wenalen; Louisiana, 1874 ***4981.45*** *p134*
Whaits, Thomas; America, 1772 ***1220.12*** *p830*
Whaland, Thomas; Boston, 1766 ***1642*** *p37*
Whale, John; Virginia, 1753 ***1220.12*** *p859*
Whale, William; Maryland, 1736 ***1220.12*** *p859*
Whalebone, John; Virginia, 1723 ***1220.12*** *p859*
Whalen, Danual 53; Ontario, 1871 ***1823.21*** *p389*
Whalen, Margeret 60; Ontario, 1871 ***1823.21*** *p389*
Whalen, Martin 28; Ontario, 1871 ***1823.21*** *p389*
Whalen, Michael 50; Ontario, 1871 ***1823.21*** *p389*
Whalen, Patrick 55; Ontario, 1871 ***1823.21*** *p389*
Whalen, Thomas; Illinois, 1860 ***6079.1*** *p15*
Whalen, Thomas 50; Ontario, 1871 ***1823.21*** *p389*
Whalen, William 60; Ontario, 1871 ***1823.21*** *p389*
Whales, Richard; America, 1719 ***1220.12*** *p859*
Whaley, Alexander; America, 1736 ***1220.12*** *p859*
Whaley, George; America, 1764 ***1220.12*** *p859*
Whaley, Isaac 60; Ontario, 1871 ***1823.21*** *p389*
Whaley, John; America, 1755 ***1220.12*** *p859*
Whaley, John 37; Ontario, 1871 ***1823.17*** *p173*
Whaley, Samuel 60; Ontario, 1871 ***1823.17*** *p173*
Whaley, William; America, 1753 ***1220.12*** *p859*
Whaley, William 38; Ontario, 1871 ***1823.21*** *p389*
Whalihan, Thomas; Louisiana, 1836-1841 ***4981.45*** *p209*
Whalim, Martin; Louisiana, 1874 ***4981.45*** *p134*
Whalin, Edward; Boston, 1766 ***1642*** *p37*
Whally, W. S. 46; Ontario, 1871 ***1823.21*** *p389*
Whalock, James; America, 1749 ***1220.12*** *p859*
Whalon, Pevice; America, 1772 ***1220.12*** *p859*
Wharley, John; America, 1740 ***1220.12*** *p859*
Wharton, Benjamin; Maryland, 1725 ***1220.12*** *p859*
Wharton, Cuthbert; Virginia, 1721 ***1220.12*** *p859*
Wharton, James; America, 1764 ***1220.12*** *p859*
Wharton, James; Virginia, 1622 ***1220.12*** *p859*
Wharton, Jane; Barbados, 1665 ***1220.12*** *p859*
Wharton, John; Annapolis, MD, 1733 ***1220.12*** *p859*
Wharton, Katherine; Maryland, 1730 ***1220.12*** *p859*
Wharton, Robert; America, 1772 ***1220.12*** *p859*
Wharton, Sarah; America, 1738 ***1220.12*** *p859*
Wharton, Susannah; America, 1733 ***1220.12*** *p859*
Wharton, Thomas; America, 1771 ***1220.12*** *p859*
Wharton, William; America, 1770 ***1220.12*** *p859*
Wharton, William; America, 1771 ***1220.12*** *p859*
Whateley, Henry 35; Ontario, 1871 ***1823.21*** *p389*
Whately, Charles 36; Ontario, 1871 ***1823.21*** *p389*
Whately, Hannah 37; Ontario, 1871 ***1823.21*** *p389*
Whatman, William; America, 1741 ***1220.12*** *p859*
Wheable, Alfred 35; Ontario, 1871 ***1823.17*** *p173*
Wheadon, Albert; Canada, 1904 ***9228.50*** *p653*
*Brother:*Wm.
*Brother:*Rall
*Brother:*Thomas
*Brother:*Percy
Wheadon, Amanda Mahy *SEE* Wheadon, Lloyd H.
Wheadon, Hilda Becket *SEE* Wheadon, Percy
Wheadon, Lloyd H.; Oregon, 1900-1923 ***9228.50*** *p653*
*Wife:*Amanda Mahy
Wheadon, Percy; Canada, 1900 ***9228.50*** *p653*
Wheadon, Percy *SEE* Wheadon, Albert
Wheadon, Percy; Seattle, 1910-1950 ***9228.50*** *p653*
*Wife:*Hilda Becket
Wheadon, Rall *SEE* Wheadon, Albert
Wheadon, Rolland; Saskatchewan, 1900-1983 ***9228.50*** *p653*
Wheadon, Ruth; British Columbia, 1900-1983 ***9228.50*** *p653*
Wheadon, Thomas; California, 1885-1983 ***9228.50*** *p653*
Wheadon, Thomas *SEE* Wheadon, Albert
Wheadon, Wm. *SEE* Wheadon, Albert
Whealan, Patrick; Boston, 1753 ***1642*** *p47*
Wheat, John; Virginia, 1718 ***1220.12*** *p859*
Wheatfield, George; America, 1764 ***1220.12*** *p859*
Wheatherhead, Joseph; Virginia, 1736 ***1220.12*** *p859*
Wheatland, Mary; America, 1763 ***1220.12*** *p859*
Wheatley, Albert 21; Indiana, 1880-1886 ***9076.20*** *p71*
Wheatley, Ann; America, 1767 ***1220.12*** *p859*
Wheatley, Elizabeth; America, 1746 ***1220.12*** *p859*
Wheatley, George; America, 1774 ***1220.12*** *p860*
Wheatley, Henry; Potomac, 1729 ***1220.12*** *p860*
Wheatley, Herbert 52; Indiana, 1881-1888 ***9076.20*** *p72*
Wheatley, Hester; Potomac, 1729 ***1220.12*** *p860*
Wheatley, John 57; Ontario, 1871 ***1823.17*** *p173*
Wheatley, John; Virginia, 1735 ***1220.12*** *p860*
Wheatley, Mary; America, 1757 ***1220.12*** *p860*
Wheatley, Mary; America, 1770 ***1220.12*** *p860*
Wheatley, Mary; Barbados, 1663 ***1220.12*** *p860*
Wheatley, Michael; America, 1730 ***1220.12*** *p860*
Wheatley, Peter; America, 1656 ***1220.12*** *p860*
Wheatley, Richard; America, 1774 ***1220.12*** *p860*
Wheatley, Robert; America, 1739 ***1220.12*** *p860*
Wheatley, Robert; Barbados or Jamaica, 1684 ***1220.12*** *p860*
Wheatley, Thomas; America, 1767 ***1220.12*** *p860*
Wheatley, Thomas; Canada, 1775 ***3036.5*** *p67*
Wheatley, William; America, 1732 ***1220.12*** *p860*
Wheatley, William; America, 1741 ***1220.12*** *p860*
Wheatly, John; America, 1744 ***1220.12*** *p860*
Wheatly, Patrick 33; Ontario, 1871 ***1823.17*** *p173*
Wheatly, Robert 59; Ontario, 1871 ***1823.21*** *p389*
Wheatly, Thomas 20; Ontario, 1871 ***1823.21*** *p389*
Wheaton, Fred 23; Indiana, 1874-1875 ***9076.20*** *p68*
Wheaton, Thomas 23; Indiana, 1858-1859 ***9076.20*** *p65*
Wheatone, Alfred 39; Ontario, 1871 ***1823.21*** *p389*
Wheelas, John; America, 1745 ***1220.12*** *p860*
Wheeldon, Benjamin; America, 1741 ***1220.12*** *p852*
Wheeldon, Elias; America, 1733 ***1220.12*** *p852*
Wheeldon, William; America, 1740 ***1220.12*** *p852*
Wheeldon, William; America, 1741 ***1220.12*** *p852*
Wheeler, Absolom 34; Ontario, 1871 ***1823.17*** *p173*
Wheeler, Alfred 33; Ontario, 1871 ***1823.21*** *p389*
Wheeler, Ann; America, 1730 ***1220.12*** *p860*
Wheeler, Ann; America, 1738 ***1220.12*** *p860*
Wheeler, Ann; America, 1767 ***1220.12*** *p860*
Wheeler, Barnabas 62; Ontario, 1871 ***1823.21*** *p389*
Wheeler, Bridget; Philadelphia, 1852 ***8513.31*** *p428*
Wheeler, Charles; America, 1769 ***1220.12*** *p860*
Wheeler, Dora 28; Ontario, 1871 ***1823.21*** *p389*
Wheeler, Edward; America, 1683 ***1220.12*** *p860*
Wheeler, Edward; America, 1759 ***1220.12*** *p860*
Wheeler, Edward; Died enroute, 1731 ***1220.12*** *p860*
Wheeler, Edward 29; Ontario, 1871 ***1823.17*** *p173*
Wheeler, Elinor 23; Ontario, 1871 ***1823.21*** *p389*
Wheeler, Ferdinand 33; Ontario, 1871 ***1823.21*** *p389*
Wheeler, Henry; America, 1701 ***1220.12*** *p860*
Wheeler, Henry 52; Ontario, 1871 ***1823.21*** *p389*
Wheeler, Henry 53; Ontario, 1871 ***1823.17*** *p173*
Wheeler, Henry; Virginia, 1767 ***1220.12*** *p860*
Wheeler, Isaac; America, 1782 ***8529.30*** *p17*
Wheeler, James; America, 1731 ***1220.12*** *p860*
Wheeler, James; America, 1760 ***1220.12*** *p860*
Wheeler, James; Virginia, 1738 ***1220.12*** *p860*
Wheeler, Joan; Barbados, 1711 ***1220.12*** *p860*
Wheeler, John; America, 1734 ***1220.12*** *p860*
Wheeler, John; America, 1736 ***1220.12*** *p860*
Wheeler, John; Barbados, 1684 ***1220.12*** *p860*
Wheeler, John; Barbados, 1686 ***1220.12*** *p860*
Wheeler, John; Barbados or Jamaica, 1699 ***1220.12*** *p860*
Wheeler, Lawrence; America, 1742 ***1220.12*** *p860*
Wheeler, Mary; America, 1741 ***1220.12*** *p860*
Wheeler, Mary; America, 1773 ***1220.12*** *p860*
Wheeler, Mary; Virginia, 1735 ***1220.12*** *p860*
Wheeler, Oscar G. 35; Ontario, 1871 ***1823.21*** *p389*
Wheeler, Ralph; America, 1745 ***1220.12*** *p860*
Wheeler, Richard; America, 1680 ***1220.12*** *p860*
Wheeler, Richard; America, 1767 ***1220.12*** *p860*
Wheeler, Robert; America, 1732 ***1220.12*** *p860*
Wheeler, Robert; Potomac, 1731 ***1220.12*** *p860*
Wheeler, Roger, Jr.; Barbados, 1698 ***1220.12*** *p861*
Wheeler, Rose; America, 1677 ***1220.12*** *p861*
Wheeler, Samuel; America, 1685 ***1220.12*** *p861*
Wheeler, Susanna; Maryland, 1722 ***1220.12*** *p861*

550 *FOR A COMPLETE EXPLANATION OF ENTRY, SEE "HOW TO READ A CITATION" SECTION*

Wheeler, Susannah; America, 1743 ***1220.12*** *p861*
Wheeler, Thomas; America, 1771 ***1220.12*** *p861*
Wheeler, Thomas; Barbados, 1693 ***1220.12*** *p861*
Wheeler, Thomas; Ohio, 1809-1852 ***4511.35*** *p58*
Wheeler, William; America, 1766 ***1220.12*** *p861*
Wheeler, William; America, 1773 ***1220.12*** *p861*
Wheeler, William; America, 1774 ***1220.12*** *p861*
Wheeler, William; Maryland, 1737 ***1220.12*** *p861*
Wheelhouse, Chas 37; Ontario, 1871 ***1823.21*** *p389*
Wheelhouse, John; America, 1745 ***1220.12*** *p861*
Wheelock, William, Sr.; America, 1769 ***1220.12*** *p861*
Whelan, Daniel 56; Ontario, 1871 ***1823.21*** *p389*
Whelan, Edward; Toronto, 1844 ***2910.35*** *p113*
Whelan, Esther; New Orleans, 1850 ***7242.30*** *p156*
Whelan, Francis; Halifax, N.S., 1827 ***7009.9*** *p61*
Whelan, James; New Orleans, 1850 ***7242.30*** *p156*
Whelan, John; Boston, 1740 ***1642*** *p45*
Whelan, John; New Orleans, 1850 ***7242.30*** *p156*
Whelan, Maria 24; Ontario, 1871 ***1823.21*** *p389*
Whelan, Mary; New Orleans, 1850 ***7242.30*** *p156*
Whelan, Peggy; New Orleans, 1850 ***7242.30*** *p156*
Whelan, Sarah; New Orleans, 1850 ***7242.30*** *p156*
Whelan, Thomas; New Orleans, 1850 ***7242.30*** *p156*
Whelan, Thomas 34; Ontario, 1871 ***1823.21*** *p389*
Whelan, Thomas 38; Ontario, 1871 ***1823.21*** *p389*
Whelan, William; New Orleans, 1850 ***7242.30*** *p156*
Wheldrake, John; Barbados, 1699 ***1220.12*** *p861*
Whelpley, Robert; Virginia, 1768 ***1220.12*** *p861*
Whelpton, William 47; Ontario, 1871 ***1823.21*** *p389*
Whepson, William; America, 1741 ***1220.12*** *p861*
Wherrett, John; America, 1774 ***1220.12*** *p861*
Whetcomb, Sarah; Annapolis, MD, 1723 ***1220.12*** *p861*
Whetland, John; America, 1746 ***1220.12*** *p861*
Whetley, William; America, 1739 ***1220.12*** *p861*
Whetstone, John; America, 1752 ***1220.12*** *p861*
Whetten, John; America, 1746 ***1220.12*** *p861*
Whetter, Francis 51; Ontario, 1871 ***1823.21*** *p390*
Whetter, Stephen; Barbados or Jamaica, 1684 ***1220.12*** *p861*
Wheymark, Elizabeth; America, 1755 ***1220.12*** *p848*
Whiat, John; America, 1733 ***1220.12*** *p905*
Whibby, Simon; America, 1697 ***1220.12*** *p861*
Whicker, Benjamin; America, 1685 ***1220.12*** *p869*
Whicker, John; America, 1685 ***1220.12*** *p869*
Whiddon, Henry; America, 1746 ***1220.12*** *p861*
Whiddon, John; America, 1730 ***1220.12*** *p861*
Whidler, John; Barbados, 1686 ***1220.12*** *p861*
Whietley, George; America, 1761 ***1220.12*** *p867*
Whiffen, John; America, 1768 ***1220.12*** *p861*
Whiffen, Thomas 55; Ontario, 1871 ***1823.17*** *p173*
Whiffin, William; America, 1746 ***1220.12*** *p861*
Whilan, John 20; St. Johns, N.F., 1811 ***1053.20*** *p20*
Whiley, John; America, 1772 ***1220.12*** *p871*
Whilihan, John 45; Ontario, 1871 ***1823.21*** *p390*
Whims, Thomas; America, 1767 ***1220.12*** *p861*
Whinney, Robert 25; Indiana, 1864-1871 ***9076.20*** *p67*
Whipple, Florentine; Ohio, 1809-1852 ***4511.35*** *p59*
Whipple, Frances; Barbados, 1683 ***1220.12*** *p861*
Whippy, Edward; Maryland, 1720 ***1220.12*** *p861*
Whiskin, Richard; America, 1757 ***1220.12*** *p861*
Whiskord, Thomas G. 36; Ontario, 1871 ***1823.21*** *p390*
Whiston, Jane; America, 1736 ***1220.12*** *p861*
Whiston, John; America, 1725 ***1220.12*** *p861*
Whiston, John Christopher; Nova Scotia, 1784 ***7105*** *p27*
Whitackre, Grace; America, 1766 ***1220.12*** *p861*
Whitaker, Andrew; America, 1750 ***1220.12*** *p861*
Whitaker, Ann; America, 1774 ***1220.12*** *p861*
Whitaker, Annie 6; Ontario, 1871 ***1823.21*** *p390*
Whitaker, Charlotte 34; Ontario, 1871 ***1823.21*** *p390*
Whitaker, David; America, 1766 ***1220.12*** *p861*
Whitaker, George 36; Ontario, 1871 ***1823.21*** *p390*
Whitaker, John; America, 1750 ***1220.12*** *p861*
Whitaker, John; America, 1754 ***1220.12*** *p862*
Whitaker, Robert; New York, NY, 1821 ***3274.55*** *p67*
Whitaker, Thomas; America, 1727 ***1220.12*** *p862*
Whitaker, William; America, 1754 ***1220.12*** *p862*
Whitaker, William; Philadelphia, 1778 ***8529.30*** *p7A*
Whitall, Daniel; America, 1766 ***1220.12*** *p862*
Whitall, John; Maryland, 1723 ***1220.12*** *p862*
Whitby, Henry 21; Ontario, 1871 ***1823.21*** *p390*
Whitby, Thomas; America, 1757 ***1220.12*** *p862*
Whitby, William; America, 1747 ***1220.12*** *p862*
Whitby, William; America, 1752 ***1220.12*** *p862*
Whitchelo, William; America, 1722 ***1220.12*** *p862*
Whitcher, Thomas; America, 1733 ***1220.12*** *p862*
Whitcherley, Thomas; America, 1724 ***1220.12*** *p862*
Whitchurch, Thomas 72; Ontario, 1871 ***1823.21*** *p390*
Whitcliff, Richard; America, 1751 ***1220.12*** *p862*
Whitcoft, William 65; Ontario, 1871 ***1823.17*** *p173*
Whitcomb, Daniel 52; Michigan, 1880 ***4491.36*** *p24*
Whitcomb, George 51; Ontario, 1871 ***1823.17*** *p173*
Whitcomb, Matilda 21; Michigan, 1880 ***4491.36*** *p24*
Whitcroft, Thomas 50; Ontario, 1871 ***1823.17*** *p173*
White, Abraham *SEE* White, Philip
White, Alan 16; Ontario, 1871 ***1823.17*** *p173*
White, Alexander; America, 1751 ***1220.12*** *p862*
White, Alexander 65; Ontario, 1871 ***1823.17*** *p173*
White, Amelia 31 *SEE* White, John
White, Ann; America, 1747 ***1220.12*** *p862*
White, Ann; America, 1748 ***1220.12*** *p862*
White, Ann; America, 1755 ***1220.12*** *p862*
White, Ann; America, 1767 ***1220.12*** *p862*
White, Ann; America, 1772 ***1220.12*** *p862*
White, Ann; America, 1773 ***1220.12*** *p862*
White, Ann 37; Ontario, 1871 ***1823.21*** *p390*
White, Ann 60; Ontario, 1871 ***1823.21*** *p390*
White, Arthur; New Orleans, 1851 ***7242.30*** *p156*
White, Benjamin; America, 1754 ***1220.12*** *p862*
White, Cath 21; Ontario, 1871 ***1823.21*** *p390*
White, Catherine; America, 1764 ***1220.12*** *p862*
White, Catherine; Annapolis, MD, 1723 ***1220.12*** *p862*
White, Catherine Maria; America, 1734 ***1220.12*** *p862*
White, Charles; America, 1766 ***1220.12*** *p862*
White, Charles; America, 1773 ***1220.12*** *p862*
White, Charles 29; Ontario, 1871 ***1823.21*** *p390*
White, Charles 30; Ontario, 1871 ***1823.17*** *p173*
White, Charles 33; Ontario, 1871 ***1823.21*** *p390*
White, Charles 70; Ontario, 1871 ***1823.21*** *p390*
White, Christopher; America, 1766 ***1220.12*** *p862*
White, Daniel; America, 1757 ***1220.12*** *p862*
White, David; Louisiana, 1841-1844 ***4981.45*** *p211*
White, David 33; Ontario, 1871 ***1823.21*** *p390*
White, David 36; Ontario, 1871 ***1823.17*** *p174*
White, Donald 82; Ontario, 1871 ***1823.21*** *p390*
White, Duncan 82; Ontario, 1871 ***1823.21*** *p390*
White, Edward; America, 1749 ***1220.12*** *p862*
White, Edward; America, 1771 ***1220.12*** *p862*
White, Edward; Annapolis, MD, 1733 ***1220.12*** *p862*
White, Eleanor; America, 1736 ***1220.12*** *p862*
White, Elizabeth; America, 1700 ***1220.12*** *p862*
White, Elizabeth; America, 1740 ***1220.12*** *p862*
White, Elizabeth; America, 1745 ***1220.12*** *p862*
White, Elizabeth; America, 1747 ***1220.12*** *p862*
White, Elizabeth; America, 1751 ***1220.12*** *p862*
White, Elizabeth; America, 1761 ***1220.12*** *p863*
White, Elizabeth; America, 1764 ***1220.12*** *p863*
White, Elizabeth; America, 1775 ***1220.12*** *p863*
White, Elizabeth; Annapolis, MD, 1725 ***1220.12*** *p862*
White, Elizabeth 40; Michigan, 1880 ***4491.39*** *p32*
White, Elizabeth 15; Ontario, 1871 ***1823.21*** *p390*
White, Elizabeth; Virginia, 1739 ***1220.12*** *p862*
White, Frances; Virginia, 1741 ***1220.12*** *p863*
White, Gabriel; Virginia, 1763 ***1220.12*** *p863*
White, George; America, 1721 ***1220.12*** *p863*
White, George; America, 1737 ***1220.12*** *p863*
White, George; America, 1740 ***1220.12*** *p863*
White, George; America, 1756 ***1220.12*** *p863*
White, George; America, 1763 ***1220.12*** *p863*
White, George; America, 1766 ***1220.12*** *p863*
White, George; America, 1767 ***1220.12*** *p863*
White, George; America, 1771 ***1220.12*** *p863*
White, George; Annapolis, MD, 1726 ***1220.12*** *p863*
White, George 34; Ontario, 1871 ***1823.21*** *p390*
White, George 38; Ontario, 1871 ***1823.21*** *p390*
White, George 40; Ontario, 1871 ***1823.21*** *p390*
White, George 46; Ontario, 1871 ***1823.17*** *p174*
White, George 63; Ontario, 1871 ***1823.21*** *p390*
White, Gerrard; Barbados, 1664 ***1220.12*** *p863*
White, Hannah; America, 1743 ***1220.12*** *p863*
White, Hannah; America, 1768 ***1220.12*** *p863*
White, Hannibal; America, 1700 ***1220.12*** *p863*
White, Henery 26; Ontario, 1871 ***1823.21*** *p390*
White, Henry; America, 1685 ***1220.12*** *p863*
White, Henry; America, 1719 ***1220.12*** *p863*
White, Henry; America, 1726 ***1220.12*** *p863*
White, Henry; America, 1731 ***1220.12*** *p863*
White, Henry; America, 1739 ***1220.12*** *p863*
White, Henry; America, 1743 ***1220.12*** *p863*
White, Henry; America, 1745 ***1220.12*** *p863*
White, Henry; America, 1772 ***1220.12*** *p863*
White, Henry; Louisiana, 1874-1875 ***4981.45*** *p130*
White, Henry 44; Ontario, 1871 ***1823.17*** *p174*
White, Isaac 56; Ontario, 1871 ***1823.17*** *p174*
White, J.; Quebec, 1870 ***8364.32*** *p26*
White, James; America, 1722 ***1220.12*** *p863*
White, James; America, 1743 ***1220.12*** *p863*
White, James; America, 1745 ***1220.12*** *p863*
White, James; America, 1750 ***1220.12*** *p863*
White, James; America, 1766 ***1220.12*** *p863*
White, James; America, 1768 ***1220.12*** *p863*
White, James; America, 1769 ***1220.12*** *p863*
White, James; America, 1770 ***1220.12*** *p863*
White, James; Maryland, 1736 ***1220.12*** *p863*
White, James; Maryland, 1741 ***1220.12*** *p863*
White, James; New Orleans, 1850 ***7242.30*** *p156*
White, James; New York, 1778 ***8529.30*** *p17*
White, James; North Carolina, 1813 ***1088.45*** *p37*
White, James 21; Ontario, 1871 ***1823.21*** *p390*
White, James 26; Ontario, 1871 ***1823.21*** *p390*
White, James 41; Ontario, 1871 ***1823.17*** *p174*
White, James 42; Ontario, 1871 ***1823.21*** *p390*
White, James 49; Ontario, 1871 ***1823.21*** *p390*
White, James 85; Ontario, 1871 ***1823.21*** *p390*
White, Jane; America, 1740 ***1220.12*** *p863*
White, Jane; Barbados, 1663 ***1220.12*** *p863*
White, Jane; Jamaica, 1717 ***1220.12*** *p863*
White, Jane; Philadelphia, 1854 ***8513.31*** *p318*
White, Jane E.; Quebec, 1833-1915 ***9228.50*** *p546*
White, Jas.; Louisiana, 1874 ***4981.45*** *p297*
White, Joan; Barbados, 1672 ***1220.12*** *p863*
White, John; America, 1675 ***1220.12*** *p863*
White, John; America, 1682 ***1220.12*** *p863*
White, John; America, 1684 ***1220.12*** *p863*
White, John; America, 1685 ***1220.12*** *p863*
White, John; America, 1715 ***1220.12*** *p864*
White, John; America, 1721 ***1220.12*** *p864*
White, John; America, 1723 ***1220.12*** *p864*
White, John; America, 1730 ***1220.12*** *p864*
White, John; America, 1738 ***1220.12*** *p864*
White, John; America, 1740 ***1220.12*** *p864*
White, John; America, 1745 ***1220.12*** *p864*
White, John; America, 1748 ***1220.12*** *p864*
White, John; America, 1750 ***1220.12*** *p864*
White, John; America, 1752 ***1220.12*** *p864*
White, John; America, 1753 ***1220.12*** *p864*
White, John; America, 1754 ***1220.12*** *p864*
White, John; America, 1759 ***1220.12*** *p864*
White, John; America, 1764 ***1220.12*** *p864*
White, John; America, 1765 ***1220.12*** *p864*
White, John; America, 1768 ***1220.12*** *p864*
White, John; America, 1771 ***1220.12*** *p864*
White, John; America, 1774 ***1220.12*** *p864*
White, John; America, 1775 ***1220.12*** *p864*
White, John; Annapolis, MD, 1733 ***1220.12*** *p864*
White, John; Barbados, 1668 ***1220.12*** *p863*
White, John; Barbados or Jamaica, 1677 ***1220.12*** *p863*
White, John; Charles Town, SC, 1719 ***1220.12*** *p864*
White, John; Died enroute, 1721 ***1220.12*** *p864*
White, John; Illinois, 1855 ***6079.1*** *p15*
White, John; Maryland, 1725 ***1220.12*** *p864*
White, John *SEE* White, Philip
White, John 46; Michigan, 1880 ***4491.39*** *p32*
White, John; New Jersey, 1700-1799 ***9228.50*** *p653*
White, John; New York, 1778 ***8529.30*** *p7*
White, John 36; Ohio, 1880 ***4879.40*** *p258*
*Wife:*Amelia 31
White, John 22; Ontario, 1871 ***1823.21*** *p390*
White, John 23; Ontario, 1871 ***1823.21*** *p390*
White, John 23; Ontario, 1871 ***1823.21*** *p390*
White, John 26; Ontario, 1871 ***1823.21*** *p390*
White, John 27; Ontario, 1871 ***1823.21*** *p390*
White, John 31; Ontario, 1871 ***1823.17*** *p174*
White, John 31; Ontario, 1871 ***1823.21*** *p390*
White, John 45; Ontario, 1871 ***1823.21*** *p391*
White, John 51; Ontario, 1871 ***1823.17*** *p174*
White, John 75; Ontario, 1871 ***1823.17*** *p174*
White, John 17; Quebec, 1870 ***8364.32*** *p26*
White, John 18; St. John, N.B., 1834 ***6469.7*** *p4*
White, John; Virginia, 1722 ***1220.12*** *p864*
White, John; Virginia, 1741 ***1220.12*** *p864*
White, John; Virginia, 1763 ***1220.12*** *p864*
White, John; Virginia, 1769 ***1220.12*** *p864*
White, John; Virginia, 1773 ***1220.12*** *p864*
White, John A. 32; Ontario, 1871 ***1823.21*** *p391*
White, Jonathan; Barbados, 1673 ***1220.12*** *p864*
White, Jonathan; Maryland, 1674 ***1236.25*** *p50*
White, Jos; St. John, N.B., 1847 ***2978.15*** *p38*
White, Joseph; America, 1733 ***1220.12*** *p864*
White, Joseph; America, 1751 ***1220.12*** *p864*
White, Joseph; America, 1763 ***1220.12*** *p864*
White, Joseph 36; Ontario, 1871 ***1823.21*** *p391*
White, Joseph 55; Ontario, 1871 ***1823.21*** *p391*
White, Joseph; Virginia, 1769 ***1220.12*** *p864*
White, Katherine; Barbados or Jamaica, 1689 ***1220.12*** *p862*
White, Laurence; Barbados or Jamaica, 1686 ***1220.12*** *p864*
White, Leon; Texas, 1889 ***6015.15*** *p30*
White, Leonard; America, 1774 ***1220.12*** *p864*
White, Margaret; America, 1772 ***1220.12*** *p864*
White, Margret 75; Ontario, 1871 ***1823.17*** *p174*
White, Mary; America, 1679 ***1220.12*** *p864*
White, Mary; America, 1723 ***1220.12*** *p864*
White, Mary; America, 1734 ***1220.12*** *p864*
White, Mary; America, 1736 ***1220.12*** *p864*
White, Mary; America, 1742 ***1220.12*** *p864*
White, Mary; America, 1743 ***1220.12*** *p865*
White, Mary; America, 1751 ***1220.12*** *p865*
White, Mary; America, 1752 ***1220.12*** *p865*

White, Mary; America, 1759 ***1220.12*** *p865*
White, Mary; America, 1765 ***1220.12*** *p865*
White, Mary; America, 1766 ***1220.12*** *p865*
White, Mary; America, 1767 ***1220.12*** *p865*
White, Mary; America, 1769 ***1220.12*** *p865*
White, Mary; Barbados, 1677 ***1220.12*** *p864*
White, Mary 42; Barbados, 1664 ***1220.12*** *p864*
White, Mary; Charles Town, SC, 1719 ***1220.12*** *p864*
White, Mary; Maryland, 1737 ***1220.12*** *p864*
White, Mary 55; Ontario, 1871 ***1823.21*** *p391*
White, Matthias; America, 1740 ***1220.12*** *p865*
White, Michael; America, 1765 ***1220.12*** *p865*
White, Michael 27; Ontario, 1871 ***1823.21*** *p391*
White, Michael 70; Ontario, 1871 ***1823.21*** *p391*
White, Nathaniel 40; Ontario, 1871 ***1823.21*** *p391*
White, Nehemiah; America, 1748 ***1220.12*** *p865*
White, Oliver 35; Ontario, 1871 ***1823.21*** *p391*
White, Orlando; America, 1734 ***1220.12*** *p865*
White, Patrick 51; Ontario, 1871 ***1823.21*** *p391*
White, Patt; New Orleans, 1851 ***7242.30*** *p156*
White, Peregriene *SEE* White, Wm.
White, Perry; America, 1684 ***1220.12*** *p865*
White, Peter 43; Ontario, 1871 ***1823.17*** *p174*
White, Peter 45; Ontario, 1871 ***1823.21*** *p391*
White, Philip; Massachusetts, 1700 ***9228.50*** *p653*
*Relative:*Zachariah
*Relative:*John
*Relative:*Abraham
White, Philip; Salem, MA, 1720 ***9228.50*** *p653*
White, Randall; America, 1772 ***1220.12*** *p865*
White, Rebecca; Virginia, 1721 ***1220.12*** *p865*
White, Resolved *SEE* White, Wm.
White, Richard; America, 1732 ***1220.12*** *p865*
White, Richard; Annapolis, MD, 1719 ***1220.12*** *p865*
White, Richard; Virginia, 1723 ***1220.12*** *p865*
White, Richard; Virginia, 1736 ***1220.12*** *p865*
White, Richard; Virginia, 1765 ***1220.12*** *p865*
White, Robert; America, 1685 ***1220.12*** *p865*
White, Robert; America, 1729 ***1220.12*** *p865*
White, Robert; America, 1751 ***1220.12*** *p865*
White, Robert; America, 1766 ***1220.12*** *p865*
White, Robert; Jamaica, 1778 ***8529.30*** *p14A*
White, Robert 35; Ontario, 1871 ***1823.21*** *p391*
White, Robert; Virginia, 1742 ***1220.12*** *p865*
White, Samuel; America, 1726 ***1220.12*** *p865*
White, Samuel; America, 1752 ***1220.12*** *p865*
White, Samuel; Marston's Wharf, 1782 ***8529.30*** *p17*
White, Samuel 37; Ontario, 1871 ***1823.21*** *p391*
White, Samuel 41; Ontario, 1871 ***1823.21*** *p391*
White, Samuel 45; Ontario, 1871 ***1823.17*** *p174*
White, Sarah; America, 1763 ***1220.12*** *p865*
White, Sarah 56; North Carolina, 1774 ***1422.10*** *p55*
White, Sarah; Ontario, 1871 ***1823.21*** *p391*
White, Sarah; Virginia, 1727 ***1220.12*** *p865*
White, Scott 61; Ontario, 1871 ***1823.21*** *p391*
White, Sophia; Virginia, 1739 ***1220.12*** *p865*
White, Susana *SEE* White, Wm.
White, Susanna; America, 1757 ***1220.12*** *p865*
White, Susanna; Virginia, 1734 ***1220.12*** *p865*
White, Thomas; America, 1700 ***1220.12*** *p865*
White, Thomas; America, 1714 ***1220.12*** *p865*
White, Thomas; America, 1733 ***1220.12*** *p865*
White, Thomas; America, 1740 ***1220.12*** *p865*
White, Thomas; America, 1742 ***1220.12*** *p865*
White, Thomas; America, 1746 ***1220.12*** *p865*
White, Thomas; America, 1747 ***1220.12*** *p865*
White, Thomas; America, 1749 ***1220.12*** *p865*
White, Thomas; America, 1751 ***1220.12*** *p865*
White, Thomas; America, 1753 ***1220.12*** *p865*
White, Thomas; America, 1755 ***1220.12*** *p865*
White, Thomas; America, 1761 ***1220.12*** *p865*
White, Thomas; America, 1771 ***1220.12*** *p865*
White, Thomas; Barbados, 1679 ***1220.12*** *p865*
White, Thomas; Illinois, 1858-1861 ***6020.5*** *p133*
White, Thomas; North Carolina, 1822 ***1088.45*** *p37*
White, Thomas 23; Ontario, 1871 ***1823.21*** *p391*
White, Thomas Christianson; Washington, 1882 ***2770.40*** *p136*
White, William; America, 1688 ***1220.12*** *p866*
White, William; America, 1723 ***1220.12*** *p866*
White, William; America, 1728 ***1220.12*** *p866*
White, William; America, 1729 ***1220.12*** *p866*
White, William; America, 1739 ***1220.12*** *p866*
White, William; America, 1750 ***1220.12*** *p866*
White, William; America, 1751 ***1220.12*** *p866*
White, William; America, 1755 ***1220.12*** *p866*
White, William; America, 1762 ***1220.12*** *p866*
White, William; America, 1766 ***1220.12*** *p866*
White, William; America, 1767 ***1220.12*** *p866*
White, William; America, 1772 ***1220.12*** *p866*
White, William; America, 1774 ***1220.12*** *p866*
White, William; Annapolis, MD, 1731 ***1220.12*** *p866*
White, William; Annapolis, MD, 1733 ***1220.12*** *p866*
White, William; Barbados, 1664 ***1220.12*** *p866*
White, William; Boston, 1718 ***1220.12*** *p866*
White, William; New Orleans, 1851 ***7242.30*** *p156*
White, William; North Carolina, 1829 ***1088.45*** *p37*
White, William 26; Ohio, 1880 ***4879.40*** *p258*
White, William 65; Ontario, 1871 ***1823.21*** *p391*
White, William 66; Ontario, 1871 ***1823.21*** *p391*
White, William; Philadelphia, 1777 ***8529.30*** *p5A*
White, William; Quebec, 1870 ***8364.32*** *p26*
White, William 18; Quebec, 1870 ***8364.32*** *p26*
White, William; Rappahannock, VA, 1726 ***1220.12*** *p866*
White, William; Virginia, 1749 ***1220.12*** *p866*
White, Wm.; Louisiana, 1874-1875 ***4981.45*** *p130*
White, Wm.; Plymouth, MA, 1620 ***1920.45*** *p5*
*Relative:*Susana
*Relative:*Resolved
*Relative:*Peregriene
White, Zachariah *SEE* White, Philip
Whitebourn, John; America, 1724 ***1220.12*** *p866*
Whitebread, Jane; America, 1702 ***1220.12*** *p866*
Whitecake, John; America, 1772 ***1220.12*** *p866*
Whitecer, Septamus 56; Ontario, 1871 ***1823.21*** *p391*
Whitefoot, Edward; America, 1744 ***1220.12*** *p866*
Whitefoot, John; Salem, MA, 1678 ***9228.50*** *p653*
Whitefoot, Thomas; America, 1773 ***1220.12*** *p866*
Whitefoot, Walter F.; New York, 1921-1974 ***9228.50*** *p120*
Whiteford, A. 19; Ontario, 1858 ***9228.50*** *p558*
Whitehair, Christian; West Virginia, 1790 ***1132.30*** *p146*
Whitehall, Stephen; Barbados or Jamaica, 1684 ***1220.12*** *p866*
Whitehall, William 24; Ontario, 1871 ***1823.21*** *p391*
Whitehand, William; Barbados, 1671 ***1220.12*** *p866*
Whitehart, Richard; Barbados, 1671 ***1220.12*** *p866*
Whitehart, Richd.; Maryland, 1672 ***1236.25*** *p47*
Whitehead, Abraham; America, 1743 ***1220.12*** *p866*
Whitehead, Charles; Annapolis, MD, 1730 ***1220.12*** *p866*
Whitehead, Daniel; America, 1740 ***1220.12*** *p866*
Whitehead, Daniel; Jamaica, 1716 ***1220.12*** *p866*
Whitehead, Elizabeth; Barbados, 1677 ***1220.12*** *p866*
Whitehead, Elizabeth; Maryland, 1736 ***1220.12*** *p866*
Whitehead, Isaac; America, 1747 ***1220.12*** *p866*
Whitehead, John; America, 1753 ***1220.12*** *p866*
Whitehead, John; America, 1773 ***1220.12*** *p866*
Whitehead, John; Ohio, 1836 ***3580.20*** *p33*
Whitehead, John; Ohio, 1836 ***6020.12*** *p23*
Whitehead, John, Jr.; Ohio, 1836 ***3580.20*** *p33*
Whitehead, John, Jr.; Ohio, 1836 ***6020.12*** *p23*
Whitehead, Joseph; America, 1761 ***1220.12*** *p866*
Whitehead, Mary; America, 1720 ***1220.12*** *p866*
Whitehead, Richard; America, 1742 ***1220.12*** *p866*
Whitehead, Robert 30; New York, NY, 1835 ***5024.1*** *p137*
Whitehead, Rose; Barbados, 1668 ***1220.12*** *p867*
Whitehead, Thomas; America, 1743 ***1220.12*** *p867*
Whitehead, Timothy; Annapolis, MD, 1733 ***1220.12*** *p867*
Whitehead, W. H. 61; Ontario, 1871 ***1823.21*** *p391*
Whitehead, William; America, 1764 ***1220.12*** *p867*
Whitehead, William; Barbados, 1683 ***1220.12*** *p867*
Whitehill, James; Iowa, 1893 ***1211.15*** *p20*
Whitehorn, John; Annapolis, MD, 1723 ***1220.12*** *p867*
Whitehorne, Nicholas; Carolina, 1724 ***1220.12*** *p867*
Whitehorne, Stephen; Barbados or Jamaica, 1684 ***1220.12*** *p867*
Whitehouse, James; America, 1774 ***1220.12*** *p867*
Whitehouse, Jeremiah; America, 1739 ***1220.12*** *p867*
Whitehouse, John; America, 1769 ***1220.12*** *p867*
Whitehouse, Joseph; America, 1773 ***1220.12*** *p867*
Whitehouse, Joseph; America, 1774 ***1220.12*** *p867*
Whitehouse, Joseph; America, 1775 ***1220.12*** *p867*
Whitehouse, Mary 68; Ontario, 1871 ***1823.17*** *p174*
Whitehouse, Samuel; America, 1764 ***1220.12*** *p867*
Whiteing, Daniel; America, 1749 ***1220.12*** *p868*
Whiteing, James; America, 1728 ***1220.12*** *p868*
Whiteing, Mary; Virginia, 1734 ***1220.12*** *p868*
Whiteing, Thomas; America, 1729 ***1220.12*** *p868*
Whiteing, Thomas; Barbados, 1665 ***1220.12*** *p868*
Whitelaw, Alexr 61; Ontario, 1871 ***1823.21*** *p391*
Whiteley, Jonathan 57; Ontario, 1871 ***1823.21*** *p391*
Whiteley, Samuel 47; Ontario, 1871 ***1823.17*** *p174*
Whiteley, William 55; Ontario, 1871 ***1823.17*** *p174*
Whitelock, John; America, 1758 ***1220.12*** *p868*
Whitely, Mary; America, 1770 ***1220.12*** *p867*
Whitely, Robert; Virginia, 1768 ***1220.12*** *p867*
Whiteman, Ann; America, 1756 ***1220.12*** *p867*
Whiteman, Sarah; America, 1760 ***1220.12*** *p867*
Whitemarsh, James; America, 1700 ***1220.12*** *p867*
Whitenail, Thomas; America, 1763 ***1220.12*** *p867*
Whitenit, William; America, 1678 ***1220.12*** *p867*
Whiteoake, Thomas; Barbados or Jamaica, 1664 ***1220.12*** *p867*
Whiteside, Theophilus 32; Ontario, 1871 ***1823.17*** *p174*
Whiteside, Thomas; America, 1753 ***1220.12*** *p867*
Whitesides, Henry; America, 1734 ***1220.12*** *p867*
Whitesides, John; North Carolina, 1813 ***1088.45*** *p37*
Whiteway, William; Barbados or Jamaica, 1694 ***1220.12*** *p867*
Whitewood, John; America, 1773 ***1220.12*** *p867*
Whitewood, Thomas; Marston's Wharf, 1779 ***8529.30*** *p17*
Whitfield, Barthia; America, 1746 ***1220.12*** *p867*
Whitfield, Charles; America, 1775 ***1220.12*** *p867*
Whitfield, Daniel; America, 1768 ***1220.12*** *p867*
Whitfield, Henry; America, 1772 ***1220.12*** *p867*
Whitfield, John; America, 1758 ***1220.12*** *p867*
Whitfield, John; Barbados or Jamaica, 1686 ***1220.12*** *p867*
Whitfield, Joshua; America, 1764 ***1220.12*** *p867*
Whitfield, Joshua; America, 1766 ***1220.12*** *p867*
Whitfield, Richard; America, 1770 ***1220.12*** *p867*
Whitfield, Thomas; America, 1765 ***1220.12*** *p868*
Whitfield, Thomas; Barbados, 1665 ***1220.12*** *p867*
Whitford, George 73; Ontario, 1871 ***1823.17*** *p174*
Whitham, Hanna F. 18; Michigan, 1880 ***4491.30*** *p32*
Whitham, Henry T. 42; Michigan, 1880 ***4491.30*** *p32*
Whitham, John J. 13; Michigan, 1880 ***4491.30*** *p32*
Whitham, Margrett 35; Michigan, 1880 ***4491.30*** *p32*
Whithier, Arthur; America, 1752 ***1220.12*** *p868*
Whiting, Ellen 50; Ontario, 1871 ***1823.21*** *p391*
Whiting, George; Died enroute, 1730 ***1220.12*** *p868*
Whiting, Henry 60; Ontario, 1871 ***1823.21*** *p391*
Whiting, James 40; Ontario, 1871 ***1823.17*** *p174*
Whiting, James 43; Ontario, 1871 ***1823.21*** *p391*
Whiting, James 65; Ontario, 1871 ***1823.21*** *p391*
Whiting, John 38; Ontario, 1871 ***1823.21*** *p391*
Whiting, John 73; Ontario, 1871 ***1823.21*** *p391*
Whiting, Letitia 78; Ontario, 1871 ***1823.21*** *p391*
Whiting, Niles 38; Ontario, 1871 ***1823.21*** *p391*
Whiting, Richard 36; Ontario, 1871 ***1823.21*** *p392*
Whiting, Richard 52; Ontario, 1871 ***1823.17*** *p174*
Whiting, Samuel; America, 1756 ***1220.12*** *p868*
Whiting, Thomas; America, 1738 ***1220.12*** *p868*
Whiting, Thomas; America, 1763 ***1220.12*** *p868*
Whiting, William 26; Ontario, 1871 ***1823.17*** *p174*
Whiting, William 36; Ontario, 1871 ***1823.21*** *p392*
Whitles, Anne; New Orleans, 1851 ***7242.30*** *p156*
Whitley, Ann; America, 1736 ***1220.12*** *p867*
Whitley, James; America, 1774 ***1220.12*** *p867*
Whitley, James 44; Ontario, 1871 ***1823.21*** *p392*
Whitley, Joseph; Died enroute, 1723 ***1220.12*** *p867*
Whitley, Joseph 67; Ontario, 1871 ***1823.21*** *p392*
Whitling, John H. 33; New York, NY, 1812-1845 ***3274.55*** *p44*
Whitlock, John 60; Ontario, 1871 ***1823.21*** *p392*
Whitlock, Robert; America, 1731 ***1220.12*** *p868*
Whitlock, William; America, 1734 ***1220.12*** *p868*
Whitlock, William; Virginia, 1729 ***1220.12*** *p868*
Whitlow, William; America, 1768 ***1220.12*** *p868*
Whitman, John 60; Ontario, 1871 ***1823.17*** *p174*
Whitman, William; America, 1736 ***1220.12*** *p867*
Whitmill, Ann; America, 1713 ***1220.12*** *p868*
Whitmill, Richard; America, 1746 ***1220.12*** *p868*
Whitmore, Delia 19; Ontario, 1871 ***1823.21*** *p392*
Whitmore, Francis; America, 1753 ***1220.12*** *p868*
Whitmore, John; America, 1770 ***1220.12*** *p868*
Whitmore, Lydia; America, 1749 ***1220.12*** *p868*
Whitmore, Robert; America, 1739 ***1220.12*** *p868*
Whitmore, Thomas; America, 1678 ***1220.12*** *p868*
Whitmore, William; America, 1773 ***1220.12*** *p868*
Whitmore, William; Annapolis, MD, 1735 ***1220.12*** *p868*
Whitnall, Henry 52; Ontario, 1871 ***1823.21*** *p392*
Whitney, Elizabeth; America, 1740 ***1220.12*** *p868*
Whitney, Henry F.; Washington, 1886 ***2770.40*** *p24*
Whitney, James; America, 1752 ***1220.12*** *p868*
Whitney, John; America, 1770 ***1220.12*** *p868*
Whiton, Henry; America, 1763 ***1220.12*** *p868*
Whitose, Mr. 40; Port uncertain, 1842 ***778.6*** *p344*
Whitsett, Benjamin 46; Ontario, 1871 ***1823.17*** *p174*
Whitson, James; Ohio, 1809-1852 ***4511.35*** *p59*
Whitson, John 63; Ontario, 1871 ***1823.17*** *p174*
Whitson, Thomas; Ohio, 1809-1852 ***4511.35*** *p59*
Whittaker, David 36; Ontario, 1871 ***1823.17*** *p174*
Whittaker, George; Barbados, 1692 ***1220.12*** *p861*
Whittaker, James; America, 1768 ***1220.12*** *p861*
Whittaker, James 41; Ontario, 1871 ***1823.21*** *p392*
Whittaker, Joseph 57; Ontario, 1871 ***1823.21*** *p392*
Whittaker, Mary Ann; America, 1767 ***1220.12*** *p862*
Whittaker, Richard 28; Ontario, 1871 ***1823.21*** *p392*
Whittaker, Thomas; Rappahannock, VA, 1729 ***1220.12*** *p862*
Whitten, George 44; Ontario, 1871 ***1823.17*** *p174*
Whitten, Mathew; Maryland or Virginia, 1719 ***1220.12*** *p868*
Whittenbury, Mary; America, 1665 ***1220.12*** *p868*
Whitter, Richard 47; Ontario, 1871 ***1823.21*** *p392*

552 *FOR A COMPLETE EXPLANATION OF ENTRY, SEE "HOW TO READ A CITATION" SECTION*

Whittier, Elizabeth 62; Ontario, 1871 ***1823.21*** *p392*
Whittiingham, William E.; Illinois, 1918 ***6007.60*** *p9*
Whittimore, Eliza 79; Ontario, 1871 ***1823.21*** *p392*
Whittimore, George; America, 1764 ***1220.12*** *p868*
Whitting, George 55; Ontario, 1871 ***1823.17*** *p174*
Whitting, John 29; Ontario, 1871 ***1823.21*** *p392*
Whittinger, P.; Louisiana, 1874 ***4981.45*** *p297*
Whittingham, John; America, 1748 ***1220.12*** *p868*
Whittingham, Joseph; Maryland or Virginia, 1738 ***1220.12*** *p868*
Whittingham, Samuel; Rappahannock, VA, 1728 ***1220.12*** *p868*
Whittington, Edmund; America, 1727 ***1220.12*** *p868*
Whittle, Anne 71; Ontario, 1871 ***1823.21*** *p392*
Whittle, Giles; America, 1685 ***1220.12*** *p868*
Whittle, Samuel; America, 1718 ***1220.12*** *p868*
Whittle, William; America, 1748 ***1220.12*** *p868*
Whittles, Austin; America, 1731 ***1220.12*** *p868*
Whittock, Joseph; Barbados, 1700 ***1220.12*** *p868*
Whitton, Henry; America, 1770 ***1220.12*** *p868*
Whitton, John; Annapolis, MD, 1731 ***1220.12*** *p868*
Whitton, Matthew; Annapolis, MD, 1719 ***1220.12*** *p869*
Whitwell, John; America, 1675 ***1220.12*** *p869*
Whitwell, William; America, 1755 ***1220.12*** *p869*
Whitwham, William; Boston, 1774 ***8529.30*** *p3*
Whitwick, Edward; Barbados, 1681 ***1220.12*** *p869*
Whitwood, Ann; Barbados or Jamaica, 1689 ***1220.12*** *p867*
Whitwood, Katherine; Barbados or Jamaica, 1689 ***1220.12*** *p867*
Whitworth, Alice; America, 1775 ***1220.12*** *p869*
Whitworth, Peter; America, 1740 ***1220.12*** *p869*
Whood, James; America, 1675 ***1220.12*** *p895*
Whorewood, Sarah; America, 1756 ***1220.12*** *p869*
Whorrall, Mary; America, 1765 ***1220.12*** *p901*
Whoulfrey, John; America, 1773 ***1220.12*** *p900*
Whytall, William; America, 1766 ***1220.12*** *p862*
Whyte, George; Ohio, 1809-1852 ***4511.35*** *p59*
Whyte, John 31; Ontario, 1871 ***1823.21*** *p392*
Whyte, John T.; Colorado, 1881 ***1029.59*** *p94*
Whyte, John T.; Colorado, 1888 ***1029.59*** *p94*
Whyten, William 27; Ontario, 1871 ***1823.21*** *p392*
Whyttie, Thomas; America, 1685 ***1220.12*** *p894*
Wiatt, John; America, 1694 ***1220.12*** *p905*
Wiber, Mary 40; Ontario, 1871 ***1823.21*** *p392*
Wiberg, Carolina N.; St. Paul, MN, 1888 ***1865.50*** *p105*
Wiberg, E.; New York, NY, 1847 ***6412.40*** *p149*
Wibird, Sarah; New Hampshire, 1703-1788 ***9228.50*** *p148*
Wicard, Charles 31; Louisiana, 1848 ***778.6*** *p344*
Wicha, Klemens; Detroit, 1929-1930 ***6214.5*** *p70*
Wichert, Jean; New Castle, DE, 1817-1818 ***90.20*** *p154*
Wichman, Chas 39; Ontario, 1871 ***1823.17*** *p174*
Wichmann, Carl Christian; America, 1857 ***7420.1*** *p175*
With wife & 3 sons
Wichmann, Carl Christian Wilhelm; America, 1883 ***7420.1*** *p341*
Wichmann, Carl Ludwig Philipp *SEE* Wichmann, Carl Wilhelm Ludwig
Wichmann, Carl Wilhelm Ludwig; America, 1870 ***7420.1*** *p286*
*Brother:*Carl Ludwig Philipp
Wichmann, Charles 39; Ontario, 1871 ***1823.17*** *p175*
Wichmann, Christine Wilhelmine Eleonore; America, 1856 ***7420.1*** *p156*
Wichmann, Conrad; America, 1856 ***7420.1*** *p156*
Wichmann, Engel; America, 1856 ***7420.1*** *p156*
Wichmann, Wilhelm; America, 1883 ***7420.1*** *p341*
Wichowski, Ignacy 16; New York, NY, 1911 ***6533.11*** *p9*
Wichtendahl, Auguste Luise Adele Wilhelmine *SEE* Wichtendahl, Carl Friedrich Ludolf
Wichtendahl, Carl Friedrich Ludolf; America, 1881 ***7420.1*** *p326*
*Wife:*Marie Dorothea Beathe Seebaum
*Daughter:*Auguste Luise Adele Wilhelmine
Wichtendahl, Marie Dorothea Beathe Seebaum *SEE* Wichtendahl, Carl Friedrich Ludolf
Wick, Anne 22; Ontario, 1871 ***1823.21*** *p392*
Wick, Catha. 53; America, 1846 ***778.6*** *p344*
Wick, Elisabeth 24; America, 1846 ***778.6*** *p344*
Wick, Jane; America, 1742 ***1220.12*** *p869*
Wick, Johann 38; New Orleans, 1848-1849 ***778.6*** *p344*
Wick, Matthew; America, 1773 ***1220.12*** *p869*
Wick, Michel 54; America, 1846 ***778.6*** *p345*
Wick, Nickless; New Jersey, 1764-1774 ***927.31*** *p2*
Wickborn, J.; Venezuela, 1843 ***3899.5*** *p547*
Wicke, Mr.; America, 1854 ***7420.1*** *p132*
Wickedal, Martin; Ohio, 1809-1852 ***4511.35*** *p59*
Wickenden, David; America, 1753 ***1220.12*** *p869*
Wickens, George 23; Ontario, 1871 ***1823.21*** *p392*
Wicker, John; America, 1753 ***1220.12*** *p869*
Wicker, John; Annapolis, MD, 1722 ***1220.12*** *p869*
Wickers, John; Barbados, 1671 ***1220.12*** *p869*
Wickerson, Henry 25; Ontario, 1871 ***1823.21*** *p392*
Wickert, Henry 34; Ontario, 1871 ***1823.21*** *p392*
Wickes, George 37; Ontario, 1871 ***1823.21*** *p392*
Wickett, Daniel; Potomac, 1743 ***1220.12*** *p869*
Wickett, John; America, 1751 ***1220.12*** *p869*
Wickett, John C.; Colorado, 1877 ***1029.59*** *p94*
Wickett, Richard 39; Ontario, 1871 ***1823.21*** *p392*
Wickham, Catherine; America, 1752 ***1220.12*** *p869*
Wickham, John; America, 1746 ***1220.12*** *p869*
Wickham, Joseph; America, 1685 ***1220.12*** *p869*
Wickham, Matthew; America, 1764 ***1220.12*** *p869*
Wickham, Thomas; Maryland, 1723 ***1220.12*** *p869*
Wickhans, Margaret; St. Johns, N.F., 1825 ***1053.15*** *p7*
Wicking, Richard; America, 1749 ***1220.12*** *p869*
Wicklund, John; Cleveland, OH, 1892-1894 ***9722.10*** *p128*
Wickman, Is.; New York, NY, 1845 ***6412.40*** *p148*
Wicks, Charles; America, 1757 ***1220.12*** *p869*
Wicks, Edmund; America, 1738 ***1220.12*** *p869*
Wicks, Edward; Annapolis, MD, 1725 ***1220.12*** *p869*
Wicks, Henry; America, 1753 ***1220.12*** *p869*
Wicks, John; America, 1734 ***1220.12*** *p869*
Wicks, John; Maryland, 1740 ***1220.12*** *p869*
Wicks, Joseph; America, 1753 ***1220.12*** *p869*
Wicks, Mary; Annapolis, MD, 1729 ***1220.12*** *p869*
Wicks, Richard; America, 1688 ***1220.12*** *p869*
Wicks, Thomas; America, 1738 ***1220.12*** *p869*
Wicks, William; America, 1774 ***1220.12*** *p869*
Wicksey, Roger; America, 1684 ***1220.12*** *p869*
Wicktorin, John W.; Chicago, 1880 ***1865.50*** *p113*
*Wife:*Margareta C. Erickson
Wicktorin, Margareta C. Erickson *SEE* Wicktorin, John W.
Wiczlinski, Rudolph; Wisconsin, 1878 ***6795.8*** *p53*
Widdel, August; America, 1854 ***7420.1*** *p133*
Widdel, Justine; America, 1867 ***7420.1*** *p267*
Widdis, Robert 34; Ontario, 1871 ***1823.17*** *p175*
Widdis, Thomas 37; Ontario, 1871 ***1823.17*** *p175*
Widdowson, Richard; Barbados, 1683 ***1220.12*** *p869*
Widdup, Paul; America, 1753 ***1220.12*** *p869*
Widen, Elvira; St. Paul, MN, 1886 ***1865.50*** *p114*
Widen, John; Minnesota, 1887-1889 ***1865.50*** *p114*
Widerikson, Peter Johnson; Iowa, 1896 ***1211.15*** *p20*
Widerington, Oswald; America, 1764 ***1220.12*** *p893*
Widgeon, Sarah; America, 1773 ***1220.12*** *p869*
Widgeon, William; America, 1745 ***1220.12*** *p869*
Widger, James; Maine, 1618 ***9228.50*** *p654*
Widger, John; America, n.d. ***9228.50*** *p654*
Widger, Peter; America, n.d. ***9228.50*** *p654*
Widger, William; America, n.d. ***9228.50*** *p654*
Widing, Mathilda; St. Paul, MN, 1883 ***1865.50*** *p114*
Widlake, Jabez, Jr.; America, 1749 ***1220.12*** *p869*
Widmann, Carol. Maria 8; Chile, 1852 ***1192.4*** *p52*
Widmann, Christian; America, 1892 ***179.55*** *p19*
Widmark, Anna Sophia; St. Paul, MN, 1891 ***1865.50*** *p114*
Widmark, Frederick; Texas, 1886-1887 ***1865.50*** *p114*
Widra, Gersh; Detroit, 1929-1930 ***6214.5*** *p61*
Widrow, Jean; New York, 1740 ***8277.31*** *p120*
Wie, Magdalaine; Boston, 1769 ***9228.50*** *p48*
Wie, Magdalaine; Boston, 1769 ***9228.50*** *p654*
Wiebe, Aron 27; New York, NY, 1893 ***1883.7*** *p40*
Wiebe, Justine 2; New York, NY, 1893 ***1883.7*** *p40*
Wiebe, Justine 24; New York, NY, 1893 ***1883.7*** *p40*
Wiebe, Susanna; New York, NY, 1893 ***1883.7*** *p40*
Wieben, John; Iowa, 1908 ***1211.15*** *p20*
Wieberig, Julius; Valdivia, Chile, 1850 ***1192.4*** *p49*
Wiebker, Agnes 30; New York, NY, 1864 ***8425.62*** *p196*
Wiebker, Chr. Heinr. 26; New York, NY, 1864 ***8425.62*** *p196*
Wiebusch, Joh. H.; Galveston, TX, 1855 ***571.7*** *p17*
Wiechard, Anne; Rappahannock, VA, 1729 ***1220.12*** *p869*
Wiechmann, Sophie; America, 1852 ***7420.1*** *p100*
Wiechowna, Julia; Detroit, 1929 ***1640.55*** *p115*
Wiedeman, Child; America, 1840 ***778.6*** *p345*
Wiedeman, Barb 21; America, 1840 ***778.6*** *p345*
Wieder, Elisabetha; America, 1870 ***2526.42*** *p133*
Wiederich, Anna 28; Louisiana, 1847 ***778.6*** *p345*
Wiederich, Mathias 26; Louisiana, 1847 ***778.6*** *p345*
Wiedler, Anna Marie 22; Missouri, 1848 ***778.6*** *p345*
Wiedler, Blazin 45; New Castle, DE, 1817-1818 ***90.20*** *p154*
Wiedler, Jacob 47; Missouri, 1848 ***778.6*** *p345*
Wiedmann, Gottlieb Friedrich; America, 1891 ***179.55*** *p19*
Wiedmann, Jakob; America, 1882 ***179.55*** *p19*
Wiegand, Anna Barbara; America, 1867 ***7919.3*** *p535*
With 4 children
Wiegand, Ferdinand; America, 1867 ***7919.3*** *p530*
Wiegand, G. Joseph; New York, 1860 ***358.56*** *p3*
Wiegand, Gustav Otto; America, 1867 ***7919.3*** *p525*
Wiegand, Heinrich Elias; America, 1867 ***7919.3*** *p534*
Wiegand, Wilhelm; America, 1857 ***7420.1*** *p175*
With wife
Wiegel, Friedrich 17; Portland, ME, 1911 ***970.38*** *p82*
Wieggrefe, Catharine Sophie Eleonore; Fort Wayne, IN, 1846 ***7420.1*** *p50*
*Daughter:*Catharine Sophie Eleonore W.
Wieggrefe, Catharine Sophie Eleonore W. *SEE* Wieggrefe, Catharine Sophie Eleonore
Wiegmann, Carl; America, 1854 ***7420.1*** *p133*
Wiegmann, F. C.; Louisiana, 1874 ***4981.45*** *p134*
Wiegmann, Heinrich; America, 1868 ***7420.1*** *p278*
*Son:*Heinrich Dietrich Gottlieb
With wife & 2 daughters
Wiegmann, Heinrich Conrad; Port uncertain, 1855 ***7420.1*** *p143*
Wiegmann, Heinrich Dietrich Gottlieb *SEE* Wiegmann, Heinrich
Wiegmann, Joseph; Louisiana, 1874 ***4981.45*** *p134*
Wiel, David; North Carolina, 1858 ***1088.45*** *p37*
Wiel, Gottlieb 26; Halifax, N.S., 1902 ***1860.4*** *p42*
Wiel, Solomon; North Carolina, 1853 ***1088.45*** *p37*
Wieland, Christian; America, 1890 ***179.55*** *p19*
Wieland, Georg; America, 1884 ***179.55*** *p19*
Wieland, Georg Friedrich; America, 1879 ***179.55*** *p19*
Wieland, Georg Johann F.; America, 1868 ***179.55*** *p19*
Wieland, Gottlieb Friedrich; America, 1883 ***179.55*** *p19*
Wieland, Gottlob; America, 1891 ***179.55*** *p19*
Wieland, Jacob; Ohio, 1809-1852 ***4511.35*** *p59*
Wieland, Johannes Georg; America, 1867 ***179.55*** *p19*
Wieland, Karl; America, 1894 ***179.55*** *p19*
Wieland, Karoline Regine; America, 1875 ***179.55*** *p19*
Wieland, Rosine; America, 1870 ***179.55*** *p19*
Wielczewski, Victor 21; New York, NY, 1920 ***930.50*** *p49*
Wielengowski, Emma Adeline; Wisconsin, 1888 ***6795.8*** *p68*
Wielgurz, Francis; Wisconsin, 1900 ***6795.8*** *p130*
Wieller, Menett 18; Port uncertain, 1844 ***778.6*** *p345*
Wiemann, Heinrich; America, 1854 ***7420.1*** *p133*
Wiemers, Andrew; Missouri, 1903 ***3276.1*** *p3*
Wiemers, Wilhelm; New York, 1859 ***358.56*** *p53*
Wien, Johannes; Philadelphia, 1854 ***170.15*** *p47*
Wienand, Ursula 20; Galveston, TX, 1844 ***3967.10*** *p371*
Wiener, Elisabeth; America, 1859 ***5475.1*** *p504*
Wiener, Gottfried; New York, 1859 ***358.56*** *p100*
Wiener, Jacob; Louisiana, 1874-1875 ***4981.45*** *p130*
Wienke, Anna Maria Louise; Wisconsin, 1897 ***6795.8*** *p150*
Wienke, Ernestine Wilhelmine; Wisconsin, 1897 ***6795.8*** *p150*
Wienold, Johann Georg Franz; America, 1883 ***2526.43*** *p184*
Wier, Thomas; Ohio, 1836 ***3580.20*** *p33*
Wier, Thomas; Ohio, 1836 ***6020.12*** *p23*
Wier, William; America, 1758 ***1220.12*** *p906*
Wierauch, Leonard; Ohio, 1809-1852 ***4511.35*** *p59*
Wierima, John 35; Minnesota, 1923 ***2769.54*** *p1381*
Wierimaa, Dan 43; Minnesota, 1923 ***2769.54*** *p1381*
Wiersma, Severine Laurence; New York, NY, 1906 ***3331.4*** *p12*
Wieruszewska, Stella; Detroit, 1890 ***9980.23*** *p97*
Wies, George; Ohio, 1809-1852 ***4511.35*** *p59*
Wiese, Anton Friedrich; America, 1872 ***7420.1*** *p298*
Wiese, Friedrich; America, 1850 ***7420.1*** *p77*
With 2 brothers & sister
Wiese, Heinrich Carl; America, 1885 ***7420.1*** *p349*
Wiesel, Peter; America, 1869 ***5475.1*** *p120*
Wiesemann, Christian; Illinois, 1851 ***6079.1*** *p15*
Wiesen, A. Maria Michely *SEE* Wiesen, Johann
Wiesen, Anna *SEE* Wiesen, Johann
Wiesen, Anna Maria 6 *SEE* Wiesen, Mathias
Wiesen, Anna Maria 31 *SEE* Wiesen, Mathias
Wiesen, Barbara Schmitz *SEE* Wiesen, Jakob
Wiesen, Barbara *SEE* Wiesen, Johann
Wiesen, Franz; America, 1881 ***5475.1*** *p250*
Wiesen, Jakob; America, 1881 ***5475.1*** *p258*
*Wife:*Barbara Schmitz
*Son:*Johann
*Son:*Michel
Wiesen, Johann *SEE* Wiesen, Peter
Wiesen, Johann *SEE* Wiesen, Jakob
Wiesen, Johann; America, 1881 ***5475.1*** *p315*
*Wife:*A. Maria Michely
Wiesen, Johann *SEE* Wiesen, Johann
Wiesen, Johann 49; Pittsburgh, 1872 ***5475.1*** *p354*
*Wife:*Magdalena Thies 45
*Son:*Johann
*Daughter:*Maria
*Daughter:*Barbara
*Son:*Nikolaus
*Daughter:*Anna
Wiesen, Katharina Kimmlinger *SEE* Wiesen, Mathias
Wiesen, Katharina 65; America, 1864 ***5475.1*** *p348*

Wiesen, Magdalena Thielen 57 *SEE* Wiesen, Peter
Wiesen, Magdalena Thies 45 *SEE* Wiesen, Johann
Wiesen, Margarethe 4 *SEE* Wiesen, Mathias
Wiesen, Maria *SEE* Wiesen, Johann
Wiesen, Mathias; America, 1881 ***5475.1*** *p517*
*Wife:*Katharina Kimmlinger
Wiesen, Mathias 33; America, 1857 ***5475.1*** *p248*
*Wife:*Anna Maria 31
*Daughter:*Anna Maria 6 months
*Daughter:*Margarethe 4
Wiesen, Michel *SEE* Wiesen, Jakob
Wiesen, Michel 40; America, 1843 ***5475.1*** *p348*
Wiesen, Nikolaus; America, 1843 ***5475.1*** *p295*
Wiesen, Nikolaus *SEE* Wiesen, Peter
Wiesen, Nikolaus *SEE* Wiesen, Johann
Wiesen, Peter *SEE* Wiesen, Peter
Wiesen, Peter 54; America, 1856 ***5475.1*** *p270*
*Wife:*Magdalena Thielen 57
*Son:*Johann
*Son:*Nikolaus
*Son:*Peter
Wiesen, Rudolph; Illinois, 1856 ***6079.1*** *p15*
Wiesenthall, Charles Frederick; America, 1757 ***1220.12*** *p870*
Wiesenthall, Israel 22; New York, NY, 1894 ***6512.1*** *p228*
Wieser, Charles; Ohio, 1840-1897 ***8365.35*** *p18*
Wieser, Johannes; America, 1854 ***2526.43*** *p158*
Wiesler, Abraham; New Castle, DE, 1817-1818 ***90.20*** *p155*
Wiesler, Johann; New Castle, DE, 1817-1818 ***90.20*** *p155*
Wiesler, Johann Alb.; New Castle, DE, 1817-1818 ***90.20*** *p155*
Wiesmann, Katharina 47; America, 1874 ***2526.42*** *p168*
Wiesner, Vilem; Texas, 1856-1906 ***2853.20*** *p64*
Wiessler, Johann; New Castle, DE, 1817-1818 ***90.20*** *p155*
Wiessmann, Adam 6 *SEE* Wiessmann, Adam
Wiessmann, Adam 35; America, 1846 ***2526.42*** *p203*
With wife
*Daughter:*Barbara 3
*Son:*Adam 6 months
*Son:*Georg 10
Wiessmann, Barbara 3 *SEE* Wiessmann, Adam
Wiessmann, Elisabetha 7 *SEE* Wiessmann, Philipp
Wiessmann, Georg; America, 1854 ***2526.42*** *p179*
Wiessmann, Georg 10 *SEE* Wiessmann, Adam
Wiessmann, Georg 16; America, 1882 ***2526.42*** *p171*
Wiessmann, Heinrich; America, 1883 ***2526.42*** *p171*
Wiessmann, Jakob; America, 1854 ***2526.42*** *p203*
Wiessmann, Johann; America, 1856 ***2526.42*** *p171*
Wiessmann, Johann Nikolaus; America, 1858 ***2526.42*** *p179*
Wiessmann, Johannes; America, 1854 ***2526.42*** *p171*
Wiessmann, Johannes 3 *SEE* Wiessmann, Philipp
Wiessmann, Margaretha 1 *SEE* Wiessmann, Philipp
Wiessmann, N.N.; America, 1753 ***2526.42*** *p171*
With 3 daughters
Wiessmann, Nikolaus; America, 1857 ***2526.42*** *p171*
Wiessmann, Philipp; America, 1854 ***2526.42*** *p203*
With wife
*Daughter:*Margaretha
*Daughter:*Elisabetha
*Son:*Johannes
Wiessner, Joh. Gottl.; Valdivia, Chile, 1852 ***1192.4*** *p54*
Wiessner, Konrad; Pennsylvania, 1849 ***170.15*** *p47*
With wife
With child 5
With child 11
Wiesweiler, Julius; Madison, WI, 1853 ***5475.1*** *p11*
Wigand, Sophie Dorothe Justine; America, 1854 ***7420.1*** *p133*
Wigert, A.; New York, NY, 1844 ***6412.40*** *p147*
Wiggan, Joseph; America, 1765 ***1220.12*** *p870*
Wigger, Anna; America, 1893-1950 ***8023.44*** *p380*
Wiggin, Lawrence; Maryland, 1742 ***1220.12*** *p870*
Wiggin, William; America, 1752 ***1220.12*** *p870*
Wiggington, John; America, 1772 ***1220.12*** *p870*
Wiggington, William; America, 1767 ***1220.12*** *p870*
Wiggins, Frank E. 14; Ontario, 1871 ***1823.21*** *p392*
Wiggins, George R. 12; Ontario, 1871 ***1823.21*** *p392*
Wiggins, Hariat 73; Ontario, 1871 ***1823.17*** *p175*
Wiggins, Henry 39; Ontario, 1871 ***1823.17*** *p175*
Wiggins, James; America, 1775 ***1220.12*** *p870*
Wiggins, John; America, 1753 ***1220.12*** *p870*
Wiggins, Mary; America, 1772 ***1220.12*** *p870*
Wiggins, Richard; America, 1678 ***1220.12*** *p870*
Wiggins, Robert; America, 1740 ***1220.12*** *p870*
Wiggins, Thomas; America, 1740 ***1220.12*** *p870*
Wiggins, Thomas; Annapolis, MD, 1719 ***1220.12*** *p870*
Wiggins, Thomas 65; Ontario, 1871 ***1823.21*** *p392*
Wiggins, William; America, 1727 ***1220.12*** *p870*
Wigginson, Peter; America, 1767 ***1220.12*** *p870*
Wigglesworth, Mrs. 65; Ontario, 1871 ***1823.21*** *p392*
Wigglesworth, Anthony 76; Ontario, 1871 ***1823.21*** *p392*
Wigglesworth, John 47; Ontario, 1871 ***1823.21*** *p392*
Wigglesworth, Joshua 65; Ontario, 1871 ***1823.21*** *p392*
Wigglesworth, William 29; Ontario, 1871 ***1823.21*** *p392*
Wiggmore, Richard; Virginia, 1732 ***1220.12*** *p870*
Wiggs, Francis; America, 1750 ***1220.12*** *p870*
Wigham, William; Barbados, 1682 ***1220.12*** *p870*
Wight, Samuel; Rappahannock, VA, 1728 ***1220.12*** *p865*
Wight, Stuart 62; Ontario, 1871 ***1823.17*** *p175*
Wight, Thomas; America, 1773 ***1220.12*** *p865*
Wight, William; America, 1774 ***1220.12*** *p866*
Wightman, James 34; Ontario, 1871 ***1823.21*** *p392*
Wigley, Edward 54; Ontario, 1871 ***1823.21*** *p392*
Wigley, Elizabeth; America, 1774 ***1220.12*** *p870*
Wigley, Elizabeth; Jamaica, 1716 ***1220.12*** *p870*
Wigley, John; America, 1748 ***1220.12*** *p870*
Wigley, John 33; Ontario, 1871 ***1823.21*** *p392*
Wigmore, A.; Iowa, 1887 ***1211.15*** *p20*
Wigmore, Betsy 20; Ontario, 1871 ***1823.21*** *p392*
Wigmore, Catherine; America, 1767 ***1220.12*** *p870*
Wigmore, Catherine; America, 1775 ***1220.12*** *p870*
Wigmore, Henry; Washington, 1889 ***2770.40*** *p81*
Wigmore, John; America, 1756 ***1220.12*** *p870*
Wigmore, Richard 44; Ontario, 1871 ***1823.21*** *p392*
Wigmore, William; America, 1669 ***1220.12*** *p870*
Wigmore, William 68; Ontario, 1871 ***1823.21*** *p392*
Wignall, James; America, 1750 ***1220.12*** *p870*
Wignall, Thomas; Maryland or Virginia, 1738 ***1220.12*** *p870*
Wignauer, John; Ohio, 1809-1852 ***4511.35*** *p59*
Wiita, Frank 34; Minnesota, 1926 ***2769.54*** *p1382*
Wiita, Mary 29; Minnesota, 1926 ***2769.54*** *p1382*
Wikes, Francis; America, 1768 ***1220.12*** *p906*
Wikidal, Joseph; Ohio, 1809-1852 ***4511.35*** *p59*
Wikidal, Julius; Ohio, 1809-1852 ***4511.35*** *p59*
Wiklander, John; Cleveland, OH, 1868-1889 ***9722.10*** *p128*
Wikstrom, Fredrik; New Orleans, 1851 ***6412.40*** *p153*
Wikstrom, Lars; Colorado, 1885 ***1029.59*** *p94*
Wikstrom, Lars; Iowa, 1869 ***1029.59*** *p94*
Wiktor, Margaret; Detroit, 1929 ***1640.55*** *p113*
Wil, Joseph 22; America, 1846 ***778.6*** *p345*
Wilbers, Henry; Ohio, 1840-1897 ***8365.35*** *p18*
Wilbert, William; Virginia, 1734 ***1220.12*** *p870*
Wilbois, Josef; America, 1881 ***5475.1*** *p280*
Wilbourne, John; America, 1755 ***1220.12*** *p870*
Wilburn, Sarah; Annapolis, MD, 1723 ***1220.12*** *p870*
Wilchd, Maria 46; Ontario, 1871 ***1823.21*** *p392*
Wilcke, Carl Hermann; America, 1865 ***7420.1*** *p238*
Wilcke, Julius; America, 1864 ***7420.1*** *p228*
Wilcock, David; America, 1729 ***1220.12*** *p870*
Wilcocks, John; Virginia, 1767 ***1220.12*** *p870*
Wilcocks, Philip; America, 1735 ***1220.12*** *p870*
Wilcocks, Robert; America, 1772 ***1220.12*** *p871*
Wilcocks, Saml 36; Ontario, 1871 ***1823.17*** *p175*
Wilcocks, Samuel; Barbados or Jamaica, 1692 ***1220.12*** *p871*
Wilcocks, Walter; America, 1752 ***1220.12*** *p871*
Wilcockson, Thomas; America, 1749 ***1220.12*** *p870*
Wilcox, Charles; Ohio, 1809-1852 ***4511.35*** *p59*
Wilcox, Daniel; America, 1692 ***1220.12*** *p870*
Wilcox, Edward; America, 1765 ***1220.12*** *p870*
Wilcox, Elizabeth; America, 1740 ***1220.12*** *p870*
Wilcox, Jane 17; Ontario, 1871 ***1823.21*** *p393*
Wilcox, John; America, 1765 ***1220.12*** *p870*
Wilcox, John; America, 1766 ***1220.12*** *p870*
Wilcox, John; America, 1773 ***1220.12*** *p870*
Wilcox, John; Virginia, 1721 ***1220.12*** *p870*
Wilcox, Lyman 57; Michigan, 1880 ***4491.42*** *p28*
Wilcox, Mary; America, 1760 ***1220.12*** *p870*
Wilcox, Mary 66; Ontario, 1871 ***1823.21*** *p393*
Wilcox, Peter; America, 1766 ***1220.12*** *p870*
Wilcox, Richard; America, 1685 ***1220.12*** *p871*
Wilcox, Robert 19; Ontario, 1871 ***1823.21*** *p393*
Wilcox, Sophia 40; Ontario, 1871 ***1823.21*** *p393*
Wilcox, Thomas; America, 1696 ***1220.12*** *p871*
Wilcox, Thomas; America, 1748 ***1220.12*** *p871*
Wilcox, Thomas; America, 1756 ***1220.12*** *p871*
Wilcox, Thomas; America, 1765 ***1220.12*** *p871*
Wilcox, Thomas; Potomac, 1731 ***1220.12*** *p871*
Wilcox, William J. 13; Ontario, 1871 ***1823.17*** *p175*
Wilczynski, Walter; Detroit, 1929-1930 ***6214.5*** *p67*
Wild, Abraham; America, 1766 ***1220.12*** *p871*
Wild, Anna *SEE* Wild, David Brickel
Wild, Caroline 7; New York, NY, 1885 ***1883.7*** *p46*
Wild, Catharine 8; New York, NY, 1885 ***1883.7*** *p46*
Wild, Catharine 32; New York, NY, 1885 ***1883.7*** *p46*
Wild, Christine 2; New York, NY, 1885 ***1883.7*** *p46*
Wild, Christopher *SEE* Wild, David Brickel
Wild, David Brickel; Philadelphia, 1871 ***8513.31*** *p432*
*Wife:*Anna
*Child:*Christopher
Wild, Edward; America, 1770 ***1220.12*** *p871*
Wild, Elizabeth; Virginia, 1732 ***1220.12*** *p871*
Wild, Francis; America, 1738 ***1220.12*** *p871*
Wild, Georg; America, 1854 ***179.55*** *p19*
Wild, H. 29; America, 1840 ***778.6*** *p345*
Wild, Henry; America, 1720 ***1220.12*** *p871*
Wild, Jacob; Ohio, 1809-1852 ***4511.35*** *p59*
Wild, Jacques 24; Louisiana, 1847 ***778.6*** *p345*
Wild, Jakob 44; America, 1800-1899 ***5475.1*** *p453*
With family of 7
Wild, Jakob 5; New York, NY, 1885 ***1883.7*** *p46*
Wild, Jane; Maryland, 1744 ***1220.12*** *p871*
Wild, Johann 35; New York, NY, 1885 ***1883.7*** *p46*
Wild, Johann Jakob; America, 1843 ***5475.1*** *p463*
With wife
With 6 children
Wild, John; America, 1775 ***1220.12*** *p871*
Wild, John; Virginia, 1724 ***1220.12*** *p871*
Wild, Jonathan H.; Philadelphia, 1855 ***8513.31*** *p432*
Wild, Joseph; America, 1775 ***1220.12*** *p871*
Wild, Joseph; Louisiana, 1874-1875 ***4981.45*** *p130*
Wild, Magdal. 4 months; New York, NY, 1885 ***1883.7*** *p46*
Wild, Maria 29; America, 1840 ***778.6*** *p345*
Wild, Peter; America, 1769 ***1220.12*** *p871*
Wild, Robert; America, 1743 ***1220.12*** *p871*
Wild, Sophie 1; America, 1840 ***778.6*** *p345*
Wild, Stephen; America, 1756 ***1220.12*** *p871*
Wild, Thomas; America, 1744 ***1220.12*** *p871*
Wild, Thomas; Maryland, 1741 ***1220.12*** *p871*
Wild, Thomas; Ohio, 1843 ***9228.50*** *p228*
Wildaw, Richard; New York, 1783 ***8529.30*** *p17*
Wildberger, Friedrich Wilhelm; America, 1863 ***5475.1*** *p542*
Wildberger, Heinr.; America, 1882 ***5475.1*** *p34*
Wildberger, Ludwig; Chicago, 1883 ***5475.1*** *p36*
Wildberger, Maria Luise; America, 1856 ***5475.1*** *p541*
Wildblood, Thomas; America, 1687 ***1220.12*** *p871*
Wilde, Ferdinand A.; Wisconsin, 1866 ***6795.8*** *p77*
Wilde, John; Virginia, 1756 ***1220.12*** *p871*
Wilde, Karl August; Wisconsin, 1869 ***6795.8*** *p78*
Wilde, Leopold; Wisconsin, 1878 ***6795.8*** *p78*
Wilder, Ann; America, 1744 ***1220.12*** *p871*
Wilder, Roger; Plymouth, MA, 1620 ***1920.45*** *p5*
Wilder, Sarah; America, 1758 ***1220.12*** *p871*
Wilder, Thomas; America, 1738 ***1220.12*** *p871*
Wilder, William; America, 1754 ***1220.12*** *p871*
Wilder, William; America, 1758 ***1220.12*** *p871*
Wildfeuer, Carl Friedrich; America, 1868 ***7919.3*** *p530*
Wildhage, Anton Wilhelm; America, 1856 ***7420.1*** *p156*
With son & 2 daughters
Wildhahn, Catharine Engel Sophie; America, 1868 ***7420.1*** *p278*
Wildhahn, Cord Heinrich; America, 1871 ***7420.1*** *p293*
*Wife:*Engel Marie Sophie Meyer
*Son:*Johann Otto
*Son:*Hans Heinrich
Wildhahn, Engel Marie Sophie Meyer *SEE* Wildhahn, Cord Heinrich
Wildhahn, Hans Heinrich *SEE* Wildhahn, Cord Heinrich
Wildhahn, Johann Otto *SEE* Wildhahn, Cord Heinrich
Wildi, Hans Ulrich 34; New Castle, DE, 1817-1818 ***90.20*** *p155*
Wildicke, Joseph; Virginia, 1741 ***1220.12*** *p871*
Wilding, Henry; America, 1774 ***1220.12*** *p871*
Wilding, Jacob; America, 1769 ***1220.12*** *p871*
Wilding, James; America, 1764 ***1220.12*** *p871*
Wilding, John; Barbados or Jamaica, 1704 ***1220.12*** *p871*
Wilding, Robert; New York, 1775 ***8529.30*** *p17*
Wildman, John; America, 1767 ***1220.12*** *p871*
Wildman, William; America, 1773 ***1220.12*** *p871*
Wilds, Hannah; America, 1772 ***1220.12*** *p871*
Wilds, Thomas; Ohio, 1843 ***9228.50*** *p228*
Wildt, Henry; Ohio, 1809-1852 ***4511.35*** *p59*
Wildy, Joan; America, 1738 ***1220.12*** *p871*
Wile, Bernhard 23; Indiana, 1852-1857 ***9076.20*** *p65*
Wile, Thomas; America, 1762 ***1220.12*** *p871*
Wile, Thomas; Ohio, 1843 ***9228.50*** *p228*
Wiles, Charles; America, 1766 ***1220.12*** *p871*
Wiles, Hannah 52; Michigan, 1880 ***4491.36*** *p24*
Wiles, Henry; America, 1753 ***1220.12*** *p871*
Wiles, James 32; Ontario, 1871 ***1823.21*** *p393*
Wiles, John 40; Ontario, 1871 ***1823.21*** *p393*
Wiles, Stephen 52; Michigan, 1880 ***4491.36*** *p24*
Wiley, Andrew 50; Ontario, 1871 ***1823.21*** *p393*
Wiley, Betty; Boston, 1766 ***1642*** *p36*
*Relative:*Jane
Wiley, David 62; Ontario, 1871 ***1823.21*** *p393*
Wiley, Hugh 45; Ontario, 1871 ***1823.21*** *p393*
Wiley, James; Boston, 1766 ***1642*** *p36*
With wife & 2 sisters
Wiley, Jane *SEE* Wiley, Betty
Wiley, John; America, 1759 ***1220.12*** *p871*

Wiley, John 63; Ontario, 1871 ***1823.21*** *p393*
Wiley, Mary; Boston, 1766 ***1642*** *p36*
Wiley, William 30; Ontario, 1871 ***1823.17*** *p175*
Wilford, Anthony; America, 1769 ***1220.12*** *p872*
Wilford, Eleanor; Maryland, 1736 ***1220.12*** *p872*
Wilford, Hannah; America, 1768 ***1220.12*** *p872*
Wilford, John; Ohio, 1836 ***2763.1*** *p22*
Wilford, John; Ohio, 1843 ***2763.1*** *p22*
Wilford, Joseph; America, 1766 ***1220.12*** *p872*
Wilford, Rachel; Potomac, 1743 ***1220.12*** *p872*
Wilharm, Miss; America, 1874 ***7420.1*** *p304*
Wilharm, Mr.; America, 1863 ***7420.1*** *p221*
Wilharm, Widow; America, 1871 ***7420.1*** *p293*
Wilharm, Carl Friedrich Wilhelm; America, 1875 ***7420.1*** *p306*
Wilharm, Catharina Engel Sophie Schermer *SEE* Wilharm, Johann Heinrich Philipp
Wilharm, Friedrich Conrad; America, 1854 ***7420.1*** *p133*
Wilharm, Friedrich Heinrich Carl; America, 1891 ***7420.1*** *p364*
Wilharm, Heinrich; America, 1852 ***7420.1*** *p100*
Wilharm, Heinrich; America, 1852 ***7420.1*** *p100*
With family
Wilharm, Heinrich; America, 1856 ***7420.1*** *p156*
Wilharm, Heinrich Friedrich Wilhelm; America, 1887 ***7420.1*** *p355*
Wilharm, Johann Christoph Philipp *SEE* Wilharm, Johann Heinrich Philipp
Wilharm, Johann Conrad; America, 1860 ***7420.1*** *p201*
Wilharm, Johann Conrad; America, 1867 ***7420.1*** *p267*
With family
Wilharm, Johann Heinrich Philipp; America, 1847 ***7420.1*** *p57*
*Wife:*Catharina Engel Sophie Schermer
*Son:*Johann Christoph Philipp
Wilhchiner, Mr. 31; America, 1846 ***778.6*** *p345*
Wilhchiner, Fred. 6; America, 1846 ***778.6*** *p345*
Wilhdriner, Mr. 31; America, 1846 ***778.6*** *p345*
Wilhelm, Barbara 59; America, 1865 ***5475.1*** *p388*
With children
Wilhelm, Carl; Chile, 1852 ***1192.4*** *p52*
With wife & child
With child 1
With child 8
Wilhelm, Caroline; America, 1867 ***7919.3*** *p530*
Wilhelm, Christian; Ohio, 1809-1852 ***4511.35*** *p59*
Wilhelm, Dorothea Colling *SEE* Wilhelm, Johann Nikolaus
Wilhelm, Friedrich; Chile, 1852 ***1192.4*** *p52*
With wife & child
With child 3
With child 8
Wilhelm, Georg; America, 1891 ***5475.1*** *p407*
Wilhelm, Georg 29; Portland, ME, 1911 ***970.38*** *p82*
Wilhelm, Jacob; Wisconsin, 1868 ***6795.8*** *p101*
Wilhelm, Jakob; America, 1867 ***5475.1*** *p544*
Wilhelm, Jakob; America, 1868 ***5475.1*** *p289*
Wilhelm, Jakob; America, 1871 ***5475.1*** *p171*
Wilhelm, Johann; America, 1864 ***5475.1*** *p370*
Wilhelm, Johann; America, 1868 ***5475.1*** *p330*
Wilhelm, Johann; America, 1873 ***5475.1*** *p212*
Wilhelm, Johann *SEE* Wilhelm, Johann
Wilhelm, Johann; America, 1881 ***5475.1*** *p332*
*Son:*Mathias
*Daughter:*Maria
*Son:*Nikolaus
*Son:*Johann
Wilhelm, Johann Nikolaus; America, 1847-1899 ***6442.17*** *p69*
*Wife:*Dorothea Colling
With 7 children
Wilhelm, Louise; Ohio, 1879 ***7420.1*** *p313*
*Granddaughter:*Marie
Wilhelm, Maria Reiter *SEE* Wilhelm, Mathias
Wilhelm, Maria; America, 1833 ***5475.1*** *p466*
Wilhelm, Maria *SEE* Wilhelm, Johann
Wilhelm, Maria 45; America, 1849 ***5475.1*** *p415*
Wilhelm, Marianne; America, 1867 ***7919.3*** *p534*
Wilhelm, Mathias; America, 1800-1899 ***5475.1*** *p440*
*Wife:*Maria Reiter
With 5 children
Wilhelm, Mathias; America, 1868 ***5475.1*** *p330*
Wilhelm, Mathias *SEE* Wilhelm, Johann
Wilhelm, Nikolaus *SEE* Wilhelm, Johann
Wilhelm, Peter; America, 1872 ***5475.1*** *p209*
Wilhelm, Pierre 19; Mississippi, 1847 ***778.6*** *p345*
Wilhelm, Reinhard; America, 1867 ***7919.3*** *p530*
Wilhelm, Richard; Chicago, 1884 ***5475.1*** *p515*
Wilhelmi, Wolrad; Valparaiso, Chile, 1850 ***1192.4*** *p50*
Wilhelmsen, Catharine Marie Charlotte Schrage *SEE* Wilhelmsen, Johann Conrad
Wilhelmsen, Johann Conrad; America, 1846 ***7420.1*** *p51*
*Wife:*Catharine Marie Charlotte Schrage
With 4 children
Wilhem, Pierre 28; America, 1846 ***778.6*** *p345*
Wiliamson, Hugh 57; Ontario, 1871 ***1823.21*** *p393*
Wilik, Joseph 48; New York, NY, 1920 ***930.50*** *p49*
Wilines, Jean 35; New York, NY, 1894 ***6512.1*** *p181*
Wilk, Joseph; Detroit, 1929 ***1640.55*** *p115*
Wilk, Karol 24; New York, NY, 1912 ***8355.1*** *p16*
Wilke, Bertha Maria Caroline; Wisconsin, 1897 ***6795.8*** *p228*
Wilke, Carl Julius; Wisconsin, 1884 ***6795.8*** *p78*
Wilke, Gottfried Samuel; Wisconsin, 1858 ***6795.8*** *p143*
Wilke, Heinrich August; Illinois, 1880 ***7420.1*** *p319*
Wilke, Hermann Emil; Wisconsin, 1892 ***6795.8*** *p28*
Wilke, Johann Friedrich Christoph; America, 1854 ***7420.1*** *p133*
Wilken, Fra.; Jamestown, VA, 1633 ***1658.20*** *p211*
Wilkening, Mr.; America, 1854 ***7420.1*** *p133*
With wife son & 4 daughters
Wilkening, Anne Marie Dorothee *SEE* Wilkening, Friedrich Justus
Wilkening, August; Port uncertain, 1907 ***7420.1*** *p383*
Wilkening, Carl Friedrich Ernst; America, 1893 ***7420.1*** *p370*
Wilkening, Charlotte Louise; America, 1860 ***7420.1*** *p202*
Wilkening, Christoph; America, 1852 ***7420.1*** *p100*
Wilkening, Conrad; America, 1852 ***7420.1*** *p100*
Wilkening, Dorothea; America, 1856 ***7420.1*** *p156*
Wilkening, Engel Marie; America, 1852 ***7420.1*** *p101*
Wilkening, Engel Marie Sophie *SEE* Wilkening, Engel Sophie Marie
Wilkening, Engel Marie Sophie Charlotte; America, 1853 ***7420.1*** *p113*
Wilkening, Engel Sophie Marie; America, 1881 ***7420.1*** *p326*
*Son:*Johannes Gottlieb
*Daughter:*Sophie Dorothea
*Daughter:*Engel Marie Sophie
Wilkening, Ernst Heinrich; Indiana, 1882 ***7420.1*** *p333*
Wilkening, Friedrich; America, 1852 ***7420.1*** *p100*
Wilkening, Friedrich Justus; America, 1856 ***7420.1*** *p156*
*Daughter:*Anne Marie Dorothee
Wilkening, Georg Wilhelm; America, 1883 ***7420.1*** *p341*
Wilkening, Hans Heinrich Friedrich; America, 1884 ***7420.1*** *p346*
Wilkening, Heinrich Conrad *SEE* Wilkening, Johann Heinrich Conrad
Wilkening, Heinrich Conrad Otto; America, 1867 ***7420.1*** *p267*
Wilkening, Heinrich Conrad Wilhelm; America, 1866 ***7420.1*** *p252*
Wilkening, Johann Conrad; America, 1852 ***7420.1*** *p101*
With 2 sons & daughter
Wilkening, Johann Friedrich; America, 1852 ***7420.1*** *p101*
Wilkening, Johann Heinrich; America, 1850 ***7420.1*** *p77*
Wilkening, Johann Heinrich; America, 1885 ***7420.1*** *p349*
Wilkening, Johann Heinrich Conrad; America, 1882 ***7420.1*** *p334*
*Son:*Heinrich Conrad
With wife & mother-in-law
Wilkening, Johann Heinrich Conrad; America, 1885 ***7420.1*** *p350*
Wilkening, Johanna Louise; America, 1860 ***7420.1*** *p202*
Wilkening, Johannes Gottlieb *SEE* Wilkening, Engel Sophie Marie
Wilkening, Otto; America, 1904 ***7420.1*** *p401*
Wilkening, Sophie Dorothea *SEE* Wilkening, Engel Sophie Marie
Wilkening, Sophie Eleonore; America, 1846 ***7420.1*** *p45*
Wilkening, Thrine Engel; America, 1848 ***7420.1*** *p59*
Wilkening, Thrine Engel; America, 1850 ***7420.1*** *p77*
*Daughter:*Thrine Sophie
Wilkening, Thrine Sophie *SEE* Wilkening, Thrine Engel
Wilkening, Wilhelmine Caroline Charlotte; America, 1870 ***7420.1*** *p286*
Wilkens, Henry 39; Ontario, 1871 ***1823.21*** *p393*
Wilkens, William; Illinois, 1852 ***6079.1*** *p15*
Wilkerson, Charlotte 34; Ontario, 1871 ***1823.21*** *p393*
Wilkerson, Elizabeth 16; Ontario, 1871 ***1823.21*** *p393*
Wilkerson, Ruth 10; Ontario, 1871 ***1823.21*** *p393*
Wilkerson, Sarah 12; Ontario, 1871 ***1823.21*** *p393*
Wilkerson, Selina 8; Ontario, 1871 ***1823.21*** *p393*
Wilkerson, William 45; Ontario, 1871 ***1823.21*** *p393*
Wilkes, Albert 37; Ontario, 1871 ***1823.17*** *p175*
Wilkes, Catherine; America, 1766 ***1220.12*** *p873*
Wilkes, Catherine 40; Ontario, 1871 ***1823.17*** *p175*
Wilkes, Charles; America, 1769 ***1220.12*** *p873*
Wilkes, Edward; America, 1755 ***1220.12*** *p873*
Wilkes, Elizabeth; America, 1745 ***1220.12*** *p873*
Wilkes, Francis; America, 1722 ***1220.12*** *p873*
Wilkes, Isaac; America, 1763 ***1220.12*** *p874*
Wilkes, Joseph; America, 1768 ***1220.12*** *p874*
Wilkes, Mary; America, 1750 ***1220.12*** *p874*
Wilkes, Nathaniel; America, 1752 ***1220.12*** *p874*
Wilkes, Robert 51; Michigan, 1880 ***4491.42*** *p28*
Wilkes, William; America, 1773 ***1220.12*** *p874*
Wilkes, William 55; Ontario, 1871 ***1823.21*** *p393*
Wilkes, William; Virginia, 1768 ***1220.12*** *p874*
Wilkeshire, William; America, 1755 ***1220.12*** *p890*
Wilkeson, William; North Carolina, 1792-1862 ***1088.45*** *p37*
Wilkey, John; Annapolis, MD, 1719 ***1220.12*** *p874*
Wilkie, Alexander 42; Ontario, 1871 ***1823.21*** *p393*
Wilkie, James 54; Ontario, 1871 ***1823.17*** *p175*
Wilkie, James 56; Ontario, 1871 ***1823.21*** *p393*
Wilkie, Robert 68; Ontario, 1871 ***1823.17*** *p175*
Wilkin, David; Utah, 1891 ***1211.45*** *p130*
Wilkin, George 46; Ontario, 1871 ***1823.21*** *p393*
Wilkin, Isabella; California, 1877 ***1211.45*** *p130*
Wilkin, James F.; Ohio, 1877 ***3580.20*** *p34*
Wilkin, James F.; Ohio, 1877 ***6020.12*** *p23*
Wilkin, Johann; Chicago, 1888 ***5475.1*** *p290*
Wilkin, Josephine 24; Michigan, 1880 ***4491.30*** *p32*
Wilkins, Anna; Philadelphia, 1860 ***8513.31*** *p321*
Wilkins, Charles; North Carolina, 1856 ***1088.45*** *p37*
Wilkins, Francis; America, 1750 ***1220.12*** *p872*
Wilkins, Henry; America, 1680 ***1220.12*** *p872*
Wilkins, Henry; America, 1772 ***1220.12*** *p872*
Wilkins, Henry; New York, NY, 1831 ***3274.55*** *p23*
Wilkins, Jane; America, 1747 ***1220.12*** *p872*
Wilkins, Jessie 73; Ontario, 1871 ***1823.21*** *p393*
Wilkins, John; America, 1744 ***1220.12*** *p872*
Wilkins, John; America, 1775 ***1220.12*** *p872*
Wilkins, John; New York, NY, 1828 ***3274.55*** *p22*
Wilkins, Joseph; Annapolis, MD, 1725 ***1220.12*** *p872*
Wilkins, Martha; America, 1736 ***1220.12*** *p872*
Wilkins, Mary; America, 1772 ***1220.12*** *p872*
Wilkins, Nicholas; Died enroute, 1730 ***1220.12*** *p872*
Wilkins, Phebe; America, 1773 ***1220.12*** *p872*
Wilkins, Philis; Virginia, 1738 ***1220.12*** *p872*
Wilkins, Richard; America, 1687 ***1220.12*** *p872*
Wilkins, Robert; America, 1685 ***1220.12*** *p872*
Wilkins, Samuel; America, 1737 ***1220.12*** *p872*
Wilkins, Samuel 33; Ontario, 1871 ***1823.21*** *p393*
Wilkins, Stephen; America, 1728 ***1220.12*** *p872*
Wilkins, Thomas; America, 1743 ***1220.12*** *p872*
Wilkins, Thomas; America, 1759 ***1220.12*** *p872*
Wilkins, Thomas; America, 1770 ***1220.12*** *p872*
Wilkins, Thomas; America, 1772 ***1220.12*** *p872*
Wilkins, Thomas; Washington, 1883 ***2770.40*** *p137*
Wilkins, William; America, 1743 ***1220.12*** *p872*
Wilkinson, Alice; Carolina, 1724 ***1220.12*** *p872*
Wilkinson, Arch'd 36; Ontario, 1871 ***1823.17*** *p175*
Wilkinson, Benjamin; Barbados or Jamaica, 1683 ***1220.12*** *p872*
Wilkinson, Catherine; America, 1768 ***1220.12*** *p872*
Wilkinson, Edward; America, 1750 ***1220.12*** *p872*
Wilkinson, Eleanor; America, 1722 ***1220.12*** *p872*
Wilkinson, Elisha; America, 1769 ***1220.12*** *p872*
Wilkinson, Eliza; America, 1765 ***1220.12*** *p872*
Wilkinson, Elizabeth; America, 1745 ***1220.12*** *p872*
Wilkinson, Elizabeth; America, 1755 ***1220.12*** *p872*
Wilkinson, Elizabeth; America, 1756 ***1220.12*** *p872*
Wilkinson, Elizabeth; America, 1762 ***1220.12*** *p872*
Wilkinson, Elizabeth; Barbados, 1681 ***1220.12*** *p872*
Wilkinson, Elizabeth; Boston, 1767 ***1642*** *p39*
Wilkinson, Finely 38; Ontario, 1871 ***1823.17*** *p175*
Wilkinson, Francis; America, 1764 ***1220.12*** *p872*
Wilkinson, Frank 33; Indiana, 1881-1884 ***9076.20*** *p70*
Wilkinson, George; America, 1763 ***1220.12*** *p872*
Wilkinson, George; America, 1765 ***1220.12*** *p872*
Wilkinson, George 31; Ontario, 1871 ***1823.17*** *p175*
Wilkinson, George 40; Ontario, 1871 ***1823.21*** *p393*
Wilkinson, George 46; Ontario, 1871 ***1823.17*** *p175*
Wilkinson, Henry; America, 1770 ***1220.12*** *p872*
Wilkinson, Henry 22; Ontario, 1871 ***1823.17*** *p175*
Wilkinson, J. 30; Ontario, 1871 ***1823.21*** *p393*
Wilkinson, James; America, 1771 ***1220.12*** *p873*
Wilkinson, James 26; Ontario, 1871 ***1823.17*** *p175*
Wilkinson, James 42; Ontario, 1871 ***1823.21*** *p394*
Wilkinson, John; America, 1754 ***1220.12*** *p873*
Wilkinson, John; America, 1756 ***1220.12*** *p873*
Wilkinson, John; America, 1764 ***1220.12*** *p873*
Wilkinson, John; America, 1767 ***1220.12*** *p873*
Wilkinson, John; Annapolis, MD, 1725 ***1220.12*** *p873*
Wilkinson, John; Jamaica, 1716 ***1220.12*** *p873*
Wilkinson, John; Maryland, 1741 ***1220.12*** *p873*
Wilkinson, John 36; Ontario, 1871 ***1823.21*** *p394*
Wilkinson, John 38; Ontario, 1871 ***1823.17*** *p175*
Wilkinson, John 42; Ontario, 1871 ***1823.21*** *p394*
Wilkinson, John; Philadelphia, 1778 ***8529.30*** *p5A*
Wilkinson, John; Virginia, 1739 ***1220.12*** *p873*
Wilkinson, Joseph; Died enroute, 1726 ***1220.12*** *p873*
Wilkinson, Joseph 33; Ontario, 1871 ***1823.21*** *p394*
Wilkinson, Joseph 41; Ontario, 1871 ***1823.21*** *p394*

Wilkinson, Joseph W.; Washington, 1885 *2770.40 p194*
Wilkinson, Joshua; America, 1746 *1220.12 p873*
Wilkinson, Margaret; Annapolis, MD, 1729 *1220.12 p873*
Wilkinson, Mary; America, 1747 *1220.12 p873*
Wilkinson, Mary; America, 1751 *1220.12 p873*
Wilkinson, Mary; America, 1752 *1220.12 p873*
Wilkinson, Mary; America, 1756 *1220.12 p873*
Wilkinson, Mary; America, 1758 *1220.12 p873*
Wilkinson, Mary; Boston, 1767 *1642 p39*
Wilkinson, Nicholas; America, 1758 *1220.12 p873*
Wilkinson, Nicholas; America, 1767 *1220.12 p873*
Wilkinson, Reuban 44; Ontario, 1871 *1823.21 p394*
Wilkinson, Richard; America, 1737 *1220.12 p873*
Wilkinson, Richard; Virginia, 1724 *1220.12 p873*
Wilkinson, Robert; Virginia, 1736 *1220.12 p873*
Wilkinson, Samuel; Annapolis, MD, 1733 *1220.12 p873*
Wilkinson, Thomas; America, 1698 *1220.12 p873*
Wilkinson, Thomas; America, 1740 *1220.12 p873*
Wilkinson, Thomas; America, 1764 *1220.12 p873*
Wilkinson, Thomas; America, 1765 *1220.12 p873*
Wilkinson, Thomas; Barbados, 1665 *1220.12 p873*
Wilkinson, Thomas; Barbados or Jamaica, 1702 *1220.12 p873*
Wilkinson, Thomas 31; Ontario, 1871 *1823.21 p394*
Wilkinson, Thomas 58; Ontario, 1871 *1823.17 p175*
Wilkinson, Thomas 59; Ontario, 1871 *1823.21 p394*
Wilkinson, Thompson 34; Ontario, 1871 *1823.17 p175*
Wilkinson, Timothy 26; Michigan, 1880 *4491.42 p29*
Wilkinson, William; America, 1732 *1220.12 p873*
Wilkinson, William; America, 1764 *1220.12 p873*
Wilkinson, William; America, 1767 *1220.12 p873*
Wilkinson, William; Barbados, 1664 *1220.12 p873*
Wilkinson, William; Barbados, 1682 *1220.12 p873*
Wilkinson, William 30; Ontario, 1871 *1823.17 p175*
Wilkinson, William 32; Ontario, 1871 *1823.17 p175*
Wilkinson, William 38; Ontario, 1871 *1823.17 p175*
Wilkinson, William 48; Ontario, 1871 *1823.21 p394*
Wilkinson, William 61; Ontario, 1871 *1823.21 p394*
Wilkinson, William; Potomac, 1731 *1220.12 p873*
Wilkinson, Wm 47; Ontario, 1871 *1823.17 p175*
Wilkson, Robert 32; Ontario, 1871 *1823.21 p394*
Wilks, Edward; Died enroute, 1725 *1220.12 p873*
Wilks, Emanuel; America, 1726 *1220.12 p873*
Wilks, Francis; America, 1758 *1220.12 p873*
Wilks, Henry; America, 1726 *1220.12 p874*
Wilks, Henry; New York, 1778 *8529.30 p5A*
Wilks, Thomas; America, 1742 *1220.12 p874*
Wilks, Thomas; Maryland, 1725 *1220.12 p874*
Wilkshire, William 48; Ontario, 1871 *1823.21 p394*
Wilkson, Robert; Virginia, 1736 *1220.12 p874*
Wilky, Adam *SEE* Wilky, Nikolaus
Wilky, George 38; Ontario, 1871 *1823.21 p394*
Wilky, Helena *SEE* Wilky, Nikolaus
Wilky, Katharina Meiers *SEE* Wilky, Nikolaus
Wilky, Mathias; America, 1860 *5475.1 p253*
Wilky, Mathias *SEE* Wilky, Nikolaus
Wilky, Nikolaus *SEE* Wilky, Nikolaus
Wilky, Nikolaus; America, 1872 *5475.1 p254*
  *Wife:*Katharina Meiers
  *Son:*Mathias
  *Son:*Adam
  *Daughter:*Helena
  *Son:*Nikolaus
Will, Agnes; America, 1868 *7919.3 p526*
Will, Albert Ferdinand; Wisconsin, 1908 *1822.55 p10*
Will, Anna Marie; America, 1840 *8115.12 p325*
Will, Balthasar; America, 1799-1832 *8115.12 p325*
Will, Caspar; America, n.d. *8115.12 p325*
Will, Elisabeth 44; America, 1864 *5475.1 p544*
Will, H.; New York, 1859 *358.56 p101*
Will, Henry; New Orleans, 1845 *471.10 p88*
Will, M. Barbara; America, 1854 *5475.1 p459*
Will, Mary 34; Louisiana, 1848 *778.6 p345*
Willafore, John; Maryland, 1672 *1236.25 p46*
Willar, Jordan 40; America, 1840 *778.6 p345*
Willard, Alex 25; Ontario, 1871 *1823.21 p394*
Willard, Nicholas; America, 1751 *1220.12 p874*
Willberg, Daniel; Illinois, 1861 *4487.25 p76*
Willcock, Hendry 21; Ontario, 1871 *1823.17 p175*
Willcock, Samuel 24; Ontario, 1871 *1823.17 p175*
Willcock, Thomas 59; Ontario, 1871 *1823.21 p394*
Willcocks, Henry; Virginia, 1772 *1220.12 p870*
Willcocks, Saml 60; Ontario, 1871 *1823.17 p175*
Willcox, Margaret; Annapolis, MD, 1732 *1220.12 p870*
Wille, Miss; America, 1860 *7420.1 p190*
Wille, Mr.; America, 1860 *7420.1 p202*
Wille, Mr.; Illinois, 1848 *7420.1 p63*
  With wife
  With child 5
  With child 8
Wille, Albertine 3; Portland, ME, 1911 *970.38 p82*
Wille, Augusta 16; Portland, ME, 1911 *970.38 p82*

Wille, Catharine Marie Becker *SEE* Wille, Johann Heinrich Christoph
Wille, Christoph; America, 1860 *7420.1 p202*
  With father
  With wife & 4 sons & 2 daughters
Wille, Conrad; America, 1853 *7420.1 p113*
Wille, Emilia 10; Portland, ME, 1911 *970.38 p82*
Wille, Engel Dorothea; America, 1854 *7420.1 p127*
Wille, Engel Dorothee Flentge *SEE* Wille, Johann Heinrich Christoph
Wille, Engel Maria Dorothea *SEE* Wille, Johann Conrad Daniel
Wille, Engel Marie Caroline Wilhelmine; America, 1857 *7420.1 p173*
  *Daughter:*Ilse Marie Dorothee
  *Son:*Johann Heinrich Conrad Christoph
  *Son:*Heinrich Philipp
Wille, Engel Marie Charlotte; America, 1864 *7420.1 p222*
Wille, Engel Marie Dorothee; America, 1857 *7420.1 p164*
Wille, Engel Marie Duhlmeyer *SEE* Wille, Hans Heinrich
Wille, Engel Marie Soph. Eleon. Katze *SEE* Wille, Johann Heinrich Conrad
Wille, Engel Marie Sophie; America, 1857 *7420.1 p171*
Wille, Engel Marie Sophie; America, 1857 *7420.1 p175*
Wille, Friedrich Conrad *SEE* Wille, Johann Conrad Daniel
Wille, Gustav 61; Portland, ME, 1911 *970.38 p82*
Wille, Hans Heinrich *SEE* Wille, Johann Conrad Daniel
Wille, Hans Heinrich; America, 1854 *7420.1 p133*
  *Wife:*Engel Marie Duhlmeyer
  *Son:*Johann Heinrich
Wille, Hans Heinrich Conrad *SEE* Wille, Johann Heinrich Christoph
Wille, Johann 19; Portland, ME, 1911 *970.38 p82*
Wille, Johann Conrad; America, 1845 *7420.1 p41*
  With son 14
  With son 10
Wille, Johann Conrad Christoph *SEE* Wille, Johann Heinrich Christoph
Wille, Johann Conrad Daniel; America, 1853 *7420.1 p113*
  *Son:*Friedrich Conrad
  *Daughter:*Engel Maria Dorothea
  *Son:*Hans Heinrich
Wille, Johann Heinrich *SEE* Wille, Hans Heinrich
Wille, Johann Heinrich; America, 1854 *7420.1 p133*
Wille, Johann Heinrich Christoph; America, 1853 *7420.1 p113*
  *Wife:*Engel Dorothee Flentge
  *Son:*Karl Wilhelm Rud.
  *Son:*Johann Konrad Christian
  *Son:*Hans Heinrich Conrad
  *Son:*Johann Conrad Christoph
Wille, Johann Heinrich Christoph; America, 1868 *7420.1 p278*
  *Wife:*Catharine Marie Becker
Wille, Johann Heinrich Conrad; America, 1851 *7420.1 p83*
Wille, Johann Heinrich Conrad; America, 1857 *7420.1 p175*
  *Wife:*Engel Marie Soph. Eleon. Katze
  With 2 sons & daughter
Wille, Johann Heinrich Otto; America, 1845 *7420.1 p35*
Wille, Johann Konrad Christian *SEE* Wille, Johann Heinrich Christoph
Wille, Johann Otto; America, 1855 *7420.1 p143*
Wille, Johann Otto; America, 1867 *7420.1 p267*
  With wife
Wille, Johann Otto; America, 1868 *7420.1 p278*
Wille, Johann Philipp; America, 1844 *7420.1 p34*
Wille, Johanna 22; Portland, ME, 1911 *970.38 p82*
Wille, Justina 38; Portland, ME, 1911 *970.38 p82*
Wille, Karl Wilhelm Rud. *SEE* Wille, Johann Heinrich Christoph
Wille, Otties 7; Portland, ME, 1911 *970.38 p82*
Wille, Paulina 13; Portland, ME, 1911 *970.38 p82*
Wille, Thrine Engel *SEE* Wille, Thrine Marie Sophie
Wille, Thrine Marie *SEE* Wille, Thrine Marie Sophie
Wille, Thrine Marie Sophie; America, 1854 *7420.1 p133*
  *Sister:*Thrine Engel
  *Sister:*Thrine Marie
Wille, Thrine Sophie Charlotte; America, 1849 *7420.1 p68*
Willemann, Elisabetha; America, 1881 *2526.42 p158*
Willemann, Johann Georg; America, 1881 *2526.42 p158*
Willemann, Johannes; America, 1771 *2526.42 p165*
  With wife & 7 children
Willemann, Peter; America, 1881 *2526.42 p158*
Willems, Jakob *SEE* Willems, Jakob

Willems, Jakob; America, 1882 *5475.1 p35*
  *Wife:*Maria Kaufmann
  *Son:*Josef
  *Son:*Peter
  *Son:*Jakob
Willems, Josef *SEE* Willems, Jakob
Willems, Karl *SEE* Willems, Margaretha Beuriger
Willems, Margaretha; America, 1886 *5475.1 p243*
  *Son:*Karl
  *Son:*Peter
Willems, Maria Kaufmann *SEE* Willems, Jakob
Willems, Nikolaus; New York, 1886 *5475.1 p243*
Willems, Peter; America, 1860 *5475.1 p387*
Willems, Peter *SEE* Willems, Jakob
Willems, Peter *SEE* Willems, Margaretha Beuriger
Willems, Pierre; Port Huron, MI, 1872 *1494.20 p12*
Willenborg, Henry; Ohio, 1809-1852 *4511.35 p59*
Willer, Blazin 45; New Castle, DE, 1817-1818 *90.20 p154*
Willer, Thomas 37; Ontario, 1871 *1823.17 p175*
Willers, Robert; America, 1761 *1220.12 p874*
Willershauser, Georg Andreas *SEE* Willershauser, Marie Katharine
Willershauser, Johannes *SEE* Willershauser, Marie Katharine
Willershauser, Ludwig *SEE* Willershauser, Marie Katharine
Willershauser, Marie Katharine; America, 1840 *8115.12 p323*
  *Child:*Georg Andreas
  *Child:*Ludwig
  *Child:*Johannes
Willert, William; Annapolis, MD, 1723 *1220.12 p874*
Willes, Elizabeth; America, 1759 *1220.12 p884*
Willes, Elizabeth; Annapolis, MD, 1758 *1220.12 p884*
Willes, Theodore; America, 1772 *1220.12 p884*
Willesmore, Thomas; Barbados, 1664 *1220.12 p874*
Willett, Ann; America, 1773 *1220.12 p874*
Willett, Arthur 40; Ontario, 1871 *1823.17 p175*
Willett, Edith Young *SEE* Willett, George Leon
Willett, George Leon; Massachusetts, 1911 *9228.50 p408*
Willett, George Leon; Panama, 1911 *9228.50 p408*
  *Wife:*Edith Young
Willett, Humphry; America, 1770 *1220.12 p874*
Willett, Jonas; America, 1736 *1220.12 p874*
Willetts, Samuel; America, 1740 *1220.12 p874*
Willey, Elizabeth; America, 1748 *1220.12 p874*
Willey, John; America, 1685 *1220.12 p874*
Willey, John; America, 1732 *1220.12 p874*
Willey, Scot 66; Ontario, 1871 *1823.21 p394*
Willford, David; Maryland, 1721 *1220.12 p872*
Willgohs, C. F. H.; Ohio, 1809-1852 *4511.35 p59*
Willhelm, . . .; New Orleans, 1840 *778.6 p345*
Willhelm, Francois; New Orleans, 1840 *778.6 p345*
William, David; America, 1673 *1220.12 p874*
William, David; America, 1749 *1220.12 p874*
William, James 50; Ontario, 1871 *1823.21 p394*
William, John; America, 1737 *1220.12 p874*
William, John; America, 1749 *1220.12 p874*
William, John; Colorado, 1873 *1029.59 p94*
William, Lewis; America, 1775 *1220.12 p874*
William, Morgan; America, 1701 *1220.12 p874*
William, Phillips 70; Ontario, 1871 *1823.17 p175*
William, Warren 24; Ontario, 1871 *1823.17 p175*
Williamhurst, Alice; America, 1772 *1220.12 p874*
Williams, Abel; America, 1738 *1220.12 p874*
Williams, Abraham 50; Ontario, 1871 *1823.21 p394*
Williams, Adam 38; Ontario, 1871 *1823.21 p394*
Williams, Alice; America, 1662 *1220.12 p874*
Williams, Alice; America, 1678 *1220.12 p874*
Williams, Alice; America, 1749 *1220.12 p874*
Williams, Andrew; America, 1762 *1220.12 p874*
Williams, Ann; America, 1742 *1220.12 p874*
Williams, Ann; America, 1750 *1220.12 p874*
Williams, Ann; America, 1757 *1220.12 p874*
Williams, Ann; America, 1762 *1220.12 p874*
Williams, Ann; America, 1768 *1220.12 p874*
Williams, Ann; America, 1772 *1220.12 p874*
Williams, Ann; Maryland, 1740 *1220.12 p874*
Williams, Ann *SEE* Williams, William
Williams, Ann *SEE* Williams, Thomas
Williams, Ann Jones *SEE* Williams, Morgan
Williams, Ann *SEE* Williams, Thomas J.
Williams, Ann 80; Ontario, 1871 *1823.21 p394*
Williams, Anna; Massachusetts, 1773 *1642 p116*
Williams, Anne; America, 1677 *1220.12 p874*
Williams, Anne Phillips *SEE* Williams, Anne
Williams, Anne; Ohio, 1838 *4022.20 p280*
  *Wife:*Anne Phillips
  *Child:*David
  *Child:*John
  *Child:*Winnie

*Child:*Thomas J.
*Child:*Lewis
Williams, Anne; Rappahannock, VA, 1729 ***1220.12*** *p874*
Williams, Arthur B. 49; Quebec, 1910 ***2897.7*** *p8*
Williams, Barbara; America, 1734 ***1220.12*** *p875*
Williams, Barbara; Barbados or Jamaica, 1685 ***1220.12*** *p874*
Williams, Benjamin; America, 1682 ***1220.12*** *p875*
Williams, Benjamin; America, 1760 ***1220.12*** *p875*
Williams, Benjamin G. *SEE* Williams, George D.
Williams, C.; Quebec, 1870 ***8364.32*** *p26*
Williams, C. Thomas 70; Ontario, 1871 ***1823.17*** *p175*
Williams, Catherine; America, 1769 ***1220.12*** *p875*
Williams, Catherine *SEE* Williams, William
Williams, Catherine *SEE* Williams, David, Sr.
Williams, Cecile 30; America, 1843 ***778.6*** *p345*
Williams, Charles; America, 1662 ***1220.12*** *p875*
Williams, Charles; America, 1722 ***1220.12*** *p875*
Williams, Charles; America, 1756 ***1220.12*** *p875*
Williams, Charlotte 11; Quebec, 1870 ***8364.32*** *p26*
Williams, Charlotte Anne 32; Ontario, 1871 ***1823.21*** *p394*
Williams, Chas 38; Ontario, 1871 ***1823.21*** *p394*
Williams, Christian; Annapolis, MD, 1730 ***1220.12*** *p875*
Williams, Christopher; America, 1735 ***1220.12*** *p875*
Williams, Christopher; Barbados, 1668 ***1220.12*** *p875*
Williams, Christopher 24; Ontario, 1871 ***1823.21*** *p394*
Williams, Cornelius; Colorado, 1873 ***1029.59*** *p94*
Williams, Daniel; America, 1725 ***1220.12*** *p875*
Williams, Daniel; America, 1775 ***1220.12*** *p875*
Williams, Daniel *SEE* Williams, Thomas J.
Williams, David; America, 1699 ***1220.12*** *p875*
Williams, David; America, 1762 ***1220.12*** *p875*
Williams, David; America, 1764 ***1220.12*** *p875*
Williams, David; America, 1766 ***1220.12*** *p875*
Williams, David; America, 1767 ***1220.12*** *p875*
Williams, David; America, 1774 ***1220.12*** *p875*
Williams, David *SEE* Williams, William
Williams, David *SEE* Williams, Anne
Williams, David *SEE* Williams, David D.
Williams, David *SEE* Williams, George D.
Williams, David; Ohio, 1840 ***3580.20*** *p34*
Williams, David; Ohio, 1840 ***6020.12*** *p23*
Williams, David; Philadelphia, 1855 ***9228.50*** *p654*
Williams, David, Sr.; Ohio, 1838 ***4022.20*** *p292*
*Wife:*Catherine
*Child:*David D.
Williams, David D. *SEE* Williams, David, Sr.
Williams, David D.; Ohio, 1838 ***4022.20*** *p292*
*Father:*David
With mother
Williams, David G. *SEE* Williams, Robert
Williams, David Lewis; Colorado, 1903 ***1029.59*** *p95*
Williams, David Lewis; Nebraska, 1869 ***1029.59*** *p95*
Williams, Dennis 60; Ontario, 1871 ***1823.21*** *p394*
Williams, Ebenezer *SEE* Williams, William
Williams, Edward; America, 1734 ***1220.12*** *p875*
Williams, Edward; America, 1735 ***1220.12*** *p875*
Williams, Edward; America, 1758 ***1220.12*** *p875*
Williams, Edward; America, 1765 ***1220.12*** *p875*
Williams, Edward; America, 1767 ***1220.12*** *p875*
Williams, Edward; America, 1769 ***1220.12*** *p875*
Williams, Edward; America, 1772 ***1220.12*** *p875*
Williams, Edward; Barbados, 1663 ***1220.12*** *p875*
Williams, Edward; Barbados or Jamaica, 1702 ***1220.12*** *p875*
Williams, Edward; Long Island, 1781 ***8529.30*** *p10A*
Williams, Edward; Rappahannock, VA, 1729 ***1220.12*** *p875*
Williams, Edward; Virginia, 1718 ***1220.12*** *p875*
Williams, Edward; Virginia, 1740 ***1220.12*** *p875*
Williams, Eleanor; America, 1764 ***1220.12*** *p875*
Williams, Eleanor; America, 1765 ***1220.12*** *p875*
Williams, Eleanor *SEE* Williams, William
Williams, Eliz.; Maryland, 1674-1675 ***1236.25*** *p51*
Williams, Eliz.; Maryland, 1674-1675 ***1236.25*** *p52*
Williams, Elizabeth; America, 1662 ***1220.12*** *p875*
Williams, Elizabeth; America, 1697 ***1220.12*** *p875*
Williams, Elizabeth; America, 1722 ***1220.12*** *p875*
Williams, Elizabeth; America, 1741 ***1220.12*** *p876*
Williams, Elizabeth; America, 1746 ***1220.12*** *p876*
Williams, Elizabeth; America, 1750 ***1220.12*** *p876*
Williams, Elizabeth; America, 1754 ***1220.12*** *p876*
Williams, Elizabeth; America, 1755 ***1220.12*** *p876*
Williams, Elizabeth; America, 1756 ***1220.12*** *p876*
Williams, Elizabeth; America, 1757 ***1220.12*** *p876*
Williams, Elizabeth; America, 1761 ***1220.12*** *p876*
Williams, Elizabeth; America, 1765 ***1220.12*** *p876*
Williams, Elizabeth; America, 1767 ***1220.12*** *p876*
Williams, Elizabeth; America, 1772 ***1220.12*** *p876*
Williams, Elizabeth; America, 1774 ***1220.12*** *p876*
Williams, Elizabeth; Annapolis, MD, 1725 ***1220.12*** *p876*
Williams, Elizabeth; Barbados, 1664 ***1220.12*** *p875*
Williams, Elizabeth; Barbados, 1668 ***1220.12*** *p875*
Williams, Elizabeth; Barbados, 1674 ***1220.12*** *p875*
Williams, Elizabeth; Carolina, 1724 ***1220.12*** *p875*
Williams, Elizabeth Isaac *SEE* Williams, John
Williams, Elizabeth; Rappahannock, VA, 1726 ***1220.12*** *p876*
Williams, Elizabeth; Virginia, 1735 ***1220.12*** *p876*
Williams, Elizabeth; Virginia, 1736 ***1220.12*** *p876*
Williams, Elizha; America, 1746 ***1220.12*** *p876*
Williams, Essex; America, 1753 ***1220.12*** *p876*
Williams, Evan; America, 1774 ***1220.12*** *p876*
Williams, Evan; Iowa, 1895 ***1211.15*** *p20*
Williams, Evan *SEE* Williams, William
Williams, Evan *SEE* Williams, John
Williams, Frances; America, 1736 ***1220.12*** *p876*
Williams, Frances; America, 1767 ***1220.12*** *p876*
Williams, Frances; Jamaica, 1717 ***1220.12*** *p876*
Williams, Frances H. 53; Ontario, 1871 ***1823.21*** *p394*
Williams, Francis; America, 1738 ***1220.12*** *p876*
Williams, Francis; America, 1742 ***1220.12*** *p876*
Williams, Francis; Annapolis, MD, 1733 ***1220.12*** *p876*
Williams, Francis; Barbados, 1669 ***1220.12*** *p876*
Williams, George; America, 1661 ***1220.12*** *p876*
Williams, George; America, 1715 ***1220.12*** *p876*
Williams, George; America, 1759 ***1220.12*** *p876*
Williams, George; America, 1763 ***1220.12*** *p876*
Williams, George; America, 1764 ***1220.12*** *p876*
Williams, George; America, 1782 ***8529.30*** *p17*
Williams, George; Died enroute, 1734 ***1220.12*** *p876*
Williams, George; Maryland, 1720 ***1220.12*** *p876*
Williams, George *SEE* Williams, George D.
Williams, George 23; Ontario, 1871 ***1823.17*** *p175*
Williams, George 46; Ontario, 1871 ***1823.17*** *p175*
Williams, George 46; Ontario, 1871 ***1823.21*** *p394*
Williams, George 49; Ontario, 1871 ***1823.21*** *p394*
Williams, George 57; Ontario, 1871 ***1823.21*** *p394*
Williams, George D.; Ohio, 1839 ***4022.20*** *p292*
*Wife:*Hannah D.
*Child:*William
*Child:*Benjamin G.
*Child:*David
*Child:*George
Williams, George W.; Colorado, 1901 ***1029.59*** *p95*
Williams, Grace; America, 1736 ***1220.12*** *p876*
Williams, H. W.; Louisiana, 1874-1875 ***4981.45*** *p130*
Williams, Hannah; America, 1767 ***1220.12*** *p876*
Williams, Hannah *SEE* Williams, William
Williams, Hannah; Ohio, 1847-1850 ***4022.20*** *p277*
Williams, Hannah D. *SEE* Williams, George D.
Williams, Henry; America, 1680 ***1220.12*** *p876*
Williams, Henry; America, 1765 ***1220.12*** *p876*
Williams, Henry; America, 1767 ***1220.12*** *p876*
Williams, Henry; America, 1768 ***1220.12*** *p876*
Williams, Henry 20; New York, NY, 1883 ***8427.14*** *p44*
Williams, Henry 29; Ontario, 1871 ***1823.21*** *p394*
Williams, Henry 30; Ontario, 1871 ***1823.21*** *p394*
Williams, Henry 50; Ontario, 1871 ***1823.21*** *p394*
Williams, Hester; America, 1761 ***1220.12*** *p876*
Williams, Hugh; North Carolina, 1832 ***1088.45*** *p37*
Williams, Isabella; Virginia, 1725 ***1220.12*** *p876*
Williams, J.; Quebec, 1870 ***8364.32*** *p26*
Williams, J.S.; Quebec, 1870 ***8364.32*** *p26*
Williams, James; America, 1738 ***1220.12*** *p877*
Williams, James; America, 1739 ***1220.12*** *p877*
Williams, James; America, 1741 ***1220.12*** *p877*
Williams, James; America, 1745 ***1220.12*** *p877*
Williams, James; America, 1752 ***1220.12*** *p877*
Williams, James; America, 1758 ***1220.12*** *p877*
Williams, James; America, 1762 ***1220.12*** *p877*
Williams, James; America, 1770 ***1220.12*** *p877*
Williams, James; Barbados, 1701 ***1220.12*** *p876*
Williams, James; New York, 1832 ***3274.55*** *p23*
Williams, James 55; Ontario, 1871 ***1823.17*** *p175*
Williams, James 55; Ontario, 1871 ***1823.21*** *p394*
Williams, James 60; Ontario, 1871 ***1823.21*** *p394*
Williams, James 74; Ontario, 1871 ***1823.21*** *p395*
Williams, James; Virginia, 1727 ***1220.12*** *p876*
Williams, James C.; Colorado, 1895 ***1029.59*** *p95*
Williams, James H.; Colorado, 1883 ***1029.59*** *p95*
Williams, James H.; Colorado, 1894 ***1029.59*** *p95*
Williams, James L. 45; Ontario, 1871 ***1823.21*** *p395*
Williams, Jane; America, 1708 ***1220.12*** *p877*
Williams, Jane; America, 1734 ***1220.12*** *p877*
Williams, Jane; America, 1751 ***1220.12*** *p877*
Williams, Jane; Barbados or Jamaica, 1692 ***1220.12*** *p877*
Williams, Jane; Virginia, 1750 ***1220.12*** *p877*
Williams, Jarratt; America, 1773 ***1220.12*** *p877*
Williams, Jervis; America, 1772 ***1220.12*** *p877*
Williams, John; America, 1675 ***1220.12*** *p877*
Williams, John; America, 1710 ***1220.12*** *p877*
Williams, John; America, 1718 ***1220.12*** *p877*
Williams, John; America, 1720 ***1220.12*** *p877*
Williams, John; America, 1722 ***1220.12*** *p877*
Williams, John; America, 1723 ***1220.12*** *p877*
Williams, John; America, 1724 ***1220.12*** *p877*
Williams, John; America, 1727 ***1220.12*** *p877*
Williams, John; America, 1730 ***1220.12*** *p877*
Williams, John; America, 1731 ***1220.12*** *p877*
Williams, John; America, 1734 ***1220.12*** *p877*
Williams, John; America, 1737 ***1220.12*** *p877*
Williams, John; America, 1738 ***1220.12*** *p877*
Williams, John; America, 1738 ***1220.12*** *p878*
Williams, John; America, 1739 ***1220.12*** *p878*
Williams, John; America, 1744 ***1220.12*** *p878*
Williams, John; America, 1747 ***1220.12*** *p878*
Williams, John; America, 1749 ***1220.12*** *p878*
Williams, John; America, 1750 ***1220.12*** *p878*
Williams, John; America, 1751 ***1220.12*** *p878*
Williams, John; America, 1752 ***1220.12*** *p878*
Williams, John; America, 1753 ***1220.12*** *p878*
Williams, John; America, 1754 ***1220.12*** *p878*
Williams, John; America, 1755 ***1220.12*** *p878*
Williams, John; America, 1758 ***1220.12*** *p878*
Williams, John; America, 1759 ***1220.12*** *p878*
Williams, John; America, 1760 ***1220.12*** *p878*
Williams, John; America, 1761 ***1220.12*** *p878*
Williams, John; America, 1762 ***1220.12*** *p878*
Williams, John; America, 1763 ***1220.12*** *p878*
Williams, John; America, 1765 ***1220.12*** *p878*
Williams, John; America, 1766 ***1220.12*** *p878*
Williams, John; America, 1767 ***1220.12*** *p878*
Williams, John; America, 1768 ***1220.12*** *p878*
Williams, John; America, 1769 ***1220.12*** *p878*
Williams, John; America, 1771 ***1220.12*** *p878*
Williams, John; America, 1773 ***1220.12*** *p878*
Williams, John; America, 1774 ***1220.12*** *p878*
Williams, John; America, 1775 ***1220.12*** *p878*
Williams, John; America, 1775 ***1220.12*** *p879*
Williams, John; America, 1782 ***8529.30*** *p17*
Williams, John; Annapolis, MD, 1722 ***1220.12*** *p877*
Williams, John; Barbados, 1664 ***1220.12*** *p877*
Williams, John; Barbados, 1671 ***1220.12*** *p877*
Williams, John; Barbados, 1700-1710 ***1220.12*** *p877*
Williams, John; Barbados or Jamaica, 1693 ***1220.12*** *p877*
Williams, John; California, 1868 ***1131.61*** *p89*
Williams, John; Carolina, 1719 ***1220.12*** *p877*
Williams, John; Charles Town, SC, 1719 ***1220.12*** *p877*
Williams, John; Maryland, 1725 ***1220.12*** *p877*
Williams, John 57; Maryland, 1724 ***1220.12*** *p877*
Williams, John 30; North Carolina, 1774 ***1422.10*** *p54*
Williams, John *SEE* Williams, Anne
Williams, John; Ohio, 1838 ***4022.20*** *p281*
*Wife:*Elizabeth Isaac
*Child:*Sarah
*Child:*Evan
Williams, John 17; Ontario, 1871 ***1823.21*** *p395*
Williams, John 24; Ontario, 1824 ***9228.50*** *p450*
Williams, John 26; Ontario, 1871 ***1823.21*** *p395*
Williams, John 27; Ontario, 1871 ***1823.21*** *p395*
Williams, John 30; Ontario, 1871 ***1823.21*** *p395*
Williams, John 31; Ontario, 1871 ***1823.21*** *p395*
Williams, John 37; Ontario, 1871 ***1823.21*** *p395*
Williams, John 42; Ontario, 1871 ***1823.21*** *p395*
Williams, John 48; Ontario, 1871 ***1823.21*** *p395*
Williams, John 50; Ontario, 1871 ***1823.21*** *p395*
Williams, John 62; Ontario, 1871 ***1823.17*** *p176*
Williams, John; Potomac, 1761-1793 ***9228.50*** *p21A*
Williams, John 8; Quebec, 1870 ***8364.32*** *p26*
Williams, John; Rappahannock, VA, 1741 ***1220.12*** *p878*
Williams, John; St. John, N.B., 1848 ***2978.15*** *p41*
Williams, John; Virginia, 1729 ***1220.12*** *p877*
Williams, John; Virginia, 1738 ***1220.12*** *p878*
Williams, John; Virginia, 1740 ***1220.12*** *p878*
Williams, John; Virginia, 1762 ***1220.12*** *p878*
Williams, John, Jr.; America, 1685 ***1220.12*** *p877*
Williams, John, Sr.; America, 1685 ***1220.12*** *p877*
Williams, John Daniel; Colorado, 1891 ***1029.59*** *p95*
Williams, John Daniel; Colorado, 1894 ***1029.59*** *p95*
Williams, John David; Colorado, 1891 ***1029.59*** *p95*
Williams, Jonathon 61; Ontario, 1871 ***1823.21*** *p395*
Williams, Joseph; America, 1742 ***1220.12*** *p879*
Williams, Joseph; America, 1752 ***1220.12*** *p879*
Williams, Joseph; America, 1765 ***1220.12*** *p879*
Williams, Joseph 35; Ontario, 1871 ***1823.21*** *p395*
Williams, Judy; Annapolis, MD, 1726 ***1220.12*** *p879*
Williams, Katherine; America, 1678 ***1220.12*** *p875*
Williams, Katherine; America, 1750 ***1220.12*** *p875*
Williams, Katie 60; Ontario, 1871 ***1823.21*** *p395*
Williams, Lewis; America, 1772 ***1220.12*** *p879*
Williams, Lewis; America, 1774 ***1220.12*** *p879*
Williams, Lewis; America, 1775 ***1220.12*** *p879*
Williams, Lewis; Barbados, 1683 ***1220.12*** *p879*
Williams, Lewis *SEE* Williams, Anne
Williams, Louesia 14; Ontario, 1871 ***1823.21*** *p395*
Williams, Louisa 11; Quebec, 1870 ***8364.32*** *p26*
Williams, Margaret; America, 1754 ***1220.12*** *p879*

Williams, Margaret; Annapolis, MD, 1731 *1220.12 p879*
Williams, Margaret; Maryland, 1720 *1220.12 p879*
Williams, Margaret *SEE* Williams, William
Williams, Margaret *SEE* Williams, William
Williams, Margaret; Ohio, 1838 *4022.20 p285*
Williams, Margaret; Ohio, 1838 *4022.20 p289*
Williams, Margaret; Ohio, 1857 *4022.20 p291*
  *Husband:*Robert
Williams, Margaret; Pennsylvania, 1860 *8513.31 p293*
Williams, Margaret 7; Quebec, 1870 *8364.32 p26*
Williams, Margery; America, 1731 *1220.12 p879*
Williams, Martha; America, 1727 *1220.12 p879*
Williams, Mary; America, 1673 *1220.12 p879*
Williams, Mary; America, 1682 *1220.12 p879*
Williams, Mary; America, 1726 *1220.12 p879*
Williams, Mary; America, 1738 *1220.12 p879*
Williams, Mary; America, 1741 *1220.12 p879*
Williams, Mary; America, 1750 *1220.12 p879*
Williams, Mary; America, 1752 *1220.12 p879*
Williams, Mary; America, 1756 *1220.12 p879*
Williams, Mary; America, 1757 *1220.12 p879*
Williams, Mary; America, 1758 *1220.12 p879*
Williams, Mary; America, 1759 *1220.12 p879*
Williams, Mary; America, 1760 *1220.12 p879*
Williams, Mary; America, 1764 *1220.12 p879*
Williams, Mary; America, 1765 *1220.12 p879*
Williams, Mary; America, 1766 *1220.12 p879*
Williams, Mary; America, 1767 *1220.12 p879*
Williams, Mary; America, 1771 *1220.12 p879*
Williams, Mary; America, 1772 *1220.12 p879*
Williams, Mary; America, 1773 *1220.12 p879*
Williams, Mary; America, 1775 *1220.12 p879*
Williams, Mary; Barbados, 1663 *1220.12 p879*
Williams, Mary; Barbados or Jamaica, 1693 *1220.12 p879*
Williams, Mary; Barbados or Jamaica, 1697 *1220.12 p879*
Williams, Mary; Barbados or Jamaica, 1700 *1220.12 p879*
Williams, Mary; Died enroute, 1734 *1220.12 p879*
Williams, Mary; Maryland, 1730 *1220.12 p879*
Williams, Mary *SEE* Williams, William
Williams, Mary Jones *SEE* Williams, Robert
Williams, Mary; Ohio, 1841 *4022.20 p279*
Williams, Mary *SEE* Williams, William J.
Williams, Mary; Ohio, 1854 *4022.20 p290*
Williams, Mary; Ohio, 1855 *4022.20 p292*
Williams, Mary 45; Ontario, 1871 *1823.21 p395*
Williams, Mary 74; Ontario, 1871 *1823.21 p395*
Williams, Mary; Virginia, 1726 *1220.12 p879*
Williams, Mary Ann 24; Philadelphia, 1855 *9228.50 p654*
Williams, Mary Ann; Utah, 1856-1857 *9228.50 p518*
Williams, Mary Therese; Illinois, 1930 *121.35 p101*
Williams, Matilda 40; Ontario, 1871 *1823.21 p395*
Williams, Michael 27; Ontario, 1871 *1823.21 p395*
Williams, Michael; Virginia, 1772 *1220.12 p879*
Williams, Morgan; America, 1763 *1220.12 p880*
Williams, Morgan *SEE* Williams, William
Williams, Morgan; Ohio, 1838 *4022.20 p292*
  *Wife:*Ann Jones
Williams, Morgan M.; Washington, 1884 *2770.40 p193*
Williams, Morris 36; Ontario, 1871 *1823.17 p176*
Williams, Nancy 72; Ontario, 1871 *1823.17 p176*
Williams, Paul; Maine, 1684 *9228.50 p339*
Williams, Peter; America, 1730 *1220.12 p880*
Williams, Peter; Barbados, 1683 *1220.12 p880*
Williams, Phila; America, 1722 *1220.12 p880*
Williams, Philip; America, 1750 *1220.12 p880*
Williams, Philip; Barbados or Jamaica, 1690 *1220.12 p880*
Williams, Pleasant; America, 1768 *1220.12 p880*
Williams, R.; Louisiana, 1874 *4981.45 p297*
Williams, Randolph; Virginia, 1721 *1220.12 p880*
Williams, Rebecca; America, 1727 *1220.12 p880*
Williams, Rebecca; America, 1769 *1220.12 p880*
Williams, Rees; America, 1769 *1220.12 p880*
Williams, Rees; Ohio, 1853 *4022.20 p293*
  With wife
Williams, Rich 51; Ontario, 1871 *1823.17 p176*
Williams, Richard; America, 1688 *1220.12 p880*
Williams, Richard; America, 1692 *1220.12 p880*
Williams, Richard; America, 1729 *1220.12 p880*
Williams, Richard; America, 1749 *1220.12 p880*
Williams, Richard; America, 1755 *1220.12 p880*
Williams, Richard; America, 1757 *1220.12 p880*
Williams, Richard; America, 1765 *1220.12 p880*
Williams, Richard; America, 1766 *1220.12 p880*
Williams, Richard; America, 1768 *1220.12 p880*
Williams, Richard; America, 1773 *1220.12 p880*
Williams, Richard; Annapolis, MD, 1726 *1220.12 p880*
Williams, Richard; Barbados, 1670 *1220.12 p880*
Williams, Richard; Ohio, 1844 *2763.1 p22*

Williams, Richard; Virginia, 1758 *1220.12 p880*
Williams, Richard; Washington, 1882 *2770.40 p136*
Williams, Robert; America, 1686 *1220.12 p880*
Williams, Robert; America, 1760 *1220.12 p880*
Williams, Robert; America, 1761 *1220.12 p880*
Williams, Robert; America, 1769 *1220.12 p880*
Williams, Robert; America, 1773 *1220.12 p880*
Williams, Robert; America, 1870 *9076.20 p68*
Williams, Robert; Barbados, 1666 *1220.12 p880*
Williams, Robert; Barbados, 1671 *1220.12 p880*
Williams, Robert; Barbados, 1674 *1220.12 p880*
Williams, Robert; Maryland, 1674-1675 *1236.25 p52*
Williams, Robert; Maryland, 1735 *1220.12 p880*
Williams, Robert; Ohio, 1836 *4022.20 p293*
  *Wife:*Mary Jones
  *Cousin:*David G.
  With 2 children
Williams, Robert *SEE* Williams, Margaret Thomas
Williams, Robert 43; Ontario, 1871 *1823.21 p395*
Williams, Robert 44; Ontario, 1871 *1823.17 p176*
Williams, Robert P.; Iowa, 1894 *1211.15 p20*
Williams, Roger; America, 1745 *1220.12 p880*
Williams, Roger; Massachusetts, 1630 *117.5 p157*
  With wife
Williams, Roger 44; Ontario, 1871 *1823.21 p395*
Williams, Roger S. 72; Ontario, 1871 *1823.21 p395*
Williams, Rotherick; America, 1683 *1220.12 p880*
Williams, Samuel; America, 1684 *1220.12 p880*
Williams, Samuel; America, 1741 *1220.12 p880*
Williams, Samuel; America, 1762 *1220.12 p880*
Williams, Samuel 32; Indiana, 1865-1866 *9076.20 p66*
Williams, Sarah; America, 1733 *1220.12 p880*
Williams, Sarah; America, 1754 *1220.12 p880*
Williams, Sarah; America, 1761 *1220.12 p880*
Williams, Sarah; America, 1770 *1220.12 p880*
Williams, Sarah; America, 1774 *1220.12 p881*
Williams, Sarah; Barbados, 1699 *1220.12 p880*
Williams, Sarah *SEE* Williams, John
Williams, Sarah Jones *SEE* Williams, Thomas
Williams, Sarah 64; Ontario, 1871 *1823.21 p395*
Williams, Sarah; Philadelphia, 1855 *9228.50 p654*
Williams, Sarah; Rappahannock, VA, 1728 *1220.12 p880*
Williams, Simon; Barbados, 1671 *1220.12 p881*
Williams, Stephen 35; Ontario, 1871 *1823.17 p176*
Williams, Stephen 40; Ontario, 1871 *1823.21 p395*
Williams, Suntra 42; Minnesota, 1925 *2769.54 p1383*
Williams, Susan; America, 1744 *1220.12 p881*
Williams, Susan; America, 1769 *1220.12 p881*
Williams, Susanna; America, 1755 *1220.12 p881*
Williams, Susanna; America, 1757 *1220.12 p881*
Williams, Susanna; America, 1764 *1220.12 p881*
Williams, Susanna; Maryland or Virginia, 1733 *1220.12 p881*
Williams, Susannah; Virginia, 1740 *1220.12 p881*
Williams, Thomas; America, 1658 *1220.12 p881*
Williams, Thomas; America, 1685 *1220.12 p881*
Williams, Thomas; America, 1691 *1220.12 p881*
Williams, Thomas; America, 1693 *1220.12 p881*
Williams, Thomas; America, 1700 *1220.12 p881*
Williams, Thomas; America, 1721 *1220.12 p881*
Williams, Thomas; America, 1726 *1220.12 p881*
Williams, Thomas; America, 1729 *1220.12 p881*
Williams, Thomas; America, 1730 *1220.12 p881*
Williams, Thomas; America, 1732 *1220.12 p881*
Williams, Thomas; America, 1734 *1220.12 p881*
Williams, Thomas; America, 1735 *1220.12 p881*
Williams, Thomas; America, 1743 *1220.12 p881*
Williams, Thomas; America, 1744 *1220.12 p881*
Williams, Thomas; America, 1748 *1220.12 p881*
Williams, Thomas; America, 1750 *1220.12 p881*
Williams, Thomas; America, 1752 *1220.12 p881*
Williams, Thomas; America, 1753 *1220.12 p881*
Williams, Thomas; America, 1754 *1220.12 p881*
Williams, Thomas; America, 1756 *1220.12 p881*
Williams, Thomas; America, 1764 *1220.12 p881*
Williams, Thomas; America, 1765 *1220.12 p881*
Williams, Thomas; America, 1765 *1220.12 p882*
Williams, Thomas; America, 1766 *1220.12 p882*
Williams, Thomas; America, 1767 *1220.12 p882*
Williams, Thomas; America, 1768 *1220.12 p882*
Williams, Thomas; America, 1772 *1220.12 p882*
Williams, Thomas; America, 1773 *1220.12 p882*
Williams, Thomas; America, 1774 *1220.12 p882*
Williams, Thomas; America, 1775 *1220.12 p882*
Williams, Thomas; Annapolis, MD, 1723 *1220.12 p881*
Williams, Thomas; Annapolis, MD, 1725 *1220.12 p881*
Williams, Thomas; Barbados or Jamaica, 1702 *1220.12 p881*
Williams, Thomas; Colorado, 1883 *1029.59 p95*
Williams, Thomas; Colorado, 1888 *1029.59 p95*
Williams, Thomas; Louisiana, 1836-1840 *4981.45 p213*
Williams, Thomas; Maryland, 1719 *1220.12 p881*
Williams, Thomas; Maryland, 1724 *1220.12 p881*

Williams, Thomas; Ohio, 1832 *4022.20 p293*
Williams, Thomas; Ohio, 1837 *4022.20 p293*
  *Wife:*Ann
Williams, Thomas; Ohio, 1866 *4022.20 p293*
  *Wife:*Sarah Jones
Williams, Thomas 36; Ontario, 1871 *1823.21 p395*
Williams, Thomas 58; Ontario, 1871 *1823.21 p395*
Williams, Thomas; Philadelphia, 1778 *8529.30 p5A*
Williams, Thomas; Plymouth, MA, 1620 *1920.45 p5*
Williams, Thomas; Potomac, 1731 *1220.12 p881*
Williams, Thomas 11; Quebec, 1870 *8364.32 p26*
Williams, Thomas; Virginia, 1758 *1220.12 p881*
Williams, Thomas; Virginia, 1768 *1220.12 p882*
Williams, Thomas; Washington, 1883 *2770.40 p137*
Williams, Thomas B. *SEE* Williams, William
Williams, Thomas H.; Illinois, 1858-1861 *6020.5 p133*
Williams, Thomas H. 24; Indiana, 1872 *9076.20 p67*
Williams, Thomas J. *SEE* Williams, Anne
Williams, Thomas J. *SEE* Williams, Thomas J.
Williams, Thomas J.; Ohio, 1841 *4022.20 p293*
  *Wife:*Ann
  *Child:*Thomas J.
  *Child:*Daniel
Williams, Thomasin; America, 1752 *1220.12 p882*
Williams, Tutor; Virginia, 1726 *1220.12 p882*
Williams, William; America, 1685 *1220.12 p882*
Williams, William; America, 1702 *1220.12 p882*
Williams, William; America, 1710 *1220.12 p882*
Williams, William; America, 1715 *1220.12 p882*
Williams, William; America, 1718 *1220.12 p882*
Williams, William; America, 1727 *1220.12 p882*
Williams, William; America, 1739 *1220.12 p882*
Williams, William; America, 1740 *1220.12 p882*
Williams, William; America, 1747 *1220.12 p882*
Williams, William; America, 1748 *1220.12 p882*
Williams, William; America, 1749 *1220.12 p882*
Williams, William; America, 1750 *1220.12 p882*
Williams, William; America, 1752 *1220.12 p882*
Williams, William; America, 1756 *1220.12 p882*
Williams, William; America, 1764 *1220.12 p882*
Williams, William; America, 1764 *1220.12 p883*
Williams, William; America, 1766 *1220.12 p883*
Williams, William; America, 1767 *1220.12 p883*
Williams, William; America, 1768 *1220.12 p883*
Williams, William; America, 1770 *1220.12 p883*
Williams, William; America, 1771 *1220.12 p883*
Williams, William; America, 1772 *1220.12 p883*
Williams, William; America, 1773 *1220.12 p883*
Williams, William; Annapolis, MD, 1722 *1220.12 p882*
Williams, William; Barbados, 1665 *1220.12 p882*
Williams, William; Barbados, 1668 *1220.12 p882*
Williams, William; Barbados, 1681 *1220.12 p882*
Williams, William; Barbados, 1688 *1220.12 p882*
Williams, William; Barbados or Jamaica, 1685 *1220.12 p882*
Williams, William; Barbados or Jamaica, 1700 *1220.12 p882*
Williams, William; Colorado, 1899 *1029.59 p95*
Williams, William; Colorado, 1903 *1029.59 p95*
Williams, William; Died enroute, 1851 *9228.50 p192*
Williams, William; Illinois, 1834-1900 *6020.5 p133*
Williams, William; Maryland, 1721 *1220.12 p882*
Williams, William; Maryland or Virginia, 1731 *1220.12 p882*
Williams, William 52; Michigan, 1880 *4491.42 p29*
Williams, William; Ohio, 1818 *4022.20 p293*
  *Wife:*Margaret
  *Child:*Hannah
  *Child:*Ebenezer
  *Child:*Mary
  *Child:*Thomas B.
  *Child:*Margaret
  *Child:*Ann
  *Child:*David
  *Child:*Eleanor
  *Child:*Morgan
Williams, William; Ohio, 1837-1840 *4022.20 p293*
  *Wife:*Catherine
  *Child:*Evan
  With daughter
  With relatives
Williams, William *SEE* Williams, George D.
Williams, William 25; Ontario, 1871 *1823.17 p176*
Williams, William 29; Ontario, 1871 *1823.21 p395*
Williams, William 35; Ontario, 1871 *1823.21 p395*
Williams, William 36; Ontario, 1871 *1823.21 p395*
Williams, William 66; Ontario, 1871 *1823.21 p395*
Williams, William; Washington, 1882 *2770.40 p136*
Williams, William, Sr.; Marston's Wharf, 1781 *8529.30 p17*
Williams, William Geo; Colorado, 1901 *1029.59 p95*

Williams, William J.; Ohio, 1841 4022.20 p294
*Wife:*Mary
With 5 children
Williams, Winnie *SEE* Williams, Anne
Williams, Zechariah 49; Ontario, 1871 1823.21 p395
Williamsen, Peter; Louisiana, 1874-1875 4981.45 p130
Williamson, Andrew; North Carolina, 1775 1422.10 p57
Williamson, Andrew 30; Ontario, 1871 1823.17 p176
Williamson, Ann; America, 1761 1220.12 p883
Williamson, Anthony; America, 1764 1220.12 p883
Williamson, Benjamin; South Carolina, 1800-1899 6155.4 p19
Williamson, Catherine; America, 1739 1220.12 p883
Williamson, David; America, 1768 1220.12 p883
Williamson, David 46; Ontario, 1871 1823.17 p176
Williamson, David 55; Ontario, 1871 1823.17 p176
Williamson, David 66; Ontario, 1871 1823.21 p395
Williamson, E. 31; Ontario, 1871 1823.17 p176
Williamson, Edward; America, 1745 1220.12 p883
Williamson, Eleanor; America, 1766 1220.12 p883
Williamson, Henry; America, 1722 1220.12 p883
Williamson, Henry 56; Ontario, 1871 1823.17 p176
Williamson, James; America, 1746 1220.12 p883
Williamson, James; Annapolis, MD, 1726 1220.12 p883
Williamson, James; Potomac, 1731 1220.12 p883
Williamson, James; South Carolina, 1808 6155.4 p19
Williamson, James; Virginia, 1735 1220.12 p883
Williamson, Jane 55; Ontario, 1871 1823.21 p395
Williamson, John; America, 1693 1220.12 p883
Williamson, John; America, 1718 1220.12 p883
Williamson, John; America, 1739 1220.12 p883
Williamson, John; America, 1754 1220.12 p883
Williamson, John; America, 1755 1220.12 p883
Williamson, John; America, 1764 1220.12 p883
Williamson, John; America, 1775 1220.12 p883
Williamson, John 36; Ontario, 1871 1823.21 p395
Williamson, John 40; Ontario, 1871 1823.21 p395
Williamson, John 47; Ontario, 1871 1823.17 p176
Williamson, John 48; Ontario, 1871 1823.17 p176
Williamson, John 61; Ontario, 1871 1823.17 p176
Williamson, John; South Carolina, 1807 6155.4 p19
Williamson, John; Toronto, 1844 2910.35 p113
Williamson, Joseph; America, 1715 1220.12 p883
Williamson, Joseph; America, 1719 1220.12 p883
Williamson, Joseph; America, 1756 1220.12 p883
Williamson, Mary; America, 1769 1220.12 p883
Williamson, Richard 60; Ontario, 1871 1823.17 p176
Williamson, Robert; America, 1750 1220.12 p883
Williamson, Sarah; America, 1743 1220.12 p883
Williamson, Shadrack; America, 1764 1220.12 p883
Williamson, Thomas; America, 1765 1220.12 p883
Williamson, Thomas; America, 1770 1220.12 p883
Williamson, Thomas; Maryland, 1726 1220.12 p883
Williamson, William; America, 1738 1220.12 p883
Williamson, William; America, 1755 1220.12 p883
Williamson, William 40; Ontario, 1871 1823.21 p395
Williamson, William 52; Ontario, 1871 1823.17 p176
Willicks, David; New York, 1778 8529.30 p17
Willicomb, William; Maryland, 1735 1220.12 p883
Willier, Elianor; West Indies, 1686 1220.12 p883
Willinborg, Francis; Ohio, 1809-1852 4511.35 p59
Willing, John; America, 1730 1220.12 p884
Willing, Matthew 29; Ontario, 1871 1823.21 p395
Willinger, Richard; America, 1716 1220.12 p884
Willingham, John; America, 1768 1220.12 p884
Willington, John; America, 1767 1220.12 p884
Willington, Thomas; America, 1766 1220.12 p884
Willington, William; Charles Town, SC, 1719 1220.12 p884
Willins, Sarah; America, 1754 1220.12 p884
Williquet, Marie Jos.; Wisconsin, 1856 1495.20 p56
Willis, Anthony; Barbados, 1664 1220.12 p884
Willis, Arnessa 40; Ontario, 1871 1823.21 p395
Willis, Benjamin; America, 1768 1220.12 p884
Willis, C.; Quebec, 1870 8364.32 p26
Willis, Dulick; America, 1750 1220.12 p884
Willis, E.; Quebec, 1870 8364.32 p26
Willis, Eleanor; America, 1736 1220.12 p884
Willis, George; America, 1766 1220.12 p884
Willis, George 60; Ontario, 1871 1823.17 p176
Willis, Henry; Quebec, 1870 8364.32 p26
Willis, Israel; America, 1726 1220.12 p884
Willis, Jacob; America, 1768 1220.12 p884
Willis, James; America, 1735 1220.12 p884
Willis, James; America, 1740 1220.12 p884
Willis, James; America, 1759 1220.12 p884
Willis, James; Virginia, 1652 6254.4 p243
Willis, Jane; America, 1769 1220.12 p884
Willis, John; America, 1685 1220.12 p884
Willis, John; America, 1746 1220.12 p884
Willis, John; America, 1756 1220.12 p884
Willis, John; America, 1770 1220.12 p884
Willis, John; America, 1775 1220.12 p884
Willis, Leonard; Virginia, 1762 1220.12 p884
Willis, Lydia; America, 1757 1220.12 p884
Willis, Mary; America, 1747 1220.12 p884
Willis, Richard; America, 1721 1220.12 p884
Willis, Richard 55; Ontario, 1871 1823.17 p176
Willis, Robert; America, 1685 1220.12 p884
Willis, Robert 66; Ontario, 1871 1823.17 p176
Willis, Samuel; America, 1739 1220.12 p884
Willis, Samuel; St. Augustine, FL, 1777 8529.30 p10A
Willis, Sarah; America, 1752 1220.12 p884
Willis, Sarah; America, 1754 1220.12 p884
Willis, Sarah; America, 1761 1220.12 p884
Willis, Tho. 19; Virginia, 1635 1183.3 p31
Willis, Thomas; America, 1768 1220.12 p884
Willis, Thomas; Barbados, 1683 1220.12 p884
Willis, Thomas; Maryland, 1670-1699 9228.50 p655
Willis, William; Barbados, 1668 1220.12 p884
Willis, William; Boston, 1776 8529.30 p5A
Willis, William; Maryland, 1744 1220.12 p884
Willis, William 54; Ontario, 1871 1823.21 p396
Willison, William; America, 1719 1220.12 p884
Willkomm, Nikolaus; America, 1881 5475.1 p343
Willman, Gustaf; Illinois, 1864 4487.25 p76
Willmore, Sarah; America, 1695 1220.12 p885
Willmott, Derry; Died enroute, 1734 1220.12 p885
Willmott, Jonas; Barbados or Jamaica, 1694 1220.12 p885
Willmott, Thomas; Virginia, 1732 1220.12 p885
Willms, Fridrich 55; Indiana, 1885-1887 9076.20 p71
Willnose, John; America, 1765 1220.12 p884
Willoghs, C. F. H.; Ohio, 1809-1852 4511.35 p59
Willoughby, Elizabeth 84; Ontario, 1871 1823.17 p176
Willoughby, Francis 41; Ontario, 1871 1823.17 p176
Willoughby, Frank 45; Ontario, 1871 1823.17 p176
Willoughby, John; America, 1732 1220.12 p884
Willoughby, Mary; Charles Town, SC, 1719 1220.12 p884
Willoughby, Thomas; America, 1767 1220.12 p884
Willoughby, Thomas 52; Ontario, 1871 1823.17 p176
Willoughby, Thomas 54; Ontario, 1871 1823.17 p176
Willoughby, William; America, 1763 1220.12 p884
Willows, Thomas 28; Ontario, 1871 1823.21 p396
Willpponen, Otto 39; Minnesota, 1923 2769.54 p1384
Wills, Benjamin; America, 1757 1220.12 p884
Wills, Ezechiel; Barbados, 1681 1220.12 p884
Wills, F. S. 25; Ontario, 1871 1823.21 p396
Wills, Henry 56; Ontario, 1871 1823.21 p396
Wills, Hugh; America, 1734 1220.12 p885
Wills, Johann Friedrich; America, 1884 7420.1 p346
Wills, Joseph; America, 1733 1220.12 p885
Wills, Joseph; America, 1741 1220.12 p885
Wills, Mary; America, 1734 1220.12 p885
Wills, Richard; America, 1760 1220.12 p885
Wills, Richard; America, 1773 1220.12 p885
Wills, Robert; America, 1742 1220.12 p885
Wills, Samuel; America, 1760 1220.12 p885
Wills, Stephen; Louisiana, 1874 4981.45 p134
Wills, Thomas; America, 1748 1220.12 p885
Wills, Thomas; Virginia, 1740 1220.12 p885
Wills, Thomas; Virginia, 1741 1220.12 p885
Wills, William; America, 1685 1220.12 p885
Wills, William; America, 1775 1220.12 p885
Willshire, James 37; Ontario, 1871 1823.17 p177
Willshire, Mary; Rappahannock, VA, 1729 1220.12 p890
Willshire, Thomas; America, 1749 1220.12 p890
Willson, . . . 45; Ontario, 1871 1823.21 p396
Willson, Amanda 23; Ontario, 1871 1823.21 p396
Willson, Andw.; Prince Edward Island, 1771 3799.30 p41
Willson, Ann; America, 1742 1220.12 p885
Willson, George 40; Ontario, 1871 1823.21 p396
Willson, James; Potomac, 1731 1220.12 p886
Willson, Jane 80; Ontario, 1871 1823.17 p177
Willson, John; America, 1770 1220.12 p887
Willson, John; Barbados, 1698 1220.12 p887
Willson, John 30; Ontario, 1871 1823.21 p396
Willson, John 50; Ontario, 1871 1823.21 p396
Willson, John 63; Ontario, 1871 1823.21 p396
Willson, Joseph; America, 1741 1220.12 p887
Willson, Margaret 49; Ontario, 1871 1823.21 p396
Willson, Roger; New York, 1782 8529.30 p17
Willson, Thomas; America, 1755 1220.12 p889
Willson, Thomas; Long Island, 1781 8529.30 p10A
Willson, Thomas 48; Ontario, 1871 1823.21 p396
Willson, Thompson 80; Ontario, 1871 1823.21 p396
Willson, William 35; Ontario, 1871 1823.21 p396
Willson, William 35; Ontario, 1871 1823.21 p396
Willy, Elizabeth; America, 1775 1220.12 p874
Wilmann, Mr.; America, 1866 7420.1 p252
With father & family
Wilmart, Dieudonne; Wisconsin, 1854-1858 1495.20 p66
*Wife:*Marie Francoise Vince
*Daughter:*Marie Josephe
*Daughter:*Marie Antoinette
*Daughter:*Marie Desiree
Wilmart, Marie Antoinette *SEE* Wilmart, Dieudonne
Wilmart, Marie Desiree *SEE* Wilmart, Dieudonne
Wilmart, Marie Francoise Vince *SEE* Wilmart, Dieudonne
Wilmart, Marie Josephe *SEE* Wilmart, Dieudonne
Wilmer, Charles; America, 1675 1220.12 p885
Wilmes, Sophia; America, 1923 8023.44 p380
Wilmore, Charles T.; Colorado, 1891 1029.59 p96
Wilmore, Edward 50; Ontario, 1871 1823.21 p396
Wilmore, Elizabeth; America, 1741 1220.12 p885
Wilmore, Emma; Colorado, 1889 1029.59 p96
Wilmore, George F.; Colorado, 1891 1029.59 p96
Wilmore, George T.; Colorado, 1891 1029.59 p96
Wilmore, John; America, 1756 1220.12 p885
Wilmore, Joseph; America, 1720 1220.12 p885
Wilmore, Sarah; America, 1750 1220.12 p885
Wilmot, Cuckold; America, 1768 1220.12 p885
Wilmot, Elizabeth; America, 1763 1220.12 p885
Wilmot, Henry; America, 1768 1220.12 p885
Wilmot, James; America, 1738 1220.12 p885
Wilmot, Maximillian; Ohio, 1809-1852 4511.35 p59
Wilmot, Servatus; Ohio, 1809-1852 4511.35 p59
Wilmot, William; America, 1764 1220.12 p885
Wilmott, Edward; America, 1685 1220.12 p885
Wilmott, Elizabeth; Virginia, 1729 1220.12 p885
Wilmott, John; America, 1726 1220.12 p885
Wilmott, Stephen; Maryland, 1737 1220.12 p885
Wilmott, Thomas; Maryland, 1731 1220.12 p885
Wilmott, William; Barbados, 1676 1220.12 p885
Wilniski, Charley; Texas, 1886 6015.15 p30
Wilpers, Heinrich 32; Galveston, TX, 1845 3967.10 p377
Wilse, John; America, 1756 1220.12 p885
Wilse, Thomas; America, 1675 1220.12 p885
Wilsenbeck, Leonhard; America, 1700-1899 179.55 p19
Wilshere, Sarah; Jamaica, 1661 1220.12 p890
Wilshire, Thomas; Annapolis, MD, 1723 1220.12 p890
Wilson, Alexander; America, 1769 1220.12 p885
Wilson, Alexander; North Carolina, 1827 1088.45 p37
Wilson, Alexander 55; Ontario, 1871 1823.17 p177
Wilson, Alexander 73; Ontario, 1871 1823.17 p177
Wilson, Alma Ch.; Minnesota, 1883-1885 1865.50 p114
Wilson, Anderson; Ohio, 1844 2763.1 p22
Wilson, Andrew 60; Ontario, 1871 1823.21 p396
Wilson, Ann; America, 1695 1220.12 p885
Wilson, Ann; America, 1733 1220.12 p885
Wilson, Ann; America, 1740 1220.12 p885
Wilson, Ann; America, 1750 1220.12 p885
Wilson, Ann; America, 1775 1220.12 p885
Wilson, Ann; Annapolis, MD, 1731 1220.12 p885
Wilson, Ann; Maryland, 1737 1220.12 p885
Wilson, Ann; Potomac, 1743 1220.12 p885
Wilson, Ann; St. Johns, N.F., 1825 1053.15 p7
Wilson, Ann; Virginia, 1758 1220.12 p885
Wilson, Anne; Annapolis, MD, 1725 1220.12 p885
Wilson, Anne; St. Johns, N.F., 1825 1053.15 p6
Wilson, Arth; Jamestown, VA, 1633 1658.20 p211
Wilson, Aurthur 77; Ontario, 1871 1823.21 p396
Wilson, Benjamin; America, 1766 1220.12 p885
Wilson, Benjamin; America, 1766 1220.12 p886
Wilson, Benjamin 37; Ontario, 1871 1823.17 p177
Wilson, C.; Louisiana, 1874-1875 4981.45 p130
Wilson, Casper; St. Johns, N.F., 1825 1053.15 p6
Wilson, Catharine; New York, 1852 8513.31 p435
Wilson, Catharine 48; Ontario, 1871 1823.21 p396
Wilson, Cecilia; America, 1742 1220.12 p886
Wilson, Charles; America, 1754 1220.12 p886
Wilson, Charles; America, 1774 1220.12 p886
Wilson, Charles 25; Ontario, 1871 1823.17 p177
Wilson, Charles 27; Ontario, 1871 1823.17 p177
Wilson, Charles 31; Ontario, 1871 1823.21 p396
Wilson, Charles 42; Ontario, 1871 1823.17 p177
Wilson, Charles 50; Ontario, 1871 1823.21 p396
Wilson, Christopher; America, 1734 1220.12 p886
Wilson, Clara; St. Louis, 1895-1983 9228.50 p476
Wilson, Darby; St. Johns, N.F., 1825 1053.15 p6
Wilson, David; America, 1721 1220.12 p886
Wilson, David; America, 1763 1220.12 p886
Wilson, David; Missouri, 1903 3276.1 p4
Wilson, David 38; North Carolina, 1774 1422.10 p54
Wilson, David 18; Ontario, 1871 1823.21 p397
Wilson, David 68; Ontario, 1871 1823.17 p177
Wilson, Donald 55; Ontario, 1871 1823.21 p397
Wilson, Edward; America, 1694 1220.12 p886
Wilson, Edward; America, 1753 1220.12 p886
Wilson, Edward; America, 1754 1220.12 p886
Wilson, Edward; America, 1757 1220.12 p886
Wilson, Edward; America, 1761 1220.12 p886
Wilson, Edward; America, 1767 1220.12 p886
Wilson, Edward; America, 1773 1220.12 p886
Wilson, Edward 34; Ontario, 1871 1823.21 p397
Wilson, Edward 55; Ontario, 1871 1823.17 p177

Wilson, Edward F. 26; Ontario, 1871 ***1823.17*** *p177*
Wilson, Edwin 16; Quebec, 1870 ***8364.32*** *p26*
Wilson, Eleanor; America, 1753 ***1220.12*** *p886*
Wilson, Elizabeth; America, 1741 ***1220.12*** *p886*
Wilson, Elizabeth; America, 1767 ***1220.12*** *p886*
Wilson, Elizabeth; America, 1773 ***1220.12*** *p886*
Wilson, Elizabeth; Barbados, 1668 ***1220.12*** *p886*
Wilson, Elizabeth; Barbados or Jamaica, 1686 ***1220.12*** *p886*
Wilson, Elizabeth; Barbados or Jamaica, 1691 ***1220.12*** *p886*
Wilson, Elizabeth; Barbados or Jamaica, 1698 ***1220.12*** *p886*
Wilson, Elizabeth 44; Ontario, 1871 ***1823.17*** *p177*
Wilson, Ephraim 51; Ontario, 1871 ***1823.17*** *p177*
Wilson, Ezekiel; America, 1766 ***1220.12*** *p886*
Wilson, Fleming 42; Ontario, 1871 ***1823.17*** *p177*
Wilson, Francis 50; Ontario, 1871 ***1823.21*** *p397*
Wilson, Francis E. 35; Ontario, 1871 ***1823.21*** *p397*
Wilson, George; America, 1719 ***1220.12*** *p886*
Wilson, George; America, 1744 ***1220.12*** *p886*
Wilson, George; America, 1767 ***1220.12*** *p886*
Wilson, George; America, 1775 ***1220.12*** *p886*
Wilson, George; Barbados, 1677 ***1220.12*** *p886*
Wilson, George 62; Michigan, 1880 ***4491.42*** *p29*
Wilson, George 2; Ontario, 1871 ***1823.21*** *p397*
Wilson, George 26; Ontario, 1871 ***1823.17*** *p177*
Wilson, George 42; Ontario, 1871 ***1823.17*** *p177*
Wilson, George 48; Ontario, 1871 ***1823.21*** *p397*
Wilson, George; Texas, 1900-1980 ***9228.50*** *p476*
Wilson, George W.; Washington, 1884 ***2770.40*** *p193*
Wilson, Gilbert; Maryland, 1719 ***1220.12*** *p886*
Wilson, Gilbert 55; Ontario, 1871 ***1823.21*** *p397*
Wilson, Grace 44; Ontario, 1871 ***1823.17*** *p177*
Wilson, Hannah; America, 1754 ***1220.12*** *p886*
Wilson, Hannah; Virginia, 1741 ***1220.12*** *p886*
Wilson, Harvey 39; Ontario, 1871 ***1823.17*** *p177*
Wilson, Henry; America, 1734 ***1220.12*** *p886*
Wilson, Henry; America, 1757 ***1220.12*** *p886*
Wilson, Henry; America, 1760 ***1220.12*** *p886*
Wilson, Henry; America, 1774 ***1220.12*** *p886*
Wilson, Henry; Colorado, 1863 ***1029.59*** *p96*
Wilson, Henry 46; Ontario, 1871 ***1823.21*** *p397*
Wilson, Hugh 20; Ontario, 1871 ***1823.21*** *p397*
Wilson, Isaac 49; Ontario, 1871 ***1823.21*** *p397*
Wilson, Isabella 44; Ontario, 1871 ***1823.17*** *p177*
Wilson, James; America, 1733 ***1220.12*** *p886*
Wilson, James; America, 1752 ***1220.12*** *p886*
Wilson, James; America, 1754 ***1220.12*** *p886*
Wilson, James; America, 1755 ***1220.12*** *p886*
Wilson, James; America, 1757 ***1220.12*** *p886*
Wilson, James; America, 1773 ***1220.12*** *p886*
Wilson, James; Annapolis, MD, 1719 ***1220.12*** *p886*
Wilson, James; Barbados, 1675 ***1220.12*** *p886*
Wilson, James; Canada, 1774 ***3036.5*** *p41*
Wilson, James; Iowa, 1909 ***1211.15*** *p20*
Wilson, James; Maryland, 1737 ***1220.12*** *p886*
Wilson, James 44; Michigan, 1880 ***4491.39*** *p32*
Wilson, James; North Carolina, 1841 ***1088.45*** *p37*
Wilson, James 18; North Carolina, 1774 ***1422.10*** *p54*
Wilson, James 34; Ontario, 1871 ***1823.17*** *p177*
Wilson, James 40; Ontario, 1871 ***1823.21*** *p397*
Wilson, James 46; Ontario, 1871 ***1823.17*** *p177*
Wilson, James 48; Ontario, 1871 ***1823.17*** *p177*
Wilson, James; Port uncertain, 1720 ***1220.12*** *p886*
Wilson, James 48; South Carolina, 1812 ***3476.30*** *p13*
Wilson, Jane; America, 1723 ***1220.12*** *p886*
Wilson, Jane; America, 1768 ***1220.12*** *p887*
Wilson, Jane; America, 1772 ***1220.12*** *p887*
Wilson, Jane; St. Johns, N.F., 1825 ***1053.15*** *p6*
Wilson, Jane; St. Johns, N.F., 1825 ***1053.15*** *p7*
Wilson, Jasper; America, 1744 ***1220.12*** *p887*
Wilson, Jennie 18; Ontario, 1871 ***1823.21*** *p397*
Wilson, Jeremiah; America, 1754 ***1220.12*** *p887*
Wilson, John; America, 1685 ***1220.12*** *p887*
Wilson, John; America, 1687 ***1220.12*** *p887*
Wilson, John; America, 1727 ***1220.12*** *p887*
Wilson, John; America, 1733 ***1220.12*** *p887*
Wilson, John; America, 1740 ***1220.12*** *p887*
Wilson, John; America, 1741 ***1220.12*** *p887*
Wilson, John; America, 1743 ***1220.12*** *p887*
Wilson, John; America, 1746 ***1220.12*** *p887*
Wilson, John; America, 1750 ***1220.12*** *p887*
Wilson, John; America, 1755 ***1220.12*** *p887*
Wilson, John; America, 1757 ***1220.12*** *p887*
Wilson, John; America, 1764 ***1220.12*** *p887*
Wilson, John; America, 1767 ***1220.12*** *p887*
Wilson, John; America, 1769 ***1220.12*** *p887*
Wilson, John; America, 1771 ***1220.12*** *p887*
Wilson, John; America, 1772 ***1220.12*** *p887*
Wilson, John; America, 1773 ***1220.12*** *p887*
Wilson, John; America, 1775 ***1220.12*** *p887*
Wilson, John; Annapolis, MD, 1725 ***1220.12*** *p887*
Wilson, John 31; Baltimore, 1775 ***1220.12*** *p887*
Wilson, John; Barbados, 1677 ***1220.12*** *p887*
Wilson, John; Barbados, 1692 ***1220.12*** *p887*
Wilson, John; Barbados or Jamaica, 1690 ***1220.12*** *p887*
Wilson, John; Barbados or Jamaica, 1712 ***1220.12*** *p887*
Wilson, John; Cleveland, OH, 1869-1879 ***9722.10*** *p128*
Wilson, John; Marston's Wharf, 1782 ***8529.30*** *p17*
Wilson, John; Missouri, 1894 ***3276.1*** *p4*
Wilson, John 17; New York, NY, 1821 ***6178.50*** *p75*
Wilson, John; North Carolina, 1828 ***1088.45*** *p37*
Wilson, John; North Carolina, 1838 ***1088.45*** *p37*
Wilson, John; Ohio, 1809-1852 ***4511.35*** *p59*
Wilson, John; Ohio, 1833 ***3580.20*** *p34*
Wilson, John; Ohio, 1833 ***6020.12*** *p23*
Wilson, John; Ohio, 1836 ***2763.1*** *p22*
Wilson, John 23; Ontario, 1871 ***1823.21*** *p397*
Wilson, John 27; Ontario, 1871 ***1823.17*** *p177*
Wilson, John 28; Ontario, 1871 ***1823.21*** *p397*
Wilson, John 30; Ontario, 1871 ***1823.17*** *p177*
Wilson, John 32; Ontario, 1871 ***1823.21*** *p397*
Wilson, John 35; Ontario, 1871 ***1823.17*** *p177*
Wilson, John 40; Ontario, 1871 ***1823.17*** *p177*
Wilson, John 42; Ontario, 1871 ***1823.21*** *p397*
Wilson, John 42; Ontario, 1871 ***1823.21*** *p397*
Wilson, John 45; Ontario, 1871 ***1823.21*** *p397*
Wilson, John 47; Ontario, 1871 ***1823.21*** *p397*
Wilson, John 49; Ontario, 1871 ***1823.17*** *p177*
Wilson, John 50; Ontario, 1871 ***1823.17*** *p177*
Wilson, John 59; Ontario, 1871 ***1823.21*** *p397*
Wilson, John 60; Ontario, 1871 ***1823.17*** *p177*
Wilson, John 60; Ontario, 1871 ***1823.21*** *p397*
Wilson, John 64; Ontario, 1871 ***1823.21*** *p397*
Wilson, John 72; Ontario, 1871 ***1823.21*** *p397*
Wilson, John; St. Johns, N.F., 1825 ***1053.15*** *p6*
Wilson, John; Virginia, 1723 ***1220.12*** *p887*
Wilson, John; Virginia, 1760 ***1220.12*** *p887*
Wilson, John; Virginia, 1771 ***1220.12*** *p887*
Wilson, John; Washington, 1882 ***2770.40*** *p136*
Wilson, John L. 35; Ontario, 1871 ***1823.17*** *p177*
Wilson, John M. 48; Ontario, 1871 ***1823.17*** *p177*
Wilson, Johnston 50; Ontario, 1871 ***1823.21*** *p397*
Wilson, Joseph; America, 1726 ***1220.12*** *p887*
Wilson, Joseph; America, 1749 ***1220.12*** *p887*
Wilson, Joseph; America, 1752 ***1220.12*** *p887*
Wilson, Joseph; America, 1757 ***1220.12*** *p887*
Wilson, Joseph; America, 1761 ***1220.12*** *p887*
Wilson, Joseph; America, 1770 ***1220.12*** *p887*
Wilson, Joseph; America, 1773 ***1220.12*** *p887*
Wilson, Joseph; America, 1775 ***1220.12*** *p888*
Wilson, Joseph 24; Ontario, 1871 ***1823.21*** *p397*
Wilson, Joseph 31; Ontario, 1871 ***1823.21*** *p398*
Wilson, Joseph; Philadelphia, 1858 ***8513.31*** *p433*
*Wife:*Phebe Marshall
Wilson, Lars Christian; Iowa, 1909 ***1211.15*** *p20*
Wilson, Laurence 50; Ontario, 1871 ***1823.21*** *p398*
Wilson, Little 36; Ontario, 1871 ***1823.21*** *p398*
Wilson, Margaret; America, 1721 ***1220.12*** *p888*
Wilson, Margaret; America, 1739 ***1220.12*** *p888*
Wilson, Margaret; America, 1747 ***1220.12*** *p888*
Wilson, Margaret; America, 1775 ***1220.12*** *p888*
Wilson, Margaret; Annapolis, MD, 1722 ***1220.12*** *p888*
Wilson, Margaret 49; Michigan, 1880 ***4491.42*** *p29*
Wilson, Margaret; Philadelphia, 1852 ***8513.31*** *p310*
Wilson, Margaret; Philadelphia, 1852 ***8513.31*** *p310*
Wilson, Margaret; Virginia, 1721 ***1220.12*** *p888*
Wilson, Maria; America, 1770 ***1220.12*** *p888*
Wilson, Maria; St. Johns, N.F., 1825 ***1053.15*** *p6*
Wilson, Maria; St. Paul, MN, 1882 ***1865.50*** *p115*
Wilson, Martha; Barbados or Jamaica, 1692 ***1220.12*** *p888*
Wilson, Mary; America, 1733 ***1220.12*** *p888*
Wilson, Mary; America, 1744 ***1220.12*** *p888*
Wilson, Mary; America, 1752 ***1220.12*** *p888*
Wilson, Mary; America, 1754 ***1220.12*** *p888*
Wilson, Mary; America, 1756 ***1220.12*** *p888*
Wilson, Mary; America, 1757 ***1220.12*** *p888*
Wilson, Mary; America, 1770 ***1220.12*** *p888*
Wilson, Mary; America, 1771 ***1220.12*** *p888*
Wilson, Mary; Charles Town, SC, 1719 ***1220.12*** *p888*
Wilson, Mary; Jamaica, 1716 ***1220.12*** *p888*
Wilson, Mary; Maryland, 1674-1675 ***1236.25*** *p51*
Wilson, Mary; Maryland, 1719 ***1220.12*** *p888*
Wilson, Mary; Maryland, 1744 ***1220.12*** *p888*
Wilson, Mary; Maryland or Virginia, 1738 ***1220.12*** *p888*
Wilson, Mary 49; Ontario, 1871 ***1823.17*** *p177*
Wilson, Mary 52; Ontario, 1871 ***1823.21*** *p398*
Wilson, Mary 87; Ontario, 1871 ***1823.21*** *p398*
Wilson, Mary A. 6; Ontario, 1871 ***1823.17*** *p177*
Wilson, Matthew; America, 1764 ***1220.12*** *p888*
Wilson, Michael 15; Quebec, 1870 ***8364.32*** *p26*
Wilson, Morgan 46; Ontario, 1871 ***1823.21*** *p398*
Wilson, Moses 40; Ontario, 1871 ***1823.21*** *p398*
Wilson, Moses 43; Ontario, 1871 ***1823.21*** *p398*
Wilson, Nathaniel; America, 1752 ***1220.12*** *p888*
Wilson, Nicholas 44; Ontario, 1871 ***1823.21*** *p398*
Wilson, Owen; America, 1739 ***1220.12*** *p888*
Wilson, Peter; Maryland, 1721 ***1220.12*** *p888*
Wilson, Peter 50; Ontario, 1871 ***1823.21*** *p398*
Wilson, Phebe Marshall *SEE* Wilson, Joseph
Wilson, Richard; America, 1675 ***1220.12*** *p888*
Wilson, Richard; America, 1735 ***1220.12*** *p888*
Wilson, Richard; America, 1772 ***1220.12*** *p888*
Wilson, Richard; Barbados, 1665 ***1220.12*** *p888*
Wilson, Richard; Maryland, 1734 ***1220.12*** *p888*
Wilson, Richard 38; Ontario, 1871 ***1823.21*** *p398*
Wilson, Richard 50; Ontario, 1871 ***1823.17*** *p178*
Wilson, Richard 54; Ontario, 1871 ***1823.21*** *p398*
Wilson, Richard 68; Ontario, 1871 ***1823.17*** *p178*
Wilson, Richard; Virginia, 1735 ***1220.12*** *p888*
Wilson, Richard; West Indies, 1686 ***1220.12*** *p888*
Wilson, Robert; America, 1738 ***1220.12*** *p888*
Wilson, Robert; America, 1740 ***1220.12*** *p888*
Wilson, Robert; America, 1746 ***1220.12*** *p888*
Wilson, Robert; America, 1749 ***1220.12*** *p888*
Wilson, Robert; America, 1767 ***1220.12*** *p888*
Wilson, Robert; Barbados, 1682 ***1220.12*** *p888*
Wilson, Robert; Ohio, 1843 ***2763.1*** *p22*
Wilson, Robert 25; Ontario, 1871 ***1823.21*** *p398*
Wilson, Robert 31; Ontario, 1871 ***1823.17*** *p178*
Wilson, Robert 62; Ontario, 1871 ***1823.21*** *p398*
Wilson, Robert; St. Johns, N.F., 1825 ***1053.15*** *p6*
Wilson, Robert; St. Johns, N.F., 1825 ***1053.15*** *p7*
Wilson, Robert; Virginia, 1734 ***1220.12*** *p888*
Wilson, Robert; Virginia, 1736 ***1220.12*** *p888*
Wilson, Robert A.; Washington, 1887 ***2770.40*** *p25*
Wilson, Rosa 40; Ontario, 1871 ***1823.17*** *p178*
Wilson, Samuel; America, 1722 ***1220.12*** *p888*
Wilson, Samuel; America, 1772 ***1220.12*** *p889*
Wilson, Samuel; America, 1774 ***1220.12*** *p889*
Wilson, Samuel; Barbados, 1671 ***1220.12*** *p888*
Wilson, Samuel; Maryland, 1725 ***1220.12*** *p889*
Wilson, Samuel 15; Ontario, 1871 ***1823.21*** *p398*
Wilson, Samuel 22; Ontario, 1871 ***1823.21*** *p398*
Wilson, Samuel 23; Ontario, 1871 ***1823.17*** *p178*
Wilson, Samuel 44; Ontario, 1871 ***1823.17*** *p178*
Wilson, Samuel 54; Ontario, 1871 ***1823.21*** *p398*
Wilson, Sarah; Rappahannock, VA, 1741 ***1220.12*** *p889*
Wilson, Silas R.; Ohio, 1851 ***3580.20*** *p34*
Wilson, Silas R.; Ohio, 1851 ***6020.12*** *p23*
Wilson, Sophia 50; Ontario, 1871 ***1823.21*** *p398*
Wilson, Stephen; America, 1727 ***1220.12*** *p889*
Wilson, Susan; Barbados or Jamaica, 1688 ***1220.12*** *p889*
Wilson, T. J. 28; Ontario, 1871 ***1823.21*** *p398*
Wilson, Tebay; America, 1750 ***1220.12*** *p889*
Wilson, Thomas; America, 1735 ***1220.12*** *p889*
Wilson, Thomas; America, 1740 ***1220.12*** *p889*
Wilson, Thomas; America, 1742 ***1220.12*** *p889*
Wilson, Thomas; America, 1745 ***1220.12*** *p889*
Wilson, Thomas; America, 1750 ***1220.12*** *p889*
Wilson, Thomas; America, 1765 ***1220.12*** *p889*
Wilson, Thomas; America, 1767 ***1220.12*** *p889*
Wilson, Thomas; America, 1768 ***1220.12*** *p889*
Wilson, Thomas; America, 1769 ***1220.12*** *p889*
Wilson, Thomas; America, 1774 ***1220.12*** *p889*
Wilson, Thomas; Canada, 1774 ***3036.5*** *p41*
Wilson, Thomas; Died enroute, 1731 ***1220.12*** *p889*
Wilson, Thomas; Long Island, 1781 ***8529.30*** *p10A*
Wilson, Thomas; Ohio, 1836 ***2763.1*** *p22*
Wilson, Thomas 30; Ontario, 1871 ***1823.17*** *p178*
Wilson, Thomas 32; Ontario, 1871 ***1823.17*** *p178*
Wilson, Thomas 56; Ontario, 1871 ***1823.21*** *p398*
Wilson, Thomas; Philadelphia, 1777 ***8529.30*** *p7*
Wilson, Thomas 19; Quebec, 1870 ***8364.32*** *p26*
Wilson, Thomas; St. Johns, N.F., 1825 ***1053.15*** *p7*
Wilson, Thomas; Virginia, 1727 ***1220.12*** *p889*
Wilson, Thomas; Virginia, 1734 ***1220.12*** *p889*
Wilson, Thomas Kay; Detroit, 1868 ***7710.1*** *p162*
Wilson, Thos 43; Ontario, 1871 ***1823.21*** *p398*
Wilson, Tycho H.; St. Paul, MN, 1889 ***1865.50*** *p115*
Wilson, William; America, 1687 ***1220.12*** *p889*
Wilson, William; America, 1690 ***1220.12*** *p889*
Wilson, William; America, 1729 ***1220.12*** *p889*
Wilson, William; America, 1733 ***1220.12*** *p889*
Wilson, William; America, 1741 ***1220.12*** *p889*
Wilson, William; America, 1752 ***1220.12*** *p889*
Wilson, William; America, 1754 ***1220.12*** *p889*
Wilson, William; America, 1756 ***1220.12*** *p889*
Wilson, William; America, 1759 ***1220.12*** *p889*
Wilson, William; Annapolis, MD, 1720 ***1220.12*** *p889*
Wilson, William; North Carolina, 1822 ***1088.45*** *p37*
Wilson, William; North Carolina, 1837 ***1088.45*** *p37*
Wilson, William 38; North Carolina, 1774 ***1422.10*** *p54*
Wilson, William; Ohio, 1836 ***2763.1*** *p22*
Wilson, William 26; Ontario, 1871 ***1823.21*** *p398*
Wilson, William 30; Ontario, 1871 ***1823.21*** *p398*
Wilson, William 43; Ontario, 1871 ***1823.21*** *p398*

Wilson, William 50; Ontario, 1871 *1823.17 p178*
Wilson, William 67; Ontario, 1871 *1823.21 p398*
Wilson, William 71; Ontario, 1871 *1823.17 p178*
Wilson, William; Potomac, 1729 *1220.12 p889*
Wilson, William; Virginia, 1772 *1220.12 p889*
Wilson, William, Jr.; Ohio, 1843 *2763.1 p22*
Wilson, William Erwin; Texas, 1886-1966 *9228.50 p476*
Wilson, William M. 24; Indiana, 1881-1882 *9076.20 p70*
Wilson, William Wallace 39; Ontario, 1871 *1823.17 p178*
Wilson, Willis 7; Quebec, 1870 *8364.32 p26*
Wilson, Wm D. 48; Ontario, 1871 *1823.17 p178*
Wilson, Zacariah 45; Ontario, 1871 *1823.17 p178*
Wilson Family ; Virginia, 1804 *9228.50 p21A*
Wilsted, Christian; Washington, 1888 *2770.40 p26*
Wilt, Barbara 15 days; America, 1846 *778.6 p345*
Wilt, Certus 2; America, 1846 *778.6 p345*
Wilt, Marie 33; America, 1846 *778.6 p345*
Wilt, Michel 4; America, 1846 *778.6 p345*
Wilt, Rose 6; America, 1846 *778.6 p345*
Wilt, Xavier 36; America, 1846 *778.6 p345*
Wilthy, George; America, 1736 *1220.12 p889*
Wilton, Daniel 43; Ontario, 1871 *1823.17 p178*
Wilton, James; America, 1767 *1220.12 p889*
Wilton, John 49; Ontario, 1871 *1823.21 p398*
Wilton, John; Virginia, 1767 *1220.12 p889*
Wilton, Richard S. 30; Minnesota, 1923 *2769.54 p1378*
Wilton, Samuel; America, 1772 *1220.12 p889*
Wilton, Thomas 19; Minnesota, 1923 *2769.54 p1378*
Wiltshear, George; America, 1742 *1220.12 p889*
Wiltshire, David; America, 1769 *1220.12 p889*
Wiltshire, Henry; America, 1752 *1220.12 p889*
Wiltshire, Isaac; Virginia, 1744 *1220.12 p889*
Wiltshire, James; Virginia, 1773 *1220.12 p889*
Wiltshire, John; America, 1736 *1220.12 p890*
Wiltshire, John; America, 1756 *1220.12 p890*
Wiltshire, John; America, 1769 *1220.12 p890*
Wiltshire, John; Maryland, 1743 *1220.12 p890*
Wiltshire, Jonathan; Virginia, 1767 *1220.12 p890*
Wiltshire, William; America, 1773 *1220.12 p890*
Wiltshire, William; Barbados, 1703 *1220.12 p890*
Wiltshire, William; Virginia, 1758 *1220.12 p890*
Wiltson, John 43; Ontario, 1871 *1823.21 p398*
Wiltz, Abraham; Ohio, 1809-1852 *4511.35 p59*
Wiltz, Albert *SEE* Wiltz, Georg
Wiltz, Anna 2 *SEE* Wiltz, Nikolaus
Wiltz, Barbara *SEE* Wiltz, Georg
Wiltz, Barbara *SEE* Wiltz, Georg
Wiltz, Georg; America, 1882 *5475.1 p228*
  *Wife:*Barbara
  *Daughter:*Barbara
  *Son:*Albert
  *Son:*Nikolaus
Wiltz, Jacob; Ohio, 1809-1852 *4511.35 p59*
Wiltz, Margarethe 8 *SEE* Wiltz, Nikolaus
Wiltz, Margarethe Kiefer 34 *SEE* Wiltz, Nikolaus
Wiltz, Maria 6 *SEE* Wiltz, Nikolaus
Wiltz, Nikolaus; America, 1867 *5475.1 p195*
  *Wife:*Margarethe Kiefer
  *Son:*Peter
  *Daughter:*Anna
  *Daughter:*Margarethe
  *Daughter:*Maria
Wiltz, Nikolaus *SEE* Wiltz, Georg
Wiltz, Peter 3 *SEE* Wiltz, Nikolaus
Wiltz, Sebastian; Ohio, 1809-1852 *4511.35 p59*
Wilzig, Eugenie 21; New Orleans, 1848 *778.6 p345*
Wilzig, Jacques 22; New Orleans, 1848 *778.6 p345*
Wilzig, Jean Jacques 27; New Orleans, 1848 *778.6 p346*
Wilzinsky, Stanislas 38; New York, NY, 1894 *6512.1 p182*
Wimbleton, William; America, 1733 *1220.12 p890*
Wimer, John; Illinois, 1858 *6079.1 p15*
Wimpisinger, John; Colorado, 1881 *1029.59 p96*
Winafeldt, Valentine; Ohio, 1809-1852 *4511.35 p59*
Winberg, Ida 28; Minnesota, 1925 *2769.54 p1382*
Winberg, William 37; Minnesota, 1925 *2769.54 p1382*
Winblad, Holger; Miami, 1920 *4984.15 p38*
Winch, Ellis; America, 1751 *1220.12 p890*
Winch, Isaac; America, 1769 *1220.12 p890*
Winch, John; America, 1765 *1220.12 p890*
Winchelsea, Donbarty; America, 1766 *1220.12 p890*
Winchester, Henry; Washington, 1888 *2770.40 p26*
Winchester, Thomas; America, 1722 *1220.12 p890*
Winchurch, John; America, 1751 *1220.12 p890*
Winckles, James; America, 1679 *1220.12 p890*
Winckles, Thomas; Ohio, 1840 *2763.1 p22*
Wincks, Joseph; America, 1742 *1220.12 p890*
Winckworth, John; America, 1737 *1220.12 p891*
Winckworth, Nathaniel; Barbados, 1694 *1220.12 p891*
Winckworth, Stephen; America, 1752 *1220.12 p891*
Wind, Mary; America, 1752 *1220.12 p890*
Windall, James 53; Ontario, 1871 *1823.21 p398*

Windeatt, Enoch; Virginia, 1765 *1220.12 p890*
Windel, Carl Wilhelm Christian; America, 1860 *7420.1 p202*
Windell, Elizabeth; America, 1755 *1220.12 p890*
Windell, Samuel 29; Ontario, 1871 *1823.21 p398*
Windemuth, Wilh.; Valdivia, Chile, 1852 *1192.4 p54*
Winder, Edward 59; Ontario, 1871 *1823.21 p398*
Winder, George; Barbados or Jamaica, 1693 *1220.12 p890*
Winder, Henry 16; Quebec, 1870 *8364.32 p26*
Winder, John; America, 1765 *1220.12 p890*
Winders, Henry 15; Quebec, 1870 *8364.32 p26*
Windett, John; Vermont, 1837 *3274.55 p24*
Windham, John; America, 1744 *1220.12 p890*
Windham, Sarah; America, 1719 *1220.12 p890*
Windheim, Heinrich Friedrich Wilhelm *SEE* Windheim, Johann Heinrich
Windheim, Johann; America, 1854 *7420.1 p133*
Windheim, Johann Heinrich; America, 1872 *7420.1 p298*
  *Son:*Heinrich Friedrich Wilhelm
  With wife 2 daughters & parents
Windheim, Johann Otto; Port uncertain, 1853 *7420.1 p113*
Windheim, Johann Tonnies Gottlieb; America, 1872 *7420.1 p298*
Windle, Francis; America, 1764 *1220.12 p890*
Windler, Christine; America, 1853 *7420.1 p113*
  With son & daughter
Windler, Heinrich Christian; America, 1851 *7420.1 p83*
  With sister
Windmill, Benjamin; Barbados, 1693 *1220.12 p890*
Windmill, John; America, 1721 *1220.12 p890*
Windmill, John 44; Indiana, 1881-1888 *9076.20 p72*
Windnagel, Alb.; Valdivia, Chile, 1852 *1192.4 p54*
Windon, Elizabeth; America, 1770 *1220.12 p890*
Windorn, G. B. 30; Ontario, 1871 *1823.17 p178*
Windover, Flora 12; Ontario, 1871 *1823.17 p178*
Windover, Mary; America, 1740 *1220.12 p890*
Windows, William; America, 1747 *1220.12 p890*
Windram, John; America, 1724 *1220.12 p890*
Windrufva, J.; New York, NY, 1845 *6412.40 p149*
Windsor, Bacon; America, 1743 *1220.12 p890*
Windsor, Geo 47; Ontario, 1871 *1823.21 p398*
Windsor, Jas 49; Ontario, 1871 *1823.21 p398*
Windsor, Joane; Maryland, 1673 *1236.25 p48*
Windsor, Thomas; America, 1768 *1220.12 p890*
Windsor, William; America, 1750 *1220.12 p890*
Windsor, William 47; Ontario, 1871 *1823.21 p399*
Windt, Albert; Wisconsin, 1885 *6795.8 p237*
Windwright, Anne; Barbados, 1675 *1220.12 p890*
Windy, John; Virginia, 1729 *1220.12 p890*
Wineberg Family ; West Virginia, 1850 *1132.30 p147*
Winegar, George; Long Island, 1781 *8529.30 p10A*
Winegarden, Ella 3; Ontario, 1871 *1823.17 p178*
Winegartner, Gustave; Ohio, 1840-1897 *8365.35 p18*
Wineholdt, George; Ohio, 1809-1852 *4511.35 p59*
Winepress, Catherine; America, 1749 *1220.12 p890*
Winer, John 42; Ontario, 1871 *1823.21 p399*
Winermute, Richard 33; Michigan, 1880 *4491.30 p33*
Winfield, Henry; Colorado, 1893 *1029.59 p96*
Winfield, Richard; Annapolis, MD, 1736 *1220.12 p890*
Winfield, William; America, 1764 *1220.12 p890*
Winfield, William; Annapolis, MD, 1722 *1220.12 p890*
Wing, Daniel; America, 1765 *1220.12 p891*
Wing, Fernando 39; Ontario, 1871 *1823.17 p178*
Wing, John; Virginia, 1729 *1220.12 p891*
Wing, Mary 42; Ontario, 1871 *1823.21 p399*
Wing, Tabitha; America, 1700 *1220.12 p891*
Wingar, William; Barbados, 1663 *1220.12 p891*
Wingarden, William 40; Maryland, 1721 *1220.12 p891*
Wingart, John; Ohio, 1809-1852 *4511.35 p59*
Wingate, Dorothy Burwell *SEE* Wingate, Roger
Wingate, Roger; Jamestown, VA, 1633 *1658.20 p211*
  *Wife:*Dorothy Burwell
  With son & daughter
Wingate, Thos 65; Ontario, 1871 *1823.21 p399*
Wingater, Anna 6; Halifax, N.S., 1902 *1860.4 p41*
Wingater, Christian; Halifax, N.S., 1902 *1860.4 p41*
Wingater, Henrich 32; Halifax, N.S., 1902 *1860.4 p41*
Wingater, Melanie 33; Halifax, N.S., 1902 *1860.4 p41*
Wingater, Wandelon 4; Halifax, N.S., 1902 *1860.4 p41*
Wingatt, Dorothy Burwell *SEE* Wingatt, Roger
Wingatt, Roger; Jamestown, VA, 1633 *1658.20 p211*
  *Wife:*Dorothy Burwell
  With son & daughter
Wingcot, Philip; America, 1752 *1220.12 p891*
Wingert, Christian; Ohio, 1809-1852 *4511.35 p59*
Wingert, Joseph; Colorado, 1904 *1029.59 p96*
Wingert, Peter; Ohio, 1809-1852 *4511.35 p59*
Wingertszahn, Barbara *SEE* Wingertszahn, Peter
Wingertszahn, Elisabeth Hesch *SEE* Wingertszahn, Peter
Wingertszahn, J. Baptist *SEE* Wingertszahn, Peter
Wingertszahn, K. Anton *SEE* Wingertszahn, Peter

Wingertszahn, Karl; South America, 1858 *5475.1 p542*
Wingertszahn, Katharina *SEE* Wingertszahn, Peter
Wingertszahn, Peter; America, 1867 *5475.1 p543*
  *Wife:*Elisabeth Hesch
  *Daughter:*Barbara
  *Daughter:*Katharina
  *Son:*K. Anton
  *Son:*J. Baptist
Winget, Sarah 36; Ontario, 1871 *1823.21 p399*
Winget, Wm 39; Ontario, 1871 *1823.21 p399*
Wingfield, James; America, 1746 *1220.12 p891*
Wingfield, James; America, 1765 *1220.12 p891*
Wingfield, Robert; America, 1621 *1220.12 p891*
Wingler, Pierre 28; Texas, 1848 *778.6 p346*
Wingrove, John; America, 1756 *1220.12 p891*
Wingrove, John; America, 1773 *1220.12 p891*
Wingrove, John; America, 1775 *1220.12 p891*
Wingrove, Thomas; America, 1741 *1220.12 p891*
Winholdt, George; Ohio, 1809-1852 *4511.35 p59*
Winholtz, Alfred; St. Paul, MN, 1867-1874 *1865.50 p115*
Winholtz, Mrs. Alfred; St. Paul, MN, 1874 *1865.50 p115*
Winholtz, Peter Adolph; St. Paul, MN, 1869 *1865.50 p115*
Winiarz, Apolonia 25; New York, NY, 1904 *8355.1 p15*
Winino, Henry 43; Ontario, 1871 *1823.17 p178*
Wink, Johannes 38; New Castle, DE, 1817-1818 *90.20 p155*
Wink, R.inhard 21; America, 1846 *778.6 p346*
Winkauf, Christopher; Wisconsin, 1856 *6795.8 p45*
Winke, John 33; Ontario, 1871 *1823.21 p399*
Winkel, Anna; America, 1882 *5475.1 p167*
  *Daughter:*Anna
  *Son:*Anstreicher
  *Daughter:*Elisabeth
  *Son:*Jakob
Winkel, Carl; Valdivia, Chile, 1850 *1192.4 p49*
Winkel, Maria; San Francisco, 1857 *5475.1 p255*
Winkelhake, Widow; America, 1855 *7420.1 p134*
Winkelhake, Widow; America, 1855 *7420.1 p143*
  With family
Winkelhake, Engel Charlotte Wilhelmine *SEE* Winkelhake, Johann Heinrich Christoph
Winkelhake, Johann Friedrich Christian; America, 1850 *7420.1 p78*
Winkelhake, Johann Heinrich Christoph; America, 1845 *7420.1 p41*
  *Daughter:*Engel Charlotte Wilhelmine
  *Wife:*Wilhelmine Dorothee Louise Giseke
Winkelhake, Johann Heinrich Christoph; America, 1846 *7420.1 p51*
  With family
Winkelhake, Wilhelmine Dorothee Louise Giseke *SEE* Winkelhake, Johann Heinrich Christoph
Winkelmeger, Wilhelm 28; America, 1846 *778.6 p346*
Winkett, James; America, 1740 *1220.12 p891*
Winkler, . . .; West Virginia, 1865-1879 *1132.30 p150*
Winkler, Alois; West Virginia, 1871 *1132.30 p149*
Winkler, August de; Miami, 1920 *4984.15 p38*
Winkler, Caroline *SEE* Winkler, Casper
Winkler, Casper; New York, 1872 *1132.30 p150*
  With brother
  *Sister:*Elizabeth
  *Sister:*Wilhelmina
  *Sister:*Mary
  *Sister:*Caroline
Winkler, Christian; North Carolina, 1837 *1088.45 p37*
Winkler, Christopher P.; North Carolina, 1841 *1088.45 p37*
Winkler, Denis 29; Galveston, TX, 1844 *3967.10 p372*
Winkler, Eduard; Valdivia, Chile, 1850 *1192.4 p49*
Winkler, Elizabeth *SEE* Winkler, Casper
Winkler, Franziska 8; Galveston, TX, 1844 *3967.10 p373*
Winkler, Franziska 35; Galveston, TX, 1844 *3967.10 p373*
Winkler, Genovefa 30; Galveston, TX, 1846 *3967.10 p378*
Winkler, Jakob 32; Galveston, TX, 1844 *3967.10 p373*
Winkler, Jakob 67; Galveston, TX, 1846 *3967.10 p378*
Winkler, Joseph 29; Galveston, TX, 1846 *3967.10 p378*
Winkler, Josephine 2; Galveston, TX, 1846 *3967.10 p378*
Winkler, Lisette; America, 1868 *7919.3 p532*
  With 5 children
Winkler, Maria Anna 1; Galveston, TX, 1844 *3967.10 p373*
Winkler, Mary *SEE* Winkler, Casper
Winkler, Wilhelmina *SEE* Winkler, Casper
Winkworth, Hugh; America, 1747 *1220.12 p891*
Winkworth, Jane; America, 1740 *1220.12 p891*
Winlund, O.G.; Cleveland, OH, 1891-1893 *9722.10 p128*
Winmeister, Fohgnner 5; Halifax, N.S., 1902 *1860.4 p41*
Winmeister, Heinrich 1; Halifax, N.S., 1902 *1860.4 p41*

Winmeister, Johannes 28; Halifax, N.S., 1902 ***1860.4*** *p41*
Winmeister, Lisbet 30; Halifax, N.S., 1902 ***1860.4*** *p41*
Winmeister, Marie 3; Halifax, N.S., 1902 ***1860.4*** *p41*
Winn, Alice; Potomac, 1743 ***1220.12*** *p906*
Winn, David; Canada, 1774 ***3036.5*** *p42*
Winn, Katherine; North Carolina, 1710 ***3629.40*** *p9*
Winn, Rosamund; America, 1753 ***1220.12*** *p906*
Winn, Sampson; America, 1769 ***1220.12*** *p906*
Winn, Thomas; America, 1751 ***1220.12*** *p906*
Winn, William; Canada, 1774 ***3036.5*** *p42*
Winne, Anne; America, 1679 ***1220.12*** *p906*
Winne, Christian; Wisconsin, 1880 ***6795.8*** *p108*
Winnegar, George; Long Island, 1781 ***8529.30*** *p10A*
Winnell, Thomas; America, 1751 ***1220.12*** *p891*
Winnet, Henry 40; Ontario, 1871 ***1823.21*** *p399*
Winnett, Jane 43; Ontario, 1871 ***1823.21*** *p399*
Winnett, John 66; Ontario, 1871 ***1823.21*** *p399*
Winnett, Thomas 38; Ontario, 1871 ***1823.21*** *p399*
Winnick, Elizabeth; Potomac, 1729 ***1220.12*** *p891*
Winnicki, Stanislaw; Detroit, 1929 ***1640.55*** *p117*
Winnington, Nathan; Virginia, 1736 ***1220.12*** *p891*
Winnington, Robert; Virginia, 1745 ***1220.12*** *p891*
Winny, Corn's; Ontario, 1787 ***1276.15*** *p231*
Winolem, Georg 50; America, 1841 ***778.6*** *p346*
Winroth, Herman 44; Kansas, 1880 ***777.40*** *p21*
Winsborough, Elizabeth; Virginia, 1763 ***1220.12*** *p891*
Winsey, Harriet; Bridgeport, CT, 1850-1851 ***9228.50*** *p195*
Winship, Thomas 26; North Carolina, 1774 ***1422.10*** *p55*
Winslett, John; America, 1766 ***1220.12*** *p891*
Winslett, Samuel; America, 1766 ***1220.12*** *p891*
Winslow, Edward; Plymouth, MA, 1620 ***1920.45*** *p5*
*Wife:*Elizabeth
Winslow, Elizabeth *SEE* Winslow, Edward
Winslow, George; Virginia, 1741 ***1220.12*** *p891*
Winslow, Gilbart; Plymouth, MA, 1620 ***1920.45*** *p5*
Winslow, Henry; New Jersey, 1864 ***8513.31*** *p433*
*Wife:*Margaret McConnell
Winslow, Jacob B. 51; Ontario, 1871 ***1823.21*** *p399*
Winslow, James 40; Ontario, 1871 ***1823.21*** *p399*
Winslow, James 44; Ontario, 1871 ***1823.21*** *p399*
Winslow, Leslie 19; Quebec, 1910 ***2897.7*** *p7*
Winslow, Margaret McConnell *SEE* Winslow, Henry
Winslow, William 62; Ontario, 1871 ***1823.21*** *p399*
Winson, John; America, 1764 ***1220.12*** *p891*
Winson, William; America, 1728 ***1220.12*** *p891*
Winstanley, Francis; America, 1769 ***1220.12*** *p891*
Winstanley, James; America, 1739 ***1220.12*** *p891*
Winstanley, Peter; America, 1766 ***1220.12*** *p891*
Winstanley, Peter; America, 1770 ***1220.12*** *p891*
Winston, Richard; America, 1727 ***1220.12*** *p891*
Winston, Thomas; Annapolis, MD, 1725 ***1220.12*** *p891*
Winten, Mr.; America, 1853 ***7420.1*** *p113*
With family
Winten, Christine Philippine *SEE* Winten, Friedrich Christian Gottlieb
Winten, Friedrich Christian Gottlieb; America, 1852 ***7420.1*** *p101*
*Sister:*Christine Philippine
Winter, Adelheid *SEE* Winter, Else
Winter, Albert; Louisiana, 1874-1875 ***4981.45*** *p130*
Winter, Ambrose; America, 1685 ***1220.12*** *p891*
Winter, Anton; America, 1882 ***5475.1*** *p221*
Winter, Bernard; America, 1876 ***5475.1*** *p219*
Winter, Bernhard; Wisconsin, 1885 ***6795.8*** *p197*
Winter, Carl Friedrich; Port uncertain, 1861 ***7420.1*** *p210*
Winter, Catherine; America, 1752 ***1220.12*** *p891*
Winter, Conrad; New York, 1860 ***358.56*** *p5*
Winter, Daniel 13; New York, NY, 1894 ***6512.1*** *p231*
Winter, Daniel 48; New York, NY, 1894 ***6512.1*** *p231*
Winter, David 21; Portland, ME, 1906 ***970.38*** *p82*
Winter, Else; Argentina, 1939 ***8023.44*** *p380*
*Sister:*Frieda
*Sister:*Adelheid
*Sister:*Therese
Winter, Ernst; America, 1892 ***2526.42*** *p127*
With relative
Winter, Ernst; America, 1892 ***2526.42*** *p133*
With brother
Winter, Frederick; Ohio, 1809-1852 ***4511.35*** *p59*
Winter, Frieda *SEE* Winter, Else
Winter, Friedrich; America, 1854 ***7420.1*** *p133*
With wife & 3 daughters
Winter, Georg 26; Portland, ME, 1906 ***970.38*** *p82*
Winter, Gotlieb; Ohio, 1809-1852 ***4511.35*** *p59*
Winter, Gottfried; Wisconsin, 1875 ***6795.8*** *p208*
Winter, Gotthilf 15; New York, NY, 1894 ***6512.1*** *p231*
Winter, Gustave; Wisconsin, 1879 ***6795.8*** *p208*
Winter, Herm.; Valdivia, Chile, 1852 ***1192.4*** *p55*
Winter, James; America, 1748 ***1220.12*** *p891*
Winter, Johannes 18; Portland, ME, 1906 ***970.38*** *p82*
Winter, John; America, 1751 ***1220.12*** *p891*
Winter, John; America, 1758 ***1220.12*** *p891*
Winter, John; America, 1767 ***1220.12*** *p891*
Winter, John; New York, 1859 ***358.56*** *p102*
Winter, Justina 47; New York, NY, 1894 ***6512.1*** *p231*
Winter, Kaspar; America, 1882 ***5475.1*** *p166*
Winter, Leopold; Ohio, 1809-1852 ***4511.35*** *p59*
Winter, Lorenz; New Castle, DE, 1817-1818 ***90.20*** *p155*
Winter, Margaret; America, 1758 ***1220.12*** *p891*
Winter, Maria 17; New York, NY, 1894 ***6512.1*** *p231*
Winter, Mathias; America, 1882 ***5475.1*** *p137*
Winter, Michael; America, 1881 ***5475.1*** *p150*
Winter, Michael 45; Ontario, 1871 ***1823.21*** *p399*
Winter, Patrick; Louisiana, 1874 ***4981.45*** *p297*
Winter, Peter; America, 1882 ***5475.1*** *p137*
Winter, Philip; Ohio, 1809-1852 ***4511.35*** *p59*
Winter, Richard; America, 1663 ***1220.12*** *p891*
Winter, Samuel; America, 1748 ***1220.12*** *p891*
Winter, Samuel; America, 1754 ***1220.12*** *p891*
Winter, Therese *SEE* Winter, Else
Winter, Thomas; America, 1734 ***1220.12*** *p892*
Winter, Thomas; America, 1756 ***1220.12*** *p892*
Winter, Thomas; America, 1759 ***1220.12*** *p892*
Winter, Thomas; Annapolis, MD, 1725 ***1220.12*** *p892*
Winter, Thomas; Barbados or Jamaica, 1687 ***1220.12*** *p891*
Winter, Thomas; Maryland, 1740 ***1220.12*** *p892*
Winter, Thomas 21; North Carolina, 1774 ***1422.10*** *p55*
Winter, Thomas; Virginia, 1772 ***1220.12*** *p892*
Winter, William; America, 1736 ***1220.12*** *p892*
Winter, William; America, 1741 ***1220.12*** *p892*
Winter, William; America, 1750 ***1220.12*** *p892*
Winter, William; America, 1764 ***1220.12*** *p892*
Winter, William; America, 1775 ***1220.12*** *p892*
Winterbottom, John; North America, 1750 ***1640.8*** *p233*
Winterbottom, John; Pennsylvania, 1828 ***8513.31*** *p434*
Winterbottom, John; Philadelphia, 1778 ***8529.30*** *p5A*
Winterbottom, Joseph; America, 1720 ***1220.12*** *p892*
Winterbottom, Margaret; America, 1757 ***1220.12*** *p892*
Winterbourne, Elizabeth; America, 1677 ***1220.12*** *p892*
Winterburn, John; America, 1764 ***1220.12*** *p892*
Winterfeld, D.; Venezuela, 1843 ***3899.5*** *p547*
Winterhalter, Alis; Ohio, 1809-1852 ***4511.35*** *p59*
Winterhalter, George; Ohio, 1809-1852 ***4511.35*** *p59*
Winterhalter, Jacob; Ohio, 1809-1852 ***4511.35*** *p59*
Winterhalter, Joseph; Ohio, 1809-1852 ***4511.35*** *p59*
Winterholter, Alis; Ohio, 1809-1852 ***4511.35*** *p59*
Winterholter, Anthony; Ohio, 1809-1852 ***4511.35*** *p59*
Winterholter, Jacob; Ohio, 1809-1852 ***4511.35*** *p59*
Winters, Edward; America, 1775 ***1220.12*** *p892*
Winters, Joseph P.; Colorado, 1891 ***1029.59*** *p96*
Winters, Thomas 55; Ontario, 1871 ***1823.21*** *p399*
Winters, Thomas 65; Ontario, 1871 ***1823.21*** *p399*
Wintersale, Joseph; America, 1768 ***1220.12*** *p892*
Winthrop, Thomas; America, 1768 ***1220.12*** *p892*
Wintle, Samuel; America, 1693 ***1220.12*** *p892*
Winton, Peter; America, 1741 ***1220.12*** *p892*
Wintour, William; America, 1720 ***1220.12*** *p892*
Winwood, Mary; Potomac, 1731 ***1220.12*** *p892*
Winyard, William; Annapolis, MD, 1731 ***1220.12*** *p892*
Winzenburg, Dorothea 56; America, 1852 ***5475.1*** *p74*
Winzenburg, Friedrich; America, 1852 ***5475.1*** *p73*
With family
Winzer, Anna Maria; Venezuela, 1843 ***3899.5*** *p540*
Wiore, Ant. 35; America, 1844 ***778.6*** *p346*
Wipper, Wilhelm; America, 1874 ***8023.44*** *p380*
Wipps, Sebastian 18; Galveston, TX, 1846 ***3967.10*** *p377*
Wir, Henry 43; America, 1845 ***778.6*** *p346*
Wir, Susan 50; America, 1845 ***778.6*** *p346*
Wirch, Bertha; Wisconsin, 1891 ***6795.8*** *p95*
Wirmer, Conrad Friedrich; America, 1840 ***7420.1*** *p21*
Wirmer, Henry J.; Ohio, 1809-1852 ***4511.35*** *p59*
Wirsching, Christoph; America, 1868 ***7919.3*** *p525*
Wirsching, Traugott; America, 1867 ***7919.3*** *p532*
Wirth, Anna 20; Halifax, N.S., 1902 ***1860.4*** *p40*
Wirth, Anna Eva Magdalena; Venezuela, 1843 ***3899.5*** *p542*
Wirth, Anton; Venezuela, 1843 ***3899.5*** *p540*
Wirth, Anton; Venezuela, 1843 ***3899.5*** *p540*
Wirth, Anton; Venezuela, 1843 ***3899.5*** *p542*
Wirth, Barbara *SEE* Wirth, Nikolaus
Wirth, Bertha; Halifax, N.S., 1902 ***1860.4*** *p40*
Wirth, Georg Friedrich Eduard; America, 1871 ***7420.1*** *p293*
Wirth, Heinrich 9; Halifax, N.S., 1902 ***1860.4*** *p40*
Wirth, Helene; Venezuela, 1843 ***3899.5*** *p540*
Wirth, Herman 3; Halifax, N.S., 1902 ***1860.4*** *p40*
Wirth, Josef; America, 1849 ***5475.1*** *p489*
Wirth, Karl 59; Halifax, N.S., 1902 ***1860.4*** *p40*
Wirth, Karolina 4; Halifax, N.S., 1902 ***1860.4*** *p40*
Wirth, Karoline; America, 1892 ***5475.1*** *p39*
*Child:*Klara
*Child:*Alfred
*Child:*Hedwig
Wirth, Kaspar; Venezuela, 1843 ***3899.5*** *p542*
Wirth, Katharina *SEE* Wirth, Nikolaus
Wirth, Margarehte Renkes *SEE* Wirth, Nikolaus
Wirth, Margarethe *SEE* Wirth, Nikolaus
Wirth, Maria *SEE* Wirth, Nikolaus
Wirth, Marianna; Venezuela, 1843 ***3899.5*** *p540*
Wirth, Mathias *SEE* Wirth, Nikolaus
Wirth, Mathilde 17; Halifax, N.S., 1902 ***1860.4*** *p40*
Wirth, Michel *SEE* Wirth, Nikolaus
Wirth, Nikolaus; America, 1880 ***5475.1*** *p213*
*Daughter:*Maria
*Wife:*Margarehte Renkes
*Son:*Michel
*Daughter:*Margarethe
*Daughter:*Katharina
With daughter
*Daughter:*Barbara
*Son:*Mathias
Wirth, Nikolaus 18; America, 1800-1899 ***5475.1*** *p478*
Wirth, Peter; America, 1866 ***5475.1*** *p138*
Wirth, Peter 10; Halifax, N.S., 1902 ***1860.4*** *p40*
Wirth, Regina 49; Halifax, N.S., 1902 ***1860.4*** *p40*
Wirthale, Emil 17; New York, NY, 1894 ***6512.1*** *p182*
Wirths, William; Colorado, 1873 ***1029.59*** *p96*
Wirtnan, John 41; Minnesota, 1925 ***2769.54*** *p1379*
Wirtz, Clementine 2 *SEE* Wirtz, Jacob
Wirtz, Elisabeth 23; America, 1864 ***5475.1*** *p370*
Wirtz, Frances 10 *SEE* Wirtz, Jacob
Wirtz, Frances *SEE* Wirtz, Jacob
Wirtz, George 7 *SEE* Wirtz, Jacob
Wirtz, Jacob; New York, NY, 1904 ***609.10*** *p14*
*Wife:*Johanna
*Child:*George
*Child:*Frances
*Child:*Clementine
Wirtz, Jacob; Uruguay, 1895 ***609.10*** *p13*
*Wife:*Johanna Berger
*Daughter:*Frances
Wirtz, Johanna *SEE* Wirtz, Jacob
Wirtz, Johanna Berger *SEE* Wirtz, Jacob
Wirtz, Katherine Boehm *SEE* Wirtz, Melchior
Wirtz, Melchior; North Dakota, 1905 ***609.10*** *p15*
*Wife:*Katherine Boehm
*Son:*Steve
Wirtz, Steve *SEE* Wirtz, Melchior
Wis, Christian; Ohio, 1809-1852 ***4511.35*** *p59*
Wischofer, Mr.; America, 1844 ***7420.1*** *p34*
With wife 2 sons & 3 daughters
Wisdom, William; America, 1692 ***1220.12*** *p892*
Wise, Abraham; America, 1758 ***1220.12*** *p892*
Wise, Benjamin 51; Ontario, 1871 ***1823.17*** *p178*
Wise, Charles; Illinois, 1858-1861 ***6020.5*** *p133*
Wise, Conrad; Ohio, 1809-1852 ***4511.35*** *p59*
Wise, Edward; America, 1738 ***1220.12*** *p892*
Wise, Edward; America, 1767 ***1220.12*** *p892*
Wise, Edward; Barbados, 1664 ***1220.12*** *p892*
Wise, Edward; Virginia, 1745 ***1220.12*** *p892*
Wise, Elizabeth; Charles Town, SC, 1718 ***1220.12*** *p892*
Wise, Emilie; Wisconsin, 1901 ***6795.8*** *p232*
Wise, George; Ohio, 1836 ***3580.20*** *p34*
Wise, George; Ohio, 1836 ***6020.12*** *p23*
Wise, J. B.; North Carolina, 1855 ***1088.45*** *p37*
Wise, Jacob; Ohio, 1809-1852 ***4511.35*** *p59*
Wise, Jacob; Ohio, 1839 ***3580.20*** *p34*
Wise, Jacob; Ohio, 1839 ***6020.12*** *p23*
Wise, James 28; Ontario, 1871 ***1823.21*** *p399*
Wise, John; America, 1741 ***1220.12*** *p892*
Wise, John; America, 1748 ***1220.12*** *p892*
Wise, John; Boston, 1834 ***3274.55*** *p73*
Wise, John; Died enroute, 1721 ***1220.12*** *p892*
Wise, John; Virginia, 1765 ***1220.12*** *p892*
Wise, Peter; America, 1699 ***1220.12*** *p892*
Wise, Richard; America, 1726 ***1220.12*** *p892*
Wise, Sarah; America, 1758 ***1220.12*** *p892*
Wise, Stephen; Maryland, 1723 ***1220.12*** *p892*
Wise, Stephen; New York, 1776 ***8529.30*** *p5A*
Wise, Susanna; America, 1727 ***1220.12*** *p892*
Wise, Thomas; America, 1749 ***1220.12*** *p892*
Wise, Thomas; America, 1763 ***1220.12*** *p892*
Wise, Thomas; America, 1767 ***1220.12*** *p892*
Wisedale, Roger; Maryland, 1719 ***1220.12*** *p892*
Wiseley, Thomas; America, 1762 ***1220.12*** *p892*
Wiselogle, George; Ohio, 1809-1852 ***4511.35*** *p59*
Wiselogle, Michael; Ohio, 1809-1852 ***4511.35*** *p60*
Wiseman, Elizabeth; America, 1754 ***1220.12*** *p892*
Wiseman, Henry; Annapolis, MD, 1719 ***1220.12*** *p893*
Wiseman, Howard 79; Ontario, 1871 ***1823.17*** *p178*
Wiseman, James; America, 1748 ***1220.12*** *p893*
Wiseman, James 36; Ontario, 1871 ***1823.21*** *p399*
Wiseman, John; America, 1701 ***1220.12*** *p893*
Wiseman, John; Barbados, 1673 ***1220.12*** *p893*
Wiseman, John; Maryland, 1673 ***1236.25*** *p48*
Wiseman, Margaret; America, 1755 ***1220.12*** *p893*

Wiseman, Margaret 19; Ontario, 1871 ***1823.21*** *p399*
Wiseman, Margaret 28; Ontario, 1871 ***1823.21*** *p399*
Wiseman, Mary 29; Ontario, 1871 ***1823.21*** *p399*
Wiseman, Richard; America, 1685 ***1220.12*** *p893*
Wiseman, Thomas; America, 1767 ***1220.12*** *p893*
Wiseman, Thomas 34; Ontario, 1871 ***1823.21*** *p399*
Wisemiller, Emanuel; Ohio, 1809-1852 ***4511.35*** *p60*
Wisemoore, Jacob; North Carolina, 1710 ***3629.40*** *p7*
Wisenueski, John; Texas, 1892 ***6015.15*** *p11*
Wiser, Michael; Ohio, 1809-1852 ***4511.35*** *p60*
Wish, Margaret; America, 1720 ***1220.12*** *p893*
Wisham, Robert; America, 1683 ***1220.12*** *p893*
Wisherd, William 26; Ontario, 1871 ***1823.21*** *p399*
Wiske, John; Wisconsin, 1882 ***6795.8*** *p166*
Wiski, John; Wisconsin, 1883 ***6795.8*** *p119*
Wiski, Wilhelmine; Wisconsin, 1884 ***6795.8*** *p143*
Wismer, Friedrich; America, 1847 ***7420.1*** *p58*
With wife
With daughter 18
With son 23
With son 13
Wismer, Jacob; North Carolina, 1710 ***3629.40*** *p7*
Wismer, Johnes; North Carolina, 1710 ***3629.40*** *p7*
Wisnecski, Charlie; New York, NY, 1884 ***6015.15*** *p30*
Wisner, Harriett 36; Michigan, 1880 ***4491.30*** *p33*
Wisner, Ludwig; Wisconsin, 1877-1977 ***1822.55*** *p10*
Wisner, Maggy E. 25; Michigan, 1880 ***4491.30*** *p33*
Wisniewski, Anton 42; New York, NY, 1920 ***930.50*** *p49*
Wisniewski, Charlie; New York, NY, 1884 ***6015.15*** *p30*
Wisniewski, John; Texas, 1892 ***6015.15*** *p11*
Wisniewski, Joseph 23; New York, NY, 1920 ***930.50*** *p49*
Wisnisoski, John; Texas, 1892 ***6015.15*** *p11*
Wisniwski, John; Texas, 1892 ***6015.15*** *p11*
Wisnoski, John; Texas, 1892 ***6015.15*** *p11*
Wisocki, Mike; Texas, 1895 ***6015.15*** *p30*
Wisocky, Jan; Detroit, 1929-1930 ***6214.5*** *p69*
Wisrock, Barbara 12; America, 1843 ***778.6*** *p346*
Wisrock, Margaretha 12; America, 1843 ***778.6*** *p346*
Wisrock, Margaretha 47; America, 1843 ***778.6*** *p346*
Wisrock, Maria 7; America, 1843 ***778.6*** *p346*
Wisrock, Michel 57; America, 1843 ***778.6*** *p346*
Wisrock, Nicolas 18; America, 1843 ***778.6*** *p346*
Wisrock, Theresia 5; America, 1843 ***778.6*** *p346*
Wiss, Jerome; Ohio, 1809-1852 ***4511.35*** *p60*
Wisse, Andreas 21; Mississippi, 1847 ***778.6*** *p346*
Wissel, Carl Christoph Wilhelm; America, 1881 ***7420.1*** *p326*
Wisselqvist, J.G.; New York, NY, 1846 ***6412.40*** *p149*
Wissen, John; America, 1752 ***1220.12*** *p893*
Wisserist, Benedict; Ohio, 1809-1852 ***4511.35*** *p60*
Wisslander, O.; Boston, 1847 ***6412.40*** *p150*
Wissner, Carl Heinrich; America, 1857 ***7420.1*** *p175*
Wissner, Mathilde; America, 1856 ***7420.1*** *p156*
Wissner, Philippe 25; Missouri, 1845 ***778.6*** *p346*
Wist, Caroline 20; New York, NY, 1893 ***1883.7*** *p40*
Wist, Gottlieb 21; New York, NY, 1893 ***1883.7*** *p40*
Wist, Jean 28; Port uncertain, 1842 ***778.6*** *p346*
Wistrom, Alfred; St. Paul, MN, 1882 ***1865.50*** *p115*
Wistrom, Anna; St. Paul, MN, 1884 ***1865.50*** *p49*
Wiswede, H.; Valdivia, Chile, 1850 ***1192.4*** *p49*
Wiswede, Mathilde; Valdivia, Chile, 1850 ***1192.4*** *p49*
Wit, Christian; Ohio, 1809-1852 ***4511.35*** *p60*
Witaker, Mary; America, 1753 ***1220.12*** *p862*
Witalis, Jozef 18; New York, NY, 1911 ***6533.11*** *p9*
Witbredt, Hein. 17; New York, NY, 1864 ***8425.62*** *p197*
Witbredt, Marie 20; New York, NY, 1864 ***8425.62*** *p197*
Witchall, Elizabeth; Marblehead, MA, 1705 ***9228.50*** *p165*
Witchell, Daniel; America, 1758 ***1220.12*** *p893*
Witchett, Elizabeth; America, 1770 ***1220.12*** *p893*
Witchingham, Mary; America, 1731 ***1220.12*** *p893*
Withager, Christine Wilhelmine Giseke *SEE* Withager, Johann Friedrich
Withager, Johann Friedrich; America, 1852 ***7420.1*** *p101*
*Wife:*Christine Wilhelmine Giseke
Withall, Thomas; America, 1773 ***1220.12*** *p893*
Withall, Thomas; America, 1774 ***1220.12*** *p893*
Witham, Henry; Annapolis, MD, 1730 ***1220.12*** *p893*
Witham, John; America, 1665 ***1220.12*** *p893*
Witham, John; America, 1750 ***1220.12*** *p893*
Witham, Samuel; America, 1754 ***1220.12*** *p893*
Witherell, Gabriel; America, 1671 ***1220.12*** *p858*
Witherell, Robert; America, 1735 ***1220.12*** *p858*
Witheridge, Isaac; Virginia, 1743 ***1220.12*** *p893*
Witheridge, Joan; America, 1734 ***1220.12*** *p893*
Witheridge, John; America, 1743 ***1220.12*** *p893*
Witherington, Anne; Barbados, 1668 ***1220.12*** *p893*
Witherington, Elizabeth; America, 1758 ***1220.12*** *p893*
Witherington, Henry; America, 1747 ***1220.12*** *p893*
Witherington, Jane; America, 1758 ***1220.12*** *p893*
Witherow, William; America, 1731 ***1220.12*** *p893*
Withers, John; America, 1737 ***1220.12*** *p893*
Withers, John; America, 1770 ***1220.12*** *p893*
Withers, Nathaniel; America, 1774 ***1220.12*** *p893*
Withers, Rebecca; Virginia, 1721 ***1220.12*** *p893*
Withers, Richard 65; Ontario, 1871 ***1823.21*** *p399*
Withers, Sarah; America, 1743 ***1220.12*** *p893*
Withers, Sarah; America, 1758 ***1220.12*** *p893*
Withers, Sarah; Maryland, 1740 ***1220.12*** *p893*
Withers, Thomas; America, 1744 ***1220.12*** *p893*
Withers, Thomas; Barbados or Jamaica, 1683 ***1220.12*** *p893*
Witherspoon, Robert; America, 1773 ***1220.12*** *p893*
Withey, Daniel; Annapolis, MD, 1719 ***1220.12*** *p893*
Withey, Thomas; America, 1727 ***1220.12*** *p893*
Withrington, Thomas; America, 1748 ***1220.12*** *p893*
Withyman, C. 32; Halifax, N.S., n.d. ***1833.5*** *p7*
*Wife:*Charlotte 32
Withyman, C. 32; Halifax, N.S., n.d. ***8445.10*** *p7*
*Wife:*Charlotte 32
*Relative:*Morgan R. 36
*Relative:*E. 38
*Relative:*M. 5
Withyman, Charlotte 32 *SEE* Withyman, C.
Withyman, Charlotte 32 *SEE* Withyman, C.
Withyman, E. 38 *SEE* Withyman, C.
Withyman, M. 5 *SEE* Withyman, C.
Withyman, Morgan R. 36 *SEE* Withyman, C.
Witkorn, Bernard; Texas, 1851 ***3435.45*** *p37*
Witkowski, Gabriel; Detroit, 1930 ***1640.60*** *p78*
Witkowski, Simon 17; New York, NY, 1852 ***7710.1*** *p156*
Witox, Catherine 19; America, 1745 ***778.6*** *p346*
Witox, Madeleine 27; America, 1745 ***778.6*** *p346*
Witox, Maria 66; America, 1745 ***778.6*** *p346*
Witox, Nicolas 56; America, 1745 ***778.6*** *p346*
Witox, Therese 22; America, 1745 ***778.6*** *p346*
Witsford, Tho; Virginia, 1652 ***6254.4*** *p243*
Witt, Carl; Iowa, 1898 ***1211.15*** *p20*
Witt, Christian; Ohio, 1809-1852 ***4511.35*** *p60*
Witt, James; America, 1754 ***1220.12*** *p893*
Witt, Johann Aug.; Wisconsin, 1885 ***6795.8*** *p143*
Witt, K.; New York, 1859 ***358.56*** *p101*
Witt, Mathews; Louisiana, 1836-1841 ***4981.45*** *p209*
Witt, Xavier; Ohio, 1809-1852 ***4511.35*** *p60*
Wittam, John; America, 1765 ***1220.12*** *p893*
Wittas, Thomas; America, 1744 ***1220.12*** *p894*
Wittbart, Mr.; America, 1853 ***7420.1*** *p113*
With family
Witte, Christine; America, 1842 ***7420.1*** *p26*
Witte, Friedrich; America, 1867 ***7420.1*** *p267*
Witte, Friedrich Adolf; America, 1873 ***5475.1*** *p31*
Witte, Johanne Louise; Philadelphia, 1855 ***8513.31*** *p410*
Witte, Mathilde; South Dakota, 1886 ***8023.44*** *p380*
Witte, Sophie Wilhelmine; America, 1845 ***7420.1*** *p37*
Witteck, Antoine; Illinois, 1852 ***6079.1*** *p15*
Wittemund, Klothilde; America, 1925 ***8023.44*** *p381*
Wittenberg, Mrs.; California, 1868 ***1131.61*** *p89*
With 2 child
Wittenberg, Ehregott Max; America, 1867 ***7919.3*** *p529*
Wittens, Sara; Barbados or Jamaica, 1697 ***1220.12*** *p894*
Wittensloe, Elizabeth; America, 1764 ***1220.12*** *p894*
Witter, Pierre 42; America, 1846 ***778.6*** *p346*
Witters, John 29; Ontario, 1871 ***1823.21*** *p399*
Wittey, Elizabeth; America, 1764 ***1220.12*** *p894*
Witthuhn, Carl; Wisconsin, 1887 ***6795.8*** *p154*
Wittich, Christian *SEE* Wittich, Sophie Katharina Hoffmann
Wittich, Friedrich *SEE* Wittich, Sophie Katharina Hoffmann
Wittich, Jakob *SEE* Wittich, Sophie Katharina Hoffmann
Wittich, Johannes *SEE* Wittich, Sophie Katharina Hoffmann
Wittich, Sophie Katharina; America, 1854 ***5475.1*** *p459*
*Son:*Jakob
*Son:*Johannes
*Son:*Friedrich
*Son:*Christian
Wittie, Adolphe Eugene Napoleon; Louisiana, 1874 ***4981.45*** *p134*
Witting, C. C. A.; Ohio, 1809-1852 ***4511.35*** *p60*
Witting, Frederick E. C.; Ohio, 1809-1852 ***4511.35*** *p60*
Wittingham, George; America, 1764 ***1220.12*** *p894*
Wittings, Sara; Barbados or Jamaica, 1697 ***1220.12*** *p894*
Wittings, Uriah; America, 1677 ***1220.12*** *p894*
Wittkohl, Carl Ludwig *SEE* Wittkohl, Sophie Louise
Wittkohl, Friedrich Wilhelm *SEE* Wittkohl, Sophie Louise
Wittkohl, Johann Friedrich Ludwig *SEE* Wittkohl, Sophie Louise
Wittkohl, Sophie Louise; America, 1872 ***7420.1*** *p298*
*Son:*Johann Friedrich Ludwig
*Son:*Friedrich Wilhelm
*Son:*Carl Ludwig
Wittkop, Carl Friedrich Wilhelm *SEE* Wittkop, Johann Georg Wilhelm
Wittkop, Caroline Margarethe Constantia *SEE* Wittkop, Johann Friedrich
Wittkop, Johann Friedrich; America, 1861 ***7420.1*** *p210*
*Sister:*Caroline Margarethe Constantia
Wittkop, Johann Georg Wilhelm; America, 1865 ***7420.1*** *p238*
*Wife:*Sophie Louise Latwesen
*Son:*Carl Friedrich Wilhelm
Wittkop, Johanne Louise Justine; America, 1861 ***7420.1*** *p210*
Wittkop, Sophie Louise Latwesen *SEE* Wittkop, Johann Georg Wilhelm
Wittkugel, Friedrich Christian; America, 1858 ***7420.1*** *p183*
Wittkugel, Wilhelm; America, 1856 ***7420.1*** *p156*
Wittman, Amalia 11; Portland, ME, 1911 ***970.38*** *p82*
Wittman, Friedrich 25; Portland, ME, 1911 ***970.38*** *p82*
Wittman, Ildefons; Chicago, 1887 ***2853.20*** *p431*
Wittman, J. Friedrich; New Castle, DE, 1817-1818 ***90.20*** *p155*
Wittman, Katerina L. 23; Portland, ME, 1911 ***970.38*** *p82*
Wittman, Katerine 3; Portland, ME, 1911 ***970.38*** *p82*
Wittman, Konrad 4; Portland, ME, 1911 ***970.38*** *p82*
Wittock, Marie 16; New York, NY, 1885 ***1883.7*** *p45*
Witton, John; America, 1758 ***1220.12*** *p868*
Witton, Mary; America, 1729 ***1220.12*** *p868*
Witton, William; America, 1756 ***1220.12*** *p869*
Witts, Elizabeth; America, 1767 ***1220.12*** *p894*
Witts, Stephen; America, 1738 ***1220.12*** *p894*
Wittstein, Em.; New York, 1860 ***358.56*** *p4*
Wittung, Jakob; America, 1863 ***5475.1*** *p541*
Wittup, William 37; Ontario, 1871 ***1823.21*** *p399*
Witty, Sarah A. 45; Ontario, 1871 ***1823.17*** *p178*
Witty, Thomas; America, 1677 ***1220.12*** *p894*
Witwicka, Katherine; Detroit, 1929-1930 ***6214.5*** *p63*
Witworth, Richard; Philadelphia, 1778 ***8529.30*** *p5A*
Witzel, Carl L. C.; America, 1885 ***7420.1*** *p350*
With wife 4 children
Witzel, Martin; America, 1838 ***170.15*** *p47*
Witzgall, Lewis; Ohio, 1809-1852 ***4511.35*** *p60*
Witzig, Jacques Pierre; Illinois, 1852 ***6079.1*** *p15*
Witzig, Jean Jacques; Illinois, 1852 ***6079.1*** *p15*
Witzke, Johann 54; New York, NY, 1885 ***8425.16*** *p32*
Witzki, Fried. 32; New York, NY, 1893 ***1883.7*** *p43*
Wixedell, Johann; North Carolina, 1710 ***3629.40*** *p9*
Wlety, Joseph 27; New Orleans, 1847 ***778.6*** *p346*
Wloch, Stanley; Detroit, 1930 ***1640.60*** *p76*
Woadam, William; America, 1725 ***1220.12*** *p898*
Wobbeking, Mr.; Fort Wayne, IN, 1851 ***7420.1*** *p84*
With wife
Wobbeking, Heinrich Wilhelm; Iowa, 1892 ***7420.1*** *p367*
Wobedo, Barbara 16 *SEE* Wobedo, Nikolaus
Wobedo, Barbara Haupental 44 *SEE* Wobedo, Nikolaus
Wobedo, Jakob 14 *SEE* Wobedo, Nikolaus
Wobedo, Karoline 9 *SEE* Wobedo, Nikolaus
Wobedo, Margarethe; Brazil, 1867 ***5475.1*** *p505*
Wobedo, Nikolaus 44; Brazil, 1865 ***5475.1*** *p521*
*Wife:*Barbara Haupental 44
*Son:*Jakob 14
*Daughter:*Karoline 9
*Daughter:*Barbara 16
Wobig, Friedrich Wilhelm Erdmann; Wisconsin, 1870 ***6795.8*** *p78*
Wobito, Johann; America, 1850 ***5475.1*** *p486*
Wobking, Carl Heinrich; America, 1890 ***7420.1*** *p362*
Wobking, Carl Heinrich Wilhelm; Illinois, 1881 ***7420.1*** *p326*
Wobking, Friedrich Wilhelm; America, 1851 ***7420.1*** *p84*
Wobscha, Helena; Wisconsin, 1893 ***6795.8*** *p164*
Wobschal, Helena; Wisconsin, 1893 ***6795.8*** *p164*
Wobschall, Carl Ferdinand; Wisconsin, 1890 ***6795.8*** *p35*
Wocker, August 29; Ontario, 1871 ***1823.17*** *p178*
Wockley, Margaret; Maryland or Virginia, 1738 ***1220.12*** *p894*
Wodsworth, Thomas 49; Ontario, 1871 ***1823.21*** *p399*
Woehrle, Anna Maria; Venezuela, 1843 ***3899.5*** *p544*
Woelk, Abraham 46; New York, NY, 1893 ***1883.7*** *p45*
Woelk, Anna 6; New York, NY, 1893 ***1883.7*** *p45*
Woelk, Elisabeth 8; New York, NY, 1893 ***1883.7*** *p45*
Woelk, Elisabeth 48; New York, NY, 1893 ***1883.7*** *p45*
Woelk, Helena 14; New York, NY, 1893 ***1883.7*** *p45*
Woelk, Isaak 16; New York, NY, 1893 ***1883.7*** *p45*
Woempner, Carl Georg Julius; America, 1881 ***7420.1*** *p326*
Woesner, John George; Ohio, 1809-1852 ***4511.35*** *p60*
Wohes, Louise; Wisconsin, 1894 ***6795.8*** *p237*
Wohlfarth, Johann 21; Galveston, TX, 1846 ***3967.10*** *p378*
Wohling, Carl Heinrich; America, 1864 ***7420.1*** *p228*
Wohling, Maria Dorothea; America, 1864 ***7420.1*** *p228*

Wohlleb, Jacob 47; New Castle, DE, 1817-1818 *90.20 p155*
Wohlt, Johanna 60; New York, NY, 1885 *1883.7 p45*
Wohlvend, Georg 27; America, 1847 *778.6 p346*
Wohlwend, John; Wisconsin, 1897 *6795.8 p101*
Wohnenburger, Johann 18; Galveston, TX, 1844 *3967.10 p370*
Wohnlich, Marya; New York, 1859 *358.56 p99*
Woiliguen, Charles 29; New Orleans, 1843 *778.6 p346*
Woitena, Stanislaus 46; Texas, 1880 *9980.22 p17*
Woitkowicz, John; Detroit, 1930 *1640.60 p82*
Woiton, Simon; Baltimore, 1879 *6015.15 p30*
Wojahn, Rudolf Julius; Wisconsin, 1881 *6795.8 p53*
Wojciechowska, Mary; Detroit, 1929-1930 *6214.5 p63*
Wojciechowski, Frank Joseph; Detroit, 1929 *1640.55 p114*
Wojciechowski, Julian; Detroit, 1930 *1640.60 p82*
Wojciechowski, Viola; Detroit, 1930 *1640.60 p83*
Wojcik, Frank 35; New York, NY, 1920 *930.50 p49*
Wojciuk, Franciszek 30; New York, NY, 1911 *6533.11 p9*
Wojtowicz, Felix; Detroit, 1930 *1640.60 p82*
Wojtusik, Jozef 4; New York, NY, 1911 *6533.11 p9*
Wojtusik, Julian 2; New York, NY, 1911 *6533.11 p9*
Wojtusik, Katarzyna 29; New York, NY, 1911 *6533.11 p9*
Wolbrecht, Friedrich; America, 1855 *7420.1 p143*
Wolcott, Allen E.; Ohio, 1836 *3580.20 p34*
Wolcott, Allen E.; Ohio, 1836 *6020.12 p23*
Wolcott, Christopher *SEE* Wolcott, Henry
Wolcott, Elizabeth *SEE* Wolcott, Henry
Wolcott, George *SEE* Wolcott, Henry
Wolcott, Henry *SEE* Wolcott, Henry
Wolcott, Henry; Massachusetts, 1630 *117.5 p155*
  *Wife:*Elizabeth
  *Son:*Christopher
  *Son:*George
  *Son:*Henry
Wold, Stephen 39; Ontario, 1871 *1823.21 p399*
Wolden, John; Philadelphia, 1778 *8529.30 p7A*
Wolf, . . . 7; Baltimore, 1889 *8425.16 p36*
Wolf, . . . 15; Baltimore, 1889 *8425.16 p35*
Wolf, Mr.; America, 1853 *2853.20 p49*
  With wife
Wolf, Adam; Illinois, 1856 *6079.1 p15*
Wolf, Albert; New York, NY, 1907 *3331.4 p11*
Wolf, Andreas; Baltimore, 1889 *8425.16 p35*
Wolf, Andreas 25; Baltimore, 1889 *8425.16 p36*
Wolf, Angela; America, 1874 *5475.1 p258*
Wolf, Anna; America, 1881 *5475.1 p151*
  *Son:*Johann
Wolf, Anna 10 *SEE* Wolf, Johann Leonhard
Wolf, Anna 31; Baltimore, 1889 *8425.16 p35*
Wolf, Anna; Detroit, 1929 *1640.55 p114*
Wolf, Augustin 31; America, 1840 *778.6 p346*
Wolf, Barbara *SEE* Wolf, Peter
Wolf, Barbara Quirin *SEE* Wolf, Peter
Wolf, Benjamin 34; New York, NY, 1893 *1883.7 p40*
Wolf, Benjamin 34; New York, NY, 1893 *1883.7 p47*
Wolf, Bernard 23; Louisiana, 1848 *778.6 p346*
Wolf, Bernhard; America, 1900 *2526.42 p134*
Wolf, Miss C. 5; New Orleans, 1834 *1002.51 p113*
Wolf, Miss C. 7; New Orleans, 1834 *1002.51 p113*
Wolf, Carolina 19; Baltimore, 1889 *8425.16 p36*
Wolf, Christian Bernhard; America, 1867 *7919.3 p527*
Wolf, Christina 9; Baltimore, 1889 *8425.16 p35*
Wolf, Clara 6; Baltimore, 1889 *8425.16 p35*
Wolf, Conrad; America, 1868 *7919.3 p530*
  With wife & 3 children
Wolf, Detlef; North Carolina, 1842 *1088.45 p37*
Wolf, E..e 2; Baltimore, 1889 *8425.16 p35*
Wolf, Elisabeth *SEE* Wolf, Peter
Wolf, Elisabetha 20 *SEE* Wolf, Johann Leonhard
Wolf, Eugen 1 months; Baltimore, 1889 *8425.16 p35*
Wolf, Eva Katharina Muller 59 *SEE* Wolf, Johann Leonhard
Wolf, Eva Margaretha; America, 1852 *2526.42 p137*
Wolf, Francis; Ohio, 1809-1852 *4511.35 p60*
Wolf, Franz; America, 1842 *2526.42 p198*
  With wife
  With child 2
  With child 4
Wolf, Franz 36; Baltimore, 1889 *8425.16 p35*
Wolf, Frederick; Illinois, 1855 *6079.1 p15*
Wolf, Georg; America, 1841 *2526.42 p134*
Wolf, Georg *SEE* Wolf, Paul
Wolf, Georg Jakob; America, 1847 *5475.1 p537*
Wolf, George 29; Mississippi, 1846 *778.6 p346*
Wolf, Gertrud *SEE* Wolf, Paul
Wolf, Heinrich; Ohio, 1907 *2526.42 p134*
Wolf, Heinrich; Port uncertain, 1841 *7420.1 p23*
Wolf, Helen 9; Baltimore, 1889 *8425.16 p36*
Wolf, J. 35; America, 1842 *778.6 p346*

Wolf, J.; Louisiana, 1874 *4981.45 p297*
Wolf, J. 3; New Orleans, 1834 *1002.51 p113*
Wolf, J. 38; New Orleans, 1834 *1002.51 p113*
Wolf, Jacob; Illinois, 1852 *6079.1 p15*
Wolf, Jakob *SEE* Wolf, Peter
Wolf, Jakob; America, 1886 *3366.30 p70*
Wolf, Jakob 14 *SEE* Wolf, Johann Leonhard
Wolf, Joel 17; America, 1847 *778.6 p346*
Wolf, Joh. Peter *SEE* Wolf, Paul
Wolf, Johann *SEE* Wolf, Paul
Wolf, Johann *SEE* Wolf, Peter
Wolf, Johann 4; Baltimore, 1889 *8425.16 p35*
Wolf, Johann Adam; America, 1871 *2526.43 p158*
Wolf, Johann Leonhard 56; America, 1883 *2526.43 p158*
  *Wife:*Eva Katharina Muller 59
  *Daughter:*Maria 25
  *Daughter:*Elisabetha 20
  *Son:*Jakob 14
  *Daughter:*Anna 10
Wolf, Johann Wilhelm; America, 1854 *7420.1 p133*
Wolf, Johannes 6 months; Baltimore, 1889 *8425.16 p36*
Wolf, John; Louisiana, 1836-1840 *4981.45 p213*
Wolf, Josef 31; America, 1840 *778.6 p347*
Wolf, Joseph 20; America, 1847 *778.6 p347*
Wolf, Joseph 18; Baltimore, 1889 *8425.16 p36*
Wolf, Joseph 19; New Orleans, 1848 *778.6 p347*
Wolf, Joseph; New Orleans, 1848 *778.6 p347*
Wolf, Justine 28; Louisiana, 1848 *778.6 p347*
Wolf, Karl; Ohio, 1905 *2526.42 p134*
Wolf, Katharina *SEE* Wolf, Peter
Wolf, Leonhard; Ohio, 1901 *2526.42 p134*
Wolf, Levi; Ohio, 1809-1852 *4511.35 p60*
Wolf, Louis 30; New Orleans, 1848 *778.6 p347*
Wolf, Ludwig; America, 1865 *5475.1 p30*
Wolf, Ludwig 1; Baltimore, 1889 *8425.16 p35*
Wolf, Miss M. 27; New Orleans, 1834 *1002.51 p113*
Wolf, Margaretha; America, 1871 *2526.43 p158*
Wolf, Margaretha 4; Baltimore, 1889 *8425.16 p35*
Wolf, Margarethe *SEE* Wolf, Paul
Wolf, Margarethe Kohl *SEE* Wolf, Peter
Wolf, Margarethe *SEE* Wolf, Peter
Wolf, Maria 25 *SEE* Wolf, Johann Leonhard
Wolf, Maria Mang 40 *SEE* Wolf, Paul
Wolf, Maria 58; America, 1867 *5475.1 p201*
Wolf, Maria 36; Baltimore, 1889 *8425.16 p35*
Wolf, Melchior 12; Baltimore, 1889 *8425.16 p35*
Wolf, Nikolaus; New England, 1869 *170.15 p47*
Wolf, Ottillie 15; Baltimore, 1889 *8425.16 p36*
Wolf, Paul *SEE* Wolf, Paul
Wolf, Paul; America, 1873 *5475.1 p231*
  *Wife:*Maria Mang
  *Son:*Paul
  *Son:*Johann
  *Son:*Joh. Peter
  *Daughter:*Georg
  *Daughter:*Gertrud
  *Son:*Peter
  *Daughter:*Margarethe
Wolf, Peter *SEE* Wolf, Paul
Wolf, Peter; America, 1880 *5475.1 p59*
  *Wife:*Margarethe Kohl
  *Son:*Johann
Wolf, Peter *SEE* Wolf, Peter
Wolf, Peter; America, 1884 *5475.1 p69*
  *Wife:*Barbara Quirin
  *Daughter:*Margarethe
  *Son:*Jakob
  *Son:*Peter
  *Daughter:*Barbara
  *Daughter:*Elisabeth
  *Daughter:*Katharina
  *Son:*Jakob
Wolf, Peter 11; Baltimore, 1889 *8425.16 p35*
Wolf, Peter; Illinois, 1852 *6079.1 p15*
Wolf, Peter; Illinois, 1854 *6079.1 p15*
Wolf, Samuel; North Carolina, 1847 *1088.45 p37*
Wolf, Valentin 36; Baltimore, 1889 *8425.16 p35*
Wolf, Valentin, II; America, 1848 *5475.1 p538*
Wolfanger, Christian; Kentucky, 1886 *5475.1 p461*
Wolfanger, Magdalena; America, 1835 *5475.1 p457*
Wolfe, Elizabeth; Barbados, 1694 *1220.12 p894*
Wolfe, John; America, 1754 *1220.12 p894*
Wolfe, John; Barbados, 1677 *1220.12 p894*
Wolfe, John; New Orleans, 1851 *7242.30 p156*
Wolfe, Joseph; America, 1763 *1220.12 p894*
Wolfe, Saunders; America, 1765 *1220.12 p894*
Wolfe, Solomon; America, 1774 *1220.12 p894*
Wolfelschneider, Anna Margaretha 15 *SEE* Wolfelschneider, Jakob
Wolfelschneider, Anna Maria; America, 1850 *2526.42 p183*

Wolfelschneider, Balthasar; America, 1888 *2526.42 p117*
  *Wife:*Elisabeth Meyer
  With mother-in-law
Wolfelschneider, Dorothea 18 *SEE* Wolfelschneider, Jakob
Wolfelschneider, Elisabeth Meyer 23 *SEE* Wolfelschneider, Balthasar
Wolfelschneider, Eva 9 *SEE* Wolfelschneider, Jakob
Wolfelschneider, Jakob; America, 1850 *2526.43 p136*
  With wife
  *Daughter:*Dorothea
  *Daughter:*Eva
  *Son:*Wilhelm
  *Daughter:*Anna Margaretha
Wolfelschneider, Konrad; America, 1836 *2526.42 p117*
Wolfelschneider, Wilhelm 7 *SEE* Wolfelschneider, Jakob
Wolfermann, Anton; Galveston, TX, 1855 *571.7 p17*
Wolfersberger, Catharina 32; America, 1843 *778.6 p347*
Wolfersberger, Franz 2; America, 1843 *778.6 p347*
Wolfersberger, Martin 40; America, 1843 *778.6 p347*
Wolff, Albert; America, 1853 *7420.1 p133*
Wolff, Anna Margaretha; Port uncertain, 1865 *170.15 p47*
  With family
Wolff, Benjamin; America, 1878 *5475.1 p191*
Wolff, Catharine 17; America, 1847 *778.6 p347*
Wolff, David Alex; North Carolina, 1859 *1088.45 p37*
Wolff, Eva 5; America, 1847 *778.6 p347*
Wolff, Frederick 22; America, 1746 *778.6 p347*
Wolff, Friederic 31; America, 1846 *778.6 p347*
Wolff, Georg 45; America, 1847 *778.6 p347*
Wolff, George 14; America, 1847 *778.6 p347*
Wolff, Isidor; America, 1893 *5475.1 p149*
Wolff, Jan 2; America, 1847 *778.6 p347*
Wolff, Johannetta; America, 1881 *5475.1 p273*
Wolff, Margaretha 19; America, 1847 *778.6 p347*
Wolff, Marie 40; America, 1847 *778.6 p347*
Wolff, Oskar August Franz; America, 1872 *7420.1 p298*
Wolff, Otto; Washington, 1883 *2770.40 p137*
Wolff, Toby; Louisiana, 1836-1841 *4981.45 p209*
Wolffe, Catherine 50; Ontario, 1871 *1823.17 p178*
Wolfgang, Johann 28; Louisiana, 1848 *778.6 p347*
Wolfington, Abraham 60; Ontario, 1871 *1823.17 p178*
Wolfington, Henry; America, 1750 *1220.12 p894*
Wolfington, James 28; Ontario, 1871 *1823.17 p178*
Wolford, John D.; Ohio, 1809-1852 *4511.35 p60*
Wolford, John Dewalt; Ohio, 1809-1852 *4511.35 p60*
Wolfrath, Carl Wilhelm; America, 1836 *7420.1 p12*
Wolfrath, Engel Marie Sophie Caroline; America, 1866 *7420.1 p246*
Wolfrath, Friedrich; America, 1847 *7420.1 p58*
  With son 16
  With daughter 3
  With daughter 4
  With daughter 15
  With daughter 11
  With daughter 7
  With daughter 9
  With daughter 22
Wolfrath, Friedrich Ludwig; America, 1847 *7420.1 p58*
Wolfrath, Johann Friedrich Christian; America, 1852 *7420.1 p101*
Wolfrath, Johann Friedrich Christoph; America, 1865 *7420.1 p238*
Wolfrey, Charles James *SEE* Wolfrey, William Henry
Wolfrey, Lucy; Barbados, 1674 *1220.12 p894*
⟨lv11⟩**Wolfrey,** William Henry; America, 1887 *9228.50 p655*
  *Son:*Charles James
Wolfsbergen, Nicolas 70; Mississippi, 1846 *778.6 p347*
Wolfsberger, George; Ohio, 1809-1852 *4511.35 p60*
Wolfsohn, Julius; Kansas, 1889 *1447.20 p63*
Wolken, Henry; Ohio, 1840-1897 *8365.35 p18*
Wolker, Barbara 42; America, 1747 *778.6 p347*
Wolker, Eva 6; America, 1747 *778.6 p347*
Wolker, Lorent 42; America, 1747 *778.6 p347*
Wolker, Maria 12; America, 1747 *778.6 p347*
Wolker, Martin 3; America, 1747 *778.6 p347*
Wolker, Michel 8; America, 1747 *778.6 p347*
Woll, Mr.; America, 1837 *5475.1 p399*
  *Wife:*Anna Maria Nau
  *Daughter:*Katharina
  With daughter-in-law 27
  *Daughter:*Barbara
  *Daughter:*Margarethe
  *Son:*Georg
  *Son:*Andreas
  *Son:*Johann
Woll, A. Maria 13 *SEE* Woll, Jakob
Woll, Andreas; America, 1837 *5475.1 p400*
Woll, Andreas 21 *SEE* Woll, Mr.
Woll, Anna Maria Nau 51 *SEE* Woll, Mr.
Woll, Barbara 9 *SEE* Woll, Jakob

FOR A COMPLETE EXPLANATION OF ENTRY, SEE "HOW TO READ A CITATION" SECTION

Woll, Barbara 14 *SEE* Woll, Mr.
Woll, Christian; America, 1860 ***5475.1*** *p412*
Woll, Conrad; America, 1836 ***5475.1*** *p399*
Woll, Friedrich; America, 1880 ***5475.1*** *p415*
Woll, Georg; America, 1837 ***5475.1*** *p385*
Woll, Georg 24 *SEE* Woll, Mr.
Woll, Jakob; America, 1836 ***5475.1*** *p410*
Woll, Jakob; America, 1865-1870 ***5475.1*** *p412*
Woll, Jakob 5 *SEE* Woll, Jakob
Woll, Jakob 37; America, 1826 ***5475.1*** *p409*
*Wife:*Kath. Diwersi 35
*Daughter:*Barbara 9
*Son:*Jakob 5
*Daughter:*Katharina 1
*Son:*Johann 3
*Daughter:*A. Maria 13
*Son:*Michel 11
Woll, Johann; America, 1837 ***5475.1*** *p400*
Woll, Johann; America, 1843 ***5475.1*** *p463*
With wife
With 6 children
Woll, Johann 3 *SEE* Woll, Jakob
Woll, Johann 22; America, 1880 ***5475.1*** *p456*
Woll, Johann 27 *SEE* Woll, Mr.
Woll, Johann 46; America, 1800-1899 ***5475.1*** *p453*
With family of 7
Woll, Karl; America, 1884 ***5475.1*** *p407*
Woll, Kath. Diwersi 35 *SEE* Woll, Jakob
Woll, Katharina 1 *SEE* Woll, Jakob
Woll, Katharina 11 *SEE* Woll, Mr.
Woll, Katharina 46; America, 1846 ***5475.1*** *p386*
Woll, Konrad; America, 1837 ***5475.1*** *p400*
Woll, Leonard 20; America, 1833 ***5475.1*** *p399*
Woll, Margarethe 25 *SEE* Woll, Mr.
Woll, Maria 66; America, 1836 ***5475.1*** *p394*
Woll, Michel; America, 1849 ***5475.1*** *p402*
Woll, Michel 11 *SEE* Woll, Jakob
Woll, Peter; America, 1836 ***5475.1*** *p399*
Woll, Peter; America, 1837 ***5475.1*** *p399*
Woll, Peter Claudius; America, 1861 ***5475.1*** *p404*
Wollacott, John; America, 1734 ***1220.12*** *p900*
Wollan, Louis A.; Washington, 1887 ***2770.40*** *p25*
Wollben, Edward L. 52; Ontario, 1871 ***1823.21*** *p399*
Wollbrecht, Carl Friedrich Julius; America, 1868 ***7420.1*** *p278*
Wollenberger, Paul; New York, NY, 1896 ***5475.1*** *p18*
Wollenweider, Amelie 22; New Orleans, 1848 ***778.6*** *p347*
Wollenweider, Augustine 5; New Orleans, 1848 ***778.6*** *p347*
Wollenweider, Marie 45; New Orleans, 1848 ***778.6*** *p347*
Wollet, . . .; Ontario, 1871 ***1823.21*** *p399*
Wolley, James; America, 1747 ***1220.12*** *p900*
Wolley, James; New Jersey, 1668 ***9228.50*** *p656*
Wollf, Benjamin 9; Port uncertain, 1844 ***778.6*** *p347*
Wollf, Benjamin 44; Port uncertain, 1844 ***778.6*** *p347*
Wollf, Josephine 10; Port uncertain, 1844 ***778.6*** *p348*
Wollf, Josephine 42; Port uncertain, 1844 ***778.6*** *p347*
Wollmann, Andrew; New York, NY, 1875 ***3366.30*** *p70*
Wollmann, Theresia 22; Valdivia, Chile, 1852 ***1192.4*** *p54*
Wollmeiner, Joseph; New York, 1859 ***358.56*** *p101*
Wollscheidt, Peter; America, 1863 ***5475.1*** *p338*
Wolock, Louis; Detroit, 1930 ***1640.60*** *p77*
Wolph, John; Virginia, 1768 ***1220.12*** *p894*
Wolsberger, Andrew; Ohio, 1809-1852 ***4511.35*** *p60*
Wolscht, Theresia 28; America, 1882 ***5475.1*** *p155*
Wolsey, George; America, 1770 ***1220.12*** *p894*
Wolsey, John H. 35; Ontario, 1871 ***1823.17*** *p178*
Wolsey, Thomas 60; Ontario, 1871 ***1823.17*** *p178*
Wolston, John; Maryland, 1671 ***1236.25*** *p46*
Wolston, Walter 26; Ontario, 1871 ***1823.21*** *p399*
Wolter, Carl; America, 1854 ***7420.1*** *p133*
Wolter, Caroline Wilhelmine Dalbsmeier *SEE* Wolter, Jacob Johann Friedrich
Wolter, Eduard; Valdivia, Chile, 1852 ***1192.4*** *p55*
Wolter, Engel Marie Dorothea; America, 1867 ***7420.1*** *p267*
*Son:*Hans Heinrich
Wolter, Gottlieb; Dakota, 1859-1918 ***554.30*** *p26*
*Wife:*Susanna Burgstahler
Wolter, Hans Heinrich *SEE* Wolter, Engel Marie Dorothea
Wolter, Heinrich Friedrich *SEE* Wolter, Jacob Johann Friedrich
Wolter, Jacob Johann Friedrich; America, 1882 ***7420.1*** *p334*
*Wife:*Caroline Wilhelmine Dalbsmeier
*Son:*Heinrich Friedrich
Wolter, Johann Jacob; Port uncertain, 1855 ***7420.1*** *p143*
Wolter, Karoline 34; Brazil, 1865 ***5475.1*** *p524*
Wolter, Katharina 23; America, 1854 ***5475.1*** *p57*
*Sister:*Margarethe 21
Wolter, Margarethe 21 *SEE* Wolter, Katharina
Wolter, Susanna Burgstahler *SEE* Wolter, Gottlieb
Woltert, Engel Marie Dorothea; America, 1867 ***7420.1*** *p267*
*Son:*Hans Heinrich
Woltert, Ernst Heinrich Gottlieb; America, 1865 ***7420.1*** *p238*
Woltert, Hans Heinrich *SEE* Woltert, Engel Marie Dorothea
Woltert, Thrine Sophie Charlotte; Minnesota, 1873 ***7420.1*** *p302*
Woltmann, Elise Dorothea Wilhelmine; America, 1862 ***7420.1*** *p216*
Woltmann, Justine Sophie Caroline; America, 1861 ***7420.1*** *p210*
Wolverton, Anna 28; Michigan, 1880 ***4491.33*** *p24*
Wolz, Samuel 17; America, 1846 ***778.6*** *p348*
Wompner, . . .; Port uncertain, 1880 ***7420.1*** *p319*
Wompner, Ernst; America, 1852 ***7420.1*** *p101*
Wondel, Joseph 28; America, 1845 ***778.6*** *p348*
Wondel, Peter 25; America, 1842 ***778.6*** *p348*
Wonderlich, John 40; America, 1841 ***778.6*** *p348*
Wonderlin, Joseph; Ohio, 1809-1852 ***4511.35*** *p60*
Wonderzcher, Charles 22; America, 1746 ***778.6*** *p348*
Wonn, Johann Wilhelm; Wisconsin, 1869 ***6795.8*** *p143*
Wonnell, James; Annapolis, MD, 1719 ***1220.12*** *p894*
Wonocotte, Thomas 29; Ontario, 1871 ***1823.21*** *p399*
Wonshaw, Elizabeth 10; Ontario, 1871 ***1823.21*** *p399*
Wood, Abraham; Ohio, 1809-1852 ***4511.35*** *p60*
Wood, Ann; America, 1732 ***1220.12*** *p894*
Wood, Ann; America, 1743 ***1220.12*** *p894*
Wood, Ann; America, 1768 ***1220.12*** *p894*
Wood, Ann 52; Ontario, 1871 ***1823.21*** *p399*
Wood, Anne 65; Ontario, 1871 ***1823.21*** *p399*
Wood, Benjamin; Barbados, 1663 ***1220.12*** *p894*
Wood, Benjamin; Virginia, 1741 ***1220.12*** *p894*
Wood, Brittania; Rappahannock, VA, 1741 ***1220.12*** *p894*
Wood, Catherine; America, 1743 ***1220.12*** *p894*
Wood, Catherine; America, 1746 ***1220.12*** *p894*
Wood, Charles; America, 1771 ***1220.12*** *p894*
Wood, Charles 37; Ontario, 1871 ***1823.21*** *p400*
Wood, Charlotte 9; Ontario, 1871 ***1823.21*** *p400*
Wood, Daniel; America, 1740 ***1220.12*** *p894*
Wood, Daniel; Annapolis, MD, 1731 ***1220.12*** *p894*
Wood, Dorothy; America, 1742 ***1220.12*** *p894*
Wood, Dorothy; Barbados, 1663 ***1220.12*** *p894*
Wood, Eady; Annapolis, MD, 1729 ***1220.12*** *p894*
Wood, Edward; America, 1655 ***1220.12*** *p894*
Wood, Edward; America, 1768 ***1220.12*** *p894*
Wood, Edward; Ohio, 1827 ***3580.20*** *p34*
Wood, Elizabeth; America, 1715 ***1220.12*** *p895*
Wood, Elizabeth; America, 1739 ***1220.12*** *p895*
Wood, Elizabeth; America, 1772 ***1220.12*** *p895*
Wood, Elizabeth; Annapolis, MD, 1725 ***1220.12*** *p895*
Wood, Elizabeth; Barbados, 1664 ***1220.12*** *p895*
Wood, Elizabeth; Virginia, 1735 ***1220.12*** *p895*
Wood, Emily 5; Quebec, 1870 ***8364.32*** *p26*
Wood, Enoch; America, 1742 ***1220.12*** *p895*
Wood, Francis; Maryland, 1720 ***1220.12*** *p895*
Wood, Fred; Illinois, 1918 ***6007.60*** *p9*
Wood, George; America, 1665 ***1220.12*** *p895*
Wood, George; America, 1721 ***1220.12*** *p895*
Wood, George; America, 1770 ***1220.12*** *p895*
Wood, George 16; Quebec, 1870 ***8364.32*** *p26*
Wood, George A. 36; Ontario, 1871 ***1823.21*** *p400*
Wood, Grace; Maryland, 1725 ***1220.12*** *p895*
Wood, Hannah; America, 1741 ***1220.12*** *p895*
Wood, Henry 46; Ontario, 1871 ***1823.17*** *p178*
Wood, Henry 15; Quebec, 1870 ***8364.32*** *p26*
Wood, J. 40; America, 1848 ***778.6*** *p348*
Wood, James; America, 1736 ***1220.12*** *p895*
Wood, James; America, 1740 ***1220.12*** *p895*
Wood, James; America, 1750 ***1220.12*** *p895*
Wood, James; America, 1752 ***1220.12*** *p895*
Wood, James; America, 1765 ***1220.12*** *p895*
Wood, James; America, 1766 ***1220.12*** *p895*
Wood, James 18; Ontario, 1871 ***1823.21*** *p400*
Wood, James; South Carolina, 1811 ***6155.4*** *p19*
Wood, James H. 43; Ontario, 1871 ***1823.17*** *p179*
Wood, Jane; America, 1743 ***1220.12*** *p895*
Wood, Jane; America, 1755 ***1220.12*** *p895*
Wood, Jane; Annapolis, MD, 1725 ***1220.12*** *p895*
Wood, Jane; Potomac, 1729 ***1220.12*** *p895*
Wood, Joane; Charles Town, SC, 1719 ***1220.12*** *p895*
Wood, John; America, 1737 ***1220.12*** *p895*
Wood, John; America, 1744 ***1220.12*** *p895*
Wood, John; America, 1747 ***1220.12*** *p895*
Wood, John; America, 1749 ***1220.12*** *p895*
Wood, John; America, 1756 ***1220.12*** *p895*
Wood, John; America, 1758 ***1220.12*** *p895*
Wood, John; America, 1765 ***1220.12*** *p895*
Wood, John; America, 1768 ***1220.12*** *p895*
Wood, John; America, 1771 ***1220.12*** *p895*
Wood, John; America, 1772 ***1220.12*** *p895*
Wood, John; America, 1774 ***1220.12*** *p895*
Wood, John; Boston, 1828 ***3274.55*** *p74*
Wood, John; Charles Town, SC, 1719 ***1220.12*** *p895*
Wood, John; Maryland, 1728 ***1220.12*** *p895*
Wood, John; Virginia, 1620 ***1220.12*** *p895*
Wood, John; Virginia, 1718 ***1220.12*** *p895*
Wood, John; Virginia, 1721 ***1220.12*** *p895*
Wood, Jonathan; Barbados, 1673 ***1220.12*** *p896*
Wood, Joseph; America, 1737 ***1220.12*** *p896*
Wood, Joseph; America, 1765 ***1220.12*** *p896*
Wood, Joseph; America, 1766 ***1220.12*** *p896*
Wood, Joseph; America, 1772 ***1220.12*** *p896*
Wood, Knightly; America, 1738 ***1220.12*** *p896*
Wood, Margaret; America, 1665 ***1220.12*** *p896*
Wood, Margaret; America, 1741 ***1220.12*** *p896*
Wood, Margaret; America, 1769 ***1220.12*** *p896*
Wood, Martha; America, 1738 ***1220.12*** *p896*
Wood, Mary; America, 1736 ***1220.12*** *p896*
Wood, Mary; America, 1740 ***1220.12*** *p896*
Wood, Mary; America, 1765 ***1220.12*** *p896*
Wood, Mary; America, 1771 ***1220.12*** *p896*
Wood, Mary; America, 1773 ***1220.12*** *p896*
Wood, Mary; Annapolis, MD, 1720 ***1220.12*** *p896*
Wood, Mary; Barbados or Jamaica, 1697 ***1220.12*** *p896*
Wood, Mary 25; Ontario, 1871 ***1823.21*** *p400*
Wood, Mathew 43; Ontario, 1871 ***1823.17*** *p179*
Wood, Michael; America, 1773 ***1220.12*** *p896*
Wood, Obadiah; America, 1760 ***1220.12*** *p896*
Wood, Paul; America, 1754 ***1220.12*** *p896*
Wood, Peter; America, 1758 ***1220.12*** *p896*
Wood, Rebecca; America, 1766 ***1220.12*** *p896*
Wood, Richard; America, 1736 ***1220.12*** *p896*
Wood, Richard; Barbados, 1698 ***1220.12*** *p896*
Wood, Richard; Charles Town, SC, 1719 ***1220.12*** *p896*
Wood, Richard; Virginia, 1732 ***1220.12*** *p896*
Wood, Richard; Virginia, 1754 ***1220.12*** *p896*
Wood, Robert; America, 1750 ***1220.12*** *p896*
Wood, Robert; America, 1761 ***1220.12*** *p896*
Wood, Robert; Barbados, 1668 ***1220.12*** *p896*
Wood, Robert; Jamaica, 1661 ***1220.12*** *p896*
Wood, Robert 45; Ontario, 1871 ***1823.17*** *p179*
Wood, Robert 50; Ontario, 1871 ***1823.17*** *p179*
Wood, Samuel; America, 1736 ***1220.12*** *p896*
Wood, Samuel; America, 1742 ***1220.12*** *p896*
Wood, Samuel; America, 1756 ***1220.12*** *p896*
Wood, Samuel, II 30; Worcester, MA, 1825-1840 ***3274.55*** *p70*
Wood, Solomon; America, 1771 ***1220.12*** *p896*
Wood, Susan; Barbados or Jamaica, 1699 ***1220.12*** *p896*
Wood, Susannah; America, 1768 ***1220.12*** *p896*
Wood, Thomas; America, 1664 ***1220.12*** *p896*
Wood, Thomas; America, 1680 ***1220.12*** *p896*
Wood, Thomas; America, 1687 ***1220.12*** *p896*
Wood, Thomas; America, 1700 ***1220.12*** *p896*
Wood, Thomas; America, 1750 ***1220.12*** *p896*
Wood, Thomas; America, 1760 ***1220.12*** *p896*
Wood, Thomas; America, 1763 ***1220.12*** *p896*
Wood, Thomas; America, 1768 ***1220.12*** *p897*
Wood, Thomas; America, 1771 ***1220.12*** *p897*
Wood, Thomas; Barbados, 1701 ***1220.12*** *p896*
Wood, Thomas; Marston's Wharf, 1782 ***8529.30*** *p17*
Wood, Thomas 41; Ontario, 1871 ***1823.17*** *p179*
Wood, Thomas 41; Ontario, 1871 ***1823.21*** *p400*
Wood, Thomas; Virginia, 1745 ***1220.12*** *p896*
Wood, Timothy; America, 1756 ***1220.12*** *p897*
Wood, Walter; America, 1739 ***1220.12*** *p897*
Wood, William; America, 1685 ***1220.12*** *p897*
Wood, William; America, 1719 ***1220.12*** *p897*
Wood, William; America, 1730 ***1220.12*** *p897*
Wood, William; America, 1737 ***1220.12*** *p897*
Wood, William; America, 1738 ***1220.12*** *p897*
Wood, William; America, 1753 ***1220.12*** *p897*
Wood, William; America, 1758 ***1220.12*** *p897*
Wood, William; America, 1763 ***1220.12*** *p897*
Wood, William; America, 1766 ***1220.12*** *p897*
Wood, William; America, 1769 ***1220.12*** *p897*
Wood, William; Annapolis, MD, 1729 ***1220.12*** *p897*
Wood, William; Barbados, 1683 ***1220.12*** *p897*
Wood, William 32; Ontario, 1871 ***1823.21*** *p400*
Wood, William 42; Ontario, 1871 ***1823.21*** *p400*
Wood, William 45; Ontario, 1871 ***1823.17*** *p179*
Wood, William; Utah, 1900 ***1211.45*** *p136*
Woodamore, William; America, 1656 ***1220.12*** *p897*
Woodar, Mary; Barbados or Jamaica, 1702 ***1220.12*** *p897*
Woodard, William; America, 1697 ***1220.12*** *p897*
Woodason, Richard; America, 1738 ***1220.12*** *p897*
Woodbegood, Mary; America, 1755 ***1220.12*** *p897*
Woodbourne, William; America, 1736 ***1220.12*** *p897*
Woodbridge, Edward; America, 1765 ***1220.12*** *p897*
Woodburn, Thomas 32; Ontario, 1871 ***1823.21*** *p400*
Woodburn, William 60; Ontario, 1871 ***1823.21*** *p400*
Woodburne, James; America, 1755 ***1220.12*** *p897*

Woodbury, Mary 43; Michigan, 1880 ***4491.42*** *p29*
Woodcock, Diana; America, 1744 ***1220.12*** *p897*
Woodcock, Edward; America, 1774 ***1220.12*** *p897*
Woodcock, James; America, 1742 ***1220.12*** *p897*
Woodcock, John; America, 1734 ***1220.12*** *p897*
Woodcock, John; America, 1764 ***1220.12*** *p897*
Woodcock, John A. 35; Ontario, 1871 ***1823.17*** *p179*
Woodcock, Robert; America, 1750 ***1220.12*** *p897*
Woodcock, Samuel; Marston's Wharf, 1782 ***8529.30*** *p17*
Woodcock, Sarah; Virginia, 1739 ***1220.12*** *p897*
Woodcock, William; America, 1685 ***1220.12*** *p897*
Woodcock, William; America, 1743 ***1220.12*** *p897*
Woodcock, William; Barbados, 1699 ***1220.12*** *p897*
Woodcocke, John; America, 1686 ***1220.12*** *p897*
Woodcocke, Nicholas; America, 1683 ***1220.12*** *p897*
Woodcocke, Thomas; Barbados, 1678 ***1220.12*** *p897*
Wooden, Elizabeth; America, 1741 ***1220.12*** *p897*
Woodey, Thomas; America, 1758 ***1220.12*** *p897*
Woodfield, Jane; America, 1771 ***1220.12*** *p897*
Woodfield, John; Maryland, 1723 ***1220.12*** *p897*
Woodfield, Maria; America, 1771 ***1220.12*** *p897*
Woodfield, Thomas; Virginia, 1670 ***1220.12*** *p897*
Woodford, Charles; America, 1741 ***1220.12*** *p897*
Woodford, Richard; America, 1740 ***1220.12*** *p897*
Woodford, Robert; America, 1740 ***1220.12*** *p898*
Woodgate, James R. 36; Ontario, 1871 ***1823.21*** *p400*
Woodger, James; America, 1758 ***1220.12*** *p898*
Woodhall, Edward; America, 1773 ***1220.12*** *p898*
Woodhall, John 40; Ontario, 1871 ***1823.21*** *p400*
Woodhall, Thomas 55; Ontario, 1871 ***1823.21*** *p400*
Woodham, George; America, 1773 ***1220.12*** *p898*
Woodham, Richard; Charles Town, SC, 1718 ***1220.12*** *p898*
Woodhouse, George; America, 1775 ***1220.12*** *p898*
Woodhouse, George; Iowa, 1914 ***1211.15*** *p20*
Woodhouse, George 40; Ontario, 1871 ***1823.17*** *p179*
Woodhouse, Henry 50; Ontario, 1871 ***1823.21*** *p400*
Woodhouse, John; America, 1730 ***1220.12*** *p898*
Woodhouse, John; Died enroute, 1726 ***1220.12*** *p898*
Woodhouse, John 82; Ontario, 1871 ***1823.21*** *p400*
Woodhouse, Mary; Annapolis, MD, 1731 ***1220.12*** *p898*
Woodhouse, Samuel; America, 1663 ***1220.12*** *p898*
Woodhouse, Thomas; America, 1753 ***1220.12*** *p898*
Woodhouse, Thomas; America, 1762 ***1220.12*** *p898*
Woodhouse, William T. 33; Ontario, 1871 ***1823.21*** *p400*
Woodhull, Ambrus 66; Ontario, 1871 ***1823.21*** *p400*
Woodhull, Maria 65; Ontario, 1871 ***1823.21*** *p400*
Woodhull, Mary 30; Ontario, 1871 ***1823.21*** *p400*
Woodin, John; America, 1766 ***1220.12*** *p898*
Woodin, Michael; America, 1737 ***1220.12*** *p898*
Wooding, John; America, 1749 ***1220.12*** *p898*
Woodington, Dorothy; America, 1751 ***1220.12*** *p898*
Woodl, Edward; Ohio, 1827 ***6020.12*** *p23*
Woodland, Christopher; America, 1754 ***1220.12*** *p898*
Woodland, Lydia; America, 1756 ***1220.12*** *p898*
Woodland, Matthew; America, 1685 ***1220.12*** *p898*
Woodland, Samuel; America, 1764 ***1220.12*** *p898*
Woodley, Benjamin; America, 1772 ***1220.12*** *p898*
Woodley, John; America, 1748 ***1220.12*** *p898*
Woodley, John; Barbados, 1668 ***1220.12*** *p898*
Woodley, John 37; Ontario, 1871 ***1823.17*** *p179*
Woodley, William; America, 1775 ***1220.12*** *p898*
Woodliffe, Nathaniel; America, 1748 ***1220.12*** *p898*
Woodlock, John 40; Ontario, 1871 ***1823.21*** *p400*
Woodly, Mary; America, 1735 ***1220.12*** *p898*
Woodman, Asshia 73; Ontario, 1871 ***1823.21*** *p400*
Woodman, Edw 45; Ontario, 1871 ***1823.21*** *p400*
Woodman, Henry 45; Ontario, 1871 ***1823.21*** *p400*
Woodman, John 52; Ontario, 1871 ***1823.21*** *p400*
Woodman, Mary 44; Ontario, 1871 ***1823.21*** *p400*
Woodman, Phillis; America, 1764 ***1220.12*** *p898*
Woodman, Thomas; Maryland, 1719 ***1220.12*** *p898*
Woodman, William; America, 1741 ***1220.12*** *p898*
Woodman, William; America, 1768 ***1220.12*** *p898*
Woodmanson, Richard; Barbados, 1672 ***1220.12*** *p898*
Woodmason, Mary; Virginia, 1750 ***1220.12*** *p898*
Woodnoth, William; America, 1719 ***1220.12*** *p898*
Woodridge, William; America, 1760 ***1220.12*** *p898*
Woodrooffe, Emma 33; Ontario, 1871 ***1823.17*** *p179*
Woodrow, Anthony; America, 1685 ***1220.12*** *p898*
Woodrow, John; America, 1685 ***1220.12*** *p898*
Woodrow, Matthew; Virginia, 1740 ***1220.12*** *p898*
Woodruff, Ephraim 55; Ontario, 1871 ***1823.21*** *p400*
Woodruff, James; America, 1742 ***1220.12*** *p898*
Woodruff, Thomas; America, 1740 ***1220.12*** *p898*
Woods, Abraham 39; Ontario, 1871 ***1823.17*** *p179*
Woods, Alexander 58; Ontario, 1871 ***1823.21*** *p400*
Woods, Alexander 70; Ontario, 1871 ***1823.21*** *p400*
Woods, Allan 41; Ontario, 1871 ***1823.21*** *p400*
Woods, Anthony; America, 1732 ***1220.12*** *p898*
Woods, Caleb; America, 1740 ***1220.12*** *p898*
Woods, Caroline 55; Ontario, 1871 ***1823.21*** *p400*
Woods, Charles 52; Ontario, 1871 ***1823.21*** *p400*
Woods, Charles; Washington, 1882 ***2770.40*** *p136*
Woods, Edward; America, 1757 ***1220.12*** *p898*
Woods, Eliza 43; Ontario, 1871 ***1823.21*** *p401*
Woods, Elizabeth 32; Ontario, 1871 ***1823.21*** *p401*
Woods, Elizabeth 70; Ontario, 1871 ***1823.17*** *p179*
Woods, George; America, 1763 ***1220.12*** *p899*
Woods, Iset 19; Ontario, 1871 ***1823.21*** *p401*
Woods, James 22; Ontario, 1871 ***1823.21*** *p401*
Woods, James *SEE* Woods, Robert
Woods, John; America, 1780 ***8529.30*** *p17*
Woods, John; Iowa, 1884 ***1211.15*** *p20*
Woods, John; New Orleans, 1850 ***7242.30*** *p156*
Woods, John 31; Ontario, 1871 ***1823.21*** *p401*
Woods, John 45; Ontario, 1871 ***1823.21*** *p401*
Woods, Martha; Maryland, 1720 ***1220.12*** *p899*
Woods, Mary Savage *SEE* Woods, Robert
Woods, Mary 32; St. John, N.B., 1834 ***6469.7*** *p4*
Woods, P.; New Orleans, 1850 ***7242.30*** *p156*
Woods, Peter; Iowa, 1888 ***1211.15*** *p20*
Woods, Robert; America, 1760 ***1220.12*** *p899*
Woods, Robert; America, 1761 ***1220.12*** *p899*
Woods, Robert; America, 1774 ***1220.12*** *p899*
Woods, Robert; North Carolina, 1802 ***1088.45*** *p37*
Woods, Robert; Ohio, 1827 ***3580.20*** *p34*
Woods, Robert; Ohio, 1840 ***6020.12*** *p23*
Woods, Robert 39; Ontario, 1871 ***1823.21*** *p401*
Woods, Robert; Philadelphia, 1868 ***8513.31*** *p434*
*Wife:*Mary Savage
*Child:*James
Woods, Robert B. 30; Ontario, 1871 ***1823.21*** *p401*
Woods, Samuel; Boston, 1775 ***8529.30*** *p5A*
Woods, Samuel; Jamaica, 1777 ***8529.30*** *p14A*
Woods, Stainsby; America, 1757 ***1220.12*** *p899*
Woods, Susanna; America, 1752 ***1220.12*** *p899*
Woods, Thomas; America, 1768 ***1220.12*** *p899*
Woods, Thomas 36; Ontario, 1871 ***1823.17*** *p179*
Woods, Thomas; Virginia, 1767 ***1220.12*** *p899*
Woods, William; America, 1686 ***1220.12*** *p899*
Woods, William; America, 1736 ***1220.12*** *p899*
Woods, William; America, 1773 ***1220.12*** *p899*
Woods, William 32; Ontario, 1871 ***1823.17*** *p179*
Woods, William 38; Ontario, 1871 ***1823.21*** *p401*
Woods, William 42; Ontario, 1871 ***1823.17*** *p179*
Woods, William 45; Ontario, 1871 ***1823.21*** *p401*
Woodside, James; Maine, 1718 ***1642*** *p22*
Woodside, James; Prince Edward Island, 1771 ***3799.30*** *p41*
Woodthey, John; America, 1769 ***1220.12*** *p899*
Woodward, Alexander; Barbados or Jamaica, 1690 ***1220.12*** *p899*
Woodward, Ann; America, 1754 ***1220.12*** *p899*
Woodward, Bessey 50; Ontario, 1871 ***1823.21*** *p401*
Woodward, Catherine; Annapolis, MD, 1736 ***1220.12*** *p899*
Woodward, Christopher; America, 1686 ***1220.12*** *p899*
Woodward, Elizabeth; America, 1743 ***1220.12*** *p899*
Woodward, Elizabeth; America, 1756 ***1220.12*** *p899*
Woodward, Elizabeth; America, 1761 ***1220.12*** *p899*
Woodward, Elizabeth; Died enroute, 1731 ***1220.12*** *p899*
Woodward, George; Jamaica, 1717 ***1220.12*** *p899*
Woodward, Henry; America, 1721 ***1220.12*** *p899*
Woodward, Henry 48; Ontario, 1871 ***1823.21*** *p401*
Woodward, James; America, 1738 ***1220.12*** *p899*
Woodward, James; America, 1774 ***1220.12*** *p899*
Woodward, John; America, 1685 ***1220.12*** *p899*
Woodward, John; America, 1722 ***1220.12*** *p899*
Woodward, John; America, 1738 ***1220.12*** *p899*
Woodward, John; America, 1747 ***1220.12*** *p899*
Woodward, John; America, 1756 ***1220.12*** *p899*
Woodward, John; America, 1768 ***1220.12*** *p899*
Woodward, John; Maryland, 1719 ***1220.12*** *p899*
Woodward, John 30; Ontario, 1871 ***1823.21*** *p401*
Woodward, John 37; Ontario, 1871 ***1823.21*** *p401*
Woodward, John 47; Ontario, 1871 ***1823.21*** *p401*
Woodward, Mary; America, 1741 ***1220.12*** *p899*
Woodward, Mary *SEE* Woodward, Ralph
Woodward, Mary 73; Ontario, 1871 ***1823.21*** *p401*
Woodward, Ralph; Hingham, MA, 1636 ***1642*** *p87*
*Wife:*Mary
With daughter
Woodward, Richard; America, 1739 ***1220.12*** *p899*
Woodward, Robert 31; Ontario, 1871 ***1823.21*** *p401*
Woodward, Samuel; America, 1761 ***1220.12*** *p899*
Woodward, Thomas; America, 1730 ***1220.12*** *p899*
Woodward, Thomas; America, 1764 ***1220.12*** *p899*
Woodward, Thomas; Barbados, 1664 ***1220.12*** *p899*
Woodward, Thomas 72; Ontario, 1871 ***1823.21*** *p401*
Woodward, William; America, 1766 ***1220.12*** *p899*
Woodward, William; Barbados or Jamaica, 1698 ***1220.12*** *p899*
Woodward, William 29; Ontario, 1871 ***1823.17*** *p179*
Woodwork, John 32; Ontario, 1871 ***1823.21*** *p401*
Woofe, James; America, 1757 ***1220.12*** *p894*
Woolard, John; Died enroute, 1729 ***1220.12*** *p900*
Woolard, Michael; America, 1756 ***1220.12*** *p900*
Woolben, George 16; Quebec, 1870 ***8364.32*** *p26*
Woolcock, John; America, 1747 ***1220.12*** *p900*
Woolcock, John; America, 1749 ***1220.12*** *p900*
Woolcock, John 47; Ontario, 1871 ***1823.21*** *p401*
Woolcock, Richard; America, 1747 ***1220.12*** *p900*
Woolcott, George; America, 1771 ***1220.12*** *p900*
Woolcott, Samuel; America, 1764 ***1220.12*** *p900*
Wooldridge, William; America, 1768 ***1220.12*** *p900*
Woolen, Sarah; America, 1748 ***1220.12*** *p900*
Woolener, William; America, 1745 ***1220.12*** *p900*
Wooler, George; Jamaica, 1661 ***1220.12*** *p900*
Wooley, James; Ohio, 1839 ***3580.20*** *p34*
Wooley, James; Ohio, 1839 ***6020.12*** *p23*
Wooley, Joseph; Ohio, 1836 ***3580.20*** *p34*
Wooley, Joseph; Ohio, 1836 ***6020.12*** *p23*
Wooley, Richard; America, 1771 ***1220.12*** *p900*
Wooley, Simeon 24; Indiana, 1876-1878 ***9076.20*** *p69*
Wooley, William; America, 1775 ***1220.12*** *p900*
Woolf, Charles Henry; Illinois, 1858-1861 ***6020.5*** *p133*
Woolfe, Barbara; Barbados or Jamaica, 1689 ***1220.12*** *p894*
Woolfenden, Roger; America, 1765 ***1220.12*** *p900*
Woolfitt, Frances A. 24; Michigan, 1880 ***4491.39*** *p33*
Woolfitt, Hannah 72; Michigan, 1880 ***4491.39*** *p33*
Woolfitt, Jane 60; Michigan, 1880 ***4491.30*** *p33*
Woolfitt, John 76; Michigan, 1880 ***4491.30*** *p33*
Woolford, Henry; Annapolis, MD, 1720 ***1220.12*** *p900*
Woolford, Sarah; Virginia, 1768 ***1220.12*** *p900*
Woolford, Thomas; Virginia, 1768 ***1220.12*** *p900*
Woolfry, Lucy; Maryland, 1674-1675 ***1236.25*** *p52*
Woolgan, Albert; Missouri, 1894 ***3276.1*** *p3*
Woolgan, John Thomas; Missouri, 1884 ***3276.1*** *p3*
Woolham, John; America, 1700 ***1220.12*** *p900*
Woolhouse, Jonathan; America, 1767 ***1220.12*** *p900*
Woolisay, Mary 70; Ontario, 1871 ***1823.21*** *p401*
Woolisay, Richard 70; Ontario, 1871 ***1823.21*** *p401*
Woollam, John; Died enroute, 1729 ***1220.12*** *p900*
Woollard, James; America, 1746 ***1220.12*** *p900*
Woollard, William; America, 1769 ***1220.12*** *p900*
Woollaway, William; America, 1773 ***1220.12*** *p900*
Woollen, Ann; America, 1757 ***1220.12*** *p900*
Woollens, Isaac; Barbados or Jamaica, 1690 ***1220.12*** *p900*
Wooller, James; America, 1766 ***1220.12*** *p900*
Wooller, John; America, 1765 ***1220.12*** *p900*
Woollestone, Samuel; America, 1665 ***1220.12*** *p900*
Woolley, Isaac 41; Indiana, 1878-1883 ***9076.20*** *p70*
Woolley, James; New Jersey, 1668 ***9228.50*** *p656*
Woolley, James; Ohio, 1836 ***3580.20*** *p34*
Woolley, James; Ohio, 1836 ***6020.12*** *p23*
Woolley, James 70; Ontario, 1871 ***1823.17*** *p179*
Woolley, Joseph; America, 1765 ***1220.12*** *p900*
Woolley, Rebecca; America, 1746 ***1220.12*** *p900*
Woolley, Richard; America, 1770 ***1220.12*** *p900*
Woolley, Richard; Maryland, 1737 ***1220.12*** *p900*
Woolley, Robert; America, 1769 ***1220.12*** *p900*
Woolley, Thomas 53; Ontario, 1871 ***1823.21*** *p401*
Woolls, William; America, 1767 ***1220.12*** *p900*
Woolmer, John; America, 1731 ***1220.12*** *p900*
Woolner, William; America, 1754 ***1220.12*** *p900*
Wooloin, Richard T.; North Carolina, 1802 ***1088.45*** *p37*
Woolrich, Sophia 71; Ontario, 1871 ***1823.21*** *p401*
Woolridge, Roger; America, 1752 ***1220.12*** *p900*
Woolridge, William; America, 1685 ***1220.12*** *p900*
Woolridge, William; America, 1760 ***1220.12*** *p900*
Woolrych, Humphrey; America, 1782 ***8529.30*** *p17*
Wools, Richard; Virginia, 1731 ***1220.12*** *p900*
Woolstonecraft, Brittania; Rappahannock, VA, 1741 ***1220.12*** *p900*
Woolway, Gilbert 24; Ontario, 1871 ***1823.21*** *p401*
Woolway, Giles 28; Ontario, 1871 ***1823.21*** *p401*
Woolway, John 45; Ontario, 1871 ***1823.21*** *p401*
Woon, Stephen; America, 1749 ***1220.12*** *p900*
Woon, Thomas; Colorado, 1881 ***1029.59*** *p96*
Woone, Benjamin; America, 1749 ***1220.12*** *p900*
Woore, John; America, 1754 ***1220.12*** *p901*
Wooten, Robert; Barbados, 1694 ***1220.12*** *p901*
Wooton, John; New York, 1783 ***8529.30*** *p17*
Wooton, Paul; America, 1771 ***1220.12*** *p901*
Wootton, Alice; America, 1775 ***1220.12*** *p901*
Wootton, James; Virginia, 1775 ***1220.12*** *p901*
Wootton, Margaret; America, 1770 ***1220.12*** *p901*
Wootton, Mary; America, 1688 ***1220.12*** *p901*
Wootton, Mary; Virginia, 1736 ***1220.12*** *p901*
Wootton, Richard; America, 1677 ***1220.12*** *p901*
Wopschall, Carl Ferdinand; Wisconsin, 1890 ***6795.8*** *p35*
Worcester, Andrew; Maryland, 1758 ***1220.12*** *p901*
Worden, John; America, 1751 ***1220.12*** *p840*
Worden, John; Ohio, 1843 ***2763.1*** *p22*
Worden, Liney B. 6; Ohio, 1880 ***4879.40*** *p258*
Worder, Henry; Marston's Wharf, 1782 ***8529.30*** *p17*

Wordly, William; America, 1759 ***1220.12*** *p901*
Worgan, William; America, 1744 ***1220.12*** *p901*
Worker, Nathaniel 25; North Carolina, 1774 ***1422.10*** *p55*
Workman, Dr.; Toronto, 1844 ***2910.35*** *p111*
Workman, Aaron 66; Ontario, 1871 ***1823.17*** *p179*
Workman, Daniel; Virginia, 1746 ***1220.12*** *p901*
Workman, Elizabeth 50; Ontario, 1871 ***1823.17*** *p179*
Workman, John; Ohio, 1838 ***3580.20*** *p34*
Workman, John; Ohio, 1838 ***6020.12*** *p23*
Workman, John 53; Ontario, 1871 ***1823.17*** *p179*
Workman, Robert 51; South Carolina, 1812 ***3476.30*** *p13*
Workman, Sam'l; Toronto, 1844 ***2910.35*** *p111*
Workman, Samuel; America, 1765 ***1220.12*** *p901*
Workman, Samuel 50; Ontario, 1871 ***1823.17*** *p179*
Worle, Charlotte 6 *SEE* Worle, Christina Elisabetha
Worle, Christina Elisabetha 25; America, 1855 ***2526.43*** *p202*
*Daughter:*Charlotte 6
*Daughter:*Katharine Elisabethe 4
*Father-In-Law:*Ferdinand
Worle, Ferdinand *SEE* Worle, Christina Elisabetha
Worle, Katharine Elisabethe 4 *SEE* Worle, Christina Elisabetha
Worle, Valentin; America, 1830 ***2526.43*** *p185*
Worledge, Samuel; Barbados, 1678 ***1220.12*** *p901*
Worley, Henry; New Jersey, 1737-1774 ***927.31*** *p3*
Worley, John; America, 1755 ***1220.12*** *p901*
Worley, Thomas; America, 1754 ***1220.12*** *p901*
Worly, Francis; Ohio, 1809-1852 ***4511.35*** *p60*
Worly, Henry; Ohio, 1809-1852 ***4511.35*** *p60*
Worm, Johann Wilhelm; Wisconsin, 1869 ***6795.8*** *p143*
Worme, Joseph 29; America, 1840 ***778.6*** *p348*
Wormelayton, Robert; Barbados, 1668 ***1220.12*** *p901*
Wormensley, George; Philadelphia, 1827 ***3274.55*** *p66*
Wormer, William; America, 1684 ***1220.12*** *p901*
Worms, Thomas 17; Quebec, 1870 ***8364.32*** *p26*
Wormsbecker, Heinrich 17; New York, NY, 1877 ***6954.7*** *p39*
Wormsbecker, Johann 19; New York, NY, 1877 ***6954.7*** *p39*
Wormser, Abraham; America, 1860 ***2526.43*** *p185*
Wormser, Michael; America, 1862 ***2526.43*** *p185*
Worn, Edward; America, 1770 ***1220.12*** *p841*
Wornell, George; Barbados, 1679 ***1220.12*** *p901*
Worner, Christian Leonhard; America, 1852 ***179.55*** *p19*
Worner, Karl; America, 1881 ***179.55*** *p19*
Wornoll, John; America, 1751 ***1220.12*** *p901*
Worral, Margaret Ann; America, 1767 ***1220.12*** *p901*
Worral, Thomas; America, 1765 ***1220.12*** *p901*
Worrall, Charles; America, 1662 ***1220.12*** *p901*
Worrall, Charles; America, 1743 ***1220.12*** *p901*
Worrall, John; America, 1685 ***1220.12*** *p901*
Worrall, Mark; America, 1771 ***1220.12*** *p901*
Worrall, Stephen 65; Ontario, 1871 ***1823.21*** *p401*
Worrell, Frances; America, 1753 ***1220.12*** *p901*
Worrell, Francis; America, 1752 ***1220.12*** *p901*
Worrell, Francis; America, 1754 ***1220.12*** *p901*
Worrell, Sarah; Barbados or Jamaica, 1686 ***1220.12*** *p901*
Worrell, Thomas; Rappahannock, VA, 1728 ***1220.12*** *p901*
Worrill, Henry; Maryland, 1734 ***1220.12*** *p901*
Worrill, William; America, 1761 ***1220.12*** *p901*
Worsfold, Thomas; America, 1773 ***1220.12*** *p901*
Worsley, Alice; America, 1755 ***1220.12*** *p901*
Worsley, Joseph 36; Ontario, 1871 ***1823.17*** *p179*
Worsley, William; America, 1723 ***1220.12*** *p901*
Worster, Andrew; Maryland, 1758 ***1220.12*** *p901*
Worsthorn, Joseph 21; New Castle, DE, 1817-1818 ***90.20*** *p155*
Worters, Thomas; Marston's Wharf, 1782 ***8529.30*** *p17*
Worth, Andrew; Virginia, 1772 ***1220.12*** *p901*
Worth, James; Barbados, 1677 ***1220.12*** *p901*
Worth, John 54; Ontario, 1871 ***1823.21*** *p401*
Worth, Mary; America, 1773 ***1220.12*** *p901*
Worth, Michael; Virginia, 1736 ***1220.12*** *p901*
Worth, Robert; America, 1746 ***1220.12*** *p901*
Wortherthing, James 50; Ontario, 1871 ***1823.21*** *p401*
Worthing, Thomas; America, 1720 ***1220.12*** *p902*
Worthing, William; America, 1764 ***1220.12*** *p902*
Worthington, John; Barbados, 1664 ***1220.12*** *p902*
Worthington, Thomas; America, 1751 ***1220.12*** *p902*
Worthington, William; America, 1764 ***1220.12*** *p902*
Wortzers, . . .; West Virginia, n.d. ***1132.30*** *p151*
Wosk, Louis David 22; San Diego, 1921 ***1029.59*** *p96*
Wostendale, John; America, 1726 ***1220.12*** *p902*
Wotenden, Ralph; America, 1675 ***1220.12*** *p902*
Wotton, Ann; America, 1774 ***1220.12*** *p901*
Wotton, Joseph; America, 1774 ***1220.12*** *p901*
Wotton, Michael; Virginia, 1731 ***1220.12*** *p901*
Wotton, Thomas; America, 1769 ***1220.12*** *p901*
Wourzaszak, August 25; New York, NY, 1920 ***930.50*** *p49*
Woyda, Carl; Wisconsin, 1897 ***6795.8*** *p32*
Wozcsinski, Frank; Wisconsin, 1900 ***6795.8*** *p53*
Wozniak, John; Detroit, 1929-1930 ***6214.5*** *p65*
Wozniak, Jos.; Texas, 1893 ***6015.15*** *p29*
Wozniak, Madaline; Wisconsin, 1898 ***6795.8*** *p53*
Wrangham, George; New York, NY, 1778 ***8529.30*** *p3*
Wrase, Minna; Wisconsin, 1885 ***6795.8*** *p153*
Wrasse, Minna; Wisconsin, 1885 ***6795.8*** *p153*
Wrathall, John 48; Ontario, 1871 ***1823.17*** *p179*
Wray, George 35; Ontario, 1871 ***1823.17*** *p179*
Wray, Jacob; America, 1757 ***1220.12*** *p902*
Wray, John; America, 1756 ***1220.12*** *p902*
Wray, John 55; Ontario, 1871 ***1823.17*** *p179*
Wray, William; Louisiana, 1836-1841 ***4981.45*** *p209*
Wray, William 31; Ontario, 1871 ***1823.21*** *p401*
Wray, William 45; Ontario, 1871 ***1823.17*** *p179*
Wrbitzky, Edmund; St. Louis, 1891 ***2853.20*** *p33*
Wreathcocke, William; Maryland, 1736 ***1220.12*** *p902*
Wrecknorth, John; America, 1774 ***1220.12*** *p902*
Wren, Samuel 63; Ontario, 1871 ***1823.21*** *p402*
Wren, Susan; Barbados, 1664 ***1220.12*** *p902*
Wrench, Frederick; Missouri, 1892 ***3276.1*** *p4*
Wrenn, Sarah; America, 1720 ***1220.12*** *p902*
Wrenshaw, Elizabeth; Barbados, 1699 ***1220.12*** *p902*
Wrentmore, Henry; America, 1685 ***1220.12*** *p902*
Wresle, John; America, 1710 ***1220.12*** *p902*
Wressell, George 45; Ontario, 1871 ***1823.21*** *p402*
Wrexham, Charles; America, 1694 ***1220.12*** *p902*
Wreziona, A.; Galveston, TX, 1855 ***571.7*** *p18*
Wride, John; America, 1754 ***1220.12*** *p902*
Wrigglesworth, Joseph; America, 1742 ***1220.12*** *p902*
Wrigglesworth, Samuel; America, 1748 ***1220.12*** *p902*
Wright, Mrs. 45; Ontario, 1871 ***1823.21*** *p402*
Wright, Mrs.; Toronto, 1844 ***2910.35*** *p114*
Wright, Abraham; America, 1750 ***1220.12*** *p902*
Wright, Abraham; America, 1773 ***1220.12*** *p902*
Wright, Alice; Barbados, 1679 ***1220.12*** *p902*
Wright, Amos; Illinois, 1834-1900 ***6020.5*** *p133*
Wright, Andrew 16; Quebec, 1870 ***8364.32*** *p26*
Wright, Ann; America, 1747 ***1220.12*** *p902*
Wright, Ann; America, 1758 ***1220.12*** *p902*
Wright, Ann; America, 1762 ***1220.12*** *p902*
Wright, Ann; America, 1770 ***1220.12*** *p902*
Wright, Ann; Died enroute, 1776 ***1220.12*** *p902*
Wright, Anne; America, 1725 ***1220.12*** *p902*
Wright, Anne 62; Ontario, 1871 ***1823.21*** *p402*
Wright, Ben; Minnesota, 1923 ***2769.54*** *p1383*
Wright, Benjamin; America, 1774 ***1220.12*** *p902*
Wright, Catherine 43; Ontario, 1871 ***1823.17*** *p179*
Wright, Charles; America, 1767 ***1220.12*** *p902*
Wright, Charles; America, 1774 ***1220.12*** *p902*
Wright, Charles; America, 1775 ***1220.12*** *p902*
Wright, Charles 25; Ontario, 1871 ***1823.21*** *p402*
Wright, Curtis 3; Ontario, 1871 ***1823.17*** *p179*
Wright, Daniel; Jamaica, 1774 ***8529.30*** *p14A*
Wright, David; America, 1770 ***1220.12*** *p902*
Wright, Edgar 16; Ontario, 1871 ***1823.21*** *p402*
Wright, Edward; America, 1774 ***1220.12*** *p902*
Wright, Edward; Maryland, 1721 ***1220.12*** *p902*
Wright, Edward 32; Ontario, 1871 ***1823.21*** *p402*
Wright, Edward 57; Ontario, 1871 ***1823.21*** *p402*
Wright, Elizabeth; America, 1675 ***1220.12*** *p902*
Wright, Elizabeth; America, 1756 ***1220.12*** *p903*
Wright, Elizabeth; America, 1760 ***1220.12*** *p903*
Wright, Elizabeth; America, 1763 ***1220.12*** *p903*
Wright, Elizabeth; Annapolis, MD, 1725 ***1220.12*** *p902*
Wright, Elizabeth; Barbados, 1668 ***1220.12*** *p902*
Wright, Elizabeth; Barbados or Jamaica, 1697 ***1220.12*** *p902*
Wright, Elizabeth; Charles Town, SC, 1719 ***1220.12*** *p902*
Wright, Elizabeth; Maryland, 1722 ***1220.12*** *p902*
Wright, Elizabeth 35; Ontario, 1871 ***1823.17*** *p179*
Wright, Elizabeth; Virginia, 1735 ***1220.12*** *p903*
Wright, Frances; Barbados, 1676 ***1220.12*** *p903*
Wright, Francis; Annapolis, MD, 1730 ***1220.12*** *p903*
Wright, Frank 25; Ontario, 1871 ***1823.17*** *p179*
Wright, George; America, 1751 ***1220.12*** *p903*
Wright, George; America, 1756 ***1220.12*** *p903*
Wright, George; America, 1769 ***1220.12*** *p903*
Wright, George 32; Ontario, 1871 ***1823.17*** *p179*
Wright, George 35; Ontario, 1871 ***1823.17*** *p179*
Wright, Giles; Maryland, 1723 ***1220.12*** *p903*
Wright, Gladduce; Virginia, 1759 ***1220.12*** *p903*
Wright, Hannah; America, 1755 ***1220.12*** *p903*
Wright, Henry; America, 1763 ***1220.12*** *p903*
Wright, Henry 78; Ontario, 1871 ***1823.21*** *p402*
Wright, Huckvill; America, 1690 ***1220.12*** *p903*
Wright, Hugh 35; Ontario, 1871 ***1823.21*** *p402*
Wright, Isobel 36; North Carolina, 1774 ***1422.10*** *p60*
Wright, Isobel 36; North Carolina, 1774 ***1422.10*** *p62*
Wright, James; America, 1661 ***1220.12*** *p903*
Wright, James; America, 1763 ***1220.12*** *p903*
Wright, James; America, 1764 ***1220.12*** *p903*
Wright, James; America, 1767 ***1220.12*** *p903*
Wright, James; America, 1768 ***1220.12*** *p903*
Wright, James; America, 1774 ***1220.12*** *p903*
Wright, James 30; Ontario, 1871 ***1823.21*** *p402*
Wright, James 31; Ontario, 1871 ***1823.21*** *p402*
Wright, James 40; Ontario, 1871 ***1823.21*** *p402*
Wright, James 40; Ontario, 1871 ***1823.21*** *p402*
Wright, James 18; Quebec, 1870 ***8364.32*** *p26*
Wright, James; South Carolina, 1808 ***6155.4*** *p19*
Wright, James A.; North Carolina, 1855 ***1088.45*** *p37*
Wright, Jane 26; Ontario, 1871 ***1823.21*** *p402*
Wright, Jane 11; Quebec, 1870 ***8364.32*** *p26*
Wright, John; America, 1687 ***1220.12*** *p903*
Wright, John; America, 1728 ***1220.12*** *p903*
Wright, John; America, 1739 ***1220.12*** *p903*
Wright, John; America, 1741 ***1220.12*** *p903*
Wright, John; America, 1747 ***1220.12*** *p903*
Wright, John; America, 1751 ***1220.12*** *p903*
Wright, John; America, 1752 ***1220.12*** *p903*
Wright, John; America, 1753 ***1220.12*** *p903*
Wright, John; America, 1754 ***1220.12*** *p903*
Wright, John; America, 1757 ***1220.12*** *p903*
Wright, John; America, 1759 ***1220.12*** *p903*
Wright, John; America, 1760 ***1220.12*** *p903*
Wright, John; America, 1765 ***1220.12*** *p903*
Wright, John; America, 1766 ***1220.12*** *p903*
Wright, John; America, 1767 ***1220.12*** *p903*
Wright, John; America, 1769 ***1220.12*** *p904*
Wright, John; America, 1774 ***1220.12*** *p904*
Wright, John; Annapolis, MD, 1726 ***1220.12*** *p903*
Wright, John; Barbados, 1664 ***1220.12*** *p903*
Wright, John; Barbados, 1667 ***1220.12*** *p903*
Wright, John; Barbados, 1681 ***1220.12*** *p903*
Wright, John; Barbados, 1684 ***1220.12*** *p903*
Wright, John; Barbados or Jamaica, 1692 ***1220.12*** *p903*
Wright, John; Carolina, 1719 ***1220.12*** *p903*
Wright, John; Illinois, 1856 ***6079.1*** *p15*
Wright, John; Maryland, 1672 ***1236.25*** *p47*
Wright, John; New York, 1776 ***8529.30*** *p5A*
Wright, John; North Carolina, 1842 ***1088.45*** *p37*
Wright, John; Ontario, 1871 ***1823.21*** *p402*
Wright, John 30; Ontario, 1871 ***1823.21*** *p402*
Wright, John 44; Ontario, 1871 ***1823.17*** *p179*
Wright, John 51; Ontario, 1871 ***1823.21*** *p402*
Wright, John 57; Ontario, 1871 ***1823.17*** *p179*
Wright, John; Virginia, 1723 ***1220.12*** *p903*
Wright, John; Virginia, 1726 ***1220.12*** *p903*
Wright, John; Virginia, 1734 ***1220.12*** *p903*
Wright, John; Virginia, 1736 ***1220.12*** *p903*
Wright, John W. 22; Ontario, 1871 ***1823.21*** *p402*
Wright, Jonas; Barbados, 1663 ***1220.12*** *p904*
Wright, Joseph; America, 1725 ***1220.12*** *p904*
Wright, Joseph; America, 1755 ***1220.12*** *p904*
Wright, Joseph; America, 1759 ***1220.12*** *p904*
Wright, Joseph; America, 1760 ***1220.12*** *p904*
Wright, Joseph; Annapolis, MD, 1725 ***1220.12*** *p904*
Wright, Joseph; Annapolis, MD, 1730 ***1220.12*** *p904*
Wright, Joseph; Barbados, 1679 ***1220.12*** *p904*
Wright, Joseph 26; Ontario, 1871 ***1823.21*** *p402*
Wright, Josiah 34; Ontario, 1871 ***1823.21*** *p402*
Wright, Katherine 19; Barbados, 1664 ***1220.12*** *p902*
Wright, Lucretia; America, 1764 ***1220.12*** *p904*
Wright, Lydia; America, 1736 ***1220.12*** *p904*
Wright, Margaret; Barbados, 1662 ***1220.12*** *p904*
Wright, Mariah 63; Ontario, 1871 ***1823.21*** *p402*
Wright, Marianne 49; Ontario, 1871 ***1823.21*** *p402*
Wright, Martha; America, 1732 ***1220.12*** *p904*
Wright, Martha; America, 1757 ***1220.12*** *p904*
Wright, Martin; America, 1736 ***1220.12*** *p904*
Wright, Martin; America, 1758 ***1220.12*** *p904*
Wright, Martin; Maryland or Virginia, 1738 ***1220.12*** *p904*
Wright, Mary; America, 1746 ***1220.12*** *p904*
Wright, Mary; America, 1766 ***1220.12*** *p904*
Wright, Mary; America, 1767 ***1220.12*** *p904*
Wright, Mary; America, 1769 ***1220.12*** *p904*
Wright, Mary; Died enroute, 1718 ***1220.12*** *p904*
Wright, Mary; Died enroute, 1720 ***1220.12*** *p904*
Wright, Mary; Maryland, 1725 ***1220.12*** *p904*
Wright, Mary 24; Ontario, 1871 ***1823.21*** *p402*
Wright, Mary 35; Ontario, 1871 ***1823.21*** *p402*
Wright, Mary 66; Ontario, 1871 ***1823.17*** *p179*
Wright, Mary; Virginia, 1734 ***1220.12*** *p904*
Wright, Mary; Virginia, 1736 ***1220.12*** *p904*
Wright, Mary; Watertown, MA, 1732 ***1642*** *p112*
Wright, Meade N. 37; Ontario, 1871 ***1823.21*** *p402*
Wright, Misael; America, 1758 ***1220.12*** *p904*
Wright, Norah 39; Ontario, 1871 ***1823.21*** *p402*
Wright, Peter; America, 1750 ***1220.12*** *p904*
Wright, Phoebe Adelaide; Minnesota, 1835-1904 ***9228.50*** *p207*
Wright, Rachel 44; Ontario, 1871 ***1823.21*** *p402*
Wright, Richard; America, 1695 ***1220.12*** *p904*

Wright, Richard; America, 1745 *1220.12 p904*
Wright, Richard; America, 1752 *1220.12 p904*
Wright, Richard 45; Ontario, 1871 *1823.21 p402*
Wright, Robert; America, 1735 *1220.12 p904*
Wright, Robert; America, 1762 *1220.12 p904*
Wright, Robert; America, 1772 *1220.12 p904*
Wright, Robert; Boston, 1775 *8529.30 p5A*
Wright, Robert; Ontario, 1881 *9228.50 p657*
Wright, Robert 40; Ontario, 1871 *1823.21 p402*
Wright, Samuel; America, 1774 *1220.12 p904*
Wright, Samuel; Barbados or Jamaica, 1710 *1220.12 p904*
Wright, Thomas; America, 1700 *1220.12 p904*
Wright, Thomas; America, 1750 *1220.12 p905*
Wright, Thomas; America, 1751 *1220.12 p905*
Wright, Thomas; America, 1752 *1220.12 p905*
Wright, Thomas; America, 1753 *1220.12 p905*
Wright, Thomas; America, 1756 *1220.12 p905*
Wright, Thomas; America, 1760 *1220.12 p905*
Wright, Thomas; America, 1763 *1220.12 p905*
Wright, Thomas; America, 1765 *1220.12 p905*
Wright, Thomas; America, 1775 *1220.12 p905*
Wright, Thomas; Annapolis, MD, 1720 *1220.12 p904*
Wright, Thomas; Charles Town, SC, 1718 *1220.12 p904*
Wright, Thomas; Maryland, 1721 *1220.12 p904*
Wright, Thomas 29; Ontario, 1871 *1823.21 p402*
Wright, Thomas 42; Ontario, 1871 *1823.21 p402*
Wright, Tobias; America, 1699 *1220.12 p905*
Wright, Tobias; Barbados, 1669 *1220.12 p905*
Wright, William; America, 1687 *1220.12 p905*
Wright, William; America, 1690 *1220.12 p905*
Wright, William; America, 1701 *1220.12 p905*
Wright, William; America, 1758 *1220.12 p905*
Wright, William; America, 1766 *1220.12 p905*
Wright, William; America, 1772 *1220.12 p905*
Wright, William; America, 1774 *1220.12 p905*
Wright, William; America, 1775 *1220.12 p905*
Wright, William; Barbados, 1665 *1220.12 p905*
Wright, William; Barbados, 1668 *1220.12 p905*
Wright, William; Barbados, 1671 *1220.12 p905*
Wright, William 29; Michigan, 4491.36 *p25*
Wright, William 17; Ontario, 1871 *1823.21 p402*
Wright, William 28; Ontario, 1871 *1823.17 p179*
Wright, William 50; Ontario, 1871 *1823.21 p402*
Wright, William 61; Ontario, 1871 *1823.21 p402*
Wright, William 70; Ontario, 1871 *1823.17 p179*
Wright, William Henry; Pennsylvania, 1838-1938 *9228.50 p657*
Wright, William John 52; Ontario, 1871 *1823.21 p402*
Wright, William K.; Colorado, 1885 *1029.59 p96*
Wright, Willison 40; Ontario, 1871 *1823.17 p179*
Wright, Wm 71; Ontario, 1871 *1823.21 p402*
Wrighte, Philip; America, 1753 *1220.12 p904*
Wrigley, Catharine Wilson SEE Wrigley, James
Wrigley, James; New York, 1852 *8513.31 p435*
  *Wife:*Catharine Wilson
  *Child:*Sarah Jane
  *Child:*Thomas Francis
Wrigley, John; Ontario, 1871 *1823.21 p402*
Wrigley, Sarah Jane SEE Wrigley, James
Wrigley, Thomas Francis SEE Wrigley, James
Wrimelt, Edward 45; Ontario, 1871 *1823.21 p402*
Wrinkle, Joseph 33; Ontario, 1871 *1823.21 p402*
Writt, Patrick; Toronto, 1844 *2910.35 p115*
Writus, Thomas; America, 1768 *1220.12 p905*
Wrobel, Aleksandra 17; New York, NY, 1912 *8355.1 p16*
Wroblewski, Joseph; Detroit, 1929-1930 *6214.5 p61*
Wroblewski, Wicenty; Detroit, 1929-1930 *6214.5 p63*
Wroe, Thomas; Boston, 1722 *9228.50 p200*
Wroth, Francis; America, 1695 *1220.12 p905*
Wroth, William; America, 1742 *1220.12 p905*
Wrubel, Wojciech; Detroit, 1929 *1640.55 p115*
Wruck, August; Wisconsin, 1899 *6795.8 p237*
Wruck, Daniel J.; Wisconsin, 1905 *6795.8 p178*
Wrzesinski, Frank; Wisconsin, 1900 *6795.8 p53*
Wucherer, Gottlob; Ohio, 1856 *3580.20 p34*
Wucherer, Gottlob; Ohio, 1856 *6020.12 p23*
Wuchner, . . .; West Virginia, 1865-1879 *1132.30 p150*
Wuchner, Ludwig; New York, 1872 *1132.30 p150*
Wudke, Augusta; Wisconsin, 1886 *6795.8 p91*
Wuelfe, Francis; Illinois, 1852 *6079.1 p15*

Wufskoff, Casha 25; America, 1841 *778.6 p348*
Wufskoff, Louis 36; America, 1841 *778.6 p348*
Wulf, Eberhard; Valdivia, Chile, 1851 *1192.4 p51*
Wulf, Johannes; Iowa, 1906 *1211.15 p20*
Wulf, Maria; America, 1905 *8023.44 p381*
Wulff, John; Colorado, 1889 *1029.59 p96*
Wull, Anna; North Carolina, 1710 *3629.40 p7*
Wullie, Theodor 28; America, 1848 *778.6 p348*
Wunderli, Fridolin; New Castle, DE, 1817-1818 *90.20 p155*
Wunderlich, Hermann Erdmann; America, 1867 *7919.3 p528*
Wunn, Amalie 27; America, 1864 *5475.1 p45*
Wunn, Joh. Georg; New York, 1894 *5475.1 p41*
Wunnacott, Robert 25; Ontario, 1871 *1823.21 p402*
Wunsch, Adam; America, 1836 *2526.42 p165*
  With wife
  With daughter 12
  With son 16
Wunsch, Franz; New York, 1859 *358.56 p99*
Wuolas, Hugo 38; Minnesota, 1925 *2769.54 p1380*
Wuolas, Sandra 34; Minnesota, 1925 *2769.54 p1380*
Wuorinen, Auro; Minnesota, 1925 *2769.54 p1379*
Wurch, Edward; Wisconsin, 1895 *6795.8 p95*
Wurch, Juliana; Wisconsin, 1903 *6795.8 p159*
Wurcherpfenig, Charles F. 36; Texas, 1848 *778.6 p348*
Wurdig, W.; Venezuela, 1843 *3899.5 p546*
Wurgelin, Joseph 29; Missouri, 1846 *778.6 p348*
Wurlot, Frederic 26; America, 1845 *778.6 p348*
Wurm, Anna; America, 1874 *8023.44 p379*
Wurmela, Jac.; New York, 1860 *358.56 p3*
Wurmser, Jean 28; Louisiana, 1848 *778.6 p348*
Wursch, Friedrich 25; New York, NY, 1899 *6406.6 p47*
Wursch, Johann 1; New York, NY, 1899 *6406.6 p47*
Wursch, Lydia 24; New York, NY, 1899 *6406.6 p47*
Wursch, Rosa 3; New York, NY, 1899 *6406.6 p47*
Wurst, Israel; Ohio, 1809-1852 *4511.35 p60*
Wurst, John; Ohio, 1809-1852 *4511.35 p60*
Wurster, Matthias; Ohio, 1809-1852 *4511.35 p60*
Wurtenberger, Martin 58; America, 1859 *2526.42 p203*
Wurth, Anna Eva Magdalena; Venezuela, 1843 *3899.5 p542*
Wurth, Anton; Venezuela, 1843 *3899.5 p540*
Wurth, Marianna; Venezuela, 1843 *3899.5 p540*
Wurtz, Anna 18; America, 1840 *778.6 p348*
Wurtz, George; Ohio, 1809-1852 *4511.35 p60*
Wurtz, Johann Konrad; America, 1880 *5475.1 p533*
Wurtz, Johannes 19; America, 1840 *778.6 p348*
Wurtz, Leonhard; America, 1880 *5475.1 p533*
Wurtz, Magd. 16; America, 1840 *778.6 p348*
Wurtz, Michel 22; America, 1747 *778.6 p348*
Wurz, Jakob; America, 1844 *5475.1 p471*
Wurz, Johann; America, 1844 *5475.1 p471*
Wusan, Andrew; Illinois, 1834-1900 *6020.5 p133*
Wuschner, Peter 26; New York, 1882 *5475.1 p413*
Wusckka, Edward 15; Portland, ME, 1911 *970.38 p82*
Wusckka, Fred 10; Portland, ME, 1911 *970.38 p82*
Wusckka, Gustav 18; Portland, ME, 1911 *970.38 p82*
Wushen, Madeleine 26; Missouri, 1845 *778.6 p348*
Wuske, John; Wisconsin, 1893 *6795.8 p37*
Wust, G. A.; Chile, 1852 *1192.4 p52*
  With son 23
Wustenfeld, August Ludwig Anton; America, 1867 *7420.1 p267*
Wustenfeld, Caroline Dorothea; America, 1866 *7420.1 p252*
Wustenfeld, Catharina Sophia Stege SEE Wustenfeld, Cord Heinrich Christoph
Wustenfeld, Cord Heinrich Christoph; America, 1845 *7420.1 p41*
  *Wife:*Catharina Sophia Stege
  With child 4
  With child 1
Wustenfeld, Engel Marie Sophie Eleon.; America, 1850 *7420.1 p70*
Wustenfeld, Heinrich Otto; America, 1854 *7420.1 p133*
Wustenfeld, Johann Conrad; America, 1855 *7420.1 p143*
Wustenfeld, Johann Heinrich; America, 1852 *7420.1 p101*
Wustenfeld, Johann Hermann; America, 1851 *7420.1 p84*
Wustreik, Henrich Frederich; Wisconsin, 1893 *6795.8 p229*

Wyandt, Jacob; Ohio, 1809-1852 *4511.35 p60*
Wyant, Jacob; Ohio, 1809-1852 *4511.35 p60*
Wyat, Katherine; Barbados, 1672 *1220.12 p905*
Wyatt, Benjamin; Barbados, 1698 *1220.12 p905*
Wyatt, Edward 57; Ontario, 1871 *1823.21 p403*
Wyatt, Elizabeth; America, 1745 *1220.12 p905*
Wyatt, Henry; Barbados, 1686 *1220.12 p905*
Wyatt, John; America, 1688 *1220.12 p905*
Wyatt, John; America, 1742 *1220.12 p905*
Wyatt, John; America, 1773 *1220.12 p905*
Wyatt, John; Annapolis, MD, 1731 *1220.12 p905*
Wyatt, Martha; America, 1721 *1220.12 p905*
Wyatt, Mary; Nevis or Jamaica, 1722 *1220.12 p905*
Wyatt, Richard; America, 1750 *1220.12 p905*
Wyatt, Richard; Barbados, 1668 *1220.12 p905*
Wyatt, Thomas; America, 1744 *1220.12 p905*
Wyatt, Thomas; America, 1752 *1220.12 p906*
Wyatt, Thomas; Barbados or Jamaica, 1688 *1220.12 p905*
Wyatt, William; America, 1729 *1220.12 p906*
Wyatt, William; America, 1739 *1220.12 p906*
Wyatt, William; America, 1751 *1220.12 p906*
Wyatt, William 22; Ontario, 1871 *1823.21 p403*
Wyatt, Wm.; Maryland, 1672 *1236.25 p48*
Wybel, John; Ohio, 1809-1852 *4511.35 p60*
Wyborn, John; America, 1739 *1220.12 p906*
Wycech, Stefan; Detroit, 1929-1930 *6214.5 p71*
Wye, Ann; America, 1772 *1220.12 p906*
Wye, George W. 32; Ontario, 1871 *1823.21 p403*
Wyer, John; America, 1755 *1220.12 p906*
Wyer, John; Maryland, 1720 *1220.12 p906*
Wyer, William; America, 1754 *1220.12 p906*
Wyers, Richard; America, 1724 *1220.12 p906*
Wyeth, William 50; Ontario, 1871 *1823.21 p403*
Wyke, Edward; America, 1699 *1220.12 p906*
Wykes, Richard; America, 1767 *1220.12 p906*
Wyld, Abel; Annapolis, MD, 1723 *1220.12 p871*
Wyld, Elizabeth; Barbados, 1669 *1220.12 p871*
Wyld, John; America, 1771 *1220.12 p871*
Wylde, Jesse; Ohio, 1844 *2763.1 p22*
Wyles, William; Barbados or Jamaica, 1680 *1220.12 p871*
Wylett, Ann; America, 1766 *1220.12 p906*
Wyley, John 38; Ontario, 1871 *1823.21 p403*
Wylie, John 44; Ontario, 1871 *1823.21 p403*
Wylie, John 74; Ontario, 1871 *1823.21 p403*
Wylie, John; Virginia, 1734 *1220.12 p906*
Wylkinson, James 26; Ontario, 1871 *1823.17 p179*
Wyllis, David 52; Ontario, 1871 *1823.21 p403*
Wyman, Michael; Maryland, 1729 *1220.12 p906*
Wymath, Samuel 45; Ontario, 1871 *1823.21 p403*
Wymer, Peter; Ohio, 1840-1897 *8365.35 p18*
Wyncott, Ann 16; Virginia, 1635 *1183.3 p31*
Wyncott, Dorothie 40; Virginia, 1635 *1183.3 p31*
Wynd, John; America, 1738 *1220.12 p890*
Wynde, Samuel; America, 1764 *1220.12 p890*
Wynn, Benjamin; America, 1753 *1220.12 p906*
Wynn, Benjamin; North Carolina, 1792-1862 *1088.45 p37*
Wynn, Francis; Annapolis, MD, 1722 *1220.12 p906*
Wynn, Henry; America, 1725 *1220.12 p906*
Wynn, Isaac; New York, NY, 1841 *3274.56 p99*
Wynn, John; America, 1775 *1220.12 p906*
Wynn, John 55; Ontario, 1871 *1823.17 p180*
Wynn, Mary; America, 1736 *1220.12 p906*
Wynn, Priscilla; America, 1681 *1220.12 p906*
Wynn, William; Annapolis, MD, 1731 *1220.12 p906*
Wynne, Abel; Ohio, 1837-1840 *4022.20 p294*
Wynne, Bacon; Annapolis, MD, 1725 *1220.12 p906*
Wynne, David; Ohio, 1837 *4022.20 p294*
Wynne, James; Barbados, 1664 *1220.12 p906*
Wynne, John 65; Ontario, 1871 *1823.17 p180*
Wynne, Richard; Virginia, 1724 *1220.12 p906*
Wynne, William; America, 1721 *1220.12 p906*
Wyre, Abraham; America, 1750 *1220.12 p906*
Wyrrall, Ann; America, 1701 *1220.12 p906*
Wysocki, Mike; Texas, 1895 *6015.15 p30*
Wyss, John V.; Ohio, 1809-1852 *4511.35 p60*
Wytherell, Joseph; America, 1685 *1220.12 p858*
Wythyman, John, Jr.; America, 1685 *1220.12 p893*

FOR A COMPLETE EXPLANATION OF ENTRY, SEE "HOW TO READ A CITATION" SECTION

X-Y

Xalter, Agata 23; America, 1846 *778.6 p348*
Xalter, Chretien 39; America, 1846 *778.6 p348*
Xalter, Joseph 1; America, 1846 *778.6 p348*
Xalter, Lisabeth 63; America, 1846 *778.6 p348*
Xalter, Louis 20; America, 1846 *778.6 p348*
Xalter, Mad. 29; America, 1846 *778.6 p348*
Xalter, Sendelin 2; America, 1846 *778.6 p348*
Xavier, Bernhard 24; Port uncertain, 1847 *778.6 p348*
Xavier, Francois 2; Missouri, 1847 *778.6 p348*
Xavier, Francoise 1; Missouri, 1847 *778.6 p348*
Xavier, Marie, I 29; Missouri, 1847 *778.6 p348*
Xavier, Marie, II 28; Missouri, 1847 *778.6 p348*
Yaerasin, Mr. 20; Port uncertain, 1844 *778.6 p349*
Yager, Peter 19; Halifax, N.S., 1902 *1860.4 p42*
Yahn, Henrey 32; Ontario, 1871 *1823.17 p180*
Yalden, John; America, 1775 *1220.12 p907*
Yallopp, Robert; Barbados, 1664 *1220.12 p907*
Yamyezeszki, Marian; Galveston, TX, 1885 *6015.15 p11*
Yamyezeszky, Marian; Galveston, TX, 1885 *6015.15 p11*
Yanisezski, Marian; Galveston, TX, 1885 *6015.15 p11*
Yaniyezesky, Charley; New York, NY, 1893 *6015.15 p11*
Yaniyezesky, Frank; Galveston, TX, 1885 *6015.15 p11*
Yaniyezesky, Ignatz; New York, NY, 1896 *6015.15 p12*
Yaniyezeszky, Marian; Galveston, TX, 1885 *6015.15 p11*
Yanizsewski, Marian; Galveston, TX, 1885 *6015.15 p11*
Yanizsewski, Marian; Galveston, TX, 1885 *6015.15 p11*
Yansen, August; Colorado, 1873 *1029.59 p97*
Yapp, Hareiett 34; Ontario, 1871 *1823.21 p403*
Yard, Henry 30; Ontario, 1871 *1823.21 p403*
Yarde, Yard; Barbados, 1675 *1220.12 p907*
Yardley, Elizabeth; America, 1750 *1220.12 p907*
Yardley, John; America, 1770 *1220.12 p907*
Yardley, Mary; America, 1750 *1220.12 p907*
Yardley, Nathaniel; America, 1752 *1220.12 p907*
Yardley, Richard; America, 1754 *1220.12 p907*
Yardsey, John; Barbados, 1679 *1220.12 p907*
Yardsley, Robert; Barbados, 1677 *1220.12 p907*
Yarema, Albert; Detroit, 1930 *1640.60 p81*
Yarlett, Thomas; America, 1725 *1220.12 p907*
Yarmouth, Edward; America, 1751 *1220.12 p907*
Yarmouth, John; America, 1732 *1220.12 p907*
Yarner, Benjamin; Virginia, 1768 *1220.12 p907*
Yarner, William; Ohio, 1809-1852 *4511.35 p60*
Yarpe, John; Barbados, 1674 *1220.12 p907*
Yarpe, John; Maryland, 1674-1675 *1236.25 p52*
Yarrall, Matthew; Barbados, 1669 *1220.12 p907*
Yarrington, Dorothy; America, 1678 *1220.12 p907*
Yarrington, Jasper; America, 1743 *1220.12 p907*
Yarum, Thomas; America, 1753 *1220.12 p907*
Yarwood, John; America, 1724 *1220.12 p907*
Yate, James; America, 1753 *1220.12 p907*
Yate, John; Barbados, 1664 *1220.12 p907*
Yates, . . .; Ontario, 1871 *1823.21 p403*
Yates, Alice; America, 1755 *1220.12 p907*
Yates, Alice; Barbados or Jamaica, 1688 *1220.12 p907*
Yates, Ann; Barbados or Jamaica, 1691 *1220.12 p907*
Yates, Anne; Barbados or Jamaica, 1688 *1220.12 p907*
Yates, Charles; America, 1720 *1220.12 p907*
Yates, Elizabeth; America, 1737 *1220.12 p907*
Yates, James 42; Ontario, 1871 *1823.17 p180*
Yates, John; America, 1721 *1220.12 p907*
Yates, John; America, 1726 *1220.12 p907*
Yates, John; America, 1727 *1220.12 p907*
Yates, John; Virginia, 1768 *1220.12 p907*
Yates, Joseph; America, 1768 *1220.12 p907*
Yates, Mary; America, 1743 *1220.12 p907*
Yates, Mary 24; Annapolis, MD, 1721 *1220.12 p907*

Yates, Ralph; America, 1700 *1220.12 p907*
Yates, Richard; America, 1697 *1220.12 p907*
Yates, Richard; America, 1737 *1220.12 p908*
Yates, Samewell; America, 1739 *1220.12 p908*
Yates, Sarah; Annapolis, MD, 1758 *1220.12 p908*
Yates, Susannah; America, 1766 *1220.12 p908*
Yates, Thomas; America, 1734 *1220.12 p908*
Yates, Thomas 42; Ontario, 1871 *1823.21 p403*
Yates, Willdy; America, 1730 *1220.12 p908*
Yates, William; America, 1737 *1220.12 p908*
Yates, William; America, 1750 *1220.12 p908*
Yates, William; Died enroute, 1728 *1220.12 p908*
Yates, William 36; Ontario, 1871 *1823.17 p180*
Yawdell, Mabel; Barbados, 1683 *1220.12 p908*
Yaxley, Stephen; America, 1758 *1220.12 p908*
Yaxley, William; America, 1765 *1220.12 p908*
Ydelary, Marie; California, 1889 *3276.8 p19*
Yeager, . . .; West Virginia, 1850-1860 *1132.30 p149*
Yeagle, Henry; Ohio, 1809-1852 *4511.35 p60*
Yeagley, John W.; Ohio, 1873 *3580.20 p34*
Yeagley, John W.; Ohio, 1873 *6020.12 p23*
Yeakle, Louis; Illinois, 1858-1861 *6020.5 p133*
Yealand, Edmund 46; Ontario, 1871 *1823.21 p403*
Yeaman, Felton; Philadelphia, 1853 *5720.10 p381*
Yearby, John; America, 1744 *1220.12 p908*
Yeardly, Willis; Virginia, 1652 *6254.4 p243*
Yearwood, Joseph; America, 1760 *1220.12 p908*
Yeast, William; America, 1755 *1220.12 p908*
Yeate, John; America, 1742 *1220.12 p907*
Yeates, Charles; America, 1746 *1220.12 p907*
Yeates, Elizabeth; America, 1756 *1220.12 p907*
Yeates, George; America, 1765 *1220.12 p907*
Yeates, Mary; America, 1740 *1220.12 p907*
Yeates, Robert; America, 1741 *1220.12 p908*
Yeates, William; America, 1754 *1220.12 p908*
Yeavsley, Thomas; Barbados, 1683 *1220.12 p908*
Yeck, Anna 9; Halifax, N.S., 1902 *1860.4 p39*
Yeck, Ewald 6; Halifax, N.S., 1902 *1860.4 p39*
Yeck, Ewald 45; Halifax, N.S., 1902 *1860.4 p39*
Yeck, Fritz 14; Halifax, N.S., 1902 *1860.4 p39*
Yeck, Hedwig 15; Halifax, N.S., 1902 *1860.4 p39*
Yeck, Lina 45; Halifax, N.S., 1902 *1860.4 p39*
Yeck, Ois; Halifax, N.S., 1902 *1860.4 p39*
Yeck, Rudolf 11; Halifax, N.S., 1902 *1860.4 p39*
Yehle, John Christian; Ohio, 1809-1852 *4511.35 p60*
Yejarrski, Peter; New York, NY, 1881 *6015.15 p30*
Yelland, Rice 40; Ontario, 1871 *1823.21 p403*
Yellowly, Joseph; North Carolina, 1809 *1088.45 p38*
Yellox, Thomas; Potomac, 1729 *1220.12 p908*
Yelverton, Matthew; America, 1685 *1220.12 p908*
Yemm, John; America, 1752 *1220.12 p908*
Yener, William; Ohio, 1809-1852 *4511.35 p60*
Yenn, Adam; Ohio, 1809-1852 *4511.35 p60*
Yentz, Alois; Ohio, 1840-1897 *8365.35 p18*
Yeo, Elizabeth; America, 1730 *1220.12 p908*
Yeo, George; Barbados, 1698 *1220.12 p908*
Yeo, John; America, 1724 *1220.12 p908*
Yeo, John; Barbados, 1698 *1220.12 p908*
Yeo, Nicholas 31; Ontario, 1871 *1823.21 p403*
Yeo, Samuel; Maryland, 1720 *1220.12 p908*
Yeo, William; Maryland, 1720 *1220.12 p908*
Yeol, Thomas 20; Ontario, 1871 *1823.17 p180*
Yeoman, John; America, 1752 *1220.12 p908*
Yeoman, John; America, 1756 *1220.12 p908*
Yeoman, Joseph; America, 1772 *1220.12 p908*
Yeoman, Richard; Charles Town, SC, 1718 *1220.12 p908*
Yeoman, Samuel; America, 1736 *1220.12 p908*
Yeoman, William; North Carolina, 1835 *1088.45 p38*

Yeomans, Margaret; Virginia, 1721 *1220.12 p908*
Yeomans, Mary; America, 1722 *1220.12 p908*
Yeomans, Mathew Heath; North Carolina, 1853 *1088.45 p38*
Yeomans, Samuel; America, 1708 *1220.12 p908*
Yeomans, Thomas; America, 1752 *1220.12 p908*
Yerk, Mary Louise; Wisconsin, 1888 *6795.8 p78*
Yerrell, Thomas 47; Ontario, 1871 *1823.21 p403*
Yessen, Jesse; Colorado, 1888 *1029.59 p97*
Yessler, Johann 37; Halifax, N.S., 1902 *1860.4 p40*
Yeter, Jerome; New York, 1860 *358.56 p150*
Yetman, Joseph 40; Ontario, 1871 *1823.21 p403*
Yetts, John; Virginia, 1740 *1220.12 p908*
Yin, Chung; Washington, 1886 *6015.10 p16*
Yler, Carl 20; New Orleans, 1848 *778.6 p349*
Yoblonski, Frank; Galveston, TX, 1901 *6015.15 p11*
Yock, Ludwick; Ohio, 1809-1852 *4511.35 p60*
Yockey, Henry; Illinois, 1858-1861 *6020.5 p133*
Yockey, John; Ohio, 1809-1852 *4511.35 p14*
Yockey, Philip; Ohio, 1809-1852 *4511.35 p60*
Yodder, Christian; Ohio, 1809-1852 *4511.35 p60*
Yodder, Joseph; Ohio, 1809-1852 *4511.35 p60*
Yoder, Christian; Ohio, 1809-1852 *4511.35 p60*
Yoder, Christian; Ohio, 1809-1852 *4511.35 p61*
Yoe, William 32; Ontario, 1871 *1823.21 p403*
Yollard, Robert; Barbados, 1668 *1220.12 p908*
Yong, Matthews; Newbury, MA, 1696 *1642 p74*
Yonger, Antoine; Louisiana, 1874 *4981.45 p297*
Yonker, Anton; Louisiana, 1767 *1220.12 p908*
York, John; America, 1767 *1220.12 p908*
York, John; Colorado, 1880 *1029.59 p97*
York, Ludwick; Ohio, 1809-1852 *4511.35 p60*
York, Richard; America, 1753 *1220.12 p909*
York, Samuel; Virginia, 1765 *1220.12 p909*
York, Sarah; Nevis or Jamaica, 1722 *1220.12 p909*
York, William; America, 1757 *1220.12 p909*
York, William; Virginia, 1733 *1220.12 p909*
Yorke, Richard; Barbados, 1664 *1220.12 p908*
Yorke, William; America, 1691 *1220.12 p909*
Yorkshire, Thomas; America, 1772 *1220.12 p909*
Yorpe, John; Maryland, 1674-1675 *1236.25 p52*
Yost, Adam; Ohio, 1809-1852 *4511.35 p60*
Yost, Frederick; Pennsylvania, 1888 *1029.59 p97*
Yost, Frederick; Pittsburgh, 1888 *1029.59 p97*
Yost, George; Ohio, 1809-1852 *4511.35 p60*
Yost, Jacob; Ohio, 1809-1852 *4511.35 p60*
Yost, Philip; Ohio, 1809-1852 *4511.35 p61*
Yotter, Christian; Ohio, 1809-1852 *4511.35 p61*
You deLa Decouverte, Pierre; Quebec, 1677 *2314.30 p172*
Youens, Richard; Marston's Wharf, 1782 *8529.30 p17*
Youings, Richard; Marston's Wharf, 1782 *8529.30 p17*
Youins, Rachael; America, 1740 *1220.12 p909*
Youk, Charles; Illinois, 1852 *6079.1 p15*
Youlans, Francis 33; Ontario, 1871 *1823.21 p404*
Youlans, Margaret; Ontario, 1871 *1823.21 p404*
Youle, Robert; North Carolina, 1813 *1088.45 p38*
Youle, Thomas; North Carolina, 1813 *1088.45 p38*
Youlton, John; America, 1768 *1220.12 p909*
Youman, Susanna; America, 1761 *1220.12 p908*
Young, Abraham 31; Ontario, 1871 *1823.21 p404*
Young, Adam; America, 1767 *1220.12 p909*
Young, Alice 7; Quebec, 1870 *8364.32 p26*
Young, Andrew; America, 1765 *1220.12 p909*
Young, Andrew Henry SEE Young, Josias Richard
Young, Angus W.; Washington, 1885 *2770.40 p194*
Young, Ann; America, 1771 *1220.12 p909*
Young, Ann 58; Ontario, 1871 *1823.21 p404*

Young, Anna; Detroit, 1885 *9228.50 p369*
Young, Archibald 65; Ontario, 1871 *1823.17 p180*
Young, Bartholomew; America, 1729 *1220.12 p909*
Young, Benjamin 48; Ontario, 1871 *1823.21 p404*
Young, Brigham Joseph *SEE* Young, Josias Richard
Young, Catherine 22; Ontario, 1871 *1823.21 p404*
Young, Catherine; Virginia, 1732 *1220.12 p909*
Young, Charles 37; Ontario, 1871 *1823.17 p180*
Young, Charles P.; Illinois, 1860 *6079.1 p15*
Young, Christian; Illinois, 1852 *6079.1 p15*
Young, Daniel; America, 1737 *1220.12 p909*
Young, David; Worcester, MA, 1730-1776 *1642 p114*
Young, Deborah; America, 1770 *1220.12 p909*
Young, Edith; Panama, 1911 *9228.50 p408*
Young, Edward; America, 1745 *1220.12 p909*
Young, Edward; Ohio, 1840-1897 *8365.35 p18*
Young, Edward 39; Ontario, 1871 *1823.17 p180*
Young, Elizabeth; America, 1743 *1220.12 p909*
Young, Elizabeth; America, 1759 *1220.12 p909*
Young, Elizabeth; America, 1772 *1220.12 p909*
Young, Elizabeth; America, 1773 *1220.12 p909*
Young, Elizabeth Esther Canivet *SEE* Young, Josias Richard
Young, Elizabeth Jane *SEE* Young, Josias Richard
Young, Ellen 12; Quebec, 1870 *8364.32 p26*
Young, Esther 17; Quebec, 1870 *8364.32 p26*
Young, Frederick; America, 1765 *1220.12 p909*
Young, George; America, 1770 *1220.12 p909*
Young, George; Ohio, 1809-1852 *4511.35 p61*
Young, George; Ontario, 1871 *1823.21 p404*
Young, George 48; Ontario, 1871 *1823.21 p404*
Young, George Henry; Ohio, 1809-1852 *4511.35 p61*
Young, Gilbert; New York, 1903 *1766.20 p36*
Young, Hellen 12; Ontario, 1871 *1823.21 p404*
Young, Henery 78; Ontario, 1871 *1823.17 p180*
Young, Henry; America, 1772 *1220.12 p909*
Young, Henry; Ohio, 1809-1852 *4511.35 p61*
Young, Honor; America, 1759 *1220.12 p909*
Young, Hugh John; America, 1762 *1220.12 p909*
Young, Jacob; Ohio, 1809-1852 *4511.35 p61*
Young, James; America, 1749 *1220.12 p909*
Young, James; America, 1755 *1220.12 p909*
Young, James; America, 1767 *1220.12 p909*
Young, James; America, 1769 *1220.12 p909*
Young, James; Barbados, 1701 *1220.12 p909*
Young, James 38; Ontario, 1871 *1823.21 p404*
Young, James 42; Ontario, 1871 *1823.21 p404*
Young, James 63; Ontario, 1871 *1823.21 p404*
Young, James D. 60; Ontario, 1871 *1823.17 p180*
Young, James M.; Washington, 1885 *2770.40 p194*
Young, Jane; America, 1761 *1220.12 p909*
Young, Jane; America, 1762 *1220.12 p909*
Young, Jessie 10; Quebec, 1870 *8364.32 p26*
Young, Job 45; Ontario, 1871 *1823.17 p180*
Young, John; America, 1730 *1220.12 p909*
Young, John; America, 1744 *1220.12 p909*
Young, John; America, 1749 *1220.12 p909*
Young, John; America, 1751 *1220.12 p909*
Young, John; America, 1753 *1220.12 p909*
Young, John; America, 1759 *1220.12 p909*
Young, John; America, 1762 *1220.12 p909*
Young, John; America, 1764 *1220.12 p909*
Young, John; America, 1772 *1220.12 p909*
Young, John; America, 1775 *1220.12 p909*
Young, John; Annapolis, MD, 1719 *1220.12 p909*
Young, John; Barbados, 1662 *1220.12 p909*

Young, John; New York, 1779 *8529.30 p17*
Young, John; North Carolina, 1856 *1088.45 p38*
Young, John; Ohio, 1809-1852 *4511.35 p61*
Young, John 40; Ontario, 1871 *1823.21 p404*
Young, John 63; Ontario, 1871 *1823.21 p404*
Young, John; Salem, MA, 1713 *9228.50 p656*
Young, John; Salem, MA, 1713 *9228.50 p656*
Young, John; Virginia, 1742 *1220.12 p909*
Young, John; Virginia, 1750 *1220.12 p909*
Young, John; Worcester, MA, 1730-1776 *1642 p114*
Young, John Eldridge; America, 1774 *1220.12 p910*
Young, John Jacob; Ohio, 1809-1852 *4511.35 p61*
Young, Joseph 29; Ontario, 1871 *1823.21 p404*
Young, Joseph 35; Ontario, 1871 *1823.21 p404*
Young, Joseph M. 40; Ontario, 1871 *1823.21 p404*
Young, Josiah 27; Ontario, 1871 *1823.21 p404*
Young, Josias Richard *SEE* Young, Josias Richard
Young, Josias Richard; Utah, 1855 *9228.50 p656*
   *Wife:*Elizabeth Esther Canivet
   *Child:*Susan Oliver
   *Child:*Louisa Sarah
   *Child:*Josias Richard
   *Child:*Andrew Henry
   *Child:*Brigham Joseph
   *Child:*William John
   *Child:*Elizabeth Jane
Young, Louisa Sarah *SEE* Young, Josias Richard
Young, Lucq; St. Kitts, n.d. *9228.50 p656*
Young, Margaret; America, 1731 *1220.12 p910*
Young, Martha; America, 1769 *1220.12 p910*
Young, Mary; America, 1756 *1220.12 p910*
Young, Mary; Died enroute, 1721 *1220.12 p910*
Young, Mary 89; Ontario, 1871 *1823.17 p180*
Young, Mary Catherine 40; Ontario, 1871 *1823.21 p404*
Young, Matthew; America, 1737 *1220.12 p910*
Young, Matthew; America, 1757 *1220.12 p910*
Young, Michael; Louisiana, 1874 *4981.45 p134*
Young, Michael; Ohio, 1809-1852 *4511.35 p61*
Young, Michel; Kansas, 1888 *1447.20 p64*
Young, Nathaniel; Maryland, 1726 *1220.12 p910*
Young, Nicholas; New York, 1777 *8529.30 p5A*
Young, Peter; Ohio, 1809-1852 *4511.35 p61*
Young, Peter 35; Ontario, 1871 *1823.17 p180*
Young, Philip; Ohio, 1809-1852 *4511.35 p61*
Young, Richard; America, 1685 *1220.12 p910*
Young, Richard; America, 1731 *1220.12 p910*
Young, Richard W. 54; Ontario, 1871 *1823.21 p404*
Young, Robert; America, 1723 *1220.12 p910*
Young, Robert; America, 1743 *1220.12 p910*
Young, Robert; America, 1767 *1220.12 p910*
Young, Robert; Ohio, 1840-1897 *8365.35 p18*
Young, Robert 27; Ontario, 1871 *1823.17 p180*
Young, Robert 29; Ontario, 1871 *1823.21 p404*
Young, Robert 37; Ontario, 1871 *1823.21 p404*
Young, Robert 45; Ontario, 1871 *1823.21 p404*
Young, Robert 70; Ontario, 1871 *1823.17 p180*
Young, Robert 26; South Carolina, 1812 *3476.30 p13*
Young, Sarah; America, 1729 *1220.12 p910*
Young, Simon 55; Ontario, 1871 *1823.21 p404*
Young, Stephen; America, 1764 *1220.12 p910*
Young, Susan Oliver *SEE* Young, Josias Richard
Young, Susanna; Rappahannock, VA, 1729 *1220.12 p910*
Young, Thomas; America, 1744 *1220.12 p910*
Young, Thomas; America, 1761 *1220.12 p910*
Young, Thomas; America, 1767 *1220.12 p910*
Young, Thomas; Annapolis, MD, 1731 *1220.12 p910*

Young, Thomas 21; North Carolina, 1774 *1422.10 p57*
Young, Thomas 60; Ontario, 1871 *1823.21 p404*
Young, Thomas; Virginia, 1764 *1220.12 p910*
Young, Timothy; America, 1731 *1220.12 p910*
Young, William; America, 1727 *1220.12 p910*
Young, William; Colorado, 1886 *1029.59 p97*
Young, William 30; Ontario, 1871 *1823.17 p180*
Young, William 35; Ontario, 1871 *1823.17 p180*
Young, William 40; Ontario, 1871 *1823.17 p180*
Young, William 41; Ontario, 1871 *1823.17 p180*
Young, William 60; Ontario, 1871 *1823.21 p405*
Young, William Arthur 32; Ontario, 1871 *1823.21 p405*
Young, William B.; Philadelphia, 1848 *7074.20 p133*
Young, William John *SEE* Young, Josias Richard
Young, Winnfret 63; Ontario, 1871 *1823.21 p405*
Youngberg, Augusta; St. Paul, MN, 1874-1905 *1865.50 p115*
Youngberg, Clara Albin; Minnesota, 1885-1887 *1865.50 p115*
Youngblood, John Philip; Mississippi, 1852 *7710.1 p156*
Youngblood, Nicholas; Ohio, 1809-1852 *4511.35 p61*
Youngblood, Peter; Ohio, 1809-1852 *4511.35 p61*
Youngbluth, John; Ohio, 1809-1852 *4511.35 p61*
Younge, Mary; America, 1720 *1220.12 p910*
Younger, James; America, 1773 *1220.12 p910*
Younger, Margaret; America, 1760 *1220.12 p910*
Younger, Sarah; Virginia, 1773 *1220.12 p910*
Younger, Thomas; America, 1772 *1220.12 p910*
Younghusband, Mary; America, 1745 *1220.12 p910*
Younglow, Loe; Washington, 1886 *2770.40 p24*
Youngman, Andrew; Ohio, 1844 *2763.1 p22*
Youngman, Edmund; America, 1744 *1220.12 p910*
Youngman, Joseph; Illinois, 1854 *6079.1 p15*
Youngquist, Carl Magnus; St. Paul, MN, 1869-1875 *1865.50 p115*
Youngquist, Emil W.; St. Paul, MN, 1888 *1865.50 p115*
Youngquist, Fritz A.; St. Paul, MN, 1874-1899 *1865.50 p115*
Youngquist, Lovisa; Wisconsin, 1885-1888 *1865.50 p115*
Youngqvist, Carl Magnus; St. Paul, MN, 1869-1875 *1865.50 p115*
Youngqvist, Emil W.; St. Paul, MN, 1888 *1865.50 p115*
Youngqvist, Fritz A.; St. Paul, MN, 1874-1899 *1865.50 p115*
Youngqvist, Lovisa; Wisconsin, 1885-1888 *1865.50 p115*
Youngs, John; America, 1758 *1220.12 p910*
Youngs, Richard; America, 1751 *1220.12 p910*
Youngs, Royal 33; Ontario, 1871 *1823.21 p405*
Yow, John 54; Ontario, 1871 *1823.21 p405*
Yowell, John; America, 1746 *1220.12 p910*
Yowens, Richard; Marston's Wharf, 1782 *8529.30 p17*
Yriarte, Felix 5; America, 1889 *3276.8 p20*
   *Father:*Patricio
   *Mother:*Pascuala Arrese
Yriarte, Pascuala Arrese *SEE* Yriarte, Felix
Yriarte, Patricio *SEE* Yriarte, Felix
Yserloh, . . .; Pennsylvania, 1838 *170.15 p47*
Yturi, Marcelina; California, 1860-1890 *3276.8 p21*
Yule, Jean; Ohio, 1843-1876 *5024.1 p139*
Yungbluth, John; Ohio, 1809-1852 *4511.35 p61*
Yungmeier, Adam; Illinois, 1855 *6079.1 p15*
Yungmeier, Joseph; Illinois, 1855 *6079.1 p15*
Yunker, Rev. Mr. 27; America, 1842 *778.6 p349*
Yuppier, Claude; Illinois, 1852 *6079.1 p15*
Yvon, Francois; Quebec, 1656 *9221.17 p348*
Yvon, Jeanne 32; Quebec, 1652 *9221.17 p255*

Z

Zabcik, Jan; Texas, 1855 *2853.20 p78*
Zabel, Albert; Port uncertain, 1885 *7420.1 p399*
Zabel, August Fredrick Wilhelm; Wisconsin, 1870 *6795.8 p124*
Zabel, Ferdinand; Wisconsin, 1874 *6795.8 p208*
Zabel, Frederich A.; Wisconsin, 1868 *6795.8 p188*
Zabloudil, Jan; Nebraska, 1878 *2853.20 p189*
Zachar, Jan; Wisconsin, 1854 *2853.20 p304*
Zacharias, Paul Gustav; Wisconsin, 1900 *6795.8 p62*
Zachee, Francoise; Quebec, 1670 *4514.3 p379*
Zacher, Adam 7; New York, NY, 1898 *7951.13 p43*
Zacher, Catharina 7 months; New York, NY, 1893 *1883.7 p37*
Zacher, George 3 months; New York, NY, 1898 *7951.13 p43*
Zacher, George 32; New York, NY, 1898 *7951.13 p43*
Zacher, Johann 10; New York, NY, 1898 *7951.13 p43*
Zacher, Johann 26; New York, NY, 1898 *7951.13 p42*
Zacher, Johanna 21; New York, NY, 1898 *7951.13 p42*
Zacher, Katherina 32; New York, NY, 1898 *7951.13 p43*
Zacher, Magdalena 15 months; New York, NY, 1898 *7951.13 p42*
Zacher, Magdalena 22; New York, NY, 1893 *1883.7 p37*
Zacher, Martin 2; New York, NY, 1898 *7951.13 p43*
Zacher, Peter 4; New York, NY, 1898 *7951.13 p43*
Zacher, Peter 23; New York, NY, 1893 *1883.7 p37*
Zacher, Theresia 6; New York, NY, 1898 *7951.13 p43*
Zacherby, Ann; Annapolis, MD, 1726 *1220.12 p911*
Zacherias, H.F.; Wisconsin, 1895 *6795.8 p143*
Zachrisson, Julius; Cleveland, OH, 1903-1905 *9722.10 p128*
Zack, Joseph; Detroit, 1929 *1640.55 p115*
Zacker, David 19; New York, NY, 1885 *1883.7 p46*
Zacobie, Joseph 21; America, 1846 *778.6 p349*
Zadala, Adalbert Boleslaw; Detroit, 1929 *1640.55 p113*
Zade, Christian; Wisconsin, 1879 *6795.8 p78*
Zadrzynski, Stanislaw; Detroit, 1930 *1640.60 p81*
Zagel, Juliane; London, Eng., 1850 *7420.1 p78*
Zahajecky, Josef; Iowa, 1854 *2853.20 p230*
Zahe, Dorothea; America, 1881 *5475.1 p332*
Zahm, Johann 30; Port uncertain, 1846 *778.6 p349*
Zahn, Johann 30; Port uncertain, 1846 *778.6 p349*
Zahn, Maximilian Georg; America, 1887 *7420.1 p355*
Zahn, Simon; America, 1888 *2526.43 p202*
Zahner, . . .; America, 1883 *170.15 p47*
  With family
Zahner, Johannes; America, 1883 *170.15 p47*
  With family
Zahorik, Alois M.; Iowa, 1889 *2853.20 p223*
Zahradnik, Jakub; Wisconsin, 1890-1899 *2853.20 p339*
Zahrt, Elisabeth; America, 1870 *2526.43 p185*
Zaih, John; New York, 1860 *358.56 p4*
Zaionc, Jacob; Texas, 1853-1872 *9980.22 p16*
Zaiontz, John; Texas, 1855-1886 *9980.22 p16*
Zajac, Jacob; Texas, 1853-1872 *9980.22 p16*
Zajac, John; Texas, 1854-1873 *9980.22 p16*
Zajac, Ludwig; Texas, 1854-1872 *9980.22 p16*
Zajic, Antonin; America, 1880-1889 *2853.20 p534*
Zajicek, Frantisek; Chicago, 1867 *2853.20 p391*
Zajicek, Josef; Nebraska, 1869 *2853.20 p188*
Zak, Frantisek; Chicago, 1866 *2853.20 p68*
  With parents
Zak, Karel C.; Cincinnati, 1893 *2853.20 p152*
Zak, Vaclav; Cleveland, OH, 1852 *2853.20 p475*
Zakrzewska, Anna 19; New York, NY, 1911 *6533.11 p9*
Zakrzewski, Johann Gottlieb; Wisconsin, 1887 *6795.8 p196*
Zaleski, Joseph; Galveston, TX, 1900 *6015.15 p12*

Zaleski, Walter; Galveston, TX, 1900 *6015.15 p12*
Zalesky, Frantisek E.; Iowa, 1845-1910 *2853.20 p240*
Zalesky, Walter; Galveston, TX, 1900 *6015.15 p12*
Zalewski, Frank; Detroit, 1929-1930 *6214.5 p67*
Zaloudek, Jan; St. Louis, 1865-1867 *2853.20 p27*
Zalud, Frantisek; Lincoln, NE, 1893 *2853.20 p170*
Zamba, Erza 22; New York, NY, 1894 *6512.1 p232*
Zambelle, Frederich; Louisiana, 1836-1841 *4981.45 p209*
Zampedri, Elorna SEE Zampedri, Fidenzie
Zampedri, Fidenzie; Colorado, 1926 *1029.59 p97*
  Wife:Maria
  Child:Elorna
Zampedri, Maria SEE Zampedri, Fidenzie
Zanarthe, Bartholomew 25; Missouri, 1846 *778.6 p349*
Zander, Anna; America, 1881 *5475.1 p75*
Zander, August; Wisconsin, 1881 *6795.8 p53*
Zander, Carl August Hermann; Wisconsin, 1889 *6795.8 p68*
Zander, Charles Christian SEE Zander, Christian F.
Zander, Christian F.; Philadelphia, 1867 *8513.31 p435*
  Wife:Sophia D. Niesche
  Child:Charles Christian
  Child:Dorothea F. H.
Zander, Dorothea F. H. SEE Zander, Christian F.
Zander, Henriette; Port uncertain, 1880 *7420.1 p318*
Zander, Sophia D. Niesche SEE Zander, Christian F.
Zander, W.; New York, NY, 1844 *6412.40 p148*
Zane, Simon; America, 1758 *1220.12 p911*
Zang, Elisabeth; America, 1870 *5475.1 p211*
  Son:Peter
  Son:Johann Peter
Zang, Georg; America, 1880 *5475.1 p173*
Zang, Johann; America, 1880 *5475.1 p173*
  Wife:M. Elisabeth Rupp
Zang, Johann Peter SEE Zang, Elisabeth
Zang, M. Elisabeth Rupp SEE Zang, Johann
Zang, Margarethe; America, 1870 *5475.1 p211*
Zang, Maria 49; America, 1861-1900 *5475.1 p71*
Zang, Maria Eisvogel 65 SEE Zang, Nikolaus
Zang, Nikolaus 72; America, 1867 *5475.1 p211*
  Wife:Maria Eisvogel 65
Zang, Peter SEE Zang, Elisabeth
Zanga, John; Washington, 1884 *2770.40 p193*
Zangarle, Anthony; Ohio, 1809-1852 *4511.35 p61*
Zangerle, Jakob; America, 1847 *5475.1 p475*
Zanker, Joseph; Ohio, 1809-1852 *4511.35 p61*
Zankie, Charles 41; Ontario, 1871 *1823.17 p180*
Zann, Adel 22; New Orleans, 1847 *778.6 p349*
Zant, Anna Eva; North Carolina, 1710 *3629.40 p8*
Zant, Johannes; North Carolina, 1710 *3629.40 p8*
Zant, Katherine; North Carolina, 1710 *3629.40 p8*
Zapaglia deRessan, Octave; Quebec, 1668 *2314.30 p171*
Zapalac, Frantisek; Texas, 1856-1906 *2853.20 p64*
Zapp, Barbara SEE Zapp, Peter
Zapp, Elisabeth Muhsler 37 SEE Zapp, Peter
Zapp, Jakob SEE Zapp, Peter
Zapp, Johann SEE Zapp, Peter
Zapp, Katharina SEE Zapp, Peter
Zapp, Peter SEE Zapp, Peter
Zapp, Peter 39; America, 1860 *5475.1 p251*
  Wife:Elisabeth Muhsler 37
  Son:Peter
  Son:Jakob
  Son:Johann
  Daughter:Barbara
  Daughter:Katharina
  With daughter

Zarbuck, Mariha Louise Johanne; Wisconsin, 1896 *6795.8 p66*
Zaretzky, Karl Wilhelm; America, 1884 *7420.1 p346*
Zarfer, Jean Louis; Louisiana, 1874 *4981.45 p297*
Zaringher, Francis; Ohio, 1809-1852 *4511.35 p61*
Zarth, Katharina SEE Zarth, Michel
Zarth, Magdalena SEE Zarth, Michel
Zarth, Michel; Brazil, 1882 *5475.1 p518*
  Daughter:Magdalena
  Daughter:Katharina
Zaruba, Cenek; Pennsylvania, 1869 *2853.20 p119*
Zarzer, Rudolf; Iowa, 1887 *1211.15 p20*
Zastrow, Emily; Wisconsin, 1892 *6795.8 p86*
Zaugg, Johannes; North Carolina, 1710 *3629.40 p8*
Zautier, Antoine 18; New Orleans, 1848 *778.6 p349*
Zautin, Johannes; North Carolina, 1710 *3629.40 p8*
Zavadil, Ludvik Vaclav; St. Louis, 1871 *2853.20 p397*
Zavitz, Thomas; Ontario, 1871 *1823.21 p405*
Zawacki, John; New York, NY, 1885 *6015.15 p13*
  Wife:Josephine
Zawacki, Josephine SEE Zawacki, John
Zawadzki, John; New York, NY, 1885 *6015.15 p13*
  Wife:Josephine
Zawadzki, Josephine SEE Zawadzki, John
Zawadzki, Martin; Washington Co., TX, 1906 *6015.15 p13*
Zawar, Mrs.; America, 1847 *5475.1 p475*
Zawar, Johann Jakob; America, 1880 *5475.1 p484*
Zawar, Josef; America, 1846 *5475.1 p472*
Zawidzki, Paul; Detroit, 1929 *1640.55 p116*
Zblewski, John; Wisconsin, 1875 *6795.8 p53*
Zbornik, Matej; Iowa, 1854 *2853.20 p230*
Zdebska, Konstantyna 26; New York, NY, 1911 *6533.11 p10*
Zdrubek, Frantisek B.; Texas, 1872 *2853.20 p63*
Zdrubek, Frantisek Boleslav; Chicago, 1867 *2853.20 p391*
Zdvoracek, Jakub; Ohio, 1881 *2853.20 p505*
  With family
Zeah, Adam; Ohio, 1842 *2763.1 p22*
Zeal, Edward 34; Ontario, 1871 *1823.21 p405*
Zeanell, Phillip; America, 1724 *1220.12 p911*
Zearinger, Joseph; Ohio, 1809-1852 *4511.35 p61*
Zech, Carl; Wisconsin, 1873 *6795.8 p28*
Zech, Carl Friedrich; Wisconsin, 1904 *6795.8 p119*
Zeck, Margarethe; America, 1881 *5475.1 p161*
Zedaker, Lydia J. 40; Ohio, 1880 *4879.40 p259*
Zeeb, George; Illinois, 1858-1861 *6020.5 p133*
Zeeble, John; California, 1868 *1131.61 p90*
Zeer, Elizabeth 22; America, 1747 *778.6 p349*
Zeer, Valentin 28; America, 1747 *778.6 p349*
Zeerorzier, Eva 20; Portland, ME, 1906 *970.38 p82*
Zeerorzier, Georg 6 months; Portland, ME, 1906 *970.38 p82*
Zeerorzier, Johann 24; Portland, ME, 1906 *970.38 p82*
Zeh, Anna Maria; Venezuela, 1843 *3899.5 p544*
Zeh, Eva; Venezuela, 1843 *3899.5 p543*
Zehenter, John Daniel; Ohio, 1809-1852 *4511.35 p61*
Zehler, Nathalie 45; America, 1871 *5475.1 p442*
Zehnder, . . .; West Virginia, 1865-1879 *1132.30 p150*
Zehner, . . .; America, 1883 *170.15 p47*
  With family
Zehner, Johannes; America, 1883 *170.15 p47*
  With family
Zehnerter, Lucien 21; Port uncertain, 1846 *778.6 p349*
Zehren, A. Maria Niedercorn 56 SEE Zehren, Anton
Zehren, Anna 26 SEE Zehren, Anton

Zehren, Anton 72; America, 1856 ***5475.1*** *p374*
*Wife:*A. Maria Niedercorn 56
*Daughter:*Anna 26
Zehren, Eva Lumma 31 *SEE* Zehren, Nikolaus
Zehren, Katharina 6 *SEE* Zehren, Nikolaus
Zehren, Katharina; San Francisco, 1857 ***5475.1*** *p255*
Zehren, Magdalena 3 *SEE* Zehren, Nikolaus
Zehren, Nikolaus 33; America, 1857 ***5475.1*** *p374*
*Wife:*Eva Lumma 31
*Daughter:*Magdalena 3
*Daughter:*Katharina 6
Zeider, George; Ohio, 1809-1852 ***4511.35*** *p61*
Zeidler, J. G.; Valdivia, Chile, 1850 ***1192.4*** *p49*
With wife
With child 1
Zeidler, Joh. Christian; Valdivia, Chile, 1850 ***1192.4*** *p49*
Zeidler, Joh. Gottl.; Valdivia, Chile, 1850 ***1192.4*** *p49*
With wife
Zeier, Elisabeth; America, 1882 ***5475.1*** *p494*
Zeiger, Elisabeth; Chicago, 1875 ***5475.1*** *p384*
*Son:*Johann
*Daughter:*Barbara
*Daughter:*Elisabeth
Zeigler, Ambrose; Ohio, 1809-1852 ***4511.35*** *p61*
Zeigler, Conrad; Ohio, 1809-1852 ***4511.35*** *p61*
Zeigler, Frederick; Ohio, 1809-1852 ***4511.35*** *p61*
Zeigler, Gotleib; Ohio, 1809-1852 ***4511.35*** *p61*
Zeimet, Elisabeth; America, 1871 ***5475.1*** *p262*
Zeiner, William; New York, 1860 ***358.56*** *p4*
Zeis, Louise; America, 1857 ***7420.1*** *p175*
Zeiter, Conrad; Ohio, 1809-1852 ***4511.35*** *p61*
Zeitlin, Henoch; Miami, 1920 ***4984.15*** *p38*
Zeitner, Franz; New York, 1859 ***358.56*** *p55*
Zelimer, August; Wisconsin, 1890 ***6795.8*** *p91*
Zelinka, Josef; Cleveland, OH, 1852 ***2853.20*** *p475*
Zell, Jacob; Ohio, 1809-1852 ***4511.35*** *p61*
Zell, Thomas; America, 1746 ***1220.12*** *p911*
Zelle, Christian Heinrich Wilhelm *SEE* Zelle, Sophie Wilhelmine Dreier
Zelle, Heinrich Friedrich Christian; America, 1886 ***7420.1*** *p352*
Zelle, Sophie Wilhelmine; America, 1886 ***7420.1*** *p352*
*Son:*Christian Heinrich Wilhelm
With son
Zeller, Andreas; Washington, 1887 ***6015.10*** *p16*
Zeller, Charles 29; New Orleans, 1843 ***778.6*** *p349*
Zeller, Christian; New Orleans, 1840 ***471.10*** *p62*
Zeller, Christian; New Orleans, 1840 ***471.10*** *p88*
Zeller, Johann Christian; America, 1860 ***5475.1*** *p412*
Zeller, Johann Henrich; America, 1838 ***170.15*** *p47*
Zeller, John; Ohio, 1809-1852 ***4511.35*** *p61*
Zeller, John C.; North Carolina, 1855 ***1088.45*** *p38*
Zeller, Paul 66; New Orleans, 1847 ***778.6*** *p349*
Zeller, Ulrich; Kansas, 1917-1918 ***1826.15*** *p81*
Zeller, Wilhelm; America, 1844 ***5475.1*** *p410*
Zeller, Wilhelm; America, 1860 ***5475.1*** *p412*
Zelliquitte, Auguste; Louisiana, 1836-1840 ***4981.45*** *p213*
Zellmer, Martin; Wisconsin, 1859 ***6795.8*** *p143*
Zellmer, Wilhelm; Wisconsin, 1871 ***6795.8*** *p127*
Zellmer, Wilhelm Ferd; Wisconsin, 1899 ***6795.8*** *p153*
Zellmer, William Ferdinand; Wisconsin, 1912 ***6795.8*** *p173*
Zellnek, Elizabeth 35; America, 1747 ***778.6*** *p349*
Zellnek, Ignatz 4; America, 1747 ***778.6*** *p349*
Zellnek, Ignatz 40; America, 1747 ***778.6*** *p349*
Zellnek, Jean 7; America, 1747 ***778.6*** *p349*
Zellnek, Julie 2; America, 1747 ***778.6*** *p349*
Zellnek, Lorenz 9; America, 1747 ***778.6*** *p349*
Zellnek, Pauline 3; America, 1747 ***778.6*** *p349*
Zellner, Johann; America, 1882 ***5475.1*** *p137*
Zelmer, Wilhelm Ferd; Wisconsin, 1899 ***6795.8*** *p153*
Zeltner, Georg; America, 1886 ***2526.43*** *p158*
Zelybek, Jakub 41; New York, NY, 1920 ***930.50*** *p49*
Zelynski, John 30; New York, NY, 1920 ***930.50*** *p49*
Zembruski, Anthony; Detroit, 1930 ***1640.60*** *p78*
Zeme, Malky Pomper; Detroit, 1929 ***1640.55*** *p117*
Zempel, Reinhold; Wisconsin, 1884 ***6795.8*** *p143*
Zen, Casper; Louisiana, 1874 ***4981.45*** *p297*
Zenber, Anthony; Ohio, 1809-1852 ***4511.35*** *p61*
Zendalski, John; Galveston, TX, 1895 ***6015.15*** *p12*
Zender, . . .; West Virginia, 1865-1879 ***1132.30*** *p150*
Zendler, Christina 15; Michigan, 1880 ***4491.36*** *p25*
Zendler, John 37; Ontario, 1871 ***1823.21*** *p405*
Zendolski, John; Washington Co., TX, 1895-1900 ***6015.15*** *p13*
Zener, Helena Muller *SEE* Zener, Josef
Zener, Josef; America, 1865 ***5475.1*** *p49*
*Wife:*Helena Muller
With stepchild
Zengerle, Bendedict; Ohio, 1809-1852 ***4511.35*** *p61*
Zengerly, Benedict; Ohio, 1809-1852 ***4511.35*** *p61*
Zenisek, Cyrill; Chicago, 1901 ***2853.20*** *p434*
Zenisek, Jakub; Iowa, 1854 ***2853.20*** *p216*
Zenisek, Josef; Iowa, 1853 ***2853.20*** *p216*
Zenisek, Josef; Iowa, 1855 ***2853.20*** *p211*
Zenkler, Appoline 32; Mississippi, 1846 ***778.6*** *p349*
Zenkler, Joseph Louis 39; Mississippi, 1846 ***778.6*** *p349*
Zenkler, Madalain 1; Mississippi, 1846 ***778.6*** *p349*
Zenkler, Marie 3; Mississippi, 1846 ***778.6*** *p349*
Zenner, Barbara; America, 1843 ***5475.1*** *p295*
Zenner, Gertrud 49; America, 1857 ***5475.1*** *p296*
*Son:*J. Philipp
*Son:*Mathias
Zenner, J. Philipp *SEE* Zenner, Gertrud Schmitt
Zenner, Johann; America, 1863 ***5475.1*** *p284*
Zenner, Mathias *SEE* Zenner, Gertrud Schmitt
Zens, A. Maria 7 *SEE* Zens, Jakob
Zens, Adam 4 *SEE* Zens, Jakob
Zens, Elisabeth Sehn *SEE* Zens, Jakob
Zens, Franz 2 *SEE* Zens, Jakob
Zens, Jakob 11 *SEE* Zens, Jakob
Zens, Jakob 38; America, 1837 ***5475.1*** *p410*
*Wife:*Elisabeth Sehn
*Daughter:*A. Maria 7
*Daughter:*Franz 2
With father-in-law
*Son:*Adam 4
*Son:*Jakob 11
*Son:*Konrad 17
*Daughter:*Katharina 13
*Son:*Kaspar 15
Zens, Kaspar 15 *SEE* Zens, Jakob
Zens, Katharina 13 *SEE* Zens, Jakob
Zens, Konrad 17 *SEE* Zens, Jakob
Zensius, Peter 20; New York, 1854 ***5475.1*** *p235*
Zensmeister, John; Ohio, 1809-1852 ***4511.35*** *p61*
Zentner, John; Illinois, 1860 ***6079.1*** *p15*
Zentsmaster, John; Ohio, 1809-1852 ***4511.35*** *p61*
Zenzius, Peter; America, 1866 ***5475.1*** *p238*
Zeorge, Jakob; North Carolina, 1710 ***3629.40*** *p8*
Zepherin, Edward; New York, NY, 1856 ***1494.20*** *p13*
Zeplin, Ludwig; Nebraska, 1905 ***3004.30*** *p46*
Zeppenfeld, Carl; Valdivia, Chile, 1851 ***1192.4*** *p51*
Zerbel, Julius; New York, 1860 ***358.56*** *p5*
Zerbel, Ottilie; Wisconsin, 1887 ***6795.8*** *p32*
Zerkey, Frederick; Ohio, 1809-1852 ***4511.35*** *p61*
Zerkowski, Golde 6 *SEE* Zerkowski, Lore
Zerkowski, Lore 21; New York, NY, 1878 ***9253.2*** *p45*
*Child:*Golde 6 months
Zero, Frank; Texas, 1884-1908 ***6015.15*** *p27*
Zerr, Anna Maria 8; Galveston, TX, 1846 ***3967.10*** *p378*
Zerr, Barbara 10; Galveston, TX, 1846 ***3967.10*** *p378*
Zerr, Elizabeth 30; America, 1747 ***778.6*** *p349*
Zerr, Johann 9; America, 1747 ***778.6*** *p349*
Zerr, Johann Baptist 43; Galveston, TX, 1846 ***3967.10*** *p378*
Zerr, Joseph 2; America, 1747 ***778.6*** *p349*
Zerr, Katharina 16; Galveston, TX, 1846 ***3967.10*** *p378*
Zerr, Katharina 44; Galveston, TX, 1846 ***3967.10*** *p378*
Zerr, Louis 3; America, 1747 ***778.6*** *p349*
Zerr, Louis 38; America, 1747 ***778.6*** *p349*
Zerr, Valentin 4; America, 1747 ***778.6*** *p349*
Zerrlant, F. E.; Louisiana, 1836-1840 ***4981.45*** *p213*
Zerwes, Peter; Brazil, 1857 ***5475.1*** *p441*
With wife & 6 children
Zerzan, Josef; Nebraska, 1848-1910 ***2853.20*** *p144*
Zeschka, Gotfried; Iowa, 1882 ***1211.15*** *p20*
Zettelmeyer von Furstenau, Maria Eva; Nova Scotia, 1751 ***2526.43*** *p208*
Zetterstrom, G.T.J.; Philadelphia, 1848 ***6412.40*** *p150*
Zetterstrom, Mathilda; St. Paul, MN, 1883 ***1865.50*** *p50*
Zetzmann, Michael; America, 1867 ***7919.3*** *p526*
With wife & 4 children
Zeuner, Christiane; America, 1868 ***7919.3*** *p530*
With child
Zeurbuchen, Ulrich; Ohio, 1809-1852 ***4511.35*** *p61*
Zeve, Joseph; Texas, 1885 ***3435.45*** *p37*
Zevinski, Edward 39; New York, NY, 1920 ***930.50*** *p48*
Zewe, A. Maria 4 *SEE* Zewe, Wilhelm
Zewe, Anna Maria Fuss 40 *SEE* Zewe, Wilhelm
Zewe, Jakob; America, 1837 ***5475.1*** *p454*
Zewe, Jakob; America, 1837 ***5475.1*** *p462*
With wife
With child
Zewe, Jakob; America, 1879 ***5475.1*** *p465*
Zewe, Johann 6 *SEE* Zewe, Wilhelm
Zewe, Johann 21; America, 1880 ***5475.1*** *p406*
Zewe, Johann 30 *SEE* Zewe, Wilhelm
Zewe, Katharina 3 *SEE* Zewe, Wilhelm
Zewe, Margarethe; America, 1879 ***5475.1*** *p386*
Zewe, Nikolaus 25 *SEE* Zewe, Wilhelm
Zewe, Wilhelm 54; America, 1837 ***5475.1*** *p385*
*Wife:*Anna Maria Fuss 40
*Son:*Johann 6
*Daughter:*Katharina 3
*Daughter:*A. Maria 4
*Son:*Johann 30
*Son:*Nikolaus 25
Zeyer, Friedrich L.; America, 1863 ***5475.1*** *p12*
*Wife:*Margarethe Luise Schmidt
Zeyer, Georg; America, 1847 ***5475.1*** *p28*
Zeyer, Johann Emmerich; America, 1841 ***5475.1*** *p27*
With family
Zeyer, Joseph 26; Galveston, TX, 1844 ***3967.10*** *p373*
Zeyer, Margarethe Luise Schmidt *SEE* Zeyer, Friedrich L.
Zeyer, Wilhelm Heinrich; America, 1841 ***5475.1*** *p27*
With family
Ziarck, Joseph 31; New York, NY, 1920 ***930.50*** *p48*
Ziarko, Jan 19; New York, NY, 1912 ***8355.1*** *p16*
Zibell, Leopold; Wisconsin, 1888 ***6795.8*** *p231*
Zicher, David 52; Halifax, N.S., 1902 ***1860.4*** *p41*
Zicher, Jacob 10; Halifax, N.S., 1902 ***1860.4*** *p41*
Zicher, Marie 58; Halifax, N.S., 1902 ***1860.4*** *p41*
Zick, Friedrich Herman; Wisconsin, 1885 ***6795.8*** *p87*
Zidzheck, Marg.; New York, 1860 ***358.56*** *p4*
Ziebell, Frederike; Kansas, 1870 ***777.40*** *p21*
Ziebler, Johann 50; Galveston, TX, 1846 ***3967.10*** *p377*
Ziecher, Anna 20; Halifax, N.S., 1902 ***1860.4*** *p41*
Ziecher, David 20; Halifax, N.S., 1902 ***1860.4*** *p41*
Zieger, Nicolas 28; America, 1840 ***778.6*** *p349*
Ziegler, Andrew 8; Halifax, N.S., 1902 ***1860.4*** *p43*
Ziegler, Anna 11; Halifax, N.S., 1902 ***1860.4*** *p43*
Ziegler, Charles; Philadelphia, 1875 ***8513.31*** *p435*
*Wife:*Fredericke Vollmer
Ziegler, David; Ohio, 1840-1897 ***8365.35*** *p18*
Ziegler, Erich; Port uncertain, 1908 ***7420.1*** *p385*
Ziegler, Felicia; Venezuela, 1843 ***3899.5*** *p541*
Ziegler, Felise 4; Halifax, N.S., 1902 ***1860.4*** *p43*
Ziegler, Franzisca 17; New York, NY, 1885 ***1883.7*** *p45*
Ziegler, Fredericke Vollmer *SEE* Ziegler, Charles
Ziegler, Georg; New York, 1891 ***5475.1*** *p38*
Ziegler, Georg; Venezuela, 1843 ***3899.5*** *p541*
Ziegler, Johann *SEE* Ziegler, Johann
Ziegler, Johann; America, 1877 ***5475.1*** *p408*
*Wife:*Margarethe Jochum
*Son:*Mathias
*Daughter:*Katharina
*Son:*Johann
Ziegler, Josepf 51; Halifax, N.S., 1902 ***1860.4*** *p43*
Ziegler, Katharina *SEE* Ziegler, Johann
Ziegler, Magdalene 50; Halifax, N.S., 1902 ***1860.4*** *p43*
Ziegler, Manana 14; Halifax, N.S., 1902 ***1860.4*** *p43*
Ziegler, Margarethe Jochum *SEE* Ziegler, Johann
Ziegler, Margartha 21; Halifax, N.S., 1902 ***1860.4*** *p43*
Ziegler, Mathias *SEE* Ziegler, Johann
Ziegler, Peter 17; Halifax, N.S., 1902 ***1860.4*** *p43*
Ziehres, Johannes; America, 1858 ***2526.42*** *p203*
Zielinski, Bartlomiej; Detroit, 1929-1930 ***6214.5*** *p70*
Zielinski, Mary; Detroit, 1929-1930 ***6214.5*** *p69*
Zielinski, Zygmund; Detroit, 1929 ***6214.5*** *p69*
Zielman, Joseph; West Virginia, 1869 ***1132.30*** *p151*
Zielonka, Jan 28; New York, NY, 1920 ***930.50*** *p49*
Zieman, William; Iowa, 1913 ***1211.15*** *p20*
Ziemer, Albert; Wisconsin, 1885 ***6795.8*** *p228*
Ziemer, Albert Johann; Wisconsin, 1888 ***6795.8*** *p224*
Ziemer, Ferdinand; Wisconsin, 1881 ***6795.8*** *p228*
Ziemke, Wilhelm; Wisconsin, 1885 ***6795.8*** *p208*
Ziems, F.; Venezuela, 1843 ***3899.5*** *p546*
Zieprecht, Heinrich; Chile, 1852 ***1192.4*** *p52*
With wife
With child 5
With child 7
Ziereck, Conrad; Long Island, 1781 ***8529.30*** *p10A*
Ziergobel, Jakob; America, 1848 ***2526.42*** *p114*
With wife
With child 2
Zierke, Elisabeth; Venezuela, 1843 ***3899.5*** *p546*
Zierke, Emilie; Wisconsin, 1882-1883 ***6795.8*** *p35*
Zierke, Hermann; Wisconsin, 1898 ***6795.8*** *p224*
Zierke, John; Wisconsin, 1881 ***6795.8*** *p53*
Zierke, Julius Friedrich August; Wisconsin, 1893 ***6795.8*** *p228*
Zies, Barbara; New York, 1859 ***358.56*** *p100*
Ziesenis, Heinrich; America, 1856 ***7420.1*** *p156*
Zieseniss, Engel Marie Dorothee Bovers *SEE* Zieseniss, Johann Friedrich Wilhelm
Zieseniss, Johann Friedrich Wilhelm; America, 1846 ***7420.1*** *p51*
*Wife:*Engel Marie Dorothee Bovers
Zieseniss, Johann Philipp; America, 1854 ***7420.1*** *p133*
Zigler, Henry; Ohio, 1840-1897 ***8365.35*** *p18*
Zigler, William; Ohio, 1809-1852 ***4511.35*** *p61*
Zika, Frantisek; Iowa, 1855 ***2853.20*** *p211*
Zika, Matej; Wisconsin, 1853 ***2853.20*** *p303*
Zika, Matej 13; Wisconsin, 1853 ***2853.20*** *p291*
With parents
Zila, Karel; Wisconsin, 1898 ***2853.20*** *p302*
Zile, Josephine 41; Ontario, 1871 ***1823.21*** *p405*

Zilki, Adolf 21; New York, NY, 1893 *1883.7 p43*
Zilligen, Henry A.; Colorado, 1882 *1029.59 p97*
Zilligen, Joseph; Colorado, 1882 *1029.59 p97*
Zilligen, Joseph; Colorado, 1884 *1029.59 p97*
Zima, Frantisek; Nebraska, 1873 *2853.20 p171*
Zima, Josef; Milwaukee, 1848-1849 *2853.20 p308*
Zimbelmann, Karl 25; Halifax, N.S., 1902 *1860.4 p42*
Zimerle, Ludwig 22; America, 1747 *778.6 p349*
Zimmer, John 46; Ontario, 1871 *1823.17 p180*
Zimmerman, John 46; Ontario, 1871 *1823.21 p405*
Zimmer, Adam *SEE* Zimmer, Adam
Zimmer, Adam; America, 1872 *5475.1 p384*
  *Wife:*Maria Marg. Haas
  *Son:*Adam
  *Daughter:*Katharina
  *Daughter:*M. Katharina
  *Daughter:*Sophie
Zimmer, Adam; South America, 1846 *5475.1 p531*
Zimmer, Angela *SEE* Zimmer, Peter
Zimmer, Anna Gornich 21 *SEE* Zimmer, Michel
Zimmer, Anna Maria; Brazil, 1878 *5475.1 p431*
Zimmer, Barbara Klein 29 *SEE* Zimmer, Johann
Zimmer, Bartholomew; Ohio, 1809-1852 *4511.35 p61*
Zimmer, Caroline 24; America, 1847 *778.6 p350*
Zimmer, Christian; America, 1846 *5475.1 p530*
Zimmer, Conrad; America, 1846 *5475.1 p530*
Zimmer, Daniel; Ohio, 1809-1852 *4511.35 p61*
Zimmer, Elisabeth; America, 1856 *5475.1 p520*
Zimmer, Elisabeth Kiefer 42 *SEE* Zimmer, Nikolaus
Zimmer, Frank; Colorado, 1903 *1029.59 p97*
Zimmer, Frank 21; Kansas, 1903 *1029.59 p97*
Zimmer, Franz *SEE* Zimmer, Nikolaus
Zimmer, Friedrich 4 *SEE* Zimmer, Friedrich
Zimmer, Friedrich 5 *SEE* Zimmer, Philipp
Zimmer, Friedrich 38; Brazil, 1865 *5475.1 p521*
  *Wife:*Katharina Bohnenberger 30
  *Son:*Friedrich 4
  *Daughter:*Philippine 1
  *Daughter:*Katharina 5
Zimmer, Jakob; America, 1861 *5475.1 p533*
Zimmer, Jakob *SEE* Zimmer, Johann
Zimmer, Jakob *SEE* Zimmer, Nikolaus
Zimmer, Jakob 19; America, 1849 *5475.1 p514*
Zimmer, Jakob; Brazil, 1854 *5475.1 p440*
  *Wife:*Maria Lermen
  With 6 children
Zimmer, Jakob 1 *SEE* Zimmer, Philipp
Zimmer, Jakob 37; New York, 1872 *5475.1 p533*
Zimmer, Johann; America, 1846 *5475.1 p514*
Zimmer, Johann *SEE* Zimmer, Nikolaus
Zimmer, Johann; America, 1882 *5475.1 p175*
Zimmer, Johann 25; America, 1860 *5475.1 p310*
  *Wife:*Barbara Klein 29
Zimmer, Johann 28; America, 1871 *5475.1 p72*
  *Wife:*Katharina Nest 25
  *Son:*Peter
  *Son:*Jakob
Zimmer, Johann; Wisconsin, 1873 *6795.8 p98*
Zimmer, Johann Jakob; America, 1846 *5475.1 p547*
Zimmer, Johann Nikolaus; America, 1847 *5475.1 p547*
Zimmer, Josef *SEE* Zimmer, Nikolaus
Zimmer, Karl 33; New York, 1880 *5475.1 p533*
Zimmer, Katharina *SEE* Zimmer, Adam
Zimmer, Katharina; America, 1882 *5475.1 p168*
Zimmer, Katharina Nest 25 *SEE* Zimmer, Johann
Zimmer, Katharina 58; America, 1843 *5475.1 p529*
Zimmer, Katharina 5 *SEE* Zimmer, Friedrich
Zimmer, Katharina 7 *SEE* Zimmer, Philipp
Zimmer, Katharina Bohnenberger 30 *SEE* Zimmer, Friedrich
Zimmer, Katharina Werner 34 *SEE* Zimmer, Philipp
Zimmer, M. Josef *SEE* Zimmer, Peter
Zimmer, M. Katharina *SEE* Zimmer, Adam
Zimmer, Margarethe 28; America, 1800-1899 *5475.1 p451*
Zimmer, Maria Lermen *SEE* Zimmer, Jakob
Zimmer, Maria *SEE* Zimmer, Peter
Zimmer, Maria Katharina 58; America, 1843 *5475.1 p529*
Zimmer, Maria Marg. Haas *SEE* Zimmer, Adam
Zimmer, Mathias 63; America, 1847 *778.6 p350*
Zimmer, Michel; America, 1864 *5475.1 p284*
  *Wife:*Anna Gornich
  *Son:*Peter
Zimmer, Nicholas; Louisiana, 1841-1844 *4981.45 p211*
Zimmer, Nicolas 19; America, 1840 *778.6 p350*
Zimmer, Nicolas; Colorado, 1897 *1029.59 p97*
Zimmer, Nicolas 24; Kansas, 1891 *1029.59 p97*
Zimmer, Nikolaus; America, 1843 *5475.1 p383*
  With wife & 3 children
Zimmer, Nikolaus; America, 1856 *5475.1 p520*
Zimmer, Nikolaus; America, 1872 *5475.1 p292*

Zimmer, Nikolaus; America, 1880 *5475.1 p325*
  *Wife:*Elisabeth Kiefer
  *Son:*Josef
  *Son:*Johann
  *Son:*Franz
  *Son:*Jakob
  *Son:*Peter
Zimmer, Nikolaus; Buffalo, NY, 1880 *5475.1 p325*
Zimmer, Peter; America, 1846 *5475.1 p546*
Zimmer, Peter; America, 1849 *5475.1 p514*
Zimmer, Peter *SEE* Zimmer, Michel
Zimmer, Peter *SEE* Zimmer, Johann
Zimmer, Peter *SEE* Zimmer, Nikolaus
Zimmer, Peter; Ohio, 1880 *5475.1 p378*
  *Wife:*Angela
  *Son:*M. Josef
  *Daughter:*Maria
Zimmer, Philipp 10 *SEE* Zimmer, Philipp
Zimmer, Philipp 40; Brazil, 1865 *5475.1 p521*
  *Wife:*Katharina Werner 34
  *Son:*Friedrich 5
  *Son:*Jakob 1
  *Son:*Philipp 10
  *Daughter:*Katharina 7
Zimmer, Philippine 1 *SEE* Zimmer, Friedrich
Zimmer, Sophie *SEE* Zimmer, Adam
Zimmerer, Anselm; New York, 1860 *358.56 p148*
Zimmerly, Edward; New York, 1872 *1132.30 p150*
Zimmerly, Karl Frederick; Missouri, 1903 *3276.1 p4*
Zimmerman, Antoine 8; Missouri, 1845 *778.6 p350*
Zimmerman, Barba 19; New York, NY, 1894 *6512.1 p232*
Zimmerman, Barbara 11; Missouri, 1845 *778.6 p350*
Zimmerman, Edward 6; Missouri, 1845 *778.6 p350*
Zimmerman, Fitteld; Ohio, 1809-1852 *4511.35 p61*
Zimmerman, Frederick; Ohio, 1840-1897 *8365.35 p18*
Zimmerman, Gaspar; North Carolina, 1710 *3629.40 p7*
Zimmerman, George; Ohio, 1856 *3580.20 p34*
Zimmerman, George; Ohio, 1856 *6020.12 p23*
Zimmerman, John; Ohio, 1809-1852 *4511.35 p61*
Zimmerman, Joseph; Louisiana, 1874 *4981.45 p134*
Zimmerman, Joseph; Ohio, 1809-1852 *4511.35 p62*
Zimmerman, Josephine 3; Missouri, 1845 *778.6 p350*
Zimmerman, Jul; Nebraska, 1905 *3004.30 p46*
Zimmerman, Lewis; Ohio, 1856 *3580.20 p34*
Zimmerman, Lewis; Ohio, 1856 *6020.12 p23*
Zimmerman, Louis 7; Missouri, 1845 *778.6 p350*
Zimmerman, Peter; Washington, 1889 *2770.40 p81*
Zimmerman, Theresa; Kansas, 1917-1918 *1826.15 p81*
Zimmerman, Wilhelm Erich; Wisconsin, 1896 *6795.8 p78*
Zimmerman, William 35; Ontario, 1871 *1823.17 p180*
Zimmermann, Agathe 12; Galveston, TX, 1844 *3967.10 p376*
Zimmermann, Alexander 12; Galveston, TX, 1844 *3967.10 p376*
Zimmermann, Anna *SEE* Zimmermann, Mathias
Zimmermann, Anna 3 *SEE* Zimmermann, Mathias
Zimmermann, Anna; Wisconsin, 1892 *6795.8 p84*
Zimmermann, Anna Christine; America, 1868 *7919.3 p525*
Zimmermann, Anna Christine *SEE* Zimmermann, Joseph
Zimmermann, Antoine 34; Missouri, 1845 *778.6 p350*
Zimmermann, Auguste; America, 1867 *7420.1 p267*
  *Daughter:*Emma
Zimmermann, Barbara 1 *SEE* Zimmermann, Mathias
Zimmermann, Barbara 38; Missouri, 1845 *778.6 p350*
Zimmermann, Carl Rinteln; America, 1853 *7420.1 p113*
  With wife & son
Zimmermann, Carl Wilhelm Ludwig; America, 1855 *7420.1 p144*
Zimmermann, Dorothea Wilhelmine Korf *SEE* Zimmermann, Joseph
Zimmermann, Elise *SEE* Zimmermann, Ferdinand
Zimmermann, Emma *SEE* Zimmermann, Auguste Hepke
Zimmermann, F.; New York, 1859 *358.56 p55*
Zimmermann, F.; Venezuela, 1843 *3899.5 p546*
Zimmermann, Ferdinand; America, 1852 *7420.1 p101*
  *Sister:*Elise
Zimmermann, Frank August Ferdinand; Wisconsin, 1884 *6795.8 p78*
Zimmermann, George 28; New Orleans, 1846 *778.6 p350*
Zimmermann, Gustav 11 months; Galveston, TX, 1844 *3967.10 p376*
Zimmermann, Heinrich 17; Galveston, TX, 1844 *3967.10 p375*
Zimmermann, Hubert; America, 1924 *8023.44 p381*
Zimmermann, Jakob; America, 1884 *2526.43 p159*
Zimmermann, Jakob; America, 1884 *2526.43 p162*
  *Mother:*Katharina Bach
Zimmermann, Johann; America, 1881 *5475.1 p260*

Zimmermann, Johann Baptist 5; Galveston, TX, 1844 *3967.10 p376*
Zimmermann, Johann Gottlieb; Wisconsin, 1883 *6795.8 p78*
Zimmermann, Johann Heinrich *SEE* Zimmermann, Joseph
Zimmermann, Joseph; America, 1870 *7420.1 p288*
  *Wife:*Dorothea Wilhelmine Korf
  *Daughter:*Anna Christine
  *Brother:*Johann Heinrich
Zimmermann, Joseph 22; Galveston, TX, 1844 *3967.10 p375*
Zimmermann, Joseph 47; Galveston, TX, 1844 *3967.10 p375*
Zimmermann, Karoline; America, 1867 *5475.1 p508*
Zimmermann, Karoline Peters 33 *SEE* Zimmermann, Mathias
Zimmermann, Karoline 15; Galveston, TX, 1844 *3967.10 p375*
Zimmermann, Katharina Bach *SEE* Zimmermann, Jakob
Zimmermann, Maria Anna 19; Galveston, TX, 1844 *3967.10 p375*
Zimmermann, Maria Anna 45; Galveston, TX, 1844 *3967.10 p375*
Zimmermann, Mathias; America, 1870 *5475.1 p145*
  *Wife:*Mathilde Rival
  *Daughter:*Anna
Zimmermann, Mathias 7 *SEE* Zimmermann, Mathias
Zimmermann, Mathias 40; America, 1856 *5475.1 p352*
  *Wife:*Karoline Peters 33
  *Son:*Peter 5
  *Daughter:*Anna 3
  *Daughter:*Barbara 1 months
  *Son:*Nikolaus 8
  *Son:*Mathias 7
Zimmermann, Mathilde Rival *SEE* Zimmermann, Mathias
Zimmermann, Michael; America, 1831 *2526.43 p158*
  With wife & 2 children
Zimmermann, Minnie Louise Bertha; Wisconsin, 1886 *6795.8 p84*
Zimmermann, Nikolaus 8 *SEE* Zimmermann, Mathias
Zimmermann, Peter; America, 1868 *5475.1 p145*
Zimmermann, Peter 5 *SEE* Zimmermann, Mathias
Zimmermann, Peter; Wisconsin, 1875 *5475.1 p275*
Zimmermann, Susanna; America, 1883 *5475.1 p24*
Zimmermann, Tibot 19; Galveston, TX, 1844 *3967.10 p375*
Zimmermann, Wilh.; Portsmouth, NH, 1925 *8023.44 p381*
Zimmermann, Wilhelmine; America, 1857 *7420.1 p175*
Zimpel, Friedrich; Wisconsin, 1872 *6795.8 p28*
Zinck, Joseph 30; Louisiana, 1848 *778.6 p350*
Zinck, Melanie 1; Louisiana, 1848 *778.6 p350*
Zinck, Therese 36; Louisiana, 1848 *778.6 p350*
Zind, Barbe 34; America, 1846 *778.6 p350*
Zind, Jean 42; America, 1846 *778.6 p350*
Zind, Joseph 2; America, 1846 *778.6 p350*
Zind, Theresa 1; America, 1846 *778.6 p350*
Zindt, Antoinette Greff *SEE* Zindt, Mathias
Zindt, Eugenie *SEE* Zindt, Mathias
Zindt, Julius *SEE* Zindt, Mathias
Zindt, Leopold *SEE* Zindt, Mathias
Zindt, Louis *SEE* Zindt, Mathias
Zindt, Mathias; America, 1883 *5475.1 p131*
  *Wife:*Antoinette Greff
  *Daughter:*Eugenie
  *Son:*Leopold
  *Son:*Louis
  *Son:*Julius
Zingre, John; Illinois, 1855 *6079.1 p15*
Zingre, Theodore E.; Illinois, 1858 *6079.1 p15*
Zininger, Christian; Ohio, 1809-1852 *4511.35 p62*
Zink, Andreas 27; America, 1847 *778.6 p350*
Zink, Caroline 50; Ontario, 1871 *1823.17 p181*
Zink, Elisabetha; America, 1867 *2526.43 p193*
Zink, Therese 54; Mississippi, 1847 *778.6 p350*
Zinker, Bertha 16; New York, NY, 1885 *1883.7 p45*
Zinn, Johann Georg; America, 1868 *7919.3 p526*
Zinner, Ernst Joseph Ludwig; America, 1882 *179.55 p19*
Zinner, Josephine; America, 1882 *179.55 p19*
Zinner, Karl; America, 1882 *179.55 p19*
Zinner, Louise; America, 1882 *179.55 p19*
Zinner, Maria; America, 1882 *179.55 p19*
Zinner, Max F.; America, 1882 *179.55 p19*
Zins, Jean 23; New Orleans, 1845 *778.6 p350*
Zins, Marianne 27; New Orleans, 1845 *778.6 p350*
Zins, Marie 21; New Orleans, 1845 *778.6 p350*
Zint, John P.; Ohio, 1809-1852 *4511.35 p62*
Zintsmeister, Jacob; Ohio, 1809-1852 *4511.35 p62*
Zionien, Benedict; North Carolina, 1710 *3629.40 p8*
Zionien, Michael; North Carolina, 1710 *3629.40 p8*
Zions, Ludwig; Texas, 1854-1872 *9980.22 p16*

Ziontz, John; Texas, 1854-1873 *9980.22 p16*
Zior, Ludwig; America, 1853 *2526.43 p192*
Zior, Peter; America, 1860 *2526.43 p192*
Zior, Peter; America, 1865 *2526.43 p192*
Ziorien, Michael; North Carolina, 1710 *3629.40 p8*
Ziorjen, Benedicht; North Carolina, 1710 *3629.40 p8*
Ziorjen, Jakob; North Carolina, 1710 *3629.40 p8*
Zipfel, Francois 16; St. Louis, 1847 *778.6 p350*
Zirhut, Matous Karel; Omaha, NE, 1798-1898 *2853.20 p144*
Zirke, John; Wisconsin, 1881 *6795.8 p53*
Zirpolo, Guiseppi 37; Minnesota, 1925 *2769.54 p1384*
Zischbacher, Carolina 36; New Orleans, 1848 *778.6 p350*
Zischbacher, Magdalena 74; New Orleans, 1848 *778.6 p350*
Zishka, Carl F.; Iowa, 1894 *1211.15 p20*
Ziske, Daniel 16; New York, NY, 1893 *1883.7 p41*
Ziske, Wilhelm 36; New York, NY, 1893 *1883.7 p41*
Zistel, Bruno 33; Indiana, 1892-1894 *9076.20 p73*
Zitka, Josef; South Dakota, 1871-1910 *2853.20 p247*
Zitko, Jan; Wisconsin, 1852 *2853.20 p303*
Zitzmann, Ottokar; America, 1867 *7919.3 p533*
Ziud, Barbe 34; America, 1846 *778.6 p350*
Ziud, Jean 42; America, 1846 *778.6 p350*
Ziud, Joseph 2; America, 1846 *778.6 p350*
Ziud, Theresa 1; America, 1846 *778.6 p350*
Zizik, Isadore; Texas, 1855-1871 *9980.22 p16*
Zizka, Jan; Minnesota, 1863 *2853.20 p267*
Zizkovsky, Vojtech; America, 1887 *2853.20 p287*
    With parents
Zlab, Vaclav; Milwaukee, 1848-1849 *2853.20 p307*
Zlebcik, Jan; Iowa, 1869 *2853.20 p238*
Zlebcik, Jan Bedrich; Iowa, 1869 *2853.20 p224*
Zlobrouski, Frank 36; New York, NY, 1920 *930.50 p48*
Zloczowski, Paul; Detroit, 1929-1930 *6214.5 p65*
Zobel, Anton 41; Port uncertain, 1846 *778.6 p350*
Zobel, Hermann; Wisconsin, 1878 *6795.8 p62*
Zoble, Julius; South Carolina, 1878 *6155.4 p19*
Z'Obrist, Caspar; North Carolina, 1710 *3629.40 p8*
Zobrist, Caspar; North Carolina, 1710 *3629.40 p8*
Zoehler, Peter; New York, 1886 *5475.1 p293*
Zohnecker, D. 25; Port uncertain, 1846 *778.6 p350*
Zohnrogh, John 22; Ohio, 1880 *4879.40 p257*
Zolbeiss, Caspar; North Carolina, 1710 *3629.40 p8*
Zolenski, Ignac; Galveston, TX, 1896 *6015.15 p12*
Zolenski, Walent; Galveston, TX, 1896 *6015.15 p12*
Zoleski, Joseph; Galveston, TX, 1900 *6015.15 p12*
Zoleski, Kostyn; Galveston, TX, 1900 *6015.15 p12*
Zoleski, Walter; Galveston, TX, 1900 *6015.15 p12*
Zoller, Mrs. Jakob; America, 1842 *2526.42 p198*
    With child 24
    With child 19
Zollner, Henri 28; Louisiana, 1848 *778.6 p350*

Zollner, Henry; Illinois, 1852 *6079.1 p15*
Zollner, Margarethe Braun *SEE* Zollner, Mathias
Zollner, Mathias; America, 1883 *5475.1 p174*
    *Wife:*Margarethe Braun
    *Son:*Michel
Zollner, Michel *SEE* Zollner, Mathias
Zonga, Andrew; Washington, 1887 *2770.40 p25*
Zonnefrank, John; Virginia, 1777-1804 *9228.50 p615*
Zopf, Augustus; Ohio, 1809-1852 *4511.35 p62*
Zorn, Charles; Louisiana, 1874 *4981.45 p134*
Zorn, Emilie Hulda; Wisconsin, 1885 *6795.8 p124*
Zorn, Katharina; Venezuela, 1843 *3899.5 p542*
Zorn, Maria 22; Brazil, 1852 *5475.1 p500*
Zorn, Maria Ursula; Venezuela, 1843 *3899.5 p543*
Zorr, Michel 42; America, 1747 *778.6 p350*
Zorr, Wieldsurga 38; America, 1747 *778.6 p350*
Zouch, Elizabeth; Barbados, 1681 *1220.12 p911*
Zouch, Miles; Barbados, 1670 *1220.12 p911*
Zouginpus, L. 25; New Orleans, 1843 *778.6 p350*
Zowurka, Catharina 34; Galveston, TX, 1855 *571.7 p16*
Zowurka, Euphenia 7; Galveston, TX, 1855 *571.7 p16*
Zowurka, Eva 5; Galveston, TX, 1855 *571.7 p16*
Zowurka, Johanna 8 months; Galveston, TX, 1855 *571.7 p16*
Zowurka, Peter 37; Galveston, TX, 1855 *571.7 p16*
Zrust, Frantisek; Nebraska, 1869-1910 *2853.20 p181*
Zryescheck, Michael; Miami, 1935 *4984.12 p39*
Zrzan, Josef; Nebraska, 1848-1910 *2853.20 p182*
Zuber, Ester Ottilie 14; New York, NY, 1864 *8425.62 p198*
Zuber, Ferdinand; Ohio, 1809-1852 *4511.35 p62*
Zuber, Kunigunde 22; New York, NY, 1864 *8425.62 p198*
Zuccalotto, Umberto; Illinois, 1918 *6007.60 p9*
Zucher, Jean. 18; America, 1747 *778.6 p351*
Zucker, H.; New York, 1859 *358.56 p101*
Zuehlke, August; Wisconsin, 1888 *6795.8 p64*
Zuehlke, Gustav; Wisconsin, 1894 *6795.8 p145*
Zuelke, August Friedrick; Wisconsin, 1893 *6795.8 p119*
Zuerbucher, Ulrich; Ohio, 1809-1852 *4511.35 p62*
Zuetlow, Bertha Maria Therese; Wisconsin, 1898 *6795.8 p84*
Zugage, Elisabeth 20; America, 1868 *5475.1 p282*
Zugler, Felicia; Venezuela, 1843 *3899.5 p541*
Zugler, Georg; Venezuela, 1843 *3899.5 p541*
Zuhlke, Wm.; Nebraska, 1905 *3004.30 p46*
Zuinberger, Henry; Ohio, 1840-1897 *8365.35 p18*
Zujor, Barbara 15 months; New York, NY, 1898 *7951.13 p42*
Zujor, Elisabeth 32; New York, NY, 1898 *7951.13 p42*
Zujor, Jacob 9; New York, NY, 1898 *7951.13 p42*
Zujor, Katherina 11; New York, NY, 1898 *7951.13 p42*
Zujor, Peter 7; New York, NY, 1898 *7951.13 p42*
Zujor, Peter 32; New York, NY, 1898 *7951.13 p42*

Zujor, Phillip 4; New York, NY, 1898 *7951.13 p42*
Zukowski, Anthony; Detroit, 1929-1930 *6214.5 p61*
Zulauf, Jacob; Ohio, 1809-1852 *4511.35 p62*
Zulke, Gustav Wilhelm; Wisconsin, 1896 *6795.8 p145*
Zulkowski, Philip; Texas, 1884 *6015.15 p28*
Zulkowski, Phillip; New York, NY, 1881 *6015.15 p28*
Zuloski, John; Texas, 1892 *6015.15 p30*
Zumstein, Jacob; Ohio, 1809-1852 *4511.35 p62*
Zumwalde, Bernard; Ohio, 1840-1897 *8365.35 p18*
Zupp, Christian; Ohio, 1809-1852 *4511.35 p62*
Zurcher, Dorothea 47; Galveston, TX, 1844 *3967.10 p373*
Zurcher, Hortense 3; Galveston, TX, 1844 *3967.10 p373*
Zurcher, Johann Ulrich 47; Galveston, TX, 1844 *3967.10 p373*
Zurcher, Magdalena 36; Galveston, TX, 1844 *3967.10 p373*
Zurcher, Maria 21; Galveston, TX, 1844 *3967.10 p373*
Zurcher, Nikolaus 38; Galveston, TX, 1844 *3967.10 p373*
Zuriki, Melchoir 31; Missouri, 1845 *778.6 p351*
Zurmuhl, Joseph 40; Louisiana, 1848 *778.6 p351*
Zurn, Elisabeth 22; New York, NY, 1893 *1883.7 p42*
Zurn, Friedrich 1; New York, NY, 1893 *1883.7 p42*
Zurn, Jacob 15; New York, NY, 1893 *1883.7 p42*
Zurn, Johann 3; New York, NY, 1893 *1883.7 p42*
Zurn, Johann 28; New York, NY, 1893 *1883.7 p42*
Zurn, Katharina; Venezuela, 1843 *3899.5 p542*
Zuruda, Martin 31; Galveston, TX, 1855 *571.7 p16*
Zusseman, Peter; North Carolina, 1710 *3629.40 p8*
Zuttermeister, Christian; America, 1853 *7420.1 p114*
    With wife & 2 sons
Zuttermeister, Heinrich; America, 1852 *7420.1 p102*
Zuwallen, Christian; Ohio, 1809-1852 *4511.35 p62*
Zvolanek, Josef Jan; 1849-1859 *2853.20 p59*
Zvonecek, Jan; Nebraska, 1874 *2853.20 p157*
Zvonecek, Josef; Nebraska, 1874 *2853.20 p157*
Zwahle, Christian; Ohio, 1809-1852 *4511.35 p62*
Zwaig, Dorothy; Detroit, 1929 *1640.55 p117*
Zweigle, Jakob; New York, NY, 1891 *3366.30 p70*
Zweigle, Wilhelm; New York, NY, 1892 *3366.30 p70*
Zwicker, Carl; Illinois, 1852 *6079.1 p15*
Zwikowsky, Josef 23; New York, NY, 1890 *1883.7 p48*
Zwilling, Joseph; Ohio, 1809-1852 *4511.35 p62*
Zwilzenski, Frank; Washington, 1888 *2770.40 p26*
Zwoll, Heinrich; America, 1867 *7919.3 p528*
    With 4 children
Zych, John; Detroit, 1929 *1640.55 p113*
Zygmon, Walter; Detroit, 1929-1930 *6214.5 p70*
Zygmontowski, Walter; Detroit, 1929-1930 *6214.5 p70*
Zymann, Cathe. 28; New York, NY, 1885 *1883.7 p45*
Zymann, Marie 3; New York, NY, 1885 *1883.7 p45*
Zyne, William; Barbados, 1669 *1220.12 p911*
Zzarzay, F.; Galveston, TX, 1855 *571.7 p18*

FOR A COMPLETE EXPLANATION OF ENTRY, SEE "HOW TO READ A CITATION" SECTION